EMPIRE FILM GUIDE

PICTURE CREDITS

A-Z films: American Beauty (United International Pictures); Beauty and the Beast (Buena Vista); Crouching Tiger, Hidden Dragon (Columbia Tristar); Deerhunter (Columbia/EMI/Warner); E.T. (Universal Pictures); Fight Club (20th Century Fox); The Graduate (Momentum Pictures); Harry Potter (Warner Brothers); The Incredibles (Buena Vista); Jerry Maguire (Columbia Tristar); Kill Bill (Buena Vista); The Ladykillers (Lumiere Pictures Limited); Manhattan (United Artists); North by Northwest (MGM); One Flew Over the Cuckoo's Nest (Warner Home Video); Planet of the Apes (20th Century Fox); Quiz Show (Buena Vista); The Rocky Horror Picture Show (20th Century Fox); The Shawshank Redemption (Rank Film Distribution); Titanic (20th Century Fox); The Usual Suspects (TBC); The Virgin Suicides (Pathe); Withnail and I (Handmade Films); X-Men (20th Century Fox); Young Guns (20th Century Fox); Zoolander (United International Pictures).

Top 10s: Page 19: The Night Of The Hunter (MGM Home Entertainment); page 83: Austin Powers: International Man Of Mystery (Guild Pathe Cinema); page 171: Carry on Cowboy (TPC/The Portman Conspiracy); page 295: Annie Hall (BFI); page 489: Life Is Beautiful (Buena Vista Home Entertainment); page 591: LA Story (Momentum Pictures) page 651: The Terminator (MGM Home Entertainment); page 681: Die Another Day (Bond Board); page 711: Say Anything (20th Century Fox Home Entertainment); page 820: Trainspotting (Universal Pictures); page 849: Some Like It Hot (MGM Home Entertainment); page 879: Basic Instinct (Momentum Pictures); page 909: Star Wars Episode II: Attack Of The Clones (20th Century Fox/Lucas Film); page 937: Full Metal Jacket (Warner Bros); page 959: Galaxy Quest (Universal Pictures); page 985: Halloween (Anchor Bay Entertainment); page 1008: Groucho Marx (Moviestore Collection); page 1023: Clockwork Orange (Warner Bros); page 1029: Shaft (BFI); page 1043: The Lord Of The Rings: The Fellowship Of The Ring (Entertainment Film Distributors); page 1057: Raiders Of The Lost Ark (Paramount/Lucasfilm): page 1072: A Nightmare On Elm Street (Entertainment In Video); page 1093: Gangs Of New York (Entertainment Film Distributors)

Images courtesy of Empire.

First published in Great Britain in 2006 by
Virgin Books Ltd
Thames Wharf Studios
Rainville Road
London
W6 9HA

A catalogue record for this book is available from the British Library.

ISBN 0 7535 1046 4
9 780753 51046 9

The paper used in this book is a natural, recyclable product made from wood grown in sustainable forests. The manufacturing process conforms to the regulations of the country of origin.

Typeset by Phoenix Photosetting, Lordswood, Chatham, Kent
Printed and bound in Great Britain by William Clowes Limited, Beccles, Suffolk

CONTENTS

INTRODUCTION

As we speed towards a bold broadband world of peer review networks, downloaded samples and average user ratings, the role of the plain old movie critic has taken a bit of a bashing recently. By reputation at least, critics are a curmudgeonly, complacent lot – shouting from the sidelines, never getting in the game.

Of course, it's plain to discerning folk that a great many fantastic writers have picked up the critic's cudgel in the ceaseless fight against mediocrity but that fact alone should not prevent regular re-examination of the role of the critic.

Naturally, we like to think that *Empire* has performed the necessary health checks every month for seventeen years.

Conceived as Project Odeon and supported by some dismal market research, *Empire* – 'The Modern Guide To Screen Entertainment' – was launched on a gambler's hunch at the Cannes Film Festival in May 1989. Our then Editorial Director, David Hepworth, summed up *Empire*'s fresh approach with this pithy manifesto – 'Movies can sometimes be art. They should always be fun.'

While the word 'fun' is too insubstantial to adequately describe some of the masterpieces you will encounter in this volume, that mission statement has remained our guiding principle over more than 200 issues that have seen *Empire* become not just the biggest movie magazine in the UK, but one of the most trusted brands in the film industry.

Empire's traditional heartland is perhaps best described as 'intelligent mainstream' but in broad terms our team of reviewers are perennially charged with finding the reasons to go and see a film, whatever its type.

We passionately believe that an individual looking to make the right movie choice on any given night does not base that decision on how a *Star Wars* movie compares to *Citizen Kane*, say, but on how it fares against rival attractions. Does it deliver on that cool trailer? Is it better than the disappointing previous one? Those are the key questions for a typical *Empire* reader.

Providing correct answers – or at least inspired guesses – is a responsibility we take very seriously. Our readers are all committed moviegoers spending hard-earned cash every week and they are very quick – frighteningly quick – to tell us when our recommendation proved poor.

It is this plain consumer advice that gives *Empire* reviews, collected here for the first time, their unique flavour. What you have in your hands is a contemporary Film Guide built to last, not a musty volume of academic argument gathering dust.

Of course, *Empire*'s unshakeable optimism has sometimes led us into flings we quickly came to regret (issue one's four star review of *Fletch Lives* is merely the first of many examples) and indeed one of the feature attractions of this particular guide is that it includes dozens of revised reviews completed with, shall we say, a cooler head.

However, don't expect *Empire* to stop having unwise movie crushes any time soon – as ever we remain utterly, foolishly, completely in love with movies. We hope you are too.

Colin

Colin Kennedy
Editor-In-Chief
EMPIRE

HOW TO USE THIS GUIDE

8 1/2 (1963) 1
(OTTO E MEZZO) 2
Starring: *Marcello Mastroianni (Guido Anselmi), Claudia Cardinale (Claudia), Anouk Aimee (Luisa Anselmi, Guido's Wife), Sandra Milo (Carla), Rossella Falk (Rossella), Barbara Steele (Gloria Morin)* 3
Director: *Federico Fellini*
Screenwriters: *Federico Fellini, Tullio Pinelli, Ennio Flaiano, Brunello Rondi, based on a story by Federico Fellini and Ennio Flaiano* 4
5 15/ 6 140 mins./7 Drama/8 Italy

9 **Awards:** *Academy Awards - Best Foreign Language Film, Best Black And White Costume*

10 **Director Guido Anselmi retreats to a spa. Between memories of his past, daydreams that turn nightmarish and the demands of wife, mistress and hangers-on, Guido can't concentrate on the science fiction film he is supposed to be making.**

11 Among the most important and influential films of the 1960s.

1 – Year of release
2 – Alternative title
3 – Cast and Character names
4 – Key credits
5 – Certificate
6 – Running time
7 – Genre
8 – Country of origin
9 – Awards info
10 – Plot summary
11 – Review

Films are listed alphabetically (ignoring definite and indefinite articles) by the titles by which we feel they are best known in the UK. While many foreign language films are listed under their English translation, others are listed by their original title. Alternative titles are placed in brackets.

The films are rated according to the following (scientifically tested) system

★★★★★ – Classic
★★★★ – Excellent
★★★ – Good
★★ – Fair
★ – Tragic

The awards information lists only the winners of the following awards ceremonies; The Academy Awards, The British Film And Television Academy Awards (The Baftas), The Cannes Film Festival, The Berlin Film Festival, The Venice Film Festival, The Golden Globes, The Golden Raspberry Awards ('The Razzies') and The Empire Film Awards.

All ratings refer to the most recent rating supplied by the BBFC, the British Board Of Film Classification. The ratings break down like this: U (suitable for audiences aged four years and over) PG (suitable for general viewing, but some scenes may be unsuitable for young children) 12/12A (suitable for 12 years and over. No one younger than 12 may see a '12A' film in a cinema unless accompanied by an adult) 15 (suitable only for 15 years and over) 18 (suitable only for adults). Some of the titles remain uncertificated and are identified by Unrated.

The genre designation is meant to provide some indication to the type of film but is by no means definitive (something like *Donnie Darko*, for example, defies easy categorisation, traversing countless genres from sci-fi to teen flick to mystery movie). The year provided is the year of copyright. The running time refers to the theatrical release only.

We welcome your criticisms, corrections and contributions. Please send your brickbats (and bouquets) to filmguide@empireonline.com or by snail mail to EMPIRE, Mappin House, 4 Winsley Street, London W1W 8HF.

*Other uses for this book include a paperweight, a draught excluder, a place you can hide a gun in like in spy films, a breeze block and a handy step you can use as part of any keep fit regime.

LIST OF CONTRIBUTORS

Gavin Bainbridge (GB)
Steve Beard (SBe)
Liz Beardsworth (LB)
Rob Beatty (RB)
Jo Berry (JB)
Darren Bignell (DB)
Amie Bolissian (AB)
Justin Bowyer (JBo)
Lloyd Bradley (LBr)
Simon Braund (SB)
Kat Brown (KB)
Phillipa Bloom (PB)
Deborah Brown (DBr)
Emma Cochrane (EC)
Andrew Collins (AC)
Clark Collis (CC)
Mark Cooper (MC)
Simon Crook (SC)
S C Dacy (SCD)
David Cavanagh (DC)
Jeff Dawson (JD)
Nick Dawson (ND)
Mark Dinning (MD)
Nick De Semlyen (NDS)
Tom Doyle (TD)
James Dyer (JD)
David Eimer (DE)
Angie Errigo (AE)
Miles Fielder (MF)
Rob Fraser (RF)
Ian Freer (IF)
Charles Gant (CG)
Andy Gill (AG)
Danny Graydon (DG)
Ed Halliwell (EH)
Jake Hamilton (JH)
Genevieve Harrison (GH)
Michael Hayden (MH)
Chris Heath (CH)
Christopher Hemblade (CHe)
David Hepworth (DH)
Chris Hewitt (CHe)
Tom Hibbert (TH)
David Hodges (DHo)
Mark Honigsbaum (MH)
Jane Howdle (JHo)
David Hughes (DHu)
Neil Jeffries (NJ)
Dan Jolin (DJ)
Colin Kennedy (CK)
Julian Ketchum (JK)
Robyn Karney (RK)
Will Lawrence (WL)
Trevor Lewis (TL)
Dorian Lynskey (DL)
Kenny Matheson (KM)
Bob McCabe (BM)
Jane McLuskey (JM)
Karen McLuskey (KM)
Barry McIlheney (BMc)
Kirsty McNeill (Kmc)
Colette Maude (CM)
Alan Morrison (AM)
Monika Maurer (MM)
John Mount (JM)
Matt Mueller (MMu)
Giala Murray (GM)
Ian Nathan (IN)
John Naughton (JN)
Kim Newman (KN)
Dee Nkabu (DN)
Andrew Osmond (AO)
Steve O'Hagen (S O'H)
Helen O'Hara (H O'H)
Lawrence O'Toole (LO'T)
David Parkinson (DP)
Patrick Peters (PP)
Elissa Van Poznak (EVP)
Pat Reid (PR)
Anthony Quinn (AQ)
Tony Quinn (TQ)
Alex Raynor (AR)
Olly Richards (OR)
Scott Russon (SR)
Mark Salisbury (MS)
Matt Snow (Msn)
Charles Shaar Murray (CSM)
Adam Smith (AS)
Anna Smith (ASm)
Andrew Stone (ASt)
Torene Svitil (TS)
Philip Thomas (PT)
William Thomas (WT)
Anne Thomson (AT)
Sam Toy (ST)
Marcus Trower (MT)
Tom Tunney (TT)
Matthew Turner (Mtu)
Caroline Westbrook (CW)
Patricia Wilson (PW)
Damon Wise (DW)
Richard Wiseman (RW)
Alex Yates (AY)
Jack Yeovil (JY)

EMPIRE Editor-In-Chief Colin Kennedy
Compiled and edited: Emma Cochrane, Ian Freer
Art Director: Ian Stevens
Art Editor Susan Carey
Picture Editors: Debi Berry, Stephanie Seelan, Kelly Preedy
Thanks to: Dan Jolin, Chris Hewitt, Olly Richards, Helen O'Hara, John Hitchcox, Liz Beardsworth, Nick de Semlyen, James Dyer, Amar Vijay, Sam Toy, Kat Brown, Pav Basra, Amie Bolissian, Nick Knowles
Special thanks: Emma Cochrane, Andrew Collins, Angie Errigo, Ian Freer, Barry McIlheney, Mark Salisbury, Adam Smith, Phil Thomas and Caroline Westbrook
Extra Special Thanks: Ian Nathan, Kim Newman and David Parkinson, without whom this book would not have been possible.

A BOUT DE SOUFFLE (BREATHLESS) (1959)

Starring: *Jean-Paul Belmondo (Michel Poiccard/Laszlo Kovacs), Jean Seberg (Patricia Franchini), Daniel Boulanger (Police Inspector), Jean-Luc Godard (Informer)*
Director: *Jean-Luc Godard*
Screenwriter: *Jean-Luc Godard*
15/89 mins./Crime/France

Stylishly alienated petty hood Michel Poiccard hares about Paris on a tear – impersonating a journalist, killing a cop, hanging out with his American girlfriend and collecting debts.

In 1959, a group of enthusiasts who had worked as critics before lifting up cameras got together and made this quick, cheap picture, dedicating it to Monogram, the Poverty Row studio which churned out Bela Lugosi or Charlie Chan Bs in the 40s. *A Bout De Souffle* started several major screen careers and kicked off the French *nouvelle vague*, the most exciting and influential film movement of the early 1960s. Before the decade was out, the jump-cuts and dizzying camerawork of this movie, partly the result of shooting with very little film stock, had percolated into the gene pool of Hollywood, eventually becoming the stuff of TV adverts and pop videos its makers would despise.

Jean-Paul Belmondo cops a Bogart attitude as a charismatic but vicious petty crook (first line: 'I'm a cunt, okay'), while Yankee gamine Jean Seberg sports a serious haircut as the hood's ironic, intellectual, ultimately treacherous girlfriend. Godard makes a tawdry anecdote exciting with unorthodox edits, improvisational jazz, actuality footage of bustling streets, film buff references (courtesy of co-scripter Francois Truffaut) and cool clothes. It stops for a lengthy spell as the main characters are shut up in a room and argue with each other for a subjective eternity, but even this sequence (the epitome of what you're not supposed to do in a first film) finds a rhythm and becomes gripping.

Mostly fast and loose, with a buzzing sense of cinematic potential, this is at once a homage to the American gangster film, and an attack on the very ideas of Americans, gangsters and films. ★★★★★ **KN**

A NOUS LA LIBERTÉ (1931)

Starring: *Henri Marchand (Emile), Raymond Cordy (Louis), Rolla France (Jeanne), Paul Olivier (Paul Imaque), Jacques Shelly (Paul)*
Director: *René Clair*
Screenwriter: *René Clair*
U/104 mins./Musical Satire/France

Emile escapes from prison and takes a job at the phonography factory founded by fellow fugitive Louis. However, both come to recognise that neither love nor fortune matters as much as friendship and being true to oneself.

Originally entitled Liberté Chérie, this scathing musical satire on the dehumanising effect of industrialisation was inspired by some wall-flowers that René Clair saw growing in a factory-pocked Parisian suburb. His hero, Emile, was based on that universal everyman, Charlie Chaplin (who returned the compliment in *Modern Times*), while the tycoon who exploits him, Louis, was modelled on another cinematic titan, Charles Pathé, who had first conceived of producing films on a conveyor belt principle in the early 1900s.

Although he was keen to rescue Talking Pictures from becoming animated radio by restoring the fluidity of silent cinema, Clair's primary purpose was to acknowledge the importance of labour, while championing the cause of the worker's dignity. Consequently, he emphasised the similarities between the employees at Louis's mechanised dystopia and the inmates at the prison where the boss had first encountered Emile. As in Clair's previous outing, *Le Million*, Lazare Meerson's sets were crucial to his design and they garnered the first Academy Award nomination ever accorded a French film.

Clair was also determined to lampoon the greed, corruption and pomposity of the capitalist élite and, thus, he presents nearly everyone not involved on the shop floor as a grasping schemer willing to scramble in the dust for a free franc – hence the unedifying cash scramble at the grand re-opening of the now fully automated phonograph plant that affords Louis and Emile the opportunity to quit the rat race and return to nature.

Managing to enrage sensitive souls on either side of the class divide, *A Nous La Liberté* disappointed at the box-office. Indeed, it was even banned in Hungary as 'an instrument of dangerous propaganda for the social order and peace among the classes'. Yet it now stands as a monument to cinematic humanism and represents the musical's first masterpiece. ★★★★★ **DP**

A PROPOS DE NICE (1930)

Directors: *Jean Vigo, Boris Kaufman*
Screenwriter: *Jean Vigo*
U/26 mins./Documentary/France

With Boris Kaufman shooting with a camera hidden beneath a blanket as he's pushed around Nice in a wheelchair, this is an avant-garde city symphony that contrasts the affluence of the tourist hot spots with the miserable poverty of those confined to the resort's backstreets.

Jean Vigo was working as an assistant to cinematographer Léonce-Henri Burel when he bought a Debrie camera with money donated by his father-in-law. While in Paris, taking a crash course in the city's cinemas, he met Boris Kaufman (Dziga-Vertov's brother) and, together with their wives, they conceived the outline for a documentary about Nice, where Vigo was living because of his fragile health.

Shooting on scraps of discarded film stock, the resulting short brought a political dimension to experimental cinema by spurning travelogue banality to concentrate on the ennui of the rich and the desperate struggle for survival of the Riviera's underclass. Barred from shooting in upmarket locations, Vigo quickly abandoned the calculated logic of his scenario and focused instead on the visceral impact of his subject matter, confident that audiences would make the intellectual leap between the juxtaposed images. But even if viewers had missed the contrasts between the hotels and the tenements, the lounging tourists and the forlorn urchins, the casinos and the gambling dens, the direct comparison between Nice's visitors and its residents was readily apparent in the climactic carnival sequence.

With his early death prompting many to lament what might have been, Vigo is the Buddy Holly of cinema. He made just three more films, amassing less than three hours screen time in his entire career. Yet *Taris* (1931), *Zéro De Conduite* (1933) and *L'Atalante* (1934) proved the missing link between the experimentation of the silent era and the golden age of talking pictures. With their naive energy and occasionally clumsy symbolism, they amalgamated the anarchic comedy of Max Linder and Charlie Chaplin, the revolutionary zeal of Dziga-Vertov and Sergei Eisenstein, the audacity of Surrealists like Luis Buñuel and the humanism of René Clair to forge a unique style that continues to inspire filmmakers around the world. ★★★★ **DP**

Jean Vigo (1905–1934)

Who was he: The *enfant terrible* of early French cinema. Completed three shorts and one feature.

Hallmarks: A magical poetic realism marked by radical experimentation.

If you see one film, see: *L'Atalante* (1934)

A.I. ARTIFICIAL INTELLIGENCE (2001)

Starring: *Hayley Joel Osment (David), Frances O'Connor (Monica Swinton), Sam Robards (Henry Swinton), Jude Law (Gigolo Joe), Brendan Gleeson (Lord Johnson-Johnson), William Hurt (Professor Hobby), Ben Kingsley (Narrator), Robin Williams (Voice of Dr. Know)*
Director: *Steven Spielberg*
Screenwriter: *Steven Spielberg, based on a screen story by Ian Watson and a short story 'Super-Toys Last All Summer Long' by Brian Aldiss*
12/145 mins./Sci-fi/Drama/USA

A robot boy programmed to experience human emotions embarks on a journey of self-discovery.

Whatever the backstory, that Stanley Kubrick implored Spielberg to make his long-cherished, existential sci-fi epic, or Spielberg hitched a lift on the late master's heritage, it doesn't matter. Sure, the film is loaded with Kubrickian touches (it commences with a cold, eloquent style, it refuses to be rushed, it's brimming with enormous, philosophical debate, its ending is potty), but this is the work of a living, breathing master – and, boy, is he good.

Taking Kubrick's nurtured sapling, Spielberg adds love, ILM miracle-grow and a fierce intellect so often overlooked (he scripted, remember), unfurling his imagination on a dazzling blend of *Pinocchio*, *Blade Runner*, *2001* and a whole lot more besides.

Big time sci-fi from a (not really) child's POV it may be, but forget a comforting *E.T.*-like fable. The film seethes with an edgy coldness that must have been born in the Kubrick vaults. Opening up with a familial drama, there is the nascent creepiness of a horror movie, as forlorn couple Monica and Henry are selected to take on David, a 'mecha' (robot) child capable of love. But once you encode the love circuits there's no going back. Naturally, Monica is freaked out, but her instincts to love take hold, even as she dares the irreversible.

These are weighty questions, indeed: What does it mean to be real? What does it mean to love? Does the power to love make us real? What is the price of loving? Gulp.

Osment is staggering. In a mesmerisingly controlled performance he creates a perfect balance between charm and otherworldliness, defying but imploring the watcher to empathise. This is a mighty old talent for one so young. Following a traumatic sequence between 'mother' and 'child', the film shifts gear as David journeys to the 'real' world. Accompanied by a groovy talking teddy bear, he pals up with sex-mecha Joe, escapes from a Flesh Fair (where humans gleefully exterminate mechas – very Schindleresque) and ventures to the noirish Oz of Rouge City.

Time to mention the CGI. *A.I.* is the finest example to date of the application of computer graphics to a storyline. In the ramshackle mechas of the Flesh Fair there are seamless half-faces, eyeless holes, actors' faces that split open to reveal their inner workings. Better still is the creation of a schizo near-future, equally antiseptic utopia and sleazy dystopia: Rouge City is Las Vegas gone mad, a neon-soaked dreamscape that beggars belief. David's quest concludes in the near-submerged Manhattan, a flawless vision of a drowned metropolis. There's half an argument to sit back and let the sheer beauty of the film wash over you. But it has somewhere else to take you, entirely. To the 'ending'.

Perplexing, infuriating, mind-blowing: it's a voyage into a wonderland where the fairy-tale motif becomes inseparable from the cool future-vision. You've got to admire Spielberg's daring – ditching the intellectual backbone for a spiritual send-off – but it doesn't sit easy. Some people might reject that wholesale; the majority might balk at the overlong and 'out there' ending. Perhaps that is the point. *A.I.* will have you debating until the landlord threatens to call the police. It's that kind of movie. Thank God for that. ★★★★★ **IN**

ⓓ ABBOTT AND COSTELLO MEET FRANKENSTEIN (1948)

Starring: *Bud Abbott (Chick Young), Lou Costello (Wilbur Grey), Lon Chaney Jr (Lawrence Talbot/The Wolf Man), Bela Lugosi (Dracula), Glenn Strange (The Monster)*
Director: *Charles Barton*
Screenwriters: *Robert Lees, Frederic L. Rinaldo, John Grant, based on the novel* Frankenstein *by Mary Shelley*
U/83 mins./Comedy/Horror/USA

Deliverymen Chick and Wilbur transport the Frankenstein Monster to a Florida castle where Dracula plots to give the creature dimwit Chick's brain. The Wolf Man enlists the comedians' aid in battling the vampire.

In *Frankenstein Meets The Wolf Man*, *House Of Frankenstein* and *House Of Dracula*, Universal Pictures teamed their various monsters in messy, enjoyable gothic scrambles. By 1948, the horror saga had run out of steam and the series that had begun with Dracula and Frankenstein in 1931 wound up pitting the studio's copyrighted famous monsters against the hugely popular comedy team of Abbott and Costello. The result was such a hit that Bud and Lou went on to mix it with Boris Karloff, the Mummy, Jekyll and Hyde and the Invisible Man.

Actually, it's not one of Abbott and Costello's better vehicles – they do a lot of annoying whining and slapping business, often in routines where a babyish Lou tries to convince the grumpy Bud that there's a monster approaching, but not much of the 'who's on first'-style vaudeville crosstalk that made them popular in the first place. It misses an obvious comic possibility: Dracula's plan to put Lou's brain in the Monster's body is thwarted, which means no scene in which the flatheaded giant bawls and bellows like Costello.

Bela Lugosi, in one of the few A-grade productions of his later career, makes a dignified return to the role that had made (and cursed) his career, but the most doggy enthusiasm comes (aptly) from the try-anything-for-a-laugh Lon Chaney Jr as Larry Talbot, his character from *The Wolf Man*. There are a few funny exchanges: Chaney: 'you don't understand, every night when the moon is full, I turn into a wolf!' Costello: 'Yeah, you and thirty million other guys!' ★★★ **KN**

ⓓ THE ABOMINABLE DR PHIBES (1971)

Starring: *Vincent Price (Dr Anton Phibes), Joseph Cotton (Dr Vesalius), Virginia North (Vulnavia), Terry Thomas (Dr Longstreet), Sean Bury (Lem Vesalius), Susan Travers (Nurse Allen)*
Director: *Robert Fuest*
Screenwriters: *James Whiton, William Goldstein*
15/94 mins./Horror/USA

After a team of doctors fail to save his beloved wife after a car crash, insane fellow practitioner Dr Anton Phibes concocts an elaborate revenge, murdering each of them in the style of the Biblical plagues of Egypt: rats, locusts' blood etc.

Very much the centrepiece of Vincent Price's third term as the creepy tsar of horror – following the traditional gloom of the '50s (see *House Of Wax*) and the lurid, Roger Corman directed flamboyance of the '60s (see *Fall Of The House Of Usher*) – this madcap revenge flick is a gothic hoot. Hammer horror in its gaudy, over-bearing, art deco stylings (although, it isn't from that stable) it is a haughty, highly entertaining entry in British horror (it was actually financed by MGM) that blends, almost imperceptibly, gallows humour and genuine fright.

Although set in the 1920s, director Robert Fuest transports the whodunit devices of Agatha Christie and a modern droll humour into Phibes twisted conniving. On his trail is a classic British plod, slow but unshakable, in Inspector Trout (Peter Jeffery) puzzled by the deranged features of the case. Phibes, you see, is in possession of the perfect alibi – he's dead ('perishing' in another car crash rushing to be by his wife's side). This also grants a scabby, proto-Freddie make-up job for Price just to add a supernatural gauze over what is essentially a flowery slasher movie.

What makes the film as rich as it is silly, is both Price's smoked-ham performance (it is moot to criticise such camp revelries, he's a half-dead, pucker-faced, diabolical genius who speaks through a mechanical voice-box – can that be overplayed?) and the sheer imagination applied to the death sequences (which make up the body of the film). For the 'rats' stage of the plot, ravenous rodents are snuck into the cockpit of one sorry doctor, another has their skull crushed by a 'frog mask'. There is even a trace of subtlety no less, in the gradual shift from sympathy to reviling in our opinion of Phibes' actions.

The language, too, matches the exotic sets and baroque deaths, with a mock-Shakespearean pomposity that Price milks for every strident syllable: 'My precious jewel, I will join you in your setting. We shall be reunited forever in a secluded corner of the great Elysian field of the beautiful beyond!' Such barmy cadences are sorely missed from the genre that has since taken itself far too seriously. ★★★★ **IN**

ⓓ ABOUT A BOY (2002)

Starring: *Hugh Grant (Will), Toni Collette (Fiona Brewer), Rachel Weisz (Rachel), Nicholas Hoult (Marcus Brewer), Sharon Small (Christine)*
Directors: *Paul Weitz, Chris Weitz*
Screenwriters: *Peter Hedges, Paul and Chris Weitz, based on a novel by Nick Hornby*
12/102 mins./Drama/Comedy/UK/USA/Germany/France

Awards: *Empire Awards – Best Actor*

Will, a self-centred 38-year-old, discovers the joys of responsibility when he is forced to spend time with an outcast 12-year-old.

Based on a hugely successful book by Nick Hornby, peppered with British acting talent and boasting the Midas touch of Tim Bevan and Eric Fellner, it comes as something of a shock to note that what appears to be an archetypal Working Title production is directed by the New York siblings behind *American Pie*, and was developed by Robert De Niro's company, Tribeca.

Indeed, after the celluloid version of Hornby's *High Fidelity* made a smooth transatlantic transplant, it's a wonder that De Niro and co. didn't seriously consider relocating shallow man-boy Will from Hornby's native Finsbury to somewhere cooler like, well, Manhattan. The reason can be found in the actor Tribeca picked to play Will (before Working Title became attached) – Hugh Grant. In his native country, there exists a vocal minority who resist – or perhaps resent – the comedic charms of Hugh Grant. But Grant is as fine a light-comic actor as these shores have produced since another Grant (Cary) showcased his gossamer talents for RKO some 60 years ago. In those days of great studio product, Grant (Cary) was mostly spared criticism for endless takes on his patented patter – Grant (Hugh) has not been so lucky. If we happily admit that Grant's range is limited, the calibration he employs seems endlessly fine.

About A Boy's funniest scenes do allow him to once more riff on the embarrassed English, but he has carefully picked out a new melody line. The scruffy haircut and North London-ish accent are clues – this is not a well-intentioned fop, but a selfish, Seinfeldian character (George with hair, Jerry with better trainers), who lands in endless trouble entirely of his own making. And, once again, Grant showcases consummate skill with occasionally modest material. Watching him work an under-written punch-line around his face – eyes darting, nose twitching – is to watch a master craftsman employing – and enjoying – all the tools at his disposal. Simply put: when Grant is on screen, the movie is a joy. Sadly, at least nominally, this is a two-hander.

Nicholas Hoult is an okay child actor who enjoys a small share of the gags, but when his character wistfully wishes he was Haley Joel Osment (and had his money), you may be tempted to agree. Poor Hoult has a lot to carry – including part of the narration and most of the emotional range – and at times you can feel the strain. Effortless these episodes are not.

There are other problems, too. When Will's voice-over slices neatly into the dialogue – a sarcastic subconscious – you get a sense of Hornby's playful narration. Too often, however, the twin voice-overs are bland and unnecessary. And while Collette and Weisz provide solid support, the movie misses the raft of British eccentrics who made Notting Hill and Four Weddings such breakout hits.

Ultimately, however, the plusses outweigh the minuses. The restraint shown by the brothers Weitz might disappoint those who know them solely from home-baked goods, but they tell this simple story with admirable clarity, employing fluid camera strokes and imaginative framing. Better yet, Badly Drawn Boy's song-based score is a triumph, a musical meta-narrative, adding character without threatening cohesion. ★★★★ **CK**

ABOUT SCHMIDT (2002)

Starring: *Jack Nicholson (Warren Schmidt), Kathy Bates (Roberta Hertzel), Hope Davis (Jeannie Schmidt), Dermot Mulroney (Randall Hertzel)*
Director: *Alexander Payne*
Screenwriters: *Alexander Payne, Jim Taylor, based on the novel by Louis Begley and the screenplay* The Coward *by Alexander Payne.*
15/125 mins./Comedy/Drama/USA
Awards: *Golden Globes – Best Actor, Best Screenplay*

Insurance-risk calculator Warren R. Schmidt retires from work and prepares for a long, uneventful journey to the grave. When his wife dies, however, he feels compelled to stop his daughter from marrying a loser.

In the year Jack Nicholson turned 65, while tabloids still persisted in focusing on his Lothario ways, this thoughtful, understated black comedy proved there was more to him than a raised eyebrow and rakish laugh.

Fat and frustrated, with a fetching comb-over, his Warren Schmidt is a man who has reached the scrapheap of retirement and is wondering where his life went. To settle his conscience, Schmidt sponsors an African child by post and, in the movie's first great laugh-out-loud moment, spills out all his venom about his dissatisfaction with his lot.

This is not simply a golden-years crisis movie, however, and when his homely but irritating wife Helen dies, director Payne expertly sets Schmidt on his path to fulfilment, which he believes will happen if he sabotages his daughter's marriage to a dull mattress salesman (a hilarious Mulroney).

Dealing with Middle America's lost dreams and its tacit class system, this taps perfectly into Nicholson's wonderfully dry comic talents. Payne has crafted a superb follow-up to 1999's *Election*. ★★★★ **DW**

ABSOLUTE BEGINNERS (1986)

Starring: *Eddie O'Connell (Colin), Patsy Kensit (Crepe Suzette), James Fox (Henley Of Mayfair), David Bowie (Vendice Partners), Ray Davies (Arthur), Mandy Rice-Davies (Flora)*
Director: *Julian Temple*
Screenwriters: *Richard Burridge, Terry Johnson, Don MacPherson, Christopher Wicking, based on the novel by Colin MacInnes*
15/108 mins./Musical/UK

1958. Low-level photographer Colin must climb the fashion tree pretty quickly if he's going to keep the love of model Crepe Suzette whose affections tend to be career-orientated.

Now notorious for being a great big waste of British money, talent and time, this featherbrained musical-drama certainly never held back on ambition. Julian Temple, moving on from his video-director stroke punk chronicler role of the late 70s, attempts to attach a caustic edge to a grand slab of self-satisfied, over directed pop-nonsense.

Any film that attempts to out-flamboyance Orson Welles, by hanging on longer than *Touch Of Evil*'s fabled four-minute opening tracking shot, is up to no good. From there on, the great lumbering, look-at-me style proceeds to dance all over the meagre mewling of the plot. The song and dance numbers are so overcooked they bleed into a mild form of bedlam – with the sole exception of Bowie's snazzy title song (the best thing the movie gives us). Temple, wrestling his way through a mightily troubled production, is trying to evoke the colour and energy that accompanied the emergence of teenage rebellion, but his cast haplessly flounder with the mock-street speak and cardboard ideas of youth and identity. And mixing in a pot-pourri of trendy faces does not credibility grant: Ray Davies, Mandy Rice-Davies, Edward Tudor-Pole and a glassy-eyed Bowie all look as if they've been sold a pup.

Little of it actually recalls MacInnes' socially minded novel. That is until Temple, clearly struck by the very evident shallowness of his endeavours, decided to hastily paste on a race riot sequence at the end. It's a forlorn attempt to fool us into thinking that this was anything more than just a ragged attempt to resurrect both the ailing British film industry and the dusty musical format. It failed on both counts. ★★ **IN**

THE ABYSS (1989)

Starring: *Ed Harris (Bud Brigman), Mary Elizabeth Mastrantonio (Lindsey Brigman), Michael Biehn (Lt Coffey), George Robert Klek (White), John Bedford Lloyd ('Jammer' Willis)*
Director: *James Cameron*
Screenwriter: *James Cameron*
15/146 mins./Sci-fi/USA
Awards: *Academy Award – Best Visual Effects*

A diving crew, investigating a deep underwater trench, discover a mysterious space ship.

James Cameron, it's said, is prone to nightmares. And people who agree to appear in his films tend to wind up sharing them. In the case of *The Abyss*, his fourth movie, the nightmare was of a towering tidal wave rolling across an endless ocean. But the nightmare he inflicted on his cast and crew would not happen on the sea's surface, but 40 feet under pitch black water in a half completed nuclear power station cooling pond in Gaffney, South Carolina. It was, in a precursor of the immense tank he would build for Titanic, the largest underwater set ever constructed. And it made Ed Harris cry.

Tales of the making of *The Abyss* (or 'The Abuse' as key grips bleakly wisecracked) are legion. There was the over-chlorinated water that made actor's hair turn green then white. There were the crew dives so long and deep that hours of depressurisation was required. There was Cameron himself, dangling upside down in a depressurisation tank to relieve the pain inflicted by his diving helmet while watching dailies through an inches thick glass porthole. And there was Ed Harris, pulling his car over on the way back to the hotel after another day in the tank and suddenly bursting into tears. 'Life's abyss,' read the inevitable, sarcastically daubed crew tee-shirt. 'And then you dive.'

But if the garish stories surrounding the *Abyss*' hellish incubation are entirely typical of Cameron, then the movie that emerged is equally so. Bombastic, spectacular, loud, ambitious and flawed, it's Cameron at his exuberant, crowd-pleasing best. Mention the word 'subtlety' to the crazed Canuck and he might well look at you as if you'd just suggested he and his sister get down and beat out the rhythm of love (after all this is the man who announced 'Merchant Ivory can kiss my ass!' when quizzed on the period detail of *Titanic*). But no living director, with the possible exception of Steven Spielberg, works so hard to utterly involve an audience, put the budget on the screen and deliver a deliriously good time.

Essentially *The Abyss* bolts the wondrous lightshows of *Close Encounters Of The Third Kind* to the humanist message of *The Day The Earth Stood Still* and transplants the resulting cocktail to a disabled undersea drilling rig thousands of feet beneath the ocean on the cusp of a fathomless trench where an American nuclear submarine has recently run aground. Trapped in a glorified leaky tin can with the oxygen running out, Cameron's cast of hardbitten grease-monkeys led by Virgil 'Bud' Brigman (Harris) witness spectacular, ephemeral glowing creatures floating in the inky blackness while they battle both the rapidly expiring time and the increasingly schizoid American military, represented by SEAL Michael Biehn, who are bent on nuking the watery critters.

Grouchy critics whinged that Cameron's movie seemed to be more interested in technology than people and indeed this is science fiction at the nuts and bolts level. Cameron's camera drifts lovingly over the meticulously researched sub-aquatic sets delivering a kind of hard-core techno-porn. Mini-subs (designed by Cameron's brother, who not only pioneered the technology required for the *Titanic* shoot but essays the challenging role of 'dead sailor with crab crawling out of mouth') glide around the drilling rig; live rats are submerged in oxygenated fluorocarbons (for real, much to the chagrin of the British censors who snipped the scene even though none of the five rodents dunked suffered any ill-effects) and in a CG sequence that was, given the newness of the technology, breathtaking, the water itself forms into a snaking, glistening tentacle. But like the majority of Cameron's work, there is a human element. Melodramatic and overblown perhaps, but it's there most obviously in the sequence where Virgil has to watch his wife (Mary Elizabeth Mastrantonio) drown and be revived in front of him. Here he delivers the kind of cash-and-carry bulk buy emotion with which he habitually fills the screen. As we said, subtlety is not Cameron's forte; impact is.

Which leads us to the much maligned ending. Or rather couple of endings since Cameron, stung by criticisms of the original conclusion forced on him by the studio, released a special edition with an extended final sequence. In truth, neither of them are any good; the second only adding some cod-motivation for the underwater aliens' revealing themselves (that hoary old cliché: stock newsreel footage of concentration camps and H-Bomb blasts – well that'll justify the destruction of humanity then) as well as some distinctly dodgy tidal wave effects to conclude.

The problem is that, direct rip-off of *Close Encounters* that it is, it requires the one emotion that Cameron simply can't put on celluloid: innocent wonder. As it would be if Spielberg tried to direct a 200-pound muscle-bound cyborg blowing seven shades of guano out of a police station, director and sequence simply don't gel. Many audiences tumbled out of multiplexes bemoaning the final daft ten minutes rather than reeling at the preceding 136. Ironically enough it is *The Abyss*' attempt to go deep that is it's only flaw. ★★★★ **AS**

Movie Trivia: The Abyss

The drowned sailor out of whose mouth a crab crawls is James Cameron's brother, Mike. Due to water over-chlorination, many actors and crew saw their hair turn green. Because of the tough shoot, the crew started wearing T-shirts bearing the legend: 'Life's An Abyss . . . And Then You Dive.'

ACCATONE (1961)

Starring: *Franco Citti (Vittorio Accatone), Franca Pasut (Stella), Silvana Corsini (Maddalena), Paola Guidi (Ascenza)*
Director: *Pier Paolo Pasolini*
Screenwriters: *Pier Paolo Pasolini, Sergio Citti*
15/120 mins./Drama/Italy

Vittorio, a Roman street hood – known to his mates as Accatone – falls in love with Stella when he attempts to recruit her as a prostitute. He vows to go straight, but is soon forced to commit increasingly risky crimes.

Twenty-seven year-old Pier Paolo Pasolini was already a published poet by the time he arrived in Rome in 1949 as a gay, Marxist country boy whose poverty quickly reduced him to an association with the ragazzi or slum punks with whom he identified and from whom he would continue to purchase sexual favours until he was murdered by one in 1975.

In addition to participating in a gas station robbery, Pasolini also helped a bandit escape from the police and he had achieved a certain notoriety before he published his first novel, *Ragazzi Di Vita*, in 1955. Fending off a charge of obscenity, he followed this with *Una Vita Violenta* , which served as the basis for *Accatone*.

Having started screenwriting in 1954, Pasolini hoped to use his contacts to fund the film. But Federico Fellini withdrew his support when he saw some test footage, which bore a naive resemblance to Carl Theodore Dreyer's *The Passion Of Joan Of Arc*. However, another previous collaborator, Mauro Bolognini, was more impressed and he persuaded Alfredo Bini to produce and Sergio Citti not only to co-script, but also to enlist his brother, Franco, for the title role.

Bernardo Bertolucci, who served as an assistant director, claimed that Pasolini was more influenced by Renaissance painting than cinema in seeking 'an absolute simplicity of expression'. Yet several critics have proclaimed that Pasolini's intuitive artistic sensibilities shaped the iconic, if anti-heroic Accatone's squalid pilgrimage around a city of seemingly redundant religious reliquery to the strains of Bach's *St Matthew's Passion*. However, traces of René Clair, Jean Renoir, Vittorio De Sica and Roberto Rossellini can be detected both in the occasionally sentimental humanism, its use of authentic locations and non-professional players and in the unsophisticated style, whose raw realism was to remain a feature of Pasolini's cinema. ★★★★ **DP**

THE ACCUSED (1988)

Starring *Kelly McGillis (Kathryn Murphy), Jodie Foster (Sarah Tobias), Bernie Coukon (Kenneth Joyce), Leo Rossi (Cliff Albrecht)*
Director: *John Kaplan*
Screenwriter: *Tom Topor*
18/110mins./Drama/USA

Awards: *Academy Awards – Best Actress (Jodie Foster), Golden Globes – Best Actress*

Having failed to bring her attackers to justice, a young rape victim goes to court to take on the witnesses who encouraged their crime.

In the United States of America, a rape is reported every six minutes. One of every four rape victims is attacked by two or more assailants. These are the grim statistics against which *The Accused* is played out, and it's to the credit of Kaplan and his cast that this dark and bitter pill has not been sweetened by the Hollywood bubblegum machine.

Jodie Foster, of course, won an Oscar for her extraordinary portrayal of rape victim Sarah Tobias – a role which was originally offered to, and turned down by, Kelly McGillis, herself the survivor of a rape. Instead, McGillis elected to play Kathryn Murphy, the deputy D.A. who takes on Sarah's case.

What's astonishing is how quickly and easily Sarah is marginalised by a legal and social structure which simply isn't geared to handle anyone like her. She's too loud, too complex. She smokes dope, drinks, hangs out with a biker, waits tables and likes to 'fool around'. When she is brutally raped by three men in a bar, Sarah is considered by Murphy to be too unreliable a witness to take the stand, and as a result the men get off on a lesser charge. Outraged, she shames McGillis into trying to convict the onlookers who, she says, were clapping and cheering and who would therefore be guilty of 'criminal solicitation'.

Kaplan and scriptwriter Tom Topor use McGillis' development to track some uncomfortable and complex social issues – the way Sarah's world collides with the sleazy plea-bargaining world of her lawyers; the way she has to fight against Murphy's initial distaste; the way she finds herself laughing outside a record store with a guy who turns out to have been at the bar that night.

Foster is simply fantastic as the tough Sarah, unshakeable in her belief that justice has not been done and that she has a right to demand it. McGillis, from a slow start, builds beautifully and by the time the action has switched to the courtroom, she has shed her starchy persona for a true advocate's passion. Her coaxing of Foster's testimony results finally in each sentence from Sarah ending with 'was inside of me', and it's enough to break your heart.

When it comes, almost at the end of the film in flashback, the rape scene is devastating, harrowing and utterly convincing; the suggestion that it's either gratuitous or voyeuristic is, frankly, nonsense. Rather, it's the point towards which the film hurtles from the opening scene in which Sarah emerges screaming from the bar, clutching her torn blouse.

The Accused received phenomenal critical acclaim and success at the box-office. If you missed it at the cinema, do yourself a favour. Don't miss it now. ★★★★★ **RB**

ACE IN THE HOLE (1951)

Starring: *Kirk Douglas (Charles 'Chuck' Tatum), Jan Sterling (Lorraine Minosa), Robert Arthur (Herbie Cook), Porter Hall (Jacob Q. Boot)*
Director: *Billy Wilder*
Screenwriters: *Billy Wilder, Lesser Samuels and Walter Newman*
Drama/U/111 mins./USA

Hired by a New Mexico paper, unprincipled big-city reporter Charles Tatum not only cajoles the national media into covering the story of a man trapped in a cave, but also lures the townsfolk into competing for their moment in the spotlight.

Screenwriters Lesser Samuels and Walter Newman were Oscar nominated for this hard-nosed, fact-based Billy Wilder melodrama, which dared to suggest that American life more closely resembled the cold, cynical core of a Frank Capra picture than the cornball, feel-good finale.

Robert Riskin, who had scripted such Capra classics as *Mr Deeds Goes To Town* and *Meet John Doe*, had already hinted that the American Dream was going sour in *Magic Town*, a 1947 satire, in which a homely burgh is corrupted when James Stewart proclaims it the embodiment of US universality. But, Wilder took such coy irony to its logical extremes in this savage follow-up to *Sunset Blvd.* and audiences who had only just seen Kirk Douglas betray the badge in William Wyler's *Detective Story* knew exactly what to expect when his New York hack walked into the office of an Albuquerque newspaper which proudly hung the hand-embroidered motto 'Tell the Truth' on its wall.

The very fact that *Ace In The Hole* (which Paramount re-issued as *The Big Carnival*, hoping to recoup some of its box-office losses) is one of the innumerable movies to have been lampooned by *The Simpsons* proves that this neglected classic has only grown in relevance since it first exposed the pernicious underside of celebrity culture. But in the early 1950s, audiences were appalled to see both decent, small-town folk cashing in on the misfortune of Leo Minosa and the undisguised relish with which Tatum approaches his work, which begins with him delaying the rescue for publicity purposes and ends with him exploiting the plight of the victim's already stressed wife, Lorraine (Sterling).

Douglas is chillingly superb, as he manipulates the amorality of his neighbours, whose ghoulish fascination with his 'human interest' story will be familiar to anyone addicted to tabloid tittle-tattle. ★★★★ **DP**

ACE VENTURA: PET DETECTIVE (1993)

Starring: *Jim Carrey (Ace Ventura), Courtenay Cox (Melissa), Sean Young (Lieutenant Lois Einhorn), Tone Loc (Emilio)*
Director: *Tom Shadyac*
Screenwriters: *Jack Bernstein, Tom Shadyac, Jim Carrey, from a story by Jack Bernstein*
12/85 mins./Comedy/USA

Ace is an unorthodox private detective in that he specialises in looking for animals. When the dolphin mascot of the Miami football team disappears just before the Superbowl, Ace is called in to track down the thief.

A surprisingly massive hit at the US box office, this private detective spoof marked the feature breakthrough of American comedian Jim Carrey whose act, on this evidence at least, seemed to consist solely of facial contortions, manic mannerisms and rubber-limbed goofyness. As Ace Ventura, Pet Detective, Carrey is a latterday Doctor Dolittle by way of *Naked Gun*'s Lt. Drebin, an animal sniffer-outer who specialises in returning pets to their owners.

The plot is almost absurdly funny – almost. When Snowflake, the Miami Dolphins' mascot, is kidnapped a fortnight before the side's Superbowl appearance, Ace is called in by flaky Dolphins executive Melissa (Cox) to track the mammal down. Ace deduces that the kidnapper must be a Dolphins player, eventually narrowing his search down to Ray Finkle, a former Miami kicker who lost his side the championship at the '84 Superbowl, and won himself a trip to the loony bin.

Tagline
He's the best there is. (Actually, he's the only one there is.)

Carrey gags his way through proceedings like a poor man's Jerry Lewis, stooping so low as to talk out of his rectum (honest) in his pursuit of a laugh. There's one good *Crying Game* gag and a number of minor moments of mirth, but nowhere near enough to sustain a 90-minute movie. American football fans might go all wobbly at the sight of quarterback Dan Marino and sundry other real-life Dolphins in bit parts, but most folk over school-age will just gape open-mouthed at the inanity of it all. ★★ **JK**

ACE VENTURA: WHEN NATURE CALLS (1995)

Starring: *Jim Carrey (Ace Ventura), Ian McNeice (Fulton Greenwall), Simon Callow (Vincent Cadby), Maynard Eziaski (Ouda), Bob Gunton (Burton Quinn), Sophie Okonedo (The Wachati Princess)*
Director: *Steve Oedekerk*
Screenwriter: *Steve Odekerk, based on characters created by Jack Bernstein*
Producer: *James G. Robinson*
PG/90 mins./Comedy/USA

Ace Ventura is called on to help prevent a tribal war in Africa by finding a sacred white bat.

In 1993, a movie based on the unlikely premise that a pet detective could scrape a decent living in the world of big business, burst onto the scene to unprecedented box office, paving the way to eight-figure salaries and world domination for a little-known comedian by the name of Jim Carrey. The inevitable sequel took $40 million in its opening US weekend and while Ace Ventura is still not the best way to utilise Carrey's talents, this follow-up kept Carreymania on the boil.

Set in Africa (although filmed in America), this kicks off with a brilliant lampoon of *Cliffhanger* involving Carrey and a cute racoon. Sadly nothing that follows is quite as inspired – the grief-stricken Ace retreats to a Tibetan monastery, only to be summoned by British emissary Fulton Greenwall to help prevent a tribal war by rescuing a stolen sacred white bat. And that's about it really, with minimal plot taking a back seat to the wild face-pulling antics of our hero as he journeys to Africa, japes about with the two opposing tribes, and attempts to crack the case in his own inimitable style.

As expected the gags come faster than the man's bank balance accumulates, the consequence being that too many fall flat, too often. And all but the most devoted fans of Carrey's elastic phizog will find his frenzied display of mugging wears thin way too soon. However, it is saved by some preposterously silly set-pieces (in particular, one which proves just how much fun you can have with bunny shapes and a slide projector and, ahem, a rhino giving birth to the bequiffed hero) that prove to be so childishly ridiculous you'd have to be made of stone not to find yourself giggling.

Ace may not be as pant-soilingly hysterical as *Dumb And Dumber*, and the character hasn't *The Mask*'s dazzling charm, but there's enough low-brow entertainment here to entertain. ★★★ **CW**

ADAM'S RIB (1949)

Starring: *Katharine Hepburn (Amanda Bonner), Spencer Tracy (Adam Bonner), Judy Holiday (Doris Attinger), Tom Ewell (Warren Francis Attinger), Jean Hagen (Beryl Caighn)*
Director: *George Cukor*
Screenwriters: *Ruth Gordon, Garson Kanin*
PG/101 mins./Romance/Comedy/USA

After a wife attempts to murder her philandering husband, their case is taken up by married attorneys, Adam and Amanda Bonner. Albeit, each on opposing sides of the courtroom.

It is based on a true story of marital crisis, written by a husband and wife duo (Gordon and Kanin) and performed by one of Hollywood's most dynamic on- and off-screen couples (Hepburn and Tracy), so George Cukor's spiky, playful, motor-mouthed comedy was never going to stint on home truths. You can't help but catch the tracerfire of previous bickering in Hepburn's beady eyes as she unleashes another volley toward her partner. The real and the fictional blur to salty effect in this minor classic, which, alongside *The Philadelphia Story* (far less of a screwball), is the high-water mark of Cukor's attempts to bottle up the battle of the sexes.

His film is very stagey, Cukor prefers to lock his camera in place and let his actors fill the frame with energy. Hepburn revs herself into such a sense of righteous indignation, taking aim at the male archetypes being upheld by her laidback husband, she threatens to slip into imbalance. But she is too good an actress to let Amanda lose her way – the script's bites and barbs leap fully-formed from her mouth without a slip or a gabble. Tracy, by contrast, eases back on the gears, wearing a wry look of uncaring. Her gales blow right over him. Little wonder, she's so het up.

The danger is we could take sides, but she is too much fun. Amanda's case seems to hinge on the dubious legality of sexual stereotyping: if the sexes in the case were reversed the husband would be found innocent. No matter, the point is whatever can fuel the fire that is all but incinerating their marriage, has comedy value. ★★★★ **IN**

ADAPTATION (2002)

Starring: *Nicolas Cage (Charlie Kaufman/Donald Kaufman), Meryl Streep (Susan Orlean), Chris Cooper (John Laroche), Tilda Swinton (Valerie), Brian Cox (Robert McKee), Judy Greer (Alice the Waitress), Maggie Gyllenhaal (Caroline)*
Director: *Spike Jonze*
Screenwriters: *Charlie Kaufman, Donald Kaufman based on the novel* The Orchid Thief *by Susan Orlean*
15/114 mins./Comedy/Drama/USA
Awards: *Academy Award – Best Supporting Actor (Chris Cooper), BAFTA – Best Adapted Screenplay, Golden Globes – Best Supporting Actor, Best Supporting Actress (Meryl Streep)*

Commissioned to adapt a non-fiction novel into a screenplay, screenwriter Charlie Kaufman ends up writing himself into the story with bizarre results.

Now here's an oddity: an Oscar-nominated screenwriter is asked to write an adaptation of *The Orchid Thief*, journalist Susan Orlean's bestselling novel about a horticultural poacher, but instead delivers a script about him trying to write said screenplay. His twin is credited as co-author, even though he only exists in the film. The author of the book and its protagonist become involved in a romantic subplot that has little to do with the content of the book, but is written about by the screenwriter in his film. And several alligators show up along the way. Confused yet?

Welcome to the world of Spike Jonze and Charlie Kaufman, who follow up *Being John Malkovich* with another dose of inspired lunacy that is set to baffle and dazzle moviegoers in equal measures.

Cage is as good as he has ever been in the dual roles of Charlie Kaufman and his 'twin brother', Donald. While the latter is a brash, confident irritant who also embarks upon a screenwriting career after attending a course by screenwriting guru Robert McKee, Charlie is a bag of neuroses – stricken with writer's block and convinced he is incompetent, physically revolting and socially inept.

Streep, as Orlean, and Cooper, as Laroche, both excel as similarly desperate people nursing their own personal heartache. However much Kaufman may have embellished the truth about his own personality, there's no denying the fact that his self-deprecating self-portrait is superb. What's more, he taps into the nuances of the tortured artist – from writer's block and insomnia, to the sheer frustration of having one's train of thought interrupted – with razor-sharp accuracy. And, in a way, that's almost the film's downfall; at times it assumes its audience knows more than it does, and its dependence on jokes about McKee, the film industry and the pressures of screenwriting may well pass over the heads of some viewers. The climax, especially, is a rather sour satire of narrative conventions that will leave most of the audience either baffled or patronised. ★★★★ **CW**

THE ADDAMS FAMILY (1991)

Starring: *Anjelica Huston (Morticia Addams), Raul Julia (Gomez Addams), Christopher Lloyd (Uncle Fester Addams/Gordon Craven), Dan Hedaya (Tully Alford), Christina Ricci (Wednesday Addams)*
Director: *Barry Sonnenfeld*
Screenwriter: *Caroline Thompson*
PG/99 mins./Comedy/Horror/USA

A loan shark and his crooked accountant plan to steal the Addams Family's fortune by introducing a fake Uncle Fester into the household.

This is the holiday treat for people whose idea of a Christmas film is one that opens with merry carollers about to be splatted with a pot of boiling oil from the ramparts of Chez Addams. Summing up what passes for a plot in this lavishly mounted wheeze might not spoil the pivotal 'twist' that anyone over the age of reason will rumble speedily. But it would surely be a waste of time, since the feeble effort to impose a storyline on Charles Addams' wittily macabre New Yorker cartoon creations merely gets in the way of the jokes.

Taken as a Big Film it may disappoint because, after all, it isn't 'about' anything. Taken as a string of ghoulish gags with some hilarious one-liners, delivered in a wonderfully spooky, kooky manor set, it's quite ridiculous but fun. Magnificent Anjelica Huston might have been born for Addams' Morticia. She's like a long drink of contaminated water as the chalk-faced, black-shrouded vamp dubbed, with absurd inappropriateness, 'Tish' by her doting, wild-eyed Gomez (hammy Julia). Christopher Lloyd is also a hoot as the psychopathic Fester, but 11-year-old Christina Ricci (Cher's swimming sprog in *Mermaids*) gives them both a run for their money with some of the best lines and biggest laughs as weird little Wednesday. 'We're going to play a game,' she explains to repugnant sibling Pugsley as she straps him into an electric chair, 'It's called Is There A God?'

The hand they call Thing has more interesting things to do here than it did in the TV series thanks to matte magic, but apart from that it's not wildly superior or different in tone, just a lot more expensive and a bit more bizarre. The more perverse quips – 'Don't torture yourself, Gomez. That's my job.' – should escape younger members of the audience, for whom all of it but the knockabout gore gags may well seem bewildering. But there are enough deliciously sick moments to amuse the more, er, sophisticated. **★★★ AS**

THE ADDICTION (1995)

Starring: *Lili Taylor (Kathleen Conklin), Christopher Walken (Peina), Annabella Sciorra (Casanova), Edie Falco (Jean), Professor (Paul Calderon)*
Director: *Abel Ferrara*
Screenwriter: *Nicholas St John*
18/82 mins./Drama/Horror/USA

An anthropology student is bitten by a vampire and finds her thirst for human blood unquenchable.

In *Bad Lieutenant*, Abel Ferrara suggested drug addicts were like vampires; here, he shows vampires in the grip of an addiction. Since *Driller Killer*, Ferrara has been American cinema's most irredeemable maverick, as much for his commitment to arthouse intensity as for his willingness to be more extreme in his vision of violence and despair than anyone working in the straight horror film.

Postgraduate student Taylor is dragged into an alleyway by a well-dressed Sciorra and bitten; she survives, but finds herself a junkie for human blood. She battens on others in a weirdly ethical way (always giving victims a chance to tell her to go away) and grapples with philosophical and spiritual issues as evil threatens to envelop her life. Finally, after a blood-drenched graduation party, Taylor achieves a strange sort of redemption.

In a performance even stronger than her committed turn in *I Shot Andy Warhol*, Taylor takes more risks than any other leading lady in recent memory, delivering a profoundly moving and subtly frightening study of a victim who turns predator. Perhaps the most seriously intended horror film of the 90s, *The Addiction* dares to tackle the personal roots of the large-scale atrocities Taylor is studying for her thesis. As haunting in its fluent verbals as in its striking black and white visuals this was one of the most challenging, unforgettable pictures of 1997. And some people will hate it a lot. You be the judge. **★★★★ KN**

THE ADVENTURES OF BARON MUNCHAUSEN (1988)

Starring: *John Neville (Baron Munchausen), Eric Idle (Desmond/Berthold), Sarah Polley (Sally Salt), Oliver Reed (Vulcan), Jonathan Pryce (Horatio Jackson), Bill Paterson (Henry Salt)*
Director: *Terry Gilliam*
Screenwriters: *Charles McKeown, Terry Gilliam, based on the stories by Rudolph Erich Raspe*
PG/126 mins./Fantasy/Adventure/UK/Germany
Awards: *BAFTA – Best Costume Design, Best Make-up Artist, Best Production Design*

The vastly improbably tale of the 17th century baron and his attempts to rescue a town from being overrun by Turks. A task that will take him to the depths of the ocean, to the moon, all the way to a confrontation with the Grim Reaper. To be taken with a sizable pinch of salt.

For a film that is a tribute to the telling of tall tales, there are more than a few gigantic myths that surround the making of this, Terry Gilliam's grand folly. Arguments with the studio, budget overruns, and tempestuous edits have all contributed to the notoriety that has stalked the movie like a shadow. It is typically ironic then that those exaggerations confined to the story itself make for a vivid and extraordinary, if not wholly satisfying, epic.

As scientists could tell you 'Munchausen Syndrome' relates to the telling of outrageous lies and the real Baron was an aristocrat drenched in myth, a reputed fantasist of the highest order. He and Gilliam would have appreciated one anothers' similar talents, the director decorates this trippy picaresque with startling far-fetched set-pieces ranging from Robin Williams warbling 'King of the Moon' removing his own head to Uma Thurman's Venus dancing in the air. Gilliam is in his element, building set upon astonishing (and bankrupting) set the size of cathedrals across his plump Rome soundstages, trying to outdo no one but himself.

Characterisation is hardly a great concern (Neville is a blank in the lead role) although there are some splendidly hammy cameos from Williams, Idle and a fulminating Reed as Vulcan, God of Fire. And so too, the burdens of story fall secondary to the director's incessant visual verve; the film is best read as a greatest hits package loosely rooted in a battle between the forces of imagination and magic and the looming age of reason. The unmistakable strains of Pythonesque satire are hard to ignore, a delight to fans but they only contribute to the nagging sense of the unbelievable. **★★★ IN**

THE ADVENTURES OF PRISCILLA QUEEN OF THE DESERT (1994)

Starring: *Terence Stamp (Bernadette), Guy Pearce (Adam/Felicia), Hugo Weaving (Tick/Mitzi), Bill Hunter (Bob), Sarah Chadwick (Marion)*
Director: *Stephan Elliott*
Screenwriter: *Stephan Elliott*
15/99 mins./Musical/Drama/Comedy/Australia

Awards: *Academy Awards – Best Costume, BAFTA – Best Costume, Best Make-up/Hair*

Three drag artists take a road trip across the Australian outback.

Any film which opens with a heavily tracked and greasepainted cross-dresser lip-synching his heart out to Charlene's seminal classic 'I've Never Been To Me' can't be dismissed as a total disaster. Indeed, Priscilla is, for the most part, a hugely entertaining romp through the Australian outback which, if it fails to sustain its rather thin plot through to the end, still has enough outrageously camp costumes and even more outrageous dialogue to keep the flighty comedy going.

Three drag artists, the secretive Tick/Mitzi (Weaving), the overbearing Adam/Felicia (Pearce) and the cool sophisticate transsexual Bernadette (Stamp) travel from Sydney to Alice Springs in a lavender-painted school bus – the Priscilla of the title – to bring their own brand of outlandish cabaret to the locals. En route, they manage to infuriate and delight just about everybody from lame-brained hicks to aborigines, experiencing the kind of unique bonding rituals which only happen in the movies.

Writer-director Elliott keeps things flowing nicely with a script built around consistently amusing bitchy one-liners, mostly the result of the hilariously prickly relationship between the mourning and world-weary Bernadette and the rebel-rousing Felicia. Stamp brings warmth and sympathy to a role which sees him boldly cast against type, and former *Neighbours* heart-throb Pearce is a major rediscovery, almost out-acting his sparring partners to prove that there is life beyond soap opera.

The film only falters after the trio arrive at their destination, forsaking its earlier sharpness in favour of inconclusive, life-affirming drama and a final effort to squeeze in as many feathery garments as possible. The many incidental pleasures on offer, however, make it more than worth viewing, if only for the sight of the three frock-adorned queens performing 'I Will Survive' in the shadow of Ayers Rock. ★★★★ **CW**

THE ADVENTURES OF ROBIN HOOD (1938)

Starring: *Errol Flynn (Sir Robin of Locksley/Robin Hood), Olivia de Havilland (Maid Marian), Basil Rathbone (Sir Guy of Gisbourne), Claude Rains (Prince John), Melville Cooper (High Sheriff of Nottingham), Ian Hunter (King Richard the Lion-Hearted)*
Directors: *Michael Curtiz, William Keighley*
Screenwriters: *Norman Reilly Raine, Seton I. Miller, Rowland Leigh (uncredited)*
U/104 mins./Action/Adventure/USA

Awards: *Academy Awards – Best Film Editing, Best Score, Best Interior Decoration/Art Direction*

Sir Robin of Locksley becomes outlaw Robin Hood in an attempt to defeat kingdom robbing Prince John and Sir Guy of Gisbourne.

The outlaw Robin Hood, who stole from the rich to give to the poor, was an established English folk-figure by 1377, when he was mentioned in William Langland's poem *Piers Plowman*. His legend inspired scores of mediaeval ballads, most importantly the epic collection *A Lytell Geste Of Robyn Hode* (1510). That Robin was a contemporary of King Richard The Lion-Hearted (1157–99) and his brother King John (1167–1216) was suggested in the 14th century and is the premise of Anthony Munday's plays *The Downfall Of Robert, Earl Of Huntingdon* and *The Death Of Robert, Earl Of Huntingdon* (both 1601) and Sir Walter Scott's *Ivanhoe* (1819). The character was appearing in films as early as 1908, when there were competing American and British movies, *Robin Hood* and *Robin Hood And His Merry Men* respectively. Douglas Fairbanks starred in a hugely expensive *Robin Hood* in 1922, an early blockbuster featuring pageantry, the Crusades, a vast castle set and typically athletic stuntwork.

The silent epic was so well remembered that no studio thought it worth considering another version for a decade and a half, until Warner Brothers employee Dwight Franklin, an advisor on the period details of *Captain Blood*, sent studio head Jack L. Warner a memo saying, 'Don't you think Cagney would make a swell Robin Hood?' It might seem an absurd suggestion now, but James Cagney had just played Bottom in *A Midsummer Night's Dream* and Warners, alongside the gangster pics, was working up a sideline in swashbucklers. Michael Curtiz's *Captain Blood* established Errol Flynn (a replacement for the unavailable Robert Donat) as an action-romance-adventure star, and showed that the no-nonsense, all-action Warners style played as well on the Spanish Main as it did in tommy-gun turf wars down on the East Side. Warner thought Franklin's suggestion sound and bought the rights to several Hood-related properties and scripts. He then assigned writer Rowland Leigh to work on a screenplay. It wound up substantially rewritten by many hands and was finally credited to Norman Reilly Raine and Seton I. Miller.

Along the way, Cagney left the studio in a contract dispute and the just-breaking Flynn landed what would become his signature role. And with Flynn on board, Olivia de Havilland and Basil Rathbone (respectively, the star's love interest and duelling partner from *Captain Blood*) were shoo-ins for Maid Marian and Sir Guy of Gisbourne. David Niven wasn't available for Will Scarlet so the forgettable Patric Knowles got the gig. But the remainder of the Merry Men and the Norman dastards were perfectly cast: bluff Alan Hale as Little John, croaky Eugene Pallette as Friar Tuck and cockney Herbert Mundin as Much The Miller's Son. And ranged against this motley band, a sly, suggestive ('any more complaints about the new tax from our Saxon friends?') Claude Rains as Bad Prince John.

Shooting began in 1937 under the direction of William Keighley, with costly Technicolor marking this as a significant step up from previous Warner action pics. But the production fell behind schedule and Curtiz stepped in to finish the movie, which bears no trace of the awkward hand-over.

Regardless of Richard Todd (who donned the green tights in 1952), a cartoon Fox for Disney, Richard Greene and Michael Praed on television or Kevin Costner and Patrick Bergin in competing 1991 projects, Errol Flynn remains the definitive Robin Hood (not yet the American-pronounced Robinhood). Our hero struts magnificently in dayglo lime pantyhose, tosses back his goateed head to laugh in the face of danger and clambers nimbly up the ivy to woo the lovely de Havilland (whose peachy complexion is as good an ad for Technicolor as her wardrobe). But Flynn could also muster the requisite gravitas when stirring the Men of Sherwood to revolt and in abusing the rightful king for abandoning England to the mercies of Rotten John.

The Adventures Of Robin Hood is an evergreen classic, as exciting, romantic and entertaining now as it always was. The lovely pastels and vivid red of three-strip Technicolor in the Californian greenwood and the pageantry of the duplicitous archery contest; an exuberant Erich Wolfgang Korngold score that makes John Williams sound like Leonard Cohen on a rainy day; stuntwork that integrates perfectly into the cut-and-thrust of the dialogue and a subliminal contemporary relevance (for John and the Normans read Adolf and the Nazis) all add up to a universal declaration that rulers should take lessons from rogues. ★★★★★ **KN**

THE ADVENTURES OF SHERLOCK HOLMES' SMARTER BROTHER (1975)

Starring: *Gene Wilder (Sigerson Holmes), Madeleine Kahn (Jenny Hill/Bessie Bellwood/Opera Singer), Marty Feldman (Sgt Orville Sacker), Dom De Luise (Eduardo Gambetti), Leo McKern (Moriarty), Roy Kinnear (Moriarty's Assistant), John Le Mesurier (Lord Redcliff), Douglas Wilmer (Sherlock Holmes), Thorley Walters (Dr Watson)*
Director: *Gene Wilder*
Screenwriter: *Gene Wilder*
PG/91 mins./Comedy/Mystery/USA

Determined to prove that he's every bit as brilliant as his older sibling, Sigerson Holmes stumbles across the clues connecting a blackmail case to a cache of missing government papers.

Having cut his screenwriting teeth with Mel Brooks on *Young Frankenstein* (1974), for which they shared an Oscar nomination, Gene Wilder made his debut as actor-writer-director with this affectionate, if scattershot comedy. He wisely steers clear of tinkering with the myth of 221B Baker Street's most famous resident, as that had already been done with acerbic wit and astute insight by Billy Wilder in *The Private Life Of Sherlock Holmes*. But he then spends so much time paying tribute to his mentor (who crops up in an unseen cameo involving a tiger and a door) that the film too frequently feels like a Brooks pastiche rather than a slapsticking satirical homage to the world created by Sir Arthur Conan Doyle.

As was to be the case with Thom Eberhardt's *Without A Clue*, in which Holmes turns out to be wholly Dr Watson's invention, the idea that Sherlock (or 'Sheer luck', as Sigerson calls him) has an envious younger brother is potentially intriguing. What's more, Terry Marsh's 1890s designs are splendidly excessive and Wilder has surrounded himself with notable members of Brooks's stock company – including the inimitable Madeline Kahn as Foreign Secretary John Le Mesurier's ditzy daughter and Dom DeLuise as her duplicitous opera-singing fiancé – as well as such British dependables as Leo McKern as Professor Moriarty and Marty Feldman as a retired Scotland Yard flatfoot with photographic hearing.

However, the case afoot fails to seize the imagination, despite a laboured attempt to invest it with a twist. Moreover, too many of the gags seem one rewrite undercooked or overdone. There are several wince-inducing moments of cod Holmesian embarrassment and some choice smut. The operatic finale, involving a drugged chorus, is also executed with gusto. But Wilder never feels in total directorial control, especially of his own over-eager performance. ★★★ **DP**

THE ADVENTURES OF SHERLOCK HOLMES (1939)

Starring: *Basil Rathbone (Sherlock Holmes), Nigel Bruce (Dr Watson), Ida Lupino (Ann Brandon), Alan Marshall (Jerold Hunter), George Zucco (Prof Moriarty)*
Director: *Alfred J. Werker*
Screenwriters: *Edwin Blum, William A. Drake, based on the play by William Gillette and the works of Sir Arthur Conan Doyle*
U/85 mins./Crime/thriller/Mystery/USA

Along the foggy streets of Old London Town, Sherlock Holmes must unravel his archival Moriarty's challenge of an unsolvable case. It soon becomes clear that all is not what it seems. The game is afoot.

The second case for Rathbone's classic incarnation of Arthur Conan-Doyle's big-brained detective was still set in the appropriate – if pleasingly clichéd – lamppost-lit London of 1894. The following adventures were to fast-forward to the 20s, somewhat polluting the formula by replacing the carriages and walking sticks with revolvers and car chases. And here, also, the chiding relationship between an arch Holmes and his dogged sidekick Dr Watson (Bruce) was less about comic interludes than thoughtfully dismantling what transpires to be two cases for the price of one.

At the opening, Holmes has narrowly missed convicting the dastardly Moriarty (played without the later theatricals by Zucco) and in a taut cab-ride from the court the great foes draw intellectual swords for the ensuing muddle of clues and red herrings. Moriarty's fiendish plan is to throw the detective off the scent by concocting a false plot, while he attempts to steal an emerald from the Crown Jewels. Thus Holmes becomes embroiled with a murder mystery imperilling a beautiful young woman. Given his tendency to offer assistance foremost to the fairer sex, he is naturally diverted.

A little creaky in its bones, the action is delivered in rash plumes of melodrama, but there is still a definitive air to Rathbone's swaggering genius and director Werker attends to all the required intricacies with due diligence. It's a marvel how developed a plot, struck through with comedy and peril, a straight-up entertainment used to be able to muster. Even though it was only based on a stageplay by William Gillette (and not an actual Conan Doyle story), this still stands as one of the finest Holmes' incarnations put to screen. ★★★★ **IN**

AN AFFAIR TO REMEMBER (1957)

Starring: *Cary Grant (Nickie Ferrante), Deborah Kerr (Terry McKay), Richard Denning (Kenneth Bradley), Neva Patterson (Lois Clark), Cathleen Nesbitt (Grandmother Janou)*
Director: *Leo McCarey*
Screenwriters: *Delmer Daves, Donald Ogden Stewart, Leo McCarey*
PG/119 mins./Romance/Drama/USA

Suave man-of-the-world Nicky Ferrante meets beautiful nightclub singer Terry McKay on a European tour and, despite both being engaged to another, they inexorably fall in love. Wrestling with their dilemma, they decide to leave things for six months and then meet at the top of the Empire State Building.

Something of a soppy legend, thanks to being heavily referenced by Meg Ryan's aw-shucks dreamer from *Sleepless In Seattle*, Leo McCarey's slight but effective weepy is, in fact, a remake of his own 1939 movie *Love Affair*. And was to be subsequently remade again, with Warren Beatty and Annette Bening, as *Love Affair* in 1994. Which is a lot of attention for a fairly light piece of mid-Hollywood melodrama.

McCarey's film rests, effectively, on a single, probing question: when you are in love, can you still fall in love? Well, according to his movie, cruelly and sentimentally, yes, you can. Pristine couple, Grant and Kerr, meet cute on a picturesque cruise of Europe, hold fire on their impulses as they are both attached to another, before recognising the inevitable. The crux is their pact – to meet six months hence atop that famous New York skyscraper – and what exactly is the right thing to do. Loyalty will contend with passion, and the fluffier (and better) romcom elements will drift into sluggish romdram. Hankies at the ready.

This is a film from a definite age; full of unrequited lust that is expressed in tight smiles and distant looks, and is inevitably headed for a righteous but sorrowful conclusion. It was the 50s, someone was bound to do the right thing. On that level, while no *Brief Encounter*, it plays its shallow hand with skill. Yet, Grant, with his crisp delivery and crisper suits, never cuts it as a tragic figure, he's too in control, ever clad in irony. Kerr, so light and attractive at first, becomes hemmed in by some dreadful songs (dubbed by Marni Nixon) and makes do, in most scenes, with a furrowed brow as if contending with lunch options rather than her emotional future.

It's most likely the sheer hopeless romance of the finale that keeps the film alight in fans' hearts, as if Grant is still up there awaiting his unanswered dream. Sob. ★★★ **IN**

AFFLICTION (1997)

Starring: *Nick Nolte (Wade Whitehouse), James Coburn (Glen Whitehouse), Sissy Spacek (Margie Fogg), Willem Dafoe (Rolfe Whitehouse), Mary Beth Hurt (Lillian)*
Director: *Paul Schrader*
Screenwriter: *Paul Schrader, based on the novel by Russell Banks*
15/84 mins./Drama/USA

Awards: *Academy Awards – Best Supporting Actor (James Coburn)*

A disaffected small-town cop investigates a possible murder case while wrestling with the realisation that he is turning into his monstrous father.

In a triple team-up that seems so natural you wonder why they haven't got together before, this offers Paul Schrader writing and directing an adaptation of a novel by Russell Banks with Nick Nolte in the lead. All three artists specialise in delving into the darks of American manhood, and this snowbound combination of family drama/rogue cop picture gets right to the heart of the matter of its title, showing how the abuse poured onto the hero since birth by his monstrous drunken dad has slowly turned him into a tragic reincarnation of the Old Man.

Wade Whitehouse is an apparently genial fixture in a small town in New

Hampshire, a combination of handyman and traffic cop, who is trying to get his life back together by hooking up with loving waitress Margie so he can qualify for custody of his daughter. He has a long-distance phone relationship with his intellectual brother Rolfe, who shares the scars of being brought up by hulking drunk Glen. When a visitor to the town dies in a hunting accident, Wade – egged on by Rolfe – starts to piece together a murder conspiracy that suggests a morass of corruption, but he is diverted from the investigation by an acute toothache (those with sensitive teeth may not enjoy the DIY dentistry scene), the death of his beloved mother and the tensions that inevitably occur when he and Margie move back in with the still-vicious but near-senile Glen.

Though it shares its snowy look with *The Sweet Hereafter* – the last film adaptation of a Banks novel – this is far from a chilly movie. Nolte, one of the underappreciated greats of contemporary cinema, delivers yet more astonishing work, sensitively inhabiting the shambling form of a man whose tragedy is that he can see exactly what a beast he is becoming and yet can do little to stop himself sliding. A marvel of the performance is the way that Nolte slowly settles into imitating the tics and snarls Coburn – in the best thing he has done since Sam Peckinpah – died employs to create the fearsome yet complicated role of the monster father.

It might be that Dafoe's narration is too precious, and some will be frustrated at the abandonment of the murder mystery to penetrate the mystery of one man's torment, but this is a powerhouse picture that comes to grips with some horrific home truths. ★★★★ **KN**

THE AFRICAN QUEEN (1951)

Starring: *Humphrey Bogart (Charlie Allnut), Katharine Hepburn (Rose Sayer), Robert Morley (Rev Samuel Sayer), Peter Bull (Captain)*
Director: *John Huston*
Screenwriters: *James Agee, John Huston, based on the novel by C.S. Forester)*
U/105 mins./Adventure/Romance/War/USA
Awards: *Academy Awards – Best Actor*

During WWI, in East Africa, cranky steamboat captain Charlie Allnut is asked to ferry forthright missionary Rose back to civilisation. Along the way they will form an unlikely alliance against the German enemy.

The first, and only, time Katharine Hepburn and Humphrey Bogart shared a screen – despite being arguably the most talented stars of their generation – is more charming curio than Hollywood event. Perhaps, that's what drew them in – the cut against the grain that John Huston's adaptation of C.S. 'Hornblower' Forester's story clearly offered.

Bogart, who was awarded with an Oscar for his transformation, shakes off the scowling loner, for a boozy old salt quick to prickle but deep down a decent cove. It's clichéd in concept, but Bogart fills him with a weathered charm, a man unable to drink away his innate morality. For Hepburn, Rose's chatterbox spinster with religious convictions as deep as Lake Victoria, was a closer match, but given they were shooting on location in Africa, she sure seems out of place in the sweaty equatorial soup that lends the film an authentic sickly gleam. It's admirable to note how willing they are to rough up their lustrous images.

Huston is on good form here. Excited by the fierce light of Africa, his film works as road movie (by river) as the mismatched duo negotiate German patrols, rapids and swarms of flies; as romance with the mismatched duo slowly come to love one another; as comedy as the mismatched duo really rile one another; and thriller, as the mismatched duo concoct a plan to blow a hole in a German gunboat at the head of the river. A plan that could prove to be suicide. That the film succeeds on so many counts, primarily as a character piece, is down to a simple equation: a great story enlivened by great actors sparking off one another and a director keen enough to just let it flow. ★★★★★ **IN**

AFTER DARK MY SWEET (1990)

Starring: *Jason Patric (Kevin 'Kid' Collins), Rachel Ward (Fay Anderson), Bruce Dern (Uncle Bud), George Dickerson (Doc Goldman), James Colton (Charlie)*
Director: *James Foley*
Screenwriters: *James Foley, Robert Redlin, based upon the novel by Robert Redlin*
18/114 mins./Crime/USA

Ex-boxer and lonely drifter Kevin 'Kid' Collins wanders into town, to hook up with an equally disenfranchised widow Fay. As their awkward relationship gathers heat, her corrupt uncle lures them into a kidnapping plot designed to net them millions.

A fairly underrated shimmy of modern noir, based on a 1955 novel by Jim Thompson, loaded with the required ingredients: slow, dogged misery shot in a softly beautiful twilight and interrupted by bursts of naked violence and eroticism. It's exactly the kind of brooding formula that has remained so fashionable in filmmakers' minds since Thompson was bottling up for his potboliers. Indeed, director Foley has been at his best when dabbling in poetic longeurs and burnt-out lives, sprinkling essence of noir over *At Close Range*, *Glengarry Glen Ross*, and *Confidence*.

None of those, however, were quite as cloaked in gloom and carnal edginess as this seedy thriller lost somewhere in the Dustbowl. Patric, also at his best with the time-honoured breed of deadbeat, near silent anti-heroes, grants Collie a disconcerting mental instability, and we learn he has just absconded from an institute, a retired pugilist slugged-out and punch-drunk, the guilt of a dead opponent resting on his soul. Hence, empty lush Fay makes a perfectly imperfect match, and Ward, with her weird, wired sexuality, gives her a restless, doomed longing that hooks straight into Collie's hollow heart.

It takes the arrival of Uncle Bud, a schemer and lowlife, and former cop, to install the necessary criminal element – a loose-hinged plan to kidnap the son of a local dignitary that requires Collie's brawn – and rather inevitably played by crank-for-hire Bruce Dern.

As the drama circles their inaction, this trio of excellent performances fills the screen with a form of spiritual exhaustion, and the film slumps into noir's typically happy-clappy comeuppance of failure, betrayal and ruin. But the mood has caught on, and the film, stamped with a stunning visual emptiness, haunts the memory for long after its sour close. ★★★★ **IN**

AFTER HOURS (1985)

Starring: *Griffin Dunne (Paul Hackett), Rosanna Arquette (Marcy), Verna Bloom (June), Tommy Chong (Pepe), Linda Fiorentino (Kiki) Teri Garr (Julie), John Heard (Tom), Cheech Marin (Neil)*
Director: *Martin Scorsese*
Screenwriter: *Joseph Minion*
15/96 mins./Comedy/USA

When computer programmer Paul picks up Marcy so begins the most insane night of his life. Lost in the netherworld of New York's SoHo, Paul yearns to get home but must first negotiate sadomasochists, cat burglars, kooks, angry cabbies, ice cream truck drivers and an angry mob that may just want to kill him.

Spoken of as a lesser Scorsese, a quick-fire, low-budget spin across the tiles of lower Manhattan having grown disaffected with working with studios, *After Hours* is sneakily one of the master's best. There is something liberated in the caffeinated hyperkinetic style he lends the movie, as if the grand moral poems he had become acclaimed for were a heavy burden, and finally he had a chance to cut loose.

That is not strictly speaking the case, for the sake of keeping things moving Scorsese ended up cutting 45 minutes from his working cut of

Joseph Minion's script (already lightened of its mobster elements). This was every bit a labour of love as *Raging Bull*, a thrilling dance of caustic genius, a morally energised screwballer in which a working drone steps out of his formulated life for a fix of something darker. Bad move.

Dunne's growing exasperation, and terror, in failing to achieve the simplest of tasks in just going home is the anchor for the Wonderland style freakshow of bohos and nutcases that stand in his path. The surreal swirl of women alone, chimes a note from the director's own turbulent romantic life. From Arquette's madly swinging moods, to Linda Fiorentino's quirky artist, to Teri Garr's beehived weirdo, the women are presented as mouse traps for this innocent sap who only wanted to get laid.

With his camera giddy and wild, Scorsese concocts a streetlife as demented as *Mean Streets* is grounded. An excursion into a sadistic, unhinged quasi-Manhattan. 'Different rules apply when it gets late,' warns Dick Miller in a cameo. It's a shame Scorsese hasn't returned to them, this is the blackest funniest comedy he's ever given us. ★★★★★ **IN**

AGAINST ALL ODDS (1984)

Starring: *Jeff Bridges (Terry Brogan), Rachel Ward (Jessie Wyler), James Woods (Jake Wise), Jane Greer (Mrs Grace Wyler), Swoosie Kurtz (Edie)*
Director: *Taylor Hackford*
Screenwriter: *Eric Hughes, based on a screenplay by Daniel Mainwaring*
15/128 mins./Romance/Drama/Thriller/USA

Ex-football star Terry Brogan is hired by dubious bookie Jake Wise to go in search of his absconded girlfriend Jessie Wyler. Travelling into Mexico, he not only finds her but falls for her, but it becomes increasingly unclear just who is manipulating who.

Any film that contests to belonging to that fabled cinematic genus of knotted intrigue and cold hearted betrayal called noir, and yet still has Phil Collins croon a bloated love song over the credits may have got its wires crossed. Taylor Hackford was fresh off a massive hit with *An Office And A Gentleman* and endeavoured to imbue something of its overblown romantic spirit into a long-desired chance to remake a 1947 noir hit called *Out Of The Past*, resplendent with old-fashioned beefcake machismo in Robert Mitchum and Kirk Douglas. The strange concoction he ends up with, proud with an 80s sheen of macho aesthetic (Jeff Bridges and James Woods), could be unique – if nonsensical – high concept noir.

Rachel Ward was hot off *The Thorn Birds* mini-series, brown-eyes the size of beach balls, she slipped about with a lost-girl allure, but this wiry bundle of nerve-ends hardly embodies the forbidding history of supple temptresses the genre holds so dear. The men in her life do better. Bridges carries a gloomy insouciance of the fallen idol as the PI betraying his paymaster for his quarry, and possibly being played by both. Woods, the best actor in the vicinity, has the decency to suggest there is more to his crooked bookie than piqued horniness, you do get a sense he is wrestling with genuine emotions.

The film really has very little to do with the original, its high-gloss veneer coupled with a pumped sound-track, idealised steamy sex and car chases in flashy motors provides less a sense of a world stripped of meaning than a triplet of over-privileged, self-serving brats having a long-distance tiff. Jane Greer, who played the centre of the 1947 triangle, pops up as Jessie's cynical mother to add a touch of credibility, but the cause is lost. This is about as noir as *Pete's Dragon*, best to accept its superficiality as a boon – Hackford, at least, gives it a slick exterior – and enjoy it is a vacuous thriller and extended Phil Collins video. ★★ **IN**

L'AGE D'OR (THE GOLDEN AGE) (1930)

Starring: *Lya Lys (The Woman), Gaston Modot (The Man), Max Ernst (Bandit Chief), Pierre Prevert (Bandit)*
Director: *Luis Buñuel*
Screenwriters: *Luis Buñuel, Salvador Dali*
15/60 mins./Drama/France

A man and a woman compulsively get together despite the forces of society, indulging in apparently perverse acts of love.

Two years after their seminal short, *Un Chien Andalou*, director Luis Buñuel and painter Salvador Dali reteamed to make a talking feature, then quarrelled, leaving Buñuel to make up most of the film on his own, delivering not just shocking surrealism but a sustained series of extreme images and outright blasphemies.

Buñuel's wry, black wit – even the cast list provokes sinister chuckles (best-ever character description, 'Defenestrated Bishop') – which couches the most outrageous assault on bourgeois sensibilities in an elegant, devilishly charming manner. It begins with found footage of scorpions attacking rats and each other from a 1912 documentary (with the perfectly surreal title, *Le Scorpion Languedocien*), then shows human scorpions, with churchmen who are as bad as bandits. It's a celebration of revolutionary love in an imperial Rome which looks like modern Paris, with a couple who roll in the mud (or worse), are separated by dour cops, chomp enthusiastically on each other's fingers, get diverted from necking to suck the toes of a marble statue and make declarations like 'oh, what joy in having killed our children!' A government minister makes a telephone call to the hero, who doesn't care about a breaking scandal; the minister shoots himself, and his corpse lies on the ceiling.

The most conceptually violent business is saved for an epilogue which offers a scene from the Marquis de Sade's *120 Days In The City Of Sodom* as doddering aristocrats stagger away from an orgy of sexual violence – led by Sade's Duc de Blangis (Lionel Salem), who is here the image of Jesus Christ. Jesus stabs to death a wounded girl, and the scalps of the degenerates' victims hang from a cross. There were organised riots in the cinemas. ★★★★★ **KN**

THE AGE OF INNOCENCE (1993)

Starring: *Daniel Day-Lewis (Newland Archer), Michelle Pfeiffer (Countess Ellen Olenska), Winona Ryder (May Weiland), Geraldine Chaplin (May Weiland), Mary Beth Hurt (Regina Beaufort), Richard E. Grant (Larry Lefferts), Miriam Margolyes (Mrs Mingott), Robert Sean Leonard (Ted Archer)*
Director: *Martin Scorsese*
Screenwriters: *Jay Cocks, Martin Scorsese, based on the novel by Edith Wharton*
PG/139 mins./Drama/Romance/USA

Awards: *Academy Awards – Best Costume Design, BAFTA – Best Supporting Actress*

New York, 1870, and Newland Archer is contentedly engaged to May Welland, when he meets her unconventional cousin Countess Olenska, a social outcast having been estranged from her husband. Having befriended her, he slowly starts to fall in love, something that could ruin his position in a world ruled by strict social conventions.

When Martin Scorsese, who'd earned his reputation charting the violent rigours of the criminal underworld, decided upon Edith Wharton's novel of repressed emotions and glittering balls as his next movie, the reaction was one of complete shock. Could two more opposing forces be found? Yet, as the canny director was well aware, her world and his were not so different, sharing many thematic facets albeit clad in utterly contrasting cloth.

This New York, older and grander than the *Mean Streets Of Little Italy*, was every bit as hierarchical and violent and as ruled by as many secret codes of behaviour, but here was a violence less of blood than the icy cut of rumour and social position. It was another opportunity for Scorsese to express his acute ear for human conditioning and his breathtaking eye for the sumptuous detail of a milieu.

How the director luxuriates in the fabric and fashion of the day; the ball scene alone, his camera granting a God's eye view of the Dervish-like couples, is a triumph of observational craft, of the rich dressing that hides the coldest of centres. These were gangsters of the glitterati, who could shun and destroy all those who don't comply with their rules. In another dazzling aside, Scorsese shoots a street of workers in the slightest of slow motion, a dizzying mass of bowler hats floating to the camera – a world of suffocating social conformity.

Daniel Day-Lewis, a master of full immersion, is presented with the challenge of subsuming his natural flourishes into what is not said, not expressed. He is like a tragic time bomb that can never explode. Michelle Pfeiffer, equally, locks herself up as tight as a girdle. Their passion is everywhere and nowhere at once.

However, the performance of the movie is that of Winona Ryder, who with the flick of her hand, the soft rise of an empty smile, establishes a million meanings; a wronged woman who reaps a revenge as subtle as it is final. The audience is left with a tale that is implied rather than told, but is devastating all the same. ★★★★ **IN**

◎ AGUIRRE, WRATH OF GOD (1972)

Starring: *Klaus Kinski (Don Lope de Aguirre), Ruy Guerra (Don Pedro de Ursua), Del Negro (Brother Gaspar de Carvajal), Helena Rojo (Inez), Cecillia Rivera (Flores)*
Director: *Werner Herzog*
Screenwriter: *Werner Herzog*
PG/100 mins./History/Drama/West Germany

Deep in the Amazon, in the 16th Century, an advance party of conquistadors attempts to locate the fabled city of El Dorado, only to be destroyed by internal conflict, the forbidding power of nature and the madness of their assumed leader Aguirre.

A legend of madness, of conflict and of foolish men miles from home, pitching their wits against the might of the Amazon jungle – thus was the making of *Aguirre, Wrath Of God* let alone the story itself. The monumental ego that was Klaus Kinski, not to forgo his talent either, was never quite as demonic as during this nightmare shoot, presided over by Werner Herzog hellbent on pushing everyone to breaking point. That such a masterful study of man and nature was the result could be method over madness, but more likely a whole lot of each.

The themes are writ large – how man's greed will drive him to destruction, here personified by the band of conquistadors, sent ahead by their general Pizzaro to find a path to the fabled treasure. Aguirre, played with less histrionics in front of the camera than were perhaps going on behind (he demanded the cinematographer always keep him in shot), his pale blue eyes glaring through the lens and his cheekbones jutting like the prongs of the Andes, offered a stunning study of man both ruthless and lost to himself. That his men turn on him is treated as much as tragedy as comeuppance.

Herzog shoots the jungle, whose vastness rises to scrape the heavens and reduces the figures of Aguirre and his men to the scale of insignificant insects, as a teeming metaphor in itself. 'Civilised man', represented by the foolish conquistadors, are cowed and destroyed by nature – our lust for gold driving us to grand folly and ultimately death. It's hardly subtle stuff, but breathtaking to behold. ★★★★ **IN**

◎ AI NO CORRIDA (1976)

Starring: *Tatsuya Fuji (Kichizo Ishida), Eiko Matsuda (Sada), Aoi Nakajima (Toku), Yasuko Matsui (Tagawa Inn Manager), Meika Seri (Matsuko)*
Director: *Nagisa Oshima*
Screenwriter: *Nagisa Oshima*
18/105 mins./Erotic/Drama/France/Japan

Japan, 1936. A maid named Sada and her married lover Kichizo quit his wife's inn and enter a geisha house to conduct an intense and, ultimately, destructive, sexual liaison.

Throughout his career, Nagisa Oshima had used actual events to confront contentious issues (like the racial mistreatment of Koreans in *Death By Hanging*, 1968) and this cause célèbre was inspired by the story of Sada Abe, who in 1936 was jailed for the murder of her lover after she was found wandering the streets with his severed penis tucked into her kimono. However, the sheer fact that she committed this 'ecstatic gesture of individual liberation' and received only a six-year sentence at a time of militaristic intransigence and moral conformism led to her becoming a folk heroine.

By showing how Sada assumed the dominant role in her relationship with the socially superior Kichizo, Oshima intended to question how far the reversal of male totalitarianism had progressed in the intervening 40 years. Yet it was not the film's bold political stance that earned it notoriety, but its graphic depiction of penetrative sex. Despite blocking out all images of pubic hair (to meet the strict censorship regulations that had forced the director to have the negative processed in Paris), Oshima was charged with obscenity and spent four years arguing his case before the courts.

There's no denying that the pair make love with obsessive compulsion in private and in public, sitting and standing, smoking and eating, singing and strangling. Yet, Oshima records their actions with a documentary detachment that gradually reveals the desperation of their coupling, as what they initially saw as their only release from a world of regimented repression becomes increasingly ritualistic and leaves them with only one, drastic escape from such intolerable pleasure.

There's undoubted sensuality and sensitivity here. But Oshima also mines Kabuki theatre, classical prints and the long-established traditions of voyeurism, exploitation and sado-masochism in Japanese pornography to expose the brutality, cowardice and hypocrisy of the nation's recent history. ★★★★ **DP**

◎ AIR FORCE ONE (1997)

Starring: *Harrison Ford (President James Marshall), Glenn Close (Vice President Kathryn Bennet), Gary Oldman (Ivan Korshunov), Wendy Crewson (Grace Marshall), William H. Macy (Major Caldwell), Dean Stockwell (Defense Secretary Walter Dean), Tom Everett (National Security Advisor Walter Dean)*
Director: *Wolfgang Petersen*
Screenwriter: *Andrew W. Marlowe*
15/124 mins./Action/Drama/USA/Germany

When hijackers take over the plane carrying the President of the United States, the President, an ex-soldier, decides to fight back.

The potential was mouthwatering: director Wolfgang Petersen returning to the politically charged thriller genre he made his own with *In The Line Of Fire*; action icon Harrison Ford in the role he was clearly destined to play – a President of the USA who kicks arse; and a scenario that ups the ante on any 'Die Hard On A Plane' variations by placing the most prominent world leader in dire jeopardy. Happily, *Air Force One* fulfils all its early promise, delivering a well oiled, no-nonsense, supremely entertaining crowd pleaser.

Following an impassioned speech in which he takes a hardline stance against terrorism, President James Marshall, together with his wife and their 12-year-old daughter, boards the titular jet to return to the States from Moscow. Midflight, however, the plane is taken hostage by an extremist nationalist Russki faction, led by bearded baddie Kurshonov. The group's demands are clear cut and brutal: the release of their imprisoned leader General Radek (Jurgen Prochnow) or they will kill a passenger every half-an-hour.

In the melee, Marshall eludes the hijackers, feigns escape in an emergency pod and begins to wage a one-man guerrilla war to gain control of the plane. This clears the decks for some taut-as-piano-wire cat and mousery as the pumped-up Prez – who it turns out is a decorated Vietnam vet – plays hide and seek with the bad guys, knocking them off one by one in a manner that more befits Clint than Clinton. Indeed, in this age of post-Rambo sophistication, there is still something incredibly enjoyable about international incidents being resolved by two men slugging it out.

Forsaking the MTV dynamism and ironic spin of *Con Air*, *Air Force One* deals in more traditional forms of action blockbusterdom: the events at least aspire to a semblance of realism, the special effects are used sparsely to powerful ends and the jokey kiss-off lines are kept to a minimum. Moreover, Petersen – an old hand at milking maximum tension from confined spaces via his submarine masterpiece *Das Boot* – orchestrates the compelling predicament with consummate mastery, escalating the spectacle from inflight fisticuffs to an amazing aborted landing set-piece and then some: from frame one, his grip does not falter and it feels good to be in such safe hands.

Be it handling difficult dilemmas or squaring up to monstrous evil, no one cuts it better in the action stakes than Ford: infusing all his stock in trade – stoic machismo, moral dignity, dyed in the wool decency – into the have-a-go politician. *Air Force One* benefits much from a blissful marriage between star persona and character spec. Oldman brings a genuine chill to his callous, intelligent terrorist, compared to his cartoony turn in *The Fifth Element*. Although Close, as the vice-president on the ground negotiating with him, has little to do except bark orders and chew scenery.

As with most actioners, the killjoys will find faults. The film is hokey on minutiae – the most security conscious aircraft in the world is effortlessly infiltrated and, much like ID4, almost every scene overflows with undiluted Yank jingoism – from a candlelit vigil outside the White House to the brazen nobility of Jerry Goldsmith's music – and the idea that 'America is ace!' screams from every pore. Still, when it is served up with such pulpy panache, old-fashioned expertise and a hero so easy to root for, come the end credit scroll, it is virtually impossible not to stand up and salute. ★★★★ **IF**

③ AIRPLANE! (1980)

Starring: *Robert Hays (Ted Striker), Julie Hagerty (Elaine), Kareem Abjul-Jabbar (Murdock), Lloyd Bridges (McCroskey), Peter Graves (Capt. Oveur), Leslie Nielsen (Dr Rumack), Lorna Patterson (Randy)*
Directors: *Jim Abrahams, David Zucker, Jerry Zucker*
Screenwriters: *Jim Abrahams, David Zucker, Jerry Zucker*
PG/86 mins./Comedy/USA

In the middle of a passenger flight, all the aircraft crew are taken ill. Only one man can fly the plane – but he had vowed never to fly again.

There's a story that when Mel Brooks – until then acknowledged king of the movie spoof with the likes of *Blazing Saddles*, *High Anxiety* and *Young Frankenstein* behind him – first saw *Airplane!* his heart sank. There were, he realised, some new kids on the block playing Mel's game, and they seemed to be playing it as well and sometimes better than he did. The experience was a pivotal one. Over the next few years Brooks would vainly struggle to retrieve the send-up mantle with insipid pastiches such as *Spaceballs* and *Robin Hood: Men In Tights*, but his spirit was mortally wounded and he retired from the fray shortly after *Dracula: Dead And Loving It* (1995). He probably did the right thing.

The brothers Jerry and David Zucker and Jim Abrahams had first met in the 70s and, as 'ZAZ' founded the Kentucky Fried Theatre Company, a sketch troupe specialising in spoofs of bad TV commercials. To gather material they used to leave an old VCR taping the telly through the wee small hours. Some time in 1974 they were spinning through the ads when they came across a terrible 1957 disaster movie *Zero Hour* based on a novel by Arthur Hailey (who would also pen the novel *Airport*, the film of which is often mistaken for *Airplane!*'s main inspiration). They immediately saw the comedic potential of the story of a shell-shocked ex-navy pilot having to land a jetliner packed with food poisoned passengers and started writing gags. Not that the trip from page to screen was easy. One studio wanted it as a 20-minute sketch at the heart of *Kentucky Fried Movie 2*; ZAZ saw the movie as set in 1957 aboard a twin prop, but were dissuaded. And the movie was originally written with commercial breaks, into which ZAZ would bung some of their ad spoofs. Finally these were stripped out entirely. What emerged six years later was quite simply the *Citizen Kane* of zany comedies. The distinguishing feature of what many people consider to be the funniest movie ever made is the sheer number of gags. They say you can't analyse humour. *Au contraire* my friends, here's a quick statistical breakdown of a one-minute sequence towards the start of the film with the timing of each joke marked: A man in a captain's uniform walks to a news rack marked with 'fiction, non-fiction, whacking material' (5.14); he picks up a magazine titled Modern Sperm (5.15); a tannoy announces 'Captain Clarence Oveur (5.20) white courtesy phone'; he picks up the red courtesy phone and a voice says 'no, the white phone' (5.30); he picks it up and the tannoy continues to page him, 'I've got it!' he yells (5.35); at the other end is a Dr Brody at the Mayo clinic with a live heart for transplant beating in a petri dish (5.50); we cut away, and when we cut back the heart keeps bouncing into shot (6. 05); the operator interrupts saying there's an urgent call from a Mr. Hamm. 'All right,' Captain Oveur orders, 'give me Hamm on five, hold the Mayo.' (6.14.).

That's a grand total of eight gags in one minute; a jph (joke per hour) rate of 480, and even if that section was particularly joke-rich, a best estimate for the whole movie (and taking into account that ZAZ initiated their policy of keeping the laughs coming through and after the end credit crawl) is well over 600. Frankly, if you're not laughing, get checked out for lockjaw.

But it's not only the gag density which elevates *Airplane!* to the pantheon of truly great movies. ZAZ populated the cast not with established comedy actors, but with newcomers such as the criminally underused Julie Hagerty and big screen heavyweights noted for their macho gravitas, mostly new to comedy. Lloyd Bridges is outstanding as McCroskey ('Looks like I picked the wrong week to quit sniffing glue') and would establish a whole new comedy career on the back of the movie, as would Leslie Nielson as Dr. Rumack ('I am serious, and don't call me Shirley') and Peter Graves, who initially dismissed – the script as, 'the worst piece of junk I'd ever seen,' before immortalising Captain Oveur with a gag you simply couldn't get away with these days ('Joey, have you ever been in a Turkish prison?'). But then the original line, 'Billy, have you ever sucked a grown man's cock?' was rapidly rejected as beyond the pale even then. Even the background characters delivered, most memorably Stephen Stucker – who sadly died in 1986 – as the unutterably surreal Johnny 'The tower, the tower ... Rapunzel, Rapunzel ...' Thankfully Zucker Abrahams Zucker turned down the immensely inferior *Airplane 2*, leaving their flight of comedic genius unsullied and making the asinine parpings of today's comic duo, the Farrelly Brothers, look distinctly grounded. ★★★★★ **AS**

AIRPLANE II: THE SEQUEL (1982)

Starring: *Robert Hays (Ted Striker), Julie Hagerty (Elaine Dickinson), Lloyd Bridges (Steven McCroskey), Chad Everett (Simon Kurtz). Peter Graves (Capt. Clarence Oveur), William Shatner (Cdr Buck Murdock)*
Director: *Ken Finkleman*
Screenwriter: *Ken Finkleman*
PG/85 mins./Comedy/USA

Breaking out of a mental hospital, Ted Striker races to stop the launch of the new Lunar Shuttle passenger ship, as he knows of the faulty computer ROK 9000. Failing that, he must get onboard and try to land it. And also deal with his ex-girlfriend Elaine.

While the team behind spoof masterpiece *Airplane!* declined to return, this inferior sequel, at least, lands as many jokes as it crashes. Mainly because director-writer Ken Finkleman, who'd previously failed to grasp the obvious with *Grease 2*, is sensible enough not to tamper with the jet-propelled (sorry) mania of the first.

Less of a direct parody, and thus loosening its grip on the genuine phobia of flying, this is, if anything, more demented still. It simply doesn't stop. While its stars maintain the strategy of playing it dead straight, we are assaulted by a Blitzkrieg of sight-gags, one-liners, in-jokes, scatological mummery and spoof references to other movies (*Rocky*, *2001* and *ET* most obviously) many of them with the stale whiff of leftovers.

The cameos, too, have less resonance and care taken with them: Lloyd Bridges, Raymond Burr and Peter Graves feel sidelined, the joke no longer about who they used to be, but just that they've turned up again. Only William Shatner is given room to truly undermine his status, something he has continued for the rest of his career.

Yet, when it hits it really hits and can boast quite possibly the finest sight-gag in film history, when Shatner's face, seemingly on a screen, turns out to be the real thing on the other side of door. And who can't resist a smirk at the confusion caused in a conversation between Captain Oveur, Mr Under and Mr Dunn? Indeed, you have to respect the skill in writing a script that continuously self-detonates: 'Ted Striker? Never heard of him. That's not exactly true. We were like brothers.' ★★★ **IN**

AIRPORT (1970)

Starring: *Burt Lancaster (Mel Bakersfield), Dean Martin (Capt. Vernon Demerest), Jean Seberg (Tanya Livingston), Jaquelline Bisset (Gwen Meighen), Helen Hayes (Ada Quonsett)*
Directors: *George Seaton, Henry Hathaway*
Screenwriters: *George Seaton, based on the novel by Arthur Haley*
PG/137 mins./Disaster/USA

Awards: *Academy Awards – Best Actress in a Supporting Role (Helen Hayes)*

As snow incapacitates Lincoln International Airport, manager Mel Bakersfield has to contend not only with frozen runways, but with a seething wife and a girlfriend who may move to San Francisco. But that's nothing to the problems facing his brother-in-law pilot Vern Demerest; he's got a stowaway, a madman with a bomb, a pregnant girlfriend and nowhere to land.

The first and foremost of the Airport movies, based on Arthur Hailey's distinctly on-the-nose attempts to write the perfect 'airport novel', here we have the trailblazer for that criminally stupid but splendidly watchable fusion of thriller dynamics with soapy melodrama, crammed with derelict stars. In suspect ways *Airport* is also one of the progenitors of the blockbuster concept – a film driven by its potential in the market rather than creativity, but being the cheesy antithesis of the frowning, arty groundswell of the seventies, gives it a certain magnificent cache.

Here, the acting is as preposterous as the set-up, although Helen Hayes was granted an Oscar for her sweetie pie, old dame routine as the repeat offender stowaway. The men, although slack around the middle, are square of jaw and face the increasingly fraught circumstances with stoic determination. The ladies, forgoing every tenet of the feminist movement, are either naggy harridans or beautiful young replacements that our chubby middle-aged heroes obviously deserve. After all they do go by such chunky and courageous WASPy monikers as Mel Bakersfield and Vern Demerest.

You have to give George Seaton his due, he and Henry Hathaway who was uncredited for directing the snowy exterior scenes where gung-ho mechanic George Kennedy shifts the stalled jet off the runway to give himself a role for life, really wrack up the tension. Cross-cutting between the earnest moral dilemmas and sweaty disaster elements, they defined a template that – despite *Airplane!*'s best attempts to sabotage it – is evident in everything from *Armageddon* to *Titanic*. Although, the sad, individualistic motivation behind Van Helfin's bombing attempt (and what was going on at airport security?) seems a tad tame by the shocking realities of subsequent history.

Still, there's an unshakeable sense that the film feeds less on any latent paranoia of flying than a secret desire to see a lot of good-looking Hollywood folk go up in flames.

The original was followed by three sequels; *Airport '74* (1974), *Airport '77* (1977) and *The Concorde: Airport '79* (1979) – all followed the same formula but to ever diminishing returns. ★★★ **IN**

AKIRA (1988)

Starring: *the voices of: Mitsuo Iwata, Nozomu Sasaki, Mami Koyama, Taro Ishida*
Director: *Katsuhiro Omoto*
Screenwriters: *Katsuhiro Otomo, Izo Hashimoto, from the graphic novel by Otomo*
12/124 mins./Animated/Action/Japan

A biker gang member, turned raging psychopath by a military experiment, escapes into Neo-Tokyo. Only two teenagers stand between him and the destruction of the city.

The written language of Japan consists of ideographs, which are mostly stylised pictures; because of this, comic strip art (manga) has never been marginalised as the kiddie-level art form it mostly remains in the West. And alongside the huge manga industry, which puts out strips about everything from baseball and cookery to Samurai action and hardcore porn, there is an equivalent animated movie (anime) business, which produces high-profile cinema films (often based on successful manga), direct-to-video series, tossed-off quickies and a great deal of television. Once, the only profile this form had in the West came from a few poorly dubbed series about Lolita-cum-Barbarella space heroines or boys who were best friends with giant robots. That the situation has changed at all, to the point where every video retail outlet has a crowded anime section, is down to the international success of one film, Katsuhiro Omoto's *Akira*.

Omoto is unusual if not unique in coming to film after establishing himself as a manga artist-writer, and *Akira* is a story he first told as a lengthy serial that began in 1982 and continued for eight years. Surprisingly, he took a break from regular production of the comic book series from 1986 to 1988 in order to write, direct, supervise and design the film version, which was therefore finished before the printed story could run its course and represents a fairly different version of the same basic plot.

The film opens on 16 June 1988, with a strange silent explosion devastating Tokyo and leaving a vast crater where the city once stood. Then, we cut to 2019, 31 years after World War III, and visit Neo-Tokyo, the new metropolis built atop the ruins. Otomo's future city is a richly detailed backdrop, imagined and designed from the huge buildings down to the smallest details of vehicles or police uniforms, and it is also a summation of every future city depicted in comics and on screen, taking in the Metropolis

Worst Movie Hairstyles

1. Cameron Diaz, Being John Malkovich (1999)
2. Jack Nance, Eraserhead (1976)
3. Demi Moore, St Elmo's Fire (1985)
4. Orlando Bloom, The Lord of the Rings (2001)
5. Julia Roberts, Full Frontal (2002)
6. Elsa Lanchester, The Bride of Frankenstein (1935)
7. Kevin Costner, 3000 Miles to Graceland (2001)
8. John Travolta, Battlefield Earth (2000)
9. Harrison Ford, Presumed Innocent (1990)
10. Robert De Niro, Taxi Driver (1976)

of Fritz Lang, DC Comics, the ad-blitzed dystopia of *Blade Runner* and many other imaginopoli. In return, Otomo's vision has been endlessly copied and 'homaged' by subsequent filmmakers.

The plot focuses on the relationship between a pair of disaffected teenagers who have grown up together in a harsh orphanage: the slight, resentful, uptight Tetsuo, and the more confident, breezy and heroic Kanada. Both kids run with a cycle gang who seem markedly less vicious than either their rivals or the city cops, but trouble is brewing between them because Tetsuo resents the way Kanada always has to rescue him.

Stepping back from this personal story, the film establishes a conspiratorial layer as a group of scientists, military men and politicians ponder what to do with a collection of withered children with enormous psychic powers, especially the mysterious and rarely-seen Akira, whose awakening to full potential might well have caused the end of the old world. While Kanada is being drawn into a relationship with Kay, a girl who is with an underground activist movement, Tetsuo has been visited by the children, who have triggered in him the growth of psychic and physical powers that might make him a superman or a super-monster and which transport the film into an area of Cronenbergian surrealism.

As befits a distillation of 1,318 pages of the story so far, *Akira* the film is teeming with incident and detail. Some themes and sub-plots get short shrift and are lost in the mix, and Akira himself only makes it to the screen in the vaguest sense. However, the film keeps piling up sequences that manage to out-astonish the last: the action chases and shoot-outs of the juvenile delinquent plot benefit from an attention to minute detail that extends to the surprised, shocked faces of the tiniest extra; the onset of Tetsuo's metamorphosis (which inspired Shinya Tsukamoto's live-action Tetsuo films) takes in nightmarish scenes of giant, animated playthings that represent repressed portions of his psyche; and the finale, which combines flashbacks with a destruction of Neo City and the creation of a new universe, is one of the most mind-bending in all sci-fi cinema. Tetsuo becomes a constantly shifting monster that alternately looks like a billion-gallon scrotal J sac or a Tex Avery mutation of the monster from *The Quatermass I Experiment*. Still, Otomo never loses sight of the tragic human character inside. ★★★★ **KN**

Anime

What is it: Japanese animated cinema — most commonly science fiction and fantasy in the internationally-exported examples, but covering everything from porno to baseball at home in Japan.

Hallmarks: Giant robots; big eyed schoolgirls; amazing fantasy landscapes; lecherous tentacles; messianic adolescent heroes; geysers of blood from sword-wounds; white-haired wizard times; dragons.

Key Figures: Hayao Miyazaki, Katsuhiro Ôtomo, Osamu Tezuka, Satoshi Kon

If you see one film, see: *Spirited Away* (2001)

ALADDIN (1992)

Starring: voices of: *Robin Williams (Genie), Scott Weinger (Aladdin), Linda Larkin (Jasmine), Jonathan Freeman (Jafar), Frank Welker (Abu/Narrator)*
Directors: *John Musker, Ron Clements*
Screenwriters: *John Musker, Ron Clements, Ted Elliott. Terry Rossio, based on a story by Roger Allers, James Fujii, Francis Glevas, Kirk Hanson, Kevin Harkey, Daan Jippes, Larry Lekr, Kevin Lima, Burny Mattinson, Sue Nichols, Brian Pimental, Rebecca Rees, Darrell Rooney, Chris Sanders, David S. Smith, Patrick A.Ventura*
U/90 mins./Animation/Comedy/Musical/USA

Awards: *Oscars – Best Original Score, Best Original Song, Golden Globes – Best Original Score, Best Original Song, Special Award (Robin Williams for his vocal work)*

A homeless boy's luck changes when he finds a magic lamp and the genie inside offers him three wishes.

At the beginning of the 90s, Disney's animation division was fully enjoying its time at the top, contentedly tanning itself in the glow of a new golden age. *The Little Mermaid* had dragged it back from the tedium of *The Black Cauldron* and *Oliver & Company*, while *Beauty And The Beast* had heralded Disney's most adoring reviews since a pasty princess shacked up with seven midgets – not to mention the only ever Best Picture Academy Award nomination for an animated film, a feat which will likely never be repeated due to the new Best Animated Film category.

Yes, the Mouse House was justifiably brimming with confidence. So something was bound to go wrong. Right? Enter Ron Clements and John Musker – the animation directors responsible for starting the Disney revolution with *The Little Mermaid* – who came in and screwed up *Aladdin* with astonishing panache. Suggested as a project by composers Alan Menken and Howard Ashman, the directors' take on the story about a street boy who finds a magic lamp was an undeniable mess. The title character's pubescent naivety sat uncomfortably with the determined sensuality of the princess, his exasperated mother sapped the film's energy and the villain was upstaged by his parrot. It was as clumsy and aimless as all the 80s trash the studio had been trying to sweep under the carpet . . .

Fortunately, Disney animation head Jeffrey Katzenberg was no longer prepared to accept such shoddy workmanship, and that particular version never limped past storyboard stage. Katzenberg had been brought to Disney in 1984 and told by Michael Eisner as they passed an unprepossessing building: 'That's the animation department. It's your headache now.' After the analgesia of recent success, he wasn't going to let it start thumping again. On what came to be known among the *Aladdin* animators as Black Friday, Katzenberg told the team to scrap virtually everything they'd been working on for months and start again. And to further add to their Arabian nightmare, he refused to move the movie's release date. Musker and Clements were faced with blank storyboards and the imminent arrival of the animation A-team from *Beauty And The Beast*, who'd have nothing to do but sharpen their pencils.

With the only other possible option to shut the production down, the directors bit the bullet and with the help of their crack team completely reinvented the feature in eight days. Writers Terry Rossio and Ted Elliott (who would go on to pen *Shrek* and *Pirates Of The Caribbean*) were brought in to work on the script and iron out the many plot flaws. Aladdin was aged a few years, in line with Katzenberg's request to make him 'more Tom Cruise, less Michael J. Fox', his mother was bumped off and the assembled team were sharply reminded to 'bring the funny'.

One element, however, remained constant: Robin Williams. Celebrity voices were nothing new to animation – Phil Harris and George Sanders were stars of their day when they voiced *The Jungle Book* – but the trend had died off as the material declined in quality. The directors had the former stand-up in mind as the only person who could inhabit the Genie from the early stages of development, and lured Williams in by presenting a test animation of the Al Hirschfield-inspired blue spirit lip-synching part of his *Reality – What A Concept* album. Through tears of laughter, the actor happily signed up for what would become animation's single greatest vocal performance. Williams' inability to stick to a script carried his scenes off on tangents of vaudevillian bizarreness that inspired supervising animator Eric Goldberg and upturned the Disney ethos of some 55 years.

Up until Williams let rip with a dizzying repertoire of pop-culture gags and celebrity impressions, Disney's fairy-tales had refused to acknowledge a world outside the land surveyed by Sleeping Beauty's castle. Each took place in a parallel universe where men wore tights, women had eyes that made Bambi look beady and animals chatted away like furry little housewives. That was all well and good for selling dreams and duvet covers to little girls, but in a film industry where superheroes were becoming the big draws and computer effects were starting to provide animated dazzle in live-action films, Disney needed to bring itself up to date to secure a larger audience – which, crucially, would include more boys.

Of course, Musker and Clements didn't want to alienate their core female audience, and they were very clever in hiding from males the fact that this was the greatest musical that Disney had yet made.

In the past, the song-and-dance numbers that were the studio's touchstone had often become small productions in their own right, not necessarily serving the story. Even *Beauty And The Beast*, certainly a more ambitious and technically superior film, put the plot on hold for showstoppers like 'Gaston' and 'Be Our Guest' – wonderful, witty creations both, but not key to the plot.

Aladdin, however, uses every song – bar the Genie's 'Friend Like Me' – to move the plot along. They serve as bridges between scenes and locations: the thunderous Prince Ali marching Aladdin from his isolated street life to the opulent bombast of the palace, or the soaring 'A Whole New World' carrying the romantic leads away from their troubled lives to a place alone above the clouds. The numbers don't just dance, they run.

Boys, however, didn't come for the hummable tunes. Some perhaps came for the slightly unsettling sexuality of Princess Jasmine, a royal dressed like a theme hooker, but primarily they came for the action – best exemplified by the knuckle-bleaching cave escape scene – and for a comedy of unpredictable wit. It had De Niro, Nicholson and Rodney Dangerfield impressions thrown in with confident casualness and maintained a tone that poked fun at itself, referencing past Disney films (and even a couple of future projects, with nods to *Mulan* and *Hercules* during 'A Whole New World').

Yes, Aladdin was the big-screen family animation that boys introduced to the world of 'mature' cartooning by *The Simpsons* would happily admit to liking, and that adults could go and see without feeling the need to have a five-year-old in tow.

It's not going too far to say that Aladdin is the progenitor of the current big-screen 'toon boom, being enjoyed everywhere but Disney's traditional animation department, which took a downturn thanks to a neglect of story rather than any failings in the medium. Pixar's sparkling output may not have come along as soon had Aladdin not primed an adult audience to look at animation as a genre as exciting as any other, and shown that Simpsonian sophistication could work when stretched to feature length. If you need to test its influence, just try to think of five live-action films of the last ten years as consistently funny as the *Toy Story* or *Shrek* movies. Post Aladdin, animation has become the breeding ground for great comedy writing talent and lays claim to the highest hit-rate of any genre. It's just a shame more of the magic didn't rub off on Disney. ★★★★★ **OR**

THE ALAMO (1960)

Starring: *John Wayne (Col. David Crockett) , Richard Widmark Col. James Bowie), Laurence Harvey (Col. William Travis), Frankie Avalon (Smithy), Patrick Wayne (Capt. James Butler Bonham)*
Director: *John Wayne*
Screenwriter: *James Edward Grant*
PG/192 mins./Western/USA
Awards: *Academy Awards – Best Sound*

San Antonio, Texas, 1836 – as Generalissimo Santa Anna's Mexican forces march toward the contested territory of Texas, a ragtag bunch of veterans and heroes, including Davy Crockett, Jim Bowie and their greenhorn leader William Travis, make a stand at old missionary known as the 'Alamo'. For 13 days they hold out, buying time for Texan general Sam Houston to pull together an army to defeat the enemy.

As much a vanity project for John Wayne, at the height of his popularity, as a chance to take this fabled slab of American folklore (although, technically speaking Texas was not part of the Union at the time), this flabby, inconsistent attempt at a Western epic (although, strictly speaking, this is too early to be a Western) is an expensive misfire.

Wayne, despite harkening from one of cinema's most enduring partnerships with the mighty John Ford, was not a natural director. The film dawdles and ruminates but never comes alive, and despite various cuts attempting to fillet a dramatic core out of its swollen running time, all eventually failed. Wayne, sensibly enough, borrows devotedly from Ford in the grand scope (he built an Alamo to scale from scratch) and earthy detail, but never manages to figure out where the drama lies. His performers are uniformly at sea. Indeed, his own Davy Crockett is so tailored to showing the star in a grand light, it seems more like Crockett, coonskin cap in place, doing his best Wayne impression.

With his own money tied up in the production, he also wasn't going to squander the chance to coat an often misunderstood part of history with his own right-wing agenda. These doomed men are fighting the cause of justice and republicanism, whereas in truth the stand is often considered a folly and needless sacrifice. Determinedly one-dimensional, the folly starts to feel all Wayne's own

The only time it sets about stirring our blood is with the arrival of Santa Anna's glorious battalions onto the battlefield, granting, finally, a luminous splendour to the arid settings. Although, this may have been more about the management of second unit director Cliff Lyons who reputedly took over the directorial reigns. Seven Oscar nominations, a spurious nod for sound, were his only reward, audiences stayed away and his great trumpet blast of a personal project would lapse into best forgotten. ★★ **IN**

ALEXANDER (2005)

Starring: *Colin Farrell (Alexander), Angelina Jolie (Olympias), Anthony Hopkins (Old Ptolemy), Val Kilmer (Philip), Rosario Dawson (Roxane), Jared Leto (Hephaistion), Jonathan Rhys Myers (Cassander), Christopher Plummer (Aristotle)*
Director: *Oliver Stone*
Screenwriters: *Oliver Stone, Christopher Kyle, Laeta Kalogridis.*
15/175 mins./HistoryWar/Biography/USA/UK/Netherlands/Germany

The life story of the legendary Macedonian hero who conquered much of the known world by the age of 25.

When Oliver Stone announces he's making another film, it's not so much a case of taking notice as taking cover. His is not the cinema of clinking teacups and subtle interplay; this is cinema as blitzkrieg: elemental, outrageous and barely tamed. And when Oliver Stone announces he's making a film of the life of Alexander The Great, the Macedonian king who trampled over half the known world, by Zeus, you'd better be prepared. Alexander looks and sounds glorious, depicting a far-off world spread with intricate detail and expansively scored by the aural grandeur of Vangelis. The battle scenes extraordinarily reconstruct the horror of war in a time when seeing the whites of your enemy's eyes was a tactical necessity. If Troy was tame and bloodless, Alexander is wild and drenched in carnal violence.

It takes three tours of duty in Vietnam to understand such visceral madness, and Stone takes his camera tight into Alexander's demented eyeballs before pulling back and letting the blood spill. In what must be the most monumental scene of any career, described in arch slow-motion from about 62 camera angles, Alexander on his faithful steed rears up before a similarly rearing armoured elephant. It's a tremendous surge of purest spectacle; the film never feels so alive as when it's immersed in death.

And yet! And yet! This is no *Spartacus*, or even a *Braveheart*. Stone's determination to bang home big themes, crackling with Freudianism, unsettles his storytelling. There's something overbearing, almost bullying, about this abbreviated tour through a decade-long campaign, pinpointing loud, emotional moments rather than dramatically satisfying ones.

The first hour is spent prying on the younger Alexander's fractious relations with his demented parents, the psychological fuel to his all-conquering mania. With hints of incest or worse, Jolie joyously chews it all up and spits it out with sexy vigour – it appears her son may have swallowed up nations just to shut his mother up.

Just as in *JFK* or *Nixon*, Stone once again ponders the blurring of history and myth. The story is weaved in flashback by Hopkins' elderly Ptolemy, who judges the frailties of the real man before carefully omitting such details from the record. These, though, are truths still hotly disputed, so the script keeps fretfully explaining itself. Alexander's bisexuality, for example, is dealt with maturely, but repeatedly.

It's convienient to note the parallels between the director's over-ambition and that of his subject, but the comparison fits. Stone pushes too far just as Alexander did, aiming to give us a leader of contradictions: tyrant and diplomat, lover and killer, god and man. Poor Colin Farrell is presented with having to turn a marble icon into a fleshy sprawl of personal issues. You can feel him strain every sinew to get it right, but with his blond locks out of whack with his heavy stubble and his Dublin accent awkwardly unchanged, he is too earthy, that one-of-the-boys persona unshakeable. Where is that spark of glory that drove men 10,000 miles from home? Where is the colossus? Yes, this is a movie of spectacularly brutal battle scenes and intense attention to detail, but, as wowed as you are, you come away never truly tasting the immensity of Alexander. ★★★ **IN**

⦿ ALEXANDER NEVSKY (1938)

Starring: *Nikolai Cherkassov (Prince Alexander Yaroslavich Nevsky), Nikolai Okhlohopov (Vassily Buslai), Andrei Abrikosov (Gavrilo Olexich)*
Directors: *Sergei Eisenstein, D.I. Vassillev*
Screenwriters: *Sergei Eisenstein, Peter Pavlenko*
PG/107 mins./History/USSR

With 13th-century Russia under attack from both the Teutons and the Tartars, the Prince of Nevsky assembles an army and confronts the Germans knights at Lake Peipus.

Returning to filmmaking after six years of inactivity, Sergei Eisenstein was keen to put into practice theories he had been developing since the arrival of sound. In his silent masterpieces, Eisenstein had championed the cause of the mass hero and explored the cinematic and political potential of montage. But, Alexander Nevsky saw him focus on a single, iconic figure, while also embracing the technique known as *mise-en-scène*, in which meaning was conveyed by composition in depth within the frame rather than the juxtaposition of colliding images.

Eisenstein didn't wholly abandon his montagist past, however, as he called his integration of sound and image 'vertical montage'. By combining visuals more indebted than previously to art and literature with Prokofiev's magisterial score, Eisenstein aimed to arouse emotional as much as intellectual patriotism and, so, while the famous Battle of the Ice primarily had propagandist purposes, it's also impossibly poetic and, therefore, makes an even more indelible impact.

Although the film ostensibly resembled a traditional movie narrative, this was still very much a revolutionary work. The notional romantic subplot was subordinated to the grander notion of sacrifice for the Motherland and Eisenstein shunned Hollywood characterisation and kept the viewer concentrated on his nationalist themes by employing symbolic types rather than identifiable individuals.

The obvious exception, however, is Nevsky himself. Clearly modelled on Stalin, he's a man of the people, who is first seen fishing and retains his common touch in all his dealings with his soldiers, who are themselves frequently presented in heroic poses that gave the populace a stake in a picture that was essentially designed to bolster Stalin's cult of personality.

Not surprisingly, the Kremlin was delighted with the film. But, within months of its release, it was shelved, as anti-German rhetoric became unexpectedly inappropriate after Stalin stunned Europe by forging the Pact of Steel with his implacable enemy, Adolf Hitler. ★★★★★ **DP**

⦿ ALFIE (1966)

Starring: *Michael Caine (Alfie Elkins), Shelley Winters (Ruby), Millicent Martin, Julia Foster (Gilda), Jane Asher (Annie), Shirley Ann Field (Carla), Eleanor Bron (The Doctor), Denholm Elliott (Abortionist)*
Director: *Lewis Gilbert*
Screenwriter: *Bill Naughton, based on his own stage play*
15/114 mins./Drama/UK

Awards: *BAFTA – Most Promising Newcomer (Millicent Martin)*

The life, times and philosophy of swinging sixties lothario Alife Elkins who works his way through a series of casual affairs without daring to commit, but as time moves along it becomes increasingly clear his idle manner and amorality may be about to catch up with him.

Now something of a landmark, or at least a famous signpost, of London's free'n'easy living in the mid-sixties and the consequent price to be paid for them, Lewis Gilbert's intelligent and funny, if obvious, satire rests entirely upon the easy, earthy charm of its star. Thankfully, Caine is equal to the pressure, holding Alfie in an equipoise between an over-sexed narcissist and a genuine, likeable man trying to make sense of the times and opportunities all about him.

Bill Naughton, who wrote a gem of a stageplay and then converted it to the screen, is also charting a fine line between moral indignation and a chirpy admiration for Alfie's breezy antics. There is a spiky wit, not to say postmodern texture, to Alfie's straight-to-camera musings, immortalised by his shrugging, if unconcerned, 'What's it all about?' The question the film asks is, 'Why not?' Surely life is to be enjoyed? The answer is grimmer than you expect.

The shadows that eventually fall across Alfie – no just universe could stand this amount of sex, charm and bluster without recompense – give the film a deeper meaning than its fizzy-cool reputation might suggest. Alfie will have a health scare, get a woman pregnant and have to witness the scuzzy backstreet abortion care of Denholm Elliott's seedy 'doctor' and finally, will find love only to have it taken away.

TOP10

Directors Who Made Only One Film

1 Charles Laughton – *The Night of the Hunter*, 1955, psychological thriller with Robert Mitchum as a psychotic preacher man.

2 Marlon Brando – *One Eyed Jacks*, 1961, a sombre Western about duelling outlaws

3 Jack Lemmon – *Kotch*, 1971, family drama starring old sparring partner Walter Matthau as the titular seventysomething.

4 Saul Bass – *Phase IV*, 1973, scary sci-fi from Hitchcock / Scorsese title designer, featuring a swam of hardnut ants.

5 Marty Feldman – *The Last Remake of Beau Geste*, 1977, 'hilarious' foreign legion spoof combining the talents of Feldman, Michael Yorke and, er, Irene Handl.

6 Steve Gordon – *Arthur*, 1981, comedy combining Dudley Moore's drunk schtick with wisecracking English butler.

7 Norman Mailer – *Tough Guys Don't Dance*, 1987, a Chandler parody starring – the kiss of death – Ryan O'Neal.

8 Robert Englund – *976-EVIL*, 1988, a surreal teen horrorfest featuring a devil summoned up by telephone.

9 Bill Murray – *Quick Change*, 1990, a farcical comedy about a getaway gone wrong starring Murray, Geena Davis and Randy Quaid.

10 Jennifer Lynch – *Boxing Helena*, 1993, the only film in which Julian Sands keeps an amputee in a box.

Lewis Gilbert has given us a moral fable that may not quite be the sum of its iconic value – thanks to endless posters and pub-imitators (a perpetual Caine problem) – but remains a defining point in Caine's career, such that Jude Law's callow remake seemed very foolish indeed. ★★★ **IN**

ALFIE (2004)

Starring: *Jude Law (Alfie), Susan Sarandon (Liz), Omar Epps (Marlon), Nia Long (Lonette), Sienna Miller (Nikki), Marisa Tomei (Julie)*
Director: *Charles Shyer*
Screenwriters: *Elaine Pope, Charles Shyer, based on the screen play by Bill Naughton*
15/105 mins./Comedy/Drama/Romance/USA/UK

A womaniser with the gift of the gab begins to see the error of his ways.

As a remake, *Alfie* doesn't so much invite comparisions with the original as rap on its front door and demand an RSVP. Well, if you wanted a post-new-lad, metrosexual, insert-achingly-trendy-style-mag-buzz-word-here Alfie for the Noughties, then director Shyer certainly doesn't get it disastrously wrong.

Despite some odd visual decisions (like the 'message' billboards screaming words like 'DESIRE', 'WISH' and 'SEARCH'), Shyer maintains a respectfully nostalgic style throughout, keeping the to-camera monologues, plonking Alfie on a retro moped and peppering the movie with jump cuts and split-screen montages.

Although, of course, this is supposed to be an update. So we have some inter-racial intercourse and a less heavy approach to the abortion scene (it doesn't require a nip down a backstreet, for one thing), while Alfie's health scare mutates from tuberculosis to a lump on the penis – the kind of thing Caine's 66 gadabout would never have let a doctor poke at.

Shyer shows remarkable restraint by not mentioning 9/11 once and keeping STDs out of the picture. But his decision to sidestep melodrama does mellow the consequences of Alfie's actions for the women he dallies with – a stronger set of characters than their 60s equivalents – which in turn lessens the impact their reactions have on our protagonist. Though, these being more touchy-feely times, Jude Law's slick, pretty-boy reincarnation is less icy and insensitive than Caine's wide-boy original, so we still have all the painfully confused 'What's it all about?' soul-searching. Caine's Alfie may not have been as likeable as Law's, but his reality-check was undeniably more poignant, especially considering the period context; where Caine was shagging away under the ever-present threat of nuclear fall-out and trying to square his kid-in-a-candy-shop reaction to the sexual revolution with the impact of Women's Lib, Law is operating in a world of equal opportunity where therapy is everyday. His epiphanies, therefore, smack a little too much of whiney navel-gazing.

Still, the actor is adept enough to keep us engaged even through the more wallowy moments, while the female cast is consistently strong – especially Susan Sarandon and brassy newcomer Sienna Miller, whose topless zucchini-hacking (with a meat cleaver, no less) provides the most memorable scene. Ouch! ★★★ **DJ**

ALI (2001)

Starring: *Will Smith (Cassius Clay/Muhammad Ali), Jamie Foxx (Drew 'Bundini' Brown), Jon Voight (Howard Cosell), Mario Van Peebles (Malcolm X), Jada Pinkett Smith (Sonji)*
Director: *Michael Mann*
Screenwriters: *Stephen J. Rivele, Christopher Wilkinson, Eric Roth, Michael Mann, based on a story by Gregory Allen Howard*
15/159 mins./Biography/Sports/USA

A biopic focusing on a decade of boxer Muhammad Ali's life, from 1964 to 1974.

In between the years 1964 and 1974, Cassius Clay wins the heavyweight boxing championship of the world, gets embroiled with Malcolm X, refuses the draft, fights the Rumble In The Jungle against George Foreman, and changes his name to Muhammad Ali.

Muhammad Ali and the movies have so far enjoyed a tempestuous relationship that has encompassed both the sublime – Leon Gast's Oscar-winning documentary, *When We Were Kings* – and the ridiculous – the self-serving Ali autobiography, *The Greatest*.

Happily, Michael Mann's biopic falls heavily towards the former. Epic yet focused, ambitious but controlled, worthy without the dull bits, Ali manages the neat trick of celebrating the man's innate strength – sporting, political and spiritual – without ever feeling like a manufactured PR job. Much to his credit, Mann creates boxing set-pieces that have nothing to do with the over-the-top histrionics of *Rocky* or the stylised brutality of *Raging Bull*. These scenes are sustained (the dust-up with Sonny Liston (Michael Bentt) is over ten minutes long), punishing and real. While the only tricksiness occurs as Mann throws in a gloves-eye-view of the blows, the footage is infused with a rough-hewn, almost DV-like quality that feels bruisingly immediate, rather than designer raw.

Occasionally the director's grip falters. The sinister subterfuge of Ali's relationship with Malcolm X and the Nation Of Islam feels fudged and, in nobly avoiding a sensationalist approach, there is a lack of dramatic fireworks in a middle section that should really crackle – Ali's refusal of the draft, and his first wife's rejection of his Muslim customs, feel somewhat flatter than they should. But around the hilarity of Ali's press conferences and weigh-ins, there are moments of sublime power.

Witness Ali pulling over in his car on learning of Malcolm X's death as the streets teem with people; a bravura opening montage cross-cutting his training with a young Ali travelling on a segregated bus and a dynamite performance from soul legend Sam Cooke (David Elliott); and the fantastically realised entrance to the Rumble In The Jungle that feels right in a way that huge, sporting spectacles recreated on screen rarely do. Surrounding Ali are various characters pushing and pulling for ownership of his soul – shady Malcolm X, promoter Don King, his friend Howard Bingham, spiritual guru Drew Brown – but the most affective relationship sits between Ali and TV pundit Howard Cosell (an unrecognisable Voight). Played to a tee by both actors, Mann teases out a friendship of mutual dependence – Ali needed Cosell to provide a mouthpiece, Cosell needed Ali to spice up ratings – and masked affection.

Watch Ali pull the toupee off Cosell's head mid-interview. But, perhaps, ultimately, the buck stops with Will Smith, and he succeeds magnificently. While much of the attention surrounding his performance will undoubtedly centre on the bulking up and pugilistic proficiency, where Smith really impresses is in the stuff that cannot be taught. Completely at home with the rapid fire banter, the swagger and the poise of the man, this is inhabiting, rather than impersonating, a real life. An honest and fearless performance, not once does Smith invoke that skinny rapper 'getting jiggy with it'. ★★★★ **IF**

ALI G INDAHOUSE (2002)

Starring: *Sacha Baron Cohen (Ali G/Borat), Kellie Bright (Me Julie), Michael Gambon (Prime Minister), Charles Dance (David Carlton), Martin Freeman (Ricky C), Rhona Mitra (Kate Hedges), Barbara New (Nan), Emilio Rivera (Rico), Jackeline Castro (Mum)*
Director: *Mark Mylod*
Screenwriters: *Sacha Baron Cohen, Dan Mazer*
15/88 mins./Comedy/UK/Germany

Ali G is unknowningly set up to overthrow the Prime Minister by the evil Chancellor of the Exchequer.

Kevin and Perry did it – why shouldn't it work for the self-appointed style guru of the Westside Staines Massive? Sacha Baron Cohen's comic creation makes the jump from 'yoof' TV send-up to big screen star with typically mixed results. When it's good, it's tears-in-the-eyes funny; but when it has to develop the story, some weak spots begin to appear.

Although the plot allows for some political satire, the general tone aims low. Smutty, crude and knob-obsessed, Ali G is a day-glo cartoon who might well have bounced from the pages of *Viz*. When he first stepped into the media spotlight, the joke was on those who, unsuspecting, took him seriously as pop culture interviewer. Now that the mask has been removed, the joke is on him. He's the by-word for every pasty-faced kid with street-cred aspirations, and the film thrives on the juxtaposition of his gangsta fantasies with the suburban reality of crap cars and turf wars over playground climbing frames. By lifting Ali G from the Staines 'hood and plonking him down in Westminster, the film finds a fish-out-of-water scenario that has fun with both sides of the equation.

His 'Keep It Real' manifesto carries about as much weight as Reagan's 'Just Say No' campaign, but surrounding him are politicians grasping at anything that will boost their standing in the polls – even if that means an immigration policy that only allows 'fit' refugees to enter the country. Because the film fills in missing elements of the Ali G myth (he's Alistair Leslie Graham and he met 'me Julie' in his Goth days at a local disco), the character might now have nowhere left to go. But that doesn't matter because Ali G Indahouse strikes while the iron is hot and the jokes are still funny. ★★★ **AM**

ALICE (NECO Z ALENKY) (1988)

Starring: *Krystina Kohoutova (Alice), Camilla Power (Voice of Alice)*
Director: *Jan Svankmajer*
Screenwriter: *Jan Svankmajer, based on* Alice's Adventures In Wonderland *by Lewis Carroll*
U/85 mins./Fantasy/ Switzerland/UK/West Germany

Having watched a stuffed white rabbit break free from its mounting and disappear through a drawer in her desk, Alice follows and embarks on a series of bizarre adventures in a wondrous, but occasionally perilous land.

Anyone familiar with Sir John Tenniel's original illustrations for Lewis Carroll's books about Alice's adventures in Wonderland and through the Looking Glass will have noted a sinister element to them that chimes in with the text's disconcerting surrealism. This dark tone should have rendered this beloved fable the perfect vehicle for master Czech animator Jan Svankmajer to make his feature debut. However, rather than proving an inspiration, Carroll's eccentric chronicle seems to inhibit Svankmajer's imagination and, on several occasional, it even exposes his limitations as a storyteller.

As ever, the texture and colours of Eva Svankmajerova's art direction are impeccable and her husband admirably resists the temptation to follow film precedent and resort to casting heavily disguised guest stars as the Queen of Hearts's subjects. Moreover, as one would expect of the artist who had already re-imagined the Jabberwocky in 1971, Svankmajer does come up with some eye-catching Carrollian moments. But they tend to come when he allows his imagination to soar and he introduces creatures of his own devising, such as the menacing flying bed, the skeletal hybrids (which anticipate vicious Sid's experiments in *Toy Story*) and the partially feathered chicks. That said, the Frog Footman who can't resist shooting out his tongue to catch flies, the Doormouse who sets up camp in Alice's hair and the taxidermied White Rabbit who has to keep gobbling sawdust to replace that oozing from his torn stomach are all memorably grotesque.

The attempt at some underwater sequences (which is notoriously difficult in stop-motion animation) is also laudable. But Svankmajer entrusted much of the puppetry to his assistant, Bedrich Glaser, who isn't always as meticulous as his mentor. Consequently, he seems content to settle for ingenious unreality rather than irresistible illusion and, so, while this is an intriguing adaptation it's never as compelling as it promises to be. ★★★ **DP**

ALICE DOESN'T LIVE HERE ANYMORE (1974)

Starring: *Ellen Burstyn (Alice Hyatt), Kris Kristofferson (David), Alfred Lutter (Tommy Hyatt), Billy 'Green' Bush (Donald Hyatt), Diane Ladd (Flo), Harvey Keitel (Ben Everhart), Jodie Foster (Audrey)*
Director: *Martin Scorsese*
Screenwriter: *Robert Getchell*
15/112 mins./Drama/USA
Awards: *Academy Awards – Best Actress*

Alice Hyatt sets off across the South-West with her young son Tommy, intending to resume her career as a singer. Along the road, she finds work as a waitress, and is torn between settling into a relationship or pursuing her ambitions.

An odd item in Martin Scorsese's filmography since its main character is neither ItalianAmerican nor a man played by Robert De Niro, this is nevertheless one of his major works. Scripted by Robert Getchell, it has a mildly feminist streak in its attempt to show a woman cast adrift by the death of her boorish trucker husband ('Green' Bush) and struggling to make her own decisions.

Ellen Burstyn, a deserved Oscar winner, is the youngish widow, managing heartbreak and falling-down humour in the same scene. The scenes with her irreverent, annoying, amazingly credible son are especially priceless – there's a masterly improv on one of the many long driving to nowhere sequences as the boy tries over and over to tell her a joke ('Shoot the dog! Shoot the dog!') she stubbornly doesn't get (watch her face crumple as he starts up again).

Harvey Keitel imports the Scorsese touch, albeit with a scorpion bolo tie and a convincing Western accent, as a suave suitor who turns violent when thwarted, while Kris Kristofferson, with white streaks in his beard, is an interesting take on the Ideal Man as caring but not soft-headed. The son's unconventional girlfriend is a very young, already-outstanding Jodie Foster ('weird!') and the feisty waitress who clashes with, then warms up to, Alice is Diane Ladd (look out for her little daughter, Laura Dern, eating ice-cream during the final scene).

Alternating gritty realism and redhued fantasy, this is one of those 70s films that wears well, universal in its heart while picking out specifics which are exactly of their time. ★★★★ **KN**

ALIEN (1979)

Starring: *Tom Skerritt (Dallas), Sigourney Weaver (Ripley), Veronica Cartwright (Lambert), Harry Dean Stanton (Brett), John Hurt (Kane), Ian Holm (Ash), Yaphet Kotto (Parker)*
Director: *Ridley Scott*
Screenwriter: *Dan O'Bannon, based on a story by O'Bannon and Ronald Shusett*
18/124 mins./Horror/Sci-fi/USA
Awards: *Academy Awards – Best Visual Effects, BAFTA – Best Production Design, Best Sound Track*

A mining ship investigating an SOS call from a distant planet find a colony of Alien eggs and – too late – realise the signal was a warning not a distress call.

Let's face it, most sci-fi movie posters are rubbish, melodramatic montage paintings designed to give you a quick visual precis of the film. (Would you like the *Star Wars* poster if it wasn't *Star Wars?*) *Alien*, however, was different. Even today its poster stands as a model for high-class movie artwork: the black background, the single nobbly egg with a v-shaped crack forming, the spaced-out letters of the title, and a tagline that must have earned the marketing team the rest of the day off: 'In space no-one can hear you scream.' It is perhaps a little too convenient to say that Alien's seismic effect on the genre was prefigured by its stark, minimalist poster, but the sheer come-and-get-it confidence gave a clue that something was about to explode.

The people who developed *Alien* did so in the shadow of *Star Wars* and *Close Encounters*, the films that had proved that, post-Vietnam, cinema audiences had a new appetite for cosmic escapism. But where these were feelgood family films, *Alien* marked a return to the malevolent flying-saucer flicks of the 50s – with a dash of John Carpenter's *Halloween* thrown in. Writer Dan O'Bannon and co-storyman Ron Shusett intended *Alien* to be a low-budget affair, like *Halloween* – in fact, like *Dark Star*, O'Bannon's previous film. Over three months, a modest script emerged from a half-finished O'Bannon story about a distress signal in space called 'Memory'. It was retitled Star Beast and finally *Alien*. When a draft was handed to artist Ron Cobb for preliminary sketchwork, he described it thus:

'A small, modest little ship with a small crew land on a small planet. They go down a small pyramid and shake up a medium-sized creature. That's about it.'

And that was about it, except with 'small, modest, little' replaced by 'fucking huge': the ship, commercial towing vehicle *Nostromo*, ended up being 800 feet long, and the 'small pyramid' became a derelict spacecraft as big as a skyscraper. However, the crew stayed small (seven, plus cat), the alien stayed medium-sized (no bigger than the man who played him, supple Masai tribesman Bolaji Badejo) and the story stayed simple: ship lands on planet in response to an SOS that turns out to be a warning; alien infects one of the crew; alien kills the rest of the crew one by one. It's *Ten Little Indians* in space. So why is it so ground-breaking? What's so special about it? Easy. The look.

Like the space tug itself, all fantasy films carry in their wake a warehouseful of weird and wonderful production paintings. Sci-fi fans eat them up. *Alien* is no different; a book of sketches was published to coincide with the film, and the journey it describes from doodle to storyboard to screen is compelling, taking in spacesuit drawings by French comic book legend Moebius, *Nostromo* interiors by Cobb, and airbrushed alien designs by H.R. Giger. It was Giger who cracked *Alien*, not just with the creature itself (rarely seen in full anyway), but with the organic innards of the derelict ship and its ghostly egg chamber. It's no surprise to learn that Giger works surrounded by animal skeletons. To describe *Alien* as a triumph chiefly in terms of its look is not to underplay its dramatic strengths, it's just that ordinary filmgoers tend to nod off if you pay tribute to designers (art directors Roger Christian and Les Dilley, production designer Michael Seymour, FX team Brian Johnson, Nick Allder, Carlo Rambali ... wake up!) and thus it's easier to praise Ridley Scott's command of the corridors, or the offbeat cast for giving the crew crumpled life. But it is *Alien*'s unique, tactile world that made it so amenable to sequels: there is little crossover in personnel from one *Alien* film to the next, yet it seems to have a life all of its own.

Alien set a new blueprint for sci-fi horror: the claustrophobia, the crew class system, and the inevitable scene where someone goes after a cat. Some favour James Cameron's gung-ho sequel, but in duplicating the alien for shoot-'em-up potential, it serves only to highlight the reserve and purity of the original. There are thrills of the highest order – Dallas (Skerritt) in the air shaft while a blip on the tracker closes in; and, of course, the famous chest-burst – but the beauty of Alien remains ... its beauty. ★★★★★ **AC**

Movie Trivia: Alien

Screenwriter Dan O'Bannon's original title was Star Beast. It's said the thin layer of mist that notified the eggs was created using a pulsar and smoke — borrowed from the band The Who. The face part of the alien's costume head is made from a cast of a real human skull.

ALIEN AUTOPSY (2006)

Starring: *Declan Donnelly (Ray Santilli), Anthony McPartlin (Gary Shoefield), Bill Pullman (Morgan Banner), Götz Otto (Voros), Morwenna Banks (Jasmine), Harry Dean Stanton (Harvery)*
Director: *Jonny Campbell*
Screenwriter: *Will Davies*
12A/95 mins./Comedy/Sci-fi/UK

It's 1996, and on a trip to Cleveland to buy Elvis trinkets for his London market stall, Ray meets the mysterious Harvey, who sells him real footage from a 1947 alien autopsy at Roswell. When Ray and pal Gary return to England and find the film has corroded, they set about making their own version to show the world.

Are Ant and Dec attempting global domination? They've been child stars, pop stars, ITV's most popular hosts, and now – with the help of *Shameless* and *Phoenix Nights* director Jonny Campbell – they've made this, their enjoyable first feature.

While it's not as hilarious as you might have hoped, it's a decent lark that begins as their two characters, Gary and Ray, agree to be interviewed by documentary-maker Morgan Banner. He has no idea who they are, but becomes interested as their story about buying genuine alien autopsy footage unfolds, and they tell how they eventually find themselves having to fake an autopsy in Gary's sister's living room.

The best scenes, of course, are the ones in which the boys are faking the autopsy with the help of an eclectic bunch of friends – an undertaker, a mannequin-maker (who is dating Ray's nan), a butcher (who provides the haggis that doubles for an alien brain), and kebab shop owner Melik (Omid Djalili) – it's like a Morecambe and Wise sketch as Nan interrupts offering biscuits, the clock falls off the wall and Gary panics as blood drops on his sister's carpet.

It's too slow in the build-up to the boys' acquisition of the film, and there's predictable rivalry between the pair later on, but once this gets going, the laughs are consistent. ★★★ **JB**

ALIEN NATION (1988)

Starring: *James Caan (Det. Sgt Matthew Sykes), Mandy Patinkin (Det. Samuel 'George' Francisco), Terence Stamp (William Harcourt), Kevyn Major Howard (Rudyard Kipling)*
Director: *Graham Baker*
Screenwriter: *Rockne S. O'Bannon*
15/91 mins./Sci-fi/USA

It's 1991 and 100,000 aliens, known as Newcomers, have unexpectedly landed on Earth, and swiftly become integrated into human society. Although the victims of prejudice and forced into menial jobs, Sam Francisco has become the first Newcomer cop, partnered with tough, racist human Matthew Sykes whose previous partner happened to be killed by Newcomers.

Given the punning title, and not-so subtle subtext of racism and immigration issues, this superficially sci-fi movie squanders the simple opportunity to be a juicy creature feature by fooling itself it has got something important to say. In fact, despite the wilting satire around the edges – Newcomers get boozed up on sour milk, silt up their innards with bad junk food and fail to comprehend human, or, at least, Californian humour – this is no more than the creaky buddy cop formula given the once over by a screenwriter with a single idea, *48 Hours* meets *E.T.*

Hence, once you get past the giant, slug skinned craniums of the Newcomers, known derisively as 'slags', the film bottoms out as two mismatched cops trace a murder which leads to a drug ring and the most obviously signalled villain since Darth Vader. Oh, and along the way they come to respect one another. As directed by the man who made *Star Trek V* – the really bad one.

Mandy Patinkin, at least, works hard to give Francisco a dopey warmth, which stands in stark contrast to James Caan who could play the hard-bitten bullyboy, boozy loner, and maverick cop type in his sleep, which he seems to be doing. The action is bitty and seldom thrills, the science fiction hastily shunted to the fringes because of budget constriction – the hint that these genetically engineered space slaves were created by some more formidable super alien is frustratingly unexplored.

Instead the film saunters along, making vague comments about the way America treats its immigrant fringes, until they confront the Newcomer baddie. You can spot him as the one doing awfully well. Still, Francisco gets the hang of jokes and over his fear of salt water and Sykes gets a another buddy. A television series briefly followed, but no one noticed. ★★ **IN**

AVP: ALIEN VS. PREDATOR (2004)

Starring: *Sanaa Lathan (Alexa Woods), Raoul Bova (Sebastian de Rosa), Lance Henriksen (Charles Bishop Weyland), Ewen Bremner (Graeme Miller), Colin Salmon (Maxwell Stafford)*
Director: *Paul W. S. Anderson*
Screenwriter: *Paul W.S. Anderson, from a story by Paul W. S. Anderson, based on characters created by Dan O'Bannon, Ronald Shusett, Jim Thomas and John Thomas*
15/101 mins./Sci-fi/Horror/Action/ USA/Canada/Czech Republic/ Germany

During an archaeological expedition in Antarctica, a scientific team accidentally stumble on a battle between Aliens and Predators.

Few franchises boast taglines so indicative as those of the *Alien* saga. Ridley Scott's chilling first instalment intoned, 'In space, no one can hear you scream' – surely the most alluring horror tag ever – while James Cameron's action-classic sequel offered the no-mess, gravelly bark of 'This time it's war.' Then Fincher's grim, part three mis-step delivered the brutal cough of 'The bitch is back', with Jeunet's sloppy Resurrection apologetically muttering, 'Witness the resurrection.' Consider, then, the strap for Paul W S Anderson's kinda-prequel: 'Whoever wins – we lose.' Yes, you guessed it, the 'we' here refers to the audience. Or, at least, an audience which doesn't entirely consist of freshly pubescent boys.

Naturally, for those who still have a bit of freshly pubescent boy, or even tomboy, in us (so to speak), there is a twinge of a thrill at the prospect of seeing the rastaphibian hunters of the *Predator* movies getting scrap-happy with H R Giger's acid-drooling xenomorphs. And Anderson's been smart enough to keep the cool species-pairing concept first suggested by the *Alien Vs. Predator* comic book: Predators breed Aliens in order to hunt them, then some unwitting humans get stuck in the middle. Neat.

Problem is, the originals were savvy enough to make sure their human element was something we could latch onto, whether it was watching an Arnie-at-his-peak outgunned and outmuscled by a mostly unseen supernatural foe, or chewing fingernails for Ripley as her destiny became agonisingly entwined with that of her nightmarish nemeses. Plus, those films offered a group dynamic which amped the suspense as the extraterrestrial stalkers picked their prey off one by one.

But Anderson is a director in a perpetual state of rush, so blindly keen to shove his early-teen audience into the front row of this intergalactic royal rumble that he's forgotten the dramatic importance of building anticipation – and along the way denied us the small luxury of any characters. Sanaa Lathan's plucky guide is nothing more than a shrug-worthy Ripley-lite, Lance Henriksen's Company-man Weyland only serves as an over-stretched plot-umbilical to the other Aliens, and poor Ewen Bremner's stumbly science-bod is a mere patsy for a string of sick jokes.

It's tempting to see Anderson's choice of setting – a gargantuan, Indiana Jones-style box of tricks, complete with sliding walls, trapdoors and shifting blocks – as an attempt to distract us from the dearth of humanity. Either that, or proof he's just played too many platform games.

So, what of the xeno-smackdown, then? Well, even that's something of a disappointment. It's certainly a treat to watch one Predator dismissively deface one of his toothy enemies with a single claw swipe in one scene, while the portrayal of the Alien Queen as a screeching version of *Jurassic Park*'s T-Rex set loose on the Antarctic surface briefly pinches the adrenal glands.

But, pressured to deliver a kid-friendly rating, the director reduces his clash sequences to a morass of clumsy cuts and juddery mis-framing; you're pushed so close to the action, it's hard to see what's going on.

It's obvious Anderson has great love for the franchises he's cross-breeding, and he peppers the movie with little in-jokes and knowing winks. But watching him reference the likes of Scott, Cameron and McTiernan is like watching a loud-mouth kid trying to join in with the grown-ups: initially entertaining, then embarrassing, and finally just plain annoying. Unless, of course, you're a loud-mouth kid yourself. ★★ **DJ**

ALIEN RESURRECTION (1997)

Starring: *Sigourney Weaver (Ellen Ripley), Winona Ryder (Annalee Call), Dominique Pinon (Vriess), Ron Perlman (Johner), Gary Dourdan (Christie)*
Director: *Jean-Pierre Jeunet*
Screenwriter: *Joss Whedon, based on characters created by Dan O'Bannon and Ronald Shusett*
15/109 mins./116 mins.(special edition)/Sci-fi/Thriller/Horror/USA

A cloned Ripley is brought back to life and ends up defending earth, once again, from flesh munching Aliens.

When French whizz Jean-Pierre Jeunet signed up to direct a fourth Alien movie there was clearly one overriding remit impressed upon him as he took pen in hand. Whatever you do, don't make *Alien³*. That he certainly has not done.

Alien Resurrection, suitably Gothic and biological, nests at the other end of the sci-fi-horror spectrum entirely, played broadly, accessibly and too often hamfistedly for a peculiar black humour.

Gone is the portentous gloom and slow build. Gone too is the vicelike tension of *Aliens*, and the bogeyman suspense of *Alien*. Instead we get the wild flourishes of *The City Of Lost Facehuggers*, *Delicatessen In Space*. So, very French.

Joss Whedon's script, which feels heavily rejigged, serves up a delicious premise: the reincarnation of Ripley spliced with a few Alien genes. So Weaver get to play it teasingly amoral, slithering out her 'I died' one-liners with a genuine raptor's smile. The plot surrounding her comeback is much more direct than previous incarnations – a bunch of anarchic scientists grow their own Aliens from an illicit cargo of humans as delivered by a band of truculent brigands. Bad idea. Through an exotic powwow, the Aliens hatch an escape plan – acid blood works a treat – and start chowing down on the crew. The ship goes Mayday and heads for Earth.

These elements established, *Resurrection* reverts to standard procedure – a scattering of survivors, in this case the pirate band plus the diffident Ripley – endeavour to escape the Alien peril by scampering through dingy corridors with flamethrowers.

What hampers this surest of sure things is Jeunet's ridiculous largesse. When tension is required he delivers gags. Where restrained mystery would turn the screws, he gives it to us straight. The Aliens, upfront from the beginning, are not the unthinking, killing machines we know and love, but idiot pet poodles with a fiercesome overbite. Characters, invitingly rangy, are dispatched with inconsistent stupidity while others suffer improbably personality changes: Ron Perlman's lascivious knucklehead turning good guy, Winona Ryder's squeaky Call making her 'dark secret' abundantly apparent. Elsewhere, Jeunet cooks up some perviness with Ripley, an Alien Queen and the pottiest birth scene in movie history. It's a consistent flaw throughout: terror replacing gunge – this is easily the goriest (at times insensibly so) Alien movie.

What rescues *Resurrection* from the margins of disaster is the sheer weight of the Alien mythology. The visuals, by *Seven*'s cinematographer Darius Khondiji, are electrifying, adhering to the space grunge atmos laid down by Ridley Scott, but adding to the low-lit, dry-iced claustrophobia with Jeunet's trademark expressionism. An extraordinary underwater sequence, although artlessly contrived, takes the breath away. The Aliens, ephemerally, have never been so gracefully defined, with hissing, steaming close-ups and willowy CGI full-body shots turning Giger's slavering extra-terrestrial to a thing of beauty. There is a thrusting, charged nature to the chase, never with Cameron's canon of adrenaline rushes, but with a brash, yucky violence that aims to shock rather than thrill. Once you've bought into Jeunet's sicko-funky style, the middle hour offers some of the choicest Alien hijinkery of the series – a stunning topsy-turvy ladder shoot-out. Ripley's nonchalant brutality (and basketball skills), Brad Dourif eyeballing a captive. Alien from behind acid-proof glass.

And there is, of course, the fabulous Weaver. As with every film in the series she is the holding force, relishing Ripley/Clone 8's molten amorality, turning the earnest, fulminating human into a vital, sexy, animalistic cross-breed with the ultimate identity crisis.

So there is not the rank dejection of having witnessed *Alien3*, just a bewildering feeling that this should have been much more considered and that, perhaps, Danny Boyle – who just missed out on the gig – was really the man for the job. ★★★ **IN**

⦵ ALIEN³ (1992)

Starring: *Sigourney Weaver (Ellen Ripley), Charles S. Dutton (Dillon), Charles Dance (Clemens), Paul McGann (Golic), Brain Glover (Andrews)*
Director: *David Fincher*
Screenwriters: *David Giler, Walter Hill and Larry Ferguson*
18/114 mins./Sci-fi/Horror/Action/USA

Ripley and her crew are escaping from Aliens when they crash onto a prison colony planet. Soon, it becomes clear the colony is also inhabited by an Alien – and it may not be alone.

This retread puts its foot wrong during the credits, as awkward exposition brings Ripley and a handy alien egg to a prison planet populated by religious fanatics who think they're either in *Porridge* or *Lock-Up*, killing off all the other left-over characters from Aliens in computer read-out asides.

The film never recovers, and busily hurries towards its absurd 'transcendent' finale – which owes more than a little to James Cameron's *T2* ending – by having interchangable characters run around dark corridors while a fish-eye lens monster chases them. The shaven head theme allows Weaver to look striking and do Joan of Arc poses, but also serves to render the rest of the cast, in contrast with the well-fleshed monster munchies of the earlier films, totally anonymous, so that by the time the death-filled finale arrives it is impossible to tell who is still alive and who has just been killed.

Write in and tell us when Paul McGann dies. On second thoughts, don't. What few attempts at character there are – Charles Dance gets one emotional speech to lull you into a false sense of security before the thingie drops on his head – come off as unfortunately gigglesome, and even Weaver, who took the two-dimensional character from *Alien* and gave her real depth for the sequel, is just going over old ground with a new haircut, being required by an idiotic script not to tell anyone that she thinks there's a monster on the loose until well after heads have been crunched to pulp and acid-blood dripped all over the show.

Originally conceived by Vincent Ward (one of many writers and directors to have come and gone on the project), as a mediaeval space epic, the story has been scaled down so it can be shot in a familiar disused ironworks of the future and filmed, by rock video grad Fincher, with a grainy brown sludginess that tries for atmosphere but comes off as simply murky.

Alien³ – which looks as if it's really called Alien Cubed – would probably not be so disappointing if it were Alien 2. After all, if it were judged alongside *Robocop 2*, *Another 48 HRs*, *Jaws 2* or *Beverly Hills Cop 2*, it would seem no better nor worse than the usual sequel. However, it's stuck with being the follow-up not only to Ridley Scott's *Alien*, one of the most-imitated and rememered s-f films of the last 15 years, but also to James Cameron's *Aliens*, that rare sequel that expands and improves upon the original. With the raising of the stakes between the first two films and coming after Cameron's all-out war with hundreds of monsters, it is now hard to get too scared by the spectacle of one lone dog-shaped alien on the loose, especially since the beast seems to have come not from the finale of the last film but from some script conference in the development hell that has been going since Renny Harlin was going to direct from a script by William Gibson.

In a back-hander of spectacular grumpiness we finally get to meet someone from the Head Office of that evil company which has been casually wasting human life for three films and incarnating all the rapacious monstrousness of corporate scumminess, and – guess what? – he's Japanese. ★★★ **KN**

⦵ ALIENS (1986)

Starring: *Sigourney Weaver (Ripley), Michael Biehn (Cpl Hicks), Carrie Henn (Newt), Bill Paxton (Pvt. Hudson), Paul Reiser (Burke), Lance Henrkison (Bishop)*
Director: *James Cameron*
Screenwriter: *James Cameron, based on a story by Cameron, David Giler and Walter Hill and on characters created by Dan O'Bannon and Ronald Shusett*
15/137 mins./Sci-fi//Horror/Action/USA/UK
Awards: *Oscars – Best Sound Effects Editing, Best Visual Effects, BAFTA – Best Visual Effects*

Ripley and a team of space marines battle a group of Aliens – and this time they've brought their mother.

Aliens is the perfect sequel. *The Empire Strikes Back*, while certainly a better film than *Star Wars*, was more a polished segment in a longer story than a stand-alone adventure. But *Aliens* is the model for every potential sequel-maker: it connects irrefutably with the events of the original (even to the point of starting exactly where the drama left off, albeit 57 years later) and expands on all the ideas and themes while simultaneously differentiating itself. The same, yet entirely different. Perfect.

It also stands as testament to the unwavering vision and icy nerve of James Cameron (here directing only his third movie). Utilising the bombed out skeleton of Battersea Power Station to create the vast industrio-grim colony/hive setting for events, he was faced with a veteran British crew who had worked on *Alien* and worshipped the ground Ridley Scott walked on. What could this Canadian punk kid know? Well, for starters that in this case more is, indeed, more. Not just a single, ruthless, unbeatable killing machine but an army of them. On home turf.

Writing as well as directing, Cameron posited a simple premise. The planet LV-426, where the first Alien was unwittingly discovered has been colonised by the *Nostromo*'s mother company Weyland-Yutani. And now communication has been lost. Time to send in a crack team of space marines and enlist the help of a traumatised Ripley. There you have it – Marines (plus the ever resourceful Ripley) versus Aliens (plus mum). This was genre splicing a la carte: the war movie fused inextricably with science fiction. A factor highlighted by Cameron's hardware fetish – he drools lavishly over the future technology of weaponry.

He was also fascinated with Ripley and understood straight away this was her story. It is her resourcefulness and ability to rationalise the crisis that enables survival (Newt is a perfect junior model – someone who has survived by her wits). Courage, for Ripley, is an acceptance of fear and dealing with it with intelligence. Weaver deservedly got an Oscar nomination.

What also counts here is execution. Cameron accepted Scott's (and, of course, H. R. Giger's) design ethic – gloop, scaly bits, loadsa teeth and long, dark, dingy, dripping corridors – but reinterpreted them as a battleground rather than a haunted house. The point he grasped straight away is that you can't win against this foe or the stigma, the sheer terror that this endomorph engenders would be lost. You can only escape. He replaced Scott's 'behind-you' tension with a muscular fury, unrelenting, sweaty-palmed, pant-filling movie intensity. Nothing before or since has locked the viewer in with such an all-consuming sense of peril (audiences and critics actually complained of physical discomfort even illness upon exiting the auditorium).

Thematically *Aliens* also expounds the set-up further. Central is a continuation of Scott and Dan O'Bannon's (the original screenwriter) bogey man hypothesis – what if a lifeform was so attuned to survival it became the perfect killing machine and as such garnered a degree of Darwinisitic respect, even from its prey? Ash in *Alien*, lunatic android though he was, praised the monster for its 'purity'. even Ripley, confronted by the duplicity of company man Burke (Paul Reiser), has to admit that 'You don't see them fucking each other over for a goddamn percentage!' Then it really gets going: Alien as giant phallus (and now there's a whole army of them) versus feminist heroine. The feminist subtext is hardly 'sub' at all, Ripley is one of the strongest female characters in movie history.

Closer to Cameron's heart, and a theme that recurs throughout his work, is the preservation of the nuclear family. With Newt rescued and Ripley taking on the role of surrogate mother we only need add Hick's gentlemanly (but by no means dominant) father to complete our model of perfect family unit (the other survivor, the android Bishop, well, he's either a kindly uncle or the pet dog or something). This whole notion is finally boiled down to a remarkable battle of maternal instincts – Ripley defending her child Newt; the queen Alien defending (or, at least, avenging) her children – summed up memorably in Ripley's battle call: 'Get away from her, you bitch!' The biology of the species has been developed to the point where empathy if not sympathy is acceptable. And if you want to keep this up there is the 'Nam in space metaphor: unseen 'gooks' mounting stealth attacks and the retreating Yanks totally undone by a tactic and mindset they cannot comprehend (a metaphor for US foreign policy?).

Tagline
This time it's war

Yet none of such academic noodling is ever at the expense of the thrills. Cameron understood fundamentally the basis here was a gut reaction. *Aliens'* construction of action scenes, its build-up of tension and its final execution of combat is a marvel to behold (the film literally provokes a physical reaction). These are characters we care about, headed up by a resourceful heroine who is pitted against a formidable enemy in a thoroughly believable environment. Pure movie. ★★★★★ **IN**

ALIVE (1993)

Starring: *Ethan Hawke (Nando Parrado), Vincent Spano (Antonio Balbi), Josh Hamilton (Roberto Canessa), Bruce Ramsay (Carlitos Paez), John Newton (Antonio 'Tintin' Vizintin), Illena Douglas (Liliana Methol)*
Director: *Frank Marshall*
Screenwriter: *John Patrick Shanley, based on a novel by Piers Paul Reid*
15/126 mins./Drama/Biography/USA

A young rugby team take desperate measures to survive after being involved in an air crash that leaves them stranded in the Andes for ten weeks.

Pity the poor marketing types condemned to work with Frank Marshall. For his feature debut, the longtime Spielberg producer opted for a tale about very large, very hairy spiders and called it *Arachnophobia*, potentially alienating the millions who suffer from that condition. And in this film he tackles the tale of the survivors of an air crash who resort to eating the corpses of their deceased fellow passengers – cannibalism, of course, being one of the last terrible taboos and not a staple of a jolly trip to the movies.

In fact, *Arachnophobia* went on to make huge amounts of money, and, as those who have read Piers Paul Read's stunning account of this story will testify, this is not about cannibalism at all; rather it is about one of the most extraordinary feats of human courage and dogged survival ever recorded.

In 1972, a young Uruguayan rugby team (most in their late teens) were heading for a tour of Chile when their hopeless ex-Uruguayan Air Force plane came down in the Andes. Many of the passengers survived with horrific injuries, staying alive for ten weeks on top of a freezing glacier by eating the dead – an action that was, incredibly, condemned by a number of their Godfearing countrymen on their return.

Marshall succeeds excellently in capturing a sense of the things that dominated the survivors' lives during those months of horror – fear, hunger, despair, cold – and proves adept at characterisation, as leaders emerge, the weak go to the wall, and the members of the audience try valiantly to be honest about how they would cope in such a testing situation. The most gripping moment, naturally enough, is when the starving survivors, knives at the ready, head for the frozen bodies – and once again Marshall doesn't flinch, depicting the incident with gruesome realism.

Where he may have gone awry, however, is in his decision to concentrate exclusively on the crash site (in the book, Reid frequently cuts back to the families and the rescue attempts), so that there are far too many shots of people sitting about outside the wrecked fuselage or huddling for warmth within it. Indeed, the entire movie is a good half-hour too long, with one too many failed attempts to get over into the Chilean valleys coming before the last, heroic trek to safety. This does, however, include some extraordinary action sequences, with the initial air crash ranking as one of the most realistic and terrifying ever filmed. And one cannot but marvel at what surviving such an incident – and the following months and years – must do to a human being. ★★★★ **PT**

ALL ABOUT EVE (1950)

Starring: *Bette Davis (Margo Channing), Anne Baxter (Eve Harrington), George Sanders (Addison Witt), Celeste Holm (Karen Richards), Marilyn Monroe (Miss Casswell)*
Director: *Joseph L. Mankiewicz*
Screenwriter: *Joseph L. Mankiewicz, based on the story* The Wisdom Of Eve, *by Mary Orr*
U/138 mins./Drama/USA
Awards: *Academy Awards – Best Supporting Actor (George Sanders), Best Director, Best Screenplay, Best Cinematography, Best Costume Design, Best Sound Recording. BAFTA – Best Film. Cannes Best Actress (Bette Davis), Jury Special Prize (Joseph L. Mankiewicz)*

Trading on the vanity and insecurity of ageing actress Margo Channing, Eve Harrington becomes her indispensable confidante in an attempt to launch her own bid for Broadway immortality.

With cinema losing its battle with television, it was no coincidence that two such rancorous exposés of Hollywood and Broadway as *Sunset Blvd.* and *All About Eve* should have been up against each other for the Best Picture of 1950. Eve landed 14 nominations, a record that was not equalled until *Titanic* in 1998. Its four female stars were all cited – Bette Davis and Anne Baxter for Best Actress and Celeste Holm and Thelma Ritter for Best

Supporting – and although they all lost out (to Judy Holliday in *Born Yesterday* and Josephine Hull in *Harvey*, respectively), the picture was successful in six other categories, notably bagging a brace for writer-director, Joseph L. Mankiewicz.

Having seen his brother Herman win an Oscar for his screenplay for *Citizen Kane*, Mankiewicz borrowed elements from its winning, flashbacking formula for this showbiz bitchfest, which sought to understand what drove aspiring actress Eve Harrington to clamber to the top over the corpse of her supposed idol, Margo Channing.

Based on Mary Orr's short story and radio play, *The Wisdom Of Eve*, this has none of the enduring class of Kane, as Joseph is nowhere near as dextrous a writer as his older sibling (with too many of his stinging bon mots sounding handcrafted rather than raspingly spontaneous) nor as inventive a director as Orson Welles. But this is still a rousing and endlessly amusing melodrama whose merciless demythologising of the tawdry trappings of fame remains acutely relevant in these days of transient celebrity.

Returning to the screen after two years away and injecting each epigram with real venom, Davis (who was only cast after Claudette Colbert damaged her back) gives a magisterial performance that seems founded upon the realisation that her own time in the spotlight was short. But she could never have anticipated that the film's future star was not to be Baxter, but a cameoing Marilyn Monroe. ★★★★ **DP**

⦿ ALL ABOUT MY MOTHER (TODO SOBRE MI MADRE) (1999)

Starring: *Cecilia Roth (Manuela), Marisa Paredes (Human Rojo), Candela Pena (Nina), Penélope Cruz (Sister Rosa), Antonia San Juan (Agrado)*
Director: *Pedro Almodovar*
Screenwriter: *Pedro Almodovar*
15/101 mins./Drama/Spain
Awards: *Oscars – Best Foreign Language Film, BAFTA – Best Film not in the English Language, David Lean Award for Direction*

Traumatised by the death of her son, a Spanish mother leaves for Barcelona where she seeks out old acquaintances.

For his 13th feature, Pedro Almodovar returns to his private but highly accessible world. The title echoes *All About Eve*, and *All About My Mother* embraces some of the plot (turned inside-out) of the great Bette Davis vehicle while exploring its thesis, that all women are great actresses but their skill at emoting in public doesn't mean that they hurt any the less inside.

Manuela promises to tell her teenage son who his father is, but he is killed by a car while pursuing an actress for an autograph. Manuela, whose job at a hospital includes playing the part of a bereaved mother in seminars to teach students how to approach a patient's relatives to get permission for organ donation, has to go through the business of letting her own son's body be harvested. She then heads for Barcelona in search of her son's father, a chick-with-a-dick hooker who has skipped town after robbing their oldest friend Agrado and impregnating (and infecting with HIV) a mixed-up nun, Rosa.

One of the film's many pleasures is that Almodovar constantly reshuffles the plot, making fresh connections, so that everything seems to turn out properly in the end after oceans of tears. In the past, he has often erred on the side of the smirk, but here he truly goes for the heartstrings without losing the absurdist humour.

With magnificent performances all around, especially from Roth and the agonisingly beautiful Cruz, this is one you just don't want to end. ★★★★★ **KN**

⦿ ALL QUIET ON THE WESTERN FRONT (1930)

Starring: *Louis Wolheim (Katczinsky), Lew Ayres (Paul Baumer), John Wray (Himmelstoss), Slim Summerville (Tjaden), Russell Gleason (Muller)*
Director: *Lewis Milestone*
Screenwriters: *Maxwell Anderson, George Anderson, Del Andrews, based on the novel by Erich Maria Remarque*
PG/145 mins./War/USA
Awards: *Academy Awards – Best Picture Best Director*

An adaptation of Eric Maria Remarque's legendary novel, in which a class of idealistic young Germans are inspired to enlist for the trenches of WWI. There the horrors of war eat away at their idealism, their political certainties struck dumb by a very real confrontation with death.

Few films, to this day, have struck as powerful an anti-war message as Lewis Milestone's extraordinary evocation of the tragic folly of war. Arguably, still the greatest WWI movie, his tender portrayal of innocent German youth is juxtaposed with the harrowing immediacy of trench warfare, shot with a telling verisimilitude many modern filmmakers, with all their tools, have failed to match.

Even more than the visceral evocation of trench life, with all its wanton squalor, the philosophical underpinnings of the film reach deep into the heart and head. At the opening, in the dreamy almost fairy-tale safety of their school life, they are resolved, thanks to the stirrings of their teacher, to sign up and fight the good fight. What becomes hastily clear amongst the mud and blood of fellow comrades and shadowy enemies alike is that there is no good fight to be fought, only a terrible one, where victory is a pointless as defeat.

Such a determined, for the time radical message, the soul of Remarque's novel, finds its most focused point in the scene where Paul, whose eyes we follow to the battlefront, is trapped in a bomb crater in no-man's land with a French solider, dying from the wound he gave him. Assaulted by remorse, he vainly tries to save him, prying through his clothes to find a name, a person beneath the victim.

The dialogue may feel arch and stagy by today's standards, the verbose speeches over fallen comrades are hardly realistic, but they are telling, and no concessions are ever made to moral notions of good versus evil (especially as we are seeing it from the German point of view). All is madness, chaos and inescapable loss, captured with poetic and perfect simplicity in the motif of a butterfly watched by Paul from his trench, a reminder of the butterflies he would trap and pin in a glass case as a boy. ★★★★★ **IN**

⦿ ALL THAT HEAVEN ALLOWS (1955)

Starring: *Jane Wyman (Cary Scott), Rock Hudson (Ron Kirby), Agnes Moorehead (Sara Warren), Conrad Nagel, (Harvey), Virginia Grey (Alida Anderson)*
Director: *Douglas Sirk*
Screenwriter: *Peg Fenwick, based on a story by Edna L. Lee and Harry Lee*
U/89 mins./Drama/USA

New England widow Cary Scott rejects the honourable advances of an old friend and proceeds to appal her well-heeled peers and snobbish offspring by falling for Ron Kirby, a gardener who is not only her junior, but also her social inferior.

A prominent intellectual in Germany before he fled the Nazis, Douglas Sirk worked as a director for hire in Hollywood before he and producer Ross Hunter hit upon a brand of high-class soap that made a fortune for Universal and established Sirk as the role model for such maverick auteurs as Rainer Werner Fassbinder, who remade this film as *Fear Eats The Soul* in 1974.

Although he dismissed such later outings as *Written On The Wind* and *Imitation Of Life* as 'kitsch craziness', Sirk was the master of the woman's picture, as he managed to subvert the conventions of the sub-genre while also offering stinging critiques of bourgeois morality and middlebrow culture. Here, Sirk and cinematographer Russell Metty use Alexander Golitzen and Eric Oborn's meticulously decorated sets to trap Jane Wyman in the apparently perfect lifestyle to which many in the audience would have aspired. Moreover, by using graceful long takes, Sirk reinforces both the soullessness of her solitude and the all-embracing exhilaration of her unexpected romance with Rock Hudson (with whom Wyman had teamed the previous year in Sirk's *Magnificent Obsession*).

As ever, Sirk makes miraculous use of reflective surfaces – windows, mirrors, furnishings and even the TV set – to present Wyman as a spirit trapped in a ethereal false idyll, while contrasting colours capture the emotional texture of both the scenes and the characters' psyches. Watch the play of light and hue on the weeping Gloria Talbott's face as she returns home having been humiliated by her friends because of her mother's dalliance. The rainbow effect may be melodramatic and unsubtle. But it conveys her confusion and misery with dazzling simplicity.

Even if it was viewed as novelettish nonsense, this would still make deliciously illicit entertainment. But, thanks to Sirk's eye for an image, it's also enthralling cinema. ★★★★ **DP**

⊙ ALL THE KING'S MEN (1949)

Starring: *Broderick Crawford (Willie Stark), Joanne Dru (Anne Stanton), John Ireland (Jack Burden), John Derek (Tom Stark), Mercedes McCambridge (Sadie Burke)*
Director: *Robert Rossen*
Screenwriter: *Robert Rossen, based on the novel by Robert Penn Warren*
U/109 mins/Drama/USA

Awards: *Academy Awards – Best Picture, Best Actor, Best Supporting Actor (Mercedes McCambridge)*

Pillar of the community Willie Stark is duped into standing in a gubernatorial election. However, he gets a taste for politics and the high life and, once in office, he abandons his principles and begins lining his pockets.

The easiest way to get a handle on this bitingly cynical political picture is to imagine a *Mr Smith Goes To Washington* in which James Stewart becomes corrupted by the very power he believed could only be used for good. Robert Penn Warren's Pulitzer Prize-winning source novel was based on the career of just such a character, Huey Long, the 'Kingfish' of Deep Southern politics in the 1920s, who so abused his position as Governor of Louisiana that he was assassinated by Baton Rouge physician, Carl Austin Weiss, in 1935.

In the book, Willie Stark's rise from small-town laywer to state legislator is presented in a series of Kane-like flashbacks, as journalist Jack Burden takes stock of his life and times. But director Robert Rossen relegated Burden to a supporting role (although John Ireland still attempts to act as Stark's conscience and provides the film's narration) in order to concentrate on Stark, whose rise and fall is now presented chronologically, so as not to distract the audience from the hard-hitting political realities with which they're about to be confronted.

Shooting on location in rundown Stockton, California, enhanced the action's authenticity. But the whole conceit could have collapsed had the Oscar-winning Broderick Crawford (until then a character actor and occasional B-movie lead) not been able credibly to portray Stark's passage from a greenhorn doing a correspondence course to better serve his clients into a monstrous power-addled grafter.

Mercedes McCambridge similarly earned herself a Best Supporting Oscar as scheming political aide, Sadie Burke. But it's Crawford who dominates proceedings and his tour de force performance has prevented *All The King's Men* from dating over the intervening half century, as every subsequent era has had its own man of the people who Jekylls into a self-serving Hyde once in office and begins championing his own demagoguery over democracy. ★★★★ **DP**

⊙ ALL THE PRESIDENT'S MEN (1976)

Starring: *Robert Redford (Bob Woodward), Dustin Hoffman (Carl Bernstein), Jack Warden (Harry Rosenfeld), Martin Balsam (Howard Simons), Jason Robards (Ben Bradlee), Ned Beatty (Dardis), Stephen Collins (Hugh Sloan, Jr), Hal Holbrook (Deep Throat)*
Director: *Alan J. Pakula*
Screenwriter: *William Goldman, based on the book by Carl Bernstein and Bob Woodward.*
15/138 mins./Political/Drama/USA

Awards: *Academy Awards – Best Supporting Actor (Jason Robards); Best Screenplay; Best Sound; Best Art Direction*

Two *Washington Post* journalists, Bob Woodward and Carl Bernstein, investigating a routine break-in at the Democratic Party Headquarters at the Watergate Building, happen upon the story of the century. A dirty tricks campaign that may lead all the way to the Oval Office.

Taking such a detailed, realistic, and unshowy approach to Woodward and Bernstein's dry account of their fateful investigation, was a risky venture for Alan J. Pakula, a sturdy enough director of middle-brow Hollywood thrillers. With a narrative so resolutely shorn of subplots and characterisation; two stars striving to shed their glamorous skins to reveal ordinary, hard-working men; and a gloomy, intricate, talky plot – audiences were likely to be heard falling over themselves to get away from the cinema.

That was the risk, the result is one of modern American film's most intelligent and provocative accounts of a nation's political failings, and a near-perfect depiction of journalism at its purist and most inspired. To be more succinct, it is quite brilliant.

Tension strains and tears at our nerves from the off as the two reporters are hardly well-matched as they spar and nag at each other, until the cause strips bare all notions of professional ego. The story also strains with a detail that is near impossible to follow as they trace the chain of corruption, aided and abetted by Hal Holbroook's growly supergrass Deep Throat, but that just adds to the sense of import. You couldn't and shouldn't trivialise this material.

Pakula's hardnosed verite texture reaches beyond just the mundane gathering of information – a process so deglamorised it feels like drudgery – to the thrilling interplay of the *Post*'s bustling, factory-like office. Here, such epoch-making events are tellingly poked and prodded by grizzly old editorial salts played by Robert Walden, John McMartin and an Oscar winning Jason Robards. Indeed, his portrayal of executive editor Ben Bradlee gives the film such a powerful injection of humour and pathos it offsets any potential drift into pomposity. And yet, it is also his voice that truly echoes what remains the most significant, vital record for the necessity of the fourth estate: 'Nothing's riding on this except the first amendment to the Constitution, freedom of the press, and maybe the future of the country. Not that any of that matters, but if you guys fuck up again, I'm going to get mad.' Pretty much, essential. ★★★★★ **IN**

⦿ ALL THE RIGHT MOVES (1983)

Starring: *Tom Cruise (Stef), Lea Thompson (Lisa Litski), Craig T. Nelson (Nickerson), Charles Ciofi (Pop), Chris Penn (Brian)*
Director: *Michael Chapman*
Screenwriter: *Michael Kane*
15/91 mins./Drama/Romance/Sport/USA

Smalltown football star Stef Djordjevic dreams of getting a football scholarship that will get him out of the narrow town confines and offer him the chance for a proper education. First though, he must deal with his hardnosed coach and the pressures of being young.

Back when Tom Cruise was still a spindly wetback with a glean of superstardom in his baby-blues, he took on the symbolic role of a young jock with dreams of something better. And while it would be overstating matters to identify this film as a mirror of Cruise's rise to glory, there is a tender resonance in its cheesy sports drama operating with all the obvious moves.

Anyway, it transpired America was really in the mood for such aspirational twaddle, as in the very same year *Flashdance* played an identical game replacing this Western Pennsylvanian steeltown with Pittsburgh and a welder with dreams of being a dancer. There is, at least, with Michael Chapman's less glossy designs, a sense of reality in the rundown town offering little more than unemployment and poverty once the hallowed days of school are done.

The school too, tackles genuine tribulations rather than the soap operatics of the similarly minded *Varsity Blues*: Stef's relationship with his girlfriend (Thompson) is complicated and honest (she is terrified if he gets out he will never return), while the kids in general are caught up with the awkward embarrassments and emotions of growing up. The central message, tied up both in the football and in the school body, is, 'What am I worth?' when the world around convinces them, not much at all.

That said, we are not talking about profound revelations. Cruise, at just 22, is doggedly one-dimensional and his sparring with overbearing Nelson's Coach Nickerson is as hoary a set of clichés as they come. And despite all its working-class, quasi-socialist trappings, the film is finally flogging the ragged old tale of following the American Dream. ★★ **IN**

⦿ ALLIGATOR (1980)

Starring: *Robert Forster (David Madison), Robin Riker (Marisa Kendall), Michael Gazzo (Chief Clark), Dean Jagger (Slade)*
Director: *Lewis Teague*
Screenwriter: *John Sayles*
15/89 mins./Comedy/Sci-fi/USA

Chicago is terrorised by a giant mutant – an unwanted pet baby alligator flushed down the toilet in 1968, which has been eating dumped experimental animals dosed with a growth hormone. Balding cop Madison and herpetologist Marisa Kendall set out to destroy the monster.

Thanks to a witty John Sayles script, solid performances, effective effects and Lewis Teague's spirited B-level direction, this formulaically-plotted monster movie crawls out of the creature feature pack and delivers old-fashioned entertainment with comic and satirical footnotes.

Typically for Sayles, the horror turns out to be the fault of a corrupt establishment conspiracy (a surprising amount of the plot resurfaces in his later, more serious *Silver City*) and there's a deal of natural justice as the toothy creature chomps down on the various venal types responsible for its gigantism, from the pet-abductor (Sidney Lassick) who supplies stolen dogs to unethical vivisectors, through the rotten Mayor (Jack Carter) who gets the hero thrown off the force, to the patronising business tycoon (Dean Jagger) who runs the crooked pharmaceuticals company and wants to ensure no link is made between his products and the giant gator.

The finale finds the monster following the delicious barbecue smell and invading a society wedding reception where it satisfyingly chomps down on the tuxedoed guests, making an especial snack of the bridegroom. It has plenty of in-jokes, from the 'Harry Lime Lives' sewer graffiti to the identification of a victim as Edward Norton (the character played by Art Carney on the sit-com *The Honeymooners*), and even the lesser victims, like Henry Silva's smug great white hunter who stalks ghetto alleys with local hoods as 'native bearers', are given a little more meat than found in most monster munchie movies. *Alligator II: The Mutation* is less a sequel than a lacklustre remake. ★★★ **KN**

⦿ ALMOST FAMOUS (2000)

Starring: *Patrick Fugit (William Miller), Frances McDormand (Elaine Miller), Billy Crudup (Russell Hammond), Kate Hudson (Penny Lane), Jason Lee (Jeff Bebe), Zooey Deschanel (Anita Miller), John Fedevich (Ed Vallencourt), Michael Angarano (Young William), Noah Taylor (Dick Roswell), Mark Kozelek (Larry Fellows), Philip Seymour Hoffman (Lester Bangs), Jimmy Fallon (Dennis Hope)*
Director: *Cameron Crowe*
Screenwriter: *Cameron Crowe*
15/123 mins./Comedy/Drama/Biography/USA

Awards: *Academy Awards – Best Original Screeplay, BAFTA – Best Original Screenplay, Best Sound, Golden Globes – Best Comedy/Musical, Best Supporting Actress (Kate Hudson)*

William Miller is a 15-year-old aspiring music writer in the 1970s. Given the dream assignment of going on the road with band Stillwater for a *Rolling Stone* feature, he embarks on the trip with enthusiasm, much to the chagrin of his mother. Once on the road, he finds his life changing forever.

God bless Brad Pitt. His last-minute decision not to play the leader of fictional band Stillwater made way here for the genuinely almost famous Billy Crudup, and ensured the story of writer/director Cameron Crowe's adolescent affair with rock is a manifesto for misfits rather than an advertisement for charisma. At its centre is an unknown 15-year-old (Patrick Fugit) and not a superstar. This is how it should be. The senior writer says to the kid, 'The only true currency in this bankrupt world is what you share with someone else when you're uncool.' Not an image that would survive proximity to Brad.

Crowe shot his own script based on his adventures as a teenage rock writer in the era of The Allman Brothers, Lynrd Skynyrd and The Eagles. His film is a thank you to those who made him: his perplexed mother, played by Frances McDormand; the late rock critic Lester Bangs; depicted with an inch too much charm by the majestic Philip Seymour Hoffman, and Penny Lane, the tender spirit at the head of the swaggering army of groupies (or,

Movie Trivia: Almost Famous

Other suggested movie titles included The Uncool and Stillwater, the name of the band in the movie. The music for *Almost Famous* was written and co-composed by Nancy Wilson, Crowe's wife and member of 80s soft group Heart. The part of Russell Hammond, the Stillwater guitarist played by Billy Crudup, was originally intended for Brad Pitt.

as they prefer 'band aids'), following the denim infantry as they scale the heights of the nascent rock industry.

It's a good-hearted film and sentimental with it: a busload of longhairs singing along with Elton John's Tiny Dancer; a rock god turning up on a young writer's doorstep; a boy gently deflowered by three groupies; a farcical crisis on a plane. Crowe gets away with it because he doesn't try to be smart; he catches every detail perfectly (the brilliant opening montage, the sleeping band shots modelled after old Rolling Stone pics, the kid attempting to compose his first review by flashlight as the band play) and lets the music as rich and off-centre as The Beach Boys' 'Feel Flows' and 'The Allmans' One Way Out' take the strain.

It's the most convincing account yet of what rock and roll felt like to the people backstage as it turned from a movement into a career. Those who were there will love the detail. Those who weren't, well, they'll wish they had been. ★★★★★ **DH**

ALPHAVILLE (1965)

Starring: *Eddie Constantine (Lemmy Caution), Anna Karina (Natasha Von Braun), Akim Tamiroff (Henri Dickson), Laszlo Szabo (Chief Engineer), Howard Vernon (Professor Von Braun – aka Leonard Nosferatu), Jean Pierre Leaud (Bellhop)*
Director: *Jean-Luc Godard*
Screenwriter: *Jean-Luc Godard*
PG/99 mins./Sci-fi/France/Italy
Awards: *Berlin Film Festival – Golden Bear*

Private eye Lemmy Caution is dispatched to a sinister futuristic metropolis to liberate its enslaved citizens by destroying the controlling Alpha 60 computer.

Borrowing a character from Peter Cheyney's cult novels, Jean-Luc Godard has cross-generic fun throughout this dark political allegory, as he blends lowbrow pulp with intellectual paranoia and hypocrisy. Sci-fi, comic books, hard-boiled paperbacks, B movies and serials are all referenced as Godard turns Eddie Constantine into a Bogartesque anti-hero who operates in a supposedly futuristic city that can only be reached through intersidereal space.

But, in fact, it can be accessed by crossing a bridge, as Alphaville is none other than contemporary Paris, which is given the soulless feel of a distant dystopia by cinematographer Raoul Coutard's inspired use of its bleak modernist architecture and nocturnal illumination.

Godard shrewdly anticipates the omniscience of computers and the dehumanisation of a near-robotic humanity through such Orwellian strategies as the suppression of art, love, thought and individuality. But his concerns lie more in the present than the future.

The Nazi Occupation was still a recent memory in the 1960s and Godard suggests that a nation that had already succumbed to one totalitarian regime was predisposed towards accepting another with equal meekness, especially as it had so readily come to trust science and technology as forces for good. Thus, it's no accident that the nefarious mastermind is called Von Braun or that he's a boffin (in keeping with *Dr Strangelove*'s satirical demonisation of academic megalomania). What's more disturbing is the fact that the residents all bear tattooed numbers and that Godard filmed in the Gestapo's Parisian headquarters, the Hotel Continental. It's sinisterly ironic, therefore, that the picture won the Golden Bear at the Berlin Film Festival.

For all its populism, the action is also packed with learned allusions to Cocteau, Kafka and the myths of Eurydice and Lot's wife. Such is Godard's genius that these highbrow references never overwhelm the pulp and that the disposable is prevented from trivialising the valuable – unlike in Alphaville or, unfortunately, our own dumbed-down times. ★★★★★ **DP**

ALTERED STATES (1980)

Starring: *William Hurt (Professor Eddie Jessup), Blair Brown (Emily Jessup), Bob Balaban (Arthur Rosenberg), Charles Haid (Mason Parrish)*
Director: *Ken Russell*
Screenwriter: *Paddy Chayefsky, based on his own novel*
18/102 mins./Sci-fi/USA

Wrestling with the idea of God after the death of his father, Professor Eddie Jessup obsessively researches the idea of altered human states by partaking of hallucinatory drugs and locking himself in a sensory deprivation tank. Gradually his weird visions lead to a physical change.

Not one to let slow-building tension and mystery get in the way of wild flourishes of extremism and shock, Ken Russell hit upon a story that more or less handled his structural excesses and tendency toward blasphemy. The story, based on a novel by Paddy Chayefsky, who also provided the script before completely disowning the film, is, frankly nuts, but delivered with such a gloriously outrageous sense of visual abandon its like a grand, daft paean to 2001's psychedelic showpiece by way of *Dr. Jekyll And Mr. Hyde*.

The idea that lurks behind all the sensory lunacy, is that man will literally regress without all the outward elements of life be they love, science or even God. William Hurt, who is determinedly po-faced throughout even when required to parade about like a rabid monkey (the primal state he reverts to), is the scientist who mixes ramped up Peyote with sensory deprivation and experiences a special effects light show that still looks pretty out-there decades later. Russell wants the screen to assume the outer limits of human experience, although one might suggest Jessup could have achieved his goal just as easily by watching an incessant loop of the director's back catalogue.

Religious iconography, defiled and horrendous (a seven eyed goat?), seethe before our eyes just to make sure beyond its preposterous science there is still enough to offend people. An effective enough style that has been remixed for everything from *Jacob's Ladder* to *Event Horizon*. Look out too for a weenie Drew Barrymore, still shy of *E.T.*

When back in 'reality' the film manages to maintain a classically doomladen sense of tampering with forces beyond our control, and Russell plays with the formula with a naughty wit – even framing a proposal scene, between Hurt and Blair Brown (who spends most of the film without her clothes on) in a psychiatric ward as a truculent loon is force-fed hallucinogens. It's just that kind of movie. ★★★ **IN**

ALWAYS (1989)

Starring: *Richard Dreyfuss (Pete Sandich), Holly Hunter (Dorinda Durston), John Goodman (Al Yackey), Brad Johnson (Ted Baker), Audrey Hepburn (Hap)*
Director: *Steven Spielberg*
Screenwriters: *Jerry Belson and Frederick Hazlitt Brennan, adapted from the screenplay A Guy Named Joe by Dalton Trumbo, based on a story by Chandler Sprague and David Boehm*
PG/123 mins./Drama/Romance/USA

When a forest-fire fighter crashes and dies, his spirit comes back to watch his former lover, and to mentor his replacment.

Always is probably Steven Spielberg's most idiosyncratic movie, in that it stands as the only example of the filmmaker ever remaking someone else's work, in this case Victor Fleming's 1943 ghostly WWII melodrama, *A Guy Named Joe*.

Among Spielberg devotees there are those that feel he falls into two camps as a filmmaker – a deeply personal director who chronicled his feelings regarding his parents' divorce through *E.T.*, and spectacularly remade his early childhood movies (and childhood obsessions) with the likes of

Close Encounters Of The Third Kind, and the later obligated father figure he seems to have become – a man who acknowledges his responsibilities and sets out to make concentration camps, America's history of African slavery and the D-Day landings a visceral and educational experience for the audience he has both lulled and culled.

Always falls between these two stools – it is at once a homage to all the movies and the styles of movies he ever loved growing up, and in many ways his own sad personal goodbye to the pure and honest flights of fancy those movies allowed him. It is consequently a movie made by a man who found himself caught between a sense of personal history and an obligation to what he felt was his wider role in history. Ironically, this makes it one of his most personal films.

Spielberg first saw *A Guy Named Joe* as a suburban child. He later recalled that, 'it was the second movie, after *Bambi*, that made me cry. I didn't understand why I cried. But I did.' While shooting *Jaws*, the emergent filmmaker discovered a fellow devotee in his star Richard Dreyfuss. Both huge Spencer Tracy fans (Tracy starred as 'Joe' in the original) Dreyfuss joked that if Spielberg ever remade it, he had to play the lead.

Spielberg began seriously playing with the notion as early as 1980, retaining the film's original title and, over the ensuing years, making his way through 12 drafts of the screenplay. He later said, 'I think it all came down to the fact that I really wasn't ready to make it.' A smart observation, because at that time Spielberg simply wasn't mature enough to give the emotional basis it needed.

Always is a pivotal film in the Spielberg canon because in many ways it marks his own quiet goodbye to his childhood. The previous year's *Indiana Jones And The Last Crusade* was his ultimate Boys' Own adventure, his final Saturday morning hurrah. *Always* was his transitional movie. (Okay, he briefly paused on *Hook* to assess why a grown man can't be a child again, but floundered.)

Always – at a domestic box office gross of $43 million – remains one of Spielberg's least successful movies financially, but it's almost impossible to see him progressing as a filmmaker without having made it.

A Guy Named Joe's WWII setting was transposed here to a group of pilot forest firefighters, a group that John Goodman's character Al Yackey tellingly views as akin to those World War II flying aces. Key among the group is Spielberg's 'Joe', here named Pete (and, true to his promise, played by Richard Dreyfuss, the closest the director has to an onscreen alter-ego.) Pete is wild, reckless and in love with fellow pilot Dorinda, perfectly played by Holly Hunter. But when Pete dies on the job, his spirit is forced to face up to her grief – he must learn to love her enough to let her love another – in this case flying dufus Ted (Brad Johnson – the film's weak link.)

Where often before Spielberg found his visual strength in the use of his self-named 'God light', here he delights in the notion of visual juxtaposition right from the opening shot a small fishing boat about to be eaten by the (*Jaws*-like?) maw of a water guzzling plane. It's a motif that plays throughout the film – the diminutive Hunter leaving the frame as Goodman's bulk bursts in; soot covered fireman's feet retreating in awe of Dorinda's virgin white-shoed elegance. In many ways this is Spielberg at his most visually playful and inventive.

But more importantly this is a film about loss. And for those that claim the director dabbles in faux sentimentalism, (or earnest historical guilt) this is a film about real emotions, spurred in part by his own recent divorce (from Amy Irving), and his ultimate acceptance of adulthood.

It is also, however, a film about moving on – Pete has to let go of Dorinda to free her to live and love again, just as Spielberg had to give up his own love of childhood, in this case one of his favourite films, *A Guy Named Joe*.

These feelings of loss were, of course, accentuated by the delightful final screen appearance of Audrey Hepburn as Pete's afterlife guide/angel, Hap (a role, curiously, originally offered to Sean Connery). Heavenly sequences shot with otherworldly grace in woodland glades and vast, golden corn fields. Not his most successful movie, by any means, but a transitional, poignant delight nonetheless. ★★★ **BMc**

AMADEUS (1984)

Starring: *F. Murray Abraham (Antonio Salieri), Tom Hulce (Wolfgang Amadeus Mozart), Elizabeth Berridge (Constance Mozart), Simon Callow (Emanuel Schikaneder), Roy Dotrice (Leopold Mozart)*
Director: *Milos Forman*
Screenwriter: *Peter Shaffer, based on his own play*
15/140 mins./Drama/USA

Awards: *Academy Awards – Best Picture, Best Director, Best Actor, Best Screenplay, Best Art Direction, Best Costume Design, Best Sound. BAFTA, Best Editing, Best Cinematography, Best Make-up, Best Sound*

Locked away in an asylum, former court composer Antonio Salieri recounts his tale of bitter jealousy and revenge toward the upstart genius Wolfgang Amadeus Mozart, who rose to fame before his eyes and the eyes of the Viennese aristocracy.

Few historical, Oscar washed epics have as fully grasped the intricacies of man's capacity to destroy himself as Peter Shaffer's adaptation of his own stageplay. Hence, Milos Forman's extraordinarily sumptuous, witty, dark, moving and majestic movie has a texture very much its own, a shadowy intimacy that transcends even the scope and splendour. In a mid-80s governed by bombastic, inch-deep action-comedies, this film stood, head and shoulders, above the masses, the masterpiece of its time. To this day, it remains up in the Gods.

Akin to Shakespeare with his turmolic spurts of history, it is the characters who bite deep into our hearts. As Mozart, Tom Hulce, jabbers and warbles like a lunatic, a bumptious, unpleasant, self-centred man blessed with a blazing talent, a 'diction from God'. He looks as if he is fit to burst, the burden of these angelic voices too much for his meagre spirit to bare. Forman craftily invited his actors to retain their American accents, liberating the film from the rigid confines of RSC eloquence and opening it up for audiences. There is something punk rock about Mozart's giddy excess, and echoes of Hollywood's own bratty talents.

Yet, the film's dark heart, its poise and class, all stem from his less-talented rival Salieri. Here is a man consumed by envy and a furious religious piety demanding that surely, he, the devoted disciple, should be able to access such dizzying musical creations. For it is he alone, beyond even Mozart himself, who recognises the true genius of those creations, a conflict that will drive him to a moral dementia – to destroy a beauty he adores. As required, F. Murray Abraham gives the performance of a lifetime: brooding, soul-deep, an Iago of seething passion, who always keeps the audience close, intimate to his plans.

The film, so magnificent and ornate, is posing very human conflicts on a grand scale: self-aware mediocrity versus blind talent, liberated creativity versus the establishment. Shaffer, trimming the over-explanatory aspects of his play, fills the film with very modern preoccupations without ever breaking the spell: homoeroticism, ego, creative rivalry, the nature of identity and evil all bubbling and boiling to the surface.

A longer 'director's cut' adds twenty minutes, solidifying some of the backstories and adding a few grim afterthoughts, but slows the natural pace too much, drying out the story. These are relatively minor grumbles, whichever cut you view, Forman's period piece is worth ever second it demands of you. The music's pretty good, too. ★★★★★ **IN**

LES AMANTS (1958)

Starring: *Jeanne Tournier (Jeanne Moreau), Jean-Marc Bory (Bernard Dubois-Lambert), Judith Magre (Maggy Thiebaut-Leroy)*
Director: *Louis Malle*
Screenwriter: *Louise de Vilmorin, based on the novel* Point de Lendemain *by Dominique Vivant*
15/86 mins./Drama/France

Bored housewife Jeanne Tournier stuns both her husband and her lover by running away from home with the archaeology student who offered assistance when her car broke down.

François Truffaut called Louis Malle's second feature 'the cinema's first night of love'. Yet, despite winning the Special Jury Prize at Venice and proving a huge commercial success, it was denounced as 'diabolical' by the Vatican newspaper, *L'Osservatore Romano*, and led to a cinema owner in Cleveland, Ohio having to resort to the Supreme Court to quash a charge of peddling obscenity.

Seen today, it's hard to understand how so delicate a sex scene could have caused such uproar. But even though France had been seduced by the cult of youth that had enlivened its postwar austerity and was supposedly revelling in the existential optimism of a new government, it wasn't quite ready for a latterday *Madame Bovary*, which exposed the emptiness of provincial life and established Jeanne Moreau as an emblem of emancipated womanhood.

The irony, of course, is that most viewers would have accepted the fact that Moreau periodically left Dijon for a Parisian rendezvous with her best friend or occasional dalliances with her polo-playing lover. It wasn't the adultery that shocked the hypocrites, but the fact that Moreau could reject the trappings of bourgeois existence and risk everything for reckless passion with a younger man.

Malle, however, was thrilled by Moreau's surrender to 'the kind of love everybody has a right to dream about' and rather than castigating her for betraying her class and sex by driving off into an uncertain future he lionised her for espousing 'the higher morality of self-realisation'. There's no question that Malle naively romanticises Moreau and Bory's Brahms-scored assignation, with Henri Decaë's photography lending a novelettish air to the couple's moonlight walk and boat trip across the lake. But, Malle's use of nudity and the close-ups of Moreau in the throes of passion were a revelation and it's only now that their sensitivity and discretion can be fully appreciated. ★★★★ **DP**

AMARCORD (1973)

Starring: *Magali Noel (Gradisca), Bruno Zanin (Titia Biondi), Pupella Maggio (Miranda Biondi), Amando Brancia (Aurelio Biondi)*
Director: *Federico Fellini*
Screenwriters: *Federico Fellini, Tonino Guerra*
18/124mins./Comedy/Drama/Italy/France

Awards: *Academy Award – Best Foreign Film*

The lives and loves of the residents of a seaside town in the Romagna have a profound effect on Titta, an impressionable teenager more atuned to his own obsessions and observations than the political and social realities of 1930s Italy.

The winner of the Academy Award for Best Foreign Film and a clear influence on Woody Allen's equally episodic *Radio Days*, this bittersweet slice of nostalgia is set in the Adriatic seaside town of Battipaglia. Yet, despite its similarities to the Rimini of his youth, Federico Fellini always denied that this was an autobiographical outing. However, with the title translating as 'I remember' in the local dialect, it's hard not to see the teenage Titta as anything but Fellini's alter ego, as he endures domestic discord and scholastic farce to devote his time to observing his neighbours and fantasising about the female anatomy.

Although the action is set in 1935, its division into seasons embracing a childhood's worth of recollections gives the film a timeless universality, which suggests that Italy is still very much labouring under the delusions of grandeur devised by Il Duce. Religion, politics, education, the family, love and sex are all explored during incidents which come to rely less on whimsical humour as Titta discovers the serious side of life. Yet while Fellini stages such memorable set-pieces as the Fascist rally, the arrival of the luxury liner and the spring wedding, he's more interested in the idealised and exaggerated characters whose psyches he probes in a series of caricature studies – the nymphomaniac who flirts shamelessly with everyone she meets; the teacher humiliated by his class; the Hollywoodised hairdresser who seduces a visiting nobleman; the crazed uncle who leaves an asylum and has to be coaxed down from a tree by a dwarf nun; the simple-minded peasant who claims to have satisfied an Arab potentate's entire harem; and the innocently promiscuous tobacconist who gives Titta his first taste of forbidden flesh.

Shot at great expense over a year at Cinecitta, this may not be Fellini's most prescient or satirical film. But it's certainly his most slyly elegiac. ★★★★ **DP**

AMÉLIE (LE FABULEUX DESTIN D'AMÉLIE POULAIN) (2001)

Starring: *Audrey Tautou (Amelie), Mathieu Kassovitz (Nino Quicampoix), Rufus (Raphael Poulain – Amelie's Father), Yolande Moreau (Madeleine Wallace – Concierge), Arthus De Penguern (Hipolito – The Writer), Urbain Cancelier (Collignon – The Grocer), Isabelle Nanty (Georgette), Serge Merlin (Dufayel), Mauric Benichou (Brestodeau – The Box Man)*
Director: *Jean-Pierre Jeunet*
Screenwriters: *Guillaume Laurant, Jean-Pierre Jeunet*
15/120 mins./Romance/Fantasy/USA

Awards: *BAFTA – Best Production Design, Best Original Screenplay*

Amélie, a waitress in a Montmartre café, decides to try and help those around her feel happier with their lives, including a reclusive man who collects discarded photo booth pictures.

Paris: city of light, city for lovers swept up by the air of romance. It's the perfect setting for Jean-Pierre Jeunet's wonderful Amélie, a film with a golden, glowing heart. This massive hit at the French box office is the very dictionary definition of 'feel-good' – its irresistible charms will dispel the heaviest clouds hanging over the head of the gloomiest misanthrope.

Freed from the darker imagination of Marc Caro (with whom he collaborated on *Delicatessen* and *The City Of Lost Children*) and the restraints Hollywood thrust upon him during *Alien Resurrection*, Jeunet has created one of the most joyous films of recent years. With its gallery of affectionately drawn grotesques and eccentrics, *Amélie* is filled with sunshine.

As in *Delicatessen*, Jeunet's characters are essentially lonely individuals drawn together by geography; here, however, he brightens their lives

Movie Trivia: Amelie

The part of Amelie was originally written for British actress Emily Watson. Emily declined the role as she couldn't speak French. Jean Pierre Jeunet allegedly cast Tautou after seeing her on a poster for Venus Beaute outside his Paris flat. In contrast to her cute performance in the film, Tautou originally wanted to be a scientist.

with the positive force that is Amélie, adorably played by Audrey Tautou. Jeunet encourages us to share sympathy with these people, as his balanced approach finds humour in their disappointments and a note of sadness in their funny little quirks.

In France, *Amélie* was attacked for depicting a Montmartre without ethnic diversity. But to criticise this film on racial grounds is like complaining that Beethoven's 5th Symphony is a bit too loud – it's just carping for the sake of it. Anyway, the whole film is filtered through the imagination of its central character, a woman who withdrew into her private little world as a child cut off from her peers. This allows Jeunet to pass off some gently bizarre observations as Amélie's own and to bathe the film in the 'magic realism' that had become tarnished by inferior films. ★★★★★ **AM**

AMERICAN BEAUTY (1999)

Starring: *Kevin Spacey (Lester Burnham), Annette Bening (Carolyn Burnham), Thora Birch (Jane Burnham), Wes Bentley (Ricky Fitts), Mena Suvari (Angela Hayes), Peter Gallagher (Buddy Kane), Allison Janey (Barbara Fitts), Chris Cooper (Colonel Fitts)*
Director: *Sam Mendes*
Screenwriter: *Alan Ball*
18/122 mins./Drama/USA

Awards: *Academy Awards – Best Actor, Best Cinematography, Best Director, Best Picture, Best Original Screenplay, BAFTA – Anthony Asquith Award for Music, Best Cinematography, Best Editing, Best Film, Best Actor, Best Actress, Golden Globes – Best Director, Best Drama, Best Screenplay*

A suburban man starts to re-evaluate his life with dramatic effects for his family and neighbours.

Released in America to a tumult of superlatives and Oscar glory, British director Sam Mendes' exceptional take on pre-millennial American ordinary people going nuts is simultaneously achingly funny and bitingly moving. It also presents he-who-can-do-no-wrong, Kevin Spacey, with the kind of richly-textured, grandstanding centrepiece that he just devours, rocking the screen with scintillating comic timing while instilling the film with an understated sadness that beautifully expresses its magical but troubled heart. It should be a career defining role, but for Spacey it's another in a canon of 'career bests'. Still, when you consider he is surrounded by brilliant turns from Annette Bening, Chris Cooper, Thora Birch and new boy Wes Bentley, you start to see how much more this is than just a sophisticate's soap opera.

Curiously furrowing similar turf to the more testosterone-heavy *Fight Club*, *American Beauty* is about male empowerment and self-discovery, with mid-life as coma where the only answer is a Zen-themed search for 'whatever makes you happy'. Both films share super-charged fire-me-if-you-dare sequences and quasi-profound diatribes against household goods. Where *Beauty* surpasses the Brad/Ed battery pack, however, is in its devotion to humanity and, ultimately, love as the prizes so frustratingly out of reach.

Spacey's human punchbag Lester Burnham finds rebirth after his daughter's jailbait buddy Angela zings his long-buried sexual antennae. Immediately he starts pumping iron, develops a range of taking-no-more-shit retorts and drops out of his dronehead job to flip burgers at the local drive-thru. Alongside his freefall are his wife Carolyn's more direct self-destruction and his estranged daughter Kate's own sexual awakening.

Alan Ball's cynically-charged script plants this dysfunctional satire in a community so off-balance it is borderline David Lynch weirdo-Americana – the Burnhams' new neighbour, ex-military man Chris Cooper, heads a regimented household, which is a terrifyingly real depiction of an utterly inert family deadened by emotional tyranny.

Unusual for such people-focused comedy-drama is the vivid visual style. In among Burnham's sexual and human reawakening are dreamy visions of Suvari sumptuously smothered with nothing but scarlet rose petals. Mendes also paints his affluent Anywhereville with a worndown quality, all saturated colours and blank walls, throwing in outlandish angles to evoke the skewed normality of these fractured lives. Oddball teen neighbour Wes Bentley, clinically romantic about Burnham's daughter and chief preacher of the film's look-for-the-true-beauty philosophy, constantly Camcords the world around him, allowing Mendes to play cool games with shots within shots.

A contrived framing device forces the ending into whodunnit silliness it doesn't need, and caricatures float around the edges – Peter Gallagher's smarmbucket real estate king hastily shagging Bening's tormented wife is funny but depthless, although these are minor imperfections. ★★★★★ **IN**

Movie Trivia: American Beauty

The American Beauty rose is classified as a hybrid perpetual and is susceptible to mildew. Kevin Spacey's real surname is Fowler.

THE AMERICAN FRIEND (DER AMERIKANISCHE FREUND) (1977)

Starring: *Bruno Ganz (Jonathan Zimmerman), Dennis Hopper (Tom Ripley), Gerard Balin (Raoul Minot), Lisa Kreuzer (Marianne Zimmermann), Nicholas Ray (Prokasch, aka Derwatt), Samuel Fuller (The American*
Director: *Wim Wenders*
Screenwriter: *Wim Wenders, based on the novel* Ripley's Game *by Patricia Highsmith*
15/126 mins./Mystery/Thriller/Germany/France

Sociopath Tom Ripley manipulates picture-framer Zimmerman into carrying out a murder contract. As always with Ripley and his victims, a semi-symbiotic relationship develops and the American steps in to help the patsy carry out a second, more problematic killing.

A fascinating mix of director Wim Wenders and author Patricia Highsmith, this also offers a collision between the acting styles of improvisational Hollywood maverick Hopper and buttoned-down Swiss-German stage star Ganz. The result is an almost hypnotic suspense film set in an international blur of subway stations, hotels, trains, empty streets, beaches and concrete flyovers, populated by enigmatic, haunted, suspicious and suspect characters.

Adapted from *Ripley's Game*, the third of Highsmith's series about cold-hearted crook Tom Ripley (with a tiny, important bit lifted from the second book, *Ripley Under Ground*), this harps on Highsmith's habitual themes of a transference of criminal identities that involves a supposedly ordinary man in murder.

Wenders, always a contemplative director, does strange things with the noir aspects (casting a lot of fellow directors as the bad guys) but the observational, character-based approach makes the suspense-thrill sequences extremely powerful when they show up. The stalking on the metro and the assassination on the train are perfect Hitchcockian set-pieces, and the finale – which involves a red Volkswagen and a sudden, unexpected but inevitable end to the friendship – remains a kicker.

But the film gains power from its quieter moments, often putting its two leads on screen alone, Hopper fiddling with snooker balls on a plastic-covered table or Ganz tinkering with gold leaf in his shop. By refusing to explain Ripley, this gets closer to Highsmith's character than any other film version – though Hopper adds enough detail of his own to make his Tom a distinctive character quite unlike the one in the books. ★★★★ **KN**

AMERICAN GRAFFITI (1973)

Starring: *Richard Dreyfuss (Curt Henderson), Ron Howard (Steve Bolander), Paul Le Mat (John Milner), Charles Martin Smith (Terry The Toad), Cindy Williams (Laurie Henderson), Wolfman Jack (XERB Disc Jockey), Harrison Ford (Bob Falfa)*
Director: *George Lucas*
Screenwriters: *Willard Huyck, Gloria Katz, George Lucas*
PG/109 mins./Comedy/Drama/USA

On one long summer night in a small Californian town, four friends, aged between 17 and 20, reach a turning point in their life.

Four years before he became Mr Star Wars, George Lucas created the kind of modest little character piece that his all-conquering blockbuster was supposed to have signed the death knell on. A genuine sleeper hit, *American Graffiti* came out of nowhere, earned well over $100 million in the US and a clutch of Oscar noms (but no wins). It's a movie that's subsequently become a landmark film of the 70s – it gave Lucas the muscle to create *Star Wars*, it launched a raft of acting talent (particularly Howard, Dreyfuss and Ford) onto bigger things and created a template for the teen movie genre that's still prevalent today – but, revisiting *Graffiti*, it feels a small, personal intimate experience, perhaps at odds with its rep and the subsequent persona of its creator.

After his debut sci-fi picture *THX-1138* flopped, pigeonholing Lucas as an esoteric, cold fish of a director, he took producer Francis Coppola's advice to create the opposite, a warm, autobiographical slice of his own life. Drawing on his own reminiscences of cruising the strip in his home town Modesto, Lucas and screenwriters Willard Huyck and Gloria Katz serve up funny, touching, telling vignettes that grow organically out of character rather than feel grafted on.

Through skilful writing and editing, Graffiti interweaves its four story strands into a unified mosaic of teen turmoil. Stolid citizen Steve is forced to choose between going to college and his steady girlfriend, Laurie. Wannabe intellectual Curt, also due to leave for college, chases a mysterious blonde in a T-Bird and joins a street gang. Meanwhile, in a sub-plot fizzing with great banter, drag racer John Milner is tricked into babysitting mouthy 13-year-old Carol while geek Terry The Toad picks up ditzy blonde Debbie in the car Steve has entrusted to him. Few films have been able to amplify and dramatise the painful transition from adolescence to adulthood with such generosity of spirit, unflinching truth (Lucas never belittles his teen's concerns) and emotional finesse.

For a director often derided for the performances in his films, Lucas draws across-the-board terrific performances from his cast. These characters are archetypes – The Class President, The Brain, The Nerd, The Greaser – yet it is astonishing the extent they become rounded complex individuals since we mostly glimpse them behind the wheels of cars. Particular standouts are Dreyfuss, all nervous energy and growing maturity and the underrated Charles Martin Smith who imbues the stock geek character with vulnerability and dignity. It is a film that has genuine affection for these kids and its hard not to get sucked into their predicaments.

Shot over 28 days pretending to be one eternal summer night before college or Vietnam beckons, the action is bathed in a warm nostalgic hue, the characters surrounded in the golden burnished glow of a jukebox. Yet this is counter pointed by the nervous documentary shooting style, a verité vitality that enhances the feel we are grabbing urgent moments. If the camera lingers on anything it is the cars. *American Graffiti* is suffused with literal autoeroticism, devoting lengthy tracking shots to cars parading and preening, choreographing the ballet with real love and care.

The script was written with Lucas' old rock and roll 45s playing in the background and the film remains an object lesson in how to match up and enrich story with music. From the opening blasts of Bill Haley's 'Rock Around The Clock' as Terry The Toad ineptly draws his Lambretta into a Drive-In, the music frames and counterpoints (but rarely apes) the action; Curt joins a street gang to the sounds of The Platters' 'The Great Pretender'; John and Carol ambush a car of squealing girls to Chuck Berry's 'Johnny B Goode'. The soundtrack is glued together by the ever present disc jockey Wolfman Jack, father figure and circus master of the whole teen drama .It also marks a transition in music as the traditional rock 'n'roll of Bill Haley gives way to the surfing sounds of The Beach Boys. As the Wolfman howls 'We're gonna rock'n'roll ourselves to death baby!!' a musical era dies on screen as well.

Not only is *Graffiti* a terrific teens-goof-off movie, it's also a valuable piece of anthropology that captures (perhaps idealises) both the rituals of 50s adolescents and a golden point in US history just before Vietnam, JFK and Watergate soured a national mood (an unsatisfying sequel *More American Graffiti* tried and failed to document the darker times). If all this feels strange to have come from the man behind *Star Wars*, it shouldn't. Both Curt and co. and Luke Skywalker are asked to leave the safety of their small town lives and take personal responsibility for their own actions in a much larger world. Both films also highlight Lucas' unerring ability to read the zeitgeist. He identified a vein of instant nostalgia – *Graffiti* is nostalgic for a time that is only ten years before it came out and spawned the likes of *Happy Days* – that has subsequently become a dominant mode across all culture. But few films captured it as exquisitely and poignantly as Graffiti. ★★★★★ **IF**

AMERICAN HISTORY X (1999)

Starring: *Edward Norton (Derek Vinyard), Edward Furlong (Danny Vinyard), Beverly D'Angelo (Doris Vinyard), Fairuza Balk (Stacey), Stacy Keach (Cameron Alexander)*
Director: *Tony Kaye*
Screenwriter: *David McKenna*
18/119 mins./Drama/USA

A former Neo-Nazi skinhead tries to prevent his brother falling in with the same crowd.

And so, after all the studio palaver Brit director Tony Kaye's debut has finally hit the screen – and what emerges is that by dissociating himself totally from the studio cut finally released, Kaye may well have been guilty of taking a switchblade to his own schnozz. Because *American History X* is a fine film, which has at its dark centre a towering performance that establishes Edward Norton as the most promising character actor of his generation.

Told through the eyes of his admiring brother (a perfectly cast Furlong), *American History X* charts the rise, if that's the right word, of Derek Vinyard, a fiercely intelligent young man who, after the shooting of his father by a black man, and encouraged by sinister good ol' boy Cameron, shaves his head, has a swastika tattooed on his chest and proceeds to galvanise the local disenchanted youth into forming a racist gang before murdering two black men who were attempting to steal his car. When Derek returns on parole after three years of his sentence, his brother David, whose doe-eyed puppyish looks bely his own gestating violent racism, is horrified to find that his brother has been reformed in jail and has not only grown back his mane but is determined to redress some of the harm he has done. Which is not a policy popular with his gang, which has gathered to welcome him back as a conquering hero.

Neo-Nazidom has a short though distinguished history on the big screen. Alan Clarke's *Made In Britain* and Australian director Geoffrey Wright's *Romper Stomper* both took an uncomfortable look inside the heads of racist thugs. Yet *American History X*'s strength is not its subject matter but Edward Norton's ballistic performance. Despite a weak backstory (Derek's rage apparently having its genesis in childhood after a few bigoted comments uttered by his dad, while his equally implausible moral reversal comes from 'meeting a nice black fella' in jail), Norton manages to deliver one of the most convincing racists ever while retaining his character's humanity. Even after he kills – and in doing so commits to celluloid one of the most sadistically shocking acts of violence in the medium's history (if, that is, all the footage of this pre-release cut survives the attentions of the BBFC) – Norton manages to preserve the shred of humanity that carries us through his redemption and prevents us from simply dismissing him as worthless scum.

Kaye's direction occasionally veers a little too close to his advertising roots; extensive use of slo-mo – particularly, for some reason, in showers that begin to resemble shampoo ads – and black-and-white lend a chic patina, which some may think is a little overcooked. And, in between set pieces, he flounders slightly, though this may be a symptom of the re-edit. Another may be the ending, in which Kaye seems to lose faith with the power of his own movie and delivers what could be seen as a cheap twist in place of a considered conclusion.

But in themselves the set-pieces are astonishing. A brutal attack on a convenience store, a gruelling prison rape sequence, and a dinner party argument that erupts into violence are all edited with sustained barnstorming energy. ★★★★ **AS**

AMERICAN MOVIE: THE MAKING OF NORTHWESTERN (1999)

Starring: *Mark Borchardt (Filmmaker), Tom Schimmels (Actor in 'Cove'), Monica Borchardt (Mark's Mom), Alex Borchardt (Mark's Brother), Chris Borchardt (Mark's Brother), Ken Keen (Friend/Associate Producer), Mike Schank (Friend/Musician), Matt Weisman (Casting Director), Bill Borchardt (Mark's Uncle/Executive Producer), Cliff Borchardt (Mark's Dad), Joan Petrie (Mark's Girlfriend/Associate Producer)*
Director: *Chris Smith*
15/104 mins./Documentary/USA

A struggling amateur filmmaker tried to complete his latest horror epic – *Coven*.

If Mike Myers' long-haired, smalltown opportunist geeks Wayne and Garth existed in real life, they'd probably be something like *American Movie*'s long-haired, smalltown opportunist geeks Mark Borchardt and Mike Schank. In fact, Smith's delightful documentary boasts a gallery of characters so eccentric that at times it feels like a spoof.

At the centre of it all is Borchardt, whose directorial ambitions are hampered by his lack of funds, to say nothing of the fact he lives in Menomonee Falls, Wisconsin. It's his determination to make his movie that impresses more than anything else, and when he runs out of cash to finance his semi-autobiographical film, *Northwestern*, he decides to finish and turn a profit on uncompleted horror pic *Coven*.

Aside from his endearingly vacant buddy Schank, a man so slow-witted you can practically hear him think, those involved include his parents, his pal Keen, an assortment of unknown actors and his financier, 82-year-old Uncle Bill, who inexplicably lives in a trailer park despite having over a quarter of a million dollars in the bank.

The standard talking heads footage is snappily intercut with film of Borchardt coercing his decrepit uncle into coughing up cash, bemoaning his financial and personal life and going to frequently hilarious lengths to get his vision on screen. What does become apparent is that for all his grand pretensions, Borchardt is a far more talented filmmaker than the numerous clips from his early work (including his slasher 'franchise', *The More The Scarier: Parts 1 – 4*, and the inspired *I Blow Up*) suggest; on the evidence shown here, *Coven* isn't half bad. And in telling his story, director Smith's skill as a documentarian comes to the fore, veering between poignant realism and out-and-out comedy, and finding unlikely stars in Borchardt and Schank, the latter playing up his skewed philosophies and lottery ticket fanaticism to scene-heisting effect.

The entertaining documentary proves once again that some ordinary people have the most fascinating lives of all. ★★★★ **CW**

AMERICAN PIE (1999)

Starring: *Jason Biggs (Jim), Mena Suvari (Heather), Shannon Elizabeth (Nadia), Alyson Hannigan (Michelle), Chris Klein (Oz), Tara Reid (Vicky), Eugene Levy (Jim's Dad), Eddie Kaye Thomas (Finch), Natasha Lyonne (Jessica), Thomas Ian Nicholas (Kevin)*
Director: *Paul Weitz*
Screenwriter: *Adam Herz*
15/96 mins./Comedy/USA

Four teenage boys try to lose their virginity before Prom night and endure plenty of humilation along the way.

American Pie arrived on screens with something of a misguided rep. *There's Something About Mary* with acne. A *Porky's* for the 90s. But while the film owes much to the spirit of early 80s lame-brained, low-budgeted yoof fare, there's something else at work here: chiefly, in between the jizz jokes and pastry intercourse, *American Pie* boasts an unremitting freshness and beguiling sweetness that easily mark it as the most enjoyable teen flick of the late 90s.

Part of the *Pie*'s winning formula is that it is built on a premise totally devoid of spin. Four teenage lads make a pact to jettison their virginity – 'Valid consensual sex. No prostitutes' – by prom night. That's it. No Shakespearean backbone or Dawson-esque irony, just an eternal adolescent dilemma pared down to enticing purity and played out with a keen comedic eye for teen torments; Jim giggles in front of nearly every girl he fancies; Kevin is 'going steady' yet seeks his brother's handwritten sexual bible in order to go all the way; macho lacrosse player Oz joins the choir to get close to Heather and learn to play 'the sensitive angle' and, finally, the bow-tie-sporting Finch tries to maintain his legendary prowess all the while harbouring a dark defect. Refreshingly these kids are not John Hughes stereotypes – nerds, jocks, brains etc. – but recognisably average kids merely anxious for action.

En route to potential sexual fulfilment, sibling directors Paul and Chris Weitz (uncredited) serve up a litany of embarrassing rites of passage scenarios with pace and surefootedness. Hats off to Biggs who embraces Jim's ever decreasing predicaments – cleaning his pipe as his dad walks in, screwing an apple pie as his dad walks in and, best of all, hilariously stripping in front of a foreign exchange student (Shannon Elizabeth) as the school tunes in on the internet – with a real skill for squirm-inducing shtick.

Although the film does indulge in calculated grossness – a spunk in beer glass gambit, an incredibly unfunny episode involving literal toilet humour – there is, more often than not, a poignancy to the schlock: even funnier than the infamous pie pokage is the aftermath, when Jim and his father hold a postmortem over the shagged out pastry, deliberating over how to tell mom. (It should be stressed that Eugene Levy's 50s-style repressed dad is a sparely used creation of comic genius).

Moreover, one of the unexpected surprises of *American Pie* is its gallery of well-written gals; the stand outs being Natasha Lyonne's gossipy sage Jessica and Alyson Hannigan as band camp obsessed dweeb Michelle who, with a single killer line of dialogue (and we're not telling), manages to steal the entire movie. Keeping the testosterone in check, the film does not deny its chicks a personality or libido and emerges all the more likeable for it.

Where *American Pie* really pays off, however, is in its conclusion. Of course, the randy little upstarts have lessons to learn about lust vs. love but it is all done with a gossamer touch, big laughs – look out for *The Graduate* rip off – and a surprising emotional punch, the quartet having crept into your affections without you really knowing.

You may go in for the sicko laughs but you'll exit with a big goofy grin and warmed cockles. The best of both worlds. ★★★★ **IF**

⑮ AMERICAN PIE 2 (2001)

Starring: *Jason Biggs (Jim), Mena Suvari (Heather), Alyson Hannigan (Michelle), Chris Klein (Oz), Tara Reid (Vicky), Eugene Levy (Jim's Dad), Eddie Kaye Thomas (Paul Finch), Natasha Lyonne (Jessica), Thomas Ian Nicholas (Kevin), Seann William Scott (Steve Stifler)*
Director: *JB Rogers*
Screenwriter: *Adam Herz, from a story by David H. Steinberg, Adam Hertz*
15/105 mins./Comedy/USA

The friends from *American Pie* meet up after their first year at college, but the same old rivalries and sex hang-ups still linger.

As great Chinese philosopher once say: 'If it ain't broke, don't fix it.' It's wisdom that the folks behind the camera here seem to have taken to heart, for *American Pie 2* is not so much a sequel as a re-bake. Every element of the original is so faithfully – some might carp cynically – reproduced, you'd be forgiven for suffering a sense of déja vu. But you'll probably be laughing too much to notice.

It's almost unprecedented in sequels to get the whole cast back together again, but – through the miracle of contractual obligation – absolutely everyone is present and correct, right down to the kid with the monkey. The excuse for the reunion (apart from the small fact that the first movie cost $11 million to make and grossed $150 million) is that it's now summer vacation after the first year of college, and the kids have rented a house at the lake. To dodge the holiday blues, they're amusing themselves by partying, hopefully pursuing lesbians and getting their hands glued to their penises.

Pie 2 ruthlessly riffs on the original set-ups, mostly with success. Liked Jim's internet strip? Witness his bizarre 'retard trombone performance'. Enjoyed Stifler quaffing jizz at his party? Then you'll probably get a kick out of Stifler getting pissed on at his party. It's the kind of shameless repetition that would be damning if the sequences weren't so well-handled and the ensemble cast as goofily likeable as ever.

With J. B. Rogers (a veteran first assistant director of smut on the likes of *Dumb & Dumber*, *There's Something About Mary* and the first *American Pie*) taking over directing duties, writer Adam Herz has tweaked the comedy graphic equaliser a little. Ratcheted up are Seann William Scott's testosterone-addled Stifler, and the majestic Eugene Levy – possessor of cinema's finest comedy eyebrows – as Jim's incredibly excruciating dad. More muted is Chris Klein's Oz, whose attempts at phone sex are a rare low point.

There has also been a slight softening of the vulgarity, although those of a politically sensitive nature may detect a faint whiff of unwelcome homophobia during a sequence in which the boys are invited to fondle, kiss and generally molest each other by a pair of porn-mag 'lesbians'. That said, the scene is certainly redeemed by being so damned funny. Whether our appetites will stretch to a third slice remains to be seen, but for the moment, seconds are very welcome indeed.

How you react to a second helping of the pie will really depend on how you feel about the image of a young man with a trumpet wedged up his arse. If for you this is the height of comedic sophistication, get ye to the DVD store. ★★★★ **AS**

⑮ AMERICAN PIE: THE WEDDING (2003)

Starring: *Jason Biggs (Jim Levenstein), Alyson Hannigan (Michelle Flaherty), Seann William Scott (Steve Stifler), Eddie Kay Thomas (Paul Finch), Thomas Ian Nicholas (Kevin Myers), January Jones (Cadence Flaherty), Eugene Levy (Jim's Dad), Angela Paton (Grandma)*
Director: *Jesse Dylan*
Screenwriter: *Adam Herz*
15/96 mins./Comedy/USA

Old friends and family gather for Michelle and Jim's wedding, but first they have to survive the bachelor party.

Before anyone actually had an opportunity to see it, the participants and the publicity machine tried to convince us that this was the funniest slice of pie yet. They were either lying or self-deluded. What is now an alleged rites-of-passage trilogy began as a cleverly disarming combination of outrageous gross-out comedy and believable characters. With dispiriting predictability, it has devolved into this – a series of scatalogical skits loosely connected in a stale *Meet The Parents*/*Father Of The Bride* (only here it's the groom) affair. The sole surprise is that the wedding itself is rather sweet, swapping a few 'eeeewwws' for 'aaaawwws', a thing that has made the *American Pies* a tad more endearing than, say, the *Porky*'s oeuvre. Of course if you just like people with their pants around their ankles, you won't be disappointed either.

Half the original cast haven't been invited to the wedding, which is fine since someone in that town would have had to grow up. Biggs' agreeable Jim is now less a victim of his hormones than he is of Scott's ageing vulgarian Stifler, whose retarded atrocities this time include an unoriginal dog poop sequence and sex with Jim's geriatric granny. Jim's accidental humiliations include covering the wedding cake with his pubic hair and an inter-species foursome onto which his prospective in-laws obligingly stumble. High points – and we're stretching here – involve time-honoured bachelor party farce with strippers and a chocolate-coated Finch.

And much as we all love Jim's dad, surely the brilliant comedic point of his existence was to be uncomfortable with his son's lurches into manhood. Now he's so enthusiastically involved, he even participates in the excruciating marriage proposal. Director Dylan, son of Bob, does a routine job, which is as much as can be expected with a script lacking in fresh gags.

Unless you desperately want to believe anyone could mistake dog doo for chocolate truffles, and that delighted ingestion of same is hilarious, you'll probably want to steer clear. ★★ **AE**

⑫ THE AMERICAN PRESIDENT (1995)

Starring: *Michael Douglas (President Andrew Shepherd), Annette Bening (Syndey Ellen Wade), Martin Sheen (A.J. MacInerney), Michael J. Fox (Lewis Rothschild), Samantha Mathis (Janie Basdin), David Paymer (Leon Kodak), Richard Dreyfuss (Senator Bob Rumson)*
Director: *Rob Reiner*
Screenwriter: *Aaron Sorkin*
12/120 mins./Comedy/Drama/Romance/USA

The President of the United States falls for a political lobbyist but press and political speculation threaten to thwart the romance before it gets off the ground.

The formerly unimpeachable Rob Reiner may have come a cropper with the ill-conceived and deservedly ignored North, but there's no doubting he got back on track with this. It's a commercial offering with classy performances, snappy, intelligent writing, and good old-fashioned romance turned up to 11. It's easily his best film since *When Harry Met Sally*, even if it requires the audience to accept the notion of an American president being the embodiment of wholesome, moral-valued Americana. But, heck, it's the movies.

The plot is simple. Widowed US premier Andrew Shepherd enjoys glowing public support and ribbing his fraught White House staff, then, at a meeting with an ecological lobby group, he is confronted with sassy, plain-talking, lovely Sydney Ellen Wade. The result is love, and a series of wonderful set-pieces as the president has to convince a sceptical Wade he's actually asking her out on a date – albeit to a White House banquet for the new president of France.

As romance blossoms with convincing sparkle between the politically opposed couple, events are complicated, naturally enough, by politics. Being the president and falling in love proves no easy combination. A debut clinch is rudely interrupted when the Libyans bomb Israel, and as Shepherd's political opponent (a smarmy Republican Richard Dreyfuss cameo) starts to attack Sydney for political gain and his popularity slips, the wheels and deals of modern politics threaten to ruin everything, leaving time for Shepherd's knock-'em-dead rallying call and the throat-thickening happy ending.

Of course it's hokey and silly, but Reiner really knows how to skirt potential schmaltz and there is a political backbone to the piece which gives it reassuring depth. Scriptwriter Aaron Sorkin (who went on to adapt this premise into the TV series *The West Wing*) has done a polished job of injecting a viewpoint without letting it dominate, or have the political vernacular suffocate the comedy. And the performances Reiner has elicited from the cast are uniformly terrific: Sheen's calm, guiding right-hand man, Fox's flustering spin doctor are stand-outs. The film, however, belongs to Douglas and Bening with two marvellously straight performances without psychotics or emotional blow-outs, giving the most credible couple ever to inhabit the White House. ★★★★ **IN**

AMERICAN PSYCHO (2000)

Starring: *Christian Bale (Patrick Bateman), Willem Dafoe (Donald Kimball), Jared Leto (Paul Allen), Josh Lucas (Craig McDermott), Samantha Mathis (Courtney Rawlinson), Reese Witherspoon (Evelyn Williams), Chloe Sevigny (Jean)*
Director: *Mary Harron*
Screenwriters: *Guinevere Turner, Mary Harron, Roberta Hanley, based on a novel by Bret Easton Ellis*
18/101 mins./Thriller/USA

An immaculately groomed Wall Street yuppie likes to indulge in his evening hobby of serial killing.

Published in 1991, Bret Easton Ellis' third novel was greeted by howls of hatred more appropriate to a small war in the Third World or another Golan-Globus *Lemon Popsicle* sequel. A first person report from inside the mind of Patrick Bateman, who epitomises the ills of the 1980s by combining the professions of Wall Street broker ('mergers and acquisitions') and serial killer ('murders and executions'), the book was widely misinterpreted as a hideously misogynist tract that used explicit violence to draw attention to a thinly plotted pretend thriller with dollops of surface-level satire.

There had always been the threat of a film, with such scary names as Oliver Stone, Brian De Palma and David Cronenberg in the ring – but the project fell to Mary Harron, the ex-BBC documentarian who made an underrated debut with *I Shot Andy Warhol*, who cannily brought aboard the apparently unlikely Guinevere Turner (the lesbian icon from *Go Fish*) to co-write and play the funniest victim. The result is the best imaginable film of very difficult material; it doesn't say much more than, 'The 80s were shit,' but manages exactly to catch the all-surfaces, dazzlingly obsessive tone of the novel, making its points by treating all subjects – nouvelle cuisine, MOR rock music, fitness kicks, clothes, personal grooming – with exactly the same pornographic attention to detail as the sex and violence.

Like the book, the film makes a point of not having a real plot: a smooth PI (Dafoe) seems set to nail the killer for the murder of a rival trader (Leto), but fades into the wallpaper along with the crime itself. Bateman, played with dead-inside charm and mounting hysteria by an astonishing Christian Bale, invites us into his world of reservations at exclusive restaurants and competitions over the quality of business cards. His detours into murder – prefaced by detailed speeches about now-embarrassing musical enthusiasms ('You actually own a Whitney Houston CD?' gasps Turner through contemptuous laughter. 'More than one?') – are hardly more bizarre and tasteless as everything else in his life. In the end, the scariest thing about Bateman is not that he's a Lecter-like freak – his crack-up in the last act brings him horribly closer to humanity – but that he is no worse than everyone else in his world, except humane-but-dim office minion Sevigny, whose role is to make the film bearable.

As for the horror: Harron is mostly very discreet, but delivers one terrific apartment-of-grue sequence as Bateman's life falls to pieces along with many victims, featuring a truly nerve-shredding chainsaw sound effect.

Often laugh-out-loud funny, conveying the cruelty of its world through persistent mistakings of identity among the well-scrubbed young men and details like the all-sharp-edges interior decor and elaborate but tiny meals, it's cool in the sense of remote rather than hip. And you wouldn't want to be seen dead with the soundtrack album. ★★★★ **KN**

AMERICAN SPLENDOR (2003)

Starring: *Paul Giamatti (Harvey Pekar), Hope Davis (Joyce Brabner), Judah Friedlander (Toby Radloff), James Urbaniak (Robert Crumb), Madylin Sweeten (Danielle), Harvey Pekar (Real Harvey), Jolyce Brabner (Real Joyce), Toby Radloff (Real Toby), Danielle Batone (Real Danielle)*
Directors: *Shari Springer Bergman, Robert Pulcini*
Screenwriters: *Shari Springer Berman, Robert Pulcini, based on the comic books* American Splendor *and Our Cancer Year by Harvey Pekar and Joyce Brabner*
15/101 mins./Comedy/Drama/Biography/USA

A mix of drama and documentary is used to tell the true story of Harvey Pekar, a Cleveland hospital file clerk who was inspired to turn his mundane, odd lifestyle into the cult comic book *American Splendor* after a chance meeting with artist Robert Crumb.

For decades, Cleveland-based file clerk and grouch Harvey Pekar has written an autobiographical comic. This film version samples anecdotes and routines, picking up a plot thread in Harvey's third marriage to an equally marginal character (the excellent Hope Davis) and rushing through the medical traumas chronicled in *My Cancer Year*, with an emphasis on how he turned the experience into art rather than give in to sickness.

Paul Giamatti, one of the great contemporary supporting players, grabs a rare lead with a snarl and a slouch, managing to co-exist on film with many illustrated versions of the character and Pekar himself. A typical strategy is the introduction of Harvey's best friend Toby, who reveres *Revenge Of The Nerds* the way others swear by *Apocalypse Now*, played by Judah Friedlander as what seems to be an outrageous, though heartfelt, caricature. Then the real Toby Radloff shows up, demonstrating that the performance is exactly true to life. With ingenious use of semi-animation and editing – oddly parallelling Ang Lee's approach to *The Hulk* – this shambles rather than slices, but manages to make heard a unique voice.

If you can get through the confusing goings-on of the first reel, then this is a satisfying experience – funny, touching and tragic by turns. And Giamatti deserved every award going. ★★★★ **KN**

AMISTAD (1997)

Starring: *Morgan Freeman (Theodore Joadson), Anthony Hopkins (John Quincy Adams), Djimon Hounsou ('Cinque' Sengbe), Nigel Hawthorne (Martin Van Buren), Matthew McConaughey (Roger Baldwin), David Paymer (US Secretary of State Forsyth), Pete Postlethwaite (Holabird), Stellan Skarsgard (Lewis Tappan), Razaaq Adoti (Yamba), Abu Bakaar Fofanah (Fala)*
Director: *Steven Spielberg*
Screenwriters: *David Franzoni, Steve Zaillan*
15/154 mins./History/Drama/USA

Based on the true life events of 1839, when African slaves took over the slave ship *Amistad*, and the trail that followed.

The 17th film of Steven Spielberg's career (his first for DreamWorks) remains an interesting, underrated curio. A further illustration of

Spielberg's desire to grapple seriously with history (witness *The Color Purple*, *Empire Of The Sun*, *Schindler's List*, *Saving Private Ryan*), it was dismissed on release either as a dry civics lesson (which is partially true) or as a kind of 'Schindler's Roots', an attempt by Spielberg to hijack someone else's cultural heritage to win critical kudos (which is patently untrue). It has been relegated, alongside *The Sugarland Express* and *Always*, to the ranks of Spielberg Films No One Ever Talks About – which is a shame as there is much more going on here than first meets the eye.

Originally, Spielberg was going to segue from *The Lost World* straight to *Private Ryan*. Yet, slipping in a project initiated by producer Debbie Allen (of *Fame* fame), he took a stripped-down crew from the *Jurassic* sequel and shot *Amistad* on the fly in just 46 days. The subject of a highly publicised (and ultimately unsuccessful) plagiarism lawsuit after respected author Barbara Chase-Riboud claimed that DreamWorks stole that interpretation of history described in her novel *Echo Of Lions*; the source material centres on the aftermath of a mutiny by 53 African captives aboard the Spanish slave ship *Amistad*. As the mutineers, led by Cinque (Hounsou), are captured in American waters, a series of courtroom trials begins to determine ownership of the slaves, the case finally ending up in the Supreme Court with ex-President John Quincy Adams (Hopkins) fighting for the Africans' freedom.

On its opening, even the most die-hard Spielberg aficionado had trouble defending its merits. Yet this dislocation for the real-life Dawson Leerys could have arisen because, on first impressions, this is the most un-Spielberg film that Spielberg has ever made. Storytelling briskness is replaced by ponderous pacing. Spectacle is sidelined by an abundance of dialogue. Visual dynamism is usurped by painterly tableaux, a series of static, muted, distanced compositions aeons away from *The Color Purple*'s prettification of black culture.

However, *Amistad* echoes around Spielberg's movies in more ways than were first apparent. It shares with *Temple Of Doom*, *Empire Of The Sun* and *Schindler's List* themes of incarceration and survival and, as lawyer Roger Baldwin (McConaughey) tries to discover who the Africans are, the film elaborates on a striving for communication that has traversed much of Spielberg's work, in particular *Close Encounters* and *E.T.*

Moreover, all the typical directorial nous is present and correct, only this time you had to search for it; the massive close-ups of Cinque's features in the opening insurrection; the colour scheme of the courtroom which progresses from an overblown messy look highlighting the prisoners' limbo through to the pristine velvety elegance of the Supreme Court as a verdict is finally delivered. The images depicting the slave ship drownings – an infant raised above the tortured bodies in the ship's hold, the chains of Africans pushed to their death – are among the most shocking, sorrowful yet strangely beautiful Spielberg has ever committed to film, the brutality perfectly counterpointed by the tinkling of a music box. In a year when *Titanic* won the Academy award for Best Picture, the filmmaking finesse Spielberg brought to *Amistad* looked positively arthouse.

A further demonstration of Spielberg's ability to tap into the Zeitgeist, the release of *Amistad* coincided with a reinvestigation into America's relationship with slavery. President Clinton held a 'town meeting' with prominent authors to ponder race debates, schools named after slave owners underwent moniker changes and debates raged over whether Americans should formally apologise for slavery (as Germany did for Nazism), and pay billions of dollars in reparations to descendants of slaves.

Into this hotbed, *Amistad* came under attack from certain historians as a misleading brand of 'infotainment' – DreamWorks literature surrounding the film quoted conversations between Adams and Cinque when in reality the pair never met – but was generally perceived to respect the complexities in the issues of slavery and race. From Cinque battling Baldwin to infighting between African tribes through the congressional sparring of Adams, this is a film full of conciliation but, importantly, not reconciliation. Spielberg has no easy solutions to the race problem: just a sensible awareness of cultures, language and dialects intermingling in the New World.

That race is such an open wound stateside may have contributed to the markedly different reception afforded *Amistad* than *Schindler's List*: while the horrors of the Holocaust happened thousands of miles away, the spectre of slavery happened right on their own doorstep, boring a hole in the US soul. Not only was Spielberg's meditation on homegrown atrocity under-appreciated, it may also have been largely unwanted. ★★★★★ **IF**

THE AMITYVILLE HORROR (1979)

Starring: *James Brolin (George Lutz), Margot Kidder (Kathy Lutz), Rod Steiger (Father Delaney), Don Stroud, (Father Bolen), Murray Hamilton (Father Ryan), John Larch (Father Nuncio)*
Director: *Stuart Rosenberg*
Screenwriter: *Sandor Stern, based on the book by Jay Anson*
18/118 mins/Horror/USA

The Lutz Family – George, Kathy and a brood of kids – move into a suspiciously affordable mansion, the scene of a recent multiple murder, and are persecuted by supernatural phenomena. George seems to become possessed by a malevolent spirit.

Supposedly based on fact – though Jay Anson's paperback best-seller seems to be a pack of lies – this put clichés found in a dozen 1970s made-for-TV films like Steven Spielberg's *Something Evil* onto the big screen and raked in huge box office returns. It took Stephen King and Stanley Kubrick to show in *The Shining* that the old scary-house-possessed-Dad gambit could be something extraordinary, but journeyman director Stuart Rosenberg (*Cool Hand Luke*) just shouts 'boo' every few minutes. It is endearing in its silliness – with Rod Steiger overdoing it wildly as a priest pestered by demonic flies, a good shock with a pig-like thing in the closet, slime pouring from the walls at every opportunity, a rare ghost smart enough to grab a sackful of cash, muttering about Indian burial grounds and cursed places, Margot Kidder fetchingly getting aerobic in her underwear and that memorably ominous façade of the Amityville Horror House with the eye-like gable windows. It founded a franchise – *Amityville II: The Possession* is a prequel with *Exorcist* elements and Amityville 3-D has stereoscopic effects and a drowned Meg Ryan. After that, theatrical outings for Amityville dried up until the 2005 remake, but straight-to-video racks were littered with quickies like *The Amityville Curse*, an adaptation of one of the many paperback cash-ins. A run of films feature items bought at an Amityville yard sale which spread the curse – a lamp in *Amityville: The Evil Escapes*, a clock in *Amityville 1992: It's About Time*, a mirror in *Amityville: A New Generation* and a dollhouse in *Amityville: Dollhouse*. ★★★ **KN**

THE AMITYVILLE HORROR (2005)

Starring: *Ryan Reynolds (George Lutz), Melissa George (Kathy Lutz), Jesse James (Billy Lutz), Jimmy Bennett (Michael Lutz), Chloe Moretz (Chelsea Lutz), Rachel Nichols (Lisa), Philip Baker Hall (Father Callaway)*
Director: *Andrew Douglas*
Screenwriter: *Scott Kosar, based on a novel by Jay Anson and a screenplay by Sandor Stern*
15/90 mins./Horror/Drama/USA

A family move into a house that was once the site of a mass murder and are soon tormented by the grisly spirits that still haunt the grounds.

Some films should never be remade – the resulting retreads are often so inferior they forever tarnish the original. *The Amityville Horror*, happily, isn't one of those films. The 1979 first stab, though hugely successful, squandered a strong, and allegedly true, story with hokey jumps and dialogue. This remake still ends up losing its nerve and resorting to predictable shocks and loud noises but stands as marginally superior to its predecessor.

The haunted house horror is one of the hardest to make consistently scary, since there's no actual monster to be vanquished and if one is concocted, it'll only end up ruining the third act with tiresome rather than terrorsome CGI. A rattled chandelier or creaking floorboard can maintain a sense of creeping terror if a director uses them confidently, allowing the audience to play with its own fears of what may be lurking in darkened corners. But after an hour of well maintained shivers, making the most of the titular residence's murky expanses with the Lutz family huddled in dimly lit rooms, director Andrew Douglas evaporates the scares by visualising everything that was previously only suggested and substituting slow build for rapid demolition.

Still Reynolds and George are interesting choices for the leads. Initially they seem far too young to play the mother and stepfather of a 12-year-old child, but are in fact of a similar age to the real-life Lutzes. Reynolds proves particularly unsettling, beginning the film in his familiar cocksure joker mode, before slowly breaking down into paranoid sociopath as the house takes a grip on him (madness helpfully signposted by bloodshot contact lenses, for those audience members who find axe wielding and shouting too ambiguous). George is given little to do, though, other than harangue the worst exorcist ever (Philip Baker Hall), but in the final stages gives a good shriek.

If *Amityville* could keep its tongue from occasionally creeping into its cheek it would be more effective, but feels the Scream-a-like need to constantly reference other horror movies. Nods to *The Exorcist*, *Halloween* and a virtual headbang at *The Shining* may be sly and post-modern, but reminding audiences of classics of the genre rather draws attention to the movie's own shortcomings.

It lacks its own identity, too often coming off as a dim imitation of *The Shining*, but as a standard shocker it does its job well enough to keep you jumping throughout. ★★★ **OR**

AMONG GIANTS (1998)

Starring: *Pete Postlethwaite (Raymond 'Ray'), Rachel Griffiths (Gerry), James Thornton (Steven 'Steve'), Lennie James (Shovel), Andy Serkis (Bob)*
Director: *Sam Miller*
Screenwriter: *Simon Beaufoy*
15/95 mins./Romance/Comedy/UK

A team of men, assigned to paint a five-mile stretch of electric pylons, is disrupted when a woman joins the crew.

Fact: regardless of what anyone may claim, nobody saw the success of *The Full Monty* coming. Indeed, when screened to the fourth estate, only a few registered large enthusiasm and no one predicted record-breaking international business. So when approaching another British comedy drama, also featuring homegrown talent and coloured with a dour tinge by the pen of *TFM* scripter Beaufoy, a certain wariness is inevitable. But this film's fate was more inevitable.

Forever struggling to maintain a sunny disposition in the face of inclement conditions both meteorological and financial, Ray and his misfit team of 'handy' men accept a lunatic gig slapping gallons of Dulux One Coat on five miles of electricity pylons before the juice goes back on at the end of August. Grubby days of banter, hard graft and hanging precariously at 100 feet are considerably enlivened by the arrival of antipodean backpacker Gerry, a game sort willing to muck in, earn a few quid and begin a salty fling with Ray while flirting with the feckless Steven, Ray's youthful best mate.

And so a few saucy shenanigans unfold – one startlingly involving Postlethwaite and Griffiths in the buff – played with reasonable conviction against the backdrop of severe landscape and the inconsistent comic relief of Ray's bodge-it-and-scarper merchants. There's a surprising weakness in the writing, however, with a plot striving for fearless relationship reality but regularly turning at standard, dramatic signposts, and the lead trio are frequently let down by poor dialogue. ★★ **DB**

AMORES PERROS (2000)

Starring: *Emilio Echevarria (El Chivo, 'The Goat'), Gael Garcia Bernal (Octavio), Goya Toledo (Valeria), Alvaro Guerrero (Daniel), Vanessa Bauche (Susana), Jorge Salinas (Luis)*
Director: *Alejandro González Iñárritu*
Screenwriter: *Guillermo Arriaga Jordán*
18/154 mins./Drama/Mexico

A devastating car accident connects three stories, all involving love, loss and regret.

Amores Perros opens with chaos, as Octavio and a friend drive away from the latest dogfight with the injured canine on the back seat and enemies in hot pursuit, then hops back, forward and sideways in time. It's a risky device, delaying crucial plot points for over an hour, but the individual stories, which weave in and out of each other with true-life untidiness, are so gripping you'll go along with them until everything becomes clear.

This film will get people's backs up before they've even seen it, by paying not entirely unsympathetic attention to a 'sport' that stands as a working definition of cruelty to animals. The last filmmaker to try something like this was Monte Hellman, whose *Cockfighter* spun him into a career limbo, but *Amores Perros* shows very little bloody pooch action, using the contrasting dogs in the car crash (Octavio's killer canine, Valeria's pet) to show the different, desperate situations of the three leads.

Octavio's story, which comes first, is the most obvious, the youth in love with the apparently saintly wife of his abusive brother, but the inevitability of its outcome doesn't make it any less affecting. Stories two and three are of stranger loves. Confined to her apartment, recovering from injuries caused by the car crash and resentful of the lover who doesn't need to say he regrets leaving his family, Valeria focuses on the situation of her dog, who has chased a ball through a hole in the floor and not come out, though he can be heard scurrying inside. Tramp hitman El Chivo watches his estranged daughter from afar and tries to fulfill his latest contract, while nursing Octavio's dog back to health – only for it to act true to the nature that has been forced upon it, driving home a hard truth.

Brilliantly directed, written, photographed and acted, this is first-rate filmmaking, horrific and tender, raw and lyrical. Trust us, you need to see this. ★★★★★ **KN**

AN ACTOR'S REVENGE (YUKINOJO) (1963)

Starring: *Kazuo Hasegawa (Yukinojo Nakamura), Fujiko Yammato (Ohatsu), Ayako Wakao (Namiji), Eiji Funakoshi (Heima Kadokura)*
Director: *Kon Ichikawa*
Screenwriters: *Daisuki Ito, Teinosuki Kinugasa, Natto Wada, based on the newspaper serial by Otokichi Mikami*
PG/113 mins./Drama/Japan

Edo, 1836, and Yukinojo, a Kabuki actor specialising in female roles, recognises the magistrate and two merchants who were responsible for the death of his parents and allies with a mysterious bandit to eliminate them.

Coming after the partly animated Disney homage, *Being Two Isn't Easy*, this marked something of a change of pace for the ever-eclectic Kon Ichikawa. However, it wasn't an assignment of his own choosing, as he had been ordered to accept it by the Daiei studio following a string of commercial misfires.

It was the second filming of Otokichi Mikami's newspaper serial, although Teinosuke Kinugasa's three-part 1935 adaptation had also been condensed into a single feature in 1952. Kinugasa (who had himself been an onnagata or oyama) acted as an adviser behind the scenes. But his star, Kazuo Hasegawa (himself a former oyama), reprised the dual role he had played 28 years earlier and it speaks volumes for the 55-year-old's longevity and skill that he was even more effective in what was his 300th film than he had been in the original monochrome version.

This is a film of constant contrast, with the clashes between artifice and reality, life and death, love and hate, stage and film, gentility and violence, and masculinity and femininity imparting a thematic richness that is complemented by visuals of such artistic depth and dexterity that they demand repeated viewings. The influence of classical Japanese prints, widescreen cinema, comic books, stage atmospherics and silent era special effects are all evident. But it's the way in which Ichikawa consistently disrupts the viewer's perspective (just as he aurally disconcerts with the jarring mix of jazz, folk music and exaggerated ambient sounds) that makes this so compelling.

Of course, the whole conceit could have collapsed into a camp catastrophe. But the screenplay, (co-written by Ichikawa's wife, Natto Wada,) is so laced with irony that Hasegawa is able to play the piece as the pulp pantomime that it has always been considered to be by Japanese audiences. Yet it remains a masterclass in both stage and screen techniques. ★★★★ **DP**

AN AMERICAN WEREWOLF IN LONDON (1981)

Starring: *David Naughton (David Kessler), Griffin Dunne (Jack Goodman), Jenny Agutter (Alex Price), John Woodvine (Dr Hirsch), Brian Glover (Chess Player)*
Director: *John Landis*
Screenwriter: *John Landis*
18/93 mins./Horror/Comedy/Sci-fi/USA
Awards: *Academy Awards – Best Make-up*

Two American tourists unwisely venture onto the Yorkshire Moors during a full moon. Both are attacked by a wolf-like creature, but only one survives . . . although subsequent events make him wish otherwise.

You know you're getting old when the first X-certificate film you ever saw gets shown on Saturday morning TV. Not that this could ever happen with *An American Werewolf In London* – too much sex, far too much nasty, nasty gore – but still, this oddball comedy-horror flick can never again seem quite as hilariously funny, nor as pant-fillingly scary as it did to a generation of 80s teens clustered around the family VCR. At the time – and this is indeed a film of its time – the werewolf effects were startling, with Oscar-winning Rick Baker pre-empting Rob Bottin's efforts on *The Thing* (1982) by a good 12 months. Equally startling was the sight of Bobbie from The Railway Children (alias Jenny Agutter) embroiled in a *Don't Look Now*-sex scene with a latent werewolf.

John Landis was one of the golden boys of US cinema when he made *AWIL* at the dawn of the new decade. Having seen *National Lampoon's Animal House* become the most successful comedy of all time, he'd helmed the sprawling cinematic hell that was *The Blues Brothers*, somehow managing to make a three-hour demolition derby into a cult hit. *American Werewolf* was something else, a campus comedy this was not. The plot is simple enough. Two clean-cut American kids, David (Naughton) and Jack (Dunne), are hiking through the English countryside. After an unsettling interlude in a village hostelry named The Slaughtered Lamb, they ignore the locals' dark hint-dropping and end up getting savaged on the moors by a marauding wolfman. Jack is killed, while David comes round in a London hospital, attended to by snub-nosed Nurse Price (Agutter) and inquisitive Dr Hirsch (velvet-voiced Brit character actor John Woodvine). It's now that things begin to get weird. Really weird. In sequences that predate the nightmare visions of *Jacob's Ladder* by a decade, David is plagued by violent and horrific dreams.

Check out the terrifically unpleasant dream-within-a-dream moment, which niftily grabs an idea from the end of *Carrie* and succeeds in making it even scarier. When the dead and decomposing Jack puts in an appearance, David sensibly concludes that he's gone insane. The alternative is to believe Jack's explanation, accept that he's become a werewolf, and commit suicide before the next full moon sends him out to kill. Tough call.

When it finally ensues, the man-into-wolf transformation scene is undoubtedly a classic. After pottering about Nurse Price's house all day, twitching with boredom, David is suddenly transfixed with agony. First his hand and then the rest of his body is stretched and contorted into a hideously hairy lycanthropic killing machine. Remember, this is before CGI morphing. What you see here is good old-fashioned makeup and trickery making the incredible seem real. After the excesses of *The Blues Brothers*, *AWIL* is an exercise in restraint. David doesn't change into the wolf until a whole hour has elapsed, whereupon the movie's pace accelerates and the bodycount multiplies. Admittedly, near the end, Landis can't resist throwing in a succinct and truly nasty pile-up in Piccadilly Circus – crushing and crunching sundry hapless Londoners with a variety of vehicles – but otherwise he handles the suspense so deftly that the relatively few moments of real horror are all the more shocking for it. And then there's the comedy. When the hideously mutilated Jack first appears to a severely traumatised David, his first words are, 'Can I have a piece of toast?' Later, Jack lures David into a porn cinema and introduces him to his victims – the pompous businessman, the cheerful courting couple, three tramps – who then advise their murderer on suitable methods of suicide. The famous scene where David wakes up naked in the wolf enclosure at London Zoo has been much imitated, even in a Lion Bar advert, while the gurning grotesques at The Slaughtered Lamb include Brit-com stalwart Brian Glover and a shockingly young-looking Rik Mayall.

However, for all its fascination, American Werewolf In London presents a confusing experience for the viewer. Certainly, the horror and laughs don't always sit well side by side – no more so than in the final frame when the sight of an anguished Agutter weeping for David (shot by police marksmen) is immediately followed by The Marcels' ram-a-lama version of

Movie Trivia: An American Werewolf in London

In the Piccadilly Circus scene, Landis has a cameo as the bearded man hit by a car and thrown through a glass window. The name of the porn movie showing when David meets Jack is *See You Next Wednesday*. This phrase (originally a phrase from *2001: A Space Odyssey*) has become Landis's trademark, showing up in *The Blues Brothers* and Michael Jackson's *Thriller*. At the close of the film's credits there is a congratulatory message for the wedding of Prince Charles and Lady Diana. Like John Landis' At the end of *A.A.W.I.L.* there is written: Any similarity to persons living, dead or undead is purely coincidental.

'Blue Moon'. It's all right, folks – it was only a movie! Likewise, David's descent into post-traumatic depression seems real enough, but the dialogues with Jack's corpse are played for pure schlock value. Then there's the movie's muddled view of Britain, ladling in realism (punks on the underground, Asian hospital porters) with Hollywood stereotypes from an earlier age – blundering bobbies, conniving villagers et al. Perhaps the whole thing is a brilliant cinematic in-joke, Landis' way of pointing out the impossibility of making a convincing horror movie in the modern age. Certainly, *AWIL* is such a taut and economical production that it's hard to imagine anything in it not happening for a reason. Incidentally, the CGI-fuelled *An American Werewolf In Paris* (1997) received roughly the same critical response as *Blues Brothers* 2000. For unwilling Yankee lycanthropes, as for pork-pie hatted R&B troubadours, original is clearly best. ★★★★ **PR**

AN AUTUMN TALE (CONTE D'AUTOMNE) (1998)

Starring: *Marie Riviere (Isabelle), Béatrice Romand (Magali), Alain Libolt (Gérald), Didier Sandre (Etienne), Alexia Portal (Rosine), Stéphane Darmon (Léo)*
Director: *Eric Rohmer*
Screenwriter: *Eric Rohmer*
U/111 mins./Romance/France

Isabelle tries to find a husband for her best friend, widowed vineyard owner Magali, but Magali might have other ideas about her future husband . . .

With *Conte D'automne*, the last in Eric Rohmer's *Tales Of The Four Seasons* series, it was conceivable the director would rehash former glories with an orange glow and lots of leaves. Yet, at 78, he has found a fresh spin on old obsessions – the pursuit of romance, the differences between the sexes – turning in a sprightly, hugely enjoyable treat that renders many of his younger counterparts leaden by comparison.

Initially it does not look promising: a slow, stilted opening introduces Magali, a middle-aged vineyard owner who feels lonely since her kids left home, finding companionship in best friend Isabelle and son's girlfriend Rosine. The movie picks up immeasurably as these two get to work in finding her a bloke; Rosine by setting her up with ex-philosophy tutor Etienne; Isabelle by putting an ad in a lonely hearts column, wooing the man who replies to the ad (an outstanding Libolt) with a mind to passing him on to Magali. Things are brought to a head as all the characters converge at a wedding, where hidden agendas and subterranean passions come deliciously to the surface.

Par for the Rohmer course, the insights into favourite concerns such as friendship, fidelity, and growing old remain witty and affectionate, the visual style is uncluttered and the performances attain gobsmacking levels of naturalism. Yet where *An Autumn Tale* differs from much of Rohmer's work is in its tight, almost farce-like plotting: the empathy established in the leisurely beginning pays off handsomely as the characters machinations and desires are intertwined at a fair old lick, moving the action to an unashamedly upbeat finale that slaps a mile wide grin across your face. ★★★★ **IF**

AN IDEAL HUSBAND (1998)

Starring: *Cate Blanchett (Lady Gertude Chiltern), Minnie Driver (Miss Mabel Chiltern), Rupert Everett (Lord Arthur Goring), Julianne Moore (Mrs Laura Cheveley), Jeremy Northam (Sir Robert Chiltern), Peter Vaughan (Phipps), Lindsay Duncan (Lady Markby)*
Director: *Oliver Parker*
Screenwriter: *Oliver Parker, from the play by Oscar Wilde*
PG/98 mins./Comedy/Romance/UK/USA

When successful minister Sir Robert Chiltern is threatened with blackmail he turns to his friend, man about town Lord Arthur Goring.

While *The Importance Of Being Earnest* is generally rated as Oscar Wilde's masterpiece, the timely wit of *An Ideal Husband* is proving irresistible to modern Wilde enthusiasts, with this glamorous screen adaptation coming on the heels of acclaimed theatre revivals. Packed with an appetising international cast, not too much can go terribly wrong in an ingenious, amusing leg-pull on the earnestness of being important.

Rising political star Sir Robert Chiltern and his perfect wife Lady Gertrude are rich, happy, and the toast of the town. Enter the sophisticated adventuress Mrs Cheveley with the goods on Sir Robert's guilty past, and suddenly he finds himself blackmailed. Either he colludes in an outrageous bit of chicanery in Parliament or he sees his marriage and career destroyed. Luckily for Sir Robert, his best chum and confidant is the swellegant playboy Lord Arthur Goring, who may be 'the idlest man in London', but after years of deftly eluding maritally minded socialites (including Chiltern's clever sister Mable, aggressively played by Minnie Driver), is expert at foiling scheming women. Goring engages in a battle of wits with Mrs Cheveley.

Goring has the best and most famous bons mots in the piece ('To love oneself is the beginning of a life long romance') and the dapper Everett is delightfully right. The other standout is Moore, a conniving treat and breathtakingly worldly-wise. However, director Parker (*Othello*) gets a bit cute in his ploys to 'open out' what originally sat comfortably in a succession of drawing rooms – particularly in his fondness for cutting back and forth between conversations and parallel actions among the sneaky men and seductive women.

It's on the film's determined stylishness that it loses the original's lightness of touch and somewhat downplays sparkling repartee in favour of a forced emotional element. Still, it wears attractively for a play that's 100 years old. ★★★ **AE**

ANALYSE THIS (1999)

Starring: *Robert De Niro (Paul Vitti), Billy Crystal (Ben Sobol), Lisa Kudrow (Laura MacNamara), Kyle Sahiby (Michael Sobol), Chazz Palminteri (Sindone)*
Director: *Harold Ramis*
Screenwriters: *Peter Tolan, Harold Ramis, Kenneth Lonergan*
15/103 mins./Comedy/USA

On the eve of his wedding, a gangster about to take control of his New York crime family turns to a shrink for therapy.

Despite playing the *King Of Comedy*, Robert De Niro and the mirth-making craft were infrequent bedfellows until this point. But this changed the perception of De Niro forever while also playing to his Mafioso strengths.

Ben Sobol is a new York psychiatrist living in the shadow of his shrink father, but looking forward to settling down into suburban anonymity with fiancée Laura. Paul Vitti is about to take on some responsibilities of the family kind too, although this kind spreads across much of the Upper East Side, has a penchant for silk suits, firearms and marinara sauce. And it's giving him major gyp. A chance meeting brings the two men together, with Vitti demanding that Sobol root out the cause of his panic attacks before he makes his crucial powerplay in front of the Mafia top brass. With his customary script-tweaking, Ramis ensures a succession of roomy but organised set pieces for his leads, who both take full advantage. Without descending into total lampoon, De Niro plays carefully on his gangster tradition, and in backing off from outright parody, the film hits just the right tone. As Vitti falls apart, De Niro supplies just enough menace to keep the performance on the mark, without going over it. Meanwhile, Crystal's frenetic, shuttering shtick is employed to good effect as Sobol walks a verbal minefield in which traditional therapy – getting in touch with the inner child or the merest suggestion of Oedipal issues – is likely to get him shot. And for the most part, it's astutely judged: no gags, no direct-to-camera mugging, and not much falling over. The Naked *Goodfellas* this ain't (thankfully). Just a stream of artfully contrived scenes packing wit, bite and bona fide classy acting, blended into a picture of rewarding novelty. ★★★★ **DB**

ANALYSE THAT (2002)

Starring: *Robert De Niro (Paul Vitti), Billy Crystal (Dr Ben Sobel), Lisa Kudrow (Laura Sobel), Joe Viterelli (Jelly), Cathy Moriarty (Patti LoPresti)*
Director: *Harold Ramis*
Screenwriters: *Peter Steinfeld, Harold Ramis, Peter Tolan.*
15/95 mins./Comedy/USA

Mobster Paul Vitti is released from prison on condition psychotherapist Dr Ben Sobol continues to care for him . . .

Probably the least-eagerly anticipated of sequels, *Analyse That* has no hype to live up to, and no eager fanbase to satisfy. So why bother? Was the farcical story of panic-attack-prone mob boss Paul Vitti (De Niro) and his unwilling psychotherapist Ben Sobel (Crystal) so very good that we needed to know what happened next? Frankly, no. But since when did that have anything to do with the production of a sequel – I Still Know What You Did Last Summer, anyone?

Carrying on where *Analyse This* left off, the film finds Vitti in Sing Sing prison, where he is high on the hit list. After duping the parole board by faking serious mental deficiencies, Vitti is unsurprisingly placed in the care of poor old Sobel. Cue inevitable farce. As before, the major plot feature is a perpetual cycle of Vitti or one of his beefy buddies dragging Sobel into some ill-thought-out caper, with the stressed-out shrink invariably finding himself in the clutches of either the law or some rival bad guys. This time there's the added angle of his much-maligned father having recently conked out, leaving Sobel with a load of dad-related demons to get to grips with on top of Vitti's many problems.

All the mobster caricatures are wheeled out once again for us to chuckle at, and Lisa Kudrow returns as Phoebe, er, Laura, Ben's seriously narked wife. Understandably, she's not best pleased to have found herself married to a load of cast-offs from *The Sopranos* as well as her woefully weak-willed husband. Perpetuating this central gag, having already milked it so enthusiastically in the first film, means that *Analyse That* is somewhat lacking any genuine spark. However, this doesn't stop it being surprisingly funny at points, with De Niro and Crystal producing a comedy double act so rich in inspired facial expressions and easy humour that, in spite of yourself, you will laugh.

By no means a bad film, and as a piece of gangster comedy-lite, it does the job. However, it's devoid of originality, and that factor significantly pulls it down. ★★ **JH**

ANATOMY OF A MURDER (1959)

Starring: *James Stewart (Paul Biegler), Lee Remick (Laura Manion), Ben Gazzara (Lt Frederick Manion), Arthur O'Connell (Parnell McCarthy), Eve Arden (Maida), Kathryn Grant (Mary Pilant)*
Director: *Otto Preminger*
Screenwriter: *Wendell Mayes, based on a novel by John D. Voelker*
15/160 mins./Crime/Drama/USA

A bachelor lawyer is called on to defend a murderer who claims the crime was committed while he suffered temporary insanity after the victim raped his wife.

From Perry Mason to John Grisham, most American lawyer movies, novels and TV shows feature idealists whose clients are innocent victims. Battling valiantly against superior legal firepower and despite great personal cost, they are rewarded when the innocent accused is acquitted and the real villains exposed and rarely mention their fees. Anyone who followed the O.J. Simpson trial knows this is a polite fiction, and that the superstars of the US legal system are not altruistic crusaders but high-priced sharpshooters. Among the first insiders to admit this was Michigan Supreme Court Justice John D. Voelker, who (under the pen-name Robert Traver) wrote the 1958 best seller *Anatomy Of A Murder*. Inspired by a real-life murder at the Lumberjack Tavern in Big Bay, Michigan, the big, complex, uncompromising book was bought by the big, complex, uncompromising Otto Preminger. The director clashed with censorship bodies to make an unexpurgated film version – even if it meant frank on-screen use of then-unheard words like 'panties', 'rape' and 'spermatogenesis'. A huge hit, with a fistful of Oscar nominations, it remains the courtroom classic. Almost every subsequent lawyer movie, even if it reverts to the Perry Mason message, has been influenced by it.

From its striking Saul Bass title design (featured also on the poster) and jazzy Duke Ellington score, *Anatomy Of A Murder* takes a sophisticated approach, unusual for a Hollywood film of its vintage. Most radically, it refuses to show the murder or any of the private scenes recounted in court, leaving it up to us to decide along with the jury whether Lieutenant Frederick Manion was or was not subject to an 'irresistible impulse' tantamount to insanity when he shot dead Barney Quill, the bearlike bar-owner alleged to have raped Manion's teasing wife Laura.

Manion is lucky enough to snag as his defence counsel Paul 'Polly' Biegler, a former Iron Cliffs County District Attorney keen to get back into court to clash with the political dullard who replaced him in office, and Biegler calls on the skills of his snide secretary and boozy-but-brilliant research partner. For the prosecution, the befuddled local DA hauls in Dancer, a prissy legal eagle from the local big city (Lansing, Mich.) whose sharp-suited, sly elegance makes an interesting clash with Biegler's aw-shucks jimmystewartian conniving. On the bench is a real-life courtroom giant: playing the judge is Joseph Welch, the attorney whose quiet persistence ('Have you no shame?') literally put an end to the career of Senator Joseph McCarthy. *Anatomy Of A Murder* is simply the best trial movie ever made, far less contrived than the brilliant but stagey *Twelve Angry Men*, with a real understanding on the part of Stewart and Scott (both among the film's Oscar nominees) of the way lawyers have to be not only great actors but stars, assuming personalities that exaggerate their inner selves and weighing every outburst and objection for the effect it has on the poor saps in the jury box. Scott accuses Stewart of 'flagrant, sneaking subterfuge' and Stewart counters with 'I'm just a humble country lawyer doing the best I can against the brilliant prosecutor from the big city of Lansing'. This, of course, plays well with the small-town folks on the jury, who see the fly-fishing, jazz-playing humbler as one of their own and are only too happy to pick up on the innuendo about the uppity slicker from out of town.

The case turns on the relationship between the Manions, and Remick (cast when Lana Turner refused to wear tight slacks) and Gazzara play their parts so well that no audience can ever quite decide whose version of what happened is most likely. Gazzara, screwing cigarettes into a strange holder and burning with suppressed anger, is that rare thing in a Hollywood crime movie: violent but smart, seemingly a sociopath but also, as his war record attests, a hero. And Remick is a giggly, calculating slut whom Stewart has to coach in dressing like a dowdy housewife, insisting she wear a girdle. The end is a kick in the teeth. The jury lets Manion off, but he skips town after (it is implied) beating up his trampy wife. He leaves a note for the lawyer he has stiffed out of a fee, claiming he had an 'irresistible impulse' to leave before paying. But the canny Biegler has used a late development in the case to position his firm for future profit, administering the valuable estate of the murder victim. ★★★★★ **KN**

ANCHORMAN: THE LEGEND OF RON BURGUNDY (2004)

Starring: *Will Ferrell (Ron Burgundy), Christina Applegate (Veronica Corningstone), Paul Rudd (Brian Fantana), Steve Carell (Brick Tamland), Vince Vaughn (Wes Mantooth)*
Director: *Adam McKay*
Screenwriters: *Will Ferrell, Adam McKay*
12A/91 mins./Comedy/USA

Ron Burgundy is the number one newsman in San Diego, but the arrival of a woman on his news team throws him for a loop.

Will Ferrell is no longer just that funny one from that film with Ben Stiller/Vince Vaughn/either of the Wilson brothers. Since *Elf*, he's been anointed as one of the new kings of comedy, the big hulking dunderhead part of the 'Fratpack' – that group of near-middle-aged men who should know better but have provided the biggest guilty laughs of this year.

But *Anchorman* isn't quite Ferrell's finest creation, having the hit-and-miss quality of an extended *Saturday Night Live* sketch. His writing credit is indicative of the fact that most of what makes it to screen is clearly just Ferrell and co. making it up as they go along, plot be damned. That sometimes leads to baffling lunacy which borders on the embarrassing, but equally it offers episodes of such inspired idiocy that the only reasonable response is to laugh yourself stupid.

Ferrell's also wise enough to surround himself with a supremely gifted supporting cast. Applegate stirs many a giggle by playing it (relatively) straight in a confederacy of dunces and, mark our words, Steve Carell, who plays dim-witted weather man Brick Tamland, will be giving Ferrell trouble at the box office soon.

Certainly the silliest comedy in some time, but mainly in a good way. Not quite as inspired as Stiller's *Dodgeball*, but if it were any more manic you'd have to put it on Ritalin. ★★★ **DJ**

ANCHORS AWEIGH (1945)

Starring: *Frank Sinatra (Clarence Doolittle), Gene Kelly (Joseph Brady), Kathryn Grayson (Susan Abbott), Jose Iturbi (Himself), Dean Stockwell (Donald Martin)*
Director: *George Sidney*
Screenwriter: *Isabel Lennart, based on a story by Natalie March*
U/143 mins./Musical/USA

Awards: *Academy Awards – Best Score (Musical)*

On shore leave in Hollywood, sailors Joseph Brady and Clarence Doolittle befriend young Donald Abbott and help his movie extra guardian, Susan secure an audition with musical maestro, José Iturbi.

Having demonstrated both his star quality and his choreographic genius on loan to Columbia in *Cover Girl*, Gene Kelly returned to MGM for this breezy musical and emerged with an Oscar nomination and the reputation as the most exciting new talent on the lot. Producer Joe Pasternak wisely gave Kelly free rein, while he concentrated on showcasing his soprano protégée, Kathryn Grayson. The decision paid double dividends, as not only did it enable Kelly to mature both before and behind the camera, but it also saw the scrawny king of the bobbysoxers, Frank Sinatra, finally fulfil his filmic potential after five indifferent outings.

Kelly upstaged Sinatra in each of their numbers together, notably demonstrating considerably more bounce and brio at the conclusion of 'I Begged Her', a comic routine which climaxed with them trampolining along a row of bunks in their dormitory. Just as he would in *Take Me Out To The Ball Game* and *On The Town*, Kelly treated Sinatra as a crooning sidekick and Ol' Blue Eyes nursed his resentment for 40 years before exacting his revenge by denying Kelly a cherished role in *Robin And The Seven Hoods* (1964). Yet, Kelly ensured that Sinatra had a trio of charming ballads by Sammy Cahn and Jule Styne – one of which, 'I Fall in Love Too Easily', landed an Oscar nom – and they all slot more easily into the action than Grayson's classical interludes with Iturbi.

But Kelly undoubtedly kept the best numbers for himself. Unable to resist showboating with kids, he performed 'The Mexican Hat Dance' with Sharon McManus and took a swashbuckling tour of MGM to 'La Cumparsita!'. However, the indelible moment was his duet with Jerry Mouse in 'The King Who Couldn't Dance', a four-minute amalgam of live-action and animation that cost $100,000 and took two months to produce. ★★★ **DP**

AND GOD CREATED WOMAN (ET DIEU CREA LA FEMME) (1956)

Starring: *Brigitte Bardot (Juliette), Curt Jurgens (Eric), Jean-Louis Trintignant (Michel), Christian Marquand (Antoine), Georges Pojouy (Christian)*
Director: *Roger Vadim*
Screenwriters: *Roger Vadim, Raoul Levy*
18/92 mins./Erotic/Drama/France

Saint-Tropez teenage Juliette Hardy marries Michel Tardieuhis' brother Antoine and teases lecherous tycon Eric Carradine before she's tamed by her timid spouse.

This is a film with more sociological than artistic significance. It marked the feature debut of Roger Vadim, an assistant to director Marc Allégret and occasional reporter for *Paris Match*. Consequently, it's much more of a live-action photo opportunity than a movie, with Vadim exploiting Brigitte Bardot's lusty innocence to cash in on postwar French society's penchant for juvenile rebellion. Yet, her pouting nudity and his freewheeling approach to morality helped transform the presentation of women on screen.

Hollywood had to be content with a watching brief, as the Production Code ensured that it wouldn't be able to take similar liberties for another decade. But the pouting Bébé's cavortings earned the picture $4 million Stateside and a further $21 million around the globe. In promoting the picture, Bardot forever changed the nature of celebrity by posing as a teasingly available sex kitten rather than a star on a pedestal. Overnight, she became the most photographed woman in the world and what made her ecstatic reception all the more salacious was the fact that she was Vadim's wife.

For all its vitality, individuality, passion and eroticism, this is little more than a saucy penny dreadful. Never the most skilful of performers, Bardot is more of an icon than a character and she's easily upstaged by the men who are supposed to be helpless in her thrall. But Vadim knew how to pose her and Armand Thirard's Eastmancolor imagery evocatively captures her beauty and vibrancy against the vivid location hues and dazzling whites that show her tanned flesh to best advantage.

And God Created Woman dented the barricades of social and cinematic propriety that the nouvelle vague would later bring crashing down. But while France was happy for BB to indulge her healthy (if adulterous) sexual appetite, there was outrage two years later when wife and mother Jeanne Moreau did the same in Louis Malle's *Les Amants*. ★★★ **DP**

ANDREI RUBLEV (ANDREY RUBYLOV) (1966)

Starring: *Anatoli Solonitsyn (Andrei Rubylov), Ivan Lapikov (Kirill), Nikolai Grinko (Danil Chorny), Nikollai Sergeyev (Theophanes The Greek)*
Director: *Andrei Tarkovsky*
Screenwriters: *Andrei Tarkovsky, Andrei Mikhalikov-Konchalovsky*
15/183 mins./Drama/USSR

Icon painter Andrei Rublev loses faith in his mission and his talent as he witnesses the political and cultural desecration of 15th-century Russia.

Divided loosely into 10 chapters, this is less a monochrome chronicle of icon painter Andrei Rublev's life between 1400–25 than a meditation on the responsibility of the artist and mankind's inveterate response to war, chaos and oppression.

'I do not understand historical films which have no relevance for the present,' Tarkovsky once wrote and, thus, it's easy to see why the film was withheld from Soviet audiences after it was completed in 1966. Tarkovsky had actually begun working on the screenplay with Andrei Konchalovsky before he had finished his debut feature, *Ivan's Childhood*. But, despite its favourable reception at Cannes in 1969, Leonid Brezhnev refused to sanction Andrei Rublev's domestic release. Although some critics have suggested that the depiction of the pitiless Mongol-Tartar tyranny angered the Kremlin, a contemporary newspaper averred that the film had slandered a national hero by showing him as a self-doubting craftsman rather than an instinctive genius who had helped to spark a Russian renaissance in the face of philistinic repression.

The film has been interpreted in many ways, with some seeing it as an allegory of Tarkovsky's own struggle to produce enduring beauty in a hostile environment. But what it certainly isn't is a factual biography, as Rublev remains an elusive enigma who is as often absent from the screen as he is at the centre of events. He may feud with a rival over God's relationship to humanity and kill a man to protect a deaf-mute girl in the church that has been vandalised by barbaric iconoclasts. But Tarkovsky is more concerned with images than deeds and it's the balloon flight over the Breughelesque countryside, the pagans carrying torches through the woods, the casting of the bell and the various still life landscapes, interiors and visages that linger like the colour fragments of Rublev's frescoes in the climactic coda.

★★★★★ **DP**

THE ANDROMEDA STRAIN (1970)

Starring: *Arthur Hill (Dr Jeremy Stone), James Olson (Dr Mark Hall), David Wayne (Dr Charles Dutton), Kate Reid (Dr Ruth Leavitt), Paula Kelly (Karen Anson)*
Director: *Robert Wise*
Screenwriter: *Nelson Gidding, from a novel by Michael Crichton*
PG/131 mins./Sci-fi/Thriller/USA

A group of scientists try to stop a deadly alien virus spreading and killing Earth's entire population.

'There's a fire.' Thus runs the simple call to arms for Dr Jeremy Stone. The US air force have called a 'Wildfire alert' – a satellite has crashed from orbit into the desert town of Piedmont, New Mexico, and now everyone is dead. That satellite was part of project Scoop, designed to collect alien microorganisms from outer space. And mankind is on the verge of the ultimate nightmare scenario – an alien virus that threatens the entire population of Earth. So a team of expert scientists are recruited to isolate and contain the dreaded outbreak before it's thank you and goodnight for all concerned. Curiously, though, a tiny baby and a booze-sodden old-timer have survived.

Taken from the excellent novel by a young doctor named Michael Crichton, whose febrile imaginings of the perils and accomplishments of science were destined to make him remarkably rich, this is a cautionary fable of extra-terrestrial invasion on a microscopic level. In a remarkably focused manner the movie concentrates on creating dramatic tension from an unseen peril. Worked in a precise three-act structure, the tension sways between the depiction of intellectual pursuit and the thriller dynamic. The first act, at the desolate Piedmont, reveals the devastation and mystery culminating in a horrifc powdered blood sequence. Then to Project Wildfire and its mammoth, multi-levelled underground bunker and the stringent demands of decontamination (including the gastro-intestinal tract) and isolation of the bug – dubbed the Andromeda Strain – to discover a way to eradicate it. The final act reverts to something more formulaic as the strain breaks out in the research facility.

What *The Andromeda Strain* does so well, and almost uniquely in film, is depict scientists as just that, scientists – rational, intelligent men and women striving to answer the call of a crisis (a fact assisted by the casting of quality unknowns rather than major stars). Director Robert Wise (a versatile helmer who also gave us *The Day The Earth Stood Still* and the first *Star Trek* movie) understood that it is vital we believe in the movie as possibility rather than escapism. The team's approach is methodical and precise, a form of detective work on a hugely detailed level. It is also honest enough to depict the numbing tedium of scientific research. There is a strange true-to-life dichotomy between the urgency of proceedings and the necessary meticulousness of the process creating an unusual and highly effective inner tension.

This, not for the first time amongst the works of Crichton, makes a firm moral statement: science must be subservient to mankind. *The Andromeda Strain* offers up science overweened and flawed – the satellite, the centre's self-destruct programme, the inept communication devices that hamper their progress – and science victorious: finally, it is brainy analysis that is the only hope. Interestingly, at the time of the film's release, Wise was criticised for making a show of the technology and special effects possibilities when his central theme was to accuse society of being seduced by science.

Wise shoots the movie in an appropriately cold, clinical style with Boris Leven's elaborate but precise production design a real feature. The set was constructed from 17 feet beneath Universal's biggest sound stage and such was Wise's dedication to scientific accuracy that he insisted on every item of featured equipment (electron microscopes, computer etc.) being the real thing.

Of course, drama is required otherwise we're faced with an absolute yawn of basic scientific analysis. So the unpredictable organism mutates and learns to chow down on plastic (and therefore the protective suits). One of the team, Leavit, unpredictably (and slightly implausibly) reveals an unmentioned epilepsy and blacks out at a crucial moment. And finally, when there is a dreaded breakout – due to the Andromeda Strain eating through the seals – and the centre's self-destruct nuclear detonation kicks in, Hall goes on a good ol' race-against-time to, well, switch it off. In no less than Indiana Jones fashion he dodges darts, lasers and poisoned gas to insert the off key. For the first time the film swaps cerebral tension and discussion for genuine action. If the centre is destroyed the virus will only mutate further, possibly becoming even more destructive. Ultimately, though, the pulp origins get the better of the realism and a conspiracy involving bacterial warfare stifles the clearheadedness of the plotting, playing a typically 70s anti-authority riff. But Wise (and Crichton) have done more than enough, concocting the most absorbing, riveting take on science fiction tempered with science fact. ★★★★ **IN**

ANGEL HEART (1987)

Starring: *Mickey Rourke (Harry Angel), Robert De Niro (Louis Cyphre), Lisa Bonet (Epiphany Proudfoot), Charlotte Rampling (Margaret Krusemark)*
Director: *Alan Parker*
Screenwriter: *Alan Parker, based on the novel by William Hjortsberg*
18/113 mins./Horror/Mystery/USA

Hired by a law firm representing the sinister Louis Cyphre, private investigator Harry Angel goes in search of missing WWII veteran Johnny Favourite, amongst the sweaty slums of New Orleans. But the further he delves into the case the more the evidence makes no sense at all.

Trust Alan Parker, a master with the stippled strokes and dappled sunbeams of 80s ad-atmospherics, to coat this overwrought but memorable noir-horror nonsense in super-soupy layers of Southern Gothic window-dressing. The film oozes along with a superficial sense of unease, leaden with overcooked metaphors: from hoodoo chicken heads to the hollow clang of descending elevators. Blood is everywhere. The film looks and feels unwell.

Parker adapted William Hjortsberg's novel *Falling Angel* (the same writer who'd helped conceive the dark fantasy of *Legend* with Parker's compatriot Ridley Scott) himself and was, obviously, more tickled by the visual opportunities than any great strengths of the story. Yet, he has cast well. When you need a boozy, sleazy, loose-hinged gumshoe (think Sam Spade without the self-control) whom else to call upon than the leathery, anti-charm of Mickey Rourke? He slumps, heavy-cast, through the twisty mechanics of the plot, most of which are pretty inexplicable, bodies piling up in his wake. What, for instance, does petit Lisa Bonnet see in this lascivious lump of an anti-hero? But soon enough they are doing the carnal dance while coated in blood and viscera (it's that kind of film). And Robert De Niro, while hardly busting a gut, still has the look of a thousand secrets lurking behind his dead eyes.

The director was never going to win any points for subtlety, beyond even its sticky style, the script rests on a increasing number of really stupid fillips of wordplay – if Harry Angel had been any better at the Sunday cryptic crossword he would have saved himself a whole lot of heartache. Or, at least, got to the nub of things a bit quicker. He does, however, make it compelling, and at the big twist, he has played a confident enough game of murky hoodwinking, like Agatha Christie overdosing on Tequila and downers. ★★★ **IN**

ⓓ ANGELS WITH DIRTY FACES (1938)

Starring: *James Cagney (Rocky Sullivan), Pat O'Brien (Fr Jerry Connelly), Humphrey Bogart (Jim Frazier), Ann Sheridan (Laury Ferguson), George Bancroft (Mac Keeler)*
Director: *Michael Curtiz*
Screenwriters: *John Wexley, Warren Duff*
PG/97 mins./Crime/USA

Rocky and Jerry were best friends who grew up on the streets of Hell's Kitchen, but while Rocky drifted from reform school into crime, Jerry broke free to become a priest, working with kids just like them. Now Rocky is back and Jerry hopes he can help him reform his ways, or, at least, keep him away from his new charges.

Like any of James Cagney's procession of 'classic' gangster movies that ruled the roost in the thirties, you have to allow a fair amount of licence for the predilections of the day. Which means to say that Michael Curtiz, who went on to direct *Casablanca*, spreads the melodrama as thick as marmalade, while the stilted rhythms of the corny dialogue and one-dimensional moralism are less old-fashioned than from a different world entirely.

Yet, this is a film with a stern heart and a genuine brain, that for once used the strictures of the Hayes Code (with its strangulating hold on Hollywood) to its own advantage – a chance to examine the nihilistic heart of the criminal and the forces that shape them.

Cagney, as is his wont chewing off vast lumps of the scenery, cannot escape the grip of his past like his friend and moral opposite Pat O'Brien has managed. He does, however, grasp why he should. Actually, when you boil it down, this is far less the gangster film than appearances might suggest. It is set in New York's, then, slum-ridden Hell's Kitchen, a hive for gangsters and lowlifes, and Rocky is trying to reinvigorate his place in the racketeering game, but it is far more a character piece about the possibilities for redemption. As much a test for Father Jerry's mettle as Rocky; will he have to turn his old friend in? Does loyalty withstand questions of what is right?

The final note, as Rocky ends-up facing the consequences of his crimes (a moral outcome that the production code necessitated) carries the tragic but inspiring undertone of a man, at last, doing the right thing. ★★★★ **IN**

ⓓ ANGER MANAGEMENT (2003)

Starring: *Adam Sandler (Dave Buznik), Jack Nicholson (Dr Buddy Rydell), Marisa Tomei (Linda), Krista Allen (Stacy), January Jones (Gina), John Turturro (Chuck), Woody Harrelson (Galaxia/Security Guard)*
Director: *Peter Segal*
Screenwriter: *David Dorfman*
15/105 mins./Comedy/USA

After an altercation on an airplane a businessman is sentenced to join an anger-management programme run by a very aggressive instructor.

Like a visit to the dentist or an overdue tax demand, the arrival of any Adam Sandler film is something that strikes fear into the hearts of many – especially the discerning cinemagoer who finds his brand of humour too broad to swallow.

With a track record that includes *Mr Deeds*, *Little Nicky* and *Eight Crazy Nights*, it's easy to see why there are plenty who feel this way. But while Sandler has more than a few turkeys under his belt, it's unfair to assume he's incapable of making a good film. After all, *The Wedding Singer* was an enjoyable hit, and his creepy turn in *Punch-Drunk Love* showed that he's capable of ditching his trademark goofiness.

Such is the case with *Anger Management*, which, while not without its flaws, is far more watchable and entertaining than the films that gained Sandler his reputation in the first place. At the very least, the fact that it shot past the $100 million mark in the US after three weeks on release, dragging American cinemas out of their wartime doldrums, suggests he must be doing something right.

That said, the film's success doesn't so much hinge on Sandler's pratfalls as on his screen relationship with Jack Nicholson – and it's here that *Anger Management* hits its stride. From the genuinely hysterical airborne opening sequence – in which Sandler's simple request for a pair of headphones taps brilliantly into the paranoia of travelling in such security-conscious times – to the many other set-pieces in which the two share the screen, this is an inspired partnership that works far better than anyone ever had a right to expect.

It's hard to imagine anyone other than Nicholson playing the unorthodox doctor. Rydell is a grotesque creation whose methods to cure his patient of his so-called 'mood swings' include moving into his apartment, making inevitable moves on his girlfriend and, in one instance, encouraging Dave to sing songs from *West Side Story* in the middle of a crowded New York highway.

Sandler, for once upstaged by somebody more over-the-top than himself, is in more restrained form than usual (although it would be hard to be anything but, given he has Nicholson's frantic mugging to contend with). As such, he makes for a splendid foil, looking slightly bemused throughout but bagging enough one-liners to hold his own against his co-star. This is the kind of buddy picture where everybody – not least the two stars – seems to be enjoying themselves, something that is obvious from the first moment that Sandler and Nicholson are together on screen. It's unfortunate, then, that the pair's relationship is at the expense of everybody and everything else, with a superb supporting cast – that includes Luis Guzman, Woody Harrelson and John Turturro as Sandler's 'anger buddy' – given far too little to do.

Tomei, as the romantic interest, is also underused. And while screenwriter Dorfman wrings enough laughs out of the script, he never realises the full potential of his dark premise, opting instead for a storyline that never quite answers the question of whether Sandler really has anger management issues or not.

The ending feels lame, presumably in an effort to give audiences their feel-good fix but, as crowd-pleasers go, this delivers the goods and it won't do Sandler's reputation any harm. Besides, any film that features John C. Reilly as a sadistic Buddhist monk is likely to bring a smile to the face of even the aforementioned 'discerning cinemagoer'.

A better script and more attention to other cast members would have helped but, as it stands, this is still the best Adam Sandler comedy since *The Wedding Singer*. ★★★ **CW**

ANIMAL CRACKERS (1930)

Starring: *Groucho Marx (Captain Jeffrey Spaulding), Harpo Marx (The Professor), Chico Marx (Signor Emanuel Ravelli), Zeppo Marx (Horatio Jamison), Lillian Roth, (Arabella Rittenhouse), Margaret Dumont (Mrs Rittenhouse)*
Director: *Victor Heerman*
Screenwriter: *Morrie Ryskind, based on the play by Ryskind, George S. Kaufman, Bert Kalmar and Harry Ruby*
U/97 mins./Comedy/USA

Explorer Jeffrey T. Spaulding, his secretary Horatio W. Jamison, musician Emanuel Ravelli and his sidekick The Professor all arrive at the Long Island mansion of Mrs Rittenhouse to attend the unveiling of her latest artistic purchase.

While they were launching *Animal Crackers* on Broadway in 1929, the Marx Brothers simultaneously made their movie debut in *The Cocoanuts*. It proved to be an unhappy experience, with directors Robert Florey and Joseph Santley being compelled to clip the anarchic quartet's wings, as they insisted that the brothers remained in shot and within range of the primitive microphones. What's more, the absence of an audience affected the foursome's timing and they arrived to make their second Paramount picture at Astoria Studios in New York with considerable misgivings – a situation compounded by the fact that they had all just lost heavily in the Wall Street Crash, with Groucho down by around $250,000.

Already a screen comedy veteran, director Victor Heerman further disconcerted the Marxes by cutting swathes from George S. Kaufman and Morrie Ryskind's screenplay. But before they mutinied, they agreed to watch some test rushes and were so reassured by what they saw that they abandoned their stage showboating and settled into what would become their stock characters.

As Captain Spaulding (who was reportedly named after the studio's drug supplier), Groucho established his trademark brash, arrogant social climber, whose ability to dupe others was matched only by his own naivete. Chico similarly honed his Italianate schemer and Harpo his mute, madcap womaniser. Even Zeppo had some choice moments, during the dictation sequence with Groucho.

Reprising her stage role, Margaret Dumont proved equally invaluable to the act and it's a joy to watch her barely suppressing giggles against Groucho's torrent of insults and inanities and Chico and Harpo's antics during the bridge game with Margaret Irving. However, the highlights belong to Groucho, whether he's clowning along to 'Hooray for Captain Spaulding!' (which would become the theme for his TV show, *You Bet Your Life*) or lampooning Eugene O'Neill's *Strange Interlude* in a virtuoso monologue. ★★★★ **DP**

ANIMAL FARM (1954)

Starring: *Gordon Heath (Narrator), Maurice Denham (All Animals)*
Director: *Joy Batchelor, John Halas*
Screenwriters: *Joy Batchelor, Jospeh Bryan, John Halas, Borden Mace, Phillip Stapp, Lothar Wolff, based on the novel by George Orwell*
U/72 mins./Animation/UK

Pigs Napoleon and Snowball lead the livestock of Manor Farm in a revolution against the tyrannical Farmer Jones, only to rapidly resort to his oppressive tactics.

British animation was launched in 1899 when Birt Acres made some matchsticks dance for a Bryant & May advertisement urging people to buy matches for the troops in the Boer War. It took another 55 years for what had essentially remained a cottage industry to produce its first feature. In the mid-1940s, J. Arthur Rank had lured David Hand (who had directed *Snow White And The Seven Dwarfs*) from Disney unsuccessfully to establish an animation unit at Pinewood. Many, therefore, questioned the wisdom of presenter Louis de Rochemont (who had founded the March of Time newsreel and instigated postwar Hollywood realism with *The House On 92nd Street*, 1945), when he announced in 1951 that he was going to sponsor a cartoon version of George Orwell's lauded 1945 allegory of Stalinist brutality.

What made the project seem even more hazardous was the fact that De Rochemont's chosen directors, John Halas and Joy Batchelor, were known only for the 70+ propaganda shorts that had been commissioned by the government during the war and the raft of educational and public information films they had produced since. Yet they were able to hire a staff of 70 artists to render the 300,000 drawings required for the film's 750 scenes and they quickly hit upon a visual style that departed from Disney's quaint brand of animal graphics. However, they emulated the American studio's tactic of giving the principals identifiable characters to make them more readily accessible for younger viewers.

Two years in the making, this remains one of the finest adult animations ever made. The grafting of a happy ending has been challenged, as has the conventional nature of the artwork and the backgrounds' lack of depth. But the palette of dark colours is intelligently used and Orwell's message about the loss of freedom remains as powerful as ever. ★★★ **DP**

ANNA KARENINA (1935)

Starring: *Greta Garbo (Anna Karenina), Fredric March (Vronsky), Freddie Bartholomew (Sergei), Maureen O'Sullivan (Kitty), May Robson (Countess Vronsky), Basil Rathbone (Karenin)*
Director: *Clarence Brown*
Screenwriter: *Clemence Dane, Salka Viertel, S.N. Berhman, based on the novel by Leo Tolstoy*
U/85 mins./Drama/USA

Anna, the pampered wife of a government official, sacrifices her luxurious lifestyle and contact with her son to be with her soldier lover, Vronsky. However, his ardour cools when Russia goes to war.

Greta Garbo and John Gilbert were at the peak of their powers as cinema's principal paramours when they made *Love* in 1927. However, Edmund Goulding's updating of Leo Tolstoy's *Anna Karenina* was to prove their penultimate silent, as *The Jazz Singer* introduced Talkies later that year and Gilbert's career collapsed as his reedy voice didn't match his dashing image.

Consequently, his boots were filled by Fredric March for MGM's lavish and reasonably faithful (if much condensed) adaptation, although he was highly reluctant to embark upon another Russian venture, having just completed *We Live Again* (1934), which was based on Tolstoy's *Resurrection*. Nowadays an unjustly forgotten actor, March gives a typically accomplished performance as the swaggering swain who fails to understand the depth of Anna's passion and discards her when something more exciting comes along.

Then Hollywood's sternest villain, Basil Rathbone is equally persuasive as the coldly cruel aristocrat, who allows social convention rather than assailable emotion to dictate his actions.

But, as with each of her pictures, this was all about Garbo. Overriding producer David O. Selznick's suggestion of George Cukor, she demanded and got both her favourite director, Clarence Brown, and cinematographer William Daniels, who knew just how to light her enigmatic beauty. She even succeeded in having all her scenes filmed on a closed set. But her divaish demands were a small price to pay for her impeccable display of amour fou, which she seems to know all along is ruinously reckless, yet she's unable to resist her fate.

It's dismaying to think that Garbo was overlooked by the Academy, especially as only Bette Davis's Oscar-winning turn in *Dangerous* came even close to her magisterial exhibition, which outclassed the subsequent efforts of Vivien Leigh in Julien Duvivier's 1953 rendition and Jacqueline Bisset in Simon Langton's woefully inadequate 1985 teleplay. ★★★★ **DP**

ANNE OF THE THOUSAND DAYS (1969)

Starring: *Richard Burton (King Henry VIII), Geneviève Bujold (Anne Boleyn), Irene Papas (Queen Katherine), Anthony Quayle (Woisey), Michael Hordern (Thomas Boleyn), Katherine Blake (Elizabeth)*
Director: *Charles Jarrott*
Screenwriters: *Bridget Boland, John Hale, adapted by Richard Sokolove, from the play by Maxwell Anderson*
PG/145 mins./History/Drama/145 mins.

Awards: *Academy Awards – Best Costume Design,*

Having made Henry VIII wait six years for her favours, Anne Boleyn finds her grasp on Tudor power slipping when she fails to provide the king with a much-cherished male heir.

Released just three years after Fred Zinnemann's impeccable, multi-award-winning adaptation of Robert Bolt's *A Man For All Seasons*, this revision of Maxwell Anderson's stage play was always going to pale by comparison. Yet it managed to earn itself an impressive 10 Oscar nominations and cashed in on the period's seemingly insatiable public appetite for all things Tudor, which prompted the BBC's later series *The Six Wives Of Henry VIII* and *Elizabeth R*, each of which commanded a respectable global audience.

The production values couldn't be bettered. Yet only Margaret Furse's costumes found favour with the Academy and the design team of Maurice Carter, Lionel Couch and Patrick McLoughlin had every right to feel aggrieved at losing out to *Hello, Dolly*!

But Charles Jarrott's studied direction deprives the action of much of its momentous drama. He keeps Arthur Ibbotson's camera at a discreet, static distance and, thus, captures only the pageantry of the court rather than its passion and intrigue. This deferential attitude is all the more surprising, considering the number of liberties that the screenplay had taken with historical fact.

Furthermore, Jarrott failed to rouse Richard Burton from the lethargy that rendered Bluff King Hal as a morose bore, whose megalomania is reduced to regal grumpiness and whose lust comes across merely as repellent lechery. Consequently, it's hard to accept the sudden outburst of dynastic fury that seals Anne's fate when she only manages to provide him with another daughter.

Geneviève Bujold, however, is infinitely more impressive. She wisely allows the scheming side of Anne Boleyn's nature to triumph over her coquettishness and, thus, she creates an enticing villain whose naked ambition does not preclude us from feeling sympathy with her when she's confounded by capricious biology. Unfortunately, despite some creditable outings, Bujold has never managed to summon a performance of similarly intense subtlety since. ★★★ **DP**

ANNIE GET YOUR GUN (1950)

Starring: *Betty Hutton (Annie Oakley), Howard Keel (Frank Butler), Louis Calhern (Buffalo Bill), J. Carrol Nash (Chief Sitting Bull), Edward Arnold (Pawnee Bill)*
Director: *George Sidney*
Screenwriter: *Sidney Sheldon, based on the play and book by Herbert Fields and Dorothy Fields*
U/107 mins./Musical/Western/USA

Awards: *Academy Awards – Best Score (Musical)*

Tomboy Annie Oakley joins Buffalo Bill's Wild West Show and has to suppress her sharpshooting prowess and competitive instinct to win the heart of fellow gunslinger Frank Butler.

Dorothy Fields conceived the 1946 Broadway smash on which this lively MGM musical was based as a vehicle for Ethel Merman. Jerome Kern had been signed up to compose the score, but on his sudden death producers Richard Rodgers and Oscar Hammerstein persuaded Irving Berlin to undertake a rare book show and he responded with such enduring gems as 'Doin' What Comes Natur'lly', 'You Can't Get a Man With a Gun', 'Anything You Can Do' and the anthemic 'There's No Business Like Show Business'.

Typically overlooking the egregious Merman for the screen version, Arthur Freed secured the rights for Judy Garland, who was recovering from another bout of the mental fragility that had been exacerbated by her addiction to pills. She promptly insisted on the removal of Busby Berkeley as director (even though he had guided her and Mickey Rooney through four vibrant barnyard movies earlier in the decade) and his replacement by Charles Walters. But Garland struggled to find her way into a character that, for once, bore no resemblance to her own personality and the glimpses of her performing 'I'm an Indian, Too' in *That's Entertainment III* demonstrate just how ill-suited she was for the role.

Walters was the next casualty of this supposedly cursed project and his successor, George Sidney, had to reshoot numerous sequences after Frank Morgan died and Louis Calhern assumed the part of Buffalo Bill. However, Howard Keel (who was making his musical debut) and Betty Hutton had succeeded in establishing a rousing rapport that gave the picture its momentum. Yet, while it earned Keel the role of Bill Hickock opposite Doris Day in Warners' Western riposte, *Calamity Jane*, Annie only confirmed Hollywood's unjustified suspicions that Hutton was incapable of moderating her performance, even though her bullish comic eagerness here is exactly what the role requires. ★★★ **DP**

ANNIE HALL (1977)

Starring: *Woody Allen (Alvy Singer), Diane Keaton (Annie Hall), Tony Roberts (Rob), Carol Kane (Allison), Paul Simon (Tony Lacey), Colleen Dewhurst (Mom Hall), Shelley Duvall (Pam), Christopher Walken (Duane Hall)*
Director: *Woody Allen*
Screenwriters: *Woody Allen, Marshall Brickman*
15/93 mins./Comedy/Romance/USA

Awards: *Academy Awards – Best Actress, Best Director, Best Picture, Best Original Screenplay, BAFTA – Best Actor, Best Director, Best Editing, Best Film, Best Screenplay, Golden Globes – Best Musical/Comedy Actress*

Alvy Singer, a neurotic, insecure comedy writer falls for singer Annie Hall, but insecurity continues to blight their relationship.

Boy meets girl. Boy introduces girl to death-obsessed literature, Swedish melodrama and the analyst's couch. Boy suffocates girl. Girl goes her own way. However you describe it, *Annie Hall* remains one of the most charming, bittersweet, beautifully played, funny love stories ever committed to celluloid. Much closer in spirit to Woody Allen's prose humour and nightclub act than any of his previous films, the romance between neurotic comic Alvy Singer (Allen) and ditzy singer Annie Hall marks the intersection between The Early Funny Ones and The Later Serious Ones. As before, the one-liners flowed thick and fast but the frenetic pace and broad tone were replaced by a gravitas and a check list of concerns – the fragility of love, sex, psychoanalysis, New York vs. countryside, Jewishness – that have dominated the output of Allen's art ever since.

How autobiographical the movie is has always been a moot point. Yes, Allen dated Diane Keaton. Yes, Keaton's real name is Diane Hall. Yes, she wore her own (subsequently trend-setting) wardrobe for the role. And although it is lovely to think that Allen and Keaton really had run-ins with runaway lobsters, it's probably fair to say the autobiographical content is more in atmosphere than incident (co-writer Marshall Brickman had an equal hand in the screenplay), especially the intimate tone created by Allen's onscreen presence and direct to camera addresses.

Albums By Actors

TOP 10

	Album	Actor
1	Do You Wanna Touch Me (Oh Yeah)	Michael Caine
2	America, Why I Love Her	John Wayne
3	A Twist of Lemmon	Jack Lemmon
4	Little Joe Sure Can Sing	Joe Pesci (as Jo Ritchie)
5	A Transformed Man	William Shatner
7	Whenever I'm Away From You	John Travolta
8	The Return of Bruno	Bruce Willis
9	Jungle Rhythm	James Dean
10	Songs I Like	Dick Van Dyke

If the personal feel is a fallacy, the observations into building and sustaining a relationship ring remarkably true, be they on the awkwardness of small talk, the dread of meeting the family or the breakdown of intimacy and communication. The couple's shift from initial fumbling to terminal uncertainty is deftly mapped out by the central performances. Keaton's ditzy ingenue ('Lah-di-dah') is one of the great comedic creations, her growing self-awareness completely believable. Often overlooked as an actor, Allen handles Alvy's growing insecurity, twisting Annie's every move into an act of disenchantment, with aplomb and sensitivity, light years away from the slapstick mugging of *Bananas* and *Sleeper*.

Away from the romantic elements, *Annie Hall* is marked by dichotomy: between the Jewish and the Gentile – on their first meeting Annie tells Alvy 'You're what Grammy Hall would call a real Jew!', a sentiment later punctuated by a fabulous sight gag with the old woman seeing Alvy dressed in Orthodox get-up – and between New York and Los Angeles. If Allen is unsurprisingly satirical about LA ('They're always giving out awards! Best Fascist Dictator: Adolf Hitler'), even taking the ultimate revenge on Californians by sneezing on the coke, he is equally barbed about the pretensions of New York, a world where Academic journals *Dissent* and *Commentary* have merged to become Dissentary, and pseuds can only be silenced by Marshall McLuhan lurking behind a movie poster (Allen originally wanted Fellini to confront the bore but the maestro was filming).

After *Love And Death*, Allen's initial idea was to place two hip New Yorkers at the centre of a murder mystery, (the idea transmuted into *Manhattan Murder Mystery* but discovered he didn't want to get embroiled in the mechanics of plot. Originally entitled *15 Anhedonia* (a Greek word which describes the inability to feel joy), the movie Allen subsequently shot was a mosaic portrait of a 40-year-old man harassed by the pressures of modern living. Only finding out the concept didn't hang together in the cutting room, Allen zeroed in on the love story aspect, re-shot more footage and reshaped the material into something that is at once classically structured yet refreshingly freewheeling.

Working with cinematographer Gordon Willis for the first time, *Annie Hall* marked Allen's maturation as a filmmaker. Eschewing the flat look of most comedies, the movie has a distinct colour scheme – golden for Alvy's childhood memories, dazzling bright light in California and muted greys and browns for New York – that perfectly delineates each section of the picture. Moreover, Allen laces the love story with an endless parade of cinematic devices to up the humour ante: subtitles (deliciously conveying what Alvy and Annie are really thinking), split screens (contrasting Alvy and Annie's diverging perspectives to their shrinks), Alvy's conversations with passers-by who are totally aware of his predicaments, Annie, high on marijuana, moving out of her own body as Alvy makes love to her, even an animated section where Alvy confronts the Queen from *Snow White*, the root of his problems with women. For the first time, Allen wasn't just filming staged pratfalls; he was using the medium to its fullest extent to enhance his comic vision.

Towards the end of the movie, Alvy turns his relationship with Annie into a play, giving the affair a happy outcome that has been denied the pair in real life. By contrasting the fiction and the fact, it reminds us that reality (and love) can be unpredictable, uncontrollable and painful. But this is precisely why Woody Allen in general and *Annie Hall* in particular are important: they keep the whole sorry mess perfectly in perspective. ★★★★★ **IF**

ANOTHER 48 HOURS (1990)

Starring: *Eddie Murphy (Reggie Hammond), Nick Nolte (Jack Cates), Brion James (Ben Kehoe), Kevin Tighe (Blake Wilson), Ed O'Ross (Frank Cruise)*
Director: *Walter Hill*
Screenwriters: *John Fasano, Jeb Stuart, Larry Gross*
18/93 mins./Comedy/Action/Crime/USA

Guess what? With a day left to serve on his sentence, Reggie Hammond is approached by old 'pal', cop Jack Cates to help him crack another case. Now things are even more complicated: Jack is trying to clear his own name, Reggie wants the $500k Jack was looking after for him, and all these bikers are trying to kill them.

That the ream of screenwriters and spurious honourees with 'characters by' credits, not least Eddie Murphy's own dubious 'story by' notation, totals eight reveals what a hotchpotch of a sequel this was from the conceptual stages. Not that they had any greater aspiration than a greatest hits package of the first film. Although, where the original – hardly a pillar in the cathedral of cinema itself – set-about its purpose with a directness and punchy wit, here the plot, much like its stars, is over-fed, under-willing and noticeably plumper round the middle.

The simple Xeroxed process of liberating Reggie from the clink – where his sentence was dubiously extended due to a prison safe being emptied – seems tortuously long-winded, finally requiring a pair of evil bikers to force his prison bus off the road. Once back in the guardianship of Jack, it's like eight years had never passed. At least, that is what director Walter Hill desperately hopes for. So, as they track down the mysterious criminal mastermind known as the 'Iceman', they must jockey for male dominance (again), come to respect one another (again) and even do a replica run round a redneck bar – the original's sparkiest concoction, nothing like as funny here.

Murphy, especially, seems out of sorts. He still lands the lines with that familiar groove of petty exasperation and put-upon indignation, but he looks ill-at-ease, nursing his wounds in safe formula after the failure of his dream project *Harlem Nights*. He's hardly helped by Hill's greater emphasis on action over comedy. By comparison, Nolte is far more content to go over old ground. Cates has, to some degree, moved on: giving up the booze, losing his girlfriend, turning out, if anything, more of system twisting maverick and Nolte shambles through it, a big, ugly bear with a sore head. Again.

The bigger budget pays for plenty more mechanical carnage, shot with the brash polish the best technicians grant you, but this is just 'another' wearisome example of Hollywood's pointless idolatry of bleached out sequels. ★★ **IN**

⦾ ANTZ (1998)

Starring: *the voices of: Woody Allen (Z-4195), Sharon Stone (Princess Bala), Dan Aykroyd (Chip), Anne Bancroft (Queen), Jane Curtin (Muffy), Danny Glover (Barbatus), Gene Hackman (General Mandible), Jennifer Lopez (Azteca), Sylvester Stallone (Weaver), Christopher Walken (Cutter)*
Directors: *Eric Darnell, Tim Johnson*
Screenwriters: *Todd Alcott, Chris Weitz, Paul Weitz*
PG/83 mins./Animated/Family/Fantasy/USA

Bemoaning his lot in life, a lowly worker ant becomes an unwitting revolutionary.

While Disney's similarly themed *A Bug's Life*, released within a few months of this, took the upper hand in light, child-friendly entertainment, visually *Antz* was more compelling and, strangely, more adult. For *Antz*, a dark tale destined to whiz right over the head of the average four-year-old, is simply breathtaking to look at, its seamless bug's-eye view of the world easily compensating for any mild inconsistencies in the storyline.

Having delivered an opening shot and title sequence among the year's best, the action hones straight in on Z-4195, a worker ant living a blue-collar existence among a colony of millions, who is none too happy with his lot in life (cue hilarious sequence in which our hero relates his problems to his shrink with all the neurotic schtick his human counterpart can muster). Possible escape comes in the form of the lovely Princess Bala, with whom he becomes smitten after an impromptu dance at a bar, only for a string of mishaps to occur in his attempts to impress her: 'Z' becomes a war hero, a revolutionary, and finally kidnaps Bala, stranding the pair in the outside world. Meanwhile, it becomes increasingly clear that Bala's fiancé, General Mandible, is one untrustworthy ant.

This is not your average cute cartoon romp – there are no original song-and-dance numbers (just some fabulous musical sequences), little in the way of knockabout comedy, and some scenes (in particular a termite/ant battle curiously reminiscent of *Starship Troopers*) which might prove too intense for tots.

That said, *Antz* delivers handsomely in many departments; its voice cast, with the exception of Stone's thanklessly starchy royal, is uniformly excellent (especially Allen, Stallone as his best pal Weaver the soldier ant and Christopher Walken as Mandible's flying sidekick Cutter), and the script, one or two slow patches aside, is a winner. But it's the animation that wins out here, from the fleshy, lifelike contours of the principal players to the individuality of even the smallest background ant. In fact, it's so well done that only Z and Bala's outdoor adventure, complete with human intervention and other members of the insect family (check out Dan Aykroyd and Jane Curtin as a delightful wasp couple), serves to remind the audience just how microscopic the characters really are. ★★★★ **CK**

⦾ ANY GIVEN SUNDAY (1999)

Starring: *Al Pacino (Tony D'Amato), Cameron Diaz (Christina Pagniacii), Dennis Quaid (Jack 'Cap' Rooney), James Woods (Dr Harvey Mandrake), Jamie Foxx (Willie Beamen), LL Cool J (Julian Washington), Matthew Modine (Dr Ollie Powers), Aaron Eckhart (Nick Crozier), Elizabeth Berkley (Mandy Murphy), Charlton Heston (Commissioner)*
Director: *Oliver Stone*
Screenwriters: *John Logan, Oliver Stone, based on a screen story by Daniel Pyne and John Logan*
15/156 mins./Drama/Sport/USA

Al Pacino's gung-ho football coach must pull an American football team out of their league table tailspin.

'Listen up team, this is the play. Us white guys are gonna blast through the middle with a mixture of youthful machismo and world-weary substance-fuelled middle-aged angst. And all the action's gonna be captured on a frenetically edited range of different film stocks! Got that? Hup! Hup! Hup! . . .'

Okay, so it's easy to make fun of Oliver Stone, but then, the guy does keep on making basically the same movie. This time the subject is the brutal world of fictitious American football team the Miami Sharks. Possibly the most 'Oliver-Stoney' Oliver Stone movie to date, Pacino essentially plays the director himself, as a hard-drinking football coach who must reverse the Sharks' losing streak, while the predictably underwritten ice maiden comes in the form of Diaz' ball-breaking club owner.

One of the film's principal critiques of the game is that, while most of the players are black, the people in control are white. Of course, this would have had more substance were it not for the fact that the best lines go to Pacino and James Woods, the latter plumbing new depths as the team's drug-dispensing doctor.

Yet, despite the film's multifarious faults, which also include a truly rotten cameo from Stone himself as a sports commentator, there can be no argument that this is one of the most visually exciting experiences of Stone's career, as the audience is dragged so close to the action that it is possible to hear every grunt, feel every injury and almost taste every drop of spilt blood.

The timidly disposed in the audience will be praying for a time out long before that climactic impossible-to-win game rolls around. It hardly needs pointing out – this being an Oliver Stone movie – that they will be doing so in vain. ★★★★ **CC**

⦾ ANY WHICH WAY YOU CAN (1980)

Starring: *Clint Eastwood (Philo Beddoe), Sondra Locke (Lyn Halsey-Taylor), Geoffrey Lewis (Orville Boggs) William Smith (Jack Wilson), Ruth Gordon (Ma Boggs)*
Director: *Buddy Van Horn*
Screenwriter: *Stanford Sherman*
PG/116 mins./Comedy/USA

Bare-knuckle boxer Philo Beddoe aims to retire from the game. But when the Mafia kidnap his ex-girlfriend, and force him to take part in the illegal championship of the world, he and orang-utan pal Clyde must set off in their pick-up truck to set things right.

No actor with a career quite as exulted and varied as Clint Eastwood, can, at the same time, boast an aberration as bizarre as his orang-utan years. Chimp-friendly Ronald Reagan may have become president but he never directed *Unforgiven*. And, while there may have been something perversely pleasurable in the original's knockabout gusto, did we really need a sequel? The powers that be thought so, and thus we got this, about the dumbest movie Clint Eastwood ever put his name to.

Just counting off the gumbo of ingredients gives you an idea of what kind of madcap thinking was or, indeed, wasn't going on around here. Again, we have our sturdy, do-the-right-thing kinda hero who happens to be a bare-knuckle boxer, getting by on the dustier side of the tracks. He also owns an orang-utan called Clyde, both cute and memorable, but actually not exactly the point. Although, this does grant us the thinly comic exercise of veteran actress Ruth Gordon, as the cuss-ready Ma Boggs, berating Clyde's lack of house-manners. The gang of idiot Hell's Angels are back and, following a mishap involving tar, now have to don wigs. There's also the re-smouldering of Philo's lurve for country and western crooner Lyn, cameos from Fats Domino and Ray Charles and a bare-knuckle fight that seems to go on forever, even though the participants have become fast friends. Any which way you can, it seems, was both title and ethos for director Buddy Van Horn. As long as it's delivered with a quick-grin, yeehaw sensibility that demands they're only messing about with a camera.

Something the original did actually pull off, as there was a sense of commitment to its own oddity. Now, after *Every Which Way But Loose* became a big hit, that oddity is being treated like process. The jokes are contrived, where before they eagerly slipped out of the rough-hewn situations. Eastwood, meanwhile, is at his sleepiest, leaving any emoting to Clyde, who proves the only one who manages to get a grip. ★★ **IN**

THE APARTMENT (1960)

Starring: *Jack Lemmon (C.C. Baxter), Shirley MacLaine (Fran Kubelik), Fred MacMurray (J.D. Sheldrake), Ray Walston (Mr Dobisch), David Lewis (Mr Kirkeby)*
Director: *Billy Wilder*
Screenwriters: *Billy Wilder, I.A.L. Diamond*
PG/125 mins./Comedy/USA

Awards: *Academy Awards – Best Art Direction/Set Direction, Best Director, Best Film Editing, Best Picture, Best Original Screenplay, BAFTA – Best Film from any Source, Best Foreign Actor, Best Foreign Actress, Golden Globes – Best Comedy, Best Actor, Best Actress*

Bud Baxter lends out his apartment so his company superiors can conduct their illicit affairs discreetly and he can earn their good will. But he risks losing his standing in the film when he falls for his boss's mistress.

When Billy Wilder saw David Lean's *Brief Encounter* an idea began to take shape in his head. He made a note of it: 'Movie about a guy who climbs into the warm bed left by two lovers.' Had Wilder's notebook fallen into the hands of a lesser director, who knows what angst and unrequited lust we might have been subjected to. Thankfully, Wilder kept close hold of it. Fourteen years later, with cryogenic attitudes to sex beginning to thaw, he and writing partner I.A.L. Diamond spun this evocative fragment into the most bittersweet urban comedy of the pre-Woody era.

The Apartment is the story of C.C. 'Bud' Baxter, a grey-flannel drone at the Consolidated Life of New York insurance company. Consolidated in a monolithic corporation whose home office has 31,259 employees, 'more than the entire population of Natchez, Mississippi,' notes Baxter in the voiceover that accompanies Joseph LaShelle's opening montage of New York (the shot that settles on Baxter, adrift in a sea of identical desks, is a homage to King Vidor's *The Crowd*. Like most big companies, Consolidated is rife with sexual intrigue, and Baxter is right in the thick of it, although not as a participant. Bud Baxter is a pimp. In exchange for periodic hikes up the corporate ladder, he loans his West Side apartment to office lotharios so they can carry on extra-marital affairs without the cost or inconvenience of a hotel room. It's a sordid existence, as Baxter comes to realise when he discovers that Fran the elfin elevator girl he adores, is flattening his mattress twice a week with Head of Personnel J. D. Sheldrake (MacMurray, magnificently loathsome.)

It's a also a pretty sordid premise on which to build a comedy. That Wilder pulls it off, treading a perilously thin line between cynicism and sentimentality, is a tribute to the man's deft touch. And Lemmon, an actor who when not guided by a firm hand can stray into disastrously mawkish excess (see *Days Of Wine And Roses*), turns in a performance that perfectly mirrors this delicate balancing act. On the surface Baxter's behaviour is pretty deplorable, and yet, because Lemmon invests him with a precisely calibrated measure of pathos, we're rooting for him all the way.

Wilder and Diamond are also instrumental here, cleverly entering the story way after Baxter's opening deposit in the favour bank has got out of hand. Throughout he's more sinned against than sinning. '[Lemmon] beautifully maintains the appearance of the lamb among ravening wolves,' was how *New York Times* critic Bosley Crowther put it. In the cannon of Billy Wilder comedies, *The Apartment* will always be overshadowed by *Some Like It Hot*, and that's perhaps as it should be. What is interesting, though, is that although the films were made barely a year apart, they appear to come from entirely different eras. Compare the innocent, giddy eroticism of *Some Like It Hot* to the jaundiced take on human relationships that runs through *The Apartment*. Banging one's secretary is still quaintly referred to as 'the old ring-a-ding-ding' and, a half-decade before the 60s began to swing in earnest, martinis are the preferred sexual lubricant. But when one oiled-up exec demands the use of Baxter's pad for a hasty tryst, the time specified is 45 minutes – adequate, but without much room for the niceties of romance. On Christmas Eve when Sheldrake, in a moment of sublime callousness, stuffs a 100 dollar bill into Fran's handbag with the line: 'You go and buy yourself something,' the truth of their 'love affair' is laid bare: she's a whore, he's her john. It's an ugly scene, but Wilder's brittle humour is up to the task. 'You'd think I would have learned by now,' sniffs Fran, 'when you're in love with a married man, you shouldn't wear mascara.'

After Sheldrake leaves, Fran notices a bottle of Seconal in Baxter's closet and ODs. Baxter saves her in the nick of time, but even though the following scenes are full of tenderness, they are never cloying. They are, however, surprisingly shocking (Fran having her stomach noisily pumped in the bathroom gets a nod in Cameron Crowe's *Almost Famous*) and desperately sad ('Why can't I ever fall in love with somebody nice like you?' asks Fran. 'Yeah, well, that's the way it crumbles, cookie-wise,' shrugs Baxter, his heart breaking.) And yet, thanks to the interjections of Baxter's neighbours, who think he's the fast living Don Juan, they're also absolutely hilarious.

Quite how Wilder marshals these disparate strands without suffering either schmaltz meltdown or terminal Bergmanitis remains a mystery. But the film has the courage of its wry convictions right up to the fade out. When Fran ditches Sheldrake in the midst of a New Year's Eve party and runs to Baxter, the embrace never comes. Instead, Baxter declares his love over an interrupted game of gin rummy. As a last line 'Shut up and deal' might lose by a nose to 'Well, nobody's perfect' but in place of another corny lip-lock it's right on the money: perfectly-tuned, bittersweet urban comedy-wise. ★★★★★ **SB**

APOCALYPSE NOW (1979)

Starring: *Marlon Brando (Col. Kurtz), Robert Duvall (Lt Col. Kilgore), Martin Sheen (Capt. Willard), Frederic Forrest (Chef), Sam Bottoms (Lance), Larry Fishburne (Clean), Dennis Hopper (Photojournalist), Harrison Ford (Colonel), Scott Glenn (Civilian)*
Director: *Francis Ford Coppola*
Screenwriters: *John Milius, Francis Ford Coppola, Michael Herr (narration), from a novel by Joseph Conrad*
15/153 mins./War/USA

Awards: *Academy Awards – Best Cinematography, Best Sound, BAFTA – Best Direction, Best Supporting Actor (Robert Duvall), Golden Globes – Best Director, Best Supporting Actor (Robert Duvall), Best Original Score*

At the height of the war in Vietnam, Captain Benjamin Willard is ordered to assassinate a rogue Colonel.

During the Vietnam War Captain Benjamin L. Willard (Martin Sheen), a special operative (i.e. assassin), is ordered by military intelligence to find a Special Forces commander who has flipped out and established his own maniacal army in Cambodia, Colonel Walter E. Kurtz (Marlon Brando), and 'terminate with extreme prejudice.' Willard's journey upriver through Vietnam is superficially an action adventure, but equally obviously an allegory of war's insanity and a metaphor for the journey into one's self. In the last 30 minutes, when Brando makes his appearance as the crazy Kurtz, the film becomes a bewildering philosophical search through improvisation and chaos – for answers and a resolution to the mysteries of madness and evil.

Francis Ford Coppola's astonishing Vietnam epic was conceived in 1969 and developed over five years by gung-ho, pro-war writer John Milius with Coppola's Zoetrope colleague and fellow anti-war guilty liberal George Lucas (originally set to direct) as a loose adaptation of Joseph Conrad's *Heart Of Darkness*, made pertinent to the war then being fought. The novella is about a man's journey up the Congo to find Kurtz, a cultured man who intended to bring civilisation to the jungle and instead became a savage. Milius' other main source of inspiration was Homer's epic poem about Odysseus's 10-year voyage home from the Trojan War, *The Odyssey*, prompting Coppola in a moment of levity amid his exhausting travails to dub his movie 'The Idiocy.'

The struggles and disasters of filming what became Coppola's obsession are legend, the subject of several books and the fascinating documentary *Hearts Of Darkness: A Filmmaker's Apocalypse*. A 16-week shoot in the Philippines became 238 days of principal photography between early 1976 and summer 77. In the first month Harvey Keitel was fired as Willard because his performance was not sufficiently impassive. The Filipino army kept recalling its helicopters in the middle of takes to chase Marxist rebels. A typhoon destroyed sets, forcing a hiatus. Stress, frustration, heat, booze and drugs did in people's heads. In March, 1977, Sheen, only 36, suffered a near-fatal heart attack, but returned to the fray five weeks later. Brando showed up overweight and unprepared, forcing yet another re-think of how the hell to end the picture before it killed them all.

Flawed but staggering cinema, the unforgettable *Apocalypse Now* set pieces are extraordinary (and so ingrained in the popular consciousness they've been lampooned in *The Simpsons* and *Duckman*), as is Vittorio Storaro's Oscar-winning cinematography.

The film opens (to The Doors 'The End') with an electrifying seven-minute montage of nightmare, memory and foreshadowing as the broken and wasted Willard's demons overwhelm him in a Saigon hotel room. (His indispensable and highly quotable narration, an afterthought during editing, was written by Michael Herr, whose definitive Vietnam reportage in *Dispatches* had provided another valuable source for Milius.)

Heading for the river aboard the PER (a naval patrol boat) crewed by Chief, Chef, Clean and Lance, Willard and the men rendezvous with their Air Cavalry escort, commanded by one of the great military loonies of all time, Col. 'I love the smell of napalm in the morning' Kilgore. Oblivious to shooting, explosions and a cow being airlifted behind him as he barks, Kilgore is a demented, charismatic Duke Wayne in a Stetson who orders a dawn raid and napalm drop on a Viet Cong-held coastal village because 'Charlie don't surf,' whereas he does. Cue the 15-minute tour de force. The chopper unit takes off at sunrise as the bugler blows the traditional cavalry charge. Kilgore blasts Wagner's 'The Ride Of The Valkyries' from his chopper tape deck and dispenses, 'Death from Above' in fountains of lurid smoke and fire. The scene concludes through a sickly haze of red dust, green and orange smoke with Col. Kilgore's notorious panegyric to jellied gasoline: 'It smelled like ... victory'.

This is but the first of surreal, nightmarish, stoned rock 'n' roll encounters vividly evoking fatal culture clash and the psychoses of war. The nearly mute witness Willard watches, chews gum and empathises with his quarry Kurtz as the boat snakes upriver by way of a meeting with a tiger, Playboy bunnies gyrating for the boys, the berserk and finally cold-blooded massacre of a boat family – lest we begin warming to Willard and the crew – to the 'Gates of Hell', an engagement at the Do Long compound await. Even more horrifically, so do the gibbering photo-journalist (Hopper) and the diatribes of the ranting Brando, whose butchering is feverishly inter-cut with the sacrificial slaughter of an ox before Coppola surrenders to an unnervingly ambiguous ending. The ultimate horror ('The horror. The horror.') of this hypnotically strange trip is as close as a film has ever come to crystallising the reality of the Vietnam War. ★★★★★ **AE**

⓪ APOLLO 13 (1995)

Starring: *Tom Hanks (Jim Lovell), Kevin Bacon (John L. Swigart), Bill Paxton (Fred W. Haise), Ed Harris (Gene Kranz), Gary Sinise (Ken Mattingly), Kathleen Quinlan (Marylin Lovell)*
Director: *Ron Howard*
Screenwriters: *William Broyles Jr, John Sayles (uncredited), Al Reinert, based on the book* Lost Moon *by James A. Lovell Jr and Jeffrey Kluger*
PG/140 mins./Drama/History/USA

Awards: *Academy Awards – Best Film Editing, Best Sound, BAFTAs – Best Sound, Best Production Design*

When the third NASA mission to land on the moon goes wrong, the crew are stranded in space, while the American's back home can only pray for their safe return.

There's no denying the power and exhilaration pumping through the heart of Ron Howard's truly excellent docu-drama detailing the incredible story of NASA's ill-fated third lunar landing mission in 1970. Hanks plays Jim Lovell, the commander of Apollo 13 whose childhood dream of setting foot on the moon was so cruelly obliterated by an unfortunate accident three days into the mission. A routine stirring of the oxygen tanks on board the spacecraft, caused an explosion which left the Apollo 13 effectively crippled, and the three astronauts – Lovell, Fred Haise and Jack Swigert – in serious danger of not making it home.

It took the combined efforts of the crew in the ship and the hundreds of NASA staff back in Mission Control Houston to get the men safely – and against all odds – back to earth, their improvisational brilliance turning what looked on the face of it to be a national disaster into perhaps the greatest triumph in US space exploration history. From such rich, stirringly heroic source material, Ron Howard – working from a jargon-heavy, yet surprisingly comprehensible script by William Broyles Jnr. and Al Reinert, based on Lovell's memoirs – has constructed a dynamic, urgent tale that grips despite prior knowledge of the eventual outcome. And any liberties taken with accuracy – and there are only a few – are taken solely to increase the film's dramatic tension.

Hanks' determined, square-jawed portrayal is the film's solid centre around which the rest of the cast orbit, but it's a film that hinges less on his performance than on the succession of tricky and mostly untried manoeuvres needed to pilot the ship home. And in the confines of the spacecraft, Hanks, Paxton (never better) and Bacon (very good) operate like a real team, the Oscar-winner graciously sharing the best lines with his co-stars rather than hogging them all to himself. Down in Mission Control, Ed Harris – who missed a best supporting actor nod – stands out as resolute mission controller Gene Kranz who barks, 'No American has ever died in space, and they're sure as hell not going to on my watch!' with spine-tingling conviction.

Tagline
Houston, we have a problem

Howard is a director known for his excess sentimentality, and while there are a few too many cuts back to the Lovell household – where his wife, children and friends sit praying in front of the telly – he comes up trumps, managing to keep the domestic drama pretty much in check, never losing sight of the gripping story unfolding in space.

Without using even a single frame of NASA footage, Howard has crafted an authentic, awe-inspiring visual spectacle, from the explosive launch of the Saturn 5 rocket, through to the zero gravity footage filmed on board the appropriately named 'Vomit Comet'.

The film is certainly made of the right stuff, and even though the tension dissipates ever so slightly towards the end, this is an exhilarating and believable journey to the dark side of the moon and (thankfully) back again. A blast. ★★★★★ **MS**

⦿ THE APOSTLE (1997)

Starring: *Robert Duvall (Euliss 'Sonny' Dewey – The Apostle E.F.), Farrah Fawcett (Jessie Dewey), Miranda Richardson (Toosie), Billy Bob Thornton (Troublemaker)*
Director: *Robert Duvall*
Screenwriter: *Robert Duvall*
12/148 mins./Drama/USA

Sonny, a Pentacostal preacher spends too much time away from home and finds his wife is having an affair. After violently avenging this betrayal he flees in shame to Louisiana where he re-establishes an old church.

Independently produced by Duvall himself, who also found time to write, direct and garner a Best Actor Oscar nomination, this is an enthralling look at the oft-imitated but rarely studied world of evangelism.

Duvall stars as Texan 'Sonny', a charismatic Pentecostal preacher whose celebrity keeps him too long away from his wife and fellow church member (Fawcett). When she has an affair with a younger preacher (Todd Allen) and forces Sonny not only out of the church he helped to set up, but also apart from the two children he loves, he tempers his rage with his faith until one day he lamps his rival in the face with a baseball bat. Sonny, you see, may be a man of god but he's no angel.

Wracked with guilt, he flees to Louisiana to start a new life and does so as a self-baptised apostle, arriving at a poor black bayou backwater community. There, with help from a tiny radio station and a retired preacher, Sonny sets about re-establishing an old church, using a mixture of his 'Holy Ghost power' and his practical skills as a mechanic.

Therein lies the film's strength. Nothing can make an agnostic squirm like full-on religion but by loading his central character with lay weaknesses as well as spiritual strengths, Duvall invests the near-documentary style film with an everyman appeal. Preaching, his power is a match for anything Linda Blair displayed in *The Exorcist*. Away from the church, he is as vulnerable as a child. He ranges from fire and brimstone to phoning home to learn his mother is dying, to trying to woo Toosie (the brilliant Richardson, as Texan as cow pie). Rising above sparkling turns from non-actors, Country singers and Billy Bob Thornton as a racist bigot out to destroy his new church, Duvall's is a spellbinding performance that even the most miserable sinner won't fail to be converted by. ★★★★ **NJ**

⦿ APT PUPIL (1997)

Starring: *Brad Renfo (Todd Bowden), Ian McKellen (Kurt Dussander), Joshua Jackson (Joey), Mickey Cottrell (Sociology Teacher), David Schwimmer (Edward French), Elias Koteas (Archie)*
Director: *Bryan Singer*
Screenwriter: *Brandon Boyce, from the novella by Stephen King*
15/111 mins./Drama/Thriller/USA/Canada/France

An unusual relationship springs up between an all-American high school teenager and an ageing Nazi war criminal.

The always-vexing question of what to make after your breakthrough movie is answered here with confidence by Bryan Singer. It would have been easy to take the Tarantino route and follow *The Usual Suspects* (Singer's second film after *Public Access*) with a similar but bigger-budget ensemble crime drama. Instead, the director takes advantage of a larger canvas to tell a more intimate, even claustrophobic story, essentially focusing on two characters.

Like the Stephen King novella on which it is based (which is as long as many novels by other authors), the film gets its most implausible turn out of the way very swiftly as small-town high schooler Todd Bowden recognises mild-mannered immigrant retiree Arthur Denker as Kurt Dussander, formerly the commandant of a Nazi extermination camp. Todd threatens Dussander with exposure, but proposes not to turn him in to the authorities if the old man helps him with a nebulous school history project on the nature of evil by telling stories about his part in the Holocaust. Dussander, whom Todd sometimes dresses up in a theatrical costumier Nazi uniform, is reluctant to dig up the past, but gradually begins to exert a snakelike fascination on the kid, clearly enjoying the opportunity of reliving his old crimes and perhaps getting his hooks into a fresh, young brain to warp a new generation of monster.

With another powerful and suggestive performance from McKellen as a retired monster who reaches out to connect with an all-American youth, *Apt Pupil* feels a little like the dark mirror image of *Gods And Monsters*. It's a nuanced reading of a role that requires the actor to play undiluted evil, gaining power from the way McKellen shows us that the frail Dussander is still a monster manipulator and at heart a stone killer. The inevitable gay subtext, stretching to an extraordinary seduction-murder scene with Elias Koteas as a would-be blackmailing tramp, is unstressed as the film goes beyond sexuality to plumb even deeper waters. Like *The Usual Suspects*, *Apt Pupil* is readable as an interrogation of the Devil. David Schwimmer wears an unfortunate moustache as a nosy school counsellor and not all the plot developments ring true, but moments carry a real chill – even in a coma, McKellen can terrify a fellow patient almost to death. ★★★★ **KN**

⦿ THE APU TRILOGY (1952/1957/1959) (PATHER PANCHALI/APARAJITO/APUR SANSAR)

Starring: *Subit Bannerjee (Apu), Urma Das Gupta (Durga), Chunibala Devi (Indir Thakrun), Runki Bannerjee (Little Durga), Reba Devi (Seja Thakrun)/Kanu Bannerjee (Harihar Ray), Karuna Bannerjee (Sarbojaya Ray), Pinaki Sengupta (young Apu), Smaran Ghosal (adolescent Apu), Ramani Sengupta (Bhabataran)/ Soumitra Chatterjee (Apurba Roy), Sharmila Tagore (Aparna), Alok Chakravarty (Kajal), Swapan Mukherjee (Pulu)*
Director: *Satyajit Ray*
Screenwriter: *Satyajit Ray, based on the novel by Bibhutibhushan Bandyopadhyay*
PG/115 mins./110 mins./117 mins./Drama/India

In Pather Panchali, Apu roams the forests and fields of his village while his hard-working mother and naive father struggle to make ends meet. In Aparajito, Apu wanders through the holy city of Benares to the banks of the River Ganges, until a family death again pushes him back to the countryside . . . Finally, in The World Of Apu, he dreams of being a writer, gets married and suffers the most terrible trauma of his life.

When it premiered at the Cannes Film Festival in 1956, *Pather Panchali* – Satyajit Ray's debut and the opening chapter of Apu's life story – opened Western eyes to an Indian cinema they had never seen before. This wasn't the song-and-dance, studio-set, romantic fantasy of Bollywood; this was an authentic, almost documentary-like depiction of a family's struggle against poverty in a rural Bengali village. The direct inspiration here was the Italian neo-realist cinema that had produced the likes of *Bicycle Thieves*.

In India in 1950, Satyajit Ray was able to meet French director Jean Renoir, who was in the country shooting *The River*. Inspired by Renoir's humanist touches, Ray set to work writing a script from a famous book he had been asked to provide illustrations for some years previously – Bibhutibhushan Bandyopadhyay's (yes!) novel, Pather Panchali.

In October 1952, Ray sunk all of his savings into buying film stock and hiring a camera, persuaded friends to become his crew, and began shooting with a cast of mainly non-professional actors . . . But with about 5,000 feet in the can, the money ran out. Indian film producers were not interested in financing such a non-mainstream film from within their industry. It was only after a high official in the West Bengal Government watched the footage that Ray was able to receive a grant to complete the movie.

Even while *Pather Panchali* was triumphing at Cannes, Ray was already at work on a sequel, *Aparajito* (*The Unvanquished*). It went one better when it played the Venice Film Festival in 1957, winning the top prize, the Golden Lion. Ray directed two other films before completing *The Apu Trilogy* in 1959 with *The World Of Apu* (*Apur Sansar*; for some reason the third film, unlike the other two, is best known in the West by its translated title).

Basically, the films follow Apu from infancy to fatherhood. In *Pather Panchali*, he roams the forests and fields of his village while his hard-working mother and naive father struggle to make ends meet. In *Aparajito*, the country paths have become city lanes, as Apu wanders through the holy city of Benares to the banks of the River Ganges, until a family death again pushes him back to the countryside ... Finally, in *The World Of Apu*, he dreams of being a writer, gets married and suffers the most terrible trauma of his life.

With such a simple storyline, what is it that makes these three films so special and unforgettable? It isn't plot; it's the meaningful detail that Ray pours into every frame. At first glance, some of this might seem irrelevant to audiences used to watching movies where each element is included in order to drive on the narrative. But Ray's details are the essence of his films – they convey the mood of the location and the relationship of the characters to the world around them.

The Apu Trilogy is a great work because it richly documents Bengali life in the earlier part of the 20th century, but does so using themes that are timeless and universal. These are genuinely moving films that never resort to sentiment; they're character stories where all the nuances play out on the actors' faces, not in dialogue. The great Japanese director Akira Kurosawa certainly had nothing but praise for his Indian counterpart: 'Not to have seen the cinema of Ray,' he once said, 'means existing in the world without seeing the sun or the moon.' It's as essential as that. ★★★★★ **AM**

Satyajit Ray (1921–1992)

Who he was: India's art movie maestro.

Hallmarks: A lack of the musical numbers usually found in Bollywood movies; suffering peasants; observation of minute social interactions; slow and apparently uneventful films that pack in a world of feeling.

If you see one movie, see: *Pather Panchali* (1969)

⓪ ARACHNOPHOBIA (1990)

Starring: *Jeff Daniels (Dr Ross Jennings), Harley Jane Kozak (Molly Jennings), John Goodman (Delbert McClintock), Julian Sands (Doctor James Atherton)*
Director: *Frank Marshall*
Screenwriters: *Don Jakoby and Wesley Strick, based on a story by Don Jakoby and Al Williams*
PG/109 mins./Comedy/Sci-fi/Horror/USA

A deadly South-American spider arrives in America and starts to claim its victims.

Somehow, with a none too catchy title and villains that create a genuine terror in many people – sharks and aliens are one thing, a spider could well be in your bath when you get home – *Arachnophobia* just about held its own in 1990's summer in the great US box office stampede. This is, no doubt, due to two important factors: it's scary and it's funny.

The devastatingly wooden Julian Sands is an entomologist striding around Venezuela, the better to catch and catalogue his beloved creepy crawlies, accompanied by a bumbling and very-soon-dead photographer. The monstrously lethal spider that caused the hapless lensman's death hitches a ride in the coffin back to his parents in Canaima, a small town in Northern California, while simultaneously, a new fresh-faced doctor is setting up home with his young and wholesome brood. By hook, by crook and, as it happens, by rook, the large, hairy and deeply unnattractive octopod joins the young family in the bedroom-bagging, mates with a local, and starts off the dynasty that will soon reduce Canaima to a gibbering shadow of its former self.

Relying heavily on the clean-cut humour of his mentor Mr Spielberg, director Marshall nevertheless racks up the squeal-factor as the new doctor's patients start mysteriously croaking and our lethal little chums scuttle around the town stamping their mark on its history. So far, it's fun and scary in a you'll-jump-out-of-your-seat-but-you-won't-have-nightmares way – with Daniels once again proving that he should be a lot more famous than he is, and a supporting cast as confident as they are likeable. Indeed, it is with the entrance of Delbert the bug exterminator that the movie really picks up, with the big man at his awesome best.

The question, of course, is whether or not the spider sequences can be stomached by the faint of heart. And, when the inevitable show-down with the multitudinous arachnoids comes, the spider-haters in the audience were indeed cheering a tad hysterically for two legs to overcome eight. ★★★★ **PT**

⓪ L'ARGENT (1983)

Starring: *Christian Patey (Yvon Targe), Sylvie van den Elsen (Old Woman), Michel Briquet (The Woman's Father), Caroline Lang (Elise Targe), Vincent Risterucci (Lucien)*
Director: *Robert Bresson*
Screenwriter: *Robert Bresson, based on the story 'The False Note' by Leo Tolstoy*
PG/90 mins./Crime/France/Switzerland

The lives of shop assistant Lucien and delivery man Yvon are plunged into a downward spiral when two youths foist a forged 500-franc note on an equally duplicitous photographer.

First drafted in 1977, Robert Bresson's 11th and final feature was based on Leo Tolstoy's novella 'The False Note'. He later described it as the film 'with which I am most satisfied or – at least it is the one where I found the most surprises when it was complete – things I had not expected'. Yet, to the casual viewer, there's a daunting inevitability about this almost Victorian morality tale in which a childish prank leads to mass murder.

Ostensibly, it's an indictment of the materialism and amorality of modern life, in which Bresson demonstrates both how cash has replaced conscience and emotion as humanity's stock currency and the ease with which wealth contaminates the soul of everyone seduced by its false promises. But by stripping down the characters to their bare essentials (and frequently presenting them in isolation to emphasise their detachment from society), Bresson makes them difficult to empathise with. Yet, they're also hard to judge, as Bresson challenges us to consider how we would act when tempted in similar circumstances. However, for all its moral rigour and fixation with predestination (which prompted many critics to accuse Bresson of Jansenism), the film is still able to offer a glimpse of drastic redemption, as Yvon confesses to his second slaughter in the final frames.

Although they hailed from different Christian traditions, cinematically Bresson is the heir of Carl Theodor Dreyer, both in his minimalism, devotion to detail and his fascination with the extent to which human actions are the result of either our own flawed natures or the intervention or absence of a divine power. Consequently, this demanding picture is less a study of corrupted innocence than a bid to understand why someone would sin when they had the choice to do otherwise. It's a theme that becomes increasingly prescient as consumerism's grip grows tighter. ★★★★ **DP**

⦿ ARMY OF DARKNESS (1993)

Starring: *Bruce Campbell (Ash), Embeth Davidtz (Sheila), Marcus Gilbert (Lord Arthur), Ian Abercrombie (Wiseman), Richard Grove (Duke Henry The Red), Bridget Fonda (Linda), Theodore Raimi (Cowardly Warrior/Second Supportive Villager/S-Mart Clerk)*
Director: *Sam Raimi*
Screenwriters: *Sam Raimi, Ivan Raimi*
15/81 mins./Comedy/Horror/USA

Ash is zapped back in time after tampering with the *Book Of The Dead* and finds himself in the middle ages, wooing a princess and leading an army of heroic knights against the army of darkness, which is led by his evil doppelgänger.

It's hard not to feel there's something jarringly wrong when an *Evil Dead* movie gets a '15' certificate and this third entry in Sam Raimi's lively horror series is not the non-stop splat rollercoaster that the earlier instalments were. Like *Evil Dead II*, it opens with a digest-cum-remake of the first film, taking geeky Ash back out to that cabin in the woods where he is beset by demons who do away with his girlfriend (blink and you'll miss Bridget Fonda), then sending him back in time to confront 'the Mediaevil Dead'.

Though it starts quite zippily, with Campbell's grimly funny clod of a hero commanding the screen, a sort of dullness sets in as magical events pile up. Ash is attacked by Liliputian versions of himself, one of whom incubates in his stomach and grows out of his shoulder to be his evil twin and, after being dismembered and buried, rises from the dead to command a zombie army. At least half the film is a big battle scene in which rotted warriors (nine mouldy extras in masks for every one Harryhausen-style impressive animated skeleton) besiege a cardboard cut-out castle.

There are lots of action jokes, marginal doodles and a few funny lines, but the whole thing is so bloodless and parodied it's hard to get worked up about. Released in several different cuts, with wildly different endings. The *Evil Dead* was authentically scary and *Evil Dead II* was authentically funny, but this is just authentically ordinary. ★★★ **KN**

⦿ AROUND THE WORLD IN EIGHTY DAYS (1956)

Starring: *David Niven (Phileas Fogg), Cantinflas (Passepartout), Shirley MacLaine (Princess Aouda), Robert Newton (Inspector Fix), Charles Boyer (Monsieur Casse)*
Director: *Michael Todd*
Screenwriters: *S.J. Perelman, John Farrow, James Poe, based on the novel by Jules Verne*
U/175 mins./Adventure/USA

Awards: *Academy Awards – Best Colour Cinematography, Best Film Editing, Best Dramatic or Comedy Score, Best Picture, Best Adapted Screenplay, Golden Globes – Best Drama, Best Comedy/Musical Actor (Catinflas)*

An English gentleman wagers that he can travel around the world within 80 days.

When showman producer Mike Todd put on a show – he put on a show! This scenic spectacle, and winner of a now seemingly inexplicable five Academy Awards, was directed by Briton Michael 'Dambusters' Anderson and shot in 16 countries. It is still entertaining, and has perfectly amusing leads in David Niven as Jules Verne's unflappable globetrotter Phileas Fogg and beloved Mexican comedian Cantinflas as his servant Passepartout, but has lost some of its charm over the years.

Fun includes the ballooning duo scooping snow off the Alps to chill the champagne, flamenco great José Greco doing his stuff, the rescue of (unlikely) Indian maharani Shirley MacLaine from a funeral pyre, a Sioux raid, every conceivable mode of 19th century transport and a zingy score.

The film is most famous for its then novel gimmick of cameos – a term actually coined by Todd. Eyes peeled, then, for Frank Sinatra, Marlene Dietrich, Buster Keaton, Noél Coward, Charles Boyer and many more.

Entertaining Sunday afternoon stuff and superior to the more recent remake. ★★★ **DP**

⦿ AROUND THE WORLD IN 80 DAYS (2004)

Starring: *Jackie Chan (Passepartout/Lau Xing), Steve Coogan (Phileas Fogg), Jim Broadbent (Lord Kelvin), Ewen Bremner (Inspector Fix), Cécile De France (Monique La Roche), Richard Branson (Balloon Man), Macy Gray (Sleeping French Woman), Arnold Schwarzenegger (Prince Hapi), Luke Wilson (Orville Wright), Owen Wilson (Wilbur Wright), Mark Addy (Steamer Captain), Kathy Bates (Queen Victoria)*
Director: *Frank Coraci*
Screenwriters: *David N. Titcher, David Benullo, David Goldstein, based on the novel by Jules Verne*
PG/120 mins./Adventure/Comedy/Action/Romance/Germany/Ireland/UK

After stealing a valuable jade Buddha from the Bank of England, Chinese thief Lau Xing disguises himself as French valet Passepartout and teams up with Phileas Fogg, an eccentric inventor who has made a wager that he can circumnavigate the globe within 80 days.

Given its status as a classic novel whose previous adaptation won the Best Picture Oscar in 1956, remaking *Around The World In Eighty Days* was always going to be a tricky task. That, however, is a poor excuse for what *Wedding Singer* director Frank Coraci has come up with: a leaden version of Jules Verne's classic, which tries to turn up the comedy factor yet offers only occasional flashes of inspiration. More than anything, it feels like yet another excuse for a frantic Jackie Chan kung fu-a-thon, only this time dressed up in 19th century costumes and set against various exotically painted backdrops.

Of course, no Chan movie can get away without giving the man himself a chance to show off his stunt work, and here he gets to take on legions of Chinese warriors and other enemies using all manner of improvised weaponry. But his antics feel oddly out of place in what is, after all, supposed to be a literary adaptation, and ultimately the action overshadows the central story rather than enhancing it. The poor script doesn't help either, littered with double entendres and borderline toilet gags that would be more at home in a high school comedy.

On the plus side, it looks pretty, with Coraci making the most of the foreign locations and period detail. Coogan is engaging enough as the eccentric Fogg (although his cut-glass English accent soon gives way to a long string of Victorian-era Alan Partridge-isms), and De France does her best with the love interest role. But bad guy Broadbent seems to spend much of his screen time shouting rather than being truly villainous, while Bremner reaches a career nadir as the Cocker-nee cop who forms the basis of a running gag that quickly wears thin.

What's really missing from this, ultimately, is the magic that any adaptation of this story so desperately needs, while the conveyor belt of cameo appearances (Arnold Schwarzenegger as a Turkish prince, Kathy Bates as Queen Victoria etc. etc.) gives it the feel of one of those mid-70s movies where the main priority was to shoehorn in as many famous faces as possible, rather than make a decent movie. It livens up a bit in the last reel when Fogg's inventive brain pulls out all the stops to try to win the bet, but by that point you'll be too jaded to care. ★★ **CW**

⦿ ARSENIC AND OLD LACE (1944)

Starring: *Cary Grant (Mortimer Brewster), Raymond Massey (Jonathan Brewster), Priscilla Lane (Elaine Harper), Josephine Hull (Abby Brewster), Jean Adair (Martha Brewster), Jack Carson (O'Hara), Peter Lorre (Dr Einstein)*
Director: *Frank Capra*
Screenwriters: *Julius J. Epstein, Phillip G. Epstein, based on the play by Joseph Kesseiring*
PG/118 mins./Comedy/USA

Calling on his elderly aunts to inform them of his impending nuptials, Mortimer Brewster not only discovers that Abby and Martha have murdered 13 gentlemen with their elderberry wine, but also has to prevent his psychotic brother Jonathan from finding the bodies in the basement.

It's often said that this frantic black comedy (which continues to divide critics) is wholly out of keeping with Frank Capra's canon of cornball feel-good. But it should not be forgotten that he started out in movies as a gag writer for slapstick kings Hal Roach and Mack Sennett and that two of his three Oscars for Best Direction were awarded for the screwball comedy *It Happened One Night* and that irresistibly manic muddle, *You Can't Take It With You*.

So, it was hardly surprising that Capra should have rushed backstage after seeing Joseph Kesselring's macabrely comic Broadway hit in the hope of securing the rights. When he discovered that Warners had beaten him to it, Capra offered to make the picture on a reckless schedule with a shoestring budget of $400,000 (a quarter of which went on Cary Grant's salary). Consequently compelled to operate on just a couple of sets, Capra instructed the cast to put everything into their performances both to sustain the story's cockeyed momentum and disguise the production's poverty. What resulted was a farce of deliciously dubious taste and an example of ensemble scenery-gnawing that has yet to be surpassed.

Josephine Hull and Jean Adair are delighfully dotty as the lethal landladies, while Peter Lorre and Raymond Massey (in a role originated by Boris Karloff) exude menace as their unwanted guests. John Alexander hurls himself into his hilarious depiction of the deluded brother whose conviction that he is President Theodore Roosevelt enables him to rationalise his sisters' murderous mercifulness. But it's Cary Grant who steals the show, as his double takes, deliberate delivery and pantomimic commotions allow just a whisper of sanity to seep into this gloriously eccentric scenario.

Although completed in 1941, the film had to be withheld for three years until the play finally ended its New York run. ★★★★ **DP**

Frank Capra (1897–1991)

Who he was: Sicilian immigrant who taught Hollywood the art (and heart) of feel-good filmmaking.

Hallmarks: Large ensemble casts; big emotions; clean-cut heroes triumphing over the system. Has an often overlooked dark side (the dream sequence in *It's A Wonderful Life* (1946), *Meet John Doe* (1941)).

If you see one movie, see: *It's A Wonderful Life*

AS GOOD AS IT GETS (1997)

Starring: *Jack Nicholson (Melvin Udall), Helen Hunt (Carol Connelly), Greg Kinnear (Simon Bishop), Cuba Gooding Jr (Frank Sachs), Skeet Ulrich (Vincent)*
Director: *James L. Brooks*
Screenwriters: *James L. Brooks, Mark Andrus, based on a story by Mark Andrus*
15/138mins/Romance/Comedy/Drama/USA

Awards: *Academy Awards – Best Actor, Best Actress, Golden Globes – Best Comedy/Musical, Best Actor, Best Actress*

An inveterate sourpuss learns the value of love and charity when he is forced to care for a neighbour's dog.

Meet Melvin Udall, the Archie Bunker of the 90s. Melvin is the dysfunctional darling of this outrageous, politically incorrect comedy from the wag who brought us *Broadcast News* and produces *The Simpsons*, James L. Brooks. Brooks also steered Jack Nicholson to an Oscar in *Terms Of Endearment*, and he repeated the favour here.

Nicholson is on top of his sneering, eyebrow-arching game as Melvin The Misanthrope, obnoxious and offensive to everyone who crosses his path. He's racist, xenophobic, anti-Semitic, homophobic, misogynistic and, for good measure, nasty to a small dog. The only excuse offered is that he suffers – ripely so – from obsessive-compulsive disorder. Ergo he's nutty as a fruitcake – which gives him licence to howl such disgraceful one-liners as would probably get a real person (or an actor less devilishly delicious than Nicholson) beaten up or arrested. Melvin earns his crust, absurdly, writing cheesy romance novels, and lives as reclusively as he can in a Manhattan apartment. One of his obsessive rituals is breakfasting daily at a cafe where only salty waitress Carol – a single mother with her own stressful woes – will tolerate Melvin's diatribes and sass him back.

When Simon, the gay artist who lives across the hall, is hospitalised, old misery-guts Melvin is coerced by Simon's agent into caring for his despised neighbour's ugly but endearing mutt and – you betcha! – bonding is soon afoot as the pooch wags its way into Melvin's corroded heart. Thus softened up, Melvin is reluctantly but irrevocably goaded into a series of grudging good deeds which are entirely motivated by self-interest but which inch him in the general direction of humanity and improbable but superb redemption.

Hunt, long a top TV sitcom star in the US, is wonderfully adept at comic repartee as the long-suffering Carol, dishing it out as well as she takes it, but she's also genuine and moving, while former chat show host Kinnear is surprisingly effective in the teary, somebody-needs-a-hug portion of the nicely plotted and well-paced proceedings. The lead trio get amusing back-up from Gooding Jr, Yeardley Smith (a.k.a. the voice of Lisa Simpson), veteran Shirley Knight as Carol's mother and Skeet Ulrich as the street hustler who brings disaster into Melvin and Simon's building. ★★★★ **AC**

ASHES AND DIAMONDS (POPIOL I DIAMENT) (1958)

Starring: *Zbigniew Cybulski (Maciek), Ewa Krzyzewski (Krystyna), Adam Pawlikowski (Andrzej), Waclaw Zastrzezynski (Szczuka), Bogulmil Kobeiela (Drewnowski)*
Director: *Andrzej Wajda*
Screenwriters: *Andrzej Wajda, Jerzy Andrzejewski, based on the novel by Andrzejewski*
18/105 mins./Drama/Poland

Maciek, a veteran of Poland's anti-Marxist Home Army, is plagued by doubts when he's ordered to assassinate Szczuka, the district secretary appointed by the new Communist government, who is himself a war hero.

In his first two features, *A Generation* and *Kanal*, Andrzej Wajda challenged the conventions of state-approved Socialist Realism and questioned the sacrifices the Polish people had made during the Second World War. This tension between romantic patriotism and pragmatic scepticism resurfaced in the final part of his 'Resistance trilogy', *Ashes And Diamonds*.

Adapted from the acclaimed novel by Jerzy Andrzejewski and set on the day marking the Nazi capitulation, the action centres on Maciek's crisis of conscience after he receives an order he feels bound to obey even though it goes against the spirit of the hard-won peace. He's permitted a brief dalliance with Krystyna in a bomb-scarred church, but fate decrees that he must accept his mission and he is fatally wounded and dies on a rubbish dump.

Attacked by some for its baroque fatalism and hyberbolic symbolism, the film was instantly hailed as a national epic. Yet it's also an intimate study of the effects of contradictory forces on two implacably opposed men with much in common. Maciek and Szczuka are from different generations, with the former being primarily a patriot, while the latter had fought for the red flag in Spain. Yet, each is fully committed to his cause and his comrades and each believes in doing his duty. However, in the course of the film, they're forced to confront the realisation that they cannot live up to their high expectations. Szczuka learns that he is not suited to governance and, thus, feels he has betrayed those he represents, while Maciek is tempted to put conscience before conviction.

Attired more like James Dean than a freedom fighter, Zbigniew Cybulski gives a remarkable peformance as the rebel doubting his cause and he remained the pin-up boy of Polish cinema until his untimely death in a train accident in 1967. ★★★★★ **DP**

ASOKA (2001)

Starring: *Shahrukh Khan (Asoka), Kareena Kapoor (Kaurwaki), Danny Denzongpa (Virat), Rahul Dev (Bheema), Hrishtaa Bhatt (Devi)*
Director: *Santosh Sivan*
Screenwriters: *Saket Chaudhary, Santosh Sivan, Abbas Tyrewala*
12/176 mins./Drama/Action/Romance/India

Charts the bloody rise and remorseful fall of Emperor Asoka in third century BC.

Santosh Sivan first caught the eye of the UK arthouse audience with his astonishingly visual film, *The Terrorist*. His follow-up, *Asoka*, provided a rare instance of an elusive Indian crossover hit – an exciting, colourful and, above all, commercial movie that delighted fans of world cinema and even won over some of the multiplex crowd.

Its retelling of Indian history does make small assumptions of knowledge but not to the extent of disturbing the enjoyment of the story for the uninitiated. A prince in disguise, lovers who are born enemies, political assassinations, devious relatives – all universal elements in a sweeping epic.

Historically, Asoka was seen as one of the most significant converts to the faith of Buddhism, and the violence of this film has been criticised as being derogatory to the faith. But Asoka's conversion would not have been so impactful had he been a man of faith from the beginning. The fact that he was such a bloody warrior is no more ably demonstrated than when the battle scenes kick in near the end, it's like Kurosawa goes Bollywood. ★★★★ **IF**

THE ASPHALT JUNGLE (1950)

Starring: *Sterling Hayden (Dix Handley), Louis Calhern (Alonzo D. Emmerich), Jean Hagen (Doll Conovan), James Whitmore (Gus Ninissi), Marilyn Monroe (Angela Phinlay)*
Director: *John Huston*
Screenwriters: *Ben Maddow, John Huston, based on the novel by W.R. Burnett*
PG/112 mins./Crime/USA

Erwin 'Doc' Riedenschneider leaves jail and assembles a gang to execute a long-planned jewellery heist. However, no one trusts fence-lawyer, Alonzo D. Emmerich, and suspicion and caprice ensure that the meticulous scheme soon begins to unravel.

John Huston is widely credited with bringing film noir to American screens with *The Maltese Falcon* in 1941. In that same year, he adapted W.R. Burnett's pulp novel *High Sierra* as a vehicle for Humphrey Bogart and he returned to the same author (who had also helped script *Little Caesar* and *Scarface*) for this prototype heist movie.

Co-scripting with Ben Maddow, Huston achieved a tangible sense of postwar anxiety and urban grit by borrowing from both the noir tradition and the voguish brand of ultra-realist problem picture exemplified by the 1949 race drama *Intruder In The Dust* (which Maddow had adapted to considerable acclaim from William Faulkner's novel).

Yet while the settings and dialogue were abrasively authentic, Huston couldn't resist empathising with the various losers against whom fate was about to conspire. Dix Handley is portrayed as a big lug who wants to buy back his father's Kentucky horse ranch; cat-loving getaway driver Gus Ninissi is a hunchback; while cracksman Louis Ciavelli has a family to feed. Similarly, the crooks' women – Hayden's girlfriend, Calhern's wife and mistress and Caruso's spouse – are anything but the usual femmes fatale.

Thus, the law-breakers are presented as anti-heroes rather than villains and their crime is considered more an act of desperation than greed. Yet once Doc's plan begins to fall apart, there proves to be little honour among the thieves and their cameraderies turn out to be as brittle as the morality of the cops set to watch over this hopelessly corrupted society.

A seminal influence on crime pictures to this day, *The Asphalt Jungle* has been remade three times (but never well), as a Western (*The Badlanders*), a caper (*Cairo*) and a blaxploitation thriller (*Cool Breeze*). ★★★★★ **DP**

THE ASSASSINATION OF RICHARD NIXON (2004)

Starring: *Sean Penn (Samuel J. Bicke), Naomi Watts (Marie Anderson Bicke), Don Cheadle (Bonny Simmons), Jack Thompson (Jack Jones), Brad William Henke (Martin Jones)*
Director: *Niels Mueller*
Screenwriters: *Kevin Kennedy, Niels Mueller*
15/95 mins./Drama/Thriller/U.S.

Based on the true story of a down-on-his-luck businessman who decides the only way to improve his lot is to attempt to assassinate the President.

Well-meaning comparisons can sometimes do more harm than good. Equating *The Assassination Of Richard Nixon* with one of the best plays ever written and some of the best movies ever made places a heavy burden of expectation upon this little film's shoulders – but they are valid reference points. This is no A-list star vehicle for Sean Penn; instead, it's a politically daring, psychologically troubling, based-on-fact American tragedy that took years to secure funding and only got made because of the artistic integrity of those involved.

Like a 70s version of Willy Loman in Arthur Miller's classic play *Death Of A Salesman*, Sam Bicke is the average Joe, ground down by the broken promises of the American Dream. He had the perfect family, but it's been taken from him. His wife won't entertain the thought of reconciliation and his children won't even pose properly for a photograph. When he's refused a bank loan for a tyre business he'd like to start with his best friend, Sam blames the bank's racism. We know, however, that it's really because he presents himself as such a desperate, unreliable figure.

As Sam's breakdown descends into paranoia and, in turn, into political scheming, the obvious cinematic touchstones are the key movies that were made around the time that this one is set – *Taxi Driver*, *The Conversation*, *All The President's Men*. The sweaty, untrustworthy face of Richard Nixon haunts Sam from nearby TV screens.

To Sam's decaying logic, this man becomes symbolic of the forces that have destroyed his life. A twice-elected yet deeply unpopular President conning the voters about a foreign war in order to further his private agenda? This film might look like the 70s and share that era's political concerns, but its relevance is here and now.

With a startling performance as the bleary Bicke, Penn also bridges cinematic past and present, winning audience sympathy for this pathetic, defective man against all odds. Arguably the best actor of his generation, he again proves he's a modern-day match for De Niro, Hackman, Hoffman and Keitel at their peak. ★★★★ **AM**

⦶ ASSASSINS (1995)

Starring: *Sylvester Stallone (Robert Rath), Antonio Banderas (Miguel Bain), Julianne Moore (Electra), Antatoli Davydov (Nicolai Tashlinkov)*
Director: *Richard Donner*
Screenwriters: *Andy Wachowski, Larry Wachowski, Brian Helgeland*
15/127 mins./Action/Thriller/USA

An assassin, targeted by his younger counterpart, teams up with a computer hacker to try to save his skin.

This hitmen-in-competition thriller promised much but delivered rather less at the cinema. On paper, casting ageing action king Stallone as the ageing world-weary number one professional assassin Robert Rath opposite Johnny-come-lately heartthrob Banderas as the Johnny-come-lately number two Miguel Bain was a stroke of genius. Sadly, casting was the only area of true genius involved in *Assassins* and the area of the script suffered most in comparison.

But strangely, the lack of any meaningful dialogue – most of the lines are keyed into or mumbled at lap-top computers – adds to the atmosphere. Stallone and Banderas are, after all, cold-hearted professional killers and not hot-to-trot cocktail party guests. The film moves through three locations – New York, Seattle and Puerto Rico. The opening scenes in the Big Apple, where Banderas terminates Stallone's 'mark' before the master has even taken aim and is then taken on the taxi ride of his life, are superb. The climax in Puerto Rico is almost as good, although overlong and blurring the line between fiction and believability a little too much. But the Seattle portion, unfortunately, is slower and too confused as it introduces Julianne Moore as Electra the (only slightly) mysterious feline fancier-cum-surveillance-expert-cum-computer-hacker-cum-thief who (surprise) becomes Stallone's partner and his aide-de-camp in the inevitable final shoot-out/battle of wits with Banderas.

A subplot juxtaposing Stallone's current dilemma with his assassination, 15 years ago, of Russia's former world number one, provides far less of a diversion than wondering just how Banderas' character, who spends most of his screentime sweating and twitching like a full-blown homicidal psychotic, still walks the streets as a free man – never mind as the world's number two assassin. It's more James Bond than Leon, more *Day At The Races* than *Day Of The Jackal*, but for most of its lengthy running time, *Assassins* is an amusing and often stylish diversion. ★★ **NJ**

⦶ ASSAULT ON PRECINCT 13 (1976)

Starring: *Austin Stoker (Lt Ethan Bishop), Darwin Joston (Napoleon Wilson), Laurie Zimmer (Leigh), Martin West (Lawson), Tony Burton (Wells), Charles Cyphers (Officer Starker), Nancy Loomis (Julie)*
Director: *John Carpenter*
Screenwriter: *John Carpenter*
18/91 mins./Action/US

On its final night, the soon to be abandoned police station in Los Angeles' Precinct 13 is targeted by a savage local gang seeking vengeance. The skeleton staff not only has to deal with the violent attack, the electricity being shut off, but also the unforeseen delivery of several death-row prisoners.

At his best, no one musters localised claustrophobia like John Carpenter. Especially, when he's not distracted by a budget of any sort. Working for next to zero for this second film, he openly crossed *Rio Bravo* with *Night Of The Living Dead*, for this highwire urban Western, pitching street hoodlums against a paltry crew of low-level police officers and high-ranking criminals headed for death row.

The beauty of the piece lies in Carpenter's succinct screenwriting. There is no slack, no need to keep iterating plot points, everything works within his exaggerated comic book universe governed by a very real violence. Why would a crew of death row inmates be in the heart of the LA ghetto? Why, because they are in transit and one falls sick, so the transit officer stops at the nearest police station.

The pace, at the start, is slow, setting a mood of hot, irritable streets brewing tension (this was a long time before the Rodney King riots and looks nastily prescient). A gang slaying is the touch paper, and once all his pieces are in place, Carpenter crosses over into bloody action – an ice cream van killing is shockingly memorable – so skilfully choreographed it totally belies the limitations of the sets and no-name actors.

Since remade with bigger names (Ethan Hawke and Laurence Fishburne) and much more money, replacing the sweltering heat with snow, its ordinariness just made the original stand out even more. Cloying dialogue aside, the twists and transitions – especially the conundrum of having to turn to prisoner Napoleon Wilson for help – are an object lesson in masterful tension. Most modern directors, including an older John Carpenter long past his best, would do well to learn something about simplicity. When you care about the characters, as we do this clutch of no mark cops and cold killers, and you believe in their nightmare, half the work is done. Carpenter's thriller also covers the other half with just as much ease. ★★★★ **IN**

⦶ ASSAULT ON PRECINCT 13 (2005)

Starring: *Ethan Hawke (Sgt Jake Roenick), Laurence Fishburne (Marion Bishop), Gabriel Byrne (Marcus Duvall), Maria Bello (Alex Sabian), Drea de Matteo (Iris Ferry), John Leguizamo (Beck), Brian Dennehy (Jasper O'Shea), Ja Rule (Smiley)*
Director: *Jean-Francois Richet*
Screenwriter: *James DeMonaco, based on earlier film by John Carpenter*
15/109 mins./Action/Crime/Drama/U.S./France

On a snowstormy New Year's Eve, Sergeant Roenick is left in charge of a nearly defunct police station in downtown Detroit. After taking an unwanted delivery of crooks – including ganglord Bishop – who need cells for the night, Roenick's precinct is suddenly attacked by a squad of well-armed assailants.

Between the scruffily satirical sci-fi spoof *Dark Star* and the lean machine of *Halloween*, John Carpenter made *Assault On Precinct 13*, a thriller which transplanted elements of the Wild West (especially *Rio Bravo*) into gang-overrun Los Angeles. A cult hit in Europe, the first *Assault* was barely released in the US and never quite gained the following of Carpenter's other early hits. So it seems a less obvious candidate for a modern makeover than other genre items from the 70s like *The Texas Chain Saw Massacre* and *Dawn Of The Dead*. It's such a patchwork of bits and pieces from other movies that it already seems like a radical remake – therefore, a new version ought to need a pressing reason to exist.

Oddly, this suspenseful and entertaining redo bypasses those expectations. Like the new *Dawn* and *Texas*, it tweaks and rethinks rather than updates. If it misses the shock and awe of the 1976 *Assault* (no gutshot little girl here, and, sadly, no sparse, nervewracking Carpenter score), the remake is still a solid cop-and-crook exercise, with plentiful gunplay and jagged character acting.

An added 20 minutes means more plot and a slightly bigger cast of besieged characters. In place of zombie-like gangbangers, the besiegers are a well-motivated and equipped team, and the supercool criminal who happens to be in the near-derelict cop shop overnight is linked to the attack rather than an 'innocent' bystander. It's good stuff, but also more conventional, and some of Carpenter's Hawksian licks have been imitated so many times that doing them again here gets *Naked Gun*-ish laughs.

Hawke, with tattoos and twitches, holds down the fort, and Fishburne channels Chow Yun Fat's impeturbability (Marion Bishop is a long way from Jimmy Jump of *King Of New York*). But the most fun comes from unpredictable support players like John Leguizamo as a motormouth junkie who always has something unhelpful to say, Maria Bello as a therapist who cracks, Brian Dennehy as the near-retirement veteran (uh-oh) and, especially, Drea DeMatteo as a gun-toting secretary in fishnets who's resolved to give up both smoking and bad boys for the New Year. Somebody give her a whole movie, please. ★★★ **KN**

THE ASTRONAUT'S WIFE (1999)

Starring: *Johnny Depp (Commander Spencer Armacost), Charlize Theron (Jillian Armacost), Joe Morton (Sherman Reese, NASA Rep.), Clea DuVall (Nan), Nick Cassavetes (Capt. Alex Streck), Samantha Eggar (Dr Patraba)*
Director: *Rand Ravich*
Screenwriter: *Rand Ravich*
15/109 mins./Sci-fi/Thriller/Horror/USA

Jillian lovingly greets her space-rocketeer husband home from a mission, but after a mishap she soon begins to think things are not what they seem and fears she may have been impregnated by an alien.

Don't be too surprised if this piece of weary hokum resurfaces on video renamed Rosemary's Space Baby, as there are only two significant differences between Ravich's debut movie and Polanski's 1968 opus:

(1) In *The Astronaut's Wife* a woman fears that she has become impregnated not by Satan but by an alien.

(2) *Rosemary's Baby* is a good movie.

The wife in question is Jillian Armacost, a sweet Southern schoolma'am with a history of some mental instability and a haircut just like the one Mia Farrow sported in – Anyone? Anyone? – *Rosemary's Baby*.

Meanwhile, Depp plays her rocketeer hubby Spencer in a good old boystylee ripped straight from the pages of Tom Wolfe's *The Right Stuff*.

At first all is sunshine chez Armacost, but following a mission mishap, Things Begin To Turn Sour – notably for Spencer's ill-fated co-pilot and his pregnant wife – followed by some increasingly dire warnings from scenery-chowing NASA bigwig, Sherman Reese.

When Jillian too suddenly finds herself expecting, it is only a matter of time before she comes to believe that Spencer's *Dukes Of Hazzard* accent may not be the only odd thing about him. Is she really going out with The Thing? Or is she just as mad as a three-cornered hat? Sadly, by the time we find out, no one cares.

While the cast do their best – particularly Depp, in what may prove to be that release year's most thankless role – the entire enterprise is itself so devoid of atmosphere that the film's attempts to show the empty airless truth about space flight seem quite redundant. ★★ **CC**

AT THE EARTH'S CORE (1976)

Starring: *Peter Cushing (Dr Abner Perry), Doug McClure (David Innes), Caroline Munro (Princess Dia), Cy Grant (Ra), Godfrey James (Ghak)*
Director: *Kevin Connor*
Screenwriter: *Milton Subotsky, based on the novel by Edgar Rice Burroughs*
PG/89 mins./Sci-fi/Adventure/UK/US

When a test drive of his new drilling machine, The Mole, goes awry, Victorian scientist Dr Abner Perry and his boisterous American backer David Innes, end up in the underground world of Pellucidar. Here they find a race of humans enslaved by a telepathic parrot-dinosaur combos called Meyhas.

On the back of Hammer's success in polishing up the horror genre, fellow British filmmakers decided it would be awfully good fun to transpose the similar thinking to a bit of Victoriana sci-fi, very loosely borrowed from authors like Edgar Rice Burroughs. They made sure their American backers were kept happy by always casting podgy American lunk Doug McClure as the hero, while Peter Cushing was on hand to play the necessary eccentric English genius, who never went anywhere without an umbrella.

This hugely limited set of fantasy adventure movies reached their nadir with *At The Earth's Core*, in which our intrepid duo tunnels beneath the mantle to rescue an enslaved tribe, chiefly because one of their number was Caroline Munro. While the budget was slim, this was still not a time of creative ingenuity – ILM has yet to make their mark – the evil Meyhas fly by evident wires, their spring powered beaks snapping like garden shears. And let's not even talk about the marmalade-powered lava effects.

And how is it this tribe speak such good English, yet still name themselves such primitive things as Gak and Ra? The trick here is to take pleasure in its clunky limits and cheapness, something assisted by the gusto with which director Kevin Connor lets it all tumble along with. How can one not find a smidgeon of love for a film where a snotty Cushing, hamming for all his worth, defies his mouldy avian foe by shouting, 'You cannot mesmerise me. I'm British!'? However, a word to the wise – if there's one rule in a spirited Z-movie such as this, it's don't trust anyone called Hoojah the Sly One. ★★ **IN**

L'ATALANTE (1934)

Starring: *Michel Simon (Le Pere Jules), Dita Parlo (Juliette), Jean Daste (Jean), Gilles Margaritis (Le Camelot), Louise Lefebvre (Le Gosse)*
Director: *Jean Vigo*
Screenwriters: *Jean Vigo, Jean Guinee, Albert Riera*
PG/85 mins./Comedy/Drama/Romance/France

After moving onto a ship with her new husband Jea, Juliette soon tired of life at sea and slips off into the Paris nightlife. Furious Jules sets off, leaving her behind, but beomes overcome by the longing for his wife, while shipmate Pere goes searching for her.

The only feature directed by the tragically short-lived Jean Vigo, this is a haunting romantic fable about a young couple who spend their life on a battered barge on the Seine.

Not much happens, and what 'show' there is is there to be stolen by wise old salt Michel Simon with a mixture of song, bawdy humour and improvisational acting. It all has a genuinely weird feel, combining dingy realism with an almost magical eroticism. This is the reason it is worth seeking out, this unique combination was one of the key influences on the New Wave directors in the 1950s and this dreamlike quality is there to be found in the films of Francois Truffaut, Jean-Luc Godard, Eric Rohmer, Claude Chabrol and Jacques Rivette.

It has improved with age, its occasional fuzziness adding a further patina to its strange texture. Vigo, who had made the shorts *A Propos De Nice* and *Zero De Conduite*, died at 29 just when the film was coming out. ★★★★ **DP**

ATLANTIC CITY, U.S.A. (1980)

Starring: *Burt Lancaster (Lou), Susan Sarandon (Sally), Kate Reid (Grace), Michel Piccoli (Joseph), Hollis McClaren (Chrissie)*
Director: *Louis Malle*
Screenwriter: *John Guare*
15/Crime/104 mins./USA/Canada

Awards: *BAFTA – Best Actor, Best Director*

Old-time hood Lou gets mixed up with the hippie husband of would-be croupier Sally. The husband is killed by the gangsters he's ripped off, and Lou enjoys his late-in-life wealthy streak, having an affair with Sally and finally becoming the killer he always wanted to be.

Louis Malle's drama of petty crime and faded dreams observes the effects of a cache of stolen drugs on the lives of a group of leftovers from both the organised crime of the 1940s and the counterculture of the 1960s as they struggle to escape the crumbling, redeveloping former gambling capital of America.

Lancaster, in his last great starring role, is infinitely patient longtime loser Lou (his gangland nickname was 'Numb-Nuts'), still looking after his mob boss's widow and running numbers, watching from his shadows as Sally goes through a provocative nightly ritual of rubbing lemon into her breasts by an open window. The reason for this is that she works at a seafood counter and has to kill the fish stink, suggesting how skewed Lou's fantasies are. Sally's useless husband (Robert Joy) and dippy pregnant sister ('I want acid, so we can learn from the baby's wisdom ... and I want his face to be tattooed') show up with stolen cocaine and Lou shifts the merchandise as the rightful owners violently close in.

Like *The King Of Marvin Gardens*, this makes great use of America's east coast gambling capital in decline, with Robert Goulet serenading at a benefit in the hospital's Frank Sinatra wing as Sally tries to place a reverse-charges call to her murdered husband's uncaring parents. Beautifully written by playwright John Guare (*Six Degrees Of Separation*) and played by a superb cast (Hollis McLaren is memorable as the fractured waifsister), this is wry, sad, erotic, funny, shocking and thoughtful. ★★★★★ **KN**

ATLANTIS: THE LOST EMPIRE (2001)

Starring: *the voices of: Michael J. Fox (Milo James Thatch), Corey Burton (Gaetan 'The Mole' Moliere), Claudia Christian (Helga Katrina Sinclair), James Garner (Commander Lyle Tiberius Rourke), John Mahoney (Preston B. Whitmore), Leonard Nimoy (King Kashekim Nedakh)*
Directors: *Gary Trousdale, Kirk Wise*
Screenwriters: *Tab Murphy, with additional material from David Reynolds, treatment from Joss Whedon and a story by Kirk Wise, Bryce Zabel and Jackie Zable*
U/95 mins./Animation/Fantasy/Action/Adventure/USA

A wealthy philanthropist funds an expedition to Atlantis, on which enthusiast Milo, and a ragtag band of mercenaries, find out why the lost city remained undiscovered.

Blame Buzz Lightyear. If he hadn't burst onto the scene in *Toy Story*, all brand-spanking new and CG-shiny, then movies like *Atlantis* would still be perfectly acceptable animation fare.

Directors Trousdale and Wise were responsible for *Beauty And The Beast*, so they obviously know their way around the animation block. Yet in attempting ambitious action sequences, *Atlantis* smacks of a medium playing catch-up with its pixellated cousin. Also sadly lacking is the sense of wonder one would expect from a movie about the Atlantean legend, while the characters are dragged from the Big Book Of Disney Stereotypes, from the comedy double act to the determined, charming hero. Collect them all! Stir in a daffy New Age plot, and – bizarrely – elements of *Stargate*, and it's clear that Trousdale and Wise have considerably overcooked the broth.

It's not a total washout, though. The design ethic – if not quite as innovative as, say, *Hercules* – is strong throughout, the Jules Verne-inspired technology nicely juxtaposed with the Inca-esque visual splendour of Atlantis itself. There's a commendable lack of musical numbers, thus sparing us the warblings of Phil Collins (or worse); the voice cast is excellent, Fox in particular; and at times, proceedings are altogether darker than the usual Mouse House fare – one early set-piece wipes out half of the explorers in seconds. Sadly, it says much about the jack-of-all-trades tone that, soon after, we're back to comic buffoonery, lest any watching kiddiewinkles require counselling.

A lost opportunity. ★★ **SC**

THE ATOMIC CAFÉ (1982)

Starring: *as themselves: Rep. Lloyd Bentsen, Vice Admiral W.H.P Blandy, Sen Owen Brewster,Frank Gallop (Newsreel Narrator), Sen Lyndon B. Johnson, Maurice Joyce (Newsreel Narrator), Nikita Khrushchev*
Directors: *Jayne Loader, Kevin Rafferty, Pierce Rafferty*
12/92 mins./Documentary/USA

A collage of instructional films, period newsreels and government-sponsored propaganda that seeks to show how Washington not only prepared the American people for a possible Armageddon, but also attempted to convince them that it would win a post-nuclear peace.

Little dates an era faster than its propaganda. Yet many of the attitudes informing the clips in this ghoulishly amusing Cold War compilation still appear to have a fundamental part to play in the selling of contemporary American foreign policy.

The project started out as a documentary about American propaganda in general and directors Jayne Loader and Kevin and Pierce Rafferty had trawled through 10,000 films before they decided to focus on what started out as an ideological crusade against the Soviet Union and finally turned into an apocalyptic terror campaign that had citizens of all ages and political persuasions convinced of the Red Menace's intention to nuke the States to the Stone Age.

Initially, the trio was pressurised by its backers into including talking head material to bring stories up to date, but this idea was eventually dropped in favour of a vérité approach to the footage, which was edited according to the principles of photomontage artists like John Heartfield and Robert Coover and such film-makers as Emile de Antonio, Bruce Conner and Philippe Mora. Consequently, the viewer is bombarded with excerpts, which become evermore chillingly preposterous in their arrogance, rectitude and naivete.

Nuclear proliferation is, of course, a deadly serious issue. But it's impossible to avoid the unintentional humour in the jingoistic platitudes and patronising exhortations contained in shorts that range from the hectoringly sombre to the absurdly upbeat. Yet while messages like 'Duck and Cover' (which came complete with a catchy theme tune) now seem risibly ineffectual, they nevertheless demonstrate the ease with which regimes can exploit the trust of imperilled peoples in order to manipulate opinion. Watching this film in conjunction with more recent outings like *Outfoxed: Rupert Murdoch's War On Journalism* and *Orwell Rolls In His Grave* will soon wipe the smile off your face. ★★★ **DP**

AU HASARD, BALTHASAR (1966)

Starring: *Annie Wiazemsky (Marie), Francois Lafarge (Gerard), Phillippe Asselin (Marie's Father), Nathalie Joyaut (Marie's Mother), Walter Green (Jacques), Jean-Claude Guilbert (Arnold)*
Director: *Robert Bresson*
Screenwriter: *Robert Bresson*
PG/95 mins./Drama/France

As he passes between various owners, a donkey named Balthazar is alternately adored and abused in a cycle which mirrors that experienced by Marie, the farmer's daughter who named him.

Inspired by Dostoevsky's *The Idiot*, this is the story of two souls – one animal, one human – who have no control over their treatment at the hands of wicked men. Robert Bresson claimed it was the film 'in which I've put most of myself', while Jean-Luc Godard (who would later marry Anne Wiazemsky) described it as 'the world in an hour and a half'. Some have proclaimed it a masterpiece of allegorical intelligence and cinematic restraint, while others have castigated it for its symbolic calculation and melancholic naivete. Clearly, those who have rejected the picture have taken exception to its Christian overtones. But *Au Hasard, Balthazar* is just as much about morality as spirituality and its warnings about the consequences of abandoning any form of ethical code are as relevant as ever in our increasingly secularised and self-centred society.

There's no denying that religious references abound. Balthazar was one of the Wise Men who visited Mary and her child among the livestock of a Bethlehem stable, while it's possible to recognise Christ in some of the alcoholic Arnold's actions and both Satan and Judas in the thuggish behaviour of Gérard, the biker who not only beats and rapes Marie, but who also causes Balthazar's death on a smuggling mission. Indeed, Balthazar's life is made up of episodes emblemising the Seven Deadly Sins. Thus, Bresson is as interested in the bestiality to which humanity could stoop as the perceived sanctity of the innocent, trusting donkey, who bears each vicissitude with patience and humility.

As in all his work, Bresson refuses to pass judgement on his characters and avoids sentimentality by the rigid formalism of his shooting style and the sobering dispassion of the performances. Yet, he does intimate here that a sin or failing can be quantified by the transgressor's degree of freedom. ★★★★★ **DP**

AU REVOIR LES ENFANTS (1987)

Starring: *Gaspard Manesse (Julien Quentin), Raphael Fejto (Jean Bonnet), Francine Racette (Mme Quentin), Stanislas Carre de Malberg (Francois Quentin), Phillippe Morier-Genoud (Father Jean)*
Director: *Louis Malle*
Screenwriter: *Louis Malle*
PG/104 mins./Drama/France

Fontainbleau, 1944 and unpopular Catholic schoolboy Julien Quentin cautiously befriends the equally bookish Jean Bonnet. However, he slowly comes to suspect that the newcomer is not who he seems and his final realisation has tragic consequences.

Louis Malle's first French-language film in a decade was proclaimed by many as his best. Based on an incident in his own childhood, it explored a boy's gradual appreciation of the harsh injustices of life as his classroom innocence is destroyed by the horrific realities of the Nazi Occupation. The film completed a loose trilogy that began with *Le Souffle Au Coeur* and *Lacombe Lucien*, in which youths were forced to make moral choices in moments of crisis. Each was refreshingly free of the cloying nostalgia that blights so many American memoirs of supposedly less tainted times. Yet, while the first two caused considerable controversy in France, this admirably restrained drama – which won the Golden Lion at Venice and received an Oscar nomination – escaped much of the censure that continues to greet studies of the Vichy era.

Perhaps, this is because Malle is careful to sustain a balance between his characters, so that schoolboys and collaborators alike are seen taunting Jews, while a soldier and a priest are shown defending them. Indeed, similar tensions consistently underpin the episodic storyline, which is punctuated with acts of searching and concealment, with the Gestapo's pursuit of Jews, freedom fighters and criminals contrasting with the boys' bid to find themselves in their rivalries, games and perusal of erotica.

Renato Berta's muted cinematography helps establish the sense of creeping oppression and deepening foreboding that pervades Julien's stumbling passage towards understanding. But it's Malle's handling of Gaspard Manesse and Raphael Fejto (who rather drift into friendship out of necessity) that keeps their fate from becoming melodramatic, as – like Brigitte Fossey and Georges Poujouly in René Clément's remarkable study of the impact of war on young minds, *Jeux Interdit* – they're never allowed fully to appreciate the seriousness of their situation until it's too late. ★★★★ **DP**

AUDITION (ODISHON) (1999)

Starring: *Ryo Ishibashi (Shigeharu Aoyama), Eihi Shiina (Asami Yamazaki), Tetsu Sawaki (Shigehiko Aoyama), Jen Kunimura (Yashuhisa Yoshikawa)*
Director: *Takashi Miike*
Screenwriter: *Dasiuke Tengan, based on the novel by Ryu Murakami*
18/115 mins./Drama/Horror/Romance/Thriller/South Korea/Japan

Japanese executive runs into a spot of genuinely scary bother when he goes in search of a second wife and meets a young woman with a toolkit.

This remarkable, evocative and disturbing picture opens as if it might develop into a sentimental romance – the audition montage is a neat little series of mostly comic vignettes that lulls you into expecting charm and a happy ending – but gradually shifts into literal nightmare mode and pays off with a haunting sequence of physical and mental torture.

The serene Eihi Shiina makes an astonishing psycho, clicking 'kiri kiri kiri' (Japanese for 'deeper deeper deeper') as she wields acupuncture needles and a toolkit in ways many audiences will find hard to watch, but there's a real tragic weight to the hero's belief that he deserves this treatment.

It's a creepy film that slowly develops its real scariness, but it also explores the battle of the sexes in ways that may be specifically Japanese, but have a distinctly universal relevance. Add to that an innovative narrative turn that manages to both revitalise that tired old 'maybe it's all a dream' gambit and pose some truly unsettling questions (What is real, what is hallucination and what is psychological just-desserts?), and the result is a cerebral assault guaranteed to linger – for an equally unsettling length of time – in the memory.

Takashi Miike, a prolific and versatile director who is a safe bet to make a big international impact, handles brilliantly the early stretches, which are light and poignant, allowing the omens to accumulate. Especially chilling is the vision of Asami hanging her head in her bare apartment, waiting for Aoyama to call, which sets up one of the most shocking frights since the punchline of *Carrie*.

Though intense to the point of unbearability, the transgressive climax almost comes as a relief after the slow ratcheting of tension that turns the introverted world of the hero into a hell where everything may turn and assault him. Unlike most US horror flicks, here is one that, by eschewing the easy thrill, goes for terror in a much more deep-seated form. And, as such, stays with you after the projector bulb has dimmed. ★★★★★ **KN**

AUSTIN POWERS IN GOLDMEMBER (2002)

Starring: *Mike Myers (Austin Powers/Dr Evil/Fat Bastard/Goldmember), Beyonce Knowles (Foxxy Cleopatra), Michael Caine (Nigel Powers), Seth Green (Scott Evil), Michael York (Basil Exposition), Robert Wagner (Number Two), Mindy Sterling (Frau Farbissinia), Verne J. Troyer (Mini Me), Fred Savage (Number Three)*
Director: *Jay Roach*
Screenwriters: *Michael McCullers, Mike Myers*
12/94 mins./Comedy/Spy/USA

After Austin's spy dad is kidnapped, Dr Evil explains that only the Dutch metallurgist Goldmember could be responsible. Zipping to 1975 and back, Austin and Foxxy Cleopatra must stop a molten asteroid of pure gold from melting the polar ice caps.

The world's biggest comedy franchise reaches episode three with a film that loudly signals its intent from the get-go: brasher, flashier, starrier, funnier. Faced with the challenge of topping the $300-million grossing *The Spy Who Shagged Me*, Goldmember opens its account with an instant, 'Wow!': a surprise-packed pre-credits sequence that glides into an explosive dance number. Comedy is film's most precarious genre, but Myers & Co. have bought maximum insurance against audience ennui.

AUSTIN POWERS: THE SPY WHO SHAGGED ME

Sequels must innovate or die, and Myers keeps on adding to his already rich recipe. This time, he throws in Austin's dad Nigel Powers (a well-cast Caine), plus latest curvaceous sidekick Foxxy Cleopatra (Knowles clearly enjoying her role), an ass-kicking F.B.I. agent who makes the most of her generic dialogue and 1970s wardrobe.

The price to be paid is the inevitable loss of focus: really, every minute of screen time where Dr Evil isn't unleashing withering disdain is a minute wasted. In particular, skin-peeling, Dutch perv Goldmember struggles to make a mark, just as Fat Bastard was an unwelcome addition last time around.

With Austin Powers movies, plotting is beside the point, the film's real essence being a succession of meticulously constructed comic interludes. Several of the ones on offer here showcase Myers at his very best – and the physical abuse repeatedly meted out to Mini-Me is a very successful running gag. But without the compensation of a narrative that truly engages, less successful jokes are left to flail in a vacuum. *Goldmember* revels in its own fabulosity, but we don't care about that – we just want to laugh. ★★★ **CG**

AUSTIN POWERS: THE SPY WHO SHAGGED ME (1999)

Starring: *Mike Myers (Austin Powers/Dr Evil/Fat Bastard), Heather Graham (Felicity Shagwell), Michael York (Basil Exposition), Robert Wagner (Number Two), Rob Lowe (Young Number Two), Seth Green (Scott Evil), Mindy Sterling (Frau Farbissinia), Verne J. Troyer (Mini-Me), Elizabeth Hurley (Vanessa)*
Director: *Jay Roach*
Screenwriters: *Mike Myers, Michael McCullers*
12/95 mins./Comedy/USA

Dr Evil goes back in time to steal Austin's 'mojo' – the secret to the agent's invincibility – so Austin will be powerless when Evil holds the world to ransom.

Sensible enough to invest in the strongest aspects of the original (i.e. Dr Evil is far funnier than Powers so we get way more of the camp Blofeld and curling pinky), this as-good-as sequel plays satisfyingly to the Identikit grooves of a terrifically funny original. The elaborate and potty storyline takes Evil back in time to 1969 to steal Powers' mojo (his sex drive) and the snaggle-toothed swinger zings back to retrieve his all important potency.

From there on in, it's a re-run of the same routines played out with more money and greater confidence. Dr Evil threatens to destroy the world with his giant moon-based 'laser' known as The Alan Parsons Project. Powers drapes himself over the deliciously sexy but less-than-funny Graham (as Felicity Shagwell). Elizabeth Hurley, Robert Wagner, Rob Lowe and Tim Robbins all crop up for hammy cameos. And it flies by. It could have been bettered. Myers' unflagging career shtick of glancing complicitly to camera as a fail-safe for weak jokes is just wearing. The intercut dance numbers carry none of the fizz they did in the first. And the third Myers-played character, a hefty Scottish dribbler known as Fat Bastard concealing the actor in swathes of sweaty prosthetic, is a failure. But, as soon as you worry it won't hold together like the first and minutes pass by without a gag, it pulls something joyous out of the comedy bag and wins you over.

Mostly it is in the most obvious, crudest gags. Powers supping from a steaming cup of boiling crap, leaving a squirm-inducing rim of shit on his upper lip. Mini Me, Evil's one-eighth-sized clone, is an inspired non-stop dwarf gag, triumphing in the most ludicrous fight scene (with Powers) in movie history. A penis-euphemism riff involving an endless array of folks spotting Evil's dubious shaped space rocket so inspired it even works twice. And there is still that artful application of the 60s spy-ethos satire to 90s affectation – cue Dr Evil going psycho on Jerry Springer; and the magnificent return of Scott Evil, Evil's dysfunctional love-child.

There is something effortlessly inviting about the Powers' franchise, as well as his vast comic talent (and much of this stuff was improvised on set), Myers possesses an innate warmth that draws in the audience. It's his deprecating grin, as he delivers another of Powers' wild pick-ups, or Dr Evil's all too evident human weariness ('Throw me a frickin' bone here, people'). ★★★★ **IN**

AUSTIN POWERS: INTERNATIONAL MAN OF MYSTERY (1997)

Starring: *Mike Myers (Austin Powers/Dr Evil), Elizabeth Hurley (Vanessa Kensington), Robert Wagner (Number Two), Michael York (Basil Exposition), Mimi Rogers (Mrs Kensington), Seth Green (Scott Evil), Fabiana Udenio (Alotta Fagina), Mindy Sterling (Frau Farbissina), Will Ferrell (Mustafa)*
Director: *Jay Roach*
Screenwriter: *Mike Myers*
15/94 mins/Comedy/USA

Sixties Secret Agent Austin Powers is defrosted in the nineties, when his evil nemesis returns to hold the earth hostage.

Impassioned anglophile Mike Myers is granted leave to indulge his Brit fancy with this all-singing, all-dancing comic homage to the 60s Bondian spy genre, resulting in a garish, unsubtle, completely OTT movie trip delivered with no small amount of guile, wit and genuine affection for the object of its ritual abuse.

Leaving no reference untapped, Myers reworks his Wayne's World camera-winkage into a vintage turn, throwing in two fine-tuned roles for the price of one – the rakish, incisor-abundant superspy Austin Powers and his scheming Blofeld-flavoured nemesis Dr Evil hoisting nefarious little pinky to lips after each despotic delivery. They're pitted together in a carnival of spoofery, the pair cryogenically frozen in 1967 then redeposited in 1997 to be faced with sexual politics, redefined caddishness and all the dry-docked fish antics their 60s hippie/megalomaniac personas can muster in the po-faced 90s. Meanwhile, Hurley is the natural foil. Sending herself up with surprising willingness, she's still drop-dead sexy in figure-hugging catsuits struggling to keep the randy Powers at arm's length.

The task at hand is a gleeful undermining of the staple cliches of spy culture – the cliffhanger escape sequences, the nutty global threat, the gadgets and gimmickry all brought down to size. While 007 is the main port-of-call, Myers' joyously ironic script fiddles with the pop-camp of all those slick 60s spy jaunts from *The Persuaders* to *Matt Helm*, against a general send-up of London's swinging decade – the opening salvo is a shimmering pop dance routine with the ever-velvet clad Powers strutting his groove alongside cheery Beefeaters, smiling bobbies, scarlet phoneboxes and his Union Jack E-type, clearly dumped on a studio backlot.

There are moments of overindulgence, a hankering to fill every frame with (occasionally repetitive) humour which upsets the film's rhythm. And referencing yourself smacks of conceit – buffooning around in his Y-fronts

Movie Trivia: Austin Powers International Man of Mystery

It's said that Dr Evil is based on Mike Myers' former boss, *Saturday Night Live* producer Lorne Michaels. Austin's video phone ring is the same as that of the hotline phone in 1965's *Our Man Flint*. General Borchevsky and Commander Gilmore are named after Toronto Maple leaf hockey stars and Mike Myers' dogs.

has become an irritating Myers 'motif'. But there's enough inspiration to counter the desperation – sporadic cutaways to the jangly timbre of psychedelic Powers-starred musical numbers; cameos from kitsch icons (Rob Lowe, Carrie Fisher, Michael York, Robert Wagner); a trippy soundtrack rewired for modern tastes and a set of puerile penis-breast cover-up routines which are, sadly, unavoidably hysterical. ★★★★ **IN**

ⓞ AUTO FOCUS (2002)

Starring: *Greg Kinnear (Bob Crane), Willem Dafoe (John Carpenter), Rita Wilson (Anne Crane), Maria Bello (Patricia Crane), Ron Leibman (Lenny)*
Director: *Paul Schrader*
Screenwriter: *Michael Gerbosi, based on the book* The Murder of Bob Crane *by Robert Graysmith*
18/104 mins./Biography/Crime/USA

Californian DJ Bob Crane becomes a 60s TV star off the back of US sitcom *Hogan's Heroes* and, hooking up with techno wizard John Carpenter, embarks on a downward spiral of seedy sex, wrecked marriages, dinner theatre and gruesome death.

At various points throughout *Auto Focus*, Bob Crane utters, 'A day without sex is a day wasted.' It's a cheery aphorism that masks a sad, compulsive life, and it is precisely this mixture of comedy and desperation that infects Paul Schrader's brilliant biopic.

A huge star in the 60s via the title role in POW sitcom *Hogan's Heroes*, Crane's subsequent sex odyssey is fashioned into fabulous filmmaking by a director near the top of his game. This film is a further demonstration of Schrader's uncanny ability to mine real-life subject matter (Yukio Mishima, Patty Hearst) for the obsessions that also infuse his creations (*Taxi Driver*'s Travis Bickle, *American Gigolo*'s Julian Kay).

Auto Focus continues his fascination with sex as a substitute for an interior life, the pull of pornography, and characters who spectacularly participate in their own downfall. Mounting the sexcapades that passed for Crane's life, Schrader's gaze is unflinching and non-judgemental, clinically carving open Crane's addictions (fame and technology as well as sex) like an autopsy.

What stops this from becoming an unwatchable nosedive into degradation is a career-best performance from Greg Kinnear. The actor makes Crane endlessly likeable, never soliciting sympathy for his painfully unaware sleazebag. He is ably supported by Dafoe, an old hand at pathetic seediness and insidious neediness. If Crane provides the star power, Carpenter lends the man power, and their mutual dependency becomes the core of the movie – a moment where Crane berates Carpenter for a stray hand on his butt during a 'group grope' is priceless.

Around the central pairing, there are excellent incidental pleasures: a jazzy title sequence straight out of a Rock Hudson-Doris Day picture, some great recreations of ersatz US sitcom, Crane's truly appalling appearance on a 70s cookery show. But it is Schrader's cool, cinematic intelligence that makes *Auto Focus* as sharp as it is superior. ★★★★ **IF**

ⓞ AVALON (1990)

Starring: *Leo Fuchs (Hymie Krichinsky), Eve Gordon (Dottie Kirk), Lou Jacobi (Gabriel Krichinsky), Armin Mueller-Stahl (Sam Krichinsky), Elizabeth Perkins (Ann Kaye), Joan Plowright (Eva Krichinsky), Kevin Pollack (Izzy Kirk), Aidan Quinn (Jules Kaye), Israel Rubinek (Nathan Krichinsky), Elijah Wood (Michael Kaye)*
Director: *Barry Levinson*
Screenwriter: *Barry Levinson*
U/126mins./Drama/USA

Account of how several generations of a middle-class immigrant family adapts to life in Baltimore.

Baltimore is one of the least celebrated of major American cities. Barry Levinson was brought up there and *Avalon* is the third occasion – after *Diner* and *Tin Men* – on which he has attempted to redress this imbalance by using it as a setting for his work. Indeed, were Levinson not coming off *Rain Man* it is doubtful that he would have been able to finance such a commercially unlikely project as this sober but quietly spectacular film with no room for stars, this tale of how one family moves from Eastern Europe to the Eastern United States and there, over a couple of generations, disintegrates.

The Krichinskys are not the huddled masses of New York's Lower East Side but the industrious lower middle classes who move to the suburbs on the back of the postwar consumer boom, making their money selling discount fridges, cookers and, significantly, televisions. They have little sentiment to spare for the old country. Sam, the grandfather whose reminiscences provide the spine of the film, recalls arriving in Baltimore on 4 July 1914 as fireworks illuminated the night sky: 'It was the most beautiful place I had seen in my entire life.' He settles in the new Utopia of the Avalon district.

The Krichinskys start off as a cliche-extended family, ceaselessly cooking and eating, squabbling and retailing old anecdotes, three and four generations under the one roof; they finish up as a bunch of nuclear units, picking at TV dinners with Milton Berle and failing to turn up to funerals. Their disintegration is wrought not by crime, war or disaster; instead the Krichinsky family is sundered by prosperity, time and television.

The art direction is superb throughout, notably in the opening sequence as young Sam wanders the streets of Baltimore like a dazzled pilgrim entering paradise, while Randy Newman, who has been in this era before with *Ragtime*, contributes excellent music. Thanks to uniformly splendid performances (particularly from Mueller-Stahl as Sam) Levinson elicits poignant humour from the inconsequential specifics of family life, many culled from the reminiscences of earlier Levinsons: the uncle storming out because the Thanksgiving turkey was carved in his absence; the boy disturbing a wasp's nest; the ambitious young cousins shooting TV commercials for their own discount warehouse; and, best of all, the aged brothers wracking their brains to remember the name of a favourite John Wayne movie. That's the one about the stagecoach. ★★★ **CC**

ⓞ AVANTI! (1972)

Starring: *Jack Lemmon (Wendell Armbruster, Jr), Juliet Mills (Pamela Piggott), Clive Revill (Carlo Carlucci), Edward Andrews (JJ Blodgett)*
Director: *Billy Wilder*
Screenwriters: *I.A.L. Diamond, Billy Wilder, based on the play by Samuel A. Taylor*
12/140 mins./Comedy/USA

A grieving Wendell Ambruster Jr arrives on the Italian island of Ischia to learn that his venerable father died in a car crash alongside his English mistress, whose daughter, Pamela Piggott, has also come to do her filial duty.

Billy Wilder was never particularly fond of this comedy of continental manners. Yet it echoed themes he had already explored with much hilarity in *A Foreign Affair* and *One, Two, Three*, in which he demonstrated that much more than the Atlantic Ocean divided Europe from America. Perhaps his disillusion was born of the fact that he was prevented by Paramount from making the picture he wanted, in which Jack Lemmon discovered not only that his father had been having annual assignations with a lover, but that his sleeping companion had been the hotel's bellboy.

Nevertheless, such is Lemmon's practised sense of wounded propriety that he's just as comically indignant about the fact that his father had been canoodling with Juliet Mills's mother. Wilder and co-scenarist I.A.L.

Diamond laced Wendell's character with facets of *The Apartment*'s C.C. Baxter, although it's also easy to recognise *The Odd Couple*'s Felix Ungar in Brewster's slavish devotion to detail and his discomfort around women.

Lemmon is expertly supported by Mills, who piled on the pounds to play the pert Miss Piggott, who comes more quickly to realise that the resort is exerting the same romantic pull on them that it did on their parents. But their mid-life liaison would not seem so charming without the complicity of the locals, whose fondness for the deceased prompts them to matchmake their offspring. Clive Revill does particularly well as the hotel manager, who manages to make reams of expository information seem quaintly conversational.

But while the human comedy is thoroughly engaging, Wilder never lets it blunt his satirical purpose, as he contrasts the mildly corrupt customs of the laconic Italian bureaucrat and the ardent American diplomat. However, the humour is gently in keeping with the leisurely pace that makes this guilty pleasure all the more delicious. ★★★ **DP**

THE AVENGERS (1998)

Starring: *Ralph Fiennes (John Steed), Uma Thurman (Emma Peel), Sean Connery (Sir August de Wynter), Patrick Macnee (Invisible Jones), Jim Broadbent (Mother), Fiona Shaw (Father), Eddie Izzard (Bailey), Keeley Hawes (Tamara), Shaun Ryder (Donavan)*
Director: *Jeremiah Checnik*
Screenwriter: *Don MacPherson, based on the television series created by Sydney Newman)*
12/90 mins./Action/Adventure/USA

John Steed teams up with Mrs Peel to battle the evil fiend known as 'The Weatherman', but can Mrs Peel really be trusted?

Remember the episode in which Diana Rigg's Emma Peel found herself in a country house built like an M.C. Escher drawing, with identical corridors that kept leading back to the same landing? Well, that sequence is included here – only this time we're sort of supposed to think it's a drug-induced hallucination and Uma Thurman's Mrs Peel gets out of the trap by simply smashing a window. That's pretty typical of *The Avengers* movie, which resurrects the wonderful trappings of the original TV series but handles them with the sort of clumsiness you, perhaps, should expect from director Chechik, the man who remade French classic *Les Diaboliques* with Sharon Stone.

Clocking in at a brisk hour-and-a-half, which suggests whole chunks of plot were pared away after previews, the film sets out to bring together John Steed and Mrs Peel for the first time in a plot which pits them against a madman out to control the weather, Sir August De Wynter. For a while, there's an attempt to suggest Mrs P. is playing for both teams, though it's obvious from the outset that there's an evil clone in the mix, paving the way for the attraction between the two to go further than it ever did on TV just so the idiots in the audience can't fail to get the message.

A bunch of stooges – the crippled Mother, the blind Father, a silent thug (an unconvincing Eddie Izzard), even Patrick Macnee as an Invisible Man – remind you that the TV series only relied on eccentrics when Linda Thorson had to be surrounded by interesting people while she learned to act.

Fiennes and Thurman look fine in the familiar outfits, but aren't very good at banter, adventure or romance: Fiennes seems uncomfortable and on the point of tears throughout (not an incredibly alluring trait on an unflappable hero); Thurman's waxy face and voice-coached English vowels just don't cut it. And Connery, in a kilt or a teddy bear suit, is disastrous, the sort of baddie even Adam West would sneer at.

There are neat sets, cool cars and nice costumes, but this Molotov champagne cocktail fizzles and goes flat very swiftly. It's not in the *Batman And Robin* ghastliness league, but it is more disappointing than hashes like *Godzilla* and *Lost In Space*. After all, they weren't based on anything as good as *The Avengers* used to be. This is a major missed opportunity. Diana Rigg, you're needed. ★★ **KN**

L'AVVENTURA (1960)

Starring: *Monica Vitti (Claudia), Gabriele Ferzetti (Sandro), Lea Massari (Anna), Dominique Blanchar (Giullia), James Addams (Corrado)*
Director: *Michelangelo Antonioni*
Screenwriters: *Michelangelo Antonioni, Ello Bartolini, Tonino Guerra, based on a story by Antonioni*
PG/142 mins./Drama/ Italy/France

While on a yachting trip to the islands off Sicily, Anna mysteriously goes missing and her architect boyfriend Sandro and closest confidante Claudia form an uncomfortable attachment while searching for her.

When *L'Avventura* premiered at Cannes in 1960, it was greeted with howls of derision for its seemingly wilful obscurantism. Yet 35 critics rallied to Michelangelo Antonioni's cause and published a defence which slowly began the film's elevation to acceptance as a masterpiece of European art cinema.

Despite struggling with budgets and having to shoot out of season, Antonioni had succeeded in fashioning a new filmic language that bound image and meaning ever more closely together, just as the characters were so intrinsically linked to the landscape of the volcanic Aeolian Islands. Evidence of this evolving methodology can be detected in both *Le Amiche* and *Il Grido*, but they couldn't match the austerity of *L'Avventura*, which saw the narrative reduced to near-insignificance and the fate of the characters left so resolutely unresolved.

Such was his indifference towards Lea's fate and the status of Sandro and Claudia's relationship that Antonioni denied the audience the orthodox opportunities of identifying with them. Every bit as lost as Lea, the searchers scarcely communicate and their lack of inter-action forces the viewer to abandon their traditional attachment to the stars and take a more intellectual approach to the meticulously measured proceedings. In other words, Antonioni was forcing us to contemplate the physical and metaphorical manner in which these determinedly modern figures have become so detached from the world around them that all they have to console themselves are their materialism, anxiety, boredom and alienation.

He did this by setting them within a barren, hostile environment in a way that emphasised their isolation. So, in spite of its title, this was anything but an adventure, as the search for Anna rapidly became an irrelevance as Antonioni became inceasingly preoccupied with the party's social dislocation and, in the process, he created a kind of chic realism which exploited the harsh poetry of the location to express the characters' moral and spiritual poverty. ★★★★★ **DP**

Michelangelo Antonioni (born 1912)

Who he is: Major Italian filmmaker.
Hallmarks: Poised elegance and sophistication; ambiguity; plots structured around unsolved and insoluble mysteries; modern urban alienation; innovatively lengthy shots.
If you see one movie, see: L'Avventura (1960)

Author Cameos In Films Of Their Own Books

1. Irvine Welsh (Trainspotting)
2. J.G. Ballard (Empire Of The Sun)
3. Arthur C. Clarke (2010)
4. Stephen King (Pet Sematary)
5. Mickey Spillane (The Girl Hunters)
6. James Ellroy (Stay Clean)
7. S.E. Hinton (Rumblefish)
8. John Irving (The World According To Garp)
9. Pat McCabe (The Butcher Boy)
10. Paul Bowles (The Sheltering Sky)

THE AVIATOR (2004)

Starring: *Leonardo Di Caprio (Howard Hughes), Cate Blanchett (Katharine Hepburn), Kate Beckinsale (Ava Gardner), John C. Reilly (Noah Dietrich), Alec Baldwin (Juan Trippe), Alan Alda (Sen. Ralph Owen Brewster), Ian Holm (Professor Fitz), Gwen Stefani (Jean Harlow), Jude Law (Errol Flynn)*
Director: *Martin Scorsese*
Screenwriter: *John Logan*
12A/166 mins./Drama/Biography/USA
Awards: *Academy Awards – Art Direction, Cinematography, Costume Design, Editing, Supporting Actress (Cate Blanchett), BAFTAs – Film, Best Make-up/Hair, Supporting Actress, Production Design, Golden Globes – Drama, Score, Actor*

A sweeping account of billionaire Howard Hughes' (DiCaprio) life in Hollywood, and how he indulged his passions for both aviation and the movie business before madness engulfed him.

Few, if any, filmmakers could hit a decade-long losing streak like Scorsese and still have us breathless with anticipation whenever a fresh project is announced, champing at the bit to see whether he's finally rediscovered the incandescent form of *Taxi Driver*, *Raging Bull* and *GoodFellas* – and whether his latest will be the picture that finally bags him an Academy Award.

But, while *The Aviator* was his strongest Oscar bid since *GoodFellas* (it is, after all, a movie about Hollywood), it couldn't withstand comparisons with Scorsese's masterworks. It's a great story well told, but we expect more than good storytelling from the man who gave us Travis Bickle.

Scorsese excels at exploring characters in whom he feels a deep personal resonance, those who, like him, have done battle with their own demons. It's through misfits like Bickle, La Motta, Henry Hill and even *The King Of Comedy*'s excruciating Rupert Pupkin that he's sought to dig out the truths of the human condition. But it's difficult to imagine the son of striving immigrants having much affinity with Howard Hughes who, despite his fascinating, tragic arc, wasn't even a self-made man, and who funded his outlandish endeavours by milking the inexhaustible cash cow of his family's machine tool business. Perhaps this is why he fails to get under the skin of his subject.

Nevertheless, Hughes' story is fascinating. It begins with the Hollywood arriviste lavishing his recent inheritance on his twin passions simultaneously, amassing the world's largest private air force and sinking an unprecedented $4 million of his own money into *Hell's Angels*, his tribute to World War I fighter pilots. Given Scorsese's infallible eye – abetted here by production designer Dante Ferreti and costumer designer Sandy Powell – the recreation of 20s Hollywood is immaculate. There are also several magnificent set-pieces to savour, among them Hughes' heroic orchestration of the *Hell's Angels* dogfight sequences from the open gun turret of a bomber and, later, a spectacular plane crash in which Hughes, flight-testing one of his own designs, rips through the rooftops of Beverly Hills.

Tagline
Some men dream the future. He built it.

In between, mustering every ounce of his stylistic verve, Scorsese chronicles Hughes' stormy romantic dalliances with Katharine Hepburn and Ava Gardner, and his draining, dragged-out fight with Pan Am chief Juan Trippe, who was determined to put his TWA airline out of business. As the visual tone shifts to keep pace with the times – the pastel hues of the 20s giving way to the oversaturated Technicolor 40s – Hughes himself transmogrifies from a brazen young mogul into a twitchy, paranoid obsessive who, against the backdrop of failed relationships and a besieged business empire, struggles to keep a grip on his failing sanity.

It's in these later scenes that Leonardo DiCaprio shines, dispelling fears that he hasn't the weight to carry such a complex, forceful role. He's mesmerising in the moment when Hughes rears back from the brink of madness to face down a corrupt senator (a superb Alan Alda) over allegations that he cheated the US Air Force.

Yet in spite of the lush production values, absorbing narrative and outstanding performances, the question of what, exactly, made this extraordinary man tick remains unanswered. When he's pulled from the flaming wreckage of his plane, the only words he manages to croak are, 'I'm Howard Hughes, the aviator'. And we know precious little more of him than that.
★★★★ SB

AWAKENINGS (1990)

Starring: *Robert De Niro (Leonard Lowe), Robin Williams (Dr Malcom Sayer), Julie Kavner (Eleanor Costello), Ruth Nelson (Mrs Lowe), John Heard (Dr Kaufman), Penelope Ann Miller (Paula)*
Director: *Penny Marshall*
Screenwriter: *Steven Zaillian, based on the book by Oliver Sacks*
12/121 mins./Drama/USA

At the tail end of the 60s, post-encephalitis patients were prescribed a drug that awoke them from comas – some of which have lasted several years – but the drug was not without side effects.

To those who know the outline of the story – that Robert DeNiro is in a coma and Robin Williams winkles him out of it – it may come as something of a surprise, mid-way through *Awakenings*, to realise that the hero of the piece is not really Robin Williams' caring Dr Malcolm Sayer, nor indeed the human spirit itself. It is, instead, a white powdery substance called L-Dopa, the drug that, in 1969, helped Leonard Lowe and his fellow patients throw off the chronic immobilisation they had endured for decades through a condition known as post-encephalitis, and suddenly start to move, talk and live once again. And, not unlike a drug itself, *Awakenings* the movie is a curiously clinical affair – often amounting to little more than an artificial exercise in the manipulation of the full range of human emotions.

The story – true, more or less, and based on Dr Oliver Sacks' 1973 book of the same name – is a gift, and has inspired numerous documentaries and dramas, including a play by Harold Pinter. And, as Randy Newman's stupendously sentimental score makes clear from the off, dry eyes are not something the filmmakers intend to tolerate, with Love and Caring and Warmth being pushed well to the fore, almost at the expense of any realistic examination of the horrific sense of shock these patients must have experienced after their various awakenings.

There are, however, major plus-points here. DeNiro, in diligent Oscar-baiting mode, is typically awesome, Robin Williams tolerable as the deeply human, yet bashful doctor, and many an opportunity is certainly offered for a hankie-soddening situation to develop in the darkness. *Awakenings* finally suffers, however, from its pronounced sense of forced emotions, suggesting a shade too much calculation from the filmmakers in what they feel will most effortlessly move their audience. And as many of the bum-shufflers in the audience at this reviewer's screening would no doubt confirm, nothing misfires to quite such a degree as badly misplaced sentimentality. ★★★ **PT**

AY, CARMELA! (1990)

Starring: *Carmen Maura (Carmela), Andres Pajares (Paulino), Gabino Diego (Gustavete), Maurizio De Razza (Lt Ripamonte), Jose Sancho (Capitan)*
Director: *Carlos Saura*
Screenwriters: *Rafael Azcona, Carlo Saura, based on the play by Jose Sanchis Sinisterra*
15/102 mins./Drama/Spain/Italy

At the height of the Spanish Civil War, Republican troubadours Carmela and Paulino, captured by Franco's forces, agree to perform for an audience of Fascist soldiers and condemned prisoners of war.

Using showbusiness as the prism through which to view the atrocities of the Spanish Civil War, Carlos Saura's rousing musical comedy has much in common with Ernst Lubitsch's 1942 masterpiece, *To Be Or Not To Be*. Unlike Joseph and Maria Tura in occupied Poland, Carmen and Paulino are devoted to one another. But, despite billing themselves as the 'Tip-Top Variety', they are under no illusions about their talent and are far more concerned with self-preservation than performance. Indeed, it's pragmatism rather than patriotism that keeps them on the road in their rickety truck, as neither seems particularly wedded to the Republican cause when we first encounter them and their mute jack-of-all trades, Gustavete (Diego).

Indeed, when they're captured by a combined force of Spanish and Italian Fascists outside Valencia and interned in a POW camp, Carmen and Paulino prove amenable to the idea of putting on a show, even if it means tweaking their lyrics to give them a pro-Franco slant. However, Carmen's burgeoning friendship with a Polish officer in the International Brigade (Zentaro) changes her perspective.

Ay, Carmela! is strewn with coarse comedy, with gusts of wind and references to Carmela's menstrual problems jostling for position with homophobic snipes and double entendres. Yet, Carmen Maura's refusal to perform anti-Republican propaganda before volunteers who were willing to die to preserve her liberty is intensely moving and there is an immense dignity in the way in which this blowsy dame comes to embody the spirit of resistance by baring her breasts and belting out the rallying anthem before she's felled by an assassin's bullet.

This may not be Saura's tautest film and there are occasional uncertainties of tone. But the performances are impeccable and it still has a power that has eluded many weightier treatises on the futility of war. ★★★★ **DP**

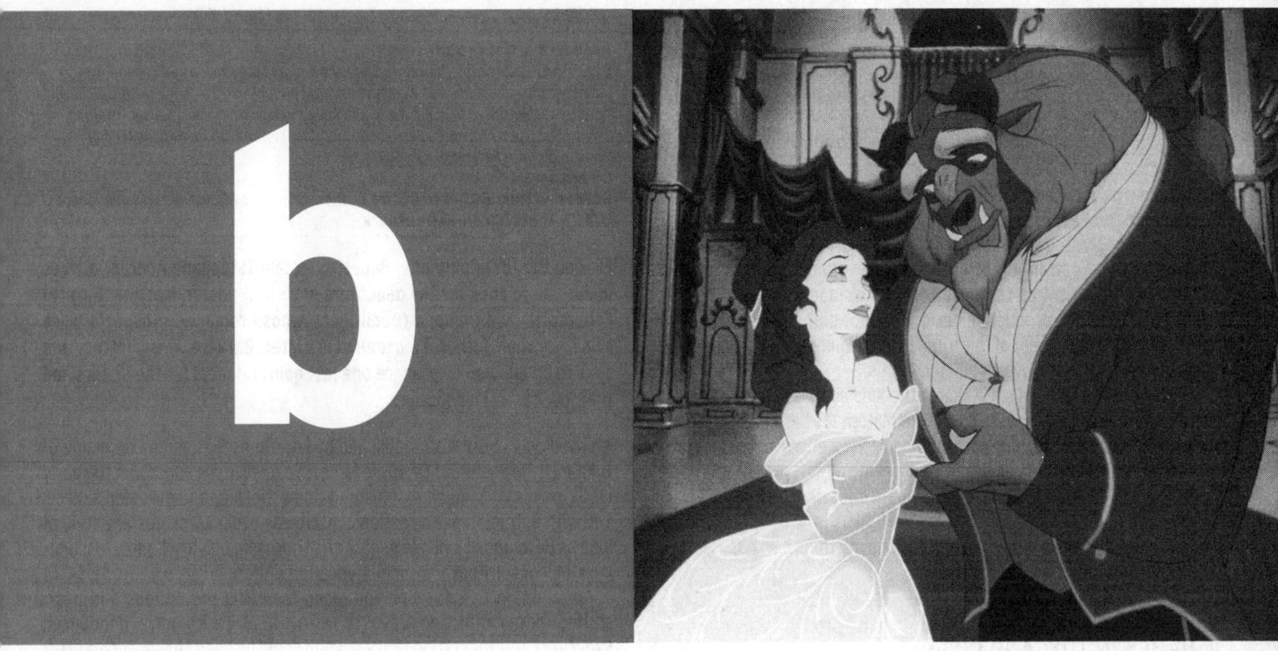

BABE (1995)

Starring: *James Cromwell (Arthur Hoggett), Magda Szubanski (Mrs Esme Hoggett) Voices: Christine Cavanaugh (Babe), Miriam Margolyes (Fly), Hugo Weaving (Rex), Danny Mann (Ferdinand)*
Director: *Chris Noonan*
Screenwriters: *George Miller, Chris Noonan, based on the novel* The Sheep-Pig *by Dick King-Smith*
U/94 mins./Fantasy/Children's/Comedy/Australia
Awards: *Academy Award – Best Visual Effects, Golden Globes – Best Comedy/Musical*

A piglet dreams of being a sheep dog, but first he must escape the farmer's wife's plans to serve him for Christmas roast.

However twee this farmyard adventure – in which the principal roles are filled by 'talking' animals – sounds, it proves so wildly hilarious and absolutely captivating that hitherto unrepentant carnivores will come out seriously entertaining vegetarianism. Babe is an innocent, frankly irresistible piglet, whisked from breeding pen to village fete to the barnyard of Farmer Hoggett whose fat, rosy wife is planning a Christmas dinner of roast pork. But Babe has 'an unprejudiced heart' and loads of pluck, affecting the lives of everyone on the farm and altering the little porker's destiny.

Adapted superbly from British writer Dick King-Smith's charming children's book *The Sheep-Pig* by producer and co-writer, George Miller, whose ten-year labour of love this is, the film boasts meticulous blending of real livestock with animatronic doubles and seemlessly plausible dubbed voice performances, notably from Christine Cavanaugh as Babe and Miriam Margolyes and Hugo Weaving as Hoggett's sheepdogs Fly and Rex. Longtime Miller colleague Chris Noonan makes his feature debut with witty invention, delightful pace and, apparently, the serenity of St Francis in choreographing his four-footed and feathered company to magnificently funny and exciting effect.

Tagline
A little pig goes a long way.

The story itself, narrated by Roscoe Lee Browne and a zany chorus of singing mice, has a sweet, touching simplicity that will enchant children, while operating just as nicely on a more mature level with it's gentler echoes of Orwell's *Animal Farm*. The impulses of human behaviour, from generosity and selflessness to bigotry and foolishness, are all on display through incidents that encompass a violent death and such comic highlights as a burglary carried out by the piggy and a neurotic duck.

Babe's heroic triumph at the climax brought a spontaneous eruption of cheering at an early preview from an audience that ranged from toddlers to grandparents in addition to the crustier critical contingent.

This reviewer for one, hasn't been able to face a pork chop in the years since, and is still laughing at the vibrant joyousness of this delicious comic fable. ★★★★★ **AE**

BABE: PIG IN THE CITY (1998)

Starring: *Magda Szubanski (Mrs Esme Cordelia Hoggett), James Cromnwell (Farmer Hoggett), Mary Stein (The Landlady), Mickey Rooney (Fugly Floom) Voices: Elizabeth Daily (Babe), Steven Wright (Bob), Glenne Headley (Zootie), Danny Mann (Ferdinand/Tug/Additional voices), James Cosmo (Thelonius)*
Director: *George Miller*
Screenwriters: *George Miller, Judy Morris, Mark Lamprell, based on characters created by Dick King-Smith*
U/98 mins./Family/Fantasy/Comedy/Australia

When Babe is separated from his owners in a sprawling metropolis, he has to rally other homeless animals to help him save the farm.

Avengers-style suspicions were aroused when a print was not available until three days before it opened. Whispers filtered back about small children fleeing test screenings in tears. Had they turned a rich silk purse into a twitching sow's ear?

Sad to say, yes. The very people who made our Christmas in 1995 have pissed on the mince pies. *Babe: Pig In The City* is wrong, wrong, wrong. In the original, a piglet escapes a 'cruel and sunless world' and brings cheery, cross-species innocence to a storybook farm. Here, circumstance takes him to a world even crueller: the composite urban sprawl of Metropolis.

When Farmer Hoggett has a nasty accident and Mrs Hoggett is arrested, Babe gets entangled in the local animal netherworld. It's a logical enough narrative extension – environmental change exerts further tests on Babe's innocent nature, providing plenty of opportunity for anthropomorphic fun (guard dogs voiced as Italian-American wise guys, a poodle as a hooker). Even the singing mice are back. So why isn't this an engaging second chapter in the life of cinema's best-loved pig?

Because director Miller (writer of *Babe* but of *Mad Max* heritage) lets the dark side run away with him. Rightly observing that fairy-tales are quite nasty, he wrongly throws all manner of unsavoury baggage at our rural innocents abroad – an airport strip-search, street punks, guns, drugs, and an even scarier variant on *Lady And The Tramp*'s dog-catchers – and the effect, combined with production design that out-glooms Orson Welles, is one of incessant defilement of the original, the audience, and the creatures forced to perform in this overpopulated circus.

God knows what dreams it will give the kiddies: the twitching leg of a dying Jack Russell, Babe with his head on a platter. It's hard to spot the animatronic join. And it's not all technical perfection either: a scene where Ferdinand the duck flies with pelicans is as convincing as Harry Hill's badgers.

How did this happen? Where *Babe* brought deep-rooted joy, the sequel brings fidgety depression. And save us from films in which chimpanzees dress in human clothes. Didn't we ban that or something? ★ **AC**

BABES IN TOYLAND (1934)

Starring: *Stan Laurel (Stannie Dum), Oliver Hardy (Ollie Dee), Charlotte Henry (Bo Peep), Felix Knight (Tom-Tom), Henry Kleinbach (Silas Barnaby)*
Directors: *Gus Meins, Charley Rogers*
Screenwriters: *Nick Grinde, Frank Butler, based on the musical comedy of Victor Herbert*
U/77 mins./Comedy/USA

Ollie Dee and Stannie Dum help keep Little Bo Peep out of the clutches of the wicked Barnaby, so she can marry Tom-Tom Piper.

With the Depression biting, movie theatres began showing double features in a bid to offer greater value to cash-strapped patrons. Consequently, the comedy short began to go out of vogue and its masters, Laurel and Hardy, were forced into full-length pictures. Built around Victor Herbert's 1903 operetta, this blend of nursery rhyme and pantomime almost didn't get made, as Stan Laurel loathed producer Hal Roach's original storyline – which had the duo playing Simple Simon and the Pieman defeating a spider-man who infuses hatred into the wooden soldiers in a bid to destroy Toyland – and both he and Ollie were knee-deep in marital difficulties.

Even the revised script was pretty much jettisoned, as Stan improvised situations on the spot in his customary manner and the rest of the cast tried to keep pace with his restless imagination. As a consequence, writer-director Ray McCarey walked out and shooting was further delayed by a series of illnesses and injuries, including Laurel tearing ligaments in his leg and Babe needing his tonsils removed during post-production.

But none of these troubles are reflected in the picture, which, for once, pits Stan and Ollie into a world as innocent as they are. The fairy-tale sets were enchanting, while the stop-motion work used to animate the soldiers was ingenious. But there was also something sinister about the Bogeymen that Barnaby unleashes in the finale and the mix of mayhem and menace made the film a firm pantomimic hit with younger audiences. Moreover, Laurel and Hardy themselves revel in several amusing set-pieces, one of which had Ollie being wrapped in a giant gift box, while another saw Stan disguised as a bride to ruin Barnaby's wedding day.

Disney tried a remake in 1961 and Keanu Reeves featured in a 1986 teleplay, but neither reproduced a modicum of the original's charm. ★★★★ **DP**

BABETTE'S FEAST (1987)

(Babette's Gastebud)
Starring: *Ghita Norby (Narrator), Stéphane Audran (Babette Hersant), Jean-Phillippe Lafont (Achile Papin), Gudmar Wivesson (Lorenz Lowenhielm as a young man), Jarl Kulle (Lorenz Lowenhielm as a young man), Bibi Andersson (Swedish Court Lady-in -Waiting), Hanne Stensgaard (Young Phillipa), Bodil Kjer (Old Phillipa), Vibeke Hastrup (Young Martina), Birgitte Federspiel (Old Martina)*
Director: *Gabriel Axel*
Screenwriter: *Gabriel Axel, based on the short story by Isak Dinesen (Karen Blixen)*
U/102 mins/Drama/Denmark

Fleeing the 1871 Commune, Babette Hersant (Stéphane Audran) arrives in Jutland to cook for the daughters of a strict pastor, Martina (Birgitte Federspiel) and Philippa (Bodil Kjer), whose romantic prospects were ruined by their father. Fourteen years later, Babette wins a lottery and asks to be allowed to prepare one last gourmet meal for the sisters and their puritanical neighbours.

Based on a short story published by Isak Dinesen (the nom de plume of Karen Blixen, of *Out Of Africa* fame) in *Ladies Home Journal* in the early 1950s, this is very much a film about domestic duty and a woman's place. Yet, with Gabriel Axel's direction consciously evoking the austere style of Ingmar Bergman, it's also a deeply affecting religious tract and a fascinating study of spiritual and secular vocation.

In addition to criticising the menu for being pretentious and overstuffed with conflicting flavours, many food critics have denounced *Babette's Feast* for stating that a woman could be head chef at such a prestigious restaurant as the Café Anglais in the mid-19th century. However, such culinary snobbery completely misses the point of this exquisite treatise on talent and the artist's choice to put their God-given gifts to the purpose they best see fit.

Martina and Philippa (who were named after the Protestant icons, Martin Luther and Philip Melancton) were respectively blessed with beauty and a glorious singing voice, but each elected to spurn romance with dashing soldier Lorenz Lowenhielm and opera star Achille Papin in order to minister to their father's congregation. Yet, neither believed that she had wasted her life in servitude and Babette feels the same way about dedicating her gastronomic genius to the service of the charitable sisters who gave her refuge after her husband and son were killed during the Commune – probably on the orders of the same General Gallifet who treated Lowenhielm to the dinner that he recalls with almost religious fervour during the feast.

Emphasising the simplicity of the Danish everyday, the repast and its preparation (which was lovingly photographed by Henning Kristiansen) has been taken by some as a contrast between Catholic and Protestant forms of worship. But, whatever its denominational symbolism, this is clearly a Last Supper, during which Babette sacrificially puts her soul into the food and drink and its consumption proves the salvation of a community whose puritanism has become a petty piety pursued more to earn the approbation of their hypocritical peers than to praise the Lord. ★★★★ **DP**

BACK TO SCHOOL (1986)

Starring: *Rodney Dangerfield (Thornton Melon), Sally Kellerman (Dr Diane Tucker), Burt Young (Lou), Keith Gordon (Jason Melon), Robert Downey Jr (Derek), M. Emmet Walsh (Coach Turnbull), Adrienne Barbeau (Vanessa), Ned Beatty (Dean Martin)*
Director: *Alan Metter*
Screenwriters: *Steve Kampmann, Will Porter, Peter Torokvei, Harold Ramis*
15/96 mins./Comedy/USA

When self-made millionaire Thornton Melon discovers that his mixed-up son Jason wants to drop out of college, he convinces the kid to stay on by enrolling himself as a freshman and promising to catch up on the education he never had.

As vehicles for fat comedians who were big in the States but never exported well go, this self-proclaimed slob comedy is nearly a masterpiece and certainly much better than the comparable *Revenge Of The Nerds* films. Dangerfield was an old pro who could wring chuckles out of the most ancient double entendres, but when given inspired schtick he could put himself up with Steve Martin and Eddie Murphy and the multi-authored script is crammed with relishable one-liners and bits of character business. Dangerfield, for instance, describes his high school football team with 'they were so tough that when they sacked the quarterback, they went after his family' and manages the all-time great chat-up line when asking a coed for help with his poetry studies by asking 'can you help me straighten out my Longfellow?'

Unlike many other star comedians, Dangerfield – who wrote the storyline – isn't afraid to let anyone else be funny in his vehicles, so watch out for Burt Young as the ultimate thug bodyguard ('in his family, he's only the second generation to walk upright'), Sam Kinison as a Vietnam veteran history lecturer ('while you were all in grade school, I was up to my waist in a rice paddy'), Robert Downey Jr as a rebellious punk ('it's all in this book, Proletarian Chicks in Bondage by Karl Marx'), Adrienne Barbeau as the ultimate slutty bitch ex ('your wife was just showing us her Klimt'/'oh, she does that to everybody') and Kurt Vonnegut Jr as himself. Later the inspiration for an outstanding *Simpsons* episode, and remade with *Cedric the Entertainer*. ★★★★ **KN**

BACK TO THE FUTURE (1985)

Starring: *Michael J. Fox (Marty McFly), Christopher Lloyd (Dr Emmett Brown), Lea Thompson (Lorraine Baines), Crispin Glover (George McFly), Thomas F. Wilson (Biff Tannen), Claudia Wells (Jennifer Parker)*
Director: *Robert Zemeckis*
Screenwriters: *Robert Zemeckis, Bob Gale*
PG/116 mins./Action/Adventure/Comedy/Sci-fi/USA

Awards: *Academy Awards – Best Sound Effects Editing*

Teenager Marty McFly has to travel back in time to save his future.

It could all have been so different. In fact, it could all have been a disaster. At the end of 1984 director Robert Zemeckis, who had been shooting his second movie, *Back To The Future*, for over a month was not a happy man. He was saddled with a lead actor who just didn't cut it as a happy-go-lucky, wisecracking teen. He was more like an angst-ridden 40-year-old struggling to make sense of existence in a godless universe. To make matters worse he'd seen a young actor perfect for the role. Michael J. Fox, then the star of TV sitcom *Family Ties* radiated youthful joie de vivre and frankly, for a movie with a solid teen base, was just gosh-darned cuter. Something had to be done. Eric Stoltz was out. Fox was in. And they started all over again. But if *Back To The Future* was the product of a fractured shoot, what emerged was well worth the agony. An almost perfectly wrought slice of old-fashioned escapist fantasy, it not only announced the celluloid arrival of the finest light-comedy actor of his generation, but was one of the very few films made in the avaricious, style-challenged 80s that transcended and survived the ugly extremes of its era (skintight stonewashed jeans which, one unkind critic remarked, 'look like they've been masturbated over by a troupe of boy scouts' excepted) and which remains an utterly beguiling little gem. To put it bluntly: if you don't like *Back To The Future*, it's difficult to believe that you like films at all.

Among the plethora of innocent charms on offer, there's the near perfect script by Zemeckis and Bob Gale which not only negotiates its time travel paradoxes with deft, exuberant wit but invests the light-hearted plot machinations with a seasoning note of honest drama (Doc's death within the first 10 minutes throws the comedy into pleasing relief and provides welcome dramatic release when we find, at the end, that the worst isn't true). There's Alan Silvestri's Williamsesque score; a plethora of memorable set-pieces – Marty's premature invention of the skateboard as he rips the top of a young kid's box-cart; his introduction of rock 'n' roll which develops into an anachronistic, Hendrix-style guitar solo ('Maybe you're not ready for that,' McFly admits, 'but trust me, your kids are going to love it.') as well as nods to other sci-fi movies – an innovation in the mid-80s when Tarantino was still re-racking the late-returns. When Marty has to convince his not-yet-dad to ask his not-yet-mom out he poses as Darth Vader (a variation on the joke appears in Part III when he calls himself Clint Eastwood) and claims to have come from the planet Vulcan. And then there's the tastefully handled Oedipal riff which, in less talented hands, might have been uncomfortable, if not downright nauseating. But at the heart of *Back To The Future* is the towering talent of the diminutive (his least favourite word, 'Why can't they just call me short?') Michael J. Fox. Thrust into the spotlight recently as a result of his illness, Fox established himself here as quite simply the most charming screen presence of the 80s. Weirdly, shortly after the massive success of the *BTTF* trilogy, it became de rigueur to bash the actor. Obviously his enormous talent for light comedy didn't sit well with the hip-cynicism of the 90s. Applying anything approaching rigorous criticism to *Back To The Future* would be like taking a jack-hammer to a perfectly risen souffle, but there are a number of intriguing readings to Zemeckis' movie, particularly since hostile critics of the directors' subsequent work, *Forrest Gump* and *Contact*, have detected in him a Capra-esque conservatism. You could make the case that *BTTF* is a manipulative critique of the 80s through the prism of an airbrushed version of the 50s that owes more to George Lucas' *American Graffiti* than the turmoil of the decade itself (the burning crosses and blacks dangling from trees are presumably 'just out of shot'). Zemeckis seems to be accusing the 80s of betraying the American Postwar dream; Marty's frumpy, nervous, bullied family are not the way things were meant to turn out (next to them at the dinner table you wonder if Marty ever inquired whether he was adopted) in the same way that the grasping 80s are not the legitimate offspring of the 'innocent' 50s.

Of course this is all a bit speculative. But if *Back To The Future* doesn't hold big ideas well, it remains like its star – small, but perfectly formed. ★★★★★ **AS**

Movie Trivia: Back to the Future

Eric Stoltz was the original choice to play Marty McFly. He was replaced two weeks into shooting the film but he is still visible in one scene, diving into the Delorean escaping the incensed Libyans. Robert Zemeckis cameos as the Jeep driver with whom Marty hitches a ride on his skateboard. Before filming began the time machine went through a lot of variations, from a laser device to a refrigerator, and finally the Delorean.

BACK TO THE FUTURE PART II (1989)

Starring: *Michael J. Fox (Marty McFly/Marty McFly Jr/Marlene McFly), Christopher Lloyd (Dr Emmett Brown), Thomas F. Wilson (Biff Tannen, Griff Tannen), Lea Thompson (Lorraine Baines/McFly/Tannen), Elisabeth Shue (Jennifer Parker/McFly), Billy Zane (Match)*
Director: *Robert Zemeckis*
Screenwriters: *Robert Zemeckis, Bob Gale*
PG/104 mins./Action/Comedy/Sci-fi/USA

Awards: *Bafta – Best Special Effects*

Marty and Jennifer travel forward in time to straighten out the future but Biff steals the time machine and they have to find a way to get back and stop him from changing the course of history.

Ending with a big tease sequence of highlights for *Back To The Future Part III*, this was always going to be the longest movie trailer in Hollywood history. Emphatically episode two of a three-part serial, this second instalment doesn't make much sense unless you're familiar with the plot of the original film, calling into question as it does all the personal histories so tidily resolved there.

We begin in 1985 with Marty just about to give his girlfriend Jennifer (Thompson, cast in the role after Claudia Wells' illness forced her off the project) a spin in his new pick-up. Suddenly hyperactive inventor Doc is on the scene with the DeLorean time machine warning that Marty's future son needs help in the year 2015. A zip forward into a world of aerial skateboards and self-fastening shoes has unexpectedly disastrous results when the old man version of Biff (Wilson, the bad guy from the first film) borrows the time machine and gives his younger 1955 self a 50-year sports almanac which enables him to bet his way to untold riches, bump off Marty's Pop and not only marry his mom but force her to have breast enlargement surgery. The radically different 1985 that Marty returns to has thus become an amoral, violent mess with the only solution being another trip back to 1955 ...

Directed and played with terrific verve, this moves so fast from one special effects set-piece to the next that there's no time at all to reflect on the basic ridiculousness of its Chinese box of a plot. At the same time there's also quite a strong undercurrent of bleakness. The shopping mall Consumerville of 2015 – all video screens, holograms and a middle-aged Marty being fired by his Japanese boss – is hardly enviable for all its hi-tech trimmings. 1955, however, is still a golden age of innocence where anything is possible and it's one of the film's slickest achievements that it manages to successfully bind an entirely new angle to the rock'n'roll finale of the original film without at all suggesting a mere rehash of the old material. Glossy, high-energy escapism, *BTTF2* easily gets the job done, even if it does now tend to look more and more like an expedient bridge between two much bigger movies. ★★★ **TT**

⦾ BACK TO THE FUTURE PART III (1990)

Starring: *Michael J. Fox (Marty McFly/Seamus McFly), Christopher Lloyd (Dr Emmett Brown), Mary Steenburgen (Clara Clayton), Thomas F. Wilson (Burford 'Mad Dog' Tannen/Biff Tannen), Lea Thompson (Maggie McFly/Lorraine McFly), Elisabeth Shue (Jennifer Parker)*
Director: *Robert Zemeckis*
Screenwriters: *Bob Gale and Robert Zemeckis*
PG/118 mins./Action/Adventure/Comedy/Sci-fi/Western/USA

Doc Brown has been left stranded in 1885. Now Marty must go back to save Doc, before bad guy Burford Tannen murders him.

As a trilogy, the *Back To The Future* films make a lot more sense strung together than, say, the *Star Wars* trio. *Back To The Future Part II* teed off a lot of critics by not being a remake of the first film, and for daring to be a) complicated, b) very fast and c) heartless. Part III, which is slightly less fleet of foot, restores the heart interest of the first film and has a satisfying complete storyline.

At the end of the second film Doc Brown was stranded in 1885 while young Marty McFly was in 1955; now, learning Doc is due to be backshot by a varmint of the Old West, Marty returns to the 1880s and we get a hugely enjoyable science-fiction Western packed with Jules Verne-style steam engines and plenty of neat jokes.

Arriving in 1885, dressed in an absurd set of fringed buckskins that accurately reflect a 1950s Roy Rogers idea of a cowboy outfit, Fox swiftly changes into a muddier, more realistic set of Western duds, and adopts the most cowboy-sounding name he can think of, one 'Clint Eastwood'. The villain is Burford Tannen, the thuggish outlaw ancestor of the bullies who terrorised Marty in various periods in the earlier films, and the movie constantly plays clever reprises of the highpoints of the series but in 1885 terms – with a chase around main street on horses replacing the skateboard stuff, a shooting match replacing video games and a community hoe-down instead of a school dance. And if you've been paying attention in the series to date, you'll get plenty of fun out of quirks like the brief appearance of the solemn child who'll grow up to be the oppressive principal or the reference to a the clip from *A Fistful Of Dollars* as seen in Part II.

This time, in a reversal of the first film, Fox buzzes around keeping the plot on the move while Lloyd softens up and has a funny romance with schoolmarm Mary Steenbergen, and it all winds up with another great suspense-action sequence as a locomotive and the DeLorean head towards the ultimate precipice. Neatest of all is a coda, which features one of the best time machines in the cinema, promising that this is indeed the very last in the series and neatly wrapping it up for everybody. ★★★★ **KN**

⦾ BACKBEAT (1994)

Starring: *Stephen Dorff (Stuart Sutcliffe), Ian Hart (John Lennon), Sheryl Lee (Astrid Kirchherr), Gary Bakewell (Paul McCartney), Chris O'Neill (George Harrison)*
Director: *Iain Softley*
Screenwriters: *Iain Softley, Michael Thomas, Stephen Ward*
15/100 mins./Musical/Biography/UK

Awards: *BAFTA – Anthony Asquith Award for Film Music*

The story of legendary 'fifth Beatle' Stuart Sutcliffe from the band's early Hamburg days. His affair with German photographer Astrid Kirchherr and untimely death would have a profound effect on both his best friend John Lennon and the band as a whole.

Tackling the glorious edifice that is The Beatles is not for the foolhardy – you're messing around with some of the most iconic imagery in history, while the music is untouchable, locked away in Michael Jackson's closet. Iain Softley clearly is no fool, taking their story head-on is just asking for it, but by opting to view the humble birth of the Liverpudlian quartet through the prism of lost member Sutcliffe, Lennon's soul mate who could barely play a note, he avoids bringing the heavens down upon him and, actually, says a heck of a lot more about the famous band. At that time Lennon and McCartney hadn't written a song, they were covering R&B and Motown hits in edgy, shake-it-all live shows. Softley captures the atmosphere of these gigs with an immediacy that recalls punk more than Sgt. Pepper.

The film splits its drama between the proto-Beatle gravitation from Liverpool art school to the rathskellers of Hamburg, a neon-lit, smoke-veiled underworld somewhere between Bohemia and Gomorrah, and Sutcliffe's own tragic journey away from the band. Bursting with spit and spunk these kids are fuelled as much by anger as ambition. McCartney (doppelgänger Bakewell) fumes at Lennon that they're carrying the useless Sutcliffe, a rage spilling onto stage. Lennon fumes at Sutcliffe as he becomes entwined with arty photographer Kirchherr (a not-so luminous Lee), suggesting a homoerotic tug. Harrison (another uncanny line up in O'Neill) is barely a boy, while drummer Pete Best can hardly utter a word and will soon be confined to the dumpbin of history himself.

Softley manages all this with a crisp authenticity, his Hamburg of the early 60s is both threatening and alive, an unlikely Petri dish for a music that would change the world. Above all, though, he lets his two lead actors cut loose. Stephen Dorff is okay with the accent, but he really captures the beautiful Sutcliffe's swaggering rock'n'roll spirit dead-on; Lennon understood that for his lack of musical ability he was the image they needed, something they kept with them long after he had died tragically of a brain haemorrhage. The winner, however, is Ian Hart's Lennon, who had a head-start having already played him in Christopher Munch's excellent *The Hours And The Times* – while no look-alike, Hart truly captures the naked wit and insecurity of a man destined for greatness. ★★★★ **IN**

BACKDRAFT (1991)

Starring: *Kurt Russell (Stephen 'Bull' McCaffrey/Dennis McCaffrey), Robert De Niro (Donald 'Shadow' Rimgale), William Baldwin (Brian McCaffrey), Scott Glenn (John 'Axe' Adcox), Donald Sutherland (Ronald Bartel), Rebecca De Mornay (Helen McCaffrey), J.T. Walsh (Aderman Marty Swayzak)*
Director: *Ron Howard*
Screenwriter: *Gregory Widen*
15/132 mins./Action/Drama/Thriller/Mystery/USA

Two warring fire-fighting brothers have to learn to work together to defeat a local arsonist.

With a script by a former fireman that invites the taunt 'Don't give up the day job', this by-the-numbers drama of estranged brothers reconciled would be mighty poor stuff but for special effects to thrill the secret pyromaniac in everyone.

Russell and Baldwin are the hot-headed firefighting sons of a fireman who died a hero in the line of duty. Kurt's is the elder, macho, unforgiving type; William's (a sexy replica of elder brother Alec, down to the chest hair pattern) is the feckless, scaredy-cat rookie.

Thenceforth the plot is so hokey that every time the siren sounds you'll be laying odds at seven to five on who'll fry next, who'll save whom, who's going to redeem himself with heroics, etc. Robert De Niro, who appears initially to have stumbled onto the wrong film set, perks up the proceedings no end when he takes centre stage as an obsessed fire investigator in a promising mystery sub-plot that sadly fizzles out.

There's even a nod to Hannibal Lecter in Donald Sutherland's cameo as a crazed, incarcerated arsonist to whom the good guys turn for tips on how to catch their current firestarter. All this, however, is just kindling for the main attraction, which is fire. According to De Niro's sage 'The only way to kill fire is to love it a little', and Howard's love affair with the element here is delirious: an ominous musical theme greets every lick of flame until fire becomes as sentient and exciting an adversary as the shark in *Jaws*; choking actors clutch tiny children and stagger manfully in slow motion through sensationally rendered conflagrations; fire hoses assume the role of laser guns in thrilling action set pieces. ★★★ **AE**

THE BAD AND THE BEAUTIFUL (1952)

Starring: *Lana Turner (Georgia Lorrison), Kirk Douglas (Jonathan Shields), Walter Pidgeon (Harry Pebbel), Dick Powell (James Lee Bartlow), Barry Sullivan (Fred Amiel), Gloria Grahame (Rosemary Bartlow)*
Director: *Vincente Minnelli*
Screenwriter: *Charles Schnee, based on a story by George Bradshaw*
PG/113 mins./Drama/USA

Awards: *Academy Awards – Best Actress, Best Black and White Set Decoration, Best Cinematography, Best Black and White Costume, Best Screenplay*

Director Fred Amiel, acclaimed screenwriter James Lee Bartlow and actress Georgia Lorrison explain in flashbacks to Hollywood mogul Harry Pebbel why they're so reluctant to work again with producer Jonathan Shields.

In the same year that *Singin' In The Rain* celebrated the cosy kitsch aspect of Hollywood, this brooding *Citizen Kane* clone sought to descend into its seedier side to expose Tinseltown in all its vainglory. The Academy was politely impressed, with all but Kirk Douglas converting their nomination into an Oscar. Yet, director Vincente Minnelli was overlooked and the film was omitted from the Best Picture shortlist, which suggests that *The Bad And The Beautiful* might have struck more raw nerves than it intended.

There was certainly considerable speculation about who had inspired which character. Jonathan Shields supposedly bore elements of David O. Selznick, Darryl F. Zanuck, Orson Welles and Val Lewton, while Georgia Lorrison bore an uncanny resemblance to Diana Barrymore. Harry Pebbel recalled Kane scribe Herman Mankiewicz, while James Lee Bartlow drew on William Faulkner and F. Scott Fitzgerald. Even minor figures like Henry Whitfield and Von Ellstein purportedly mirrored Alfred Hitchcock and Erich von Stroheim and Josef von Sternberg respectively.

Minnelli was always prone to melodrama. But this is a laudably unsentimental portrait of the picture business, in which the principals come to realise that while Shields has scarred them emotionally, he had also enhanced their careers. The choice between love and art is a key Minnelli theme and, as ever, his inspired use of visual symbolism and contrast reinforces the psychological mood. Robert Surtees's monochrome photography is particularly effective in the sequence in which Shields explains how the unseen is crucial to horror and in Georgia's nocturnal dash through the driving rain in a blaze of suicidal self-pity. But, Minnelli's use of sound is also impressive, most notably during the Beverly Hills party in which he uses overlapping dialogue to convey the cacophony of colliding egos.

In 1962, Minnelli revisited the intricacies and iniquities of movie-making to lesser effect in *Two Weeks In Another Town*. ★★★★ **DP**

BAD BOY BUBBY (1993)

Starring: *Nicholas Hope (Bubby), Claire Benito (Mam), Ralph Cotterill (Pop), Carmel Johnson (Angel), Syd Brisbane (Yobbo)*
Director: *Rolf De Heer*
Screenwriter: *Rolf De Heer*
18/112 mins./Comedy/Drama/Australia/Italy

35-year-old Bubby, a slapheaded mooncalf, has been raised in one filthy room and used as a sex-object-cum-whipping-boy by a monstrous Mum who claims the air outside is poisonous. Bubby's life gets worse when his long-lost Dad, a bogus clergyman, shows up. After innocently killing his parents with clingfilm, he ventures a new life in the world outside.

The first reels of Bad Boy Bubby are an endurance test for the easily depressed, but once Bubby gets out of the horrible family home, the film segues from extraordinary and unbearable to extraordinary and exciting. Wandering away from the fridge-ready corpses of his parents (and a cat) into a storyline reminiscent of *Being There* or *The Enigma Of Kaspar Hauser*, Bubby imitates others' behaviour to sometimes disastrous ends, and pursues his ideal woman, who turns out to be a large, good-natured nurse. In the city, he encounters brutality, indifference, sex (seduced by a svelte Salvation Army singer and brutally raped in jail), patronage, showbiz success and camaraderie (when he is adopted by a punk group who incorporate his cat-killing rants), notoriety (as the police seek the clingfilm killer), love and a religious revelation.

Dutch-Australian director Rolf De Heer uses techniques which seem like gimmicks (employing 31 different directors of photography, recording all the sound through tiny mikes hidden in the star's ears) which somehow don't get in the way of the disorienting story. One scene, as Bubby hugs a handicapped girl whose love he can't return, is among the most wrenchingly honest thing in the movies. Hope gives an astonishing performance, while the film manages marvellously to weave grotesque humour from the indefensible. It's a one-off weirdie, offputting for whole stretches but unforgettable, not for everyone but highly recommended to the discerning. ★★★★ **KN**

⊙ BAD BOYS (1995)

Starring: *Martin Lawrence (Det. Marcus Burnett), Will Smith (Det. Mike Lowry), Téa Leoni (Julie Mott), Tchéky Karyo (Fouchet). Joe Pantoliano (Captain C. Howard), Theresa Randle (Theresa Burnett)*
Director: *Michael Bay*
Screenwriters: *Michael Barrie, Jim Mullholland, Doug Richardson, based on a story by George Gallo*
18/118 mins./Action/Comedy/Crime/Thriller/USA

Two LA supercops must swap lifestyles to take down a drugs baron.

Fans of the slam-bang cop action comedy will have their entertainment glands solidly squeezed by this racy party popper of a movie in the line of *48 Hrs*, *Lethal Weapon* and *Beverly Hills Cop*, produced by the Cop megabuck duo of Simpson and Bruckheimer. A sizeable spring hit in the States, it's already made cinestars of two American TV favourites, comic Martin Lawrence and Fresh Prince Of Bel-Air Will Smith, whose teaming as wisecracking Miami Vice detectives makes a hot partnership.

Lawrence, a hyper hoot in the days before he became annoying, is family man Marcus; Smith, a studly dish, is Mike, a glamour boy with rich folks and a Porsche. Following the elaborately exciting heist of $100 million worth of heroin by arch European villain Tchéky Karyo, the motor-mouthed twosome have 72 hours to recover it before Internal Affairs shuts down their very own, disgraced drugs squad.

Setting about it with appropriate dispatch, they tear through various glossy, violently efficient set-pieces (shoot 'em ups, chases, explosions, the familiar drill), pick through grossly dead people and engagingly uphold the time-honoured bickering buddy tradition – they even have a shrieking boss (Joe Pantoliano) to chivvy them along.

Comic complications come courtesy of a *Comedy Of Errors*-style swapped-identity charade. Frightened eyewitness Julie will only spill her guts to the partner with the ladies' man rep – Smith's Mike. But he's unconscious somewhere at the time, so Marcus takes over Mike's persona and bachelor pad to babesit Julie, leaving Mike to move in with Mrs Marcus and the kiddies as a surrogate man of the house.

Rest assured, we've seen it all a million times before, but there are abundant (foul-mouthed) funnies, and debut director Michael Bay shows his commercials expertise propelling the noisy nonsense into a frantically slick and thoroughly enjoyable extravaganza. ★★★ **AE**

⊙ BAD BOYS 2 (2003)

Starring: *Martin Lawrence (Det. Marcus Burnett), Will Smith (Det. Mike Lowrey), Jordi Molla (Hector Juan Carlos 'Johnny' Tapia), Gabrielle Union (Syd), Peter Stormare (Alexei), Theresa Randle (Theresa), Joe Pantoliano (Captain Howard), Henry Rollins (TNT Leader)*
Director: *Michael Bay*
Screenwriters: *Ron Shelton, Jerry Stahl, based on a story by Marianne Wibberley, Cormac Wibberly, Ron Shelton and characters created by George Gallo*
15/147 mins./Action/Comedy/Thriller/USA

Wisecracking cops Mike and Marcus are assigned to stop a drug lord from flooding Miami with deadly Ecstasy. Complications arise when Marcus' sister Syd, an undercover DEA who also happens to be romancing Mike, gets caught in the crossfire.

Whether the original *Bad Boys* merited a sequel is a moot point – with worldwide takings of over $180 million on a $23 million budget, it was inevitable.

However, a gap of eight years – an age in cinematic terms – means that the hardly indelible characters have fallen off the movie-going radar and need to make quite a noise to recapture an audience now more enamoured with CG, kung fu and fantasy than bullets and fireballs. While not wanting for bangs, as a film *Bad Boys II* makes more of a dull thud.

Smith and Lawrence are an agreeable comic pairing when given the right material and a reason for their incessant bickering – otherwise their sniping is irritating rather than hilarious.

The 'killer Ecstasy' plot (which causes precisely one fatality and seems to do very nicely for Lawrence in one jarring comedy sequence) on which their antics are hung might have passed muster in the 80s, but seems a little 'so what?' now – like warning against the perils of CFCs.

The pair do have their moments (especially an amusing interrogation of Marcus' daughter's terrified date), but much of what's here is offensive (corpse tossing, anyone?) without being funny. Smith in particular, though a master of the buddy comedy genre, could do with being pickier with his material, having starred in nothing consistently hilarious since the original *Men In Black*.

Even in the face of leaden material, Michael Bay still manages to pull some impressive directorial tricks out of the bag. The first car chase down a Miami highway beats the overloaded freeway free-for-all of *The Matrix Reloaded* hands down, and his use of the camera is occasionally dazzling. But for what?

Circling a shootout in one continuous tracking shot looks jaw-dropping, but when the villains have no apparent motive or relevance, you might as well watch it with the sound off. By the time the film hits the two-hour mark, with a needless trip to Cuba and yet another car chase/shootout, what was once invention has long since dulled into pointless repetition. There's some 'bad', meaning good, here; there's also a lot of plain bad. Frankly, there's just far too much of everything. ★★ **DH**

⊙ BAD DAY AT BLACK ROCK (1955)

Starring: *Spencer Tracy (John L MacReedy), Robert Ryan (Reno Smith), Anne Francis (Liz Wirth), Dean Jagger (Tim Horn), Walter Brennan (Doc Velie)*
Director: *John Sturges*
Screenwriters: *Dom McGuire, Millard Kaufman, based on the story by Howard Breslin*
PG/81 mins./Drama/Thriller/USA

Just after World War II, John J. Macready gets off the train at a one-horse desert town and stirs up trouble with hostile locals by asking after a Japanese-American farmer who hasn't been seen since 1941.

A hugely influential widescreen Western, with a *High Noon*-like plot that plays out over one crowded day in the middle of nowhere, mixing straight-up suspense mechanics with editorialising about the gutlessness of all-American communities. It was one of the first movies to look at the modern-day West, with jeeps bouncing along the old horse trails and a sense that the frontier values have dribbled away in economically depressed times and in any case concealed fairly unpalatable attitudes to outsiders.

Stiff-armed, city-suited Spencer Tracy, stolidly middle-aged and unthreatening, wanders about the small town, provoking hostile reactions from all and sundry as he probes into the local guilty secret. Robert Ryan, always a complicated villain, is the neurotic cattle baron who did the dirty deed everyone is trying to cover up, while Lee Marvin and Ernest Borgnine are memorably fiendish as the cowboy thugs who keep getting in Tracy's way. Dean Jagger's drunken weakling Sheriff and Walter Brennan's grumbling cynic town doctor want to do the right thing, but still won't stick their necks out to help the stranger. Anne Francis is slightly improbable as a glamourpuss in blue jeans, though she plays a less-stereotyped role in the procedings than expected.

In the American cinema's first major martial arts sequence, Borgnine pours too much ketchup into Tracy's chili and the crippled hero lays him out with swift judo moves. The Important Social Message (about wartime racial prejudice against Japanese-Americans) pops up late in the day but doesn't spoil the simmering suspense, and John Sturges does his best-ever job of direction as the slow-burning plot explodes into CinemaScope action. ★★★★ **KN**

⓪ BAD EDUCATION (2004) (LA MALA EDUCACION)

Starring: *Gael Garcia Bernal (Angel/Juan/Zahara), Fele Martinez (Enrique Goded), Javie Carmara (Paquito), Daniel Gimenez Cacho (Father Manolo), Lluis Homar (Mr Berenguer)*
Director: *Pedro Almodovar*
Screenwriter: *Pedro Almódovar*
15/109 mins./Thriller/Spain

Years after their intense schoolboy relationship ended, Ignacio calls filmmaker Enrique, leaving him a manuscript. Reading it, Enrique recognises events from their boyhood and is moved to re-investigate the past.

Pedro Almodóvar's cinematic preoccupation with profoundly kooky women's crises is so over. *Talk To Her* marked the departure, with its two male protagonists. Now this intriguing, intimate, deliriously disturbing film noir – la Pedro has virtually no women in it, unless you count the drag queens. Or the glimpses of Spanish screen icon Sara Montiel (she and those film clips are real, believe it or not), who fuels the fantasies and desires of the juvenile movie buffs finding refuge from choir practice and pederasty at their Catholic boys' school in the local cinema.

But Mexican heart-throb Gael García Bernal not only makes striking personality transformations into multiple characters (Angel, Juan and Montiel-impersonator Zahara), he's also mighty pretty in a dress and the *femme fatale* of the piece. Fele Martínez, who was in *Talk To Her* and Amenobar's *Open Your Eyes*, has the more subdued role, and is watchfully effective as the guy you want to take for Almodóvar's alter ego.

It goes without saying that this is an audacious business. It's gay with a vengeance and a bold mix of art, trash and accomplished homage. The structure is what fascinates, unsurprisingly, since Almodóvar worked on it for over ten years. Not only do we get films within a film, but stories that open up into other stories, real and imagined. It's all the same story, really – one of child molestation and its aftermath of faithlessness, creativity, despair, passion, blackmail, murder and deception – told from different perspectives of truth and fiction.

Since Almodóvar is the exact contemporary of his two main characters – Enrique and Ignacio were schoolboys together in the early 60s and meet again in 1980 when Enrique has a few big pictures under his belt – it's inviting to grasp for 'facts'. Almodóvar's own experiences with priestly paedophiles are well known, but this is a far more complex affair – about destiny and choice – than an autobiographical payback.

It's probably more significant that the character who is a film director is not only essentially the narrator, but the one who observes, questions and lets things play out to see how far into danger and emotional turbulence he will let them take him. ★★★★ **DW**

⓪ BAD INFLUENCE (1990)

Starring: *Rob Lowe (Alex), James Spader (Michael Boll), Lisa Zane (Claire), Christian Clemenson (Pismo Bell), Kathleen Wilhoite (Leslie)*
Director: *Curtis Hanson*
Screenwriter: *David Koepp*
18/99 mins./Mystery/Thriller/USA

Rob Lowe plays a devilish charmer who gives yuppie James Spader a taste of the real high life.

One of Curtis Hanson's earlier directorial efforts, *Bad Influence* hints at the visual flair and sharp intelligence that would emerge in *L.A. Confidential* and *8 Mile*, but lacks the heart and substance of his later work.

In part this is thanks to its late 80s sensibilities, with Rob Lowe's psycho charmer and James Spader's yuppie geek (again!) only interested in the pursuit of big money, shallow highs, empty sex and hard liquor.

That said, as Lowe systematically dismantles Spader's antiseptic existence, Hanson and writer David Koepp handle the thriller plot well, with Lowe effective as the plastically beautiful but deeply dangerous bad influence of the title. At the time of the release, Rob Lowe's video exploits with under-age girls had just become national news that added extra frisson to certain scenes involving a camcorder in the movie. ★★★ **LB**

⓪ BAD LIEUTENANT (1992)

Starring: *Harvey Keitel (The Lieutenant), Victor Argo (Bet Cop), Paul Calderon (Cop One), Leonard Thomas (Cop Two), Robin Burrows (Ariane), Frankie Thorn (Nun)*
Director: *Abel Ferrara*
Screenwriters: *Zoe Tarmarlaine Lund, Abel Ferrara*
18/96 mins./Crime/Thriller/USA

A New York cop self-destructs on booze, drugs and gambling, but salvation possibly awaits following the rape of a nun – the $50,000 reward could pay off his debts and his soul may find some spiritual solace along the way.

Abel Ferrara out-sleazes even his own grubby oeuvre with this powerful if overbearing study of a soul swallowed by depravity.

Co-written with Lund, he plays the Lieutenant's junkie mistress here and previously collaborated with Ferrara on cult hit *MS.45*, *Bad Lieutenant* was met with howls of outrage on release.

In truth, the intensity is more implied than real and far less bloody than any of the accompanying controversy at the time suggested.

Still, there's every form of narcotic imbibing going and Keitel beats off in front of two girls he's pulled over for a minor traffic violation and later staggers about bollock-naked mewing like a sick cat.

Stunningly he never even received an Academy nomination as the cussedly vile nameless New York cop spiralling out of control – the role he was born to play. Which is a strange kind of compliment. ★★★★ **IN**

⓪ THE BAD NEWS BEARS (1976)

Starring: *Walter Matthau (Coach Morris Buttermaker), Tatum O'Neal (Amanda Whurlitzer), Chris Barnes (Tanner Boyle), Vic Morrow (Roy Turner)*
Director: *Michael Ritchie*
Screenwriter: *Bill Lancaster*
PG/102 mins./Sports /Comedy/USA

Cantankerous former minor league player Morris Buttermaker, who now prefers his beer to his baseball, is bribed into coaching Little League losers the Bears, a team without any talent at all. With the sly addition of star pitcher Amanda Whurlitzer and a local punk kid Kelly Leak, the Bears are about to prove their bouncebackability.

Who better than Walter Matthau, his face drooping like Deputy Dawg, his sandpapery voice perpetually tinged with sarcasm, his lolloping stride that of a man who left his enthusiasm in his unmade bed, to lend this knockabout joy mixing kids, sports and nihilism, the appropriate note of doleful reality? Coach Buttermaker, part-time pool cleaner, is a no-hoper, he's on the make, a 'cruddy alky' slipping slurps of bourbon into his beer can and giving his impressionable team the rough edge of his worldly wisdom. They can see right through him. He's a bum.

But that's why Michael Ritchie's comedy is easily in the top ten kids movies. His direction and Bill Lancaster's snarky script purposefully takes the triumph-over-the-odds blather of a thousand sports movies and transforms it into a caustic attack on America's empty-headed win-at-any-cost ethos. Dignity, this Little League riot espouses, means a hell of a lot more than a tin trophy.

The brawling, cussing, frankly lumpy pack of kids are so magnificently unsentimental, they remind you of nothing more than genuine 12-year-olds with that irritating habit of cutting right to the truth of the matter. 'All we got on this team are a buncha Jews, spics, niggers, pansies, and a booger-eatin' moron!' wails Chris Barnes' Tanner Boyle, whose mouth should be sealed with a parental warning sticker. Tatum O'Neal, as cute as a button and as rough as a squaddie, shines as star-pitcher Amanda caught on the cusp of womanhood, or, at the very least, can make it out on the horizon. Her surrogate father-daughter relationship with Buttermaker has an air of swallowed tenderness. It's one the film's great skills, these kids, and adult-kids, are people we care about all the way down to the big hearts bursting in their yellow clad chests. Ritchie has won us over, and by the final show-down with the weasely Yankees, the message is clear. We'll allow poet and philosopher Tanner Boyle to elucidate: 'Hey Yankees… you can take your apology and your trophy and shove 'em straight up your ass!' ★★★★ **IN**

BAD NEWS BEARS (2005)

Starring: *Billy Bob Thornton (Morris Buttermaker), Greg Kinnear (Roy Bullock), Marcia Gay Harden (Liz Whitewood), Sammi Kane Kraft (Amanda Whurlitzer), Ridge Canipe (Toby Whitewood)*
Director: *Richard Linklater*
Screenwriters: *Bill Lancaster, Glenn Ficarra, John Requa, based on the 1976 screenplay by Bill Lancaster*
12A/113 mins/Comedy/Sports/USA

New year, new Little League and, thanks to some polite but firm bribery, a lawyer mom has blagged her son's inept baseball team a supposed trophy in the form of former pro and permanent drunk Morris Buttermaker. Can he slap his brats into shape to beat rivals The Yankees, or will the ankle-biter encounter prove too much?

If Tim Burton's *Planet Of The Apes* tried to avoid the remake tag by pompously referring to itself as a 'reimagining', what to call a movie so twinned to its source you're left ducking the sparks of déjà vu? If you're looking for a pat tag for Richard Linklater's film, 'action replay' fills the gap.

With its anti-PC buffoonery, the 1976 *Bad News Bears* provided the template for every renegade-team sports movie since, and it's also given *Bad Santa* scriptwriters Glenn Ficarra and John Requa an easy life: structure, characters, even score have all been ported over. Question is, if it ain't broke…?

Luckily, Bears' predictability works in its favour. From training montage to loser salvation, this is unapologetic comfort viewing. On a gags-to-laughs ratio, it's certainly the comedy to beat this season, thanks mostly to Billy Bob Thornton's twinkly, ragged Buttermaker. Still, for a movie so up on its genre smarts, it's odd Linklater should pitch a dipper for the climax, with the final game way too laidback to truly excite. As such, you leave your seat with a microwaved glow, not the atomic high you think you're owed. ★★★ **SC**

BAD SANTA (2003)

Starring: *Billy Bob Thornton (Willie), Tony Cox (Marcus), Brett Kelly (The Kid), Lauren Graham (Sue), Bernie Mac (Gin), John Ritter (Bob Chipeska), Cloris Leachman (Grandma)*
Director: *Terry Zwigoff*
Screenwriters: *Glenn Ficarra, John Requa*
15/91 mins./98 mins. (director's cut)/Comedy/Crime/USA/Germany

Alcoholic safe-breaker Willie uses his cover as a department store Santa to rob the very same stores. But his living is thrown into jeopardy by a corrupt shop detective and a dimwitted small boy.

Developed from an original idea from the Coen brothers, *Bad Santa* is a seasonal confection of vomit, piss, crime, snot, suicide, alcoholism and vigorous anal sex. Perfect counter-programming, then, against the saccharine bilge usually secreted by studios at Christmas and a positive tonic for those of us who see this time of year as a toxic chore rather than a period imbued with 'Yuletide enchantment'.

Essentially, this is a one-joke movie: Santa is not an avuncular, present-delivering grandfather figure, but a dyspeptic misanthrope who we first meet vomiting against an alley wall, and who pursues his real calling as a safe-breaker aided by an only slightly less angry dwarf (brilliantly played by Tony Cox, who's adorned with a Caucasian pair of elf-ears; a sly comment, presumably, on the institutional racism rampant at the North Pole). But the joke is a good one and, more importantly, is delivered by Billy Bob Thornton, one of modern cinema's natural comic actors, while the often literally scatological dialogue is inventive and varied enough to help. On one occasion, for example, Santa listens to a child's Christmas wish before advising him, 'Why don't you shit in one hand and wish in the other, see which fills up first?'

Surprisingly, there's something reminiscent of the Ealing comedies about *Bad Santa*. Like the best Ealings, its tale of cynical criminality terminates a (sort of) moral point. And it's here that Zwigoff pulls off a minor miracle – Santa's growing relationship with The Kid, a snot-faced tweenie with weight issues and limited intelligence, should be the moment that the movie caves in to the truly vulgar sentimentality against which it apparently stood. Instead, *Bad Santa*'s unorthodox sweetness creeps up on you unannounced.

It wafts you out of the cinema grinning not only at lines such as, 'You're not going to shit right for a week,' delivered by Father Christmas during a particularly exhausting bout of bottom sex with a lady in a changing room, but because Zwigoff has actually managed to slip you a Mickey of that Christmas spirit while you weren't looking. Bastard. ★★★★ **AS**

BAD TASTE (1987)

Starring: *Peter Jackson (Derek/Robert), Terry Potter (Ozzy), Pete O'Herne (Barry), Craig Smith (Giles), Mike Minett (Frank), Doug Wren (Lord Crumb)*
Director: *Peter Jackson*
Screenwriters: *Peter Jackson, Tony Hiles, Ken Hammon*
18/91 mins./Comedy/Sci-fi/Horror/New Zealand

When aliens arrive in a remote corner of New Zealand, with the sole intent of turning humans into hamburgers for their fast food joint, Crumb's Crunchy Delights, the authorities send the 'boys' to investigate and hopefully rescue Giles, a local door-to-door charity collector taken captive by the aliens.

Now venerated as being the debut of *Lord Of The Rings* director Peter Jackson, this scuzzbucket splatter movie is unlikely to win anyone over on production values – there aren't any – or plot logic – there isn't any – but it just might with its sicko, genre-bending humour and gleeful awareness of its own nuttiness. Jackson was 25 when he made it, at the same age Orson Welles made *Citizen Kane*, comparisons tend to blur a bit after that. It took the Kiwi four years to complete, cost him $150,000 and he stars, directs, produces, writes, shoots and most likely did the on-set catering to boot. Hence this film will tell you a whole lot more about the filmmaker than his magnificent fantasy trilogy.

To start with he's got a strange sense of humour, and a true love of horror's sticker confines. The film is an anarchic mess of a story, intent on jumping to the gloopy effect sequences as quickly as possible. A staccato rhythm rather dictated by the wind-up camera they were using unable to film for more than 30 seconds at a time. The rubbery aliens, disguised as humans for much of the film, are desperate for human flesh, especially the 'chunky bits' and at one particularly gruesome juncture a ravenous invader cracks open a human skull and eats the brains with a spoon. A crackpot scenario, that wobbles its way to the grand finale when a town house launches into space.

The acting is desultory, dictated by the collection of Jackson's friends and compatriots being totally untrained. The director himself crops up in twin roles of alien and human. Especially as 'Derek', he has a rollicking time staggering about the rough seaside locations, an alien who keeps reinserting an errant slab of brain. Gandalf was a long way off, but the formative talent is on show if you look closely, there is a crude sense of wonder, a richness of experimenting with tricky effects and flamboyant camera angles, and an engaging sense of having a really great time just making a movie. Welles would have loved it. ★★★ **IN**

BAD TIMING (1980)

Starring: *Art Garfunkel (Alex Linden), Theresa Russell (Milena Flaherty), Harvey Keitel (Inspector Netusil), Denholm Elliott (Stefan Vognic)*
Director: *Nicolas Roeg*
Screenwriter: *Yale Udoff*
18/123 mins./Drama/USA

In Vienna, Milena is admitted to hospital after a suicide attempt. While doctors try to save her life, a police inspector tries to find out what happened between Milena and her lover, psychologist Alex, during an unaccounted-for period of time. Alex remembers his relationship with the girl, eventually confronting his own criminal actions.

Also known as *Bad Timing: A Sensual Obsession*, this mosaic-like mystery (it's almost like a Burroughsian cut-up of a *Columbo* episode) intercuts the investigation of the circumstances surrounding the suicide attempt of good-time girl Theresa Russell and her earlier, troubled relationship with withdrawn American psychology lecturer Art Garfunkel.

One of a remarkable run of time-bending exercises conducted by director Nicolas Roeg between *Performance* and *Eureka*, this tackles the whodunit and continental romance genres as unconventionally and savagely as his earlier films dealt with coming of age drama (*Walkabout*), the ghost story (*Don't Look Now*) and science fiction (*The Man Who Fell To Earth*). Hallucinatory, kaleidoscopic flashes follow the growth and disintegration of the central affair while unconventionally obsessive Viennese policeman Keitel tries to piece together a puzzle that leads to a truly shocking revelation of what these people have done to each other.

Everything in the film has the status of a clue (a picture of a maze, significant books, snippets of music), but the disturbing parallels between Keitel and Garfunkel (who specialises in the study of curiosity) lead the audience finally to sympathise with Russell's scribbled plea 'I wish you'd know me less and love me more'. As he showed with Mick Jagger and David Bowie, Roeg can get amazing work from pop singers you'd think couldn't act, making Garfunkel interestingly withdrawn, quizzical and edgy – but he also draws a career-best performance from the young Russell as the captivating but maddening Milena. ★★★★★ **KN**

BADLANDS (1974)

Starring: *Martin Sheen (Kit), Sissy Spacek (Holly), Warren Oates (Father), Ramon Bieri (Cato), Alan Vint (Deputy), Gary Littlejohn (Sheriff)*
Director: *Terrence Malick*
Screenwriter: *Terrence Malick*
18/94 mins./Crime/Drama/USA

Dramatisation of the Starkweather-Fugate killing spree of the 1950s, which left a trail of bodies throughout the Dakota badlands.

At the heart of Terrence Malick's astonishing debut – a fictionalised account of Charles Starkweather's 1950s killing spree – is a trio of paradoxes.

The film is a meditation on the banality of evil, but features an incredibly handsome and charismatic protagonist in Martin Sheen's psychotically self-deluded garbage man, Kit.

His relationship with lonely schoolgirl Holly (Sissy Spacek) is depicted as disturbing and mutually destructive, yet granted genuinely romantic interludes – including a moonlight smooch to the sound of Nat King Cole.

And the natural world – typically for Malick – is painted as a thing of idyllic beauty, yet constantly corrupted with stark images of dead animals, fallen trees and, of course, the bullet-riddled bodies of Kit's victims.

Such confident complexity is beyond the reach of lesser movies – the superficially similar *Bonnie And Clyde* feels, well, superficial in comparison. For all the heat generated by that film's blood-spattered shootouts, its stylised brutality pales next to the sudden bouts of violence which occur whenever Kit is backed into a corner.

His sense of Southern good manners – calling his victims 'Sir', asking humbly, 'Suppose I shot you, how'd that be?' – makes the crimes all the more chilling.

Both central performances are amazing, but only Spacek went on to become one of the most in-demand stars of the 70s. *Apocalypse Now* aside, Sheen had to wait until becoming a middle-aged character actor before roles worthy of his talent came along. Observant fans of *The West Wing*, however, may notice that Kit snaps on his denim jacket in the same over-the-shoulder, both-arms-at-once way in which President Bartlet dons a tux. ★★★★★ **RF**

BAISE-MOI (2000)

Starring: *Karen Lancaume as Karen Bach (Nadine), Raffaela Anderson (Manu), Céline Beugnot (Blonde at Billiards), Adama Niane (Boy at Billiards)*
Director: *Virginie Despentes, Coralie*
Screenwriters: *Coralie, Virginie Despentes, from the novel by Despentes*
18/77 mins./Adult/Drama/Thriller/France

A couple of murderous outsiders hook up on a killing spree. Before the final credits roll, they've done away with a woman at a cash till, various blokes they bed, and anyone who happens to get in their way.

When asked what he was rebelling against in *The Wild One* (1954), Brando answered, 'What've you got?' Almost 50 years on, the theme of teenagers kicking against the system remains as potent as ever. But unless there's a motive for the mayhem, it simply becomes mindless – and this is pretty much the problem with *Baise-Moi*.

'Rape Me', 'Screw Me' and 'Fuck Me' have all been suggested as English translations of the title, but none of them carries the nihilistic anger of the original. This is primarily a film about fury. Yet its sheer amorality and reckless exploitation corrupts its message by misdirecting the focus. It was pulled from French cinema screens within just three days of its release after protests were made about its graphic depiction of sex and violence. In their wisdom, the censors here have removed an explicit seven-second shot from the rape sequence. But, that part aside, they have allowed the film to be released in its grungy, sordid, digital-videoed entirety, presumably with the thinking that potential psychos are allergic to subtitles.

The mock-scandalised media hungrily feasted upon the film's content and the fact that it was written and directed by two women (indeed, it's based on ex-prostitute Despentes' bestselling novel) and features a couple of porn stars. However, this emphasis on the gyrating and bloodletting allows the filmmakers to escape without explaining their motives. Had this Gallic *Thelma And Louise* been out for revenge against men following their rape, there would have been a purpose to their slaughter. But they don't just kill men, nor do they only kill men who've bedded them. So what is Despentes and Trinh Thi's agenda? Apparently, the impetus behind this 'feminist warrior vision' was to be 'so in your face that we will end up on your mind'. So now you know. ★★ AM

BAMBI (1942)

Starring: *the voices of: Bobby Stewart (Bambi), Peter Behn (Thumper), Paula Winslowe (Bambi's Mother), Stan Alexander (Flower), Cammie King (Faline)*
Director: *David D. Hand*
Screenwriters: *Perce Pearce, Larry Morey, based on a story by Felix Salten*
U/70 mins./Animated/Family/USA

A young fawn named Bambi makes friends with a gap-toothed bunny and a coy skunk, loses his mother and finally grows to maturity.

To say that *Bambi* is about frolicking woodland animals is like saying *The Lord Of The Rings* is about little men blowing smoke and combing their hairy feet. There are the cute bits everyone knows; baby Bambi stuck on a fallen tree-trunk (actually one of the test animations that convinced Walt to make the film) and the seduction of Thumper by a girl bunny, his runaway libido physically displaced to one helplessly peddling paw. Yet Disney's film uses these cuddly moments as grounding for a natural-world opus that, in its own way, is almost as ambitious as Peter Jackson's Middle-earth epic.

Walt was suspicious of artiness – 'We're selling corn and I like corn,' he once said – but he was devoted to pushing into new territories. *Fantasia* had presented full-blown diabolism with the topless witches and monster devil of the Night On Bald Mountain segment. *Bambi*, meanwhile, returned to the traditional animal cartoon and twisted it into negative space.

The backgrounds took their lead from Tyrus Wong, a lowly Chinese animator whose sketches encouraged other artists to soften and blur the branches and grasses of Bambi's world, putting the focus squarely on the beautifully drawn animals (just watch Thumper's little-boy mannerisms). Impressionism blends with expressionism in stunning bursts of colour. The forest fire is a shivering yellow painting; the screen brightens to a red-orange as the deer herd flees man; Bambi's fight with a rival stag is all struggling silhouettes, livid golds and icy blues.

The Lion King, Disney's attempt to emulate *Bambi* 50 years on, can't reach such highs. In fact, its outgoing wonder has been better captured in Brad Bird's *The Iron Giant* (which also has a key scene with a deer) and Hayao Miyazaki's *My Neighbour Totoro*, a cartoon that goes for exquisite detail rather than Bambi's rarefied impressionism.

Essentially Bambi is a one-off, something the studio seems to have forgotten with plugs for a bland-looking video sequel on the otherwise excellent Collector's Edition DVD. It underlines how much Disney has lost since its glorious best-and-worst of times, six decades ago.

After all, this is a Disney cartoon where scene flows to scene with an absolute simplicity, where the terrifying villain never appears, and where the death of Bambi's mother – undoubtedly one of the most traumatic in film history – is restricted to a gunshot, the bleakest of snowscapes and a heartbreaking tear. That Walt can cut from this straight to the silliest of spring-themed symphonies (with twittering bluebirds modelled on a 1933 Disney short, *Birds In The Spring*) shows his mastery of a medium that can turn on a dime in a way unimaginable in live-action.

We laugh and we grieve, but mostly we marvel, at Bambi's introduction to a little April shower, to the miracles of snow and ice, and to the magnificent herd that represents the mystery of adulthood, bounding over Bambi's head with the clash of cymbals. Disney's point, admirably unspoken but transparent to a child, is that this is all of a piece. ★★★★★ AO

BANANAS (1971)

Starring: *Woody Allen (Fielding Melish), Louise Lasser (Nancy), Carlos Montalban (Gen. Vargas), Natividad Abascal (Yolanda), Jacobo Morales (Esposito)*
Director: *Woody Allen*
Screenwriters: *Woody Allen, Mickey Rose*
15/82 mins./Comedy/USA

In a bid to impress an intense activist named Nancy, gadget-tester Fielding Mellish fakes a fascination with Third World politics and finds himself enmeshed in the civil disturbances splintering the South American republic of San Marcos.

Loosely based on Richard Powell's novel *Don Quixote USA* and originally entitled *El Weirdo*, Woody Allen's second outing as writer-director-star is an erratic concoction that overcomes its lack of continuity and coherence to pack in satirical, surreal and slapstick gags at a frantic pace. The first cut ran for two hours, but Ralph Rosenblum persuaded Allen to excise some 37 minutes of footage (with the casualties including an attack on the guerillas' camp by a rhumba band and a parody of Bob Hope entertaining the troops) and the celerity and brevity go some way to disguising the mediocrity of some of the material.

Opening and closing with sequences in which sportscaster Howard Cosell commentates upon the assassination of the President of San Marcos and the consummation of Fielding Mellish and Nancy's marriage, this is a film about America's tendency to trivialise everything for mass consumption, whether it's the advertising of cigarettes or the reporting of a major political story.

It's also a satire about dissemblance in a society in which nothing lives up to expectation and no one fulfils their promises. Like the Execusisor machine, revolution seems to offer an easy solution to the problems of a developing country, but President Vargas's pledge to reform simply results in the imposition of twice-hourly underwear changes and Swedish as the national language. Only in such a cockamamie world could a man in a fake Castro beard (who couldn't even successfully buy a porn mag, let alone deter subway muggers back in New York) become an icon.

Although there are fine homages to Chaplin, Buster Keaton, Eisenstein and Harold Lloyd here, this is a scattershot offering full of apolitical mockery. Yet, Allen frequently patronises Latin America and not even the scathing assaults on the State Department quite atone for his careless choice of clichés and caricatures. ★★★ DP

BANDE A PART (1964)

Starring: *Anna Karina (Odile), Daniel Girard (English Teacher), Louisa Colpeyn (Madame Victoria), Chantal Darget (Arthur's Aunt), Sami Frey (Franz), Jean-Luc Godard (The narrator)*
Director: *Jean-Luc Godard*
Screenwriter: *Jean-Luc Godard, based on the novel* Fool's Gold *by Dolores Hitchens*
15/97 mins./Crime/Drama/France

Bored with life and besotted with pulp culture, English language students Arthur and Franz compete for the affections of Odile, a naive classmate who has tipped them off about a stash of cash at her aunt's suburban home.

Jean-Luc Godard's seventh feature fame rests largely in prompting Tarantino to call his production company Band Apart. But this pastiche of the Hollywood crime thriller is as entertaining as it's inventive and, while not a patch on François Truffaut's *Shoot The Piano Player*, it is one of the most fascinating films of the late-New Wave.

Loosely based on Dolores and Bert Hitchens' pulp novel, *Fool's Gold*, this is far from a standard adaptation. Godard is more interested in such intangibles as youth, sexual attraction, boredom, the Americanisation of France and the unique atmosphere of Paris to bother with trivialities like narrative.

But his main preoccupation is the untapped potential of cinema. All the stylistic gimmickry that characterised the Nouvelle Vague is present and correct. But rather than just extolling the virtues of film, he actively denounces its artistic cousins, which, while visually striking, lack cinema's energy and freedom. It's all about action and its presentation in a vibrant and original way.

Godard is so smitten with all things cinematic that he constantly draws your attention to them. In amidst the countless references to the Hollywood B movie, he toys with narrative conventions (inserting such asides as the café dance sequence), technology (removing background sound during the minute's silence), screen grammar (cutting according to the rhythms of Michel Legrand's score rather than the usual dramatic cues) and the proscenium illusion (using the film's noir voiceover to announce details of a colour '[Cinema]scope sequel'). Ultimately, this is Godard-lite. But it still contains more ideas than most directors can summon in a lifetime. ★★★★ **DP**

⑩ BANDITS (2001)

Starring: *Bruce Willis (Joe Blake), Billy Bob Thornton (Terry Lee Collins), Cate Blanchett (Kate Wheeler), Troy Garity (Harvey Pollard)*
Director: *Barry Levinson*
Screenwriter: *Harley Peyton*
12/123 mins./Comedy/Crime/Drama/Romance/USA

After a daring jailbreak, bank robbers Joe and Terry embark on a crime spree. They smoothly empty a bank vault, but the arrival of housewife Kate to the crew threatens to split them apart.

There's something reassuringly reliable about Barry Levinson's movies. He's the cinematic equivalent of a mid-range Volvo. You're not going to have a life-changing experience, but neither are you likely to have to call Watchdog. *Bandits* is no exception to the 'generally quite good' rule, finessing its way slickly through a well-built script and showcasing two reasonably entertaining performances and one standout one.

The central appeal of the movie are Willis and Thornton who, as a comedy duo, display the ease and familiarity of Butch and Sundance. They're served by a screenplay which delivers enough honed repartee to keep at bay the potentially unpleasant fact that these two make their living terrorising innocent people. Cate Blanchett is serviceable as the Thelma-esque frustrated housewife with a liking for power ballads who hooks up with the boys. But it's Thornton who, as is increasingly the case, is the real crowd-pleaser – a hypochondriac host of tics, twitches and dubious medical insight who snaffles the best lines with all the expertise of a high street pickpocket.

The good generally outweighs those parts that lack imagination. A fantastic jailbreak in a cement mixer (complete with an ingenious and witty helicopter shot of the massive truck rumbling through suburban back gardens) makes up for a pretty redundant 'Real Crime TV' framing device. Meanwhile, the eclectic soundtrack and Dante Spinotti's high-gloss cinematography covers over a rather obvious plot twist. There's also the slight problem that the heists themselves aren't quite as exciting as they should be, and the ménage à trois doesn't resolve itself in a particularly satisfying, or credible, way.

But all this is made up for by the general bonhomie and an array of the most entertainingly unpleasant hairpieces to appear on the big screen since Burt Reynolds' career imploded. ★★★★ **RF**

⑩ BARBARELLA (1967)

Starring: *Jane Fonda (Barbarella), John Phillip Law (Pygar), Anita Pallenberg (The Great Tyrant), David Hemmings (Dildano), Milo O'Shea (Concierge/Duran Duran), Marcel Marceau (Professor Ping), Claude Dauphin (President of Earth), Veronique Vendell (Captain Moon), Sierge Marquand (Captain Sun)*
Director: *Roger Vadim*
Screenwriters: *Claude Brule, Terry Southern, Roger Vadim, Vittorio Bonicelle, Clement Biddle Wood, Brian Degas, Tudor Gates, from the comic by Jean-Claude Forest*
15/98 mins./Adventure/Sci-fi/Fantasy/France/Italy

In the year 400000 Barberella is called upon to save the earth from warmongering scientist Duran Duran.

This is the first of three colourful, sexy, trivial, endearing Dino De Laurentiis productions adapted from popular comic strips – the others being Mario Bava's superthief epic *Diabolik* (1968) and Mike Hodges' delirious remake of *Flash Gordon* (1980). All these films are literally episodic, preserving the plot lurches of a medium given to introducing new characters and settings every week, and have a bubbly, pop-art sensibility that spends more time on the art direction, the costuming and the psychedelic music track than the plot (though it took seven credited writers to script Barbarella, including Terry Southern). Set beside *Barbarella*, the staid *2001: A Space Odyssey* and the sexless *Star Wars* seem pretty stuffy; actually, when Jane Fonda's orgasm blows all the fuses of an 'excessive pleasure machine,' Barbarella makes Flash Gordon seem pretty stuffy.

Barbarella is cheerfully catch-all in its mix of notional sci-fi elements (spaceships, other planets, super-weapons) with even more fantastical fairytale gambits (angels, suits of living leather, invisible keys) and bits of business taken from genres as far afield as the swashbuckler, the avant garde art movie ('psychedelic' and decadent imagery courtesy of Fellini and Godard) and even the porno film (Fonda does a zero-g strip under the credits and has bizarre sex with most of the male characters). Jean-Claude Forest's original comic strip, to which the multi-authored film is surprisingly faithful, was a witty, teasing homage to Alex Toth's famous Flash Gordon strips, replacing the iron-jawed space pilot Flash with a blonde 'five star double-rated astro-navigatrix.' The Frenchman Forest based his heroine on the cinema's reigning sex kitten, Brigitte Bardot. De Laurentiis signed up Bardot's ex-husband/sometime Svengali to direct his expensive Barbarella, and he brought along his current wife as star. In 1967, Jane Fonda was at the height of her adorability, well before her political commitments of the 70s and work-out obsessions of the 80s. In America, she had not overcome the stigma of being the daughter of screen legend Henry and had endured a series of fluffy co-ed roles before having a hit and gaining a sexy image in amazingly tight jeans as the wholesome outlaw heroine *Cat Ballou*. She brings to Barbarella a strange, saluting squareness that is as big-sisterly as it is sirenlike ('Oh, how darling', she exclaims over cute children, nice dollies or pretty little birds – all of which then try to kill her), but she wears (and unwears) a succession of truly amazing fashion creations with all the confidence of a generation that thought sex was, above all, fun. Over 30 years on, there is still an irresistible sexiness to Barbarella's post-coital langours, as she sings her own theme song ('Barbarella, Psychedelia!') while stroking her face with an angel-feather plucked during passion.

The plot, which everyone treats as a joke ('a good many dramatic situations begin with screaming'), has Earth girl Barbarella despatched to Tau Ceti in search of missing scientist Duran Duran (yes, that's where those 80s gits got their name from) and his deadly 'positronic ray' ('Why would anybody want to invent a weapon?'). Earth has been civilised and harmonious for centuries, but Tau Ceti exists 'in a primitive state of neurotic insensitivity' and the naïve heroine runs into a succession of oddballs who want to kill her or have sex with her or both. Among the Tau Cetians we meet are a horde of appealing but murderous feral children (their steel-mouthed dolls nibble Barbarella's thighs), the hairy-chested 'Catchman' Mark Hand (Ugo

Tognazzi, who introduces Barbarella to old-fashioned physical sex and makes a notable convert), underground revolutionaries Professor Ping and Dildano (David Hemmings, who has hand-touching new-fashioned mental sex with our girl), the concierge (Milo O'Shea, who plays a sonata for 'Executioner And Various Young Women' with Barbarella and the excessive pleasure machine), Pygar the blind angel (John Phillip Law, doing for female audiences what Jane Fonda did for the men) and the svelte Great Tyrant Of Sogo (Anita Pallenberg of *Performance* fame, dubbed with the deeply sexy croak of Joan Greenwood).

Rather like the central character of a Fellini movie (De Laurentiis produced *Nights Of Cabiria* and *La Strada*), Barbarella's journey brings her to a big city which turns out to be hideously decadent underneath its attractive bustle. Sogo, dedicated to evil pleasures, is built on top of a living lake called the Matmoss that feeds off the citizens' rottenness, as represented by such depraved pleasures as ladies lolling about smoking 'essence of man' from a giant bong in which a man is drowning, and the crucifixion of the innocent angel. The finale has everything blow up as the Matmoss overwhlems Sogo, the revolutionaries are callously zapped into nowhere by the usurping concierge (who turns out to be the fugitive Duran Duran) and only Barbarella's innocence protects her from the evil goo, which makes a bubble in itself to avoid touching her. Finally, Pygar saves both Barbarella and the wicked queen, proclaiming quite reasonably that an angel has no memory. ★★★★ **KN**

BARBERSHOP (2002)

Starring: *Ice Cube (Calvin Palmer), Anthony Anderson (J.D.), Cedric The Entertainer (Eddie), Sean Patrick Thomas (Jimmy James), Eve (Terri Jones), Troy Garity (Issack Rosenberg)*
Director: *Tim Story*
Screenwriters: *Mark Brown, Don D. Scott, Marshall Todd*
12A/102 mins./Comedy/Drama/USA

Calvin Palmer has inherited his father's barbershop, the social centre of his Chicago neighbourhood. But when he is offered a deal by the local hustler, who has diabolical plans for the place, he is tempted to betray his friends and close down the shop for good.

Barbershops in the UK are more often associated with Brylcreem and lengthy soliloquies on the state of the Premiership than raucous laughter and good times. That's apparently not the case in the Chicago projects – at least, according to this rambling comedy, in which Calvin must decide whether to put his community first, or follow his dreams and sell the shop that provides his neighbours with somewhere to hang out.

Cube is as likeable as ever, and the magnificently monikered Cedric The Entertainer is delightful as a particularly eccentric barber. But the script really should have been given a trim, as it tries to cram in so many characters that few are given the time and space to develop. It is also hampered by a woeful subplot, involving two inept crooks trying to break into a stolen ATM, that makes *Home Alone 2* seem like a work of high art. ★★ **RW**

BARCELONA (1994)

Starring: *Taylor Nichols (Ted Boynton), Chris Eigeman (Fred Mason), Tushka Bergen (Montserrat), Mira Sorvino (Marta Ferrer), Pep Munne (Ramon)*
Director: *Whit Stillman*
Screenwriter: *Whit Stillman*
12/101 mins./Comedy/Romance/Political/USA

Two very different cousins try to find true love in Barcelona, but find their preconceptions of the 'ideal woman' sorely tested.

Whit Stillman's debut film *Metropolitan* showed such a distinctive vision and possessed such an offbeat feel that it seemed highly probable that he might only have one film in him.

But not only does this second effort carry over a couple of that film's stars and much of its unique tone, it progresses from the achievements of *Metropolitan* by being more than just a re-run of its WASPish riffs that worked so well.

Living in the eponymous city in the 'last decade of the Cold War', Ted, sales manager at an American Corporation, searches for romantic and spiritual fulfilment, hung up on the idea that he should date only homely girls because beauty is an illusion. His cousin, the shallower Fred, is a junior Naval officer with a vague diplomatic function, bristling at the anti-Americanism of many Spaniards and only interested in beautiful girls. Ted's philosophy is severely strained when he falls in love with Montserrat, an exceptionally beautiful girl. Romantic and political complications ensue, and an underlying friction exists between the cousins – which has its roots in childhood – surfaces.

Stillman waxes romantic as he chronicles the foibles and lifestyles of well-meaning, well-born, slightly intellectual, wealthy folk. And while there is something of Woody Allen in the endless philosophising over matters of the heart, Stillman is a more genuinely passionate filmmaker.

With wry performances from all concerned, including a baffling gaggle of Spanish girls deliciously showing up the adsurdities of the Yanks, this may not be quite as fresh as *Metropolitan*, but it's a thoroughly charming, subtly serious and sneakily captivating movie. ★★★★ **KN**

BARRY LYNDON (1975)

Starring: *Ryan O'Neal (Barry Lyndon), Marisa Berenson (Lady Lyndon), Patrick Magee (Chevalier de Balibari), Hardy Kruger (Captain Potzdorf), Steven Berkoff (Lord Ludd), Gay Hamilton (Nora), Leonard Rossiter (Captain Quinn)*
Director: *Stanley Kubrick*
Screenwriter: *Stanley Kubrick, based on the novel by William Makepeace Thackeray*
PG/184 mins./Historical Drama/UK

Awards: *Academy Awards – Best Art Direction, Best Cinematography, Best Costume Design, Best Score, BAFTA – Best Director, Best Cinematography.*

A young Irish rogue Redmond Barry, a relentless social climber determined to join the aristocracy, joins the British army. Over 25 years, he goes from spy to con-artist to snaring a rich widow, Lady Lyndon, and finally taking his place at the top table. But with it come the seeds of his downfall.

Shot over two years with the kind of obsessive detail only Stanley Kubrick could muster up from his typically unbreakable research, this costume drama is so stately it appears to be operating under a spell.

The great director was adapting William Thackeray's fairly disregarded debut novel, a picaresque centring on a selfish prig who saunters through 19th century European history, but, as ever, his focus is the ritualised behaviours that dehumanise us and push us toward solitude. Indeed, the book is filleted to a spare series of events, then spread over three sumptuous hours of decoration and absolute poise. Reputedly there is one line in his script that translated to ten minutes of screen time.

Thus his actors become pieces in a chess game, beautiful philosophical constructs to be moved hither and thither, more automatons than humans. Still, there's no doubting the quality of Kubrick's eyes, Ryan O'Neal and former model Marisa Berenson were technically the most beautiful people on the planet at the time. Their performances feel more like echoes.

Their tableau, haunted by the lush paintings of Constable and Watteau, is so richly decorated it almost becomes static. It's a world that functions almost subliminally as if you are absorbing the images rather than simply seeing them. Kubrick borrowed a satellite camera from NASA, possessing the world's largest aperture, to capture the natural light of a thousand candles. With barely perceptible zooms it takes in this place of order and design, a history, for all its duels, betrayals, and loveless manipulations, built on conformity. The individual is a sham, a selfish mask, who will be engulfed by the system.

It is also a film so divorced from easy emotion, it is hard to measure on any kind of entertainment scale. This may be the landscape of the swashbuckler, but it is bathed in deep melancholy. The result is pure art, that all but locks the watcher out. ★★★★ IN

BARTON FINK (1991)

Starring: *John Turturro (Barton Fink), John Goodman (Charlie Meadows), Judy Davis (Audrey Taylor), Michael Lerner (Jack Lipnick), John Mahoney (W.P. Mayhew), Tony Shalhoub (Ben Geiser)*
Director: *Joel Coen*
Screenwriters: *Ethan Coen, Joel Coen*
15/116 mins./Comedy/Drama/USA

An idealistic New York playwright soon sells out his ideals when he is enticed to Hollywood to write screenplays for movies. However, when he develops writers' block, his world becomes more sinister . . .

The brilliant John Turturro is, of course, the Barton of the title, a self-pitying, self-absorbed, self-conscious 1940s playwright whose patronising homilies to The Common Man have done him proud in New York's theatrical circles, and who is now in being feted by Hollywood.

Once he's effortlessly sold out his 'art' to take a contract at Capitol Pictures, however, he finds himself holed up in a very bizarre hotel with John Goodman for a neighbour and a blank piece of paper for company. As he desperately tries to get going on the B-picture wrestling opus he's been commissioned to write ('It's a wrestling picture – whaddya want, a road map?'), Barton's world gradually closes in, with everything becoming not what it seemed to be – from whether Goodman is who he says he is, to whether Barton's novelist hero actually writes his own books.

Finally, in the utterly Coen-esque and violently compelling denoument, nothing, of course, is neatly resolved. Apart from the usual enticements you'd expect from Joel and Ethan Coen – performances to knock your block off from Turturro, Goodman, Lerner as the horrendous studio chief and Judy Davis as the love interest; visual flourishes aplenty; a literate, witty screenplay – what we have here is a subtle assault on the arrogant obsessions of certain kinds of writers.

Unwilling to really listen to the 'common man' he professes to champion, pathetically convinced of his own talent, Barton Fink is too busy making up stories to actually live any. Barton Fink is the ultimate in intellectual ballast, and with him the Coens have created a genuinely believable and multi-faceted character, while giving us a thumping good story that never lets up in its humour, pathos and intrigue ★★★★ PT

BASEKETBALL (1998)

Starring: *Trey Parker (Joseph Cooper), Matt Stone (Doug Remer), Robert Vaughn (Baxter Cain), Ernest Borgnine (Theodore Denslow), Dian Bachar (Kenny 'Squeak' Scolari), Yasmine Bleeth (Jenna Reed), Jenny McCarthy (Yvette Denslow)*
Director: *David Zucker*
Screenwriters: *David Zucker, Robert LoCash, Jeff Wright, Lewis Friedman*
15/95 mins./Comedy/Sports/USA

Two nerds invent a new sport that's a cross between baseball and basketball which suddenly takes off in America in a big way.

Battered in the sick flick stakes by *There's Something About Mary* during the 1998 US Summer season, *BASEketball* never obtained a cinema release in the UK. Which is a crying shame, as its high gag quotient would have thrived in a packed multiplex auditorium: mixing the velocity and lunacy of the *Naked Gun* series (step forward director Zucker) with the sickness and stupidity of *South Park* (step forward the stars Parker and Stone), and adding an element of satire that is absent from both *BASEketball* has more than enough laughs to make it top notch Friday night fodder.

Perhaps one of the reasons the movie tanked so badly in the States – thus condemning it to the DVD shelves here – is that it takes the piss out of so much that America holds dear. As nerds 'Coop' and Remer invent a hybrid of baseball and basketball that emerges out of the suburban driveways to sweep the nation, we are treated to a full-on lampooning of US sports culture encompassing team names (the New Jersey Informants, the LA riots), corporate sponsorship, the complex rules and statistics-obsessed commentary, with a pointed intelligence that belies the film's dumbass appearance. The mickey taking reaches its zenith with the inspired notion of 'psyche outs' in which players put off their opponents by any means necessary – be it sleeping-with-your-dead-mother insults or Stone sipping the fat from Marlon Brando's liposuction with a straw – an idea so perfect it is amazing it hasn't found its way into real sport.

Weaved around BASEketball set-pieces, there are subplots involving Stone and Parker trying to bed Yasmine Bleeth's charity worker, and rival team owner Robert Vaughn's plan to corrupt the homespun sport into something more lucrative. But these rarely provide a hiatus in the laughs, which practically cover every comedy base; gross out (Kremer licking an old biddy's dildo), slapstick (a blind kid gets a ball straight in the mush), sight gags (an American football team celebrates a touchdown by breaking into Riverdance), and media skits (look out for the hilarious TV show *Road Kill – Caught On Tape*, in which cuddily animals are mowed down by an out of control car).

Of course, some of it misses by a mile – Ernest Borgnine singing 'I'm Too Sexy' (don't ask), anything featuring McCarthy as Borgnine's money grabbing wife – but there's always a gag that lands soon after. Out of the central twosome, Parker's geniality is far more appealing than Stone's dudedom, yet the movie is stolen by Dian Bachar as Squeak, the duo's pint-sized punchbag. All in all, a slam dunk. Or is that a home dunk? ★★★★ IF

BASIC (2003)

Starring: *John Travolta (Hardy), Connie Nielsen (Osborne), Samuel L. Jackson (West), Timothy Daly (Styles), Giovanni Ribisi (Kendall), Taye Diggs (Pike), Harry Connick Jr (Vilmer), Margaret Travolta (Nurse #1)*
Director: *John McTiernan*
Screenwriter: *James Vanderbilt*
15/98 mins./Thriller/Drama/Mystery/USA

While out on a training exercise, three American Rangers, including their much hated sergeant, are killed in a mysterious shooting incident. Investigator Tom Hardy is called in to interview the survivors, and begins to realise that things are not as they seem.

Oh, as someone once wrote, how the mighty have fallen. If, a decade or so ago, you had informed action fans that John McTiernan – creator of two of the best octane-delivery systems of all time in *Predator* and *Die Hard* – would have turned out not just two bad films in a row, but two films so noxiously awful that the McTiernan brand would be forever soiled, we'd have laughed you out of the multiplex.

But McTiernan has indeed now scored a double whammy of hooey. While the execrable *Rollerball* may perhaps have been forgiven as an aberration, *Basic* seals the deal. McTiernan has lost it – big time.

Essentially Kurosawa's *Rashomon* as reimagined by cretins, *Basic* plays on the same event as remembered and re-remembered by different characters, all of whom seem to have something to hide. Sadly, it's pretty much impossible to tell the scenarios apart through the cacophonous sound mix, which obscures (probably thankfully) much of the dialogue. And whereas *Rashomon* probed the nature of truth and *Basic*'s other forbear, *The Usual*

Suspects, dazzled with an intelligent, finely-honed screenplay, this simply gets hopelessly lost in its tedious plot while its cast labours unanimously to deliver career-worst performances.

The only smidgen of anything that might come close to being described as entertaining is Giovanni Ribisi's wildly eccentric turn as a bed-bound gay marine whose fruity accent suggests Clay Shaw from *JFK* via elocution lessons from Loyd Grossman. But even this tiny pleasure is obliterated, as James Vanderbilt's screenplay doesn't so much just stretch credibility, as strap it to a medieval rack and start spinning the handle. Travolta is not exempt: a rather desultory attempt at his usual cool schtick is punctured by a hilariously gratuitous shot of the bare-chested, post-shower star. (He really is too old for this kind of narcissistic swaggering).

Vanderbilt's hopelessly knotted script piles reversal upon reversal until, when the 'truth' is finally revealed, it's hard to care as it's just another dumbly implausible scenario. ★ **AS**

◎ BASIC INSTINCT (1992)

Starring: *Michael Douglas (Detective Nick Curran), Sharon Stone (Catherine Tramell), Jeanne Tripplehorn (Dr Beth Gardener), George Dzundza (Gus)*
Director: *Paul Verhoeven*
Screenwriter: *Joe Eszterhas*
18/122 mins./Erotic/Thriller/USA

A detective goes on the trail of a female serial killer, who despatches her victims with an ice-pick after having sex with them.

Few movies capture their 'moment' as well as *Basic Instinct*. This was the Hitchcockian thriller updated, the coming-of-age of Michael Douglas, the screen immortalisation of Sharon Stone, the zenith of the writer as money-maker, and, in its own small way, the legitimisation of the softcore porn thriller.

Basic Instinct was the movie where Euro-sleaze met Hollywood cliche, where boundaries were redefined, and where legs were spread and knickers found absent. It would be easy to dismiss *Basic Instinct* as a trash movie but the truth is that what Paul Verhoeven delivered was in fact the kind of movie Hitchcock would have made had he ever allowed himself to damn the ratings board and indulge all the sexual peccadilloes he hinted at but always obliquely obscured. Verhoeven didn't so much take the gauze away from the camera as whip the panties off the leading lady, a noticeably Hitchcockian icy blonde in the form of been-around-the-block-a-bit Sharon Stone, whom Verhoeven had 'discovered' making *Total Recall*.

Verhoeven – a cinematic sensualist if ever there was one – recognised something in Stone, whether it be the stuff of stardom or a ruthless determination to access the stuff of stardom (there's a difference) and all he asked her to do to attain some was leave her knickers at the door. She acquiesced, and then spent years claiming she didn't realise where the camera was gonna be (yeah right!). Whatever the background details, Stone became a star simply by baring all to camera and also – in what retrospectively remains one of the most surreal moments in cinema history – to 'Newman' (Wayne Knight) from *Seinfeld*!! The ghost of Hitchcock permeates every frame of Verhoeven's thriller. He's there in the way the film-maker focuses on his cast, prominently framed against an almost fake-looking background; he's there – or at least Bernard Herrman is – in every note of Jerry Goldsmith's effective score. And he's there in the twisted, confused sexuality of the male protagonist – in this case cop Nick Curran (Douglas) a target for Catherine Tramell (Stone) both as a writer and a possible killer.

Long in the shadow of his father Kirk, Michael Douglas first established himself in movies as a producer – winning an Oscar for *One Flew Over The Cuckoo's Nest* in 1975. He finally found his reward on screen by playing the morally dubious card – a cheating husband in *Fatal Attraction* and a corporate vampire in *Wall Street*. Douglas was well on his way to becoming a poster child for the morally bankrupt post-yuppie American dream; *Basic Instinct* confirmed that journey and the destination.

Here he was offered the chance to all but rape a colleague (Jeanne Tripplehorn, in the film's most controversial scene) and then convert a black widow murderess from her path of crime, purely on his ability in the sack. He calls her the 'fuck of the century' but when she puts that ice-pick down in favour of a good seeing to, it's clear that Det. Nick knows how to wield the night stick. Male fantasy ran rampant and Douglas lapped up such a smug, conceited role. Joe Eszterhas, a former writer for *Rolling Stone* magazine, had parlayed journalism into Hollywood success with the likes of *F.I.S.T.* and *Jagged Edge*. His desire to push the boundaries of how Hollywood viewed sex netted him millions for the screenplay of *Basic Instinct* and proved to be something of a career high for the hack last seen penning *Burn Hollywood Burn*. Verhoeven established his credentials in the sci-fi genre with the brutal *RoboCop* and the success of *Total Recall*.

But *Basic Instinct* was a turning point for all concerned – and ironically for some it became a point of no return.

Verhoeven and Eszterhas went on to make the much pilloried *Showgirls*, before the former returned to the sci-fi genre with *Starship Troopers*, and the latter went on to pen memoirs that had much to say about Sharon Stone's knicker-less state.

Stone herself has yet to duplicate the success of this one role. Even Douglas hasn't had a role to equal this since.

Some movies define their time in every way – and, more than anything, *Basic Instinct* represents a brief moment in Hollywood history when excess was openly celebrated. When a hack writer could pick up $3 million for a screenplay, when a nobody actress could leap to the top of the Hollywood pile by showing her pussy, when a Euro-director with a penchant for satire was clever enough to seize that moment. ★★★★ **BM**

◎ BASIC INSTINCT 2: RISK ADDICTION (2006)

Starring: *Sharon Stone (Catherine Davis Tramell), David Morrissey (Dr Michael Glass), Charlotte Rampling (Milena Gardosh), David Thewlis (Roy Washburn), Hugh Dancy (Adam Towers)*
Director: *Michael Caton-Jones*
Screenwriters: *Leora Barish, Henry Bean, based on characters created by Joe Eszterhas*
18/114 mins./Drama/Thriller/Germany/Spain/UK/USA

Following the suspicious death of her latest lover, Catherine Tramell is diagnosed with 'risk addiction' by psychiatrist Michael Glass. She enters therapy with Michael, who becomes obsessed with his patient. His career, sanity and life are pulled apart when a string of murders prompt suspicions and accusations.

In 1992, *Basic Instinct* established Sharon Stone as a psychosexual superstar and, not incidentally, 'fuck of the century'. A decade-and-a-half on, in a new century, here's a London-set sequel. Paul Verhoeven, whose overkill sold the first movie's silly story, is replaced by the measured, considered Michael Caton-Jones. And the dim, horny, out-of-control cop played by Michael Douglas (whose fate is sadly not revealed) gives way to a smart, icy, control-freak psychiatrist played by the luckless David Morrissey.

Screenwriter Joe Eszterhas isn't getting huge paydays for rejigging *Jagged Edge* any more and this new (if distinctly familiar) script is crafted by Leora Barish (*Desperately Seeking Susan*) and Henry Bean (*The Believer*, *Deep Cover*, *Internal Affairs*). A while back, when David Cronenberg was set to direct, the *Basic Instinct 2* script got a buzz as being cleverer, deeper, sharper and sexier than the original (which, given the writers' track record, is credible). Somewhere in years of development (many directors and co-stars were mooted), it must have been rewritten too many times, because this is a bland, silly, play-by-play redo of *Basic Instinct* without even the original's Gothic, over-the-top bravado. And, no, there's no scene here that will get as much attention as the underwear-free police interrogation of 1992 – even if Caton-Jones does riff on his own backlist by having Stone pose in one shrink session like Joanne Whalley as Christine Keeler in the poster for his movie *Scandal*.

There ought to have been a way to do more with the fascinating, ambiguous Catherine Tramell, but *Basic Instinct 2* just reprises her previous act, as a professional man gets unwisely involved and squirms deeper and deeper into her trap as he's set up to take several nasty falls. Elsewhere, good British actors (David Thewlis, Charlotte Rampling) are laden with duff lines (Thewlis' Welsh-accented delivery of, 'I want that cunt in jail' is priceless) and footballer Stan Collymore gets drowned.

There is one clever variation on the original's action as Dr. Glass snoops around a ladies' loo in a Soho club, driven by moans coming from a stall to suspect he's about to catch Catherine in a girl-on-girl clinch with his ex-wife (Indira Varma), only to receive a nasty, very different surprise. Otherwise, you've been here before when it was fresher. ★★ **KN**

BASIL, THE GREAT MOUSE DETECTIVE (1986)

Starring: *the voices of: Barrie Ingham (Basil), Val Bettin (Dr David Q. Dawson), Vincent Price (Professor Ratigan), Susanne Pollatschek (Olivia Flaversham) Candy Candido (Fidget)*
Directors: *Ron Clements, Burny Mattinson, David Michener, John Musker*
Screenwriters: *Ron Clements, Burny Mattinson, David Michener, John Musker, based on the novel by Paul Galdone and Eve Titus*
U/73 mins./Animation/USA

After a small girl's toymaker father is kidnapped, Basil, the mouse equivalent of Sherlock Holmes, picks up the case, which leads first to a rather deficient bat and then to a deadlier foe entirely Professor Ratigan.

A better then you remember entry from the corridors of Disney animation during their wan years following Walt's death and before the success of *The Little Mermaid*. The film is often written off as it failed at the box-office, but it reveals a rare vibrancy and attention to detail, not to forgo its daring leanings toward a *Looney Tune* style mania, that had all but been stamped out due to growing costs and a general lack of effort.

The emergence of computers is one reason that the backgrounds zing again, a tasty Victoriana touching base with all a tourist guide's worth of London memorabilia. Two of the tumble of directors, Ron Clements and John Musker, were forging ahead, twisting the enemy microchips to their own uses and measuring up a future for the medium. They would become very much its guiding lights with *The Little Mermaid* and *Aladdin*. What they grasped was that kids had changed a bit from Uncle Walt's day, and while they wanted a good story, they also wanted zany. This Basil works less in the Basil Rathbone mould than the Basil Fawlty, a hyperactive pipsqueak, never quite in control. One dazzling helter-skelter escape sequence has the rodent hero defy any number of choppers and anvils, to catch a photo-op with perfect precision at the end. It's also good to hear the sonorous thrum of Vincent Price's immortal voice as twisted Moriarty-alike Professor Ratigan.

The music is never forced on us, leaving it the story to whisk us along, actually a bit too briefly, to its climax in and about Big Ben, a sequence in no short supply of genuine thrills. Compared to the lumpy, over-laden efforts that finally put paid to Disney's animated arm a second time around, this is a real treasure. ★★★★ **IN**

BASKET CASE (1982)

Starring: *Kevin Van Hetenryck (Duane Bradley), Terri Susan Smith (Sharon), Beverly Bonner (Casey), Robert Vogel (Hotel manager), Diana Browne (Dr Judith Kutter), Lloyd Pace (Dr Harold Needleman), Bill Freeman (Dr Julius Lifflander), Joe Clarke (Brian 'Mickey' O'Donovan), Ruth Neuman (Aunt)*
Director: *Frank Henenlotter*
Screenwriter: *Frank Henenlotter*
18/90 mins./Horror/USA

Duane checks into a Skid Row hotel in New York, hauling a wicker basket which contains Belial, his deformed, separated Siamese twin. Duane unleashes the twisted Belial on the careless doctors who made a botch of the operation to separate them, but also tries to make a relationship with a girl that excites his telepathic brother to homicidal jealousy.

Wearing its sleaze with pride, this New York splatter movie is the one about the monster in the basket. Made in 1982 by Frank Henenlotter, who later gave the world *Brain Damage* and *Frankenhooker* – not to mention *Basket Case 2* and *3* – it was one of the first films to try on purpose for that mix of horror and humour predecessors like Herschell Gordon Lewis (to whom the film is dedicated) only managed by accident and ineptitude.

Basket Case has the look of an on-the-streets underground slice-of-life or *Deep Throat* era hardcore, with ugly pictures of uglier places and even uglier people (the nearest the script has to a romantic line is 'you're cute when you slobber') and the monster/gore effects are at once laughably fake and genuinely repellant until an ill-judged climactic rape spoils the fun. Nevertheless, it's a hard film to forget: they may not be given much to do by the sloppy script but the protagonists are somehow interesting and, if only for a moment – Belial clawing his way out of a twist-tied garbage bag after being disposed of as medical waste – affecting.

Now that the cheapest, most disreputable films look like professionally shot TV movies, there's something invigorating about a film that goes all out for grottiness. The sequels, which feature Van Hentenryck and British jazz singer Annie Ross, are slicker and have better effects, but miss that before-the-streets-were-cleaned-up New York vibe. ★★★ **KN**

BASKETBALL DIARIES (1995)

Starring: *Leonardo DiCaprio (Jim Carroll), Lorraine Bracco (Jim's Mother), Marilyn Sokol (Chanting Woman), James Madio (Pedro), Patrick McGaw (Neutron), Mark Wahlberg (Mickey), Juliette Lewis (Diane Moody), Ernie Hudson (Reggie)*
Director: *Scott Kalvert*
Screenwriter: *Bryan Goluboff, based on the novel by Jim Carroll*
18/102 mins./Biography/Drama/USA

Four Catholic school boys, whose lives revolve around basketball, find their rebellious natures leading them towards less savoury pursuits.

Although the title conjures up images of another no-hopers-to-world-beaters type movie, this is the very antithesis of the predictable all-you-need-is-team-spirit genre. In fact, it focuses on four rebellious Catholic boys, in particular charismatic diarist Jim Carroll, whose adolesence becomes an inexorable downward spiral into drug addiction and crime.

Of the four, only Neutron hauls his life back on track and gains a basketball scholarship, while the others throw away their sporting talents, descending into hustling to finance their habits. The physical Mickey develops a penchant for violent robbery, Pedro's carelessness inevitably gets him arrested, and Jim's diary entries turn surreal as his life collapses into vagrancy and squalor.

Without rising star DiCaprio and Mark Wahlberg this would have been considerably more turgid and unappealing. But their charm allows sympathy and involvement with the characters, despite their efforts towards self-destruction. DiCaprio's performance is further evidence of great things to come, taking Carroll convincingly from schoolboy pranks to harrowing sequences of addiction and cold turkey.

This long-planned adaptation of Carroll's semi-autobiographical best-seller has suffered somewhat in the telling, not least in the rather hackneyed creation of Reggie Porter as Jim's worldly-wise, one-on-one partner. And while never glamorising the effects of drugs, the message remains slightly ambiguous as Carroll finally emerges a sensitive, thoughtful young man as a result of his experiences. The effect is like a John Hughes movie with a monkey on its back. ★★★ **DB**

BASQUIAT (1996)

Starring: *Jeffrey Wright (Jean Michel Basquiat), Michael Wincott (Rene Ricard), Benico Del Toro (Benny Dalmau), Claire Forlani (Gina Cardinale), David Bowie (Andy Warhol), Dennis Hopper (Bruno Bichofberger), Gary Oldman (Albert Milo), Christopher Walken (The Interviewer), Willem Dafoe (The Electrician), Jean-Claude La Marre (Shenge), Parker Posey (Mary Boone)*
Director: *Julian Schnabel*
Screenwriter: *Julian Schnabel, based on a story by Lech Majewski and John F. Bowe, with story development by Michael Holman*
15/108 mins./Biography/Drama/USA

The meteoric rise and fall of 1980s graffiti artist Jean-Michel Basquiat.

A New York ghetto in 1981, enter a young black kid with a talent for graffiti. The art world gets wind and makes him a star. The rich and famous go wild for him. Andy Warhol becomes his buddy and he dates Madonna. By 1988, he's world famous but it's too late, because the lonely kid tragically dies of a drug overdose. On this evidence, the short life of pop artist Jean-Michel Basquiat should make for gripping viewing.

Sadly, given the biopic treatment by writer-director Schnabel, an artist friend of Basquiat, the media circus that shaped his life is completely shunned in favour of uneasy pretension, and the refusal to treat its title character as anything other than a misunderstood genius. Wright makes for a wonderful Basquiat, with his Bambi eyelashes and dazed smile, and there are some spicy cameos from Gary Oldman, Christopher Walken and Dennis Hopper.

But as Schnabel has explicitly gone for the real Basquiat slant, it's puzzling that Wright is given all of 30 lines throughout the entire film, the origins of Basquiat's blazing talent are snubbed, his sexual orientation and Herculean drug intake are totally bypassed, and his web-like graffiti art is used only as background furniture.

True, there is some fine photography and some imaginative images, but Schnabel's elitist snobbery turns almost every scene into overblown tragedy (highlighted by one audacious vision of Basquiat crowned with gold in front of Picasso's *Guernica*).

Oddly enough, the film scores with Bowie's spellbinding take on the ageing Warhol. Without this comedic but beautiful performance and an off-beat soundtrack, this is little more than wet paint. ★★ **JH**

BATMAN (1989)

Starring: *Michael Keaton (Batman/Bruce Wayne), Jack Nicholson (Joker/Jack Napier), Kim Basinger (Vicki Vale), Pat Hingle (Commissioner Gordon), Billy Dee Williams (District Attorney Harvey Dent), Michael Gough (Alfred), Jack Palance (Carl Grissom), Jerry Hall (Alicia)*
Director: *Tim Burton*
Screenwriters: *Sam Hamm, Warren Skaaren, based on a story by Sam Hamm and characters created by Bob Kane*
12/121 mins./Adventure/Action/Fantasy/USA

Awards: *Academy Awards – Best Set Decoration*

A millionaire turns himself into a vigilante super-hero after his parents are shot.

The Batman, night-time identity of orphaned billionaire Bruce Wayne, made his debut in *Detective Comics* in 1939, the creation of artist Bob Kane and often-unrecognised writer Bill Finger. Along with Superman and Wonder Woman, he is at the heart of *DC*'s superhero empire, not to mention the Justice League Of America, and appears in more comics now than he ever did before. There were a couple of baggy-tights Batman and Robin serials in the 1940s, with sped-up scraps sending slouch-hatted stuntmen flying, but for decades the Dark Knight was literally in the shadow of the Man of Steel, never quite becoming the American icon that the red-caped Superman was.

When that finally happened, the craze for Batmania almost killed off the character – Batman really took off because of the camp 1960s TV show with square-jawed-but-podgy Adam West in the cowl and a succession of flamboyant guest star baddies. *DC* abandoned the 'holy radioactive shark!' business soon after the show's three-year run, and spent 20 years trying to take the Bat seriously again, with a great, gothic 70s run from artist Neal Adams and some inspired writing in the 1980s from artist-scripter Frank Miller Jr (whose *Batman: The Dark Knight Returns* and *Batman: Year One* completely rebuilt the character and Gotham City) and Alan Moore (whose major contribution, *Batman: The Killing Joke*, did the same for Bruce's arch-nemesis the Joker, and incidentally put Batgirl in a wheelchair for life).

Ever since the big-screen success of the Superman movies from 1978, a big-budget Batman was in development. When Tim Burton was first approached, his reaction was 'I used to love that show', doubtless remembering longtime idol Vincent Price's role as Egghead, but a look at how far the comics had come since helicopter umbrellas and 'same bat-time, same bat-channel' persuaded him to take a darker, more Miller-influenced approach. Comics fans were at first appalled at the casting of Michael Keaton, then best-known as a comedian, as Batman, reasoning that his wobbly jaw would look silly under the mask and dreading the return of Adam West's Bat-buffoon. And you didn't even have to be a comics fan to think the idea of sticking in a soundtrack album's worth of songs from Prince was a desperate idea – in the event, Burton did his best to bury them in the aural background and rely on a suitably shivery, dark-heroic score from Danny Elfman.

What Burton and scripter Sam Hamm did was start all over again, with a fantastical Gotham City of art-deco skyscrapers, an abandoned cathedral (think about it), cavernous mansions and caves, and crime-blighted alleyways. Even the regular citizens wear modified 1940s clothes, and everyone else is ready for a dangerous costume party.

In the comics, Bruce Wayne's parents were gunned down by a petty hood named Joe Chill, but the script opts for plot symmetry by making the murderer who sets Bruce on the path to become a masked vigilante, the young Jack Napier. Batman later semi- accidentally knocks him into a vat of chemicals that bleach his skin, turn his hair green and fix a facial bullet wound into an eternal grin. Thus, Michael Keaton's Batman and Jack Nicholson's Joker have created each other, and the film follows their nightmare pas de deux as they struggle over various prizes, from newsgirl Vicki Vale (Kim Basinger) to the admiration of the whole city (the Joker gives away free money). The top-billed Nicholson is perilously close to Cesar Romero or Frank Gorshin in the 60s, but retains a monstrous/pathetic core that would be the mainstay of Burton's Bats.

Oddly, the aspect Burton is least comfortable with is the action. Much of it was staged by second-unit man Peter MacDonald (*Rambo III*), and includes the expected aerial acrobatics, Bat-gadgets and punch-ups (without those ZAP! and KA-BOOMM! signs). But what Burton does best is to brood on fractured identities – his Bruce Wayne is as much Citizen Kane or Jay Gatsby, a host unnoticed at his own party (when Vicki asks him if he knows who Bruce Wayne is, he honestly responds, 'I really don't'), and his Joker is the fiend that was always inside Jack Nicholson, exploding as the, 'First fully-functional homicidal artist' (he kills his best friend).

A huge hit, the movie spun off *Batman: The Animated Series* and a cartoon feature *Batman: Mask Of The Phantasm*, which have done some extraordinary things with the characters. And Burton went darker still with *Batman Returns*, a family event movie that opens with Pee-Wee Herman celebrating Christmas by letting his deformed baby float away into a sewer. In contrast, Schumacher's first *Batman* opens with a tie-in plug for McDonald's. Splat! ★★★★ **KN**

BATMAN AND ROBIN (1997)

Starring: *Arnold Schwarzenegger (Mr Freeze/Dr Victor Fries), George Clooney (Batman/Bruce Wayne), Chris O'Donnell (Robin/Dick Grayson), Uma Thurman (Poison Ivy/Dr. Pamela Isley), Alicia Silverstone (Batgirl/Barbara Wilson), Michael Gough (Alfred Pennyworth), Pat Hingle (Commissioner Gordon), John Glover (Doctor Jason Woodrue) Elle Macpherson (Julie Madison), Vivicia A. Fox (Ms B. Haven)*
Director: *Joel Schumacher*
Screenwriter: *Akiva Goldsman, based on characters created by Bob Kane*
PG/125 mins./Action/Adventure/Fantasy/USA

This time Batman has to battle two foes; Mr Freeze and Poison Ivy, but now he also has two sidekicks to 'help' him – Robin and a fledgling Batgirl.

The Batsuit is wrapped around Clooney; O'Donnell returns as Robin; Arnie is Mr Freeze and Thurman is Poison Ivy. The only other thing you need to know is that Wayne's Uncle Alfred is unwell and Alicia Silverstone arrives not to nurse him but to free him from his life of servitude.

So much for social conscience, but is it fun? Well, for the first half-hour it is: close-ups of the bat and the bird getting suited and booted; chilling with Mr Freeze in a wham-bam set-piece; introducing bad-guy Bane; and fertilising fantasies as Poison Ivy turns from nerdy botanist to vengeful sadist. It all leaves you ready for more. But then more is exactly what you get. Rather too much more, as both plot and audience attention span stretch to breaking point.

Schumacher has learnt a little from *Batman Forever* and has reined in the vertigo-inducing crash-cuts making *Batman And Robin* a lot easier on the eye. But with the change of pace comes a change in emphasis, the target audience now perhaps a little younger and more receptive to cornball wisecracks. The overall impact is more like the 60s TV series than anything envisaged by *D.C. Comics'* Bob Kane (whose consultancy credit must be largely contractual) or Tim Burton (whose gloomy architecture of the first two films is the sole remnant of his Dark Knight vision).

In place of Gothic pathos, Schumacher has a simple three-point plan. One: never let anyone say anything profound when there's an excruciating pun to be made. Two: never let anyone use a doorway when there's a wall to smash through. And, three: never ever get the good guys into a situation that can't be solved by a Bathook-and-wire firing thingy. Actually, there is another, unwritten rule; never let the good guys upstage the talent. And so they don't. O'Donnell's independent-streak strop soon wears thin and although Clooney is cool in the suit, his Wayne is too laconic, too angst-free, and given to unseemly smirking. *Batman And Robin* therefore is once more about the nemeses: about Arnie looking like a cross between Gary Glitter and the Lloyd's building, Uma as a set of French curves squeezed deliciously into a green Lycra body-stocking, and er, Bane (her grunting muscleman sidekick who grunts and, yup, has muscles).

Silverstone, in particular, is a major disappointment; though apparently fresh from 'Oxbridge', she's not even asked to attempt an English accent, and sulks the whole movie until, in the finale, the bat and the bird finally get a bat-bird but by that point the audience will have ceased to care. ★★ **NJ**

BATMAN BEGINS (2005)

Starring: *Christian Bale (Bruce Wayne/Batman), Michael Caine (Alfred), Liam Neeson (Henri Ducard), Katie Holmes (Rachel Dawes), Gary Oldman (Jim Gordon), Cillian Murphy (Dr Jonathan Crane), Tom Wilkinson (Carmine Falcone), Rutger Hauer (Earle)*
Director: *Christopher Nolan*
Screenwriters: *Christopher Nolan, David S. Goyer, based on a story by Goyer and characters by Bob Kane*
12A/141 mins./Action/Fantasy/USA

Billionaire down-and-out Bruce Wayne, traumatised since the murder of his parents, is recruited by The League Of Shadows, ninja assassins devoted to eradicating society's ills. Rejecting their methods, he returns to Gotham and embarks on a one-man war against crime.

As the title suggests, this sets out to be radically different from the series inaugurated by Tim Burton's *Batman* in 1989 and trashed by Joel Schumacher's *Batman And Robin* in 1997. Indeed, director Christopher Nolan gets even further than Burton from the camp of the 1960s TV show, to the point where you wonder how cartoonish Bat-foes like the Penguin could ever appear in Nolan's rusty, economically desperate Gotham City.

Whereas Burton sketched an Art Deco hell and shoved Michael Keaton on screen in a Bat-suit in the first minutes, Nolan puts off the moment when Christian Bale dons the mask for almost an hour. Influenced by the look and feel of the *X-Men* films, *Batman Begins* spends a lot of time in a world only just removed from reality before getting to the superheroics.The first act finds Wayne in a Chinese prison and a Himalayan monastery, transforming from bearded brawler to black-clad ninja as he flashes back to a lifetime of trauma that – in this version – began even before his parents' deaths, as he falls down a well and is terrorised by the bats which later inspire his night persona. Burton had Wayne's mom and pop killed by the hoodlum who would become The Joker, but Nolan reverts to earlier comics and makes the murderer a panicky no one named Joe Chill, blurring the set-up so young Bruce and even Wayne Sr (Linus Roache) must take some blame for the killings.

The Nolan who made *Memento* and *Insomnia* is at home with extreme psychological states – this might complete a Three Colours Of Neurosis trilogy by following memory loss and sleeplessness with phobia. It's certainly a smart move to cast the former Patrick Bateman as a Batman who always seems about to crack up. Bale even makes the old playboy-idiot act work, suggesting – as Michael Caine's dry Alfred notes – a man who needs to pretend to have fun because he might accidentally enjoy himself.

Batman maintains a secret identity, but he's recruiting an army for a war – forming alliances with Gordon, the only honest cop in Gotham, and Wayne Enterprises' R&D man Lucius Fox (Morgan Freeman), while treating childhood sweetheart/Assistant D. A. Rachel Dawes as much as an informant as love interest (she takes the role played in comics by Harvey Dent, who becomes the disfigured villain Two-Face, suggesting a possible career-changing stretch for Holmes if this thread carries through).

With a city that looks less fantastical than Burton's, Nolan hits the streets and slums of Gotham to show a horrific escalation of evil that demands Batman's presence even as Gordon suggests he might make it worse; old-fashioned Mob guys (Tom Wilkinson) are edged out by masked freaks (Cillian Murphy, starily creepy even before he pulls on his Scarecrow hood) and a fanatical force run by the bastard sons of Fu Manchu and Osama bin Laden. Unlike Burton, Nolan doesn't skimp on action either, with brutal fights, vehicle chases and, in one great sequence, a mass escape from Arkham Asylum of serial killers and maniacs doped up with the Scarecrow's fear serum.

In terms of big-screen comic-adaptation triumphs, it's recently been Marvel who've been ahead (*X-Men*, *Blade*, *Spider-Man*); but, by learning several tricks from Marvel franchises, *Batman Begins* undoubtedly gets rival comics house *DC* back in the game. ★★★★★ **KN**

⊙ BATMAN FOREVER (1995)

Starring: *Val Kilmer (Batman/Bruce Wayne), Tommy Lee Jones (Two-Face/Harvey Dent), Jim Carrey (Riddler/Edward Nygma), Nicole Kidman (Dr Chase Meridian), Chris O' Donnell (Robin/Dick Grayson), Michael Gough (Alfred Pennyworth), Pat Hingle (Commissioner James Gordon), Drew Barrymore (Sugar), Debi Mazar (Spice)*
Director: *Joel Schumacher*
Screenwriters: *Lee Batchler, Janet Scott Batchler, Akiva Goldsman, based on characters created by Bob Kane*
12/122 mins./Action/Fantasy/Adventure/USA

Batman takes on a new sidekick as he goes toe-to-toe with Two-Face and The Riddler.

The rage that greeted Schumacher's ruination of the bat-franchise, *Batman And Robin*, and the director's alleged penitence, is well recorded. But a look back at his first bash at the bat-franchise reveals all the elements that scuppered the second: gloomy Gothicism is replaced with sexy campery, action is mostly mishandled and Robin is in full possession of the infamous nipples. What makes *Forever* at least watchable is Jim Carrey's frenetic Riddler (blowing Tommy Lee Jones' Two-Face off the screen, much to his rumoured chagrin) and a script that makes some sense.

But Val Kilmer's Batman is the blandest of the bunch and Nicole Kidman as the sexed-up psychologist looking for the man behind the bat is no more than a clothes horse. And if that wasted star power wasn't enough check out Drew Barrymore as token moll Sugar.

Difficult, in retrospect, to see why this was the biggest hit of 1995. **★★ AS**

⊙ BATMAN RETURNS (1992)

Starring: *Michael Keaton (Batman/Bruce Wayne), Danny De Vito (Penguin/Oswald Cobblepot), Michelle Pfeiffer (Catwoman/Selina Kyle), Christopher Walken (Max Shreck), Michael Gough (Alfred Pennyworth), Michael Murphy (Mayor), Christi Conway (Ice Princess), Andrew Bryniarski (Chip), Pat Hingle (Commissioner Gordon)*
Director: *Tim Burton*
Screenwriter: *Daniel Waters, from a story by Daniel Waters and Sam Hamm, characters created by Bob Kane*
12/126 mins./Action/Crime/Fantasy/Thriller/Romance/USA/UK

A corrupt businessman and the Penguin plot to take over Gotham. Only Batman can see their true motives, but he, too, is distracted by a confusing new adversary – Catwoman.

And so *Batman Returns* with a vengeance that must surely tax even the most optimistic Warner executive's credulity. Having created one of the biggest-grossing movies of all time, the hope must have been that, with any luck, *Batman Returns* would do the expected sequel trick and pull in 75 per cent of the original's take.

Instead, of course, Tim Burton pulled it off once again, smashing Batman's opening weekend record of $42 million with a $47.7 million take in the US. In fact, the extraordinary success of both movies comes as something of a surprise, since these are intensely personal affairs, with *Batman Returns* coming across as even more of a Tim Burton film than did the original.

Gothic architecture, adorned with bizarre gargoyles, is constantly powdered with snow (*Edward Scissorhands*), the Danny Elfman score swells around the action like a tempestuous sea (*Edward*, *Batman*) and the oddball characters are constantly preoccupied with their outsider status (*Edward*, *Batman*, *Pee Wee's Big Adventure*). Indeed, despite Burton's professed irritation at having his work described as 'dark', it is hard to conceive of film being any darker than *Batman Returns* if the audience are to see anything on the screen at all.

Despite the absence of the late Anton Furst's set designing skills, Gotham City is if anything more impressive here, with the soaring buildings brilliantly created via special effects and the street-level sets immaculately detailed and strangely compelling. Jack Nicholson's Joker is, of course, replaced by Danny De Vito's hideous Penguin as Batman's nemesis, with the little man frankly doing a far better job, at once sadly pathetic and evil-minded. Meanwhile, the mousey Selina Kyle (the excellent Pfeiffer) is transformed into Catwoman in a uniquely Burton moment (i.e. it's never explained why or how she does it), and between them they succeed in getting up The Dark Knight's nose, with The Penguin allying with the evil Max Shreck in a bid for the office of Mayor of Gotham and Catwoman perpetrating athletic revenge on the arrogant, patronising and (in Walken's case) murderous men in her life.

Despite some tortuous one-liners, the shock here is the remarkable lack of any humour, as if Burton and screenwriter Daniel Waters are somehow taking the whole thing too seriously, a surprise since Burton has proved himself a highly competent director of comedy. He does, however, once again prove himself as a filmmaker of rare vision here, with the atmosphere of a city on the brink expertly created by a man who knows exactly what he wants to say. That so many people seem prepared to listen is a testament not to Warner's vast marketing machine but to Tim Burton's twisted vision. **★★★★ PT**

⊙ BATMAN: THE MOVIE (1966)

Starring: *Adam West (Bruce Wayne/Batman), Burt Ward (Dick Grayson/Robin), Lee Meriwether (The Catwoman/Comrade Kitanya 'Kitka' Irenya Tantanya Karenska Alisoff), Cesar Romero (The Joker), Burgess Meredith (The Penguin), Frank Gorshin (The Riddler), Alan Napier (Alfred), Neil Hamilton (Commissioner Gordon), Stafford Repp (Chief O'Hara), Madge Repp (Aunt Harriet O'Cooper), William Dozier (Narrator – uncredited)*
Director: *Leslie H. Martinson*
Screenwriter: *Lorenzo Semple Jr, based on characters by Bob Kane*
U/105 mins./Action/Comedy/USA

Batman and Robin take on the combined forces of Catwoman, The Joker, The Penguin and The Riddler.

The shark repellent Batspray. Everyone remembers the shark repellent Batspray.

But it's only on re-watching the campy, tongue-super-glued-in-cheek 60s take on Batman that its true genius can be appreciated.

For two generations this was 'the Batman' – and then Frank Miller went all Dark Knight and Batman suddenly had to be serious again. But the proceeding two decades was the reign of the 'fun' caped crusader, when Adam West and Burt Ward donned their ridiculous Technicolor suits – both on TV and the big screen – to wage war in an alternate universe of subtitled fights, 'holy' exclamations and 'old school' movie stars turned supervillains.

To be fair, there's not much that's cinematic about the feature film outing – veteran TV series director Martinson just uses it as an excuse for a bigger budget for stunts (a bat boat and helicopter!), a longer running time and a larger cast – as all four of Batman's chief nemesises unite to take over the world.

Credit to West and Ward whose straight faces and comic timing allow the concept to work – and stretch the joke further than would seem possible. Their final sprint to save the planet is exactly that – running against an obviously fake moving backdrop they utter the following immortal exchange – Robin: 'Holy marathon! I'm getting a stitch Batman.' Batman: 'Let's hope it's a stitch in time, Robin, that saves nine – the nine members of the United Nations Security Council.'

And there's plenty more of those where that came from! **★★★★ EC**

1 ***Seven*** **– Supremely creepy and unsettling credit sequence that gives us a glimpse into the mind of the film's killer – not that we realise that until later.**

2 ***The Naked Gun*** **– We follow a cop car siren as it races along the city streets, and then, in a turn to the surreal, through a ladies' changing room onto a rollercoaster.**

3 ***Austin Powers*** **– Our hero dances his way through swingin' 60s London in a witty and colourful introduction to spying's most shagadelic star.**

4 ***Spider-Man 2*** **– Neatly recaps all the key moments of the previous film in a series of fantastic paintings by comic book artist Alex Ross.**

5 ***The Spy Who Loved Me*** **– the most Bond of all the Bond credit sequences, this has naked girls and big guns and Russian hats galore.**

6 ***Vertigo*** **– Saul Bass' dreamy and slightly disturbing opening for Hitchcock's psychological masterpiece mixes psychosis and, of course, vertigo to good effect.**

7 ***Catch Me If You Can*** **– Better than the Pink Panther credits that inspired it, the film's cop and con man chase each other through a stylised, jazzy world.**

8 ***Mission: Impossible*** **– All the movie's key moments are hidden in machine-gun flashes here, as a fuse burns and *that* theme tune plays.**

9 ***Intolerable Cruelty*** **– Greeting card cherubs fall in love and beat each other up in this animated 50s pastiche.**

10 ***Superman: The Movie*** **– A young boy reads aloud from Superman's comic book debut, before we slide into space, to Krypton, as the theme kicks in. Magic.**

◑ *BATTERIES NOT INCLUDED (1987)

Starring: *Hume Cronyn (Frank Riley), Jessica Tandy (Faye Riley), Frank McRae (Harry Noble), Elizabeth Pena (Marisa Esteval), Michael Carmine (Carlos)*
Director: *Matthew Robbins*
Screenwriters: *Brad Bird, Matthew Robbins, Brent Maddock, S.S. Wilson*
PG/106 mins./Sci-fi/USA

With their building under threat of demolition from unscrupulous developers, who even stoop as low as hiring a local gang of youths to intimidate them, a group of vulnerable tenants have no one to turn to. That is until diminutive mechanised aliens fly in the window.

Add equal parts of *Cocoon*'s octogenarian revamp and *E.T.*'s genial alien therapy, the merest sprinkling of trite robot-as-human prattling *Short Circuit*, undercook on a low creative heat and serve mentioning the fact Steven Spielberg is, unfathomably, involved at some blueprint stage. Thus, you end up with this perky but pointless rehash of the cute alien format that became embedded in the late 80s.

Makeweight director Matthew Robbins, running with an idea from Spielberg, is working on the basis that making things smaller will always make them far more endearing. These flying electric tin-lids with blue headlamps for eyes are supposedly alive in some respect. At one point, they even multiply producing even weenier hovering pie dishes, on which to lavish our aw-shucks reactions. Are we really that susceptible to sentimental prodding that we'll buy into a family of alien frisbees with a heart?

They are, to be fair, assisted by some talented human beings, Hume Cronyn and Jessica Tandy as the elderly couple who need saving by these hard-wired pie-dishes, give it a strange sense of plausibility, or at least, a sense of purpose. After all, it is just a silly fairy-tale set in a bullying modern New York of scowling real-estate developers, where the magic of these winking micro-bots is enough to send them packing.

Although pitched at kids' love of gadgetry, and the effects are convincing (although, you suspect, with plenty of batteries involved) the film is rather heavy-handed, and suspiciously racist, with its Hispanic hoodlums, recycling the wan platitudes of do-gooder aliens being just a wish away. ★★ **IN**

◑ BATTLE BEYOND THE STARS (1980)

Starring: *Richard Thomas (Shad), Robert Vaughn (Gelt), John Saxon (Sador), George Peppard (Cowboy), Darlanne Fluegel (Nanelia), Sybil Danning (Saint-Exmin), Sam Jaffe (Dr Hephaestus)*
Director: *Jimmy T. Murakarmi*
Screenwriter: *John Sayles*
PG/104 mins./Sci-fi/USA

When a pacifist farm colony is threatened with being turned into a sun by the evil Sador, the young emissary Shad is sent out to recruit some hard-nosed warriors to save them.

A quick glance at the talent behind this sci-fi B-movie might give you the wrong impression – John Sayles writes the scripts, James Horner does the score and a young James Cameron fiddles with the special effects. That its director, Jimmy T. Murakarmi, was never heard from again and Roger Corman is the producer clears matters up. This is a daft rejig of *Seven Samurai*, or rather *The Magnificent Seven*, set in space, a quickie knock-off bumping along the money-spinning wake of *Star Wars*.

Yet, if you're found wanting for some unassuming, cheesy sci-fi fun there is enough bumbling charm here to make-do. Corman was a dab hand at making nothing stretch into something, and if you accept most the explosions are the same one recycled again and again, it motors along with a barmy gusto. They dropped by the better end of rent-a-hasbeen department to fill the obligatory gang of ageing cowboys, if not the name department: Shad? Gelt? Shador? Poor old space cowboy George Peppard is simply called Cowboy. Still, having Robert Vaughn virtually reprise the exact role he had in John Sturges' 1962 classic, albeit in space, is a small victory.

Sayles, long before his socio-political subtexts, is having a whale of time reworking the seven whacky warriors – Sybil Danning is a riot as the Valkyrie-themed Saint Exmin. You can tell because they call her a Yalkyrie. While Cayman of the Lamdda Zone is a green lizard who wants to eat Nanelia whose father is just a head on a box with flashing lights. Best of all are the Nestor, six telepathic beings who share the same consciousness and feel each other's pain. For what it lacks in special effects, which are ropey at best, it makes up for imagination. And, both Lucas and Kurosawa resisted suing. ★★★ **IN**

◑ BATTLE FOR THE PLANET OF THE APES (1973)

Starring: *Roddy McDowall (Caesar), Claude Akins (General Also), Natalie Trundy (Lisa), Severn Darden (Governer Kolp), Paul Williams (Virgil)*
Director: *J. Lee Thompson*
Screenwriters: *John William Corrington, Joyce Hooper Corrington, Paul Dehn*
PG/93 mins./Sci-fi/USA

The last part of the ape-saga, finds a new generation of chimps' uncertain hold on power being undermined from within and without. Their pacifist leader Caesar is trying to maintain a fragile peace, but the warrior gorillas threaten civil war, and a surviving band of mutant humans are readying an attack on the ape city.

The fifth and final gasp in the series of talking-ape movies that has long since abandoned its satirical verve and Charlton Heston. The only survivor in the cast list is Roddy McDowall, but now he's playing the son of his famous rubber-masked hero Cornelius. What does remain is a limp and humourless B-movie that really hasn't got its ideas to line up.

On the one hand we have the prattling chimps and orang-utans debating philosophy and whether it is better to live in harmony with humans or just have-done and enslave them. The gorillas make their views in no uncertain terms, but they are still just here to be hulking, snarling bad guys on horseback. There is way too much talking going on, as if the film is struggling to find a clever point, aware what the series has achieved. But to no avail. It just forces the plot to become increasingly knotted up with Caesar trekking to the previously nuked mutant city to find a video message from his parents, and the gorillas dropping his spying son from a high branch.

Meanwhile, a new gang of mutant madmen, another set of bad guys led with some fervour by Severn Darden's maniacal leader, prepare to eradicate the highly-synapsed Simian population, just so we can get to the battle bit of the title. J. Lee Thompson, who should know his way around a straight-up war-movie as the man behind *The Guns Of Navarone*, but neither he, nor his screenwriters, can find any good reason for keeping the franchise hobbling along. Even the action, when it finally turns up, is clunky and repetitive, limited by a reduced budget, a problem that horrifyingly also afflicts the vital ape make-up now far more restrictive and unconvincing than it was five years previously. The end was nigh. ★★ **IN**

◑ THE BATTLE OF ALGIERS (MAARKARAT ALGER) (1965)

Starring: *Yacef Saadi (Kader), Jean Martin (Colonel), Brahim Haggiag (Ali La Pointe), Tommaso Neri (Captain), Sammia Kerbash (One of the girls), Ugo Paletti (Captain), Fusia El Kader (Halima)*
Director: *Gillo Pontecorvo*
Screenwriters: *Gillo Pontecorvo, Franco Solinas*
15/120 mins./War/Italy/Algeria

Awards: *Golden Lion Venice*

Over the course of three years, a cynical French colonel pits his wits against the freedom fighters of Algeria's National Liberation Front.

Based on actual events – although not without its moments of dramatic licence – Gillo Pontecorvo's film chronicles three years of insurrection and repression with such cine-veracity that the producers felt the need to append a caption at the end of the opening titles assuring viewers that 'not one foot' of documentary material had been included.

Released just four years after Algeria had secured its independence from France, this technical and dramatic masterclass has lost none of its power to shock and provoke. American critic Pauline Kael compared its propagandist impact with Leni Riefenstahl's *The Triumph Of The Will* and even accused Pontecorvo of being that 'most dangerous kind of Marxist, a Marxist poet'. Kael may have had a point about socialist agit-prop being afforded a cinematic and socio-political respectability that has always been denied right-wing filmmaking. But surely a more useful comparison could be made with Roberto Rossellini's *Rome, Open City* (1945), which was also made on location, with a largely non-professional cast in a neo-realistic style that owed more to newsreel than studio artifice.

However, Pontecorvo avoids the melodramatics of Rossellini's film by presenting the victims of both the bomb blasts and the reprisals as genuine innocents rather than the faceless casualties of a revolutionary or imperialist cause. Consequently, the lingering shots of unsuspecting individuals before the carnage are every bit as disturbing as those depicting the rebels being tortured by Jean Martin's military. Pontecorvo's sympathies may be evident, but his conviction and condemnation are not devoid of compassion.

Despite winning the Golden Lion at Venice and being nominated for three Academy Awards, *The Battle Of Algiers* was banned in France for five years. It's this contentiousness on which its reputation still rests. But it also has a vigour, a commitment and an intelligence that is absent from too much modern cinema. ★★★★★ **DP**

BATTLE OF BRITAIN (1969)

Starring: *Harry Andrews (Senior Civil Servant), Michael Caine (Squadron Leader Canfield), Trevor Howard (Air Vice Marshall Keith Park), Curt Jurgens (Baron Von Richter), Ian McShane (Sgt Pilot Andy), Kenneth More (Group Capt. Baker), Laurence Olivier (Air Chief Marshal Sir Hugh Dowding), Nigel Patrick (Group Capt. Hope), Christopher Plummer (Squadron Leader Harvey), Michael Redgrave (Air Vice Marshal Evill)*
Director: *Guy Hamilton*
Screenwriters: *James Kennaway, Wilfred Greatorex*
PG/133 mins./War/UK

In 1940, the British Royal Air Force fights a desperate battle against the German Air Force for control of British air space to prevent a Nazi invasion of Britain.

'Never, in the field of human conflict, was so much owed by so many to so few ...' Churchill may have bagged the best lines, but in 1940 it was the RAF that grabbed the glory. The battle was over just 29 years old when this film was released. Now, years later still, it begins to look like ancient history with stunning aerial sequences, filmed from the cockpits of droning Heinkel bombers and dogfighting Spitfires. Purists will note, most of the latter are late models and complain there are nowhere near enough Hurricanes, but the Luftwaffe hardware is there in strength, as it was until a bunch of under-trained, over-worked and outnumbered RAF and allies beat the odds and the threat of invasion with tally-ho heroism and much stiff upper lippery.

The planes took up most of Bond producer Harry Saltzman's budget but he also assembled such a large all-star cast that at times all of 'the few' seem to pass before the camera. Indeed, there are so many familiar faces that even Michael Caine gets shot down, to the dismay of his faithful black dog. The hound is marginally more credible than the Susannah 'Don't you yell at me, Mr Warwick' York subplot and some of the music grates, but Olivier is on fine form as Air Chief Marshall Dowding outwitting Curt Jurgens' Baron Von Richter. It's a long way from *Top Gun*, but it's still stirring stuff. ★★★★ **NJ**

BATTLE ROYALE (BATORU ROWAIARU) (2000)

Starring: *Beat Takeshi (Kitano), Tatsuya Fujiwara (Shuya Nanahara – Boys #15), Aki Maeda (Noriko Nakagawa – Girls #15), Taro Yamamoto (Shougo Kawada – Boys #5), Masanobu Ando (Kazuo Kiryama – Boys #6), Kou Shibasaki (Mitsuko Souma – Girls #13)*
Director: *Kinji Fukasaku*
Screenwriter: *Kenta Fukasaku, based on the novel by Koushun Takami*
18/122 mins./Drama/Thriller/Action/Horror/Japan

In the near future, Japan institutes a programme to cope with rising youth crime, by selecting a random class of 14- and 15-year-olds and packing them off to an island, where they are given weapons and three days to eliminate each other until a sole survivor remains.

William Golding's *Lord Of The Flies* has always been a popular set text in schools because it makes young readers wonder what they would do in the same situation. *Battle Royale* does exactly the same thing, but with even harder choices for its school-uniformed characters.

With a level of violence that restricts it to adult cinemagoers, this will really play when seen by audiences the same age as its characters. The censorious might feel a fantasy like this encourages teen violence, but director Kinji Fukasaku actually does a wonderful job of making the horrors alien and degrading, as a few sympathetic characters rail against the adult system that forces them to act like a conservative's nightmare of rebel youth.

The film deftly establishes its unlikely premise and allows enough glimpses of regular school life to explain why teacher Kitano (played to world-weary perfection by a wry Beat Takeshi) is fed up with his class. Then, the kids are gassed on a bus trip and wake up on an isolated island, where Kitano is empowered to throw a knife into the skull of a girl who talks during a lecture and blow the head off the chief troublemaker to make a point.

Then, for three days, 42 children are on their own, dying in comic-horrific vignettes that often ring uncomfortably true, and showing nobility as often as beastliness. By the time you've worked out who the kids are, most of them have gone, in a succession of surprising, disturbing, touching, horribly funny or deeply upsetting ways. It's impossible to guess which of these neatly-uniformed youngsters is secretly a serial killer, a self-sacrificing hero, a born victim or simply another body count statistic.

Indeed, it's a movie that never lets you settle down, zipping between satire and splatter, offering moments that will make the most hardened viewer cringe and snatches of quiet melancholy that will haunt you for a long time. ★★★★ **KN**

BATTLEFIELD EARTH (2000)

Starring: *John Travolta (Terl), Barry Pepper (Jonnie Goodboy Tyler), Forest Whitaker (Ker), Kim Coates (Carlo), Sabine Karsenti (Chrissy), Michael Byrne (Parson Staffer), Kelly Preston (Kirk), Christian Tessier (Mickey), Sylvain Landry (Sammy), Richard Tyson (Robert The Fox), Christopher Freeman (Processing Clerk)*
Director: *Roger Christian*
Screenwriters: *Corey Mandell, J.D. Shapiro, based on the novel by L. Ron Hubbard*
12/118 mins./Sci-fi/USA

In the year 3000, a human slave rises up against the alien oppressors who have colonised a post-apocalyptic earth.

Given the relationship between the stars and the original Earth author, L. Ron Hubbard of Scientology fame, *Battlefield Earth* bares more than a passing whiff of a dubious vanity project. After all, Travolta's been trying to get the screen version of the mammoth novel off the ground for a decade. What has finally emerged is a peculiar paradox, science fiction that feels old-fashioned, its nominal alien overlords must die set-up and B-movie ideas outmoded by the onrush of Matrixes and Phantom Menaces.

Shot in a murky twilight, possibly to hide the sloppy fusion of CGI and modelwork, we are in a familiar desolate futurescape (3000) of crumbling ruins and isolated tribes. The Psychlos – really daft lanky, dreadlocked Tefal heads with rank complexions and hefty codpieces – are a sinister, genocidal race of manipulators and sadists, exploiting Earth for mineral assets, principally gold. Travolta's Terl is a maniacal security chief with a greedy personal agenda (to get off this forsaken world as rich as possible). Pitted against him is Jonnie Goodboy Tyler (*Saving Private Ryan*'s Barry Pepper), a wild human refusing to submit to alien thraldom, who through Terl's misguided subterfuge gets mind-zapped with Psychlo know-how and plots an uprising of the backward Earthlings. And that's about it.

Director Roger Christian, once a set decorator on *Star Wars*, keeps getting confused as to which film he's ripping off, fudging his way through various slices of *Blade Runner*, *The Matrix*, *Planet Of The Apes* and even TV's long, lamented invasion hit, *V*. His wannabe cool, foggy noirish look is at odds with all the comic-book broadness and the action, especially the nuke-the-baddies crescendo, and it's edited with such crashing fury that most of it is plain incomprehensible.

Bizarrely, the film that actually springs to mind, upon looking at Travolta's plump, rubbery claws and preposterous giant forehead, is *Carry On Screaming*. Which just about says it all. There is nothing in *Battlefield Earth* you can take seriously. While the producer/star certainly tries his darnedest to give it some flavour, playing Terl with the same raspy-cool badness he threw into *Face/Off*, the script remains ropey no matter how much relish it's given. It's also shot through with floppy logic: the Psychlos' non-comprehension at human cunning, even though the former defeated 'civilised' man, or post-apocalyptic cavemen learning to fly a secret store of Harriers in ten minutes flat.

With the exception of Trek's comical nastiness, none of the other characters even register. Barry Pepper has nothing to work with in Tyler, so he hulks about moodily as if trying to get the whole thing over without being noticed. Forest Whitaker, lost in Psychlo prosthetic, as Trek's fumbling evil sidekick, Ker, is given nothing more than the occasional cackle, while Richard Tyson, Kelly Preston and Kim Coates do no more than turn up. As for Scientology ... to be fair, there isn't anything sinister going on here, with nary a blipvert or allusion to be found. The sensible option would be to distance themselves from such irksome rubbish entirely. ★ **IN**

◑ BATTLESHIP POTEMKIN (BRONENOSETS POTYOMKIN) (1925)

Starring: *Aleksandr Antonov (Grigory Vakulinchuk, Bolshevik Sailor), Vladimir Barksy (Commander Golikov), Grigori Aleksandrov (Chief Officer Giliarovsky), Ivan Bobrov (Young Sailor, flogged while sleeping), Mikhail Gomorov (Militant Sailor)*
Directors: *Sergei M. Eisenstein, Grigori Aleksandrov*
Screenwriters: *Nina Agadzhanova, Sergei M. Eisenstein, intertitles by Nikolai Aseyev, Sergei Tretyakov*
PG/75 mins./Drama/History/War/Soviet Union

When Russian naval staff are given rotten meat to eat on top of the squalor they already suffer, there's call for mutiny, and riots ensue, which bring about great bloodshed.

Denied a certificate by the British censors in 1926 and so frowned upon by the government that a distributor who tried to secure the film was 'visited' by Scotland Yard, *Battleship Potemkin* was seen almost exclusively in Britain at film societies and workers' clubs until the advent of DVD. Eisenstein's masterpiece is a film that many like to discuss knowledgeably, but surprisingly few have seen.

Don't be put off by the fact that it's an old silent movie or by the highbrow pronouncements that will undoubtedly herald its standing as a cinematic masterpiece. Simply remember that without it the shower scene in *Psycho* would have been messy but not masterly and Kevin Costner would never have chased a pram down a staircase in *The Untouchables*.

Potemkin was originally planned as a brief aside in a multi-episode history of the 1905 Russian Revolution. However, bad weather prevented Eisenstein from shooting any other scenes and while on location in Odessa, he became obsessed with the story of the mutiny on board the battleship and the brutal assault on the citizens who came to welcome it into port. From this distance, it's hard to appreciate the effect Potemkin had on contemporary viewers. The complexity was impressive enough, but Potemkin's greatness lay in the fact it proved that symbolic imagery could have the same emotional and intellectual impact on an audience as narrative logic. Cliché perhaps, but cinema never would be the same again. The plate smashing, the fog scene, the Odessa steps massacre and the roaring lion are among the most famous images ever committed to celluloid. If you only ever see one silent, this is the one it should be. ★★★★★ **DP**

Silent Russian Cinema

What it is: State-sponsored, post-Revolution cinema, wedding cutting-edge technical innovations with propagandist intent.
Hallmarks: Montage; strict adherence to whatever view of contemporary Russia the authorities held that week; revolutionary fervour; striking silhouettes; hideous-looking capitalist baddies; noble crowds of heroic revolutionary goodies.
Key figures: Sergei Eisenstein, Dziga Vertov, Alexander Dovzhenko.
If you see one movie, see: *Battleship Potemkin* (1925)

◑ BATTLESTAR GALACTICA (1978)

Starring: *Richard Hatch (Captain Apollo), Dirk Benedict (Lieutenant Starbuck), Lorne Greene (Commander Adama), Noah Hathaway (Boxey), Jane Seymour (Serina)*
Directors: *Richard A. Colla, Alan J. Levi*
Screenwriters: *John Ireland, Glen A. Larson*
PG/119 mins./Sci-fi/USA

With the 12 colonies of man all but destroyed by the evil Cylon Alliance, and the battle fleet in ruins, the sole remaining battlestar, Galactica, leads a ragtag convoy of ships in search of the mythical planet of Earth. The first stop is Carillon, where the Cylons have laid a trap.

Although a pilot for a subsequent American TV series, *Battlestar Galactica* was released as a full theatrical movie in Britain to cash in on the demand for sci-fi cowboy movies in the mould of George Lucas' magnificent *Star Wars*. Although evidently a rip-off – there were hints of Lucas even taking the matter to the courts – this spacebound wagon train, whose limits are readily apparent, is great fun.

That is down to creator Glen A. Larson's keen nose for a story, and grasp that what made Lucas' blockbuster sing was fundamentally a punchy set of memorable characters with really cool names. Larson fully obliges here: Richard Hatch as the noble, straight-faced hero Apollo, the splendid Dirk Benedict as smart-tongued Han Solo clone Starbuck, and leathery Lorne Greene lending his wise basso-tones to their leader Adama. John Ireland's dialogue even manages a sly reflexive irony: 'Ten thousand light years from nowhere, our planet shot to pieces, people starving, and I'm gonna get us in trouble?' smarts the ever-chirpy Starbuck.

Their adventure rattles on at a great pace, dividing its attentions between the initial escape after human betrayal leads the forbidding Cylons, with their oscillating red eye-bulb, warbling computer speak and shiny metal hides, to crash the human party, and a pitstop on decadent planet Carillon. Here, the plot hides a particularly nasty about-face for the do-gooder heroes.

It may just be a launching pad for the popular series that jetted onto BBC2, but there is thoroughness to the script that allows the pilot to stand-alone. The effects too, while never touching *Star Wars*' galactic ballet, are vigorous and exciting, the human's spacecraft designed with natty Aztec motifs. The head-rush whoosh as the fighters launch along glittering tubes into the battle was just ace. ★★★ **IN**

BEACHES (1988)

Starring: *Bette Midler (CC Bloom), Barbara Hershey (Hillary Whitney Essex), John Heard (John Pierce), Spalding Gray (Dr Richard Milstein), Lainie Kazan (Leona Bloom), James Read (Michael Essex), Grace Johnston (Victoria Cecillia Essex), Mayim Bialik (CC Bloom, aged 11), Marcie Leeds (Hilary Whitney Essex, aged 11).*
Director: *Garry Marshall*
Screenwriter: *Mary Agnes Donoghue, based on the novel by Iris Rainer Dart*
15/123 mins./Drama/USA

Singer CC Bloom is summoned from the Hollywood Bowl to the bedside of Hillary Whitney Essex, and flashes back over their thirty-year friendship. CC goes from brash singing telegram girl to brash Broadway star to brash down-and-out to brash recording sensation, while Hillary progresses from rich radical student through rich ACLU lawyer to rich housewife to rich divorcee single mother to rich terminally ill invalid.

Adapted by Mary Agnes Donoghue from Iris Rainer Dart's novel, and produced by Bonnie Bruckheimer-Martell and Margaret Jennings South, *Beaches* epitomises the sort of triple-strength, three-hankie work you can expect from American women with three names and gives the lie to those who thought they stopped making women's pic heartstring-tuggers like *Old Acquaintance* or *Mr Skeffington* in the 1940s.

Midler is more often given to singing comic songs about brassieres than Bette Davis or Greer Garson used to be, but her character is given just as many chances to have emotional crises, overcome her innate selfishness and egomania and put down a succession of foils with waspish remarks. And Barbara Hershey, fresh from a series of silicone implants which did a Dorian Gray trick to her face, models tasteful high fashions, swings her gorgeous hair and dies with utmost dignity. Husbands, lovers and business associates pop up and then disappear from their lives, but they still have each other, and are finally able to share in the raising of Hillary's daughter. John Heard gets stuck with the Claude Rains role, standing about devotedly and letting the women get all the big scenes.

The bravura performances are undeniably watchable even during the inevitable fade-away-and-die finale, and the early, comic stretches – particularly an Atlantic City sequence starring the astonishing Mayim Bialik as the 11-year-old Midler – are refreshingly breezy. ★★★ **KN**

BE COOL (2005)

Starring: *John Travolta (Chili Palmer), Uma Thurman (Edie Athens), Vince Vaughn (Raji), Cedric the Entertainer (Sin LaSalle), Christina Milian (Linda Moon)*
Director: *F. Gary Gray*
Screenwriter: *Peter Steinfeld, based on the novel by Elmore Leonard*
12A/118 mins/Comedy/Crime/USA

Chili Palmer has had enough of being a movie producer — now he's moving into the music industry. With the help of a record label owner, he's set on making a new musical discovery a star.

For a sequel to criticise sequels is to play a very dangerous game indeed. Even those with the humour and originality to back up their knowing winks have to be careful to stay the right side of smug. Those as wandering and witless as *Be Cool* should know not to provide snarky film critics with extra ammo.

Ironically, it's the first scene, in which Chili Palmer and a cameoing James Woods riff on how sequels are cash-ins with no real value, that provides the only real moment of clever comedy. From thereon in, F. Gary Gray's follow-up to Barry Sonnenfeld's *Get Shorty* saunters where its forbear swaggered, mumbles where the other zinged. Gray fails to differentiate *Be Cool*'s music biz from the movie industry we saw in *Get Shorty*, so the archetypes he sends up (clueless managers, jumped-up stars) are merely poor imitations of the characters in Chili's first outing. There's no individual as extravagantly entertaining as *Shorty*'s Danny DeVito (although he does have a bit-part here), Gene Hackman or Dennis Farina, just a roll-call of famous faces so exhaustive that it's difficult to pick any of them out of the starry crowd.

The number of names onscreen is dazzling, but it's a case of 'never mind the quality, feel the cast', with Gray apparently too overwhelmed by the calibre of his actors to reign in their performances or cut their big moments to keep the plot trim. Travolta whispers his way through the film with no authority and fails to reignite any chemistry with Thurman, bland as a record label owner – which is astonishing given their history. The ill-advised retread of their lusty dance routine in *Pulp Fiction* is a sexless labour, making these two icons of cool look like in-laws drunkenly grinding to convince the kids they've still got it.

Meanwhile, Milian is fine as the aspiring singer of whom everyone wants a piece (though her pretty-but-thin voice rather begs the question: why?), Harvey Keitel disappears in the mix and it's kindest to ignore Vince Vaughn's embarrassing mugging as the faux-ghetto manager altogether. It's a solitary hooray, then, for The Rock, who hoards the few laughs there are with a game turn as a gay bodyguard, taking on everything with such a lack of ego that you forgive the stereotype. ★★ **OR**

THE BEACH (2000)

Starring: *Leonardo DiCaprio (Richard), Tilda Swinton (Sal), Virginie Ledoyen (Françoise), Guillaume Canet (Etienne), Robert Carlyle (Daffy), Paterson Joseph (Keaty)*
Director: *Danny Boyle*
Screenwriter: *John Hodge, based on the novel by Alex Garland*
15/119 mins./Drama/Adventure/Thriller/USA

Richard acts on the word of a crazed traveller and goes to seek out paradise in Thailand. What he finds is a society cut off from civilisation, which at first seems idyllic, but the stong characters and various weaknesses in the group bring about its own destruction.

Getting away from it all on an unspoilt tropical beach is not the idyll of your lottery winning dreams in this unnerving drama of a hidden Eden where obsessive travellers disassociate from the world.

DiCaprio is backpacker Richard, who thinks he's worldly-wise, but is so 'the young American abroad' when he seeks adventure and danger in Thailand. A strange encounter with crazed Daffy, who rants of a perfect, secret beach, seems the travel tip for him. And he recruits a French girl he fancies rotten and her amiable boyfriend to join him on a mysterious, funny, scary journey to the spectacularly beautiful (take a bow, cinematographer Darius Khondji) haven.

There Sal holds sway over a community of drop-outs who are kind of a cross between the Swiss Family Robinson and an apocalyptic water sport cult. Like Garland's novel, the film will be compared with *Lord Of The Flies* as the absence of societal constraints and concerns creates a moral vacuum for wild things to rumpus mightily. *The Beach* is more a microcosm of the modern world, though, with a more experienced gang and their alternative attempts to connect with one another riven by their secrets, desires, jealousies and competitiveness. They import their own serpents into this paradise.

Richard is more than a little disturbed, as we learn from a voiceover that borders on intrusive but underlines his alienation. His fixation with 'Nam movies could be spelled out more clearly to explain his solitary stint in the jungle turning into a pathological commando game, *Heart Of Darkness* for the Sega generation.

DiCaprio's perfect as the smartarsed thrill-seeker and the more wry narrator with hindsight, but he works very hard for his reputed $20 million fee when required to turn into a bug-eating nutter. Despite the dodginess of this interlude, however, Boyle's direction holds a true line between allure and horror, and Hodge's script is intriguing and forceful. It's much better than rumoured: entertaining, engrossing, and ripe for discussion – somewhere civilised – afterwards. ★★★★ **AE**

BEAN (1997)

Starring: *Rowan Atkinson (Mr Bean), Peter MacNicol (David Langley), Sir John Mills (Chairman), Pamela Reed (Alison Langley), Harris Yulin (George Grierson), Burt Reynolds (General Newton), Larry Drake (Elmer), Danny Goldring (Security Buck), Johnny Galecki (Stingo Sheelie), Chris Ellis (Det. Butler), Peter Capaldi (Gareth)*
Director: *Mel Smith*
Screenwriters: *Richard Curtis, Robin Driscoll, from characters created by Rowan Atkinson, Richard Curtis*
PG/90 mins./Comedy/USA

As an attempt to get him out of the country, security guard Mr Bean is sent to Los Angeles to help watch over a precious painting. But the gallery mistake him for an art expert – and foolishly increase his responsibilities.

Mr Bean, the accident-prone, faintly irritating goon who gives Rowan Atkinson the chance to use his rubber-faced, nay bodied abilities to full effect, barely sustains the laughs over a 30-minute sketch show, never mind a movie. So the fact that the result is not only consistently entertaining, but frequently laugh-out-loud funny, comes as a very pleasant surprise.

The plot has Mr Bean working as a security guard at the National Gallery, where unsurprisingly, he's not much cop. When an opportunity arises to get rid of him by packing him off to Los Angeles, the gallery seizes it eagerly. There he is to work at a monumental unveiling ceremony for a painting worth $50,000,000.

Once in the City Of Angels, Bean soon crushes the idyll of his host family (MacNicol, Reed) and charges around with all the finesse of a liberated zoo animal. But the LA gallery reps (who mistakenly believe him to be London's finest art scholar) put his bizarre behaviour down to genius and foolishly leave him alone with the painting. Given the sheer number of visual gags, it's inevitable that some of them fall flat. But thanks to a decent script, other characters are given room to breathe rather than just letting the latex-mugged protagonist take centre stage.

Tagline
The ultimate disaster movie.

The set-pieces are for the most part hilarious (Bean's attempt to dry his trousers after an accident in the men's room proves a high point), and the sensibly short running time prevents things from wearing thin.

Atkinson performs to perfection, giving his alter ego some much needed personality (Mr Bean turns out to be rather smarter than in previous outings and even gets a few lines) and making him strangely likeable. ★★★★ **CW**

THE BEAST FROM 20,000 FATHOMS (1953)

Starring: *Paul Christian (Professor Tom Nesbitt), Paula Raymond (Lee Hunter), Cecil Kellaway (Prof. Thurgood Elson), Kenneth Tobey (Col. Jack Evans), Donald Woods (Capt. Phil Jackson), Lee Van Cleef (Capt. Stone)*
Director: *Eugene Lourie*
Screenwriters: *Fred Freiberger, Eugene Lourie, Louis Morheim, Robert Smith, based on a story by Ray Bradbury*
PG/80 mins./Sci-fi/USA

Nuclear testing in the Arctic awakens a prehistoric rhedosaurus which has been frozen in the ice. The radioactive dinosaur returns to wreak havoc in its ancient spawning grounds – now New York City.

One of the key titles in the 1950s science-fiction boom, this was conceived as an atom age equivalent of *King Kong* – which had enjoyed a successful re-release in 1952 – and became the breakout film for rising effects man Ray Harryhausen.

Beast sets the pattern for many subsequent creature features, opening with an A-bomb test that releases a dinosaur from its million-year-sleep in the arctic ice, then has the monster destroy a few ships at sea and an isolated lighthouse while the nuclear scientist hero (Christian) who glimpses the thing in the blizzard tries to convince the authorities that he isn't crazy. Also typical is the tight-suited lady boffin (Raymond) with a masculine name ('Lee Hunter'), the bristling military man (Tobey) who keeps asking how to kill the thing, and the older specialist (Cecil Kellaway) whose diving bell gets swallowed (presumably at 20,000 fathoms).

The rousing climax brings the monster ashore in New York to chomp down on big city cops, trample through familiar streets and send crowds fleeing in panic before it takes a last stand amid burning rollercoasters on Coney Island as a sharpshooter (bit player Lee Van Cleef) takes the beast down with an isotope missile.

Purportedly based on a tiny Ray Bradbury story ('The Foghorn'), it owes quite a bit to *King Kong* – but was then homaged itself in the first *Godzilla* movie, which is more or less a remake. There was no such beast as a 'rhedosaurus' (the 'rh' comes from the animator's initials), but the catlike carnivorous quadruped is one of the greatest dinosaurs in the movies. ★★★ **KN**

THE BEASTMASTER (1982)

Starring: *Marc Singer (Dar), Tanya Roberts (Kiri), Rip Torn (Maax), John Amos (Seth), Josh Milrad (Tal), Rod Loomis (King Zed), Ben Hammer (Young Dar's Father)*
Director: *Don Coscarelli*
Screenwriters: *Don Cscarelli, Paul Pepperman*
15/118 mins/Fantasy/Adventure/USA/West Germany

In a far off land at a far off time, heir to the throne Dar is transferred to the belly of an ox by evil priest Maax because a prophecy decided that this child will end up killing him. Rescued by a kindly family, he grows up to discover he has the power to communicate with animals and begins a quest for revenge.

A dirt cheap Conan clone stripped of gore for the young viewer, this is swords and sorcery at its most banal. Although being conceived and directed by Phantasm's Don Coscarelli, his world never comes to life, just a bog standard pre-medieval landscape as shot in Southern California. A mild mysticism hangs over it as Rip Torn's maniac priest ducks and dives between prophecies predicting his demise, but there is little in the way of redolent magic. It's a budget thing (there wasn't one) granting us no special effects to speak of, and leaving a hacked-out quest for revenge, stocked with B-rate actors in leather costumes (Singer and Roberts) and Torn caught on a career downswing.

Dar (were consonants on the pricy side?)'s natty ability to telepathically commune with animal-kind gives him a menagerie of beasts to fight his cause: a hawk (for its eyes), a pair of comedy ferrets (for their cunning) and a black panther (for its strength). Thus we get all the cuteness we could want. He also gets a bit steamed up over his cousin Tanya Roberts, just to make sure dads don't drop off to sleep.

Coscarelli requires no more of his cast, two and four-legged, to look lean and tanned, and read (or squawk) their sparse and corny lines in lazy American accents, then leap from boulder to boulder in over-choreographed and unconvincing fight scenes. There is a mild satisfaction when hammy Torn reaps his comeuppance – why didn't he just fire his soothsayer? – but the film scores no points on style, wit or pleasingly framed shots. Eleven-year-olds deserve better. ★★ **IN**

BEAUTIFUL GIRLS (1996)

Starring: *Matt Dillon (Tommy 'Birdman' Rowland), Noah Emmerich (Michael 'Mo' Morris), Annabeth Gish (Tracy Stover), Lauren Holly (Darian Smalls), Timothy Hutton (Willie Conway), Rosie O'Donnell (Gina Barrisano), Martha Plimpton (Jan), Natalie Portman (Marty), Michael Rapaport (Paul Kirkwood), Mira Sorvino (Sharon Cassidy), Uma Thurman (Andera), Sam Robards (Steve Rossmore), David Arquette (Boddy Conway)*
Director: *Ted Demme*
Screenwriter: *Scott Rosenberg*
15/112 mins./Drama/Comedy/Romance/USA

A piano player unsure about the choices in his life returns home to his family and friends to take stock.

Following the wave of bubbling, group-hug chick-flicks, came an emotionally charged chum movie from the bloke's perspective: sort of a male *Now And Then* with Demme defying all the odds with a gently entertaining charmer.

For bar pianist Hutton, thoughts of a steady job and marriage to Annabeth Gish (*Mystic Pizza*) are inducing palpitations. So when his high school reunion conveniently fudges the issue, he hotfoots it to snowy Knight's Ridge. Still ensconced in his hometown are four childhood friends – Dillon's ex-campus superstar turned snow plough driver, his sidekick Kev, family man Mo and supermodel-obsessed Paul – and in their company, he's more confused than ever.

Many so-called ensemble pieces provide little more than a host of unknowns backing one or two minor stars, but this is a rare and worthy exception. With no one big enough to swamp matters, the familiar cast convince by gelling instantly into a group of old friends. No small credit goes to Mira Sorvino as Dillon's loyal and long-suffering girlfriend, Holly as his self-centred ex, and Uma Thurman as bartender Stinky's (Priutt Taylor Vince) cousin and girl.

Hutton makes for a winning guide through this unassuming take on camaraderie and adult responsibility, but the stand out is Natalie Portman, who added to a reputation well-earned in Leon, as a smart, beguiling 13-year-old. ★★★★ **DB**

A BEAUTIFUL MIND (2001)

Starring: *Russell Crowe (John Nash), Ed Harris (Parcher), Jennifer Connelly (Alicia Nash), Christopher Plummer (Dr Rosen), Paul Bettany (Charles), Adam Goldberg (Sol), Josh Lucas (Hansen)*
Director: *Ron Howard*
Screenwriter: *Akiva Goldsman, based on the book by Sylvia Nasar*
12/130 mins./Drama/USA

Awards: *Academy Awards – Best Supporting Actress, Best Director, Best Picture, Best Screenplay based on Previously Published Material, BAFTA – Best Actor, Best Supporting Actress, Golden Globes – Best Drama, Best Supporting Actress, Best Actor (Drama), Best Screenplay*

John Nash is a mathematical whizz struggling to come up with a truly original idea with which to make his name. Later in life, however, a stint code-breaking for the government results in creeping paranoia and a gradual slide into schizophrenia.

Playing the mentally ill has always been a fast-track to critical and Oscar success. Here Russell Crowe stood on the shoulders of Geoffrey Rush (*Shine*), Daniel Day-Lewis (*My Left Foot*) and Dustin Hoffman (*Rain Man*) in trying to attract the Academy's attention for the third year running, with yet another crowd-pleaser of a performance. That he missed out on the final gong probably had more to do with his personal behaviour (punch up at the BAFTAs!) than his acting talent.

Essentially it's that old chestnut the inspirational biopic and Ron Howard skilfully yomps us along the well-worn path of early promise (success at sums!), catastrophic downfall (going bonkers!), and a final, emotionally charged triumph over adversity (winning the Nobel Prize!). The problem is that, even if you haven't read the book on which it's based, you're left with the niggling suspicion that this is all too neat to be anything near the whole story. As indeed turns out to be the case.

Nash's bisexuality, a child out of wedlock and a divorce are all AWOL, while the feel-good ending neatly skips over the horrible, irreparable reality of a professional and personal life effectively ruined by insanity. Of course, any biopic smoothes the edges and has to construct a story out of the messy realities of life, but here there's a sense that the manipulation borders on dishonesty.

None of which is to deny that there are very good things as well. Crowe marshals his tics with showy aplomb, Howard displays his usual facility for smoothly engineered filmmaking, and Akiva Goldsman's (yup, he of *Batman And Robin*) screenplay delivers the necessary dramatic wallop and a craftily shocking reversal.

Support is generally good, especially from Paul Bettany, previously seen whooping it up as Geoffrey Chaucer in *A Knight's Tale*. But in the end, Howard's film's undoubted effectiveness conceals a disappointingly cynical heart. ★★★ **AS**

BEAUTY AND THE BEAST (1991)

Starring: *the voices of: Paige O'Hara (Belle), Robby Benson (Beast), Rex Everhart (Maurice), Richard White (Gaston), Angela Lansbury (Mrs Potts), Jerry Orbach (Lumiere), David Ogden Stiers (Cogsworth/Narrator)*
Director: *Kirk Wise*
Screenwriters: *Linda Woolverton, from a story by Kelly Asbury, Brenda Chapman, Tom Ellery, Kevin Harkey, Robert Lence, Burny Mattinson, Brian Pimental, Joe Ranft, Christopher Sanders and Bruce Woodside*
U/84 mins./Animated/Fantasy/Family/USA

Awards: *Best Original Score, Best Original Song, Golden Globes – Best Comedy/Musical, Best Original Score, Best Original Song*

When Belle's inventor father goes missing, she tracks him down to a castle owned by a fearsome beast. She then agrees to take her father's place as hostage and soon begins to feel affectionately towards the Beast.

Back in October 1991, New York Film Festival audiences were treated to something rather different. For the first time, Disney screened an unfinished version of its latest project, *Beauty And The Beast*. This, remember, was in the days before DVD 'making of' material, when even film students were limited in their access to films as works-in-progress. So the print that audience saw was a revelation: a mixture of polished animation, black-and-white basics and inspirational sketches.

But even more eye-opening was the film itself. Here was a musical that heralded Disney's return to classic form, and that went on to become the first (and, thanks to the new category, last) animated film to be nominated for an Academy Award in the Best Film category. The standing ovation that *Beauty And The Beast* received at the New York Film Festival, and the critical acclaim that followed, was just the start of the film's success story.

The top brass at Disney knew full-well the statement they were making with the festival screening. Since Walt's death in 1966, the standard-setting animation arm had lost its way. The magic was kept alive through re-releases of films like *Bambi* and *Snow White And The Seven Dwarfs*, but more recent efforts – from the bland *The Fox And The Hound* to the forgettable *The Black Cauldron* – weren't doing them any favours. What's more, the saccharine, kid-friendly approach of Disney was out of favour in a cinema world where, even in U-certificate films, swearing, single-parented kids befriended aliens (*E.T.*), and heroes had to confront the fact their father murdered half the universe (*The Empire Strikes Back*).

Finally, in 1989, the studio got back on track with *The Little Mermaid*. It had the flavour of much-loved, old-style Disney – memorable musical numbers, loveable animal sidekicks – but a more up-to-date approach to storytelling. If this was a gentle hint that Disney was once more a force to be reckoned with, then *Beauty And The Beast* was a sirens-blaring, flashing-lights announcement that the studio was not only back, but heading for the big league. This was when it suddenly became fashionable to call such movies 'animated features' rather than 'cartoons' – and this particular one was to be geared as much to the adult audience as the kids they would be accompanying. The kid-free screening at the New York Film Festival – and the unfinished state in which the film was screened – made this grown-up approach very clear. As did the content. The visual references alone – from the *Battleship Potemkin* pram running down the stairs in the final castle battle, to the Jackie Gleason-style Honeymooners facial expression of the Beast as Belle turns down his invitation to dinner – were for the buffs, not the under-eights.

The key to making this new version of *Beauty And The Beast* work lay in the way the makers approached the fairy-tale source material. Walt Disney had tried to adapt the story twice himself (once in the 1930s and again in the 1950s), but had stumbled over how to expand it to feature length. This time, the studio decided to engage a scriptwriter (Linda Woolverton) who was a novice to the animated world, but had a very 90s take on the story. For the Beauty who would learn to love the Beast, Woolverton created Belle – a feminist heroine who was more rounded than previous Disney characters. The writer also poured the foibles of her ex-boyfriends into the villain, the vain Gaston, who tries to woo Belle for himself and destroy the Beast. The results were hilarious. To Woolverton, the characters were written as real people, not cartoons.

Howard Ashman and Alan Menken, the musical team who had been re-engaged after their success on *The Little Mermaid*, had no problem finding songs for such characters. But these weren't just songs for the sake of it. Each was there to move the story on, either physically bridging gaps during which the characters travel between locations ('Kill The Beast'), or fleshing out the character without slowing up the narrative ('Gaston'). Ashman and Menken were at first worried that their approach might be too theatrical for Disney. The irony is that not only was their first attempt (Belle's opening number) adored by the team working on the project, but the theatrical approach paid off when *Beauty And The Beast* became Disney's first Broadway stage musical and paved the way for a whole new division at the studio. Ashman's energy was astounding, considering he was dying of AIDS even as they recorded the final soundtrack. In the end, despite being bed-ridden in New York, he stayed on the phone as the final songs were recorded, directing operations. The film is dedicated to him.

Humour also played a major part in the film's success – visual gags for the kids and sly asides for the adults were another Disney first. Without this testing ground, *Toy Story* wouldn't have been half as funny. *Beauty And The Beast* also paved the way for the new digital style of animation. Important sequences, such as the ballroom dance scene, were handed over to the digital division to give the movie a 3-D life and depth.

But what appeals most to film fans is that those who made it clearly loved movies. The film references – and there are many – are not random. They reference films, or moments in films, that are truly great. Cocteau's visual masterpiece, *La Belle Et La Béte*, is a clear influence throughout, but throw in a bit of Busby Berkeley choreography (for tableware, of course!), a *Gone With The Wind* backdrop and even a nod to *Bambi*, and you can be sure almost every member of the audience will have picked up on at least one. ★★★★★ **EC**

Movie Trivia: Beauty and the Beast

Mary Kay Bergman (Bimbette) voiced most of the female characters in *South Park*. She committed suicide in 1999. Walt Disney originally tried to adapt *Beauty and the Beast* in the 1930s and 1950s, but the project never took off.

BEAVIS AND BUTT-HEAD DO AMERICA (1996)

Starring: *voices of: Mike Judge (Beavis/ Butt-head/ Tom Anderson/Mr Van Driessen/Principal McVicker), Cloris Leachman (Old Woman on Plane and Bus), Richard Linklater (Tour Bus Driver), Demi Moore (Dallas Grimes), Bruce Willis (Muddy Grimes), Greg Kinnear (AFT Agent Bork)*
Directors: *Mike Judge, Yvette Kaplan*
Screenwriters: *Mike Judge, Joe Stillmand*
12/81 mins./Adventure/Animation/Comedy/Crime/USA

After Beavis and Butt-head's beloved TV is stolen, the pair decide to venture into the outside world to get in back.

This, they must have repeated like a production meeting mantra, is never going to work. While America's favourite pair of duo-dimensional delinquents may have captured what remains of the MTV generation's shredded imagination when delivered in couch potato friendly 40-second chunks, with a dire rock promo never more than two minutes away, the idea of giving what is essentially a one-joke cartoon strip 81 minutes of big-screen time must have had the folks at Disney snorting into their Crayolas. Which made it something of a surprise when Beavis and Butt-head turned out to be a serious contender for funniest film of 1997.

For those terminally disconnected to the *Zeitgeist*, Beavis and Butt-head are two hormonally crazed teenager morons who spend the majority of their time staring at MTV and mining the language for unlikely double entendres. In their first movie outing their low-rent idyll is disrupted when their precious TV is stolen and the boys set off on a road trip to retrieve the tube and inevitably to 'score'. What follows is essentially a series of sketches, almost all of which hit their mark, with highlights being the boy's first plane trip (violently disrupted by Beavis raiding an old lady's handbag for pep pills that transform him into screeching alter ego Cornholio) together with the two lying near death from thirst in the desert only to launch into trademark guffaws when a pair of vultures start shagging in front of them.

What also emerges is a new and surprising likeability in the characters. Cretinous and sex-obsessed they may be – what 14-year-old isn't? – but there's an innocence about them summed up in Beavis's big speech in which he shrieks to a bemused busful of passengers that: 'We're never gonna score, never! It's not fair!' And with a final shot of the boys hoiking their beloved TV into the sunset it becomes clear who the unlikely inspiration for this duo are. Ladies and gentlemen, Beavis and Butt-head, Tom and Huck for the 90s. ★★★★ **AS**

◑ BEDAZZLED (2000)

Starring: *Brendan Fraser (Elliot Richards/Jefe/Mary), Elizabeth Hurley (The Devil), Frances O'Connor (Alison Gardner/Nicole Delarusso), Miriam Shor (Carol/Penthouse Hostess), Orlando Jones (Danile/Dan/Danny, Esteban, Beach Jock, Lamar Garrett, Dr Ngegitigegitibaba)*
Director: *Harold Ramis*
Screenwriters: *Larry Gelbart, Harold Ramis, Peter Tolan, based on a screenplay by Peter Cook and Dudley Moore and a story by Peter Cook.*
12/93 mins./Fantasy/Comedy/USA/Germany

Elliot Richards is a social misfit, lonely, romantically inept, mocked by his work colleagues and hopelessly in love with co-worker Alison Gardner. When the devil turns up and offers him seven wishes in return for his soul, Elliot accepts in order to snag the girl of his dreams.

Master screenwriter and all round grouch William Goldman once remarked that screenplays are all about structure, they're pieces of engineering rather than art; bridges rather than sculptures, if you will. It's a lesson that writer-director Harold Ramis obviously took to heart when he penned his 1993 comic masterpiece, *Groundhog Day*; in engineering terms it's near perfect, a positive Sydney Harbour Bridge of an achievement that withstands viewing after viewing without so much as a wobble. Unfortunately, *Bedazzled* is more like London's much-mocked Blade Of Light. It looks fantastic on paper, but once you're on it, it bounces you around for a while before throwing you off feeling slightly nauseous.

What Ramis' film does share with *Groundhog Day* is the element of repetition. Essentially a series of linked sketches, it has lonely, cubicle-bound technical support advisor Elliot Richards adopting various guises, courtesy of Beelzebub, in an attempt to woo love of his life, Alison. He becomes, among other archetypes: a Colombian drug baron (with an audacious ten minutes of the film conducted in Spanish with subtitles); a sensitive 'new man' who has difficulty looking at the sunset without bursting into tears; and an underendowed basketball star. Inevitably in each instance, Lucifer throws a curve ball and things don't work out. When he asks to be rich, sophisticated and well-endowed, he also happens to be gay. When he's a sensitive guy, she turns out to prefer a bit of rough. And so on.

There are enough genuinely funny moments in *Bedazzled* to keep you gently amused, and certainly more than its inspiration, the Peter Cook/Dudley Moore movie of 1967, can boast. Brendan Fraser, who's been threatening to blossom for a while now, is a comic revelation, fashioning six utterly different riffs on his geekish central character and showing a facility for a more sophisticated brand of comedy than he hinted at with the cute-but-dumb lug act he employed in *California Man* (1992), *George Of The Jungle* (1997) and *Blast From The Past* (1999). Elizabeth Hurley is as one-dimensional as ever, but not enough to do any real damage.

What does hobble the movie is an ending which drives straight off a cliff. While in *Groundhog Day* the central character can credibly be seen to have 'learned something' from the constant repetition by the end of the movie, here Ramis tries the same trick and it simply doesn't come off. There is absolutely no-reason for Fraser's character's transformation and the conclusion is simply baffling. Not exactly dazzling, then, but bright enough to deserve a few hours of your time. ★★★ **WT**

◑ BEDKNOBS AND BROOMSTICKS (1971)

Starring: *Angela Lansbury (Eglantine Price), David Tomlinson (Emelius Browne), Roddy McDowall (Mr Jelk), Sam Jaffe (Bookman), Cindy O'Callaghan (Carrie Rawlins), Ray Snart (Paul Rawlins), Ian Weighill (Charlie Rawlins)*
Director: *Robert Stevenson*
Screenwriters: *Ralph Wright, Ted Berman, Bill Walsh, Don DaGradi, based on the novel by Mary Norton*
U/117 mins./Fantasy/USA
Certificate: G/U
Awards: *Academy Awards – Best Special Visual Effects*

During WWII three evacuee children are sent to live with Eglantine Price, who turns out to be a trainee witch. From there they embark on a series of adventures, travelling using a magic bed, in search of the mystical words that will enable Price to help with the war effort.

From the team that brought you *Mary Poppins* comes a whole lot more of the same. And while the songs have none of the enduring catchiness of 'A Spoonful Of Sugar' or 'Chim-Chim Cher-ee', the blend of real-life action and deliciously elaborate animation is fabulous.

Angela Lansbury, one of those actors who arrived fully middle-aged, takes over from Julie Andrews as the kooky, genial pseudo-mother figure – here a proto-witch on a magical correspondence course rather than a flying nanny – and does a fair job with the necessary blend of the ethereal and stoical English pragmatism. As was the modus operandi of this early '70s brand of Disney wish-fulfilment, the trio of kids are simply bland ciphers for the nipper audience, travelling by an enchanted bedstead to magical worlds characterised by being gloriously cartoon. Such lavish animation threaded with flesh and blood characters is a wonderful, transporting idea for children, a lost art amongst the clever-clever majesty of CGI.

An underwater number, in which the human's sing through bubbles, boasts a wild assortment of anthropomorphised sea critters, but the highlight is a soccer match staged by the lion king of Naboomland. With perennially stiff-uppered Poppins-remainder David Tomlinson as ref, the rules are more a matter of royal decree, and a scuffling, baffling, riotously fun game ensues between all manner of elephants, lions, bears, hogs, rhinos and cheetahs.

It's an irritation then that the film feels the need to return to the threat of the war. Lansbury's plan, and the overarching plot device, is to complete a spell to animate an army of hollow suits of armour to take on the invading Nazis. A heavy concept for kids to take hold of, especially given how faceless the enemy are, and the strange dashes of jingoistic pride are almost distasteful: 'We have driven the Hun into the sea,' the good witch declares with some satisfaction. ★★★ **IN**

◑ BEETLEJUICE (1988)

Starring: *Alec Baldwin (Adam Matiland), Geena Davis (Barbara Maitland), Michael Keaton (Betelgeuse), Catherine O'Hara (Delia Deetz), Glenn Shadix (Otho), Winona Ryder (Lydia Deetz), Robert Goulet (Maxie Dean)*
Director: *Tim Burton*
Screenwriters: *Michael McDowell, Warren Skaaren, based on a story by McDowell, Larry Wilson*
15/92 mins./Comedy/Horror/USA
Awards: *Academy Awards – Best Makeup*

A ghostly couple find their beloved New England home taken over by particularly revolting yuppies. In an effort to get rid of them they hire a 'freelance bio-exorcist' named Beetlejuice.

Tim Burton's outlandish horror comedy has newlydeads Alec Baldwin and Geena Davis hiring trouble-shooting zombie Michael Keaton to keep their home from human habitation. At first this seems to offer a solution to their problems – the new inhabitants do indeed seem to be more scary than the ghosts – but rapidly Beetlejuice's manic 'solutions' descend into chaos.

There is loads to revel in – a young Winona Ryder as the estranged daughter of the new family, Harry Belafonte music, a glorious closing gag – and, despite the delightfully demented visuals on offer, little to contend with Keaton's full-on comedic whirling dervish.

At the time, it seemed like a one-off oddity; now it seems like a Burton blueprint: surreal sensibility (check), nutty energy (check) and an acute feel for the pangs of the outsider (check). Amazingly, it all still feels fresh, even though Burton has since become something of his own franchise since. ★★★★ **IF**

⊙ BEFORE SUNRISE (1995)

Starring: *Ethan Hawke (Jesse), Julie Delpy (Celine), Andrea Eckert (Wife on the train), Hanno Poschi (Husband on the train), Karl Bruckschwaiger (Guy on the bridge), Tex Rubinowitz (Guy on the bridge)*
Director: *Richard Linklater*
Screenwriters: *Richard Linklater, Kim Krizan*
15/97 mins./Romance/Comedy/Drama/USA

Two travellers meet on a train in Europe as they are about to begin their journeys home. They decide to spend their last 24 hours together talking about life and love.

When was the last time you saw a leading man ask his onscreen love interest what she might begin to hate about him, were they to stay together? Probably never, actually – unless you happen to have seen *Before Sunrise*, an overlooked-at-the-cinema but utterly charming blend of romance and realism that breathes new life into the genre.

Two strangers, Jesse, and Celine, meet on a train bound for Vienna: he is heading for Austrian turf to fly back to the States; she is on the way home to Paris, a plan disrupted when Jesse successfully charms her off the train. The pair proceed to spend the entire night wandering around the Austrian capital, sharing cerebrally charged anecdotes and gradually falling in love. And as the sun comes up and the time for them to go their separate ways grows ever closer, the possibility of them ever seeing each other again becomes steadily more remote.

Director Richard Linklater earned his hip-directorial stripes with *Slacker* and *Dazed And Confused*, but with this intelligent, witty and poignant tale he really comes of age, replacing romantic stereotypes with fleshed-out, believable characters and giving Delpy the kind of sassy, spirited role that most actresses can only dream of. The glamour effect, too, is played down, focusing on the glorious Austrian scenery instead, and at times even slipping into fly-on-the-wall documentary mode.

But what really transforms what is fundamentally two people walking the streets nattering into something utterly irresistible is a script that crackles with wit and wisdom, that allows the pair to weigh up the pros and cons of prolonged coupledom instead of drenching them in hearts and flowers sentiment. Just five minutes of screen time in the company of Hawke and Delpy provides more insight into relationships than a dozen romantic comedies could ever muster up between them. A rare treat indeed. ★★★★ **CW**

⊙ BEFORE SUNSET (2004)

Starring: *Ethan Hawke (Jesse), Julie Delpy (Celine), Veron Dobtcheff (Bookstore Manager), Louise Lemonie Torres (Journalist #1), Rodolphe Pauly (Journalist #2), Mariane Plasteig (Waitress)*
Director: *Richard Linklater*
Screenwriters: *Richard Linklater, Julie Delpy, Ethan Hawke, from a story by Richard Linklater and Kim Krizan, based on characters created by Richard Linklater and Kim Krizan*
15/80 mins./Drama/Romance/USA

Awards: *Empire Awards – Best Actress*

Nine years after they said goodbye in Vienna, Jesse and Celine bump into each other in Paris at a reading from his new novel. Shocked but delighted to see each other, they spend the next few hours before he has to fly home.

Back in 1995, Richard Linklater – until then best-known for *Slacker* and *Dazed And Confused* – left Kevin Smith to chronicle America's waster youth and made a small, offbeat romance called *Before Sunrise*. A deeply appealing two-hander about an American backpacker (Hawke) and a French student (then-unknown Delpy) who meet on a train and talk their way around Vienna, *Before Sunrise* charmed romantically inclined twenty-somethings everywhere. The crux of the matter in that film, of course, is that at the end the pair agree to meet six months on. Would they be there? Would they live happily ever after? It was fun to daydream, but ultimately, was that even the point?

It is now. A decade later, Linklater – rejoined by his two stars, who share the writing credits – has produced a 'real-time' sequel, catching up with Jesse and Celine nine years down the road – a prospect that must strike both joy and trepidation into the hearts of devotees. Have they spoilt it all? Conversely, will it mean anything to those new to the pair? Should it ever have been made? The answers to these are broadly no, yes (there are even helpful flashbacks to the first film – but oh don't they show how shockingly gaunt Hawke has become!) and, well, the third could generate debates to rival those of our spirited protagonists.

Certainly there are problems with the film. A mere 80 minutes long, like *Before Sunrise* the structure of *Before Sunset* – two people wander aimlessly, arguing, flirting, ultimately rejoicing in each other – is not on paper the stuff of high drama, and some will find the lack of a definite story arc undisciplined and unengaging. Potentially more damaging is the abruptness of the ending which, coupled with the short running time, could leave some viewers wondering if the last reel slipped down the back of a filing cabinet. Teasingly frustrating in its ambiguity, the final scene – languid, heady, sexy as hell – eschews a solid, conventionally dramatic conclusion, instead taunting us with yet more questions – some will love this, but after the building tension of the preceding moments, others will demand more.

That said, there is still so much to love about Linklater's literate, candid, and this time necessarily more sombre film. Jesse and Celine, now in their early 30s and in theory older and wiser, are still as delightfully real as they were ten years ago. All credit to Hawke and Delpy, who hardly seem to be acting; they just are these characters. Meeting up by (almost) chance in Paris with mere hours until Jesse has to leave, the shell-shocked pair walk the streets of Le Marais and the Latin Quarter, stumbling from awkwardly polite niceties to heartfelt confessions and anxieties touching the very core of their 'grown-up' lives – the poignancy of regret, the loneliness of failing relationships, the agonising conflict between desire and duty – universal subjects that extend beyond the parameters of Jesse and Celine's story and will strike a chord even with those unfamiliar with the first film.

While some might balk at such wordiness, the film is far from earnest or depressing, full of humour and joy – and the three writers counter any chance of boredom by dropping mini bombshells at regular intervals; tiny ripples on the Richter Scale, perhaps, but hugely important twists in the context of this couple. Set against the beauty of Paris – cinematographer Lee Daniel hardly has to try! – it's near impossible not to be seduced by this picture, the director nevertheless cranking up the aesthetics by filming the city in long, golden-dappled tracking shots that soothe the eye just as he tightens the emotional screws. An involving and all too fleeting joy. ★★★★ **AE**

⊙ BEFORE THE REVOLUTION (PRIMA DELLA RIVOLUZIONE) (1964)

Starring: *Adriana Asti (Gina), Francesco Barilli (Fabrizio), Allen Midgette (Agostino) Morando Morandini (Cesare – Teacher), Domenico Alpi (Fabrizio's Father), Giuseppe Maghenzani (Fabrizio's mother), Clelia (Cristina Pariset)*
Director: *Bernardo Bertolucci*
Screenwriters: *Bernardo Bertolucci, Gianni Amico*
15/112 mins./Drama/Italy

Rejecting his bourgeois background, Fabrizio falls under the spell of Marxist intellectual Cesare and into the bed of his Aunt Gina before returning to his roots and his materialistic fiancée Clelia.

Bernardo Bertolucci was only 22 when he embarked on this follow-up to his auspicious debut, *The Grim Reaper*. Inspired by Stendhal's *The*

Charterhouse Of Parma, it's a rattlebag of borrowings and homages. Among the other literary antecedents are Shakespeare, Wilde and Pavese, while Bertolucci's touchstones Verdi and Freud also provide key inspiration, as does the 18th-century French politician Talleyrand, who provided the film's title in his epithet about those living before the revolution being the only ones to appreciate the full benefits of liberty.

A self-professed cinéaste, Bertolucci references numerous heroes in a visual style that was, nevertheless, beginning to assume a recognisable identity. The rose-tinted realism comes from Roberto Rossellini, the operatic intensity from Luchino Visconti and the Marxist dialect from Pier Paolo Pasolini (whom he had served as an assistant director). The integration of the characters within their environment owes much to Michelangelo Antonioni, the use of elegant, fluid sequence shots recalls both Max Ophuls and Alain Resnais, while the resort to jump cuts, structural fragmentation and knowing narration is unmistakably Godardian.

Yet, this is also very much a personal project, with an element of autobiographical self-analysis informing Fabrizio's odyssey, and it's fascinating to note how the visual poet in Bertolucci triumphs over the dilettante idealogue. Indeed, the film's emotional intensity is more affecting than its muddled message, which seems to be that it's easier to play the angry young man who can shock his complacent peers than an activist wholly committed to lasting change.

Bertolucci would regularly return to the theme of the naive firebrand who champions the ideals of an older guide only to discover that he's neither politically nor psychologically strong enough to pursue them. But while his later work would be more structurally and intellectually mature, there's still an earnest honesty about *Before The Revolution*'s precocious zeal. ★★★★ **DP**

⦸ THE BEGUILED (1971)

Starring: *Clint Eastwood (Corporal John McBurney), Geraldine Page (Martha Farnsworth), Elizabeth Hartman (Edwina Dabney), Jo Anne Harris (Carol)*
Director: *Don Siegel*
Screenwriters: *Albert Maltz, Irene Kamp, based on the novel by Thomas Cullinan*
15/105 mins./Drama/USA

A wounded Union soldier is found by a pupil of a nearby Confederate girls boarding school. As he heals, he starts to seduce the girls one by one, plotting his escape, and the harmonious mood of school is overcome by jealousy and bitterness, finally boiling over into evil.

Possibly the oddest of all Clint Eastwood's westerns in that,despite its Civil War setting, it has more in keeping with Tennessee Williams' sweaty Gothic melodramas, with an injection of Freudian paranoia, than the stolid Old West of John Ford. As directed with Don Siegel's 70s-type knack for reworking genre staples with an austere, edgy unpredictable style.

Eastwood has rarely played such an ambiguous loner, before or since, nothing about this man is reliable as he works his subtle games on this love-struck female world, run with icy restraint by the great Geraldine Page. She can smell trouble in the air and wants rid of this man, and the film takes the first of its u-turns away from a standard anti-war stance of immediate problems overcoming political conflict. That is not the point, the war is only a backdrop, here it is about the destructive powers of sexual energy and, through it, the real civil war that exists between the sexes. Eastwood's escape attempts are spoiled and the harmony sours, as various green-eyed minxes try to keep him put and keep their rivals at bay. A switch from male dominance into female empowerment; this manipulative, cruel soldier is transformed into a victim of his own creating.

Siegel, however, is far from finished, taking the film to the vestiges of horror. When she sees her frail school plunge into a kind of testosterone-kicked dementia, she takes drastic and unforgettable action. With seething Freudian undercurrents, they elect to amputate Dirty Harry's injured leg – a castration metaphor powerful enough to send men retching with its preternaturally calm female attendees, brandy anaesthetic and rusty hacksaw. It's enough to spin this taut character piece into the realms of the *Grand Guignol*, and make this one of Eastwood's least inspected but most daring films. ★★★★ **IN**

⦸ BEHIND ENEMY LINES (2001)

Starring: *Owen Wilson (Lt Chris Burnett), Gene Hackman (Admiral Leslie McMahon Reigart), Gabriel Macht (Stackhouse), Charles Malik Whitfield (Capt. Rodway, USMC), David Keith (Master Chief Tom O'Malley)*
Director: *John Moore*
Screenwriters: *David Veloz, Zak Penn, based on a story by Jin Thomas, John Thomas*
15/106 mins./Action/War/Drama/Thriller/USA

During the Bosnian conflict, an American pilot goes off-mission and witnesses war atrocities before being shot down in hostile territory. America's attempts to rescue him are stymied by NATO and he is left to fend for himself.

As every schoolboy knows, truth is the first casualty of war. Hence the main Hollywood trend post-September 11 seems to be towards skewed events in American military actions. Ridley Scott's *Black Hawk Down* takes patriotic liberties with events in Somalia, while *Behind Enemy Lines* has Bosnia as the background against which a true story is given a triumphal spin.

In this case it's the tale of Scott O'Grady (fictionalised as Lt Chris Burnett), a US fighter pilot who was shot down in Bosnia and daringly rescued by American forces against NATO wishes. But there the history lesson ends, and what William Goldman would no doubt refer to as 'Hollywood bullshit' is shovelled in by the cartload. But as long as you know that you're being comprehensively frogmarched up the garden path, it's a hell of a ride. Newcomer John Moore steals from all the right places, topping and tailing the movie with 'homages' to *Top Gun*, lifting a *Saving Private Ryan* one-man-to-rescue motif, while his post-*Matrix* shooting style owes a lot to *Three Kings*.

The action sequences are superlative: a missile/jet chase scene is hold-your-breath-'til-you-turn-blue good. There's even the occasional hint of intelligence, as in a scene where the frustrated NATO commander points out to a fuming Hackman that the American army risking the whole peace process for the sake of one soldier is patently batty.

But – and perhaps this element was injected after the World Trade Center attacks – it soon settles, plot-wise at least, into standard Hollywood war movie territory, with swarthy Bosnians in Bad Guys position and the clean-cut Wilson as our golden-haired, all-American hero. So, although the creeping hand of propaganda is in evidence, as long as you're inoculated against the flag-waving histrionics, *Behind Enemy Lines* is a great deal of brash, ballistic fun. ★★★★ **AS**

⦸ BEING JOHN MALKOVICH (1999)

Starring: *John Cusack (Craig Schwartz), Cameron Diaz (Lotte Schwartz), Catherine Keener (Maxine), Orson Bean (Dr Lester), Mary Kay Place (Floris), John Malkovich (John Horatio Malkovich)*
Director: *Spike Jonze*
Screenwriter: *Charlie Kaufman*
15/112 mins./Comedy/USA

Awards: *BAFTA – Best Screenplay*

A dishevelled puppeteer discovers a portal leading into the body of actor John Malkovich and decides to put it to commercial use.

OK, so the movie debut of Spike Jonze, the pop video veteran best known for Fatboy Slim's remarkable 'Praise You' clip, was never exactly going to be run-of-the-mill stuff. Even so, nothing prepares you for just how dazzlingly original *Being John Malkovich* actually is. Taking an idea which could have been stretched beyond breaking point or simply fallen flat in the wrong hands, Jonze turns it into one of the most startling pictures to grace the screen in a long time, a film that manages to be hysterically funny and achingly poignant, while making the possibility of living life as a crotchety, pompous movie star seem like the most attractive prospect in the world.

Cusack is Craig Schwartz, a straggly-haired, poverty-stricken puppeteer goaded by his animal-fixated wife (Diaz, almost unrecognisable under a gigantic brown wig) into getting a proper job, which he does, as a filing clerk on the seventh-and-a-half floor (a gag which really has to be seen) of a nondescript office building. It's here, while working for a dotty centenarian boss and lusting after colleague Maxine that he stumbles upon the hidden portal that sucks unsuspecting parties straight into Malkovich's brain, thus giving the person the opportunity to literally 'be' Malkovich for 15 minutes, before being spewed out beside the New Jersey turnpike. But what starts out as a money-spinning novelty quickly descends into insanity, as Diaz discovers the joys of the portal, Keener discovers the joys of Malkovich, and Malkovich (giving possibly the performance of a lifetime as, well, himself), slowly begins to twig that a bunch of complete strangers are messing with his head.

While the premise is an attention-grabber in itself, *Being John Malkovich* offers more than just a neat gimmick to win over its audience. Kaufman's script is an absolute winner, playing up the absurdity of the situation and sustaining the joke with a steady stream of new twists, yet giving its characters an abiding sense of humanity, and even explaining why it is that Malkovich's bonce should boast this unique feature. And the performances shine – Cusack and Diaz have rarely been better, while Keener is as splendid as ever as the opportunistic Maxine. But this is Malkovich's movie, and it's a constant joy to see him send himself up on such an alarming scale, coming over as the kind of obnoxious, self-obsessed idiot no actor would ever want to appear to be (the scene in which he, too, decides to try the portal into his brain is a masterpiece). At times it all becomes a little too surreal for its own good (a sequence in which a chimp regresses into its own childhood is, frankly, beyond the pale), but otherwise the multi-talented Jonze has created an outstanding piece of work, an off-kilter vision curiously reminiscent of the Coen Brothers, that isn't easily forgotten. ★★★★ **CW**

BEING THERE (1979)

Starring: *Peter Sellers (Chauncey Gardiner), Shirley MacLaine (Eve Rand), Melvyn Douglas (Benjamin Turnball Rand), Jack Warden (President Bobby), Richard Dysart (Dr Robert Allenby)*
Director: *Hal Ashby*
Screenwriters: *Jerzy Kosinski, Robert C. Jones, based on the novel by Kosinski*
15/130 mins./Comedy/USA

Awards: *Academy Awards – Best Supporting Actor (Melvyn Douglas), BAFTA – Best Screenplay*

After his master dies, simpleton gardener Chauncey Gardiner, known as Chance, is left to fend for himself. Taken in by an ailing businessman and his wife, Chance's bizarre utterances gleaned only from television and gardening are taken as profound and he starts to have an influence all the way to the White House.

For eight years Peter Sellers urged author Jerry Kosinski to grant him the right to play the touching savant at the heart of his novel, a kind of Forrest Gump without the homespun platitudes. He knew it was the role of a lifetime, a role that cleaved closest to the empty vessel of his own persona.

Meanwhile, Hal Ashby had proven skilful at interpreting the vagaries of human dependence in *The Last Detail* and *Coming Home*, and hones in on our desperation to divine meaning where none seems apparent.

Thus, when Chance tumbles unwittingly into the real world of New York society, his barely audible utterances take on the cadence of grand wisdom. There is a natural gag at the heart of the device – such homilies as, 'As long as the roots are not severed, all is well' are purest twaddle yet start to come across as insightful. The audience are invited to become believers; the film a test of universal gullibility. And given how the world has since been overtaken by the quick-buck blather of endless self-help gurus and the bottleneck of 'reality' TV, Ashby's satire has grown more relevant with time.

There is a wonderful synergy between the glazed, beatific performance from Sellers, cutting a vehement u-turn away from tumbling down staircases and karate chopping Kato, and Ashby's slow, mannered direction. The film never ruffles its feathers, even as the ranks of the FBI and CIA begin to feel threatened by this weird being undetectable on their files. Even his name is given to him. Shirley MacLaine and Melvyn Douglas give excellent support to Sellers remarkable performance, representatives of society's callow hunger for truth. And while the final twist may tug too hard at suspensions of disbelief, it's a haunting note that registers religion as much as a human necessity as a divine placebo. ★★★★ **IN**

BELLE DE JOUR (1967)

Starring: *Catherine Deneuve (Severine Serizy), Jean Sorel (Pierre Serizy), Michel Piccoli (Henri Husson), Genevieve Page (Madame Anais), Pierre Clementi (Marcel), Francisco Rabal (Hippolyte)*
Director: *Luis Bunuel*
Screenwriters: *Luis Bunuel, Jean-Claude Carriere, based on the novel by Joseph Kessel*
18/101 mins./Drama/Comedy/France/Italy

While contentedly married to a doctor, Severine cannot bring herself to commit sexually. Instead, she indulges in wild erotic fantasies, leading her, unbeknownst to her husband, to become a prostitute in the afternoons.

This is surrealist director Luis Bunuel's most accessible movie, which is a relative argument, as it is hardly a standard romance, but it is an easier narrative to take hold of than his usual flourishes, offering up more redolent, if exotic, emotions. You also get the magnificent porcelain beauty of Catharine Deneuve instead of eyeball-slitting. There's a lot to be said for that.

In fact, it is the key to the film's sly blasphemy – that such a delicate beauty would harbour such carnal desires. Bunuel enjoys contrasting the vivid suggestions of Deneuve's brothel-life with flashbacks of her first communion and irreligious dreams. And the film is hardly explicit in anything more than suggestion, and even those for all their masochism are made up of sniggeringly firstbase naughtiness, usually involving a trussed Deneuve being whipped by a man in livery.

Luis Buñuel (1900–1983)

Who he was: Blistering Spanish surrealist, who most often worked in France and Mexico.

Hallmarks: Extreme anti-clericalism; icily beautiful women; outwardly respectable but inwardly perverse, bourgeois characters; moments of real shock – see the eyeball slitting in *Un Chien Andalou* (1928)

If you see one movie, see: *The Discreet Charm Of The Bourgeoisie* (1972)

As is the Spanish director's want, there is lightness, a quasi-comedy, rather than degradation, to this creature's descent into apparent sordidness. The point is that sexual deviancy is perfectly at home in everyday people with perfect marriages. Indeed, giving it freedom could be the key to perfecting marriage. Whenever her handsome husband, Jean Sorel, draws her from her perverse reveries, she replies, 'About you.' It is both lie and cure to their sexless harmony.

With its neatly judged performances – Genevieve Page is wonderful as the madam – and effortless style, the film takes on a paradoxical guise as the classiest of masochistic sex comedies. ★★★★ **IN**

LA BELLE NOISEUSE (1991)

Starring: *Michel Piccoli (Edouard Frenhofer), Jane Birkin (Liz), Emmanuelle Béart (Marianne), Marianne Denicourt (Julienne), David Bursztein (Nicolas)*
Director: *Jacques Rivette*
Screenwriters: *Pascal Bonitzer, Christine Laurent, Jacques Rivette, inspired by the novella* Le Chef-d'oeuvre inconnu *by Balzac*
15/240 mins./Drama/France/Switzerland

Blocked artist Edouard Frenhofer battles with his demons and the proud spirit of his reluctant model, Marianne, while seeking the inspiration for her portrait.

Critic-turned-auteur, Jacques Rivette has never been one to hurry. *L'Amour Fou* runs for four hours and 12 minutes. *Out One* lasts for 13 hours, with the 'abridged' version, *Out One: Spectre*, clocking in around 270 minutes. Even the more accessible *Celine* and *Julie Go Boating* (192 mins) and *Secret Defence* (170 mins) took their own good time. But rarely have 240 minutes been better spent than in the company of this magisterial study of the agonising process of creation.

Basically, this is an art-house investigation into the *Indecent Proposal* idea, as a young artist offers up his girlfriend to spark the inspiration of a painter who hasn't worked in the decade since abandoning a nude study of his wife, 'La Belle Noiseuse' (Quebecois slang for a woman who drives men to distraction).

What follows is a battle of wills between Michel Piccoli's aging artist, spurned spouse Jane Birken, envious disciple David Bursztein and reluctant model, Emmanuelle Béart. The marital duel is the more emotionally intense. But Piccoli's determination to capture the essence of the proud Béart is the more compelling, as it's enacted in real time in the tactile terms of ink sketches, charcoal outlines and watercolour washes.

If the hand of Bernard Dufour provides the on-screen finesse, then Piccoli supplies the artistic passion, as he contemplates Béart's flesh not only as an artistic challenge, but also as a means of freeing himself from Birkin's stifling affection and, thus, of reviving his career. Rarely has so cerebral a film been so brutal.

Rivette also released a 120-minute version of the film, which he dubbed a 'Divertimento'. Despite being shorn of the creative sequences, this is more than a simple precis, as it appears between alternative bookends and shifts the emphasis on to Birkin and her acceptance of her husband's relationship to his work and his model. ★★★★ **DP**

THE BELLES OF ST TRINIANS (1954)

Starring: *Alastair Sim (Millicent Fritton/Clarence Fritton), George Cole ('Flash' Harry), Joyce Grenfell (Policewoman Ruby Gates), Hermione Baddeley (Miss Drownder), Betty Ann Davies (Miss Waters), Renee Houston (Miss Brimmer), Beryl Reid (Miss Wilson), Irene Handl (Miss Gale), Joan Sims (Miss Dawn), Sid James (Benny), Barbara Windsor (Schoolgirl)*
Director: *Frank Launder*
Screenwriters: *Sidney Gilliat, Frank Launder, Val Valentine, based on the characters created by Ronald Searle*
U/91 mins./Comedy/UK

The daughter of an Arab racehorse owner finds herself the centre of a plot for control of St Trinian's, a unique private school for girls where betting, drinking and gambling are positively encouraged.

A bastion of school holiday morning TV viewings (and sickies), the St Trinian's saga (a sequence of four movies: *Belles*, *Blue Murder*, *Pure Hell*, *Train Robbery*, plus a latter-day disaster *Wildcats* in 1980) holds a special place in the pantheon of British comedy. Be it the hockey -sticked anarchy, the suspender-belted allure of the 'older' girls, the motherly exasperation of Alastair Sim in a wig or the genial bumbling of the outside authorities, they are whimsical and darkly funny movies encased in a warm, fuzzy England that probably never existed.

Artist Ronald Searle first invented the horde of unruly schoolgirls in 1941 while serving in World War II, producing a series of acerbic cartoons for satirical magazines *Lilliput* and *Punch* right through to 1953. This wasn't the innocent public school japery of broken windows and dodging prep as depicted in *Just William* or the *Jennings* series. This amoral, pre-pubescent rabble were the punkettes of their day; smoking, gambling, fighting and running riot over their slipshod educational establishment like prototype Mafiosa in ill-fitting gymslips.

The duo of Frank Launder and Sidney Gilliat (director and producer and co-writers), hot off the relatively tame school comedy *The Happiest Days Of Your Life*, honed in on the delicious possibilities for mayhem and satire to first make *Belles*. In so-doing, they provided a template for the paradoxically quaint but subversive style of British comedy that worked its way into the *Doctor* and *Carry On* franchises.

St Trinian's School For Girls, a less than august public school in countrified England, seems to be made up of only two discernible years (although others are mentioned in passing they never appear). We get the sexually predatory, self-serving sixth form (assayed by girls 25 if a day) and the disreputable force of nature that is the fourth form (characterised by a signature banshee wailing every time they move en masse). While the girls are portrayed more as a huddle than individuals – we only get to properly meet sixth form boss Bella (Vivienne Martin), fourth form leader Jackie (Diana Day) and resident school snitch Florrie (Jill Braidwood) – it is the teaching staff and extras who are the central comedy figures.

Immediately, it's Alastair Sim's show. He is the wonderfully stoic epicentre of the movie as headmistress Miss Fritton – a sterling mix of benign, if misplaced pride ('We're one big happy family'), dubious fiscal habits and creative cunning. Although ostensibly a man-in-drag, the role is written straight; the humour isn't about the wig or false chest but the richly invented character and the slippery charm Sim applies to her. It is implicit that it's a bloke in a skirt but somehow irrelevant. Miss Fritton's preternatural ability to sidestep and overlook the various mantraps and madnesses that ricochet around her is one of the film's central comedic hooks. Sim also plays her twin brother, the crooked Clarence. Hot on the trail of insider racing tips – new girl Princess Fatima's father has top horse Arab Boy running in the Cheltenham Gold Cup – he exhorts his sister to reinstate his oft-expelled daughter Bella. Unforgettable too is George Cole as cockney spiv Flash Harry, a silver-tongued, pencil-'tached rogue who seems to dwell in the bushes in the school grounds, abetting the girls in various nefarious pursuits (bootleg gin, racing bets). Characterised by the shiftiest walk in film history, Cole made an entire career out of this under-the-law persona (Flash grew up to be Arthur Daley).

The teaching staff are a dissolute bunch of wrecks, alcoholics, ex-cons, ingenues and insinuated – but not openly declared (this was 1954) – lesbians, played by a cadre of (underused) great British funny-ladies. Into the mix that includes Irene Handl, Beryl Reid, and Joan Sims strides Joyce Grenfell as the bumbling undercover police officer Ruby Gates whose precision-timed horsy exuberance and pratfalling is about the only genuine innocence on show.

Events – and the plot is tidily lean – crescendo into ribald farce as the fourth formers kidnap Arab Boy to stop the sixth formers (in league with Clarence) knobbling him. Meanwhile Miss Fritton goes into business with Harry, betting the school funds on the outcome of the race, before war breaks out when the fourth form (plus Arab Boy) are besieged in their dorm by Clarence's bower boys and the errant sixth. The day is saved by the timely arrival of the Old Girls (a formidable mass viewed from their ankles down). Launder delivers the knockabout thrills with real vigour, cutting back to Miss Fritton's long-suffering eyes, Harry's padded-shoulder shrug and Ruby's lanky ineptitude. The school is, of course, saved from disaster and the natural disorder of things resumes.

What endures and still beguiles about the St Trinian's movies is a mythic Englishness of wood-panelled public school nicety and eccentric 'grown-ups' completely sabotaged by a pack of street-wise urchins and long-legged lovelies in a hail of flour bombs and lacrosse sticks. It's kind of radical when you think about it. ★★★★★ **IN**

⊙ BELLEVILLE RENDEZ-VOUS (LES TRIPLETTES DE BELLEVILLE) (2003)

Starring: *voices of: Béatrice Bonifassi (Triplets singing voice), Lina Boudreault (Triplets), Michele Caucheteux, Jean-Claude Donda, Mari-Lou Gaughier (Triplets)*
Director: *Sylvain Chomet*
Screenwriter: *Sylvain Chomet*
12A/78 mins./Animation/Comedy/Adventure/France/Belgium/Canada/UK

During the Tour De France, ace cyclist Champion is kidnapped by the Mafia and taken to the megalopolis of Belleville. Mme Souza, Champion's doting grandmother, mounts a daring rescue mission, aided by three ageing music hall stars.

While it does not feature any sex or violence, Belleville Rendez-Vous is animation solely for adults. Shot through with sadness and satire, nostalgia and complexity, French animator Chomet's first full-length feature mixes a cracking, comedic (practically dialogue-free) adventure yarn with a hymn for times lost into something unique and cherishable.

From the opening musical number, Chomet throws in terrific set-pieces (Mme Souza chasing an ocean liner on a pedalo, a last reel getaway that would put Hollywood to shame), subtle cultural commentary (Belleville is a thinly-disguised America), great supporting characters (the sad-faced cyclists, the hulking mobsters), and, best of all, an emotionally resonant core.

A Portuguese old dear with a clubfoot, Mme Souza is the most unlikely cartoon hero for decades, but her implacable, resourceful spirit and indomitable desire to protect her grandson is enormously winning. ★★★★ **IF**

⊙ BEND IT LIKE BECKHAM (2001)

Starring: *Parminda Nagra (Jess Bhamra), Keira Knightley (Jules Paxton), Jonathan Rhys Meyers (Joe), Anupam Kher (Mr Bhamra), Archie Panjabi (Pinky Bhamra), Shaznay Lewis (Mel), Frank Harper (Alan Paxton), Juliet Stevenson (Paula Paxton)*
Director: *Gurinda Chadha*
Screenwriters: *Paul Mayeda Berges, Gulhit Bindra, Gurinda Chadha*
12/112 mins./Comedy/Drama/Sports/UK/Germany

Jess is desperate to be a footballer, but her parents have other ideas. When friend Jules convinces her to join a local team, she has to keep it a secret – especially when the final falls on the day of her sister's wedding.

Anything *East Is East* can do, *Bend It Like Beckham* can do better. Like that runaway hit, Gurinder Chadha's football-themed comedy is set in Britain's Indian community, but has wide appeal. It, too, is about the tight (some say protective) restrictions imposed by family and tradition, and how the younger generation address this while trying to fit into the modern, multi-cultural world.

Regardless of ethnic background, all teenagers have run-ins with their parents. And, like Jess in the film, if they can't talk to their elders, they'll discuss their dreams with the posters on their bedroom walls. Perhaps Chadha shows more confidence handling the domestic comedy-drama and Bollywood-lite music, dance and colour of the wedding scene than the football footage, but she marshals together the many elements of her film and sustains an infectiously buoyant mood.

As *Bhaji On The Beach* and *What's Cooking?* revealed, she has an amazing touch with people. She's on the side of the kids and their parents, never turning the older generation into out-of-touch, stereotypical tyrants. Nagra is tremendously appealing in the lead role, while Knightley and Rhys Meyers add to the sex appeal. As Jules' mum, Juliet Stevenson seems to have wandered straight in from the set of a Mike Leigh movie, confidently telling her tomboy daughter (whom she fears is a lesbian), 'There's a reason why Sporty Spice is the only one without a fella.'

A feel-good movie with issues relevant to everyone in the audience, *Bend It Like Beckham* is a real word-of-mouth crowd pleaser. The in-jokes will be lapped up by Asian viewers but, given that *Goodness Gracious Me* is one of the funniest British comedies on TV, they won't fly over the heads of everyone else. It might yet qualify for the champions' league. ★★★★ **LB**

⊙ BENEATH THE PLANET OF THE APES (1969)

Starring: *James Franciscus (Brent), Kim Hunter (Zira), Maurice Evans (Dr Zaius), Linda Harrison (Nova), Paul Richards (Mendez), Victor Buono (Fat Man)*
Director: *Ted Post*
Screenwriter: *Paul Dehn*
15/95 mins./Sci-fi/USA

Searching for missing astronaut Taylor and his crew, new arrival Brent goes from the ape village into the forbidden zone, where he finds an underground civilisation, peopled by telepathic mutants. As the apes prepare to annihilate mankind, Brent discovers the answer to his search.

A fair fist of a sequel to the hit sci-fi parable which closed with a fuming Charlton Heston riding off into the distance with his mute paramour Linda Harrison. With a reduced budget and Heston's reluctance to put on his loincloth, turning up only for the briefest of cameos at the end, Ted Post set about finding a new angle on the future Earth populated by latex monkeys with mixed feelings about humanity's rights.

Kicking off with a rescue mission was a smart move, it gives the film a chance to start with more or less the same designs as the original – man's shock at discovering intelligent Simians in charge. Now, though, it is the warlike gorillas who have the upper paw, urging an attack on the Forbidden Zone where a tribe of sentient if mutant humans (including their own variation on latex face tissue) dwell with their precious nuclear bomb. It is here, also, where diffident Heston-clone James Franscicus, along with talk-free sex-bomb Hamilton, will locate the expensive services of Charlton Heston. Roddy McDowell, who had excelled as genial chimp Cornelius, had scheduling problems, but packing David Watson in an indentikit monkey mask at least keeps the continuity if not the acting talent.

It is, in all, a far lesser film. In place of the sharp satire on racism and class, as well as the pontificating over science and religion, is a bullish sci-fi opera, far more gothic and unrestrained. The Forbidden City itself is a splendidly overworked mishmash of future-world and New York Subway station, setting the scene for a thrilling burst of bloody action. The original's shock ending is replaced with a massive downer. It is, finally, an attempt to sound a similar clarion call at man's self-destructive folly, but the effect is more whimper than bang. We've been there, done that, and bought the plastic orang-utan figurines. A franchise was on the march, all the same. Goddamn you all to hell. ★★★ **IN**

BEN-HUR (1959)

Starring: *Charlton Heston (Judah Ben Hur), Stephen Boyd (Messala), Jack Hawkins (Quintas), Haya Harareet (Esther), Hugh Griffith (Sheik Ilderim), Martha Scott (Miriam), Sam Jaffe (Simonides)*
Director: *William Wyler*
Screenwriter: *Karl Tunberg, from the novel by Lew Wallace*
U/212 mins./History/Region/USA

Awards: *Academy Awards – Best Picture, Best Actor, Best Supporting Actor (Hugh Griffith), Best Director, Best Colour Cinematography, Best Film Editing, Best Art Direction, Best Score (Drama or Comedy), Best Costume Design (Colour), Best Sound, Best Special Effects, BAFTA – Best film from any source, Golden Globes – Best Motion Picture – Drama, Best Director, Best Supporting Actor (Stephen Boyd), Special Award for directing chariot race (Andrew Marton)*

In biblical times, a Jewish prince is betrayed by a friend and sent into slavery but he returns to extract his revenge.

In an age of widescreen epics, Ben-Hur was consciously designed to be the biggest and best of them all. Producer Sam Zimbalist spent five years planning the project. It was to cost an unprecedented $15 million. It would contain the most expensive action sequence ever filmed, while among its 300 locales would be the biggest single set ever created. There would be a record 365 speaking parts, 73 of which would be credited. Its director, William Wyler, would collect the largest sum ever paid to an individual for a motion picture and go on to shoot a phenomenal 1,125,000 feet (about 213 miles) of footage, of which all but 23,838 feet would end up on the cutting-room floor. So determined was Wyler to outdo the master of spectacle, Cecil B. DeMille, that he even selected Moses, from his 1956 *The Ten Commandments*, for the title role.

Yet much of this was a speculative show of bravura, as MGM was in a financial crisis. Ultimately, this calculated risk would become the biggest first-run grosser to date and land an unheard of 11 Oscars (a feat only matched since by *Titanic*). But it all could have been a different story, especially after Zimbalist died on location in Rome.

Lew Wallace began writing *Ben-Hur* just after the Civil War. The biggest American bestseller of the 19th century, it was adapted for the stage in 1899, with future cowboy legend William S. Hart as Messala. Sidney Olcott directed a screen version for Kalem in 1907, which famously employed the services of the Brooklyn Fire Department for the chariot race. But nothing could have prepared film folk for the blockbuster rendition filmed in Italy and released by MGM in 1925.

Yet the newly formed studio nearly had a disaster on its hands, as the rise of Mussolini and the incompetence of director Charles Brabin and his star, George Walsh, brought the production to a standstill. But wunderkind producer Irving G. Thalberg stepped in to rescue the project by appointing Fred Niblo as director and casting Ramon Novarro in the lead.

A young William Wyler acted as an assistant director on the chariot sequence and, so, when Zimbalist offered him the remake 33 years later, he seized the opportunity – even though he was taking a monumental risk, as his reputation rested on intense (and some would say rather arty) melodramas. His main concern was the screenplay. Karl Tunberg's original was unusable, yet he was to retain sole credit and achieve the unwanted distinction of being the film's only failed Oscar nominee. Novelist Gore Vidal was brought in for a rewrite, only to be shuffled along after Wyler nixed his notion of a homoerotic undercurrent to Judah and Messala's rivalry (thus depriving us of a queer hero for a whole year, before a bathing Laurence Olivier asked Tony Curtis if he preferred oysters or snails in Spartacus).

Instead, British playwright Christopher Fry came on board, much to Charlton Heston's relief. Not that he was the first choice for the pivotal role. Burt Lancaster, Kirk Douglas and Rock Hudson had all been considered after Paul Newman announced, following his disastrous debut in *The Silver Chalice* (1954), that he would, 'Never again act in a movie in a cocktail dress.' But, viewed today, who else could have carried the picture with such physical prowess and moral dignity?

Despatched by his former childhood friend into the imperial galleys, Judah Ben-Hur returns to Jerusalem as a Roman citizen, having rescued the admiral, Quintus Arrius, from a pirate attack. Intent on avenging himself on Messala, he duels to the death with him in a chariot race at the Circus Antioch before seeking his mother and sister in the leper caves, following his encounter with the crucified Christ.

Ben-Hur is a hero without a cause whose motive for action can, perhaps, be found in Marlon Brando's 'Whaddyagot?' retort in *The Wild One* (to paraphrase the question, 'What are you fighting for?')

Initially he feuds with Messala out of spurned friendship, albeit with a little bruised national pride on the side. Then he exhibits a well-honed survival instinct and sense of military duty, during the sea battle. Revenge is now his prime justification and pure hatred drives him on during Yakima Canutt's impeccably staged chariot race. But then he gets a touch of religion and his quest to locate his kin is inspired by new-found humanity and filial love. It's kneejerk stuff of course, but a tad more complex than your average muscle-bound, gun-toting thuggery.

No wonder Wyler said when the movie wrapped: 'Well Chuck. Thanks a lot. I'll try to give you a better part next time.' ★★★★★ **DP**

BERLIN: SYMPHONY OF A GREAT CITY (DIE SINFONIE DER GROBSTADT) (1927)

Director: *Walter Ruttmann*
Screenwriter: *Karl Freund, Carl Mayer, Walter Ruttmann*
U/65 mins./Documentary/Germany

A day in the life of the German capital that opens with the sun rising and the citizens going about their business and concludes with a panoply of nocturnal activity and a spectacular firework display.

Although he acknowledged its technical virtuosity, John Grierson (who is widely credited as 'the father of the documentary') criticised Walter Ruttmann's landmark film for its formalism and beauty. Like many a pioneer, Grierson believed that an actuality had to have a socio-political purpose and he felt that this was blunted by Ruttmann's emphasis on the activities of Berlin's citizens rather than their attitudes.

However, Grierson seems to have misunderstood the underlying message of this hugely influential avant-garde impression of everyday Berlin, as Ruttmann always protested that he was less intent on highlighting the differences between the classes at work, rest and play than in extolling what united them and how the city's prosperity was dependent upon this continued collaboration.

Yet this turned out to be a dismayingly optimistic prospectus, as the vitality of the Weimar era was soon dissipated and Berlin proved not to be an amorphous metropolis but a city riven by countless prejudices.

Yet, Ruttmann always prioritised the film's aesthetics and vouched that it was more about the kinetic interplay of surfaces, shapes and rhythms than politics. This symphony was a celebration of modernity and mechanisation and Ruttmann was keener to showcase the city in its diverse entirety than its individual citizens (whom he called his 'living material'). Therefore, animate and inanimate objects alike were abstracted to form images whose content and context were less important than their ornamental and metric potential.

However, critics like Siegfried Kracauer accused Ruttmann of dehumanising those captured by his camera and censured his juxtaposition of shots of people eating with those of ravenous lions and those in phoneboxes with chattering monkeys. These might once have been laughed off as clumsily comic attempts at associational montage, but, as Ruttmann went on to become a prominent Nazi propagandist, their significance takes on a chilling new meaning. ★★★★ **DP**

BEST IN SHOW (2000)

Starring: *Christopher Guest (Harlan Pepper), Parker Posey (Meg Swan), Michael Hitchcock (Hamilton Swan), Eugene Levy (Gerry Fleck), Catherine O'Hara (Cookie Fleck), Coolidge (Sherri Ann Ward Cabot), Fred Willard (Buck Laughlin)*
Director: *Christopher Guest*
Screenwriters: *Christopher Guest, Eugene Levy*
12/80 mins./Comedy/USA

From the *Spinal Tap* boys, this 'documentary' is set behind the scenes of a dog show in America's Midwest. Quirky characters, clueless commentators and pampered pooches prevail as the competition reaches its peak.

Christopher Guest's third foray into the world of 'mockumentary' – an area in which he's had plenty of practice – owes more to 1996's *Waiting For Guffman* than it does to *This Is Spinal Tap*, given that it's focused on ordinary people doing something extraordinary in order to hog the limelight. While *Guffman*, however, was set in the world of amateur dramatics, *Best In Show* instead concentrates on a Crufts-like dog trial, which, if Guest is to be believed attracts some of the maddest contestants in the world.

Thus we have O'Hara as the terrier trainer who seems to have had a fling with every man she encounters; Levy as her long-suffering hubby who is, literally, blessed with 'two left feet'; Posey as the uptight New Yorker whose much-cosseted pet even has its own psychiatrist; Coolidge as the ultra-rich trophy wife complete with decrepit sugar daddy – and so the list goes on. Anybody who has seen *Tap* or *Guffman* will be familiar with the territory – the difference being that it's all a bit hit and miss this time around.

Guest taps into the absurdities of his characters with the kind of satirical wit and accuracy you might expect, but too many of them are one-dimensional, stereotypical or (in the case of Posey, for example), just plain annoying. Things liven up in the final act, thanks to the commenting double-act of Jim Piddock and Fred Willard, and the pooches, all of them gloriously silky-haired and healthy-looking, nab enough of the limelight to keep dog fanciers happy. While it's refreshing to come across a comedy that offers gentle, subtle humour as opposed to the more popular outrageous variety, the overriding sense of déjà vu prevents this from scaling the heights of Guest's previous efforts. ★★★ **CW**

BEST LAID PLANS (1999)

Starring: *Alessandro Nivola (Nick), Reese Witherspoon (Lissa), Josh Brolin (Bryce), Gene Wolande (Lawyer), Jonathan McMurtry (Vet), Father Terrance Sweeney (Priest), Rebecca Klinger (Diner Waitress), Rocky Carroll (Bad Ass Dude), Kate Hendrickson (Bar Waitress)*
Director: *Mike Barker*
Screenwriter: *Ted Griffin*
15/93 mins./Crime/Drama/Thriller/USA

A small-town slacker tries to sting an old friend in order to pay off his mob debts.

Despite hinging on such indie staples as failed heists, small town dreams and slacker lovers, there is something undeniably fresh about *Best Laid Plans*. Buzzing with the thrill of defying convention, Brit director Barker's stylish, agreeably dark, twisty-turny fest certainly impales the viewer on tenterhooks yet lacks the substance to turn the enjoyably good into the memorably great.

Griffin's screenplay centres on Nick, ensconced in a dreary job and needing to raise some cash to pay off a local villain. The action intercuts between how Nick met his predicament and his complicated solution – persuading his girlfriend Lissa to seduce long lost college buddy Bryce out of his valuable coin collection, then cry rape. The plan goes belly up when Bryce holds Lissa hostage and calls in Nick to garner advice. There follows mucho cat and mousery as the clock runs down before Nick has to pay up or else.

Bettering his uneven debut *The James Gang*, Barker displays a confident handling of the shifting time frame, lacing the action with well-judged shocks – a moment when Nick and Lissa appear in a TV commercial before Bryce's very eyes is heart stopping – and vibrant visuals, all saturated colours and skewy camera angles. Witherspoon, if low on things to do, is appealing, Brolin is believably boorish yet this is Nivola's movie, injecting his scheming dreamer with edgy charm and understated sex appeal.

Yet where *Best Laid Plans* falls short is in its hollow centre. The motivations and morals of the characters are sacrificed at the altars of style and plot. Moreover, when the final turn becomes apparent, it leaves you deflated rather than uplifted. ★★★ **IF**

THE BEST YEARS OF OUR LIVES (1946)

Starring: *Myrna Loy (Milly Stepenson), Fredric March (Al Stepehenson), Dana Andrews (Fred Derry), Teresa Wright (Peggy Stephenson), Virginia Mayo (Marje Derry), Harold Russell (Homer Parrish)*
Director: *William Wyler*
Screenwriter: *Robert E. Sherwood, based on the novella* Glory For Me *by MacKinlay Kantor*
U/172 mins./Drama/USA

Awards: *Academy Awards – Best Picture, Best Actor (Fredric March), Best Supporting Actor (Harold Russell), Best Director, Best Screenplay, Best Film Editing, Best Film Score, Honorary Award (Harold Russell). BAFTA – Best Film From Any Source*

Al Stephenson, Fred Derry and Homer Parrish return to Boone City after their Second World War service and struggle to acclimatise to life with loved ones who have changed as much as they have.

Based on MacKinley Kantor's blank verse novel, *Glory For Me* (which was itself inspired by an article in *Time* magazine), this sincere, if occasionally melodramatic study of the problems facing America's returning service personnel landed eight Academy Awards, with the debuting Harold Russell becoming the first actor to win two Oscars for the same performance.

But while producer Samuel Goldwyn was instrumental in its commissioning, director William Wyler always considered this an intensely personal project, as he knew something of the psychological pressures of readjusting to civvy street, having seen action with the US Army Air Corps while making the documentaries, *Memphis Belle* (1944) and *Thunderbolt* (1945).

Like so many Hollywood veterans returning to studio duty, Wyler was determined to make a statement that proclaimed the changed nature of society. Consequently, he challenged both established visual and storytelling conventions in this audacious achievement, whose cinematic worth has always been overshadowed by its sentimental reception.

The opening segment of the film is almost devoid of plot, as Wyler concentrates on the spaces inhabited by the returning trio to show how three men of contrasting ages, classes and expectations, and who had fought very different wars (Homer had lost his arms in the Navy, Al had been a sergeant in the Army and Fred had participated in bombing raids over Germany), were temporarily more closely bonded together by the common experience of confronting the enemy than they were to the families and friends they had left behind.

However, from the moment they're deposited by taxi, the trio are shown in all the inglorious isolation involved in adjusting from combat to domesticity. What's more, America soon proves to be a land unfit for heroes and their fraught situations are made all the more uncompromising by the fact they're presented in long, deep-focus takes which both enhance the action's realism and keep the audience unwaveringly involved in it.

French theorist André Bazin hailed *Best Years* a masterpiece of mise-en-scène cinema and its influence would be felt around the world. ★★★★ **DP**

LA BETE HUMAINE (1938)

Starring: *Jean Gabin (Jacques Lantier), Simone Simon (Severine), Fernard Ledoux (Robaud), Julien Carette (Pecqueux), Blanchette Brunoy (Flore), Jean Renoir (Cabuche)*
Director: *Jean Renoir*
Screenwriter: *Jean Renoir, based on the novel by Emile Zola*
PG/105 mins./Drama/France

Séverine seduces engine driver Jacques Lantier to prevent him from reporting her guardian's murder at the hands of her stationmaster husband, Roubard. But, before long, she's suggesting another crime passionel.

Jean Renoir's first major commercial success came about largely because Jean Gabin wanted to fulfil a childhood ambition to drive a train. Basing his screenplay on a cursory perusal of Emile Zola's 1869 novel, Renoir played down the Lantier family's history of alcoholism and concentrated instead on the intensity of the lovers' passion and the authenticity of the rail workers' environs. Thus, he not only captured the spirit of his source, but by shooting on location around Le Havre and Paris's Gare Saint-Lazare, he also achieved a grimy naturalist lyricism that heightened the picture's emotive potency.

Yet while Renoir was more interested in the authenticity of the setting than the mechanics of the plot, the film still contains several standout set-pieces, including the killing of Grandmorin (Jacques Berlioz) behind the train compartment blinds, Gabin and Simone's assignation in the rail sheds during a downpour, and Gabin's final acts of uncontrollable rage and bitter regret.

Leaving Gabin to essay his trademark flawed everyman, Renoir lavished attention on his female leads. But, while he reined in Simone Simon's feline sensuality to emphasise the lethal innocence of her femme fatality, he highlighted the locomotive's sexual symbolism and lit La Lison as though it was a lissom diva.

Fritz Lang was permitted no such latitude when he remade *La Bête Humaine* as *Human Desire* in 1954, by which time it had already exerted a considerable influence on Hollywood film noir. But, this was very much a feature that reflected its times. Along with another 1938 Gabin vehicle, Marcel Carné's *Quai Des Brumes*, it exuded the pre-war pessimism of a nation that could see its impending fate in that of Gabin's doomed tragic heroes.

However, Renoir captured the anxiety of a society teetering on the brink with even more power and prescience in his next feature, *La Règle Du Jeu*. ★★★★ **DP**

BETTY BLUE 37.2 LE MATIN (1986)

Starring: *Beatrice Dalle (Betty), Jean-Hugues Anglade (Zorg), Gerard Damon (Eddy), Consuelo De Haviland (Lisa), Clementine Celarie (Annie), Gerard Damon (Eddy), Clementine Celarie (Annie)*
Director: *Jean-Jacques Beineix*
Screenwriter: *Jean-Jacques Beineix, based on the novel by Phillippe Dijan*
18/120 mins./Drama/France

Easy-going handyman and unpublished author Zorg, hooks up with volatile beauty Betty, who is determined to get his books into print. When the rejections pile up, her fury leads them on a self-destructive spiral into and out of Paris and to the vestiges of sanity.

Much celebrated for its fraught sexuality, rampant nudity and frothy, stylised direction, not to forget a poster that bedecked a million student walls as some kind of emblem of intellectual as well as hedonistic fervour, *Betty Blue* is a marvel of sheer verve over any kind of sensible substance. It is a teenage dream of curvy, indolent sirens fuelling stalled creativity with tip-top shagging and near dementia.

The opening alone is a magnificently dolly shot into a beachside shack to discover Beatrice Dalle, whose pouting air of carnal need makes Angelina Jolie resemble a prudish great-aunt, and whippet skinny Jean Hugues Anglade making the beast with two backs with some abandon. Director Jean-Jacques Beineix isn't one for pussy footing around, his quasi-noir flourishes grant the film a heated energy it never pulls away from.

In fact, it just grows ever more hysterical as Dalle hones in on some kind of nuclear breaking point, the rejection of her lover's prose taken as a personal assault. It is a memorable performance, mostly minus her underwear, as torrid as her director's panting camerawork. The script is hardly taking it easy either, with its sub-Chandler epithets pretending to be profound remarks: 'She was a flower with psychic antennae and a tinsel heart.' Poor Anglade understandably seems to be reeling for the entire film, a dope caught in a maelstrom.

How you take such fulminating erotica depends on how seriously you take it. There is a pleasing sense that Beineix is leaving to us to decide whether this is pure parody, fully aware of its loopy overtones, or blunderbuss wish fulfilment, an artist's ultimate concoction that his muse would turn up with great breasts, an insatiable itch and a willingness to do the paperwork. ★★★ **IN**

BEVERLY HILLS COP (1984)

Starring: *Eddie Murphy (Detective Axel Foley), Judge Reinhold (Detective Billy Rosewood), John Ashton (Detective Sergeant John Taggart), Lisa Eilbacher (Jeanette Summers), Steven Berkoff (Victor Maitland)*
Director: *Martin Brest*
Screenwriter: *Daniel Petrie Jr*
15/105 mins./Comedy/Crime/USA

After his friend is killed in front of his eyes, cocksure Detroit detective Axel Foley heads to Beverly Hills in search of the killer. Teamed up with a pair of sceptical local detectives, Foley prises open a major drugs conspiracy governed by psychotic kingpin Victor Maitland.

After *Trading Places* introduced the world to the rat-a-tat tongue and slacker cool of Eddie Murphy and *48 Hours* had shown a tough, ethnic core, he hit upon the role that would turn him into a superstar – fast-talking, rule dodging cop Axel Foley. With a name like that how could it fail, especially as Daniel Petrie Jr's script was a terrifically deliberate reworking of the fish-out-water formula, peppered with prize one-liners and shaped by tidy plotting, and director Martin Brest gave it some real zip by blurring the divides between action and comedy. An idea that went on to define the 80s. It may be shallow and crassly commercial, but this is blunt-nosed entertainment of rare quality.

Brest's smartest move was the casting of Murphy; everyone from Al Pacino to Sylvester Stallone had been circling the project, ready to play it dead straight. Once Murphy's ripe smile and easy tread were injected into what was a well-oiled but standard policier, everything changed. The plot, involving Steven Berkoff's pay-the-rent baddie's drug ring, falls to the background, a sturdy framework for the star's ribald energy.

What matters here is Murphy bouncing his salty Detroit attitude off the empty-headed Beverly Hills platitudes, and his teasing, but quite touching, relationship with local cops Judge Reinhold and John Ashton, leaning the film into comedy. Poking holes in Hollywood's housing estate is an evergreen opportunity, and Murphy gives it a real charge.

That said, there's little effort given to human cost, the violence is carried off with a typically brute indifference. There's not much here to believe in, rather than simply soak up, the embodiment of an era's devotion to high concept. Harold Faltermeyer's beeping synth riff 'Axel F' reminding you exactly where the movie came from. ★★★★ **IN**

⊙ BEVERLY HILLS COP II (1984)

Starring: *Eddie Murphy (Detective Axel Foley), Judge Reinhold (Detective Billy Rosewood), John Ashton (Detective Sergeant John Taggart), Jurgen Prochnow (Maxwell Dent), Dean Stockwell (Charles 'Chip' Cain), Paul Reiser (Det. Jeffrey Friedman)*
Director: *Tony Scott*
Screenwriters: *Larry Ferguson, Warren Skaaren, David Giler, Dennis Klein*
15/100 mins./Comedy/Crime/USA

Alex Foley, the smart-talking Detroit cop, returns to Beverly Hills when he discovers his friend Captain Andrew Bogomil has been shot and injured. There he teams up with former partners detectives Rosewood and Taggart to solve a series of 'alphabet robberies' that may be connected with the shooting.

Sensibly made within touching distance of the original hit, with Murphy's growing influence according him the right to conceptualise the story for the sequel, this is a suitably pumped, fish-back-out-of-water facsimile of what came before. Although, getting big gun director Tony Scott to take up where Martin Brest let drop, puts the emphasis on a darker shade of violence, which sits uneasily with the flip dialogue and localised satire.

The new badguys, and such is their hammy scowling they might as well wear t-shirts exclaiming 'evil gun runner and family,' are populated by the stiff-jawed trio of Jurgen Prochnow, Dean Stockwell and giantess Brigitte Nielsen, but their labyrinthine schemes are damn near incomprehensible. Once again, that isn't really the point. Scott's slick camera must rest on the exuberant fizzog of Mr Murphy, rapping out his foul-mouthed jive to the general irritation of the stiff locals and inept police department. And being an outta-towner, our loveable wag gets to play pretend as a Caribbean psychic, a blabbering building inspector and the man in charge of Hugh Hefner's pool maintenance. Shamefully, as trite and mechanical as all this blather most certainly is, it works. Murphy, for a decade, nestled happily in the exalted glow of superstardom – as long as he plied his energised shtick.

Scott does get to have some fun with the set-pieces, concocting heady chases, shot with the luxuriant sheen that was the trademark of uber-producers Don Simpson and Jerry Bruckheimer. They, of all people, knew the sequel should do more.

The second sequel left things far too late, coming seven years later with John Landis at the helm. Murphy seemed drained of fizz and the plot a clunky and cheap-looking riff on *Die Hard* set in a theme park. They had forgotten that when it comes to the ready gloss of the action-comedy, God is in the padding. ★★★ **IN**

⊙ BEWITCHED (2005)

Starring: *Nicole Kidman (Isabel Bigelow/Samantha), Will Ferrell (Jack Wyatt/Darrin), Shirley MacLaine (Iris Smythson/Endora), Michael Caine (Nigel Bigelow), Jason Schwartzman (Ritchie)*
Director: *Nora Ephron*
Screenwriters: *Nora Ephron, Delia Ephron, based on the TV series by Sol Saks*
PG/102 mins./Comedy/Fantasy/USA

On-the-skids movie star Jack Wyatt attempts a comeback as Darrin Stephens in a remake of classic sit-com *Bewitched*, unknowingly casting a real witch as Samantha . . .

The formula for transferring TV shows to the big screen is pretty much set in stone by now. Snap up the rights, round up a few lower-tier A-listers with a passing resemblance to the original cast (Ben Stiller is David Starsky!), pop into Plots-R-Us, put your faith in the almighty god of brand recognition, then tune out the snide reviews and wait for the nostalgia boom to kick in at the box office. Okay, it's hit and miss – *Charlie's Angels 2*, anyone? – but certainly less risky than doing something, hush-our-mouths, original. And in the rare instances where system-bucking does occur (*Josie And The Pussycats*, for instance: a throwaway Saturday morning cartoon elevated to wicked pop-culture satire) the financial returns have been predictably dire.

We should be happy, then, that writer-director Nora Ephron throws the dog-eared playbook defiantly out the window with her adaptation of beloved re-run fodder *Bewitched*. In essence it's a prolonged meta-joke on the whole recycling trend itself, involving a narcissistic movie star attempting to revive his flagging career via a remake of the classic sit-com and inadvertently casting a real witch in the process. Great idea. The trouble is, if there was ever a TV show begging for straight treatment, it's *Bewitched*. A charming, evergreen treat, itself a coy lift from subversive, gay-coded play *Bell, Book And Candle*, it was kitschy high concept personified: suburbanite everyman marries a going-straight witch. Adorable hijinks ensue. So while you can admire Ephron's chutzpah, it's less easy to like her movie, which simply tries far too hard.

The same can be said of Ferrell who takes his usually infallible shtick to uncomfortably manic levels. Still, it's not all bad: Kidman is delicious, all wide-eyed and breathy, dithering at the prospect of her new life in the real world. And it does have its moments – a swoony sequence where Ferrell and Kidman fall in love, larking about on a deserted soundstage; Ferrell wailing, 'Am I going to get pregnant?' when Kidman finally comes clean. But it's too clever for its own good and, with apologies for hitting a sitter, the magic just isn't there. ★★ **SB**

⊙ BEYOND THE MAT (1999)

Starring: *As themselves: Mick Foley, Jake Roberts, Terry Funk, Vince McMahon, Tony Jones, Michael Modest, Roland Alexander, Darren Drozdov, Vickie Funk, Stacey Funk, Brandee Funk, Paul Heyman, Brandy Smith*
Director: *Barry W. Blaustein*
Screenwriter: *Barry W. Blaustein*
15/102 mins./108 mins (director's cut)/Documentary/USA

A documentary taking a look at the men behind the spandex, both in and out of the wrestling ring.

For those of us for whom wrestling means memories of Kendo Nagasaki grappling in front of salivating grannies on a rainy Saturday afternoon, the World Wrestling Federation, with all its attendant camp hooplah, may appear to be a 'sport' populated by lunatic egomaniacs intent on enacting bizarre S&M fantasies in front of an audience of whom a fair proportion are bedding their own cousins.

But *Saturday Night Live* writer Blaustein's sensitive documentary reveals the human beings behind the brawling, a set of alternately desperate, damaged and, in one case, surprisingly well-adjusted performers who, like the stars/victims of the old Hollywood studio system, swirl round the edges of celebrity after the ruthless machine that is WWF slams them to the mat for the last time. ★★★★ **AS**

⊙ BEYOND THE VALLEY OF THE DOLLS (1970)

Starring: *Dolly Read (Kelly MacNamara), Cynthia Myers (Casey Anderson), Marcia McBroom (Petronella (Danforth), John LaZar (Ronnie 'Z-Man' Barzell), Michael Blodgett (Larry Rocke)*
Director: *Russ Meyer*
Screenwriter: *Roger Ebert, based on a story by Meyer and Ebert*
18/109 mins./Erotic/Drama/USA

The Carrie Nations, a three-girl band, come to Hollywood and get mixed up in heartbreak, showbiz success, drugs, sex and a psychopathic hermaphrodite rock star who throws a party which turns into a massacre.

Not a sequel to the bland film of Jacqueline Susann's trashy best-seller, this is more like a demented remake, alternating modish psychedelia with deliberately square moralising. 20th Century-Fox, seeing how things were going in 1970, hired sexploitationer Russ Meyer, fresh from cheap masterpieces like *Faster, Pussycat, Kill! KILL!* and *Vixen*, and gave him a healthy budget, soliciting the sleaziest mainstream film made in Hollywood til that point.

Beyond is light on the nudity and enormous breasts for which Meyer's films are known, but zips astonishingly through bizarre insanities (co-scripted by critic Roger Ebert) with movie in-jokes (a lawyer villain named after shifty character actor Porter Hall), recurrent Meyer obsessions (a cameo from Martin Borman), caricatures of celebrities ('Randy Black', the heavyweight champion of the world), exploitable hot topics presented with all the sensitivity and understanding of a supermarket tabloid (rock 'n' roll, lesbianism, LSD, 'wild parties'), a soundtrack that alternates girlie pop and oompah band music, overheated dialogue ('you shall drink the black sperm of my vengeance!') and lovingly deployed cliché film techniques (the animated line on a map as the girls drive West).

Everyone gets a quotable signature line: Edy Williams, as hot-to-trot starlet Ashley St Ives, rounds on a guy who takes her fancy with 'you're a groovy boy – I'd like to strap you on some time'; John Lazar, as Jagger lookalike superstar and incipient gender-confused mass murderer Ronnie 'Z-Man' Barzell, screams 'this is my happening, and it freaks me out!'; and David Gurian, as temporary paraplegic Harris Allsworth, declares 'I want it, I need it, I love it when a beautiful woman licks between my toes.' ★★★ **KN**

BHAJI ON THE THE BEACH (1993)

Starring: *Kim Vithana (Ginder), Jimmi Harkishin (Ranjit), Sarita Khajuria (Hashida), Mo Sesay (Oliver), Lalita Ahmed (Asha), Surendra Kochar (Bina)*
Director: *Gurinda Chadha*
Screenwriter: *Meera Syal, based on a story by Meera Syal and Gurinda Chadha*
15/100 mins./Comedy/Drama/UK

A group of Asian women descend on Blackpool for a day out where they begin to realise they have more in common than it first appears.

Modest in budget but ambitious in scope, this lively ensemble piece has the Saheli Asian Women's group hitting Blackpool in their rickety old minibus for a day out, with director Chadha exploring the tensions in the lives of a group of carefully differentiated female characters. This is no right-on fantasy of idealised Asian women, however, with Chadha instead giving us warm but honest thumbnail sketches of, among others, doddery unreconstructed oldsters with unrefined prejudices, a middle-aged woman of tasteless glamour, and two boy-mad teenagers.

Contrasting the general egg-and-chips English realism with intriguing fantasy sequences, Chadha lifts the piece some way from its workaday premise, yet her main method of generating dramatic sparks and laughs, by bringing cultures into head-on collisions – such as when the oldsters watch a male strip show at a nightclub – is too obvious to really engage. Indeed, it's with the introduction of male characters that the film really lets itself down. Chadha's men are stereotypes. Eager to get his wife Ginder and son back, violent father Ranjit and his two brothers track the women down leading to the film's climax, a rather hysterical tug-of-love stand-off – a bargie, if you will – on the beach in which Ranjit behaves true to his stereotype.

Not a bad film, this is, however, too heavily steeped in that tradition of British filmmaking that says cinema is a place where minority issues should be off-loaded, not a majority entertained. ★★ **MTr**

BICENTENNIAL MAN (1999)

Starring: *Robin Williams (Andrew Martin), Embeth Davidtz (Little Miss Amanda Martin/Portia Charney), Sam Neill ('Sir' Richard Martin), Oliver Platt (Robert Burns), Kiersten Warren (Galatea), Wendy Crewson ('Ma'am' Martin), Hallie Kate Eisenberg (7-year-old 'Little Miss' Amande Martin)*
Director: *Chris Columbus*
Screenwriter: *Nicholas Kazan, based on a short story by Issac Asimov and the novel* The Positronic Man *by Issac Asimove and Robert Silverberg.*
PG/132 mins./Sci-fi/Drama/Romance/USA/Germany

A domestic robot who develops emotions strives to become human over the course of two centuries.

Following a well-crafted opening credit sequence in which we see the titular robot being assembled, the action kicks off in the year 2005 – throughout the film the future looks like 2000, save a few matte paintings and the obligatory flying cars – in which well-to-do Mr Martin surprises his wife and two daughters by introducing a new addition into the household: a robot, fully programmed to cook, clean, record *Who Wants To Be A Millionaire*, whatever. In totally predictable fashion, the automaton irks the older daughter he names 'Miss', endears himself to the younger sprog he dubs 'Little Miss' – she mispronounces 'android' as 'Andrew', hence giving the droid his family name – and, encouraged by Martin, begins to develop a creative, human side that takes the form of reading books, carving ickle horses and making topnotch clocks that would shame the Swiss.

The notion of robots wanting to be human is a well-worn SF conceit yet *Bicentennial Man* has little that is fresh to bring to the party: indeed, the design of the robot itself is formula stuff. The plot uneasily spins out over 200 years – cue dollops of ageing make-up – focusing on the relationship between Andrew and the grown up Little Miss (Davidtz), who teaches the droid the meaning of love and liberty, then sends him off into the big wide world to find his robot brethren and fall in love with Little Miss' daughter Portia (also Davidtz). Ah, bless.

Eschewing the non-stop gag routes (if you want real comedy robots, stick with 1973's *Sleeper*), this trades in a schmaltzy humanism. If the studios were worried that Williams would be lost under a ton of prosthetics, they needn't have: behind the mask Williams is dignified; once he gets his own skin, however, he falls into his old mawkish ways.

Despite a strong score by James Horner and some effective moments, Columbus never creates anything other than mechanical characters and scenarios, never really delivering the emotional wallop the story dictates. Sci-fi at its sappiest. ★★ **IF**

BICYCLE THIEVES (1948)

Starring: *Lamberto Maggiorani (Antonio Ricci), Lianella Carell (Maria Ricci), Enzo Staiola (Bruno Ricci), Elena Altieri (The Fortune Teller), Vittorio Antonucci (The Thief)*
Director: *Vittorio De Sica*
Screenwriters: *Cesare Zavatinni, Vittorio De Sica, Oreste Biancoli, Susie D'Amico Adolfo Franci, Gherardo Gherandhi, Gerardo Guerrieri, from a story by Cesare Zavatinni, based on the novel by Luigi Bartolini*
U/89 mins./Drama/Italy

Awards: *Academy Awards – Honorary Award (for most outstanding foreign language film), BAFTA – Best Film, Golden Globes – Best Foreign Film*

Bruno Ricci accompanies his father Antonio on a desperate quest around Rome to retrieve the stolen bicycle that Antonio needs to keep the bill-sticking job on which his impoverished family depends.

It's often stated that the casting of Cary Grant in this seminal work of neo-realism would have fatally undermined Vittorio De Sica's intention of presenting an authentic snapshot of everyday life in postwar Italy. Yet, non-professionals Lamberto Maggiorani and Enzo Staiola were both selected according to typage and such deliberation reveals the care which De Sica lavished on this meticulous recreation of backstreet Rome. Nothing was left to chance in his pastiche of spontaneity, with the extras being choreographed as rigidly as the leads to ensure that every expression and gesture illuminated the director's precise deep-focus compositions.

Inspired by a Luigi Bartolini novel, *Bicycle Thieves* is clearly a product of its times, with unemployment, poverty and the dejection of defeat very much to the fore. Yet, for all its political ramifications, its enduring appeal lies in the very human story at its heart, which focuses on a father's proud determination to sustain his household and a son's crisis of faith in his hero. By emphasising the absurdity and fatalism of daily life, De Sica questions the validity of competing contemporary solutions to society's problems. The pious, the bourgeois and the proletarian alike leave Antonio and Bruno to their fate, as they are each fully aware that everyone's first duty is to themselves in such dire circumstances. Indeed, De Sica consistently stresses the impotence of socialism by showing the pair being shunned and menaced by crowds and mobs of people who acquiesce in and exploit the uncontrollable cyclical misery of their neighbours.

It's no accident that Antonio is searching for a Fides ('Faith') bicycle, as the film draws inspiration from both the New Testament and Dante's *Divine Comedy*. Yet, De Sica insists that family unity is more crucial to social rejuvenation than any religious or political creed. Nevertheless, he still undercuts the surface sentimentality of the climactic reunion by reminding us that Antonio has lost both his bike and his job and that inevitably tougher times lie ahead. ★★★★★ **DP**

Italian Neo-Realism

What is it: Although first applied to Visconti's *Ossessione* (1942), The Italian Neo-Realist movement flourished after World War II, building a reputation on raw, intimate movies that depicted the harshness and humanity of everyday Italian life.

Hallmarks: Plot-lines pulled from reality; shooting on real-life locations, often with available light, scraps of film stock and non-professional actors; personal lyricism.

Key figures: Roberto Rossellini, Vittorio De Sica, Luschino Visconti, Aldo Vergana.

If you see one movie, see: *Bicycle Thieves* (De Sica, 1948)

⑮ BIG (1988)

Starring: *Tom Hanks (Josh), Elizabeth Perkins (Susan), Robert Loggia (MacMillan), John Heard (Paul), Jared Rushton (Billy)*
Director: *Penny Marshall*
Screenwriters: *Gary Ross, Ann Spielberg*
PG/104 mins./Comedy/Drama/Fantasy/USA

Having made a rash wish at a fairground booth, 12-year-old Josh awakens in an adult body, but still very much the child within. Unable to explain the transformation, he escapes to the big city to find employment at a toy company and the romantic attentions of a woman far too old for him, at least on the inside.

The finest in the spate of body-swap comedies of the late eighties, this is the film that revealed that Tom Hanks was capable of much more than just doltish comedy. His transformation into the jagged lope and wide-eyed enthusiasm of a prepubescent boy is a marvel of physical acting. The whole film rests on the realisation of that one idea, and the curly-haired everyman, here everyboy, makes it sing from the rafters.

The conceit, for all its inevitable sentiment, is that the world makes a whole lot more sense through the eyes of a child. Adults needlessly complicate, they lose touch with what matters. So this child behind-enemy-lines, dressed in adult skin, takes on the guise of idiot savant. Josh is a proto-Gump, but with the engaging street smarts of a neighbourhood kid. The bond between Hanks and Jared Rushton as Josh's best mate Billy is seamlessly carried from boy to man.

Director Penny Marshall handles the more complicated proposals of the script with some subtlety: the terror of his first night in the big city is so realistic (and miraculously performed) we lose sight of Hanks as a thirtysomething man; the sexual interaction with Elizabeth Perkins avoids any kind of crass outfall; and there is a satisfying gradient as Josh absorbs adulthood all-too-swiftly laying the groundwork for his undoing. Life has its natural pace, don't tamper. There's also no need to examine the magic at work, it is a transformative power granted by the writers.

Then the film is sprinkled with a particularly movie kind of magic – a succession of simple, joyous moments that lift off the screen and into the consciousness like stolen treasure. Hanks and Robert Loggia dancing chopsticks across an oversized keyboard, Perkins letting go of her grown-up inhibitions and trampolining for all she's worth, the soft, knowing look she gives Josh as they must finally separate. It's a purely Hollywood design, but that in a sense is what makes it so wonderful. Watch it through a kid's eyes. ★★★★ **IN**

⑮ THE BIG BLUE (LE GRAND BLEU) (1988)

Starring: *Jean-Marc Barr (Jacques Mayol), Jean Reno (Enzo Molinari), Rosanna Arquette (Johana Baker), Paul Shenar (Dr Laurence), Sergio Castellitto (Novelli)*
Director: *Luc Besson*
Screenwriters: *Luc Besson, Robert Garland, Marilyn Goldin, Jacques Mayol, Marc Perrier*
15/119 mins./Drama/France

Two childhood friends, Enzo and Jacques, long since grown apart but still sharing their passion for free-diving, will reunite at a championship in Italy. In the meantime American scientist Johana has become fascinated with Jacques' almost dolphin-like physiognomy beneath the water. He is the only one who can threaten Enzo's hold on the world championship. Love and rivalry will push them into dangerous places.

Luc Besson, he of the cinema du look, if not cinema du think, reached a kind of Zen-like apotheosis with this tale of men-fish, slowing down their heart-rates so that they can plunge into the amniotic glory of the deep and commune with nature. It's a spiritual glaze: achingly beautiful, haunted by the tender strains of Eric Serra's keyboards, but, at heart, pure showing off. Unsurprisingly, then, it has become a cult champion, lost to the exigencies of plot.

What, Mr Besson, are we to make of Jacques' somnolent, inhuman persona? Jean-Marc Barr, as handsome as an Alpine dawn, simply fills the vacuum of his character with long-looks and moody indifference. Quite why kooky Rosanna Arquette falls for him, demanding to have his children even if they might have webbed feet, is anyone's guess. The script's not helping, it's all subtext – man, nature, the great unknowables. It's probably his magnificent cheekbones and the quirky fact he has pictures of his dolphin family in his wallet.

Jean Reno helps shifts things along, his long-face has a diffident, ironic quality, but we are so engulfed in enigma, we are kept nonplussed if not completely irked by these child-cod-men who dream of spending their lives in the drink.

What's left is a world-spanning, ocean-diving aesthetic nearly peerless in its visual appetite. Nature takes on a sublime, dreamlike quality in cinematographer Carlo Varni's hands; Besson is much happier communing than telling a story. There's a lot to be said for just letting it wash over you, you might just detect traces of the spiritual salve it strains for (there's a 168 min. director's cut that could replace the need for goldfish). But try fathoming its depths and you'll just get washed ashore. ★★★ **IN**

THE BIG CHILL (1983)

Starring: *Glenn Close (Sarah), Tom Berenger (Sam), William Hurt (Nick), Jeff Goldblum (Michael), Mary Kay Place (Meg), Kevin Kline (Harold), Meg Tilly (Chloe), Don Galloway (Richard), JoBeth Williams (Karen), James Gillis (Minister), Alex (Kevin Costner) (uncredited)*
Director: *Lawrence Kasdan*
Screenwriters: *Lawrence Kasdan, Barbara Benedek*
15/103 mins./Comedy/Drama/USA

Seven members of a close-knit college group of friends are reunited fifteen years later after the eighth commits suicide. The funeral and reception lead to an extended weekend for all as they decide to spend time together pondering the recent events.

The Big Chill is actually remarkably similar to John Sayles' 1980 effort, *The Return Of The Secaucus Seven*, an original, spot-on look at a group of 60s college friends and erstwhile radicals reunited for a weekend of reminiscences, revelations and regrets.

Sayles' movie cost only $60,000, however, had no names attached to it, and so petered about the arthouse circuit, well regarded but little seen.

Lawrence Kasdan, coming off *Body Heat*, had more resources and promptly spun a box-office hit with his own story of a generation and a wonderful acting ensemble whose wage bill would be staggering to meet now (Tom Berenger, Glenn Close, Jeff Goldblum, William Hurt, Kevin Kline, Mary Kay Place, Meg Tilly and JoBeth Williams).

Goldblum is a hustling, cynical journalist, Hurt's tragi-comic drugs dealer yo-yos on chemical All-Sorts, Place's lawyer seeks a volunteer to impregnate her, Kline's entrepreneur treats everyone to new trainers, Close's earth mother doctor is subjected to everyone's sob stories and Tilly's much younger, aerobicising Merry Widow reminds them of their age. Meals, jogs, unexpected couplings and confessions in the kitchen provide hilariously interwoven vignettes of the group's lifestyles and concerns, all to a wittily used soundtrack of Motown classics.

The now famous forehead and extremities of Kevin Costner make cameo appearances as the much talked-about corpse, Alex. ★★★★ **IF**

THE BIG CLOCK (1948)

Starring: *Ray Milland (George Stroud), Charles Laughton (Earl Janoth), Maureen O'Sullivan (Georgette Stroud), George Macready (Steven Hagen), Rita Johnson (Pauline York), Elsa Lanchester (Louise Patterson)*
Director: *John Farrow*
Screenwriter: *Jonathann Latimer, based on the novel by Kenneth Fearing*
PG/95 mins./Crime/USA

Tyrannical publisher Earl Janoth murders his mistress by stabbing her with a toy sundial, then uses all the resources of his organisation to pin the crime on a mystery man seen in the vicinity. George Stroud, editor of *Crimeways* magazine, is in charge of tracing the man, which is problematic since he is himself the likely fall guy.

An outstanding Paramount film noir, directed by the dependable, underrared John Farrow, this is a Hitchcockian 'wrong man' movie, based on the novel by Kenneth Fearing. With an absurd splash of moustache and a scary mean little boy presence, Laughton makes an impressive, self-loathing, megalomaniac villain (based on publisher Henry Luce). As in many noirs, the villains are all sexually strange: scarfaced George Macready as Laughton's coded-as-gay right-hand-man and usually loveable Harry Morgan as an all-in-black masseur-murderer.

Early on, the film establishes the *Crimeways* technique for tracking absconders, a lo-tech blackboard to which more and more clues are added as the picture of the unknown man becomes more detailed, then Milland squirms as the description comes more and more to resemble him. There are domestic time-outs that ought to add tension but become tiresome, wasting Maureen O'Sullivan in the draggy role of the wife who is always on the point of leaving Milland because he spends too much time at work.

Elsa Lanchester has a funny bit as an eccentric painter with a brood of fatherless kids who is commissioned to do a sketch of the culprit she glimpsed and turns in a Picasso-esque abstract. In its fiendishly brilliant plot construction and media empire milieu, it is far more memorable than the remake *No Way Out*, which uses a Washington political backdrop and adds a gilding-the-lily plot twist that undoes the still-potent premise. ★★★★ **KN**

BIG DADDY (1999)

Starring: *Adam Sandler (Sonny Koufax), Joey Lauren Adams (Layla Maloney), Jon Stewart (Kevin Gerrity), Cole Sprouse/Dylan Sprouse (Julian 'Frankenstien' McGrath), Rob Schneider (Nazo), Kristy Swanson (Vanessa), Steve Buscemi (Homeless Guy), Tim Herlily (Singing Kangeroo)*
Director: *Dennis Dugan*
Screenwriters: *Steve Franks, Tim Herlihy, Adam Sandler*
12/93 mins./Comedy/Drama/USA

A lovable oaf adopts a five-year-old boy in order to impress a girlfriend. Misguided parenting techniques are applied and found wanting.

From hooligan golfer to drinks carrier, via wedding reception crooner and grown-bloke-back-at-school hijinks, perhaps the most remarkable thing about *Saturday Night Live* comedian Sandler's burst to box office heights is that it's all been done off the back of the same routine – a dysfunctional but lovable loser learns a few life lessons, gets the girl and saves whatever requires saving. But, hey, if it ain't broke ...

Here's how the pertinent details bolt to formula this time around: professional layabout Sonny has reached the age of 32 without getting married or using his law school degree. In an ill-judged effort to impress his departing girlfriend, Vanessa, Sonny reaches an agreement with his flatmate, Kevin, to take custody of his illegitimate five-year-old son, Julian. The (new) girl is snowed-under attorney, Layla. The lesson is taking responsibility for one's actions and in this case, that means Julian's childhood.

It's a sweet construct in which, as ever, the world is that safe, cartoonish version of reality – hurling logs in the path of speeding roller-bladers is satisfyingly amusing, while the American legal and social services systems seem to operate on a chaotically arbitrary and scarily trusting basis. But it manages to be quite consistently funny, with each juvenile gag balanced by the odd spark of wit and outrageousness – although a courtroom finale allowing Sandler and his writers to get their father-son relationship themes out of their systems, is predictably and excruciatingly hamfisted.

Kevin Smith fave Adams is delightful and never really had the roles her talent deserved after this; and on the cute kid(s) front, the Sprouse siblings manage quite a winning and irritation-free performance. But this, of course, is Sandler's show, once again held together by his curious yet addictive everyman charm: noisy, American loutishness played with just the right blend of vigour and humility. ★★ **DB**

⊙ THE BIG EASY (1986)

Starring: *Dennis Quaid (Remy McSwain), Ellen Barkin (Anne Osborne), Ned Beatty (Jack Kellom), Ebbe Roe Smith (Detective Dodge), John Goodman (Detective DeSoto)*
Director: *Jim McBride*
Screenwriter: *Daniel Petrie Jr*
15/108 mins./Crime/Thriller/USA

Slightly corrupt but wholly charming New Orleans cop Remy McSwain investigates a burgeoning gang war between old guard mafiosi and voodoo-worshipping drug dealers. The case is complicated by Internal Affairs investigator Anne Osborne, who unprofessionally has an affair with her chief suspect.

This opens with a real grabber: under the credits, the camera swoops low over the Louisiana swamps while fast Cajun music plays, then zooms through built-up New Orleans at dead of night to come to rest on a corpse floating face-down in front of a mob-owned building. For four-fifths of its running time, *The Big Easy* is much better than the average cop movie: the script bristles with wittily tough talk, while fast-pattering Quaid works up a nice double act romance-feud with Barkin (his cheeky grin is well-matched with her lopsided smile).

It's a funny, exciting, touching, sexy movie and climaxes several times with bravura sequences – a convincingly awkward love scene interrupted when a radio-pager sounds from a pile of discarded clothes, a nice bit of courtoom squirming as Quaid tries to get off the corruption hook, and expertly edited outbursts of straight action.

However, the film falters in the home stretch, introducing a rather too-obvious surprise villain and reducing the initially interesting plot to an over familiar set of betrayals and compromises. Originally scripted as Windy City, and set in Chicago, the film really works because of the locale change, allowing director Jim McBride, in his brief mainstream career between underground art (*David Holzman's Diary*) and bland TV movies (*Blood Ties*), to take advantage of New Orleans' picturesque architecture, great music (the soundtrack is outstanding), terrific food and convivial yet decadent atmosphere.

As in a run of late 80s films, big, genial John Goodman plays the sweaty sidekick who could be convicted of repeatedly trying to steal any scenes that aren't nailed down. **★★★★ KN**

⊙ BIG FISH (2003)

Starring: *Ewan McGregor (Young Ed Bloom), Albert Finney (Senior Ed Bloom), Billy Crudup (Will Bloom), Jessica Lange (Senior Sandra Bloom), Alison Lohman (Young Sandra Bloom), Helena Bonham Carter (Jenny/The Witch), Robert Guillaume (Senior Dr Bennett), Danny DeVito (Amos Calloway)*
Director: *Tim Burton*
Screenwriter: *John August, based on the novel by Daniel Wallace*
PG/110 mins./Drama/Fantasy/USA

After returning home to be at his dying father's bedside, Will Bloom is once again forced to listen to the tall tales of his larger-than-life dad that plagued his youth. Frustrated by the barriers these fanciful yarns put in their relationship, Will tries to uncover the facts behind the fiction.

From scissorhanded misfits to headless horsemen via Z-grade filmmakers... if any undercurrent has coursed through Tim Burton's work, it is that real life is frankly not good enough and needs embellishing. It is something of a surprise, therefore, that it took the filmmaker until his 11th effort to make this conceit explicit.

In the novel *Big Fish* by Daniel Wallace, Burton has found a vehicle to express his fascination with the fantastical and its relationship to reality. Whimsical without being twee, freewheeling without being messy, moving without being schmaltzy, *Big Fish* aligns Burton's visual virtuosity and offbeat sensibility to a story that, for once, has more than one foot in the real world. It's a charming piece of witty, warm-hearted filmmaking. After the soulless *Planet Of The Apes*, Burton has scaled down the logistics but broadened the thematic and emotional scope, crafting a tale that feels grandiose yet homespun. Part-*Baron Munchausen*, part-*Forrest Gump*, the approach of visualising the exaggerated tales of a dying man relayed to his dubious adult son echoes the storytelling traditions of Americana, yet recasts it in Burton's unique tone of voice.

In Bloom's fantastical universe, Burton is on familiar territory – a sleepy '50s-looking town recalls Edward Scissorhands, a spider-filled forest hints at *Sleepy Hollow* – serving up vignettes that, if occasionally rambling and unfocused, are marked with boundless visual imagination that hints at the darker currents in wholesome Americana. Bloom's fanciful adventures with conjoined Korean cabaret singers, a werewolf and a misunderstood giant are suffused with an affection for the bizarre, tapping into an affinity with the outsider that is a touchstone in Burton's work. Moreover, *Big Fish* is also Burton's funniest film in ages. From Edward's birth, shooting between his mother's legs and down a hospital corridor, to his run in with the kung fu fighting Korean military, Burton delivers a steady stream of laugh-out-loud absurdity.

A by-product of this is that the characters sometimes feel more like ciphers than rounded individuals. That said, McGregor gives young Edward a winning amiability and maximum sparkle, his extravagant courtship of wife-to-be Susan (Alison Lohman plays a young Jessica Lange with creepy accuracy) – involving skywriting planes and an impromptu field of daffodils – emerging as intoxicatingly sweet. Finney inhabits rather than reveals his bigger-than-life figure.

Surrounding the main players, Burton has assembled a starry-ish line-up that enriches the tapestry without ever feeling like stunt cameos. Danny DeVito is a conniving circus ringleader; Helena Bonham Carter takes a dual role, including a one-eyed witch who looks bizarrely like Faye Dunaway; and Steve Buscemi relishes a turn as a small-town poet-turned-bank robber-turned-Wall Street baron.

Ultimately, *Big Fish* is much more than a compendium of Timbo's greatest hits. For the first time since Ed Wood, Burton has transcended his hermetically sealed world and connected with wider concerns. He has moving things to say about kids accepting their parents' foibles and how emotional truths sometimes supersede factual veracity. In anchoring the whimsy to something more heartfelt, Burton is greatly aided by Billy Crudup, who underplays potentially cringeworthy bedside scenes with his dying dad. If the ending muddles its message, it'll take a hard heart not to feel touched come the close of Bloom's picaresque adventures. And that's no lie. **★★★★ OR**

⊙ THE BIG LEBOWSKI (1998)

Starring: *Jeff Bridges (Jeffrey Lebowski – The Dude), John Goodman (Walter Sobchak), Julianne Moore (Maude Lebowski), Steve Buscemi (Theodore Donald 'Donny' Kerabatos), David Huddleston (Jeffrey Lebowski – The Big Lebowski), Philip Seymour Hoffman (Brandt), Tara Reid (Bunny), Peter Stormare (Nihilist #1), Flea (Nihilist #2), John Turturro (Jesus Quintana)*
Director: *Joel Coen*
Screenwriters: *Ethan Coen, Joel Coen*
18/117 mins./Comedy/Crime/Mystery.USA/UK

Geoffrey 'The Dude' Lebowski has his routine of bowling and dope-smoking rudely interrupted when debt collectors mistake him for the millionaire Geoffrey Lebowski and piss on his rug. A host of crossing and double crossing ensues.

Academy Awards, box office dividends, the trappings of fame and fortune, the Coen Brothers have been dancing with the devil of late with Fargo's successes – supposedly introducing the brothers grim to the rapt world of the commercial big time. Their immediate reaction, naturally, was to laugh in the face of populism and follow Fargo's black on white trickery with a film as peculiar, original and unstintingly inventive as any on their twisted CV. Hollywood will be as perplexed by their genius as ever, this is a movie that will only make perfect sense if you happen to possess Coen genes. No need to trouble yourself, mind. Just sit back and let The Dude be your guide.

The Dude Lebowski is 'a man in whom casualness runs deep', a 70s fall-out, hippy-child grown old but not wise as he gets unwittingly caught up in a wifenapping drama after being mistaken for a millionaire, The Big Lebowski. Egged on by his brute buddy, the ineptly psychopathic Vietnam vet Walter (Goodman having the time of his life) – one third of the Dude's bowling triumvirate, made up by the sappy Donnie (Steve Buscemi playing way against type) – he seeks reparation and becomes one of the multitude of parties that wheel in and out of the ensuing vortex of double-cross, treble-cross, extortion, carpet pissing and torture by marmot.

It's a pastiche of Raymond Chandler's labyrinthine noir, anchored not in the hard-bitten Bogart but the quixotic pothead Bridges (perfectly cast), floating (quite literally in the magnificent Busby Berkeley style dream sequences) from one nexus of disaster to the next. All the familiar Coenisms are present and correct: the delicious ear for the nuance of language, the humdrum milieu (Venice Beach, LA) transformed into an ethereal alternate-world of lavish detail and a set of characters that rests comfortably between excess and insight, each as rich and unforgettable as anything from their previous odysseys. Try Julianne Moore's pseudo-European feminist art freak, Peter Stormare's German synth rocker-cum-porn star nihilist or John Turturro's outrageous convicted child-molester turned bowling alumnus Jesus (as presented in slo-mo to the twangs of a Latino trilled Hotel California) for character novelty.

Visually director Joel has surpassed himself, surreally complementing the fervid script with a trippy beauty. The film's central motif, the leisurely pursuit of ten pin bowling, is transformed into something lyrical and wondrous in a stream of elegant longeurs. The man even sticks a micro-camera inside a bowling ball to dizzy the whole audience momentarily.

For those who delight in the Coens' divinely abstract take on reality, this is pure nirvana (cross *Blood Simple* with *Raising Arizona* if you must), yet beyond the hysterical black comedy, scattered violence and groovy dialogue, there sounds the same song to human goodness which enriched *Fargo*. In The Dude's easy-riding, people-loving approach to the mess of his life, you are witness to something no end of $200 mill sinking tubs could touch upon. In a perfect world all movies would be made by the Coen brothers. ★★★★★ **IN**

BIG NIGHT (1996)

Starring: *Marc Anthony (Cristiano), Tony Shalhoub (Primo), Stanly Tucci (Secondo), Andre Belgrader (Stash), Minnie Driver (Phyllis), Peter McRobbie (Loan Officer), Isabella Rossellini (Gabriella), Liev Schreiber, Christine Tucci (Woman Singer), Ian Holm (Pascal), Allison Janney (Ann), Campbell Scott (Bob)*
Directors: *Campbell Scott, Stanley Tucci*
Screenwriters: *Joseph Tropiano, Stanley Tucci*
15/107 mins./Drama/USA

In 50s New Jersey two Italian-American brothers struggle to keep their restaurant afloat.

Mamma mia, this is a tasty delight, a captivating, bittersweet culinary comedy drama of brotherhood and the American dream.

Primo and Secondo Pilaggi are hopeful Italian immigrant brothers struggling to make a go of their little restaurant, The Paradise, in 1950s New Jersey. Primo is a master chef, a culinary artist who lives by the creed 'To eat good food is to be close to God'. His younger sibling Secondo, who yearns for success and its trappings – a flash car and fancy women being priorities – is the matre d' and business brain exasperated by his brother's refusal to pander to the locals' lowbrow preferences for spaghetti and meatballs or steak and fries. Across the street, rival Pascal is prospering by what the outraged Primo denounces as 'the rape of cuisine'.

In a last ditch bid to publicise their fare, Secondo persuades Primo to prepare a sumptuous banquet for singing star Louis Prima and his band. It is to be quite a night, one the community will remember for the romantic complications, alarming revelations and furious confrontations served up between the antipasto and the dolci.

Written by Tucci (the unforgettable Prince Of Darkness, Richard Cross, in *Murder One*) and his cousin Joseph Tropiano, this is a richly detailed picture of the fraternal relationship, coloured by their emotionality, contrasting ambitions and ethnicity. Tucci and his actor buddy Campbell Scott, who also appears as a Cadillac salesman, have with panache evoked the Italian-American neighbourhood and the period while orchestrating superb ensemble playing. Shalhoub is just beautiful, slinging skillets and wistfully eyeing the spinster florist down the street. He and Tucci's dapper wannabe, out of his depth in his efforts to assimilate and conquer, present authentic Italian-Americans with subtlety and real humour, without toppling over into exaggeration and cliché. But everyone is just right, from Holm, the knowing Rossellini to the Paradise's quiet young waiter (Marc Anthony). Collectively they dish up beautifully observed vignettes of blood ties, conflicting desires, and how to make an omelette.

Charming, funny, poignant and mouth-watering, this is most wisely seen well fed beforehand or you'll be drooling. ★★★★ **AE**

THE BIG PICTURE (1989)

Starring: *Kevin Bacon (Nick Chapman), Emily Longstreth (Susan Rawlings), J.T. Walsh (Allen Habel), Jennifer Jason Leigh (Lydia Johnson), Michael McKean (Emmet Summer), Kim Miyori (Jenny Summer), Teri Hatcher (Gretchen), Jason Gould (Carl Manknik), Stephen Collins (Attorney), Roddie McDowell (Judge), John Cleese (Bartender Frankie)*
Director: *Christopher Guest*
Screenwriters: *Michael Varhol, Christopher Guest, Michael McKean, Martin Short (Neil Sussman, Nick's Agent) (uncredited)*
12/100 mins./Comedy/Drama/Music/Romance/USA

The winner of a student film competition is whisked away to Hollywood where he gradually finds his life's dreams are watered down.

Having co-written and starred (as the Great Nigel Tufnell) in *This Is Spinal Tap*, director Christopher Guest here turns the same wonderfully accurate eye to the movie business and turns out a razor sharp, very funny and loonily endearing skit on the Hollywood studio system. The overwhelming lack of enthusiasm for the film in the US was perhaps down to a reluctance among the American movie-going public to believe that their beloved industry could actually be anything like this.

Opening with a series of horribly believable student films – a Napoleonic widescreen epic revealing the incipient megalomania of its auteur, a daffy bit of performance art madness from Jennifer Jason Leigh (who entered into the spirit of the whole thing by making her own character's film), and a ghastly amateurish courtroom drama made by the son of a bigshot agent who is thus able to get a big name cast (Elliott Gould, June Lockhart, Roddy McDowell) to appear in his film – Guest then goes on to spotlight a succession of spot-on funny-nasty caricature Hollywood characters, among them J.T. Walsh as the scheming producer, Martin Short (uncredited in his best-ever screen work) as a grasping gay agent and even John Cleese, in a micro-gag as a bartender.

The eventual winner out of this dreadful bunch is student director Nick Chapman (Bacon), who is, of course, immediately sucked into the morass that is Hollywood, seduced onto the books of a voracious agent, and lured into a series of wonderfully staged pitch meetings with various producers. Somewhere along the way, Chapman's original idea for a black and white 'relationships film' gradually turns into *Beach Nuts*, a no-holds-barred nerd comedy. Not surprisingly, the whole thing starts to affect his mind, and he swaps his devoted girlfriend for a murderously ambitious bikini girl starlet, while becoming more and more desperate to see his film – no matter how badly mutilated it may be by this stage – up there on the screen. And so it goes on.

The whole thing does tend to run out of steam towards the end, but *The Big Picture* is likely to be much-loved by anyone with more than a passing fascination with how Hollywood works. ★★★★ **JY**

THE BIG RED ONE (1980)

Starring: *Lee Marvin (Sergeant), Mark Hamill (Griff), Robert Carradine (Zab), Bobby Di Cicco (Vinci), Kelly Ward (Johnson), Siegfried Rauch (Schroeder), Stephane Audran (Walloon), Serge Marquand (Rasonnet), Charles Macaulay (General Captain), Alain Douey (Broban)*
Director: *Samuel Fuller*
Screenwriter: *Samuel Fuller*
15/113 mins./158 mins. (reconstructed version)/War/Action/Drama/USA

A US Army sergeant who participated in the First World War now leads his former rifle squad, the First Infantry, through the major battles of the Second World War.

Writer, producer and director Sam Fuller was a unique, idiosyncratic voice in Hollywood, whose raw, unrefined, uncompromising perception of the world was somewhat embarrassing to the business men and the bourgeoisie. His work was often disdained as B-movie actioners or melodramas. But he is revered by many filmmakers (Scorsese, Wenders, Tarantino to name but a few who acknowledge his influence) and a major cult of devotees because his films pack real punch. They are full of emotional truth and authentic life experience, none more so than war films including *The Steel Helmet*, *Merrill's Marauders* and his autobiographical masterpiece, *The Big Red One*. Fuller's boast, 'Any war picture I made, you're in the war!' is the simple truth.

Well travelled and well seasoned, Fuller had been a crime reporter, political cartoonist and pulp novelist by the time America entered World War II. At 31 he enlisted and as a rifleman in the legendary Fighting First, the Big Red One, fought in North Africa, Sicily, Normandy, Belgium and Czechoslovakia. He kept a diary of sketches, recording the weather, his mental state, his health and the killing. These experiences inform all his war movies, but this is the most personal in detail and tersely eloquent passion.

This is the journey of four 'wet noses' – Griff, Johnson, Vinci, Zab (Carradine as the Fuller character, a narrator who repeatedly hits the nail on the head in a stream of concise observations) – and the Sergeant marching them through hell, keen only on getting through it. You can smell the smoke of battle and the sweat of men trapped and outnumbered, feel the stomach-knotting fear awaiting an enemy's move, the gag-making horror of liberating a concentration camp and coming eye to eye with real evil.

The film opens in France, November 1918, on a weary Marvin picking his way through bodies and stabbing a stray German beneath a giant crucifix, unaware that the war is over. A piece of cloth from the dead man's hat, a numeral one, becomes the insignia of the First Infantry Division and a quarter of a century later they're about to land in North Africa under the gaze of the veteran, now a sergeant. Although these are the stock characters of war drama – the sage, grizzled Sarge, the farm boy, the street kid, the nice guy who doesn't want to kill anyone and the witness – Fuller's are particularly credible – when men next to them die, all they allow themselves to feel is fleeting relief. The closest they get to a group hug is a surprise reunion with Sarge, whose escape from a German field hospital in Tunis in tattered Arab dress to shepherd his men to Sicily is handled with determined humour; Fuller pulls back to a long shot before anybody is tempted to go misty-eyed as the squad runs towards him.

Fuller's depiction of D-Day is intimate, economical and tersely eloquent. The action is relentless, paced and varied in order to capture a full range of experiences, human and inhuman. The squad's first engagement is an accidental attack when Vichy French troops are trying to throw their lot in with the Americans. Their first encounter with Germans is a nightmare of confusion and panic. From that point they become wiser and warier, more efficient at killing, through scenes of madness (literally, in a raid on a German-occupied mental asylum) and mayhem; punctuated with surprises and snipings for which there is no preparation, only luck or mischance. Only fleetingly does Fuller leave the squad, to visit equally disenchanted Germans echoing the same sentiments (about the distinction between murdering and killing).

While the squad is pinned down on Omaha Beach, losing man after man, wrestling with equipment and terror, he keeps cutting to a wristwatch on a dead soldier in the water. As the remaining First make it through the wire and away, the last shot of the watch shows the water red with blood. The action culminates in, 'the final joke of the whole goddam war', a cosmic bit of synchronicity that underlines everything the film has told us: that men never know what it's really all about except to shoot and not get shot. ★★★★★ **AE**

THE BIG SLEEP (1946)

Starring: *Humphrey Bogart (Phillip Marlowe), Lauren Bacall (Vivian), John Ridgely (Eddie Mars), Louis Jean Heydt (Joe Brody), Elisha Cook Jr (Jones), Regis Toomey (Bernie Ohls)*
Director: *Howard Hawks*
Screenwriters: *William Faulkner, Jules Furthman, Leigh Brackett, based on the novel by Raymond Chandler*
PG/118 mins./Mystery/Crime/USA

Private eye Philip Marlowe is hired to find the missing son-in-law of an ailing millionaire, and gets mixed up with his client's daughters, femme fatale Vivian and nymphet Carmen, not to mention a dirty book racket, organised crime, blackmail and several murders.

Less effective as a Raymond Chandler adaptation than *Murder, My Sweet*, this skirts around the nymphomania, pornography and drug addiction that are central to the novel's plot. Bogart's hardboiled Marlowe extends his own wry, insolent image rather than tries to play Chandler's character, while the sexual crackle of his scenes with Bacall obviously follows up their romantic teaming in Hawks's *To Have And Have Not* and their real-life marriage. These sequences were reshot with sexier dialogue after a preview, when Hawks decided audiences would rather have fun than a story they could follow.

Nevertheless, it remains a classic, wholly lovable movie, deploying Chandler's large and picturesque supporting cast to exceptional effect: Vickers's rich tramp is one of the great movie sluts, trying to sit on Marlowe's lap while he's standing up; Charles Waldron sits pickled in alcohol in his oppressively hot greenhouse amid the orchids he loathes, reminiscing about his wild life; Elisha Cook Jr delivers a definitive loser weasel role, forced to drink poison by a blankly malevolent hood; and Dorothy Malone pops in as a provocative bookstore clerk who offers Marlowe clues about a rare edition of *Ben-Hur* and an afternoon's solace.

Famously impossible to understand, this is less a jigsaw than a mystery tour, presenting great scenes in which Bogart faces down a series of strange characters. Decades before the self-referential, self-mocking tone became mandatory in would-be cool thrillers, Hawks delivers almost a parody of the private eye genre, using the mystery as a blatant excuse for visual and verbal pleasures. ★★★★★ **KN**

Film Noir

What it is: Hardboiled, cynical, romantic strain of Hollywood crime movie that flourished in the 40s.
Hallmarks: Stark black-and-white cinematography; haunted and trapped protagonists; slinky femme fatales; doomed minor characters; flashback structures; wisecracks; gunplay; trenchcoats; rain; the city at night.
Key figures: directors Billy Wilder, Robert Siodmak, Jules Dassin, John Huston; writers Raymond Chandler, James M. Cain, Cornell Woolrich
If you see one movie, see: *Double Indemnity* (1944)

BIG TROUBLE IN LITTLE CHINA (1986)

Starring: *Kurt Russell (Jack Burton), Kim Cattrall (Gracie Law), Dennis Dun (Wang Chi), James Hong (David Lo Pan), Victor Wong (Egg Shen), Kate Burton (Margo)*
Director: *John Carpenter*
Screenwriters: *Gary Goldman, David Z Weinstein, W.D. Richter*
15/99 mins./Action/Adventure/USA

Two-fisted meathead Jack Burton helps out his Chinese friend Wang Chi when Wang's green-eyed fiancée is kidnapped, in rapid succession, by a San Francisco street gang, a band of martial artists and three evil spirits in the service of David Lo Pan, the two-thousand-year-old godfather of Chinatown, who needs to marry or sacrifice the girl if he is to lift an ancient curse and rule the universe.

An American tribute to the Hong Kong sword and sorcery genre, in the spirit of efforts like Tsui Hark's *Zu: Warriors From Magic Mountain* (practically unseen outside of ethnic theatres and film festivals in 1986), this is one of John Carpenter's more amiable pictures, taking its tone from Kurt Russell's John Wayne-influenced performance as the confident leading man who reverses the Green Hornet-and-Kato white hero/Asian sidekick tradition by bungling every task he is called upon to do (he's the sort of guy who shoots at the ceiling and then is surprised when lumps fall on his head) while super-efficient Chinese fighters get him out of trouble.

Set mostly in a magical world under San Francisco which is populated by monsters, magicians and masters of mystic martial arts, it mixes straight he-man heroics and kung fu action with wonderful weapons, acrobatic stunts and special effects trickery. In addition, Russell strikes some sparks with Lois Lane-like heroine Kim Cattrall, who is also a potential bride for the Fu Manchu-like Lo Pan. It falters a little in its confusing climactic battle, but is breathlessly paced, wittily scripted, amusingly played, action-packed and relentlessly spooky.

Like Carpenter's *The Thing*, this was a commercial misfire on its first release but has picked up a cult following. It now seems well ahead of the game in introducing Chinese-style wirework and mythology to the Hollywood action film. ★★★ **KN**

BIG WEDNESDAY (1978)

Starring: *William Katt (Jack), Gary Busey (Leroy), Jan-Michael Vincent (Matt), Patti D'Arbanville (Sally), Lee Purcell (Peggy Gordon), Sam Melville (Bear), Robert Englund (Narrator, Fly)*
Director: *John Milius*
Screenwriters: *Dennis Aaberg, John Milius, Joel Chernoff (uncredited)*
PG/114 mins./Comedy/Drama/USA

Three friends, whose lives have always revolved around surfing, find their dreams of endless waves encroached on by looming adult responsibilities and the Vietnam war.

Made in 1978 and set on the beaches of California between 1964 and 1974, John Milius's autobiographical movie opens as a coming-of-age film, with three board-toting buddies hitting the seas at every opportunity and cutting loose with beer and broads between the waves. Then, after a riotous trip to Tijuana has established their characters, the film segues into a semi-melancholy meditation on the gradual congealing of the American Dream, as brushes with Vietnam, adulthood and existential angst sour the endless summer of the protagonists.

Milius, whose politics might kindly be labelled 'individualist' and unkindly 'barbarian', is, if nothing else, not enamoured of compromise, and so he neglects the chance to make a surfer's *American Graffiti* in favour of an approach that combines the expected yahoo-isms of the crushed beer-can school of cinema with a surprising sensitivity and a mystic affinity for the seas that *Point Break* was laughably unable to equal.

A commercial wipe-out on its first release, the film has never quite gathered the cult reputation it deserves, perhaps because director Milius has never proved as audience-friendly a figure as his movie brat contemporaries Steven Spielberg, George Lucas or Francis Ford Coppola, with whose careers his own has inter-twined.

Big Wednesday boasts perfectly judged performances from William Katt, Jan-Michael Vincent and Gary Busey and, with eerie aptness, the flare of promise and descent into direct-to-video gloom shared by the director and stars underlines the film's theme; that these suntanned demigods with a built-in sell-by date, last seen watching a younger boardman surf rings around their old records, are doomed to disappointment no matter how big their big day may be.

A worthy reissue in 1992, with the incredible surfing scenes overpowering on the big screen, this is also a reminder that Milius, who has retreated to scripting blockbusters like *Patriot Games* after the crash of a run of projects culminating with *Flight Of The Intruder*, is one of the few filmmakers in Hollywood crazy enough to be worth arguing about. ★★★★★ **JY**

BIGGIE AND TUPAC (2001)

Starring: *as themselves: The Notorious B.I.G. (archive footage), Tupac Shakur (archive footage), Nick Broomfield, Russell Poole, David Hicken, Billy Garland, Voletta Wallace, Mopreme, Kevin Hackie, Reggie Wright Snr.*
Director: *Nick Broomfield*
15/108 mins./Documentary/Music/UK

Friends who fell out, rappers Tupac Shakur and Christopher Wallace (aka The Notorious BIG) ultimately both became victims of drive-by shootings. Years later, documentary filmmaker Nick Broomfield investigates.

As the title suggests, *Biggie And Tupac* functions as a companion piece to Nick Broomfield's previous film, *Kurt And Courtney*. Again, the British documentary maker is intrigued by the untimely demise of an American musician – in this case, a pair of twinned, unsolved murders – and again he holds little faith in the official version of events. However, if you thought that Broomfield had provoked a formidable foe in Courtney Love, just wait till you see his jailyard showdown with fearsome rap mogul Suge Knight.

Persistent critics contend that Broomfield's documentaries are exercises in self-promotion, and certainly the first half of this movie is littered with investigative dead-ends included for (often funny) comic respite. However, soon enough you get the feeling that he is really onto something – a tangled web of racism, money and ego that takes you deep into the dark heart of L.A..

Unlike *Kurt And Courtney*, Broomfield has more than mere conspiracy theories to chew on this time around, and once his tenacity starts to yield real breakthroughs, the second half builds to a compelling climax. Since

Broomfield patented his affable English patter – Miss Marple with a mic – this alien-abroad territory has been further mapped by Jon Ronson and Louis Theroux amongst others, and yet Broomfield remains an investigative irritant without peer.

Despite the fact that *Biggie And Tupac* – in common with all Broomfield films – is subjective and uneven, the results are entertaining, charming, shocking and oddly affecting. While he might lack the righteous indignation of a crusader (see Michael Moore), Broomfield has rediscovered the persistent instincts of a yard dog. Good for him. ★★★★ **CK**

BILL AND TED'S BOGUS JOURNEY (1991)

Starring: *Alex Winter (Bill S. Preston, Esq/Granny Preston/Evil Bill), Keanu Reeves (Ted Logan/Evil Ted), William Sadler (Grim Reaper/English Family Member), Joss Ackland (Chuck De Nomolos), Pam Grier (Ms Wadroe), George Carlin (Rufus), Amy Stock-Poynton (Missy Logan)*
Director: *Peter Hewitt*
Screenwriters: *Ed Solomon, Chris Matheson*
PG/93 mins./Aventure/Comedy/Fantasy/Sci-fi/USA

A tyrant from the future sends evil android doubles back in time to assassinate Bill and Ted and take their places, but being 'dead' isn't going to stop the heroes from saving the planet.

One very satisfying aspect of *Bill & Ted's Excellent Adventure* was its refusal to redeem the pair, allowing them to depart as stupid as they arrived. Useful for a sequel too, as without any acquired wisdom Bill & Ted's dedicatedly dumb surfer cool (the characters' central joke) can remain impervious to accepted logic and the first film's lunatic humour need not be diminished.

Bogus Journey begins with what was hinted at in *Excellent Adventure* – that in the future Bill & Ted culturally dominate the planet. (It presumes a more-than-working knowledge of the first film, and so wastes no time.) However, the wicked DeNomolus is about to travel back to 1990 (where Bill & Ted have left school and dream of stardom with their awful heavy metal band), kill the guys and replace them with looklike, thoroughly nasty androids, 'the evil robot usses'.

While this creates confusion in town, Bill & Ted appear to be breezing through the hereafter: they, literally, gamble with death and beat the Grim Reaper at parlour games like Twister and Cluedo; hang out in Hell ('Just like an Iron Maiden album cover'); visit Heaven to get help in making their own androids ('the good robot usses'); and return to 'save the babes'. All with the same idiot expressions of perplexed optimism and still unable to play their guitars. Every bit as acutely observed as its predecessor – all sorts of verbal asides and background visual gags supplement the free-flowing main jokes, Winter & Reeves (Bill & Ted) achieve new levels as teenage morons and the supporting cast (notably Sadler as the foppish Grim Reaper) play out the ridiculousness with the dryest of Pythonesque straight faces. ★★★ **LB**

BILL AND TED'S EXCELLENT ADVENTURE (1989)

Starring: *Keanu Reeves (Ted Logan), Alex Winter (Bill. S. Preston), George Carlin (Rufus), Terry Camillleri (Napoleon)*
Director: *Stephen Herek*
Screenwriters: *Chris Matheson, Ed Solomon*
PG/90 mins./Sci-fi/Comedy/USA

Doofus double-act Ted 'Theodore' Logan and Bill S. Preston, are in grave danger of flunking out at high school, if they don't pass their history presentation. Thankfully, a dude from the future turns up with a time machine, pointing out the good of mankind depends on their passing. Borrowing the phone-box-shaped time machine, they skit about time getting some first-hand research done.

A shoddy but personable teen comedy easily outgunned by its later sequel, but still managing the not inconsiderable tasks of making Keanu Reeves a star, turning air-guitar twiddles into a universal motif for, well, something cool, and reinterpreting the pronunciation of Socrates as 'So-Crates.' It's a lot less funny than you remember, but has charm in spades, so let it roll.

The central shtick is that California's lowest achievers (they think Joan of Arc was Noah's wife), who only dream of hitting it big with their rock band The Wyld Stallions, mix it up with the great thinkers of history. Care of some dilapidated special effects (the budget was paltry), this inept duo of 'dudes' make-nice with Napoleon, Genghis Khan, Lincoln, Beethoven, Freud (the 'Frood-dude') and, of course, So-Crates, co-opting them back to the future for the big presentation cum rock show.

It is widely considered, and mostly true, that Reeves has played Ted Logan for his entire career. His trademark flabbergasted lunk routine was born out of Ted's blissful, floppy headed ignorance. Winter matches him lummox for lummox. Their partnership, with its threads of affection, is the best thing about the film. And their Valley-patter of backward pointing sentences and goofball delivery has become the Lingua Franca for idiot-comedy being bastardised by everyone from Brendan Fraser to *Wayne's World*. This film is seminal (snark!). Its jokes, however, are scattershot and intermittently funny, shouting either 'bodacious' or 'excellent' a lot. The general air of chaos is not wholly welcome.

Still, how can you be too curmudgeonly about a film whose central philosophy is, 'to be excellent to one another'? Party on. ★★★ **IN**

BILLY ELLIOT (2000)

Starring: *Jamie Bell (Billy Elliot), Julie Walters (Mrs Wilkinson), Jamie Draven (Tony), Gary Lewis (Dad), Jean Heywood (Grandma), Stuart Wells (Michael), Mike Elliot (George Watson)*
Director: *Stephen Daldry*
Screenwriter: *Lee Hall*
15/111 mins./Drama/UK

Awards: *BAFTA – Alexander Korda Award for Best British Film, Best Actor, Best Supporting Actress, Empire – Best British Actress, Best British Film, Best Debut (Jamie Bell)*

A miner's son dreams of becoming a ballet dancer.

A film about a pre-teen, would-be ballet dancer – set against the gritty backdrop of the 1984 Miners' Strike – doesn't at first sound like an enticing prospect. So it's all credit to director Daldry that he created the first genuinely exhilarating Brit flick of the new millennium, a no-holds-barred triumph which, minus the current staples of drugs, violence, gangsters and pop stars-turned-actors, shines out like a beacon among the recent sea of homegrown mediocrity.

The key to *Billy Elliot*'s success is its deceptive simplicity; in telling this story of a boy who wants to swap his boxing gloves for ballet tights, Daldry has eschewed the regular dance movie clichés – debilitating illness, disability etc. – to create a triumph-over-adversity tale of a different kind. Here, the only obstacle Billy has to overcome is the opposition of his widowed father – a tragic figure who is having to cope not only with single parenthood, but the daily grind of the picket line in the ongoing miners' strike.

Yet, for all its grittiness, this is never a depressing film, instead one which treats its year's turbulent history as set dressing for the central story. There is a great deal of comedy here too, as our pint-sized hero shakes off his two left feet and starts to display his potential, ably backed by dance teacher Mrs Wilkinson – Walters in her best role for years. Along the way he gets into scrapes, discovers his burgeoning sexuality via his two best mates – the cross-dressing Michael and precocious pre-teen Debbie (Nicola Blackwell) – and has the audience rooting for him at every turn and pirouette.

Where this really scores and tugs the emotions, though, is in the dance sequences themselves, set largely to a medley of 80s hits and comprising unorthodox moves guaranteed to blow away the stereotypes of ballet – with one particularly glorious set-piece guaranteed to have even the most stoic of viewer complaining of something in their eye. Bell is as accomplished a dancer as he is an actor, carrying the movie with astonishing aplomb and turning in a star-making performance, which is nothing short of astonishing. ★★★★★ **CW**

BILLY LIAR (1963)

Starring: *Tom Courtenay (Billy Fisher), Julie Christie (Liz), Wilfred Pickles (Geoffrey Fisher), Mona Washbourne (Alice Fisher), Ethel Griffies (Florence), Finlay Currie (Duxbury), Rodney Bewes (Arthur Crabtree), Leonard Rossiter (Shadrack)*
Director: *John Schlesinger*
Screenwriters: *Keith Waterhouse, Willis Hall, based on their play*
PG/98 mins./Drama/UK

Billy is a dreamer who works at a funeral parlour. But his tendency to drift into a dream world creates problems at work and in his relationships with three women.

Charlie Chaplin once defined the three key ingredients for a comedy as a park, a policeman and a pretty girl. In the case of 60s classic, *Billy Liar*, one might suggest instead a hill, a councillor and a neurotic undertaker's clerk. Together they make one of the defining scenes in one of British film's most enduring comedies.

Said clerk, Billy Fisher, is finding his life in a small Northern town swiftly unravelling: his struggle to share one engagement ring between two fiancées is becoming unequal. He fancies someone else anyway and his funeral parlour boss refuses to accept his resignation to allow him to take up a job with a London-based comedian (itself a fiction) until he can explain the whereabouts of some unsent company calendars and the accompanying missing postage money.

Addressing this latter problem, he walks out onto the moors to dispose of some calendars but instead encounters his employer, Councillor Duxbury. Over the course of their conversation Courtenay moves from nervousness to thinly concealed hysteria at the prospect of his crime being uncovered. When the subject of the calendars is finally broached he lapses into an unconscious gibberish, mimicking the older man's broad Yorkshire accent, finally declaring, 'I'm just aboot thraiped wi' thees place,' before receiving a curt comeuppance. Deftly played by Courtenay, it reveals all the subtle strengths of John Schlesinger's influential film. The subject matter is the forerunner of Monty Python's Yorkshireman sketch, Courtenay's nervous Northerner is the template for Alan Bennett's schtick while the imitative impulse is pure Zelig. For director John Schlesinger the scene represented a triumph over adversity.

'Finlay arrived on location,' he recalls of the veteran actor, 'and he said, 'I hope you'll understand, but I lost my last daughter two nights ago.' So we went to great lengths to hide the hearse from him but he was playing an undertaker, of course. He was terribly sporting and very professional about it all but he couldn't remember any lines.'

Billy Liar began life as a novel, under the working title, The Young Man's Magnificat. Its author, Keith Waterhouse, then a freelance journalist, later wrote of his work, 'Pretty soon I had 10,000 words. They were as pretentious as the title itself.' The manuscript was drunkenly left in the back of a taxi but undaunted, Waterhouse began again. After a further rewrite, the novel was published to international acclaim. 'An English Salinger has burst upon the scene,' being one fairly typical review.

Presently, working with the writer Willis Hall, a friend from his hometown Leeds, Waterhouse adapted it into a successful West End play featuring Albert Finney in the lead. Producer Joe Janni and director Schlesinger who had previously collaborated on *A Kind Of Loving* (for which Waterhouse and Hall wrote the screenplay) felt it would make an ideal follow-up.

Courtenay, who had succeeded Finney in the West End role, was cast in the lead and Schlesinger assembled a fine cast of solid English character actors in supporting roles, most notably Leonard Rossiter pitch perfect as the oleaginous, technology-obsessed undertaker Shadrack. The role of free spirit Liz, eventually taken by Julie Christie, proved more problematic, however. Initially, an actress called Topsy Jane was cast in the part, but some weeks into the shoot, as she suffered a breakdown, Schlesinger realised he had made a mistake. 'We'd tested Julie twice, but I'd been against casting her because she didn't seem to me to be Earth Mother enough,' laughs Schlesinger. 'When we ran into difficulties we looked at the tests again and I said, "We must be crazy not to have cast Julie Christie in the first place." '

Christie looked the part and brought an enormous vivacity to her character, impressing Schlesinger sufficiently to cast her – against studio wishes – for her Oscar-winning role in *Darling*. Nevertheless, it remains Courtenay's film. He confesses to feeling chronically shy at the time despite the success of *The Loneliness Of The Long Distance Runner*. 'I'd come into the business and all of a sudden I was one of the most famous actors in England,' he recalls. 'And I hadn't done anything.' He was also grieving the loss of his mother, who died a week before shooting began. Nevertheless, his grasp of Billy's beguiling mixture of naivety and duplicity is a comic *tour de force*.

'Billy is in every molecule of my body,' he reflects. 'Everyone has a particular gift and mine I suppose is a directness of feeling and I think that's what made my role work. It's direct and it's honest. That's why people still identify with Billy today.'

Indeed. *Billy Liar* has worn far better than its more serious-minded contemporaries. It manages to make the same points about class and opportunity as more bombastic kitchen-sink dramas without recourse to tub-thumping. Shot in Schlesinger's beloved black and white and in CinemaScope it remains a pleasure to look at. For anyone, anywhere who has ever felt thraiped it remains an unalloyed, imperishable joy. ★★★★★ **JN**

THE BIRDCAGE (1996)

Starring: *Robin Williams (Armand Goldman), Gene Hackman (Senator Keeley), Nathan Lane (Albert), Dianne West (Louise Keeley), Dan Futterman (Val Goldman), Calista Flockhart (Barbara Keeley), Hank Azaria (Agador), Christine Baranski (Katharine)*
Director: *Mike Nichols*
Screenwriter: *Elaine May, based on the screenplay* La Cage Aux Folles *by Jean Poiret, Francis Verber and Marcello Danon, adapted from the stage play by Jean Poiret*
15/118 mins./Comedy/USA

A gay cabaret owner and his drag queen companion agree to put up a false straight front so that their son can introduce them to his fiancée's right-wing moralistic parents.

As Hollywood continues its fascination with translating foreign classics and dressing blokes in an ever-wider selection of feminine attire, it seemed inevitable that along would come a film which combined the two. And indeed, 1978's Gallic institution *La Cage Aux Folles* was that very candidate. The original was a farce of pant-wetting proportions that spawned two sequels and a musical. The remake offers glitz, glamour and Robin Williams. The results, while overly sincere, are for the most part satisfying.

Williams, all gaudy suits and preposterous facewear, is nightclub owner Armand Goldman who lives in Miami Beach in a flat full of artefacts that would make a porn star blush, with over-emotional drag queen beau Albert, convinced his other half is up to no good. Then Armand's son announces his upcoming marriage to the daughter of a senator embroiled in a political scandal, and the impending in-laws head cross-country to meet their new family. All the stops are pulled out to convince the right-wingers that normality and heterosexuality reign chez Goldman. It doesn't work.

The build-up gradually piles on layers of comedy before giving way to all-out farce in the final reel, but all too often allowing political correctness to impede on the good humour. What is refreshing, though, is to see Williams' mugging taking a back seat, allowing him to play, appropriately enough, straight man to Lane's frequently hysterical histrionics. Meanwhile Hank Azaria provides frenzied hilarity as the couple's neurotic housemaid and Hackman shows unexpected comic dexterity. Reservations aside, this has a winning charm which stands it head and shoulders above its more patronising cross-dressing companions. ★★★ **CW**

THE BIRDS (1963)

Starring: *Rod Taylor (Mitch Brenner), Tippi Hedren (Melanie Daniels), Jessica Tandy (Lydia Brenner), Suzanne Pleshette (Annie Hayworth), Veronica Cartwright (Cathy Brenner), Ethel Griffies (Mrs Bundy)*
Director: *Alfred Hitchcock*
Screenwriter: *Evan Hunter, based on the book by Daphne du Maurier*
15/115 mins./Horror/USA

Awards: *Golden Globes – Most Promising Newcomer (Tippi Hedren)*

The romantic dramas of Bodega Bay, where bored socialite Melanie is pursing lawyer Mitch, are interrupted when thousands of birds start attacking the area.

Three years after *Psycho*, Alfred Hitchcock was casting about for more suitably disturbing entertainment. He hit on a story by Daphne Du Maurier, then threw it away, essentially keeping only the title and the idea of birds attacking people. The picture is a slow, deliberate, technically ingenious exercise in blind fear, as mysterious massed bird attacks strike at a small community and a smug heroine. 'All you can say about *The Birds* is nature can be awful rough on you,' was Hitchcock's summation of his film's theme, but an inspiration, he revealed, came from his own memories of wartime bombings. 'The helplessness of the people [in *The Birds*] is no different than people in an air raid with nowhere to go ... You don't know where to go. Where can you go? You're caught. You're trapped.'

Typically, horror films in which critters attack, feature beasts that are dangerous to begin with (sharks, snakes, velociraptors), or that have become big and nasty because of radiation, pollution, genetic engineering, sorcery or mutation (giant mutant killer ants, giant mutant killer bunnies, giant mutant killer tomatoes etc). Pseudo-scientific rationales are usually *de rigueur*. The concept Hitchcock and screenwriter Evan Hunter arrived at was deliciously different: a 40s screwball comedy-romance superimposed over an inexplicable tale of terror.

Suave lawyer Mitch Brenner and spoiled little rich girl Melanie Daniels meet in a San Francisco pet shop – after Hitch's customary cameo, quickly exiting the shop with two dogs on leads – where Mitch wants a pair of love-birds for his kid sister's birthday. ('How did you know my name?' she chirps. 'A little birdy told me.') Impulsively Melanie follows him to his – weekend getaway, the family home up the coast in Bodega Bay, to pursue a mischievous flirtation. (Hitchcock's habitual delight in visual incongruity is in evidence as mink-clad Melanie climbs aboard a skiff with a birdcage.)

For nearly an hour the audience is strung along by Mitch and Melanie's light banter as she becomes embroiled in his decidedly strange situation which involves a much younger little sister (Veronica Cartwright, who 16 years later would face terror anew as Lambert, the crew member who sobs 'I say we abandon this ship' in *Alien*), a possessive mother (Tandy), and the village schoolteacher (Pleshette) who still has the hots for him. It is only because the film is called *The Birds* that we are alert to odd notes (like Lydia's lengthy telephone conversation about chicken feed), gradually increasing in severity, that occur before the first mass avian attack at young Cathy's birthday party.

The air of normality makes the horror to come all the more real and effective. Another ominous clue before Hitchcock lowers the boom is the complete absence of music. His favourite composer, Bernard Herrmann, served as sound consultant but the 'score' is an experimental electronic melange of peeps, caws and cries from ever-present, agitated birds. The most famous sequence endures as one of the creepiest ever concocted. Melanie sits smoking outside the school while the children inside sing a repetitive nursery rhyme. Behind her a crow alights on the jungle gym. She smokes, oblivious. Then there are four crows ... a fifth ... a sixth and seventh. She smokes a while, notices a bird overhead, turns her head ... and there are hundreds perched on the jungle gym, on rooftops, all around the playground. Waiting silently. Gulp. When Melanie and Annie hurry the children quietly away it is the waiting birds that we're compelled to watch. We hear what they hear, the sudden sound of the children's feet, running away. The birds take to the sky and the savage attack begins.

A highlight is the 13-minute scene at The Tides Restaurant, which functions like a one-act play, bringing together a group including an ornithologist, a Bible-quoting barfly, a fisherman and an anxious mother to air speculations and bear witness to the most spectacular set-piece, an attack in which a man is immolated, fiery panic ensues, seagulls bear down from far above the town (a ten-second shot on which matte artists spent three months painting in the birds), and Melanie is trapped – like a caged bird – in a phone booth.

Hedren, making her film debut as the last of Hitchcock's cool blondes, nearly lost an eye in another great sequence: the climactic attic siege during which birds were repeatedly flung at her for a montage attack, strikingly like Psycho's shower scene. But for an audience the most unnerving revelation is that they never regain emotional control after her ordeal. What occurs in *The Birds* is never explained or resolved. Theories, ornithological, biblical and psychological, are hinted at. But in the end we're left with the birds, watching as the people abandon the house to them. Dawn rises, and a final expectation is confounded: the words The End do not appear on the screen. ★★★★ **AE**

BIRTH (2004)

Starring: *Nicole Kidman (Anna), Cameron Bright (Young Sean), Danny Huston (Joseph), Lauren Bacall (Eleanor), Alison Elliott (Laura), Michael Desautels (Sean), Anne Heche (Clara), Peter Stormare (Clifford)*
Director: *Jonathan Glazer*
Screenwriters: *Milo Addica, Jean-Claude Carriere, Jonathan Glazer*
15/100 mins./Drama/Mystery/USA

Ten years after her husband's death, as she announces her impending second nuptials, wealthy New Yorker Anna is visited by a boy who claims to be her former spouse.

Squeezed somewhere into Nicole Kidman's impossibly busy schedule, this lofty meditation on grief, love, resurrection and the world's most famous actress taking a quick dunk with a small boy was never exactly going to flow in the mainstream. Stranger still, Jonathan Glazer's claustrophobically slow waltz through a shivering New York sees the director impressively shedding the sunny glaze and macho swagger of 2000's *Sexy Beast* for something more hypnotically morose, more European in flavour and Kubrickian in style.

It's simplest to read *Birth* as a ghost story, albeit one where the supernatural elements are brushed under the divan for a metaphysical romance where a woman, never fully recovered from losing her husband, may have conjured his spirit in boy's form. The suggestion is that this new 'husband' is more an embodiment of her passionate ideals than the real man who was hardly the prince that death has made him.

Meanwhile, her family and understandably narked fiancé Danny Huston (who cascades from bemused, to stunned, to a delightful outburst of indignant pique where he attempts to spank his love rival) look on in abject confusion. Thank heavens, then, that her mother is none other than Lauren Bacall, whose imperturbable features signal she's seen plenty weirder than a grown daughter hooking up with a wee scamp who, by rights, should be keener on Tekken 4.

It is she who reminds you that Glazer is treading a perilously thin line between good and bad taste, and you can't help but wonder whether *Birth* might have made a great little black comedy. Yet, as close as it comes to collapsing into its own absurdity, it clings on. In fact, this very high-wire act only adds to the discomfort; you're never quite sure where we'll end up.

Glazer's success is to lend such sombre, abstract material a granite conviction, similar in tone if not thrill to M. Night Shyamalan's work, ably assisted by Kidman's gift for icy fragility. Her eyes red-rimmed, her hair shorn to a tight, asexual crop, the entire film slips dreadfully toward the moment when she'll finally shatter. ★★★ **SC**

THE BIRTH OF A NATION (1915)

Starring: *Lillian Gish (Elsie Stoneman), Mae Marsh (Flora Camereon), Henry B. Walthall (Col. Ben Cameron), Miriam Cooper (Margaret Cameron), Mary Alden (Lydia Brown)*
Director: *D.W. Griffith*
Screenwriters: *D.W. Griffith, Frank E. Woods, Thomas F. Dixon Jr, based on the novel and play* The Clansman *by Dixon Jr and* The Leopard's Spots *by Dixon Jr*
15/192 mins./Drama/USA

Respectively hailing from the North and the Old South, the Stoneman and the Cameron families are torn apart by the American Civil War. However, they are reunited by romance and the Ku Klux Klan during the Reconstruction.

Erich von Stroheim claimed that D.W. Griffith put 'beauty and poetry into a cheap and tawdry sort of entertainment'. But Griffith was always a refiner and extender of existing techniques rather than an innovator and the conventions of Victorian art, literature and melodrama always counted for more than cinema in his storytelling style. Consequently, sentimentality, pretentiousness and political naivete permeate much of Griffith's work.

Yet few contemporaries could have attempted to produce a film of such scope and significance as *The Birth Of A Nation* and it remains among the most ambitious pictures ever produced. However, it exposed more of Griffith's weaknesses than his strengths and its intellectual poverty has continued to haunt it since its contentious release over 90 years ago.

Adapted from two Civil War novels by the negrophobic Thomas Dixon Jr *The Clansman* and *The Leopard's Spots*, the film was constructed from 1544 individual shots into a laudably coherent series of imposing tableaux. But while the authenticity of battle sequences inspired by Matthew Brady's celebrated photography prompted President Woodrow Wilson to opine that the action was tantamount to 'history written in lightening', the picture's racist rhetoric was condemned by many viewers (not least for the fact that its success helped rejuvenate the moribund Ku Klux Klan), who lamented the presentation of the 'good' blacks as Uncle Toms as much as they did the degenerate depiction of the villains.

Yet opponents proved to be very much in the minority, as this monumental epic earned greater profits in proportion to its cost ($100,000) than any film in history. By 1931, it had taken $18 million and by 1946 (the last date for which accurate records exist) it had been seen by over 200 million worldwide. It's not surprising, therefore, that some consider *The Birth Of A Nation* to be the source of the more pernicious myths that have since sustained America's self-image. ★★★ **DP**

BITTER MOON (1992)

Starring: *Hugh Grant (Nigel), Kristen Scott Thomas (Fiona), Emmanuelle Seigner (Mimi), Peter Coyote (Oscar), Victor Banjeree (Mr Singh)*
Director: *Roman Polanski*
Screenwriters: *Gerard Brach, John Brownjohn, Roman Polanski*
18/138 mins./Drama/France/UK

Onboard an ocean liner headed for Istanbul, British couple Nigel and Fiona meet a strange French woman called Mimi who is travelling with her crippled husband Oscar. Oscar proceeds to tell a story of how he met this girl in Paris, and how their obsessive affair led him to this place.

Very much indicative of Roman Polanski's skittish middle years, post *Chinatown* and before his return to glory with *The Pianist*, this sordid tale of sexual obsession, told with blithering complexity through a series of flashbacks, would be too terrible for words if you didn't notice the blackly comic edge. How else to swallow such preposterous caterwauling about love gone wrong, which reduces Polanski's poor actress wife, Emmanuelle Seigner, and aging American actor Peter Coyote, to acts of such depravity neither have recovered much of their poise since.

The set-up has us compare the prudish, and by association, sexless marriage of Hugh Grant and Kristen Scott Thomas (some 2 years before *Four Weddings*), with this severely het-up couple's episodic tapestry of kinky bed-hopping. Memoirs so laughably overwrought they make *Last Tango In Paris* seem the soul of credibility. There is crassness rather than danger in the G-strings and pig-mask role-playing that Polanski unveils as the ultimate debasement of romance. If low on urge, try whips, psychological torture and physical violence. Don't they believe in divorce in Paris?

In the director's head, this is some Grand Guignol parable on modern marriage, part film noir, part porn movie, but it creeps along painfully slowly barely mustering a turn of events let alone a solid twist. Mimi, of course, is the other player in the tryst, and Nigel (Grant doing what he does best – twittering) is drawn to her both in person and through the extremities of her story. Of course, without giving too much away, this nasty game is still ongoing, the entrapping of this priggish couple, the very next move. As it all ends with a preposterous last gambit, you really become convinced Polanski just wants to have a big old laugh. ★★ **IN**

THE BITTER TEA OF GENERAL YEN (1933)

Starring: *Barbara Stanwyck (Megan Davis), Nils Asther (Gen. Yen), Toshia Moria (Mah Li), Walter Connolly (Jones), Gavin Gordon (Dr Robert Strife)*
Director: *Frank Capra*
Screenwriter: *Edward E. Paramore Jr, based on the story by Grace Zaring Stone*
PG/88 mins./Drama/USA

Arriving in Shanghai to marry childhood sweetheart Robert Strike, missionary Megan Davis falls into the hands of Chinese warlord General Yen and remains loyal to him as his enemies close in.

Frank Capra helped make Barbara Stanwyck a star in *Ladies Of Leisure*, *The Miracle Woman* and *Forbidden*. Thus, having failed to win an Oscar for the calculatingly patriotic *American Madness*, he called upon her again for this adaptation of Grace Zaring Stone's bestselling novel.

Flying in the face of opposition from Columbia's notoriously difficult chief, Harry Cohn, Capra achieved a surprising opulence and stylisation in this Von Sternbergian drama that persuaded the mean-spirited mogul to afford him the creative independence that resulted in the string of Capracorn classics on which his reputation now largely rests.

Scripted by Edward Paramore, rather than Capra's usual collaborator Robert Riskin, the film is somewhat naive and patronising in its characterisation, as Stanwyck's New England prude is seduced by the sensuality of Nils

Asther's Oriental in much the same way that Lillian Gish had been by Richard Bathelmess in *Broken Blossoms* (1919) and Deborah Kerr would be by Yul Brynner in *The King And I* (1956). Yet, the action contains considerably more eroticism than either D.W. Griffith or Walter Lang's films, with the dream sequence in which Stanwyck imagines herself about to be ravished by Asther among the items that persuaded America's moral guardians that Hollywood could only proceed under the strictures of an inflexible Production Code.

However, it's fascinating to compare this feature's attitudes with those in *The Battle Of China* (1944), one of the seven documentaries that Capra produced for the World War II series, *Why We Fight*. Presenting China as an ancient civilisation heroically resisting the pitiless Japanese, this makes no mention of warlords whose rejection of Christianity and indifference to the plight of orphans renders them barbarians. Yet, both films shared Capra's emigrant conviction that America needed to be made more aware of the world away from its isolationist shores. ★★★ **DP**

◎ BLACK CAT, WHITE CAT (CRNA MACKA, BELI MACOR) (1998)

Starring: *Bajram Severdzan (Matko Destanov), Doctor Kolja (Matko Destanov), Florijan Ajdini (Zare Destanov), Jas'ar Destani (Grga Major), Adnan Bekir (Little Grga), Zabit Mehmedovski (Zarije Destinov), Sabri Sulejmani (Grga Pitic), Srdan Todorovic (Dadan), Salija Ibraimova (Afrodita), Stojan Sotirov (Bugarski Carinik)*
Director: *Emir Kusturica*
Screenwriters: *Gordan Mihic, Emir Kusturica*
15/129 mins./Comedy/France/Germany

Two ageing gypsy gangsters agree to arrange a marriage between their children. But their wilful offspring have other ideas.

Although it won Emir Kusturica his second Palme D'Or at Cannes, *Underground* caused such a furore in the former Yugoslavia that the Bosnian filmmaker announced his retirement. However, he was lured back behind the camera after his production staff came up with this riotous blend of crime, comedy and romance.

Grga is a gypsy godfather and rubbish dump tycoon. Also in his 80s, his best pal, Zarije owned a cement works until he sold it off to Dadan, a coke snorting mobster who has just tricked Zarije's doltish son, Matko, out of his petrol train heist. Unaware of the duplicity, Matko agrees to compensate him by marrying his son, Zare, to Dadan's diminutive sister, Afrodita, even though he's besotted with Ida, a waterfront waitress.

The web of relationships takes a while to weave. But once the characters are in the place for the wedding, the fun begins. Both octogenarians conk out and are kept on ice in the attic, Afrodita escapes and falls for Grga's towering grandson (while disguised as a tree stump) and Dadan gets his comeuppance in a chainsawed privy.

There is a political subtext if you look hard enough at the age gap angle. But Kusturica has determinedly set out to produce a joyous romp in the company of the people with whom he clearly has an affinity, the gypsies. With goats, geese and the eponymous felines rarely out of shot and played to the frantic strains of a gypsy band, the gleeful farce is a scattershot affair, with offbeat hilarity vying with clumsy slapstick. But there are lyrical moments too, most notably a seduction in the sunflowers. ★★★★ **DP**

◎ BLACK HAWK DOWN (2001)

Starring: *Josh Hartnett (Eversmann), Ewan McGregor (Grimes), Tom Sizemore (McKnight), Eric Bana (Hoot), William Fichtner (Sanderson), Ewen Bremner (Nelson), Sam Shepard (Garrison), Gabriel Casseus (Kurth), Kim Coates (Wex), Hugh Dancy (Schmid)*
Director: *Ridley Scott*
Screenwriter: *Ken Nolan, based on the book by Mark Bowden*
15/150 mins./War/USA
Awards: *Academy Awards – Best Sound, Best Editing*

Mogadishu, 1993. At war with a Somalian warlord, in the longest sustained ground battle since Vietnam, U.S. troops set out on a mission to capture his senior advisors. When two of their helicopters – the Black Hawks of the title – are shot down, the surviving troops are trapped in a terrifying firefight.

Would-be historians and contributors to the *Daily Mail* letters page, put your pens down now. Don't even think about it. Because for all its on-paper parallels – American troops in a real-life military conflict, Josh Hartnett looking a little forlorn – this is no *Pearl Harbor 2*. Better luck next time. Indeed, if it's gung-ho jingoism and overblown sentimentality you're after, you're pissing up entirely the wrong flagpole. On this evidence, at least, the dastardly Jerry Bruckheimer appears to have learnt his lesson.

That's not to say that he and Ridley Scott have scrimped any on the style – the spectacular helicopter footage, particularly the first seismic crash, almost lives up to *Harbor*'s 'bomb p.o.v.' money shot. It's more the case that style and substance are here given equal billing. Yes, the Somali enemy has one sequence of particularly brutal savagery. And yes, their Muslim faith is highlighted with a shot of the call to prayer, which could – and no doubt will – be cited as containing a not-so-subliminal, post-September 11 poignancy. But, by and large, Scott abandons a black and white stance for an exposé of the unilateral tragedy of war.

In doing so, he subjects his audience to a barrage of uneasily believable horrors, a relentless assault on the senses that continually drums home the chaotic intensity of conflict. If his initial pitch was, 'It's the opening 30 minutes of Saving Private Ryan – except for two hours,' he's comfortably fulfilled his brief. Naysayers will claim that the net result is one of confusion, and to an extent they have a point. Arguably throwing his implausibly good-looking ensemble (at times it's as if the kids from the Gap ads have taken up arms) into the fray too soon, Scott never gives the viewer time to bond with his heroes.

There's a vague sense of pre-recognition. Bloom is the naive new recruit. McGregor struggles with an unlikely accent as the reluctant desk clerk. Bana (fully justifying his casting as The Hulk with the only standout turn on display) is a maverick tough-nut. And a better-than-usual Hartnett plays the recently promoted sergeant leading his men out for the first time. But these are merely sketched characters. Do we care when one of them bites the bullet? Not really. Can we sometimes not even make out exactly what's going on? This is fair comment. But then, just maybe, that's the point. You can forget cartoon action sequences; this is as honest a depiction of the heat of battle as you're likely to find.

It's an admirable move, casting aside standard war movie clichés in favour of gritty realism. Structurally, though, there's seldom a sense of narrative coherence. Act One's 'men on a mission' segues into a claustrophobic, Zulu-esque Act Two, and then an, erm, claustrophobic, Zulu-esque Act Three. Fine, so real events may not have lent themselves to a traditional dramatic arc, but the lack of a discernible climax may leave some feeling shortchanged. ★★★ **MD**

◎ BLACK NARCISSUS (1946)

Starring: *Deborah Kerr (Sister Clodagh), Sabu (Dillip Raj), David Farrar (Mr. Dean), Flora Robson (Sister Phillipa), Jean Simmonds (Kanchi), Esmond Knight (Gen.Toda Raj), Kathleen Byron (Sister Ruth), Jenny Laird (Sister Honey), Judith Furse (Sister Briony), May Hallatt (Angu Ayah)*
Directors: *Michael Powell and Emeric Pressburger*
Screenwriters: *Michael Powell and Emeric Pressburger, based on the novel by Rumer Godden*
PG/100 mins./Drama/1946
Awards: *Academy Awards – Best Colour Cinematography, Best Art Direction-Set Decoration*

A group of nuns attempt to set up a convent high in the Himalayan mountains. But the enterprise is undone a growing sexual tension and madness within the increasingly fragmented sisterhood.

Fitting into a creative white hot streak between *A Matter Of Life And Death* and *The Red Shoes*, this Michael Powell and Emeric Pressburger masterpiece takes all the preconceptions you have about British cinema and blows them out of the water. About as far away from the talk-driven, stiff-upper-lipped dramas that held sway at the time, *Black Narcissus* is as bold and inventive a piece of moviemaking as you are ever likely to see.

If the high concept – English nuns go bonkers with sexual tension and jealousy setting up a mission in the Himalayas – isn't a strong enough reason to make *Black Narcissus* essential viewing, then its across-the-board performances and flights of cinematic daring take the film into the realm of unqualified masterpiece. Deborah Kerr excels as the young ambitious Sister who becomes bewitched by the climate, the natives and her powerful feelings for Government agent Mr. Dean (an equally excellent David Farrar). But the Nun Of The Match award goes to Kathleen Byron as the increasingly demented Sister Ruth – the moment when she appears in a vibrant crimson dress and shocking red lipstick is as startling as any in cinema

Mountains have been written about the film's technical virtuosity – Powell and art director Alfred Junge built the Himalays in the home counties and the effect is still jawdropping – and Jack Cardiff's use of colour in general and Technicolour in particular is an object exercise in how to use a camera to enhance subtext rather than merely record events. As such, it is easy to see why Powell has been such a big influence on filmmakers, in particular Martin Scorsese who in the likes of *Mean Streets*, *Taxi Driver* and *Cape Fear* borrows numerous riffs from the *Black Narcissus* playbook.

But perhaps it's best to ignore the film buffery and wallow in its heavy atmosphere and rawest of emotions. It is that genuine cinematic rarity – an erotic British film – and as such it should be at the top of any must-see list. ★★★★★ **IF**

BLACK RAIN (1989)

Starring: *Michael Douglas (Detective Sergeant Nick Conklin), Andy Garcia (Detective Charlie Vincent), Ken Takakura (Assistant Inspector Masahiro Mastsumoto), Kate Capshaw (Joyce)*
Director: *Ridley Scott*
Screenwriters: *Craig Bolotin, Warren Lewis*
18/125 mins./Crime/Drama/USA

Having captured a scowling emissary from the Japanese Yakuza, New York detectives Nick Conklin and Charlie Vincent escort the villain back to Osaka. There they manage to lose their captive, and must descend into an alien underworld embroiled in a savage war between rival gangs, to retrieve him.

This is the film, above all the various throws of his aesthetic genius, that best embodies the tricky cult of Ridley Scott. It is a standard issue fish-outta-water cop thriller, but transposed to Osaka's glistening towers, and possesses everything that intoxicates and infuriates about the director's predilections. Of course, it looks fabulous, fixing the neon-noir deco dreadscape of his masterpiece *Blade Runner*, into a real context – Japan's sprawling urban civility – that feels, if anything, more exotic still. It also centres on a typically gutsy Michael Douglas performance; he was at the height of his fame, post *Wall Street*, an American hero with rough edges and big hair. Yet, no matter how well dressed, the movie can't escape the gravitational pull of formula. Douglas is the maverick kind, street-smart, out for revenge on the enemy's turf, and lumbered with stiff-necked Ken Takakura, a buddy-up that melts from friction to mutual respect. It's *Beverly Hills Cop* without the jabber, but plenty of Sushi.

Away from the exuberances of its bloody violence – if the American policier makes its points with bullets, the Japanese variety is all knife edges – Scott is aiming to comment on postwar cross-cultural lack-of-relations. Casual resentments that hover teasingly over racism pepper the film, supposedly fed by the brutish attitudes of character (Douglas' Conklin is no saint – Internal Affairs are about to cook his ass back in the Apple). Americans are defined as individuals bucking the system, their Japanese equivalent systemised drones confined by tradition.

It's a problematic gesture, as it becomes increasingly indistinct whether the film is commenting on or just joining in such prejudice – there is a daft preponderance of inscrutable Eastern glances. Thankfully, and vitally, Takakura gives a terrific turn as the deskbound detective babysitting these livewire New Yorkers. His becalmed Samurai leanings have a genuine effect on Conklin, enough to pause his brute punch-'em-and-they'll-tell-you approach to detection and grasp something of this poised foreign culture. They make a good duo, once Andy Garcia is helpfully removed from proceedings.

In shorthand – it's fittingly involving, if overcooked, pulp given the uber-sheen by Scott's multi-layered palette (you know: smoke stacks, neon blurs, all blacks, purples and smudged greys) as shot by soon-to-be-promoted Jan De Bont the soon-to-be director of *Speed*. ★★★ **IN**

THE BLACKBOARD JUNGLE (1955)

Starring: *Glenn Ford (Richard Dadier), Anne Francis (Anne Dadier), Louis Calhern (Jim Murdock), Margaret Hayes (Lois Judby Hammond), John Hoyt (Mr Warneke), Sidney Poitier (Gregory W. Miller)*
Director: *Richard Brooks*
Screenwriter: *Richard Brooks, based on the novel by Evan Hunter*
12/100 mins./Drama/USA

Idealist teacher Richard Dadier gets a job in an inner city school. Among the junior hoodlums in his class are a knife-wielding gang leader and an alienated but redeemable smart black kid.

Based on a novel by Evan Hunter, this is a broad-strokes torn-from-the-headlines 'social problem' picture. The story of the tough, sensitive teacher in a school without hope who reaches out to a class of troublemakers and wins them over has become a Hollywood staple (*Class of 1984*, *Dangerous Minds*, *Dead Poets Society*) but this original version still packs a punch. Ironically, it was a hit in 1955 at least partially because it was the first mainstream film to tap into rebel youth attitudes condemned in the story, using Bill Haley's 'Rock Around the Clock' as a theme tune and littering the dialogue with hipster speak (bad boy Morrow is 'hopped up on sneaky pete').

Director Richard Brooks stages effective scenes of kids running wild: an attempted rape in the school library, a well-organised gang attack in an alley, a moment of anarchy as thugs smash a music-loving teacher's irreplacable collection of jazz 78s and the final face-off in the classroom between switchblade-waving Morrow and English teacher Ford. It isn't afraid to go all-out for big emotions, contrasting Haley's rocking with Poitier's choir doing 'Go Down Moses', reaching for the American flag in the corner of a classroom to clobber a snivelling delinquent. Anne Francis is stuck with the stiff role of Ford's wavering wife, but the leads are great (insolent maniac Morrow is the anti-James Dean and Poitier smoulders with charisma) there's good work from character actors Louis Calhern, Emile Meyer and John Hoyt, plus snarling in class from future director Paul Mazursky and future M*A*S*H regular Jamie Farr (billed as Jameel Farah). ★★★ **KN**

BLACKMAIL (1929)

Starring: *Amy Ondra (Alice White), John Longden (Frank Webber), Donald Calthrop (Tracy), Cyril Ritchard (The Artist), Sara Allgood (Mrs White), Charles Paton (Mr White)*
Director: *Alfred Hitchcock*
Screenwriters: *Alfred Hitchcock, Benn W. Levy, Charles Bennett, based on the play by Bennett*
PG/75 mins./Crime/UK

Despite being jilted, Scotland Yard detective Frank Webber helps ex-girlfriend Alice White pin the blame for the murder of her artist admirer on a blackmailing stranger named Tracy.

Despite the oft-repeated assertion, this was not Britain's first Talkie. That honour goes to the Edgar Wallace adaptation, *The Clue Of The New Pin*, although it's obvious from the longevity of Alfred Hitchcock's picture which was the superior. Adapted from a play by Charles Bennett, *Blackmail* was originally filmed as a silent and then wholly reshot with sound when recording technology became available. Both the mute and the talking versions were released, as few British cinemas had been wired for sound, and there are visual differences between the two. However, it was the spectacle of the cast speaking that drew the curious and gave Hitch his biggest box-office hit to date.

Dispensing with the services of Eliot Stannard, who had scripted eight of his nine previous features, Hitchcock co-opted Benn Levy to sharpen the dialogue. However, the idea for the British Museum finale – which established the Hitchcock tradition of staging set-pieces on famous landmarks – came from Michael Powell (although John Longden had recently starred in Maurice Elvey's 1928 drama, *Palais De Danse*, which had included a building with a glass dome). The sequence was achieved using the Schüfftan Process – which Hitchcock had probably first seen on his sojourn in Germany and which allowed live action to be combined with paintings and/or models via a mirror placed at 45° to the lens – and it instigated a fascination with technology that would enable the Master of Suspense to keep conducting visual experiments to the end of his career.

Over 75 years on, *Blackmail* now feels a little creaky. But Hitchcock's intuitive use of sound remains remarkable. Music is employed as source rather than as a novelty and the sequence in which Alice is lacerated by the repeated use of the word 'knife' by her gossiping neighbours on the morning after the murder has lost none of its devastating psychological power. **★★★★ DP**

BLACULA (1972)

Starring: *William Marshalll (Prince Mamuwalde/Blacula), Vonetta McGee (Tina), Denise Nicholas (Michelle) Thalmus Rasulala (Gordon Thomas), Gordon Pinsent (Lt Peters)*
Director: *William Crain*
Screenwriters: *Joan Torres, Raymond Koening*
18/92 mins./Horror/USA

In the 18th Century, Prince Mamuwalde visits Castle Dracula to ask the Count to sign a petition against the slave trade. Dracula turns Mamuwalde into a vampire and chains him into a coffin. In 1972, gay antique dealers bring the coffin to Los Angeles and Mamuwalde pursues the reincarnation of his lost love while spreading vampirism through the city.

One of the great gimmick crossovers, this blends the then-popular blaxploitation movie with the classical vampire film.

William Marshall, after a career playing African leaders on spy or jungle shows brings his rich voice and Shakespearean dignity to the role of the vampire prince, swanning through contemporary Los Angeles in a cloak lined with white silk. It suffers from reusing that tiresome mummy plot in which the monster bothers the reincarnation of his old girlfriend, but it has some of the excitement of the wave of vampire movies with modern settings – *Dracula AD 1972, Count Yorga – Vampire, The Night Stalker* – common in the early 1970s.

Perennial loser Elisha Cook Jr gets an especially memorable death ('lifted' by Stephen King in *Salem's Lot*) as a morgue attendant who gets a nasty shock when a murdered lady cab driver rises from the slab to attack. It struggles to include the mandatory blaxploitation digs at 'the Man', as the black Van Helsing type (Rasulala) complains to the white cop on the case 'it's amazing how much sloppy police work involves black victims' but there's a certain aptness in the depiction of Count Dracula (a very hammy Macaulay) as an arrogant racist swine.

It was followed by a run of similar black horror pictures, including the inevitable *Blackenstein*, the more imaginative *Dr Black And Mr Hyde* and a superior sequel (with Pam Grier as a voodoo priestess) *Scream, Blacula, Scream!* **★★ KN**

BLADE (1998)

Starring: *Wesley Snipes (Blade/Eric Brooks/'The Daywalker'), Stephen Dorff (Deacon Frost), Kris Kristofferson (Abraham Whistler), N'Bushe Wright (Dr Karen Jenson), Traci Lords (Racquel)*
Director: *Stephen Norrington*
Screenwriter: *David S. Goyer*
18/120 mins./Horror/Action/USA

Blade is half man half vampire, and is on a mission to rid the world of his fang-bearing brethren.

However traditional Van Helsing's crucifix-waving, mythology-spouting vampire-hunting histrionics may be, there's something altogether more reassuring about a pumped-up Wesley Snipes kicking six kinds of undead crap out of the undead bloodsuckers.

Meet Blade. From the outset it's clear this is a troubled hero – a precredit sequence has him enter the world shortly after his mother's fatal encounter with a pointy-toothed demon of the night. Hardly your model birth. But every superhero has their dark side to wrestle with and being half vampire just leaves you with an aggravating desire for meat cooked very, very rare. With a nifty serum suppressing such cravings and equipped with weaponry by grizzled armourer Abraham Whistler, Blade launches a one-man crusade to rid the world of vampires, forsaking the classic cross and holy water combo for a more forthright reliance on weighty darts, bullets capped with garlic essence and a sword edged in silver.

As ever in comic book translations, the film is tasked with carrying the conviction of big screen entertainment, while remaining true to its escapist fantasy origins. But although *Blade* is occasionally uneven, it treads the line rather more successfully than most by halting its tongue halfway into the cheek, and ladling a swathe of sicko shocks and enough whirling combat to keep serious horror and action fans satisfied. Snipes' formidable presence is crucial to selling this, his strength as an actor just about excusing some ludicrous lines; his martial arts expertise allowing close-up coverage of the flashy choreography. And wisely trading on charisma and implied menace in the face of his adversary's physical might, Dorff is a worthy nemesis as the seductive Deacon Frost, cooking up a suitably megalomaniac and blood-soaked plot involving ancient vampire lore and the subjugation of the human race.

Director Norrington's music video background is evident but turns out to be highly effective in energising the concept – his stall is set out in a thrilling opener in which pounding techno fills an abattoir night club and assembled corpuscle-quaffers are driven into further frenzy by blood piped through the sprinkler system. The party comes to a premature end when Blade gatecrashes in rather spectacular fashion. Norrington's ability with stuntwork, fight sequences and positing CGI are unquestionable.

Movie Trivia: Blade

Director Stephen Norrington has a cameo as a vampire feasting on a girl during the chase with officer Krieger. LL Cool J was the first choice to play Blade. When Blade is chased to the subway and the train is passing by, all the passengers are cardboard cutouts.

In film terms, the superhero genre is only ever entered into if a franchise is in the offing and even before a postscript that couldn't have heralded a sequel more blatantly if 'Blade will return ...' ran as a subtitle, it's clear that this is planned merely as an opening act. Given the participation of his production company, Amen Ra Films, Snipes has made a knowing investment. ★★★ **DB**

BLADE II (2002)

Starring: *Wesley Snipes (Blade/Eric Brooks/'The Daywalker'), Kris Kristofferson (Abraham Whistler), Ron Perlman (Reinhardt), Leonor Varela (Nyssa), Luke Goss (Nomak), Matt Schulze (Chupa), Danny John Jules (Asad)*
Director: *Guillermo del Toro*
Screenwriter: *David S. Goyer, characters created by Marv Wolfman, Gene Colan*
18/117 mins./Action/Thriller/Horror/USA

The underground vampire community, and the world at large, are threatened by a mutated, deadly new strain of badass bloodsuckers – the Reapers. And so Blade must reluctantly team up with The Bloodpack – a team of assassins originally trained to kill him.

Pow! There goes another limb. Oof! And a head. Aaargh! Is that a pancreas? Squelch! Nope, think it's a kidney. Welcome, boys and girls, to the cartoon carnage of *Blade II*. Thought the first one was violent? Trust us, you ain't seen nothin' yet. And, frankly, hallelujah for that because, as horror sequels go, Guillermo Del Toro's gore-drenched follow-up to Stephen Norrington's vastly underrated 1999 cult hit is up there with the best of them.

Infused with a frenetic, manga-esque tempo that actually outdoes its predecessor for pace (you won't draw breath for the first 30 minutes, guaranteed), a balls-to-the-wall gallows humour, and some of the most inventive effects choreography this side of, erm, *Blade*, fans of stylised comic book mayhem need look no further.

Picking up the action (quite literally) immediately after the events of part one, Snipes' eponymous anti-hero finds himself in Prague, persevering on his quest to eradicate the world of those 'blood-guzzling motherfuckers'. He's also keen to track down old buddy/father figure Whistler, a man whom everyone – not least Kristofferson, who spends much of the two hours looking rather bewildered – thought had bitten the bullet last time around. (This is a movie about resurrecting the dead, after all.) Here, though, Blade has very much accepted his lot as the baddest ass on the block. Gone are his philosophical musings and pensive stares, replaced by an insatiable bloodlust. Look out, vampire bad guys, he's really starting to enjoy this now.

Goss as Nomak, meanwhile, is a joy. No, seriously. Continuing the Stephen Dorff, pretty-boy-turned-nasty trend of the original, his turn as Blade's newfangled nemesis is by turns terrifying and intentionally camp. As the leader of vicious new strain, The Reapers, he does of course have some truly exceptional special effects to fall back on in the rare moments when shades of *Drop The Boy* briefly shine through. And oh, those Reaper effects. An ingenious blend of *Predator* (their jaws opening out into gaping voids), *Salem's Lot* (think the teeth) and *Alien* (as if all that weren't enough, they're equipped with a mouth within a mouth), this new breed is a consistent technological marvel.

Minor downsides are, arguably, The Bloodpack's underwritten individual characterisations (surely an issue of time constraints) and a bizarre credit sequence monologue, which sets the scene with much the same crassness as *Knight Rider*'s 'lone crusader' opening salvo. But ultimately, Del Toro marks his return to the big budget arena he has avoided since *Mimic* with aplomb. Think what James Cameron did with *Aliens*, and you're about there. ★★★★ **MD**

BLADE RUNNER (1982)

Starring: *Harrison Ford (Rick Deckard), Rutger Hauer (Roy Batty), Sean Young (Rachael), Daryl Hannah (Pris), M. Emmet Walsh (Bryant)*
Director: *Ridley Scott*
Screenwriters: *Philip K Dick, Hampton Fancher, David Webb Peoples, Roland Kibbee*
15/114mins./Sci-fi/Thriller/USA
Awards: *BAFTA – Best Cinematography, Best Costume, Best Production Design/Art Direction*

Blade runner, Deckard, is tasked with hunting down four replicants. But his attraction to one of them begins to cloud his judgement.

'I think some – a lot – of people enjoy it, and that's their prerogative,' said a grumpy Harrison Ford of *Blade Runner* in the *Boston Globe*, 1991. 'I played a detective who did no detecting. There was nothing for me to do but stand around and give some focus to Ridley's sets.' Ah well, he didn't much enjoy being in Star Wars either, and some – a lot – of people enjoyed that, too. The truth is, few actors come off well in sci-fi movies if they feel that it's them versus the sets or them versus the director's imagination. As it is, Harrison Ford's apparent bemusement works perfectly within Ridley Scott's framework; his former blade runner Rick Deckard, though expert at 'retiring' the almost-human androids known as replicants, spends most of the film bemused. As he tracks down four escaped replicants (a detective doing 'no detecting'?) in a darkly malevolent, incongrously rainy 2019 Los Angeles, he falls in love with *femme fatale* Rachel (Young), who is a replicant. And it's this tentative, enigmatic relationship that drives the film.

Blade Runner is possibly the most talked-about sci-fi movie ever made. It achieved this honour by being a failure on its original release, thus attaining the valuable sheen of a true cult (something that could never be said about *Star Wars*, despite the rapacity of its followers). When re-released theatrically in the form of a Director's Cut in 1992, it was reappraised by formerly sniffy critics, and more people paid to see it. The irony of this belated legitimisation is that the Director's Cut is more cryptic and ambiguous than the original, and – crucially to the sort of fan who roams the Internet – supported the popular theory that Deckard himself is a replicant.

There are actually only minor differences between the original and the Director's Cut (indeed, the tag is misleading, as it's actually a compromise between director and studio). Scott removed the explanatory voice-over and happy ending, both of which had been added after disastrous sneak previews. He also introduced a 12-second dream sequence involving a unicorn, which helps explain the significance of an origami unicorn that appears in the final sequence. Oddly, some of the extra frames of violence in the video version are now excised. While obsessive aficionados hotly debate the merits of each version (and whether Deckard is a replicant or not), the casual fan will glean enough pleasure just watching the film – any bloody version – and admiring its astonishing production values.

In a poll of the members of the 1992 World Science Fiction Convention, *Blade Runner* was voted the third best sci-fi film of all time behind *Star Wars* and *2001: A Space Odyssey*. What it shares with those films – and it's sexier than the former, and deeper than the latter – is influence. *Blade Runner* rewrote the rulebook, and altered the way sci-fi movies looked forever.

Scott's advertising background has given him a unique sixth sense for overdoing it, hence the dusty light shafting through Venetian blinds; the pounding, backlit rain; and the kaleidoscopic colours, now the basic grammar of any filmmaker. The look of *Blade Runner* can be credited to production designer Lawrence G. Paull, 'visual futurist' Syd Mead, art director David L. Snyder, cinematographer Jordan Cronenweth and ubiquitous FX man Douglas Trumbull. But the overall vision was Scott's: 'a film set 40 years hence, made in the style of 40 years ago.' (Note, by the way, how much warmer its pre-CGI effects are than those which dominate today.)

In H.G. Wells' *The Time Machine*, Earth was divided into a clean, Aryan paradise above ground and a hellish, primitive netherworld beneath, a division that recurs constantly in movie sci-fi. In *Blade Runner*, the sleek and the ugly, the ancient and the modern, co-exist, just as they do in any big city today (the Ancient Egyptian grandeur of the Tyrell Corporation versus the dilapidated, leaky hulk of J.E Sebastian's building). Perhaps this is why *Blade Runner*'s future is so compelling, and why it's still duplicated ad nauseum in rock videos and bank adverts.

But *Blade Runner* is more than a collection of stunning pictures. It oozes the type of allegory that will keep stoners up all night for years to come. Try this one for size: Batty (Hauer) is Jesus – after all, he sticks a nail through his hand and dies, releasing a dove as he does so – and Tyrell (Joe Turkel), referred to by Batty as his 'maker', is God. This theory makes the replicants us. Well, humans are programmed, like replicants, to die from birth, a paradox encapsulated in the last line of the film: 'It's too bad she won't live! But then again, who does?' ★★★★★ **AC**

BLADE TRINITY (2004)

Starring: *Wesley Snipes (Blade), Kris Kristofferson (Abraham Whistler), Dominic Purcell (Drake), Jessica Biel (Abigail Whistler), Ryan Reynolds (Hannibal King), Paker Posey (Danica Talos)*
Director: *David S. Goyer*
Screenwriters: *David S. Goyer, based on characters created by Marv Wolfman, Gene Colan*
15/113 mins./Horror/Action/USA

Tired of their war against the half-human, half-vampire Blade, vampire leaders devise a final solution: resurrect Dracula, while simultaneously framing Blade for a human massacre.

As the character that arguably revamped the comic book movie genre, Wesley Snipes' Daywalker deserved a good send-off with this, the third and final *Blade* movie. Unfortunately, as with the last trilogy to invoke 'Trinity', it's a crushing disappointment.

Sadly, the blame can be laid squarely at the feet of David Goyer who, after writing the first two instalments, pulls double duty here, and makes a right old balls of it, lacking the directorial skills to redeem his surprisingly shoddy script, instead overloading the action sequences with MTV editing, while hanging his actors out to dry. What with Blade hanging up his sword, *Blade Trinity* was meant to serve as a franchise-continuing introduction to the Nightstalkers. However, Biel has precious little to do, while Reynolds' usual razor-sharp comic instincts are buried beneath a barrage of one-liners so bad they come complete with tumbleweed.

So if the Nightstalkers aren't worthy, then it's up to Blade himself to redeem matters. However, try as he might, the always-slick Snipes is allowed no room to shine, and ultimately – notably in his face-offs with Dominic Purcell's appallingly anaemic Dracula – ends up simply retreading past triumphs.

The *Blade* films, previously, have been extraordinarily divisive – fans tend to either like the first *Blade* and hate Part II, or vice versa. At least with *Blade Trinity*, Goyer has made a movie that everyone will agree sucks. ★ **JD**

THE BLAIR WITCH PROJECT (1999)

Starring: *as themselves: Heather Donahue, Michael Williams, Joshua Leonard, Bob Griffin, Jim King, Sandra Sanchez, Ed Swanson, Patricia Decou*
Director: *Eduardo Sanchez*
Screenwriter: *Eduardo Sanchez*
15/87 mins./Horror/USA

Three film students travel to Maryland to make a student film about a local urban legend – The Blair Witch – but they never return. One year later, the students camcorder was found in the woods. This film is the footage that was in the camera.

By the time *The Blair Witch Project* opened in Britain on October 22, 1999 there can hardly have been a film fan who was unaware of the extremely strange story behind its making.

Few are those who hadn't heard about the pair of Florida film school graduates who had persuaded three twentysomething actors to spend a week videoing themselves in the Maryland woods. Of how the two directors had repeatedly terrified the beleaguered trio in a successful attempt to capture real fear on their faces. And of how they expertly manipulated the internet to make the result one of the most successful horror flicks of all time. Indeed, when the film finally hit British screens several months after its American opening it could be argued that audiences here knew far more about the film than was good for them, and certainly anyone who hasn't seen it already would be better off rectifying that egregious situation before reading any further.

For *The Blair Witch Project* is one of those movies where ignorance is bliss – or, to be more accurate, terror. Ostensibly the last testament of a film crew who, as the opening credits inform us, disappeared off the face of the planet, the movie resembles a genuine documentary so closely it makes the likes of *This Is Spinal Tap* and *Drop Dead Gorgeous* look like David Lean epics. Certainly it fooled many of those American college students who were shown the film prior to its release – the ruse in this case was aided by a profusion of apparently genuine 'Missing' posters which sought information relating to the whereabouts of the supposedly long-lost youngsters.

Such screenings would help generate the positive word-of-mouth that real-life directors Daniel Myrick and Eduardo Sanchez knew was absolutely essential if their film was going to be a success. Certainly, its air of mystery was by far the film's strongest selling point – featuring, as it did, little in the way of stars, special effects or even competent camera work. Nor could the directors claim much of a cinematic track record. Indeed, their most high profile previous experience had been making videos to be shown inside Planet Hollywood restaurants. But the pair shared a love of 70s horror flicks and decided to pool their meagre resources for a film that would attempt to recapture the visceral terror that they felt on first viewing William Friedkin's *The Exorcist* or Larry Cohen's *It's Alive*.

'We were after complete realism,' recalls co-director Sanchez. 'We knew that if we did it with a crew it wouldn't work. From the beginning we wanted to do *Blair Witch* as an improvised film. We were basically going to leave the actors for certain amounts of time on their own, tell them what was happening and let them shoot it for a couple of hours at a time. Then we'd come back, review the footage and go on to the next scene.'

What really put the project on a one-way track to Horrorsville, however, was the input of Gregg Hale – a onetime Special Forces sergeant who had previously worked with the duo on a portmanteau horror film called *Black Chapters*. 'Gregg said, "When I was in Special Forces training they put us through this POW camp scenario,"' explains Sanchez. '"And after about two or three days of being in that camp surrounded by these guys hitting you, and yelling at you in Russian, and not letting you sleep, and hosing you down with water, you start to believe that it's really happening." He said, "You know, we could do this to the actors." Dan and I were like, Yeah!'

So it was that a group of unsuspecting, unknown actors Heather Donahue, Michael C. Williams and Joshua Leonard found themselves pretending to make a film about an ancient woods-dwelling witch while being genuinely terrified as the film crew deposited ominous-looking stick men in their path or played them tapes of children crying in the middle of the night. 'We were the Blair Witch,' says Myrick. 'We had to get up at three in the morning and run around their tent. We had to hike through the woods to drop off directing notes. Then we'd review Heather's video tapes at the end of the day to see how it was reading on camera.'

The end product, which was painstakingly hyped by both the distributors Artisan and the filmmakers' own website, would prove to be a genuinely unnerving cinematic experience. The film also produced 1999's most enduring image – the close-up of a wigged-out Donahue talking to her own camera as (and there's really no point in beating around the bush here) liquid snot poured out of her nose. 'That was my own snot,' laughs Donahue. 'I've never done stunt snot in my life. I'm anti-glycerin.' ★★★★ **CC**

BLAST FROM THE PAST (1999)

Starring: *Brendan Fraser (Adam Webber), Alicia Silverstone (Eve Rustikoff), Christopher Walken (Calvin Webber), Sissy Spacek (Helen Thomas Webber), Dave Foley (Troy)*
Director: *Hugh Wilson*
Screenwriters: *Bill Kelly, Hugh Wilson, from a story by Bill Kelly*
12/112 mins./Comedy/Drama/Romance/USA

A thirtysomething innocent emerges from a nuclear bomb shelter to take on life in the hostile 90s.

Since her breakthrough in 1995 with *Clueless*, Alicia Silverstone has struggled to find a suitable vehicle for her undoubted charms. *Blast From The Past*, a good-natured romantic comedy that teams her with Brendan Fraser, wasn't the answer even if it is a significant step up from 1997's *Excess Baggage*. More than anything, though, it's further proof that while young actors may rule Hollywood at the moment, they're still only as good as the scripts they get. Not that the film is unfunny, it's just that there aren't enough jokes to disguise the improbable set-up.

Silverstone plays Eve, a cynical LA girl tired of 90s men and their inconsiderate, selfish ways. Fraser is Adam, a 35-year-old who's spent his entire life living in a nuclear bomb shelter after his paranoid parents (played by Walken and Spacek) mistook a 1962 plane crash for the start of World War III. Cocooned in a cosy world of cheesy 50s sitcoms and endless Perry Como, Adam is understandably frustrated and so jumps at the chance to get out and re-supply the shelter.

Almost immediately he meets Eve, and from then on the comedy is meant to flow from the clash between her street-smart twentysomething and Adam's impeccably-mannered, old-school gent. The problem is that just isn't enough and despite appealing performances from both the leads, it's left to Walken and Spacek (virtually unrecognisable from her 70s classics *Badlands* and *Carrie*) to inject a much-needed dose of real humour into the goings-on. It was inspired casting on the part of director Hugh Wilson to enlist them to play Adam's apple-pie parents and as Walken potters around the shelter with a mad glint in his eye and Spacek's quietly hysterical housewife hits the cooking sherry, you get the feeling that the movie might have been better if everyone had stayed underground. ★★★ **DE**

BLAZING SADDLES (1974)

Starring: *Cleavon Little (Bart), Gene Wilder (Jim), Slim Pickens (Taggart), David Huddleston (Olson Johnson), Liam Dunn (Reverend Johnson), Alex Karras (Mongo), Mel Brooks (Governor Lepetomane/Indian Chief)*
Director: *Mel Brooks*
Screenwriters: *Mel Brooks, Norman Steinberg, Andrew Bergman, Richard Pryor, Alan Uger, based on a story by Andrew Bergman*
15/93 mins./Comedy/Western/USA

A black sheriff is hired to drive people away from a town so speculators can build a railroad through without paying too much for the land.

In July of 1974, Mel Brooks sat in the screening room at Warner Bros anxiously watching the assembled executives who were about to view his recently completed Western spoof, *Blazing Saddles*. He was desperately in need of a hit. His debut movie, *The Producers*, had been a minor success despite being decried by some critics as 'too Jewish' and 'over manic', but his follow-up, *The Twelve Chairs*, had been an unmitigated flop. The film suffered as Mel held his wildly inventive humour in check and audiences had rejected it. Brooks wasn't about to make the same mistake twice; *Blazing Saddles* was nothing if not zany and totally out of control. Together with screenwriters Norman Steinberg and Alan Uger, with input from Richard Pryor, Brooks transformed the material into a gag-saturated spoof. Between them, the writers generated enough material for an eight-hour movie which, like a fine comic consommé, they reduced down to about an hour-and-a-half. Brooks might have expected disapproval for the lewdness of some of his jokes, but not finding something to laugh at was surely not an option.

Ninety or so minutes of glacial silence later, after the blank-faced big wigs had exited the screening room, Brooks reasoned that he was in big trouble. The critical response on the film's release was hardly more encouraging. 'To sit frozen-faced among the press show audience, which was convulsed with laughter, was a disconcerting experience,' wrote a baffled Dilys Powell. 'What I found amazing was that, in one of our better theatres, a civilised-looking audience laughed loudest and longest at a scene in which a bunch of cowboys sit around a campfire eating beans,' declared a horrified John Simon. 'One after another, they raise their backsides a bit and break wind, each a bit louder than his predecessor. If this is what makes audiences happiest, all future for the cinema is gone with the wind.' (All fart gags in Simon's view being equal, but some apparently more equal than others).

Of course, it was exactly what delighted audiences. Brooks' wholehearted embracing of rank vulgarity, together with his innovative quickfire sketch structure, titillated crowds more used to sophisticated Hollywood humour and, with its sheer quantity of gags, left them breathless; if one zinger misfired, there was sure to be another mere seconds away. It was a style that not only established the modern spoof (*Airplane* or *Naked Gun* are unthinkable without *Blazing Saddles*, as is *National Lampoon*), but which continues to reverberate through the new generation of low comedies.

But there's more to *Saddles* than an object lesson in the comedic possibilities of intestinal gas. As the more perceptive critic Kenneth Tynan, himself no stranger to the expert employment of vulgarity, remarked, *Blazing Saddles* is 'low comedy in which the custard pies are disguised hand-grenades'. Uniquely for a spoof, and certainly unique in Mel Brook's oeuvre, it has a darkly angry heart. It is a film about real bigotry, a phoney West and the unreliability of movies as repositories for a shared history.

'It was time to take two eyes, the way Picasso had done it, and put them on one side of the nose,' he explained to one journalist on being asked what his intentions were. 'The official movie portrait of the West is simply a lie. I figured my career was finished anyway, so I wrote berserk, heartfelt stuff about white corruption and racism and Bible-thumping bigotry.' It's hardly surprising that, as a Jew, Brooks felt the Western to be an alienating genre. In an industry with a high percentage of Jewish people, from screenwriters to execs to studio owners, the Western was unique in allowing no place for the wit or sensibility that had helped define the industry, let alone for Jewish characters. Equally it grievously misrepresented the role of black people in the culture of the Old West, with the 9,000 black ranchworkers, cattle-hands and cowboys thoroughly invisible in the classics of the genre. It was hardly surprising, then, that, from the film's very first joke, Brooks lays his cards on the table. A bunch of redneck qangmasters demand that the black workers engage in 'a good old nigger worksong'; the assembled grafters respond with an incongruously sophisticated rendition of Cole Porter's classic, 'I Get No Kick From Champagne', while the potato heads wind up singing 'Camptown Races'. It's a nifty and very funny reversal, but Brooks can't help following it up with a gag in which our black hero winds up neck-deep in sinking sand. It's this scattershot juxtaposition of heartfelt, angry satire with dumbass slapstick, all seasoned with a fair measure of vulgarity, that gives *Blazing Saddles* a tone unique to film – a tone shared by the most successful comedy magazine of the times. It is, quite literally, political correctness gone *Mad*.

This juxtaposition of the intelligent and sophisticated with the crass is one of Brooks' main weapons throughout the movie. Take the schoolmistress' letter of complaint to the Governor, which concludes, 'The fact that you have sent this sheriff here just goes to show that you are the leading asshole in the state.' In Mel's world, respectable figures of authority have to have their pompousness revealed as fake; they have to be brought down to our level.

But if the bulk of the characters are bigoted or dumb or both, the movie is given its much-needed humanity by Gene Wilder and Cleavon Little as The Waco Kid and Sheriff Bart respectively. Wilder's career never flourished aqain as it did under Brooks' direction, and Little delivers an irresistible laid-back charm as a man who has to cope with little old ladies shouting, 'Up yours, nigger!' at him.

Towards the end of the movie, Brooks' disciplined indiscipline runs out of control. The chase through various movie sets, as the plot of *Blazing Saddles* erupts into the 'real' world, is an audacious idea that doesn't guite come off (though it is fun to see Harvey Korman buying his Raisinettes and rushing into Grauman's Chinese to see what happens to him). But he manages to pull it back together and flick a final defiant V at the phoniness of the Western genre when, in the final shot of our heroes riding into the sunset, they suddenly dismount and climb into a limousine. Everything about the romantic Western is a lie it seems, including the happy ending. As Brooks said, he just wanted to 'use every Western cliche in the book and perhaps, if we were lucky, kill some of them in the process'. For him, it seemed to be personal, and perhaps it's for that reason he would never make anything as funny again. ★★★★★ **AS**

BLEAK MOMENTS (1971)

Starring: *Anne Raitt (Sylvia), Sarah Stephenson (Hilda), Eric Allan (Peter), Joolia Cappleman (Pat), Mike Bradwell (Norman), Liz Smith (Pat's Mother), Malcolm Smith (Norman's Friend), Donald Sumpter (Norman's Friend), Christopher Martin (Sylvia's Boss)*
Director: *Mike Leigh*
Screenwriter: *Mike Leigh*
PG/111 mins./Drama/UK

Sylvia, a typist with a deep frozen firm of chartered accountants, lives a sherry-soaked life of quiet desperation in a South London semi. Her only human contact comes from her mentally handicapped sister Hilda, her frumpish malteser-addicted workmate Pat, her terminally meek teacher boyfriend Peter and a stuttering hippie Norman who plays the guitar hesitantly in the garage.

With a cast who seem perpetually on the point of tears, and an improvised scenario that seems to consist mainly of embarrassed pauses, *Bleak Moments* is at once warmly, gently funny and the most depressing 111 minutes you'll ever spend in front of a motion picture.

Made in 1971, when it was too much for anyone to take, it displays much of the brilliance that was confirmed by Mike Leigh's TV work in the 1970s and early 80s, but put him off making theatrical films for at least a decade. Leigh displays an uncanny rapport with his unfamiliar but outstanding cast, an ability to turn a disastrous Chinese meal or an awkward 'come back to my place for coffee' situation into the subtlest kind of comedy, a precise feel for the nuances of life in contemporary Britain (Streatham, actually) and a complete lack of cruelty towards his pathetic characters.

As often in Leigh's work, ordinary, repressed, miserable folk are allowed to show glimpses of deep chasms of despair or longing – this can make lines that could come from a Robin Askwith movie ('I'd like you to take off your trousers') come over like Chekhov. While the film's quality is undeniable, its relentless vision of trivial miseries requires a great deal of patience and understanding on the part of an audience. Too good to pass over on its rare revivals, but see it with someone who will cheer you up afterwards. ★★★ **KN**

BLONDE VENUS (1932)

Starring: *Marlene Dietrich (Helen Faraday), Herbert Marshall (Edward Faraday), Cary Grant (Nick Townsend), Dickie Moore (Johnny Faraday), Francis Sayles (Charlie Blaine)*
Director: *Josef Von Sternberg*
Screenwriters: *Jules Furthmann, S.K. Lauren, based on a story by Von Sternberg*
15/92 mins./Drama/USA

Devoted mother Helen Faraday becomes a nightclub singer in order to afford medical treatment for her husband, Edward. However, she risks losing her son when she takes up with smooth operator Nick Townsend.

Fresh from the critical and commercial triumph of *Shanghai Express*, Josef von Sternberg submitted an original scenario for Marlene Dietrich's next picture, only for the Paramount front office to consider it immoral and demand wholesale changes. When Von Sternberg refused, he was suspended and the project was handed to Richard Wallace. However, Dietrich refused to work with him and Von Sternberg was reinstated on the provision he toned down the screenplay.

Ostensibly, *Blonde Venus* is a morality tale, in which, from the best of motives, a model wife and mother sinks ever deeper into depravity before managing to recover her virtue on attaining international celebrity. But its wildly melodramatic storyline was merely an excuse for Von Sternberg to exhibit Dietrich in a series of increasingly stylised set-pieces.

Some, like the 'Hot Voodoo' number (in which Dietrich emerges from a gorilla suit sporting a blonde fright wig) were purely provocative. Yet, while few filmmakers placed more objects between their camera and the star, each prop, wisp and shadow was meticulously placed to enhance the visual and psychological texture of the image. Consequently, thanks to art director Wiard Ihnen and cinematographer Bert Glennon, the locales through which Dietrich drags her son, as she flees from the sleazy New York backstreets to the sweltering and scarcely more salubrious dives of Galveston, are impossibly atmospheric and confirm Von Sternberg as much more than an exotic pictorialist.

Indeed, some critics have suggested that he was attempting something of a feminist treatise here in revealing how Dietrich is abused by the various lecherous, exploitative, officious, priggish and self-serving men she encounters. Yet, this is actually a paean to the underdog in general, with even the black characters being presented in a more sympathetic and less stereotypical light than they were in the majority of other Golden Age features. ★★★ **DP**

BLOOD AND WINE (1996)

Starring: *Jack Nicholson (Alex Gates), Stephen Dorff (Jason), Jennifer Lopez (Gabriela 'Gabby'), Judy Davis (Suzanne), Michael Caine (Victor 'Vic' Spansky), Harold Perrineau Jr. (Henry)*
Director: *Bob Rafelson*
Screenwriters: *Nick Villiers, Alison Cross, from a story by Nick Villiers, Bob Rafelson*
15/101 mins./Thriller/Crime/Drama/US/UK

A diamond robbery leads to complications and spilt blood for a Miami wine merchant and an ailing safe cracker.

Bob Rafelson and Jack Nicholson have a history: they first collaborated in 1968 when Rafelson directed and Nicholson wrote the Monkees' art movie *Head*. In the 70s, they made the moment-catching *Five Easy Pieces* and the even more brilliant *The King Of Marvin Gardens*. If their *The Postman*

Always Rings Twice remake was disappointing, their previous collaboration (1992's *Man Trouble*) suggested irrevocable decline. It's bittersweet to report that *Blood And Wine*, by no means a disaster, was a long way from being a return to form.

Miami wine merchant Alex is married to a limping drudge, whose grown-up son Jason divides his time between shark fishing, working in the family business and hating his stepfather. Through his girlfriend, a Cuban maid, Alex gains entry to a wealthy household, which is robbed by his friend Victor, a terminally ill burglar. Various cock-ups lead to Alex losing the booty to Jason, several people getting brutally killed, an unconvincing relationship developing between Jason and the chiquita, and ironic fate closing in.

It's especially sad to see acknowledged greats imitating younger talents, as Rafelson fumbles with the sort of set-up that the Coen Brothers have mastered; *Blood And Wine* comes off poorly set beside *Blood Simple* or *Fargo*. Nicholson and Caine may be living legends, but they coast here with puffy faces and lazy mannerisms. Nicholson, in particular, is threatening to join Sean Connery and Gene Hackman in that class of movie star whose greatness we have to take on trust as they lope non-committally through yet another movie they manifestly don't give a damn about.

This feels old-fashioned, with stars who eclipse their characters, and miss the point of the traps of plot and personality that power the Coens' films. Dorff is a nonentity supporting hero, leaving Davis and Lopez to etch the only fully rounded characterisations. Though the plot ambles sunnily around Florida, neither the specific regional background nor the title-justifying but irrelevant oenological milieu connects with the crime plot. ★★ **KN**

THE BLOOD OF A POET (1930)

Starring: *Enrique Rivero (Poet), Elizabeth Lee Miller (Statue), Jean Desbordes (Louis XV Friend), Feral Benga (Black Angel)*
Director: *Jean Cocteau*
Screenwriter: *Jean Cocteau*
PG/55 mins./Drama/France

Unwilling to endure the solitude required for creativity, a poet attempts to pass his Muse to a statue, which exacts its revenge by condemning him to a series of disconcerting adventures.

When Jean Cocteau's film debut first played in America, a $25 reward was offered to anyone who could explain its meaning. Yet, while *The Blood Of A Poet* continues to defy precise interpretation, it has come to be recognised as both a pioneering work of art and a foretaste of the themes and images that would come to dominate Cocteau's cinema.

Having dallied with infeasible success in everything from verse to fiction, theatre to ballet and tapestry to typography, Cocteau came to film convinced it was an artisanal pursuit wholly unsuited to conveying the poet's rarified impressions. Yet, despite his belief that poetry was more atuned to the realities of life and death than any other artform, he soon discovered that the moving image was also an infinitely subtle and deeply personal mode of communication.

Despite being sponsored by the same Vicomte de Noailles who had patronised Luis Buñuel and Salvador Dali, Cocteau vehemently denied that his film was in any way influenced by the Surrealists. Yet, his disregard for narrative convention and intuitive grasp of cine-lyricism clearly tapped into the Second Avant-Garde's experimental audacity. His use of mirrors, trick perspectives, reversed footage and animation to approximate the dream state is inspired and it's tempting to disregard his anti-allegorical protestations and seek intellectual significance in the stream of narcissistic images that elongates the time it takes for a building to collapse to explore the agony and the ecstasy of creation.

Yet even if this is only a reverie on the illogicality of the subconscious, it's still a triumph of the imagination and provides invaluable insights into Cocteau's artistic vision. However, it isn't quite the work of a polymathematic amateur, as the exquisite monochrome photography was fashioned by George Périnal (who regularly collaborated with René Clair and Alexander Korda), while the music was composed by Georges Auric, who scored 100+ films over the next 40 years. ★★★★ **DP**

BLOOD SIMPLE (1984)

Starring: *M. Emmet Walsh (Private Detective Visser), Frances McDormand (Abby), Dan Hedaya (Julian Marty), John Getz (Ray), Samm-Art Williams (Maurice)*
Director: *Joel Coen*
Screenwriters: *Ethan Coen, Joel Coen*
18/97 mins./Crime/Thriller/USA

A detective is hired to despatch a man's wife and her lover, but instead fakes the hit and puts a bullet in the man. The lover, assuming the wife tried to despatch her husband, attempts to "clean up" the mess.

Most movie mysteries are told from the inside. We, the audience, along with a detective character, are confronted with baffling circumstances and gradually piece together the clues, finally learning the truth just as the hero or heroine does, walking away unscathed from the last-reel revelations. *Blood Simple*, the 1983 debut feature of the Coen Brothers, is not like that. For a change, we're in a privileged position, always knowing more than the characters we're following, understanding their wrong-headed thought processes, appreciating the ironies they miss, seeing where a slightly different bit of behaviour would have saved lives or led to happier endings.

Typical of the Coen approach is the handling of a traditional thriller gimmick (cf: the finale of *Strangers On A Train*) of the incriminating item left at the scene of the crime, which forces the killer to return and imperil himself to cover up. Murderous private eye Loren Visser (M. Emmet Walsh) leaves his distinctive Man Of The Year cigarette lighter under a clump of fresh-caught fish in the office where he has put a bullet into bar-owner Julian Marty (Dan Hedaya), and later assumes lovers Abby (Frances McDormand) and Ray (John Getz) know he is a killer because they have this vital clue. But the lighter remains unnoticed under the fish throughout the film, and Visser isn't even a killer, having left Marty wounded only for Ray to come along and, under the impression that Abby has tried to do away with her husband, finish him off by burying him alive. At every turn of this complex plot tangle, we know what's going on – but none of the characters ever get the big picture, except (perhaps) Visser on the point of death after he has been shot by Abby under the mistaken impression that he is her husband. 'I'm not afraid of you, Marty,' she says. Chortling, Visser responds, 'Well, ma'am, if I see him, I'll sure give him the message.'

The title is an expression the Coens found in the stories of hard-boiled writer Dashiell Hammett, who would later inspire their gangster epic *Miller's Crossing*, and refers to a state of mind whereby a person is so caught up in the need for violence – or sex, money, revenge, status – that he or she loses his or her wits and is destroyed. The setting is Texas, but not the wide-open state of numberless Westerns. This is a world of dark, dark desert nights, where unlit roads cross empty spaces. Marty, proprietor of a bar named Neon Boots, has hired Visser to prove that his wife is an adulteress, though it's possible that it's only this paranoia that drives her to get together with dim-bulb bartender Ray. Humiliated when Abby breaks his 'pussy finger' (more relevantly, his trigger finger) and walks out, Marty hires Visser to kill the lovers, but the PI opts for the lower-risk strategy of collecting the fee and shooting Marty.

When Ray thinks Abby has shot her husband, he makes a botch of cleaning up the blood with his windbreaker, and can't even bury the corpse without imperilling himself, as the dying Marty points a gun out of his grave. An alleged theft, a doctored photograph in a safe, tensions between the lovers and suspicions that won't go away complicate an intricate but always clear pattern.

Less obviously comic than the Coens' subsequent films, this has a degree of beyond-black humour but is mostly a study of the way things always go wrong when people don't use their heads. 'Who looks stupid now?' is an appropriate send-off line delivered by a murderer to a victim, as all the dumbness naturally leads to death. The last reel, with Abby attacked by a man she doesn't know for reasons she can't understand, is a great monster-and-the-girl face-off, as M. Emmet Walsh, in a career-best performance as the sweaty thug in a yellow leisure suit and huge straw cowboy hat, shoots holes through a wall to free his knife-pinned hand. It's a cruel picture, in which all four main characters get to be possible or actual murderers or murder victims and anyone is capable of doing the worst to anyone else. Later, in *Fargo*, the Brothers would add a humane, caring figure, promoting McDormand to detective, and set this murderous anthill in context; but here, at the beginning, they were much more ruthless. ★★★★★ **KN**

⦾ THE BLUE ANGEL (DER BLAUE ENGEL) (1930)

Starring: *Emil Jannings (Prof. Immanuel Rath), Marlene Dietrich (Lola Frohlich), Kurt Gerron (Kiepert, a Magician), Rosa Valetti (Guste, his Wife), Hans Abers (Mazeppa)*
Director: *Josef von Sternberg*
Screenwriters: *Robert Liebmann, Karl Vollmoeller, Carl Zuckmayer, based on the novel Professor Unrat by Heinrich Mann*
PG/99 mins./Drama/Germany

Professor Rath, a middle-aged schoolmaster, visits a cabaret where his pupils have been wasting time, and becomes smitten with Lola, a singer. Dismissed from his position, Rath marries the girl and becomes a humiliated, abused clown.

A masochistic melodrama spotlighting what was considered great screen acting in 1930 from Emil Jannings and a first, raunchy glimpse of a plump-thighed, throaty-voiced Marlene Dietrich in the role that made her career. It owes something to the silent circus-themed dramas of Lon Chaney (*He Who Gets Slapped*) and in turn sketches several ideas developed in Hollywood in the horror classic *Freaks*, with Jannings – who was often cast as pompous, pathetic individuals who lose the last scraps of their dignity – at his best when he becomes a grotesque clown.

While acting as assistant to a sadistic stage magician, Jannings has eggs repeatedly smashed over his forehead and cracks himself, grunting cock-a-doodle-doo as he attacks his wife and her strongman lover, then shambles like a refugee from Dr Caligari's Cabinet back to the schoolroom where he dies grasping his old desk.

This was a last hurrah for Jannings, who (despite that terrifying rooster impersonation) was essentially a silent actor – but it was a beginning for Dietrich, who would later be polished into inscrutability by the Svengali-like director Joseph von Sternberg. Here, she's much more like a real person, and Lola is far more complex than the evil, scheming sluts of silent melodrama. Dietrich shows Lola's compassion for her degraded husband as well as her estrangement from him, and (of course) is stunning on stage.

It was made in two versions – a German language film and a shorter, part-English talkie; on the whole, the German film is stronger, but Dietrich's songs ('Falling In Love Again', 'They Call Me Naughty Lola') sound better in English. ★★★★ **KN**

⦾ BLUE IN THE FACE (1995)

Starring: *Victor Argo (Vinnie), Lou Reed (Man With Strange Glasses), Michael J Fox (Pete Maloney), Roseanne (Dot), Mel Gorham (Violetta), Jim Jarmusch (Bob), Lily Tomlin (The Waffle Eater), Madonna (Singing Telegram), Harvey Keitel (Auggie)*
Directors: *Paul Auster, Wayne Wang*
Screenwriters: *Paul Auster, Wayne Wang*
15/83 mins./Comedy/USA

Vinnie, owner of the Brooklyn Cigar Company, is thinking of selling out to a health food store, but is eventually dissuaded by the ghost of baseball star Jackie Robinson (!) and the reminder of the blow that was the defection of the Brooklyn Dodgers team.

An add-on to *Smoke*, shot in six days after the main feature wrapped, with Paul Auster providing situations for his cast to shoot the breeze with and Wayne Wang pulling in vox pop chats with various Brooklynites, facts and figures about the borough and perhaps a greater sense of place than *Smoke*, which was more intent on the characters' arcs.

It's a unique film that gives Victor Argo, a familiar tough guy face in *Abel Ferrara* and other NYC pictures, a couple of musical numbers, but there's a nice thread in which the chatter in the store often seems to turn musical, even to the extent of RuPaul showing up to lead an impromptu party or Harvey Keitel's love interest (Mel Gorham, glimpsed in *Smoke*, highlighted here) doing a strip in front of the mirror.

There are sketch-like turns from Michael J. Fox as a slightly cracked (bogus?) researcher asking odd questions of Giancarlo Esposito, Lily Tomlin as a male bum, Madonna as a grumpy singing telegram girl, Roseanne as Argo's love-hungry neglected wife (more affecting than funny), Mira Sorvino as a passerby who won't press charges against a 12-year-old pickpocket Keitel has run down (he gives the kid her bag and tells her to run), Mailk Yoba as a rapper/conman who has a different act every time he shows up, Lou Reed talking about cigarettes and his glasses and Jim Jarmusch as a man sharing his last cigarette with the store-keeper who sold him all the others. ★★★ **KN**

⦾ THE BLUE LAGOON (1980)

Starring: *Brooke Shields (Emmeline), Christopher Atkins (Richard), Leo McKern (Paddy Button), William Daniels (Arthur Lestrange), Elva Josephson (Young Emmeline), Glenn Kohan (Young Richard)*
Director: *Randal Kleiser*
Screenwriter: *Douglas Day Stewart, based on the novel by Henry De Vere Stacpoole*
15/104 mins./Drama/USA

Two children shipwrecked on a tropical island, slowly grow-up learning all the lessons of life at first hand – from fishing techniques to childbirth.

Titter-worthy tosh contending we'd all have had a much more enlightened puberty if we'd been left to fend for ourselves on a desert island. Let nature have its way implores the dotty narrative as prettified quislings Brooke Shields and Christopher Atkins learn about the exciting side of bodily function, inspired by the strange sproutings each other is suddenly sporting. The constant asides to take in the lush tropical locations a nod to the instinctual processes God intended all along.

At least, director Randal Kleiser, late of *Grease* fame, had the good sense to employ the highly talented Nestor Alemendros as his cinematographer, who provides a gorgeous sense of tranquillity amongst the heady jungle greens and crystal clear ocean blues provided by their Fiji locations. The two stars, with body doubles on-hand for the naughtier moments (sorry, perfect expressions of human love), flit about their idyll with perpetually dumbfounded expressions. The idea is a glorious awakening untrammelled by outside influence, but it comes across like a Bacardi advert populated by special needs kids.

Eyepatch Wearers — TOP10

1 Snake Plissken, *Escape from New York* – Kurt Russell
2 Captain Franky Cook, *Sky Captain and the World of Tomorrow* – Angelina Jolie
3 Number Two, *Austin Powers* – Robert Wagner and Rob Lowe
4 Elle Driver, *Kill Bill* – Daryl Hannah
5 Mrs Taggart, *The Anniversary* – Bette Davis
6 Rochefort, *The Three Musketeers* – Christopher Lee
7 Fearless Leader, *The Adventures of Rocky and Bullwinkle* – Robert De Niro
8 Emilio Largo, *Thunderball* – Adolfo Celi
9 Peter Gatien, *Party Monster* – Dylan McDermott
10 Nick Fury, *Nick Fury: Agent of Shielf* – David Hasselhoff

Another problem, beyond the handling of biological tug, is the entire lack of threat. We are shown a nearby tribe into human sacrifice, a hint toward some ghastly peril in store for our acne-free lovebirds. But Kleiser declines to break the placid surface of his homily to gorgeousness and nowt happens. Everything is idealised, their island survival a matter of building a natty hut and Shields getting through childbirth without mussing up her lovely hair.

It's based on a 1903 novel by the grandly monikered Henry De Vere Stacpoole, and Jean Simmons availed herself for a 1949 version. She, at least, wasn't stuck with such deranged dialogue as Emmeline's excruciatingly silly: 'You're always staring at my buppies!' Welcome to the real world, love. ★★ **IN**

THE BLUE LAMP (1949)

Starring: *Jack Warner (PC George Dixon), Jimmy Hanley (PC Andy Mitchell), Dirk Bogarde (Tom Riley), Robert Flemyng (Sgt Roberts), Bernard Lee (Insp. Cherry), Peggy Evans (Diana Lewis), Dora Bryan (Maisie),*
Director: *Basil Dearden*
Screenwriter: *T.E.B Clarke, Alexander Mackendrick*
PG/84 mins./Drama/UK

Awards: *BAFTA – Best British Film*

New recruit Andy Mitchell leads the manhunt when his mentor, PC George Dixon is gunned down by reckless crook Tom Riley.

Although it's best known for its mildly subversive comedies, Ealing Studios under Michael Balcon also had a pronounced social conscience. Throughout the war, it had emphasised the importance of community action to defeating the Nazis and Basil Dearden's film takes a similar attitude towards cracking crime. The public provides several significant leads as Inspector Cherry Lee and his bobbies track down the thugs responsible for shooting George Dixon and it even plays its inadvertent part in Tom and Spud's apprehension at the dog track.

Moreover, the criminal fraternity also does its bit, rallying to shop the outsiders who had dishonoured their code, in much the same way that the Berlin underworld united to capture Peter Lorre's child killer in Fritz Lang's *M*.

Yet, there's something quaintly old-fashioned about the scenario by ex-copper T.E.B. Clarke. The intention is clearly to highlight the emergence of a new breed of trigger-happy criminals, who had become enured to violence during the war and whose lack of discipline reflected a dangerous challenge to traditional morality. But what results is a uniquely English police procedural, which has none of the grit and authenticity of such contemporary American crime dramas as Jules Dassin's *The Naked City* or Elia Kazan's *Panic In The Streets*. Clarke has little ear for street argot and were it not for Dirk Bogarde's edgy performance, this would have been forgotten as quickly as any quota quickie.

The BBC was so impressed with the picture that it starred Jack Warner in *Dixon Of Dock Green* (1955-76), which similarly portrayed plods as ordinary blokes with a pronounced sense of duty. But when Clarke attempted to introduce some moral ambiguity to the policier in *Gideon's Day*, he succeeded only in presenting the great John Ford with one of his dullest films. ★★★ **DP**

THE BLUE MAX (1966)

Starring: *George Peppard (Bruno Stachel), James Mason (General Count von Klugermann), Ursula Andress (Countess Kaeti von Klugermann), Jeremy Kemp (Willi von Klugermann), Karl Michael Vogler (Otto Heidermann)*
Director: *John Guillermin*
Screenwriters: *Ben Barzman, Basillio Franchina, David Pursall, Jack Seddon, Gerard Hanley, based on the novel by Jack Hunter*
PG/156 mins./War/USA

Awards: *Bafta – Best British Art Direction*

Bruno Stachel, a lower-class hotshot pilot, rises through the ranks of the German air force in World War One, earning the hatred of his own comrades as much as the enemy, and romancing the aristocratic wife of his commanding general.

An epic-length WWI flying drama, based on the best-selling novel by Jack Hunter, directed on the ground by journeyman John Guillermin but coming to life mostly in the second-unit aerial sequences directed by Anthony Squire. Flying ace movies had come and gone in the 1930s, and this was the first attempt to revive the genre in widescreen and colour, with lovingly restored vintage planes got into, then blasted out of the air.

Its story owes something to the bastard-makes-good-but-winds-up-unhappy genre popular in the 1960s (*Room At The Top*, *Hud*) as blond upstart Peppard focuses so intently on winning the *pour le merite* or 'Blue Max' medal automatically handed out after twenty victories ('I'm afraid it's a rather small medal,' admits offhand General James Mason, 'but it's the highest Germany can give') that he becomes a national hero while the rest of his squadron bite the dust one by one, usually in incidents for which he is responsible.

In 1966, it was sold not only on its dogfight and stunt-flying action but on 'three steamy bedroom scenes', in which the glacial Andress wears only a towel and tries to get a reaction from the unresponsive Peppard. The supporting cast mixes familiar German exports (Anton Diffring, Karl Michael Vogler) with accent-sporting Brits (Jeremy Kemp, Derren Nesbitt), but Mason, as the puppet-mastering senior officer who sets Bruno up for his final crash, walks away with the whole film.

An afternoon television perennial, it's surprisingly watchable nonsense – and the daredevil flying-under-the-bridge sequence remains a classic air action sequence. ★★★ **KN**

⦿ BLUE STEEL (1990)

Starring: *Jamie Lee Curtis (Megan Turner), Ron Silver (Eugene Hunt), Philip Bosco (Frank Turner), Louise Fletcher (Shirley Turner), Clancy Brown (Nick Mann), Elizabeth Pena (Tracy Perez)*
Director: *Kathryn Bigelow*
Screenwriters: *Kathryn Bigelow, Eric Red*
18/98 mins./Action/Thriller/USA

On her first night on the job a rookie cop breaks up a supermarket robbery and kills the gunman. The gun ends up in the hands of a deranged Wall Street broker who starts to obsess about the cop.

A complete commercial non-event on its theatrical release, *Blue Steel* still managed to tickle the fancy of quite a few critics, naturally intrigued by the notion of a woman director and a leading female star together tackling the traditional men-only preserve of the tough cop thriller. Throw in the fact that this is an Oliver Stone production and the box office bellyflop is – on paper – yet more difficult to understand.

On DVD viewing, however, *Blue Steel* adds up to little more than a faintly hysterical version of what is a fairly dull blueprint to start off with. Rookie cop Megan Turner (Curtis) finds herself first the date then the prey of commodities broker-cum-psycho Ron Silver and chases him all over town while trying to fend off various accusations that she isn't much cop at this sort of thing because she's not Clint Eastwood. Curtis and Silver both know how to do this sort of thing with their eyes shut and the first half-hour has some genuine class about it, but too often Bigelow presses the overkill button, reducing Silver's initially intriguing mix of sharp suits and bullets to a simple blood-crazed voices-in-the-head sort of nutter while Curtis' attempts to prove herself all on her own seem simply stupid and worthy of that much-feared return to pushing pencils.

By the time Curtis – after what must be five days without sleep – suddenly decides to dive into bed for sexual gymnastics with a grouchy Philip Bosco, only to be violently, some may say, gratuitously interrupted by old stock exchange Satan himself, all attempts at creating a genuine alternative to the buddy cop thriller appear to have been long since buried under the need for a suitably frenzied climax. Bigelow is big here on fetishism, heavily stylised images and the look of the city at night. A little restraint would, however, have made this entertaining enough thriller a considerably bigger and better proposition. ★★★ **BMc**

⦿ BLUE VELVET (1986)

Starring: *Kyle MacLachlan (Jeffrey Beaumont), Isabella Rossellini (Dorothy Vallens), Dennis Hopper (Frank Booth), Laura Dern (Sandy Williams), Hope Lange (Mrs Williams), Dean Stockwell (Ben)*
Director: *David Lynch*
Screenwriter: *David Lynch*
18/120 mins./Mystery/USA

In a seemingly picture perfect American town a college lecturer finds a severed ear and enlists the help of a high school girl to help him find the body to which it once belonged.

The mid-1980s did not represent a golden age of American filmmaking. The great directors of the previous decade were not on top of their game: Marty was drained, Francis bankrupt, Friedkin burnt out, Altman washed up, Roman on the run and Spielberg, seemingly having peaked with *E.T.*, was in his literary adaptation period. Spike Lee and Jim Jarmusch were starting to produce interesting work in the low-budget, independent sector, but the medium was crying out for a figure with a distinctive vision and voice. David Lynch answered the call with *Blue Velvet*.

Lynch was an unlikely saviour. He'd made his breakthrough in 1977 with *Eraserhead*, a deeply disturbing, surreal nightmare of a movie. It was a cult favourite on the late-night circuit and with student film societies, and secured Lynch a switch to the mainstream with prestigious period flick *The Elephant Man*, which in turn earned him a Best Director Oscar nomination. It seemed Lynch would be assimilated onto the Hollywood A-list, especially when he was given the reins of big-budget, long-gestating sci-fi epic, *Dune*. The resulting film, however, was a disaster, a turkey as unappealing as the one which came to life and bled all over the table in *Eraserhead*. Lynch's moment in the sun was over, but *Dune* did see him establish two key relationships – with producer Dino De Laurentiis and young actor Kyle MacLachlan. While lesser moguls might have retreated to lick their wounds and blame their director, De Laurentiis hailed Lynch as a talent to rank alongside Fellini (with whom he had also worked) and bankrolled his next film to the tune of six million dollars. Much happier working from his own script, Lynch delivered the film on time and within budget, without compromising his vision.

Blue Velvet established the Lynchian style, introducing themes he would explore obsessively throughout much of his future career. With MacLachlan as his seemingly clean-cut alter ego, the former Eagle Scout from Missoula, Montana, probed the dark heart of small-town America. Jeffrey Beaumont lives in a neighbourhood of white picket fences and manicured lawns, but when taking a shortcut home from visiting his hospitalised father, young Jeff finds a severed human ear. The model citizen takes said ear to the local police station but, though this satisfies his sense of civic duty, his innate curiosity is awakened and eager to know more. As Jeffrey tells Sandy, the sweet-natured high school girl and daughter of local cop Detective Williams, 'I believe there are opportunities in life for gaining knowledge and experience, but sometimes that means taking a risk.' Soon, this fresh-faced couple are conspiring to sneak into the apartment of nightclub chanteuse Dorothy Valens, hoping to find clues that will help them solve the mystery: 'Nobody would think two people like us would be crazy enough to do something like this,' they cheerily decide. In fact, Jeffrey's knowledge and experience arrives in the form of sadomasochistic sex with Dorothy and a life-threatening confrontation with her psychotic lover, Frank.

In a film of extreme characters and daring performances, no one is wilder than Frank, no characterisation more 'out there' than that delivered by Dennis Hopper. Nearly two decades on, and with a string of self-parodic rent-a-nut job gigs from Hopper to taint the viewer's perception, Frank remains an astonishing creation. He is a terrifying individual, perverse and brutal, with the attention span and tantrum capacity of a small child. Hopper seizes the role with relish, somehow avoiding going over the top despite screaming lines like, 'Let's fuck – I'll fuck anything that moves,' or responding to Jeffrey's reguest for a particular brand of beer with the immortal riposte, 'Heineken? Fuck that shit! Pabst Blue Ribbon.' After many drug-addled years in the wilderness, this represented a significant comeback for Hopper, and his work was honoured by festivals and critics' circles around the world (though the good people at the Academy preferred to bestow a Best Supporting Actor nomination on his far more heart-warming performance in the period basketball movie, *Hoosiers*). The Academy couldn't ignore Lynch, however, and he was given his second Best Director nomination. Film-lovers the world over breathed a sigh of relief – finally, in a time dominated by such eyesores as *Top Gun* and *Flashdance*, here was a great film made by a great director, we thought. But watching *Blue Velvet* again two decades on, it's clear we were only half right.

The truth is, *Blue Velvet* isn't perfect. Yes, it's compelling and exciting, and were it not for *Raging Bull* and *GoodFellas* at either end of the decade you could make a case for it being the best American film of the 1980s. You can watch it now and, alongside terrific stuff from Hopper, MacLachlan and Laura Dern, marvel at Isabella Rossellini's heartbreaking *femme fatale*, or drink in the heady cocktail of cinematography and production design. The problem with *Blue Velvet* is David Lynch or, more specifically, the fact that David Lynch went on to do better work.

MacLachlan's wide-eyed Jeffrey is in marked contrast to Dennis Hopper's deeply disturbed Frank. *Twin Peaks* is a more inventive subversion of small-town Americana, and in Leland Palmer possesses a villain more threatening than Frank since he hides his own corruption, rather than glorying in it. If Frank walked into a bar you'd walk – or run – out; if Leland Palmer asked you to pass the beer nuts, you'd probably strike up a conversation with him. The good citizens of Lumberton only get into trouble by straying into the wrong neighbourhood, getting mixed up with the wrong kind of people; in *Twin Peaks* – and this is a far more chilling notion – evil lurks in your home, your family. As for the other Lynchian chords first struck in *Blue Velvet* – sexual obsession, ideas of identity, electrifying musical numbers – these would all resurface to more satisfying effect in his masterpiece, Mulholland Dr.

Instead, think of this not as the definitive David Lynch movie; but instead, as the best Hitchcock movie Alfred himself never made. Many Hitchcockian elements are present and correct: the lush, Bernard Herrmann-esque score Angelo Badalamenti provides over the opening credits, the MacGuffin of the severed ear, the small-town milieu lifted from *Shadow Of A Doubt*. The curious, voyeuristic hero comes straight out of *Rear Window*, only to take a shift into *Vertigo* territory when Jeffrey becomes sexually obsessed with Dorothy Valens. When Sandy looks across the table in the diner and says to Jeffrey, 'I can't figure out if you're a detective or a pervert,' she is basically articulating the question which underscored Hitchcock's finest cinematic hours. ★★★★ **RF**

ⓑ THE BLUES BROTHERS (1980)

Starring: *John Belushi (Joilet Jack), Dan Aykroyd (Elwood), Aretha Franklin (Soul Food Café Owner), James Brown (Rev. Cleophus James), Cab Calloway (Curtis), Ray Charles (Ray), Carrie Fisher (Mystery Woman), Henry Gibson (Nazi Leader), John Candy (Burton Mercer)*
Director: *John Landis*
Screenwriters: *John Landis, Dan Aykroyd*
15/133 mins./Comedy/USA

Two brothers set out on a 'mission from God' to raise funds for their old orphanage. Their plan – to reunite their old band for a gig to end all gigs.

The Blues Brothers opens like a Walter Hill movie. Wide, unpeopled views of Joliet Penitentiary. A prisoner being escorted to release. A confederate waiting outside in the wasteland by the prison. A criminal reunion. The music doesn't even cut in for five minutes. Like *Wayne's World* – and, um, *Coneheads, It's Pat, Stuart Saves His Family* and *Superstar* – *The Blues Brothers* is a spin-off from the American TV comedy institution, *Saturday Night Live*, which drew personnel from the media arm of *National Lampoon* magazine and the Canadian Second City improv comedy troupe.

National Lampoon's Animal House (1978), directed by John Landis, had already established the SNL style as a screen staple, incidentally making a break-out star of fat slob comic John Belushi. Dan Aykroyd missed being in *Animal House*, though the character of 'motorhead' D-Day was based on him. Belushi and Aykroyd shared an interest in urban American soul, blues and rhythm and blues, and created the characters of orphans Jake and Elwood Blues – brothers by choice not birth – as a way of indulging their craze, more intent on the music than the comedy. *The Blues Brothers* appeared on SNL, and as a live act opening for Steve Martin. Then, at that precise moment when Hollywood was willing to countenance such excess (ie: *1941* was being greenlit too), Aykroyd produced a script the size of a phone book and Landis climbed aboard.

Like *1941*, *The Blues Brothers* wasn't much liked when first released. It was too long, too expensive, too wasteful. Besides, everyone was into disco and didn't want to hear from John Lee Hooker, James Brown, Aretha Franklin, Ray Charles or Cab Galloway. Unlike the much-maligned *1941*, *The Blues Brothers* has survived, reinventing itself as a slow-burning cult hit in the decade before films were written off after their opening weekend. Among the first wave of major movies available on rental video, and riding a resurgence of interest in the soundtrack album, the film has become some sort of classic. It's one of those 'Oh, my God, look who's in it!' pictures – besides guest stars Carrie Fisher and Twiggy, you get micro-bits from Bill Murray, Frank Oz, Paul Reubens and, famously, Steven Spielberg, and that's not even counting all the musical greats worked into the tapestry. By the turn of the century, the film had finally passed the true test of lasting success and yielded a disappointing sequel, *Blues Brothers 2000*.

One of the reasons *The Blues Brothers* didn't immediately click is that it's hard to work out what it's supposed to be – a comedy, an action movie, a musical? There may have been a groovy atmosphere but getting served was a nightmare. Belushi and Aykroyd (in identical black suits, porkpie hats and Raybans) are a classic tall/fat, deadpan/explosive double act to set beside Laurel and Hardy, Abbott and Costello, Hope and Crosby, Tom and Jerry and Martin and Lewis. But they're also unusual in the tradition in that they are never at cross-purposes, always focused on their twin goals of saving the orphanage and getting the band back together, and rarely argue. Most comedy teams bicker and batter each other until the outside world intervenes and they turn against a bullying cop or landlady. But the Blues Brothers are solid, inhabiting their own world and getting laughs from the way they are always in tune with each other – improvising a cowboy music set ('Rawhide!') when they unwisely book themselves into a bar that has 'both kinds of music, country and western.'

In the end, this is a 1980s mutation of the 1930s Warner Brothers musicals, with car chases instead of Busby Berkeley dance routines. The setting is realistic, observed with affection (it's a great showcase for Chicago without glamorising the city) and the showbiz characters are torn between their art and the practicalities of earning a living. Landis, who has a real feel for American music, puts songs everywhere (even the elevator musak and overheard radio licks are significant) and goes beyond the posings of *Fame* to give the music back to the people.

Belushi and Aykroyd dance like cartoon characters, with backflips and body-stretches, but everyone else moves like a real person. In the 'Twistin'' number, a pen clatters onto the ground as a group of bystanders jive, and Landis lets the detail stand in the edit.

There's an echo of those hideous all-star chase films – *The Great Race, It's A Mad Mad Mad Mad World, Monte Carlo Or Bust, The Cannonball Run* – in Landis' love of cameos, multi-car pile-ups and marauding extras. The finale, as the Brothers rush to give Spielberg the money to save the orphanage, throws in cops, state troopers, a country and western band (The Good Ole Boys), Illinois Nazis (The American Socialist White Peoples' Party, whose acronym sounds a lot like 'asswipe'), the National Guard, firemen, SWAT teams, the army and Carrie Fisher.

There's a lot of destruction, but as in *Bugs Bunny*, no one really gets hurt. Stories of on-set excess, mostly revolving around Belushi's ultimately suicidal drug intake, are legion. But for such a huge picture it's surprisingly tight, with Landis' unerring instinct for the right funny shot (Belushi leaning over the line to sign for his possessions, the hand-moves for 'Stand By Your Man') and the constant thrum of great music to keep it going. It ends where it began, in prison – with the band behind bars performing 'Jailhouse Rock', and baton-wielding bulls running in to batter them senseless. Hell, that's America. ★★★★ **KN**

⦿ BLUES BROTHERS 2000 (1998)

Starring: *Dan Aykroyd (Elwood Blues), John Goodman (Mighty Mack McTeer), Joe Morton (Cab Chamberlain), Nia Peeples (Lieutenant Elizondo), Kathleen Freeman (Mother Mary Stigmata), J.Evan Bonifant (Buster Blues), Frank Oz (Warden), Steve Lawrence (Maury Sline), Darrell Hammond (Robertson), Erykah Badu (Queen Mousette)*
Director: *John Landis*
Screenwriters: *Dan Aykroyd, John Landis*
PG/123 mins./Comedy/Musical/USA

Elwood Blues comes out of retirement following the death of his brother, reforming the legendary R&B duo with newcomer John Goodman in order to raise money for an orphan brat.

Some movies you just have to ask 'why?'. What on earth would possess apparently sane movie producers that a sequel to a film which was critically mauled, flopped disastrously, is over 18 years old, and has had half its putative comedy duo drop dead of a drugs overdose over a decade ago was a halfway decent idea? And yet the green light flickered on.

How you react to *Blues Brothers 2000* really depends on your take on the first movie – since it is essentially a straight remake with John Goodman slipping recklessly under and behind the late John Belushi's hat and shades. We also have the introduction of a Culkin-alike in the shape of 'J. Evan Bonifant', here a refugee from the orphanage for which Elwood and the gang intend to raise money by, ho hum, getting the band back together and taking part in a Battle Of The Bands competition.

On the way all the 'old favourites' such as Aretha Franklin (who belts out her old hit 'R.E.S.P.E.C.T.') are brought back from the dead. The roadhouse mini-concert is replaced by a monster-truck show, and they are no longer 'on a mission from God' but rather declare that 'God works in mysterious ways'. Given the fact that this film exists at all, we can be in no doubt about that.

This is a warmed-up corpse of a movie, having neither the courage to do anything new or the wit to make a joke out of its own unoriginality. To be fair, a couple of the songs are what your gran would no-doubt call toe-tapping, and for those of a musical bent the final battle, which turns into an extended jamming session, is impressive simply in terms of the number of famous faces up there on the same stage. ★★ **AS**

⦿ BODY DOUBLE (1984)

Starring: *Craig Wasson (Jake Scully), Melanie Griffith (Holly), Gregg Henry (Sam), Deborah Shelton (Gloria), Guy Boyd (Jim McLean), Dennis Franz (Rubin), David Haskell (Drama Teacher)*
Director: *Brian De Palma*
Screenwriters: *Robert J Avrech, Brian De Palma*
18/114 mins./Thriller/USA

Jake Scully, an actor who suffers from claustrophobia, house-sits in an incredible apartment as a favour to a friend. From this vantage point, he spies on a sexy neighbour, then witnesses her being gruesomely drill-murdered by a Red Indian hit man. Traumatised, he begins to think he's been set up, and has to impersonate a porn actor to get close to hardcore queen Holly Body who might have an answer to the mystery.

A typical Brian De Palma effort from the 1980s, borrowing ideas from Hitchcock even as it goes all-out for the kind of effects only De Palma would even consider.

Undigested chunks of the plots of *Vertigo* and *Rear Window* are stirred into a defiantly downbeat, grim and perverse storyline in which objectionable characters slaughter each other, and even the hero is branded as a panty-sniffing loon by the cops. DePalma does everything to excess, with long tracking shots that tend to pay off sexually: prowling like a stalker as Shelton shops for underwear, wandering into a labyrinthine apartment as Jake finds his girlfriend screwing another guy or marching onto a porn movie set to the tune of Frankie Goes to Hollywood's much-banned 'Relax'. A pre-chubby Melanie Griffith is wonderfully slutty-mysterious as the bleached blonde star of *Holly Does Hollywood* (the name 'Holly Body' was later taken up by a real pornstar) who has been employed as part of a sinister scam.

Once you get past the deliberately ridiculous story, it's a fine example of the director's lush overkill style from the days before his 'Hollywood hired gun' hackwork and offers a redeeming thread of silly sick humour. The Nicolas Cage movie *Vampire's Kiss* takes its title from the punk exploitation film, directed by a bullying Dennis Franz, which Craig Wasson is supposed to be starring in here. ★★★ **KN**

⦿ BODY HEAT (1981)

Starring: *William Hurt (Ned Racine), Kathleen Turner (Matty Walker), Richard Crenna (Edmund Walker), Ted Danson (Peter Lowenstein), JA Preston (Oscar Grace), Mickey Rourke (Teddy Lewis)*
Director: *Lawrence Kasdan*
Screenwriter: *Lawrence Kasdan*
18/113 mins./Thriller/USA

When smalltown Florida lawyer Ned Racine falls for the sultry but very married Matty Walker, a torrid affair begins. They then hatch a plot to murder her rich husband, but things may not be what they seem.

Openly intending to reinvent the seething amorality of film noirs heyday in the 40s and 50s, Lawrence Kasdan gets his two key ingredients dead on: the cold heart of his screenplay and the sheer heat of his leading lady. It's not for nothing that Kathleen Turner, who was making her debut, would be the prototype for Jessica Rabbit, she starts every conversation with her body, finishing them off with the razor edge of her tongue: 'You're not too smart, I like that in a man.'

As with noir's abiding tenets, William Hurt's offbeat bottom-dwelling lawyer deserves everything he's going to get, but, thanks to the actor's skill in giving him a human strain, we still catch the note of his despair. He's seedy, an over-aged bachelor priding himself on his womanising skills. It's his judgement that's well off. After a night of this kind of passion – and Kasdan revolves his plot around the landmark va-va-voom of their sexual encounter – who wouldn't get a bit cock-eyed. He's just a normal, greedy, lust-driven guy, she's got things going on.

Thus, when they plot the perfect murder, of Richard Crenna's weasley but loaded husband, you just know something dark and complicated will unfold in the background. Kasdan fuses the traditions of old into his contemporary setting with some subtlety – the intricacies of legalese and America's obsession with real estate are keynotes in the wiring of the set-up.

In an inspired creative move, the director takes the basic visual motifs of the genre – turn down the lights and let the shadows fall long – and adds stark humidity. The film is set during the sweltering prelude to a storm, a heated mirror to their illicit passions. And, as events so inevitably collapse around Racine's ears, the natural recompense for the sordidness of his life, so Kasdan achieves his goal, creating a film to sit proudly in the legacy of those nihilistic standard bearers of the past. ★★★★ **IN**

⦿ BODY OF EVIDENCE (1992)

Starring: *Madonna (Rebecca Carlson), Michael Forest (Andrew Marsh), Joe Mantegna (Robert Garrett), Charles Hallahan (Dr McCurdy), Anne Archer (Joanne Braslow), Willem Dafoe (Frank Dulaney), Julianne Moore (Sharon Dulaney)*
Director: *Uli Edel*
Screenwriter: *Brad Mirman*
18/101 mins./USARomance/Thriller

Awards: *Razzie – Worst Actress*

An art gallery owner, accused of killing her lover through excessive sex, is soon engaged in similar activity with her defence lawyer.

The subject of much derision at the time, Madonna's offering arrived on these shores having flopped across the pond, but no doubt hoping to bask in the glow of a *Basic Instinct*-style sexual controversy.

La Ciccone is art gallery owner Rebecca Carlson who lives on an impossibly lavish and improbably stable houseboat, and has a rich older lover with a dodgy ticker. After a bout of strenuous sex involving bondage and nipple clamps, he winds up dead from a cardiac arrest, leaving district attorney Joe Mantegna to bring in Madonna for her lover's murder, claiming she, er, fornicated him to death – 'she's the murder weapon' – aided by a dash of cocaine in his nasal spray, for the $8 million she's set to inherit in his will.

With defence lawyer Willem Dafoe on her case, what follows is a courtroom drama of mounting tedium interspersed by scenes of Madonna pouring hot candle wax over Dafoe's chest and genitalia, and masturbating with Enya-like musak twinkling away in the background. 'That's what I do – I fuck,' she purrs at one point, just in case we don't quite get it.

The main problem here, however, is that whereas *Basic Instinct* – which this tries so desperately to emulate – had a healthy dose of self-deprecating humour (you always felt director Paul Verhoeven's tongue was well embedded in his cheek), *Body Of Evidence* takes itself far too seriously, its actors spouting Brad Mirman's stilted dialogue with the stony-faced sincerity of people wishing they were somewhere else altogether.

And while Madonna is constantly presented as a beautiful young woman of mystery, the fact is that here she looks far from young, far from beautiful and – for anyone who checked out the previous year's literary offering, *Sex* – very far from mysterious. Willem Dafoe, a particularly fine actor when the script takes him and sometimes when it doesn't, is here treading water, desperately out of his depth, grinning like a Cheshire cat on heat, whether he's humping his wife ('You're great when you've got a big case,' she moans) or having his head stuffed into Madonna's crotch (no stand-ins here) while she's posed on the bonnet of a limo. ★★ **MS**

BODY SNATCHERS (1993)

Starring: *Terry Kinney (Steve Malone), Meg Tilly (Carol Malone), Gabrielle Anwar (Marti Malone), Billy Wirth (Tim Young), Christine Elise (Jenn Platt)*
Director: *Abel Ferrara*
Screenwriters: *Stuart Gordon, Dennis Paoli, Nicholas St John, based on a screen story by Raymond Cishteri, Larry Cohen and the novel by Jack Finney.*
15/87 mins./Sci-fi/Horror/Thriller/Mystery/USA

With a slight variation on the usual story, an environmentalist is investigating toxic waste on an army base and it is left to his daughter to save the day from the evil aliens who victimise humans by ridding them of their 'essence' and taking over their bodies.

Addressing the universal personal and political fear that individuals or society can easily lose the essentials of humanity and become soulless 'pods', the body snatching concept is one of the great pop myths. Jack Finney's 1955 novel *The Body Snatchers* was famously filmed by Don Siegel in 1956 as *Invasion Of The Body Snatchers*, and again by Phil Kaufman in 1978. On the strength of the earlier versions and this 1993 reworking, it seems the scary story is a property which could usefully be redone every 15 years as long as films are made.

Sticking less to Finney's plot than the earlier films, Abel Ferrara's take on the story is set on an army base. Rather than a medical-scientific investigator hero, the protagonist is Marty (Anwar), teenage daughter of an Environment Protection Agency boffin who is investigating the storage of toxic materials in an army installation. The military setting, which has already imposed an uncomfortable degree of conformity on characters, is a bold stroke which increases the political resonance and allows for gung ho action with helicopters and missiles, including a marvellously ambiguous and hollow triumph at the finale.

On the assumption that the audience already knows the premise, *Body Snatchers* doesn't explain the alien invasion, it simply shows it with gloopily effective special effects. Ferrara, in a rare medium-budget excursion, shows he can make a smooth-looking, well-paced film, while his acute ear for character tensions deftly captures the untidy human emotions that the pods live without. The writing and acting are way above average for a sci-fi quickie: note how a 'truth' game between Anwar and soldier hero Billy Wirth sets up resonances that pay off throughout the film. ★★★★ **KN**

THE BODYGUARD (1992)

Starring: *Kevin Costner (Frank Farmer), Whitney Houston (Rachel 'Rach' Marron), Gary Kemp (Sy Spector), Bill Cobbs (Bill Devaney), Ralph Waite (Herb Farmer)*
Director: *Mick Jackson*
Screenwriter: *Lawrence Kasdan*
15/121 mins./Romance/Thriller/Mystery/Music/USA

Frank Farmer is hired as a bodyguard for international pop singer Rachel Marron, but soon finds himself falling for her.

Originally penned by Lawrence Kasdan for Steve McQueen back in the late 60s, this absurd piece of entertaining fluff passed through a number of hands over the last 25 years – at one stage nearly turning into yet another Madonna disaster – before ending up in the firm grip of one Kevin Costner and his merry men at TIG Productions. True to form, Costner insisted on the unlikely figure of Whitney Houston in the central diva role, opted for the unflattering *Presumed Innocent* crewcut, brought in a relatively low-profile director in L.A. Story's Mick Jackson, and – hey presto! – yet another enormous worldwide hit rolled out of the factory gates.

The story is, of course, preposterous. Top pop singer Rachel Marron receives death threats, reluctantly hires ace bodyguard Frank Farmer to look after her, singer meets bodyguard, bodyguard sleeps with singer, singer and bodyguard fall out, fall in again, go to a log cabin in the snow, go to the Oscars, and it all sort of ends happily ever after, except for Gary Kemp.

Along the route of this eminently predictable nonsense, however, a number of less obvious developments occur. Houston, for instance, is really rather excellent in her first movie role, entirely convincing as the bitch-cow-diva-from-hell-with-customary-heart-of-gold, and singing throughout with a voice that sounds as if it was manufactured some place close to heaven. Similarly, Costner is here less punchable than on recent outings, his customary weary air of resignation sitting well on this particular character's broad shoulders, while even the well-signposted ending, a tremendous exercise in movie cliché, still manages to stir the heart as the strains of the longest-running chart-topping ditty blast across the runway.

If that particular song, that particular image, tend to stick in the throat, then the whole thing is very likely not for you. If, on the other hand, you still find yourself humming along at the oddest moments, then *The Bodyguard* will have you laughing and crying into your takeaway. ★★★ **BMc**

THE BONE COLLECTOR (1999)

Starring: *Denzel Washington (Lincoln 'Linc' Rhyme), Angelina Jolie (Amelia Donaghy), Queen Latifah (Thelma), Michael Rooker (Captain Howard Cheney)*
Director: *Phillip Noyce*
Screenwriter: *Jeremy Iacone, based on the book by Jeffery Deaver*
15/118 mins./Mystery/Drama/Thriller/USA

Lincoln Rhyme is a bed-ridden forensic expert drafted in to solve a serial killer case. He takes on reluctant, able-bodied cop Amelia Donaghy to act as his 'legs on the ground' and together they start to see a horrific pattern in the murders.

The days when serial killer movies aspired to be *Silence Of The Lambs* or *Seven* are a distant memory; now there are films out there that would be happy to be compared with *Copycat, Kiss The Girls* or *The January Man*. To wit, *The Bone Collector* – which takes a couple of appealing stars, a half-way interesting premise and some of the shoddiest plotting ever attempted in a serious major studio picture, and comes up with an overlong, too-often giggly exercise in hunt-the-psycho.

Lincoln Rhyme, a hotshot New York police forensics expert, is paralysed after a beam falls on him at the scene of a crime. The weekend he finally persuades his doctor friend to assist his suicide when he gets back from holiday on Monday, his old colleagues come to him with a puzzling case. Unlikely cop Amelia Donaghy (Jolie), a child model-turned-beat-pounder, has come across a property developer buried in a railway yard, the flesh of his forefinger skinned away and a turn-of-the-century iron bolt lying significantly nearby in a pile of clues. Despite seizures that might leave him a vegetable, Rhyme gets on the case, manipulating his computer mouse with the forefinger that is his only moving part below the neck, and feeding the timorous Amelia instructions as she combs various subterranean, rat-infested, dripping holes where subsequent victims may or may not be still alive.

All you really need to know about the script, from a novel by Jeffery Deaver, is that it thinks 'Lincoln Rhyme' is a creditable character name, that you'll believe Angelina Jolie in uniform, that soap opera snippets ('My psychiatrist says you're not giving me what I want out of this relationship') are real dramatic depth, that a superfluity of clues makes for a real plot and that lone-chick-exploring-infernal-gloom scenes always work. Only the last proposition, demonstrated with the usual low-wattage torchlight and cascading water sounds, makes sense.

Phillip Noyce's *Dead Calm* established him as a master of the exciting thriller, but – too many dumb Hollywood pictures like *Patriot Games* and *The Saint* later – his credit has come to be a virtual guarantee of ordinariness, and *The Bone Collector* duly pays off with the the most sick-making, happy families/affirmative values final scene that's come along in many a month. Silly, but not quite demented enough to be much fun. ★★ **KN**

THE BONFIRE OF THE VANITIES (1990)

Starring: *Tom Hanks (Sherman McCoy), Bruce Willis (Peer Fallow), Melanie Griffith (Maria Ruskin), Kim Cattrall (Judy McCoy), Saul Rubinek (Jed Kramer), Morgan Freeman (Judge Leonard White)*
Director: *Brian De Palma*
Screenwriter: *Michael Cristofer, based on the novel by Tom Wolfe*
15/125 mins./Comedy/USA

Sherman McCoy, 'Master of the Universe' and his mistress take the wrong turn off the highway, end up in the wrong neighbourhood, and make the wrong move by scarpering after knocking over a black teenager. When tabloid hack Peter Fallow gets hold of the story, events spiral into a citywide scandal.

A cause célèbre of ignominiously huge proportions, a humbling tale of grand names undone by ego and faulty thinking, a debacle thick with controversy and misspent money: how the making of this adaptation of this most famous modern novel, echoes the satirical throes of the book itself. Shame, so little of it ended up in the actual movie. The glare of attention, where every one of poor Brian De Palma's decisions was run through the court of public opinion, proved too much – the result was an insipid comedy of manners, miscast, edgily directed and neutered of the novel's scabrous misanthropy. Tom Wolfe hooted with derision, how ironically apt.

People had complained of the choice of De Palma from the very beginning. Wasn't he a man for thrillers? More a Hitchcock than the Billy Wilder-type required. The naysayers, for once, were right. He is unable to set a tone for the piece, taking it way too deep into broad comedy; it borders on outright parody. The sting of the book was in the swollen realities of the 80s it was truffling up from Central Park. The casting doesn't help. Tom Hanks as a Master of the Universe, this Wall Street general plump on success and self-regard? He comes across as a foolish dolt out of his depth. How can we savour his undoing? He's one of us.

Bruce Willis as booze-sodden reporter Peter Fallow, merely the book's narrative catalyst, is granted too much room. He obliges by hamming it all up, doing an appalling drunk dodging the accent, and barely leaving a mark on the movie's surface.

The girls fare mildly better: Melanie Griffith, as the gold-digging mistress is all bust and bubblehead, while Kim Cattrall is deliciously icy as Wolfe's 'Social X-Ray', the designer draped skeletons who ruled over Park Avenue. But the burble of the plot, which amplifies into a cacophony of bellowing sides by the courtroom finale, has nothing to offer them.

Sure, De Palma fills it with his inventive camera trickery, including taking us on a 14-minute tracking shot through an entire building, but the film wasn't in need of visual fillips, it needed an edge. By the whitewashed finale, missing the whole point by a country mile, the game is truly up. A bonfire, indeed, in all but flame. ★★ **IN**

BONNIE AND CLYDE (1967)

Starring: *Warren Beatty (Clyde Barrow), Faye Dunaway (Bonnie Parker), Gene Hackman (Buck Barrow), Michael J. Pollard (C.W. Moss), Estelle Parsons (Blanche), Gene Wilder (Eugene Grizzard)*
Director: *Arthur Penn*
Screenwriters: *David Newman, Robert Benton*
18/111 mins./Crime/USA

Awards: *Academy Awards – Best Actress in a Supporting Role (Estelle Parsons), Best Cinematography, BAFTA – Most Promising Newcomer Female (Faye Dunaway) Most Promising Newcomer Male (Michael J. Pollard)*

A young couple go on a killing spree during the American Depression.

Given that Arthur Penn's gorgeously photographed, ecstatically bloody folk tale hit the screens in an era when the previous milestone in movie violence was Jimmy Cagney squashing a grapefruit into a broad's face, the furore that *Bonnie And Clyde* stirred up among critics and public alike is easily appreciated. Ironically though, if studio head Jark Warner had had his way, it would not have caused a ripple. Warner, over whose latter day stable of screen hoods Cagney reigned supreme, hated the film so much he attempted to bury it in a chain of Texas drive-ins. And Warner, a studio system dinosaur whose fate was sealed the moment *Bonnie And Clyde* went into production was not alone. Typical of the old guard's reaction to the film was the legendary panning it received from *New York Times* critic Bosley Crowther after it premiered at the 1967 Montreal Film Festival. And with every Crowther acolyte across America following the old blowhard's lead, an early bath was assured.

It opened in a handful of theatres in the autumn of 1967 and closed before Christmas. But the producer-star Beatty, who had allegedly gone down on his knees himself before the Warner brass – even, it's said, calling their bluff with an outrageously ambitious offer to buy the rights out of his own pocket – begging them to give it another chance. No doubt the film's ignominious demise put the dent in his notorious ego, but he was also well aware of which way the wind was blowing. The soundtrack album, featuring banjo pickers Flatt and Scruggs, has already become a hit and Faye Dunaway's beret and maxi-skirt look had sparked an international vogue for depression-era chic. Most significantly though, *Newsweek* critic Joseph Morgenstern took the unprecedented step of admitting that his original review was completely wrong and publishing a revised version praising the film to the skies.

In the end, *Bonnie And Clyde* re-opened. It became one of Warner Brothers biggest ever money-spinners and earned itself 10 Oscar nominations (it won two: Estelle Parsons for Best Supporting Actress and Burnett Guffey for Best Cinematography). In the process, of course, it turned the entire American movie industry on its head.

Naturally, the violence in *Bonnie And Clyde* was a sizeable bone of contention. But what really divided audiences was its moral ambiguity – its glamorising of two vicious killers and the easy manner in which it blended slapstick humour, overt eroticism and vivid bloodletting.

To the section of society that had choked on its collective martini over *Guess Who's Coming To Dinner*, it was the final nail in the coffin of common decency. To another, busy tuning in, turning in and dropping out, the anti-establishment image of two outlaw lovers on the run struck a resounding chord. The scene in which a cocksure Clyde offers his gun to a poor black sharecropper so he can shoot holes in the foreclosure sign erected by the bank that has evicted him, encapsulates the mood of the film perfectly. The criminal-as-folk-hero has been a theme intrinsic to American cinema ever since, and the Barrow gang's whole, dizzy crime spree is a defiant finger to the forces of law and order.

What distinguishes *Bonnie And Clyde* from the later slew of movies celebrating nonconformity – *Easy Rider* et al – is that alongside the life-affirming thrill they get from thumbing their noses at the law, both Bonnie and Clyde know that ultimately their fate is to die a violent death. This certainty haunts the film, and the moments where it bursts in on the gang's devil-may-care attitude are painful and sad. In one high-spirited sequence the outlaws have some fun by taking the nervy Eugene Grizzard (Gene Wilder in his first big screen role) for a ride. The scene is hilarious, with Wilder in top near-hysteria form, but it turns instantly dark when Bonnie learns that he is an undertaker and they kick him out of the car. Another beautifully shot, achingly melancholy set-piece is the one in which Bonnie, now a celebrity outlaw, goes home to visit her mother. With the light diffused by the swirling dust bowl, she talks about marrying Clyde and settling down close to her family. But she's fantasising about a future she knows she doesn't have. And her mother knows it too. 'You live within a mile of me, honey, and you'll be dead,' she says, and the flat, weary sadness in her voice is her daughter's death knell.

Tagline

They're young … they're in love … and they kill people.

The point where time finally runs out for *Bonnie and Clyde* is one of the most shocking and memorable death scenes in the history of cinema. And the horrifically prolonged hail of bullets pummelling their bodies, which writhe obscenely long after the life has left them, is probably closer to the truth than anything else in the film. Overall it's a romanticised, revisionist picture, and even in the finale Penn can't resist ramming his point home with iconic slow motion. But in reality, Bonnie Parker and Clyde Barrow were ambushed by police near Arcadia, Louisiana, in late May, 1934 and lawmen fired so many rounds into their car that Barrow's shirt was cut in half. Later, crowds paid to see their mutilated corpses in the morgue.

For better or worse, American cinema changed forever the day *Bonnie And Clyde* was released. Almost every aspect of it was revolutionary: the debt to the French New Wave (it was offered to Truffaut before Penn); the championing of the anti-hero; the free-wheeling camera work and cinematography; the use of unknown stage actors in supporting roles; and, of course, the painfully rendered violence, all were enormously influential. Even Beatty's – some say grudging – agreement to portray Barrow as impotent was a brave move; for a romantic leading man of his stature to play a sexually dysfunctional character was absolutely unheard of. Critic Patrick Goldstein has called it 'the first modern American film'. Anyone remember what Bosley Crowther called it? ★★★★★ **SB**

⦿ BOOGIE NIGHTS (1997)

Starring: *Mark Wahlberg (Eddie Adams/Dirk Diggler), Burt Reynolds (Jack Horner), John C. Reilly (Reed Rothchild), Julianne Moore (Amber Waves), Heather Graham (Rollergirl), Philip Seymour Hoffman (Scotty J.), Don Cheadle (Buck Swope), William H. Macy (Little Bill)*
Director: *Paul Thomas Anderson*
Screenwriter: *Paul Thomas Anderson*
18/156 mins./Drama/USA
Awards: *Golden Globes – Best Supporting Actor (Burt Reynolds)*

The rise and fall of porn-star Dirk Diggler, his sizeable schlong and the 70s sex industry itself.

'To get 'em in the theatre you've got to have big tits and big dicks and they don't want to spurt joy in the first five minutes,' says porn director Jack Horner (a compelling Reynolds, who, bizarrely distanced himself from this project) explaining why his porno films, first made on film and then on the cheaper videotape, were a prolific success.

Beginning in 1977 and ending in '84, Anderson's follow-up to the *Hard Eight* traces the life of Eddie Adams the small town boy with a very big bean-pole, and his odyssey to the priapic-obsessed San Fernando Valley, detailing his evolution from pot washer and occasional exhibitionist to porn pin-up Dirk Diggler, a character inspired by famed giant-dicked pornster John Holmes.

Ex-rap star and former Calvin Klein philanthropist Marky Mark (previously known as cheeky 'n' cocky, now simply as Mr Wahlberg), though noticeable in *Fear*, has metamorphosed into something much more impressive here. And Moore lends substantial support as his porn co-star Amber Waves, at once surreally mothering him while gently suggesting he should 'try and cum on my stomach and tits'.

There are memorable set-pieces: the behind-the-scenes portrayal of a porn shoot – where the nervous Diggler is desperate to please; an unhinged William H. Macy (as crew member Little Bill) trailing through a poolside party (cocaine, cocaine everywhere, and not a nasal hair intact) while his wife is being rigorously pumped by some unknown stud in full view of everyone.

With films such as Ang Lee's *The Ice Storm* settling on a 70s milieu – oil crisis-era styling is suddenly hip, and with the flared hipsters, boob tubes, crimped hair and incandescent make-up of the porn ingenues, this is a spot-on visual evocation of the time. Even down to the music. But Anderson doesn't blow it all on style over content: while Milos Forman's *The People Vs. Larry Flynt* (which dealt with similar subject matter) looked good but didn't sound right, this develops cleverly and offers more of an eviscerating full frontal – you do see Dirk Diggler's 13-inch thwacker, rather unnecessarily in fact. Anderson delivers full-on hedonism and then makes you wrestle with what is an unsanctimonious hangover.

Boogie Nights nearly allows itself damned brilliance but tries too hard as it falls prey to an excessive running time, burdening itself with some largely unnecessary subplots and scenes – one of which misfires as a faltering love letter to Tarantino. ★★★★ **AS**

⦿ BOOK OF SHADOWS: BLAIR WITCH 2 (2000)

Starring: *Kim Director (Kim Diamond), Jeffrey Donovan (Jeffrey Patterson), Erica Leerhsen (Erica Geerson), Tristine Skyler (Tristen Ryler), Stephen Barker Turner (Stephen Ryan Parker)*
Director: *Joe Berlinger*
Screenwriters: *Dick Beebe, Joe Berlinger, from characters by Daniel Myrick, Eduardo Sanchez*
15/90 mins./Horror/Thriller/USA

One year on from the original, five young people venture into the Black Hills to further explore the legend and visit the sites made famous by the film. Led by Jeff Patterson and helped along by beer and dope, things soon get out of hand.

While it would be difficult to match the media mayhem that surrounded the release of *The Blair Witch Project* (1999), it's fair to say that *Book Of Shadows* was one of the more eagerly awaited sequels of 2000.

As co-writer/director Berlinger has acknowledged, satisfying both fans and critics of the original was never going to be easy, not least since the production had to be squeezed into an extremely tight schedule to meet the simultaneous US/UK Halloween release date. Sadly, that *Blair Witch 2* is something of a rush job is all too evident in the resulting film.

Eschewing the 'shakycam' technique that nauseated so many cinemagoers first time around, Berlinger wisely chose to go his own way, fusing genuine TV footage with documentary-style interviews and more 'conventional' techniques. The first 20 minutes are very strong, developing the is-it-real-or-is-it-pretend? theme of the first film by recapping on the furore surrounding TBWP in a montage of real clips and interviews with so-called Burkittsville locals, the sequence shot through with a dry humour that niftily pokes fun at the phenomenon. So far so good.

The director maintains the pace as he slips into the main plot of the film – and fans of gore who felt let down by the original can rest assured that the blood and guts quotient is suitably high. In look it's all very slick, and Berlinger at times evokes the haunting beauty of Sanchez and Myrick's original film, bleaching most of the colour from the film to sinister effect.

What lets it all down is a deeply confused plot and an, at times, embarrassingly cheesy script. Once the group have decamped to Jeff's spooky warehouse lair it's as if the writers feel the need to increasingly rely on schlock tactics and lame surprises to liven up an increasingly dull story. Interesting themes are touched upon – collective illusion, group hysteria and society's persecution of the loner – but they are not developed, Berlinger instead opting for a hackneyed possession sub-plot, and a series of clumsy non-sequiters that suggests the witch can change what's been filmed (yes, you get to see the witch this time), but never really explains what her motivation might be.

The whole enterprise starts to feel amateurish, finally grinding to an abrupt conclusion, as if the filmmakers themselves have run out of ideas and enthusiasm. But while the actors gamely give it their all, it is disappointing that a film with so much potential has apparently been sacrificed to the demands of the marketing department. ★★ **LB**

BORN ON THE FOURTH OF JULY (1989)

Starring: *Tom Cruise (Ron Kovic), Bryan Larkin (Young Ron), Raymond J. Barry (Mr Kovic), Caroline Kava (Mrs Kovic), Josh Evans (Tommy Kovic), Sean Stone (Young Jimmy), Anne Bobby (Susanne Kovic), Jenna von Oy (Young Susanne)*
Director: *Oliver Stone*
Screenwriters: *Oliver Stone, Ron Kovic, based on Ron Kovic's autobiography*
18/140 mins./Drama/War/USA

Awards: *Academy Awards – Best Director, Best Editing, Golden Globes – Best Director, Best Picture, Best Drama Actor, Best Screenplay*

The second film in Oliver Stone's Vietnam trilogy sees Ron Kovic, a patriotic young American, reduced to life in a wheelchair by a sniper bullet. Initially wallowing in his physical and mental impotence – he drinks, he fights, he uses prostitutes – Ron recovers his energies and makes his way to the front of the Anti-War movement.

Marine Ron lets go another round at the hidden Viet Cong snipers, an unshakeable belief in his own invincibility evident in his every action, fanatical pride in his corps and country driving him on over the brink. Suddenly, the entire beat of the action switches from observing this foolhardy act to a position inside Kovic as the fateful bullet rips through his spinal cord. Ever so slowly you arc up and over with him, collapsed onto the ground in a crumpled heap, the final thud bringing the blood up from the lungs and out through the mouth. It is a sickening, brutal, wholly unforgettable moment and just one of many that linger long after *Born On The Fourth Of July* has run its epic course.

The true story of Vietnam veteran Ron Kovic, originally told in his 1976 book *Born On The Fourth Of July*, could have easily lost its impact on the screen, reduced to the unfortunate plight of an unlucky whinger who bit off more than he could chew. Instead, it translates quite magnificently into a thoroughly moving tale of one man's extraordinary life, depicting the awful sense of impotence that comes with a young body trapped in a wheelchair while all the time supplying the fascinating backdrop of three of the most turbulent decades in American history.

And then there is Tom Cruise. Impressive enough in the fairly traditional role of the all-American boy preparing himself for glory, he is literally unrecognisable as the postwar paraplegic, displaying a depth and range never previously even hinted at in a remarkable performance that immediately lifts him out of his previous cheesecake category and places him smack at the front of a whole generation of American actors. The scene in which he rips out his catheter to rage against a wholly redundant penis, while his mother looks on suitably aghast, is at once deeply affecting and barely watchable, while the tears streaming down his face as he finally finds some sort of desperate comfort in a Mexican brothel have already been shared by audiences throughout America. Willem Dafoe supplies strong support, but this is Cruise's movie, wheeling around like a madman, looking like a thinner David Crosby and barking at the world for reducing him to this sorry state. The closest parallel would be Daniel Day Lewis in *My Left Foot*, a fair indication of the quality of work on display here.

The gradual politicisation of this former gung-ho patriot is less skilfully handled by Stone, with no real explanation of why exactly Cruise switches tack so dramatically. The film is overlong and overwrought and there is also a distinct sense of having travelled some of these paths before, via *The Deer Hunter* (early hometown scenes), *Coming Home* (vet in a wheelchair) and, of course, this director's own *Platoon*. And yet in a film this big, none of these flaws seem to add up to a hill of beans. Few 'Nam movies had covered so much ground with such aplomb, fewer still have packed such a punch to the heart. ★★★★ **AE**

BORN ROMANTIC (2000)

Starring: *Craig Ferguson (Frankie), Ian Hart (Second Cab Driver), Jane Horrocks (Mo), Adrian Lester (Jimmy), Catherine McCormack (Jocelyn), Jimi Mistry (Eddie), David Morrissey (Fergus), Olivia Williams (Eleanor), Kenneth Cranham (Barney), John Thomspson (First Cab Driver), Paddy Considine (Ray), Hermione Norris (Carolanne), Sally Phillips (Suzy), Jessica Stevenson (Libby)*
Director: *David Kane*
Screenwriter: *David Kane*
15/96 mins/Comedy/UK

Six lonely thirtysomethings search for love in London, their courtships played out against the backdrop of a salsa club. Meanwhile, minicab driver Jimmy quietly watches their romantic drama unfold from the driver's seat.

From the writer-director of 1999's *This Year's Love* comes this equally lightweight but enjoyable confection, again focusing on the romantic trials and tribulations of that most unfortunate of creatures – the thirtysomething single Londoner. Echoing the structure of his first film, Kane tracks six largely unconnected characters whose lives, in fatalistic manner, overlap, this time thanks to the twin poles of their existence – a salsa club and the local minicab firm (Kismet Cabs, named after the film's production company), which ferries them from one drama to the next.

Refreshingly, Kane's female characters make more of an impression –

icy Eleanor, frumpy freak Jocelyn (an unrecognisable McCormack) and Mo, who covers up devastating betrayal by sleeping with any man who'll have her. Vying for their affections are love rat Fergus, the dapper Frankie and Eddie, a would-be criminal played with disarming charm by *East Is East*'s Mistry. Meanwhile, pulling this dysfunctional crew together is minicab driver Jimmy, quietly fighting his own heartbreak.

Underscored with a gentle, almost whimsical humour – thanks largely to minicab drivers Hart and Thomson, whose pseudo-philosophical musings on women and relationships punctuate the main drama – yet suitably gritty, *Born Romantic* will no doubt appeal to the legions of *Cold Feet* fans who are missing their weekly fix (as well as Thomson, look out for *Cold Feet*'s Hermione Norris as, coincidentally, an embittered ex-wife).

But herein, to an extent, lies the problem, as Kane's film fails to measure up to the high standards set by recent TV forays into the same themes. The limitations of the running time – 96 minutes to develop three complicated relationships isn't long – means empathy is correspondingly limited. Yes, there are laughs, but *Born Romantic* isn't quite as funny or endearing as it would like to be, and while this prevents a descent into sentiment, it makes the action less involving than you would hope. ★★★ **LB**

BORN YESTERDAY (1950)

Starring: *Judy Holliday (Billie Dawn), Broderick Crawford (Harry Brock), William Holden (Paul Verrall), Howard St John (Jim Devery), Frank Otto (Eddie)*
Director: *George Cukor*
Screenwriter: *Albert Mannheimer, based on the play by Garson Kanin*
U/103 mins./Comedy/USA

Awards: *Academy Awards – Best Actress*

Embarrassed by the ignorance of his moll, Billie Dawn, crooked junk tycoon Harry Brock hires Paul Verall to give her a crash course in culture and etiquette. But, in the process, she learns to think for herself.

George Cukor was renowned for his ability to coax career-best performances out of Hollywood's star actresses. Yet, he seems to have been overawed by the reputation that Judy Holliday forged in Garson Kanin's stage show, as he allows her to play Billie Dawn pretty much as she had on Broadway. Shooting in long takes to accommodate the debutant's familiarity with the role, Cukor permits her to retain many theatrical traits that seem too calculated for the screen. A little advice on playing to the camera rather than the circle might have made what is an already enchanting turn all the more accomplished.

Yet, Holliday very nearly didn't get to repeat her triumph at all, as Columbia boss Harry Cohn spent four years trying to find a bigger name to carry the movie version. He did succeed, however, in replacing Paul Douglas with Broderick Crawford, who was hot off the back of his Oscar victory for *All The King's Men*, and there's more than a little Willie Stark in his portrayal of Harry Brock, a seemingly buffoonish character who proves to have a resistibly ruthless streak.

This is essentially a *Pygmalion* story, in which a brassy ex-chorine is taught how to harness her intuitive smartness to America's founding principles. Thus, Billie is as much a Capra character as a screwball heroine and there's a subtle difference between her twisted logic and that of the dumb blondes later played by the likes of Marilyn Monroe.

But, unfortunately, the empowered Billie is nowhere near as interesting as the word-mangling innocent and the action loses much of its zip once she comes to realise that there's more to life than being a kept woman. That said, it's only when she falls in love with Paul that she begins to appreciate what he is teaching her. Thus, she merely replaces the influence of one dominant male with another rather than becoming fully emancipated. ★★★ **DP**

BOTTLE ROCKET (1996)

Starring: *Luke Wilson (Anthony Adams), Owen C. Wilson (Dignan), Ned Dowd (Dr Nichols), Shea Fowler (Grace), Haley Miller (Bernice), Robert Musgrave (Bob Maplethorpe), Andrew Wilson (John Mapplethorpe – 'Future Man')*
Director: *Wes Anderson*
Screenwriters: *Wes Anderson, Owen C. Wilson*
15/92 mins./Comedy/Crime/USA

Alienated rich boy Anthony Adams pretends to escape from the mental home to which he has voluntarily committed himself, to join his hyperactive best friend Dignan in a career of crime that begins with burgling his parents' home. The third man on the team is Bob Maplethorpe, an even richer kid who is bullied by his jock brother 'Future Man' and gets to be the getaway driver on the grounds that he's the only one who has a car.

A smart little first feature from Wes Anderson, made in collaboration with writer-star Owen C. Wilson (and several Wilson brothers). In an era not exactly short of quirky bungled heist movies, Anderson and Wilson take an interesting tack – coming in late on lifelong relationships, and showing us the pay-offs to friendships and resentments that have been simmering for years: note the scene as Dignan tries to explain his detailed scheme while Maplethorpe just wants to play with the guns bought with his money and Adams has to equivocate between the two.

James Caan pops up late, in a wry, tough guy role as a shady character who rips the kids off but is still a better parent than the other nonentities – telling Future Man off at a country club for picking on Bob, dishing out double-edged advice. The Wilsons in the leads play perfectly, with slightly goofy grins and a real sense of oddball friendship: Adams holds himself back a little because he knows where Dignan will drag him, while Dignan is really really trying (too hard) not to screw up this time, and a lot of the script has the ring of authenticity if only because all the private jokes and references that pass by are plainly embedded in the real lives of the creators. ★★★★ **KN**

BOUDO SAUVE DES EAUX (BOUDU SAVED FROM DROWNING) (1932)

Starring: *Michel Simon (Boudo), Charles Granval (Monsieur Lestingois), Marcelle Hainla (Mme Lestingois), Severine Lerczynska (Anna-Marie), Jean Daste (Student)*
Director: *Jean Renoir*
Screenwriter: *Jean Renoir, based on the play by René Fauchois*
PG/84 mins./Comedy/France

Suicidal hobo Priapus Boudu is rescued from the Seine by affable bookseller Edouard Lestingois, who allows him to remain as his guest even after he seduces both his prudish wife, Emma, and his uppity maid, Anne-Marie.

Bouyed by the reception of *La Chienne*, Jean Renoir and Michel Simon reteamed on this adaptation of René Fauchois' boulevard comedy, in which Simon had starred on stage in 1925. Always a fan of Charlie Chaplin's *Tramp*, Renoir was keen to explore how an inveterate vagabond would respond to traditional bourgeois values. But while the intention was clearly satirical, this is not the declaration of class warfare that some critics have claimed.

Charles Grandval plays Lestingois as a thoroughly decent idealist, with a reverence for culture and a genial humanism that inspires him to seek the best for Boudu, even when he's at his most boorish. Indeed, this is a classic example of Renoir's pet theory that everyone has reasons for their actions and he resolutely refuses to judge, either the Lestingois's affectations or Boudu's inability to come to terms with an entirely alien lifestyle.

Renoir slyly suggests how easy it is to be seduced by comfort, but he is much more interested in celebrating non-conformism than condemning middle-class cosiness – hence Fauchois's hearty disapproval of Renoir changing the ending to allow Boudu to resume his life as a child of nature. Perhaps he would have been better disposed towards Paul Mazursky's remake, *Down And Out In Beverly Hills* (1986), which panders to American audiences by reducing the characters to more obviously recognisable anti-heroes and villains.

A vein of Greek mythology runs through Boudu. But there's nothing fantastical about the location shooting, which uses long, fluid, deep-focused takes to capture the flavour of both the Seine around the Pont des Artes and the Marne countryside. Looking out on to the neighbouring rooftops, the Lestingois apartment similarly feels like the scene of real life and this contextualising of the household within its milieu adds authenticity to Renoir's wry observations on contemporary society. ★★★★ **DP**

BOUND (1996)

Starring: *Jennifer Tilly (Violet), Gina Gershon (Corky), Joe Pantoliano (Caesar), John P. Ryan (Mickey Malanto), Christopher Meloni (Johnny Marconi)*
Directors: *Larry Wachowski, Andy Wachowski*
Screenwriters: *Larry Wachowski, Andy Wachowski*
18/104 mins./Crime/Thriller/USA

Corky, a tough female ex-con and her lover Violet concoct a scheme to steal millions of stashed mob money and pin the blame on Violet's crooked boyfriend Caesar.

This has exactly the plot that served in such films noirs as *Out Of The Dark* and *Angel Face*. And Jennifer Tilly, with her oriental eyes, Monroe voice, purple lipstick and sheath dresses, is a perfect modern equivalent for the man-traps who used to be played by Barbara Stanwyck, Jane Greer or Jean Simmons.

The radical stroke of Bound, however, is that the part that would have once gone to Robert Mitchum is here taken by Gina Gershon. Tattooed, leather-jacketed and smiling crookedly, Gershon may be the first unapologetically gay lead in what is essentially a commercial thriller rather than niche market arthouse erotica.

Though there's one sax-worthy sex scene, this cannily plays down top shelf writhings in favour of complex relationships and tightly scripted suspense. Corky, a heist woman, and Violet are bystanders when Violet's boyfriend Caesar has to launder (literally) two million dollars in bloody cash reclaimed from an unwise ex-Mafioso who tried to rip off the family.

Between them, they cook up a scheme to grab the money and get out of town. Lovingly designed in black and white, and played with a nice sense of irony, this offers the not unappealing spectacle of gorgeous, funny, clever women making fools of hard-boiled Mafia guys.

It works perfectly as a *Blood Simple*-style retro thriller, and was an early hint that the writing-directing team of the Brothers Wachowski would be names to watch. ★★★★ **KN**

BOUND AND GAGGED: A LOVE STORY (1992)

Starring: *Ginger Lynn Allen (Leslie), Karen Black (Carla), Chris Denton (Cliff), Elizabeth Saltarrelli (Elizabeth), Mary Ella Ross (Lida), Chris Mulkey (Steve)*
Director: *Daniel B. Appleby*
Screenwriter: *Daniel B. Appleby*
18/94 mins./Drama/USA

Free-spirited lesbian Elizabeth decides her two closest friends need extricating from destructive relationships: beer buddy Cliff has just bungled a suicide attempt after some serious, mainly sexual humiliation at the hands of his faithless wife, while housewife Leslie, her occasional lover, keeps crawling back to her bullying thug husband Steve. A kidnapping and road trip ensue.

In a fairly low-key way, *Bound And Gagged* hits a lot of bases, taking a road movie trip across country with the bandaged Cliff whinging like Stan Laurel as the ever-more-manic Elizabeth resorts to more and more severe stratagems to keep the object of her affections under her complete control.

Especially in Mulkey's evil husband character, the spectres of *Thelma And Louise* seem to haunt this highway, while the literal bondage-of-love plot echoes Pedro Almodovar's *Tie Me Up! Tie Me Down!*.

The results are a little too familiar for their own good, especially since writer-director Daniel Appleby would obviously like to be considered quirky and original even as he combines family value violence and free-spirited escaping into the heartland.

There are the usual cameo oddballs and frustrated escape attempts, tastelessly typified by the passer-by who notices the tied-up Leslie's pleas for help and attempts to molest her. The comedy interludes about adultery and suicide are somewhat bungled, but the performances – of the subsequently underused Saltarrelli and 'adult' veteran Ginger Lynn Allen, especially – are peppy enough to get the vehicle through the rutted terrain and over the bumpy plot stretches. ★★ **KN**

THE BOUNTY (1984)

Starring: *Mel Gibson (Fletcher Christian), Anthony Hopkins (William Bligh), Laurence Olivier (Admiral Hood), Edward Fox (Captain Greetham), Bernard Hill (William Cole), Liam Neeson (Charles Churchill), Daniel Day-Lewis (John Fryer)*
Director: *Roger Donaldson*
Screenwriter: *Robert Bolt, based on the book by Richard Hough*
15/132 mins./History/Drama/UK/USA

The legendary tale of William Bligh, whose cruelty forced his crew, led by his first mate Fletcher Christian, to mutiny and cast their overthrown leader, and those loyal to him, adrift in the Pacific. As Christian evades British retribution, Bligh begins an epic voyage to take his tiny boat to some kind of safety.

With David Lean overcome by ill health and creative prevarication, Robert Bolt's script, a third retelling of the true-tale of Mutineers on the triple-rigged ship The Bounty, fell into the disappointingly serviceable hands of Roger Donaldson. The result is what you might expect given the ingredients, an impressively researched, speculated and psychologically evaluated script solidly handled by a director without the visual gifts to take it quite where Lean might have.

Certainly, the film takes a more even hand with a story made straightforwardly Hollywood by two previous adaptations in 1935 and 1962. For instance, William Bligh was never a captain, his humble origins prevented it and such precision provokes issues of class resentment between Anthony Hopkins' complicated Bligh and Mel Gibson's Christian, an upper-class dilettante, driven less by reason than a sensual self-purpose. Their conflict, the absolute heart of the story, is not one of innate good versus the crushing effects of abused power, but one of two diverging viewpoints between former friends.

An intense Hopkins grasps Bligh's immediate dichotomy: a repressed and inflexible man disposed to rash bouts of temper, but at the same time a brilliant seaman aware that necessity can outpace decency. His devotion to Queen and country, the strict guidance of his orders, also reveals Bolt's familiar themes of imperialistic civilisation versus native disorder. Gibson, in one of his best performances, interprets Christian not as natural leader but a fool to the moment, his love of a Tahiti princess one of his guiding motives. And unusually the script goes on to compare the subsequent effects of the mutiny as Christian's earthly paradise breaks down through disease and lack of leadership, while Bligh finds his way, by some miracle, to safety and the Admiralty.

Such quality and intelligence, however, is undermined by Donaldson's rather measured technique. His film is elegant but never beautiful, a pretence at Lean's magnificence contradicted by a lavish but anachronistic Vangelis score. It is the words and performances, including a crew of soon-to-be famous British actors, which excite; their director is out of his depth. ★★★ IN

THE BOURNE IDENTITY (2002)

Starring: *Matt Damon (Jason Bourne), Frank Potente (Marie), Chris Cooper (Conklin), Clive Owen (The Professor), Brian Cox (Ward Abbott), Adewale Akinnuoye-Agbaje (Wombosi), Gabriel Mann (Zorn), Julia Stiles (Nicholette)*
Director: *Doug Liman*
Screenwriter: *Blake Herron, based on the novel by Robert Ludlum*
12A/113 mins./Thriller/USA/Czech Republic

A bullet-ridden amnesiac is rescued from drowning by a fishing trawler, only to find himself the unwitting target of enemies. Is he really the ruthless assassin they think he is? And will he even live long enough to figure it out?

With a two-year shooting schedule, a script that was redrafted more times than the cast care to remember, and Matt Damon making at least two movies (*Ocean's 11* and *Spirit*) in the middle of all that mess, this thriller comes to the cinemas as much a marked man as its central character. Some of the joins do show, especially towards the end of the film, when a couple of minor characters disappear completely, but by then it has been too much fun to start picking holes.

From the moment Jason Bourne discovers his true powers – taking out in blistering style two cops who accuse him of loitering – a new hero is created. Damon plays Bourne as a man of cat-like instinct; he can make a weapon out of a fountain pen and sense danger at the most innocent of signals.

On the run across Europe with beatnik Potente, his quest to find himself becomes more involving since he is the opposite in nature to his physical appearance. This blue-eyed, innocent-looking American wants to be just that – and yet, much to his horror, he can't help using calculated efficiency to dispose of anyone who represents a challenge to him.

Doug Liman (*Swingers*, *Go*) seemed an unlikely choice as an action director, but his hand-held camera style and the improvisational work he does with actors clearly paid dividends here. However ridiculous the situation (and there are some extremely ridiculous situations), he maintains an air of heightened realism about his treatment of Bourne's predicament.

Pumped-up sound effects add to the gruesomeness of the fight sequences. Listen for that moment when the pen is pulled out of a would-be assailant's hand – it's a beaut! ★★★★ EC

THE BOURNE SUPREMACY (2004)

Starring: *Matt Damon (Jason Bourne), Franka Potente (Marie Kreutz), Brian Cox (Ward Abbott), Julia Stiles (Nicolette), Karl Urgan (Kirill), Gabriel Mann (Danny Zorn), Joan Allen (Pamela Landy)*
Director: *Paul Greengrass*
Screenwriter: *Tony Gilroy, based on the novel by Robert Ludlum*
12/120 mins./Action/Thriller/USA

Awards: *Empire – Best Actor, Best Film*

Since the events of *The Bourne Identity*, amnesiac former CIA hit man Jason Bourne has been living under the radar and off the map. But, his violent, covert past catches up with him, so, instead of running, he decides to take the fight to them.

Who'd have thought it? While James Bond was undergoing constant reinvention, little Tommy Cruise was gallivanting about on *Missions: Impossible*, and Vin Diesel was boasting that *xXx* was da bomb, the spy franchise to beat them all went about its business quietly – rather like its hero. *The Bourne Identity* was a welcome surprise, a captivating, twisting thriller with (gasp) an interesting lead character. *The Bourne Supremacy* builds on and exceeds the original, delivering, quite simply, one of the finest big-budget thrillers in years.

Not that you'd ever notice the budget – this is in many ways an anti-blockbuster. There are stunts here, fight scenes and car crashes there (with the final crunching pursuit through and under the streets of Moscow vying for a spot in the cinematic auto-wreck Top Ten), but no glib one-liners, no pat love interests and none of the CG-augmented new laws of physics that Hollywood loves so much.

There's never a sense that director Paul Greengrass and returning screenwriter Tony Gilroy are ticking off boxes; instead, Greengrass, building on both the promise and aesthetic of *Bloody Sunday*, revitalises standard action licks with Tommy-gun editing and constantly whipping cameras. Fans of *24* will love it.

Storywise, we're not in corkscrewing, M:I territory here. In fact, the plot runs out of steam well before the end, allowing Greengrass to explore – and inflict – the emotional trauma suffered by Bourne. And so we end as we began, not with a bang, but with a quiet moment of vulnerable, and genuinely touching, reflection for an already exposed hero.

It's a risky strategy for an 'action' movie, but happily it works thanks to Matt Damon's astute, underplayed performance, through which he totally eschews movie star vanity (and that toothy grin) to stand close-cropped head and shoulders above a strong cast. Damon's Bourne is cold yet not emotionless, lethal yet not invincible – a very human hero, racked by emotional and physical pain. It's a brave performance and, by the end, there will be few who won't want to see Bourne on the run again soon in *The Bourne Ultimatum*. ★★★★ CH

BOWFINGER (1999)

Starring: *Steve Martin (Bobby Bowfinger), Eddie Murphy (Kit Ramsey/Jiffernson 'Jiff' Ramsey), Heather Graham (Daisy), Christine Baranski (Carol), Jamie Kennedy (Dave), Terence Stamp (Terry Stricter), Robert Downey Jr (Jerry Renfro)*
Director: *Frank Oz*
Screenwriter: *Steve Martin*
12/97 mins./Comedy/USA

Kid row filmmaker Bobby Bowfinger must sign reluctant megastar Kit Ramsey in order to get his latest project off the ground but who needs the real Kit when you can use a perfectly good look-a-like?

He may be regarded as one of the world's funniest laughter merchants, but there's no denying that Steve Martin's movie career has been on the downswing of late. Aside from a superb, against-type role in *The Spanish Prisoner*, a dearth of decent movies since 1991's *LA Story* have left him floundering. So it's something of a relief that *Bowfinger*, a Martin-penned poke at the film industry, is such a splendidly funny piece of work.

When small-time director Bobby Bowfinger asks Hollywood's hottest agent to give his latest movie a shot, the answer is yes – provided he can sign action star Kit Ramsey in the lead. For the opportunistic Bowfinger, the small matter of Ramsey turning down the script (a dismal sci-fi horror epic entitled *Chubby Rain*) doesn't pose a problem. Hiring Kit lookalike Jiff (Murphy, in a dual role), a nerd who couldn't punch his way through a damp paper bag, Bowfinger scrapes together a motley cast, led by fading diva Carol and fresh-faced ingénue Daisy who's not averse to sleeping her way through the crew. He then launches an elaborate scheme to snare the paranoid Ramsey, thanks to concealed cameras and his cast interacting with him at key moments.

It's a wildly original idea and one that could have failed dismally, but Oz builds up the comedy gradually rather than going for all out mirth in the first half. By the time Murphy mark II appears, the action has switched into high gear, unleashing a string of frenetic set-pieces (Kit's involvement in a

Scientology-like cult, Jiff's hysterical attempts to cross the LA freeway) and allowing the cast to enjoy themselves immensely. And even if it gets a bit too ridiculous at times, and its take on Hollywood is just a little too cynical for its own good, *Bowfinger* still provides a refreshing antidote to the formulaic studio comedies of late. ★★★ **EC**

BOWLING FOR COLUMBINE (2002)

Starring: *as themselves: Michael Moore, Charlton Heston, Marilyn Manson, Dick Clark, James Nichols, Matt Stone, Barry Glassner, Richard Castaldo*
Director: *Michael Moore*
Screenwriter: *Michael Moore*
15/119 mins./Documentary/US/Germany/Canada

Awards: *Academy Awards – Best Documentary*

Sparked into action by the shootings at Columbine High School, TV Nation presenter Michael Moore investigates the state of gun control in the USA.

Forget record tokens and a competitive interest rate – there's a bank in Michigan that will give you a free gun if you open an account. 'Only in America,' say the Brits, chuckling and shaking our heads. But laughs turn to tears on a daily basis in the States, where the incidence of death by gunshot wounds has escalated to epidemic proportions.

Investigative filmmaker Michael Moore's heartfelt documentary – as entertaining as it is politically damning – looks deep into America's love affair with firearms. Guns aren't just part of daily life in the States; they're a legal part of the Constitution. And this – combined with an ingrained fear of enemies without and within – is a fatal attraction.

Moore's arguments are passionate and factually sound, but he's never dry. At his best, he embraces the absurdity of a given situation, twisting it in on itself, shaming the callous and greedy into facing up to their responsibilities. For example, in a genius move, he takes a wheelchair-bound victim of the Columbine High School shooting – a boy who has inoperable bullets lodged in his body – to the headquarters of K-mart, the company who supplied the ammunition so readily over the counter to the teenage killers. The boy is only, Moore contends, returning their merchandise. The supermarket chain's reaction is a surprise for both audience and filmmaker, as thrilling a cinematic experience as many a clever plot twist.

The film even has an inbuilt climactic showdown, as NRA member Moore and NRA President Charlton Heston meet up to discuss the issues at hand. As ever, Moore gets a foot in the door using a combination of intelligence, research and charisma, before playing the emotional card. Moore never forgets that all of these political debates and legal details have a tragic, personal cost. As Heston slinks off, we realise it may be impossible to watch *Ben-Hur* in the same light again. ★★★★ **OR**

BOX OF MOONLIGHT (1996)

Starring: *John Tuturro (Al Fountain), Sam Rockwell ('The Kid', aka Buck Bucky), Catherine Keener (Floatie Dupre), Lisa Blount (Purlene Dupre), Dermot Mulroney (Wick)*
Director: *Tom DiCillo*
Screenwriter: *Tom DiCillo*
15/112 mins./Comedy/Drama/USA/Japan

Taking a break from his stressful city job, a construction foreman befriends a crazy country boy.

This offering from the man behind *Johnny Suede* and *Living In Oblivion* is a road movie that mixes the weird with the wonderful in equal measures.

The action circles around Al Fountain, an anally retentive construction boss whose well-maintained wires short circuit when he discovers his first grey hair and begins to visualise surreal images. Although he tries to maintain a semblance of normality with his wife and son, Bobby, during their daily telephone conversations, he is clearly a man in need of a break. When his construction crew is called off their current contract, he decides to break off from the main group, hire himself a car and embark on an adventure. And that's when he meets and bonds with a modern day forest dwelling hermit, Bucky.

DiCillo is superbly astute at creating an edgy sense of foreboding in his films (the middle American OAPs who carry an axe on country walks in this film are as creepy as the dwarf in his movie-within-a-movie in *Living In Oblivion*). And the extraordinary Turturro is put to good use with measured support from spunky Rockwell and the luscious Keener as a phone sex operator.

An all-talking touchy-feely road movie of sorts, this perfectly utilises the isn't-life-shit-this-decade motif that characterises many of the best movies of the moment with a melancholy tone. ★★★★ **CH**

THE BOXER (1997)

Starring: *Daniel Day-Lewis (Danny Flynn), Emily Watson (Maggie), Gerard McSorley (Harry), Brian Cox (Joe Hamill), Ciaran Fitzgerald (Liam), Ken Stott (Ike Weir), Kenneth Cranham (Matt MaGuire)*
Director: *Jim Sheridan*
Screenwriters: *Jim Sheridan, Terry George*
15/113 mins./Drama/Sport/USA/Ireland

Danny Flynn is separated from his sweetheart for 14 years for being involved in IRA terrorist activity. When he gets out he finds she is married with a child, though her husband has also gone away for 'The Cause'. What ensues is the tale of a man trying to rebuild his life in the face of so many contemporary pressures.

Amid a cacophony of cack-handed hijacks of Irish politics for Hollywood again, Jim Sheridan's clear, intelligent directorial voice once again hits the strident notes of realism. After the towering ramifications of *In The Name Of The Father*, he returns to Belfast (although films in Dublin) to tell a wonderful love story and paint the starkest picture of life under the shadow of The Troubles since *Harry's Game*. He's also brought along frequent collaborator and muse Daniel Day-Lewis to deliver the kind of all-encompassing central performance that makes a mockery of the big 'acting' that is reeled in and out of the multiplexes every week.

The axis of the story is an unbreakable love-bond between Danny Flynn and Maggie, teenagers torn apart by Flynn's arrest for IRA activity and 14-year stretch (symbolically the same term of incarceration as Gerry Conlon). Flynn is released days before the ceasefire will sow confusion into the community and restless ranks of the paramilitarists, and returns home to seek out his two lifelong loves: Maggie and boxing. Maggie, though, has a husband (now, too, imprisoned for 'The Cause') and a young son, Liam, while Flynn's sacred gym has long since fallen to disuse with former coach Ike Weir now preaching sucker punches from a bottle.

What transpires is the tale of a man trying to rebuild his shattered life against the pressures of tribalism, taboo (to interfere with the wife of a 'POW' grants a bullet in the head) and political unrest – matters doubly complicated by Maggie's father Joe Hamill being the local IRA honcho – and a community that has lived by fear and some kind of belief trying to come to terms with the notion of peace.

Filming with subtle menace, Sheridan is mindful of how the big political picture and token media coverage bear little relevance to the deep-seated social divide of Ulster's capital. This is a daily life punctuated by the shudder of explosions, sniper shots and children hurling Molotov cocktails at advancing riot police. Yet the film's power rests in its concentration on the human costs. After renouncing his IRA past, Flynn is an outcast, his only solace found in the bloodied exertions of the ring. The sheer intensity of the couple's rediscovery is so awkward and pregnant with forbidden desire it is rendered almost unbearable.

Sheridan gets caught directing in shorthand – nominally touching on ideas that are never coaxed to fruition and his 'love conquers all' subtext feels overly cosy. But with performances as piercing as these (Watson, Cox, Stott and, of course, Day-Lewis, each faultless to a person) you can forgive overreaching ambitions. And in one unforgettable scene of the young Liam breaking through an army cordon to cradle a possibly booby-trapped dead body, he has imprinted cinema's most searing image of Belfast's bitter legacy. Peace, he reminds us, will never come cheaply. ★★★★ **IN**

BOXING HELENA (1993)

Starring: *Julian Sands (Doctor Nick Cavanaugh), Sherilyn Fenn (Helena), Bill Paxton (Ray O'Malley), Kurtwood Smith (Doctor Alan Palmer), Art Garfunkel (Doctor Lawrence Augustine), Betsy Clark (Anne Garrett)*
Director: *Jennifer Chambers Lynch*
Screenwriter: *Jennifer Chambers Lynch*
18/107 mins./Drama/Thriller/USA

Distraught and unable to cope with a break-up from the beautiful Helena, surgeon Nick Cavanaugh is surprised to find her at his mercy after a terrible accident. He proceeds to remove her limbs one by one, leaving her to live in a box.

It's a salutary lesson that a film that hopes to be accorded some gasping notoriety for its twisted sexuality and violence, all wrapped up in a weird sub-sub-comedy, is better known for its behind-the-camera shenanigans. According to the case, Kim Basinger was due to play the heartless and finally limbless Helena, but pulled out of her contract (understandably in hindsight given the risible result) causing a stew of writs and tiresome legality which left the film playing a sad second-fiddle with its own hoped for controversy.

Sherilyn Fenn took over as the object of Julian Sands unnatural obsession, and she looks unsure what she's just stepped into, overcooking what should be a fiery, demented victim of her own self-hatred as much as the doctor's cracked love. Jennifer Chambers Lynch has clearly looked to her father David and his offbeam Americana liberated from textual logic, but she has none of his sly humour and visual intoxication.

Daddy was all subtext, daughter forces it all onto the surface, robbing the film of a much-needed ambiguity. Cavanaugh, played with Sands usual giddy imbalance, is a Freudian mishmash tormented by unnatural desires for his deceased harpy of a mother, transferring his affection onto the dreadful Helena, a ridiculous concoction of curves and carnality. How she torments the befuddled doc. Even after a car crash forces him to amputate both her legs, and traps her in his home, she wheels about in an ancient wheelchair, flinging things at him and screeching like a car alarm. If the film wasn't so painfully unwatchable, it might have taken on a splashy, crackpot humour of its own. No luck, Lynch has no control of her own filmmaking limbs, and what should be an arch parable of dark sexual fantasy teeming with possession, control, and revenge, its dopey castration metaphors and despicable characters leave unmanned, unwomanned and entirely unlikable. ★ **IN**

BOYS DON'T CRY (1999)

Starring: *Hilary Swank (Brandon Teena), Chloe Sevigny (Lana), Peter Sarsgaard (John), Brendan Sexton III (Tom), Alison Folland (Kate)*
Director: *Kimberly Peirce*
Screenwriters: *Kimberly Pierce, Andy Bienan*
18/114 mins./Drama/Biography/USA

Awards: *Academy Awards – Best Actress, Golden Globes – Best Actress*

Small-town sensibilities are exposed when a new arrival turns out to be more than he appears.

The (loosely based on a) real-life tale of a lesbian transvestite con-person who gets mixed up with an alcoholic, two psychotic ex-cons and an out-and-out fruitloop: it's clear from the gloomy start that *Boys Don't Cry* is going to be far from pretty. Bleak, uncompromising and at times plain unpleasant, the film takes for its source material the true story of Brandon Teena (Swank), a girl who, well, just wants to be a boy. A sex-changing (getting her hair cut and sticking a dildo down her pants) credit sequence sees our hero(ine) at first on the pull, duping a local girl into a bit of nookie, and then on the run, when the truth about her sexuality rears its bizarre head.

She is a fugitive of the law, as well as a few irate townsfolk, and a twist of fate leads to her befriending a bunch of trailer-trash misfits and, temporarily, enjoying a new-found freedom under her manly guise. Of course, it's all going to go horribly wrong – particularly when she falls in love with the local girlie sweetheart – and, on this level at least, it does not disappoint.

Where the film does go slightly awry is in granting its principle characters such a sparse background depth that insufficient insight is given into many of their motives, and a marginally overlong running time occasionally loses a degree of momentum. Minor quibbles aside, an array of dazzling performances (including an absolute barnstormer from Swank) and Peirce's taut direction (the rape scene in particular is captured with brutal flair) conspire to produce a genuinely harrowing experience. ★★★★ **MD**

THE BOYS FROM BRAZIL (1978)

Starring: *Gregory Peck (Doctor Josef Mengele), Laurence Olivier (Ezra Lieberman), James Mason (Eduard Seibert), Lilli Palmer (Esther Lieberman), Uta Hagen (Frieda Maloney), Rosemary Harris (Mrs Doring), Steve Guttenberg (Barry Kohler)*
Director: *Franklin J. Schaffner*
Screenwriter: *Heywood Goulds, based on the novel by Ira Levin*
18/123 mins./Drama/War/USA/UK

Based on the Ira Levin thriller, a young Nazi hunter comes across a meeting of old SS members in Paraguay, led by Josef Mengele, and overhears the beginnings of a strange plan. When relaying to his superior Ezra Leiberman, the old master slowly uncovers a dreadful secret the result of which means the birth of a Fourth Reich.

When confronted with a novel so far-fetched and potentially dubious as Ira Levin's old-Nazis up-to-no-good potboiler, the best approach is to populate it with proud old actors guaranteed to lend it a credibility it doesn't wholly deserve. The weather-worn faces and grand elocution of Gregory Peck and Laurence Olivier does keep Franklin J. Schaffner's dark thriller just about on an even keel, and by the laughable revelation carried in its denouement you are gripped enough not to gag with derision. In fact, for much of its slowburn build there is a classy, intelligent thriller at work, something closer in tone to *The Odessa File*. Still, you must remain guarded to how over the top and quasi-horror events will finally turn.

Now, due to concerns of being a Nazi Party-pooper, the crazed schematics at the heart of this twisty not-to-say twisted plot must remain hidden. It involves the fermenting of a new Reich through some scientific excesses even Bond's arch-villainy would consider overreaching, although the duo of elderly thesps (both 65 at the time) were never going to be up for a good chase scene no matter how many Dobermans you set on them. Peck, in one of his scant few deviations from Atticus Finch's strident moralism, snarls and sneers with relish as Mengele, a man of reason if not sanity. Olivier, loosely basing Lieberman on legendary Nazi-hunter Simon Wiesenthal, has always been able to switch sides with aplomb – he even played a variation on the evil German doctor two years previously in *The Marathon Man* – and their final confrontation does manage the electric buzz of those rare face-offs between screen greats. In the meantime, Peck-Mengele instructs his cronies to hotfoot it about the globe to execute a hit list of 94 ageing men, a psychological down payment on the outcome.

Having Jerry Goldsmith stir up another gothic score, as brazen and operatic as his clarion call of his *Omen* soundtrack, adds an appropriate layer of Wagnerian doom to proceedings. But, no matter how well-groomed, there's no escaping the thinness and exploitation tendencies of Levin's trite writing. ★★★ **IN**

BOYZ N THE HOOD (1991)

Starring: *Larry Fishburne (Furious Styles), Ice Cube (Dougboy Baker), Cuba Gooding Jr (Tre Styles), Nia Long (Brandi), Morris Chestnut (Ricky Baker), Tyra Ferrell (Mrs Baker), Angela Bassett (Reva Styles)*
Director: *John Singleton*
Screenwriter: *John Singleton*
15/107 mins./Drama/USA

Three black teenagers living in the South Central LA consider their prospects.

Arriving to pre-publicity involving riots, looting sprees and a body count, it's easy to suppose *Boyz N The Hood*'s appeal lies in an easily accessed glamorisation of violence. Happily such assumptions are without substance. The film not only lives up to its 'Increase The Peace' subtitle but by refusing to overtly moralise puts its concerns across with astonishing impact.

The 'Boyz' are three kids looking for very different things as they pass out of their teens: university; doing nothing yet not returning to jail; and a career on the football field. The 'Hood' (neighbourhood) is the gang-law killing fields of South Central LA. And the story, such as it is, observes their lives in two chunks, at age six and, mainly, 11 years later.

This well-worn coming of age theme is given no special treatment (the kids' extraneous worries involve parents, girls, cars and having fun), and the series of minutely detailed everyday incidents opens participants' lives to the point at which you feel part of them. It's once you know the area's vibrant cross-section of personalities, attitudes and ambitions – very few of them gang affiliated – that the increasingly obvious background takes on genuinely shocking proportions. A girl's concentration on her homework is repeatedly broken by gun fire; helicopter searchlights illuminate living rooms as families watch TV; and unfamiliar cars prompt panic on porches. When tension finally spills over into the inevitable pointless murder, attention is focused not on the act but (rarely bothered with in comparable films) on the immediate effect on the family of the bloody death of a 17-year-old boy. The scenes are a horribly damning indictment of the situation, but the film as whole goes further.

Singleton's portrait of local residents as exactly what you'd find in any other part of town, just less wealthy, affords a dignity and air of normality to black life. But more importantly, their self-containedness (characters and lives are not seen merely as relative to white people) allows the underlying message of their need to take responsibility for themselves to be perceived as able to offer a solution. ★★★★★ **LB**

THE BRADY BUNCH MOVIE (1995)

Starring: *Shelley Long (Carol Brady), Gary Cole (Mike Brady), Christine Taylor (Marcia Brady), Christopher Daniel Barnes (Greg Brady), Jennifer Elise Cos (Jan Brady), Paul Sutera (Peter Brady), Oliver Hack (Cindy Brady), Jesse Lee (Bobby Brady), Henriette Mantel (Alice Nelson), David Graf (Sam Franklin), Florence Henderson (Grandma)*
Director: *Betty Thomas*
Screenwriters: *Laurice Elehwany, Rick Copp, Bonnie Turner, Terry Turner, characters created by Sherwood Schwartz*
12/90 mins./Comedy/USA

Whilst everyone else has dragged themselves into the 90s, the Bradys are still rooted in the 70s and holding on to their sitcom values. However, evil neighbour Mr Ditmeyer is determined to destoy their utopia by demolishing the family home and building a mall.

While the initial idea of bringing the 70s most whiter-than-white family to the big screen might invoke suicidal thoughts in anyone who saw *The Beverly Hillbillies*, this TV to movie leaper is an unexpected treat. It manages to retain its eye-straining outfits, hummable theme tune and all-round feelgood persona without ever feeling dated or laboured.

The main joke is that while the outside world has dragged itself into the 90s, chez Brady things are still very much as they were on 70s TV – flared of trouser, pointy of collar, and distinctly rose-coloured, with an inherent chirpiness that defies such modern niceties as smog warnings or car-jackings. Over the fence, however, things ain't so perfect: their neighbour, Mr. Ditmeyer (McKean) wants to demolish the family home to make way for a shopping mall, and is prepared to go to any lengths to see they submit.

Things may look bleak for the Bradys, but their ability to apply their duff homespun wisdom to every crisis carries the film to its almost inevitable conclusion, while the world of 70s sitcom-land dishes up a plethora of sub-plots for the Brady siblings to wrestle with. Bad nose days and ghastly hippy love songs are both on the agenda, but it's truly middle-child Jan Brady's paranoid schizophrenia which gets the giggle motor going.

And here you have the movie's true, deliciously subversive, cunning. The scriptwriters have taken an almost post-modern glee in dissecting the glossy, moralistic world of this family of eight, running a range of real-life issues – homosexuality, school shrinks, modelling, food fadism, teenage sex – by way of their plastic sensibilities. It's more a tribute to the Bradys than a film about them, backed up by appearances from a number of the original cast.

A bizarre juxtaposition of forgettable Friday night fluff and a wicked attack on sitcom values, this is enormous fun, one of the best TV adaptations to date, and guaranteed to provoke a nostalgic misty eye and mischevious grin in anybody who's ever owned a crimplene tank top. The sequel continued in very much the same spirit. ★★★ **CW**

BRAINDEAD (1992)

Starring: *Timothy Balme (Lionel Cosgrove), Diana Peñalver (Paquita Maria Sanchez), Elizabeth Moody (Mum – Vera Cosgrove), Ian Watkin (Uncle Les), Brenda Kendall (Nurse McTavish), Stuart Devenie (Father McGruder)*
Director: *Peter Jackson*
Screenwriters: *Stephen Sinclair, Fran Walsh, Peter Jackson*
18/97 mins./Comedy/Fantasy/Horror/New Zealand

On a trip to the Zoo, a young man's mother is transformed into a flesh eating zombie. At first he tries to cover up her 'change', but with the body count mounting, it's clear someone will have to take action . . .

Set in a genteel 1957 New Zealand, where a strain of rabies-like zombiehood is imported by a Sumatran rat-monkey, this is one sick, sick horror comedy.

While spying on her intimidated son (Balme) and his 'unsuitable' ethnic girlfriend (Penalver) as they take a trip to the zoo, an interfering and snobbish Elizabeth Moody is bitten by the truly repulsive beast, turning into a ravenous cannibal creature. Initially Balme tries to conceal his mother's infirmity, but the plague spreads and soon he has to deal with a zombified nurse, priest and juvenile delinquent.

In the early stretches, Jackson juxtaposes grotesque comedy – Moody eats her own ear with custard, the nurse has a china bird embedded in her forehead, a splattery conflict is played out against an episode of *The Archers* – but, like Balme, loses control entirely when the nurse and the priest mate to produce a hideous zombie baby who needs barbed wire over his pram to keep him down.

The gore comedy of Romero's *Living Dead* trilogy and Raimi's *Evil Dead* is here plagiarised and taken to a point of no return, yielding a parade of comic atrocities which is astonishing, but eventually monotonous. It has trace elements of a plot in Balme's well-intentioned but disastrous attempts to look after his monstrous mother, but Jackson soon jettisons characterisations and story development in favour of an orgy of tasteless effects.

Unfortunately, the film works best in its occasional, almost subtle touches, such as the squirming pile of constricting intestines seen preening itself in a bathroom mirror. ★★★ **KN**

BRAM STOKER'S DRACULA (1992)

Starring: *Gary Oldman (Count Vlad Dracul/Dracula), Winona Ryder (Mina Murray/Elisabeta), Anthony Hopkins (Professor Abraham Van Helsing), Keanu Reeves (Jonathan Harker), Richard E. Grant (Dr Jack Seward), Cary Elwes (Lord Arthur Holmwood), Sadie Frost (Lucy Westenra), Monica Bellucci (Dracula's Bride)*
Director: *Francis Ford Coppola*
Screenwriter: *James V. Hart, from the novel by Bram Stoker*
18/130 mins./Horror/Romance/Fantasy/USA

Awards: *Academy Awards – Best Make-up, Best Costume Design, Best Sound Effects Editing*

In Ford Coppola's Dracula, the Count turned his back on God after his wife committed suicide thinking her husband died in battle. Then some 400 years later he becomes obsessed with Mina who bears an uncanny resemblance to his late wife.

Oh, for olden times when all that happened in a vampire/Dracula movie was some Transylvanian coach driver would go (in an ill-suited Dorset accent, usually), 'Oh, no, don't go up to the castle tonight, master, there's evil afoot!' Oh, for Bela Lugosi or the lusty fangs of Christopher Lee. Oh, particularly, for the bit in the Hammer Drac-fests where Francis Matthews (worst actor ever) opens the creaky coffin lid and reels back in preposterous 'terror'. Coppola has made some excellent films, it cannot be denied: *The Conversation*, *Apocalypse Now* and of course the *Godfather Part I* and *II*. Gothic horror, however, is evidently not his forte. He fails to make his Dracula laughably lovable, à la Terence Fisher (Hammer supremo) and he fails to make it in any way frightening; he simply manages to make it terribly, terribly dull – an achievement in itself.

Gary Oldman's Count turns into a skinless bat and green mist and a strange old git and a festival of rats; Keanu Reeves, as the weedy Jonathan Harker, struggles with his Anglo-toff accent. There's sex: Sadie Frost has it off with a werewolf (Dracula in crafty Mr Disguise kit); mad baby-feasting vampirellas provide Keanu with painful-looking 'blow' jobs. There's death: slow-motion decapitations aplenty and men stuck on sticks. There are irksome discussions on the meaning of love within the Goth heavy metal-styled settings of foggy castles, and the special effects – ranging from the gory to the patently absurd – are ladled over the whole like an impossible soup. There's even Sir Anthony Hopkins as Dracula's nemesis, Van Helsing, sniffing away dementedly like Hannibal Lecter all over again.

The film is a calamity, a muddle, a mish-mash, nothing but blood spouting from the mouths of the undead. Fake accents steal up upon you without warning – does Gary Oldman really say, 'I am the last of the Formica?' Probably not, but it makes little difference so laboured is the plot. Bram Stoker's Dracula is all style, no content (though Tom Waits as the insect-craving crackpot Renfield is rather marvellous), so if 'horror' hokum is your particular cup of tea, might we direct you instead to *The Abominable Dr Phibes*. You know where you are with Vincent Price. ★★ **TH**

BRASSED OFF (1996)

Starring: *Pete Postlethwaite (Danny), Tara Fitzgerald (Gloria), Ewan McGregor (Andy), Stephen Tompkinson (Phil), Jim Carter (Harry), Philip Jackson (Jim), Sue Johnston (Vera)*
Director: *Mark Herman*
Screenwriter: *Mark Herman*
15/103 mins./Comedy/Drama/Romance/Music/UK/USA

A Yorkshire pit faces closure but the colliery band still want to compete for band of the year at the National championships.

Despite a comparatively quiet cinema release, astounding word of mouth steered *Brassed Off* into the money-making zone, its blend of political drama and light-hearted comedy striking a chord with cinemagoers. However, now that it's all over bar the faint parp of a wind instrument, did it actually deserve the sleeper success? Yes and no, as it happens.

Grimley Colliery is a fictional Yorkshire pit about to close its doors for the last time depending on the vote from its miners. But in the face of impending unemployment, the colliery's brass band – led by Danny – keeps playing on, reaching the semi-finals of the National Championships and heading for the great play-off at the Royal Albert Hall. There's even an unlikely new addition to the musicians – in the shape of local girl made good Gloria – who wins the affections of fellow bandsman Andy. But as is par for the course, the road to trumpeting glory is paved with unexpected obstacles.

The tone proves problematic – after all, pit closures and the knock-on effect of forced redundancy was never going to be the stuff that knock-about comedies are made of. And the film is unsure whether to be a spirited political puff piece or a light-hearted comedy, so goes for a mixture of both, the result being that many of the more light-hearted vignettes fall flat, giving rise to an unbelievably fantastical denouement

The unexpected saviour of the movie proves to be the brass band music itself, which provides a solid backdrop to much of the action (one set-piece, featuring dejected miners and protesters leaving the colliery, is all the more poignant for the tune which accompanies it).

More predictably, the acting is top-notch. McGregor breathes life into a less-than-interesting role, Fitzgerald shines and Tompkinson is excellent as a man on the brink of cracking up. But Postlethwaite takes top honours as his dad, the bandleader for whom everything takes second place to music. Not an unqualified success then, but well-meaning and enthusiastic enough to warrant attention. ★★★ **CW**

BRAVEHEART (1995)

Starring: *Mel Gibson (William Wallace), Patrick McGoohan (Longshanks – King Edward I), Sophie Marceau (Princess Isabelle), Catherine McCormack (Murron), Brendan Gleeson (Hamish), James Cosmo (Campbell), Angus MacFadyen (Robert The Bruce), Ian Bannen (The Leper), Peter Hanly (Prince Edward)*
Director: *Mel Gibson*
Screenwriters: *William C de Mille, Mary O'Hara*
15/171 mins./History/Drama/Adventure/USA

Awards: *Academy Awards – Best Cinematography, Best Director, Best Sound Effects Editing, Best Makeup, Best Picture, BAFTAs – Best Cinematography, Best Costume Design, Best Sound, Empire Awards – Best Film, Golden Globe – Best Director.*

In the 13th century, Scot William Wallace raises an army to lead a bloody revolt against English invaders.

Braveheart is that rarest of things: a film which reawakened a nation's interest in its own history. The story began when American screenwriter Randall Wallace was visiting Edinburgh. Intrigued to see an impressive statue of William Wallace, the writer asked who his namesake icon was. 'He's our greatest hero,' replied a tour guide. The rest is history – or, at least, the best tribute Hollywood can pay to it.

Returning home, Wallace became obsessed with the Scottish rebel, who battled to throw off the yoke of English oppression in the late 13th century. His passion was infectious. When Mel Gibson read the resultant script, he immediately felt a powerful identification with the central figure. 'He's completely uncompromising,' said Gibson of the man who was to provide his greatest screen role, 'Which is why he's such an extraordinary character.' Determined to retain his own vision of what Braveheart should be, Gibson insisted on directing the project as well as starring in it. The result was not so much a film as a phenomenon.

Inspired by the great movie epics – notably Kubrick's *Spartacus* – Gibson threw himself into the project. From the rain-soaked, mud-splattered shoot near Inverness, to the fields of Ireland (employed for the sweeping battle scenes), the star found himself evolving a no-frills, rapid-fire directing technique which he described as, 'Hopping in front of the camera, doing the scene, and if it's not a complete disgrace getting the hell out.' Cast, crew and many hundreds of extras were treated to the sight of their leading man commanding the action in full William Wallace wig and blue face paint.

In Gibson's version of events, William Wallace is an educated commoner who turns outlaw in 1290s Scotland after the English slay his sweetheart Murron (played by the hauntingly beautiful Catherine McCormack), Taking command of the Scottish rebel effort brings Wallace into direct conflict with the fearsome English King, Edward I – also known as the Hammer Of The Scots or simply Longshanks.

Sticking fairly closely to historical events (although Gibson plays merry hell with chronology), *Braveheart* depicts Wallace's victory over the English forces at Stirling, his betrayal and defeat at Falkirk and his final capture, subsequent show trial and brutal execution in London.

Taking the villain's role as Longshanks, Patrick McGoohan, in an all-too-rare big screen outing, is a malevolent revelation. If the rest of the English are depicted as either murderous thugs or hopelessly effete, McGoohan's gleeful portrayal of pure evil is a crucial counter-balance to the essential goodness of Wallace. 'Not the archers,' is Longshanks' superbly nasty battle order. 'Arrows cost money. Use up the Irish – their dead cost nothing.'

Fleeting romantic interest comes from Sophie Marceau, playing the luminous French beauty trapped in a loveless marriage to the homosexual Prince Of Wales, who attempts to intercede on Wallace's behalf. Also making a strong impression is Angus MacFadyen as Robert The Bruce, the Hamlet-like figure who, unlike Wallace, will one day be king of Scotland. 'He's constantly drawn to the dark side,' noted MacFadyen, 'of compromise and wealth and preserving the castles and land which he has.' Randall Wallace went so far as to suggest that the dynamic between Wallace and the Bruce may be the 'true heart' of his story. 'He (The Bruce) wanted to do the right thing, but also tried to face the realities of life and make the compromises that were necessary,' he explained. Historical context aside, a major factor of the *Braveheart* sensation was the scale and ferocity of its battle scenes. Marshalling 1600 extras from the Irish army and employing mechanical horses to perform stunts far too dangerous for real animals, Gibson recreated the brutality of medieval combat to breathtaking effect. And it's in the heat of battle that Wallace the man of peace is transformed into a butchering beserker.

'Wallace was truly interested in liberty,' said Gibson. 'He loved his country and wanted freedom for his fellows. But at the same time he was kind of a savage. This is the dichotomy of the man.'

Of course, the defining characteristic of Gibson's Wallace is heroism. His patriotism is backed by boundless reserves of courage; his natural leadership and military brilliance ensure that his men will follow him into hell. Gibson embodies this with absolute conviction – it's no wonder that in Scotland they've started erecting statues of Wallace that bear his features.

Braveheart has been criticised for its strongly – some would say rabidly – anti-English sentiments, and for playing fast and loose with Anglo-Scottish history (Randall Wallace's 'don't-let-the-facts-get-in-the-way-of-a-good-story' attitude to his subject matter provoking the most ire). But does the movie really distort Scottish history any more than Shakespeare did with Macbeth? At any rate, *Braveheart* has provoked a massive resurgence of interest in the history of Scotland and its national identity. William Wallace may have been 'kind of a savage', but there's no doubt he would have approved. ★★★★ **PR**

Movie Trivia: Braveheart

After seeing the movie, the RSPCA were convinced that the horses were real and investigated Gibson. James Horner's music score has been used for countless commercials promoting Scotland and in the *Cast Away* trailer starring Tom Hanks. The realism of the battles was enhanced by using extras from the Irish Territorial Army.

BRAZIL (1985)

Starring: *Jonathan Pryce (Sam Lowry), Kim Greist (Jill Layton), Robert De Niro (Tuttle), Michael Palin (Jack Lint), Ian Holm (Kurtzmann), Bob Hoskins (Spoor), Ian Richardson (Warrenn), Peter Vaughan (Helpmann), Jim Broadbent (Dr Jaffe)*
Director: *Terry Gilliam*
Screenwriters: *Terry Gilliam, Tom Stoppard, Charles McKeown*
15/142 mins./Fantasy/Sci-fi/UK

Awards: *BAFTA – Best Production Design, Best Special Visual Effects*

A statistician in a grimy future world tries to correct a computer error and comes under scrutiny of the State.

Terry Gilliam never read George Orwell. Sure, he knew about *1984*. 'But the knowledge I had was just general knowledge, the stuff you get from college. And then there was the simple fact that 1984 – the year! – was approaching. So I thought we've got to do 1984Y2.'

With Alice somewhere near the back of his mind, former Python animator Gilliam held a distorted looking glass up to Orwell, transcontinental bureaucracy, his own personal history, his outrage at the world around him, and – in doing so – created one of the most universally accessible, deeply personal future visions that cinema had ever known. Only, it wasn't a future vision. *Brazil* – named a 30s Latin American hit song – was not set in that titular country, or the future. It was instead set in 'every part of the 20th century', or 'the other side of now'. For a movie awash with a timeless set of images, that were both retro-futuristic and futuristically-retro, *Brazil* was, possibly more than any other film released round or about 1984, the most contemporary film of its day. And its triumph is that it still is.

'It allowed me to get out of my system something that had been bothering me for a long time,' Gilliam later recalled 'the frustrations of living in the second half of the 20th century.'

Brazil began life on a beach in Port Talbot of all places. While on location for his first solo outing as director, *Jabberwocky*, in 1976, Gilliam found himself on the coal-dust encrusted beach, watching a lone figure picking up the strains of Ry Cooder's 'Maria Elena' on his transistor radio. Around the same time he chanced upon a book at the home of noted historian and fellow Python Terry Jones that detailed how, in the Middle Ages, those accused and convicted – i.e. burned to death – of witchcraft, had to pay their torturers for the privilege of being tortured. Add to this some personal reminiscences – Gilliam's own inadvertent participation in the LA police riots of 1967 and his father's misguided belief in an acid-wielding plastic surgeon – and the nucleus of *Brazil*, then called *The Ministry* – or even *19841/2* – was formed.

Gilliam began writing the movie in 1979. It would take five years and several collaborators before it made it to the screen – in several different cuts. His first co-writer was Charles Alverson, a long-time friend from Gilliam's early days working on the cult satirical magazine, *Help!*, in New York. Tom Stoppard subsequently took a few passes at it, followed by actor-writer Charles McKeown. 'I was the one who had this thing in his head, and probably had to use quite a few people to get it out,' Gilliam later said.

Gilliam set about casting his movie: Jonathan Pryce as – for want of a better word, the 'hero' – Sam Lowry beat out the likes of Val Kilmer and a then desperate to be in it Tom Cruise. The female lead Kim Greist snatched her role from the eager jaws of hot stars Kelly McGillis and Madonna to less lasting effect.

The shoot itself proved problematic when, 12 weeks in, Gilliam and McKeown were forced to cut nearly half the film's fantasy sequences. Gilliam responded to such drastic cuts in his deeply personal vision by losing the ability to walk. 'I don't know what happened,' he said. 'My brain just went catatonic. I couldn't get up. I couldn't move. I just went catatonic.'

A week later, the director left his sick bed and completed a masterful film of neo-futuristic-retro chaos. With Robert De Niro cast as a subversive plumber, Brazil was always going to be a hard sell. But this was just the beginning of its long and troubled journey to finding an audience.

Universal Pictures in the US refused to release Gilliam's cut. He re-cut it and they still refused. He then took an ad out in film industry trade bible *Variety* questioning the studio 's decision and the LA Film Critics subsequently named it Best Film Of The Year. An Oscar nomination for Best Screenplay followed and Universal's hand was well and truly forced.

And in a strange way it's right that *Brazil*, the relatively little film about the cog in the wheel who dreamed of a better world, should have fought the fight it did. A film about oppression overcame its own and in doing so took a personal film and turned it into a universal (no pun intended) event. Gilliam took Lewis Carroll's mirror and held it up to Hollywood and in the process discovered that he was indeed in one hell of a funhouse. ★★★★★ **BM**

BREAKDOWN (1997)

Starring: *Kurt Russell (Jeffrey 'Jeff' Taylor), J.T. Walsh (Warren 'Red' Barr, Gang Truck Driver, Kathleen Quinlan (Amy Taylor), M.C. Gainey (Earl, Gang Member), Jack Noseworthy (Billy, Gang Member), Rex Linn (Sheriff Boyd), Ritch Brinkley (Al, Gang Member), Moira Harris (Arleen Barr, Red's Wife)*
Director: *Jonathan Mostow*
Screenwriters: *Jonathan Mostow, Sam Montgomery*
15/95 mins./Action/Thriller/USA

Kurt Russell searches for his missing wife, who disappeared when their car broke down on a desert highway.

Blend Steven Spielberg's *Duel* with John Boorman's *Deliverance* and chuck in a touch of yuppie-retribution movie and the end result is not, surprisingly, the expected hotchpotch but an incredibly tense, gripping, white-knuckle treat, which eschews high concept in favour of strong plotting and nail-chewing tension.

Director Mostow's impressive take on the road movie is a brief dip into everyone's nightmare – Russell and Quinlan are a married couple driving cross-country when their car breaks down. Friendly trucker Walsh stops and offers them a lift to the nearest phone. She accepts while Russell opts to stay and look after their precious wheels. When the desert equivalent of the AA fails to show, he manages to make his way to the next truck-stop, only to find no sign of his wife. Worse still, trucker Walsh claims he's never seen Russell before in his life, let alone his wife. With the police doing a damn fine impression of doubting people named Thomas and the locals seemingly uninterested, Russell takes things into his own hands in order to uncover what's become of his missus.

The great thing about *Breakdown* is simply that what you see is what you get. Want 90 minutes of edge of the seat tension? You got it. Want an unravelling nightmare that stays with you long after the movie? You got it. Want a decent performance from Kurt Russell, here firmly playing the ordinary man in an extraordinary situation? You even get that. By knowingly acknowledging the influence of *Duel* and *Deliverance*, Mostow fully delivers on all his promises, with a film that knows how to both rely on and build genuine suspense in favour of tired action set-pieces. ★★★★ **BM**

BREAKER MORANT (1980)

Starring: *Edward Woodward (Lieutenant Harry 'Breaker' Morant), Jack Thompson (Major J.F. Thomas), Bryan Brown (Lieutenant Peter Handcock), John Waters (Captain Alfred Taylor)*
Director: *Bruce Beresford*
Screenwriters: *Jonathan Hardy, David Stevens, Bruce Beresford, based on a play by Kenneth Ross*
PG/107 mins./Drama/Australia

In the midst of the Boer War, three Australian officers, upon orders, execute their prisoners. Put on trial by a General Staff hoping to keep their distance from the atrocities of war, they put up a surprisingly strong defence, bringing into question the whole idea of military culpability.

This remarkable, superbly mounted anti-war movie from Australia dallies in none of the absurdities of similar themed material that tends to dress war as a surrealist horror. Bruce Beresford at his most measured, tackles a true story of three devoted Aussie lieutenants court-marshalled for executing a Boer prisoner and a German missionary for no good reason other than some form of revenge, without extraneous detail or exterior subplots. Not that his film is thin, indeed, it is heavy with period detail, well organised and powerfully, intelligently acted by the four leads.

The focus for the screenplay, based on Kenneth Ross' play, is the debate of where responsibility lies, and where the act of murder rests in the context of war. If these three men were following orders, given by their shadowy British commanders, then how are they to blame? A brilliant, vividly infuriated Jack Thompson as their determined defence lawyer Major Thomas, mounts his case around this very dilemma. Surely, if these men are guilty, then the firing squad they ordered should equally be on trial.

Edward Woodward, ably supported by Bryan Brown and Lewis Fitzgerald, doesn't portray Breaker Morant as a good or just man, in a fierce, moody performance he creates the idea that straightforward morality is a quality unaffordable by men at war. Beresford lifting the microcosm of this localised story to question the very legal and moral boundaries of warfare itself. Can a soldier killing an enemy, even by execution, be committing murder? He also sensibly realises that pat and obvious answers to such contentions don't exist – the film concludes with a pessimistic note of failure on all counts. And his film, richly shot and so stirringly acted, remains one the most telling and moving parables of war's grand folly that cinema has ever given us. ★★★★★ **IN**

ⓓ BREAKFAST AT TIFFANY'S (1961)

Starring: *Audrey Hepburn (Holly Golightly), George Peppard (Paul Varjak), Patricia Neal (2-E), Buddy Ebsen (Doc Golightly), Martin Balsam (O.J. Berman), Mickey Rooney (Mr Yunioshi)*
Director: *Blake Edwards*
Screenwriter: *George Axelrod, based on the novella by Truman Capote*
PG/115 mins./Drama/USA
Awards: *Academy Awards – Best Song, Best Score*

Writer Paul Varjak moves into a New York apartment building and becomes captivated by his neighbour, Holly Golightly. Each has a wealthy benefactor keeping them and both find they have to accept some home truths.

It's with good reason that 40 years after appearing as Holly Golightly, Audrey Hepburn – cigarette-holder in hand, subtly streaked hair pinned high – is still a poster icon for those aspiring to the kind of classy romance that doesn't seem to exist anymore.

The surprise to those who know the image but not the film, is that in the world of *Breakfast At Tiffany's*, this character is just as much of a dream for Holly. She's a fake. Someone who lies so well she believes her own spin. Paid to deliver 'weather reports' by a mobster she visits in jail, collecting $50 a time to 'go to the powder room', she acts with such dignity, it would seem impertinent to question her cover stories. But as Paul becomes drawn into her world, he realises he's going to have to knock her fantasy just a little bit if there's any future for them as a couple.

But then, Paul is just as much a fake, a one-trick-pony writer, kept by a richer older woman while he struggles with his career. Peppard, far from the tough-talking A-Team leader he was later to become, is almost unrecognisable as the blond, square-jawed hero. He has little more to do here than be a solid rock, there to catch Holly when she eventually falls, and his acting talents are eclipsed not only by Hepburn's but by the strong supporting cast.

In Blake Edwards' hands the story is lighter than the Truman Capote novel on which it was based, but he manages to add some trademark humour (sadly including the sore thumb of Rooney as a squawking Japanese neighbour) and keep the romance sweet. And it's the romantic scenes that stand out; Holly crooning 'Moon River' to her cat, as Paul listens above; the day they decide to do things they've never done before and the rain-soaked climax. ★★★★ **EC**

ⓓ THE BREAKFAST CLUB (1985)

Starring: *Emilio Estervez (Andrew Clark), Paul Gleason (Richard Vernon), Anthony Michael Hall (Brian Johnson), John Kapelos (Carl), Judd Nelson (John Bender), Molly Ringwald (Claire Standish), Ally Sheedy (Allison Reynolds)*
Director: *John Hughes*
Screenwriter: *John Hughes*
15/97 mins./Drama/USA

A rag-tag bunch of unruly kids are ordered into school on a Saturday for an extra special morning detention. Defiant at first, they eventually find a camaraderie when the principal buggers off and leaves them to entertain themselves.

'When the causes of the Decline Of Western Civilization are finally writ, Hollywood will surely have to answer why it turned over one of man's most significant art forms to the self-gratification of high-schoolers ...' Industry rag *Variety* didn't so much greet *The Breakfast Club* with open arms as crunch it into an armpit-lock and squeeze until the jerking stopped. In retrospect, this violent reaction to such a vanilla-flavoured piece of cinema reads like a badly informed dad's rants. Or maybe an allergic reaction to Emilio Estevez's dancing. *Variety* was cruel at the time but, over 20 years on, has time been cruel to the *Club*? In the spirit of adolescent indecision, that's a definite yes-no.

Calling it radical would be a stretch, yet in 1985 *The Breakfast Club* dressed differently from all the other teen comedies flying down the chutes. Director John Hughes wrote the script in a fortnight, constructing a simple, one-location talkie that brought a generation's submerged angst to the surface. The result was a movie that's confused, impatient, indulgent, naive, clumsy, unintentionally funny and prone to random outbursts of energy. Rather like the audience that lined the blocks to tune in and angst out.

To Shermer High, then, where five Kellogg's Teen Pack archetypes – jock, weirdo, nerd, rebel, prom queen – are assembled for an all-Saturday detention. Over the course of eight hours, they pick at each other's defences (fun) until an existential maelstrom hits and they come to learn some universal teen-truths (less fun). Estevez, Ally Sheedy and Judd Nelson are all volume, the last blasting out his bothers like a WWE wrestler, but Molly Ringwald and Anthony Michael Hall are great, even during the film's more pompous moments.

The style might be flying in from another decade (Sheedy's makeover from chic Goth to Bridesmaid Of Minnie Mouse is as laugh-out-loud as it ever was), but the emotional baggage has survived the journey. Really – and this is a compliment – it's a movie for anyone who's ever had zits. Which means all of us at some point. So, if you had zits in the 80s, there's guilty retro-pleasures aplenty, like Estevez's dance moves, an extraordinary piece of performance art that combines harassment by persistent wasp (arms) with prostate-popping squat thrusts (legs). And if you have zits now? There's just about enough truth behind the banalities to still strike discord.

Hughes has made funnier (*Ferris Bueller*) and better (*Pretty In Pink*), but this is the only one you could get away with calling iconic. Good and bad, it's still the definitive 80s teen movie – and, to paraphrase Simple Minds, don't you forget about it. ★★★★ **SC**

ⓓ BREAKING THE WAVES (1996)

Starring: *Emily Watson (Bess), Stellan Skarsgard (Jan), Katrin Cartlidge (Dodo), Jean-Marc Barr (Terry), Udo Kier (Man on the Trawler), Adrian Rawlins (Doctor Richardson)*
Director: *Lars Von Trier*
Screenwriters: *Lars Von Trier, Peter Asmussen*
18/156 mins./Drama/Denmark/Sweden/Norway/Netherlands/Finland/France/U.S./Iceland
Awards: *Cannes Film Festival – Jury Prize*

A paralysed oil rig worker urges his wife to engage in sexual encounters with strangers.

Danish filmmaker Lars von Trier's work has been distinctive for his sardonic outlook and his gimmicky preoccupation with arty technique. This, his English language debut, which won the 1996 Jury Prize at Cannes, arouses more emotion. You'll leave weeping or arguing, but certainly not bored by a tale that ranges between the weird, the wonderful and outrageous.

Despite the pursed lips of relations and church elders in a remote Scottish village in the 1970s, devout, innocent young Bess marries oil rig worker Jan. The austerity of her environment is contrasted sharply with Bess's warmth, affection, and the rapture she finds in sex with her Scandinavian husband. Then we realise the reason for everyone's concern; Bess is a sweet, happy girl but definitely not right in the head. She is unable to bear separation from Jan, and when he is brought back from the rig paralysed after an accident, her obsession adds to his despair. They arrive at a bizarre arrangement; he urges her to take a lover, she interprets this as a spiritual mission.

The development of their bond from misunderstanding to tragic, twisted sacrifice is, frankly, creepy and infuriating. Bess's conversations with God, especially, resemble a clumsy *Exorcist* spoof, and one is tempted to side with the contingent who reckon she should be in a padded cell. The perverse convolutions of the second hour are also particularly hard going.

It's here that credulity and patience become strained to breaking point. But von Trier is intent on the miraculousness inherent in love and faith, and miracles are duly provided in a daring and exalting send-off – repayment with interest for the ordeal by which it has been obtained. ★★★★ **AM**

⓪ BRIDE OF CHUCKY (1998)

Starring: *Jennifer Tilly (Tiffany), Brad Dourif (Chucky – voice), Katherine Heigl (Jade), Nick Stabile (Jesse), Alexis Arquette (Howard Fitzwater/Damien Baylock), John Ritter (Police Chief Warren Kincaid)*
Director: *Ronny Yu*
Screenwriter: *Don Mancini*
18/89 mins./Comedy/Horror/Thriller/USA

Chucky gets hitched to his old girlfriend, her soul transported into a demonic dolly.

If ever a horror franchise was written off entirely, it was the *Child's Play* series. Though a ludicrous boondoggle made it a tabloid hot potato, *Child's Play 3* was about the mildest, most redundant splatter sequel ever made. Therefore, it's a voodoo miracle that this belated fourth entry, which wisely doesn't have a number in the title, pulls all the pieces together, gives them a couple of unusual spins, and goes all out for yocks and yucks that, for the most part, it delivers.

Serial killer Charles Lee Ray, whose spirit (the Nicholsonesque voice of Brad Dourif) moved into the body of a killer doll ('The story is so long that if it were a movie it would take several sequels to tell it all,' Chucky sneers), had a hitherto-unknown trailer trash girlfriend, Tiffany. She claims the leftover scraps of the doll from that police evidence lock-up where they also keep Jason's mask and Freddy's glove and performs a ritual out of Voodoo For Dummies that gets the now pretty-mangled Chucky walking around again.

Tagline
Chucky gets lucky.

After a lover's argument, the doll electrocutes the babe by tossing a TV set (screening *Bride Of Frankenstein*) into her bath, and her spirit is transmitted into another doll. The toys have to get to Ray's grave in New Jersey to retrieve a macguffin amulet, so high school runaways Jade and Jesse are conned into driving them across country and, incidentally, getting a Mickey-and-Mallory reputation by taking the blame for the escalating body count!

The commitment to upping the quality is evident in the choice of ex-Hong Kong superstar director Yu (*Bride With White Hair, The Phantom Lover*), which brings some much-needed atmosphere and action. With an appealing mix of innocence, smarts and homicidal mania, Tilly is a valuable addition to the franchise, and has even more fun when turned into a killer slut Lady Penelope. The real reversal is that producer-writer Don Mancini, who has been behind the whole series, has suddenly learned to write sharp dialogue (even the traditionally irksome teenage leads are appealing, and the squabbling dolls are wonderful) and toss off subtler-than-*Scream* frame-breaking jokes about how dated Chucky (who died in 1989) is and how much he has to live down. It ends with an atmospheric graveyard face-off and, of course, a set-up for *Son Of Chucky*. ★★★★ **KN**

⓪ THE BRIDE OF FRANKENSTEIN (1935)

Starring: *Boris Karloff (The Monster), Colin Clive (Baron Henry Frankenstein), Elsa Lanchester (Mary Wollstonecraft Shelley/The Monster's Mate), Ernest Thesiger (Dr Septimus Pretorius), Gavin Gordon (Lord Byron), Douglas Walton (Percy Bysshe Shelley)*
Director: *James Whale*
Screenwriters: *William Hurlbut, John L Balderston, based on the novel by Mary Shelley*
PG/80 mins./Horror/USA

A dual narrative sees Mary Shelley continuing the story of Frankenstein from where her novel finished, while, in the fictional counter-part she creates, the monster searches for a wife.

After the enormous success of *Frankenstein* in 1931, Whale was, apparently, oddly unwilling to add a second chapter to his tale of Promethean arrogance run amok. We have reason to thank whoever persuaded him to change his mind then, since *Bride* not only outstrips his original foray into horror in terms of invention and visual splendour, but stands as one of the most beguiling American films ever made. Packed with Whale's impish humour and sly subversion (both well documented in Bill Condon's excellent 1998 biopic *Gods And Monsters*), it also features characterisations of a subtlety seldom, if ever, witnessed in the horror genre and a clutch of acting performances to match.

The story picks up loosely where Frankenstein left off. The village mob, having seen the dreaded monster burn to death in the windmill and Frankenstein himself fall to his doom, head back to town safe in the knowledge of a job well done, their flaming torches extinguished and pitchforks stowed ready to brandish another day. Yet one couple remain, the parents of the little girl accidentally drowned by the monster in the previous film. They won't be satisfied until they see the corpse with their own eyes. Unfortunately, the creature is far from dead, a point made abundantly clear when it consigns the father to his own watery grave after he is foolish enough to venture inside the gutted building. Helped from the wreckage by the unwitting mother – who thinks the outstretched hand protruding from the rubble belongs to her husband – the monster shambles off into the forest to wreak customary havoc in a fruitless search for companionship.

Meanwhile, back at the castle, Henry Frankenstein (Clive – another brilliant essay in barely controlled mania) who also survived the mob's vengeance, is visited by the mysterious Dr Pretorius (Thesiger), an alchemist whose hobby is also the creation of artificial life, albeit on a much smaller scale. In one of the film's most memorable scenes he shows off his Lilliputian handiwork to an appalled Frankenstein who has vowed never to play God again. Nevertheless, Pretorius outlines his plan to create a mate for the monster and later succeeds in persuading Henry, via blackmail and kidnap, to partner him. Thus, in a perfectly realised riot of thrumming generators and flailing arcs of electrical current, high up in the castle rafters, the Bride is brought to life.

The film is stocked with similarly arresting moments – the monster, pursued through the forest finding shelter in the house of a blind, violin-playing hermit, himself as lonely as the misbegotten creature; Pretorius encountering the monster in an abandoned crypt, offering false friendship in order to lure him back to Frankenstein's castle; the monster pleading with a reluctant Frankenstein to give life to his longed for mate.

Charles D. Hall's art direction and John Mescall's glowing cinematography combine to brilliant effect, seamlessly merging surrealist fantasy with classic Hollywood gothic, garnished here and there with Expressionist flourishes. Note for instance how the forest changes from lush realism to a nightmare landscape of stunted tree trunks and tangled undergrowth as the monster takes flight from the huntsmen, his fear and panic mirrored in the unearthly, swirling vista around him. But it is the performances of Karloff, Lanchester and Thesiger that are the real heart of the film. Karloff, here receiving above-the-title billing, discovers new heights of pathos and rage, again investing the monster with a remarkable degree of humanity. The scene in which he rails against his repulsive appearance reflected in a lake is both touching and sad. And Lanchester, who also plays the young Mary Shelley in the film's prologue, is a worthy adversary. Her darting, angular movements, reminiscent of the automaton Maria in Fritz Lang's *Metropolis*, are beautifully controlled and, in contrast to Karloff's hulking gait, strangely elegant. Her appearance – deathly pallid skin with streaks of white hair highlighting her mountainous bouffant – is another triumph for makeup artist Jack Pierce and an image as instantly recognisable as Karloff's monster. And the shriek of horror she emits on seeing her intended for the first time rivals Fay Wray's piercing

Movie Trivia: The Bride of Frankenstein

The success of this sequel spawned six sequels by Universal pictures but none were directed by James Whale. The village prison set would be used again for Bela Lugosi's lair in *The Raven*, also starring Boris Karloff. To set up this sequel all prints of the 1931 *Frankenstein* were pruned of a last scene that contradicted the opening of the new film. Elsa Lanchester's look was modeled on a bust of Egyptian queen Nefertiti.

response to King Kong as the most famous scream in cinema history. But it's Thesiger who almost walks away with the film. Manipulative, camp, with ambiguous sexuality akimbo (only the director's supremely deft touch could have got that past the Hays office) and an erudite way with a thinly veiled blasphemy, it's impossible not to see him as an expanded version of Whale himself. And in the end it's Whale's erudite genius that brings it all together. He sculpts every nuance of self-parody, social satire, horror, humour, wit and whimsy into a dazzling whole, keeping every one of his fantastical plates spinning until the tragic, inevitable finale. Rejected by his bride and shunned by the world, the monster brings down the laboratory, burying his bride and the evil Pretorius in the debris. 'We belong dead' he moans.

In the original script Henry and his young wife Elizabeth also perished but at the last moment Whale saw fit to spare them. It seems an odd about face given his take on traditional relationships throughout the film. *Bride* has been seen, with some justification, as a thinly veiled attack on heterosexual values. Still, in 1935, if you could get away with showing a deformed monster (the ultimate rough trade?) settling down in domestic bliss, albeit short-lived, with another man, you could afford to throw the odd diversionary sop the censor's way. ★★★★★ **SB**

THE BRIDGE ON THE RIVER KWAI (1957)

Starring: *William Holden (Major Shears), Jack Hawkins (Major Warden), Alec Guinness (Colonel Nicholson), Sessue Hayakawa (Colonel Saito), James Donald (Major Clipton)*
Director: *David Lean*
Screenwriters: *Carl Foreman, Michael Wilson, based on the novel by Pierre Boulle*
PG/161 mins./War/USA

Awards: *Academy Awards – Best Picture, Best Director, Best Actor (Alec Guinness), Best Screenplay, Best Cinematography, Best Editing, Best Music Score; BAFTA – Best Film, Best British Film, Best British Actor (Alec Guinness), Best British Screenplay*

A squad of British soldiers arrive at a Japanese POW camp in the Burmese jungle, and after some conflict between their respective leaders, they are co-opted into building a railway bridge across the River Kwai. Meanwhile, the Allies plan a mission to blow-up the bridge before it can be used.

The first in David Lean's epic phase, this proud and accomplished war movie boasts all the qualities that made the British director a true great: lavish cinematography, meaty performances, and a psychologically complex script. It went on to soak up all the major Oscars, which has often skewed popular opinion into thinking of it as a grand, old-school opera of the British at war. However, this is to downplay the daring structure, the near absence of out-and-out warfare, and the fierce investigation of cultural divides be they Japanese, British or American, as personified by William Holden's brashly heroic Shears who will become the true enemy of Alec Guinness, in one of his most legendary roles as the indefatigable Colonel Nicholson.

Beyond the rash of subplots and beachside longeurs that take the story away from the POW camp, it is Nicholson's gradual breakdown into madness that occupies Lean's closest attentions. Guinness fills him with an absurdist stridency that is at once utterly heroic, masochistic and damn near demented, standing up to the speculative cruelty meted out by Hayakawa's irate camp commander Sessue. That they generate a form of respect is down to a kind mutual understanding of military bearing. A contest at which Lean nags and tests, contending that war is not a clean matter of following the rules. When Sessue demands the British prisoners partake in the building of a bridge, Nicholson sees this as a chance to keep his men in order, to show-off a British pride in work. What he so glaringly loses sight of, is that he is abetting the enemy.

When Shears, who has escaped from the camp, returns to destroy the bridge, giving the film a burst of lively adventure, the extent of Nicholson's madness becomes clear. The messiness of war has destroyed the order of his mind, even to the point of abusing his own men. His realisation of the bridge's doom, and his own with it, is as powerful a rendition of the unbidden, psychological damage of war than any amount of coughed-up T.S. Eliot by a hairless Brando. ★★★★★ **IN**

Movie Trivia: The Bridge On the River Kwai

This would be Alec Guinness and Jack Hawkins' third collaboration, as they worked previously together in *Malta Story* and *The Prisoner*. While the bridge in the story was built by prisoners in two months, the one constructed in Sri Lanka (then Ceylon) for filming took eight months. In some prints of this movie, Alec Guinness' surname is written Guiness.

A BRIDGE TOO FAR (1977)

Starring: *Anthony Hopkins (Lt. Col. John Frost), Edward Fox (Lt General Brian Horrocks), Michael Caine (Lt Col. J.O.E. Vandeleur), Sean Connery (Maj General Roy Urquhart), Robert Redford (Major Julian Cook), Elliot Gould (Col Robert Stout), Dirk Bogarde (Lt General Browning)*
Director: *Richard Attenborough*
Screenwriter: *William Goldman, based on the novel by Cornellius Ryan*
PG/176 mins./War/UK/USA

Awards: *BAFTA – Best Supporting Actor (Edward Fox), Best Soundtrack, Anthony Asquith Award for Film Music*

A multi-faceted telling of Operation Market-Garden, the Allies failed attempt to capture and hold a series of bridges that offered a perfect springboard to attack Germany.

For this wildly ambitious WWII epic, Richard Attenborough assembled one of the starriest male casts in cinema's long years, and set them to work try trying to wrestle a satisfying narrative out of the sprawling Allied misadventure that was Operation Market-Garden. An unusual and courageous choice for a war movie as it centres on marked failure.

There is an ironic equivalence between the British director's long, worthy and detailed film falling just short of its objective and the original mission's overreaching endeavours to gain a bridgehead into Nazi Germany. Neither succeeded, but both were a stirring effort all the same.

Attenborough's dilemma, despite sterling assistance from his screenwriter William Goldman, is the bitty nature of the narrative. Rather than concentrate on one particular facet of the history, he endeavours to capture snatches and starts from a host of different generals, colonels and privates dotted up and down the Rhine, all being co-ordinated by Dirk Bogarde's stuffy Lieutenant General. It's less a matter of a cast than a candy store of sparkling cameos.

The stand-out, or at least the most memorable, sequence involves the taking of Arnhem by Anthony Hopkins' Johnny Frost. The interminable stalemate of frontline combat is powerfully rendered: the strafed streets, the lack of supplies, the drift to inevitable surrender. It's one of the few occasions the ruthless exposure of troops is fully evinced.

While the film gets bogged down trying to extract the appropriate exactitude of the era – you can imagine how weighed down the set was by nodding historical advisors – the stiff-upper-lipped gallantry amongst the host of million dollar generals still carries a great sense of its own magnitude. Just chalk 'em up – Redford! Caan! Connery! Caine! Olivier! Hackman! – and watch the calamities tumble about them. The cross-hatched leadership with their endless table-talk and prevarication, plants the seeds of their own failure. In the end they were aiming too high, pushing one bridge too far. War and moviemaking share a lot in common. ★★★ **IN**

THE BRIDGES OF MADISON COUNTY (1995)

Starring: *Clint Eastwood (Robert Kincaid), Meryl Streep (Francesca Johnson), Annie Corley (Carolyn Johnson), Victor Slezak (Michael Johnson), Jim Haynie (Richard Johnson)*
Director: *Clint Eastwood*
Screenwriter: *Richard LaGravenese, based on the novel by Robert James Waller*
12/135 mins./Romance/Drama/USA

Robert Kincaid arrives in Iowa to take picture of the area. He bumps into neglected wife and mother Francesca and, with Francesca's family away for the week the pair indulge in a short but intense romance that lasts in their memories long after it is over.

The young, the smart alec, and those invulnerable to the contemplation of paths not taken in life, are likely to hold cheap the qualities that have made this handsomely crafted tearjerker the class, romantic weepy of 1995 in America – where 36 per cent of moviegoers are over 40.

It seems there is money (and Oscar nominations) to be gained from the sensitive, tasteful affirmation that there is a sex life to be had after the bloom is off the bod. Adapted from the phenomenally successful (and to this reviewer, ghastly) novel of the same name by Robert James Waller, Fisher King scripter Richard LaGravenese has pared the tale of its worst pseudo dribblings about taut muscles and 'the molecular space between male and female' with grace and some good humour. The film shifts the focus of the book from shaman-like *National Geographic* photographer Robert Kincaid (played by Eastwood) to Meryl Streep's Francesca, a robust but dreamy, Italian-born, taken-for-granted farmer's wife in Iowa.

With Francesca's corn-fed family conveniently out of the picture for a whole week at a cow show, she's ripe for a brief encounter when Kincaid pulls up in his pick-up truck in 1965 and ambles out in search of the nearest photogenic bridge. He proceeds to stick around to dispense enough quotes from Byron, cold beer and hot love to last a lifetime.

Playfully incorporating the inability of children, however old, to acknowledge their parents' sexuality, the story is intercut by present day episodes in which the recently deceased Francesca's adult son and daughter discover the history of this passionate interlude with envious shock that 'between bake sales Mom was Anais Nin!'.

As director, Eastwood goes for the slow burn in an unhurried, measured rhythm of visual details and silences that say more than the sometimes overly literary dialogue. And although some of the blubbing provoked is grief at Eastwood suddenly looking 100 years old, that unpredictable thing called chemistry is abundantly present, with Eastwood and Streep's artistically-lit couplings magically stirring. Discretionary warnings should be posted, however: 'This film is not suitable for guys.' ★★★★ **AE**

BRIDGET JONES' DIARY (2001)

Starring: *Renée Zellweger (Bridget Jones), Colin Firth (Mark Darcy), Hugh Grant (Daniel Cleaver), Jim Broadbent (Bridget's Dad), Gemma Jones (Bridget's Mum), Sally Phillips (Sharon – 'Shazza'), Shirley Henderson (Jude), James Callis (Tom), Embeth Davidtz (Natasha), Celia Imrie (Una Alconbury)*
Director: *Sharon Maguire*
Screenwriters: *Helen Fielding, Andrew Davies, Richard Curtis, based on the novel by Helen Fielding*
15/132 mins./Comedy/Romance/UK/France
Awards: *Empire – Best British Film*

Helen Fielding's infamous journal-keeper makes her big-screen debut, armed with Chardonnay, fags and a king-size bar of chocolate. And with gorgeous boss Daniel and hunky barrister Mark vying for her affections.

The cinematic adaptation of Helen Fielding's chick-lit classic was an endeavour fraught with pitfalls: the first person narration was never going to be an easy crossover to movies; the potential to alienate the male cinema-goer was massive; and the selection of Texan Zellweger to play Britain's favourite neurotic raised further suspicions. However, what first-time director Maguire, the writers and the perfectly pitched cast have created is another great British rom-com that manages to be even funnier and more romantic than Notting Hill.

The film's success is thanks in no small part to the three leads. Grant, as the deliciously dastardly Daniel, has never been better – far sexier as a posh cad and bounder than the usual foppish sweetie. Devilish and charming in equal measure – and with a dash of the Rupert Everetts about him – it's easy to see why Bridge can't resist his sleazy charms. Firth, meanwhile, is less of a showman, but appropriately revisits the haughty yet smouldering Mr Darcy of the BBC's *Pride And Prejudice*, the subject of so much girlie lusting in the original diary; as aloof barrister Mark Darcy, he's six-foot of repressed passion just waiting to be unleashed. Zellweger, meanwhile, who rarely lets the accent slip, more than answers her critics, lurching from one disaster to the next, but still managing to balance her endearing daffiness with an irresistible sauciness – no wonder Daniel and Mark are fighting to get into her control-top knickers.

Admittedly there are moments when her more embarrassing gaffes make you cringe, yet the character is in a sense the victim of her own success; it's easy to forget that, as much as she is an icon of modern womanhood, she is also a satirical, albeit deeply affectionate, take on that same creature. Large tracts of the diary – and no doubt many readers' 'best bits' – have, by necessity, been omitted. Moreover, Bridget's wonderful 'urban family', Tom (James Callis), Jude (Shirley Henderson) and Shazzer, are greatly underused, and a sub-plot featuring Bridget's parents' troubled marriage seems truncated.

But these are minor quibbles, and with at least one laugh-out loud moment every five minutes, several stand-out scenes (Geoffrey and Una's tarts 'n' vicars party and Daniel's boating accident, to name but two), a swooningly romantic denouement and the sort of top-class support that you only seem to get in British comedies, what you have is an above-average chick-flick that even blokes will tolerate (cf. Renée's bunny outfit). V.g., as Bridget might say. ★★★★ **LB**

BRIDGET JONES – EDGE OF REASON (2004)

Starring: *Renée Zellweger (Bridget Jones), Colin Firth (Mark Darcy), Hugh Grant (Daniel Cleaver), Jacinda Barrett (Rebecca), Jim Broadbent (Bridget's Dad), Gemma Jones (Bridget's Mum), Sally Phillips (Shazzer), James Callis (Tom), Shirley Henderson (Jude), James Faulkner (Uncle Geoffrey)*
Director: *Beeban Kidron*
Screenwriters: *Richard Curtis, Andrew Davies, Helen Fielding, Adam Brooks, based on the novel by Helen Fielding*
15/108 mins./Comedy/Romance/UK/France/Germany/Ireland/US

Now she's found love with Mark Darcy, it looks as though Bridget's singleton days are over – until an apparent love rival threatens to put a dampener on their relationship.

If you were to list the most likely sequels ever, this one would surely come just after *Harry Potter And The Chamber Of Secrets* and *Batman Begins*. After all, the movie adaptation of *Bridget Jones's Diary* was a huge hit with both public and (surprised) critics alike, while the source material already existed in the shape of Helen Fielding's follow-up book. But that doesn't mean we're looking at a surefire success – sadly, Bridget's latest big-screen adventures represent more of a retread than any kind of progression.

While there's still some amusement to be had from our hapless heroine's quirky approach to life, the film feels light on plot and often struggles to fill its near two-hour running time, defaulting to schmaltz mode when something, dare we suggest it, funny would have worked so much better.

Nowhere is this more apparent than during the first half, when Bridget, having settled into a life of cosy coupledom with Mark Darcy, becomes convinced he's up to no good behind her back, her insecurities all but killing their perfect relationship. Which is all very well, but it's dragged out to such an extent as to become frustrating to watch. Things pick up considerably once Grant returns as Bridget's sleazy ex – now working as a TV reporter for a trashy travel show – while the heroine herself, through a series of contrivances, winds up in a Thai prison and is forced to rethink her actions while behind bars.

Much of the humour is confined to a handful of set-pieces and keeps the same showy, slapstick mood established in the first movie – so we have Bridget sky-diving out of a plane into a pigsty, Bridget teaching a cell-load of Thai convicts to sing Madonna songs and, in one admittedly hilarious sequence, Bridget realising that skiing isn't nearly as easy as it looks. Zellweger, who has settled comfortably into the role, shines here, relishing the chance to show off her comic talents, while Grant once again proves he's much more fun to watch when playing a bad guy. Firth, however, is wasted – Mark Darcy is so dull that it's almost a relief when their relationship starts to unravel – while other returning cast members, including Sally Phillips, Shirley Henderson and Jim Broadbent, are given so little to do that you wonder why they bothered coming back at all.

We're not talking total washout, though. It's a serviceable sequel, which will please the less demanding crowd. Plus, to the film's credit, it does look better than its predecessor, even if this should come as no surprise given that director Beeban Kidron has more of a track record than *Diary*'s Sharon Maguire. Kidron really makes the most of her locations, interspersing the action, for example, with beautifully shot views of London and Thailand that help liven things up considerably. But beyond that, *Edge Of Reason*'s overwhelming filmmaking-by-numbers feel rankles, with Kidron wheeling out warmed-over versions of jokes from the first pic (there's even a fight sequence between Firth and Grant, would you believe) and resorting to standard-issue rom-com clichés and radio-friendly pop tunes to plug the gaps.

Perhaps if it had relied more on the book than the first movie, things might have been different; the sequence in the novel in which Bridget interviews Colin Firth, for example, would have made for very interesting viewing – clearly the filmmakers agreed because it later appeared as a DVD extra. As it stands, it's little more than a hit-and-miss attempt to replay its predecessor's cinematic triumphs. ★★ **CW**

BRIEF ENCOUNTER (1945)

Starring: *Celia Johnson (Laura Jesson), Trevor Howard (Alec Harvey), Cyril Raymond (Fred Jesson), Stanley Holloway (Albert Godby), Joyce Carey (Myrtle Bagot), Valentine Dyall (Stephen Lynn)*
Director: *David Lean*
Screenwriters: *Noel Coward, David Lean, Anthony Havelock-Allan, based on Noel Coward's play Still Life*
PG/86 mins./Romance/UK

Middle-class housewife Laura meets Dr Alec Harvey when she gets grit in the eye at the railway buffet, who skilfully removes the dirt in question only to fill her heart with longing and hope. Gradually they fall in love, though they know that their love, in a middle-class England of strict sensibilities, is impossible.

Skilfully set to Rachmaninov's *Second Piano Concerto*, this account of a passionate yet unconsummated relationship between a married woman and a married doctor created a great impression both here and abroad. Its value lies above all in its realistic description of provincial, middle-class English life: the couple's cluttered suburban home; Saturday shopping in the small town; the tea room; the lock-keeper's home; and, especially, the railway buffet that's the centre of the affair. Under her silly hat, Celia Johnson is undeniably moving, while Howard is everything a 'proper' man should be. There is also effective support (and some comic relief), from even the most minor of characters.

Full credit should be given to cinematographer Krasker, whose beautiful monochrome rendering of a love that cannot be, gave the film an oft imitated look, and a sense of realism that struck a chord with audiences at the time – and with romantics ever since. ★★★★ **CW**

David Lean (1908–1991)

Who was he: Editor turned director of masterful Noel Coward and Charles Dickens adaptations before becoming cinema's definitive large-canvas dramatist.

Hallmarks: Epic sweep; mixture of spectacle and intelligence; astonishing craft; bum-numbing running times.

If you see one film, see: *Lawrence of Arabia* (1962)

BRIGADOON (1954)

Starring: *Gene Kelly (Tommy Albright), Van Johnson (Jeff Douglas), Cyd Charisse (Fiona Campbell), Elaine Stewart (Jane Ashton), Barry Jones (Mr Lundie), Hugh Laing (Harry Beaton)*
Director: *Vincente Minnelli*
Screenwriter: *Alan Jay Lerner, based on the musical play by Lerner and Frederick Loewe*
U/108 mins./Musical/USA

Tommy and Jeff, Americans on a grouse-hunting holiday, wander through a Scotch mist into the enchanted village of Brigadoon, which remains as it was in 1754, existing for only one day in every century. Tommy falls for local girl Fiona.

Though Alan Jay Lerner and Frederick Lowe's score includes the standard hit 'Almost Like Being in Love', this is one of MGM's more grotesque musical efforts. In 1953, Vincente Minnelli made *The Band Wagon*, in which Jack Buchanan plays a director of musicals who runs away with himself and delivers a pretentious, overly-wrought flop – a year later, Minnelli made *Brigadoon*, which seems exactly like the comically dud production glimpsed in the earlier film.

A widescreen reproduction of a Broadway hit, *Brigadoon* runs to acres of face-frozen grins, billows of smoke machine mist, stiff supporting performances (with bogus Scots accents that make James Doohan sound like Robert Carlyle), a pompous and tasteless script and a kitsch vision of Scotland which is long on tartan tights and choreographed lynchings.

The long-legged Charisse, in ridiculous costumes, is the major attraction from the past, tempting cynical modern American Kelly to disappear into the magical village, and a far more convincing reason for surrendering to the fantasy than the somewhat embarrassing 'social comment' sequences.

The film tries to sell the frozen-in-1754 village as a magical utopia like Shangri-La, but it's hard not to sympathise with the one bad-tempered villager who hates the ridiculously-contrived spell a pastor has brought down on Brigadoon to protect it from the outside world – the rest of the happy folks hunt this poor loser down and bring about his death, all the while singing a song about it.

Based on a Japanese ghost story, the film later inspired Herschell Gordon Lewis's splatter classic *Two Thousand Maniacs*! ★★ **KN**

BRIGHTON ROCK (1947)

Starring: *Richard Attenborough (Pinkie), Carol Marsh (Rose Brown), Hermione Baddeley (Ida Arnold), William Hartnell (Dallow), Nigel Stock (Cubit), Wylie Watson (Spicer)*
Director: *John Boulting*
Screenwriters: *Graham Greene, Terence Rattigan, based on the novel by Greene*
PG/92 mins./Crime/UK

An adaptation of Graham Greene's classic novel, about a small-time Brighton hoodlum Pinkie, whose attempts to cover up a murder become ever more complicated. To silence one particular witness, the naïve and lovestruck Rose, he ensnares and marries her.

While so many authors suffer the translation to the big screen, their words too sprawling to whittle down to some sensible filmic order, Graham Greene's wiry, evocative fiction makes the journey more or less intact. Alongside *The Third Man* and *The Fallen Idol*, this strident, shadowy seaside noir is a further mark of excellence in his adapted canon.

The trick seems to be to grasp first and foremost the complex natures of his characters, then let the plot spill about them. Getting Pinkie right was essential, he stands as possibly Greene's most memorable character, a lowlife gang leader barely beyond his teens, shirking his good Catholic upbringing, his soul lost to small ambitions and petty crime. Richard Attenborough, then so fresh-faced, gives him real edges, driven by an uncomfortable urgency he can never settle. There's an unreachable itch in his Pinkie, but he has charisma, albeit a stern, violent kind of magnetic force.

Into his deadly orbit falls the lithe naïf Rose, a waitress dappy for love, determinedly upholding her Catholic dues carrying an unbidden knowledge that could sink Pinkie. So he works her vulnerability, offering her the sham of true love, which she buys wholesale. Carol Marsh exposes both her vulnerability and stalwart heart.

The film is cast well across the board – William Hartnell, Nigel Stock and Wylie Watson as Pinkie's weasley band, and Hermione Baddeley as Ida, the brassy broad who is onto Pinkie.

Director John Boulting brings the fabled Greeneland, that vile landscape ripened on sin and betrayal at the black heart of all his novels, to sensuous life. You feel the throb of Brighton's cramped summer streets, the raddled squawks of hungry gulls, and the sizzle of frying food. Yet beneath this papered veneer of normality, lurks a seething underworld, shorn of glamour, where righteousness will finally usher the film to its fateful, cruel conclusion. ★★★★ **IN**

BRING IT ON (2000)

Starring: *Kirsten Dunst (Torrance Shipman), Eliza Dushku (Missy Pantone), Jesse Bradford (Cliff Pantone), Gabrielle Union (Isis), Clare Kramer (Courtney)*
Director: *Peyton Reed*
Screenwriter: *Jessica Bendinger*
12/105 mins./Comedy/USA

With the help of gymnastics genius Missy Pantone, Torrance, the captain of cheerleader champs the Toros, drives her team to create an original routine, skirts around romance with Missy's brother and squares up to Isis, the head girl of rivals the Clovers.

So overflowing with lithe young totty – shot in languorous slo-mo – that local divisions of the Dirty Mac Brigade are already stocking up on multiply tissues, *Bring It On*, for the rest of us, is a spirited cartwheel through cheerleading and teen comedy grooves without ever getting to the heart of how ridiculous parading with pom poms actually is.

As the opening sequence kicks in – a direct-to-camera cheerleading routine that takes the piss out of every one you've ever seen – the stage is set for a sharp satire on high school rituals. Yet, the edgy tone soon dissipates and the movie swiftly blands out into more conventional fare, ticking all the boxes in the teen flick checklist: laboured girlie bitching, drippy romance, smart-aleck little brother as comic relief, the alternative rock soundtrack, the easy moral (being yourself is what counts) and an ending as predictable as anything on 90210 are all here and accounted for.

Still, there's lots to like about *Bring It On*. The dialogue contains a smattering of sassy lines ('Your ass is so big it could form its own web site'), the look is bright and cartoony and the film throws the occasional quirk into the formula: a high school that roots for the cheerleaders rather than the team, and a funny, bizarre scene in which Torrance and Cliff try to outdo each other in a teeth-cleaning face-off.

As she proved with the superior *Drop Dead Gorgeous*, Dunst can simultaneously inhabit, yet slyly lampoon, the all-American stereotype, and is rapidly becoming the most interesting of the young set. Reed, meanwhile, injects the proceedings with a surfeit of energy: the staging of the cheerleading sequences is particularly dynamic and inventive, the direction finding myriad ways to film the umpteen scenes of cavorting.

Fun and lively, then, but lacking the requisite intelligence to make it anything else. ★★★ **IF**

BRINGING OUT THE DEAD (1999)

Starring: *Nicolas Cage (Frank Pierce), Patricia Arquette (Mary Burke), John Goodman (Larry Verber), Ving Rhames (Marcus), Tom Sizemore (Tom Wall), Marc Anthony (Noel), Mary Beth Hurt (Nurse Constance)*
Director: *Martin Scorsese*
Screenwriter: *Paul Schrader, based on novel by Joe Connelly*
18/121 mins./Drama/USA

Nicholas Cage plays a despairing paramedic buckling under the pressure of attending casualties in Hell's Kitchen, dragged further into hell by a succession of manic partners, but possibly saved by an ex-junkie whose dad is dying from a heart attack.

For his 18th feature film as director, Martin Scorsese went back to his roots. After dilly dalai-ing with Eastern spirituality in Kundun, the world's most vital film director has returned to New York, damaged heroes and the filmmaking fireworks that got the world excited about the man in the first place. And if *Bringing Out The Dead* is not vintage Scorsese, it's still an original, blistering slice of virtuoso moviemaking.

Riding shotgun with old writing cohort Schrader, Scorsese's adaptation of Joe Connelly's novel fairly fizzes on kinetic energy as it follows haunted paramedic Frank Pierce (Cage, reining in the histrionics) through three nights and two days working for New York's Emergency Medical Service. As Pierce and partners – food obsessed Larry, bible-bashing soul brother Marcus and borderline psycho Tom (a terrifically manic Sizemore) – revive cardiac arrests, bring overdosers back from the brink and attend a virgin birth (kind of), Scorsese's breathless directorial mastery is at full tilt: finding fantastic variety in a film rooted around the exteriors/interiors of an ambulance, we are treated to an onslaught of breakneck pans, funky framing, crackerfire editing and perfectly deployed music that tangibly articulates the in-your-face brutality and adrenaline rush of the graveyard shift.

By comparison, the less successful daytime sequences are eerily sedate yet unmoving as Pierce hooks up with Mary Burke, the daughter of one of Pierce's patients, whose withdrawn drug-dependent life mirrors his own. In the latter stages, as Pierce seeks solace in narcotics, Scorsese goes into overdrive – speeded-up imagery, spectres emerging from the streets – underlining his unparalleled genius at depicting troubled psychosis through searing visuals.

This could all be unrelentingly unwatchable, but it isn't. In fact, it is the funniest Scorsese movie since *After Hours*, plying a nifty trade in pitch-black humour: be it Pierce begging his boss to fire him or the cracking dialogue exchanged en route to accidents. But far from being insensitive, it is abundantly clear that their caustic worldview preserves the paramedics' sanity. With its plotline of a troubled loner cruising NY's streets in a metal box, *Dead* strongly echoes *Taxi Driver*. It may never attain the feverish intensity and staying power of the earlier film, but a slightly off colour Scorsese is better than 98 per cent of most directors firing on all cylinders.

★★★★ IF

⦿ BRINGING UP BABY (1938)

Starring: *Katharine Hepburn (Susan Vance), Cary Grant (David Huxley), Charlie Ruggles (Maj. Horace Applegate), May Robson (Aunt Elizabeth), Barry Fitzgerald (Mr Gogarty)*
Director: *Howard Hawks*
Screenwriters: *Dudley Nichols, Hagar Wilde, based on a story by Hagar Wilde*
U/102 mins./Comedy/USA

A palaeontologist becomes mixed up with crazy socialite and ends up on the trail of a lost leopard.

Screwball comedy is defined by the eccentric characters, unconventional situations, slapstick, mishaps, sexual chemistry and snappy repartee of this landmark jape. Staples of the genre – an absent-minded professor, a madcap heiress, a contrary animal (or three in this case), a large sum of money being sought, pratfalls, cocktails, false identity, a pursuit, a car crash, an unwanted fiancée, and absurd confusion – are all present in mint condition in Howard Hawks' breakneck-paced, maniacally funny picture; written by one of the top screenwriters of the 30s, Dudley Nichols (an Oscar winner for the John Ford drama *The Informer* (1935).

The earnest, easily muddled palaeontologist in need of some fun, Dr David Huxley is awaiting the last bone to complete the brontosaurus he has laboured four years to reconstruct. It is to arrive on the morrow, his wedding day. Fiancée and assistant Alice Swallow (Virginia Walker), a prim bluestocking scold, sends him off to play golf with the lawyer of a potential benefactor, to schmooze for a million-dollar grant to continue his project at the natural history museum. But Huxley's efforts on the golf course become a shambles when he encounters blithe and playful, 'conceited, spoiled little scatterbrain' Susan Vance. And that's just the first five minutes. Give her 24 hours and disaster instigator Susan is going to turn David's life upside down.

Baby is the tame leopard Susan's brother has shipped from his hunting expedition in Brazil (just the sort of thing the idle rich do in 30s films). The only information that comes with him is that Baby likes dogs (whether as food or for companionship poses a later relevant question) and music, particularly 'I Can't Give You Anything But Love'. He also likes mauling the hapless professor Huxley, as does Susan, who is determined to have him and keep him near when she discovers how handsome he is without his academic specs on.

Thus he is shanghaied to convey Baby to Susan's aunt's farm in Connecticut where – after the obligatory collision with a poultry truck, car theft and the swiping of David's clothes – she is revealed as the wealthy philanthropist. Meanwhile, her fiendish fox terrier George steals and buries the brontosaurus clavicle (somewhere in a 26-acre garden), Susan frees a man-killing leopard she's mistaken for the missing Baby and most of the ensemble are jailed in noisy pandemonium.

Countless films have imitated *Bringing Up Baby*, most famously Peter Bogdanovich's homage *What's Up, Doc?* (1972), but it is futile to look for its equal. Hawks, a master of any genre, was one of the innovators of deliriously frantic, overlapping dialogue; only *His Girl Friday* (1940 – also Hawks) can claim faster talking. Hepburn and Grant, who made four films together, are a peerless partnership in the departments of good looks, charm and comic timing, throwing themselves down slopes, into water holes, atop a dinosaur and into love like no one else. Highlights include Susan, unaware David's foot is on her hem, stomping off minus the back of her lamé gown, forcing a tandem silly walk out of a club to cover her exposed drawers; Susan and David harmonising 'I Can't Give You Anything But Love' to a sulking Baby on the roof, over a Viennese psychiatrist who's already convinced they're insane; and the enraged David aggressively accosting stately Aunt Elizabeth (May Robson) while he's wearing nothing but a marabou-trimmed negligee.

The special effects, devised by Linwood Dunn, deserve a mention since, even today, the interplay between Grant, Hepburn, the pooch, the recalcitrant Baby, and his deadly double, looks hilariously real. The leopard was filmed separately and put together with his co-stars by means of a travelling matte, blended split-screen technique. Look very closely when Hepburn drags the snarling beast into the police station (actually she was heaving a prop man tied to her rope), and you may just glimpse the ghost image of another rope (the underlay footage of the trainer pulling the leopard).

Bringing Up Baby, which cost about a million dollars to make, did not find favour with audiences on its first release and actually lost about $365,000. Hepburn's latest of several flops, it ended her work at RKO. She moved back to New York for two years, returning in possession of the rights to film *The Philadelphia Story*, for which she chose Grant to partner her in a triumphant comeback – at MGM. Ironically, as RKO declined, *Bringing Up Baby*'s popularity grew alongside its reknown as 'the definitive screwball comedy'. And so did Hepburn's fortune. The savvy star owned a piece of it.

★★★★★ AE

Howard Hawks (1896–1977)

Who he was: Former pro car racer who, over four decades, became Hollywood's most versatile craftsman, working with practically every major star (Wayne, Monroe, Bogart, Hepburn) and mastering every genre.

Hallmarks: Unobtrusive camera movements; overlapping dialogue; feisty heroines; camaraderie among men in confined spaces; comedies often the inverse of his action flicks.

If you see one film, see: *His Girl Friday* (1940)

BROADWAY DANNY ROSE (1984)

Starring: *Woody Allen (Danny Rose), Mia Farrow (Tina Vitale), Nick Apollo Forte (Lou Canova), Sandy Baron (himself), Corbett Monica (himself), Jackie Gayle (himself), Morty Gunty (himself)*
Director: *Woody Allen*
Screenwriter: *Woody Allen*
PG/84 mins./Comedy/USA

Over dinner a group of New York agents try to best one another with stories of Danny Rose, Broadway's least successful agent. The winning tale involves Danny babysitting comeback singer Lou Canova's girlfriend – when he starts to fall for her, two mobsters come to pay a visit.

Back when there was loveableness to Woody Allen's work, when he bordered his philosophising and quaint studies of losers in the game of romance, with traces of parody, he delivered this slight but delightful tale of an all-count loser. Danny Rose is all heart but no talent, which could equally go for his muddle of novelty acts including xylophonists, milk bottle players ('Never had a lesson!') even a bird that can get a tune out of a piano. He's a nonsense, the punchline to his peers jokes. Even his sole credible act is an aging singer with a booze problem and a mistress who needs managing in her own right. Nothing goes well for Danny, but then he's played with all Allen's magnificent gusts of neurotic jabber, forever hunched and apologetic, but the master performer never lets us forget he's a human being.

The plot, relayed by a gabble of well-oiled fellow agents (played by the real deal) at the Carnegie Deli, has Danny forced to play partner to Nick Apollo's aging but reasonably talented crooner's latest squeeze-on-the-side. When they have a fight, it transpires she's also got a Mafioso on the go. Next thing you know, hyper-nervous Danny is staring down the barrel of a mobster's gun. And this being in the classic Allen mould, where the real heart gets the girl, he falls for this brassy headache himself.

Mia Farrow, for once, works firmly against her typical chiselled, intellectual waifs, Tina is set with sunglasses, attitude and an ever-present puff of cigarette smoke. She's so far out of Danny's reach, he might as well not exist. Apollo is a good discovery, he plays Lou Canonva louche and loud, but soft, sticking by this schmuck of an agent even when better offers could have sent him flying, These are the touchstones for Allen's slender, rascally comedy: loyalty over success, love over social status. It's a fairy-tale, a glittering New York fable told in a silvery black and white, laden with nostalgia for times and oddities long gone from the hallowed halls of Broadway. **★★★★ IN**

BROKEBACK MOUNTAIN (2005)

Starring: *Heath Ledger (Ennis Del Mar), Jake Gyllenhaal (Jack Twist), Randy Quaid (Joe Aguirre), Anne Hathaway (Lureen Newsome), Michelle Williams (Alma)*
Director: *Ang Lee*
Screenwriters: *Larry McMurtry, Diana Ossana, based on a short story by Annie Proulx*
15/134 mins./Drama/USA

Awards: *Academy Awards – Best Director, Best Score, Best Adapted Screenplay, BAFTA – Best Film, Best Supporting Actor (Jake Gyllenhaal), Best Adapted Screenplay, Best Director, Golden Globes – Best Director, Best Drama, Best Original Song, Best Screenplay*

The year is 1963 and two jobbing farmhands take a gig tending sheep on a remote mountain. During their months alone, they form a bond that extends to a sexual relationship, but once the job is finished they return to their daily lives. However, the attraction remains, and will haunt them over the next two decades.

When word first reached us that, after the critical opprobrium heaped on *Hulk*, Ang Lee was turning his attention to what was only ever described in the press as a 'gay Western', we thought he'd taken leave of his senses – and, indeed, sensibility. A director with a remarkably broad palette, Lee had trademarked a devastating understatement in films as controlled and anguished as *The Ice Storm*, while *Crouching Tiger* revealed his magic touch extended to action too. Now there was a sense that maybe he was about to overreach himself, or (worst-case scenario) had lost all sense of identity and was about to over-indulge himself. Then, when stories leaked that the Cannes Film Festival had given it the thumbs-down this year – in favour of a line-up that consisted of directors we'd definitely consider to be his peers – it really seemed that the shit was about to hit Lee's fans.

We needn't have worried. *Brokeback Mountain* may even be Lee's finest film to date, an amalgamation of the work he's done before but pushed forward into the realms of, well, something we've never seen before. Though the opening half-hour is dream-like and idyllic, recalling the more beautiful landscapes in Gus Van Sant's most mainstream movies (*My Own Private Idaho* specifically), Lee's film takes arthouse conventions and absorbs them into a style that, while never approaching commercial, is both romantic and accessible. Much of this is down to the two leads – neo-Hollywood heartthrobs playing, to one degree only, against type – but Lee is careful with his framing and the first half hour – that ominous lead-up to the first graphic fumble – is suffused with rare beauty and an almost palpable sense of place.

Half an hour of mountains, sheep, changing seasons and minimal dialogue may seem a leap for most audiences, but Lee's touch is light instead of stately, and he leads us slowly into an affair that would otherwise seem forced and clumsy. As he says himself, *Brokeback Mountain* itself is a key supporting player in the film, a place where nobody else matters – or, more importantly, is. It's a vital part of the movie that prepares us for the inevitable day when Jack Twist (Jake Gyllenhaal) and Ennis Del Mar (Heath Ledger) come down from their idyll and try to pick up their lives where they'd left off. Both enter into half-hearted marriages, have children and take shitty jobs, but the memory of the time on the mountain lingers. Could it last in the real world? Jack, ever the idealist, thinks so; Ennis, the fatalist and the realist, knows otherwise, shrinking back into his armour of plaid and leather.

It's here that Lee's film truly announces its intentions, and for a good portion of the drama Jack and Ennis are far apart; in fact, they don't even communicate for four years. In the meantime, they settle into drudgery and roles they resent, but Lee's masterstroke is to pull the camera back from their interior world. What sounds on paper like a traditional gay independent movie does not follow the usual formula and actually gives voice to its audience's prejudices and apprehensions. We hear their Brokeback boss, Joe Aguirre (Randy Quaid), snidely pass judgment ('You boys sure found a way to make the time pass up there'), and when Ennis' wife (a poignant Michelle Williams) sees exactly what the score is with Jack, her confusion – and indeed revulsion – is key to the film's climax, if it can be said to reach one in the usual sense.

But enough of Lee and his dexterity and subtlety – we've known about it all along, even in *Hulk*, which, for all the kerfuffle and despite a lumpy ending, was a sensitive sins-of-the-father story wrapped up in genre clothing. Jake Gyllenhaal, too, is something of a known quantity, a lugubrious presence whose big blue eyes will make Brokeback a paradoxically compelling object of morbid passion for teenage girls the whole world over. And we'll forget the terrific marketing strategy of having *The Princess Diaries*' star Anne Hathaway make her topless debut. No, the real revelation here is Heath Ledger as the bruised and sometimes brutal Ennis.

His tortured secret is the tragedy and the ecstasy of this powerful and moving film, a smart study of relationships that could but can't and never will be. **★★★★★ DW**

ⓢ BROKEN ARROW (1996)

Starring: *John Travolta (Major Vic Deakins), Christian Slater (Captain Riley Hale), Samantha Mathis (Terry Carmichael), Delroy Lindo (Colonel Max Wilkins), Frank Whaley (Giles Prentice)*
Director: *John Woo*
Screenwriter: *Graham Yost*
15/108 mins./Action/Thriller/USA

When stealth bomber pilot Vic Deakins reveals his dark side stealing two nuclear missiles (or 'Broken Arrows') for an elaborate slice of extortion, it is up to his co-pilot Riley Hale and local park ranger Terry Carmichael, to track him down on foot and save Utah from annihilation.

The first sign that John Woo's transfer from his Hong Kong haunts was not going to be quite as exalted as hoped for, this crackpot thriller features John Travolta exaggerating every gesture and smirk, like John Wayne jacked on amphetamines, and a loose collection of cranked-up action scenes, but scant else. There is something flabby and wasteful about this thriller looking to Western motifs for its spin, the action sprawling across an arid piece of Utah scrub where the despicable 'Deak' has stashed his stolen nukes.

We start with the partners, Deak and Riley, a father-son, teacher-pupil, bully-victim concoction represented by the fact they commence proceedings by pummelling each other in a boxing ring. Just for giggles really. It's swiftly apparent Deak is a win-at-all-costs kinda guy, Hale may have a decent core. That's it for characterisation, now just stand back as Travolta hits full throttle and Woo goes to his store cupboard of iconic imagery – twin revolvers, ticking bombs, bumpy car chases, all pumped slightly higher, slightly longer.

The reason for the desert setting, and it supplies a nifty subterranean nuclear explosion throbbing a ripple across the surface scenery, is that is where Deak has ditched their jet to nab the missiles to commence his complicated plan for extorting money out of the government or he'll light the blue touch paper. There's some comedy mined here, Woo never allows us to take his giddy actioners very seriously. Travolta is certainly in on the joke, he pretty much is the joke, but no one seems to have told Christian Slater who is horribly earnest and never sits right in the hero mould. The film stops dead whenever he wanders in.

Of course, it throttles along, gathering enough momentum to carry you to next overblown action sequence, but no matter how high wire the stunts, or brash and cavalier the acting, it never escapes the feel of an over-budgeted B-movie drunk on its own pointless excesses. **★★ IN**

ⓢ BROKEN BLOSSOMS (1919)

Starring: *Lillian Gish (Lucy Burrows), Richard Barthelmess (Cheng Huan), Donald Crisp (Battling Burrows), Arthur Howard (Burrows' manager), Edward Pell (Evil Eye)*
Director: *D.W. Griffith*
Screenwriter: *D.W. Griffith, based on the story* The Chink And The Child *by Thomas Burke*
PG/90 mins./Drama/USA

Frustrated in his mission to bring peace to the English, Chinese aristocrat Cheng Haun wallows in opium addiction until he determines to rescue Lucy from her abusive father, Battling Butler.

Based on the sensitively titled story 'The Chink and the Child' from Thomas Burke's collection *Limehouse Nights*, this initially seems like a typical silent melodrama. But, there's actually little traditional action in this profound study of character and mood, which devotes more time to the cinematic emoting of Lillian Gish and Richard Barthelmess than it does to the theatrical histrionics of Donald Crisp. Moreover, D.W. Griffith relaxes his strict Victorian morality to explore such contentious issues as opium eating, sado-masochism and inter-racial romance.

This was Griffith's first studio-bound feature and he tailors his lighting and décor to enhance both the authenticity and intensity of the scenario. He was greatly aided in this by Hendrik Sartov (who assisted Billy Bitzer with the numerous close-ups) and editor James Smith, who achieves a trance-like metre that was wholly commensurate with the idyllic seclusion in which Gish and Barthelmess cocoon themselves and the temperament of a world still in the throes of recovering from global conflict.

Gish initially refused to play the waif and missed some of the six-week rehearsal period with influenza. Yet, she was to give one of her finest performances, with the delicacy of the sequence in which she fixes a smile with her fingers contrasting with the visceral terror she exhibits while cowering in the closet from the axe-wielding Crisp. Barthelmess similarly excels himself, although he borrowed many of the 'Yellow Man''s mannerisms from George Fawcett, who had developed the part during pre-production.

Forced to buy the picture back for $250,000 from Paramount's Adolph Zukor, Griffith released it through the newly formed United Artists and used tints, live prologues, orchestras and choirs to boost its box-office prospects. It made a fortune, but its filmic influence was most keenly felt among French Impressionists like Louis Delluc, Germaine Dulac and Marcel L'Herbier and German 'street realists' like Karl Grune and G.W. Pabst. **★★★★ DP**

ⓢ BROKEN FLOWERS (2005)

Starring: *Bill Murray (Don Johnston), Julie Delpy (Sherry), Heather Simms (Mona), Sharon Stone (Laura), Alexis Dziena (Lolita Miller)*
Director: *Jim Jarmusch*
Screenwriter: *Jim Jarmusch*
15/106 mins./Comedy/Drama/USA/France

When an anonymous letter arrives at his door telling him he has a grown-up son who may be searching for him, Don Johnston – egged on by his wannabe-detective neighbour Winston – goes on a cross-country journey in search of the old flames who could possibly be the mother.

However you prefer your Bill Murray to be served – *Lost In Translation*'s sad, worldweary blend or *Groundhog Day*'s wryly cynical cuppa – this sharply observed comedy-drama from writer-director Jim Jarmusch should slip down nicely. Here Murray portrays Don Johnston, a middle-aged former Don Juan (although rather a cackhanded one, as constantly referenced with riffs on his near-namesake) confronted by his past, who half-heartedly embarks on a tour on which he learns as much about himself as about the women who may have borne him a son.

Broken Flowers shares much of the tone of *Translation*, slightly disconnected yet full of heart. There's also an autumn-years quirkiness and exasperation with American suburbia that's reminiscent of *About Schmidt*, as Don travels from one ex-girlfriend's home town to another in a series of nondescript rental cars, arriving with a bunch of pink flowers each time (a suggestion from enthusiastic neighbour Winston, who thinks the colour of the bouquet may get a reaction since the anonymous letter was on pink paper).

His revisited conquests are a disparate bunch, in keeping with our hero's muddled emotional state. There's an affectionate meeting with Laura (Sharon Stone) and her daughter Lolita (who truly lives up to her name), then a bizarre one with prim and proper Dora (Frances Conroy) and her husband (played by the wonderful Christopher McDonald, most remembered as Geena Davis' irritating hubby in *Thelma And Louise*). Most enjoyable, though, is Don's visit with Carmen (Jessica Lange, simply lovely), an ex-lawyer-turned-animal communicator. In fact, all the actresses (including Tilda Swinton as ex number four) give wonderful performances in the short screen time each of them is allowed.

But the most inspired teaming is that of Murray, terrific throughout, and director Jarmusch (the pair previously worked together on *Coffee And*

Cigarettes, which shares this movie's episodic tone). Jarmusch has already displayed an empathy for the outsider and the loner in movies like *Dead Man* and *Stranger Than Paradise*, and in Murray he has a perfect foil, a melancholy, still man who holds this journey into mid-life crisis with a bemused loveability and makes it a trip truly worth joining him on. **★★★★ JB**

THE BROOD (1979)

Starring: *Oliver Reed (Dr Raglan), Samantha Eggar (Nola), Art Hindle (Frank), Cindy Hinds (Candice), Nuala Fitzgerald (Julianna), Henry Beckman (Barton Kelly), Susan Hogan (Ruth)*
Director: *David Cronenberg*
Screenwriter: *David Cronenberg*
18/91 mins./Horror/Canada

Frank Carveth is worried that his ex-wife Nola is being driven crazier by Psychoplasmics, a form of therapy invented by pop psychologist Dr Hal Raglan in which patients' neuroses manifest physically on their bodies. Child-sized, deformed creatures murder Nola's parents, and Frank traces them back to Raglan's institute.

David Cronenberg's third above-ground science fiction/horror movie is more controlled than *Shivers* or *Rabid*, narrowing focus from a community going insane to a single, troubled family.

An intensely acted, cleverly written mystery, this methodically sets out an absurd premise – that mad Nola's rage is given shape in an exo-womb which produces the Brood, who go out into the world to kill according to her conscious and unconscious desire – with such conviction that it seems to make perfect sense.

Barrel-shaped Oliver Reed is an ambiguous mad scientist, a confrontational shrink who employs extreme roleplay technique in therapy sessions that sometimes seem like improv drama and seem as liable to drive his patients deeper into insanity as pull them out of it. Though it's a serious picture about a surprisingly well-played broken marriage and custody case, Cronenberg is always playful with the scary stuff.

The Brood, wrapped up in bright parkas and scarves, are unsettling monsters, and their attacks are memorably nasty: battering an abusive mother to death in a well-appointed kitchen with a meat-tenderiser, dragging a drunken father into the dark under the bed like a childhood nightmare made flesh and murdering a kindergarten teacher with building blocks in front of her terrified pupils.

Hindle seems appropriately numbed by the whole experience, stuck with the deadloss assignment of representing normality, but Eggar does a great deal with the role of the mad mother, lifting a white ceremonial robe, chewing through the birth sac, licking her newborn monster clean of blood. **★★★★ KN**

BROTHERHOOD OF THE WOLF (LE PACTE DES LOUPS) (2001)

Starring: *Samuel Le Biihan (Gregoire de Fronsac), Vincent Cassel (Jean Francois de Morangias), Emilie Dequenne (Marianne de Morangias), Monica Bellucci (Sylvia)*
Director: *Christophe Gans*
Screenwriters: *Stephane Cabel, Christophe Gans*
15/142 mins./Action/Horror/History/France

It may be the Age Of Reason, but the peasants in a far-flung rural region of France are convinced they're being stalked by a supernatural monster. A famed warrior-naturalist and his Mohawk Iroquois sidekick come seeking the truth.

While shooting *Citizen Kane*, Orson Welles announced that the paraphernalia of moviemaking was the best train set a boy could ever have. Clearly Christophe Gans (*Crying Freeman*) shares this sense of awe at the possibilities. Lap dissolves, match cuts, slow motion, freeze frames, top shots, distortion, superimposition. Not since the New Wave has a French director used narrative devices with such gleeful self-regard.

It's a dizzyingly bravura attempt to reproduce the visual energy of a computer game, while attempting to remain true to the realities of pre-revolutionary France. But how to assess a film that is so ambitious yet so flawed, so original and yet so slavishly derivative?

By far its most fascinating aspects are its borrowings. Gans has rifled through the archives for ideas, right down to the furnishings in the Brotherhood's lair, which owe a huge debt to the castle trappings in Jean Cocteau's *Beauty And The Beast*. But there are also references to the noble savage, celebrated in both the philosophical writings of Rousseau and fiction like *The Last Of The Mohicans*. There are homages to the Spaghetti Western, the martial arts movie, anime quests like *Princess Mononoke* and the Gothic revelries of Tim Burton. And then, tucked in the margins, there's the whole Enlightenment debate about reason and religion.

Had Gans been able to rein in the stylistic excess, this might have been more compelling. That said, it's quirky enough to entertain and complex enough to challenge. But arthousers beware: this is more *Crimson Rivers* than *Ridicule*. **★★★ DP**

THE BROTHERS GRIMM (2005)

Starring: *Matt Damon (Wilhelm Grimm), Heath Ledger (Jacob Grimm), Lena Headey (Angelika), Monica Bellucci (Mirror Queen), Mackenzie Crook (Hidlick)*
Director: *Terry Gilliam*
Screenwriter: *Ehren Kruger*
12A/118 mins./Adventure/Fantasy/UK/Czech Republic/USA

French-occupied Germany, 1812. Bogus witch-hunters Wilhelm and Jacob Grimm are sent by psychotic French general Delatombe – who has discovered their scam – to uncover another suspected ersatz spook plot involving missing children – one whose terrors turn out to be all too real . . .

Terry Gilliam's always had something of a Grimm sensibility – his early movies had a grimy, cruelly comical fairy-tale feel, something that's infected much of his work ever since. So the pairing of Gilliam with the titular story-weaving siblings should have formed the perfect match for the director's long-awaited return to the big screen.

Gilliam die-hards may be pleased to hear that this fanciful fictionalisation of the Grimms' early years couldn't have been made by anyone else – it's as 'Gilliam' a movie as *Sleepy Hollow* was a 'Burton'. But, with its deliberately filth-slathered historical setting, its overly mannered comedy performances and its regular bursts of violent slapstick, this feels more like Gilliam circa 1980 than 2005; replace Heath Ledger and Matt Damon with Michael Palin and Eric Idle, switch the (frankly dire) CG with budget-defying physical effects and you have the movie he never made between *Jabberwocky* and *Time Bandits*.

It's a fitfully entertaining affair. Ledger and Damon prove a great double act, their banter and bicker-work eliciting most of the laughs, Damon's Will being the dashing braggard, Ledger's Jake the awkward romantic. But every chuckle dies once Peter Stormare's faux-Italian goon Cavaldi blunders into frame, spitting every line with such elaborate gesticulation that you wonder why Gilliam didn't point out that this is a film, not a panto, even if it does refer to magic beans and eldritch mirrors.

Such references are, thankfully, neatly inserted, the idea being that Jake and Will were inspired to write their tales based on these 'real' events. Less neat, though, is this tale's structure, which forever hops in and out of the dark, enchanted forest where Monica Bellucci's undead queen has been abducting children, to such a degree that any suspense gradually evaporates.

Yet despite its flaws *The Brothers Grimm* is no disaster. With slyly anachronistic references to special effects and budgets, scripter Ehren Kruger takes satirical swipes at Hollywood. And Gilliam has a ball when it comes to the more horrific scenes – among those sure to haunt you are one involving a child-swallowing horse that spews spider-web from its mouth, and another in which a portly mud-monster steals a kiddie's face. You just can't help wishing that the whole movie was as effective as its better moments ... ★★★ **DJ**

◑ THE BROTHERS MCMULLEN (1995)

Starring: *Shari Albert (Susan), Maxine Bahns (Audrey), Catharine Bolz (Mrs McMullen), Connie Britton (Molly McMullen), Edward Burns (Barry/Finbar McMullen), Mike McGlone (Patrick McMullen), Jack Mulcahy (Jack McMullen)*
Director: *Edward Burns*
Screenwriter: *Edward Burns*
15/98 mins./Comedy/Drama/USA

Three New York Irish Catholics attempt to deal with the various romantic problems thrown up by their personal and religious baggage.

Written, directed by and starring an erstwhile US TV entertainment show's production assistant and shot at the weekend in his mum's house, this is yet another no-budget success story, having won the Sundance Festival Grand Jury Prize. And deservedly so.

The three siblings in question are New York Irish Catholics, thrown together for a few months in their childhood home. The film concentrates on their attempts to deal with the various romantic problems thrown up by their personal and religious baggage. Youngest brother Patrick is just out of college, a by-the-book God-fearing Catholic; middle sibling Barry is a boho scriptwriter for whom any relationship that lasts longer than one date constitutes a serious commitment; Jack is the eldest, happily married until he's tempted by the offer of a sex-only affair.

Despite its twentysomething preoccupations, its no-expense-spent finances and young, inexperienced cast, this has none of the slacker affectations of, say, *Clerks*. Instead, it's a surprisingly mature film resting entirely on the quality of the script and performances. It's funny, penetrating and coolly cynical in its handling of the boys' mounting emotional crises, without ever falling into the melodramatic depths of soap opera. Love, Barry explains to his kid brother, is merely an excuse for women to drag men into the emasculating, stifling conspiracy of marriage. This is a subtle and witty film with more to say to the so-called 'Generation X' audience than all of Hollywood's mainstream efforts put together. When Burns got enough money to shoot a movie outside his mum's living room, he sadly never reached the same beautifully rendered heights. ★★★ **DHo**

◑ BRUCE ALMIGHTY (2003)

Starring: *Jim Carrey (Bruce Nolan), Morgan Freeman (God), Jennifer Aniston (Grace Connelly), Philip Baker Hall (Jack Baylor), Steve Carell (Evan Baxter)*
Director: *Tom Shadyac*
Screenwriters: *Steve Koren, Mark O'Keefe. Steve Oedekerk*
12A/101 mins./Comedy/Drama/Fantasy/Romance/USA

Despite having just about as perfect a life as it's possible to have, TV news reporter Bruce Nolan thinks God has it in for him. To show him how absurdly blessed he really is, God gives him omnipotent power.

This is Bruce Nolan: an affluent guy with an astonishingly undemanding job in the media, a beautiful apartment in a spotless backlot neighbourhood, and a doting girlfriend who looks like Jennifer Aniston. And all he does is bitch to the man upstairs about how crappy his life is. We're actually supposed to care about this ungrateful prick? Well, it's a good job he's funny. There are, in fact, few comic actors around who can touch Carrey when he's on solid, high-concept ground – and there's a limited number of altitudinous adjectives available to describe the dizzying heights of this concept: Carrey plays God. Ker-ching!

Projecting a soft-pedalled version of his stock Ace Ventura character, he mines the set-up for all its worth. And thanks to canny writing and snappy direction, he's given plenty to work with, creating a miniature Red Sea scenario in a bowl of soup and exacting revenge on a gang member dumb enough to utter, 'When monkeys fly out of my butt.'

But while the laughs come thick and fast, it's difficult to find the film anything like as charming as it thinks it is. For a start, you can't help feeling that, rather than granting such an over-privileged yuppie whiner supreme power, any self-respecting deity might teach him a lesson with some good old-fashioned smiting. Getting bogged down in theology would, perhaps, ruin the fun. But then, so does a pervading aura of smugness and an over-arching conviction that, not only does God exist, he fully endorses the aspirations of rich, white, self-satisfied Americans whose prayers are primarily concerned with their stock portfolios.

Ask yourself this: if you were in Bruce's shoes, after you'd whisked up a few girls' skirts, taught your dog to pee in the toilet, changed your car into a Ferrari and made your girlfriend's tits bigger, wouldn't you – as he conspicuously doesn't – spare a thought for the blind homeless person who hangs out in front of your office? ★★★ **SR**

◑ BUCK ROGERS IN THE 25TH CENTURY (1979)

Starring: *Gil Gerard (William 'Buck' Rogers), Erin Gray (Wilma Deering), Tim O'Connor (Dr Huer), Pamela Hensley (Princess Ardala), Henry Silva (Kane), Felix Silla (Twiki – body)*
Director: *Daniel Haller*
Screenwriters: *Glen A. Larson, Leslie Stevens*
PG/89 mins./Sci-fi/USA

Base on the classic serials of the 1930s, Captain Buck Rogers is accidentally put in suspended animation during a 1987 space launch. He wakes up 500 years later to find Earth under attack from the Draconians. Earth's Terrans suspect he may be an enemy spy.

With his eyes on the *Star Wars* prize, producer Glen A Larson had already devised the pulp sci-fi adventure *Battlestar Galactica*, but didn't rest there, re-inventing the classic space ace Buck Rogers as created by author Philip Francis Nowlan and first personified by Buster Crabbe in the late 30s. In modernising the idea of this time-travelling astronaut well out-of-his-water in a far-flung future Earth, he kept strictly to the Lucas formula: dogfights galore, a screwy semi-aristocratic social structure and bleeping, comedy robots. It was also, akin to *Galactica*, the launching pad for a mildly successful television series.

Larson, with his rented director Daniel Haller, does retain something of the flavour of the 30s or, better, the 50s – the bad guys, the Draconians, are pseudo-Mongols, stand-ins for the yellow peril of Communist China, and the film has daft dance sequences and social restraints, making the film feel absurdly old-fashioned. Elsewhere it is simply a cheap *Star Wars* knock-off. The smug Gil Gerard, painfully sucking in his gut for the skin-tight white future-suit, dashes about, a plank with a haircut, hoping to echo the swagger of Harrison Ford's Han Solo and missing by light years. The wobbly, copper-plated midget droid Twiki is fun for about three scenes then just irritates. And the sets and space action are just restricted by its lack of budget, something that could have emboldened a more comic -book knowingness, but the creators are playing even the comedy dead straight.

The only redeeming facet in the whole sappy adventure, is Erin Gray's schoolboy fantasy Wilma Deering, a tough, gorgeous space pilot. But even here the script is too coy and childish to allow sex appeal to reach the stars. ★★ **IN**

Fake Bands TOP10

1. Spinal Tap (This Is Spinal Tap)
2. The Blues Brothers (The Blues Brothers)
3. Autobahn (The Big Lebowski)
4. The Commitments (The Commitments)
5. Filgrin D'an And The Modal Nodes (Star Wars)
6. Hey That's My Bike (Reality Bites)
7. Citizen Dick (Singles)
8. Marvin Berry And The Starliters (Back To The Future)
9. Sweet Sue And Her Society Syncopators (Some Like It Hot)
10. Wyld Stallyns (Bill And Ted's Excellent Adventure)

A BUCKET OF BLOOD (1959)

Starring: *Dick Miller (Walter Paisley), Barboura Morris (Carla), Amthomy Carbone (Leonard de Santis), Julian Burton (Maxwell H. Brock). Ed Nelson (Art Lacroix), John Brinkley (Will)*
Director: *Roger Corman*
Screenwriter: *Charles B. Griffith*
15/66 mins./Comedy Horror/USA

Terminally untalented artist wannabe Walter Paisley hailed as a genius by the beatniks who hang out at the café where he works as a bus-boy when he coats a dead cat in clay and is hailed as a great sculptor. Naturally, if he wants to stay a success, Paisley has to find more subjects, turning out works with titles like 'Severed Head' and 'Murdered Man'.

Roger Corman's quickie masterpiece, much more satisfying than its better-known semi-remake *The Little Shop Of Horrors*, this mixes the old favourite *House Of Wax* business of coating corpses to create artworks with cool satire of the then-current beatnik scene. Dick Miller, one of the most prolific bit-players in the movies, gets a rare leading role as a whining, initially good-natured schmuck who so desperately wants to be creative that he's willing to commit murder and so hooked on acclaim that he becomes a serial killer to keep the masterpieces coming.

Also funny is Anthony Carbone as the beret-wearing art dealer who catches on early and is torn between avarice and disgust, but unwilling to turn the killer in to the cops while his gruesome sculptures are making his gallery hot. Screenwriter Charles Griffith has a knack for spot-on beat dialogue, especially when pretentious poet Max Brock composes a hilarious ode to Walter's genius, accompanied by freeform jazz – 'A master sculptor is in our midst,' Brock tells his acolytes, 'hands of genius have been carrying away the empty cups of your frustrations. His is the silent voice of creation within the dark, rich soil of humility, he blossoms as the hope of our nearly sterile century . . . bring me an *espresso*, Walter.'

A near-perfect miniature, shot fast and cheap and imaginative, with a mix of macabre humour and surprising melancholy. ★★★★★ **KN**

THE BUENA VISTA SOCIAL CLUB (1999)

Director: *Wim Wenders*
Starring: *as themselves: Luis Barzaga, Joachim Cooder, Ry Cooder, Juan de Marcos Gonzalez, Julio Alberto Fernandez, Ibrahim Ferrer, Carlos Gonzalez, Ruben Gonzalez, Salvador Repilado Labrada, Pio Leyva, Manuel 'Puntillita' Lopez*
Screenwriter: *Wim Wenders*
U/105 mins./Documentary/Music/USA/UK

This documentary traces guitarist Ry Cooder's collaboration with a troup of veteran Cuban musicians.

Buena Vista Social Club was a Grammy-winning 1996 Ry Cooder album, which has since given its name to the band of musicians he employed to make it although, considering the age of most concerned, they are perhaps better suited to the Cuban epithet 'Super-Abuelos' (the super grandads). Cooder was so enamoured of the musicians that, while scoring Wim Wenders' *The End Of Violence*, he passed on the bug to the director, who asked if he could document Cooder's return trip to the island for a follow-up session.

What Wenders found is a musical education for pupils of all ages, but beneath its rich soundtrack it also paints a very human picture, using such characters as Ruben Gonzalez – an 80-year-old pianist, beautifully captured playing free-form while a children's ballet class rehearses around him – and Compay Segundo, now 92, with a voice like Nat King Cole.

Given stars like these, nobody needs actors and so Wenders is left free to effortlessly transfer the magic of sound to the medium of moving pictures. Apart from the studios, homes and other locales of Havana, the ensemble are also filmed performing in Amsterdam and New York and, in one memorably touching moment, strolling the Big Apple's streets slack-jawed in joy and amazement.

So much more than a stream of talking heads, Wenders delivers a fly-on-the-wall/Steadicam viewpoint that allows us to enjoy seeing old-timers reeling back the years through the simple pleasure of singing and playing, doing what comes naturally. ★★★★ **KN**

BUFFALO 66 (1998)

Starring: *Vincent Gallo (Billy Brown), Christina Ricci (Layla), Ben Gazzara (Jimmy Brown), Mickey Rourke (The Bookie), Rosanna Arquette (Wendy Balsam), Jan-Michael Vincent (Sonny), Anjelica Huston (Jan Brown)*
Director: *Vincent Gallo*
Screenwriters: *Vincent Gallo, Alison Bagnall*
15/110 mins./Comedy/Drama/USA

Just out of prison, Billy Brown recruits a tap dance student, Layla, to pose as his wife in an attempt to impress his parents.

Only an actor in his first feature as a writer-director-star would insert a gratuitous line of dialogue in an early scene to make sure the audience knows he has a really big penis. As this shows, Gallo, a strong-jawed supporting hood in *The Funeral* and *Palookaville*, certainly isn't short of confidence (or ego). The major problem of following this generally enjoyable little picture is believing Gallo's script when it has the heroine, abducted and abused by the Gallo character, fall genuinely and sincerely in love with him in the space of a few miserable hours.

Billy Brown, just out of prison, returns to his grim hometown of Buffalo, New York, and impulsively grabs Layla, a tap dance student, because he has told his parents he is away on government work and needs someone to pretend to be the wife he claims to have married. Surprisingly, Layla goes along with the scheme and works hard to impress Billy's weird parents, football-obsessed mom and brutal crooner dad. Her understanding of the comical grimness of Billy's life increases as they revisit scenes from his pre-prison life, including a trip to the bowling alley where he was hailed as a champion and an encounter with the former prom queen he fantasised was his girlfriend.

Gallo is clearly well up on his US indies and borrows freely from *Pulp Fiction* and *The Big Lebowski*, but his East Coast post-industrial setting allows for a distinctive and genuine grimness. Ricci, with heavy eye make-up and bowling ball breasts, passes for 28 (wasn't she 14 the year before?) and struggles to make the vacuum of her character credible. Bits and pieces are arresting and audacious, but it has a shaggy dog feel that prevents it from being first-rate. ★★★ **KN**

BUFFALO SOLDIERS (2001)

Starring: *Joaquin Phoenix (Ray Elwood), Ed Harris (Col. Berman), Scott Glenn (Sgt. Lee), Anna Paquin (Robyn Lee), Elizabeth McGovern (Mrs Berman)*
Director: *Gregor Jordan*
Screenwriters: *Eric Weiss, Nora Maccoby, Gregor Jordan, based on the book by Robert O'Connor*
15/98 mins./Comedy/Drama/War/UK/Germany

On an American army base in West Germany at the time of the fall of the Berlin Wall, Ray Elwood is making a killing refining incoming heroin for the base's drug dealers, until the unbendable Sergeant Lee arrives to bring the troops in line.

After two-and-a-half years of mysteriously going awol, Australian director Gregor Jordan's military satire finally yomped onto the big screen. Set firmly in the tradition of *M*A*S*H* and *Catch 22*, *Buffalo Soldiers* is a deliriously dark, caustic romp, which gleefully depicts the American army as venal, corrupt, incompetent and stupid. And that's just for starters.

Unsurprisingly, it was less than well received in the United States. At its Sundance premiere, one enraged patriot lobbed a bottle at the screen, though, like a smart bomb, it went awry and hit an old gentleman in Row 3 on the head. They obviously didn't get the joke then, because *Buffalo Soldiers* is a sharp, hip and funny film.

Essentially *Bilko* meets *Trainspotting*, Jordan's second film (falling between Heath Ledger vehicles *Two Hands* and *Ned Kelly*) features a troika of vigorous performances. The always reliable Ed Harris takes the role of loveable but inept Battalion Commander Wallage Berman, a myopic officer more interested in establishing his genealogical connection to a war hero with the appealing monicker 'The Iron Boar', while Scott Glenn is a terrifying picture of grinning, self-righteous sadism as hard-ass Sgt Robert Lee. But it's Joaquin Phoenix, rapidly becoming one of cinema's most versatile and likeable actors, who manages to defuse a little of the bleakness as Ray, the battalion secretary who appropriates most of the supplies for himself and spends his spare time providing pharmacological R&R for the bored GIs. Think Radar O'Reilly with added heroin.

Certainly there's the odd uncertain moment. The movie has difficulty switching gears between its lighter, almost sitcom-ish moments and the nihilistic orgy it becomes towards the end. And a few of the set pieces – such as a tank going out of control and ploughing through a German town – though entertaining, may be a little too 'John Landis' for some people's tastes. But despite these minor wobbles, *Buffalo Soldiers* remains a piece of glorious, provocative mischief. ★★★★ **CW**

A BUG'S LIFE (1998)

Starring: *the voices of: Dave Foley (Flik), Kevin Spacey (Hopper), Julia Louis-Dreyfus (Princess Atta), David Hyde Pierce (Slim), Hayden Panettiere (Dot), Phyllis Diller (Queen), Richard Kind (Molt), David Hyde Pierce (Slim), Denis Leary (Francis)*
Directors: *John Lasseter, Andrew Stanton*
Screenwriters: *Andrew Stanton, Donald McEnery, Bob Shaw*
U/94 mins./Animation/Family/Adventure/USA

An ant goes on quest to find warriors to defend his colony, but recruits a circus troop by mistake.

A Bug's Life had the misfortune of having to follow two tough acts. As the second effort from John Lasseter's Pixar outfit, it had to live in the shadow of the highly successful *Toy Story*, and as the second CGI insect fable to hit the screens in 1998, it inevitably offered up characters and scenes very like those you saw in *Antz*.

However *Antz*, produced by ex-Disney top man Jeffrey Katzenberg's DreamWorks, aspired to a certain level of adult sophistication which is matched in *A Bug's Life* only in a wittily animated skit on those end credits sequences that include outtakes from the movie. As a proper Disney production, *A Bug's Life* instead goes all out for kid-friendliness with a lot of slapstick (including a literal gag where a stick insect gets slapped), a simple goodies versus baddies, underdog-comes-through storyline and a batch of appealing, comical characters.

As in *Antz*, the setting is an anthill where a foul-up misfit has a crush on the princess, but the plot here is more clear-cut, poaching the set-up from *The Seven Samurai/Magnificent Seven* as crossed with the fable of *The Grasshopper And The Ant*. An isolated ant colony strives all season to assemble an offering of food for a roving band of tyrannical grasshoppers under the leadership of the glowering Hopper. Flik (Foley, a stalwart of ace Canadian comedy troupe *Kids In The Hall*), an ant dreamer whose inventions never quite work, sets out to save the day by recruiting a band of warrior insects from a nearby bug city. He gets his antennae crossed and hires instead a broken-down flea circus who have to save the day using their performance skills.

Adults might experience a certain degree of impatience with the highly-guessable storyline, which is disappointingly straightforward after the multi-level cleverness of Pixar's other efforts, but children will respond not only to the bug-level knockabout but to the broad-strokes, loveable characters: a fat caterpillar who yearns to transform into 'a beautiful butterfly', a pair of chortling Hungarian pillbug acrobats (both voiced by Michael McShane), the gentle-hearted but fearsome looking rhino-nosed beetle (Brad Garrett), a male ladybug (Denis Leary) who resents being taken for a girl, and the cowardly rantings of David Hyde Pierce's stick insect.

If Flik isn't quite up to the Woody Allen character in *Antz*, Julia Louis-Dreyfus' neurotic, hyperactive ant princess is more interesting than Sharon Stone's take on the same part.

A Bug's Life is not quite as all-round great as *Toy Story*, or *Finding Nemo*, or *The Incredibles*, but in offering a lot of charm and imagination, some scary moments (the vertical take-off 'hoppers), excellent animated action and plenty of comedy, it ensures that it's still light years ahead of most live-action comedy output. And it saves its one Randy Newman song for the end so you don't have the action hobbled by musical numbers the way traditional Disney 'toons have been in the last ten years. It's just a shame that, set against the rest of the Pixar output, it offers nothing new. ★★★★ **KN**

BUGSY (1991)

Starring: *Warren Beatty (Benjamin 'Bugsy' Siegel), Annette Bening (Virginia Hill), Harvey Keitel (Mickey Cohen), Ben Kingsley (Meyer Lansky), Elliott Gould (Harry Greenberg), Joe Mantegna (Geroge Raft), Bebe Neuwirth (Countess di Frasso)*
Director: *Barry Levinson*
Screenwriter: *James Toback, from the book* We Only Kill Each Other: The Life And Bad Times of Bugsy Siegel *by Dean Jennings*
18/135 mins./Crime/Biographical/Romance/USA

Awards: *Academy Awards – Best Art Direction/Set Decoration, Best Costume, Golden Globes – Best Drama*

Mobster 'Bugsy' Siegel moves to Hollywood where his dreams and penchant for indulgence land him in trouble with his peers.

Despite its Best Picture, Best Actor etc., honours from the LA Critics, one has the sneaking suspicion that younger, hip cinema-goers, fed up to the back teeth with American gangster nostlagia, will receive this Ode on a Dead Hood as a handsome bore. For those longer of tooth – at least, old enough to remember when Warren Beatty was a beauty rather than the Richard Nixon lookalike he has dismayingly become – *Bugsy* is a grand, old-fashioned Big Hollywood Picture.

In a lavish, gorgeous recreation of the 40s – heavenly nightclubs, big bands with crooners, women in gold lamé – Beatty gives us a terrifically watchable portrait of Benny 'Bugsy' Siegel as a vain, dapper man with an obsessional craving for glamour and fame, unpredictably veering from genial charmer to viscious nut. For the sake of presenting Bugsy as this figure of intrigue and charisma, director Levinson and screenwriter James Toback effectively concentrate on two elements: the mutual fascination between the underworld and showbusiness, underscored by Bugsy's lifelong friendship with George Raft (Joe Mantegna), his splash in Hollywood's café society, and his big thing with devious, slinky 'starlet' Virginia Hill (Bening); and Bugsy's 'invention' of Las Vegas, a mission invested with the mythic qualities of a visionary's quest.

Historically there's a lot of romanticised tosh. Bugsy made his big entrance in Tinsel Town nearly a decade before depicted; a murder charge given a key position here happened before Bugsy met Virginia, and the psychotic Siegel's day-to-day doings included rape, heroin pushing and massive extortion from every major film studio by Bugsy's various filthy rackets. Taken as a fable of a bloody American dream in which crime, sex and movie fantasy are inextricably mixed, though, it's a compelling story. Everything is first-rate, too, from entrancing visuals to the Ennio Morricone score to the great cast – among whom Ben Kingsley steals the show with his brilliant turn as Syndicate mastermind Meyer Lansky and the late rock impresario Bill Graham proves surprisingly good as Lucky Luciano. ★★★★ **AE**

BUGSY MALONE (1976)

Starring: *Scott Baio (Bugsy Malone), Florrie Dugger (Blousey Brown), Jodie Foster (Tallulah), John Cassisi (Fat Sam), Martin Lev (Dandy Dan), Paul Murphy (Leroy Smith)*
Director: *Alan Parker*
Screenwriter: *Alan Parker*
PG/93 mins./Comedy/Musical/UK

Awards: *BAFTA – Best Newcomer (Jodie Foster), Best Supporting Actress (Jodie Foster), Best Screenplay, Best Production Design, Best Soundtrack*

Set in a mythical Prohibition America, freewheeling hero Bugsy Malone finds himself in the middle of a gang war between Fat Sam and Dandy Dan. As things hot up, he corals a bunch of down-and-outs to fight the cause, while trying to impress Blousey Brown, a new girl in town desperate to make it as a singer.

It is always funny to note that Alan Parker, who would go on to be best known as a director of full-blooded, archly styled dramas, began his career with this sprightly gangster-themed musical cast entirely with kids albeit representing adult counterparts. That it works so well is down to the high quality, low-mawkishness of his chosen youngsters, the elaborate production design built across Pinewood stages, and an excellent set of songs by Paul Williams. Easy as that, except when most others try such a hazardous concept they come skidding off the road.

Good thinking goes on from the top down – replacing lethal Tommy guns with the splurge equivalent (firing globules of what looks like gloopy wallpaper paste), having pedal-powered sedans, and keeping the script thrumming with cod-period dialogue all work a treat. The film is wryly mocking its sources, but with a sense of easy love. The host of whippersnappers draped in adult cloth, in Jodie Foster's case brazenly sexualising her, live up to the test of carrying this hybrid off. Foster is the stand out, saucily experimenting with the role of Fat Sam's moll, but Scott Baio, Florrie Dugger and John Cassisi's plaintive Fat Sam are all decent. Parker had a knack splicing youth and music he would utilise with *Fame* and *The Commitments*.

Clearly as well as his good eye, he has a very good ear. The songs slip easily into the gangster drama in miniature: 'My Name Is Tallulah', 'So You Wanna Be A Boxer' and 'Down And Out' all served up with drama school gusto. The big finale, when all splurge has been spent, is close to magnificent – a thumping piano chord silencing the battleground and the gentle strains of 'I Could Have Been Anything That I Wanted I Be' begins, segueing into the entire cast joining together for a rendition of 'You Give A Little Love'. Of course, its cheesy as hell, but the film has earned its send off. You can't help but smile along. ★★★★ **IN**

BULL DURHAM (1988)

Starring: *Kevin Costner (Crash Davis), Susan Sarandon (Annie Savoy), Tim Robbins (Ebby Calvin 'Nuke' LaLoosh), Trey Wilson (Joe 'Skip' Riggins)*
Director: *Ron Shelton*
Screenwriter: *Ron Shelton*
15/108 mins./Comedy/USA

A small-town baseball groupie who takes a different ball-player from the local team under her wing and into her bed each season, chooses the super-talented youngster one year only to find herself drawn to the veteran nearing the end of his career.

Contradicting the accepted wisdom that sports movies are box office poison, *Bull Durham* was a winner with both critics and audiences in the USA, incidentally giving the garter trade a quite unexpected fillip.

Writer Ron Shelton, who previously scripted the war correspondent movie *Under Fire*, brought his own experience as a minor league ballplayer to this witty comedy and uses his directorial debut to share his passion for baseball, lusty women and small-timers with big hearts. The central character isn't a baseball player, but a baseball groupie, Annie, the unlikeliest woman you could hope to find in a spot like Durham, North Carolina. Annie's kind of a happy Blanche Dubois, devoted to screwing, baseball and amateur philosophy, imparting wisdom via one-liners like 'the world is made for people who are not cursed with self-awareness'.

Each season Annie zeroes in on one player from the Durham Bulls to share her bed and benefit from her knowledge of baseball and life. This year she selects dim-witted young Ebby 'Nuke' LaLoosh, a pitcher with a 'million dollar arm and a five cent brain', not to mention a horrible hair style and a Motley Crue T-shirt, as her protégé. But she really fancies the veteran at the end of his career, Crash Davis.

Crash is also occupied with teaching Nuke what's what and his cynical efforts provide several of the film's best laughs as he wearily instructs the twit in How To Talk To The Press and not to let fungus grow in his shower shoes, and holds curt seminars mid-game on the pitcher's mound. Naturally, by the end of the season everyone has learned a little something about the Big Game Of Life and Nuke even gets a good haircut.

Kevin Costner gets to deliver a Classic Speech about what he believes in – the small of a woman's back, good scotch, high fibre, prolonged foreplay and chocolate cookies, among other things – and the soundtrack veers engagingly from Edith Piaf to Sixty Minute Man. Ultimately what will determine how this fares with non-baseball fans is not so much how you feel about baseball as whether you could like a woman who ties men to the bed while reading them the poems of Walt Whitman. ★★★★ **AE**

◎ BULLET IN THE HEAD (DIE XUE JIE TOU) (1990)

Starring: *Tony Leung Chiu Wai (Ben/Ah Bee), Jacky Cheung (Frank/Fai), Waise Lee (Paul/Little Wing), Simon Yam (Luke), John Woo (Police Inspector)*
Director: *John Woo*
Screenwriters: *Janet Chun, Patrick Leung, John Woo*
18/136 mins./Drama/Thriller/Hong Kong

After a run in with the Triads, three crooks head to Vietnam, hoping to make a living as smugglers.

Connoisseurs rate this 1990 epic as the greatest of John Woo's bullet ballets, though perhaps because regular star Chow Yun-Fat is absent it hasn't had the success of *The Killer* or *Hard-Boiled*. Without Chow it's hard to get a moral fix, so you'll be genuinely surprised when some of the cast go bad and others reveal a deeper heroism. All are driven mad with fear and pain, and scream hysterically through set-pieces as alienating as they are visceral.

After upsetting the Triads on their home turf in 1967, a trio of criminals flee to Vietnam and attempt to make a killing as smugglers. But their first contraband is destroyed by the Vietcong and they are sucked into a cycle of casual violence. Falling in with another crook, the group is torn apart as a terrible incident explains the title, winding up – naturally – in a Woo-style holocaust.

But *Bullet* is let down by various elements that are impossible to take seriously because they lack any ironic edge; such as the irritating bubblegum score. It tries to be a Chinese take on *The Deer Hunter*, but transports Michael Cimino's meditation on Americanism and savagery into a world where nationality and insanity seem equally absurd. If you weren't moved by 'Nam vets singing 'America The Beautiful', you might be more stirred by the sight of Woo's characters waving British passports in panic as they try to evade execution. ★★★★ **AS**

◎ BULLETS OVER BROADWAY (1994)

Starring: *John Cusack (David Shayne), Jack Warden (Julian Marx), Chazz Palminteri (Cheech), Joe Viterelli (Nick Valenti), Jennifer Tilly (Olive Neal), Rob Reiner (Sheldon Flender), Mary-Louise Parker (Ellen), Dianne Wiest (Helen Sinclair), Harvey Fierstein (Sid Loomis), Jim Broadbent (Warner Purcell)*
Director: *Woody Allen*
Screenwriters: *Woody Allen, Douglas McGrath*
15/99 mins./Comedy/USA

Awards: *Academy Awards – Best Supporting Actress (Dianne Wiest), Golden Globes (Dianne Wiest)*

Broadway playwright David is delighted to have his latest play in production but less so with his mobster backer and the moll his backer wants to take the place of the leading lady.

Any coolness Hollywood may have showed Woody Allen as a result of his domestic situation is clearly at an end with seven Oscar nominations for this comedy of art representing a collective Tinseltown hug. They were also much deserved as this was a delightful diversion, if not one to get that hysterical about. As character rich as any of his comedies, it features another remarkable ensemble and an avalanche of brilliant gags.

In 1920s New York tortured playwright David accepts the backing of a gangland boss to put on one of his productions. But in return for his benevolence, Mr Big wants a role for his screeching chorus girl moll Olive. She is duly cast as a psychiatrist in David's turgid drama, alongside other eccentric players including Eden Brent and Warner Purcell, and the neurotic, over-the-top, over-the-hill leading lady Helen Sinclair (Wiest in her Oscar-winning role).

Wiest is screamingly funny as the fading Broadway diva who manipulates her awed writer-director at every turn, accelerating his betrayals of art and heart. Meanwhile, David's intellectual buddies – including Rob Reiner, ever useful as his wisecracking best friend – debate sex, love and creativity from their cafe table vantage point. The dizzying twist in this comic collision of Runyonesque gangsters, Greenwich Village pseuds and Broadway darlings is that the soul of the only true artist dwells in the least likely beast, as, lurking in the stalls, Olive's hoodlum minder (Palminteri) begins to make suggestions about improving the play.

Allen can't be topped at craftily insinuating ideas into wacky, witty scenarios, but this doesn't have the lingering satisfactions of an *Annie Hall* or *Manhattan*. For Allen buffs craving their annual fix of funnies, however, it teems with vividly beautiful period atmosphere, sparkling vignettes, wicked dialogue and detail, making it a charming, clever addition to his already considerable canon. ★★★★ **CK**

◎ BULLITT (1968)

Starring: *Steve McQueen (Bullitt), Robert Vaughn (Chalmers), Jacqueline Bisset (Cathy), Don Gordon (Delgetti), Robert Duvall (Weissberg), Simon Oakland (Capt. Bennett)*
Director: *Peter Yates*
Screenwriters: *Alan R. Trustman, Harry Kleiner, based on the novel* Mute Witness *by Robert L. Pike*
15/131 mins./Action/Crime/Thriller/USA

Awards: *Academy Awards – Best Film Editing,*

An unorthodox cop is assigned to protect a government witness but when the witness is murdered the cop goes on the trail of his killers.

If the late, extremely great Steve McQueen ever played cops and robbers when he was growing up then it seems safe to assume that the *Great Escape* star was never to be found on the side of the rozzers. One of Hollywood's most defiantly anti-authoritarian figures, the actor delighted in breaking the law, be it smoking dope or exceeding the speed limit on his beloved bikes. Indeed, if there was ever an actor designed for the 60s then it was McQueen, and by the time of *Bullitt* he had become, to all intents and purposes, the most highly-paid flower child in town. Even if that town happened to be hippie Mecca San Francisco.

'Steve would come up to me and say things like, "Hey, you're a soul chick, and you go up to these dudes and, man, you really dig the scene," ' said his co-star Jacqueline Bisset. 'I would think, "What on Earth is he talking about?"' In fact, given that the film required McQueen to play a Frisco policeman investigating the brutal murder of a witness about to testify against 'the organisation', it seems somewhat surprising that he signed on for *Bullitt* at all. 'I'd never felt easy around cops,' he would later recall. 'As a kid running the streets I'd been hassled a lot by the police and I'd always figured they were one side of the fence with me on the other.' But *Bullitt* was the first production by his own company, Solar, and McQueen knew that the combination of his pulling power and the thriller genre stood an above average chance of setting the cash tills ringing. Moreover, when McQueen began hanging out with San Francisco's finest to research the role, he discovered that his erstwhile tormentors weren't quite as bad as he had imagined: 'It was a real eye-opener. The guys I rode with were straight, honest guys with a mean job to do. They really won my respect.' And, in turn, McQueen had wholeheartedly won theirs.

'Steve's cops tested him,' explained McQueen's co-star and friend Don Gordon. 'They took him to the morgue. But he showed up eating an apple.'

Yet, while *Bullitt* was for its time an incredibly realistic and at times quite gruelling policier, its initial success was in large part due to the film's 12-minute car chase in which McQueen's Detective Frank Bullitt chases a pair of mob hitmen across San Franicsco. Traditionally, such sequences had been filmed by second units but,for *Bullitt*, director Peter Yates himself

Coolest Character Names — TOP 10

1. Snake Plissken, *Escape from New York*
2. Han Solo, *Star Wars*
3. The Dude (His Dudeness, El Duderino), *The Big Lebowski*
4. Johnny Utah, *Point Break*
5. Xenia Onatopp, *GoldenEye*
6. Memphis Raines, *Gone in Sixty Seconds*
7. Holly Golightly, *Breakfast At Tiffany's*
8. Ming the Merciless, *Flash Gordon*
9. Sick Boy, *Trainspotting*
10. Sidney J. Mussburger, *The Hudsucker Proxy*

took charge. A wise move, given that McQueen intended to perform his own stunts. The actor had previously been forced to admit that his *The Great Escape* motorbike leap, which most people assumed he had done himself, had actually been performed by stuntman Bud Ekins. It was an embarrassment that McQueen didn't want to repeat on *Bullitt*. At first, all went well. Then came a shot where McQueen was required to swing fast around a narrow side street, clip a stationary car, then peel away at breakneck speed.

'When I reached the corner I overcooked it completely and smashed right into the parked car,' McQueen subsequently confessed. 'Just wrote it off entirely and bounced into another one next to it. We'd got a lot more realism than we'd bargained for.'

Following this incident McQueen's then-wife Neile begged Yates to start using stuntmen. Which is why the star reported for duty one morning only to discover Bud Ekins driving Bullitt's Mustang down the hill while wearing his character's jacket and sunglasses.

'McQueen was mad,' said Ekins. 'He said, "You fucker, you're doing it to me again." '

Despite such problems, the resulting sequence was a *tour de force* which, with Yates' superb eye for detail and McQueen's brooding presence, would help create one of the classic thrillers of all time. But, even though its chase scene has been left in the proverbial dust by subsequent generations of filmmakers, *Bullitt* is still remembered as the film that broke new ground when it came to what could be done with two cars and a lot of burning tarmac. ★★★★ **CC**

THE 'BURBS (1989)

Starring: *Tom Hanks (Ray Peterson), Carrie Fisher (Carol Peterson), Bruce Dern (Mark Rumsfield), Rick Ducommun (Art Weingartner), Corey Feldman (Ricky Butler)*
Director: *Joe Dante.*
Screenwriter: *Dana Olsen*
PG/102 mins./Comedy/Horror/Thriller/USA

A newcomer to a surburban neighbourhood has a hard time convincing his family and the rest of the locals that his suspicions about sinister goings on next door are anything more than paranoia.

Set in Hinckley Hills, America, *The 'Burbs* (the title, one of many film in-jokes, being a reference to *The Birds*) has a suburban hero Ray Peterson taking a relaxing vacation at home. This is disturbed when his neighbours (Dern, Ducommun) encourage Ray in his fantasies about the Klopeks, a seldom-seen family of newcomers whose bizarre habits include digging in the garden and operating unidentifiable but noisy machinery after midnight during thunderstorms.

Various sinister incidents nudge Ray towards a confrontation with the Charles Addams-style Klopeks. In its twisted comic-horrific approach to suburbia, the film goes along with the trend (*Parents*, *Meet The Applegates*, *White Of The Eyes*, *The Stepfather*, *Life On The Edge*) to go against the nostalgic, happy family vision of contemporary America by finding madness and monstrosity in the heart of the ideal home. Like most of its contemporaries, it is not just an interesting attempt at subverting the normality centred likes of *Parenthood* or *Look Who's Talking*, but a wickedly inventive comedy, crammed full of sly gags and bizarre characterisations. The funniest scene in the film is a parody of *Once Upon A Time In The West* with composer Jerry Goldsmith spoofing Ennio Morricone on the soundtrack as the camera homes in on the squinting eyes of all the residents of the close, including a distressed poodle.

For the most part, *The 'Burbs* follow director Dante's *Explorers* in its unusual (and unpopular) narrative strategy – presenting a situation filled with threat and mystery which turns out to be entirely innocent, thus forcing the audience to reassess its attitudes to the 'normal' point-of-view. The key speech, marvellously delivered by Hanks at the climax of another apparently effortless but actually marvellous performance, has Ray turning on his jovially paranoid neighbours as the Klopek house burns with 'Don't you see, we're the ones who are acting suspiciously!'

Shot on the same lot as the archetypal retro sitcom *Still The Beaver* with a cameo from Lucille Ball's perennial boss Gale Gordon to underline the connection, *The 'Burbs* deliberately evokes that artificial world in which nobody seems to go out to work because only one major set exists. It fumbles at the last moment and can't quite make the final break with traditional menace-dominated storylines in the way *Explorers* does, but this is still mainly a pleasantly nasty delight that was strangely overlooked in the cinema. ★★★★ **KN**

THE BURNING (1981)

Starring: *Brian Matthews (Todd), Leah Ayres (Michelle), Brian Backer (Alfred), Larry Joshua (Glazer), Jason Alexander (Dave), Ned Eisenberg (Eddy)*
Director: *Tony Maylam*
Screenwriter: *Peter Lawrence*
18/91 mins./Horror/USA/Canada

A prank misfires at an upstate New York summer camp, and caretaker Cropsy is horribly burned. He lurks in the woods and murders the next generation of camp counsellors.

Though an obvious imitation of *Friday The 13th*, this is actually based on the tale of 'Cropsy', one of the more persistent American campfire legends (as was a competing, even more ordinary slasher, *Madman*).

Directed by Brit Tony Maylam, following his sleeper success with *Riddle Of The Sands* and en route to not much else, *The Burning* often pops up on lists of 'early, embarrassing credits' thanks to Holly Hunter in a one-line bit ('Hey Todd, over here!'), Jason Alexander (*Seinfeld*) as the flamboyant fat slob and Fisher Stevens (*Short Circuit*) as 'Woodstock'.

In addition, the story was co-written by future Miramax supremo and Oscar magnet Harvey Weinstein. It was briefly notorious in the 1980s when it landed on the Department of Public Prosecution's 'video nasties' list, because a mix-up at the distributors meant that the version available on video was sixteen seconds or so bloodier than the BBFC-approved theatrical cut. It may be the tamest of all the video nasties, despite some finger-scissoring and shears-slashing from special effects make-up superstar Tom Savini.

The only real deviation from the *Friday The 13th* template is that the put-upon virgin who gets persecuted throughout but becomes almost the sole survivor of the massacre is a nerdy guy (Brian Backer) rather than the usual Jamie Lee Curtis-type 'final girl'. Quite apart from all the *Friday The 13th* sequels and *Don't Go In The House* (which was also called *The Burning* for a while), this tends to blur in the memory, getting mixed up with slasha-likes *The Campsite Massacre, Body Count, Terror Train, Pledge Night, Slaughter High, Don't Go In The Woods*, etc. ★★ **KN**

BUTCH CASSIDY AND THE SUNDANCE KID (1969)

Starring: *Paul Newman (Butch Cassidy), Robert Redford (Sundance Kid), Katharine Ross (Etta Place), Strother Martin (Percy Garris), Henry Jones (Bike Salesman), Jeff Corey (Sheriff Bledsoe), Cloris Leachman (Agnes)*
Director: *George Roy Hill*
Screenwriter: *William Goldman*
PG/112 mins./Western/USA

Awards: *Academy Awards – Best Cinematography, Best Score, Best Song, Best Original Screenplay, BAFTA – Anthony Asquith Award for Music, Best Actor (Robert Redford), Best Actress, Best Cinematography, Best Directions, Best Film, Best Film Editing, Best Sound Track, Golden Globes – Best Score*

Butch and Sundance are two outlaws who rob trains in the Old West. As the country gets more civilised, a special posse is hired to hunt them down – so the pair, and their girl, flee to a new life in Bolivia.

Before he became a screenwriting essayist, William Goldman won an Oscar at the fag end of the 60s for his screenplay that presents legendary outlaws Butch and Sundance, not so much in a revisionist light, as a sepia tone. His playful script mixes historical detail with a great degree of leniency, resulting in a Western that aims to reinvent the West not as it was, but as the place we all wanted it to be.

Newman, his dazzling blue eyes never more piercing, is Butch, leader of the notorious Hole In The Wall Gang and a visionary bank robber. Redford, famously held in close-up by director George Roy Hill to establish his presence, broods with all the good nature of the Fastest Gun In The West, staring the camera down and providing a perfect foil – both comic and serious – for Newman. (And to think, Warren Beatty turned down the role, Steve McQueen bailed at the 11th hour and Newman was originally down to play the Kid until he suggested swapping roles with Redford – which just goes to show how haphazard making a classic movie can be.) Ross, meanwhile, fresh from *The Graduate*, radiates as the woman behind – and often between – the two outlaws, providing both a physical and mental romantic interest for our two decidedly heterosexual heroes.

Movie Trivia: Butch Cassidy and the Sundance Kid

Besides Steve McQueen and Warren Beatty, the studio also considered Marlon Brando and Dustin Hoffman to play the roles of Butch Cassidy and the Sundance Kid. Bob Dylan was allegedly asked to sing the famous theme song but sadly declined. Katherine Ross married Sundance cinematographer Conrad Hall when filming was finished.

Coming as it did at the end of Hollywood's love affair with the romantic notion of the West, and on the cusp of its later dissection of the Western archetype, *Butch Cassidy And The Sundance Kid* avoids falling between these two stools; instead it finds the Western, like its central characters, in transition. Hell, it's kept William Goldman in work for over three decades, even though he's only written a handful of decent screenplays since. *Year Of The Comet*, anyone?

There are, of course, the points against: Newman's bike riding to B. J. Thomas redefines the word 'twee', and George Roy Hill could be held singlehandedly responsible for begetting what we now perceive as the 'buddy movie' (with the director and his star re-teaming for *The Sting* a mere four years later), and its influence can still be felt today in everything from the *Lethal Weapon* franchise, to *Thelma And Louise* and beyond.

But along the way Butch and Sundance take the time to provide us with cinema's greatest waterfall leap (and how many Sunday afternoons have been defined by Redford yelling 'Shiiiiitttt!!!!' – in a family film, no less?), and one of cinema's most memorable and elegiac endings, as Butch and Sundance literally fade into a photo memory. In fact, it's hard to imagine that a movie with the Burt Bacharach career low of 'Raindrops keep falling on my head/And just like the guy whose feet are too big for his bed' could ever feel this good. ★★★★★ **BM**

BYE BYE BIRDIE (1963)

Starring: *Janet Leigh (Rosie DeLeon), Dick Van Dyke (Albert F. Peterson), Ann Margret (Kim McAfee), Maureen Stapleton (Mama Mae Peterson), Bobby Rydell (Hugo Peadbody), Jesse Pearson (Conrad Birdie)*
Director: *George Sidney*
Screenwriter: *Irving Brecher, based on the play by Michael Stewart*
U/112 mins./Musical/USA

Publicist Albert arranges a stunt whereby, rock'n'roll star Conrad Birdie will kiss Kim, one of his teenage fans, on the Ed Sullivan Show the night before he is inducted into the army. Conrad and the television production team descend on a small town and cause chaos, especially with Kim's parents and boyfriend. Meanwhile, Albert tries to defy his smothering Mom and marry his secretary.

A very underrated musical, adapted from the Broadway musical, but entirely transformed into an energetic film experience by veteran director George Sidney. A satire of the Elvis Industry, it also gets laughs from its 60s *MAD* magazine style jabs at the insanities of the ordinary American family.

The score, matching memorable tunes from Charles Strouse with witty lyrics by Lee Adams, is outstanding, but the songs are put over by a very enthusiastic cast. Ann-Margret, so frisky she probably needed to be tethered between takes, is incredible as the sweater-filling teenage temptress, holding centre screen during dynamite dance numbers choreographed by Onna White, while Paul Lynde (the unmistakable voice of the Hooded Claw) is memorably demented as her television-worshipping father (he had a novelty hit with the bitter, funny song 'Kids').

The calm centre of the film is Janet Leigh, at her most lovely, who duets with Dick Van Dyke in 'Put on a Happy Face', while the sole weak spot is Pearson's insufficiently-Elvisoid Conrad Birdie (though his songs, 'Honestly Sincere' and 'One Last Kiss' are very funny). The film has several lasting legacies in pop culture – that 'we love you [fill in the blank]' chant still heard on football terraces comes from the song 'We Love You Conrad' and Oasis's 'What's The Story, Morning Glory' is titled after the opening line of the song 'The Telephone Hour'. ★★★★ **KN**

CABARET (1972)

Starring: *Liza Minnelli (Sally Bowles), Michael York (Brian Roberts), Helmut Griem (Maximillian von Heune), Joel Grey (Master Of Ceremonies), Fritz Wepper (Fritz Wendell), Marisa Berenson (Natalia Landauer)*
Director: *Bob Fosse*
Screenwriter: *Jay Presson Allen, based on the stage play by Joe Masteroff, the stage play I Am A Camera by John Van Druten*
PG/124 mins./Musical/USA

Awards: *Academy Awards – Best Actress, Best Supporting Actor (Joel Grey), Best Director, Best Cinematography, Best Film Editing, Best Song Score, Best Art Direction-Set Decoration, Best Sound*

Berlin in the 1920s. American Chanteuse Sally Bowles has a fling with bisexual British writer Brian Roberts and tries to carve out a career as a gold-digger, putting the moves on a handsome aristocrat, while the ascendant Nazis put a crimp in their madcap lifestyle.

As Germany swings darkly through the inflationary 1920s and brownshirts take over the streets, Minnelli's émigré entertainer Sally Bowles waves her painted fingernails ('divine decadence') and does weird jazz with venomous MC Joel Grey. Christopher Isherwood's autobiographical Berlin stories (previously filmed as *I Am A Camera*, with Julie Harris as Sally) were turned into a play and then a Broadway musical, and are here wrestled into movie shape by choreographer Bob Fosse, who contributes an incredible razzle-dazzle which landed the film up to its rolled stockings in Oscars.

It tries a little too hard to cross *The Gold Diggers* of 1933 with *The Rise Of The Third Reich* to be comfortable, but stands as a hugely enjoyable, occasionally chilling, musical.

The terrific score by John Kander and Fred Ebb includes showstoppers like 'Cabaret', 'Money Makes the World Go Around', 'If You Could See Her Though My Eyes' and, as repopularised by Spitting Image's Margaret Thatcher in the late 1980s, the second most-famous Nazi anthem (after 'Springtime for Hitler') written by Jews, 'Tomorrow Belongs to Me'. Few movie musicals since the Busby Berkeley days have managed so well the trick of presenting musical numbers as self-contained set-pieces – sketches rather than pop videos – that comment upon rather than advance the 'story'.

Liza Minnelli, whose subsequent career has been spotty at best, gets her one great moment centre-screen in a Louise Brooks haircut and fabulous 20s fashions, while the face-painted, sing-song Grey is amazing as a cross between Leonard Sachs, David Bowie and Dracula. ★★★★ **KN**

CABIN FEVER (2002)

Starring: *Rider Strong (Paul), Jordan Ladd (Karen), James DeBello (Bert), Cerina Vincent (Marcy), Joey Kern (Jeff), Robert Harris (Old Man Cadwell), Arie Verveen (Henry – The Hermit)*
Director: *Eli Roth*
Screenwriters: *Eli Roth, Randy Pearlstein*
15/93 mins./Horror/Thriller/USA

Five kids rent a cabin in the wilds for a grad party, but bad things happen when a hermit blunders past and infects one of them with a deadly and contagious flesh-eating bug.

As tabloid frenzies go, necrotising fascitis (the so-called 'flesh-eating bug') is such a natural for a horror movie, it's a surprise it took so long to happen. *Cabin Fever*, though, is at least as much an entry in the backwoods menace cycle as it is an epidemic movie.

Early on, the urban interlopers are creeped out by the *Deliverance*-like atmosphere of the local store shack, where an albino lad sits outside biting strangers. In the woods, the bug cues memorably gruesome moments (especially the leg-shaving scene). It plays not only on the fear of disease but the way attitudes to the infected become ruthless, as the kids who dump their friend in the woodshed are turned on by rifle-toting townsfolk. There's a fine line between homage and simply stealing, but writer-director Eli Roth mostly manages the former, threading in 1970s-style elements (even the songs from *Last House On The Left*) while doing interesting things with some unexpected character arcs and left-field developments. ★★★ **KN**

⓪ THE CABINET OF DR CALIGARI (DAS KABINETT DES DOKTOR CALIGARI) (1919)

Starring: *Werner Krauss (Dr Caligari), Conrad Veidt (Cesare), Friedrich Feher (Francis), Lil Dagover (Jane), Hans Heinrich von Twardowski (Alan), Rudolf Lettinger (Dr Olsen)*
Director: *Robert Wiene*
Screenwriters: *Hans Janowitz, Carl Mayer*
U/71 mins./Horror/Thriller/Germany

Francis tells the story of his friend, Alan, who meets a hypnotist Cesare who predicts Alan will die. When Alan is murdered Cesare is the prime suspect.

Several claims have been made on behalf of Robert Wiene's silent classic – few of which can actually be sustained. Even the credits are disputed, with nigh on every key contributor keen to aggrandise their role in what has long been acclaimed a watershed production. What can't be gainsaid is that the screenplay was written by Czech poet Hans Janowitz and Austrian artist, Carl Mayer, who drew on a murder case and a mutual suspicion of psychiatric assessment to concoct the tale of a fairground barker who misuses his hypnotic powers to compel a mournful cipher into doing his evil bidding.

That arch fabulist, Fritz Lang, who was briefly assigned to direct the film, insisted that he had worked extensively on the script and devised its controversial coda, in which it transpires Caligari is far from the deranged director of a lunatic asylum living out a sinister fantasy, but a benevolent philanthropist striving to save our hero from his own dangerous imaginings. Lang's dishonesty is matched only by Janowitz's disingenuity. Postwar he tried to disassociate himself from the framing device after it assumed an unwelcome political significance.

The recently discovered copy of the original shooting script, which includes a variation on the bookend idea, also disproves Janowitz's contention that the film's remarkable visual appearance had been devised by the writers. Having failed to persuade Czech artist Alfred Kubin to design the stylised decor, Robert Wiene hired Deck's own Hermann Warm, Walter Rohrig and Walter Reimann, who turned to the paintings of Edvard Munch and the Expressionist stage designs of pioneering impresario Max Reinhardt for the inspiration for their cramped, crooked town of Holstenwall.

On a more pragmatic level, an electricity shortage meant it was more efficient to paint in the lighting effects than waste precious power. Similarly, Werner Krauss and Conrad Veidt (who played Caligari and his sidekick Cesare) were both Reinhardt alumni and were able to fashion their own grotesque make-up and exaggerated gestures. By no means the first German horror film to make an international impact (Paul Wegener's *The Student Of Prague* and *The Golem* did that), *Caligari* has always been credited with inspiring an Expressionist boom in German filmmaking, thanks to its angular painted sets, mannered performances and psychologically daring themes.

But, in fact, it was a stylistic one-off – or at least it is now, as Hans Kobe's feature, *Torgus* (1921), and other slavishly Expressionist 'homages' which no longer exist. Other films of the period certainly included examples of Expressionist design, but the physical aspect of Wiene's experiment remained unique. Consequently, it's even pushing it to state that any of the other *schauerfilme* (shadow films) made in Germany in the 1920s were Expressionist in the truest sense. Certainly pictures like *Warning Shadows*, *Waxworks* and *Metropolis* reflected the troubled national psyche, but they drew on the popular artistic strategy of *stimmung* (atmosphere), which owed more to the gothic.

Similarly, the suggestion that the film preconditioned the German people for the acceptance of Nazi rule is also hard to justify. In *From Caligari To Hitler*, his seminal study of cinema's influence on the dark Teutonic soul, theorist Siegfried Kracauer argued that Caligari was a bogus Messiah whose outward displays of strength merely masked tyranny, while Cesare the victim, hypnotised into doing his evil bidding, stood for the mesmerised German people who were complicit in Nazi atrocities.

Read in 1948, with the guilt of World War II still haunting the newly divided populace, such scapegoating might have seemed persuasive. But now, it's as fanciful as it is understandable. Defeat and despair hang heavily over *Caligari*, but surely the collapse of an empire, the suppression of a militarist tradition, the failure of a socialist revolution and the penury of a Depression had a more profound influence on the advent of Nazism than Friedrich Feher raving about proto-zombies.

Most damningly, 80 years after its release provoked heated analytical debate, *Caligari* has even lost its critical kudos and is now considered more a curio than a bold advance towards a new horizon of cinema art. So if it didn't really achieve any of the things it's famous for, why has this contrived, distorted, stilted film retained such an intense fascination? Forget the fact it heralded in an era of studio perfectionism in 20s Germany or inspired an unprecedented decade of avant-garde experimentation around Europe. ★★★★★ **DP**

⓪ THE CABLE GUY (1996)

Starring: *Jim Carrey (The Cable Guy), Matthew Broderick (Steven M. Kovacs), Leslie Mann (Robin Harris), Jack Black (Rick), George Segal (Steven's Father), Ben Stiller (Sam Sweet/Stan Sweet), Janeane Garofalo (Medieval Times Waitress), Andy Dick (Medieval Times Host), Owen Wilson (Robin's date)*
Director: *Ben Stiller*
Screenwriter: *Lou Holtz Jr*
12/96 mins./Comedy/Drama/Thriller/USA

When mild-mannered Steven slips Chip, the cable guy, $50 for free cable, he lets himself in for a world of trouble, as Chip decides to become Steven's new best friend.

'I gave you free cable, what have you ever done for me?' What began life as the film that scooped Carrey the title of Hollywood's highest paid actor, ended as being the movie that wiped out his winning streak. Yet for all the debate about whether it was too dark, too radical a departure, or just too crap, *The Cable Guy* was, let's face it, never going to out-gross Ace Ventura at the box office. A pet detective speaking out of his arse is one thing, but a cable man who buys his buddies prostitutes (having previously checked them out first) or plucks the eyebrows from a love rival, is a whole new comedic ball game.

It was a bold decision by Carrey to eschew his loveable goofball image to such a degree, and as Chip Douglas, the psychotic cable TV engineer who inveigles his way into the life of architect Steven, you actually believe he could do some serious damage. The film begins with Steven, having just moved into his new bachelor pad after splitting with his girlfriend Robin, offering Chip a $50 bribe to chuck in a few extra channels, not realising that this lonely, seriously unhinged guy desperately wants a friend, to the extent that he will take over his life.

As the lisping, TV-obsessed Chip, Carrey is at his most maniacal to date – witness his karaoke version of Jefferson Airplane's 'Somebody To Love'. He could, we feel, go both ways. And does. So too the film veers from the wildly comic to the uncomfortably nasty – the scene in which Chip beats the daylights out of a prospective suitor of Robin is almost too horrible to watch. Only at its denouement does the film lack the courage of its blackly comic convictions; otherwise, this could well be seen as Carrey's most interesting work. ★★★ **NJ**

⓪ THE CAINE MUTINY (1954)

Starring: *Humphrey Bogart (Capt. Phillip Francis Queeg), Jose Ferrer (Lt Barney Greenwald), Van Johnson (Lt Steve Maryk), Fred MacMurray (Lt Tom Keeler), Lee Marvin (Meatball)*
Director: *Edward Dmytryk*
Screenwriters: *Stanley Roberts, Michael Blankfort, based on the novel and play by Herman Wouk*
U/124 mins./Drama/War/USA

During World War Two, martinet Captain Queeg takes command of the USS Caine and tries to whip the slobbish misfit crew into shape, but shows signs of dangerous, obsessive instability. During a storm, Queeg's nerve breaks and junior officer Maryk, egged on by malcontented troublemaker Keeler, leads a mutiny. Later, the mutineers are put on trial.

Somewhat stodgily directed by Edward Dmytryk, this adaption of Herman Wouk's well-regarded novel remains a gripping drama, thanks to a crewful of unforgettable performances. Fred MacMurray (always better as a shifty creep than in his usual family man roles) is the psycho-babbling stirrer who foments the mutiny but tries to cover his ass in court, Van Johnson the conscience-stricken junior officer who winds up on trial, Jose Ferrer the showy lawyer who comes up trumps at the court martial and Lee Marvin the slobbiest soldier in the US Navy are all spot-on. But the show belongs to Humphrey Bogart in one of his latter-period, craggy psychopath roles as Captain Queeg, the ball-bearing rattling maniac who accuses his men of stealing strawberries, cracks under pressure and continually snipes and sneers at everyone on deck.

The meat of the drama comes after the mutiny, in the courtroom finale where Queeg is put on the stand and is prodded into revealing his insanity, as Bogart turns the unstable villain into an almost-sympathetic, tragic figure. There's a deadweight romantic subplot between the young, uncharismatic ensign (Robert Francis) and May Wynn (who took her screen name from the Wouk character), which feels like a contractual obligation, and – as with *From Here To Eternity*, *Peyton Place* and many other 1950s book-to-film transfers – there's quite a bit of manoeuvring to appease the censors by balancing the film's indictment of the US Navy with scenes that show Queeg is a freak rather than typical. ★★★★ **KN**

CALAMITY JANE (1953)

Starring: *Doris Day (Calamity Jane), Howard Keel (Wild Bill Hickock), Allyn McLerie (Katie Brown), Phillip Carey (Lt Danny Gilmartin), Dick Wesson (Francis Fryer)*
Director: *David Butler*
Screenwriter: *James O'Hanlon*
U/101 mins./Musical/USA
Awards: *Academy Awards Best Song ('Secret Love')*

Frontier tomboy Calamity Jane is sent to Chicago to bring a chanteuse back to entertain the folks of Deadwood, but brings the star's maid Katie Brown instead. Under Katie's influence, Calamity starts acting more female, and the two girlfriends form an eternal square with Wild Bill Hickock and a handsome army officer Danny Gilmartin.

1950s sock 'em entertainment, with Doris Day bright as a brass button and 'fizzy as a busy sarsparilla' as Calamity Jane, the rough and tumble braggart in fringed leathers who learns to dress and act like a real girl.

The plot is a blatant imitation of *Annie Get Your Gun*, but this luridly colourful musical earns its place in the classics file for Day's spirited gunwoman, and an unbeatable album's worth of showstoppers from Sammy Fain and Paul Francis Webster, ranging from the lively 'Deadwood Stage' through the witty 'Just Blew in From the Windy City' and the lyrical 'Take Me Back to the Black Hills' to Day's best-ever romantic torch ballad 'Secret Love' (a Best Song Oscar-winner).

Hailed decades later as a seminal feminist fantasy, this is more likely to appeal for its vibrant silliness, though only Keel's manly baritone on 'My Heart is Higher Than a Hawk' prevents it seeming like the greatest lesbian date movie of all time as cross-dressing Calamity and ultra-femme Katie set up home together in a cabin – the climax of the story rushes through the male-female pairings and depends on Calamity riding headlong across country to bring back the girl she has accidentally run out of town on the stage.

A moment for connoisseurs: Keel's underplayed first look at Day dressed up in white feminine finery at the officers' dance, followed by Day's puzzlement as she is besieged by cavalrymen who want to fill in her dance card. ★★★★ **KN**

CALENDAR GIRLS (1993)

Starring: *Helen Mirren (Chris Harper), Julie Walters (Annie Clarke), John Alderton (John Clarke), Linda Basset (Cora), Annette Crosbie (Jessie), Philip Glenister (Lawrence Sertain), Ciaran Hinds (Rod Harper), Celia Imrie (Celia), Geraldine James (Marie), Penelope Wilton (Ruth Reynoldson)*
Director: *Nigel Cole*
Screenwriters: *Tim Firth, Juliette Towhidi*
12A/108 mins./Comedy/Drama/UK/USA

Chris and Annie are two of the more rebellious women of the Knapely W.I. When Annie's husband's dies of leukaemia, Chris comes up with the novel idea of cajoling fellow members into posing for a calendar to raise money for leukaemia research – but the catch is, they'll pose naked.

The true story of the Yorkshire Women's Institute members who stripped for charity was crying out for cinematic treatment. A female alternative to *The Full Monty* would be welcome news to tabloids, not to mention the many actresses decrying the lack of decent parts for ladies of a certain age. And whatever criticisms are levelled at the resulting movie, there can be no complaints about 'decent female parts' in both senses of the phrase.

The cast is faultless, with Julie Walters and Helen Mirren both playing against type. Mirren, as the voluble instigator of the calendar, is softer and more extrovert than usual, while Walters brings a gentle restraint to the recently bereaved Annie, but still retains some much- needed humour. The warmth of friendship portrayed in this close-knit community is genuine and gives the film moments of real resonance. There are many laugh-out-loud moments, as well as real tear-wellers, such as when letters from similarly bereaved women start to flood in to the 'calendar girls'.

It's clear that the filmmakers wanted to portray what happened to this group of women with respect and integrity. However, it is this vital aspect that makes the last third of the film such dull viewing. The natural climax would seem to fall at the moment Annie and Chris first realise the calendar's impact, walking into a room full of camera-flashing press corps. But the story continues beyond this, trying to show the impact of its success on the women involved, and on Annie and Chris' friendship in particular. An extended trip to America seems to be tagged on for the benefit of overseas audiences, and minor character arcs are lost in what follows.

There is no doubt that *Calendar Girls* is appealing, but there is a lingering sense of dissatisfaction with its conclusion, which seems so unnecessary given the high-points that have occurred before. ★★★★ **EC**

CALIFORNIA MAN (1992)

Starring: *Sean Astin (Dave Morgan), Brendan Fraser (Link), Pauly Shore (Stoney Brown), Megan Ward (Robyn Sweeney), Robin Tunney (Ella), Jonathan Ke Quan (Kim)*
Director: *Les Mayfield*
Screenwriter: *Shawn Schepps*
PG/88 mins./Comedy/USA

While having a pool dug out in his backyard, Dave Morgan and his best mate, and fellow loser, Stoney Brown discover a frozen caveman. Thawing him out, they decide to introduce this Ice Age kid to life in modern day California and gain a touch of much needed credibility in the process.

This vacuous teen comedy was entitled *Encino Man* for its US release, after the specific Los Angeles suburb seemingly populated by a modern candour of Cro-Magnon man – The Wayne-Bill-Ted man. Hankering after a quick buck in the wake of those successes, Les Mayfield fails to equip the surface idiocy with the appropriate tickle of knowingness; the contrast between such innocent under-achieving and the burdens of knowledge. *California Man*, as it was understandably rechristened for foreign climes, is a tale of fools clamouring for cool rather than betterment. And more fool them for it.

The joke here, for what it's worth, contends that this double act of Valley ignoramuses, refitted Bill and Ted's without the floppy necked charm, are every bit as caveman as their new pet. There was a glimmer of light on the horizon for Sean Astin, who doesn't fully fit the dude-cake role; a decade hence he would leave for Middle-earth, Pauly Shore making his debut, shrivelled in the sun of immediate attention, his frittered dude-speak holding forth in playgrounds and malls for no more than a summer. His name, like his sprawling perm, is now utilised as a notation for abject loss of fashion. Anyway, his hyper-spaced jargon was completely incomprehensible: buff, grindage, chillin', gnarling, flamage. The art, if you will, is to hasten the clips of regular speech, not to just burp out abstract words.

The lump they defrost from their pool excavations is Brendan Fraser, who has the good grace to look stupid. And as the buds refit him for High School, tutoring him in their clouded philosophy, it becomes clear he is far more equipped for the dangers of this world than are the duo of dips. He eats like a starving wolf, does wheelies in a car and mimics, mimicking a routine damn near as crusty as him, rappers and movie heavies he sucks up for television. Thus he leads Pauly and Seany on the path to cool and to be themselves or somesuch prattling gesture toward morality. The path to funny, however, was in the opposite direction. ★★ **IN**

◎ CALIFORNIA SUITE (1978)

Starring: *Alan Alda (Bill Warren), Michael Caine (Sidney Cochran), Bill Cosby (Dr Willis Panama), Jane Fonda (Hannah Warren), Walter Matthau (Marvin Michaels), Elaine May (Millie Michaels), Richard Pryor (Chauncy Gump), Maggie Smith (Diana Barrie)*
Director: *Herbert Ross*
Screenwriter: *Neil Simon, based on his play*
15/103 mins./Comedy/USA
Awards: *Academy Awards – Best Supporting Actress (Maggie Smith)*

Four episodes chronicle the discussions and misadventures of five couples staying at the Beverly Hills Hotel.

Few playwrights have been translated to the screen so frequently or so consistently successfully as Neil Simon. Seven years after shaping a trio of New York vignettes into Plaza Suite, he sought to repeat the formula with this all-star West Coast collection. The attempt earned him an Oscar nomination, but this is a messy misfire, which lurches uneasily between moments of earnest drama and crass slapstick. It's at its best when it sticks to the comedy of manners that Simon does best. But, even then, the laughter is often strained.

The opening meeting between the Manhattanite Jane Fonda and Californian Alan Alda to decide the future of their daughter is better played than it's written. Despite the recriminations, it's apparent that nine years of divorce have done little to heal the wounds or diminish the couple's feelings. But Simon allows the encounter to descend into a tale of two seaboards, with the result that the pair's personalities are soon submerged beneath bon mots more suited to Masterpiece Theatre than an emotional showdown.

The byplay between Maggie Smith and Michael Caine, as she prepares for the evening's Oscar ceremony, is more suitably stylised and quips trip off the duo's tongues with acid precision. Smith, ironically, snagged a Best Supporting statuette for her sly insight into the insecurities of an ageing Oscar loser. But the ever-underestimated Caine is infinitely more courageous, as he lays his image on the line to reveal the heartache of the repressed Hollywood gay.

As the only returnee from Plaza Suite, Walter Matthau sleepwalks through being caught with a comatose hooker in his bed by trusting wife, Elaine May. But Bill Cosby and Richard Pryor have to endure the nightmare of playing doctors whose rivalry erupts into a series of catastrophes, which are supposed to be madcap and hilarious, but are actually cacophonic and racially dubious. ★★ **DP**

◎ CAMELOT (1967)

Starring: *Richard Harris (King Arthur), Vanessa Redgrave (Guenevere), Franco Nero (Lancelot Du Lac), David Hemmings (Mordred), Lionel Jeffries (King Pellimore), Laurence Naismith (Merlyn)*
Director: *Joshua Logan*
Screenwriter: *Alan Jay Lerner, based on his own play adapted from the novel The Once And Future King*
U/226 mins./Musical/USA
Awards: *Academy Awards – Best Art Direction-Set Decoration, Best Costume Design, Best Music, Scoring Of Music, Adaptation or Treatment*

Inspired by love for his new bride, Guenevere, King Arthur establishes the Round Table. But its ideals are compromised when the queen begins an affair with the bravest of the knights, Sir Lancelot.

Hollywood had always been in awe of Broadway. Why else would a director with so little cinematic imagination as Joshua Logan be entrusted with three such prestigious musicals as *South Pacific*, *Camelot* and *Paint Your Wagon*. Influenced by the Russian theatrical theorist, Constantin Stanislavsky, Logan always placed greater emphasis on text and performance than he did on visuals. So, it's a wonder that the Academy bestowed Oscars on John Truscott for his art direction and costume design, as his meticulously recreated neverland was scarcely seen behind the insistent close-ups with which Logan chose to tell this tale of betrayal and broken ideals.

The original stage show had totalled 873 performances, with Richard Burton, Julie Andrews and Robert Goulet in the leads. But Alan Jay Lerner and Frederick Loewe's last musical collaboration had never recovered structurally from the need to trim it down from its initial five-hour running time. Consequently, it lacked the fluidity of their earlier work and while songs like 'How to Handle a Woman' and 'If I Ever Would Leave You' were well integrated into the storyline, they were far less memorable than the hits from such recent outings as *My Fair Lady* and *Gigi*.

However, its run coincided with the emergence of the new Camelot being formed around John F. Kennedy in the White House and this cachet helped ensure its success. But that new age optimism had long since evanesced and America was beset by the social unrest provoked by Vietnam and the Civil Rights movement by the time Logan's lacklustre film version was released.

Richard Harris brought a melancholic vulnerability to Arthur and he delivered his songs with unassuming passion. But off-screen lovers Vanessa Redgrave and Franco Nero (who was dubbed by Gene Merlina) were woefully miscast and the $18 million production became one of the biggest commercial disasters of the 1960s. ★★ **DP**

◎ CAMILLE (1937)

Starring: *Greta Garbo (Marguerritte), Robert Taylor (Armand), Lionel Barrymore (Duval), Elizabeth Allan (Nichette), Jessie Ralph (Nanine), Henry Daniel (Baron de Varville)*
Director: *George Cukor*
Screenwriters: *Zoe Akins, Frances Marlon, James Hilton, based on the novel and play* Le Dame Aux Camelias *by Alexander Dumas fils*
PG/108 mins./Romance/USA

Risking the comfortable life afforded her by the Baron de Varville, courtesan Marguerite Gautier falls for handsome innocent Armand Duval, only for his father to forbid the liaison.

This was the fifth screen adaptation of Alexandre Dumas fils's novel, *La Dame Aux Camélias*, after silent versions starring Clara Kimball Young (1915), Theda Bara (1917), Alla Nazimova (1921) and Norma Talmadge (1927). It proved to be the last production supervised by MGM wünderkind, Irving G. Thalberg. But it survived the bombastic opulence with which he draped it to become one of the most genuinely moving romantic dramas Hollywood ever produced.

This is almost entirely due to the majestic presence of Greta Garbo. Ever since Dumas transferred his story to the stage in 1852, the part of Camille had been deemed the female equivalent of Hamlet. Sarah Bernhardt, Eleanora Duse, Tallulah Bankhead and Lillian Gish, among others, had risen to its challenges. But it's impossible to imagine that any of these divas could have matched Garbo as the impossibly refined demimonde, who radiates the passion she feels for her dashing swain before succumbing gracefully to the pain of parting. Rarely has prostitution been presented with such insight, tact and cultivation. Yet, there's an almost ironic perversity about Camille's willing abandonment of her pampered existence to sample once again the thrill of young flesh and Garbo captures this with a disarming honesty that enables her to relish each joy with unsurpassed rapture and to suffer each reversal with exquisite agony.

Taylor is clearly in awe of his co-star, but this gives his otherwise lunkish display of devotion a puppyish appeal. Henry Daniell is more cynically persuasive as Camille's spurned patron and Leonore Ulric exudes poisonous envy as Olympe. But George Cukor allowed Lionel Barrymore to play Duval as another of his peppery curmudgeons and the unrepentant Americanness of his performance is one of the film's few failings.

Hollywood, however, committed a more grievous faux pas by overlooking Garbo and awarding the Best Actress Oscar to Luise Rainer for *The Good Earth*. ★★★★★ **DP**

CANDYMAN (1992)

Starring: *Virginia Madsen (Helen Lyle), Tony Todd (The Candyman/Daniel Robitaille), Xander Berkeley (Trevor Lyle), Kasi Lemmons (Bernadette 'Bernie' Walsh), Vanessa Williams (Anne-Marie McCoy)*
Director: *Bernard Rose*
Screenwriters: *Bernard Rose, based on a story by Clive Barker*
18/99 mins./Drama/Fantasy/Horror/USA

Helen Lyle is a student who decides to write a thesis about local legends and soon discovers the myth of Candyman – a killer called into existence by chanting his name while looking in a mirror. She decides to put the myth to the test ...

Alright, quieten down at the back, get out your exercise books and pens and concentrate. We're going to do a little film theory. It won't take long – but there may be a test. *Candyman* is an almost perfect example of what film boffins call a 'recursive' horror movie. Recursive horror is horror about horror. Think Wes Craven's *New Nightmare*, where 'real' Freddy is conjured up by bad movie sequels, or *Fright Night* where cheesy horror movie presenter Roddy McDowell is confronted with 'real' vampires. They're movies that talk about themselves; movies that vanish up their own arses – in a good way. They also have the power to be uniquely scary. Because they admit that some horror is in our imaginations, they imply that some isn't. They're about what's real and what's not; about what's part of the story and what's waiting at home in the shadows. So telling yourself 'It's only a movie' won't save you from them. And it definitely won't save you from *Candyman*.

Candyman was born in the imagination of Clive Barker, arguably Britain's most successful modern horror writer, in a short story entitled 'The Forbidden', first published in his seminal collection *The Books Of Blood* (1984-1985). Originally set on a deprived Liverpool housing estate, it was about local residents attempting to investigate the legend of a local serial killer. Bernard Rose, British director of the underestimated, visually startling *Paperhouse* (1988), transferred the action to Chicago, not only making the story more Yank-friendly, but actually improving it (the squalor of the housing projects outstrips anything even Toxteth has to offer), as well as bolstering the movie with a fascinating social and racial subtext.

Helen Lyle and Bernadette Walsh are precocious university researchers investigating local urban legends. When they hear about Candyman, the son of a slave viciously murdered for having it off with a white woman (in a fantastic monologue delivered by Rose himself we find out that a mob hacked his hand off, before smearing honey all over him and throwing him naked into an apiary, so they must have been serious) they investigate, tremulously heading off to the hooked one's stomping ground, the crime-infested, and almost entirely black, housing projects of Cabrini Green. There they find a community terrified by the spectre of Candyman, and who find a focus for their fears of violence, sudden death and grinding poverty in the mythical figure. But, in attempting to prove the non-existence of Candyman, Helen conjures up the real deal (in the shape of Todd, who delivers a terrifying, almost entirely vocal performance). 'You were not content with the stories', he intones, 'so I was obliged to come'. He needs a new victim to revive the myth and, appropriately enough, has decided that it will be the academic who tried to puncture it. 'Our names will be written on a thousand walls. Our crimes told and retold by our faithful believers,' he announces. Not quite the quiet life of academe she had been planning on but hey, these things happen.

Tagline
We dare you to say his name five times!

Rose's movie is a triumph on many levels. Not only does it deliver a plethora of visually imaginative, shocking scenes – Candyman floating horizontally above Helen bound in a straitjacket, a psychologist being 'split from his crotch to his gullet', not to mention an end sequence which required both actors to be covered with swarms of live bees – there's the score by American minimalist composer Philip Glass, which moves from a nursery rhyme tinkle to melancholic, melodic choral histrionics as the true grand guignol erupts. There's Jane Ann Stewart's fantastic production design, which brilliantly juxtaposes the middle class pastel-drenched academic's apartment with the graffiti splashed, crack-pipe riddled wasteland of Cabrini.

Many horror films have subtexts. *Frankenstein* is about man's irresponsible dabbling with nature, *Dracula* about men's unease with female sensuality, while some have even found cheapo slashers like *Friday The 13th* and *The Burning* to have hidden texture in their pro-authority leanings (disobey your parents and you won't get grounded, you'll get dismembered).

The nightmare surroundings of Cabrini Green that Helen enters are very real (and, in a nice touch, are the inverse of her own – her swank apartment block is a tarted up housing project) and it is, Rose seems to be proposing, people like her who are responsible for the existence of Candyman. Not just by reviving him in the supernatural passages of the story, but out of the need for a myth like him in the first place. Whether you happen to agree with his views on race issues or not, it's a powerful and intelligent idea in a genre not popularly known for them. We get, he intimates, the nightmares we deserve. Sometimes, it appears, we even invent them for ourselves. ★★★★ **AS**

CANNIBAL! THE MUSICAL

Starring: *Trey Parker (Alferd Packer/Voice Of Old Man/Voice Of Indian No.2), Matthew Stone (James Humphrey/Woman On Porch), Toddy Walters (Polly Pry) Dian Bachar (George 'California' Noon), Stephen Blackpool (Black Cat)*
Director: *Trey Parker*
Screenwriter: *Trey Parker*
18/95 mins./Horror/Musical/USA

In Colorado in the 1880s, Alferd Packer, sole survivor of a party of miners, stands trial for murder and alleged cannibalism.

The first feature from Trey Parker and Matt Stone, later the auteurs of *South Park* and *Team America: World Police*. Made on a minimal budget under the title *Alferd Packer: The Musical* but retitled for release by the tasteful folks at Troma Pictures, it's a period Western horror musical comedy based on a true story (prefiguring *Ravenous*) about Alferd Packer (whose spellcheck-defying name is printed wrongly in many, many sources), the only man ever convicted of cannibalism in the United States.

It opens with a quite impressive gore sequence in bleached-out snowy wastes, which turns out to be the version of the story told by the prosecutor. In jail, Packerd (Parker, acting as 'Juan Sanchez') tells his story to reporter Polly Pry, placing the blame on another member (Ian Hardin) of the party of miners he was guiding through Colorado in the 1880s. There's a witty subplot about Packerd's relationship with his unfaithful horse Liane, and winds up with a whole town singing 'Hang the Bastard, Hang Him High'. It has its longeurs but there's an air of genial enthusiasm, tempered by sick humour, that is surprisingly engaging. Incidentals include a tribe of Japanese Indians, a pus-squirting Confederate cyclops, a deliberately pathetic dream ballet in the style of *Oklahoma!*, a cameo from avant-garde filmmaker Stan Brakhage (who was the filmmakers' professor at Colorado University) and the inevitable 'fudge, Packer?' joke. The score offers very clever Rodgers and Hammerstein pastiches ('It's a Schpedoinkel Day'), prefiguring the surprisingly sophisticated if crass musical parodies of *South Park: Bigger, Longer & Uncut* and *Team America*). The US DVD also has one of the most entertaining, if drunken filmmaker commentary tracks ever recorded. ★★★ **KN**

Ⓓ THE CANNONBALL RUN (1981)

Starring: *Burt Reynolds (J.J. McClure), Dom DeLuise (Victor Prinzim), Farrah Fawcett (Pamela Glover), Roger Moore (Seymour Goldfarb Jr), Dean Martin (Jamie Blake), Sammy Davis Jr (Morris Fenderbaum), Jackie Chan (Jackie Chan)*
Director: *Hal Needham*
Screenwriter: *Brock Yates*
PG/95 mins./Comedy/USA

A bizarre bunch of multi-national entrants gather to take part in a trans-American motor race. The idea, highly illegal as it is, is to reach California first, by any means necessary. The dirty tricks of this bunch of racers, however, threatens to all but destroy the competition entirely.

Like a retirement home for seventies, if not even earlier, icons, this big screen, real-peopled (well, kind of) reworking of TV's cartoon *Whacky Racers* is a burbling nonsense, but at least one obvious enough in its intentions. Hence, it's hard to sneer, there's a loopy charm to its episodic, action-orientated comedy.

The antecedents are obvious. Casting Burt Reynolds, at his most drolly exasperated, tips its forelock to the *Smokey And The Bandit* movies. The sheer drum roll of tattered greats suggests the lengthy star-packed hi-jinks of *A Mad Mad Mad Mad Mad World*. And any number of Roger Moores and Jackie Chans identify former glories and or contemporary references. Farah Fawcett, as the lovely caught up with Reynolds ambulance bound – to siren their way through the traffic – hurtle for victory, is yesterday's sex bomb.

Then Hal Needham, a former stunt driver himself, isn't looking for sophistication. The aging superstars turn up, do their thing – Dean Martin and Sammy Davis Jr, dressed as priests, simply play gags off their own booze problems – and allow the movie to throttle its way to the end. The general tone of the humour possesses a lurid sexism, as creased and worn-out as much of the cast. Adrienne Barbeau simply unzips her cleavage to slip away from traffic cops about to cite her for speeding. The limited stunts too, bare the hallmarks of low budgeting, missing the opportunity for some fender-bending fun.

What saves the movie is its relaxed sense of self-awareness. Reynolds all but winks at the audience with his collection of Dick Dastardly sneaks and dodges, but holds onto that winning, hangdog warmth that got him to the top of the pile in the seventies. Who can blame him, his doofus sidekick Dom DeLuise, to be fair about the funniest thing in the movie, is convinced he is superhero Captain Chaos ready to answer the call of duty at the most inopportune of times. And that it was obviously a (cannon)ball to make is revealed via the collection of outtakes of gaffs and corpsing relayed over the end-credits.

A less-important film you would be hard pressed to find, but there remains a place for Z-grade fluff like this, such that they managed to undercut themselves with a truly dreadful sequel. ★★★ **IN**

Ⓓ A CANTERBURY TALE (1944)

Starring: *Eric Portman (Thomas Colpeper, JP), Sheila Sim (Alison Smith), Dennis Price (Peter Gibbs), Sergeant John Sweet (Bob Johnson), Esmond Knight (Narrator/Seven-Sisters Soldier/Village Idiot), Charles Hawtrey (Thomas Duckett)*
Directors: *Michael Powell, Emeric Pressburger*
Screenwriters: *Michael Powell, Emeric Pressburger*
U/124 mins./Drama/UK

When Land Girl Alison Smith has glue poured into her hair in wartime Kent, British Tommy Peter Gibbs and American GI Bob Johnson help her track down the culprit.

In his autobiography, *A Life In Movies*, Michael Powell explained that he and Emeric Pressburger had made *49th Parallel* to show America that World War II was its concern as much as Europe's, and *One Of Our Aircraft Is Missing* and *The Life And Death Of Colonel Blimp* to demonstrate the respective indomitability of the continent and the UK. *A Canterbury Tale*, therefore, was intended to reaffirm the spiritual values and traditions binding the Allies together. However, wartime audiences were baffled by such lyrical mysticism and this undeniably curious film became the Archers' first critical and commercial setback.

Pressburger's bid to turn the search for the Glueman of Chillingbourne into a detective mystery doesn't really come off. But the depiction of the Kent countryside and the heartfelt discussion of the central trio's hopes and fears is genuinely moving, as are the climactic sequences, in which the pilgrims receive their Canterbury blessings.

Powell himself had mixed feelings about the filmic quality of this quietly passionate statement of national pride, although he retained a fondness for its themes and tone. Admittedly, he'd been unable to secure his chosen cast, but it's hard to imagine that the reception would have been any more positive had Deborah Kerr and Roger Livesey essayed the roles of Alison and the eccentric squire, Thomas Colpepper. Preoccupied with the invasion of France, viewers had no time for either a story populated by latterday Chaucerian pilgrims or its allegorical allusions.

However, few got to see the film in its original form over the next 30 years, as the only available print was the 1949 American version, which reduced the length from 124 to 95 minutes and removed Powell's elegiac opening and replaced it with shots of John Sweet atop a New York skyscraper, as he recalls his experiences to new bride Kim Hunter. ★★★ **DP**

Powell & Pressburger

Who they were: Michael Powell (director) and Emeric Pressburger (screenwriter), aka The Archers. British film's most imaginative, cinematic double act.
Hallmarks: Bold Technicolor images; stiff-upper-lipped soldiers; a playful sense that movies can do anything.
If you see one film, see: *The Red Shoes* (1948)

CAPE FEAR (1962)

Starring: *Gregory Peck (Sam Bowden), Robert Mitchum (Max Cady), Polly Bergen (Peggy Bowden), Lori Martin (Nancy Bowden), Telly Savalas (Charles Sievers)*
Director: *J. Lee Thompson*
Screenwriter: *James R. Webb, based on the novel* The Executioners *by John D. MacDonald*
15/105 mins./Thriller/USA

Ex-convict Max Cady turns up in Florida and stalks upright lawyer Sam Bowden, whom he blames for his recent jail term, plotting horrible revenge on Bowden by terrorising his family. Sam goes to the police for help, but is forced outside the law to protect his womenfolk.

Later remade by Martin Scorsese and as a 'Sideshow Bob' episode of *The Simpsons*, this imitation Hitchcock thriller is a classic almost by default, with an appropriately uptight hero performance from Peck and merely good direction by long-time journeyman J. Lee Thompson outweighed by a sure-fire thriller premise (from John D. MacDonald's novel *The Executioners*) and the second-best-ever (after *Night Of The Hunter*) Robert Mitchum villain performance.

Mitchum is seething but subtle as the insolent, insouciant animal, smiling and chomping on a cigar as he flaunts legal smarts picked up in the joint, laying out plans for a diabolical revenge against Peck and his squeaky-clean wife and daughter, carefully harassing the family with lurking menace that doesn't actually break the law but making it perfectly clear that he intends to rape either or both of the women into catatonia.

People disturbed by Robert De Niro's mania in the remake might be even more creeped out by Mitchum's bare-chested presence as he explains the precise legal definition of 'consent' to Bergen, cracking an egg in his hand and rubbing it into her chest.

The climax, set in a conveniently named river, is an especially exciting mano-a-mano pay-off to all the ratcheted-up tension, but it's Mitchum's sly craziness which raises it to cult heights.

Bernard Herrmann's pounding score (reused in the remake) has sterling support provided by a post-Psycho Martin Balsam (like Herrmann, one of several Hitch hold-overs on the cast and crew) and a pre-bald Telly Savalas. ★★★★ **KN**

CAPE FEAR (1991)

Starring: *Robert De Niro (Max Cady), Nick Nolte (Sam Bowden), Jessica Lange (Leigh Bowden), Juliette Lewis (Danielle Dowden), Robert Mitchum (Lieutenant Elgart), Gregory Peck (Lee Heller), Illeana Douglas (Lori Davis)*
Director: *Martin Scorsese*
Screenwriter: *Wesley Strick, based on the 1962 screenplay by James R Webb, based on the novel* The Executioners *by John D. MacDonald*
Cinematography: *Freddie Francis*
18/128 mins./Thriller/USA

Just-released convict Max Cady persecutes lawyer Sam Bowden, who deliberately botched his defence, setting out to get revenge in a campaign of terror against Bowden's family.

By 1991, Martin Scorsese was the most distinctive and talented film-maker working at the peak of his powers but had still never quite had the mega-hit which would give him the Hollywood clout to go along with his abilities.

As a payback to Universal for supporting his tricky *Last Temptation Of Christ* project, Scorsese unashamedly applied himself to a big-scale quickie thriller, built on the skeleton of the well-remembered 1962 suspense thriller. Scorsese enters into the spirit of the thing, reusing Bernard Herrmann's score to melodramatic effect, calling upon Saul Bass for a suitably ominous credit sequence, and respectfully casting the stars of the earlier film (Robert Mitchum, Gregory Peck, Martin Balsam) in telling cameos.

Nolte and DeNiro are superb as the antagonists, a compromised lawyer and a self-educated white trash supervillain, and Juliette Lewis and Jessica Lange are outstanding as Nolte's imperilled family.

The first hour presents a quietly scary logic as Max, barely breaking the law, reduces Sam's life to shreds. However, Scorsese abandons subtlety with an all-stops-out gothic finale in a swamp that finally answers the question of what a *Friday The 13th* movie would look like starring and directed by Academy Award nominees.

The suspense rises in a crescendo as the demented Cady – certainly the most loathsome character De Niro has ever played – invades the Bowden houseboat during a storm, finally transformed into a Freddy-faced monster as he is burned and battered but keeps crawling out of the waters to attack again, and finally dragged under while speaking in tongues.

Despite provocative debate on legal and family ethics, it's just a horror picture, but it is at least a damn good horror picture. ★★★★ **KN**

CAPOTE (2005)

Starring: *Philip Seymour Hoffman (Truman Capote), Catherine Keener (Harper Lee), Clifton Collins Jr (Perry Smith), Chris Cooper (Alvin Dewey), Bruce Greenwood (Jack Dunphy)*
Director: *Bennett Miller*
Screenwriter: *Dan Futterman, based on the book by Gerald Clarke*
15/114 mins./Drama/Canada/USA

Awards: *Academy Awards – Best Actor, BAFTA – Best Actor, Golden Globes – Best Actor*

It's 1959, and celebrated author Truman Capote decides to make his next project the shocking murders of the Clutter family in a small, conservative Kansas town where nothing usually happens. Then, researching his project, the author becomes fascinated with one of the killers, Perry Smith.

Long ago, Hollywood realised that the trouble with making biopics of writers is that their lives tend to be dull – it's 75 per cent sitting down scribbling and 25 per cent worrying about money, neither activity particularly exciting to watch. But an early writer biopic that clicked was *The Life Of Emile Zola*, the 1937 Best Picture Oscar winner. This skimped over decades of dreary novel-production to concentrate on the author's involvement with the Dreyfus case, in which a French-Jewish army officer was wrongly convicted of treason. Zola got an editorial and a catchphrase ('J'accuse!') out of his advocacy, but the Warner Bros. winner was more concerned with the intricacies of the famous miscarriage of justice and sufferings endured on Devil's Island. Capote follows almost exactly the same course as the Zola movie, but for two things: Capote wrote his most enduring book, the 'factual novel' *In Cold Blood*, about the Clutter Murders of 1959; and Perry Smith, who languishes Dreyfus-like on Death Row for half the film, was guilty.

Directed by Bennett Miller and written by Dan Futterman, *Capote* is distilled from Gerald Clarke's like-titled biography, which covers all of the author's life. It plays not as a full-on birth-to-death account of Truman Capote's career or even a third dramatisation (after the famous 1967 movie and a TV remake) of *In Cold Blood*. The film is, like Mike Leigh's *Topsy-Turvy*, a biopic of a work of art (here, art-cum-journalism), following *In Cold Blood* from conception (shotgun blasts in Kansas, a small headline read in New York) through its seven-year development to publication, spotlighting the demands it makes on a writer who'll never complete anything again and the way the writing process affects people, like the cops and killers, who have other things on their mind. There are very few of those tear-a-page-out-of-the-typewriter-and-throw-the-crumpled-paper-in-a-wastebasket scenes that fail to convey what writing a book is actually like, but no movie has ever done better by the process of complicated creation, especially that home-stretch wish that the thing were finally done.

Aside from being a foot-and-a-half too tall, which is brilliantly concealed from the camera, Philip Seymour Hoffman is miraculously well-cast as Capote, a man who devoted his life to becoming an apparent caricature of himself. Hoffman does that cartoon voice (Capote sounded a lot like Tex Avery's forlorn mutt Droopy) perfectly, but shows the canny, cold, compulsive brain working behind the sparkling eyes. Note how Capote, at first sight and sound the sort of flamboyant queen you'd expect to be tarred and feathered in middle America in 1959, gets close to key players in the case, wooing witnesses and befriending the cop on the case (Chris Cooper) through his literary-inclined wife (Amy Ryan). Though he becomes ambiguously smitten with the 'sensitive' Perry, Capote can calmly lie through the cell-bars about the judgmental title he has chosen for the book he hopes will clear his pal's name.

While the film is about *In Cold Blood*, the frame allows exploration of Capote's relationships with longtime/long-suffering companion Jack Dunphy and childhood friend/research assistant/fellow author Nelle Harper Lee.

In Cold Blood divides Capote's life, but *Capote* the movie shows the before (cocktail-party celebrity on the back of *Breakfast At Tiffany's*) and after (a slide to alcoholism and writer's block) mingling as the writer wrestles with his material, desires, conscience and perhaps-necessary artistic callousness. ★★★★★ **KN**

CAPRICORN ONE (1978)

Starring: *Elliot Gould (Robert Caulfield), James Brolin (Colonel Charles Brubaker), Brenda Vaccaro (Kay Brubaker), Sam Waterston (Lieutenant Col. Peter Willis), O.J. Simpson (Commander John Walker)*
Director: *Peter Hyams*
Screenwriter: *Peter Hyams*
PG/123 mins./Thriller/USA/UK

When a NASA mission to Mars fails to get off the ground, and their funding is threatened, they decide to fake a landing. But as the fakery threatens to come to light, the lives of the astronauts forced to act out the journey, is threatened as the government try to cover things up.

An excellent, if forgotten, late seventies conspiracy thriller which takes the existent fable of the faked moon landing and runs with it. Certainly, you have to forgive the whacking great lumps of far-fetchedness. Shadowy political trickery is one thing, fabricating an entire NASA mission is near impossible to credit. Get over that and it's a whole lot of fun watching Hal Halbrook's – who played supergrass Deep Throat in *All The President's Men* – wicked scheming unravel thanks to the gutsy work of Elliot Gould's tatty hack.

It is he, one of the seventies great unrecognised joys, who gives the film its ironic fizz, as if it is almost parodying the seriousness of the eras moody suspicions. As he pieces together the factual anomalies, tipped off by his soon-to-die insider buddy Robert Walden, and dodges various attempts on his life (the most immediate form of verification) the film spins into life. The second half is pure chase movie, a race against time as the trio of heroic spaceman escape their desert prison and are gradually hunted down. That they are played by James Brolin, Sam Waterston and O.J. Simpson, who gets to drink from a dead snake, tells you just what era this film harkens from.

Director Peter Hyams, a hack himself who veers between the outright crap and expertly handled B-movies like this, plays around with some loopy helicopter shots in search of a resonant style. He needn't have worried, the set-up is strong enough, a truly original focus for a thriller – for a while the astronauts are unaware they haven't gone to Mars! Employing composer Jerry Goldsmith, who delivers one of his most stirring scores helps no end, as does a hilarious cameo from Telly Savalas as a crop-dusting pilot who Gould ropes into his rescue mission. In a strange way, it's well worth a remake. ★★★★ **IN**

CAPTAIN BLOOD (1935)

Starring: *Errol Flynn (Dr Peter Blood), Olivia de Havilland (Arabella Bishop), Lionel Atwill (Col. Bishop), Basil Rathbone (Captain Levasseur), Ross Alexander (Jeremy Pitt)*
Director: *Michael Curtiz*
Screenwriter: *Casey Robinson, based on the novel by Rafael Sabbatini*
PG/119 mins./Adventure/Historical/USA

Having been sold into slavery for a supposed treachery to the King, English gent Dr Peter Blood hatches an escape that leads him to stealing a Spanish galleon. In so doing, he turns from gent to pirate, taking on the mantle of Captain Blood, scourge of the high seas, but soon enough he is drawn back to rescue Port Royal from a French attack.

Errol Flynn and his swaggering gait were unheard of before director Michael Curtiz plucked him from the veils of obscurity for this splendid piratical jaunt. It proved the call of destiny, the film launched a career of grandiose and high flung swashbuckling, a new form of heroism that struck its time, Depression-hit America, like a bolt of electricity. Yet, to put the success of this tale of sweet revenge down to the star alone is to ignore Curtiz's lavish shots of the sun-caressed Caribbean seas and the ease with which Casey Robinson relays Rafael Sabatini's novel with all its Defoe-like textures.

This is shaggy dog history, of course, the pirate captain as dashing rogue, as tanned as a teak deck. A further cry from the scheming brutes of reality you could not reach. Yet, in Flynn's hands, Blood becomes a more complex roustabout than you might expect. This is a man wronged in the past and broken free from slavery – that he was owned by Olivia de Havilland's arch and spoiled Arabella Bishop and would eventually revisit her adds a deft sexual power game to all the polished spills of swordplay. Life has led to Blood, he swaggers because he is proud, he flaunts the rules because they have turned against him, but his moral core, nestled close to his heart, will ignite when a just cause is shown. He is certain, a magnificent, unironic gleam of old Hollywood.

And Curtiz, who would go on to make a dozen films with Flynn despite rumours of mutual hatred, matched his star's flamboyance with a gorgeous sense of spectacle very much his own. The film is constantly spoiling for a fight, and Flynn's glorious talents with a blade are shown to full effect, especially when he duels nefarious rival Basil Rathbone. That pair would join Curtiz for the splendour of *The Adventures Of Robin Hood*, the signature film of the age, but in many ways *Captain Blood* is a more layered and memorable film. ★★★★ **IN**

CAPTAIN CORELLI'S MANDOLIN (2001)

Starring: *Nicolas Cage (Captain Corelli), Penelope Cruz (Pelagia), John Hurt (Dr Iannis), Christian Bale (Mandras), Irene Papas (Drosoula), Gerasimos Skiadaressis (Mr Stamatis), Aspasia Kralli (Mrs Stamatis), Michael Yannatos (Kokolios)*
Director: *John Madden*
Screenwriter: *Shawn Slovo, based on book by Louis de Bernieres*
15/131 mins./War/Romance/UK/France/USA

Cephallonia, 1941. Village beauty Pelagia is betrothed to simple, boyish Mandras, who has gone off to fight in Albania. But as the Italians invade the island, Pelagia is drawn to the charming, musical, life-embracing 'enemy', Captain Corelli.

A publishing phenomenon, Louis de Berniere's bestselling tale of love and war, music and innocence lost in bloodshed and remorse, had to be made into a movie. Yet it's no small task tackling a beloved saga that is reckoned to nestle in one out of every 20 British households.

Fans will argue it's not as good as the book, but John Madden has delivered a pretty mooch around rustic, tranquil Cephallonia. The prospective

Brit Baddies TOP10

1. Christopher Lee (Dracula, The Man With The Golden Gun, Lord Of The Rings, Star Wars prequels)
2. Alan Rickman (Die Hard, Robin Hood, Prince Of Thieves)
3. Gary Oldman (True Romance, Leon)
4. Sir Laurence Olivier (Marathon Man)
5. Brian Cox (Manhunter)
6. Basil Rathbone (The Adventures Of Robin Hood)
7. Donald Pleasence (You Only Live Twice)
8. Steven Berkoff (Beverly Hills Cop, Rambo: First Blood Part 2)
9. Anthony Hopkins (Hannibal Lecter)
10. Jason Isaacs (The Patriot)

lovers exchange guilty looks and barbs; gentle Antonio and his good-humoured company of soldiers perform opera and demonstrate they are lovers, not fighters; invaders and occupied tentatively celebrate their shared culture, all of them bathed in endless sunshine. When we hear the Allies have taken faraway Rome, it's a case of, 'Oh, right, there's a war on.'

It's an hour and a half before the conflict really impacts, the bigger picture sacrificed in Shawn Slovo's screenplay in favour of the central love story and the journeys of a fistful of characters, including Bale's – from amorous, carefree fisherman to hardened guerrilla – and Morrissey's, whose 'good' German is particularly affecting, while Hurt pieces characters and the narrative together as doctor/witness with his customary, formidable flair.

The execution of a dozen Italians is the most powerful climax in a scenic, old-fashioned affair, but in reality, 10,000 of them were murdered, which makes the small-scale human story threads here rather thin, however tenderly spun out.

Cruz is sweet in her 40s frocks and, undone by Corelli's string plucking, registers distress prettily. Cage is appropriately charming, lovable and impassioned. The insoluble problem is the accents, creating a seriously unfortunate air of absurdity. Those playing Greeks (and Papas, who, rather amazingly, got in this picture even though she really is Greek) affect lusty booming as though auditioning for a Zorba re-make, though extras around the village square carry on in Greek, which seems very obdurate of them. Actors playing principal Italians speaka da English like Chico Marx – including Cage (real name Coppola), who has a firmer grip on the famous mandolin than on his vowel sounds – but chorus boys sing and march in Italiano.

They actually sing 'Santa Lucia', too. You half expect a gondolier to appear singing, 'Just-a one Cornetto.' But no, it's the Nazis who pitch up, which is when the film really gets going. Where would war movies be without those bastards, eh? Once the Huns get beastly and the fighting and suffering kick in, you can unfurl the tissues without feeling sheepish. ★★★ **AE**

CAPTURING THE FRIEDMANS (2003)

Starring: *Arnold Friedman (Father), Elaine Friedman (Mother), David Friedman (Eldest Son), Seth Friendman (Middle Son), Jesse Friendman (Youngest Son), Howard Friedman (Arnold's brother), John McDermott (Postal Inspector), Frances Galasso, Detective (Ret. Director, Sex Crimes Unit)*
Director: *Andrew Jarecki*
15/107 mins./Documentary/USA

Andrew Jarecki's documentary uses archive footage shot by the Friedman family – as well as contemporary interviews – to tell the bizarre, harrowing story of how a family ripped itself apart when its father was accused of a string of sexual assaults on young boys.

The known facts, such as they are, are these: in 1987, Arnold Friedman, a respected school teacher and father of three boys, had his home raided after being caught ordering a pederastic magazine from Denmark. Local families were soon being questioned by the police about computer classes that Friedman had been holding in his basement, and within days lurid allegations of sustained sexual abuse against neighbourhood boys emerged.

Friedman was charged by police, his youngest son was also implicated, and the family imploded. And, owing to another son's newfangled video camera, it's all on tape. As a harrowing family drama, *Capturing The Friedmans* is pretty much without parallel. Jarecki invites us to watch aghast as tragedy piles upon tragedy. One of the most shocking and upsetting moments in the film is not recorded visually at all, but on audio tape. A shot of the cassette reels winding is held seemingly interminably as we hear a screaming match over the family dinner table, in which the three brothers round viciously on their mother for failing to support their father after his arrest.

But at a deeper level it's an object lesson in the occasional elusiveness of truth. It leaves you not knowing what to think. And that's the point. Jarecki's film brilliantly illustrates the fallibility of memory, the slippery nature of 'facts' and even people's invention of events that may never have taken place.

A policewoman describes the piles of pornography that supposedly littered the Friedman's home, while on the screen we see the original police snapshots of the raid itself, in which the home is distinctly porn-free apart from a small stash of magazines hidden behind a piano in the basement. One of the alleged victims describes a grotesque episode of group abuse in the basement, before contradicting himself in the same interview and revealing that he hadn't had the memory at all until he was subjected to hypnosis. Other alleged victims come tantalisingly close to admitting that – under extraordinary pressure from inept police – they made the whole thing up (in one of the film's occasional grimly funny moments, one of the parents points out that the whole community had always been incredibly competitive, leading to bizarre 'if your son was abused five times, mine was abused six' kinds of boasting). ★★★★★ **CW**

CARLITO'S WAY (1993)

Starring: *Al Pacino (Carlito Brigante), Sean Penn (David Kleinfeld), Penelope Ann Miller (Gail), John Leguizamo (Benny Blanco), Ingrid Rogers (Steffe), Viggo Mortensen (Lalin)*
Director: *Brian De Palma*
Screenwriter: *David Koepp, from the novels* Carlito's Way *and* After Hours *by Edwin Torres*
Producer: *Martin Bergman, Willi Baer, Michael Scott Bergman*
18/141 mins./Crime/Drama/USA

Carlito Brigante has just left jail after a decade, and is determined to go straight. But everything around him conspires to pull him back into a cycle of violence and crime.

It's 1975 in New York: hot pants have replaced mini-skirts, disco dancers have forsaken pot for cocaine, the O'Jays are on the soundtrack and crime is a going business. Carlito Brigante is out of jail and on the streets in his calf-length leather coat after smarmy lawyer Kleinfeld has busted the government's case against him. Carlito takes over the management of a club in Spanish Harlem, pockets loose cash that comes his way after he's accidentally mixed up in a shoot-out, gets non-commitally together with old gang buddies, and makes a play for his ex-girlfriend.

Everyone wonders when Carlito will get back into the rackets, but he insists he wants to save up enough money to invest in a legitimate business – a car rental firm in the Bahamas. Slowly, the pressure builds up on the ex-gangster to get back into crime. When Kleinfeld's dealings with the Mafia threaten meltdown unless a mob boss is sprung from a prison barge, Carlito feels a terrible obligation to the man who gave him his second chance, and so agrees to go along on a midnight cruise to fish the godfather out of New York harbour. With De Palma and Pacino back together in an Hispanic-flavoured gangster epic ten years after Scarface, the expectation here is for wall-to-wall death-o-rama. While De Palma is never one to stint on the blow and the broads, *Carlito's Way*, adapted by David Koepp from novels by Judge Edwin Torres, is comparatively light on the blood. Unusually, the film resurrects the post-Hays Code gangster movie plot of the former hoodlum desperately trying to stay straight, allowing the hero to be as tough a mother as he used to be, but also enough of a good guy to be sympathetic.

Pacino's Carlito is a wonderfully haggard, desperately reformed man. Quietly ashamed of his former excess and flawed by his lack of cold-hearted viciousness, he narrates in flashback from a first scene shooting (which recalls *Serpico*), aware that his attempt to stay clean is doomed. Though the relationship with Miller, a Broadway wannabe working as a topless dancer, is formulaic, everything else in the movie clicks perfectly. Penn, with a receding wire-wool haircut, redeems his career as a lawyer slime spinning out of control, and there are gems of strutting Latino villainy from Luis Guzman, John Leguizamo and Viggo Mortensen.

De Palma, still atoning for *Bonfire Of The Vanities*, demonstrates here that when he's in the mood he can be a virtuoso show-off but still tell a story. An early scene in a poolroom as a drug deal goes wrong while Pacino performs a trick shot is an absolute model of suspense, and the final chase, through the New York subway to Grand Central Station, chews your nerves for nearly 15 minutes of near-misses and shocks before the actual violence. A gangster biggie, this one is there with a bullet. ★★★★★ **KN**

◑ CARMEN JONES (1954)

Starring: *Dorothy Dandridge (Carmen Jones), Harry Belafonte (Joe), Olga James (Cindy Lou), Pearl Bailey (Frankie), Joe Adams (Husky Miller), Nick Stewart (Dink Franklin)*
Director: *Otto Preminger*
Screenwriter: *Harry Kleiner, based on the book by Oscar Hammerstein II*
U/103 mins./Musical/USA

On leave to see his fiancée, Cindy Lou, trooper Joe falls for Carmen, a worker in a Jacksonville parachute factory who is stringing along prize-fighter, Husky Miller.

Oscar Hammerstein was struggling with this updating of Bizet's 1875 opera when he was invited by Richard Rodgers to collaborate on *Oklahoma!* The success of both shows resurrected the lyricist's flagging career, but in neither case did the ensuing screen version do the electrifying original much justice. Where *Carmen Jones* was concerned, many were outraged by the stereotypical depiction of the African-American characters, while others lamented the fact that so many principals had their vocals dubbed. Yet, without the much-maligned Otto Preminger, the picture might never have been made at all.

Previous all-black musicals, like *Hallelujah*, *Cabin In The Sky* and *Stormy Weather* had been commercial calamities, largely because audiences in the Deep South refused to watch them. Yet, Preminger persuaded Fox supremo Darryl F. Zanuck to stump up a budget of $800,000 and consent to the casting of the relatively unknown Dorothy Dandridge over more established stars like Joyce Bryant and Elizabeth Foster. Seduced by Dandridge's feisty screen test, Preminger became her lover and, despite a tempestuous on-set relationship, he guided her to the distinction of becoming the first African-American to be nominated for Best Actress. However, his preoccupation with Dandridge (who nearly resigned because of her concerns that the part presented black women in a negative light) meant that he neglected the miscast Harry Belafonte, who looks consistently uncomfortable with both Joe's demeanour and having to mime to a playback.

Yet there was little that Preminger could have done about this situation. Bizet's estate had never been entirely happy with Hammerstein's revision of Meilhac and Halévy's libretto and its insistence that the film resembled a folk opera rather than a Broadway entertainment did much to undermine its integrity. Nevertheless, songs like 'Stand Up and Fight', 'Dat's Love' and 'Beat Out That Rhythm on a Drum' still pack a punch and such moments of gaudy passion and pizzazz come close to atoning for the occasional melodramatics and lapses in political taste. ★★★ **DP**

◑ CARNIVAL OF SOULS (1962)

Starring: *Candace Hilligoss (Mary Henry), Frances Feist (Mrs Thomas, Landlady), Sidney Berger (John Linden), Art Ellison (Minister), Stan Levitt (Dr Samuels)*
Director: *Herk Harvey*
Screenwriter: *John Clifford*
15/91 mins./Horror/Thriller/USA

Mary and her two friends plough off a bridge onto a river when involved in a drag race. She appears to be the only survivor, and after recovering, accepts a job in a new town as a church organist, only to be dogged by a mysterious phantom figure that seems to reside in an old run-down pavilion.

We start with a road crash. A car hurtles off a bridge into a silt-choked river and vanishes. Rescue attempts seem futile until, in one of the film's first starkly surreal images, a young woman is seen standing, bewildered and bedraggled on a sandbank. It appears she is the only survivor but after taking up her new job as a church organist she is strangely drawn to an abandoned carnival palace out of town. Things start to get weirder when she starts to see strange, pale-faced ghouls and people fail to notice her (a gimmick later used in *The Sixth Sense*) before, in a climactic final sequence, she returns to the palace and dances with the ghouls. Back at the river the car is found. A final shot shows her corpse still in the passenger seat.

Until the runaway success of *The Sixth Sense* in 1999, ghost stories have pretty much been horror movies' poor relation. There are the occasional classics such as *The Legend Of Hell House* (1973), *The Haunting* (1962), *Jacob's Ladder* (1990) and, arguably, *The Shining* (1980), but generally directors have steered clear of the sub-genre, put off perhaps by the qualities required to produce a really good, haunting yarn. Unlike other kinds of fright movie, the ghost story can't rely on mind-blowing special effects or inventive new ways of dismembering the human body, but rather on those most difficult of effects of all to achieve: precision storytelling and molasses thick atmosphere.

Luckily these are qualities that don't require gargantuan budgets, a good thing for Herk Harvey, a maker of industrial training films for Kansas commercials company Centron, and intent on producing his first feature. He had only $33,000 seed money, a cast of friends and colleagues (with what can only be described as limited acting experience) and a tight schedule having taken a leave of absence from his job. What he also had was a great idea, and even more important, a fantastic location. *Carnival Of Souls* is one of those very rare films whose set is as important as its content.

The film's twist ending is now a cliché (it's used in *Jacob's Ladder* but was probably coined originally by American writer Ambrose Bierce whose story *Incident At Owl Creek* was adapted as a short in 1961) but at the time packed a terrific punch. It's difficult to overstate how important *Carnival Of Souls* is in the history of the independent horror movie. In 1962 American horror was in a pretty dismal state, dominated by the cheesy drive-in fare provided by American International Pictures (*I Was A Teenage Frankenstein*, *How To Make A Monster*) and the, admittedly superior, work of Roger Corman (*Pit And The Pendulum*). The only recent innovation of any note had been *Psycho* in 1960 (and Harvey nods towards the film with his tense driving scenes, as well as some risque bathroom sequences that would have been unthinkable before Hitch had his leading lady butchered in the shower). But other than that serious, bleak horror that didn't rely on pantomime makeup or schlock gothery and cruddy references to the stalwart monsters of the 30s was pretty much non-existent.

Legions of subsequent micro-budget horror directors owe Harvey (who sadly died in 1996 without ever making another feature) a debt of gratitude. From George A. Romero, who openly acknowledges the visual influence that *Carnival* had on his black and white classic *Night Of The Living Dead*, to Tobe Hooper with his pretty much DIY *Texas Chain Saw Massacre*, Sam Raimi with *The Evil Dead* and John Carpenter's *Halloween*, independent horror filmmakers are all treading in Harvey's footsteps. For that matter when Daniel Myrick and Eduardo Sanchez took their video cameras into the woods for *The Blair Witch Project* in 1999 they were repeating, in part at least, the technique of Harvey and cinematographer Maurice Prather who used location shooting with their lightweight 16mm Arriflex cameras to give the movie a unique, mobile feel. (Dennis Hopper would use the same technique to shoot seminal 60s flick *Easy Rider* a full seven years later. *Carnival* has worn better.)

In the dance sequences themselves, the huge space festooned with rotting streamers is reminiscent of the ballroom sequences in Kubrick's *The Shining* (1980). As with many indie horror movies it exists in a number of cuts from 80 mins to a possibly mythical two-hour version. ★★★★★ **AS**

CARRIE (1976)

Starring: *Sissy Spacek (Carrie White), Piper Laurie (Margaret White), Amy Irving (Sue Snell), William Katt (Tommy Ross), John Travolta (Billy Nolan), Nancy Allen (Chris Hargenson), Betty Buckley (Miss Collins), P.J. Soles (Norma Watson), Sydney Lassick (Mr Fromm), Stefan Geirasch (Principal Morton)*
Director: *Brian De Palma*
Screenwriter: *Larry Cohen, based on Stephen King's novel*
18/97 mins./Horror/USA

Carrie is the outsider of her class, bullied by them and by her mother, a religous fanatic who walks around in a black cape. But on the night of the school prom, Carrie decides to avenge all those who have persecuted her.

Carrie is not a horror film. At least, not according to Brian De Palma. 'Horror films are Hammer films, vampires and Frankenstein,' he said at the time of *Carrie*'s release. 'I love those pictures but I don't feel it's exactly what I'm doing.'

Carrie is not even a horror novel. At least, not according to its author Stephen King. 'It's largely about how women find their own channels of power,' he wrote in *Danse Macabre* in 1981. 'And what men fear about women and women's sexuality.' There you go. Not about a teenager who kills everybody on prom night after all. *Carrie* may be no ordinary horror film or horror novel, but horror it certainly is, exemplifying what some call De Palma's 'red period' (*Sisters* (1972) to *Body Double* (1984). As King's debut, written while working for $1.60 an hour in an industrial laundry, *Carrie* set him on the way to becoming one of the most successful living authors – and to be fair to this commendably unpretentious man, he describes his own attempts at subtextualising *Carrie* as 'heavy, turgid stuff'.

The reason why both book and film worked was that the action took place in a familiar setting, high school. Since *Carrie*, there have been more high school horror movies than you can shake a pom-pom at, but in 1976, after the success of *Carnal Knowledge* (1971), *American Graffiti* (1973) and on television *Happy Days*, awareness of high school culture was at a new high. Time to tip a bucket of pig's blood all over it. *Carrie* is a bloody film, but not in the traditional slasher sense. It begins with the sight of menstrual blood and pivots on the blood of an unfortunate porker, but very little human blood is spilt before our eyes (electrocution and burning do for most of Carrie's victims) – except, that is, for the kitchen utensil 'crucifixion' of Carrie's mom.

For all the morbid, vicarious, popcorn-munching fun to be had from De Palma's first – and arguably only – true cinematic masterwork, *Carrie* is loaded with subtext for those who seek it. When, in the film's memorable opening sequence, Carrie (a perfectly cast Sissy Spacek) is taunted over her first period in the communal showers, the religious connotations are implicit – the over-the-top notion of the female 'curse of blood' dates back to original sin in The Bible and is reinforced at home by Carrie's mom, a self-flagellating, man-hating, fundamentalist nutcase whose own-brand Baptism in the book becomes extreme Roman Catholicism in the film. Plenty to get your teeth into, especially as Mrs White gets comeuppance for her fervent beliefs.

Is this King and De Palma's revenge against oppressive authority, religion as a whole or – paging Dr Freud! – against dear old Mom? It's easy to read under the surface of the blood, the curse, the crucifixion, even the pagan, ritualistic slaughter of the pig. De Palma's skill inhabits three unforgettable set-pieces in Carrie: the shower scene, prom night and the dream-sequence ending. De Palma's decision to play the first in soft-pornographic slow-motion (soft focus implied by steam) is unsettling, especially when it snaps back to real-time on Carrie's discovery. The prom is a true tour de force and actually Hitchcockian in its understanding of suspense (we know the bucket of blood is suspended above the stage; Carrie does not). More slo-mo ups the impact as Carrie and suitor William Katt approach their fate, and the famous split-screen payoff – which took De Palma six whole weeks to cut together – is a rare case of gimmickry well employed in the name of narrative.

The 'Carrie White burns in Hell' finale, as dreamt by a guilt-ridden Sue (Amy Irving), which involved Spacek being buried in a coffin under rocks, has entered the annals of the All-Time Great Movie Endings. It's one of the few tricks screenwriter Laurence D. Cohen did not glean from the novel. It's fitting that such an influential film should have effectively patented the dummy ending that is now an obligation of every two-bit slasher. Not exactly the first time a hand had emerged from a grave, admittedly, but the tactic was skilfully executed – it works every time, like Ben Gardner's head in *Jaws*.

The film's $1.8 million budget prevented De Palma from depicting Carrie's walk home as it appears in the book (by the time she gets there, half the city of Chamberlain is ablaze), but the route from King novel to the screen would not be as carefully trodden again until Frank Darabont went to work. ★★★★★ **AC**

CARRY ON ABROAD (1972)

Starring: *Sid James (Vic Flange), Kenneth Williams (Stuart Farquhar), Charles Hawtrey (Eustace Tuttle), Joan Sims (Cora Flange), Bernard Bresslaw (Brother Bernard), Barbara Windsor (Sadie Tomkins)*
Director: *Gerald Thomas*
Screenwriter: *Talbot Rothwell*
PG/88 mins/Comedy/UK

The *Carry On* team, in usual guises, head for the Spanish resort of Elsbels to find the hotel unfinished and weather atrocious. Soon enough their hijinks will be curtailed by the very collapse of the building.

CARRY ON AGAIN DOCTOR

In which Sid James is married to Joan Sims but still busy trying to get giggly Barbara Windsor into bed, while Kenneth Williams is uptight, and Charles Hawtrey lurches about a fair bit. It's *Carry On* carrying on without an ounce of inspiration, fresh thinking, but a reassuring good measure of familiar set-ups, awful entendres and crazy gags.

The situation is the classic British cheap package holiday, a satire of the ugly attitudes of Brits abroad. Thus, eternal gag-writer Talbot Rothwell takes aim at foreign food, racial bigotry, and a weird elixir that turns everyone randy as their hotel comes crashing down around them. But, especially for one so late in the series, the funny quotient is surprisingly high and, for once, they all seem to be having a really good time. Rothwell, with director Gerald Thomas, keeps the jokes tumbling at a much faster rate than before; a pace bordering on spoof. It's a touch naughtier as well – we're in the more prurient 70s now – with that famous glimpse of a sudsy Babs' bottom. The stand-outs, however, are those two plump doyens of the series: Hattie Jacques and the all too underrated Joan Sims as the ever-nagging wife to Sid James. ★★★ **IN**

CARRY ON AGAIN DOCTOR (1969)

Starring: *Sid James (Gladstone Screwer), Kenneth Williams (Frederick Carver), Charles Hawtrey (Doctor Ernest Stoppidge), Jim Dale (Doctor Jimmy Nookey), Joan Sims (Ellen Moore), Barbara Windsor (Goldie Locks)*
Director: *Gerald Thomas*
Screenwriter: *Talbot Rothwell*
PG/89 mins./Comedy/UK

Dr Nookey is shipped off to a remote island by arch rival Frederick Carver. But there he discovers a miracle tonic that could change his fortunes...

The eighteenth *Carry On* and third medical instalment sees Jim Dale (in his last outing) being sent into exile onto the tawdry tropical isle of Beautific to be corrupted by witchdoctor Gladstone Screwer.

Half the film is set on the island, where he discovers a miracle slimming tonic – and Sid James steals all the best lines – and the rest back in Blighty where his luck takes a turn for the better and romance with Barbara Windsor beckons, if he can better hissing enemy Kenneth Williams and his stooge Charles Hawtrey. There are also inevitable appearances by 'Matron' Hattie Jacques, endowed with a name (Miss Soaper) for the first time and Joan Sims as the millonairess with whom he sets up business.

The fast-moving plot and changing locations keep the show moving, and makes this one of the more successful entries in the series. Although the nearest the film crew got to the tropics was Maidenhead, the locations were more in tune with the saucy seaside postcard humour of Rothwell's script. ★★★ **EC**

CARRY ON AT YOUR CONVENIENCE (1971)

Starring: *Sid James (Sid Plummer), Kenneth Williams (W.C. Boggs), Charles Hawtrey (Charles Coote), Joan Sims (Chloe Moore), Hattie Jacques (Beattie Plummer), Bernard Bresslaw (Bernie Hulke)*
Director: *Gerald Thomas*
Screenwriter: *Talbot Rothwell*
PG/90 mins/Comedy/UK

W.C. Boggs, as may be apparent, are fine purveyors of lavatories and bathroom equipment, but they are assailed by industrial disputes, led by shop foreman Sid Plummer. Funny that when it comes to the day of the work outing, no one is on strike.

One of the most involved of all the *Carry On* plots, even bordering on the political (a first) in its comedy of unionised shop floors and frustrated businessmen (personified by an arch and devious Kenneth Williams, of course, as W.C. Boggs himself) trying to keep the work force in place, but deep down is still a silly farce boasting every possibility of toilet gag. For once, Sid James takes a more fatherly role as perpetual union irritant Sid Plummer, it's his daughter Myrtle (a pretty Jacki Piper) who is busy playing the bosses son Lewis (Bill Maynard) off against young union rep Vic (Kenneth Cope). Strikingly (no pun, intended) this is one of the least lurid and the film suffers accordingly.

Elsewhere the usual faces (but no Barbara Windsor) are caught up in numerous subplots involving Charles Hawtrey playing strip poker with Vic's mom (why?), Sid's budgie picking the racing winners, and a good lot of familiar slapstick on the works outing. But it's too fussy and flat, too preoccupied with its setting, to rank highly in the series. ★★ **IN**

CARRY ON BEHIND (1975)

Starring: *Elke Sommer (Prof. Anna Vrooshka), Kenneth Williams (Prof. Roland Crump), Bernard Bresslaw (Arthur Upmore), Joan Sims (Daphne Barnes). Kenneth Connor (Major Leep), Jack Douglas (Ermie Bragg), Windsor Davies (Fred Ramsden), Peter Butterworth (Barnes), Liz Fraser (Sylvia Ramsden)*
Director: *Gerald Thomas*
Screenwriter: *Dave Freeman*
PG/90 mins/Comedy/UK

The discovery of Roman remains next to a run-down campsite sees archaeologists – in particular Prof. Anna Vrooshka and Prof. Roland Crump – mix with happy-go-lucky holidaymakers. The results equal chaos.

Basically a retread of *Carry On Camping* modernised to cash in on the 70s explosion in caravanning, *Carry On Behind* – the tagline ran 'We gave you *Loving*, we gave you *Dick*, now we give you *Behind*' – throws up the usual assortment of henpecked husbands, innuendo, nagging wives, more innuendo battle-axe-mother-in-laws, even more innuendo and dolly birds with little in the way of tampering with the formula.

The only differences this time round is that it features a Hollywood starlet in Elke Sommer, star of *A Shot In The Dark*, who enjoys some entertaining cavorting with Williams as two randy archaeologists. (Interestingly enough, Sommers was paid 5 times more than series regular Williams). And also, in the scenes of romantic reconciliation at the end of the film – particularly in the reunion of Joan Sims and Peter Butterworth – the film aims for the heartfelt, something that few *Carry Ons* truly do.

But, despite the exotic co-star and stabs at emotion, there is something depressingly 70s about *Behind*. Set in the height of summer but shot in the depths of winter, the whole film is a grey, overcast reminder of a Britain shot through with retarded sexual politics and bad domestic holidays. Yet there is also something grim about the series trotting on when its glory days are long behind it. By the point in the movie when the caravan site begins to sink into the soggy ground. It is a beautiful metaphor for the franchise itself. ★★ **IF**

CARRY ON CABBY (1963)

Starring: *Sidney James (Charlie Hawkins), Hattie Jacques (Peggy Hawkins), Kenneth Connor (Ted Watson), Charles Hawtrey (Terry 'Pintpot' Tankard), Esma Cannon (Flo Sims), Liz Fraser (Sally), Bill Owen (Smiler), Milo O'Shea (Len), Jim Dale (Expectant Father), Amanda Barrie (Anthea)*
Director: *Gerald Thomas*
Screenwriter: *Talbot Rothwell*
PG/91 mins./Comedy/UK

Charlie Hawkins is so obsessed with his taxi business ('Speedee Cabs') that he neglects his wife Peggy, which drives her to set up her own rival firm ('Glam Cabs'), employing dolly-birds in tailored uniforms to undercut the likes of Ted Watson and 'Pintpot' Tankard.

Perhaps because it was scripted by Talbot Rothwell as a standalone script entitled *Call Me A Cab* and then reworked as a *Carry On*, this is a rare entry in the popular series with more interest in having a proper plot than tossing off gags every line. It's the friendliest of the films, built around the relationship between a cackling but good-hearted Sid James and an unusually touching Hattie Jacques. Some of the later *Carry Ons* go beyond saucy postcard humour to become grumpily misogynist, but this has what could almost be labeled a feminist story-line – with Jacques given more to do than be the butt of hefty battleaxe jokes.

Among the expected *Carry On* bits: Kenneth Connor in drag, Jim Dale as a nervously expectant father, Amanda Barrie in a corset, Charles Hawtrey in a leather jacket as a devout rambler ('we like to go as far as we can'), Liz Fraser as Connor's perky intended. Kenneth Williams is missed, but his role as the obnoxious shop steward (*Carry On* producer Peter Rogers never missed a chance to be nasty about the unions) is ably taken by Norman Chappell. With familiar faces Bill Owen, Peter Gilmore (*The Onedin Line*), Milo O'Shea, Peter Byrne (*Dixon Of Dock Green*), Renee Houston and Michael Ward as the tweedy businessman who has apparently left a pearl earring in the back of Connor's cab. ★★★ **KN**

CARRY ON CAMPING (1969)

Starring: *Sid James (Sid Boggle), Charles Hawtrey (Charlie Muggins), Joan Sims (Joan Fussey), Kenneth Williams (Doctor Kenneth Soaper), Barbara Windsor (Babs), Hattie Jacques (Miss Haggard), Bernard Bresslaw (Bernie Lugg)*
Director: *Gerald Thomas*
Screenwriter: *Talbot Rothwell*
PG/88 mins./Comedy/UK

Sid and Bernie's plans to take their girlfriends to a nudest camp come a cropper when they end up in Paradise Holiday Camp populated by a very strange bunch indeed. Although, the naughty, not-to-say over-sized schoolgirls certainly improve the view.

Whatever your take on the *Carry On* series there is no doubting their cultural impact, they have never been forgotten, a sprawl of impish, cheeky comedies fixated both with British repression and British randiness. *Camping*, a later entry so-to-speak, is possibly the least ambitious, all but free of plot merely a series of vignettes barely held together by the overarching idea of a camping holiday. Yet, here, with the heady pursuit of recreation its target, is the *Carry On* formula at its essence – that ribald mix of eccentricity and sexual failure. Camping, with its overt double meaning, is like soft porn draped in the companionable cloth of sitcom, another voyage through British small-mindedness.

So, what do we get for our 90 minutes spent with the team of such familiar faces – and this is the A-list on show: James, Windsor, Hawtrey, Sims, Williams and Jacques? The answer is a scattershot of both slapstick – Windsor's bikini top 'ba-dooinggging' through the air has become an iconic image of a sort – and Talbot Rothwell's trademark double entendres (he scored well on names: Fussey, Haggard, Boggle) as Sid tries to work his way in to those matching bottoms of the giggly blonde (Windsor, starting to look a bit stretched as a schoolgirl). Interestingly, given the title, Hawtrey plays it straight fumbling around in a tent with Valerie Leon, although Williams keeps to his neurotic, pinched face distaste for all things biological.

Overall it's a sloppy entry into the cannon, including that comedy staple of undercranking the film for sped-up antics, a little closer to the bone sex-wise with the odd knee trembler, but still with a wry, easy familiarity that keeps us returning to tick off the regulation gags ad infintum. ★★ **IN**

CARRY ON CLEO (1964)

Starring: *Sid James (Mark Antony), Kenneth Williams (Julius Caser), Kenneth Connor (Hengist Pod), Charles Hawtrey (Seneca), Joan Sims (Calpurnia), Jim Dale (Horsa), Amanda Barrie (Cleopatra), Julie Stevens (Gloria), Sheila Hancock (Senna Pod), Jon Pertwee (Soothsayer)*
Director: *Gerald Thomas*
Screenwriter: *Talbot Rothwell, based on the play by William Shakespeare*
PG/92 mins./Comedy/UK

A strange and not entirely accurate retelling of the fabled story of Antony and Cleopatra, as seen through the eyes of two British slaves, Hengist and Horsa.

Unique in the pantheon of *Carry On* movies, this is the only one of those chirpy, uneven comedies to be based on a Shakespearean play. Perhaps, that is why it is considered one of, if not the, finest of the bunch. However, both these statements should be qualified. Being the best *Carry On* movie does not test the likes of *Some Like It Hot* or *Annie Hall* in the ranks of classic comedy, nor is it necessarily the best *Carry On*, you could just as easily argue *Khyber*, *Spying* or *Screaming*. And as far as Will the Bard is concerned, no matter how hard you search the original text, you will find no trace of Senna Pod or, indeed, Sosages.

Yet, there is a rare genius in screenwriter Talbot Rothwell's rewiring of one kind of British wordplay into an entirely different one, although scholars could tell you Shakespeare was equally adept at bawdy farce if not quite up to the inspired gasp of Kenneth William's Caesar: 'Infamy! Infamy! They've all got it in for me!' This is *Carry On* working in top gear. The team, including the trio behind the camera of director Gerald Thomas, writer Rothwell and producer Peter Rogers, found greater purchase for their muse when pushing against some historical or generic baseline. Here, splurging both the bard and the swords'n'sandals bluster of Roman epics.

It looks splendid, dressed in the gaudy colours of countless costume houses; the likes of Williams, Sid James and the rest obviously thrilled to be dressing-up, as if it added an air of dignity to their formula sacking of political correctness. Hence the performances bubble and thrum with more than just winking efficiency, Williams especially gives a shrill, put-upon frustration to the campest Caesar in all history. Amanda Barrie, lately of *Coronation Street* fame, adds fluttery sexy glitter to Cleo, giving it just a bit more dimension and life than the series' regular giggly sex-bomb Barbara Windsor might have. It's still evidently a *Carry On* movie, but one that reminds you there was certainly talent at work. ★★★★ **IN**

CARRY ON COLUMBUS (1992)

Starring: *Jim Dale (Christopher Columbus), Bernard Cribbins (Mordecai Mendoza), Maureen Lipman (Countess Esmerelda), Peter Richardson (Bart Columbus), Alexei Sayle (Achmed), Rik Mayall (The Sultan), Nigel Planer (The Wazir), Leslie Phillips (King Ferdinand), June Whitfield (Queen Isabella). Julian Clary (Don Juan Diego)*
Director: *Gerald Thomas*
Screenwriters: *Dave Freeman. John Antrobus*
PG/91 mins./Comedy/UK

1492. Christopher Columbus persuades King Ferdinand and Queen Isabella to finance his expedition to find a new trade route to the East by sailing West and accidentally discovering America.

If you've seen all the other *Carry On* films, you'll probably want to collect the set by clocking the last gasp, though it's a fairly horrible experience. In 1992, the quincentenary of Columbus's voyage was commemorated by three disappointing-to-disastrous films. On a budget-to-income basis, *Carry On Columbus* was probably more of a hit than Ridley Scott's *1492: The Conquest Of Paradise* or the Salkinds' *Christopher Columbus: The Discovery*.

Fourteen years after the series fizzled out with the fairly poor *Carry On Emmanuelle*, all the greats (Sid James, Kenneth Williams, Charles Hawtrey) were gone, though director Gerald Thomas got back in harness for his last job, bringing to a sad close the series he had begun with *Carry On Sergeant*. Leftovers like Jim Dale, Bernard Cribbins and Kenneth Connor had to put up with being lumped in with a load of alternative comics like Julian Clary ('I'll come up your end in the night'), Tony Slattery and Rik Mayall. Others who crowd into the movie solely so they can claim to have been in a *Carry On* include Sara Crowe, Alexei Sayle, Maureen Lipman, Keith Allen, Danny Peacock, Peter Richardson, Nigel Planer, Martin Clunes, Chris Langham, Don Henderson and Burt Kwouk (as 'Wang'). It has one funny sequence, involving Native Americans played by Larry Martin and Charles Fleischer who talk like Martin Scorsese characters, but is mostly just a cheaper alternative to pantomime. Barbara Windsor was approached to star, but wisely opted to do end-of-the-pier in Blackpool instead.

The script somehow misses out on the *Carry On*-friendly historical fact that Columbus's real name was Colon. ★ **KN**

CARRY ON CONSTABLE (1960)

Starring: *Sid James (Sergeant Frank Wilkins), Eric Barker (Inspector Mills), Kenneth Connor (P.C. Charlie Constable), Charles Hawtrey (P.C. Timothy Gorse), Kenneth Williams (P.C. Stnaley Benson), Leslie Phillips (P.C. Tom Potter), Joan Sims (W.P.C Gloria Passworthy), Hattie Jacques (Sergeant Laura Moon), Shirley Eaton (Sally Barry), Cyril Camberlain (Thurston)*
Director: *Gerald Thomas*
Screenwriter: *Norman Hudis, based on an idea by Brock Williams*
U/86 mins./Comedy/UK

Sergeant Wilkins is charged with mentoring four new recruits when the police station is left short-staffed by a flu epidemic. But this hapless bunch are more likely to help the criminals than hinder them...

The fourth film in the *Carry On* series marked two debuts. It was the first to feature the excellent Sid James and it was the first to feature nudity (the recruits four bare buttocks). James had been shipped in as a replacement for *Carry On Teacher*'s Ted Hayes, when Hayes decided not to continue in the series and proved to be note perfect casting from here on in.

Constable faced other struggles on the way to the screen. Originally Peter Rogers had planned this as the third film, but after writer Norman Hudis was sent off to Slough police station for research he came back gloomily reporting that policing did not appear to be a very funny business. In fact, it was the TV series *Dixon of Dock Green* that provided the eventual inspiration needed, and this was as more a spoof of that popular show than anything else.

The larks of the new recruits – Williams, Phillips, Hawtrey and Connor, provide much humour of the physical sort, especially when Williams and Hawtrey diguise themselves as 'Ethel' and 'Agatha'. But the undoubted scene-stealers are the raft of British character actors, including Irene Handl and Esma Cannon, who typify that uniquely British eccentricity so prevalent in the films of the time.

Surprisingly, this was the last appearance (for 32 years) for eternal playboy Leslie Phillips. Although very much associated with the series, he was in fact better known from the equally popular Rank 'Doctor' films. He did pop up again in Columbus. ★★★ **EC**

CARRY ON COWBOY (1965)

Starring: *Sid James (Johnny Finger, the Rumpo Kid), Kenneth Williams (Judge Burke), Jim Dale (Marshal P. Knutt), Charles Hawtrey (Chief Big Heap), Joan Sims (Belle Armitage), Angela Douglas (Annie Oakley), Bernard Bresslaw (Little Heap)*
Director: *Gerald Thomas*
Screenwriter: *Talbot Rothwell*
PG/94 mins./Comedy/UK

English sanitary engineer Marshall P. Knutt is mistaken for a lawman when Judge Burke sends for help to rid Stodge City of the Rumpo Kid and his gang of desperadoes.

Following the success of *Carry On Cleo*, Talbot Rothwell began work on another movie pastiche, while director Gerald Thomas, producer Peter Rogers and regulars Sid James, Joan Sims and Jim Dale took a busman's holiday on the sub-Ealing crime caper, *The Big Job*. This nine-month hiatus gave Rothwell the leisure to produce a polished screenplay whose lampoons demonstrated an obvious knowledge of and affection for the Western. Indeed, over the series as a whole, only its immediate successor, *Carry On Screaming* revealed a surer sense of genre.

Cowboy is easily the franchise's darkest hour. Gone is the cartoonish socko of Cleo and in its place comes real violence, with the Rumpo Kid blithely gunning down those who stand in his path, while Annie Oakley (Angela Douglas) harbours tangible hatred in her determination to avenge her father's murder. Consequently, the standard of the acting is higher than usual, with the cast maintaining credible American accents throughout (although Charles Hawtrey and the debuting Bernard Bresslaw respectively resort to patronising parody as Big and Little Heap). Indeed, Sid and his fellow outlaws even learned to ride – although they had to be content with galloping across Chobham Common in Surrey rather than the wild frontier. Black Park (a favourite Hammer location) stood in for the Reservation, while the Stodge City set at Pinewood had to be constructed with a right turn at the end of the main street to disguise the fact that a motorway and some studio outbuildings lay behind it rather than the open plains.

Although they had been primarily associated with comedy since they'd first teamed on radio's *Hancock's Half Hour*, James and Williams were respected character actors and they clearly responded to the film's challenges, as did Joan Sims, who gives one of her best performances as the glamorous Belle. ★★★ **DP**

CARRY ON CRUISING (1962)

Starring: *Sid James (Captain Wellington Crowther), Kenneth Williams (First Officer Leonard Marjoribanks), Kenneth Connor (Doctor Arthur Binn), Liz Fraser (Glad Trimble), Dilys Laye (Florence 'Flo' Castle), Esma Cannon (Bridget Madderley), Lance Percival (Wilfred Haines)*
Director: *Gerald Thomas*
Screenwriter: *Norman Hudis*
U/89 mins./Comedy/UK

Captain Crowther despairs when he discovers that he'll be accompanied on his 10th anniversary cruise aboard the SS *Happy Wanderer* by novices Leonard Marjoribanks, Arthur Binn and Wilfred Haines.

Fresh off *Carry On Regardless*, Gerald Thomas and Peter Rogers embarked on the musical comedy, *Raising The Wind*, which featured many series regulars, as well as Eric Barker, whom they had previously encountered on the nautical romp, *Watch Your Stern* (1960). Indeed, it was Barker's suggestion that the next franchise outing should be set aboard a luxury liner and he received a story credit, although the screenplay was again produced by Norman Hudis.

Much to everyone's surprise, Rogers managed to secure a budget of £140,000 and the announcement that the picture was to be made in colour convinced many of the cast that they were finally going to shoot on a glamorous location. However, they were summoned to Pinewood, as usual, with the notable exception of Charles Hawtrey.

A veteran of British screen comedy, Hawtrey resented the fact that he was billed below Sid James and Kenneth Williams and he not only demanded that Rogers rectified the situation, but also placed a silver star on his dressing-room door. The producer's response was to replace him as the seasick chef with an eccentric taste for the exotic with Lance Perceval, who acquitted himself admirably in his only *Carry On* appearance.

As with Hudis's previous five scripts, the emphasis is very much on community, although there's still time for some deliciously skittish scene-stealing by the inimitible Esma Cannon and for ship's doctor Kenneth Connor to fall for Dilys Laye's singularly unimpressed passenger before the company rally to celebrate the captain's anniversary.

The film ends with Crowther rejecting a commission with another line, which became all the more ironic when Hudis announced that he was decamping to Hollywood – much to the fury of Williams, who always believed that the *Carry Ons* were beneath him and he despaired for a further 16 years of his continued involvement. ★★★ **DP**

CARRY ON DICK (1974)

Starring: *Sid James (Dick Turpin/Reverend Flasher), Kenneth Williams (Captain Desmond Fancey), Hattie Jacques (Martha Hoggett), Joan Sims (Madame Desiree), Kenneth Connor (Constable), Barbara Windsor (Harriet/Harry), Bernard Bresslaw (Sir Roger Daley), Peter Butterworth (Tom 'Doc' Scholl), Jack Douglas (Sergeant Jock Strapp)*
Director: *Gerald Thomas*
Screenwriter: *Talbot Rothwell, from a story by George Ewart Evans and Lawrie Wymar*
PG/91 mins/Comedy/UK

Randy and dandy highwayman Dick Turpin terrorises the countryside around Upper Dencher with Bow Street Runners Captain Fancey and Sergeant Jock Strapp hot on his heels.

For true fans of the franchise, this is the last real *Carry On* flick as it is the final film to feature series legends Sid James (who died in 1976), Barbara Windsor and Hattie Jacques and also the last one to be scripted by Talbot Rothwell, who provided the series' unique mixture of risqué charm and wit. Mining the bawdy historical atmosphere, Rothwell delivers a feel good romp that if not classic *Carry On* is enjoyable middle order stuff.

After a slow start, Rothwell's script throws in some choice innuendo ('All this talk of Big Dick. I've had enough of it!') and gives every one of the regulars a chance to shine. In the dual role of Turpin and Reverend Flasher, James has lots of opportunity to give off his trademark throaty cackle and has some good chemistry with Windsor as a member of his highway gang Williams and Douglas (in his first major dialogue role) do nice variations on the characters Williams and Peter Butterworth did in *Don't Lose Your Head*. Peter Butterworth gets some great comedy business as, dressed up in drag, he tries not to ogle Joan Sims' bosoms. Even some of the smaller cameos register: Hattie Jacques as a nosey housekeeper listening at the door, Kenneth Connor as an ageing copper more interested in totty than Turpin.

As a 'historical' *Carry On* it is perhaps better than *Henry*, not as good as *Cleo* and has a sheen of poignancy around it as the last time this Brit Institution would work together in their most famous line up. ★★★ **IF**

CARRY ON DOCTOR (1967)

Starring: *Frankie Howerd (Francis Bigger), Sid James (Charlie Roper), Charles Hawtrey (Mr Barron), Kenneth Williams (Doctor Kenneth Tinkle), Jim Dale (Doctor Jim Kilmore), Barbara Windsor (Nurse Sandra May), Joan Sims (Chloe Gibson), Bernard Bresslaw (Ken Biddle), Hattie Jacques (Matron)*
Director: *Gerald Thomas*
Screenwriter: *Talbot Rothwell*
PG/94 mins./Comedy/UK

When the popular Dr Kilmore is sacked after being discovered in a compromising position on the roof of the nurses' home, the patients plot to get him reinstated.

Were hospitals ever really like this? Nurses are either battle-axes or stocking clad minxs. None of the doctors are fit to be trusted with a scalpel and the patients all seem to have taken up permanent residence.

The latter was probably just as well for Sid James, having suffered a heart attack in real life, a bed-ridden role for the fifteenth film in the series suited him fine.

Dr Kilmore (Jim Dale – the closest the series came to a male sex symbol) is the dedicated doctor loved by his malingering patients and loathed by the all-seeing Matron and his superior Dr Tinkle. Their chance to discredit him comes when Kilmore attempts to rescue a barely clothed nurse (Windsor) from the roof of a nursing home. Chaos inevitably ensues, which climaxes with the patients storming the operating theatre.

But the scene-stealing on this occasion is done by guest-starring Frankie Howerd, a quack who mistakenly believes he only has a week to live. He has the bonus of being the one who gets to reference the memorable 'daffodil thermometer' scene from the earlier *Carry On Nurse*, fending a nurse off with the offending flower with the words, 'Oh no you don't! I saw that film!' ★★★ **ECe**

CARRY ON DON'T LOSE YOUR HEAD (1966)

Starring: *Sid James (Sir Rodney Effing), Kenneth Williams (Citizen Camembert), Jim Dale (Lord Darcy Pue), Charles Hawtrey (Duc de Pommfrit), Peter Butterworth (Citizen Bidet), Joan Sims (Desirée Dubarry)*
Director: *Gerald Thomas*
Screenwriter: *Talbot Rothwell*
PG/90 mins./Comedy/UK

Fiddlesome fop Sir Rodney Effing assumes the guise of the Black Fingernail to rescue French aristocrat the Duc de Pommfrit from the big cheese of the Revolutionary police, Citizen Camembert.

In 1967, Peter Rogers severed his links with Anglo Amalgamated and signed a lucrative new deal with the Rank Organisation. However, furious at losing its sole source of guaranteed income, Anglo refused him permission to continue using the 'Carry On' prefix and this spoof of The Scarlet Pimpernel was initially released simply as *Don't Lose Your Head*. Eventually, however, it came to be accepted as the 13th entry in the long-running series and remains one of its best.

Keen to return to the historical antics of *Carry On Cleo*, screenwriter Talbot Rothwell sold the project as an opportunity for Sid James and Kenneth Williams to recreate the swashbuckling rivalry that had existed between Errol Flynn and Basil Rathbone in the 1930s. Williams acquiesced with his usual indifferences, but James was particularly enthused by the prospect of some derring-do and proved himself to be an accomplished swordsman, alongside Jim Dale as his sidekick, Lord Darcy.

He was less enamoured, however, at having to don drag for one of his escapades and he endured Williams and the crew taunting him about his complexion and curvaceous figure with seething ill grace. Yet Sid got his own back on Rothwell, who usually allowed no ad-libbed additions to his screenplays, by devising Charles Hawtrey's business with the letter on the guillotine.

Flushed with a budget of £200,000, Rogers spent lavishly on costumes and rented Waddesdon Manor, Clandon Park and Cliveden for his 18th-century backdrops. But, for all its fey opulence, this is still a gloriously vulgar romp, which boasts such memorable characters as Citizen Bidet (the ever-reliable Peter Butterworth) and the Duke and Duchess de la Plume de ma Tante, with the latter enabling Joan Sims to turn in another of her peerless displays of coarse refinment, as Camembert's social-climbing sister, Desirée DuBarry. ★★★ **DP**

⓪ CARRY ON EMMANNUELLE (1978)

Starring: *Kenneth Connor (Leyland), Kenneth Williams (Emile Prevert), Suzanne Danielle (Emmannuelle Prevert), Joan Sims (Mrs Dangle), Jack Douglas (Lyons), Peter Butterworth (Richmond), Beryl Reid (Mrs Valentine)*
Director: *Gerald Thomas*
Screenwriter: *Lance Peters*
15/88 mins/Comedy/UK

The horny wife of a French Diplomat, Emmannuelle Prevert shags her way through a host of Brit based VIPs including the PM and the American Ambassador. Everyone, in fact, except her own husband.

Or when two dying franchises collide. The juxtaposition of Britain's favourite comedy institution and Europe's most famous soft porn character was always going to signal the death knell for both series and so it came to pass (although the *Carry On* title added an extra N in the name to avoid copyright problems). Suzanne Danielle slips into the title character's body hugging outfits and waltzes through a witless scenario in which her character's indiscretions lead to a national scandal (the only one immune to her charms is her diplomat husband, Kenneth Williams in full on camp, shrieking mode).

While most *Carry Ons* were shot in 6 weeks, *Emmannuelle* was made in just over a month and badness abounds at every level. A Concorde nose cone gag is risible. A snazzy 70s theme song ('Love Crazy') is terrible. But worst of all is the mistaken belief that T&A is, of its own accord, funny and that the subtle use of double entendre, sly innuendo and wit has long fallen by the wayside. The regular Carry Oners tried their best – Peter Butterworth has fun as a dithering old fart, Joan Sims does her best po-faced battle-axe until she finds sexual enlightenment and this is a rare *Carry On* where Jack Douglas doesn't do that shake and quiver thing – but it was too little too late. It's almost impossible to think that over the pond, Woody Allen had just made *Annie Hall* and we were subjected to this – right down there with *Carry On England* vying for the worse of the series. ★ **IF**

⓪ CARRY ON ENGLAND (1976)

Starring: *Kennth Connor (Captain. S. Melly), Windsor Davies (Sergeant-Major 'Tiger' Bloomer), Judy Geeson (Sergeant Tilly Willing), Patrick Mower (Sergeant Len Able), Jack Douglas (Bombardier Ready)*
Director: *Gerald Thomas*
Screenwriters: *David Pursall, Jack Seddon*
PG/89 mins/Comedy/UK

Blighty, 1940. Stuck up Captain S. Melly becomes the new commanding officer at an experimental mixed sex air defence base where the platoon are far more interested in each other than any enemy attack. As Melly tries to quell the randy behaviour, he becomes the target of an attack on his straight-laced ideals.

Number 28 in the series and *Carry On* is rapidly approaching moribund status. A slow action replay of *Carry On Sergeant*, *England* misjudges the saucy seaside charm of the original and, in an attempt to keep pace with 'modern' comedy trends, replaces it with on-the-nose smut and low-level sex action. With new cast members and a new crew – crucially established screenplay writer Talbot Rothwell had been replaced by witless newbies David Pursall and Jack Seddon – the old magic had been replaced by bad puns (Sgts Ready, Willing and Able?) and a flush of toilet gags that jettison the film into the realms of the unwatchable.

Only four of the *Carry On* mainstays made it onto the cast list; Kenneth Connor eschews his little man persona to become a jumped up little dictator, Peter Butterworth does a brief nice essay in pompous stiff upper lippedness, Jack Douglas reprises his jerk and twitch schtick for the umpteenth time and Joan Sims is sidelined as an overbearing Private with barely ten lines to deliver. But TV 'favourites' Windsor Davies (retreading his overbearing Sgt Major routine from *It Ain't Half Hot Mum*), Patrick Mower and Judy Geeson are barely replacements for Sid James, Kenneth Williams and Barbara Windsor and England has the whiff of a bad sitcom. In short, it represented the beginning of the end. ★ **IF**

⓪ CARRY ON – FOLLOW THAT CAMEL (1967)

Starring: *Phil Silvers (Sergeant Nocker), Kenneth Williams (Commandant Maximilian Burger), Jim Dale (Betram Oliphant 'Bo' West), Charles Hawtrey (Captain Le Pice), Joan Sims (Zig-Zig), Angela Douglas (Lady Ponsonby), Peter Butterworth (Simpson), Bernard Bresslaw (Sheikh Addul Abulbul), Anita Harris (Corktip), John Bluthal (Corporal Clotski)*
Director: *Gerald Thomas*
Screenwriter: *Talbot Rothwell*
PG/95 mins./Comedy/UK

With his reputation unjustly in tatters after a cricketing mishap, Betram Oliphant West, along with his stalwart manservant Simpson, joins the French Foreign Legion. Here, amongst a ragtag and lackadaisical bunch, trouble looms with the Arab locals and the arrival, albeit heavily disguised, of West's ladylove Lady Jane Ponsonby.

With the series lagging and losing fans, and inspiration in short supply, the *Carry On* franchise looked to revamp its ailing formula. They did this first by foolishly ditching the 'Carry On' prefix (reinstating it in 1968) and, to no great gain or loss, adding a famous American, also on his uppers, to its troupe of ageing eccentrics. Phil Silvers, from TV's *Bilko*, made an effervescent addition to this thin tale of dappy legionnaires made on the well-disguised Camber Sands, but still seems to inhabit an entirely different brand of sassier humour that sits awkwardly with the pun-rich antics of this mob. Still, Gerald Thomas was in experimental mode all round adding montages, stabs of physical comedy and strands of remarkably dark humour. Monty Python was making waves and Thomas wasn't eager to be seen as old-fashioned.

The result must be the oddest *Carry On* of them all, and a big failure at the box office. Not that it is entirely a creative failure, far more effort has been put into the visual look of the film (on this level it is the best directed), with seasoned regulars like Kenneth Williams (possibly the most reliable of them all) and Charles Hawtrey relishing the chance to both break free of the prattling closet dwellers they usually play (Williams is transformed into a sadistic brute). Jim Dale and the hard-working Peter Butterworth also make for an appealing pair in the lead, giving the film a sense of greater purpose than the next gag.

Silvers, his bald pate gleaming like a bowling ball, has such an easy manner, the slippery, jovial conman he made a career out of, but he just slips on the Bilko mantle and trudges to the finish line to claim his cheque. Little surprise, then, that the film feels so burdened with confusion, and no amount of heaving bosoms and revealed rumps can return it to former glories. Still, the respite in experimentation was soon to be abandoned, *Up The Khyber*, the series last great hurrah, was next on the list. ★★ **IN**

⓪ CARRY ON GIRLS (1973)

Starring: *Sidney James (Sidney Fiddler), Barbara Windsor (Hope Springs), Joan Sims (Connie Philpotts), Kenneth Connor (Mayor Frederick Bumble), Bernard Bresslaw (Peter Potter), June Whitfield (Augusta Prodworthy), Valerie Leon (Paula Perkins)*
Director: *Gerald Thomas*
Screenwriter: *Talbot Rothwell*
PG/88 mins./Comedy/UK

In the seaside resort of Fircombe (snicker), Sid Fiddler proposes a beauty contest to boost the local economy, bullying the ineffectual Mayor into supporting him even though scheming feminist Augusta Prodworthy is dead set against such sexism.

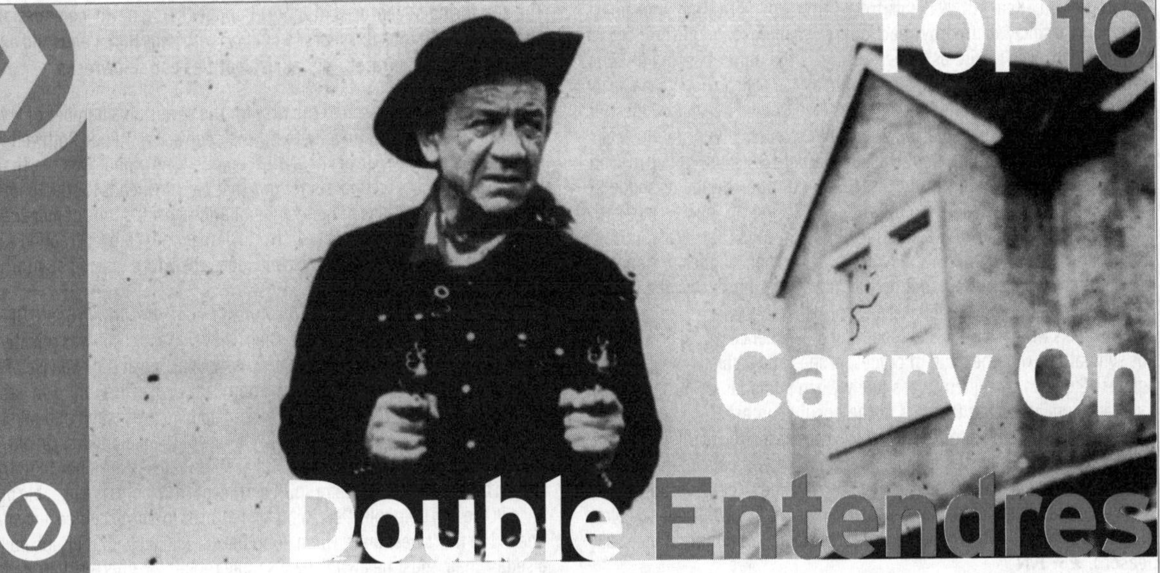

1 Henry VIII: 'After six months of married life, the only thing I'm having off is her head.' – *Carry On Henry*

2 **Matron: 'Young birds may be soft and tender but the older birds have more on them'**
Sid: 'Yes, and take a lot more stuffing'. – *Carry On Matron*

3 Lady Binder to Sir Rodney at one of his famous functions: 'You've always had magnificent balls.' *Carry On – Don't Lose Your Head*

4 **Daphne Honeybutt, after a quick draw demonstration by Simpkins: 'I'm sure I'll never get my draws off as slickly as that!' – *Carry On Spying***

5 Policewoman Passworthy to a prisoner shocked as four naked policemen walk past her cell: 'Well, you did ask for a cell with southern exposure.' – *Carry On Constable*

6 **The Khasi: 'May the benevolence of the good Shivoo bring blessings on your house.'**
Sir Sidney Ruff-Diamond: 'And on yours.'
The Khasi: 'And may his radiance light up your life.'
Sir Sidney: 'And up yours.' – *Carry On Up The Khyber*

7 Biddle: 'Nurse, I dreamed about you last night.'
Nurse Clark: 'Did you?'
Biddle: 'No, you wouldn't let me.' – *Carry On Doctor*

8 **Mrs Fussey: 'Joan may think you're a gentleman but personally I've got sore misgivings.'**
Sid Boggle: 'You ought to put some talcum powder on them.' – *Carry On Camping*

9 Lady Evelyn Bagley: 'There is my reputation to think of. You would need to be very circumspect.'
Prof. Inigo Tinkle: 'Oh, I was. When I was a baby.' – *Carry On Up The Jungle*

10 **Belle Armitage (admiring a gun): 'My, that's a big one.'**
Johnny Finger: 'I'm from Texas, ma'am. We've all got big ones down there.' – *Carry On Cowboy*

A late-period, Kenneth Williams-free *Carry On*, with the smuttiness embarrassingly diluted by reactionary moaning, though the jibes at 'Women's Lib' aren't quite as embarrassing as the union-bashing of *Carry On at Your Convenience*. With Robin Askwith as 'Larry Prodworthy' and a lot of girls glimpsed in mild undress, it edges close to the British sex film style that was about to render the *Carry Ons* anachronistically prim. However, most of it is familiar routines, with hulking Bernard Bresslaw got up in drag, Kenneth Connor repeatedly losing his trousers (though he seems suddenly old and pathetic) and Sid's lecherous larceny ticking off long-term steady Joan Sims but clicking with biker chick Hope Springs (Barbara Windsor). The finale is oddly confused: as often, a regimented performance is wrecked for slapstick effect, but here feminist saboteurs ruin the beauty contest with itching powder bikinis and sprinklers.

This feels wrong: it's not that funny and the audience would presumably not sympathise with the gang of prudes, prunes and lesbians wrecking the oglefest Sid is so commited to. It's funny when pompous dullards or venal fools are humiliated, but the girls of the beauty contest – who get a hard enough time in the film – are never established as deserving of this treatment.

It's the film that most sets up James and Windsor as a couple, in that she's the only woman who finds his non-stop leching endearing, but thanks to 1970s hairstyling and fashions, Babs looks more like Whitfield and Sims than the 'crumpet' (Valerie Leon, Margaret Nolan, Marianne Stone, Sally Geeson). ★★ **KN**

CARRY ON HENRY (1970)

Starring: *Sid James (King Henry VIII), Kenneth Williams (Thomas Cromwell), Charles Hawtrey (Sir Roger de Lodgerly), Joan Sims (Queen Marie), Terry Scott (Cardinal Wolsey), Barbara Windsor (Bettina)*
Director: *Gerald Thomas*
Screenwriter: *Talbot Rothwell*
PG/89 mins./Comedy/UK

King Henry VIII has grown tired with his new wife Queen Marie of Normandy, who refuses to have sex (and eats too much garlic anyway, but he is loathe to remove her head in case it starts a war with their neighbour. Thus he concocts a plan to force her into an affair, he can then uncover.

It is a widely considered rule of thumb that the *Carry Ons* are so much better when inhabiting a period scenario, as if somehow the old crew could convince themselves they were doing something a touch more dignified. However, a play on the habits of debauched King Henry VIII presented problems. How could a king's avaricious designs, particularly on the buxom Bettina, daughter of the Earl of Bristol (snark!) ever be denied him (the central tenet of the whole series – Sid James trying, and failing, to get his end away) if he is the king? The answer director Gerald Thomas and screenwriter Talbot Rothwell muster is a limp series of slapstick routines in which the gnarly king occupies himself in Benny Hill-style chases.

Again confusingly, Kenneth Williams and Charles Hawtrey, play heterosexuals, the later even making the garlic scented queen pregnant. There is much too-ing and fro-ing around the king's devious plotting, but aside from tight fitting bodices and some well-worked art direction, and Sid James really working his end of things (!) it suffers the lack of working-class charm that lies at the heart of the series. ★★ **IN**

CARRY ON JACK (1964)

Starring: *Bernard Cribbins (Albert Poop-Decker), Kenneth Williams (Captain Fearless), Juliet Mills (Sally), Charles Hawtrey (Walter), Donald Houston (First Officer (Jonathan Howett), Percy Herbert (Mr Angel), Jim Dale (Carrier), Patrick Cargill (Spanish Governor)*
Director: *Gerald Thomas*
Screenwriter: *Talbot Rothwell*
PG/91 mins/Comedy/UK

The sea-faring adventures of Albert Poopdecker, a newly commissioned Midshipman (he took 8½ years to qualify) who joins HMS *Venus* and experiences a mutiny, pirates, mistaken identities and shipwrecks.

Carry On Jack represented the first for the series on a number of levels; it was the first to officially feature screenwriter Talbot Rothwell who became the gatekeeper of the series' unique tone, And it was the first to feature a historical setting, something that paid dividends for the team for, despite the distinct lack of budget, it not only provided tons of mileage for punning and farce, it also set their worldview at one remove, creating a universe that exists by its own laws and logic, therefore making any form of ludicrousness acceptable

Originally titled *Carry On Up The Armada* – until the British Board Of Film Censors insisted on a title change, then *Carry On Sailor* (this was rejected to avoid confusion with *Carry On Cruising* – *Jack* has fun at the expense of C.S. Forrester's Hornblower yarns, as Poop-Decker has his uniform stolen inside a house of ill repute then is picked up by a pressgang and taken to the ship that he was due to serve on. The lack of the major *Carry On* players (no Sid, no Babs) is a problem but Juliet Mills' Sally attacks her temptress turned heroine with maximum spirit and Bernard Cribbins is a likeable presence in the Jim Dale role. Dale, himself, features in a brief cameo and snags one of the film's best lines; when Poop-Decker suggests that his job pulling a sedan chair 'must be awful', Dale simply replies. 'It's better than walking the streets.' ★★ **IF**

CARRY ON LOVING (1970)

Starring: *Sid James (Sidney Bliss), Kenneth Williams (Percival Snooper), Charles Hawtrey (James Bedsop), Joan Sims (Esme Crowfoot), Hattie Jacques (Sophie Plummett), Terry Scott (Terence Philpot), Richard O'Callaghan (Bertrum Muffet), Bernard Bresslaw (Gripper Burke)*
Director: *Gerald Thomas*
Screenwriter: *Talbot Rothwell*
PG/88 mins./Comedy/UK

Sid and Sophie Bliss are supposedly married proprietors of a computer dating agency. But their computer's claim of accurately matching couples is as much of a sham as their marriage.

In the wonderfully named Much-Snogging-In-The-Green, romance is in the air. But it's not going to have much chance to flourish if Sid and Sophie Bliss' computer system has much to do with it. This low-tech matching service involves a card being shoved in a slot by one of the couple and the other picking one out of the filing system and pushed back through another slot, all while the client marvels at the wonders of modern technology. This leads to some classic comedy mismatching, but then clients like sex-starved Terry Scott and milk-bottle top model maker Richard O'Callaghan hardly deserve better.

There's far too little of James and Jacques as the Agency bosses who aren't what they seem and too much forced coupling, but then the ads at the time emphasised this as a 'sex' comedy. And while the 'sex' may seem tame now, at the time it was enough to drive up the box office.

Worth watching for Kenneth Williams' delicious marriage councillor and the welcome wheeling out of some British acting verterans for cameo roles (especially Joan Hickson as the aged Mrs Grubb) but Rothwell was clearly running dry of endings for this, the 19th of the series, as the climax food-fight shows.

The impressive looking (if not functioning computer) was a left over from the TV series *UFO*. Jokes it seems, were not the only thing the *Carry On* crew recycled. ★★ **EC**

➂ CARRY ON MATRON (1972)

Starring: *Sid James (Sid Carter), Kenneth Williams (Sir Bernard Cutting), Charles Hawtrey (Dr Francis A. Goode), Joan Sims (Mrs Tidey), Hattie Jacques (Matron), Bernard Bresslaw (Ernie Bragg), Kenneth Connor (Mr Tidey), Kenneth Cope (Cyril Carter), Terry Scott (Dr Prodd), Barbara Windsor (Nurse Susan Ball)*
Director: *Gerald Thomas*
Screenwriter: *Talbot Rothwell*
PG/87 mins./Comedy/UK

A gang of thieves plan to steal some contraceptive pills from a hospital by disguising one of their number as a nurse . . .

The fourth medical adventure, and one of the funnier of the later *Carry Ons* saw gang of crooks Ernie, Freddy, Sid and his son Cyril trying to infiltrate Finisham Maternity Hospital in search of contraceptive pills to sell abroad.

Inexplicably, Cyril, the least convincing transvestite in history, is nominated to be disguised as a nurse to check out the lay of the land and immediately attracts the attentions of serial groper Dr Prodd and befriends room-mate student Nurse Ball, who naturally enjoys sleeping nude. Soon he/she is front page news after successfully delivering a movie-star's triplets and the Matron is beginning to get suspicious.

It's all completely ridulous in a lovable way and culminates in a chase scene through the nurses' home. Along the way there's fun to be had from 'eating machine' overdue expectant mother Joan Sims, sexually confused Dr Cutting and the wonderful Hattie Jacques, whose dominance of the hospital *Carry Ons* is finally acknowledged in the title. ★★★ **EC**

➂ CARRY ON NURSE (1959)

Starring: *Kenneth Connor (Bernie Bishop), Shirely Eaton (Nurse Dorothy Denton), Charles Hawtrey (Humphrey Hinton), Hattie Jacques (Matron), Terence Longdon (Ted York), Bill Owen (Percy 'Perc' Hickson), Leslie Phillips (Jack Bell), Joan Sims (Nurse Stella Dawson), Kenneth Williams (Oliver Reckitt), Wilfred Hyde-White (The Colonel)*
Director: *Gerald Thomas*
Screenwriter: *Norman Hudis, from the play* Ring For Catty*, by Patrick Cargill, Jack Searle*
PG/86 mins./Comedy/UK

Haven Hospital is anything but thanks to the iron rule of the Matron, so the long serving patients decide to take over and run things their way.

This second *Carry On* film was an even bigger hit than the first, dominating the UK Box Office of 1959 and making an impact in the States too. It led to a five-year contract for producer/director team Gerald Thomas and Peter Rogers to turn out similar films – which they did at the rate of at least two a year ad naseum.

The main plot revolves around the romance of soon-to-be golden girl Shirley Eaton and Terence Longdon, but the future stars of the series were already making their presence felt. So while Kenneth Williams was only booked in a supporting role as a sneering intellectual and Hattie Jacques was sparsely used as the over-bearing matron, it was these characters that were to come to the fore in later episodes.

Interesting too to watch one of the longest lasting players Joan Sims, cast for the first time here in the 'pretty girl' role and then see her 24 films down the line, when other prettier young things had taken her place, transmuted into a Jacquesite. Time was less kind to the *Carry On* females than the males.

The humour is less bawdy than it became – although the daffodil rectal thermometer joke probably troubled the censors (and was rumoured to have bothered Hyde-White's agent too). The sketch-like nature of the various goings-on in the hospital meant it was consistently funny and it is with good reason that this remains one of the most fondly remembered outings for the gang. ★★★ **EC**

➂ CARRY ON REGARDLESS (1961)

Starring: *Sid James (Bert Handy), Kenneth Connor (Sam Twist), Charles Hawtrey (Gabriel Dimple), Joan Sims (Lily Duveen), Kenneth Williams (Francis Courtenay), Bill Owen (Mike Weston), Liz Fraser (Delia King)*
Director: *Gerald Thomas*
Screenwriter: *Norman Hudis*
PG/90 mins./Comedy/UK

Bert Handy runs the Helping Hands agency, and his motley crew claim to able to tackle any job . . .

The fifth *Carry On* had only just enough plot to hang a series of gags on, as Bert Handy's Helping Hands agency took on a bizarre series of jobs, whose only link is that they're ripe with comic opportunity.

So we have Kenneth Williams babysitting a chimp, Kenneth Connor in a *39 Steps* parody, Joan Sims getting sizzled at a wine-tasting, wimpy Charles Hawtrey winning a boxing match and the whole team demonstrating the Ideal Home Show to destruction.

In the background dubious gobbledegook talking Stanley Unwin hangs around, obviously up to no good, but happy endings beckon for everyone.

Watch out for cameo roles from the future Miss Marple Joan Hickson, *Last Of The Summer Wine*'s Bill Owen and *Just A Minute*'s Nicolas Parsons.

Not a classic in the series, but a great showcase for some of its stars and worth seeking out for that reason. ★★★ **EC**

➂ CARRY ON SCREAMING (1966)

Starring: *Harry H. Corbett (Detective Sidney Bung), Kenneth Williams (Doctor Orlando Watt), Jim Dale (Albert Potter), Charles Hawtrey (Dan Dann), Fenella Fielding (Valeria Watt)*
Director: *Gerald Thomas*
Screenwriter: *Talbot Rothwell*
PG/97 mins./Comedy/UK

Evil is afoot in 19th Century London, someone is kidnapping pretty young women and turning them into wax mannequins for storefronts. Hot, well lukewarm, on the trail in Detective-Sergeant Sidney Bung, whose investigations lead him to the sinister Doctor Orlando Watt.

By the twelfth entry into the *Carry On* series, the team was well into its stride but showing signs of being stuck in its ways, success was reducing inspiration rather than firing it. Kudos, then, should be given for this successful attempt to enrich the basic tenets of the *Carry On* ethos with a new flavour. *Screaming* is most certainly a *Carry On* film, with its pungent innuendo and sheepish sexism, but its exploration of a genre – in this case, the lurid fillips of Hammer Horror – reveal genuine skill and appreciation. There was the sense, seldom sought out post-*Screaming*, that *Carry On* could become a satirical tool.

Most obvious of *Screaming*'s small triumphs, is that between its bouts of bawdy humour, it is actually scary. Referencing the fog-bound traditions of *House Of Wax*, *Frankenstein* and *Dr Jeykll And Mr Hyde* as well as more unusual combo-horrors like *Frankenstein Meets The Wolfman*, the schemes of evil Doctor Watt, played with Williams' writhing high-pitched gusto, and meted out by his lugubrious duo of hirsute ghouls Oddbod and Oddbod Junior, have a squirmy sense of awfulness. The joke is sailing as close to the genre as possible, aided by some excellent low-budget, and rather gruesome special effects work. The corpse count may not be as high as the gaudy *Carry On* period pieces, but it carries an effective sense of finality. 'Frying tonight,' drools Williams nastily, as he plunges his victims into a vast vat of boiling wax.

It is still a comedy and a very funny one at that. Harry H. Corbett,

Steptoe himself, made a one-time entry into the series and of the quartet of famous one-off players (otherwise add Bob Monkhouse, Ted Ray, Phil Silvers) made the most of the opportunity, giving dopey Detective-Sergeant Bung a sturdy, formal quality. He sort of feels like a real hero. Credit too, for Thomas' gleeful mocking of the Eastmancolor hues of Hammer, the glaring, sickly palette can be seen to best effect amongst the pipes and pipettes of Watt's flamboyantly clichéd lab. As with all the best parodies, there was love amongst its naughtiness. ★★★★ **IN**

CARRY ON SERGEANT (1958)

Starring: *William Hartnell (Sgt Grimshawe), Bob Monkhouse (Charlie Sage) Shirley Eaton (Mary Sage), Eric Barker (Captain Potts), Dora Bryan (Norah), Bill Owen (Cpl Bill Copping), Charles Hawtrey (Peter Golightly), Kenneth Connor (Horace Strong), Kenneth Williams (James Bailey), Norman Rossington (Herbert Brown), Hattie Jacques (Captain Clark), Cyril Chamberlain (Gun Sergeant)*
Director: *Gerald Thomas*
Screenwriter: *Norman Hudis, based on the novel* The Bull Boys *by R.F. Delderfield*
U/84 mins./Comedy/UK

Sergeant Grimshaw, on the point of retirement, wants to leave the army on a high note by winning the Star Squad prize for the best-drilled platoon of National Servicemen. However, he has the misfortune to be put in charge of a group of misfits and foul-ups who seem very unlikely soldier material. After comic failures, the platoon learns how much the prize means to their sergeant and shape up to do him proud.

The foundation stone of a great British institution, this is only a *Carry On* in embryo. Based on *The Bull Boys*, a novel by R.F. Delderfield, it's a collection of all the jokes and anecdotes that accrued during a decade or so of peacetime National Service, and is at once a parody of the gung ho American basic training picture (Take the High Ground, etc) and a sketch of the foul-ups-who-get-in-shape plot endlessly reused since (*Police Academy*, etc).

Hartnell, typecast as a tough guy before becoming the BBC's first Doctor Who, is the incarnation of every unwilling conscript's worst nightmare, shouting and growling at soldiers who don't know how to button their uniforms or hold their guns, but showing that sentimental streak which motivates them to become parade-ground smart in the finale. Bob Monkhouse takes the light leading man role that Jim Dale would later specialise in, and key players (Sid James, Barbara Windsor) aren't yet in place, but the direction of the series can be discerned in the scene-stealing bits by Charles Hawtrey and Kenneth Williams as blithely camp idiots and Kenneth Connor as the hypochondriac 'Horace Strong'. Hattie Jacques is in there in a bit part, but the cast is filled out by Britfilm names who wouldn't go on to be associated with the *Carry Ons* – Shirley Eaton, Dora Bryan, Norman Rossington and Bill Owen. ★★★ **KN**

CARRY ON SPYING (1964)

Starring: *Kenneth Williams (Desmond Simpkins), Barbara Windsor (Daphne Honeybutt), Bernard Cribbins (Harold Crump), Charles Hawtrey (Charlie Bind), Eric Barker (The Chief), Dilys Lane (Lila), Jim Dale (Carstairs)*
Director: *Gerald Thomas*
Screenwriters: *Talbot Rothwell, Sid Colin*
U/87 mins./Comedy/UK

After a top secret formula is stolen by STENCH (Society for the Total Extinction of Non-Conforming Humans), not-so-top but still secret Agent Simpkins of the British intelligence and three inept trainees set about retrieving it, before it falls into the hands of the dastardly Dr Crow.

It was as sure as taxes that the *Carry On* team would end-up taking a few pot-shots at the Bond series, that it took such an early punch, only two years after 007's cinematic conception, reveals a rare prescience on their behalf. This is the last of the black and white *Carry Ons* and still in touch with the more genial comedy of its early years, less caught up with bawdy farce than a spry pastiche sighting everything from Bond's emerging prowess to the tinkle of the zither score from *The Third Man*. While never as exuberant or self-aware, Austin Powers' wry inspection of the genre owes plenty to this frothy top-line *Carry On*.

The set-up with its ring of plaintive British cost-cutting, presents a British intelligence organisation having to send its least-able operative, the bumbling, ignorant Agent Simpkins (a rare lead for Kenneth Williams) and his tottering trio of spies in training (Barbara Windsor, Bernard Cribbins, and, inevitably, that ribcage on legs Charles Hawtrey) across the globe – ably produced on Pinewood soundstages – to get back the precious formula (possessed of a great punchline). Naturally, this is a process fraught with idiocy, and thus prolonged from success, until we end up in the bowels of Crow's secret layer. It will take a double agent, secretly working for SNOG (Society for the Neutralisation of Germs), to save the day.

More sprightly and less encumbered with the need to titillate that would ring-fence the *Carry Ons* in later life, there is a youthfulness about *Spying* that still remains fresher than the colour films. The characters, assuredly potty as they are, are all likeable rather than ridiculous caricatures of British life. Again, in these formative, more elegant early days of *Carry On* there is none of the growing disgust that their director and writer grew for the wheedling conformity of their later characters. In that it is something to treasure. ★★★★ **IN**

CARRY ON UP THE JUNGLE (1970)

Starring: *Frankie Howerd (Prof. Inigo Tinkle), Sid james (Bill Boosey), Terry Scott (Jungle Boy), Charles Hawtrey (Tonka/Walter Bagley), Joan Sims (Lady Evelyn Bagley (Kenneth Connor), Bernard Bresslaw (Upsidasi)*
Director: *Gerald Thomas*
Screenwriter: *Talbot Rothwell*
PG/89 mins/Comedy/UK

In deepest Africa, an expedition led by Lady Evelyn Bagley to find her long lost son is hindered by Professor Inigo Tinkle's attempts to find the rare Oozalum bird, run-ins with wildlife, a tribe called the Lubby-Dubbys and a Tarzan-like savage.

The first *Carry On* of a new decade saw the team start on good, if, not great form. Originally going to be called *Carry On Tarzan* until producer Peter Rogers couldn't get the rights to use the name, *Carry On Up The Jungle* uses the not particularly convincing plot strand of an exotic African adventure (filmed not in Kew Gardens as in popular belief but on Pinewood soundstages) to string together a series of skits, parodies and bawdiness that for the most part hit the mark.

Jungle does what the *Carry Ons* do best (see *Carry On Up The Khyber*), placing a group of British eccentrics in a hostile alien environment and sitting back to watch how they cope. The sparring between James' bumbling white hunter (he shoots sherpas instead of lions) and Howard's fey ornithologist is sparkling stuff, more than compensation for the aimless plotting. Yet the big laugh getter is Terry Scott (in a role turned down by Jim Dale) as the wannabe Tarzan type, swinging through the jungle like a klutz, being child-like in his sexual awakening by *Carry On* crumpet Jacki Piper and almost enjoying carnal relationship with his mother (Sims). The action fizzles out in the end when the gang are captured by an all female tribe from Aphrodisia and marks should be deducted for a blacked up Bernard Bresslaw as a lazy servant but this is *Carry On* working at its natural state; cheap, charming and funny. ★★★ **IF**

◎ CARRY ON UP THE KHYBER (1968)

Starring: *Sid James (Sir Sidney Ruff-Diamond), Kenneth Williams (Rhandi Lal, the Khasi of Kalabar), Charles Hawtrey (Private Jimmy Widdle), Roy Castle (Captain Keene), Joan Sims (Lady Joan Ruff-Diamond), Bernard Bresslaw (Bungdit Din), Terry Scott (Sergeant Major MacNutt), Angela Douglas (Princess Jelhi)*
Director: *Gerald Thomas*
Screenwriter: *Talbot Rothwell*
PG/88 mins./Comedy/UK

A crisis is created in the Raj when it is revealed that the British occupiers actually wear underpants under their kilts (the absence of which had terrified the natives into submission), prompting a mission to reclaim said undergarments and restore peace.

There is a tendency to look back at British cinema in the 1960s as the era of earnest kitchen-sink dramas and angry young men. But in terms of box office at least, this is something of a myth. Two British films made the UK top five in 1960: *Doctor In Love* and *Carry On Constable*. In 1965, the big money-spinners were *Those Magnificent Men In Their Flying Machines* and *Carry On Cleo*. In 1968, *Carry On Up The Khyber* topped the British box office, as did *Carry On Camping* a year later. In fact, take out the Bond movies and the bawdy comedies, and British product barely registers on the commercial radar during the swinging decade.

Yet the *Carry Ons* never won any awards (not a sniff of BAFTA recognition in 20 years) and were treated mostly with indifference by the critics. Some would argue that this is no more than the series deserved. Silly. Smutty. Sexist. Oh yeah? And how would you describe the American gross-out comedies of the 90s? The fact is, the cream of *Carry On* represents some of the finest and most joyful middlebrow entertainment this country has ever produced; *Cleo*, *Cowboy*, *Screaming*, and *Khyber* are prime examples of what a good repertory cast, a prohibitive budget and a British sense of fun can achieve.

While it's true that the *Carry Ons* started to tail off in quality around *At Your Convenience*, and reached an unhappy nadir with *Emmannuelle* edged into a corner by the more frank and fleshy *Confessions* series the 60s gems remain enjoyable on a far more concrete basis than just camp kitsch. *Up The Khyber* is a genuinely original, resourceful and funny film. No surprise that it is producer Peter Rogers' favourite out of a series which, if played back to back, would run for 44 hours and 36 minutes. Even *Variety* liked it.

Shakespeare had his history plays, and so did *Carry On*. As a general rule of thumb, if a *Carry On* has period costumes, it's one of the good ones even during the 70s decline, only *Henry* and *Dick* stand up. *Khyber*, with costumes by regular Emma Selby Walker, is set in India in 1895, during the days of the Raj. Action centres around Scots Guards regiment, the Third Foot And Mouth – cue central gag about what's under their kilts, which was less of a hackneyed notion in 1968. But this is not a *Carry On* you have to make apologies for 30-odd years later.

If the innuendo smacks of a more prudish, repressed era and shows how far away the Summer Of Love really was from Pinewood this adds to the film's innocent charm. The punnish character names are still delightful (The Khasi Of Kalabar, Private Jimmy Widdle, Princess Jelhi, Bungdit Din), the cut-price Snowdonia locations are effective (the same mountain pass filled in for China in *The Most Dangerous Man In The World* starring Gregory Peck, shot directly after the *Carry On* team had left) and Talbot Rothwell's script includes some killer set-pieces – not least the oft-cited besieged dinner party, which is an all-time golden great; thanks in no small part to the combined comic intuition of diners Sid James, Joan Sims, Julian Holloway, Roy Castle and Peter Butterworth. (Butterworth, veteran of 16 *Carry Ons*, was never better than as lecherous missionary Brother Belcher, but, like so many other fine regulars, his loyalty to the franchise saw his reputation as an actor unfairly dulled by repetition.)

Archly subtitled The British Position In India, *Up The Khyber* is not all lavatory humour and overuse of the term 'tiffin'. Rothwell slips in a rare topical joke (Khasi: 'They will die the death of a thousand cuts!'; Princess Jehli: 'Oh no, that's horrible!'; Khasi: 'Nonsense, child, the British are used to cuts!'), and there's a sly reference to the fact that Peter Rogers had struck a deal with Rank film distributors: after a gong is banged, the Khasi describes it as 'rank stupidity'. For further layered intrigue, composer Eric Rogers slips in a musical reference to Tchaikovsky's *Letter Song* (from Eugene Onegin) when Sid James dictates a letter. It's smarter than any seaside postcard.

But the reason the *Carry On* costume dramas are more durable than contemporary romps like *Loving* and *Girls* is that they speak less of the turbulent times in which they were made, coming off less quaint and dated. *Up The Khyber* does not have 'late 60s' written all over it compare it with the lame hippy festival denouement in *Carry On Camping* (1969), which looks desperate.

As *Carry On* chronicler Robert Ross says, *Khyber*, 'almost gets its foot in the door as a classic of respectable British cinema'. To deny it such legitimacy would be to take a very stiff British position indeed. ★★★★ **AC**

◎ CARS (2006)

Starring (voices): *Owen Wilson (Lightning McQueen), Paul Newman (Doc Hudson), Bonnie Hunt (Sally), Larry the Cable Guy (Mater), Tony Shalhoub (Luigi), Guio Quaroni (Guido), John Ratzenberger (Mack), Michael Keaton (Chick Hicks), Richard Petty (The King Strip Weathers)*
Director: *John Lasseter*
Screenwriters: *Dan Fogelman, Dan Gerson, Robert L. Baird, John Lasseter based on a story by Philip Loren, Kiel Murray, Joe Ranft*
PG/121 mins/Animation/USA

Arrogant race car Lightning McQueen is on the verge of superstardom, until a highway crash leaves him stranded in sleepy town Radiator Springs and sentenced to community service. Initially desperate to leave, he comes to appreciate the quiet life thanks to the town's inhabitants.

There is no question that *Cars*, Pixar supremo John Lasseter's first time behind the wheel since *Toy Story 2*, is the animation studios greatest visual achievement. Those geniuses chez Lightyear have long recognised that the best computer animation is not obsessed with realism but detail. Everything in *Cars* is clearly of a bulbous, shiny cartoon world, but is so exquisitely crafted that the reflection off the hood of a speeding racer or the neon miasma bathing a midnight town is almost enough to make you openly weep in the cinema. There is not a single flaw on the face of this film; it's like Angelina Jolie with hubcaps.

It starts lean and energetic. The opening featuring cocksure racer Lightning McQueen whizzing around the track is a breakneck action sequence that could sit happily in any live-action film. When a later motorway mishap lands McQueen in derelict town Radiator Springs where the most spectacular auto is an emotionally unstable fire engine and a day when holidaying people carriers pop through is considered eventful, it's hard not to yearn for the heady roar of the race track.

It's not that McQueen's cohorts in the town are dull; it's just that they're not especially funny. With the possible exception of rust bucket tow-truck Mater, it's unlikely you'll remember any of them after the closing credits in the same way you do such incidental characters as *Toy Story*'s Rex, mini-Incredible Jack-Jack or that stoned surfer turtle from *Finding Nemo*. Pixar without funny is like Disney without animal sidekicks or Miyazaki without that bit you didn't really understand but still kinda liked - It just doesn't quite run with the smooth hum of fun we've come to expect of history's greatest animation house.

In contrast with the film's message, Radiator Springs is a nice place to hang out for a while, but you wouldn't want to live there. Which makes it a great relief when the movie's ending turns out to be such a humdinger.

Bringing the slow and fast lanes together in glorious fashion, it makes sense of the movie's duller sections and uses them to invest the action with emotion. It's a finale so full of joy, imagination and technical brilliance that you forgive Lasseter the previous storytelling flaws and, teamed with what might be the greatest Pixar credits gag to date, means you'll leave the movie on a petrol-induced high. ★★★ **OR**

CASABLANCA (1942)

Starring: *Humphrey Bogart (Richard 'Rick' Blaine), Ingrid Bergman (Ilsa Lund Laszlo), Paul Henreid (Victor Laszlo), Claude Rains (Capt. Louis Renault)*
Director: *Michael Curtitz*
Screenwriters: *Julius J. Epstein, Philip G. Epstein, Howard Koch, based on the play Everybody Goes To Rick's by Murray Burnett and Joan Alison)*
U/102 mins./Drama/War/USA

Awards: *Academy Awards – Best Director, Best Picture, Best Screenplay*

Rick is the solitary, aloof owner of the most popular bar in wartime Vichy-run Casablanca when the woman who broke his heart walks in . . . along with her hero husband. Only Rick can help them escape the Nazis . . . but will he?

On paper, perhaps it doesn't sound so much: the woman who broke a man's heart walks into his bar – 'of all the gin joints in all the world' – with her husband. But 'the problems of three little people' are compounded by wartime intrigue in a dangerous, mysterious locale. You must remember this: you can't trust anyone who doesn't love *Casablanca*. Never mind that screen writing mavens use it as a model for structure and narrative, or that it received Academy Awards for Best Picture, Director and Screenplay. The fundamental thing is that everything in the film's magical, melodramatic combination of patriotic wartime sentiments, desperate refugees and star-crossed lovers works beautifully, every time.

Casablanca is almost certainly – to the astonishment of those involved in its somewhat chaotic production – the most enjoyable wannasee-again-and-again picture ever made. As *Philadelphia Inquirer* critic Carrie Rickey once wrote, 'Though not the best movie ever, it's the best friend among American films.' Every time you see it, one or another gem of dialogue from the treasure store of worldly witticisms and ironic exchanges strikes you anew. (Rick: 'I came to Casablanca for the waters.' Renault: 'What waters? We're in the desert.' Rick: 'I was misinformed.')

Casablanca began as a play, *Everybody Comes To Rick*'s, by Murray Burnett and Joan Alison. Burnett got the idea from a European trip in 1938, when he became aware of refugees in flight from Nazism and observed the colourful crowd in a nightspot in the South of France – the inspiration for Rick Blaine's French-Moroccan 'gin joint' (an expression Bogie himself substituted for 'cafe').

In the first of many twists of fate, the play came into a Warner Bros studio reader's hands on 8 December 1941, the day after Pearl Harbor. As the US declared itself at war. studios raced to get patriotic pictures into production. Two weeks later, Warners' executive in charge of production, Hal Wallis, decided to make the film, changed the title to evoke the exotic romanticism of the studio's hit *Algiers*, and announced it as a done deal before contracts were signed (Burnett and Alison reputedly receiving a record $20,000 for the rights to an unproduced play).

Contrary to myth and some curious publicity ploys, Humphrey Bogart was always in Wallis' mind for Rick, and sibling screenwriters Julius J. and Philip G. Epstein were briefed to tailor it to him. When the Epsteins went to work on Frank Capra's *Why We Fight* documentary series, they were only half done with *Casablanca*, to which they would return. Howard Koch (who had scripted the most famous radio broadcast in history, the panic-inducing adaptation of *The War Of The Worlds* for Orson Welles) was brought in.

The self-sacrificing love story that is the soul of the film was the Epsteins' providence. So, too, was the smart, cynical humour that brings the supporting cast and background figures to extraordinarily vivid life. Uncredited, Casey Robinson (screenwriter of several hits, including *Now, Voyager*) re-wrote the Paris flashback sequences that reveal Rick's love affair with Ilsa Lund and his heartache. But the plot of *Casablanca* is a political thriller, and it was Koch (whose literate liberalism later saw him blacklisted) who dealt with that. He tackled Bogart's concerns about Rick's background, fleshing out the embittered, enigmatic, idealistic but ultimately heroic character that Bogie personified with immortal style.

Ilsa was another problem. Originally she was an American gold-digger who wrecked Rick's marriage but dumped him for the richer Victor, to whom she was mistress, not wife. The censors would have gone bananas, and the filmmakers wanted her sympathetic, hence the notion of a vulnerable, dispossessed European duty-bound to her husband. *Algiers* beauty Hedy Lamarr was unavailable, so Wallis negotiated with David O. Selznick to borrow Ingrid Bergman (in exchange for Warners actress Olivia de Havilland). With the script still incomplete, Bergman fretted that she didn't know which man she would end up with. But it is one of those rare miraculous accidents that Bogie and Bergman, although he was standoffish to her off-camera, are sublime together on screen.

Paul Henreid, then starring with Bette Davis in *Now, Voyager*, was less than thrilled about what he saw as the preposterousness of playing a Czech Resistance leader who would escape a concentration camp to turn up in Morocco, elegantly dressed for sophisticated sparring with Nazi officials. However, he gritted his teeth and did it in return for prominent billing and Warners' help with his visa status. Conrad Veidt, an outspoken opponent of Nazism who had narrowly escaped Germany, far from resenting typecasting as Major Heinrich Strasser actually had it in his contract that he exclusively play villains, so adamant was he that playing suave Nazi fiends would help the war effort.

Émigré director Michael Curtiz, not so much an artist as a supremely skilled craftsman who imposed himself in many genres, had a perfectionist – some said tyrannical – personality on sets. He also had an infatuation with Americana and its emotional sentiments that unified all of *Casablanca*'s elements and creative talents into its fast-paced, atmospheric, utterly captivating whole. Warners' boast that people of 34 nationalities collaborated on the film may have been an exaggeration, but it certainly embraced a great many. There is no better example than *Casablanca* of the Hollywood melting pot. The film created a world in miniature, in which basic universal desires, sins and impulses, for bad and good, are enveloped in glamour, suspense and style.

Casablanca is universally beloved because it presents the most admirable, inspirational myth of Americana in its romantic idealism: Rick's redemptive surrender of Ilsa for the greater good, and his departure to join the fight for right. The first time you see it is just the beginning of a beautiful friendship. ★★★★★ **AE**

CASSHERN (2004)

Starring: *Yusuke Iseya (Casshern/Tetsuya Azuma), Kumiko Aso (Luna Kozuki), Akira Terao (Kotaro Azuma-hakase), Kanako Higuchi (Midori Azuma), Fumiyo Kohinata (Kozuki-hakase)*
Director: *Kazuaki Kiriya*
Screenwriter: *Kazuaki Kiriya, based on characters by Dai Sato, Shotaro Suga, Tatsuo Yoshida*
15/141 mins./Sci-fi/Japan

In a world ravaged by war and pollution, scientist Dr Azuma struggles to save humanity with self-healing 'neo-cells'. But when his lab is struck by lightning, his experiments come to life and launch an offensive on humanity . . .

One of the joys of *The Matrix* was that it was the nearest we'd yet come to seeing a live-action animé. This Japanese sci-fi epic, directed, shot, cut and co-written by debut filmmaker Kazuaki Kiriya, comes even nearer. Yet, with its 'digital backlot' shooting method and retro-fitted, 40s-future setting, its nearest Western equivalent is *Sky Captain And The World Of Tomorrow* – given the dark shadings of Terry Gilliam's *Brazil*.

Visually, it's astounding. Rejecting the hyper-realistic burnish of Lucas-like CGI, Kiriya dirties his images, saturating colours in some scenes, bleaching them to harsh black-and-white in others, all the while embracing fantastic impossibility. In one sequence, the clunky, spike-helmed robot hordes march along as red-and-black Communist-poster cut-outs. In another, an immense brick building takes to the skies, aided only by a rickety array of propellers.

Being an adaptation of a 35-episode 70s cartoon show, though, Casshern struggles in its storytelling. Overlong and overedited, the film clumsily attempts to make connections between every character. Still, like much animé, it's an experience of the imagination rather than intellect, so the story's confused, agitated operatics are at least balanced out by Kiriya's impressive aesthetic flourishes. ★★★ **DJ**

CASINO (1995)

Starring: *Robert De Niro (Sam 'Ace' Rothstein), Sharon Stone (Ginger Mckenna), Joe Pesci (Nicky Santoro), James Woods (Lester Diamond), Don Rickles (Billy Sherbert), Alan King (Andy Stone), Kevin Pollack (Phillip Green)*
Director: *Martin Scorsese*
Screenwriters: *Nicholas Pileggi, Martin Scorsese, based on Nicholas Pileggi's book.*
18/183 mins./Drama/Crime/USA

Awards: *Golden Globes – Best Actress (Sharon Stone)*

Ace Rothstein and Nicky Santoro are two mobsters who move to Las Vegas to make their fortunes. But they come into conflict when Ace falls for a pushy showgirl, Ginger, and Nicky falls into a cycle of drugs and violence.

If you like to know where you are with a director, *Casino* is the movie for you. Placing *The Age Of Innocence* and *Cape Fear* to one side for a moment, here we have Scorsese returning to what he knows best, and to the people he loves.

Co-written with *GoodFellas* screenwriter Nicholas Pileggi, and starring the usual suspects in the form of Bobby De Niro and Joe Pesci, you also have the warm reassurance of the presence of many of *GoodFellas'* character actors, grizzled of visage and twitchy of trigger-finger, Scorsese's mum doing a cameo, Elaine and Saul Bass producing the opening credits, and many recognisable directorial flourishes. Even better for Scorsese fans, within 15 minutes Joe Pesci is stamping on some schmuck's head in a bar, screaming obscenities as a bewildered Robert De Niro looks on with that great quizzical expression of his.

GoodFellas Part II? Well, sort of. Scorsese insisted this isn't a mob film, and you can see his point. It tells the – slightly embellished – true story of Sam 'Ace' Rothstein, a brilliant Mid-West gambler recruited by the wiseguys to run their casino in Vegas, which he proceeds to do with ruthless efficiency. It all sours when his old buddy Nicky Santoro (Pesci in fantastic psycho mode) comes to town and starts throwing his weight around at more or less the same time as Ace makes the one big reckless gamble of his life: persuading sex-bomb hustler Ginger McKenna to marry him. This head-strong twosome just add too many maybes into the comfortable set-up, and slowly the easy money-making machine starts to malfunction. Then the baseball bats come out.

Tagline
No one stays at the top forever.

This is De Niro's finest hour certainly since *GoodFellas* and maybe since *The King Of Comedy*. Onscreen for nearly the whole three-hour running time, he is chillingly logical about his life at first, slowly descending into panic, frustration and violence as things go wrong. He plays it perfectly from start to finish, as indeed do the entire cast. Sharon Stone is a revelation, Pesci is his usual mesmerising self, and if at times the story drags – with too much voiceover and quasi-documentary – the three of them refuse to let go of your nether regions for a second.

If the violence is even more stomach churning than in *GoodFellas* (check out Pesci's creative use of a vice) and if Scorsese isn't making huge strides in terms of his filmmaking lexicon, this is still a powerful, disturbing and entirely fascinating examination of a specific time and place, and of the nature of the deals we do – with our employers, with our friends, with our lovers. ★★★★★ **PT**

CASINO ROYALE (1967)

Starring: *Peter Sellers (Evelyn Tremble), Ursula Andress (Vesper Lynd/007), David Niven (Sir James Bond), Orson Welles (Le Chiffre), Joanna Pettet (Mata Bond), Dallah Lavi (The Detainer), Woody Allen (Jimmy Bond, Dr Noah), Deborah Kerr (Agent Mimi, Lady Fiona McTarry), William Holden (Ransome), Charles Boyer (Le Grande)*
Directors: *John Huston, Ken Hughes, Robert Parrish, Val Guest, Joseoh McGrath*
Screenwriters: *Wolf Mankowitz, John Law, Michael Sayers, Billy Wilder, Val Guest, Joseph Heller, Ben Hecht, Terry Southern, based on the novel by Ian Fleming*
PG/131 mins./Comedy/Adventure/UK

Sir James Bond is called out of retirement when the world is threatened by mysterious mastermind 'Dr Noah'. Meanwhile, the British secret service recruit and train various other operatives who are code-named 'James Bond 007', notably baccarat expert Evelyn Tremble, who is required to take on SMERSH chief Le Chiffre at the Casino Royale.

With five directors, at least seven 007s (including Joanna Pettet, Terence Cooper and Woody Allen!), more spot gags than a *MAD* Magazine article and a panoply of astonishingly beautiful women, this spoof of the Bond films is overpopulated, overstuffed, wildly inconsistent, episodic and a total mess. But it's so expensively insane that it can't help but be entertaining.

For the money, you get … a terrific Burt Bacharach score (and Dusty Springfield singing 'The Look of Love'); trendy psychedelic sets (you'll love Ursula Andress's bedroom); stretches of inspired lunacy (Deborah Kerr's Scots routine, Peter Sellers insulting Orson Welles over a baccarat table); Dave Prowse as the Frankenstein Monster; a flying saucer in Trafalgar Square; comedy cameos from British institutions like Richard Wattis and Ronnie Corbett; more 60s lovelies (Ursula Andress, Dahlia Lavi, Jacqueline Bisset, Joanna Pettet) in more outlandish frocks than any other picture (it's more sophisticatedly sexy than the official Bonds); Woody Allen before a firing squad ('my doctor says I mustn't allow bullets to enter any part of my body'); and an orgy of excess that tides over the let-the-fire-extinguishers-off-and-have-the-cowboys-ride-in slapstick. Too often written off as a disaster – and admittedly a total mess (Sellers walked off the set in mid-film, and the contrivances used to cover this are glaringly obvious) – it is arguably a more engaging, appealing film than 75% of the 'official' 007 films. ★★★★ **KN**

CAST AWAY (2000)

Starring: *Tom Hanks (Chuck Noland), Helen Hunt (Kelly Frears), Nick Searcy (Stan), Chris Noth (Jerry Lovett), Lari White (Bettina Peterson), Geoffrey Blake (Maynard Graham)*
Director: *Robert Zemeckis*
Screenwriter: *William Broyles Jr*
12/143 mins./Adventure/Drama/USA

Awards: *Golden Globes – Best Actor*

Leaving girlfriend Kelly behind just before Christmas, FedEx engineer Chuck Noland sets off troubleshooting. Disaster strikes when his plane comes down and Noland is washed up on an uninhabited shore. Bereft of modern comforts, Noland attempts to cope with his prison of solitude.

The first collaboration between Robert Zemeckis and Tom Hanks since the Oscar-winning *Forrest Gump*, *Cast Away* had been hyped as Oscar bait, but actually aims for something more than an overly emotional prestige picture.

Never opting for the cheap laugh or quick sentiment, Zemeckis tackles all sorts of desert island risks, making a minimalist premise and (for the most part) solitary actor play credibly over a two-hour-plus storyline.

After an unremarkable let's-meet-the-characters introduction, Zemeckis pulls out all the stops, creating a terrifying plane crash, mostly through a hand-held depiction of Noland's terror. Once Noland is alone in his tropical hell, what follows is expertly sustained, wordless moviemaking.

If the film invokes all sorts of Robinson Crusoe-styled clichés – the initial lack of hunting skills, the inability to generate fire – they are elevated by Hanks' ability to convince and Zemeckis' commitment to putting the character through the mill: stones rip into the soles of Noland's naked feet; the discovery of the aircraft's drowned pilot; and, most gut-wrenching of all, a DIY act of dentistry involving an ice skate that would have even the most strong-stomached viewer turning away.

Occasionally Zemeckis' grip falters – a subtle hint of a suicide attempt is later bowlderised by blatant spelling out. But what stops the good becoming great, however, is the lack of emotional wallop on Noland's return to the mainland – they don't work hard enough in making us care about the characters, so our sense of investment in the relationship is dulled.

To his credit, Zemeckis never cops out by cutting back to middle America to follow rescue attempts or grieving relatives. Hanks commands attention throughout and, as Noland starts talking to a washed-up volleyball (dubbed Wilson after its brand name), makes a relationship between an increasingly unhinged man and a plastic sports object not only believable, but bizarrely moving. ★★★★ **IF**

◎ CASUALTIES OF WAR (1989)

Starring: *Michael J. Fox (Eriksson), Sean Penn (Sgt Tony Meserve), Don Harvey (Cpl Thomas E. Clark), John C. Reilly (PFC. Herbert Hatcher), Thuy Thu Le (Tran Thi Oahn), Ving Rhames (Lt Reilly)*
Director: *Brian De Palma*
Screenwriter: *David Rabe, based on the article by Daniel Lang*
18/113 mins./War/USA

The outsider in a rough squad of American troopers in the Vietnam war, Eriksson is deeply disturbed when they rape and murder a local girl. Such that he decides justice is far more important than comradeship and turns in his fellow soldiers.

Despite the lurking amorality of his previous films, Brian De Palma delivered an about face with this staunchly moral, serious and moving tale of the atrocity of war. Not the grand sin of war in general, but the specific destruction of order amongst soldiers far from home who have lost sight of their own humanity.

Meserve, played with Penn's usual rugged intensity and brute force, is a man whose survivalist impulses have come askew; the death that surrounds him has allowed him to reinvent himself. He's dominant but cartoonish, recklessness has overtaken him and his men follow him, struck that such masculinity could keep them alive. When he decides, during a long-range reconnaissance, they can have their way with a Vietnamese girl, they run into an unforeseen problem – the relative innocence, and hence intact morality, of new recruit Eriksson.

In one of Michael J. Fox's few serious roles, he injects this blinkered young man with a naiveté, a yet to be crushed sense of basic goodness. It is this that drives him to oppose the dreadful actions that follow. De Palma mixes up these elements with extraordinary skill, reeling in his familiar gimmickry he exposes the conflicting pressures of warfare. Survival requires a shedding of natural behaviours, to find something animalistic, but where does it stop? How does a solider, in the shocking daily loss of comrades, retain who he is? Meserve may be beyond reach. Eriksson is on a journey into disillusionment.

Tightly structured, the film is told in flashback from the stone-faced Eriksson on a San Francisco-bound train catching sight of a girl who resembles their victim. From here it builds through a series of concentrated vignettes, from the almost comic spill of violence and the surreal periods of quiet, toward the crime at its centre. This brutal act is examined with a brazen, desperate logic – that Meserve has been denied leave (his channel to local whores), that the sudden loss of their radio man has stirred a natural anger. But De Palma, at his most personal, remains staunch, there are no extenuating factors, war is no excuse, and his film remains a telling damnation of man's capacity for evil. ★★★★ **IN**

◎ THE CAT AND THE CANARY (1939)

Starring: *Bob Hope (Wallie Campbell), Paulette Goddard (Joyce Norman), John Beal (Fred Blythe), Douglass Montgomery (Charlie Wilder), Gale Sondergaard (Miss Lu)*
Director: *Elliott Nugent*
Screenwriters: *Walter DeLeon, Lynn Starling, based on the play by John Willard*
PG/72 mins./Comedy/Mystery/USA

In a Louisana swamp mansion, the relatives of millionaire Cyrus West gather to hear the reading of his will. West decrees that if his chosen heir goes mad before dawn, a mystery second heir will inherit. A warder from a nearby insane asylum shows up and reveals that a homicidal maniac known as 'the Cat' has escaped and is in the area.

A remake of the stage-derived silent hit which epitomised the old-dark-house sub-genre of comedy mystery, this boosted Bob Hope as a major screen comedian and reminded the studios that sliding secret panels, disguised killers lurking in hidden passageways, wills read at midnight and gatherings of suspicious heirs never fail to raise a creaky chill.

In too many later films, star comedians just play scared or stupid (witness: Lou Costello); here, Hope's smart lines come through what seems to be a real fear for his life and the fast-talking comic is also clever enough to handle the detective work rather than haul on a colourless leading man to take the strain.

The visuals are less extravagantly gothic than the 1927 Paul Leni version, but it makes its claw-gloved and masked killer a genuinely unpleasant threat, frequently reaching out of the shadows to clutch at the lovely Paulette Goddard or staring out through the eyes of a portrait hanging in the gloomy Louisiana swamp mansion where everyone is confined for the duration.

The cast includes fine red herring work from perennial villains George Zucco (as the lawyer whose corpse tumbles from a secret nook in a textbook scare) and Gale Sondegaard (as the slinky, sinister and somehow sexy housekeeper). The mystery was never that mysterious, but the jokes remain snappy – 'Don't these big old empty houses scare you?' 'Not me, I was in vaudeville.' ★★★★ **KN**

◎ CAT BALLOU (1965)

Starring: *Lee Marvin (Kid Shelleen/Strawn), Jane Fonda (Catharine Ballou), Michael Callan (Clay Boone), Dwayne Hickman (Jed), Nat 'King' Cole (Sam The Shade), Stubby Kaye (The Sunrise Kid)*
Director: *Elliot Silverstein*
Screenwriters: *Walter Newman, Frank Pierson, based on the novel by Roy Chainslor*
PG/97 mins./Comedy Western/USA

Awards: *Academy Awards – Best Actor (Lee Marvin); BAFTA – Best Foreign Actor (Lee Marvin)*

Seeking revenge after her father is shot dead and her farm about to be taken by the railroad barons, Cat Ballou turns to famed gunfighter Kid Shelleen. The problem is, he is a drunkard, long past his glory days, who can hardly hold a gun, while his horse is in an even worse state.

Prising open the pomp and gravity of the Western tradition, this whacky, often hilarious comedy is testament to the fact most things have been done before. It's like a prelude to all the schoolboy antics of the Farrelly brothers and the silly spoofing of the Zucker team. And, actually, it also remains a delightful if limited piece of genre spinning in its very own right. Mainly because Lee Marvin, in two separate roles (one with a tin nose) concocts an Oscar winning roustabout, a booze-ankled has-been who hasn't exactly gone to seed rather than passed out on the way.

A young, flirty Jane Fonda, back when she played everything with a perky gusto, a squeak or two from being irritating, but spirited and gorgeous enough to get away with it, is the damsel in distress required to figure it out for herself. Her father has been murdered, her outlaw friends the very definition of useless, let alone this blotto gunman wobbling about the place. This is the central joke, that as the bad guys close in, at some point he will awaken from his stupor and save the day. He's just taking forever to do it.

Marvin thrills in being able to dismantle his rigid, tough guy persona, but he's too good an actor to simply play straight drunk adding an air of faded glory to Kid Shelleen. He's a real joke, rather than a spoof, complete with languid horse who has a habit of trotting sideways. But he also gets to play the cold-hearted, metal-nosed killer Tim Strawn, a stiff representation of the Marvin we know.

The plot, held together by balladeers Nat King Cole and Stubby Kaye playing chorus to events (an idea later stolen by the Farrellys), forces this woeful gang into playing outlaw, robbing the scurrilous railroads, but their day will come. Before it does there are plenty of wry cracks about Western myth (a washed-up Butch Cassidy makes an appearance), a suitably superficial and glossy glow about its variations on the genre's visual tenets, and about the funniest horse ever put on screen to soak up. ★★★★ **IN**

THE CAT FROM OUTER SPACE (1978)

Starring: *Ken Berry (Dr Frank Wilson), Sandy Duncan (Dr Elizabeth Bartlett), Harry Morgan (Gen. Stilton), Roddy McDowall (Mr Stallwood), McLean Stevenson (Dr Norman Link)*
Director: *Norman Tokar*
Screenwriter: *Ted Key*
U/104 mins./Sci-fi/Comedy/USA

After the US authorities find a crashed spaceship, its pilot, a cat with a miraculous collar that allows it to communicate with humans, goes on the run. He finds help in the shape of Frank Wilson, who may have the skills to mend the craft and allow him to escape.

Disney, in the late 70s, seemed up for anything, as long as they could hawk it to minors on some cutesy content – a possessed VW beetle, psychic kids, mother-daughter body swapping. This conceptual ballast reached an all-time absurd with this sci-fi blather about an alien pussy complete with that hoariest of stalwarts telepathic powers. Talk about covering your bases, you get a furry star 'and' slapstick antics as Jake the interstellar cat flies a bi-plane. Still, this does predate *ET* by four years.

It's very slight, flushed with that identikit suburban Disney gloss, but is handled by Norman Tokar with an easy charm. Jake (voiced by Ronnie Schell) has a likable nonchalance and mild disgust at humankind's antics. The writing isn't exactly first base, but is still clutching for second. But there is some intelligence in the idea of Jake's downed saucer needing $120,000 worth of gold before it can take off. The only answer his surrogate keeper, Ken Berry playing a helpful scientist, can come up with is to hit the casino, where the cat's psychic powers can stack the odds in their favour.

The effects are dotty and obvious, but sensibly not too ambitious. A cello playing itself care of Jake's talents is patently strung up with wire, but the budget was slim and the miracles of digital manipulation must have seemed about as likely as a talking cat. Yet, there's enough here to capture the imaginations of the smallest viewers, animals with personalities always work a treat in that department, but the film's rewards will always have to be measured by the simple proposal of its title. ★★★ **IN**

CAT PEOPLE (1942)

Starring: *Simone Simon (Irena Dubrovna), Kent Smith (Oliver Reed), Tom Conway (Dr Judd) Jane Randolph (Alice Moore), Jack Holt (Commodore), Alan Napier (Carver), Elizabeth Dunne (Miss Plunkett), Elizabeth Russell (The Cat Woman)*
Director: *Jacques Tourneur*
Screenwriter: *DeWitt Bodeen*
PG/73 mins./Horror/USA

Irena, a fashion artist living in New York City marries an average-Joe American. Their marriage suffers though, as Irena believes that she suffers from an ancient curse – whenever emotionally aroused, she will turn into a killer panther.

In the early 40s, a horror movie was supposed to be something hairy and melodramatic like Universal's hit *The Wolf Man*. That picture introduced all the clichés and conventions of the werewolf legend to the cinema and confirmed the genre stardom of Lon Chaney Jr a bearlike fellow willing to sit still for the makeup ordeal whereby Jack P. Pierce glued enough yak-hair to his face to stuff a sofa. With Chaney stalking Universal's back lot version of the Welsh moors, *The Wolf Man* might not have been art, but it was creepy fun in a childish sort of way and set the box-office afire. Naturally, other studios wanted a slice of the pie.

In 1942, RKO Pictures, still reeling from a feud with newspaper tycoon William Randolph Hearst over their backing of Orson Welles' veiled Hearst biopic *Citizen Kane*, took another body blow from Welles' follow-up *The Magnificent Ambersons*. Executives were fired and a new regime took over, instituting a policy of 'showmanship, not genius'. Val Lewton – formerly a sidekick of arch-tyrant David O. Selznick – was hired to command a brisk, efficient unit whose ostensible job was to turn out horror movies just like they made 'em over at Universal. There were left-over sets and costumes from the Welles movies, both of which featured old dark houses just as suitable for prowling Karloffs and Lugosis as Kanes and Ambersons. Studio head Charles Koerner tested out a jim-dandy title for the first of Lewton's proposed quickies, *Cat People*. If the public went for guys who turned into wolves, then it stood to reason they'd be even happier with girls who turned into cats. It was the kind of slam-dunk project that had the publicity department turning out a lurid fang-and-claw poster even before there was a film to go with it.

However, Lewton was secretly ambitious. His background was schizoid, torn between the pulp of *Weird Tales* magazine (for which he had once written a cat-werewolf story) and the *Reader's Digest* classiness of Selznick (who once had Lewton read Dickens to him as he sat on the toilet). If he had to make a film about a woman who turned into a cat, then Lewton intended to make the best possible cat person movie imaginable. To top off the whole thing, he would go all out to be scary in a way *The Wolf Man*, for all its growling, couldn't manage. Assessing the sorry state of the once-great genre, mired as it was in fairytale European settings and third-hand plots, Lewton opted for a subtle, innovative movie. He brought the monster home literally and figuratively by setting the action in contemporary New York (*Cat People* is among the first supernatural horror films to take place in a world its audience was familiar with) and by making an unusual stab at psychological depth.

Having guided DeWitt Bodeen through a solid script, Lewton hired young French director Jacques Tourneur (who would later helm horror classic *Night Of The Demon*, and set about finding an unusual cast. The kittenish Simone Simon stars as frigid Serbian refugee Irena Dubrovna, unable to consummate her marriage to 'plain Americano' Oliver Reed

(Smith) because she is afraid orgasm will transform her into a giant panther. When her frustrated husband is tempted into an affair and her creepy psychoanalyst Dr Judd (Conway) comes on to her, her fingernails sharpen (in an unforgettable shot, she strokes a sofa to leave parallel scratches in the material) and some sort of change comes over her. Is she a were-panther or just disturbed? The answer doesn't come until the last scene, and is all the more unsettling because of it. The stalking sequences – as 'other woman' Jane Randolph is pursued through Central Park or menaced in a swimming pool by an almost-unseen force – are still chilling, but the power of the film is in Simon's uniquely appealing performance. In one ominous little vignette in a Serbian restaurant, she is struck silent by the sight of a mysterious beauty (Elizabeth Russell) who seems to be another passing cat woman.

Lewton allegedly got the job because someone misheard his claim to have written 'horrible novels' as 'horror novels'. A man of taste, he opted to paint the screen with shadows, knowing the audience would imagine far worse horrors than an effects man could create. It was a huge hit, and Lewton delivered eight more strange and frightening little movies, first with Tourneur (*I Walked With A Zombie*, *The Leopard Man*; then Mark Robson (*The Seventh Victim*, *The Ghost Ship*, *Isle Of The Dead*, *Bedlam*; and Robert Wise (*Curse Of The Cat People*), *The Body Snatcher*. Lumped together they represent one of the most impressive and unnerving bodies of work in the field. ★★★★★ **KN**

CAT PEOPLE (1982)

Starring: *Nastassja Kinski (Irena Gallier), Malcolm McDowell (Paul Gallier), John Heard (Oliver Yates), Annette O'Toole (Alice Perrin), Ruby Dee (Female), Ed Begley Jr (Joe Creigh)*
Director: *Paul Schrader*
Screenwriter: *Alan Ormsby, based on a story by DeWitt Bodeen*
18/118 mins./Horror/USA

Irena Gallier comes to New Orleans to live with her strange preacher brother Paul, who tells her that they are the last of the cat people and can only have sex with each other if they want to avoid turning into panthers.

In 1982, Paul Schrader seemed a very odd choice to remake Val Lewton's classic 1943 horror movie. The original was a model of restraint and subtlety and the remake, frankly, isn't.

In an overheated New Orleans, sister and brother Nastassja Kinksi and Malcolm McDowell are the last survivors of a race of humans who transform into leopards when sexually aroused. While McDowell rips the legs off hookers, Kinski more delicately becomes obsessed with gentle zoo-keeper John Heard, who is marked out as the man for her because of his sensitive handling of a caged leopard in his care.

The script redoes all the set-pieces of the original, including a cameo from another cat lady that scuppers the whole 'last of the cat people' premise, but Schrader seems to throw most of them away – the menacing of Annette O'Toole in a swimming pool is especially ordinary – in favour of an understandable, obsessive lingering on the pouting face and frequently naked form of the lissom Kinski, who is involved in the weirdest bondage scene in the movies.

It has the sort of slimy transformation scenes that were de rigueur in early 1980s werewolf movies, with the big cat faces erupting from beneath the smooth human ones, and stretches of dreamlike wandering that become either fascinating or sleep-inducing depending on your mood. It's not exactly good, and it has some very bad scenes indeed, but the performances sometimes sparkle and the unusual happy ending – scored with David Bowie's 'Putting Out the Fire With Gasoline' – is surprisingly moving. ★★★ **KN**

CATCH ME IF YOU CAN (2002)

Starring: *Leonardo DiCaprio (Frank Abagnale Jr), Tom Hanks (Carl Hanratty), Christopher Walken (Frank Abagnale), Martin Sheen (Roger Strong), Nathalie Baye (Paula Abagnale), Amy Adams (Brenda Strong), James Brolin (Jack Barnes)*
Director: *Steven Spielberg*
Screenwriter: *Jeff Nathanson, based on the book by Frank Abagnale Jr with Stan Redding*
12/141 mins./Biography/Crime/USA
Awards: *BAFTA – Best Supporting Actor (Christopher Walken)*

Devastated by his parents' divorce, 16-year-old Frank runs away from home and embarks on an audacious career as a conman. Travelling across the globe, Frank tries his hand by turns as an airline pilot, doctor and lawyer, all the while pursued by dogged FBI agent Carl Hanratty.

Frank Abagnale Jr, the real-life subject of Steven Spielberg's breezy feature, never dreamed that he would be the subject of a movie. How do you condense five eventful years into two hours? he has asked. And, bearing in mind that this practical concern comes from the man who saw no great difficulty in scamming $2.5 million in forged cheques before he'd even reached his 21st birthday, it's an interesting worry. Actually, although Spielberg allows himself a further 20 minutes' grace in the running time, the result suffers from an unlikely dichotomy of feeling both overlong (a slight sag around its midriff) and detail-light (having sacrificed many of the book's more intriguing nuances).

Were this not inspired by real events, but rather a fictional screenplay, Spielberg would surely have drawn a red line through certain chapters for sheer momentum's sake. As it is, slightly hamstrung by factual accuracy, we occasionally find ourselves meandering through scenes that serve little purpose. Also, certain chronological jumps (Hanratty finds Frank in France) arrive somewhat out of the blue, as if a couple of scenes of explanatory preamble have been left on the cutting room floor.

Then again, contrary to expectation, this is not the frothy, superficial caper we'd been led to believe. Forget that trailer; what we have here is a deeply moving, quite wonderfully acted coming-of-age black comedy, packed with equal measures of pathos and plain fun. In focusing on the lovely Leo accompanied by a girdle (collective noun) of trolley-dollies, early teasers have rather missed the point: this is as sophisticated as modern moviemaking gets, Spielberg's most deft handling of comedy to date, and a shot of pure class straight into the heart of cinema. Thought *Ocean's 11* was cool and sexy? Trust us, this is too.

While in different hands Abagnale's adventures would have lingered far more on the hedonistic aspects of what, let's face it, must have been one damn fine foray into manhood (picture for just a second an Oliver Stone version of the stewardess sequence), for Spielberg the focus is elsewhere. In fact, his obsession with the themes of fatherhood has arguably never been more heartbreakingly realised than in *Catch Me If You Can*'s telling incidentals: Frank watching Mr and Mrs Strong do the washing up, Franks Jr and Sr's lunch meeting: these are powerful touches that will stay with you long after the end credits roll.

Considerably darker than anticipated – abortion and infidelity simmer under a deceptively glossy sheen – the film requires the highest calibre of acting talent, and in his casting Spielberg delivers an unprecedented ensemble. For DiCaprio fans, this is the best reason to go to the cinema since he went down on the *Titanic* – he is back at his blistering, finest-of-his-generation standard. Hanks devotees, meanwhile, will rejoice at yet another subtly distinct variation on the Everyman; and obsessives of TV series *Alias* will be positively cock-a-hoop at Jennifer Garner's erotically supercharged cameo. As for Walken, well, if you make it through his performance without shedding a tear, then there's a fiver here with your name on it. ★★★★ **MD**

CATS & DOGS (2001)

Starring: *Jeff Goldblum (Professor Brody), Elizabeth Perkins (Mrs Brody), Alexander Pollack (Scotty Brody), Miriam Margolyes (Sophie the Castle Maid), the voices of: Tobey Maguire (Lou the Beagle), Alec Baldwin (Butch), Sean Hayes (Mr Tinkles), Susan Sarandon (Ivy), Michael Clarke Duncan (Sam) Jon Lovitz (Calico), Charlton Heston (The Mastiff)*
Director: *Lawrence Guterman*
Screenwriters: *John Requa, Glenn Ficarra*
PG/87 mins./Family/Comedy/USA
Awards: *Razzie – Worst Supporting Actors (Charlton Heston)*

Mr Tinkles, a despot cat, is scheming to interfere in Prof. Brody's work on a cure for dog allergies. After the cat-napping of the Brodys' dog, a worldwide canine organisation arranges for a secret agent pup to be infiltrated into the family, but Mrs Brody picks Lou, an untrained beagle, instead. Retaliating, Mr Tinkles sends cat ninjas to attack Brody and conquer the world.

Cats & Dogs has an irresistibly funny idea, cross-breeding the talking animals of *Babe* with the retro-Bond skittery of *Spy Kids*, and at its best, it delivers charm and laughs, with miraculous use of trained pets, animatronics, CGI and fake faces on real animals to make an entire cast of felines and canines come to life.

There is solid voicework from Tobey Maguire as Lou, the ordinary pup who yearns for adventure but learns that all he needs is the love of a human master, with Alec Baldwin and Susan Sarandon gruff and sly as Buddy and Ivy, the veteran agent dogs. But the runaway success of the film is the fluffy megalomaniac Mr Tinkles, voiced by Sean Hayes and benefitting from amazingly detailed and expressive fur and whisker-work.

The human characters are less fully-realised, with gawky eccentric Goldblum and briskly mommish Perkins well aware that their scenes without the animals are potential fast-forward fodder, and Pollock is a cookie-cutter cute-but-neglected kid (traumatised because Dad doesn't show up for his soccer try-outs) whose dialogue consists of exclamations like 'cool!' and 'sucks!'

The script has the feel of something that's been overcrafted, with all the characters stuck with positive and empowering arcs, and homilies to family values delivered as the score burbles in that way that is supposed to warm the heart but tends to turn the stomach. Setting itself up as a dog film, it's the sort of movie that prefers dumb doggedness over catty wit, though the cat characters tend to get all the big laughs, and there's even a wonderful, Nuremberg rally-style finish with a horde of quisling mice and terrific stuntwork. ★★★ **KN**

CATWOMAN (2004)

Starring: *Halle Berry (Patience Phillips/Catwoman), Benjamin Bratt (Tom Lone), Sharon Stone (Laurel Hedare), Lambert Wilson (George Hedare), Frances Conroy (Ophelia)*
Director: *Pitof*
Screenwriters: *John D. Brancato, John Rogers, Michael Ferris, from a story by Theresa Rebeck, John D. Brancato, Michael Ferris, characters created by Bob Kane*
12A/104 mins./Action/Crime/Fantasy/USA
Awards: *Razzies – Worst Actress, Worst Director, Worst Picture, Worst Screenplay*

After being resurrected by an ancient Egyptian cat, cosmetics industry designer Patience Phillips turns from shy, badly dressed punchbag into the vengeful, powerful Catwoman. Employing her feline powers, Phillips seeks rough justice for those who killed her. . .

This isn't the slinky anti-heroine of the *Batman* comic books or Tim Burton movie. It isn't even a tongue-in-cheek tribute to any of the Catwomen (Julie Newmar, Eartha Kitt) from the campy 60s TV show. In the hands of Halle Berry and French visual effects whizz-turned-director Pitof, Catwoman is a new breed of feline. And not an attractive one.

Starting from scratch, with no connection to the previous incarnations, this Catwoman has more in common – storywise, at least – with undead avenger The Crow. Halle Berry does all she can to sex up the stale proceedings once she's transformed from frowzy wallflower into lithe whip-cracker. Sadly, despite her still undeniable screen presence and poised intensity, Berry fails to break out of the formulaic Hollywood summer movie routine. Patience tests out her new abilities (She has keen senses! She's supernaturally agile! She drinks milk! She hisses at dogs!) and squeezes into a ludicrous costume to, sort of, fight crime, before embarking on a mewling rampage of revenge. Fetish-freak-reject wardrobe aside, the biggest problem here is the logic-starved plot, revolving around a cosmetics conspiracy in which Lambert Wilson and his scheming spouse, Sharon Stone, invent a face cream which dissolves your skin if you stop using it.

It doesn't really matter that Catwoman '04 is so distant from a character who's been around for six-odd decades – in fact, a new, inventive take would have been welcome – but this wannabe blockbuster is far from original. We don't get a narrative line here, only excuses for shoddily executed action scenes (the bad CG renders the pouncing Berry weightless and unconvincing), a forced romantic subplot (why Benjamin Bratt's do-gooder cop falls for Patience is anyone's guess) and a laughable, OTT climax. Here, Berry catfights bitchy make-up doyenne Stone, now a superpowered chick herself with hard-as-steel skin. And why does she have hard-as-steel skin? Because she slaps on pumped-up face cream. Oh yes, it really is that silly. ★ **OR**

CECIL B. DEMENTED (2000)

Starring: *Melanie Griffith (Honey Whitlock), Stephen Dorff (Cecil), Alicia Witt (Cherish), Adrian Grenier (Lyle), Maggie Gyllenhaal (Raven), Mink Stole (Mrs Sylvia Mallory), Patricia Hearst (Fidget's Mom)*
Director: *John Waters*
Screenwriter: *John Waters*
18/87 mins./Comedy/France/USA

Appallingly egotistical film star Honey Whitlock spends most of her time emotionally torturing her assistant, until she is kidnapped by cinematic terrorist Cecil B. Demented and force to make a 'real film' – and learn the 'true meaning' of cinema.

With bad taste pretty much everywhere in mainstream movies these days, John Waters may be forgiven for feeling more than a tad ripped off. After all, this is the man who pretty much invented cinematic vileness as a legitimate art form, delivering, among other deviant delights, a gargantuan transvestite devouring dog excrement (*Pink Flamingos*), which quite frankly makes *Road Trip* and its 'prostate milking' look positively respectable. It's no surprise, then, that the target of his latest assault on decency should be directed at Hollywood itself. And while its walls may not take a Jericho-like tumble, there's a lot of fun to be had in watching The Pope of Trash's hysterical attack.

The film melds all the usual Waters ingredients: high campery, bitch-queen movie stars, surreal terrorism kidnap (always his favourite crime) and really bad hair. But this time, unlike the director's previous outing, *Pecker*, there's a palpable anger to the gleefully grotesque gumbo.

Demented resembles a deranged Dogme director, not only shooting on the streets, but enlisting the help of porno and bad action movie fans when confronted by an enraged establishment. Cinemas showing 'Patch Adams: The Director's Cut' are trashed; the set of 'Forrest Gump II: Gumped Again' is bloodily disrupted, and all the while Whitlock (Griffith brilliantly sending up her 'difficult' rep) is seduced like some latter-day, celluloid Patty Hearst, with the Sprockets as the Symbionese Liberation Army, the film building to a quite literal orgy of sex and violence.

Cecil B. is unlikely to win Waters any new fans. It has all the flaws of his best work: pretty much inept technical direction; some acting which more than borders on ropey; and more than the occasional comedic longeur. As one character remarks, 'I walk out of your movies even on airplanes'. For Waters this would be the ultimate compliment. ★★★★ **AS**

CELEBRITY (1998)

Starring: *Melanie Griffith (Nicole Oliver), Kenneth Branagh (Lee Simon), Winona Ryder (Nola), Judy Davis (Robin Simon), Dylan Baker (Priest at Catholic Retreat), Charlize Theron (Supermodel), Joe Mantegna (Tony Gardella) Famke Janssen (Bonnie), Leonardo Di Caprio (Brandon Darrow), Gretchen Mol (Vicky), Hank Azaria (David)*
Director: *Woody Allen*
Screenwriter: *Woody Allen*
18/113 mins./Comedy/Drama/USA

Lee and Robin divorce, and he makes it his mission to seek out fame, celebrity and riches. Meanwhile she has a chance meeting with a new man, and finds happiness – and fame – almost by accident.

To the tones of Beethoven's Fifth, a single-seater fighter writes the word HELP in its vapour trail in the Manhattan sky. It's a great opening. Minutes later, Melanie Griffith is giving Kenneth Branagh a blow job in her childhood bedroom. Yes, we're in New Woody territory.

The self-loathing of *Deconstructing Harry* has been toned down, but there's no stinting on the sex, drugs and swearing – with Gershwin and urban neuroses present and correct, too. Celebrity is set within the worlds of filmmaking, publishing, fashion and TV, and the vehicle that carries Allen's wry examination of the human condition this time out is fame – in all its cruel and unpredictable glory.

Branagh plays Lee Simon, a self-absorbed celebrity hack whose early mid-life crisis prompts him to dump his frumpy wife Robin, buy an Aston Martin and take off in search of the high life. What he finds, through a series of shallow affairs (cue: Charlize Theron, Winona Ryder and Famke Janssen) and increasingly desperate attempts to get his screenplay read, is that the pursuit of fame can be a dispiriting business, and that even a BJ from Melanie Griffith is simply icing on a very shitty cake. Robin, on the other hand, left dithering in the ruins of her marriage, has her life transformed through a chance meeting with a suave TV executive (Joe Mantegna) and ends up happy, fulfilled and famous almost despite herself.

Celebrity is Woody nearly on top form – poignant, touching, profound. And, thank God, it's funny. Which is good, because if it wasn't so gracefully executed, Branagh's prodigiously bad performance would have dragged it under. His slavish impersonation of Allen, grotesquely amplifying every vocal mannerism and behavioural tick, is as inexplicable as it is annoying. That the film survives – triumphs, in fact – is testament to how good it really is. ★★★★ **SB**

CELINE AND JULIET GO BOATING (CELINE AND JULIET VONT EN BATEAU) (1974)

Starring: *Juliet Berto (Céline) Dominique Labourier (Julie), Bulie Ogier (Camille), Marie-France Pisier (Sophie), Barbet Schroeder (Olivier), Phillippe Clevenot (Gulio), Nathalie Asner (Madlyn)*
Director: *Jacques Rivette*
Screenwriters: *Jacques Rivette, Eduardo de Gregorio, Juliet Berto, Dominique Labourier, Bulie Oglier, Marie-France Pisier*
12A/193 mins./Drama/Fantasy/France

Meeting by chance in a Parisian park, Montmartre magician Céline befriends occult-fixated librarian Julie and they soon find themselves at the centre of a murderous melodrama being staged in a possibly haunted house.

Frustrated at having to abandon his variation on *The Phantom Of The Opera*, Jacques Rivette teamed with his proposed Phénix star, Juliet Berto, to concoct a scenario for her and her friend, Dominique Labourier. Working in tandem with screenwriter Eduardo de Gregario, the trio conceived this freewheeling epic as a series of seemingly improvised, but in fact meticulously planned episodes, which explored such contrasting issues as magic and myth, fantasy and memory, time and place, and identity and duality.

Infused with the spirit of *Alice In Wonderland*, the action also alluded to the writings of Proust, Borges and Pirandello, as well as the films of Louis Feuillade, Jean Cocteau and Alfred Hitchcock. But, while some critics protested at the three-hour running time and lack of obvious meaning, others recognised it as Rivette's most mesmerising offering and it has since acquired cult status (thanks in no small part to the fact that the heroines constantly have to consume enchanted candy to make sense of their experiences in the possibly haunted mansion).

Closing with an inversion of its opening, this is a consistently mischievous picture that's best appreciated by surrendering to its meandering flow of images and ideas. In true New Wave style, Rivette endlessly subverts narrative convention and by having Céline and Julie slip in and out of fiction, he challenges the very nature of authorship. Consequently, we're left to wonder whether they are spectators of or participants in 'Phantom Ladies Over Paris' (the film-within-the-film, which was based on a couple of short stories by Henry James) and the fact that they ultimately find themselves in custody of young Madlyn (the child that Bulle Ogier and Marie-France Pisier seem prepared to murder in order to wed her widowed father, Barbet Schroeder) only further blurs the line between the real and the imagined, the lived and the dreamed. ★★★★ **DP**

CENTRAL STATION (CENTRAL DO BASIL) (1998)

Starring: *Fernanda Montenegro (Dora), Marilia Pera (Irene), Vinicius de Oliveira (Josue), Soia Lira (Ana), Othon Bastos (Bastos), Otavio Augusto (Pedrao)*
Director: *Walter Salles*
Screenwriters: *Joao Emanuel Carneiro, Marcos Berstein, based on an original idea by Walter Salles*
15/115 mins./Drama/Brazil

A former schoolteacher works in the Central Station in Rio, writing and mailing letters from illiterate customers. While she despises her customers, she is moved to take care of one, a young boy whose mother is killed in an accident. Together, they set off to find his long-lost father.

This poignant road movie from documentary filmmaker Salles was nominated for two Oscars, having already won Berlin's Golden Bear (best film) and Silver Bear (best actress) gongs. Featuring the unlikely pairing of an old bat of a retired teacher and a newly orphaned nine-year-old boy, the film keeps the audience engrossed in their yo-yoing relationship as it offers insights into the underbelly of Brazilian life.

The odd couple meet at Rio's main railway station where Dora makes a meagre living writing letters for illiterate travellers; one of these is Josue's mother, who is trying to contact the boy's father. Although Dora has become hard and cynical about life, when the boy's mother is run over, she takes him home – seeing in him a reflection of her own sad childhood. While it never overshadows the central characters' story, the reality of Brazilian poverty is brought into sharp relief when Dora sells Josue to a so-called adoption agency, only to kidnap him back when she learns that it's only his internal organs that will be adopted. Forced to flee the city, the two take off by bus to find Josue's absentee father.

The barbed humour is a delight, with the duo bickering constantly, yet Dora never loses audience sympathy as the misfortunes pile up. She's an offbeat heroine: plain, bad-tempered, hard-drinking, but also vulnerable as she tries to conceal her yearning for love and happiness. Josue is smart without losing his childish innocence, not a Hollywood-style mini adult.

Against a backdrop of beautifully shot roadside vistas, both actors deliver captivating performances in this touching, spiky tale that's also rich in social detail. ★★★★ **JB**

CHANGING LANES (2002)

Starring: *Ben Affleck (Gavin Banek), Samuel L. Jackson (Doyle Gipson), Kim Staunton (Valerie Gipson), Toni Collette (Michelle), Sydney Pollack (Stephen Delano)*
Director: *Roger Michell*
Screenwriters: *Chap Taylor, Michael Tolkin, from a story by Chap Taylor*
15/99 mins./Drama/Thriller/USA

Rushing to make a vital court appointment, lawyer Gavin Banek has a minor collision with Doyle Gipson, a man equally rushed to appear at a hearing to establish child custody. After a vital file accidentally swaps hands, the two engage in an escalating spiral of revenge.

Buried deep in the lower strata of Hollywood's sub-sub-genres is the 'really shitty day' movie. Previous examples include Joel Schumacher's *Falling Down*, Walter Hill's *The Warriors* and Martin Scorsese's underrated *After Hours*. The rules are simple: take one or more characters whose plans for the next 24 hours seem pretty simple, add one random and apparently insignificant element into the mix – a lost bank note, a traffic jam – and watch their lives unravel like so many loose-knit sweaters in a briar patch.

Changing Lanes is a superior example of the species. Here the hubristic characters are a father who is pursuing the last hope of his otherwise kaput marriage, and an ambitious young lawyer, desperate to impress his intimidating boss. The catalyst for their downfall is a minor fender-bender on a rainy New York morning.

Screenwriters Taylor and Tolkin (respectively, Woody Allen's production assistant and screenwriter of *The Player*) have wrought an intricate screenplay full of misdirection and surprising hairpin twists. Michell's direction is precise and understated, a world away from the cloying sentiment he drizzled over *Notting Hill*. But what's really impressive about the film is that the two central characters being put through the emotional wringer are neither all-hero nor all-villain, as might be expected from a studio movie with two big-name stars. Instead, Banek and Gipson are stressed, flawed human beings trying to survive the urban pressures of New York at different ends of the social spectrum.

Jackson gives an intense, discomforting edge to a character which otherwise could easily have been a cardboard cut-out 'recovering alcoholic with issues'. At one point he brutally beats a couple of two-bit racists, seeming not to know or care when to stop, and giving the audience cause to wonder whether his wife's decision to abandon him might have been the right one: he's a cloud of nebulous rage.

Equally, Affleck's character is not a stereotyped grasping yuppie. His depiction of a youthful WASP-ish attorney draws on the slight sleaziness he showed in *Boiler Room* and *Mall Rats*, but it's tempered by an increasingly horrified awareness of his dizzying spiral into corruption and vengeance. It may be the best performance of his career so far and he, together with Amanda Peet as his wife, deliver one of the movie's high-points – a restaurant scene in which he discovers his marriage is not built on the foundations he thought. It's as icy a representation of cynical corruption as anything by Neil LaBute, and one of the best scenes in any movie this year.

But, like its protagonists, *Changing Lanes* has a flaw – a precision-tooled Hollywood ending which has all the sophistication of a *Sesame Street* homily. Look, it says, if we could only just all sit down and talk, maybe we could learn to co-operate ... It's a pity, since the film has otherwise watched – with an ironic, appalled fascination – what otherwise sane individuals are capable of doing to each other *in extremis*, and this too-neat ending has the necrotic whiff of focus group response cards and studio cowardice. Apart from that probably inevitable disappointment, this is a gripping, intelligent film. ★★★★ **AS**

CHAPLIN (1992)

Starring: *Robert Downey Jr (Charlie Chaplin), Geraldine Chaplin (Hannah Chaplin), Paul Rhys (Sydney Chaplin), John Thaw (Fred Karno), Moira Kelly (Hetty Kelly/Oona O'Neill), Anthony Hopkins (George Hayden), Dan Aykroyd (Mack Sennett), Marisa Tomei (Mabel Normand), Penelope Ann Miller (Edna Purviance), Kevin Kline (Douglas Fairbanks)*
Director: *Richard Attenborough*
Screenwriters: *William Boyd, Bryan Forbes, William Goldman, from a story by Diana Hawkins, based on the biography* Chaplin: His Life And Art *by David Robinson and* My Autobiography *by Charles Chaplin*
12/144 mins./Biography/Drama/UK/USA
Awards: *BAFTA – Best Actor*

The life of silent film star Sir Charles Chaplin, from his arrival in Hollywood in the 1920s to the final recognition of his talents at the 1972 Oscars.

Sir Richard Attenborough's long-in-the-making account of the life of Sir Charles Chaplin is a film you desperately want to like, but it emerges as a big, shiny, old-fashioned biopic that ultimately fails either to illuminate the genius of its subject or to excite as a story. It is, in fact, a rather uneven and unfocused plod through a long, eventful life, from tousle-haired tyke singing his little heart out for the pennies of a cockney crowd to frail 83-year-old weeping on stage at the 1972 Oscar ceremony.

En route Robert Downey Jnr's impersonation of Chaplin is always impressive – physically he's superb and the voice is not bad – as a horde of actors known and unknown flit through. Geraldine Chaplin plays her own sad, mad grandmother, Charlie's mother; Dan Aykroyd has fun as Keystone king Mack Sennett; and Paul Rhys is good as Charlie's brother Sydney. Many an expensively dressed cipher is variously announced as Stanley (Laurel), Edna Purviance, William Randolph Hearst or J. Edgar Hoover, though they are seldom given dialogue or traits to distinguish their significance in Chaplin's professional or private life.

An exception is Kevin Kline, obvious and effective casting for swashbuckling Douglas Fairbanks, whose exuberance, dash and sad decline briefly enliven an otherwise dull picture of Hollywood. As a somewhat clumsy structural device, Anthony Hopkins is little seen but oft heard as a fictitious book editor, prodding the aged Chaplin to elaborate on sections of his 1964 autobiography. Along with captions of the Seven Years Later variety, he exists to bridge the years with unnatural remarks like, 'So, Charlie, at that time you were married to Lita Grey, your second wife, who bore you two sons, Sydney and Charlie Jr, within 13 months,' while a shot of Charlie's notorious Lolita clutching two infants gives way to Diane Lane's approximation of the vivacious beauty Paulette Goddard.

There are some delightful and striking scenes here: Charlie and Sydney in flight from the police in legally disputed possession of the negatives of *The Kid*, done in the style of a *Keystone Kops* comedy; Charlie in the dark, watching himself, or preparing for *The Great Dictator* by railing before footage of Adolf Hitler, "I know you, you bastard!" For all the love and money that went into Chaplin, one cannot fail to note that the big laughs and choicest bits come with the excerpts of the real Chaplin at his best in *The Kid*, *City Lights*, *Modern Times* and others, inescapably suggesting that the only thing one really needs to know about him is his inimitable work. ★★★ **AE**

CHARADE (1963)

Starring: *Cary Grant (Peter Joshua), Audrey Hepburn (Regina Lampert), Walter Matthau (H. Bartholemew), James Coburn (Tex Panthollow), George Kennedy (Herman Scobie)*
Director: *Stanley Donen*
Screenwriter: *Peter Stone, based on the story* The Unsuspecting Wife *by Stone and Marc Behm*
PG/113 mins./Thriller/USA

When her husband is murdered, not that she was too keen on him, Regina Lampert finds herself alone in Paris without a penny to her name and

stalked by various men who seem to think she knows the location of a stolen WWII payroll. Only the charming Peter Joshua seems to be on her side, but he does keep changing his name.

This is what happens when the director of *Singin' In The Rain* chances his skilful arm at a Hitchcockian thriller. It's glossy, charming, silly, and far too self-aware to be at all thrilling. If he'd added songs it would have been magnificent, as it stands it's a slight piece of star-caressed capering.

Everything seems too playful, there is no peril, even for the waifish Audrey Hepburn bobbing about on a sea of deception after her no-good husband goes and gets himself murdered. With this tone set, the film's procession of murders and rigorous twists are delivered with a breezy nonchalance, punchlines to giddy jokes. It would be macabre, if Donen didn't shoot Paris like an elegant dream. This film is so light it borders on the featherbrained, but the writing is witty and if you have Cary Grant you might as well make full use of him.

Grant was never as fully Grant as in this picture, his dented swagger, his pursed look of wounded pride, his teasing sense of being able to get exactly what he wants if he could just spare the effort. When one particular hoodlum, out of a flock of such thugs, forces him to the roof of a Parisian office block with the aim of teaching him to fly, Grant just shrugs: 'All right, but the view better be worth it.' He's magnificent, but stoppers up the plot like a champagne bottle, no fizz escapes past his prankish grin.

Hepburn is a good match, all jerks and sighs, carrying the sort of exasperated why-me candour of an Earthbound Barbarella, although she's far more chaste. The best thing about the movie is watching them fall in love, a process that would be greatly sped up if he could figure out which side he's on. There is a muddle of secrets and lies to work themselves out, and the whereabouts of a cache of cash her late husband seems to have stolen from his friends (played with offhand callousness by James Coburn, George Kennedy and Ned Glass). But the plot is just motions, it's the wilting of Hepburn's distrust that counts, and the mooring of Grant's waywardness. Just drink in the smooth romance of the movie's most famous line, as a drunk Regina splits open her heart: 'Do you know what's wrong with you?' she asks of Peter. 'Nothing.' ★★★ **IN**

THE CHARGE OF THE LIGHT BRIGADE (1968)

Starring: *Trevor Howard (Lord Cardigan), Vanessa Redgrave (Clarissa Morris), John Gielgud (Lord Raglan), Harry Andrews (Lord Lucan), Jill Bennett (Mrs Fanny Duberly), David Hemmings (Captain Nolan)*
Director: *Tony Richardson*
Screenwriters: *Charles Wood, John Osborne*
12/139 mins./War/UK

The 1855 events that led up to Britain's involvement in the Crimean War against Russia, culminating the Battle of Balaclava, and the strokes of madness that led to the infamous, suicidal charge made by the British Light Brigade against the enemy artillery.

A satirical take on the epic format made popular in the sixties, in that it bitterly concentrates on the mismanagement and upper-class hubris that led to the unnecessary slaughter of five regiments of British cavalrymen in a frontal attack on Russian canons. Tony Richardson, a caustic voice from the left of British cinema, lays the blame firmly at the huddle of inexperienced aristocrats who saw war more as an opportunity for glory than a matter of sound tactics, viewing enlisted men as fodder for their aspirations.

It's so determined to take its vehement antiwar stance, that the narrative tends to lack a driving through line, it keeps ponderously circling the brusque conferences between Lords Cardigan, Raglan and Lucan (an ancestor of that absconded seventies murderer) played with brutish authority by Trevor Howard, John Gielgud and an excellent Harry Andrews respectively.

If there is a hero of the piece it is David Hemmings' young Captain Nolan, whose understanding and experience of the battlefield draws him to contend with the stupidity of his superiors. They, naturally, dismiss his calls to sense – why should they listen to an underling? And with history's inevitable irony, Nolan was killed before the charge even began, and Richardson laps up the symbolism of a hero who is denied even a glorious martyrdom.

It's a long, good-looking film, rich in the detail of the era, taking much of its running time charting the reasons, often dubious, for Britain's presence on this baren outcrop in the Black Sea. War was a rite of passage, an opportunity for fame, directed by fools in big hats, unencumbered by self-doubt.

The final attack is breathlessly mounted, the thunder of shells bursting with horrid power overheard, a constant, thrumming sense of momentum toward death. Finally the camera lingers on a dead horse, a symbol of absolute waste. Heavy-handedness aside, Richardson makes a telling point. ★★★★ **IN**

CHARIOTS OF FIRE (1981)

Starring: *Ian Charleson (Eric Liddell), Ben Cross (Harold Abrahams), Nigel Havers (Lord Andrew Lindsay), Nicholas Farrell (Aubery Montagne), Ian Holm (Sam Mussabini), Cheryl Campbell (Jennie Liddell), John Gielgud (Master of Trinity)*
Director: *Hugh Hudson*
Screenwriter: *Colin Welland*
U/123 mins./Sports/Drama/UK

Awards: *Academy Awards – Best Picture, Best Screenplay, Best Costume Design, Best Score (Vangelis); BAFTA – Best Film, Best Supporting Artist (Ian Holm), Best Costume Design*

The journey of two young British sprinters, marked by contrast, to Olympic glory in 1924. One, Eric Liddell, is a devout Christian running for God and refuses to race on Sunday, the other, Harold Abrahams, is a Jew, who runs to escape prejudice by means of adulation.

It is strange to consider that Oscar glory probably did *Chariots Of Fire* a disservice. The film went from a vibrant, original and brilliantly executed period drama, with one of the most instantly recognisable scores of all time, to being unfairly cast in the bombastic mould of the fastidiously uncool epics. Writer Colin Welland's verbose cheer, 'The British are coming!' would lie across the film like a shadow. In many respects the power and artistry of Hugh Hudson's gem has been clouded by fashion.

The knack that Welland's screenplay pulls off is using the sporting framework of the film as a study of human nature, in particular the conflicts between devotion and identity. Are these men defined by their talents, the speed in their narrow limbs, or are they simply blessed with them? He also uses their level playing field to contrast the humble background of Ian Charleson's Liddell, a man troubled that he should turn to missionary work rather than run, and the privilege of Ben Cross's Abrahams. Thus we are caught up with the characters so deeply their triumphs become vital, and Hudson fills the scenes of running with an exhilaration, a kind of spiritual ecstasy.

This is a film of fire, not a staid period piece trying to pick its way through the niceties of society. The thrill of Vangelis' magnificent score with its paradoxical modernist classicism, energises the ready finery and splendour that Hudson can't help but pour into the film. A scene of the team of runners sprinting through the morning surf accompanied by the composer's soaring piano riff, is a moment of transcendence; images taking on a poetic harmony.

Yet, it is not at all hippish, the detailed performances from Charleson and, especially Cross as the complicated Abrahams, give the film a gritty truth. Heroics are not a matter of purity, they are a matter of out-doing oneself. ★★★★★ **IN**

CHARLIE AND THE CHOCOLATE FACTORY (2005)

Starring: *Johnny Depp (Willy Wonka), Freddie Highmore (Charlie Bucket), David Kelly (Grandpa Joe), Helena Bonham Carter (Mrs Bucket), Noah Taylor (Mr Bucket), James Fox (Mr Salt)*

Director: *Tim Burton*

Screenwriter: *John August, based on the book by Roald Dahl*

PG/115 mins./Family/Fantasy/USA

Awards: *Empire Awards – Best Actor*

Charlie Bucket subsists in poverty, fixating on the town's chocolate factory to disguise the taste of endless cabbage soup. Winning one of five golden tickets to tour the confectionery-creation facility, Charlie meets his idol Willy Wonka and the four other grotesque winners on a journey through the chocolatier's bizarre world.

It's a strange thing, taste. There are those who will tell you, under the misty-eyed delusion of nostalgia, that Mel Stuart's fun but heavily flawed *Willy Wonka & The Chocolate Factory* is an indisputable classic. But where the 1971 Gene Wilder vehicle left a feeling of emptiness after a brief saccharine high, Tim Burton's vision of Roald Dahl's fable of cavities and calamities has the same rich sweetness shot through with the acidic wit that's kept kids turning the novel's pages and ruining their appetites for 40 years.

Charlie And The Chocolate Factory deliciously melds the director's two favoured styles: Grimm Goth-lite and pop-art gaudiness. Burton hasn't been so visually jubilant since he upped sticks from Gotham. Wonka's fantastical factory, pregnant with vibrancy and mischief, stands like a twisted Taj Mahal over the anytime-anytown that's home to little Charlie Bucket, a boy who can but dream of a pot to piss in.

Burton establishes an early mood of cosy poverty; warm comedy and familial snugness shining through the elegant wintry gloom. But when the doors to Wonka's works open, the senses are subject to a rapturous assault that doesn't let up 'til the credits roll.

There's so much imagination flying around – Dahl's, Depp's, Burton's, Alex McDowell's exquisite production design – that a pre-cinema Aspirin is advised to prevent migraines. Oompa-Loompas, the Mr Whippy-headed factory short-arses, sing infanticidal ditties in styles ranging from Busby Berkeley to The Darkness by way of *Hair*. A hot-pink dragon boat careens down a hellish, disco-lit tunnel. A precocious brat is trapped in a Kubrick homage. And as for Depp – well, chalk another one up for Mr Mentalist.

The trust built up between Depp and Burton allows the former free rein to craft a hilarious, yet sinister, yet loveable man-child. Worries that the Michael Jacksonesque appearance denotes squirming undertones should be allayed.

This candyman can't stand children, watching with horror as his factory is overrun, then with glee as, one by one, his junior tour party (an enjoyably gruesome bunch with faces like Quentin Blake scribblings and hearts calcified by sugar and indulgence) meet their comeuppance, before spitting barbs at those who remain.

But a warm heart and a playful intelligence anchor the madness. It's unusual to be moved by a children's movie, but in casting *Finding Neverland*'s Highmore as his guide, Burton finds a soul for his film.

Never has a bottom lip been quite so emotive as when trembled by Highmore, and rarely has such sweetness in a child performance failed to incite a desire to lock them in a cupboard until they learn a little cynicism.

John August's script has taken the fantasy of the book and grafted it to a distinctly unsickly moral of family and hard work over imperiousness and entitlement. And he's added some meat to the novel, too. In particular, Wonka is given a wonderfully macabre backstory, with a dentally fascist father (Christopher Lee) who has left him trapped in eternal childhood, whey-faced and fright-wigged from years locked up with no more than midgets for company.

While there are noticeable omissions from the story – the removal of Charlie's mild rebellion making him possibly too saintly – all are made with respect for the source and on focused course for an ending of August's own invention that wraps up this sweet treat with great satisfaction. ★★★★ **OR**

CHARLIE'S ANGELS (2000)

Starring: *Cameron Diaz (Natalie), Drew Barrymore (Dylan), Lucy Lui (Alex), Bill Murray (Bosley), Sam Rockwell (Eric Knox), Kelly Lynch (Vivian Wood), Tim Curry (Roger Corwin), Crispin Glover (Thin Man), John Forsythe (Voice Of Charlie), Matt LeBlanc (Jason), Luke Wilson (Pete Komisky), Tom Green (Chad)*

Director: *Joseph McGinty Nichol*

Screenwriters: *Ryan Rowe, Ed Solomon, John August, based on the television series by Ivan Goff and Ben Roberts*

15/98 mins./Action/Comedy/Thriller/USA

Three female detectives – nutty Natalie, daring Dylan and ass-kicking Alex – investigate a case that may threaten their boss – an elusive Charlie.

Few of 2001's films had as much pre-release baggage as *Charlie's Angels*, with its unsubstantiated tales of on-set rivalry, hissy fits and slapping. Away from the negative publicity, however, and ignoring the adage that no finished product can survive such hype untainted, is the movie actually worth your while? Well, yes and no, really. While the project's curious must-see factor should rescue it from plummeting to the level of obscurity associated with 1998's *The Avengers* (and, indeed, there's a pungent whiff of that misguided venture about this), the end result is muddled, to say the least; visually stylish, sporadically entertaining, yet all-too-frequently painful.

From the opening sequence, when Barrymore dons one of the most implausible disguises known to man, it's obvious where this is heading: straight down the road marked 'self-parody'. Somewhere along the line, someone has hit upon the notion that all things 70s are so gleefully kitsch and ironic that they deserve to be treated as such. Thus the ensuing action is peppered with one-liners and bon mots, usually offset with a self-congratulatory wink to camera. Yet the script is so unashamedly clunky, you have to wonder how much better this could have been had it focused more on the action side rather than trying to send itself up the whole time. Quite aside from anything else, only Murray – easily the best thing in the movie – truly rises above the level of the material.

As for the girls, it's all too clear that there's a fine line between substance and set-dressing here, given that any attempt by the perky threesome to do the action heroine thing is offset by endless gratuitous buttock close-ups and slow-motion tossing of hair. For the record, Liu stops swinging her raven locks just long enough to emerge with the most dignity, and while Diaz kicks some impressive butt, the rest of the material's hardly a stretch; both she and Barrymore are confined to disco-pratfalls, topless tree-tumbling and solving impossible clues that seem to have come from the Scooby-Doo school of logic.

That's not to say *Charlie's Angels* is without its moments; the fight set-pieces are fast and furious, there's a nicely judged red herring, and the last half-hour, full of beat-'em-up, blow-'em-up shenanigans finally gives the blockbuster-hungry audience its money's worth. But in the end, *Charlie's Angels* comes across as little more than a $90 million pantomime, all but lacking audience participation and a comedy cow costume.

The sequel *Charlie's Angels: Full Throttle* continued in a similar vein, but this time with a bikini-clad Demi Moore as the villain, Bernie Mac replacing Murray as Bosley and cameos from Bruce Willis, John Cleese, the Olsen twins and original Angel Jaclyn Smith. ★★ **DB**

CHARLOTTE GRAY (2001)

Starring: *Cate Blanchett (Charlotte Gray), Billy Crudup (Julien Levade), Michael Gambon (Levade), James Fleet (Richard Cannerly), Abigail Cruttenden (Daisy), Charlotte McDougall (Sally), Rupert Penry-Jones (Peter Gregory)*
Director: *Gillian Armstrong*
Screenwriter: *Jeremy Brock, from a novel by Sebastian Faulks*
15/121 mins./War/Romance/Drama/UK/Australia/Germany

In 1943, Charlotte is recruited by the Special Operations Executive and, after her pilot lover, Peter, is shot down, volunteers to go into France as an undercover agent.

As was the case with *Captain Corelli's Mandolin*, this is a reverent, scenic and problematic adaptation of a bestselling novel (this time by Sebastian Faulks) and a love story amid wartime action and suspense.

The role of Charlotte is exceptional because she gets to combine intelligence with derring-do and moral righteousness. She also has to convey the psychological tension of sustaining a masquerade, as Charlotte 'becomes' Dominique Gilbert, complete with dyed hair, foreign underwear and behavioural tics. Director Armstrong has always done her best work illuminating women who want more from their lives, but this bites off more than a gal can chew. The book's emphasis is on Charlotte's internal journey; on film, she is less self-contained and busier with collaborators and Nazis.

Ultimately this exposes how largely ineffectual her war efforts have been while she's been exploring her identity and heart. Fans of the book will regret that the script misses a few tricks; those who haven't read it may be left baffled by an abrupt denouement. The film has appealing chemistry between Blanchett and Crudup, as well as strong moments – the Resistance cell walking into a trap, Dominique's rendezvous with her disaffected Brummie contact, Mirabel – but it can't escape a melodramatic phoniness.

It wants to be moving and inspiring, but doesn't deliver the emotional punch of those no-frills, black and white, post-War films about underground heroines Violette Szabo and Odette Churchill. Or, indeed, of Faulks' documentary series about the S.O.E. blunders and betrayals that doomed over half its courageous agents to lonely deaths. ★★★ **AE**

CHASING AMY (1997)

Starring: *Ethan Suplee (Fan), Ben Affleck (Holden McNeil), Scott Mosier (Collector), Jason Lee (Banky Edwards), Casey Affleck (Little Kid), Joey Lauren Adams (Alyssa Jones), Matt Damon (Shawn Oran – Executive #2), Jason Mewes (Jay), Kevin Smith (Silent Bob)*
Director: *Kevin Smith*
Screenwriter: *Kevin Smith*
18/113 mins./Comedy/Romance/USA

Holden and Banky are best friends and comic book collaborators. But when Holden falls for another artist, Alyssa, who turns out to be a lesbian, all three find that they still have a lot to learn.

A young, bearded Ben Affleck heads the cast here as a comic book creator who falls for fellow scribbler Alyssa, only to discover she prefers the company of women. Undeterred, he still sets out to win her heart, but finds himself running the risk of losing not just Alyssa but also his best friend and collaborator Banky as well.

While this bears all the hallmarks of a Kevin Smith comedy – from the inevitable appearance of Jay and Silent Bob, through to conversations about *Star Wars* (the Darth Vader / African-American analysis is screamingly funny) and sex – it also has a poignant, thought-provoking side which renders it a cut above your average bland rom-com.

So while the Smith touches are as filthy and funny as ever, there's a deeper, more emotional level to this film that sets it apart from his earlier films. ★★★★ **CW**

CHICAGO (2002)

Starring: *Catherine Zeta-Jones (Velma Kelly), Renee Zellweger (Roxie Hart), Richard Gere (Billy Flynn), John C. Reilly (Amos Hart), Christine Baranski (Mary Sunshine), Queen Latifah (Matron Mama Morton), Lucy Lui (Kitty Baxter), Taye Diggs (Bandleader), Colm Feore (Martin Harrison), Dominic West (Fred Casely)*
Director: *Rob Marshall*
Screenwriter: *Bill Condon, based on the musical by Bob Fosse and Fred Ebb, and the play by Maurice Dallas Watkins*
12/113 mins./Musical/Crime/USA/Germany
Awards: *Academy Awards – Best Supporting Actress (Catherine Zeta-Jones), Best Art Direction/Set Decoration, Best Costume Design, Best Editing, Best Picture, Best Sound, BAFTA – Best Supporting Actress, Best Sound, Golden Globes – Best Musical/Comedy, Best Actor in Musical/Comedy, Best Actress in Musical Comedy (Renée Zellweger)*

1920s Chicago, a hotbed of jazz, sex and murder. Velma Kelly, top showgirl, is sent to prison for murder, and is closely followed by cheating housewife Roxie Hart, who's main aim is to use her prison sentence as a ticket to celebrity.

Chicago is no *Moulin Rouge*. Okay, so perhaps that's slightly unfair. Not every musical post-MR is going to reinvent the wheel, and *Chicago* – the first out of the blocks – sure as hell doesn't. But it is rousing, sassy and hugely entertaining – and that ought to be enough to ensure that musicals stick around for a while yet.

A film version of *Chicago* has been almost inevitable since the show – which was originally directed by Bob Fosse in 1975 – was revived recently on Broadway and in the West End, and it's easy to see why. Every musical ultimately lives and dies by the quality of its songs, and there Chicago holds all the aces. A pure musical, in that there's a song practically every two or three minutes (indeed, the acerbic dialogue scenes are almost rushed through with indecent haste), Chicago is packed with great tunes, from the opening 'All That Jazz', to 'All I Care About Is Love', to John C. Reilly's plaintive 'Mr Cellophane'. Each of these subtly expands upon the movie's preoccupations with the American justice system (where celebrity talks and bullshit walks), female empowerment and the fickle nature of stardom, without beating you over the head. That, for the most part, they're toe-tapping classics, doesn't hurt either.

Yet good songs demand a good cast. At first glance, Chicago's experimental line-up doesn't bode well. Happy to report, though, everyone acquits themselves in style. The guys – Gere, very funny as the impossibly suave lawyer, and John C. Reilly, breaking hearts as Roxie's put-upon husband, croon with the best of them, but this is all about the original Spice Girls, Roxie and Velma. Catherine and Renée.

Zeta-Jones may have started out in the West End, but the singing and dancing skills she unveils are still surprising, strutting her stuff with the confidence of a woman who knows that she's now Hollywood royalty. Her man-eating Velma fair burns up the screen, and to live with that Zellweger – very much the unproven Nicole Kidman of the equation – needs to be on her game. Thankfully, she is. Although lacking the raw sexuality you might expect of Roxie, Zellweger instead concentrates on the character's vulnerability, using her little girl lost voice to great effect. And yes, she can belt out a tune, her singing voice stronger than you might expect.

Overall, there are problems, of course: it's far too stagey, and for a film where the female cast spend 90 per cent of their time in bras and knickers, it's strangely unsexy. But it's first-timer Marshall who threatens to derail proceedings, his TV background manifesting itself in his addiction to stifling close-ups, uninventive camerawork and a strange adherence to the choreography of the stage show. He does try to open out the play Dennis Potter-style, but where a bolder director might have slowly merged the fantasy and reality worlds, Marshall's frenzied intercutting rapidly loses impact. Yet armed with that cast, those songs, and a budget large enough to recall glorious Technicolor MGM memories, even Ken Loach could make this fly. And Marshall is savvy enough to ensure this is a lavishly mounted high time, just waiting to be had. ★★★ **CH**

CHICKEN LITTLE (2005)

Starring: *the voices of: Zach Braff (Chicken Little), Garry Marshall (Buck Cluck), Don Knotts (Mayor Turkey Lurkey), Patrick Stewart (Mr Woolensworth), Amy Sedaris (Foxy Loxy), Steve Zahn (Runt of the Litter), Joan Cusack (Abbey Mallard)*
Director: *Mark Dindal*
Screenwriters: *Steve Bencich, Ron Friedman*
U/81 mins./Family/Animation/USA

Chicken Little has become a figure of fun for the animal inhabitants of Oaky Oaks after creating panic with his bizarre insistence that the sky is falling. But the big-headed bantam's paranoia eventually proves well-founded . . .

The held breath over whether Disney can succeed commercially in computer animation without Pixar has already been exhaled with immense relief, with *Chicken Little* easily flapping its way past $100 million in America. The question over whether it has succeeded artistically doesn't have quite such an emphatic answer.

Disney has, of course, already dabbled in CGI with 2000's *Dinosaur*, which was every bit as visually awesome and ploddingly brainless as its subjects. *Chicken Little*, however, represents its first time taking on the same comic-caper style as its on-off stablemate. It's far from having any of the ingenuity or dazzle of even Pixar's early efforts, but then, it's not really trying to.

Nowhere in this spunky little movie will you find a shot designed to make you marvel at the things they can do with those newfangled computers these days. You could criticise it for lack of ambition, for not trying to compete on Pixar's level. But your average eight-year-old, at whom this is squarely aimed, will be giving that little thought, so much the better to enjoy it for the Saturday-morning silliness that it does so well.

The story's essential slightness is improved no end by the large number of off-the-wall twists it manages to cram into its brief running time (if you've managed to avoid the spoilerising trailer, at one point you'll genuinely be scratching your head wondering what the hell is going on – quite an achievement for a Disney kids' movie), culminating in an excellent action set-piece. The solid dialogue is pepped up by terrific background visual gags and the assembled voice cast is impressive.

Braff, Cusack and Zahn are all perfect for voiceover roles, and that the likes of Catherine O'Hara, Fred Willard and Patrick Warburton fill the smallest roles speaks of the general quality. They may not have the best material to work with, but they do wonderfully with what they have.

Pixar has set the standard for cartoons that offer as much, or more, to adults as children, and anything that doesn't swell with wry wit seems to be now rejected as a failure. Judged by those criteria, *Chicken Little* disappoints. Judged as the children's film it is, it punches winningly above its bantam-weight. ★★★ **OR**

CHICKEN RUN (2000)

Starring: *the voice of: Mel Gibson (Rocky), Julia Sawalha (Ginger), Miranda Richardson (Mrs Tweedy), Jane Horrocks (Babs), Lynn Ferguson (Mac), Imelda Staunton (Bunty), Benjamin Whitrow (Fowler), Tony Haygarth (Mr Tweedy), Timothy Spall (Nick), Phil Daniels (Fetcher)*
Directors: *Nick Park, Peter Lord*
Screenwriter: *Karey Kirkpatrick, based on an original story by Nick Park and Peter Lord*
U/84 mins./Animation/Comedy/UK

Ginger the hen is determined to escape from the battery farm where she and her fellow chickens live. She's held back by her meek comrades – until Rocky, a wisecracking rooster, shows up and inspires them to new heights.

Don't anticipate any promotional tie-ins with KFC for an animated comedy in which chickens, forced to lay eggs or get the chop, plot to escape a farm where they are penned in behind barbed wire in conditions that definitely flout the Geneva Convention. Yes, it's a remarkably well-sustained spin on the popular P.O.W. camp movie, with a touch of The Squawkshank Redemptions about it, too.

With three Oscars for Park's shorts and a barrow load of awards between them, Lord, Park and the team at Bristol's Aardman can claim world supremacy in stop-motion clay animation. Hollywood money has enabled them to create a first full-length feature that is big and ambitious. That it is also very funny and imaginative owes more to love than finance, however.

The film is a tribute to the inspired lunacy that drives people to wave aside CGI, doggedly crafting models and moving them painstakingly through 24 poses for each second of film. *Chicken Run* has 563 feathered and costumed puppets, tons of plasticine, and meticulously constructed sets to set off the kind of ingenious details, endearing characters and riotous gags that made *Wallace And Gromit* international stars.

It also has a smart mix of nostalgia, sweetness and flip modernity in design and dialogue, playing with time-honoured types – a pair of rats to act as spies and scroungers, an old rooster named Fowler who constantly drones on about his days in the RAF and tut-tuts, 'Cock-a-doodle-do-what-what' – situations and plotting. Puns also abound: Rocky is the self-styled Lone Free Ranger, Fowler claims the rank of Wing Commander.

Even the most hardened audience will erupt into cheers and applause for a dandy set-piece inside the pie making machine – a sequence that recalls Indiana Jones fleeing the booby-trapped treasure chamber – and the hilariously spiffy climax. You can't help but love the delicious absurdity and dedication in a film that boasts a 'mouth and beak replacement co-ordinator' among the crew credits. In the same spirit that has enshrined *Babe* as the *Citizen Kane* of talking pig movies, *Chicken Run* is definitely the *Casablanca* of chick flicks. ★★★★★ **CW**

Movie Trivia: Chicken Run

The filmmakers used 3,500 kilos of Plasticine during production and in an average week they managed to shoot 90 seconds of animation.
The Plasticine puppet of rooster Rocky has the most facial expressions (18), whereas Bunty has only a paltry (get it? Poultry!) 11.

⊙ UN CHIEN ANDALOU (AN ANDALUSIAN DOG) (1929)

Starring: *Simonne Mareuil (Girlfriend), Pierre Batcheff (Man) Luis Bunuel (Man In Prologue), Salvador Dali (Seminarist), Robert Hommet (Young Man), Marval (Seminarist), Fano Messan (Hermaphrodite)*
Director: *Luis Buñuel*
Screenwriters: *Salvador Dali, Luis Buñuel*
15/17 mins./Surrealist/Fantasy/France

A man takes a straight razor to a woman's eye. Then, a young man struggles with obsessive desires, hampered by absurd interventions from ants, an androgyne playing with a severed hand, pianos, clergymen, dead donkeys and a doppelgänger. The hero walks happily along a beach with his girlfriend but, in Spring, they are sprouting out of the ground.

In 1929, aspiring director Luis Buñuel and painter Salvador Dali collaborated on a seventeen-minute short which would become the most important film manifestation of the surrealist movement.

It is at once a parody of conventional Hollywood narrative, seeming to end with a happy couple strolling into the sunset, and an aggressive deconstruction, trumping the fade-out shot with a grotesque image of the couple transformed into grotesque human trees. It opens with an archetypal caption, 'once upon a time', and a sequence which remains shocking in the 21st Century – probably more than its imitation in Lucio Fulci's *Zombie Flesh Eaters* – as Buñuel himself sharpens a straight razor, tests its edge on his thumbnail, holds open a woman's eye and, in unflinching close-up, sinks the blade into an eyeball. It's an editing trick, using an animated shot of clouds slashing across the moon and an insert of a dead calf's aqueous humour being sliced, but it's still a seminal moment of film splatter. Buñuel and Dali claimed that they arrived at the scenario, which of course features no dog, by drawing on their dreams and impulses, then throwing out anything which might be interpreted as having a meaning.

This has not prevented generations of audiences and critics from interpreting it as the story of a man struggling with sexual desire and frustration, with his own psychological hang-ups and the forces of society (cops, priests) getting in the way. ★★★★★ **KN**

⊙ CHILD'S PLAY (1988)

Starring: *Catherine Hicks (Karen Barclay), Chris Sarandon (Detective Mike Norris), Alex Vincent (Andy Barclay), Brad Dourif (voice of Chucky), Dinah Manoff (Maggie Peterson)*
Director: *Tom Holland*
Screenwriters: *Dan Mancini, John Lafia, Tom Holland*
15/87 mins./Horror/USA

When young Andy Barclay gets a doll for his birthday little does he know that it has been possessed by the spirit of serial killer Charles Ray Lee, who transferred it at the point of death via voodoo. He also has a deadly plan to escape his plastic confines.

There is something just impossible to buy about this silly horror movie – not that a plastic doll has been possessed by the spirit of the Lakeside Strangler, but that anyone would purchase such an ugly looking toy for a kid anyway. Chucky with his bulbous blue eyes, outsized egg of a head, and blank face is the least appealing friend a child could want. A boy doll? Come on.

Okay, so onto to the schlocks, now so veiled in notoriety that the Bulger case cited a second sequel. But when you look at the original it really is rather tame. The first half, as Chucky (voiced with sinuous petulance by Brad Dourif) reveals his black purposes to his new owner, all happens second hand. He grimaces, and snarls, or grins with lascivious hunger, but the murders are off screen. Were they really thinking they might get a young audience?

Tom Holland does inject a strain of humour into proceedings, and he balances it well with keeping a spooky tone of voice. There are fun movies references (look out for *The Shining*) remixing horror's iconography with this midgity thing. You know where all this is headed, but that it becomes mildly discomforting is credit to Holland for actually framing it all within the genre's well-worn apparatus. Look out (and down) behind you. With its success, a batch of sequels followed that drifted ever closer to outright parody. ★★★ **IN**

⊙ CHILDREN OF THE CORN (1984)

Starring: *Peter Horton (Burton Stanton), Linda Hamilton (Vicky), R.G. Armstrong (Diehl), John Franklin (Isaac Chroner), Courtney Gains (Malachi)*
Director: *Fritz Kiersch*
Screenwriter: *George Goldsmith, based on the short story by Stephen King*
18/93 mins./Horror/USA

In the isolated town of Gatlin, the children have turned to a strange religion, murdering all the adults, and worshipping, 'He who walks behind the rows.' When a young couple witness a murder they head into town to report it, soon to discover something even worse.

Based on a Stephen King short story, this dirt-cheap horror tale of eerie kids and their mysterious worship has a certain piquancy going for it. King was always good at playing on more sensitive notes, and the idea of evil children carries quite a punch. It is a fairly original set-up in a genre dogged by formula, but one that is finally bedevilled by the constraints of budget and a ludicrous monster movie denouement.

Up until then, these hick pickaninnees conjure up a creepy little gothic pleasure. Led by the doom-dealing Isaac (played with fierce confidence by John Franklin) and ably assisted by the blood thirsty Malachi keen with a scythe, they feed off of King's religious context (just listen to those names); loosely the film conducts an inspection of the lurid influence religion can have on inexperienced minds. Linda Hamilton and Peter Horton do well in pretty standard roles, the couple who step off the beaten track and right into Hell's high school. Trapped by these knife-clad peddlers of arch mumbo-jumbo, they vainly try to run for it, but those fields, ripe with corn, don't look too safe.

It's ragged round the edges, but then Fritz Kiersch is working with a budget Roger Corman would laugh at, and he does a good job. Keeping the big reveal until late, he uses POV shots to plot the movement of 'He', there is an icy dread in the flailing attempts of this couple to best a group of children. But, sad to say, it will all come crashing down around his ears, no pun intended, when he has to bring it all to a heart-stopping crescendo.

The effects are phoney, anticipated by the weakest storm in movie history, a rubbery beastie that tunnels in the earth – it might have been better to keep him hidden. You tune out laughing, and all the hard work is undone. King sneered and ignored it. But, its success on video would lead to no fewer than six sequels, none of which are worth watching. ★★★ **IN**

⊙ CHIMES AT MIDNIGHT (1966)

Starring: *Orson Welles (Sir John 'Jack' Falstaff), Keith Baxter (Prince Hal), John Gielgud (King Henry IV), Margaret Rutherford (Mistress Quickly), Jeanne Moreau (Doll Tearsheet), Norman Rodway (Henry Percy – Hotspur)*
Director: *Orson Welles*
Screenwriter: *Orson Welles, based upon the plays* Henry IV Parts I and II, Henry V, Richard III and The Merry Wives Of Windsor *by William Shakespeare and* The Chronicles Of England *by Raphael Holinshed*
U/116 mins./Drama/Spain/Switzerland

Although insurrection threatens the throne of his father, Henry IV, Prince Hal devotes himself to carousing with shiftless knight Sir John Falstaff. But when power comes within his grasp, he cruelly abandons the old man to his fate.

Orson Welles first played Falstaff in a school production and his fascination with the incorrigible rogue inspired the bold attempt to meld eight

Shakespearean plays into the stage epic *Five Kings*, which bankrupted the Mercury Theatre in 1939. Twenty-one years later, Welles opened in Belfast with the equally ambitious *Chimes At Midnight*, which combined elements from *Richard II*, both parts of *Henry IV*, *Henry V* and *The Merry Wives Of Windsor* with extracts from Holinshed's *Chronicle* to create a lament for the passing of Merrie England.

However, this study of maverick potential being crushed by Machiavellian pragmatism was very much about Welles himself, who clearly equated the Lancastrian monarchy with the Hollywood studio system that had cast him adrift. Moreover, it's possible to draw comparisons between Welles's final triumph and his first, as the disappointment and dejection that Falstaff feels in his old age recalls that of Charles Foster Kane after the failure of his bid to mentor Susan Alexander.

What's even more apparent is that, despite his customary battles with budgets and schedules, Welles had lost none of his vitality, either as an actor or director. Having burst through the screen as the reckless roister-doister, his display of quiet dejection as Hal severs his ties is deeply touching, while the use of a moving, deep-focused camera around the Spanish sets and locations is sublime. What's more, the depiction of the confusion and carnality of combat in the Battle of Shrewsbury sequence (which took three weeks to edit) ranks alongside anything achieved by Eisenstein or Kurosawa.

Yet, there are flaws here. The soundtrack is often indistinct and the poor synchronisation is as distracting as the stylistic clashes between the meticulously mannered John Gielgud, the laconic Keith Baxter, the fulsome Margaret Rutherford (as Mistress Quickly) and the anachronistically modern Jeanne Moreau (as Doll Tearsheet). But nothing detracts from the melancholic majesty of this maligned masterpiece. ★★★★★ **DP**

THE CHINA SYNDROME (1979)

Starring: *Jane Fonda (Kimberly Wells), Jack Lemmon (Jack Godell), Michael Douglas (Richard Adams), Scott Brady (Herman De Young), James Hampton (Bill Gibson), Peter Donat (Don Jacovich)*
Director: *James Bridges*
Screenwriters: *Mike Gray, T.S. Cook, James Bridges*
PG/122 mins./Drama/USA

Awards: *BAFTA – Best Actor, Best Actress*

Covering a simple story about alternative energy sources at a nuclear power plant, TV reporter Kimberly Wells witnesses what could be a safety breach. But, as she strives to bring the story to light, she finds herself caught up in a conspiracy to cover up the incident.

Thirteen days after this meaty conspiracy thriller, with both the mismanagement of risky power sources and the responsibility of the media in its sightlines, came out it became eerily prophetic. Disaster struck for real at the nuclear plant at Three Mile Island, and the film shifted from paranoid to realistic virtually overnight. An event that has skewed the general view of James Bridges' toward being something of a disaster movie. It isn't really, having more in common with such testy modern parables as *Network* and *The Insider*.

Hence, it owes most of its power to the seriousness of the performances. Jane Fonda, at the height of her political clamouring, works beautifully as the anchorwoman stuck in dead donkey stories, hoping to pick up some hard news credentials with a series on new energy sources. When she, and freelance cameraman Michael Douglas, surreptitiously capture a breach of safety standards – beautifully shot through rippling coffee cups and urgent red lights – she thinks she's hit career paydirt.

The clincher for her story is Jack Lemmon's nervy plant manager. In one of his great straight roles, with that sharp-flavoured mix of hangdog and justly determined, Lemmon is the true believer confronting the cracking of his faith – his slow turn to whistle-blower one of the main dramatic strands.

The 70s may have been ebbing away, but Bridges keeps the film in tune with the era's air of mistrust, shooting the movie with documentary stillness and clarity, mixing this with the futuristic sterility of the plant itself. Technology, as ever, is examined through a pessimistic prism, but the script is equipped with enough jargon and detail to expose the work and responsibility of the filmmakers. The underlying message is that it is human complacency more than anything that undoes noble scientific endeavour.

The final third captures an emotional power, ironically every bit as powerful as the nuclear equivalent, as the humanity both fights the cause and ushers in deception and cover-up. ★★★★ **IN**

CHINATOWN (1974)

Starring: *Jack Nicholson (J.J. Gittes), Faye Dunaway (Evelyn Mulwray), John Huston (Noah Cross), Perry Lopez (Escobar), John Hillerman (Yellburton), Diane Ladd (Ida Sessions), Roman Polanski (Man With Knife)*
Director: *Roman Polanski*
Screenwriter: *Robert Towne*
15/131 mins./Mystery/USA

Awards: *Academy Awards – Best Screenplay, BAFTA – Best Actor, Best Direction, Best Screenplay, Golden Globes – Best Director, Best Drama, Best Actor, Drama*

A private detective investigating an adultery case stumbles on to a scheme of murder that has something to do with water.

Screenwriter Robert Towne's status as a Hollywood sage was achieved largely through his reputation as a script doctor and consultant. But a trio of breakthrough, credited scripts – written specifically for two actor friends – remain his most tangible achievement. These were *Shampoo* for Warren Beatty, and, for Jack Nicholson, *The Last Detail* and *Chinatown*.

Chinatown, Towne's finest two hours (for which he won the film's only Oscar, Best Original Screenplay, in a year dominated by *The Godfather Part II*), is an LA story of the 1930s, a political conspiracy noir thriller and a complex, hard-boiled detective mystery in the Raymond Chandler/Dashiell Hammett line. A sophisticated film that covered everyone involved in glory, including the audiences who responded appreciatively to the dense, demanding and dark story line. Private eye J.J. 'Jake' Gittes ('Discreet Investigations') is more dapper with his centre parting and snappy suits than Chandler's Phillip Marlowe or Hammett's Sam Spade. He's also more humorous, physical and prosperous (with associates Duffy and Walsh as well as the obligatory good secretary). At the same time he is more alienated. Jake is a former cop haunted by the veiled past which climaxed in an unspecified crisis when he worked LA's Chinatown. Elusive references to the district dot the film, but the most that is drawn from Jake on the subject is that, 'I was trying to keep someone from being hurt. I ended up making sure that she was hurt.' Thus the enigmatic title – only in the film's final five minutes do the principal characters in a fateful convergence, get to Chinatown – stands for failure, bad luck, and being out of your depth in something you don't understand.

Jake is hired by a dolled-up broad (Diane Ladd) to get the goods on her allegedly philandering husband, Hollis Mulwray, prominent chief engineer for the city's water and power department. He gets Page One scandal snaps of Mulwray and a young girl in their 'love nest', but the backslapping comes to an abrupt halt when the real Mrs Evelyn Mulwray appears in his office. Jake persists in investigating further as intimidation and corpses mount, because he doesn't like being made a fool of, and he doesn't like duplicity. ('I make an honest living,' he says proudly.) Mulwray and a homeless man living in a storm drain are found drowned in the middle of a drought, Jake sees water secretly diverted and discovers a property scam in which nursing home residents and dead men are the nominal owners of a new empire.

Towne was a native Los Angelino and informed his script with a love for the town and a nostalgia for its coming-of-age, a time when the desert city grew in order to come to where the water was. And water is everywhere throughout the film, from the ocean where tons of it are being dumped to the reservoirs Jake circuits, the garden pond that holds a vital clue and the tap dripping in a murdered woman's kitchen. It is the key to great power and wealth, the tool of insatiable greed and ambition.

It was Roman Polanski's genius, however, that made the film not merely an intelligent and intricate narrative but a great, disturbing vision. Polanski, with his tragically intimate experience of evil, toughened the script up, most crucially in changing Towne's happy-ish ending (in which Evelyn and Katherine got away) to the bitter but unforgettable conclusion which leaves Jake pole-axed, led away in shock by his partners (urging 'Forget it, Jake; it's Chinatown').

John Huston's bluff tycoon not only thinks he can get away with anything – he can. It was also Polanski who observed with a vividly humane perception those collected oddballs, miscreants and victims: the coroner with a hacking cough; the distressed farmers; the snotty little clerk at the Hall of Records; the burly client who weeps at evidence, the weaselly little spiv ('Where'd you get the midget?', played, of course, by Polanski himself) who slits Jake's nose.

That it is very firmly 'A Roman Polanski Film' as billed was completely verified by the belated and nigh unfathomable 1990 sequel *The Two Jakes*, scripted by Towne and directed by Nicholson revisiting his Gittes in 1948 (it, too, is well-acted, complicated and polished-looking, but sadly lacking in the unifying magic). Faye Dunaway, whose neurasthenic quality has never been exploited to better advantage than by Polanski (who gave her – and got – a rough time in the process) is beautifully nuanced as the cool, elegant, Marcel-waved Evelyn whose birthmark, 'a flaw in the iris' represents the heart of darkness in the film. She is presented as a high-class *femme fatale* and indeed her suspect motives enhance the menace and jeopardy until both her anxiousness and her glowing seduction scene are suddenly cast in a different light by the most shocking of the revelations. It is still Nicholson's show, though – his fatalistic glamour and presence as the cynical, wisecracking, impulsively decent snoop, dented not a bit by the ignominy of sporting a substantial bandage over his nose for much of the film. ★★★★★ **AE**

A CHINESE GHOST STORY (SINNUI YAUWAN) (1987)

Starring: *Leslie Cheung (Ning Tsai-Shen), Wong Tsu Hsien (Nieh Hsiao-Tsing), Ma Wu (Yen Che-Hsia), Dawei Hu, Jin Jianf, Wai Lam, Siu-Ming Lau*
Director: *Ching Siu-Tung*
Screenwriter: *Kai-Chi Yun*
15/98 mins./Action/Adventure/Hong Kong

Ning Tsai-Shen, a humble tax collector, is forced to spend the night in the notoriously haunted Lan Ro Temple. There, he incurs the wrath of ghost-busting Taoist swordsman Yen Che-Hsia and falls in love with the mysterious and lovely ghost girl Nieh Hsiao-Tsing.

The first Chinese horror film to get much of a release in the West, though it's a summation of its genre rather than a truly innovative picture. A simple story of a decent young man in love with a ghost gets more complicated when it turns out that Hsiao-Tsing is bound in fealty to a 100-year-old hermaphrodite tree spirit with a deadly mile-long tongue, and is forced to entrap passing men so the killer tree can suck them of their yang elements (turning them into withered zombies who lurk in the basement). The evil tree has promised Hsiao-Tsing in marriage to a particularly unpleasant demon, Lord Black, and that Tsai-Shen has to go to Hell to rescue her.

Chinese ghosts leap around, bouncing off walls and trees like pinballs, and are possessed of ridiculous but deadly appendages like the fearsome tongue featured here or the cloud of long-haired, voraciously gnawing severed heads Lord Black unleashes against our hero. Director Ching Siu-Tung also delivers touching romance, spotlighting the winsome charm and very sexy ankles of Wong Tsu Hsien, gorgeous imagery as twenty-foot veils flutter in supernatural winds while ghosts flit hither and yon, some farcical comedy involving cowardly humans, more-or-less useless sub-titles on the export version (for instance, 'she's in danger' is translated as 'she's dangerous') and even a handful of songs. It isn't quite as completely demented as *Mr Vampire*, but it is truly strange. The film inspired several sequels, including an animated version, and many, many imitations. ★★★★ **KN**

CHITTY CHITTY BANG BANG (1968)

Starring: *Dick Van Dyke (Caractacus Potts), Sally Ann Howes (Truly Scrumptious), Lionel Jeffries (Grandpa Potts), Gert Frobe (Baron Bomburst), Benny Hill (The Toymaker), Robert Helpmann (the Child Catcher), James Robertson Justice (Lord Scrumptious), Heather Ripley (Jemima), Barbara Windsor (Blonde)*
Director: *Ken Hughes*
Screenwriters: *Roald Dahl, Ken Hughes, Richard Maibaum, based on the novel by Ian Fleming*
U/144 mins./Fantasy/Musical/UK

Based on Ian Fleming's children's favourite, this is the tale of inventor Caractacus Potts, who turns a rusted wreck into the titular super car, ready for an adventure into the mysteriously childless barony of Vulgaria.

This justly celebrated and ever-faithful kids movie works so well because it possesses a good deal of everything: light, catchy musical numbers; madcap technology; fairy-tale kingdoms; cheeky, adult-mocking comedy; and genuine scariness. It's an object lesson for purveyors of young cinema – be silly, be clever, but always, no matter how much nonsense is on show, be real.

Divided into two near-equal halves, we begin watching the slow birth of Chitty, a car with hidden secrets, that manages to not only bring pretty aristocrat Sally Ann Howes into the orbit of eccentric single father Dick Van Dyke, but also whisk them off on an adventure into a Germanic backwater run by the demented, but really rather loveable Gert Frobe (who'd made his name as prime Bond villain Goldfinger). And there are those songs to keep things buzzing, Disney-esque ditties that have a calming quality on the breezy mayhem. It's always a surprise, no matter how many times the film is revisited, how anchored it feels. At the heart, it is about forming a family.

The second half, where the car, to be fair, takes a back seat, is pure fantasy. In this tinpot realm, where Frobe's babyish mindset has banned children and demanded that his disconsolate people provide him with magnificent toys for his birthday. Growing up, hereabouts, is something youngsters do not adults. Naturally, he's got his sights set on Chitty, and has sent out his child catcher to capture Caractacus' bleating kids. Robert Helpmann's Dickensian' snatcher, crooked top hat and protruding nose, taps such a primal vein, he has become an iconic emblem of a child's latent fear; the bogeyman of a million nightmares. He's almost too much, but the film triumphs with a riotous crescendo, as hidden packs of urchins are freed to bring everything crashing down the upper classes' idiotic ears – the film is interestingly class critical.

A vivid, splendid ride, director Ken Hughes washes the tale in primary colours, delicious scenery and an easy eccentricity. The names alone – Caractacus Potts, Truly Scrumptious, Baron Bomburst – carry the kind of rich, onomatopoeic tickle of Roald Dahl, who not coincidentally lent a hand with the screenplay. ★★★★ **IN**

CHOCOLAT (2000)

Starring: *Juliette Binoche (Vianne Rocher), Lena Olin (Josephine Muscat), Johnny Depp (Roux), Judi Dench (Armande Voizin), Alfred Molina (Comte de Reynaud), Peter Stormare (Serge Muscat), Carrie-Anne Moss (Caroline Clairmont), Leslie Caron (Madame Audel)*
Director: *Lasse Hallström*
Screenwriter: *Robert Nelson Davis, based on the novel by Joanne Harris*
12/121 mins./Romance/Comedy/Drama/USA

In 1959, single mum Vianne Rocher arrives in a small French village and opens a confectionery specialising in chocolate. Although the mayor, Comte de Reynaud, opposes the scandalous candy, it has an inspirational effect on the sleepy town.

The daughter of an adventurous but conformist French pharmacist and a wandering Mayan shamaness, the heroine of Joanne Harris' novel *Chocolat* represents two literary traditions mixed together – the tale of French provincial manners (cf: *Clochemerle*) and South American magical realism (cf: *Like Water For Chocolate*). Lasse Hallström has recently hit his international stride by making films of slightly off-beat literary efforts: his last was John Irving's *The Cider House Rules*, and *Chocolat* was followed by E. Annie Proulx's *The Shipping News*. Here, he brings a delicate touch to a blend of comedy, soap, romance and magic that feels at first like a souffle, but turns out to be more substantial.

The broad strokes are familiar, and might even come from *A Fistful Of Dollars*: a mysterious stranger arrives in town and inspires the downtrodden to rise against the local bosses, who resort to duplicity and – in the end – violence to hang on to power. Vianne's chocolate has a lot of work to do: Judi Dench is estranged from her uptight daughter; kleptomaniac Olin is at risk of being battered by her drunkard husband; lovestruck pensioner John Wood is still unsure about asking out an old lady; and there's the sexual inactivity of peasant Ron Cook to tackle.

As all these stories turn for the better in wry, charming, understated asides, arch-puritan Molina bullies the Presley-loving priest into preaching ever more explicit anti-chocolate sermons, even as he is tempted to more drastic measures.

The comedy, expertly played, segues into romance as Johnny Depp turns up with an Irish accent and a guitar to give the independent Binoche a little love interest, but the heart of the film is the criticism of the heroine voiced by her daughter, who isn't exactly happy with the life mission of wandering chocolate benevolence that has been foisted on her. It's an unusual insight into a familiar story, and complicates the film's path to a satisfying, if not entirely unexpected, ending. ★★★★ **KN**

CHOPPER (2000)

Starring: *Eric Bana (Mark Brandon 'Chopper' Read), Simon Lyndon (Jimmy Loughnan), David Field (Keithy George), Daniel Wyllie (Bluey), Bill Young (Det. Downie)*
Director: *Andrew Dominik*
Screenwriters: *Andrew Dominik, based on the books by Mark Brandon Read*
18/94 mins./Biography/Drama/Thriller/Australia

A biopic of Mark 'Chopper' Read, Australia's answer to Britain's gangland criminal big boy, Reggie Kray. The film traces Chopper's time both behind bars and as he trawls the underbelly of the villain's world, in his personal quest to achieve worldwide notoriety.

Six years of controversy precede Andrew Dominik's debut feature. Two thousand two hundred-odd days of "Ban this sick film!" brouhaha and censorship politics. And as to whether the result was worth the wait, the answer comes as a resounding 'yes'.

Misguidedly being heralded along *Natural Born Killers* lines, this bleak character study in fact owes credit to an altogether more sinister inspiration. For while admittedly adopting Oliver Stone's stance of 'non-judgmentalism', Dominik discards the colour-saturated, stylistic pyrotechnics for a gritty feel far more reflective of John McNaughton's unsparing, unrelenting exercise in abject objectivity, *Henry: Portrait Of A Serial Killer*.

In each film, events stem from fact not fiction, rendering them even more horrifying. Yet by treating his eponymous, real-life antihero with exactly the same documentary technique as McNaughton, Dominik dispenses with comment and opinion – simply sitting back and allowing the camera and its, frankly insane, subject free rein (and rope to hang himself). After all, let's make no mistake, 'Chopper' is mad.

Portrayed by Australian comic Bana – a brave casting decision that pays off admirably – with an understated neurosis bordering on split-personality disorder, the shameless self-publicist – now with no fewer than ten books to his name – goes about his business with brutal efficiency. Indeed, even if he does apologise to his victims in the bloody aftermath (usually too late for them to actually hear it), he justifies himself as being a self-styled vigilante ridding the underworld of its less desirable clientele.

Bana – who underwent a reverse Tom Hanks/*Cast Away* rapid weight gain before filming the post-prison second half – is a genuine tour de force. But, in the suspense stakes, as his physique balloons, so too does the story's focus. A lean first half – containing the infamous 'ear-slicing' sequence (think *Reservoir Dogs* and then some) – is superb, often lingering on the action far too long to be comfortable, whereas a final reel padded with extraneous exposition manages to somewhat dull an otherwise polished package. ★★★★ **MD**

CHRISTINE (1983)

Starring: *Keith Gordon (Arnie Cunningham), John Stockwell (Dennis Guilder), Alexandra Paul (Leigh Cabot), Robert Prosky (Will Darnell), Harry Dean Stanton (Rudolph Junkins)*
Director: *John Carpenter*
Screenwriter: *Bill Phillips, based on the novel by Stephen King*
18/110 mins./Horror/USA

School misfit Arnie Cunningham falls under the influence of a sleek, red, murderous '50s Plymouth Fury, a supernaturally-empowered car which regenerates itself when trashed and enjoys tormenting its victims with blasts of rock 'n' roll.

Adapted from the Stephen King 'killer car' novel, this John Carpenter film is more like an assembly line vehicle than a customised job, but is nevertheless a slick, entertaining piece of work. Keith Gordon, whose transformation from tongue-tied, bespectacled zit factory to smooth girl-getter is weirdly reminiscent of Jerry Lewis in *The Nutty Professor*, brings a much-needed touch of humanity to the formulaic horror-in-high-school plotline (which King reprised from *Carrie*), in which a succession of slobbish, nasty, dislikable characters who pick on poor Arnie or dare to inconvenience his car are gorily done away with by the supercool, super-malicious Christine.

Robert Prosky, Alexandra Paul (with a fluffy 80s do), John Stockwell and Harry Dean Stanton (as the inevitable puzzled cop) head a good supporting cast, but the car, of course, steals the picture, rolling off the production line to the tune of *Bad To The Bone* and periodically recovering from write-off accidents via impressive special effects. Made back when every single King best-seller was turned into a violent, profane mid-budget movie directed by a horror hotshot rather than a blanded-out TV mini-series, this is one of those films which seemed ordinary in the cinema, but plays much better on TV, DVD or video.

It is at least a well-made, well-played, satisfyingly gruesome thoroughly ordinary picture – and is certainly far better than latterday Carpenter films like *Vampires* or *Ghosts Of Mars*.

You also get a compilation album's worth of great blasts from the past to go along with the death and destruction, including witty gags like the car thief blasted away with *You Keep A-Knocking But You Can't Come In*. ★★★ **KN**

◑ THE CHRONICLES OF NARNIA (2005)

Starring: *Georgie Henley (Lucy Pevensie), Skandar Keynes (Edmund Pevensie), William Moseley (Peter Pevensie), Tilda Swinton (White Witch), James McAvoy (Mr. Tumnus, the Faun), Jim Broadbent (Professor Kirke)*
Director: *Andrew Adamson*
Screenwriters: *Ann Peacock, Andrew Adamson, based on the book by C.S. Lewis*
PG/140 mins./Fanstasy/Adventure/Family/USA
Awards: *Academy Awards – Best Make-up, BAFTA – Best Hair/Make-up*

To escape the horrors of the Blitz, the Pevensie children are packed off to live with eccentric Professor Kirke. While playing in his mansion, they discover a wardrobe that provides a portal to the magical world of Narnia. Cue wicked witches, Turkish Delight, talking wolves and a huge smack down to decide the fate of a kingdom.

Bombarded by a whole blitzkrieg of meeja attention positing, 'Is it the new *Potter/Rings/Krull*?' (delete where applicable), it comes as something of a surprise that Disney's take on C. S. Lewis' kiddie classic is its own beast entirely. More streamlined than *Potter* and less compelling than *Rings* (let's not mention *Krull*), *Narnia* hits all the right bases, but ultimately doesn't fuel the blood and fire the imagination enough to create the movie *Narnia* of our dreams.

Unlike the directors of the *Potter* flicks, director/co-writer Andrew Adamson isn't bogged down by having too much plot to wade through, and there is a sense of directness and narrative neatness about *Narnia* that Rowling's cinematic outings have lacked. Indeed, he takes more chances with his source material. Some of the additions come off a treat – as Peter boards the train for the country, his shared moment with a young World War II Tommy is a touching foreshadow of his own destiny as a warrior – although others, like an action set-piece in which our heroes have to cross an iced-over waterfall while being pursued by the lupine secret police, feel more perfunctory. Still, there is less a sense of ticking off Everybody's Favourite Scene From The Book, more a sense of getting on with a story.

The warmest surprise about Adamson's *Narnia* is that the things that caused the greatest concern pre-movie are the things that have come off most smartly. The kids give across-the-board strong performances, with younger Pevensies Georgie Henley and Skandar Keynes in particular displaying impressive subtlety and restraint. James McAvoy finds vulnerable charm as the potentially awful faun Mr. Tumnus, and the mixture of decent CGI and Liam Neeson's Qui-Gon Jinn-ness have lent lion king Aslan a noble, credible presence. Thankfully, there's no aura of tweeness and the film lacks a sense of BBC-teatime-serial quaintness.

If anything, it's too understated. Tilda Swinton is chillingly effective in her quieter moments as Jadis, luring Edmund to the dark side, but has no real grandstanding, scenery-chewing scenes to etch the White Witch as a truly memorable big-screen villain. Her best moment, the film's highlight, is the sacrifice of Aslan at the stone table, played as part primal scene, part occult ritual, finding an emotional gravitas – check the big close-up of Aslan's eye – that the rest of the movie never matches.

What is strangely absent is a real sense of scale and wonder, at least until the climactic battle. Early doors, the ambition is set high – the movie opens onboard a German plane dropping bombs on the Pevensies' house – but Adamson's directorial colour soon goes mysteriously AWOL. Early scenes in the woods feel studio-bound, the queen's castle looks more bland fridge-freezer than magisterial ice palace and, as the journey progresses – from a run-in with salt-of-the-earth Cockernee beavers (Ray Winstone and Dawn French, not as annoying as they sound) to a meeting with Santa Claus (James Cosmo) – there is little to provoke outright awe.

Like most modern blockbusters boasting 1,500 effects shots, the effects quality varies from the great, to the middling, to the poor. But it is only when the movie reaches its final (bloodless) battle that it feels like imagination run riot; minotaurs, giants and dwarves face off against centaurs, satyrs and rhinos, while phoenixes and gryphons strafe the skies. Meanwhile, Adamson doesn't lose sight of the smaller stories within the big conflict. Unlike *Troy* or *Alexander*, this is actually a big battle that you can follow and in which you can invest emotion. If the rest of the movie had the same untethered flights of fantasy, it might have been a masterpiece. **★★★ IF**

◑ THE CHRONICLES OF RIDDICK (2004)

Starring: *Vin Diesel (Riddick), Colm Feore (Lord Marshal), Thandie Newton (Dame Vaako), Judi Dench (Aereon), Karl Urban (Vaako), Alexa Davalos (Kyra), Linus Roache (Purifier)*
Director: *David Twohy*
Screenwriters: *David Twohy, characters by Jim Wheat, Ken Wheat*
15/135 mins./Adventure/Sci-fi/Action/Thriller/USA

Outlaw antihero Riddick is back and standing in the way of a galaxy-wide crusade by all-out scumbags the Necromongers, who are so evil even their haircuts are scary. In the meantime, there is an old face to rescue: Kyra, the girl he saved and then abandoned.

Those without the benefit of having caught *Pitch Black*, the muscular predecessor to this hulking new blockbuster, should be warned that Richard B. Riddick is not a man in touch with his feminine side. In fact, he's a pumped-up sour-puss with surgically reconfigured night vision, dashing around reaping mayhem because in this ghastly far-flung future, popping a chill pill is not on the itinerary. And isn't it always the way? As you're striving to be the ultimate badass in the galaxy, you keep getting roped in to save the day.

Such is Vin Diesel's lot as this beefcake Snake Plissken replica five years after fighting off a herd of alien-bat thingees, now thoroughly irritated to find himself at the epicentre of an inter-planetary crisis. Meanwhile, his director, David Twohy, is busy ramping up the scope of the franchise with demented levels of creative abandon.

There is no end of snazzy art direction, with impressive worlds built out of slabs of baroque CGI providing the playground for a potty-load of sci-fi hogwash about dastardly Necromongers on a quest for the Underverse – an evil nirvana where Chris Waddle mullets are all the rage.

Twohy's universe is a scattershot of cod-mythology refracted from Tolkien, *2000AD*, Frank Herbert and the upper echelons of L. Ron Hubbard's featherbrained cyber-cult, Scientology.

Not that the film is entirely devoid of value. An inspired riff involving an oven-baked planet, with Riddick and crew sprinting to keep ahead of a molten sunrise, plus a sexy bad-girl spin on Lady Macbeth from Thandie Newton, temporarily lift the turgid ping-pong between mouthfuls of prophetic mumbo-jumbo and bloodless head-cracking. The combat is oddly techno-spare, opting for mano-a-mano physicality rather than zappy space opera.

And it does, at least, get its viewers thinking. Why was the hero christened Richard when everyone else goes by such tongue-swallowing sobriquets as Vaako and Irgun? And was that really our treasured Dame Judi enlisting her noble brow to this heavy metal fray? The pay day must have been sweet, as she now has to set Aereon, an incorporeal Elemental who wisps in and out of shape to explain the plot, alongside Queens Victoria and Elizabeth. **★★ IN**

⊙ CHUCK & BUCK (2000)

Starring: *Mike White (Buck O'Brien), Chris Weitz (Charlie 'Chuck' Sitter), Lupe Ontiveros (Beverly Franco), Beth Colt (Carlyn Carlson), Paul Weitz (Sam), Maya Rudolph (Jamilla)*
Director: *Miguel Arteta*
Screenwriter: *Mike White*
15/96 mins./Comedy/Drama/USA

Following the death of his beloved mother, Buck invites his boyhood friend Chuck to the funeral. Buck subsequently transforms a casual invite to visit Chuck in Los Angeles into a full-scale stalking.

A sensation at 2000's Sundance Festival, *Chuck & Buck* is thrilling in the most straightforward sense: you dare not guess what happens next. Like an embarrassing aunt at a wedding, watching the criminally naive Buck track down his childhood best friend, now happily married and unwilling to act like a ten year-old again, is an uncomfortable but compulsive experience for the viewer.

Like some of the year's most thought-provoking movies – *Timecode, Dancer In The Dark* – *Chuck & Buck* is shot on digital video; however, it's not the dim lighting or director Miguel Arteta's shaky camera work which makes for occasionally difficult viewing. The subject matter – stalking, preteen sexual experimentation, social inadequacy – will leave you squirming in your seat, even if you manage a hearty laugh.

It comes as a pleasant surprise to see the Weitz brothers, who scored big as director and producer of *American Pie* (1999), showcase altogether different talents here. Chris handles the difficult role of Chuck by leading with a strong chin and steady gaze, while big brother Paul grabs all the best lines and biggest laughs as Sam, the nice-but-dim actor Buck hires to play his stage version of Chuck.

But this is Mike White's movie all the way. As a screenwriter he has written himself a bold, indelible character, and matches it with a bug-eyed, lollipop-sucking performance, redolent of childhood wonder. The innocent Buck knows no shame and no boundaries, and as his attempts to convince Chuck of their 'special friendship' grow more desperate – and hilarious – he manages to draw the audience in. This is sympathy with the stalker.

While the more politically correct may wonder if the story-line is implicitly homophobic, writer and actor White invests Buck with such unquestioning tenderness that the salient point is surely not his sexual orientation, but his stunted development. He is simply too pure for this world.
★★★★ CK

⊙ CHUNGKING EXPRESS (CHONGQING SENLIN) (1994)

Starring: *Brigitte Lin (Woman in blonde wig), Tony Leung Chiu Wai (Cop 633), Faye Wong (Faye), Takeshi Kaneshiro (He Zhiwu, Cop 223), Valerie Chow (Air Hostess)*
Director: *Wong Kar-Wai*
Screenwriter: *Wong Kar-Wai*
12/100 mins./Drama/Comedy/Romance/Hong Kong

Told in two distinct halves, this mood piece from Wong Kar-Wai follows two cops, who are both on the rebound from failed relationships. Both meet mysterious women and are drawn to them.

'People say a dog is a man's best friend, so why does mine refuse to share my sorrow with me?' Wong Kar-Wai, aided by cinematographer Chris Doyle, emerged as the most distinctive filmmaker of the late 1990s with this elliptical essay on love and mystery.

It's very much a film of two parts, following two distinct threads as neon-lit, night-time stories bleed into each other. The plot, such as it is, follows two just-ditched policemen, who are drawn to contrasting women, Brigitte Lin as a femme fatale and Faye Wong as a less dangerous but equally unusual waitress.

Wong's dreamlike tone and Doyle's stunning cinematography make this strange love story a joy to watch. **★★★★ KN**

⊙ CINDERELLA MAN (2005)

Starring: *Russell Crowe (Jim Braddock), Renee Zellweger (Mae Braddock), Paul Giamatti (Joe Gould), Craig Bierko (Max Baer), Paddy Considine (Mike Wilson)*
Director: *Ron Howard*
Screenwriters: *Cliff Hollingsworth, Akiva Goldsman*
12A/144 mins./Drama/USA

Caught in the grip of the Depression, one-time boxing contender Jim Braddock is forced to support his family – wife Mae plus kids – by working in a dockyard. When his former manager, Joe Gould, gets him a lucrative break as dead meat for a heavyweight challenger, it kickstarts one of the most remarkable career revivals in sporting history.

It would be easy to write off *Cinderella Man* sight-unseen. Co-written by Akiva Goldsman (still wanted for crimes against screenwriting in more than 40 states following *Batman & Robin* and *Lost In Space*) for genial journeyman Ron Howard, this tale of an underdog who triumphs over adversity is, on paper, noble, worthy, dull awards-season fodder. But, like Howard's *Apollo 13*, this pugilistic powerhouse is a beautifully modulated showcase for the director's ability to take a yarn where the outcome is a given and spin the inevitable into dramatic gold. It's a neat, enviable trick, delivered with gravitas, danger and an emotional uplift long overdue after the darkness of summer.The real-life Braddock's rise (the film opens with the boxer in punishing form), fall (the Braddock family battling poverty after the Wall Street Crash) and slow climb back to the top seemingly invented The Boxing Movie Cliché Handbook – from pressure on Braddock to throw a fight to the Raging Bull Flashbulb And Body-Punch Combo™, it's all here – but Howard's artistry pulls you through. This is confident craftsmanship, peaking in the last-reel showdown between Braddock and human bear Max Baer; Howard knows that, by this time, he's won your investment, and has the assurance to play out the final bout at brutal, compelling length.Allied to the filmmaking know-how is Howard's unstinting commitment to the values of his hero and the story's emotional truth. When Braddock gives back the welfare handout after he picks up a huge fight purse, or forces his son to return a stolen salami, Howard – who, don't forget, played that apex of dignity, Richie Cunningham – understands these values intuitively. He doesn't know how to be flippant, ironic or over-sentimental about such ideals – just genuine.

Where the director is less successful is in trying to graft a fairy-tale patina onto the grim reality of Depression-era America, washing what should be down and dirty in nostalgic, fable-esque hues. Elsewhere, the plotting loses sight of Paddy Considine's down-at-heel stockbroker, who befriends Braddock on the docks before transforming into a bitter political activist. More successfully, Howard manages to evoke the mood in telling period detail – Mae (good work from Zellweger in a tricky supporting role) and kids stealing the wood from an Esso sign after their electricity has been cut off; Gould's once opulent apartment a hollow shell, emptied of all the trappings of wealth.Yet what really lifts *Cinderella Man* head and shoulders above genre convention is the one-two combination of Crowe and Giamatti. The latter, as Braddock's corner man, allies his energetic scrappy-schlep likeability to raw, excitable emotions, nailing Gould in funny, moving, proud colours. But the film belongs to Crowe, still the best synthesis of movie star and actor working today. His restraint and sad reluctance turns Braddock from a too-good-to-be-true shining saint into an unshowy, introspective everyman. When Braddock is forced to go before the boxing bigwigs and beg for money to keep his family afloat, you can almost hear the applause of the Academy Awards audience as Crowe sits in his little splitscreen box. His scenes with Giamatti feel like a privilege to watch, and when they're together, Cinderella Man transforms from a good film into a great one. ★★★★ **IF**

CINEMA PARADISO (NUAVO CINEMA PARADISO) (1988)

Starring: *Jacques Perrin (Toto as an adult), Salvatore Cascio (Toto as a child), Philippe Noiret (Alfredo), Nino Terzo (Peppino's Father), Roberta Lena (Lia), Nicolo di Pinto (Madman), Pupella Maggio (Older Maria)*
Director: *Giuseppe Tornatore*
Screenwriter: *Giuseppe Tornatore*
PG/123 mins./Comedy/Drama/Italy/France

Awards: *Academy Award – Best Foreign Language Film, BAFTA – Best Actor, Best Supporting Actor, Best Original Film Score, Best Original Screenplay, Golden Globe – Best Foreign Language Film*

A famous filmmaker returns to the Sicilian village where he grew up. He reminisces about the projectionist at the local cinema, his best friend as a child, who taught him to love cinema . . .

Hands up who's seen *Cinema Paradiso* on the big screen? You may have heard of it, a cheery Italian art film about the friendship between a gruff projectionist and a cute young boy, set in a dusty, WWII Sicilian village. And that it's meant to be quite good. For a foreign film, like. Well, here's a second chance to bathe in the graceful, moving simplicity of one of cinema's great love songs to cinema.

Tornatore hit upon something miraculous when he wrote this tale of romance, between a young man and the movies, and friendship, between a wise, wry projectionist Alfredo and the cheeky urchin Salvatore who wiles his way into the booth. Peppered with moments from film greats – the lyrical syntax of this love affair – the film grows up with Salvatore, slipping from moment to cherishable moment.

Not a false note is struck among the sunkissed Sicilian locations, gentle, humorous performances, and tinkling soundtrack. Assembled with a wide-eyed, childlike wonder, Tornatore taps themes of bonding, nostalgia, community, history and the power of film to transport man into a world of dreams.

Transcending boundaries of arthouse and subtitle, *Cinema Paradiso* wraps you in a tender embrace and refuses to let go. And if you haven't blubbed by the time a fortysomething Salvatore plays Alfredo's long-hidden gift, then you're most likely dead. Don't sniff at its foreignness – this is food for the weary soul. ★★★★★ **DP**

CITIZEN KANE (1941)

Starring: *Orson Welles (Charles Foster Kane), Joseph Cotton (Jedediah Leland), Dorothy Comingore (Susan Alexander), Everett Sloane (Mr Bernstein), Ray Collins (Boss J.W. "Big Jim" Gettys), George Coulouris (Walter Parks Thatcher), Agnes Moorehead (Mary Kane)*
Director: *Orson Welles*
Screenwriters: *Orson Welles, Herman J, Mankiewicz*
Producer: *Orson Welles*
U/119 mins./Drama/USA

Awards: *Academy Awards – Best Original Screenplay*

Media mogul Charles Foster Kane dies in his mansion, Xanadu. His last word is "rosebud", and the quest to find out what it means drives a newspaper reporter to interview his ex-wives and friends . . .

Even people who have never seen *Citizen Kane* know it's the greatest film of all time. Orson Welles' debut has become an undisputed cultural benchmark – the celluloid equivalent of *War And Peace*, the *Mona Lisa*, *Hamlet*, *Moonlight Sonata*, or *Sergeant Pepper's Lonely Hearts Club Band* (the Beatles album, not the Bee Gees movie). But how did it achieve and maintain this exalted position as a cinematic sacred cow?

From the start, the critics were on Orson's side. The Hearst press refused to carry ads or reviews for the film, thus fatally damaging its box office potential (Kane losing something in the region of $150,000), but elsewhere the notices seemed to recognise an instant classic. 'The most surprising and cinematically exciting motion picture seen in many a month . . . it comes close to being the most sensational film ever made in Hollywood,' gushed *The New York Times*. 'Belongs at once among the great screen achievements,' opined the *New York World-Telegram*. Other journalists placed Welles in the revered company of legendary figures Charles Chaplin and D. W. Griffith, saying, 'This one film establishes him as the most exciting director now working.'

However, such hoopla, coupled with a relative lack of Oscars, made little difference to Welles in the years immediately following *Citizen Kane*. Attendant ticket sales and industry cachet would have justified the free hand Welles was given to make his debut, and placed him in a far stronger bargaining position in subsequent battles with the studios. But with neither box office dollars nor gold-plated statuettes for protection, Welles was vulnerable: follow-up picture *The Magnificent Ambersons* was taken away from the director and given an upbeat ending, and his bold ideas for future projects were treated with a mixture of suspicion and contempt.

But as the next generation of filmmakers ascended to positions of influence, they tipped their collective hat to Welles at every opportunity, with Alan Yentob, for example, commissioning a feature-length *Arena* documentary on the great man for BBC TV (which is, incidentally, the best programme of its kind ever made). A critical canon was established with Kane firmly placed in the top spot. The film was named the best ever made in *Sight & Sound*'s 1962 poll, a position it has held with stubbornness ever since.

Perhaps this is because although it was made in 1941, it still feels remarkably modern. Indeed, that it centres on the power of media moguldom generations before Murdoch; takes on numerous genre meldings (detective story, biopic, backstage musical, film noir and a stunning newsreel parody) and rejects linear storytelling (yet still remains both clear and gripping) make it more 90s than 40s. Yet, what separates it from modern multiplex fodder is its old-school magic – showmanship, intelligence and risk-taking crafted into perfectly realised, stunning cinema.

Devoid of the pretension that usually permeates critics' choices, *Kane* unravels with intelligence, biting wit and a real sense of playful ambiguity. The big themes – the perversion of idealism, the corrupting nature of success, the impenetrability of human beings – are carried off with the lightest touch as Kane descends from vibrant newspaper man to manipulative Svengali to bloated, distant husband. While all the cast turn in great work – Cotten is breathtaking as Kane's cohort Leland – it is Welles' own performance (often overlooked in lieu of his other talents) that really grounds the directorial razzle-dazzle with substance.

To re-visit *Citizen Kane* is to experience the infinite possibilities of movies being realised right before your very eyes. The sheer audacity and delight Welles takes in flouting conventions and inventing new ones is what keeps it fresh. It is that unique movie, chocker with great bits – the breakfast table marriage montage, Leland's "girl on a ferry" reminiscence, that camera ascent to the theatre rafters – that solidifies into a totally satisfying whole.

Considering all its appended academic apparatus (be sure to work 'deep focus cinematography'; 'revolutionary use of ceilings' and 'he was only 25!' into the pub conversation), it remains a gloriously entertaining classic. ★★★★★ **RF**

① CITY LIGHTS (1931)

Starring: *Charlie Chaplin (A Tramp), Virginia Cherrill (A Blind Girl), Florence Lee (The Blind Girl's Grandmother), Harry Myers (An Eccentric Millionaire), Al Ernest Garcia (The Eccentric Millionaire's Butler), Hank Mann (A Prizefighter)*
Director: *Charles Chaplin*
Screenwriter: *Charles Chaplin*
U/87 mins./Comedy/Drama/USA

Having dissuaded a drunken millionaire from committing suicide, The Little Fellow sets out to raise the funds for an operation to restore the sight of a blind flowergirl.

Charles Chaplin began shooting *City Lights* in 1928. Convinced that sound was a passing fad, he determined to stick with the pantomimic style that had made him cinema's first superstar. However, the continued success of the Talkies persuaded him to close the picture down and consider whether he should let The Tramp speak. Resuming in silence, Chaplin was further hindered by the Wall Street Crash, which made the risk of bucking a commercial trend seem all the more precarious. Yet, his courage was fully vindicated when this precision blend of slapstick and sentiment was proclaimed his masterpiece.

The symbolism of the movie's moral message was hardly subtle. When he's blind drunk, the millionaire treats the Little Fellow like a bosom buddy, but the moment he's sober, he denies all knowledge of him. These temporary lapses in prejudicial distinction contrast with the girl's total acceptance, as her blindness forces her to base her judgments on personality not appearance. Indeed, it's her innate goodness that prompts the charitable act which ultimately enables her to recognise her benefactor through touch.

Yet, while he implies this happy ending, Chaplin leaves us wondering whether The Tramp is actually going to settle down and embrace bourgeois society. He had already exploited this ambiguity in *The Gold Rush* (1925) and *The Circus* (1928) and would resort to it again in his last 'silent', *Modern Times* (1936), as though he was hedging his bets about if or when the character would return. However, some critics have suggested that the finale's chastity relates to the Little Fellow's Messianic aspect, as he undergoes variations on baptism, denial, miracle-working and persecution in the course of his unrivalled display of selflessness.

Such attempts at interpretation shouldn't, however, obscure the fact that this is a frequently hilarious comedy, with the boxing sequences and the elevator gag ranking amongst Chaplin's most inspired pieces of clowning. ★★★★★ **DP**

⑮ CITY OF GOD (CIDADE DE DEUS) (2002)

Starring: *Alexandre Rodrigues (Rocket), Leandro Firminio da Hora (Lil' Ze), Phellipe Haagensen (Benny), Douglas Siva (Lil'Dice), Jonathan Haagensen (Shaggy), Matheus Nachtergaele (Carrot), Seu Jorge (Knockout Ned)*
Director: *Fernando Meirelles*
Screenwriter: *Braulio Mantonvani, based on the novel by Paulo Lins*
18/130 mins./Crime/Drama/Action/Brazil/Germany/France
Awards: *BAFTA – Best Editing*

In the 1960s, Cidade De Deus is already the most violent favela – neighbourhood – of Rio De Janeiro. Over the years, drugs and guns flood the area, making all-out gang war inevitable. Aspiring photographer Sandro must try to survive and stay clean if he is to escape.

It would be rather cheap to tag *City Of God* 'the South American *Goodfellas*', as if every region of the world is somehow entitled to at least one gangster masterpiece in the freewheeling Scorsese tradition. (Where, you might ask, is the British *Goodfellas*?) However, since the audience for a two-hour-plus Brazilian movie might not show without some strong encouragement, let's make this clear: *City Of God* is the South American *GoodFellas*.

And not just because of the episodic flashback structure, or the controlling voiceover based on a first-hand account of real events. Nor even because in gurning, gun-toting Zé Pequeno, *City Of God* boasts a jabbering psychotic every bit as compelling and unpredictable as Joe Pesci's Tommy. No, *City Of God* is the South American *Goodfellas* simply because it's more-or-less in the same class. And only a handful of movies can make that claim.

Based on Paulo Lins' eyewitness testimony of the bloody turf war which for years raged in Rio De Janeiro's most notorious slum, *City Of God* contains enough indelible characters and unforgettable stories to fill several good films. After some five years of preparation, director Meirelles marshals this wealth of material in a dizzying variety of ways, finding – even after two hours of gun battles – new ways to shoot and edit a sequence.

However, if *City Of God* were notable chiefly for inventive editing, then it would be merely a remarkable technical achievement; but the film's real ace is the kids. Through an exhaustive series of open auditions and workshops, Meirelles and co-director Lund not only unearthed dozens of non-professionals right out of the favelas, they also encouraged them to improvise large sections of the script. The results are right and true in a way that Harry Potter can never be. The scene in which two young kids must decide whether they want to be shot in the hand or the foot contains some of the most powerful acting ever committed to celluloid. Devastating. ★★★★★ **CK**

⑮ THE CITY OF THE LOST CHILDREN (LA CITE DES ENFANTS PERDUS) (1995)

Starring: *Ron Perlman (One), Daniel Emilfork (Krank), Judith Vittet (Miette), Dominque Pinon (Diver/Clones/Stocle), Jean-Claude Dreyfus (Marcello, Flea Tamer)*
Directors: *Jean-Pierre Jeunet, Marc Caro*
Screenwriters: *Gilles Adrien, Jean-Pierre Jeunet, Marc Caro*
15/112 mins./Fantasy/France

Krank, an evil inventor incapable of dreaming, kidnaps children hoping to steal their dreams – but can only retract their nightmares. But when the adoptive younger brother of circus strongman One is taken, One teams up with thief Miette to stage a daring rescue.

Delicatessen, the feature debut of Jeunet et Caro, was such a one-of-a-kind cult item, it would seem almost impossible to follow. Happily, given a larger budget and huge sets, the team dreamed up a worthy successor in this more expansive though no less weird picture. Like *Delicatessen*, the setting is a fantastical alternate world located somewhere between Terry Gilliam's *Brazil* and Jules Verne's France, but this has a more fairy-tale-like narrative. The film hangs on a touching team-up between a good-hearted but dim-witted side-show strongman and a waif-like orphan thief as they search for Perlman's missing younger brother.

On an offshore rig, a renegade clone and his four identical younger siblings (all *Delicatessen*'s Dominique Pinon) tap into the dreams of stolen children, taking the advice of a brain in a tank with the voice of Jean-Louis Trintignant. Meanwhile, in a waterfront city of rusted metal and grotesque down-and-outs, Siamese twin sisters known as 'The Octopus' run a Fagin-like operation, forcing children onto the streets to steal before selling not their ill-gotten gains, but the children themselves to the Nosferatu-ish Emilfork.

Also mixed up in it all is the broken-down opium-addicted owner of a flea circus, played by *Delicatessen* star Jean-Claude Dreyfus, and a sect of one-eyed revivalist cyborgs. Unlike Gilliam, who is clearly a major influence, Jeunet and Caro take care with their storyline and characters, hanging their cherished bits of astonishing business – a flea-cam trip from head to head, the chaos caused by a tear striking a cobweb, Emilfork's attempt to impersonate Santa Claus – on an involving, moving plot. *The City Of Lost Children* is as great a film as you thought *Chitty Chitty Bang Bang* was when you were five years old. ★★★★★ **KN**

◑ CITY ON FIRE (LUNG FU FONG WAN) 1987

Starring: *Chow Yun-Fat (Ko Chow), Danny Lee (Fu), Yueh Sun (Inspector Lau/Uncle Kung), Carrie Ng (Huong), Roy Cheung (John Chan), Maria Cordero (Lounge Singer), Victor Hon (Bill), Kong Lau (Inspector Chow)*
Director: *Ringo Lam*
Screenwriters: *Ringo Lam, Tommy Sham, Jack Maeby (English version)*
18/101 mins./Action/Crime/Drama/Thriller/Hong Kong

Intrepid guilt-ridden copper Ko Chow wants to get out of undercover work and get married, but his obsessive boss gets him to go after a gang who have carried out a series of violent jewel robberies.

Years ago, *Empire* pointed out similarities between *Reservoir Dogs* and a then obscure Hong Kong crime movie *City On Fire*. With the belated British release of the 1987 film, audiences have a chance to see for themselves. You may, however, find the first hour of *City* surprising, in that it has no more in common with *Dogs* than it does with *Deep Cover* or *White Heat*.

The finale, however, is familiar: a raid, Ko gets gutshot, guns get pointed, accusations get hurled. With Yun-Fat as Tim Roth, Lee takes Harvey Keitel's role and there are equivalents to Lawrence Tierney and Chris Penn as internal bleeding segues into a bullet festival.

Aside from the *Dogs* fuss, it's an impressive thriller that lays to rest the rumour that all Hong Kong has to offer is John Woo. Ringo Lam has a different, less cool, more frenetic style of gun-waving and betrayal, with more politicking on the part of the cops and crooks. If you're used to Yun-Fat's calm in Woo movies, it's a revelation to see him here, hyperactive and neurotic.

In the end, Tarantino took no more from this than he did from The *Killing*, *The Taking Of Pelham 123* and *Day Of The Wolves* (a real obscuro), but if hokey controversies are what it takes to get outstanding movies noticed, then it is important to note that French psycho movie *36:15 Code Père Noel* is an exact and superior template for *Home Alone*. ★★★★ **KN**

◑ CITY SLICKERS (1991)

Starring: *Billy Crystal (Mitch Robbins), Daniel Stern (Phil Berquist), Bruno Kirby (Ed Furillo), Patricia Wettig (Barbara Robbins), Helen Slater (Bonnie Rayburn), Jack Palance (Curly Washburn), Jake Gyllenhaal (Danny Robbins)*
Director: *Ron Underwood*
Screenwriters: *Lowell Ganz, Babaloo Mandel*
12/112 mins./Adventure/Comedy/Western/USA

Businessmen Phil, Ed and Mitch are each having a midlife crisis. They decide to go on a two week break to the wild west where they meet Curly who teaches his reluctant new charges how to become real cowboys.

Mitch, Phil and Ed are not entirely at home on the range. This trio of mid-life, middle-class, middlingly-successful city folk have signed on as temporary cowpokes to drive a herd of cattle through untamed New Mexico as some sort lesiure activity (last year's vacation was bull running in Spain).

However, this year the threesome have more on their minds than merely an adventure, as their everyday circumstances have taken unforseen turns: regular guy Mitch feels his life and marriage have stagnated; perennial bachelor Ed is about to get hitched; and the mild-mannered, hen-pecked Phil has been caught doing the wild thing with a teenage employee.

Thus notion of an innocents abroad-ish slapstick gets replaced by the prospect of a voyage-of-self-discovery and the deeply less-than-amusing *Thirtysomething* landscape looms worryingly large. Mercifully though, *City Slickers* chooses to focus on the absurdities of their situations both at home – Mitch's major worry is hair in his ears – and on the prairie – the mumblingly self-conscious 'Yee-hahs' as they set off are a joy to watch.

While this sending up of onset of middle age angst is hardly Allenesque in aridity, it's enough to afford less-sensitive types a good laugh, but still give those looking for a deeper message something to over-analyse, and means that our heroes' eventual coming to terms with life and its values, thanks to weatherbeaten trail boss Curly (Jack Palance in necessarily overly-weatherbeaten mode), can remain a reasonably dry-eyed affair.

Of course, interwoven with this strand of, er, thoughtful comedy, the moments of sheer stupidity are manifold. Every western cliché comes under the cosh – the stampede, the disrespectin' of womenfolk, the fording a swollen stream, the drunken chuck wagon driver, the birth of a calf etc, etc.

And, lest we forget that these guys who Mitch describes as looking like 'one of The Village People' should have more than just tender feet, the scene after the first riding lesson involves icepacks on groins. ★★★★ **LB**

◑ A CIVIL ACTION (1988)

Starring: *John Travolta (Jan Schlichtmann), Robert Duvall (Jerome Facher), Tony Shalhoub (Kevin Conway), William H. Macy (James Gordon), John Lithgow (Judge Walter J. Skinner), Kathleen Quinlan (Anne Anderson), James Gandolfini (Al Love), Stephen Fry (Pinder), Dan Hedaya (John Riley), Sydney Pollack (Al Eustis)*
Director: *Steven Zaillian*
Screenwriter: *Steven Zaillian, based on the novel by Jonathan Harr*
15/112 mins./Drama/USA

A group of parents, whose children have died via pollution, enlist Jan Schlichtmann, a hot-shot lawyer, to fight their case against two huge corporations. But Schlichtmann soon realises that he may have met his match in opposing lawyer, Jerome Facher, with defeat possibly spelling financial ruin for him and his firm.

Studious, ever-so mature and firmly grounded in the eternal combat between big legal issues and moral backbone, dead serious filmmaker Steven Zaillian (who made *Innocent Moves* and scripted *Schindler's List*) determinedly knocks the Grisham out of the chunky Hollywood courtroom tussle.

Commendable certainly, but with the pop novelist's sweaty lawyer sideshows goes much of the fun. *A Civil Action* is all moody debate and weighty performance, deadpan and weirdly unmoving, jabbing uneasily at the frothy betes noires of the courtroom thriller – the moral redemption of the money-grabbing lawyer; the downfall of the soulless corporate no-gooder; the teasing examination of the fallibility of the justice system. True case or not, it's a mystery why Hollywood was fussed about it at all.

The ambulance chaser at the nub is Travolta's Jan Schlichtmann, a hot-shot personal liability litigator who uncovers a potential goldmine in the case of Woburn, Massachusetts, the snowy hamlet whose water supply was contaminated by industrial solvents leading to the deaths of eight children from leukaemia. The movie's opening half plays to form – Schlichtmann and his besuited scene-stealing cronies (Shalhoub, Macy, Zelijko Ivanek) rattling ethical sabres at the devious co-defendants: lawyers Jerome Facher and William Cheesman. Witnesses are uncovered, emotionally charged depositions delivered from bereaved parents (Quinlan is especially prickly) and preliminary legalese bandied about in John Lithgow's voluminous Gothic courtroom.

Then Zallian turns his thriller into a stodgy drama, the case taking a back seat to the trials of Schlichtmann's company's financial woes, the mellow wisdom Duvall beautifully instils in sly old fox Facher and the fudged moral awakening in Schlichtmann's slick suit. You long for the big hammy show-down, all those crafty cross-examinations and lightning quick objections, but it's a no-show – the case is actually dismantled in the complex process of real-life legality. It is a government watchdog that eventually slams the miscreants while Schlichtmann is left broke and spiritually beaten.

Travolta struggles to give the leading man life, never getting to the kernel of his obsession or receiving any emotional outlet to express a troubled mind. Director Zaillian just can't handle the truth, his direction, although magnificently shot by Conrad L. Hall, is stiff and muddled, unable to balance the meaty power of real law with the need for some movie excitement. He ends up relying on the array of top class actors (and a pointlessly oddball Stephen Fry cameo) to develop a human story. And it saps the movie of fizz.

With the dissatisfying fade out, through a half-dozen false promise finales, there comes an insatiable craving for a last ditch surprise witness, the emergence of some concealed evidence, the killer closing speech with all those deviously unorthodox courtroom theatrics. Something satisfyingly cheesy and cliched to take home with you. Zaillian's adherence to the facts is commendable, but sometimes the truth can be such a bore. ★★ **IN**

THE CLAIM (2000)

Starring: *Peter Mullan (Daniel Dillon), Milla Jovovich (Lucia), Wes Bentley (Dalglish), Nastassja Kinski (Elena Burn/Elena Dillon), Sarah Polley (Hope Burn), Shirley Henderson (Annie)*
Director: *Michael Winterbottom*
Screenwriters: *Frank Cottrell Boyce, based on the novel* The Mayor of Casterbridge *by Thomas Hardy*
15/115 mins./Drama/UK/France/Canada

California, 1840s and Dillon, a young prospector, sells his wife and daughter in return for a gold claim. Twenty years later and he has become mayor of a struggling pioneer town. Dillon is desperate for a young visiting surveyor, Dalglish, to bring the railway to his town, but it is the return of his wife and daughter that holds the key to Dillon's future.

Winterbottom's wintry western, as a visual spectacle, is an excellent companion piece to Robert Altman's equally bleak *McCabe And Mrs Miller*. The sense of time and place is brilliantly encapsulated – this feels like a moment in history we have not visited before, and it's recalled in marvellous detail, much of it overturning 'Old West' cliches, to wit: the best realised whorehouse in Hollywood history.

The atmosphere is well sustained. Michael Nyman's score is wonderfully evocative, the sets and scenery spectacular, while the stunning photography, by cinematographer Alwin Kuchler (*Ratcatcher*), is simply chilling: you can actually feel the cold.

Unfortunately, if you spend too long in the cold, after a while you'll long fora cup of cocoa, and there's nothing here to warm the hands or the soul. Winterbottom keeps his characters at such a remove that we are not given a chance to really feel for them. Bentley's Dalglish is impressively complex, but unfortunately he still falls far short of a hero. As an actor Mullan would make for a fine King Lear, but his Daniel Dillon lacks that tragic dimension. As for the women, two generations of Euro beauty – Nastassja Kinski and Milla Jovovich – are apparently sharing one generation of acting talent. Only Sarah Polley, as the bartered child Hope Dillon, opens herself up enough to make you actually care what happens to her.

Winterbottom seems so afraid of melodrama that he always errs on the side of caution, underplaying every scene. In the BBC version they would be emoting until the corsets burst. It's a shame really, because in all other respects, this is fine, fine filmmaking, it's just hard to feel very involved. ★★★ **CK**

CLAIRE'S KNEE (LE GENOU DE CLAIRE) (1970)

Starring: *Jean-Claude Brialy (Jérôme), Aurora Cornu (Aurora), Beatrice Romand (Laura), Laurence De Monaghan (Claire), Michèle Montel (Mme Walter)*
Director: *Eric Rohmer*
Screenwriter: *Eric Rohmer*
Producer: *Pierre Cottrell, Barbet Schroeder*
PG/105 mins./Drama/France

Vacationing before his marriage, Jérôme is encouraged by his novelist friend Aurora to flirt with Laura, her host's teenage daughter. However, the thirtysomething diplomat is more intrigued by her capricious sister, Claire.

As a critic at *Cahiers du Cinéma*, Eric Rohmer had acquiesced in the house denunciation of the literate style of French film-making that François Truffaut had branded 'cinéma du papa'. Yet, the fifth of Rohmer's six Moral Tales is tantamount to a filmic novel. Gone is the spirit of improvisation that had inspired the dialogue in *La Collectionneuse* and in its place comes a sense of meticulous manipulation, as Rohmer appears to preside over proceedings like an author assembling notes and sketches to achieve a fuller understanding of his characters.

Yet, this delicious comedy of manners never feels like a formal exercise, even though Jérôme and Aurora clearly approach their intellectual game from a professional perspective. Having set the intrigue in motion, Aurora sits back to observe like the novelist she is, while the diplomat in Jérôme rises to the challenge of satisfying Aurora's curiosity, managing Laura's crush and proving his own contention that a physical gesture can be stripped of erotic or emotional meaning – all while remaining faithful to Lucinde, the fiancée he loves, but for whom he feels little passion.

Rohmer's genius for naturalistic conversation and the relaxed performances of his exemplary ensemble ensure that this deliciously illicit situation remains charming instead of becoming arch. But an equally significant factor is Nestor Almendros' seductive cinematography, whose greens and blues sustain the heady summer mood that separates this month by Lake Annecy from real life and, thus, ensures that Brialy's potential indiscretions (with all their fetishistic overtones) remain frivolously harmless.

Rohmer pokes gentle fun at Jérôme's attempts to find a rational justification for his absurd contention that touching Claire's knee will not only improve his relationship with her, but also assuage his doubts about marriage. But he never judges him because, unlike other Rohmer protagonists, he's fully aware of his folly. ★★★★ **DP**

CLASH OF THE TITANS (1981)

Starring: *Harry Hamlin (Perseus), Judi Bowker (Princess Andromeda), Burgess Meredith (Ammon), Laurence Olivier (Zeus), Maggie Smith (Thetis), Ursula Andress (Aphrodite), Claire Bloom (Hera)*
Director: *Desmond Davis*
Screenwriter: *Beverley Cross*
PG/118 mins./Adventure/Fantasy/UK

A retelling of the Greek myth in which the young hero Perseus embarks on a quest to stop the Kraken from killing his beloved Andromeda, a dreaded fate decreed by the Gods. The secret to which may be gaining the head of the awful Medusa whose hideous look can turn a man to stone.

The swansong of Ray Harryhausen's stop-motion genius, made shortly before the style was shuffled out of the mainstream into cultdom, and he was too old to spend weeks creating seconds of film. Hence, this long-winded yarn gets away with mangling mythology and some clunking acting from its leads, with the sheer joy of the master's work. Painstaking performances from the likes of the Medusa, the Kraken, a clockwork owl, giant scorpions and Calibos, the be-tailed bad guy, are far more worthy of our attention than the near stop-motion acting of Harry Hamlin.

The reason for giving *Titans* the time of day, is simply to sit back and marvel at its model work – maybe with nothing quite as downright iconic as the skeleton army from *Jason And The Argonauts*, but splendid all the same. The tricky battle with the pug-ugly Medusa (hint: polish your shield!) has a heavy cast of genuine terror. It's a fun ride in that respect, familiar fable takes on a finely wrought detail, assisted by some strong production work from designer Frank White, although he gets rather confused about his historical periods with Romanic-style armour and Biblical looking peasants.

The plot is standard issue questing – solve this bit to get to that, the task-tenets of a computer adventure game with helpful hints from those Gods pro Perseus, and trickery from those against. In a cute visual motif, the white-clad divines move clay figures across a board, playing humanity like a giant chess game. And while not giving it their all, this spread of aging theatrical gods – including Laurence Olivier as Zeus – manage to avoid putting their noble tongues anywhere near their cheeks. ★★★ IN

CLEAR AND PRESENT DANGER (1994)

Starring: *Harrison Ford (Jack Ryan), Willem Dafoe (CIA Field Contractor Mr. Clark), Anne Archer (Dr. Cathy Ryan), James Earl Jones (Admiral James Green), Benjamin Bratt (Captain Ramirez)*
Director: *Phillip Noyce*
Screenwriters: *Donald Stewart, Steve Zaillian, John Milius, based on the novel by Tom Clancy*
12/142 mins./Action/Thriller/Drama/USA

A close friend of the President and his family are murdered aboard their yacht in the Caribbean, setting off a chain of events that leads Jack Ryan, Deputy Director of the C.I.A., into a dangerous confrontation with the Colombian drug cartel.

The third outing for Tom Clancy's CIA hardman Jack Ryan, *Clear And Present Danger* has a much meatier centre than preceding cinematic Ryan adventures *The Hunt For Red October* (with Alec Baldwin playing Ryan) and *Patriot Games* (Harrison Ford stepping into the breach). Overcoming author Tom Clancy's reservations regarding *Patriot Games* – not only did the curmudgeonly scribe object to Ford for being too old, he also dubbed Noyce 'a B-movie director at best' – Phillip Noyce's politically-tinged blockbuster manages to be complex yet surefooted.

Rejecting the simplistic linearity of *Patriot Games, Clear And Present Danger* interweaves two Jack Ryan yarns in one film: one sees Ryan investigate covert operations (known as Operation Reciprocity) to destroy drug cartels in Colombia, the other follows Ryan investigating the subsequent cover-up in the Oval Office. Along the way, Ryan is crossed, double-crossed, sees friend and CIA Director Greer pass away, is nearly blown to bits in ambush and joins forces with soldier Willem Dafoe to rescue the Operation Reciprocity troops who have been abandoned by a change in Goverment policy. (The title derives from the section of US law that prohibits the commitment of American military power except to situations where there exists 'a clear and present danger to the national security of the United States.')

In adapting *CAPD* for the screen, some of Clancy's murky subterfuge has been simplified – Clancy concludes with Ryan agreeing to a cover-up of the operation. Here, Ryan embarks on a rescue mission, distilling the film's intricate machinations to a punch-up – but the dense, arguably over-talky screenplay by (among others) John Milius and Steven Zaillian makes surprisingly few concessions to popcorn munching bozos for a late summer blockbuster. Indeed the sensibilities of the latter two writers make for a good guide to the film's nature, a curious hybrid of intelligent (particularly 70s) conspiracy thriller (Zaillian's influence) and gung-ho, let's-rescue-the-troops actioner (Milius' influence). Politically the film wants to have its cake and eat it as the flag-waving (Yanks quash Johnny drug baron) is buttressed with Watergate-style implications that the corruption in American society goes right to the top.

Throughout, the film's ideology is ambiguous – the montage intercutting Greer's funeral with ambushing troops can be taken as either a condemnation of Greer's principles or an embodiment of his values – but even that is to be lauded in a studio-financed Harrison Ford vehicle. Both visually and thematically, the White House has rarely been painted in such a multitude of greys, unlike the high contrast look of Colombia with its more obvious sense of danger. If the most riveting moments of *Patriot Games* saw Ryan stand before a bank of monitors in a CIA observation theatre watching satellite images of a British SAS hit on the Irish terrorists, *CAPD* is equally enthralled by the notion of hi-tech hardware as a conduit for surveillance and action. Technological ambience seeps through the whole film – the CIA Large Room included the StorageTek data storage unit, a robotic machine capable of storing information equivalent to 50,000 years of The *Wall Street Journal* – but also in one fantastic nail-biting scene in which Ryan taps at a computer to prevent a Presidential minion deleting files on Operation Reciprocity.

However, the film contains superbly crafted sequences of the more regular kind of action. A Colombian hacienda is destroyed by an American's smart bomb. But, best of all, is the ambush on Ryan's American convoy on the back streets of Bogota. Expertly crafted by Noyce, the grenade launcher-inspired melee is brilliantly orchestrated, totally believable and augmented by the powerful use of (Academy Award-nominated) sound effects to heighten the impact.

Yet the film's biggest boon is its action hero. Older, more subdued than Baldwin's hot shot, Ford's Ryan is the antithesis of James Bond: wholesome, clean-cut, a model of suburban virtues. In certain senses, he is a cross-section of characters Ford had played to date; the sensitive family man of *Regarding Henry*, the man-about-town of *Working Girl*, the soldier of fortune of *Indiana Jones*, the dogged lawyer of *Presumed Innocent* all coalesce as Ford serves up his own brand of dignity and moral gravitas. As President Bennett berates Ryan for questioning the latter's judgment – 'How dare you come in here and lecture me!' shouts Bennett, 'How dare you, Sir!' barks back Ryan – it is difficult to think of another actor who could go toe-to-toe with a US President and get away with it. Marked by Ford's ability to make quizzical and harassed suggest gloomy introspection, examples of virtue and integrity under fire don't come much better than this. ★★★★ IF

CLEOPATRA (1963)

Starring: *Elizabeth Taylor (Cleopatra), Marc Anthony (Richard Burton), Rex Harrison (Julius Caesar), George Cole (Flavius), Roddy McDowell (Caesar Augustus), Martin Landau (Rufio)*
Director: *Joseph L. Mankiewicz*
Screenwriters: *Sidney Buchman, Ben Hecht, Ranald MacDougall, Joseph L. Mankiewicz*
15/95 mins/Drama/History/UK/USA/Switzerland

Awards: *Academy Awards – Best Art Direction, Best Cinematography, Best Costume Design, Best Effects*

The life, times and love affairs of the famed Egyptian queen confronting the might of the Roman Empire, first in the noble guise of Julius Caesar, then a passionate Marc Anthony. But in a swirl of politics and murder, tragedy will finally undo her.

Its reputation as a megabucks disaster (it cost $44 million), so lavish you can almost smell the polish, there is no doubting the effort and pomp on display, but Joseph L. Mankiewicz loses track of any human drama amid his giant sets and equally elaborate superstars. The press may have haunted its Italian soundstages, rumours spilling out of an affair to match that of Cleopatra and Marc Anthony betwixt Elizabeth Taylor and Richard Burton, but the film arrived inert, rubbed clean of sensation by the clamour that surrounded it. Things do start promisingly, with Rex Harrison relishing the chance to fill the sandals of the great Caesar arriving in Egypt to claim both queen and country. He ís swaggering and arrogant, and enunciates like only Professor Higgins aught. When the Ides of March bring their unforeseen bad tidings, both empire and movie lose their prize possession. From here Mankiewicz slows the pace down to a crawl. Taylor looks more concerned with keeping her giant head dresses in place than creating some inner life in her Cleopatra, while Burton does that really irritating pinched face thing, as if the woes of the now turbulent world, or maybe constipa-

Trailer Cliches TOP10

1 'In a world...'
2 'In a time...'
3 'In a place...'
4 Romantic comedy trailers that give away the ending
5 'This summer.../ This holiday season...'
6 'Expect the unexpected.'
7 Black screens and brief flashes of attacks to make horror trailers scarier
8 'Get ready for the white-knuckle thrill ride of the year!'
9 'Disney [or whoever] invites you to join them for a...'
10 The music from *Requiem for a Dream, Clear and Present Danger* or *A Few Good Men*

C

tion, were stifling his movement. Their great and, inevitably, tragic affair should be torrid and heartbreaking, bringing kingdoms crashing down around their feet, not this dozy trawl through some epic scenery.

There you have it, Mankiewicz opts for splendour – not least Cleopatra's arrival in Rome on a giant golden Sphinx, a wonderful splash of excess – over action and real drama. The complex political backstory is vague and imprecise, the battles dawdling, the reasons why disaster will be met upon the classical lovers difficult to fathom. The script ran through the hands of a host of writers, but none found a heart (and Taylor would need more than makeup to give Cleo some kick). For four hours this moody, glossy pantomime leadenly plods on, saying much more about the hubris and excess of old-time Hollywood thinking than the burnished glories of an ancient world. ★★ **IN**

⓪ CLERKS (1994)

Starring: *Brian O'Halloran (Dante Hicks), Jeff Anderson (Randal), Marilyn Ghigliotti (Veronica Loughran), Lisa Spoonhauer (Caitlin Bree), Jason Mewes (Jay), Kevin Smith (Silent Bob)*
Director: *Kevin Smith*
Screenwriter: *Kevin Smith*
18/92 mins./Comedy/USA

A day in the life of two convenience store clerks.

Life is hard when you're a wunderkind. Writer/director/ actor Kevin Smith made *Clerks* for $27,575 scraped together after he dropped out of film school. Since then, he's had decent budgets and bankable stars to play with for but none of these films have come anywhere near to matching the low-budget brilliance of his debut feature. Shot in black and white on a 16mm camera, and featuring a cast of unknowns, *Clerks* is easily the cleverest and funniest comedy of the 90s.

Set in the Quick Stop convenience store at 58 Leonard Avenue in Leonardo, New Jersey, *Clerks* tells the story of a day in the life of Dante Hicks. Overeducated, underpaid, apathetic and yet likeable, Dante is Generation X made flesh, agonising over his tangled personal life, while marking time in a brain-numbing dead-end job. If Basil Fawlty was funny because he was an hotelier who hated his guests, then Dante is funny because he's a convenience store clerk who hates his customers. And what a bunch they are.

From the chewing gum salesman who whips up an anti-smoking mob, to the oldster who borrows a porno mag to read in the employees-only john; from the weirdo on a quest to find the perfect dozen eggs, to the musclebound meathead who cruises chicks while ridiculing Dante's physique, all human life is to be found at the Quick Stop. Next door at RST Video lurks the scabrous Randal. While Dante takes whatever the customers dish out, Randal is forever launching pre-emptive strikes, lacerating them with razor-wire wit before they've even had a chance to bore him with their stupidity.

Usually, this is unconscionably cruel, but highly funny, as when a young mother asks for her kiddie's favourite cartoon, and is given a run-down of exceptionally disgusting hardcore porn titles. Outside, friendly neighbourhood drug dealers Jay and the accurately-named Silent Bob trawl for business, with Jay occasionally wandering into the Quick Stop to shoplift or aim friendly insults at the woeful Dante.

The one thing Dante has going for him is Veronica, the feisty girlfriend who patently gives a damn sending the anti-smoking rioters packing, bringing her man lasagne for lunch, and urging him to go back to college. Dante, however, is still hung up on Caitlin, the high school sweetheart who cheated on him 'eight and a half times' and whose engagement to an Asian design major, reported in the local paper, is causing him great distress. The deliciously self-assured Caitlin returns home to tell Dante that she's not really engaged, but ends up having sex in the darkened men's room with the porn mag-borrowing old guy, in the mistaken belief that he's Dante.

To make matters worse, the pensioner is revealed to have been dead for some time before his liaison with Caitlin. As Caitlin is hauled off to the nuthouse, the hapless Dante is dumped by Veronica, just as he has been made to realise, by Silent Bob of all people, that it's she who he loves. After a store-trashing fight with Randal, he finally achieves the blessed relief of closing the store. And the supreme irony? This is his day off, as Dante continually bemoans, 'I'm not even supposed to be here today!'

As an assemblage of weird and twisted scenes from the butt-end of American life (appropriately enough, Smith named his production company View Askew), *Clerks* has been much imitated but never equalled. Typical US 'indie' efforts like *SubUrbia* and *Empire Records* don't even come close. Smith may have merely been drawing on his own experiences of working at the Quick Stop, but the comic vignettes are so cunningly interwoven, and the classic lines are deployed with such unhinged abandon, that you have to concede his current reputation as the Quentin Tarantino of comedy is a richly deserved one.

Tagline
Just because they serve you doesn't mean they like you.

Despite containing no scenes depicting sex or violence (unless you count Dante and Randal's truly pathetic tussle), Clerks has perhaps the most unrelentingly offensive dialogue you've ever heard (seriously, it's that good) and this was enough to win it a dreaded NC-17 rating in the States. Usually reserved for porno flicks, the rating was eventually reduced after the all-powerful Miramax picked up the flick and hired hotshot attorney Alan Dershowitz to argue their case.

Rudeness intact, Smith's dialogue is a thing of comic wonder. As a one-stop catchphrase shop, it trounces even *Spinal Tap*. From Dante's 'My girlfriend sucked 37 dicks!' (Customer: 'In a row?') to the roofer who asserts, 'Any contractor working on that Death Star knew the risk involved'.

Ultimately the film's philosophy is perhaps best expressed in the words of one of the Quick Stop's more articulate customers: 'It's important to have a job that makes a difference, boys. That's why I manually masturbate caged animals for artificial insemination.' ★★★★ **PR**

THE CLIENT (1994)

Starring: *Susan Sarandon (Reggie Love), Tommy Lee Jones ('Reverend' Roy Foltrigg), Mary-Louise Parker (Dianne Sway), Anthony LaPaglia (Barry 'The Blade' Muldano), J.T. Walsh (Jason McThune), Anthony Edwards (Clint Von Hooser), Brad Renfro (Mark Sway), Will Patton (Sergeant Hardy), William H. Macy (Dr Greenway)*
Director: *Joel Schumacher*
Screenwriters: *Akiva Goldsmith, Robert Getchell, based on the novel by John Grisham*
15/124 mins./Crime/Thriller/USA
Awards: *BATFA – Best Actress*

Mark, an 11-year-old boy, witnesses a gruesome suicide, just after the victim has confessed his involvement in an underworld murder. Soon, he finds out that a little knowledge can be a dangerous thing.

The Client was the third of John Grisham's legal thrillers to be adapted for the screen within 18 months. As such, it is inescapably viewed as the latest episode of a publishing movie phenomenon: less starry and glitzy than the previous two, shorter on action, longer on legal wrangling and substantially stronger on characterisation. With its abundance of juicy performances and Schumacher's grip on what made it a page-turner, it's a taut suspense thriller.

The Client of the title is an 11-year-old boy, the poor but spunky Mark Sway, disadvantaged dweller in a Tennessee trailer park with his single mother and little brother. The boys witness a gruesome suicide, but not before the self-terminator spills his guts about his involvement in an underworld murder to the terrified, reluctant Mark. Before long the cops, Feds, press, self-publicising US prosecutor (Jones, serving up his delicious ham) and the mobsters in question all get wind of the boy's incriminating knowledge, and the chase is on. Enter Susan Sarandon, marvellous as lawyer Reggie Lowe, a dried-out drunk in need of redemption, to fight imperilled Mark's case for staying out of the hot seat as a star witness who doesn't want to talk.

Trying to control at least 47 fiends running around, Schumacher does an efficient job at keeping them sorted. Helpfully, they all look like baddies – with Anthony LaPaglia taking the cake as principal mob meanie. Far from being cute, the boy is a pain in the arse, but this is Sarandon's show in which she strikes just the right notes from tough, smart and sassy to vulnerable and touching. ★★★ **AE**

CLIFFHANGER (1993)

Starring: *Sylvester Stallone (Gabe Walker), John Lithgow (Eric Qualen), Michael Rooker (Hal Tucker), Janine Turner (Jessie Deighan), Caroline Goodall (Kristel, Jetstar Pilot), Leon (Kynette), Craig Fairbrass (Delmar)*
Director: *Renny Harlin*
Screenwriters: *Michael France, Sylvester Stallone, from a story by France*
15/112 mins./Action/Thriller/U.S./Netherlands

Gabe is an expert climber, but hasn't climbed since an accident left a friend dead. However, he is called back to help a group stranded in the mountains – unaware that they are actually armed, dangerous and searching for a fortune in stolen money.

A reminder of the days in which Sly's muscle matched his box office clout (those in any doubt consider for a moment the calamity of his *Get Carter* re-make). A superb pre-credit sequence – so brilliantly parodied by Jim Carrey in *Ace Ventura: When Nature Calls* – plays out into the solid action template: from explosive, tense and at times vertigo-inducing set-pieces, to a script chock full of classic one-line clangers.

Lithgow is clearly modelling his devilishly effete, quasi-intellectual antics as head bad guy on those of Alan Rickman in *Die Hard* – the sequel which saw Harlin cut his action teeth – but an overall mood of taut suspense and some nice backstory more than mask his theatrical flamboyance. Worth a look also for an appearance by *EastEnders*' Craig Fairbrass and for arguably being the inspiration behind Tom Cruise's block-busting bravado in *M:I-2*.

Action filmmaking at its best – a career high for director Harlin and arguably Stallone as well. ★★★★ **MD**

CLOCKERS (1995)

Starring: *Harvey Keitel (Det. Rocco Klein), John Turturro (Det. Larry Mazilla), Delroy Lindo (Rodney Little), Mekhi Phifer (Ronald 'Strike' Dunham), Isaiah Washington (Victor Dunham), Keith David (Andre the Giant), Regina Taylor (Iris Jeeter)*
Director: *Spike Lee*
Screenwriters: *Richard Price and Spike Lee, based on the book by Richard Price*
18/128 mins./Drama/Crime/Mystery/USA

Strike is a young city drug pusher whose brother carries the can when a night man at a fast-food restaurant is found with four bullets in his body. But the cop assigned to the case doesn't buy his guilt.

Spike Lee reportedly took over directorial duties on this collaboration with writer Richard Price and producer Martin Scorsese with reluctance when Scorsese decided to pass and make *Casino*. It is hard to imagine Lee was completely thrilled to helm another drama of inner city anger and despair when he is keen to move black cinema out of the ghetto, but he pulls this off, belatedly.

The central character is Strike (Phifer making his debut), a clocker (a street-level, 'around the clock' drug seller), all purpose bad boy and one of a set who dispense dope, brandish guns and have conversations in which 'Yo, man' is the most intelligible remark.

The set-up is a murder mystery. Strike's evil drugs boss, controlling father figure and neighbourhood king-pin Rodney wants a man dead. When the guy is killed, detective Rocco Klein (Keitel, partnered almost silently by John Tuturro) has a surprisingly ready-to-hand suspect in Strike's brother, Victor. But Victor is a responsible, hard-working, aspirational citizen; Rocco doesn't like the way things add up, and keeps investigating.

Why he should put himself to the trouble is the question Strike finally asks for us. And the answer, never articulated, gives us something to chew on. This comes – after an hour and a half of wearyingly familiar clocking, trash talking bad asses, gun swapping, bent cops prowling and general menace – when a series of interrogation sequences dramatically pick up the pace, feeling and meaning to accompany Lee's atmospheric style throughout. The most interesting aspect, however, is the diversity of attitudes and lives Lee and co-writer Price suggest in the community beyond Rodney's druggies – including a mother anxious that her son not be sucked into the clocking world and a black neighbourhood cop continually on Strike's back. Not Lee's finest but intriguing nonetheless. ★★★ **AE**

A CLOCKWORK ORANGE (1971)

Starring: *Malcolm McDowell (Alexander 'Alex' de Large), Patrick Magee (Mr. Alexander), Michael Bates (Chief Guard), Warren Clarke (Dim), John Clive (Stage Actor), Adrienne Corri (Mrs. Alexander), Paul Farrell (Tramp), Clive Francis (Lodger)*
Director: *Stanley Kubrick*
Screenwriter: *Stanley Kubrick, based on the novel by Anthony Burgess*
18/137 mins./Sci-fi/UK

In a futuristic Britain, a gang of thugs (droogs) controlled by one young man, Alex, run rampant – perpetrating rape, muggings, beatings galore. Eventually Alex is captured, subjected to experimental treatment to cure him of his anti-social tendencies, and released back into polite society …

Now it can be seen again, perhaps the nonsense talk that has surrounded Kubrick's adaptation of Anthony Burgess' dystopian novel will finally evaporate. From the controversy, you'd think the film was like, say, *Romper Stomper*: a glamorisation of the violent lifestyle of its teenage protagonist, with a hypocritical gloss of condemnation to mask delight in rape and ultra-violence. Actually, it is resoundingly both fable-like and abstract.

Alex, juvenile delinquent of the future, gets a brief 20 minutes anarchic rampage before his apprehension by brutal authorities, whereupon he changes from defiant thug into cringing boot-licker, volunteering for a behaviourist experiment that removes his capacity to do evil. The 'cured' Alex finds he has made sadistic monsters of his former victims, and is paid back in full. Alexander, the last decent man in a corrupt world, is transformed by Alex's assault on his home into a freak, toted about in a wheelchair by Dave Prowse (speaking with his own Bristol voice, for a change). Even more appalling is the realisation that Alex's old 'droogs' have gone straight by joining the police, channelling brutishness into the service of the state.

It's all stylised, from Burgess' invented pidgin Russian to 2001-style slow tracks, through sculpturally-perfect sets (like many Kubrick movies, the story could be told through decor alone) and exaggerated, grotesque performances (on a par with those of *Dr. Strangelove*).

Made in 1971, based on a novel from 1962, *A Clockwork Orange* resonates across the years. Its future is quaint now, with Alexander pecking out 'subversive literature' on a giant IBM typewriter, 'lovely, lovely Ludwig Van' on vinyl, and Alex stranded alone in a vast and empty National Health hospital ward. However, the world of 'Municipal Flat Block 18A, Linear North' is very much with us: a housing estate where classical murals are obscenely vandalised, passersby are rare and yobs loll about with nothing better to do than hurt people. ★★★★★ **KN**

CLOSE ENCOUNTERS OF THE THIRD KIND (1977)

Starring: *Richard Dreyfuss (Roy Neary), François Truffaut (Claude Lacombe), Teri Garr (Ronnie Neary), Melinda Dillon (Jillian Guiler), Bob Balaban (David Laughlin), J. Patrick McNamara (Project Leader)*
Director: *Steven Spielberg*
Screenwriter: *Steven Spielberg*
PG/135 mins./Sci-fi/USA

Awards: *Academy Award – Best Cinematography, BAFTA – Best Production Design/Art Direction*

A string of strange occurrences suggest that aliens are about to visit earth, and an ordinary man – Roy – is one of the many drawn to visit the site where they will land.

Steven Spielberg has made a number of masterpieces: *Jaws*, *Schindler*, *Raiders*, and *E.T.* spring readily to mind. He has, though, never made a more complete film than *Close Encounters*.

Released in the same year as *Star Wars*, in many ways it did more to enhance the genre, and in the landing of the mothership produced one of the great moments of cinema history. Originally titled *Watch The Skies*, the source material was Dr. J. Allen Hynek's *The UFO Experience: A Scientific Enquiry* (he was the first to establish the three stages of close encounter) and hints of *The Day The Earth Stood Still*. And while the likes of Paul Schrader and Matthew Robbins worked on various drafts and conceptual ideas, the screenplay is credited solely to Spielberg and to all intents it reflects his vision entirely.

Although *E.T.* ranks high, *Close Encounters* is Spielberg's most personal film. Its inspiration harks back to watching a meteor shower as a sci-fi obsessed young boy in Phoenix and his 1964 home movie, the alien-themed *Firelight*, was undoubtedly the precursor. The director himself later described this film as encapsulating, 'My vision, my hope and philosophy'.

It was an arduous shoot. They had six rap parties since endings were constantly revised when the director was inspired to go back and expand his vision (he kept watching *The Searchers* throughout the shoot, which did and didn't help). Overbudget and way overschedule, he completely missed his release date, allowing buddy George Lucas to get ahead of him in the change-movies-forever stakes with *Star Wars*. It was worth the trauma though.

Every detail of Spielberg's vaunting ambition is reflected in the finished product. Typical of Spielberg (and, indeed, redolent of his heroes Hitchcock and Capra) this is a film that focuses on average people: the extraordinary occurring within the heart of the ordinary. Roy Neary is an electrical engineer touched by the hand of God (well, shiny happy people from deep space) thrusting him onto to a spiritual quest that tugs beneath reason and delivers him finally to the iconic shape of Devil's Tower, Wyoming. Alongside his journey is that of François Truffaut as Claude Lacombe (based on famed French UFO expert Jacques Valle), the scientific team leader whose more pragmatic investigations lead him eventually to the same place – but without the interplanetary spiritual connection ('I envy you,' he whispers to Neary, when he is preparing to embark on the ultimate encounter).

Also drawn to Devil's Tower is Jillian Guiler who is seeking the return of her kidnapped child Barry. On a fundamental level this is a film about faith, the need to 'believe'. As with most Spielberg films, the message is powerfully and anti-cynical. Innocence and optimism prevail – the aliens are angelic, childlike, non-threatening. And it is the innocence, Neary's inner child, that the alien beings finally choose (just as they would have chosen Spielberg himself). This is a film without bad guys, the drama constructed out of yearning and mystery not peril.

And no account of *Close Encounters* can pass by without mention of that staggering finale – the arrival of the mothership. In these days of CGI, there remains a holy aura around this sequence. Douglas Trumbull (who did all the trippy stuff for *2001*) created something that tested the boundaries of both the cinema screen and the audience capacity for wonder as the city-sized craft is lowered into the frame and locks itself somewhere deep within the memory.

There are other notations to chalk up. The debate between the two versions – Spielberg laid on a special edition in 1980, although its interior shots of the mother ship added little to the mood of the original. It is the first Spielberg film to truly encompass his preoccupations: children, family, suburbia, and the emotionally abandoned. And then there is the music: the chord progression that John Williams masterfully inserted as the theme to universal communication.

Nearly thirty years on and the approach to alien visitation has come full circle. *The X-Files*, *Independence Day* and numerous aggressive additions to contact philosophy have returned to the paranoid notions of yore, where conspiracy and threat are the abiding themes. Here, in the film that forever sealed Spielberg's reputation as one of cinema's great directors, dwells something else entirely: a sense of wonder, that the unknown can reveal joy, and – akin to the overarching hope of *Schindler's List* – that humanity may actually have a chance of succeeding. ★★★★★ **IN**

Movie Trivia: Close Encounters Of The Third Kind

For the scene where the little boy (Cary Guffey) cries out 'Toys!', Spielberg was in his eye-line displaying a brand new toy car. Amongst the details on the mothership are R2-D2, a cemetery and models of the plane abducted by the craft. The mothership was inspired by an oil refinery that Spielberg saw in India, lit up with a profusion of light.

⑮ CLOSELY OBSERVED TRAINS (1966)

Starring: *Vaclav Neckar (Trainee Milos Hrma), Jitka Bendova (Condictor Masa), Josef Somer (Train Dispatcher Hubicka), Vladimir Valenta (Stationmaster Max), Vlastimil Brodsky (Counselor Zednicek), Jiri Menzel (Dr Brabek)*
Director: *Jiri Menzel*
Screenwriters: *Jiri Menzel, Bohumil Hrabal based on his own novel*
15/89 mins./Drama/Czechoslavakia
Awards: *Academy Awards – Best Foreign Language Film*

Some time towards the end of the Second World War, Milos Hrma, the latest in his family's long line of nobodies, begins work at a provincial Czech station, with his mind more firmly fixed on losing his virginity than doing his duty.

After both Evald Schorm and Vera Chytilova turned down the chance to direct this adaptation of Bohumil Hrabal's acclaimed novel, feature debutant Jiri Menzel accepted with alacrity and won an Oscar for his pains.

Right from the opening sequence, in which Milos describes the misadventures of his hapless ancestors while proudly donning the uniform of a minor railway official, Menzel succeeds in both invoking the spirit of Jaroslav Hasek's seminal anti-war novel, *The Good Soldier Schweik*, and establishing a subversive sense of the absurd that would continue to characterise his cinema.

Played by pop star Vaclav Neckar, Milos is a genial innocent, whose wide-eyed incomprehension of the world around him contrasts with the cheerfully corrupt opportunism of the womanising guard, Hubicka (Josef Somer), and the blustering hypocrisy and subservience of Max (Vladimir Valenta), the stationmaster who is never happier than when tending his pigeons. Yet neither is depicted in an unsympathetic light. Indeed, even the Nazis shown ogling a trainload of nurses are merely presented as adolescent conscripts. Only Zednicek, the collaborationist controller, is denied any humanity and Menzel superbly deflates his pomposity during the scene in which he seeks to redefine a string of Wehrmacht setbacks as strategic triumphs.

Wartime resistance was a sacrosanct subject in 1960s Czechoslovakia and Menzel risked official ire by suggesting that combat was absurd and that heroism was as much a matter of chance as courage. Yet, there is still something deeply moving about the way in which Milos accepts his mission from Viktoria Freie (Nada Urbankova), the circus performer-turned-partisan, who had relieved him of the ignoble virginity that had earlier driven him to attempt suicide in a brothel. Yet, even in the midst of tragedy, Menzel can't help resorting to the surreal phallic imagery with which the action is studded, by showing the erect signal penetrating the billowing clouds of smoke. ★★★★ **DP**

⓪ CLOCKWISE (1986)

Starring: *John Cleese (Brian Stimpson), Alison Steadman (Gwenda Stimpson), Sharon Maiden (Laura), Nadia Sawalha (Mandy Kostal),*
Director: *Christopher Morahan*
Screenwriter: *Michael Frayn*
PG/96 mins./Comedy/UK

When fastidious comprehensive headmaster Brian Stimpson is called upon to travel to Norwich to deliver a keynote speech to a group of elite school headmasters, his tightly wound world will start to unravel. Disaster will follow disaster, shattering his regimented world, but in the long run maybe, finally, granting him some inner peace.

There's no escaping the spectre of Basil Fawlty looming over this well-written, tightly constructed comedy of very British manners, he's right there in Brian Stimpson's righteous indignation and not-so-paranoid assumption that the fates are conspiring against him; the world being just there only to crush his well-earned dignity. Cleese works wonders with Stimpson, giving him a measure of truth beneath the riduclous veneer, but he is pure Basil rumbling with fury as his simple journey to East Anglia becomes a comedy of errors.

Playwright Michael Frayn has a gift with the crisp rhythms of the English language, those fundaments of the ordinaire. Just listen to the names – Stimpson, Leatherbarrow, Wisely, Trellis – they ring perfectly true, even as the nightmare drifts into the absurd. The film rests upon the strain between Stimpson's punctiliousness – he watches over his pupils with the cruel gaze of a Nazi commandant bellowing punishments though his loud speakers – and the chaos of the world that he has held at bay for so long. His own emotions included. The point is to collapse under pressure may be the first step to harmony.

Once launched on his journey, Frayn and director Christopher Morahan are basically playing classical farce: his train will be delayed, he hitchhikes a ride with an errant older pupil (Sharon Maiden), before various farmers, mad old biddies, rival teachers and a touching reunion with an old flame will stand before him and his goal of toadying up to his betters. This is Frayn's home turf, the ruinous twists of fate, he established with the play *Noises Off*.

It is funny in a familiar, comforting way. The gags are obvious but slyly presented, allowing a clever undertow commenting on such local foibles as class, masculinity, ambition, and self (all tribulations set before the great British male) to emerge between the slings and arrows of outrageous travel plans. It is predictable, but in one delicious scene as Cleese eases himself into a warm bath at a monastery (don't ask) and his agony temporarily evaporates, the film presents an elegant philosophy for life – get out of the damn rat race. ★★★★ **IN**

⑱ CLOSER (2004)

Starring: *Natalie Portman (Alice), Jude Law (Dan), Julia Roberts (Anna), Clive Owen (Larry), Nick Hobbs (Taxi Driver), Colin Stinton (Customs Officer)*
Director: *Mike Nichols*
Screenwriter: *Patrick Marber, based on his play*
18/98 mins./Romance/Drama/USA

Awards: *BAFTA – Best Suppporting Actor (Clive Owen), Golden Globes – Best Supporting Actor (Clive Owen), Best Supporting Actress (Natalie Portman)*

Dan helps Alice after a minor accident. After using her in his novel, he's photographed by Anna. Through an internet prank, Dan gets Anna together with Larry, before Larry finds Alice in a strip-club . . .

Mike Nichols has always been drawn to the mysteries of sexual entanglement as expressed in rich, theatrical dialogue. In *Who's Afraid Of Virginia Woolf?*, he stuck close to Edward Albee's play about a nastily complex two-couple evening; in *Carnal Knowledge*, he shot cartoonist Jules Feiffer's original script about two men and their contrasting attitudes to women over the decades.

Closer, scripted by Patrick Marber from his own play, could just have been a smart scrambling of these two earlier films. But it's far more than that, thanks to its fiercely distinctive voice and a powerhouse ensemble more than capable of holding its own against the much-lauded teams of *Virginia Woolf* (a film where the entire cast was Oscar-nominated) and *Carnal Knowledge*.

After the lightweight Lothario of *Alfie*, Jude Law's Dan is a much more involving character; restless and pathetic, sad and sadistic (his internet come-on to Clive Owen's Larry is horribly comic) and an always-crushed romantic. It's Law's best screen work to date, and he provides the anchor for awards-calibre scenes from Owen (who played Dan in the West End stage version) and an astoundingly sensual Portman (playing a pole-dancer and fulfilling the fantasies of too many sad *Star Wars* fans).

As for Roberts, if she's the palest of the quartet, it's because one of the most desirable women in the world invests her role with such a haunted chill you can't imagine Law leaving Portman for her or Owen being driven to such hilariously fiendish lengths to get her back. Nichols and Marber both have a background in comedy double acts, Nichols having exchanged neurotic barbs with former collaborator Elaine May and Marber having been Alan Partridge's all-purpose chat show guest. So *Closer* is a succession of tart two-hander sketches, strung together by wild sex and steady relationships, which skips over the months to see only the meet-cute and dissolve-ugly moments in the romantic square dance of these four people. ★★★★ **KN**

CLUELESS (1995)

Starring: *Alicia Silverstone (Cher Horowitz), Stacey Dash (Dionne), Brittany Murphy (Tai), Paul Rudd (Josh), Dan Hedaya (Mel Hamilton), Donald Faison (Murray), Elisa Donovan (Amber), Breckin Meyer (Travis Birkenstock)*
Director: *Amy Heckerling*
Screenwriter: *Amy Heckerling*
12/97 mins./Comedy/Romance/USA

Jane Austen's *Emma* meets *Beverley Hills 90210* as US teen, Cher, match makes for her friends, little realising where her own heart lies.

On the surface, Amy Heckerling's 90s spin on Jane Austen's novel *Emma* appears to be merely another frothy coming-of-age flick. Scratch below the shiny exterior, though, and what emerges is something altogether more clever, as much a sharp, satirical parody of the affluent as it is hip, sassy entertainment dressed in designer labels.

Silverstone, whose hot status would shame most thermonuclear reactors, plays Cher, 15 years old going on 35, daughter of a widowed, irascible but loaded lawyer and blessed with beauty and popularity superseded only by the enormity of her wardrobe. For her, life is a stream of shopping, gossiping on a mobile phone with best friend Dionne, and using her assets to be top dog at school.

However, while her head may be a vacuum, her heart is in the right place and she endeavours to do good wherever she sees fit: first by uniting two single, lonely teachers (coinciding, nicely, with her attempts to bribe her way to better school grades); and second by transforming new student Tai from dumpy hippy to LA airhead. Only when it transpires that Cher might have sacrificed her own happiness (and potential romantic entanglements) at everybody else's expense does her carefree world come crashing in around her.

Silverstone, complete with pseudo-philosophical voice-overs and a frenetic lexicon of teen dialect ('surfing the crimson wave' may yet pass into common usage) has just the right amount of dizzy charm to carry off lead duties. A spoiled brat her character may be, but a loveable one all the same. And the conclusion, obvious as it is, is heart-warming.

The one drawback is that the teenage leads seem a little too sure of themselves given their tender years, with such dilemmas as nose-jobs replacing more traditional adolescent woes. Fortunately the film is good-natured and smart enough to overcome such foibles, and stands out as a respectable, if alternative, addition to the all-conquering Jane Austen canon. ★★★★ **CW**

COACH CARTER (2005)

Starring: *Samuel L. Jackson (Coach Ken Carter), Rob Brown (Kenyon Stone), Robert Ri'chard (Damian Carter), Rick Gonzalez (Timo Cruz), Nana Gbewonyo (Junior Battle), Antwon Tanner (Worm)*
Director: *Thomas Carter*
Screenwriters: *Mark Schwahn, John Gatins*
12/136 mins./Drama/Sports/USA/Germany

Ken Carter is an unorthodox high-school basketball coach, but while his methods raise eyebrows, the results can't be argued with. However, when Carter benches his entire team after discovering how abysmal their grades are, controversy is stirred . . .

'Formulaic!' is not a word you often see screaming at you from movie posters. It is, however, an apt – and almost entirely non-disparaging – description of this hardworking sports flick that finds Samuel L. Jackson in feisty bread-and-butter mode as a hard-ass high-school basketball coach who moulds his ramshackle team of ghetto toughs into a finely-tuned winning machine.

It's join-the-dots fare but, as any mad scientist will tell you, formulae can yield surprising results. There's added zip here in that Carter's overriding ambition is not for his kids to win the pennant (or whatever it is American high school basketball teams compete for) but to keep them out of prison, insisting they dress smart and maintain academic grades necessary for college admission.

There'll be no surprises if you've seen *Hoosiers* or, indeed, any other sports movie (and there won't be many if you haven't, to be honest). But it's a good story, well told, the on-court action is thrilling and authentic and, let's face it, you'd pay to watch Sam Jackson play a hard-ass clockmaker, let alone a hard-ass high-school basketball coach who turns boys into men with words of wisdom, a necktie and a big old padlock. ★★★ **SB**

A COCK AND BULL STORY (2005)

Starring: *Steve Coogan (Tristram Shandy/Walter Shandy/Steve Coogan), Rob Brydon (Toby Shandy/Rob Brydon), Dylan Moran (Dr. Slop/Dylan Moran), Keeley Hawes (Elizabeth Shandy/Keeley Hawes), Gillian Anderson (Widow Wadmaker/Gillian Anderson)*
Director: *Michael Winterbottom*
Screenwriter: *Frank Cottrell Boyce, based on the novel by Laurence Sterne*
15/94 mins./Comedy/UK

Steve Coogan stars in an adaptation of Laurence Sterne's 'unfilmable' 18th century novel, *The Life And Opinions Of Tristram Shandy, Gentleman*, playing a man who sets out to narrate the story of his life and affairs but finds it hard to get past his messy birth.

Just when you think you've got a fix on Michael Winterbottom, he's made three more completely different films. A downside to this hyperactivity is that many of his quickie experiments (*9 Songs*) just don't come off, but this reteaming (after *24 Hour Party People*) with Steve Coogan is one of Winterbottom's most entertaining pictures, even though it's still an ambitious and intelligent effort to cope with a novel that's one of the cornerstones of English literature.

It cannily tackles Sterne's book by dramatising choice extracts, finding a film equivalent for its deliberately self-defeating detours and stirring in a thread about making the movie to add yet more layers of critical and comical discourse.

Steve Coogan plays Tristram and his father Walter, while Rob Brydon (*Marion And Geoff*'s Keith Barret) takes the role of the unassertive Uncle Toby – but both also play funny versions of themselves. Coogan constantly complains that people who make fun of him get him confused with Alan Partridge, but this only makes him appear more like his pathetic, self-defeating sit-com character, especially when his family-man act is undermined by revelations about his night with lap-dancer 'Hedda Gobbler'. The shift of power between the stars is deftly, hilariously handled, with a major unsaid fact (that Coogan hasn't read the book) setting up a nastily delightful late development involving a game Gillian Anderson.

The behind-the-scenes sections have the feel of a Christopher Guest mockumentary, affording funny or poignant moments to edge-of-frame characters like the historical adviser (Mark Williams) campily fuming over the rampant inaccuracies in the battle scenes, the Fassbinder-worshipping runner Coogan fancies (Naomie Harris), or the quietly downtrodden director (Jeremy Northam).

Meanwhile, the Shandy scenes, played at several levels of exaggeration (one turns out to be a Coogan nightmare, in which Brydon sounds like Roger Moore), perfectly catch Sterne's free-association way of telling a tale, so that the telling comes to the fore and the story itself repeatedly gets lost. The film shifts through epitomising, deconstructing and parodying the English heritage drama movie genre (to which Winterbottom contributed *Jude*) and pokes gentle fun at the film business, with petty power-struggles on location and everyone fumbling towards a picture they know isn't going to turn out well.

A successful mix of literary adaptation, meta-fictional discourse and inside-showbiz comedy. Both funny and clever. ★★★★ **KN**

COCOON (1985)

Starring: *Don Ameche (Arthur Selwyn), Wilford Brimley (Benjamin Luckett), Hume Cronyn (Joseph Finley), Brian Dennehy (Walter), Jack Gilford (Bernie Lefkowitz), Steve Guttenberg (Jack Bonner), Maureen Stapleton (Marilyn Luckett), Jessica Tandy (Alma Finley)*
Director: *Ron Howard*
Screenwriters: *Tom Benedek, David Saperstein*
PG/117 mins./Sci-fi/Comedy/USA

Awards: *Academy Awards – Best Supporting Actor (Don Ameche), Best Special Effects*

When a group of octogenarians steal into a private swimming pool, they happen upon a recent store of alien cocoons, and gain a new lease of life. But when the aliens discover their eggs sapped of life power, the elderly bunch elect to help them to retrieve the ancient batch from the bottom of the ocean.

Imagine *ET*'s genial alien ethos hooked up with the evident, if sappy, comedy of a coterie of Floridian retirees rejuvenated to youthful bluster, as directed by the audience pleasing, if sappy, tendencies of Ron Howard – who was clearly on a fairy-tale jag having only just delivered a major hit with mermaid comedy *Splash*. How you react to the sum total of that equation – nausea, mild discomfort or an easy smile of acceptance (some movies are just entertainment after all) – should warn you how to approach this broad, effective, but nailed on sentimental load of sprightly old tosh. That said, this is a positive review.

To start with, it's not often a team of actors on the wrinklier side get to be the heart of a movie, and that those actors – Don Ameche the stand-out was granted an Oscar for his generous, detailed performance – manage to whittle out the knowing humour as well as the japery from the set-up. The gag, away from the film's elaborate hokey sci-fi set-up (Atlantean aliens in the guise of Brian Dennehy come back to retrieve a batch of cocoons stored for a millennia at the bottom of the ocean), is that old folk regain youthful vigour. Cue: sporting prowess and renewed sexual appetites. It's obvious silliness, but they give it a rarefied dignity; the entire film operating as a give-OAPs-a-chance campaign call.

Steve Guttenberg, as the friendly face of the pre-30 age bracket, helps the aged and the alien alike, and gets it on with a female ET (embodied by Tahnee Welch, Raquel's daughter) in a major piece of tantric-style shagging. And it all revs up with a race-against-time style ending, with some fancy UFO effects and the offer of eternal life albeit on a planet far weirder than Florida. Howard, as a director, is astute enough to concentrate on the sparkle of character rather than the nerdy fabric of alien landings, his film far more a comedy parable than a sci-fi adventure. ★★★ **IN**

UN COEUR EN HIVER (1992)

Starring: *Daniel Auteil (Stéphane), Emmanuelle Béart (Camille) Andre Dussolier (Maxime), Elisabeth Bourgine (Helene), Brigitte Catillon (Régine), Maurice Garrel (Lachaume)*
Director: *Claude Sautet*
Screenwriter: *Yves Ulmann, Claude Sautet*
12/104 mins./Romantic/Drama/France

Stéphane and Maxime run a violin repair business. However, their partnership is jeopardised when Maxime leaves his wife for Camille, a beautiful musician who becomes obsessed with breaking down Stéphane's evasive reserve.

Claude Sautet was a master of middle-class mores, who deftly dissected the pettiness and hypocrisy of his characters in a series of intense melodramas that never quite found the international audience they deserved. He was particularly fascinated by threesomes and had already explored their subtle dynamics in *Les Choses De La Vie*, *César et Rosalie*, *Vincent, François, Paul Et Les Autres* and *Une Histoire Simple* before he embarked on this stylish romantic ménage that is as refined as the classical music world against which it is set.

The action opens as a study of mutual dependence, in which the gregarious Maxime exploits the undemonstrative Stéphane's expertise, while the latter lives vicariously through his partner's hectic social life. But this delicate balance (based as much on acceptance as affection) is disturbed by the intrusion of Camille, who views Stéphane's reserve as a challenge that becomes an obsession as she falls in love with him.

Un Coeur En Hiver's discussion of social and sexual convention relies heavily on ambiguity and misconception, as Camille is convinced that Stéphane's interest in her art and indifference to her personality is some sort of intellectual come on. But his fascination with people precludes sentiment and, so, while he is content to observe and analyse their behaviour, he is unwilling to make an emotional investment in them.

In the hands of a lesser director, the symbolism of a craftsman who can fine tune an instrument but no longer has the soul to play could have appeared crass. But, such are Sautet's insight, compassion and finesse that the drama intrigues and involves throughout. Adding to its frisson was the fact that Daniel Auteuil and Emmanuelle Béart were then an item. Yet it was Dussolier who, along with Sautet, won a César for his work. ★★★★ **DP**

COFFEE AND CIGARETTES (2003)

Director: *Jim Jarmusch*
Starring: *as themselves: Roberto Benigni, Steven Wright, Joie Lee, Cinqué Lee, Steve Buscemi, Iggy Pop, Tom Waits, Joseph Rigano, Vinny Vella, Vinny Vella Jr., Renee French, E.J. Rodriguez, Alex Decas, Isaach De Bankole, Cate Blanchett, Mike Hogan, Jack White, Meg White, Alfred Molin, Steve Coogan, Katy Hansz, Genius/GZA, RZA, Bill Murray, William Rice, Taylor Mead*
15/95 mins./Comedy/Music/Drama/USA/Japan/Italy

Starting life as a *Saturday Night Live* sketch in 1986, Jim Jarmusch's compendium of 11 short films sees various actors/musicians as fictionalised versions of themselves in caffeine and nicotine fuelled conversations.

With coffee now taken on the run in cardboard beakers and cigarettes relegated to an anti-social, only-on-the-pavement habit, there's an almost nostalgic air to Jim Jarmusch's hymn to java, smokes and quirky conversations.

Delighting in throwing people together in unexpected combinations, this anthology of 11 vignettes may be uneven, but throws up enough laughs, smiles and cool moments to stave off the accusations of self-indulgence. Being part of a project that Jarmusch fits around his feature films, three of the episodes here have appeared before.

The first sees verbal hurricane Roberto Benigni meeting withdrawn Steven Wright, each missing the point of the other. In the second, Steve Buscemi explains to Spike Lee's siblings Cinqué and Joie how Elvis was replaced by a twin brother. But the best of this old bunch features Tom Waits and Iggy Pop, who play passive-aggressive games of one-upmanship about their songs on the nearby jukebox.

Enjoyable new entries include Bill Murray exchanging herbal remedies with the Wu-Tang Clan's RZA and GZA, and Jack and Meg White of The White Stripes discussing the physics of the Tesla Coil. The real treats, however, are movie-based; Steve Coogan and Alfred Molina deliver a terrific meditation on insincere actors, career climbing and the impossibility of having a normal conversation in Hollywood, while a virtuoso Cate Blanchett, playing both herself and her white-trash cousin, whips up an 11-minute soap opera, spinning on the pomposity of success and the ugliness of envy.

Some of the episodes are unfocused and lose their way – Bill Rice and Taylor Mead pretending their coffee is Champagne; Alex Descas and Isaach de Bankolé talking around anxiety and comfort – and not everyone will slide into the film's relaxed, ruminative rhythms. But Jarmusch makes gentle points about the difficulty of making connections and how epiphanies often occur in idle moments. Also, considering how talky the concept is, he manages to jimmy in some cinematic brio, with lovely high contrast black-and-white imagery and snatches of music, from Mahler to doo-wop, perfectly punctuating the pauses in patter. ★★★ **JB**

COLD MOUNTAIN (2003)

Starring: *Jude Law (Inman), Nicole Kidman (Ada Monroe), Renee Zellweger (Ruby Thewes), Donald Sutherland (Reverend Monroe), Ray Winstone (Teague), Brendan Gleeson (Stobrod), Philip Seymour Hoffman (Veasey), Natalie Portman (Sara), Kathy Baker (Sally Swanger))*
Director: *Anthony Minghella*
Screenwriter: *Anthony Minghella, based on the novel by Charles Frazier*
15/155 mins./Drama/Romance/War/USA
Awards: *Academy Awards – Best Supporting Actress (Renee Zellweger), BAFTA – Best Supporting Actress (Renee Zellweger), Anthony Asquith Award for Film Music, Golden Globe – Best Supporting Actress (Renee Zellweger)*

Late in the American Civil War, wounded Confederate soldier Inman deserts, embarking on an epic journey back to his despairing sweetheart, Ada. Meanwhile Ada, with the help of indomitable farm hand Ruby, is fighting her own battles against hunger, ruin and terrorisation by local villain Teague.

The problem with *The English Patient* is that to enjoy it, you have to be either English or patient. So said Joe Queenan, as he delivered his pithy proscription on director Anthony Minghella's multiple Oscar-winner. Well, Minghella was at it again last year, chiding those who are neither patient, nor, in this case, American; those unable to endure the ponderous, painful roads down which his characters invariably wander.

Here, the director's casualty of wartime love is Inman, a Confederate deserter who's travelling home to his love, Ada, whom – this being a distinguished Miramax literary adaptation – he has never really known. Like *The English Patient* and the Lasse Hallström brace *The Cider House Rules* and *Chocolat*, *Cold Mountain* emerged from Weinstein's production line primed to tap on Oscar's shoulder, brimming with literary pedigree, lavish scenery, weighty emotions and an eminent cast. Alas for Miramax, the only shoulder offered by Oscar was as cold as the film's mountain. That, however, should not really matter: Minghella's movie – a soft-yet-savage folk tale – is, in fact, so self-congratulatory it should be able to survive without plaudits from other quarters. It revels in its deliberate delicacy, painting gnarled characters against a vast, snowy backdrop framed by menacing mountains.

This epic canvas might not inspire the Academy – he has done it all before – but it lets Minghella adapt another poetically composed novel, where the plot is of less importance than an immersion in the landscapes and the characters' inner conflicts. The love between Inman and Ada is that of a folk tale; the two have barely met, yet during their separation each wields the memory of the other as a weapon in their own personal battles, their affection serving as salvation from their circumstances, rather than recalling a longing for times past. So too the main narrative structure, employed by every scribe from Homer to Hartman (Phil, in *Pee-Wee's Big Adventure!*), which sees the hero's journey punctured by encounters that act as their own self-contained fables.

Kidman's porcelain beauty, Renée Zellweger's spikey sidekick, Jude Law's distant hero – all the elements that so annoyed more acerbic critics are valuable ingredients of a fairy-tale, and it is only within this context that the delicate love story blossoms, detached from the harsh realism of the world in which it plays.

Of course, by design, fairy-tales lack the desert heat and fiery passion that helped *The English Patient* connect with a wide audience (the central affair is, by comparison, rather cold) and it's safe to say Minghella never quite wrestles his part-odyssey, part-survival story structure into submission, but his journey boasts enough wonders to woo even the most jaded critic. ★★★★ **WL**

COLLATERAL (2004)

Starring: *Tom Cruise (Vincent), Jamie Foxx (Max Durocher), Jada Pinkett (Annie), Mark Ruffalo (Fanning), Peter Berg (Richard Weidner), Bruce McGill (Pendrosa), Debi Mazar (Young Professional Woman)*
Director: *Michael Mann*
Screenwriter: *Stuart Beattie*
15/120 mins./Thriller/USA
Awards: *BAFTA – Best Cinematography*

Max is an LA taxi driver who dreams of a better life. Smooth-talking Vincent is in town for one night, with five stops to make. Max agrees to provide the ride, but soon finds that his passenger is an assassin and all the stops are targets . . .

Heat, Michael Mann's meditation on the crime movie, was a dialogue between two people who breathed the same intoxicating air but rarely shared the same physical space. *Collateral*, his latest unholy visitation on the City Of Angels, reverses this dynamic. Professionally mild cabbie Max and professional assassin Vincent travel roads that should never cross, but for one night they're boxed together, reluctant chauffeur and ruthless killer.

If *Heat* explored the harmonics between equal but opposite forces – cop vs. thief; Pacino vs. De Niro – this investigates a very different relationship between the strong and the seemingly helpless. It is fitting, then, that it pits the world's biggest star against a young actor then still best known as a comedian. And in the same way that Max must tap hidden talents if he's to survive, Jamie Foxx enters the cab with promise and exits as the equal of a Cruise operating at the very top of his own A-game.

Cruise, perverting that trademark salesman charm into something altogether sinister, and Foxx, his natural exuberance pinched into quiet confidence, play *Collateral* as a buddy movie. It's Vincent who dresses as a lone wolf, but until this night both men have operated as one, and some welcome comedy is occasioned by the odd couple adjusting to each other. Vincent insinuates himself into Max's comfortable routine – in one memorable diversion, the killer makes nice with his hostage's mom – and challenges his liberal assumptions. In return, Max gradually chips away at Vincent's carefully constructed cynicism, inadvertently turning what should be a routine assignment into a bloodbath.

Cruise (and Foxx) hogged the headlines for playing against type, but *Collateral* is every inch Mann's movie. Historical baggage weighed the director down on *Ali*, but like many auteurs before him, he's more comfortable, and more effective, working within the confines of a genre movie. Or, to be more accurate, redefining what those very limitations can be. Just as young Turks are making a mark by brazenly stealing from the Michael Mann playbook, the master stylist pulls ahead of the pack once more. The musical cues are still bold, the location scouting typically inspired, but Mann's weapon of choice this time around is digital video, a tool that allows him to see farther and go deeper into the night than any previous director has dared. The electrifying result is an entirely new type of noir, one not defined by high contrast but by colour, an ever-shifting palette of purples, blues, browns and blacks. By night, Mann's LA is a bruise.

Meticulously constructed it may be, but *Collateral* is not without structural problems. After a jack-in-the-box first hour, when Max's cab swings right every time you are convinced it must turn left, the last act does slide inexorably towards convention. In place of surprise we are offered mere plot devices, the kind of cosmic coincidences only screenwriters truly believe in. And even as we demand the only possible conclusion – a showdown – we understand that it can never really satisfy.

Those who can recall *Heat*'s airport climax will immediately identify the malaise. Not that Mann could ever consciously mount a lazy set-up, but he is understandably reluctant to let his film get out of the cab. After all, for as long as Foxx is at the wheel, Cruise is in the back and Mann's giving directions, this is a movie at its best. ★★★★ **IN**

⓪ THE COLOR OF MONEY (1986)

Starring: *Paul Newman (Fast Eddie Felson), Tom Cruise (Vincent Lauria), Mary Elizabeth Mastrantonio (Carmen), John Turturro (Julian), Bill Cobbs (Orvis), Keith McCready (Grady Seasons)*
Director: *Martin Scorsese*
Screenwriter: *Richard Price based on the novel by Walter Tevis*
15/119 mins./Sports/Drama/USA

Awards: *Academy Awards – Best Actor (Paul Newman)*

Aged pool hustler Fast Eddie Felson discovers a punk kid Vincent bubbling with talent and attitude and decides to mould him into a hustler just like he used to be. But Vincent's mouthy lack of restraint may spoil a perfect partnership.

It wouldn't be like Martin Scorsese to pick up the tabs on a simple sequel, and this glossy, hard-spoken pool drama, a follow-on from *The Hustler*, never aligns to the simple organising principle of repeat value. This is an original film based around an old character in Paul Newman's rusted former pool-hustler, who can still think it, but has drunk away most of his table tricks. Scorsese, very much a fan of Robert Rossen's grabby energy in the original, is after a relationship movie, a father-son style conflict, and divides his attention between Eddie's cantankerous weariness, and Vincent's loose grin and youthful spite, echoing the vim of Eddie of old.

There are the traits of a road movie in the film's drift from pool hall to hall, and stabs of the sports genre as Newman plays coach to the puckish skills of Cruise (who does much of the ball blitzing himself). It has a measured spirit, shot to the lurid colour schemes of these tobacco stained second-floor hollows with their spectrum of clicking, gleaming balls. Scorsese, with his furtive camera, is not after a wholly real world, but a movie slanted one where emotions ping and slice like their tabletop equivalent.

Newman, somehow inevitably, was awarded an Oscar for this firebrand turned to smouldering with age, oily and suspect in demeanour, but still staunch enough to spark into rage at his protégé's bullish stupidity. It is often forgotten, in the face of his blockbustering excesses, how Cruise matches the old master. He's alive with thrusting youth, naïve but strong and equally as fiery as this imposing guru. The sight of Cruise's Vincent twirling his pool cue like a strutting Samurai to the howling joys of Warren Zevon's *Werewolves Of London* has the excitable appeal of talent's doltish requirement to reveal itself. Something of little use to a hustler.

Between them resides Mary Elizabeth Mastrantonio's Carmen, the girlfriend and manager of Vincent. Played with tough control, she's got the measure of Eddie, but they share an understanding of Vincent.

Swirling with crunching, hard-balling dialogue by novelist Richard Price, the film finally is Eddie's journey, his casting-off of former glories, and rejuvenation of inner spirit. You're never too old Scorsese grins, but you could be too young. ★★★★ **IN**

⓪ THE COLOR PURPLE (1985)

Starring: *Danny Glover (Albert), Whoopi Goldberg (Celie), Margaret Avery (Shug Avery), Oprah Winfrey (Sofia), Willard Pugh (Harpo), Akosua Busia (Nettie)*
Director: *Steven Spielberg*
Screenwriter: *Menno Myjes, based on the novel by Alice Walker*
15/152 mins./Drama/USA

Awards: *Golden Globes – Best Actress (Whoopi Goldberg)*

The life of Celie, a young black girl growing up in the early 1900s. The first time we see Celie, she is 14 – and pregnant – by her father. We stay with her for the next 30 years of her tough life . . .

Were *The Color Purple* to be released today Steven Spielberg might respond to all the flak by quoting the poet Ali G: "Is it because I is black?"

For *The Color Purple* is Spielberg's black film. The one that's inside so many white, liberal American filmmakers but rarely transpires in such brazen, unapologetic form. Wracked, we may assume, with the subliminal national guilt of slavery, many white directors have tackled black issues, not least, among Spielberg's immediate forbears, the Canadian Norman Jewison, who made *In The Heat Of The Night* (1967) and later *A Soldier's Story* (1984), and only relinquished *Malcolm X* to Spike Lee when he realised he wasn't black enough to tell the tale. Brave decision.

So what was Spielberg doing, after *The Temple Of Doom*, with his pale mitts on Alice Walker's 1983 Pulitzer Prize-winning novel *The Color Purple*? Firstly, this was a symptom of the director's self-intellectualising phase, which may have been an entree to a mid-life crisis – he was 38, and anticipating his first kid with Amy Irving – or simply a reaction to almost a decade of Academy snubs, sidelining him as some kind of Barnum figure. Having given literature a wide berth in childhood (he turned his school copy of *The Scarlet Letter* into a flick book), he was now making up for lost time – also acquiring the rights to *Empire Of The Sun* and *Schindler's Ark*.

Taking place between 1909 and 1946 in Georgia, *The Color Purple* (as in, 'It pisses God off when you walk by the colour purple in a field and don't notice') is the story of Celie (debutante Whoopi Goldberg), a young black girl forced into a marriage of convenience with a cruel, unfaithful widower, 'Mister' (Danny Glover). As if to accelerate the merry-go-round of misery that is her life, Celie is separated from her beloved sister Nettie and must also endure the knowledge that her two children (sired by who else but her own father) were sold at birth to a local reverend.

Unlike so many other films dealing with blacks in the South, racism is barely touched upon (not a burning cross in sight). Whites are largely absent from the picture – save for the local mayor and his wife, pompous rather than evil. Spielberg simply treats the community as a microcosm for life, even an extended family. So we get good blacks and bad blacks – a refreshing realism supplied by the book – and in that respect *The Color Purple* isn't about race issues at all.

It is sentimental though, for both a mythic past (the painter Andrew Wyeth has a lot to answer for here), and the simplicity of rural life on the porch in a pair of dungarees. How very different from the home life of our own dear Steve. The 'Spielbergisation' of Walker's book can be seen in the toning down of its explicit lesbian tryst between Celie and Mister's mistress Shug Avery (the fabulous Margaret Avery). Alice Walker herself curtailed other more potentially damaging decisions, such as the casting of Diana Ross in the Shug role. 'We had to make it clear,' Walker said afterwards, 'that authenticity means not having Diana Ross! The final cast list must seem like they have stepped straight from the pages of the book.'

Well, true to Spielberg's enduring sixth sense, *The Color Purple* is perfectly and quietly cast. (It made Goldberg and Danny Glover stars, and launched Chicago talk show host Oprah Winfrey to national acclaim.) That said, the film ultimately groans under the weight of its desire to do good. Spielberg was all too conscious of his unsuitability for the job. He'd tried to turn it down when associate producer Quincy Jones had first approached him, and later admitted, 'I wanted to do this book because I was scared I couldn't.' As a result, he allowed too many cooks to advise him, and the broth was duly spoiled. Not only I did hands-on 'Project Consultant' Walker hover over his right shoulder, but Jones also spent a lot of time on set and in the editing room, on the grounds that he needed to be close to the material for which he was composing the score. (An awful, sugary score, by the way – bring back John Williams.)

Spielberg even enrolled Gordon Parks, director of *The Learning Tree* (1969) and *Shaft* (1971), to guide him during filming, gathering images as a stills photographer, assisting him with the 'vibe' and, in effect, playing his uncredited black Jiminy Cricket.

None of this helped in the end. It's a beautifully shot, overlong piece of afternoon I schmaltz, which, biographer John Baxter notes, was 'edited in the glow of new fatherhood.' It enraged African-American pressure groups for showing black men as brutes and suggesting blacks lived in too much comfort, and pissed off lesbians who felt 'their' story had been airbrushed out.

It made about $140 million and won a grand total of ... no Oscars (from 13 nominations). Best Film that year? *Out Of Africa*. About white people. **★★★ AC**

THE COLOUR OF POMEGRANATES (SAYAT NOVA) (1968)

Starring: *Sophico Chiurelli (Poet As A Youth), Melkon Aleksanyan (Poet As A Child), Vilen Galstan (Poet In The Cloister), Giorgi Gegechkori (Poet As An Old Man), Spartak Bagashvili (Poet's Father), Medea Djaparidze (Poet's Mother)*
Director: *Sergei Paradjanov*
Screenwriter: *Sergei Paradjanov based on the poems by Sayat Nova*
U/73 mins./Drama/USSR

Starting out as a humble weaver, Sayat Nova (Sophico Chiurelli) serves as the king's minstrel and as a cloistered monk before being martyred for his faith by invading infidels.

In 1968, Sergei Paradjanov was arrested for supporting Ukrainian dissidents and exiled to the Amo-Bek-Nazarov Studios at Yerevan in Armenia. As part of his punishment, the Soviet authorities rejected numerous film scripts before finally passing *The Colour of Pomegranates*. However, the censors clearly didn't realise what a politically and culturally contentious picture they were sanctioning.

Ostensibly, the film was based on the life of the Armenian poet Aruthin Sayadin (1712–95), the weaver who became known as 'Sayat Nova' or the King of Song on becoming court minstrel to King Heracle II of Georgia. However, his career looked over when he was sent to a monastery for seducing the king's sister, Anna. But he rose through the ecclesiastical ranks and was Archbishop of Tiflis when he was martyred on the steps of his cathedral by the invading Persians.

However, Paradjanov wasn't interested in the sacrifice of a national hero or his status as an artist. He was fascinated by the psychological and intellectual shifts that enabled a peasant to become a troubadour and then a saint and the part that was played in these transformations by fate, love and soul. Consequently, he spurned dialogue and confined Sayadin's verses to a handful of captions in order to present an expressionist reverie that was acted out to classical Armenian music. Logic mattered less than lyricism and the sumptuous tapestry of rich colours, stylised movements and innovative symbols that Paradjanov concocted remains without parallel in world cinema.

Without realising that Paradjanov had slipped numerous allusions to Armenian nationalism into his iconoclastic tableaux, the Kremlin banned the film for its formalism (shorthand for the fact that anything of such dazzling beauty and ambiguity had to be subversive and/or self-indulgent). However, it now stands as a monument to the vision and courage of a remarkable artist. **★★★★★ DP**

COME AND SEE (IDI I SMOTRI) (1985)

Starring: *Aleksei Kravchencko (Florya Gaishun), Olga Mironova (Glasha), Liubomiras Lauciavicius (Kosach)*
Director: *Elem Klimov*
Screenwriters: *Ales Adamovich, Elem Klimov based on* The Story Of Khatyn And Others
15/146 mins./War/USSR

As the Nazis penetrate ever further into his country, Byelorussian peasant boy Florya discovers a buried German rifle and leaves home to join the army. But as he witnesses atrocities first hand his innocence is shattered and very nearly his sanity.

Properly considered one of the most powerful and disturbing war movies ever made, Elem Klimov's hallucinogenic journey into the vile inhumanity of war, especially as perpetrated by the Reich as they invaded Russia, this is a film of great craft, courage and a deep seated compassion. Although made under the auspices of Soviet controlled cinema, the film rages against oppression, the terrible price that is paid by the humble and poor in the face of political conflict. It is a vision of hell on earth, contrasted with moments of unearthly beauty, that spiral of haunting majesty and lunacy of *Apocalypse Now*, but with its own deterministic grit.

Rumours abound that Klimov used hypnosis on his fledgling actor Aleksei Kravchencko, the twisted soul of his story, to extract the emotional, even existential, shock of reaction to unknowable things. Whatever the case, it must stand as one of the greatest child performances. Through a series of intense close-ups, reaction shots to death's myriad forms, Kravchencko's face is a map of terror and incipient madness, but there is a gradual closing up, a sealing off from horror. It is one of the film's pressing themes – how humans become inured to extremity, how the annihilation of innocents can become the norm.

The physical representation of war, not of battle but of the Nazi's genocidal sweep across the pastoral plains of Byelorussia, is shot with a raptured precision like a netherworld from a Grimm Brother fairytale. But none of their moral nightmares, for all their trippy gloom, could compare to the carnival of abhorrence as the Nazis hound an entire village into a barn ready to burn them alive. Spielberg for *Schindler's List* borrowed their clapping, deranged, subhuman enjoyment of the process. Klimov's guile is to offer up, all-too briefly, moments of emotional connection as Florya escapes in the company of a luminous peasant girl, played with a mild delirium by Olga Mironova, through those desolate woods – they shower by shaking sodden tree branches and when she quicksteps on his case top it is like a moment stolen from a dream. War's unbearable reality forces humanity into surreal pastures, and this landscape, fogged and unending, feels like nowhere on Earth.

Unforgettable and deeply traumatic – while never forcefully gruesome, the death rent across the screen tests you to the limits – *Come And See* is an extraordinary piece of filmmaking. More than that, though, it is a cry of indignant force: how could something so indisputably wrong ever come to pass? **★★★★★ IN**

THE COMMITMENTS (1991)

Starring: *Robert Arkins (Jimmy Rabbitte), Michael Aherne (Steven Clifford, Piano), Angeline Ball (Imelda Quirke, Backup Singer), Bronagh Gallagher (Bernie McGloughlin, Backup Singer), Andrew Strong (Deco Cuffe), Colm Meaney (Jimmy Rabbitte, Sr.), Andrea Corr (Sharon Rabbitte)*
Director: *Alan Parker*
Screenwriters: *Ian LaFrenais, Dick Clement, Roddy Doyle, from his novel*
15/120 mins./Comedy/Drama/Music/USA/UK

Awards: *BAFTA – Best Director, Best Editing, Best Film, Best Adapted Screenplay*

A Dublin wide-boy tries to put together a soul group for a shot at the big time.

Given the chance to manage a combo who specialise in Radio 2 crap at weddings, Dublin hustler Jimmy Rabbitte is struck with a vision, and resolves to transform the group into The Commitments, a powerful force who plan to short circuit all that revisionary U2 and Sinead O'Connor nonsense by doing something that will really put Irish music on the map.

With his conviction that the Irish are the blacks of Europe and Dubliners the blacks of Ireland, Jimmy decides their niche lies in old soul standards, calls in a piss-headed bus conductor to sing, and a weird assortment of musicians – from a guru-like oldie who claims to have played trumpet with Elvis and Otis to a medical student who switches between church organ and rocking piano – plus three girls to do backing vocals who look pretty. Despite arguments and ordeals, the group gets on stage, and the film pretty much becomes a succession of favourite numbers, topped off with an ironic and hilarious version of the *American Graffiti* where-are-they-now-type ending.

Having made *Fame* – marvellously punctured here by a skinhead who bawls 'Fame, I'm Going to Live Till Tuesday' – Parker here turns out a rethink of the young talents-on-the-make musical, the no-hope misfits following the eternal showbiz tradition of clicking onstage and coming apart behind the scenes. With plenty of gritty Dublin humour, albeit rather too much of the Derek and Clive badmouth variety, and a succession of very funny vignettes, almost in the Bill Forsyth tradition, *The Commitments* has a sense of fun that had been missing from Parker's mainly dreary and miserabilist films of the late 80s. A pop musical in the way Cliff's films or Elvis' 50s vehicles were, this is one liable to sneak by even the most committed Parkerphobe. Highly recommended. ★★★★ **JY**

THE COMFORT OF STRANGERS (CORTESIE PER GLI OSPITI) (1990)

Starring: *Christopher Walken (Robert), Rupert Everett (Colin), Natasha Richardson (Mary), Helen Mirren (Caroline), Manfredi Aliquo (The Concierge)*
Director: *Paul Schrader*
Screenwriter: *Harold Pinter from the novel by Ian McEwan*
18/107 mins./Drama/UK

To succour their ailing relationship, British couple Colin and Mary holiday in Venice. Having lost their way one evening, they are rescued by the mysterious Robert, who proceeds to lure them into the dangerous fantasies of his own life.

The pedigree on show here is without question, the icy, macabre storytelling grace of Ian McEwan as adapted with the crisp, loquacious dialogue of Harold Pinter and directed with Paul Schrader's gloomy ruminations on human frailty. Place them in the murky underbelly of Venice's backstreets, a nightmare milieu forever echoing with the distraught clamour of *Don't Look Now*, and you can lay claim to a provocative, if pretentious, sub-horror movie.

Shot by famed cinematographer Dante Spinotti, who gives the film a seeping, feverish texture, a gothic atmosphere of creeping abhorrence, Schrader hones, with his familiar snail's pace approach to plot, in on an effective erotic strangeness where this dissolving English couple, played with a due mix of yearning and restraint by Natasha Richardson and Rupert Everett, are lured into a Venetian aristo's warped relationship with his wife Caroline. And if you're looking for a sexual deviancy hovering just out of reach, then coupling the oddball phraseology of Christopher Walken with the cool intelligence of Helen Mirren is the best place to start.

The encounter, rapt with potential risk, re-enflames the carnal desires in this shuttered couple, with its peculiar voyeurism, malevolence and elusive purpose. Why do Walken's Robert and Mirren's Caroline steal their guests' clothes having put them up for the night? To what awful use are they ultimately being put? This is all the stuff of payoff, but this being the work of Paul Schrader, who would rather concern himself with religious symbolism and the tracer-fire of evil, the outcome is unsure and incomplete. Frustratingly so, as if atmosphere, and it fair drips from every twisting corner and forgotten square, will suffice. Evidently Robert is up to no good, Walken is pulling out all the stops on his creepzoid persona, an endless almost ludicrous flutter of tics, but his performance kind of sums the film up – it's all furtive gesture and little gripping plot. ★★★ **IN**

THE COMPANY OF WOLVES (1984)

Starring: *Sarah Patterson (Rosaleen), Angela Lansbury (Granny), David Warner (Father), Tusse Silberg (Mother), Micha Bergese (Huntsman), Brian Glover (Amorous Boy's father), Stephen Rea (Young Groom)*
Director: *Neil Jordan*
Screenwriters: *Angela Carter, Neil Jordan, based on a collection of short stories by Carter*
18/95 mins/Horror/Fantasy/UK

A young girl dreams she is Rosaleen, who, wearing a red cape, carries her basket through the woods to Granny's house. Along the way, she meets and flirts with a werewolf in the guise of a man, and promises him a kiss if he reaches Granny's house before her.

The late feminist novelist Angela Carter had a peculiar if not downright potty take on literature. Her predilection was to take familiar, classical fairytales and suffuse them with sexual references, building on the inherent suggestive metaphors until they are almost screaming for mercy. Little Red Riding Hood? Well, the hood can be taken for the female hymen and the wolf male lust ... Nursery tales a la Sigmund Freud. Lavish, dark and abstract, they were exotic, subversive fantasies seemingly beyond the reach of conventional cinema. Irish director Neil Jordan, a novelist himself who began his film career as a creative assistant on John Boorman's *Excalibur* in 1981, first met Carter at a writer's conference and it was she who expressed an interest in bringing her short stories to the screen.

The short story called *The Company Of Wolves* (from the collection *The Bloody Chamber*), which forms the basis for the film, was a meagre 12 pages long so Carter and Jordan (they wrote the script together) built it up in layers, inserting imagery from classical fairytales into a deliberately dreamlike and episodic format (there is virtually no running narrative), with only Angela Lansbury's genial grandmother bestowing cautionary fables on her enraptured granddaughter Rosaleen to string the various elements together. Shedding virtually all the features of a classical werewolf story, the film seems to exist entirely within Rosaleen's imagination. Its horror – such as it is – is conveyed through creeping revulsion and menace. The setpieces that pepper the film are startlingly, even gleefully, nasty hinting at the brash excesses of Ken Russell but delivered with immeasurably more elegance.

A long lost husband (played by Jordan faithful Stephen Rea) returns home and, on finding his bride remarried, proceeds to tear off his own face. As he does so, the snarling jaws of a wolf are revealed. Later, at a lavish wedding party, the debauched guests are transformed into ravening wolves by a gatecrashing (and heavily pregnant) witch. Finally, Rosaleen herself enters the fray of her own dreamscape, enacting Little Red Riding Hood with a handsome huntsman whose eyebrows happen to meet in the middle – the film did few favours for the self-respect of the more hirsute gentleman. All the while the story weaves in and out of the 'real' world as Rosaleen's older sister Alice falls foul of a wolf (read: she has already succumbed to the male dominated sexual world) and the devil himself makes an appearance in a Rolls-Royce.

It is a complex and at times infuriating structure – it often helps to conceive of the film as the book of short stories it stems from – but simultaneously vivid and disturbing. The production design is extraordinary, belying the film's shoestring budget. The late Anton Furst (who later worked on Tim Burton's *Batman* creates a storybook idyll laced with sinister delights, a world laden with primal symbolism: mist-shrouded forests stocked with phallic mushrooms, giant dollhouses, forbidden fruit ripe for the plucking. In turn the werewolf sequences boast highly original and appropriately hideous transformations by makeup specialist Christopher Tucker. Wolves literally climb out from inside ('The worst kind of men are hairy on the inside', the huntsman's face splitting open to reveal the snout; at the changeling banquet a woman rips open her bodice to display hairy breasts; the lost husband tears off his skin and his skull transforms into a wolf's: all grim, bloody and blackly funny – although by current standards they are showing their age.

As a horror film it is immediately metaphorical. In fact, it acts as one giant allusion in which reality is simply an afterthought. Jordan always saw it as a meditation on the ways society teaches young women to look at themselves sexually and to recognise the things to be afraid of. Company certainly centres on Rosaleen's sexual awakening, a kind of phantasmagoric representation of puberty where men, quite literally, are beasts. ★★★ **IN**

CON AIR (1997)

Starring: *Nicolas Cage (Cameron Poe), John Cusack (U.S. Marshal Vince Larkin), Monica Potter (Tricia Poe), Landry Allbright (Casey Poe), M.C. Gainey (Swamp Thing), Steve Buscemi (Garland 'The Marietta Mangler' Greene), Dave Chappelle (Joe 'Pinball' Parker), Ving Rhames (Nathan 'Diamond Dog' Jones), John Malkovich (Cyrus 'The Virus' Grissom), Colm Meaney (DEA Agent Duncan Malloy)*
Director: *Simon West*
Screenwriter: *Scott Rosenberg*
15/115 mins./Action/Thriller/USA

Cameron Poe is on his way home to his adoring wife and daughter after serving years in prison for manslaughter. He's travelling on a plane full of supremely dangerous prisoners on their way to a new super-prison – but when the inmates take over the plane, only Cameron can stop their plans.

Action movies have a tendency to become victims of their own stupidity, taking themselves oh-so-seriously when they are obviously preposterous. *Con Air*, on the other hand, works a treat, because rather than merely acknowledging its ridiculousness, it glorifies it, magnifying every excess to previously untapped levels.

This is the kind of film in which criminals haven't just committed a misdemeanour, they've butchered 37 people and used their body parts as headgear; a plane doesn't just take off, it does so with the loading ramp down and a car attached by a rope; and a single car is not blown up when there are six armoured vehicles which can be demolished in a much noisier fashion. Yes, disbelief is required not so much to be suspended as removed altogether, but it barely matters as this is an adrenaline blast of the highest order.

Transporting dangerous criminals anywhere by air is a Very Bad Idea – but where would dramatic potential be without it? The lifers are being flown to a new maximum security unit in Alabama. Naturally though, even before the seatbelt sign has been switched off, the psychos – led by a shaven-headed Malkovich as Cyrus 'The Virus' Grissom – have launched an awesome escape bid.

Fortunately, parolee Cameron Poe happens to be on board; off home to his wife and the daughter he's never met. He is an all-round decent bloke, who was framed and lives out his seven year sentence behind the opening credits (the Zucker brothers couldn't have done it better). It's down to him to reign in the crims while on the ground, cop Cusack blusters about trying to prevent his colleagues from shooting the plane down.

Thus is the scene set for a barrage of blistering set pieces, each more over-the-top than the last and hardly allowing pause for breath. High-speed chases are played out, things are gleefully smashed to smithereens or ignited in balls of flame, and Cage is curiously compelled to strip down to his vest. But its jocular nature aside, on an action level this delivers in spades – tautly edited, pacily directed and guaranteed to cause shocked gasps and blanching of knuckles.

And the cast enjoy themselves immensely. Ving Rhames isn't quite as scary here as in *Pulp Fiction*, but Malkovich spits out his lines with relish, and Buscemi, as the stark raving bonkers Marietta Mangler, is a marvel despite only having about ten lines in the entire movie. There are weak links – Colm Meaney's screeching cop seems strangely out of place, and the obligatory soggy ending pushes all the wrong buttons – but both are brief enough not to mar things. ★★★ **CW**

CONAN THE BARBARIAN (1982)

Starring: *Arnold Schwarzenegger (Conan), James Earl Jones (Thulsa Doom), Max von Sydow (King Osric), Sandahl Bergman (Valeria), Ben Davidson (Rexor), Cassandra Gava (The Witch), Gerry Lopez (Subotai), Mako (The Wizard/Narrator)*
Director: *John Milius*
Screenwriters: *John Milius, Oliver Stone, based on the stories by Robert E. Howard*
15/129 mins./Action/Adventure/Fantasy/USA

When his mother and father are killed in a raid by the evil sorcerer Thulsa Doom, Conan is sent to a slave camp. As the years pass, he develops into a powerfully-built man, determined to get revenge for his parents' death.

Given the mythic nature of *Conan The Barbarian*'s eponymous muscle-bound hero it is perhaps not surprising that the film itself has generated a greater than average mythology. There is the story, for example, of toy company Mattel who were intending to market a range of Conan action figures until they saw the blood-soaked final product and opted out. By then, however, they were lumbered with several hundred thousand effigies of Arnold Schwarzenegger. Desperate to recoup some money, Mattel revamped the dolls and came up with a very different kind of icon: He-Man.

Then there's the one about how Schwarzenegger and *Conan* producer Dino De Laurentiis first met. At the time the Italian was trying to cast the lead of *Flash Gordon* and believed that the then largely unknown body-builder might be just the man for the job. As Schwarzenegger biographer Nigel Andrews later wrote, 'The meeting is said to have lasted one minute 40 seconds. According to Arnold, Dino had time only to comment, "You have an accent! I cannot use you for Flash-a Gordon! Nah! Flash-a Gordon has no accent!" Arnold retorted, "I have an accent? I can't even understand you!" ' De Laurentiis, however, is not a man to bear a grudge – at least not when doing so might stand in the way of making money – and had few problems with the casting of Arnold as the decidedly un-American Conan. Ironically, Sam J. Jones, who was eventually cast as Flash Gordon, had his entire part dubbed by another actor.

The original Depression-era *Conan* comic had been written by Robert E.

Howard who, like Schwarzenegger, transformed himself through body-building from skinny pup into an adult hulk before blowing his brains out at the age of 30. By then, however, Conan's rampaging his way through ancient lands, beating to a pulp as many people as he could get his hands on, had captured the public's imagination.

And who better to put him there than John Milius, who had already proved his empathy for myth with films like *Dillinger* and *The Wind And The Lion*. But, after showing initial interest, Milius disappeared to make his surf epic *Big Wednesday*. For a while *Conan* co-writer Oliver Stone was in the frame to direct. Other names considered included completed work on *Big Wednesday*, the director re-attached himself to the project. Filming eventually began in January 1981.

But the shoot would prove to be a difficult one, in part due to the number of stunts involved but also because, as De Laurentiis had feared years before, Schwarzenegger's accent rendered some passages of dialogue virtually incomprehensible. Ultimately, many of the actor's lines were redubbed or cut completely. Moreover, the Austrian Oak's swordplay proved too much for Ralph Bakshi, Ridley Scott and even Hal Needham who directed Schwarzenegger in *The Villain*. 'I read the script,' recalls Needham, 'I didn't understand it. I said, "Shit Arnold, I can't do this." Big mistake. 'Cos I haven't been asked back to do anything else.'

Needham's loss would prove to be Milius' gain when, having impressive, his foes tended to be less so, in particular a giant snake that, even in pre-CGI times, couldn't have looked less realistic if it had 'Made in Taiwan' stamped across its scales. Yet, the seriousness with which Milius took proceedings – a good indication of which is his prefacing the whole shebang with a quote from Nietszche – elevated the enterprise far beyond both its pulp origins and technical limitations. The result, which finds Schwarzenegger tracking down the snake cult leader who killed his parents, may at times border on camp but it is never tongue-in-cheek. In fact, the director had originally planned on making a film, 'As serious as *Star Wars*,' and, even if he never quite achieved those lofty heights, the end product remains a truly epic piece of action-heavy myth-making. Indeed, seen today, Conan eerily resembles such epics as *El Cid*, *Ben-Hur* or virtually any other vintage Charlton Heston movie you'd care to mention – a similarity that is by no means coincidental.

'I told Arnold, "Look at Charlton Heston," ' says Milius. ' "He's always bigger than life. And if you look at his career he was very smart in picking things to play that way. In *The Greatest Story Ever Told* he's John The Baptist – and he plays him like Conan!" ' ★★★ **CC**

◎ CONAN THE DESTROYER (1984)

Starring: *Arnold Schwarzenegger (Conan), Grace Jones (Zula), Wilt Chamberlain (Bombaata), Mako (Akiro The Wizard), Tracey Walter (Malak), Olivia D'Abo (Princess Jehnna), Sarah Douglas (Queen Taramis), Pat Roach (Man-Ape-Toth Amon)*
Director: *Richard Fleischer*
Screenwriter: *Stanley Mann*
15/103 mins./Fantasy/Adventure/USA

Ancient hero Conan leads a curious band of warriors and thieves to rescue a princess held prisoner by a sorcerer on an island in a chamber of mirrors. But it soon becomes clear the whole thing is a set-up by the evil Queen Taramis, who plots to resurrect a terrible monstrosity.

While no one was really expecting the brute philosophy of John Milius' original Conan adventure – still one of the most stirring fantasy movies about – we still expected more from veteran director Richard Fleischer (who'd lent a fleet-footed, visionary thrill to Disney's *20,000 Leagues Under the Sea*) than this by-rote swords and sorcery twaddle. Riddled with the usual genre clichés – rescue the princess, defeat the evil sorcerer (ever known any good ones?), quell the rubbery beast – it's 101 muscularity, watchable in a guiltily lowbrow kind of way, but entirely devoid of Milius' brimstone, Nietzschean gusto.

Arnie, still keeping distance from the script, still looks the part. His walnut body is so exaggerated he feels meta-human, a distortion of what we consider even heroic, and teaming him up with Grace Jones, as an Amazonian spear carrier, lends the film an extraordinary, if hilarious, sense of the body brutal. Elsewhere in his ragtag gang conjoined to rescue Olivia D'Abo's rather bland princess of blonde hair and squeaky voice, is former basketball star Wilt 'The Stilt' Chamberlain, and Mako, who returns from the first film as the irascible nearly-wizard Akiro.

And where Milius sensibly restrained the temptation to give in to the outright supernatural, Fleischer throws himself in wholesale. A big risk when your budget is snared by locations and the growing stature of the main man. Thus when evil queen (ever known any good ones?) Taramis (Sarah Douglas, who does have the perfect physiognomy for such a role: oversized eyes bulging over pointed cheekbones) plans to resurrect big, green, be-horned god Dagoth (name department on a go slow?) we are sure to discover there's a man in an unconvincing rubber suit (actually Pat Roach) ready to play pull the sinew with Conan the Inexpressive. Still, credibility has long since departed the ancient land of Cimmeria, with the transformation of sorcerer Toth Amon into a kind of walking frog (actually Pat Roach).

Elsewhere, Fleischer does well with locations, poorly with sets, and dreadfully with script. Robert E. Howard aficionados pretend it never happened. ★★ **IN**

◎ CONDORMAN (1981)

Starring: *Michael Crawford (Woody Wilkins), Oliver Reed (Krokov), Barbera Carrera (Natalia), James Hampton (Harry Oslo), Jean-Pierre Kalfon (Morovich), Dana Elcar (Russ Devlin), Vernon Dobtcheff (Russian Agent), Robert Arden (CIA Chief)*
Director: *Charles Jarrott*
Screenwriters: *Mickey Rose, Marc Stirdivant*
PG/90 mins./Action/Adventure/USA

After assisting his CIA buddy with a simple bit of couriering, comic book artist Woody Wilkins is enamoured with Russian beauty Natalia, desperate to defect. Thus he gains the chance to turn his two-dimensional creation into three-dimensional reality, and the hero Condorman is born for real.

What strange confluence of events led to the existence of this superhero spoof is probably beyond reasoning, but at one point in the history of cinema Disney, on their creative uppers in the early 80s, decided they needed to make an expensive adventure spectacle for kids centred on Michael Crawford, lately star of pratfalling sitcom *Some Mothers Do 'Ave 'Em*. The result, while hardly insulting, is just wearily dumb and obvious, a near-but-not-quite-comedy crow-barred out of Robert Shecky's novel, itself straightforwardly a Bond parody.

Shot across heartily clichéd European locations – we're in gay Paris, so shoot at the Eiffel Tower why don't you? – the story is a dotty fusion of espionage, with various acronymic organisations lining up to work or hinder a star defection, with mock superheroics. Condorman isn't real, he's a spoof within a spoof, offering scant pleasure for the eager tots who want to buy into this nonsense.

Michael Crawford seems unsure what director Charles Jarrott wants from him, and fixes on what he is best known for – falling over a lot. Granted a budget by his CIA operatives, he even gets to add condorcars, condorchutes, and assorted condorparaphernalia (adding untold unsold toys to superstore shelves) to swell the whole confused mix of Bondian action, comic book heroics and knockabout comedy. Meanwhile, Oliver Reed doesn't exactly phone in his bad guy ham-it-ups rather than send a disorientated carrier pigeon. ★★ **IN**

➂ CONFESSIONS OF A DANGEROUS MIND (2002)

Starring: *Sam Rockwell (Chuck Barris), George Clooney (Jim Byrd), Julia Roberts (Patricia) Drew Barrymore (Penny, Rutger hauer (Keeler), Maggie Gyllenhall (Debbie), Kristen Wilson (Loretta), Jennifer Hall (Georgia)*
Director: *George Clooney*
Screenwriter: *Charlie Kaufman, based on the book* Confessions Of A Dangerous Mind: An Unauthorised Autobiography *by Chuck Barris*
15/108 mins/Comedy-Drama/USA/Germany
Awards: *Berlin Film Festival – Silver Bear (Sam Rockwell)*

TV producer/host Chuck Barris leads a double life. When not creating the cult anti-talent search series *The Gong Show* or *The Dating Game* (the inspiration for *Blind Date* in the UK), he's a globe-trotting CIA assassin. But falling ratings and murderous treachery make him wonder just who he can trust. Based on a true story – but is it real?

While shooting his directorial debut, Orson Welles said it was like playing with the world's biggest train set. *Confessions Of A Dangerous Mind* may not be in the *Citizen Kane* class, but George Clooney's first foray behind the camera does boast similarly bravura technique and an infectious sense of joy in the filmmaking process. Hilarious and thrilling, playfully sexy and emotionally involving, this is sophisticated entertainment and, along with *Good Night And Good Luck*, confirms Clooney's status as a director to watch.

Like his regular collaborators Soderbergh and the Coens, Clooney gleefully draws upon every cinematic trick in the book to make every frame count. This wizardry isn't a case of auteur-poseur, however. The film's eclectic style is ideally suited to its schizophrenic content, as hero Chuck Barris reflects on his dual life as game show czar and CIA assassin. It's the kind of bizarre tale you'd expect from Charlie Kaufman, but this isn't an *Adaptation*-style adaptation: the screenplay is actually pretty faithful to the autobiography in which Barris first made his outlandish claims.

The movie triumphs by giving equal dramatic weight to the ratings war and the Cold War – the network and the wet work. Sam Rockwell is compelling as Barris ('A nice guy, even though he's a prick'), but sometimes seems dazzled by the sheer star wattage assembled around him. As the CIA handler, Clooney plays it as straight as possible when sporting a quiff and beautifully groomed moustache, while Barrymore is hugely endearing as the sexually adventurous, emotionally vulnerable woman who shares Chuck's life but not his secrets.

Even Rutger Hauer shines, escaping straight-to-video hell to remind the world just how good he was in *Blade Runner*. Best of all, however, is Julia Roberts, a revelation as cynical, glamorous, decadent femme fatale Patricia – her idea of flirting is to inform Barris, 'You're not like the other murderers.' Under normal circumstances, you might say she steals the movie, but there's no doubt that the plaudits here belong to the director. ★★★★ **RF**

➂ CONFETTI (2006)

Starring: *Martin Freeman (Matt), Jessica Stevenson (Sam), Jimmy Carr (Antoni), Olivia Colman (Joanna), Stephen Mangan (Josef), Meredith MacNeill (Isabelle), Robert Webb (Michael)*
Director: *Debbie Isitt*
Screenwriter: *Debbie Isitt*
15/104 mins./Comedy/UK

Bridal magazine *Confetti* offers a luxury home for the couple with the most original wedding of the year. The finalists – whose nuptial themes are a Broadway musical, a tennis match and a nudist rite – find that pre-marital jitters and family tensions are exacerbated by competitive pressures.

Here's a cute, silly affair that may be just the ticket if you are in need of visual aid to deter a crazed intended from plotting wedding overkill. A hundred-odd minutes of the ludicrous matrimonial mania on show here makes a quick, quiet little registry office ceremony look like the height of taste and class.

Confetti owes most of its laughs (the tone here suggests a conscious effort to progress from the 'niceness' of Working Title's genre dominance) to a seasoned company of 'cringe comedians' that enfolds stand-ups and British TV comedy sparks, many of them familiar from *Peep Show*, *The Office*, *Spaced*, *Alan Partridge*, *Green Wing* et al, as well as improvisational veteran Alison Steadman in its ensemble.

And who doesn't get a kick out of a kooky mockumentary? But ever since *This Is Spinal Tap* nailed the rock documentary, the bar has been mighty high for faux fly-on-the-wall parody, with Christopher Guest still pre-eminent in the field. Whereas Guest's documentary-like structures and improvs foster sharp but fundamentally affectionate observations of real human behaviour, however absurdly extreme, director Debbie 'Nasty Neighbours' Isitt is having more of a satirical crack at the unreality of TV-type 'reality' – from the surreal Bridezilla series on down.

The trigger is conniving publishing folk (Jimmy Carr, Felicity Montagu) who need a stunt to boost their bridal-style mag, and duly interview a string of ridiculous couples. The three pliant pairs they settle on are pretty lame themselves. Most believable are couple number one, Matt and Sam (Martin Freeman and Jessica Stevenson). These two are sweeties who love musicals and want to play Fred Astaire and Ginger Rogers on their big day – if they can nudge mother-of-the-bride Steadman and Sam's pushy cruise entertainer sister out of the spotlight for once.

Couple number two, jealous, controlling Josef and put-upon Isabelle (Stephen Mangan and Meredith MacNeill), are highly-strung, aggressive tennis enthusiasts whose ceremony on a mocked-up court with ball boy attendants and an umpire celebrant involves rather a lot of puns about balls. Mangan shines as the most unpleasant contender and delivers the best petulant outbursts: 'Please get it into your thick head how much I respect you!'

Couple number three, Michael and Joanna (Robert Webb and Olivia Colman, who deserve some kind of a prize for letting it all hang out with such seeming nonchalance), are dippy naturists whose hopes for a dignified and spiritual experience au naturel seem doomed the minute *Confetti*'s editor realises that nudes on the cover sell mags of the upper-rack variety, but not one pushing satin Cinderella gowns and out-of-control consumerism.

Upstaging all of them are the squealing, wildly enthusiastic wedding planners, Gregory and Archie (Jason Watkins and Vincent Franklin), a dandy duo who appear to have been styled sartorially on eccentric artists Gilbert and George but as characters are very much in the queenie panto tradition of the two camp dudes that Martin Short and B. D. Wong played in the Steve Martin *Father Of The Bride*. That they are fairly hilarious is probably something we should be heartily ashamed of, since swishy cinematic wedding planners/interior decorators/choreographers are as stereotypical as the fey hamsters in that bizarro credit card advert. But hey, satire and sensitivity, not a good match.

The expected highlight – the actual weddings, performed one after another before judges – falls a little short since the clearly modest budget delivers something closer to a school revue than parodic spectacle. It also dawdles long enough to set you wondering about details, like, 'Why don't the tennis players have any friends?' and, 'How is it that when performing her vows, Sam suddenly has a pair of pipes like Ruthie Henshall when she was previously tone deaf?' We'd argue that their efforts would be funnier if the singing and dancing were more toe-curling – like Round One of *X Factor* auditions. In this respect, *Confetti* doesn't quite manage to keep up the courage of its convictions.

Apparently, having established the concept and situations, Isitt had the cast improvise all the dialogue; now we know why Mike Leigh improvises before shooting but has a script down cold when the cameras actually roll. The actors riffing here are funny up to a point; their body language and expressions are more eloquent than the dialogue. A wordsmith honing the better ideas would have trimmed the flab, and since Isitt is a playwright one would have hoped for tighter content, more pointed and more consistent in tone. Still, it's cheerfully daft enough to be good fun, and even if you won't be quoting it the next day, it'll keep you laughing from start to finish. ★★★ **AE**

⦾ THE CONFORMIST (IL CONFORMISTA) (1969)

Starring: *Jean-Louis Trintignant (Marcello Clerici), Stefania Sandrelli (Giulia), Dominique Sanda (Anna Quadri), Pierre Clementi (Lino Semirama – the chauffeur), Gastone Moschin (Manganiello), Enzo Tarascio (Professor Quadri)*
Director: *Bernardo Bertolucci*
Screenwriter: *Bernardo Bertolucci based on the novel by Alberto Moravia*
18/107 mins./Drama/Italy/France/West Germany

Paris, 1938 and Fascist agitator Marcello Clerici is ordered to assassinate his mentor, Professor Quadri, whose bisexual, socialist spouse Anna has designs on Marcello's glamorous, but unloved wife, Giulia.

Adapted from Alberto Moravia's novel, this study of a man trapped between convention and rebellion could be called Bernardo Bertolucci's *5*, as not only was it his fifth feature (the half being his contribution to *Love And Anger*, 1967), but it also revealed as much about its maker as it did its protagonist. No wonder Bertolucci once averred, '*The Conformist* is my most difficult film ... because it is the simplest one.'

Ostensibly, it's a reworking of the structure and themes of *Before The Revolution*, in which the hero was torn politically (between Marxism and his bourgeois upbringing) and sexually (between marriage, incest and homosexuality) before accepting his fate. Jean-Louis Trintignant's Fascist foot soldier is similarly trapped: firstly by what he presumed to be the fatal ramifications of the childhood assault that caused him to repress his sexual identity, and secondly by his inability to respond to his attraction to Dominique Sanda, who he feels betrayed him in attempting to seduce Stefania Sandrelli during their scorching tango.

But this complex, multi-layered drama pits Bertolucci in a ethical-creative crisis of his own, as he establishes an aura of decadence he isn't quite able to denounce. Following his New Wave instincts, the action is elliptical and lyrical. But Bertolucci was as keen to recreate both the social and cinematic opulence of 1930s Paris. Consequently, he and cinematographer Vittorio Storaro made extensive use of elaborate camera movements, vibrant colours, dramatic angles and delicate contrasts of light and shade consciously to evoke the stylisation of Josef von Sternberg, Max Ophuls and Orson Welles. Yet, perhaps Bertolucci's reluctance to pursue his natural Godardianism derived from the fact that Jean-Luc Godard had criticised his decision to accept Paramount coin to complete the picture? He certainly made his resentment known, however, by giving Enzo Tarascio (who is brutally murdered in the snowy woods) Godard's exact address and phone number. ★★★★★ **DP**

⦾ CONGO (1995)

Starring: *Laura Linney (Dr. Karen Ross), Dylan Walsh (Dr. Peter Elliot), Ernie Hudson (Captain Munro), Tim Curry (Herkermer Homolka), Grant Heslov (Richard, Elliot's Assistant), Joe Don Baker (R.B. Travis, TraviCom CEO), Lorene Noh (Amy), Mary Ellen Trainor (Moira), Mista Rosas (Amy The Gorilla)*
Director: *Frank Marshall*
Screenwriter: *John Patrick Shanley, based on the novel by Michael Crichton*
12/109 mins./Fantasy/Adventure/USA

A team of diamond hunters go missing in the jungles of the Congo, prompting another team to fly in after them, searching for their missing compatriots. Inevitably, however, things go badly wrong.

Jurassic Park and *Disclosure* may have joined the megabucks hall of fame, but this screen adaptation of a Michael Crichton novel shows that plundering the science-as-thriller guru's back catalogue is not always a surefire way to success. While *Jurassic Park* made the idea of dinosaurs plausible, *Congo* takes an equally far-fetched idea but only serves to make the concept all the more ludicrous with the end result.

The action gets under way with an explorer hunting for diamonds in the jungle, only to have his organs rearranged by a creature bearing a strong resemblance to an Old English sheepdog with problem skin. Almost immediately, his scientist fiancée heads off to look for him, joined by a mad Romanian (Curry, making his contribution to great accent travesties of our time) convinced of the existence of the gems, and a weedy primatologist returning his pet gorilla Amy to the jungle having taught the creature to talk.

It transpires that this particular primate's vocals aren't just restricted to parrot-fashion mimicking. Amy (in truth, an impressive Stan Winston animatronic creation) can spout lucid sentences with the help of a verbal translator, and as such provides some of the movie's best acting, as the trio, joined by a wisecracking Ernie Hudson, try to establish just what it is that's been scattering bits of explorer everywhere.

What begins as mildly intriguing stuff with some genuinely unsettling moments, quickly melts into a plot so confusing that it almost begins to look as though the editor was taking some mind-altering substance. Scientific mumbo-jumbo and dialogue of the 'But doc, I don't understand' variety is wheeled out to a worrying extent. *Congo* stops quite far short of delivering any truly mind-blowing thrills, and when it finally spills the beans on just what is hiding in the jungle, it's more of a predictable anti-climax than a shocking revelation. The weakest Crichton adaptation to date. ★★ **CW**

⦾ CONSPIRACY THEORY (1997)

Starring: *Mel Gibson (Jerry Fletcher), Julia Roberts (Alice Sutton), Patrick Stewart (Dr Jonas), Cylk Cozart (Agent Lowry), Steve Kahan (Mr. Wilson)*
Director: *Richard Donner*
Screenwriter: *Brian Helgeland*
15/135 mins./Thriller/Romance/Drama/USA

Jerry Fletcher is a paranoid New York cab driver who sees conspiracy theories everywhere, and reports them to a busy DA, who he has a crush on. When one of his theories turns out to be right, they are both put in danger.

With some movies, it's hard not to have that creepy feeling you've been here before. Here's Mel Gibson indulging in the brand of mentally unhinged heroism perfected in all those *Mad Max* and *Lethal Weapon* movies. There's Julia Roberts as the lawyer with the lips of an angel and the uptake of a sloth, slowly realising all those paranoid fantasies are true, as in *The Pelican Brief*. And at the helm is Richard Donner, also of the *Lethal* series, who can probably direct star vehicle comedy thrillers in his sleep (indeed, that's the only acceptable explanation for *Assassins*) and clearly isn't interested in listening to a pitch unless a cadre of evil super-agents in black helicopters are after the heroes.

Jerry Fletcher is the epitome of an obsessive nutcase, a New York cab driver with the compulsion to purchase a copy of *The Catcher In The Rye* when he gets a panic attack, and whose hobby is compiling bizarre conspiracy theories which he then writes up in a loony newsletter. Alice Sutton is the Justice Department chick to whom Jerry takes his insane notions, setting up a relationship that see-saws unsettlingly between smart-talking romantic comedy and stalker-stalkee menace.

Given that it's established early on that Alice is the daughter of a mysteriously-murdered judge and Jerry's neuroses run a lot deeper than they seem, it's a certainty that there will indeed turn out to be a conspiracy to get the both of them. And with Stewart doing a *Marathon Man* act as the CIA psychiatrist, Dr. Jonas, with a needle of truth serum ready and, after his first encounter with Gibson, a half-bitten nose, it's not too much of a strain to figure out who'll be behind everything rotten in the plot.

Though it tries to be different, with hair's-breadth escapes that don't depend on implausible stunts or Bondian-scale explosions, *Conspiracy Theory* is an uneasy mix of laughs and thrills; suspense and soap. While Gibson makes something of a role that plays cleverly with his inability to be entirely likeable, Roberts is dragged along for the ride and does little but toss her hair and listen to garbled explanations. The script unwisely goes out of its way to identify its maguffin as '*Manchurian Candidate* stuff', reminding you how effective this could have been if it weren't too lazy to cap all its fake explanations with a satisfying real one. ★★★★ **AC**

THE CONSTANT GARDENER (2005)

Starring: *Ralph Fiennes (Justin Quayle), Rachel Weisz (Tessa Quayle), Hubert Kounde (Arnold Bluhm), Danny Huston (Sandy Woodrow), Bill Nighy (Sir Bernard Pellegrin)*
Director: *Fernando Meirelles*
Screenwriter: *Jeffrey Caine, based on the novel by John le Carré*
15/129 mins./Drama/Germany/UK/

Awards: *Academy Awards – Best Supporting Actress, BAFTA – Best Editing, Golden Globes – Best Supporting Actress*

After his radical wife is found savagely murdered in the Kenyan bush, low-ranking British diplomat Justin Quayle begins to suspect this was no simple bandit attack but the result of a conspiracy much closer to home. Retracing her path, he unearths a terrible secret and the legacy of a woman he never truly knew.

Those au fait with the icy vibe of spymaster John le Carré may be surprised to hear that this latest adaptation of one of his labyrinthine novels is not set among the rusting cracks of the Iron Curtain but the sun-baked shanty towns of Kenya. And neither is it concerned with the shenanigans of secret agents. At least, not directly. This is haunting romance, a ruminating thriller and a depiction of modern Africa a million moons from the grandeur of Meryl Streep's 'faahhrm' in the veldt.

What won't surprise is that Jeffrey Caine's script is a demanding beast. We have to grasp the origins of the marriage between impassioned Tessa and an inert – except when tending his florid garden – Quayle after it has been horribly sundered. Through a series of extended flashbacks, Weisz gives Tessa such irrepressible spirit she looms ghost-like over the rest of the movie. We have to pick up the threads of a typically fiddly le Carré conspiracy involving the dark practices of drug companies testing medicines in the desperate backwaters of Nairobi – something Tessa was on to and hid from her husband, a man sequestered on the bottom rung of the diplomatic ladder. Plus, there hangs a doubt over Tessa's fidelity; an oily Danny Huston, as Quayle's haughty superior, was obsessed with her.

City Of God's fireball Fernando Meirelles (who replaced the *Potter*-bound Mike Newell) restrains the whiplash pans and hyper-space tracking shots of his first outing to moodily tread among such multi-layered and slow-burning material. As the film stretches out its limbs to expose the weighty political subtext – aid as a poisoned chalice – he finds his feet, shooting the street poverty and arid Kenyan expanses with a bold, unsentimental eye while revealing a sensitivity for character.

Fiennes, inch by delicate inch, awakens Quayle from his torpor to feel what his wife so badly felt about the injustice meted out to the Third World. Meirelles has also managed a very literary concept – the inversed plot. This is a love story told in its aftermath, a rites-of-passage drama flowing from middle-aged stasis into youthful passion and a thriller where the outcome is preordained, but devastating all the same. ★★★★ **IN**

CONSTANTINE (2005)

Starring: *Keanu Reeves (John Constantine), Rachel Weisz (Angela Dodson/Isabel Dodson), Shia LaBeouf (Chas Kramer), Djimon Hounsou (Midnight), Max Baker (Beeman)*
Director: *Francis Lawrence*
Screenwriters: *Kevin Brodbin, Frank A. Cappello, based on the comic book* Hellblazer *by Jamie Delano, Garth Ennis*
15/121 mins./Fantasy/Horror/USA/Germany

John Constantine is a man gifted – or rather cursed – with the ability to see the 'half-breed' demons and angels that walk the Earth. More interested in exorcising demons, he's reluctant to help police detective Angela investigate the suicide of her sister, but when full-on demons start fighting their way into our plane, he reconsiders.

Keanu Reeves does a good 'pissed off'. He may be an actor of, shall we say, limited range, but when a look of slight confusion and handsome disgruntlement is needed, he's your man. As such, he slips easily into the role of netherworld-weary demon-slayer John Constantine. Or, at least, the movie version of John Constantine.

Those familiar with the caustic, mouthy blond Liverpudlian of the *Hellblazer* comic-book series may be disappointed with this moodier, more laconic Californian version. But to those who couldn't care less about graphic-novel faithfulness, he's a terrifically miserable sod. His demon-slaying is merely to facilitate his entry into Heaven and avoid a trip downstairs as punishment for the mortal sin of suicide (from which he was unwillingly resuscitated), and if he should improve the lives of mankind along the way, well, that can't be helped.

The fact that he's an inhabitant of abstinent LA who smokes like George Burns after a three-day orgy, leaving him riddled with lung cancer, is the icing on the rotten cake. He makes Batman look like a highly caffeinated *T4* presenter. Reeves plays Constantine as Neo minus the self-importance. He is, for the most part, humourless, only occasionally hurling the odd dagger of wit, which he throws away with louche abandon, rather than delivering it Arnie-style over a bullet-ridden corpse.

In fact, rather than the all-action, quick-talking demon apocalypse you'd think this storyline demands, this is more a movie of mood than moment. Set-pieces are effectively brief and scattered rather than constant CGI aggressions, while interest is maintained by both a persistent fear that something wicked this way comes and a plot that, while sometimes confusing, is always inventive. Where other movies might dwell on a holy water-drenched battle with half-human/half-demon hordes, or the dispatching of screeching, winged evils, Constantine keeps them short and sharp, in a way befitting an anti-hero who'd rather not be there if he didn't absolutely have to.

Through the sweeping lens of Francis Lawrence (the music video director behind Britney Spears' sweaty-walled *I'm A Slave 4 U*, among others), *Constantine*'s world is eerily beautiful to behold. Hell is a parallel dimension, accessed via a cat and a puddle (the script is full of such welcome quirks), scorched and teeming with spindly, half-decapitated nasties. The real world is only a little better, imbued with a sense of stylish, Fincher-esque dankness. To complement the overall sombre tone, there's tremendous wit in the details, particularly in the antihero's choice of weaponry, be it crucifix-etched knuckle-dusters or a cross-shaped shotgun.

However, all the sophistication of the presentation isn't quite enough to cover up shortcomings in the script, which could have delved more into the lives of the footsoldiers embroiled in this battle between the forces of good and evil. The characters disrupting Constantine's life are enticing, yet in most cases distant. Weisz crumbles gently as the detective who's haunted by her sister's death, but the character is undeniably flimsy, while Swinton's elegant, androgynous Gabriel could do with more flesh on his/her/its wings. One part should have been completely jettisoned, and that's the glaringly misjudged comedy sidekick, Chas. He disrupts the tone whenever he's on screen, his presence making no sense alongside a confirmed loner like John Constantine.

Slender supports aside, though, Constantine is a wry pleasure, thankfully free of much of the redemptive cuddliness that can blight even the darkest blockbuster. You can't go too far wrong with a movie where the hero would much rather kiss up to a Marlboro than the leading lady. ★★★ **OR**

CONTACT (1997)

Starring: *Jodie Foster (Eleanor Arroway), Matthew McConaughey (Palmer Joss), James Woods (Michael Kitz), Angela Bassett (Rachel Constantine), John Hurt (S.R. Hadden), David Morse (Ted Arroway), Jena Malone (Young Ellie), Rob Lowe (Richard Rank)*
Director: *Robert Zemeckis*
Screenwriters: *Michael Goldenberg, James V. Hart, based on the novel* Contact *by Carl Sagan, and a story by Carl Sagan and Ann Druyan*
PG/142 mins./Sci-fi/USA

Ellie is determined to find out if we are alone in the universe. When her satellite array picks up a message from space, she is determined to be the person to make first contact with the mysterious callers.

What you get out of *Contact* will depend much on your take on humankind's quest for proof either that we are not alone, or that there is a god (the two are tantalisingly opposite sides of the *Contact* coin). But you need not to have read Carl Sagan's book, only to have gazed at the stars and wondered ...

The story is of Ellie Arroway, orphaned and single, but refusing to believe we are alone in the universe. Inspired by her father's memory, she now works as an astronomer sifting through deep space radio waves with a small team (including a fine William Fichtner as blind astronomer Dr. Kent Clark – ouch) financed by reclusive billionaire S.R. Hadden. Ellie and the team are viewed as outcasts by much of the establishment, including her ex-boss Drumlin until an E.T. calls and Arroway tunes in ecstatically.

But reaction to her discovery disappoints her: the national security advisor takes a dim view; Drumlin takes the credit; and only presidential advisor Constantine (an excellent Bassett) takes the sensible middle ground. While the world goes nuts, and the nuts go religious, the signal is dissected but not understood. Then Hadden intervenes and it is decoded as the blueprint for a giant machine that promises transport, contact and the ultimate truth ... for one person only.

Zemeckis redeploys all the brilliant stylistic tricks that made *Forrest Gump* such a visual treat: digital magic (giving President Clinton almost as much screentime as some co-stars); beautiful cinematography (by Don Burgess, painting stunning pictures of New Mexico satellite dishes), and an opening sequence (pulling back from Earth to deep space) that could just be the Greatest Movie Beginning Of All Time.

In places (as in *Gump*) the film seems a little long and too deep in sentiment – especially in developing the romance between Arroway and McConaughey's religious scholar-cum-government advisor. Strangely, McConaughey drifts in and out more as the film's moral conscience than Arroway's hunk on the side, but plays as well as he looks, with a presence far outweighing his years. And with Foster as his focus Zemeckis can hardly fail. She is brilliant (and more beautiful than ever), as the forceful individual whose idealism leads the whole planet towards a giant leap.

There are few laughs, no *Men In Black*-style monsters and only a little sci-fi hokum (Hurt's barking Hadden – an airborne Howard Hughes – and NASA's over-familiarity with the technology of the alien machine) because *Contact* delivers on more than a pure visual level, reiterating the idea that greatest progress is made taking 'small steps' towards enlightenment. We've long grown accustomed to the movies telling us we are not alone, but *Contact* is the first film to take the answer as seriously as the question. ★★★★ **NJ**

Movie Trivia: Contact

The doctored footage of President Clinton resulted in CNN banning the use of their logo in fictional movies. Jodie Foster's real name is Alicia Christian Foster. Her siblings dubbed her Jodie. Ralph Fiennes and Sidney Poitier were considered to star but were not cast.

THE CONVERSATION (1974)

Starring: *Gene Hackman (Harry Caul), John Cazale (Stan), Allen Garfield (William P. 'Bernie' Moran), Frederic Forrest (Mark), Cindy Williams (Ann), Teri Garr (Amy), Harrison Ford (Martin Stett)*
Director: *Francis Ford Coppola*
Screenwriter: *Francis Ford Coppola*
15/113 mins./Drama/USA
Awards: *BATFA – Best Film Editing, Best Sound Track*

Surveillance expert Harry Caul uncovers a murder plot via his eavesdropping.

The same year Francis Coppola made *The Godfather Part II*, he also wrote and directed another great landmark American film of the 70s. A tense, paranoia thriller, *The Conversation* is also a disturbing exploration of privacy and personal responsibility in the age of technological intrusion. Gene Hackman finds bittersweet poignancy in solitary surveillance expert Harry Caul, indifferent to the subjects of his eavesdropping until the furtive confidences of illicit lovers arouse guilt and longings that draw him into a murder plot and corporate conspiracy.

Groundbreaking sound design by Walter Murch and the know-how of advisor Hal Lipset (who examined the notorious gap in Nixon's White House tapes) enhance the realism; compelling dialogue and Hackman's finely portrayed internal struggle give it the fascination of a recurring dream.

A masterful study in psychology that touches on issues accutely prevelant today. ★★★★★ **AM**

CONVOY (1978)

Starring: *Kris Kristofferson (Rubber Duck), Ali MacGraw (Melissa), Ernest Borgnine (Sherriff Lyle Wallace), Burt Young (Love Machine/Pig Pen), Madge Sinclair (Widow Woman)*
Director: *Sam Peckinpah*
Screenwriter: *B.W.L. Norton*
12/106 mins./Action/Comedy/USA

Free-spirited trucker 'Rubber Duck' is pursued by traffic cop Lyle Wallace as he leads a convoy of trucks across the USA. The chase becomes a big media event and Rubber Duck becomes a counterculture rebel hero.

Even in the tiny genre of films based on songs (*Ode to Billy Joe*, *Purple People Eater*, *The Crossing Guard*), Convoy is a strange effort. C.W. McCall's 1977 CB radio-themed novelty hit was just a collection of trucker slang, but here it is gussied up by Sam Peckinpah (no less) as a big rig reprise of *The Wild Bunch*.

Kris Kristofferson is perfectly cast as trucker outlaw Rubber Duck, while a wonderfully oversized Ernest Borgnine goes all out as 'Dirty Lyle', the 'bear' who hates 'breakers' and finally decides to call in the National Guard to help him enforce traffic laws with machine guns. The plot is almost invisible, with Rubber Duck and his breaker buddies just up and deciding to trundle their lorries across the Western States in a dash for Mexico (no one ever mentions delivering their loads to intended destinations) and becoming such a folk hero that the creepy governor (Seymour Cassell) tries to cash in. Kristofferson and Borgnine were old Peckinpah hands, as is heroine Ali MacGraw (a characterless photographer) and sidekick Burt Young ('Love Machine' aka 'Pig Pen'), and there's a lot of business about cops and outlaws who mirror each other, but the main attraction is the visuals – huge trucks rolling across desert roads in clouds of dust, police cars crashing through billboards, trucks demolishing a corrupt small town. There are traces of road movie melancholia in the depressed cafes, jails and laybys where free spirits are broken, but it's still mostly a cash-in on *Smokey and the Bandit* with a few rags of poetry tossed into the mix. ★★★ **KN**

COOGAN'S BLUFF (1968)

Starring: *Clint Eastwood (Deputy Sheriff Walt Coogan), Lee J. Cobb (Det Lt. McElroy), Susan Clark (Julie Roth), Tisha Sterling (Linny Raven), Don Stroud (James Ringerman), Betty Field (Mrs. Ellen Ringerman), Tom Tully (Sheriff McCrea)*
Director: *Don Siegel*
Screenwriters: *Herman Miller, Dean Riesner, Howard Rodman*
15/93 mins./Crime/USA

Arizona Deputy Sheriff Walt Coogan is sent to New York to pick up hoodlum prisoner James Ringerman who has escaped from a prison hospital. Though well out of his jurisdiction and patronised by the big city cops, Coogan sets out to bring in his man.

'A man's gotta do what a man's gotta do,' sneers cigar-chomping urban cop Lee J. Cobb at tight-lipped Deputy Coogan when he declares his intention to track down a runaway hippie troublemaker as if he were pursuing an outlaw in the desert.

This is a key movie in the evolution of the cop picture and of Eastwood's star image, offering an odd parallel with *Midnight Cowboy* as the straight-looking, cowboy-hatted hero is treated as a joke by the kooks, deadbeats and freaks of the city, who sneer at his John Wayne values, prehistoric sexual attitudes and faintly campy boots. Don Siegel's second great New York cop picture, following *Madigan*, this is also a rough draft for the San Francisco-set *Dirty Harry*.

It's a transformed Western, with Eastwood's straight-shooting but uptight cowboy policeman stalking in a stetson through the Pigeon-Toed Orange Peel freak-out club (one of the great 1960s scenes – featuring psychedelic lighting effects and bikini girls dancing in cages with peace symbols written on their tummies), casting disapproving sneers at social workers and flower children, and corraling his fugitive after an exciting motorbike chase in Central Park.

He proves that his old-style heroism still plays in the 60s, but softens his dead right values enough to show some sympathy for his battered captive. The cowboy cop-out-of-water theme was reprised, in more gentle mode, in the Dennis Weaver TV series *McCloud*, but has been reworked, in increasingly bizarre disguises, in the likes of *The French Connection II*, *Brannigan*, *Cruising*, *Beverly Hills Cop*, *Red Heat* and *Black Rain*. ★★★★ **KN**

THE COOK, THE THIEF, HIS WIFE AND HER LOVER (1989)

Starring: *Richard Bohringer (Richard Borst), Michael Gambon (Albert Spica), Helen Mirren (Georgina Spica), Alan Howard (Michael), Tim Roth (Mitchel), Ciaran Hinds (Cory), Gary Olsen (Spangler)*
Director: *Peter Greenaway*
Screenwriter: *Peter Greenaway*
18/124 mins./Drama/France/Netherlands/UK

Georgina Spica embarks on a pantry-enclosed affair with another regular customer of her favourite restaurant, shunning her bulldog of a husband. He, the Thief of the title, meanwhile, plots tortuous acts of revenge.

It comes as no surprise to learn that it took director Peter Greenaway a very long time to find a film company that would consider his script for more than 30 seconds, since the film opens with a close-up of dogs gorging on hunks of bloody carcass and then pans to the Thief force-feeding dogshit to a naked man. The cold artiness of Greenaway's previous films (*The Draughtsman's Contract*, *The Belly Of An Architect*) is thoroughly subordinated here.

Shot entirely on Elstree's stage six, the story unfolds during several evenings at an exclusive French restaurant where the Thief hangs out with his scummy gang of cut-throats, regaling them with his obscene vanities and diabolic table manners, and casually brutalising his long-suffering Wife.

The Wife meanwhile is intrigued by a quiet, fastidious diner and embarks on a series of fatal sexual liaisons with him, starting in the ladies' lavatory and progressing through the restaurant's various well-stocked pantries. The Cook assists the couple and ignores the Thief's escalating violence. Eventually, the Thief tumbles and carries out a hideous revenge.

From the astonishing studio sets and (Gaultier-designed) costumes to Gambon's performance (so ferociously wicked that it beggars description), Greenaway attacks his targets with a sadistic obsession that is, frankly, terrifying. Many people will be profoundly offended by this film – by the monstrous misanthropy that Greenaway lays bare through it, by the spiteful images of women in a vicious world – but some may appreciate it for what it certainly is: the most startling depiction of intellectual cruelty and evil for many years. ★★★★ **JM**

COOL HAND LUKE (1967)

Starring: *Paul Newman (Luke), George Kennedy (Dragline), J.D. Cannon (Society Red), Lou Antonio (Koko), Robert Drivas (Loudmouth Steve), Strother Martin (Captain)*
Director: *Stuart Rosenberg*
Screenwriters: *Donn Pearce, Frank Pierson based on the novel by Pearce*
15/126 mins./Drama/USA

Luke drunkenly vandalises parking meters. This minor offence leads to a light custodial sentence that he manages to screw up into something tantamount to the death penalty by resisting all attempts to grind him down.

A big hit in 1967, this combines the then-popular rebel-against-the-system and America-is-rotten themes with the pleasures of the good ole boy hellhole prison farm/chain gang genre. It also affords Paul Newman – at the height of his blue-eyed superstar charisma – one of his best roles as Luke, a mooncalf vandal first seen striking out against 'the Man' by drunkenly decapitating parking meters.

Landed on a Deep South prison farm ruled by a smiling tyrant (the unforgettable Strother Martin), Luke's downright mule-headed attitude brings him into major conflict with the grinning guards (Clu Gulager as a sadist in mirrorshades) and makes him a heroic martyr for the other cons (bullyboy George Kennedy, who learns to 'respect' the loon). Finally, he takes on the Christ-like qualities associated with other rebel-in-the-jug heroes like Jack Nicholson in *One Flew Over the Cuckoo's Nest* and Tim Robbins in *The Shawshank Redemption* and inspires one final break-out.

Cool Hand Luke is one of those movies everybody remembers Great Moments from: the egg-eating contest (with Newman's uncomfortably bloated belly), the card game that gets out of hand, Gulager's sunglasses getting stepped on, Martin's catchphrase (the poster line) 'what we've got here is a failure to communicate'. Fans of sweaty redneck character actors get a treat, what with an unbeatable array of J.D. Cannon, Anthony Zerbe, Joe Don Baker, Clifton James, Harry Dean Stanton, Dennis Hopper and Morgan Woodward all in one film. Stuart Rosenberg, hardly a directorial star but a solid talent, shepherds the great cast through the solid story, but adds a distinctive sun-drenched, slow-burning atmosphere to this wryly comic allegory. ★★★★ **KN**

⦿ COP LAND (1997)

Starring: *Sylvester Stallone (Sheriff Freddy Heflin), Harvey Keitel (Ray Donlan), Ray Liotta (Gary 'Figgsy' Figgis), Robert De Niro (Lt. Moe Tilden), Janeane Garofalo (Deputy Cindy Betts), Michael Rappaport (Murray 'Superboy' Babitch), Annabella Sciorra (Liz Randone)*
Director: *James Mangold*
Screenwriter: *James Mangold*
18/104 mins./116 mins (director's cut)/Drama/USA

Freddy Heflin always wanted to be a cop, but because he is partially deaf, can go no higher than being a local sheriff in a town where many cops live. Gradually, however, Freddy begins to realise that some of the cops he idolises are not as honest as he is.

Perhaps unfairly, *Cop Land* reached Brit screens loaded with all the baggage of a long-touted movie. This is the film that represented the first demonstration of 'real' acting from Sylvester Stallone after years of mumbling machismo and, of course, the film that enticed a troika of top thesping talents to take the minimum wage and a 'supporting' role. The result is an honourable attempt to return the mainstream thriller to a more serious, intelligent vein, yet ultimately lacks the complexity of characterisation, dense subterfuge and overall feeling of weightiness that separates the great from the good.

The title refers to Garrison, New Jersey, a New York satellite town that is home to cops who service the Big Apple and is presided over by slow-witted, overweight, partially deaf Sheriff Freddy Heflin. Heflin is an innocent officer totally unaware of the scandal that envelops the town – chiefly an inner circle of corrupt lawmen, lead by Ray Donlan, who are using the town to hide Donlan's nephew and fellow cop Murray Babitch, in the frame for killing two joyriders.

However, Heflin's senses begin to be shaken, firstly by Gary 'Figs' Figgis (an excellent Liotta) an ex-member of Keitel's sanctum, then by the arrival of Internal Affairs agent Moe Tilden to investigate Babitch's disappearance. Soon the convoluted events spiral out of control – Figgis' house is burnt to the ground in an arson attack, Donlan attempts to bump off Babitch to cover his tracks – and Heflin is forced to choose between head in the sandom and taking a stand against those he has previously idolised.

It is not difficult to see why so many acting heavyweights took pay cuts to constitute the stellar cast: director James Mangold's screenplay has a stimulating set-up, characters that owe more than a nod to real people and is prepared with meaty, dramatic confrontations – an argument involving Liotta sticking a dart up his tormentors' nose is winceworthy in the extreme. Equally fascinating is the Smallsville milieu, the siege mentality of the cop ghetto being evoked with considerable realism.

Unsurprisingly, much of the pleasure is derived from the Clash Of The Acting Titans. Just watching these icons strutting their stuff in the same screen space – De Niro chewing scenery with a voracious appetite, Keitel's simmering intensity ready to blow at any moment – creates a filmic frisson par excellence. Appealingly placed between the two giants is Stallone's Heflin, his dumb lug demeanour providing an effective, sympathetic centre to the occasionally overwrought action. It is also incredibly enjoyable (and ironic) watching the wannabe serious thesp Stallone bowing and kow-towing to the method godheads of De Niro and Keitel.

Leaning heavily on the lone sheriff/dirty town motif and concluding with a pump-action bloodbath, *Cop Land* owes more to the simplicity of a Western than, say, Sidney Lumet's powerhouse police corruption dramas. There is just so much glossed-over backstory – Liotta's relationship with Keitel revolving around a murdered partner, Stallone's relationship with unattainable love Annabella Sciorra – that the broad-stroke storytelling eventually becomes confusing and insubstantial. Which is a shame, as somewhere buried in *Cop Land* is a first rate policier. ★★★ **IF**

⦿ CORPSE BRIDE (2005)

Starring: *the voices of: Johnny Depp (Victor Van Dort), Helena Bonham Carter (Corpse Bride), Emily Watson (Victoria Everglot), Tracey Ullman (Nell Van Dort/Hildegarde), Paul Whitehouse (William Van Dort/Mayhew/Paul the Head Waiter)*
Directors: *Tim Burton, Mike Johnson*
Screenwriters: *John August Pamela Pettler, Caroline Thompson*
PG/76 mins./Animation/Comedy/UK/USA

Victor Van Dort, while memorising wedding vows in the woods, accidentally finds himself married to Emily, who dwells in the land of the dead. Emily is delighted with her new husband, but Victor still wants to marry his original fiancée, Victoria.

The reason Tim Burton is an always-in-work A-list director, while the comparably talented Terry Gilliam struggles to get compromised films made, is that he has an uncanny knack of adapting famous material by other people – whether the Batman comics, a Roald Dahl children's book or *The Legend Of Sleepy Hollow* – into films that are at once value-for-money crowd-pleasers balancing charm and chills and oddly personal little exercises in his own obsessions. Very occasionally, he takes a chance and tries something which feels completely his own.

If *Charlie And The Chocolate Factory* was Burton's big picture for 2005, this is his miniature. With its brief running time, tight little story and sweet/sad Gothic fairy-tale feel, it's more like the live-action *Edward Scissorhands* than Burton's previous animated venture, *The Nightmare Before Christmas*. Design elements are held over from *Nightmare*, which was directed by Henry Selick, and Danny Elfman returns with more songs (livelier than they are memorable), but *Corpse Bride*, which Burton co-directed with animator Mike Johnson, is a different prospect, maybe a trickier sell to a holiday audience even at Hallowe'en, although finally as affecting.

The Johnny Depp-voiced, long-legged, shock-haired Victor is yet another of Burton's film alter egos, demonstrating his inner sensitivity with piano duets, but this is the first Burton film since *Batman Returns* to give much space to female yearnings.

Victor might seem like a hesitant, Scissorhanded misfit in the drab world of the living, but the title character is the blue-skinned, fish-lipped, mostly-rotted Emily. Despite the fact that one eyeball is frequently popped by a chatty maggot, Emily is an alluring creation – cute and repulsive at the same time, and invested with a lot of heart. And the Corpse Bride's rival, Victoria, who could easily get squeezed out of our affections, is as lovingly characterised.

The central irony is that the living world is cold, bitter, restrictive and self-interested, while the underworld is warm, colourful, frivolous and generous. This means that the story is controlled until Victor is dragged under the graveyard, when it makes way for gruesome gags about detached body parts. Thankfully, it does get back to a properly Victorian finish at the altar, with melodramatic villainy, sacrifice and a happy resolution. ★★★★ **KN**

⦿ COURAGE UNDER FIRE (1996)

Starring: *Denzel Washington (Lt. Colonel Nathaniel Serling), Meg Ryan (Captain Karen Emma Walden), Lou Diamond Phillips (Staff Sergeant John Monfriez), Matt Damon (Specialist Ilario), Bronson Pinchot (Bruno), Regina Taylor (Meredith Serling), Scott Glen (Tony Gartner, Washington Post), Sean Astin (Patella)*
Director: *Edward Zwick*
Screenwriter: *Patrick Sheane Duncan*
15/117 mins./War/Drama/USA

Gulf War veteran Serling is assigned by the Army to research a proposed posthumous Medal of Honor for Karen Walden. But as he tries to find out what happened to her, he comes up against a web of lies and cover-ups.

Apart from a scattershot of video-hell gung ho nonsense (mostly starring Rob Lowe), this was the first movie to tackle the subject of the Gulf

War. It was also the first to encompass that moral-itch of an issue which that conflict brought to the public eye: the phenomenon of 'friendly fire' (i.e. being killed by your own side). Yet instead of the expected dose of post-traumatic Vietnam-type war-is-hell psycho-babbling, this is a compelling drama and mystery story in one, and still intelligent enough to carry its share of wartime demons and semi-meaningful issue-making.

There are two strands at work. First, the framework plot of Colonel Nat Serling whose tank is seen mistakenly blowing up one of America's own in the mayhem of Operation: Desert Storm at the film's start. Secondly, in the post-Gulf future, this troubled (see: sneaky alcohol binges, fractious marriage etc.) officer is put in charge of researching a posthumous Medal Of Honor, that of Karen Walden, the first ever woman to be awarded the medal – surrounding the whole event in a media frenzy. However, as he delves into the circumstance of her courageous demise – the rescue of under-fire troops by a lone soon-to-be-downed chopper crew – he is bedevilled by lies, cover-up and downright nastiness. In classic movie tradition, only in unearthing the shattering truth can Colonel Serling exorcise his own ghosts.

Seen entirely in a set of flashbacks replaying the same event from different perspectives as various grunts give their slant, Ryan – an odd but actually quite satisfying choice – acts up a storm of swear-laced military lingo and tough-girl posturing. As with the intense *Flesh And Bone* or *In The Cut*, Ryan is far more accomplished when she ditches the dippy romance.

The recreation of the Gulf's desert combat is solidly realistic without venturing into the sledgehammer photorealism of, say, Oliver Stone – the action, for once, the slave of the story. After the ridiculous *Legends Of The Fall*, Zwick has rediscovered the touch that made *Glory* so measured. And the very nature of friendly fire punctures any possibility of unpalatable star-spangled jingoism. This is – gasp! – a Hollywood movie actually daring to bare its teeth at silly American flag-waving.

The kernel (no pun intended), however, is Washington's riveting performance. As the going gets tougher, the red tape denser, you can see him palpably shed his clouded mien into a hidden nobility. While the uniform defines Walden, Serling uses it for cover.

Apart from some scattered pottiness (drunken stupors, manic suicides) the film's only big failing is in the big twist. After so many red-herring takes on the 'incident', the real one somehow doesn't ring true, leaving you pondering what all the fuss had been about anyway. The journey, though, is worth every penny, packing gravitas, food-for-thought and prickles of familiarity (this is one war we all remember) into every turn. Brain, as well as brawn, can still be part of the big movie ethos. ★★★ **IN**

◎ THE COURT JESTER (1956)

Starring: *Danny Kaye (Hubert Hawkins), Glynis Johns (Maid Jean), Basil Rathbone (Sir Ravenhurst), Angela Lansbury (Princess Gwendolyn), Cecil Parker (King Roderick I)*
Directors: *Melvin Frank, Norman Panama*
Screenwriters: *Melvin Frank, Norman Panama*
U/101 mins./Comedy/Musical/USA

Ye Olde England and Hawkins poses as a jester to help the Black Fox overthrow the usurpacious King Roderick. However, his mission is complicated by the affections of Princess Gwendolyn and the enmity of ruthless baron, Sir Ravenhurst.

Even after a decade in Hollywood, during which time he had scored with *The Secret Life of Walter Mitty* and *White Christmas*, Danny Kaye was still concerned that the energy and spontaneity of his cabaret performances didn't come across on screen. He had been performing live since he was 14 and a rapport with his audience was key to his appeal. So, he formed Dena Productions to attempt some uniquely Kayesque vehicles. Although it remained his favourite picture, his initial venture, *Knock On Wood*, had only done moderate business. But it at least it made money. *The Court Jester* lost $1.8 million. Yet, it has since become one of Kaye's best-loved outings.

As ever, there were some amiable songs and plenty of pantomimic tomfoolery. But Kaye was always more verbally than physically dexterous and his tongue-twisting ingenuity during the scene in which he, Mildred Natwick and Glynis Johns lace a goblet of wine gave rise to perhaps his most famous line, 'The pellet with the poison's in the vessel with the pestle; the chalice from the palace is the brew that's true.'

Yet, while Kaye sought to steal every scene, the film's success owed much to the excellence of the supporting cast. Cecil Parker essays another of his genial dupes, while Angela Lansbury revels in the rare opportunity to be glamorous and coquettish, as the amorous princess. Indeed, only Glynis Johns is short-changed, as Kaye never got the hang of love scenes and the romantic subplot is something of a dud. But the pivotal performance came from Basil Rathbone, who not only excelled at such hissable villainy, but whose presence also linked the movie to the very swashbuckling costumers, like *The Adventures of Robin Hood*, that it was seeking to lampoon.
★★★★ **DP**

◎ LES COUSINS (1959)

Starring: *Gérard Blain (Charles), Jean-Claude Brialy (Paul), Juliette Meyniel (Florence), Claude Cerval (Clovis), Genevieve Clury (Genevieve), Michelle Meritz (Yvonne)*
Director: *Claude Chabrol*
Screenwriter: *Claude Chabrol, Paul Gégauff*
18/109 mins./Drama/France
Awards: *Berlin Film Festival – Golden Bear*

Arriving in Paris to complete his law studies, Charles lodges with his cousin Paul. However, their respective diligence and decadence appeals equally to Florence a free spirit whose indecision will prove their downfall.

Made for a mere $160,000, Claude Chabrol's second feature won the Golden Bear at Berlin. In many ways, it's a mirror image of his debut, *Le Beau Serge* – although its scenario was actually devised first – in which Jean-Claude Brialy returns to his rural village to have his life destroyed by his alcoholic childhood friend, Gérard Blain. Indeed, Chabrol slips another sly reversal into *Les Cousins*, by casting Claude Cerval, who had previously played the priest, as the irredemably wicked Clovis.

But such doublings and inversions were all part of Chabrol's grand design to contrast Blain's self-deceiving dullard with Brialy's decadent dastard and Cerval's cynical schemer with Guy Decomble's priggish bookseller. It's a typically Hitchcockian tactic. But Fritz Lang also seems to have been an influence on the film's sense of foreboding and its expressionist lighting. Indeed, the use of Wagner and the fascistic nature of the cousins' apartment (which belongs to their unseen Uncle Henry) only reinforces the action's Germanic aspect.

Yet, Chabrol's own distinctive voice and vision clearly emerge in the way in which he employs compositional harmony and smooth camera movements to depict a fragmenting situation. Moreover, he also dispenses with the *Cahiers du Cinéma* checklist of ticks and preoccupations that still infatuated his fellow New Wavers, although, rather than being a conscious rejection, this could reflect the input of co-scenarist Paul Gégauff (who would become Chabrol's most effective collaborator).

The emphasis on duality and reversal continues in the cousins' attitude to Juliette Meyniel, as neither she nor Blain is prepared to change their entrenched natures to embark on a potentially beneficial relationship. Thus, she remains footloose and slips into Brialy's bed before succumbing to Cerval. And it's the sight of them together than prompts Blain to commence the accidental game of Russian Roulette that provides the picture's fatal final pairing of action and reaction. ★★★★ **DP**

◎ COYOTE UGLY (2000)

Starring: *Piper Perabo (Violet Sanford), Adam Garcia (Kevin O'Donnell), John Goodman (Bill Sanford), Maria Bello (Lil), Tyra Banks (Zoe), Bridget Moynahan (Rachel), Melanie Lynskey (Gloria), Del Pentecost (Lou the Bouncer), Michael Weston (Danny), LeAnn Rimes (Herself)*
Director: *David McNally*
Screenwriters: *Gina Wendkos*
12/100 mins./Drama/Romance/Music/USA

Against her father's wishes, Violet leaves her comfortable life in New Jersey to follow her songwriting dream in the Big Apple. However, she's quickly forced to take a job in a bar – a bar where the waitresses are expected to do much more than pull a swift pint.

Hands up anyone who, while greedily gobbling up the endless explosions of *The Rock* and *Armageddon*, secretly yearned for Jerry Bruckheimer to forsake mindless violence (and fun), return to his roots and make a *Flashdance* for the millennium? Anyone? Anyone?

Okay, how about an easier question: what is *Coyote Ugly*? Well, it's a real-life raucous bar in New York City for a start. It would like to be a feminist fable (yeah, right). Beyond that, the expression refers to those mornings-after-the-night-before when you find yourself coiled around a stranger so hideous you would, like a coyote caught in a trap, prefer to chew your arm off rather than spend another second spooning. And with this charming metaphor in mind, 'Coyote Ugly' could become a new term in the critical lexicon, because after half an hour of this film, gnawing flesh begins to look like a pretty good option.

If only they had stayed in the bar. While the antics of the Coyote Ugly barmaids – They dance! They strip! They're exploited! – form an admittedly attractive backdrop, the table-dancing soon gives way to a 'plot' which follows drippy ingenue Violet as she pursues a drippy songwriting dream and an equally drippy romance with drippy male lead, Adam Garcia. Yuck.

To illustrate just how shallow the dramatic ambition on display is, we need refer to but one scene: a bar brawl in which our stagestruck heroine persuades sailors (sailors!) to down stools (stools!) by singing karaoke. In that moment, we are asked to believe, a star is born. If you swallow that, you'll swallow anything – including one of the cocktails mixed by the patently unprofessional Coyote Ugly staff. ★ **CK**

◎ CRADLE WILL ROCK (1999)

Starring: *Hank Azaria (Marc Blitzstein), Ruben Blades (Diego Rivera), Joan Cusack (Hazel Huffman), John Cusack (Nelson Rockefeller), Cary Elwes (John Houseman), Phillip Baker Hall (Gray Mathers), Angus Macfadyen (Orson Welles), Bill Murray (Tommy Crickshaw), Vanessa Regrave (Countess LaGrange), Susan Sarandon (Margherita Sarfatti), John Turturro (Aldo Silvano), Emily Watson (Olive Stanton)*
Director: *Tim Robbins*
Screenwriter: *Tim Robbins*
15/132 mins./Drama/USA

A sprawling ensemble piece, set in Depression-era New York. The main focus is on the staging of a controversial, socialist play by Orson Welles' theatre group, but other strands of the plot follow a starving actress, and Nelson Rockefeller's commissioning of a mural by Diego Rivera.

Tim Robbins' third film as a director dramatises a theatre anecdote about the attempted suppression of Marc Blitzstein's socialist musical, *Cradle Will Rock*, the premiere of which was directed by boy wonder Orson Welles.

The story expands Altman-style to take in several other political-artistic strands from the 30s, as Nelson Rockefeller commissions a mural for the lobby of his skyscraper from Diego Rivera, Jewish fascist Margherita Sarfatti peddles great works of art to American industrialists to get backing for Mussolini, and reactionaries mount hearings on communist influence in the publicly-funded theatre as a way of attacking President Roosevelt's New Deal.

All this is there, as well as thumbnail sketches of economic desperation (Emily Watson starving on the streets), high society decadence, a steel strike that parallels the plot of the play, fantasies in which Blitzstein is visited by the ghostly figures of his dead wife and Bertolt Brecht and a bizarre almost-love affair between washed-up ventriloquist Murray (as good here as in *Rushmore*) and anti-communist agitator Joan Cusack (also on top form).

Bits of it don't work – Macfadyen has the bluster of a young Welles but crucially misses the voice, scenes of Rockefeller partying with Rivera are fun but unlikely, not enough is made of the irony of a pro-union play being banned by a union, and Blitzstein's show doesn't look that hot – and you probably need to know a lot of cultural and political history to sort out what is going on.

But there's important meat here. Given the amount of actual history worked in, it's amazing Robbins has time to make things up, but there are intriguing conspiracy scenes with Philip Baker Hall, Sarandon and Vanessa Redgrave (as a Marxist Margaret Dumont), and a wonderful thread about Murray's despair at political theatre ('Reds aren't funny') that climaxes when he commits professional suicide by having his dummy sing the *Internationale* before an anti-commie crowd. ★★★★ **KN**

◎ THE CRAFT (1996)

Starring: *Robin Tunney (Sarah Bailey), Fairuza Balk (Nancy Downs), Neve Campbell (Bonnie), Rachel True (Rochelle), Skeet Ulrich (Chris Hooker), Christine Taylor (Laura Lizzie), Breckin Myer (Mitt)*
Director: *Andrew Fleming*
Screenwriters: *Peter Filardi, Andrew Fleming, based on a story by Peter Filardi*
15/101 mins./Genre Horror/Drama/Fantasy/USA

Real witch Sarah is new in town, and wants to blend in. However, she is quickly spotted by a wanna-be-witch trio who function as the generic school misfits. Things start getting interesting when their black magic begins to work, with murderous consequences.

If awards were bestowed upon films for far-fetchedness, this latest variation on the careworn teen angst theme – a coming-of-age tale garnished with black comedy and OTT horror – would surely have accumulated a hatful. That said, for all its stupidity, the second effort from *Threesome* helmer Andrew Fleming provides plenty of schlocky fun.

Troubled teen Sarah falls in with a misfit trio immediately recognisable as outcasts due to their extraordinary eye makeup, skin deformities and fondness for doctoring their school uniforms. They also happen to be into witchcraft, as Sarah discovers when she is inaugurated into their magic circle. But while the quartet's initial bouts of spell-casting – levitation, alopecia imposed upon the school's queen bitch (*The Brady Bunch*'s Christine Taylor) – are amusing, things take a turn for the sinister when head 'witch' Nancy uses her powers to murderous effect, and Sarah decides enough is enough.

For the first two-thirds this comes across as a lightweight cross between *Heathers* and *The Witches Of Eastwick*. There's plenty of dark humour to savour too (mainly courtesy of the snarling, deliciously mean Balk) although the conscious efforts to capture an adolescent audience mean *The Craft* is never quite as warped as it could have been.

What lets the film down badly, though, is its over-reliance on flashy special effects, giving way to a final reel showdown that becomes increasingly ridiculous by the second and culminates in an unexpectedly malicious pay-off. Still, with suitable suspension of disbelief this makes for agreeable enough nonsense. ★★★ **CW**

CRASH (1996)

Starring: *James Ballard (James Spader), Holly Hunter (Helen Remington), Elias Koteas (Vaughan), Deborah Kara Unger (Catherine Ballard), Rosanna Arquette (Gabrielle), Peter MacNeil (Colin Seagrave)*
Director: *David Cronenberg*
Screenwriter: *David Cronenberg, based on the novel by J.G. Ballard*
18/100 mins./Drama/USA/Canada

After he is involved in a car crash, James becomes strangely sexually aroused by crashes and fellow victims. He discovers an entire sub-culture built around his obsession, and tries to pull his wife into it with him.

Herman Hesse's *Steppenwolf* opens with the epigraph 'Not for Everybody'. That goes triple for David Cronenberg's adaptation of J.G. Ballard's 1973 novel, which tackles such extreme subject matter that the mere idea of the film will be a major turn-off for many. However, as with *Dead Ringers*, Cronenberg approaches a touchy concept with a mixture of icy tact and cinematic daring, always informing the wilfully perverse material with a penetrating intelligence and (almost subliminally) very black wit.

James Ballard and his wife Catherine try to keep their marriage alive through shared infidelities and machine fetishes. Ballard survives a major car crash and finds himself aroused in his new car with Helen, a survivor whose husband was killed in the wreck. The charismatic Vaughan, an obsessive explorer of the erotic potential of road accidents, draws Ballard and Helen into his sub-culture, where the fatal smashes of James Dean or Jayne Mansfield are staged as lethally pornographic performance art.

Ballard is fascinated with Vaughan and his acolytes (including a remarkable Rosanna Arquette in leg-irons) and joins with them sexually, all the while looking for a way to bring Catherine up to speed on the fixation, plotting that she should eventually be blessed with her own crash.

It's a very strange road travelled here, yielding a movie that seems like porno from a parallel world. It achieves its strangeness by having apparently realistic characters react in a consistently 'off' way. Without using slo-mo or other obvious tricks, the film fetishises crashed cars (and scarred bodies), as its characters ignore the life-and-limb threatening side of automotive excess and are turned on by write-offs and pile-ups as if that were entirely normal.

It ought to be shocking (one scene has Spader making love to Arquette by penetrating a crash-caused wound in her thigh) but its matter-of-fact tone and concentration on nuance of character in frank sex scenes renders it moving and involving rather than lurid and gratuitous. ★★★★ **KN**

CRASH (2004)

Starring: *Sandra Bullock (Jean), Don Cheadle (Graham), Matt Dillon (Officer Ryan), Jennifer Esposito (Ria), William Fichtner (Flanagan). Terrence Howard (Cameron), Thandie Newton (Christine), Ryan Phillippe (Officer Hanson)*
Director: *Paul Haggis*
Screenwriters: *Paul Haggis, Robert Moresco, based on a story by Paul Haggis*
15/113 mins./Drama/Crime/USA/Germany

Awards: *Academy Awards – Best Editing, Best Picture, Best Original Screenplay, BAFTA – Best Supporting Actress (Thandie Newton), Best Screenplay*

Set over the course of two nights and one day, this multi-stranded ensemble drama dissects the turbulent state of race relations in LA as disparate lives career into each other with unexpected results.

In the prologue to Paul Haggis' ambitious directorial debut, Los Angeles police detective Graham Waters, dazed after a traffic accident, muses distractedly over whether the denizens of LA subconsciously engineer the odd fender-bender as a means of making contact with their fellow citizens. It's a fleeting, almost dream-like moment, one of many that Haggis (screenwriter of *Million Dollar Baby*) juxtaposes with gritty realism and high drama, to paint a highly personal portrait of this unique city.

The metropolis itself doesn't interest Haggis so much as the labyrinthine matrix of race relations it fosters. Crash opens proper with two African-American youths strolling late at night through a smart shopping mall, one of them pontificating on the suspicious glances and instinctive wariness their presence elicits from the rich white folks. It's a familiar spiel and your heart sinks at the prospect of a wordy, didactic seminar from a director out to prove he's down with the brothers. A moment later, however, the rug is pulled smartly out from under us. The character is wordy and didactic, yes, but not the film. He is also – as he proves when he and his partner carjack a young District Attorney and his wife – everything he despises white people for suspecting he is.

It's a feature of the brilliant screenplay that first impressions are constantly knocked sideways. When the taint of tokenism threatens to creep in, it's invariably dispelled by a deeper insight or a veer into tragedy, occasionally even farce, that lays naive preconceptions mercilessly bare. The robbery sets in train a narrative of escalating complexity through which Haggis attempts to put a human face on LA's multicultural plight via a cast of characters drawn from every facet of the city's diverse ethnic spectrum, whose lives intersect at various incendiary junctures over an intense 36-hour period.

It's the human drama, laced so poetically into its cultural context, that makes *Crash* such riveting viewing. And when, as happens on occasion, Haggis stretches credibility to breaking point or ladles on the pathos, he is saved by his universally outstanding cast. It's unfair to single anyone out, but Matt Dillon is superb as the ostensibly standard-issue LAPD redneck, as are Terrence Dashon Howard as a self-satisfied TV producer facing a life-changing identity crisis, and Bullock as a scared rich bitch retreating into loneliness and paranoia behind the walls of her Beverly Hills mansion.

Of course, Los Angeles serves as more than a mere backdrop. Crucial to Haggis' depiction of life in the City Of Angels are its sprawling infrastructure; its near-total reliance on hermetically sealed automobiles; its ghettoising freeway system that carves unbridgeable psychological gulfs between rich neighbourhoods and poor; its desolate sidewalks, deserted subway stations and monolithic parking lots, all of which contribute to a pall of mistrust that hangs as heavy in the air as smog.

If the message in this electrifying film is not overtly one of optimism, it is at least one of hope. There's no plea for peace, love and understanding here – Haggis is too honest for that. Still, Crash depicts not so much a population failing to live in harmony, but one somehow just about succeeding – in spite of a grimly stacked deck, as well as its own myopia, stupidity and knee-jerk intolerance. ★★★★ **SB**

CRAZY/BEAUTIFUL (2001)

Starring: *Kirsten Dunst (Nicole Oakley), Jay Hernandez (Carlos Nunez), Bruce Davison (Tom Oakley), Herman Osorio (Luis), Miguel Castro (Eddie)*
Director: *John Stockwell*
Screenwriters: *Phil Hay, Matt Manfredi*
12/99 mins./135 mins. (director's cut)/Drama/Romance/USA

Carlos is a poor Latino straight-A student who attends school in an upscale part of LA. There he meets wild child Nicole, with whom he falls in love. But her destructive behaviour threatens their future.

The set-up is as formulaic as they come: wild child rich kid Nicole falls for studious, impoverished Carlos, and thus ensues the typical round of tensions and break-ups before a saccharine finale undoes any goodwill the film has built up.

With Stockwell adding a style that is more rough-hewn than the typical studio project, it's good to see a teen pair portrayed as recognisable human beings rather than sex-fuelled stereotypes, and Dunst and Hernandez make a likeable couple.

But the arc of their romance, played out to the obligatory US indie pop soundtrack, has nothing in the way of surprises or quirks to lift it out of the ordinary. ★★★ **IF**

CREATURE FROM THE BLACK LAGOON (1954)

Starring: *Richard Carlson (David Reed), Julie Adams (Kay Lawrence), Richard Denning (Mark Williams), Antonio Moreno (Carl Maia), Nestor Paiva (Lucas), Whit Bissell (Dr Thompson), Bernie Gozier (Zee), Henry Escalante (Chico)*
Director: *Jack Arnold*
Screenwriters: *Harry Essex, Arthur A. Ross*
PG/79 mins./Horror/Adventure/USA

An expedition to the Upper Reaches of the Amazon disturbs the natural habitat of the Gill Man, a prehistoric human-fish hybrid. Scientists attempt to capture the valuable specimen, but the creature is smitten with a svelte ichthyologist.

Directed by sometimes-inspired journeyman Jack Arnold (*The Incredible Shrinking Man*), this is one of the best-loved monster movies of the 50s. Whereas many of its rivals drag until the monster shows up and turn ridiculous afterwards, this establishes an atmosphere of unease and magic in the early stretches, as the monster is glimpsed as a 3-D clutching hand accompanied by its memorable blaring theme tune. When it slinks on screen, the Creature is not some stuntman in a waterlogged sack with ping-pong-ball eyes but a truly impressive make-up creation – a fish-faced humanoid in a scaly wetsuit, which even has its own unique swimming style.

The backlot is covered in foliage to create an impressive jungle hell, and the good ship *Rita* chug chugs across the glassy surface of the Black Lagoon in true *African Queen* fashion. The underwater scenes remain definitive, with the curvy Adams floating on the surface and dangling her long white legs above the Creature's claws, and the Gill Man performing a serpentine underwater ballet beneath her pin-up form.

Few 1950s science fiction films bothered with sex, but this swimming flirtation remains as classic an image of impossible love as King Kong and his tiny blonde.

This element of 'mad love', harking back to classic horror, is at odds with 50s trends and was the single ingredient that made *Creature From the Black Lagoon* more than just another fun monster romp for the kids.

The monster has been merchandised ever since, and was instantly popular enough to return in Arnold's *Revenge of the Creature* and Jack Sherwood's *The Creature Walks Among Us*. ★★★★ **KN**

CREEPSHOW (1982)

Starring: *Hal Holbrook (Professor Henry Northup), Adrienne Barbeau (Wilma Northup), Leslie Nielsen (Richard Vickers), Carrie Nye (Sylvia Grantham), E.G. Marshall (Upson Pratt), Ed Harris (Hank Blaine), Ted Danson (Harry Wentworth), Stephen King (Jordy Verrill)*
Director: *George A. Romero*
Screenwriter: *Stephen King*
15/120 mins./Horror/USA

Five tales of horror assembled into one movie. In the first an old man returns from the grave to visit the daughter who murdered him; in the second, a dumb farmer inspects a meteor that has landed in his yard; in the third, a husband seeks revenge on his wife and her lover; in the fourth, a college is tormented by a creature delivered in a crate; and in the final episode, a fastidious millionaire has a spot of cockroach trouble.

A jaunty and well-mounted portmanteau of five gleefully silly horror tales inspired by the drugstore traditions of the E.C. Comics and adapted by native master of the genre Stephen King who even stars in one episode as a hick farmer who picks up an alien fungus. What makes the series so rich and memorable is George A. Romero, who angled his legendary zombie films with a satirical twist, and presents these stories as icky parables. Each of the tales redresses some kind of moral imbalance, as if nature, or, indeed, supernature, seeks to keep its world in order.

The film is framed by a small boy's chagrin at having his comic book collection thrown away – he plots evil fantasies of revenge that plug into the unfolding quintet of macabre comedy – granting the lurid perspective of a pubescent boy, the favoured slant for horror's wicked practitioners. We start with the least of the crew, *Father's Day*, telling of a zombie father revisiting his vile family as they squabble over the inheritance. It's the least imaginative, and most schlocky. *The Lonesome Death Of Jordy Verrill*, starring a woefully hammy King, is much more fun, and really rather tragic, as this lonely hillbilly inspects a fallen meteor only to be riddled with alien plant life.

From there the film has picked up a head of steam, and springs into a lively rhythm. Leslie Nielsen gives the vengeful cuckold of *Something To Tide Over You* a lustful nastiness, as he buries his wife and lover up to the necks on a beach with the tide coming in – typical of King's situational punch. The Crate, with the always worthwhile Hal Holbrook, spins the idea of ageing professors' avaricious inquiry consuming them as finally they get a discovery that bites back – hell, the box did say, 'Danger: Do Not open.' And lastly, the best of all, a Howard Hughes parody as E.G Marshall's ultra-rich (King's own swelling coffers offered their own guilty muse) recluse hermetically seals his New York penthouse from infection. The cockroaches, in a fabulous piece of gross-out, find a better place to hide.

It's all brushed with camp, which tends to sap the film of genuine fear, but that is Romero and King's aim; the splashy, often giddy, and childish thrill of the yuck. ★★★★ **IN**

CRIES AND WHISPERS (VISHKNINGAR OCH ROP) (1972)

Starring: *Ingrid Thulin (Karin), Liv Ullmann (Maria/Her Mother), Harriet Andersson (Agnes), Karl Sylwan (Anna), Erland Josephson (Doctor), Georg Arlin (Fredrik)*
Director: *Ingmar Bergman*
Screenwriter: *Ingmar Bergman*
18/90 mins./Drama/Sweden

Awards: *Academy Awards – Best Cinematography*

In a remote Swedish mansion, Agnes hopes that her lingering death will reunite her feuding sisters, Karin and Maria. But the only person affected by her suffering is her maid, Anna, whose compassion is rooted in memories of her dead baby and her faith in God.

Having fallen from critical and commercial favour in the early 1970s, Ingmar Bergman struggled to raise the $400,000 needed for this intense study of the pain of solitude, disappointment, godlessness and death. However, both his star trio and cinematographer Sven Nykvist agreed to defer payment until a distribution deal had been secured and the film proved to be a significant success. Indeed, in addition to being nominated for five Academy Awards, it also went some way to re-establishing a reputation undeservedly tarnished by *The Rite* and *The Touch*.

Bergman later revealed that all three sisters represented facets of his mother's personality, with Agnes being principled but ineffectual, Karin aloof and egotistical, and Maria cold and testy. Yet, by confining them within the stifling mansion, he also suggested that they were part of the same soul – a concept engendered by Bergman's childhood conviction that the soul was a red monster whose insides were hideously membranous.

Red is, indeed, the feature's dominant colour, with the oppressive décor being reinforced by the bloodiness of Karin's hands and lips after she mutilates her labia before her uncomprehending husband Fredrik (Georg

Arlin) and the stomach wound Maria's spouse Joakim (Henning Moritzen) inflicts upon himself at the dining table, while his wife looks on with contemptuous indifference.

Yet, Bergman had also been inspired by a more recent vision of three women in white whispering together in a red room – hence the concluding image of the sisters sat together on the garden swing, as Anna reads Agnes' journal and imagines her to be at peace. Indeed, it's fitting that the maid should be permitted this reverie, as she alone had shown her mistress any real pity, as she cradled her in a conscious evocation of the *Pièta* on the night when she appeared to rise temporarily from the dead in a last desperate bid to bring Karin and Maria together. ★★★★★ **DP**

LE CRIME DE M. LANGE (THE CRIME OF MONSIEUR LANGE) (1936)

Starring: *René Lefèvre (Mons. Amédée Lange), Odette Florelle (Valentine), Henri Guisol (Meunier), Marcel Levesque (Bessard), Odette Talazac (Mme. Bessard)*
Director: *Jean Renoir*
Screenwriters: *Jean Castanier, Jean Renoir, Jacques Prévert*
PG/90 mins./Comedy/Drama/France

When scheming magazine boss Batala is presumed killed in a train wreck, pulp writer Amédée Lange persuades his tenement neighbours to help him publish his Western stories about Arizona Jim. But, just as their enterprise looks likely to become a success, Batala returns for his cut.

Having returned from Italy, where he had laid the foundations of neorealism with Toni, Jean Renoir assumed the reins of a project named *Sur la Cour*, which had been been conceived by Catalan artist Jean Castanier as a project for Renoir's three-time assistant director, Jacques Becker. However, this was very much a collaborative affair and although Jacques Prévert was brought in to polish the screenplay, many scenes were improvised during the 28-day shoot by a cast that included several members of the left-wing theatrical troupe, Groupe Octobre.

Capturing the informality and optimism of the Popular Front era, when a coalition government seemed to have the answers to France's domestic and diplomatic problems, this is an unashamedly political film. Yet, apart from its championing of the co-operative spirit, its message is never propagandised. Indeed, Renoir is more interested in character and community than in rhetoric or narrative and he once claimed that the story would make an excellent basis for a musical, in which everyone had an aria describing how their profession contributed to the general good.

But, this underrated feature remains closer in tone to a Western. It begins on the Belgian frontier, as the locals recognise Lange from a wanted poster, before settling into a prolonged flashback about socio-economic pioneers, which ends with Lange gunning down the baddy (who is one of the few wholly unsympathetic characters in Renoir's humanist canon).

The closing sequence returns to the border to show Lange and Valentine (Odette Florelle) crossing to presumed happiness, just as the killer in *La Chienne* got away with their crime. But, the film also harks back to *Boudu Sauvé des Eaux*, in which Michel Simon was similarly allowed to escape his life sentence. Indeed, Renoir reinforced the link with the 360° pan before Lange shoots Batala, which recalled Boudu's view of the countryside before he slipped into the River Marne. ★★★★ **DP**

Jean Renoir (1894–1979)

Who was he: Son of Impressionist painter Pierre-Auguste, the Godfather of French cinema and arguably the greatest filmmaker cinema has ever seen.
Hallmarks: Compassionate humanism; elegant camera moves; deep focus and naturalistic acting, often by non-professionals.
If you see one film, see: *La Règle Du Jeu* (1939)

CRIMES AND MISDEMENORS (1989)

Starring: *Caroline Aaron (Barbara), Alan Alda (Lester), Woody Allen (Cliff Stern), Anjelica Huston (Dolores Paley), Mia Farrow (Halley Reed), Martin Landau (Judah Rosenthal), Jerry Orbach (Jack Rosenthal)*
Director: *Woody Allen*
Screenwriter: *Woody Allen*
15/107 mins./Drama/USA

In two separate stories of adultery; a New York doctor resorts to desperate measures to cover up his long-term adulterous affair. An unhappily married documentary filmmaker fights an adulterous temptation while making his latest movie on a TV producer.

On paper, *Crimes And Misdemeanors* doesn't exactly play like a big fat barrel of laughs. Respected pillar of the community has hysterical lover bumped off, big questions about God and morals and right and wrong and all that sort of existential tackle are promptly raised and then, er, it's all tied up neatly at the end.

Thankfully, the task of blowing all this potentially dullsville material up on to the screen is in the hands of Woody Allen.

This is, in effect, two movies for the price of one. The first follows the fortunes of eye specialist Judah Rosenthal as he attempts to shake off the increasingly unwanted passion of mistress Dolores, a passion that threatens to destroy the cosy well-appointed life of Judah and his inevitably tight-knit Jewish family and circle of dinner party friends.

The second tracks the typically shambolic career and love life of failed TV documentary maker Clifford, as he attempts to woo Mia Farrow by a mixture of afternoon trips to the cinema and thinly-concealed antagonism towards ghastly brother-in-law Lester (Alan Alda in his finest hour to date).

These two apparently separate threads are superbly woven together by Allen through the character of rabbi Sam Waterston, brother of Lester and confidant of the desperate Judah.

Aside from the formidable feat of managing to address such vast issues as murder, retribution and original sin and making it seem like a fun kind of thing to talk about, what makes *Crimes And Misdemeanors* such a rare treat is the sheer quality of performance on display and the memorable dialogue. 'The last time I was inside a woman was when I visited the Statue of Liberty,' cracks Woody in his undisputed role as king of the schmucks.

And, later, 'A man defecated on my sister,' he says, bewildered, to the wife he hasn't slept with in over a year. 'Well, I have to get up at seven,' she replies, turning over, as people always do. Lovely. ★★★★★ **BMc**

CRIMEWAVE (1985)

Starring: *Louise Lasser (Helene Trend), Paul L. Smith (Faron Crush), Brion James (Arthur Coddish), Shree J. Wilson (Nancy), Edward R. Pressman (Ernest Trend), Bruce Campbell (Renaldo 'The Heel')*
Director: *Sam Raimi*
Screenwriters: *Ethan Coen, Joel Coen, Sam Raimi*
PG/83 mins./Crime/Comedy/USA

In a Detroit jail, innocent Vic Ajax is being dragged to the electric chair. He flashes back to the strange circumstances that have brought him to this fate, which involve a pair of rodent exterminators who freelance as hit men.

Sam Raimi has disowned his second film, co-written with Joel and Ethan Coen, mostly because producer interference meant he had to use the bland Birney in the lead rather than his preferred star, Bruce Campbell – who nevertheless cops many of the best lines as the slimy gigolo 'Renaldo the Heel' ('Hey, baby why don't ya come on over to my pad – we'll have a scotch and sofa'). Surprisingly, it's quite an entertaining little effort, combining the craziest aspects of classic Hollywood screwball comedy with the kind of fresh insanity found in the great cartoons – one sequence in which Louise Lasser is chased through seemingly dozens of coloured doors is up there with the best of Looney Toons. Though cheaply made, which gives it an odd look somewhere between low budget tat and stylised gloss, *Crimewave* is a more inventive, engaging and, above all, funnier comedy than most big studio films of the mid-80s. Much of the comic weight is given to sustained slapstick chases and battles, but the film's charm comes from its performances – particularly, hulking Paul L. Smith and ratlike Brion James as Faron Crush and Arthur Coddish, who seem like the live-action equivalents of the Tasmanian Devil and Wile E. Coyote down to the Mel Blanc-type funny voices. With a terrific 40s big band score (occasioning one marvellous gag about a dance contest), a loving approach to its own stereotypes, and a sense of its own peculiarity, *Crimewave* is never going to be anybody's favourite movie, but deserves a small but fanatical cult following. ★★★ **KN**

THE CRIMSON PIRATE (1952)

Starring: *Burt Lancaster (Captain Vallo), Nick Cravat (Ojo), Eva Bartok (Consuelo), Torin Thatcher (Humble Bellows), James Hayter (Professor Prudence)*
Director: *Robert Siodmak*
Screenwriter: *Roland Kibbee*
U/105 mins./Action/Adventure/USA

A wry, somewhat acrobatic pirate, Captain Vallo, discovers there is nefarious double-dealing on the high seas, and becomes embroiled in rebellion against the colonial government in the Caribbean.

Something of a cross between parody and tribute to the dash of Errol Flynn, particularly in *Captain Blood* (even the title was echoed), this delightfully upbeat, cartoonish adventure story was the template for the tone and style of *Pirates Of The Caribbean*. In many ways it is a much better film. There is a more striking, believable gusto to Burt Lancaster's swaggering Captain Vallo. This is a rogue in love with the amoral splendour of his life, his dreamy grin is as wide as the ocean.

Partnered by the mute Ojo, (the gypsy-looking Nick Cravat, who lands punchlines and one-liners by pulling derisive faces), they are about to find their carefree approach being pulled up with a dose of responsibility. Naturally, given the era this movie hails from, this will arrive in the very comely shape of a good lady. Eva Bartok's Consuela is the daughter of the revolutionary leader, somewhat obviously names El Libre (Fredrick Lesiter, all stoic cause and righteousness), and will force the inconstant Vallo to mend his ways, or, at the very least, bend them a little.

Robert Siodmak utilises the heightened buzz of the pirate genre to play the film close to outright comedy, skirting the serious points of the plot as swiftly as possible while the action springs and rattles with more style than evident danger. Lancaster was a gymnast before he became an actor, as was Cravat, and their spring-heeled antics harken towards the slapstick of silent cinema rather than the heroic verve of Flynn's swashbuckling; Lancaster never feels noble rather than enthusiastic. A balletic double-act that never let the film stick in its shoes as they twirl like monkeys through knots of rigging and about the decks of the glorious galleons.

It is a breeze to watch, lacking the demands of real drama, but in its fabulous settings and wry tribute to the pleasures of pure escapism is truly a minor classic. ★★★★ **IN**

CRIMSON TIDE (1995)

Starring: *Denzel Washington (Lt. Commander Ron Hunter), Gene Hackman (Capt. Frank Ramsey), George Dzunda (Chief of the Boat), Viggo Mortensen (Lt. Peter 'WEAPS' Ince), James Gandolfini (Lt. Bobby Dougherty), Rick Schroder (Lt. Paul Hellerman), Steve Zahn (William Barnes)*
Director: *Tony Scott*
Screenwriter: *Michael Schiffer, from a story by Michael Schiffer and Richard P. Henrick*
15/116 mins./War/Thriller/Action/USA

When Russian rebels get hold of one of their government's old nuclear bases, a US nuclear submarine is ordered to fire, and then immediately receives an incomplete counter-order. As the tension grows, the captain and executive officer come into conflict about which order to follow.

Equipped with liberal helpings of square-jawed top quality Hollywood thespianism, and that expensive, highly commercial Tony Scott gloss-finish, this submarine-set mutiny thriller is about as good as it gets. A high profile movie that, for once, dispenses with the pile-driver effects of your everyday blockbuster, to trade in high voltage characters, visceral claustrophobia and a tension you can chew on. A nail-nibbling plot resting on what could happen rather than what does.

On a big, big sub, hot with nuclear potency, trouble brews. Up on the surface, the scriptwriters have contrived a suitable, if rather forced, global crisis with fascist Russian rebels getting into that broom cupboard filled with nuclear missiles and threatening the new world order. Down below, all hell breaks loose and the alert shifts to DEFCON 3. Then, provided by a magnificent duo of performances, an already simmering relationship between old school, plain-talking Captain Ramsey and his new executive officer – the bright Hunter – goes ballistic when orders come through to blast the Russkies before they blast us, closely followed by a second, incomplete counter order.

What it boils down to is Washington's thinker says hold off, wait and confirm, while the scalp scratching, orders-are-God Hackman is for pressing the big button. The script (written by a host of scribes including an uncredited Quentin Tarantino) delivers a series of screen-shaking face-offs before Washington takes matters into his own hands and usurps his cantankerous boss. Events are heightened to fever pitch by Scott's pulsating tick-tock rhythm as they inch toward the brink of nuclear war while, between the lines, the burdens of responsibility and duty are duly examined – the film taking an intelligently neutral stance over the two main protagonists' contrasting ethics.

Tarantino's script doctoring works to mixed effect; he grooms the final confrontation scene to perfection, but the pop-culture references (*Star Trek, The Silver Surfer*) stick out like bilge water in a Perrier factory. The film is also masculine to the hilt, a feast for hardware junkies and action freaks alike, with female roles kept to the barest of minimums. But as Washington and Hackman pout and fume like masters, awash in Scott's trademark super-slick direction and Hans Zimmer's stirring score, the effect is mesmerising. ★★★★ **IN**

CRITTERS (1986)

Starring: *Dee Wallace Stone (Helen Brown), M. Emmett Walsh (Harv), Billy Green Bush (Jay Brown). Scott Grimes (Brad Brown), Nadine Van der Velde (April Brown), Billy Zane (Steve Elliot)*
Director: *Stephen Herek*
Screenwriters: *Stephen Herek, Domonic Muir, Don Opper*
15/82 mins./Sci-fi/Horror/USA

A bunch of Krites – furry tumbleweeds with a lot of teeth – escape from an intergalactic prison farm and head for the universal backwater planet, Earth. Down on a Kansas farn, the Brown family find themselves under attack from the hungry, dangerous nuisances and it's down to a bratty kid to fend them off with fireworks.

This is a typical 1980s attempt to recapture the feel of 1950s s-f monster movies like *It Came From Outer Space* or *Invaders From Mars*, with slightly higher-tech effects than the originals, and a slightly tongue-in-cheek script which deploys deliberately stereotypical characters (M. Emmett Walsh as the sceptical Sheriff, Don Opper as the village idiot who thinks aliens are communicating with him through the fillings in his teeth) and ominous mumblings about the threat from 'out there'.

The lead monsters are sort of endearingly nasty (their gremlin-like burblings are given pithy sub-titles) and the movie has fun with its small town setting, but the film is perhaps a little too derivative to pass muster with the best of retro-chic s-f (*Strange Invaders, Alligator*) because it concentrates on serving up the recipe as before with more obvious humour, rather than straining for the mix of paranoia, black and white anxiety and pulp poetry that distinguishes the best of the originals.

Grimes and Opper pop up again in *Critters 2: The Main Course*, with Mick Garris replacing Stephen Herek as director; that had a bigger effects budget – unlike a pair of cheaper, back-to-back, direct-to-video follow-ups, *Critters 3* and *Critters 4*.

Opper, who had a hand in writing the series, co-stars in the latter pair with whatever-happened-to-them? losers Leonardo DiCaprio and Angela Bassett, tangling with Krites in a run-down apartment building and a cramped spaceship. ★★★ **KN**

◎ CROCODILE DUNDEE (1986)

Starring: *Paul Hogan (Michael J. 'Crocodile' Dundee), Linda Kozlowski (Sue Charlton), John Meillon (Walter Reilly), Mark Blum (Richard Mason), Michael Lombard (Sam Charlton)*
Director: *Peter Faiman*
Screenwriters: *John Cornell, Paul Hogan, Ken Shadie*
15/98 mins./Comedy/Australia

When New York reporter Sue Charlton brings Australian hunter Mick Dundee from the Outback to the Big Apple, he becomes an instant hit. Treating the uptight city as he would the wilds of his homeland, he adapts with ease, although matters of the heart prove more complicated.

Life and art blurred when this likeable comedy became a blockbusting hit in America. Its star Paul Hogan, with his leathery, implacable Aussie charm, was an overnight superstar, directly mirroring the shrugging enthusiasm of Crocodile Dundee his briefly iconic character who won over the country in similar fashion. There's nothing too clever about the idea, just landing a different kind of fish out of water in a familiar comic landscape – the trilling pretension of New York City. And Hogan's gift for self-aware understatement, as he picks not-so innocently at the luxuries and pointlessness about him, fits the bill as much as it plays a dopey cliché of thickset Australian manners. Are we really meant to believe this cogent man is truly this ignorant of the greater world like some kind of alien? Yet you easily forgive it the shakiness of concept with the crispiness of delivery. The film, for all its obviousness is hugely funny and entertaining.

Out-blading a potential mugger, the conundrum of the bidet, transsexual encounters, all the flabby vicissitudes of city life are swung across the curious simple-minded attitude of Dundee. And he meets them all with a flash of his grin and the warble of his antipodean wisdom: 'Imagine seven million people all wanting to live together.' The film sags when it moves into gassy routines of the romcom.

Dundee doesn't fit the troubled heart of romantic dilemma, he's too strong and pragmatic for us to believe in his mooning. Kozlowski, who would marry Hogan in life, does a good job with the melting rich girl enticed by his earthy charms, and it is her who holds the film just about in place when it threatens to unravel into sappiness.

Two sequels were to follow, but there was nowhere left for Dundee to go once he had become acclimatised to the American dream. The first brought the couple back to Oz for a confrontation with evil poachers, and after a gap of 13 years, tried out LA, but the joke was as flat and dated as his croc-toothed jacket. ★★★ **IN**

◎ CROSS OF IRON (1977)

Starring: *James Coburn (Hauptmann Stransky), Maximilian Schell (Feldwebel Rolf Steiner), James Mason (Oberst Brandt), David Warner (Hauptmann Kiesel)*
Screenwriters: *Julius J. Epstein, James Hamilton, Walter Kelley*
18/143 mins./Action/Drama/War/UK/West Germany/Yugoslavia

A platoon of war-toughened German soldiers must endure not only the deprivations and dangers of the Eastern Front, but also a new commander obsessed with earning a Cross of Iron, German military's highest medal, to maintain his family's honour.

That a director so steeped in a Western folklore of violence and nihilism, would make such a telling piece of antiwar politic as this rending tale of German soldiers on the Russian Front, could be construed as a strange thing. Yet, when you look closely at *Cross Of Iron*, to place it within the greater context of Sam Peckinpah's career, it starts to make a whole lot of sense. This is a tale of fading antiheroes facing up to the realities of war; a war they are losing. This is not a film of heroism, but of survival. And Peckinpah metes out death here with the same glorious, spasmodic poetry – slow-motion, jabbing cuts, the rash splatter of countless squibs – as he had done with *The Wild Bunch*, his signature film.

Indeed, in so many ways Peckinpah even outdoes the brazen, unblinking violence of his Westerns with the sheer ferocity on show here. This was the first time he had tackled war head-on, and it was just like the great antagonist to cajole us into sympathising with German soldiers, the cold enemy of cinema. James Coburn, in towering form, is the good face of the unit, Stransky, determinedly brave and moralistic, willing to face up to his callow new commander. He is so identified with war, when injured and recovered, he returns to the front rather than goes home. 'Do you love the war so much or are you afraid of what you'll become without it?' inquires Senta Berger's nurse. Classic Peckinpah, men defined by their actions at the expense of all else.

Another of his favoured themes is the clash between men of the establishment and his earthy true-men like Stransky. Maximilian Schell plays this obstruction to true duty, an aristo so determined to pick up that elusive, titular medal he is willing to lie for it, to steal another man's heroism. Ideals though have long been lost in the face on the Russian onslaught, the very structure of command is breaking down, it is to death they march. Peckinpah knows of nowhere else. ★★★★★ **IN**

◎ CROUCHING TIGER, HIDDEN DRAGON (WU HU ZANG LONG) (2000)

Starring: *Chow Yun-Fat (Li Mu Bai), Michelle Yeoh (Yu Shu Lien), Zhang Ziyi (Jen Zu), Chang Chen (Lo), Lung Sihung (Sir Te), Cheng Pei Pei (Jade Fox), Li Fa Zeng (Governor Yu)*
Director: *Ang Lee*
Screenwriters: *James Schamus, Wang Hui Ling, Tsai Kuo Jung, based on the novel by Wang Du Lu*
12/119 mins./Martial Arts/Romance/History/USA

Awards: *Academy Awards – Best Art Direction, Best Cinematography, Best Foreign Language Film, Best Original Score, BAFTA – Anthony Asquith Award for Music, Best Costume, Best Film not in the English Language, David Lean Award for Direction, Golden Globes – Best Director, Best Foreign Language Film*

Set in a mythical China of the early 19th century, a romantic epic is spun about the theft of an ancient sword known as Green Destiny. The owner, renowned warrior Li Mu Bai, and female fighter, Yu Shu Lien, discover the culprit is a young aristocrat, Jen.

Having proven himself a black belt of versatility with unsung US Civil War drama *Ride With The Devil*, Ang Lee's venture into the world of martial arts may prove the diminutive Taiwanese director has no limitations whatsoever.

With kung fu so gloriously choreographed, shot and edited that it literally has you gasping for breath, an epic canvas of stunning Chinese scenery and a set of beautifully measured characters trading genuine emotions, it's *The Matrix* spliced with David Lean, seasoned with the late 70s Oriental TV series, *The Water Margin*. Oh, and it's in Chinese.

Events begin with a tease – ten minutes of poised dialogue, elegantly shot and pristinely acted, building up the undercurrent of unrequited passion between Li and Yu. All very formal and cunningly misleading. Seemingly from nowhere, the movie then explodes into action, as a masked thief steals Li's famous sword and Yu gives chase across the rooftops of Beijing in an extraordinary display of high flying wire-work, edited to a surging staccato drumbeat.

So dazzling is its visual craft and breathless momentum, you have to swallow the urge to cheer out loud. Not since *Jurassic Park* has filmmaking joyously thundered through the boundaries of its own medium. And there's not a pixel in sight.

Over the succeeding two-hour span, Lee and legendary martial arts coordinator Yuen Wo Ping offer up increasingly astounding fight sequences, involving everything from the most elaborate bar room brawl in history, to a dazzling tree-top duel allowig the camera to dip and bend woozily with the flexing branches. The kung fu on show grants its masters a mystical weightlessness, and its director crafts it all like volcanic ballet, as graceful as it is brutal.

It is still an Ang Lee joint, though, and he gives his characters credence, making their romantic entanglements as real as their chopsocky is fantastical, and injecting a sly humour. Chow Yun-Fat and Michelle Yeoh move seamlessly between feats of physical prowess and nuances of emotion. However, the fire at the heart of the movie is the stunning Ziyi. Ostensibly this is Jen's rites-of-passage and, as she rejects an arranged marriage, driven by an insatiable desire for self-expression, Ziyi fills her with furious, exciting fervour.

This is the story of true female empowerment, where the ladies revel in kick-arse glory and the men opt for calm consideration. On just about every level, it needs to be seen to be believed. ★★★★★ **IN**

Movie Trivia: Crouching Tiger, Hidden Dragon

Jet Li was originally offered the role taken by Chow Yun-Fat but turned it down to make *Romeo Must Die*. Neither Michelle Yeoh nor Chow Yun-Fat were fluent in Mandarin, so the script had to be presented to them phonetically. The title of the movie refers to an ancient Chinese proverb meaning 'To hide your strength from others'.

CROUPIER (1988)

Starring: *Clive Owen (Jack Manfred), Nick Reding (Giles Cremorne), Nicholas Ball (Jack Snr.), Alexander Morton (David Reynolds), Barnaby Kay (Car Dealer), Gina McKee (Marion Nell)*
Director: *Mike Hodges*
Screenwriter: *Paul Mayersberg*
15/91 mins./Crime/Drama/Germany/U.K./France/Ireland

Jack Manfred is set up by his gambling-crazed father to take a job as a dealer in a London casino. This puts a strain on his relationship with his day-working girlfriend, especially when he has a succession of flings.

Croupier was first released in the UK in 1999 and did very little business. The film then opened to some success in America, and at least a dozen other, mostly lesser, British crime films came and went (in one, *Essex Boys*, Alex Kingston essentially redoes her *Croupier* role, albeit with a different accent). In a rare instance of the film business admitting they might have been wrong, *Croupier* scored a proper re-launch, a re-release at the cinema and a string of award nominations for Owen.

If it's not quite a missing masterpiece – Owen's cool central performance gets a bit too blank for comfort at times, and the last reel has two or three twists too many as vital plot elements, like who-killed-whom and who-has-the-money, get dropped – it is still a strong London thriller, with a lot of good stuff about an unfamiliar dusk-'til-dawn world.

Scripted by Mayersberg, who directed 1986's similarly strange *Captive*, *Croupier* has a nugget of a creepy, paranoid mystery, but is as interested in the odd details of working in a semi-legitimate casino: relationship-ruining hours, the inviolable-but-often-ignored rules, the potentially violent dim-wit clients, the sharpies with schemes to rook an already-rigged game.

With a writer hero, whose only other option is ghosting a novel to be ascribed to a football star, and a plot that might or might not be made up just to give him something to write about, there's a lot of distancing going on. But, as in *Get Carter*, Hodges has a way with suspicious supporting characters and strange women – especially funny fatale Kingston and the oddly sexy Hardie. And all the places are caught exactly: the hero's basement flat, the cramped but luxurious gambling hell, and a country house where a gambling-and-adultery-break turns sour. ★★★★ **BMc**

THE CROW (1994)

Starring: *Brandon Lee (Eric Draven), Rochelle Davis (Sarah), Ernie Hudson (Sergeant Albrecht), Michael Wincott (Top Dollar), Bai Ling (Myca), Sofia Shinas (Shelly Webster)*
Director: *Alex Proyas*
Screenwriters: *David J. Schow, John Shirley, based on the comic book and comic book series by James O'Barr*
18/100 mins./Horror/Thriller/USA

Eric Draven and his fiancée are brutally murdered on Devil's Night, a night when the henchmen of crime-boss Top Dollar traditionally indulge in wanton acts of violence and arson. A crow brings Draven's restless soul back from the dead and he sets out to wreak revenge upon his killers.

In March, 1993 *The Crow* had been shooting in Wilmington, North Carolina (later home of *Dawson's Creek*) for nearly two months. The production was on a tight schedule and strapped for cash. Allegedly, the completion bond company was in town. It was no surprise then that when a gun required some dummy bullets, instead of buying a set for the princely sum of $20, the props department asked a special effects technician to knock some up from a box of real ammunition. This he did by removing the bullets with a pair of pliers, emptying the shell of explosive and firing the percussion cap with a hammer before reinserting the bullet into the empty shell casing. While he was at it he made some quarter load blanks but somehow a bullet got reinserted into the blank's shell casing.

When the gun came to be mock fired, in the din of the scene no one heard the tell-tale slight popping sound as a missed percussion cap fired with just enough force to propel a bullet into the barrel, where it stuck. It stayed there until, in a later scene, the gun was prepped with full-load blanks (requested by Proyas for the muzzle flare they provided) and fired in the direction of Brandon Lee by actor Michael Massee (Funboy). Lee slumped to the ground as planned. Proyas called cut. But Lee didn't get up.

And so the making of *The Crow* ended in tragedy. Which is bleakly appropriate, because in the mid 1970s it began with one.

James O'Barr, a troubled young man with a childhood spent being shuttled between orphanages and foster parents, was enjoying one of the few happy periods in his life. For three years he had been going out with a girl he had met when he was 16 years old. By the late 70s they were engaged. Two weeks before her 18th birthday she was run down and killed by a drunk driver. The result was Eric Draven. 'It just poured out,' O'Barr says. 'My character is able to return from the grave because some things just cannot be forgiven.'

In fact Draven is a continuation of a cinematic archetype – the revengeful spirit returned to earth to set wrongs right, going back to Clint Eastwood's character in *High Plains Drifter* and Boris Karloff in *The Walking Dead*. Alex Proyas, an Egyptian-born but Australia-based commercials director, was attracted to the melancholy material and considered it perfect for the rock-gothic visual style he favoured and had employed in his debut *Spirits Of The Air, Gremlins Of The Clouds*.

Design-wise The Crow is like a comic book brought to life. While some critics ridiculed the stylised model work (which he reprised in his subsequent movie *Dark City*) it is, in fact, entirely appropriate to the heightened, deliberately overcooked nature of the piece. Equally, the dialogue remains trapped, in tone at least, in comicbook speech bubbles. Unlike *Superman* or Tim Burton's *Batman*, there's no attempt to transform it into 'naturalistic' movie dialogue. *The Crow* revels shamelessly in its pulpish roots, thus legitimising what would otherwise be over-ripe verbiage such as, 'Mother is the name for God on the lips and hearts of all children,' or the quoting of Edgar Allen Poe ('Suddenly there came a tapping, as of someone gently rapping, rapping at my chamber door') and Milton's *Paradise Lost* ('Abashed the Devil stood, And felt how awful goodness is').

Draven's enemies aren't super villains like The Joker, but ordinary street scum with The Crow as a kind of supernatural vigilante. He takes no particular satisfaction in his killings, but more a resigned appreciation of destiny. 'They're all dead,' he remarks, conjuring haunting overtones of his own rapidly approaching demise. 'They just don't know it yet.'

Though both Christian Slater and River Phoenix had been offered the role, Proyas' final casting decision turned out to be a masterstroke. Embodying the new 'sensitive' breed of action hero, later to provide rich pickings for the likes of Leonardo DiCaprio and Keanu Reeves, Lee not only delivers spectacularly in the martial arts sequences (he is co-credited as fight-choreographer) but spends much of the movie in black leather trousers, stripped to the waist and drenched with the perpetual *Blade Runner*-esque rain.

The question is, would *The Crow* be the cult movie it is today without Lee's untimely death? Possibly not, although interest in the character was strong enough to generate a dire sequel with Vincent Perez in the title role, as well as a TV series with chopsockey C-lister Mark Dacascos. What is certain though is that, like River Phoenix and James Dean, Lee entered the grim pantheon of fast-lived good-looking corpses and thus gained a morbid immortality which no doubt adds to his popularity among his adolescent, angsty fan base. It's a popularity significantly reinforced by Lee's eerie musing on mortality during his final screen interview just days before his death. 'Because we do not know when we will die we get to think of life as an inexhaustible well,' he said. 'It all seems limitless.' ★★★★ **AS**

⓪ THE CRUCIBLE (1996)

Starring: *Daniel Day-Lewis (John Proctor), Winona Ryder (Abigail Williams), Paul Scofield (Judge Thomas Danforth), Joan Allen (Elizabeth Proctor), Bruce Davison (Reverend Parris)*
Director: *Nicolas Hytner*
Screenwriter: *Arthur Miller, based on his play*
Producer: *Robert A. Miller, David V. Pokorny*
12/124 mins./Drama/USA

Awards: *BAFTA – Best Supporting Actor (Paul Scofield), Empire Awards – Best Actress (Joan Allen)*

A 17th-century Salem woman accuses an ex-lover's wife of witchery in an adaptation of the Arthur Miller play.

The Salem witch trials have to a large degree entered the Heritage Tourism arena, put down by many laypeople as a quirk of the past, thought of as a bizarre historical aberration that resulted in the hanging of 19 innocent people in a little Massachusetts town in 1692. What Arthur Miller did in the early 1950s with his play was to relentlessly pick away at the story in an attempt to get to its heart.

The facts are simple, if astonishing. In the puritanical, superstitious world of 17th century America, several young girls started behaving strangely, with some falling into unconsciousness. Baffled, the physicians concluded that Satan was to blame and the hunt for the witches who had possessed the girls began. Soon, the West Indian slave of the village pastor was forced into a confession, and suddenly petty jealousies erupted, vendettas were settled, and anyone whose behaviour didn't conform to the social and religious norm was accused.

Their defence? They had none. The only way to avoid the noose was to confess to being a witch and face utter estrangement, which many heroically refused to do. After nine months of terror, the trials were called to a halt and a kind of sanity returned.

Miller, who admits that the McCarthy witchhunts were the inspiration for his play, took the tough route in an age of black-and-white heroes and villains, and refused to simplify his characters. John Proctor, for instance, is the voice of reason in the village, but here is a central character who adulterates, beats women, and refuses to take responsibility for his actions. Likewise, Scofield's Judge Danforth, an individual more interested in the majesty of the law than in seeing justice done, is often seen as a misguided man of God, attempting to do what he feels is best.

After his success with *The Madness Of King George*, Hytner directs the stellar cast with great skill, and they do him proud, particularly Day-Lewis as the passionate but confused Proctor, Ryder as the scheming accuser Abigail and Joan Allen as the injured and upright Elizabeth Proctor. The absolute standout, though, is Scofield, whose performance is, yes really, worth the rental price alone, a mesmerising, dark presence throughout the film.

If there is a criticism it is that by opening the play out into a movie, all the original sense of buttoned-down claustrophobia is lost. What happened in Salem was a combination of selfishness, hysteria and pig ignorance, but at its core were a group of young women sent almost literally insane by the repressed piety of the Puritan community which denied them any pleasures, including simply dancing. In the play, this comes over loud and clear. ★★★★★ **PT**

⓪ CRUEL INTENTIONS (1999)

Starring: *Sarah Michelle Gellar (Kathryn Merteuil), Ryan Phillippe (Sebastian Valmont), Reese Witherspoon (Annette Hargrove), Selma Blair (Cecile Caldwell), Joshua Jackson (Blaine Tuttle)*
Director: *Roger Kumble*
Screenwriter: *Roger Kumble, based on the novel* Les Liaisons Dangereuses *by Choderlos de Laclos*
15/97 mins./Drama/Romance/Thriller/USA

Kathryn and Sebastian are amoral step-siblings. Kathryn bets Sebastian a night with her that he can't bed Annette, the headmaster's daughter who is sworn to have no sex before marriage.

It's a little presumptuous to say that *Cruel Intentions* is 'suggested' by Choderlos De Laclos' novel *Les Liaisons Dangeureuses* (as the opening credits tell us). However much this modernisation may want to distance itself from the French classic, it's as accurate a replication as you could hope to find, with cellphones and uplift bras replacing the corsetry and ugly smallpox deaths of the original. In fact, anybody who's seen the fabulous *Dangerous Liaisons* will be on familiar territory; the similarities, from character names to Phillippe's failed attempt to out-smooth *Liaisons*' John Malkovich, stand out a mile.

Gellar and Phillippe are wealthy New York step-siblings Kathryn and Sebastian; the former given to snorting coke out of a modified crucifix and shagging her way around the Upper East Side, the latter just given to shagging his way around the Upper East Side. In a bet to settle their lust for each other, however, they make a wager, involving virginal new headmaster's daughter Annette. If Sebastian fails to pop her closely-guarded cherry before the start of the new term, Kathryn gets his vintage Jaguar. If, however, he succeeds, he gets Kathryn for the night. Cue: saucy shenanigans and subplots galore (mainly involving innocent pawn Cecile – a wildly mugging Blair), before Sebastian, deciding he quite fancies the hymeneally-blessed Annette, develops a moral centre.

With its parade of double entendres (coming across as a kind of *Carry On Teens*), hysterical adults, stupendously OTT performances and preposterous climactic 'tragedy', this is the kind of movie which purists will dismiss as a mockery of the original.

Leaving aside the classy roots it has so shamelessly mangled, however, this is a lot of fun; Gellar does well, pouting and preening and throwing hissy fits all over the shop, as does Witherspoon, whose character seems remarkably eager to bed Phillippe given her strict stance on virginity (the woman has, clearly, been saving herself for Ryan's privates). And if Phillippe's acting extends only as far as an ability to convincingly put on his shades, and if the plot takes some swallowing, it doesn't stop this from being glossily enjoyable nonsense, the sort which will happily entertain for an hour-and-a-half without troubling the old grey matter too much. ★★★★ **CW**

THE CRUEL SEA (1953)

Starring *Jack Hawkins (Commander Ericson), Donald Sinden (Lockhart), John Stratton (Ferraby), Denholm Elliott (Morel), John Warner (Baker), Stanley Baker (Bennett)*
Director: *Charles Frend*
Screenwriter: *Eric Ambler*
PG/126 mins./Drama/War/UK

The story of HMS Compass Rose, a 'Corvette' consigned to protect the convoys of merchant shipping from German U-Boats, from the point of view of both its noble Commander Ericson and his inexperienced crew members.

Made while the memories of WWII were still fresh in audiences' minds, this adaptation of Nicholas Monsarrat's famous novel of enduring the Atlantic run, leans toward the glorification rather than penetration of history. Yet, still Charles Frend, with a background in documentaries, endeavours to inject genuine emotion into the doings of an inexperienced crew thrust into the heat of battle, all the while alluding to, rather than tackling head on, the futility of their conflict.

Not that film is entirely liberated from a staunch Britishness of design, There are fewer more stiff-upper-lipped than Jack Hawkins' stalwart Captain Ericson, faced with the numinous pressures of command in the roiling waters of the North Atlantic. He too, though, is not just the typical rod of command. In one searing sequence he must order depth-charges to be let off to destroy a lurking U-Boat, even though there are his own men in the water. A necessity he greets with angry tears.

Structurally, the film is loose, more of a dark soap opera than a purposeful plot. Monsarrat's book was written as a snapshot of life at war, and the film is guided by his detail on individual lives rather than the particulars of a mission. Officers, including John Stratton's Ferraby, turn to drink and are pushed to breaking point. Elsewhere it is adulterous wives, bereavements and various personal issues that dog the crew, including debuts for Donald Sinden and Denholm Elliot, as much as the cold pursuit of U-Boats.

Technically, it has the tang of authenticity, as the Admiralty, encouraged by its dedication to idealism, co-operated fully, although most of the Corvette ships had been scraped at the end of the war; a rather rundown vessel, the *Coreopsis*, was eventually located in Malta.

For most of the audience, only eight years past the ending of WWII, such a gruelling but stirring saga must have had a towering effect. ★★★★ **IN**

CRUMB (1994)

Starring: *Robert Crumb (Himself), Aline Kominsky (Herself – Robert's wife), Charles Crumb (Himself – Robert's older brother), Max Crumb (Himself – Robert's younger brother), Robert Hughes (Himself – Time Magazine Art Critic), Martin Mueller (Himself – Owner of Modernism Gallery)*
Director: *Terry Zwigoff*
15/121 mins./Docudrama/USA

This documentary biopic looks at revolutionary US comic book artist Robert Crumb, and his tortured family.

This seemingly placid doc on the life and career of cult comic book artist Robert Crumb, who debunked superhero traditions with satire and psychedelic absurdity, is loaded with despair.

For what unfolds from director Terry Zwigoff's inspired shuffle through the patterns and patter of a visionary American eccentric, weighed down by a carnival of sexual peccadilloes (piggybacks are his thing), is a biting exploration of family dysfunction and artistic catharsis.

Unlike his brothers, shell-shocked into near-catatonia by childhood trauma, Crumb spilled his tormented psyche into his art, creating brilliant, deformed attacks on American life. Which, of course, is exactly what Zwigoff is up to.

No ordinary biopic, or documentary for that matter, this is a rare glimpse into the twisted mind of a visionary artist. ★★★★ IN

CRY-BABY (1989)

Starring: *Johnny Depp (Wade 'Cry-Baby' Walker), Amy Locane (Allison Vernon-Williams), Susan Tyrrell (Ramona Rickettes), Polly Bergen (Mrs Vernon-Williams, Allison's Grandmother), Iggy Pop (Uncle Belvedere Rickettes), Ricki Lake (Pepper Walker), Traci Lords (Wanda Woodward), Kim McGuire (Hatchet-Face, Cry-Baby gang aka Mona Malrovawski)*
Director: *John Waters*
Screenwriter: *John Waters*
15/85 mins./Comedy/Musical/Romance/USA

A good girl square who desperately wants to be bad falls for a crooning Dean-like bad-boy who gets sent to juvie.

It is unlikely that supporters of the John Waters' school of bad taste – those among you who relished every disgusting moment of *Pink Flamingos* and *Female Trouble* – will quite be prepared for *Cry-Baby*, easily the Pope Of Trash's most mainstream up to *Serial Mom* which followed. Anyone, however, who has studiously avoided the more notorious of Waters' films is likely to be pleasantly surprised at this original, well played and blackly humourous piece of entertainment that only occasionally shows any evidence of the director's penchant for more outrageous behaviour.

Johnny Depp – who was at the time a major teen heart-throb in the US thanks to his role in the TV series *21 Jump Street* – successfully parodies his real-life image in his role here as Wade 'Cry-Baby' Walker, a hip 'drape' from the wrong side of the tracks in 50s Baltimore who falls for 'square' Allison Vernon-Williams.

The ensuing madness of Drapes versus Squares (with Waters' regulars Ricki Lake and Mink Stole plus notorious names like Iggy Pop, Troy Donahue and the Patty Hearst) moves from the Drapes' Jukebox Jamboree where

Cry-Baby teaches Allison to French kiss amid much exaggerated tongue-waving to an unusual version of that old favourite, the chicken race. On his way through this merry romp – peppered with some splendid dialogue ('You've made me the happiest juvenile delinquent in Baltimore!') and great period tunes – Waters sends up every 50s movie from *Grease* to *Jailhouse Rock*, with Depp well cast as his hollow-cheeked Presley.

The supporting cast are equally impressive, most notably first-time actress Amy Locane as the square who is transformed into a vamp and Kim McGuire as the appropriately-named Hatchet-Face ('Her face was her fortune – and she was broke!').

Great stuff, in a pleasantly distasteful sort of way. ★★★★ **JB**

THE CRYING GAME (1992)

Starring: *Stephen Rea (Fergus), Jaye Davidson (Dil), Miranda Richardson (Jude), Forest Whitaker (Jody), Adrian Dunbar (Maguire), Jim Broadbent (Col)*
Director: *Neil Jordan*
Screenwriter: *Neil Jordan*
18/112 mins./Drama/Romance/Thriller/UK
Awards: *Academy Awards – Best Screenplay, BAFTA – Alexander Korda Award for Best British Film*

Fergus, a member of the IRA and Jody, a British soldier develop a friendship. When the hostage situation goes wrong, Fergus heads to London to seek out Dil, Jody's lover. Dil has no idea about Fergus' IRA background, but there's something Fergus doesn't know as well . . .

The shock sleeper hit to top them all, *The Crying Game* arrived on video while still making Oscar-propelled box office history in the US as the most successful non-genre independent movie of all time. Here in the UK, of course, Neil Jordan's low-budget production met with a rather less favourable commercial and critical reaction, the hapless victim of the double sucker punch caused by the collapse of Palace Pictures and the stifling parochialism of large parts of the English media. Now, thanks to the miraculous rewriting-of-history facility made available by the VCR, and now DVD, a more considered second opinion can be offered.

Oddly enough, the typically gushing hosannahs from the US maybe went a bit far, with too little attention being paid to Forest Whitaker's hopeless Tottenham accent, Jaye Davidson's unnatural stiffness, the bizarre and outmoded Essex Man caricature, and the inherent problem within the basic premise that – hey! – all these IRA chaps need is a spot of male bonding and the love of a good woman – or not – and everything will turn out just fine.

Set against the sheer harrowing power of Jordan's screenplay and Stephen Rea's memorable performance as Fergus, however, none of the above can stop *The Crying Game* from being one of those rare films that has a genuinely haunting quality, a film that lingers in the imagination long after apparently more accomplished and considerably more expensive pieces of work have forever disappeared, a film that – dammit – dares to actually try to say something, and say it with wit, bravado, flair and a basic disregard for the supposed rules of timorous moviemaking in the 90s.

Tagline
Play at your own risk.

That Neil Jordan does all of this is remarkable enough. What elevates this little gem of a movie into a different dimension is that he does it with the twin taboos of Northern Ireland and adult sexuality and he does it with the aid of Stephen Rea, a great Irish stage actor blessed with a quite extraordinary sense of grief about everything he does. 'I'm not good for much,' sighs Rea, as the full, desperate nature of his sorry plight takes hold, and, like so much about *The Crying Game*, it really is enough to break the hardest of hearts. ★★★★ **BMc**

CUBE (1997)

Starring: *Nicole de Boer (Joan Leaven – The Math Student), Nicky Guadagni (Helen Holloway – The Doctor), David Hewlett (David Worth – The Architect), Andrew Miller (Kazan – The Autistic Man), Julian Richings (Alderson – The First Victim), Wayne Robson (Rennes – The Fugitive), Maurice Dean Wint (Quentin – The Cop)*
Director: *Vincenzo Natali*
Screenwriters: *Andre Bijelic, Vincenzo Natali, Graeme Manson*
15/90 mins./Drama/Fanatsy/Horror/Sci-fi/Canada

Seven total strangers awaken one day to find themselves alone in a cubical maze. Once they meet, they work together using their given skills and talents to survive the deadly traps which guard many of the coloured cubic rooms.

Alderson, a nervous, bald man in prison clothes, walks through a strange square-shaped room, and is surprised by a descending razor-wire grille that turns him into a man-shaped tower of cubes that fall apart in disgusting fashion.

Before its credits, *Cube* has shown us the only set we're going to see and established that hideous abuses can befall its human characters. It's an eye-opening kick-start and clues the audience in to who is really behind the vast trap machine in which the cast are struggling. We later learn that every one of the subjects has a predestined part to play in the drama of escape, and poor Alderson's role was to make a dramatic point for us.

Early on, as the characters argue about whether their situation has been engineered by the military-industrial complex ('Only the government could build something this ugly'), space aliens or 'Some rich sicko' the canniest of them advises 'Take a good, long look-see . . . because I've got a feeling it's looking at us.' Those unseen watchers, who never show up on screen, are – of course – the audience; and the elusive point of the exercise is to provide us with an hour and a half of puzzlement and entertainment as we watch human rats battle a fiendish maze.

Director-writer Vincenzo Natali warmed up by making *Elevated*, a short film about three people trapped in a lift. *Cube* expands the scale with four extra characters and a single set that can be cannily relit to stand in for an assortment of the estimated 17,576 rooms within the master cube.

The plot is simple: seven people wake up within a vast maze that resembles (more closely than it at first seems) a giant Rubik's Cube. Each room is a cube within a cube, with six doors opening to other rooms, but a percentage of the rooms are equipped with deadly booby traps which soon claim the life of renowned prison-escapee Rennes. Each of the surviving group has a talent: cop Quentin is obsessive about making it to freedom, student Leaven is a maths prodigy; loser Worth was unknowingly part of the design team who assembled the cube; conspiracy theorist Holloway is a doctor with the right mindset to expect this sort of thing ('Nobody's ever going to call me "paranoid" again'); and autistic Kazan is a savant who can out-calculate Leaven when the stakes rise.

As they try to solve problems, alternating between co-operation and conflict, they gradually make their way towards the perhaps-mythical exit, and learn about their own resources and failings along the way. *Cube* was one of two 1998 science fiction movies named after three-dimensional shapes, and cost roughly nothing next to Barry Levinson's inflated Michael Crichton movie *Sphere*, which falls into all the traps that the off-Hollywood effort knows to avoid: Natale sidesteps the big let-down that comes when the purpose of the artefact is laboriously explained in *Sphere* by simply not explaining who was behind the whole thing, and trusting us to concentrate on the character drama and the mind-puzzle at the heart of the script. It was also one of two 1997 independents to apply itself to mathematics as a well-spring of mystery and imagination, making for a stimulating double-bill with Darren Aronofsky's *Pi*.

The cast are the sort of faces who show up in Canadian-shot (*South Park* fans will notice a high 'aboot' rate in the dialogue) trash TV like *The Outer Limits*, *Forever Knight* and *The Hunger*, and sometimes aren't quite up to scenes that call for subtlety as well as hysteria. But the non-star ensemble ensures a level of surprise about who of these characters – all named after various prisons – will make it through, with a couple of last-minute, against-the-cliché sacrifices. There's a clever arc as the very qualities – take-charge indomitability, quickness to action, determination to survive – that mark Quentin (the only black character) out as a hero at the beginning then turn him into the psychopathic menace who has to be ditched and bested so that the others can make it to freedom. Inspired two inferior sequels – *Hypercube* and *Cube Zero*. ★★★★ **KN**

CUL-DE-SAC (1966)

Starring: *Donald Pleasence (George), Françoise Dorléac (Teresa), Lionel Stander (Richard), Jack MacGowran (Albert), Iain Quarrier (Christopher), Geoffrey Sumner (His Father), Renée Houston (His Mother)*
Director: *Roman Polanski*
Screenwriters: *Gerard Brach, Roman Polanski*
15/11 mins./Comedy/Thriller/UK
Certificate: /15

George and his younger French wife Teresa have retreated to a castle off the coast of Northumbria. Their home is invaded by Richard and Albie, gangsters fleeing after a robbery, and a shifting balance of power among the group leads to farcical, yet dangerous situations.

As a follow-up to *Repulsion*, Roman Polanski was allowed to step further beyond the bounds of the kind of sexploitation his British producers at Compton-Cameo (home of *Confessions of a Windmill Girl* and *Mini-Skirt Weekend*) usually specialised in and make this black comedy, which shows the influence of Harold Pinter and Samuel Beckett.

Set on the bleak but picturesque Lindisfarne Island, the film enters the private world of a squabbling married couple marvellously played by Pleasence (in shrill, mincing, bald mode) and Dorléac (who does sulky, sexy and unpredictable).

Their endless round of private quarrels and kinks is interrupted, just as Teresa has dressed George up in her nightdress and painted his face, by the frog-voiced American hood Stander, who can barely contain his prurient disgust at these 'normal' folks, and his bleeding, dying, mouselike sidekick MacGowran.

The getaway Volkswagen is stranded on a causeway by the rising waters, a memorably surreal image, and the crooks have to wait not for Godot but a similarly-tardy master criminal named Katelbach.

At first, the gangsters intimdate their unwilling hosts, but horrible day-trippers show up (including one of the most deliberately obnoxious children in the movies) and Richard has to pose as a butler and take his share of humiliation.

There's an advance over *Repulsion* as Polanski, with a superb (if combustive) cast, realises the subtler, funnier uses of English, which adds a touch of farce to the nightmarish vision of cruel people struggling in absurd traps. ★★★★ **KN**

THE CURSE OF FRANKENSTEIN (1957)

Starring: *Peter Cushing (Baron Victor Frankenstein), Hazel Court (Elizabeth), Robert Urquhart (Paul Krempe), Christopher Lee (The Creature), Melvyn Hayes (Young Victor), Valerie Gaunt (Justine)*
Director: *Terence Fisher*
Screenwriter: *Jimmy Sangster, based on the novel* Frankenstein *by Mary Shelley*
12/82 mins./Sci-fi/Horror/Drama/UK

Baron Victor Frankenstein, in prison for murder and trying to evade the guillotine, tells a priest how he and his mentor, Paul Krempe, had performed many scientific experiments, eventually leading to the resurrection of a dead body.

Frankenstein was the biggest name in horror from 1931 until 1948 when Universal's flathead met Abbott and Costello, at which point the tragic, fearsome Monster became a laughable goon. In the early 50s, horror was out of fashion (save for a 3D blip around the time of *House Of Wax* in 1953) and monsters came from outer space or A-bomb test sites. Then Hammer Films, a small British production company, had an unexpected hit with *The Quatermass Experiment* (1956) and cast around for another monster. They seized on the idea of remaking the original science-gone-mad property, in bloody colour and with as much bodice-ripping and eyeball-in-a-jar action as the censors would allow.

Hammer assigned Jimmy Sangster to come up with a script that had as little as possible to do with Shelley's original novel or Universal's copyrighted film, and handed the job of direction to Terence Fisher. Fisher abandoned the monochrome documentary look of *Quatermass* in favour of the lovely pastels and lurid primaries of Eastmancolor, and the half-modern/half-fairytale world of the James Whale version gave way to a meticulous mid-Victorian Switzerland, complete with elaborate sets, hairstyles and costumes. Whale's Henry Frankenstein might as well be a sorcerer, but Hammer's Baron is a chilly scientist, forerunner of the conscience-free obsessives who pioneered rocketry under the Nazis and nuclear weapons throughout the Cold War.

Like the 1931 film, Hammer's first *Frankenstein* made its leading man into a horror star. Indeed, it went one better by making both its leading men into horror stars. To play Victor Frankenstein, an icy rake who seduces the maid and bumps off a cuddly professor in order to continue his monster-making, Hammer selected Peter Cushing, then famous for a string of roles on BBC TV that ranged from Winston Smith in *1984* to Mr. Darcy in *Pride And Prejudice*. Cushing dominates the film with a performance that ranges from fanatical coldbloodedness to hysterical raving. His masterstrokes are telling gestures: absent-mindedly wiping bright blood on the plush lapel of a well-tailored coat, dashing about his laboratory pulling levers as his creature stirs in his tank, briskly asking his lovely fiancée for the marmalade just after he has locked his cast-off mistress in with the raging Monster.

Universal's Frankensteins concentrate on the Monster, but the star here is the Baron. Cushing returned in numerous sequels: all those directed by Fisher – *The Revenge Of Frankenstein* (1958), *Frankenstein Created Woman* (1967), *Frankenstein Must Be Destroyed* (1969), *Frankenstein And The Monster From Hell* (1974) are worth a look with the actor expanding his performance as a succession of experiments go disastrously awry.

For the Monster, Hammer were torn between *Carry On* stalwart Bernard Bresslaw and multilingual bit player Christopher Lee. Bresslaw's agent wanted too much money, so Lee won both the role and a place in the horror firmament, a position confirmed in 1958 by a star-making turn as *Dracula*.

Though intended to have a sculptor's hands and a physicist's brain, the creature is malformed because Victor's insufferably moralistic assistant Paul Krempe smashes the brain's bottle in a fierce tussle over the ethics of body-snatching. For too long, Lee has been criticised for not imitating Karloff's performance. Actually, he does wonders with the role of a monster who is almost a scripted afterthought to the rottenness of his creator. Laced tight like a silent movie whiteface clown, the creature periodically explodes into terrifying bursts of homicidal rage. There's a gruesome moment amid lush Berkshire greenery where half his head has been shot away, and he displays a sickening, yet oddly touching, streak of vanity by attempting to conceal a fresh brain-surgery scar among all his other grotesque deformities when Frankenstein exhibits him to the still-appalled Krempe.

It's far from Hammer's best horror – the first half is bogged down with chat around the dinner table, and Krempe is a scowling plot device who wears out his welcome rather too quickly – but it is the first, and sets the template for all the gothics the company would turn out over the next 15 years. In 1957, the film was a great commercial success and widely harangued by the press on the grounds of its (now mild-mannered) gore and sleaze. ★★★ **KN**

Teen Movie Clichés

TOP10

1 The hero's well-off parents just don't understand!
2 The only people who understand even less are the teachers.
3 The 'ugly' girl is actually a supermodel hidden under glasses and bad hair.
4 The high school jock hero is actually sensitive beneath that studly exterior.
5 The spotty nerd loses his virginity to a scorchingly sexy older woman.
6 Nasty, snobby girls and moronic thugs are always humiliated by the end.
7 The valedictorian heroine doesn't do nudity, but it's OK – her cheerleader friend does.
8 The crappy school band suddenly gets good on prom night.
9 The grown-up narrator intones, 'After that summer, nothing would ever be the same again …'
10 Teenage girls dress in outfits a Las Vegas showgirl would find demeaning and which the Duchess of Devonshire couldn't afford.

THE CURSE OF THE CAT PEOPLE (1944)

Starring: *Simone Simon (Irena Reed, Oliver's dead wife), Kent Smith (Oliver Reed), Jane Randolph (Alice Reed), Ann Carter (Amy Reed), Eve March (Miss Callahan, Amy's teacher)*
Directors: *Robert Wise, Gunther von Fritsch*
Screenwriter: *DeWitt Bodeen*
U/70 mins./Drama/Fantasy/Horror/USA

Amy, a child who lives too much in a world of her own imagining, is visited by an apparition who seems to be the ghost of her father's first wife. She is also drawn to the house of a dotty old lady who has driven her own daughter to the point of homicidal insanity.

An unexpected sequel to producer Val Lewton's hit *Cat People*, this brings back key cast and characters but tells a very different story. Kent Smith and Jane Randolph, the dull hero and heroine of the first movie, have moved to upstate New York (near Washington Irving's Sleepy Hollow) and are raising a lonely misfit daughter whose 'imaginary playmate' is the original cat girl, reincarnated in a form-fitting mediaeval nightgown as a ghostly fairy godmother.

Less an outright horror film than a study in child psychology, it manages to chill as it shows how Amy's childish eccentricities might lead her to an adulthood as tragic as that of the mother and daughter who live in a nearby old house, the old lady insisting that the younger woman isn't her daughter and the spinster turning murderously jealous of the younger visitor.

Carter gives the most natural, affecting and complex child performance in any 1940s film, and co-directors Robert Wise (who went on to a major career) and Gunther von Fritsch (who didn't) evoke the magical and nightmarish world of a clever misfit child.

There's an especially unsettling recital of the legend of the Headless Horseman, whose imagined hoofbeats drive Amy towards a real danger. The climax is as frightening and emotional as anything in the horror canon, with a moment of catharsis – prefiguring the more famous finish of *The Searchers* – as the would-be killer's resolve breaks and she comforts rather than throttles the little girl. ★★★★★ **KN**

CUTTER'S WAY (1981)

Starring: *Jeff Bridges (Richard Bone), John Heard (Alex Cutter), Lisa Eichhorn (Mo Cutter), Ann Dusenberry (Valerie Duran), Stephen Elliott (J.J. Cord)*
Director: *Ivan Passer*
Screenwriter: *Jeffrey Alan Fiskin based on the novel* Cutter And Bone *by Newton Thornburg*
18/105 mins./Thriller/USA

Wandering downtown LA late at night, Richard Bone glimpses a man stuffing something which turns out to be the horribly abused corpse of a runaway girl into a trashcan. Alex Cutter, Bone's best friend, leaps on flimsy evidence to the conclusion that the culprit is oil billionaire J.J. Cord and sets out to avenge the girl and punish the villain's many crimes.

One of the great overlooked American movies, with career-highlight work from director Ivan Passer (adapting Newton Thornburg's novel *Cutter and Bone*) and stars Jeff Bridges as ex-radical gigolo Bone, John Heard as one-eyed, one-legged, drunk Vietnam veteran Cutter and Lisa Eichhorn as Cutter's hardboiled waif wife Mo, who wishes both men would grow up but still gets horribly involved when her husband initiates a blackmail scam supposedly to determine whether or not oil billionaire J.J. Cord is guilty before setting out on a mission of vengeance.

Released in 1981, this is almost the last '1970s-style' film, a character study revolving around a mystery which is never really resolved. Cord, who represents to him everything evil and poisonous about America, is the sort of American monster found in *Citizen Kane*, *Chinatown* and Howard Hughes' biography (the name derives from the Hughes substitute in *The Carpetbaggers*), but his actual guilt or innocence is beside the point – which is to compare and contrast the psychically and physically mutilated leftovers from the era of war, protest and dropping out. Lisa Eichhorn, who should have had a much bigger career, is luminous as the sad-eyed heroine and her exit is among the most shocking and tragic in the cinema.

John Heard pulls off his showiest role – especially in a climax which finds him charging after the dragon on a white horse, rampaging through a posh party at the Cord estate in search of justice. ★★★★★ **KN**

CYRANO DE BERGERAC (1990)

Starring: *Gérard Depardieu (Cyrano de Bergerac), Anne Brochet (Roxane), Vincent Perez (Christian de Neuvillette), Jacques Weber (Count DeGuiche), Roland Bertin (Ragueneau)*
Director: *Jean-Paul Rappeneau*
Screenwriters: *Jean-Claude Carrière, Jean-Paul Rappeneau, based on the play by Edmond Rostand*
U/135 mins./Romance/Drama/France

Awards: *Academy Awards – Best Costume, BAFTA – Best Cinematography, Best Costume, Best Makeup (Jean-Pierre Eychenne, Michele Burke), Best Original Film Score, Golden Globes – Best Foreign Language Film*

Cyrano is an accomplished poet, playwright, soldier and duellist – but his abnormally large nose means that he is unlucky in love. Harbouring an unrequited crush on his cousin Roxane, he agrees to help her – even when that means helping the object of her affections to win her heart.

Cyrano De Bergerac arrived in the UK already laden with a Best Actor Award for Gérard Depardieu, scooped at last May's Cannes, and the 1990 European Film Awards' gong for Production Designer Of The Year. These early indicators, suggesting that Jean-Paul Rappeneau's version of the century-old Edmond Rostand classic play is something really rather special indeed, prove to be absolutely correct. This epic tale – several leagues away from Steve Martin's *Roxanne* version of the same story – has Depardieu in fine swashbuckling form as the flamboyant Gascon swordsman and inspired poet with the astonishingly large nose who, shining and suffering by turns, lives for the love of his gorgeous cousin Roxane (a bright interpretation by Brochet), but who – alas! – only has eyes for the pretty but dim-witted Christian de Neuvillette. Too hung up about that conk ever to make his real feelings known to the lady, Cyrano finally decides to woo Roxane through Christian, penning his billets-doux, and even seducing her on Christian's behalf in a balcony scene à la *Romeo And Juliet*. After much verbal lovemaking, Christian and Roxane (she still blissfully unaware of the duplicity) eventually marry, but far from living happily ever after, the couple arouse the vengeful jealousy of Roxane's other admirer the Count DeGuiche (Weber), Christian and Cyrano are packed off to battle as punishment and – affairs of the heart being what they are – it all, of course, goes horribly wrong. Rappeneau has said that this version of *Cyrano* combines the Rostand play with Errol Flynn's *Robin Hood* recalled from his childhood and, indeed, this faithful but fantastic adaptation – which even has the characters speaking in the original verse form (superb English sub-titles courtesy of Anthony Burgess) – positively bursts with all the wonder and excitement of a world as seen through a child's eyes: larger-than-life characters, the richest colours and the minutest, most sumptuous details, all of which are lovingly captured by cinematographer Pierre Lhomme in scenes as disparate as the stately magnificence of the Paris opera and the chaos of battle at Arras. For all its spectacle and splendid all-round performances, however, *Cyrano De Bergerac* is without doubt Gérard Depardieu's film. His is the gentle giant, at times a spellbinding entertainer juggling words and his sword with equal ease, at others, a vulnerable, tongue-tied romantic in Roxane's presence. This is a moving performance which puts the heart firmly back into romance and surely guarantees much hanky-wringing in the aisles. Truly the Greatest Love Story Ever Told.

★★★★★ **PB**

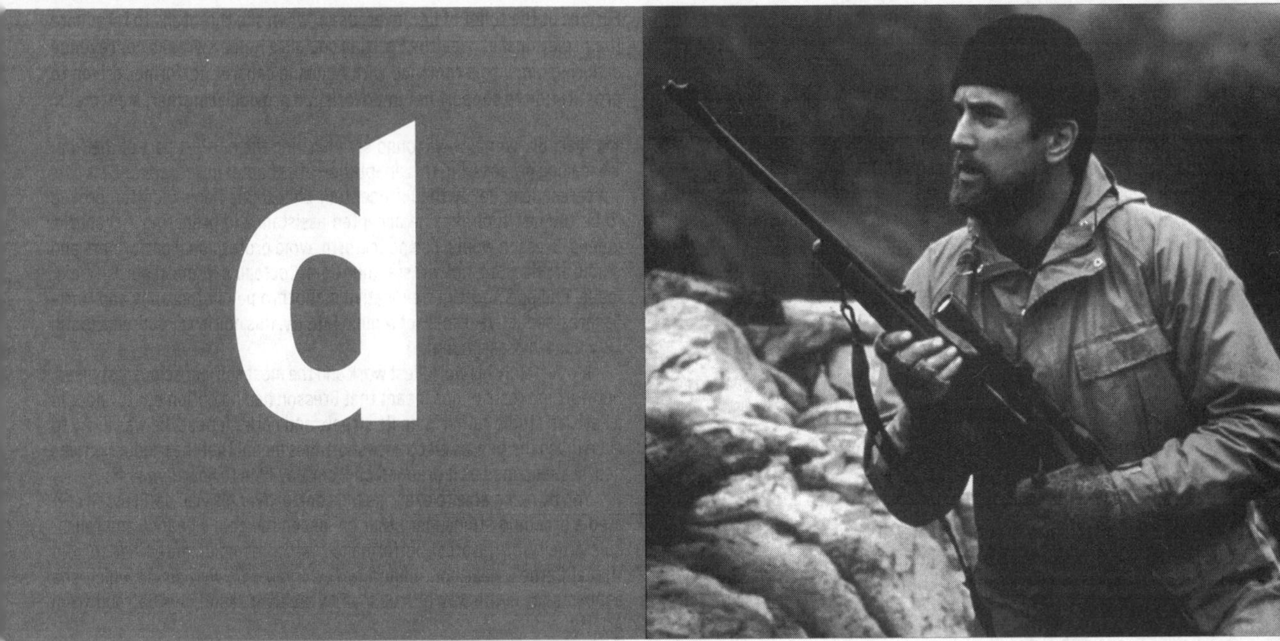

⦾ THE DA VINCI CODE (2006)

Starring: *Tom Hanks (Robert Langdon), Sophie Neveu (Audrey Tatou), Ian McKellen (Sir Leigh Teabing), Jean Reno (Captain Fache), Paul Bettany (Silas), Alfred Molina (Bishop Aringarosa), Jurgen Prochnow (Andre Vernet)*
Director: *Ron Howard*
Screenwriter: *Akiva Goldsman, based on the novel by Dan Brown*
12A/149 mins/Thriller/USA

Following the savage murder of Louvre curator Saunière, Harvard symbology professor Robert Langdon is embroiled in a plot involving a sexy police cryptologist, a jet-setting bishop, an albino monk assassin and the French rozzers that could lead to the discovery of the Holy Grail.

Much of the talk surrounding the success of Dan Brown's *The Da Vinci Code* concerned how cinematic it was: linear storytelling, short chapters, constant movement punctuated by sporadic violence, all set against a heady backdrop of Big Religious questions. All the adaptation needed to do was put Ext or Int at the front of every scene and it was a sure thing. So how Ron Howard, whose middle-brow sensibility would seem a perfect fit for the book's high-minded populism, managed to come up with something so wide of the mark is a bigger mystery than anything dreamed up by Brown.

A movie so dependent on exposition that there is no room for anything else, be it character, atmosphere, or even action set-pieces, the storytelling operates not through character motivations and desires but through a series of puzzles and clues. So as Langdon and Neveu lurch from mystery to mystery – a Countdown conundrum here, an olde worlde Rubik's Cube there – there is no sense of solving the mystery along with the heroes as they unravel impenetrable riddles ('So Dark The Con Of Man') with ease, if little logic – whenever it gets complex, Tautou pops up with an 'I don't understand' to induce further plot clarifications.

After an hour of Langdon and Neveu prattling around, McKellen's entry into the proceedings as a doddery Grail authority gives it a real boot up the backside, lending a real zest and twinkle to his difficult scenes of yet more explanation. Also on the plus side, Bettany's mad albino henchman – half zealot, half Sith – has some effective moments (wince as he flagellates himself). But the film's biggest surprise is the lack of engagement of its two major players. With any attempts at character sidelined by the sheer volume of plot, Hanks is a remote, detached presence, devoid of his trademark energy and charisma (he's also the only Harvard professor to lecture via the *Question Of Sport* numbers board).

Equally hesitant, Howard's trademark assurance eludes him – he botches one of the few action sequences through incomprehensible editing as Langdon and Neveu evade the police in a Smart car – and he never hits the right tone to make this hooey digestible. By the time third act comes round with its big revelations that throw up more questions than resolutions, the director feels just too drained to care. And so will you. ★★ **IF**

⦾ DALEKS' INVASION EARTH 2150 A.D.

Starring: *Peter Cushing (Dr. Who), Bernard Cribbins (Tom Campbell), Ray Brooks (David), Andrew Keir (Wyler), Roberta Tovey (Susan), Jill Curzon (Louise)*
Director: *Gordon Flemyng*
Screenwriters: *Terry Nation, Sydney Newman, Milton Subotsky, David Whitaker*
U/81 mins./Sci-fi/UK

Constable Tom Campbell blunders into a police telephone box, and finds himself whisked off to the future by the time-travelling Dr. Who. In 2150, London is in ruins, and occupied by an invasion force of evil aliens intent on scooping out the Earth's core and turning the planet into a giant spaceship.

A superior sequel to *Dr. Who and the Daleks*, the first big-screen adaptation of the BBC's flagship science fiction series, this stuck with Peter Cushing's talcum-in-the-hair dotty old loon interpretation of Doctor Who but has a semi-sumptuous widescreen look, a nice sense of World War II reconfigured as sci-fi adventure, memorable theme music, a splendid flying saucer landed in Sloane Square and excellent action scenes.

It lacks the grey desperation of 'The Dalek Invasion of Earth', Terry Nation's original TV serial, but its cherry-and-metal-flake colour scheme is appealingly gaudy. And, of course, it has the Daleks, the cult creatures of the 1960s, patrolling the ruins of London, barking 'exterminate', puffing deadly smoke at squirming humans, emerging eerily from the waters of the Thames and finally sucked to their doom by a realignment in Earth's magnetic core.

Bernard Cribbins replaces Roy Castle in the leading sidekick role, doing some comedy business when he tries to fit in with Daleks' corps of the PVC-clad, motorcycle-helmeted zombie RoboMen, but also has a lot of fun doing the sort of action heroics he was never asked to perform in any of his other work.

A solid supporting cast take the whole thing with deadly seriousness – Ray Brooks, Andrew Kier and Godfrey Quigley as pea-jacketed Resistance fighters organising against the Daleks as if they were Nazi invaders, and a memorable bit from the untrustworthily suave Philip Madoc as a double-crossing black marketeer who fully deserves his overkill extermination. ★★★★ **KN**

Ⓓ THE DAM BUSTERS (1954)

Starring: *Richard Todd (Wing Commander Guy Gibson), Michael Redgrave (Dr. Barnes N. Wallis), Derek Farr (Group Captain J.N.H. Whitworth) Ursula Jeans (Mrs Wallis)*
Director: *Michael Anderson*
Screenwriter: *R.C. Sherriff based on the book* Enemy Coast Ahead *by Guy Gibson and* The Dam Busters *by Paul Brickhill*
U/124 mins./War/UK

Dr Barnes Wallis struggles to convince the Air Ministry of the merits of a bouncing bomb attack on the dams of the industrial Ruhr, but a Lancaster squadron under Wing Commander Guy Gibson is eventually entrusted with the mission.

Michael Anderson spent two years researching this adaptation of Paul Brickhill's eponymous bestseller and Guy Gibson's memoir, *Enemy Coast Ahead*. However, he shifted the emphasis away from the heroics of the 617 Squadron, which lost 56 men in the raid on Germany's industrial heartland, and on to the unsung ingenuity of the backroom boffins who kept the forces supplied with potentially war-winning weaponry.

The tone very much reflected that established during the Second World War itself, when the likes of *San Demetrio, London* and *Fires Were Started* boosted the morale of British audiences without whipping them into the flagwaving frenzy that so many Hollywood combat pictures sought to arouse. This insistence on authenticity partly explains Anderson's decision to shoot in black and white, although the clincher was the availability of original footage of the bomb tests (which was augmented elsewhere by the superb special effects, which earned Gilbert Taylor an Oscar nomination).

Mention *The Dam Busters* today and most people will burst into Eric Coates' famous march. But the attack on the Möhne and Eder dams only occupies a fraction of the running time. Anderson and screenwriter R.C. Sherriff (who had written that seminal study of life in the trenches, *Journey's End*) were acutely aware of the sacrifice made by Gibson's unit, which lost eight of its 14 planes, and paid handsome tribute in the sequences in which it trains for the mission.

However, they were more concerned with the ethical conundrum facing Barnes Wallis, who was torn between professional perfectionism, staunch patriotism and sickening guilt at the human cost his munitions would exact. Consequently, Michael Redgrave is able to give a more nuanced performance than Richard Todd, whose Gibson maintains his stereotypically stiff upper lip whether he's facing the loss of his beloved dog or the prospect of breaking bad news to the 617's loved ones. ★★★★ **DP**

Ⓓ LES DAMES DU BOIS DE BOULOGNE (1945)

Starring: *Paul Bernard (Jean), Maria Casarès (Hélène), Elina Labourdette (Agnès), Lucienne Bogaert (Mme D.), Jean Marchat (Jacques)*
Director: *Robert Bresson*
Screenwriters: *Robert Bresson, Jean Cocteau based on the novel* Jacques le Fataliste, *by Denis Diderot*
PG/83 mins./Drama/France

Furious at the relief of her lover, Jean, when she threatens to terminate their relationship, wealthy Parisian socialite Hélène wreaks her revenge by luring him into a romance with Agnès, a cabaret performer driven to prostitution to support her impoverished provincial mother, Madame D.

Robert Bresson always found scriptwriting the hardest part of the film-making process. But this adaptation of a chapter in *Jacques Le Fataliste*, a picaresque novel by the 18th-century philosophe Denis Didertot, proved to be the last time that he accepted assistance in preparing a scenario. Indeed, Bresson would also henceforth avoid professional performers and studio artifice. But, notwithstanding Jean Cocteau's formal if abrasive dialogue, Philippe Agostini's evocative monochrome photography and Maria Casarès' seductive display of femme fatality, this noirish melodrama is still very much a Bresson film.

It's certainly his worldliest work and the most self-consciously stylised. But wartime restrictions meant that Bresson had no option but to shoot in a Parisian studio rather than its streets and parks. Indeed, he was lucky to even finish the film, as electricity shortages meant that the production was nearly abandoned as it dragged on from May 1944 to February 1945.

Yet, by being able to exercise full control over his visuals, Bresson created a brooding atmosphere that enhanced the cool elegance and relishable cruelty of Casarès' performance, which complemented her turn in Marcel Carné's near-contemporary *Les Enfants Du Paradis*, in which she again stands in the way of true love by stealing Jean-Louis Barrault from Arletty.

Both films were intended to be rallying cries to the occupied nation (with Jean-Luc Godard later declaring *Les Dames* to be 'the only film of the French Resistance'). But audiences preferred Carné's period ebullience and rebelled against Bresson's austere visuals (which he later disowned as excessively theatrical) and sombre story, even though it actually ended on an optimistic note, for by refusing to allow Hélène's wedding day declaration that he had married a slut to sully the purity of his love, Jean destroys the only power she has over him and, thus, he and the nobly valorous Agnès are now as free as France. ★★★★ **DP**

Ⓓ DAMIEN: OMEN II (1978)

Starring: *William Holden (Richard Thorn), Lee Grant (Ann Horn), Jonathan Scott-Taylor (Damien Thorn), Robert Foxworth (Paul Buher), Nicholas Pryor (Dr. Charles Warren)*
Director: *Don Taylor*
Screenwriters: *Harvey Bernhard, Stanley Mann, Mike Hodges*
18/107 mins./Horror/USA

Damien Thorn, the Antichrist, is now 13 years old and under the supervision of his rich uncle Richard Thorn and attending a military school. Here he contends growing into manhood and his father's inheritance to reap evil upon mankind.

A fairly well-thought out sequel to Richard Donner's famous Satanic thriller *The Omen*, as in it's sensible enough to retain Jerry Goldmsith's splendidly overwrought operatic score, the procession of freakish deaths as basic plot mechanic, and even develops a interesting identity crisis for the young demon spawn. The Antichrist is about to go through puberty and that's not going to be pretty.

Don Taylor, who replaced an irked Mike Hodges (creative differences) is certainly not up to pushing any major boundaries, rather than simply transfer the gothic apparatus of the original – Biblical cant, booming choirs, whacky slabs of pre-ordained death – to the plush confines of New England. And instead of Gregory Peck (who, if you recall, never made it to the credits of *The Omen*) we have another prime American star drifting into age, William Holden as the uncle who has taken charge, blindly, of this precursor to the end times.

With these changes in place, the plot follows its predecessor almost verbatim. As various people catch on to the true makeup of this teen, they are eradicated by hideously bizarre methods, as augured by the presence of (as applicable) a slavering black dog or demented raven. One poor soul is trapped beneath ice, and, in the film's oft-cited echo of David Warner's celebrated beheading in Damien's debut, a scientist (who has tested Damien's unusual blood) is trapped in a lift then sliced spectacularly in half. The message: it is dad, down below, who is the perpetrator.

Jonathan Scott-Taylor does a fine job with lifting Damien to another level, adding a human dimension to the icy stare of Harvey Stephens' baby-faced assassin. In one powerful scene, Taylor confronts his own self by finding the triple sixes on his scalp and runs, tormented by the truth, into a wood to scream, 'Why me?' to the heavens, make that, Hell. It takes Lance Henrickson's scowling sergeant at his school to point him in the right direction of Revelation for some good advice. Once he's swallowed the bitter pill of destiny, the film has nowhere to go than through the motions of a grand, quite effective slasher movie.

The story was to be picked up by the inferior *Omen III: The Final Conflict* with Sam Neil taking over, and there was also a fourth episode, a complete nonsense about a female progeny that doesn't even have the good grace to follow the Biblical template. ★★★ **IN**

DANCER IN THE DARK (2000)

Starring: *Bjork (Selma), Catherine Deneuve (Kathy), David Morse (Bill), Peter Stormare (Jeff), Udo Kier (Dr. Porkorny), Joel Grey (Oldrich Novy), Vincent Paterson (Samuel)*
Director: *Lars von Trier*
Screenwriter: *Lars Von Trier*
15/140 mins./Musical/Drama/Denmark/U.S./Sweden/Germany/Norway/Netherlands/France

Single mother Selma works two different jobs and scrapes by, in order to save enough money to give her son an eye operation that will save the deteriorating sight that she suffers. But when her landlord tries to steal her money, a tragedy unfolds.

Lars Von Trier continues to make films that shouldn't really work, but are nevertheless amazingly powerful. At once a musical and a meditation upon musicals (a bit like *Pennies From Heaven*), this is mostly shot *Dogme*-style, with edgy camerawork and improv-seeming performances, but segues into fantasised musical numbers.

The video blur look is brighter than the film's 'reality', but still not MGM glam, and the tunes grow out of rhythmic factory or scratch noises into Bjork songs that are nothing like conventional film music.

Sometime in the 60s in America (shot in Europe, because Von Trier won't fly), Czech single mum Selma works in a basin factory so her son can have an operation which will prevent the hereditary blindness that has already put her in the dark. She goes to the movies with Kathy, who explains the images to her, and gently if devastatingly resists nice guy Jeff ('I don't want a boyfriend'). Selma dreams of an unreal world, but her 'real' life is just as fable-like. Cop Bill, Selma's self-hating wicked landlord, steals her cash stash and forces her to desperate acts that beg for an unhappy ending.

Bjork (whose accent easily passes for Czech) is marvellous in a difficult role, locking herself into real and symbolic prisons for a love she can barely express in words ('I just wanted to hold the little baby'). The songs work in context, though Bjork's extraordinary voice – perhaps best appreciated by those blessed with the auditory register of a dog – doesn't really sit well with the needs of even a musical as off-beat as this. Nevertheless, she's a star. In a sub-plot, Selma rehearses for a performance of *The Sound Of Music*, so Bjork even reinterprets *My Favourite Things* in her own style, at first comically but eventually to heartbreaking effect. ★★★★★ **KN**

DANCES WITH WOLVES (1990)

Starring: *Kevin Costner (Lt. John Dunbar), Mary McDonnell (Stands With A Fist), Graham Greene (Kicking Bird), Rodney A. Grant (Wind In His Hair), Floyd 'Red Crow' Westerman (Ten Bears)*
Director: *Kevin Costner*
Screenwriter: *Michael Blake, based on Blake's novel*
12/181 mins/Adventure/Drama/Western/USA

Awards: *Academy Awards – Best Cinematography, Best Director, Best Film Editing, Best Original Score, Best Picture, Best Sound (Russell Williams II, Jeffrey Perkins, Bill W. Benton, Gregory H. Watkins), Best Screenplay based on material from another medium, Golden Globes – Best Director, Best Drama, Best Screenplay*

Lt. John Dunbar is dubbed a hero after he accidentally leads Union troops to a victory during the Civil War. He requests a position on the western frontier, but finds it deserted. He soon finds out he is not alone, but meets a wolf he dubs 'Two-socks' and a curious Indian tribe. Dunbar quickly makes friends with the tribe, and discovers a white woman who was raised by the Indians. He gradually earns the respect of these native people, and sheds his white-man's ways.

An idealistic Union soldier with a romantic dream of the fast-vanishing frontier is rewarded for an act of heroic gallantry in the Civil War with the posting of his request, a remote fort in the Dakotas. There he is befriended by a tribe of the Lakota Sioux and goes native, only to be caught up in the encroachment of the white man, seeing the twilight fall on the great horse culture of the Plains.

Kevin Costner's directorial debut was ambitious, epic and, most worryingly, a Western – chunks of it actually in Lakota Sioux with English subtitles – at a time when only Clint Eastwood was daring the unfashionable grand old genre with any success. Industry wags gleefully predicting disaster dubbed it 'Kevin's Gate'. Costner had the last laugh in a personal, artistic and commercial triumph when it rode away with seven Oscars, including Best Picture and Director. It was the first Western to win Best Picture since *Cimarron* (1931).

Dances With Wolves is a captivating adventure and wistful elegy that sprung from a fascination Costner and his buddy, writer Michael Blake, shared with an entire Baby Boomer generation who grew up with the cavalry and Indians in Saturday matinees and on primetime TV but were later affected by the 60s-born movements for Native American rights and the environment. Its South Dakota locations and exciting action sequences were ideally suited to Australian cinematographer Dean Semler's talents, the *Mad Max* veteran at home with both awesome landscapes and rootin' tootin' action. Together they created a lyrical, warmly evocative prairie odyssey which refuses to stint on rich detail, as in the time and space given to Dunbar's strange journey to the abandoned fort and his introduction to the Indians – by stages his terror, curiosity and notions of formal diplomacy giving way to his complete captivation by his feather-decked neighbours and their way of life.

As director Costner was sufficiently savvy to take lingering elegiac, mystical, sentimental, comic or romantic chapters in Dunbar's story to a series of vivid action climaxes. The film draws you in from the outset on a Tennessee battlefield with wounded Lt. John J. Dunbar courting death, galloping straight across a line of Confederate riflemen, finishing his wild ride on trusty steed Cisco unscathed. And he does it again, his arms outstretched in a sacrificial attitude, unwittingly inspiring a Union rout of the Southerners and becoming 'a living hero'. Conventional Indian attacks are largely avoided since the film is specifically a love affair with 'The People', portrayed as proud, quick and humorous: 'I had never known a people so eager to laugh, so devoted to family, so dedicated to each other. And the only word that came to mind was harmony.'

McDonnell's Stands With A Fist remembers in a flashback the massacre on her family's homestead. The muleteer is slaughtered by a Pawnee hunting party looking for some action. And Dunbar/Dances With Wolves' ordeal when ultimately he is taken prisoner by an Army detachment is ended by an archetypally whooping band of braves in a gruesome flurry of arrows and tomahawks – with the unique distinction that it is the Indians who are the good guys charging to the rescue and the blue coats who are the savage baddies. Otherwise the most memorable action set pieces are in keeping with the majestic pace of the film. The earth-shaking passing of the buffalo that awakens Dunbar to a dreamlike glimpse of the mighty herd leads to the stately buffalo hunt. Beginning with ritual body painting and horse decorating, building to the gallop into the racing herd, the chase with its whoosh of arrows, whump of spears, cracks of Dunbar's rifle and thuds of crashing buffalo, Dunbar's rescue of the boy Smiles A Lot from a wounded beast's charge and the eating of its heart is an extraordinary eight-minute sequence that is spectacular but also furthers the story by elaborating the significance of what they are doing.

Tagline
Inside everyone is a frontier waiting to be discovered.

The same is true of the ferocious Pawnee assault on the village. The Lakota war party away and the raiders spotted, Dances With Wolves casts off Dunbar by giving his Army rifles to his friends and leading the frantic defence: 'As I heard my Sioux name being called over and over, I knew for the first time who I really was.' A year after its release Costner presented the 'special edition' version of *Dances With Wolves* with nearly an hour of additional material. Almost all of this is seamlessly inserted snippets of dialogue here, a bit more snogging there, and still more ravishing scenery.

The most important 'new' scene is Dunbar's discover that the Lakota have caught, tortured and slain the ignoble white buffalo hunters. But there is no new major action scene and the added length, while handsome and involving for devotees, does drag the pace. Action fans are likely to be happier with the arguably superior, inarguably likeable, original 'short' version. ★★★★★ **AE**

DANGEROUS LIAISONS (1988)

Starring: *Glenn Close (Marquise de Merteuil), John Malkovich (Vicomte de Valmont), Michelle Pfeiffer (Madame de Tourvel), Swoosie Kurtz (Madame de Volanges), Keanu Reeves (Chevalier Danceny), Uma Thurman (Cécile de Volanges)*
Director: *Stephen Frears*
Screenwriter: *Christopher Hampton, based on his play and novel* Les Liaisons Dangereuses *by Choderlos de Laclos*
15/120 mins./Drama/USA

Awards: *Academy Awards – Best Art Direction/Set Decoration, Best Costume Design, Best Screenplay based on material from another medium, BAFTA – Best Supporting Actress (Michelle Pfeiffer), Best Adapted Screenplay*

Vicomte de Valmont and the Marquise de Merteuil enjoy a relationship of equal parts desire and disdain. They constantly try and outdo the other in their morally reprehensible acts, which usually involve the deflowering of young socialites.

This story has been creating a stir since it was published as a novel in Paris in 1782. Condemned as a work of 'revolting immorality', it was promptly banned by the very society it described, which of course didn't stop it being voraciously devoured for the next 200 years. The stage version, adapted by British playwright Christopher Hampton, won the 1986 Olivier Award. And then, of course, comes the film.

Malkovich and Close are at it immediately. When she asks him to seduce naive teenager Cécile de Volanges, to massively humiliate her prospective husband, he refuses as he's otherwise engaged attempting to bed the highly moralled Mme de Tourvel, just for the hell of it. As he tries it on he locks horns with her chum, Cécile's mother, and decides that deflowering the latter's daughter is, after all, a good idea. Meanwhile, de Merteuil has sorted out an alternative operative (a callow music teacher) who she ends up taking to bed herself. And so the permutations continue until the almost entirely unexpected ending.

The main characters' devotion to this sexual and social point-scoring is absolute – after the time and trouble they put into it, success becomes an end in itself – and the film could so easily have fallen apart due to this sheer ludicrousness. However, magnificently subtle playing of the lead roles by Close (twisted in the extreme), Malkovich (reptilian charm) and Pfeiffer (tormented beyond endurance) involves the viewer so completely that the entire business becomes not only possible but probable. They operate on the principle that everybody concerned is as barking mad as only the fabulously wealthy can be, therefore nothing needs justifying, and energy can be spent on the details that bring the film so vividly to life. ★★★★★ **LB**

DANGEROUS MINDS (1995)

Starring: *Michelle Pfeiffer (Louanne Johnson), George Dzundza (Hal Griffith), Courtney B. Vance (George Grandey), Robin Bartlett (Carla Nichols), Beatrice Winde (Mary Benton)*
Director: *John N. Smith*
Screenwriter: *Ronald Bass based on the book by LouAnne Johnson*
Costume Design: *Bobbie Read*
15/90 mins./Drama/USA

Former marine, Louanne Johnson, turns to teaching in a deprived Los Angeles high school. Detecting intelligence in her class of students, held back by social conditioning, she strives to find a way to communicate and then inspire them to better things.

You can understand why such tuned-in producers as Jerry Bruckheimer and Don Simpson would rehash the evergreen formula of an idealistic teacher turning their recalcitrant students to do their homework and hence have a better life (see everything from *To Sir With Love* to *Dead Poets Society*), but it still baffles why the commercially minded duo changed the name of the real Louanne Johnson's memoirs – *My Posse Don't Do Homework*. That it turned out to be a big hit, could be less down to its tired execution (lame work by makeweight TV director John N. Smith) than a hugely popular supporting video combining a deadpan Michellle Pfieffer, back-to-front on a chair, with rap star Coolio singing *Gangsta's Paradise*.

The film itself, built around Pfeiffer's then major stardom, is a fairly witless rerun of the aforementioned teacher-who-toughs-it-out scenario. That we already know she is an ex-marine, nine years in the service, means she can handle herself and possesses the required zeal to transform this set of clichéd misfits into real students (i.e. those who step up to the academic plate and express themselves). The chosen method, that hook by which she must snare their socially deprived minds, is poetry. Not the high-falutin' verses of Walt Whitman as prescribed to that bunch of wilful toffs in *Dead Poets Society*, but the earthy lines of Bob Dylan's *Tambourine Man*.

How much of this trite piffle bares any resemblance to the real story of Johnson who played the unconventional card (isn't it about time they abandoned conventional teaching, it clearly doesn't work) in an LA high school, is open to question. What is certain is that it delivers it in a flat, mechanical, unengaging manner (even Pfeiffer seems listless in her own vehicle) patronising its subjects in a way the script's philosophy assumes to detest – the undeveloped kids might as well come with labels perched in their fashionable haircuts: 'violent father', 'hidden talent' etc., etc. John N. Smith, a plodder at best, shoots without any context, the film barely escaping the confines of the classroom to present us with an idea of where these kids are coming from. But, then, they don't really matter when you've got Coolio on tap. ★★ **IN**

ⓓ DANTE'S PEAK (1997)

Starring: *Pierce Brosnan (Harry Dalton), Linda Hamilton (Rachel Wando), Charles Hallahan (Paul Dreyfus), Jamie Renee Smith (Lauren Wando), Jeremy Foley (Graham Wando)*
Director: *Roger Donaldson*
Screenwriter: *Leslie Bohem*
12/104 mins./Drama/USA

Vulcanologist Harry Dalton and town mayor Rachel Wando become convinced that nearby Dante's Peak is about to erupt. But can they convince the townspeople before the mountain goes ballistic?

The battle of the volcano movies commenced with this $100 million-plus effort, first out of the melting pot – ahead of rival pic *Volcano* – eager to alert audiences of the dangers of living too close to a really big smoking mountain. Or, to put it a bit more simply, this is yet another one of those mindlessly enjoyable outings which eschews such unimportant details as plot or characterisation in favour of the biggest, flashiest special effects money can buy. *Twister* with lava, if you will.

Brosnan is vulcanologist-with-a-past Harry Dalton, who, in a confusing opening sequence, fails to save his girlfriend from being fatally clonked on the head by a piece of stray volcanic rock (who said *Cliffhanger* at the back?). Cut to four years later, and said lonely eruption expert is dispatched to self-advertised nice-place-to-live Dante's Peak to investigate the rumblings of a hitherto long-dormant mountain. There he falls for local mayor-cum-coffee-shop-owner Rachel (Hamilton) and her two kids. When he detects signs of an imminent eruption but is shouted down by his boss, you just know it's only going to be a matter of time before the mount pours forth its contents, which it does in quite spectacular fashion.

And here is where the film really kicks in. After taking what seems like a volcanic age to get going, concentrating instead on peppering Brosnan and Hamilton's inevitable courtship with appalling dialogue ('Making love is like riding a bicycle – you never forget,' coos Brosnan with all the seductive charm of a rutting rhino), the special pyroclastic effects are definitely worth the wait. Ash falls from the heavens like snow, buildings crumple as though fashioned from matchsticks, cars and bridges are dramatically swept away, and every cliché in the disaster movie rule book is dragged out – from second-rung characters meeting untimely ends through to Rocky the heroic dog who may or may not make it through the mayhem.

Impressive though all this may be, what the film lacks is a sense of panic. Apart from a couple of brief post-eruption sequences, those who aren't buried under a ton of the hot stuff seem largely to be going through the motions. Still, the leads are likeable enough (Brosnan displaying the kind of square-jawed heroics with which he breezed through *Goldeneye*), the claustrophobic finale suitably tense, and despite a prevailing sense of the ridiculous, with suspension of disbelief this works just well enough to land it comfortably in the Saturday night special bracket. It does, however, serve as a cautionary reminder that the effects-are-everything formula is starting to wear thin. ★★★ **CW**

ⓓ DAREDEVIL (2003)

Starring: *Ben Affleck (Matt Murdock/Daredevil), Jennifer Garner (Elektra Natchios), Colin Farrell (Bullseye), Michael Clarke Duncan (Wilson Fisk/The Kingpin), Jon Favreau (Franklin 'Foggy' Nelson), Derrick O'Connor (Father Everett), David Keith (Jack Murdock)*
Director: *Mark Steven Johnson*
Screenwriter: *Mark Steven Johnson*
15/103 mins./133 mins. (director's cut)/Action/Thriller/Crime/Fantasy/USA

Awards: *Razzie – Worst Actor*

An accident blinds young Matt Murdock but heightens his remaining senses. As an adult, he fights for justice as a lawyer by day and superhero by night – until a romance with Elektra, martial artist daughter of a tycoon, brings him up against New York crime boss Kingpin and assassin-for-hire Bullseye.

The fourth major Marvel Comics franchise to make it to the screen – following *Blade*, *X-Men* and *Spider-Man* – *Daredevil* works hard to establish an identity separate from those series, limiting the fantastical elements by endowing its leather-clad players with preternatural rather than the supernatural abilities. It pitches straight in with a wounded, suited-up Daredevil (Affleck) clinging like a gargoyle to a church steeple, then zooms into his blind eye to kick off a complicated set of flashbacks that cover even more comics history than was crammed into the slightly roomier *Spider-Man* script.

As is typical with superheroes, the cool powers – demonstrated by snappy, imaginative visuals that show how the blind man 'sees' through soundwaves – are balanced by more than his fair share of traumas and harsh life lessons. Oddly, the childhood section of the film puts less emphasis on quasi-science fiction stuff about the poor kid from Hell's Kitchen blinded by a spray of radioactive goop and gifted with reflexes beyond the normal than it does on a rerun of 1940s noir boxing melodramas (*Body And Soul*, *The Set-Up*). Matt's dad, Jack 'The Devil' Murdock (David Keith), refuses to take a dive in the ring and is murdered outside the arena by a rose-throwing shadowman who, as in Burton's *Batman* film, will clearly wind up as our hero's arch-nemesis.

Sensibly, we skip some years to avoid crossover with the *Batman* and *Spider-Man* on-the-job superhero training scenes. When we pick it up, Matt's night-time alter ego is established as an urban legend, with newshound Ben Urich – who sadly no longer works alongside Peter Parker at the *Daily Bugle*, because the franchises are with different studios – determined to unmask the vigilante. Affleck does well in a charming/unnerving meeting with Garner's asskickette heroine, first pulling fake disabled pick-up moves on her in a coffee shop then getting down to serious foreplay in an impromptu punch-up in a playground.

Things fray when the villains are introduced. Michael Clarke Duncan's cigar-smoking megalomaniac Kingpin and Colin Farrell's venomous Irish hitman Bullseye are fun characters with neat gimmicks (Bullseye can kill anyone with anything, including paperclips and peanuts). Even the enmities that swirl between the characters are serviceable (after a first encounter with Daredevil, Bullseye is incensed – 'You made me miss!'). What isn't seamless is the way the villains are yoked into the Matt-Elektra story and, after a couple of Hong Kong-style one-on-one wire-strung battles, there's little room to develop, prompting a drop-off after the movie comes out of flashback mode. A supposed final confrontation between the hero and his father's killer fizzles because the film can't bring itself to commit to any of the possible outcomes.

Writer-director Mark Steven Johnson over-relies on an album's worth of songs to underscore emotion and excitement, when he ought to trust his mostly fine writing and effective casting. Affleck, the good guy equivalent of his legal shark in *Changing Lanes*, is a more convincing hero than in his earlier leading man outings, and everyone else is on form. But the initial good impression dissipates by the fade-out. ★★ **CH**

ⓓ DARK CITY (1998)

Starring: *Rufus Sewell (John Murdoch), Kiefer Sutherland (Dr. Schreber), Jennifer Connelly (Emma Murdoch), Richard O'Brien (Mr. Hand), Ian Richardson (Mr. Book), William Hurt (Inspector Frank Bumstead)*
Director: *Alex Proyas*
Screenwriters: *Alex Proyas, Lem Dobbs, David S. Goyer, from a story by Alex Proyas*
15/103 mins./Science Fiction/Thriller/Fantasy/USA

John Murdoch is tortured by strange memories and visions that the people around him don't seem to share. Is he going mad? Or is there something in the sunless city where he lives that can explain what is happening to him?

Proyas' previous work was *The Crow* – a movie that the majority of its audience went to see to try to catch the point at which Brandon Lee checked out – but which turned out to be a satisfyingly dark and melancholic comic book piece showcasing Proyas' unique visuals. With *Dark City* we get the same gloomy pop Gothery but this time with less of the emotional content. And no one bought it on set. Bummer.

John Murdoch wakes up in the bath only to find that the metropolis around him is in the process of being physically remodelled by a bunch of pale-faced floating blokes in terrifying hats who look like the kind of thing Salvador Dali might have nightmares about. Not only that, but they're swapping people's personalities over, and Murdoch has wound up as a murderer pursued by the cops. He must persuade Inspector Bumstead that there is something afoot with the city while Dr. Schreber (Sutherland in an enjoyably over-the-top Peter Lorre impression) tries to track him down to administer the painful head injection that will make him forget.

If this all sounds beyond ludicrous that's because it is. Proyas appears to have been so distracted with his gloomy vision of the city that he forgot to actually write anything approaching a coherent story. Which is why, while the majority of the performances are serviceable, it's the sheer overwhelming style that gets *Dark City* through. Proyas drenches each shot in a unique feel and delivers a movie with a visual sense with all the inventive, poetic power of Ridley Scott or Terry Gilliam firing on all cylinders. ★★★ **AS**

THE DARK CRYSTAL (1982)

Starring: *the voices and puppet performances of: Jim Henson (Jen/High Priest), Frank Oz (Augha/Chamberlain), Kathryn Mullen (Kira), Dave Goelz (Fizzgig/General/Dying Emperor), Louise Gold (Gourmand)*
Directors: *Jim Henson, Frank Oz*
Screenwriters: *Jim Henson, David Odell*
PG/93 mins./Fantasy/Adventure/USA/UK

As the prophesy foretold, the three suns have come into conjunction for the first time in a 1000 years, and the chance has finally come to find the missing shard of the Dark Crystal and end the chaotic rule of the evil Skekses. It is the tiny Gelfling Jen, the last of his race eradicated by the cruelty of the Skekses, who sets out on the dangerous quest.

When The Muppets' creative duo of Jim Henson and Frank Oz decided to stretch their puppetry into the reaches of feature films, they proved more than merely zany puppetmasters. Here was a pair of hugely imaginative purveyors of quirky fantasy mythos. *The Dark Crystal* has an ethereal alien quality to its startling visions, far removed from the Earth-bound contours of traditional fairy-tales. It is a hippyish dreamlike movie that entirely succeeds as a children's adventure. A feat they would continue, with marginally less wonder, in *Labyrinth*.

The choice of removing all humans from the structure of the film – a first for Henson and Oz – was inspired. It liberated the film from attesting to its structural limitations (i.e. revealing the strings), in this quaint realm of innocent Gelflings, gentle, sorrow-burdened Mystics and the squawking, detestably brilliant birdlike Skekses. Of course, the imprimatur of Professor Tolkien is fully evident: diminutive saviours facing impossible odds, with the Gelfling Jen, a simpering do-gooder, out to trace the origins of the missing shard of the fabled all-powerful crystal, and so save his world in process, but it is less the straightforward plot than the extraordinary execution which dazzles.

The design concepts are a marvel. Utilising the talents of celebrated fantasy illustrator Brian Froud, the film has a life and feel all its own, the puppets given vital energy by Henson's brilliant workshop, their movements while not exactly human are free of the jerky obvious motions of a puppet. This is most delightful and energetic with the Skekses, this world's ripe villains, who come loosely based on the seven deadly sins. These memorably vile entities, creating a cacophony of rueful bleats like rabid dinner ladies, prevent the film from ever drifting into sappy moralism by inviting an enquiry on the avaricious nature of evil. ★★★★ **IN**

DARK STAR (1974)

Starring: *Brian Narelle (Lt. Doolittle), Cal Kuniholm (Boiler), Dre Pahich (Talby), Dan O'Bannon (Pinback), Joe Sanders (Powell)*
Director: *John Carpenter*
Screenwriter: *John Carpenter*
PG/83 mins./Sci-fi/USA

The crew of the Dark Star are on a 20-year mission to clear a path in space by destroying planets that are in the way of navigation routes. After a series of mishaps Mother, the ships computer, can no longer persuade Bomb not to detonate. Even the dead captain is of little help in arguing with Bomb who is bound to do his duty.

Comedy and sci-fi rarely mix, and when they do it's usually in the inferior form of spoof (*Spaceballs, Airplane II*). Woody Allen's *Sleeper* probably comes closest to a true sci-fi comedy but even here the jokes emerge from a 20th Century man's perceptions of the future and its odd technologies (orgasmatrons, orbs and nostrilectomies).

John Carpenter's debut movie *Dark Star* is almost unique in getting its laughs naturally from the desperate situation of its protagonists and their conflicting characters. But alongside the gags *Dark Star* has at its heart a strangely touching sense of the loneliness and isolation that must accompany space travel. It also originated the grungy, 'realistic' look to the future which would influence both *Blade Runner* and *Alien*. Which is not surprising since it is, amongst many other things, a riposte to the sleek techno-worship and impenetrable philosophical ponderings of Stanley Kubrick's *2001: A Space Odyssey* which was released six years earlier.

Dark Star has four astronauts aboard the titular craft which, after 20 years in deep space carrying out its relatively pointless mission of blowing up unstable planets, is falling to pieces. The original commander is dead (though still talking from his cryogenic suspension chamber in the hold) after his seat exploded, the sleeping quarters have been destroyed and since the crew can't be bothered to do anything about it they bed down in a detritus-strewn storage locker. 'Storage area 9 self-destructed last week,' notes commander Doolittle (Narelle) wearily in his log, 'destroying the ship's entire supply of toilet paper.' Not only that but the ship's computer ('Mother', voiced by Cookie Knapp, the only member of the cast excluding Carpenter and screenwriter Dan O'Bannon to have any kind of future in the movies, she's a set teacher now) spends most of its time trying to persuade Bomb number 20 to desist from exploding and return to the bomb bay.

Meanwhile the crew – comprising space hippy Talby who simply gazes at the stars; Boiler who uses bits of the collapsing ship for target practice; and Finback who bitches about the state they're in and, in one of the film's virtuoso sequences, is attacked by the ship's mascot alien (which closely resembles a beach ball) – bicker, slob around and pass the endless hours as best they can.

Originally made as a University Of Southern California film-school graduation project, *Dark Star* ran a mere 45 minutes until producer Jack H. Harris spotted the movie's cult potential and kicked in extra funding taking the running time to feature length and the budget to a total of $60,000, a paltry amount for any movie, let alone science fiction, traditionally an expensive genre simply because of the demands of special effects. But Carpenter brilliantly turns his lack of funds into an asset, directly poking fun at Kubrick's state-of-the-art futurescapes with his own tatty sets and straggly-bearded space cowboys.

The Kubrick baiting is pursued through the music. Whereas the distinguished *2001* helmer famously used carefully selected classical pieces, Carpenter invokes tacky country and western (*Benson, Arizona* is the film's main theme), rock and roll, and in a wicked dig at Kubrick's esoteric selections, has the computer play *When Twilight Falls On NGC-891* which turns out to be unendurable muzak. Even the movie's final shot of a sun rising above a planet is a reference to the *Space Odyssey*.

But *Dark Star* is far more than a cheap gag at another movie's expense. Firstly it explore several themes and motifs that would appear in both Carpenter and O'Bannon's subsequent work: the O'Bannon-scripted *Alien* owes not only its computer's moniker (Mother) to *Dark Star* but its theme (isolated astronauts dealing with an alien intruder) could simply be seen as *Dark Star* played without the laughs, while Carpenter would take that self-same theme, relocate it to the Antarctic and call his intruder The Thing (it isn't only movies that owe a debt of gratitude, TV's *Red Dwarf* is unthinkable without Carpenter's antecedent). And secondly, it is permeated with an almost poetic sense of melancholy and loneliness. At one point Doolittle plays an odd musical instrument he has constructed out of water filled bottles, while up in his viewing capsule Talby simply stares in wonder at the stars.

The whimsical ending which has Bomb No. 20 developing a God complex and destroying the ship (another *2001* nod, this time towards Hal) leaves Doolittle surfing into an alien planet's atmosphere to end life as a shooting star, while Talby joins The Phoenix Asteroids to glow and circle the galaxy forever (it's an ending that displeased sci-fi author Ray Bradbury who accused Carpenter of cribbing it wholesale from his short story *Kaleidoscope*). And in a treat for pedants, Carpenter manages to commit what is probably the first and only philosophical flub in film history – the subject Doolittle discusses with the bomb is epistemology, not phenomenology. The high-minded Kubrick may have had the last laugh after all. ★★★★★ **AS**

DARK VICTORY (1939)

Starring: *Bette Davis (Judith Traherne), George Brent (Dr. Frederick Steele), Humphrey Bogart (Michael O'Leary), Geraldine Fitzgerald (Ann King), Ronald Reagan (Alec Hamlin)*
Director: *Edmund Goulding*
Screenwriter: *Casey Robinson based on the play by George Emerson Brewer Jr and Bertram Bloch*
PG/105 mins./Drama/USA

Socialite Judith Traherne is nursed through her losing battle with a brain tumour by loyal friend, Ann King, and specialist Dr Frederick Steele, who falls in love with his plucky patient.

'Who wants to see a dame go blind?' opined the ever-sensitive Jack Warner, after Bette Davis begged him to persuade independent producer David O. Selznick to release the rights to George Emerson Brewer Jr. and Bertram Bloch's minor stage hit. Yet, despite the mogul's pessimism, millions faced with the darkening world situation wept their way through this three-hankie melodrama, almost as an act of catharsis. Indeed, Davis viewed the project in much the same way, as she sought suitable showcases to compensate for missing out on Scarlett O'Hara in *Gone With the Wind*. Ironically, Vivien Leigh would pip her to the Best Actress Oscar, but Davis always regarded this as her favourite role.

Yet she had misgivings about her ability to handle Judith Traherne's graceful demise. But director Edmund Goulding cleverly decided to shoot in sequence to allow Davis to gain confidence from playing against type as the gregarious socialite, whose joie de vivre gives way to some trademark bitching (in the superbly played drunk scene, in which Judith accuses Ann and Dr Steele of conspiring to keep her negative prognosis a secret) before she settles down to some exquisite suffering.

Davis channelled her off-screen emotions into the part, as not only was she going through a divorce, but she was also on the rebound from affairs with William Wyler and Howard Hughes. But she drew solace and inspiration from George Brent (who was himself newly divorced from actress Ruth Chatterton) and their romance clearly colours their latter scenes together, although his bland charm barely registers against Davis' powerhouse performance, which is only matched in insensity by Max Steiner's occasionally intrusive score.

Elsewhere, the debuting Geraldine Fitzgerald provides some serviceable support, as does Humphrey Bogart, who belies miscasting to lend some earthy intrigue as an Irish Mellors to Davis' lachrymose Lady Chatterley. ★★★ **DP**

DARK WATER (HONOGURAI MIZU NO SOKO KARA) (2002)

Starring: *Hitomi Kuroki (Yoshimi Matsubara), Rio Kanno (Ikuko Matsubara), Mirei Oguchi (Mitsuko Kawai), Asami Mizukawa (Ikuko Hamada)*
Director: *Hideo Nakata*
Screenwriters: *Hideo Nakata, Takashige Ichise*
15/101 mins./Horror/Japan

Aiming to make a new start, single mother Yoshimi and her young daughter Ikuko move into a new apartment in a run-down part of town. Their harmony is soon disrupted by strange goings on, especially a nasty water stain on the ceiling that seems to grow every day. Then a small child keeps appearing.

While still working his icy chills in his homeland of Japan – he's now installed in Hollywood remaking his own work – Hideo Nakata directed a series of effective, idiosyncratic ghostly tales that positioned the horror genre away from the glare of schlock. His notion of fear is a slow creep, a stain on the ceiling, the blur of a video image, the insidious tremor caused by a momentary image of a small Japanese child with lank hair and dead eyes. In this style, his most famous films, *Ring* and *Ring 2*, might as well have been squealing up Elm Street way compared to the subtle strains of this ghost story that uses reticence, a flat refusal to fully expose its evil schemes, to invoke a very redolent fear.

Thus you have one of the slowest, and often most infuriating, horror movies ever made. *Dark Water*, as its name suggests, works most of its dread through the expanding image of an iron-brown water stain, and the unending drip-dripping of its torment. The ethereal backstory here tells of a missing girl (a staple of Japanese horror) in ghost form haunting the scene of her downfall in search of a new mother, and Yoshimi, with her own child, fits the bill. In the meantime she'll 'make friends' with little Ikuko.

Nakata, however, keeps the supernatural shards of his story at one remove, allowing them to glimmer sullenly in the background – repeated glimpses of this spooky kid – building a small soap opera in the foreground. We learn Yoshimi (played with dancing nerves by Hitomi Kuroki) has escaped from a brutal marriage, leaving her frayed and open to suggestion; one being that her paranoia over this strange vision of a girl is being manipulated by her ex-husband aiming to regain custody of their daughter. The film, at this stage, never fully commits to the outright alien, allowing Nakata to insinuate it could all be in her head, the mucky glower of that stain representing the state of her mind.

Things do tip finally in the direction of genuine weirdness, if not toward an ending that wholly explains itself, but the impression lasts, proving that oft-regaled saw in horror parts that less is so often more. Especially when it comes to the itchy terror of pre-pubescent Japanese children. ★★★★ **IN**

⑮ DARK WATER (2005)

Starring: *Jennifer Connelly (Dahlia), John C. Reilly (Mr. Murray), Tim Roth (Jeff Platzer), Dougray Scott (Kyle), Pete Postlethwaite (Veeck)*
Director: *Walter Salles*
Screenwriter: *Rafael Yglesias, based on the film Honogurai mizu no soko kara by Hideo Nakata, Takashige Ichise and the novel by Koji Suzuki*
15/105 mins./Drama/Horror/USA

Troubled divorcée Dahlia Williams moves into a rundown apartment with her young daughter Ceci, desperately seeking solace from an acrimonious custody battle with her ex-husband. But the damp patch in the bedroom ceiling is only the start of her problems, which include mysterious thumps from upstairs and the arrival of Ceci's sinister imaginary friend . . .

With *The Grudge* and two *Ring* movies translating their shrieks into kerchings at the US box office, it's hardly surprising that Hollywood's been peering hard at the Japanese horror genre in search of further decent remake material. And Disney could have done far worse than plunge its chunky white gloves into *Ringu* director Hideo Nakata's *Dark Water*. With its dank, overcast urban setting, Nakata's original is an effective little mix of chills and intrigue – even if it does lack *Ringu*'s outright scares while pretty much offering more of the same (circular threats, watery motifs, sinister ghost girls with lank, inky hair). Put simply, it's good enough to warrant a fresh take, but flawed enough for improvements to be made.

Combine that with an American pedigree that reeks of quality and, at first glance at least, *Dark Water* should be the strongest Asian-horror remake to date. We have Oscar-winning actress Jennifer Connelly taking the lead as the fraught, haunted mother, supported by some cast-iron character actors: John C. Reilly as a patronising, sleazy landlord, Tim Roth as a hobo lawyer, Pete Postlethwaite as a surly, monosyllabic caretaker. Most excitingly, helming duties have gone to Walter Salles, the Brazilian brain behind arthouse breakouts *Central Station* and *The Motorcycle Diaries* (not to mention his producing credit on *City Of God*), here making his North American movie debut.

Treating *Dark Water* as an intimate and sensitively sustained human drama, one which concerns the travails of a single mother in a harsh environment, Salles has proven himself the perfect man for the job. He's certainly a good match for his leading lady. Dahlia is a woman with issues, specifically abandonment issues, and under Salles' steady guidance Connelly keeps her overprotectiveness on the right side of mania. With the vein in Connelly's worry-line-etched forehead looking fit to burst throughout, the neurosis is apparent as an acute, internal throb which occasionally mutates into a migraine (accompanied by a discomfiting screech on the soundtrack) – not as the kind of twitchy, shouty performance you'd expect from a lesser actress.

But is she a scream queen? Well, therein lies *Dark Water*'s key problem: it's just not scary, so there's little to warrant any screaming. Connelly's done misery many times before (*Requiem For A Dream, House Of Sand And Fog, A Beautiful Mind* – she even spent most of *Hulk* weeping), and it would have been refreshing to see her exercise her lungs in a big, fun, jump-out-of-your-skin Hollyhorror. Yet that's not what she or anyone else involved has set out to do. That it consciously avoids most genre-cliché pitfalls is both *Dark Water*'s greatest strength and its biggest weakness. On the one hand, it's intelligent and beautifully bereft of any cats leaping out of shadows to orchestral blasts; on the other, it's just not entertaining, at least not in the popcorny, audience-pleasing sense.

Of course, ghost stories don't have to be out-and-out horrors, but even, say, *The Sixth Sense* summoned up a few gut-freezing set-pieces. Here it's more a case of atmosphere-building, from the gloomy, snot-green-and-grey set dressing, to the harsh, ghost-child whispers. Yet there's no overwhelming sense of threat, of the kind of primal terror that you'd imagine would come from encountering a malevolent supernatural entity in a rundown apartment block. Salles is undoubtedly a great director, but if *Dark Water* makes one thing clear, it's that he just isn't a great horror director.

★★★ **DJ**

⑮ DARKMAN (1990)

Starring: *Liam Neeson (Peyton Westlake), Frances McDormand (Julie Hastings), Colin Friels (Louis Strack Jr.), Larry Drake (Robert G. Durant), Nelson Mashita (Yakitito), Ted Raimi (Rick)*
Director: *Sam Raimi*
Screenwriters: *Sam Raimi, Ivan Raimi, Chuck Pfarrer, Daniel Goldin, Joshua Goldin*
15/96 mins./Action/Science Fiction/USA

Left for dead after gangsters drop him in a vat of acid and blow up his lab, scientist Peyton Westlake is hideously scarred beyond recognition. When doctors remove his neurons he can no longer feel pain and gains incredible strength, and using his own skills creates a synthetic skin to cover his deformity. Thus he sets out for revenge as Darkman.

Long before he turned his exuberant methodology – a breezy, elastic style both in camerawork and storytelling – to the high-gloss of *Spider-Man*, Sam Raimi did a dry-run by inventing his own superhero for this off-beam comic book movie. It is unmistakably the work of Raimi, managing that strange commingling of the upbeat and superficial with a caustic, often bleak sense of humour. *Darkman* has a nasty, unwelcoming core, a biproduct of the shadowy story and nonchalant style. Hence, it is his least likeable film, including the ranks of *Evil Deads*, but there's no doubting the imagination on show.

The twitch of the idea, its yucky hook, is that Darkman's shifting identities – he can construct any face to fit his own scorched mien, including his own – can only last for a couple of hours before disintegrating to reveal the mishmash beneath. The sources for this shifting anti-hero are obvious: Gaston Leroux's *Phantom Of The Opera*, H.G. Wells' *Invisible Man*, Andre De Toth's *House Of Wax*. Men who wear masks to hide themselves not to become things: an interesting reverse angle on standard superhero psychology.

Part of what makes Raimi's execution of this keen idea so leaden, is miscasting. Liam Neeson, a strikingly tall man so good for noble idealists, doesn't fit the form of a superhero, especially one as doubly messed up as this. You need a scene filling personality, a propensity for camp flourishes, to make this character work; Raimi's alter-ego Bruce Campbell would have thrilled to the part. Frances McDormand too, although an excellent actress, doesn't gel with the downtrodden girlfriend role, and despite putting in hard work as the attorney caught up with shady property dealers, she too seems adrift. The film offers little to root for working through the straightforward delivery of revenge.

The bad guys, inevitably, have more fun. Raimi's exaggerated style allow snarly gangsters Colin Friels and a splendidly vindictive turn from Larry Drake as a finger-collecting henchman, to cut loose. There is, though, little room allowed for morality, visually Raimi is playing it for all its worth: the swooping camera, the synthetic lighting, the splash of loud special effects. A grab-bag of giddy exaggeration, working hardest for laughs rather than thrills, this is the superhero genre executed as B-movie freakshow. ★★ **IN**

◎ DARLING (1965)

Starring: *Laurence Harvey (Miles Brand), Dirk Bogard (Robert Gold), Julie Christie (Diana Scott), Roland Curram (Malcolm), Jose-Luis de Villalonga (Cesare), Alex Scott (Sean Martin)*
Director: *John Schlesinger*
Screenwriter: *Frederic Raphael based on a story by Raphael, Schlesinger and Joseph Janni*
15/128 mins./Drama/UK

Awards: *Academy Awards – Best Actress, Best Original Screenplay, Best Costume Design, BAFTA – Best British Actor (Dirk Bogard), Best British Actress, Best British Art Direction, Best British Screenplay*

London model Diana Scott becomes an overnight celebrity when she moves in with married TV commentator Robert Gold, only to drift into movies and dead-end relationships with PR maven Miles Brand and Italian nobleman, Cesare.

In some ways, *Darling* appears to be a film 40 years ahead of its time, as only now is the public so fully aware of the luvviness and sham glamour of the fame game. But for all its dogged determination to hold up a mirror to the Swinging Sixties, this has more in common with 'angry young men' movies like *Room at the Top* and *This Sporting Life* than such chic contemporary pictures as *Georgy Girl* and *Blow-Up*.

Director John Schlesinger and Oscar-winning scenarist Frederic Raphael sought to shock with their discussion of promiscuity, homosexuality, infidelity and abortion. But *The Wednesday Play* on the BBC was then addressing similar issues with considerably more grit and insight. Indeed, there's a smug satisfaction about the cynicism and satire, which undermines potentially excruciating sequences like the suburban dinner party and the charity ball at which liggers and wannabes gorge themselves in the cause of famine relief.

Schlesinger's visual style is equally out of step with its trendy ambitions. Apeing the nouvelle vague, he employs handheld camera, accelerated motion, freeze frames and jump cuts, but the Hollywood montage sequence chronicling Robert and Diana's social whirl feels like a relic from the 1930s. Moreover, the soundtrack is positively antedeluvian in its avoidance of pop music.

It's as though Raphael and Schlesinger were attempting different things with the same story. The former seems content to set up celebrity clichés and caricatures solely for the amusement of knocking them down, while the latter takes a less sardonic approach by striving to show that this world of frivolity and exploitation actually damages those who can't hack its excesses and cruelties. Yet, even though the Oscar-winning Christie and the bored-looking Bogard are ultimately casualties of the spiritedly amoral Harvey's PR machine, it's hard to feel much pity for them. ★★★ **DP**

◎ DAS BOOT (THE BOAT) (1981)

Director: *Wolfgang Petersen*
Starring: *Jurgen Prochnow (Captain), Herbert Gronemeyer (Lt. Werner/Correspondent), Klaus Wennemann (Chief Engineer), Hubertus Bengsch (1st Lt./Number One), Martin Semmelrogge (2nd Lt./Number Two), Bernd Tauber (Chief Quartermaster), Erwin Leder (Johann), Martin May (Ullman), Heinz Hoenig (Hinrich), Uwe Ochsenknecht (Chief Bosun)*
Screenwriter: *Wolfgang Petersen, based on the novel by Lothar G. Buchheim*
15/150mins./War/Drama/West Germany

Set aboard a German U-boat in 1942, this follows the crew's attempts to survive the Battle of the Atlantic, and understand the regime that they serve.

Anyone who thinks spending three-and-a-half hours trapped in a darkened room might be a tough call should be made to watch *Das Boot* – and count themselves lucky. Lucky on two counts as it happens: first, that they never had to set to sea in a submarine in war time; and second, that they've just seen the most awesome war movie ever made.

And yet *Das Boot* also carries a poignant anti-war message as you live and breathe with the crew of U-96 on one incredible voyage in 1941. When released in 1982, it became the most successful foreign movie ever in the US and was nominated for six Oscars. This colour-rich reprinted version, complete with restored footage and re-designed digital sound is, simply, even better.

It is impossible to watch without empathising with the men on board, learning which of them sleeps or works behind each bulkhead. Most of them long for the taste of sea air and spray only the privileged few (of officers and audience) get after climbing the conning tower to scan the horizon. Such is the sense of documentary realism that it becomes almost impossible to believe any of the cast ever left the set.

Petersen (who went on to direct In *The Line Of Fire* and *Air Force One*) uses a handheld camera to astonishing effect, but as stunning as the visuals are, most critical in this is the sound. Listen (because your life depends on it) for overhead enemies dropping depth charges, hold your breath (because it may be your last) as each silent running takes you to excruciating depths. And for God's sake, duck when the pressure of a metre too far causes the already straining hull to give up its rivets in nerve-shredding explosions of surround sound. We've all seen war and submarine films before but we've never seen anything like *Das Boot*. ★★★★★ **KN**

Tagline
When the hunters become the hunted.

Movie Trivia: Das Boot

Many feel that with *Das Boot* Petersen launched his sea trilogy with *The Perfect Storm* (2000) and *Poseidon* in 2006. The submarine models were also used in *Raiders Of The Lost Ark*. The entire cast were kept indoors for the duration of the shoot so they would all have a pale complexion. The film was widely criticised in Germany for depicting the crew in a good light. Ironically when it was shown in America, it got a standing ovation.

◎ DAVE (1993)

Starring: *Kevin Kline (Dave Kovic/Bill Mitchell), Sigourney Weaver (Ellen Mitchell), Frank Langella (Bob Alexander), Ving Rhames (Duane Stevenson), Ben Kingsley (Vice-President Nance), Laura Linney (Randi), Bonnie Hunt (White House Tour Guide), Oliver Stone (Himself), Arnold Schwarzenegger (Himself)*
Director: *Ivan Reitman*
Screenwriter: *Gary Ross*
12/110 mins./Comedy/Romance/USA

With the President of America recovering from a stroke, the White House track down his spitting image, and force him to make public appearances before the public notice. Only Dave has a mind of his own and soon the White House begin to realise their mistake.

Amiable is the defining word for this comedy in which Kevin Kline adds to the comic tradition of VIPs swapped with doppelgangers, doing double duty as a despicable President of the United States and the lookalike Everyman, Dave Kovic, who is drafted to stand in for the Pres when the real one is felled by an ill-timed stroke. Ill-timed, that is, for conniving politicos and White House chief of staff Frank Langella who has duped Dave into this masquerade to a heinous end, but rather fortuitous for the country. For Dave is an impersonator with a conscience who decides to 'share a couple of ideas with the country', addressing himself to the nation's moral and economic ills.

This sweetly funny farce perpetuates the common but erroneous belief that the President of the United States actually runs things. Filmed in the run-up to the-then presidential election (with, by the way, very good reconstructions of the White House and its South Lawn) and informed by the public's loathing of politicians, it derives its best moments from bringing Dave's normal guy's point-of-view to bear upon corruption and bureaucracy. Dave's approach to tackling the budget deficit, for instance, is an absolute hoot, but also appeals to Joe Normal's gut feeling that a little decency and common sense could perform miracles in Washington.

Kline works wonders here with a captivating comic performance that sustains even when the sharper humour of the first half gives way to increasingly cutesy, dewy-eyed developments. The ensemble around him is excellent, too, from corgi-toting First Lady Weaver and Langella to Ben Kingsley as the Vice-President. Cameos from dozens of real politicians, newsreaders, reporters, law-makers and celebrities as themselves add to the fun, including an appearance from Oliver Stone to expound a conspiracy theory that gives the film its hippest gag. Flimsy, yes, but warmly recommended for light-hearted likeability. ★★★ **AE**

DAVID COPPERFIELD (1935)

Starring: *W.C. Fields (Micawber), Lionel Barrymore (Dan Peggotty), Maureen O'Sullivan (Dora), Frank Lawton (David Copperfield), Madge Evans (Agnes)*
Director: *George Cukor*
Screenwriters: *Howard Estabrook, Hugh Walpole based on the novel by Charles Dickens*
U/133 mins./Drama/USA

David Copperfield survives the cruelty of his stepfather Murdstone and the scheming of Uriah Heep to befriend Mr Micawber and romance both Dora and Agnes Wickstone.

Mention MGM's adaptation of Charles Dickens' masterpiece and most people will immediately recall W.C. Fields' scene-stealing performance as Mr Micawber. But, the real heroes of this enterprise are Howard Estabrook and Hugh Walpole, who captured the spirit of the source novel with a fidelity and finesse that Hollywood has all-too-rarely emulated.

That said, the film would never have been made at all without the persistence of producer David O. Selznick, who cherished the book from childhood readings by his emigrant film distributor father, Lewis, who had used the book to learn English on first arriving in the States. However, Selznick's father-in-law, Louis B. Mayer, mistrusted classics, as they invariably disappointed aficionados and bored lowbrows. However, a year's worth of memos browbeat Mayer into assigning a $1 million budget and Selznick and director George Cukor embarked on the crucial task of casting.

Some choices were offbeat, others inspired. Lionel Barrymore reined in his testiness as Dan Peggoty, Roland Young surpassed himself as the obsequious Uriah Heep and Basil Rathbone excelled as the cynically malevolent Murdstone, while the likes of Edna May Oliver (Aunt Betsey), Elsa Lanchester (Clickett), Lennox Pawle (Mr Dick) and Una O'Connor (Mrs Gummidge) turned in typically assured character displays.

But Fields and Freddie Bartholomew came aboard in more fortuitous circumstances. The latter was spotted on a location-scouting tour of England and Freddie's parents and aunt had to settle a custody battle before he was confirmed over Mayer's preference, Jackie Cooper. Fields had initially lost out to Charles Laughton in pre-production. But masses of research failed to ease the notoriously temperamental Laughton into the role and he quit after a week of fluffed lines and growing desperation. His successor completed his scenes in a fortnight, blending Dickens with his own unique screen persona to deliver an unforgetable performance, in which he even managed to ad lib in character.

Selznick's gamble paid off with box-office takings of $3.8 million, but the curmudgeonly Mayer still tried to trim the running time until dissuaded by protesting punters. ★★★★★ **DP**

DAWN OF THE DEAD (1978)

Starring: *David Emge (Stephen), Ken Foree (Peter), Scott T. Reiniger (Roger), Gaylen Ross (Francine), David Crawford (Dr. Foster), David Early (M. Berman), George A. Romero (Television Director)*
Director: *George A. Romero*
Screenwriter: *George A. Romero*
18/125 mins./Horror/USA

The dead are walking the earth, and four survivors of the zombie plague take refuge in a deserted shopping mall. Once inside however, they are trapped by hordes of the dead and a gang of militant bikers.

With Zack Snyder's stylish *Dawn Of The Dead* remake, the excellent 'rom-zom-com' *Shaun Of The Dead*, and a new *Resident Evil* all appearing recently, the zombie movie is clearly back from the grave. So there's no better time to revisit the original *Dawn Of The Dead*, George A. Romero's belated follow-up to his seminal 1968 *Night Of The Living Dead*, in which survivors of the zombie plague (among them Gaylen Ross, David Emge and Ken Foree) hole up in a shopping mall to fight off the undead horde that's closing in on them. When the going gets tough, Romero suggests, the undead go shopping.

Although a 139-minute full-screen travesty claiming to be the 'Director's Cut' is already available on DVD in the UK (tacitly endorsed by splatter FX-man Tom Savini's agreement to provide a commentary – for shame), the Special Edition features Romero's uncut 125-minute version, a perfect mix of shock and satire. It's not only the most gratuitously gory film ever to come out of Pittsburgh (courtesy of Savini's splatty effects), it's also as brilliantly subversive an attack on mindless consumerism as you're ever likely to see. Just go down to any shopping centre and observe the similarities between the shambling shoppers and Romero's pasty creations . . .

Surmounting with consummate ease that, 'Difficult second walking dead movie' problem, George A. Romero here equals, maybe surpasses, *Night Of The Living Dead* with a bleak, pessimistic allegory of modern consumer society. Grim, gruelling but beautifully shot, this is intelligent, sophisticated horror. ★★★★★ **DHu**

THE DAY AFTER TOMORROW (2004)

Starring: *Dennis Quaid (Jack Hall), Jake Gyllenhaal (Sam Hall), Emmy Rossum (Laura Chapman), Dash Mihok (Jason Evans), Jay O'Sanders (Frank Harris), Sela Ward (Dr. Lucy Hall)*
Director: *Roland Emmerich*
Screenwriters: *Roland Emmerich, Jeffrey Nachmanoff, based on a story by Roland Emmerich, suggested in part by* The Coming Global Superstorm
12/124 mins./Disaster/Adventure/USA

Awards: *BAFTA – Best Visual Effects*

Palaeoclimatologist Jack Hall fears that global warming could eventually precipitate another ice age but the US government won't listen. Fools. Hall is not only right, the ice age happens so fast that his estranged son gets trapped in NY's public library, and only his dad can save him . . .

Roland Emmerich, as even his critics would concede, has a flair for destruction. *Independence Day*, and to a lesser extent his whole canon, from *Stargate* through to *The Patriot*, is an expert exposition of the slow build/big bang theory of devastation. Emmerich can be relied upon to prolong the inevitable cataclysm, steadily cranking up the tension as dead-meat mortals struggle to understand forces that the audience already knows will consume them – the 'money shot', after all, is always in the trailer.

The problem with *ID*, and to a greater extent *Godzilla*, is that when the storm finally passes and the fight-back begins, Emmerich appears to lose interest, as if the German only really came to America to tear down the White House. The second half of those movies, which should theoretically contain all the surprise, issue none. With *The Day After Tomorrow*, *DAT* if you will, Emmerich does not exactly correct this imbalance (the movie clearly climaxes with the New York tidal wave familiar from the trailers), but he does find a genre which provides an even better showcase for destruction and sustains his interest until the bittersweet end: the disaster movie.

DAT cleaves much closer in structure and spirit to *The Poseidon Adventure* (Emmerich's personal favourite disaster movie) than to *ID*. It is, in effect, The Poseidon Planet, and once disaster strikes with an incalculable cost to off-screen human life, the raggedy bunch of comically mixed survivors must simply hold out long enough for the rescue helicopters to arrive.

DAT may willingly, and often knowingly, reheat the hoariest chestnuts of the disaster genre, but mercifully survival-by-cliché never threatens to occasion the kind of flag-waving, grandstanding jingoism that so spoiled *ID*. Indeed, divorced from American producing partner Dean Devlin, Emmerich finally reveals his true colours here jabbing the red, white and blue until it bleeds bright green.

Disaster movies have always been an implicitly political genre. They flourish, as they did during the early 1970s, during times of economic uncertainty, and serve to expose hubristic mankind's misplaced faith in technology – and, by extension, capitalism itself. In that sense, *DAT*, a project that the writer-producer-director developed himself away from studio interference, is as much a personal picture as a cookie cutter blockbuster, and the green European could not have chosen a better time to land a blow against American arrogance.

Of course, just because the director takes his politics seriously – the Kyoto Accord is name-checked in the first five minutes – doesn't mean that we have to, and the level of political debate on display in Emmerich's phoney UN conference is hardly more convincing than the shonky scientific explanations cribbed from that famous authority, alien abductee Whitley Strieber. Luckily, Emmerich has always cast actors rather than stars, and here he is well served by his B-list leading men. Character moments still represent thin ice for the director, but with Quaid spreading grit and gravitas and Gyllenhaal gamely skating the comic margins of the material, the movie just about keeps its footing as it slides inexorably towards the holy devastation we all came to see.

Three truly unmissable sequences – the tornados tearing through LA, the drowning of New York and the final superfreeze – set the benchmark for the summer of special effects and create a template for the onslaught of CG-driven disaster movies that will doubtless follow. The CGI may not always be entirely photo-realistic, but these sequences have sweep and power and, in places, an almost eerie beauty. And it is here that the director finds himself on surer ground, finding space amid the mayhem for the deft touches and cruel wit so often lacking from the dialogue scenes. Everybody is good at one thing, they say; for Emmerich, it's destruction.

★★★★ AE

A DAY AT THE RACES (1937)

Starring: *Groucho Marx (Dr. Hugo Z. Hackenbush), Chico Marx (Tony), Harpo Marx (Stuffy), Alan Jones (Gill), Maureen O'Sullivan (Judy), Margaret Dumont (Mrs. Upjohn)*
Director: *Sam Wood*
Screenwriters: *Robert Pirosh, George Seaton, George Oppenheimer based on a story by Pirosh and Seaton*
U/109 mins./Comedy/USA

Veterinarian Hugo Z. Hackenbush poses as a doctor at a society hospital, which is under threat from the owner of the neighbouring racetrack, where jockey Stuffy and tipster Tony make their equally shady living.

As they were coming off the back of their best two pictures, *Duck Soup* and *A Night At The Opera*, the Marx Brothers can be forgiven here for slipping slightly from such high standards. Yet, this typically anarchic farce contains their finest single routine, while two more rank amongst their funniest.

Countless writers contributed to the diverse plotlines that were discarded and plundered during pre-production. Groucho later claimed 18 different screenplays were involved, as stories about an anti-noise device, travelling players reducing a mansion to chaos and strangers renovating a rundown guest house came to nothing. Eventually, a concoction about a sanitorium and a racetrack was cobbled together and the trio took the rough draft on tour, where it took 141 stage performances to hone the gags and perfect the pacing.

However, shooting was halted after just 12 days, as Irving G. Thalberg, the exec who had lured the brothers to MGM from Paramount, died at the age of just 37. The picture was closed down for three months while Thalberg's envious employer, Louis B. Mayer, restructured the studio around himself and gave the Marxes notice that he now called their tune.

But the threesome rose above adversity and animosity to produce their longest-ever picture, with Alan Jones's solo slot and Dave Gould's Oscar-nominated aqua-pastiche of Busby Berkeley padding out the running time. Harpo also fronted an uncomfortable sketch with some shanty blacks, which was supposed to reinforce his Everyman appeal, but wound up a patronising burlesque.

However, he chipped in with typical enthusiasm to the sequences in which he and Chico disrupt first Groucho's examination of Mrs Rittenhouse (Margaret Dumont) – in which he brilliantly lampoons the pomposity of Sig Rumann's Dr Leonard Z. Steinberg – and then his attempted seduction of Esther Muir's buxom blonde. But nothing could top the 'Tutsi Frutsi Ice Cream' routine, in which Chico dupes Groucho into buying the paraphernalia required to cash-in on a racing tip and, in the process, exposes the flummery and fast-bucking greed that his social superiors simply fail to notice.

★★★★ DP

DAY FOR NIGHT (LA NUIT AMERICAINE) (1973)

Starring: *François Truffaut (Ferrand), Jacqueline Bisset (Julie Baker), Jean-Pierre (Alphonse), Valentina Cortese (Séverine), Jean-Pierre Aumont (Alexandre)*
Director: *François Truffaut*
Screenwriter: *François Truffaut, Suzanne Schiffman, Jean-Louis Richard*
15/120 mins./Drama/France

Neurotic star Julie Baker, ageing homosexual Alexandre, alcoholic diva Séverine and reckless juvenile Alphonse gather on the Riviera to shoot *Meet Pamela* with hard-of-hearing French director, Ferrand.

Within two weeks of finishing the ill-starred *Une Belle Fille Comme Moi*, François Truffaut began shooting this highly personal paean to film and the communality of film-making. The idea first came to him as he passed the Parisian set for Bryan Forbes' *The Madwoman of Chaillot* at Victorine Studios in Nice and his intention was to show how movies often have to overcome insurmountable problems in order to reach the screen.

Yet, he was also keen to pay tribute to the unseen and unsung crew members without whom a project would founder. Moreover, as ever, Truffaut couldn't resist hommages to his heroes and references to Jean Cocteau, Jean Renoir, Orson Welles and Françoise Dorléac are complemented by the picture's dedication to silent stars Lillian and Dorothy Gish.

The plot for *Meet Pamela* came from a British news story. But the on-set incidents were based on Truffaut's own experiences (the recalcitrant cat, for example, came from *La Peau Douce*) and those of his friends. Thus, the documentary authenticity of the production sequences is reinforced by anecdotal truth. But, the very fact that the film is called *Day for Night* confirms that it is also something of an illusion, as this is the name given to the technique (whose French equivalent is *La Nuit Américaine*) of covering the lens with a filter to shoot nocturnal sequences in broad daylight.

The excellent ensemble deserves credit for entering so fully into the spirit of this debunking of actorly egotism and capriciousness. But it's obvious from Truffaut's own performance as Ferrand that he adores his cast and is prepared to indulge their follies and failings to achieve his cherished family atmosphere. Yet, by sporting a hearing aid, Truffaut also highlights the director's isolation and the fact that while filming may be a collaborative process, the completed picture represents the vision of a single artist. ★★★★★ **DP**

Ⓓ DAY OF THE BEAST (EL DIA DE LA BESTIA) (1995)

Starring: *Alex Angulo (Padre Angel Beriatrua), Armando De Razza (Professor Cavan), Santiago Segura (Jose Maria), Nathalie Sesena (Mina), Maria Grazia Cucinotta (Susan)*
Director: *Alex de la Iglesia*
Screenwriters: *Jorge Guerricaechevarria, Alex de la Iglesia*
18/103 mins./Comedy/Horror/Thriller/Spain/Italy

A Basque priest becomes convinced, after intense study of the Bible, that the Anti-Christ is going to be born in Madrid on Christmas Day. Desperate to find the child, he tries to summon the Devil by committing a steadily escalating series of sins . . .

Alex De La Iglesia's first film *Accion Mutante* was one of those near miss efforts that would really like to be a cult movie but tries just a tad too hard. This follow-up, though, is a vast improvement – a comedy which manages to parody *The Omen*, indulge in well-timed farcical running-around and take pot-shots at everything from Satanic Heavy Metal through TV paranormal hucksterism to Spanish modern architecture.

After close textual study of the Bible and a brush with a falling crucifix, a gentle priest Angel realises that the Anti-Christ is due to be born in Madrid this Christmas Day. In order to be best placed to destroy the Beast, Angel resolves to get in with the Devil by becoming a major league sinner, but his trail of escalating crimes – stealing the wallet of a dying man while giving him his last rites – fails to provoke an infernal manifestation. However, Angel soon hooks up with hulking biker Jose Maria, and Professor Cavan, a TV psychic, both of whom are eventually persuaded to join the crusade.

The situations get nicely crazier, but perhaps the film overdoes the pell-mell pacing of the gags – like when Angulo botches his attempt to shed the virgin blood of his landlady's hysterical daughter or when our three heroes (The Three Stupid Men in this inversion of the Nativity) dangle from a huge neon sign tripping on LSD having been driven out of the window by a demonic presence. ★★★★ **KN**

Ⓓ THE DAY OF THE JACKAL (1973)

Starring: *Edward Fox (The Jackal), Terence Alexander (Lloyd), Michel Auclair (Colonel Rolland), Alan Badel (The Minister), Tony Britton (Inspector Thomas), Dennis Carey (Casson)*
Director: *Fred Zinnemann*
Screenwriter: *Kenneth Ross based on the novel by Frederick Forsyth*
15/142 mins./Thriller/France

Awards: *BAFTA – Best Film Editing*

A telling, partly based on truth, of the hiring of a nameless assassin, known only as The Jackal, to murder French president De Gaulle. Through the intricacies of his preparations we follow him to Paris with the French police slowly picking up his trail.

Fredrick Forsyth had already sought out the framework of a real assassination attempt on De Gaulle by dissidents infuriated at his dissolution of the French Foreign Legion, and transformed it into an excellent, brilliantly researched if pulpish thriller, thus providing Fred Zinnemann (best known for *High Noon*) with the perfect template for this exhaustive procedural. In many ways, this outstanding piece of filmmaking marks the apotheosis of a certain style of thriller that has since fallen out of fashion – the mind game. Built with the minutiae of a Swiss watch, without any direct showiness but an arch precision, it is about the coldness of purpose, the amoral planning of Edward Fox's Jackal and the diligence of the man out to stop him, played with wry intelligence by British actor Tony Britton.

What may sound obvious, a clearly linear plot, is made infinitely complex by the portrayal of this empty vessel of a killer by Fox. He is boyish, very charming, a ruthless, soulless man who takes in everyone, including the watcher. That is Zinnemann's cleverest ploy, he allows us to root for The Jackal, to pine for him to succeed. Morality is thrown awry. Yet, he is a ghost, we know nothing about him except the role he has assumed. An actor playing an actor; as a theme the film exposes the strange shell of moviemaking itself, the lure of its obvious deception.

On the other side of this cloudy moral divide, lies the investigation. Hampered by the lack of identity for the quarry, it is fascinating picture of sheer resolves, painstaking research, they inch toward this elusive assassin. The question, which drives the plot at a heady pace, is will they reach him time? A strange, but real, kind of tension given we know, factually, that De Gaulle died peacefully in his bed. How The Jackal will come to fail is blindingly unforeseen, for all the detail, his near-perfect planning, fate will assert its own reckoning.

There is true beauty in the realism at the heart of what could come across a fanciful movie plot, with its documentarian coolness of execution, the crisp rhythms of Zinnemann's direction, we feel we are staring through a window into the shadowy recesses of history. ★★★★ **IN**

Ⓓ THE DAY OF THE TRIFFIDS (1962)

Starring: *Howard Keel (Bill Masen), Nicole Maurey (Christine Durrant), Janette Scott (Karen Goodwin), Kieron Moore (Tom Goodwin), Mervyn Johns (Prof. Coker)*
Directors: *Steve Sekely, Freddie Francis (uncredited)*
Screenwriter: *Bernard Gordon based on the novel by John Wyndham*
15/93 mins./Sci-fi/UK

A meteor shower blinds almost all humanity, just as a space-borne strain of ambulatory killer plants ('Triffids') begins to proliferate. Bill Masen wakes up in hospital after an eye operation to discover that he is one of the few sighted people left.

The 1962 film version of *The Day of the Triffids* remains a TV staple, more probably because of the lasting reputation of John Wyndham's classic original novel than its own qualities. The premise is strong, but the realisation is frankly messy. It opens well, sticking close to the book, as Howard Keel makes his way through a bewildering world of blind panic and creeping, stinging greenery. There are unsettling, effective bits with a plane literally flying blind and the beginnings of panic among the fumbling survivors, and one good triffid encounter in a fog before the monsters start looking like foul-tempered Christmas trees. After the first act, the film is strangely compelled to stray all over the map, with trips to France and Spain that have no discernible purpose and a new bunch of characters (veteran Mervyn Johns, child actress Janina Faye, cutie Carole Ann Ford) dragged on and written off. Ford has an especially good exit, blindly feeling her way along a wall towards an evil plant which lashes her with its phallic sting. Director Steve Sekely's original cut was judged to be so disastrous that an uncredited Freddie Francis was brought in to shoot a whole new sub-plot, featuring Keiron Moore and Janette Scott in a vine-besieged lighthouse, to thread through the old footage: this allows for one of those hokey happy endings later parodied in *Mars Attacks!* as plain old seawater kills the monsters. A lot less satisfying than the later BBC serial adaptation, it still has some solid end-of-the-world and killer-plant material. ★★ **KN**

THE DAY THE EARTH STOOD STILL (1951)

Starring: *Michael Rennie (Klaatu/Carpenter), Patrica Neal (Helen Benson), Hugh Marlowe (Tom Stevens), Sam Jaffe (Prof. Jacob Barnhardt), Billy Gray (Bobby Benson)*
Director: *Robert Wise*
Screenwriter: *Edmund H. North, based on a story by Harry Bates*
U/92 mins./Drama/Sci-fi/Thriller/USA
Awards: *Golden Globes – Best Film Promoting International Understanding*

An alien with his mighty robot land their spacecraft on cold war Earth just after the end of World War II. They bring an important message for the planet but communications turns out to be difficult.

Extraordinary for its great intelligence, sophistication and acuity. An admonishment for the Atomic Age, its insistent message – 'Pursue your present course and face obliteration' – carries even more urgency 50 years on than it did when internationalists and anti-nuclear lobbyists were regarded (and often persecuted) as un-American kooks and subversive stooges of the Red Menace.

The film's enduring popularity is a tribute to the strength of its idea, its thoughtful, articulate screenplay by Edmund H. North (a former army officer who years later shared Academy Award honours with Francis Ford Coppola for their *Patton* screenplay) and the quality of the acting (all enhanced by composer Bernard Herrmann's understated but much-imitated mood score and Leo Tover's eerily lit black-and-white cinematography), rather than its minimal action and modest if effective visual tricks. Director Robert Wise's inexpensive but ingenious realisation of the world-wide power cut sequence that gives the film its title is the icing on a perfectly-baked cake.

Although its basis comes from the imaginative story *Farewell To The Master* by Harry Bates, published in *Astounding Science Fiction* in 1940, *The Day The Earth Stood Still* is quite a differently developed, cautionary fable assuming the guise of pulp science fiction. Immediately, the serious, unspectacular tone engineered by Wise renders the fantastic tale grippingly credible. After an unidentified craft circling the Earth at impossible speed is tracked by radar, an astonished, fearful populace and an armed-to-the-teeth military contingent greet its landing in Washington D.C. From the prototypical silvery domed saucer a humanoid figure calmly emerges. 'We have come to visit you in peace and with good will,' he says and is promptly shot by a nervous soldier with an itchy trigger finger.

It would almost be funny if it weren't so easy to believe that this is exactly what would happen if such a scenario ever happened for real. And what the over-eager sniper took to be a weapon, held out by the visitor, was actually a pressie, a gizmo for studying life on other planets, smashed beyond repair. Shame! The recovering alien, Klaatu, whose embarkation point remains a mystery – 'Let's just say we're neighbours' – shows enviable forbearance by still wanting to meet with representatives from all the nations of the earth to deliver a message.

He receives a string of politically-motivated excuses for the impracticality of this and decides instead to mingle with the ordinary folk in an attempt to understand such 'strange, unreasoning' stupidity. Posing as one Mr. Carpenter he befriends widowed secretary Helen Benson and her son Bobby while his robot companion Gort (big, quiet type with a visor face, emits a disintegration ray when provoked) stands sentry at the saucer. It's interesting, Bobby tells Klaatu, who is in search of an ally with some influence, that the greatest man in America is scientific genius Professor Earnhardt (Sam Jaffe, playing an amiable Einstein stand-in). A contemporary 10-year-old would almost certainly have to direct him to a basketball player or TV talk show host.

Klaatu's concept for a drastic demonstration of force to get a hearing – 'Something dramatic but not destructive' – is brilliant: he neutralises all electrical impulses, everywhere, with the considerate exceptions of hospitals and planes in flight. For half an hour the world (cue stock shots of New York, London, Paris and Moscow at a standstill) is brought to a halt. Again, plausibly, Klaatu's disappearance and display of technological superiority are attended by neatly delineated tensions: spiralling hysteria, Monster From Mars headlines, an accelerating hunt, betrayal from Helen's venal, self-serving fiancé (Hugh Marlowe, typifying the segment of mankind begging to be exterminated) and violence. Only the dying Klaatu's message, which Helen must deliver to Gort – 'Klaatu barada nikto!' – can prevent the robot from turning the planet into a burnt-out cinder.

Invested with this responsibility, Neal's Helen is practically unique in 50s drama, sci-fi or otherwise. She's a working mother raising a bright, open child. She doesn't fall and twist her ankle and she doesn't scream once even though she shows a healthy respect for the robot. She stands up to her weasely man. She doesn't have a trust issue, and she's not there for smooches, insidious mind control or getting her clothes alluringly torn. Very impressive.

Wise is most often acknowledged as the Academy Award-winning director of *West Side Story* and *The Sound Of Music*, but this is his signature masterpiece, suffused with the understanding he showed as editor of *Citizen Kane* and the command of moody atmosphere demonstrated in his directorial debut *Curse Of The Cat People* and honed in his classic horror-thriller *The Body Snatcher*. ★★★★★ **AE**

DAYS OF HEAVEN (1978)

Starring: *Richard Gere (Bill), Brooke Adams (Abby), Sam Shepard (The Farmer), Linda Manz (Linda), Robert Wilke (The Farm Foreman), Jackie Schultis (Linda's Friend)*
Director: *Terrence Malick*
Screenwriter: *Terrence Malick*
PG/95 mins./Drama/USA
Awards: *Academy Awards – Best Cinematography; BAFTA – Anthony Asquith Award for Film Music (Ennio Morricone)*

1916. With the Depression yet a chill on the wind, a drifter Bill, his lover, Abby, and sister, Linda, arrive to work the fields of the Texan Panhandle. There, disguising their relationship as a brother-sister bond, the couple hoodwink a rich but ailing farmer who marries Abby before realising what has happened.

The films of Terrence Malick, only four of them to date over a thirty-year career, are visual poems, testaments to his enflamed passion for natural beauty, but emotionally elusive and reluctant to directly engage the heart. *Days Of Heaven*, his second film, and his shortest, is a work of furtive gesture, a love-triangle set amongst the miraculous plains of wheat in that stretch beyond vision across the Mid-West. Tossing out his script, Malick required his cast, led by Richard Gere but dominated by young Linda Manz, the film's soulful observer (she gives a hauntingly literary narration), to invent their own lines, to feel out the story. It is a story told in small, obtuse movements where even dialogue is reduced to tiny fragments of a holistic whole.

Malick's is a captivating modus, one so beautiful it almost transcends the simple purposes of film. Over a year of shooting, he coalesced his storyline into his themes, ever-present preoccupations about man's frailty in the face of nature's power and God's indifference to our petty concerns. The romantic travails of the three leads (a trio filled out by a doleful Sam Shepard and subdued romance of Brooke Adams) and the moral cost that will be meted out, is constantly contrasted with the sun-burnished ocean of corn swept by languid breezes; the habitual drift of animals and birds, and the spare existence of these hermit workers flitting across a continent, an itinerant augur of the Depression to come. Rarely has a film bared itself to simple majesty (unless you count Malick's other work), it feels epic yet runs barely over and hour and a half.

Nothing is ever truly said in Malick's oblique approach, it is felt, sensed along its dreamlike path. True, if you fail to fall under his spell, it will likely translate as prettified pretension, gaseous, even wanky. But for converts, drugged out on his imagery, by the Biblical surge of its finale, a plague of locusts arriving like damnation, swallowing up the crop as these the heavenly days are consumed by hellfire, this is the towering, unconventional power of a true artist. ★★★★★ **IN**

◑ DAYS OF THUNDER (1990)

Starring: *Tom Cruise (Cole Trickle), Robert Duvall (Harry Hogge), Nicole Kidman (Dr. Clare Lewicki), Randy Quaid (Tim Daland), Cary Elwes (Russ Wheeler), John C. Reilly (Buck Bretherton), Don Simpson (Aldo Bennedetti)*
Director: *Tony Scott*
Screenwriter: *Robert Towne*
12/107 mins./Sports/Drama/USA

Hot-headed stock car driver Cole Trickle strives to succeed on the Nascar circuit but his attitude could well ruin his chances. Teamed with seasoned old trainer Harry Hogge he could just have a chance, but falling for his doctor, Clare Lewicki, isn't going to help.

A study in the purification of American moviemaking into something preordained for success. This shiny great Hollywood machine is built of matchless commercial rivets: Tom Cruise, risen into the zenith of his stardom; the sharp instincts of producers Don Simpson (who takes a cameo) and Jerry Bruckheimer; a concept fusing the brash machsimo of *Top Gun* and the pupil-mentor tutelage of *The Color Of Money*; and the preternatural good looks of Tony Scott's filmmaking applied to the grunt and muscle of Nascar racing. It is a movie designed within an inch its life, failure was not an option. That it does fail, so awfully, is also unwittingly written into its very DNA. There was no room to breath inside the brusque deliberateness of its execution. It is a film so thought out, so measured in its shallowness, that it is totally incapable of surprising anyone.

Tom Cruise, who had been pushing away from the template that was making him massive – this petulant youth with father issues, a hot head coasting on charm – through the rank desperation of *Born On The Fourth Of July* and the testing ground of *Rain Man*, but this was a stumble back into the unbending straits of formula. Chalk them up: the brash youth (his good self) who must learn to tame himself to succeed; the wise mentor (Robert Duvall) who must impart the legend; the strong female love interest (Nicole Kidman) who nudges the emotion to the surface; the rival as friend (Michael Rooker); the indigestible winner-ethos, where only victory can complete the journey.

There is no doubting the technical skill in putting this construction together, but it bares no trace of romance or heart or basic humanity. Just listen to the syllabic nonsense of the names: Cole Trickle, Harry Hogge, Clare Lewinski; they have the preformed rhythms of a scriptwriter's smug invention. Every motion, from the clamour of the racetrack to the sparring of teacher and pupil, has been worked out for audience satisfaction and grants none. This is not a real film, it is an automaton, a pod-movie, and, thankfully, proved the death nail for such high-concept filmmaking. ★★ **IN**

◑ DAZED AND CONFUSED (1993)

Starring: *Jason London (Randall 'Pink' Floyd), Rory Cochrane (Ron Slater), Sasha Jenson (Don Dawson), Wiley Wiggins (Mitch Kramer), Michelle Burke (Jodi Kramer), Parker Posey (Darla)*
Director: *Richard Linklater*
Screenwriter: *Richard Linklater*
18/97 mins./Comedy/Drama/USA

It's the last day of the school year in 1976, and everyone's ready for a party. First, however, the incoming freshmen students must go through bizarre initiation rituals organised by the soon-to-be-seniors, while everyone does their best to get stoned or get laid.

Writer-director Richard Linklater's second feature after *Slacker* is a funkier, more focused and much funnier movie than his original twentysomething micro-drama. A commercial failure in the US, despite generally good notices, it hung around in limbo waiting for a UK release for more than a year. Characterised in some quarters as the *American Graffiti* for the slacker generation, this is in fact a very clever piece of retro 70s anti-nostalgia which scrupulously avoids sentimentality. It just wants to tell us how genuinely strange the 70s were.

Tracking 18 hours in the lives of a bunch of high school juniors and incoming freshmen as they quit school and prepare for a party that evening, it jumps around between different characters (the Stoner, the Jock, the Intellectual, the Cool Guy) and events – including some truly horrific high school initiation rituals – to give an impressionistic account of what it was really like to be a 70s American suburban teen. Its approach is mosaic and non-linear, exactly like *Slacker*, but whereas that first film was devoted to the excavation of a number of tiny obsessions, this attempts to archive a whole culture.

In this it is largely successful. Linklater has gone back to 1976 and marked it as the defining year for the beginnings of slacker culture. There is the same aimlessness, the same bog cult games, the same complex irony, only purged of fear and loathing. Back in the 70s, according to *Dazed And Confused*, it was still possible to be optimistic about the future. ★★★★ **SBe**

◑ DEAD CALM (1989)

Starring: *Sam Neill (John Ingram), Nicole Kidman (Rae Ingram), Billy Zane (Hughie Warriner), Rod Mullinar (Russell Bellows), Joshua Tilden (Danny), George Shevtsov (Doctor), Micheal Long (Specialist Doctor)*
Director: *Phillip Noyce*
Screenwriter: *Terry Hayes, based on the novel by Charles Williams*
15/96 mins./Horror/Thriller/Australia

John and Rae are enjoying a miniature cruise when they stumble upon an apparently marooned mariner, Hughie. John's worst fears are quickly realised as Hughie promptly steals the cruiser, with John's wife still on board.

Orson Welles originally bought the rights to *Dead Calm* (from a novel by thriller writer Charles Williams) in the mid-60s, only for it to become one of his many unfinished projects (although according to co-star Jeanne Moreau, it was completed and remains unseen under Welles' orders). It is intriguing to imagine the results: Welles had one of the boldest, most recognisable of stylistic touches, whereas Phillip Noyce's interpretation is defined only by the glossy competence of the advertising agency.

Australian navy officer John Ingram is on a yachting trip with his young wife Rae to recover from the death of their child. They pick up Hughie, a distraught survivor from a nearby vessel whose other crew members, he says, have died of food poisoning. Reluctant to believe this story, Ingram rows out to the schooner where he finds evidence to confirm his suspicions. Hurrying back to his wife and his yacht, he sees it departing, Hughie at the helm and an unsuspecting Rae at his mercy. Ingram then gives chase: the strong, competent man of the sea battling with the element he has mastered for 25 years, and slowly losing control.

Initially, the film works well as a tense, teasing suspense vehicle displaying, for instance, none of the cinema's customary sentimentality in its dealings with animals and children: in the opening minutes, the couple's baby is catapulted head-first through a windscreen and later a small dog is impaled on a harpoon. But one of *Dead Calm*'s major problems is that it brings to mind ideas and plot similarities from so many other films that you are constantly being reminded of its own rather humble status.

Even more of a problem, though, is the film's ever-more desperate search for shocks, capped by the type of absurd 'false ending' that was tagged on to every horror film released in the five years after *Carrie* and which was reprised by the likes of *Fatal Attraction*. ★★★ **IN**

⦿ DEAD MAN WALKING (1995)

Starring: *Susan Sarandon (Sister Helen Prejean), Sean Penn (Matthew Poncelet), Robert Prosky (Hilton Barber), Raymond J. Barry (Earl Delacroix), R. Lee Ermey (Clyde Percy)*
Director: *Tim Robbins*
Screenwriter: *Tim Robbins, based on the book by Sister Helen Prejean, C.S.J*
15/120 mins./Crime/Drama/USA

Awards: *Academy Awards – Best Actress*

Sister Helen Prejean is a nun in Louisiana who becomes the spiritual advisor of a man on Death Row. Unquestionably guilty of the crime for which he is accused, Matthew Poncelet nevertheless gradually opens up to her attempts to communicate — even as she also tries to comfort the families of his victims.

Based on the real experiences and insights of Sister Helen Prejean, a Catholic nun in Louisiana whose community service took her into the state penitentiary's death house, the film explores moral truth, the consequences of murder, and the human need for revenge. Sister Helen replies to a letter from lonely, frightened Matthew Poncelet, a condemned rapist and murderer awaiting execution. Despite her own misgivings and outside pressure to distance herself from him, she becomes his visitor, spiritual advisor and friend.

For nun and killer it is a remarkable journey. Poncelet is not charming or even likeable, nor is he a victim of injustice. His crime was heinous. He is repellent, bigoted trash. But Sister Helen is a woman centred on faith in God and humanity. Confronting his demons, she hopes to move him to take responsibility for his life, to face death with honesty.

Sarandon, as ever, is superlative. Penn is beyond superlatives.

Unflinchingly he presents a cold, hard, despicable individual, then rips him inside out until the monster is revealed to be a human being. Their dual achievement is the true intimacy they develop despite the prison barriers of wire and window, Robbins skilfully working with the space between them.

Beyond these two and Sister Helen's fight for Poncelet's soul, Robbins gives enormous weight to the victims of the crime. The ordeal of the young couple murdered is glimpsed and, finally, remembered. The pain, grief and rage for vengeance in those who mourn them are dutifully respected. It may be regarded as a failing that Robbins' apparent lack of certainty in the ethical conflict laid out prevents him from verbalising an unequivocal pro or con answer. Instead, he very effectively forces the viewer to ask, with no little distress, is it ever right to kill? ★★★★ **AE**

⦿ DEAD MAN'S CURVE (1998)

Starring: *Matthew Lillard (Tim), Michael Vartan (Chris), Randall Batinkoff (Rand), Keri Russell (Emma), Tamara Craig Thomas (Natalie), Anthony Griffith (Detective Shipper)*
Director: *Dan Rosen*
Screenwriter: *Dan Rosen*
15/91 mins./Comedy/Drama/Thriller/USA

Urban legend has it that, if your college roommate commits suicide, you will then get perfect grades for the rest of the year. Chris and Tim decide to put this theory to the test.

Best known as the screenwriter of *The Last Supper*, Rosen has fashioned a jet-black comedy that, for once, lives up to and surpasses the 'acclaimed at the Sundance Film Festival' epithet routinely dished out to every non-studio film to reach these shores.

Dead Man's Curve takes its cue from a prime slice of American college mythology – that is, if a student commits suicide, the bereaved roommates will immediately garner a straight-A term average to ease them through the grieving process. Two students, manipulative Tim and sensitive Chris, are struggling to reach the requisite grades to guarantee a spot at Harvard. So they select their third roommate, the boorish Rand, as their ticket to academic excellence: the elaborate plan sees them plant evidence to imply that Rand is suicidal, get him drunk, then throw him off a cliff. After the college counselling process, the pair achieve their perfect grades before cracks begin to appear in their unlikely alliance.

Rosen imbues the clever plotting – Rand's body is never found, Tim begins to move in on Chris' girlfriend Emma – with involved twists, augmented by large helpings of dark humour, a spot-on soundtrack featuring the best in miserable music (The Smiths, naturally, plus a sublime use of *Bela Lugosi's Dead* by Bauhaus) and an unnerving, slightly askew visual style that perfectly mirrors the subject matter.

The young cast – eye candy to a man – are uniformly excellent (particularly Lillard, who plays everything with a maniacal glint) and Rosen displays a keen, sardonic eye for the pressures and cliqueiness of US dorm life. While the whole thing may need a credibility check and the twist-in-the-tale endings go one step too far, the whole thing is so sharp, witty and breathlessly cool that such qualms are easily forgotten. Indeed, Rosen seems to be that rare commodity within American low-budget movie circles – a director who keeps the audience in mind, has a cracking story to tell and the requisite skill and intelligence to spin it. ★★★★ **IF**

⦿ DEAD MAN'S SHOES (2004)

Starring: *Paddy Considine (Richard), Gary Stretch (Sonny), Toby Kebbell (Anthony), Emily Aston (Patti), Neil Bell (Soz), Craig Considine (Craig), Matt Considine (Matt)*
Director: *Shane Meadows*
Screenwriters: *Shane Meadows, Paddy Considine, Paul Fraser*
18/90 mins./Thriller/UK

Awards: *Empire Awards – Best British Actor*

Army-trained Richard returns to his hometown with his mentally-challenged younger brother, Anthony, in tow. Anthony has been used and abused by a raggedy bunch of local drug dealers, and Richard plans to teach the bullies a deadly lesson ...

Shane Meadows' raw revenge flick should be called *Sympathy For The Bogeyman*, because the director dusts off the invincible-killer-picks-off-teens routine and tells it from the bogeyman's point of view. The result is a thoughtful, possibly controversial, horror that offers none of the easy comforts typical of the genre – these victims are far from innocent, but do they deserve to die?

The film is so pure of purpose that it feels like a zero-budget debut; after the sprawling *Once Upon A Time In The Midlands*, that may have been Meadows' intention. Its first steps are, in fact, faltering, with the supporting cast struggling to improvise necessary exposition – but whenever Considine is onscreen, the movie has a magnetic centre around which the others can happily orbit.

Potentially Britain's answer to De Niro, the actor made a searing debut in Meadow's *A Room For Romeo Brass*, a film that boldly changed gear halfway through. This is even more fearless – genre conventions are trashed, key characters summarily dispatched and liberal niceties squashed. Meadows may not offer genuine insight into the psychology of monsters, but here he has created a memorable movie bogeyman. ★★★★ **DJ**

DEAD OF NIGHT (1945)

Starring: *Mervyn Johns (Walter Craig), Roland Culver (Eliot Foley), Mary Merrall (Mrs Foley), Frederick Valk (Dr, Van Straaten), Renee Gadd (Mrs Craig), Anthony Baird (Hugh Grainger)*
Directors: *Alberto Cavalcanti ('The Ventriloquist's Dummy', 'The Christmas Story') Basil Dearden ('The Linking Story', 'The Hearse Driver'), Robert Hamer ('The Haunted Mirror') Charles Crichton ('The Golfing Story')*
Screenwriters: *John Baines, Angus Macphail, T.E.B. Clarke (based on the stories by H.G. Wells, E.F. Benson, John Baines and Angus Macphail)*
PG/104 mins./Horror/UK

Architect Walter Craig arrives for a weekend party at the home of a potential client, and astounds the company by claiming to have a recurring dream about the weekend which seems to be coming true. Each guest, in turn, recounts their own tale of the supernatural.

Still the greatest multi-story ghost/horror picture, this uncharacteristic Ealing film -directed by Robert Hamer, Charles Crichton, Basil Dearden and Alberto Cavalcanti – came out in 1945 and can still spook audiences. The least successful tale is Crichton's token Ealing comedy, about golfing ghosts with Basil Radford and Naunton Wayne, but the other four stories are near-perfect and there's an unsettling wraparound about the genteel weekend party that gets scarier with each story.

Dearden directed the linking material and the opener, an anecdote often included in 'true spook story' anthologies in which a hospital patient has a precognitive dream involving jovially sinister undertaker Miles Malleson ('room for one more inside, sir').

Cavalcanti directed a delicate, chilly little anecdote in which Sally Ann Howes runs into a ghost child during a game of hide and seek at a Christmas party, but also the showstopper finale with Michael Redgrave (in an outstanding performance) as a ventriloquist whose dummy develops an independent personality and threatens to ditch him for a more outgoing partner. Hamer contributes a nasty little anecdote about Googie Withers buying a haunted mirror which sometimes reflects a cluttered Victorian room rather than her smartly modern flat, and which influences her weak-willed husband (Ralph Michael) towards murderousness.

Each of the episodes has been endlessly imitated by later anthology movies and TV shows – the seeds of about a dozen *Twilight Zone* episodes alone can be found here.

It's terribly British, with crusts-cut-off politeness around the dinner table, but undercurrents seething in every barbed dialogue exchange and terrors growing in the shadows. ★★★★★ **KN**

DEAD POETS SOCIETY (1989)

Starring: *Robin Williams (John Keating), Robert Sean Leonard (Neil Perry), Ethan Hawke (Todd Anderson), Josh Charles (Knox Overstreet), Gale Hansen (Charlie Dalton)*
Director: *Peter Weir*
Screenwriter: *Tom Schulman*
PG/128 mins./Drama/USA
Awards: *Academy Awards – Best Original Screenplay, BAFTA – Best Film, Best Original Score*

English teacher John Keating returns to the 50s prep school where he was once a student. His unorthodox teaching methods shock his fellow staff members, but inspire his pupils to think beyond the dull, white collar careers ahead of them. But their experiments with freedom come at a price . . .

The success at the US box office of Peter Weir's evocative drama about youthful dreams and self-discovery is a tribute to the pulling power of Robin Williams at the height of his success since it is unusual to see a 'quality film' rubbing receipts with comic book heroes and horror fiends.

Those attracted by his participation were not disappointed, although Williams is in fact not the busiest character in the role of charismatic English teacher John Keating. As the kind of teacher everyone wishes they'd had, inspiring his students with passion and joy, he is the catalyst for the actions of the teenagers he has enthralled. Much of the story's telling devolves on a cast of then newcomers (Robert Sean Leonard, Ethan Hawke, Gale Hansen and Josh Charles particularly), acquitting themselves very well as the classmates in a strictly traditional New England private school in 1959 who are moved to dream and to dare by Keating's encouragement.

Williams makes of Keating an immensely sympathetic presence that suffuses the film even when he is off-screen. Renowned for his improvisational flights, his performance here is controlled – warm rather than whacky, stirring rather than wild. His facility at letting rip is used judiciously to marvellous effect in classroom scenes in which he soars: exhorting the boys to tear up their texts, circling a shy student to squeeze a poetic outburst from the startled boy, impersonating John Wayne playing Macbeth.

Spellbound by Keating and on fire to emulate him, a group of the boys form the Dead Poets Society in imitation of a secret club led by their hero in his own schooldays at the academy. The boys' clandestine nocturnal meetings in a cave are innocent enough adventures during which they spout poetry and tackle deep and meaningful matters like girls, booze and life.

Unfortunately the plot takes a bumpy diversion into the anticipated clash with authority, concentrating on the trouble between one of Keating's most promising boys and his ambitious, insensitive father. A tragedy – semaphored way before it finally occurs – leads to hysterical recriminations and reprisals that cruelly chill the film's previously celebratory tone, revived at the last with a corny but spirit-lifting end.

As one would expect from the director of such films as *Picnic At Hanging Rock*, *Gallipoli* and *Witness*, Peter Weir, accompanied by his regular director of photography, John Seale, distinguishes himself by creating a strong sense of the time, place and people while imbuing even simple acts with beauty and mystery. A long shot of the boys walking in the dark to their secret place, for example, is a magical image of their excitement, fear and high spirits. This film radiates intelligence, humanity and warmth through many such small moments. ★★★★ **AE**

DEAD PRESIDENTS (1995)

Starring: *Larenz Tate (Anthony Curtis), Keith David (Kirby), Chris Tucker (Skip), Freddy Rodriguez (Jose), Rose Jackson (Juanita Benson), N'Bushe Wright (Delilah Benson), Terrence Howard (Cowboy)*
Directors: *Albert Hughes, Allen Hughes*
Screenwriters: *Michael Henry Brown, based on a story by Allen Hughes, Albert Hughes, Michael Henry Brown, suggested by the story* Specialist No.4 Haywood T *by Wallace Terry*
18/119 mins./Action/Crime/Drama/USA

Returning from Vietnam, Anthony finds himself disillusioned by the life he left behind. Desperate to provide for his young family, he turns to crime in an attempt to find a better life.

Dead Presidents may sound like an attempt by Oliver Stone to tell simultaneously the story of Roosevelt, Truman, Eisenhower and Johnson, but, in fact, turns out to be another entry into the world-consuming genre that is the heist movie. Actually, this second outing from the directors of *Menace II Society* is half robbery flick and half war film although anyone expecting *The Return Of Kelly's Heroes* is probably in for a shock.

Kicking off in 1968 we zero in on naive high school kid Anthony Curtis who fulfils the film's early coming-of-age feel by being, despite a small flirtation with a local hood, pretty much obsessed with sex, sex, cool soul music and sex. Eventually Curtis succeeds in bedding – and impregnating – childhood sweetheart Juanita Benson but subsequently enlists for a tour of Vietnam where he sees most of his mates become either corpses or basket cases.

Returning to something less than a hero's welcome, the now fully trained-up killing machine makes a stab at a normal life with Juanita but finally comes to the decision that stealing a van-load of used currency would be a more profitable use of his time (the title refers to the faces of deceased US leaders found on American dollar bills).

While the final result may occasionally try to cover a hundred topics when perhaps 99 would have sufficed, there is no doubt that *Dead Presidents* is a very impressive, if often jaw-droppingly violent, piece of work. ★★★★ **KN**

DEAD RINGERS (1988)

Starring: *Jeremy Irons (Beverly Mantle\Elliot Mantle), Genevieve Bujold (Claire Niveau), Heidi Von Palleske (Cary), Barbara Gordon (Danuta), Shirley Douglas (Laura)*
Director: *David Cronenberg*
Screenwriters: *David Cronenberg, Norman Snider based on the book* Twins *by Bari Wood, Jack Geasland*
18/115 mins./Horror/Canada

Identical twin gynaecologists Beverly and Elliot Mantle work together. While the suave, outgoing Elliot is accepting awards and research fellowships, the retiring, more overtly neurotic Beverly is doing the actual graft and taking care of the patients. When the twins begin a relationship with a patient, actress Claire Niveau, they are exposed to emotional dangers that ultimately lead to disaster.

Based on a tabloid headline ('Twin Docs Found Dead in Posh Pad'), this icy drama could almost play as a sophisticated farce, and the sequence in which Genevieve Bujold confronts the Mantle twins in a restaurant, tumbling to the fact that the man she has been having an affair with is actually two people, marvellously skirts the ridiculous and the chilling.

It's not a comedy but an uncompromised and uncompromising film which contains moments of horror and physicality far more shattering than the goriest special effects gimmick. It deals with questions of identity, the mystique of surgery, and male inability to come to terms with the mysterious folds of women's minds and bodies. In the home stretch, it's a profoundly depressing, yet deeply moving, study in addiction and degradation. With an unhappy outcome a foregone conclusion, it's astonishing that the film is as suspenseful as it is as Beverly becomes a drug addict and Elliot follows him into hell, perhaps to rescue him, perhaps to join him.

The special effects are invisible, with Jeremy Irons doing far more to create the illusion of duality than any optical splicing and the direction is remarkably tactful and assured.

David Cronenberg gets away from the horror/science fiction genre in which he had established his style, presenting the inhuman condition without recourse (one slightly too blatant dream sequence apart) to flesh-stretching special effects, borrowings from earlier horror films and the trappings of conventional melodrama. ★★★★ **KN**

THE DEAD ZONE (1983)

Starring: *Christopher Walken (Johnny Smith), Brooke Adams (Sarah Bracknell), Tom Skerritt (Sheriff Bannerman), Herbert Lom (Dr. Sam Welzak), Anthony Zerbe (Roger Stuart) Colleen Dewhurst (Henrietta Dodd), Martin Sheen (Greg Stillson)*
Director: *David Cronenberg*
Screenwriter: *Jeffrey Boam based on the novel by Stephen King*
18/103 mins./Horror/USA

Johnny Smith awakens from a five-year coma to discover he has psychic abilities. After helping a small-town Sheriff catch a serial killer, Johnny is convinced that crusading politician Greg Stillson is a potential danger to the world.

One of a wave of Stephen King adaptations from the early 1980s, this was a step towards the mainstream for weirdo auteur David Cronenberg. It has some of that episodic 'compressed miniseries' feel which a lot of King pictures get stuck with (the book was later redone as a TV serial with Anthony Michael Hall) but still manages a lot of powerful material. Walken has one of his signature roles as stiff-legged outsider Johnny Smith, alienated by the loss of his entire life (his girlfriend Brooke Adams has married someone else) who foresees disasters wherever he goes.

There's a mini-psycho picture as Smith helps the cops in King's small town of Castle Rock root out the killer in their midst, which prompts the film's few straight shock sequences (a scissors suicide, a mad performance from Colleen Dewhurst as the monster's mother), but the dramatic meat of the piece comes when Johnny tangles with up-and-coming politico Stillson, a folksy homicidal maniac who now looks horribly like a young George W. Bush. Cronenberg gets a lot out of the wintry Canadian locations passed off as King's haunted Maine, and works hard with his actors – weaving between the s-f/horror stuff is a great deal of underplayed emotion, especially in the heartbreaking business between Walken and the underrated Adams.

Familiar supporting players like Skerritt, Herbert Lom and Anthony Zerbe – who are usually asked to turn up and read their lines – get a little more meat, and rise to the occasion. And *West Wing* fans who think Sheen ought to be President should check out his political villainy here. ★★★★ **KN**

DEATH BECOMES HER (1992)

Starring: *Meryl Streep (Madeleine Ashton), Bruce Willis (Dr Ernest Menville), Goldie Hawn (Helen Sharp), Isabella Rossellini (Lisle Von Rhoman), Ian Ogilvy (Chagall)*
Director: *Robert Zemeckis*
Screenwriters: *Martin Donovan, David Koepp*
PG/104 mins./Comedy/Fantasy/USA

Helen and Madeleine have hated each other for years, ever since Madeleine stole Helen's boyfriend Ernest and married him. Helen plots her revenge, but after Madeleine discovers a drink that provides eternal youth, their problems are only just beginning.

Improving with age, Robert Zemeckis' black fantasy sees Goldie Hawn and Meryl Streep play bitchy actresses battling it out for the secret of eternal youth. Years after Streep steals dumpy Hawn's man, Hawn returns in improbably youthful form to win him back. In trying to get to the root of her former friend's sudden makeover, Streep too discovers the secret to staying young and beautiful in Hollywood – and the strange price that you pay for it.

Charged with a baroque cartoony feel, ILM's groundbreaking CGI effects and Zemeckis' filmmaking flair are expected. The blackness of the tale and Bruce Willis' skill at playing a henpecked husband is not.

Both leading ladies display great willingness to send up themselves and Hollywood, and Willis' quiet nervous breakdown showcases his previously unguessed-at comic skills. But it's the pitch-black comedy and celebrity satire that make this so enjoyable. ★★★ WT

DEATH LINE (1972)

Starring: *Donald Pleasence (Inspector Calhoun), Norman Rossington (Detective Sergeant Rogers), David Ladd (Alex Campbell), Sharon Gurney (Patricia Wilson), Hugh Armstrong (The Man)*
Director: *Gary Sherman*
Screenwriter: *Ceri Jones*
18/87 mins./Horror/UK

A series of disappearances on the London Underground Railway are traced back to the inbred, cannibal descendants of navvies trapped by a cave-in during the building of the tunnels.

Also known, aptly, as *Raw Meat*, this is one of the best British horror films of the 1970s, competing with the wave of stronger American splatter with its clever, gruesome premise, dollops of grue, lots of cynicism and nice, down-at-heel London locations.

A human monster (Armstrong) who looks like a scabrous tramp haunts the Piccadilly Line, picking off and eating the odd commuter, trying to keep alive his diseased wife. Tea-drinking copper Inspector Calhoun (Donald Pleasence, in the performance of a lifetime) is called into the case with his sidekick sergeant (Norman Rossington) when the latest victim (James Cossins) turns out to be a high-ranking civil servant fresh from a neon-lit sleaze spree in Soho, and has to cut through bureaucratic red tape (represented by Christopher Lee in a bowler hat). Meanwhile, down in the tunnels, the last of the monsters lives out his pathetic, horrid leftover life, expressing himself through the only words he knows, 'mind the doors'. It includes a wonderful, apparently-improvised drunk scene from Pleasence and a breathtaking 360° pan around the cannibals' dripping, dank, corpse-strewn underground lair.

Less makeshift than a lot of its rivals from the 1970s, it has solid, witty dialogue, a memorably funky music score and the sort of urban legend premise that people will swear is based on truth rather than newly minted for the movie. American writer-director Gary Sherman also made the cloying New Seekers 'I'd Like to Buy the World a Coke' ads, and used his share of the fee from that to finance this gutsy, gritty debut; sadly, his subsequent works – *Poltergeist III*, *Wanted Dead or Alive* – have not fulfilled his promise. ★★★★ KN

DEATH ON THE NILE (1978)

Cast: *Peter Ustinov (Hercule Poirot), Jane Birkin (Louise Bourget), Lois Chiles (Linnet Ridgeway Doyle), Bette Davis (Marie Van Schuyler), Mia Farrow (Jacqueline De Bellefort), Jon Finch (James Ferguson), Simon MacCorkindale (Simon Doyle), Maggie Smith (Miss Bowers), David Niven (Colonel Johnny Race)*
Director: *John Guillermin*
Screenwriter: *Anthony Shaffer, based on the novel by Agatha Christie*
PG/140 mins./Thriller/UK

Awards: *Academy Awards – Best Costume Design; BAFTA – Best Costume Design*

On board a steamer S.S. Karnak heading down the Nile there is murder most foul when a rich heiress turns up minus her mortal coil. Luckily, although not for the culprit, the brilliant Belgian detective Hercule Poriot is also a passenger.

If you exercise those 'leettle grey cells' and ponder the vast filmic output based upon the books of Agatha Christie, those teasing whodunits cast from an unchanging mould, none embody the easy (taxing of brain is purely optional) treats of the formula as perfectly as this middle-order star packed vessel (literally) from the Ustinov era. Ustinov, a garrulous and watchable, if limited, actor, made Hercule Poirot an avuncular charmer who seemed to happen upon solutions as if they were punchlines to long winded anecdotes. He was fun, but lacked the edges, the cold brilliance of Christie's most famous creation. The previous twirler of his moustache, Albert Finney, in *Murder On The Orient Express*, gave him bite and bustle, a cantankerous determination.

The plot here follows Christie's eloquent mechanics to the tee. An exotic circumstance lubricated by money – here a boat trip down the Egyptian chapter of the Nile – populated by a set number of suspects of varying aspects (all with a credible motive) and the addition of our portly homemade detective. As became the fashion for these get-togethers, they took on the guise of Hollywood retirement homes, filling their casts with former greats up for the easy glide of Christie's stock characters. Here it's an especially good selection of has-beens at the murder-mystery party: Bette Davis, David Niven, Maggie Smith, a young Mia Farrow, and a rare sighting of Jane Birkin. In a curious side order of trivia, Angela Lansbury, who would become Ustinov's bland equivalent as Miss Marple, takes a small but memorable role as a dotty old flirt.

If you feel obliged you can follow the trail of clue and red herring alike, to figure out the murder of an heiress (who wants all that money?). Alternatively, you can soak up legendary cinematographer Jack Cardiff's lush views of the Egyptian shores and watch this gaggle of weathered old luvvies hamming up Anthony Shaffer's witty translation of Auntie Agatha's death fixation. There are few more relaxed pleasures in the movie game. ★★★ IN

DEATH RACE 2000 (1975)

Starring: *David Carradine (Frankenstein), Simone Griffeth (Annie), Sylvester Stallone (Machine Gun Joe Viterbo), Mary Woronov (Calamity Jane)*
Director: *Paul Bartel*
Screenwriters: *Robert Thorn, Charles B Griffith based on a story by Ib Melchior*
18/78 mins./Action/Sci-fi/USA

In the futuristic year of 2000, a fascist America supports a transcontinental road race in which drivers score extra points for murdering pedestrians. The rebel underground plant an assassin on the crew of racer Frankenstein, but it turns out the champion has his own agenda.

A distinctively crass, hugely enjoyable sick satire from director Paul Bartel, working for uber-producer Roger Corman – allegedly, Bartel kept thinking up more and wilder jokes, while Corman insisted more and more people got run over.

It has a comic strip premise which is neverthless wholly credible in a sick sort of way, with character-themed race car drivers – the leather-clad and purportedly scarfaced Frankenstein, snarling hood Machine Gun Joe Viterbo, cowgirl killer Calamity Jane and fun-loving Nazi valkyrie Matilda the Hun – who seem to have inspired generations of wrestlers and TV gladiators, and hilarious work from Don Steele and Joyce Jameson as the smarmy, hypocritical, fanatical sports commentators who alternately harass and hail the automotive killers ('of course it's violent, that's how we like it, violent, violent, violent!').

Shot obviously on the cheap, with carny-look custom cars (with hood-mounted bullhorns or monster teeth) and dollops of ketchupy splat, it includes many *Looney Tunes*-style gags as rebel forces attack the race, prompting a great running joke as the state-controlled news media refuse to admit the existence of American dissidents and blame all revolutionary acts on the French (who have apparently wrecked the United States' economy and once-great postal service).

Among the crassest laugh-lines in the cinema is the reveal that Frankenstein has had his hand replaced with a detachable bomb ('What do you call that?' 'A hand grenade'), and there are deservedly classic performances from Stallone ('loved by thousands, hated by millions') and Woronov as the craziest of the racers. ★★★★ **KN**

THE DECLINE OF WESTERN CIVILISATION (1981)

Starring: *Alice Bag Band (Themselves), Alice Bag (Herself), Black Flag (Themselves), Don Bolles (Himself), Circle Jerks (Themselves), Philo Cramer (Himself), Darby Crash (Himself), John Doe (Himself)*
Director: *Penelope Spheeris*
Screenwriter: *Penelope Spheeris*
R/100 mins./Documentary/USA

A non-fiction chronicle of the late 1970s Los Angeles punk scene, highlighting major bands (X, Black Flag, Fear) and no-hopers alike.

'This is a fucking movie representing fucking LA, so dance,' shouts a singer at his audience, 'you want people in Philadelphia to see a bunch of fucking deadbeats!' Before embarking on the highs (*Wayne's World*) and lows (*The Beverly Hillbillies*) of her career as a director of fiction films, Penelope Spheeris made this loud, funny, horrific and frighteningly innocent rock documentary. She films bands doing their stage acts and talks with them in their hovels, but it's a selection of chilling to-camera interviews with young fans that are scariest ('Michael X-Head' explains that he beats people up because 'I feel like I'm doing something I'm good at').

Among the performers, Exene Cervenka of X (later Mrs Viggo Mortensen) and Claude Bessy of Catholic Discipline are the most articulate, and their songs are notably more complicated and intelligent than, say, the efforts of The Circle Jerks or Alice Black Bag. But you get the true rebarbative, obnoxious punk spirit from the abusive, macho, (satirically?) homophobic rants of Lee Ving of Fear or the mumbling, blatantly self-destructive and incapable Darby Crash of the Germs (dead before the film came out). Nicole Olivieri, manager of the Germs, could be working with Spinal Tap when she explains 'it's like being the mother of four three-year-olds.'

The music ranges from the excellent to the frankly appalling – the song titles probably say it all, 'Depression', 'Revenge', 'Nausea', 'We're Desperate', 'Back Against the Wall', 'Wasted' and 'I Don't Care About You'. Followed by *The Decline of Western Civilisation, Part II: The Metal Years* and *The Decline of Western Civilisation, Part III*, both of which are similar mixes of valuable musicological document, social history, eardrum abuse and pre-The Osbournes lives-of-the-rich-and-fucked-up. ★★★★ **KN**

DECONSTRUCTING HARRY (1997)

Starring: *Woody Allen (Harry Block), Richard Benjamin (Ken), Kirstie Alley (Joan), Billy Crystal (Larry/The Devil), Judy Davis (Lucy), Bob Balaban (Richard), Elisabeth Shue (Fay), Demi Moore (Helen), Robin Williams (Mel), Caroline Aaron (Burt), Mariel Hemingway (Beth Kramer), Amy Irving (Jane), Julie Kavner (Grace)*
Director: *Woody Allen*
Screenwriter: *Woody Allen*
18/96 mins./Comedy/USA

Harry is a novelist who has always used the lives of those around him for inspiration. But as he prepares to receive an award from the college that expelled him, his latest ex marries a friend and he suffers writer's block, he has to face up to the damage he has caused.

Woody Allen's 27th film as writer-director, his 24th comedy, is his most nakedly self-confessional work yet. Unnervingly, it is both hilariously funny and quite disturbing, with Allen's neuroses and fixations manifested in some shocking ugliness and intimately personal revelations we'd rather not have seen confirmed.

Allen's screen alter ego is writer Harry Block, whose career has been spun out of turning his neurotic and erotic misdeeds into thinly disguised fiction. Six analysts and three wives down the line, Harry still hasn't grown up and knows it, admitting he likes prostitutes because 'you don't have to talk about Proust and films' with them, and deceiving himself with regard to his inappropriate relationship with a 25-year-old. Harry's life, with emphasis on his sexual kinks and emotional inadequacy, is explored by contrasting extracts from his writing with the 'reality' – with Demi Moore, Julia-Louis Dreyfus, Richard Benjamin, Robin Williams, Stanley Tucci and Tobey Maguire playing, respectively, the fictional counterparts of Harry's second ex (Alley), his third ex (Amy Irving)'s sister (Davis), and four different Harrys.

Comedy and drama collide in some surreal heights, as when Harry's literary creations begin appearing in his 'real' life to confront him, and Harry's rival for Shue, Larry appears as the Devil in Harry's dream of descent into hell. In the most brilliant conceit, Harry's short story character movie star Mel (Williams) goes out of focus in real life and everyone has to accommodate his distortion by wearing funny glasses.

What's deeply awful here is that after all these years giving the impression that he loves women, Allen airs a rage and loathing (we're interpreting Alley and Davis, at least, as Mia Farrow stand-ins) unprecedented in his work, and hateful obscenities directed at the women that are all the more appalling coming so unexpectedly from his mouth. Even with its abundance of pithy one-liners and honest insight, most viewers are likely to be discomfited by such autobiographical obsession, and bound to agree with Woody Harry's anguished climactic screech 'I'm OD-ing on myself!' Too true. ★★★ **AE**

THE DEEP (1977)

Starring: *Robert Shaw (Romer Treece), Jacqueline Bisset (Gail Berke), Nick Nolte (David Sanders), Louis Gossett Jr. (Henri Cloche), Eli Wallach (Adam Coffin)*
Director: *Peter Yates*
Screenwriters: *Peter Benchley, Tracy Keenan Wynn based on the novel by Benchley*
15/123 mins./Adventure/Thriller/USA

Discovering a secret way into a sunken wreck, two amateur scuba-divers find themselves threatened by some Bermudan thugs. There is more than treasure at stake, with a stock of morphine ampoules buried with the very same sunken ship. Thus Gail Berke and David Sanders turn to wizened salt Romer Treece for help.

In the wake of *Jaws*' great success, Peter Yates adapted another of author Peter Benchley's submerged novels. On the surface it looked good: sunken galleons, Caribbean locations, voodoo, treasure, wicked drug runners and a sexy lead couple. There was even the return of Robert Shaw as another booze-reddened sea salt if anything even crustier than Quint (but nowhere near as memorable). Just one thing missing – a ruddy great shark. This empty-headed thriller relies on little more than good locations, some quality underwater photography and Jacqueline Bisset in a wet t-shirt. Which isn't all bad.

Actually, for the first hour, it drums up a goodly amount of tension. Happening upon a wreck, and dodging a Jurassic-sized electric eel, this sexy couple (Bisset as kept in see-through t-shirts, Nolte shaggy and tanned) think they've hit the mother lode. Enter sinister Lou Gosset Jr. who rather than simply follow them to the wreck (where there is also, as is usual for this kind of pulp, a secret drug haul) he kidnaps the couple to retrieve the glass ampoule they've brought up from below, just to make sure he checks underneath Bisset's bikini top. Well, you have to be sure. Later, he intimidates her by dressing as a voodoo skeleton and dragging a bird's foot across her belly. 'I've been painted!' she wails.

Even Shaw's presence, joining the couple to salvage the wreck and make his fortune, fails to revive the film's fortunes. Yates goes through the motions doggedly, staging underwater fights and plot twists, but is left to pad out such 'thrills' with endless yakking about 'provenance' (the security required for a legal salvage) and the boys (Bisset is left in the boat) hoovering of the seabed before, finally the bad guy gets his caught between eel and highwater. ★★ **IN**

DEEP BLUE SEA (1999)

Starring: *Thomas Jane (Carter Blake), Saffron Burrows (Dr. Susan McCallister), LL Cool J (Sherman 'Preacher' Dudley), Michael Rapaport (Tom Scoggins), Stellan Skarsgård (Jim Whitlock), Samuel L. Jackson (Russell Franklin)*
Director: *Renny Harlin*
Screenwriters: *Duncan Kennedy, Donna Powers, Wayne Powers*
15/105 mins./Action/Horror/Thriller/USA

A team of scientists on a sea-based research station enhance sharks' brains in an attempt to find a cure for Alzheimer's disease. However, when the sharks get loose, they must find their way back to safety past perfect predators who can now reason and plan ...

Whopping great sharks with oversized brains taking sizeable chunks out of a bunch of stroppy, eclectic, overfamiliar character types desperately searching for the surface of the fragmenting frame of a deep sea research centre. We were never going to be talking high art with Renny Harlin's dutifully overblown and grin-forming return to the ocean wave.

After a protracted set-up, locating us in a labyrinthine marine lab with a team of potty scientists obsessed with the idea that protein extracted from a shark's cortex can cure Alzheimer's (don't ask), an argumentative shark and some problematical weather leave the facility crippled and its three mentally dextrous cartilaginous inhabitants on the loose. The result is a dynamic, often thrilling mix of dumb-arse horror-disaster movie staples and borderline parody.

The major problem is that the point where Harlin crosses over into satire is hard to gauge. At its most outrageous, *Deep Blue Sea*'s clunky dialogue starts to dally at the edges of smartness; facility owner Sam Jackson's literally snigger-inducing tale of ancient horrors with its crowning punchline is a delicious subversion of Quint's USS *Indianapolis* speech from *Jaws* (which acts as a template of in-jokery for Harlin), and the movie seems to be constantly wagging its B-movie tail as if to keep telling us, 'It's meant to be daft, okay?'

However, between some truly terrifying performances (Burrows, chief meddler with nature, convinces on precisely no levels whatsoever), churning predictability and huge contrivance, much of the badness is just plain badness. You're never entirely sure whether you're laughing at or with *Deep Blue Sea*.

Harlin is, though, a director who can pace and co-ordinate action. The set-pieces are mounted with increasing bizarreness (a shark switching on an oven?) and a real sense of playfulness; one towering knee-jerker is so good you half expect an instant replay in slo-mo. Newcomer Jane, as the macho shark wrangler Carter Blake, gives proceedings a dependable heroic centre and this is one of the first effects-driven movies to effectively meld CGI with modelwork to the best advantage of both. ★★★ **IN**

DEEP IMPACT (1998)

Starring: *Robert Duvall (Capt. Spurgeon 'Fish' Tanner), Tea Leoni (Jenny Lerner), Elijah Wood (Leo Beiderman), Vanessa Redgrave (Robin Lerner), Morgan Freeman (President Tom Beck), James Cromwell (Alan Rittenshouse), Jon Favreau (Dr. Gus Partenza), Mary McCormack (Andrea 'Andy' Baker)*
Director: *Mimi Leder*
Screenwriters: *Bruce Joel Rubin, Michael Tolkin*
12/120 mins./Drama/Sci-fi/Thriller/USA

A comet is heading for Earth – and it's big enough to spell disaster for all life on the planet if it strikes. As the US president launches a desperate last-minute bid by NASA to blow up the comet, Earth prepares for the worst, taking refuge in caves and where they can ...

Pairing George Clooney and trail-blazing director Mimi Leder (longtime collaborators on *ER*) on *The Peacemaker* seemed about as close to a surefire hit as possible for DreamWorks SKG's debut production in 1997. But the result somehow failed to light up the sky. Which rather left the studio still anxious to score. This time, though, while the planet's plight may be even bleaker, a plot of high drama dripped through intensely personal strata provides Leder with much more scope.

Lovelorn teen Leo Beiderman joins his high-school astronomy class after going starry-eyed over fellow student Sarah Hotchner, only to spot a heavenly body that'll make the earth move for everybody. All at once. In the wake of volcanoes and alien invasions, the cinematic theme du jour has careering comets on collision course: Earth. And before Bruce Willis tried his luck in *Armageddon*, US President Morgan Freeman announces Uncle Sam's fail-safe measures.

First up, careworn and improbably named astronaut Spurgeon Tanner has been fished out of retirement to join the comet-cracking crew of a joint Russo-American spaceship dubbed *Messiah*. As their mission entails an unprecedented landing on the rock to bury nukes, further contingencies are planned. Namely, a warren of caves back on Earth loaded with tuck, designed to sustain a million people for two years while the dust settles – 200,000 boffins already selected plus 800,000 lucky Americans who'll be joining the chosen through a national lottery.

Tagline
Heaven and Earth are about to collide.

Blending the epic with the intimate is never an easy feat, and to achieve sufficient emotional impact amid the widescale issue of entire species snuff-out, the audience has to care about the characters by the time doom looms. Despite solid enough stuff from Freeman, Wood and Duvall, only Tea Leoni's rising reporter – who springs the story – enjoys enough screen time to make any sort of connection. But such failure is nevertheless largely admirable, symptomatic of an attempt to meld graphic realisation of the Extinction Level Event, while asking whether mankind would lose its humanity under the shadow of apocalypse, and doing all of this within a tight two-hour movie, not a sprawling, self-indulgent butt-buster.

Around the serious 'issues' of course, special effects do have their place, and these are sometimes awesome, sometimes pretty ordinary. A spectacular bundle of tricks is unleashed in the finale, guaranteed to prompt jaw/carpet interface but a questionable comet-surface scene has our doughty defenders attempting to plant nukes by leaping about an original series *Star Trek* set streaming with dry ice. And while straining for the most part to preserve scientific credibility, NASA's highly trained team go about their illogical rescue bid with a gung-ho attitude to maximise viewer thrills. ★★★ **DB**

DEEP RISING (1998)

Starring: *Treat Williams (John Finnegan), Famke Janssen (Trillian St. James), Anthony Heald (Simon Canton), Kevin J. O'Connor (Captain Atherton), Jason Flemyng (Mulligan)*
Director: *Stephen Sommers*
Screenwriter: *Stephen Sommers*
15/106 mins./Action/Horror/Thriller/Sci-fi/USA

A gang of jewel thieves board an apparently deserted liner in the South China Seas, only to find that the passengers and crew have been killed off by some strange monster, that sucks the water from its victim's bodies.

Godzilla used state-of-the-art CGI to decommission the man in a suit. *Deep Rising* seeks to consign the rubber octopus to the special effects museum (with a sign beneath it no doubt, saying, 'Last used in *Warlords Of Atlantis*, 1978'). However, unlike *Godzilla*, this monster B-movie doesn't have ideas above its station.

The set-up mixes *Beyond The Poseidon Adventure* with *Under Seige*: a motley squad of piratical armed mercenaries in the South China Sea – transported, no-questions-asked, by a wisecracking sea dog and his whining 'grease monkey' – boards luxury liner *Argonautica* in order to fleece its rich passengers. However, what they find is a ghost ship and just three survivors: a jewel thief in a red dress, the vessel's captain and shifty owner. Williams utters that threadbare cue: 'I've got a really bad feeling about this', and the claustrophobic *Alien*-blueprint battle begins – dark corridors, big guns, half-glimpsed tentacles, individuals picked off one by one.

Like the previous year's *Anaconda* and *The Relic*, *Deep Rising* gives it the full *Blue Peter*, making a lot out of very little. It's nothing we haven't seen before, and as a scriptwriter, director Sommers is no David Mamet ('There's something down here,' warns Williams, before our first octopoid sighting; 'An island!' exclaims Heald when he spies land), but there is an unmistakable air of knowing self-parody about the square-jawed heroics and the *Ten Little Indians* framework, and it is possible to laugh with the film and not at it. Tragically, the worst lines are hogged by the Brits, a miscast Jason Flemyng machine-gunning tentacles with an unconvincing, 'Have some of this, you wankers!'

The creature effects, by *Total Recall*/*The Thing* supremo Rob Bottin, are not bad, and, while only the lily-livered will actually find the it's-behind-you tactics scary, it rattles along at a fair lick. ★★★ **AC**

THE DEER HUNTER (1978)

Starring: *Robert De Niro (Michael Vronsky), John Cazale (Stanley 'Stosh'), John Savage (Steven), Christopher Walken (Nikonar 'Nick' Chevotarevich), Meryl Streep (Linda), George Dzundza (John)*
Director: *Michael Cimino*
Screenwriter: *Deric Washburn, based on a story by Michael Cimino, Deric Washburn, Louis Garfinkel, Quinn K. Redeker*
18/183 mins./Drama/War/USA

Awards: *Academy Awards – Best Supporting Actor (Christopher Walken), Best Director, Best Film Editing, Best Picture, Best Sound, BAFTA – Best Cinematography, Best Editing, Golden Globes – Best Director*

A group of friends who work in steel mills prepare to go to war by taking a trip into the mountains to kill deer. Their slow-paced life is shoved into the stark reality of warfare and the psychological effects of such a shocking contrast prevent them from slotting back into society.

The Deer Hunter, Cimino's second movie following the pleasingly throwaway *Thunderbolt And Lightfoot*, can, and should, be read as an epic treatise on endurance, and, in particular, the indomitable spirit of the American male. The near three-hour narrative tracing the classic human parabola from wedding bliss to funeral blues.

We open in the hellish heat and sulphurous fumes of the Pennsylvania steel mills, where friends and co-workers Michael, Nick, Stan, Steven and Axel endure inhuman conditions for meagre pay, night after night.

These are tough men, we are told. The weekly reward for the steelworkers is escape into the cool mountains, and Michael in particular is soon scampering across snow-capped peaks with a gazelle's grace. But, lest we forget that a ticket to heaven comes at a prix fixé, Michael tracks and kills a beautiful stag, as if nature itself must pay his tithe.

It's a film of striking and often startling contrasts, and Cimino doesn't once flinch from an unpromising gear change. Indeed, *The Deer Hunter* is distinguished by quite audacious transitions from high to low, light to dark.

At one point, Michael, abandoned in his motel room at night, suddenly appears at the other side of the frame, still shrouded in darkness; only when he steps forward into the light do we realise that it is now daytime and he is outside, standing in the shade, hiding from his friends.

And, famously, there is the sudden jolt into Vietnam. The hunting buddies, exhausted and exhilarated from a successful trip, come to rest around a piano played by George Dzundza's loveable bar owner; dimly, the rhythm of what sound like rotor blades underscore the pretty melody. Without warning we are in another world, helicopters rain napalm down on a green forest.

If, as Dante maintained, hell is composed of seven levels, we have just slipped down several stages at once.

At a time when patience was a given rather than a virtue, 70s audiences were happy to endure the inevitable longueurs – a 40-minute wedding production number that fails to forward the plot – because word-of-mouth had assured them that all hell would soon break loose.

And for cinemagoers who had yet to be fed money shots and special effects, the notorious Russian Roulette sequence – where POWs Michael, Nick and Steven must face off against each other for the amusement of their Viet-Cong captors – which takes place early in the second hour, was the equivalent of a must-see, water-cooler moment.

Simply one of the most terrifying scenes in celluloid history, this sequence alone ensured that *The Deer Hunter* would become perhaps the most unlikely blockbuster of all time. When the film went on to dominate the 1978 Oscars – taking five awards including Best Film and Best Director – Cimino was heralded as the poster-child for the brave new world of American cinema. A man, it was supposed, who could do no wrong.

On his return from Vietnam, Michael's failure to reconnect with friends whom he once openly patronised is lent a genuinely tragic dimension. There is no way Michael could explain what he has seen, what he has lived through, even if he wanted to.

And in a movie that is practically spoilt for stand-out performances – Meryl Streep's luminous debut, John Cazale's last screen appearance, Christopher Walken's Oscar-winning breakthrough – De Niro is always central, manfully shouldering the film just as Michael carries the crippled Steven to safety. His work with Scorsese is more expansive, more celebrated, but Michael is De Niro's signature performance: the enigmatic, stoic, thoroughly Nietzschean hero who has not only appeared in various forms (see *Heat*'s Neil McCauley) throughout his career, but one that we mere mortals can easily imagine is a close relation of the great man himself.

The Deer Hunter is a gruelling film, an upsetting experience, as much an endurance test for the audience as it was for cast and crew fighting a private war on location in Thailand. And yet, from the justly ubiquitous theme music to Vilmos Zsigmond's rich and lyrical cinematography, *The Deer Hunter* is a film of enormous, if mostly melancholy, beauty.

As such, it contains a raw power to move, and in some cases, bait, audiences to extremes of emotion almost unparalleled in cinema. At the time this was an astonishingly ambitious attempt to dress a wound in the American psyche that was still fresh and weeping; years on, *The Deer Hunter* deserves to be reclaimed as one of the most powerful humanist tracts ever committed to celluloid. ★★★★★ **CK**

THE DEFIANT ONES (1958)

Starring: *Tony Curtis (John Jackson), Sidney Poitier (Noah Cullen) Theodore Bikel (Sheriff Max Muller), Charles McGraw (Captain Frank Gibbons), Lon Chaney Jr (Big Sam)*
Director: *Stanley Kramer*
Screenwriters: *Nedrick Young, Harold Jacob*
PG/97 mins./Drama/USA

Bigoted white convict John Jackson and angry black convict Noah Cullen escape from a prison farm chained together at the wrist, and argue, brawl and co-operate their way across country, learning to understand and help each other along the way.

This Stanley Kramer messageathon plays better as a high-concept thriller than a statement about race relations or the human condition. Too much of it involves Curtis' Joker, who dreams of becoming a wealthy

'Charlie Potatoes', squabbling with Poitier's Cullen, who bristles whenever he's called 'boy', but the good stuff is physical – the cons trying to get across a river or out of a mud pit, with much symbolic hand-clasping. Along the trail there are one-act-play-like encounters with lynch mob leader Claude Akins who is defied by sympathetic old lag Lon Chaney Jr, and with abandoned farmwife Cara Williams, who comes on hysterically strong to Curtis and directs Poitier off to drown in a swamp, prompting the white man finally to admit kinship with his fellow downtrodden escaped con.

There's the inevitable bit where Curtis smears mud on his face, is mistaken for a black man and learns something of what it's like being Poitier, but this is somehow less powerful than the unaddressed, just-the-way-it-is murderous racism of the poor white trash folks they encounter on the run.

Behind a front, the screenwriter was blacklistee Nedrick Young, which explains some of the anger at the failings of America. The ending is nicely understated, as Curtis is too weak to go on but Poitier stays with him as humane sheriff Theodore Bikel, having defied straining-at-the-leash state trooper Charles McGraw (who wants to send in the Dobermans), just quietly arrests the runaways. The leads are too pretty for their roles, and neither is well-cast as an underclass convict, but Bikel, McGraw, Chaney, Akins and the others do good work. ★★★ **MH**

ⓓ DELIVERANCE (1972)

Cast: *Jon Voight (Ed Gentry), Burt Reynolds (Lewis Medlock), Ned Beatty (Bobby Trippe), Ronny Cox (Drew Ballinger), Ed Ramey (Old Man), Billy Redden (Lonny)*
Director: *John Boorman*
Screenwriter: *James Dickey based on his own novel*
18/109 mins/Adventure/USA

Taking a weekend canoeing trip down a backwater river in deepest Georgia, four urbanites and friends, find themselves caught up in a nightmare when set upon by some very unfriendly locals.

After the nihilistic violence of *Point Blank*, British director John Boorman took on another story of American machismo in peril, swapping the unyielding urban landscape of his earlier thriller for the feverish wilds of America's untamed void. This is a land unconquered, a squalid, treacherous place where city slickers are set upon by demented locals for daring to believe they are equal to nature's demands. It is a magnificent, gruelling test of a movie, visceral, raw, drawing easy comparison with Sam Peckinpah's *Straw Dogs* (which plied a similar tack in rural Cornwall) and Walter Hill's later tale of men lost in the bayou, *Southern Comfort*.

Boorman, taking James Dickey's novel and script as his basis, is having a fine time subverting the hokey traditions of the American backwoodsmen built by such soft icons as Davy Crockett and Daniel Boon. In this febrile neighbourhood, it ain't the guffawing yokel Clampet-style Hillbillies, but deranged, twisted versions of the noble American myth, inbred and remorseless. That the film is not about to hold back, is signalled when Ned Beatty is brutally raped, an act of shocking humiliation and unmanning. *Deliverance* is ruggedly tearing down accepted concepts of machismo. On that level, its reputation is misleading, it is not a tale of man against nature, but of man destroyed, crushed, by forces they cannot come to terms with. Beatty is being punished for his clumsy attempts to communicate with the locals, his apparent condescension. As for Ronny Cox's doomed character, seemingly the most reasonable of the quartet, who famously has the banjo duel with a freakily deformed local child, his ruin is ordained by his foolish attempts to apply 'civilised' logic to their nightmare.

For all its thematic fire, the heart of what is Boorman's best film is in its powerful physicality. Shot with tremendous vitality along the Chattooga River, the director forces the film into the spume and hellwater of the treacherous rapids, where the real actors (including two of the biggest stars of the seventies in Jon Voight and Burt Reynolds) – insurance be damned – were manfully doing their own navigation. Voight even had to scale a two hundred foot cliff. Ultimately, the remaining members will have to fight back to endure, and the film completes its conception of violence as man's primal state. 'Survival,' growls Reynolds, 'is the name of the game.' ★★★★ **IN**

ⓓ DEMOLITION MAN (1993)

Starring: *Sylvester Stallone (John Spartan), Wesley Snipes (Simon Phoenix), Sandra Bullock (Lt. Lenina Huxley), Nigel Hawthorne (Dr. Raymond Cocteau), Benjamin Bratt (Alfredo Garcia)*
Director: *Marco Brambilla*
Screenwriters: *Daniel Waters, Robert Reneau, Peter M. Lenkov, based on a story by Peter M. Lenkov, Robert Reneau*
Producer: *Howard G. Kazanjian, Michael Levy, Joel Silver*
15/115 mins./Action/Sci-fi/Comedy/Crime/USA

A particularly malicious criminal is cryogenically frozen along with a top policeman to keep him under control if ever they are released. Come the year 2032, that's exactly what happens, with Snipes on the rampage and only Stallone with the ability to stop him.

'Send a maniac to catch a maniac!' yells Sly, launching himself back into muscleman mode and possibly the maddest, baddest, most enjoyably silly action flick of 1993. It's 1996: anarchy rules, Los Angeles is up in flames, and Stallone is the crack LAPD cop and titular Demolition Man, so-called 'cause he blows up buildings, who is sentenced to an eternity in the cooler (literally, as he's cryogenically frozen) when a hostage rescue goes horribly wrong and innocent townsfolk die. Banged up with him in cryoprison is the man behind the crime – Wesley Snipes, bleach-blond, crazy as hell, with a real bad attitude – and the two serve out their time until parole comes up, Snipes escapes and Stallone is defrosted to snare him.

And here's where the riot really starts, as the pair – a dynamite screen combination – explode into the brave new world of San Angeles, 2032: squeaky clean, law-abiding, much, much too good to be true, urged to its state of Utopia under the seemingly benevolent rule of founder Dr. Cocteau (Hawthorne, quietly megalomanic) and troubled only occasionally by an underground Resistance hankering after good old-fashioned 20th Century pleasures like swearing, booze and sex. Little wonder the new age is utterly unprepared for Snipes (rehabbed in cryo as an even more homicidal maniac with the strength of a small army) and Stallone (rehabbed as, er, a seamstress who can knit a mean jumper but fortunately hasn't lost all his muscular faculties) blasting their way through the action.

There's a thin plot to be had of the World Domination kind – Dr. Cocteau is mad and wants to take over the world, and uses Snipes to help him kill the leader of the Resistance; Snipes gets madder and wants to take over the world, and the leader of the Resistance rebels; Stallone gets caught in between – but what really makes this movie swing is the sheer sense of fun in making it which is conveyed to the screen.

Snipes and Stallone clearly had a blast, and you can't help but share the joke: from the 20th Century memorabilia collected by 21st Century cop Sandra Bullock (including a poster for *Lethal Weapon 3*), to in-references like the Schwarzenegger Presidential Library ('Don't tell me,' groans Stallone, 'I don't want to know'). Snipes gets to quote *Scarface* and Sly sends himself up something rotten. The techno-gadgetry is just brilliant, and there's even sort of a message in here somewhere ('Hurting people is not a good thing,' chides our Sly, 'well, sometimes it is').

First-time director Brambilla delivers the ultraviolence with spectacular comic book results and the panache of a pro, managing from a running start to build-up the mind-boggling action into a climactic special effects frenzy so stupendous as to freeze any criticism in its tracks. If ever there was a movie equivalent to the one-night stand this is it – not necessarily something you'll remember next day but fast, furious and damn good fun while it lasts. ★★★★ **PB**

⊙ DERSU UZALA (1975)

Starring: *Maxim Munzuk (Dersu Uzala), Yuri Solomine (Capt. Vladimir Arseniev), Schemeiki Chokmorov (Jan Bao), Vladimir Klemena (Turtwigin), Svetlana Danielchanka (Mrs. Arseniev)*
Director: *Akira Kurosawa*
Screenwriter: *Akira Kurosawa, based on the journals by Vladimir Arseniev*
U/137 mins./Adventure/USSR/Japan

Awards: *Academy Awards – Best Foreign Language Film*

As Russian soldier Vladimir Arseniev searches for the grave of Dersu Uzala, the Gold tribesman he befriended in the Siberian wilderness in 1902, he thinks back to the encounters that led to nomad's demise.

Following the debacle of *Tora! Tora! Tora!* and the box-office failure of *Dodes'kaden*, Akira Kurosawa attempted suicide. Yet, he was ready to resume his career within a year and accepted funding from Mosfilm for this imposing adaptation of the memoirs of soldier-explorer Vladimir Arseniev. However, Arseniev's friendship with Dersu Uzala mattered less to Kurosawa than the opportunity to lament the unstoppable march of progress that was destroying areas of untouched wilderness and corrupting the peoples who had lived there undisturbed for centuries.

Kurosawa shot in 70mm to convey the vastness of the Siberian taiga. But the scale also served to detach the director from his subject and, while this is often an achingly beautiful and deeply moving film, it's not one of Kurosawa's more heartfelt efforts.

The Ussuri landscape is often idealised and Dersu's understanding of it is similarly romanticised. Indeed, there were critics who accused Kurosawa of patronising Dersu by presenting him as a latterday version of Rousseau's noble savage. Yet, he is clearly more akin to a Siberian samurai, whose code is rooted in respect for nature and co-existence with even menacing beasts, like tigers.

Conversely, Kurosawa's depiction of life in Khaboravsk is naively pessimistic, with domestic comforts and technical advances being considered equal evils with the claustrophobic enclosure and commercial exploitation of urban existence.

Compositionally, Kurosawa tends towards aloof pictorialism (note the use of telephoto lenses and the scarcity of close-ups). Yet his use of colour and light and the manner in which he binds his characters into their environment is masterly. What's more, there are also several memorable set-pieces, including the montages of the tree branches and the nocturnal cacophony, and the contrasting rescues, in which Dersu first saves Arseniev from the blizzard and then the Russians deliver Dersu from the rapids.

Five years later, Kurosawa would achieve a more complete fusion of theme and image in *Kagemusha*. ★★★ **DP**

⊙ THE DESCENT (2005)

Starring: *Shauna Macdonald (Sarah), Natalie Jackson Mendoza (Juno), Alex Reid (Beth), Saskia Mulder (Rebecca), MyAnna Buring (Sam), Nora-Jane Noone (Holly)*
Director: *Neil Marshall*
Screenwriter: *Neil Marshall*
18/100 mins./Horror/UK

Awards: *Empire Awards – Best Horror*

Under the guidance of adrenaline junkie Juno, a sextet of spunky spelunker-ladies rappel into the depths of an Appalachian pothole seeking adventure – or at least some good stories they can tell back home. But, when things start to go wrong, it looks unlikely that any of them are ever going to see home, or indeed daylight, ever again . . .

Neil Marshall sure knows how to get your attention. Mere minutes into *The Descent*, he'll have made you jump half out your seat, sent your popcorn cascading ceilingward and left nervous titters bubbling around the theatre. Here's a man who truly, deeply, horribly knows his horror. Welding a fanboy mentality to a masterful grasp of genre-filmmaking, Marshall goes all-out to disturb, upset and downright terrify his audience for a relentless 100-odd minutes, pausing only occasionally to allow us the odd twitchy laugh or indulge in a bit of visual-reference in-jokery (*Aliens* and *Carrie* are just two of the more obvious homaged movies).

The Geordie shockmeister first got our attention back in 2002 with his gruey, boisterous squaddies-versus-werewolves debut *Dog Soldiers*. Scrappy and shoestringy it may have been, but it marked Marshall out as a British talent to keep our beadies on. *The Descent* represents a logical progression. It's bigger-budget (or, at least, it looks it), better-looking, far scarier and will, no doubt fling small-fish Marshall into a much bigger pond – one ringed with tinsel.

Much of *The Descent*'s success is due to the beautiful economy of the concept: six girls, one cave and a whole lotta pain. The subterranean setting is conducive to horror and Marshall grinds every last wince out of it. Even before the screams begin and the bones start snapping, the claustrophobia will get you, with the women elbowing and puffing their way through cheese-press tunnels, their hardhats scraping disconcertingly against stone, the rockdust snaking through the dank, stale air in the torchlight . . . And once we're all down in the dark, we're down there for the rest of the movie. There's no respite, no moment to sit back and breathe easy.

Thankfully, Marshall's inventive enough to make this work for, rather than against him. Some scenes are lit by the eerie crimson glow of a flare, others washed in the green of a glowstick, while in a few we can only see through the fuzzy, black-and-white nightsight of a camcorder. And when there's no light at all, he lets his creepy sound-design do all the dirty work.

Naturally there's far more to this than the vacation-gone-wrong set-up. For a start, there's the strained character dynamics, played out effectively by the cast as Sarah's (Macdonald) mental state becomes worryingly fragile, while Juno's (Mendoza) ballsiness soon teeters into recklessness. Then, even worse there's ... Well, it's probably best we don't go there. The less you know, the more you'll enjoy. If, of course, being scared shitless is what you consider enjoyable. ★★★★ **DJ**

⊙ DESPERADO (1995)

Starring: *Antonio Banderas (El Mariachi), Salma Hayek (Carolina), Joaquim de Almeida (Bucho), Cheech Marin (Short Bartender), Steve Buscemi (Buscemi), Carlos Gomez (Right Hand), Quentin Tarantino (Pick-up Guy)*
Director: *Robert Rodriquez*
Screenwriter: *Robert Rodriquez*
18/106 mins./Action/Drama/Thriller/USA

Musician El Mariachis true love is killed and the criminals responsible for her death leave him maimed. Now he carries a guitar case full of weapons and comes to a new town in search of those responsible.

Bigger, better, faster; *Desperado* is a spiritual, and spirited remake of director Rodriguez's $7,000 *El Mariachi*, proof positive that throwing millions of dollars at what was by itself something of a small budget gem can actually result in a better movie.

It's not the smartest career move for a director's second film to be a scene-by-scene remake of his first, but with Rodriguez it's clearly a declaration of intent. Not content with the relatively small audience that saw his Spanish language original, he decided to take what Hollywood was only too keen to give him and recast his movie as a *High Plains Drifter* for the post-Tarantino audience.

The plot is straightforward enough. The mysterious Mariachi (this time played to the hilt by Banderas), wanders into town with a guitar case and vengeance in his heart. His entrance is preceded by that of the perennially weasel-like Steve Buscemi, busily recounting a tale from the original movie. The Eastwood-like Mariachi is out to get the big cheese drug lord, willing to blow away everyone and everything in his path to get it.

What really counts, though, is Rodriguez's assured abilities. This is Peckinpah crossed with John Woo on speed, full of souped-up action pieces that defy anything even approaching credibility in their wanton lust for pure cinematic destruction, but more than make up for it in Rodriguez's skilful editing and delicately perverse sense of humour. And it's not just action – it's hard to imagine anyone of any sexual persuasion or inclination not finding something to fantasise over in the eventual coupling of Banderas and the luscious Hayek. ★★★★ **BM**

DESPERATE HOURS (1990)

Starring: *Mickey Rourke (Michael Bosworth), Anthony Hopkins (Tim Cornell), Mimi Rogers (Nora Cornell), Lindsay Crouse (Chandler), Kelly Lynch (Nancy Bryers), Elias Koteas (Wally Bosworth), David Morse (Albert)*
Director: *Michael Cimino*
Screenwriters: *Lawrence Konner, Mark Rosenthal, Joseph Hayes, from the novel and play by Joseph Hayes*
15/105 mins./Drama/Crime/USA

Michael is a psychotic criminal who seduces his lawyer and persuades her to help him to escape prison. Once outside, he and his accomplices take a family hostage to wait out the manhunt. But things begin to go wrong when the father of the family becomes determined to fight back.

When Michael (Rourke – in mean and moody mode) breaks out of prison with the help of pretty lawyer Nancy, he and two accomplices need a place to hide until they can flee to Mexico. They select a suburban house, home to Jim and Nora Cornell, and their two children.

When Nora opens the door to Michael, the family's nightmare begins. Held captive by the escaped murderer, his brother and dim-witted sidekick, they are forced to become dependent on their captors, relying on Michael's assurance that no one will be harmed if they co-operate. But ex-soldier Jim determines to fight back, alienating his family who see him as the person whose heroics could cost them their lives. Meanwhile, Nancy is being questioned by the police and FBI agent Brenda Chandler, who believe they can use her to finally catch the escaped criminal. The police manipulate Nancy, and while Michael also uses her, the family and his buddies as pawns – but for how long?

A tried and tested story (first a Broadway play and then a film starring Humphrey Bogart), this thriller seemed a perfect vehicle for director Cimino, but it suffers from a slow middle and some chronic miscasting. You may swallow the fact Welsh-accented Hopkins fought in Vietnam, but it's harder to believe he's also married to much younger Mimi Rogers. The toughest pill to swallow, though, is Kelly Lynch. Tottering around in mini skirt and three-inch stillettoes, she does not immediately bring to mind a high-powered lawyer. Surprisingly, the most credible character is Michael, played by a convincingly menacing Rourke, who fulfils the promises he made in *Body Heat* at the beginning of his career. ★★ **JB**

DESPERATELY SEEKING SUSAN (1985)

Cast: *Rosanna Arquette (Roberta Glass), Madonna (Susan), Aidan Quinn (Dez), Mark Blum (Gary Glass), Laurie Metcalf (Leslie Glass), Robert Joy (Jim), Anna Levine (Crystal), Bill Patton (Nolan), Peter Maloney (Ian), Steven Wright (Larry)*
Director: *Susan Seidelman*
Screenwriter: *Leora Barish, Floyd Byars*
15/104 mins/Romantic/Comedy USA

Awards: *BAFTA – Best Actress in a Supporting Role (Rosanna Arquette)*

A housewife, weary of her humdrum life, follows a personal ad, 'Desperately Seeking Susan' to New York where she discovers the untamed Susan herself. Intrigued, she ends up buying Susan's jacket, and discovers someone else is also seeking Susan.

That the first of Madonna's screen performances, captured slightly before she took on the trappings of an icon, remains her finest comes down to an equal draw between the paucity of her work since and the vibrant, intuitive variation on her 'real-life' persona she created here. Susan, the real Susan, is a wild child, the free spirited embodiment of Madonna's, then, musical ethos, draped in whacky threads, smears of rouge and pure attitude. It's little wonder that disillusioned housewife Roberta (the excellent Rosanna Arquette), who has built a fantasy about her from a series of personal ads in a newspaper, goes as far as taking on her identity. When she gets clobbered on the head, she wakes up believing she is actually Susan.

Susan Seidelman, giving her movie a breezy pout, enjoys the galloping nonsense of the plot, its spin on identity and image, a play on the shifting sands of pop culture. It is a shame that her film has no great point to make about its make up, in all senses of the term. Appropriately enough, it is all surface, a glistening mix of potty thriller and screwballing comedy, filled with clichéd mobsters, mistaken identities and that stock convenience, amnesia. Even on this level, there is little care given to its structure, Seidelman just lets it bubble up into an incomprehensible muddle of reverses and twists and reveals. With Aidan Quinn turning up to fall for the pseudo Susan (that is Arquette) and give the film a mild romance to drive it to the close.

The right tactic to take with *Desperately Seeking Susan* is to just take in its easy jaunt about a New York that even a recently as the mid-eighties looks like a different world, gaudy and messy, an underground realm of neon-lit sleaze-holes, not the pristine Manhattan of today. It's entertaining, because of the bright, likeable performances, and with Madonna's subsequent rise in stature, remains something of a pop artefact. ★★★★ **IN**

DESTINATION MOON (1950)

Starring: *John Archer (Jim Barnes), Warner Anderson (Dr Charles Cargraves), Tom Powers (General Thayer), Dirk Wesson (Joe Sweeney), Erin O'Brien Moore (Emily Cargraves)*
Director: *Irving Pichel*
Screenwriters: *Rip Van Ronkel, R.A. Heinlein, James O'Hanlon, based on the novel* Rocketship Galileo *by R.A. Heinlein*
U/92 mins./Sci-fi/USA

An American businessman, worried that the government is leaving space exploration to less altruistic nations, funds a moon mission. A four-man crew pilot a rocketship to the moon, and explore the satellite.

Co-scripted by novelist Robert A. Heinlein (*Starship Troopers*), this colourful George Pal production was ground-breaking science fiction in its day. An attempt to get away from the comic strip conventions of *Flash Gordon*, it's a rare serious, monster-free trip into outer space, which deserves its historical place but has worn less well than its scrappier, pulpier competition.

Rocketship XM, a black and white quickie rushed into release as a spoiler while Pal was crafting the effects work of *Destination Moon*, now plays a lot better, and not just because it includes a woman on the crew and heads off to Mars to run into a fallen civilisation and radioactive mutants. In lieu of mutants and space babes, the film offers elaborate special effects, cardboard characters (the crew consists of three square-jawed scientists and a jerk from Brooklyn the others explain things to) and cliché crises that have cropped up in many subsequent films (spies from 'an unfriendly power' try to sabotage the launch, the rocket needs in-flight repairs which require a space-walk, there's a last-minute need to lose luggage so the ship can come home). It tries for scientific accuracy by 1950 standards and features a cartoon sequence with Woody Woodpecker explaining the ins and outs of rocket propulsion, but now seems on the quaint, slow and unexciting side.

A great deal of the detail turned out to be on the nose when NASA launched actual moon missions, but the elements that stand out tend to be those Heinlein and Pal got wrong – like the private industry-funded space programme and the use of a gleaming single-stage lava lamp-style rocket to get to the moon. ★★ **KN**

DESTRY RIDES AGAIN (1939)

Starring: *Marlene Dietrich (Frenchy), James Stewart (Tom Destry), Mischja Auer (Boris Callaghan), Charles Winninger, ('Wash' Dimsdale), Brian Donlevy (Kent)*
Director: *George Marshall*
Screenwriters: *Felix Jackson, Henry Myers, Getrude Purcell based on the novel by Max Brand*
PG/94 mins./Western/USA

Saloon chanteuse Frenchy swaps sides when mild-mannered lawman Tom Destry vows to rid Bottleneck of Kent, the gambler who's been cheating locals out of their ranches.

Mr Smith Goes to Washington transformed James Stewart into a symbol of American decency. Around the time of its release, he issued a statement proclaiming that 'a James Stewart picture must have two vital ingredients: it will be clean and it will involve the triumph of the underdog over the bully'.

Based on the novel by Max Brand, *Destry Rides Again* ticked both boxes. Yet it also quietly subverted Stewart's stance, as his iconographic integrity was being exploited to relaunch the career of Marlene Dietrich, who had been branded 'box-office poison' following the failure of *Angel* in 1937. Indeed, she was only Universal's second choice for the assignment and returned from Europe following the collapse of Julien Duvivier's *The Image* to replace Paulette Goddard. But Dietrich would have further scuffed Stewart's escutcheon if she had succeeded in her quest to seduce him, which lasted for much of the production.

Director George Marshall reckoned that Westerns had more elements of audience appeal than any other type of movie. But, just to be on the safe side, he stuffed this rattling yarn with plenty of slapstick, wisecracks, songs and melodrama. He even got Dietrich to indulge in a cat fight with Una Merkel that ended with Stewart dousing them both with water.

Yet, this was about as macho as Destry got during the opening sequences, as Marshall went out of his way to label him a sissy. He descended the stagecoach carrying a parasol and a canary cage, while he preferred milk or tea to hard liquor. Yet, even though Frenchy hands him a mop and bucket when he announces that he's going to clean up the town, Destry eventually proves that ingenuity can be just as lethal as gunfire (although he's finally reduced to drawing in anger). All of which was a far cry from the darker kind of cowboy that Stewart would play in Anthony Mann's psychological Westerns of the 1950s. ★★★★ **DP**

DEUCE BIGALOW: EUROPEAN GIGOLO (2005)

Starring: *Rob Schneider (Deuce Bigalow), Eddie Griffin (T.J. Hicks), Jeroen Krabbe (Gaspar Voorsboch), Til Schweiger (Heinz Hummer), Douglas Sills (Chadsworth Buckingham, III)*
Director: *Mike Bigelow*
Screenwriters: *Rob Schneider, David Garrett, Jason Ward, from characters created by Schneider and Harris Goldberg*
15/83mins./Comedy/USA
Awards: *Razzie Awards – Worst Actor*

Following the death of his wife, the retired manwhore goes to visit his pimp friend T.J. in Amsterdam – just as a crazed killer is knocking off the gigolos of Europe . . .

Rob Schneider's he-ho sequel shares the slapdash feel of its predecessor, as if it's been made by people who can't believe they've been given money to goof around for a few weeks with a camera. But, despite being shot in the endlessly distracting Amsterdam, *Deuce Bigalow 2* is more focused and funnier than the original.

In the past, Schneider has seemed unwilling to let anyone else share the spotlight, but this time around he's generous to a fault, practically playing straight man to the excellent Eddie Griffin, who provides most of the big one-liners and, in one hilarious riff about being falsely outed, the film's funniest running gag.

Naturally, it's patchy as hell, but there's arguably inspiration here, from the wonderfully inventive gigolo vocabulary – we have no idea what a Chilean rainbow is, and we're not entirely sure we want to find out – to a near-heroic effort to insult every minority group under the sun. It's also surprisingly sweet, in that strange way that only a movie that features a girl with a penis for a nose 'sneezing' into soup can be . . . ★★★ **CH**

DEUCE BIGALOW: MALE GIGOLO (1999)

Starring: *Rob Schneider (Deuce Bigalow), William Forsythe (Detective Chuck Fowler), Eddie Griffin (T.J. Hicks), Arija Bareikis (Kate)*
Director: *Mike Mitchell*
Screenwriters: *Harris Goldberg, Rob Schneider*
15/88 mins./Comedy/USA

Deuce Bigalow is a fishtank cleaner, until he is asked to housesit for a professional gigolo. However, when he accidentally wrecks the house, he must turn to 'manwhoring' himself in order to raise the money to repair the damage.

Another loud, boisterous tale that trades in lowest-common-denominator humour and drags its (supposedly) loveable loser through one hectic scrape after another, before pitching him up into a gets-the-girl finale and none-too-considered moral: that most human folk, no matter how fat, black, tall, impotent or deviant, are basically alright. Unfortunately, much like its central character, the movie seems to spend much of its modest running time floundering on its rear.

It is often said of knockabout, low-brow comedies that all the best bits are in the trailer, and this is certainly true here. But *Deuce Bigalow* has managed to carve out a further distinction: not only does the trailer hold the best bits, but by the time they're surrounded with all the other guff in the film, most of the comic value has been sucked clean out of them. Even a timely *Matrix* lampoon isn't quite converted and many other gags, both visual and verbal, are executed with the panache of a blunt guillotine.

Held in slightly lower esteem than the pond scum he regularly scours, Deuce is an affable, wide-eyed creation, but he's no Happy Gilmore, and failing to fully emulate Adam Sandler is a telling shortfall. It's unsurprising, given the film's prevailing mood (slapstick, pants-falling-down, farty), to find Sandler's name bearing an executive producer credit, but his involvement behind the scenes is clearly no form of guarantee.

This, in fact, is perhaps the most revealing eye-opener yet on why Sandler himself is successful: when centre stage, he can somehow make a loutish performance gel with a crude but sentimental script and pull laughs from it. *Deuce Bigalow*, meanwhile, merely misfires all over the place, never really getting off the ground. ★ **DB**

◑ DEVDAS (2002)

Starring: *Shahrukh Khan (Devda Mukherjee), Madhuri Dixit (Chandramukhi), Aishwarya Rai (Parvati), Jackie Shroff (Chunnilal), Kiron Kher (Sumitra), Smita Jaykar (Kaushalya)*
Director: *Sanjay Leela Bhansali*
Screenwriters: *Sanjay Leela Bhansali, Prakash Kapadia based on the novel by Saratchandra Chatterjee*
PG/182 mins./Romance/Drama/Musical/India

When prodigal son Devdas returns to India from his studies in England, his plans to marry childhood sweetheart Paro are dashed. But even when he's finding comfort at the bottom of a bottle and living with a courtesan, the flame of their love never truly goes out . . .

The first Bollywood film to be invited into the Official Selection of the Cannes Film Festival brought a riot of colour and choreography to the artier end of the film spectrum. It then received a high-profile U.K. cinema release at a time when Bollywood movies were very much in the spotlight. An Oscar nomination for Lagaan brought international credibility for what had been a specialist market; but given that Bollywood movies regularly find themselves in the U.K. box office top ten and themed exhibitions are popping up across the country, it's time to stop treating these movies as curiosity items and start enjoying them as the pure cinematic experiences they so often are.

As far as mainstream audiences are concerned, the groundwork for Devdas has been provided by *Moulin Rouge* as much as by other Indian films. The literate script, rich colour schemes and wonderfully energetic song-and-dance set-pieces grow naturally out of the sumptuous style of the story, which is familiar enough to Western eyes with its *Romeo And Juliet*-style approach to neighbouring lovers kept apart by social standing.

Those familiar with the novel on which this and many other earlier films are based will discover deeper levels as the characters reflect the mythological lovers, Krishna and Radha. Everything looks absolutely gorgeous, from the ornate sets, to the intricate costumes, to the lead actors themselves. After *Kabhi Khushi Kabhie Gham* and *Asoka*, Shahrukh Khan collected his third U.K. hit in a row, while former Miss World Aishwarya Rai proves she has the acting talent to back up her flawless looks. It's a long haul, of course, but every inch of the screen is packed with detail. This is cinematic spectacle to the power of ten. ★★★★ **OR**

Bollywood

What is it: The world's most prolific film industry, an unparalleled outpouring of Hindi-language cinema from the western Indian city of Bombay (hence 'Bollywood'; even those who transliterate Bombay into English as Mumbai tend not to call it 'Mollywood').
Hallmarks: Long running time; steamy but chaste romance; elaborate musical numbers every reel or so; lots of suffering en route to a happy ending; big spectacular crowd scenes.
If you see one movie, see: *Mother India* (1957)

◑ DEVIL IN A BLUE DRESS (1995)

Starring: *Denzel Washington (Easy Rawlins), Tom Sizemore (DeWitt Allbright), Jennifer Beals (Daphne Monet), Don Cheadle (Mouse Alexander)*
Director: *Carl Franklin*
Screenwriter: *Carl Franklin, based on a book by Walter Mosley*
15/102 mins./Crime/Mystery/Thriller/USA

A 1940s Afro-American private detective is hired to find a woman and gets mixed up in a murderous political scandal.

Carl Franklin's likeable take on Walter Mosley's nostalgic 40s LA-set pulp fiction proves another chip off the noir(ital) block from the director of the more contemporary, and frankly better, *One False Move*. The latest in a series of private eye movies which descend from *Chinatown*, *Devil* attempts to recreate the labyrinthine cynicism of a bygone genre and although not without class ends up substituting blurry period feel for the contemporary grit of the films it evokes.

Ezekial 'Easy' Rawlins, handsomely played by Washington, is a just-fired ex-GI who needs to keep up payments on his LA tract home. He is hired by a suitably shady character to locate Daphne Monet, the missing girlfriend of a mayoral candidate. Daphne likes blue dresses and black men and Easy's search for her turns up two corpses in as many days. The case, and the film, proceed predictably until Easy calls in Mouse, a friend from back home whose comical but frightening violent streak livens things up considerably.

This is a very seductive picture, with Washington posing in a vest or a snappy hat, a cool jazz soundtrack, lots of vintage cars and hopping dialogue. Franklin expresses a genuine nostalgia for the neatly lawned and folksy black LA communities that would turn into the urban wasteland of John Singleton. However, the resolution of the mystery – which depends on a pathos Beals isn't allowed to evoke – prompts a strong shrug of 'is that all there is?' leaving you expecting a bigger finale than the one you've had. In all, it's of considerable interest, but can't cut it with the trenchcoat classics.
★★★ **KN**

◑ THE DEVIL RIDES OUT (1968)

Starring: *Christopher Lee (Duc de Richelieu), Charles Gray (Mocata), Nike Arrighi (Tanith Carlisle), Leon Greene (Rex Van Ryn), Patrick Mower (Simon Aron), Gwen Ffrangcon Davies (Countess), Sarah Lawson (Marie Eaton), Paul Eddington (Richard Eaton)*
Director: *Terence Fisher*
Screenwriter: *Richard Matheson based on the novel by Dennis Wheatley*
PG/95 mins./Horror/UK

The Duc de Richelieu discovers that his young friend Simon Aron has fallen in with a Satanic cult led by the sinister Mocata. The Duc and his friends try to rescue Simon, but Mocata summons up the forces of darkness to get revenge.

A spirited bit of demon-busting, with a solid Richard Matheson script that streamlines Dennis Wheatley's once-popular but deeply stodgy novel into a pacy occult thriller, this is a more ambitious effort than the average Hammer horror film.

Christopher Lee is cast against type in the Van Helsing role of the heroic, authoritarian goateed wise man who clashes with Charles Gray's suave, sneaky Satanist. Set in the 1920s rather than the 1880s, it has a Bulldog Drummond touch as heroes dash about the home counties in period cars while decadent aristocrats worship the goat-headed one in decorous mass rituals.

The exotic-looking Nike Arrighi is Tanith, predestined to be groped and stabbed on the black altar by the villain, and there's an early example of the revoked plot development as she is killed, then resurrected when white magic rolls back time to provide a happy ending. Terence Fisher, the most prolific of Hammer's in-house directors, does especially well underlining the religious aspects of the epic conflict.

As often happened, an inadequate but heroic hunk (Leon Greene) was dubbed by voice-of-all-work Patrick Allen, but the two-fisted secondary hero still spends most of the film being patronised or shouted at ('you fool, Rex!') by the pompous Duc.

In an unforgettable climax, the heroes (including Sarah Lawson and a young Paul Eddington) huddle in a mystic circle while demon entities rage all around and Lee barks out magic gibberish ('the Unknown Last Line of the Saaamaaa Ritual') to see off the skull-headed Fourth Horseman. Also known as *The Devil's Bride*. ★★★★ **KN**

⊙ THE DEVIL'S ADVOCATE (1997)

Starring: *Keanu Reeves (Kevin Lomax), Al Pacino (John Milton), Charlize Theron (Mary-Ann Lomax), Jeffrey Jones (Eddie Barzoon), Judith Ivey (Mrs. Alice Lomax), Connie Nielsen (Christabella Andreoli)*
Director: *Taylor Hackford*
Screenwriters: *Jonathan Lemkin, Tony Gilroy based on the novel by Andrew Neiderman*
18/144 mins./Drama/Thriller/USA/Germany

Top lawyer Kevin is lured to the big city for the job of a lifetime. He brings his wife Mary-Ann and, at first, everything seems perfect. But soon Kevin starts to get suspicious about his boss.

Eschewing the current trend for CGI by the bucketload, director Hackford convinced Pacino to star by steering away from the effects-laden monster movie of original conception to a more classic struggle, with a villain so old school he's practically the headmaster. There's hell to pay for hot-shot lawyer Kevin Lomax, who's lured by the big bucks/flash pad seduction of a top firm, and ups sticks for NYC with wife Mary-Ann in tow. Also into the bargain comes the rather warm mentorship of fiery-eyed boss John Milton, but despite obvious pointers (constant furnace motifs, 'odd things' happening), Lomax fails to suss that Milton's 'firm' extends a lot further than the office block, and traditionally has need for large toasting forks.

Such implements, however, are not required when the levers of power, sex and prestige can turn a human soul – the film taps into recognisable, viewer-friendly desires. Likewise, Pacino's Dark Prince is wily, lusty and persuasive, but ultimately quite a subtle version of a scheming Old Nick. That said, he wildly over-acts towards the end, but by this stage it's both appropriate and hugely enjoyable and Reeves is just about up to the job as the straight foil. ★★★ **DB**

⊙ THE DEVIL'S OWN (1997)

Starring: *Harrison Ford (Tom O'Meara), Brad Pitt (Rory Devaney/Francis Austin McGuire), Margaret Colin (Sheila O'Meara), Ruben Blades (Edwin Diaz), Treat Williams (Billy Burke), Natascha McElhone (Megan Doherty)*
Director: *Alan J.Pakula*
Screenwriters: *David Aaron Cohen, Vincent Patrick, Kevin Jarre, based on a story by Kevin Jarre*
15/111 mins./Action/Drama/Thriller/USA

After Frankie Maguire sees his father murdered he becomes an IRA activist. On the run and on a mission he stows away with street cop Tom O'Meara and moves to cause havoc, in the form of large numbers of missiles, in New York totally unbeknown to his kind father-figure friend.

With the rare old brouhaha that blew up during shooting – overruns, creative clashes, general script jiggery-pokery and lead actors venting spleen in public – it is hard to be clear-headed about this IRA-themed pot-boiler from *All The President's Men*'s Pakula. For all the smoke there's got to be fire. But while this is by no means the movie it should have been, there is still much to appreciate amid the weaving of plot, the trilling of Gaelic pipes and the blunderbuss approach to evaluating Northern Ireland's eternal conflict. The emphasis on character in *Rambo* scribe Kevin Jarre's screenplay (aided by Vincent Patrick and David Aaron Cohen) gives the film unexpected maturity.

An eight-year-old Frankie Maguire (later played by Pitt) watches his pa take a sectarian bullet and grows up to be an inflamed activist for the IRA. He has no qualms about killing, indeed, barely has the commencing flash-back wilted, than Brad Pitt is spraying dank Ulster streets with ludicrous automatic gunfire. On the run and on a mission, he ships to New York, and a safe haven with unknowing Irish street cop Tom O'Meara. The crux of the matter is that cop and undercover terrorist bond – with Freudian loopiness, O'Meara is touted as some kind of surrogate father figure. All is just too peachy, mind. And as the moralistic cop shares hearth and home, his Provo tenant finalises a shipment of missiles for the cause with shady, clichéd arms dealer Billy Burke. Soon enough, the emerald hued excrement hits the Big Apple fan and the film gets on with being a thriller (as the Burke deal sours, balaclava'd thuggery enters the mix).

Pakula is one for the slow build. Too much time is spent showing what a do-gooder Ford is – his expert human characterisation has already done the trick – with extraneous policing sub-plots and twee family gatherings. However, in keeping the terrorism to the sidelines it becomes harder and harder to accept Pitt as the cold-hearted killer and the jolt into the closing chase sequence is effectively harsh. Predictably, as Pitt flips and hits the street it is the big-hearted cop who elects to bring him in alive, never quite shaking those son-he-never-had feelings. What the film really gets arse-about-face is its political bearing.

It's a tasty moral conundrum – true killers can have a human side; what do you do if you love them? Choosing to hang it round the mess of Northern Ireland was foolishness. Big movies have rarely grasped the political sensitivity of the region (for every *Michael Collins* there is a *Blown Away*), and here the naiveté is rife. Yes, it's more switched on than *Patriot Games*' maddo IRA faction, and Pitt does better with the accent than you'd expect, but turning the whole thing into a dogged Western and offering an idiotic redemption for the confused terrorist will leave a bad taste in many mouths.

Better, then, to keep your mind open, shrug off the controversy, dismiss the scuttlebutt and bad-mouthing and enjoy a couple of zinger performances in a solid if uneven game of movie cat and mouse. ★★ **IN**

⊙ LES DIABOLIQUES (DIABOLIQUE) (1955)

Starring: *Simone Signoret (Nicole Horner), Vera Clouzot (Christina Delasalle), Paul Meurisse (Michel Delasalle), Charles Vanel (Inspector Fichet), Jean Brochard (Plantiveau)*
Director: *Henri-Georges Clouzot*
Screenwriters: *Henri-Georges Clouzot, Jerome Geronimi, Frédéric Grendel, René Masson, from the novel* Celle Qui N'était Pas *by Pierre Boileau, Thomas Narcejac*
15/92 mins./Horror/Mystery/Thriller/France

The wife and mistress of a sadistic boarding school headmaster plot to kill him. They drown him in the bathtub and dump the body in the school's filthy swimming pool. But when the pool is drained, the body has disappeared – and subsequent reported sightings of the headmaster slowly drive his 'killers' crazy.

Banish all memories of the Sharon Stone remake – Henri-Georges Clouzot's original is the real deal.

The scheming mistress of a callous school headmaster team persuades the headmaster's heiress wife (also wife of the director) that murdering him would be a solution to all their problems. But their plan appears to have backfired when his body goes missing and school children report seeing the victim alive and well.

Clouzot plays deftly with audience expectation and as the story unfolds so the suspense deepens.

In its brilliant handling of horror-thriller conventions, *Les Diaboliques* is to European cinema what *Psycho* is to Hollywood, with an ending that provides the superb climax to an atmospheric chiller. ★★★★ **PW**

⊙ DIAL M FOR MURDER (1954)

Starring: *Ray Milland (Tony Wendice), Grace Kelly (Margot Wendice), Robert Cummings (Mark Halliday), John Williams (Chief Inspector Hubbard), Anthony Dawson (Captain Swan Lesgate), Leo Britt (The Narrator)*
Director: *Alfred Hitchcock*
Screenwriter: *Frederick Knott based on his own play*
PG/105 mins./Thriller/USA

Margot Wendice is framed for murder when she stabs the hitman hired by her cuckolded husband, Tony. However, he hadn't counted on the

tenacity of her whodunit-writing lover Mark Halliday and Chief Inspector Hubbard of Scotland Yard.

Alfred Hitchcock was struggling with a project called *The Bramble Bush*, a mistaken identity yarn about a crook who steals a murderer's passport, when he agreed to direct Frederick Knott's adaptation of his own stage success. He was never particularly fond of the film. Yet it remains one of his most bleakly amusing and it also reveals a good deal about his approach to film-making.

Knott's play had premiered on the BBC in March 1952 before running for 425 performances in the West End and a further 552 on Broadway. It was a neatly constructed affair, although hardly original, as it bore the influence of both the real-life case of ex-RAF officer Neville Heath (who had been executed for the murder of two women) and St John L. Clowes's thriller, *Dear Murderer*, which had been filmed by Arthur Crabtree with Eric Portman in 1947.

Warners had acquired the rights for £30,000 from Sir Alexander Korda (who had originally paid a mere £1,000 for them) and Hitchcock made few alterations to Knott's screenplay. Indeed, Hitch seemed to be more interested in setting himself technical difficulties than in teasing the audience. As he had demonstrated with *Rope* (1948) and would do again with his next picture, *Rear Window* (1954), Hitchcock saw no need to open out the action for the sake of it and relished the chance to play claustrophobic games with the décor of a single set. Such confinement intensified the action and he further heightened it here by his mischievous use of 3-D. Whereas most directors settled for hurling a few objects towards the camera to give the viewer a visceral thrill, Hitch used the extra dimension to highlight props and angles and, thus, create a more dislocated atmosphere. He employed colour in a similar way, gradually removing warmer hues to emphasise the chill of reality closing in around Grace Kelly.

Ray Milland oozes suburban malice. But Kelly simpers occasionally as the abused adulteress, while Robert Cummings is blandness personified as her beau. The star turn, however, is John Williams' disarmingly dapper detective. ★★★ **DP**

DIAMONDS ARE FOREVER (1971)

Starring: *Sean Connery (James Bond), Jill St. John (Tiffany Case), Charles Gray (Ernst Stavro Blofeld), Lana Wood (Plenty O'Toole), Jimmy Dean (Willard Whyte), Bruce Cabot (Saxby)*
Director: *Guy Hamilton*
Screenwriters: *Richard Maibaum, Tony Mankiewicz based on the novel by Ian Fleming*
PG/118 mins./Spy/Adventure/UK

Thinking he has, at last, ridden the world of his archenemy Ernst Stavro Blofeld, James Bond follows the case of a large amount of stolen diamonds where all the smugglers who handle the gems are being bumped off. As he follows the plot, it turns out Blofeld might not be so dead.

After the minor débâcle of George Lazenby's momentary tenure as 007, the Bond producers offered Connery a hefty paycheck to return to the fold for one last hurrah. The result, while never losing Bond's populist streak (it was another big hit), reveals more cracks than it ought. Connery ageing quickly, his hairline indeterminately assisted, doesn't fully recapture the swagger of his halcyon adventures. The plot, one of Ian Fleming's better, is effectively unusual for its first half – a genuine piece of global policing for the British agent as he traces the diamond-studded clues from Amsterdam to Las Vegas (this remains the most Americanised of all the films), but here it founders with the re-appearance of Charles Gray, the third and least of the actors to play Blofeld. He's too smug and comic, with none of the deep freeze of Donald Pleasence. The big finale, wastefully spilling about an oilrig off the Californian coast, is a washout compared to the glorious, Ken Adams-designed uber-bases we were accustomed to.

Cubby Broccoli and Harry Saltzman, Bond's guiding lights, were furiously trying to recapture the glory of *Goldfinger*, Bond's high-water mark, corralling its director Guy Hamilton, writer Richard Maibaum and Welsh diva Shirley Bassey for a second opportunity to roll her tonsils around a theme song (a good one). But it feels distant, an echo of the elegance and restraint of *Goldfinger*, with too much emphasis on action (a dumb moonbuggy chase through the Nevada desert is a limp effort) and acute violence (Bambi and Thumper, two sexy acrobats, beat seven bells out of poor 007 in a scene that slips dangerously outside of the fantasy milieu). Only, the cool frisson in having Bond play the gaudy tables of Vegas, a reverse of the lavish world of Monte Carlo; Jill St John's sassy redhead and the camp duo of henchmen, Mr. Kidd and Mr. Wint (Putter Smith and Bruce Glover), assassins with a horribly leery modus operandi, stand the test of time. The main-man Connery is evidently back against his better judgment and no amount of John Barry scoring, and fierce pyrotechnics could finally reignite the lustre of his heyday. ★★★ **IN**

DIARY OF A COUNTRY PRIEST (1950)

Starring: *Claude Laydu (Priest of Ambricourt), Jean Riveyre (Count), André Guibert (Priest of Torcy), Nicole Maurey (Louise), Nicole Ladmiral (Chantal), Marie Monique Arkeil (Countess)*
Director: *Robert Bresson*
Screenwriter: *Robert Bresson based on the novel by Georges Bernanos*
U/120 mins./Drama/France

Suffering from stomach cancer, a young priest arrives in the godless parish of Ambricourt in northern France and becomes mired in the complex domestic discord involving a disaffected count, his tormented wife, his scheming daughter Chantal and his governess mistress, Louise.

Thwarted in his bid to film a life of St Ignatius Loyola, Robert Bresson embarked on this faithful adaptation of Georges Bernanos' novel. The late author had already rejected treatments by both the celebrated screenwriters Jean Aurenche and Pierre Bost, and by Fr. Raymond Brückberger, but his estate approved Bresson's austere approach, which retained the journalistic structure, while removing the lengthy theological and sociological diatribes delivered by the Priest of Torcy.

Indeed, the dialogue was taken almost verbatim from the text. But this was not so much a movie than a meditation on the curé's quest for salvation for both himself and his flock. Bresson offers us reflections on events rather than the incidents themselves, hence his emphasis on the voice-over narration and pages from the diary, which lead us into elliptical sequences which present only the dramatic essentials so as not to distract us from the interiority of the action.

This was a new kind of film-making, in which Bresson moved away from traditional 'cinema', with its focus on externals, to champion 'cinematography', which attempted to chronicle a character's inner life. To achieve this he conducted an extensive search for a Catholic non-actor, whose performance he could completely control. Claude Laydu was a 22-year-old Swiss, who met with Bresson every Sunday for a year and even spent time in a monastery to assume the mien and mannerisms of a conflicted cleric. But, he is as much a prop as the simple objects which Bresson uses to define the priest's humble, rootless existence, in which we are forced to share by the insistent close-ups.

This absence of establishing shots, the scarcity of camera movements and the stylistic purity of scenes limited to fundamental information stunned the cinematic establishment. But, like Carl Theodor Dreyer before him, Bresson succeeded in combining asceticism with spirituality and although the priest's journey recalls the Stations of the Cross, its simple humanity makes this much more than a mere religious experience. ★★★★★ **DP**

Bands Inspired by Movies — TOP 10

	Band	Film	Inspiration
1	Duran Duran	Barbarella	Villain played by Milo O'Shea
2	Travis	Paris, Texas	Antihero played by Harry Dean Stanton
3	Black Rebel Motorcycle Club	The Wild One	A posse of bike-riding hooligans
4	Black Sabbath	Black Sabbath	1963 horror movie with Boris Karloff
5	Mogwai	Gremlins	A gremlin before he turns nasty
6	Moloko	A Clockwork Orange	A milk drink
7	Nerfherder	The Empire Strikes Back	A creature mentioned in Princess Leia dialogue
8	Mudhoney	Mudhoney	A 1965 Russ Meyer film
9	They Might Be Giants	They Might Be Giants	A 1971 Sherlock Holmes movie
10	McFly	Back To The Future	Surname of the hero played by Michael J Fox

THE DIARY OF ANNE FRANK (1959)

Starring: *Millie Perkins (Anne Frank), Joseph Schildkraut (Otto Frank), Shelley Winters (Mrs Van Daan), Richard Beymer (Peter Van Daan), Gusti Huber (Edith Frank)*
Director: *George Stevens*
Screenwriters: *Francis Goodrich, Albert Hackett based on the play and autobiography* Anne Frank: Diary Of A Young Girl
U/170 mins./War/USA
Awards: *Academy Awards – Best Supporting Actress (Shelley Winters), Best Art Direction-Set Decoration, Cinematography*

Thirteen year-old Anne Frank begins keeping a record of her experiences after her family joins the Van Daans and an ageing dentist in the attic sanctuary provided by an Amsterdam merchant and his wife.

George Stevens led a US Army Film Unit during the Second World War, becoming the first to record the horrors of the Nazi death camps when he entered Dachau in 1945. His colour footage of the survivors and the pitiful conditions in which they had been incarcerated remains chilling in its stark realism and it's easy to understand why he would have felt moved to make this adaptation of Frances Goodrich and Albert Hackett's play. What's less comprehensible, however, is why he would have opted to shoot the film in black and white and widescreen.

Presumably, he felt (much as Steven Spielberg would later do with *Schindler's List*) that monochrome brought a sense of gravitas to proceedings that were already laudably sombre. But whatever sense of place or suspense he sought through Oscar-winning cinematographer William C. Mellor's artful manipulation of light and shade is dissipated by the clumsy use of CinemaScope. Any feeling of claustrophobia and the desperate endurance required to remain in such close confinement for two years is lost in compositions that make the attic space above the spice shop at 263 Prinzengracht seem positively cavernous.

The tone of the film similarly tends to the grandiose. Anyone familiar with *Anne Frank: The Diary of a Young Girl* will know that its impact lies as much in her charming naiveté as much as in the portent of the situations she describes. But Goodrich and Hackett's screenplay is less concerned with the alternate optimism and uncertainty of a teenage girl and focuses instead on the contrasting temperaments of her companions. Thus, everyone is given their set-piece moment and, as a consequence, blowsier performances like Shelley Winters' Mrs Van Daan are allowed to overshadow more considered work by the likes of Joseph Schildkraut, Gusti Huber and Diane Baker as Otto, Edith and Margot Frank.

For all its faults, this remains a moving tribute to some quietly heroic victims of barbarism. But, even in its restored 170-minute version, it only tells part of the story. ★★★ **DP**

DICK TRACY (1990)

Starring: *Warren Beatty (Dick Tracy), Charlie Korsmo (Kid), Glenne Headly (Tess Trueheart), Madonna (Breathless Mahoney), Al Pacino (Big Boy Caprice), Dustin Hoffman (Mumbles), William Forsythe (Flattop), Charles Durning (Chief Brandon), Mandy Patinkin (88 Keys), Paul Sorvino (Lips Manlis)*
Director: *Warren Beatty*
Screenwriters: *Jim Cash, Jack Epps Jr based on the characters created by Chester Gould*
PG/103 mins./Action/Crime/Fantasy/USA
Awards: *Academy Awards – Best Art Direction/Set Decoration, Best Makeup, Best Original Song (Sooner or Later (I Always Get My Man) by Stephen Sondheim), BAFTA – Best Makeup, Best Production Design*

Straight cop Dick Tracy has his hands full tracking down the mob connection of Big Boy Caprice and his army of wise guys – but he also has to deal with the attentions of singer Breathless Mahoney, who threatens his relationship with his girl, Tess Trueheart.

Boasting astonishing visual pizzazz – courtesy of production designer Richard Sylbert and cinematographer Vittorio Storaro – every scene offers optical overload as Beatty's yellow-clad crimefighter walks through astonishingly realised comic book gangster locales to battle mob boss Al Pacino. Virtually every frame looks like it came straight from a comic book, with Beatty's noble hero facing a Who's Who of villains.

Sure, the plotting is no great shakes, but there's enough to keep you going between showdowns with some of Hollywood's finest, and some pretty decent torch songs by Madonna's Jessica Rabbit-like Breathless Mahoney. ★★★ **IF**

DIE ANOTHER DAY (2002)

Starring: *Pierce Brosnan (James Bond), Halle Berry (Jinx), Toby Stephens (Gustav Graves), Rosamund Pike (Miranda Frost), Judi Dench (M), John Cleese (Q), Michael Madsen (Damian Falco), Emilio Echevarria (Raoul), Colin Salmon (Charles Robinson), Samantha Bond (Miss Moneypenny), Madonna (Verity) (Uncredited)*
Director: *Lee Tamahori*
Screenwriters: *Neal Purvis, Robert Wade, based on characters created by Ian Fleming*
12/133 mins./Action/Adventure/Thriller/UK/USA
Awards: *Empire Awards – Best Newcomer (Rosamund Pike), Razzie – Worst Supporting Actress (Madonna)*

Betrayed by an MI6 mole, James Bond is captured by the North Koreans, tortured and exchanged for an enemy agent. Out for revenge, 007 heads first to Havana, where he meets American agent Jinx, then to London and Iceland to investigate flamboyant entrepreneur Gustav Graves, who has created a satellite with deadly purposes.

While everyone has been busy getting all misty-eyed about 40 splendid years of indentured service, Kiwi bright spark Tamahori had the onerous task of shifting Bond into the new cinema order while not tampering with still very capable circuitry. Mission: unresolved, for this is a strange and unfulfilling beast, neither a reinvention nor a celebration of the dutiful gadgets/girls/cars/fruitcake-billionaire-imperils-the-world formula, but an intermittently entertaining patchwork of both.

The plot-line undoubtedly sounded hip and risky at brain-storming meetings: adding a detective element, being daring enough to lock Bond up over the opening credits, making Halle Berry a partner for the leading man rather than a simpering bed-fellow. However, there are just too many twists and extraneous strands for the running time to cope with. It's not a lack of effort but a lack of restraint that makes it such a muddle; Tamahori flooding the screen with good intentions, idea upon idea piling up like a car crash.

Ironically, that's exactly what is missing – the clarity and expertise to pull off a simple car chase, or exploding military hovercraft, or kung fu fight on a ditching cargo plane. The blunted, hectic editing leaves the film agitated and graceless. The execution is so complex, so riddled with afterthought, it makes a mess of the clean linear lines that made the formula so successful. And CGI this poor is embarrassing.

But before you lose faith and head for your *Dr. No* special edition, amid the desperation to fend off such brash, leadless newcomers as *xXx*, the grand traditions and great scenes emerge. Bond duels with Graves in a posturing fencing match, crashing through a starchy gentlemen's club with magnificent gusto. Leering henchman Rick Yune has diamonds embedded in his scarred mug, and multiple *Goldfinger*-style laserbeams turn a punch-up into a freaky dance number. They make you want to cheer with relief.

Die Another Day is also very sexy. Berry, restricted by a one-dimensional character, makes no bones about which gadgets she has at her disposal. All told, the camera spends more time perusing her chest than it does the sleek bonnet of the new Aston Martin, while Pike makes for an enticing contrast, an ice-cold MI6 agent throwing frosty barbs in the direction of Bond's libido. In fact, all the cast more than pass muster.

Toby Stephens proves the most buoyant and happily hammy of all Brosnan's foes, recast by a madcap gene therapy into a dapper splice of Richard Branson and Hugh Grant's evil twin. Although, when you boil down his motive, he is a tad conflicted as to whether capitalism or communism is the raw material for his devilry. Let's forget Madonna's cameo, it's as half-witted as her dreadful theme song.

And throughout it all, Brosnan is the glue that keeps the film from descending into parody. He is now so confident flipping from gritty determination to louche chauvinism, you can feel him slip nuances beneath his director's nose. As his films get more chaotic, he gets subtler. 007 even gets his first orgasm for 40 years; no wonder he's got a spring in his step. ★★★ **IN**

⓪ DIE HARD (1988)

Starring: *Bruce Willis (John McClane), Reginald VelJohnson (Sgt. Al Powell), Bonnie Bedelia (Holly Gennero McClane), Alexander Godunov (Karl), Alan Rickman (Hans Gruber)*
Director: *John McTiernan*
Screenwriters: *Jeb Stuart, Steven E. de Souza*
18/131 mins./Action/Crime/Thriller/USA

When German terrorists invade the Nakatomi Plaza Hotel and take the occupants hostage only man – New York City Cop John McClane – can stop them.

A critically-acclaimed character actor best known for his performances in such erudite BBC fair as *Smiley's People* and *The Barchester Chronicles*, Alan Rickman raised more than a few eyebrows when he crossed the pond to play *Die Hard*'s skyscraper-hijacking German super-criminal Hans Gruber. 'I'd never picked up a machine gun before, or even a handgun,' he said, shortly after the movie's release. 'But I thought it could turn out to be a fabulous film. Something like the best ride at the funfair. That's why I did it.'

He was right, and then some. A thrill-packed *Boy's Own* adventure that follows New York cop Bruce Willis' shirtless (and agonizingly shoeless) John McClane as he attempts to rescue wife Bonnie Bedelia from the clutches of Rickman and his gang of heavily armed robbers. It is no small irony, therefore, that the book which provided *Die Hard*'s inspiration, *Nothing Lasts Forever*, was written by detective Roderick Thorp, a man who knew all too well that the average copper's daily grind tends not to feature an excess of international villain-oriented skullduggery. 'Really, police work is just grinding it out,' the author subsequently explained. '[In a movie] usually the first thing that happens is our hero arrives on the scene, gets out of the car, runs up the steps past the uniformed guard on the door and picks up the phone. The phone hasn't been dusted for fingerprints yet! He already screwed up! And they don't get the dead bodies right at all. A corpse is a horrifying thing. The glazed eyes. The frozen fingers. The smile, which is a matter of the muscles tightening and the teeth being exposed – you never see that.'

Indeed, Thorp's hero – called Joe Leland in the books – had previously been portrayed by Frank Sinatra in the gritty 1968 movie *The Detective*. When producer Joel Silver decided to adapt *Nothing Lasts Forever* for the big screen, however, it wasn't just the names he decided to change. Silver had already struck gold on *Lethal Weapon* (1987), transforming the up-and-coming Mel Gibson into a superhero with a badge. He decided to repeat the trick with *Die Hard* by recruiting Bruce Willis. At the time Willis was still considered very much a TV star thanks to his stint on the hugely successful but hardly action-packed *Moonlighting*. *Die Hard*'s original poster did not even feature the actor's likeness because it was feared that this might actually put cinemagoers off. In retrospect, of course, there is no doubt that the perennially smirking Willis contributed mightily to the film's enormous success as he traded blows and quips with equal assurance.

Actually, the script is so heavy with yucks that even the smallest of characters, like the pair of humourless FBI agents, are handed lines infinitely superior to those spoken by most action movie leads. The film's real star, though, is director John McTiernan whose demolition-heavy vision – brilliantly shot by future *Speed* helmer *Jan de Bont* – marked him out as, arguably, second only to James Cameron in the pure action stakes. The result even pleased author Thorp, despite the liberties which McTiernan and Silver had taken. 'What they wanted to make was what you saw, which was a slam-bang action film,' the detective concluded. 'I'm very happy with it. Minor quibbles – but you can nit-pick anything if you want to.'

One group of people who didn't nit-pick were the studio execs who, inspired by the film's boffo box office returns, began greenlighting a slew of knock-offs including *Die Hard On A Boat (Under Siege)*, *Die Hard In A Sports Stadium (Sudden Death)*, *Die Hard On A Train (Under Siege II)* and *Die Hard On A Bloody Big Mountain (Cliffhanger)*. Meanwhile, the franchise itself would spawn two sequels: Renny Harlin directed the fairly duff *Die Hard II* before McTiernan returned for the substantially better third instalment. Rumours also persist that a fourth movie is on its way, with the most recent

---

Movie Trivia: Die Hard

The teddy bear that John McClane is carrying with him on the plane in the opening scenes when he is in the airport is the same one that Jack Ryan (William Baldwin) carries with him on the plane in *The Hunt For Red October*. The bodycount in *Die Hard* is 18 in comparison with 164 for *Die Hard 2*. The Nakatomi Plaza is actually the 20th Century Fox building based in Century City, California.

---

scenario finding John McClane battling villainry in the South American jungle. Incidentally, McTiernan's original film proved just as popular in Germany as everywhere else following the decison to transform Rickman's gang of thieves from Teutonic terrormongers into the far less contentious 'Europeans.' ★★★★★ **CC**

DIE HARD 2 (1990)

Starring: *Bruce Willis (John McClane), Bonnie Bedelia (Holly McClane), William Atherton (Richard Thornburg), William Sadler (Col. Stuart)*
Director: *Renny Harlin*
Screenwriters: *Steven E. de Souza, Doug Richardson, based on the novel* 58 Minutes *by Walter Wager*
15/124 mins./Action/Adventure/Thriller/USA

Christmas time again. John McClane is at Dulles Airport in Washington, waiting for his wife to arrive for Christmas with their families, when he discovers a plot to take control of the airport. Soon, a new group of mercenaries are making demands, holding the circling planes hostage while McClane sets off to find and stop them.

Pretty much an object lesson in sequel making, Renny Harlin's follow up to the action classic delivers just enough knowing nods ('How can the same thing happen to the same guy twice?' wails Willis), while notching up the explosion quotient. Only William Sadler as villain Col. Stuart lets it down somewhat, delivering a serviceable performance but one that nowhere near rivals Alan Rickman's sneering incarnation of pure evil.

It's entertaining nonsense that doesn't quite manage to recapture the magic of the original. Still, there are some nice moments here, and Willis is on solid ground as the iconic McClane. ★★★ **AC**

DIE HARD WITH A VENGEANCE (1995)

Starring: *Bruce Willis (John McClane), Samuel L. Jackson (Zeus Carver), Jeremy Irons (Simon Gruber), Graham Greene (Joe Lambert), Colleen Camp (Cannie Kowalski)*
Director: *John McTiernan*
Screenwriters: *Jonathan Hensleigh, Roderick Thorp*
15/131 mins./Action/USA

Another very bad day begins in the life of Detective John McClane, when a bomb goes off on the streets of New York. Then a man named 'Simon' calls the authorities demanding McClane joins in a game of Simon Says otherwise more bombs will go off.

While most of us were pondering the next urban cage in which John McClane will be reduced to his vest, facing off against some nefarious criminal scheme (shopping mall? Subway train? Oilrig?) original director John McTiernan and the writer of *Die Harder* decided to spin the basic idea on its head. For the third, and to date final, *Die Hard* the boundaries are New York itself, McClane's home turf, and the deadly game is entirely personal. It was considered thinking, but partnering McClane with irascible Harlem shop owner Samuel L. Jackson immediately reduced the lone wolf qualities of one of Hollywood's most worthwhile franchises. This is a buddy-buddy romp of good order but scant inspiration and not quite the *Die Hardest* we were looking for.

The idea is that the villain of the first (and still best) blitzkrieg of action, Alan Rickman's Hans Gruber, has left a brother keen on exacting revenge. McClane is forced into dashing about Manhattan, picking up Jackson as a passenger in the process, to solve various riddles. It's a structural conceit that keeps the film hurtling along, and McTiernan ably contrasts the nightfall of the previous film with the sweltering glare of a New York summer day (a better reason to get down to that vest). This is *Die Hard* inverted. Therefore, for all its consummate actioneering, and the film opens dramatically with a sudden screen-shuddering explosion like a gung-ho calling card – we're back! – it lacks the vital claustrophobia and that wry notion that, more than the baddies' devilry, the fates themselves are aligned against Bruce Willis' plaintive hero.

The soap opera that is McClane's life remains in full gear, he's back on the booze, suspended from the force and his marriage is in tatters – although Bonnie Bedelia, his on-off wife, opted out of a third film and her absence is felt. *Vengeance* lacks the spare design of before, that McClane must overcome these ridiculous odds ultimately to mend his relationship. And while Willis has the role down pat and Jackson does his loud, proud thing, Jeremy Irons' sneering and snorting Euro-git is long way shy of Rickman's gleaming villainy. It's fun, in that crazy-hectic, no-expense spared approach of good action movies, McClane remains a very likeable hero, he has Indiana Jones' why-me exasperation, a man who would rather be anywhere else. It's just that this time, his day just got that bit too complicated. ★★★ **IN**

DIG! (2004)

Starring: *As themselves: Anton Newcombe, Courtney Taylor-Taylor, Joel Gion, Matt Hollywood, Peter Holmstrom, Zia McCabe, Brent DeBoer, Eric Hedford, Dean Taylor*
Director: *Ondi Timoner*
Screenwriter: *Ondi Timoner*
15/107 mins./Documentary/Music/USA

Seven years in the making, this documentary tracks then-unknown, US bands The Dandy Warhols and The Brian Jonestown Massacre as they launch their musical careers. Pretty soon the Dandys make it big, while Jonestown start to crumble under the weight of their frontman's ego . . .

You've heard about the successful band that implodes in a frenzy of clashing egos and copious drugs. Now hear about the unsigned band that reaches rock meltdown way ahead of widespread recognition and fat paycheques. Our troubled troubadours are retro-psychedelics The Brian Jonestown Massacre, and this rock opera of a documentary follows them as they kick-start a 'musical revolution' along with soulmates The Dandy Warhols.

Thing is, while the Dandys bugger off to Europe and make it big, the apparently more talented Jonestown achieve devolution, not revolution, shedding band members like confetti, and the only thing lead man Anton Newcombe kicks is a punter's face after he's heckled on stage. But what filmmaker Ondi Timoner is left with is a gripping record of creative angst and deteriorating relationships.

DiG! is a dizzying collage, thrumming with the energy of a live performance; a jam session of colour and monochrome, a medley of performances, arguments and parties. With its epic timeframe – Timoner cut from 1,500 hours of footage – this is the documentarian's equivalent of the Method. Living, touring and partying with her subjects, Timoner puts us centre-front for the gig.

We're there as Jonestown get busted for drugs, as their manager deserts mid-tour, as they hoover narcotics from the coffee table. And the spectacle of the unfolding inter-band schism is grimly hilarious, culminating with Newcombe delivering shotgun shells to the Dandys' dressing room. In equal measure, moments of pathos permeate, such as when a maudlin Joel Gion (the band's scene-stealing Bez figure) reflects on how he's wasted four years being little more than a drug-addled tambourine man.

As riveting as this mêlee of spiralling egos is, *DiG!* earns its fifth and final star as a microcosm of 'indie' music on the cusp of corporate takeover. Stupendous serendipity has gifted Timoner the perfect parable of the 1990s music industry. While Newcombe's deranged commitment to the indie spirit precludes his success, The Dandys trigger a new, thoroughly modern mechanism of music marketing, becoming huge off a mobile phone advert. Where once plugging a product would be the death-knell for artistic credibility, in these days of corporate cool-hunters and sponsored tours, it's almost a prerequisite. ★★★★★ **S O'H**

③ DINOSAUR (2000)

Starring: *the voices of: D.B. Sweeney (Aladar), Alfre Woodard (Plio), Ossie Davis (Yar), Max Casella (Zini), Hayden Panettiere (Suri), Samuel E. Wright (Kron), Julianna Margulies (Neera), Joan Plowright (Baylene), Della Reese (Eema)*
Director: *Eric Leighton, Ralph Zondag*
Screenwriters: *John Harrison, Robert Nelson Jacobs, from a story by Robert Nelson Jacobs, Ralph Zondag, from an earlier screenplay by Walon Green, with story by Thom Enriquez and John Harrison, with additional story by Tamara Lusher, Shirley Pierce, Rhett Reese*
PG/82 mins./Animation/Family/Adventure/USA

The late Cretaceous era. A stray egg hatched by lemur-like apes grows to be a humane-but-rebel dinosaur Aladar. After a meteor storm holocaust, Aladar and his family join an exodus across the desert in seach of the perhaps illusory 'nesting grounds'.

Though it doesn't add up to much more than a photo-realistic redo of that regular cartoon *The Land Before Time* (1988), this prehistoric trek follows the *Toy Story* movies (1995, 1999) and *A Bug's Life* (1999) by being another major advance in the field of CGI animation, with entirely convincing backgrounds – including tricky stuff like water, fire, leaves and fur – as well as easy-peasy desert and rocks.

Sadly, the personal strands that emerge along the trek aren't too interesting and are hindered by thin vocal characterisations. Moreover, there are no songs to leaven the journey for the kiddies, resulting in a tone that is far more downbeat than most Disney summer output. However, augmented by a typically bombastic James Newton Howard score that owes more than a nod and a wink to *The Lion King* (1994), the sweeping visions are often astonishing, with as many tiny felicities as the bigthinks moments.

It is a long way from both the fantasies of *One Million Years BC* (1966) or *When Dinosaurs Ruled The Earth* (1969), in which great lizards and cavemen live at the same time, but its commitment to palaeontological credibility still takes a back seat to storytelling, with a lot more disaster and conflict than leaf-munching and hibernating. ★★★ **KN**

③ DIRTY DANCING (1987)

Starring: *Jennifer Grey (Frances 'Baby' Houseman), Patrick Swayze (Johnny Castle), Jerry Orbach (Dr. Jake Houseman), Cynthia Rhodes (Penny Johnson), Jack Weston (Max Kellerman), Jane Brucker (Lisa Houseman), Kelly Bishop (Marjorie Houseman)*
Director: *Emille Ardolino*
Screenwriter: *Eleanor Bergstein*
12A/100 mins./Romance/Drama/Musical/USA

Awards: *Academy Awards – Best Original Song ('(I've Had) The Time Of My Life')*

In the summer of 1963, Baby goes to a mountain holiday resort with her parents and sister. There, she meets dance teacher Johnny Castle, who teaches her how to move, and with whom she falls in love. But things are never quite that simple . . .

Dirty Dancing's standing as one of the 80s most memorable teen movies is due as much to the phenomenon than the film itself. Virtually every twenty-something woman in the modern world watched it as a pre-teen (drawn in by that slightly naughty title) and was won over by the film's sweet-but-not-schmaltzy vision of first love. Then, of course, there are the many otherwise normal people out there who can recite the entire script, sing all the songs and have watched the film an unhealthy number of times. But the film's appeal isn't just down to the hype that surrounds it.

The story of the girl (Grey) who gets lessons in dance – and lurve – amounts to little more than feel-good fluff. But both leads give it their best shot, with Swayze on fine hip-swinging form and Grey acting and actually looking like Jane Average, rather than a supermodel in a pair of glasses. And then there's that cheesy yet perfect dialogue. 'No one puts Baby in the corner'; 'I carried a watermelon?'; 'You're wild!' – it ain't Shakespeare, but thanks to a strange sort of alchemy, it goes through so-bad-it's-good territory and back out into the clear waters of genius.

But perhaps the film's real staying power comes from the fact that, while everyone remembers the dancing and the (many) comic moments, there are touches of real darkness here too – racism, backstreet abortions, infidelity. It's that dark background that allows the love story to shine more brightly, and provides that huge emotional high when the dancing begins.

Endlessly quotable, strangely fascinating and immensely charming, there's a reason that this retains an evergreen appeal. And it takes a hard heart not to grin at the final, euphoric dance number. The fact that it spawned one of the biggest-selling soundtracks ever (yes, people paid good money to own something featuring Patrick Swayze singing), a sell-out concert tour, a (lesser) sequel and a stage musical shows how people have taken it to their hearts. ★★★★ **CW**

③ THE DIRTY DOZEN (1967)

Starring: *Lee Marvin (Maj. Reisman), Ernest Borgnine (Gen. Worden), Charles Bronson (Joseph Wladislaw), Jim Brown (Robert Jefferson), John Cassavetes (Victor Franko), Richard Jaeckel (Sgt. Bowren), George Kennedy (Maj. Max Armbruster), Trini Lopez (Pedro Jiminez), Ralph Meeker (Capt. Stuart Kinder), Robert Ryan (Col. Everett Dasher-Breed)*
Director: *Robert Aldrich*
Screenwriters: *Lukas Heller, Nunnally Johnson, based on the novel by E.M. Nathanson*
15/149 mins./War/Drama/Action/UK

Awards: *Academy Awards – Best Sound Effects*

It is 1944 and the Allied Armies stand ready for a major invasion of Germany from bases in England. As a prelude to D-Day, US Army Intelligence orders a top secret mission where convicted criminals will be offered a pardon in return for parachuting into the Reich on a suicide mission.

Dirty Dozen director Robert Aldrich once commented, 'I wouldn't win the Academy Award if I filmed the Second Coming.' Of course, what he failed to mention was that any Aldrich-directed religious event would doubtless have featured more shooting, fighting and all-round machismo-fuelled mayhem than even the most apocalyptic of doomsayers could predict. For, although Aldrich did direct a handful of movies which focused on women not least *Whatever Happened To Baby Jane?* (1962) he is best remembered for such testosterone-infused ventures as *Kiss Me Deadly* (1955), *Flight Of The Phoenix* (1965), *The Longest Yard* (1974) and *The Dirty Dozen*.

'If my films have any central theme it is that a man is bigger than the things around him,' Aldrich explained towards the end of his career. 'You can measure him not by his success but by the way he struggles.' Certainly *The Dirty Dozen* featured its fair share of struggles, both on-screen and off. What on paper looked like pure gold – the tale of an American major who convinces 12 army prisoners to join him on what is virtually a suicide mission behind enemy lines, with pretty much every member of the cast a star in his own right – often threatened to deteriorate into trash as those stars came into conflict with each other during the shoot in Borehamwood.

Notably fractious was the relationship between Charles Bronson and notorious hell-raiser Lee Marvin. 'Bronson was in the sequence where he and Lee, in a giant weapons carrier, go across the bridge after the big explosion,' producer Kenneth Hyman later recalled. 'Well, Lee didn't show up. I drove to London, straight to the Star Tavern in Belgravia. Lee was hanging on at the end of the bar apparently as drunk as a skunk. Now he is the man who has to drive that vehicle across the bridge. I get him into the car and feed him like a child from a flask of coffee. We arrived on the set and got out of the car. Bronson was standing at the back of the chateau where he'd been waiting for Marvin to show. We pulled in and Lee sort of fell out of the car. Charlie says, "I'm going to fucking kill you, Lee!" And I go through my routine: "Don't hit him, Charlie – don't punch him."'

Remarkably, according to Hyman, once Bronson had been mollified,

Marvin did drive the weapons carrier across the bridge: 'He always came through. There were several moments in the production when he probably couldn't have articulated his own name. But you'd never know it from the sure way in which he moved.'

Further problems were caused by the sheer volume of sound coming from the production. Eventually, Aldrich was given 14 days' notice to make less noise after Borehamwood resident Mrs Helen James complained, 'For three weeks we've been kept awake by machine-gun fire, explosions and I don't know what.' Over three decades after the event it has to be said that Mrs James' inconvenience seems like a small price to pay.

It is here that we learn to recognise, if not necessarily identify with, such characters as John Cassavetes' surly Franko, or Telly Savalas' downright psychotic Maggott as they outwit again and again Marvin's arch enemy, the by-the-book Colonel Breed (Robert Ryan). There is no doubt, though, that *The Dirty Dozen* belongs to the granite-faced Marvin himself who, although often very funny, never looks anything other than the WWII vet that he actually was. *The Dirty Dozen* would not win an Academy Award for Aldrich, who died in 1983. But it remains a high watermark for movies about tough-guys-being-tough-together, as director Joe Dante recognised when he recruited surviving cast members Ernest Borgnine, Clint Walker, Jim Brown and George Kennedy to voice characters in his tough-toys-being-tough-together movie *Small Soldiers* (1998).

Such recognition would doubtless have pleased Aldrich, although not as much as the fact that his film proved to be one of MGM's most successful movies of all time. For, as the director pointed out after its release in typically hard-nosed style, 'My first duty is to those who put up the money. Everyone would like an artistic triumph. But it doesn't do a director any good to be arty as hell and wind up with a product that's not much more than a damned expensive home movie.' ★★★★★ **CC**

DIRTY HARRY (1971)

Starring: *Clint Eastwood (Harry Callahan), Reni Santoni (Chico), Harry Guardino (Bressler), Andy Robinson (Scorpio), John Mitchum (DeGeorgio), John Larch (Chief), John Vernon (Mayor)*
Director: *Don Siegel*
Screenwriters: *Harry Julian Fink, Rita M. Fink, John Milius (uncredited), Dean Riesner, based on an unpublished story by Rita M. and Harry Julian Fink*
18/102 mins./Crime/USA

A San Francisco cop with little regard for rules (but who always gets results) tries to track down a serial killer who snipes at random victims.

Thank heavens for masturbation. Had it not been for Frank Sinatra's sprained wrist (okay, so sadly it is only speculation that this was due to an RSI), Dirty Harry Callahan would have turned out a very different incarnation indeed. In fact, having been turned down by Ol' Blue Eyes himself, the role was subsequently offered to both John Wayne and then Paul Newman before Josey Whales blasted into town. And so it was that Clint Eastwood became Dirty Harry, the renegade detective ('He doesn't break murder cases. He smashes them,' boasted the poster) with his heart in the right place and pistol pressed firmly to the temple of San Francisco's grimy underworld. Loosely based on the still unsolved real-life case of the 'Zodiac Killer' – a serial killer who had terrorised the city since the 1960s and continued to do so as filming started – the plot sees our titular SFPD maverick track infamous psychopath Scorpio (Robinson) and try, in vain as it turns out, to save his latest victim, a 14-year-old girl who has been buried alive. But while Eastwood delivers a virtuoso performance – one that would spawn four sequels – Robinson steals a fair share of his thunder, turning in a display of visceral intensity.

Not that it came easy, thanks to the combination of his deep-seated pacifism, and a personal phobia of guns which would make him flinch every time he had to pull a trigger (to the point that Siegel was eventually forced to shut down production for nearly a week and enlist a firearms expert to teach him to realistically fire a gun). Couple this with the death threats he later received and Robinson may well have wished in hindsight that the part had gone to first choice Audie Murphy, an American war hero who was killed in a plane crash before he could accept.

Regardless, the end result was landmark cinema. A violent (it was banned in Finland for over a year) Western-set-within-city-walls, laced with homage – look out for a theatre in the background featuring a *Play Misty For Me* (1971) billing; a wall which bears the graffiti 'Kyle', the name of Eastwood's son; and the final scene, in which Harry throws his badge into the river, that is a deliberate nod towards *High Noon* (1952). It is also, of course, quite unrelentingly cool. To wit the oft-repeated, eternally adored: 'I know what you're thinking. Did he fire six shots or only five? Well, to tell you the truth, in all this excitement, I've kinda lost track myself. But being as this is a 44 Magnum, the most powerful handgun in the world, and would blow your head clean off, you've only got to ask yourself one question: "Do I feel lucky?" Well, do ya punk?'

Most notable, however, was *Dirty Harry*'s timing. Tapping into the public's pervading mistrust of the authorities – principally courtesy of the massive NYPD corruption scandal that was ripping through the US police force at the time – Siegel's ambivalent masterpiece laid down a template (1. Kill someone in the first five minutes 2. Stage your finale near water 3. End with a pull shot – usually helicopter – away from the action) that would not only be strictly adhered to by its own sequels, but, generally, by copycats ad infinitum.

It's been referenced in everything from *Ferris Bueller's Day Off* (1986) to *Die Hard With A Vengeance* (1995). It's been spoofed well in *The Naked Gun* (1988), and not in *Stop! Or My Mom Will Shoot* (1992). And it marked the continuation of a beautiful mentor/protégé friendship between Siegel and Eastwood. A friendship which saw them work together a total of seven times, and one which would finally be commemorated in 1992 when Eastwood dedicated *Unforgiven* to his lifelong compadre.

Tagline
You don't assign him to murder cases. You just turn him loose.

As idols go, Eastwood chose well with Siegel, the Cambridge university-educated director who started out as an editor, before helming classics such as *Invasion Of The Body Snatchers* (1956). He developed a penchant for cameos (here he is credited as 'man running down street') and along with Robert Totten became the first to be credited with the Director's Guild Of America's universal pseudonym Alan Smithee – for *Death Of A Gunfighter* (1969). Of all his 38 films, though, *Dirty Harry* is up there with the best of them. A perfect blend of Bruce Surtees' stark, grainy cinematography, Lalo Schifrin's original score, in a real sense, Harry Callahan gets stitched up oscillating between twangy pseudo-porn and haunting melodies, and Siegel's own, undisputed knack for orchestrating action that would forever establish its hero as the toughest cookie ever to grace the screen. As for anyone in any doubt, well, they can always ask themselves one question. ★★★★★ **MD**

DIRTY PRETTY THINGS (2002)

Starring: *Chiwetel Ejiofor (Okwe), Audrey Tautou (Senay), Sergi Lopez (Sneaky), Sophie Okonedo (Juliette), Benedict Wong (Guo Zi), Zlatko Buric (Ivan)*
Director: *Stephen Frears*
Screenwriter: *Steven Knight*
15/97 mins./Drama/Thriller/USA/UK

Illegal alien Okwe – a Nigerian doctor with tragic secrets – works two jobs and rents sofa space from Turkish refugee Senay. When he makes a gruesome discovery he cannot go to the police, but risks sleuthing himself, while trying to protect Senay and evade immigration authorities.

This unconventional, compelling thriller pulls off a complicated trick neatly – combining social observation and political comment entertainingly, with an original mystery at the fore. It is set in an as yet little-explored London scene – that of the new, invisible workforce of asylum-seeking chamber maids, seamstresses, minicab drivers and night porters who have converged on the UK from far-flung countries and cultures, bringing with them sad histories and humble hopes.

It's hard to believe its writer was one of the 'creators' of *Who Wants To Be A Millionaire?*, but then, greed and humiliation are reliable staples of human interest – and both certainly play their part in this story.

Tautou is the audience bait for *Amélie* fans and she is again enchanting, and very touching, as the vulnerable but proud girl trying to maintain personal standards, prepared to do almost anything to survive except admit her feelings. But at the head of the international cast is charismatic British actor Ejiofor, who has already earned notice at the Royal National Theatre. As the conscience of the story, he carries the weight of the film, and he does so with authority and poise.

While it's essential to the plot that the characters inhabit a seedy London shadow-world of sleazy hotels and backstreet enterprises, this is by no means as bleak or depressing as one might think. It's beautifully filmed by the Oscar-winning Chris Menges, and there is considerable humour springing from the colourful but utterly believable array of outsiders, hustlers, creeps, dreamers and schemers. Our favourite is the dry Chinese hospital morgue attendant, who plays chess with Okwe, dispensing romance and survival tips, along with purloined medicines.

As for the shocking riddle Okwe stumbles upon, it's a chiller: the kind of macabre crime that makes an urban legend and serves well here to put the sympathetic protagonist into peril and an almighty moral pickle. **★★★★ AE**

DIRTY ROTTEN SCOUNDRELS (1988)

Starring: *Steve Martin (Freddy Benson), Michael Caine (Lawrence Jamieson), Glenne Headly (Janet Colgate), Anton Rogers (Inspector André)*
Director: *Frank Oz*
Screenwriters: *Dan Launer, Stanley Shapiro, Paul Henning*
PG/110 mins./Comedy/USA

Two con-men of differing styles, who prey upon on women's good nature, find their Mediterranean town isn't big enough for the both of them. So, they decide on a plan: the first one to extract $50,000 from a chose female target gets to stay, the loser leaves.

It was a great example of winning casting, everything subtly back to front, with eternal salt-of-the earth Michael Caine slick as an oyster as the debonair crook, and chirpy, sarky Steve Martin as a small fry in the con-game, a grifter who bottom feeds but is seeking to up his game. They've landed in the prettified setting of Beaumont-sur-Mer on France's Côte D'Azur and the camera just laps it up. It's a glorious white-washed postcard-perfect playground for these sleazebags, right down to the pomade smarming back Caine's boisterous head of hair, gullible women taking in the sea air.

Frank Oz, reworking a Marlon Brando/David Niven double-header called *Bedtime Story* from 1964, gives the film a gleeful amorality, framing this pair of scoundrels' sly wickedness as a delightful form of tomfoolery. We're on their side through and through, from Lawrence's tutelage of Freddie's rogue on the higher reaches of conning, to their rivalry over the apparently feeble Glenne Headly. Oz, with his trio of screenwriters, is interested in the allure these men offer, not simply a sexual enticement, but, with Lawrence especially, that they take on the guise of a female fantasy of adventure, a caddish gleam in the eye. Caine is wonderful as Lawrence, a magnificent slimeball, honed to a perfection with the local police in his pocket.

Little wonder he's so discomforted by the rude games played by Martin's Freddie. He lacks the grace, the charm, the savoir-faire. And now he's cutting in Lawrence's turf. When they form, for a while, a double-act, the film is at its funniest. Martin playing Freddie disguised as the idiotic Prince Ruprecht, royal retard at the classiest tables in the Riviera, recalls the comedian's heyday mixing the herky-jerky style of old slapstick with his nuthouse of characters of the 80s. When they set about each other, the film slips back into the obvious, with a predictable comeuppance on its way for the pair of them. But Headly keeps up, lost in the breezy corners of her pretty skull, and with its light touch, handsome locations and comfort with letting the characters flow rather than pelt us with a succession of madcap set-ups, *Dirty Rotten Scoundrels* prospers on an old-fashioned kind of charm. **★★★★ IN**

DIRTY WEEKEND (1993)

Starring: *Lia Williams (Bella), Rufus Sewell (Tim), Michael Coles (Norman), David McCallum (Reggie), Christopher Ryan (Small One), Sean Pertwee (The Quiet One), Ian Richardson (Nimrod)*
Director: *Michael Winner*
Screenwriters: *Michael Winner, Helen Zahavu based on the novel by Zahavi*
18/102 mins./Comedy/UK

Having been spied on and harassed by a local pervert, Bella finally has enough. She transforms herself into an avenging angel equipped with a hammer, eradicating the world of problem men.

Justly vilified on release as a piece of asinine exploitation trumped up as a feminist tract, this is an ugly movie indeed. Helen Zahavi's novel had already stirred furious debate as to whether it is simply a vile piece of wish fulfilment or a genuine exploration of female predicament in a world fraught with male-orientated peril. That it was picked up by controversial director Michael Winner, best known for his own series of vigilante operas, the *Death Wish* films, and derided as a filmmaker of little subtlety and, often, grave misjudgment, was never going to end well. He made of this deranged tale of a victimised woman's violent revenge amongst the low-lit streets of Brighton, a horrible, lurid film made all the more indigestible by its pretence at relevance.

If you were going to try and disinter some meaning from its procession of nasty images, you could assemble an argument that Bella (played with befuddled intent by Lia Williams) tormented by Rufus Sewell's vile peeper, and his hideous intentions, is on an extreme form of feminist retribution – to castrate all men and leave the world a better place. But, in Winner's hands, there feels little difference in the behaviour of the men and her rebirth as a vigilante. The film is incapable of shifts in tone, everything feels equally as grubby and indistinct, just rubbing our faces in the indecency of human nature. Where does Winner get off? Is he daring to expose us to feelings we don't want to admit to, or is he titillated by his own outrageousness? Bella's empowerment is to transform herself into the equivalent of the hungry, pathetic, dangerous men who cross her path. How is that any kind of betterment? The film, with its bitter examination of depravity, is a depressing event.

A coterie of good actors seem willing to humiliate themselves, including Michael Coles as a fat professor ridiculed for his premature ejaculation until he turns on Bella and David McCallum as a dentist who forces her to give him a blowjob. Both are dealt with, their sordid behaviour answered. Winner, however, is merely juggling the book's jagged idea, shooting in a flat, unappealing light, so that even stylistically the film can't even flare into the deliberate ghastliness of a horror film. He fails – or is that refuses? – to engage with the shock value of this liberation fantasy, to test its boundaries, only shoving it roughly into your face. **★ IN**

d

⦿ DISCLOSURE (1994)

Starring: *Michael Douglas (Tom Sanders), Demi Moore (Meredith Johnson), Donald Sutherland (Bob Garvin), Caroline Goodall (Susan Hendler), Roma Maffia (Catherine Alvarez)*
Director: *Barry Levinson*
Screenwriters: *Paul Attanasio, based on the novel by Michael Crichton*
18/128 mins./Drama/Thriller/USA

A computer specialist is sued for sexual harassment by a former lover turned boss who initiated the act forcefully, which threatens both his career and his personal life.

Having recreated dinosaurs in *Jurassic Park* and taken a wholehearted swipe at Japanese corporations with *Rising Sun*, blockbusting author Michael Crichton turned his money-raking muse to the subject of sexual harassment. But here's the rub: *Disclosure* focuses on a woman sexually harassing a man. Published to much furore and no end of dinner party jabber, the novel, about a female boss demanding favours beyond the call of duty from her male underling at a hi-tech computer firm, was a massive best-seller and Hollywood duly forked out piles of cash for the movie rights.

However, after burning his fingers on previous movie adaptations of his work, Crichton kept tight control of this one, with final approval on those filling the critical roles. As director he chose Barry Levinson, a once major talent gagging for a commercial venture to breathe life back into his flagging career after *Toys* and *Jimmy Hollywood*. As Tom Sanders, the production executive at Seattle computer firm DigiCom on the verge of a lucrative merger, he had always had Michael Douglas in mind. While as Meredith Johnson, the blonde-haired, voluptuous power babe who beats Sanders to his expected promotion and then lands him in the soup with her major league come-on, came the surprising choice of the auburn-locked, not-terribly-unsexy, Demi Moore.

After refusing a sexual tryst many red-blooded men would kill for, Sanders finds himself beaten to the punch when she claims he harassed her. He naturally refutes the charges, turns to arch-harassment lawyer Roma Maffia for help, kicks up no end of fuss and, in threatening to collapse the merger, loses just about every friend he's got.

All this segues into some deeper, devilish corporate deception involving Crichton's current pet topics – virtual reality and hyper-speed disc-drives – though it's best not to bother trying to understand the buckets of techno-babble, since this is ultimately little more than splendid piece of high-spec trash, about as profound as a knees-up at Butlins. And as a supposed hotbed of controversy, the message-making arrives as a slice of only-in-America tittle-tattle rather than some earth-shattering exposé of the latest social ill.

The performances are well up to scratch, with Douglas replaying his male-in-peril thing with predictable ease, brewing up a fine chemistry with the vampish Moore as they U-turn from sexual heat to a frost you could ski on. All of which adds up to a glossy, tightly directed caboodle that entertains in a way that only Tinseltown can muster and is guaranteed to have you talking for weeks to come. ★★★ **IN**

THE DISCREET CHARM OF THE BOURGEOISIE (LE CHARME DISCRET DE LA BOURGEOISIE) (1972)

Starring: *Fernando Rey (Don Raphael – Ambassador of Miranda), Delphine Seyrig (Simone Thévenot), Stéphane Audran (Alice Sénéchal), Bulle Ogier (Florence), Jean-Pierre Cassel (Henri Sénéchal)*
Director: *Luis Buñuel*
Screenwriter: *Luis Buñuel, Jean-Claude Carrière*
15/101 mins./Comedy/Drama/Italy/Spain
Awards: *Academy Awards – Best Foreign Language Film. BAFTA – Best Actress, Best Original Screenplay*

A variety of bizarre occurrences conspire to prevent the Thévenots, the Sénéchals, Madame Thévenot's lover, Ambassador Rafael Acosta, and her sister, Florence, from dining together.

Having declared that *Belle de Jour*, *The Milky Way* and *Tristana* were all to be his final film, Luis Buñuel was inspired to produce this scathing satire by producer Serge Silberman's recollection of an occasion when guests arrived for a dinner party he'd forgotten he was hosting. It proved to be the 72 year-old's most artistically complete and commercially successful feature and earned him the Oscar for Best Foreign Film (although he was less than enamoured to be given an award by '2500 idiots').

The Discreet Charm of the Bourgeoisie is a *L'Age d'Or* for the 70s. The protagonists turn out to be neither discreet nor charming, with the ambassador being a fascistic drug dealer, Madame Thévenot an adulteress and the gardening bishop a murderer. Yet, Buñuel conceded that 'I now say with humour what I used to say with violence', and while he mocked the characters on political, religious, sociological and psychological levels, the quality of his mercilessness is somewhat strained.

The searing ingenuity of his imagery, however, is undiminished. Directing via a prototype video link because of his sciatica, Buñuel replaced his customary close-ups and constricted camera movements with tracking shots and zooms. Yet, he edited largely in the camera and spent just over a day in the cutting room. This economy renders the complexity of the action all the more remarkable, as Buñuel plays games with planes of reality throughout and, such is their absurdity, that its impossible to distinguish between actual events, the dreams and anecdotes that punctuate them, and the scenes on the open road.

By forestalling the meal with increasingly sinister interruptions, Buñuel derides his directionless fools for their decadence, class consciousness, indolence and desperate attachment to a collapsing patriarchal order. Moreover, by keeping them on the move, this mordant masterpiece reveals just how little he cares about their ultimate destination. ★★★★★ **DP**

⦿ THE DISH (2000)

Starring: *Sam Neill (Cliff Buxton), Kevin Harrington (Ross 'Mitch' Mitchell), Tom Long (Glenn Latham), Patrick Warburton (Al Burnett), Genevieve Mooy (May McIntyre), Tayler Kane (Rudi Kellerman), Bille Brown (Prime Minister)*
Director: *Rob Sitch*
Screenwriters: *Santo Cilauro, Tom Gleisner, Jane Kennedy, Rob Sitch*
12/101 mins./Comedy/Drama/Australia

1969, and as the world counts down the days to Apollo 11's moon landing, the citizens of a tiny Australian town have more reason than most to be excited. A huge satellite receiver built in a sheep field has been selected to beam the moonwalk around the globe.

From the Australian team behind neglected comedy gem *The Castle* comes a heart-warming, true-life tale of small town folk caught up in the biggest television event of the last century.

Neither as raucous nor as funny as *The Castle*, *The Dish* is deceptively slight. However, following a honey-slow start, a power cut crisis cranks the plot into motion and the characters into focus. Suddenly we appreciate the sense of living history, and the technical skills of the unlikely heroes assembled to bring it off. From thereon in, the pleasure offered by this calorie-free confectionery is entirely in rooting for the underdog, and no less enjoyable for the certain knowledge that one way or another, the end will warm the cockles.

Indeed, rarely has a film featured a more likeable cast of characters. Possible dark spots, like the interfering NASA busybody, are very quickly ushered into the circle of friends. As the pipe-smoking hub of operations,

Cliff Buxton is so solid and dependable that grown men will want him for an uncle.

Elsewhere, delightful character actors abound, all of them painting in broad enough strokes to raise a smile, but investing enough warmth to keep the small town eccentrics the right side of caricature.

Australia seems to have made such miniature delights a specialist subject, and *The Dish* plays to the nerdish, space-loving teenager inside many an adult male, in exactly the same way that the similarly-toned *Muriel's Wedding* stirred up soft and squishy sentiments in any girl who ever played dress-up or felt left out.

That's not to say that both sexes won't get a kick out of *The Dish*, but it's surprising to find such a purely feel-good film which relegates notions of romance and family life to secondary place, and celebrates instead the joys of the workplace, mathematics and gadgetry. ★★★★ **CK**

DJANGO (1966)

Starring: *Franco Nero (Django), Jose Bodalo (Gen. Hugo Rodriguez), Loredana Nusciak (Maria), Angel Alvarez (Nataniele), Jimmy Douglas (Jonathan), Eduardo Fajardo (Maj. Jackson)*
Director: *Sergio Corbucci*
Screenwriters: *Bruno Corbucci, Sergio Corbucci, Jose Gutierrez Maesso, Franco Rosetti, Piero Vivarelli*
18/91 mins./Western/USA

Django arrives in a Western border town where Mexican bandidos are feuding with scarlet-hooded Klansmen. A super-skilled gunman, he hires himself out to various villains and brings about the destruction of both evil factions.

Made in 1966, this was unreleased in Britain at the time because of its excessive violence: for decades, all that could be seen of the film were the excerpts seen in *The Harder They Come*, where Jimmy Cliff's Jamaican bandit models himself on Nero's lone gunfighter. It is at once an imitation of Sergio Leone's *A Fistful Of Dollars* and an extension of Leone's spaghetti western style into even more baroque and bizarre areas. The blue-eyed Django (Nero) walks into town across a muddy plain, painfully dragging a coffin behind him, accompanied by his memorably wailing theme song. Tiring of jokes about how he's going to need that wooden box if he keeps sassing the baddies, Django arranges to meet the villain's hundred top guns on main street and, as they gallop wildly towards him, calmly unpacks a machine gun from the coffin and mows them down. Thereafter, it gets more grotesque and gothic as a hypocritical priest is forced to eat his own severed ear. Django, his hands smashed and unusable, has to chew off the trigger guards of his pistols and use a grave marker to work the guns in a graveyard shoot-out climax. After Leone, Sergio Corbucci was the genius of the spaghettis, following this up with a run of gritty, political greats: *Companeros*, *A Professional Gun*, *The Hellbenders* and *The Great Silence*. *Django*, a box office sensation in Europe, inspired dozens of official and unofficial sequels, including *Django the Bastard* (which has the same ghost gimmick as *High Plains Drifter*) and the surreal *Django, Kill!*; Nero returned to the role in 1987 in *Django Strikes Again*. ★★★★ **KN**

DO THE RIGHT THING (1989)

Starring: *Danny Aiello (Sal), Ossie Davis (Da Mayor), Ruby Dee (Mother Sister), Giancarlo Esposito (Buggin' Out), Spike Lee (Mookie), Bill Nunn (Radio Raheem), John Turturro (Pino), Rosie Perez (Tina)*
Director: *Spike Lee*
Screenwriter: *Spike Lee*
18/120 mins./Comedy/Drama/USA

Buggin' Out, a black activist, demands the black community boycott Sal's pizzeria. Though this call to arms is laughed off, it unearths racist attitudes in Sal's workforce and in the police, which contribute, along with rising discontentment among the local black community, to an unavoidably bloody finale.

One sweltering New York day the residents of a block in a black area take to the street, some having more on their minds than enjoying the weekend sunshine. Black activist Buggin' Out seeks to raise awareness; Raheem stalks the street blasting 'Public Enemy' from a massive hi-fi; while Mookie delivers for Sal's Famous Pizzeria – owned and run by Aiello and his two sons. The restaurant has been a neighbourhood focal point for 25 years. People drift in and out in buoyant humour until Buggin' Out notes the lack of black faces among the Italian-American celebrities on Sal's Wall Of Fame.

Unsurprisingly his call for a boycott by the folk who 'grew up on Sal's pizzas' goes unheeded and life goes on. Mookie skives, amiable drunk Da Mayor elegantly courts the block's matriarch, three old boys set patio furniture on the corner and lie about the 'ass kickings' they once gave a local lad called Mike Tyson and a fire hydrant provides an impromptu wet T-shirt contest. But there's palpable tension back at Sal's: son Tino is openly racist, the police are casually so, Buggin' Out is on a crusade, stuttering retard Smiley is becoming more persistent with the Xeroxed snaps of Dr. King and Malcolm X that he habitually touts and Raheem's radio is getting louder and louder. When the latter three team up, it leads to disaster for Sal and a fatality for the neighbourhood.

Lee's acute observation distils humour from accuracy rather than caricature but his growth as a filmmaker is impressive. He subtly steps up the pressure, releasing it after each incident and then returning to it at an elevated level and as the mood changes and the good-natured crowd turn into a rampaging mob, sympathies are pulled in several directions. The finale debunks the we-all-live-in-harmony myth by bluntly stating that much as most people oppose racism, if you push anybody too far they tend to choose sides. This might not sit comfortably with much of the potential audience, but both factions emerge with equal dignity and blame, and it's the only honest view Lee could have taken. ★★★★ **LB**

DOC HOLLYWOOD (1991)

Starring: *Michael J. Fox (Dr. Benjamin Stone), Julie Warner (Vialula/'Lou'), Barnard Hughes (Dr. Aurelius Hogue), Woody Harrelson (Hank Gordon), David Ogden Stiers (Major Nick Nicholson), George Hamilton (Doctor Halberstrom), Bridget Fonda (Nancy Lee Nicholson)*
Director: *Michael Caton-Jones*
Screenwriters: *Jeffrey Price, Peter S. Seaman, Daniel Pyne, based on the novel* What? ... Dead Again? *by Neil B. Shulman, adapted by Laurian Leggett*
15/104 mins./Comedy/Romance/USA

Benjamin Stone is a young high-flying doctor on his way to LA to take up his new post as a plastic surgeon. After a car crash he is given a community service order, forced to spend a few days in the small town of Grady as an assistant to the GP.

This is a straightforward tale: the slick young Dr Stone is driving across America to an outrageously well-paid post as a Los Angeles cosmetic surgeon, forced to spend a few days in a tiny town in Georgia he succumbs to its rural charms and starts to doubt whether a life of ease and plenty is for him.

The storyline is both over-obvious and highly unlikely – with no twists, surprises or secondary plots. But most disappointing of all is the desire for simplicity resulting in the 'comedy' losing out badly to the 'romantic'. In spite of a few neat running gags – a pig, a belligerent nurse and a soap opera style episodic letter – the laff level is far below par.

Fox has made his name playing a clever blend of high farce and low-down cynicism, yet the edge he could be relied on to cut through any mush with is almost completely missing. Likewise the possibilities for extraneous lunacy by supporting characters is woefully underused (notably Woody Harrelson as a super-macho insurance salesman). ★★★ **LB**

DODGE CITY (1939)

Starring: *Errol Flynn (Wade Hatton), Olivia de Havilland (Abbie Irving), Ann Sheridan (Ruby Gilman), Bruce Cabot (Jeff Surrett), Frank McHugh (Joe Clemens), Alan Hale (Algernon 'Rusty' Hart), Henry O'Neill (Col. Dodge)*
Director: *Michael Curtiz*
Screenwriter: *Robert Buckner*
PG/104 mins./Western/USA

Trail boss Wade Hatton comes to Dodge City and is shocked by the all-round violence and corruption. He reluctantly puts on a Sheriff's badge to make the wide-open Kansas town safe for womenfolk and children.

One of the primal myth Westerns, this colourful, rip-roaring, action-packed Errol Flynn vehicle is based on the story of Wyatt Earp. The dashing Flynn and his brawling pals clean up the lawless frontier town by getting rid of the bad guys (smug Bruce Cabot, snarly Victor Jory) who have been running the place only to feel suffocated when Dodge City becomes so decent it ain't fit for a man to live in and head off in a joke finish for the still-wild Virginia City, which Flynn tamed in an unconnected follow-up.

Directed by Michael Curtiz, who stages the best-ever barroom brawl in the movies as a fistfight explodes through the wall of the huge saloon and into the meeting of the Pure Prairie League next door. Various people have claimed to have had the idea for the scene in Curtiz's *Casablanca* where the patriots drown a German song with 'La Marseilleise', but here, four years earlier, good-guy ex-rebels drown out 'Marching Through Georgia' with 'Dixie' in exactly the same way.

Flynn, ably sidekicked by Alan Hale and Guinn 'Big Boy' Williams and romancing the Technicolor loveliness of Olivia de Havilland, struts and smiles with the best of them, showing his *Robin Hood* sincerity when the baddies kill a little kid but mostly taking it all in fun as 'the most movin-on man you ever saw'.

Made in the same year as *Stagecoach*, this is another super-Western, cramming in as many cowboy themes (iron horse, wagon train, cattle drive, heroic Sheriff, saloon-running varmints, march of civilisation, Civil War) as possible in one hugely entertaining package. ★★★★ **KN**

DODGEBALL: A TRUE UNDERDOG STORY (2004)

Starring: *Vince Vaughn (Peter LaFleur), Christine Taylor (Kate Veatch), Ben Stiller (White Goodman), Rip Torn (Patches O'Houlihan), Justin Long (Justin), Stephen Root (Gordon), Joel Moore (Owen), Chris Williams (Dwight), Alan Tudyk (Steve the Pirate), Missi Pyle (Fran), Gary Cole (Cotton McKnight), Jason Bateman (Pepper Brooks), Hank Azaria (Young Patches O'Houlihan)*
Director: *Rawson Marshall Thurber*
Screenwriter: *Rawson Marshall Thurber*
12A/96 mins./Comedy/Sport/USA

Faced with losing his gym to a corporate chain, Peter LaFleur enters his rag-tag clientele in the Vegas Dodgeball Tournament. But Globo Gym's White Goodman is hip to their plan, entering his Purple Cobras to stop them . . .

Dodgeball's subtitle – 'A True Underdog Story' – couldn't be more apt. When the film first appeared, it was a true underdog indeed, written off as a lesser offering from Ben Stiller's Frat Pack. Once it hit, though, it was clear that this was arguably the most quotable – and funniest – dumb comedy since *The Naked Gun*.

On release, all the plaudits went to Stiller's preening villain White Goodman, but this is, in truth, an ensemble movie, with the likes of Rip Torn's foul-mouthed Patches O'Houlihan ably supporting him. The movie's secret weapon, though, is Vince Vaughn's sardonic protagonist Peter LaFleur, who keeps the craziness grounded in a manner reminiscent of a young Bill Murray.

So many ideas and gags crash into each other that some are bound to miss, and there are one or two patchy spells, but it's in the melding of styles that *Dodgeball* works, as director Rawson Marshall Thurber blends character-based comedy with gross-out and an excellent deployment of cameos (Norris! Shatner! Hasselhoff!). Most of all, it's a tribute to the joys of physical comedy – watching people being hit in the balls has never been so much fun. ★★★★ **CH**

DOG DAY AFTERNOON (1975)

Starring: *Al Pacino (Sonny Wortznik), John Cazale (Sal), Charles Durning (Det. Egt. Moretti), Chris Sarandon (Leon), Sully Boyer (Mulvaney), Penny Allen (Sylvia), James Broderick (Sheldon), Carol Kane (Jenny)*
Director: *Sidney Lumet*
Screenwriter: *Frank Pierson, based on a magazine article by P.F. Luge, Thomas Moore*
15/Crime/130 mins./USA
Awards: *Academy Awards – Best Original Screenplay, BAFTA – Best Acting, Best Editing*

A man robs a bank to pay for his lover's sex change operation but it turns into a hostage situation and then a media circus.

In The Dorchester Hotel in London, sometime in January 1974, Al Pacino told director Sidney Lumet and screenwriter Frank Pierson (*Cool Hand Luke*) that he categorically would not play the part of Sonny Wortznik in *Dog Day Afternoon*. It was not the news they had wanted to hear. Not only had they flown over just for this meeting, the part had been written with Pacino in mind. But he was adamant. He had just finished shooting *The Godfather Part II*, which had left him, in his own words, 'Exhausted and infinitely depressed' and just didn't fancy taking on a role that would, given his famous dedication to The Method, have him working himself up to a state of near hysterical anxiety on a daily basis. Apologies were made, hands were shaken and Lumet dispatched the script to Dustin Hoffman. But when Pacino heard that his rival in the diminutive acting genius stakes was showing interest he did an about face and demanded another shufti. The result was not only the granddaddy of all heist-gone-wrong films, but one of his finest performances in the decade he, De Niro and the crime movie made their own.

There was something about the 70s that threw up not only consistently great movies of all kinds, but crime movies in particular – and all sub-genres were covered. There was the grand opera of *The Godfather* films, noirish gumshoe action with *Chinatown*, political chicanery with *All The President's Men*. In most crime genres the 70s delivered the 'best of' category. And that includes the heist-gone wrong-movie. It's been a staple of crime cinema since *The Asphalt Jungle* in 1950 and *Rififi* in 1955. Recent efforts such as *Reservoir Dogs* and *The Usual Suspects* show that it remains an audience pleaser as, when well-written and directed, it grants the audience permission to enjoy criminal shenanigans, and to identify with the perpetrators, without condoning them. Then there's the natural human delight in seeing things unravel disastrously. And in terms of plans assuming the appearance of a pear it would be difficult to beat what happened at the First Brooklyn Savings Bank on August 22nd, 1972.

Lumet and Pierson's recreation of Sonny Wortzick's botched attempt to steal thousands of dollars to fund his boyfriend's sex-change operation moves deftly from farce to tragedy with things going catastrophically wrong from the start. There's the third member of the gang who bottles out within minutes of the robbery kicking off and inquires whether he can use the getaway car to go home, the sarcastic bank teller (played brilliantly by Penelope Allan, 'Did you ever have a plan or what? I mean, did you just barge in on a whim?' she asks witheringly at one point) and there are hungry husbands waiting for dinner phoning the bank to ask when Sonny 'thinks he'll be done by'. It's a brilliantly handled crescendo into chaos with Lumet, a past master of directing claustrophobic movies (*Fail Safe*, *Twelve Angry Men*), building the sense of oppressive heat, tension and ultimately surreal action as various pressure groups arrive outside to cheer or decry the bisexual bank robber in front of the impotent NYPD.

And here's where *Dog Day* becomes more than just another heist movie. It's a gripping picture of a city close to meltdown. From Lumet's dazzling opening montage in which we see scenes of a city about to boil over in more ways than one, sweltering 70s New York becomes a raucous character in the movie. 1972's cultural mêlée is perfectly invoked as the heist transforms into a counter-cultural jamboree with a botched bank robbery as its central piece of performance art. Only, as they say, in the 70s.

Apart from the opening titles, Lumet uses no music, adding to the realistic, documentary feel while his camera in the opening minutes of the heist hurtles round his confined set before slowly settling down as Sonny and Sal hunker down for the long haul. It's a triumph of controlled direction and fantastic editing (by Dede Allen, whose Oscar-winning scalpel work includes *Bonnie And Clyde*, *The Hustler* and, weirdly enough, *The Breakfast Club*).

The film is also filled with outstanding performances from Pacino, Cazale (cast at Pacino's insistence, the part was originally written for a 14 year-old boy, as Sal was in real life) and Charles Durning as the harassed police chief trying not only to prevent a bloodbath inside the bank but also to control his own trigger-happy cops. Chris Sarandon delivers an effective turn as wannabe woman Leon and the film's handling of gay issues, though it looks dated today, is remarkably advanced for the mid-70s – though Pacino balked at a kiss outside the bank and the scene was re-written as an amazingly effective telephone conversation. And while in the tradition of the heist movie, crime doesn't pay – Sonny was sent down for 20 years – signing movie waivers obviously does. In 1973 Warner Brothers paid him $7,500, the exact price of a sex-change operation. Leon is now Liz Eden, and lives in New York. ★★★★★ **AS**

DOG SOLDIERS (2002)

Starring: *Sean Pertwee (Sgt. Harry G. Wells), Kevin McKidd (Pvt. Cooper), Emma Cleasby (Megan), Liam Cunningham (Capt. Ryan), Thomas Lockyer (Cpl. Bruce Campbell), Darren Morfitt ('Spoon' Witherspoon)*
Director: *Neil Marshall*
Screenwriter: *Neil Marshall*
15/105 mins./Action/Horror/UK/Luxembourg

Six happy-go-lucky soldiers, stranded in remote woodland, see their training mission go 'belly up' when the full moon rises and a pack of bloodthirsty werewolves start to hunt them down. Can they make it to daybreak?

For some reason or other, 2002 seemed to be 'raid Romero' year in the UK. Danny Boyle and Alex Garland pilfered freely from the maestro of the undead for *28 Days Later* and, in box office terms at least, scored a hit. But for genre buffs, it is this micro-budgeted lupine caper that should attract their attention and their pocket money.

Lifting enthusiastically from *Night Of The Living Dead* as well as *Assault On Precinct 13* (together with more than a soupcon of *The Evil Dead* and a dash of *Aliens*), *Dog Soldiers* gleefully goes walkies through the standard genre trappings – full moons, howlings in the dark, shredded guts and a bunch of squaddies trapped in a house straight out of a fairy-tale. Writer-director Neil Marshall's screenplay does, however, show evidence of being written by a graduate magna cum laude of the Shane Black School Of Excellence In Movie Dialogue ('If Little Red Riding Hood should show up with a bazooka and a bad attitude, I expect you to chin the bitch!' – Anita Brookner this ain't), and the acting occasionally has a slight prefab quality to it.

But these minor flaws are more than made up for with energy, wit and inventive gore, and the jokes are good – a tug of war between Pertwee and a dog over his exposed guts is a standout. Marshall treads the line between laughs and tension expertly, and makes a virtue of his negligible FX budget by keeping his excellently designed (and thankfully non-CG) man-dogs where they belong: in the shadows. Pedigree stuff. ★★★★ **AS**

DOGFIGHT (1991)

Starring: *River Phoenix (Eddie Birdlance), Lili Taylor (Rose), Richard Panebianco (Berzin), Anthony Clark (Oakie), Mitchell Whitfield (Benjamin), Holly Near (Rose Sr.)*
Director: *Nancy Savoca*
Screenwriter: *Bob Comfort*
15/94 mins./Comedy/Drama/Romance/USA

1963, the night before the 18-year-old 'Birdlace' Eddie and his friends are shipped to Vietnam. They play a dirty game called 'Dogfight': all of them seek a woman for a party, and who finds the most ugly one, wins a prize.

This post-*My Own Private Idaho* romantic comedy pairs possibly a man who was destined to be one of Hollywood's finest young leading men (until a fatal drugs overdose) with Lili Taylor, who came to fame alongside Julia Roberts in 1988's *Mystic Pizza*.

Given only a shockingly limited release in the US – two theatres in all – and zinging straight to video in the UK, *Dogfight*, if no modern classic, certainly deserves a wider audience than the handful of zealots singing its praises to date.

Phoenix is Edward Birdlace, the teenage marine on his last night in San Francisco before setting off to 'Nam, egged on by his army buddies to take part in the Dogfight, a local eve-of-war ritual involving picking up the worst-looking girl in town – hence the rather offensive name – and parading her in front of the gang.

Taylor, in one of the more hideous dresses in the movies, is Phoenix' choice, and is, not surprisingly, less than thrilled when she correctly divines what is going down.

What elevates this slight tale above the ordinary is a stunning performance from Taylor, investing her character with sensitivity and wit, while Phoenix yet again displays all the signs of a potential master at work. Savoca, last heard of on *True Love*, displays a sure touch, particularly in one wonderful wardrobe crisis scene that will strike a chord with all female viewers, turning this particular Dogfight into an interesting anecdote, and one that is well-told and well-performed. ★★★ **JB**

DOGMA (1999)

Starring: *Ben Affleck (Bartleby), George Carlin (Cardinal Ignatius Glick), Matt Damon (Loki), Linda Fiorentino (Bethany Sloane), Salma Hayek (Serendipity), Jason Lee (Azrael), Jason Mewes (Jay), Kevin Smith (Silent Bob), Alan Rickman (Metatron), Chris Rock (Rufus), Alanis Morissette (God)*
Director: *Kevin Smith*
Screenwriter: *Kevin Smith*
15/130 mins./Adventure/Comedy/Fantasy/USA

Bethany is an ordinary woman who learns that she is the last descendant of Christ, and is destined to save the world. Two renegade angels are attempting to re-enter Heaven – and if they succeed, it will mean that God is fallible and the universe will end. With a motley crew of religious figures, Bethany sets off to stop them.

This, next to Smith's usual standards, is a Simpson/Bruckheimer epic, complete with 'proper' Hollywood stars and a special effects budget.

But what surprised the far-Christian right – opposed to the film before they even saw it – was that this was not a satire or a Python-style skit on organised religion; *Dogma* was a sometimes touching, sometimes incredibly funny, often confusing attempt to convey the last 2,000 years of Catholicism in one, easy-to-digest communion.

The movie starts with Cardinal Glick offering absolution to anyone who passes under the archway in his cathedral as part of his 'Catholicism Wow!' campaign to get people back into church. Unfortunately, Loki and Bartleby, two fallen angels who have been banished to Earth, get wind of the Cardinal's intentions and hatch a plan: if they cut off their wings they will become human, and if their sins are absolved they will be allowed back into heaven. But there's a technical hitch. If this happens, it means God will be unbanishing the angels he banished. Which means that God made a mistake – and goodbye civilisation as we know it.

Something must clearly be done about this, so we meet Bethany, a lapsed Catholic visited by the gloriously jaundiced Metatron, the official voice of God, who charges her with the task of heading off the rogue pair before the damage can be done. Setting off on her Oz-style journey, she hooks up with an increasingly oddball cast of characters – black apostle Rufus, a muse called Serendipity and, inevitably, Smith regulars Jay and Silent Bob – as the end of the world looms nearer. And if it all sounds like a lot of information to process, it is.

Which is the film's chief failing. With so many characters and such a complicated storyline, Smith frequently gets bogged down, culminating in a film that seems unable to work out quite where it ends and who its heroes are.

That said, there are plenty of wonderful and unexpected scenes – not least Alanis Morissette's first appearance in a Hollywood movie – and one-liners to satisfy Smith's aficionados, including a beautiful scene in which Affleck seems to good-humouredly poke fun at the rumours about his friendship with Matt Damon ('Do I come off as gay?'). It's too long and doesn't quite work, but as a marketing campaign for a fresh look at religion it's certainly food for thought. Or as Metatron puts it: 'You people. If there isn't a movie about it, it's not worth knowing.' ★★★ **DW**

DOGS IN SPACE (1987)

Starring: *Michael Hutchence (Sam), Saskia Post (Anna), Nique Needles/Deanna Bond (The Girl), Tony Helou (Luchio), Chris Hayward (Chainsaw Man), Peter Walsh (Anthony), Laura Swanson (Clare), Adam Briscomb (Grant)*
Director: *Richard Lowenstein*
Screenwriter: *Richard Lowenstein*
18/103 mins./Drama/Australia

Melbourne, 1978. A bunch of people share a house: Sam, the permanently stoned and irresponsible lead singer of a punk rock group, Anna, his blonde and occasionally in-work girlfriend, Luchio, a student who is actually studying amid the chaos, some surplus hippies, several hopeless musicians, and untold vermin, human and otherwise.

This doesn't really have a plot, though someone dies in the last reel to fool you into thinking there's been a story in there somewhere. Instead, we have an almost ciné vérité chronicle of the day-to-day lives of deadbeats. Someone comes by to explain at length how a chainsaw works. Sam's mother delivers a home-cooked meal and clean washing to her catatonic son.

A wild party upsets the neighbours, and leads to mass devastation. The gang burn a TV set in the hope of passing it off as a piece of Skylab, which has just fallen on Australia. Despite its downer ending, it lacks the kind of mock-tragic overtones that give Penelope Spheeris' similar *Suburbia* a sort of dignity. Instead, we have a film that's as loud, rude, annoying, anarchic and opportunist as its characters. There's no question that it's is an uncannily convincing depiction of life with a bunch of drop-out scumbags, but there's also a slight problem that it's hard to care about their eventual sufferings.

However, much of it very funny, and even if the lead characters make you want to throttle them, the minor cameos are spot on. Note, for instance, the friendly policeman who went to school with one of the household and performs a minimal search of the house while trying to seem desperately in tune with the punks, or the junior politico who tries to talk the uninterested band into doing a benefit gig and gets lost in the party. ★★★ **KN**

DOGTOWN AND Z BOYS (2001)

Starring: *Sean Penn (narrator), as Themselves: Jay Adams, Tony Alva, Jeff Ament, Bob Biniak, Steve Caballero, Paul Constantineau, 'Baby' Paul Cullen, Skip Engblom, Tony Friedkin, Glen E. Friedman, Marty Grimes, David Hackett, Tony Hawk, Jeff Ho*
Director: *Stacy Peralta*
Screenwriters: *Stacy Peralta, Craig Stecyk*
15/91 mins./Documentary/Sport/USA

In run-down Dogtown, the Zephyr Team skate empty swimming pools after the surf blows out. This documentary traces the development of skateboarding from the early '70s through to the fame, fortune and eventual fall of some of the team's teenage members.

There are those who believe that documentary's place is on the small screen. *Dogtown And Z Boys* effortlessly proves them wrong – factual movies can be as exciting, slick and accessible as any other species of celluloid.

Stacy Peralta's film is an exuberant, nostalgic paean to a time, place and a lifestyle. A founding member of the Zephyr Team (Z Boys), Peralta traces the history of the skateboard from its early years as a stalled 60s fad, through to his friends' reinvention of it as an extreme sport with marketing deals and corporate sponsorship. Quite a trip for an activity that only began when the inventive beach-bums found themselves with nothing to do when the surf blew out mid-morning.

There's an engaging rebelliousness to the use of California's infrastructure – the towering waves of playground asphalt and the empty swimming pools of the vacationing middle classes – for a purely hedonistic kick. Peralta matches that kinetic creativity with dynamic, imaginative use of his archival material.

His camera hurtles across the still images, while Sean Penn's deadpan narration, complete with coughs and splutters, is perfectly pitched. It's hardly an unbiased film – it concludes with a sell-out to corporate America and the gentrification of Dogtown's once seedy beachfront. But who doesn't re-edit their own history?

What comes across most poignantly in Peralto's minor masterpiece is the sheer joy of being a member of the coolest gang on the beach, as remembered – and embellished – by a generation of fortysomethings for whom, you suspect, life has never been anywhere nearly as good. A genuine must-see. ★★★★★ **CK**

DOGVILLE (2003)

Starring: *Nicole Kidman (Grace Margaret Mulligan), Harriet Andersson (Gloria), Lauren Bacall (Ma Ginger), Jean-Marc Barr (The Man with the Big Hat), Paul Bettany (Tom Edison), Blair Brown (Mrs. Henson), James Caan (The Big Man), Patricia Clarkson (Vera), Jeremy Davies (Bill Henson), Ben Gazzara (Jack McKay), Philip Baker Hall (Tom Edison Sr.), John Hurt (Narrator)*
Director: *Lars von Trier*
Screenwriter: *Lars von Trier*
15/178 mins./Drama/Thriller/Mystery/Denmark/Sweden/U.S./Netherlands/U.K./Germany/France

On the run from city gangsters, Grace seeks shelter in the small mining town of Dogville. At first, her willingness to take on any amount of hard work wins over the townsfolk; but as they grow greedy and exploitative, they risk betraying her and bringing a terrible tragedy down on their own heads.

Forget the detailed locations of *The Lord Of The Rings* or the built-to-scale replica of 19th Century Manhattan in *Gangs Of New York*. All you need to reconstruct a Depression-era town in a remote corner of America are a few white lines on a black floor – but only if you possess the artistic daring of Lars von Trier.

Stylistically, the shadow of playwright Bertolt Brecht looms large over *Dogville*, and not just because the story is inspired by his song lyric, 'Pirate Jenny'. Von Trier approaches his latest film like a Brecht play, adhering to the German's theories in near-textbook fashion by always emphasising the artifice and theatricality of the action.

Von Trier's detractors – and there are many – will argue that this is nothing more than filmed theatre. On a very basic level, perhaps so; although if this cast were assembled on Broadway or in London's West End, the show would be a complete sell-out months in advance, so we should be thankful for any opportunity to share the experience. But Anthony Dod Mantle's digital video camera isn't simply documenting a performance. It restlessly and fearlessly intrudes into this place and into these lives. Its close-ups – capturing key emotions as they flicker across the characters' faces – are vital to describing the moral arc of the story. This is something that can only be achieved cinematically, an intensity that's impossible to render elsewhere, not even from the front row of a playhouse's stalls.

The bare 'stage' on which von Trier presents his action is also thematically relevant. If *Dogville* brings to mind another play, it is Thornton Wilder's *Our Town*, with its nostalgic chronology of a close American neighbourhood and its inhabitants. In *Dogville*, though, there can be no hiding place behind a white picket fence or a twitching lace curtain. Von Trier strips away walls, doors and windows. Later, he strips away the characters' niceties and social politeness.

When a rape occurs at an important point in the story, neither the viewers nor the Dogville residents – washing their hands of their guilt in the comfort of their own homes – are allowed any barrier to help them avert their eyes from the harsh truth. Everyone and everything is exposed for what it truly is inside.

Another criticism frequently flung at von Trier (and one that quite often sticks) is that his treatment of female characters is almost hateful. In *Breaking The Waves*, *The Idiots* and *Dancer In The Dark*, sexual humiliation, unjust suffering and heart-wrenching sacrifice are all in a day's work for his heroines. So too in *Dogville*, although after the townsfolks' betrayal of Grace, this time there is a stronger sense of moral retribution on the guilty rather than on the innocent.

At the beginning of the film, Tom is keen to prove that the values of a tight community are essentially good, and so persuades his neighbours to open their doors and their hearts to Grace while she flees from danger. Although America is a country that historically has prided itself on giving shelter to the oppressed, von Trier's attack on a society that will hypocritically exploit the weakest among it is surely aimed at a wider target than his supposed nemesis across the Atlantic. He is criticising anyone who knowingly turns his or her own disappointments and shortcomings into the persecution of an outsider.

In this light, *Dogville* raises issues that are perhaps more vital in today's world than at any other point in history, then presents them in an intellectually stimulating style. And so by all means argue that von Trier's latest is theatre and not cinema. But at least acknowledge that *Dogville*, in a didactic and politicised stage tradition, is a great play that shows a deep understanding of human beings as they really are. ★★★★★ **AM**

LA DOLCE VITA (1960)

Starring: *Marcello Mastroianni (Marcello Rubini), Anita Ekberg (Sylvia), Anouk Aimée (Maddalena), Yvonne Furneaux (Emma), Magail Noel (Fanny), Alain Cuny (Steiner)*
Director: *Federico Fellini*
Screenwriters: *Federico Fellini, Ennio Flaiano, Tulio Pinelli, Brunello Rondi*
15/174 mins./Drama/Italy

Disinterested in his suicidal girlfriend, Emma, and bored with his latest conquest, Maddalena, gossip writer Marcello Rubini tours Rome with a sensual starlet before winding up, more disillusioned than ever, at a seaside orgy.

Federico Fellini approached peak form with this parody of both the socialites and celebrities who bask in cheap publicity and the parasites who report their antics as though they were of world-shattering import.

The film coined the term 'paparazzi' and it's intriguing to note how little the morality of the glory-seeking shutterbug has changed since Fellini scandalised the chattering classes with this cynical, satirical study of a Rome that had become starstruck following the success of such Hollywood runaways as *Three Coins In The Fountain* and *Roman Holiday*.

Cobbled together from contemporary headlines, discarded screenplays (*Moraldo In The City* and *A Journey With Anita*) and superfluous fragments (the beached sea monster incident came from *I Vitelloni*), the episodic storyline showed an Eternal City overrun by social movers and showbiz shakers and Fellini couldn't resist exposing them as the wannabes, has-beens and never-wouldbes they were.

Paul Newman was reportedly keen to be participate in this denunciation of faux glamour. But Fellini insisted on Marcello Mastroianni as his alter ego, especially having failed to land either Peter Ustinov or Walter Pidgeon for Steiner (Alain Cuny), Silvana Mangano for the heiress Maddalena (Anouk Aimée) or Edwige Feuillère, Greer Garson or Luise Rainer for Nadia (Nadia Gray). It proved to be a wise decision, as Mastroianni's insouciant charm only highlights the indolence of those around him.

Fellini also struck lucky with his choice for Sylvia the Tinseltown starlet, as Monroe-esque Swede Anita Ekberg's pneumatic cavorting in the Trevi Fountain became one of the iconic images of the 1960s.

Producer Dino De Laurentiis predicted that this 'incoherent, false and pessimistic' picture would prove a calamity. But its banning by the Catholic Church as atheist, Communist and treasonable filth made it a cause célèbre. Moreover, by his brilliant use of a shallow depth of field on a sprawling CinemaScope canvas, Fellini had single-handedly rebranded and repositioned Italian cinema and earned himself the creative freedom that would result in yet another masterpiece, *8 1/2*. ★★★★ **DP**

DOMINO (2005)

Starring: *Keira Knightley (Domino Harvey), Mickey Rourke (Ed Mosbey), Edgar Ramirez (Choco), Riz Abbasi (Alf), Delroy Lindo (Claremont Williams), Mo'Nique (Lateesha Rodriguez)*
Director: *Tony Scott*
Screenwriters: *Richard Kelly, based on a story by Kelly and Steve Barancik*
15/127 mins./Action/Crime/France/USA

A 'biopic' of Brit ex-pat Domino Harvey who, bored with her life as a model, became a bounty hunter. She and her two co-workers pursue their prey while being followed by reality TV cameras. When an associate tries to pull a fast one to raise emergency cash, she ends up in an interrogation room, recounting her tale.

Nobody shoots and cuts quite like Tony Scott. Now in his 60s, the man has enough panache to burn off any of Hollywood's new top guns. So long as he's armed with a strong narrative, you're guaranteed a good time, regardless of how over-the-top he goes. In theory then, the pairing of Scott and *Donnie Darko* scribe Richard Kelly should make for an intriguing sound-clash, but in practice, once you pile Scott's visual jazz on top of Kelly's post-modern pop culture riffs, the end product is too often simply noise.

On the upside, the details work well. Individual sequences are all impeccably assembled, Rourke's grizzled vet chips in some memorable deadpan dialogue and there's a scene involving a shoulder joint that might just qualify as the 'holy shit!' moment of the year. But like the playing pieces of the title, these sequences are balanced precariously – close but never exactly strung together by the script – and it only requires one of them to fall to send all of the others crashing down.

Fair enough, from the get-go Scott backs away from asserting that this is anything like an honest biopic, which should leave us free to enjoy the ride, but the scattershot screenplay also makes life very tough for Knightley (hot but not hard) in the title role. The assorted veterans fare better in supporting parts – Mickey Rourke wears bounty-hunting boss Ed Moseby like a comfortable leather jacket, and Delroy Lindo makes the most of his limited screen time as a shonky bail bondsman. The standout, though, is Walken, who waltzes into the entertaining second act as a 'reality TV producer' and single-handedly makes us forget we were half-way through a 'sort of' biopic.

Alas, Walken's thin plot-thread soon unravels, and for her third act *Domino* – both the woman and the movie – morphs again, into a metaphysical morality tale with delusions of grandeur. Scott tries to snatch our attention back with a big gun battle, but bizarrely it's just a photocopy of *True Romance*'s climax. Ultimately, nothing here brings us any closer to Domino, and you begin to wonder if Scott would have been a better choice for a standard treatment of the same subject. ★★★ **ST**

DON JUAN DE MARCO (1995)

Starring: *Marlon Brando (Dr. Jack Mickler), Johnny Depp (Don Juan), Faye Dunaway (Marilyn Mickler), Geraldine Pailhas (Dona Ana), Bob Dishy (Dr. Paul Showalter), Rachel Ticotin (Dona Inez), Talisa Soto (Dona Julia)*
Director: *Jeremy Leven*
Screenwriter: *Jeremy Leven, based on the character Don Juan partly created by Lord Byron*
15/97 mins./Comedy/Drama/Romance/USA

A young man commits one last seduction, then attempts to kill himself by throwing himself from a billboard. A psychologist is called in to talk him down, and spends the next ten days trying to learn if the man is, as he claims, Don Juan De Marco, the world's greatest lover.

In one of the most inspired pieces of casting in many a year, the devilishly handsome Depp takes on the part of a young man who believes he is Don Juan De Marco, the legendary Latin lover and seducer of more than one thousand women. It's a role Depp was born to play, his beauteous looks and doe-eyes the perfect accompaniments to a lifetime of seduction and loving.

The story unfolds with Don Juan, bedecked in Zorro mask, flowing cloak and brandishing a shiny blade, embarking upon a final fling before perching himself atop a billboard in an attempt to end his own life, having lost his one true love. The police call in Dr. Mickler, a psychiatrist on the cusp of retirement, who talks him down and has him committed to a mental hospital where he has the next ten days to prove whether Depp is, in fact, certifiable, or whether he can be unleashed once again upon the female population.

Over the course of the next week-and-a-half, Depp spins his life 'story', from his childhood in Mexico to his time in an Arab harem where his favours were taken by 1,500 women during an understandably exhausting two-year period. It's a poetic catalogue of erotic adventures that are more sensual than sexual. Within moments of his arrival, however, the hospital's female staff have turned into gibbering wrecks, while Brando's relationship with his wife seems to gain added spice as he gradually realises that Don Juan is truly who he says he is.

Slight but undoubtedly sweet, this is a comic confection of innocence and charm. Depp is again a revelation as the dream lover whose acceptance of his fantasy world shows a firmer grasp on his own 'reality' than the saner folks around him. Brando meanwhile, straining at the girth but never really shown head-to-toe, fills the screen with as much charisma, but doesn't allow himself to dominate Depp. His cheeky reproach to a colleague for putting on weight is a terrific moment, a wink at the audience. The rest of the film is equally wonderful. ★★★★ **MS**

DON'T LOOK NOW (1973)

Starring: *Julie Christie (Laura Baxter), Donald Sutherland (John Baxter), Hilary Mason (Heather), Clelia Matania (Wendy), Massimo Serato (Bishop), Renato Scarpa (Inspector Longhi)*
Director: *Nicolas Roeg*
Screenwriters: *Allan Scott, Chris Bryant, based on a short story by Daphne Du Maurier*
18/110 mins./Mystery/UK/Italy
Awards: *BAFTA – Best Cinematography*

After the tragic death of their daughter, Laura and John Baxter take a trip to Venice in an attempt to save their marriage. While there they encounter a strange couple of old ladies, one of whom claims to have second sight. Meanwhile, John catches a glimpse of a figure in a red coat, as Venice is terrorised by a serial killer.

Few films can as efficiently induce an attack of the screaming heebie-jeebies as Nicolas Roeg's classic supernatural thriller. Based on a Daphne Du Maurier short story and made in 1973, it's one of the most haunting, enigmatic and, in the final moments, bloodily shocking movies ever made – and it showcases, in Roeg, one of Britain's most distinctive voices who, sadly, was reduced to tatty American TV mini-series and, last year, a documentary about Claudia Schiffer.

It's difficult to pin down exactly what makes *Don't Look Now* so effective. From its opening, in which we witness the sudden drowning of the Baxters' daughter (brilliantly shot with pre-Steadicam hand-held by cinematographer Anthony Richmond), the film starts to creep into the subconscious. Images of water permeate the movie; red is associated both with overwhelming grief and danger. Shattered glass and empty dining rooms are equally regular symbolic motifs, while Venice, deserted and wintry, is a suitably chilly setting for the enigmatic riddle.

But, if the technical feats of the movie are impressive, it's Sutherland and Christie who give the movie its mournful, deeply moving heart. They're a heartrendingly believable couple struggling to survive the pressures that the tragic loss of their daughter has put on their marriage. The infamous sex scene, intercut with their post-coital getting ready to go out, all to Pino Donaggio's poignantly lyrical score, remains the single most brilliantly realised erotic sequence in cinema. And the ending is still as much of an horrific jolt as it was nearly three decades ago, managing to terrify and move simultaneously – more than you can say for Claudia Schiffer. ★★★★★ **AS**

◎ DONNIE BRASCO (1997)

Starring: *Al Pacino (Lefty Ruggiero), Johnny Depp (Donnie Brasco/Joe Pistone), Michael Madsen (Sonny Black), Bruno Kirby (Nicky), James Russo (Paulie), Anne Heche (Maggie Pistone)*
Director: *Mike Newell*
Screenwriter: *Paul Attanasio, based on the book* Donnie Brasco: My Undercover Life In The Mafia *by Joseph D. Pistone, with Richard Woodley*
18/127 mins./Crime/Drama/Thriller/USA

Joe Pistone is an undercover FBI agent ordered to infiltrate the mob as Donnie Brasco. He befriends a small-time hoodlum called Lefty, who he forms a genuine friendship with – although he knows that his actions will cost Lefty his life . . .

As if setting out to disprove the commonly-held theory that only Martin Scorsese can make based-on-fact tales of corruption and betrayal with a Mafia background, here's a movie that seems to be almost a Greatest Hits package of material from the Scorsese catalogue – *Mean Streets, GoodFellas, Casino* – done in a far less operatic, slightly more credible fashion. It may lack Scorsese's obvious relish for the milieu, but that at least leaves it less open to charges of glamorising horrible people doing terrible things in a ghastly business.

In the late 1970s, small-time New York wiseguy known as Lefty befriends young-blood Donnie Brasco, and brings him into the mob, schooling him in how to dress and talk and in the minutiae of the family's intricate power structure. But Donnie is actually Joseph Pistone, a deep-cover FBI agent on a long-term assignment to infiltrate the cosa nostra. The job is already a strain on Pistone's marriage and family life, and gets even more complicated when he begins to feel a genuine friendship for the deadbeat Lefty, though he knows that as soon as the operation is over his friend will be murdered for being taken in by him.

Screenwriter Paul Attanasio, a veteran of *Quiz Show* and TV's *Homicide: Life On The Street*, crafts a showcase for actors: no matter how one might want to fast-forward through the repetitive scenes of Pistone having trouble with his wife (an ill-used Anne Heche), the material soars whenever the men are left alone. Pacino, as hunched and battered here as he was smooth and powerful as *The Godfather*, is remarkable, and Depp manfully keeps up with him. You also get wiseguy action from such reliable types as Michael Madsen, James Russo and Bruno Kirby.

Mike Newell sometimes directs it too much as if it were a soap opera, rarely using Donnie-Joe's situation for suspense and not quite matching the intensity of the similarly-plotted *Deep Cover*. However, Pacino's outstanding work elevates this to the crime movie pantheon. It even has at least one new line destined to enter the Gangster Catchphrase Hall Of Fame: 'Remember, when they send for you, it's your best friend that does it.' ★★★★ **KN**

◎ DONNIE DARKO (2001)

Starring: *Jake Gyllenhaal (Donnie Darko), Jenna Malone (Gretchen Ross), Drew Barrymore (Mrs. Karen Pomeroy), Mary McDonnell (Rose Darko), Katharine Ross (Dr. Lilian Thurman), Patrick Swayze (Jim Cunningham), Noah Wyle (Dr. Monnitoff), Maggie Gyllenhaal (Elizabeth Darko)*
Director: *Richard Kelly*
Screenwriter: *Richard Kelly*
15/188 mins./Drama/Mystery/Sci-fi/Thriller/USA

A rabbit-headed figure, Frank, informs American teen Donnie Darko that the world is coming to an end. School hysteria is also proving to be dangerously life-threatening.

On a shadowy, non-existent street in Weirdsville, USA, first-time writer-director Richard Kelly lives next door to David Lynch and Greg Araki. In order to keep up with the neighbours, he has crafted his own magnificently bizarre hybrid of suburban paranoia and apocalyptic teen angst.

Of course, there could be a 'logical' explanation for the disturbing nightmares and time-travelling episodes that central-character Donnie undergoes. He's a sharply intelligent but world-weary boy, and the fact that he avoids taking his medication hints that what we're seeing – including his imaginary giant rabbit friend – is the by-product of some form of schizophrenia.

But Kelly leaves plenty of room for dark and playful ambiguity, and it's the casting of Jake Gyllenhaal that makes these bold moves succeed. A black sheep triplet to Tobey Maguire and Elijah Wood, Gyllenhaal's exquisite comic timing and laidback personality create a wonderful tension with the odd events surrounding Donnie. Donnie is a walking storm of complex human emotions, trapped in a world where teachers, parents and other adults want to simplify everything into twin extremes – fear and love, right and wrong, Republicans and Democrats.

If the New Age gurus and grown-ups in the film who try to ban books do so because they want everyone to conform, then Donnie is a rebel with a cause and Gyllenhaal a pin-up star for the 'Doom Generation'. Even the name – Donnie Darko – sounds like a comic book superhero and, in a beautifully twisted way, he might be the only one who can save the world.

Kelly deftly tickles the eye and the ear, particularly during Donnie's visual and aural hallucinations. He also makes great use of a 1980s soundtrack. When the camera pans, *Magnolia*-style, across the cast to a version of Tears For Fears' 'Mad World', the lyrics perfectly sum up Donnie's gloriously skewed state of mind: 'The dreams in which I'm dying are the best I've ever had.' ★★★★★ **AM**

◎ THE DOOR IN THE FLOOR (2004)

Starring: *Elle Fanning (Ruth Cole), Jeff Bridges (Ted Cole), Kim Basinger (Marion Cole), Jon Foster (Eddie O'Hare), Larry Pine (Interviewer)*
Director: *Tod Williams*
Screenwriter: *Tod Williams, based on the novel by John Irving*
15/111 mins./Drama/USA

Eccentric children's writer Ted Cole and his wife Marion have been ripped apart by the deaths of their two sons. When aspiring author Eddie O'Hare is employed as Ted's assistant one summer, he becomes their reluctant go-between.

John Irving's busy, quirky novels have proven tough to adapt for the big screen as there's often too much going on. Tod Williams deals with this by tackling only the first third of Irving's *A Widow For One Year*, his *The Door In The Floor* combining a coming-of-age tale with a cryptic study of how grief can dismantle a family.

In a sense, it's a detective story, with Eddie the wide-eyed outsider trying to figure out what happened to the Coles' sons, and why exactly Ted has hired him. Even the casting seems designed to wrongfoot. Jeff Bridges has the most likeable face in Hollywood: big, friendly and rumpled like an unmade bed. The sight of him shambling around in a tatty dressing gown, flashing his wry grin, recalls *The Big Lebowski*'s The Dude, but Ted is a much trickier customer. Meanwhile, Basinger, whose beauty gets deeper and sadder with age, makes Marion glassy with grief and impossible to read.

Ruthlessly plotted and aching with emotional alienation, it's intelligent and intriguing, but frostier than *The Ice Storm*. Even the moments of sexual farce (Eddie is the unluckiest masturbator since Jim in *American Pie*) are more melancholy than funny. If you're in the mood, though, this better-than-the-book adaptation casts quite a spell. ★★★ **DL**

THE DOORS (1991)

Starring: *Val Kilmer (Jim Morrison), Meg Ryan (Pamela Courson), Kathleen Quinlan (Patricia Kennealy), Michael Madsen (Tom Baker), Josh Evans (Bill Siddons), Dennis Burkley (Dog), Billy Idol (Cat), Kyle MacLachlan (Ray Manzarek)*
Director: *Oliver Stone*
Screenwriters: *Randall Jahnson, Oliver Stone*
18/140 mins./Biography/Drama/Music/USA

The rise and decline of the late 1960s band The Doors.

Oliver Stone's hallucinatory psychodrama biopic of rock god/poet Jim Morrison goes further than most cinematic memoirs of artists in confronting its subject's destructive impulses while glorifying his creative energy.

Val Kilmer is extraordinary as Morrison, holding the centre with a demonic charisma, while Stone recreates the late 60s milieu with vibrant versimilitude.

The coming together of The Doors (with Kyle MacLachlan particularly strong as the disciplined organist Ray Manzarek), their rise and Morrison's star power are conveyed with fond exhilaration. But there's also a constant undercurrent of awareness that the permissiveness and excess of the day will fuel Morrison's horrific physical decline and his erratic, obnoxious behaviour, bringing about his pitiable death in 1971.

The clear intent is to equate the acid experience, the quest for inner knowledge and Jim's creepy sado-masochism with the dark, nightmare side of The American Dream. In this, the film is fairly successful. But the attempts to plumb Morrison's sensitive side, his (pretentious) philosophical bent and his struggle to channel his considerable talents positively are something of a blur in the trippy kaleidoscope. Great soundtrack, though! **★★★ AE**

DOUBLE INDEMNITY (1944)

Starring: *Fred MacMurray (Walter Neff), Barbara Stanwyck (Phyllis Dietrichson), Edward G. Robinson (Barton Keyes), Porter Hall (Mr. Jackson), Gig Young, billed as Byron Barr (Nino Zachette)*
Director: *Billy Wilder*
Screenwriters: *Raymond Chandler, Billy Wilder, based on the novel by James M. Cain*
PG/106 mins./Crime/USA

Walter Neff, a smooth-talking insurance agent, and Phyllis Dietrichson, the wife of one of his clients, are instantly attracted to one another. They plot to murder her old man and make off with his life insurance money, but all does not go to plan . . .

It's become a cliché to mention Great Oscar Injustices when celebrating classic movies, but *Double Indemnity* is such a prime example of the phenomenon, it's impossible to resist. Billy Wilder's hard-boiled masterpiece lost out to its polar opposite, cosy priest drama *Going My Way* – given a choice between Barbara Stanwyck in a fetishised anklet and Bing Crosby in a dog collar, the Academy plumped for the padre. Maybe they figured World War II America deserved something with more of a feel-good factor.

For his first thriller, Wilder took a break from his regular screenwriter Charles Brackett, calling upon no less a talent than Raymond Chandler to help him adapt James M. Cain's sleazy (in a good way) tale of an insurance salesman seduced into murder by a suburban femme fatale. The two men didn't get on – Chandler's drinking trying Wilder's patience on numerous occasions – but the resulting script is a beautiful hybrid. The director gives his comic instincts full rein in the exchanges between sucker Fred MacMurray and dogged investigator Edward G. Robinson, while the novelist finds room for sinister poetics in the voice-over – 'Murder smells like honeysuckle.' With the whole thing enriched by Cain's fatalistic worldview, it all (to quote Edward G.'s character) 'fits together like a watch'.

Arguably the least pretentious of cinema's great directors, Wilder distanced himself from claims that the movie represented an early foray into film noir, only grudgingly accepting that some of the lighting had a certain style to it and, yes, he was a fan of Fritz Lang's German expressionist work. Regardless of stylistic considerations, *Double Indemnity* does boast an undeniable 'noir' element in Stanwyck's über-bitch, Phyllis Dietrichson. Phyllis is a stunning creation, opportunistic yet calculating, remote yet passionate, world-weary yet as petulant as a spoiled child. She's on screen a relatively short amount of time, certainly far less than MacMurray, yet it's an iconic performance from the moment she appears at the top of the staircase wearing only a towel and a seductive sneer. She's also granted some of the best lines in a film packed with memorable dialogue, culminating in a moment of shockingly frank self-awareness – 'I never loved you, Walter, not you or anybody else – I'm rotten to the heart.' Guess what – this dynamic villainess didn't win an Oscar, either. She lost out to Ingrid Bergman's vulnerable victim from *Gaslight*. **★★★★★ RF**

Tagline
From the moment they met it was murder!

THE DOUBLE LIFE OF VÉRONIQUE (LA DOUBLE VIE DE VERONIQUE) (1991)

Starring: *Irène Jacob (Veronique/Veronika), Halina Gryglaszewska (Aunt), Kalina Jedrusik (Gaudy Woman), Aleksander Bardini (Orchestra Conductor), Wladyslaw Kowalski (Veronika's Father)*
Director: *Krzysztof Kieslowski*
Screenwriter: *Krzysztof Kieslowski, Krzysztof Piesiewicz*
15/97 mins./Drama/Fantasy/France/Poland

Awards: *Cannes Film Festival – Best Actress*

Although oblivious to the other's existence, Veronika, an aspiring Polish soprano, and Véronique, a Parisian music teacher, gradually become aware that they are connected to a spiritual twin.

Krzysztof Kieslowski's first film outside his native Poland is meticulously balanced between the mystical and the mysterious to enable viewers to decide for themselves whether the lives of two women sharing several physical, cultural and psychological traits are linked by pure coincidence or a grander design.

Divinely photograped through golden filters by Slawomir Idziak, to emphasise the warmth of the worlds inhabited by Veronika in Krakow and Véronique in Paris, this is a film of great fragility and beauty, with the delicacy of the puppet theatre and Zbigniew Preisner's score being embellished by the surfeit of reflective surfaces that project the imagery back on itself and, thus, reinforce the overall sense of duality.

Irène Jacob is simply sublime and thoroughly merited the Best Actress prize at Cannes. However, she wasn't Kieslowski's first choice for the role and it's hard to imagine how the film might have turned out had Andie MacDowell been cast.

It would have retained its experimental abstraction, however, as Kieslowski seems to be rehearsing the transcendent style he would employ on the *Three Colours* trilogy. As she would be in the concluding part, Jacob is swathed in red throughout, as though she is cocooned by the forces controlling her destiny and Kieslowski is celebrating the use of a shade that had now lost its political overtones, with the fall of Communism. The star is also rescued from its Soviet associations, as it's suggested that Veronika's journey parallels that of the Magi (whose story is mentioned early in the action by her mother) as they made their way to Bethlehem.

Kieslowski permitted a considerable amount of ambiguity to cloud the conclusion. But the audience at the New York premiere didn't understand the significance of Véronique's reverie by the tree and so Kieslowski shot an additional minute, in which her father (Claude Duneton) comes out to call to her and she runs into his arms.

Compelling, challenging and irresistibly beautiful, this delicate metaphysical masterpiece only emphasises how much cinema lost through Krzysztof Kieslowski's tragically early death. ★★★★★ **DP**

DOWN WITH LOVE (2003)

Starring: *Renee Zellweger (Barbara Novak), Ewan McGregor (Catcher Block), Sarah Paulson (Vikki Hiller), David Hyde Pierce (Peter MacMannus), Tony Randall (Theodore Banner), Jeri Ryan (Gwendolyn), Melissa George (Elkie)*
Director: *Peyton Reed*
Screenwriters: *Eve Ahlert, Dennis Drake*
12A/101 mins./Comedy/Romance/USA/Germany

New York, 1963, and author Barbara Novak's feminist guide, *Down With Love*, is a huge success. Celebrity playboy journalist Catcher Block disguises himself as a well-mannered innocent in an attempt to make her fall in love and expose her as a hypocrite. But he finds himself falling for her, too.

Let's face it, the world isn't exactly crying out for a tribute to the Rock Hudson/Doris Day capers of the late 50s/early 60s. America certainly isn't, if this film's disappointing US box office is anything to go by. Nonetheless, director Reed (*Bring It On*) has lovingly recreated the kitsch style and innuendo-charged wit of comedies like *Pillow Talk* in this fluffy little frippery, and with moderate success.

Drawing its romantic obstacles from a burgeoning sexual revolution (Barbara's theory for female empowerment champions sex over romantic love), this revels in the changing political climate of its time. Catcher woos simpering air hostesses only to face rejection once they've read Barbara's man-bashing tome, *Down With Love*, while her publisher Vikki makes mincemeat of Catcher's smitten boss, Peter.

The fluidity of the sexual dynamics drives the plot forward while permitting nudges and winks aplenty – Catcher and Barbara are both trying to stick to their guns (she mustn't fall in love, he mustn't have sex if he's to win her heart), while the effeminate Peter is attempting to convince Vikki that he's all man. To lay on the farce further, the two men swap flats for the purposes of wooing their women. So while Peter is fumbling with the hi-tech controls of a kitted-out bachelor pad, Catcher is using his boss' more traditional quarters to convince Barbara of his worth as a long-term prospect.

Casting-wise, McGregor is no Rock Hudson, but he glides through his role as a dapper poseur with the requisite charm and lightness of touch, as does Hyde Pierce in a near-reprisal of his regular role as Frasier Crane's uptight brother Niles in the long-running US sitcom. Zellweger, however, may act the part but does not look it, her bony frame appearing out of place amidst the curvy 60s stylings.

This, along with a few clumsy scenes and a slight overdose of knowing humour, makes *Down With Love* more of a pleasant little diversion than a truly confident comedy. ★★★ **LB**

DOWNFALL (UNTERGANG, DER) (2004)

Starring: *Bruno Ganz (Adolf Hitler), Alexandra Maria Lara (Traudl Junge), Corinna Harfouch (Magda Goebbels), Ulrich Matthes (Joseph Goebbels), Julian Kohler (Eva Braun), Heino Ferch (Albert Speer)*
Director: *Oliver Hirschbiegel*
Screenwriter: *Bernd Eichinger, based on the books* Inside Hitler's Bunker *by Joachim Fest and* Until the Final Hour *by Traudie Junge and Melissa Muller*
15/156 mins./Drama/History/War/Germany/Italy/Austria

In 1945, as Berlin falls to the Russians, Adolf Hitler and his inner circle retreat to a bunker for a futile last stand. Hitler's secretary Traudl looks on as the Fuhrer veers between depression and delusion and finally marries his long-term girlfriend, Eva Braun, before putting a bullet in his brain . . .

Most dramatic versions of the fall of Berlin and the simultaneous events within Hitler's bunker end with the suicides of Adolf Hitler and Eva Braun. But Oliver Hirschbiegel's impressive epic is notable for soldiering on grimly after the main character has left the stage, presenting the complete collapse of the Third Reich.

It keeps us in the company of the last remaining guilty parties, the time-serving minions and misplaced idealists, as they spill out of the bunker into the rubble of the city, struggling to find a place in the strange new world without the monster who's shaped their lives and wrecked an entire continent.

We get thumbnail sketches of the supporting monsters: Eva Braun desperately organising parties in the rubble; Himmler talking undying loyalty then scarpering to pitch some hopeless deal to the Allies; and, worst of all, Magda Goebbels, who gently murders her six children while her husband finds his preparations for suicide are upstaged by the Führer getting there first and doing it with more style.

At the centre of it all is Bruno Ganz, easily one of the screen's great Hitlers. He performs in German with an exact recreation of that rasping accent, depicting with shocking conviction a mercurial tyrant who pats dogs and children, refuses to listen to the bad news and throws those famous tantrums – especially when told that the dauntless armies he has been counting on are largely imaginary. The telling strokes, though, are the callous asides which show how estranged from reality he is; when told young officers have been wiped out, he remarks, 'That's what young men are for.' One priceless moment, too dreadful to be invention, sees the official summoned to perform a hasty marriage obliged by Nazi law to ask whether Hitler or Braun have Jewish ancestors before proceeding with the pathetic ceremony.

Having made subterranean suspense film *The Experiment*, Hirschbiegel is an imaginative choice of director. Throughout, we get a real sense of the enclosed, insane world of the bunker – but the director never allows us to lose sight of the dreadful plight of the rest of the battered city, where the citizens are caught between Nazi death squads and the onrolling Soviet tanks. ★★★★ **S O'H**

DOCTOR DOLITTLE (1967)

Staring: *Rex Harrison (Doctor John Dolittle), Anthony Newley (Matthew Mugg), William Dix (Tommy Stubbins), Portia Nelson (Sarah Dolittle), Samantha Eggar (Emma Fairfax), Richard Attenborough (Albert Blossom)*
Director: *Richard Fleischer*
Screenwriter: *Leslie Bricusse, based on stories by Hugh Lofting*
U/152 mins./Musical/USA
Awards: *Academy Awards – Best Special Effects, Best Original Song ('Talk To The Animals')*

Doctor Dolittle, a world famous veterinarian who can speak most known animal languages, sets off to find the legendary Great Pink Sea Snail. Along the way he engages in dialogue with the Pushmee-Pullyu and the Giant Moon Moth.

A hugely expensive (for its time) and overly lengthy family adventure based on Hugh Lofting's treasured series of novels, that emerges, just, as an adequate genial diversion. With Rex Harrison lightly reworking his Professor Higgins routine from *My Fair Lady* as the upper-crust vet with a knack for animal linguistics, the film takes a leisurely tone of voice, relying on a procession of rather flat songs and good animatronics, as well as animal training, to carry it. The wan, meandering storytelling hampers the escapist slant, while Harrison's smoothness, not even stirring himself to vigour for the Oscar wining song, 'Talk To The Animals' (as with playing Higgins, he talks his way through his songs rather like The Pet Shop Boys), is too distant to give the film a strong centrepiece.

Washed in Technicolor, the film is as bright as a button, but its lack of any great peril – it is a buoyant picaresque, globe trotting in search of rare species – leaving it a matter of whimsy rather than thrill. The biggest burden Dolittle faces is to raise the finance for is latest expedition – not the stuff of ripe drama. With *Mary Poppins* a recent hit, the idea clearly is a lighthearted not-to-say lightheaded parable of a man who understand animal and therefore is much more in-tune with what the world needs. It's a green dream, with songs and giddy children. And there is a mild appeal in watching Harrison's deadpan boffin blow bubbles to converse with goldfish and invent eyeglasses for a myopic horse. Although, too many of the animal scenes revert to a chaotic slapstick as they try to cram as many furred and feathered friends into them as possible. The set must have smelled rotten.

Richard Fleischer was a consummate craftsman of big budget fantasy adventures after *20,000 Leagues Under The Sea* and *Fantastic Voyage*, but is less sure how to combine his exotic style with a burlesque musical. ★★ **IN**

DOCTOR DOLITTLE (1998)

Starring: *Eddie Murphy (Doctor Dolittle), Ossie Davis (Archer Dolittle), Oliver Platt (Dr. Mark Weller), Peter Boyle (Calloway), Raven (Charisse Dolittle)*
Director: *Betty Thomas*
Screenwriter: *Nat Mauldin, based on the stories of Hugo Lofting*
PG/85 mins./Comedy/USA

After a car crash, Doctor Dolittle finds he can understand everything that animals say. First he has to accept his new skill, then learn to use it . . .

Given the recent track record of chattering creature movies, remaking the 1967 Rex Harrison starrer (based on Hugo Lofting's children's charmer) about a doctor who could talk to animals must have seemed such a good idea. Add to that a director with an able track record in comedies (*The Brady Bunch*, *Private Parts*), and Murphy, and the results should really have spoken for themselves. And in terms of box office – enough to spawn a pitiful sequel – they did. But no amount of talent can disguise what a lacklustre vehicle this is.

As John Dolittle, Murphy is a respected medic, whose ability to converse with the animal kingdom has been buried since childhood when, in a dreary prologue, his chats with his dog (voiced by Ellen DeGeneres) are curbed by an 'exorcism'. But it only takes a quick bang on the bonce one night, while swerving his car to avoid a stray dog, for it all to come flooding back.

Cue problems with Murphy and movie alike; while word gets round and he finds himself doling out treatment to the furry and feathered clients that flock to him, the movie seems unsure of where to go after its one joke is spent.

Thus we are left with a beautifully crafted animatronic menagerie (courtesy of Jim Henson's Creature Shop) who, presumably because their natter is regarded as enough of a selling point, are given nothing to do but fire off cheap one-liners and irritate their human star. The staples of an arch villain and strong storyline are absent, leaving merely a display of frantic, forced Murphy mugging and a mawkish subplot about a suicidal circus tiger that'll have 'em vomiting in the aisles.

There's no denying *Doctor Dolittle* is slickly put together – the set pieces featuring man and animal are impressive – unspoilt by any evidence of blue-screening or special effects wizardry – but it's just too bad everything else is such a bland disappointment. ★★ **CW**

DR. JEKYLL AND MR. HYDE (1932)

Starring: *Fredric March (Dr. Henry Jekyll/Mr. Hyde), Miriam Hopkins (Ivy Pearson), Rose Hobart (Muriel Carew), Holmes Herbert (Dr. Lanypn), Edgar Norton (Poole), Halliwell Hobbes (Brog-Gen Carew)*
Director: *Rouben Mamoulian*
Screenwriters: *Samuel Hoffenstein, Percy Heath based on the novella* The Strange Case Of Dr. Jekyll And Mr. Hyde *by Robert Louis Stevenson*
15/90 mins./Horror/USA
Awards: *Academy Awards – Best Actor*

Victorian researcher Dr. Jekyll takes a serum that unleashes the wicked side of his nature as the ape-like Mr. Hyde. While Jekyll is engaged to a prim miss, Hyde gets involved with a Soho slut. Jekyll tries to quit the drug, but involuntarily becomes the murderous Hyde.

Certainly the best all-round film adaptation of the much-remade Robert Louis Stevenson novella, this offers March in Oscar-winning form as the handsome, romantic Jekyll and the neanderthal prankster Hyde. This version suggests Dr. J devises his potion to deal with the sexual frustration he feels during his long engagement, which prompts Hyde to lope lecherously after good-time girl Champagne Ivy.

Made before the Hays Code was in force, there are daring moments of semi-nudity and suggestiveness, plus a still-unsettling progression of violence as the degenerate Hyde becomes more depraved with each new transformation. March's Hyde is a daring, teasing villain, a fanged ape trussed up in an opera hat and evening clothes. Hyde enjoys a faceful of rain, and snatches the opportunity to grope a passing music hall girl or trip up a waiter with his silver-handled cane. He snarls and threatens then giving an almost-winning grin before pouncing, condemns Jekyll as a hypocrite who likes to ogle a girl's leg but talk about her circulation, and finally scales the laboratory shelves like Kong in a temper when the police come for him. Rouben Mamoulian, one of the least-remembered of great early Hollywood directors, uses a great deal of then-daring technical trickery – lengthy subjective camera scenes, set-piece transformations, striking symbolic images – but the film still buzzes thanks to the peppy performances of March and Hopkins. Also worth catching are the versions with John Barrymore (1920) and Spencer Tracy (1941). ★★★★★ **KN**

DOCTOR MABUSE, THE GAMBLER (1922)

Starring: *Rudolf Klein-Rogge (Dr. Mabuse), Aud Egede Nissen (Cara Carozza, die Tanzerin), Getrude Welcker (Gräfin Dusy Told), Bernhard Goetzke (Chief Inspector Norbert von Wenck)*
Director: *Fritz Lang*
Screenwriters: *Fritz Lang, Thea von Harbou based on the novel by Norbert Jacques*
PG/242 mins./Crime/Germany

Dr. Mabuse is a Machiavellian mastermind whose ruthless gang exploits the weakness of such corrupt fools as Edgar Hull and Count Told. However, Chief Inspector von Wenck is determined to get his man.

Brilliantly played with flamboyant dastardliness by Rudolf Klein-Rogge, psychoanalyst Dr. Mabuse is a criminal mastermind, whose genius for hypnotism and disguise enable him to defraud the Stock Exchange, steal treaties, run crooked gambling dens, abduct women and murder anyone who stands in his way. Yet, when he's finally brought to book, he disintegrates into insanity.

As is clear from the subtitles appended to each episode – 'The Great Gambler: A Portrait of the Age' and 'Inferno: A Play About People of Our Time' – Fritz Lang and his co-scenarist and wife-to-be Thea von Harbou (who had just divorced Klein-Rogge) intended this epic thriller to be a condemnation of Weimar decadence and amorality and contemporary critics lauded its exposé of societal excess.

Yet theorist Siegfried Kracauer could later suggest that the film anticipated the nation's seduction by a similarly mesmeric malevolent, Adolf

Hitler, who masked his crimes with a cloak of political expediency. It certainly shared the brooding atmosphere of another Expressionist classic that Kracauer claimed prepared the German psyche for tyranny, Robert Wiene's *The Cabinet of Dr. Caligari*, whose theme of malleable madness would recur in the 1932 sequel, *The Testament of Dr. Mabuse*, in which the maniacal villain grooms asylum director Dr Baum (Oscar Beregi) as his alter ego.

However, by the time he produced a third instalment, *The Thousand Eyes of Dr. Mabuse* in 1960 (in which a madman claims to be a reincarnation of the fiend and turns out to be his son), Lang was no longer able to temper his melodramatic instincts with the visual authority he had displayed in the original, where the use of lighting effects, décor and multiple exposures was unerring and masterly.

Yet Lang still occasionally succumbs to excess here, and there are sluggish passages filled with interminable intertitles. But, overall, the plotting is assuredly mature and far less serialised than it was in his earlier two-parter, *The Spiders*. ★★★★ **DP**

German Expressionism

What is it: Prevalent in Germany after World War I, this was a style of filmmaking that sought to reveal inner experience through the use of overt stylisation and metaphor.

Hallmarks: Obviously artificial lighting (marked by deep shadows); crime/horror stories; distorted, artificial sets; extremely stylised acting; disorienting camera angles.

Key figures: Directors Fritz Lang, Robert Wiene, F.W. Murnau.

If you see one movie, see: *The Cabinet of Dr. Caligari* (Wiene, 1919)

DR. NO (1962)

Starring: *Sean Connery (James Bond), Jack Lord (Felix Leiter), Joesph Wiseman (Dr. No) Ursula Andress (Honey Ryder), Eunice Gayson (Sylvia), Lois Maxwell (Miss Moneypenny), Bernard Lee (M)*
Director: *Terence Young*
Screenwriters: *Richard Maibaum, Johanna Harwood, Berkely Mather based on the novel by Ian Fleming*
PG/110 mins./Spy/UK

James Bond investigates the murder of a British agent in Jamaica and discovers a plot by the megalomaniac villain Dr. No to scupper the US space programme.

The beginning of the super-successful franchise, this remains one of the most satisfying Bond films. Connery, with only a hint of irony, is the suave secret agent, introduced at a gaming table while lighting an expensive fag, enjoying an expense account Caribbean holiday that must have seemed like unparalleled hedonism to British audiences who'd only just got over rationing.

The licence to kill gets several endorsements as Bond efficiently and brutally sees off dastardly baddies who are threatening world peace, and – in another fantastical touch – Britain holds the key to the balance of power. Dr. No, a German-Japanese genius with metal hands, is about as credible as Fu Manchu, but Joseph Wiseman mints all the Bond villain clichés, from the gorgeously-designed island lair (courtesy of art director Ken Adam) with built-in nuclear power plant (and a then-famously-stolen portrait of the Duke of Wellington hung on the wall) through to purred threats and attempts to convince 007 to sell out and join his evil organisation ('I thought you had some style, Mr. Bond, but I see you're just a stupid policeman').

And, of course, there's Ursula Andress as prototypical Bond girl Honey Ryder, emerging from the seas in a bikini with a knife strapped to her thigh, with her own reasons for wanting to see Dr. No's scheme for world conquest thwarted.

That twangy guitar theme and the gunsight-iris titles sequence are in place already. Series regulars Bernard Lee and Lois Maxwell make their debuts, but Peter Burton plays Q (to be replaced by Desmond Llewellyn) and Jack Lord is CIA agent Felix Leiter (to be replaced by a succession of stooges). ★★★★ **KN**

DR. PHIBES RISES AGAIN (1972)

Starring: *Vincent Price (Dr. Anton Phibes), Robert Quarry (Darius Biederbeck), Peter Jeffrey (Inspector Trout), Fiona Lewis (Diana Trobridge), John Thaw (Shavers), Peter Cushing (Ship's Captain), Beryl Reid (Miss Ambrose), Terry-Thomas (Lombardo)*
Director: *Robert Fuest*
Screenwriters: *Robert Fuest, Robert Blees*
15/89 mins./Horror/UK

Dr. Anton Phibes returns from the grave and sets off for Egypt in search of the river of eternal life, with which he can revive his beloved wife. Competing with the doctor is Biederbeck, an archaeologist who has his own reasons for seeking out the mystic waters.

A lively, spirited sequel to *The Abominable Dr. Phibes*, which misses the *Se7en*-like rigour of a plot structured around the Plagues of Egypt but still manages to come up with a succession of gruesome, black comic death scenes.

Price returns as the skull-faced, white-robed Phibes, who eats and speaks through a hole in his neck and wears a wax Price mask over his mutilated face, and redecorates a pyramid in art deco style to serve as his Egyptian HQ, complete with clockwork orchestra and cinema organ. Quarry, fresh from a pair of *Count Yorga* films, was being built up as a horror star at the time, and is rather a swish, nasty leading man, but the supporting cast is sterling – Peter Cushing in a bit as a ship's captain, John Thaw as an archaeologist slashed by a killer hawk, Hugh Griffith as a drunk thrown overboard in a giant gin bottle, Beryl Reid as a grieving relative, big bald Milton Reid as a bodyguard killed by a trick telephone, Caroline Munro in a literal Rolls-Royce of coffins as the temporarily-dead Mrs. Phibes, Peter Jeffrey and John Cater as bumbling Scotland Yard men and Fiona Lewis in lovely 20s fashions as an imperilled bright young thing.

The most elaborate murder involves a His Master's Voice ceramic dog full of scorpions, but director-writer Robert Fuest, also returning from the first film, concentrates as much on art deco fripperies as the blood-letting. The climax features Price's inimitable cover version of 'Somewhere Over the Rainbow'. ★★★★ **KN**

DR. STRANGELOVE OR: HOW I LEARNED TO STOP WORRYING AND LOVE THE BOMB (1964)

Starring: *Peter Sellers (Group Capt. Lionel Mandrake/President Merkin Muffley/Dr. Strangelove), George C. Scott (Gen. 'Buck' Turgidson), Sterling Hayden (Gen. Jack D. Ripper), Keenan Wynn (Col. 'Bat' Guano), Slim Pickens (Maj. T.J. 'King' Kong), James Earl Jones (Lt. Lothar Zogg)*
Director: *Stanley Kubrick*
Screenwriters: *Stanley Kubrick, Terry Southern, Peter George, based on the novel* Red Alert *by Peter George*
PG/102 mins./Science Fiction/Comedy/War/UK

Awards: *BATFA – Best British Art Direction, Best British Film, Best Film from any Source, UN Award*

U.S. Air Force Colonel Jack Ripper goes completely and utterly mad, and sends his bomber wing to destroy the U.S.S.R. The U.S. president meets with his advisors, where the Soviet ambassador tells him that if the U.S.S.R. is hit by nuclear weapons, it will trigger a 'Doomsday Machine' which will destroy all plant and animal life on Earth.

2*001: A Space Odyssey* is usually cited as Stanley Kubrick's sole contribution to science fiction. Wrong. *Dr. Strangelove* is a black comedy. It's a savage, surreal political satire. It's a cautionary Cold War tale. It's a suspense farce. And it is also science fiction. Sci-fi is not confined to stories of space exploration, the future, or extra-terrestrial life. Science fiction is speculative fiction about human beings exploring themselves and their possibilities.

Crucially – and this is the science bit – it often does this by dealing with humans dealing with technology. Technology running away with us is the basis of *Dr. Strangelove*. When a fanatical U.S. general launches a nuclear attack on the U.S.S.R. the president has his hands full recalling bombers, calming Russians, contending with his advisors and a twisted scientist. The thriller plot comes from a serious novel by RAF officer Peter George, published in the U.S. as Red Alert, in the U.K. as *Two Hours To Doom* under the pseudonym Peter Bryant.

Kubrick loved it but thought people were so overwhelmed by the threat of annihilation that they were in denial, apathetic to nuclear documentary or drama. His goal – brilliantly realised – was to surprise audiences into reacting to the very real prospect of global extermination.

His means was the cinematic equivalent of a political cartoon, outrageously funny and deceptively provocative. It was in Kubrick's nature to disdain leaders as madmen. Co-writer Terry Southern was a satirist with a penchant for sexual mania. Together they contrived a cast of caricatures whose grotesque concerns and absurd fixations, by their very incongruity, play up the harsh, precise realism in which they are set.

The opening narration of the film, about intelligence of a doomsday device, is factual. The Strategic Air Command operations: fact. The interior of the B-52 bomber: accurate; the responses of its crew: out of the flight manual. The computers that take the situation beyond human intervention: more capable of doing just that with every passing year. Be afraid. Be very afraid.

The action is confined to three locations, each stricken by a failure to communicate. At Burpelson Air Force Base Gen. Jack D. Ripper, obsessed with bodily fluids and commie conspiracy, circumvents Fail-Safe protocol and orders a bomber wing to nuke the 'Russkies'. An RAF gallant on an exchange programme, Group-Capt. Lionel Mandrake is held captive by this genocidal maniac, then has to convince his hostile 'rescuer', Col. 'Bat' Guano and a disbelieving telephone operator that he has to speak to the president.

Aboard the B-52, code-named 'Leper Colony', moronic but dogged Maj. T.J. 'King' Kong and his crew (including James Earl Jones making his screen debut as Lt. Luther Zogg, Bombardier) experience radio failure and are oblivious to frantic efforts to recall them. In the War Room at The Pentagon ('Gentlemen, you can't fight in here. This is the War Room!'), sane but ineffectual President Merkin Muffley, rampant, gum-chomping Gen. Buck Turgidson, Soviet Ambassador de Sadesky and demented Dr. Strangelove (Kubrick's nod to *Metropolis*' mad scientist Rotwang, complete with mechanical arm, with Sellers parodying Werner Von Braun and Edward Teller) are gathered in a desperate, futile attempt to stop the machinery of an automatic Armageddon being activated.

After paying Sellers a million dollars ('I got three for the price of six,' Kubrick quipped) the director still had enough for production designer Ken Adam to create an awesome, nightmare set for Gilbert Taylor's superior black-and-white cinematography. Sellers' side-splitting, three-way display is legend but the ensemble is a wow of exaggerated, perfectly-timed, acutely-shot posturing. While two images are never forgotten – Kong astride the hydrogen bomb, yee-hawing all the way down, and Strangelove, unable to control his mechanical arm flying into the Nazi salute and throttling himself.

Every viewing is a reminder that the film is stuffed with sparkling dialogue: Kong taking inventory of the B-52 survival kits, which include money, chewing gum, nylon stockings, lipsticks and condoms, exclaiming 'Shoot, a fella can have a pretty good weekend in Vegas with all that stuff!'; Guano, sizing up Mandrake as a 'Deviated prevert', Muffley breaking it to Soviet Premier Kissoff that one of his base commanders 'Went and did a silly thing' in a classic Sellers monologue; Strangelove, so aroused by mass slaughter he rises from his wheelchair shrieking 'Mein Führer, I can walk!' ★★★★★ **AE**

d

Movie Trivia: Dr Strangelove

Peter Sellers was originally cast in four roles but had difficulty in developing the American accent for the fourth character Major T.J. 'King' Kong. After Sellers broke his leg, Slim Pickens was cast as the gung ho pilot. A giant custard pie fight finale in the war room was shot but later discarded. Peter Sellers based Dr. Strangelove's sinister accent on that of famous photographer Weegee.

DR. WHO AND THE DALEKS (1965)

Starring: *Peter Cushing (Dr. Who), Roy Castle (Ian), Jennie Linden (Barbara), Roberta Tovey (Susan), Barrie Ingham (Alydon), Geoffrey Toone (Temmosurus)*
Director: *Gordon Flemyng*
Screenwriters: *Terry Nation, Milton Subotsky*
U/82 mins./Sci-fi/UK

Dr. Who, an eccentric inventor, travels to the planet Skaro in his police box/time machine. The Doctor and his companions get involved in a war between the pacifist humanoid Thals and the evil cyborg Daleks.

A big-screen adaptation of the BBC's enormously successful TV franchise, this was an early example of dumbing-down and pumping-up. The Doctor, played on television by William Hartnell (and others) as a mysterious alien, is turned – in one of Peter Cushing's rare terrible performances – into a childish, daffy, thoroughly human scientist (whose surname actually seems to be 'Who'), first seen chuckling over the adventures of Dan Dare in the *Eagle* comic, and much-given to pottering about the laboratory overdoing the eccentric mannerisms. The crew of the TARDIS makes room for kids' entertainer Roy Castle and the Doctor's granddaughter is de-aged from a sulky, sultry teenager into a cheery little girl.

The Thals, the heroic humanoid race persecuted by the Daleks, are the weediest alien guerillas in the movies, a crew of Julian Clary lookalikes with drama school accents who have reverted to a tribal level of pre-industrial civilisation but kept their eye makeup skills honed. Nevertheless, for a generation of behind-the-sofa fans, the film is beyond criticism – simply for getting the Daleks (the great British monsters of the 1960s) on cinema screens in lovely glowing colours, and having hordes of the things trundle evilly around their metal city barking 'ex-ter-min-ate' and puffing killer smoke at cringing victims.

The skeleton of Terry Nation's H.G. Wells-derived story is still workable, with a suspenseful countdown-to-doom finale ('that's my lucky number!') and the sort of sets, music and monster-choreography impossible on a 1960s TV budget. *Daleks' Invasion Earth 2150 AD*, the sequel, is even better, but the two *Who* films still make an engaging kiddie matinee double bill. ★★★ **KN**

⊙ DOCTOR ZHIVAGO (1965)

Starring: *Omar Sharif (Doctor Yuri Zhivago), Julie Christie (Lara Antipova), Tom Courtenay (Pasha), Alec Guinness (General Yevgraf Zhivago), Ralph Richardson (Alexander Gromeko) Geraldine Chaplin (Tonya), Rod Steiger (Victor Komarovsky), Rita Tushingham (The Girl),*
Director: *David Lean*
Screenwriter: *Robert Bolt based on the novel by Boris Pasternak*
PG/193 mins./Drama/USA

Awards: *Academy Awards – Best Screenplay, Best Art Direction, Best Cinematography, Best Costume Design, Best Score*

An adaptation of Boris Pasternak's famous Russian novel, following the two romances that shape poet-doctor Yuri Zhivago, first with his childhood sweetheart Tonya, then the passionate liaison with Lara Antipova, whose own life is intricately caught up with the revolution that is sweeping their country.

This is the point for many critics where David Lean's ambition – seemingly to create the biggest movies in history – finally overtook his filmmaking craft. And certainly, by comparison with both *The Bridge On The River Kwai* and *Lawrence Of Arabia*, it is less incisive, it's hero less brittle. However, this is less down to a dulling of Lean's art or screenwriter Robert Bolt's ability to glean a strong narrative out of a long-winded book, than the more romantic leanings of the story itself. Which meant the script, as rich and intelligent as it is, did work to Lean's worst tendencies – he was a sucker for a beautiful face and in Julie Christie found a beauty that could fell a nation. She is the equivalent of Peter O'Toole's Lawrence, but he was more complex a character, much more so than Omar Sharif's swoony Zhivago. That said, this is a film, achingly long, that has power in its veins, a story told with vivid colour, pain, texture and a ravishing sense of the romance of film.

When compared to the so-called epics of the modern era, to criticise *Zhivago* for shallowness seems absurd. Its tale of twin loves, and of a nation tearing itself apart – the parallel lies within Zhivago, a man conflicted between two passions as his country is conflicted between two futures – has a real majesty. This is not just down to Lean's poetic camera, and never has catastrophic starvation looked quite this gorgeous, but to the strength of the performances. Christie and Sharif have to carry the film's longing, the magnetic need between them is palpable, but Bolt's barbed screenwriting is most alive in two other characters. Firstly, Tom Courtney's stoic, unshakable Pasha, rapt with revolutionary zeal ('He's the kind of man the world pretends to look up to, and in fact despises'). Secondly, the standout, the dark face of bitter realism that ultimately keeps the film from slipping into a distant rapture, is Rod Steiger's brilliantly callous Komarovsky. He is twisted, hungry, a cruel manipulator, whose vivid commentary is the counterpoint to the wanton sweeps of poets and warriors. He's the film's true human.

It requires effort, stamina through its long hours, but Lean creates moments of cinema for history (if not quite the vice versa) – Klaus Kinski's cameo on the gruelling train journey; the staggering ice palace sequence; the bloody quelling of the revolutionaries in Moscow). And if Maurice Jarre's soaring score, a landscape in itself, doesn't move you then you have ice in your veins as cold as a Siberian winter. ★★★★ **IN**

⊙ DRACULA (1931)

Starring: *Bela Lugosi (Count Dracula), Helen Chandler (Mina Seward), David Manners (Jonathan Harker), Dwight Frye (Renfield), Edward Van Sloan (Dr. Van Helsing)*
Director: *Tod Browning*
Screenwriters: *Tod Browning, Dudley Murphy, Garrett Ford, based on the novel by Bram Stoker and the 1927 stage play by Hamilton Deane and John Lloyd Balderston*
PG/84 mins./Horror/USA

Estate agent Renfield travels to the Carpathian mountains and is met by a mysterious coachman who delivers him to Castle Dracula for the worst night in the history of the tourist trade.

There have been many Draculas. But the one against which all others are measured is Bela Lugosi. Tod Browning's 1931 film is stagey and creaky, but it also has wonderful, unforgettable moments. Lugosi's performance is, on one level, high camp. Yet when he says 'I am Dracula,' by God he means it. When we're talking about the blood-sucking undead, he simply is the man. Stoker's novel, published in 1897, has proved as irresistible for dramatisation as his vampire's magnetic power over his victims. Stoker himself (business manager of London's Lyceum Theatre) turned it into a play which was never produced. Then in 1921 a Hungarian silent film, *Drakula's Death* (now lost), used a different plot entirely but borrowed the name. F.W. Murnau's *Nosferatu* is the eeriest version of all and bequeathed Max Schreck's repulsive, ratlike vampire to our collective nightmares.

In 1924 in London, Hamilton Deane wrote an authorised stage version of the book which pared down both plot and characters. It was critically derided but was nevertheless a hit. And it's to this version that we owe the image of the vampire as a suave man-about-town decked in immaculate evening dress. When it reached Broadway in 1927, re-written by John Balderston, it provided the big break for Hungarian émigré Bela Blasko. Bela's exotic accent and sinister charisma regularly had women fainting in the aisles. Universal's plans for a faithful adaptation of Stoker's novel were abandoned in favour of the simplified play when the Great Depression left them strapped for cash. They were also strapped for a star. It was intended as a vehicle for Lon Chaney by his favourite director, Browning, whose flair for the macabre had been amply demonstrated in the Chaney-starring *London After Midnight* (1927). Sadly, Chaney died of cancer in 1930. Enter Lugosi.

Ill at ease with sound, Browning often deferred to cinematographer Karl Freund, whose credits included Fritz Lang's *Metropolis* (he would go on to direct *The Mummy* in 1932). Nevertheless, Browning achieved a pervasively creepy atmosphere with long periods of silence and stylised movement, massive, decayed staircases, dank dungeons, giant spider webs, squeaking bats, howling wolves, and Lugosi's tortured delivery ('Listen to them, children of the night. What music they make').

That it is Lugosi's presence that makes this film a classic is easy to demonstrate thanks to the early sound era practice of making different language versions of the same movie. Using the same script and sets, Universal produced a Spanish-speaking *Dracula* simultaneously, its cast and crew working through the night to make way for Browning's unit by day. In many ways it is technically superior, with more interesting, more fluid camera work. But its *Dracula*, Carlos Villarias, is as hokey as Lugosi but signally fails to create the deliriously tingling unease. Lugosi's unnaturalness is strangely perfect. He sported no fangs. He had no special effects makeup other than dark lipstick and light green greasepaint. Pencil spotlights were shone on his eyes to emphasise his hypnotic stare.

Later Draculas have always been determinedly un-Lugosi-like: tall, smooth Christopher Lee in Hammer's handsome cycle, Jack Palance's twisted victim figure, Frank Langella's rakish seducer, tortured Gary Oldman in Coppola's spectacle, Klaus Kinski sensationally disgusting in Herzog's remake of *Nosferatu* (1979). But from the Universal horror cycle through scores of derivative B-movies, parodies, remakes and spinoffs (including *Sesame Street*'s numerate instructor The Count), it is the image of Lugosi that endures as the iconic vampire. So inseparable did he become from the role of Dracula that he ended up parodying the role in ever more degrading vehicles, the last and lowest being Ed Wood's notorious *Plan 9 From Outer Space*. ★★★★ **AE**

◑ DRACULA (1958)

Starring: *Peter Cushing (Dr. Van Helsing), Christopher Lee (Count Dracula), Michael Gough (Arthur Holmwood), Melissa Stribling (Mina Holmwood), John Van Eyssen (Jonathan Harker)*
Director: *Terence Fisher*
Screenwriter: *Jimmy Sangster, based on the novel by Bram Stoker*
15/82 mins./Horror/UK

After Jonathan Harker attacks Dracula at his castle, the vampire travels to a nearby city, where he preys on the family of Harker's fiancée. The only one who may be able to protect them is Dr. van Helsing, Harker's friend and fellow-student of vampires, who is determined to destroy Dracula, whatever the cost.

It's increasingly difficult now to convey the excitement of a film being shown on television. There was a time – pre-Sky, pre-digital, pre-DVD even – when you were at the mercy of the programmers' whim. Hell, there were only three channels and they were off half the time. In light of this, respect is due to the BBC for what must be one of the great innovations in the history of television. No, we're not talking ground-breaking, thought-provoking documentaries, or even *Big Brother*. What the Beeb did, in the halcyon days of the 70s, was to turn their weekend late-night slot into a horror movie double bill. Thus it was possible to see Karloff's *Frankenstein*, followed by Christopher Lee's take on the same role. The next week it might be Bela Lugosi's *Dracula* and, in sharp contrast, Christopher Lee, in the 1958 version. It was Universal versus Hammer and at the time, that colour stuff sure looked good.

'Hammer' is now a word synonymous with the history of horror movies. Hammer Films, the films that fuelled the fantasies and nightmares of several generations, began as a distribution outfit in the 1930s. William Hinds – the 'Hammer' of vaudeville act Hammer & Smith – lent his name to the company, although it was initially Enrique Carerras, and later his son James, who ran the operation at Bray Studios. They made a variety of movies (including cinematic spin-offs from the popular Dick Barton radio show) hitting on the perfect formula in the mid 50s. *The Quatermass Experiment*, based on the BBC TV serial, showed Hammer that audiences craved horror.

What Hammer did – and this shouldn't be under-estimated – was bring colour to the horror genre. Even two years later in *Psycho*, Alfred Hitchcock was using chocolate syrup to simulate blood in the shower because it looked better in black and white. But when Christopher Lee sucked neck in *Dracula*, you saw the lush delights of Eastmancolor etched indelibly on his teeth. Casting, of course, played a huge part in the success of the Hammer cannon. Having cast Peter Gushing as the icy Baron in the previous year's *Curse Of Frankenstein*, they remoulded him as the urbane man with a conscience – Van Helsing, the vampire hunter, a role later tackled, to lesser effect, by the likes of Laurence Olivier and Anthony Hopkins. But the real casting coup was Christopher Lee. Previously seen opposite Cushing as the Monster in *Curse Of*, Lee was here allowed to display his haunting looks, imperious manner and blood sucking-charm.

In the hands of writer Jimmy Sangster and director Terence Fisher, however, this incarnation of the Count deviated sharply from Stoker's original almost from the outset. Jonathan Harker (John Van Eyssen) travels to the Count's castle – a fine example of production designer Bernard Robinson's distinctive style – not to work on his books, but as an agent of Van Helsing, who is intent on destroying him. Similarly, Lee's majestic interpretation of the undead owed little to Bela Lugosi's performance. He opted instead to play Dracula as a cool, debonair aristocrat, whose charm adds to the sexual undercurrents and inherent eroticism of the vampire myth, something that director Fisher was eager to explore (and something that would become a mainstay of the increasingly sexed-up Hammer output).

Cushing returned as Van Helsing in 1960's *Brides Of Dracula*, but Lee didn't don the fangs again until 1965's *Dracula: Prince Of Darkness*. He played the role for Hammer a further five times, well into the 70s (taking a break briefly to play the role in Italy for Jess Franco's *El Conde Dracula* (1970)), but no subsequent outings matched the sheer visceral delight of this original.

When Tim Burton decided to make 1999's *Sleepy Hollow* in the guise of the great British horror movies, he clearly showed how well he understood the impact of Terence Fisher's direction, James Bernard's magnificently excessive scores and the fact that if the gore looks like jam – it doesn't matter. Just feel the beautiful melodrama. ★★★★★ **BM**

◑ DRACULA (1979)

Starring: *Frank Langella (Count Dracula), Laurence Olivier (Prof. Abraham Van Helsing), Donald Pleasence (Dr. Jack Seward), Kate Nelligan (Lucy Seward), Trevor Eve (Jonathan Harker), Jan Francis (Mina Van Helsing), Sylvester McCoy (Walter)*
Director: *John Badham*
Screenwriter: *W.D. Richter, based on the play by Hamilton Deane and John L. Balderston and the novel by Bram Stoker*
15/109 mins./Horror/UK/USA

Whitby, Yorkshire. Count Dracula pays court to independent-minded Lucy Seward. Dr. Van Helsing, father of the murdered Mina, diagnoses vampirism.

One of three *Draculas* released in the same month in 1979, in competition with *Love at First Bite* and *Nosferatu the Vampyre*, this was the lushest, highest-budgeted vampire movie made up to that date.

It was produced as a setting for Langella's bubble-permed, disco-look Dracula, a role he had played with great success on Broadway. Scripted by W.D. Richter, who had just reworked *Invasion Of The Body Snatchers*, and directed by John Badham, hot off *Saturday Night Fever*, the film throws all the expected elements and characters in the air, then has them fall in new, unexpected, not-always-workable ways.

Well before Gary Oldman, Langella played Dracula as a romantic as much as a monster, with his influence proving liberating for the frustrated heroine, casting her usually heroic fiancé Jonathan (an understandably grumpy Trevor Eve) as a smothering drag and making Van Helsing (Olivier, doing one of his accents) a fussy old killjoy. It boasts wonderful gothic art direction, with Dracula as a spider in the centre of a deep-focus cobweb in his ruined abbey, and unexpected bits of humour, courtesy of Donald Pleasence's always-hungry doctor and Tony Haygarth as the lunatic Renfield. However, the busy chase scenes, John Williams' overblown score and many pompous smoochy interludes don't quite fit with the leftover Hammer horror stuff about a fanged bride of Dracula (Jan Francis) attacking in catacombs beneath the graveyard. It's nevertheless entertaining.

Badham has insisted most DVD and video releases present the film with the colours bleached almost completely – muting the lavish look the film had in theatres. ★★★ **KN**

◑ DRAGNET (1987)

Starring: *Dan Aykroyd (Sgt. Joe Friday), Tom Hanks (Pep Streebeck), Christopher Plummer (Reverend Jonathan Whirley), Harry Morgan (Captain Gannon), Alexandra Paul (Connie Swail)*
Director: *Tom Mankiewicz*
Screenwriters: *Dan Aykroyd, Alan Zweibel, Tom Mankiewicz based on the Radio and TV series by Jack Webb*
PG/106 mins./Comedy/USA

Sergeant Joe Friday, nephew of a legendary by-the-book Los Angeles cop, is partnered with Pep Streebeck, a rule-breaking loose cannon. Their first case brings them up against a malign anarchist cult.

A stab at a comedic/parodic remake of a classic television show, a full decade before the ironic revivals like *The Brady Bunch Movie* and

Starsky & Hutch, this highlights Dan Aykroyd's spot-on impersonation of deadpan Jack Webb in the role of the supposed nephew of Webb's clipped Joe Friday, hero of the seminal 1951-59 police procedural *Dragnet* (famous for its dum-dah-DUM-dah theme) and a slightly less seminal hippie-busting 1967 revival. Tom Hanks, before he grew serious acting muscles, plays fast and loose as the easygoing 80s policeman whose modern attitudes (including a willingness to torture a suspect) contrast with the uptight, hat-wearing conservatism of Friday (he also gets to do a lot of schtick – impersonating Freddy Krueger and the like).

Harry Morgan, a sputtering veteran of the original series, is promoted to a desk job, barking orders to the mismatched cops, and Alexandra Paul is an unusually funny heroine, a 'Republican virgin from Orange County' who is even more stranded out of time than Friday.

The most fun supporting turn comes from a game Christopher Plummer as a giggling 'moral majority' televangelist who dons goat-leg britches to officiate at the ceremonies of the wonderfully-named PAGAN (People Against Goodness And Normalcy) cult (their catchy chant is 'Kill the good! Kill the good!').

Aykroyd's script has more than its share of clever, witty ideas, but the film still feels the need to descend way too often to *Police Academy*-style heroes-dress-up-like-idiots sequences (Aykroyd and Hanks get into 80s punk gear to infiltrate a concert). Despite this lampoon, *Dragnet* returned seriously to television in 1989 and again in 2003. ★★★ **KN**

DRAGONHEART (1996)

Starring: *Dennis Quaid (Bowen), David Thewlis (King Einon), Pete Postlethwaite (Gilbert of Glockenspur), Dina Meyer (Kara), Jason Issacs (Lord Felton)*
Director: *Rob Cohen*
Screenwriters: *Charles Edward Pogue, based on a story by Patrick Read Johnson, Charles Edward Pogue*
PG/103 mins./Action/Adventure/USA

A dragonslayer encounters the last of the dragons and, both facing extinction, agree to put their enmity aside. Instead, they turn upon a tyrannical King, who the dragon saved from death many years before.

With the likes of *Hawk The Slayer*, *Krull* and *Willow* having been laughed out of cinemas the length and breadth of this fair land, any film venturing into fairy-tale fantasy arrives laden with trepidation. Give or take the odd *Conan* movie, sword and sorcery malarkey never had it good on celluloid before *The Lord of the Rings* changed everything. And even with the addition of its awesome computer-generated dragonmelding artifice, *Dragonheart* isn't about to set the world alight and alter preconception.

Too childish to deliver any satisfying yuks and written without enough conviction to support either the characters or storyline, the film's interest rests solely on the merits of the CGI dragon, Draco, which, thankfully, is superb.

This grungy fairy-tale is ridiculously convoluted in the set-up for such a one-note affair – pernicious kinglet comes a cropper in battle, benevolent dragon donates half his ticker to keep the kid alive, with the understanding that he will grow up to be kind and noble and an all round top king (unlike the last one). The curio feature of this deal is that any pain felt by either dragon or king – who naturally grows up to be a snotty, malevolent git – is felt by the other. One dies, they both buy it.

At the heart of such Grimm-lite moralising is the last known knight – who botched the upbringing of the newly despotic Thewlis – wandering the land dispensing dragons to the big cave in the sky. Then he meets his match in the last dragon, Draco (voiced with laconic skill by Connery) – they find common ground in mutual near-extinction and unite to form a travelling vaudeville routine of mock dragon-slaying, before happening upon the enslaved run-down kingdom (populated by about 37 people), and rousing the yokels to overthrow the dastardly regal.

Having set out its mythic stall, the straightforwardness of the plot proper could be written on the back of the proverbial fag packet. And among the bland Slovak pastoral decor the likes of Pete Postlethwaite (travelling priest), pretty Dina Meyer (impassioned babe villager) and, even, the too-long absent Julie Christie (majestic queen mum) are lost in nothing roles. The crux, and the quality, of this thin fable is in the quirky and well-played relationship between Quaid's knight and Connery's dragon.

Humorous, delicate and at times touching, it's aided ten-fold by the sheer detail expressed in the movement and Conneryesque shape of the pixel-made reptilian visage, they make for a delightful screen partnership. ★★★ **IN**

DRAGONSLAYER (1981)

Cast: *Peter MacNicol (Galen), Caitlin Clarke (Valerian), Ralph Richardson (Ulrich), John Hallam (Tyrian), Peter Eyre (Casiodorus Rex), Albert Salmi (Greil), Sydney Bromley (Hodge), Chloe Salaman (Princess Elspeth), Emrys James (Simon), Roger Kemp (Horsnik)*
Director: *Matthew Robbins*
Screenwriters: *Matthew Robbins, Hal Barwood*
PG/108 mins/ Fantasy Adventure/USA

The Dark Ages. A king staves off the threat of a nearby dragon by sending him virgins as sacrifice, each selected by a random lottery. In search of a solution, a group of villagers seeks out ageing wizard Ulrich to help kill the dragon, but with his untimely death it is left to his apprentice Galen to face the beast.

A forgotten gem of fantasy filmmaking from the early 80s, which pioneered an approach to the genre for which Peter Jackson would later be feted – gritty realism. This is a world, ours most likely, where magic is slipping away in the face of religion's stranglehold, where politics and prejudice have snarled up the old ways, and caked in that Pythonesque stew of muck and mildew. Director Matthew Robbins wants us to feel his ancient realm as pungent and alive, free of the shiny, angled sets and polished armour of cliché. And when it comes to his dragon, in these days long before the arrival of CGI, he is a triumph of hideous might: animalistic, ancient, brimming with fire and power. ILM were behind his creation and they work the ardent magic with aplomb, but in keeping with Robbins' earthy sense of scale.

You can accuse the screenplay of borrowing a little too freely from the standard texts. Tolkien's wizened sage Gandalf is reworked as Ralph Richardson's splendid codger Ulrich, who then takes a surprise early bath, to return Obi-Wan style to look over his protégé's progress. But Peter MacNicol, who might ring a few bells for Ally McBeal fans, is likeably non-heroic, curly haired and stick-thin, he is the geek who must face unfaceable odds. A rite of passage literally through the inferno, and by the final confrontation with the fiery beast, through its excellently Dante-esque lair, the film stirs up a real sense of wonder.

And it doesn't dispense with intelligence to get there. The idea of political control is examined in Peter Eyre's conniving king playing both the oppression and the defeat of the dragon as a form of spin for his own rule. There is also a clever play on sexual identity in Caitlin Clarke disguising herself as a man to escape the dragon's fire. Worth rediscovering. ★★★★ **IN**

DREAMCATCHER (2003)

Starring: *Morgan Freeman (Col. Abraham Curtis), Thomas Jane (Dr. Henry Devlin), Jason Lee (Joe 'Beaver' Clarenden), Damian Lewis (Gary 'Jonesy' Jones), Timothy Olyphant (Pete Moore), Tom Sizemore (Lt. Owen Underhill), Donnie Wahlberg (Douglas 'Duddits' Cavell)*
Director: *Lawrence Kasdan*
Screenwriters: *William Goldman, Lawrence Kasdan, based on the novel by Stephen King*
15/136 mins./Drama/Fantasy/Horror/Sci-fi/USA/Canada

Four childhood buddies sharing a mysterious telepathic bond find their annual hunting trip is about to go horribly wrong. Engulfed by unseasonable blizzards, they realise that a deadly alien is in the woods with them, taking a keen interest in their powers. Meanwhile, a special army unit is intent on eradicating all evidence of alien activity.

Alien vegetables with sentient powers? Insane military commanders with hair-triggers and crypto-fascist pronouncements? Four life-long buddies with fraying lives and telekinetic foreheads? Snow, trees and flashbacks to a golden past of forgotten promise? We can only be tromping around in the genre-bending brain of Stephen King, whose mammoth novel Lawrence Kasdan has bravely elected to fillet down to a manageable movie, for a directorial U-turn away from sturdy ensemble dramedies.

As is too often the case, King proves no easy beast to wrestle. This sprawling, frequently unfathomable monster movie may kick off with some serious shock value, but it soon putters out into a scattershot of interesting ideas hastily smothered by a giant slab of soul-draining CGI.

Let's start with the good stuff. The setting is perfect. Shot in the dense, snowy forests of British Columbia, the cabin in the woods cliché is presented in an otherworldly white-out, muffling sound and disorientating vision.

Two of our heroes – Lewis and Lee – rescue a delusional stranger wandering lost among the trees. That he has a distended stomach and is emitting acrid, sonorous farts should be cause for concern, as should the itchy patch of red mould on his cheek. Cue a razor-teethed riff on *Alien*. Fair play to Kasdan: he holds the scene in check as it treads a tightrope between the schoolboy gross-out and something terrifyingly primal. The tension genuinely starts to claw at your brain cells, and it's not long before some of the name-cast are reduced to a pulpy mess.

The actors' performances are crisp and inviting. Kasdan is a dab-hand at the rhythms and rituals of friendship, and we get an immediate sense of the tests the years have placed on the guys' bond. Lee and Timothy Olyphant have smaller but distinctive roles, leaving it to Jane and *Band Of Brothers* star Lewis (a Brit, no less) to bear the brunt of the movie. Lewis, especially, rises to the challenge of not only pulling off a pitch-perfect American accent, but also being possessed by an alien and doing a fidgety rendition of Gollum-esque double talk. Kasdan, in a daring but only semi-successful move, also depicts the real Jonesy trapped within his own head in a vast memory depository.

Then the army turns up and the plot descends into anarchy. Without the room, or indeed skill, to contain all of King's disparate elements – alarmist conspiracy theories, postmodern giggles (the mould is dubbed 'Ripley'), psychic powers – the film resorts to lumbering action scenes and a baffling surge of story points shuffled into the ending. Finally we have to endure a pathetic rush-job of totally unexplained, rubbery-looking CGI monstrosities roaring at each other like something from those barking mad Toho creature features.

Given that this is the sum-total of the hot scriptwriting combo of William Goldman and Lawrence Kasdan, 'could do better' doesn't get halfway there. Make 'em watch *Children Of The Corn* on loop until they've learned their lesson. ★★★ **IN**

DRIVING MISS DAISY (1989)

Starring: *Jessica Tandy (Miss Daisy Werthan), Morgan Freeman (Hoke Colburn), Dan Aykroyd (Boolie Werthan), Patti LuPone (Florine Werthan)*
Director: *Bruce Beresford*
Screenwriter: *Alfred Uhry, based on his play*
U/99 mins./Comedy/Drama/USA

Awards: *Academy Awards – Best Actress, Best Makeup, Best Picture, Best Screenplay based on material from another medium, BAFTA – Best Actress, Golden Globes – Best Comedy/Musical, Best Actor, Best Actress*

Jessica Tandy is Miss Daisy, an elderly, stubborn and wealthy Jewish resident of 1948 Atlanta, whose steady life is shaken when her gentle businessman son, worried about her increasingly nonsensical roadsense, engages Hoke as her driver.

For *Driving Miss Daisy*, as for his previous tales of the American South, *Tender Mercies* and *Crimes Of The Heart*, Australian director Bruce Beresford has clearly given great thought to the casting of the principals. Unlike those movies, however, the extraordinary performances in *Driving Miss Daisy* are merely an accompaniment, albeit a delicious one, to a film suffused with quality – from the screenplay (adapted by Alfred Uhry from his Pulitzer prize-winning play) to the magnificent period settings and minute attention to detail.

'I wouldn't be in your shoes if the sweet Lord Jesus came down and asked me himself,' warns Daisy's maid on Hoke's first day, and inevitably the old lady gives him a terrible time.

But their relationship inches closer over following years, often to laugh-out-loud effect, and the story follows them as they, and the South, move into the 50s, the 60s, the 70s. The passing years are beautifully heralded by the two of them climbing in and out of a series of ever-modernising cars, a subtlety echoed by the subdued representation of the underlying theme of racial inequality. There are no blazing crosses or fat, murderous racists in *Driving Miss Daisy*, but Hoke's insistence on stopping the car to pee with the explanation that 'You know coloureds can't use the restrooms in the gas stations, Miss Daisy', or the look of horror on Daisy's face when told of the unseen bombing of her synagogue, are worth a dozen *Mississippi Burning*-style lynchings and beatings.

Then there are the performances. Morgan Freeman, who reprises the role he made his on stage, exudes dignity, humility and humanity with magnificent ease. And Jessica Tandy somehow plays that Hollywood invention, the cantankerous Jewish mother, with utter conviction. ★★★ **PT**

DROP DEAD GORGEOUS (1999)

Starring: *Kirsten Dunst (Amber Atkins), Ellen Barkin (Annette Atkins), Allison Janney (Loretta), Denise Richards (Rebecca 'Becky' Ann Leeman), Kirstie Alley (Gladys Leeman), Sam McMurray (Lester Leeman), Mindy Sterling (Iris Clark), Brittany Murphy (Lisa Swenson), Amy Adams (Leslie Miller)*
Director: *Michael Patrick Jann*
Screenwriter: *Lona Williams*
15/97 mins./Comedy/USA/Germany

In a small Minnesota town, some parents – and girls – will stop at nothing – including murder – to win the annual beauty pageant.

From the moment front-runner Tammy Curry is blown to pieces on her sabotaged tractor, it's clear this beauty pageant will be fought tooth and nail. And it ain't gonna be pretty. In the small Midwest community of Mount Rose, Minnesota, the Sarah Rose Miss Teen Princess America contest is into the final furlong. But for all the sugar-coated spoutings of world peace and harmony hairspray, it's a question of victory by any means necessary – as a roving documentary film crew discovers.

In the Blue Ribbon rhubarb pie corner is Becky Leeman, rich kid daughter of former winner and rabidly proud officiating beauty pageant President Gladys. And in the red, trailer-trash corner is morgue makeup artist Amber Atkins, championed by her boozy mother Annette and her mother's morally suspect best friend Loretta.

Casting-wise it's spot on, as Alley launches with smiley, viper spitefulness into a beacon of single-minded hypocrisy, and is well matched by Richards, even if she looks the least convincing high school teenager since Stockard Channing's Rizzo enrolled in Rydell High. Dunst meanwhile is blossoming into a very accomplished actress, and – together with Barkin and Janney – claims most of the prize lines.

The dark laughs are consistent, and the parody of middle America's bizarre beauty contest fixation is spiked with some jolting shock tactics – from the nurse-assisted wheelchair dance by the reigning anorexic crown holder to Richards' hilarious (not too mention blasphemous) love song for Jesus – but such blackness never obstructs rooting for Dunst's likeable teen. ★★★ **DB**

DRUGSTORE COWBOY (1989)

Starring: *Matt Dillon (Bob), Kelly Lynch (Dianne), James Le Gros (Rick), Heather Graham (Nadine), James Remar (Gentry), William S. Burroughs (Tom the Priest)*
Director: *Gus Van Sant*
Screenwriters: *Gus Van Sant, Daniel Yost, based on the novel by James Fogle*
18/100 mins./Crime/Drama/USA

Faithfully based on the written experiences of James Fogle, imprisoned on a 22-year sentence for narcotics charges, the story focuses in on the drug-stealing and drug-taking exploits of junkie Bob Hughes, his junkie wife Dianne and their junkie friends Rick and Nadine.

This is the sort of film that the art of movie rental was designed for. A minor critical triumph on its theatrical release in 1989, *Drugstore Cowboy* never quite hit home commercially, its potentially bleak subject matter perhaps not the best guarantee of a good night out.

On video or DVD, however, this tale of a merry band of early 70s junkies deserves a much wider audience and, at just a couple of squid for nearly 100 minutes of gripping viewing, is about as good value for money as it's possible to get. What sets this apart from the usual tripe spewed out about the so-called drug culture is the overriding sense it gives of actually having been there, taken that, and thoroughly enjoyed it at the time.

Set in beautiful Portland, Oregon rather than the token ghetto, and peppered with everyday dialogue and everyday events rather than the usual moralising hysteria that tends to come with this territory, the acute air of realism only flags in the last half-hour with Bob's unexplained and wholly unexpected conversion to a quieter and drug-free way of life. And while his attempt to kick the habit is never portrayed as a simple act of willpower, it's hard to avoid a suspicion that this Damascus-like turnaround is a late attempt by Van Sant and company to balance the overwhelming impression built up so far – namely, that taking drugs can be a whole lot of fun if you happen to like that sort of thing.

Best of all in this intriguing little film is Matt Dillon, the perfect cool cat of the day, governed by all sorts of odd superstitions and the driving force behind the whole operation. And special mention too for William S. Burroughs – yes, that one – as the veteran junkie priest, still hoping for the ultimate fix to such an extent that it's hard not to share his glee when Dillon presents him with a neat little bottle of just what he's always wanted. A minor gem. ★★★★ **BMc**

DUCK SOUP (1933)

Starring: *Groucho Marx (Rufus T. Firefly), Harpo Marx (Pinky), Chico Marx (Chicolini), Zeppo Marx (Lt. Bob Roland), Raquel Torres (Vera Marcal) Louis Calhern (Ambassador), Margaret Dumont (Mrs. Gloria Teasdale)*
Director: *Leo McCarey*
Screenwriters: *Bert Kalmar, Harry Ruby, Arthur Sheekman, Nat Perrin*
U/68 mins./Comedy/Musical/USA

Rufus T. Firefly, a cynical reprobate, is foolishly appointed president of Freedonia when his rich sponsor Mrs. Teasdale bales out the bankrupt nation. However, when neighbouring ambassador Trentino, from Sylvania, attempts to woo her away from him, Firefly declares war.

Arguably, alongside *A Day At The Races*, the Marx Brothers' zenith, this brief satire-in-extremis packs more into its 68 minute examination of international politicking than subsequent comedies do with another hour. The genius of the Brothers' infectious routines, a febrile mix of deranged slapstick (none of Chaplin's arty body-balletic, thank you) and the snap and sting of Groucho's wordplay ('Remember, you're fighting for this woman's honour, which is probably more than she ever did'), is the pace at which it spills forth. Any slower and the cracks would show, their policy is that if you tell it fast enough it will always be funny. They were right.

The film reaches a state of frenzy that is almost ecstatic as Rufus T. Firefly, Groucho at is most snappily assured with those hydraulic eyebrows permanently banked at sarcastic, determines to send his new plaything, the nation of Freedonia, off to war with its neighbour. After all, their ambassador had called him an, 'upstart!'

What raises this particular episode of their mania above all others, is twofold. It was the only time they teamed up with legendary director Leo McCarey, who tidied up their loose edges and encouraged them to seek loftier targets to spoil. And here was the second triumph of *Duck Soup*, although they denied it, it remains one of the most incisive anti-war satires ever made, a film that rivals *Dr. Strangelove* and betters Chaplin's haughty *The Great Dictator* for caustic verve. It is down to the grinning hooligan persona they concoct, as if nothing in the world matters. As one dopey brother is sent to press the lines of a besieged building, Groucho's rabbit-mouthed Firefly sends him on his way in typical fashion: 'You're a brave man. Go and break through the lines. And remember, while you're out there risking your life and limb through shot and shell, we'll be in here thinking what a sucker you are.' The world can be so dark that laughter is the only option. ★★★★★ **IN**

DUDE, WHERE'S MY CAR? (2000)

Starring: *Ashton Kutcher (Jesse Montgomery III), Seann William Scott (Chester Greenburg), Jennifer Garner (Wanda), Marla Sokoloff (Wilma), Kristy Swanson (Christie Boner)*
Director: *Danny Leiner*
Screenwriter: *Philip Stark*
15/83 mins./Comedy/Sci-fi/USA

A pair of bargain bin Bill and Teds wake up after a bender and, unable to recall anything that happened the night before, set out to retrace their wasted steps and find their misplaced ride. In the process the knuckle-headed stoners encounter alien invaders, marauding ostriches and a plot to destroy the universe.

Never mind the wheels, whatever happened to the plot? Mistaking repetition of dialogue for a fruitful means of laughter grabbing, the misadventures of two stoners searching aimlessly for their missing motor takes in witless and painfully unfunny in equal measures, without ever throwing in an original idea in its 82-minute running time.

On paper there is an engaging simplicity to the premise and the restriction of forcing the action into the compressed timespan of one night often forces filmmakers to get creative – witness *Ferris Bueller's Day Off*, *American Graffiti*, *After Hours*, *Three O'Clock High*. Yet director Leiner and writer Stark have crafted a wasteland of jokes that missed the mark where the occasional laughs die of loneliness.

That the visiting aliens give the dudes jewellery that makes girls' 'hoo haas' (the film's patois) bigger is a perfect barometer for the level of humour involved. Moreover, one of the two funny gags in the movie, the boys' discovery that they both have tattoos – 'Dude! What's mine say?' 'Sweet! What's mine say?' – appears in the trailer.

Given better material, it's not unthinkable that Kutcher and Scott could work very well as a comedic twosome: the former boasts an amiable goofy quality and the latter has proved in *American Pie* and *Road Trip* that he knows how to deliver a punchline. Along the way, the pair encounter Fabio (in the film's other decent joke), Brent Spiner as a Frenchman and Kristy Swanson as the obligatory teen babe.

The dumb buddy comedy has a noble lineage stretching back to Laurel and Hardy and beyond. This stream of celluloid inanity could draw a chalk outline round its corpse. All together: 'Dude, where's my refund?' ★★ **MD**

DUEL (1971)

Starring: *Dennis Weaver (David Mann), Jacqueline Scott (Mrs. Mann), Eddie Firestone (Café Owner), Lou Frizzell (Bus Driver), Gene Dynarski (Man in Café)*
Director: *Steven Spielberg*
Screenwriters: *Richard Matheson*
PG/90 mins./Action/Mystery/Thriller/USA

David Mann is trying to drive his car across California. When he tries to pass a gas tanker, the driver somehow takes offence and an increasingly deadly driving duel begins.

In August 1978, after ITV showed an episode of seemingly innocuous comic book adaptation *The Incredible Hulk* – apparently, you won't like him when he's angry – the station's switchboard was jammed with irate viewers. Rather than moaning about the poster-paint green prosthetics or Bill Bixby's balsa wood acting, the indignation arose because the episode had purloined a wealth of car chase footage from Steven Spielberg's *Duel* which the channel had screened earlier that year.

In retrospect, it was a pretty dumb idea to plunder from *Duel*. Built on a skilful ebb and flow axis of surprise and suspense, it has few rivals when it comes to sustaining an action agenda throughout the full running time. To be sure it's a slender story – mild-mannered suburbanite David Mann is chased along desert highways by a malevolent truck – but the film thrives on the lean meanness of its (road) rage against the machine. Not only is the vehicle never ascribed a simplistic motivation (like the shark or velociraptor of future Spielberg hits, it simply exists to kill) but the driver is never ever revealed. Tension and terror, not characterisation and plot, are what matter here.

The genesis of *Duel* can be traced to celebrated sci-fi writer Richard Matheson, author of *The Shrinking Man* and regular contributor to the *Twilight Zone*. Shortly after the JFK assassination Matheson and writing partner Jerry Sohl were driving through a narrow canyon when a truck began tailgating them with reckless abandon. 'Partially we were terrified,' the screenwriter recalled, 'and partially infuriated, turning our rage about the Kennedy assassination into rage at the truck driver. We were screaming out of the window but the truck driver's window was closed and he couldn't hear it. My friend had to pull up, skidding onto one of these dirt places in the road. In the writer's mind, once you survive death, you start thinking of a story.'

With the subsequent yarn published in *Playboy*, the resulting movie adaptation is a masterclass in how to shoot and cut a car chase. Plotting the action and camera placements on a map, Spielberg fashioned stunning variations on the cat and mouse theme, pepping up the pursuit with bizarro camera angles (big close-ups of Mann captured with a telephoto lens) and sound effects (the truck's heavy duty rumble, the car's pathetic engine whine) all knitted together into stunning editing patterns.

If the casting of Mann was vitally important – Spielberg approached Gregory Peck, Dustin Hoffman and David Janssen before Universal closed down the shooting of *McCloud* to free up Dennis Weaver – perhaps more crucial was the casting of the truck. Presented with a line-up of vehicles, Spielberg opted for a Peterbilt gasoline tanker truck, partly due to its strangely human aspect suggested by a small snout at the front and two ear-like hydraulic tanks by the doors. Over the meagre 16-day shoot, the stunt drivers – *Bullitt*'s Carey Loftin in the truck, Dale Van Sickle in Mann's red Valiant – put the pedal to the metal, achieving top speeds of 135mph, while Spielberg emphasised the pace and scale of the vehicles by placing the camera low to the road.

The compositions are amazingly dynamic and diverse, but so is the tone. From the black humour of Mann mistaking a train horn for a blast from the truck to his paranoia at a roadside diner trying to guess the identity of his tormentor; from the full-on spectacle of the truck chasing Mann around a snake farm, to the strangely beautiful finale, *Duel* is a far more protean experience than it had any right to be. Extended from 73 minutes on TV to 90 minutes in the cinema, some of its best moments are only viewable in the theatrical version: the POV shots from the bonnet of Mann's car, which skilfully chart his journey from suburbia to sticks; the truck's attempts to push Mann in front of a train, the darkly comic moment in which the truck comes to the aid of a school bus after Mann has been unable to help them.

The big screen version also features one of the greatest faux pas in recent movie history – due to the change in screen shape, glimpsed briefly but clearly in Mann's rear view mirror is a youthful Steven Spielberg directing from the back seat. He is not the only one undertaking the ride of a lifetime. ★★★★ **IF**

THE DUKES OF HAZZARD (2005)

Starring: *Johnny Knoxville (Luke Duke), Seann William Scott (Bo Duke), Jessica Simpson (Daisy Duke), Burt Reynolds (Boss Hogg), Willie Nelson (Uncle Jesse), Lynda Carter (Pauline)*
Director: *Jay Chandrasekhar*
Screenwriter: *John O'Brien, based on a story by O'Brien and Jonathan L. Davis and characters by Gy Waldron*
12A/106 mins./Action/Comedy/USA

Makin' their way the only way they know how (that's just a little bit more than the law will allow) the irrepressible Duke Boys, aided and abetted by Cousin Daisy and Uncle Jesse, run predictable rings around Boss Hogg and his hapless cronies.

With a rebel yell, the General Lee rides again. And, for viewers of a certain age, it's an undeniable thrill to see the legendary tangerine Charger back in action, barelling down dusty backroads, executing impossible handbrake turns and shrugging the bonds of gravity to sail majestically through the air as the familiar strains of its melodious klaxon declaim the ante bellum glory of the South.

Would that other elements of this by-the-book retread had anything like as much mojo, suffering as it does from a plot with less meat on its bones than a worked-over rack of ribs. Johnny Knoxville and Seann William Scott may be a tight fit for the raunched-up Bo and Luke (here they're moonshine runners for real, rather than the wimpy reformed characters of the TV series). And the choice of C&W icon Willie Nelson for irascible old goat Uncle Jesse and Burt Reynolds, the king of Southern-fried farce, for Boss Hogg verges on genius.

But they're just not given anything remotely interesting to do. As it is, some piffle about fixing up the General Lee to defeat Boss Hogg in an auto race makes for tiresome interludes of hollering and brawling that simply get in the way of the car chases. Far too much ho-hum and not nearly enough yee-haw. ★★ **SB**

DUMB AND DUMBER (1994)

Starring: *Jim Carrey (Lloyd Christmas), Jeff Daniels (Harry Dunne), Lauren Holly (Mary Swanson), Mike Starr (Joe 'Mental' Mentaliano), Karen Duffy (J.P. Shay), Victoria Rowell (FBI Special Agent Beth Jordan), Teri Garr (Helen Swanson)*
Director: *Peter Farrelly*
Screenwriters: *Peter Farrelly, Bennett Yellin, Bobby Farrelly*
12/106 mins./Comedy/USA

Lloyd is a nice-but-dim taxi driver, who tries to return a suitcase full of money to a beautiful woman passenger. He and his friend Harry journey cross-country to find her in Aspen, where they start to fight for her affections.

As soon as the opening credits inform the audience that *Dumb And Dumber* was 'wrote by The Farelly Brothers', it's obvious that a brain-stretching experience is not on the cards. Cringe not at its apparent terribleness, however, for what follows is a delight: 102 minutes of non-stop, toilet-fixated, pant-wettingly daft humour that has charmed Americans into auditoria in droves and looks set to cause similarly huge bouts of laugh-induced incontinence among UK cinemagoers.

The plot, such as it is, takes road movie form: Lloyd, a chauffeur with more room upstairs than the Goodyear blimp, drives the babelicious Mary Swanson to the airport, and is instantly smitten. When she leaves her briefcase in the terminal, he retrieves it, and soon he and his equally brain-deprived bud Harry are journeying halfway across America to return the case to the object of his desire.

The scene is thus set for a jokefest of such preposterous proportions that calling it infantile over-estimates the sophistication level by about a squillion miles. Extra-strong laxatives, swaggering homosexual cowboys and urine-quaffing are all trotted out in the name of comedy, while a subplot involving a heavy mobster after the briefcase (left at the airport on purpose, naturally) threatens to ruin everything for the air-headed twosome.

Debut director Farelly and his cast romp through proceedings with real gusto and impeccable comic timing, meaning the next jaw-jamming surge of giggles is never more than a moment away, with the normally staid Daniels displaying hitherto untapped comic talent and almost stealing the show from under the nose of his habitually imbecilic co-star. This is by no means the best film ever made, but as an any-night-of-the-week crowd-pleaser it's indisputably the funniest film since *Airplane!*, and perform further miracles for Carrey's status as one of the world's biggest stars. ★★★★★ **CW**

DUMBO (1941)

Starring: *the voices of: Edward Brophy (Timothy Mouse), Herman Bing (Ringmaster), Verna Felton (Elephant), Sterling Holloway (Stork), Cliff Edwards (Jim Crow)*
Director: *Ben Sharpsteen, Norman Ferguson (Segment Director), Wilfred Jackson (Segment Director), Bill Roberts (Segment Director), Jack Inney (Segment Director), Sam Armstrong (Segment Director)*
Screenwriters: *Joe Grant, Dick Huemer based on a book by Helen Aberson and Harold Pearl*
U/64 mins./Animation/USA
Awards: *Academy Award Best Score (Musical)*

Dumbo, a circus elephant born with freakishly large ears, rises from miserable ugly ducklinghood to superstardom when it is discovered that he can fly. For a while, he believes his abilities come from a magic feather but eventually he learns that it's down to his own inherent abilities.

Initially rushed through production to compensate for the box-office failure of *Fantasia*, *Dumbo* is the most underrated of Walt Disney's cartoon features. Just over an hour long and refreshingly free of artistic pretension, it is (along with *Pinocchio*) the most timelessly perfect cartoon in the Disney backlist, embodying the typical fable of an orphan outsider (whose mother is humiliatingly penned in a madhouse for trying to protect him) who finds out that he is secretly special and is rewarded with a happier family life.

With a genuinely cute animal hero (compare the phoney cute of *An American Tail* or *The Land Before Time*) and an appealing storyline, the film is exactly right for younger children, with its humour and charm and reassuring finish, but it's not too milk-soppy for anyone over eight, and has always played as well to parents as kids.

Given that it's a 'talking animal' film, it's daring to have the title character be mute – most of the talking is handled by Dumbo's manager-sidekick Timothy Q. Mouse (familiar gangland actor Ed Brophy) but Dumbo himself is an amazingly expressive character (it's as much in the eyes as the ears). Song highlights: the 'Pink Elephants on Parade' psychedelic hallucination sequence, which is years before its time; 'Baby Mine', one of the sweetest songs ever recorded; and 'When I See an Elephant Fly?', a witty batter number ('I've seen a needle that winked its eye') performed by four crows who are the sharpest, most fondly created black characters in any 1941 movie. ★★★★★ **KN**

DUNE (1984)

Starring: *Kyle MacLachlan (Paul Atredies), Francesca Annis (Lady Jessica), Kenneth MacMillan (Baron Harkonnen), Patrick Stewart (Gurney Halleck), Sean Young (Chani)*
Director: *David Lynch*
Screenwriter: *David Lynch based on the novel by Frank Herbert*
PG/190 mins./Sci-fi/USA

Based on the best-selling sci-fi epic by Frank Herbert, this far-flung tale tells of planet Dune, the only source of spice in the galaxy and the necessary ingredient for interstellar travel. After the Atredies family are sent to govern the desert planet, tragedy befalls them when their Duke Leto is assassinated, and his son Paul barely escapes with his life, soon to fulfil a remarkable destiny.

Derided, disowned, and debated endlessly, David Lynch's weird venture into big budget sci-fi spectacle (having turned down the chance to make *Return Of the Jedi*) is a most fascinating disaster of genre making. On a storytelling level Frank Herbert's swollen book, a thinly disguised allegory of the Arab control of oil supply, proved far too intricate and unwieldy to cohere into a sensible film. And Lynch wasn't about to worry about it, wrapping the film in swathes of religious symbolism, and letting it devolve into a rare form of highly expensive gibberish. No matter which, of many, extended cuts you watch the yarn retains no holding logic. Even lovers of the book's dense arcana – a universe of squabbling aristocratic families, mystical witches, messiahs, and emperors all vying for control of the necessary Spice – found it impossible to follow.

Yet, on another level, it isn't without artistic merit. Story was never going to concern Lynch for long (making him a foolish choice for director), but he lends Herbert's crowded mythos with its low-level fusion of the hi-tech and the Biblical, a vivid design. From the red-stained deserts (it was shot in Mexico) to the industrial horror of Harkonnen, to the great worms, giant phallic beasts coursing through Dune's outback, the film has a surreal grace that draws you in. And the characters, as is Lynch's wont, are rich and wild and amongst his funniest. While MacLachlan's hero-messiah Paul is bland, a good looking trope for the film's peculiar destiny, Kenneth MacMillan has a whale of a time as the corpulent villain Baron Harkonnen, coated in suppurating boils as if his whole body oozed with his avaricious evil. Although, Sting in naught but a codpiece might have been an extravagance too far – the singer turned actor never fully recovered from the look.

Thus, it is hard to truly punish *Dune*. As a version of the book it remains hopeless (John Harrison's TV mini-series made in 2000 does a far better job in adapting the book) but as a piece of outrageous sci-fi art, thrilling to its own excess, it is far more of a piece with Lynch's idiosyncratic career than he has made out. ★★★ **IN**

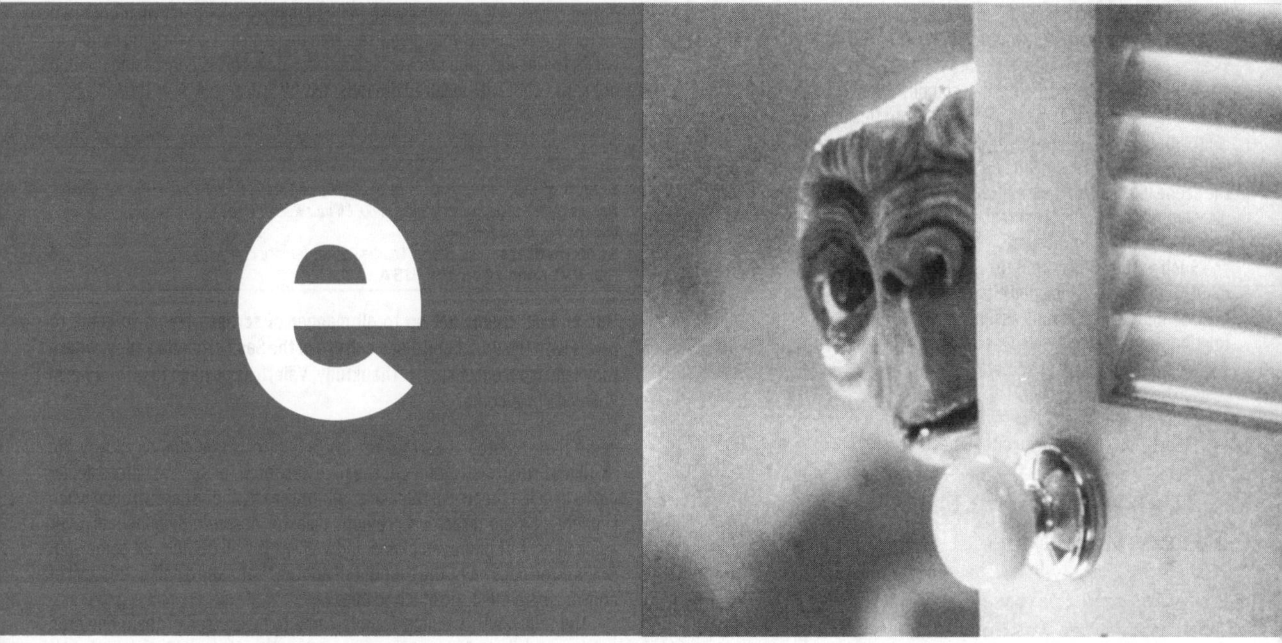

E.T. THE EXTRA-TERRESTRIAL (1982)

Starring: *Dee Wallace (Mary), Henry Thomas (Elliott), Peter Coyote (Keys), Robert MacNaughton (Michael), Drew Barrymore (Gertie), Erica Eleniak (Pretty Girl)*
Director: *Steven Spielberg*
Screenwriter: *Melissa Mathison*
U/115 mins./Sci-fi/Fantasy/USA

Awards: *Academy Awards – Best Sound Effects Editing, Best Visual Effects Editing, Best Original Score, Best Sound, BAFTA – Best Score, Golden Globes – Best Drama, Best Score*

A group of Earth children help a stranded alien botanist return home.

Thanks to greetings cards, poseable figurines and those British Telecom commercials, the world has long since absorbed E.T. – the character – as an icon of icky sentimentality. The movie, however, is founded on an altogether more troubled view of the world: more specifically, the young Spielberg's experience of adult dysfunction. In countless ways – its suburban setting, the similarities between Elliott (Thomas) and Roy Neary, the encroaching presence of the secret state, aliens – E.T. is of a piece with *Close Encounters*. The thematic link, however, goes way deeper.

The latter film was inspired by the night Spielberg's father showed him a meteor shower; *E.T.* – by contrast, is informed by the desolation felt when his parents divorced and his dad exited the family home. He was 17 at the time, yet there is the occasional inference that, when dad left, he took the last vestiges of childhood wonder with him. 'Dad would believe me,' mutters Elliott when his mother quietly rejects his belief that he's clapped eyes on something deeply strange. In its own way, it's the most revealing line in the movie.

After the comic-book bravado of *Raiders Of The Lost Ark*, one gets the distinct sense that Spielberg felt duty-bound to return to contemporary middle America. Moreover, this shrinking of vistas was even further intensified by two strokes of genius: the fact that the lion's share of the film is shot from a child's perspective – the teacher, for example, is allowed no more exposure than the maid in *Tom & Jerry* – and the recurrent contrast between what unfolds in the movie and the altogether more otherworldly province of sci-fi. *Star Wars* references abound; better still, when Elliott finally comes clean to his brother's BMX gang, we get a shard of *Star Trek*.

'He's a man from Outer Space and we're taking him to his spaceship,' says Elliott, matter-of-factly.

'Well, can't he just beam up?' replies one of the youthful troupe.

'This is REALITY, Greg,' Elliott shoots back. To anyone in the same age bracket, this was truly thrilling stuff: sci-fi where the 'fi' aspect was in grave danger of withering away.

It was François Truffaut who put the notion of child-meets-alien in Spielberg's mind. Seizing on Cary Guffey's wonder-struck role in *Close Encounters*, he made his suggestion with an almost missionary zeal: 'Kids! You must make a movie with kids'. From there, however, the route to *E.T.* was by no means simple. Spielberg returned to an ongoing project entitled *Night Skies*, a borderline horror movie in which a gang of aliens terrorise the residents of an isolated farmhouse – but seized on the anomalous presence of a sensitive extra-terrestrial named Buddy and his fleeting friendship with an autistic child. In cahoots with the screenwriter Melissa Mathison, then the partner of Harrison Ford, he thus came up with a modern *Peter Pan*.

And how modern it was. The divorce subtext reflected Hollywood's acknowledgement that marital breakdown was starting to define US society (the pioneering *Kramer Vs. Kramer* was released two years before). Equally importantly, the shadowy role given to government agents had its roots in the aftershocks of Watergate – and the sense that, under Ronald Reagan, the State's more sinister aspect was as strong as ever. Agents bug Elliott's bedroom, break into his home and finally announce their presence via the sound of post-Vietnam paranoia: whirring helicopter blades.

In the midst of it all, however, childhood remains inviolate. Indeed, the character of E.T. has the power to pull people back from the brink of cynical adulthood; in that sense, Robert MacNaughton's portrayal of big bro' Michael is one of the movie's more overlooked masterstrokes. He begins the film in a fug of cigarette smoke, ordering Elliott to fetch pizza and affecting the pose of a grown-up. By the end, he and his younger brother see the world through identical eyes.

It's some token of the film's accomplishment that the same transformation was wreaked on its audience, and – to this day – the Western world is crowded with people who, at the first stirrings of John Williams' theme, will come over all Pavlovian and start fighting back the tears. Show them the scene in which E.T. lies, half-dead, in the river, and they will all but crumble; remind them of his resurrection in the government's ice-box, and you ought to send out for tissues.

Such is the explanation for *E.T.*'s eternal place in our hearts. As ever, mind you, Spielberg included elements that no purveyor of schmaltz would ever go near. One can only assume that the makers of birthday cards and telephone ads have passed over this dialogue: Michael: 'Maybe it was a pervert or a deformed kid or something.'

Gertie: 'A deformed kid.'

Michael: 'Maybe an elf or a leprechaun.'

Elliott: 'It was nothing like that, penis-breath!' ★★★★★ **JH**

Movie Trivia: E.T. The Extra-Terrestrial

Harrison Ford was cast as Elliot's school headmaster. Sadly his small part was left on the cutting room floor. E.T.'s face was an amalgam of Albert Einstein, poet Carl Sandburg and a pug dog.

THE EAGLE HAS LANDED (1976)

Starring: *Michael Caine (Colonel Kurt Steiner), Donald Sutherland (Liam Devlin), Robert Duvall (Colonel Max Radl), Jenny Agutter (Molly Prior), Donald Pleasence (Heinrich Himmler), Anthony Quayle (Admiral Canaris), Larry Hagman (Colonel Pitts)*
Director: *John Sturges*
Screenwriter: *Tom Mankiewicz based on the novel by Jack Higgins*
15/135 mins./War/UK

A platoon of heavily disguised Nazis, led by the noble Colonel Kurt Steiner, parachute into a small English village soon to be visited by Winston Churchill, their plan being to abduct the leader.

One of the more preposterous of that breed of pulp war movies that populated the late sixties and seventies, this adaptation of the Jack Higgins thriller is lent a sturdy complexion by the craftsmanlike talents of John Sturges (a director who specialised in beefy bravado: *The Great Escape*, *The Magnificent Seven*) and a memorable about-face in having Michael Caine play a Nazi, albeit one who was down on the whole killing Jews part of the war. This was a film never turning full face to the reality of its set-up; look, they're goodish Nazis. However, as a piece of energetic gung-ho, it's just that bit slyer and more intriguing than the by-rote men-on-a-mission brigade.

With its idyllic country setting, fully embodying that prettified view Hollywood have of Blighty, the film is innately restricted in terms of action. So, Sturges allows his characters to simmer that bit longer. Caine, accent apart, lends this noble man a grim certainty, and his legacy of straight-up good-guys makes it a natural response to side with him. Donald Sutherland is excellent as the IRA spy whose anti-Brit stance has him betray both town and Jenny Agutter. JR himself, Larry Hagman, turns up for an extended cameo as a wisecracking yank Colonel catching a sniff of wrongdoing. And Donald Pleasence has a delicious time as Himmler complete with maniacal cackle.

It plays, rather cunningly, more as a mystery than an out-an-out war movie. Will the villagers catch on before it's too late? Actually, the big reveal is terrific as a German trooper jumps into a rushing stream to save a drowning girl. A word to the wise for scheming Nazis – don't wear your real uniform underneath your disguise. From there on in it's a thrilling bundle of twists to the victorious close. Indisputably daft, this is engrossing enough nonsense shot with assured obviousness by Sturges. ★★★ **IN**

EARTH GIRLS ARE EASY (1988)

Starring: *Geena Davis (Valerie Dale), Jeff Goldblum (Mac), Jim Carrey (Wiploc), Damon Wayans (Zebo), Julie Brown (Candy Pink), Charles Rocket (Ted)*
Director: *Julien Temple*
Screenwriters: *Julie Brown, Charlie Coffey, Terence E. McNally*
PG/100 mins./Comedy/USA

Mac and his chums get up to all manner of scrapes trying to come to terms with the donut and disco culture of the San Fernando Valley, where they land from outer space. Thankfully, Valerie is on hand to offer a warm Valley Girl welcome.

The first minutes of *Earth Girls Are Easy* offer some clue as to why the film's British distributors at the time hesitated for so long before deciding to give it a theatrical release at all. The credits have barely rolled when suddenly it's the director's previous disaster *Absolute Beginners* all over again, a host of bug-eyed aliens and Valley Girls all belting out some sub-B-52s dirge and really, the thought of another hour and a half of this sort of nonsense is almost too much to bear.

Mercifully, either Julien Temple came to his senses or the money ran out, because *Earth Girls Are Easy* gradually settles down into a mildly diverting tale of what happens when three visitors from outer space land in the San Fernando Valley and become adopted by those equally strange creatures known as Valley Girls. Led by Mac, the furry trio get some radical haircuts courtesy of Valley Girl supreme Candy Pink (Julie Brown, who also co-wrote the screenplay) and, predictably enough, Mac is soon in a major clothes-off situation with Valerie.

Perhaps the most surprising element in this bizarre tale, however, is the very presence of then rising stars Geena Davis and hubby Jeff Goldblum in such a lightweight production. It's an unlikely addition to the joint c.v, and difficult to avoid the suspicion that neither would be in the starting line-up two years on. She displays few signs of the zany charm that won her the Best Supporting Actress Oscar for *The Accidental Tourist* while he somehow manages to clumsily combine both of his most famous roles in one package, *Fly*-like as the pre-shave alien, goofy *Tall Guy* afterwards.

The ensemble singalongs aside, Julien Temple shows signs of a new discipline to rein in his more excessive tendencies and displays a neat understanding of both Valley culture and the kitsch side of 50s Hollywood sci-fi flicks. But now it's more watchable for the 'spot-the-future-stars-under-the-fur-game'. Jim Carrey, for instance, barely registering. ★★ **BT**

EARTH VS THE FLYING SAUCERS (1956)

Starring: *Hugh Marlowe (Dr. Russell A. Marvin), Joan Taylor (Carol Marvin), Donald Curtis (Maj. Huglin), Morris Ankrum (Brig. Gen John Hanley), John Zaremba (Prof. Kanter)*
Director: *Fred F. Sears*
Screenwriters: *George Worthing Yates and Bernard Gordon based on the book* Flying Saucers From Outer Space *by Major Donald E. Keyhoe*
U/83 mins./Sci-fi/USA

Invaders arrive on Earth en masse, attacking the US space programme and then launching an assault on Washington DC. Heroic inventor Russell Marvin comes up with a sound-based weapon that brings down the alien spaceships.

Not quite on the classic level of *The Thing From Another World*, *Invasion Of The Body Snatchers* or *The Day The Earth Stood Still*, this archetypal, enjoyable black and white 50s s-f item delivers scenes of mass devastation which are still often excerpted (in Orson Welles' *F for Fake*, for instance) or homaged (in *Mars Attacks!* and *Independence Day*).

As the tabloid headline-style title indicates, it's the definitive collection of 1950s UFO legends, and as such a key source for *Close Encounters* and *X-Files* to come: 'foo fighters', abduction and mind-probe, buzzed airliners, etc. Flying saucers, brilliantly animated by Ray Harryhausen, attack the Earth, and we get lots of great scenes of the buzzing machines smashing up Washington landmarks or blasting away at the army with ray guns.

The stubby, helmeted aliens sometimes emerge from their sleek ships and zap people with death-rays, but it's the saucers that are the main attraction. There are a few too many 'scientific' talks with wooden hero Marlowe explaining things in the laboratory and paranoid modern audiences might be disturbed by the high-handed attitude of the authorities in suspending all personal freedoms in order to wage interplanetary war (one of the uncredited screenwriters was blacklisted Bernard Gordon).

However, the aliens are genuinely eerie, the battles are exciting and it has enjoyable blustering from a cast of familiar B stalwarts like Morris Ankrum, giving his 87th reading of the part of the uptight general who heads up the Earth defence forces ('when an armed and threatening power lands uninvited in our capital, we don't greet it with tea and cookies!'). **★★★ KN**

EARTHQUAKE (1974)

Starring *Charlton Heston (Stewart Graff), Ava Gardener (Remy Royce-Graff), George Kennedy (Sergeant Slew Slade), Lorne Green (Sam Royce), Genevieve Bujold (Denise Marshall), Richard Roundtree (Miles Quade)*
Screenwriters: *George Fox, Mario Puzo*
PG/123 mins./Disaster/Thriller/USA

Awards: *Academy Awards – Best Sound*

Focusing on the marital dilemmas of construction engineer Stewart Graff, we follow the catastrophic effects of a major earthquake on a cross section of Los Angelinos, as their city is reduced to ruins.

Whatever else you may say about Irwin Allen's boldest effort as purveyor of fire and brimstone for the mass market, the sound was great. Heralded from its posters, the film came fully equipped with Sensoround, a process that would, hopefully, give the audience a three dimensional experience as the crunching of concrete and the twisting of steel reverberate through our very backsides. This was, however, rather dependant on the quality of the speakers at your local fleapit. And a sensational buzzing through the bottom apart, this remains a big, bloated piece of empty spectacle hoping its could-happen concept would give it a spiky resonance.

While earlier entries into Allen's cannon of disaster movies confined their spread of labouring has-beens to a single location (boat, skyscraper, et al) here it must sprawl across a whole city. It's like Altman's *Short Cuts* meets the apocalypse. As damns break, buildings shatter, and power lines fry Angelinos, we also have to deal with Lorne Greene as boozy Ava Gardner's father (despite only seven years' difference); as her husband, sturdy hero Charlton Heston (two years younger) plays away with Genevieve Bujold. It's all a muddle of soap operatics with none of the rich-kids up in flame spice of *The Towering Inferno*. Only Walter Matthau's blithering drunk is in any way interesting, as he stumbles about oblivious to the falling masonry.

What can you say of the effects? Well, they are ground-breaking, but only in a literal way. Time and endless we-were-there-with-a-camera 'When Nature Bites Back' type documentaries have exposed the shuddering city blocks as the disintegrating models they clearly are. Some of the set building, a morass of ruined civilisation, can be impressive, but when we go up-close with the actors you get more than a hint of that old wobbling camera routine. Anyway, the quake doesn't even last that long, this is more a movie about the survival for a bunch of idiotic grumble-mouths you would rather see crushed beneath a fallen lamppost. **★★ IN**

EAST IS EAST (1999)

Starring: *Om Puri (George Khan), Linda Bassett (Ella Khan), Jordan Routledge (Sajid Khan), Archie Panjabi (Meenah Khan), Emil Marwa (Maneer Khan), Chris Bisson (Saleem Khan), Jimi Mistry (Tariq Khan)*
Director: *Damien O'Donnell*
Screenwriter: *Ayub Khan-Din, based on his play*
15/96 mins./Comedy/Drama/UK

Awards: *BAFTA – Alexander Korda Award for Best British Film, Empire Awards – Best Debut (Damien O'Donnell)*

1971 Salford, and chip shop owner George Khan expects his children to follow his strict Muslim ways. However, after his eldest son flees an arranged marriage, the cracks in the behaviour of the others begin to show, and family strife breaks out . . .

A towering performance from Om Puri anchors this finely wrought adaptation of Ayub Khan Din's celebrated stage play, about a mixed-race family wrestling with their cultural identity in 1971 Salford.

Puri plays chip shop owner George Khan, a proud Pakistani married to an English woman who is attempting to bring up his seven recalcitrant children as good Muslims. An overbearing patriarch, known as 'Ghengis' by his kids, he is devastated when his eldest son, Nazir, flees from an arranged marriage.

Disowning him, Khan redoubles his efforts to maintain Pakistani traditions but, needless to say, his remaining offspring – with the exception of Maneer, a dedicated scholar of the Koran – are no keener than Nazir to adopt their father's values. As an arranged marriage looms large, for the first time, the family openly opposes him and George's frustrations finally erupt.

Puri is superb as the beleaguered George, conveying perfectly the contradictions of a man who wants the best for his children, but whose stubbornness and faith in his cultural identity blind him to exactly what that is. Bassett is similarly effective as his wife Ella, a Salford woman born and bred, who is torn between her love for her husband and her desire to see her children happy. Casting of the anarchic Khan clan is also perfect – the constant mix of bickering and affection are right on the money; you could almost believe they were a real family.

The film skilfully avoids most Asian-Britain clichés and by confining proceedings to the Khan family, it gives the exploration of culture-collision issues a tight focus. That said, you're never in any doubt about its theatrical origins, and whether it might have been more comfortable on the small screen is open to debate. Some quite brutal scenes of domestic violence don't sit well with the comic, often farcical, overtones and certain scenes lack momentum. But for the most part, it's a funny, astute and quietly moving piece of work. **★★★★ SB**

EASY RIDER (1969)

Starring: *Peter Fonda (Wyatt/Captain America), Dennis Hopper (Billy/Wolfman), Jack Nicholson (George Hanson), Phil Spector (Connection), Toni Basil (Mary)*
Director: *Dennis Hopper*
Screenwriters: *Dennis Hopper, Peter Fonda, Terry Southern*
18/94 mins./Drama/USA

Two free-wheelin' bikers set out from Los Angeles for New Orleans and Mardi Gras. Along the way they encounter a wild variety of weird and not-so wonderful characters who come to sum up the clash of cultures in America.

Justly celebrated as the film that truly channelled that whole counter-cultural thing along the downward slope of the sixties, Dennis Hopper's experimental mishmash of a road movie is flawed by its own concept. It was such a product of its time it feels vacuous and aloof, its so-called greatness exaggerated all out of proportion. So, in approaching the bumpy adventures across the heart of America, or at least its leathery Southern belt, of Captain America (the heroic-looking Peter Fonda) and Wolfman (Dennis Hopper looking like he would dance with any devil given the chance) context is everything. This was 1969, the year of Woodstock, the Vietnam War, and the growing discontent in American youth.

What is most apparent is its flagrant deconstruction of what was considered popular cinema. The film is shapeless, a picaresque squall of bizarre encounters between the chopper-riding heroes of freedom as they bounce between communes of 'shroomed hippies, suspicious yokels, to the famous fireside encounter with a booze-riddled lawyer played by Jack Nicholson. To be fair, the film isn't a dope session, for each woozy slab of drop-out bliss the film counters with a growing sense of dysfunction. These easy riders are looking for an answer that can't ever be located. They harken to the call of doom.

The open depiction of drugs and drug culture drenched the film in controversy, but what irritates is not the moral dimension more than using such an alternative lifestyle as an excuse to labour the intelligent design with wafty, pointless psychedlia. The New Orleans section, where they are tripping on LSD and hook up with Toni Basil and Karen Black, is a near unwatchable wobble through the filmmakers' genuine whacked-out adventures shot a year prior to the rest of the film. Hopper probably felt it was outrageously daring, but it drives a huge spoke into the film's spinning wheels. Thus, while you cannot dismiss its place in history, its power is in what it represented rather than what it did. ★★★ **IN**

Movie Trivia: Easy Rider

The lead characters are named after Wyatt Earp and Billy the Kid. Jack Nicholson's role was originally written for Rip Torn. Peter Fonda actually designed his captain America jacket which he wears all throughout the movie. Fonda had flu during the nude swim sequence — all the shots of him were taken later and spliced in.

L'ECLISSE (1962)

Starring: *Alain Delon (Piero), Monica Vitti (Vittoria), Francisco Rabal (Ricardo), Louis Seigner (Ercoli), Lilla Brignone (Vittoria's Mother), Rosanna Rory (Anita), Mirella Ricciardi (Marta)*
Director: *Michelangelo Antonioni*
Screenwriters: *Michelangelo Antonioni, Tonino Guerra, Elio Bartolini, Ottiero Ottieri*
PG/124 mins./Drama/Italy/France

Having broken up with Riccardo, Vittoria meets her mother at the Roman Stock Exchange and is smitten by dashing broker Piero.

Pauline Kael once dubbed this austere drama 'Some Like It Cold'. But the concluding part of the 'alienation' trilogy that commenced with *L'Avventura* and *La Notte* was never likely to be a study in emotional warmth.

At a time when French New Wavers were romanticising Paris, Michelangelo Antonioni was intent on showing that even a city as eternally vibrant as Rome could dehumanise inhabitants with seemingly everything to live for. Consequently, the setting becomes as important a character as Monica Vitti's commitment-shy translator or Alain Delon's suave stockbroker and Antonioni packs scenes of frantic activity (at the Stock Exchange and the blackface dance) or intense contemplation (Vitti's broken engagement and the aeroplane ride) with a symbolic significance that makes the isolation imposed by modernity all the more tragic.

It takes artistic courage to make a film about tedium. Federico Fellini ultimately failed to do so in *La Dolce Vita*, as he couldn't resist making the ennui he was satirising seem fascinating. But Antonioni is more disciplined, as the precise formalism of the opening sequence demonstrates. The juxtaposition of figure and prop is almost fanatically meticulous, with both the shifts in perspective and the contrasts between Vitti and Francisco Rabal and the décor being used to reflect the state of their relationship.

Yet, if Antonioni's style occasionally borders on abstraction, his motifs to suggest the breakdown of communication couldn't be clearer, as he utlises architecture to keep his characters apart. Moreover, he frequently films them through doors, hallways, gates, fences and windows.

But his masterstroke is the non-ending, in which Gianni Di Venanzo photographs people, places and things associated with Vitti and Delon and their designated rendezvous. Antonioni even ends this allusional montage with a lookalike couple to confound our expectations before closing on a close-up of a street lamp, as if to suggest that artificiality has eclipsed what was once real. It's a deliberately ambiguous ending, as Antonioni shatters our passivity and forces us to speculate as to the couple's future. ★★★★ **DP**

ED WOOD (1994)

Starring: *Johnny Depp (Ed Wood), Martin Landau (Bela Lugosi), Sarah Jessica Parker (Dolores Fuller), Patricia Arquette (Kathy O'Hara), Vincent D'Onofrio (Orson Welles), Bill Murray (John 'Bunny' Breckinridge)*
Director: *Tim Burton*
Screenwriters: *Scott Alexander, Larry Karaszewski*
15/127 mins./Biography/Comedy/Drama/USA

Awards: *Academy Awards – Best Supporting Actor (Martin Landau), Best Makeup, Golden Globes – Best Supporting Actor*

Edward Wood Jr. was the legendary 50s director famed as the world's worst, and this biopic charts his friendship with faded horror icon Bela Lugosi, his transvestism and his unswerving determination to make films.

A black-and-white biopic of Edward D. Wood Jr., arguably the world's worst filmmaker, the cross-dressing director of such Z-grade cult classics as *Plan 9 From Outer Space* and *Glen Or Glenda*, was always going to be a tough sell. And so it proved – reflected by its disastrous box office performance in the US from a director who had previously been blessed with the Midas touch.

Which is a shame, because this is perhaps one of Tim Burton's finest films, a delightful, funny, bizarre, touching, magical, moving insight into one of cinema's most maligned filmmakers from a director whose work has always shown him to have a true affinity with the outsider. And, in Hollywood terms at least, they came no more outside than Ed Wood, a charming auteur with Orson Welles aspirations and a dearth of talent who died in 1978, and whose films only truly gained their infamy and cult status in the early 80s.

The film follows the inept, if ever optimistic Ed through the production of three films – *Glen Or Glenda*, *Bride Of The Monster* and *Plan 9* – and finishes on the most upbeat note possible, with Ed driving away from the premiere of *Plan 9* believing he's made his masterpiece, when in reality his life from that point on only became more tragic.

Episodic in structure and more than a tad liberal with the truth, the film is more character study than Tinseltown exposé (though Burton deliciously recreates the filming of Wood's three most infamous movies), focusing on the delusional director and his bizarre coterie of hangers-on and wannabes, among them the Swedish wrestler Tor Johnson, TV horror host Vampira and failed transsexual Bunny Breckinridge, and succeeds in the main due to its performances. In particular an Oscar-winning turn from Martin Landau as Bela Lugosi, the morphine-addicted star of Universal's 1930 *Dracula*, who Ed resurrected at the tail end of his career, helping him stave off destitution and addiction.

And it's their relationship that's the core of the film. Depp himself gives a truly mesmerising performance, both in and out of drag, notching up another distinctly oddball role that again reveals the measure of the actor's talents.

The script by Larry Karaszewski and Scott Alexander crackles with witty one-liners and is often laugh out loud funny, playing up Ed's transvestism and fondness for angora sweaters, but never stooping to being nasty or judgmental. Burton shows a lightness of touch and a healthy sense of humour in his direction, and gets from his cast the most fleshed-out, rounded performances in any of his films to date. There's no doubt Burton loves these characters. The surprise is you will too. ★★★★ **KN**

EDUCATING RITA (1983)

Starring: *Michael Caine (Dr. Frank Bryant), Julie Walters (Rita, aka Susan), Michael Williams (Brian), Maureen Lipman (Trish), Jeananne Crowley (Julia), Malcolm Douglas (Denny)*
Director: *Lewis Gilbert*
Screenwriter: *Willy Russell based on his own play*
15/110 mins./Drama/UK

Award: *BAFTA – Best Actor, Best Actress, Best Screenplay*

An adaptation of the celebrated stageplay, in which a young working-class hairdresser decides to better herself by completing her education. But her growing relationship with her tutor Dr. Frank Bryant, a morose soul inspired by her dedication, threatens her marriage.

While it's easy to sneer at the familiar gauze of little people and their little lives, British cinema's damp whiff of used teabags, Lewis Gilbert, and two career best performances from his leading actors, give this film such energy it leaves the pleasant aroma of life and possibility.

Educating Rita is a gem, created by the fertile pen of Willy Russell who dresses the downtrodden in layers of self-respect rather than Mike Leigh's forced caricatures. She is emerging from the fog of routine, becoming aware the limits and destinies of her life might be overcome. She wants to be more than this prescribed version of herself, a gobby hairdresser anchored by a drab husband and negative friends, but she has a way to go. The key to Julie Walters' splendidly rich interpretation is a form of demand, she is bursting with need but stymied by circumstance. Yet, her abridged reactions to the traditions of English Lit carry the caustic brilliance of true intelligence, a shattering of blithe pretension, starting with her anatomic reading of the title of *Howards End*.

Frank is equally in need, but he's smothered his failings in whiskey. Caine, during his slow transition from leading man to classy character actor, checked in with this leaning tower of an academic: spiky, self-destructive, drunk. The electric jolt of Rita, from the moment she tiptoes into his messy study, is a life-giver. She is ready with questions that have long been taken for granted, like why he stopped writing poetry. They make a beautifully odd couple, in a love story at one remove.

Lewis Gilbert is doing a realist spin on *Pygmalion*, replacing the songs with a maudlin edge. But it is effective, and finally optimistic, Willy Russell's angry message that people are trapped by their environment not their abilities, is salved by the sweetness of the final parting. ★★★★ **IN**

EDWARD SCISSORHANDS (1990)

Starring: *Johnny Depp (Edward Scissorhands), Winona Ryder (Kim), Dianne Wiest (Peg), Anthony Michael Hall (Jim), Kathy Baker (Joyce), Vincent Price (The Inventor), Alan Arkin (Bill)*
Director: *Tim Burton*
Screenwriters: *Caroline Thompson, Tim Burton*
PG/105 mins./Fantasy/Romance/USA

Awards: *BAFTA – Best Production Design*

An artificial man with scissors for hands lives alone in a dilapidated manor above his town. Lured down by a kindly Avon lady, he at first produces a sensation among the townspeople, impressed by his skills at topiary and hairdressing. However, when he falls in love with a cheerleader, things become more complicated ...

Once upon a time there was a young director who made two wonderfully imaginative films before really finding the pot of gold at the end of the rainbow with *Batman* in 1989. Instead of cashing in on his biggest success to date, however, Tim Burton's follow-up here was about as far from a mainstream blockbuster as it is possible to get. Instead, *Edward Scissorhands* is a touching and decidedly left-of-centre fairytale, and, even from the man who has previously brought you *Pee-Wee's Big Adventure* and *Batman*, his most whimsical film to date.

Tagline
His story will touch you, even though he can't.

The Edward of the title is not a man, but a creation of The Inventor (an all-too fleeting cameo from Vincent Price). Edward looks human enough, except for one detail – he has scissors instead of hands – and lives alone in a crumbling mansion high above a street of pastel-coloured houses. Kind-hearted Avon lady Peg (a marvellous turn from Wiest) miraculously discovers Edward's hiding place and brings him down to the 'real' world, where he is soon embraced by her neighbours when they discover the boy's frustrated scissorhands are equally talented whether shaping hedges or creating outlandish hairstyles. Life is further complicated when Edward falls for Peg's cheerleader daughter and it is not long before the trusting innocent is coerced into committing a crime.

One of the many successes Burton pulls off in this delightfully odd film was to cast his various players against type in this dreamlike world. Anthony Michael Hall, for example, best known for playing the nerd in *The Breakfast Club*, succeeds here in showing a far nastier side in his role as oafish boyfriend Jim, while Winona Ryder brings a delicate touch to her underdeveloped role as the nice girl on the block. It is Johnny Depp, however, who was previously confined to standard bad boy roles, who surprised the most, creating a character trapped by his incomplete body, accurately conveying Edward's frustration without using many words, his pale, scarred face showing the hurt on discovering that even the gentlest touch with his Freddy Krueger-like blades can cause pain.

Edward Scissorhands certainly has its flaws, dwelling too long on Edward's talent for scissorwork and leaving a number of characters too thinly sketched for comfort. It remains, however, an ambitious and quite beautifully conceived fairy-tale. ★★★★★ **JB**

EIGHT LEGGED FREAKS (2002)

Starring: *David Arquette (Chris McCormick), Kari Wuhrer (Sheriff Samantha Parker), Scott Terra (Mike Parker), Scarlett Johansson (Ashley Parker)*
Director: *Ellory Elkayem*
Screenwriters: *Jesse Alexander, Ellory Elkayem, based on a story by Ellory Elkayem, Randy Korfield*
12/99 mins./Action/Comedy/Horror/Sci-fi/USA

Toxic waste creates giant spiders in Arizona. People are attacked, cob-web-cocooned, liquidised and eaten. Prodigal son Chris McCormick and Sheriff Sam Parker, advised by the latter's spider-obsessed brat, rally

survivors. And so the townsfolk fight back with guns, chainsaws, perfume, methane, a mobile phone and raw courage.

No coming attraction of 2002 created as much buzz as the trailer for *Eight Legged Freaks* (previously known as *Arach Attack*), with its excellent tagline, 'Do you hate spiders? Do you really hate spiders? Well, they don't like you either!' We're happy to report that the film delivers everything the promo promised, sneaking in under the radar and emerging as the best unpretentious genre movie in many a moon.

While the similarly-themed *Arachnophobia* stuck too close to reality with its regular-sized villains, this goes the whole hog by spilling enough toxic waste to bulk up the spiders to sizes ranging from four to 20 feet across. In the 1950s, classic B-movies like *Them!* and *Tarantula* made big bugs a science-fiction staple, capitalising on our near-universal queasiness about creatures with more eyes and legs than seem reasonable. Those quickies proved that the feeblest rubber puppets rampaging in a sandbox could raise a healthy chill, so it's surprising it took so long to revisit the they're-crawling-to-get-you sub-genre with state-of-the-art effects.

Ellory Elkayem, insect-obsessed auteur of the short parody, *Larger Than Life*, and the cockroach quickie, *They Nest*, respects the traditions of the genre in everything from setting (a western town about to go bankrupt), to character type (a Harry Potter-like kid who knows grown-ups won't believe his monster-spider stories). The plot also follows the expected lines – an escalation of attacks as the mutated spiders strike first in the desert by day, then invade the town by night, driving the survivors into a failing mall and a played-out gold mine.

Perhaps not as smartly scripted as the similarly retro *Alligator* or *Tremors*, this is still a well-put-together film, showing that the Dean Devlin-Roland Emmerich team is capable of much better monster stuff than *Godzilla*, if they call in more screwball collaborators.

The opening reel has a fine cameo from Tom (*The Tooth Fairy*) Noonan as the creepy spider-farmer, while the leads are actors you wouldn't necessarily want to see in a picture without giant spider co-stars but are still painless company for the duration. Unassuming hero Arquette and cute sheriff Wuhrer rise to the occasion by providing a nicely thrown-away romantic sub-plot in between the cobweb crises. Then there's sprightly ham from Leon Rippy, Doug E. Doug and Scarlett Johansson in the traditional roles of mayor-whose-fault-it-all-is, paranoid-shock-jock-who-turns-out-to-be-right and stun-gun-wielding-teen-princess.

But this isn't a people movie. It's a spider movie, and its web-spinners are on great form. Noonan's lecture on arachnid behaviour sets up effects sequences the phobic won't abide, but which will delight others. A horde of giant, leaping spiders pursue teenagers on dirt-bikes, trapdoor spiders suck townsfolk under the street, human victims are liquidised, and hordes of the things crawl over the roof as Arquette tries to get a mobile phone signal.

The mostly-CGI spiders work well on screen, splatting with satisfying bursts of green goo, extending pipe-cleaner legs around an old codger's armchair, cocooning grannies and generally exciting yelps of pleasurable revulsion whenever they scuttle on screen. With a witty score that keeps playing variations on 'Itsy Bitsy Spider' and a title likely to enter the language, this is a real scream from beginning to end. ★★★ **CH**

⦿ 8 ½ (OTTO E MEZZO) (1963)

Starring: *Marcello Mastroianni (Guido Anselmi), Claudia Cardinale (Claudia), Anouk Aimée (Luisa Anselmi, Guido's Wife), Sandra Milo (Carla), Rossella Falk (Rossella), Barbara Steele (Gloria Morin)*
Director: *Federico Fellini*
Screenwriters: *Federico Fellini, Tullio Pinelli, Ennio Flaiano, Brunello Rondi, based on a story by Federico Fellini and Ennio Flaiano*
15/140 mins./Drama/Italy
Awards: *Academy Awards – Best Black and White Costume, Best Foreign Language Film*

Director Guido Anselmi retreats to a spa. Between memories of his past, daydreams that turn nightmarish and the demands of wife, mistress and hangers-on, Guido can't concentrate on the science fiction film he is supposed to be making.

Among the most important and influential films of the 1960s. Fellini's stand-in is Mastroianni, a blocked director with the coolest sunglasses in Europe whose fantasy life and actual reality keep devolving into a circus-like infernal parade. Multi-layered and wonderfully adept in its mix of the meaningful and the trivial, this should be annoyingly self-involved (as when American directors like Woody Allen and Bob Fosse have copied it), but it's enchanting and trenchant, with an outstanding cast of Euro-beauties (Barbara Steele, Anouk Aimée, Claudia Cardinale) and grotesques, plus an amazing score from Nino Rota (incorporating classical snippets) and luminous widescreen monochrome cinematography from Gianni Di Venzano.

Though blatantly autobiographical, the film is also merciless about its subject – incorporating a wizened, carping critic who tags along behind Guido pointing out what's wrong with his films and his fantasies and, by implication, the movie we're watching (in one funny bit, Guido imagines having this annoying fellow hanged).

Fellini's outrageous fantasies of masculine empowerment all turn around and bite: the major set-piece is Guido's vision of himself as the pampered master of a harem of all the women in his life, but even in this daydream there's a revolution and the abused beauties rebel against the whip-wielding tyrant; more subtle but as affecting is the reaction of Guido's wounded, brave, tough wife (Aimée) to seeing his version of their marital problems up on the screen in tests for the film he's making. The title refers to the number of films (including a short) Fellini had made up to and including this one. ★★★★★ **KN**

Federico Fellini (1920–1993)

Who he was: Switched from neo-realism to become Italian cinema's greatest fantasist.

Hallmarks: Often eschewed conventional plots for dream-like atmosphere and 'life is a circus' metaphors. Obsessed with clowns, spaghetti and big-breasted women.

If you see one film, see: *La Dolce Vita* (1960)

⦿ EIGHT MEN OUT (1988)

Starring: *Jace Alexander (Dickie Kerr), John Cusack (Buck Weaver), Gordon Clapp (Ray Schalk), Don Harvey (Swede Risberg), Charlie Sheen (Hap Felsch)*
Director: *John Sayles*
Screenwriter: *John Sayles, based on a book by Eliot Asinof*
PG/119 mins./Sports/Drama/USA

In 1919, eight ball players from the Chicago White Sox were approached by a gambling syndicate to throw the Series against the Cincinatti Reds. The terrible pay and harsh times contributed to the players' decision to betray their game and fans.

Of course, *Eight Men Out* was never going to achieve commercial success theatrically in the UK. Why? It's about baseball. And it's not a baseball movie in the guise of a romantic comedy, a heartwarming fantasy, a biopic in which the misfits pull off a miracle, or a male weepie. But if it was just about baseball, Sayles wouldn't have been interested either.

Specifically, *Eight Men Out* is a meticulously detailed period drama about the Black Sox scandal of 1919, when eight players from the Chicago White Sox, then the finest in the game, were tried on charges of conspiracy.

They were accused of throwing the sport's premier championship event, the World Series. Events surrounding the affair not only brought the game into disrepute, they had a lasting impact on the business of professional sport.

Even if you couldn't care less about baseball, there is a fascinating story well told here. It represents a clash between athletes, big business interests and the media, adapted from the definitive book on the scandal by Eliot Asinof (who appears in the film as a team owner).

As conspiracies go it was a muddled, even farcical business. In 1919 a lot of big money was being placed on the imminent series, with the odds heavily on the Sox, the poorly paid team owned by skinflint Charles Comiskey. Two small-time Philadelphia gamblers approached a player about tanking the best-of-nine-games series. These gamblers went to notorious New York 'financier' Arnold Rothstein (immortalised in *The Great Gatsby* and here played by Michael Lerner) to bankroll their con. Rothstein turned them down but made his own deal with Boston gambler 'Sport' Sullivan.

So two sets of rival gamblers were negotiating with a couple of not-very-bright players. These in turn recruited team-mates, some of whom agreed to go along for a variety of reasons. Some never took any money and played well; others were oblivious to the scheme and watched in fury as they went down in humiliating defeat.

A legendary Chicago reporter himself, Studs Terkel plays pioneering sports writer Hugh Fullerton, and Sayles plays Fullerton's protégé Ring Lardner, to whom he actually bears a strong resemblance (Lardner, by the way, became a celebrated satirist and was the father of Ring Lardner Jr., Oscar-winning screenwriter of *Woman Of The Year* and *M*A*S*H*). Fullerton and Lardner sniffed something fishy, eventually pieced together the sorry story and broke the bad news to heartbroken fans.

For anyone who appreciates artistic integrity and is interested in genuinely independent films, the prolific and highly personal work of John Sayles is essential viewing. ★★★★ **AE**

ⓘ 8 MILE (2002)

Starring: *Marshall 'Eminem' Mathers (Jimmy), Brittany Murphy (Alex), Kim Basinger (Stephanie), Mekhi Phifer (Future), Evan Jones (Cheddar Bob), Omar Benson Miller (Sol George)*
Director: *Curtis Hanson*
Screenwriter: *Scott Silver*
15/110 mins./Drama/USA
Awards: *Academy Awards – Best Original Song*

It's 1995 and Jimmy Smith Jr. desperately wants to be a rapper but the trials and tribulations of Detroit working class life seem set to destroy his ambition.

Let's get this over with: *8 Mile* is the rap *Rocky*, the hip-hop *Saturday Night Fever*. But just because comparisons are easily made does not make them uninstructive. Lest we forget, both *Rocky* and *Saturday Night Fever* were instant pop classics, shrewdly engineered yarns of personal triumph set against a harsh, blue-collar landscape.

And, like boxing in *Rocky* and dancing in *Saturday Night Fever*, rapping in *8 Mile* possesses redemptive power – raw talent will always out. In fact, the chief difference in this case is that the charismatic leading actor is not in need of an iconic moment. Eminem is a star already.

As Jimmy, Eminem's (or rather Marshall Mathers; there's none of the bluster of Eminem, or Slim Shady, here) internalised performance does not invite sympathy easily. Often hooded and perpetually wearing a cap and scowl of some description, he keeps the audience at a safe distance. The camera does not love him (Rodrigo Prieto's unforgiving camera loves little in the steely, blue bleakness of Detroit) because his power must be carefully guarded, much like the music which we hear only fitfully for most of the movie.

Of course, in the best *Rocky* tradition, *8 Mile* demands a climactic showdown. However, when Jimmy is called to 'battle' against a rival rapper, the punches cannot be pulled; for the movie to work at all, Eminem's natural skills must finally break free. Without giving anything away, the manner of Jimmy's triumph is one of the most exhilarating scenes you will see all year.

And yet Curtis Hanson has crafted too nuanced a movie to close on an unambiguous high. This is not *The Karate Kid*. Indeed, in the closing moments, it becomes clear that the organising myth of *8 Mile* is perhaps not *Rocky*, but Shakespeare's *Henry IV Part I*. Jimmy is Prince Hal, the king in waiting, who must stop slumming in low company and strike out on his own if he is to ascend to his rightful throne. From *Rocky I* to *Henry IV* – it really is that good. ★★★★ **CK**

ⓘ 8 MM (1999)

Starring: *Nicolas Cage (Tom Welles), Joaquin Phoenix (Max California), James Gandolfini (Eddie Poole), Peter Stormare (Dino Velvet) Anthony Heald (Daniel Longdale)*
Director: *Joel Schumacher*
Screenwriter: *Andrew Kevin Walker*
18/123 mins./Mystery/Thriller/USA

A private detective becomes obsessed with finding out if a 'snuff' film is genuine.

If there is a key image at the black heart of 8mm, it is Nicolas Cage's face, squirming in disbelief and terror at unbridled violence depicted off-screen accompanied by a projector whirr. In many ways the shot embodies the film's chief limitation – for although a serious, occasionally absorbing look into the phenomenon of snuff movies, it never really peers far enough into the darkness to be requisitely scary and subversive.

Turning in his most restrained performance since bagging the Oscar for *Leaving Las Vegas* (whereupon he immediately delved into action heroism), Cage gives the film a solid, empathetic centre as Tom Welles, a surveillance supervisor hired by a rich widow to discover the whereabouts of a young girl seemingly slaughtered in a (not particularly disturbing) snuff movie found within her dead husband's estate.

Indeed, it is as an old fashioned detective story that *8mm* works best; Schumacher and *Se7en* scribe Andrew Kevin Walker allow Welles to piece the puzzle together logically – mundane detective work builds believably to one-on-one enquiries to surveillance work – creating the impression that the 'tec is really earning his breaks without script contrivance or coincidence.

As the hunt gets more obsessive Schumacher deftly sketches the ripples on normal life, firstly through the ever excellent Catherine Keener as Welles' increasingly neglected wife and more movingly, in touching scenes in which Welles quietly interrogates the missing girl's mother (Amy Morton).

Schumacher laces the trail with mordant humour – Welles watches two snuff movies to see the same actress 'murdered' in different movies – fleeting obscenity (check out the weird enema porn) and some bone-crunching violence, all to an intermittently successful Middle Eastern-flavoured score. Indeed, as the investigation storyline seems to run out of steam, the movie is given a huge boost by Joaquin Phoenix who adds zip and humour as Max California, a fast-talking adult bookstore worker who guides Welles through the seedy underworld.

Yet, once the full abhorrent truth is uncovered, the film enters into more conventional thriller territory as Welles goes on a personal crusade to right the wrongs. Schumacher attempts to play the denouement with a hard edge – a sequence where Cage explores a deserted house, the soundtrack dominated by the repetitive click of needle on vinyl, is creepily effective – yet an obvious twist in the yarn, some sub-*Batman* villains (Peter Stormare with a dodgy accent and a masked S&M fetishist named Machine) and some overwrought attempts to define character motivations manages to dissipate the tension and intensity entirely.

Moreover, the skills Walker displayed in *Se7en* for telling nuance and crackling dialogue are absent here: the film never really gets under the skin of its central character – even Cage is unable to transmute Welles' descent from polite private eye to driven avenging angel into anything other than a by-the-numbers character corruption – or fully realises the seedy, grimy milieu of hardcore porn (and beyond) the characters inhabit. Indeed, for a film that unravels in the shadowy recesses of artistic and human morality, there is little that unnerves.

Such an intoxicating, lurid, sordid underbelly would seemingly fire Schumacher's imagination, yet he adds little in the way of atmosphere – opting instead for cold, muted colour, perhaps wary of over-egging the brutal subject matter. Ultimately, the film never gets close to the complexities snuff raises – why are people drawn to such material? Why do we need it to exist? – offering risible conclusions in a hollow finale.

Foreshadowing his return to basics with the likes of *Tigerland* and *Phone Booth*, this post *Batman & Robin* outing for Schumacher overdoes the scuzziness, but is an occasionally compelling odyssey into darkness. ★★★ **IF**

---

8 WOMEN (HUIT FEMMES) (2001)

Starring: *Catherine Deneuve (Gaby), Isabelle Huppert (Augustine), Emmanuelle Béart (Louise), Fanny Ardant (Pierrette), Virginie Ledoyen (Suzon), Danielle Darrieux (Mamy), Ludivine Sagnier (Catherine), Firmine Richard (Madame Chanel), Dominque Lamure (Marcel)*
Director: *François Ozon*
Screenwriters: *François Ozon, Marina de Van, freely adapted from a play by Robert Thomas*
15/113 mins./Comedy/Mystery/Musical/France/Italy

Eight female family members reunite in a remote mansion in the snowy countryside of 1950s France. But what should in fact be a glamorous, social affair becomes a dramatic cutthroat murder mystery as the women discover their beloved patriarch has been killed, and they are the suspects.

The enfant terrible of French cinema, François Ozon's brave foray into the mind of not one, but eight, women is a gloriously-executed examination of what lies beneath the manicured façade of the female species.

From the outset, the film plays like Agatha Christie meets Douglas Sirk, and is shot like a sumptuous 1950s Technicolor melodrama. However, with content exquisitely linked to form, all is not as it seems; as the plot thickens, the veneer cracks and the genre subtly twists its way to kitsch theatricality.

Meanwhile, the women spiral to reveal unexpected intentions – sexual, murderous, dishonest, perverse. A body is discovered in an isolated country house and one of them must be the killer. But is it Suzon, back for college vacations, her elegant mother, her spinster aunt or the hypochondriac spinster sister? Or one of the other women?

At first cringeworthy, the sight of Catherine Deneuve clicking her heels to a tune is soon delightful. From the twitchy recluse Huppert, to the raunchy Béart, every one of this star-led cast has a chance to spin and sing her yarn to beguiling effect. ★★★★ **DP**

EL CID (1961)

Starring: *Charlton Heston (El Cid/Rodrigo Diaz de Bivar), Sophia Loren (Jimena), Raf Vallone (Count Ordonez), Genevieve Page (Princess Urraca), John Fraser (Prince Alfonso), Michael Hordern (Don Diego)*
Director: *Anthony Mann*
Screenwriters: *Philip Yordan, Fredric M. Frank, Ben Barzman*
U/182 mins./History/Drama/USA

The legendary story of Rodrigo Diaz, who became known as El Cid, the man driven by honour and unquestionable valour to lead his beloved Spain in driving the Moorish invaders from their shores in the 11th century.

The first thing to say about this epic that seems to span entire Bank Holidays with its golden-hued majesty, is that for a crowd of noble Spaniards they look distinctly Aryan. Only the Italian Sophia Loren looks in any way like she might hail from the Mediterranean regions. This is a film willing to dispense with realism as long as it adheres to that school of bulging epics, in which Charlton Heston forever wrested the world from the brink of history by glowering and twitching his bronzed jaw. You could class this as the final piece in a trilogy of epics, following *The Ten Commandments* and *Ben-Hur*, but it is much harder work than those Biblical piles, a twisting, turning, achingly slow journey to the final battle.

Heston seemed to be working his way through the big league of directors, after Cecil B. DeMille and William Wyler, he worked here with Anthony Mann whose legacy of macho Westerns seemed a good base for this tale of unflagging nobility. But neither he, nor Heston, nor the familiar ream of screenwriters, find much of interest within the armour clad soul of Diaz. He's Lawrence Of Arabia, unifying the Christian kings of Spain, but without the tormented soul. This is a man so resolute he might as well be made of marble. And Mann directs his journey like he was building a cathedral, every scene is pristine and huge, but utterly prescribed. How could the 11th century be this clean? How could the grand love between Diaz and the swooning Jimena (Loren pouting for Christendom) be so sterile? Good deeds are so bland when there are no flaws to be bridged.

Everything about the film radiates a kind of assumed glory. The battle scenes are mighty, the locations vast, but there is not enough here to grant the watcher the surge of triumph of *Ben-Hur*. The craft on show is splendiferous, the score, by Miklos Rozsa, suitably soaring, but even by the famous rousing ending where they tie El Cid's corpse to a horse to lead the charge, still feels like it's pretending. ★★★ **IN**

EL MARIACHI (1992)

Starring: *Carlos Gallardo (El Mariachi), Consuelo Gomez (Domino), Jaime DeHoyos (Bigoton), Peter Marquardt (Maurico (Moco), Reinol Martinez (Azul)*
Director: *Robert Rodriguez*
Screenwriter: *Robert Rodriguez*
15/80 mins./Action/USA

A new guitar player comes to town to play his music but is somehow mistaken for a hitman, another recent arrival. The mariachi then stumbles across the local bar and in turn the beautiful bar-owner, who takes him in, unaware the gangsters are after the wrong man.

A then twenty-four-year-old Robert Rodriguez's (*Sin City*, *From Dusk Til Dawn*) amazingly assured feature debut cost a mind-blowingly minuscule $7,000 to make but is more than just an example of brilliance over no budget. Using the well-worn theme of mistaken identity, writer-director-producer-editor-cameraman Rodriguez has here crafted an action flick infinitely more exciting than many a film costing ten thousand times as much, transcending its budgetary limitations with wonderful ingenuity, invention and sassy wit.

A lone, black-clad guitar player – the eponymous mariachi – arrives at a Mexican border town looking for employment and is mistaken for a similarly attired hitman whose own identical guitar case contains a semi-automatic arsenal. There, the mariachi falls for a beautiful bar owner who takes him in, unaware of the inevitably tragic and explosive consequences of her actions.

Shamelessly derivative – *Mad Max*, *The Terminator*, the Coen Brothers, you name it – this, much like Sam Raimi's *Evil Dead*, has an exhilarating rawness that works for, rather than against it, its kinetic pacing, visceral editing and bravura camerawork revealing the presence of a director with unbridled visual panache. A minor masterpiece. ★★★★ **MS**

⓪ ELECTION (1999)

Starring: *Matthew Broderick (Jim McAllister), Reese Witherspoon (Tracy Flick), Chris Klein (Paul Metzler), Jessica Campbell (Tammy Metzler), Mark Harelik (Dave Novotny)*
Director: *Alexander Payne*
Screenwriters: *Alexander Payne, Jim Taylor, based on the novel by Tom Perrotta*
15/120 mins./Comedy/USA

Tracy Flick is an obnoxious overachiever hated by popular teacher Mr McAllister, after she got his best friend fired. When she appears a shoo-in for student council president, he does everything he can to stop her winning . . .

It used to be the case that the Western was the genre that Hollywood turned to when it wanted to examine the state of the nation. But the oater appears to have been usurped by the high school movie. In a year overrun with classic stories reset in schools and teenage dramas as varied as *Rushmore*, *Never Been Kissed* and *American Pie*, Election still managed to be an outstanding picture of 1999, developing the John Hughes genre of the 80s into a form that might be capable of turning out films as sharply incisive about American mores as *The Man Who Shot Liberty Valance* or *Unforgiven*.

In a small Omaha community, popular teacher Jim McAllister has to supervise an election for president of the student body but is troubled by the fact that the sole candidate is ferocious overachiever Tracy Flick, who has already ruined the life of his best friend by getting him sacked after they had an affair. McAllister encourages nice guy jock Paul Metzler, sidelined from sport by a broken leg, to run against Tracy. A dark horse candidate emerges in Paul's sister Tammy, a lesbian whose dearest wish is to be expelled so she can be sent to an all-girls' catholic school, and who reacts when her girlfriend dumps her for her brother by running on an 'I don't care' platform.

Tagline
Reading.
Writing.
Revenge.

With narration from all four of the principles and a script that keeps piling on the moral dilemmas, this never settles for easy moralities. Like *Rushmore*, it's brilliantly-scripted and played, with a real sense of offbeat character. Broderick, carrying memories of Ferris Bueller into the classroom, delivers his best grown-up performance to date, while Witherspoon (switching her smile on and off like a light), Klein (endearingly dumb) and Campbell (snarling through braces) are spot-on as teen charicatures of larger political types. ★★★★ **KN**

⓪ ELEKTRA (2005)

Starring: *Jennifer Garner (Elektra), Goran Visnjic (Mark Miller), Kirsten Prout (Abby Miller), Will Yun Lee (Kirigi), Terence Stamp (Stick)*
Director: *Rob Bowman*
Screenwriters: *Zak Penn, Stu Zicherman, Raven Metzner, based on the motion picture characters by Mark Steven Johnson and the comic book characters by Frank Miller*
12A/100 mins. (director's cut)/Action/Fantasy/USA

Badass ninja hitwoman Elektra Natchios accepts a mystery assignment, and befriends a widower and his young daughter – only to learn that they are her targets. With The Hand, a band of supernatural assassins, also after the pair, Elektra must decide where her loyalties lie.

Proving – as if proof were needed – that death is no bar to a long career in comics or comic-book movies, Daredevil's love interest gets her own spin-off feature. Last seen stabbed with one of her own sais by a slaphead Colin Farrell, Elektra's back from the Other Side, and she's not happy about it. After watching this, you may not be too thrilled yourself.

From a playgirl millionaire's daughter, Elektra has metamorphosed into a cold-blooded assassin for hire. But that's not the only change she's gone through. A well-shot opening scene sees her stalk a notorious gangster and his team of guards, almost invisible apart from a flash of her trademark red sash. Jason Isaacs, as her target, talks of her supernatural abilities in awed tones, and sure enough the reborn Elektra has hitherto unguessed-at powers. She can now move instantaneously across short distances, see flashes of the future and has hearing to rival her ex-boyfriend. All of which would have come in exceedingly useful prior to her first death, but is essential when faced with her new enemies, the Hand.

These colourful baddies offer most of the film's few high points. Tattoo (Chris Ackerman) has body art that comes alive; Typhoid (Natassia Malthe) is a woman seriously in need of Listerine – her breath kills – and lead bad guy Kirigi (Will Yun Lee) focuses more on just looking menacing, but does reveal real fight skills in a showdown more than a little reminiscent of the final scenes of *Daredevil*.

Despite oozing star quality, Garner struggles to rise above the limitations of the script. While she's able to play with a few character quirks, such as her obsessive-compulsive fruit arranging, and excels in the fight scenes, she's not given a single witticism, so seriously does the film take her plight. Even the eternally gloomy Batman gets one-liners, and this lack of humour hamstrings *Elektra*, which is especially disappointing given Garner's fine comic touch.

Director Rob Bowman employs some stylistic flourishes, and the stunts and fights are impressive despite some obvious CGI. But enormous plot holes and a script that's fatally light on character mean there're few selling points beyond Jennifer Garner's corset . . . ★★ **H O'H**

⓪ ELEPHANT (2003)

Starring: *Alex Frost (Alex), Eric Deulen (Eric), John Robinson (John McFarland), Elias McDonnell (Elias), Jordan Taylor (Jordan), Carrie Finlea (Carrie)*
Director: *Gus Van Sant*
Screenwriter: *Gus Van Sant*
15/91 mins./Drama/USA

An ordinary day in an ordinary school, with students working, flirting, whining and wandering, caught up in mundane concerns. Then Alex and Eric, two of their schoolmates, show up with gym bags full of guns and set out to kill as many people as possible.

It was inevitable that someone would make a movie about the Columbine High School shootings, and it's probably inevitable that several more films will follow Gus Van Sant's low-key, blankly devastating, simple account of a day in an American high school which ends as two teenagers murder a number of their schoolfellows and teachers for reasons that will never be clear.

Some have put *Elephant*'s surprise Palme d'Or win at Cannes down to a reaction to the momentous nature of its subject rather than any inherent cinematic achievement; in fact, it's not even a movie movie but was shot for the US cable channel HBO. However, it's not a TV-style true crime exploitation picture but a restless, improvised back-and-forth that would probably be dull (like Van Sant's interminable but similarly handled *Gerry*) were it not for the foreboding that comes from the fragility of the youths (almost all well above average in looks) and the long following shots as we get time-overlapping snippets of the day of the massacre.

We latch onto a cross-section of kids, from playground demi-gods to a quietly nerdy girl, and have time to get a sense of who they are on the point of becoming before the killers (Alex Frost, Eric Deulen) show up in combat gear with their stash of internet-ordered weaponry.

The second half is about the murderers' backgrounds (the cast mostly use their real first names rather than playing the kids from Columbine), with a lot of cultural baggage (murder-spree video games, classical piano, a TV doc about Hitler, semi-gay shower clinches, automatic weapon target practice in the woodshed) that still don't 'explain' the unfathomable.

We see the note-taking and mapping prep for the atrocity, with a chilly sign-off ('The most important thing, have fun'). The massacre isn't sensationalised, with snippets of the action intercut with credible moments of people wandering around not knowing what's going on and living or dying for no fault of their own.

It's deliberately studied, with punctuating shots of the calm sky and long takes that strain patience. In the end, it's basically a statement that this happened and could too easily happen again – undiluted by the editorialising that a conventional picture, or even a Michael Moore documentary, would be compelled to add. ★★★★ **JB**

ⓞ THE ELEPHANT MAN (1980)

Starring: *Anthony Hopkins (Dr. Frederick Treves), John Hurt (John Merrick), Anne Bancroft (Mrs. Kendal), John Gielgud (Carr Gomm), Wendy Hiller (Mothershead), Freddie Jones (Bytes), Michael Elphick (Night Porter), Hannah Gorden (Mrs. Treves)*
Director: *David Lynch*
Screenwriters: *Christopher DeVore, Eric Bergen, David Lynch, based on* The Elephant Man, A Study In Human Dignity *by Ashley Montagu and* The Elephant Man And Other Reminiscences *by Sir Frederick Treves*
PG/125 mins./Biography/Docudrama/UK

Awards: *BAFTA – Best Actor, Best Film, Best Production Design/Art Direction*

A deformed man, who travels as a circus exhibit, is rescued by a doctor and introduced to high society.

In one of the most unlikely strokes of inspiration, Mel Brooks, wearing his producer's hat saw David Lynch's semi-underground first feature, *Eraserhead*, and decided Lynch was the director to handle a serious project Brooks held dear, a biopic of John Merrick, the Victorian freak, and of Frederick Treves, the philanthropic doctor who became his patron and friend.

The central performances are astonishingly subtle. John Hurt allows humanity to shine through impressive makeup as the multiply-deformed Merrick, who retains a childlike gentleness no matter how sorely he has been abused. Anthony Hopkins does wonders with self-doubt and underplaying in an apparently secondary, but actually more complex, role. The careful, literate script wavers between the melodramatic and the sentimental, just as Merrick passes through the slums and sideshows to become something of a pet for high society (another form of freakshow?).

However, Lynch imports all the cinematic strangeness of *Eraserhead*, creating a Victorian Britain of hideous industrial accidents and steam-belching machines in Expressionist black and white, and turning a trip to the theatre – a highlight in Merrick's life – into a magical celebration of the fantastical that evokes the memories of the early trick films of Georges Méliés. It's a very rich film, confident enough in its emotional core to get away with broadstrokes like the villainous performances of Freddie Jones and Michael Elphick as rotten exploiters, and a visit from Anne Bancroft as a star actress. If you thought the sweetness of *The Straight Story* was unprecedented in Lynch's work, look again at this earlier true-life tale of odd, everyday heroism. ★★★★ **KN**

ⓞ ELF (2003)

Starring: *Will Ferrell (Buddy), James Caan (Walter), Bob Newhart (Papa Elf), Edward Asner (Santa), Mary Steenburgen (Emily), Zooey Deschanel (Jovie), Amy Sedaris (Deb)*
Director: *Jon Favreau*
Screenwriter: *David Berenbaum*
PG/95 mins./Comedy/Fantasy/USA

After he creeps out of his crib at the orphanage and into Santa's bag, Buddy is raised at the North Pole and works in Santa's workshop with the elves. Shocked when he finally discovers he's human, not elf, Buddy goes to New York in search of his father, who turns out to be in need of some Christmas cheer.

An uncanny gift for physical comedy helps Will Ferrell propel this festive family movie along, even though it's barely more than a string of sketches held together by a conventional plot.

His giant-among-elves character first amuses with his mere size, but in New York he's an outcast of a different kind: a wide-eyed, relentlessly cheerful child in a man's body whose elf-talk convinces everyone he's a nutjob.

The gags swing between mildly inventive and screamingly obvious, but even the latter are performed and timed well enough to draw a laugh. The plot, however, is so overshadowed by comic set-pieces that its ending fails to deliver the emotional impact it should. And it doesn't help that the supporting characters are either overexposed (we see far too much of Buddy's father at his work, for example) or underdeveloped (love interest Jovie is likeable but sidelined). ★★★ **OR**

ⓞ ELIZABETH (1998)

Starring: *Cate Blanchett (Elizabeth 1), Geoffrey Rush (Sir Francis Walsingham), Christopher Eccleston (Duke Of Norfolk), Joseph Fiennes (Robert Dudley, Earl Of Leicester), Richard Attenborough (Sir William Cecil), Kathy Burke (Queen Mary Tudor), James Frain (Alvaro De La Quadra), Emily Mortimer (Kat Ashley), Kelly Macdonald (Isabel Knollys)*
Director: *Shekhar Kapur*
Screenwriter: *Michael Hirst*
15/124 mins./Biography/History/UK

Awards: *Academy Awards – Best Makeup, BAFTA – Alexander Korda Award for Best British Film, Anthony Asquith Award for Film Music, Best Cinematography, Best Makeup/Hair, Best Supporting Actor, Best Actress, Empire Awards – Best Actress, Golden Globes – Best Actress in a drama*

The story of Elizabeth's rise to the throne of England, avoiding execution by her sister and the politics of the court, to become Queen.

The tragedy of Queen Elizabeth I is that the more confident and powerful she grew, the weirder her hairdos became. The coiffeur theory of history is borne out in Kapur's snazzy costume drama, in which Good Queen Bess' ascension to the throne, early reign, and transformation from vivacious young woman into majestic icon are presented as a dark historical thriller.

Not your typical Tudor pageant, *Elizabeth*'s 16th century England is a sordid, deadly place, the royal court teeming with intrigues, religious fanatics and groupies. Queen Mary (Kathy Burke as a grotesque nutter) busies herself torturing Protestants. When she dies, the new queen's 'advisors' (led by Sir Richard Attenborough as Sir William Cecil) are keen on getting all Tarantinoid on errant Catholics. Fast-rising actress Blanchett makes a spirited, intelligent and attractive young princess struggling to assert herself over conniving nobles and the nation.

Essentially this is a sympathetic portrait of a smart, strong woman stretched to survive and command in a man's world, while her sense of duty conflicts with her romantic inclinations. Vying with the call of destiny for her attention, Fiennes presents a dandy distraction as Elizabeth's ambitious lover, Robert Dudley (this before she became a professional virgin). Good, too, are the impressions of regal isolation amid the pomp and decorative excess.

The slip-ups in a generally absorbing, sometimes inspired and visually potent production are some unnecessarily tittersome stunt casting – Wayne Sleep, Eric Cantona – among an otherwise class ensemble (notably Rush as the queen's coolly sinister henchman and Eccleston as perfidious Norfolk), and a decidedly arty bent. ★★★ **AE**

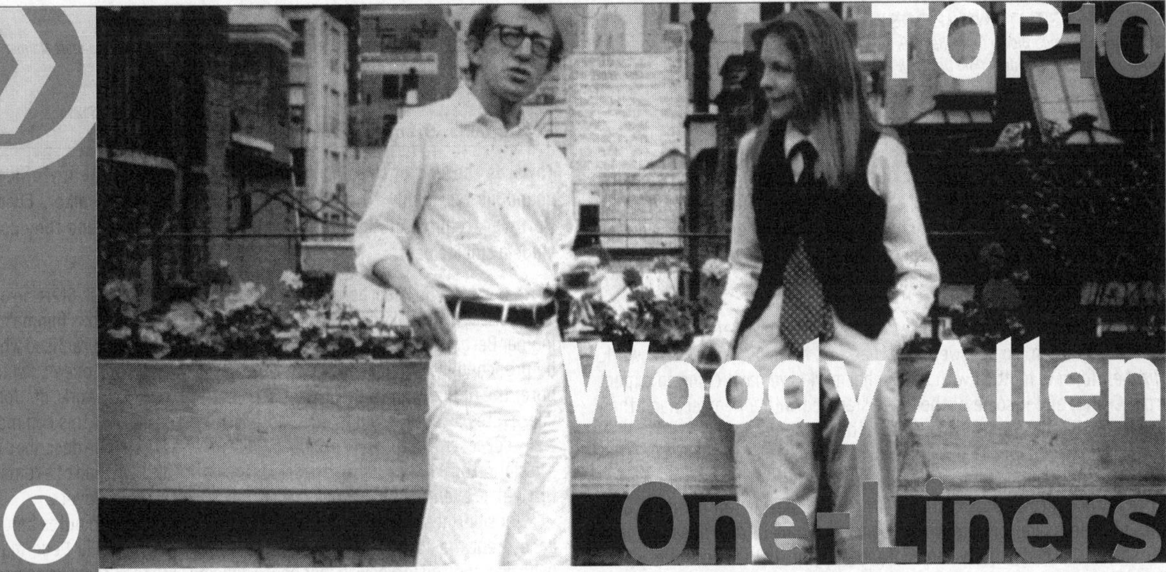

1 **Don't knock masturbation – it's sex with someone I love.** ***Alvy, Annie Hall***

2 **If it turns out there is a God, I don't think you can say he's evil. I think the worst thing that you can say about him is that he's basically an underachiever.** ***Boris, Love and Death.***

3 **The last time I was inside a woman was on a visit to the Statue of Liberty.** ***Cliff, Crimes and Misdemeanors***

4 **I just met a wonderful new man. Sure, he's fictional, but you can't have everything.** ***Cecilia, The Purple Rose of Cairo***

5 **I don't wanna bad-mouth the kid, but he's a horrible, dishonest, immoral louse.** ***Danny, Broadway Danny Rose.***

6 **The brain is the most overrated organ, I think.** ***Ike, Manhattan***

7 **I once stole a pornographic book that was printed in Braille. I used to rub all the dirty parts.** ***Fielding, Bananas***

8 **I'll get broads up here like you wouldn't believe: swingers, freaks, nymphomaniacs, dental hygienists.** ***Allan, Play It Again***

9 **I can't listen to that much Wagner, you know? I start to get the urge to conquer Poland.** ***Larry, Manhattan Murder Mystery***

10 **Sex and death. Two things that come once in a lifetime. But at least after death you're not nauseous.** ***Miles, Sleeper.***

ⓘ ELIZABETHTOWN (2005)

Starring: *Orlando Bloom (Drew Baylor), Kirsten Dunst (Claire Colburn), Susan Sarandon (Hollie Baylor), Alec Baldwin (Phil DeVoss), Jessica Biel (Ellen Kishmore)*
Director: *Cameron Crowe*
Screenwriter: *Cameron Crowe*
12/123 mins./Drama/Romance/USA

Life is not going well for Drew Baylor – he's just been fired after losing his employers millions of dollars, and then learns that his father has died. But rather than drive him further into despair, his father's passing brings him back from the brink of suicide, giving him purpose and kickstarting a romance with air stewardess Claire.

For his sixth movie as writer-director, Cameron Crowe returns, with clear determination, to the well that has fed his most distinctive work. *Elizabethtown* is mottled with all the hallmarks we have come to expect from Crowe, and if some of them are stamped with a heavier hand than usual, that hardly detracts from its affecting charm.

In the wake of *Vanilla Sky*, an uncharacteristic rush of adrenal psychedelia that baffled and infuriated much of his following, fans will be comforted to find Crowe back on familiar ground – deeply felt human drama with effortless overtones of wistful comedy. *Elizabethtown* does not have the sharply barbed narrative hook of *Jerry Maguire* or the engrossing backdrop of *Almost Famous*; it lulls you into a gentle embrace rather than grabbing you with a situational come-on.

Shorn of conceptual set-dressing and with a streamlined, propulsive plotline, *Elizabethtown* unravels in unaided accord with character arc and the emotional interplay of its major protagonists. Front and centre is Bloom's Drew Baylor, a part that requires our Orly to prove his acting mettle without the get-up and funny wigs. Cast as a put-upon everyman by Billy Wilder's biggest fan, Bloom turns in a decent Jack Lemmon (complete with American accent) in what is surely his best performance to date. Bloom is ably abetted by Kirsten Dunst, who is at her most edible as the incorrigibly meddlesome yet irresistible flight attendant.

As Claire and Drew's romance duly blossoms, the absent son is inevitably seduced by the mildly eccentric residents of Elizabethtown – who, he discovers to his amazement, harbour an unswerving possessive affection for his father – all of whom, down to the lowliest bit parts, are drawn with Crowe's keen eye for human foibles. Conspicuously absent, however, is the lurking edge of darkness that underscores the bittersweet euphoria of his most satisfying films – the fraught, borderline abusive relationships at the heart of *Say Anything*, *Jerry Maguire* and *Almost Famous*, for instance – and there are excursions into sentimentality that strike one, on first viewing at least, as unnecessarily protracted, even for a filmmaker who has shown an uncertain grip on the syrup spoon before ('You complete me' etc).

Still, real people have a great capacity for sentimentality, especially when their lives are clarified by grief, and it is to Crowe's credit that he refuses to shy away from that. In fact, it is exactly this sloppy fallibility to the proverbial slings and arrows that *Elizabethtown* celebrates, just as it does the unbreakable bonds of family and the redemptive power of love. And there is no better interpreter of these sticky, delicate, inconvenient facets of our existence than Crowe, certainly not one working in the Hollywood mainstream at any rate, and that includes his mentor, James L. Brooks.

This is also Crowe's most personal film by far. His own father died 16 years ago and absent fathers have been a recurring feature, if not a theme, of his movies ever since. *Elizabethtown* is the result of a recent visit to his father's birthplace in Kentucky, somewhere he had not visited since the funeral, and the flood of emotion that overtook him. Armed with that knowledge it is easy to forgive *Elizabethtown* both its mushy longueurs and the moments where Crowe signs his signature with a paintbrush rather than a quill. ★★★ **SB**

ⓘ ELVIRA MADIGAN (1967)

Starring: *Pia Degermark (Elvira), Thommy Berggren (Sixten Sparre), Lennart Malmer (Friend), Nina Widerberg (Little Girl), Cleo Jensen (Cook)*
Director: *Bo Widerberg*
Screenwriter: *Bo Widerberg based on a ballad by Johan Lindstrom Saxon*
PG/90 mins./Drama/Sweden

Towards the end of the 19th century, Sixten, a married army officer, abandons his family to elope with teenage tightrope walker, Elvira. However, reality sets in after an idyllic Danish summer and they conclude a suicide pact.

In many ways, Bo Widerberg is the Swedish François Truffaut. Starting out as a critic, he attacked the work of the country's most famous filmmaker, Ingmar Bergman, for shunning everyday reality. Yet, having practised what he preached in early features like *The Baby Carriage* and *Love 65*, which bore the influence of British Social Realism and the work of John Cassavetes, Widerberg adopted a more lyrical approach for this commercially successful period piece. Indeed, *Elvira Madigan* could be described as a variation on *Jules Et Jim*, with a disapproving society (instead of a romantic rival) preventing the happiness of a pair of star-crossed lovers.

Considering they were only presented with their lines minutes before each scene was shot, Thommy Berggren and 17 year-old Pia Degermark (who was spotted in a newspaper photo dancing with the Crown Prince and went on to win Best Actress at Cannes) are superb as the couple willing to risk everything for their illicit passion. But while Jorgen Persson's luminous naturally lit cinematography is invariably cited as the main reason for the enduring appeal of this fact-based melodrama, Widerberg captures the small humiliations of poverty with as much fidelity as the colours of summer, which are made all the more enchanting by the accompaniment of Vivaldi's Violin Concerto and Mozart's Piano Concerto No.21.

Widerberg intended the film to be a cautionary tale for a younger generation infused with the spirit of 60s rebellion, as he sought to show them the perils of attempting to live outside society, no matter how restrictive its attitudes appeared to be. But the picture's international success owed little to its moral message and more to the painterly pastoralism, which Widerberg consciously fashioned after the soft, diffused light achieved by the French Impressionist, Pierre-August Renoir. However, there were those who denounced the naive sentimentality of the storyline and accused Widerberg of having created an unintentionally amusing parody of high art. ★★★ **DP**

ⓘ THE EMERALD FOREST (1985)

Starring: *Powers Boothe (Bill Markham), Meg Foster (Jean Markham), William Rodriguez (Young Tommy), Yara Vaneau (Young Heather), Estee Chandler (Heather Markham), Charley Boorman (Tomme)*
Director: *John Boorman*
Screenwriter: *Rospo Pallenberg*
12/110 mins./Adventure/UK

The based-on-truth story of an American engineer who, while in the Brazilian quarter of the Amazon jungle, finds his small son kidnapped by a tribe to be raised as their own. Over the years, he continues his search to the point of obsession, until he finally discovers him.

John Boorman's eco-drama is truly authentic in the verdure of its Amazonian setting, he shoots every leaf and limb of the feverish forest with stunning intricacy almost smothering the film in nature. Look what we are losing, he screams through the dense picture, how can we allow this? Here is a director clamouring with passion, but there's something bull-headed about the inordinate amounts of beauty on show that puts you right off. Bring on the damn dam, you want to demand, suffocating on its righteousness, just make the nagging Englishman stop going on.

That he also cast his son Charley – then as blonde as an angel and thin as a twig, now thick with largesse and busy silting the world's atmosphere with motorbike fumes – presumably to give some rush of familial resonance: what if it were your child? A theme lost on everyone but the self-satisfied director. Thankfully, we do get Powers Boothe, an enormously underrated actor, brilliant as the human face of desolation. It is his journey to realisation that nature is best, that drives the film rather than a simple search for his lost boy. Structurally, the film is more involved than it appears.

The 'native' sections of Boorman's movie are as gallingly realistic as the study of trees, but there remains an air of the patronising gent about the harsh rites of passage this squeaky kid (did he have to be quite *this* blonde?) has to endure before he passes into adulthood. What does Boorman want us to make of drinking human ashes and blood – is this a better way of life? Are nature's brutal necessities a better path than the succour of his real father's devotional love? There is an interesting ambiguity in this, but Boorman chooses the path of melodrama as Boothe and son are reunited with a cloying sense of fulfilment. After all the bewailing about Mother Nature, is this really just a film about dad issues? ★★ **IN**

EMMANUELLE (1974)

Starring: *Sylvia Kristel (Emmanuelle), Alain Cuny (Marco), Daniel Sarky (Jean), Jeanne Colletin (Ariane), Mariika Green (Bee), Christine Bolson (Marie-Ange)*
Director: *Just Jaeckin*
Screenwriter: *Jean-Louis Richard based on the book by Emmanuelle Arsan*
18/105 mins./Erotica/France

The wife of a French diplomat in Bangkok, Emmanuelle embarks on a voyage of sexual discovery. And that's about it really.

Seminal (ahem) soft core porn classic, based on the autobiographical novel by actress Emmanuelle Arsan, that became a huge breakout box-office across the world, offering a less graphic, couple friendly take on the genre than the prevailing likes of *Deep Throat* and *Behind The Green Door*. First time director Just Jaeckin's film is the movie that set the clichés for the soft core films to follow; the soft focus centerfold aesthetic, the bizarrely Victorian lingerie, the soft pastel colour schemes and wicker chairs, the woodlands of potted plants and draperies blowing in a cooling breeze – it all started here.

While *Emmanuelle* had been essayed before by Erika Blanc in *IO*, Sylvia Kristel, then just 22, gives the essential take on the character, adding a sweetness and innocence, actually giving the traces of a performance in between joining the mile high club, lesbian romps and sex as a spectator sport in a Thai warehouse. Elsewhere, Alain Cuny, who was slumming it after appearing in Fellini's *La Dolce Vita*, gives a performance of over the top solemnity as Emmanuelle's aged mentor and the scenes sandwiched in between the rumpy pumpy are so serious as to border on parody.

Still it kickstarted a franchise that fostered many official and unofficial entries, not to mention many variations of spelling on the lead character's name – a Sylvia Krystel-Mia Nygren run of films, that started in 1984 with *Emmanuelle 4* spelled the character with two ms while a strand starring Laura Gemser only went with one. To add further confusion, the *Carry On* entry added a double N. ★★★ **WT**

EMPIRE OF THE SUN (1987)

Starring: *Christian Bale (Jim Graham), John Malkovich (Basie), Miranda Richardson (Mrs. Victor), Nigel Havers (Dr. Rawlins), Joe Pantoliano (Frank Demerest), Leslie Phillips (Maxton)*
Director: *Steven Spielberg*
Screenwriters: *Menno Meyjes (uncredited), Tom Stoppard, based on the novel by J.G. Ballard*
PG/152 mins./Drama/USA

Awards: *BAFTA – Best Cinematography, Best Score, Best Sound*

When the Japanese invade Shanghai in 1941, a young, pampered British boy is separated from his parents and must learn to survive on his own. He is helped by an American pilot and the adults in the prison camp where he ends up.

Along with *The Color Purple*, this marked a brief, mid-80s step into more serious territory, although the topic – the aftermath of Pearl Harbor, as affluent westerners are herded out of Shanghai by the Japanese military – is far-reaching, this is a very personal tale of the struggle for survival and the transformation of James Graham from posh, plummy mummy's boy to wily, conniving rat, bartering his way through life in the internment camps.

It becomes an odyssey of epic tone, though – mostly because John Williams' string section refuses to shut up – with triumph of will/indomitable spirit type stuff ladled on thick. Based on J.G. Ballard's novel and allegedly drawn from his own experiences, Spielberg's technical ability is very clear, with much to appreciate on close examination.

That you have eons of time for such examination is a weakness, and while Bale lets nobody down, the film's real failing is that it hangs on the viewer engaging with his adapting character – and it's very easy not to. Malkovich's domineering and self-serving Basie is a far more absorbing character – and the friction his friendship with Jim causes for Frank – but Nigel Havers' Dr. Rawlings and Miranda Richardson's reluctant mother-figure Mrs. Victor pique the interest only as identifiable window dressing. ★★★ **DB**

EMPIRE RECORDS (1995)

Starring: *Anthony LaPaglia (Joe Reaves), Maxwell Caulfield (Rex Manning), Debi Mazar (Jane), Rory Cochrane (Lucas), Johnny Whitworth (A.J.), Robin Tunney (Debra), Renee Zellweger (Gina), Brendan Sexton III (Warren), Liv Tyler (Corey Mason)*
Director: *Allan Moyle*
Screenwriters: *Carol Heikkinen*
Producers: *Tony Ludwig, Arnon Milchan, Michael Nathanson, Alan Richie*
12/90 mins./Comedy/Drama/USA

Empire Records is an independent music store under threat of takeover by a big, soulless corporate chain. As the employees try to get the money together needed to keep the store open, they learn about each other, and their personal problems come to the fore.

Set around the titular music emporium, a neon-lit outlet that bears more resemblance to a nightclub than your local Our Price, the slice-of-life stuff on display here is action packed. In just 24 hours, shop manager Joe and his staff are saddled with a personal appearance from a pompous 70s throwback crooner (Maxwell Caulfield, never better cast), a hold-up by a young vigilante and a takeover bid to turn the place into a chain store.

Then there are the personal problems of his adolescent employees: drug dependency, promiscuity and unrequited love. All are aired lightly but never investigated enough to intrude on the general bonhomie. Instead the young cast (headed by the appealing Tyler and the philosophising Cochrane), face life's trials by conducting mock funerals and ruminating on their ambitions.

Directed by *Pump Up The Volume*'s Moyle, the film's main failing is its tendency to be too self-consciously hip, with a continuous music soundtrack and much footage of consumers and cashiers alike frugging on the shop floor giving, it the feel of an elongated pop video. Meanwhile the middle section, which attempts to add a serious thread to proceedings, succeeds only in slowing them down. But after the bleak picture painted by films like *Kids*, a contemporary of this fluffier film, it is refreshing to know that, on the evidence presented here, American teenagers are still carefree, nay blemish-free individuals. ★★★ **CW**

END OF DAYS (1999)

Starring: *Arnold Schwarzenegger (Jericho Cane), Gabriel Byrne (The Man/Satan), Robin Tunney (Christine York), Kevin Pollak (Chicago), Rainer Judd (Christine's Mother), Miriam Margolyes (Mabel), Rod Steiger (Father Kovak)*
Director: *Peter Hyams*
Screenwriter: *Andrew W. Marlowe*
18/121 mins./Action/Drama/Horror/Mystery/USA

At the end of the second millennium, in the closing days of 1999, Satan visits New York in search of his bride to bear the Antichrist. Jericho Cane, a suicidal ex-cop whose family have died, begins to suspect that something is very wrong with the businessman he has been assigned to protect . . .

Jericho is a security specialist with a Martin Riggs complex, i.e. he's tragically lost his wife and daughter and he spends his off duty hours hitting the vodka and sucking on the end of his gun, never getting round to pulling the trigger. It's the end of the century in a couple of days, something that has got the Pope pretty agitated – for he knows that Satan himself is somewhere at large in the world, back to claim the woman 'chosen' for him 20 years earlier.

Rather conveniently, Satan has taken the form of a man, whom Jericho is in charge of protecting. But when a tongue-less priest starts taking pot shots at Byrne, our hero suspects that something of a Biblical nature is up. Having tracked down the girl, Jericho must keep her out of the clutches of the devil until midnight 2000 – or time's up for the rest of us.

There comes a point when watching End Of Days that you realise the plot is almost identical to that of *Terminator 2* (1991) – Arnie as hero on the run protecting a woman who holds the key to the future of the world, firing lots of cool guns at an unstoppable foe that relentlessly keeps pursuing them, before eventually revealing his/its real non-human form. And then, of course, you click why this is the case – this is not the great Arnie comeback movie as touted; Arnie wants you to think he's never been away! And here it feels like he hasn't. True, there are a few more lines than he's usually capable of, a bit of character depth that he seems uncomfortable with (Arnie in tears shocker!) but, once the action kicks in, you know exactly where you are.

End Of Days is a fun, all-out action movie with a sexy millennial edge (sell-by date, January 1). Director Hyams is as workmanlike as ever though, so some of the action moments clunk a tad, and inconsistencies in the plot are generally avoided rather than explained – why were Arnie and co. guarding Byrne in the first place? Then again, we are dealing with a movie in which the central plot is basically, 'Satan's back – and he has to get laid by midnight!' so maybe such grievances are moot. ★★★ **BM**

THE END OF THE AFFAIR (1999)

Starring: *Ralph Fiennes (Maurice Bendrix), Julianne Moore (Sarah Miles), Stephen Rea (Henry Miles), Ian Hart (Mr. Parkis), Jason Issacs (Father Smythe), James Bolam (Mr. Savage)*
Director: *Neil Jordan*
Screenwriter: *Neil Jordan, based on the novel by Graham Greene*
18/109 mins./Romance/Drama/UK/USA
Awards: *BAFTA – Best Adapted Screenplay*

Henry Miles fears his wife may be having an affair, and confides in friend Bendrix. As a one of her former lovers himself, Bendrix is unsurprised but profoundly jealous and hires a private dick to find out more about Mrs. Miles' new lover.

While his actual books tended to feature a good deal of internal angst-ridden rumination, Graham Greene was always aware that the cinematic medium requires a much snappier pace, as his screenplay for *The Third Man* amply demonstrates. Unfortunately, it is a lesson that those responsible for *The End Of The Affair* have singularly failed to take on board.

Based on Greene's roman-à-clef and told in a series of sometimes bewilderingly intricate flashbacks, the film stars Fiennes as novelist Maurice Bendrix who, after discovering bureaucrat pal Henry Miles in a distressed state, learns of his friend's fears that Mrs. Miles is playing away from home. Having spent most of World War II exchanging a good deal more than ration coupons with the lady in question, this doesn't exactly come as big news to Bendrix. Nevertheless, consumed by jealousy, the writer employs a firm of private detectives to discover the truth about his ex-mistress' new lover, thus setting off a train of events that will end in remorse, tragedy and a good deal of anti-religious railing.

Indeed, although the film is theoretically a love triangle, the entire structure has a more square-ish feel to it with God Himself occupying the fourth corner. The result is a scenario which, while intriguing on the page, rather bogs things down on the screen. Not that the result is by any means a disaster. Both Moore and Rea are excellent, as is Sandy Powell's costume design, while fans of the unclothed Fiennes derrière should have little to complain about. Best of all though is Ian Hart's turn as the world's most morally-inclined private dick – yet more proof that someone should give this guy a proper leading role again before he gets forever pigeonholed as our very own Buscemi-style cameo king. ★★★ **CC**

END OF THE CENTURY (2003)

Starring: *as themselves: Joey Ramone, Dee Dee Ramone, Tommy Ramone, Marky Ramone, CJ Ramone, Johnny Ramone, Ritchie Ramone*
Directors: *Michael Gramaglia, Jim Fields*
15/108 mins./Documentary/Music/USA

The band that kick-started the punk scene is no more. Part tribute, part journalistic exploration, this documentary is a rocket ride through the twisted history of New York's finest rockers.

'One, two, three, four . . . ' The familiar cry that provided the countdown to punk rock first erupted in a dingy New York bar, CBGB, back in 1974. Amid a blitzkrieg of three-chord guitar riffs and a swirl of bubblegum vocals, the Ramones ripped through an entire set in just under 30 minutes. They'd started as they would go on, an aggressive whirlwind of energy and emotion, two raw elements that, as *End Of The Century* demonstrates, can be found in equal parts both in the music and the band members' personalities.

Charting their history from the early days through to the death of Joey and Dee Dee, directors Gramaglia and Fields let the tale speak for itself, collecting interviews, old and new, with all the band members and those they influenced to relate a saga of creative genius, internal strife and immense disappointment.

In spite of their legacy, the band failed in their bid for commercial acclaim, and the directors leave no stone, or stoner, unturned when delving into the drug abuse, incestuous behaviour and in-fighting that came to define the band. The directors do occasionally sacrifice veracity to boost the drama – bassist Dee Dee's recollection of Tommy's contribution, for example, is misleading – but when the truth is this good, the facts usually speak for themselves. ★★★★ **WL**

ENDURING LOVE (2004)

Starring: *Daniel Craig (Joe), Samantha Morton (Claire), Rhys Ifans (Jed), Alexandra Aitkin (Natasha), Susan Lynch (Rachel), Bill Nighy (Robin), Bill Weston (Grandpa), Anna Maxwell Martin (Penny)*
Director: *Roger Michell*
Screenwriter: *Ian McEwan*
15/100 mins./Drama/Thriller/UK
Awards: *Empire – Scene of the Year (The Balloon Sequence)*

While enjoying a romantic picnic, Joe and Claire catch sight of an out-of-control hot air balloon. As they attempt to rescue those inside, they witness someone fall to their death. Afterwards Joe finds himself stalked by Jed, a man who was also at the scene.

Though it crawls into the same queasy headspace as *Fatal Attraction*, this adaptation of Ian McEwan's novel is a far cry from that movie's slick thrills. Director Roger Michell eschews bunny-boiling melodrama, relying instead on his leading man's performance to chart the victim's emotional disintegration.

Considering that the leading man in question is *Layer Cake*'s Daniel Craig, that wasn't such a bad call. By no means just a foil for Rhys Ifans' amorous stalker, Craig's Joe shares the unhinged loner's obsessive nature; as he slides ever downwards, the actor hits just the right notes of paranoia and detachment, his cobalt-blue eyes flashing with panic.

There are also some effective visual quirks. The novel's celebrated hot air balloon set-piece is converted into a truly heart-jolting sequence, the camera heaving upwards with each new blast of wind. And, as Joe's neat existence falls apart, tidily-framed shots are replaced by ones that lurch like a lovesick drunk.

While such measures help lift the story from its literary roots, the director could have trimmed the tale down further. It may also prove too cold an exercise for some, the moral ambiguity meaning there's no-one to really root for. Still, that doesn't stop it from being an effective study of deeply twisted love. ★★★ **IN**

LES ENFANTS DU PARADIS (1945)

Starring: *Arletty (Garrance), Jean Louis Barrault (Baptiste Deburreau), Pierre Brasseur (Frederick Lemaitre), Marcel Herrand (Lacenaire), Pierre Renoir (Jericho), Maria Casares (Natalie), Etienne Decroux (Anselme Deburreau), Fabien Loris (Avril), Leon Larive (Stage Doorman, 'Funambules'), Pierre Palov (Stage Manager, 'Funambules')*
Director: *Marcel Carné*
Screenwriter: *Jacques Prévert*
PG/95 mins./Drama/France

Paris, the 1840s. The strangely saintly Garance is loved by three men of the theatre, mime Baptiste Debureau, declamatory tragedian Frederick Lemaitre and criminal-cum-playwright Lacenaire.

An expensive period epic shot during the Nazi Occupation, ostensibly an act of collaboration but actually a celebration of the Free French spirit, *Les Enfants du Paradis* was not premiered until 1945, because director Marcel Carné hid bits of the film until the Germans left Paris. It is hard to convey just how important this movie is to the French; as if it were their *Gone With the Wind*, *Citizen Kane* and *Alexander Nevsky* rolled into one film (or, considering the 188 minute running time of its two parts, two films). As the love stories revolve around the reticent heroine, with everyone falling for everyone else at the wrong times, the film offers a parade of carnivals, duels, passions, performances, arguments, insults, conversations, crimes and epigrams. All the while, the main players are defined by their relationships with their rowdy, loving audiences (the title refers to the Paradis of the theatre, cheap seats thronged by the common people of Paris) and a salute to the shrugging joys of Frenchness is sneaked in past Nazi censors who were expecting a trite period romance. It's an essential piece of cinema, but from a non French perspective (or even from five decades) a slightly academic pleasure. Unlike *Kane*, you have to make allowances for what it meant to its first audiences and, while the self delighted and very French male performances remain involving, it's hard not to feel Arletty is a bit blank to represent every man's fantasy. The film equivalent of a Victorian novel, this is expansive and traditionalist in technique, a magnificent triumph of looking backwards. ★★★★ **KN**

LES ENFANTS TERRIBLES (1950)

Starring: *Nicole Stéphane (Elisabeth), Edouard Dermithe (Paul), Jacques Bernard (Gérard), Renée Cosima (Dargelos/Agathe), Roger Gallard (Gérard's Uncle)*
Director: *Jean-Pierre Melville*
Screenwriters: *Jean-Pierre Melville, Jean Cocteau based on the novel by Cocteau*
18/107 mins./Drama/France

Teenage siblings Paul and Elisabeth have a close, near-incestuous relationship. They draw others into their sphere, but set up house together. When it seems Paul will transfer his exclusive affections to another girl, Elisabeth takes drastic action.

Scripted by Jean Cocteau, from his 1929 novel, and directed by Jean-Pierre Melville, before his run of reputation-making crime films, this unsettling, near-surreal picture is one of those key works often drawn on by later artists. Peter Jackson in *Heavenly Creatures* and Bernardo Bertolucci in *The Dreamers* both take an inspiration from the private world of the young, sexually bizarre couple depicted here, as does novelist Ian McEwan in *The Cement Garden*. However, this collaboration between two very different French sensibilities has its own, distinctive, peculiar fascination.

The brawny-seeming Dermithe, protégé of the writer, is oddly cast as a sickly youth felled in the opening by a snowball to the heart thrown by the androgynous school bully (played by the actress who will resurface as his potential love interest), but delivers a remarkable double-act with the sharp-featured, unnervingly-intense Stéphane, who makes the mother-sister-lover character an ultimately terrifying force of nature.

It's no wonder this charismatic, if haggard duo lure others – devoted Gérard, a wealthy but short-lived American husband (Martin) and all-round gal pal Agathe (Cosima) – into their private world, where rooms in an abandoned theatre or the mansion Elisabeth inherits are transformed into magical, if overcrowded hidey-holes. The heavily-plotted third act has an almost Shakespearean sense of doom, underlined by the seductive, persuasive, insightful voice of the novelist, who reads extracts from the original on the soundtrack in a device that ought to be overblown (it was when Bertolucci had Paul Bowles do the same in *The Sheltering Sky*) but plays marvellously here. ★★★★ **KN**

Jean Cocteau (1889–1963)

Who he was: French poet, painter, filmmaker and all-round art figure.
Hallmarks: The myth of Orpheus; artworks incorporated into the set; simple yet amazing visual effects; fairy-tale simplicity; hymns to male beauty.
If you see one movie, see: *Orphée* (1950)

THE ENGLISH PATIENT (1996)

Starring: *Ralph Fiennes (Almasy), Juliette Binoche (Hana), Willem Dafoe (Caravaggio), Kristin Scott Thomas (Katharine Clifton), Naveen Andrews (Kip), Colin Firth (Geoffrey Clifton), Kevin Whately (Hardy)*
Director: *Anthony Minghella*
Screenwriter: *Anthony Minghella, based on the novel by Michael Ondaatje*
15/162 mins./Romance/Drama/UK/USA/Italy

Awards: *Academy Awards – Best Supporting Actress (Juliette Binoche), Best Art Direction/Set Decoration, Best Cinematography, Best Costume, Best Director, Best Editing, Best Original Score, Best Pictures, Best Sound, BAFTA – Anthony Asquith Award for Film Music, Best Cinematography, Best Editing, Best Film, Best Supporting Actress, Best Adapted Screenplay, Empire Awards – Best British Director, Golden Globes – Best Drama, Best Original Score*

At the close of WWII, a young nurse tends to a badly-burned plane crash victim. His past is shown in flashbacks, revealing an involvement in a fateful love affair.

Movie Star Phobias

1. Billy Bob Thornton (antiques)
2. Woody Allen (Showers with drains in the middle)
3. Steven Spielberg (Elevators)
4. Chevy Chase (Snakes)
5. Alfred Hitchcock (Policemen)
6. Burt Lancaster (Hydrophobia)
7. Johnny Depp (Clowns)
8. Katharine Hepburn (Fire)
9. Kim Basinger Agoraphobia
10. Drew Barrymore (Claustrophobia)

The ingredients most likely to give a critic indigestion are fatty emotions and over-ripened sentimentality. And so it was that *The English Patient* succeeded so magnificently, both critically and to the tune of £12 million at the UK box office.

And yet, in its ambition to underplay every emotional nuance (except for Ralph Fiennes' visceral outburst late in the film), it ultimately under-performs. While the film offers understatement, the critics have preferred to overstate its merits. The story recounts the journey of the mysterious Count Almasy (Fiennes), a cartographer of uncertain nationality who is dragged, badly burned and half-dead, from the wreckage of his bi-plane at the tail end of World War II. As he is placed under the care of Canadian army nurse Hana (Oscar-winner Binoche) to live out the final days of the war in a dilapidated Italian villa, a magnificent story unravels (in flashback) of his illicit love for a married woman, Katharine Clifton.

Simultaneously, Hana is completing her own emotional journey with the help of a bomb disposal officer (Naveen Andrews – with whom she shares one of the truly classic scenes in the film), and occupational thief Caravaggio appears out of nowhere to question the elusive Almasy, suspecting him of being the spy who helped the Germans to get their men into the Sahara.

There is a compelling lack of emotional involvement here: the brief flashes of unbridled feeling certainly hit home, and when they come, they excise quickly any doubt about the effectiveness of Fiennes, but still we care little for this underwhelming Count Almasy and his flighty, faintly irritating, inamorata Katharine Clifton. Some might argue that this is deliberate and is true to an 'unfilmable' novel (Booker Prize-winner by Michael Ondaatje) but on the small screen, the majestic vistas of vanilla deserts and blistering sunsets are mere Discovery Channel fodder and do not make up for the low-fat epic romance.

Here is passion that merely blisters the heart rather than blasts it asunder. After a heart-stopping, nine Academy Award-winning, six Bafta scooping and two Golden Globe-grabbing journey to classic status, there is an unthinking consensus about *The English Patient* which belies its true quality. ★★★★ **CHe**

ENIGMA (2001)

Starring: *Dougray Scott (Thomas Jericho), Kate Winslet (Hester Wallace), Saffron Burrows (Claire), Jeremy Northam (Wigram), Nikolaj Coster Waldau (Puck), Tom Hollander (Logie), Matthew Macfadyen (Dave)*
Director: *Michael Apted*
Screenwriter: *Tom Stoppard, based on the novel by Robert Harris*
15/119 mins./War/Thriller/Mystery/UK/US/Germany/ Netherlands
Awards: *Empire Awards – Best British Actress (Kate Winslet)*

At the height of World War II, mathematical genius Jericho returns to the Bletchley Park code-cracking base after a nervous breakdown following an ill-fated romance. The pressure is mounting because the Germans have mysteriously changed their code again, hinting that there may be a spy in the camp. And fingers are pointing at Jericho.

Robert Harris' expert novel is cut from the mould of the classic British spy thriller, teeming with double-crosses and red herrings, caught in a whirlpool of paranoia. It is also very wordy, bereft of traditional action scenes and set in a period groove that lends itself more to the Sunday night TV serial than Friday night multiplex viewing.

Apted, Stoppard and first-time producer Mick Jagger (spot the cameo) have worked hard at giving the story a cinematic sheen. And there is premium British acting talent on display: Scott is excellent as the nerve-shredded genius unable to let go of his unresolved past, Winslet dutifully frumps-up as his ever-eager sidekick, and Northam damn-near pickpockets the movie as the slimy, subtle Secret Service operative trying to piece it all together. Additionally, it looks the part – filmed on location at the real thing: Bletchley Park's former Station X.

Bletchley's fascinating contribution to the war effort is given full voice. The intricacies of Enigma code-cracking – based on synapse-frazzling number games – is made sensible, even riveting, during one furious sequence, as the code-breakers race against time to divine the latest key, sacrificing a shipping convoy in the process. The sheer mental pressure the war exerted on the British stiff-upper ethos is palpable amongst the clandestine maze of flashbacks and shifty sub-plots.

Tagline
Unlock the secret.

Yet, the story still slips through their fingers. Apted doesn't have enough faith that his spy games and brain-busting are dynamic enough to keep an audience attentive, and resorts to melodramatic impulses – soppy car chases, a fluffed trainbound chase – especially in the slapdash ending. It needs more room to breathe, to play on the mounting tensions and romantic misfires, to make the twists hit home as real shockers. Sorry fellas, it needs a nice, cosy slot on the goggle-box; edge of the sofa, tea and biscuits, thank heavens we won the war. ★★★ **IN**

THE ENIGMA OF KASPAR HAUSER (JEDER FUR SICH UND GOTT GERGEN ALLE) (1975)

Starring: *Bruno S (Kaspar Hauser), Walter Landergast (Dauner), Brigitte Mira (Kathe), Hans Musaus (Unknown Man), Willy Semmeltrogge (Circus Director), Michael Kroecher (Lord Stanhope)*
Director: *Werner Herzog*
Screenwriter: *Werner Herzog*
PG/110 mins./Drama/Germany

In 1828, a young man, Kaspar Hauser, who has been raised in a cellar with no human contact, is left in a Nuremberg town square, able to speak only a single sentence. The innocent youth is put on show only to be studied by scientists and interrogated by priests and philosophers.

Originally entitled *Jeder für sich und Gott gegen* Alle (*Every Man For Himself And God Against All*), this terrific movie from Werner Herzog's golden period in the 1970s is deliberately-paced, perfectly played and as moving as it is thought-provoking.

Based on a famous German case history from the 1800s, this follows Kaspar Hauser, a strange youth who appears in a small town one day, having been raised in a solitary cellar away from all other human beings, holding a mysterious letter which gives clues but no explanations, never having been taught to walk, speak (aside from the sentence 'I want to be a gallant rider, as my father was before me'), eat anything but bread or understand basic concepts like inside and outside and why cats don't walk upright.

Bruno S, a real-life schizophrenic street musician impressed to star in the film, is extraordinary as the wild-eyed, well-intentioned Kaspar whose unique background gives him a fresh, delightful, childishly wise viewpoint. Herzog examines the interaction of the odd innocent on the kindly or cruel people who look after him or exploit him, but always focuses on how Kaspar feels and thinks, creating a truly disorienting vision (even showing his dreams in flickering 8mm inserts).

Priceless moment: Kaspar's answer to the age-old schoolbook conundrum, put to him by a long-nosed and humourless logician, about how to discern the villager who always tells the truth from the villager who always lies ('I would ask him "are you a tree-frog?" '). ★★★★★ **KN**

⦿ ENTER THE DRAGON (1973)

Starring: *Bruce Lee (Lee), John Saxon (Roper), Kien Shih (Han), Ahna Capri (Tania), Angela Mao (Su Lin), Jim Kelly (Williams), Robert Wall (Ohara), Anna Capri (Tania)*
Director: *Robert Clouse*
Screenwriter: *Michael Allin*
18/99 mins./Martial Arts/USA

Trained by Shaolin monks, martial arts supreme Lee travels to an island under the guise of taking part in a tournament. His real task is to track down a renegade monk who may be running a drug operation from that very island.

Dint of the untimely death of its athletic star, and the glaring iconography of his oft-referenced yellow tracksuit, this kung-fu spectacle has taken on the air of legend, and deemed a classic of its kind. Its reputation, however, glows far greater than the film itself. Examined minus the trappings of cult, it languishes in the typically ludicrous plotting and predictably exaggerated moves of the genre, directed without mood or constancy by Robert Clouse, but elevated by the staggering prowess of its superstar.

His fourth film, made on a self-enforced hiatus in shooting *The Game Of Death*, this was the film that made Bruce Lee famous, a student poster-boy for the ages with his impossibly taut body. But how you respond to the succession of concussive fight scenes rather depends on how you take to whole nature of kung-fu movies at all. From this angle, they are stingingly rapid, a blur of skill and control, but they are also archly choreographed, like dance sequences, with no sense of the real. How one fight is won or lost remains infuriatingly obscure.

Otherwise this is a sub-Bondian muddle of bad dubbing and lathered over-direction. That, again, is what its fans delight in: the lurid overplay creating a world very much its own. But cultdom can throw a cloak over a pale body. Lee's magnetic presence aside, this is a crumbling edifice. ★★ **IN**

⦿ THE ENTERTAINER (1960)

Starring: *Laurence Olivier (Archie Rice), Brenda de Banzie (Phoebe Rice), Joan Plowright (Jean), Roger Livesey (Billy), Alan Bates (Frank), Daniel Massey (Graham), Albert Finney (Mick Rice), Shirley Ann Field (Tina), Thora Hird (Mrs. Lapford)*
Director: *Tony Richardson*
Screenwriters: *John Osborne, Nigel Kneale based on the play by Osborne*
PG/108 mins./Drama/UK

When third-rate comic Archie Rice abandons his shrewish alcoholic wife Phoebe for younger blonde, Tina Lapford, only his daughter and confidante, Jean, appreciates the real reasons for his actions.

The Entertainer was Laurence Olivier's proudest screen achievement. He had initially warmed to Archie Rice on stage in 1957, because he offered an escape from interminable classical parts. But the world's finest thespian came to recognise something of himself in this desperate ham whose embittered egotism tainted the lives of those around him and it's this identification that enabled Olivier to produce such a lived-in performance.

There was a hint of art imitating life, as Olivier would marry co-star Joan Plowright in 1961. But there's a sense in which he protested too much in his claims of kinship with Archie, as only a truly great actor could have made such mediocrity seem credible. Moreover, he also locates a dimming spark of humanity in this boorish bully and, thus, turns him into a tragic antihero, whose cruel wisecracks belie a despair and vulnerability that he refuses to acknowledge. Indeed, the coastal setting is most apt, as Rice is a Cnut-like figure desperately seeking to hold back the tide, by both bedding Tina Lapford and by persisting with music-hall schtick that was old hat when Max Miller did it in the 1930s. Yet, the irony is that Archie seems more human in his grotesque greasepaint, as he grimaces his way through the tired gags and atonal ditties that say as much about the audience that paid to see him as they do about the talentless has-been himself.

Filmed by Oswald Morris, the sights of the seaside backwater found echo in the equally morose images captured by Gilbert Taylor in Jerry Summers' *The Punch And Judy Man*, in which Tony Hancock similarly lamented the passing of the traditional seasonal entertainments. But Tony Richardson, who was making only his second feature, is clearly more comfortable with these authentic locations than he was with the studio sets used for *Look Back in Anger*, which was similarly adapted by John Osborne and Nigel Kneale from the former's Royal Court production. ★★★★ **DP**

⦿ ENTRAPMENT (1999)

Starring: *Sean Connery (Robert MacDougal), Catherine Zeta-Jones (Virginia Baker), Ving Rhames (Aaron Thibadeaux), Will Patton (Hector Cruz), Maury Chaykin (Conrad Greene), Kevin McNally (Haas)*
Director: *Jon Amiel*
Screenwriters: *Ronald Bass, William Broyles Jr., based on a story by Ronald Bass, Michael Hertzberg*
12/113 mins./Comedy/Crime/Romance/Thriller/US/UK/Germany

An insurance agent convinces her company to let her pretend to be a thief, so that she can win the trust of master burglar Robert MacDougal. But once they meet, she reveals to him that she really is a thief, and persuades him to train her up as his assistant. The only question is, who's playing who?

Though the genre dates back to Raffles and Simon Templar, the super-thief movie really got going with Hitchcock's *To Catch a Thief* in 1955, then caught on big time in the 1960s. A succession of glossy, cosmopolitan pictures featured beautiful stars, exotic locales, ingenious heists, circumvented security systems and robbers who never hurt anyone: *Topkapi, The Thomas Crown Affair, How To Steal A Million, Dead Heat On A Merry Go Round* et al.

Back then, Connery would have been perfect casting as a suave international art thief and Catherine Zeta-Jones hadn't been born. Now, both leading man and genre are wheezing creakily.

The game of deception starts with a pre-credits snatch of a valuable Rubens from a New York high rise, then insurance investigator Gin Baker poses as a thief to get close to legendary rip-off artist MacDougal (guess who?) and entraps him into stealing a Chinese mask from an English stately home. But it turns out that Gin is really a thief (or is she?), and wants Mac to help her pull off a high-tech stunt in Malaysia that depends on the

Millennium Bug (or does she?). Meanwhile, Gin's boss (Patton, hiding behind a bogus moustache) and Mac's sidekick (Rhames, doing his bit from *Mission: Impossible*) loiter on the sidelines (or do they?), setting up for more betrayals and reverses. Oh, and Mac's resolve never to get sexually involved with partners in crime – understandable in Rhames' case – crumbles at the sight of Zeta-Jones in an Emma Peel outfit.

Though not as execrable as *The Saint*, the last attempt at this sort of thing, *Entrapment* ambles lazily through its set-up and features only one (admittedly impressive) stretch of white-knuckle daredevilry as our heroes dangle off the tallest building in the world (which is in Kuala Lumpur, incidentally).

Otherwise, close-ups of Sean's hairy cheeks give him an Albert Steptoe look entirely at odds with his supposed sex-symbol image and he appears supremely uncomfortable in the romantic badinage department, especially during a lengthy postscript set on the most boring railway station in Southeast Asia. We've also seen rather too many so-called suspense sequences lately involving allegedly inaccessible computer terminals and programs downloaded from disks, and it's hard not to sympathise with Mac's lament that bank robbery just isn't fun any more without sacks of loot to cart away. ★★ **SB**

⦿ ERASERHEAD (1976)

Starring: *Jack Nance (Henry Spencer), Charlotte Stewart (Mary X), Allen Joseph (Mr. X), Jeanne Bates (Mrs. X), Judith Anna Roberts (Beautiful Girl Across the Hall), Laurel Near (Lady in the Radiator)*
Director: *David Lynch*
Screenwriter: *David Lynch*
18/89 mins./Fantasy/Horror/USA

Henry has increasingly bizarre dreams, each one more horrific than the last. He falls in love with a girl who then falls pregnant only to give birth to a mutated baby. All the while watching his lady in the radiator who sings to him.

It's hard to believe that David Lynch was in a six-year struggle to make *Eraserhead* on a piffling American Film Institute grant. It's harder still to believe that its closeted body horror and mind-blown surrealism have since almost become a part of the cultural landscape. Almost. For no matter how many cheesy pop videos or arty horror flicks rip off its (very late-70s) aesthetic of slimy industrial decay, this film remains as powerful, original and disturbing as ever.

The central conceit of boy-meets-girl-has-mutant-baby is still the stuff of American Gothic nightmares and Lynch's repertoire of soft squelches, thin skins, horrible blobs and panicky gestures remains an enduring archetype of puritan sexual disgust. What is surprising is how Jack Nance's grumpily delicate performance as the frustrated father, Henry, has become a period piece. With his trademark props – pens in breast pocket, electro-shock hair-do, white socks – he has come to resemble an old silent comedian stranded in a Buñuel twilight zone where the familiar punchlines don't work anymore. He is at once more charming and less grotesque than he used to be.

What emerges most clearly from the film, post-*Twin Peaks*, is the offbeat humour. The old black comedy is still there – Henry's crazy in-laws and their nervous tics, the mini-chickens which come alive on the plate, the final infant apocalypse – but it is now boxed in by a more insistent tone of uncanny menace which surely amounts to a put-on. Think of the smiley lady-behind-the-radiator stomping the foetal worms which are ruining her act, or the creepy, echoey sound-effects, or Nance's puzzled reaction shots – they are like that moment of blankness which precedes a surprise party. Except, with Lynch, the blankness goes on forever and the party never happens. ★★★★★ **SBe**

⦿ ERIN BROCKOVICH (2000)

Starring: *Julia Roberts (Erin Brockovich), Aaron Eckhart (George), Albert Finney (Ed Masry), Marg Helgenberger (Donna Jensen), Cherry Jones (Pamela Duncan), Peter Coyote (Kurt Potter)*
Director: *Steven Soderbergh*
Screenwriter: *Susannah Grant*
15/130 mins./Biography/Drama/USA
Awards: *Academy Awards – Best Actress, BAFTA – Best Actress, Golden Globes – Best Actress in a Drama*

An unemployed single mother blackmails her lawyer into giving her a job as a legal clerk, but goes on to discover a corporate cover-up that would become one of the biggest legal cases in US history. Based on a true story.

Your typical Julia Roberts vehicle tends to do what it says on the tin: big budget romcom shenanigans with that smile, and those legs. Cue: box office jamboree. Open up *Erin Brockovich*, though, and inside is something radically new: a superlative character piece where you actually stop thinking that Julia Roberts is, well, Julia Roberts, and immerse yourself in the travails and triumphs of trashy single mum Erin Brockovich and her legal crusade. A performance, in fact, that earned the Pretty Woman an Oscar.

Brockovich is presented initially as a terminally unlucky but doggedly determined individual wrestling with trying to bring up her kids, stymie her mounting debts by finding an elusive job and generally come to terms with the fact that her life, thus far, has come to nothing. What she has in droves is empathy for fellow victims and the steely determination to scale mountains. Usually with suits on.

Her great cause – and the movie's plot – lies in her discovery that a huge corporation's negligent pollution of a small town has resulted in a horrendous array of cancers and illness amongst the locals. Having wormed her way into a smalltime law firm as a skivvie, by sheer force of will she then cajoles her long-suffering boss Ed Masry to take up the case and let her do her stuff – you know, win over the folks, take on the dastardly big time lawyer types with her roughshod-but-real ways while neglecting her family and top new boyfriend, as she discovers someone she really likes. Herself.

Okay, so it makes no bones about going for the obvious (and you can virtually tick off the dramatic highpoints) – its basis in truth notwithstanding, the movie is certainly predictable. But it does it so well, a less showy than usual Soderbergh delivering a movie that is both intensely funny and emotionally satisfying. It may lack the gravitas of *The Insider*, whose themes of ordinary folk striving against corporate pressure it closely mirrors, but it still makes the same passionate points about the evils inherent in big business America and how an individual can still affect the system.

Brockovich is brought to life with a hitherto unseen range by Roberts, enlivening the nascent grit with a splendidly foul-mouthed wit as she delivers the film's nicely timed comic relief. Lost is the gorgeous movie star and born is a real person: vulnerable, caring, balls of brass. Finney, alongside her, gives one of those rich character turns that remind why you always loved him: a mix of exasperation, tenderness and emerging belief etched into his creased looks as he deals with this force of nature he somehow employs. ★★★★ **IN**

⦿ ERNEST SAVES CHRISTMAS (1988)

Starring: *Jim Varney (Ernest P.Worrell/Aster Clement/Auntie Nelda/The Snake Guy), Douglas Seale (Santa Claus), Oliver Clark (Joe Carruthers), Noelle Parker (Harmony Star)*
Director: *John R. Cherry III*
Screenwriters: *B. Kline, Ed Turner*
PG/95 mins./Comedy/USA

Santa Claus wants to retire and hand on his position to a child-loving TV show host. Ernest P. Worrell, a taxi driver, volunteers to help Santa on his mission – if he fails, there will be no Christmas.

Comedian Jim Varney (the voice of Slinky Dog in the *Toy Story* films) created the character of loudmouth redneck janitor Ernest P. Worrell, whose catchphrases were 'Hey, Vern!' and 'knowhutImean?', in a series of television commercials for various products. In the 1980s, Varney threw together video compilations of sketches in which he plays Ernest (and the rest of the obnoxious or cretinous Worrell family) and a TV series *Hey Vern, It's Ernest*, but the character achieved his biggest success with his bigscreen debut *Ernest Goes to Camp*, a comedy designed to appeal to those who find Pauly Shore films too intellectually demanding.

Ernest Saves Christmas, the sequel, is the only Ernest movie to have scored a UK theatrical release, presumably on the grounds that in the holiday season parents are forced to take their kids to anything.

The funniest scene, in which Santa is thrown into a jail with a crowd of tattooed toughs and instantly turns them into carol-singing softies, notably doesn't feature Ernest. Though Varney's comedy style doesn't really play outside middle America, subsequent Ernest films all became video rack-fillers or afternoon TV staples: *Ernest Goes to Jail*, *Ernest Scared Stupid* (his horror film parody), *Ernest Rides Again*, *Ernest Goes to School*, *Slam Dunk Ernest*, *Ernest Goes to Africa* and *Ernest in the Army*.

On his death in 2000, Varney left *Ernest the Pirate* unfinished. Imagine how good a film starring the Scots lady from next door who uses Flash or detailing the high seas adventures of Cap'n Birdseye would be – then watch something else. ★ **KN**

ESCAPE FROM LA (1996)

Starring: *Kurt Russell (Snake Plissken), A.J. Langer (Utopia), Steve Buscemi (Map to the Stars Eddie), Georges Corraface (Cuervo Jones), Stacy Keach (Cmdr. Malloy), Pam Grier (Hershe La Palmas),Valeria Golino (Taslima), Peter Fonda (Pipeline)*
Director: *John Carpenter*
Screenwriters: *John Carpenter, Debra Hill, Kurt Russell, based on characters created by John Carpenter, Nick Castle*
15/101 mins./Action/Adventure/Sci-fi/USA

In the future LA is an island, seperated from the mainland by an earthquake, which is home to the unwanteds of the US. Until a man with a plan and a remote control turns up . . .

In 1981, John Carpenter, then a hot director whose track record included *Dark Star*, *Assault On Precinct 13* and *Halloween*, made *Escape From New York*, a futuristic action movie starring Kurt Russell as Snake Plissken, an eyepatch-sporting, dirtbag hero. Now, a decade and a half later, Carpenter has slipped to DTV disappointments such as *Village Of The Damned* while Russell has never quite graduated from star to superstar.

Along with producer Debra Hill, the pair have got back together to knock together a screenplay for a sequel. And in so doing, they have come up with lots of neat ideas and characters, but still fall back on the same old, far from original plot.

An earthquake has turned Los Angeles into an island where President Cliff Robertson dumps the nation's undesirables. However, LA's Che Guevara wannabe supremo, Cuervo Jones has got hold of a remote control unit that can shut off all the machines in the world.

The fascist Christian regime again calls on the still shaggy, still unshaven Russell to retrieve the macguffin. Given that a fair budget has been allotted, it's a shame that the whole thing seems such a scrappy, dull-witted spectacle, with extras standing around in the dark as Snake breezes past on mini-sub, bike, helicopter or surfboard.

The stupidity of the plot can be gauged from the sequence in which the one-eyed Plissken saves his life by demonstrating his basketball skills (close one eye and try to shoot some hoops for further elucidation). There are promising characters played by decent actors – Stacy Keach as head cop, Peter Fonda as a surfer dude, Bruce Campbell as a plastic surgeon, Buscemi as a triple-crosser, Pam Grier as a transvestite – but no one has anything to do except trade insults with Snake and get left behind by the film's race to go nowhere fast. In 1981, *Escape From New York* seemed like Carpenter's least interesting film; now, *Escape From LA* makes it seem a masterpiece. ★★ **KN**

ESCAPE FROM NEW YORK (1981)

Director: *John Carpenter*
Starring: *Kurt Russell (Snake Plissken), Lee Van Cleef (Bob Hauk), Ernest Borgine (Cabby), Donald Pleasence (The President), Issac Hayes (Duke of New York), Harry Dean Stanton (Brain), Adrienne Barbeau (Maggie)*
Screenwriters: *John Carpenter, Nick Castle*
15/99 mins./Action/Adventure/Sci-fi/USA

A condemned criminal and former war hero is offered his freedom if he can rescue the President of the United States from the walled prison island of Manhattan after a terrorist brings down the President's plane in this futuristic adventure.

Far-fetched if not plain daft, there is still something enjoyably cinematic in the idea of Manhattan as a walled-in maximum security prison where the criminals swill around in their own skewed version of society. According to the screen captions the barricade went up in 1988, the events of the film occur in 1997. But if prophecy isn't Carpenter's strong suit, his concept, execution and lead character make for a fascinating acid-fairy-tale.

Carpenter's ruined Manhattan is a grim, grungy netherworld. Utilising primitive matte and modelwork to construct desolate versions of the real thing, the fragged cityscape is brought to sullen life. A bleak, nightmarish vision of the future with its own class strata, it's pertinent to note that it was created at least a year before *Blade Runner*. Into this Darwinist hell hole tumbles the US President in his Airforce One escape pod, clutching a tape of an address which will stave off an imminent world war with the USSR (this is pre-Glasnost moviemaking). To get him, and the tape, out, the ultimate self-preservationist is required. Enter Snake Plissken, ex-soldier turned bank robber turned social reprobate and ultracool sourpuss.

Russell as Plissken is magnificent. Long before the meaty actor's credibility was undone by a parade of indifferent action roles and bad romcoms, he embodied the superantihero (next he applied his infallible resourcefulness to *The Thing*) instilling a sense of can-do physicality and sneery indifference into everything he did (significantly, Tommy Lee Jones was the preferred choice). The voice raspy and laconic, Plissken's slowburning style stems directly from Sergio Leone and Clint Eastwood's legendary Man With No Name and is echoed in any number of subsequent loner-arsehole-heroes (*Mad Max*, *Waterworld*'s Mariner et al).

Tagline
1997. New York City is now a maximum security prison. Breaking out is impossible. Breaking in is insane.

Casting Lee Van Cleef as the duplicitous Hauk simply underlines the reference. Plissken, though, is more preoccupied, less loosely mercenary than Eastwood's ponchoed outsider. Mainly because he's got an explosive implant in his neck with 24 hours on the clock, a superbly direct dramatic device to give the film a real urgency.

Fuelled by a dark strain of irony, this is far less an action movie than you might expect. Drawn-out sequences, absorbing all of production designer Joe Alves' gritty realism and Carpenter's effective but dated plinky-plonky synth score, are only intermittently punctuated by bursts of Snake's indomitable machismo and fairly mediocre gunplay (revealing budget limitations). Instead, Carpenter has created a kind of apocalyptic character piece-cum-black comedy. And beyond Plissken, Borgnine as NY cabbie Cabbie, Isaac Hayes as badguy Duke, Harry Dean Stanton's Brain and Van Cleef's snidey Hauk make big comic book impressions.

This is a product of post-Vietnam/Watergate America, a world of political distrust and widespread anti-establishment fervour – the hero serves no one but himself, yet we're still invited to admire him, simply for his capability if nothing else. New York (a micrcosm of America) is a desolate, moral wasteland where only the fittest and cruellest survive. Putting the boot in on the American Dream is a theme inherent in many of Carpenter's movies. The director preceeded *EFNY* with another excellent tale of civil unrest *Assault On Precinct 13*. And it's notable that the poor *Escape From LA* manages none of this cold cynicism, born as it is out of a less caustic – less relevant? – decade. ★★★★ **IN**

ESCAPE TO WITCH MOUNTAIN (1975)

Starring: *Eddie Albert (Jason O'Day), Ray Milland (Aristotle Bolt), Donald Pleasence (Lucas Deranian), Kim Richards (Tia Malone), Ike Eisenmann (Tony Malone), Walter Barnes (Sheriff Purdy), Denver Pyle (Uncle Bene)*
Director: *John Hough*
Screenwriter: *Robert M. Young based on the novel by Alexander Key*
U/97 mins./Fantasy/USA

Two orphans, Tia and Tony, blessed with psychokinetic powers, fall under the evil charge of Lucas Deranian posing as their uncle. He wants to get these kids into the clutches of millionaire Aristotle Bolt, with desires on their powers.

What a peculiar but effective children's adventure movie this is. Peculiar because, at the time, the mid-seventies, Disney was preoccupied with making *Herbie* movies and letting its animation department go to ruin, and hatching onto Alexander Key's exciting novel showed a rare flash of forward thinking. Magical kids are all the rage these days, and this charming, perilous tale of telepathic sprogs on the run carries a similar haunted strain to the *Harry Potters* – the search for family.

The main thrust of the plot involves the mystery of these kids' origin. We are told they were somehow shipwrecked with only a 'star case' and a picture with two suns at the top to hint at some form of alien status. That and their cerebrally fired abilities: the classic 70s staples of telekinesis, levitation, manipulation of locks; nothing too tricky for the effects department to manage. Then they happen upon a map to the Witch Mountain of the title, and the race is on. Tia Mallone and Ike Eisenmann (whose freckly face became the imprimatur of all child actors of the era) give them a chatty, attractive exuberance, if not much in the way of emotional vulnerability. Still, they could be from another planet, so who are we to judge?

On the badguy side of the equation is moody capitalist Ray Milland ready to exploit their marvellous talents. How deviously American; the film seems to have stumbled upon a subtext about craven parent figures manipulating their children's talents for profit, as if Disney is undermining its entire ethos. Milland and Donald Pleasence work well as a sinister duo, and the film musters some genuine kids-in-distress terrors to infect the dreams of its impressionable target audience. Mummy, will a nasty fat American millionaire steal me away? Thankfully, friendly but emotionally wounded loner Eddie Albert turns up to aid their escape. Strangely, when you start adding it all up, it really starts to resemble a dry-run for *E.T.* ★★★ **IN**

ETERNAL SUNSHINE OF THE SPOTLESS MIND (2004)

Starring: *Jim Carrey (Joel Barish), Kate Winslet (Clementine Kruczynski), Kirsten Dunst (Mary), Mark Ruffalo (Stan), Elijah Wood (Patrick)*
Director: *Michael Gondry*
Screenwriter: *Charlie Kaufman, from a story by Charlie Kaufman, Michel Gondry, Pierry Bismuth*
15/108 mins./Comedy/Fantasy/USA
Awards: *Academy Awards – Best Original Screenplay, BAFTA – Best Editing, Best Original Screenplay, Empire Awards – Best British Actress*

Shy Joel Barish meets free-spirited Clementine and they start a rocky relationship. One day she seems not to recognise him and Barish discovers she has visited Lacuna Inc. and had all memories of him wiped. An angry Barish decides to undergo the same procedure, but begins having second thoughts.

Charlie Kaufman has a problem with endings. As a pure ideas man, the Oscar-nominated screenwriter of *Being John Malkovich* and *Adaptation* is without peer. But the third act of his *Confessions Of A Dangerous Mind* script gets tangled up in its own intrigue; and *Malkovich* also ends without conviction, limping over the line as if it has not drawn breath since that sprint start. Kaufman's problem with third acts is, in fact, so acute that it becomes the very substance of *Adaptation*'s sour last half hour.

But just as everyone (including Kaufman) was ready to conclude that Charlie's acorns simply do not develop into full-sized trees, along comes the measured growth and glorious blossom of *Eternal Sunshine Of The Spotless Mind*, his most satisfying fantasy yet. Make no mistake, *Eternal Sunshine* has a really terrific third act – it's just the first two that threaten to get in the way.

Eternal Sunshine Of The Spotless Mind is, in fact, the second Kaufman script helmed by Michel Gondry who, like previous collaborator Spike Jonze, is an acclaimed director of music videos. Their first underrated and unseen venture was *Human Nature* which – setting aside the almost obligatory 'third act problems' – simply didn't boast the sugary star coating (Rhys Ifans?) that is apparently necessary to make the patented Kaufman weirdness palatable (Cusack, Cage, Clooney). *Eternal Sunshine* has no such problems, with both an embarrassment of riches on the bench and, front and centre, the biggest star yet to be drawn to the cult of Kaufman: Jim Carrey.

Carrey, his dramatic ego keeping that famous comic id on a tight leash, will no doubt bemuse the *Bruce Almighty* crowd with his most interior, least expressive role so far – Joel Barish, a character actually described as 'close-mouthed'. But before any self-styled sophisticates start shouting 'see-ya!', *Adaptation* fans might find themselves equally discomfited, for *Eternal Sunshine* is not the headlong rush of ideas that its high-concept pitch might have you believe.

A cute but low-key and very long pre-credits sequence gives way to a potentially bewildering opening in which we share Joel's confusion at why his girlfriend is ignoring him. Once Barish discovers her visit to Lacuna Inc. and decides on a tit-for-tat strategy, the majority of the action takes place over one night in one small room and inside one man's rapidly disintegrating memory.

Part fever dream and part chamber piece, it takes a long time before any sunshine at all breaks into what is a melancholic and occasionally bitter first half. However, once Joel's subconscious decides that the procedure is a bad idea and enlists the 'memory' of Clementine (Winslet at her most winning) in a daring escape plan, the movie picks up pace and starts to explore comic areas – teenage humiliation, suppressed trauma – that play to Carrey's obvious strengths and best showcase the undoubted visual verve of Gondry. (The dazzling editing alone demands repeat viewings to unscramble.)

Even better, as Joel's situation becomes more hopeless, the tone miraculously becomes more hopeful, journeying right back to those first, deeply romantic, days with Clementine. All at once, Kaufman's master plan snaps into focus, with the true purpose of the Lacuna technical team (everyone scores in small parts, notably a disarming Dunst) revealed with an unexpected reversal.

A final, bittersweet coda seals the deal; the movie has travelled into light but the memories of darkness past can never be entirely wiped away. No movie since *Annie Hall* has better captured the entire arc of a relationship, and even Woody Allen stopped short of presenting the beginning and the end at the exact same time. ★★★★ **CK**

ETRE ET AVOIR (2002)

Starring: *as themselves: Georges Lopez (The teacher), Alize, Axel, Guillaume, Jessie, Johan, Johann, Jonathan, Julien, Laura, Letitia, Marie-Elizabeth, Nathalie, Olivier, Franck, Kevin, Jérôme, Magali, Lea, Oceane, Thomas, Valentin*
Director: *Nicholas Philibert*
Producer: *Gilles Sandoz*
U/104 mins./Documentary/France

A documentary about a tiny rural school in France, where in one classroom George Lopez teaches children ranging in age from 4 to 11.

The opening shots of this documentary linger on the frozen hills of Auvergne, a farming province in the heart of France. But the atmosphere at the local school is in stark contrast to the chill outside, since the children have Georges Lopez for their teacher. A remarkable man who's run the one-class school by himself for 20 years, Lopez exudes warmth, patience and genuine affection for his students.

Culled from 60 hours' worth of footage recorded over ten weeks in a small classroom, this is a charming exercise in consummate professionalism. Shooting on film rather than digi-video, Nicolas Philibert reclaims actuality from the sensation-seeking of reality TV as he captures the changing seasons to emphasise the unwavering support that Georges Lopez gives the four to ten year-olds in his charge.

Lopez is gentle and fair, reassurance is unceasing, and the emotion he feels at the end of term is wholly genuine (especially as he knows retirement is close after 20 years' service to a community that clearly treasures him). But Philibert is also interested in how the kids respond to Lopez and his admirably diverse curriculum, and the director is rewarded with Jojo's mischief, the day trip to the nearby 'big' school and the arrival of next year's timorous intake. ★★★★ **NDS**

EUREKA (1982)

Starring: *Gene Hackman (Jack McCann), Theresa Russell (Tracy), Rutger Hauer (Claude Maillot von Horn), Jane Lapotaire (Helen McCann), Mickey Rourke (Aurellio D'Amato), Ed Lauter (Charles Perkins), Joe Pesci (Mayakofsky)*
Director: *Nicolas Roeg*
Screenwriter: *Paul Mayersberg based on the book by Paul Mayersberg*
18/130 mins./Drama/USA

In the 1920s, prospector Jack McCann strikes it rich. Years later, Jack is a recluse in the Caribbean, annoyed that his daughter has married a gigolo and threatened by mobsters who want to take over his island.

One of the last great undiscovered movies, this is the sort of picture you could swear you'd dreamed. It opens with a long, hallucinatory prologue with a craggy Hackman lost amid the splendours and horrors of snowbound British Columbia and magically gifted with wealth in a literal golden shower (a breathtaking moment), then cuts to the 1940s and finds that the hero has become a Citizen Kane-like hollow man ('once I had it all, now I only have everything'), worried that his son-in-law is another kind of gold-digger and weirdly diffident as persuasive gangsters indicate how far they are willing to go to take his island away from him. Based on the real-life story of Sir Harry Oakes, the millionaire who was murdered in his Xanadu-like retreat during WWII, this is a film you can watch over and over: it combines visual flair and very strong acting (Mickey Rourke and Joe Pesci have early gangster roles) with ambitious and intriguing subject matter, but its precise meaning or direction are almost impossible to fathom.

Nicolas Roeg delivers a string of audacious, unforgettable scenes: the best exploding head ever seen in a non-splatter movie, Hackman's appalling death by blowtorch (the killer is Joe Spinell, of *Maniac* fame), the decadent Hauer smooching with a snake-toting voodoo priest, and a courtroom finale that turns into a bizarre love scene/acting masterclass for Russell and Hauer. It's one of those movies that defies the star rating system: according to individual taste, it veers from ★★★★★ to ★ from scene to scene, and even viewing to viewing. ★★★★ **KN**

EUROPA, EUROPA (1991)

Starring: *Marco Hofschneider (Young Solomon Perel), Julie Delpy (Leni), Andre Wilms (Robert Kellerman), Solomon Perel (Himself), Aschley Wannlinger (Eric), René Hofschneider (Isaak Perel)*
Director: *Agnieszka Holland*
Screenwriters: *Agnieszka Holland, Paul Hengge based on the book of memoirs by Solomon Perel*
15/111 mins./War/Drama/Germany

When his family is arrested by the Gestapo, Polish-Jewish teenager Solomon Perel spends the remainder of the war alternately passing himself off as a member of the Stalinist Komsomol and the Nazi Hitlerjugend in order to survive.

This tale of chance, coincidence and courage would seem like an incredible contrivance were it not based on the remarkable wartime experiences of Solomon Perel (who's latterly seen on an Israeli riverbank). Born near Braunschweig to Polish-Jewish parents on Hitler's birthday, Solly owed his survival more to his non-descript physicality and unformed personality than his calculating ingenuity and linguistic skill. Perel never thought of himself as a hero and Agnieszka Holland concurs in his verdict by depicting him as Zelig incarnate. Some critics denounced this approach for touting conformism, but Holland rejected their reading as flatly as she did that of the feminists who saw the film as a treatise on the trouble caused by penises.

First seen during his circumcision, Solly is cast adrift from his family on the day before his bar mitzvah. Yet, he undergoes a form of baptism that seemingly anoints him for preservation, as he sinks into the river at the start of his chameleonic adventures. This sequence initiates the series of cultural, spiritual and idealogical clashes that Solly experiences as he passes from being a Young Pioneer in an orphanage in Soviet-occupied Grodno to becoming Wehrmacht mascot Josef 'Jupp' Peters, a member of Poland's Germanic minority, the Volksdeutsche.

However, he constantly runs the risk of being exposed and it's telling that Zenek (Andrzej Mastalerz), the Catholic Polish patriot, attempts to betray him, while Robert (Andre Wilms), the closet gay in Nazi uniform, respects his secret. Yet, these rare intrusions of human instinct are soon replaced by ethereal irony, as Solly's attempt to defect to the Russians results in his becoming an accidental hero and more of an insider than ever.

But, even then, there are more twists of fate awaiting him, as he witnesses the Lodz ghetto where his parents will perish and is again spared unmasking by a chance bomb. However, Holland carefully maintains the balance between fact and surreality by inserting dream sequences, in which Hitler waltzes with Stalin, the Judas-like Zenek is cruficied as Christ, and Hitler cowers in an implied bid to prevent the revelation of his own racial impurity. ★★★★ **DP**

⊙ EVEN COWGIRLS GET THE BLUES (1993)

Starring: *Uma Thurman (Sissy Hankshaw), Lorraine Bracco (Delores Del Ruby), Pat Morita (The Chink), Angie Dickinson (Miss Adrian), Keanu Reeves (Julian Gitche), John Hurt (The Countess), Rain Phoenix (Bonanza Jellybean), Ed Begley Jr. (Rupert), Carol Kane (Carla), Sean Young (Marie Barth), Crispin Glover (Howard Barth), Roseanne (Madame Zoe)*
Director: *Gus Van Sant*
Screenwriter: *Gus Van Sant, based on the novel by Tom Robbins*
15/101 mins./Comedy/Romance/Drama/USA

Sissy has enormous thumbs, which she uses to hitchhike across the US. However, when she gets work as a model and is sent to a ranch in California for a photoshoot, things get really strange.

Sometime model Sissy Hankshaw has thumbs the size of jumbo hot dogs, but rather than feel cursed, she uses them to hitchhike her way across America. Countless drivers skid to a halt when they're brandished, and even planes are in thrall when she extends them skywards.

Sissy's vagrant lifestyle changes, however, when her friend The Countess (an outrageously camp performance from John Hurt) matches her with an asthmatic artist and then sends her to film a TV commercial on his ranch. This outlandish haven is staffed by butch cowgirls led by Bonanza Jellybean (Phoenix, sister of the late River) who plots the demise of the ranch's patriarchy.

Delayed for a year while Van Sant did some serious re-editing, this adaptation of Tom Robbins' novel (originally published in 1976) only serves to prove how unadaptable the book was. It aims to be a hip slice of 70s counter-culture cinema but it's hard to be moved by Sissy's psychedelic trip through political activism and the New York high-life.

The cast do their best with the stilted dialogue, and Thurman projects the right air of innocence, but the best performance is by Angie Dickinson as the ranch's uptight manager. Ultimately, not even the combined efforts of her and Hurt can rescue this film. ★ **CM**

⊙ EVENT HORIZON (1997)

Starring: *Laurence Fishburne (Captain Miller), Sam Neill (Dr. William Weir), Kathlenn Quinlan (Peters, Med Tech), Joely Richardson (Lt. Starck), Richard T. Jones (Cooper), Jack Noseworthy (Justin), Jason Issacs (D.J.), Sean Pertwee (Smith)*
Director: *Paul W.S. Anderson*
Screenwriter: *Philip Eisner*
18/96 mins./Horror/Sci-fi/Thriller/UK/USA

Seven years before, a revolutionary spaceship that used a black hole drive disappeared. Now it has reappeared in the orbit of Neptune, and a rescue ship is sent to see if there are any survivors. However, it soon becomes clear that something is onboard – but it ain't human . . .

As soon as the camera peers around the desolate spacecraft Event Horizon, circling Neptune's storm ravaged atmosphere in a decaying orbit, it's pretty obvious that director Paul Anderson spent his youth swotting up on all the right directors: Kubrick, Scott, Cameron, Hitchcock.

Superbly styled in techno-Gothic space-grunge chic, this sci-fi/horror cross-breed is a directorial triumph of reference and homage. And despite script and storyline shortcomings, is sick, nasty and gruesome enough to rattle the cages, frazzle the ganglions and jerk the patellas of those unable to boast lead-lined nervous systems. Not quite 'The Shining In Space' of its aspirations, it works more as effect than concept.

With preamble kept to a bare minimum, Captain Miller and his crew of salvage and rescue grunts are whisked to deep space to find out where Event Horizon has been since it disappeared seven years previously. The ship was a secret government project – designed by passenger Neill – which could create its own black hole and zap across the universe in no time at all. Problem is, it went somewhere it shouldn't and has brought back an incumbent 'evil force' from a place beyond our imagining etc., etc. The point is that this is not a bug movie but a ghost movie – so surrealism is allowed.

At first, this conjures up some of the most visceral tension seen in a movie since Ridley Scott first let a spiky insectoid go walkabout on the Nostromo, as the crew – Fishburne's taciturn captain, Richardson's stiff XO, Kathleen Quinlan's serious medic, Sean Pertwee's salt-of-the-earth helmsman, Richard T. Jones' wisecracking rescue king et al (all very *Alien*) – tries to fathom heinous visions, offal-strewn control decks and other crew members chucking themselves out of airlocks. It's not long before things have become so fraught that you're fit to burst. Inevitably the horror sags: invisible forces sucked from other dimensions allow too much in the way of corner-cutting, and the lack of any credible explanation leaves you unsatisfied. Things just happen and anything goes.

This, though, is never at the expense of the visual craft. *Event* doesn't just borrow from fine antecedents, it takes their future shock value to new heights, using genuinely original FX and creepy camerawork to great effect. And placing Fishburne at its heart is a fine move; the man oozes credibility, giving the potentially schlocky hellhouse nastiness an unnerving element of real fear. ★★★ **IN**

⊙ EVERY WHICH WAY BUT LOOSE (1978)

Starring: *Clint Eastwood (Philo Beddoe), Sondra Locke (Lynn Halsey-Taylor), Geoffrey Lewis (Orville Boggs), Beverly D'Angelo (Echo), Walter Barnes (Tank Murdock)*
Director: *James Fargo*
Screenwriter: *Jeremy Joe Kronsberg*
15/110 mins./Comedy/USA

A travelling prizefighter hits the road with his best buddy – an orang-utan named Clyde.

Contrary to popular belief, this film – and its much-the-same sequel *Any Which Way You Can* – from the swampier regions of the 70s are not about an orang-utan named Clyde. Certainly they include an ape by that name, guzzling beer, fouling cop cars and, at the behest of a snappy, 'Right turn, Clyde,' knocking flat a gang of bumbling, swastika-stamped bikers (seemingly, the Keystone chapter of the Hell's Angels fraternity). In truth, he's merely a secondary character, a Polonius or Banquo to the main drama, which can be summed up loosely as a redknecked, bare-knuckle-boxing movie-cum-comedy with a County & Western tang. Or, if we're talking high concept, the man with the 'tan lets his fists do the talking.

A bizarre fillip in Eastwood's transition from matinee idol to grand old man of cinema, they are free-forming episodes of commercial whackiness trading off the craggy machismo of the star as well as the loose-limbed, rootin'-tootin' chaos of *Smokey And The Bandit* (1977), *Convoy* (1978) even *The Cannonball Run* (1981). Quite frankly Clyde was the least of their oddities. Which beggars the question – what the hell was everyone thinking?

America had finally recovered from Vietnam and Nixon, so put it down to Hollywood just cutting loose and meaningless for a spell. Or, perhaps, it was the fact everyone told Eastwood not to do it, and just like the predilections of his hairy buddy, he flipped them the bird.

To recap, *Loose* is the one where Clint fights bare-knuckle, falls for slender crooner Sandra Locke and Clyde's snobbish 'tude gets on the nerves of the cuss-ready Mama Boggs. The original, by the shortest of hops is the better, at least displaying a belief in backwater togetherness. ★★★ **IN**

⦿ EVERYONE SAYS I LOVE YOU (1996)

Starring: *Woody Allen (Joe Berlin), Goldie Hawn (Steffi Dandridge), Alan Alda (Bob Dandridge), Julia Roberts (Von Sidell), Drew Barrymore (Skylar Dandridge), Edward Norton (Holden Spence), Tim Roth (Charles Ferry), Natalie Portman (Laura Dandridge), Gaby Hoffman (Lane Dandridge), Natasha Lyonne (D. J. Berlin), Lukas Hass (Scott Dandridge), Billy Crudup (Ken)*
Director: *Woody Allen*
Screenwriter: *Woody Allen*
12/101 mins./Comedy/Musical/Romance/USA

An ultra-liberal family from New York's Upper East Side swap partners and fall in and out of love – in song, and in Paris, Venice and NYC itself.

Like Christmas, birthdays and Jonathan Ross changing the title of his film show, there's something deeply comforting about the arrival of Woody Allen's annual movie. Some are splendid, others merely all right, but the cinematic year would be sadly deprived without something from one of America's leading auteurs. Here he's excelled himself: bolting the neurotic, fluffy fun of *Manhattan Murder Mystery* to the controlled sentimentality of *The Purple Rose Of Cairo*. The result is arguably his finest film of the 1990s.

It's a musical, an odd choice given the disastrous performances of recent attempts to re-invent what was once one of cinema's most popular and technically innovative genres; but having observed the abject failure of the likes of *Absolute Beginners* and *Earth Girls Are Easy*, Allen opts for a human scale song-and-dancefest, giving his celebrity assortment of a company (including regular Alda as well as Tim Roth, Norton and Hawn) the opportunity to burst into song with varying results ranging from Norton's Perry Comoesque warblings to Allen's 'old man mumbling in the shower'.

The content is the standard Allen shtick – neurotic family entangled in complex personal relationships shout and yammer at each other, usually over the dinner table while Woody himself falls hopelessly in love and makes an amusing mess of it. What differentiates it are the songs where the quavering voices of untrained singers add an almost irresistible reality and grace to what can be an occasionally overpowering and bombastic verbal style. He's not afraid to throw in a couple of production numbers either, including a masterfully choreographed hoofing outbreak in a hospital corridor and a delightful sequence in which Goldie Hawn flies over the banks of the Seine. ★★★★ **AS**

⦿ EVERYTHING IS ILLUMINATED (2005)

Starring: *Eugene Hutz (Alex), Elijah Wood (Jonathan Safran Foer), Jonathan Safran Foer (Leaf Blower), Jana Hrabetova (Jonathan's Grandmother), Stephen Samudovsky (Jonathan's Grandfather)*
Director: *Liev Schreiber*
Screenwriter: *Liev Schreiber, based on the novel by Jonathan Safran Foer*
12A/106 mins./Drama/USA

Jonathan, a neurotic American Jew, travels to the Ukraine to find a woman he believes helped his grandfather escape from the Nazis. His guide is Alex, an idealistic local with a garbled grasp of English and a similarly warped take on Western culture. Driven by Alex's anti-Semitic grandfather, they take a road trip of discovery...

Jonathan Safran Foer's debut novel, written in his early 20s, has a striking effect on those who read it. Some are impressed by its precocious talent, its whimsical collision of foreign cultures and magic-realist digressions into Jewish history. Others throw the book across the room, finding it smug, smart-arsey and borderline racist. There's really no middle ground, and Liev Schreiber's considered and surprisingly lean adaptation – his assured directing debut – will do little to upset the admirers or convince the critics.

It begins in the present day, where Jonathan, a sort-of-writer, is collating artefacts from his closed-off life. The death of his grandfather ignites a curiosity about his European roots, so Jonathan takes off to the Ukraine, equipped only with a black suit, some plastic bags and a picture of the peasant woman who may or may not have been instrumental in his grandfather's departure for the West. But when he arrives, Jonathan's romantic expectations are dashed: the villages of the past, or shtetls, are long gone, and the rustic idyll cemented over in the dying throes of Communism.

Which may sound like the opening to something turgid and mournful, but, for a novice, Schreiber plays a very bold game, stripping out the novel's folklore and committing to its modernity. Central to this is Eugene Hutz's Alex, a gangly, beady-eyed culture vulture who descends on Jonathan with an almost insatiable curiosity. Just as Jonathan backs away from reality, Alex grabs it and tackles it, creating an odd-couple chemistry that's only enhanced by Wood's generous, second-string performance, which begins inscrutably enough and in the final frames almost morphs entirely into a moving, Magritte-like enigma.

Carrying it forward, however, is Hutz, a captivating first-timer whose gypsy-punk boho band Gogol Bordello keep the movie pumping forward on a soundtrack that owes a massive but nevertheless enjoyable debt to the films of Emir Kusturica. Schreiber never quite musters the rude health of Kusturica in his prime, and his strange decision to tweak the crucial twist of the source material might wrong-foot a few viewers, but this is a creditable, and credible, adaptation of a book that many considered unfilmable. ★★★★ **DW**

⦿ EVERYTHING YOU ALWAYS WANTED TO KNOW ABOUT SEX* BUT WERE AFRAID TO ASK (1972)

Starring: *Woody Allen (The Fool/Fabrizio/Victor Shakapopulis/Sperm # 1), John Carradine (Dr. Bernardo), Lou Jacobi (Sam), Louise Lasser (Gina), Anthony Quayle (The King), Tony Randall (The Operator), Lynn Redgrave (The Queen), Burt Reynolds (Sperm Switchboard Chief), Gene Wilder (Dr. Doug Ross)*
Director: *Woody Allen*
Screenwriter: *Woody Allen based on the book by David Reuben*
18/87 mins./Comedy/USA

A series of sketches, purportedly based on Dr. David Reuben's best-selling 1970s sex manual.

One of Woody Allen's 'early, funny films', this is a rare (mostly successful) film attempt at sketch comedy, with a run of self-contained, gag-driven segments answering the questions 'Do Aphrodisiacs Work?' (Allen as a medieval jester smitten with queen Lynn Redgrave but thwarted by a chastity belt), 'What is Sodomy?' (psychiatrist Gene Wilder falls in love with a sheep), 'Do Some Women Have Trouble Reaching Orgasm?' (a smug, flat Antonioni parody), 'Are Transvestites Homosexuals?' (Lou Jacobi as a middle-aged schlub caught in women's clothes), 'What Are Sex Perverts?' (a skit on 1950s game shows as a panel of celebrities on *What's My Perversion?* try to guess the mystery kink of a guest contestant), 'Are the Findings of Doctors and Clinics Who Do Sexual Research Accurate?' (an extended joke about science fiction films, with John Carradine as a mad sex researcher who unleashes a giant breast that rampages across the countryside like The Blob) and 'What Happens During Ejaculation?' (Burt Reynolds and Tony Randall are brain-workers and Allen is a sperm in a human body run by a NASA-style mission crew).

Some sketches simply don't work (the drag skit is especially pointless), but Allen crams in many funny, crass lines (like the sci-fi hero who snaps 'I know how to handle tits') and there's one genuinely classic performance from Wilder, who is magnificent, absurd and bizarrely touching as the uppercrust shrink smitten with a sheep. Dr. Doug Ross, George Clooney's character on *ER*, is named after Wilder's wool-loving character here.

Though Allen was still a better writer and performer than director at this stage of his career, he stretches to effective parodies of early television, mad scientist horror films and high-tech Michael Crichton science fiction. ★★★★ **KN**

EVIL DEAD (1981)

Starring: *Bruce Campbell (Ash), Ellen Sandweiss (Cheryl), Betsy Baker (Linda), Hal Delrich (Scott), Sarah York (Shelly)*
Director: *Sam Raimi*
Screenwriter: *Sam Raimi*
18/85 mins./Horror/USA

Five teens go into the woods and accidentally release evil by playing a taped translation of the Necronomicon. One by one they turn into zombies – the evil dead.

Punk kids with no formal film training (and more ambition than money) have always been drawn towards low-budget horror movies, most of them destined for Kim Newman's dungeon. But Sam Raimi's *The Evil Dead* reigns supreme, the knock-off drive-thru cheapie that became an iconic, oft-imitated classic.

Its reputation is deserved. Darker, and scarier, than its hyper-kinetic remake/sequel, Raimi's movie melds chunks of *Night Of The Living Dead*, *The Texas Chain Saw Massacre* and – bizarrely – *The Three Stooges*, into a tense, gory whole. Unbound by cinematic convention, Raimi unleashed his free-range camera, and ghoulish, omnipresent sound effects to create a bleak, paranoid atmosphere and a raft of sudden, effective shocks.

There's even a hint of the grungy edge that condemned the film to the infamous Video Nasties list in the mid-80s: namely, the still-shocking tree rape sequence. And, if you can overlook the mostly lame-o acting, cheeseball effects and fumbling drama, there's enough fledgling genius here to fill another thousand horror movies. The punk kids did good. ★★★★ **CH**

EVIL DEAD II (1987)

Starring: *Bruce Campbell (Ash), Sarah Berry (Annie), Dan Hicks (Jake), Kassie Wesley (Bobby Joe), Theodore Raimi (Posessessed Henrietta), Denise Bixler (Linda)*
Director: *Sam Raimi*
Screenwriters: *Sam Raimi, Scott Spiegel*
18/85 mins./Horror/USA

A young man named Ash takes his girlfriend Linda to a secluded cabin, and plays back a professor's tape-recorded recitation of passages from the Book of the Dead, unknowingly waking the evil spirits.

It was remiss of the film geeks in *Scream 2* to overlook *Evil Dead II* when discussing the paucity of superior sequels. Alright, it's more of a remake – or remix – than a Part Two, but it's fairly unique in improving upon the promise of the original, like the new model of a household appliance with a whole rack of extra functions and twice as many flashing lights. Like its hero Ash, in fact, who, having lopped off his own infected hand, replaces it with a chainsaw ('Groovy!').

This film is a genuine case of more is more. Director Sam Raimi, producer Robert Tapert and star Bruce Campbell agreed to make a sequel to *The Evil Dead*, their own pioneering low budget gorefest of 1982 ('The Ultimate Experience In Gruelling Terror'). Raimi had just been approached by legendary Italian producer Dino De Laurentiis to helm a screen adaptation of Stephen King's *Thinner* – after all, King had raved about *The Evil Dead*: 'It was like a thunderstorm in a bottle.' Raimi eventually turned *Thinner* down, but after a more than influential nudge from King, De Laurentiis agreed instead to fund *Evil Dead II*.

Let us not underestimate the impact of the original *Evil Dead* (original title: *Book Of The Dead*). A simple tale of college kids in a cabin being taken over by demons, Raimi's full-length debut – after years of Super-8 shorts – was heavily influenced by *The Texas Chain Saw Massacre*, *Friday The 13th*, *The Hills Have Eyes* and *Night Of The Living Dead*, but managed through sheer guts and brio to find a place of its own in the horror pantheon achieving notoriety in Britain during the 'video nasty' wars. (Having topped the UK video rental charts in 1983, it was briefly banned in 1984 under the Obscene Publications Act.) Raimi, only 22 when he made the film, seemed destined for greater things. But it hasn't quite happened yet. Highlights of his 'grown up' career include *Spider-Man* and *Spider-Man 2*, the stylised western *The Quick And The Dead* and the undeserved flop *A Simple Plan*.

The iconic Campbell, like Raimi, seems destined to go to his grave as 'the Evil Dead bloke'. Why? Simple. Because *Evil Dead II* made the huge mistake of being one of the greatest horror movies of its age, and not just because it contains a scene where an eye pops out of its socket and lands in someone else's mouth. Although that does help.

The original was shot on 16mm and cost around $400,000. The sequel had a budget of $3.6 million, and this was both its blessing and its curse. The budget gave Raimi, Tapert and Campbell (the three partners in Renaissance Pictures) the chance to re-do *Evil Dead* with knock-out gore effects, more stop-frame animation, bigger monsters, moving trees and wackier camerawork (including an astonishing 'ride' through the woods in which Campbell is strapped to an unseen revolving crucifix!). And yet the budget prevented them making the ambitious, medieval sequel Raimi had envisaged – his 14th century vision is reduced to one scene at the end.

So it was that *Evil Dead II* was confined to the haunted cabin of the original. It even begins with a speeded-up recap of *Evil Dead* which should have been existing footage but had to be re-shot because it was too complicated to relicense the first film from the 50 different territories it had been sold to. Thus, *Evil Dead II* begins with *Evil Dead* in précis, effectively rendering the first film obsolete (although, of course, academic purists still cling to it as a superior work). Raimi describes the recap as 'shorthand': in it only Ash and Linda discover the fateful *Book Of The Dead* in the cabin; in the original, there were five of them (as anyone who saw the film knows). This entire sequence makes *Evil Dead II* unique, especially for a Part Two, and though Campbell himself admitted that he is 'not interested' in this preamble, it acts as a great entree for first-timers.

Once the sequel has 'kicked in' (Campbell's words), at the point where dead Linda rises from the grave and does a macabre dance, it's a true rollercoaster – the same conceits are recycled, but in such style you never feel shortchanged. ★★★★ **AC**

EVITA (1996)

Starring: *Madonna (Eva 'Evita' Peron), Antonio Banderas (Che Guevara), Jonathan Pryce (General Juan Domingo Peron), Jimmy Nail (Agustin Magaldi)*
Director: *Alan Parker*
Screenwriters: *Alan Parker, Oliver Stone, based on the musical play* Evita, *lyrics by Tim Rice and music by Andrew Lloyd Webber*
PG/135 mins./Musical/Biography/USA

Awards: *Academy Awards – Best Song, Golden Globes – Best Comedy/Musical, Best Song, Best Actress in a Comedy/Musical*

The hit musical based on the life of Evita Duarte, a B-picture Argentinian actress who eventually became the wife of Argentinian president and dictator Juan Perón, and the most beloved and hated woman in Argentina.

Madonna knocks herself out and deserves cheers for the emotional range and humanity with which she sings in Alan Parker's spectacular film. But whether you think the movie is great or grisly, rests in large part on your palate for Andrew Lloyd Webber's music.

In case you've been on Mars, *Evita* is the 20-year-old mega hit Andrew Lloyd-Webber/Tim Rice musical based on the life of Argentinian icon Eva Peron, who rose from nothing to model/starlet to powerful and revered legend by ruthless bed-hopping and self-reinvention.

There is not an instant Madonna is on screen when she is not palpitating with intense empathy for Eva and the determination to be electrifying. This is her biggest moment and she knows it. A true diva.

In contrast, Antonio Banderas just has to show up to tango away with a scene. That, is a real Movie Star. His seemingly effortless Che is sexy, surly, sneering and tuneful. And he certainly earns his salary with a virtually ubiquitous presence – here a waiter or cleaner, there a reporter or streetfighter – to provide narration. Pryce, however, has a thankless task as Col. Juan Peron, but fascist dictators have never deserved good songs. Jimmy Nail also leaps in, decidedly un-Latino, to croon a satirical ballad.

The 'screenplay' (attributed to both Parker and one-time scheduled director Oliver Stone) makes judicious cuts from the ageing show. Songs frequently serve as voiceover to montages, some of them fab: Eva dancing, screwing and climbing her way up the socio-political strata through 'Goodnight And Thank You'; soldiers and socialites expressing their derision of her in 'Dangerous Jade', Eva's indulgent sprees intercut with dancers, rioters and junta enforcers.

The outdated adherence to the show's pseudo-opera form is a problem – odd lines sung outside the defined 'numbers' should have been dumped, or spoken. The solemn pomposity of the work is another, from which Parker relieves us with some masterful staging, eye-poppingly epic set pieces ('Don't Cry For Me Argentina', and the most awesome funeral procession since *Ghandi*) and big, rhythmically varied orchestrations (from a team including Emilio Estefan). The cinematography by Darius Kondji (*Se7en*, *Stealing Beauty*, *The City Of Lost Children*) is also a superb asset. ★★★ **AE**

EXCALIBUR (1981)

Starring: *Nigel Terry (King Arthur), Nicol Williamson (Merlin), Nicholas Clay (Lancelot), Helen Mirren (Morgana), Cherie Lunghi (Guinevere), Paul Geoffrey (Perceval), Robert Addie (Mordred), Gabriel Byrne (Uther), Liam Neeson (Gawain), Corin Redgrave (Cornwall)*
Director: *John Boorman*
Screenwriters: *Rospo Pallenberg, John Boorman, based on the book* Le Morte D'Arthur *by Thomas Mallory*
15/140 mins./Action/Fantasy/USA

When boy Arthur, draws a sword out of a stone he fulfils a prophecy the makes him the next King of England. But his sorceress sister Morgana may bring about his downfall.

This John Boorman film sees him also at two extremes – helming both the age-old yarn of Arthurian legend, and a cast (including Liam Neeson, Patrick Stewart and Gabriel Byrne) who, although now well-established, were then distinctly new to the scene.

Indeed, it's a dichotomy that makes for a terrific end result, full of energy but also mysticism. All the elements (sword in stone, Holy Grail and cuckolding Guinevere) are present and correct, and even if it does descend into the confusingly symbolic towards its breathtaking climax, the combination of glorious photography and epic drama more than makes up the deficit.

Shorn of much of the sentimentality of many Arthurian adaptations – *First Knight*, we mean you – this emphasises the blood, guts and magic of England's greatest ever monarch. ★★★★ **MD**

EXECUTIVE DECISION (1996)

Starring: *Kurt Russell (Dr. Phil David Grant), Steven Seagal (Lt. Colonel Austin Travis), Halle Berry (Jean, Flight Attendant), John Leguizamo (Captain Rat), Oliver Platt (Dennis Cahill)*
Director: *Stuart Baird*
Screenwriters: *Jim Thomas, John Thomas*
15/134 mins./Action/Adventure/Thriller/USA

When terrorists take over a jumbo jet, a group of crack commandos are smuggled aboard in mid-air to try to save the day – unaware that the terrorists are also armed with enough nerve gas to take out the Eastern seaboard . . .

Forget *Sudden Death*, *Broken Arrow* and *Terminal Velocity*. Forget every one of the spate of potty high flying escapades that cavorted their way onto screens around the same time as this hostage drama with scant regard for good sense. *Executive Decision* taps such levels of preposterousness it makes *Die Hard 2* resemble a taut exercise in Ken Loach-styled social realism. It is also the most amount of ludicrous fun for many a moon.

On a speeding jumbo heading for Washington, a group of fanatical Middle Eastern terrorists (of no given address) have exercised their right to hijack. So far so typical. What makes this different is that they have smuggled aboard a bomb-rigged cache of ultra-lethal nerve gas in quantities capable of wiping out much of the continent's Eastern seaboard. And you can bet your life that their reasonable but intermittently psycho leader David Suchet (Euro villain as Middle Eastern) is on for a bit of suicide bombing.

A multitude of plot complications later and a crack team of commandos have snuck on board (care of a Stealth bomber and an almost disastrous transference procedure) ready to face a further multitude of complications in rescuing the passengers, disarming the bomb, and averting the 'executive decision' of destroying the 747 (and the 400 aboard) before it reaches the American exclusion zone. As you can gather, there is far too much plot and none of it convinces, but first-time director Baird rips-off action movie staples with such abandon that as you howl with laughter you're still tottering on the edge of your seat.

Russell is the Jack Ryan type, roped in at the last minute who spends the entire movie in a Bondian tuxedo. There's also John Leguizamo's grunt, Oliver Platt's nerdy computer whizz, Berry as the gutsy stewardess and Joe Morton as a bomb disposal expert who – shock! – is rendered paralysed as soon as they crash the plane. To top it all Steven Seagal gets an unbilled extended cameo as a hard-bitten chief commando only to buy it early on.

Every cliché in the book is turned full-throttle – even after all the *Die Hard*ery is done with, the film spends an extra 15 minutes pretending to be an *Airport*-style disaster movie. The least surprising element is that Joel Silver is credited as executive producer. ★★★ **IN**

EXISTENZ (1999)

Starring: *Jennifer Jason Leigh (Allegra Geller), Jude Law (Ted Pikul), Ian Holm (Kiri Vinokur), Willem Dafoe (Gas), Don McKellar (Yevgeny Nourish), Christopher Eccleston (Seminar Leader), Sarah Polley (Merle)*
Screenwriters: *David Cronenberg*
Director: *David Cronenberg*
15/97 mins./.Sci-Fi/Crime/Drama/Thriller/Canada/France/U.K.

Allegra Geller, the world's leading games designer, has come up with a new virtual reality game, which she is testing with a focus group. However, when an assassin attacks the gathering, she goes on the run with a young marketing man, taking the prototype game with her.

For the first time since 1983's *Videodrome*, David Cronenberg is here working from a script based on a story he originated himself, which makes it a purer work even than such thoroughly Cronenbergised efforts as *The Fly* and *Dead Ringers*, and unburdened by the schizoid feel of such literary adaptions as *The Naked Lunch* and *Crash*.

A side effect of this de facto comeback is that the cutting edge ideas Cronenberg began to explore in *Videodrome* have now become assimilated into the mainstream, rendering *eXistenZ* a little late in the day when tackling virtual reality, games-playing, near-future corporate wars and 'the realist underground'.

As with *Videodrome*, the plot breaks from 'reality' early on as a demonstration of a new game designed by Allegra Geller is interrupted by an assassin wielding an ingenious organic gun composed of mutant amphibian parts which fires human teeth as bullets. This is guessably a move in a continuing game that proceeds through layers of reality as the wounded Allegra, on the run with PR nerd/security man Ted Pikul, has to enter the world of her own game and take Ted with her, which involves having the reluctant hero fitted with a spinal implant 'bio-port' in the backwoods gas station run by treacherous Gas. Once in the game, further layers have to be penetrated Chinese box fashion as Allegra and Ted find a fantasy world disturbingly close to their reality.

Like many Cronenberg films (*Videodrome* excepted), *eXistenZ* suffers from a weak male lead, but has an unusual heroine and an array of eccentric supporting red herrings (even the dodgy accents are 'explained'). Less weighty than Cronenberg's more 'important' work, this rediscovers a pleasure in action filmmaking absent since his 'early, funny ones' and deploys the mannerisms (freak character names, invented jargon, machine-flesh interfaces) we loved in *Shivers*, *Rabid*, *The Brood* and *Scanners*. ★★★★ **KN**

⑩ THE EXORCISM OF EMILY ROSE (2005)

Starring: *Laura Linney (Erin Bruner), Tom Wilkinson (Father Moore), Campbell Scott (Ethan Thomas), Jennifer Carpenter (Emily Rose), Colm Feore (Karl Gunderson)*
Director: *Scott Derrickson*
Screenwriters: *Paul Harris Boardman, Scott Derrickson*
15/119 mins./Drama/Horror/USA

Father Moore, a small-town priest, is on trial for the negligent homicide of a young woman who died in his care during an exorcism. Defending him is Erin Bruner, an atheist lawyer who comes to doubt her own beliefs as the spooky evidence mounts up.

Laura Linney shouldn't really be in *Emily Rose* – or at least, she should only be in its courtroom-based half. She doesn't do schlocky horror, she does proper stuff with serious haircuts that gets you Oscar nominations. So her presence in this (possibly) supernatural thriller points to the fact this is more than a grip-your-armrest, knock-over-your-snacks chiller.

If director and co-screenwriter Scott Derrickson makes one great decision in his execution of this strange legal-horror hybrid, it's to never come down on a definitive side of the central argument that his movie presents: was Emily Rose, based on a real-life girl, really possessed by demons, or was her terrifying behaviour the result of a serious medical condition? We see relatively little of the actual story of Emily (ferociously played by newcomer Carpenter, with a hell of a set of lungs), instead reliving her story through the court case that followed when police decided Emily's death was down to Father Moore's negligence in not seeking medical help for his charge.

Linney's naturally fierce – but in a cuddly way – screen presence clutches the viewer as she fights for the freedom of a man who represents beliefs she doesn't hold, but gradually opens up to the possibility that darker forces may be at work. A lesser actress might have succumbed to the desire to play the spooky moments with horror-movie fright, but Linney remains consistently a defence lawyer who happens to be experiencing some freaky shit. You're never forced to take a particular viewpoint (Campbell Scott provides stoic counterpoint as the prosecution) which makes this much more of a brainteaser than it could have been.

But for all its cleverness, *Emily Rose* does have its hokey moments. The explanation of religious history and symbolism is, at times, clunky, despite Wilkinson's solid performance, and incidents like glasses smashing when things get demonic and the demise of witnesses feel like easy scares from a lesser film. Carpenter possesses the flashback scenes with unsettling intensity, and there will be times when fainter viewers will be hiding in their popcorn, but there are rarely moments of absolute terror – rather of frequent disquiet. ★★★ **OR**

⑩ THE EXORCIST (1973)

Starring: *Ellen Burstyn (Mrs. MacNeil), Max von Sydow (Father Merrin), Jason Miller (Father Karras), Lee J. Cobb (Lt. Kinderman), Jack MacGowran (Burke), Kitty Winn (Sharon), Linda Blair (Regan)*
Director: *William Friedkin*
Screenwriter: *William Peter Blatty*
18/121 mins./Horror/USA

Awards: *Academy Awards – Best Sound, Best Screenplay based on material from another medium, Empire Awards – Movie Masterpiece Award (William Friedkin), Golden Globes – Best Direction, Best Drama, Best Screenplay, Best Supporting Actress (Linda Blair)*

Regan is an adolescent girl, living with her mother in Georgetown in Washington, who starts exhibiting strange symptoms. When all medical possibilities are exhausted, her mother is sent to a priest who becomes convinced that Regan is possessed and an exorcism is necessary otherwise Regan will die.

In 1998, the year of its 25th anniversary, you couldn't avoid *The Exorcist*. There were books, a television documentary and thousands of column inches to mark its theatrical reissue. It was re-viewed and reviewed, and the general consensus was that it was as good today as it had always been.

However, in a surreal twist of events, the British Board Of Film Censors still refused to grant the film a video certificate. The then BBFC boss James Ferman said, 'The problem with *The Exorcist* is not that it's a bad film, it's that it's a very good film – one of the most powerful ever made.'

Thus, in 1998, despite this sense that *The Exorcist* was back in the public domain, you still could not rent or buy it in this country. In effect, one of the most powerful films ever made was rendered even more powerful. Like *Clockwork Orange*, *The Evil Dead* and The Beach Boys' *Surf's Up* album, *The Exorcist* attained the mythic power of unattainability. Then, in 1999, the spell was broken. The BBFC woke up, smelt the coffee, and finally saw fit to grant *The Exorcist* its requisite 18. Out it came on video, laserdisc and DVD.

Now the demon Pazuzu walks among us; he lurks in high street shops between *A Bug's Life* and *Patch Adams*, he sits on Ikea shelves the length and breadth of the country, he is seen by under-age kids, kids of 12, the same age as Regan MacNeil. The question is, does a film as powerful as *The Exorcist* lose any of its power by being as accessible as *Toy Story*? Because we can now skip to a scene, or pause for a cup of tea, or view the film while its director provides a running commentary, does that subtract from the primal fear it tapped into more than a quarter of a century ago? The answer, thankfully, is no. However much the religious aspects of the film affect you (they seem to work best on the devout and the stubbornly atheistic), *The Exorcist* is still a terrifying movie, a fact proven by the great horror litmus test: even the bits set during the day are scary.

Halloween passes this test (Michael Myers among the washing), as do *The Shining* ('All work and no play . . .') and more recently *The Sixth Sense* (the hanging bodies in the school). Although, perhaps the most traditional shock in *The Exorcist* occurs in darkness (in the attic, in fact), a disarming sense of unease begins in the autumnal streets of Georgetown as fallen leaves dance to the strains of Mike Oldfield's 'Tubular Bells'. The very thought of *The Exorcist* can produce goosebumps at any hour of the day – that's how scary it is. Why does this film retain this power to unerve and upset and how does it have the ability to drain the colour from our cheeks? It's about the Devil possessing a small child, that's horrible enough, and it contains scenes of physical degradation that would make a coroner blanch. But that's just cheap gore and facile exploitation of our fear of graveyards – you might argue that the really scary thing about *The Exorcist* is the sound.

There's the aforementioned appropriation of 'Tubular Bells', there's Jack Nitzsche's sparing but eerie incidentals (insectoid strings underscore the revealing of the words 'help me' on Regan's stomach). But put the music aside and concentrate on the actual sound edited by Robert Knudson and Chris Newman (who took home one of the film's measly two Oscars) and you will hear where the horror lies. Here's the heart of the film's subtle command over our synapses: the mysterious scuffling in the attic; the rising crescendo of wind and fighting dogs in Northern Iraq when Father Merrin faces the demon statue; the fading echo of screaming as a possession scene cuts to a more peaceful one; and the brilliant use of traffic noise: constant car horns, a deafening subway train, the plane which obscures the conversation between Karras and a younger priest in the church courtyard, overheard by Chris MacNeil.

But the film's piece de resistance, soundwise, is the demon itself, thanks in no small part to the dedication of actress Mercedes McCambridge. It is her guttural voice that provides the obscenities and her willingness to experiment with mushy apple and raw eggs that resulted in her (quite literally) coming up with the vomiting effects. A delicate blend of wild animals, loops and treated voices combined to create the full demonic chorus – so effective that it can be deeply disturbing even without the sight of Linda Blair under Dick Smith's makeup. When Karras plays back a tape recording in his apartment, we're just as spooked as he is. ★★★★★ **AC**

Movie Trivia: The Exorcist

Linda Blair's mother, who cameos as a nurse, brought her in to audition for the role. The steps used in Father Karras' death were covered in half-inch thick rubber and would be used again in *The Exorcist III*. In 1973 evangelist Billy Graham claimed there was genuine evil living in the reels of the movie.

EXORCIST II THE HERETIC (1977)

Starring: *Linda Blair (Regan MacNeil), Richard Burton (Fr. Phillip Lamont) Louise Fletcher (Dr. Gene Tuskin), Max von Sydow (Father Merrin). Kitty Winn (Sharon Spencer), Paul Henreid (The Cardinal), James Earl Jones (Older Kokumo), Ned Beatty (Edwards)*
Director: *John Boorman*
Screenwriter: *William Goodhart*
18/118 mins./Horror/USA

Former possessee Regan MacNeil, still troubled by her experience with the demon Pazuzu, participates in hypnosis-telepathy therapy. Investigating the death of Father Merrin, Father Lamont travels to Africa, where young Merrin first tangled with Pazuzu, then returns to America to save Regan.

A famously disastrous follow-up to William Friedkin's horror hit, this has never won many admirers – though it now looks like the best of the generally disastrous *Exorcist* sequels, in that it at least offers a lot of interesting material jumbled together in a frankly incoherent manner. Blair, a few years further into puberty than in her debut performance, is chubby-cheeked and astonishingly nubile as the repossessed heroine ('I was possessed by a demon. Oh, but it's okay, he's gone now!'), while Von Sydow appears mostly in makeup-free flashbacks as the young Father Merrin tangling with Pazuzu in Africa (pre-empting both versions of *Exorcist IV*) and returning bit-player Kitty Winn explains why none of the other characters are back.

However, the most entertainment value comes from Richard Burton as the new priest in town, who wears a silly headpiece for telepathic synchronisation with the patient and suffers one truly cringe-inducing horror moment as he treads on a spike that goes completely through his bare foot. John Boorman, already see-sawing between genius and lunacy, has no interest at all in the spook business, but litters the film with astonishing sights and sounds, especially in the African sequences which include incredible landscapes, an impressive plague of demon mosquitoes and James Earl Jones as a leopard-outfitted chieftain.

Rather than sample more Mike Oldfield, the film stretches to a terrific music score, mixing liturgical and African themes, from Ennio Morricone. Musing on the film's no acceptance by *Exorcist* fans, Boorman said 'I guess I didn't throw enough Christians to the lions.' ★★ **KN**

THE EXORCIST III (1990)

Starring *George C. Scott (Lt. William Kinderman), Ed Flanders (Father Joseph Kevin Dyer), Brad Dourif (The Gemini Killer/James Venamun), Jason Miller (Patient X), Nicol Williamson (Fr. Paul Morning), Scott Wilson (Dr. Temple)*
Director: *William Peter Blatty*
Screenwriter: *William Peter Blatty, based on his own novel* Legion
18/110 mins./Horror/USA

Cop Kinderman is baffled by mutilation murders which bear the trademarks of the Gemini Killer who died in the electric chair at exactly the instant exorcist Father Karras was falling to his death. In a secure hospital, Kinderman finds Patient X, who alternately looks like Gemini and Karras.

All three *Exorcist* sequels have been troubled, disappointing films which exist in multiple versions because of clashes between the studios who own the franchise and the visionaries they hire to follow up William Friedkin's hit. Here, William Peter Blatty, original author of the novel, steps up to write and direct, ignoring *Exorcist II: The Heretic* and adapting his own follow-up book, *Legion*.

Too much of the movie takes place in dark rooms where people describe horrors that might more profitably have been on the screen, and the plot is a house of cards that constantly collapses as Blatty the screenwriter poses Blatty the director challenges that he can't meet.

However, the film comes to life in a few brief, illogical flashes that deliver genuine scares – a possessed old woman crawling ignored on the ceiling, a white-robed figure with an impressive decapitation implement drifting after a doomed nurse. Examining Blatty's original cut, the producers decided an *Exorcist* sequel ought to have an exorcism in it, and so Nicol Williamson was called in for extra Bible-thumping scenes which look exactly like tacked-on additions that pad out an already-ludicrous climax ('I believe in slime,' Scott yells) to insane proportions.

Though dressed up with a lot of talk about faith and the nature of Evil, *Exorcist III* is essentially yet another variation on the cycle of movies (*The Hidden*, *Shocker*, *The First Power*) in which a cop pursues a body-hopping serial murderer, with mad-eyed Dourif doing the act he had already perfected in *Child's Play*. ★★ **KN**

EXORCIST: THE BEGINNING (2004)

Starring: *Stellan Skarsgård (Father Lankester Merrin), James D'Arcy (Father William Francis), Izabella Scorupco (Sarah), Remy Sweeney (Joseph), Julian Wadham (Major Granville)*
Director: *Renny Harlin*
Screenwriter: *Alexi Hawley, from a story by Caleb Carr and William Wisher*
15/100 mins./Horror/USA

The full story of the first encounter briefly referenced in the original between *The Exorcist*'s Father Merrin and the demon Pazuzu, set in and around an ancient church in Nairobi in 1949.

Where do you start with a cacophony like this? It involves dark powers beyond our understanding, the chill touch of evil and the death of all we have come to love and hope for. And that's just the screenplay ...

You are, no doubt, well aware of the trials and tribulations that have gone into making this prequel to one of cinema's greatest nerve-wrackers (a film already burdened with two less-than-scratch sequels), and how *The Beginning* was completely reshot, with previous incumbent Paul Schrader shown the door as rumours spread like black flies that he'd neglected to include anything that was, well, scary. This, though, is Renny Harlin's version and we should hear him out.

If Schrader's problem was restraint, then Harlin goes for broke with a murky, baroque atmosphere closer in texture to a Marilyn Manson video than William Friedkin's much-vaunted original. Cue a monstrous mishmash of rotten and rotting clichés, including blood-smeared walls, inversed crucifixes, slavering hyenas and rattling bedsteads. Harlin does achieve some arresting images amid the maggoty excess, and there is a suitably pestilent array of vile goings-on.

Alas, he also keeps hitting the CGI panic button and the film is afflicted with too many gratuitous, cheap shocks. Skarsgård manfully wrestles to maintain some dignity throughout the lurches of the barely re-animated storyline, and occasionally the ghost of what may have attracted the former director flits past: a loose parallel between the supernatural evil on show here and the more pragmatic wickedness of the Nazis.

However, it's just too much of a muddle, with whole scenes baring no explanation and whole actors looking like they've stumbled into the wrong movie (naming no names, Alan 'Snatch' Ford). As the film twists its tail like a demented serpent, you half expect Schrader to leap out – his complexion gone, literally, to hell – and yell, 'I told you so!' in that cough-drop snarl that's been the butt of too many parodies to be scary anymore. And they wouldn't even cough up for 'Tubular Bells' on the soundtrack, either. Boo, hiss all round. ★★ **IN**

DAS EXPERIMENT (2001)

Starring: *Moritz Bleibtreu (Tarek Fahd – Häftling Nr. 77/Prisoner #77), Christian Berkel (Steinhoff – Häftling Nr. 38/Prisoner #38), Oliver Stokowski (Schütte – Häftling Nr. 82/Prisoner #82), Wotan Wilke Möhring (Joe – Häftling Nr. 69/Prisoner #69) Stephan Szasz (Häftling Nr. 53/Prisoner #53), Polat Dal (Häftling Nr. 40/Prisoner #40),*
Director: *Oliver Hirschbiegel*
Screenwriters: *Mario Giordano, Christoph Darnstadt, Don Bohlinger, based on the novel* Black Box *by Mario Giordano*
18/119 mins./Drama/Thriller/Germany

Volunteers enter an underground facility and are asked to spend three weeks in a mock-up prison, playing out the randomly alotted roles of convicts and guards. But it soon becomes evident that the guards are taking their roles too seriously ...

Inspired by an actual 1971 experiment, this opens as cool, psychological drama. Undercover reporter Fahd needs the study to get out of hand to make his story sexier, so he needles mild-mannered 'guard' Berus, an incipient megalomaniac who eventually asserts his authority by imprisoning psychiatric staff who try to limit his power.

Claustrophobia and the opportunity for apparently consequence-free brutality turn the prisoners into shuffling wrecks and the guards into strutting thugs. A jolly Elvis impersonator becomes a bullying rapist, while a military man intent on quietly serving his time is forced to bond with Fahd to stage a jailbreak.

Echoing the mock-doc feel of *Blair Witch*, director Hirschbiegel takes his time with the set-up, cutting away to what seems at first the irrelevance of Fahd's new girlfriend on the outside, before delivering an unforgettably suspenseful second half. ★★★★★ **KN**

THE EXTERMINATING ANGEL (EL ANGEL EXTERMINADOR) (1962)

Starring: *Silva Pinal (Letitia – The Valkyrie), Jacqueline Andere (Senora Alicia Roc), Jose Baviera (Leandro), Augusto Benedico (Doctor), Antonio Bravo (Russell), Javier Masse (Eduardo)*
Director: *Luis Buñuel*
Screenwriter: *Luis Buñuel, Luis Alcoriza based on the play* Los Naufragos de la Calle de la Providentia *by Jose Bergamin*
12/92 mins./Comedy/Drama/Mexico

Repairing to the estate of a Mexican aristocrat after an evening's religious entertainment, a dinner party finds itself confined to a single room and, even though there seems to be nothing preventing them from leaving, they resort to increasingly primal instincts in order to survive.

Delighted by the furore created by *Viridiana*, Luis Buñuel embarked on this defiantly indecipherable satire, which was based on an idea he had harboured since 1940 and which had informed the unrealised short, The *Castaways of Calle Providencia*. However, it also bore the influence of Alain Resnais' *Last Year at Marienbad*, as it not only entrapped some bored bourgeois in a stylised setting, but also used repetition to disrupt the temporal flow and confuse the narrative logic.

Yet, as Buñuel insisted during the press conferences he gave around its release, this was a film that defied explanation and could best be defined as an accumulation of the images and ideas that had preoccupied and amused him since he'd created his Surrealist masterpieces, *Un Chien Andalou* and *L'Age d'Or*.

Certainly no attempt is made to explain why the guests prove incapable of leaving the drawing room, even though it's apparent to most of them that they are deteriorating mentally, physically and socially at an alarming rate. Russell (Bravo) dies and is crammed into the same cupboard as the suicidal lovers, Eduardo (Masse) and Beatriz (Montesco), while incestuous siblings Francisco (Loya) and Juana (Guilmain) steal morphine from a terminally ill companion, and Ana (Haro Oliva) goes into a trance and begins summoning demons. Besides such behaviour, urinating in urns, bashing holes in the wall to get at the water pipes and eating the sheep driven into the room by a bear acquired by Nobile (Rambal) the host for a post-prandial ruse seems positively normal.

Buñuel's intention is clearly to erode the veneer of civility that keeps the bourgeoisie from imploding and show how the very status, etiquette and ritual upon which their complacent privilege rests isolates them from the remainder of society and reduces them to inertia. But he's also keen to reveal both the bestial instincts that lurk beneath their smug sophistication and their inability to learn from their experiences, as the action closes with the survivors being unable to leave the local cathedral, while a riot erupts outside. ★★★★ **DP**

THE EYE (GIN GWAI) (2002)

Starring: *Angelica Lee (Wong Kar Mun), Lawrence Chou (Dr. Wah), Chutcha Rujinanon (Ling), Yut Lai So (Yingying), Candy Lo (Yee), Yin Ping Ko (Mun's grandmother), Pierre Png (Dr. Eak), Edmund Chen (Dr. Lo), Wai-Ho Yung (Mr. Ching), Wilson Yip (Taoist)*
Director: *Oxide Pang Chun, Danny Pang*
Screenwriters: *Jo Jo Yuet-Chun Hui Oxide Pang Chun, Danny Pang*
15/99 mins./Horror/Hong Kong/UK/Singapore

A young girl, blind from the age of two, has her sight restored with a cornea transplant, only to discover the unfortunate side-effect: the ability to see disgruntled spirits.

Remember the song 'Gary Gilmore's Eyes'? No? Well, the Pang brothers take The Adverts' minor punk classic and run with it, fashioning a truly unnerving tale from the idea that a blind girl, who receives an experimental cornea transplant, starts seeing more than she might care to.

Creepy as hell, *The Eye* makes *The Sixth Sense* look like *Ghostbusters*.

There is a touch of Irvin Kershner's *The Eyes Of Laura Mars* about the film, and comparisons with *The Sixth Sense* are inevitable, but the Pangs' stunning visual flourishes puts *The Eye* in a veritable class of its own.

Whilst their previous film, *Bangkok Dangerous*, was often in serious peril of swamping content with style, *The Eye* redresses the balance and delivers an intriguing and thoroughly menacing little tale.

It milks every aspect of cinema: special effects, camerawork, sound, music, editing. Hell, even the opening titles are ridiculously disturbing. One of the best horror movies of recent years. ★★★★ **AM**

ⓘ EYES WIDE SHUT (1999)

Starring: *Tom Cruise (Doctor William Harford), Nicole Kidman (Alice Harford), Sydney Pollack (Victor Zeigler), Marie Richardson (Marion), Rade Seberdzija (Milich), Alan Cumming (Desk Clerk)*
Director: *Stanley Kubrick*
Screenwriters: *Stanley Kubrick, Frederic Raphael, based on the novella* Traumnovelle *by Arthur Schnitzler*
18/160 mins./Drama/USA

Doctor Bill Harford appears to have the perfect marriage with his wife Alice. When she admits that she has been tempted to cheat on him, he is left reeling from shock, and goes out into the Manhattan night where he meets strange characters and sees another side of life.

As an epilogue to the career of Stanley Kubrick, who died aged 70, within days of delivering the finished film, *Eyes Wide Shut* is just about perfect in that it is unmistakably, definitely Kubrickian. Some will take that 'correctly' to mean it is intellectually intent, fastidiously crafted, directorially commanding and endlessly intriguing. Others, just as correctly, can read that as maddeningly portentous, laborious and remote.

Be aware that the film has been poorly served by advance speculation (most of the widely reported plot titbits prove wrong) and the overexposure of the juicy Tom and Nicole snog clip, an outrageous bit of trailer foreplay unconsummated in the event and giving the entirely erroneous impression that this film is a non-stop bonkfest. Naturally audiences obligingly stampeded first showings in the USA. Just as naturally, the box office tailed off noticeably as soon as word got round that Cruise doesn't actually get his kit off (although Kidman does, often), in what is not so much an erotic drama as a psychological probing of marriage, desire, jealousy and sexual paranoia. Adapted from Arthur Schnitzler's heavy *Dream Story*, this is about the reality of sexual love versus its illusions.

William Harford is a successful Manhattan doctor with a swank apartment, wealthy, demanding patients (including Sydney Pollack), and a lovely wife and child. Wife Alice ran an art gallery that went broke, leaving her too much time to get tipsy at parties, high on recreational pot and petulantly confrontational about a marriage that looks pretty enviable to mortal couples.

Aggrieved at being taken for granted, she picks a fight with her confident, comfortable husband, dropping a bombshell that rattles his security and sends him off into the night. In his subsequent dreamlike odyssey, he encounters a patient's daughter with a sad fixation to confide, a jazz musician with a bizarre story to tell, a costume hire shop where absurd nastiness goes on behind the racks, a streetwalker with whom he is at a loss ... All these things persuade Harford that everyone is having it off except him, while he's haunted by graphic images of his wife in flagrante.

The central set piece in his dissociative wanderings through this sinister world of secrets and sexual tension – where every location is ironically set off by a garish Christmas tree – is a mysterious, ritualistic gathering of masked swingers. The orgying (childishly 'digitally amended' in the USA to obscure close encounters of the pelvic kind) is explicit, but more theatrical than kinky, and in keeping with Schnitzler's perception of sexual adventure as a melancholy, hollow experience. The 'party' is both pretentiously bizarre and the single most striking sequence in the entire film, simultaneously evoking dream, pretence and illusion as remarkably vivid.

Cruise, as usual, was grossly underestimated in the early American reviews, with honours going to Kidman, whose character's disaffection gives her the opportunity for some showy rants. But it is Cruise, who is in virtually every scene, who lends the film an essential humanity. His palpably wounded male pride, pain and vulnerable bewilderment keep you connected to what is otherwise a cold, humourless, despairingly cynical (and thus typically Kubrickian) observation of human relationships. ★★★★ **AE**

⊙ F/X: MURDER BY ILLUSION (1986)

Starring: *Bryan Brown (Rollie Tyler), Brian Dennehy (Leo McCarthy), Diane Venora (Ellen), Cliff De Young (Lipton), Mason Adams (Col. Mason), Jerry Orbach (Nicholas De Franco)*
Director: *Robert Mandel*
Screenwriters: *Gregory Fleeman, Robert T. Megginson*
15/109 mins./Crime/Action/USA

Special makeup effects ace Rollie Tyler is hired by a government agent to fake the death of a mafia boss who is about to turn states' evidence. However, everyone is playing a double game and Rollie finds himself on the run, pursued by cops who think he's a killer and spies who want to dispose of him before he can incriminate them.

A neat little thriller, directed by Robert Mandel – who has spent most of his subsequent career in television (*The X-Files, Lost*). It doesn't have the big explosions and flip wisecracks of a typical '80s action picture, preferring to explore a high concept: the hero is a special effects technician – a veteran of *I Dismember Mama, Blood in the Basement* and *Vermin From Venus* – who finds himself in the middle of a twisty mystery where his deceptive skills come in handy.

Very cannily, the script starts out a shade predictably, with De Young's smooth-suited but incipiently twitchy federal agent an obviously duplicitous villain, lulling the audience into thinking the plot will fall obviously like a row of dominoes. Then, a few real shocks and surprises come along, taking the story into unexpected areas, though one development curtails the welcome performance of the underrated Diane Venora as the hero's girlfriend.

Bryan Brown is a relaxed, charismatic protagonist, credibly ordinary enough to be imperilled but with a twinkle in his eye as he realises how he can turn the tables. Turning up half way through the film, Brian Dennehy adds a much-needed touch of weary comedy as a seedy homicide detective who reluctantly teams with the hero.

The exciting, satisfying finale pits the effects man and his bag of tricks against a houseful of heavily-armed bad guys. Brown and Dennehy returned in a solid if unspectacular sequel directed by Richard Franklin, *F/X2* (1991). ★★★ **KN**

⊙ THE FABULOUS BAKER BOYS (1989)

Starring: *Jeff Bridges (Jack Baker), Michelle Pfeiffer (Susie Diamond), Beau Bridges (Frank Baker), Ellie Raab (Nina), Xander Berkeley (Lloyd)*
Director: *Steven Kloves*
Screenwriter: *Steven Kloves*
15/114 mins./Drama/USA

Awards: *BAFTA – Best Sound*

Two fading club musicians, Jack and Frank Baker, decide to spruce up their act by taking on sexy singer Susie Diamond. The act immediately takes off, but the growing affection between Jack and Susie threatens to destroy the entire group.

The pedigree of Steven Kloves' silken drama can be found among the smoky dives, the drafty aftermaths of weddings and club shows of the Baker Boys' act; the film is infected with faded hope, of lives turned to the faltering patter of the ordinary. These guys, not without talent, are resting at the moment their dream finally dies. And in walks Michelle Pfeiffer. If there's anything sure to give a guy a jolt it's that, and Kloves knows it. The sequence of auditions, as the irritable brothers yawn and pout over the procession of no-marks, is the perfect prelude. When Susie bursts in an hour and a half late, she is so forthright they virtually sit up and beg. When she sings, with a husky, dirty, spellbinding voice (entirely Pfeiffer's own) they, and us, are love struck.

The film, with its cool, jazzy ballads played outright, flirts with the tempo of a musical, but is too sultry for that. It moves to the slovenly, lovely drift of Susie's body, the spell she weaves on this cranky double-act. Her immaculate version of 'Makin' Whoopee' sprawled alluringly across Jack's piano top is a classic moment, and that they break out in a rash of desire was as inevitable as nightfall.

This, however, is only the touch paper for the real explosion in the film, the simmering rivalry between the brothers, the unspoken needle that Jack is a whole lot more talented than Frank (and echoed by the relative success of the fabulous Bridges boys) that must out. Their performances, perhaps more than Pfeiffer's swooning (she has the showy part), humming with petty prejudice and deep dependence, are the soul of the movie. It is a love story, but one about realising what you have, not what you've lost or gained. ★★★★ IN

FACE (1997)

Starring: *Robert Carlyle (Ray), Ray Winstone (Dave), Steven Waddington (Stevie), Julian (Philip Davis), Steve Sweeney (Weasal), Damon Albarn (Jason), Gerry Conlon (Vince), Leon Black (Robbie), Lena Heady (Connie)*
Director: *Antonia Bird*
Screenwriter: *Ronan Bennett*
18/110 mins./Crime/UK

A gang of ageing bank robbers, led by former idealist Ray, unite for one last job, but growing recriminations within the group could be the ruin of them all.

Movie heists are configured to go wrong, it's a fact of film lore. But here Antonia Bird and her screenwriter, sometime novelist Ronan Bennett, are aiming to plant a political subtext into this hoariest of thriller tenets. Ray, Robert Carlyle's resolute leader whose plan it is to raid a security firm depot, is a disillusioned socialist who has turned to crime to kick back at a system that has crushed his ideals. And the working class lives of his fellow villains, are shown shorn of glamour, a clutch of miserable, needy crooks oppressed by years of Thatcherism.

Fair enough, Brit crime films have often thrived with political underpinnings, both *The Long Good Friday* and *Get Carter* ponder the ills of capitalism, but here it is too deliberate. Even Gerry Conlon, the real man falsely imprisoned for the Guilford pub bombings (as depicted in *In The Name Of The Father*) turns up for an early cameo to add another layer of credence to their right-on credentials.

But it soon becomes apparent the political definition is not matched by depth anywhere else. *Face* is all surface, where Ray Winstone's Dave is yet another hard-nosed East End villain, and Philip Davies the inevitable nutjob in the pack. All hell is about to break lose when he gets greedy, a fact that could be read as anti-capitalist, but really is just a thumping great cliché. Things are going to get bloody, Antonia has seen *Reservoir Dogs*, there's a traitor in the group.

To grant it some latitude, the heist sequence is mounted with stunning ferocity, a pumping sense of the pure adrenaline rush of high crime, but when the haul turns out smaller than expected they just set about one another with foul mouths and crowbars. The guys are good enough actors, urgently trying to push roles they've been played to death somewhere new (Steven Waddington does a brave job with another age-old trope, the worried simpleton, and Damon Albarn doesn't embarrass himself) but in the clamour of the film's furious second half logic and nuance get smothered in implacable violence. There's an inventive twist as the remaining gang members attempt to reclaim the loot that has been stolen and ended up in a police station, but this remains the same old same old. ★★★ IN

FACE/OFF (1997)

Starring: *John Travolta (Sean Archer), Nicolas Cage (Caster Troy), Joan Allen (Eve Archer), Alessandro Nivola (Pollux Troy), Gina Gershon (Sasha Hassler), Dominique Swain (Jamie Archer)*
Director: *John Woo*
Screenwriters: *Mike Werb, Michael Colleary*
18/139 mins./Action/Crime/Sci-fi/USA

In order to discover the location of a ticking bomb somewhere in Los Angeles, cop Sean Archer undergoes a revolutionary face-swapping procedure with comatose bad egg Castor Troy. However, when Troy wakes up, he turns the tables, and assumes Archer's identity, setting the scene for a showdown between them.

A little modern movie history. In 1988 John McTiernan stuck Bruce Willis in a skyscraper, penned a few witty one-liners, distilled his plot to 100 per cent proof high concept and bought a lot of big fireworks. The result, *Die Hard*, signalled the birth of one of the most successful sub-genres of all time – the modern actioner (essentially anything to which the dismally overworked coda 'high octane' can be attached).

For the last decade or so everything in that genre has been living on its legacy – and things had started to look jaded. Until *Face/Off*. Because with *Face/Off*, ex-Hong Kong director John Woo has given the whole shooting match a much needed kick in the squibs.

John Travolta is Sean Archer, head of a covert FBI counter terrorism agency on the trail of psychotic terrormeister Castor Troy (Cage), who has planted a bomb set to detonate after he has made his getaway and reduce the population of Los Angeles to one less than, er, one. Unfortunately, in the opening firefight Archer nixes said nutcase and, with no idea where the ticking device is, takes the 'obvious' option. He has Troy's face sliced off and glued to his noggin while his own visage resides in a jar.

Needless to say such an opportunity for a concept so high you need oxygen to climb it cannot fail to be carried through and sure enough Cage, not dead after all, wakes up and appropriates Travolta's visage. The world, including Travolta's apple pie family and bosses, thinks one is the other, Travolta is slung into a futuristic version of Wormwood Scrubs while Cage porks his wife, ogles his daughter, and plans to take over the world, or at least Southern California.

It is, of course, beyond ludicrous. But Woo's strength is to positively revel in the unlikeliness of his conceit. In one of the plethora of memorable scenes Travolta (as Cage) breaks down in front of his confused wife and howls with hysterical laughter at the predicament he's in. Equally Cage (as Travolta) is not beyond dipping his toes in the self-referential water – 'This ridiculous chin . . .' he moans.

But if the knowing sharpness of the script is one strength, the action sequences – which simply set a new benchmark – are another. Shoot-outs are choreographed with the precision of a 40s musical number (quite literally in one astounding firefight, played out to the strains of 'Somewhere Over The Rainbow'), car chases assume a new intensity when jets and helicopters drift casually into shot and the final boat sequence features a shot of the two leads being hurled through the air that will leave audiences gasping.

Added to which are the performances from Travolta and Cage who try deliriously to out-do each other's lunatic badness when they get the Castor Troy role (Cage just pipping Travolta with the scene where, dressed as a priest after planting his bomb, he dances through the LA Conference Centre to the strains of the 'Hallelujah Chorus', lewdly harassing a girl in the choir singing it).

Woo's triumph, then, is to finally have realised the American-sized budget Hong Kong actioner. While *Broken Arrow* and *Hard Target* had moments of the director's inimitable style – essentially a willingness to use any and every filmic trick, especially his beloved slo mo – *Face/Off* has Woo written through it like a stick of rock. ★★★★★ IN

THE FACULTY (1998)

Starring: *Jordana Brewster (Delilah Profitt), Clea DuVall (Stokely 'Stokes' Mitchell), Josh Hartnett (Zeke Tyler), Salma Hayek (Nurse Rosa Harper), Famke Janssen (Miss Elizabeth Burke), Piper Laurie (Mrs. Karen Olson), Bebe Neuwirth (Principal Valerie Drake), Robert Patrick (Coach Joe Willis), Jon Stewart (Prof. Edward Furlong)*
Director: *Robert Rodriguez*
Screenwriter: *Kevin Williamson, based on a story by David Wechter, Bruce Kimmel*
15/104 mins./Comedy/Horror/Sci-fi/USA

A group of teenage school stereotypes find that their teachers are aliens that drain humans dry to live. As the alien epidemic spreads, so does the paranoia, which leaves the teens believing the monster-maker could be close in their midst.

Pitching a concept so high – *Invasion Of The Body Snatchers* meets John Hughes' back catalogue – it needs clearance in international airspace, this mind meld between guerrilla godhead Robert Rodriguez (*Desperado/From Dusk Till Dawn*) and slasher sultan Kevin Williamson (*Scream*) cannily proffers double-barrelled entertainment; for the Clearasil set, this is simply attractive eye candy fending off numerous schlock tactics; for anyone old enough to fondly remember Anthony Michael Hall, however, *The Faculty* becomes a blatant mixture of affectionate teen satire and sci-fi cliché that enjoyably reinforces how much you know about movies.

The plotting zeroes in on a group of school stereotypes – egghead Casey, black-clad misfit Stokely, wise-ass drug pusher Zeke, student mag ed Delilah, doubting jock Stan and Southern belle new gal Mary Beth – who discover the teaching staff in their run down high school have been taken over by squid-like alien parasites that drain humans dry to live. As the epidemic spreads into other students, family, the police, Rodriguez tangibly builds up the growing paranoia (in a fantastic comedic replay of *The Thing*'s blood test scene, the teens snort homemade nose candy to flush out the alien host), before piling on bizarro gore (punctured eyeballs, skin crawling worms, heads sprouting legs, gallons of pus) as the group discovers that the producer of the morphing monsters could come from within their number.

Despite never delivering on the promise engendered by the Rodriguez-Williamson pairing, this is corny, queasy, quick-witted fun. All the teens turn in engaging, likeable performances with Duvall and Hartnett emerging as standouts. Equally entertaining are the adroitly cast adults; Rodriguez fave Salma Hayek (throwing off the sex bomb mantle to assay a flu-stricken nurse), Robert Patrick (playing hardnut football coach) and Famke Janssen (turning heads as a predatory English teacher) all have gleeful fun as the shapeshifting educators.

The showy staples of Williamson's writing still shine through – the youngsters' familiarity with the movie rules of engagement, up-to-the-minute injokery (Zeke peddles nude video tapes of Jennifer Love Hewitt and Neve Campbell), the confidence in the audience's cine-knowledge to supplant characterisation and story detail – yet the plotting and placing lacks the assurity, invention and momentum to deliver the requisite adrenaline rush. Moreover, never really nailing the correct mix of irony and horror, Rodriguez's direction is devoid of its usual full-on fizz and manic excess. Perhaps surprisingly, he seems very much at home with the adolescent comedy aspects – the High School hierarchies and teen torments are knowingly etched, the dispirit in the underfunded establishment is humorously spot on. But he is less comfortable with the action, and is over-reliant on big CGI set pieces. For a film that should have detailed the ultimate in teen rebellion, perhaps what's missing is a real sense of anarchy. **★★★★ IF**

FAHRENHEIT 451 (1966)

Starring: *Oskar Werner (Montag), Julie Christie (Linda/Clarisse), Cyril Cusack (Captain), Anton Diffring (Fabian), Jeremy Spenser (Man With Apple), Bee Duffell (Book Woman)*
Director: *François Truffaut*
Screenwriters: *François Truffault, Jean-Louis Richard, David Rudkin, Helen Scott, based on a novel by Ray Bradbury*
12/112 mins./Sci-fi/UK

Guy Montag is a firefighter who lives in a lonely, isolated society where books have been outlawed by a government fearing an independent-thinking public. It is the duty of firefighters to burn any books on sight or said collections that have been reported by informants. After Montag falls in love with book-hoarding Clarisse, he begins to read confiscated books.

While Isaac Asimov, A.E. Van Vogt and Robert Heinlein were happy to sell to *Amazing Stories* or *The Magazine Of Fantasy* and *Science Fiction*, Ray Bradbury was appearing in *The Saturday Evening Post*. His contemporaries were lucky to meet the geeks at sci-fi conventions and be plagiarised as tacky Z-features (Heinlein's *The Puppet Masters* was ripped off as *The Brain Eaters*), but Bradbury attracted serious literary attention for collections like *The Martian Chronicles* and *The Illustrated Man*. The film of his 1953 novel *Fahrenheit 451* was directed by no less than François Truffaut.

Perhaps because it was his first film in English and he suffered a major falling-out with his *Jules Et Jim* star Oskar Werner during production, but Truffaut himself was never very fond of *Fahrenheit 451*. Most people who have written about it find it a hard movie to like, either because they feel the sci-fi elements let down Truffaut's humanist vision or because the director doesn't stick closely enough to Bradbury's. One piece of acute criticism came from George Bluestone, who noted that Truffaut could never quite work up the horror necessary to convey Bradbury's nightmare vision of a bibliophile society because, for him, the cinema was the sacred art/entertainment form.

He would have made a much more passionate film if the premise had been a world which banned and burned movies (we do glimpse *Cahiers du Cinéma* and Chaplin's autobiography going up in flames along with Sartre, Nabokov, Dickens and *MAD Magazine*). Bradbury's novel, like George Orwell's similarly-plotted *Nineteen Eighty-Four*, is less a credible depiction of a future society than it is an allegorical satire on the present. This means that its points about McCarthyism or 1950s vulgarity are well-taken, but a film adaptation has to take seriously a story that never really tries to be credible. Clearly, a fascist society based on the suppression of books is a ridiculous premise – totalitarian governments take mass media over rather than take them away.

Why does everyone in this book-hating world learn to read? How does a book-hating fireman know the names of famous authors? What about songs or plays? Who writes the scripts for the banal soap operas? And how come it is so easy to leave the city and escape to join the rebels in the idyllic countryside? – an influential non-ending followed by George Lucas' *THX-1138*, *Blade Runner* and the film of *The Handmaid's Tale*. Nevertheless, the film has a quiet creepiness that remains effective even though its future vision looks almost quaint now with its 1966 sparkliness (courtesy of cinematographer Nicolas Roeg).

There is a hint in the double-casting of Julie Christie as fireman Montag's pill-popping zombie wife Linda and the crop-haired rebel teacher Clarisse (echoed by the more audacious dual role longtime movie Nazi Anton Diffring takes as Montag's nastiest fireman comrade and Clarisse's collaborationist headmistress) that we are not supposed to take everything we see literally. The best aspects of this horrid world are shown with a satirical streak that prefigures Terry Gilliam's *Brazil*: the ambulance men who talk like plumbers and call round to calmly pump the wife out after a drugs overdose; the pillar-box red fire station with a trundling fire engine that whisks flamethrower-wielding, black-clad firemen off to start blazes of books; the dissidents who are given away because their house features no actual television aerial.

Werner may be stiff in the Winston Smith role, but Christie is interesting twice, and Bee Duffell has a great cameo as the woman who'd rather burn herself than live without her books. The finale, after Montag has rebelled by turning his flamethrower on his boss, is also more poetic than believable, as the hero joins a country commune of 'Book People', who have devoted their lives to memorising their favourite texts (Montag chooses *Tales Of Mystery And Imagination* by Edgar Allan Poe). The image of these muttering souls milling around in the snow is indelible, at once absurd and touching, acknowledging the bleakness of the present but expressing hope for the future. **★★★★ KN**

⦿ FAHRENHEIT 9/11 (2004)

Director: *Michael Moore*
Screenwriter: *Michael Moore*
15/116 mins./Documentary/Political/USA

Awards: *Razzie Awards – Worst Actor (George Bush), Worst Screen Couple (George W. Bush, Condoleezza Rice), Worst Supporting Actor (Donald Rumsfeld), Worst Supporting Actress (Britney Spears)*

Crusading documentary filmmaker Michael Moore explores the 'fixing' of the 2000 presidential elections, the Bush family's links with Saudi Arabia and the aftermath of the 2001 attacks on the World Trade Center . . .

If the devil's greatest trick was to convince mankind he didn't exist, Michael Moore went one better, convincing us that he was the most dangerous man in the universe on the basis of just six reels of film. *Fahrenheit 9/11* arrived in Cannes as the most incendiary movie ever made. Disney forced Miramax to drop it! It didn't have a US distributor!

The small print told a different story. Miramax knew from Day One that Disney's governing board couldn't release such a partisan film in election year. And as for the reason why it didn't have a distributor: could it simply have been down to the fact that Miramax was kicking up a fuss, exaggerating the need to see it and hiking up the price accordingly?

Moore's previous film, *Bowling For Columbine*, didn't exactly bode well; after a terrific first hour it slipped slyly into an ego trip, culminating in staged footage of Moore confronting the National Rifle Association's confused spokesman, Charlton Heston, in his own home. That's not journalism, that's just plain rude, so how would Moore face down the President of the United States? Walk up to the White House and shit on his doorstep, while waving a big sign that says, 'YOU ARE A C**T'?

Fortunately, Moore is smarter than that. *Fahrenheit 9/11* reveals in its first moments that he has become much more comfortable with his materials and that he knows very well his grinning mug isn't enough to swing this one. So for the bulk of its running time Moore acts mostly as a simple narrator, relishing his own scathing prose as he spins a yarn very similar to the opening chapters of last year's bestseller, *Dude Where's My Country?* And it's here that the film works best; piling up facts and figures that paint an uncanny picture of a war based on a lie propagated by a regime founded on an injustice.

The figurehead for this is George W. Bush, portrayed as a simpleton playboy groomed for the job by his old man's cronies. For Moore, this is exquisite payback for a moment when he and Bush came face-to-face for the first and only time. 'Behave yourself, will you?' sneered Bush. 'Go find real work.' And so much of this film is Moore's sarcastic reply. Real work? Like being declared President after a rigged election, decided in a state governed by your brother, then spending the first 42 per cent of your initial eight months in office on holiday? It's a testimony to Dubya's idiocy that Moore doesn't have to try too hard to make him look inept.

Moore's greatest achievement is the handling of 9/11 itself, rendered on a black screen with sound effects, followed by reaction shots of the stunned crowds nearby. He doesn't milk it, leaving you to your own revulsion at the sight of Bush sitting helplessly in a Florida schoolroom for a full seven minutes after the second plane hit the World Trade Center. This is the film's smoking gun; the unforgettable moment. After this it wavers somewhat, sidetracking itself with the vagaries of the War On Terror before settling on Iraq and the human rights abuses there.

Showmanship it may be, and in the wake of the Abu Ghraib prison scandal, the anti-war lobby is not so hard to impress, but this is still passionate filmmaking with a strong, idiosyncratic voice. It may not pose all the questions or find all the answers, but it's hard to deny Moore its right to be seen right here, right now. ★★★★ **CK**

⦿ FAIL-SAFE (1964)

Starring: *Dan O'Herlihy (Gen. Black), Walter Matthau (Groeteschele), Frank Overton (Gen. Bogan), Edward Binns (Col. Grady), Fritz Weaver (Col. Cascio), Henry Fonda (The President), Larry Hagman (Buck)*
Director: *Sidney Lumet*
Screenwriter: *Walter Bernstein, based on the novel by Eugene Burdick and Harvey Wheeler*
PG/111 mins./Drama/USA

Computer error sends a flight of bombers to attack the USSR. The President tries to avert all-out nuclear war, and is forced to make a great sacrifice to save the world.

Overlooked in 1964 because it played straight the nightmare scenario which had just been turned into comedy by Stanley Kubrick in *Dr. Strangelove*, this adaptation of the Eugene Burdick/Harvey Wheeler bestseller is still an impressive and disturbing brink-of-doom thriller.

Inevitably, *Fail-Safe* rings less true than *Strangelove* by insisting on a dignified, humane, liberal response to a situation that more aptly produces horror, hysteria and biting misanthropy, but Sidney Lumet has a knack of wringing suspense from scenes in which men in suits or uniforms sit or stand around indoors exchanging pointed dialogue. Fonda is the ideal image of what a US President should be like, and a large supporting cast includes pointed turns from Walter Matthau as a Strangelovian doomsday theorist ('these are not normal people, these are Marxist fanatics') and future funnyman Dom DeLuise as the technician heartbroken at being ordered to share vital information with the Soviets. The (understandable) withholding of US defence department co-operation means that minimal amounts of stock-footage had to be processed, used in repeated shots or even negative, to convey the far-off front line where the war is close to breaking out.

It's technically very innovative: General Dan O'Herlihy's Sarah Connor-like holocaust dreams and the minimalist destructions of major cities (unforgettably conveyed by the whine heard on the hot line when the telephone at the other end disintegrates) seem the sort of bold strokes you'd expect from a contemporary cutting edge director rather than a major 1960s motion picture. Remade interestingly as a live TV drama by Stephen Frears in 2000, with Harvey Keitel, George Clooney and Richard Dreyfuss. ★★★★ **KN**

⦿ FAILURE TO LAUNCH (2005)

Starring: *Matthew McConaughey (Tripp), Sarah Jessica Parker (Paula), Zooey Deschanel (Kit), Justin Bartha (Ace), Bradley Cooper (Demo)*
Director: *Tom Dey*
Screenwriters: *Tom J. Astle, Matt Ember*
12A/96 mins./Comedy/Romance/USA

Tripp is a 35 year-old who, despite having a successful career and a way with women, has yet to move out of his parents' home. As a last resort, his folks hire a woman whose job involves getting men to finally fly the nest. However, her latest client proves a tougher challenge than she thought, especially when romance rears its head.

Over the past few years, the perennial rom-coms that sprout in spring have become so identikit and formulaic that at times it's impossible to tell which one you're actually watching. Thus we have *Failure To Launch*, which comes along to fill the slot recently occupied by *Along Came Polly*, *Meet The Fockers* and countless others – the difference being that this one's just a tad sharper and sassier than most.

Where it succeeds is in a quirky, eccentric supporting cast who look like they're genuinely enjoying themselves – leaving the blander headline stars to play out the all-too-predictable romance bit. Deschanel is a delight as Parker's kooky roommate, who's plagued by a mockingbird that's as rooted to the tree outside her window as McConaughey's protagonist is to his parents' home. And, as Tripp's long-suffering folks, Bates and Bradshaw make for an appealing double-act.

Its main stumbling block, however, is McConaughey himself, who doesn't come across as a natural comedian – at times you find yourself wishing for Owen Wilson. But the film's uneven first half soon gives way to a likeable enough comedy which, while ultimately forgettable, fulfils its potential as acceptable date movie fare. ★★★ **CW**

◎ THE FALL OF THE HOUSE OF USHER (1960)

Starring: *Vincent Price (Roderick Usher), Mark Damon (Phillip Winthrop), Myrna Fahey (Madeline Usher), Harry Ellerbe (Bristol), Eleanor LeFaber (Ghost), Ruth Okander (Ghost), Geraldine Paulette (Ghost)*
Director: *Roger Corman*
Screenwriter: *Richard Matheson based on the story by Edgar Allan Poe*
15/79 mins./Horror/USA

Philip Winthrop tracks his missing fiancée Madeline to the decaying mansion where she is under the influence of her doom-haunted brother Roderick Usher.

With this 1960 film, released as *The House of Usher* in the States, Roger Corman persuaded Sam Arkoff and James H. Nicholson, cost-conscious heads of American International Pictures, to combine the budgets which would have covered two of the black and white monster pictures he had been making in the 1950s in order to make one colourful, decadent, widescreen gothic.

Screenwriter Richard Matheson imaginatively elaborates on Edgar Allan Poe's famous (and out of copyright) tale, and Vincent Price brings just the right degree of refined camp to his white-haired, velvet-jacketed antihero. Later, Price would be overly prone to winking at the audience, but here he plays it close to straight as the hyper-sensitive Roderick, who can hear every scratching rat in the walls of the house and the beating of his entombed sister's heart.

The plot covers burial alive, incest, monomania, a family curse and sadism, but the film is a masterly exercise in sustained weird atmosphere. Actually, four characters spend the whole film glooming around the vast interior of the decaying mansion, awaiting a last-reel fire which brings the roof down on their heads as the maddened Madeline rises from the tomb to drag her brother into the flames.

A major commercial success, this established a format which would serve Corman, Poe and Price for five years' worth of similar classics: *Pit and the Pendulum, Tales of Terror, The Haunted Palace, Masque of the Red Death, Tomb of Ligeia*. Beware pan&scan TV prints, and insist on the correct aspect ratio: Corman and cinematographer Floyd Crosby were masters at using the whole of the widescreen oblong, with off-centre compositions and nervous tracking shots that convey the sense that things are terribly wrong in this old house. ★★★★ **KN**

◎ FALLEN ANGELS (DUO LUO TIAN SHI) (1995)

Starring: *Leon Lai (Wong Chi-Ming – the Killer), Michelle Reis (The Agent), Karen Mok (Baby), Takeshi Kaneshiro (He Zhiwu), Charlie Young (Charlie), Toru Saito (Sato – the Manager), Chen Man Lei (Father)*
Director: *Kar Wai Wong*
Screenwriter: *Kar Wai Wong*
18/96 mins./Drama/Crime/Comedy/Hong Kong

A disillusioned assassin is on his last job, and is experiencing distinctly unprofessional feelings for his partner. Not wishing to give in to temptation, he sets out to find a surrogate for his affections, and meets some strange characters on the way.

The fifth feature from writer-director Kar-Wai Wong, who has been picking up awards and friends (such as Quentin Tarantino) ever since his 1988 debut *As Tears Go By*, this follows hot on the heels of *Chungking Express* and echoes much of its predecessor's style – 99 per cent shot on hand-held cameras, pop promo-style action sequences, with loosely connected characters in garish Hong Kong nightscapes moving in and out of bars and fast-food parlours as their lives meet but never quite entwine.

The central character, the assassin, wants a new life with his partner-in-crime Agent but instead employs a jukebox lyric to tell her goodbye and takes up with the live-for-the-minute Punkie after a chance encounter.

All this is punctuated by outbursts of brutal gunplay but, unlike *Chungking*, has little in the way of humour – notwithstanding mute ex-con Ho who pesters his father with a video camera and breaks into various shops then kidnaps people as his 'customers', including one poor soul he tries to shave and later drags inside an ice-cream van he has hijacked forcing him to eat and eat and eat.

Ho's antics are small reward, however, for enduring the overall sense of frustration that the characters all share, and chasing after them along Hong Kong's labyrinthine back streets. ★★ **NJ**

◎ FALLING DOWN (1993)

Starring: *Michael Douglas (William 'D-Fens' Foster), Robert Duvall (Detective Martin Prendergast), Tuesday Weld (Amanda Prendergast), Frederic Forrest (Nick, Surplus Store Owner)*
Director: *Joel Schumacher*
Screenwriter: *Ebbe Roe Smith*
18/113 mins./Crime/Drama/Thriller/USA

On a sweltering L.A. day, mild family man 'D-Fens' decides to take revenge on urban America after his car breaks down on the freeway.

'I'm going home,' states William (a.k.a. D-Fens, a.k.a. Michael Douglas) at the beginning of *Falling Down*, finally abandoning his car when the heat, frustration and sheer crapness of being stuck in an L.A. freeway gridlock overwhelms him.

The big problem for D-Fens (so called because he works in the defence industry: 'making America safe') is that, if truth be told, traffic jams are the least of it. Modern urban living adds up to a nightmare combination of gang warfare, immigrants who can't speak your language, burger joints from hell, rich bastards hoarding the best bits for themselves, unbridled selfishness and dark, depressing squalor.

And today, on his walk back home to Venice Beach from the freeway, he is not going to take it any more. Running like a California Tourist Officer's nightmare (the best credit? 'Annoying Man At Phone Booth' or possibly 'Kid With Missile Launcher'), this then proceeds like a cross between *Death Wish* and a Sergio Leone movie, with D-Fens encountering each urban irritation with a combination of long-suffering wit and machine-gun fire. A Korean shopkeeper, refusing to change a dollar for the phone, gets his shop smashed to pieces; a gang of Hispanic youths receive a taste of their own Uzi-power; and a startled burger vendor (played by Michelle Pfeiffer's sister, fact fans) is offered the option between serving breakfast and death.

Meanwhile, at the local precinct, Robert Duvall is on his very last day as a cop, deciding that the successful nailing of this fanatic would finish his career on a suitably upbeat note. Director Schumacher and screenwriter Ebbe Roe Smith are on frighteningly thin ideological ice here, of course, and their response is disappointingly cack-handed. Is the guy a fascist? Can't be: the only person he deliberately kills is a caricature of a sadistic Nazi. Is he a vigilante? Can't be: he actually says, 'I am not a vigilante.' Is he a racist? Can't be: he gives rich, white scum just as much grief as he does poor, black scum.

Schumacher, of course, is not renowned for his lightness of touch, but the obvious terror he feels at being labelled ideologically unsound does begin to grate after a time – a terror strangely not tempering the mildly misogynistic glee with which hen-pecked husband Duvall finally gives his wife an earful of abuse. Despite these reservations, this is a remarkably tense thriller and a thumping good story – like *The Swimmer*, which it often resembles, it manages to avoid the 'and then' factor that so often mars these episodic tales, largely by deftly cutting between D-Fens' antics, Duvall's last day at the office and the loony's wife (Hershey) at home in Venice with their young girl. It is also far and away Schumacher's best movie, and proves yet again that Michael Douglas, alone among the Hollywood A-list, is a genuine risk-taker. ★★★★ **PT**

Tagline
The adventures of an ordinary man at war with the everyday world.

FAMILY PLOT (1976)

Starring: *Karen Black (Fran), Bruce Dern (Lumley), Barbara Harris (Blanche), William Devane (Adamson), Ed Lauter (Maloney), Cathleen Nesbitt (Julia Rainbird)*
Director: *Alfred Hitchcock*
Screenwriter: *Ernest Lehman from the novel* The Rainbird Pattern *by Victor Canning*
PG/120 mins./Thriller/USA

Fake medium Blanche and her sidekick Lumley stumble on to a murderous plot hatched by an oleaginous jeweller named Adamson and his mistress of disguise, Fran.

Fifty years after he made his directorial debut with *The Pleasure Garden*, Alfred Hitchcock embarked on his final picture. It was somewhat apt that he transferred the action of Victor Canning's novel, *The Rainbird Pattern*, from the English countryside to California, as it symbolically marked his own journey from Leytonstone to Los Angeles.

The hunt for a missing person was a classic Hitchcock scenario and Barbara Harris and Bruce Dern's search for Eddie Shoebridge recalls the pursuits undertaken by Robert Donat in *The 39 Steps*, Michael Redgrave and Margaret Lockwood in *The Lady Vanishes*, James Stewart in *Vertigo*, Cary Grant in *North By Northwest* and Vera Miles in *Psycho*. The latter film's obsession with the influence of the dead over the living also recurs in Family Plot, as it had previously informed *Notorious* and *The Trouble With Harry*.

Karen Black's confession that she feels a sexual charge when either kidnapping her victims or collecting the diamonds that she and William Devane demand as ransom echoes the attitudes of Grace Kelly, Janet Leigh and Tippi Hedren towards illegality in *To Catch a Thief*, *Psycho* and *Marnie*. Moreover the latter shares *Family Plot*'s preoccupation with a fateful childhood occurrence, a plotline that had its antecedants in *Downhill* and *Spellbound*.

What was unique for a Hitchcock narrative, however, was the decision to take two seemingly unconnected stories and allow them to run parallel for much of the action before allowing them to converge. Hitch always insisted on warning his audience about what was going to happen, as he preferred to keep them in suspense waiting for the inevitable rather than shock them with the unexpected. But by playing out Harris and Dern's mission to locate a long-lost heir in a different plane to Black and Devane's abduction racket, Hitchcock was able to coax the viewer into jumping to their own conclusions, which he then proceeded to confound. ★★★ **DP**

THE FAMILY STONE (2005)

Starring: *Claire Danes (Julie Morton), Diane Keaton (Sybil Stone), Rachel McAdams (Amy Stone), Dermot Mulroney (Everett Stone), Craig T. Nelson (Kelly Stone), Sarah Jessica Parker (Meredith Morton), Luke Wilson (Ben Stone)*
Director: *Thomas Bezucha*
Screenwriter: *Thomas Bezucha*
PG/102 mins./Comedy/Drama/USA

Christmas at the Stone family home is a time for laughter, joy and liberal values – until eldest son Everett brings Meredith, his tightly wound girlfriend, home for the holidays. Younger brother Ben's crush on her, and the attraction between Everett and Meredith's sister Julie, add further complications.

Spending what Americans call 'the holidays' with one's own family can be traumatic enough, so it's a bit odd that anyone would want to torture themselves further by seeing movies about other people's Christmas or Thanksgiving gatherings. A decade ago, Jodie Foster assembled an eclectic cast (including, coincidentally, Claire Danes) for the hit-and-miss comedy drama *Home For The Holidays*; Thomas Bezucha aims for much the same territory with his sophomore effort as writer-director – and manages to score more hits than misses.

The Family Stone comprises bohemian parents Sybil and Kelly, devoted daughters Amy and Susannah, and three sons: a deaf gay (Tyrone Giordano) with a black boyfriend (Brian White), a feckless stoner (Luke Wilson), and an uptight businessman, Everett, whose new girlfriend rubs everyone up the wrong way from the moment she brings her uptight, Upper-West-Side attitude to the vast New England family home. The family is so close-knit, poor Meredith is virtually doomed before she steps out of the car, watched by the crowd at the kitchen window. For all their tolerant values and political correctness, the Stones have mercilessly pre-judged Meredith – much to the annoyance of Everett, who has marriage in mind.

It's a recipe with ingredients taken from everything from *Meet The Fockers* to *Sweet Home Alabama*. But Bezucha is thankfully less concerned with exploring familiar fish-out of-water themes than breathing life into multi-faceted, flawed characters, who reveal new complexities as the story progresses. Likewise, his commendable script is mostly successful at juggling elements of comedy, drama, romance, and even trickier prospects such as poignancy and farce.

Only twice does the film stretch credibility, and thus patience: first, when Meredith finally frees her 'inner freak' after a few beers with Luke Wilson's affable Ben; and later, when the arrival of her down-to-earth sister Julie sends the plot in yet another direction. And, talking of direction, Bezucha's is far less technically assured than his writing, but the uniformly high quality of the performances – Keaton and Parker in particular – smooths over the cracks. ★★★ **GH**

THE FAN (1996)

Starring: *Robert De Niro (Gil Renard), Wesley Snipes (Bobby Rayburn), Ellen Barkin (Jewel Stern), John Leguizamo (Manny), Benicio Del Toro (Juan Primo)*
Director: *Tony Scott*
Screenwriter: *Phoef Sutton, based on the book by Peter Abrahams*
15/116 mins./Thriller/USA

An all star baseball player becomes the unhealthy focus of a down-on-his-luck salesman.

Robert De Niro has, over the years, got the psycho act down to a series of chillingly controlled performances: think Travis Bickle in *Taxi Driver*, Jake LaMotta in *Raging Bull*, Al Capone in *The Untouchables* or Max Cady in *Cape Fear*. With *The Fan*, he delivers yet another obsessively honed and frighteningly realised nutcase: Gil Renard.

Renard is a West Coast door-to-door knife salesman whose sales routine involves shaving his arm and leg hairs to verify the sharpness of his blades. De Niro makes him a pressure cooker of pent-up emotion: frustrated, downbeaten, he is a man foundering in a world that no longers walks to his tune, by turns pathetic and scary, venting his anger in a barrage of expletive-driven remarks.

Divorced, alienated from his son, facing the sack from the firm his father started, Renard's only pleasure in life is baseball – more specifically his team, the San Francisco Giants, whose latest signing is hot-shot slugger Bobby Rayburn (Snipes), a $40 million acquisition with a killer swing and a money-grabbing agent (Leguizamo).

Having already lost his favourite shirt number to rival Giant Benicio Del Toro, Rayburn then loses his lucky charm in the outfield on opening day, and his home run cannon stops firing. But while most Giants supporters in the stands turn against their erstwhile hero, Renard remains loyal, going so far as to kill Del Toro in order to get Rayburn his number back.

While there is fun to be had in waiting for Renard finally to blow his fuse and use one of those knives he's so proud of, the film tries so hard to comment on the notion of celebrity that it all but forsakes the simple, old-fashioned pleasures of the thriller genre. Namely thrills. The scene in which Renard puts on one of Rayburn's uniforms while his own clothes are drying is truly chilling but generally Scott compensates by filling every frame with his pumped-up, visual razzamatazz. The opening sequence with De Niro and Snipes in separate cars talking to each other via Ellen Barkin's radio phone-in show as they plough through San Francisco's famously undulating streets is a blistering example of cross-cutting. But the rapid-fire editing and glossy cinematography cannot disguise *The Fan*'s ultimate lack of excitement.

When Renard finally explodes in a *Fatal Attraction*-style moment, launching his attack on the man he had previously supported and idolised, the effect it has on the film is almost to unbalance it, and the finale in which Renard and Rayburn face off on the pitcher's mound during a downpour at the Giants' stadium, is a washout in more ways than one. File under: majorly disappointing. ★★ **MS**

FANNY AND ALEXANDER (FANNY OCH ALEXANDER) (1982)

Starring: *Gunn Wallgren (Helena Ekdahl), Boerje Ahlsetdt (Prof. Carl Ekdahl), Christina Schollin (Lydia Ekdahl), Allan Edwall (Oscar Ekdahl), Pernilla Allwin (Fanny Ekdahl), Bertil Guve (Alexander Ekdahl)*
Director: *Ingmar Bergman*
Screenwriter: *Ingmar Bergman*
15/188 mins./Drama/France/West Germany/Sweden

Awards: *Academy Awards – Best Foreign Language Film, Best Art Direction-Set Decoration, Best Cinematography, Best Costume Design. BAFTA – Best Cinematography*

Following an idyllic Christmas, Fanny and Alexander Ekdahl lose their actor father and their mother lodges them with Jewish antique dealer, Isak Jacobi, to spare them the rigid discipline of her new husband, Bishop Edvard Vergerus.

Sixty-four year-old Ingmar Bergman announced this delightfully intimate epic as his final film. Yet, despite his insistence that movie-making was now a young man's game, he must also have been hurt by the fiscal wranglings that nearly prevented its production and required the Swedish Film Institute to persuade Gaumont and the German TV station ZDF to step in after Lew Grade withdrew because of the picture's projected length.

Ultimately, the small-screen version was to run for 300 minutes, while the theatrical release came in at just over three hours. Yet, considering it took six months to shoot and contains some 60 speaking parts and 1,200 extras, it's to Bergman's credit that he only required a $6 million budget.

The picture's impetus seems to have come from fellow director Kjell Grede's concern that Bergman always made such forbidding features when he possessed such a lust for life. But Bergman alleged that the idea came to him during an idyllic summer at his Faro home and while admitting that it contained autobiographical references, he preferred to think of the film as 'a huge tapestry, filled with masses of colour and people, houses and forests, mysterious haunts of caves and grottoes, secrets and night skies'.

Yet speculation persisted about the extent to which the action was inspired by Bergman's own childhood. Many presumed that Alexander was his alter ego, but Bergman contended that he had more in common with the martinet bishop (although he clearly bore a resemblance to the director's father, who had been a chaplain to the Swedish Royal Family). He did, however, concede that Fanny's love of puppet theatre came from his sister Margaretha, while he shared Alexander's passion for silent cinema. Moreover, Bergman also found work for two of his sons, one of his daughters and his fourth wife on the project.

Evocatively designed by Anna Asp and Susanne Lingheim, and beautifully photographed by Sven Nykvist, the film is awash with enchanting details. But its strength lies in its contrasting moods and the vivid realism of its formal set-pieces, the yuletide festivities, the funeral and the climactic baptism. ★★★★ **DP**

Ingmar Bergman

Who is he: Swedish gloom-monger used as a byword for serious, heavy drama and weighty philosophical themes.

Hallmarks: Fear; loathing; pontificating on the nature of existence and God; marital breakdown; death – you can see why Ingmar never gets invited to parties – covered in long takes in close-up.

If you see one film, see: *The Seventh Seal* (1957)

FANTASIA (1940)

Starring: *as themselves: Deems Taylor, Leopold Stokowski, The Philadelphia Symphony Orchestra*
Directors: *Samuel Armstong, James Algar, Bill Roberts, Paul Satterfield, Hamilton Luske, Jim Handley, Ford Beebe, Walt Disney, Norman Ferguson, Wilfred Jackson, T. Hee*
Screenwriters: *Lee Blair, Elmer Plummer, Phil Dike, Sylvia Moberly-Holland, Norman Wright, Albert Heath, Bianca Majolie, Graham Keid, Paul Pearse, Carl Fallberg, Leon Thiele, Robert Sterner, John Fraser McLeish, Otto Englander, Webb Smith, Erdman Penner, Joseph Sabo, Bill Peet, George Stallings*
Music: *Johann Sebastian Bach, Peter Ilich Tschaikovsky, Igor Stravinsky, Ludwig van Beethoven, Modest Mussorgsky, Franz Schubert*
U/120 mins./Animation/Family/Fantasy/Music/USA

Awards: *Academy Awards – Honorary Awards (Walt Disney, William E. Garity, J.N.A. Hawkins, Leopold Stokowski)*

A host of animated shorts set to classical music.

If you've never seen *Fantasia* you will be disappointed to discover what a remorselessly kitsch experience it actually is. If you have seen it and were on hallucinogenics at the time, remember it that way. There are, indeed, some magical sequences here, as one would certainly expect in a film made by 60 animators supervised by 11 – count 'em – directors.

Most watchable are the abstractions to Bach, ahead of their time,

Mickey Mouse, never more delightful than as The Sorcerer's Apprentice, the Chinese mushrooms dancing, the trippy flowers and the hippos in tutus – all still a hoot.

Together, these make for perhaps a maximum of 70 minutes of greatness. That leaves an awful lot of stuff in this movie that one has mercifully forgotten in the intervening years, boredom frequently relieved only by absolute incredulity at what one is seeing. Personal favourites are the nude but 'tastefully' organless fairies, while the decline of the dinosaurs to Stravinsky's *Rite Of Spring* is interminable, and the vulgar absurdity to which Beethoven's *Pastoral* is subjected takes some beating with centaurs courting centaurines coiffed in the fashion of Joan Crawford. Every time this is screened anywhere, poor Ludwig must be rolling in his resting place.

Let a child watch this at your peril: judging by the writhings and high-pitched bleatings in this reviewer's vicinity, you will probably not be thanked with warmth. ★★★ **WT**

FANTASIA 2000 (1999)

Starring: *As themselves: Leopold Stokowski, Ralph Grierson, Kathleen Battle, Steve Martin, Itzhak Perlman, Quincy Jones, Bette Midler, James Earl Jones, Penn Jillette Teller, James Levine, Angela Lansbury, the voices of: Wayne Allwine (Mickey Mouse), Tony Anselmo (Donald Duck), Russi Taylor (Daisy Duck)*
Directors: *James Algar, Gaetan Brizzi, Paul Brizzi, Hendel Butoy, Francis Glebas, Eric Goldberg, Don Hahn, Pixote Hunt*
Screenwriters: *Oliver Thomas, Joe Ranft, Elena Driskill, Hans Christian Andersen, Carl Fallberg, Joe Grant, Irene Mecchi, Pearce Pearce, David Reynolds*
U/75 mins./Family/Animation/Music/USA

Disney's original plan to update the shorts in *Fantasia* came to fruition with this film, which includes all new cartoons linked by celebrities – plus a spruced up Sorcerer's Apprentice.

When Walt Disney released *Fantasia* in 1940, he hoped to continually revise the format in order to combine new segments with old favourites. Now, some 60 years on, his nephew Roy has resurrected the idea to celebrate the millennium. But, like the original, the sequel is a curate's egg, with moments of hilarity and beauty alternating with the pompous and the banal.

The eco theme informing the opening recurs throughout the picture. But neither the sight of geometric butterflies fluttering frantically to the strains of Beethoven's *Fifth*, nor the concluding renewal fantasy enacted to Stravinsky's *Firebird* have the abstract grace of the original's *Toccata and Fugue*. Even less successful is the winsome dance of the flying whales to Respighi's *Pines Of Rome*, which is further marred by the impersonality of the computer-generated imagery.

In contrast to these more impressionistic pieces, three episodes tell simple stories. Mickey Mouse returns in a newly digitised version of The Sorceror's Apprentice, while Hans Christian Andersen's fable of the Steadfast Soldier is unfussily related to the accompaniment of Shostakovich's *Piano Concerto #2*. Finally, Donald and Daisy Duck have a charmless adventure on board Noah's Ark, which is not improved by the replacement of Donald's trademark bluster by Elgar's *Pomp And Circumstance*.

The real invention is saved for a day in the life ... segment inspired by the cartooning of Al Hirschfeld and underscored by Gershwin's *Rhapsody In Blue*. But, while this New York portmanteau exploits the urban vibrance of the music, it is also guilty of some dubious racial and sexual caricaturing. Free of any such lapses is the gleefully silly episode in which a mischievous flamingo causes havoc with a yoyo to Saint-Saens' *Carnival Of The Animals*. Dressed up in IMAX, *Fantasia 2000* is a breathtaking spectacle. But bereft of its scale, it hardly justifies the 60-year wait. ★★★ **DP**

FANTASTIC FOUR (2005)

Starring: *Ioan Gruffudd (Reed Richards), Jessica Alba (Sue Storm), Chris Evans (Johnny Storm), Michael Chiklis (Ben Grimm), Julian McMahon (Victor Von Doom)*
Director: *Tim Story*
Screenwriters: *Mark Frost, Michael France, based on the comic book by Jack Kirby and Stan Lee*
PG/106 mins./Action/Adventure/Fantasy/Sci-fi/USA

During a space mission to do something confusingly scientific, a strange storm affects reticent egghead Reed Richards, his ex-girlfriend Sue, her arrogant boyfriend Vincent, her cocky younger brother and their grouchy buddy Ben, imbuing them all with special powers.

The summer of 2005 had been strangely cloudy. We had plenty of quality gloom – the dark reawakening of a dormant knight, an earnestly enjoyable retreat from a galaxy far, far away and a socio-political alien invasion – but we've not, in the purest sense of the word, had a lot of fun. You know, big, dumb expensive fun. *Fantastic Four* is big, expensive and dumb in spades – but also unforgivably dull.

The protection of Marvel's flagship supergroup property has infused the whole movie with a sense of nervousness, leaving it unsure whether it's a pure action comedy or looking to be something deeper. It's certainly not a movie made for critics, miserable creatures that we are, but it does assume an arrogant level of idiocy in its audience. It emerges as a studio accountant's dream of product placement with a lazy eye on the early teen market, providing just enough effects shots to make a good trailer and sell some baseball caps.

Yet surely even the teeniest cinemagoer now demands more than occasional cleavage and sloppy CG? *Spider-Man*, for example, became the biggest superhero franchise because it spoke to an adolescent insecurity experienced by all, while *X-Men* deftly spliced puberty and alienation. If *Fantastic Four* has a message it's that being a celebrity is, like, super hard. Well, who cares?

Director Tim Story fails to either inject any real sense of joy into his silliness or even extend the quartet's powers, played with in a few fun asides, into a single sustained action sequence. Like the movie, his Four spend much of their time confined to safe areas, afraid to do anything that might be dangerous or upset the public.

Story's stylistic flatness also infects his (mis)cast. Gruffudd is too sweetly anonymous to emerge as a reluctant leader, McMahon too preening to be anything other than camp and then there's Jessica Alba. Expecting anyone to buy her as a 'Director of Genetic Research' was always wishful thinking of Cinderella proportions, but an acting range extending from hurt pout to scowly pout makes her the movie's low-point. Praise be, then, for Chiklis and Evans, who as The Thing and Johnny Storm inject respectively a degree of heart and humour sorely lacking whenever they leave the screen. They alone lift this above pay-per view advertising. ★★ **OR**

FANTASTIC VOYAGE (1966)

Starring *Stephen Boyd (Grant), Raquel Welch (Cora), Edmond O'Brien (General Carter), Donald Pleasence (Doctor Michaels), Arthur O'Connell (Colonel Donald Reid)*
Director: *Richard Fleischer*
Screenwriters: *David Duncan, Harry Kleiner, Jerome Bixby based on the novel by Otto Klement and Jay Lewis Bixby*
U/100 mins./Sci-fi/USA

Awards: *Academy Awards – Best Art Direction (Jack Martin Smith, Dale Hennessy, Walter M. Scott, Stuart A. Reiss), Best Visual Effects (L.B. Abbott, Art Cruickshank, Emil Kosa Jr.)*

Using a miraculous shrinking science, a team of specialists are injected into the bloodstream of a dying scientist by removing the blood clot in his brain. The problem is they only have one hour before they start to grow again.

The most celebrated of all director Richard Fleischer's exuberant B-movies that cluttered up the sixties with sunny absurdities like talking animals or humans who can talk animal, this tale of a journey through the human body by miniaturised submariners still carries the high charge of imagination. Just the idea of these trippy, gloopy representations of the body's inner workings, and their endless ghoulish fascination, stand up to the test of time, and the film, despite the cheesy excesses of its second-tier cast, is a blast.

The crew of the tiny Proteus might as well be body parts of the movie such is their lack of depth: the stiff, heroic captain (Boyd), the slightly crazed scientist (Pleasence), the more genial scientist (Kennedy) and his shapely female assistant (Welch) who has to peel down to a figure-hugging wet-suit. Who would have thought? Well, the producers, who aren't making any pretence at this being more than an expert piece of juvenilia. The nearest the film comes to a subtext is the conflict between the crew's scientists, one of whom professes a belief in a God, and the film, in a hangover from the paranoid leanings of 50s sci-fi, contains a strong anti-communist bent i.e. the Godless.

You're not really going to watch such bubbly nonsense for its political voice, the best reason to join in is the action Fleischer assembles on this whistle-stop tour of the main organs. Naturally, the mission goes awry as the ship gets caught in the rapids of the jugular vein, has to traverse the pumping heart, and awakens armies of corpuscles and antibodies that play havoc with Welch's wetsuit. It's a bright burst of silliness and wonder. ★★★ **IN**

FAR AND AWAY (1992)

Starring: *Tom Cruise (Joseph Donnelly), Nicole Kidman (Shannon Christie), Thomas Gibson (Stephen Chase), Robert Prosky (Daniel Christie), Barbara Babcock (Nora Christie), Colm Meaney (Kelly)*
Director: *Ron Howard*
Screenwriter: *Bob Dolman, based on story by Bob Dolman and Ron Howard*
15/140 mins./Adventure/Drama/Romance/USA

Joseph is a young Irish peasant facing ruin in his home country. He runs away to America with poor little rich girl Shannon. There, they hope to take advantage of the land that is apparently freely available to settlers.

Such was their seemingly constant tabloid coverage, it's hard to believe that Tom Cruise and Nicole Kidman actually only collaborated on three joint ventures during their time together. And, though blatantly no *Eyes Wide Shut*, this second on-screen pairing for the Super-A couple remains a class apart from the dross that was *Days Of Thunder*.

Ron Howard directs the epic journey of snobbish society girl, Kidman, and farmer pugilist, Cruise, from Ireland to the stark reality of a new-found America from a story apparently inspired by his own ancestors.

It involves a classic poor boy-rich girl love story (with Cruise memorably protecting his vitals with a chamberpot), flight to 'land-of-dreams' America, squalid living, bare-knuckle boxing and – most thrilling of all – the final land race.

If a touch melodramatic, and recounted for the most part in shameless Oirish accents, an assured swagger and solid storyline maintain momentum. ★★★ **MD**

FAR FROM HEAVEN (2002)

Starring: *Julianne Moore (Cathy Whitaker), Dennis Quaid (Frank Whitaker), Dennis Haysbert (Raymond Deagan), Patricia Clarkson (Eleanor Fine), Viola Davis (Sybil)*
Director: *Todd Haynes*
Screenwriter: *Todd Haynes*
12A/107 mins./Drama/Romance/France/USA

In suburban Connecticut of the 1950s, Cathy and Frank Whitaker are the perfect and popular corporate couple. But the façade crumbles when Cathy first discovers Frank's double life, and then begins a friendship with black gardener Raymond. Tongues start wagging and social ruin looms.

On one level, *Far From Heaven* is a fabulous piece of performance art – the reinterpretation of an out-of-favour genre by a witty filmmaker with hip credentials and connections (including Steven Soderbergh and George Clooney for executive producers). But when you get into it, the emotional experiences of the film's distant lives are timeless and powerfully affecting.

Anyone familiar with plush 50s Technicolor melodramas will immediately recognise Todd Haynes' inspiration for this bold experiment as Douglas Sirk. A leftist filmmaker who fled from Nazi Germany to Hollywood, Sirk's European sophistication and formal visual style elevated absurd and maudlin stories into deliriously entertaining, heightened-reality, multiple-hanky domestic dramas. Haynes has cited Sirk's *All That Heaven Allows* (middle-class widow Jane Wyman falls in love with young gardener Rock Hudson and suffers social ostracism) and *Imitation Of Life* (the daughter of Lana Turner's black housekeeper passes as white with heart-rending consequences) as two of his touchstones.

With remarkable confidence and subtlety, Haynes has taken on topics never addressed openly in their day – homosexuality, interracial love, the oppression of women – along with the hard drinking, malice, home-wrecking and tearful sacrifice that were the stuff of vintage 'women's pictures'. What is most fascinating is that Haynes does not allow a single arched brow, whiff of campness or hint of irony to break the spell. We are transported in time to see the world through the characters' eyes, attitudes and vocabulary. When, for example, Frank is shamed into seeing a psychiatrist for an uncomfortable discussion of aversion therapy, there is nothing funny about it. The hostile reception Cathy gets at her little girl's ballet recital is chilling. The tenderness between Cathy and Raymond is agonising because we realise as clearly as they do what they are up against.

Quaid, showing hitherto unsuspected depth, is ideal as the clean-cut, all-American guy who has become a self-loathing, mean drunk under the burden of his guilty secret. Haysbert, underplaying beautifully, is magnetic as the gentle man in whom the heroine finds liberating understanding and empathy. Moore is magnificent as the glamorous homemaker whose self-discovery has a painful price. What they all have in common is loneliness – isolated by taboos, repressions and niceties enforced by Cathy's 'friends' among the daiquiri-fuelled ladies who lunch and dish the dirt.

The picture looks good enough to eat, with quite exquisite art direction, costumes and cinematography all keyed to a specific and sumptuous colour palette. As autumnal New England drifts into winter, the character's clothes are toned to complement the backdrop, interior landscapes and dramatic moods. But the style serves the content.

If you're wondering quite what the point of this is, beyond reclaiming a genre, Haynes' careful observation of human nature leaves you in no doubt at all that any contemporary complacency over issues of sex and race is as naive and hypocritical in the Dubya Bush and Blair era as it was in Eisenhower and Macmillan's. ★★★★★ **EH**

FAR FROM THE MADDING CROWD (1967)

Starring: *Julie Christie (Bathsheba Everdene), Terence Stamp (Sergeant Francis Troy), Peter Finch (William Boldwood), Alan Bates (Gabriel Oak), Fiona Walker (Liddy)*
Director: *John Schlesinger*
Screenwriter: *Frederic Raphael based on the novel by Thomas Hardy*
U/168 mins./Drama/UK

Young Bathsheba Everdene, wildly beautiful and wilful, is too independent for the tastes of rural Wessex. Her tale will bring three entirely different men into orbit around her with tragedy not far behind.

The bleak social tragedy of Thomas Hardy's fiction as transformed by the perfect cheekbones and icy chic of sixties Brit cinema – a 'madding crowd' if ever there was – here was an ironic beast. In taking possibly Hardy's most famous novel, the tale of outcast Bathsheba whose determination to better herself puts her at odds with the confined society of her rural neighbours, but draws to her three different men, to reap inevitable scandal, John Schlesinger stripped the book of its morose gloom for the inevitable glamour of having Julie Christie and Terence Stamp as the romantic leads. The film is dashing, gorgeous, and romantic, but shorn of the desperate isolation of Hardy's Bathsheba that fuels her cruel ambition.

Hence, the film is smooth where it should be spiky and satirical. That said, it is still not hard to watch such period travails when you have Christie, at her most nakedly vulnerable, Stamp bearing his cold beauty like a sword edge, and Peter Finch strong and stolid as Boldwood, the older man fixated on this girl. Only Alan Bates, ironing out his louche, urban persona doesn't fully fit the shepherd Gabriel, the loyal, seemingly ideal final corner of this love-square. The Dorset hillsides are vividly shot by Nicolas Roeg (who would later direct Christie in *Don't Look Now*) with a precious, National Trust-promoting grandeur, adding to the rather idealised vision Schlesinger has created for his adaptation. Although, the stampede of sheep over the cliff edge, the mark of Gabriel's ruin, is mounted with stunning clarity. You just hope they were using stunt sheep.

The film has opted to be a moody romance, billowing with yearning and sexual desire. In the book it is her spirit and her restrictive circumstances, and the fire they fuel inside Bathsheba, that draws these men toward her. Here you rather get the sense, as fully understandable as it is, that it is the fact she's Julie Christie that has sparked such interest. It's surprising half the county haven't chanced their arm. ★★★ **IN**

FAREWELL, MY CONCUBINE (BA WANG BIE JI) (1993)

Starring: *Leslie Cheung (Cheng Dieyi), Zhang Fengyi (Duan Xialou), Gong Li (Juxian), Lu Qi (Guan Jifa), Ying Da (Na Kun), Ge You (Master Yuan), Li Chun (Xiao Si – teenager), Lei Ha Man-zhang (Xiao Si – adult)*
Director: *Chen Kaige*
Screenwriters: *Lilian Lee, Lu Wei, from the novel by Lilian Lee*
15/170 mins./History/Drama/Hong Kong

Awards: *BAFTA – Best Film not in the English Language, Cannes Film Festival – Palme D'Or, Golden Globes – Best Foreign Language Film*

Following the lives of two Chinese boys as they grow up in the early 20th century, learning to be performers in their beloved opera house. As the two mature one falls in love with the other, who then goes on to marry a woman, but despite this their friendship remains strong, with the opera they perform echoing their real lives.

Banned not once but twice in its native China, and now only showing there with the very begrudging assent of the government, Chen Kaige's fifth film, and his first since the critically acclaimed *Life On A String* in 1990, transcended bureacratic red tape to jointly win (with *The Piano*) the top prize at Cannes. And, having successfully changed its nation of origin to Hong Kong to avoid the restrictions imposed by Chinese statehood, was now not only eligible for, but also went on to win the Best Foreign Language Film Oscar.

The epic sweep of Kaige's painterly eye takes in a sumptuously detailed panorama of Chinese history through the lives of two men, inextricably linked from 1925, a time of warlords' rule and the heyday of the Peking Opera, through 1937 and the Japanese invasion, to the inexorable rise of Communism and the Cultural Revolution. Cheng Dieyi and Duan Xialou, beautifully portrayed from youth to age by Cheung and Fengyi respectively, are the central characters, set apart from the rest by their utter dedication to the Opera, a bond which weathers throughout their uncompromising childhood apprenticeship and eventual stardom, and the unrequited love Dieyi has for Xialou – mirrored, with painful foreboding of the consequences to come, by their nightly performance in a traditional opera, with Xialou as the King and Dieyi as his self-sacrificing Concubine. When Xialou marries his real-life concubine (Gong Li, mesmerising as ever), the stage is truly set for that lingering, final curtain.

More than anything, Kaige uses the relationships both to explore themes – most obviously homosexuality – and to reflect and reveal the greater turmoil taking place in Chinese politics and history, subjects still not readily recognised by his own government and culture. If Kaige's film is also about the triumph of the individual in a society given to the masses, then he too, as director of this difficult and politically dangerous film, has surely prevailed with what is ultimately a fascinating portrait of China, both beguiling and tragic to behold. ★★★★ **PB**

FARGO (1996)

Starring: *Frances McDormand (Marge Gunderson), William H Macy (Jerry Lundergaard), Steve Buscemi (Carl Showalter), Peter Stormare (Gaear Grimsrud), Harve Presnell (Wade Gustafson), John Carroll Lynch (Norm Gunderson), Steven Reevis (Shep Proudfoot)*
Director: *Joel Coen*
Screenwriters: *Ethan Coen, Joel Coen*
18/98 mins./Crime/Drama/Comedy/UK/USA

Awards: *Academy Awards – Best Actress, Best Original Screenplay, BAFTA – David Lean Award for Direction, Empire Awards – Best Actress*

A desperate businessman hires two hoods to kidnap his wife, in order to grab the ransom money for himself. However, when small-town sheriff Marge Gunderson starts to investigate, his carefully laid plan goes horribly wrong.

After the scraper-sized flop that was *The Hudsucker Proxy* (although, let it be known, it remains a work of genius) the Coen brothers returned to territory previously found fertile. Put simply, *Fargo* is *Blood Simple* with laughs and a heck of a lot of snow. But *Fargo* is far from simple, it is a deliciously convoluted tale of crime, punishment and a cowardly used-car salesman set in a white-out snowscape of Minnesota, written and directed with the verve, painstaking nuance and outrageously black humour that have become the mainstay of a Coen movie.

It opens in Fargo, a hick-town, where in a bar fogged with cigarette smoke, desperate, cash-strapped car dealer Jerry Lundegaard hires a misbegotten duo of thugs to kidnap his wife. He can then cajole her loaded pop to stump up the ransom and make a killing. The problem is, a killing is exactly what is made. Mishap follows mess-up into a brilliantly plotted farce of lies, confusion and hilarity.

This is the Coens' paean to the middle-America of their youth, and, thanks to McDormand's heavily pregnant police chief Marge Gunderson, has the most heart of any of their films. With big-hearted motherliness and a sharp nose for wrong-doing, she traces the inept brigands and fraught Lundegaard to a bloody conclusion. The Coens have such an ear and eye for the myriad quirks of human life that throughout *Fargo*'s movie-sized absurdity – events take an increasingly corpse-strewn spin out of control – there is a constant sense of plausibility to it all.

Script-wise it's an expected – by Coen reputation – joy, with not a cliché nor clunker to be had and an irrepressible playfulness with language, especially the spittle-spilling Scandinavian originated names of the region. Acting-wise, too, it hums with class. Buscemi does his finest rendition of the put-upon, whining geek yet, Stormare manages to elicit pure menace with scattered grunts and stares, and McDormand's chirruping, waddling Marge – a true original – is a career best.

Director Joel Coen recalls *Blood Simple*'s expansiveness in a solemn world of endless snow and from Marge's unfortunate class reunion to the *Psycho* reference in the kidnap scene mixes the real with the oddball without showing the joins. ★★★★★ **AS**

⊙ THE FAST AND THE FURIOUS (2001)

Starring: *Paul Walker (Brian O'Conner), Vin Diesel (Dominic Toretto), Michelle Rodriguez (Letty), Jordana Brewster (Mia Toretto), Rick Yune (Johnny Tran)*
Director: *Rob Cohen*
Screenwriters: *Gary Scott Thompson, Erik Bergquist, David Ayer, based on a screen story by Gary Scott Thompson and a magazine article* Racer X *by Ken Li*
15/106 mins./Action/Crime/Thriller/USA/Germany

On the darkened streets of LA, kids illegally race souped-up cars at speeds of over 150 mph. That's problem enough for the cops, but when a series of daring raids on moving trucks seems to be connected with the tribe of boy racers, they decide it's time to infiltrate the gangs . . .

Now here's a delightful oddity – a movie that does exactly what it says on the tin. *The Fast And The Furious* is a mindless, hellaciously hectic, borderline irresponsible drag race of a movie that flattens the accelerator in the first few seconds and doesn't let it off until the final frame. And in Vin Diesel it invents the first genuine action hero since Bruce Willis paid a visit to Nakatomi Towers. In other words, it's a gas. Lifting its title from an appropriately cheesy 1950s AIP racing flick (erstwhile creators of the classy likes of *I Was A Teenage Werewolf*) and its plot from *Point Break*, Rob Cohen's movie is the kind of determinedly dimwitted popcorn entertainment that the big studios have been throwing hundreds of millions at each summer with, for the most part, limited success. And this, implausibly, from the man who made the execrable frat flick, *The Skulls*.

For a start, *TFATF* has a plot – not a complex one, granted, but at least there's something close to a story. It has eye candy in the shape of dimwit bobby-dazzler Paul Walker (appropriately enough, a refugee from American soap *The Young And The Restless*) and Jordana Brewster. And it has Diesel, a unique brooding hulk of a man who looks as if he's either going to rip your head off or read you poetry. But most of all it has car chases. Really fast ones. Cars roar past – and even through – the camera at speeds of up to 170 mph, while in the hi-jack sequences they hurtle around and under speeding trucks – and, of course, smash into each other with satisfying regularity. In seamlessly interweaving top-notch CGI and incredible stuntwork, Cohen has delivered some of the finest auto-action ever put on screen. Sadly, the inevitable Vin Diesel-less sequels were not as strong. ★★★★ **AS**

⊙ FASTER PUSSYCAT, KILL, KILL (1965)

Starring: *Tura Satana (Varla), Haji (Rosie), Lori Williams (Billie), Sue Bernard (Linda), Stuart Lancaster (The Old Man), Paul Trinka (Kirk), Denis Busch (The Vegetable), Ray Barlow (Tommy)*
Director: *Russ Meyer*
Screenwriter: *Jack Moran, based on a story by Russ Meyer*
18/84 mins./Action/Drama/Comedy/Crime/USA

Three strippers seek new challenges in life, so they turn to murder and kidnapping, killing a man and holding his girlfriend hostage at a remote location in the desert.

From the first, Meyer's movies attracted a smattering of hip-cynical-cool college types along with the hordes of raincoats who just came to see huge tits. If you watch the entire back catalogue in one go, it becomes mind-numbing; but if you sample selectively the films are astonishing. His films celebrate and caricature a still-young country's adolescent male obsessions – babes in boots, fast cars, ultra-violence, jazzy music, really large breasts, the need for speed, small-town scandal, cheap thrills and fast sex.

Meyer was a rare sexploiter who suggested that naked girls might be ... well ... fun! Meyer made a few more nudies but the market was soon swamped by imitators with lookalike films about X-ray specs or girls' schools, so he moved on to intense, steamy, kinetic, bizarro melodramas – and in among this run of potent drive-in titles (*Lorna, MudHoney, Vixen!*) was his probable masterpiece, the immortal *Faster, Pussycat! Kill! Kill!*.

After karate-chopping an all-American drag racer to death and kidnapping his sweet teenage girlriend, psychotic go-go dancer Varla leads two equally busty, equally crazy sidekicks, Rosie and Billie, into the desert where they find the homestead of a crippled miser and his hulking, mentally challenged son 'Vegetable'. The thrill-kill kittens kick up dust as they double-cross each other, try to seduce every man in sight, search for a hidden fortune and explode with a hyperactivity that suggests they're on course for early graves and don't much care about it. 'What's your point?' asks one over-awed man, only for Varla to snap, 'It's of no return and you've just reached it.'

A cross-breed of girl-gang movies with the brand of rural gothic that would lead to *Deliverance* and *The Hills Have Eyes, Faster, Pussycat! Kill! Kill!* is arguably as much an outrageous parody of the trash-exploitation film as it is a drive-in barnstormer. Though the Russ Meyer imprimatur and the outrageous title suggest steaming, explicit sex, it is surprisingly restrained in the nudity department (leather tops are cut low but never come off), though every scene seethes with overheated, sleazy eroticism. Satana, a half-Apache, half-Japanese dancer with a pennyweight of eye makeup and sausage-skin-tight jeans, also has a way with sneery threats that makes her one of the most offbeat villains in cinema history. Her snarling, pouting, wriggling style is caught by the rest of the cast and even the driving jazz score (The Bostweeds' theme song, later covered by The Cramps, is a hoot).

The overdrive melodramatics extend to hilarious narration ('Ladies and gentlemen, welcome to violence!'), and performances are pitched so broad they make the Marx Brothers seem restrained (and strangely, Haji sounds a lot like Chico). Big breasts, fast cars, tight jeans, sudden death – what more do you want?

Va va voom! Varla and the girls may be villains, but their uncompromising grrrl-power attitudes ('I never try anything – I just do it. Wanna try me?') fuelled a whole grindhouse tradition, from those Roger Corman prison break-outs of the 1970s to Quentin Tarantino's hard-hitting heroines. If you only see one Russ Meyer, as the saying goes, this is the pick of the litter. ★★★★★ **KN**

⊙ FATAL ATTRACTION (1987)

Starring: *Michael Douglas (Dan Gallagher), Glenn Close (Alex Forrest), Anne Archer (Beth Gallagher), Ellen Hamilton Latzen (Ellen Gallagher), Stuart Pankin (Jimmy)*
Director: *Adrian Lyne*
Screenwriter: *James Dearden*
18/119 mins./Drama/Thriller/Romance/USA

Awards: *BAFTA – Best Editing*

An apparently loving husband, Dan, embarks upon a frantic one-night affair with unhinged book editor Alex, only to be made to pay for his sins with her campaign of crazed retribution.

It was the remarkable double of *Fatal Attraction* followed by *Wall Street* that vaulted Michael Douglas to the top of the A-list of desirable leading men. Adrian Lyne's slick, racy thriller was the biggest grossing hit of 1987 and was read as a timely parable about the dangers of indulging in unsafe sex. Sex certainly never came more lethal than this, when Douglas' Dan Gallagher succumbs to a one-night stand with Glenn Close's seemingly blasé book editor Alex Forrest.

Gallagher's punishment for having his fun in such places as the kitchen sink and the lift is discovering that the lady is a serious loony. An unfaithful husband's worst nightmare comes to life as the obsessional, spurned Alex winds herself up listening to *Madame Butterfly* and embarks on a vengeful reign of terror.

From the first ominous tantrum as Gallagher attempts a cheery ta-ta, the unease is wound tighter and tighter through such staples of screen psycho behaviour as destruction of property and the old mutilation of a family pet routine (rendered with an appalling difference) to outright horror. This is all wildly gripping, suspenseful stuff, with a masterfully done, heart-stopping climax, although the last Grand Guignol split-seconds are never quite as scary as the first time you see it. Poor Alex – deranged as she is – does have a point in her grievance that he's taken what he wanted and now she can get lost. The escape clause for our hero is that she not only asked for it but downright insisted, and the twist that so captured the public was the depiction of the man as the stalked victim.

Douglas is attractive and believable, but he does take a backseat to Glenn Close's spectacularly crazed performance. It would be fun to see the original ending – which American test audiences couldn't stomach – in which the Madame Butterfly motif reached a logical, very much more downbeat conclusion, with her suicide leaving him framed for murder. ★★★★ **AE**

FATHER OF THE BRIDE (1950)

Starring: *Spencer Tracy (Stanley T. Banks), Joan Bennett (Ellie Banks), Elizabeth Taylor (Kay Banks), Don Taylor (Buckley Dunstan), Billie Burke (Doris Dunstan)*
Director: *Vincente Minnelli*
Screenwriters: *Frances Goodrich, Albert Hackett, based on the novel by Edward Streeter*
U/92 mins./Comedy/USA

Stanley and Ellie Banks prepare for their daughter's wedding – Stanley more reluctantly than the rest of the family.

Although the 1950s vision of family life seems incredibly dated, the heart of this film – a father's complete bemusement at the increasingly ridiculous preparations for his only daughter's wedding – still rings true. Spencer Tracey's perfect comic timing and strength of character carry the film – and served more as a model for Robert Di Niro in *Meet The Parents*, then the substance-lite performance from Steve Martin in the 90s re-make.

Also memorable is the (seemingly now) impossibly fresh and virginal Elizabeth Taylor, whose alternating highly strung and worldly wise attitude to her future tests her dad to the limits. Don Taylor, her wonderfully named suitor Buckley, is noticeably less memorable so it's no surprise that he later found a more fulfilling career behind the camera as a director whose credits included *Omen II* and *Escape From The Planet Of The Apes*.

This also spawned (almost literally) a rare-for-its-day sequel *Father's Little Dividend* (1951) – which was more heart-warming and considerably better than Martin's *Father Of The Bride Part II*. ★★★★ **EC**

FATHER OF THE BRIDE (1991)

Starring: *Steve Martin (George Stanley Banks), Diane Keaton (Nina Banks), Kimberly Williams (Annie Banks), Kieran Culkin (Matty Banks), George Newbern (Bryan MacKenzie), Martin Short (Frank Eggelhoffer)*
Director: *Charles Shyer*
Screenwriters: *Frances Goodrich, Albert Hackett, Nancy Meyers, Charles Shyer*
PG/105 mins./Family/Comedy/USA

George and Nina Banks have a near idyllic life, until their eldest daughter, Annie, comes home from college and announces that she is engaged to be married. While Nina and Annie throw themselves into the preparations, George – unprepared to accept that his daughter is all grown up, goes a little crazy . . .

Following on from the success of American remakes of foreign classics like *Cousins* and *Three Men And A Baby*, it is hardly surprising that film-makers started rummaging through Tinseltown's vaults in search of suitable American films to update for cinemagoers in the 1990s. Scorsese's remake of *Cape Fear* may be the most talked about, but another film to recieve this treatment is Vincente Minnelli's classic 1950 comedy *Father Of The Bride*, which originally starred Spencer Tracy and a young Elizabeth Taylor as his daughter.

Funnyman Steve Martin, taking the Tracy role, is George Banks, whose daughter Annie returns home from college announcing that she is going to get married, sending George into palpitations while muttering 'but she's only a little girl', while his wife is more interested in hiring a suitable wedding caterer.

That's pretty much it with regards to the plot, with George going from moping about losing his little girl to a man he doesn't like, to George moping about the rising cost of the wedding. Perhaps the highlight is Martin Short parading about as flamboyant wedding co-ordinator Frank, spending ludicrous amounts of money on decorations and menus, while talking in an almost unintelligible foreign accent.

However, the film is still a pale imitation of the original, with Steve Martin moving further away from his whacky guy persona and more towards the mildly amusing fortysomething seen in *Parenthood*. That said, there are still some laughs to be had, including a hilarious scene in which George begins by examining the contents of his daughter's future in-laws' bathroom cabinet, and ends up falling in their pool. ★★★ **JB**

FEAR AND LOATHING IN LAS VEGAS (1998)

Starring: *Johnny Depp (Raoul Duke), Benicio Del Toro (Dr. Gonzo), Tobey Maguire (Hitchiker), Ellen Barkin (Waitress at the North Star Café), Gary Busey (Highway Patrolman), Christina Ricci (Lucy), Mark Harmon (Magazine Reporter at Mint 400), Cameron Diaz (Blonde TV Reporter)*
Director: *Terry Gilliam*
Screenwriters: *Terry Gilliam, Tod Davies, Alex Cox, Tony Grisoni, from the book by Hunter S. Thompson*
18/128 mins./Comedy/Drama/USA

A gonzo journalist and his crazed lawyer take a road trip to Vegas to cover a sporting event. Sadly, the carload of drugs that they took care to pack mean that they get somewhat distracted en route.

Put yourself in Terry Gilliam's shoes for a moment. As the director of the hugely anticipated adaptation of Hunter S. Thompson's classic counter-culture novel, you are handed a project which has been branded 'unfilmable' by Hollywood for more than quarter of a century, a budget which requires the aid of a magnifying glass, one previous owner – Brit director Alex Cox who jumped ship when the oft-cited 'creative differences' reared their ugly head – and an absentee landlord in Thompson himself, whose main interests amount to drinking heavily, firing shotguns or doing both simultaneously.

In the face of such insurmountable odds, Gilliam has bravely chosen to spike his film: it looks great, it gives you the giggles and it bends your mind. But unfortunately, when the lights go up, you're left with a headache.

The plot, which generally takes a backseat to some magnificent images, follows sports writer Raoul Duke and his Samoan attorney Dr. Gonzo travelling to Las Vegas in 1971 to cover the legendary Mint 400 desert motocross. Not that much reporting gets done: for these boys are fully-fledged, card-carrying drug enthusiasts who swallow a suitcase of illegal pharmaceuticals and wander down the Vegas strip as if it were Hell on Earth.

The fact that anywhere on Earth would resemble Hell if you digested 73 pellets of mescaline, a salt shaker full of cocaine and a pint of raw ether goes unnoticed because Gilliam has crafted scene after scene of hallucinatory brilliance, some of which – melting carpets, a literal lounge lizard attack – ranks among his most bizarre and best imagery to date.

The film itself, though, crumbles into oblivion through heavy symbolism (the American dream is blatantly represented as a wasteland of car wrecks) but still manages to maintain its shape even while melting, thanks to two exemplary performances: Depp progresses majestically through the picture like the author's clone – bald head, filtered cigarette, manic gestures – pulling out that little bit extra with a droll narration. Equally stunning, Del Toro's massive 45-pound beer gut and vomit-flecked hair goes far beyond the call of thesping duty. Both actors are world class in a film that squeezes your pleasure pads and wrings your brain but ultimately fails. ★★★ **JH**

⦿ FEAR EATS THE SOUL (ANGST ESSEN SEELE AUF) (1974)

Starring: *Brigitte Mira (Emmi), El Hedi Ben Salem (Ali), Barbara Valentin (Barbara), Irm Hermann (Krista), Peter Gauhe (Bruno), Rainer Werner Fassbinder (Eugen)*
Director: *Rainer Werner Fassbinder*
Screenwriter: *Rainer Werner Fassbinder*
15/92 mins./Drama/West Germany

Much to the disgust of her family and friends, ageing cleaning woman Emmi falls for Moroccan labourer Ali. But once they're married, the disapproving chorus seeks to re-integrate them into their circle from the most selfish of motives.

Rainer Werner Fassbinder trailed the story of *Fear Eats the Soul* in an anecdote told by the chambermaid in *The American Soldier*. It was based on a newspaper report, but the influence of Douglas Sirk's *All That Heaven Allows* is readily apparent, both in terms of narrative structure and visual style. As so often before, Fassbinder's use of angle, light and colour recalls that of his mentor. He also makes typically telling use of mirrors. The scenes in which Emmi and Ali stare at themselves in the glass intentionally reflect each other, as the ex-Nazi surrenders to her love for a Moroccan and the belittled man struggles to reconcile his beloved wife with her muddled petit bourgeois values. But the hospital mirror shot is even more pertinent, as it suggests the inescapability of reality and casts doubt on the couple's future.

For all its Sirkian influence, the film also borrows Bertolt Brecht's idea of typage in order to universalise the attitudes of those opposed to Emmi and Ali's relationship. Her children, neighbours, co-workers and even her grocer abandon her on her wedding day and Fassbinder can't resist setting the reception in Hitler's favourite Munich restaurant to emphasise the iniquity of their prejudice. Ironically, only the forces of repression and exploitation (the cops and the capitalist landlord) are prepared to live and let live.

Yet, once the pair return from their holiday, they are grudgingly accepted – albeit from selfish individual motives rather than any sense of tolerance. Emmi's offspring require her to babysit, the neighbours want to use her basement, the grocer can't afford to lose her custom in the face of supermarket competition, and the cleaners shift their ire on to their new Yugoslav workmate.

This is a highly emotive melodrama. But while Fassbinder is content for audiences to empathise with his victimised lovers, he also wants them to recognise that the social, economic and moral factors that brought Emmi and Ali together will ultimately drive them apart. ★★★★ **DP**

⦿ FEARLESS (1993)

Starring: *Jeff Bridges (Max Klein), Isabella Rossellini (Laura Klein), Rosie Perez (Carla Rodrigo), Tom Hulce (Atty. Stephen Brillstein), John Turturro (Dr. Bill Perlman), Benicio Del Toro (Manny Rodrigo)*
Director: *Peter Weir*
Screenwriter: *Rafael Yglesias, based on his novel*
15/122 mins./Drama/USA

A man's personality is dramatically changed after surviving a major airline crash.

Living without fear isn't really living an authentic life, but it's quite a good experiment. So goes the main thrust of Peter Weir's mature, thought-provoking and downright odd story of Max and Carla (the Oscar-nominated Perez), survivors of a plane crash and in their own ways scarred by it. Carla is bitter, twisted and pining for her one-year-old who perished in the conflagration. Max is elated, metaphysically inclined, and newly empowered by his lack of fear after having stared right into the eye-sockets of the Big D and survived.

Strangers before the crash, their lives intertwine as they each come to terms with what happened. Lionised by the media and by the passengers he led to safety, Max is having none of it, choosing instead to test the limits of his fearlessness by standing atop high buildings, refusing to lie to get more insurance money, ending his marriage if necessary, and putting his life in danger to help others, notably Carla. He is, throughout, a pain in the arse, refusing to let anyone in to his little world, patronising those who've never had a near-death experience and living life utterly on his own terms.

This unsympathetic character could be one of the reasons why *Fearless* was such a huge box office flop – others may include the large amounts of wailing and arguing involved, the reasonably complex (though occasionally sixth-form) metaphysical concepts, the sprinkling of thoughtful philosophy, and the lack of a decent car chase. For those happy to engage in such things, however, *Fearless* is a bravely adult film, misfiring in places with its cod psychology and occasionally dropping the philosophical ball, but having a genuine and largely successful crack at adapting a literate, intelligent novel into a literate, intelligent film. And the acting's brilliant, too. ★★★★ **PT**

⦿ FELICIA'S JOURNEY (1999)

Starring: *Bob Hoskins (Joseph Ambrose Hilditch), Elaine Cassidy (Felicia), Arsinee Khanjian (Gala), Peter McDonald (Johnny Lysaght), Gerard McSorley (Felicia's Father)*
Director: *Atom Egoyan*
Screenwriter: *Atom Egoyan, based on the novel by William Trevor*
12/116 mins./Drama/Thriller/Canada/U.K.

A lonely catering manager befriends a young girl, just arrived from Ireland and in search of her lover. But it soon becomes clear that he has more in mind than simple charity.

Cult Canadian director Atom Egoyan has a fascination with people not being what they first appear. So it should come as no surprise that the Canadian director should be drawn to William Trevor's disturbing novel about a pregnant Irish teenager who comes to England looking for the boyfriend who left her – and instead finds a sinister Brummie bachelor.

As a portrait of the banality of evil, Bob Hoskins' Hilditch is little short of brilliant. A loner whose scrupulously maintained home looks like a 50s time capsule, he conceals a hi-tech video camera (another of Egoyan's obsessions since 1987's *Family Viewing*) in his Morris Minor and uses it to record dark conversations with young homeless girls. To Cassidy's guileless Felicia, his promise to help her find her lover makes him seem nothing more than a kindly old man, a far cry from her own hateful father, blinkered in his vision of a noble Republican past. Hilditch is also trapped in the past and, as he obsessively watches his celebrity mother's TV cookery classes, we glean he has skeletons in his closet – and possibly the back garden.

Egoyan's film weaves together impressionistic flashbacks of rural Ireland with panoramic shots of the industrial Midlands, gradually narrowing the focus to reflect Felicia's entrapment. That we experience a genuine shiver of dread owes much to Cassidy's finely realised depiction of childlike naiveté within a young woman's flowering sexuality.

If there's a problem, it's surely that Egoyan's surrealist flourishes (pretty out there even by his own high standards of oddness) sit uneasily within the drama. But that's a small price to pay to see a true original at work. ★★★★ **TL**

Long Film Titles

TOP10

1 Night Of The Day Of The Dawn Of The Son Of The Bride Of The Return Of The Revenge Of The Terror Of The Attack Of The Evil, Mutant, Alien, Flesh-eating, Hellbound, Zombified Living Dead Part 2: In Shocking 2-D
2 The Persecution And Assassination Of Jean-Paul Marat As Performed By The Inmates Of The Asylum Of Charenton Under The Direction Of The Marquis De Sade
3 The Incredible Strange Creatures Who Stopped Living And Became Mixed-Up Zombies.
4 The Saga Of The Viking Women And Their Voyage To The Waters Of The Great Serpent
5 You've Got To Walk It If You Like To Talk It Or You'll Lose That Bear
6 The Heart Of A Lady As Pure As A Full Moon Over The Place Of Medical Salvation
7 I Could Never Have Sex With A Man Who Had So Little Regard For My Husband
8 Oh Dad, Poor Dad, Mamma's Hung You In The Closet And I'm Feeling So Sad
9 Gas-s-s-s! Or, It Became Necessary To Destroy The World In Order To Save It
10 Introduction To Arnold Schoenberg's Accompaniment To A Cinematographic Scene

③ FELLINI-SATYRICON (1969)

Starring: *Martin Potter (Encolpius), Hiram Keller (Ascytius), Max Born (Giton), Capucine (Tryphaena), Salvo Randone (Eumolpus), Magali Noel (Fortunata)*
Director: *Federico Fellini*
Screenwriters: *Federico Fellini, Bernardino Zapponi, Brunello Rondi based on the fragment* Satyricon *by Gaius Petronius*
18/128 mins./Drama/France/Italy

While feuding over Giton, classical youths Encolpius and Ascyltus embark on a quest for experience and, in the process, encounter such diverse Romans as imperial pimp Lichas, Oriental slave and orgy host, Trimalchio.

Federico Fellini had long considered adapting Petronius' *Satyricon*. In 1966, he announced a production with Alberto Sordi and Claudia Cardinale, but his casting ambitions soon came to encompass Mae West, Groucho Marx, Jimmy Durante, Danny Kaye and Boris Karloff. Thwarted by their reluctance, he declared that unless he could land Richard Burton, Elizabeth Taylor, Marlon Brando, Brigitte Bardot, Jerry Lewis, Peter O'Toole, Lee Marvin, The Beatles and Presidents Lyndon Johnson and Charles De Gaulle he would settle for unknowns. So, when more realistic choices Terence Stamp and Pierre Clémenti proved too expensive, Fellini hired Martin Potter (a bit parter from *The Caesars*), Chelsea hippy Max Born and New Yorker Hiram Keller, who'd had a minor slot in *Hair*.

Gleefully linking the fragments of the original text with decadent doings of his own devising, Fellini sought both to create an animated fresco and to recapture the free love aspirations of the waning Sixties. But what emerged was a photomontage of excess, whose autobiographical and satirical allusions Fellini alternately embraced and denied. The spirit of Nero's master of revels is still detectable, but Encolpius and Ascyltus' misadventures, which are undertaken with a vitality, curiosity and naiveté that only youth could afford, are primarily based on dreams and musings drawn from Fellini's infamous notebooks.

Midway through production, Fellini discovered that Alfredo Bini had completed his own take on Petronius and United Artists was forced to acquire it for $1million in order to suppress its release. But comparisons might have deflected some of the barrage of criticism to which *Fellini-Satyricon* was subjected. Some protested at the decadence, others at the depiction of grotesques and caricatures. But, while commending Danilo Donati's designs, many accused Fellini of lazily setting *La Dolce Vita* in classical dress and taking its themes to extremes. This is certainly a wildly inconsistent and occasionally incoherent work, but it's far from the intellectually bankrupt Cecil B. DeMillean orgy that some have suggested. ★★★ **DP**

③ FELLINI'S CASANOVA (1976)

Starring: *Donald Sutherland (Giacomo Casonova), Tina Aumont (Henriette), Cicely Browne (Madame D'Urfe), Carmen Scarpitta (Madame Charpillon), Clara Algranti (Marcolina), Daniela Gati (Giselda), Margaret Clementi (Sister Maddalena)*
Director: *Federico Fellini*
Screenwriters: *Federico Fellini, Bernardino Zapponi based on the autobiography* Histoire De Ma Vie *by Giacomo Casanova*
15/163 mins./Drama/Italy/USA

From his seclusion at the Castle of Dux, Casanova recalls his sexual encounters with, amongst others, an ageing Marquise, a beautiful countess, a hunchback and an automaton.

Never one to make a definitive statement, Federico Fellini declared this fantastical portrait of Giacomo Casanova to be both 'my most complete, expressive, courageous film' and 'the worst film I ever made'. Although it's studded with trademark moments, this isn't one of Fellini's finest hours. But, considering the chaotic conditions under which it was made, it's far better than it had any right to be.

Depressed by the state of his marriage to Giulietta Masina and pressing tax problems, Fellini had little enthusiasm for the project when it was mooted by Dino Di Laurentiis. He was even less taken with the producer's suggestion of Robert Redford for the title role. Similarly dismissing Marlon Brando, Al Pacino, Jack Nicholson and Michael Caine, Fellini insisted on Marcello Mastroianni, as he was not only an easy collaborator, but also something of a lothario himself. But, even after De Laurentiis withdrew, Fellini had to abandon Marcello and accept the casting of Donald Sutherland to appease his new Hollywood backers.

Fellini treated the Canadian with disdain from the off and the more he struggled to come to terms with his character, the more the director left him to his confusion. Yet, Fellini's problem lay less with the actor than with his loathing of Casanova himself.

Disregarding his achievements as an author and enterpreneur and his exploits as a gambler and spy, Fellini chose to focus on Casanova's reputation as a great lover and took sadistic delight in depicting him as a washed-out shell looking back on his past, without any appreciation of either the disdain of those who once feted him or the fact that his pursuit of pleasure had dulled his ability to feel.

Some saw Fellini's own despair in this depiction. But Sutherland's detachment from the 'braggart Fascist' of the director's jaundiced design makes this technically impressive exercise seem even more morally and intellectually barren. ★★★ **DP**

FERRIS BUELLER'S DAY OFF (1986)

Starring: *Matthew Broderick (Ferris Bueller), Alan Ruck (Cameron Frye), Mia Sara (Sloane Peterson), Jeffrey Jones (Ed Rooney), Jennifer Grey (Jeanie Bueller), Cindy Pickett (Katie Bueller), Charlie Sheen (Boy in the Police Station), Ben Stein (Economics Teacher), Kristy Swanson (Simone Adamley)*
Director: *John Hughes*
Screenwriter: *John Hughes*
15/102 mins./Comedy/USA

A high school wise guy is determined to have a day off from school, despite what the principal thinks.

'What's amazing about *Ferris Bueller*,' Jeffrey Jones told *Empire* back in 1998 (after he'd bemoaned the fact that he was likely to be better remembered for his role as nutcase headmaster Ed Rooney than his Emperor Joseph II in 1984's *Amadeus*), 'is that we're asked to, and do, sympathise with a kid whose only complaint in life is that his sister got a car for her birthday and he got a computer.' It is, indeed, a hell of an achievement. *Ferris Bueller's Day Off* is, in fact, an unadulterated celebration of what it's like to be young, white, middle class and well-heeled in mid 80s America. So it should, on paper at least, be an unbearably smug celebration of crass consumerism. Consider: Ferris' idea of a good time is bombing around in a vintage Ferrari; a visit to the Chicago stock exchange followed by lunch in the city's swankiest restaurant of posh scran for which his method of payment goes undisclosed.

It's also a hymn to capitalism and the advantages offered to a metropolitan teenager. Ken Loach this obviously ain't. Which makes the fact that it's an almost irresistibly likeable, defiantly sunny comedy all the more astounding.

There are those of course who will declare *The Breakfast Club* as the triumphant apex of John Hughes' teen oeuvre. While the detention flick certainly spoke to its pimply audience with the uncanny, unerring familiarity that Hughes made his own from his directorial debut *Sixteen Candles* in 1984 (though many previous writing efforts had gone unproduced, most notably his *Jaws* sequel: *Jaws 3 (People 0)*, in subsequent years its dour adolescent navel-gazing edges alarmingly toward the embarrassing (leading Jay in Kevin Smith's *Dogma* to acidly remark that it was in essence a movie about stupid kids who actually show up for detention).

Ferris Bueller however, has aged somewhat better, indeed Hughes seems to have considered it the best of his teen movies, abandoning the genre afterwards in favour of pre-teen laughs with the *Home Alone* movies and then the significantly less successful infant comedy *Baby's Day Out*. In charm offensive terms *Ferris Bueller's Day Off* is the storming of Omaha Beach. At its centre is an astonishing performance from a 24 year-old Matthew Broderick who, with *War Games* and *Ladyhawke* was not only rapidly establishing himself as the teen pin-up du jour but as a talented, appealing actor who promised, rightly as it turned out, a shelf life well beyond the standard 15 minutes of adolescent notoriety. It's impossible to conceive of Ferris being played by anybody else (indeed, an attempt to launch a TV spin off with the diminutive Charlie Schlatter now to be seen on daytime TV's *Diagnosis Murder* in the lead role crashed and burned despite the presence of a youthful Jennifer Aniston as his sister).

But if Broderick's performance is a gem, it can sometimes detract from the brilliance of the support. Alan Ruck as neurotic best buddy Cameron is a standout (the two had previously worked together extensively on the New York stage). Jeffrey Jones established a career-defining character much to his chagrin with crazed high school principal Ed Rooney ('When Ferris Bueller looks back on the wreck his life has become, he'll remember the name Ed Rooney!') while Jennifer Grey essays terminally pissed-off sister Jean with spiteful aplomb.

Hughes' direction has never been more assured. He describes the movie as a love letter to Chicago and, indeed, he uses many of the same locations he's used in previous movies: the expensive houses in Ferris' suburbia were used in *She's Having A Baby* and the high school is the same abandoned school used in *The Breakfast Club*. Veteran cinematographer Tak Fujimoto shoots the windy city in gloriously intense, summer colours.

But *FBDO* has a little more to it than simply delighting in the possibilities of skiving in Chicago. As critic David Thompson has pointed out, there's a slight air of premature middle-age about all of Hughes' characters. Ferris is no exception, in fact, he's impossibly wise for the 17 year-old he's meant to be; not least in the speech he gives about approaching the end of adolescence and his friendship with Cameron and about adulthood looming over the horizon. It's certainly implausible that a high schooler would have quite that level of self-awareness, but then Ferris' appeal is his preternatural savvy. And it's an element that deftly underscores the fun with a melancholic poignancy.

Tagline
One man's struggle to take it easy.

No other teen comedy either in the 80s or beyond would serve up such an innocent, generous, upbeat cheerfulness that would become unthinkable during the cynical 90s or in the slew of 00s teen movie homages. Life, as Ferris famously remarks, moves pretty fast. If you don't stop and look around you might miss it. *Ferris Bueller* is one of the things you should definitely make some time for. ★★★★★ **AS**

FESTEN (THE CELEBRATION) (1998)

Starring: *Ulrich Thomsen (Christian Klingenfeldt), Henning Moritzen (Faderen/Father Helge Klingenfeldt-Hansen), Thomas Bo Larsen (Michael), Paprika Steen (Helene)*
Director: *Thomas Vinterberg (uncredited)*
Screenwriters: *Thomas Vinterberg, Mogens Rukov, based on an idea by Thomas Vinterberg*
15/105 mins./Drama/Denmark/Sweden

When his extended family reunite for his 60th birthday, patriarch Helge finds some family secrets brought suddenly out into the open.

This head-banging drama about a bunch of nobs who gather at a stately country pad for a 60th birthday was made under a strict set of rules called Dogme 95, drawn up by a group of four Danish directors including Vinterberg and Lars Von Trier (whose *The Idiots* is another Dogme film). The 'vows of chastity', as they call them, include using only hand-held cameras in available light.

Assuming viewers aren't rendered terminally queasy by the cinematography – a gimmick resembling a demented bluebottle's eye-view of events – Festen is a fierce dissection of family life. It kicks off as the guests prepare for dinner, mixing scenes of chunks of chit-chat, frantic kitchen preparations, quickie sex and the discovery of a dead sister's suicide note. The birthday boy is Helge and the main focus is on his three children, inscrutable Christian, uncouth Michael and emotional Helene. Their stories unfold like a whodunit in darkly comical fashion, until Christian drops a bombshell.

Vinterberg adopts no obvious moral stance over the racism, brutality and self-delusions of the guests but just seeing them in documentary-like action will be enough to unsettle most viewers as it ricochets between unsavoury outbursts. While there's barely a likeable trait on display and Vinterberg courts controversy with his conclusion, there's no denying that some of the Dogme strictures inject urgency and surprise into what could have been a tediously static affair. ★★★ **JB**

FEVER PITCH (1997)

Starring: *Colin Firth (Paul), Ruth Gemmell (Sarah Hughes), Holly Aird (Jo), Mark Strong (Steve), Neil Pearson (Paul's Dad), Ken Stott (Ted, the Headmaster)*
Director: *David Evans*
Screenwriter: *Nick Hornby, based on his book.*
15/102 mins./Comedy/Romance/Sport/UK

Teacher and obsessive Arsenal fan Paul falls for Sarah, but his unhealthy interest in his team threatens to drive them apart.

Imagine being a dedicated Arsenal fan. Painful, certainly, but just try. Through the 70s and 80s they watched in awe as the Reds demolished English and European football. Unfortunately for the Gunners, that colour belonged to Liverpool and the Arsenal faithful accepted the idea of being forever the bridesmaid. When they did have their moment, though, Nick Hornby was there to relish every second of it. His famous book, documenting both Arsenal's fairytale 1988/89 season and his own stress-ridden personal life, captures all the passion and stupidity of being a football fanatic. The film, which Hornby also scripted, keeps the passion but acts a touch stupid too.

Paul, an English teacher and Arsenal obsessive, meets fellow tutor Sarah and a stormy relationship develops while the Gunners head for their first league title in 18 years. Paul lopes around contemplating the next home fixture while Sarah contemplates holding their relationship together. The couple look doomed – as do the Gunners – but as history shows, a touch of magic filled the air around Highbury that year.

David Evans' witty and occasionally touching film scores on many levels, not least from two wonderfully understated performances from Firth and Gemmell, but it's filmed like an intimate TV drama rather than the big screen romance it tries to ape. Hornby has embellished the script with plenty of male truisms, and there's also a fair whack of female skill, but the animalistic fever behind the book has been projected into a mild-mannered, faintly passionate comedy.

Despite cross 70s flashbacks where a Mecca-like Arsenal ground becomes a sanctuary from the young Paul's divorcing parents, *Fever Pitch* peaks when Firth explains the universal appeal of football to a sceptical Gemmell, a theme which implodes in the wake of the Hillsborough tragedy, which the film expertly handles. The minuscule budget may stretch the terrace-crowd sequences, but the action really kicks off in the bedroom and the classroom, where Hornby's wit is razor-sharp. ★★★ **JH**

A FEW GOOD MEN (1992)

Starring: *Tom Cruise (Lt. Daniel Kaffee), Jack Nicholson (Col. Nathan R. Jessep), Demi Moore (Lt. Cdr. JoAnne Galloway), Kevin Bacon (Capt. Jack Ross), Keifer Sutherland (Lt. Jonathan Kendrick), Christopher Guest (Dr. Stone), Noah Wyle (Cpl. Jeffrey Barnes)*
Director: *Rob Reiner*
Screenwriter: *Aaron Sorkin, based on his play*
15/138 mins./Drama/USA

Idealistic Navy lawyer Daniel Kaffee is assigned to defend two Marines accused of murder. It seems like a clear-cut case, but as Kaffee probes deeper, he uncovers murky goings-on at the soldiers' army base.

This timeless thriller acts as a reminder of how stars who have been so average elsewhere can produce excellent – some career-best – work when in the hands of a confident director (Reiner, who was then at the height of his powers following *When Harry Met Sally* and *Misery*). Nicholson and Cruise, as the grizzled old army general holding onto secrets and the idealistic young lawyer turk who 'can't handle the truth', raise the bar on performances, and where they lead, everyone else, including a surprisingly solid Demi Moore, follows.

However, it's clear now, over ten years on from the movie's release, that the real star of *A Few Good Men* is the film's de facto creator, Aaron Sorkin, the big-brained genius who wrote the initial play upon which this was based. He went on to create *The West Wing* and the sharp-witted, intelluctually-charged machine-gun dialogue that personified that show's first few seasons is on display here, as Sorkin paints a morally complex picture of the highly-charged military situation in Cuba; circumvents conventions of the genre (Moore and Cruise's characters flirt, but never get it on) and still finds the time to fit in a couple of truly classic scenes. Now that's writing. *The West Wing* proved it was no fluke. ★★★★ **EC**

FIDDLER ON THE ROOF (1971)

Starring: *Topol (Tevye), Norma Crane (Golde), Leonard Frey (Motel), Molly Picon (Yente), Paul Mann (Lazar Wolf), Rosalind Harris (Tzeitel), Michele Marsh (Hodel), Neva Small (Chava), Paul Michael Glaser (Perchik)*
Director: *Norman Jewison*
Screenwriter: *Joseph Stein, from the book of the musical, based on stories by Sholom Aleichem*
U/180 mins./Comedy/Musical/USA

Awards: *Academy Awards – Best Cinematography, Best Score, Best Sound, Golden Globes – Best Musical/Comedy, Best Actor*

Against a background of political upheavel in a Jewish settlement in pre-revolutionary Russia, Tevye deals with the disappointing marriage choices of his three daughters.

Norman Jewison's spin on Sholom Aleichem's classic tale, originally filmed in 1939 as the Yiddish-language *Tevye*, is one of the few screen musicals of the last 35 years which actually works – largely thanks to its glimpse into a long-gone culture (that of a Jewish ghetto in pre-revolutionary Russia), combined with a memorable roster of tunes ('If I Were A Rich Man', 'Sunrise Sunset' et al).

Topol is Tevye, who dreams of a better life even as his wilful daughters rebel against his plans of arranged marriages, and the prejudices of the outside world threaten to ruin his cosy existence. John Williams' adapted score was one of the pair of Oscars gleaned from the eight it was nominated for. Jerry Bock's fine songs are actually few and far between, while the plot's political undertones play second, er, fiddle to the trials and tribulations of Tevye. Look out for a pre-*Starsky And Hutch* Paul Michael Glaser.

Like many musicals, the good songs dry up in the second half, but its blend of energetic joie de vivre and social commentary sustains it through to the end. ★★★★ **NA**

FIELD OF DREAMS (1989)

Starring: *Ray Kinsella (Kevin Costner), Amy Madigan (Annie Kinsella), Gaby Hoffman (Karin Kinsella), Ray Liotta (Shoeless Joe Jackson), Timothy Busfield (Mark), James Earl Jones (Terence Mann), Burt Lancaster (Dr. 'Moonlight' Graham), Frank Whaley (Archie Graham), Dwier Brown (John Kinsella)*
Director: *Phil Alden Robinson*
Screenwriter: *Phil Alden, based on the book Shoeless Joe by W.P. Kinsella*
PG/107 mins./Sports/USA

Ploughing Iowan fields for a pittance, Ray Kinsella risks financial ruin to build a baseball diamond, convinced a voice he heard in the fields told him to do so. Soon ghosts – metaphorical and literal – from the past make their welcome way to his pitch . . .

Field Of Dreams concerns things that touch everybody (although men no longer enjoying their first flush of youth should find it most resonant) like the yearning for reconciliation, lost innocence and a second chance. Such are the themes of the unlikeliest fable Hollywood has devised since

Jimmy Stewart befriended an angel in *It's A Wonderful Life* or, indeed, a six-foot rabbit in *Harvey*.

Ray Kinsella was 18 at the end of the 60s and now, for want of a better idea, is a farmer in Iowa with a wife (the salty, vivacious Amy Madigan) and a small daughter. One day in the cornfield he hears a voice: 'If you build it, he will come.' Naturally, his reaction is to distrust his own sanity, as is his wife's when he decides that the 'it' he must build is a baseball field, right in the middle of corn acreage they cannot afford to plough under.

Impelled by instincts he can neither deny nor understand, he builds the field and waits for what will happen next. This is the sudden appearance of baseball star 'Shoeless' Joe Jackson, just as he was in 1919 when he and the rest of the Chicago White Sox baseball team were disgraced for throwing the World Series. But the quest isn't over yet: 60s writer and activist Terence Mann (James Earl Jones, a magnificent curmudgeon) is dug out of disillusioned retreat, and then he and Ray find they must then track down another former ball-player turned doctor (a bewhiskered Burt Lancaster).

That the Doc turns out to have died years before matters not; by now the idea of ghosts reclaiming their lost opportunities is comfortingly familiar. And so the story unfolds towards the healing of Ray's own big regret, a scene so evocatively played against the sun setting gold behind the corn that only the most flint-hearted will be able to restrain a sniffle.

Too idiosyncratic and witty merely to wallow in sentimentality, *Field Of Dreams* will surely stand as a classic update of what made Old Hollywood so magical. It's still a wonderful life. ★★★★★ **MS**

Movie Trivia: Field of Dreams

Despite starring in three made-for-TV roles, this would be Burt Lancaster's last film role. Tom Hanks was the first choice to play Ray Kinsella but he turned the role down.

THE FIELD (1990)

Starring: *Richard Harris ('Bull' McCabe), Sean Bean (Tadgh McCabe), Frances Tomelty (Young Widow), Brenda Fricker (Maggie McCabe), John Hurt (The 'Bird' O'Donnell)*
Director: *Jim Sheridan*
Screenwriter: *Jim Sheridan, based on the play by John B. Keane*
15/107 mins./Drama/Ireland/UK

An Irish *King Lear* – Richard Harris is a farmer obsessed with the ownership of a disputed plot of land, which leads to bloodshed and awful retribution.

Initially, Jim Sheridan's follow-up to surprise wonder *My Left Foot* looks deceptively and alarmingly like Old Hollywood's notion of Oirish whimsy. British thespians – notably John Hurt with blackened teeth as the village idiot – antic about an emerald countryside being madly colourful and tuck into some toothsome stews in quaint cottages; villagers, tinkers and a red-haired temptress brawl outside the pub while the naive, ineffectual priest wrings his hands and rolls his eyes to heaven. Inexorably, however, *The Field* builds into a mesmerising tragedy of appalling dimensions and remarkable power.

Richard Harris – who'd have thought he had it left in him? – turns in an astonishing performance, restrained, frightening and affecting to the core as Bull McCabe, a farmer whose obsession with ownership of a disputed piece of land leads to bloodshed and most awful retribution. This is an Irish *King Lear*, with old wrongs, secrets and griefs gradually revealed, longings, jealousies and greeds passed down from one generation to the next. Sheridan's screenplay (from the play by John B. Keane) touches Irish history, blood, sweat and class and inspires fine work from everyone onscreen, including Tom Berenger as the rich Irish-American intruder 'looking for his roots', Brenda Fricker as the wife McCabe hasn't touched or spoken to in 18 years, and Frances Tomelty as the Anglo-Irish widow who owns the three acres McCabe would have.

Beautifully made, the 30s period dressing, photography and Elmer Bernstein score mark this as a thoroughly distinguished production, in every way as gripping and compulsive as that other great drama of the land, *Jean De Florette*. High praise indeed. ★★★★ **AE**

FIERCE CREATURES (1997)

Starring: *John Cleese (Rollo Lee), Jamie Lee Curtis (Willa Weston), Kevin Kline (Vince McCain/Rod McCain), Robert Lindsay (Sydney Lotterby), Michael Palin (Adrian 'Bugsy' Malone), Ronnie Corbett (Reggie Sea Lions), Carey Lowell (Cub Felines), Derek Griffiths (Garry Ungulates), Cynthia Cleese (Pip Small Mammals)*
Directors: *Fred Schepisi, Robert Young*
Screenwriters: *John Cleese, Iain Johnstone*
12/93 mins./Comedy/UK/USA

When a friendly zoo is taken over by a large company, the zookeepers try to convince their new owners that their animal charges are more bloodthirsty than they really are.

According to its new owners, voracious international conglomerate Octopus, Marwood Zoo, deep in the heart of rural England, needs to turn a 20% profit or it's goodbye beasties, hello Japanese golf course.

But when hapless manager Rollo Lee's policy to exhibit only animals of a 'fierce' nature is scuppered by his reluctant staff, ambitious Octopus execs Curtis and Kline's alternative is lurid advertising and panto-style animal costumes for the keepers

Lob in innuendo, embezzlement and colossal misunderstanding and you've got the best elements of farce and sitcom rolled into one deliciously entertaining whole. Cleese is Fawlty in a zoo but it's a routine of enduring quality, Curtis is as assured and sultry as ever, and Kline has twice the fun in dual roles as obnoxious and flatulent Aussie billionaire Rod McCain, and his embittered son Vince – frequently venting bile-filled tirades, labelling Cleese 'a giraffe in drag' and 'a flamingo with a boner' among others.

Palin rounds out the reunion as insect expert Bugsy Malone, leading a wonderful ensemble cast of quirky keepers.

Measured against *A Fish Called Wanda*, which contained the same key cast, it is a disappointment, but on its own terms, it's a perfectly amiable comedy. ★★ **DB**

THE FIFTH ELEMENT (LE CINQUIEME ELEMENT) (1997)

Starring: *Bruce Willis (Korben Dallas), Gary Oldman (Zorg), Milla Jovovich (Leeloo), Ian Holm (Cornelius), Chris Tucker (Ruby Rhod), Luke Perry (Billy)*
Director: *Luc Besson*
Screenwriters: *Luc Besson, Robert Mark Kamen, based on a story by Luc Besson*
PG/127 mins./Sci-fi/France

It's 2259 and earth is attacked by a force of 'pure evil' that can only be defeated by a fifth element. The only problem is that no one knows what this fifth element is. It arrives in the form of clone Leeloo, an average-joe taxi driver Korben Dallas and priest Cornelius.

Shrouded during production in the kind of secrecy more appropriate to biological warfare research, *The Fifth Element* burst onto the screen in front of an audience which had not the slightest idea what to expect. The reason for the covert nature of the filming becomes obvious once *The Fifth Element* is seen. Because this is a film that looks unlike any you've seen before. Ever.

Director Besson jettisons the now tired *Blade Runner* vision of a foggy post-apocalyptic future for a bright, primary colour-drenched picture of New York at high noon in the year 2259 complete with thousands of flying cars, Chinese junks floating incongruously among the mêlée and in one astounding shot a vista of New York after the sea level has dropped with Manhattan perched atop a sheer cliff face. Oh, and as a bonus it also contains the largest indoor explosion ever filmed (fire crews apparently took 20 minutes to extinguish the resulting blaze at Pinewood).

Storywise, we're pretty much in by-numbers sci-fi hokum territory. Earth is attacked by a force of 'pure evil' defeatable only by the mysterious fifth element – the usual suspects earth, fire, water and air proving unequal to the task. The trouble is, nobody has the foggiest idea what that might be. Futuristic cabby Korben Dallas gets entangled in the mythical brouhaha when sexy clone Leeloo (a scorching performance from ex-model Jovovich, previously best known for, um, *Return To The Blue Lagoon*) crashes through the roof of his taxi and they rope in priest Cornelius to try and save the planet.

Occupying the Mingish bad-guy role is a loopily nasty Gary Oldman who gleefully manifests the gamut of bad guy tics from a limp to a pronounced though frankly inexplicable South Georgia accent. The rip-offs are masterfully chosen though, from the atmospheric prologue in 1930s Egypt (always a good companion to sci-fi, though wasted in the recent *Stargate*) to the Chris Foss (omnipresent 80s sci-fi paperback cover artist) style impossibly massive and impossibly gleaming spaceships. The eclecticism continues through the casting choices with the incongruous likes of Lee Evans, bedecked in a Jean-Paul Gaultier sailor suit, to Tricky and American camp comic Chris Tucker who minces about the place as the universe's most irritating DJ – a sort of interstellar Chris Evans.

Willis returns from his forays into more demanding performances (*12 Monkeys*) to deliver the familiar wise-cracking everyman complete with *Die Hard*-style ripped clothing and frantic gunplay sequences (although you've not seen a ripped shirt until you've seen a ripped shirt by Gaultier), while Jovovich is a revelation. But the strength of this film is in its visuals. Just as *Blade Runner* changed the way the future looked for a decade-and-a-half of sci-fi filmmakers, so *The Fifth Element* threatens to do the same. Besson and a team of designers including Jean 'Moebius' Giraud and Gaultier have pilfered everything from comic-strip art to the clunky colourful style of the Japanese video game to create an utterly unique visual experience.

If this suffers from any fault it's a case of conceptual overload, with Besson almost losing control of the whole shebang in the third act, laying on the comedy a little too heavily and losing grip of what there is of a story. But with a movie that looks this good, when the plot does go off a little kilter just relax and take in the view. ★★★★ **AS**

FIGHT CLUB (1999)

Starring: *Brad Pitt (Tyler Durden), Edward Norton (Narrator), Helena Bonham Carter (Marla Singer), Meat Loaf (Robert Paulsen), Jared Leto (Angel Face)*
Director: *David Fincher*
Screenwriter: *Jim Uhls, based on the novel by Chuck Palahniuk*
18/139 mins./Drama/USA

Awards: *Empire – Best British Actress*

A lonely, isolated thirtysomething young professional seeks an escape from his mundane existence with the help of a devious soap salesman. They find their release from the prison of reality through underground fight clubs.

When it opened in America to somewhat disappointing business, there was a widespread misjudgement that *Fight Club* was an action movie about underground bare-knuckle boxing contests – perhaps an inflated, star-powered version of Jean-Claude Van Damme vehicles like *Bloodsport* or *Kickboxer*.

Actually, it's a horror movie which literally begins in the fear-centre of its narrator's brain (and arguably stays there) and spins a postmodern rethink of *Psycho* with enough dizzying side-trips to pull off yet again the long-blown surprise ending that two apparent antagonists are, in fact, the same person. Adapted faithfully from Chuck Palahniuk's novel, the film follows a buttoned-down insurance minion who projects himself as flamboyant, anti-social, charismatic genius revolutionary Tyler Durden, in order to shake up his own life and, in the end, society as a whole. The splitting of one persona into 'Jack' (if that's his real name and not a convenience plucked from a *Reader's Digest*-ish magazine he finds) and 'Tyler Durden' evokes Norman Bates and his mother, but also echoes that other once-surprising revelation, that respectable Dr. Jekyll and murderous Mr. Hyde are the same person.

By externalising an alter ego as an apparent actual person played by another actor, *Fight Club* might seem to be cheating – but is merely using the device Robert Bloch did in his *Psycho* novel, where Norman and Mother have long talks. There are similar instances in not a few horror films, like the *Lucy Comes To Stay* segment of 1972's *Asylym* (which Bloch wrote) where repressed Charlotte Rampling and homicidal Britt Ekland are one person, or *The Other*, from Tom Tryon's novel, where one of a set of twins turns out to be either a ghost or an alternate personality.

This gambit, which many of *Fight Club*'s original audiences found infuriating, is actually so well established in the genre that Brian De Palma could play a joke at its expense in *Raising Cain*, where John Lithgow's imaginary father turns out to be real after all. *Fight Club* is the third and most complex in director David Fincher's loose trilogy of nightmare movies, following *Seven* (or *Se7en*, to be strictly accurate) and *The Game*. It begins in the fear-centre of a brain and spins a postmodern rethink on *Psycho*. Fincher's theme – trace elements can be found even in his compromised debut, *Alien³* – is the crisis of middle-class masculinity in a world torn between oppressive conformity and a libido-like anarchic underbelly that is at once dangerous, alluring and life-changing.

Se7en is also about an unsatisfied minion (there, Pitt) who meets his monster alter ego (Kevin Spacey) and is manipulated into murdering him, while *The Game* also strips away every trapping of success and wealth from Michael Douglas as he realises his whole life is a conspiracy whose purpose he fears and desires at the same time. The trajectory of Fincher's career is away from strict genre and into an unclassifiable twilight zone, but he takes with him an evolving, unique filmmaking style that suggests a final evolutionary form of the horror movie as a species of black satire shot through with impolite bursts of violence as terrifying as they are liberating.

Tagline
Mischief.
Mayhem.
Soap.

A chronic insomniac addicted to kibitzing at self-help groups, Jack encounters goth chick Marla, who has a similar kink, and is forced into a wilder sphere when he hooks up with Durden, whom he seems to meet on an aeroplane. When his Ikea-outfitted condo is blown up in a mysterious explosion, Jack moves into a dilapidated old house (reminiscent of the Bates Motel) with him. The pair indulge in recreational fistfights in a bar parking lot, which expands into an underground club for alienated men to take out their frustrations on each other as a homosocial and homoerotic act.

Though Durden and Maria have a noisy affair, fantasised and actualised by Jack, women almost don't impinge on the world of Tyler Durden. It's a plot feint about the overt attraction between the male leads, beautiful Brad and wiry Edward, that winds in on itself with the revelation that Jack has been fighting himself. Durden turns Fight Club into Project Mayhem, a campaign of revolutionary pranks which extends so far into the infrastructure of society that when Jack catches on to his double life and confesses, most of the cops turn out to be in on it.

There is a great deal of sick humour at the expense of masculinist ideals and white-collar society – Durden's bizarre pranks (splicing porno frames into family films, making soap of liposucked human fat) to the dizzying third act as Jack is bewildered by the escalation of the project his disciples know he has initiated, with his statements taken up as chanted slogans and seemingly every bruised man he meets in on the scheme. It culminates in real horror as Jack purges himself of Durden by shooting himself in the mouth, blowing out Durden's brains but not his own, and embracing the puzzled Maria as the skyline of financial buildings explodes. ★★★★★ **KN**

Movie Trivia: Fight Club

Meat Loaf's character had two fat suits designed, one with nipples and one without. The studio was reluctant to use the one with nipples since they felt they were abnormally prominent. The names used by the narrator in his support groups are characters from *Planet of the Apes* and Robert De Niro roles of the 70s. Ed Norton's character isn't named in the film.

FINAL DESTINATION (2000)

Starring: *Devon Sawa (Alex Chance Browning), Ali Larter (Clear Rivers), Kerr Smith (Carter Horton), Tony Todd (William Bludworth), Kristen Cloke (Ms. Valerie Lewton), Seann William Scott (Billy Hitchcock)*
Director: *James Wong*
Screenwriters: *Glen Morgan, James Wong, Jeffrey Reddick, based on a story by Jeffrey Reddick*
15/98 mins./Horror/USA

After one of them experiences a powerful vision, a group of students leave an airplane that goes on to crash, killing everyone onboard. But after the accident, strange accidents carry off members of the group, suggesting that Death, or Fate, may be holding a grudge.

Given the relative disappointment of the final part of the *Scream* trilogy, you'd have been forgiven for thinking that the cycle of wry, ironic teen-based horror flicks that Craven and his Munch-masked monster kicked off had utterly run out of steam. *Final Destination*, however, seems to demonstrate that there's life in the old sub-genre yet, as it's certainly the most inventive, funny and downright enjoyable Friday nighter ever since.

Unusually, *Final Destination* is a horror flick without a monster. After they miraculously escape an air crash that dispatches the majority of their classmates to the almighty, Alex Browning (movie buffs will already have noticed the curious pattern of the characters' surnames – they're all classic horror directors) and friends are methodically hunted down by a presumably pissed off 'fate' that intended them to exit this mortal coil via the explosive qualities of aviation fuel and the non-negotiable nature of gravity.

This set-up allows screenwriters Glen Morgan, James Wong and Jeffrey Reddick an excuse to deliver a cascade of deliriously overwrought fatal 'accidents': slippery floors and shower attachments do for one; scrap metal and an approaching train produce a devastating death for another, while a sequence involving a boiling kettle, block of knives, leaky vodka glass and an exploding computer plays like an advert made by the Royal Society For The Prevention Of Accidents.

First time director Wong (who previously directed episodes of *The X-Files*) flawlessly judges the shocks' timing – one particularly nasty road accident will leave audiences gasping with surprise – and, in the opening 15 minutes of the film, delivers the most devastating air crash sequence ever put on film (easily beating *Alive!*, the previous holder of the title).

The cast, many of whom are graduates of the late 90's tidal wave of teen flicks (Ali Larter was the wearer of the infamous whipped cream bikini in *Varsity Blues*, while Seann William Scott was teen lothario Stifler in *American Pie*), are a further indication of the sheer depth of talent now knocking around Hollywood in search of decent scripts. Sadly, the following not-quite-on-a-par sequels, for obvious reasons, couldn't make use of them. ★★★★ **CC**

FINAL FANTASY: THE SPIRITS WITHIN (2001)

Starring: *the voices of: Ming-Na (Dr. Aki Ross), Alec Baldwin (Capt. Gray Edwards), Ving Rhames (Sgt. Ryan Whitaker), Steve Buscemi (Officer Neil Fleming), Peri Gilpin (Officer Jane Proudfoot), Donald Sutherland (Dr. Cid), James Woods (General Hein)*
Director: *Hironobu Sakaguchi, Moto Sakakibara*
Screenwriters: *Al Reinert, Jeff Vintar, based on story by Hironoby Sakaguchi, with additional dialogue by Jack Fletcher*
PG/106 mins./Animation/USA/Japan

It's 2065. Earth is threatened by phantom-styled aliens unleashed by a giant meteor. As humanity holes up in barrier cities and scheming General Hein plans to destroy the aliens by annihilating the Earth, scientist Dr. Aki Ross, aided by a clutch of soldiers, struggles against the odds to neutralise the alien threat.

Heralded as the biggest advancement towards photo-realistic computer animation yet seen, *Final Fantasy: The Spirits Within* was at once a step forward into a brave new world and a step back into stale science fiction hokum. If the quality of the writing had matched the artistry of the animation it would border on masterpiece. As it is, the result – which hardly set the box office on fire on its US opening – resembles a beautifully wrought computer game, minus the interaction.

The film gets off to a powerful, wordless start as Aki Ross is pursued by the military through a fantastically realised, derelict, drizzly New York. From here on in, there are big, set-piece moments to razzle the retina: Aki caught in the middle of an alien stampede; phantoms killing off soldiers by reaching and pulling out souls from bodies.

Eschewing the gaudy game patina, the movie has an impressively detailed, muted visual sheen that is much more Ridley Scott than John Lasseter. But it is in its minutiae that *Final Fantasy* really impresses. Moments that would pass by unnoticed in a live-action flick become increasingly impressive as you witness a medium expanding its boundaries before your very eyes: Aki running her fingers through her hair (follicles previously a sticking point for CGI); the blemishes on her wan skin; the subtleties of torchlight; the 'handheld' quality of the 'camerawork'. If the photo-realistic claim is extravagant, there are flashes when *Final Fantasy* completely blurs the distinction between CGI and live action.

But while the 'wow' factor remains consistently high – there is a great set-piece as the heroes shoot their way past the phantom menace – the level of interest begins to dissipate as the one-dimensional characters, mystical mumbo-jumbo and hokey plotting simply fail to take hold. If she is stunningly realised visually, Aki lacks shading in the character stakes, her love story with Affleck-alike Gray Edwards failing to spark.

Moreover, the soldiers who assist Aki are straight out of the James Cameron Academy For Disgruntled Grunts – Buscemi's techie geek, Rhames' hard-as-nails-sarge – while James Woods hams it up mightily through gigabytes of beautifully rendered, pixellated scenery. You might have seen this story time and again in a Saturday morning cartoon but, in superseding the state of the art, *Final Fantasy* ensures it's worth another look. ★★★ **IF**

◐ FINDING NEMO (2003)

Starring: *the voices of: Albert Brooks (Marlin), Ellen DeGeneres (Dory), Alexander Gould (Nemo), Willem Dafoe (Gill), Allison Janney (Peach), Jan Ranft (Jacques), Geoffrey Rush (Nigel), Elizabeth Perkins (Coral)*
Director: *Andrew Stanton, Lee Unrich*
Screenwriters: *Bob Peterson, David Reynolds, Andrew Stanton, from a story by Andrew Stanton*
U/101 mins./Animated/Family/Comedy/USA
Awards: *Academy Awards – Best Animated Feature*

Overprotective father Marlin is horrified to witness his curious, young clownfish son Nemo's captured by a human diver. Frantic Marlin overcomes his timidity to search for Nemo, helped by his new blue friend Dory in a deep-sea CGI adventure.

No doubt there is a scientific explanation for why human eyes are always drawn to a tank full of tropical fish. Whatever the fascination is, the Pixar boys have it rumbled – so entrancing is the composition of this animated fishy tale.

On paper, a story about fish doesn't sound as engaging as a yarn about cuddlier critters or the secret life of toys. But, of course, the eye-catching marine life in *Finding Nemo* is more human than piscine. Marlin is a red-and-white clownfish at pains to correct the misconception that his species is funny. He can't tell a joke to save his life and has been a bundle of nerves since his mate and her eggs were eaten. The sole survivor was Nemo, who, in a differently-abled touch, has an under-developed fin and has been kept sheltered in the anemone they call home. Rebellious, he wanders off perilously close to a fishing boat, is caught, and gets plopped into a Sydney dentist's waiting-room aquarium, where senior prisoner Gill is plotting a great escape with the kind of ingenuity and daring immortalised in the more upbeat prisoner-of-war movies.

Anthropomorphism runs (or is that swims?) riot on Marlin's quest. One of the characters, somehow, fortuitously reads English. A toothsome trio of sharks (led vocally by Barry Humphries) have formed a Fish-Eaters Anonymous chapter which meets in a wrecked submarine to forswear cannibalism (pity we aren't told what the alternative nourishment is). And reports of the devoted father's courageous journey spread through the ocean and above it until a multiplicity of genuses are rooting him on. This passes the point of absurdity when Marlin hitches a lift to Australia with thrill-seeking stoner turtles who talk like Bill and Ted.

Yet it's all beautifully composed and consistently charming, as Disney's bacon-saving association with the inventive Pixar studio strikes gold again in a perfectly family-oriented pitch of adventure, humour and thinly-veiled life lessons for the sprats.

The voice cast is highly recognisable and the scripted characterisations capitalise on actors' familiar mannerisms – particularly Brooks' perennially neurotic, pessimistic schtick wrapped up in the anxious Marlin; DeGeneres' perky, goofy Dory (who wittily suffers from short-term memory loss and regularly has to be reminded of the story so far); Dafoe's sinister gravitas in the battered, grimly determined Gill; and Rush's uninhibited pizzazz for Nigel the pelican.

Grown-ups may experience some restlessness as sentimentality seeps in. But there are nods to adults in fun homages to *Psycho*, *Pinocchio* and *The Terminator* (the pelican getting the immortal line, 'Hop inside my mouth if you want to live'), in almost subliminal leg-pulls (a moored boat named The Surly Mermaid), and in a postscript visual gag that makes sitting through the end credits essential. The style is a triumph in the use of colour, movement and effects – notably in the detailed schools of fishes, the emergence of figures from the blurry depths and a 'swirling vortex of terror' sequence.

★★★★ AE

◐ FINDING NEVERLAND (2004)

Starring: *Johnny Depp (Sir James Matthew Barrie), Kate Winslet (Sylvia Llewelyn Davies), Julie Christie (Mrs. Emma Du Maurier), Radha Mitchell (Mary Ansell Barrie), Dustin Hoffman (Charles Frohman), Freddie Highmore (Peter Llewelyn Davies), Ian Hart (Sir Arthur Conan Doyle), Kelly Macdonald (Peter Pan)*
Director: *Marc Forster*
Screenwriter: *David Magee, based on the play* The Man Who Was Peter Pan *by Allan Knee*
PG/106 mins./Drama/Biography/USA/UK
Awards: *Academy Awards – Best Original Score, Empire Awards – Best Newcomer (Freddie Highmore)*

Handicapped by his own success, playwright J. M. Barrie is depressed by his apparent importance in the critical world. Then a meeting with a widowed mother and her four sons sparks a lasting friendship and the inspiration for his greatest work: *Peter Pan*.

Johnny Depp has never gotten around to putting away childish things. Instead he's spread them liberally across his career, delving into the farthest corners of the dressing-up box to portray everything from transvestite, to pirate, to scissor-handed boy. Which makes him not only a wow at fancy dress parties, but also the perfect choice to portray J. M. Barrie, creator of Peter Pan and eternal child himself.

Stuck in a functional marriage to a brittle social climber who wanders their darkened home like a widow in waiting, Depp's Barrie is less a tortured artist than a tethered fantasist, dimmed by the expectation of the theatrical world and awkward in the company of the fusty society types who frequent his plays. His chance meeting with Sylvia Llewelyn Davies and her four sons unshackles not only Barrie's creativity as a writer, but also Marc Forster's own visual ingenuity.

The combination of the quaint Victorian setting and Barrie's fertile imagination allows Forster to conjure up a world where fantasy leaks into the everyday as fleeting moments – a tinkling bell here, a brandished hook there – thereby sowing the seeds of Pan. It's redolent of Peter Jackson's *Heavenly Creatures*, where even the mundane seems slightly askew, lending the entire film a lush, storybook look. Forster and cinematographer Roberto Schaefer frame everything with intricate beauty, be it Sylvia sighted through a hole in a newspaper, a camera darting fairy-like over an enthralled audience, or the hazy, painterly fantasy sequences.

Depp, seemingly unable to put a foot wrong performance-wise, is both playful and judicious as Barrie. Though the script bats him between melancholia and elation as his friendship with the Llewelyn Davies family inflicts its own joys and tragedies, Depp adds an endearing eccentricity that's all his own. It's hard not to detect the actor's barmy hand in a moment where he arrives at the children's house wearing an elaborately feathered American Indian headdress with a wooden duck under his arm. Winslet, meanwhile, plays Sylvia with an earthy gutsiness in a performance that'll wring a tear from even the coldest eye. Yet, great as the two leads are, both are soundly upstaged by an actor with a fraction of their experience.

Freddie Highmore, who plays Sylvia's curmudgeonly son Peter, shows the potential to be the finest child actor since Haley Joel Osment – but without the latter's creepy air of middle age. Peter is the fractured, fluttering heart of the movie, sparking up a tentative friendship with Barrie that never hits a false note. You'd expect that a film dealing with the closeness between a grown man and small boys would suggest the kind of sinister goings-on currently associated with a certain other Neverland, but the script – adapted from Allan Knee's stageplay by David Magee – approaches it in a subtle, graceful way, painting Barrie's face with abject disgust when an acquaintance points out that the relationship has raised the suspicions of the society gossips.

It should be noted that Magee has played fast and loose with the chronology of Barrie's life, inventing and omitting events to suit the story, but this is not a by-the-numbers biopic so much as a celebration of the joy of childhood, the fleetingness of life and the birth of art. More than anything, though, it's simply a wonderful story, spun from both comedy and tragedy and told with such elegance and wit that you can't fail to be dusted by its magic. ★★★★★ **OR**

FINIAN'S RAINBOW (1968)

Starring: *Fred Astaire (Finian McLonergan), Petula Clark (Sharon McLonergan), Tommy Steele (Og The Leprechaun), Don Francks (Woody Mahoney)*
Director: *Francis Ford Coppola*
Screenwriter: *E.Y. Harburg, Fred Saidy, based on their play.*
U/180 mins./Musical/USA

Irishman Finian McLonergan steals a crock of gold from Og the leprechaun and arrives in the Southern state of Missitucky convinced that its value will grow if he plants it in the ground, as the Americans had done with Fort Knox.

Several attempts had been made to film E.Y. 'Yip' Harburg and Fred Saidy's 1947 Broadway hit before Francis Ford Coppola stepped into the breach some 20 years later. Work had commenced and been abandoned on an animated version – with vocalisations by Frank Sinatra, Judy Garland, Ella Fitzgerald and Louis Armstrong – while a Dick Van Dyke package had come to nothing in 1965. But, in truth, Hollywood had little faith in a project whose acerbic social commentary was bound to upset the guardians of the Production Code, while its depiction of a Senator changing colour and the co-mingling of black and white sharecroppers would have been too much for Southern audiences, for whom screen musicals were carefully stripped of their African-Americans so as to avoid giving offence.

To his credit, Coppola reinforced the racial satire by adding a new character, Howard, the botanist who attempts to cultivate mintolated tobacco and lampoon the servile Stepin Fetchit type that Hollywood had spent 50 years passing off as the acceptable face of black America. But he singularly failed to equate the message with the current state of the Civil Rights campaign. Thus, its contention that blacks are just the same as whites beneath the skin is not only outdated, but also positively patronising.

Coppola similarly misjudged many of the musical sequences. Petula Clark admirably handles such tunes as 'How Are Things in Glocca Morra?', but Tommy Steele is allowed to overact and his mugging spoils the likes of 'When I'm Not Near the Girl I Love'. Sixty-eight year-old Fred Astaire, in his 31st and final musical, was given greater licence to create his own routines with Hermes Pan. But much of the satirical sting was drawn from 'When the Idle Poor Become the Idle Rich' and Warners ludicrously chopped off Fred's feet when they blew the print up to 70mm, as they were so pleased with the film's glossy whimsy.

Audiences thought otherwise, however, and this promising, but compromised picture was a resounding flop. ★★★ **DP**

FIREFOX (1982)

Starring: *Clint Eastwood (Mitchell Grant), Freddie Jones (Kenneth Aubrey), David Huffman (Buckholz), Warren Clarke (Pavel Upenskoy)*
Director: *Clint Eastwood*
Screenwriters: *Alex Lasker, Wendell Wellman based on the novel by Craig Thomas*
15/136 mins./Action/Adventure/USA

When intelligence is picked up that the Soviets have invented a revolutionary new stealth fighter called Firefox, piloted using a neural connection to the brain, former Vietnam War pilot Mitchell Grant goes on a covert mission to steal it. But as he jets away from Russia, it transpires there is another prototype hot on his trail.

What was up with Clint Eastwood in the eighties? As his gruff Dirty Harry persona waned with age, he seemed willing, almost eager, to besmirch his reputation with ludicrous high concept pap typically involving apes. But even those orang-utan comedies have a semblance of credibility compared to this video-game primer, lurid with a right-wing propaganda that wouldn't have been out of place in the McCarthy era. And Eastwood even directed this one. Shame on you, Clint.

Made as the Cold War seemed so chilly it would never thaw, and based on Craig Thomas' Tom Clancy-esque techno thriller, the implication that the Russkies have developed a weapon that could blow heartland American clean out of their beds without warning, certainly held a superficial trepidation. Of course, the one man, now John Wayne was pushing up daisies, who could save them was going to be granite-faced Clint Eastwood. Half of his film, baring hints of the austere, moody style he would put to great use in later career, is a form of espionage thriller as he goes undercover, disguised with moustache and horn-rimmed glasses into the commie heartland (stand-in: Austria) to steal the Firefox (he can after all 'think' in Russian and thus steer the jet to safety). Grittiness, however intelligently meant, doesn't fit the quasi-sci-fi trappings of the novel at all. There was never any way to make the film feel real, so why not revel in its absurdity?

Yet the film methodically lurches through a series of dry undercover manoeuvres as Grant plots his way through a swathe of secret agents, including his brash CIA brothers and the scurrilous KGB on his trail. When he finally clambers into the hi-tech cockpit, after what seems an age of that grungy looking clandestine stuff, the film should rev up into an action packed finale. Time has not told well on the tin-pot effects used to simulate flying at Mach 6 (4,500 mph) and the chase between the twin Firefoxes, with their dim modernistic styling like a Lamborghini crossed with a nuke, are fake enough to be laughable. A clunky symbol of a film that should be confined to history. ★★ **IN**

FIRES WERE STARTED (1943)

Starring: *George Gravett (Dykes), Phillip Dickson (Walters), Fred Griffiths (Johnny Daniels), Loris Rey (J. Rumbold), Johnny Houghton (S.H. Jackson), William Sansom (Barrett)*
Director: *Humphrey Jennings*
Screenwriter: *Humphrey Jennings*
U/74 mins./Docu-Drama/UK

At the height of the Blitz, Barrett, a new recruit at an Auxiliary Fire Service station in London, has a day to learn the ropes before he's thrown into the front line to fight a blaze at a dockside warehouse.

His reputation enhanced by the lyrical realism of the 1942 short, *Listen to Britain*, Humphrey Jennings produced his first and only feature. In paying tribute to the disbanded Auxiliary Fire Service, which had performed heroics during the Blitz, he drew heavily on the docudramatic tradition established in films like *Target for Tonight* and *In Which We Serve*. But, Jennings sought to recreate reality by employing those who had experienced it first hand and his cast was made up of members of the newly established National Fire Service, who largely improvised their dialogue after discussion with the director.

Jennings began the project with the barest outline, which was something of a reckless tactic, considering that he had never previously attempted a drama with a linear narrative and definable, individual characters. However, he was always more at home in the editing room than on location and he imparted a poetic power to his footage that not only made it persuasive propaganda, but also ensured it has endured as a masterclass in audiovisual authenticity.

By adopting a day-in-the-life structure, Jennings was able to educate viewers about how a station went about its business. Yet, the sequences showing the crew preparing their equipment in the calm before the storm also captures the mundanity of duty and how these everyday men and women cope with the constant pressure of laying their lives on the line for their country. Images of the basking dog and the blossoming tree only reinforce this impression of a country worth fighting for. Yet, Jennings avoids a physical depiction of the Nazi enemy and resists any overt hostility towards them. Indeed, he treats the blaze that threatens the munitions ship almost as if it were a natural disaster to emphasise that the AFS would have responded with courage and professionalism regardless of the conflagration's cause.

Consequently, this is an impeccably paced, precisely edited commendation of a classless community uniting in a selfless act of defiant resistance. ★★★★ **DP**

Humphrey Jennings (1906–1950)

Who was he: Arguably Britain's greatest documentary filmmaker. Tragically lost his life after falling off a cliff while scouting locations in Greece.
Hallmarks: Poetic evocations of everyday life, captured through striking imagery; minimalist commentary and radical editing strategies.
If you see one movie, see: *Listen To Britain* (1942)

THE FIRM (1993)

Starring: *Tom Cruise (Mitch McDeere), Jeanne Tripplehorn (Abby McDeere), Gene Hackman (Avery Tolar), Hal Holbrook (Oliver Lambert), Holly Hunter (Tammy Hemphill), David Strathairn (Ray McDeere), Gary Busey (Eddie Lomax)*
Director: *Sydney Pollack*
Screenwriters: *David Rabe, Robert Towne, David Fayfiel, based on the novel by John Grisham*
15/153 mins./Thriller/Drama/USA

Having successfully graduated from Harvard law school, Mitch McDeere turns down Wall St. to work for a smaller firm with the incentive of a brand new car and house and even a generous pay rise. It's not until further down the line that McDeere begins to realise there might have been a catch.

Sydney Pollack's adaptation of John Grisham's 1991 bestseller is a big, slumbering, occasionally invigorating Star Vehicle, with most of the menace that propelled Grisham's gripping page-turner diluted in favour of a more Cary Grant-ish take on the classic Hollywood conspiracy thriller. Lacking the paranoia of Pollack's own *Three Days Of The Condor*, it's also gelatinous, sloppy and over-indulgent, yet somehow manages to make the grade as a pulpy, old-fashioned movie experience.

Tom Cruise is Mitch McDeere, a brash, grin-flashing hotshot, top in his Harvard law class and Wall Street-bound until the small Memphis law firm of Bendini, Lambert & Locke lure him down South with a stupendous salary, gorgeous house and new Mercedes. It seems too good to be true, and, of course, it is, with McDeere's more intuitive, earthy wife Abby smelling a rat when wholesome cult-like firm members start sounding like a cross between Dan Quayle and the Stepford Wives. No one has ever left The Firm alive, but McDeere isn't totally clued into the fact that he's made a Faustian career deal with a pit of wire-tapping, blue-blooded vipers until abrasive cue ball FBI agent Ed Harris fills him in on Bendini's Mafia money-laundering ways and offers him two choices: break the legal code of honour and get enough dirt to indict the firm, or prepare for 20 years in the slammer when Bendini inevitably goes down.

This is a film powered along by several meaty and flamboyant character turns. Besides Harris, the more memorable etchings are made by Hackman, brilliant, as always, as Cruise's cynical, ultimately remorseful mentor, Avery Tolar; Gary Busey as a seedy private investigator; Academy and BAFTA Award nominated Holly Hunter as Busey's tarty secretary and Cruise's partner-in-Mob-busting; and David Strathairn as McDeere's wise, soulful convict brother. Indeed, without the performances, this would mostly be a non-starter, since Pollack didn't so much direct this as blandly guide it along the safest, risk-free path to commercial bonanza, making numerous plot changes en route from page to screen. Nonetheless, Cruise fans won't be disappointed and there are enough dizzying new twists in the somewhat convoluted final act to keep Grisham fans entertained without totally alienating them. Instantly forgettable, but with undeniable pulp appeal. ★★★ **MM**

FIRST BLOOD (1982)

Starring: *Sylvester Stallone (John J. Rambo), Richard Crenna (Col. Samuel Trautman), Brian Dennehy (Hope Sheriff Will Teasle), Bill McKinney (State Police Capt. Dave Kern), Jack Starrett (Deputy Sgt. Arthur Gale)*
Director: *Ted Kotcheff*
Screenwriters: *Michael Kozoll, William Sackheim, Sylvester Stallone, based on the novel by David Morrell*
15/97 mins./Drama/Action/Thriller/USA

In a small town in Oregon, Vietnam veteran John Rambo is arrested for vagrancy by corrupt Sheriff Will Teasle. Abused by Teasle and his deputies, Rambo goes crazy, escaping into the surrounding hills, massively armed with every weapon he needs to take revenge on Teasle.

It should, on the face of it, be almost impossible to defend John Rambo. For most people the name conjures up the cartoonish excesses of *Rambo First Blood Part II* with sweaty Sylvester Stallone grunting his way through director George P. Cosmatos' kerosene-drenched excess. But times get the heroes they deserve, the erstwhile cine-hack progenitor of the likes of *The Cassandra Crossing* and *Cobra* (together with a youthful James Cameron on screenplay duty) delivered an icon utterly appropriate to the political and social overkill of the mid-80s.

The unfeasibly pneumatic Stallone, complete with ammo-decked granite-hewn pecs and an anti-tank grenade launcher slung casually over his shoulder, became a poster-boy for America's flourishing Republican right. Ronald Reagan became – entirely to his non-dismay – 'Ronbo'. The gun lobby gazed lovingly at Rambo's array of hardware like horny raincoats at the ammunitions equivalent of a fuck show. And potato-headed adolescents in Arse Springs, Arkansas, no-doubt dribbled half-chewed 'goober' as the Vietnamese were reduced to so many targets on a hi-tech human coconut shy.

It's all gloriously ironic because, in fact, the John Rambo created by novelist David Morrell is a considerably more ambivalent, anti-authoritarian figure than the steroidal stereotype of the *First Blood* sequels. In fact he's the first of a cinematic archetype – the emotionally wounded vet betrayed both then and now by his country – and of a sub genre, the confessional 'Nam film. After Rambo it would be impossible to make a gung-ho rumble in the jungle like *The Green Berets* and have it taken seriously. *Platoon*, *Casualties Of War*, *Hamburger Hill* and *Full Metal Jacket* all incorporated some element of the 'war as a personal hell' motif while Oliver Stone located Rambo's real-life counterpart in *Born On The Fourth Of July*. For American audiences at least, these post-Rambo Vietnam flicks were the ideal combination of bloody mayhem and Oprah-style emotional gush, crystallised in the poster image for *Platoon*, a soldier, arms flung heavenward with the legend 'The first casualty of war is innocence'. But Rambo got there, and lost it, first.

It's pretty obvious that *First Blood* is going to be an untriumphant take on the war from the very start when John Rambo wanders into a small, picturesque lakeside town to track down an old war buddy. There he finds that his friend has died of cancer – blamed by his widow on all that 'orange stuff' employed by the US Army. Worse, when the local Sheriff (ever dependable movie heavy Brian Dennehy) criticises him for wearing, ironically he assumes, the American flag, Rambo's response, after being abused and degraded, is to deliver a little taste of Vietnam to the small-town America that had put him there. In so doing, Dr. Frankenstein-like, he created a monster.

But as well as the sociopolitical fun to be had, and the deeply satisfying fact that once again America got hold of the wrong end of the cultural stick, there's the fact that *First Blood* is a first-rate, taught action thriller. Ted Kotcheff, an eclectic Canadian director who won an Emmy for classic British TV drama *Edna, The Inebriate Woman* before much later delivering the less critically lauded *Red Shoe Diaries 3: Another Woman's Lipstick*, paces the film superbly – the motorcycle/police cruiser chase in the opening 20 minutes is a textbook example of how to shoot one, using no musical soundtrack and long takes. Whereas cinematographer Andrew Laszlo (who the previous year had lensed backwoods drama *Southern Comfort* to which, along with *Deliverance*, *First Blood* owes at least a visual debt) shoots British Columbia in coldly evocative greys and muddy greens.

Stallone himself employs the doe-eyed, baffled innocence that served him so well in *Rocky* before he transformed himself into a laughable human caricature. He's a walking, stalking muscular martyr who half the time seems to be inviting the audience to pull a thorn out of his psychic paw. Wisely, he restricts his dialogue to the bare minimum (admirable since he shares a screenwriting credit) only erupting into what many critics felt was absurd burbling in his final touchy-feely breakdown sequence ('... he's fuckin' screaming', there's pieces of him all over me ... I'm tryin' to pull 'em off you know? And he ... My friend! It's all over me!') But to be fair, isn't the whole point of hysterically emotional incoherence that it is emotional, hysterical and, erm, incoherent?

Whatever its flaws – which include a dreadful end-title song with the cringeworthy lyric, 'It's a real war/outside your front door' as well as the creation of an early 80s adolescent vogue for cheap rip-off, 'Rambo knives' complete with compass and 'wire-saw' in the handle in case the same thing happens to you, down the Arndale presumably. All in all, not bad for the director who, seven years later, would deliver *Weekend At Bernie's* and a star who would go on to attempt the world's first arm-wrestling drama with *Over The Top*. ★★★★ **AS**

THE FIRST GREAT TRAIN ROBBERY (1978)

Starring: *Sean Connery (Edward Pierce), Donald Sutherland (Robert Agar), Lesley-Anne Down (Miriam), Wayne Sleep ('Clean Willy' Williams), Michael Elphick (Burgess)*
Director: *Michael Crichton*
Screenwriter: *Michael Crichton based on his own novel*
12/110 mins./Crime/USA

Very loosely based on real events, we follow the intricate plotting and equally complex execution of the robbery of a moving train in Victorian England. The prize is a military payroll, and the thieves, led by Edward Pierce, are rogues of very high standing.

A splendidly detailed and rousing caper movie written and directed by popular author Michael Crichton from his own novel, that flaunts historical accuracy in favour of the alluring sizzle of gentleman rogues up to no good. Sean Connery and Donald Sutherland make for an appealing pair of crooks, amoral to their core but brimming with derring-do and street smarts. We're rooting for them all the way, with their jaunty tops hats, swishing tails and landscapes of facial hair. As they are assisted by the fetching Lesley-Anne Down the deal is sealed. Never has Victorian underwear been applied with this breathtaking effect.

There are two clear halves to the efficient script (Crichton has a scientist's care for precision). First the crack-team work through the planning stages, as they gradually purloin imprints of the four keys required to open the safe, followed by the heist itself on a train hurtling through the British countryside. During this age of steam power, it seemed an impossible gambit. Tame, perhaps, by the brutal pace of modern action sequences, Crichton still instils a stirring authenticity with Connery manfully doing his own stunts as he crosses the rooftop through billows of sooty smoke, for the getaway.

All around, Crichton soaks up the weft and weave of fanciful Victoriana from the cold, brick walls of the prison for Wayne Sleep's acrobatic jailbreak to the lush, silken decor of the brothel where the sexy Down steals away a key from Alan Webb's randy bank manager. But realism is not the style, Crichton is after a giggly quality as if it's being told as a pub yarn, soaked in exaggeration and acute trickery to defeat impossible hurdles, while never far from redoubtable moral lessons. ★★★★ **IN**

FIRST KNIGHT (1995)

Starring: *Sean Connery (King Arthur), Richard Gere (Lancelot), Julia Ormond (Guinevere), Ben Cross (Prince Malagant), Liam Cunningham (Agravaine), John Gielgud (Oswald)*
Director: *Jerry Zucker*
Screenwriters: *William Nicholson, Lorne Cameron, David Hoselton*
PG/134 mins./History/USA

A retelling of the King Arthur fable, centering on a young, dashing Lancelot arriving at the court of an ageing Arthur, who is about to marry a much younger Guinevere. When the younger couple fall in love, honour and desire will come into conflict.

A horribly overwrought rendition of the old Arthurian staple, that strains to interrogate the love triangle issue at the expense of all else. What we are left with is a sappy, wounded star vehicle, big on anachronism (check out Lancelot's American drawl) and low on mythological grandeur. Never has ancient Britain looked so cleansed of identity. Camelot, with its formal, bland design (not John Box's finest hour) is recalling nothing more than the wooden sets of Errol Flynn-era swashbucklers, a flavour Jerry Zucker seems to be aimlessly harkening to.

Even away from the soapy, stilted exhumation of the bones of legend in William Nicholson's script, nothing ever relaxes. Connery, bewigged as ever, presents a sturdy mien but is so uncomfortable in the love scenes with a wan Julia Ormond, he nearly blushes. Their romance, supposedly constructed about honour rather than love, is tepid and uninteresting. But that's an irritant compared to the calamity of Richard Gere's casting.

Lancelot has been refashioned as some kind of unprincipled renegade, dishily ruffled around the edges and burdened with the stock Hollywood psychology of a troubled childhood. Frankly, compared to that rod of principle, the pure manifestation of nobelesse that rides through tradition, he's a complete berk. The idea is that love shatters apart Lancelot's identity, reducing him to nothing. Here the gooey glances this pair of twittering lovebirds share come across like playground puppy love, and Arthur should have them both beheaded on the grounds of treasonous texting.

Elsewhere, Ben Cross pays his mortgage as duff made-up badguy Malagant, a good knight who has soured, and with his pack of stunt men is responsible for giving the film some action. But it's all over-choreographed horse stunts and Gere leaping through a trial by contraption that predates Sonic the Hedgehog by centuries. ★★ **IN**

THE FISHER KING (1991)

Starring: *Robin Williams (Parry), Jeff Bridges (Jack Lucas), Mercedes Ruehl (Anne Napolitano), Amanda Plummer (Lydia), Adam Bryant (Radio Engineer)*
Director: *Terry Gilliam*
Screenwriter: *Richard LaBravenese*
15/137 mins./Fantasy/Comedy/Drama/Romance/USA

Awards: *Academy Awards – Best Supporting Actress (Mercedes Ruehl), Golden Globes – Best Actor (Robin Williams), Best Supporting Actress (Mercedes Ruehl)*

After one of his listeners opens fire on a bar, shock-DJ Jack is demoted to a life working in a record store. One night he is set upon by thugs and rescued by a homeless hero. In return the man asks Jack's help to retrieve the Holy Grail and woo the object of his desire.

The camera swoops down from the ceiling to concentrate on the head of chain-smoking, pony-tailed Jack Lucas as he hurls frantic abuse at a caller. He's a mega-successful Manhattan 'shock DJ' and in line for his own TV sitcom – until one night his world falls apart when one frustrated listener to his show opens fire in a bar, killing several people.

Three years on, Jack's life has dramatically changed, he's working in a video store with girlfriend and drinking enough to end up in a sodden heap one night, only to be rescued from a bunch of thugs by Parry, a homeless knight-in-dirty-clothes with a fascination for the Holy Grail (this is a Terry Gilliam film, after all). In return for saving him, Parry wants Jack to retrieve the Holy Grail for him (it's in the hands of a Fifth Avenue businessman), and although Jack clearly believes Parry is crazy, the two form an uneasy alliance, with Jack helping Parry in his other quest – to finally meet the woman he has been worshipping each day from afar, Lydia. But nothing is ever easy, and Parry is haunted by a threatening vision of the Red Knight, a fire-breathing monster that chases him, spectacularly galloping through Central Park.

A mixture of fantasy and everyday melodrama, *The Fisher King* is certainly, in comparison with *Baron Munchausen* or *Brazil*, one of Gilliam's more conventional movies, but it is peppered with some extraordinarily vivid set pieces – a scene in Grand Central Station where Parry spots Lydia and all the commuters suddenly begin to waltz around her is amazing to look at – and boasts four-star performances from both Bridges and Ruehl. Although there are moments when the mixture of comedy, fantasy and drama don't come off – when Williams occasionally reverts to his comedy routine his character becomes less believable – this is still an original, touching movie that is well worth the price of a ticket. ★★★★ **JB**

A FISTFUL OF DOLLARS (1964)

Starring: *Clint Eastwood (The Man With No Name), Marianne Koch (Marisol), Gian Maria Volonte (Ramon Rojo), Wolfgang Lukschy (John Baxter), Sieghardt Rupp (Estaban Rojo), Jose Calvo (Silvanto)*
Director: *Sergio Leone*
Screenwriters: *Sergio Leone, A. Bonzonni, Victor Andrews Catena, Jaime Comas Gil, Mark Lowell, Frenando Di Leo, Clint Eastwood, Duccio Tessari*
15/100 mins./Western/Italy/Spain/West Germany

A lonely gunfighter arrives in a town torn apart by rival gangs, the Rojos and the Baxters, and decides to play each side off against one another for his own gain.

The first of Sergio Leone's masterful Spaghetti Westerns is by definition a landmark – it invented a whole damn sub-genre, set Clint Eastwood upon the road to superstardom, and managed something impossible: it rejuvenated the ailing Western. In short, it was like the arrival of punk rock.

By 1964, the genre was creaking in its bones, Wayne and Ford were growing older, and along came this whacky Italian who had earned his stripes helping make quota-quickie B-movies for the European market. With no concept of tradition he flooded the screen with personality: fierce close-ups picking out every pore and pimple of faces as craggy as the Spanish landscape he transformed into an untamed America; a nihilistic disregard for morality; and music thrumming through the film like a dramatic pulse. Ennio Moricone's indelible score added a wild swagger to this oddball tale of a lone gunman's conniving plan to set two gangs of killers against one another.

The story was actually borrowed from Akira Kurosawa's *Yojimbo*, a director who had already drawn from the Western tradition of John Ford. But Leone, who's English was spare at best, isn't too concerned with the burdens of script when he can lavish his world with such style. These sweaty seething desperadoes – about the only thing that differentiates Eastwood's anonymous shooter is his marginally cleaner aspect – partake in a grungy, discordant kind of violence, an ugly strain of killing that has no room for heroics. But the action is still shot with marvellous invention. Leone makes the borders of the frame feel limitless, his camera moves striking out unpredictably as if he could barely tame his vision.

Stubbled, chewing on a cheroot cigar, and wearing that threadbare poncho, Eastwood comes short on talk (the script hadn't given him many words anyway) but presents this antihero with an aloof sense of parody. He looks like a man who has to stir himself to action, as if he'd much rather be dozing off the whiskeys, but his mind was ticking away always looking for the angles. Gone was the strident folklore of John Wayne, for a shocking, genius, caustic fusion of homage and ridicule. Leone never looked back. ★★★★★ **IN**

FITZCARRALDO (1982)

Starring: *Klaus Kinski (Brian Sweeney Fitzgerald/Fitzcarraldo), Claudia Cardinale (Molly), Jose Lewgoy (Don Auilino), Miguel Angel Fuentes (Cholo the Mechanic), Paul Hittscher (Capt. Orinoco Paul)*
Director: *Werner Herzog*
Screenwriter: *Werner Herzog*
PG/157 mins./Adventure/Drama/West Germany

In 19th century Peru, Brian Sweeney Fitzcarraldo wants to make a fortune to finance the building of an opera house in the jungle. He buys a boat and sets out on a daring mission to harvest a fortune in rubber from an inaccessible stretch of the Amazon basin – which involves hauling the huge boat over a mountain between two rivers.

One of Werner Herzog's 'mad visionary' movies, this is epic-length but at heart a simple tale. With Klaus Kinski in the lead (replacing an ailing Jason Robards) and the splendour of South American jungles all around, it is obviously a return to the territory of their earlier hit *Aguirre, Wrath of God*. But it's a surprisingly sweet-natured film, with even Kinski cracking his psychotic shell a little and showing some charm in the scenes with Fitz's indulgent mistress, jungle madame Claudia Cardinale, and setting out on his mad quest with an almost-innocent resolve simply to bring Caruso to the jungle.

It's not even a *Heart of Darkness* tale, as Fitzcarraldo finds a native tribe who are willing to help him in his vast engineering project, albeit for their own spiritual reasons that turn out to be at odds with the objective of making a huge amount of money.

The major coup is that the only way Herzog can imagine making this story is actually to do the impossible and then film it – when the boat chugs up a mountain or runs dangerous rapids, it's actually happening in front of the camera. Whereas earlier Herzog-Kinski protagonists end up irredeemably mad or dead, Fitzcarraldo is allowed a triumph – he may not achieve the goals he set out, but he pulls off something astonishing and finally does sail an entire opera company upriver to perform for the bewildered, yet moved locals. ★★★★ **KN**

New German Cinema

What is it: A wave of activity among young German directors from the early 1970s to the early 80s, which came after decades of purely low-level commercial output from an industry shattered by the War.

Hallmarks: Low-budgets; elliptical storytelling; thorough digestion of influences from Hollywood (especially Douglas Sirk and Nicholas Ray); semi-surreal vision of rainy modern Europe or historical analogues to same; daring use of kitsch pop soundtracks.

Key figures: Rainer Werner Fassbinder, Werner Herzog, Wim Wenders.

If you see one movie, see: *The American Friend* (1977)

FLASH GORDON (1936)

Starring: *Buster Crabbe (Flash Gordon), Jean Rogers (Dale Arden), Charles Middleton (Ming the Merciless), Priscilla Lawson (Princess Aura), Jack Lipson (King Vultan), Richard Alexander (Prince Barin), Frank Shannon (Dr. Zarkov)*
Director: *Frederick Stephani*
Screenwriters: *Frederick Stephani, George Plympton, Basil Dickey, Ella O'Neill, based on the comic strip by Alex Raymond*
PG/97 mins./Sci-fi/USA

Ming the Merciless, Emperor of the Planet Mongo, bombards the Earth with death rays. Flash Gordon and Dale Arden are pressganged by genius Dr. Zarkov to take a flight to Mongo in his experimental space rocket – the Earth people ferment a revolution to overthrow Ming and save two planets.

Based on Alex Raymond's famously well-drawn (and sexy) newspaper strip cartoon, this thirteen-episode 1936 serial remains one of Hollywood's most delirious fantasies, at once childish in its gosh-wow attitude and all-action business and deliriously adult in the many s-m or lust-driven sequences. Swimmer Crabbe, hair dyed blonde and wearing tights, is the perfect two-fisted serial hero, tangling with baggy-suited monsters or toiling shirtless in the mines of Mongo, but everyone is perfectly cast: the thin-lipped, bald-pated, Fu Manchu-moustached, snarling Middleton as the megalomaniac dictator of Mongo (he insists his guards address him as 'mighty potentate') who nurtures a wild lechery for peppy Earth girl Dale; and the fleshy, bare-midriffed, lazy-eyed Priscilla Lawson as Ming's sometimes-treacherous daughter Princess Aura.

The special effects, with stubby little rocketships trailing sparks, seem quaint these days, and Universal's penury is evident in the recycling of sets, music cues and even footage from the likes of *The Mummy* and *Bride of Frankenstein*. Like most serials, it's a hard slog if watched as a four-hour feature, but still plays well if you dole out a chapter or so a day, appreciating the ingenuity required to save Flash, Dale and company from various cliffhangers.

Crabbe and Middleton returned in two direct sequels, *Flash Gordon's Trip to Mars* (1938) and *Flash Gordon Conquers the Universe* (1940). Subsequently, Flash has returned several times in live-action and cartoon TV series, in the sexy parody *Flesh Gordon* and the colourful 1980 remake with Sam Jones and Max Von Sydow. ★★★ **KN**

FLASH GORDON (1980)

Starring: *Sam J. Jones (Flash Gordon), Melody Anderson (Dale Arden), Max von Sydow (The Emperor Ming), Topol (Dr. Hans Zarkov), Ornella Muti (Princess Aura), Timothy Dalton (Prince Barin), Brian Blessed (Prince Vultan), John Osborne (Arborian Priest), Richard O' Brien (Fico), Peter Duncan (Young Treeman)*
Director: *Mike Hodges*
Screenwriter: *Lorenzo Semple Jr., based on characters by Alex Raymond, adapted by Michael Allin*
PG/111 mins./Sci-fi/UK

When the Earth comes under a series of deadly attacks from outer space, American football star Flash Gordon and travel agent Dale Arden are kidnapped by a scientist and taken to the planet Mungo, origin of the attacks. There, they face the terrifying Emperor Ming . . .

Sometime in the mid-70s, a young George Lucas tried to obtain the rights to Saturday serial superfranchise *Flash Gordon* with the idea of doing a remake. Thankfully he failed, or neither *Star Wars* nor this little gem would have ever made it to the screen.

Eschewing the portentous epic feel of the *Wars* entirely, Mike Hodges (*Get Carter*) goes for comic book campery, with designer Danilo Donati (a Fellini collaborator) replicating the crazy angles, primary colour-saturated frames of the comic book source material. Standout scenes include the flight of the Hawkmen, the reception at Ming's court and the Emperor's never-bettered wedding vows.

Max Von Sydow, Brain Blessed and Timothy Dalton act at the intensity of pantomime. Jones (now confined to DTV hell) is perfect as the blond bombshell himself, while the Queen soundtrack ratchets the flamboyance levels up a couple of notches. The question mark after The End, though, promised a sequel that was, alas, not to be. ★★★★ **AS**

FLATLINERS (1990)

Starring: *Kiefer Sutherland (Nelson), Julia Roberts (Rachel Mannus), Kevin Bacon (David Labraccio), William Baldwin (Joe Hurley), Oliver Platt (Randy Steckle)*
Director: *Joel Schumacher*
Screenwriter: *Peter Filardi*
15/115 mins./Horror/Thriller/Sci-fi/USA

A group of medical students researching near-death experiences start experimenting on themselves in order to produce visions. But when these visions return to haunt them in their real lives, they reach deeper and farther to find a cure.

Joel Schumacher and a pre-*Speed* cinematographer Jan De Bont go design doolally in this ludicrously thin but fun cod-philosophical caper.

The plot doesn't deliver on its excellent premise (doctors stopping each others' hearts to voyage to the other side, then reviving themselves). The cast of bright young things poised on the brink of superstardom (or so it must have seemed to Billy Baldwin) give it their all, but are hamstrung by a lack of humour and sometimes paper-thin characterisation.

They also make the most unlikely bunch of medical students ever depicted onscreen and live in impossibly huge loft apartments.

But thankfully, there's no pretence at reality here and there's more than script and performance on offer, and when it comes to spectacular vacuous visuals, Joel's the man, so sit back and enjoy the lightshow. ★★★★ **AS**

FLESH AND BONE (1993)

Starring: *Dennis Quaid (Arlis Sweeney), James Caan (Roy Sweeney), Meg Ryan (Kay Davies), Gwyneth Paltrow (Ginnie), Scott Wilson (Elliot)*
Director: *Steven Kloves*
Screenwriter: *Steven Kloves*
15/126 mins./Drama/Crime/USA

Some thirty years after Arlis witnesses his father murdering a family, he runs into Kay, who happens to be the family's baby who was spared. Kay and Arlis suspect nothing about each other, but when Arlis' father returns, old wounds are reopened.

Firmly dumping their star appeal in the nearest dustbin, husband and wife team Quaid and Ryan pile on the imperfections and ruffle up their gorgeous complexions for this dark, moody, brilliantly written marriage of love story and thriller. A superlative flop – the masses clearly don't want to see their idols with dirty fingernails – set along sunburnt Texan roads and dead-end towns, crying out for discovery.

Things commence 30 years back with a murder. In fact, a wholesale slaughter occurs when a supposedly stray kid lets his thieving father Roy into the home of the good folks who took him in. When the amoral scoundrel is disturbed, he has no qualms in slamming bullets into the whole family, bar a screaming baby.

Spring forward to the present and to Arlis Sweeney, a drifting vending machine filler, an emotional iceberg with a deadly secret. In a fateful squall of events he meets, helps and falls for Kay, the downbeat beauty touting black-eyes and bad luck. But before he can decide that happiness may be an option, his sleazy, no-good pa, that very same Roy, arrives on the scene with a back full of scattershot, a wispy, cynical companion and the realisation that Kay is none other than that orphaned baby.

Kloves' tragic conundrum required a lot of his players, with the plot drawn out long and sinewy the characters are the driving force, and they respond in spades. Quaid has never been better as the unsmiling, introspective Arlis, Ryan gushes curses and love like a manic fountain, discolouring her whiter than white persona with agreeable ease and Caan, slightly overdoing things, delivers a rasping baddie spitting deception and threats.

And their director, too, does a masterful job in holding it all together; the pace, cool and sombre, is never rippled, the desolate landscapes are hauntingly atmospheric and the unsuspected ending a shivery note of poignancy. Hardly a barrel of laughs then, but this slowburn tale sears its way onto the synapses and then flat refuses to budge. ★★★★ **IN**

FLESH AND THE DEVIL (1926)

Starring: *John Gilbert (Leo von Harden), Greta Garbo (Felicitas), Lars Hanson (Ulrich von Eltz), Barbara Kent (Hertha von Eltz), William Orlamond (Uncle Kutowski)*
Director: *Clarence Brown*
Screenwriter: *Marian Ainslee, Benjamin Glazer, Hanns Kraly, Frederica Sagor based on the novel* The Undying Past *by Hermann Sudermann*
U/112 mins./Romantic Drama/USA

Ulrich von Eltz marries Countess Felicitas von Rhaden after his childhood friend, Leo von Harden, kills her husband in a duel. However, they're soon cocking pistols when Felicitas seduces her old flame.

In only her sixth feature, Greta Garbo became a global superstar through her performances as Felicitas, the femme fatale in MGM's adaptation of Hermann Sudermann's novel, *The Undying Past*. The film marked her first teaming with Clarence Brown, who would guide her through six more of her finest outings. But, more significantly, it also united her with John Gilbert and they quickly became Hollywood's most celebrated cinematic couple, both on and off the screen. Indeed, such was her new-found kudos that Garbo felt able to go on strike until the studio improved her contract.

Yet, *Flesh And The Devil* is a wildly melodramatic tale, with the flashback to Leo and Ulrich's blood brothers ritual on the Isle of Friendship being as corny as the Pastor's booming declaration that 'the Devil uses the flesh of women to try and tempt men' is a clumsy bid to appease the Hays Office by imposing a semblance of moral gravitas on proceedings that are littered with infidelities, killings and simmering love scenes between Garbo and Gilbert. Naturally, these now seem tame, but there's still something ineffably chic about the way in which Gilbert cups his hand to light Garbo's cigarette and something sensually sinful in her turning of the communion chalice so that she can drink from the spot touched by her lover's lips.

Indeed, to audiences in 1926, screen sex had never seemed so steamy and it's interesting to compare this ménage with that of the city woman and the country couple in F.W. Murnau's *Sunrise*, which was released the same year. William Daniels' lustrous cinematography takes the novelettish edge off the impassioned clinches, while the Austrian setting adds romance and nobility to the themes of love, loyalty and honour, thus intensifying Garbo's icy sacrifice, as she drowns trying to prevent the duel that, ironically, serves to restore the broken bond of friendship in the decidedly homoerotic finale. ★★★★ **DP**

FLESH FOR FRANKENSTEIN (ANDY WARHOL'S FRANKENSTEIN) (1974)

Starring: *Joe Dallesandro (Nicholas), Monique Van Vooren (Baroness Katrin Frankenstein), Udo Kier (Baron Frankenstein), Arno Juerging (Otto), Dalila Di Lazzaro (Female Monster), Srdjan Zelenovic (Male Monster)*
Directors: *Paul Morrissey, Antonio Margheriti*
Screenwriters: *Tonino Guerra, Paul Morrissey*
18/95 mins./Horror/Comedy/USA/Italy/France

Baron Frankenstein creates two creatures from stolen human parts, in order to breed a Serbian master race. He mistakenly uses the brain of an impotent would-be monk rather than the local stud and the resulting 'male zombie' has no sexual interest in his intended mate.

If possible, see this horror-comedy in 3-D and cringe at outthrust head-lopping scissors, dangling scarlet entrails, gouts of blood and flapping bats. Paul Morrissey, director-writer of Andy Warhol's later Factory movies, pokes fun at Hammer Films in the storyline but retains the Warholian philosophy of casting beautiful people rather than experienced actors. The cast audibly struggle with convoluted dialogue (the most-quoted line is 'to know Death, Otto, you must fuck life in the gall bladder'), but Udo Kier's mad-eyed rants as the maniacal Baron and Joe Dallesandro's dumb Brooklyn himbo mumbling as the supposed hero are all part of the fun.

The laboratory scenes are beautifully staged grand guignol, as Kier presides over ridiculous anatomical experiments – and the finale arranges a series of mangled corpses as characters meet gruesome fates, lining up the dead across the screen as if for a curtain call.

This Baron is married to his own snobbish sister (Monique Van Vooren) and their quietly creepy *Turn of the Screw*-like children scurry around in the background, observing tableaux of sex and violence and learning deadly lessons which are applied in a deliciously sinister punchline. After the vérité roughness of the Factory films, Morrissey goes for a stately, European elegance in locations, widescreen cinematography, art direction and musical accompaniment – the backdrops are all subdued, so that only the acting and the gore takes the film way over the top.

The same team followed through with the equally charming-horrid *Blood for Dracula*. ★★★★ **KN**

FLETCH (1985)

Starring: *Chevy Chase (Irwin 'Fletch' Fletcher), Joe Don Baker (Chief Jerry Karlin), Dana Wheeler-Nicholson (Gail Stanwyk), Richard Libertini (Frank Walker), Tim Matheson (Alan Stanwyk), M. Emmet Walsh (Dr. Joseph Dolan), George Wendt (Fat Sam), Geena Davis (Larry)*
Director: *Michael Ritchie*
Screenwriter: *Andrew Bergman based on the novel by Gregory McDonald*
PG/98 mins./Comedy/USA

Journalist Irwin 'Fletch' Fletcher is approached by a millionaire who claims to be dying of bone cancer and asks to be painlessly assassinated so his wife can claim the insurance money. Suspicious of the deal, Fletch digs deeper and uncovers a network of bigamy, dope-dealing and police corruption.

Though smarmy, opportunist investigative reporter Irwin ('no one calls me Irwin') Fletcher somehow became comedian Chevy Chase's signature role, this bland adaptation of Gregory MacDonald's terrific crime novel is a tired effort. The supporting suspects are played by an array of welcome 80s character faces – George Wendt (*Cheers*), George Wyner (*Hill Street Blues*), M. Emmet Walsh (*Blood Simple*) and Joe Don Baker (*Edge of Darkness*) – and a young Geena Davis is a bright spot as Fletch's Gal Friday, but Chase is miscast as McDonald's heel of a hero, and has to fall back on Peter Sellers knock-off disguises, funny false names ('Dr Rosenpenis', 'Arnold Babar', 'Mr Poon') and lame wisecracks ('Why don't we go lay on the bed and I'll fill you in?').

A large percentage of the running time is devoted to people getting in and out of cars, driving around, walking in and out of buildings, walking around or just plain sitting still that Harold Faltermeyer can cram in a fistful of forgettable musak tracks to fill out a *Beverly Hills Cop*-style soundtrack album. Director Michael Ritchie had made his reputation with brilliant, offbeat 1970s films (*The Candidate*, *Smile*, *Prime Cut*) but spent the 1980s working well below his ability on schlock like this and The Golden Child.

Though MacDonald wrote a string of sequels, Ritchie's *Fletch Lives* (1989) is an 'original' which feels more like a Bob Hope vehicle as Fletch inherits a Southern plantation and gets mixed up with bikers, the Ku Klux Klan, toxic waste and crooked televangelists. ★★ **KN**

FLIGHT OF THE NAVIGATOR (1986)

Starring: *Joey Cramer (David Freeman), Veronica Cartwright (Helen Freeman), Cliff De Young (Bill Freeman), Sarah Jessica Parker (Carolyn McAdams), Matt Adler (Jeff Freeman)*
Director: *Randal Kleiser*
Screenwriter: *Mark H. Baker, Michael Burton, Matt MacManus*
U/90 mins./Sci-fi/USA

In 1978, kid David Freeman disappears. Eight years later, he turns up only four hours older and suffering from amnesia. A government science agency link this mystery with the discovery of an alien spaceship, which it turns out David has been mind-altered to pilot.

In the mid-80s, there was a blip of teen-themed science fiction, usually featuring curly man-permed junior heroes, streamlined fantastic vehicles and rubber monsters: *Back to the Future*, *My Science Project*, *Weird Science*, *The Last Starfighter*, *Explorers*, *D.A.R.Y.L.* . . .

This is among the dullest of the cycle, pitched not at the misfit geniuses who appear in the other films but at squeaky clean pre-yuppies whose idea of hi-tech is a dog-catching-a-frisbee contest. Here, the wish fulfilment fantasy is that a child could be swept up by a boiled-sweet-shaped spaceship called Max (voiced by Paul Reubens, doing his Pee-Wee Herman act and credited as 'Paul Mall') and whizz it all over the country with the power of his mind.

A Disney movie, it features the typical Uncle Walt family in which all troubles can be dealt with by a few hugs and some declarations of yucky kid love and the traditional evil government cover-up agency, a genre staple from *E.T.* onwards, is turned into a mildly over-authoritarian but well-intentioned group of concerned adults.

The oddest side of this mostly faceless effort is that it manages to get nostalgic about – of all years – 1978, with the uncharismatic junior hero wistfully yearning for Jimmy Carter and the Bee-Gees in a manner that might have something to with the fact that 1978 was the year Randal Kleiser last had a hit movie, *Grease*. Cliff De Young and Veronica Cartwright are earnest as Mom and Dad, while a young Sarah Jessica Parker sparkles in a purely ornamental role. Painless, but unmemorable. ★★★ **KN**

THE FLIGHT OF THE PHOENIX (1965)

Starring: *James Stewart (Captain Frank Towns), Richard Attenborough (Lew Moran), Peter Finch (Captain Harris), Hardy Kruger (Henrich Dorfman), Ernest Borgnine (E. 'Tucker' Cobb),*
Director: *Robert Aldirch*
Screenwriter: *Lukas Heller*
PG/142 mins./Action/Drama/USA

When their transport plane crashes in the middle of the Sahara, the surviving passengers most bond together to build a new plane out of the wreckage of the old. But they must overcome their own personal prejudices and conflicts to do it.

A terrifically absorbing and finely tuned piece of low-key disaster moviemaking, made all the more compelling by its magnificent cast of character actors. The ingeniousness of Lukas Heller's writing, and Robert Aldrich's canny direction, is that the issue of survival, that this group of disparate has-beens must team-up to build their only hope, The Phoenix, an idea concocted by Hardy Kruger's emotionless German passenger, is as important as the issues of class, nationalism and ingrained bitterness that all the characters shoulder.

James Stewart's captain, guilt-ridden over his own error that led to the crash, distrusts Kruger's nervy plane designer, mostly because he still carries the resentments of WWII in his bones. Some things are hard to shake, no matter what the stakes. Peter Finch and Ronald Fraser, captain and private, fight a war of class oppression and bitterness that leads to tragedy. Survival, the movie supposes, first requires man to overcome himself.

Yet, subtexts aside, it surely works as one of those old-fashioned adventure tales set at a time, the fifties, when the world was still remote enough to genuinely lose people. It has the queasy sense, lost in the contemporary remake, that our grip on civilisation may not be as firm as we think. And even has time for a doozy of a twist. ★★★★ **IN**

FLIGHT OF THE PHOENIX (2004)

Starring: *Dennis Quaid (Frank Towns), Tyrese Gibson (A.J.), Giovanni Ribisi (Elliott), Miranda Otto (Kelly), Tony Curran (Rodney), Sticky Fingaz (Jeremy), Jacob Vargas (Sammi), Hugh Laurie (Ian), Scott Michael Campbell (Liddle), Kevork Malikyan (Rady), Jarek Padlecki (Davis)*
Director: *John Moore*
Screenwriters: *Scott Frank, Edward Burns, based on the 1965 screenplay by Lukas Heller*
12/113 mins./Action/Adventure/USA

After picking up a crew of oil workers, pilot Frank Towns runs into a sandstorm and crashes into the Gobi desert. Survival prospects seem dim, until a mysterious passenger announces that he's an aircraft designer and they can build a new plane from the wreckage . . .

As if lousy US box office hadn't already burdened Fox's adventure fledgling with enough excess baggage, cunning TV schedulers clipped its wings by handing Robert Aldrich's superior 1965 original a prime post-New Year slot just as the UK release beckoned. Recent history has certainly served up more egregious remakes than John Moore's plucky, if clunky, new *Phoenix*, but it is the Irish director's misfortune to have provided a textbook example of everything that studio pictures have lost, and in some places gained, during the four decades since Aldrich adapted Elleston Trevor's novel.

The gains are not insignificant, and certainly less commented upon by critics circling this holiday turkey. Aldrich's *The Flight Of The Phoenix* is talky, overlong and lacks a climax. Despite being partially shot in the Arizona desert, it also fails to generate any real sense of location – or even heat. Moore's *Flight Of The Phoenix* (note the lack of the definite article, as if the remake doesn't dare lay claim to ultimate status) is a sleeker, faster model. The third act has been rehauled and plot holes in the original papered over.

More importantly, Moore takes advantage of all the tools in the modern filmmaking kit to create an impressive – and oppressive – atmosphere. The plane crash has real weight; the sun real potency; the sand gets simply everywhere. Unlike Aldrich's Saharan set, Moore's Gobi desert actually makes you sweat – which should be half the battle.

The losses, however, are even more considerable. Aldrich's cast included four Oscar winners, with James Stewart headlining as pilot Frank Towns. Quaid in Stewart's Everyman shoes we can handle, but below him Moore is working with bit parts and nobodies. Stewart's co-pilot was Richard Attenborough; Quaid gets singer-turned-actor Tyrese ... Who would you rather fly with?

But Tyrese and company are symptoms rather than cause. The reason great actors flocked to the first *Phoenix* was because it was a true character piece, rich in eternal conflict and contemporary meaning. Trevor was a World War II RAF engineer and his principal characters are veterans scarred by both war and post-war recovery. Officers and enlisted men play out the class struggle, while Towns struggles with a guilt that knows unspoken depths and fragile minds fight losing battles with heat exhaustion.

It's not as if current socio-political circumstances have starved us of big themes, but Moore's focus-grouped movie seems to be afraid of them. The very notion of character is reduced to a node, items to be ticked off some pre-flight checklist. Where Stewart's crew fought, Quaid's squad merely bicker. No matter how hard Giovanni Ribisi works in the key role as the arrogant aircraft designer, he still lacks the one quality that made his predecessor such an irritant to old Allies: a German accent.

And where Aldrich could simply let his accomplished actors explore rewarding character interactions for a couple of hours, the remake must constantly invent incident, new things for the motley crew to do lest the (apparently quickly bored) audience see through the entire ruse. Some of the diversions are diverting enough, but several, such as the Hey Ya musical montage, are unforgivable.

What is best about Moore's model are the parts salvaged wholesale from the first *Flight* – the elements of the original design that simply could not be improved upon. So, for all its problems, *Flight Of The Phoenix* remains a cracking survival story with a distinctive feel and a surprising twist. ★★★ **CK**

FLIGHTPLAN (2005)

Starring: *Jodie Foster (Kyle), Peter Sarsgaard (Carson), Kate Beahan (Stephanie), Erika Christensen (Fiona), Sean Bean (Captain Rich)*
Director: *Robert Schwentke*
Screenwriters: *Peter A. Dowling, Billy Ray*
12A/98 mins./Drama/Thriller/USA

Aeronautics expert Kyle Pratt boards a plane with her seven-year-old daughter Julia to fly the body of her recently deceased husband from Berlin to the US. Following a small snooze mid-flight, Pratt awakes to find her daughter is missing, with no stewardesses, passengers or flight records acknowledging Julia's existence.

It is perhaps surprising that Hollywood has taken four years since 9/11 to make aircraft interiors the suspense locale du jour. Sandwiched between *Red Eye* and the upcoming *Snakes On A Plane*, *Flightplan* adds Hitchcockian enigma – think a mid-air *The Lady Vanishes* – to the already heightened fears surrounding aircraft travel and delivers an entertaining diversion that fails to stand up to closer scrutiny.

For an hour or so, this is all suspenseful fun. The premise – how can a mother lose a daughter in such a confined space? – is crackerjack and the screenplay has the confidence to wring it out in a patient build, finding conflict amid the claustrophobia. There are obvious red herrings (a run-in with an Arab passenger raises the spectre of terrorism) and diversions (Greta Scacchi pops up as a therapist who counsels Kyle), while the tension between the growing anger of the passengers and the staff's attempts to keep Kyle calm is tangibly evoked. Schwentke's camera glides between business class, cattle class and the aircraft's bowels, dynamising the space while filling the cabin with dread. Starting the movie a sallow presence, Foster grows in stature, her escalating anxiety and anger shot through with trademark steely determination.

Around Foster, the supporting cast put in solid spadework; Peter Sarsgaard makes for a genial, sympathetic air marshall, Sean Bean is professional and stoic as the pilot, Kate Beahan perhaps overplays her card as a worldweary air stewardess, while Erika Christensen is wasted as a newbie trolley-dolly.

It's only when the story has to unravel itself and solve its mystery that the turbulence kicks in. The set-up is so meticulously constructed and airtight that the writing paints itself into a corner and the final third neither has the big suckerpunch or storytelling grace to deliver a satisfying resolution. Still, part of the fun here is trying to anticipate how it will all work out, then pulling it to pieces in the pub afterwards. *Flightplan* may have more holes than a slab of Emmental but it doesn't really matter. The compelling first half and Foster's gravitas are enough to make the journey worthwhile. ★★★ **IF**

THE FLINTSTONES (1994)

Starring: *John Goodman (Fred Flintstone), Elizabeth Perkins (Wilma Flintstone), Rick Moranis (Barney Rubble), Rosie O'Donnell (Betty Rubble), Kyle MacLachlan (Cliff Vandercave), Halle Berry (Sharon Stone), Elizabeth Taylor (Pearl Slaghoople)*
Director: *Brian Levant*
Screenwriters: *Tom S. Parker, Jim Jennewein, Steven E. de Douza*
U/91 mins./Family/Fantasy/Comedy/USA

Awards: *Razzie – Worst Screenplay*

Fred Flintstone is not the brightest guy in the world but is pleased when a successful businessman wants to hire him for his company. Sadly unknown to Fred it turns out he is wanted merely as a foil for an embezzling scheme run by the boss.

One is forced to ponder, with some depression, the futility of film reviewing as an occupation in cases like this, as the enduring affection for Hanna-Barbera's prehistoric animated favourites, the hyperbolic overdrive, the burger franchise tie-ins and the avalanches of merchandising attending this release conspired to designate it a blockbuster, however unworthy.

No expense has been spared on the construction of a Bedrock where the design, deco, costumes and animal 'appliances' are identical to the amusing inventions of the source cartoon. Indeed, the best things in the film are the animatronics and puppets devised by Jim Henson's Creature Shop, notably the Flintstones' rambunctious pet Dino and Fred's office Dictabird. But this is a Bedrock in which loudness is too often confused with humour.

From the Steven Spielrock Presents banner and the opening credits sequence that is an exact duplication of the series' credits, it's relentlessly, boomingly cute and obvious. The script, meanwhile, is pitifully bereft of wit, conveying the absence of inspiration in making a live-action jape from a 30-year-old cartoon comedy despite the crediting of three scriptwriters and the rumoured toiling of up to 35 gagsters at various stages during its development.

Fred Flintstone helps neighbours Barney and Betty Rubble adopt the jungle boy Bam Bam, before Fred and Wilma turn vulgar and spend, spend, spend when the dim one is elevated to executive status at the stone quarry by baddie Cliff Vandercave and used as the fall guy in an embezzling scheme with the help of sultry, pouting secretary Sharon Stone.

Injected into this tame scenario are a few lame jokes, the embarrassing spectacle of Elizabeth Taylor as Fred's squawking mother-in-law and the BC-52s bludgeoning the theme song to death, while all the principals can do is impersonate their animated predecessors. When a pterodactyl doing what pigeons are famed for doing gets the biggest laugh, you know you're in trouble. Yabba Dabba Poo! ★★ **AE**

FLIRTING (1991)

Starring: *Noah Taylor (Danny Embling), Thandie Newton (Thadiwe Adjewa), Nicole Kidman (Nicola), Bartholomew Rose ('Gilby' Fryer)*
Director: *John Duigan*
Screenwriter: *John Duigan*
12/99 mins./Drama/Australia

Danny has been sent to boarding school, in this sequel to *The Year My Voice Broke*. Against a backdrop of bullying and sadistic teachers Danny strikes up an affair with an African girl.

'I remember the smells the most: stale lockers with fruitcakes running into the wood; crusty shoe polish; Quink ink for fountain pens; disinfectant on the floor; fresh chalk; mouldy oranges; and, on a rainy day, the deep, rank, wild smell of discarded football boots.' With this evocative olfactory enticement, writer/director John Duigan opens the second part of the trilogy which began with his 1987 rites-of-passage tale, *The Year My Voice Broke*, here drawing us back into the world of hapless teen Danny Embling.

It is now 1965, and Danny is happily ensconced in a remote Australian boys' boarding school. Here, rendered the outsider amongst his more boisterous contemporaries, Danny spends his days gazing wistfully across the lake to the neighbouring ladies' college – until he discovers a kindred spirit in the shape of the beautiful Thandie (a promising debut for Newton), and life suddenly takes on a decidedly more rosy hue.

While his beautifully observed characters (Nicole Kidman does her bit as Head Girl) and situations are immediately recognisable, Duigan never once resorts to simple stereotype. The exquisite pleasure of first love is portrayed without so much as a hint of romantic mush, while Danny's groping journey toward a meaning in life will have even the most hardened old cynics waxing nostalgic over their own adolescent years. ★★★★ **PB**

FLIRTING WITH DISASTER (1996)

Starring: *Ben Stiller (Mel), Patricia Arquette (Nancy), Tea Leoni (Tina), Alan Alda (Richard Schlichting), Mary Tyler Moore (Mrs. Coplin), George Segal (Mr. Coplin), Lily Tomlin (Mary Schlichting), Josh Brolin (Tony),*
Director: *David O. Russell*
Screenwriter: *David O. Russell*
15/92 mins./Comedy/USA

A young man, his wife, and his incompetent case-worker travel across country to find his birth parents.

Despite the exuberant effort and an attractively off-beat cast, director Russell, with his follow-up to the left-field shock tactics of *Spanking The Monkey*, upheld an unfortunate tradition. Americans don't get farce. They dress it up too shiny, they go easy when the crap should rain in torrents, and no race on earth understands the art of dignified defeat like the British. And after a cutely entertaining first 20 minutes, it gives up on replicating the underwear nuances of that doubly institution of a thousand Blighty reps and descends into an unfunny, double-speed sitcomery that keeps listening for the reassuring timbre of canned laughter.

It's a shame because the concept has legs. Hyper-neurotic New Yorker Stiller, doing a woody Woody Allen, discovers he is adopted and despite the loving attention of his wife and baby, has to enlist the suspect assistance of an agency girl (the sassy Leoni) and hit the road in search of his biological folks.

The sting is Leoni keeps messing up her sources, so Stiller rattles through a series of impossible parentage (redneck truck driver, Californian beach mum etc.) and disastrous retreats involving inadvertent structural damage to various neighbourhoods. Meanwhile, his adoptive parents (the great pairing of George Segal and Mary Tyler Moore) give chase, two closet homosexual FBI agents get on their case, and Arquette thinks he's giving the incredibly sexy Leoni (whose character's dubiousness is never explored) far too much attention.

And when he finds his 'real' parents they are stuck in some dope-fuzzed New Mexico 60s time warp, present him to a psychotically jealous dimwit brother, and are horribly overplayed by Lily Tomlin and Alan Alda. In British hands, this could have worked a treat, but Russell's take is loud and glaringly unsubtle.

The cast working their Hollywood butts off to give it life and certainly Moore delivers her delicious pouty fussing with aplomb, but after the laughs have been drained from its opening quarter, it just labours on indifferently. ★★ **IF**

THE FLY (1986)

Starring: *Jeff Goldblum (Seth Brundle), Geena Davis (Veronica Quaife), John Getz (Stathis Borans), Joy Boushel (Tawny), Les Carlson (Dr. Cheevers), David Cronenberg (Gynaecologist)*
Director: *David Cronenberg*
Screenwriters: *Charles Pogue, David Cronenberg, based on a story by George Langelaan*
18/100 mins./Drama/Horror/Sci-fi/USA

Awards: *Academy Awards – Best Makeup*

Seth Brundle, a brilliant but eccentric scientist, tests his teleport system on himself and accidentally becomes a mutant fly-man.

'I can be a sucker for a romantic story,' remarked David Cronenberg on first seeing the script for *The Fly*. Frankly it's an odd declaration from the man who delivered the sadistic, perverse, downright stunning excesses of *Shivers*, *Videodrome* and *Rabid*. But then his concept of a 'romantic story' is equally leftfield. What kind of romance has a sequence in which one of the subjects vomits milky enzymes on a doughnut before slurping up the resultant liquefying mess, or who splatters a mirror with puss squeezed from his degenerating fingertips? Or, as we find out half way through, keeps his penis in the bathroom medicine cabinet? *Jerry Maguire* this ain't.

But it's the romantic, melodramatic heart of Cronenberg's gooey fairytale that ensured that it became the Canadian native's biggest commercial hit bringing, for the first time, his work complete with all his trademark obsessions, to the attention of an audience for whom his name would call to mind a brand of imported lager more readily than one of the most challenging auteurs of modern cinema. Cronenberg's re-thinking of the original 1958 screenplay is full of imaginative innovations. While James Clavell's original screenplay has scientist Vincent Price happily married while he tinkers in the basement with his teleportation device, Cronenberg has Seth Brundle (a fantastically cast Jeff Goldblum whose bug-eyes and gangly limbs lend him a distinctly insectoid look from the start) an unmarried loner living in a detritus-strewn loft pursued by science journalist and love interest Veronica Quaife (then wife Geena Davis).

More importantly, while in the original Vincent Price emerges as a somewhat ludicrous figure with a fly claw and a cloth over his head to disguise the 'true horror' of his metamorphosis (not to mention the frankly *Twilight Zone*-esque cheapness of the end shot with a tiny man's head on a fly body squeaking 'help me.') Cronenberg has Brundle emerge from his experimental teleportation pod apparently unchanged making his metamorphosis into Brundlefly the dramatic heart of the movie and leaving Veronica, like the audience, half fascinated and half repulsed by his slow physical decay and transformation. It's a re-working of *Beauty And The Beast* remixed for a technological age with the dramatic caveat that Beauty knows from the start that the man she is falling in love with will transform into a deeply unlovable creature.

Indeed, she must remain in love with Brundlefly even as he abducts her from an abortion clinic she has booked into to rid herself of their child. Or as he vomits on ex-boyfriend Strathis Borans (John Getz, delivering a character who in his own way metamorphoses from creepy ex-boyfriend to hero of the hour) reducing his arm and leg to bloody stumps. Purists may argue that *The Fly* is not science fiction at all but a horror movie, it certainly has all the spectacular gore and prosthetics of a scarefest, but thematically it is much closer to *Frankenstein* than any other film, and *Frankenstein* is much closer to science fiction than horror taking the subject of mankind's uneasy relationship with science as its theme.

Both Seth Brundle and Baron Frankenstein create monsters through their overpowering scientific curiosity and its attendant arrogance, but in Brundle's case the twist is that it is himself that he 'creates'. There are also nods to *Dr Jekyll And Mr Hyde*, another tale with the perversion of science rather than horror at its core. Cronenberg was attracted to the material partly because it so neatly reflected his own obsessions with our uneasy relationship with our bodies and their fleshy existence. Disease and mutation crop up in almost all his films but *The Fly* expresses Cronenberg's ideas in a mainstream movie for the first time.

And while he has said that it was not intended as a movie about Aids specifically (it was made in 1986 when fear of the disease was at its height) it's difficult not to see that unease as a crucial ingredient. But *The Fly* is not only a movie of ideas, it's a collection of great elements. Howard Shore's brooding, dramatic score; Geena Davis delivering what would become one of the most quoted poster taglines of all time ('Be afraid ... Be very afraid.'); Cronenberg himself appearing in one of the movie's most intense sequences as Veronica dreams she gives birth to a huge writhing maggot (an epilogue in which she actually spawns a 'butterfly child' thus undercutting the tragedy was shot but tested badly and was discarded) and a baboon being turned inside out. But it is the end sequence in which Brundlefly, now utterly unrecognisable having been fused with the technology itself, that devastates blending as it does all Cronenberg's themes: mutation, disease, love and death into a dramatic, melancholic conclusion.

'Every love story must end tragically,' remarked Cronenberg. Brundle is betrayed not by his lover but by his own body before begging Veronica to shoot him. The movie concludes in an unimaginably grim shot of Brundle's twisted corpse, a mutilated, unconscious Borans and Veronica sobbing uncontrollably. ★★★★★ **AS**

FLY AWAY HOME (1996)

Starring: *Jeff Daniels (Thomas Alden), Anna Paquin (Amy Alden), Dana Delaney (Susan Barnes), Terry Kinney (David Alden), Holter Graham (Barry Stickland)*
Director: *Carroll Ballard*
Screenwriters: *Robert Rodat, Vince McKewin, based on the autobiography by Bill Lishman*
U/110 mins./Family/Drama/USA

A father and daughter decide to attempt to lead a flock of orphaned Canada Geese south by air.

Very occasionally a kids' film bases itself on old-fashioned moviemaking skills, classic storytelling and simple emotions, and comes up trumps.

With the children's market shattering into so many sub-categories it is less likely, one supposes, that films like this will get the go-ahead. Which is a big shame. Anna Paquin, Oscar-winner at 12 with *The Piano*, plays Amy Alden, a girl sent to live with her dad in Ontario after her mother is killed. She's withdrawn, he's hopeless, and his girlfriend is slightly more menacing than Cruella De Vil in young Amy's eyes.

Things change, however, when she finds some Canada Goose eggs and raises the young birds as her own, realising that, because she was the first living thing they clapped eyes on, they see her as their mum. Her dad is, naturally, an eccentric inventor, and when the time comes for the geese to migrate, he builds a couple of flying machines and shows them the way. It sounds appalling.

But there is a wonderful lack of mawkishness in this movie, a feeling of the real world and real people, heftily aided by, frankly, brilliant performances by Daniels and Paquin. It's largely about coming to terms with loss and conquering the fear of the future, but if that makes it sound a bit grim, be assured it's not. ★★★★ **PT**

THE FLYING DEUCES (1939)

Starring: *Stan Laurel (Stan), Oliver Hardy (Ollie Hardy), Jean Parker (Georgette), Reginald Gardiner (François), Jean Del Val (Sergeant), James Finlayson (Jailor)*
Director: *A. Edward Sutherland*
Screenwriters: *Ralph Spence, Charles Rogers, Alfred Schiller, Harry Langdon*
U/69 mins./Comedy/USA

Spurned by Georgette, the Parisian waitress he loves, Oliver Hardy persuades Stan Laurel to enlist in the Foreign Legion with him, so that he can forget. However, the Commandant assigns them to Georgette's beau, François.

Stan Laurel was a perfectionist. His eye for detail was crucial to the success of Laurel and Hardy's shorts and features alike. But his tendency to take control occasionally caused friction. Indeed, this film only came about because Stan was in dispute with producer Hal Roach over the shooting of *A Chump at Oxford* and independent newcomer Boris Morros decided to exploit the situation to arrange a loan deal.

However, Morros made the mistake of commissioning Alfred Schiller to concoct a screenplay based on the French comedy, *Les Aviateurs*, and Stan was so unimpressed that he virtually washed his hands of the project. Schiller clearly had no insight into the Laurel and Hardy dynamic and tried to turn them into competitive wiseacres along the lines of Abbott and Costello. Yet, Laurel clearly collaborated to some extent on the much-revised screenplay with Ralph Spence, Charles Rogers and onetime silent clown Harry Langdon, as the bulk of the story resembled *Beau Hunk*, while the scene in which the heartbroken Ollie contemplates suicide was a discard from *The Live Ghost*.

Stan proved more pro-active once filming began at General Studios, even though Morros had insisted on a detailed shooting script to curtail any ad libbing that might unnecessarily extend the budget. Consequently, Laurel fell foul of director A. Edward Sutherland, who was hardly a comic novice, having handled such W.C. Fields vehicles as *Mississippi* and *Poppy*.

Amidst all this incompetence, tension and indifference, it's amazing that *The Flying Deuces* has anything to recommend it. It's certainly one of the weaker features of the Roach era, but there's much to enjoy in Ollie's bashful flirting with Jean Parker, Stan's harp-playing on a bed spring, the soft shoe routine to 'Shine On, Harvest Moon' and the endurance flight that culminates in Ollie being reincarnated as a horse. ★★★ **DP**

◎ FLYING DOWN TO RIO (1933)

Starring: *Dolores Del Rio (Belinha de Rezende), Gene Raymond (Roger Bond), Raul Roulien (Julio Rubiero), Ginger Rogers (Honey Hale), Fred Astaire (Fred Ayres), Blanche Frederici (Dona Elena), Walter Walker (Senor de Rezende), Etta Moten (Black Singer)*
Director: *Thornton Freeland*
Screenwriters: *Cyril Hume, H.W. Hanemann, Erwin Gelsey based on a play by Anne Caldwell and a story by Lou Brock*
U/85 mins./Musical/USA

Belinha de Rezende is torn between Brazilian fiancé Julio Rubeiro and bandleader Roger Bond, whose father's plans to open a luxury hotel in Rio de Janeiro are being jeopardised by a trio of mysterious Greeks.

Flying Down to Rio is only remembered for one thing. But the first teaming of Fred Astaire and Ginger Rogers makes this mediocre RKO musical unforgetable. Yet no one seems to recall how this inspired partnership came about. Dorothy Jordan had been announced in the Rogers role, but married studio boss Merian C. Cooper instead and Fred was reunited with the blonde he'd once dated in New York while choreographing her 'Embraceable You' number in George Gershwin's *Girl Crazy*. They share a few bantered exchanges and Fred later reprises Ginger's song solo, 'Music Makes Me'. But they're pretty much kept apart until Ginger insists that they show the locals 'a thing or three' by joining in 'The Carioca'.

However, even this wasn't conceived as a showcase and they're off screen for much of its duration, as a white, a mulatto and a black singer respectively carry the melody. But the sight of them gyrating with their foreheads pressed together and then atop seven grand pianos prompted a dance craze across the States and made the movie a massive hit (baffling Astaire, who was so convinced he'd made his second and final feature that he took his stage show, *The Gay Divorce*, to London).

Yet, the picture's look also had much to do with its success. It's a resolutely modern affair celebrating new modes of transport and communication and the faster film stock and sharper lighting gave the sets a glistening elegance that captivated Depression audiences seeking a little escapism. Moreover, sound recording techniques had much improved since the musical become box-office poison following its initial novelty boom. Consequently, choreographer Dave Gould was able to keep his cast moving, whether it was Fred tangoing with Dolores Del Rio or a bevy of chorines wing-walking on biplanes over the city, in a title routine consciously designed to out-Buzz Busby Berkeley, who had been largely responsible for reviving the genre at Warners. ★★★ **DP**

◎ THE FOG OF WAR: ELEVEN LESSONS FROM THE LIFE OF ROBERT S. MCNAMARA (2003)

Starring: *Robert S. McNamara, Errol Morris (interviewer)*
Director: *Errol Morris*
PG/95 mins./Documentary/USA

Awards: *Academy Awards – Best Documentary*

Eighty-seven year-old Robert S. McNamara – who, as America's Secretary Of State for Defence during the Cuban Missile Crisis and the Vietnam War, was the Donald Rumsfeld of his day – looks back over his life and career and attempts to draw lessons from the tragedy of Vietnam.

Get ready for the unlikeliest documentary duo since Charlton Heston turned up in that other critically-acclaimed, box office-busting reality show, *Bowling For Columbine*.

Behind the camera is Errol Morris, the filmmaker whose extraordinary body of work (including *The Thin Blue Line*, which led to the release of a wrongly-convicted man on Death Row) effectively makes him the father of the modern documentary. In front is Robert S. McNamara, the former US Secretary Of State who was one of the architects and – publicly at least – advocates of America's involvement in the Vietnam War, which led to the deaths of 47,378 American soldiers and more than two million North Vietnamese. In World War II, he was also part of the strategy team that advocated the firebombing of 67 Japanese cities – killing 1.9 million civilians – and now admits that, had the Allies lost, he would have been tried as a war criminal.

The format is typical of Morris' less-is-more approach: much of the running time has McNamara talking directly to the camera, with Morris' occasional interjection. But the private-detective-turned-documentary-maker has also unearthed some extraordinary archive footage and – more crucially for the former Defence Secretary's own defence – recently released White House tapes that substantiate McNamara's claims that he expressed early reservations about America's involvement in Vietnam – views for which he was eventually fired.

Morris has said he came to bury McNamara, not to praise him, but the sleek-faced politico – with the nails-on-a-blackboard voice – is as crafty now as when he was the most hated man in America, and he's not about to be snared by any of Morris' traps. (In one attempt to break through McNamara's reticence, Morris calls out, 'Is it the feeling that you are damned if you do and damned if you don't?' to which the wily McNamara responds, 'Yeah, that's right – and I'd rather be damned if I don't').

There's an argument that, at a certain age and decrepitude, even the most sinister individuals become sympathetic, or at least pathetic. But however you see McNamara – misguided, misunderstood or mass murderer – the film's status as a must-see documentary is indisputable. ★★★★★ **WL**

◎ THE FOG (1980)

Starring: *Adrienne Barbeau (Stevie Wayne), Jamie Lee Curtis (Elizabeth Solley), Janet Leigh (Kathy Williams), John Houseman (Mr. Machen), Tom Atkins (Nick Castle)*
Director: *John Carpenter*
Screenwriters: *John Carpenter, Debra Hill*
15/89 mins./Horror/USA

The Centenary of the small sea town, Antonio Bay, is approaching. While the townsfolk prepare to celebrate, the victims of the crime that founded the town rise from the sea to claim retribution. Under cover of the fog, they carry out their vicious attacks, searching for what is rightly theirs.

'In France, I'm an auteur. In England, I'm a horror movie director. In Germany, I'm a filmmaker. In the US, I'm a bum.' Ladies and gentlemen, Mr. John Carpenter – at once genius and buffoon. But if on occasion circumstance has been his worst enemy (most notably when the release of *Village Of The Damned* in 1995 coincided with the death of several children in the Oklahoma bombing), he only really has himself to blame.

Boasting an 'eclectic' filmography, to say the least, this is the man who has taken us on a journey through the sublime (*Halloween*, *The Thing*), the ridiculous (*Prince Of Darkness*, *Memoirs Of An Invisible Man*) and the, frankly, crap (*Christine*, *Escape From LA*). When he's bad, he sucks. But thankfully, when he's good, he's very, very good. One of the most immediately identifiable directors of his generation – as Kurt 'Snake Plissken' Russell once told him: 'You can see ten seconds of any of your movies and know they're yours' – he can capture a mood, build tension and play his trump card all in one fell swoop. An auteur (sorry, but the French are right), indeed.

The film, however, that he cites as one of his most arduous also happens to be one of his most audacious, one of his most visually impressive and one of his most heartfelt. Not that Carpenter was initially happy with it, of course. An attempt at something 'A little bit H.P. Lovecraft,' *The Fog*'s problems were twofold. 'It's not that it was technically difficult,' said

Carpenter afterwards, 'it was – the balance that was problematic. Getting the tempo right.' Come post-production (and this is after – he'd already re-shot 'about a third of it'), the issue became exacerbated, with Carpenter so convinced of the film's 'flatness' that he hastily wrote a score (another indelible thumbprint) to save it from the critical mauling he feared would follow.

He needn't have worried. For, while the score's characteristic synth brilliance (Carpenter insits that he only employs himself as composer because he is both 'cheap and on time') helps to build a taut, chilling atmosphere, the final result is quite possibly the most criminally underrated horror film of the last two decades. Wasting no time from the get-go, a crusty old salt dispenses the plot to a group of young boys around a campfire. In a two-minute prologue, Carpenter sets a scene that would have taken most directors half an hour to deliver. Where he does stretch his legs is in the credit sequence, establishing Leigh's adage that 'This town sits around for 100 years and nothing happens, and then one night the whole place falls apart' via a number of individual scenes (with Hitchcockian references, as well as nods to Poe, *Jaws* and *Carrie*). The pirates – sort of seafaring horsemen of the apocalypse, carried inland in the glowing fog that is their harbinger – are wonderful. A silent, plodding menace out for revenge having been tricked into running their ship aground, who are as unwilling to negotiate in any way as Carpenter's previous incarnation of terror, Michael Myers.

This is neither the time nor the place for wisecracking embodiments of evil. Barbeau, meanwhile, is superb, trapped by a sense of grim responsibility in her isolated lighthouse. And it's incredibly funny. As well as a Carpenter cameo there is some priceless dialogue (Kathy: 'Sandy, you're the only person who can make "Yes, ma'am" sound like "Screw you."' 'Sandy: 'Yes, ma'am'). Many character names (Dr. Phibes, the coroner, among them) are aimed with arch precision; in particular Dan O'Bannon (Carpenter's classmate, with whom he made *Dark Star* in 1973) and Tommy Wallace (his production designer). Special effects supremo Rob Bottin also doubles as head pirate Blake, while Barbeau's last line, 'Look for the fog ...' echoes that from 1951's *The Thing From Another World* (remade by Carpenter 31 years later); and the band mentioned on air is The Coupe De Villes, Carpenter and Co.'s, as yet unsigned, rock combo.

Tagline
What you can't see won't hurt you ... it'll kill you!

Most significant, though, is the film's intention. Having publicly apologised (admittedly with tongue firmly in cheek) for the glut of misogynistic slasher fare that flowed after his original 'masked killer' feature, this is arguably Carpenter's personal antidote. Pure, clean, the flipside of its contemporaries. ★★★★ **MD**

FOLLOW THE FLEET (1936)

Starring: *Fred Astaire (Bake Baker), Ginger Rogers (Sherry Martin), Randolph Scott (Bilge Smith), Harriet Hillard (Cornie Martin), Lucille Bail (Kitty Collins)*
Director: *Mark Sandrich*
Screenwriters: *Dwight Taylor, Allan Acott based on the play* Shore Leave *by Hubert Osborne*
U/110 mins./Musical/USA

When Connie Martin falls out with sailor beau Bilge Smith over the boat she wants to buy him, her sister, Sherrie, and his best pal, Bake Baker, set about arranging a reunion.

Concerned that Fred and Ginger's appeal would wane if they remained indefinitely in the Art Deco neverland of *Roberta* and *Top Hat*, RKO producer Pandro S. Berman insisted that they played more down-to-earth characters in their fifth feature. Consequently, Astaire was cast as a gum-chewing sailor, while Rogers became a hostess in a dance hall on the San Francisco waterfront. However, in order to accommodate the change, they were forced to play second fiddle to Randolph Scott and Harriet Hilliard, as the feuding lovers who had been centre stage in Hubert Osborne's source play, *Shore Leave*. At one point, Berman considered allowing Ginger to play both sisters and it's very much to the picture's detriment that she didn't, as Hilliard is simperingly inconsequential and Irving Berlin's ballads 'Get Thee Behind Me, Satan' and 'But Where Are You?' were largely wasted on her.

The remainder of the score is hugely enjoyable, however. Astaire and a sailor ensemble breeze their way through 'We Saw the Sea' and 'I'd Rather Lead a Band', while Ginger got to do her only tap solo in the couple's 10 teamings when she reprised 'Let Yourself Go' at the audition where her singing is sabotaged by bicarbonate of soda.

But, as ever, it's the duets that make the movie, with the dance contest version of 'Let Yourself Go' and the muffed rehearsal routine to 'I'm Putting All My Eggs in One Basket' being full of comic business, as well as effortless elegance. But 'Let's Face the Music and Dance' was even more daring, as it set the trademark 'woo to win' number within a show context and risked risibility with its melodramatic content. Yet, it becomes irresistibly moving and chic because of the deceptive simplicity of the steps.

The film was a hit, but not all the critics were convinced and RKO knew never to let anyone share Fred'n'Ginger's spotlight again. ★★★★ **DP**

FOLLOWING (1998)

Starring: *Jeremy Theobald (Bill), Alex Haw (Cobb), Lucy Russell (The Blonde), John Nolan (The Policeman)*
Director: *Christopher Nolan*
Screenwriter: *Christopher Nolan*
15/70 mins./Thriller/Crime/UK

A writer starts shadowing strangers, purely out of curiosity, but gradually gets drawn into a world of crime after becoming obsessed with a burglar whom he stalks.

Made for what appears to be loose change in and around the streets of London, Nolan's first feature is by no means without promise, even though the film tries to run before it can walk with regard to its ambitious, noir-like narrative, a tortuous, convoluted mélange of flashbacks and fast-forwards that come on like Nic Roeg on acid.

Nevertheless, the central conceit is compellingly mapped, as wannabe writer Bill (Theobald) takes to 'shadowing' strangers he encounters in the streets for no other reason than his own voyeuristic curiosity. One of them is Cobb, a handsome, urbane and unnervingly cruel burglar who breaks into flats in order to analyse the owners' personal lives and play mischievous mind games with their property: 'You take it away, and show them what they had,' muses Cobb, like some sociopathic first-year philosophy student let loose at a freshers' fair.

Bill is enlisted as his understudy, but it's only when he hooks up with the girlfriend of a gangster that the gullible hero stops being a fish out of water and becomes a lamb to the slaughter in a deadly game of cross and double cross.

Shot in edgily effective monochrome and with a running time of around 70 minutes, the film can hardly be accused of overstaying its welcome, though Nolan's assembled cast of non-professional actors lack the dramatic ballast to compensate for his erratic plot elisions. Haw, to give him his due, displays a charismatic persona and does a nice line in clipped vowel villainy, but Theobald is faced with an uphill struggle in an attempt to animate or win sympathy for his colourless character. Nolan went on to direct *Memento*, *Insomnia* and the mega budget *Batman Begins*, making this film an interesting debut of a major talent. ★★★ **TL**

FOR A FEW DOLLARS MORE (PER QUALCHE DOLLARI IN PIU) (1965)

Starring: *Clint Eastwood (The Man With No Name), Lee Van Cleef (Col. Douglas Mortimer), Gian Maria Volonte (Indio), Josef Egger (Old Man Over Railway), Rosemarie Dexter (Colonel's Sister), Mara Krup (Hotel Manager's Wife), Klaus Kinski (Hunchback)*
Director: *Sergio Leone*
Screenwriters: *Luciano Vincenzoni, Sergio Leone, based on a story by Leone and Fulvio Morsella*
15/130 mins./Western/Italy/Spain/West Germany

Two bounty-hunters, the vengeance-seeking Colonel Mortimer and the purely mercenary Monco, track the flamboyantly insane outlaw El Indio who has wronged Mortimer's family. El Indio, meanwhile, plans to rob a supposedly impregnable bank in El Paso.

The second of Sergio Leone's 'Dollars' trilogy brings back Clint Eastwood as the poncho-clad, cheroot-chewing gunman from *A Fistful of Dollars*. Though he was promoted as 'the Man With No Name', the character was called 'Joe' in the first film, 'Monco' here (it means 'one-handed' in Spanish, and relates obscurely to a leather half-gauntlet which is his signature garment) and would be 'Blondy' in *The Good, the Bad and the Ugly*.

Though Eastwood takes top-billing, he actually plays a secondary role to Lee Van Cleef's hawk-eyed, pipe-puffing supercool avenger, who has so many trick guns in his saddle-blanket and such snappy clothes that he seems like 007's great-grandfather out West. With supreme irony, both naturally English-speaking leads have almost no dialogue while the Italian Volonté spots reams of maniacal talk as the near-messianic villain, who shoots babies, smokes dope, has bizarre laughing jags (as immortalised on his 'wanted' poster, which seems to have been silkscreened by Andy Warhol), kills his own men on a whim, fetishises a chiming musical watch and finally remembers the terrible thing he did to Mortimer's sister during one of Leone's greatest duel/corrida scenes.

It doesn't have the perfect plot *Fistful* poached from *Yojimbo* (which Kurosawa had stolen from Dashiell Hammett) and tends, like all subsequent Leone films, to be a serial-like string of individually outstanding scenes rather than a story. Nevertheless, it has a wealth of marvellous Western imagery, grotesque-comic business (Van Cleef striking a match on seething baddie Klaus Kinski's hunchback), Ennio Morricone's baroque score, iconic stars and unforgettable supporting faces. ★★★★ **KN**

FOR ME AND MY GAL (1942)

Starring: *Judy Garland (Jo Hayden), George Murphy (Jimmy K. Metcalf), Gene Kelly (Harry Palmer), Marta Eggerth (Eve Minard), Ben Blue (Sid Simms)*
Director: *Busby Berkeley*
Screenwriters: *Richard Sherman, Fred Finklehoffe, Sid Silvers, Jack McGowan, Irving Brecher based on the story* The Big Time *by Howard Emmett Rogers*
U/103 mins./Musical/USA

Ambitious vaudeville hoofer Harry Palmer forms a double act with the trusting Jo Hayden and a romantic attachment to established chanteuse Eve Minard in order to speed his rise to the top.

Once the king of the Hollywood musical, Busby Berkeley's career was on the slide by the time he directed this nostalgic MGM flagwaver and his diminished inspiration is all-too-readily apparent. Despite coming off a trio of 'puttin' on a show' romps with Judy Garland and Mickey Rooney, his staging of Garland solo slots like 'Oh, You Beautiful Doll' and 'Till We Meet Again' was front-on and flat, as though he were viewing her from a seat in the audience.

To an extent, this passivity was suitable for the 1910s setting. But Berkeley was notably more animated when working with Gene Kelly, who was making his screen debut. He had rather been thrown in at the deep end, having replaced George Murphy in the male lead at Garland's insistence, but the songs were all standards and he was familiar with the backstage milieu from his time on Broadway. Moreover, Harry Palmer bore a marked resemblance to Joey Evans, his breakthrough character in *Pal Joey*, who had similarly been prepared to exploit anyone and anything to get his way. He certainly strings Jo along here, as he wilfully ignores her feelings and mooches up to Eve Minard to take advantage of her social and showbiz contacts. He even resorts to smashing his hand in a trunk to defer the draft, so that he can take his shot at the big time at New York's Palace Theatre.

Kelly would come to specialise in such cocky, cynical, selfish types, but while his clumsy egotism was always tempered by romance, he retained a boyish irresponsibility that was key to his appeal. He's only afforded a single solo ('Tramp Dance') here. But he teams well with Ben Blue on 'Frenchie Frenchie' and benefits hugely from Garland's generosity on 'When You Wore a Tulip', 'Ballin' the Jack' and the timeless title number. ★★★ **DP**

FOR THE LOVE OF THE GAME (1999)

Starring: *Kevin Costner (Billy Chapel), Kelly Preston (Jane Aubrey), John C. Reilly (Gus Sinski), Jena Malone (Heather Aubrey), Brian Cox (Gary Wheeler), J.K. Simmons (Frank Perry)*
Director: *Sam Raimi*
Screenwriter: *Dana Stevens, based on the novel by Michael Shaara*
12/137 mins./Drama/Romance/Sport/USA

A veteran baseball player takes to the field for one last game – knowing that how he plays could change his future.

Following a string of rather embarrassingly high-profile flops, Costner returned to the well of grown-up rounders in the hope that it will once again sprinkle some magic over his ailing career. Garnering what can mercifully be described as mixed reviews in the States, *For Love Of The Game* isn't, unfortunately, up to the standard of either *Bull Durham* or *Field Of Dreams*. But if you can stomach the occasionally cloying sentiment, it goes a long way towards restoring his tattered reputation as a leading man.

It helps that he's perfectly cast as Billy Chapel, an aging star pitcher who arrives at the crossroads of his life on the eve of a big game. Not only is he about to be traded after 20 years as the heart and soul of the Detroit Tigers, but Jane, the love of his life, is also leaving him. Marooned on the pitcher's mound, retracing the steps that have brought him here, he achieves a kind of sporting Nirvana. Tuning out the roar of a hostile New York crowd, he realises that the fabled 'perfect game' is within his grasp.

It's all pure soap, of course. But, in America at least, baseball has always been wreathed in a sacred romantic glow, and there's no denying that Costner cuts a heroic, if somewhat quixotic, figure. Staring the end of his career in the face, with no Jane to cushion the fall and his weary arm screaming in pain, you can't help but root for him as he fights his last, lonely battle.

Director Sam Raimi, treading confidently over very unfamiliar ground compared to his usual bread-and-butter of blood-and-gore, musters a deal of visual pizazz, added to which is good support play from Preston and Reilly. But it's ultimately Costner's movie, and if it's an uneven, often overwrought piece of work, it's nevertheless compelling evidence that given the right role he can still cut it in the majors. ★★★ **SB**

FOR WHOM THE BELL TOLLS (1943)

Starring: *Gary Cooper (Robert Jordan), Ingrid Bergman (Maria), Akim Tamiroff (Pablo), Arturo de Cordova (Agustin), Vladimir Sokoloff (Anselmo), Mikhail Rasummy (Rafael)*
Director: *Sam Wood*
Screenwriter: *Dudley Nichols based on the novel by Ernest Hemingway*
U/170 mins./War/Drama/USA

Awards: *Academy Awards – Best Supporting Actress (Katina Paxinou)*

Having been brutalised by Franco's forces, Maria rediscovers a zest for life on meeting Robert Jordan, an American with the International

Brigade, who joins a Republican guerilla band in the mountains above Segovia in order to destroy a key Loyalist bridgehead.

Paramount paid a record $150,000 when it acquired the rights to Ernest Hemingway's Spanish Civil War epic. Originally, it had been earmarked for Cecil B. DeMille. But he fell by the wayside, along with Vera Zorina, who threatened to sue the studio after it dropped her on seeing the rushes of the first three weeks shooting in the Sierra Nevadas. Much to the relief of Hemingway (who had already insisted on Gary Cooper after his performance in the 1932 version of the author's classic, *A Farewell to Arms*), his personal choice, Ingrid Bergman, was awarded the role of Maria and her intense, yet naturalistic performance earned her first Oscar nomination and confirmed the superstar status that had already been conferred by *Casablanca*.

Yet, the Catholic Church and the Spanish government did everything they could to persuade the US State Department to have the picture suppressed. However, Paramount chief Adolf Zukor insisted that the film had no political agenda, even though its Republican sentiments were as clear as its exortion to all repressed peoples to rise in active resistance against Fascist tyranny.

Despite its propagandist value and air of literary prestige, the film was accorded a mixed critical reception, with many complaining of its excessive length and deriding Sam Wood's melodramatic handling of the love scenes. Yet, when the picture was reissued in the mid-1950s, it was George Coulouris and Konstantin Shayne's scenes that were cut rather than any of the interminable close-up clinches.

Bergman approaches poetic realism in the scenes in which she describes her gang rape and bids farewell to Cooper as he embarks upon his heroically doomed mission. But fellow Europeans Akim Tamiroff and the Oscar-winning Katina Paxinou bring some much-needed grit as the war-weary leader of the guerillas and the mistrusting peasant who took control of the band when she saw his purpose waning. ★★★ **DP**

FOR YOUR EYES ONLY (1981)

Starring: *Roger Moore (James Bond), Carole Bouquet (Melina Havelock), Topol (Milos Columbo), Lyn-Holly Johnson (Bibi Dahl), Julian Glover (Aristotle Kristatos)*
Director: *John Glen*
Screenwriters: *Richard Maibaum, Michael G. Wilson based on the short stories* For Your Eyes Only *and* Risico *by Ian Fleming*
PG/127 mins./Spy/UK/USA

After a British spy ship is sunk, its top secret encryption device used to launch Polaris missiles is found to be missing. If it has fallen into enemy hands the results could be catastrophic. So 007 is sent to investigate and his snooping leads him to Greece.

With *Moonraker* tipping the Bond balance into absurdity and critical derision, the knee-jerk reaction was to reel in the comedy and Flash-Harry hi-tech gumbo, for a leaner, more realistic form of 007 adventure. Sadly, the series was still encumbered with Roger Moore's portly incarnation, an actor who never found a way of playing the famous role other than with droll insincerity. The film, stylishly wired in places, still ranks as one of the most forgettable Bonds on record.

The all-new moody feel kicks in from the very beginning where we find Bond visiting the grave of his dead wife. The winking is out, in comes edge. When 007 arrives in a cloudy Greece, he hooks up with Carole Bouquet's beautiful avenging angel. It transpires, Bond's target, elusively known as 'Contact' could well be the man who killed her parents. Personal vengeance is a striking theme for this franchise, but it doesn't sit well. As the film labours to generate plot and character, only vaguely keeping tabs with the chirpy traditions, you start to wish it would cut loose and give an excruciating quip.

Moore just looks confused. He obviously wants to do his thing then hit the bar for cocktails, but John Glen is nagging him to add a roughness to the slick exterior. Equally, it just doesn't fit. The news is clear, there's only so far you can push a Bond before it breaks. These films are rigid and inflexible. And when it finally does relent to partake in standard Bondian thrills, it's like a relief. A silly car chase with Bond piloting a clapped-out 2CV is hilarious, and a terrifying cliff approach to a monastery (for the underwhelming conclusion) hints toward the glamorous sweep of location so sorely lacking. And Bouquet does make a brittle, intelligent Bond girl for once, which could be why no one remembers her either. ★★ **IN**

FORBIDDEN PLANET (1956)

Starring: *Walter Pidgeon (Dr. Edward Morbius), Anne Francis (Altaira Morbius), Leslie Nielsen (Commander John J. Adams), Warren Stevens (Lt. 'Doc' Ostrow), Jack Kelly (Lt. Jerry Farman), Richard Anderson (Chief Engineer Quinn)*
Director: *Fred M. Wilcox*
Screenwriter: *Cyril Hume, based on a story by Irving Block, Allen Adler*
U/98 mins./Sci-fi/USA

A starship crew goes to investigate the silence of a planet's colony only to find two survivors, one with a deadly secret.

For an American moviegoer in 1956 the opening minutes of *Forbidden Planet* must have been extremely comforting. While other science fiction films of the era rode the Cold War paranoia wave prevalent at the time (*The Thing From Another World*, *Invasion Of The Bodysnatchers* and *Invaders From Mars* to name but three) *Forbidden Planet* firmly established a future for America that many people at the time harboured severe doubts it had.

A voice-over informs us that 'By 2200 AD they had reached the other planets of our solar system, almost at once there followed the discovery of hyperdrive ... And so at last mankind began the conquest and colonisation of deep space.' And as we are introduced to the crew-cutted crew of the United Planets Space Cruiser C577-D we are left in no doubt whatsoever as to which country has pioneered this impressive expansion. From global policeman to galactic frontiersman it seems that America is set to triumph and prosper well into the future. Sing hosanna and break out the sarsparilla and apple pie! Plus, of course, a thinly-veiled ya-boo sucks to you Ivan.

It's hardly any wonder that, on the surface at least, *Forbidden Planet* is a futuristic fanfare for America. The studio that produced it, MGM, was among the most fervidly patriotic of the Hollywood majors, delivering American family value fare like Mickey Rooney's stultifyingly wholesome *Andy Hardy* series and spectacular though vacuous musical extravaganzas such as *Ziegfeld Follies*. However, although at first glance the film (famously and pretty loosely based on *The Tempest*) is a tale of American derring do and scientific smarts triumphing over adversity on the new interstellar frontier, deep in its psyche it's something much more intelligent, prophetic and terrifying: nothing less, in fact, than a Promethean exploration of the dangers of technology out of control and its capacity to destroy its creators. It's a theme picked up in the 60s and 70s by films as diverse as *2001: A Space Odyssey*, *The Terminal Man* and *Westworld*, and it remains frighteningly prescient in light of 21st century anxieties over AI and genetic modification. And all, believe it or not, from the guy who directed *Lassie Come Home*. Space Cruiser C577-D's mission is to search for survivors of the spaceship Bellerophon which crashed on deserted planet Altair-4 two decades earlier. However, when Commander Adams (Leslie Neilson before discovering that spoof-heavy comedy was his true métier) and his crew arrive they are greeted less than enthusiastically by Dr. Morbius, played with true mad-scientist verve by Walter Pidgeon, although his daughter Altaira is more curious about the delivery of interstellar beefcake; in one classic scene a frustrated Commander Adams bemoans her effect on his sex-starved crew, 'Oh get out of here before I have you run out of the area under guard … and then I'll put more guards on the guards!' he wails.

Morbius reveals that Altair-4 was previously occupied by a super-intelligent race, the Krell, who have not only provided the designs for the amazing robot Robby (who would become the main poster image for the movie and a celebrity in his own right, making many personal appearances and popping up, much later, on an episode of *Mork And Mindy* voiced, weirdly enough, by Roddy McDowall) but have left massive laboratories that the good doctor has been fooling around in. As the cruiser is repeatedly attacked by a mysterious invisible force – 'monsters from the id' – it eventually emerges that the fantastic power of the alien technology has liberated Morbius' subconscious from his teeming noggin and sent it on the rampage.

Forbidden Planet has its weaknesses. Hume's dialogue often creaks horribly, while Neilson and Francis are a couple so wooden you get the impression that if they ever did do the nasty the resultant progeny would resemble Pinocchio. The cutting edge special effects and cavernous sets influenced numerous other films including *Star Wars*. Robby, the robot with a personality, is an obvious ancestor of C-3PO while the concept of a militarised United Planets would mutate into *Star Trek*'s starfleet.

The soundtrack (of rather 'electronic tonalities by Lois and Bebe Barren') comprises the first use of electronic music in a mainstream film and Cedric Gibbons and Arthur Loneran's sumptuous production design makes excellent use of Technicolor (hey, a green sky … we must be in outer space!). But it is the movie's theme, that even at the heart of a Promethean exploration of technology out of control and its capacity to destroy its creators an advanced, technological society (precisely what America believed itself to be with it's endless supply of 'clean' nuclear power and a plastics-powered consumer boom) lurks the base nature of humanity that finally distinguishes it as a major work. And one that delivers a timely lesson in the decade that used science to invent aerosol cheese. ★★★★ **AS**

FORCE OF EVIL (1948)

Starring: *John Garfield (Joe Morse), Beatrice Pearson (Doris Lowry), Thomas Gomez (Leo Morse), Howland Chamberlin (Freddy Bauer), Roy Roberts (Ben Tucker), Marie Windsor (Edna Tucker), Paul McVey (Hobe Wheelock), Tim Ryan (Johnson), Sid Tomack ('Two & Two' Taylor), Georgia Baackus (Sylvia Morse)*
Director: *Abraham Polonsky*
Screenwriters: *Abraham Polonsky, Ira Wolfert, based on his novel* Tucker's People
PG/78 mins./Crime/USA

Big-time crook Ben Tucker pulls a scam which enables him to take over all his rivals in the numbers racket, while employing an unethical lawyer to agitate for the creation of legal gambling. However, before business can be resumed blood must be spilled.

A top-flight film noir, this thriller was the directorial debut of screenwriter Abraham Polonsky (*Body and Soul*), who was promptly blacklisted and didn't make another film until *Tell Them Willie Boy is Here* in 1970. Based on Ira Wolfert's novel *Tucker's People* and originally scripted in blank verse (!?), it's the story of a crooked lawyer (Garfield) who comes to question his easy lifestyle as his bookie brother (Thomas Gomez) is sucked deeper into a gambling racket that ruins his life. Extremely dark and poetic, this is an early example of the male-bonding melodrama, with Garfield and Gomez playing in an arena of fraternal ties and betrayals that would later produce *On The Waterfront* and *Mean Streets*.

Leftist Polonsky clearly intended the film to be an indictment of the ruthlessness of the capitalist system represented in its purest form by a crime syndicate whose only business is extorting and cajoling money from the poor and desperate, but is surprisingly sympathetic to low-level workers in the gambling racket who routinely get roughed up by the cops or killed by the higher-ups. This approach gives the film an angry, political edge that populates the formless shadows of noir with real meaning. For the most part, it consists of unhappy people in tawdry rooms being brutal to one another (Marie Windsor is a showstopper as Tucker's trampy, vampy wife), but the stylised finale gets outside at dawn as Garfield takes a walk down to the riverbank where his dead brother has been dumped. ★★★★ **KN**

FORCES OF NATURE (1999)

Starring: *Ben Affleck (Ben Holmes), Sandra Bullock (Sarah Lewis), Maura Tierney (Bridget Cahill), Steve Zahn (Alan), Blythe Danner (Virginia)*
Director: *Bronwen Hughes*
Screenwriter: *Marc Lawrence*
12/105 mins./Comedy/Romance/USA

A groom gets cold feet en route to his wedding – thanks in part to wild child, travelling companion Sarah.

Here we go, a virile 90s spin on the Cary Grant/Katharine Hepburn screwballers of the 40s with a hip-for-the-kids pairing of kooksome everygirl Bullock and brawny dish Affleck. A marketer's dreamboat, what with all that comedy (and these two have been known to land a gag in their time) and the added spice of some dynamic action. But who on earth left the handbrake on?

The pitch is *Plane, Trains And Automobiles* with top totty, as Affleck's fraught groom-to-be Ben Holmes endeavours to reach his Savannah wedding through raging weather and travel catastrophes, saddled with weirdo companion Sarah. She, by a procession of increasingly confused plot devices, has him masquerade as her hubby, pretend to be a doctor, do a strip at a gay joint and go on the run from the law. She's a grab-life kinda girl, he's a real stick-in-the-mud. Telegram to the audience – opposites are gonna attract this way soon.

Director Hughes does a shabby job of assembling all this obvious (but obviously attractive) stuff. There is no sense of jeopardy or panic in the farcical shenanigans, the set pieces – plane crash, car lift with loony, bus ride with octogenarian revellers – are flat and ineffectually paced at a crawl while characters gas on about the hateful world of monogamy. There is little-to-zilch chemistry between Affleck and a Bullock who fumbles to find the tenor of Sarah's kooky but soulful take on life in a script foregoing wit in favour of contriving yet another tortuous scrape. And for Hughes to do her cute special rain effect where she slo-mos up the droplets but keeps the rest of the action running at normal speed. Which, frankly, is just naff pop-promo gimmickry.

All you can say for this misfire is that the boy Affleck is a star. Even lumbered with such trite characterisation as the commitment-neurotic, he instils his pretty boy looks with the charming sense of imposed dignity that Cary Grant made a career out of. His leading man credentials are writ large but this film does his efforts few favours. What should have been light and frothy, a cutsie-pie whirlwind romance, is finally hamstrung by a leaden earnestness: today's nightmare vogue of shallow movies searching in vain for some kind of weighty moral deliberation. We slip off with such a damnably 'honest' conclusion about true love, you just want to puke. ★★ **AE**

FOREIGN CORRESPONDENT (1940)

Starring: *Joel McCRea (Johnny Jones/Huntley Haverstock), Laraine Day (Carol Fisher), Herbert Marshall (Stephen Fisher), George Sanders (Scott ffolliott), Albert Basserman (Van Meer)*
Director: *Alfred Hitchcock*
Screenwriters: *Charles Bennett, Joan Harrison, James Hilton, Robert Benchley*
U/120 mins./Thriller/USA

August, 1939. American crime reporter Johnny Jones is sent to Europe to get the low-down on this World War thing, and finds himself mixed up in a web of intrigue, assassination, impersonation and espionage.

Though it namechecks the Nazis rather than the 'agents of an unnamed power' who are the villains in *The 39 Steps* or *The Lady Vanishes*, this Alfred Hitchcock thriller is exactly the same kind of highly-wrought entertainment. The plot straggles from London to Holland as amiable, two-fisted McCrea gets into and out of a series of scrapes, aided by a sardonic, covertly-patriotic British journo and resisting the obvious deduction that the woman he's in love with is intimately involved with the conspiracy. Indulging his theory that suspense sequences should be keyed to the cliché associations of any locale, Hitchcock's visit to Holland prompts set-pieces involving rain (a fleeing assassin disturbs a sea of umbrellas) and windmills (amid a crowd of slowly-revolving mills, one is turning *the wrong way*).

In London, Edmund Gwenn has a wonderful, creepy cameo as a cheery private eye-bodyguard ('I may not be lean, sir, but I'm quick') who is actually a hit-man hired to shove the hero off a cathedral. The climax, set on the day war broke out, is a plane crash that was an effects stunner in its day and still delivers a punch.

An add-on, made after a few months' more war had convinced everyone how serious the situation was, finds McCrea broadcasting from the heart of the blitz, talking about the lights going out and calling America to arms (with the 'Star-Spangled Banner' over the end title!); it's the sort of naked, bleeding patriotism only possible in wartime, but it can still raise a tear sixty-five years on. ★★★★ **KN**

FORREST GUMP (1994)

Starring: *Tom Hanks (Forrest Gump), Gary Sinise (Lieutenant Dan Taylor), Robin Wright Penn (Jenny Curran), Sally Field (Mrs. Gump), Mykelti Williamson (Benjamin Buford Blue – 'Bubba')*
Director: *Robert Zemeckis*
Screenwriter: *Eric Roth, based on the novel by Winston Groom*
12/142 mins./Drama/Comedy/History/USA

Awards: *Academy Awards – Best Actor, Best Director, Best Visual Effects, Best Editing, Best Picture, Best Screenplay based on material from another source, BAFTA – Best Special Effects, Golden Globes – Best Direction, Best Drama, Best Actor*

Despite his seemingly ordinary heritage Forrest Gump is destined to play a big part in history through the second half of the 20th Century – only he is too naïve to realise.

The charmed and charming life journey of an innocent tossed through three decades of America's turbulent modern history makes for an original and hugely appealing story. Its mesmerising potential only falters because director Robert Zemeckis' agility with ingenious special effects occasionally outpaces his narrative judgment, as it did in *Death Becomes Her* and, to a lesser extent, in *Who Framed Roger Rabbit?*. It is still his most emotionally satisfying work to date, though, and however mildly or sharply one is struck by its dramatic flaws, there can be few who would deny the film's entertainment value or the captivation of Tom Hanks' performance as the eponymous Gump, which saw him walk off with a second Best Actor Oscar and make another overwrought speech.

Forrest Gump (the man) is short on I.Q. points but long on heart, a pure and simple soul who follows a straight path through the world, ever true to the homely advice of his mother – the source of guiding Gumpisms such as 'Stupid is as stupid does' – and to his elusive lifelong love Jenny. He begins his serendipitous skirmishes with destiny in childhood by unconsciously giving ideas to the as-yet-unknown Elvis Presley, and goes on to become, unintentionally, a football star, war hero and tycoon. State-of-the-art computer digitalised compositing enables Forrest to interact with Presidents JFK, LBJ and Nixon, pop stars like John Lennon and TV personalities galore, creating other illusions to quite astounding effect.

Less successful is the strand throughout the film in which Wright's Jenny counterpoints Forrest's naïve plod – always following his heart and his inner voice of right-doing in a country losing direction – with her extended walk on the wild side through promiscuity, drugs and loss of belief. Overlong, the film begins to slide into a sentimentalised panorama of the times with distracting, though admittedly frequently hilarious, spectacles.

Yet, for all its mush and meandering, this is among the stand-out audience pleasers of the year, a monstrous hit in the US with box office receipts that made well over the $300 million mark.

Hanks outdoes himself in the loveable dolt department with unforgettable, utterly disarming work. Just as he recaptured boyishness in *Big* without resorting to cuteness, here he brilliantly portrays slowness and dumb doggedness without being patronising. Despite its flaws, this is simply unmissable. ★★★★★ **AE**

FORT APACHE (1948)

Starring: *Henry Fonda (Lt. Col Owen Thursday), John Wayne (Capt. Kirby York), Shirley Temple (Philadelphia Thursday), Ward Bond (Sgt. Maj. Michael O'Rourke), John Agar (Lt. Michael 'Mickey' O'Rourke)*
Director: *John Ford*
Screenwriter: *Frank S. Nugent based on the story* Massacre *by James Warner Bellah*
U/127 mins./Western/USA

Faced with the insubordination of both his daughter, Philadelphia, and Captain Kirby York, Lt. Colonel Owen Thursday insists on handling the threat posed by the Apache in his own supercilious supremacist way.

This is the first instalment in John Ford's Cavalry trilogy and, like *She Wore a Yellow Ribbon* and *Rio Grande*, it was based on a short story by James Warner Bellah. The screenplay was written by debuting ex-critic Frank S. Nugent, who (at Ford's suggestion) compiled detailed background histories for each character and these dictated everything from the décor of their rooms to their response to orders and their interaction with the other inhabitants of the fort.

Ostensibly, this is a typical Ford Western, with plenty of sentimental comedy lacing the meticulously staged action. But its primary emphasis is on military etiquette, with each rank knowing its place and the importance of deference to the effectiveness of the unit. Even drinking in the mess is as subject to hierarchical acceptance as formal social events like the dance. Yet Ford is also intrigued by the manner in which army wives conduct domestic life within the confines of a front line stronghold and he uses Shirley Temple's adolescent exuberance to question Irene Rich and Anna Lee's unconditional support for such unflinching patriarchy.

Henry Fonda's chauvinism and bullet-headed arrogance set him at odds with John Wayne's careerist captain. But it's Thursday's love of ritual glory and pernicious racial hatred that prove his undoing. The Cavalry code is powerless against the iconoclasm of Cochise (Miguel Inclan), who exploits Thursday's underestimation of the Apache and disdain for his enlisted immigrants (he can never remember the Irish sergeant O'Rourke's name) to lure him to his senseless destruction.

Ford acknowledges the right of the Native Americans to resist genocide and accords them due military honour here. He also uses Wayne's encounter with the press to lionise the dutiful courage of the average soldier. Yet, even in reminding us that noble men do wicked deeds, he insists on perpetuating the myth of a system that turns the murderer of B Troop into a national hero. ★★★★ **DP**

THE FORTUNE COOKIE (1966)

Starring: *Jack Lemmon (Harry Hinkle), Walter Matthau (Willie Gingrich), Ron Rich (Luther 'Boom, Boom' Jackson), Cliff Osmond (Mr. Purkey), Judi West (Sandy Hinkle)*
Director: *Billy Wilder*
Screenwriters: *Billy Wilder, I.A.L Diamond*
U/125 mins./Comedy/USA
Awards: *Academy Awards – Best Supporting Actor (Walter Matthau)*

Shyster lawyer 'Whiplash' Willie Gingrich persuades his TV cameraman brother-in-law, Harry Hinkle, to sue for damages after he's injured in a pitch-side collision with American footballer Boom Boom Jackson while covering a game.

Billy Wilder was deeply wounded by the furious critical response to *Kiss Me, Stupid*. It was denounced by the press for being sordid rather than satirical and was branded obscene by the Catholic Legion of Decency for allowing an adulterer to go unpunished. Indeed, Wilder was so despondent that he reportedly contemplated suicide during a year in Europe spent considering his future.

Yet, he seemed thoroughly unrepentant when he returned Stateside and embarked upon another savage assault on American morality. But, Wilder's decision to sacrifice cynicism for a sugar-coated climax prompted another torrent of invective, this time from critics accusing him of having lost his nerve (perhaps he should have heeded his own fortune cookie advice, 'you can't fool all of the people all of the time').

So, even though it marked Jack Lemmon's first teaming with Walter Matthau, there's little wonder that Wilder didn't have a good word to say about a film he described as 'the beginning of my downfall'. It wasn't even an enjoyable shoot, as the production had to be closed down for several weeks after Matthau suffered a heart attack (as Peter Sellers had done on *Kiss Me, Stupid*). But, although he looked thinner than before, Matthau effortlessly resumed the bileful opportunism that was to earn him a Best Supporting Oscar. It also confirmed him as an excellent foil to Lemmon, who reprised to perfection the hesitant patsyism he'd exhibited in *The Apartment*.

Yet, perhaps, the most interesting protagonist is Boom Boom Jackson. Some have identified him as the first black character in a Hollywood movie whose colour was not of primary importance. But while his solicitousness and integrity contrast sharply with that of Willie and Harry's gold-digging ex-wife, Sandy (Judi West), the fact that he is abandoned by the Cleveland Browns to turn to the bottle (like the boxer father who once killed a man in the ring), represents the picture's most telling comment on contemporary America. ★★★ **DP**

THE 40-YEAR-OLD VIRGIN (2005)

Starring: *Steve Carell (Andy Stitzer), Catherine Keener (Trish), Paul Rudd (David), Romany Malco (Jay), Seth Rogen (Cal)*
Director: *Judd Apatow*
Screenwriters: *Judd Apatow, Steve Carell*
15/116 mins./Comedy/USA

Unassuming, toy-collecting electrical-store worker Andy is goaded by his workmates into admitting that he's never bumped uglies. His friends set to work rectifying this situation, but Andy only has eyes for Trish, who's interested in love not sex.

Steve Carell, who provided some of the best improv in *Anchorman* and has risen admirably to the impossible task of filling Ricky Gervais' shoes in the US version of *The Office*, should soon be as big a star as Will Ferrell. Director and co-writer Judd Apatow, the brilliant creator of TV series *Freaks And Geeks*, equally deserves all the success in the world. This first big project for both men is almost the wonderful movie such a pair should produce – yet it falls just short, strangely hamstrung by an overload of uncontrolled creativity.

Regardless, if you don't leave The *40-Year-Old Virgin* with a goofy grin playing across your face, it's time to stock up on Lithuanian fishing documentary DVDs and book yourself a regular slot on *Newsnight Review*.

This has many a moment of gross-out comedy par excellence, providing all manner of yuk for your buck. A bizarre speed-dating sequence with nipples making bids for freedom and a sly chat-up in a bookshop (preceded by the finest dating advice in history) will bring tears to the eyes, while a squirming, clearly improv'd waxing session will invite multiple howls. Carell has a natural gift for making the mundane uproarious and remaining loveable throughout (it's a measure of his charm that his insistence on keeping cherry firmly intact never seems pathetic) that elevates even the basest comedy moments . . . although two morning-erection jokes is pushing it.

It's in trying to be more that Apatow sadly stumbles. At the film's centre is a very sweet story about a man choosing to wait for a woman he loves rather than give it up for one of the nymphomaniacs shoved his way. It's like an older, yet less mature, version of *American Pie*. But where that balanced sweet and unsavoury, this loses its central romance amid the bodily fluids and flatulence. Catherine Keener, always watchable, is left screaming for attention as an insistent pack of testosteroney friends continually interrupt her storyline, reducing both her romantic impact and their own hilarity.

With 15 minutes edited out, this could be a terrific comedy and a possible rom-com classic. As it stands, *The 40-Year-Old Virgin* is delightfully disgusting, yet faintly disappointing. ★★★ **OR**

48 HOURS (1982)

Starring: *Nick Nolte (Jack Cates), Eddie Murphy (Reggie Hammond), Annette O'Toole (Elaine), Frank McRae (Haden), James Remar (Albert Ganz)*
Director: *Walter Hill*
Screenwriters: *Roger Spottiswoode and Walter Hill & Steven E. De Souza.*
15/96 mins./Cop/Comedy/Thriller/USA

On the trail of two cop-killers, boozy cop Jack Cates 'borrows' their former partner, the wisecracking Reggie Hammond, from jail to help him trace them. The problem is his parole is fixed at a slight two days. Oh, and Reggie has his own agenda. Oh, and they really, really don't get on.

Although dated, there is a brute edginess to this popular slice of formula odd coupling. It's not just about Eddie Murphy's foul-mouthed comebacks, although they were never as bouncy or cutting as here, or Nick Nolte's irresponsible bullyboy pose he has spent the rest of his career trying to unseat, but also the way Walter Hill pitches a ready Hollywood staple into a harder, dare-we-say more realistic world. It's as if Lemmon and Matthau had stumbled into *The French Connection*, with the added spice of race.

Indeed, there's more than a casual tip-of-the-hat in Murphy's (possibly career best) scene in which, posing as a cop, he saunters into a redneck bar, Confederate Flag pressed to the wall, humming with racist lunks, and jives his way to supremacy. It's the direct inverse of Gene Hackman's take-over of a black-filled Harlem bar in that famous thriller. 'I'm your worst fucking nightmare, man!' snaps Reggie to the dumbstruck clientele. 'A nigger with a badge.' The writing is an equal to Murphy's whiplash tongue.

As this is a film by Hill, who has busily traded in a violent, earthbound machismo (*Southern Comfort*, *The Warriors*) it hardly pulls its punches. If anything, this must surely count as the most violent 'comedy' in film history, as Hill dwells on the many bare-knuckle beatings (usually involving Nolte) that are his particular filmic peccadillo. Yet, he's also a skilled purveyor of a piquant, scuzzy atmosphere, a lurid, criminal underbelly where it takes two distrustful specimens to further the cause of good.

Real Names — TOP10

1	Dirk Bogarde	Derek Jules Gaspard Ulric Niven van den Bogaerde
2	Cary Grant	Archie Leech
3	John Wayne	Marion Morrison
4	Marilyn Monroe	Norma Jean Baker
5	Jane Seymour	Joyce Penelope Wilhemina Frankenberg
6	Albert Brooks	Albert Einstein
7	Antonio Banderas	Jose Antonio Dominquez Bandera
8	Alan Alda	Alphonse d'Abruzzo
9	Carmen Miranda	Maria do Carmo Miranda Da Cunha
10	Lauren Bacall	Betty Jean Perske

Their story is regulation potboiling, the bad-guys are simply that, bad to the bone, the good guys have the bonus of character and the two stars are having a ball. Nolte no less than the showpiece his partner grants, threads in a sense of pressing moral determination beneath his louche, jack-the-rules exterior. That the fact they come to appreciate one other, the grudging respect of a million clichés, feels so satisfying, shows just how successful the film is. ★★★★ **IN**

THE FOUR HORSEMEN OF THE APOCALYPSE (1921)

Starring: *Pomeroy Cannon (Madariaga, the Centaur), Josef Swickard (Marcello Desnoyers), Bridgetta Clark (Dona Luisa), Rudolph Valentino (Julio Desnoyers), Virginia Warwick (Chichi), Alan Hale (Karl von Hartrott)*
Director: *Rex Ingram*
Screenwriter: *June Mathis based on the novel* Los Cuatros Jinetes Del Apocalipsis *by Vincente Blasco Ibañez*
Unrated/134 mins./Drama/War/USA

Argentinian aristocrat Julio Desnoyers arrives in wartime Paris and seduces Marguerite Laurie, while her husband is away at the front. However, when he returns home blinded, she devotes herself to nursing him and Julio enlists to meet a hero's end.

Screenwriter June Mathis is usually credited with persuading the cash-strapped Metro Pictures to sponsor this adaptation of Vincente Blasco Ibañez's novel. Moreover, she also secured the director's berth for Rex Ingram and the lead for the little-known Italian immigrant actor, Rudolph Valentino.

Today, if it's remembered at all, this landmark silent is best known for Valentino's sensual tango routine. But its contemporary reputation rested on Ingram's meticulous direction.

Armed with a budget of around $1 million, he set about mounting a production to rival those of his friend, Erich von Stroheim. Guided by a batallion of technical advisers, he personally supervised every aspect of the civilian and military décor and costuming, as well as the lighting design (although here he owed a sizeable debt to the estimable John Seitz). His attention to detail paid off, with his depiction of the uncertainties of the home front and the atrocities of the trenches drawing comparisons with D.W. Griffith. Moreover, the film, which was shown in large cities with full orchestral accompaniment and live sound effects for the battle sequences, made $4 million at the box office.

Yet while it was acclaimed in the States as a realistic masterpiece (despite its uncomfortable blend of pacifism and mysticism), it was received with reservations in Europe. Cinéastes noted the Irish-born director's continental sensibilities (even though he had never visited France). But patriots everywhere complained about the depiction of their nation – with the Germans resenting the resuscitation of the beastly Hun, the French castigating the emphasis on American forces, and the British protesting about their virtual absence from proceedings (a complaint that would revive over 75 years later on the release of *Saving Private Ryan*).

Vincente Minnelli updated the story to the Second World War in 1962, with Glenn Ford in the Valentino role. But while Milton Krasner's cinematography was praised for its fluidity, it was pronounced a bore and many questioned Minnelli's pictorialist use of Nazi iconography. ★★★ **DP**

FOUR ROOMS (1995)

Starring: *Tim Roth (Ted, The Bellhop), The Missing Ingredient: Sammi Davis (Jezabel), Amanda De Cadenet (Diana), Valeria Golino (Athena), Madonna (Elspeth), Ione Sky (Eva), Lili Taylor (Raven), Alicia Witt (Kiva), The Wrong Man: Jennifer Beals (Angela), David Proval (Sigfried), The Misbehavers: Antonio Banderas (Man), Salma Hayek (TV Dancing Girl), The Man From Hollywood: Paul Calderon (Norman), Quentin Tarantino (Chester Rush), Bruce Willis (Leo) (uncredited)*
Director: *Allison Anders (The Missing Ingredient), Alexandre Rockwell (The Wrong Man), Robert Rodriguez (The Misbehavers), Quentin Tarantino (The Man From Hollywood)*
Screenwriters: *Allison Anders (The Missing Ingredient), Alexandre Rockwell (The Wrong Man), Robert Rodriguez (The Misbehavers), Quentin Tarantino (The Man From Hollywood)*
18/98 mins./Comedy/Drama/USA

Awards: *Razzie – Worst Supporting Actress (Madonna)*

A night in a hotel is seen from the perspective of a bellhop, and what he sees in four very different rooms there.

Oh dear. It must have seemed like a very good idea at the time. Take four hip young directors. Let them loose on a vanity project in which they each write and direct a segment – a room – of a film set in a hotel on New Year's Eve. The result? A dull, largely pointless, mostly boring exercise that begins badly, tests your patience as well as your endurance, and proves that all that Tarantino touches doesn't turn to gold. The four stories are linked by Ted the bellhop (an annoying Roth, like Jerry Lewis on acid) who is left alone for the evening to man the front desk.

It begins very badly indeed with *Honeymoon Suite: The Missing Ingredient*, directed by Allison Anders, in which Valeria Golino, Madonna, Sammi Davis, Lili Taylor and Ione Skye are a coven of witches determined to resurrect the spirit of the goddess Diana and reverse a spell that was perpetrated on her wedding night. To the ceremony each must bring a life fluid; only Skye swallowed hers (use your imagination), and so has to procure the missing ingredient from Roth's initially reluctant bellhop. It's a spiritless piece, tedious, lifeless, symptomatic of the film as a whole.

It quickly goes from bad to worse with *Room 404: The Wrong Man*, directed by Alexandre Rockwell, the most pointless segment, certainly the most prosaic, with Roth involved in a dispute between a bound and gagged Jennifer Beals and her gun-toting husband.

Things pick up considerably with *Room 309: The Misbehavers*, directed by Robert Rodriguez, starring Antonio Banderas as a Mexican gangster who leaves his two children in the care of Ted with the strict instruction 'Don't misbehave.' They do. And it involves cigarettes, a dead hooker, a hypodermic, and fire. It's a one-joke skit but Rodriguez's frenetic comic book style lifts the picture, only for it to implode with *Penthouse: The Man From*

Hollywood, directed by Quentin Tarantino, which comes across as a major ego exercise for its director, playing a famous comedian who offers Ted $1,000 to chop off his pal's finger if he loses their bet. The story owes a debt to Roald Dahl, who gets a name check in the credits, but lacks any sparkle or wit.

QED: anthology films never work; Tarantino is not infallible; casting Madonna as a lesbian witch and Bruce Willis in a silly party hat doesn't necessarily make for great entertainment. ★★ **MS**

FOUR WEDDINGS AND A FUNERAL (1994)

Starring: *Hugh Grant (Charles), James Fleet (Tom), Simon Callow (Gareth), John Hannah (Matthew), Kristin Scott Thomas (Fiona), David Bower (David), Charlotte Coleman (Scarlett), Andie MacDowell (Carrie), Rowan Atkinson (Father Gerald)*
Director: *Mike Newell*
Screenwriter: *Richard Curtis*
15/116 mins./Romance/Comedy/UK

Awards: *BAFTA – Best Actor, Best Supporting Actress (Kristin Scott Thomas), Best Film, David Lean Award for Direction, Golden Globes – Best Comedy/Musical Actor*

At a friend's wedding, Englishman Charles falls for a vivacious American Carrie and pursues her through a summer of weddings, helped (and hindered) by his loyal friends.

In the modern fairy-tale realm of *Four Weddings And A Funeral* the charming prince is an archetypal English, upper middle-class twitterer who struggles with himself to overcome his fears of intimacy and commitment and babbles his now classic, stammering declaration of love: 'Um, look. Sorry, sorry … I, I just wondered … I really feel … in short, to recap in a slightly clearer version, uh, in the words of David Cassidy, in fact, um, while he was still with The Partridge Family, uh, "I Think I Love You", and uh, I, I just wondered whether by any chance you wouldn't like to … uh … uh … um. No, no, no. Of course not. I'm an idiot. He's not. Excellent, excellent, fantastic, uh, I was going to say lovely to see you. Sorry to disturb. Better get on. Fuck!'

At a time when British films with a hope of succeeding internationally were almost exclusively handsome period pieces, along came writer Richard Curtis' abundantly entertaining and engaging contemporary romantic comedy. Director Mike Newell's films had met with mixed fortunes, although his 1992 period romance *Enchanted April*, made for TV, had tickled U.S. critics and become a surprise arthouse hit in America. TV comedy veteran (*Blackadder*) Curtis had already made a pleasing transition into feature film with the quirky *The Tall Guy*. Still, *Four Weddings* was a production of modest ambition and expectations, with the cast accordingly contracted at humble British scale (about £65,000 in Hugh Grant's case).

But standing out in a good ensemble turned out to be a career rocket launcher for Grant, Kristin Scott Thomas (Fiona) and John Hannah (as Matthew, with his show-stopping turn at the funeral reciting W.H. Auden's Funeral Blues: 'stop all the clocks, cut off the telephone …'). *Four Weddings And A Funeral* became the then top-grossing British film of all time, and the one a subsequent wave of British comedies aspired to equal. It also set forth the winning formula for Curtis' line of romcom: a sophisticated but boyish, bemused, self-mocking Grant, an American leading lady for the market place, a group of vulnerable, endearing chums who are witty, weird and/or whacky, and a romance fraught with mistiming and misunderstanding.

Wedding Number One, Angus and Laura's in Somerset, is introductory. Charles is late and has forgotten the rings but gives a great Best Man speech and is struck by the thunderbolt they call love when he sees Carrie, who engineers their one-nighter despite his diffidence.

The plot thickens at Wedding Number Two, Bernard and Lydia's in London. Charles is late but is outdone in the gaffe department by Rowan Atkinson's vicar, whose dismal recital of the vows ('… to be my awful wedded wife') injects a spot of Beanishness, and in the Best Man stakes by the excruciating effort of James Fleet's Tom ('I congratulated him because all his other girlfriends had been such complete dogs, although may I say how delighted we are to see so many of them here this evening!'). Charles is busy being harassed by more than half of the women he's slept with, discovering his dream girl has become engaged, and getting trapped in the bedroom where the newlyweds are going at it.

One month later Charles runs into Carrie for the film's sole non-ceremonial social encounter, long enough to gasp out the justly famous David Cassidy-citing highlight. Another month on Charles obviously is late for Carrie's rites, but not for those attending Gareth's demise, an occasion devised to provide a pause from hilarity for reflection and wit gathering. A leap of ten months takes us to what really comprises a set of three and a half weddings and a funeral; the reason for making a feature of Charles' brother David being deaf emerging in the outstanding jest of the, 'speak now or forever hold your peace' sequence conducted in sign language.

Four Weddings is comedy that knits together superior sitcom sketches. So blithely is it unencumbered by backstory or reason it doesn't bear reality checks even on first viewing but still draws you in. How did this cross-generational set, from the soignée, acerbic Fiona to Simon Callow's flamboyant, professorial Gareth and Charlotte Coleman's younger, overstated kook Scarlett, become inseparable? How can an old buddy not know that Tom's manor is the size of Blenheim Palace? Does anybody have a job? Does nobody have parents? Why would Carrie marry the pompous politician Hamish (Corin Redgrave) at all, and why invite all these people she scarcely knows to her wedding? Who can make sense of the last conversation in the rain? And on repeated viewing we're not at all sure we wouldn't have been happier if it had been the long-suffering Fiona to land Charlie, after all. (But then we couldn't have the huge laugh at Fifi's fate in the end credits wedding pictures.) It is a tribute to Newell's crisp direction and the cast's delightful performances that this good-natured jape transcends its blatant contrivance to cajole and continually amuse. ★★★★ **AE**

1492: CONQUEST OF PARADISE (1992)

Starring: *Gérard Depardieu (Christopher Columbus), Sigourney Weaver (Queen Isabella), Armand Assante (Sanchez), Loren Dean (Older Fernando), Angela Molina (Beatrix)*
Director: *Ridley Scott*
Screenwriter: *Roselyn Bosch*
15/150 mins./History/Drama/UK/USA/France/Spain

Covering 20 years of the life of Christopher Columbus, from his initial efforts to raise interest in his voyage into the unknown, through immortalising triumphs and the ultimate disillusionment of seeing Eden turned into Hell.

After the countless books, articles, TV documentaries and movies already assailing one's sensibilities, the exhausted lay person naturally looks to this to be the definitive account of Christopher Columbus' momentous journey from the coast of Spain to the Caribbean, the better to consign the rest to the bin and have Ridley Scott tell it like it is. It comes as something of a shock, then, to realise early on that reappraising Columbus' personality – he's been accused of obsessional greed, wanton murder of the natives and general megalomania – has been entirely reversed here.

Indeed, Depardieu is required to present our Christopher as a caring eco-freak implanted with a deep desire not to wreck his New World or rape any locals, meaning that the best anecdotes – like the one about him claiming to have spied land first, thus selfishly divesting the real lookout of his lifetime pension reward – do not feature here. More worryingly, Columbus' very motives for setting sail in the first place are somewhat muddied – if he didn't go for riches beyond imagining, what did he go for? Depardieu merely mutters something about not accepting the world as it is before hoisting anchor and pointing his boat westwards.

Putting aside these problems, Ridley Scott has produced a snapshot of history on a par with the very best. The atmosphere of fear, dread and ignorance in medieval Spain is brilliantly recreated, and the sheer vastness of the undertaking – bigger, surely, than the first space flight, since Columbus had literally no idea of what lay beyond the horizon – comes across loud and clear. As you'd expect from the arch visualist, he does the subject aesthetic justice too, despite the irritating use of some coloured filters left over from *The Duellists*.

It's surprising though, that in the wake of *Thelma & Louise*, the human moments of *1492* sink like cannonballs, with the assorted European thesps often making themselves less than clear in the English language department, and many a character development and relationship-building scene presumably still on some cutting-room floor. Whilst Scott lacks the genius of, say, Fred Zinnemann in bringing history to life, and while his two-and-a-half hour celebration of the discovery of the Americas sags somewhat in the middle, this is no *Revolution*. As for Gérard Depardieu, he's the standout – loping around like a particularly charismatic sore-headed bear, and playing triumph, passion and crushing disappointment with equal Gallic aplomb. ★★★ **PT**

THE FOURTH MAN (DE VIERDE MAN) (1983)

Starring: *Jeroen Krabbé (Gerard Reve), Renée Soutendijk (Christine Halsslag), Thom Hoffman (Herman), Dolf de Vries (Dr. de Vries), Geert de Jong (Ria), Hans Veerman (Begrafenisondernemer)*
Director: *Paul Verhoeven*
Screenwriter: *Gerald Soetemann based on the novel by Gerard Reve*
18/105 mins./Drama/Netherlands

Gerard, a drunken gay writer, is troubled by prophetic dreams. In a seaside town on a speaking engagement, he is so stricken with lust for hunk Herman that he romances the youth's girlfriend Christine (Renée Soutendijk), a witchlike minx who has buried three husbands and is setting her sights on a fourth.

Though he had modest international hits with *Spetters* and *Soldier of Orange*, this was the breakthrough film for Dutch director Paul Verhoeven, landing him a Hollywood career. Now, it seems like a subtler draft of *Basic Instinct* as a smitten, befuddled, frankly absurd male hero is drawn inexorably into the orbit of a blonde manipulatrice who might well be a supernaturally-powered serial murderer but could equally be a total innocent who has had tragic luck with marriages.

Based on a novel by Gerard Reve, who uses his own name for the main character, it combines bizarre multi-sexual eroticism, weird religious imagery (including a crucified gay pin-up and a guest appearance by the Virgin Mary), Argento-like horror film grue (a gouged eyeball dripping from a spyhole in a hotel door) and very sly black humour. With perfectly balanced performances from Soutendijk, whose tightly-marcelled hair and blood-red lips make her an unusual satanic seductress, and Krabbé, who persists in finding decency in his astonishingly sleazy character, it unfolds as louche fantasy, with several genuinely surprising plot reversals and one or two moments of pure shock.

Like Verhoeven, both stars earned solid international careers on the strength of their work here – but arguably have never been better. Reminiscent of the films of Harry Kumel (*Daughters of Darkness*, *Malpertuis*) in its sado-erotic atmosphere, Low Countries setting and fusion of the supernatural with comedy of manners, *The Fourth Man* is an unusual, tasty picture that leavens audacious symbolism with wicked wit. ★★★★ **KN**

FRANKENSTEIN (1931)

Starring: *Colin Clive (Henry Frankenstein), Mae Clarke (Elizabeth), John Boles (Victor Moritz), Boris Karloff (the Monster), Edward Van Sloan (Dr. Waldman)*
Director: *James Whale*
Screenwriters: *Garrett Fort, Francis Edwards Faragoh, John Balderston, Robert Florey, based on the novel by Mary Shelley and the play by Peggy Webling*
PG/71 mins./Horror/Sci-fi/USA

Dr. Frankenstein creates a simple creature from various body parts but the creature turns into a monster when Dr. Frankenstein rejects him.

Universal's *Dracula*, to which Whale's film was a follow-up, was a spooky adaptation of a Broadway play. It could easily have been a one-off, remembered only as a footnote to the drawing-room mystery. Without *Frankenstein*, there wouldn't be a genre called the horror film, and the form would never have found its greatest star.

The English Whale took the project, which had been prepped by director-writer Robert Florey as a possible vehicle for *Dracula* star Bela Lugosi, to escape being typecast as a director of World War I-themed movies like *Hell's Angels* and *Journey's End*. Later, after *The Invisible Man* and *Bride Of Frankenstein*, he regretted even more his close identification with a genre that swiftly became the most déclassé in Hollywood. But while he was putting the picture together, he exercised all his peculiar creativity, hacking out of Mary Shelley's unwieldy novel a fable of an overreaching scientist and his abused, childlike outcast of a monster.

For the role of Henry Frankenstein (as opposed to Shelley's Victor), Whale rejected Leslie Howard and cast his neurotic *Journey's End* leading man Colin Clive, whose clipped British vowels sound strange in the supposedly mid-European setting (the film seems to be set in a light opera-style no-place, no-time rather than a real country). From the cast of *Dracula*, Whale retained both Edward Van Sloan as the sceptical elder who strongly disapproves of Frankenstein's experiments, and the unforgettable Dwight Frye as the hunchbacked dwarf assistant who drops the normal brain he has been told to steal and substitutes that of a mad criminal.

However, the career break-out of the film was William Henry Pratt, a 42 year-old Englishman who had turned his back on a privileged upbringing and emigrated to become a truck driver in Canada and a jobbing bit-player in the States. Pratt had popped up in a few gangster and melodrama movies, but Whale saw something in his eyes that fitted his conception of the Monster. Universal's makeup genius Jack P. Pierce devised the flattop, the neck terminals (not bolts), the heavy eyelids and the elongated, scarred hands. Meanwhile Whale kitted the creature out with a shabby suit like those worn by the ex-soldier hobos then riding the rails, and added the clumping asphalt-spreader's boots. But it was Pratt who transformed the Monster from a snarling bogeyman into a yearning, sympathetic character whose misdeeds are accidental (drowning a little girl) or justified (hanging the dwarf who has tortured him with fire). In the opening credits, the Monster is billed as being played by '?'. Only at the end of the film were the audience told it was a fellow by the name of Boris Karloff, Pratt's stage handle, who had terrified, moved and inspired them.

The pain in Karloff's eyes is real – all the clobber was agony to wear, and the experience turned the mild-mannered actor into a militant: he helped found the Screen Actors Guild to save others from suffering for long hours under the California sun and the burning arc-lights. Modern audiences find some of the plot scenes trite and chatty, with winsome heroine Mae Clarke and stiff second lead John Boles tiresome unless the Monster is threatening them. But all of Karloff's scenes – and most of Clive's and Frye's grave-robbing – remain as compelling as ever. There are a number of wondrous theatrical set-pieces, among them the 'creation', with lightning crackling around the tower and the Monster raised to the angry sky on an operating table; the Monster's first appearance (seen from behind, he turns to show us his face and the camera stutters towards him); the heartbreaking sequence with the little girl; the primal attack on the heroine on her wedding day (one of few bits taken from the book); and the pursuit of the Monster by a mob of peasants, winding up in the old mill where creator and creation confront each other in one of the earliest horror movie inferno finales.

Originally, Clive died and Clarke paired off with Boles, but post-production tinkering saved Frankenstein for the sequels. Whale, Karloff and Clive were persuaded to come back in 1935 for *Bride Of Frankenstein*, a sequel that is more elaborate, sophisticated, cynical and entertaining than the original, if also a trifle more calculated in its sentiment and misanthropy. Oddly, Whale again tried to kill Frankenstein and again changed his mind at the last minute. Whale quit, but Karloff became the grand old man of horror. He had another spin in his best role in the spirited *Son Of Frankenstein*, then made way for lesser horror stars Lon Chaney Jr. (*Ghost Of Frankenstein*) and, sadly, Lugosi (*Frankenstein Meets The Wolf Man*) before stunt man Glenn Strange got into the boots for *House Of Frankenstein* – in which Karloff plays a mad doctor – *House Of Dracula* and the death knell wind-up *Abbott And Costello Meet Frankenstein*. ★★★★★ **KN**

ⓓ FRANKENSTEIN (1994)

Starring: *Robert De Niro (The Creature), Kenneth Branagh (Victor Frankenstein), Tom Hulce (Henry Clerval), Helena Bonham Carter (Elizabeth), Aidan Quinn (Captain Robert Walton), Ian Holm (Baron Frankenstein), Richard Briers (Grandfather), John Cleese (Professor Waldman), Robert Hardy (Professor Krempe), Cherie Lunghi (Victor's Mother), Celia Imrie (Mrs. Moritz)*
Director: *Kenneth Branagh*
Screenwriters: *Steph Lady, Frank Darabont, based on the novel by Mary Shelley*
15/123 mins./Horror/Sci-fi/UK/Japan/USA

A young doctor fatigued by the hopelessness of fatal cases decides to defy death by creating life, but not in the kinky, fun way. But the monster he creates is as destructive as it is lonely.

It was after listening to Byron and Shelley discuss the boundary between life and death and the possibilities of transgressing it through new pseudo-sciences, like galvanism, that the 19-year-old Mary Godwin (subsequently Mrs. Shelley) had the nightmare she elaborated upon to create her novel *Frankenstein*. Of course, they were all on drugs at the time, too.

Nearly 180 years later, this adolescent fairy-tale of scientific monomania and romance – the grandfather of the Mad Scientist genre in literature and film – still taps into some collective abhorred. And anticipates the medical ethic questions of the late 20th Century.

Kenneth Branagh's sumptuous version for Francis Coppola's Zoetrope, the umpteenth cinematic stab at Mary Shelley's story, is a vigorous, entertaining re-telling. Branagh's Victor Frankenstein is first seen frosted and furred in the Arctic, gasping out his cautionary tale to obsessed explorer Aidan Quinn, taking us back to his carefree youth, when the Swiss Family Frankenstein were fond of romping round their lovely chateau. Then a personal loss twisted the student doctor's soul. Bent on the reanimation of the dead, he sacrifices everything to that end, creating new life that never should have been wrought and condemning himself and his loved ones to retribution on a grand scale.

Branagh can never please everyone of course, but his performance as Victor Frankenstein is muscular, best when driven and intense. Helena Bonham Carter looks splendid as his lifelong love, Tom Hulce is charming if under-used as Victor's sunnier, concerned sidekick (Henry, not Igor), and a host of familiar British thesps do their thing big time, outshone by a quiet, completely unrecognisable John Cleese as Victor's troubled professor mentor.

For the first half of the film one wonders exactly what appeal the role of the creature could have had for Robert De Niro, unless it was a masochistic thrill to suffer in silence as his peg-legged miscreant is hanged for murder, spliced, diced, badly stitched up, dunked in goo, electrocuted, reviled and slung out to die by his insensitive, paternally challenged Victor F. But as his hideous wretch skulks yearningly around the hovel of poor-but-happy peasants (including the blind grandfather Richard Briers – a casting disaster for British audiences on titter alert), re-acquiring powers of speech, literacy and cogitation, nursing rejection into sensational revenge, one does warm to his unnatural plight.

The biggest contribution, however, is made by the extravagantly handsome production design and sequences derived from Branagh's love of Big Pictures: the discovery of a dead child, the mob lynching of an innocent, the reanimating of the corpse (an arrestingly yukky set-piece) and some ripping business with ice floes and electrical storms.

Unhappily, these are badly served by some inane dialogue that confuses camp melodrama with Gothic horror. James Whale's esteemed 1931 version, even more nominally based on the novel, is revered as much for its restraint as its Expressionist style and Boris Karloff's pitiable monstrosity.

In one's dreams, Branagh's romantic Technicolor visuals wedded to a more intellectually rigorous screenplay that defied you to snigger, might have mounted a more serious challenge to the old classic. As *Frankensteins* go it's more enjoyable than many, but will no doubt pass muster simply as an acceptable night out that could have been better. ★★★ **AE**

ⓓ FRANKENSTEIN MEETS THE WOLF MAN (1943)

Starring: *Ilona Massey (Baroness Elsa Frankenstein), Patric Knowles (Dr. Frank Mannering), Lionel Atwill (Mayor Of Vasaria), Bela Lugosi (The Frankenstein Monster), Maria Ouspenskaya (Maleva), Dennis Hoey (Insp. Owen), Lon Chaney (The Wolf Man/Lawrence Stewart 'Larry' Talbot), Don Barclay (Franzec), Rex Evans (Vazec), Dwight Frye (Rudi)*
Director: *Roy William Neill*
Screenwriter: *Curt Siodmak*
PG/74 mins./Horror/USA

Grave-robbers disturb the resting place of werewolf Larry Talbot who returns to life and travels to middle Europe in the hope that the surviving notebooks of Dr Frankenstein hold the secret of curing his affliction. However, an overcurious scientist opts to use the notes to restore the Frankenstein Monster to full strength.

This was the first great team-up monster movie, setting a precedent for everything from *King Kong vs Godzilla* to *Freddy vs Jason*. It is simultaneously a direct sequel to *The Wolf Man*, in which Chaney Jr. created his most lasting monster character, and *The Ghost of Frankenstein*, in which he had taken over from Boris Karloff as the flat-headed, big-booted Frankenstein Monster.

Since Chaney couldn't play both title roles, it was a clever, if ironic casting stroke to put the sadly aged Bela Lugosi, who missed out on playing the Monster in the 1931 James Whale film that made Boris Karloff a star, into the makeup. At the end of *Ghost*, the Monster receives a brain transplant from Ygor, a broken-necked minion played by Lugosi, and so it could be argued that Lugosi was reprising this role rather than following Karloff and Chaney – though, in the event, many of the more strenuous scenes were played by stunt-men subbing for the star.

Silly but enormous fun, complete with gypsy musical numbers and an insane battle royal finish as the monsters rip each other apart while some loon dynamites the dam and the castle is swept away in a flood. This is one of the most-often excerpted films in movie history – it's ignored by Robert De Niro and Uma Thurman while having sex in *Mad Dog and Glory* and appropriately screens in the background of an early scene in *AVP: Alien vs Predator*. ★★★ **KN**

FRANKIE AND JOHNNY (1991)

Starring: *Al Pacino (Johnny), Michelle Pfeiffer (Frankie), Hector Elizondo (Nick), Nathan Lane (Tim), Kate Nelligan (Cora), Jane Morris (Nedda)*
Director: *Garry Marshall*
Screenwriter: *Terrence McNally, based on his play* Frankie and Johnny in the Clair De Lune
15/118 mins./Drama/Comedy/Romance/USA

Awards: *BAFTA – Best Supporting Actress (Kate Nelligan)*

Recently released from the clink Johnny gets a job in a cafe beside waitress loner waitress Frankie. She resists his affections but persistent Johnny is determined that love will eventually blossom

A major dud on its theatrical release, with the expected chemistry between Pacino and Pfeiffer simply failing to materialise, the direction by *Pretty Woman* helmsman Garry Marshall being limp in the extreme and the script by Terrence McNally sticking far too closely and literally to his own hit Broadway production.

And, as if all of this were not disappointing enough, The Previously Great Al Pacino wears a wretched bandana kind of thing around his head for most of the time, surely one of the ten great sartorial disasters in the movies. Along the way, Pacino gets to have some seriously moody eye contact, a frenzied and not entirely successful bedroom romp with the frankly unrecognisable Kate Nelligan, and some of the corniest dialogue this side of *Far And Away*, a film which, in the essential conceit of its central premise, *Frankie and Johnny* faintly resembles.

And, er, that's about it, bar the rather sickly musical accompaniment every time good old Frank or John takes a quick time out from feeding the masses. Pacino and Pfeiffer end up being just about as enthralling, just as gripping, as any other cranky waitress and short-order cook one cares to mention. ★★ **BMc**

FRANTIC (1988)

Starring: *Harrison Ford (Doctor Richard Walker), Emmanuelle Seigner (Michelle), Betty Buckley (Sondra Walker), John Mahoney (Williams)*
Director: *Roman Polanski*
Screenwriters: *Roman Polanski, Gerard Brach, Robert Towne, Jeff Gross*
15/120 mins./Thriller/USA

While attending a medical conference in Paris, Dr. Richard Walker's wife mysteriously disappears. With the authorities proving no help, he takes matters into his own hands, hooking up with the awkward beautiful Michelle who knows something she's not telling.

Here's a terrific set-up. Roman Polanski does Hitchcock in Paris with Harrison Ford in the lead, and for the first half it more than lives up to its billing. Ford working well against type, ditches the macho-crap, that aura of dominant certainty, for a nerveball academic stumped that a situation like this would ever force entry into the safe confines of his life. During an early action sequence, he stumbles after the heroin-chic fatale-charms of Emmanuelle Seigner's Michelle across slippery rooftops desperately trying to quell the tide of vertigo-induced nausea. Never have we seen Indiana Jones so unmanned.

Suffused with paranoia, as Walker bounces off the faceless wall of indifference of the authorities – he traverses the usual stations of concierge, embassy and police to no avail – Polanski both references the sharp trill of the master's games and also plays with the form. Walker's xenophobic tendencies are teasingly forced back into his face. And he must sink beneath the city's glittery surface into the sordid haunts of the Parisian underworld where the film starts to hint at obviousness, swiftly exhausting its invention. This stiff doctor, his face a picture of frustration and distaste, is tugged through punkish nightclubs and across the regulation parade of weirdoes toward some kind of denouement. And this being Polanski, he gets suitably excited by the effect this sleek, sexy girl is having on Walker. Seigner, in her first film, is quite something, pouty and exotic, a livewire. You half want Walker to forgo the absconded wife for this slender flame of a girl.

The film finally collapses in its writing. Out of all this labyrinthine plotting and flirting emerges a flaccid ending so silly it threatens to ruin the film. It certainly spoils the clammy atmosphere of alien threat – that it could be this strange city itself that has stolen his wife. And from the director of *Chinatown* that is unforgivable. ★★★ **IN**

FREAKS (1932)

Starring: *Wallace Ford (Phroso), Leila Hyams (Venus), Olga Baclanova (Cleopatra), Roscoe Ates (Roscoe), Henry Victor (Hercules), Harry Earles (Hans), Daisy Earles (Frieda), Rose Dione (Madame Tetrallini), Daisy Hilton, Violet Hilton (Siamese Twins)*
Director: *Tod Browning*
Screenwriters: *Willis Goldbeck, Leon Gordon, Edgar Allan Woolf, Al Boasberg based on the short story Spurs by Clarence Aaron 'Tod' Robbins*
15/64 mins/Horror/USA

Glamorous tightrope walker Cleopatra marries a wealthy dwarf Hans and poisons him, prompting the brotherhood of freaks ('gooble gobble, one of us') to horrible revenge. This anecdote is told in a carnival to a crowd of gawkers who are eventually shown the grotesque chicken-woman Cleopatra has been turned into.

A disaster in its day and a career-scupperer for director Tod Browning, this carnival tale was glamour studio MGM's 1932 attempt to get in on the horror market recently opened up by *Dracula*, *Frankenstein* and company at Universal. Rather than calling on the makeup artistry that had transformed Boris Karloff into the Frankenstein Monster or the Mummy, Browning controversially cast real-life microcephalics, hermaphrodites and dwarves as his freaks. The film shows obvious fondness for its carny cast, filling out the fable-like plot with vignettes about the love life of Siamese twins, how the living torso gets about walking on his arms or the way an armless legless man lights a cigarette (NB: a roll-up!). It's oddly charming for much of its length, showing its human oddities as child-like innocents or heroic survivors, but pulls an unforgettably nasty nightmare ending that undermines everything else in the movie as the freaks crawl through the mud and rain to avenge the martyred midget, at last becoming the monsters the world thinks them to be.

The studio was so horrified that it sold the picture off to grindhouse distributors who appropriately toured it around sleazy tent shows under the title *Nature's Mistakes*. However, it was revived in the 1960s – when, incidentally, British Censors rescinded their ban on it. In an era when the word 'freak' had a more positive meaning, it became recognised as a one-of-a-kind bizarro masterpice.

It's also the film Lyle Lovett talks about in *The Player*. ★★★★ **KN**

FREAKY FRIDAY (2003)

Director: Mark Waters
Starring: *Jamie Lee Curtis (Tess Coleman), Lindsay Lohan (Anna Coleman), Mark Harmon (Ryan), Harold Gould (Grandpa), Chad Michael Murray (Jake)*
Screenwriter: *Leslie Dixon, based on the book by Mary Rodgers*
PG/93 mins./Comedy/USA

Quarrelling Tess and resentful 15 year-old daughter Anna are magicked into each other's bodies for a fraught Friday of unfamiliar challenges, romantic complications and new mutual understanding.

Besides the obligatory wiseacre kid brother, no teen flick is complete these days without the ingénue performing a music promo.

FREDDY GOT FINGERED

So this body swap fairy-tale climaxes in a band audition at Hollywood's House Of Blues. Happily, Jamie Lee Curtis gurning through a guitar solo (she is Lady Spinal Tap, after all) while her floundering 'mother' mimes on stage is amusing.

As is this amiable wheeze in general. Adapted from Mary Rodgers' juvenile classic of comedic life lessons, it's a sensible update of the 1976 Jodie Foster version, in which a girl not knowing how to operate a washing machine was as whacky as it got.

Now Mom, in her daughter's guise, tackles school bullying and young lurve – taking an excruciating turn when the boy is drawn to the older woman – while the teen-as-mother has fun with Mom's psychiatric patients, fending off her amorous fiancé and endangering the wedding. ★★★ **ASm**

FREDDY GOT FINGERED (2001)

Starring: *Tom Green (Gord Brody), Rip Torn (Jim Brody), Marisa Coughlan (Betty), Eddie Kaye Thomas (Freddy Brody), Harland Williams (Darren), Anthony Michael Hall (Dr. Dave Davidson), Julie Hagerty (Julie Brody), Jackson Davies (Mr. Malloy), Drew Barrymore (Mr. Davidson's Receptionist)*
Director: *Tom Green*
Screenwriters: *Tom Green, Derek Harvie*
18/87 mins./Comedy/USA
Awards: *Razzie Awards – Worst Actor (Tom Green was the first actor to turn up to accept his Razzie Award), Worst Director, Worst Picture, Worst Screen Couple (Tom Green … and any animal he abuses), Worst Screenplay*

When an unemployed cartoonist moves back in with his reluctant folks, they soon threaten to turf him out. But then he starts spreading rumours that they abused his younger brother …

Whoever thought it wise to give MTV star Tom Green his own movie should be tied down and forced to repeatedly watch the horrific result.

The plot, which has Green as a frustrated animator living with his father is irrelevant – this is just an excuse for Green to indulge his love of tasteless 'comedy' which includes jokes about child molestation and masturbating elephants. Drew Barrymore is only in it because she was dating Green at the time, and the pair couldn't face being separated (see also *Charlie's Angels* – or rather don't).

And as for this – AVOID! ★ **OR**

FREDDY VS JASON (2003)

Starring: *Robert Englund (Freddy Krueger), Ken Kirzinger (Jason Voorhees), Monica Keena (Lori Campbell), Jason Ritter (Will Rollins), Kelly Rowland (Kia Waterson)*
Director: *Ronny Yu*
Screenwriters: *Damian Shannon, Mark Swift, based on characters created by Wes Craven, Victor Miller*
18/97 mins./Horror/USA/Italy

Freddy summons Jason to Elm Street so they can team up and terrorise the local teenagers, but soon the duo are locked in their own battle.

If ever a film did what it said on the tin, this is it. Both the *Elm Street* and *Friday The 13th* franchises were last seen in interesting, offbeat, postmodern incarnations, but *FVJ* ignores any attempts at cleverness and picks up storylines dropped in *Freddy's Dead* and *Jason Goes To Hell*.

As explained in too many clunking exposition scenes, Freddy, powerless because teens have forgotten him, summons the unkillable Jason to Elm Street to make the kids afraid again. The pizza-faced knife-finger guy then gets jealous as the hockey-masked machete man eclipses his rep, and the title is dramatised as Freddy terrorises Jason in dreams/memories that go back to the long-forgotten plot of the first *Friday* then are dragged into the real world of Camp Crystal Lake for a very bloody finish. ★★★ **KN**

FREDDY'S DEAD: THE FINAL NIGHTMARE (1991)

Starring: *Robert Englund (Freddy Krueger), Lisa Zane (Maggie Burroughs), Shon Greenblatt (John Doe), Lezlie Deane (Tracy), Ricky Dean Logan (Carlos), Breckin Meyer (Spencer), Yaphet Kotto (Doc), Roseanne (Childless Woman)*
Director: *Rachel Talalay*
Screenwriter: *Michael De Luca based on a story by Rachel Talalay and characters created by Wes Craven*
18/89 mins/Horror/USA

In part six of the *Nightmare on Elm Street* series, dream monster Freddy Krueger has finally killed all the children of his hometown, and seeks to escape its confines to hunt fresh prey. To this end, he recruits the aid of his (previously unmentioned) daughter. However, she discovers the demonic origin of her father's powers and meets Dad head-on in a final showdown (originally presented in 3-D).

Given that ole' pizza face had slashed well beyond his kill-by date, this supposing concluding deathfest, which promised to be the last instalment in the *Nightmare On Elm Street* series, was timely and long overdue. However, it was hard not to feel that even the supposedly definitive death Freddy gets at the end of this movie was always going to be a temporary one. The major problem with *Freddy's Dead* is that it comes on as if it's going to be something very different, then turns out to be exactly the same. There's an entirely new title format (it's not called *A Nightmare on Elm Street, Part 6: The Dream Something*), a caption setting the action in 2001 and a declared intent to get Freddy into new locales across the USA. This apart, however, a group of cardboard cut-out (and cut-up) characters are promptly introduced, a few pathetic mysteries set in motion and it's up and away on the usual stuff. With such a ramshackle formula, it's hard not to waste time on the gimmicks; unbilled cameos from Alice Cooper, Johnny Depp and Roseanne Barr, more grindingly boring heavy metal music, a borderline tasteless dwelling on child abuse and evil father figures, and the final reel in 3-D 'Freddy vision', presumably to stop you from leaving early. Finally, the one interesting idea – what would a town be like if all the teenagers in it had been slaughtered in five movies? – is thrown away with a few cheap jokes. ★★ **KN**

FREE WILLY (1993)

Starring: *Jason James Richter (Jesse), Lori Petty (Rae Lindley), Jayne Atkinson (Annie Greenwood), August Schellenberg (Randolph Johnson), Michael Madsen (Glen Greenwood), Michael Ironside (Dial)*
Director: *Simon Wincer*
Screenwriters: *Keith A. Walker, Corey Blechman, Tom Bendek, from a story by Keith A. Walker*
U/112 mins./Family/Adventure/Drama/USA

Jesse is a young street kid who vandalises a local marine park. As a punishment, he is forced to go back to the park to clean up his graffiti and there he befriends the park Orca, Willy.

Dissect any kids-oriented Hollywood offering these days and the same clichés come away in your hands: dysfunctional child, no 'mom' or 'pop', finds a soul-mate in something no one else understands (in this case, a whale, could be E.T.), gets his act together, rejects tearaway chums, rejects then accepts father-figure, fights and triumphs over the money-grubbing baddies, makes a big sacrifice and ends up a distinctly better human being. The only thing that separates these movies is how the filmmakers tell the story, and fortunately *Free Willy* is told with an unusually truthful eye and just the right amount of blub-inducing poignancy.

Resident of an unnamed town in the Pacific North-West, Jesse (the excellent Richter – where do they find these pint-sized talents?) is the kid with no mom or pop who ends up making amends to the community by cleaning off the graffiti he sprayed all over a marine park that's home to a three-ton killer whale called Willy. Stuck with hopelessly miscast Michael Madsen and Helen Mirren-lookalike Jayne Atkinson for foster parents, Jesse begins to connect with Willy, joyfully realising that the grumpy Orca (they only ever call it an 'Orca' in the film, is that a P.C. thing?) will do tricks only for him, and not so joyfully realising that – just like himself! – all Willy needs to have a crack at happiness is to be reunited with his family, currently frolicking out in the bay.

Some of the performances are disturbingly ropey (especially from Madsen, so good as a foul-mouthed *Reservoir Dog*, so useless at saying 'Heck!'), there aren't enough proper laughs, and the whole thing follows an incredibly well-worn track, but the lad is immensely likeable, the ending's both awe-inspiring and genuinely moving, and the killer whale is great value throughout. ★★★ **PT**

FREEWAY (1996)

Starring: *Kiefer Sutherland (Bob Wolverton), Reese Witherspoon (Vanessa Lutz), Wolfgang Bodison (Detective Mike Breer), Dan Hedaya (Detective Garnet Wallace), Amanda Plummer (Ramona Lutz), Brooke Shields (Mimi Wolverton), Brittany Murphy (Rhonda)*
Director: *Matthew Bright*
Screenwriters: *Matthew Bright, Oliver Stone*
18/110 mins./Comedy/Crime/Drama/Thriller/USA

Teenager Vanessa Lutz, on her own after her mother is arrested, sets out to find her grandmother's house, and hitches a lift from apparently decent driver Bob Wolverton, who turns out to be a serial killer. She escapes, but Vanessa is arrested for assaulting Bob.

The road-crime movie is such a formula in Hollywood that almost every debuting director turns one out, but writer-director Matthew Bright rings the changes by modelling this white trash nightmare on Red Riding Hood. Reese Witherspoon, turning her career around after 'good girl' roles in the likes of *The Man in the Moon*, is hilarious as the fifteen-year-old hitchhiker ('them are some mighty big fuckin' teeth ya got there, Bob') who runs across plausible psychopath Kiefer Sutherland, who claims to be a therapist and gets her to open up to him about the abuse she has suffered from her stepfather before she realises he's getting off on her story ('take it from me, a professional, Vanessa – you are a fucking moron').

The latter stages become especially twisted, with Witherspoon having a grim time in a hellhole juvenile prison (where she is befriended by lesbian Brittany Murphy) and Sutherland showing off hideous disfigurement ('look who got hit with the ugly stick') as he sets out to get twisted revenge. There are great supporting sleaze performances from Dan Hedaya, Brooke Shields, Amanda Plummer (as Riding Hood's crack ho momma) and Bokeem Woodbine.

Bright, who is evidently a big fan of John Waters 'early, funny movies', followed up with *Confessions of a Trick Baby*, sometimes known as *Freeway 2*, which is an equally perverse take on Hansel and Gretel featuring Natasha Lyonne and Maria Celedonio as wild grrls on the run, with Vincent Gallo as a transvestite witch who runs a kiddie porn empire. ★★★★ **KN**

THE FRENCH CONNECTION (1971)

Starring: *Gene Hackman (Jimmy 'Popeye' Doyle), Fernando Rey (Alain Charnier), Roy Scheider (Buddy Russo), Tony Lo Bianco (Sal Boca), Marcel Bozzufi (Pierre Nicoli)*
Director: *William Friedkin*
Screenwriter: *Ernest Tidyman, based on the book by Robin Moore*
18/104 mins./Crime/USA

Awards: *Academy Awards – Best Actor, Best Director, Best Film Editing, Best Picture, Best Screenplay based on material from another medium, BAFTA – Best Actor, Best Editing, Golden Globes – Best Director, Best Drama, Best Drama Actor*

A pair of NYC cops in the Narcotics Bureau stumble onto a drug smuggling job with a French connection.

Almost 30 years before the Florida recount decided the US presidential race, another close-run contest between two equally popular men ended in a similar re-examination of ballot papers. The Best Actor trophy at the 1972 New York Film Critics awards was a tie between Gene Hackman for *The French Connection* and Peter Finch for *Sunday Bloody Sunday*. They conducted a recount, and Hackman clinched it. The best man won.

The role of hardball New York cop Jimmy 'Popeye' Doyle made Gene Hackman. With typical good grace, he plays down his part in the film's success: 'I really don't think I had anything to do with the quality of the film. That was a director's film. Anybody would have been good in my role.'

He's wrong, of course, though *The French Connection* might be described as a director's film. When producer Philip D'Antoni put forward 31 year-old William Friedkin for the job, 20th Century Fox swallowed hard. Friedkin had only *The Night They Raided Minsky's* and *The Boys In The Band* to recommend him, but D'Antoni (who'd previously produced *Bullitt* with the equally untried Peter Yates) fancied him for being an unconventional choice. This was not intended as a standard cops-and-robbers flick. The book, by *Green Berets* author Robin Moore, was written like a fictional potboiler but based on fact: the story of a 1962 heroin bust in New York, in which detective Eddie 'Popeye' Egan (his name was tweaked for the film) and his partner Salvatore Grosso (Buddy Russo on screen) led the swoop on $32 millions' worth of incoming brown stuff from Marseilles. For a true story – the book even has maps! – it read like a cracking movie. But all credit to creator of *Shaft*, Ernest Tidyman for an imaginative job on the screenplay (for which he won an Oscar), building in the memorable establishing sequence in which Popeye and Russo (Scheider) go undercover in a biting New York winter as Father Christmas and pretzel vendor. They chase and interrogate a vendor of less legal wares, and Popeye taunts him with his now-legendary riddle, 'Do you pick your feet in Poughkeepsie?' (Hackman was so offended at having to retake this violent assault 27 times, he threatened to walk away from the picture, but was dissuaded by the threat of legal action.)

The French Connection is a deftly-mixed cocktail of realism and dramatic licence, encapsulated in the blending of Moore's reportage and Tidyman's streetwise invention (as in the bit where a hip chemist tests the French importers' heroin for purity and describes it as 'junk of the month club'). Friedkin's hand-held documentary style was the perfect vehicle for the film's pumped-up vérité: it's since become Hollywood shorthand for 'gritty realism' to shoot long and let the camera wobble, but in 1971 this was really radical stuff for a mainstream studio film.

However, for all the sleazy authenticity (much of the action was shot in real-life junkie hotspots in Manhattan and Brooklyn, and Hackman went on patrol with Eddie Egan to research the unconventional ways of the Narcotics Bureau), the high point of *The French Connection* remains its car chase, a sequence that was added to Tidyman's screenplay when no studio would touch the script. Its inclusion was a bare-faced commercial decision, no doubt inspired by *Bullitt*'s own four-wheeled money shot. It's testament to Friedkin's commitment (and that of stunt driver Bill Hickman) that the car chase trashed all before it and has yet to be matched for visceral, brake-squealing energy.

The sequence is actually a train chase, as Doyle's Pontiac sedan pursues an elevated subway carriage containing French smuggler Nicoli (Marcel Bozzufi, star of the film's poster image). Wreaking controlled mayhem for weeks of shooting under the Stillwell Avenue Line was not enough realism for Friedkin; he wanted an uninterrupted shot of the entire chase with one camera on the bumper and one inside the car to capture Popeye's point of view. Hickman took the wheel and drove 26 blocks with a flashing light to alert the very real pedestrians and drivers. See that woman with a pram? Real woman. Real pram. Real baby.

Maverick cops are ten a penny in the cinema, as are their trusty sidekicks but there is something about the way Hackman plays Popeye that elevates him above the herd. When he first read the script he saw his chance to emulate Cagney, but he's far more than a screen-filling tough guy – he exhibits the same insouciant, grinning authority that Hackman managed to subtly invest in characters as diverse as *The Poseidon Adventure*'s Rev Scott and *Crimson Tide*'s Captain Ramsey, over 20 years apart. Popeye Doyle is Gene Hackman finding his own brand.

Maybe *The French Connection* is an actor's film after all. ★★★★★ **AC**

The French Connection

James Caan and Peter Boyle both turned down the chance to play Doyle. The real Egan and Grosso appear in the film as the detective's supervisors. Egan was also advisor on the film. Roy Scheider's character is not in the sequel *French Connection 2*.

THE FRENCH LIEUTENANT'S WOMAN (1981)

Starring: *Meryl Streep (Sarah/Anna), Jeremy Irons (Charles Henry Smithson/Mike), Hilton McRae (Sam), Emily Morgan (Mary), Charlotte Mitchell (Mrs. Tranter), Colin Jeavons (Vicar)*
Director: *Karel Reisz*
Screenwriter: *Harold Pinter, from the novel by John Fowles*
15/127 mins./Romance/UK

Awards: *BAFTA – Anthony Asquith Award for Film Music, Best Actress, Best Sound, Golden Globes – Best Drama Actress*

Anna and Mike are actors playing the roles of two 19th Century lovers, who gradually develop a similar relationship to the characters they portray.

This is a film that arrived with acclaim and has drifted into obscurity over the years. A worthy attempt to adapt John Fowles' literary experiment to the big screen, ultimately it suffers from the coldness of the narrative – with so much emotion bubbling beneath the surface, some emotional breakthrough is needed to satisfy the viewer.

Anna and Mike are bored actors, who enter into an affair as a distraction while making a film about Sarah, a Victorian English woman abandoned by her French Lieutenant lover who entrances Charles, a wealthy, principled young man. Their love stories run parallel paths throughout the film and while Jeremy Irons, and particularly Meryl Streep at her most luminous, seem perfectly cast in their dual roles – their acting technically faultless – their characters are ciphers, symbols of their respective eras, rather than flesh and blood creations.

There is one heart-stopping moment – when Sarah is standing on the quay staring out to sea and turns around to let her eyes fall on Charles (and the camera) – but the promise of what could have grown from there is never fulfilled. ★★★ **EC**

FRENZY (1972)

Starring: *Jon Finch (Richard Blaney), Barry Foster (Robert Rusk), Barbara Leigh-Hunt (Brenda Blaney), Anna Massey (Babs Milligan), Alec McCowen (Chief Inspector Oxford)*
Director: *Alfred Hitchcock*
Screenwriter: *Anthony Shaffer from the novel* Goodbye Piccadily, Hello Leicester Square *by Arthur LaBern*
18/116 mins./Thriller/UK

Murderous greengrocer Bob Rusk implicates ex-RAF hero Richard Blaney as Chief Inspector Oxford scours Covent Garden for the 'necktie killer'.

Since his departure for Hollywood in 1939, Alfred Hitchcock had only made two films in Britain and neither *Under Capricorn* nor *Stage Fright* had been particularly impressive. So, the 73 year-old Londoner clearly set out to atone with what would prove to be his penultimate picture. Opening, like *Young And Strange* exactly 40 years earlier, with a body floating down the Thames, *Frenzy* was not just a dark homage to the bustling city of Hitchcock's youth, but it was also a scrapbook of the themes and stylistic traits that had become his trademarks.

The title came from a discarded screenplay of the mid-1960s (aka *Kaleidoscope*) that Hitchcock had been developing with Howard Fast, before Universal decreed that no one would want to see a film about a gay psychopath. But the story of a necktie strangler who stalks the backstreets of Covent Garden was adapted from Arthur LaBern's novel, *Goodbye Piccadilly, Farewell Leicester Square*.

The emphasis on the mind, motives and methodology of a killer links *Frenzy* with *Shadow of a Doubt*, *Strangers on a Train* and *Psycho*. But the empathy with the innocent accused also recalled *The 39 Steps*, *I Confess*, *The Wrong Man* and *North By Northwest*. However, Hitchcock managed subtle personality twists in both Bob Rusk and Richard Blaney to ensure that neither villain nor hero was as sympathetic as Bruno Antony and Norman Bates or Richard Hannay and Roger Thornhill.

Typically, however, Hitchcock couldn't resist some grim comedy, hence the crack of Anna Massey's rigor-mortised fingers being echoed by Vivien Merchant (the wife of detective Alex McCowen) carelessly breaking crispy breadsticks while discussing the case over dinner. Hitchcock was accused of misogyny for his comparison of Foster's first on-screen victim, Barbara Leigh-Hunt, with a quick lunchtime snack and his second, Massey, with a sack of potatoes. But such callousness chillingly reflects the dog-eat-dog society in which the film is set, as well as its all-pervading atmosphere of decline, decay and disappointment. ★★★ **DP**

FRIDAY NIGHT LIGHTS (2004)

Starring: *Billy Bob Thornton (Coach Gary Gaines), Lucas Black (Mike Winchell), Garrett Hedlund (Don Billingsley), Derek Luke (Boobie Miles), Jay Hernandez (Brian Chavez)*
Director: *Peter Berg*
Screenwriter: *David Aaron Cohen, Peter Berg, based on the book by H.G. Bissinger*
12A/118 mins./Drama/Sports/USA

Based on a real-life story and book, *Friday Night Lights* follows the dramatic 1988 season of high school American football team the Permian Panthers, led by noble-minded head coach Gary Gaines. This is a season that will come to enfold all the hopes, brutal realities and personal tragedies of a hard-scrabble town called Odessa, lost among the desiccated plains of Texas.

Stop right there. If you've read the premise for this vivid, compelling movie and have immediately switched off at the thought of another story about that incomprehensible, herky-jerky US sport, you should know different. Yes, this is a film about American football, but it is so much more. It is a stark survey of the hold sport has on life, with its tribal allure and power to devastate both supporter and player. Directed by sometime actor Peter Berg through the framework of an earthy coming-of-age saga, the grunt 'n' buckle trade-offs of 'football' have never felt so profound.

There has been some criticism of the deviation from factual detail to fit a more emotionally telling template, but it is a formula as passionately reproduced as any *Rocky*, *Seabiscuit* or *Bull Durham*. The wounded star player forced to confront the end of his playing career before it has even got going is as ragged a moment of honest pain as anything Mike Leigh could cook up on a London council estate. Country and Western crooner Tim McGraw shrinks his cowboy brio into a drunken brute of a former football hero facing up to the bitter realisation he has come to mean nothing more than history. Meanwhile his son, not half the player, has to bear the brunt of his hopelessness. 'After football, it's just babies and memories,' he glumly reports, father-to-son. A hell of a thing to lay on a 17 year-old.

Which is the whole point Berg and his cousin, original author H.G. 'Buzz' Bissinger, are making – in what sane world does a tender bunch of kids in the prime of their life have to carry an entire town's neuroses?

As the team coach, Thornton is the honest-to-God kinda guy who, ironically, sees through the devotional haze; winning isn't everything, it only feels like it. This should all ring very familiar. The all-consuming obsession of Odessa, down to radio phone-ins and car park confrontations, carries the same religious patter as rabid soccer support does here. They are the heartbeat of whole communities.

Berg is smart enough to find something suspicious in this and also the absurdity that Bissinger observed: the coin-toss to decide a tournament's outcome, the real estate signs staked out on the coach's lawn after defeat, the inverse racism applied to influence referees ('zebras'). Such detail allows the film to breathe, keeping it aloft from the go-go sport-as-American-metaphor clichés too often hung on the game. The swaying emotion of the seesaw season carries a universal clarity. You want these boys to triumph. In fact, you will long for it. The action has the punching, rhythmic edits of genuine sports coverage, and in among the players' lives the handheld camerawork has the unblinking force of a documentary. Yet, Berg's delivery still possesses an essential movieness, and his film has a mythical reach, skies filled with the contrails of unattainable dreams. These are less the tones of the melodramatic sports milieu than the romantic Western, the young cowpoke's rite-of-passage transmuted from the chaparral to the stadium. And when you read the written coda of what happened to the real kids, it's a note of pure heartbreak. So stay for the closing credits, if for nothing else but to stifle your sobs. ★★★★★ **IN**

FRIDAY THE 13TH (1980)

Starring *Betsy Palmer (Mrs. Pamela Voorhees), Adrienne King (Alice Hardy), Harry Crosby (Bill), Laurie Bartram (Brenda), Jeannine Taylor (Marcie Cunningham), Kevin Bacon (Jack Burrell)*
Director: *Sean S. Cunningham*
Screenwriters: *Victor Miller, Ron Kurtz*
18/95 mins./Horror/USA

Unbeknownst to a new set of teen vacationers at Camp Crystal Lake, this was the site of two horrible murders. And now the killings are going to start again.

The film that launched a long and rusty franchise of teenage slaughter (12 episodes if you count the gimmick addition of *Freddy Vs Jason*), this cheapo horror stands as one of the principal markers for the whole slasher phenomenon. In reality it is a pallid *Halloween* rip-off, with a mediocre shock count and a botched ending. People tend to forget that this original lacks the remorseless presence of Jason himself, blanked off with a hockey mask, who we are told drowned as a small retarded boy in 1957 while his camp councillors are otherwise occupied. As the bodies pile up amongst this testy crowd of horny teens, there remains a vacant hole where someone scary should be. In a strange way, this film stands unique amongst all slasher films as one where the killer is nearly intangible.

Sean Cunningham, who never gained the reputation of a Wes Craven or John Carpenter, does muster a chilling nastiness about the ensuing cull. Various nubile girls bounce about minus their bras, encouraging the boys to get randy, and, as we've all learned from *Scream*, any consummation spells certain death. The most famous slaying has a young Kevin Bacon punctured with an arrowhead up through the mattress from beneath a bed, although the most gruesome death has an axe bite realistically through a girl's face. Comparatively *Friday The 13th* is fairly unbloody, and its fairly murky texture doesn't fit the idyllic lakeside setting, while only Mark Nelson's joker in the pack stands out as a memorable character.

And when it is exposed, the killer's true identity actually forces the film into a rather pragmatic frame. Only a lazy, unfathomable twist ending would allow the endless hulk of splattered teenagers to lurch on for 25 years. ★★ **IN**

FRIED GREEN TOMATOES AT THE WHISTLE STOP CAFE (1991)

Starring: *Kathy Bates (Evelyn Couch), Mary Stuart Masterson (Idgie Threadgoode), Mary-Louise Parker (Ruth Jamison), Jessica Tandy (Ninny Threadgoode), Cicely Tyson (Sipsey), Chris O'Donnell (Buddy Threadgoode)*
Director: *Jon Avnet*
Screenwriters: *Fannie Flagg, Carol Sobieski based on the novel by Flagge*
12/130 mins./Drama/USA

Troubled housewife Evelyn Couch, whose marriage is in tatters, forms an unlikely friendship with an old lady named Ninny Threadgoode. Ninny proceeds to tell her the story of Idgie from 1920s Alabama, a tale that inspires Evelyn to take hold of her life.

A so-called chick flick, although that is such a demeaning tag, with literary heritage (author Fannie Flagg co-wrote the screenplay), with the breathing space of interesting characters and a clever story-in-a story structure, makes for one of the better entries in the ill-served sub-genre. One of its main qualities is that it's not strictly about romance, being far more concerned with female empowerment. No one's burning their bras and preaching from the gospel according of Andrea Dworkin, but there amongst the gentle flow of its Sapphic currents, the film is a tribute to enduring sisterhood.

In the present day this is seen in the intuitive bond between broken housewife Kathy Bates (too brusque to truly convince as a downtrodden puddle of womanhood) getting some down-home nurturing from Jessica Tandy's antique Southern Belle. Her storytelling accesses the friendship between tomboy Mary Stuart Masterson and fine femininity of Mary-Louise Parker. Surprisingly, it is the younger actresses who make the biggest impression. Masterson, an underrated actress, works the free-spirit cliché with a sense of furious entitlement: drinking, gambling, pointlessly pursuing male weakness as a salvation from the chains of destiny. Never has housewifery been depicted with such brutality, which is partly Flagg's theme – break those prescribed social bonds.

And only amongst the staunch strictures of the patriarchal Deep South, is the battle for non-conformity most fraught. Which also means we've got to fitfully journey over the bumpy camber of Klansmen, downtrodden blacks, lynch mobs and brutal husbands. As the foreground is keenly intelligent, the background is a bland whistle stop tour of gruelling Southern life. ★★★ **IN**

FRIGHT NIGHT (1985)

Starring: *Chris Sarandon (Jerry Dandridge), William Ragsdale (Charley Brewster), Amanda Bearse (Amy Peterson), Roddy McDowell (Peter Vincent), Stephen Geoffreys (Evil Ed Thompson)*
Director: *Tom Holland*
Screenwriter: *Tom Holland*
18/106 mins./Horror/USA

Horror-loving teenager Charley Brewster is sure that a vampire has moved in next door, so he turns to washed-up actor Peter Vincent, now hosting a cheap TV show called *Fright Night* to help him. A firm unbeliever, Vincent only agrees for money.

Taking the John Hughes formula that broke out in the eighties like severe acne, tales of plaintive teens bucking the system while falling in love

Shocking Movie Twists (beware spoilers!) TOP10

1. It's his sledge! (Citizen Kane)
2. Dil's a boy! (The Crying Game)
3. Verbal's Keyser Soze! (The Usual Suspects)
4. They're the same guy! (Fight Club)
5. Raymond's mother had him brainwashed! (The Manchurian Candidate)
6. It wasn't Jimmy Stewart, but John Wayne! (The Man Who Shot Liberty Valance)
7. The Matrix isn't real! (The Matrix)
8. The planet is Earth! (Planet Of The Apes)
9. Janet Leigh dies! (Psycho)
10. Bruce Willis is a ghost! (The Sixth Sense)

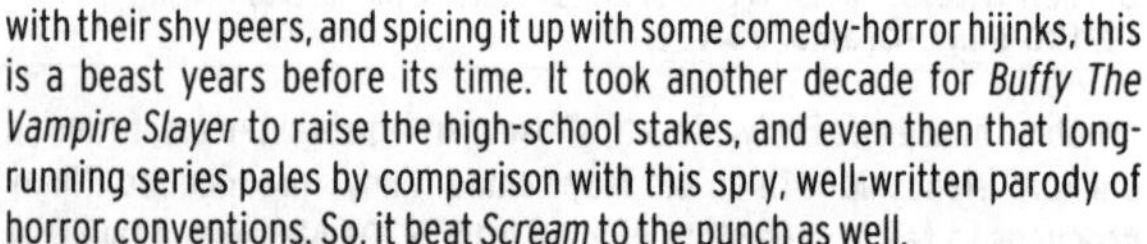

with their shy peers, and spicing it up with some comedy-horror hijinks, this is a beast years before its time. It took another decade for *Buffy The Vampire Slayer* to raise the high-school stakes, and even then that long-running series pales by comparison with this spry, well-written parody of horror conventions. So, it beat *Scream* to the punch as well.

Tom Holland got off to a flyer with his casting. William Ragsdale, who was to go on to do very little, is a likeable hero as Charley, part geek part dish, who really digs his horror movies. When he spots the vampire-like habits (for starters he drinks really Bloody Marys) of the shadowy figure who has moved into the neighbourhood, played by Chris Sarandon, part Donald Trump part Bela Lugosi, there is only one place he can turn, especially when it seems this intruder in his white-picket upbringing has designs on his girlfriend (the cute Amy Peterson). And that is to TV horror time host Peter Vincent granted the fluttering consonants and goggly eyes of a clearly coasting Roddy McDowell.

It's dotty, a little ragged (particularly in Stephen Geoffery's overbearing buddy who get a vampiric makeover) and fairly tame in the shock department, but it has a wining guile. Holland injects a light tribute to the forgotten joys of traditional horror movies, the enthralling fantasy of vampires, werewolves and Frankenstein's monster. As Vincent laments, 'Nobody wants to see vampire killers anymore, or vampires either. Apparently all they want are demented madmen running around in ski masks hacking up young virgins.' Amongst the sludge of slasher flicks and soap operas that had clogged up either genre, *Fright Night* showed real spirit. ★★★★ **IN**

THE FRIGHTENERS (1996)

Starring: *Michael J. Fox (Frank Bannister), Trini Alvarado (Dr. Lucy Lynskey), Peter Dobson (Ray Lynskey), John Astin (The Judge), Jeffrey Combs (Milton Dammers), Dee Wallace-Stone (Patricia Ann Bradley)*
Director: *Peter Jackson*
Screenwriters: *Fran Walsh, Peter Jackson*
15/110 mins./122 mins. (director's cut)/Comedy/Fantasy/Horror/ New Zealand/USA

A psychic private detective who consorts with deceased souls becomes engaged in a mystery as members of the town community begin dying mysteriously.

Having garnered such critical acclaim and respectability with *Heavenly Creatures*, New Zealand director Peter Jackson made a welcome return to the world of hectic horror hokum and delivered a deeply sick, weird and enjoyable romp.

Using his familiarity with a threesome of third-rate ghouls to haunt houses, Frank Bannister is running a spook extermination scam clearing up the mess after the ghouls have scared everyone witless. However, a series of unexplained deaths – the victims popping their clogs after massive heart attacks – draws the law's attention to Bannister, and makes him wonder if he has anything to do with the spiralling mortality rate. In fact, the culprit is a 'soultaker', an expensive-looking piece of CGI, who reaches into people's chests to give their ticker a quick squeeze.

Thrown into the brew is a serial killer, a nutty FBI agent, and a love interest in the form of recently widowed Lucy. Since Jackson was responsible for *Bad Taste* and the majestically sick *Meet The Feebles*, this may come as a shock to those who've only witnessed *Heavenly Creatures*.

But here he displays his talent for juxtaposing truly disturbing imagery (particularly in a graphical reconstructed newsreel sequence of a killing spree in a hospital) with light-hearted comedy in the form of the spook threesome. ★★★★ **AS**

FROM DUSK TILL DAWN (1996)

Starring: *Harvey Keitel (Jacob Fuller), George Clooney (Seth Gecko), Quentin Tarantino (Richard Gecko), Juliette Lewis (Kate Fuller), Ernest Lui (Scott Fuller), Cheech Marin (Border Guard/Chet Pussy/Carlos), Fred Williamson (Frost), Salma Hayek (Santanico Pandemonium)*
Director: *Robert Rodriguez*
Screenwriter: *Quentin Tarantino, from a story by Robert Kurtzman*
18/108 mins./Horror/Crime/Comedy/USA

Two Desperado-type brothers and career criminals take a preacher and his two teenage stepchildren hostage and flee to Mexico where they end up at a local strip bar that is populated by vampires.

The first script that Quentin Tarantino was paid to write, back in 1990 – for the tidy sum of $1,500 – has been dusted down and spruced up with *Desperado* director Robert Rodriguez at the helm, a biggish budget and a high profile cast led by the then superstar-in-waiting, *ER*'s George Clooney. Swelled from its obvious B-movie origins to must-see status thanks to Tarantino's near Messiah-like standing (even after *Four Rooms*) and Rodriguez's impeccable action movie credentials, and featuring the Quentmeister in his first proper acting gig, this funky fusion that is two-thirds guns'n'muthafuckas and one-third vampires'n'gore is a real (blood)blast, a rollicking, slam-bang piece of entertainment that goes for the jugular and the funny bone.

Seth and Richie Gecko are criminal brothers on the lam, heading for Mexico after a prison breakout with a bag full of moolah and the entire Texas law enforcement community on their tail, having left numerous bullet-riddled corpses in their bloody wake. Seth, the older and slightly saner of the two, with a tattoo snaking round his neck and down onto his arm, coerces his sexually deviant sibling into kidnapping faithless minister Jacob, his jailbait daughter Kate and adopted son, and using their camper van to get across the Tex-Mex border, pitching up at the aptly named Titty Twister, an open all-night bar with a fine line in hostess action to wait until dawn when Carlos, their south of the border contact, will arrive.

To their (and Carlos') surprise, the inhabitants of the bar mostly reveal themselves to be of the bloodsucking, undead, long in the tooth variety and are pretty soon chowing down on those mere mortals unlucky enough to be drinking in the bar. Cue mucho bloodletting as Rodriguez mixes John Woo with George Romero, and has a horrific hoot, hacking off limbs, heads and various other body parts with bloody abandon, as the remaining humans and vampires square up to each other in a neat variation on the Mexican standoff, with a rapidly diminishing supply of 'weapons' and dawn still some way off.

As you'd probably expect, these are no ordinary caped, pale-faced bloodsuckers, rather deformed, twisted, hideous, full-bodied monsters courtesy of the effects wizards at KNB (the 'K' of which, Robert Kurtzman, provided the story and originally paid Tarantino to write the script in return for KNB supplying the ear-slicing effect in *Dogs*). Clooney, in his first major role since hitting the big time with *ER*, proves why he went on to be huge, while, alongside, Tarantino more than holds his own as the lecherous Richie lusting after Lewis. There are cameos from Cheech Marin (thrice), makeup man Tom Savini, and Rodriguez fave Salma Hayek as a stripper with a novel way of pouring whiskey into Tarantino's gaping mouth. While certainly not for those people of the squeamish variety, if you expect to be entertained you'll have almost as good a time watching this as they obviously had making it. A real monster mash. ★★★★ **MS**

FROM HELL (2001)

Starring: *Johnny Depp (Inspector Fred Abberline), Heather Graham (Mary Kelly), Ian Holm (Sir William Gull), Robbie Coltrane (Peter Godley), Leslie Sharp (Kate Eddowes), Susan Lynch (Liz Stride)*
Directors: *Albert Hughes, Allen Hughes*
Screenwriters: *Terry Hayes, Rafael Yglesias, based on the graphic novel by Alan Moore and Eddie Campbell*
18/115 mins./Crime/Horror/History/USA

Whitechapel, 1888. Inspector Abberline investigates the Jack the Ripper case, detecting a vast conspiracy behind the murders. As the bodies pile up, he grows closer to Mary Kelly, a prostitute who seems fated to be the Ripper's final victim.

Adapting the panoramic Alan Moore-Eddy Campbell comic, the Hughes Brothers present a far-fetched 'solution' to the Jack the Ripper case that allows a dissection of the corruption behind the phrase, 'Victorian values'.

The film's cavernous Whitechapel is a teeming, threatening environment even before the Ripper begins systematic elimination of the canonical victims, with cringing whores – played at full throttle by the likes of Katrin Cartlidge and Susan Lynch – in as much danger from bullyboy gangstas as an imported toff psychopath.

Because the story is oft-told (nearly qualifying the film as a remake of 1978's *Murder By Decree*), *From Hell* runs the risk of following an elaborate set-up with a blown punchline, and the script can't quite sell its Jack as at once a purposeful assassin and a mad killer.

However, it's always fun to see Masonic conspiracies exposed, and a range of squirmingly superior British acting talent (Ian Holm, Ian Richardson, Paul Rhys) perfectly embodies double-dyed arrogance and sadistic delight in extreme surgery. Ruled over by a 'cold-eyed' queen, this world sees the poor only as specimens, its attitudes symptomised not only by eviscerated drabs but an exhibited Elephant Man and lobotomies performed as theatre. The murders take place behind the Ripper's Dracula cloak, with telling, hallucinatory, gruesome details (a torn-out heart boiled in a kettle).

Cinematographer Peter Deming (the master of unease who shot *Mulholland Dr.*) has his camera prowl gloomy alleys as sinister carriages pass and red blood seems splashed over painted London skies. Depp and Graham have peculiar characterisations (visionary junkie cop, feminist trollop), but opening and closing with its copper in an opium den allows for a reading of the film as a delirious nightmare distantly based on historical fact. ★★★★ **AM**

FROM HERE TO ETERNITY (1953)

Starring: *Burt Lancaster (Sgt. Milton Warden), Deborah Kerr (Karen Holmes), Montgomery Clift (Robert E. Lee Prewitt), Frank Sinatra (Angelo Maggio), Donna Reed (Alma Lorene), Ernest Borgnine (Sgt 'Fatso' Judson)*
Director: *Fred Zinnemann*
Screenwriter: *Daniel Taradash based on the novel by James Jones*
PG/118 mins./Drama/USA
Awards: *Academy Awards – Best Picture, Best Supporting Actor (Frank Sinatra), Best Supporting Actress (Donna Reed), Best Director, Best Screenplay, Best Cinematography, Best Film Editing, Best Sound Recording (John P. Livadary). Cannes Film Festival – Special Award*

In 1941, at Camp Schofield on Hawaii, Private Robert E. Lee Prewitt clashes with his c.o., who wants him to resume his boxing career, while the c.o.'s neglected wife has an affair with a sergeant and misfit Maggio suffers in the stockade. Meanwhile, the Japanese are about to bomb Pearl Harbor.

This big bestseller-type movie (from James Jones' novel) about life and love on a US Army base scooped an armload of Oscars in 1953. Director Fred Zinneman stages a few scenes so well that they are still imitated or parodied and, if the 'adult' themes – blunted by a censorship requirement that the army not be offended by a depiction of military sloppiness, hypocrisy, homosexuality or brutality – are less daring than they once were, it has more than enough iconic moments to make it endlessly rewatchable.

Montgomery Clift is the sensitive soul who'd rather play the trumpet than box and goes AWOL only to become a martyr-hero during the attack on Pearl, Frank Sinatra is the cocky soldier who suffers appalling abuse from bullying military policeman Ernest Borgnine (*The Godfather* presents a scurrilous theory about how the crooner won this plum role) and Donna Reed is the most decorous, sweet-tempered hooker in the cinema.

The spectacular last-reel recreation of the bombing makes this, Michael Bay notwithstanding, the Pearl Harbor film to beat, but the unquestioned highlight is the famous on-the-beach adultery scene between virile sergeant Lancaster and an unusually unladylike Kerr, with the waves crashing around them to symbolise their unrestrained passions.

Hard to take all that seriously these days, but always entertaining as gutsy soap opera. It was remade as a TV miniseries in 1979, with William Devane, Natalie Wood, Don Johnson and Kim Basinger. ★★★★ **KN**

FROM RUSSIA WITH LOVE (1963)

Starring: *Sean Connery (James Bond), Daniela Bianchi (Tatiana Romanova), Pedro Armendariz (Kerim Bey), Lotte Lenya (Rosa Klebb), Robert Shaw (Red Grant), Bernard Lee ('M')*
Director: *Terence Young*
Screenwriters: *Richard Maibaum, Johanna Harwood based on the novel by Ian Fleming*
PG/110 mins./Spy/UK

To avenge the death of their agent Dr. No, international crime cartel SPECTRE have Soviet spy-mistress Rosa Klebb and psychopath Red Grant implement a plan to assassinate British agent James Bond.

The second James Bond movie, and still one of the best. It opens with a classic piece of misdirection as Connery's super-agent is found in the middle of a dangerous mission, and then swiftly killed by hard man Robert Shaw – but this turns out to be a test run with a Bond lookalike, and we're into a diabolically clever scheme to lure 007 to his doom and only incidentally serve the strategic interests of the Soviet Union.

It's a long chase scene, studded with memorable set-pieces: the hair-pulling gypsy cat-fight between Aliza Gur and Martine Beswick, Bond tumbling to the fact that the villain is only impersonating an English officer and gentleman because he orders the wrong wine with fish (and then throttles him with a trick briefcase), Hitchcockian cat-and-mouse with an attack helicopter, and an attack by the wonderful Lotte Lenya with a poisoned shoe. Daniela Bianchi isn't one of the more memorable Bond girls, which is a shame since her character is supposed to have been selected for the mission especially to appeal to our rogue agent, but Bernard Lee and Lois Maxwell continue to develop their regular roles as M and Miss Moneypenny and Desmond Llewellyn makes his series debut as Q.

Seen only in shadow, the cat-stroking SPECTRE chief Blofeld is played by Anthony Dawson and dubbed by Eric Pohlmann – though he would be dropped from *Goldfinger*, Blofeld's enmity with Bond would serve as a continuing story arc all the way from *Dr. No* to *Diamonds Are Forever*. Monty Norman's Bond theme recurs, but we also get the first Bond hit song – Matt Monro's balalaika-scored title number. **★★★★ KN**

THE FRONT PAGE (1974)

Starring: *Jack Lemmon (Hildy Johnson), Walter Matthau (Walter Burns), Susan Sarandon (Peggy Grant), Vincent Gardenia ('Honest Pete' Hartman, Sheriff of Clark County)*
Director: *Billy Wilder*
Screenwriters: *Billy Wilder, I.A.L. Diamond based on the play by Ben Hecht and Charles MacArthur*
PG/104 mins./Comedy/USA

Cynical editor Walter Burns uses the escape of dead man walking Earl Williams to persuade ace reporter Hildy Johnson against quitting the newspaper business to marry organist, Peggy Grant.

In many ways, Ben Hecht and Charles MacArthur resembled the screen personas of Walter Matthau and Jack Lemmon, who fittingly headlined Billy Wilder's take on their 1928 Broadway smash. Reporters on rival Chicago newspapers in the 1920s, Hecht was a hard-boiled cynic, while MacArthur aspired to refinement and their contrasting temperaments clearly informed this tale of an editor who will sink to any depths to keep his star writer and beat his rivals to a scoop.

Although he had previously analysed the dismal opportunism of the media in *Ace in the Hole* and recalled the romanticised lawlessness of the Jazz Age in *Some Like It Hot*, Wilder never felt wholly comfortable with adapting this landmark screwball, which was produced, in part, to cash in on the success of *The Sting*.

The play had twice been filmed before – by Lewis Milestone in 1931 (with the Oscar-nominated Adolphe Menjou and Pat O'Brien) and by Howard Hawks as *His Girl Friday*, which starred Cary Grant and Rosalind Russell and added a sexual frisson to the action by turning Hildy Johnson into a woman. But Wilder had never been impressed with either version and was keen to restore the virile newsroom language that had been toned down to appease the Hays and Breen Offices.

Revelling in the Machiavellian scheming and acerbic quips, Matthau turned in a scathingly comic performance. But Lemmon struggled to shake off past characters like J.J. Poindexter, Harry Hinkle and Felix Ungar and, thus, he feels less like a bitten hack than David Wayne and Charles Durning.

But, while their rat-a-tat byplay still seemed slick, Watergate and Vietnam had made America a harder-nosed placed than it had been even during Prohibition and the Depression and the cutting edge of Hecht and MacArthur's satire had largely been blunted. 'The times were better, or we were a little bit more naive,' Wilder later lamented. 'We laughed easier.' **★★★ DP**

THE FUGITIVE (1993)

Starring: *Harrison Ford (Dr. Richard Kimble), Tommy Lee Jones (Marshal Samuel Gerard), Sela Ward (Helen Kimble), Julianne Moore (Dr. Anne Eastman)*
Director: *Andrew Davis*
Screenwriters: *Jeb Stuart, David Twohy, from a story by Twohy*
12/127 mins./Action/Thriller/Drama/USA

Awards: *Academy Awards – Best Supporting Actor, BAFTA – Best Sound, Golden Globes – Best Supporting Actor*

Dr. Richard Kimble is framed for the murder of his wife and goes on the run.

It was almost 40 years ago that the last episode of the long-running TV series from which this is derived was made, but the premise remains unchanged: Dr. Richard Kimble is wrongly convicted for his wife's murder, his story of a one-armed killer unsubstantiated. En route to prison, a train wreck makes his escape possible, and he is hunted relentlessly by a lawman named Gerard.

The brutal murder of Helen Kimble is gruesomely realised here as the opening credits roll, the first in a series of flashbacks that haunt Ford's Kimble and spur him on with his desperate odyssey. His adversary, Tommy Lee Jones' intense Gerard, is a pitiless federal marshal given to wisecracks and unbending in upholding the law. And while David Janssen's Kimble was the 60s version of the Western hero, Ford's man on the lam is more like a dark modern Zorro, compelled to perform feats of impossible daring, constantly courting recapture, yet unstoppable in his quest for justice.

The first half is arguably the more entertaining with its relentless action climaxing in the first face-to-face encounter between Kimble and Gerard. 'I didn't kill my wife!' protests Kimbles. 'I don't care!' retorts Gerard, setting out the imperatives, justice versus the law, that define their tense relationship. The second half, in which Kimble returns to home ground to solve the mystery, busies itself with an additional, topical but just slightly sanctimonious plot element of corruption in the medical establishment, a formulaic conspiracy, and enough fateful and fortuitous coincidences for a Dickens novel.

It's never not fun, however, and is seldom less than gripping. Director Andrew Davis, having paid his dues with Steven Seagal on *Above The Law* and *Under Siege*, proves he can play with the big boys and the big money, treating the clever screenplay with the imagination and urgency it deserves. **★★★ AE**

FULL METAL JACKET (1987)

Starring: *Matthew Modine (Private 'Joker' J.T. Davis), Adam Baldwin (Animal Mothers), Vincent D'Onofrio (Private 'Gomer' Leonard Lawrence), R. Lee Ermey (Gunnery Sergeant Hartman)*
Director: *Stanley Kubrick*
Screenwriters: *Stanley Kubrick, Michael Herr, Gustav Hasford based on the novel The Short Timers by Hasford*
18/116 mins./War/UK

The journey of one Private 'Joker' Davis, through the gruelling training regime to be a marine, fraught with its own psychological damage, to Vietnam itself. Here, as a war correspondent, he covers the Tet offensive.

Divided like a rift into two distinct halves, Stanley Kubrick's examination of the Vietnam conflict found him on unusually inconsistent form; the film is both powerful and frustratingly unengaged. In the first section, the boot camp, the great intellectual exalts in the dehumanising process of turning greenhorn boys into killing machines. R. Lee Ermey's staggering performance as a drill sergeant pounds into these young men like a bulldozer, and in the case of Private 'Gomer', (Vincent D'Onofrio – fat, dangerous, a walking powder keg) the pressure will become too much. These barrages of abusive language and intimidation are supposed to burn survival into these empty vessels, but Kubrick is divulging a process of brutality to match the moral objections of the conflict itself. In Gomer's self-destruction, the seething necessities of war are barbarities in themselves – conform or die.

Once away from the bullying of training and into the fragged cities and casual death of Vietnam itself, stunningly envisioned on an old gasworks in London's East End, Kubrick seems bereft of purpose. He's made his chilling point, that a solider must shed his humanity and become a machine, and now Modine's wide-eyed thinker contends with the battlefield itself and the film sinks into a guarded examination of muddy methodology. Is it that the state of this war is too politically messy for Kubrick's contemplative gaze? Modine's Joker has too astute a mind to be an innocent, and his cumbersome narration covers Kubrick's highly designed – it is bloody and beautiful but never surreal or horrifying – but strangely empty variation on this 'phony war'. ★★★ **IN**

THE FULL MONTY (1997)

Starring: *Robert Carlyle (Gaz), Mark Addy (Dave), William Snape (Nathan), Steve Huison (Lomper), Tom Wilkinson (Gerald), Paul Barber (Horse), Hugo Speer (Guy), Lesley Sharp (Jean), Emily Woof (Mandy)*
Director: *Peter Cattaneo*
Screenwriter: *Simon Beaufoy*
15/90 mins./Comedy/UK

Awards: *Academy Awards – Best Musical/Comedy Score, BAFTA – Audience Award, Best Film, Best Actor, Best Supporting Actor (Tom Wilkinson), Empire Awards – Best British Film*

Gaz, always on the lookout for easy money, gathers his dole-collecting mates together to do their, individual, version of the Chippendales. All manner of chaotic events ensue, as the less-than-athlectic, troubled 'dancers' attempt to rehearse and perform their special show.

A monumental smash hit, Peter Cattaneo's debut feature has become a byword for successful Brit comedy (posters are always declaring films to be the new *Full Monty*), which is surprising given its modest ambition and gag rate.

A fixture at one of Sheffield's job clubs, Gaz is always on the lookout for easy money to pay child support to his ex-wife. After seeing the Chippendales raking it in, Gaz enlists a bizarre troupe of fellow blokes to form a strip-group: including fat Dave, miserably aware of his love handles and his non-existent libido; Gerald, the ballroom dancing ex-foreman who hasn't the guts to tell his wife he's been out of work for six months; Horse, long in the tooth but a great little mover – and a plumber whose greatest asset is in his Y-fronts.

The central joke is that there's nothing funnier than a bunch of less-than athletic Englishmen prancing about in leather G-strings. Issues of the male body image are well thought out, despite the ludicrous notion that any woman would like to see this unlikely bunch with their kit off. The male characters are well 'fleshed-out', although the female roles, especially the long-suffering wives, are given too little attention. With some original comic touches – the group silently practising their routine while queueing in the DSS is a stand-out – the film put its cast (especially Carlyle, Wilkinson and Addy) on the map and gave a new lease of life to Hot Chocolate's hit 'You Sexy Thing'. ★★★ **Dbr**

FUN WITH DICK AND JANE (1977)

Starring: *Geroge Segal (Dick Harper), Jane Fonda (Jane Harper), Ed McMahon (Charlie Blanchard), Dick Gautier (Dr. Will)*
Director: *Ted Kotcheff*
Screenwriters: *David Giler, Jerry Belson, Mordecai Richler, from a story by Gerald Gaiser*
PG/99 mins./Comedy/Crime/USA

When Dick becomes unemployed he decides to enlist Jane in a criminal spree to fund their surburban lifestyle.

With an unfunny Jim Carrey/Téa Leoni-starring remake out of the blocks, it's well past time to revisit this wickedly entertaining and admirably subversive black comedy from 1977 – a time when America looked different (at least in details like the hideously floral interior design with wallpaper that matches the furniture and fashions like evening gowns that look like that inflatable suit from *Sleeper*) but had already plunged into the moral vacuum that's likely to make the new version just as horribly relevant.

Directed by underrated, versatile pro director Ted Kotcheff (best known for *First Blood*), the movie opens with children's illustrations; Dick and Jane being the American equivalents of Janet and John. These smartly demonstrate the ideal, conformist upper-middle-class life aerospace exec Richard Harper and his beautiful, poised wife Jane have achieved by doing everything they were supposed to, which extends to a dream house in the suburbs, a son named Billy and a dog named Spot. When Dick is laid off by his smarmy boss because of the post-space programme downturn in the industry, the couple fail to make the grade as 'welfare cheats' and come close to financial collapse, but getting caught up in the robbery of a usurious loan company prompts them to turn to crime to keep the swimming pool heated and gourmet food on the table.

After an hilarious sequence of armed robberies, in which 'the bickering bandits' rip off hate figures like the phone company and a greedy evangelist, the climax comes in a heist at Dick's old employer's, which skewers corporate hypocrisy as they try to steal the slush fund the company can't admit exists.

The really subversive aspect of the movie is that it depicts an appallingly cynical vision of all-encompassing corruption in the pastel tones of sitcom. Seventies icons George Segal and Jane Fonda spark sexily off each other as if the Dick Van Dyke and Mary Tyler Moore characters from *The Dick Van Dyke Show* found themselves turning into Bonnie and Clyde.

Fonda, in a rare light comic role during her run of heavier projects, is hard-boiled, wry with a put-down and disturbingly sexy as she becomes an outlaw (at the time, much was made of a discreet scene which she plays while on the toilet), even handling her slapstick scenes with elegance. Meanwhile, Segal's frazzled square, who initially can't do anything right, gradually warms to a life of outright crime which the movie makes clear is morally no worse than the white-collar crookery practised by everyone in Watergate-era America – or, indeed, now ... ★★★★ **KN**

THE FUNERAL (1996)

Starring: *Christopher Walken (Ray Tempio), Chris Penn (Chez Tempio), Annabella Sciorra (Jean), Isabella Rossellini (Clara Tempio), Vincent Gallo (Johnny), Benicio Del Toro (Gaspare), Gretchen Mol (Helen)*
Director: *Abel Ferrara*
Screenwriter: *Nicholas St. John*
18/99 mins./Crime/Drama/USA

The head of a clan of gangsters tries to come to terms with his younger brother's death.

Abel Ferrara remains the least appreciated Great American Director, committed at once to the unfashionable areas of the exploitative genre movies and all-out art filmmaking. In *The Funeral*, he flashes back to the Warner Bros-style classic gangster epic, even opening with a nippet of Bogart in *The Petrified Forest*, but his snappily dressed, wisecracking, instinctively violent 1930s hoods harbour the psychotic, philosophical and religious impulses of many Ferrara protagonists.

In the coffin is Johnny Tempo, the youngest of three gangster brothers, long reckoned to be uncontrollable because of his political radicalism and love of taunting rival crook Gaspar Spoglio. Mourners include brother Ray, shoulderer of all the agonies of a world in which he feels he is already damned, and Chez, a bloated maniac whose fiery temperament can erupt in embarrassing public blues-wailing or frightening displays of physical brutality.

Flashbacks reveal how Johnny got shot, and Ray and Chez both wonder how they should claim their revenge. The 1930s setting allows for plenty of period footnotes – the politics are exact, if obscure – but the business of the movie is finally religious.

This is a hard film to follow, with its intricate collection of flashbacks and high quality ethical debates, and eventually settles for character over plot comprehensibility, but Ferrara draws remarkable work out of Walken, who is less funky here than in *King Of New York*, and Penn who shows that his gangsters don't have to come up with an unforgettable punchline. ★★★★ **KN**

FUNNY BONES (1995)

Starring: *Oliver Platt (Tommy Fawkes), Jerry Lewis (George Fawkes), Lee Evans (Jack Parker), Leslie Caron (Katie Parker), Richard Griffiths (Jim Minty), Oliver Reed (Dolly Hopkins)*
Director: *Peter Chelsom*
Screenwriters: *Peter Chelsom, Peter Flannery*
15/128 mins./Comedy/UK

The son of a legendary American comedian arrives in Blackpool in search of new jokes to use in his act – and discovers a long lost brother.

'I never saw anything funny that didn't cause pain.' A defining quote from the script to a film that, despite the crass video packaging ('A captivating comedy treat!' it bawls), begs for more than just your laughing gear.

The last great movie about the rib-tickling art was Scorsese's *King Of Comedy*; apt, since erstwhile gurnsmith Jerry Lewis is the common link between that and this – by comparison – achingly British take on the pain beneath the clown's painted smile. And, ironically, it is the transatlantic flipside here that lends an engrossing twist to (*Hear My Song* director) Chelsom's grubby, Blackpool-anchored peek into the unspoken secrets of comedy.

The Parker Brothers (impeccably cast real-life variety comics Freddie Davies and George Carl) are a past-it circus double act, whose reputation was blackened 12 years ago by their gifted 'nephew' Jack – branded 'a known, bona fide maniac' by the authorities – in a grisly moment of madness, revealed, gradually, in black-and-white flashback.

The aforementioned narrative trump card is played when, in poles-apart Las Vegas, Blackpool-born Tommy Fawkes dies onstage at the Hilton Oasis, and is thus prompted to debunk to England in search of material to buy. Yet when reunited with his childhood acquaintances, the Parkers, umpteen skeletons are released from the cupboard, especially when Tommy's comic legend father turns up to take him back home (the star's touchdown at a dog-eared Blackpool 'airport' presents an emblematic clash between US celebrity and modest Northern English seaside hospitality).

There are subplots, too, concerning a Frenchman's feet and an egg filled with eternal life powder, plus fabulous support from Richard Griffiths as Head Of Tourism and a rich soundtrack of poignant laugh-free American blues.

Although Evans for many will be the film's selling point (and he turns in a delightfully demented performance, if a touch lax of Northern accent), it is the downbeat, timeless originality of Chelsom and Peter Flannery's story that marks it out for immortality. Not just a patronising pop at old-school vaudeville entertainers (although the freakshow audition scene is cruel fun), it is a beautifully written thesis on the in-built tragedy of laughter and the pain of nostalgia: 'Why do all the best things in life belong to the past?' A tower de force. ★★★★ **AC**

FUNNY GIRL (1968)

Starring: *Barbra Streisand (Fanny Brice), Omar Sharif (Nick Arnstein), Kay Medford (Rosa Brice), Anne Francis (Gerorgia James), Walter Pidgeon (Florenz Ziegfeld)*
Director: *William Wyler*
Screenwriter: *Isobel Lennart based on the musical by Jule Styne, Bob Merrill and Lennart*
U/151 mins./Musical/USA

Awards: *Academy Awards – Best Actress*

Gambler Nicky Arnstein helps Fanny Brice become the star of Florenz Ziegfeld's Follies. But he's intimidated by her success and jeopardises their relationship with ever-more reckless betting sprees.

Fanny Brice should have been the Talkies' first female star. However, she didn't conform to Hollywood standards of beauty and she's best known now through this musical biopic, which earned the debuting Barbra Streisand an Oscar (in a Best Actress tie with Katharine Hepburn for *The Lion in Winter*).

In many ways, Streisand's rise to the top mirrored that of Brice, whom she had played in the original stage version of Isobel Lennart's play. But, she was much more fortunate in her transition to films, as director William Wyler had guided 40 stars to Oscar-winning performances from 125 nominations. Moreover, cinematographer Harry Stradling was sufficiently skilled to find the photogenicity in her famous facial features, while costumer Irene Sharaff, choreographer Herbert Ross and co-stars Kay Medford (as mother Rose Brice) and Lee Allen (as mentor Eddie Ryan) were reprising their Broadway roles.

Streisand was even lucky in the fact that she fell in love with her leading man, Omar Sharif, and their romance certainly enhanced their on-screen chemistry. However, he was anything but first choice to play gambler Nicky Arnstein, with Frank Sinatra, Rock Hudson, Tony Curtis, Marlon Brando and Gregory Peck all passing before Columbia hired the then-hot Egyptian star of *Doctor Zhivago*.

The Cairo press were less than enamoured by the casting, however, and castigated Sharif for sharing the screen with a Jew around the time of the Six Day War. But, despite all the negative publicity, the film became one of the top 10 box-office hits of the 1960s. Streisand proved to be equally adept at comedy and drama, but she best captured Brice's gauche charm while singing Ziegfeld tunes like 'My Man' and 'Second Hand Rose' or such Jule Styne-Bob Merrill originals as 'Don't Rain on My Parade' and 'People'.

In 1975, Streisand starred in the sequel, *Funny Lady*, with James Caan as second husband, impresario Billy Rose. However, it felt very much like an afterthought. ★★★★ **DP**

A FUNNY THING HAPPENED ON THE WAY TO THE FORUM (1966)

Starring: *Zero Mostel (Pseudolus), Phil Silvers (Lycus), Jack Gifford (Hysterium), Buster Keaton (Erronius), Michael Crawford (Hero), Michael Hordern (Senex)*
Screenwriters: *Melvyn Frank, Michael Pertwee based on the book by Burt Shevelove, Larry Gelbart*
PG/99 mins./Comedy/USA
Awards: *Academy Awards – Best Adapted Score*

Geeks TOP10

1. Thomas "Neo" Anderson (Keanu Reeves), The Matrix
2. Napoleon Dynamite (Jon Heder), Napoleon Dynamite
3. Professor Julius Kelp (Jerry Lewis) The Nutty Professor
4. Dr. Egon Spengler (Harold Ramis), Ghostbusters
5. Brandon Wheeger (Justin Long), Galaxy Quest
6. Kate "Acid Burn" Libby (Angelina Jolie), Hackers
7. Gary Wallace (Anthony Michael Hall), Weird Science
8. Michelle (Alyson Hannigan), American Pie
9. Craig Schwartz (John Cusack), Being John Malkovich
10. Terry the Toad (Charles Martin Smith), American Graffiti

Roman slave Pseudolus hopes to secure his freedom from Senex by helping his son, Hero, keep brothel keeper Lycus' virginal acquisition, Philia, away from preening gladiator Miles Gloriosus.

Richard Lester had always been a devoted disciple of Buster Keaton and he gave the silent maestro his final feature role in this adaptation of Bert Shevelove and Larry Gelbart's Broadway success. Although he's primarily seen in what is literally a running gag (as Erronius traipses seven times round the Seven Hills of Rome in the hope of recovering the children kidnapped by pirates), Keaton's spirit is evident in every scene, as not only does Lester pay homage to his knockabout style, but he also fills the frame with throwaway pieces of comic business that only emerge on repeated viewing.

However, Lester's energetic editing (which owed much to the nouvelle vague) occasionally works against the practised playing of Zero Mostel, Jack Gifford and Phil Silvers by visually disrupting the verbal flow of scenes that owed as much to vaudeville patter as the trilogy of comedies penned by 3rd-century BC playwright, Plautus.

Yet Lester had been personally selected by Mostel, over the likes of Charles Chaplin, Orson Welles and Mike Nichols, for the comic skills he had honed in collaboration with The Goons and the knack for musical numbers he had developed with The Beatles. Indeed, Lester seems more assured staging such Stephen Sondheim gems as 'Comedy Tonight', 'Everybody Ought to Have a Maid' and 'I'm Lovely' than he was banter that required timing not speed. Yet, while Lester was guilty of allowing Silvers to mug shamelessly in another variation on Sgt. Bilko, he shrewdly allowed the likes of Michael Hordern and Patricia Jessel to steal scenes with their deft underplaying.

Packing the action with antiquarian clichés and caricatures, Lester anticipated Frankie Howerd's cult sitcom, *Up Pompeii*. But the scattershot approach to the often anachronistic comedy also had its influence on Mel Brooks' movie pastiches and the more cerebral lunacy of *Monty Python's Life of Brian*. ★★★ **DP**

FURY (1936)

Starring: *Spencer Tracy (Joe Wheeler), Sylvia Sydney (Katherine Grant), Walter Abel (District Attorney), Edward Ellis (Sheriff), Walter Brennan (Buggs Meyers), Bruce Cabot (Bubbles Dawson)*
Director: *Fritz Lang*
Screenwriters: *Bartlett Cormack, Fritz Lang based on the story* Mob Rule *by Norman Krasna*
Unrated/90 mins./Crime/USA

Joe Wilson is detained in a small-town jail, suspected of being involved with a kidnapping. A lynch mob burns down the jail before Joe is exonerated. Though he escapes the blaze, he lets the world think he's dead as members of the mob are put on trial for murder.

Fritz Lang's first American feature is a hybrid of social problem melodrama (complete with statistics about lynching) and twisted noir melodrama, with Spencer Tracy transformed from peanut-popping nice guy into a maniacal, croak-voiced avenger who gloats over the trial of the folks who 'murdered' him. Lang uses silent movie-style montages as rumours run around town (old ladies gossiping are intercut with cackling hens) and delivers almost comical horror moments as ordinary, decent, mild-mannered citizens turn into frenzied beasts as they attack the jail.

The second half of the film is a strained, weird courtroom drama with a non-stop barrage of 'objection sustained' and outrageous tactics from the crusading district attourney (Abel) and the shifty defence counsel (Hale), plus a climax in which Joe lurches zombie-like to the stand after the verdict is in, not to forgive the bastards who tried to burn him (and then weasel out of it by getting friends to commit perjury and give alibis) but to save his fragile, waif-like girlfriend (the big-eyed, extraordinary Sylvia Sidney) from madness. Lang, having skipped Europe to avoid the Nazi film industry, spotlights aspects of America – the story is inspired by the real hysteria around the Lindbergh kidnapping case – which reminded him too much of what he had tried to leave behind. The script has purple patches and too many unbelievable twists to be taken seriously as social comment, but the film has an overheated gothic charge that remains powerful, and the riot is a bravura action scene. ★★★ **KN**

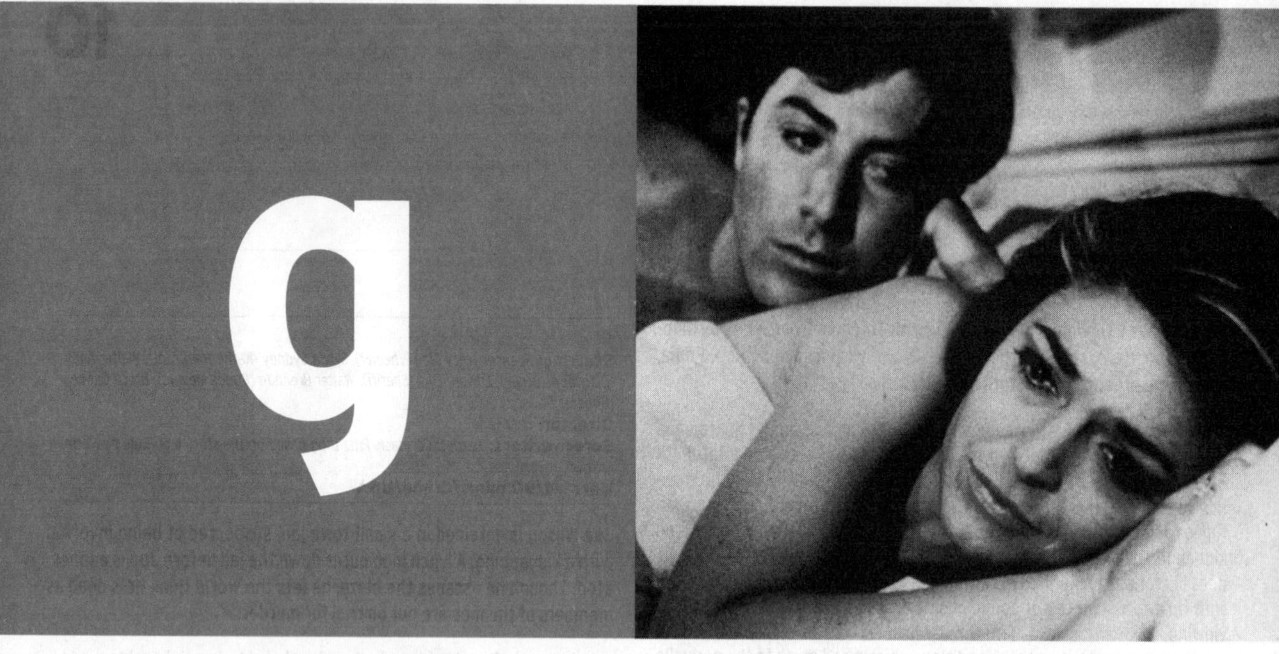

G.I. JANE (1997)

Starring: *Demi Moore (Lt. Jordan O'Neil), Viggo Mortensen (Master Chief John James 'Jack' Urgayle), Anne Bancroft (Sen. Lillian DeHaven), Jason Beghe (Royce)*
Director: *Ridley Scott*
Screenwriters: *David Twohy, Danielle Alexandra, based on a story by Danielle Alexandra*
15/124 mins./Action/Drama/USA
Awards: *Razzie – Worst Actress*

Jordan O'Neil signs up as the first female Navy SEAL but before she gets to do battle she'll have to survive training.

Private Benjamin meets *Top Gun*, with an ultra-fit, shaven-headed Demi Moore joining the ultra-tough training programme to become America's first woman Navy SEAL.

The story, however, is confused: overlong, it begins by being about a woman battling to overcome prejudice, and ends up a gun-toting Arab-killing action movie. Political intrigue is also thrown in, with Bancroft as a senator with a secret agenda, but this is soon discarded in favour of guns and explosions.

In trying to fit into this man's world, Moore overdoes the belligerence: the apotheosis of her gung-ho bonhomie being her resounding cry of 'Suck my dick!', as she is finally accepted into the all-male company. She's one of the boys, cigars and all. Her character is unsympathetic and, like everyone else, has no real depth. The only glimmer of interest is produced by Mortensen's master chief, the obligatory hard-ass with a heart of gold.

While it aims to be about women's rights, male prejudice, and political corruption, this film is really just about looks. Ace stylist Ridley Scott is in his element during the action sequences, luxuriating in the visual detail: the trademark moodicam interiors, the stark white deserts, the camera soaking up Moore's moonlit one-arm press-ups. Physically at least, Mrs. Willis certainly earns her fee – in the transformation from girly desk-bound type to paid-up army grunt, we get a good five minutes of Moore shaving her long hair down to the celebrated buzz cut.

In spite of a catalogue of downsides, including clunky dialogue, fuzzy morals and preposterous story lines, *G.I. Jane* does offer a perverse level of enjoyment. Scott's divine aesthetic interlaces the ensuing nonsense with stirring gung-ho, ever-increasing weaponry – and cigars – for shallow appeal. But for all Moore's grunting and growling, this is still a man's view of the world. Any feminist subtext has clearly gone AWOL. ★★ **DBr**

GALAXY QUEST (1999)

Starring: *Tim Allen (Jason Nesmith/Cmdr. Peter Quincy Taggart), Sigourney Weaver (Gwen DeMarco/Lt. Tawny Madison), Alan Rickman (Alexander Dane), Tony Shalhoub (Fred Kwan), Sam Rockwell (Guy Fleegman)*
Director: *Dean Parisot*
Screenwriter: *Robert Gordon, from a story by David Howard and Robert Gordon*
PG/102 mins./Adventure/Comedy/Sci-fi/USA

The stars of a *Star Trek*-a-like sci-fi show are kidnapped by aliens who mistakenly think the characters in the show are real and can save their planet.

Going boldly beyond the comic skits and lore references that have peppered popular culture for 35 years, this full-blown spoof of the *Star Trek* phenomenon is so witty and polished it will endear itself even to those who don't know a transporter beam from a phaser blast. This is a one-joke premise, affectionately and knowingly developed into a multiplicity of wonderfully amusing gags and hugely enjoyable performances.

Vain, arrogant ham Jason Nesmith and his co-stars from long-cancelled sci-fi adventure series *Galaxy Quest* make mortifying bucks appearing at conventions of avid Questers. Cast reunions are occasions for jealous rants, recriminations and laments for lost careers – from Gwen, who played the show's communications babe, the now adult Tommy, who played the boy genius navigator, the permanently stoned Fred, and the snooty Shakespearean thespian, doomed to be remembered as *Quest*'s prosthetic-headed, half-humanoid, half-reptilian science officer, Dr. Lazarus.

Approached by a group of oddballs who seem only slightly more cuckoo than the typical Questie autograph hounds, the inimical ensemble find themselves whisked into space aboard a working replica of their telly starship by the Thermians, a race who not only have monitored Earth TV transmissions, but have modelled their society and technology on *Galaxy Quest*. Now they are engaged in a desperate battle with a tentacled conquering foe, depending on their heroes to lead them to victory and save the universe. 'Uh-oh's all round, as the scared and hopelessly inadequate actors struggle to rise to the occasion.

Director Parisot (*Home Fries*) maintains a lively pace and playful tone through well-executed pastiches of every cliché in the genre, such as 'the away mission', on which the bit-part player as the crewman with no name is horribly aware he's bound to be the first casualty, the commander contrives to shed his shirt, and Gwen's uniform gets ever more revealingly shredded. The entire cast is game for the ridiculous, while Stan Winston's aliens and ILM visual effects give this the gloss of a straight-faced sci-fi spectacle. Beam on up. ★★★★ **CW**

GALLIPOLI (1981)

Starring: *Mark Lee (Archy Hamilton), Bill Kerr (Jack), Mel Gibson (Frank Dunne), Ronnie Graham (Wallace Hamilton) Harold Hopkins (Les McCann), Charles Lathalu Yunipingli (Zac)*
Director: *Peter Weir*
Screenwriters: *Peter Weir, David Williamson*
PG/110 mins./War/Australia

The story of two Australian sprinters from different backgrounds, whose potential careers as athletes are interrupted by the arrival of World War I. Both friends sign up to join the ANZACS, and are sent to fight the Turkish at Gallipoli where they will meet tragedy.

A haunting and moving tribute to the Australians who sacrificed their lives in WWI against not the Germans but the Turks at the lesser sung battle of Gallipoli from the assured hand of Peter Weir. Made not a year after the intellectual rattle of fellow Aussie anti-war movie *Breaker Morant*, Weir's film takes a more obvious but, in many ways, more affecting route – the tragic loss of innocence.

These two prettified friends are virtually an anthem for lost youth in their own right. A young Mel Gibson, free of the acerbic undertones or fanaticism of his later career, is Frank a city kid who can surely run and meets equally beautiful and fleet-footed country-boy Archy Hamilton at a track meet. It is a moment of familiar destiny as their friendship draws them toward the war as an opportunity to find honour, glory, escape, all the patented offerings of a soldier's life that tend to keep the abject horror and death to the fine print.

Here, like *All Quiet On The Western Front* and countless other observers of The Great War's great losses, is a study of the illusory and real forces that propel dreamy young men into the fields of conflict. This is as much a matter of comradeship – there are whispers here of a homoerotic bond between the two heroes – as duty, men drawn to stand alongside each other. And Weir portrays this strange calling as an intimate elegy, shot with both candour and a fascinating counterpoint between the expanse of the Outback and the limits of the hot trenches, that reveals his unerring talent for opening up the sad hearts of men. ★★★★★ **IN**

THE GAME (1997)

Starring: *Michael Douglas (Nicholas Van Orton), Sean Penn (Conrad Van Orton), Deborah Kara Unger (Christine), James Rebhorn (Jim Feingold), Peter Donat (Samuel Sutherland)*
Director: *David Fincher*
Screenwriters: *John D. Brancato, Michael Ferris*
15/128 mins./Mystery/Thriller/USA

Nick Van Orton, the man who has everything, is given a ticket by his brother to join The Game. But what at first promises to be a fun, live, interactive adventure soon turns life-threatening.

Douglas is Nicholas Van Orton, a ludicrously rich broker with a big house, a plush lifestyle and no one to share it with. His wife has left him, his father committed suicide when he was nine (in an overly stylized home movie sequence at the opening of the movie – *Flatliners* anyone?) and the result is that he's a very cold fish indeed. When his rebellious brother hands him the phone number of a company called, bizarrely, Consumer Relation Services he, quite against character, phones it, gets signed up for a mysterious 'game' and then the shit hits the fan.

Garish clown dolls turn up outside his luxury pad in cruel caricature of his dad's body, his telly starts talking to him, the house is creatively vandalized with enough UV to power a really big school disco and when he tries to stop playing a load of masked maniacs with machine guns begin taking pops at him.

There are a number of serious problems with all this. Firstly, it's shockingly derivative. There are elements of *FX Murder By Illusion*, *After Hours*, a touch of *Bad Influence*, plus a little of the surreal confusion of *The Prisoner* while Douglas joins in the reprise-fest by taking Gordon Gecko from *Wall Street* and turning him into D-Fens from *Falling Down* half way through. Oh, and the final sequence is a gag lifted from *Lethal Weapon*.

The second is that what plot there is (and it looks like a 25-minute *Twilight Zone* episode distended over a patience-wearing near two-an-a-quarter hours) makes no sense whatsoever. We are never given a clue as to why Van Orton must be put through these horrendous trials – he's not that bad a guy – nor why the person who turns out to be behind it would want him to be.

Granted, there are a couple of nice sequences, Sean Penn (in a tragically underdeveloped role) is as fine as he always is, and there's a nicely handled nightmare senario in which Douglas gets stranded miles from home with no money. But in the end, this a major disappointment. ★★ **AS**

GANDHI (1982)

Starring: *Ben Kingsley (Mohandas K. Ghandi), Candice Bergen (Margaret Bourke-White), Edward Fox (General Reginald Dyer), John Gielgud (Lord Irwin), Trevor Howard (Judge Broomfield), John Mills (Lord Chelmsford), Martin Sheen (Vince Walker), Saeed Jaffrey (Sardar Patel)*
Director: *Richard Attenborough*
Screenwriter: *John Briley*
PG/88 mins./History/Drama/UK/India

Awards: *Academy Awards – Best Picture, Best Director, Best Actor (Ben Kingsley), Best Art Direction, Best Cinematography, Best Costume Design, Best Editing, Best Writing; BAFTA – Best Film, Best Direction, Best Actor (Ben Kinglsey), Best Newcomer (Ben Kingsley), Best Supporting Actress (Rohini Hattangadi)*

The epic tale of the low-level Indian lawyer working in South Africa, who became the spiritual leader of India, inspiring the downtrodden population to rise up and overthrow the British colonialists, but by non-violent means only.

The enduring sweep of David Lean's work owes much to his poeticising of history's more mundane features into the descant of high adventure, whereas Richard Attenborough's dedicated and finely tuned biopic of that beloved nappy-clad pacifist, avers grandeur in search of truth. A tricky principal amongst the shrill intensity of the movies. For all the momentous history (the opening funeral cast just about everyone in India) and striking moments of human intimacy on show, his film is often a doze, lacking the full conviction of a good epic to cut loose.

The subject itself, the godlike Mahatma, that shrewish guru whose only worldly trapping is his pair of wire-rimmed specs, offers up a staggering accomplishment but an unassuming mythology. His passive-aggressive stance in the face of religious conflict and the rigours of both British colonialism and the Indian caste system, consummately investigated by John Briley's intelligent script, has none of the stirring action or belly-fire of a *Lawrence Of Arabia* or a *Ben-Hur*. Hence this three-hour tramp through his life is very talky and slow and deliberately unlovely as Gandhi rises from the campaigning lawyer clamouring for the rights of Indians in Apartheid-swept South Africa to an uncompromising figurehead. His determined stance of non-violent confrontation often cruelly led to violent reprisal, in one of the film's most searing moments a group of his followers are bloodily beaten down by British soldiers without even flinching.

It is obvious that Attenborough is engaged in a deeply felt labour of love and the film possesses a contained power similar to the man himself; Ben Kingsley, an unknown chosen to play him, does a fine job at assuming iconography, unwilling to epitomise a bland goodness, and exposes his irritating pigheadedness. But in the director's unwillingness to excite the tale, as if its disapproving subject was keeping a keen eye from whatever heaven he was taken to, the film remains proud but forgettable. ★★★ **IN**

GANGS OF NEW YORK (2002)

Starring: *Leonardo DiCaprio (Amsterdam Vallon), Daniel Day-Lewis (Bill 'The Butcher' Cutting), Cameron Diaz (Jenny Everdeane), Jim Broadbent (Boss Tweed), John C. Reilly (Happy Jack), Henry Thomas (Johnny Sirocco), Liam Neeson ('Priest' Vallon), Brendan Gleeson (Walter 'Monk' McGinn)*
Director: *Martin Scorsese*
Screenwriters: *Jay Cocks, Steve Zaillian, Kenneth Lonergan, from a story by Jay Cocks, suggested by* Gangs of New York *by Herbert Ashbury)*
18/165 mins./Crime/Drama/History/USA

Awards: *BAFTA – Best Actor, Golden Globes – Best Director, Best Song*

As the American Civil War rages, rival gangs battle for New York's Lower East Side. On one side are the Nativists, led by the vicious Bill The Butcher. On the other, Irish-American Amsterdam Vallon and the reviled 'foreign hordes', fighting for their place in the city.

Since 1999, when Leonardo DiCaprio signed on with America's greatest living director, expectations have slipped from 'eagerly-awaited', to 'long-awaited', to worryingly 'long-delayed', as *Gangs Of New York*'s US release moved from December 01, to July, then December 02.

It arrived here burdened with gossip of hostilities and an awareness that there's been a lot of fiddling about, all of which gave DiCaprio time to make a Spielberg movie that opened almost simultaneously.

Masterpiece or muddle, then? Truth is, Scorsese's spectacle is something of both. This dark, provocative 19th century epic – with its gorgeously sinister cinematography (by Michael Ballhaus) and stunning period detail – is signature Scorsese.

Ambitiously he extends his journey through the violence in America's social fabric back in time to argue that, to quote the poster, the great democracy was born (bloodily) in the streets, and is still kicking and screaming to this day.

This is a bold, brave look at history as it is not taught, brutally contradicting the 'melting pot' fable of the American Dream.

These huddled masses are clawing for survival in a cesspit of poverty, cruelty, corruption and greed, ultimately to be engulfed in the Draft Riots, America's worst mass explosion of civic unrest. *Gangs*' romantic fictional plot – running through the bigger, factual backdrop – is traditional. A poor urchin witnesses his father's gruesome murder by the white Anglo-Saxon Protestant lord of the 'hood, grows up in a grim institution, returns to avenge his father, falls for a tough lovely, and becomes the Moses of his squalid, barbaric patch of Manhattan.

This is unnecessarily drawn out when we all know roughly where it's going. Amsterdam's buddy, for example (*E.T.*'s Elliott, Henry Thomas, as Johnny), might as well have 'I'm going to betray you because I covet your girl' tattooed across his forehead. The second half of the film, however, feels rushed. The narrative hiccups and jumps around as peripheral characters and wider ideological, racial and religious conflicts envelop the local, personal turmoil. Bewilderment or boredom, choose one.

The film doesn't disappoint, however, in its breathtakingly cinematic – and frequently horrific – set-pieces. Most memorably, a remarkable single shot follows newly-arrived, ragged, starving immigrants disembarking, issued with citizenship, sworn into the army, thrust into uniform and marched up the gangplank of a Federal ship as coffins of the war casualties are unloaded.

Tagline
America was born in the streets.

Daniel Day-Lewis resists the temptation to twirl his handlebar moustache, but his superb impersonation of Robert De Niro (once set to play The Butcher) is sociopathic, show-stealing Grand Guignol, as he ruthlessly wields cleavers, knives and power with disturbing expertise. A xenophobic monologue he delivers seated by Vallon's bed, draped in a bloody Stars and Stripes, is absolutely hair-raising. DiCaprio, meanwhile, looks the heart-throb but also provides the vital emotional engagement. Diaz is implausibly contemporary and clean for her role, but valuable in the erotic stakes.

It has to be said that funny hats and voluminous checked pants distinguish this decade as a particularly absurd fashion era for men. The gangs look like satirical dastards in a nightmare of atavistic street fights and sadistic entertainments created by a mad Charles Dickens on a very bad trip. ★★★★ **AM**

GANGSTER NO. 1 (2000)

Starring: *Malcolm McDowell (Gangster 55), David Thewlis (Freddie Mays), Paul Bettany (Young Gangster), Saffron Burrows (Karen), Kenneth Cranham (Tommy), Andrew Lincoln (Maxie King)*
Director: *Paul McGuigan*
Screenwriter: *Johnny Ferguson*
18/103 mins./Crime/Drama/Thriller/U.K./Germany/Ireland

On the eve of his mentor's release from prison, a gangster looks back on his 1960s reign of terror.

Given the dreadful quality of most post-*Smoking Barrels* British gangster movies, plus the fact that Malcolm McDowell's recent career has been less than stellar, this 60s-set venture could easily have been lost in the shuffle.

McDowell plays ageing Cockney crook Gangster 55 who, on hearing that the mentor he betrayed three decades previously is about to be released from jail, finds himself reminiscing about the good old days. At least, they were good for the youthful 55 – a tremendous performance of icy Nietzschean emptiness by Bettany – if not for his soon-to-be-butchered contemporaries. Before long his sights have levelled on Thewlis himself, who the sexually ambivalent Bettany believes has gone soft after falling for nightclub chanteuse, Karen.

Finally, with 55 now in control of the entire operation, McDowell leads us through a brief history of the last 30 years (horse race-fixing and lots of bloodshed) before preparing to face both Thewlis and his own demons in the present day.

A stylistically superb jaunt through psychotically Swinging London – where every shoe is handmade and every transgressor a 'caaaaahnt!' – Gangster No. 1 benefits from both an ace Johnny Dankworth score and a truly demented turn from McDowell in what must be his best performance since 1971's *A Clockwork Orange*.

The real plaudits, however, should go to photographer-turned-director McGuigan, whose sharp eye succeeds in stripping away the myth of the luva-duck 60s crim while still allowing the audience to wallow in his all-too-enticing lifestyle. ★★★ CC

THE GARDEN OF THE FINZI-CONTINIS (1971)

Starring: *Dominique Sanda (Micol), Lino Capolicchio (Giorgio), Helmut Berger (Alberto), Fabio Testi (Malinate), Romolo Valli (Giorgio's Father), Raffaele Curl (Ernesto)*
Director: *Vittorio De Sica*
Screenwriters: *Cesare Zavattini, Vittorio Bonicelli, Ugo Pirro based on the novel by Giorgio Bassani*
Unrated/93 mins./Drama/Italy/West Germany
Awards: *Academy Awards – Best Foreign Language Film, Berlin Film Festival – Golden Bear*

As Mussolini's racial laws limit opportunities for the Jews of 1930s Ferrara, the aristocratic Micol and her ailing brother, Alberto, offer bourgeois student Giorgio and Communist engineer Malnate the sanctuary of their garden.

Frustrated by the interference of producer Carlo Ponti on *Sunflower* and nettled by the press' negative response to the middlebrow dramas and saucy comedies in which he now specialised, Vittorio De Sica decided to rebel. Yet, while the critical response to this adaptation of Giorgio Bassani's autobiographical 1962 novel was largely positive, the author denounced the film and later repudiated his contribution to the screenplay. However, De Sica was unfazed by what he saw as a sulky response to his decision to reduce the role of Giorgio's father (Romollo Valli) and revelled in his reputation as the comeback kid after the picture took the Golden Bear at Berlin and the Academy Award for Best Foreign Film.

De Sica had never been a Fascist, but he shared the nation's shame at the persecution of Italian Jews during the Second World War. Yet, he centres the action on Bassani's premise that the Finzi-Continis' problems lay more in the Sephardic arrogance that prompted them to shut themselves away from reality than their ethno-religious origins. Thus, it's their wealth and status as much as the walls of their manicured estate that detach them from those lesser Jews being denied access to civic rights and social amenities. But such trappings prove to be of little value in 1943, when Mussolini was persuaded by Berlin to participate in the Holocaust.

Although he shoots the authentic locations of his Edenic idyll with a nostalgic soft-focus, De Sica undermines any sense of romanticism by depicting the characters as the damned clinging to a dream that Giorgio first realises is untenable when he meets the Dachau escapee while taking money to his student brother in France. But, he also presents them as neo-realistic figures, who are as much victims of societal injustice as the boys in *Shoeshine*, the bill-sticker in *Bicycle Thieves* and the old man in *Umberto D.* ★★★★ DP

GARDEN STATE (2004)

Starring: *Zach Braff (Andrew 'Large' Largeman), Natalie Portman (Sam), Peter Sarsgaard (Mark), Ian Holm (Dr. Gideon Largeman), Armando Riesco (Jesse), Ron Leibman (Doctor Cohen)*
Director: *Zach Braff*
Screenwriter: *Zach Braff*
15/118 mins./Comedy/Drama/USA

Returning to his New Jersey home for his mother's funeral, moderately successful LA actor Andrew Largeman feels distanced and depressed by his empty life. But a few days spent with free-spirited Sam lead Andrew to reconsider whether his lot is as bad as he thought.

Like scoutmasters with moustaches or anybody holding a clipboard, actors-turned-directors should be treated with suspicion. For every Oscar-worthy Clint Eastwood or Ron Howard, there's an Ethan Hawke or Matt Dillon lurking with some pretentious bilge to throw on an undeserving public. Thankfully, despite being recognisable only from his goofy prat-falling on the US sitcom *Scrubs*, Zach Braff shows little of the self-consciousness that riddles most vanity projects, proving himself a first-time writer-director with a sophisticated eye.

Braff takes the familiar themes of hometown dislocation and middle-youth angst and refreshes them with humour, visual invention and one magic ingredient: Natalie Portman. Clichés be damned; she's a revelation. Okay, she's been a revelation before, but years of duff choices and a staccato vagueness in her *Star Wars* outings suggested her talent had ebbed as hormones set in. Playing Sam, the uninhibited optimist who wafts away Andrew's veil of melancholia and makes him realise life ain't so bad after all, she's entrancingly natural, hilarious and loveable. It was a surprise not to see her among 2004's Best Supporting Actress Oscar nominees.

The film suffers slightly when Portman's energy is absent from the screen – Andrew is a rather more sedate presence – but Braff's peculiar outlook is constantly engaging and surprising. Not only has he an ear for casually witty dialogue, but he can also compose shots of offbeat beauty, suffusing the banal with abstract frivolity (a knight at the breakfast table, an ice-skating alligator) that never come across as trying too hard. He deftly balances the singular journeys of Andrew, Sam and Andrew's aimless acquaintance Mark (the ever terrific Peter Sarsgaard), subtly plaiting them together into a moving whole.

The only time the storytelling falters is when Braff tries to say too much, hammering home what he's already articulated well enough for most of the film: that life is what you make of it. A scene between Andrew and his estranged father (an underused Ian Holm) comes across as pat and unnecessary, but its inclusion only mildly dilutes a great debut from a promising talent. ★★★★ OR

GARDENS OF STONE (1987)

Starring: *James Caan (Sgt. Clell Hazard), Anjelica Huston (Samantha Davis), James Earl Jones (Sgt. Maj. 'Goody' Nelson), D.B. Sweeney (Pvt. Jackie Wilson), Dean Stockwell (Capt. Homer Thomas), Mary Stuart Masterson (Rachel Field), Sam Bottoms (Lt. Webber), Elias Koteas (Pete Deveber), Larry Fishburne (Cpl. Flanagan)*
Director: *Francis Ford Coppola*
Screenwriter: *Ronald Bass based on the novel by Nichoias Proffitt*
15/111 mins./Drama/USA

In the late 60s, veteran sergeant Clell Hazard and ambitious recruit Jackie Willow are chosen for the US army's prestigious Washington Old Guard, burying the Vietnam dead, but Clell would rather be training boys to stay alive and Willow wishes he was off fighting the war.

After the third or fourth collapse of his career, Francis Coppola became a hired gun, emulating his heroes Howard Hawks and John Ford by directing tidy professional films on schedule and under budget. This is a familiar mix of patriotic pride in the great traditions of the American military and numbed inability to make up the national mind about the rights and wrongs of Vietnam.

If anything, the script is too balanced – with Caan being cynical about the war and getting tagged a 'peacenik' by his comrades, Anjelica Huston as a Washington Post reporter who represents the bleeding heart protester worldview and Sweeney as the gung-ho grunt doomed to die in 'Nam. As celebrations of the military go – and there's no denying this is one of those – the film works, with perfectly modulated performances from the whole cast and a fine streak of the sort of NCO hijinx and barroom eulogies found in John Ford cavalry movies.

However, a cynical viewer might remember that Coppola had been making films for five years by the period in which this one is set, and that his original idea of a film for 1968 was *You're a Big Boy Now*, a celebration of the long-haired hell-no-we-won't-go hippie free spirit sneered at by the short-back-and-sides, flag-saluting unforms who carry this movie. If Coppola really meant *Gardens of Stone*, it would have been more courageous to have made it in 1968 rather than wait for the much more conservative, hawkish year of 1987. ★★★ **KN**

GASLIGHT (1944)

Starring: *Charles Boyer (Gregory Anton), Ingrid Bergman (Paula Alquist Anton), Joseph Cotton (Brian Cameron), Dame May Whitty (Miss Bessie Thwaites), Angela Lansbury (Nancy Oliver)*
Director: *George Cukor*
Screenwriters: *John Van Druten, Walter Reisch, John Balderston, based on the play* Angel Street *by Patrick Hamilton*
PG/114 mins./Thriller/USA
Awards: *Academy Awards – Best Actress, Best Black and White Art Direction, Golden Globe – Best Actress*

Returning to the house where her aunt was murdered, Paula Anton is tormented by her husband, who perpetually reprimands her for minor thefts she can't remember committing. Then a detective takes an interest in the old murder case and the new resident of No 9, Thornton Square.

In 1944, Ingrid Bergman took home a Best Actress Oscar for her work as the neurotic, persecuted wife in this thundering Victorian melodrama, based on the play by Patrick Hamilton.

At the heart of the piece is the splendidly cruel scenario of a husband who subtly drives his wife out of her mind in a house suffocating with Victorian clutter, while rooting through the derelict upper floors for some jewels left behind by the murdered aunt.

MGM production gloss, an extra reel of romantic holiday, fussy comedy relief from Dame May Whitty and George Cukor's broad strokes direction make for a less affecting, suspenseful effort than the undervalued 1940 British film version directed by Thorold Dickinson with a magnificently nasty Anton Walbrook turning down the gas on the very frail Diana Wynyard.

If you only see one *Gaslight*, look around for Dickinson's tighter take on the piece, but there's still much to admire in the extravagantly art-directed Hollwyood remounting. Then at the peak of her talent, Bergman has a succession of big, impressive mad scenes that show off her acting muscles – and is given the full Hollywood glamour lighting and costuming to highlight her considerable personal beauty – while a coldly suave Boyer comes alive as he salivates over those jewels and thinks up new ways to make his wife feel wretched. The best work, however, comes from a teenage Angela Lansbury (in her screen debut) as an impudent, sexy-sinister maidservant, undermining her mistress at every turn and pouting to perfection. ★★★ **KN**

GATTACA (1997)

Starring: *Ethan Hawke (Vincent Freeman), Uma Thurman (Irene Cassini), Ernest Borgnine (Caesar), Tony Shalhoub (German), Jude Law (Jerome Eugene Morrow), Alan Arkin (Det. Hugo) Gore Vidal (Director Josef), Elias Koteas (Antonio Freeman), Blair Underwood (Geneticist), Mason Gamble (Vincent Freeman – Boy)*
Director: *Andrew Niccol*
Screenwriter: *Andrew Niccol*
15/101 mins./Drama/Mystery/Sci-fi/Thriller/USA

In the near future, imperfect genetic beings ('in-valids') are forbidden from partaking in the best society can offer, but in-valid Vincent manages to con his way into a top job. Then a murder investigation threatens to expose him . . .

Sci-fi written and directed by first time helmer Andrew Niccol, a vision of the 21st century when genetic engineering is the accepted norm to produce perfect people – and anyone conceived out of love is handicapped by the stigma, labelled an 'in-valid' (geddit?), and barred from social or professional advancement.

The story is the predictably simple one of an in-valid Vincent bucking the system to fulfil his romantic dream of space travel. Gattaca (pronounced gat-a-ka), is the name of the corporation that can put him on a rocket to Titan, Saturn's 14th moon. The twist: in order to escape the system Vincent must first fool it by posing as Jerome, genetically perfect but crippled by an accident, so now bitter and willing to sell his bodily fluid, and tissue samples to allow Vincent to pass the constant ID tests required to work at Gattaca.

And so against a backstory of Vincent's remembered parallel struggle against a genetically superior brother, he passes all the tests, works at Gattaca and watches rockets lift-off, longing for his turn. He falls in love with co-worker Irene and all goes well until his boss is murdered and forensics find an in-valid's eyelash, prompting a search for the cuckoo in the hitherto perfect Gattaca nest.

It's a great set-up but sadly the plot unfolds slowly and with little action, playing like a short story. Visually, Niccol's vision of the 21st century is intriguing, returning to a classically 40s style with slick haircuts, plain clothes, and electric cars that look like Citroëns. A Frank Lloyd Wright building, doubling for Gattaca H.Q., confirms the vision of a future that is sparse and functional, with only men and women as beautiful as Hawke and Thurman to look forward to. *Blade Runner* neon or *Fifth Element* chaos don't get a look-in.

Instead it's chiefly a tense head vs. heart struggle with Hawke, ironically, almost blandly perfect and Law's bitter cripple the most exciting performance. There's good support from Alan Arkin as the homicide detective but for all its style and promise, *Gattaca* is far easier to look at than actually watch. ★★★ **AC**

THE GAY DIVORCEE (1934)

Starring: *Fred Astaire (Guy Holden), Ginger Rogers (Mimi Glossop), Alice Brady (Hortense Ditherwell), Edward Everett Horton (Egbert Fitzgerald), Erik Rhodes (Rodolfo Tonetti), Eric Blore (Walter)*
Director: *Mark Sandrich*
Screenwriters: *George Marlon Jr, Dorothy Yost Edward Kaufman based on the musical play* The Gay Divorce *by Dwight Taylor and Cole Porter*
U/107 mins./Musical/USA
Academy Awards: *Best Song (The Continental)*

Mimi Glossop mistakes dancer Guy Holden for Rodolfo Tonetti when she arrives with her aunt, Hortense Ditherwell, in the English seaside resort of Brightbourne to meet the co-respondent hired to secure her divorce.

Realising they had stumbled on to a star teaming in *Flying Down to Rio*, RKO announced that Fred Astaire and Ginger Rogers would reunite in *Radio City Revels*. However, while scribes struggled to come up with a scenario to fit the title, someone in the front office suggested acquiring the rights to Cole Porter's stage hit, *The Gay Divorce*, as Fred had already scored with it on Broadway and in London. Initially, Astaire didn't think Ginger had the class to play the female lead and suggested the studio found an English type. However, he was more concerned about becoming bound into another partnership so soon after breaking with his now-retired sister, Adele. But once *The Gay Divorcee* (whose title was changed to mollify a Hays Office keen not to make marital break-up sound too attractive) became a box-office smash and RKO realised it had devised a new form of intimate musical comedy, Fred and Ginger's fates were sealed.

They only dance for around 10 minutes in the whole picture, as it adhered closely to the operetta strategy of twinning the romantic leads with a comic pair whose relationship mirrors that of the stars. Thus, Alice Brady and Edward Everett Horton (as Fred's lawyer pal, Egbert Fitzgerald) are accorded their own set-pieces, as were Erik Rhodes and Eric Blore, as a fussy waiter. Indeed, Everett Horton even got his own musical showcase, 'Let's K-nock K-neez', which he shared with the up-and-coming Betty Grable.

All but one of Porter's original songs were dropped, but 'Night and Day' remains one of Fred'n'Ginger's finest duets and established the seduction dance as his way of winning her heart. Astaire's solo, 'A Needle in a Haystack', is also memorable, as it had all the balletic grace of a slapstick routine, as he cavorted around his dressing-room. But, while 'The Continental' won the inaugural Oscar for Best Song, it was an elongated ensemble affair that lacked any of the élan that Busby Berkeley invested into his 'variation on a theme' showstoppers. ★★★ **DP**

THE GENERAL (1927)

Starring: *Marion Mack (Annablle Lee), Charles Henry Smith (Mr. Lee, Annabelle's father), Richard Allen (Annabelle's brother), Glen Cavender (Union Capt. Anderson), Buster Keaton (Johnny Gray)*
Directors: *Clyde Bruckman, Buster Keaton*
Screenwriters: *Clyde Bruckman, Buster Keaton*
U/75 mins./Comedy/Romance/War/Action/USA

When Union spies steal an engineer's beloved locomotive, he pursues it single handedly and straight through enemy lines.

'Love, locomotives and laughs' promised the posters for Buster Keaton's Civil War epic. It was a succinct and accurate summary. Buster, on incomparable form, plays dependable railroad engineer Johnny Gray, a man who is devoted to two things: his beloved locomotive, The General, and his sweetheart Annabelle. When war breaks out Johnny is keen to impress his girl by joining the Confederate army. Deemed more use as an engineer, however, he is rejected. Annabelle believes he has shirked his manly duty and refuses to speak to him. A year later a band of enemy raiders steal The General and plan to drive it into Union territory, destroying Confederate supply lines as they go. Outraged, Johnny leaps into the cab of another locomotive and sets off in hot pursuit, unaware that Annabelle is being held prisoner on board the stolen train.

What follows is, arguably, one of the greatest screen comedies ever made. In advance of a ritzy New York premiere, *The General* was previewed at the California Theatre in San José, California, on October 22, 1926. It was a star-studded event and, fittingly, the filmfolk steamed into town aboard the Lark, the legendary all-Pullman service that plied the overnight route from Los Angeles to Portland, Oregon. The Hollywood crowd were put up at the luxurious Sainte Claire Hotel where a mood of cautious optimism can well be imagined.

There was a lot riding on the San José preview. *The General* was Keaton's pet project and he had lavished enormous amounts of time and money on it. The film, among the most expensive of its day, was shot entirely on location in Oregon, which offered both magnificent scenery and stretches of the single-gauge railway track needed for the antique locomotives. The wood-burning engines were authentic in every detail, as was everything else about the production. At Buster's behest, no expense was spared. The train that crashes through a burning bridge into the riverbed below was a genuine Civil War locomotive. The scene was filmed in a single take and the mangled engine remained where it lay for many years, becoming a local tourist attraction.

Keaton based the look of the film on the haunting Civil War photographs of Mathew Brady, just as Spielberg took visual cues from Frank Capra's still photography and George Stevens' 16mm footage of WWII for *Saving Private Ryan*. The results are astounding, without doubt the most evocative and authentic depiction of the Civil War on film – D.W. Griffith's *The Birth Of A Nation* doesn't come close, and Victor Fleming's *Gone With The Wind* is a travesty by comparison.

Keaton had made features before, but never anything on this scale. It was still a comedy of course and his timeless everyman persona and supreme talents as a physical comedian shone through. But the slapstick was more gentle than usual and played out against an extravagant backdrop. The danger, and Buster knew it, was that the majestic locations, the chase scenes and the historical setting would overshadow the very thing the public came to see: him. It was a gamble, and it did not pay off. The morning after the out-of-town screening, Josephine Hughston in the San José Mercury-Herald wrote: 'There is a feeble plot of a sort and considerable rather pointless comedy, although some of it is really funny.'

Film criticism was not, as you can see, the arena of sparkling wit and insight it has since become. Nevertheless, Ms. Hughston's review, an echo of the broader audience reaction for all its clumsy phraseology, was enough to send Keaton and United Artists into a panic. Fearing that the New York premiere would elicit a similar yet more damaging response, UA took the unprecedented step of releasing the film in Japan. It debuted in December 1926 under the title *Keaton, Shogun* and did good business. However, it was a brief respite. *The General* finally opened in the United States to critical indifference and disappointing box-office.

Tagline
Love, locomotives and laughs.

Although far from the disaster historians have proclaimed it, the film's tepid reception must have been a crushing blow to Keaton. For him it had been a labour of love and he had poured his heart and soul into it. Shortly after *The General* was released he sacrificed his independent status for a contract with Metro-Goldwyn-Mayer. It was the worst decision of his career. Selling his soul to producer Joe Schenck (whose brother Nicholas ran MGM) Keaton was forced to stand by while the studio systematically shut him out of the creative process. It was a desperately unhappy union and led directly to Keaton's battle with the booze (a battle, it is seldom noted, that he won against insuperable odds).

Now that *The General* has taken its rightful place in the pantheon, it's difficult to see why contemporary audiences found it so easy to resist. The gags don't come as thick and fast as pie-in-the-face aficionados might have liked, but when they do they are perfectly choreographed and impeccably timed. And Keaton's nimble stunt work was never better. The Civil War setting was a significant stumbling block. The conflict remained in living memory and mining it for laughs was looked on as rubbing salt into wounds. Even so, Buster was careful not to address political issues – unlike Griffith, whose *Birth Of A Nation* was repulsively biased. The most credible explanation is that audiences were simply put off by the low ratio of gags to action. If so, in search of a few jokes, they tossed aside a masterpiece, the magnum opus of a man who, when Chaplin's sentimental crown finally topples, may well emerge as the finest filmmaker of the silent era. In which case, they fully deserved both the execrable *The Jazz Singer* and The Great Depression. ★★★★★ **SB**

THE GENERAL (1998)

Starring: *Brendan Gleeson (Martin Cahill), Adrian Dunbar (Noel Curley), Sean McGinley (Gary), Maria Doyle Kennedy (Frances), Angeline Ball (Tina), Jon Voight (Inspector Ned Kenny)*
Director: *John Boorman*
Screenwriter: *John Boorman, based on the novel by Paul Williams*
15/124 mins./Drama/Crime/U.K./Ireland

The real-life story of Dublin folk hero and criminal Martin Cahill, who master-minded two daring robberies in Ireland, but attracted unwanted attention from the police, the IRA, the UVF and members of his own team.

Put together for next to nothing on the good name of its writer-director-producer John Boorman, *The General*, shot in lustrous black-and-white, is the extraordinary true story of Dublin folk hero and wanted-man Martin Cahill.

Working contrary to the crateloads of wistful comedies and political deadpans that creak out of Ireland each month, this manages hard edged and comedic, a convincing character study, that doesn't concern itself with upending the political strife of that fair isle. It's easy to see how Boorman became so passionate about his subject; Cahill's short but jam-packed tenure in the world was that of a modern-day Robin Hood. He laughed in the face of the establishment in his quest for bent cash, notoriety and a nifty alibi.

Structured around two spectacular heists, the script reconstructs his greatest exploits, depicting a man loyal to family and his working class community and who, in the support of his off-centre values, was quite capable of sadistic brutality. Gleeson is superb as Cahill, allowing his incredible spirit and criminal guile while ceding the essential brazen naïvety that was his unmaking. In support, there is a host of familiar Irish faces; Maria Doyle Kennedy and Angeline Ball from *The Commitments* (as his wife and her sister, both of whom mothered his children), Adrian Dunbar and Sean McGinley leading his gang, plus Jon Voight, delivering a solid accent and lack of pretence in the foil role of Cahill's cop nemesis Ned Kennedy.

It gets cramped by its black-and-white artiness (after all, Cahill is the very epitome of a colourful character) and Boorman is never completely secure about where his moral ground lies. Minor quibbles, though. ★★★★ **IN**

GENEVIEVE (1953)

Starring: *John Gregson (Alan McKim), Dinah Sheridan (Wendy McKim), Kenneth More (Ambrose Claverhouse), Kay Kendall (Rosalind Peters),*
Director: *Henry Cornelius*
Screenwriter: *William Rose*
U/86 mins./Comedy/UK
Awards: *BAFTA – Best British Film*

Barrister Alan McKim and his wife, bicker their way to Brighton in their 1904 Darracq, as they race against insufferable advertising executive Ambrose Claverhouse and his free-spirited girlfriend, Rosalind Peters, in their 1904 Spyker.

Although it was produced by Rank, this timeless comedy coasted to success in the Ealing slipstream. Director Henry Cornelius had served a five-year apprenticeship at the studio before directing one of its legendary comedies, *Passport to Pimlico*, while John Gregson had featured in *The Titfield Thunderbolt*, another celebration of vehicular heritage, this time involving a steam train. Indeed, Cornelius even offered William Rose's screenplay to Michael Balcon, but the Ealing chief decided he had too many comedies on the go and passed (although he would learn his lesson and hired Rose for both *The Maggie*, and *The Lavender Hill Mob*).

Even Rank placed only cursory faith in the project, presenting Cornelius with such a miserly budget that he had to shoot most of the picture on the roads around Pinewood and only managed a couple of days each in London and Brighton, for the start and climax of the veteran car rally that provides the backdrop to the Darracq-Spyker wager.

Yet, what resulted was Britain's best-loved road movie, which also doubled as satire on male posturing that was made all the more amusing by the fact that the quaint antiquity of the motors undercut Alan and Ambrose's machismo and emphasised their bourgeois gentility. Ably capturing the obsessiveness of the enthusiast, Gregson is both a boor and a bore and he's perfectly complemented by Dinah Sheridan's feisty loyalty, Kenneth More's affable arrogance and Kay Kendall's maverick charm. Indeed, everything looks so relaxed, with the humour emerging from both the character contrasts and situations that remained within the bounds of probability.

Adding to this freewheeling atmosphere was Larry Adler's harmonica score (for which Muir Mathieson received an Oscar nomination, as Adler was blacklisted in Hollywood). But what makes *Genevieve* so remarkable was that it was written by an American and directed by a South African and yet its insights into the British psyche match Ealing at its best. ★★★★ **DP**

GENTLEMEN PREFER BLONDES (1953)

Starring: *Jane Russell (Dorothy), Marilyn Monroe (Lorelei), Charles Coburn (Sir Francis Beekman), Elliott Reid (Malone), Tommy Noonan (Gus Esmond), George 'Foghorn' Winslow (Henry Spofford III)*
Director: *Howard Hawks*
Screenwriter: *Charles Lederer based on the play by Anita Loos, Joseph Fields*
U/91 mins./Comedy/Musical/USA

Dorothy Shaw and Lorelei Lee are two little girls from Little Rock, whose trip to Europe is complicated by Lorelei's flirtation with Sir Francis Beekman and Dorothy's discovery that Malone is spying on her gold-digging pal for her fiancé Gus Esmond's father.

Marilyn Monroe was very nervous about this follow-up to the star-making *Niagara*, as she wasn't sure she was up to the challenge of either the musical numbers or the deadpan comedy. However, just as he had done with Katharine Hepburn on *Bringing Up Baby*, Howard Hawks guided Monroe towards her new screen persona and, in the process, subjected her to a total make-over to transform her from a pin-up into a star.

Inheriting a role for which Betty Grable was now deemed too old, Monroe departed from Anita Loos' stage character to achieve a brand of innocent sensuality that was to become her trademark. But much of the credit goes to Hawks, who moulded her curves and charm to create a new kind of sex kitten, who was much less threatening than such blonde bombshells as Jean Harlow and Mae West.

Indeed, he gave all the acerbic wisecracks to the sturdier Jane Russell, so that Monroe's humour seemed to be almost accidental (as it would do again in *How to Marry a Millionaire*). Yet, she worked hard to accomplish this spontaneity, with choreographer Jack Cole putting her through rigorous rehearsals.

However, the look of her most iconic number, 'Diamonds Are A Girl's Best Friend', came about by chance, as Monroe had attracted such negative publicity after attending an awards ceremony in the gold lamé dress she wore in the movie that Fox insisted on ditching her original costume (a flesh-coloured leotard strategically studded with gems) for the pink gown that gave the routine its kitsch class (which was hijacked by Madonna for her 'Material Girl' video).

The plot meanders once the principals reach Paris, with Russell's romance with Elliott Reed refusing to catch light. But she provides a selfless foil for Monroe's giddy scene-stealing and Charles Coburn turns in another polished display of harmless lechery. ★★ **DP**

GEORGE OF THE JUNGLE (1997)

Starring: *Brendan Fraser (George, the King of the Jungle), Leslie Mann (Ursula Stanhope), Thomas Haden Church (Lyle van de Groot), John Cleese (An Ape Named Ape – voice), Richard Roundtree (Kwame, Traveling Sidekick), Greg Cruttwell (Max), Abraham Benrubi (Thor), Keith Scott (Narrator)*
Director: *Sam Weisman*
Screenwriters: *Audrey Wells, Dana Olsen, based on a story by Dana Olsen and characters by Jay Ward*
PG/92 mins./Family/Adventure/Comedy/USA

In this spoof of Tarzan, orphan George is raised by apes in the African jungle but decides to head for the city when he's attracted to an exploring American heiress . . .

Anyone familiar with the Tarzan spoof cartoon series will remember the theme jingle's punchline, 'Watch out for that treeeeee!'. George, the eternal klutz, remains oblivious. It is one of the few irritants in a jolly wheeze that George's vine swinging invariably results in a cajones-crushing collision – a gag that runs past exhaustion. Otherwise this is a good giggle that operates efficiently on two levels, one for kids and one for those alive to irony.

From his swell treehouse, George enjoys an idyllic domain, fellowship with the wildlife, and mythic status. Enter the expedition of pretty heiress Ursula Stanhope and her environmentally unfriendly fiancé, whose hip, superior African guide (Richard 'Shaft' Roundtree) and porters sustain a hilariously smart-assed running commentary in subtitled Swahili. After the swinger and the girl get acquainted, she's charmed by his lifestyle, impressed by his, um, personality (Fraser looks pretty darn good in a buttflap) and delighted, as are we, by pets including a cute capering CGI elephant calf.

Embroiled in foiling the schemes of the fiancé, the duo also take a trip to San Francisco, providing a *Pretty Woman*-like shopping expedition in which the jungleman is pleased to learn he looks good in Armani.

The cast play it sprightly amid cartoon bright settings and snappy comedic action, with the wittier gags largely falling to narrator, who provides knowing observations and links ('Meanwhile, at a very expensive waterfall set ...'). John Cleese is an added joy as the voice of George's smarter ape brother. Fraser is comic, hunky and engaging, the CGI, puppet and real animals are a treat, and the good-natured humour seldom falters. Very amusing fun. ★★★ **AE**

GEORGE WASHINGTON (2000)

Starring: *Candace Evanofski (Nasia), Donald Holden (George), Damian Jewan Lee (Vernon), Curtis Cotton III (Buddy), Rachael Handy (Sonya), Paul Schneider (Rico Rice)*
Director: *David Gordon Green*
Screenwriter: *David Gordon Green*
12/89 mins./Drama/USA

A fragile boy refuses to let his health problems limit his career aspirations.

An accidental death and a hidden corpse provide the impetus for this determinedly offbeat study of impoverished youth. But David Gordon Green's debut is resolutely focused on character.

At the hub of events is Nasia, a precocious African-American girl who dumps her cocky boyfriend for George, a timid pre-teen who channels his presidential aspirations into being a traffic-directing superhero – in spite of the fact that his skull is so soft he risks death if he so much as gets it wet.

These are lives that have dead-ended before they've had a chance to begin and Green deserves credit if nothing else, for daring to portray American childhood with such grim resignation. ★★★★ **JB**

GEORGY GIRL (1966)

Starring: *James Mason (James Leamington), Alan Bates (Jos), Lynn Redgrave (Georgy), Charlotte Rampling (Meredith), Bill Owen (Ted), Clare Kelly (Doris)*
Director: *Silvio Narizzano*
Screenwriter: *Margaret Forster, Peter Nichols based on the novel by Forster*
15/100 mins./Comedy/Drama/UK

Resisting the advances of her parents' boss, James Leamington, virginal children's dance instructor Georgy finds herself falling for Jos, the genially shallow boyfriend of her reluctantly pregnant flatmate, Meredith.

Although the swinging London scene has come to represent the popular image of 1960s Britain, the majority of people endured a far more humdrum reality. Everyday life felt more like a Wednesday Play than an Austin Powers picture and this adaptation of Margaret Forster's novel cleverly draws on contemporary movies for its tone.

In many ways, it's the female flip side of *Alfie*, with Georgy taking a more responsible attitude to relationships, and the suburban counterbalance to *Darling*, with Georgy similarly caught between an older mentor and a younger suitor who may not be as suitable as he seems. There's even a hint of *A Taste of Honey* and such tele-dramas as *Cathy Come Home* and *Up The Junction* in the story's discussion of gender, class and morality. Yet, James Mason's presence also draws comparisons with *Lolita* and *Spring And Port Wine*, with the latter's sense of stern patriarchy recurring in Bill Owen's martinet father.

But, regardless of its myriad influences, *Georgy Girl* very much has its own character, thanks to Lynn Redgrave's Oscar-nominated performance. Her good-hearted, self-doubting acceptance of everyone else's foibles and failings makes her irresistibly attractive. Yet director Silvio Narizzano never wholly demonises the other members of the central quartet, despite the seediness of Mason's machinations, the delusional hopelessness of Alan Bates' daydreams and the selfish hedonism of Charlotte Rampling's reckless response to the baby that Redgrave ends up rearing as her own.

It may have its roots firmly in the Kitchen Sink tradition, but this also reflects the social aspiration encouraged by Harold Wilson's Labour government. Consequently, it embraces the manners and mores of the celebrity set (the debuting Rampling, for example, was dressed by happening designer, Mary Quant), while also recognising the options that newly emancipated women were becoming less afraid to take. It's certainly a film long overdue reappraisal. ★★★★ **DP**

GERRY (2002)

Starring: *Casey Affleck (Gerry), Matt Damon (Gerry)*
Director: *Gus Van Sant*
Screenwriters: *Casey Affleck, Matt Damon, Gus Van Sant*
15/103 mins./Drama/Adventure/US/Argentina/Jordan

Awards: *Cannes Film Festival – Palme D'Or*

Two nice, dumb, young Americans get lost in the desert and spend a very long time trying to find their way out, passing through sand dunes, salt flats, mountains, good humours and spite, as well as physical and mental exhaustion.

Recent winner of the Palme D'Or for *Elephant*, Gus Van Sant's other new movie tells the story of two woefully unprepared orienteers, both called Gerry.

The pair pull off the highway during a long road trip for a stint of unspecified sightseeing. They begin trekking towards said sights, deviating from the hikers' route, and strike out across a scrubby desert. They whoop and rugby tackle each other until they are completely disorientated, then try to find their way back.

They fail, of course, and spend the next hour or so trying to stave off their hunger, thirst and mutual hatred as they try to make their way back to civilisation.

Very little actually happens, but if you are patient enough to sit through it, you'll catch some stunning scenery, as well as the occasional bit of engaging improvisation and interplay from the actors. That certainly whiles away the first 45 minutes or so, but then it does drag somewhat. ★★★ **AR**

GET CARTER (1971)

Starring: *Michael Caine (Jack Carter), Ian Hendry (Eric Paice), Britt Ekland (Anna Fletcher), John Osborne (Cyril Kinnear), Tony Beckley (Peter)*
Director: *Mike Hodges*
Screenwriter: *Mike Hodges, based on the novel* Jack's Return Home *by Ted Lewis*
18/111 mins./Crime/UK

When his brother dies under mysterious circumstances in a car accident, London gangster Jack Carter travels to Newcastle to investigate.

Get Carter was intended to be very violent. Michael Caine recently remarked, 'It looks like *Mary Poppins* now.' But it doesn't. In fact, it's surprising how hard-hitting and brutal *Get Carter* still is, even in these desensitised times.

London hitman Jack Carter revisits his Newcastle upon Tyne birthplace after the mysterious death of his brother Frank. He enters a seedy world of porn, corruption and murder, eventually joining the dots between 'Mr. Big' Cyril Kinnear, slot-machine magnate Cliff Brumby and scumbag chauffeur Eric Paice. Though warned off, Carter connives and strong-arms his way to the awful truth.

Adapted from the novel *Jack's Return Home* by Ted Lewis (interestingly, set in an unnamed steel town), *Get Carter* can be viewed as a pale, drizzly imitation of Raymond Chandler – director Hodges even throws in a copy of *Farewell My Lovely* to head off facile comparisons – but in its desperately grim north-eastern setting and the casual stylishness of its cruelty, it creates a semi-mythic world all of its own. Though Caine exudes cool (only really losing his composure during the coal-cart climax), his heartlessness and contempt for women are never neatly redeemed.

This is a gangster film without the laughs of *Lock Stock And Two Smoking Barrels*, the pop of *Pulp Fiction* or the theatre of *The Godfather* – a landmark British thriller that deserves more than just kitsch appreciation for having *Corrie*'s Alf Roberts and one always-misquoted famous line in it. It's violent without buckets of blood, sexy without being explicit, and contains a revelatory sequence with a film projector that trumps *8mm*. 'Clever sod, aren't you?' says one lowlife to Carter. 'Only comparatively,' he replies. ★★★★★ **NJ**

GET SHORTY (1995)

Starring: *John Travolta (Chili Palmer), Gene Hackman (Harry Zimm), Rene Russo (Karen Flores), Danny DeVito (Martin Weir), Dennis Farina (Ray 'Bones' Barboni), James Gandolfini (Bear)*
Director: *Barry Sonnenfeld*
Screenwriter: *Scott Frank, based on the novel by Elmore Leonard*
15/105 mins./Comedy/Crime/USA

Awards: *Golden Globes – Best Comedy/Musical Actor*

A Miami loan shark heads to Hollywood hoping to make it big in the movies.

The Quentin Tarantino backlash stops here. How come? Well, although Hollywood's hip young gunslinger isn't actually named or indeed involved in *Get Shorty*, it is surely the first major motion picture to truly surf the waves of his phenomenon. In the first instance, *Reservoir Dogs* totally re-activated the old-fashioned crime caper movie in an age of sex-mad 'psychological' thrillers, and *Get Shorty*, from the novel by hard-boiled crime supremo Elmore Leonard, reverberates with a *Dogs*ian level of wiseguy humour. Second, *Pulp Fiction* totally reactivated John Travolta, whose presence in this film is ten feet tall. His character, the one-and-a-half-bit Miami loan shark Chili Palmer, may as well be Vincent Vega's down-at-heel brother for all of his essentially good-natured menace, sharp suits and nerdish attention to detail.

Palmer, despatched to Hollywood to track down missing-presumed-rich life insurance scamster Leo Devoe, becomes embroiled in the bottom end of the moviemaking business when he meets up with cheesy producer Harry Zimm. Keen to leave behind Florida and a reasonably successful career in strong-arming, Palmer begins to harbour dreams of moguldom. He romantically links himself with B-movie pumpstress Karen Flores, and subsequently schmoozes self-obsessed, cod-method superstar Martin Weir to appear in his movie based on a 'fictional' pitch about a missing-presumed rich insurance scamster etc. Palmer is a big-time film buff – in one scene, having beaten up stuntman-turned-bruiser Bear, he eagerly asks him to name what movies he's been in.

The fabulously location-rich *Get Shorty*, as likeable a slice of mob hokum as *True Romance* (but without the gruesome violence), looks wonderful, the garish pinks and yellows of Miami poignantly contrasted by *Addams Family*-man Sonnenfeld with the sun-bleached, roller-blind cool of Los Angeles. Against this sumptuous background, a complex, back-stabbing Tinseltown farce that recognises both *The Player* and *Ed Wood* is delightfully played out, not least by a cap-toothed, medallion-swingin' Hackman. Travolta, unsurprisingly, is unputdownable, nabbing all the best dialogue – he suggests a trip to see *A Touch Of Evil*, to 'go and watch Charlton Heston be a Mexican', and describes his hired vehicle as 'the Cadillac of mini-vans' so infectiously, the impressionable DeVito gets himself one.

By turns satirically glamorous and seedily dark, *Get Shorty*'s stylistic success will surely spell a deluge of Leonard adaptations. Let's hope they're as engaging and original as this one. And long may Tarantino watch over us. ★★★★ **AC**

THE GETAWAY (1972)

Starring: *Steve McQueen (Doc McCoy), Ali McGraw (Carol McCoy), Ben Johnson (Jack Benyon), Sally Struthers (Fran Clinton), Al Lettieri (Rudy Butler), Slim Pickens (Cowboy)*
Director: *Sam Peckinpah*
Screenwriter: *Walter Hill, based on the novel by Jim Thompson*
18/122 mins./Crime/USA

Doc McCoy is released from prison thanks to the influence of a big-time gangster and ordered to carry out a robbery. Doc and his wife take the money and head for the Mexican border, pursued by a vengeful thug.

This streamlined road-gangster film allows Sam Peckinpah to integrate the themes and style of his Westerns into a contemporary setting. In a modern West of motels and cactus malls, Peckinpah allows McQueen to demonstrate cowboy cool and calls on the services of a few old-time character actors (like the wonderful Slim Pickens and an uncharacteristically evil Ben Johnson).

Peckinpah's status as a poet of carnage is confirmed by abstract use of the pump shotgun as an instrument of picturesque destruction, while there are textbook incidences of suspense as McQueen hunts down a pickpocket who has stolen a suitcase full of loot or sees off the hit men who launch an assault on his seedy hotel hide-out. In adapting Jim Thompson's hard-boiled novel, Peckinpah comes close to displaying his rare sentimental streak in the understated but affecting depiction of the relationship between the bank robber hero and his devoted wife (McGraw), which captures the uneasiness of a life outside the law but also conveys the couple's commitment to each other.

Indeed, the romantic teaming is so potent that screenwriter Walter Hill (who also had a credit on the Alec Baldwin-Kim Basinger remake) has to omit the novel's cynical last chapter, in which the characters are trapped in a Mexican hell-hole which swallows their personalities, though Peckinpah's *Bring Me The Head Of Alfredo Garcia* might be seen as a feature-length elaboration of the Thompson sketch. Al Lettieri, the premier moustached brute of the 1970s, is memorably appalling as a very bad sort on the trail of the outlaw hero. ★★★★ **KN**

TOP10

Dialogue People Often Get Wrong

1 ***White Heat* (1949)**
Who Says It: *Arthur Cody Jarrett (Cagney)*
What people say: *'Look, Ma, I'm on top of the world!'*
Actual Line: *'Made it, Ma, to the top of the world, Ma!'*

2 ***Casablanca* (1942)**
Who Says It: *Rick Blaine (Humphrey Bogart)*
What people say: *'Play it again, Sam.'*
Actual line: *'Play it.'*

3 ***Taxi Driver* (1976)**
Who Says it: *Travis Bickle (Robert De Niro)*
What people say: *'Are you lookin' at me?'*
Actual line: *'Are you talkin' to me?'*

4 ***Get Carter* (1971)**
Who Says It: *Carter (Michael Caine)*
What People Say: *'You're a big man, but you're out of shape.'*
Actual line: *'You're a big man, but you're in bad shape.'*

5 ***On The Waterfront* (1954)**
Who Says It: *Terry Malloy (Marlon Brando)*
What People Say: *'I coulda been a contender. I coulda had class. I coulda been somebody.'*
Actual line: *'I coulda had class. I coulda been a contender. I coulda been somebody.'*

6 ***She Done Him Wrong* (1933)**
Who Says It: *Lady Lou (Mae West)*
What People Say: *'Come up and see me some time.'*
Actual line: *'Why don't you come up some time and see me?'*

7 ***The Virginian* (1929)**
Who Says It: *The Virginian (Gary Cooper)*
What People Say: *'Smile when you say that.'*
Actual line: *'If you want to call me that, smile.'*

8 ***The Godfather* (1972)**
Who Says It: *Michael Corleone (Al Pacino)*
What People Say: *'I made him an offer he couldn't refuse.'*
Actual line: *'My father made him an offer he couldn't refuse.'*

9 ***Star Wars* (1977)**
Who Says It: *Caption at the start of the film*
What People Say: *'Long ago, in a galaxy far, far, away ...'*
Actual line: *'A long time ago, in a galaxy far, far away ...*

10 ***Monty Python's Life of Brian* (1979)**
Who Says It: *Brian Cohen (Graham Chapman) and Reg (John Cleese)*
What People Say: *'Are you the People's Front of Judea?'; 'Fuck off! We're the Judean Peoples' Front.'*
Actual line: *'Are you the Judean People's Front?'; 'Fuck off! What? Judean Peoples' Front? We're the People's Front of Judea.'*

◑ THE GETAWAY (1994)

Starring: *Alec Baldwin (Carter 'Doc' McCoy), Kim Basinger (Carol McCoy), Michael Madsen (Rudy Travis), James Woods (Jack Benyon), David Morse (Jim Deer Jackson), Jennifer Tilly (Fran Carvey), Philip Seymour Hoffman (Frank Hansen)*
Director: *Roger Donaldson*
Screenwriters: *Walter Hill, Amy Holden Jones*
18/115 mins./Crime/Thriller/USA/Japan

Doc McCoy is released from prison thanks to the influence of a big-time gangster and ordered to carry out a robbery. Doc and his wife take the money and head for the Mexican border, pursued by a vengeful thug.

An exact remake of the 1972 Sam Peckinpah thriller, which essentially reshoots the old Walter Hill script. Roger Donaldson turns out quite an acceptable actioner, though its use of criminal outlaw heroes is more amoral than existential and the ghost of Bloody Sam is impossible to compete with.

It's at its best in the simple suspense sequences, like the supercriminal hero's pursuit of an opportunist petty crook who has happened to steal the suitcase with the loot from his wife on a train. Kim Basinger is quite often cast in the decorative-but-uninteresting way Ali McGraw was in the 1970s, but delivers a far better performance than Ali did – perhaps because Amy Jones has been brought in to do a light rewrite and punch up the woman's role. Baldwin is competent in a variation on his Miami Blues criminal role, but doesn't come within a hundred degrees of that special Steve McQueen cool. Even reliables like James Woods and Michael Madsen can't best memories of the readings of their roles given by Ben Johnson and Al Lettieri, though Richard Farnsworth does a nice homage to Slim Pickens.

A good rule of thumb is 'don't remake it if you haven't got anything new to say' and, though this is by no means an atrocious disaster, it's hard not to feel cheated by such a refried movie. ★★★ **KN**

◑ GHOST (1990)

Starring: *Patrick Swayze (Sam Wheat), Demi Moore (Molly Jensen), Whoopi Goldberg (Oda Mae Brown), Tony Goldwyn (Carl Bruner), Rick Aviles (Willie Lopez), Gail Boggs (Louise Brown), Amelia McQueen (Clara Brown), Vincent Schiavelli (Subway Ghost)*
Director: *Jerry Zucker*
Screenwriters: *Bruce Joel Rubin*
15/128 mins./Fantasy/Romance/USA

Awards: *Academy Awards – Best Supporting Actress, Best Original Screenplay, BAFTA – Best Supporting Actress, Golden Globes – Best Supporting Actress*

Sam Wheat pops his clogs, finds himself in dead-man's limbo and tries to contact his lover Molly by enlisting psychic Oda Mae.

In 1990, while Ghost and Pretty Woman battled it out at the box offices of the world, here in the UK it was an altogether very different story. Pretty Woman did indeed fare very well, grossing nearly £12 million. Jerry Zucker's Ghost, however, quite simply smashed all box office records at that time to bring in more than £22 million and become the most successful film ever to be released in the UK at that time.

It's easy to see why. Ghost has a number of elements that make it virtually irresistible, namely Zucker's deft comic touch which expertly avoids sentimentality, Whoopi Goldberg's legendary – and, of course, Oscar-winning – performance as the so-far-over-the-top-she's-down-the-other-side Oda Mae Brown and Demi Moore's ability to cry in a sexier fashion than anyone in recent history.

The story is simple, but it's not so much the tale as the telling of it that has enraptured audiences throughout the world – and it is abundantly clear that while the rest of Hollywood was trying to do a Batman, Zucker had his finger on a far more universal pulse.

And so, with chocolates, mansize tissues and, preferably, the one you love all within grabbing distance, Ghost is the film to round off that perfect evening of slush. You had, as the tagline suggests, better believe it ★★★★ **PT**

◑ THE GHOST AND MRS MUIR (1947)

Starring: *Gene Tierney (Lucy), Rex Harrison (The Ghost of Capt. Daniel Gregg), George Sanders (Miles Fairley), Edna Best (Martha), Vanessa Brown (Anna), Natalie Wood (Anna as a child)*
Director: *Joseph L. Mankiewicz*
Screenwriter: *Phillip Dunne, based on the novel by R.A. Dick*
U/104 mins./Romance/Fantasy/USA

Widow Lucy Muir escapes her smothering in-laws and rents Gull Cottage, a seaside home complete with the ghost of a former owner, Captain Gregg. The repressed living woman and the passionate spectre clash, but fall in love.

Even audiences resolutely unmoved by Patrick Swayze's undying love for Demi Moore in Ghost are liable to be reduced to helpless blubbing by the finale of this 1947 supernatural romance.

Gene Tierney's perfect face is even more gorgeous when seen through a mist of sentimental tears, while Rex Harrison is ideal as the crusty but inwardly sensitive sea dog who lurks around her rented cottage. Caddish George Sanders is the young widow's appealingly cynical living (and married) suitor, but she spends her whole life waiting for the post-mortem union with the bearded, suave soul-mate she has almost persuaded herself is only a dream.

The comic elements played up in the 1968 TV sit-com version with Edward Mulhare and Hope Lange are present in the near-knockabout first half, which emphasises mildly risqué banter between the leads and supernatural shenanigans as the ghost scares off interlopers, but director Joseph L. Mankiewicz is ultimately concerned with tugging the heartstrings with the impossible romance.

An eerily evocative Bernard Herrmann score and Charles Lang's luminous photography of a Californian imitation of the English coast add to the atmosphere of magic, but the very tasteful Mankiewicz also uses masterly art direction to characterise the ghost through the warm, appealing interiors of Gull Cottage.

Mounted with all the glamour 20th Century-Fox could muster, this is one of those movies that reminds you how good Hollywood used to be with faces, as Lang's gorgeous monochrome close-ups of Tierney and Harrison fill the screen.

A single flaw is Natalie Wood's too-American moppet, but all the other character players are perfect. ★★★★ **KN**

◑ GHOST DOG: THE WAY OF THE SAMURAI (1999)

Starring: *Forest Whitaker (Ghost Dog), John Tormey (Louie), Cliff Gorman (Sonny Valerio), Dennis Liu (Chinese Restaurant Owner), Frank Minucci (Big Angie), Damon Whitaker (Young Ghost Dog)*
Director: *Jim Jarmusch*
Screenwriter: *Jim Jarmusch*
15/116 mins./Action/Comedy/Drama/USA/France

A bird-loving hit man, finds himself distracted from his chosen career by a mob boss' daughter and his desire not to injure his feathered friends.

Jim Jarmusch makes films that can be classed as comedies, though the characters never so much as crack a smile and indeed take every little thing with the utmost seriousness, not to say solemnity. Like *Dead Man*, Jarmusch's shot at the Western, *Ghost Dog* borrows the shape of a conventional genre movie but piles oddity upon absurdity to such an extent that you have to assume it takes place in an emptier universe next door, hence no one sees the joke.

Borrowing heavily from Jean-Pierre Melville's classic *Le Samourai*, and expounding at length on the parallel between hit man and Japanese swordsman which Melville was content to leave to the title, the film introduces us to Ghost Dog, a bear-like assassin-cum-pigeon fancier. Ghost Dog lives in a shack on a roof, communicating with his mafioso 'master' Louie via messenger pigeon, and spends his off-hours studying bushido (the samurai code of honour), hanging out in the park with his ice cream man best friend – with whom he does not share a common language – and listening to fairly mellow rap.

When his latest hit is mildly compromised by the presence of a mob boss' daughter, who lends him a book, *Rashomon*, after he has shot her lover, Ghost Dog becomes the quarry as Louie's mostly geriatric hood pals come after him. Naturally he turns the tables, though he is wont to be distracted by a robin perching on his rifle barrel.

The film is full of moments of stifled hilarity, with long-time movie villains Cliff Gorman and Henry Silva especially wry as mafia men with unexpected enthusiasms (Gorman likes rap), and apart from the slobbish, inept Louie, everyone in the cast seems intent on out-weirding everyone else. Like *Dead Man*, it has enough gunplay and style to pass as an upmarket video rental gun pic, but the real action is in the pauses, when Whitaker is on screen doing nothing in an extremely expressive manner. If you don't like Jarmusch, this won't convert you, but if you're prepared to synch with his mindset there's wry amusement to be had. ★★★ **KN**

⓪ GHOST WORLD (2001)

Starring: *Thora Birch (Enid), Scarlett Johansson (Rebecca), Steve Buscemi (Seymour), Brad Renfro (Josh), Illeana Douglas (Roberta)*
Director: *Terry Zwigoff*
Screenwriters: *Daniel Clowes, Terry Zwigoff, based on the comic book by Daniel Clowes*
15/111 mins./Comedy/Drama/USA

Misfit teens Enid and Rebecca crave independence but find their options severely limited. Drifting restlessly they pour scorn on all around them, until Enid develops a fascination for oddball Seymour.

Daniel Clowes' now-classic comic art creation, *Ghost World*, has been one of the most interesting graphic novels of the last decade, capturing sarcastic teen angst and commenting on the collapse of modern culture, no less, with mordant humour, well-drawn poignance and acutely realistic dialogue.

His 18-year-old protagonists Enid and Rebecca – revolted by the cheesiness, phoniness and greyness of peers, parents and environment – are sneering, smart-aleck soul sisters to J.D. Salinger's icon of disaffected youth, Holden Caulfield.

Director Zwigoff, whose work includes acclaimed documentary Crumb, has adapted their search for a place in the world as a brightly cartoon-coloured but melancholy comedy whose tone is dangerously balanced between edgy satire and sulky despair. The first release from John Malkovich's production company, Mr. Mudd, this is a bold venture that is more admirable than, perhaps, it is appealing.

We are not expected to love these girls for their ridicule of the eccentrics, creeps and losers they perceive around them, nor for the mean pranks they conceive in their immature boredom as stalkers of the sad and lonely.

Irresistible, however, is the keenly observed awfulness of consumerism, fashion and obsessive record, comics and video collectors. Also under the microscope is half-assed feminist political correctness, in the shape of Enid's ex-hippie art teacher (a hilarious Douglas).

Performances are spot-on. Birch stretches her pouty, unhappy adolescent schtick to convey the complexities of the self-loathing Enid, while Buscemi's record enthusiast looking for love in a heinous green cardie is as touching and real as he is a comical turn-off. ★★★★ **AE**

⓪ GHOSTBUSTERS (1984)

Starring: *Bill Murray (Dr. Peter Venkman), Dan Aykroyd (Dr. Raymond Stantz), Sigourney Weaver (Dana Barrett), Harold Ramis (Dr. Egon Spengler), Rick Moranis (Louis Tully), Annie Potts (Janine Melnitz), Ernie Hudson (Winston Zeddmore)*
Director: *Ivan Reitman*
Screenwriters: *Dan Aykroyd, Harold Ramis*
PG/107 mins./Comedy/Sci-fi/USA

Awards: *BAFTA – Best Original Song (Ghostbusters)*

Three unemployed parapsychology professors set up shop as a unique ghost removal service.

Halfway through the initial release of *Ghostbusters*, director Ivan Reitman decided to run a new trailer on TV. He simply took the mock-television commercial snippet from the movie and inserted a real usable number. At the other end was a recorded message, from Murray and Akroyd, running along the lines of 'Hi, we're out catching ghosts right now, please leave a message.' The line received 1000 calls an hour, 24 hours a day for six weeks. *Ghostbusters* was more than just a groovy comedy from the *Saturday Night Live* stable, more than a special effects-driven, spoofy blockbuster, more than just a smash-hit movie. It was a bona fide phenomenon. Something that had leaked out of the cinemas straight into the public conscious as its exuberant mantra 'Who ya gonna call?' chimed from playgrounds to shopping malls.

The original idea, born in Dan Aykroyd's head, was of a set of intergalactic Ghostbusters competing with rival companies in the future. Director Ivan Reitman was the man to ground the idea, bringing it back to Earth and New York City and introducing the notion of this madcap start-up company arriving just as seriously sinister goings-on hit town. Originally, a range of different names were suggested for the main roles: John Belushi for Venkman, Eddie Murphy for Winston, John Candy for Louis Tully. But you can't imagine a more fitting trio for the bumbling, boilersuited spiritual pest control than Murray, Aykroyd and Ramis.

The characterisation and much of the comedy is constructed around the differing (and conflicting) personalities – and varying attitudes toward their science – of the three main Ghostbusters (loosely modelled on the Three Stooges). Peter Venkman (Murray – Moe) is a feast of asinine one-liners, a vessel of dominant sarcasm for whom the pursuit of knowledge is inseparably entwined with the pursuit of girls. Raymond Stantz (Ackroyd – Curly) is bumbling and loveable; brains wrapped up in a clown's clothing: science is a way of avoiding a proper job. Egon Spengler (Ramis – Larry) is nerdy and absent-mindedly professorial, for whom science is everything at the expense of common sense. Ernie Hudson's PC-friendly presence as a fourth, blue collar 'Buster' Winston feels token and underdeveloped.

Constructed with deft commercialism, the film is as about as undemanding as you can get. The supernatural element is cartoonish and barmy ('Gozer the Traveller, He will come in one of the pre-chosen forms. During the rectification of the Vuldrini, the traveller came as a large and moving Torg!') and the set pieces spectacular but credible within the confines of the story (New York is given a weird, Gothic expansiveness). The script – by Ramis and Aykroyd – skilfully grounds itself in Venkman's teasing bile ('I don't have to take this abuse from you, I've got hundreds of people dying to abuse me') as it spouts out ludicrous pseudo-rational scientific jargon ('Free-floating, full torso, vaporous apparition'). Even its plot makes some kind of sense with a park-side apartment building becoming a gateway to the nether world and the reincarnation of a Babylonian demon. Not to forget the contribution of Ray Parker Jr.'s hit theme song, adding to the joie de vivre of blockbuster success.

Vitally important to the hook, was the juxtaposition between New York's brazen cynicism and the daft supernaturalism. The Mayoral office – led by William Atherton's (Thornburg from *Die Hard*) snidely bureaucratic meddler – refuse to give credence to the phantasmagoric threat until it is almost too late. For every far-fetched episode Venkman has a snide retort – after a headlong collision with a bulbous lime-green entity, Venkman, coated in ectoplasm, just moans, 'He slimed me!' Another pivot is the combo of romantic interest cellist Sigourney Weaver and her dweeby pest of a neighbour, Rick Moranis' goofball accountant – both soon to be possessed by sinister spirits and become the focus of the impending apocalypse. Events hurtle along, leaving little room to stop and ponder why it is so many otherwordly events directly coincide with the formation of this outfit. And while the effects feel dated by today's standards (the Sta-Puft Marshmallow man stomping up the street is evidently a giant inflatable) there is a quaint charm to their limitations.

Given its hugeness, the movie was followed by an inevitable but grossly inefficient sequel – something to do with yet another evil entity knocking at the door of reality and a giant river of slime under Manhattan. Strangely though, given the popular levels *Ghostbusters* reached in the mid-80s, it has left little trace of itself. Apart from the marketing, that is, this was the birth of the movie-as-logo (everything from *Batman* to *Jurassic Park* followed suit). Yet this was the first true fusion of blockbuster and all-out comedy. ★★★★ **IN**

Movie Trivia: Ghostbusters

John Belushi was originally set to play the role of Peter Venkman (Bill Murray). Eddie Murphy was originally sought for the role of Winston Zeddemore but declined the offer. Huey Lewis and the News sued Ray Parker Jr., who sang the title theme 'Ghostbusters', as they felt the song plagiarised their hit 'I Want A New Drug'. Director Reitman provides the voice of Zuul, the evil spirit at the centre of the drama.

GHOSTBUSTERS II (1989)

Starring: *Bill Murray (Dr. Peter Venkman), Dan Aykroyd (Dr. Raymond Stantz), Sigourney Weaver (Dana Barrett), Harold Ramis (Dr. Egon Spengler), Rick Moranis (Louis Tully), Ernie Hudson (Winston Zeddemore), Annie Potts (Janine Melnitz), Peter MacNicol (Dr. Janosz)*
Director: *Ivan Reitman*
Screenwriters: *Harold Ramis, Dan Aykroyd*
PG/108 mins./Sci-fi/Comedy/Action/Adventure/USA

The boys are back in town – they never went away, but were derided as frauds, despite saving the world, and handed a bill for damages. Thankfully, another threat to civilisation is bubbling in the sewers, so the Ghostbusters can give up their humiliating day-jobs.

Since sending the Pilsbury Doughboy back to the land of Homepride, Venkman and his buddies have been hit by the city for a repair bill and are generally derided as frauds. Times are hard, Stantz and Zeddemore now guest at children's parties between the jelly and the conjuror, their earlier exploits largely forgotten: in response to the chant 'Who yuh gonna call?', the yuppie larvae shout 'He-Man!'. Venkman hosts a risible TV show for armchair psychics and Spengler has retreated into research. But they're reunited when Weaver's son Oscar becomes the victim of a playful poltergeist. She goes to Spengler for help and the trail leads them under the city where a monstrous Stygian river of pink slime is generating enough negative energy to turn the population of New York into a bunch of complete assholes.

Ramis and Aykroyd have written a sharp script with more than a casual eye on the children. The slime is OK (it likes to listen to Jackie Wilson and, in the film's most seditious moment, there's a suspicion that Spengler has been sleeping with it) and the whole affair is funny in a harmless, gloopy sort of way.

But the attempts to integrate Murray into mainstream society (he's seen cooing over baby Oscar in a way that's not entirely ironic) is uncomfortable. The character shone in the original because he was allowed to be self-centred, immature and careless; placing him in a relationship that demands genuine warmth simply doesn't work. In addition, too much action is carried by Aykroyd, Ramis and Hudson as Murray tries to rekindle his old flame, and the climax is a pale rerun of the original's classic confrontation: 'Let's show the Sumerian bitch how we do things downtown!' ★★★ **RB**

GHOSTS OF THE ABYSS (2003)

Starring: *As themselves: Bill Paxton, Dr. John Broadwater, Dr. Lori Johnston, Charles Pellegrino, Don Lynch, Ken Marschall, James Cameron, Mike Cameron, Jeffrey N. Ledda, Corey Jaskolski, Jason Paul*
Director: *James Cameron*
Producers: *John Bruno, James Cameron, Chuck Comisky, Janace Tashjian, Andrew Wright*
PG/59 mins./90 mins. (DVD version)/Documentary/USA

A documentary exploring the wreck of the Titanic.

So how exactly do you follow the highest grossing film of all time? Well, if you're James Cameron, you take your sweet time and finally revisit your biggest hit, this time in 3-D.

The director's first foray into the world of Imax goes deep down to the bowels of the Titanic with an awed Bill Paxton ('Look, it's the ship's hull!'), promising to explore previously unseen aspects of the wreck. The 3-D gimmick undoubtedly adds to the enjoyment – the huge crashing waves and the Titanic looming out of the murky depths are breathtaking – but after the novelty begins to wear off, it becomes apparent that the whole concept of searching a 90-year-old wreck is actually quite dull.

Despite Paxton's whooping every time a new artefact comes on screen, it's hard to be constantly excited about watching a bunch of rusty, decayed junk – historic and three-dimensional though it may be. ★★★ **OR**

THE GHOUL (1933)

Starring: *Boris Karloff (Professor Moriant), Cedric Hardwicke (Broughton), Ernest Thesiger (Laing), Dorothy Hyson (Betty Harlow), Anthony Harrison (Kaney)*
Director: *T. Hayes Hunter*
Screenwriter: *Roland Pertwee, John Hastings Turner, Rupert Downing, L. du Garde Peach, from the novel and play by Dr. Frank King, Leonard J. Hines*
PG/69 mins./Horror/UK

Dying Egyptologist Professor Morlant insists he be buried with a valuable jewel taped to his hand, so he can revive in the tomb and perform a ritual he believes will give him eternal life. Various parties scheme to get hold of the jewel.

Having become a horror star in Hollywood, Boris Karloff returned in triumph to Britain for the first time in decades to take the leading role – reminiscent of his just-completed turn in *The Mummy* – in this homegrown stab at taking back some of the gothic action from the upstart Americans. The opening and closing reels are the most effective, with a hollow-eyed Karloff expiring in bed surrounded by grasping Dickensian grotesques like the club-footed butler (Ernest Thesiger) and an untrustworthy lawyer

(Cedric Hardwicke) and – after sitting out too much of the middle-section of the movie – reviving in the tomb and lumbering about zombie-like as he tries to offer up the sacred scarab to a statue of Anubis.

The actual plot is a combination of proven old properties like *The Cat and the Canary* (heirs and schemers gather in an isolated house to get hold of treasure) and *The Moonstone* (knife-wielding foreigners out to reclaim the jewel stolen from their ancient culture) and has as much silly comedy, like the spinster who is overly impressed by an Egyptian on the strength of having seen Rudolf Valentino in *The Sheik* too many times, as it does proper creepy stuff. A young Ralph Richardson enjoys his screen debut as an unctuous curate who turns out to be another crook who has set enough gunpowder under Karloff's tomb to allow for an explosive finale.

Based on a novel by Frank King, which was remade in more comical mode – with Sid James, Keneth Connor and Shirley Eaton – as *What a Carve-Up!* in 1962. ★★★ **KN**

GIANT (1956)

Starring: *Elizabeth Taylor (Leslie Benedict), Rock Hudson (Jordan 'Bick' Benedict), James Dean (Jett Rink), Carroll Baker (Luz Benedict II)*
Director: *George Stevens*
Screenwriters: *Fred Guiol, Ivan Moffat, based on the novel by Edna Ferber*
PG/201 mins./Drama/USA

Texas cattleman Jordan 'Bick' Benedict marries fiery Easterner Leslie. Besides his lifelong rivalry with wildcat oil-driller Jett Rink, Bick has troubles with his rebellious children.

A prestige release in 1956, this is best-known now as James Dean's last picture – though he takes third place in the credits while the film concentrates on the family problems of Rock Hudson's stubborn cattle king. Over three hours pass as decades trudge by and the dry, empty spaces of Texas dwarf even the big personality cast as oilwells replace ranches. Based on Edna Ferber's novel, *Giant* is typical of director George Stevens: so intent on being great, it quite often forgets to be even good.

For instance, a wonderfully-played final scene with Hudson and Taylor is marred by two atrocious parting shots of big-eyed, symbolic children. But it's irresistible, epic soap opera, with many fine performances and passages. Dean's Jett begins as a wildcatting, ambitious cowboy, whooping it up covered in oil when he strikes it rich, but is less comfortable in the later stages as a slick-tached, empty-souled oil baron.

The method star masters small, telling gestures (a distinctive way of waving goodbye, a cowpoke's array of rope tricks, a cruciform pose with a rifle) but the underrated Hudson bites off the big dramatic challenges and drunken sidekick Chill Wills steals every scene that isn't nailed down.

A potentially sticky plot thread about Texan racism works much better than in most 1950s 'message' pictures because the film holds back on the big speeches in the home stretch and has Hudson wordlessly struggle with his inbuilt prejudices as he is finally compelled to stand up and fight (and take a beating) in defence of the hispanic daughter-in-law he has previously been reluctant to acknowledge. ★★★ **KN**

GIGI (1958)

Starring: *Leslie Caron (Gigi), Maurice Chevalier (Honore Lachaille), Louis Jordan (Gaston Lachaille), Hermione Gingold (Mme Alvarez), Eva Gabor (Liane D'Exelmans)*
Director: *Vincente Minnelli*
Screenwriter: *Alan Jay Lerner, based on the play by Anita Loos, from the novel by Colette*
PG/119 mins./Comedy/Musical/Romance/USA

Awards: *Academy Awards – Best Art Direction/Set Decoration, Best Cinematography, Best Costume, Best Director, Best Editing, Best Original Song (Gigi), Best Music, Best Picture, Best Screenplay based on material from another medium, Golden Globes – Best Musical, Best Direction, Best Supporting Actress (Hermione Gingold)*

In early 20th Century Paris a young courtesan, Gigi, is being coached to entertain aristocratic males by her Grandmother. But bored millionaire Gaston starts to realise he wants Gigi as more than a mistress ...

When Gigi swept the board at the Oscars, Lerner and Loewe drew much criticism for effectively rehashing their previous hit *My Fair Lady* – they even threw in one of the leftover songs from that show's theatrical run ('Say A Prayer For Me Tonight'). Nor did it help that Audrey Heburn had played the role of Gigi in the play on Broadway.

But this musical still sparkles with spirit and life of it's own thanks to memorable songs ('Thank Heavens For Little Girls', 'I Remember It Well'), a feast of Cecil Beaton costumes and the direction of Minnelli, who excelled at making his female stars look joyful. He also made the most of the Parisian locations, a wonderful extravagance after so many studio set musicals.

Tart dialogue pokes fun at the social mores of the Parisian society, which most likely also contained digs at the Hollywood set of the time too and Leslie Caron, one of the most unusual screen icons, seems to perfectly contrast this caustic set-up by being everything it is not. ★★★ **EC**

GIGLI (2003)

Starring: *Ben Affleck (Larry Gigli), Jennifer Lopez (Ricki), Al Pacino (Starkman), Christopher Walken (Det. Stanley Jacobellis), Lenny Venito (Louis), Justin Bartha (Brian), Lainie Kazan (Mother), Missy Crider (Robin)*
Director: *Martin Brest*
Screenwriter: *Martin Brest*
15/121 mins./Crime/Comedy/Romance/USA

Awards: *Razzie – Worst Actor, Worst Actress, Worst Director, Worst Picture, Worst Screen Couple, Worst Screenplay*

Two low-level mob ops kidnap a mentally challenged youth who has something to do with a court case. One of them is a New Age lesbian; the other a young buck who thinks he can 'cure' her of that.

When faced with a movie that has no redeeming qualities whatsoever, certain questions are bound to arise. The most pertinent among them is not 'why?', but 'how?'. The reason why this film got made is because, on paper at least, casting two hot Hollywood stars in a romantic comedy makes sound commercial sense. 'How' is a little more tricky.

How, for instance, throughout what was presumably a fairly standard production schedule – the impression that it was conceived, written, produced, shot, edited and marketed over a weekend is, perhaps, deceptive – did no-one notice that not a single element of it achieved a basic professional standard?

How, given the practice of screening dailies, was it not immediately apparent that Ben Affleck and Jennifer Lopez have such a catastrophic lack of screen chemistry that they appear to be from entirely different species?

How, in the long months from pitch meeting to premiere, did it escape detection that the script, if such a thing ever existed, was written by a gibbon? That Stevie Wonder was doing the lighting? That the camera was threaded with scrunched-up Izal toilet paper? That the editor had recently lost both hands in an industrial accident? That the director was absent from the set during the entire shoot? That the soundtrack had seeped in from a Saga-produced documentary on cruising the Norfolk Broads? That the best way to capitalise on Lopez's Latino bombshell image was probably not by casting her as a nouveau hippy lesbian? That even one shot of Ben Affleck's hairy, sweaty armpit is grounds for pulling the plug on anything? That deploying a mentally-challenged character for comic effect is unspeakably offensive?

How, basically, did this film ever get a release? Which is not to say how did it get a nationwide US release in over 3,000 theatres? But how did it get a release in any media format whatsoever? Beyond what we know of rampant narcissism and naked opportunism, it will remain a mystery. ★ **SB**

GILDA (1946)

Starring: *Rita Hayworth (Gilda), Glenn Ford (Johnny Farrell), George Macready (Ballin Mundson), Joseph Calleia (Obregon), Steven Geray (Uncle Pio)*
Director: *Charles Vidor*
Screenwriter: *Marion Parsonnet based on Jo Eisinger's adaptation of E.A. Ellington's original story*
PG/110 mins./Drama/USA

Buenos Aires casino owner Ballin Mundson orders henchman Johnny Farrell to keep an eye on his new wife, Gilda, unaware that the pair once enjoyed a tempestuous affair.

Rita Hayworth never forgave Virginia Van Upp for creating this crackling film noir for her. Indeed, she held her directly responsible for the fact that her subsequent lovers went to bed with Gilda and woke up with her. Yet, female co-scenarists Marion Parsonnet and Jo Eisinger were equally culpable for objectifying Hayworth as the love goddess whom both George Macready and Glenn Ford wanted to possess and control, but neither of whom deigned to cherish.

As director Charles Vidor once said, 'the picture was about hate being as exciting an emotion as love' and sparks certainly flew within a ménage à trois whose simmering sado-masochism and latent homosexuality seemed to transgress just about every item on the Production Code. It was as though the Breen Office was allowing such resistible characters to commit such despicable sins to ward the audience off the temptations of the flesh. Yet, the film confounded the critics by becoming a hit date movie for returning GIs keen to see the pin-up who had helped them get through the war.

Hayworth certainly didn't let them down, with Jack Cole's choreography having been inspired by a stripper's routines. Indeed, this motif recurred in the picture's most iconic moment, as Hayworth peeled off her long gloves while gyrating in a strapless black satin gown to Anita Ellis's dubbed rendition of 'Put the Blame on Mame'. But off screen, Hayworth was feeling anything but a femme fatale, as her marriage was collapsing across the Columbia lot as Orson Welles conducted an affair on the set of *The Stranger*, which she'd persuaded studio chief Harry Cohn to greenlight.

Rita would eventually fall into the arms of her five-time co-star, who developed a crush on her during the shoot. Yet Ford still managed to sustain the intense pessimism and world-weary cruelty (perhaps channelled from his wartime stint in the Marines) that made Farrell one of the most ambiguous anti-heroes of the 1940s. ★★★★ **DP**

GINGER SNAPS (2000)

Starring: *Emily Perkins (Brigitte 'B' Fitzgerald), Katharine Isabelle (Ginger Fitzgerald), Kris Lemche (Sam), Mimi Rogers (Pamela Fitzgerald), Jesse Moss (Jason McCardy)*
Director: *John Fawcett*
Screenwriters: *Karen Walton, based on a story by Karen Walton and John Fawcett*
18/108 mins./Drama/Horror/Canada/USA

Brigitte and Ginger, alienated teens, survive an encounter with a vicious beast, but Ginger has been bitten and begins to transform into a werewolf. Brigitte vows to help her, but soon raging sluttiness gives way to violence.

The problem with werewolf films is that they almost always seem to be structured around showing off the special effects, from the yak hair dissolves of *The Wolf Man*, through the rubberwork of *An American Werewolf In London*, to the CGI of *An American Werewolf In Paris*. This low-budget entry doesn't quite take the Cat People approach of keeping its beast entirely off-screen, but it does work harder at the character stuff than the monster-making.

Breaking with the familiar periodic full moon transformation mythology, Ginger Snaps plays out a scenario more like *The Fly*, whereby the unfortunate Ginger gradually (and perhaps permanently) shape-shifts into a big dog form. Along the way, symptoms develop, such as sharper teeth and nails, increased (and embarrassing) hairiness, becoming white streaks in her mane, and hormone-driven instincts that tear her between desires for animalistic sex and bloody carnage.

Recently, under the influence of *Buffy The Vampire Slayer*, teen-themed horror movies have been tidy satires, fliply allegorising teenage problems in hokey Gothic leftovers.

Ginger Snaps is more toothsome, as the supernatural situation serves to throw into crisis the relationship between the normally strange Fitzgerald sisters: the older and marginally more confident incipient babe Ginger and the glowering, sulky, sensitive Brigitte. The kind of girls who stage multiple mock suicides as a school project, they have sworn to be dead or out of town by the age of 16, thus Brigitte feels as threatened by Ginger's sudden interest in boys as by her wolf-like manifestations.

Karen Walton's sharp screenplay is especially strong in the family scenes, allowing performances of *Heavenly Creatures* intensity from the young leads, and a very funny turn from Mimi Rogers as their perkily callous Mom. A regulation monster of the kind seen in too many *Howling* sequels makes an unavoidable appearance in the finale, but director John Fawcett works hard to produce a truly emotional climax. ★★★★ **CH**

GIRL WITH A PEARL EARRING (2003)

Starring: *Colin Firth (Johannes Vermeer), Scarlett Johansson (Griet), Tom Wilkinson (Van Ruijven), Judy Parfitt (Maria Thins), Cillian Murphy (Pieter)*
Director: *Peter Webber*
Screenwriter: *Olivia Hetreed, based on the novel by Tracy Chevalier*
12A/100 mins./Biography/Drama/USA/UK/Luxembourg

The Delft area of Holland, 1665: 17-year-old Griet is sent to work as a servant in the troubled household of local artist Johannes Vermeer. Gradually he finds the new maid something of a muse and trouble brews as Vermeer's growing feelings for Griet become apparent.

Tracy Chevalier's novel, from which *Girl With A Pearl Earring* is adapted, attempts to solve the mystery that surrounds Vermeer's painting of the same name. Although no-one is sure of the identity of the beautiful girl who inspired the artist to produce one of the world's greatest paintings, Chevalier cobbled together a series of clues and created a bestselling novel.

Director Webber sticks firmly to the book and, in doing so, has produced a captivating film whose stunning use of set design and colour recreates Vermeer's sense of space and reality in almost every shot.

Firth's Vermeer is distant and untouchable, making his attraction to Griet all the more powerful. Johansson, meanwhile, shows a remarkable resemblance to the servant girl in the picture, and her ability to keep Griet simple and naturally beautiful (coupled with her turn in *Lost In Translation*) is a marker of good things to come. ★★★★ **LB**

GIRL, INTERRUPTED (1999)

Starring: *Winona Ryder (Susanna Kaysen), Angelina Jolie (Lisa), Brittany Murphy (Daisy), Clea DuVall (Georgina), Whoopi Goldberg (Valerie), Jeffrey Tambor (Dr. Potts), Jared Leto (Tobias Jacobs), Vanessa Redgrave (Dr. Wick)*
Director: *James Mangold*
Screenwriters: *Anna Hamilton Phelan, James Mangold, Susan Shilliday, Lisa Loomer, based on the memoirs of Susanna Kaysen*
15/127 mins./Biography/Drama/USA

Awards: *Academy Awards – Best Supporting Actress (Angelina Jolie), Golden Globes – Best Supporting Actress (Angelina Jolie)*

A sensitive girl is committed to a women-only mental asylum, after mistakenly taking too may painkillers to cure her headache. There she meets a group of girls who will change her perspective on life.

Populated with sexy stars and a tastefully furnished madhouse, *Girl, Interrupted* may well do for asylums what *Top Gun* did for the Navy. Coming on like Charlie's Angels Flew Over The Cuckoo's Nest, James Mangold's intelligent, engaging adaptation of Susanna Kaysen's real-life memoir offers a fresh spin on movie asylum clichés thanks to a spirited cast and a refreshing resistance toward heartstring pulling and obvious preaching.

Ryder is Susanna, a 60s sensitive type who commits herself to a mental institution after she takes a bottle of aspirin to cure a headache. We are then introduced to the inmates who will quickly form Susanna's clique: Daisy, an anorexic daddy's girl; Polly, whose horrifically scarred face masks her innate sensitivity; and Lisa, a free-spirited sociopath who has turned asylum escapes into an artform. Of course, the girls bond (though never in a sickly way), and have 'adventures' (midnight bowling, sneaking a peek at their psychiatric reports); yet this is never as cute as you might think, Mangold always injecting the proceedings with a slight, distinctly anti-Tinseltown edge.

The film has little new to say about the divide between rationality and lunacy, but it presents its argument with humour and persuasion. Mangold never overplays the emotional beats, having enough restraint to string together vignettes of life on the ward, and be it Susanna turning the tables on her therapist or an outing to an ice cream parlour, *Girl, Interrupted* gives you the time to care for the characters.

If the film has drawbacks, it is that it occasionally stretches belief and it resolves itself too neatly, betraying the rawness that has gone before. Yet ultimately it gets by on the strength of its double-handed performance whammy. Jolie is on fire as the wild child who knows exactly how to push everyone else's buttons while staying firmly in control of her own. Yet in many ways it is Ryder's movie, etching a journey from confusion to clarity that is both believable and moving. ★★★ **IF**

⓪ GLADIATOR (2000)

Starring: *Russell Crowe (Maximus), Joaquin Phoenix (Commodus), Oliver Reed (Proximo), Connie Nielsen (Lucilla), Derek Jacobi (Gracchus), Djimon Hounsou (Juba), Richard Harris (Marcus Aurelius)*
Director: *Ridley Scott*
Screenwriters: *David Franzoni, John Logan, William Nicholson, from a story by David Franzoni*
15/150 mins./Adventure/History/USA

Awards: *Academy Awards – Best Actor, Best Costume, Best Visual Effects, Best Picture, Best Sound, BAFTA – Audience Award, Best Cinematography, Best Editing, Best Film, Best Production Design, Empire Awards – Best Actor, Best Actress, Best Film, Golden Globes – Best Drama, Best Score*

Maximus Decimus Meridius is Commander of the Emperor Marcus Aurelius' Armies of The North in 180AD. When Caesar dies and his twisted son and daughter take over Maximus and his family suffer the consequences but will the brave soldier get his revenge?

Ben-Hur, Spartacus, Quo Vadis – that was when they made movies as big as cities, proper, meaty, swallow-an-afternoon films. Well, what may have been out of vogue for 40 years is making one hell of a comeback. In the grandest tradition of them all. Ridley Scott, together with man of the moment Russell Crowe, has enriched the legacy of sandals, swords and leather wrist thingees to create a magnificent epic. Hammering on all the touchstones of yore while utilising all the tricks the modern filmmaker has to hand, this is hardly subtle, but its impact is absolute, its performances loud and clear and its ambition all up there on screen. Commencing with a full-scale, extras unlimited, realism unabated battle sequence in a mud strewn Germanica, we are confronted by a general tired of war and an emperor, Marcus Aurelius, near death. Furious at the bond between Aurelius and his beloved warrior, his unhinged heir, Commodus, kills pop and condemns Maximus to death. Big mistake. Especially when you kill his loving wife and child, whom he yearns for, by burning and crucifixion.

And so the plot follows Maximus' rise as a gladiator – trained by a remarkably vociferous and effective Oliver Reed, whose face is peculiarly CGI'd in certain scenes from beyond the grave – driven by lust for revenge. In the meantime, Rome is in turmoil with the nutty new emperor, played with gleeful hamminess by Phoenix, attempting to dismantle the Senate while his doting sister Lucilla seems to have other plans. And just to make things more complicated, she happens to be Maximus' ex.

Russell Crowe was clearly born in a hard month, in a hard year during a freak outbreak of total hardness. The man exudes the physicality of a wild animal. Shifting testosterone like a pre-bloated Brando, he holds the screen with such assuredness and force you simply can't rip your eyes away from him. When he looks pissed off (as he does for 90 per cent of the time), the movie possesses its own gravitational pull.

Ridley Scott was also the man for the job. His trademark visual panache – making everything seem utterly glorious no matter how brutal or gritty – presents the events on a truly epic canvas of filtered light and ancient landscapes. CGI has recreated Rome's massive colosseum and the gore splattered combat sequences therein are literally stunning – the face-off between Maximus and his gladiator brothers and a stream of chariots in mid-arena makes a mockery of *Ben-Hur*'s fabled race sequence, and utilising *Private Ryan*-esque frame-jumping techniques gives the fighting a tangible realism that crashes out of the screen. There is an interesting if token commentary on the use of violent entertainment to subvert the masses, but on the whole, historical accuracy is reserved more for the technical elements than any sense of political, religious or dialectic truth (accents are all over the shop). The film also bobbles in its need to cram so much politicking in, to draw in an empire in crisis to the more personal story of one man's revenge. And while this is all grand opera, driven by sweeping gestures and pompous, overwritten dialogue, it is prone to plain silliness, especially in granting us the big showdown at the close. But the sheer dynamism of the action, coupled with Hans Zimmer's lavish score and the forcefield of Crowe, still made for a fearsome competitor in the summer movie stakes. ★★★★ **KN**

Movie Trivia: Gladiator

Mel Gibson was the first choice to play Maximus but he refused the role. In the original script Maximus' character was called Narcissus, the man who killed the real-life Emperor Commodus. Filming was marked by the death of Oliver Reed in a Malta pub. Reed spent £450 after having downed three bottles of Captain Morgan's Jamaican rum, eight bottles of German beer and numerous doubles of Famous Grouse Whisky.

⓪ GLEAMING THE CUBE (1989)

Starring: *Christian Slater (Brian Kelly), Steven Bauer (Al Lucero), Richard Herd (Ed Lawndale), Le Tuan (Colonel Trac), Min Luong (Tina Trac), Art Chudabala (Vinh Kelly)*
Director: *Graeme Clifford*
Screenwriter: *Michael Tolkin*
12/100 mins/Action/USA

Mixed-up teen Brian investigates his adopted brother's death by getting on his skateboard and whizzing about Los Angeles in search of arms dealers.

Just what the world needed, a skateboarding vigilante movie. Slater plays a punk who's no good at anything that doesn't involve a skateboard, but ignores the cop on the case (Steven Bauer) who justifiably keeps telling him not to interfere. He romances the dead kid's Asian girlfriend (Le Tuan) in an attempt to get the goods on her father – who is mixed up in the killing – and turns from a boring no-good slob into a boring clean-cut preppie. In a scene evidently supposed to be an emotional climax to compare with Ray Milland refusing a drink in *The Lost Weekend* or Gary Cooper throwing away his badge in *High Noon*, the kid even consents to leave his board at home and walk somewhere. However, he climbs back on a special model for the big chase at the end.

This is one of those movies that seems to have been stuck together like a model kit. It has enough skateboarding footage to fill out a half hour timewaster documentary, enough plot for a low-grade kiddie adventure movie, enough insight into the Californian Vietnamese community for a two-minute news filler on a slow night, enough teen pouting and angst for an MTV spot, and enough family crises for the pre-credits sequence of a suburban soap. Slater is a blandly rebellious hero, and his hymns to skateboarding as the last bastion of freedom are pretty hilarious. It gets mechanically exciting in the contrived action scene at the end, but its overall ordinariness – compounded by lacklustre villains, inoffensive rock music and nary a whiff of sex or sleaze – becomes extraordinarily wearisome long before that. ★★ **KN**

GLENGARRY GLENN ROSS (1992)

Starring: *Jack Lemmon (Shelley Levene), Al Pacino (Ricky Roma), Ed Harris (Dave Moss), Alan Arkin (George Aaronow), Kevin Spacey (John Williamson), Alec Baldwin (Blake), Jonathan Pryce (James Lingk)*
Director: *James Foley*
Screenwriter: *David Mamet, based on his play*
15/100 mins./Drama/USA

A ruthless boss sets his sales office a challenge – those who fail will lose their jobs.

Handicapped by possibly the worst movie title of 1992, James Foley's *Glengarry Glen Ross* is that rare delight, a film that works even better on the small screen. Free from the need to be cinematic and out in the open air, the full claustrophobia of David Mamet's original stage work can once again be recaptured, the full intensity of the storyline reclaimed from Hollywood's better intentions.

Mamet, as always, makes life difficult for those who would adapt his work for the screen, resolutely refusing to compromise on the overtly realistic dialogue – everybody says everything twice, a lot of it being the exact nonsense we spew forth every day – and spending more than 90 minutes ensuring that nothing really happens except for a lot of guys sitting around talking shite.

But what wonderful guys, what memorable shite. First among equals has to be The Great Jack Lemmon, one minute the very definition of oily as smooth-talkin' Shelley Levine, the next giving a fair impression of a man on the edge of total desperation as he hopelessly tries to flog some worthless real estate to people who can't afford it in the first place. Quality support, not surprisingly, is provided in the shape of Pacino, Harris, Alda and Baldwin, the latter exploding onto the screen in a blistering cameo as the bully-boy brought in from head office to pep up the troops in his own inimitable way ('First prize is the Cadillac, second prize is a set of steak knives, third prize is . . . you're fired'). So often miscast, Baldwin here uses his physical bulk and natural air of malevolence to terrific effect, producing his finest screen work in the process. Together, these poor bastards go about their soul-destroying way, gradually losing faith as each attempted deal falls through, each lead proves worthless. Pacino, the smartest by far, is also the hardest of the bunch, blatantly trying to rip off the hapless Jonathan Pryce, only to be accidentally foiled by clueless office manager Kevin Spacey, who in turn is dished out a genuinely shocking verbal assault from Pacino for his trouble. ★★★★★ **BMc**

THE GLENN MILLER STORY (1953)

Starring: *James Stewart (Glenn Miller), June Allyson (Helen Burger Miller), Charles Drake (Don Haynes), George Tobias (Si Schribman), Harry Morgan (Chummy MacGregor)*
Director: *Anthony Mann*
Screenwriters: *Valentine Davies, Oscar Brodney*
U/115 mins./Drama/USA

Spurred on by his wife Helen and best pal Chummy MacGregor, trombonist band leader Glenn Miller searches for the sound that he knows the kids will love.

Universal Studios had sizeable misgivings about this tribute to Glenn Miller, the King of Swing whose plane had disappeared ten years earlier while crossing the English Channel for a Christmas concert. Musical biopics like *The Fabulous Dorseys* had invariably failed at the box office, while musical tastes had changed considerably in the decade since Miller's demise. But the suits were equally concerned by the lukewarm reception accorded James Stewart's trio of psychological Westerns with director Anthony Mann. However, they needn't have worried, as this became the fifth highest-grossing film of 1954 and Stewart himself earned over $1 million from his share of the profits.

Miller's mother had complained when Stewart was cast that he wasn't as handsome as her son. However, he certainly made Miller more genial than many remembered him and he also brought his music to a bigger audience than the trombonist himself had managed through countless tours, radio broadcasts and movies like *Sun Valley Serenade* and *Orchestra Wives*. Although it took fewer liberties than such songwriter histories as *Night And Day* and *Words And Music*, this was still very much a rose-tinted portrait that made a hero out of a workaholic, who actually stumbled across his distinctive sound through years of trial and error rather than a moment of chance inspiration when a trumpeter's split lip led to 'Moonlight Serenade' being played on a clarinet.

But Mann sticks laudably to his plan 'to tell the story of a man who is hunting for something new and finally finds it'. To that end, he creditably captured the slog of life on the road and the exhilaration of jam sessions with the likes of Louis Armstrong and Gene Krupa (for which Stewart copied the hand movements of Joe Yukl to Murray MacEachern's accompaniment). However, Mann couldn't resist romanticising the mournful finale, as Miller had recorded 'Little Brown Jug' years before it came across the ether like a parting gift. ★★★ **DP**

GLITTER (2001)

Starring: *Mariah Carey (Billie Frank), Max Beesley (Julian Dice), Da Brat (Louise), Tia Texada (Roxanne), Valarie Pettiford (Lillian Frank), Ann Magnuson (Kelly), Terrence Howard (Timothy Walker)*
Director: *Vondie Curtis-Hall*
Screenwriter: *Kate Lanier, based on a story by Cheryl L. West*
PG/104 mins./Drama/Music/USA

Awards: *Razzies – Worst Actress*

New York,1983. Orphan Billie Frank has set her sights on a glittering musical career. When hot DJ Dice spots her in a club, the two soon enjoy more than a working relationship. But, as Billie's star rises, can their love survive the ruthless world of disco?

There is a cruel theory doing the rounds that Mariah Carey's 2001 breakdown was actually a ruse to avoid publicity duties for her first film. Here at

Empire, we are sure that Ms. Carey was genuinely exhausted and are glad that she seems to be on the mend. But, let's face it, if the ditzy diva had thrown a sickie, who could have blamed her? *Glitter*'s rhyming slang is well earned.

At times during the first hour of this 'rags to riches' story, *Glitter* appears to be the world's first Zen movie. Absolutely nothing happens. As young Billie works her way from disco clubs to Madison Square Garden, entire scenes wander past with the nutritional content of a CD case.

This is film as four-times-a-week soap opera. A world where all narrative and dramatic concerns have been replaced with illuminating exchanges such as:

'Will you sign for my label?'

'Yes, I will.'

'Good, let's sing another song.'

Naturally, director Vondie Hall would find piss-poor excuses to feature Carey's warble, but a scene which exists only to showcase the drumming talents of Max Beesley? Please. If *Glitter* had thrown up a single character with the appeal of Simon Cowell, it might have made for an average episode of Pop Idol.

Mercifully, the incident-packed climax contains moments of such stupefying silliness (just watch for the dramatic reappearance of a cat we have not seen for ten years!) that *Glitter* approaches a near-*Showgirls* camp-ness, but it is all too little, too late.

As for the question of whether Carey can act: on this evidence, who can tell? If this fluff was ever intended to be pseudo-biopic, all the good stuff was left on the floor. ★ **CK**

GLORY (1989)

Starring *Matthew Broderick (Colonel Robert Gould Shaw), Denzel Washington (Private Trip), Morgan Freeman (Sergeant Major John Rawlins), Jihmi Kennedy (Sharts) Cary Elwes (Major Cabot Forbes)*
Director: *Edward Zwick*
Screenwriter: *Kevin Jarre, based on the books* Lay This Laurel *by Lincoln Kirstein,* One Gallant Rush *by Peter Burchard and the letters of Robert Gould Shaw*
15/122 mins./War/USA

Awards: *Academy Awards – Best Supporting Actor (Denzel Washington), Best Cinematography, Best Sound.*

Based upon the actual letters of Colonel Robert Gould Shaw, this Civil War drama tells of the formation of the first fully black company of soldiers, led by this white colonel. They must face both the violence of the war itself, as well as the bigotry within their own army, but still come out triumphant.

A stirring, politically correct, glossy old epic about the Massachusetts 54th Regiment, the entirely black regiment who lead the fateful charge on Fort Wagner in the Charleston Bay, that provides a helpful shorthand for the contribution of 37,000 African-Americans in the turmoil of the Civil War. Edward Zwick, a director of often stifling earnestness, fills this layered history with a indignant self-righteousness, some terrifically stern acting (Denzel Washington picked up his first Oscar as the jaded former slave Trip), and sensibly had Brit cinematographer Freddie Francis behind the camera. The film manages the trick of feeling authentic while looking grand and operatic.

But the film's liberal-mindedness is often overbearing. Kevin Jarre's script shapes its characters as defined archetypes – the angry black man (Washington), the noble black man (Morgan Freeman), the empathetic captain (Matthew Broderick) – rather than as real men with conflicting motivations. Its message is like a trumpet blast, but we shouldn't ignore that it is an important one. Glory presents America's birth pangs with determined clarity; that racism is an ill contained in its very make-up.

And there is undoubtedly a thrilling charge to their great triumph. Filmed with blistering power, as the regiment surges down a beach through clouds of cannon-fire, it becomes starkly clear that heroism is something uninfluenced by colour. It just is. And the film's misty-eyed simplicity keeps that dead centre. ★★★★ **IN**

GO (1999)

Starring: *Sarah Polley (Ronna Martin), Katie Holmes (Claire Montgomery), Desmond Askew (Simon Baines), Nathan Bexton (Mannie), Scott Wolf (Adam), Jay Mohr (Zack), Timothy Olyphant (Todd Gaines), Jane Krakowski (Irene)*
Director: *Doug Liman*
Screenwriter: *John August*
18/103 mins./Comedy/USA

Three stories of twenty-somethings intertwine involving sex, drug dealing and gambling.

This post-Tarantino slice of LA lowlife certainly takes its cues from the structure and buzz of The Big Q but rejects his old movie/TV/pulp world for something approaching reality. Or reality as experienced by young, fringy, poor, fun-seeking Los Angelinos, anyway.

Like *Pulp Fiction*, *Go* strings three separate stories on a narrative thread, but it does a neater job of meshing them together. Three sets of characters live through the same night, colliding at specific junctures, and each story comes with a punchline that slingshots into a coda, tying everything off neatly as the survivors stagger dazed into the dawn.

Set just before Christmas, the spring of the plot is that Brit Simon, a supermarket employee who dabbles as a drug connection, exchanges shifts with financially-strapped and dog-tired Ronna, so he can head off to Las Vegas for a weekend of riotous fun while she raises cash to pay her rent. Ronna is approached by Adam and Zack, soap opera actors who are hoping to score from Simon. This prompts her to seek out Simon's connection Todd and get the drugs, leaving behind her reluctant friend Claire as collateral as she hooks up with Adam and Zack, who turn out to be amateur undercover cops run by strange narc Burke. Everyone's weekend goes wrong: all the leads end up being pursued by angry gunmen.

It's a neatly contrived piece, with good performances from a likeable, mostly unfamiliar cast. The amorality over drugs and sex is pleasingly realistic, and although they're indulged in with catastrophic consequences (while having a stoned threesome, Simon and some bridesmaids ignore a hotel fire they've started), the attractions are still not seen as evil in themselves. Director Liman, of *Swingers* fame, and writer August weave the tapestry well, using a far-better-than-average rave score and not too many gimmicks to suggest the dusk-till-dawn party vibe.

There are several great comedy sequences, notably party guy Mannie who on too much E has a subtitled conversation with the dealer's cat which segues from light banter to sheer horror ('You're going to die!'). Also clever are the multiple meanings wrung from the title, in the spirit of which, you're strongly urged to go see it. ★★★★ **KN**

GOAL! (2005)

Starring: *Kuno Becker (Santiago Munez), Alessandro Nivola (Gavin Harris), Marcel Iures (Erik Dornhelm), Stephen Dillane (Glen Foy), Anna Friel (Roz Harmison), Kieran O'Brien (Hughie McGowan)*
Director: *Danny Cannon*
Screenwriters: *Dick Clement, Ian La Frenais, Mike Jefferies, Adrian Butchart*
12A/118 mins./Drama/Sport/USA

A young Mexican immigrant spends his childhood in the barrios of LA, longing to play professional football. Years later, having been spotted by ex-agent Glen Foy, Santiago suddenly finds his dream is within shooting distance – with a trial at Newcastle United FC . . .

Lately, it's not been easy being an English footie fan. So, those mired in misery after recent results could do worse than turn to Danny Cannon's latest, a sweet-natured football fairy-tale played with heart, good humour and an irrepressible sense of fun.

Let's be clear: the screenwriters leave no cliché untried as, Billy Elliot-style, young Santiago (newcomer Kuno Becker) battles a dad who won't even countenance his ambition; fish-out-of-water antics and anxieties ensue as the Mexican-American struggles to adapt to the arcane habits and hostilities of England's North-East; and ill health threatens to destroy Santy's career before it's begun. Will he triumph over adversity to make Newcastle's first team? You'll just have to go and see.

But cheese aside, where *Goal!* succeeds is in wittily drawn, *Footballers' Wives*-style stereotypes (the cool-headed foreign manager, Alessandro Nivola's playboy soccer star), lovely performances and a satisfying emotional arc. There's also some exciting matchplay to enjoy, largely involving the Magpies and Liverpool, and the appearance of several soccer stars as themselves (Beckham, Zidane, Raul). It's a warm tribute to the beautiful game that, for two hours at least, offers an escape from football's – and life's – harsher realities. ★★★ **LB**

⊙ THE GODFATHER (1972)

Starring: *Marlon Brando (Don Vito Corleone), Al Pacino (Michael Corleone), James Caan (Sonny Corleone), Richard Castellano (Clemenza), Robert Duvall (Tom Hagen), Diane Keaton (Kay Adams)*
Director: *Francis Ford Coppola*
Screenwriters: *Mario Puzo, Francis Ford Coppola, based on the novel by Mario Puzo*
18/175 mins./Crime/Drama/USA
Awards: *Academy Awards – Best Actor, Best Picture, Best Screenplay based on Material from another Medium, BAFTA – Anthony Asquith Award for Film Music, Golden Globes – Best Director, Best Drama, Best Drama Actor, Best Original Score, Best Screenplay*

The aging patriarch of an organised-crime dynasty transfers control of his clandestine empire to his reluctant son.

A son returns from war and doesn't want to get mixed up in the family business: organised crime. When his father is gunned down, however, he commits murder and is inextricably bound by ties of blood, heritage and 'honour' to a course of vendetta and power ruthlessly maintained through fear. Eventually he inherits his father's mantle as syndicate big shot and family head, the film ending with a chilling shot of the door closing on his uncomprehending WASP wife as Michael Corleone receives the homage 'Godfather'.

It was the first event movie of the 70s, the one multitudes queued up to see, the one whose dialogue, characters and imagery instantly became ingrained in the collective consciousness. It made stars of Pacino and Caan, won Oscars for Picture, Screenplay and Brando, in a triumphant comeback. Shortly after its premiere in 1972 *Variety* reported, 'The Godfather is an historic smash of unprecedented proportions'. At the time the director, Francis Ford Coppola, was holed up in a hotel writing the screenplay for *The Great Gatsby*, a job he took to relieve his financial problems because he believed in his movie. He had only been given the film after a lengthy wish-list of veterans including Otto Preminger, Elia Kazan, Fred Zinnemann and Franklin Schaffner turned it down. He perked up when Frank Capra wrote to him, claiming it was, 'Out of this world. I cheered inwardly at scene after scene.'

People are still cheering scene after scene in one of the greatest American films ever made, and committing chunks of dialogue to memory – like the goons in TV's *The Sopranos* who adore *Godfather* impersonations and businessmen like Tom Hanks' bookseller in *You've Got Mail* who explains to Meg Ryan that *The Godfather* is the font of all wisdom for the modern man.

Not since Warner Brothers' crime cycle of the 30s had the underworld so captured the public imagination. Fingering the story's irresistability, Mario Puzo's best-selling novel was, the author considered modestly, 'A great combination, the family story and a crime story. And also I made them out to be good guys except they committed murder once in a while'. In adapting the book with Puzo, Coppola had a darker, ultimately more profound take: 'I looked at it as the story of a king with three sons.' It is pulp fiction turned into opera, an epic of gangster patriarchy, of family, of America itself. 'I believe in America,' are the first words in the film, spoken by the undertaker Bonasera, an immigrant proud of his assimilation and enrichment. But, he says, 'for justice we must go to Don Corleone.'

Puzo introduced the term godfather, now synonymous with crime family bosses. The words Mafia, Cosa Nostra, camorra and the like never occur in the film because Paramount producer Al Ruddy was paid a little visit by Joe Colombo, one of the heads of the real 'five Families', and nervously promised the crime syndicate would be referred to in non-Italian terms.

Ironically real Mafiosi later embraced the film, paying assiduous court to its principals to this day and affecting the language and style of Vito, Michael, Sonny, their lieutenants and soldiers. Original protests by Italian-Americans who deplored being defamed en masse (the Sons Of Italy, The Italian-American Anti-Defamation League and its champion Frank Sinatra, who raised funds to campaign against the film) have been overshadowed ever since the film's release by its popularity within that same ethnic group. Italian immigrants' descendants, whose assimilation and Americanisation has been complete, view with nostalgic yearning the Corleone clan happily pounding down their pasta together, celebrating and sorrowing together at the weddings, the baptism, and the inevitable funeral. Such anecdotes, the legends (Brando did not stuff his cheeks with cottonwool, but had resin blobs clipped to his back teeth; Sinatra, universally believed to be the model for crooner Johnny Fontane, did attack Puzo in a restaurant, calling him a 'stool-pigeon'), the footnotes (the baby being baptised during the climactic murder binge is Coppola's infant daughter Sofia), and the postscripts (Brando sending 'Satcheen Littlefeather' to reject his Oscar) are so abundant that there are volumes of *Godfather* lore and trivia. TV documentaries have been made of the actors' screen tests.

This landmark remains a masterly work, fully deserving of its reputation. Coppola can be credited with laying the groundwork of 70s cinema with his commanding technical engineering and his audacious, visceral and stately set-pieces (the horse's head in the bed, the slaughter of Sonny which Coppola acknowledges was inspired by Arthur Penn's climax to *Bonnie And Clyde* (1967), the interweaving of the sunny wedding party with Don Corleone's court indoors, the progress of Michael's respectful Sicilian courtship of Apollonia contrasted with Connie and Carlo's explosive domestic life, and, most unforgettably, the dazzling finale of assassinations – that will make Michael undisputed Godfather – carried out against the sacramental rites in which he assumes the role of godfather). But the film's finest qualities also reveal Coppola's fluency in the classics, from the superior pulp of the 30s, into 40s noir and social dramas. His authoritative grip on an ordered, fastidiously constructed narrative, Dean Tavoularis' richly detailed design, the weight given to a fabulous supporting ensemble (Robert Duvall, Richard Conte, John Cazale, Castellano, Alex Rocco et al.), Gordon Willis' striking cinematography, Nino Rota's beautifully melodic score.

The one enduring criticism of *The Godfather* is that it glorifies the Mafia, affection mingled with abhorrence in its expression of the acts and ethos of Vito Corleone and his extended criminal family. The identification – both Coppola's and the audience's – with Pacino's Michael is unreserved. And cold, ruthless, logical Michael is definitely not the 'pretty good guy' it amused Puzo to characterise him as.

Time and two more pictures would highlight the despair and nihilism in *The Godfather* with its burden of sins accruing beyond redemption. The 1974 sequel, *The Godfather, Part II* (which took six Oscars) is arguably even more compelling in its elaboration of power's corruption into complete moral decay. 1990's flawed *Part III* sees Michael get his with Shakespearean finality, Heaven finding a way to kill his only joy. The Godfather continues to entice and entrance, however, for its emphatically mythic exploration of family, be it one cursed in blood and ambition. ★★★★★ **AE**

Movie Trivia: The Godfather

Paramount originally wanted Laurence Olivier or Edward G. Robinson to play Don Vito. During the scene where Vito's body is carried on a stretcher, Brando added 200lb lead weights to the stretcher as a joke. Before she played Michael's daughter Mary in *The Godfather: Part III*, Sofia Coppola played a baby in Part 1 and a child in *Part II*.

THE GODFATHER: PART II (1974)

Director: *Francis Ford Coppola*
Starring: *Al Pacino (Don Michael Corleone), Robert Duvall (Tom Hagen), Diane Keaton (Kay Corleone), Robert De Niro (Vito Corleone), John Cazale (Fredo Corleone), Talia Shire (Connie Corleone), Lee Strasberg (Hyman Roth)*
Screenwriters: *Francis Ford Coppola, Mario Puzo, based on characters from Puzo's novel*
18/200 mins./Crime/Drama/USA

Awards: *Academy Awards – Best Supporting Actor (Robert De Niro), Best Art Direction/Set Decoration, Best Original Score, Best Picture, Best Adapted Screenplay, BAFTA – Best Actor*

The early life and career of Vito Corleone is portrayed while his son expands and tightens his grip on his crime syndicate in the 1950s.

The Godfather is a more important film, of course it is. But *The Godfather Part II* is a better film. It's more ambitious, it's more elegiac, it delves deeper into the soil of Italian-American myth, plus … what were they thinking of, trying to match the critical and commercial dynamite of the first film? *The Godfather Part II* was, from conception upwards, an insane project. But it worked.

When *The Godfather* premiered in New York on 14 March 1972, co-screenwriter and novelist Mario Puzo had already started work on the sequel. That's how sure Paramount were that they had a monster hit on their hands, despite some exhibitors turning up their noses at a preview screening: too little action, too much talking, and too long – proof that in no way are exhibitors a bunch of popcorn-selling philistines. After two days of release, cinema managers were being offered bribes by punters desperate to get to the front of the queues which busted the proverbial block. There was something of the Mafia about the way in which Paramount doubled ticket prices for weekend shows to squeeze extra revenue from their new cash cow.

The sequel, announced on 16 April and working-titled *Don Michael*, was a commercial inevitability ('When you've got a licence to make Coca-Cola, make Coca-Cola!' said Charlie Bluhdorn, head of Gulf & Western, who owned Paramount). *The Godfather* grossed $101 million in its first 18 weeks, and nobody was going to stop the studio having another cake and eating it. But Francis Ford Coppola, the young director whom the studio had almost fired from *The Godfather* but who was now feted by Hollywood and the world, wasn't that interested. So they offered him a million dollars plus a huge 13 per cent of the profits and total artistic control. Altogether now: it was an offer he couldn't refuse.

Thus, out of this sticky climate of money-grabbing corporate opportunism did cinema's greatest *Part II* emerge. Pub debates about the diminishing returns of the sequel usually collapse at the mention of its name. So why does it work? Why isn't it *Police Academy 2: Their First Assignment*? Much of it has to do with the unique power of its own Part I, which established its family of characters so vividly. Audiences were gagging for more of Michael, Tom, Kay, Fredo and Connie. But the Coppola-Puzo masterstroke was to develop the saga in two directions, forwards through the Faustian ascendance ol Don Michael, and backwards into the early 1900s, tracing Vito Andolini's first steps into Mafiahood (he earns the surname Corleone – the name of his home village – through a mix-up at Ellis Island's immigration control).

As with all of Coppola's best work, the casting was inspired. (And as with *The Godfather*, fans can while away hours mulling over who might have been cast. Try this one: dying Miami mobster Hyman Roth – played with precision by acting coach Lee Strasberg in the film – could have been Laurence Olivier, Elia Kazan or blacklisted screenwriter DaltonTrumbo!) Robert De Niro, plucked from the 'rising star' racks after *Mean Streets*, seems born to play the young Marlon Brando. Pacino, Coppola's wild card in casting *The Godfather*, grows into the central role of Michael in perfect parallel with his character, and Diane Keaton proves the quiet lynchpin (which is no mean feat in this necessarily male-dominated film).

Everything that was majestic and mythic about *The Godfather* is more so in *Part II*, with scenes deliberately matching the original. Author of the essential *Godfather Book*, Peter Cowie, describes the two-part saga in musical terms, as 'Coppola's suite', with bass lines, motifs and rhyming patterns. ('As a whole,' Coppola said, 'the first film ought to haunt the second like a spectre.') So instead of constantly reminding us that the first film is better, *Part II* builds on its operatic sweep and cranks up the drama, both narratively and visually. Cinematographer Gordon Willis goes into sublime sepia overdrive for the flashbacks. Production designer Dean Tavoularis tops his own evocative 1940s New York streets with a living, breathing Italian immigrant community circa 1912 (actually the Ukrainian quarter). The epic 26-minute wedding scene that opened Part I is echoed in *Part II* by the altogether tackier confirmation party at the new Corleone compound in Lake Tahoe (the lake itself claiming the life of Michael's own brother in *Part II*'s chilling climax).

Actually, claiming Part IIs superiority over Part I is like saying Lennon's better than McCartney. One cannot now exist in isolation from the other; they must be watched by anyone who loves American film consecutively (and not in the form of 1977's seven-hour TV omnibus, which, though Coppola-curated, puts the story into chronological order for dimwits). Apparently, they made a *Part III* too. ★★★★★ **AC**

THE GODFATHER PART III (1990)

Starring: *Al Pacino (Michael Corleone), Diane Keaton (Kay Adams), Talia Shire (Connie Corleone), Andy Garcia (Vincent Mancini), Eli Wallach (Don Altobello), Joe Mantegna (Joey Zasa), George Hamilton (B.J. Harrison), Bridget Fonda (Grace Hamilton), Sofia Coppola (Mary Corleone)*
Director: *Francis Ford Coppola*
Screenwriters: *Mario Puzo, Francis Ford Coppola*
15/161 mins./Crime/Drama/USA

Awards: *Razzie – Worst New Star (Sofia Coppola), Worst Supporting Actress (Sofia Coppola)*

Don Corleone, now wizened, is feeling the shadow of God and attempts to draw the family business out of the pits of immorality. When he is foiled, it is the turn of cousin Vinnie, who shares his father Sonny's hothead, to take over. Michael may let the business go that way, but he is more reluctant when it comes to his daughter.

As a nice little film about a bunch of hoods and their involvement in some complicated conspiracy involving the Vatican, *The Godfather Part III* works just fine, boasting first-rate performances from its two leading men and displaying enough clever directorial touches to suggest that this Francis Ford Coppola chap is a name to look out for. As the slavishly-awaited sequel to two of the finest films of the last 30 years, however, as the third episode in what may well be the Greatest Movie Story Ever Told, *The Godfather Part III* is, frankly, a dreadful disappointment.

It is, perhaps, unfair that this new production should be so smothered under the reputation of two films made nearly 20 years previously. By so closely adhering to the exact structure of his previous two instalments, however, and through his liberal employment of flashbacks, Coppola himself seems to beg for the comparisons, making it abundantly clear throughout that what is on offer here is no new departure, but simply part three of that old familiar tale of the familia Corleone. And as such, it simply doesn't work, lacking the strength of narrative, the menace, the sheer epic sweep of all that has gone before.

For about the first 30 minutes, however, everything seems to be very much in order. The familiar strains of Nino Rota's theme music never fail to send a shiver, the introduction of Andy Garcia as the suitably hotheaded bastard son of Sonny is a welcome addition to the ranks, while Pacino, all grey and shrunk, immediately conveys a telling portrait of immense power and obscene wealth, made all the more impressive by its confinement within such a wizened old frame. The first hint that we may be going slightly off the rails comes with the gathering of the clans and the subsequent *Die Hard*-style interruption from the skies, a badly-handled set piece more reminiscent of Bond than the beautifully understated brutality of the tollbooth.

From here on, the violence becomes increasingly cartoon, notably Garcia riding a horse through the inevitable street festival, while things go from bad to worse as it gradually becomes all too apparent just how far out of her depth Sofia Coppola really is, floundering helplessly in her vain attempts to convince as both the Garcia love interest and daughter of the Don. By the time the much-vaunted operatic climax comes along, it is hardly surprising that proceedings finally slip into near-farce, as the supposed top assassin in all of Sicily takes a good half-hour and a fair portion of Cavalleria Rusticana to line up his sights. Miss Sofia manages to provoke the giggles amidst such supposed tragedy and all that is left is a basic rerun of your actual Don Corelone coil-shuffling routine to round things off.

Fans of the first two instalments are likely to find *The Godfather Part III* an unworthy heir to the tradition. First-time voters, meanwhile, will surely wonder what on earth all the fuss was all about. ★★★ **BMc**

GODS AND MONSTERS (1998)

Starring: *Ian McKellan (James Whale), Brendan Fraser (Clayton Boone), Lynn Redgrave (Hanna), Lolita Davidovich (Betty), Kevin J. O'Connor (Harry)*
Director: *Bill Condon*
Screenwriter: *Bill Condon, based on the novel* Father of Frankenstein *by Christopher Bram*
15/105 mins./Drama/Biography/USA

Awards: *Academy Awards – Best Screenplay based on material from another medium, Golden Globes – Best Supporting Actress (Lynn Redgrave)*

A film director becomes attracted to his male gardener but will his feelings harm their developing friendship?

Though biographical movies about Hollywood stars have been common since *The Jolson Story* in 1947, only recently have real-life film directors warranted the full treatment. While Tim Burton's *Ed Wood* was a collage of the best stories about the famously eccentric Z-film director, this adaptation of Christopher Bram's novel *Father Of Frankenstein* is rooted meticulously in the last days of Dudley-born, Hollywood-resident James Whale. Through a fictional relationship, Bram speculates about the circumstances of Whale's death and weaves an impression of the specifics of his life and career.

Following his turn in *Apt Pupil*, McKellen has another Oscar-worthy role as Whale. A working class lad who reinvented himself as a gentleman amid the carnage of World War I, his surprisingly brief film career was highlighted by *Frankenstein* and *Bride Of Frankenstein* and then faded away. The frame of the film is that, in the late 50s, Whale has suffered a stroke whose side effects include a mental condition whereby he is afflicted with vivid flashbacks that prevent him from concentrating but are an excuse for visualising key moments in his life. The elderly homosexual notices the shapely shoulders of Clayton Boone (Fraser), an ex-Marine who trims his Beverly Hills lawn, and asks the young man to model for him.

Rooted in a sophisticated reworking of the emotional thread of *Bride Of Frankenstein* (the Monster wants a friend), the relationship between Whale and Boone is perfectly played, with Boone at once charmed and repulsed by the canny, wicked Whale. A melodramatic twist is a little reminiscent of the film *Agatha* in its addition of mystery to the known facts, but the heart is McKellen's performance for Fraser, and the younger man's baring of body and soul. It has a streak of waspish comedy – at a Hollywood party, Whale introduces his gardener to a plummy Princess Margaret – but, in the end, goes straight for the heart with a beautiful, fantasy-tinged finale. ★★★★ **KN**

GODZILLA (GOJIRA) (1954)

Starring, *Akira Takarada (Naval Salvage Officer Hideto Ogata), Momoko Kochi (Emiko Yamane), Akihiko Hirata (Dr. Daisuke Serizawa), Takeshi Shimura (Dr Kyohei Yamane), Fuyuki Murakami (Dr. Tabata), Sachio Sakai (Reporter Hagiwara)*
Director: *Ishiro Honda*
Screenwriters: *Takeo Murata, Ishiro Honda, based on the story by Shigeru Kayama*
PG/81 mins/Sci-Fi/Japan

As ships go missing and a remote island is terrorised following H Bomb testing in the pacific, Japanese scientists are dispatched to investigate the cause. They find the answer in a 30 storey prehistoric lizard with radioactive breathe and an appetite for destruction.

The greatest of Men In A Suit monster movies, Godzilla remains a glorious watch. A touchstone for everything from Jurassic Park to Independence Day, the power of this Giant Lizard Goes Apeshit Across Tokyo masterpiece has still not been dimmed by the numerous remakes and rip-offs that have followed in its week – hell, even the terrible Godzooki character in the cartoon spin off could not dampen its power.

In its initial US release version, Raymond Burr was integrated into the Japanese original as a reporter remembering a staggering disaster and the effect, along with the rudimentary dubbing, was unintentionally laughable. But without this add-on, the film is much more satisfying experience. Takeshi Shimura, in the same year as his iconic role in *Seven Samurai*, brings a focused assurance to his paleontologist hero, lending a weight to the scenes depicting the calm before the storm and, even though a drippy romantic sub-plot threatens to drag proceedings down, the cast do just enough to make you care come armageddon time.

Revisiting Godzilla, it is surprising to the extent that the film is dominated by a pervasive atmosphere of fear, not only of the Big G himself but the fear of the H bomb. Just ten years on from Hiroshima, the Japanese attitudes to nuclear weapons infuse the whole film – images of dead animals, gargantuan waves, radiation, fire abound – and the film has a tangible atmosphere of dread but this is leavened by a briskness in the storytelling and the demented desire to entertain. The moment Godzilla raises his head over the hill is still a moment to be transfixed by. Like *Thunderbirds*, this is a movie that revels in destruction, helped no end by Akira Ifkube's score, and as the patently fake buildings and cars are trounced, it is hard not to get caught up in the childish glee of it. In the fourteen or so sequels that followed, Godzilla becomes a less threatening figure, turning into a protector and saviour of humanity rather than its nightmare. But he was never more memorable than he was here – mad, bad and *really* dangerous to know. ★★★★ **WT**

◑ GODZILLA (1997)

Starring: *Matthew Broderick (Dr. Nick Tatopoulos), Jean Reno (Philippe Roache), Maria Pitillo (Audrey Timmonds), Hank Azaria (Victor 'Animal' Palotti)*
Director: *Roland Emmerich*
Screenwriters: *Dean Devlin, Roland Emmerich, from the story by Ted Elliott, Terry Rossio, Dean Devlin, Roland Emmerich, based on character created by Toho Co. Ltd.*
PG/132 mins./Adventure/Fantasy/USA

The story, for what it's worth, is true to the 1954 Japanese original: nuclear testing creates a mutant, 200-foot-high lizard which rampages on a city – then, Tokyo; here, New York.

Big. Expensive. Over-hyped. It was the event picture to out-event all previous event pictures. Right from that first trailer, *Godzilla* was big news. Its reputation preceded it like a German holidaymaker putting his towel on a deckchair a year in advance. In the 1970s TV ad for Chewitts, Godzilla ate everything in his path. This time out, that included his own advance publicity.

To the credit of director Emmerich – who co-writes with producer Dean Devlin – the carried-over build-up within the film is expertly handled: radars blip; ships sink; an attack survivor mouths the word 'Gojira' (respectfully enough, Godzilla's original Japanese name, misheard then as here); Broderick stands in a footprint, and a fisherman on a jetty says 'I think I gotta bite'. As with Emmerich and Devlin's *Independence Day*, the sense of foreboding is enormous, like the first rumblings of a really bad stomach upset. Although no monster movie will ever top *Jaws* for its cocktail of tension and tease, *Godzilla*'s marketing hype mixes with the mounting onscreen malarkey, and – unlike Manhattan's inhabitants – we're ready for our first sighting.

Brilliantly, it's feet-first, then there's a shapely bit of leg, climaxing with a breathtaking pan up through the lens of news cameraman Hank Azaria. From there on in, it's the full monster – and you've got to hand it to those CGI Johnnies. Godzilla is dark (the whole film takes place at night), loud, malevolent and, most importantly, agile. He even swims like the creatures in *Alien Resurrection*.

So far, so jaw-dropping. But like *Independence Day* after the Capitol building, it can only go downhill from here. And 200 feet is a long way. Arguably *Godzilla*'s money shot (a gaping hole through the old Pan-Am building) is also its turning point, after which the narrative focuses on Godzilla's eggs, which Broderick and co. discover hatching in Madison Square Garden, soon overrun with Godzookis. This glaring attempt to replicate Spielberg's velociraptors is let down – incredibly enough – by design and technology. These beasts lack elegance and precision, and the resulting siege is simply unengaging and samey, even resorting to misjudged slapstick.

Mercifully, there follows a proper, terrifying climax, in which the tragic spirit of *King Kong* is finally evoked, and any warm-blooded viewer will already be siding with the reptile (victim) over the mammals (idiots). ★★
AC

◑ THE GOLD RUSH (1925)

Starring: *Charles Chaplin (The Lone Prospector), Mack Swain (Big Jim McKay), Tom Murray (Black Larsen), Henry Bergman (Hank Curtis), Malcolm Waite (Jack Cameron), Georgia Hale (Georgia)*
Director: *Charles Chaplin*
Screenwriter: *Charles Chaplin*
U/96 mins./Adventure/Comedy/Romance/USA

The Tramp goes to the Klondike in search of gold and finds it – and more.

In 1922, after eight years of playing his baggy trousered tramp, Charlie Chaplin declared his vagabond days were over. He embarked upon *A Woman Of Paris* (1923) with the aim of becoming a great artist. But that lachrymose melodrama was a critical and commercial flop and Chaplin was forced to swallow his pretensions and throw himself into this knockabout comeback, which, ironically, was to prove his mastery of screen poetry.

Initial inspiration for this movie came from two sources: a series of stereoscopic slides, belonging to Douglas Fairbanks, depicting an 1898 Klondike stampede and a graphic account of the infamous Donner expedition, which had ultimately succumbed to cannibalism. Yet there are countless autobiographical references throughout the film (Chaplin's schizophrenic mother, for example, had been a dancing girl), while others relate to his experience in music-hall (including the opening pursuit by a bear, which hailed from traditional English panto).

But there were also significant cinematic influences. In particular, Chaplin was impressed by the comedy of thrills Harold Lloyd had patented while hanging from the hands of a tower clock in *Safety Last*. So he devised the shack teetering on the precipice edge, which dipped further towards oblivion each time the Little Fellow or fellow prospector, Big Jim McKay, made a sudden movement. If anything, this is more comedy of suspense than heartstopping thrills, as the building see-saws so often that its fate becomes less important than how long Chaplin can sustain the gag and keep it funny.

The illusion was slightly marred, however, by the fact that Chaplin relied on models rather than stunts to achieve his effect. But it had a more obviously human touch than Lloyd's brash daredevilry, as Chaplin initially thinks the lurching is down to his hangover.

With its location naturalism, Erich Von Stroheim's *Greed* (1924) also left an impression, as Chaplin took his company into the Sierra Nevada to shoot snowscapes. Some 500 hobos were hired to give the trek a sense of scale. But only a handful of location shots found their way into the finished film.

As with many of Chaplin's later films, the comedy is unashamedly worldly. The primary themes are cruelty, avarice, madness and the vagaries of fate, so it's inevitable that the Tramp should seem less frivolous than before. Indeed, he appeared to be openly inviting our pity where once he'd have encouraged us to laugh. Yet, when one considers the circumstances under which the film was made, it's a wonder there's any humour here at all.

The part of Georgia, the dance-hall girl who steals the Tramp's heart, was originally conceived for Lita Grey. However, the teenage protégé had to be replaced after Chaplin got her pregnant and she insisted on marriage. It's easy to detect resentment, therefore, in the picture's attitude to the character now played by Georgia Hale.

In the 1942 reissue (to which Chaplin made several adroit alterations and appended a score and a commentary), it's implied Georgia has genuine feelings for the Little Fellow. But this is a bitterly ironic happy ending, as there's no guarantee that the gold-digger who toyed with Chaplin's affections in a bid to enrage a scornful beau has changed one iota.

Although the film predates the Depression, Chaplin never forgot the misery of poverty and frequently used it as a basis for comedy. Melancholy pervades the movie. Yet it also contains some of the best-known set-pieces of Chaplin's whole career. Nearly all of them revolve around hunger.

Most famously, the Tramp boils his boot only to lose the topside to the aptly named Big Jim, leaving him to feast on the laces and the hobnails. The succulence he suggests at each mouthful is pure pantomimic pathos. Yet, the episode proved less enjoyable for Mack Swain, as Chaplin insisted on so many takes that the laxative qualities of the liquorice leather had a devastating effect.

Days later, the still-ravenous Jim hallucinates that his companion is a giant chicken and chases him around the shack – with Chaplin meticulously miming each barnyard jerk. This scene also includes one of the film's few all-out slapstick moments, as Charlie and Jim jostle for the gun and the axe. Another was a reworking of an incident in *A Dog's Life* (1918), when Charlie uses a rope to hold up his trousers, only to discover it's attached to a moggy-chasing mutt who hurtles him to the floor. Finally, while waiting patiently for his New Year party guests, Charlie imagines passing an idyllic evening with his beloved, for whom he performs the 'dance of the rolls' – with his head bobbing ingratiatingly behind two fork legs with their little bread shoes. It's a sublime routine that deserved more than Johnny Depp's cringingly twee reprise in Benny And Joon. ★★★★★ **DP**

THE GOLDEN CHILD (1986)

Starring: *J.L. Reate (The Golden Child), Eddie Murphy (Chandler Jarrell), Charles Dance (Sardo Numspa), Charlotte Lewis (Kee Nang), Victor Wong (The Old Man)*
Director: *Michael Ritchie*
Screenwriter: *Dennis Feldman*
PG/94 mins./Action/Adventure/Comedy/USA

Chandler Jarrell, a private dick-cum-social worker, must track down a little Buddhist boy, known as the precious lad of the film's title. Apparently, an evil sorcerer is also on his tail, so it's up to Jarrell to piece together clues before all hell breaks loose.

The Golden Child suffers from being an uneasy alloy of incompatible elements. Eddie Murphy stars, but has installed some kind of limiter into his motor mouth, leaving some scenes where he might usually zing indignantly feeling a little empty. There is Charles Dance, a perfectly respectable villain (i.e. British with a sturdy jaw and piercing eyes) who would surely have done better with darker, less family-orientated material. Then there is the plot, which is weirder than *Big Trouble in Little China*, but with none of the knowingly bad laughs.

Put specifics to one side and the film fairs no better. It tries to pitch up somewhere between a Raymond Chandler homage (Jarrell's first name is one of many hints), an *Indiana Jones*-style serial romp, and a pantomime of a family event. If there is a successful balance between such differing styles, then this film doesn't find it. ★ **GB**

THE GOLDEN VOYAGE OF SINBAD (1974)

Starring: *John Philip Law (Sinbad), Caroline Munro (Margiana), Tom Baker (Koura), Douglas Wilmer (Vizier), Martin Shaw (Rachid)*
Director: *Gordon Hessler*
Screenwriters: *Ray Harrryhausen, Brian Clemens*
U/105 mins./Fantasy/UK

Legendary sailor and adventurer Sinbad, comes into the possession of a tablet inscribed with the part of a map that was in the possession of the evil Koura who comes in hot pursuit. When it transpires Vizier has another part of the map, Sinbad embarks on a quest to solve its riddle.

In the grand pantheon of Sinbad movies, those pleasurable Arabesques of silly beasts, big swords and scantily clad maidens, this lower league Ray Harryhausen stop-motion thriller squeezes between the better *Eye Of The Tiger* and the worse *Seventh Voyage*. Genre-freaks will lap up its lumpy fantasy, the snobbier cinephile amongst us will look aghast at its dreadful B-list cast and thin plotting (island A to city B to secret cave C), but still recognise that when it comes to creating a six-armed living statue of the goddess Kali, Harryhausen is your man. Although he was coasting on past glories a bit here.

The prize for Sinbad and his loyal crew is a mystical fountain of youth guarded by anything Harryhausen can run his hand to (one eye centaurs, a griffin, a demonic homunculus (look it up!) and an enchanted ship's figurehead). The special effects are, of course, spruce and well managed, maybe not a match for the CG wonders of today, but there remains a transporting glee to such lightheaded adventures. Although the actors look a bit askance at the demands of sword-fighting modelwork foes, but then John Philip Law (of Barbarella fame) and Caroline Munro were clearly cast for their cheekbones not their intuition. At best, Tom Baker bellows with panto-villainy as requisite evil sorcerer Koura. The limits are very evident, but the cheerful hubris to this kind of curly fairy-tale will always find a welcome home. ★★★ **IN**

GOLDENEYE (1995)

Starring: *Pierce Brosnan (James Bond), Sean Bean (Alec Trevelyan), Izabella Scorupco (Natalya Simonova), Famke Janssen (Xenia Onatopp), Joe Don Baker (Jack Wade), Judi Dench (M), Robbie Coltrane (Valentin Zukovsky), Alan Cumming (Boris Grishenko), Samantha Bond (Miss Moneypenny), Desmond Llewelyn (Q), Minnie Driver (Irina)*
Director: *Martin Campbell*
Screenwriters: *Jeffrey Caine, Bruce Feirstein, based on a story by Michael France, characters by Ian Fleming*
12/130 mins./Action/Spy/Thriller/USA

Bond is back, this time with Pierce Brosnan as the British superspy. Now that the Cold War is over, Bond has new enemies to contend with.

Six years in the wilderness and Bond returned, dapper, sprightly and raring to go. The rest has done the old chap good. This is no *Goldfinger*, granted, but *Goldeneye* was so much more than any of us could have hoped for.

And there's a good reason. Director Campbell and scriptwriters Michael France and Jeffrey Caine decided to make a Bond film: there's no pretence at realism (Ian Fleming's whole ethos); the necessary 90s trappings (political correctness, the fall of communism and the changing global politics) have been imbued with humour – that knowing wink at the audience; and the stunts, girls and gadgets are to die for. Bond is back.

The plot, on close examination (the perks of DVD), is a sly amalgam of former Bondian plots: the killer satellite from *Diamonds Are Forever*, the meltdown of global money markets from *Goldfinger*, the Caribbean hangout from *Dr. No* and the Soviet game-play of *From Russia With Love*. It's 60s madcap draped in 90s hi-techery.

Brosnan does the sensible thing and never tries to touch Sean Connery. Instead he revamps that indomitable British spirit – ditching the earnestness of Dalton – plays the humour adroitly, and looks as comfortable winning at Baccarat in Monte Carlo as he is mowing down Russian extras in a Moscow prison.

Tagline
You know the name. You know the number.

The film does falter in the last third – the big finale lacks imagination – the bad guy is tepid and, at times, the whole thing seems a touch too sadistic (the body count is up there with Arnie). But that's three cons against countless pros: Scorupco and Janssen actually have legitimate plot functions, there is a wealth of interesting cameos (Judi Dench's tough-talking M, Robbie Coltrane's voluminous Russian mafioso, Alan Cumming, Joe Don Baker), and the tank chase in St. Petersburg is a new action high. There's also a great credits sequence and Tina Turner is the nearest thing to Shirley Bassey without being Shirley.

'You're a relic of the Cold War,' growls Dench's cynical M at her shaken but, most definitely, not stirred secret agent. How he has proved her wrong. ★★★★ **IN**

⓪ GOLDFINGER (1964)

Starring: *Sean Connery (James Bond), Gert Frobe (Goldfinger), Honor Blackman (Pussy Galore), Shirley Eaton (Jill Masterson), Tania Mallett (Tilly Masterson), Harold Sakata (Oddjob), Bernard Lee ('M'), Martin Benson (Solo), Cec Linder (Felix Leiter), Lois Maxwell (Moneypenny)*
Director: *Harry Saltzman*
Screenwriters: *Richard Maibaum, Paul Dehn, based on the novel by Ian Fleming*
PG/112 mins./Spy/Adventure/UK

Awards: *Academy Awards – Best Sound Effects*

The Bank of England has discovered that someone is stockpiling vast quantities of gold and suspects international bullion dealer Auric Goldfinger of being involved. The Bank requests that British agent James Bond be sent to investigate. Bond soon uncovers an audacious plan to commit 'the crime of the century' and bring economic chaos to the West.

At the beginning of *Goldfinger*, James Bond emerges from black water sporting a seagull on his head, then proceeds to shed his wet suit to reveal a snazzy tuxedo replete with buttonhole. Larger than life, faintly ridiculous, completely cool, it is perhaps the quintessential James Bond movie moment to kickstart the quintessential James Bond movie. In short, *Goldfinger* is the Bond flick where 007 really hit his stride. From the broad strokes – exotic locale, vast Ken Adam sets, a large-scale finale – to the gracenotes (this was the first Bond film where Q grumpily talks 007 through his gadgets) it solidified the template yet was fresh enough not to feel formulaic. Moreover, no other 007 flick achieves such a perfect balance between glamour and action, sex and special effects, drama and comedy.

Bond number three, after *Dr. No* (1962) and *From Russia With I Love* (1963), *Goldfinger* takes a frankly ludicrous plot conceit – bulbous gold-hoarding maniac controls Fort Knox via a team of jet-flying totty and plans Operation Grand Slam, a scheme to irradiate the bullion and give him control of the world's gold reserves – yet never undermines its silliness to the point where the heroics become unengaging. Gadgets are to the fore but do not swamp the story. Indeed, it's a rare Bond film where 007 actually gets to do some spying and survive on his wits. Rather than pure Q dept gizmology, it is Bond's smattering of knowledge concerning Operation Grand Slam that stops Goldfinger melting his nuts.

Despite its robbery plotline, *Goldfinger* is less a heist movie and more a duel between superhero and supervillain. Auric Goldfinger – the surname came from an architect acquaintance of Ian Fleming's – is one of the few Bond adversaries to pose a proper, believable threat to Bond. As inhabited by Gert Frobe and voiced by Michael Collins, Goldfinger is an expert melding of the snide and the ruthless. In fact, so successful was Frobe that, working on early drafts for *Diamonds Are Forever*, screen scribe Richard Maibaum toyed with the idea of making the villain Auric Goldfinger's twin brother who has a passion for sparklers. The idea was dropped. Happily, Goldfinger has a henchman to match his prowess: mute manservant Oddjob (Harold Sakata, a wrestler known as Tosh Togo) who establishes his credentials early on by crushing a gold ball in his hand and decapitating a statue with his razor-brimmed hat. Later he gives Bond a thorough workout in a punishing last reel punch up.

Traversing a variety of looks, from the smoky exoticism of Mexico to the glitzy environs of Fort Knox, director Hamilton etches the action with fine detail – in the opening brawl, Bond sees his assailant approaching in the reflection of his lover's eye; the corpse-in-the-car-crusher murder – yet still pulls off the huge sweep: Pussy Galore's Flying Circus spraying nerve gas as John Barry's music goes into outlandish overdrive. Some of Goldfinger's greatest action licks went through a number of incarnations: Bond's near castration by laser beam was originally death by buzzsaw until Maibaum declared the spinning blade a hoary melodramatic cliché; the now iconic customised Aston Martin DB5 (a DBS in Fleming's novel) was originally billed as a Bentley. Graced with oil slick dispenser, machine guns, front wheel scythes (born from Maibaum's fascination with Ancient Greece) and, best of all, an ejector seat deployed in a blistering getaway, it is simply the sexiest motor in movie history, both on screen and as a Corgi plaything (hands up, who lost the little ejector seat man?). If nothing else, Goldfinger got in on the ground floor as far as product placement and merchandising are concerned, both of which are now action movie staples.

If the physical stuff is top-notch, Goldfinger also scores heavily in between the set-pieces both in its less frantic beats – witness the priceless encounter in which Bond out-cheats Goldfinger over 18 holes, or 007's discovery of Jill Masterson covered head to foot in gold paint – and in its characterisation. Sidelined in the book as a lesbian gangster, Pussy Galore is here upgraded to Goldfinger's personal pilot and is perhaps the closest Bond has come to meeting a female incarnation of himself. Smart as she is sassy, Honor Blackman's 'Poosy' gives Goldfinger an edge not provided by any other Bond girl.

With Blackman offering a formidable screen presence that previous eye candy Ursula Andress and Daniela Bianchi never mustered, Connery is forced to raise his game, but looks more comfortable in the role than ever. He delivers the requisite peppering of one-liners with panache – 'Shocking, positively shocking,' he quips as he electrocutes an assailant in the bath – but never muddies Bond's identity as sexual predator, suave sophisticate or menacing murderer. For once, the bulk of the theme song's lyrics – 'Enter his web of sin/but don't go in' – apply at least as much to 007 as they do to Goldfinger. A Midas touch indeed. ★★★★★ **IF**

Goldfinger

Gert Frobe's performance as Goldfinger was actually entirely redubbed, due to his impenetrable German accent. Unlike the movie, in the novel Pussy Galore is a lesbian. The name Goldfinger stems from Ian Fleming's dislike of Hungarian architect Erno Goldfinger.

⓪ DER GOLEM (1920)

Starring: *Paul Wegener (The Golem), Albert Steinruck (Rabbi Loew), Lydia Salmonova (Miriam), Ernst Deutsch (Der Rabbi Famulus), Hans Sturm (Der Rabbi Jehuda)*
Director: *Carl Boese, Paul Wegener*
Screenwriter: *Henrik Galeen, Paul Wegener based on the novel by Gustav Meyrink*
PG/91 mins./Fantasy/Horror/Germany

When the Holy Roman Emperor orders the Jews to be expelled from 16th-century Prague, Rabbi Loew fashions a golem out of clay to protect his people and summons the demon Astaroth to bring his creation to life.

When Paul Wegener directed himself in *Der Golem* and *Der Golem Und Die Tänzerin*, German psychological cinema was wholly in thrall to Scandinavian chiaroscuro. But, by the time he completed this 1920 version – which abandoned contemporary references and adhered solely to the original Polish-Jewish myth (hence its subtitle, 'How He Came into the World') – films like Robert Wiene's *The Cabinet of Dr Caligari* had introduced a homegrown expressionism that reflected the nation's mood in the aftermath of the Great War.

Given its themes and timing, the picture has been subjected to close scrutiny by critics seeking anti-Semitic and chauvinist references. But, while good cases can be more for and against these arguments, what remains clear is that this is a film of deceptive complexity whose influence continued to be felt for many years.

The theorist Siegfried Kracauer claimed that *Der Golem* reflected post-imperial resentment at the perceived Jewish orchestration of the capitalist conspiracy that had caused the war. Thus, Wegener played his part in conditioning the German mind for the Holocaust. But, while the Famulus (Ernst Deutsch) is guilty of re-animating the statue to destroy Florian (Lothar Müthel), the knight who has stolen the heart of the Rabbi's daughter, Miriam (Lyda Salmonova), the greater evils are attempted by the emperor, whose edicts typify Christian intolerance of the Jews throughout the Middle Ages. Indeed, by contrasting Loew with Faust, Wegener and co-director Carl Boese seemed to be trying to link the story to Goethe's masterpiece, which ranked as the epitome of high German art.

Similarly, accusations of misogyny can be countered, for while it's possible to see Miriam and the Golem as the Rabbi's wayward creations, the giant's climactic rampage through the ghetto suggests a condemnation of rampant male desire (which is notably curtailed by the innocence of a young girl in a sequence with pronounced Marian overtones). What's less at issue, however, is the feature's legacy, as it influenced *Metropolis*, *Frankenstein* and *King Kong*, among many others. ★★★★ **DP**

GONE IN 60 SECONDS (2000)

Starring: *Nicolas Cage (Randall 'Memphis' Raines), Giovanni Ribisi (Kip Raines), Angelina Jolie (Sara 'Sway' Wayland), T.J. Cross (Mirror Man), William Lee Scott (Toby), Scott Caan (Tumbler), James Duval (Freb), Will Patton (Atley Jackson), Delroy Lindo (Det. Roland Castlebeck), Timothy Olyphant (Det. Drycoff), Robert Duvall (Otto Halliwell), Christopher Eccleston (Raymond Vincent Calitiri), Vinnie Jones (The Sphinx)*
Director: *Dominic Sean*
Screenwriter: *Scott Rosenberg, based on the 1974 motion picture by H.B. Halicki*
15/117 mins./Action/Crime/Thriller/USA

A genius car thief has to assemble a team to steal 50 luxury cars in one night while his brother is held hostage.

A remake in the Bruckheimer (sans Simpson) style of a minor 70s car theft/chase/crash movie (that was written, directed by and starred H.B. Halicki), this is an identikit of big-bucks action pictures still mired in the style Bruckheimer – director Dominic Sena barely registers – 'perfected' in the 80s. It brings back the actors, images, plot devices and editing tricks from such hits as *Top Gun*, *Days Of Thunder*, *The Rock and Con Air*, but rushes through its rerun without ever really coming to grips with the fact that one car theft is very much like another.

Ribisi, younger brother of retired superthief Cage, fouls up in an especially stupid way working for British nasty Eccleston (a Northern bastard rather than the usual uppercrust thug). In order to persuade the mob boss not to kill his brother, Cage gets back into the criminal life and assembles a team – crusty veteran Duvall, Silent Bob-esque The Sphinx, cuddly black Chi McBride, improbable mechanic/bartender Jolie – to mix with his brother's young crew to steal 50 luxury cars in one night.

Patton is a go-between for all the criminal parties on show here, valiantly reprising his Armageddon act by trying to suggest emotional content where none exists, while outclassed cops Lindo and Olyphant plod along in the stylish crooks' tracks, planning to nail Cage once and for all, despite the fact that in LA, 'Nobody cares about auto theft.'

Among the gimmicks required to keep the plot going is a dog which swallows crucial car keys, a particular model of classic auto about which Cage has a complex, simmering who-left-whom resentment between the brothers, Eccleston's transparent plan to off everybody anyway (the final face-off takes place in what looks rather like a leftover from the set of James Cameron's *Terminator 2*), and a traffic blockage that prompts Cage to make an Evel Knievel leap which would like to be the highlight of the picture.

It's impossible to care about Cage's mission – someone asks someone else whether they ever wonder if stealing cars is wrong, and is fobbed off with a non-answer – on any level: Ribisi is an arsehole who deserves to get crushed, Eccleston a creep who doesn't deserve the cars, and the car-owners are anonymous rich types – rather like the executives who greenlit this film, perhaps? – who presumably deserve to get ripped off. But the music is loud, the editing is fast, the cast is overqualified and the cars... Well, they're just cool. ★★ **KN**

GONE TO EARTH (1950)

Starring: *Jennifer Jones (Hazel Woodus), David Farrar (Jack Reddin), Cyril Cusack (Edward Marston), Sybil Thorndike (Mrs. Marston), Edward Chapman (Mr. James), Esmond Knight (Abel Woodus)*
Directors: *Michael Powell, Emeric Pressburger*
Screenwriters: *Michael Powell, Emeric Pressburger based on the novel by Mary Webb*
PG/110 mins./Drama/UK

In the Shropshire marches in the 1890s, free-spirited Hazel is torn between her husband, a mild parson, and a dashing aristocrat to whom she is uncontrollably drawn.

This full-blooded rural melodrama affords the gorgeous Jones, with an astonishing accent, the opportunity to inflame passions left and right. When young George Cole spots Hazel in a new dress, he leers suggestively that she is like 'j-a-a-a-m', but the trouble comes from the fox-hunting sadist who takes her for a night of 'bundling' in but is clearly not a man to put up with her hunt sabotage as she tries to protect her pet vixen from his pack of hounds.

It's plain from the first that a tragic ending is on the cards, and the film works itself into a suitable frenzy before expiring during a climactic fox hunt. *Gone to Earth* finds the Michael Powell-Emeric Pressburger team working rather unhappily with egomaniac producer David O. Selznick, who was mainly concerned with making his wife look good, and tackling a novel by Mary Webb, a forgotten bestseller of the type parodied in *Cold Comfort Farm*, splurging the screen with sex, mysticism and the countryside in glowing colours. The effect is of some weird crossbreed of Thomas Hardy and Hammer Films, frequently toppled into bathos by the performances of Jones, whose country girl would not be equalled in unlikeliness until Nastassja Kinski in *Tess*, and Farrar, who appears to be auditioning for the role of the evil squire in a Victorian bloodbath.

Nevertheless, this is a must-see film for its unashamed romanticism, its breathtaking visual delirium, the excellent performance of Cusack as the only rational person in the county and the sheer spirit with which the fundamental daftness of the plot is served up. ★★★★ **KN**

GONE WITH THE WIND (1939)

Starring: *Clark Gable (Rhett Butler), Vivien Leigh (Scarlett O'Hara), Hattie McDonald (Mammy), Leslie Howard (Ashley Wilkes), Olivia de Havilland (Melanie Hamilton), Butterfly McQueen (Prissy)*
Directors: *Victor Fleming, George Cukor, Sam Wood*
Screenwriters: *Sidney Howard, Jo Swerling, Charles McArthur, Ben Hecht, John Lee Martin, John Van Druten, Oliver H.P. Garrett, Winston Miller, John Balderstone, Michael Foster, Edwin Justus Mayer, F. Scott Fitzgerald, David O'Selznick*
PG/220 mins./Drama/Historical/Romance/USA

Awards: *Academy Awards – Best Actress, Best Supporting Actress, Best Art Direction, Best Cinematography, Best Director, Best Film Editing, Best Picture, Best Screenplay, Technical Achievement Award*

Scarlett O'Hara is besotted with Ashley, but when he marries Scarlett's cousin instead, Scarlett starts a tempestuous relationship with no-good Rhett Butler – all against the background of the Civil War in America's Deep South.

The uncomfortable truth about many a film classic, be it Orson Welles' *Citizen Kane*, Stanley Kubrick's *2001* or Jean-Luc Godard's *Breathless*, is that they're often more easily admired than genuinely enjoyed. Not so

Gone With The Wind, the classic tale of the death of the Old South and the survival of the feisty Scarlett O'Hara, which is, relatively speaking, the biggest grossing film of all time, so far notching up $6,718 million at inflation-adjusted rates.

Gone With The Wind's several virtues – which include a supremely fluent narrative, a witty script, a clutch of great performances and sheer visual splendour – are not only undiminished by the passage of time, but perhaps seem all the more remarkable for it. 1939, the year of *Gone With The Wind*'s original release, also saw the release of such films as *Wuthering Heights*, *The Wizard of Oz*, *Stagecoach* and *Of Mice and Men*.

For all that, its worth remembering that *Gone With The Wind* didn't come clean away from the marble, like some cinematic Michelangelo, but was the unlikely result of a long drawn-out production process beset by indecision, unholy strife and considerable compromise. 'No civil war picture ever made a nickel' MGM production chief Irving G. Thalberg warned producer David O. Selznick even as he was agreeing to pay $50,000 for the rights to Margaret Mitchell's original novel.

Meanwhile, Selznick agonised over the casting of the film (Susan Hayward and Katherine Hepburn were both considered for the role eventually won by Vivien Leigh, while Bette Davis would probably have been the first choice), and dismissed scriptwriters with apparent abandon. F. Scott Fitzgerald lasted two weeks, as did the original director George Cukor. The director who took over, Victor Fleming, claimed to have suffered a nervous breakdown before shooting was completed.

In the light of such torments, Selznick et al's eventual triumph may be surprising, but it's churlish to scan the finished film for signs of the chaos out of which it was born. Some of *Gone With The Wind*'s current appeal may be the result of a veneer of camp that certainly overlays it, and the film is by no means psychologically complex or original. But there's no denying its effectiveness as pure and popular entertainment, or indeed the radical and richly expressive quality of the film's overall look. Scarlett's 'As God is my witness' speech may spring few surprises first or second time round, but the way she is dramatically silhouetted against a gradually brightening, exaggeratedly colourful morning sky is still worthy of wonder. ★★★★★ **AE**

GOOD BYE, LENIN (2003)

Starring: *Daniel Bruhl (Alex), Katrin Sass (Mutter), Chulpan Khamatova (Lara), Maria Simon (Ariane Kerner), Florian Lukas (Denis), Alexander Beyer (Rainer)*
Director: *Wolfgang Becker*
Screenwriters: *Wolfgang Becker, Bernd Lichtenberg*
15/121 mins./Comedy/Drama/Romance/Germany

Staunch communist Christiane falls into a coma shortly before the fall of the Berlin Wall. When she wakes eight months later, her health is so fragile that her son Alex must convince her that nothing has changed to save her shuffling off this mortal coil.

Opening in typically Euro-miserablist fashion with an impoverished East German Communist slipping into a coma, this doesn't immediately present itself as a laugh riot.

Yet there's some great comedy to be had from unconscious Commies and civil unrest. The idea of teenage Alex keeping his newly awakened mother in the dark about the fall of the Berlin Wall is inspired and handled with a deft comic touch that shoots for delicate humour rather than all-too-obvious farce.

At two hours, it slightly overextends itself, stalling in the third act with a series of dramatic family revelations. But the understated performances by Bruhl and Sass and clever use of the historical background as metaphor for family disagreement see it through. Even the 'lets all just get along' message is subtle enough not to derail what is a charming and original tale. ★★★★ **AM**

GOOD MORNING VIETNAM (1987)

Starring: *Robin Williams (Adrian Cronauer), Forest Whitaker (Edward Garlick), Tung Thanh Tran (Tuan), Chintara Sukapatana (Trinh), Bruno Kirby (Lt. Steven Hauk)*
Director: *Barry Levinson*
Screenwriter: *Mitch Markowitz*
15/119 mins./Comedy/Drama/War/USA
Awards: *Golden Globes – Robin Williams*

In a move to boost troop morale during the Vietnam War, Chicago DJ Adrian Cronauer is sent over to conquer the airwaves. He does, but not without causing a few shockwaves – especially when he starts taking in the madness going around him.

When airman-turned-DJ Adrian Cronauer first arrived in Saigon in 1965, the military bigwigs must have thought they had a prize lunatic in their midst. Before Cronauer, the boys in the field had been subjected to a daily radio diet of Mantovani, educational programmes and public health warnings. With his very first broadcast, Cronauer ripped up the rule book and blasted out a heady mix of the Beach Boys, James Brown and zany patter between the discs. Not surprisingly, he soon became a popular hero while getting further up the noses of the top brass with each show.

In *Good Morning Vietnam*, Barry Levinson's exaggerated account of the DJ's antics, Robin Williams is Cronauer and finally gets the perfect vehicle to express his furious comic talent. For the various memorable studio scenes, Williams simply made it up as he went along with Levinson picking out the very best for his final cut. The end result of this inspired improvisation is a sense of genuine excitement every time Williams takes the mike to poke fun at the military authorities, Richard Nixon and the next person who comes to mind.

His first broadcast after arriving in from Crete is blistering stuff as he cranks the dials up to full volume and then greets the bewildered troops with what would soon become his famous trademark. 'Gooooooooood Morning Viet-naaaaam!' roars Williams. 'This is not a test, this is rock and roll, time to rock it from the Delta to the DMZ!!' The whole country appears to instantly lock into his groove, all bar his immediate superiors who stare aghast at their transistors.

It's only when Williams leaves the studio and tries to go native through his teaching lessons and his romantic interest with one of his pupils that *Good Morning Vietnam* goes off the rails. The dialogue is just as sharp but the friendship between Williams and a teenage member of the Cong is clumsily sketched and ends in an awkward confrontation which seems to be trying to tell us that not all American soldiers were kind-hearted DJs and that all wars would end if only we could all get together and play baseball.

This last half-hour aside, *Good Morning Vietnam* triumphs because of Williams, ably backed up by Forest Whitaker showing the economical acting skills he would later bring to *Bird*. Studded with memorable one-liners ('you are in more dire need of a blow-job than any white man in history') and punctuated with great 60s music. ★★★★ **BMc**

GOOD NIGHT, AND GOOD LUCK (2005)

Starring: *David Stathairn (Edward R. Murrow), Robert Downey Jr. (Joe Wershba), Patricia Clarkson (Shirley Wershba), Ray Wise (Don Hollenbeck), Frank Langella (William Paley), Jeff Daniels (Sig Mickelson), George Clooney (Fred Friendly)*
Director: *George Clooney*
Screenwriters: *George Clooney, Grant Heslov*
PG/93 mins./Drama/Japan/France/UK/USA

America, 1953. Planning their CBS news show *See It Now*, hack Ed Murrow and producer Fred Friendly hit on a combustible story: the sacking of a 'Commie' Navy pilot without trial or justification. With pitbull tenacity,

Murrow and co. put reputation, network and lives on the line as they collide with the formidable Senator McCarthy, head of the toxic House Of Un-American Activities . . .

You can take the man out of TV, but you can't take the TV out of the man. Granted, we're all children of the gogglebox, but in the case of George Clooney, the holding glare of the tube shines stronger than most. Clooney's dad, Nick, was a news anchor for some 30 years; George was five when he wobbled onto his first studio floor. Even before E. R., there was a strong cathode content fizzing in those genes.

Clooney's directorial debut, *Confessions Of A Dangerous Mind*, was a gregarious if over-styled assault on trash TV. This, his second shout through the megaphone, recreates a key moment from the medium's golden era – journalist Ed Murrow's dogged pursuit of witchfinder general, Joseph McCarthy. Curiously, both movies make the same point: that TV has a duty beyond its zombifying power to distract, delude and isolate. Otherwise, there's no comparison. By any director's standards, this is superior filmmaking.

Employing a monochrome palette that's heavy on the shadows and evocative jazz interludes that act as both mood barometer and Greek chorus, the movie's sense of a nation reduced to a sustained paranoid twitch is artfully realised. Period films often fall for the trappings of sentiment and nostalgia – not here. Clooney plays out the drama with a very modern urgency, bottling the buzz of an under-siege 50s newsroom through quick-fire improvologue before settling into a deep-pressured slow-burn. The principal action takes place in a darkened TV studio lit like a bunker, and for good reason: this is, after all, war.

Murrow clearly liked a good fight – during World War II, he risked his neck reporting from the rooftops in the thick of London's Blitz. Still, his war of words with McCarthy took true nerve, because he had more to lose than just his life.

In a climate where freedom of speech was killed by fear, if McCarthy targeted you as a 'Red', 'Commie' or even a socialist, it was instant guilt by association. It wasn't just you who was sunk – it was your colleagues, your friends, your family (rather than face allegations, one character here sees suicide as the only available option).

Which leads us to the movie's most gripping moments: the screened showdowns between Murrow and McCarthy. Murrow – a deadpan, enigmatic Strathairn – calls for tolerance and candour. McCarthy, typically, settles for insults, tarring Murrow 'the cleverest of the jackal pack'. Well, better a jackal than a Neanderthal. Tempting as it must have been to cast a McCarthy, the decision to go with archive footage is an excellent one. Not only does it lend a documentary edge to proceedings, it also exposes the hectoring senator for what he was: a ham, a bully, a coward and a thug. History's already judged him and, figuring history has a nasty habit of repeating itself, Clooney condemns him all over again. Given that a certain George W. has inherited that not-so-great US tradition of passing the buck (a McCarthy speciality), you'd be hard-pressed to call *Good Night*'s concerns redundant.

The film isn't without its bumps. This is a microcosm-of-a-moment movie, and character development simply doesn't come with the territory. Strathairn withstanding, the support feels script-sketched, if not reduced to thematic ciphers (Downey Jr. and Clarkson's clandestine marriage is used solely to reflect the era's aura of nervy secrecy). They get your respect alright; just don't expect any emotional air-punching. Then again, it's apparent Clooney doesn't want to leave you with that cosy Ron Howard feeling. He wants to leave you stimulated, talkative and, perhaps, a little combative about the current state of our corporate-badged media. A second viewing certainly promises further rewards. ★★★★ **SC**

⊙ GOOD WILL HUNTING (1997)

Director: *Gus Van Sant*
Starring: *Robin Williams (Sean Maguire), Matt Damon (Will Hunting), Ben Affleck (Chuckie Sullivan), Stellan Skarsgard (Prof. Gerald Lambeau), Minnie Driver (Skylar), Casey Affleck (Morgan O'Mally)*
Screenwriters: *Matt Damon, Ben Affleck*
15/126 mins./Drama/USA
Awards: *Academy Awards – Best Supporting Actor, Best Original Screenplay, Golden Globes – Best Screenplay*

A troubled maths genius must choose between an academic career and hanging out with his working-class friends.

Good Will Hunting may well be the Rocky story of the 90s. Two young (then unknown) actors – Matt Damon and Ben Affleck – wrote a script that dealt with the commercial double suicide that is mental health issues and genius mathematicians. Within months, their script had sold for a million dollars (plus change), the two actors were set to star, Gus Van Sant was on board to direct and Robin Williams was lending big name clout to the supporting roles. The result is a beautiful piece of filmmaking that was bound for Oscar glory and box office success.

A janitor at a technological institute, Will is a 20-year-old caught between Boston's working-class environs and its elite academia. But unlike the friends he hangs with, he also has a photographic memory and an amazing ability to solve mathematical problems of the highest order. A professor tries to nurture his talent and tame his temper, enlisting the help of jaded shrink Robin Williams – the boy knows life in abstract, the man knows the pain of the real thing. Together they find an understanding and, in some small way, a path towards redemption.

The strength of *Good Will Hunting* lies in the amazing assurance of its script, and the backing both its cast and makers give it. Director Van Sant steers well clear of unnecessary sentiment, opting instead to find the emotional reality and harshness within the story. Damon is superb, his pal Affleck equally strong. But, in a movie that exudes quality, however, it is Robin Williams that provides both its heart and its highlight. In this day and age, *Good Will Hunting* is, simply, as good as movies get. ★★★★★ **BM**

⊙ THE GOOD, THE BAD AND THE UGLY (IL BUONO, IL BRUTTO, IL CATTIVO) (1966)

Director: *Sergio Leone*
Starring: *Clint Eastwood (Joe), Eli Wallach (Tuco), Lee Van Cleef (Setenza), Aldo Giuffre, Chelo Alonso, Mario Brega, Luigi Pistilli, Rada Rassimov, Enzo Petito, Claudio Scarchilli*
Screenwriters: *Luciano Vincenzoni, Sergio Leone, based on a story by Agenore Incrocci, Furio Scarpelli, Vincenzoni and Leone*
18/161 mins./Western/Italy/Spain

The Good and the Ugly have a hate-hate relationship and take to leaving each other in deserts to save themselves. However, when they're given a map detailing the whereabouts of some treasure, they pull together for the trip. Unfortunately they end up in a Prisoner of War Camp with The Bad, who wants a piece of the action.

Amid the endless homages and the sheer adoration meted out to Sergio Leone's ambitious, pricier finale to his Spaghetti Western trilogy, it's easy to forget just how damn good the film is.

Of course, much has been written on the director's mission to recast the grand traditions of the Western genre in a bold, wry, Euro-sheen that both paid tribute and deconstructed everything it stood for; how he divested the cowboy genre of its pomp and added irony, hyperbole and a great deal of slithery twang. Yet his purposes were never trivial, and to see the film as simply an exercise in effervescent cool is to miss the point entirely.

Draped in anti-war sentiment, a deep-seated compassion as counterpoint to its superficial amorality, this is a covert condemnation of American hypocrisy dressed in a poncho and chewing cheroots with slick indifference.

The version revamped by MGM, just shy of three hours, is as close as possible to Leone's original 177-minute cut. Deemed too long to satisfy American audiences the film was reigned back to 162 mins, and circulated thus ever since.

With due reverence, Eastwood and Wallach lent their now age-worn voices to dub the reinserted scenes, which makes them simple to detect, and on the whole their initial excision never really dampened the plot. However, Leone's movies were never designed to be concise, and letting this leathery, quasi-comic-book dream roam a few more dunes in search of that cache of gold is only to be applauded. ★★★★★ **IN**

GOODBYE, MR CHIPS (1939)

Starring: *Robert Donat (Charles Chipping), Greer Garson (Katherine Ellis), Terry Kilburn (John Peter Colley), John Mills (Peter Colley, as a young man)*
Director: *Sam Wood*
Screenwriters: *R,C, Sherriff, Claudine West, Eric Maschwitz, Sidney Franklin based on the novella by James Hampton*
PG/114 mins./Drama/UK

Awards: *Academy Awards – Best Actor (Robert Donat)*

Charles Chipping arrives at Brookfield School as a junior master in 1870 and remains a cornerstone of the institution over the next 58 years, as boys come and go and he comes to terms with the loss of his wife, Katherine, in childbirth.

Inheriting a role initially destined for Charles Laughton, Robert Donat gave the performance of his career in this charming evocation of life in an English public school. Modelling his voice and mannerisms on his wife's uncle, the distinguished architect C.F.A. Voysey, Donat overcame his chronic asthma to beat Clark Gable to Best Actor in the year that *Gone With the Wind* swept the Academy Awards.

The debuting Greer Garson was also nominated for her delightful display as Katherine Ellis, whom Chips meets while walking in the Austrian Alps with his colleague Max Staefel (Paul Henreid, who was billed as Von Henreid in his first English-speaking role) and who brings the old bachelor out of himself to earn the undying affection of his charges.

James Hilton wrote the original novella in just four days to meet a magazine deadline. Although some have claimed its inspiration was his own schoolmaster father, the model for Mr Chips seems to have been one W.H. Balgarnie, who taught Hilton at a private school near Cambridge. The story became popular after literary critic Alexander Woollcott championed it on his radio show and it was snapped up by MGM for production at its UK studio at Borehamwood (although Repton stood in for Brookfield, with several teachers and pupils serving as extras).

The estimable R.C. Sheriff was among those who worked on the screenplay, which not only conveys the school's spirit, but also the intrusion of real life upon an essentially enclosed community. The sequences in which the boys and masters first meet Katherine are very sweet, while Chips's mourning for both his late wife and the alumni lost in the Great War is deeply affecting, yet as admirably unsentimental as his own deathbed scene.

MGM remade the movie as a musical in 1969. Peter O'Toole landed an Oscar nomination for his efforts in the title role and Petula Clark worked hard as Katherine. But Leslie Bricusse's mediocre songs are largely redudant and the debuting Herbert Ross's direction falls into every trap that Sam Wood's had so scrupulously avoided. ★★★★★ **DP**

GOODFELLAS (1990)

Starring: *Robert De Niro (James Conway), Ray Liotta (Henry Hill), Joe Pesci (Tommy DeVito), Lorraine Bracco (Karen Hill), Paul Sorvino (Paul Cicero)*
Director: *Martin Scorsese*
Screenwriters: *Nicholas Pileggi, Martin Scorsese, based on the book* Wise Guy *by Pileggi*
18/148 mins./Crime/Drama/USA

Awards: *Academy Awards – Best Supporting Actor (Joe Pesci), BAFTA – Best Costume, Best Direction, Best Editing, Best Film, Best Adapted Screenplay*

Henry Hill and his friends work their way up through the mob hierarchy.

In 1985, when he was in the middle of shooting *The Color Of Money*, Martin Scorsese didn't think there was much future in the gangster movie. Not only had he already visited that territory with his triumphant calling-card *Mean Streets* in 1973, but the final word seemed to have been delivered by Francis Ford Coppola with *The Godfather* the previous year. 'There's no sense in making another gangster picture, unless it's as close as possible to a certain kind of reality, to the spirit of a documentary,' he said. Nothing seemed to suggest itself. Then he was handed the galley proofs for a not-yet published book, *Wise Guy* by Nicholas Pileggi. And he changed his mind.

Pileggi's book, a non-fiction account of the life and crimes of Henry Hill based upon interviews with Hill after he entered the witness protection programme, meshed perfectly with Scorsese's early memories of peering out of his window in Little Italy and being, 'Aware of these older men who had power without lifting a finger ...' It's a child's-eye view perfectly captured in the opening act of the movie, in which a young Henry mesmerised by the money and glamour of the neighbourhood thugs is slowly sucked into the milieu of the mobster. It's a story of seduction and in one of the blackest scenes he's 'pinched' for the first time only to be greeted by a crowd of cheering hoods. These people are not only corrupt, they're worse; they rejoice in corrupting others. But there's no doubt where this path will lead. In one of the many freeze frames, which occur at the various key turning points in the film, young Henry is seen silhouetted against a bright orange cumulus of fire from an exploding car yard. You don't need to be a Catholic like Scorsese to work out where Hill is headed.

But it's in the second act that the movie really takes off. Here we see the GoodFellas in their element and Scorsese in his. There are too many great moments to list: Tommy's 'You think I'm funny?' tirade in the restaurant (all improvised); Jimmy sitting at a bar, not moving a muscle and yet somehow managing to convey with still, gimlet eyes that, by the end of Scorsese's slow zoom, he's decided to execute Morey; the breathtaking steadicam trip through a nightclub's kitchens (unplanned – Scorsese couldn't get permission to go in the front way so devised the incredible sequence on the hop). Scorsese delights in the technical possibilities of filmmaking. There are flash cuts, freeze frames, crash zooms, montage, the most systematic, brilliant use of score both over and under the action in cinema and an audacious voiceover (often the sign of lazy storytelling – here an integral part of the movie). This is look Ma, no-hands! filmmaking and as critic Pauline Kael pointed out, the reason that this movie above all others appealed to the twentysomething film enthusiasts of 1990 was that it was akin to going to a gig and wishing you were in the band. 'They don't just respond to his films,' she wrote, 'they want to be him.'

But there's much more lurking underneath the bravura direction. Unlike Coppola's *Godfather*, which elevates its characters to the level of players in some grand opera, *GoodFellas* slyly undermines the swagger of the gangsters, presenting them instead as pathetic characters trapped in a bubble of ostentatious bad taste.

There is the constant vulgar waving around of $20 bills, the grotesque soft furnishings, the mink coats and pink Cadillacs. These are loathsome yuppies with firearms, and it's surely no accident that *GoodFellas* found success in 1990, the year that this kind of garish conspicuous consumption began to be decried.

Not only that, these are criminals who carry with them the seeds of their own destruction. Their greed, ego and corruption conspire satisfyingly against them. The gang that pull off the giant airport heist are systematically murdered by Jimmy who is unable to believe that, in their idiocy, they won't give him away. He is in turn betrayed by Hill who is motivated by fear generated by his own greed (he gets into the drug trade against the explicit word of Pauly – a magnificently reserved Paul Sorvino), while Tommy has the arrogance to think he can mess with the Mafia, and pays for it by being shot in the head. Everyone gets what's coming to them and in the end Henry's fate is particularly appropriate. He may not wind up in the inferno that Scorsese suggests at the start of the movie, but he's in a perfectly-realised personal purgatory; rotting in the Witness Protection Programme, the boy who ever since he could remember, 'wanted to be a gangster', winding up as an 'ordinary schnook'.

It is of course a little too perfect to be true. In an ironic kicker, in real-life, Hill used his new identity to embark on yet more crime and was summarily kicked out of the programme a few years later. ★★★★★ **AS**

THE GOONIES (1985)

Starring: *Sean Astin (Mikey Walsh), Josh Brolin (Brand Walsh), Jeff Cohen (Lawrence 'Chunk' Cohen), Corey Feldman (Clark 'Mouth' Devereaux), Kerri Green (Andy Carmichael), Martha Plimpton (Stef Steinbrenner), Jonathan Ke Quan (Richard 'Data' Wang), John Matuszak (Lotney 'Sloth' Fratelli), Robert Davi (Jake Fratelli), Anne Ramsey (Mama Fratelli)*
Director: *Richard Donner*
Screenwriter: *Chris Columbus, based on a story by Steven Spielberg*
PG/114 mins./Adventure/Comedy/Family/USA

A bunch of kids out for an adventure, and to find money to resist the property developers, embark on pirate treasure hunt.

Pirate gold, elaborate traps, winding waterslides and the inimitable 'truffle shuffle' – could this be the most accomplished kids' adventure of all time?

Richard Donner's treasure hunt demonstrates superb crossover appeal, thrilling kids and enchanting adults with its deftly-spun tale of derring-do. Thanks to Chris Columbus' lively script, the film crackles along at a fair old pace; there's spectacle too, with Donner sparing no expense on the film's elaborate sets – impressive on a scale barely attempted in today's green-screen-dependent features.

Though the film reduces its girls to mewling liabilities and shamelessly exploits both the token ethnic character and the obligatory fat kid, who cares when everyone's having this much fun? ★★★★ **JDy**

GOSFORD PARK (2001)

Starring: *Michael Gambon (Sir William McCordle), Kristin Scott Thomas (Lady Sylvia McCordle), Alan Bates (Jennings), Helen Mirren (Mrs. Wilson), Camilla Rutherford (Isobel McCordle), Maggie Smith (Constance, Countess of Trentham), Emily Watson (Elsie), Richard E. Grant (George), Geraldine Somerville (Louisa, Lady Stockbridge), Eileen Atkins (Mrs. Croft), Ryan Phillippe (Henry Denton), Jeremy Northam (Ivor Novello), Tom Hollander (Anthony Meredith), Stephen Fry (Inspector Thompson), Kelly McDonald (Mary Maceachran), Clive Owen (Robert Parks)*
Director: *Robert Altman*
Screenwriter: *Julian Fellows, based on an idea by Robert Altman, Bob Balaban*
15/137 mins./Drama/Mystery/USA

Awards: *Academy Awards – Best Original Screenplay, BAFTA – Alexander Korda Award for Best British Film, Best Costume, Golden Globes – Best Director*

A weekend at the country estate of a nouveau riche baronet and his blue-blooded wife brings together aristocrats, arrivistes, showbiz people and servants. Everyone's class sensibilities and guilty secrets intensify when a dead body is discovered.

With films we recognise as 'Altmanesque' springing from Los Angeles, Marseilles and New Delhi, it's salutary to revel in a classic model by the master of the movie mosaic himself, as he presides over a richly-nuanced screenplay and an ensemble to die for.

While wittily referring to the manor mystery genre, this is no whodunnit, but a multi-layered tragicomedy of manners, motives and relationships within a decaying social order.

A Who's Who of British Equity proves wonderfully adroit at the idiosyncratic, improvisational Altman Experience – theatrical knights wielding and polishing the silver, great dames slinging arch glances and saucepans. Upstairs, ungracious tycoon Michael Gambon is bedevilled by in-laws. Downstairs, hostility between housekeeper Helen Mirren and cook Eileen Atkins builds to a moving, revelatory confrontation without impeding butler Alan Bates' regulation of the staff.

Holding their own in this company are Americans Bob Balaban (Altman's partner in the conception and production) as a coolly-received Hollywood producer and Ryan Phillippe, affecting a purposefully dubious accent, as his highly suspicious valet. Jeremy Northam is just divine as matinee idol Ivor Novello, whose presence provokes sniffs from the aristos but excites the housemaids.

The pivotal character is Kelly Macdonald's Mary, the new lady's maid whose quiet labours position her perfectly to observe the misbehaviour and foibles above and below stairs with perception and sympathy. And although Dame Maggie Smith's imperious countess grabs the largest share of memorable lines, everyone has his moment in this inventive and fully-detailed piece. That includes the valet protesting, 'I've washed him and I've dressed him, and if he can't find his own way to the drawing room it's not my fault!' ★★★★ **AE**

THE GOSPEL ACCORDING TO MATTHEW (1964)

Starring: *Enrique Irazoqui (Jesus Christ), Margherita Caruso (Mary, as a girl), Susanna Pasolini (Mary, as a woman), Marcello Morante (Joseph), Mario Socrate (John the Baptist), Settino Di Porti (Peter), Otello Sestilli (Judas), Ferrucio Nuzzo (Matthew), Giacomo Morante (John), Alfonso Gatto (Andrew)*
Director: *Pier Paolo Pasolini*
Screenwriter: *Pier Paolo Pasolini, based on The Gospel according To St. Matthew*
U/135 mins./Drama/France/Italy

Awards: *Venice Film Festival – Special Jury Prize*

Jesus Christ preaches a message of such spiritual and political power that he is crucified by an unholy alliance of the Roman and Jewish authorities.

Despite their obvious differences, it's surprisingly easy to draw parallels between Pier Paolo Pasolini and Christ. Both abandoned the religion of their youth and so alarmed the authorities with their outspoken views that they were charged with blasphemy. Both presented fresh interpretations of established texts – Christ the Old Testament, Pasolini the plays of Sophocles, the masterworks of medieval literature and, of course, Matthew's gospel. And both lived among society's outcasts and perished at the hands of the very people they sought to champion.

It's not difficult, therefore, to see why the gay, Marxist poet and film-maker would be drawn to the life and teachings of a Jewish carpenter. Pasolini was inspired to make the film after realising that Christ's message was as politicised as it was compassionate and he quotes directly from scripture throughout.

A dedication to the late Pope John XXIII and a visual style that astutely combined the revolutionary and the reverential went some way to deflecting Vatican criticism. The tableaux owed much to devotional art, while the restrained depiction of the miracles and the crucifixion contrasted with the sentimental pictorialism of Hollywood offerings like *King of Kings*. But the employment of handheld cameras and zoom lenses enabled Pasolini to achieve a modernity that had its roots in Carl Theodor Dreyer's *The Passion of Joan of Arc*, neo-realism and the nouvelle vague.

More contentious was Pasolini's choice of cast. Spanish architecture student, Enrique Irazaoqui was selected for Christ because of his El Greco-like demeanour (although he was dubbed by Enrico Maria Salerno), while the director's mother, Susanna, played the Virgin Mary. Other roles were taken by Calabrian peasants and notable literary figures, with Roman trucker Otello Sestili essaying Judas.

There was an inevitable Marxist backlash against the film's 'reactionary ideology' and Pasolini admitted to being ashamed of some moments of 'disgusting pietism'. Yet it won the Special Jury Prize at Venice and an award from the International Catholic Film Office. ★★★★★ **DP**

Pier Paolo Passolini (1922–1975)

Who he was: Child poet, young novelist. Maker of incendiary films, covering all the controversial bases — Marxism, atheism, fascism, homosexuality. Murdered in mysterious circumstances.

Hallmarks: Non-professional actors, natural lighting.

If you see one film, see: The Gospel According to St. Matthew (1964)

THE GRADUATE (1967)

Starring: *Anne Bancroft (Mrs. Robinson), Dustin Hoffman (Ben Braddock), Katharine Ross (Elaine Robinson), William Daniels (Mr. Braddock), Murray Hamilton (Mr. Robinson)*
Director: *Mike Nichols*
Screenwriters: *Calder Willingham, Buck Henry, based on the novel by Charles Webb*
15/105 mins./Drama/Comedy/USA

Awards: *Academy Awards – Best Director, BAFTA – Best Director, Best Film, Best Editing, Best Newcomer, Best Screenplay, Golden Globes – Best Musical/Comedy, Best Musical/Comedy Actress, Best Director, Most Promising Female Newcomer (Katharine Ross), Most Promising Male Newcomer (Dustin Hoffman)*

Recent college graduate Benjamin Braddock is trapped into an affair with Mrs. Robinson, who happens to be the wife of his father's business partner and then finds himself falling in love with her teenage daughter, Elaine.

So here's to you Mrs. Robinson – you certainly cut a swathe through Hollywood's middle-class American value system at the fag-end of the 60s. Hooking up with primordial Generation X-er, Benjamin Braddock (son of her husband's partner) stunned, appalled and excited cinemagoers (it was a huge hit) and created a classic tale of social dysfunction and trashing weddings. We're all fucked up, Nichols' bravura poem sang to us, is there any hope? This was satire at its most biting. Benjamin Braddock is a startling creation, his disassociation and disaffection carry shades of Salinger's miseryguts Holden Caulfield, but Benjamin is portrayed in a much more heart-on-sleeve fashion. He is set apart from the wealthy vacuum-packed world of his parents (summed up by Walter Brooke's terrifying single word of advice: 'plastics') and distanced from the loved-up world of his peers. Adulthood and the future beckon, but he can only float, finding solace at the bottom of the pool (water serves as a constant metaphor for separation) and escape in the clutches of Mrs. Robinson: saviour, parasite, devil.

Nichols first approached an ageing Doris Day for the part of Mrs. Robinson, but she was horrified by the subject matter, terrified of ruffling her clean-cut 50s persona. Still, it is hard to imagine anyone but Anne Bancroft in the role. In reality merely seven years Hoffman's senior, she locates the dark heart of a character consumed by self-loathing and armoured in cool cynicism. She shifts from tragic to malicious, certainly a vampiric figure but in the face of the buttoned-down platitudes of their suffocating suburban deadzone her bitterness makes her real. She represents a Benjamin or Elaine that has given in ('It's too late,' she growls at a fleeing Elaine. 'Not for me!' her daughter cruelly returns).

Hoffman was also a second choice. Nichols had mulled over Robert Redford as Benjamin but surmised that playing a bit of a loser would be a stretch for an actor that beautiful. In a career defining turn, Hoffman (then 29), filled the angsty loafer with a nasally self-absorption; equally misfit and arsehole. Katharine Ross was blessed with the ideal American sweetheart looks for Elaine – the counterpoint to all the vulgar goings-on at the Taft Hotel. As the film shifts into its more romanticised second-half, Elaine is transformed into an elusive, angelic figure – another symbol of rescue for the hangdog loner Benjamin.

Though the film frequents painful areas of life, it is very funny. The infamous seduction sequence allows Hoffman a twitching realistic terror, further exacerbated by the almost knockabout humour of the first hotel liaison ('Are you here for an affair, sir?'). In the bedroom his nerves reduce him to madly banging his head against the wall – a scene improvised by Hoffman and maintained as he noticed his director screaming with laughter. Buck Henry and Calder Willingham's adaptation of Charles Webb's novel is a bounty of observational wit from screwed-up individuals. Benjamin is forced to show off his new scuba gear at another vile parental shindig and Nichols shoots it all POV with heavy Darth Vader breathing as his dad (William Daniels) submerges him in the pool. The opening dinner party is a smear of cloying chitchat from the gauche neighbourhood zombies until the phantom presence of Mrs. Robinson beckons him to drive her home.

'Mrs. Robinson', the song that is, is never actually sung in the movie, serving only as a jangly instrumental backing to the race-to-stop-the-wedding finale (Nichols later encouraged Simon to apply the lyrics). Simon And Garfunkel's legendary songs that do feature are integral to the themes of isolation and yearning, as much a part of *The Graduate* vibe as Nichols' mannered direction. From the intro as Benjamin arrives at LAX airport (a travelator scene nabbed by Quentin Tarantino for *Jackie Brown*) to the balladeering of 'The Sound Of Silence', the songs constantly establish and fix his state-of-mind. The ending has been the cause of endless debate. Having clutched Elaine from the jaws of mediocrity, they flag down a bus and in the face of the passengers' incredulous looks make their way to the back. Here Nichols pulls his finest, radically unromanticised trick. At first they giggle and gasp at their foolhardiness, then they look apart and the movie fades away. Spiritually they have separated, the comfort has broken. This is not a fairytale ending, this is an uncertain voyage into the future: have they run away together or have they just run away? Coo-coo-ca-choo. ★★★★ **IN**

Movie Trivia: The Graduate

Robert Redford was originally cast as Benjamin but he apparently turned it down thinking he wouldn't be able to project the required naivety. Although Mrs. Robinson is supposed to be much older than Benjamin, Dustin Hoffman and Anne Bancroft are only six years apart in age. The legs that appear on the promotional poster belong to Linda Gray — most famous for playing Sue Ellen in *Dallas*.

◎ GRAND CANYON (1991)

Starring: *Danny Glover (Simon), Kevin Kline (Mack), Steve Martin (Davis), Mary McDonnell (Claire), Mary-Louise Parker (Dee), Alfre Woodward (Jane), Jeremy Sisto (Roberto)*
Director: *Lawrence Kasdan*
Screenwriters: *Lawrence Kasdan, Meg Kasdan*
15/134 mins./Drama/USA

Six characters' lives intertwine in 90s L.A. with incidents ranging from comic to soapy drama.

Touted as a *Big Chill* for the nineties, this glance at the traumas of living in the metropolis of Los Angeles does indeed centre around a group of people dealing with their individual mid-life crises, and reunites *Chill*-director Kasdan with star Kevin Kline.

Unfortunately, that's where the similarities end. In fact, the first few scenes of the movie more closely resemble *The Bonfire Of The Vanities*, with Kevin Kline taking a wrong turn in his Mercedes driving home one night, and ending up breaking down in a deserted South Central LA street. Saved in the nick of time from a gang of hoodlums by tow-truck driver Danny Glover, Kline begins to realise how threatening life in the big city really is.

The plot twists and turns between comedy and soap opera drama as new characters are introduced to show different aspects of Los Angeles: Kline's wife, the rather wooden Mary McDonnell, discovers an abandoned baby and 'adopts' it; Kline's secretary (Parker) and friend (Woodward) are coping with the loneliness of being single working women; Glover has to deal with his sister's family living in one of LA's rougher areas; and Kline's best friend, Steve Martin, a producer of violent movies, finds himself on the recieving end of the kind of violence he glorifies. Each scene produces a new catastrophe for one of the characters, and although Kasdan and his co-writer, wife Meg, manage to successfully intertwine the lives of the six characters, it often seems that they have added one disaster too many to the recipe.

Steve Martin walks away with the comic plaudits as the money-minded producer, making you wish his role was larger, and Woodward, Glover and Kline all add realism to a plot that sometimes defies belief. Although followers of *The Big Chill* and *Silverado* may be disappointed by what is essentially an amusing forty-something movie, fans of soap opera will want to go back for more. ★★★ **JB**

◎ GRAND HOTEL (1932)

Starring: *Greta Garbo (Grusinskaya), John Barrymore (Baron Felix von Galgiern), Joan Crawford (Flaemmchen), Wallace Beery (General Director Preysing), Lionel Barrymore (Otto Kringelein)*
Director: *Edmund Goulding*
Screenwriter: *William A. Drake based on Drake's stage adaptation of the novel* Menschen im Hotel *by Vicki Baum*
U/115 mins./Drama/USA

Awards: *Academy Awards – Best Picture*

Fate takes a hand in the lives of Russian ballerina Grusinskaya, gentleman thief Baron Felix von Geigern, dying accountant Otto Kringelein, grasping industrialist Preysing and gold-digging stenographer Miss Flaemmchen in a Berlin hotel.

The only film to win the Academy Award for Best Picture without receiving any other nominations was based on a novel and a play by the German author Vicki Baum, which was translated for Broadway by William A. Drake. MGM producer Irving G. Thalberg paid $13,500 for the rights and set about assembling an all-star cast. However, none of his quintet approached the project with any enthusiasm, with Greta Garbo convinced she was too old and ungainly to play a ballerina and Wallace Beery angered that such a wholly unsympathetic character as the scheming industrialist would damage his reputation for bullish geniality.

Thalberg wisely appointed Edmund 'the Lion Tamer' Goulding as director and he keeps the action under creditable control, introducing the principals with impressive efficiency in the opening scenes. He may have failed to prevent Garbo and John Barrymore from occasionally resorting to silent melodramatics during their love-making, but he did manage to keep Beery, Lionel Barrymore and Joan Crawford's notorious scene-stealing antics in check. He was less successful, however, in avoiding behind-the-scenes feuds, particularly between Crawford and Beery, although Garbo and Barrymore seem to have struck up a rapport that belied the Great Profile's casting over Garbo's companion, John Gilbert.

Despite her misgivings, Garbo gives a superb performance as the fading star who wants to be alone from the pressures of fame and the responsibilities of her art. Indeed, her entire physique seems to change as Barrymore's charlatan abandons his bid to rob her to coax her out of suicidal despair. By the time he departs to face his destiny, Garbo has ceased to be a prima diva and is simply a woman in love, whose melancholy has been replaced by the lightness and charm of a dancer.

Her co-stars have their moments, but this is Garbo's picture. It may not have aged wonderfully well, but its interweaving of individual storylines into a satisfying dramatic whole made it the first soap and its formula has been endlessly repeated ever since. ★★★★ **DP**

◎ LA GRANDE BOUFFE (1973)

Starring: *Marcello Mastroianni (Marcello), Michel Piccoli (Michel), Phillipe Noiret (Phillippe), Ugo Tognazzi (Ugo), Andrea Ferreol (Andrea), Solange Blondeau (Danielle)*
Director: *Marco Ferreri*
Screenwriters: *Marco Ferreri, Rafael Azcona*
18/124 mins./Comedy/Drama/France/Italy

An airline pilot, a chef, a TV producer and a judge meet at a French villa and vow to eat themselves to death.

Marcello Mastroianni could never be accused of playing it safe. Fresh from playing the lead in Jacques Demy's eccentric gender satire, *A Slightly Pregnant Man*, he embarked on the fourth of his seven collaborations with Marco Ferreri, which foregrounded bodily functions in order to denounce the suicidal folly of contemporary society. The film divided audiences from its premiere at Cannes, where punch-ups broke out among the assembled critics and violence continued to attend its long run in Paris. It was even said that Mastroianni's then-lover, Catherine Deneuve, was so appalled by the picture that she didn't speak to him for a week.

This is certainly a film with something to offend everyone. Its bleak, bawdy humour is anything but subtle, with each character carefully designed to reflect what Ferreri considered to be modern evils – the injustice perpetuated by the corrupt judicial system; the cultural inanity encouraged by television; the greed of the developed world when much of the planet was starving; and the restless urge to travel, both to escape from domestic reality and to bring about a global village that could be more easily conquered and exploited. No wonder Pier Paolo Pasolini was inspired by the erupting bottoms and toilets to create his own savagely scatalogical assault on the Fascist mentality in *Saló,* or *The 120 Days of Sodom*.

The ensemble performances are truly remarkable and whether they're world-wearily cursing their lots or engaging in food fights, Mastroianni, Piccoli, Noiret and Tognazzi abandon their egos and place implicit trust in Ferreri's audacious design. Yet, the impious Mastroianni inevitably stands out, as his controlling sensuality continuously overcomes his despondency and he fetishises over the statue in the garden and the Bugatti motor in the garage before indulging himself with both the prostitute and the visiting school teacher. Indeed, it's with something approaching relief that his comrades bundle his corpse into the fridge to resume their funereal repast in peace. ★★★★ DP

LA GRANDE ILLUSION (1937)

Starring: *Jean Gabin (Marechal), Pierre Fresnay (Capt. De Boeldieu), Erich von Stroheim (Von Rauffenstein), Marcel Dalio (Rosenthal), Dita Parlo (Elsa, Farm Woman)*
Director: *Jean Renoir*
Screenwriters: *Jean Renoir, Charles Spaak*
PG/95 mins./War/Prison/France

Two French officers in a POW camp during World War I befriend a Jew and begin to hatch an escape plan from the supposed impenetrable fort.

A profound examination of the nature of war, with a strong pacifist – but not appeasing – streak.

In 1916, commandant Von Stroheim runs a supposedly escape-proof German POW camp and comes to respect one of his charges, aristocratic French officer Fresnay. They share a doomed vision of honourable war that the carnage of World War I has rendered hideously obsolete, and a tragic escape attempt brings the truth home to them both.

With a letter-perfect performance from Von Stroheim, and a potent examination of the differences of class and attitude among the prisoners and the guards, this is less hectoring than most anti-war films, but nevertheless makes a lasting statement. ★★★★★ DP

THE GRAPES OF WRATH (1940)

Starring: *Henry Fonda (Tom Joad), Jane Darwell (Ma Joad), John Carradine (Casey), Charley Grapewin (Grandpa Joad), Dorris Bowdon (Rosaharn), Russell Simpson (Pa Joad)*
Director: *John Ford*
Screenwriter: *Nunnally Johnson, based on the novel by John Steinbeck*
PG/129 mins./Drama/USA

Awards: *Academy Awards – Best Supporting Actress (Jane Darwell), Best Director*

During the Depression, the Joad family are evicted from their Oklahoma farm and set out to find work in California. Experiencing social injustice, poverty and ill-treatment, Tom Joad becomes an outlaw labour agitator, while Ma keeps the family together with her strength of spirit.

Though he later liked to dismiss himself as a director of journeyman Westerns, John Ford was drawn to the works of important contemporary writers in the 1930s and 40s. For the most part, these 'respectable' Oscar-bid productions (*The Informer, How Green Was My Valley, The Long Voyage Home, The Fugitive*) wear less well than the Westerns, but *The Grapes of Wrath*, from John Steinbeck's controversial novel, is among the director's greatest films.

Steinbeck only let 20th Century-Fox have the rights on the condition that the social anger not be watered down, and the film is astonishingly frank for a production of its vintage (for the first time in an American movie, a flush toilet is heard). In some ways, just putting on screen the conditions Steinbeck wrote about gives them a greater impact, and memorable sequences depict huge caterpillar tractors ploughing under the sharecroppers' meagre homes, and hellhole conditions in transient camps or the strike-breaking workers' quarters.

Henry Fonda has one of his most iconic roles as ex-con Tom Joad, striding against the skyline, and following the example of near-crazy, yet-Christlike Preacher Casey as he is driven outside the law and resolves to do something about injustice. It shares with Ford's Westerns a sense of the struggle to build a community – as usual, a big party sequence features home-made music and exuberant dancing – but there's a high degree of specific indictments of the powerful bankers and ranchers and thuggish cops and vigilantes who give these Okies such a hard time. ★★★★★ KN

GREASE (1978)

Starring: *John Travolta (Danny Zucco), Olivia Newton-John (Sandy), Stockard Channing (Betty Rizzo), Jeff Conaway (Kenickie), Didi Conn (Frenchie)*
Director: *Randal Kleiser*
Screenwriters: *Bronte Woodard, Allan Carr, from the musical by Warren Casey, Jim Jacobs*
PG/110 mins./Musical/USA

1958. Danny has a holiday romance with squeaky-clean Australian tourist Sandy. She sticks around and ends up going to the same high school. They meet again. They tiff. They make up. They tiff again. And so on. But that's only the story — it's the songs that matter here.

If there have only been a handful of successful screen musicals since *Grease* first appeared, it's mainly because very few of them can hold a candle to the memorable song-and-dance routines and all-round exuberance on offer here. Unlike the other film from the late 70s that everyone remembers – *Star Wars*, *Grease* isn't necessarily one of those films that needs to be seen on the big screen to be appreciated fully. But the fun to be derived from going into a cinema to watch the highlights from the class of Rydell High's senior year with a like-minded audience renders this a truly unmissable experience.

However, *Grease* is a bit of a strange movie to be considered classic, given its lack of merit in other departments. The acting is hardly Oscar quality (although the gleefully mocking Channing and Conaway provide some spark), the direction is pedestrian, and it's likely that better scripts have been penned on postage stamps.

But ironically, it's this clunky kitsch quality that makes *Grease* such a perpetual joy, even after repeated viewings. There's something delightful about watching people obviously long out of school trying to play 17 again (Channing, in particular, was 32 when she took on the role of Rizzo) while they croon the likes of 'Greased Lightning' and 'Summer Nights'. The innocence of the decade is affectionately and none-too-seriously captured – though they may have dressed differently in the 1950s, 17-year-olds were rebellious too.

For it's 20th anniversary, there was a celebratory sprucing up – the sound effects are sharper, the print cleaner, the songs louder than ever before. Which is the icing on the cake for a film which almost no one will admit to liking, but is still universally adored. In short, re-release heaven. ★★★★★ CW

Movie Trivia: Grease

For the record the original Sandra Dee was a B-list 50s actress (*The Reluctant Debutante, A Summer Place*), famous for her purity and innocence. In a twist of irony, Henry Winkler (*Happy Days'* Fonzie) turned down the role of Danny Zuko in *Grease* for fear of being typecast. Due to an untimely broken zip, Olivia Newton John had to be sewn into the tight leather trousers she wears in the final sequence.

GREASE 2 (1982)

Starring: *Maxwell Caulfield (Michael Carrington), Michelle Pfeiffer (Stephanie Zinone), Lorna Luft (Paulette Rebchuck), Didi Conn (Frenchy), Eve Arden (Principal McGee), Sid Caesar (Coach Calhoun), Dody Goodman (Blance Hodel), Tab Hunter (Mr. Stuart)*
Director: *Patricia Birch*
Screenwriter: *Ken Finkleman*
PG/115 mins./Comedy/Musical/Romance/USA

1961. Geeky Englishman Michael Carrington joins Rydell High and is attracted to the leader of the Pink Ladies – Stephanie – but Stephanie wants someone more dangerous, so Michael transforms himself into a motorbike-riding hero.

This sequel to the mega-hit *Grease* was, by comparison, a disaster on release. With only a smattering of supporting cast returning, asking the newcomers Michelle Pfeiffer and Maxwell Caulfield, both making cinematic debuts, to carry the show was quite some task. Yet they are so likeable they probably could have managed it – if there'd been a respectable show to carry in the first place. But this garbled tosh about bowling alleys, mysterious motorbike riders and a school talent contest doesn't hang together. It's more an excuse to hang a load of disparately themed songs together – a seduction in a nucleur bunker? a fashion romp through the seasons? – and hope for the best.

And yet, time has been kind to it. It's a bona-fide cult classic and that's because it's so over-the-top packed with terribleness, wonderfully camp production numbers and the corniest dialogue – it actually ends up having a car crash fascination that makes it compellingly watchable. Even songs like 'Cool Rider' and 'We're Going To Bowl Tonight' drum into your head so the words linger.

File under guilty pleasures and enjoy at your own risk. ★★★ **EC**

THE GREAT DICTATOR (1940)

Starring: *Charles Chaplin (Hynkel, Dictator Of Tomania/A Jewish Barber), Paulette Goddard (Hannah), Jack Oakie (Napaloni, Dictator Of Bacteria), Reginald Gardiner (Schultz)*
Director: *Charles Chaplin*
Screenwriter: *Charles Chaplin*
U/127 mins./Comedy/War/USA

Recovered from Great War-induced amnesia, a Jewish barber returns to discover his homeland, Tomania, under the control of a dictator, Adenoid Hynkel. He's sent to a concentration camp, but his resemblance to the tyrant affords him the opportunity to prevent catastrophe.

Charlie Chaplin and Adolf Hitler were born in the same week in April 1899. But, as the opening caption of this daring satire insists, 'Any resemblance between Hynkel the dictator and the Jewish barber is purely coincidental'. This was a piercingly double-edged gag as, not only had the Reich banned Chaplin's films under the misapprehension that he was a Jew, but the rumour also persisted that Hitler himself was of Semitic extraction.

The picture certainly ruffled feathers in Germany, with the Consul George Gyssling writing to Hollywood's moral guardian, Joseph Breen, to have the project quashed when it was announced in 1939. Yet, it was later asserted that the Führer had imported a print from Portugal and had watched it twice. His reaction was never recorded, but his architect, Albert Speer, claimed that Chaplin's impersonation of Hitler's mannerisms was uncanny.

Seven years after its release, *The Great Dictator* got Chaplin into even more trouble, when his former friend and one-time Communist sympathiser Konrad Bercovici sued him for $5 million for plagiarising his original idea. Chaplin settled out of court for $90,000, although he always insisted that the producer Alexander Korda had suggested a comedy trading on his similarity to Hitler in 1937.

Moreover, it's hard to think of anyone else devising such comic business as the barber shaving to the accompaniment of Brahms's Hungarian dance, Hynkel pirouetting around his office balancing a giant floating globe or the Tomanian and Bacterian dictators fighting for supremacy in elevator chairs. The concluding speech, in which the barber appeals for world peace, was also pure Chaplin – although, by the time it was finished, the picture's primary purpose was to rouse America from its isolationist lethargy to combat the threat posed by Fascism.

The film drew a mixed critical response, but received five Oscar nominations. It remains both funny and poignant, with Chaplin excelling in his dual role, while being magnificently supported by Henry Daniell as Garbitsch, Billy Gilbert as Herring and Jack Oakie as the competitively bombastic Napolini. ★★★★ **DP**

THE GREAT ESCAPE (1963)

Starring: *Steve McQueen ('Cooler King' Hilts), James Garner ('The Scrounger' Hendley), Richard Attenborough ('Big X' Bartlett), James Donald (Senior Officer Ramsey), Charles Bronson (Danny Velinski), Donald Pleasance ('The Forger' Blythe), James Coburn ('The Manufacturer' Sedgwick), David McCallum (Ashley-Pitt), Gordon Jackson (MacDonald), John Leyton (Willie)*
Director: *John Sturges*
Screenwriters: *James Clavell, W.R. Burnett, based on the book by Paul Brickhill*
PG/169 mins./Prison/War/USA

The Nazis, exasperated at the number of escapes from their prison camps by a relatively small number of Allied prisoners, relocates them to a high-security 'escape-proof' camp to sit out the remainder of the war. Undaunted, the prisoners plan one of the most ambitious escape attempts of World War II.

There's something fundamentally British about *The Great Escape*. Obviously, it's a largely British story in the first place, even though it was made by an American studio and featured a bundle of American actors – some equipped with uncertain accents (James Coburn's Aussie number take a bow.) What's so British about it is how for several generations it has been indelibly associated with Christmas afternoon TV/Bank Holiday afternoon TV/wet Sunday afternoon TV – in fact there were times when *The Wizard Of Oz*, *The Sound Of Music* and *The Great Escape* together in one copy of the *Radio Times* just screamed 'National Holiday'. And while the others introduced us to fantasy worlds and singing nuns respectively, *The Great Escape* did something far more important.

It was for many their first introduction to war. More importantly, *The Great Escape* does not just document a dramatic and enormously significant true-life event that took place in the latter stages of World War II – an event now not experienced by anyone under the age of 60 – it humanises it. In the dog days of WWII, the Germans decided to round up all those already keen on escape into one super POW camp – Stalag Luft III. Paul Brickhill was one of those, and wrote a book in 1950 about the most audacious prison camp escape in history. John Sturges spent the next 13 years trying to make a movie of it, and it was only the success of his all-star ensemble Western *The Magnificent Seven* the previous year that allowed him to raise the $4 million needed to get the movie up and running. *The Great Escape*, shot over the course of 1962, was filmed on location in Europe, where ironically the studio-built camp was housed at Bavaria studios in Germany.

It could be argued that given their leniency in embracing the production of a film that dealt with such recent history, the German characters were appropriately mellowed. But this worked in the film's favour. Ironically, for a film about the Allies' escape methodology, *The Great Escape* often finds its heart in the performance of Hannes Messemer, the newly-appointed camp Commandant, Colonel Von Luger. His comment to flier Hilts (McQueen) that, 'We are both grounded for the duration of the war,' plus his reluctance to return the 'Heil Hitler' salute to the SS served to humanise a country that less than 20 years before had been pilloried for the actions of a rather short and deeply horrendous tyrant. No mean feat for a patriotic all-star action movie.

Sturges got his film together, his cast in place, his European locations in hand (plans to shoot in the mountains above LA were quickly abandoned.) Six weeks in, his star went AWOL. Steve McQueen, AKA Hilts, 'The Cooler King', after watching rushes for a movie that Sturges claims never had a script, decided his character wasn't strong enough. Garner and co. got him back and, one motorcycle jump later, the world was a different place. McQueen jumping that bike over the barbed wire fence remains one of the most indelible images of cinema. Who cares if McQueen didn't actually do the stunt – he tried but fell: stunt rider Bud Ekins crosses the fence.

The final act of *The Great Escape* is a masterfully sustained piece of action and tension as the various escapees struggle for freedom via train, bicycle, motorbike, rowing boat and hitchhiking. Sturges cuts between all their exploits and leads us to the inevitable tragedy as 50 of the 76 that actually escaped are shot by the Germans, their lack of uniforms allowing Nazis to treat them as spies rather than POWs.

The final element was added in post-production – Bernstein's fantastic score. 'What is so wonderful about this film is Elmer Bernstein's music,' co-star David McCallum once said. And he's right – from the opening shot of the prisoner's arrival at Stalag Luft III, it hits a defiant note. ★★★★ **BM**

Movie Trivia: The Great Escape

In the motorcycle jump scene, McQueen can be seen in costume as one of the motorbike-riding German soldiers. The motorbike ridden by McQueen is the same bike as the one used by The Fonz in *Happy Days*. Charles Bronson who played the chief tunneller had previously worked as a miner and advised Sturges on the tunnelling scenes.

GREAT EXPECTATIONS (1946)

Starring: *John Mills (Pip Pirrip), Valerie Hobson (Estella/Her Mother), Bernard Miles (Joe Gargery), Francis L. Sullivan (Jaggers), Martita Hunt (Miss Havisham), Finlay Currie (Abel Magwitch), Jean Simmons (Estella As Child), Alec Guinness (Herbert Pocket), Ivor Barnard (Wemmick)*
Director: *David Lean*
Screenwriters: *David Lean, Ronald Neame, Anthony Havelock-Allan, Cecil McGivern, Kay Walsh, from the novel by Charles Dickens*
PG/118 mins./Drama/UK
Awards: *Academy Awards – Best Art Direction-Set Decoration, Best Cinematography*

Rooming in London with Herbert Pocket, Pip is obsessed with Estella, the proud beauty he first met as a child at the home of her guardian, Miss Haversham. However, his future is bound to another figure from his past, the escaped convict, Magwitch.

This was the third screen telling of Charles Dickens's classic novel, following a 1916 version, starring Jack Pickford and Louise Huff, and a 1934 remake, with Phillips Holmes and Jane Wyatt. Written by David Lean, Ronald Neame and Anthony Havelock-Allan, the screenplay is a model of judicious pruning and compression, with characters being removed or reduced to 'a sniff' to keep the action moving and the focus firmly on the principals. Yet, not only is the story's twisting intrigue retained, but the Dickens spirit pervades every scene.

The plot is built around Pip's enduring obsession with Estella. But, as in all Dickensian dramas, justice had to be done to the vivid secondary characters and Martita Hunt was ethereally sour and brittle as Miss Haversham, Bernard Miles exuded geniality as Joe Gargery and Finlay Currie combined desperate menace with remorseful benevolence as Magwitch.

His entrance, in the Kentish churchyard, remained among Lean's finest directorial moments, although it owed much to his expertise as an editor to achieve its resounding impact. Guy Green's Oscar-winning monochrome photography was also key, as it reinforced the brooding atmosphere of the art direction by John Bryan and Wilfred Singleton, who also won Academy Awards for such masterly sets as the virtual mausoleum in which Miss Haversham mourns the demise of her romantic dreams and Mr. Jaggers (Francis L. Sullivan)'s legal office, whose walls are lined with the death masks of those he couldn't save from execution.

Always prone to stiffness, Valerie Hobson proved less alluring than her junior counterpart, Jean Simmons. But 38-year-old John Mills and 34-year-old Alec Guinness (who was making his full debut, after appearing as an extra in *Evensong* in 1934) bely their years to capture the innocence and exuberance of a youth that is remorselessly tempered by the cruel Victorian reality that undercuts any lingering certainty in the far from sentimentalised happy ending. ★★★★★ **DP**

THE GREAT MCGINTY (1940)

Starring: *Brian Donlevy (Dan McGinty), Muriel Angelus (Catherine McGinty), Akim Tamiroff (The Boss), Allyn Joslyn (George), William Demarest (The Politician)*
Director: *Preston Sturges*
Screenwriter: *Preston Sturges*
U/81 mins./Comedy/USA
Awards: *Academy Awards – Best Original Screenplay*

Hobo Dan McGinty so impresses The Boss and The Politician by managing to vote 37 times in one election that they sponsor his ascent of the political ladder from alderman to mayor and governor. However, he recovers his sense of decency on marrying Catherine and that's when his problems really begin.

Few filmmakers have struck a patch as purple as the one that Preston Sturges enjoyed between 1940-44. The pictures he produced in this period became the benchmark for American screen comedy and provided the link between the sophisticated conceits of Ernst Lubitsch and the tougher societal swipes aimed by another German emigré, Billy Wilder. So, it should come as no surprise to learn either that Sturges spent part of his youth in Europe or that he was given the latitude to launch his acerbic assault on the American Dream by the most transatlantic of all Hollywood studios, Paramount.

In 1941, Sturges won the inaugural Oscar for Best Original Screenplay for this directorial debut. On accepting, he apologised for his own absence and announced that he was happy to collect the award on Mr Sturges's behalf. He later regretted his flippancy, but it was a suitable way to receive an accolade for a script that was anything but original, as it had begun life as *The Vagrant* back in 1933 – the same year in which he broke through as a Hollywood scenarist with another exposé of graft in high places, *The Power and the Glory*. Sturges had then spent the remainder of the decade urging Paramount to produce the script and they finally agreed when he offered to sell it for just $10, on the proviso that he also directed.

Considering that the studio only gave him a budget of $35,000 and a three-week shooting schedule, the film's trenchant wit and visual subtlety are nigh on miraculous. Brian Donlevy's rise and fall is charted with a sagacious mix of silent clowning and scorching wisecracks, which were delivered with stinging precision by the likes of William Demarest, Harry Rosenthal, Frank Moran, Jimmy Conlin and Robert Warwick, who would become key members of Sturges's stock company.

Sturges would improve considerably as a director. But, this comic Kane has lost little of its venom. Indeed, in an era of floating chads, its message is more relevant than ever. ★★★★ DP

THE GREAT ZIEGFELD (1936)

Starring: *William Powell (Florenz Ziegfield), Luise Rainer (Anna Held), Myrna Loy (Billie Burke), Frank Morgan (Billings), Reginald Owen (Sampson)*
Director: *Robert Z. Leonard*
Screenwriter: *William Anthony McGuire*
U/170 mins./Musical/USA

Awards: *Academy Awards – Best Picture, Best Actress (Luise Rainer), Best Dance Direction*

Starting out with a strongman act, Florenz Ziegfeld rises to become the producer of such legendary Broadway shows as the Follies and Show Boat and the husband of French chanteuse Anna Held and actress Billie Burke.

Known as The Great Glorifier for the lavish annual revues, dubbed the Ziegfeld Follies, which showcased the charms of the American Girl, Broadway impresario Florenz Ziegfeld died before he could make an impact in Hollywood. Yet, within a year of his passing in 1932, William Anthony McGuire had pitched a biopic that Universal had been forced to reject on the grounds of cost. However, MGM, which was keen to claw back some of the ground lost to Warners and RKO (respectively home to Busby Berkeley and Fred Astaire and Ginger Rogers) in the early years of the movie musical, willingly stumped up a $2 million budget (its largest to date) and invested $250,000 of it on a single number, Irving Berlin's 'A Pretty Girl Is Like a Melody', which had become the Follies' theme tune.

The MGM publicity machine insisted that Ziegfeld's widow, Billie Burke, had personally sanctioned the casting of William Powell as her husband and was thrilled by the fact that she was to be played by Myrna Loy. However, neither Powell nor Loy resembled their characters and made little attempt to duplicate their mannerisms, as they traded on the appeal of a recurrent teaming that had been formalised in the Thin Man mysteries. Consequently, the acting laurels went to Luise Rainer, the Austrian making her US debut as Anna Held, whose display of choked misery as Powell phones to inform her of his impending nuptials secured her the Academy Award for Best Actress.

Director Robert Z. Leonard failed to prevent the narrative from dragging in places, but Seymour Felix's Oscar-winning choreography admirably captured the extravagance of Ziegfeld's stage spectacles and it's only a shame that Marilyn Miller priced herself out of a guest slot alongside such Follies alumni as Fanny Brice, Ray Bolger, Leon Errol and Ann Pennington. ★★★ DP

THE GREATEST STORY EVER TOLD (1965)

Starring: *Max Von Sydow (Jesus), Michael Anderson, Jr. (James The Younger), Carroll Baker (Veronica), Ina Balin (Martha Of Bethany), Pat Boone (The Figure In The Tomb), Victor Buono (Sorak), Richard Conte (Barabbas), Joanna Dunham (Mary Magdalene), José Ferrer (Herod Antipas), Van Heflin (Bar Amand), Charlton Heston (John The Baptist), Martin Landau (Caiphas), Angela Lansbury (Claudia), John Wayne (Centurion At Crucifix)*
Director: *George Stevens*
Screenwriters: *James Lee Barrett, George Stevens, based on Fulton Oursler's novel*
U/190 mins/Religious Drama/ USA

Judean carpenter's son Jesus Christ becomes a preacher and miracle worker. But his popularity threatens the uneasy alliance between Herod Antipas and the Roman governor, Pontius Pilate.

Fulton Oursler's 1949 novel had already been adapted for the radio by Henry Denker by the time Fox paid $100,000 for the rights in the hope that screenwriter Philip Dunne would repeat his success with *David and Bathsheba*, *The Robe*, *Demetrius and the Gladiator* and *The Egyptian*. However, Dunne had had enough of antiquarian epics and the project passed to United Artists, who paid George Stevens $1 million to produce, direct and co-script (with James Lee Barrett) a New Testament spectacular to surpass MGM's *King of Kings*.

Shooting in Ultra-Panavision 70 and Technicolor on location in Utah and Arizona, Stevens made sure all of his $20 million budget appeared on the screen. But, while the Oscar-nominated efforts of cinematographers William C. Mellor and Loyal Griggs, art director Robert Day, costumer Vittorio Nino Novarese and SFX supervisor Joseph McMillan Johnson added to the scope and scale of the piece, the film was as pompous and portentous as Alfred Newman's glutinous score.

Such was his perfectionism that Stevens squeezed the life out of his story and even after it had been cut down from 260 minutes to 238, 197 and, finally, 190 minutes, time still hung heavy as Stevens found something for his endless roster of guest stars to do. It made box-office sense to cast Charlton Heston as John the Baptist, Sidney Poitier as Simon of Cyrene and Carroll Baker as Veronica. But Angela Lansbury, Shelley Winters and Van Heflin found themselves playing completely fictitious characters who only prolonged the agony (which was ultimately compounded by John Wayne's immortally awful delivery of the line 'Truly this man was the Son of God', as the centurion at the foot of the Cross).

Max von Sydow brought some Bergmanesque intensity and mysticism to the role of Christ and Claude Rains (King Herod), Telly Savalas and José Ferrer made hissable adversaries. But nothing could prevent the picture's commercial calamity – although it eventually found an audience in church halls and schools. ★★★ DP

GREED (1924)

Starring: *Zasu Pitts (Trina), Gibson Gowland (McTeague), Jean Hersholt (Marcus), Dale Fuller (Maria), Tempe Pigott (Mother McTeague), Sylvia Ashton ('Mommer' Sieppe)*
Director: *Erich Von Stroheim*
Screenwriters: *Joseph Farnham, June Mathis, Erich Von Stroheim*
PG/140 mins./239 mins./Drama/USA

Simple-minded dentist John McTeague marries Trina after she wins $5000 on the lottery. His jealous friend Marcus accuses him of chasing the money. But she becomes obsessed with not spending her winnings, forcing the couple into penury, a fact made worse when Marcus informs the police McTeague is working without a licence. A situation that will end in murder.

No one alive has seen the full version of Eric Von Stroheim's naturalistic tale of the labours and perils of life and money. Based on Frank Norris' Depression-era novel, the immigrant director in search of a near lunatic level of reality envisioned his film to come in at nine hours long. He even screened it for critics and studio heads without a single break, before unsurprisingly, although much to his chagrin, MGM demanded he cut it. He returned with a four and a half hour version, which they chopped in half again resulting in a fistfight between a truculent Von Stroheim and Louis B. Mayer (Mayer won on all counts). The missing footage has taken on the aura of lost treasure, as various archivists and historians seek it like the Holy Grail.

But that is history, what of the film that remains, a mutilated version that is still deemed a masterpiece of silent cinema? This may be down to what it represents of the director's ambition, but there is no doubting the marshalling of intricate lives turning in the coils of money, something Stroheim sought to preserve in each delicate beat.

Trina (Zasu Pitts) reflects an ultimate absurdity in winning money then, despite falling into poverty, worshipping it, unwilling to sully her cache with spending. With rich intensity, Von Stroheim reveals the shocking effects of human pettiness, an innate absurdity of existence. It is not the girl Gibson Gowland and Jean Hersholt fight over in the film's loose love triangle, it is not even the money, it is the thought of the other besting them. It is a dance of jealousy that will spiral to a Grand Guignol of death and ruin. And to assist his vérité mood the director shot in real locations (in and around San Francisco) rather than on soundstages, a realistic tapestry that would be sliced apart and resown; many of his striking compositions, invested with emotion, were borrowed by Orson Welles.

Incidentally, there now exists a restored version made by Rich Schmidlin. He found a trove of lost material – production stills, a note book, unseen footage – and has edited it all in to give it a more documentary styled indication of what that epic original version must have attempted. ★★★★ **IN**

GREEN CARD (1990)

Starring: *Gérard Depardieu (George), Andie MacDowell (Bronte), Bebe Neuwirth (Lauren), Gregg Edelman (Phil), Robert Prosky (Bronte's Lawyer)*
Director: *Peter Weir*
Screenwriter: *Peter Weir*
15/107 mins./Comedy/Romance/Drama/Australia/France/USA
Awards: *Golden Globes – Best Comedy/Musical, Best Comedy/Musical Actor*

Frenchman George marries uptight American Bronte so he can get a Green Card, after which they go their separate ways. But when immigration come calling they have to move in together to prove that their marriage is genuine.

Green Card is a romantic comedy in reverse: it starts with the wedding, proceeds to the ups and downs of a budding relationship, and concludes with the couple falling in love. It's funny, sweet – and utterly lop-sided. Tailor-made for Depardieu (and Depardieu only) by the excellent Australian writer/director Peter Weir, *Green Card* provided the perfect bridgehead for the Gallic grandee to make his mark in the English-speaking movie marketplace. But it is precisely the red-blooded panache (yet cow-eyed sensitivity) for which Depardieu is so rightly famed that throws into wan relief the character played by MacDowell (her first movie since *sex, lies, and videotape*).

This sort of movie depends on the flying of sparks – any Tracy/Hepburn classic demonstrates the alchemy in question – and sparks do not fly when a blacksmith's hammer finds itself striking against something with all the frictive properties of a halibut. On paper it works. George Faure is French and needs a US Immigrations Green Card if he is to stay in America; Bronte Parrish is that quixotic thing, a horticulturist determined to green her fingers in New York City, and she has set her heart on an apartment requiring her to fulfil just one further condition – that she produce a husband. A mutual friend makes the introduction, the knot is tied, and all would be well but for the sudden attentions of the immigration people cracking down hard on inauthentic conjugal relations. Thus George and Bronte must live together, the better to pass muster with the government.

Constant domestic spats and disagreements about everything must be overcome for love to bloom, but to the audience with one foot still grounded in reality it's abundantly clear that the ox-like free spirit that is George would be bored silly with the precious Bronte. In fact, he would be far more likely to go for the charms of her best friend, Lauren (Neuwirth, familiar from TV's Cheers), at whose mother's snobby dinner party quite the best scene in the movie erupts as Depardieu reveals a hitherto little-recognised if idiosyncratic talent for music. ★★★ **MS**

THE GREEN MILE (1999)

Starring: *Tom Hanks (Paul Edgecomb), David Morse (Brutus 'Brutal' Howell), Bonnie Hunt (Jan Edgecomb), Michael Clarke Duncan (John Coffey), James Cromwell (Warden Hal Moores), Sam Rockwell ('Wild Bill' Wharton), Barry Pepper (Dean Stanton)*
Director: *Frank Darabont*
Screenwriter: *Frank Darabont*
18/187 mins./Drama/Fantasy/USA

John Coffey appears on death row every inch the murderer. But his huge presence is misleading as he proves himself not only a sensitive soul, but a man imbued by the power of God. When Coffey performs miraculous acts of healing, Edgecomb begins to believe he is innocent. But is that enough to keep Coffey from the electric chair?

Straight up, Frank Darabont is a 'great' in the making. The story-is-God dedication that transformed *The Shawshank Redemption* into a modern classic is much in evidence in this lavish, confident fantasy drama, but he may be hamstringing himself with his dogged devotion to pop-horror guru Stephen King's prison-inspired output. *The Green Mile* impresses, shines, awes, jabs the heart at moments, but it is no *Shawshank*. King wrote the book as an experiment in serialised fiction – six even parts each cliffhangered to the next – and at a bot-busting three-plus hours, the movie feels like watching a whole mini-series in one sitting. There's certainly a lot of great stuff here. But be warned, you'll need stamina.

Directing, Darabont was reputedly infuriatingly meticulous, every scene finessed with a Kubrick-esque repetition of takes in search of perfection. It has paid off. This slow-burn 30s-set tale of a prison Death Row (the corridor, here lime green, is known as the mile) shaken by the arrival of a dim-witted giant accused of slaughtering two baby girls, is a paragon to expert detail.

The performances are subtle, the script faithful to King's prose, the style elegant and poised and the big moments suitably grandiose. The crux of the matter is that the gentle seven-footer John Coffey has the miraculous, quasi-Holy power to heal. And heal he does, from narrator and Row boss Paul Edgecomb's graphic urinary infection, to pet mouse Mr. Jingles, squashed by the Rows bullyboy new recruit Percy Wetmore. All of which, combined with Coffey's ethereal view of what separates the good and bad, convinces the rattled Edgecomb that he must be innocent.

Over the epic running time the film inches its way through a complex soap opera of events on the Row, punctuated by three pivotal and grisly executions via 'Old Sparky', the electric chair. And, à la *Saving Private Ryan*, the story is told care of a mysterious flashback framework. All of which works brilliantly. Yet, when denouements unravel and Coffey works his magic – marked by a freaky spewing of tiny black insects into the air – it is all far less staggering than the build-up signals. In the main this is down to the sheer length – and so much of it superfluous – that patience is exhausted and drama dampened. There is also a lot less going on here than Darabont reckons, ostensibly boiling down to a simple take on the evil-that-men-do.

Polished it is, profound it ain't. A big, tasty meal that lacks the nourishment of *Shawshank*. It is harsh, though, to judge solely against such a startling debut and *The Green Mile* is about as accomplished a piece of storytelling as you'll come by. Morse, Clarke Duncan, Bonnie Hunt as Edgecomb's wife and, especially, Hutchison weave their own acting magic. Hanks' everyman routine may have become so ingrained it virtually doesn't register, but you can't imagine the movie without him. And Darabont, the real star, is a director in a classic tradition. Give him a story and he delivers a real movie. Time, though, to ditch King. ★★★★ **IN**

GREETINGS (1968)

Starring: *Robert De Niro (Jon Rubin), Jonathan Warden (Paul Shaw), Gerritt Graham (Lloyd Clay), Richard Hamilton (Pop Artist), Megan McCormick (Marina)*
Director: *Brian De Palma*
Screenwriters: *Brian De Palma, Charles Hirsch*
18/88 mins./Drama/USA

Three oddball friends – a conspiracy nut, a quiet, shy type, and a voyeuristic filmmaker – amble through 60s life, trying to figure out their place in the world.

Before he got hung up on Hitchcock, Brian De Palma seemed to want to launch an American nouvelle vague. This freewheeling satire may be the most '1968' of all the films made that year, following three long-haired drop-outs through various contemporary obsessions: sexual liberation, political paranoia, Vietnam.

Even before hitting on the thriller as his preferred genre, De Palma is fascinated by the mechanics of voyeurism, with a young Robert De Niro as a camera freak unsure whether he is an artist or a pervert, and Gerritt Graham as the snooper into the Kennedy assassination who finds himself in a sniper's crosshairs.

Messy, but lively and surprisingly funny. ★★★★ **KN**

GREGORY'S GIRL (1981)

Starring: *Gordon John Sinclair (Gregory), Dee Hepburn (Dorothy), Jake D'Arcy (Phil Menzies), Clare Grogan (Susan), Allison Forster (Madelaine), Chic Murray (Headmaster)*
Director: *Bill Forsyth*
Screenwriter: *Bill Forsyth*
PG/91 mins./Romance/Comedy/UK

Awards: *BAFTA – Best Screenplay*

Gregory is a normal teen who is infatuated with a classmate but he must work to win her affection.

Watching *Gregory's Girl* when you are still a teenager must be a tough experience; not only does it heighten all the vulnerabilities, awkwardness and hopelessness that marks out the acne years but it also denies any notion that the experience is unique and special. It may be set in Cumbernauld, Scotland – the accents were famously dubbed so cloth-eared Yanks could understand them – but Bill Forsyth's superbly judged mixture of romantic yearnings and the offside trap is so well observed and poignantly rendered it could play just as well in Mombassa as Motherwell.

Owing more to the generous, gentle approach of French filmmakers René Clair and François Truffaut than anything produced by Ealing, *Gregory's Girl* grew out of Forsyth's desire to make a young love story. Inspired by Jack Kerouac's high-school set comedy *Maggie Cassidy*, Forsyth developed the (BAFTA-winning) screenplay during workshops at Glasgow Youth Theatre layering an understated sense of social comment into the confection.

'I wanted to show someone in a very luxurious situation,' Forsyth explained of the story, 'growing up in a new town, going to a good school and who was still prepared to whine about the only thing for him to whine about – the fact that he was in love.'

Anchored around an especially useless school football team, the plot is simplicity itself: gawky Gregory struggles to earn the attention and affection of new star striker Dorothy who has relegated him to goalie in the first eleven. Forsyth barely resorts to the gal-in-a-guys'-team gambit to get laughs. Instead he offers inspired sight gags (a kid in a penguin suit is directed from classroom to classroom), endlessly quotable dialogue ('Ten years old with the body of a woman of 13') and a sense of silliness rooted in reality (the horizontal park dance).

Moreover, much of *Gregory's Girl*'s comedy is purely character-based, realised by spot-on performances. An apprentice electrician during the film's making, Sinclair (he is credited as Gordon John in the movie but switched to John Gordon for the usual Equity reasons) is probably cinema's most likeable gangly teen; a master at comedically capturing pained diffidence. By turns driven and winsome, Hepburn, who learned her football skills at Partick Thistle, neatly etches Dorothy as an unattainable yet believable goddess – her lesson in trapping a football-cum-disco dance is priceless. But she is outshone by the elusive, beret-sporting Susan, the girl Dorothy sets him up with: spotted by Forsyth working as a waitress (just as her band Altered Images were taking off) Grogan is such a likeably loopy presence, the film pulls off the neat trick of Gregory losing out on the object of his desire yet still winning.

Orbiting around the central threesome are a number of interesting teen characters – trivia-obsessed Andy, cookery expert Steve whose skill at home economics is the gentle counterpoint to the gender subversion in the main plot – that have no truck with the Jock-Nerd-Prom Queen stereotypes parodied in Kevin Williamson scripts. Forsyth's world works on a sliding scale of wisdom: it is the teachers who are the most juvenile – standouts here are the perfectly pathetic footie coach Phil Menzies and the headmaster delightfully lost in his own world playing the piano – the teens only slightly more adjusted but it is the kids who hold the monopoly over real wisdom – in particular Gregory's pre-teen sister Madelaine who adeptly coaches her dippy brother in the ways of love.

Amid the gentle frippery, *Gregory's Girl* nails the glorious pains and heartfelt highs of adolescence better than many films with more serious centres. Tapping into universal dating rituals – getting up the nerve to ask someone out, dressing up for a date, waiting for the date to arrive – the playing out of Gregory's infatuation may be comic but it is truthful. Both on and off the set. 'Gordon was actually getting on with Dee,' recalls Forsyth, in particular the sequence in which Dorothy is hit upon by the suave school reporter. 'During that scene, Gordon became jealous between takes, the other guy was chatting up Dee. And he had a car he could really drive! So the whole thing became real.'

Budgeted at under £200,000, grossing around £500,000, in the end, *Gregory's Girl* didn't prove to be a particularly influential movie: there was a brief trend in quirky Scotcom such as *Restless Natives* and *The Girl In The Picture*; *Trainspotting* practically lifted a riff from Forsyth's dialogue concerning 'a world full of wankers'; and 2000 saw the painfully dreadful *Gregory's 2 Girls* which propelled our hapless hero, now a teacher, into a frankly ludicrous plot about factory malpractice and human rights atrocities.

In the end, perhaps *Gregory's Girl* was just too darned idiosyncratic to replicate. Daft and deft, innocent yet knowing, it remains the growing up spread you never grow out of. ★★★★ **IF**

GREMLINS (1984)/GREMLINS 2: THE NEW BATCH (1990)

Director: *Joe Dante*
Starring: *Zach Galligan (Billy Peltzer), Phoebe Cates (Kate Beringer), Scott Brady (Sheriff Frank), Corey Feldman (Pete F.), Howie Mandel (Voice of Gizmo), Judge Reinhold (Gerald), Dick Miller (Murray Futterman), Gremlins 2: Christopher Lee (Dr. Catheter)*
Screenwriters: *Chris Columbus, Charlie Haas*
15/106 mins./Comedy/Fantasy/Horror/USA

A loveable but mysterious exotic pet brought home from Chinatown becomes the source of a slew of miseries for an American suburb when the 'Mogwai's' owners disobey a few basic precautions and help spawn a host of evil creatures.

A sly parody of Spielbergian cuteness, what startles about the first *Gremlins* is the courageous shifts in tone: Capra-esque warmth (the small-town locale, the glow of Christmas) switches to comedic carnage

Bald Bad Guys — TOP 10

1	Lex Luthor	Gene Hackman / Kevin Spacey, Superman films
2	Dr Evil	Mike Myers, Austin Powers films
3	Colonel Walter E. Kurtz	*Apocalypse Now*
4	Ernest Stavro Blofeld	Donald Pleasance and Telly Savalas, Bond films
5	Kingpin	Michael Clarke Duncan, *Daredevil*
6	Imhotep	Arnold Vosloo, *The Mummy*
7	Cypher	Joe Pantoliano, *The Matrix*
8	Archer Maggot	Telly Savalas, *The Dirty Dozen*
9	Graf Von Orlok	Max Schreck, *Nosferatu*
10	Max Schreck	Willem Dafoe, *Shadow of the Vampire*

(Father Christmas is gleefully throttled); Spielbergian wonder (good mogwai Gizmo trilling along with Billy's keyboard) segues into gut-wrenching violence (the gremlin zapped in a microwave). Moreover, the film's bizzaro feel is summed up by one of the film's quieter moments; taking refuge from the onslaught, heroine Kate tells Billy just exactly why she hates the festive season, a grimly funny yarn about how her father was found dead in the chimney dressed as Santa Claus. A scene Warner Bros wanted to cut, the moment typifies the film's flouting of the rules to mine humour from horror.

Inspired by writer Chris Columbus' spell living in an apartment plagued by mice, early versions of the script boasted an even meaner streak. The first drafts saw the gremlins eat a dog and cause havoc in McDonalds, eating the diners but leaving the burgers untouched. Yet, to make the script more palatable, Dante and producer Mike Finnell reverted back to the notions of Gremlins as represented in the old World War II stories: mischievous little critters who turn technology against humans. Bringing the creatures to the screen involved what was state-of-the-art technology in pre-CGI 1984. With Gizmo's brown-and-white colouring taken from Spielberg's mutt Chauncy, the look of the nastier gremlins was deemed to be reptilian. The 10-inch figures were operated via a combination of marionette puppetry, cable-operated facial/arm movements, and, in certain cases where a puppeteer was impractical, a radio-controlled version.

For gremlins guts, wheat paste, foam rubber and food colouring became the order of the day. If the *Gremlins* movies are about anything, it is loving the flotsam and jetsam of movie lore. During the first flick old movie stars (Harry Carey Jr., Dick Miller) rub shoulders with in-jokes – the local movie house shows a double bill of *Watch The Skies* and *This Boy's Life*, the working titles of *Close Encounters* (1978) and *E.T.* (1982) – and quotation: the gremlins' raucous reaction to *Snow White And The Seven Dwarfs* (1937) offers a fantastic juxtaposition of Dante and Disney. It is a tactic that is taken to untethered extremes in *A New Batch*.

Tagline
Here they grow again.

The references build up at a dizzying rate – *Batman, Apocalypse Now, Rambo: First Blood Part II, The Winged Serpent, New York, New York* just to skim the surface – often usurping regular plot conventions as the means of moving the story. Cartoons are critical in this respect. While the acknowledgements are occasionally overt – Chuck Jones cameos as a cartoonist in the first film; the sequel's opening gambit features Bugs Bunny and Daffy Duck clowning around the Warner Bros logo – the influence of animation is woven into the fabric of the film. The freeform collection of sight gags and pratfalls in both films have the unreality and pacing of the best toons – see the gremlins take over Dorry's Tavern. If the first one belongs to the inventive gaggery of Jones, the sequel is predicated on the subversive self-referencing of Tex Avery: Daffy's return to interrupt the end credits crawl ('Long, isn't it?') and, best of all, the moment where the film seemingly melts in the gate only to reveal that the gremlins have taken over the projection booth.

However, if *A New Batch* is ultimately more satisfying, it is because the nutty invention sets its sights on everything that is crap about modern culture, from automated buildings to TV chefs to intellectualism run rampant (the hilariously erudite talking gremlin riffing on Susan Sontag) to colouring old movies ('Casablanca, now in colour with a happier ending!').

In hindsight, the two movies embody a double bill of lost careers; Columbus dropped his wicked sense of humour in favour of sugar-coated sentiment (1999's *Bicentennial Man* et al); Dante's satirical edge has been blunted by the studio system, his last picture *Small Soldiers* was a kind' of Gremlins 3 without the bite; Gates' fine comedic skills have been sorely missed since being Mrs. Kevin Kline became a full-time job. Yet perhaps it is a little unfair to expect them to top this exhilarating brace of beast feasts.

★★★★ IF

GREYSTOKE: THE LEGEND OF TARZAN, LORD OF THE APES (1984)

Starring: *Christopher Lambert (John Clayton/Tarzan), Ian Holm (Capitaine Phillippe D'Arnot), James Fox (Lord Charles Esker), Andie MacDowell (Miss Jane Porter), Ralph Richardson (The Sixth Earl Of Greystoke), Ian Charleson (Jefferson Browne), Nigel Davenport (Maj. Jack Downing)*
Director: *Hugh Hudson*
Screenwriters: *Robert Towne, Michael Austin, based on the novel* Tarzan Of The Apes *by Edgar Rice Burroughs*
PG/143 mins./Drama/Adventure/USA
Awards: *BAFTA – Best Make-up*

A shipwrecked boy who is brought up by a pack of apes in deepest Africa is discovered by explorer Capitaine Phillippe D'Arnot: this man thinks he is an ape. Upon investigation it is discovered he is the descendant of the Earl Of Greystoke, although attempts to return him to civilisation prove problematic.

Returning to the grittier trail of Edgar Rice Burrough's original novel, Hugh Hudson, fresh from his *Chariots Of Fire* glory, attempts to bring a naturalism to the classic tale of the ape-man Tarzan. It's a worthy idea, but as rich in historical detail and sumptuous with earthy design as the film is, it's a story that can't take the strain of realism.

As Christopher Lambert, clutched from the banks of obscurity, rattles around the great dining room of his new home, his limbs lolloping and grunting like a constipated pig, the stiff poise Hudson adopts crashes into ruin. This film is utterly ludicrous, po-faced, and overcrowded with empty meaning, leaving you recalling the pulp days of Johnny Weissmuller like great art.

We should heed the warning of the gaggle of men-in-suits for a gorilla community, and that the re-fangled storyline (Jane doesn't even get to Africa) dodges the cool swinging through trees caterwauling stuff for a weird, interminable satirical examination of British manners. The film spends an age comparing the 'savagery' of this new arrival, who doesn't take well to table manners, with the brute bigotry of the aristocracy. For a

Tarzan film it's tortuously slow. Having grown with a kind of Simian purity, it is only natural for Clayton/Tarzan to reject 'civilisation' for the freedom of the wild. Wow, deep.

Everyone gives that kind of furrowed-brow performance, pronouncing their words like the kicking of mud off heels (except that is for Andie MacDowell's Jane, whose baby tones were dubbed over by Glenn Close), desperate to add layers of importance to what should just be a good-looking adventure movie. Lambert, of course, really goes for it in what would politely be called a physical transformation, but if we're being honest this is just a bad French actor getting away with his awful pronunciation. ★★ **IN**

THE GRIFTERS (1990)

Starring: *John Cusack (Roy Dillon), Anjelica Huston (Lilly Dillon), Annette Bening (Myra Langtry), Pat Hingle (Bobo Justus), J.T. Walsh (Cole)*
Director: *Stephen Frears*
Screenwriter: *Donald E. Westlake based on the novel by Jim Thompson*
18/119 mins./Drama/USA

A son and mother, Lilly and Roy Dillon, both hard-core conmen, or grifters, are reunited after he is landed in hospital when a job goes wrong. When his girlfriend, Myra, another trickster, turns up it transpires she and Lilly do not get along. When Myra suggests forming a partnership with Roy, excluding Lilly, things start to unravel for them all.

A deft and bleak adaptation of noir-specialist Jim Thompson's novel by versatile British director Stephen Frears, that had the added bonus of making a star out of Annette Bening as a floozy on the make. Her delightfully naughty minx, brazen with full-frontal nudity, makes one twisted corner of this triangle of bottom-dwelling grifters working the tracks, the scene, anything they can bend to their own gain, hoping for the big win that will never come. It's a sordid world, and Frears depicts it with a suitably boiled-dry sensibility, deglamourising their tired twists, before stirring up the scum of their personal lives. This could be the least sentimental film ever made, but it's sharp and knowing and a witty tribute to the great noirs of the 40s and 50s thrumming to screenwriter Donald E. Westlake's biting rejoinders and shadowy wisdom: 'You don't stand still. You either go up or down, sooner or later. Usually a down,' shrugs Anjelica Huston's tired mol, laying bets to raise the odds on horse races.

Huston's is the performance of the film. Transformed into a wiry bottle-blonde just holding age at bay, there is toughness and experience wired into her terse smile. She knows best, which means she knows how to survive, and Huston fills this cracking cookie with a burning sensuality. And when her baby-faced son (a well-cast Cusack layering this prissy player with frailty) starts pushing his luck too far, she has to confront the strange calling of maternal feelings. And they hint at the really strange.

Frears, in his own way, is playing a confidence trick. With his split screens, sharply edited beats and cool-hued America he drags before his camera, he's distracting us with a seedy tale of crime, when the story is all about family. On one level his film is cheeky, flippant, and blackly comic, but deep down, right there in its noir heart, it has the kind of clammy shudder that made *Chinatown* a great. ★★★★ **IN**

GRIZZLY MAN (2005)

Starring: *as themselves: Werner Herzog, Carol Dexter, Val Dexter, Sam Egli, Franc G. Fallico, Willy Fulton, Marc Gaede, Sven Haakanson*
Director: *Werner Herzog*
Screenwriter: *Werner Herzog*
15/103 mins./Documentary/USA

Through interviews and video-recorded footage, filmmaker Werner Herzog reveals the strange life (and death) of the bear-loving Timothy Treadwell, a man who spent every summer for the last 13 years of his life observing and filming the creatures he loved at perilously close range . . .

In some ways, *Grizzly Man* is the anti-*March Of The Penguins*. For 2005's kiddie-centric avian doc-blockbuster, the filmmakers happily anthropomorphised their cute subjects; in Werner Herzog's astonishing documentary, the director insists via his idiosyncratic, bellow-whispered voiceover that the last thing we should be doing is treating animals like people. That's what failed actor-turned-celebrity bear expert Timothy Treadwell did, and it got both he and girlfriend Amie Huguenard brutally killed and eaten.

Not that Treadwell was strictly humanising the grizzlies he 'protected' during his 13 summers in the Alaskan hinterland. Rather, while recognising, even revelling in, their inherent dangerousness, he convinced himself he'd discovered a secret connection with them, that he and they were innocent children of the universe playing together away from the evils of the modern human world.

This makes for some profoundly compelling viewing. Via Herzog's sensitively edited use of Treadwell's self-filmed adventures and observations, the man is revealed as a truly bizarre cove, the kind of hubristic, self-tortured obsessive you'd expect to attract the director of *Fitzcarraldo* and *Aguirre*.

Dressed like Chuck Norris and voiced like Pinocchio, Treadwell lives out a Disneyfied action-movie fantasy where he's a lone, maverick beast-master, one moment frothing obscenities at God (or Allah, or the 'big Hindu floaty thing') for denying the bears rain, the next talking to his cutesily monickered 'friends' in a baby-talking voice, wagging his finger chidingly after one takes a grumpy claw-swipe at his face.

Of course, it all ends in tears, and Herzog loads the film with powerful, bitter, dramatic irony. In one haunting moment, he runs a video-diary excerpt in which Treadwell whinily intones to camera, 'I will die for these animals, I will die for these animals, I will die for these animals . . .'

But is it a tragedy? Well, it's tragic that Treadwell's foolhardiness got his girlfriend killed. But, as troubled as he was, it's hard not to think that the Grizzly Man himself was asking for it – indeed, weirdly, his 100 hours of footage could even be seen as the longest suicide note ever composed. ★★★★★ **DJ**

GROSSE POINTE BLANK (1997)

Starring: *John Cusack (Martin Q. Blank), Minnie Driver (Debi Newberry), Dan Aykroyd (Mr. Grocer), Alan Arkin (Dr. Oatman), Joan Cusack (Marcella), Jeremy Piven (Paul Spericki), Hank Azaria (Steven Lardner)*
Director: *George Armitage*
Screenwriters: *Tom Jankiewicz, D.V. DeVincentis, Steve Pink, John Cusack, based on a story by Tom Jankiewicz*
15/108 mins./Crime/Thriller/Comedy/USA

Martin Blank is a professional assassin. He is sent on a mission to a small Detroit suburb, Grosse Pointe, and, by coincidence, his ten-year high school reunion party is taking place there at the same time.

As suggested by its baffling title, Grosse Ponte Blank is a real oddity, a genuine genre-hopper that veers quirkily between stylised noir, caustic satire and shamelessly romantic comedy with barely a pause for breath.

As risk-takers go, however, it succeeds admirably. Martin Q. Blank is a cucumber-cool hitman who, after years of financially rewarding homicide, wants out – until he is coerced into doing one final job, which coincides with his tenth anniversary school reunion in his home town of Grosse Pointe, Michigan. But that's not the only business he has to take care of; aside from putting on a fixed grin and filling his former classmates in on his post-education days, there's the small matter of making up with his high school sweetheart Debi whom he stood up on prom night and hasn't seen since.

Meanwhile, fellow assassin Grocer is in hot pursuit, aiming to wipe out his more proficient rival before he can get to his victim. The script, which requires its characters to talk in bullet points rather than sentences, favours superbly ironic witticisms over brash one-liners, delivering a complex story woven together so neatly it never confuses the audience.

There's much fun to be had, too, from the many incidental players who pop up, from the gallery of bores Blank once shared locker space with, to his screeching secretary (Joan Cusack, Cusack sibling Ann also makes an appearance), while the leads make an attractive, believable couple.

Add to that taut direction which steers clear of such obvious staples as gratuitous violence (the occasional showers of cartoonish gunplay are all the more effective for it), and an 80s soundtrack destined to turn the heads of nostalgics everywhere, and the result is one of the smartest, most original offerings to roll off the studio conveyor belt in a long while. Hugely recommended. ★★★★ **CW**

⓪ GROUNDHOG DAY (1993)

Starring: *Bill Murray (Phil), Andie McDowell (Rita), Chris Elliott (Larry), Stephen Tobolowsky (Ned), Brian Doyle-Murray (Buster), Rick Overton (Ralph)*
Director: *Harold Ramis*
Screenwriters: *Danny Rubin, Harold Ramis, from a story by Rubin*
PG/103 mins./Comedy/USA

Awards: *BAFTA – Best Original Screenplay*

A cynical weatherman is forced to continuously relive the worst day of his life until he learns to become a better person.

A man awakens at 6am to the alarm call of local radio station DJs prattling on about the weather. Everything is in its place: the entire lack of hot water, the landlady with a vacancy between her ears, folks gathering at Gobbler's Knob for the Groundhog festivities. Exactly like yesterday. Hold on, this is yesterday. Only today. There has been a fair amount of dispute over where *Groundhog Day*'s time-trap idea originated. Sci-fi author Richard Lupoff claimed they used his short story, 12:01pm, based around the idea of a man repeating an hour on an endless loop (it was made into a short film and a TV movie) that at least posited a scientific explanation (the hero gets an electric shock). However, in 1986 Ken Grimwood wrote the award-winning *Replay*, which has a man repeating whole lifetimes (well, 25 year spans) without any explanation.

Whatever the source, neither of these stories was exactly funny. And here Ramis and co. jump in. *Groundhog Day* is played expertly for laughs as well as philosophy, a grand pastiche of 'Capraesque' fables (by way of Dickens' Scrooge) with a cynical old sot having to locate his humanity to free himself from the conundrum of endlessly repeating the same day.

That day is February 2nd, in a snowy Punxatawney, Pennsylvania, where asinine TV weatherman Phil Connors has been sanctioned for the local ritual of Groundhog Day involving a plump beaver-like rodent predicting how soon spring will hit. Just getting through the ordeal is top of Connors' agenda. However, 'next' morning, the identical radio spiel introduces Connors and the audience (but no one else) to the fact it's Feb. 2nd. Again. And the repetition isn't going to stop.

The film is comedically richer in its first half. While coming to terms with his predicament, Connors awakens to the possibilities for exploiting the peculiar time-shifting – worming his way into women's knickers by snaffling info, guzzling junk food with abandon, flouting the law and generally being as big an ass as he can muster (exactly what Murray does best). It's fantasy fulfilment and like any drug has an almighty comedown. Depression hits, especially when his repeated attempts to charm his producer Rita consistently fail no matter how much groundwork he puts in. So much so, he ends up trying suicide but to no avail – he wakes up again to Sonny and Cher, and the dopey DJs cackling, 'It's Groundhog Day!' Then there is a breakthrough: Connors discovers himself, dedicating himself to heroically righting the same wrongs everyday. And as he never 'resets', he accumulates the wisdom and experience of age. There is the vague sense that 100s of years may have passed in this rewind fashion: Connors becomes a virtuoso piano player, an expert ice sculptor, and ultimately the genuine kind of guy that Rita will fall for. Bingo!

That the conceit is never explained is wholly the point. This is cornball metaphysics, Connors must learn the error of his egotistical ways and find compassion and love for his fellow man (God, the God, it seems, is playing a divine prank). Which sounds ghastly in concept but is immediately leavened by the casting of Murray, the master of bone-dry acerbic wit, and even as his stiff facade is worn away by the toil of endless days he doesn't let things descend into the saccharine, just a genuine sense of self-discovery. The skill in maintaining variety is extraordinary, Ramis plays around with pacing, perspective and rhythm while the script presents Connors with a progression of mind-states and purposes which will ultimately shed light on his actual quest while keeping the story invigorated. The film never repeats itself.

All the while Ramis is taking a sidelong glance at the filmmaking process itself, the idea of repeated takes altered slightly to improve them without the dramatic purpose being changed. Editing has never seemed so complex and self-reflexive – as the Groundhog Days wind ever on, we are given increasingly short snippets of their variations right down to a hail of slaps as Connors repeatedly fails to lure his beloved Rita to his bed. While Murray is sublime, taking his world-weary sourpuss delivery to new heights, the really hard work is going on in his supporting cast – they have to literally play Groundhog, enacting each 'new' take with as little variation as possible from the previous.

The term 'Groundhog Day' has almost entered common usage as a phrase for uncannily repetitive events. The real town of Punxatawney is now a major tourist attraction and Ramis tried his arm at more comedic reality, bending with the lesser cloning-themed flick *Multiplicity* (1996) starring Michael Keaton.

Of course the movie's remarkable format opens it up to all kinds of bizarre interpretations. You can theorise endlessly on the nature of Connors' predicament: for instance as a metaphor for the growth stages of man (he goes from confusion to belief in his invincibility to learning about mortality to love and fulfilment, with Rita acting as the mother figure). There is also a Buddhist take involving reincarnation and some debate that Ned Ryerson (Tobolowsky's jackass old schoolchum) may also be caught in a time loop.

Satisfactorily, we are left with a note of doubt, Connors hasn't fully recovered – as the lovey-dovey couple elect to stay in Punxatawney and search out a delightful love nest, he nervously states 'We'll rent to start . . .' ★★★★★ **IN**

⓪ THE GRUDGE (2004)

Starring: *Sarah Michelle Gellar (Karen), Jason Behr (Doug), William Mapother (Matthew), Clea DuVall (Jennifer), KaDee Strickland (Susan), Grace Zabriskie (Emma), Bill Pullman (Peter), Ted Raimi (Alex)*
Director: *Takashi Shimizu*
Screenwriters: *Takashi Shimizu, Stephen Susco, based on the films* Ju-on: The Curse, Ju-on: The Curse 2, *and* Ju-on: The Grudge, *written by Takashi Shimizu*
15/92 mins./Horror/USA

An American nurse in Tokyo is assigned to care for an elderly woman. In the eerie house she discovers a vengeful curse that haunts anyone who passes the threshold. To stop it she must discover the source of the ghostly anger that has already claimed too many victims.

The initial reaction to hearing that Takashi Shimizu has remade his own Japanese cult hit for a Western audience is: why bother? While spooky, the first of the *Ju-On* series came off as merely a cheap imitation of *Ringu*, failing to spark the same positive international reaction as its frightening forebear.

Shimizu hasn't vastly improved on the original, but he has refined it, making it its own shivering entity rather than a pale imitation. Stephen Susco's script simplifies the plot while fleshing out the characters (although Gellar's frowny nurse could still have done with a bit more on her bones) and crafting a more satisfying resolution.

The terror is upped without relying on too many clichés – we'll let the odd cat in a cupboard slide – and while the harsh, clinical look and lack of humour may not appeal to everyone, it keeps the dread simmering, with the cast in a permanent state of uncomprehending panic rather than screechy horror.

It's in the set-pieces, rather than the story, that *The Grudge* really works, and the best of these cleverly subvert the usual horror havens – daylight, public transport, your big, snuggly duvet – so that the scares reverberate long after the final jump. ★★★ **RF**

GUNCRAZY (1992)

Starring: *Drew Barrymore (Anita Minteer), Robert Greenberg (Mr. Sheets), Rodney Harvey (Tom), Jeremy Davies (Bill), Dan Eisenstein (Chuck), Joe Dallesandro (Rooney), Willow Tipton (School Girl), James LeGros (Howard), Ione Skye (Joy)*
Director: *Tamra Davis*
Screenwriters: *Matthew Bright*
15/97 mins./Crime/Drama/Thriller/USA

Anita is pure white trash, bored and used in small-town America. Developing a penpal relationship with ex-con Howard, she murders her abusive stepfather and steps out with new man Howard on a wild and murderous downward spiral.

Set against the kind of down-at-heel trailer park rarely seen in recent American cinema, this powerful and unexpectedly good low-budgeter seems decades away from the staple wish-fulfilment fantasy of most 90s teen movies. Rooted in the ambiguously doomed 70s spirit of *Badlands* or *Thieves Like Us*, with a few *Thelma & Louise* licks thrown in for good measure, this has a title no doubt intentionally identical to *Gun Crazy*, the 1949 offering that, along with *They Live By Night*, inaugurated the killer couple-on-the-road movie.

Anita, a dirt-poor schoolgirl unaffectionately known as 'the sperm bank', enters into a remarkably pure but dangerous relationship with penpal James Le Gros, a gun-happy and none-too-bright convict. After learning how to use a gun in preparation for her first meeting with her dream guy, Anita murders her mother's sexually abusive boyfriend almost for the practice, and when her parolled man comes to town, circumstances force them into further killing. In Bonnie and Clyde mode, the well-intentioned outlaws (when they try to rob a bar, the customers plead poverty and the pair feel obliged to give back the money) dash across country to find Anita's mother, a junkie hooker.

The downbeat storyline is familiar right to the gloomy ending, but the script is tough and gritty (Barrymore's most romantic line is 'you can come in my mouth') and all the supporting cast are excellent. Michael Ironside and Billy Drago, usually seen as psycho villains, here show they can act, as a probation officer and a snake-handling preacher respectively, while Ione Skye turns in another weirdly stoned cameo as Ironside's airhead daughter. Director Davis does especially good work with the pouting Barrymore, who successfully broke into the adult phase of her career. ★★★ **KN**

THE GUNS OF NAVARONE (1961)

Starring: *Gregory Peck (Captain Keith Mallory), David Niven (Corporal Miller), Anthony Quinn (Colonel Andrea Stavros), Stanley Baker (Private 'Butcher' Brown), Anthony Quayle (Major Roy Franklin), Irene Pappas (Maria Pappadimos), James Robertson Justice (Jensen), Richard Harris (Barnsby)*
Director: *J. Lee Thompson*
Screenwriter: *Carl Foreman*
U/158 mins./War/USA/UK
Awards: *Academy Awards – Best Special Effects*

A team of crack commandoes is sent to infiltrate a German-held Greek island with the aim of blowing up the twin cannons that threaten the evacuation of nearby British troops. But the mission, led by the stalwart American Captain Keith Mallory, is beset by danger both from the outside and from betrayal within.

A hardy perennial of that grand tradition of WWII men-on-a-mission movies (usually adapted, as is the case here, from gutsy Alistair MacLean novels), this conventional but thrillingly made and performed adventure in many ways symbolises the entire sub-genre. Its dedicated mechanics have been purloined by countless other movies, but never to quite the same effect.

To wit: you present a mission that is damn-near impossible – scaling a terrible cliff face in the pouring rain, hiding out amongst the Greek rebels, staving off betrayal, scheming your way inside the Nazi base, and, finally, by hook or by craftily lift-mounted booby trap, victory is achieved. You cast it with a mix of noble chins (Gregory Peck and David Niven doing what they do best – being upright and moral) and stubbly jaws (Stanley Baker and Anthony Quinn doing what they best – being tough and moody). And you shoot with an eye on spectacle rather than realism, with a lean, direct script that can boast genuine flares of emotion without crowding the mission with subplots.

J. Lee Thompson understood that precision-wrought simplicity, avoiding ambiguity like an enemy patrol, can reap glorious dividends (the film was a big hit). Although, beyond the calling of its plot, this set of likeable characters do come intelligently alive and there is real directorial skill in the growing tension of the finale – this is not just a matter of blindly going through the motions. Violently out of fashion, perhaps, but inspirational in its own tidy way. ★★★★ **IN**

GUYS AND DOLLS (1955)

Starring: *Marlon Brando (Sky Masterson), Jean Simmons (Sergeant Sarah Brown), Frank Sinatra (Nathan Detroit), Vivian Blaine (Miss Adelaide), Robert Keith (Lieutenant Brannigan), Stubby Kaye (Nicely Nicely Johnson), B.S. Pulley (Big Jule)*
Director: *Joseph L. Mankiewicz*
Screenwriter: *Josephy L. Mankiwicz, based on the musical play by Abe Burrows and Jo Sweling and the story The Idyll of Miss Sarah Brown by Damon Runyon*
PG/150 mins./Musical/Comedy/Romance/Crime/USA
Awards: *Golden Globes – Best Musical/Comedy, Best Musical/Comedy Actress*

New York gambler Sky Masterton makes a bet with rival Nathan Detroit that he can score with any woman in sight – whereupon Detroit challenges him to conquer Sarah Brown, a sergeant in the Salvation Army.

Despite its chocolate-boxy, garishly-coloured look, as producer Sam Goldwyn's vulgarity and director Joseph L. Mankiewicz's pretensions bring out the worst in each other, this film of the often-revived Frank Loesser monster stage hit (based on the stories of Damon Runyan) is largely likeable.

A snappily dressed Marlon Brando – lightening up after a run of earnest dramatic hits – and the lovely Jean Simmons are better than you'd expect as the romantic leads. Brando, probably at the peak of his physical presence, is fluent in Runyan's distinctive, idiomatic, present-tense patter ('the companionship of a doll is a pleasant thing even for a period of time running into months ... but for a close relationship that can last us through all the years of our life, no doll can take the place of aces back to back') and even makes a fist of the showstopping song-and-dance number 'Luck Be a Lady'.

Frank Sinatra, more comfortable in the genre, exercises his tonsils as rival high-roller Nathan Detroit, and there's real show-stopping from Vivian Blaine as Nathan's long-neglected girlfriend ('speaking of chronic conditions, happy anniversary') and Stubby Kaye as Nicely Nicely Johnson – a crook who unexpectedly lets rip with a gospel-style number ('Sit Down, You're Rockin' the Boat'). The wonderful score is so strong that the soundtrack album, divorced from the sometimes overblown visuals, would earn a four-star rating. Hits: 'Fuge for Tinhorns', 'I Were a Bell I'd be Ringing', 'A Person Could Develop a Cold', 'Take Back Your Mink', 'The Oldest Established Permanent Floating Crap Game in New York', 'Guys and Dolls'. **★★★ KN**

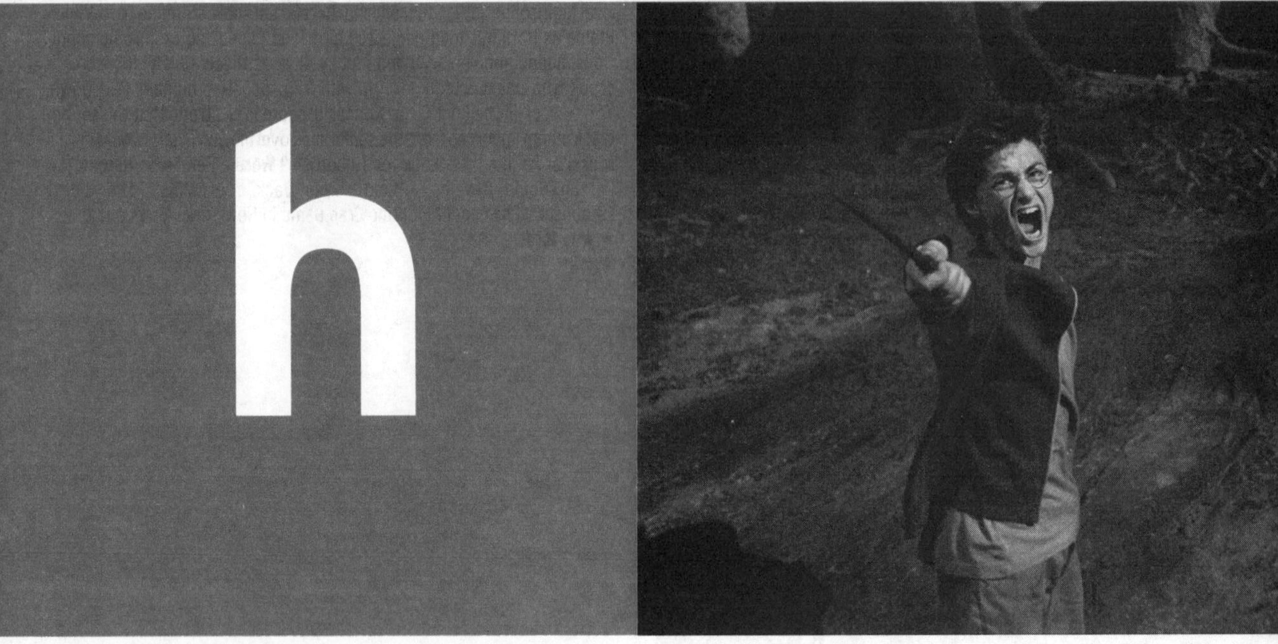

HACKERS (1995)

Starring: *Jonny Lee Miller (Dade Murphy/'Crash Override'/'Zero Cool'), Angelina Jolie (Kate 'Acid Burn' Libby), Jesse Bradford (Joey Pardella), Matthew Lillard (Emmanuel 'Cereal Killer' Goldstein), Fisher Stevens (Eugene 'The Plague' Belford aka Mr. Babbage), Alberta Watson (Lauren Murphy), Lorraine Bracco (Margo)*
Director: *Iain Softley*
Screenwriter: *Rafael Moreu*
12/107 mins./Action/Crime/Thriller/USA

When a group of high school computer hackers expose a corporate scam their lives are put at risk.

Two years after his Beatles study *Backbeat* landed Iain Softley firmly in the list of young Brit directors tipped for greatness, his follow-up effort finally appeared and – as with most tech films – it dated fast.

Having been banned from touching a computer until his 18th birthday after a hacking stunt that brought the whole of Seattle to a standstill, Dade Murphy and his mum move to New York, where he resumes his techno boffin activities and meets a gang of like-minded folk at his new school, including the dreadlocked Cereal Killer and the gutsy Kate (a closely shorn, debuting Angelina Jolie). However, when one of their number accidentally infiltrates a corporate scam masterminded by The Plague, it's down to the gang to divert computer catastrophe and the finger of suspicion pointed at them.

It's a thin plot, certainly, and one which flounders considerably in a middle third monopolised by dull technobabble and untenable teen bonding, but the young cast, who all went on to greater things, provide a welcome shot of vibrancy and enthusiasm, while Stevens' cackling panto villain snarl and tendency to get all the best lines ('there is no right or wrong, only fun or boring') helps no end. ★★★ **CW**

HAIL THE CONQUERING HERO (1944)

Starring: *Eddie Bracken (Woodrow Lafayette Pershing Truesmith), Ella Raines (Libby), Bill Edwards (Forrest Noble), Raymond Walburn (Mayor Noble)*
Director: *Preston Sturges*
Screenwriter: *Preston Sturges*
U/101 mins./Comedy/USA

Rejected by the Marines, hay fever sufferer Woodrow Lafayette Pershing Truesmith takes a shipbuilding job because he can't face his father. However, he invents war exploits and finds himself running for mayor against Everett J. Noble after Sergeant Heppelfinger persuades him to pose as a homecoming hero.

Preston Sturges found himself in Oscar competition with himself in 1945, when both *The Miracle of Morgan's Creek* and this caustic wartime satire were nominated for Best Original Screenplay. Ironically, he lost out to Lamar Trotti for *Wilson*, a biopic of the US President after whom Eddie Bracken's anti-hero was named.

Only Sturges could have got away with two such stinging assaults on the small-town America that Frank Capra had insisted had a heart even if it didn't always use its head. But what's most remarkable about this frantic farce is that the Breen Office sanctioned such a non-stop lampoon of patriotism, mother love, political corruption and bogus heroism at a time when the Second World War was far from won.

Was this really the United States that the brave boys were fighting for, with its foolish fathers, doting moms and inconstant sweethearts being ready to swallow anything they were told by anyone in authority or uniform? No wonder several contemporary critics denounced Sturges for treating his characters and their values with contempt. Indeed, some even accused him of using long, tracking shots to follow them throughout the town as though they were specimens in a laboratory.

Yet, the fluid camera style roots the citizens firmly in their cocooned environment and reinforces Sturges's contention that you can fool most of the people all of the time. Moreover, it enabled him to pack the frame with characters who all have something to say and insist on saying it very quickly and at the same time as everybody else. Only a director working with a well-drilled stock company could execute such finely tuned dialogue (which rattles between wisecracks, fortune cookie philosophising and impassioned speeches) with such precision and the likes of William Demarest, ex-boxer Freddie Steele and Raymond Walburn (who is the embodiment of plutocratic graft) all excel beside Bracken's misguided milksop. ★★★★ **DP**

LA HAINE (1995)

Starring: *Vincent Cassel (Vinz), Hubert Kounde (Hubert), Said Taghmaoui (Said), Abdel Ahmed Ghili (Abdel), Solo (Santo), Joseph Momo (Ordinary Guy)*
Director: *Mathieu Kassovitz*
Screenwriter: *Mathieu Kassovitz*
15/96 mins./Crime/Drama/France

Three friends – Vinz, Said and Hubert – meet the morning after a riot sparked by the injury in police custody of a young man from their neighbourhood. While the three kill time, the violence of the previous night threatens to well up again.

If you peer hard enough from the roofs of the Parisian suburbs where *La Haine* is set, you can just about see the tourist-friendly face of the city in the distance. Using tough, immediate, black-and-white photography, Kassovitz presents a world that's socially and ethnically (if not geographically) a million miles away from *Amélie*.

In fact, the atmosphere of boiling-over tension among restless youths reacting to police brutality is closer to Spike Lee's *Do The Right Thing* than any other French movie of the period.

Kassovitz and leading man Cassel slapped their national cinema across the face as the men to watch in 1995. And, as his portrait of an inner city, multiracial community drawn together by boredom, anger, prejudice and pounding rap music, continues to pack a punch. ★★★★★ **NDS**

HAIR (1979)

Starring: *John Savage (Claude), Treat Williams (Berger), Beverly D'Angelo (Sheila), Annie Golden (Jeannie), Dorsey Wright (Hud), Don Dacus (Woof)*
Director: *Milos Forman*
Screenwriter: *Michael Weller, based on the musical play by Gerome Ragni, James Rado and Gail McDermot*
15/118 mins./Musical/USA

Midwestern farm boy Claude comes to New York for the Vietnam draft. But, in Central Park, he meets hippies Berger and Sheila and the course of his war is irrevocably changed.

Milos Forman had seen the first off-Broadway preview of *Hair* while visiting the United States in 1967. Suitably impressed by its countercultural values and catchy pop tunes, he had hoped to stage a production in Prague, but soon found himself in exile following the Soviet crackdown.

By the time Forman arrived in Hollywood, the Great White Way's first amplified show, subtitled 'An American Tribal Love-Rock Musical', had run 1,742 performances. But his attempts to secure the rights were thwarted by a tarot reader, who advised co-writers Gerome Ragni and James Redo against the deal. However, the success of *One Flew Over the Cuckoo's Nest* gave Forman the clout to greenlight a project that chimed in exactly with his US debut, *Taking Off*, and the iconoclastic comedies he had made in Czechoslovakia.

Unfortunately, America and its music scene had moved on in the 12 years it took for Forman to mount his production. Consequently, Galt MacDermot songs like 'Aquarius' and 'Good Morning Starshine' sounded impossibly twee in a post-punk world. Yet, despite a mixed critical response, the film found an audience with a younger generation that was no better disposed towards Uncle Sam than the Summer of Love's hippies. But, Forman failed to persuade those who had smoked dope, burned their draft cards and indulged in free love to tune in, turn on and drop out all over again rather than assume their place as the Establishment-in-waiting.

Forman and screenwriter Michael Weller brought a sense of coherence to the original freewheeling structure and Twyla Tharp's choreography imparted an infectious dynamism. But the profanity, nudity and disregard for the fourth wall that had made the stage show such a sensation were lost in the translation. Moreover, neither John Savage nor Treat Williams gave particularly empathetic performances and, consequently, the denunciation of authority and the celebration of drugs, environmentalism, racial tolerance and individual freedom seemed self-consciously liberal and theatrical. ★★★ **DP**

HAIRSPRAY (1988)

Starring: *Sonny Bono (Franklin Von Tussle), Ruth Brown (Motormouth Maybell), Divine (Edna Turnblad/Arvin Hodgepile), Deborah Harry (Velma Von Tussle), Ricki Lake (Tracy Turnblad),*
Director: *John Waters*
Screenwriter: *John Waters*
PG/90 mins./Musical/USA

Baltimore, 1962. Chubby Tracy Turnblad is devoted to 'The Corny Collins Show', a local pop program in which white teens dance to cleaned-up black music. Tracy fights her way onto the show and leads a crusade for integrated television that soon sparks off riots in the local carnival.

John Waters' first near-overground feature, this feels less like a project from the sicko who made *Pink Flamingos* and his regular star Divine than something in the filmography of Baltimore's other resident director, Barry Levinson. Like *Diner* and *Tin Men*, *Hairspray* is rooted in re-creation of and affection for an early 60s when things were even more confusing than they became.

Aside from one or two teeny zit and vomit jokes, the film is remarkably clean-spirited, with all the nastiness confined to the unpleasant Von Tussle family and a racist TV station owner and the teens settling their differences in the approved Frankie and Annette fashion by dancing their feet off.

The social content is half-sent-up in a Russ Meyer sort of way, but Waters' pose as an amoral pervert slips somewhat and develops an alternate identity as a waspish, essentially moral, satirist. Meanwhile, as vital social issues are debated, the kids are more interested in shimmying, turning their heads into abstract sculptures via ever more outrageous hairstyles and showing off pre-fab 60s outfits.

This is the first Waters film to feature actual technical competence behind the cameras, and it brings on real performers rather than one-note grotesques. Divine, in one of his last appearances, is still a limited actress, but despite having two roles doesn't have enough screen time to become as annoying as he too often does in starring roles.

With cheerfully grotesque cameos from Debbie Harry, Pia Zadora and Sonny Bono. Thoroughly charming, and later a Broadway musical. ★★★★ **KN**

HALLOWEEN (1978)

Starring: *Donald Pleasence (Dr. Sam Loomis), Jamie Lee Curtis (Laurie Strode), Nancy Kyes (Annie Brakett), P.J. Soles (Lynda VanDerclork), Charles Cyphers (Sheriff Leigh Brakett)*
Director: *John Carpenter*
Screenwriters: *John Carpenter, Debra Hill*
18/91 mins./Horror/Thriller/USA

Michael Myers has been in an institution since he was a young boy, after murdering his sister. Now he's escaped and is heading back home to terrorise the quiet community that still remembers him.

John Carpenter, a young director with only two films behind him – expanded college project *Dark Star* and thriller *Assault On Precinct 13* (1976) – intended *Halloween* to be a ruthless machine of a movie, a thrill ride designed simply to leave the audience shaking with fear. He succeeded. It became the single most successful independent production at that time and changed the face of the horror movie. If Universal's 1931 *Frankenstein* is 'the most important horror movie ever made' then *Halloween* runs it a close second.

After Carpenter's film no co-ed taking a shower was safe from the legion of masked psychotics who haunted high schools, college dorms, summer camps and slumber parties. The formula was so outrageously successful that by 1981 over 60 per cent of American releases were of the stalk'n'slash genre. Without Michael Myers there would be no Jason Voorhees (*Friday The 13th*) or Freddy Krueger (*Nightmare On Elm Street*). The ripples continue to roll across horror's dark millpond with ironic horrors like *Scream* and *Urban Legend* themselves being spoofed in *Scary Movie*, while *I Know What You Did Last Summer* simply returns to the tried and tested formula. But no movie since Carpenter's has delivered the requisite shocks with such exuberant elegance. *Halloween*'s main influences are probably *Psycho* and Michael Powell's *Peeping Tom*, the tale of a voyeuristic killer who forces his victims to watch their own deaths. That element of voyeurism is present in Carpenter's lurking camera and extensive use of point-of-view (POV) shots, both from the killer and his victim's perspectives. It's a technique that dazzles from the start of the movie.

The celebrated opening sequence, in which we peer through the windows of a white clapboard house at a couple of canoodling teens, before tracking them upstairs, remains one of the greatest deployments of Steadicam (or, strictly speaking, Panaglide, Panavision's now defunct version of the system) in cinema. In fact, it's a type of shot peculiarly suited to building tension and therefore to horror, as Stanley Kubrick would demonstrate two years later in *The Shining*. What appears here to be a fluid sequence actually has at least one cut: one when the child puts the clown's mask on and another that Carpenter claims is in there but refuses to reveal where. It also audaciously compresses time – we are lead to believe that the canoodling couple have bumped uglies. Certainly the boy is pulling his shirt back on as he comes downstairs and the bedsheets show signs of some energetic romping.

But in fact they've been up there for less than two minutes. Either it's the least satisfying shag in film history or Carpenter is already putting his cards on the table. All extraneous matter is stripped away leaving a drag racer of a fright machine. The technical achievements don't end with Panaglide. If, like most people, you've only seen *Halloween* on tape then you've only actually seen about two thirds of it. Carpenter elected to shoot in widescreen, one of the first horror directors to do so, and then used the oceans of space the format offered to further unnerve his audience. Compositions are deliberately unbalanced with gaping holes into which something could jump at any time. (Normally the jumping was done by co-screenwriter Nick Castle. Billed as 'The Shape', he would go on to make his directorial debut with *TAG: The Assassination Game* in 1982).

Then there's Carpenter's insistent synth-score, certainly one of the best ever composed for a horror movie, which juxtaposes tinkling electronic piano with doom-laden organ chords and enough sudden 'stingers' to keep adrenaline levels uncomfortably high. The heart of *Halloween* is its simplicity. It establishes the rules of teen-horror – so eloquently mocked in *Scream* – and obeys them slavishly. Teens fall victim to The Shape only after they have committed some anti-authoritarian crime, usually having sex, but occasionally boozing or smoking dope. It was Carpenter's counter-intuitive discovery that adolescents, at whom the film is squarely aimed, were, by the late 70s, a deeply conservative audience who liked nothing more than to see their own kind viciously punished for supposed social transgressions.

Hardly the free spirits of the *Easy Rider* decade, but then Margaret Thatcher and Ronald Reagan were just around the corner. Much of Carpenter's success would become cliché in the following years: the lurking camera, slaughtered teens and a killer who refuses to lie down and die (indeed, like the arm bursting out of the ground at the end of *Carrie*, the shot of the 'dead' shape rising behind Laurie would become the stuff of spoof – but only because it was so effective in the first place). ★★★★★ **AS**

◑ HALLOWEEN II (1981)

Starring: *Jamie Lee Curtis (Laurie Strode), Donald Pleasence (Dr. Sam Loomis), Charles Cyphers (Sheriff Leigh Brackett), Jeffrey Kramer (Graham), Lance Guest (Jimmy Lloyd)*
Director: *Rick Rosenthal*
Screenwriters: *John Carpenter, Debra Hill*
18/92 mins./Horror/USA

Laurie Strode, having survived an encounter with psychopath Michael Myers, is taken to hospital on Halloween night. Evading the pursuing Dr Sam Loomis, Michael traces Laurie and murders the hospital night staff as he tries to get to her.

A disappointing sequel to John Carpenter's 1978 slasher film, with a drugged Jamie Lee Curtis wandering around a hospital in an unflattering wig, while the masked nutcase tries to do her in and Donald Pleasence mutters darkly in the background.

Finding that director Rick Rosenthal had entirely failed to match the suspenseful tone of the classic first picture, producer Carpenter inserted various splattery sequences to get something interesting on the screen, but the picture has very little – apart from Pamela Susan Shoop's chest and the Chordettes version of 'Mr Sandman'. Dana Carvey made his screen debut in a bit-part, but the killable orderlies, nurses and doctors are a fairly forgettable bunch of vaguely familiar faces who didn't go on to great careers.

Carpenter wrote the screenplay (and provided a reprise of his memorable theme tune), and introduced the plot element that the heroine is the long-lost sister of the maniacal multiple murderer, which makes no sense but has still become the continuing thread on which the latterday sequels have been hung. The first film, despite its open ending, was a standalone masterpiece – but this turns it into a formula that can be endlessly repeated.

To his credit, Carpenter realised that and tried something different in *Halloween III: Season of the Witch*, though he then left the series and it reverted to more formula efforts along the lines of *Halloween II*. It's a lookalike for several other hospital-set slasher films in which medical implements are used for murder: *X-Ray*, *Visiting Hours*. ★★ **KN**

◑ HALLOWEEN III: SEASON OF THE WITCH (1982)

Starring: *Tom Atkins (Dr. Daniel 'Dan' Challis), Stacy Nelkin (Ellie Grimbridge), Dan O'Herlihy (Conal Cochran), Michael Currie (Rafferty), Ralph Strait (Buddy Kupfer), Jadeen Barbor (Betty Kupfer), Brad Schacter ('Little' Buddy Kupfer Jr.)*
Director: *Tommy Lee Wallace*
Screenwriter: *Tommy Lee Wallace*
15/96 mins./Horror/USA

Conal Cochran, a pagan toy tycoon, plots to play a very nasty trick on the children of America come Halloween. Various people stumble onto his scheme and try to stop him.

The one *Halloween* sequel in which He doesn't come home, this was producer John Carpenter's attempt to get the series away from the original's psycho-on-the-loose storyline and turn it into a vehicle for more far-fetched Halloween-themed horror tales.

Though original screenwriter, Nigel Kneale (of the *Quatermass* series), removed his name from the final film after a coarsening rewrite by director Tommy Lee Wallace, his strange touch is evident in the offbeat story. The setting is an Irish-dominated Northern California company town owned by the Silver Shamrock Novelty corporation, whose Halloween masks are pushed by an amazingly irritating TV jingle you won't ever be able to get out of your head ('two more days to Halloween, Halloween, Halloween').

Tom Atkins and Stacy Nelkin are typical low-rent horror movie protagonists, dim-bulbs who hit onto an *Invasion of the Body Snatchers*-style conspiracy involving sharp-suited corporate robots and run around as the plot unfolds, but guest star Dan O'Herlihy steals the film as a Celtic joke tycoon ('the man who invented sticky toilet paper and the dead dwarf gag') who hates the way American kids are despoiling the religious spirit of Samhain and decides to teach them a nasty lesson.

His scheme, which involves a stolen Stonehenge megalith ('sure, you'd never believe how we did it') and a techno-magic spell that turns the heads of TV watchers into writhing masses of snakes and insects is value for money, and O'Herlihy mixes enough serious malice into the charm to come across as a great screen baddie. Beware the UK version, which has suffered swingeing censor cuts to the more enjoyably gruesome moments. ★★★ **KN**

HALLOWEEN 4: THE RETURN OF MICHAEL MYERS (1988)

Starring: *Donald Pleasence (Dr. Sam Loomis), Ellie Cornell (Rachel Carruther), Danielle Harris (Jamie Lloyd), Beau Starr (Sheriff Ben Meeker), George P. Wilbur (Michael Myers)*
Director: *Dwight H. Little*
Screenwriters: *Alan B. McElroy, based on a story by McElroy, Danny Lipsius, Larry Rattner, Benjamin Ruffner*
18/88 mins./Horror/Thriller/USA

Ten years after his last attack on his sister, Michael Myers escapes from a sanatorium and returns to his hometown of Haddonfield, Illinois, to stalk his young niece, slaughtering any teenager who gets in his way.

Five years after the interesting *Halloween III: Season of the Witch*, the rights to the series have passed from originator John Carpenter to producer Moustapha Akkad and *Halloween 4* corrects what *Halloween III* did 'wrong' by being precisely as unimaginative, uninspiring, predictable and dumb as the disappointing *Halloween II* or any of the other psycho sequels to the *Friday the 13th* or *A Nightmare on Elm Street* bloodbaths clogging the marketplace in the late 1980s.

Jamie Lee Curtis' career had taken off to such a degree that she wouldn't even consider appearing in a trash quickie like this (except in a photograph), but Donald Anything-for-Money Pleasence, the busiest actor in the world, didn't have such scruples and so Dr Loomis, the looney shrink Donald played in the first two films, returns with plastic scars to show he was a bit hurt by the explosion at the end of *Halloween II*, but with his raincoat and silly voice intact.

Some teenagers make out and get killed, Michael causes a power cut, the cute ickle orphan is menaced, gory things happen off screen where there's no danger that they might frighten you, and Carpenter's old synth riff is replayed plenty of times. It's incredible that a film could be so closely patterned on Carpenter's still-thrilling original and yet be so suspenseless, stupid, unscary and plodding. It opens with lumps of dull exposition, and then rushes through a story littered with annoyingly thin characters, ridiculous contrivances and wholly idiotic plot twists. Miraculously, something interesting happens in the last two minutes, but by that time it's far, far too late. ★★ **KN**

HALLOWEEN 5 (1989)

Starring: *Donald Pleasence (Dr. Sam Loomis), Ellis Cornell (Rachel Carruther), Matthew Walker (Spitz), Danielle Harris (Jamie Lloyd Carruther), Wendy Kaplan (Tina Williams), Beau Starr (Sheriff Ben Meeker), Tamara Glynn (Samantha Thomas)*
Director: *Dominique Othenin-Girard*
Screenwriters: *Michael Jacobs, Dominique Othenin-Girard, Shem Bitterman, based on characters created by John Carpenter, Debra Hill*
18/96 mins./Horror/Thriller/USA

Jamie Lloyd, Michael Myers's niece, is still traumatised by his last Halloween massacre, and further troubled when it turns out she has a psychic link with the killer.

This quinquel, sub-titled The Revenge of Michael Myers on posters but not prints, opens by taking back the single interesting sequence in *Halloween 4: The Return of Michael Myers* by revealing that Michael's nine-year-old niece has not followed in his footsteps and killed her stepmother.

Then, the semi-supernatural psycho (Donald Shanks) returns from his resting place at the bottom of a well to stalk another group of tedious teens. Harris has psychic flashes whenever Michael is about to kill, Donald Pleasence does his old ominous act ('I prayed that he would burn in hell. But in my heart, I knew that hell would not have him') and dies for the second time in the series (which wouldn't prevent him returning for *Halloween: The Curse of Michael Myers*), and a mysterious gunslinger loiters in the background, intervening to aid Michael in a jailbreak and presumably help out in future sequels (this sub-plot is left up in the air until the next film).

The story concentrates on Harris, as unkillable because of her age as Michael is because of his importance to the continuation of the series, so the mandatory make-out, practical joke and slaughter sequences seem like intrusions on their family bonding. Late in the film, director Dominique Othenin-Girard (*Omen IV: The Awakening*) tries preposterously to work up sympathy for Michael, with Pleasence speechifying about the madman's need to slake the 'rage' inside him, and Harris coaxing the killer into removing his mask so a tear can be observed leaking from his eye before business as usual resumes with the murderer ineffectually trying to carve up the girl and getting kicked into touch until the next sequel. ★ **KN**

HALLOWEEN H20: TWENTY YEARS LATER (1998)

Starring: *Jamie Lee Curtis (Laurie Strode/Keri Tate), Josh Hartnett (John Tate), Adam Arkin (Will Brennan), Michelle Williams (Molly Cartwell), LL Cool J (Ronald 'Ronny' Jones), Janet Leigh (Norma Watson), Joseph Gordon-Levitt (Jimmy Howell)*
Director: *Steve Miner*
Screenwriters: *Robert Zappia, Matt Greenberg, from a story by Zappia, characters created by Debra Hill, John Carpenter*
18/86 mins./Horror/USA

Twenty years after surviving an attack by her psychotic brother, Laurie Strode has changed her name to Keri Tate and is the headmistress of a California private school. She still has visions of Michael Myers coming to get her. One Halloween, he shows up at the school and menaces Laurie and her teenage son.

H20 can't quite pretend there haven't been *Halloween* movies since 1982 – it has to get round its heroine's death, established in *Halloween 4* – but attempts to refresh the franchise for the *Scream* generation by calling Jamie Lee Curtis back to the role that made her career.

The standard stalk-and-slash takes an *Aliens*-like turn in a crowd-pleasing last act, which gets *Scream*-like kicks from not pulling the expected revelations (at one point, it's a shock that Michael doesn't come back from the dead) and allows Curtis to do many of the things you've always wanted to see twitty horror movie heroines do. The in-jokes are subtler than usual, with a nice conversation between Curtis and her real-life mother Janet Leigh, which makes sense for the characters in this film but also applies to Leigh's sufferings in *Psycho*.

HALLOWEEN; RESURRECTION

Director Steve Miner, on board because John Carpenter passed, made two early *Friday the 13th* sequels and manages the business of the sudden knee-jerk shocks with ease, realising (as previous sequels didn't) that *Halloween* movies are supposed to be scary not violent. However, the film is cluttered with disposable supporting characters (LL Cool J as the gatekeeper deserves a swifter, more extreme fate than he gets) and is often clumsy where Carpenter used to be deft. Taken as a sequel to *Halloween*, this is just above average; taken as a sequel to *Halloween II*, which is where most of its backstory comes from, it looks terrific. ★★★ **KN**

⦾ HALLOWEEN: RESURRECTION (2002)

Starring: *Jamie Lee Curtis (Laurie Strode), Brad Loree (Michael Myers), Busta Rhymes (Freddie Harris), Bianca Kajilich (Sara Moyer), Sean Patrick Thomas (Rudy Grimes)*
Director: *Rick Rosenthal*
Screenwriters: *Larry Brand, Sean Hood, based on a story by Larry Brand, characters created by Debra Hill, John Carpenter*
15/89 mins./Horror/USA

After finally murdering his sister, masked killer Michael Myers returns to his derelict childhood home. College kids hired by an internet entrepreneur spend Halloween night in the Myers house for a spooky web-cast. Michael starts killing off the wannabe net-stars.

Halloween H20: Twenty Years Later ignored earlier dud sequels, bringing back Jamie Lee Curtis and some quality. Early in this eighth *Halloween*, we learn that Michael wasn't decapitated after all, and long-suffering Laurie finally gets killed – though that's never stopped her brother showing up in the next film so Curtis might not be as free of the series as she thinks. It's basically a join-the-dots version of *My Little Eye*, with Busta Rhymes taking on the LL Cool J role of token rapper who has it in his contract that he a) doesn't get killed and b) kicks psycho ass. A group of showoff college kids are recruited by an internet entrepreneur to spend the night of Halloween in the derelict Myers house in Haddonfield, Illinois (now large enough to have a previously-unheard-of university campus) while wearing webcams and spied on by a supposed net audience of 'thousands'.

As the kids are slaughtered by the boy who 'picked up a knife when he was six years old and never put it down', heroine Bianca Kajilich gets txt msg advice from net-nerd Sean Patrick Thomas. Originally, Kajilich was set up to be the new Jamie Lee, but test audiences most folks would disagree with responded more to Rhymes' kung fu-practising, fast-talking loon and so the rapper gets to show up and pound the killer into yet another fiery demise.

Weakly staged by Rick Rosenthal, who directed *Halloween II* back in 1980, and indifferently acted by nobodies, this is every bit as feeble as the forgotten *Halloweens 4* through *6*. ★ **KN**

⦾ HALLOWEEN: THE CURSE OF MICHAEL MYERS (1995)

Starring: *Donald Pleasance (Dr. Sam Loomis), Paul Rudd, as Paul Stephen Rudd (Tommy Doyle), Marianne Hagan (Kara Strode), Mitch Ryan, as Mitchell Ryan (Dr. Terence Wynn)*
Director: *Joe Chappelle*
Screenwriter: *Daniel Farrands, based on characters created by Debra Hill, John Carpenter*
18/88 mins./Horror/USA

Years after the disappearance of Michael Myers, the teenagers of Haddonfield, Illinois, defy a local ordnance by celebrating Halloween. Michael's niece escapes from a Druid cult with a baby who may be her uncle's, and the killer pursues her to his hometown.

'According to Celtic legend, one child from each tribe was chosen to be inflicted with the curse of Thorn,' moans Donald Pleasence, 'so after the blood sacrifices of its next of kin on the night of Samhain, Halloween, the sacrifice of one family meant sparing the lives of an entire tribe. For years, I've been convinced there must be some reason, some method behind Michael's madness.'

Another soulless, pointless rip-off, this doodles around the plot parameters of John Carpenter's *Halloween* movies with only Pleasence, who died during production, and Carpenter's theme tune as links to the series' beginnings. Like *Jason Goes to Hell: The Final Friday*, it tries to import a more supernatural element by revealing that Michael (George P. Wilbur) kills because of a Druid curse and that there's a cult out to protect him.

The mysterious cowboy-hatted figure from *Halloween 5* turns out to be Mitchell Ryan, leader of the Michael worshippers, but the plot touches on such new events as a possible child Michael might have spawned with the absentee heroine of the last two films to continue the killing tradition, while hero Tommy is the kid baby-sat by Jamie Lee Curtis back in *Halloween*.

The line that rings the most hollow sound is 'kick the audience in the face enough and they'll lick you all over.' This is certainly the weakest of the *Halloween* films. After this, the series tried to forget three whole sequels to restart the franchise with the back-to-basics *Halloween H20: Twenty Years Later*. ★ **KN**

⦾ HAMBURGER HILL (1987)

Starring: *Steven Weber (Sergeant Worcester) Anthony Braille (Vincent 'Alphabet' Languidly), Michael Boatman (Midtown), Don Cheadle (Private Washburn), Dylan McDermott (Sergeant Frantz)*
Director: *John Irvin*
Screenwriter: *James Carabatsos*
18/112 mins./War/USA

The story of the ten-day assault on Hill 937, dubbed Hamburger Hill because of the bloody cost in life, in Vietnam, as seen through the eyes of one company of American soldiers.

Out of the three Vietnam movies that arrived in quick succession in the late eighties, (after *Platoon* and *Full Metal Jacket*) John Irvin's is the most American. It is determined its men are heroes, and their endeavour honourable. The theme is the call of duty, against horrifying odds, not the rage of politics and the destruction of the human psyche that typically defines the Vietnam movie. The film champions the succour of brotherhood and dismays at the slaughter of so many men, so has far more in common with WWI sensibilities than *Apocalypse Now*.

The acerbic title refers to the GI's gallows humour nickname for their objective, Hill 937, referencing the notorious Pork Chop Hill from the Korean War. It rather graphically identifies what became of most American bodies in the hailstorm of enemy gunfire – chopped meat. The story structure itself isn't very original: a study of one company's comradeship under fire, but applying that framework to the surrealistic horrors of Vietnam is an interesting tack. With its cast of unknowns (Dylan McDermott is the only one who subsequently made something of a name for himself) these soldiers are certainly tossed and turned by doubts and fears, but they are hardly the fragmenting dropouts and psychos that seem to populate the genre.

Irvin is asking a straightforward but profound question – how do ordinary men deal with the alien necessities of what they are required to do? There is an aching ridiculousness to the gruelling, costly task of taking this hill. And the film is at its most powerful when simply evaluating individual motivation. Asked why he has volunteered for another tour of duty, Steven Weber's Sergeant Worcester gives a telling account of how America's anti-war movement has cut them adrift from the beautiful college girls meeting him at the airport with 'bags of shit' and how his wife has moved in with her hippy lover.

Irvin's action, however, lacks the shocking immediacy of Oliver Stone, and the sheer hellish grind of gaining the slopes of this damn hill in the

Shau Valley never feels quite the Sisyphean nightmare it should. But as a direct tribute to the dignity of the soldier facing attacks on both their bodies and their souls it puts things in a salutary context. ★★★★ **IN**

HAMLET (1948)

Starring: *Laurence Olivier (Hamlet), Eileen Herlie (Queen Gertrude), Basil Sydney (King Claudius), Jean Simmons (Ophelia), Norman Woodard (Horatio), Felix Aylmer (Polonius), Terrence Morgan (Laertes), Peter Cushing (Osric), Stanley Holloway (Gravedigger), John Laurie (Francisco)*
Director: *Laurence Olivier*
Screenwriter: *Alan Dent, based on the play by William Shakespeare*
U/153 mins./Drama/UK

Awards: *Academy Awards – Best Picture, Best Actor, Best Art Direction-Set Decoration, Best Costume Design (Roger K. Furse). Bafta – Best Film.*

Hamlet is informed by his father's ghost that he was murdered by Claudius, the brother who has since usurped his throne and wedded his wife, Gertrude. However, the Danish prince's quest for revenge is too easily deflected and he pays the ultimate price for his indecision.

Released in the same year as Orson Welles's *Macbeth*, the first non-American film to win the Oscar for Best Picture remains one of cinema's finest Shakespearean adaptations, although many at the time were unhappy with the liberties taken with the text by the newly knighted Laurence Olivier. Having viewed *Henry V* in terms of a colourful canvas, Olivier saw *Hamlet* as an engraving and, thus, opted for a monochrome approach that was given an additional sombre chill by Desmond Dickinson's atmospheric photography.

Having first played the Bard's most complex hero in 1937, the 41-year-old Olivier was also aware that movie audiences were not going to tolerate the full four and a half hours and so he compressed the action into 153 minutes. Among the cast casualties were Fortinbras's Norwegian forces and Rosencrantz and Guildenstern, who not only got a film of their own in 1990 (with Tim Roth and Gary Oldman as Tom Stoppard's anti-heroes), but who also became the models for Pumbaa and Timon in *The Lion King*, which is essentially *Hamlet* in animal form.

Made for £580,000, this is a decidedly Freudian interpretation of the play, with Hamlet's frustrations fuelling his Oedipal relationship with Gertrude and the sado-masochistic manner in which he treats Ophelia. But it's also a wholly cinematic vision, with the camera prowling around the Oscar-winning sets like a combination of old Hamlet's restless spirit and his son's inconstant purpose. Indeed, Elsinore almost becomes a character in itself, as it sucks the life out of those trapped inside it.

Olivier also keeps the camera moving during the famous scenes and speeches and ingeniously interiorises the 'To be or not to be' soliloquy to reinforce the impression of a man bottling up emotions he's powerless to resolve. Some critics claimed this tactic drew the play's passion, but the dignified formality of the performances only emphasise the lust, avarice, insanity and murderous intent lurking beneath the courtly façades. ★★★★ **DP**

HAMLET (1990)

Starring: *Mel Gibson (Hamlet), Glenn Close (Gertrude), Alan Bates (Claudius), Paul Scofield (The Ghost), Ian Holm (Polonius), Helena Bonham Carter (Ophelia), Nathaniel Parker (Laertes), Sean Murray (Guildenstern), Michael Maloney (Rosencrantz)*
Director: *Franco Zeffirelli*
Screenwriters: *Christopher De Vore, Franco Zeffirelli, based on the play by William Shakespeare*
PG/130 mins./Drama/USA/UK/France

The prince of Denmark is haunted by the ghost of his father the king, who claims to have been murdered by his brother in an act of high treason, and it encourages young Hamlet to avenge him. But the prince has doubts, and is torn between his allegiance and fear of madness.

Hairdressing has a certain amount to answer for in Zeffirelli's screen Hamlet for the 90s. Glenn Close's Gertrude, on first sight, keening over her husband's corpse while exchanging come-hither glances with Alan Bates' Claudius, sports enough flaxen plaits nailed to her head to kit out three Valkyries and a Swedish housekeeper on the side. Mel Gibson, meanwhile, glowers from under a ginger fringe that does absolutely nothing for him except clash with his beard.

Tonsorial peeves aside, however, Zeffirelli's choice of Gibson to tackle the greatest dramatic role in the English language is vindicated by a competent and attractive performance that has thought, vigour and humour. No noble youth, nor particularly persuasive as a scholar, Gibson is too, too stolid when soliloquising but impressive when his blood is up or feigning madness. Once the killing gets underway, he really starts cooking and few Hamlets can have been more plausible when warning, 'I have in me that which is dangerous.' Close, meanwhile looks ridiculously young to have hatched this particular Ham (in real life the actors are only 9 years apart in age), though the credit side of this freshness is an Oedipal confrontation one can readily buy.

Around Gibson and Close, Brit thesps do their stuff – with Ian Holm and Paul Scofield particularly strong. And Helena Bonham Cater, one may fairly say with surprise, is an affecting Ophelia, thanks to Zefferelli shunning the manically fey blonde clichés for a quieter and quite disturbing manifestation of madness.

Zeffirelli and script collaborator Chrisophe De Vore have done an honourable job of abbreviating the play into a coherent screen affair, and the visuals are fine, but one might have hoped for more inspiration and audacity.

The result is that those familiar with the play are likely to view this production with indifference – those less well acquainted are a little in danger of falling asleep. ★★★ **AE**

HAMLET (1996)

Starring: *Kenneth Branagh (Hamlet), Derek Jacobi (Claudius), Julie Christie (Gertrude), Richard Briers (Polonius), Kate Winslet (Ophelia), Nicholas Farrell (Horatio), Michael Maloney (Laertes), Brian Blessed (Ghost), Billy Crystal (First gravedigger – uncredited), Robin Williams (Osric – uncredited)*
Director: *Kenneth Branagh*
Screenwriter: *Kenneth Branagh, based on the play by William Shakespeare*
PG/242 mins./Drama/USA

Awards: *Empire Awards – Best British Actress (Kate Winslet)*

Hamlet is summoned home for his father's funeral and his mother's wedding to his uncle. In a supernatural episode, he discovers that his uncle, whom he hates anyway, murdered his father.

When Branagh elected to make his vision of Shakespeare's all-conquering tale into the grandest of the cinematic versions, he surely gave little mind to its ultimate fate, placed on a Blockbuster shelf between Mel Gibson and *The Hand That Rocks The Cradle*. Faced with those choices should the casual renter go for hunkdom, horror or high art?

In the end, there should be no debate, just take this and get all three. Feel the quality and get twice the width (plus an interval and recap!). True, squeezed into a letterbox format like a Sunday paper, the much-trumpeted 70mm original loses the jaw-dropping impact it had on the cinema screen, but it is no less richly coloured for its loss of scale.

The top-line performances are uniformly awesome, with Winslet in particular playing well beyond her years. There are stunning support turns too, notably from Richard Briers, Michael Maloney and Charlton Heston, plus well-paced levity from box-office carrots Gérard Depardieu, Billy Crystal and Robin Williams, and box-office turnip Ken Dodd.

So make yourself comfortable on the sofa, dig out the dog-eared paperback that saw you through English lessons, and let your finger hover over the pause button. Use it to catch up on the dialogue. Use it to savour the sheer splendour of the majestic art direction. ★★★★★ **NJ**

HANA-BI (1997)

Starring: *Beat Takeshi (Yoshitaka Nishi), Kayoko Kishimoto (Miyuki), Ren Osugi (Horibe), Susumu Terijama (Nakamura), Tetsu Watanabe (Tesuka), Hakuryu (Yakuza Hitman)*
Director: *Takeshi Kitano*
Screenwriter: *Takeshi Kitano*
18/103 mins./Thriller/Japan

When his partner Horibe is wounded during the stakeout he abandoned to visit his dying wife in hospital, world-weary cop Nishi quits the force, borrows some cash from a yakuza and plans a bank robbery in a bid to atone for his and a lawless society's failings.

Takeshi Kitano began work on this deeply personal meditation on love, violence, grief and loss before his near-fatal motorcycle accident. Echoing themes from both *Violent Cop* and *Sonatine*, its blend of death fixation and life affirmation renders it as moving as it's edgy. But this is also a wondrously cinematic exercise in the exploitation of space and stillness and it confirms Kitano as both a highly modern filmmaker and the heir to such classical directors as Yasujiro Ozu.

But, in addition to writing, directing and editing the picture, Kitano also bestrides it as the taciturn, short-fused Nishi, who is just as likely to thrust chopsticks into someone's eye as he is to repay a kindness. Considering that his face still bore the effects of his crash, Kitano's performance is incredibly courageous as well as compellingly combustible. Yet, there's also a touching sensitivity about his scenes with Kayoko Kishimoto, which contrast starkly with the methodical manner in which he plans his heist and apportions his twisted charity.

Initially adopting a fragmented structure, the action conveys the confusion Nishi feels as he tries to cope with both his wife's impending demise (having already suffered the loss of his daughter) and the paralysis of a partner who was not only protecting an undeserving society, but also acting out of friendship. But the interjected flashes of violence are contrasted with moments of disconcerting peace, which suggest both Nishi's despondency and, ultimately, the serenity he achieves before his own merciless death.

Exquisitely photographed by Hideo Yamamoto, the snowy fields, blossoming trees and idyllic seascapes have a tranquillity that is reinforced by the paintings seen in the bank and at the hospital, which, like Horibe's bizarre floral-beasts, were painted by Kitano himself.

This is very much the work of an auteur at the peak of his powers. But it's also an intrepid insight into Kitano's physical and psychological state as he embarked upon his second chance at life. ★★★★ **DP**

THE HAND THAT ROCKS THE CRADLE (1992)

Starring: *Annabella Sciorra (Claire Bartel), Rebecca De Mornay (Mrs. Mott/Peyton Flanders), Matt McCoy (Michael Bartel), Ernie Hudson (Solomon), Julianne Moore (Marlene)*
Director: *Curtis Hanson*
Screenwriter: *Amanda Silver*
15/110 mins./Thriller/USA

Peyton Flanders seemed to be the perfect nanny, but secretly she was out to wreck the lives of the family she was supposed to be helping . . .

The Hand That Rocks The Cradle certainly hits a nerve. Curtis Hanson's postmodern morality tale is a sure-footed combination of unerring commercial touch, a central storyline that strikes at – shamelessly exploits, some will say – the most basic human fears within us all, and, most impressively, two hugely enjoyable performances from its pair of leading ladies.

The back-from-the-dumper De Mornay is the oddly-named Peyton Flanders, the psycho-nanny from hell out to destroy the happily married Claire Bartel, after the said Mrs. Bartel has effectively destroyed her own marriage some years before.

Being a thoroughly modern kind of gal, however, Peyton comes armed not with a knife but with a nanny's outfit, eventually infiltrating the Bartel nest in the guise of Little Miss Goody Two Shoes, an illusion shattered forever with the memorable image of De Mornay breastfeeding the brat.

From here in, it's Peyton vs. Claire to the death, with useless hubby McCoy stuck in the background, and only good old racial stereotype Solomon and his trusty old bike of any use in an emergency situation, of which there are, of course, plenty.

And that's about it, really, except it's all done in a suitably stylish way from the man who directed *LA Confidential* and *8 mile*, and it's really quite frightening in a 'It's Behind You' kind of way, and not a little disturbing, one imagines, for parents of small babies everywhere. ★★★★ **BMc**

HANNAH AND HER SISTERS (1986)

Starring: *Woody Allen (Mickey), Michael Caine (Elliot), Mia Farrow (Hannah), Carrie Fisher (April), Barbara Hershey (Lee), Lloyd Nolan (Hannah's Father), Maureen O'Sullivan (Hannah's Mother), Daniel Stern (Dusty), Max von Sydow (Frederick), Dianne Wiest (Holly)*
Director: *Woody Allen*
Screenwriter: *Woody Allen*
15/106 mins./Drama/Comedy/USA

Awards: *Academy Awards – Best Supporting Actor (Michael Caine), Best Supporting Actress (Dianne Wiest), Best Original Screenplay, BAFTA – Best Director, Best Original Screenplay*

This is a tale of three Thanksgiving dinners and what happens in the interim to the guests – actress Hannah and her siblings Lee and Holly and the men in their lives: bored financial adviser Elliot; tortured artist Frederick; and neurotic TV executive, Mickey.

Leo Tolstoy wrote in *Anna Karenina* that 'all happy families resemble one another, but each unhappy family is unhappy in its own way' and Woody Allen always claimed the Russian's novel was his primary inspiration for *Hannah and Her Sisters*. However, its focus on three siblings recalls Allen's first straight drama, *Interiors*, while the linking of autobiography, show-business and family celebration also echoes Ingmar Bergman's late masterpiece, *Fanny and Alexander*.

Indeed, the film referencing continues when Mickey (whose neuroses and hypochondria had briefly driven him towards Catholicism) finds salvation in the Marx Brothers' *Duck Soup*. Yet, for all its screen antecedents, the use of voice-overs and the 16 chapter headings give the action a distinctly bookish feel.

The acting, however, occasionally tends towards theatricality, with Michael Caine being particularly guilty of deliberated delivery in his Oscar-winning turn. In mitigation, however, he found Allen's working methods less than conducive and was reined in when he attempted to be more overtly comic (Max von Sydow and Barbara Hershey were likewise told to stick to the grand design when they suggested an alternative reading of their showdown).

Along with Allen, Mia Farrow seems most comfortable with the tone, although she was less than amused to discover just how much of their own lives Allen had slipped into the screenplay. The brain tumour related to the director's own scare during *Manhattan*, while he conceded that Frederick, Elliot and Mickey reflected facets of his own personality. But Maureen O'Sullivan (Farrow's real-life mother) refused to play opposite her daughter unless some of the more blatant references to Mia and her sisters, Tia and Stephanie, were removed.

Several scenes involving Caine and Hershey's affair were also cut. But, ultimately, Allen had to add the climactic dinner after friends at preview screenings objected to the ambiguous *Interiors*-like ending. The resulting picture was his most mature work to date and his witty, literate screenplay deserved its Oscar as much as Dianne Wiest's superbly realised Best Supporting performance. ★★★★ **DP**

HANNIBAL (2001)

Starring: *Anthony Hopkins (Hannibal Lecter), Julianne Moore (Clarice Starling), Gary Oldman (Mason Verger – uncredited), Ray Liotta (Paul Krendler), Frankie Faison, billed as Frankie R. Faison (Barney), Giancarlo Gianni (Pazzi), Francesca Neri (Allegra Pazzi), Zeljko Ivanek (Dr. Cordell Doemling), Hazelle Goodman (Evelda Drumgo), David Andrews (FBI Agent Pearsall)*
Director: *Ridley Scott*
Screenwriters: *David Mamet and Steven Zaillian, based on the novel by Thomas Harris*
18/131 mins./Thriller/USA

Ten years after his escape, Hannibal Lecter has decamped to Florence, while Clarice Starling has been sidelined at the FBI to ponder anew her missing adversary. Then someone familiar shows up in Italy . . .

Even for a high-profile sequel such as this, the preceding ballyhoo was pretty intense. The talent behind *The Silence Of The Lambs* – director Jonathan Demme, and Clarice herself, Jodie Foster – scarpered to the hills on reading Thomas Harris' deeply disappointing sequel. Still, Hopkins returned, and the arrival of new recruits Julianne Moore and Ridley Scott, piping hot after *Gladiator*, boded well. Add the mouthwatering screenwriting talents of David Mamet and Steve Zaillian, and something special was definitely on the cards.

The resulting collaboration is, for the most part, as faithful an adaptation of a novel as you could wish. Except you wouldn't. Foster and crew were right, it was just a bad idea in the first place. Scott's leaden movie simply exacerbates all the frustrations of Harris' derided novel – it's a thriller devoid of thrill. For starters, there's just no-one to worry about, for the only person in any kind of jeopardy is Lecter himself and it's his invulnerability we all love. The much mooted combo of Mamet and Zaillian have failed to find life in the moribund book, and Lecter is allowed none of the devilish wordplay, piercing intellect or sparks of hideous violence that defined his complex persona.

As events wobble from Florence to Washington to Verger's New England estate, driven by spurious motivations, you can't help but recall the intricacy and skill that made *Silence* so riveting. There's not a single set piece in *Hannibal* to match the mind-blowing escape of Lecter or the double house twist at the end of the original, replete with its scalpel sharp editing. Maneating hogs, mobile phone chases and the odd gunfight hardly suffice.

While story ineptitudes cannot be laid at his door, the flat visual style and – staggering – lack of atmosphere are most certainly Scott's fault. Where is the florid Gothic mood of *Silence* or, for that matter, the hulking darkness of *Alien*? Florence might as well be Huddersfield. Hopkins, too, struggles to rediscover the impact he once made. The script doesn't help – apart from a lecture on fine art, you'll be hard pressed to find anything clever emanating from that mind. Outside of the cell, Lecter comes across as foppish and avuncular, a listless foodee sporting a hat at a jaunty angle. Moore is a huge misfire – perhaps Foster had just made the role too much her own. Only Liotta and Oldman have fun with the nominal bad guy roles: a slimy FBI suit and the dribbling, biscuit-faced billionaire Verger. Character piece or thriller, love story or psychodrama, Hannibal confounds and dumbfounds – an inert spectacle and a frightening waste of modern cinema's juiciest villain. ★★ **IN**

THE HAPPIEST DAYS OF YOUR LIFE (1950)

Starring: *Alastair Sim (Wetherby Pond), Margaret Rutherford (Muriel Whitchurch), Guy Middleton (Victor Hyde-Brown), Joyce Grenfell (Miss Gossage)*
Director: *Frank Launder*
Screenwriter: *Frank Launder, based on the play by John Dighton*
U/83 mins./Comedy/UK

A bureaucratic error at the Ministry of Education results in St Swithin's School for Girls having to share Nutbourne School with its all-male population, much to the consternation of respective Heads, Miss Muriel Whitchurch and Wetherby Pond.

Playwright John Dighton (who would co-script the Ealing classics *Kind Hearts and Coronets* and *The Man in the White Suit*) wrote the part of Miss Muriel Whitchurch especially for Margaret Rutherford and she's in unstoppable form in this adaptation of the 1948 West End hit. However, her natural scene-stealing proclivities were ably held in check by Alastair Sim, assuming George Howe's part of the ambitious headmaster whose promotion to a prestigious academy is jeopardised by the accidental billeting of Rutherford and her mostly colonial charges.

The stage action had been confined to the staffroom. But Frank Launder and Sidney Gilliatt opened it out to exploit both Nutbourne's classrooms and its grounds. This also enabled them to include the kids, who threw themselves into everything from pillow fights to Greek dancing and rollerskating through the corridors with St Trinian-like brio. Indeed, Launder and Gilliatt were keen to establish a link with cartoonist Ronald Searle's anarchic institution and they not only commissioned him to draw the opening credits, but also went on to produce six comedies based on his popular books. It's tempting to think that just as Joyce Grenfell's Ruby Gates bore a delicious resemblance to Miss 'Call Me Sausage' Gossage, so Sim borrowed from what the Punch critic called Rutherford's 'most disgraceful exhibition of ruthless femininity' for Miss Prism in *The Belles of St Trinian's*.

Much of the byplay between Rutherford and Sim revolves around the single central joke and it's to their eternal credit that they keep it fresh – particularly during the frantic, farcical finale in which they forge an unlikely alliance to prevent her parents from discovering the presence of the boys and his governors from realising that their school is no longer single sex. But there's also a saucy undercurrent to the references to mistresses and biology lessons and it's doubly amusing that the Nutbourne motto is 'Guard Thine Honour', bearing in mind lecherous master Hyde-Brown's collection of smut. ★★★★ **DP**

HAPPINESS (1998)

Starring: *Jane Adams (Joy Jordan), Lara Flynn Boyle (Helen Jordan), Cynthia Stevenson (Trish Maplewood), Dylan Baker (Bill Maplewood), Philip Seymour Hoffman (Allen)*
Director: *Todd Solondz*
Screenwriter: *Todd Solondz*
18/139 mins./Comedy/Drama/USA

Joy and her circle of friends and relations all seem to hide dark secrets – and the revelations of their disturbing behaviours build a disturbing picture of a certain kind of society.

Giving a film a title like *Happiness* somehow suggests that there's going to be precious little on display, and Solondz's follow-up to his indie hit *Welcome To The Dollhouse* indeed presents a cross-section of modern American agonies as an interlocked selection of characters strive for happiness in all manner of doomed ways. It's a vision of hell, but it has a truthfulness and a humanity that renders it as moving (and, in a weird way, entertaining) as it is horrific.

Striking a balance between making you laugh out loud and cringe inside, the film spirals out from the life of the ironically named Joy, fresh from killing off a disastrous relationship, introducing a tangle of people somehow related to her: her sisters Trish, a home-maker, and Helen, a poetess; Trish's husband Bill, living with unspeakable urges; the girls' parents, separating in retirement; Bill's patient Allen, an obscene phone caller obsessed with Helen; and Allen's neighbour Kristina, a heavyweight obsessed with Allen, who turns out to have another ghastly secret.

Scene after scene conjures up a potent combination of acute embarrassment, existential terror and appalled wit. Most attention is bound to be paid to the plot about Bill, a paedophile whose clumsy arrangement of the rape of his 11-year-old son's best schoolfriend is an against-the-odds masterpiece of beyond-black comedy. Solondz manages to make a paedophile into a real, sympathetic character without ever exploiting the subject or prettifying his behaviour – indeed, Baker's final scene, as he tries honestly to answer his son's questions about what he has done, is genuinely on a par with the 'coulda been a contender' speech from *On The Waterfront*.

Many of the other strands are as affecting and powerfully acted, touching on equally perverse material. Boyle works a strange pathos within a caricatured role, and Gazzara, in his fifth decade as an underrated screen great, does an enormous amount with tiny suggestions. Besides Baker, Adams, Stevenson and Hoffman (as a man so tragically dull even his shrink zones out on him) deliver the sort of work that in a just world would take home Academy Awards. Among the most ambitious, successful and shattering American films of the decade – it might not be the ideal date movie, but you have to see it. ★★★★★ **CW**

Ⓓ HARD-BOILED (LASHOU SHENTAN) (1992)

Starring: *Chow Yun Fat (Inspector Tequila Yuen), Tony Leung Chiu Wai (Tony), Teresa Mo (Teresa Chang), Philip Chan (Supt. Pang), John Woo (Mr. Woo)*
Director: *John Woo*
Screenwriter: *Barry Wong, based on a story by John Woo*
18/126 mins./Action/Crime/Drama/Hong Kong

Having gone undercover to discover his partner's killer, a cop, Yuen, manages to infiltrate a mob and meets Johnny, a hitman. Eventually they both realise the other is a cop and team up to bring in the criminals.

The first feature film from critically worshipped Hong Kong director John Woo to receive more than a cursory release in the UK, this is an explosively visceral, operatic tour de force of breathtakingly choreographed violence and blistering ballistic pyrotechnics that begins over-the-top with a teahouse shoot-out that leaves at least 30 people dead, and then escalates into a succession of even more outrageous action set pieces.

In Hong Kong, on the eve of the Communist takeover and the relinquishment of British rule, police detective Yuen loses his partner in the teahouse slaughter, and against the advice of his superior, Chan, continues his own investigation into an illegal arms consortium, determined to nail those responsible for his partner's death. Following up a brutal hit, Yuen crosses paths with an undercover cop, Tony, who, posing as a hit man, has infiltrated the gun-running operation and who, unbeknown to Yuen, passes coded messages back to Chan. When Tony is forced to betray his boss and defect to a rival gang headed by sadistic young pretender Johnny, Yuen uncovers Tony's secret.

Upon learning that a city hospital is the site of Johnny's arsenal, the pair team up for a showdown that culminates in a maelstrom of bullets and delirious destruction. With a body count well into three figures, more firepower than you can shake an Uzi at, and imaginatively realised, adrenaline-pumping action sequences to turn Hollywood's action directors green, this was Woo's most outrageous two hours to date. Mixing the frenzied pacing of kung fu flicks with a plethora of cinematic tricks – slow-motion, freeze-frames, wipes – Woo has elevated the action movie into the realm of art. Infinitely more exciting than a dozen *Die Hards*, action cinema doesn't come any better than this. ★★★★ **IN**

Ⓓ A HARD DAY'S NIGHT (1964)

Starring: *John Lennon (John), Paul McCartney (Paul), George Harrison (George), Ringo Starr (Ringo), Wilfrid Brambell (Grandfather), Norman Rossington (Norm)*
Director: *Richard Lester*
Screenwriter: *Alun Owen*
U/83 mins./Musical/Comedy/UK

Escaping hordes of fans, the Beatles board a train for London to play on a live TV show. Joined by their manager Norm and Paul's grandfather, the band groove at a nightspot before Ringo goes AWOL, throwing the whole television appearance into jeopardy.

Think about it. What transformed The Beatles into the Fab Four? The music got the girls screaming and had academics making comparisons with Mahler, but it was their quick wit that made them the loveable Mop Tops. John Lennon asking those in the audience to rattle their jewellery at the Royal Command Performance charmed the Establishment. *A Hard Day's Night* seduced the parents.

Even before the watershed conquest of America, the screenwriter (playwright Alun Owen) had accompanied the Fabs on a flying visit to Paris to witness the insanity of Beatlemania first hand. Although, whether his day-in-the-life format predated the Maysles brothers' strategy for US Beatles' documentary *Yeah Yeah Yeah* remains open to conjecture.

What's indisputable, however, was that the band was dead against the idea of making an Elvis-Cliff style musical and had already nixed Brian Epstein's enthusiasm for The Yellow Teddy Bears, as they wouldn't have been allowed to write their own songs. Indeed, it was the music that persuaded United Artists to back the movie in the first place – as not only would they make a quick killing while the group's sure-to-be short-lived popularity lasted, but they would also secure exclusive rights to a new 'soundtrack' album.

Ultimately, this was to be the only LP solely composed by Lennon and McCartney and remained at No. 1 in the UK for 23 weeks.

Ironically, the director that producer Walter Shenson attached to the project had a history of those pop musicals the Fabs so detested. But Dick Lester's use of camera in *It's Trad, Dad* (1961) and the fact he had steered the Goons through their transition from radio to television won the Beatles over. Indeed, Lester's genius for physical comedy, that had informed Spike Milligan's *The Running, Jumping And Standing Still Film* (1959), would resurface in the manic playing-field shenanigans accompanying *Can't Buy Me Love*.

More importantly, Lester was something of a movie magpie. Just as John and Paul drew on R&B, rock'n'roll and showtune ballads for inspiration, so Lester borrowed liberally from Buster Keaton, cinéma vérité, documentary style Free Cinema, Fellini and the nouvelle vague for his unconventional approach to narrative and image-making. In the process, he became the godfather of MTV, as he sought ways of breaking from the lip sync and strum approach to filming pop. Even when he had no option, as in the final TV show sequence, he managed to use angle, lighting and rapid editing to fashion an anti-performance style later followed by *Ready, Steady, Go* and *Top Of The Pops*.

His attempt to jettison traditional narrative altogether was less successful, however, as Ringo's runner and the Mack Sennettesque search for him definitely constitute a storyline. Moreover, it induces the only slackening in the breakneck pace, even though it did give Ringo a moment in the spotlight, similar to George's dismissal of the 'grotty' trend-spotting media and John's mistaken identity encounter with Anna Quayle. Sadly, Paul's backstage showdown with a Shakespearean luvvie was cut.

Similarly, Wilfrid Brambell, as Paul's Irish grandfather, was given a few Steptoe-like set pieces to cash in on his TV celebrity. But there was nothing sitcom about the rest of the film's humour. Whether scripted or ad-libbed, it managed to showcase the irreverent charm that had made the Mops the media's darlings, while also proving that, despite the fame, they were still just four likely lads from Liverpool.

Based on their now legendary performance at Kennedy Airport (which took place just weeks before shooting began), the press conference sequence is particularly revealing of their rapid-fire repartee. John later dismissed comparisons with the Marx Brothers. But there are definite similarities between their caustic combinations of sarcasm, puns, irony, insult and nonsensical deadpan, with the reporters almost becoming a collective Margaret Dumont (the stuffy comedy foil for the Marx brothers).

But Lester was keen to demonstrate both his and the group's catholic comedy influences. There's mild surrealism in the way the Fabs suddenly appear outside the train to taunt the snooty commuter and in John's unexplained disappearance from an emptying bath-tub. A hint of Chaplinesque pathos (or at least Norman Wisdom sentimentality) informs Ringo's riverside meanderings, while slapstick dominates the anarchic 'playtime' sequence, which Lester makes all the more hilarious by his use of helicopter shots, unexpected angles and variegated film speeds.

With global takings of $11 million on a £200,000 outlay, *A Hard Day's Night* changed the visual presentation of pop forever. Moreover, it gave the Beatles a taste for movies. Following the singularly undistinguished *Help!*, John co-starred in Lester's *How I Won The War*, Ringo teamed with Peter Sellers for *The Magic Christian*, George formed HandMade and saved Monty Python's *Life Of Brian*, and Paul made *Give My Regards To Broad Street* – and they don't come much funnier than that. ★★★★ **DP**

THE HARD WAY (1991)

Starring: *Michael J. Fox (Nick Lang/Ray Casanov), James Woods (Detective Lt. John Moss), Stephen Lang (Party Crasher), Annabella Sciorra (Susan), Penny Marshall (Angie, Nick's Agent), Christina Ricci (Bonnie)*
Director: *John Badham*
Screenwriters: *Daniel Pyne, Lem Dobbs, based on a story by Lem Dobbs, Michael Kozoll*
15/111 mins./Action/Comedy/Crime/USA

A Hollywood superstar, planning on playing a cop in his next movie, teams up with the real thing to learn the ropes.

New York City Cop John Moss obsessively dogging the trail of a snickering bleached-blond psychopath who calls himself the Party Crasher, is so wrapped up in his job that everything else, from his girlfriend to his mental and physical health, has to come a distant second behind his overriding need for violent justice. Hollywood heartthrob Nick Lang, tired of fantasy action films with roman numerals in the title, wants to play a tough cop just like Moss, and wangles a chance to go on the streets with the tough guy so he can get the part. Moss, of course, hates the idea, but Lang proves persuasive, sticking to it even after ghetto gangbangers steal his cell phone.

John Badham, coming off the shabby vehicle *Bird On A Wire*, takes this premise and wrings out the perfect epitome of what the script has Moss call 'Hollywood horseshit'. An exceptional escapist movie, it combines enjoyably sleazy urban thrills (listen to Woods' dialogue and you'll be able to expand your vocabulary by 38 new obscenities) with good-natured daffy Hollywood parody. The stars, effectively mismatched, play together well, with the lightweight (and shortarse) Fox tagging along amusingly behind the driven, neurosis-fuelled hardman Woods. And while Woods teaches Fox to be a psycho hero, the screen lover takes time to help the cop forge a relationship with his girl.

In addition to star chemistry and in-jokes, *The Hard Way* has all the required custom features – to wit, one excellent heroine who holds her own in fights and arguments, one superb villain who genuinely enjoys torturing and killing people, one soundtrack crammed with inventive borrowed urban sounds (L.L. Cool J. drops in for a cop cameo too) and a stunt-filled finale with the principals dangling from a giant model of Fox's face over Times Square. Highly recommended nonsense. ★★★ **KN**

HAROLD & KUMAR GET THE MUNCHIES (HAROLD & KUMAR GO TO WHITE CASTLE) (2004)

Starring: *John Cho (Harold Lee), Kal Penn (Kumar Patel), Paula Garces (Maria), Neil Patrick Harris (Neil Patrick Harris), David Krumhotz (Goldstein), Ryan Reynolds (Male Nurse)*
Director: *Danny Leiner*
Screenwriters: *Jon Hurwitz, Hayden Scholossberg*
15/88 mins./Adventure/Comedy/U.S./Canada/Germany

Harold, a Korean-American investment banker with a report to file, and Kumar, an Indian-American student facing a vital interview at medical school, smoke grass to chill out. When hunger strikes, they realise that only White Castle burgers will hit the spot and set off on a surreal all-night adventure to find some . . .

Danny Leiner's magnum opus – *Dude, Where's My Car?* – may have been awful, but there's no denying the genius in that title, and, for the follow-up, it's good to see the muse hasn't left him. In fact, it's blossomed; where Dude was a skimpy ragbag of ideas strung together by the goofy coupling of Ashton Kutcher and Seann William Scott, *Harold & Kumar* is a much better riff on the same formula, with richer characters and a tighter, though no less stupid, script.

It's also a strangely radical movie, putting two smart, white-collar ethnic guys in a genre that's designed for young, dumb Caucasians. But Leiner rarely plays the race card – yes, H&K do face racism, especially from the cops, but this cheerful romp simply satirises it into yet another thing that gets between the duo and their burgers. Like the escaped cheetah, for example, or an E'd-up Doogie Howser, who steals their car to quench his lust for more drugs and lap dancers.

Crasser gags – like the excruciatingly awful 'battleshits' scene – spoil what could have been a fantastic comedy, but this is cleverer than it looks, inviting Middle America to accept two non-WASP character actors as leads and illegal drug use as a suitable premise for a sweet, romantic comedy. For that alone, it should be applauded. ★★★ **DHu**

HARRY AND THE HENDERSONS (BIGFOOT AND THE HENDERSONS) (1997)

Starring: *John Lithgow (George Henderson), Melinda Dillon (Nancy Henderson), Margaret Langrick (Sarah Henderson), Joshua Rudoy (Ernie Henderson), Kevin Peter Hall (Harry)*
Director: *William Dear*
Screenwriters: *William Dear, Bill Martin, Ezra D. Rappaport*
PG/110 mins./Family/Comedy/USA

George Henderson, vacationing in the woods with his family, runs over a Bigfoot and takes it back to Seattle. Named Harry, the creature makes friends with all and sundry, but is pursued by a nasty French scientist.

Despite a superbly-realised monster costume from effects whiz Rick Baker (*Greystoke, An American Werewolf in London*) and the traditional fine befuddled John Lithgow performance, this Steven Spielberg production – turned out while he was backing similarly underwhelming confections like *batteries not included*, *The Land Before Time* and the *Amazing Stories* TV series – is just a gooey xerox of *E.T.: The Extra-Terrestrial* and *Splash!*, as a weird creature is accepted by middle-class WASP suburbia but persecuted by a nasty scientist who wants to do experiments on it.

Melinda Dillon reprises her wide-eyed mom act from *Close Encounters*, Don Ameche does his spirited codger bit from *Cocoon* and M. Emmet Walsh reins in his habitual sleaziness to play Lithgow's eccentric old dad – everyone gets to do multiple doubletakes when confronted by the eight-foot-tall friendly monster. In his early screen career, Bigfoot was usually found in appalling pseudo-documentaries (*Legend of Boggy Creek*, *Sasquatch*) or video nasties (*Shriek of the Mutilated*, *Night of the Demon*). This, his big budget breakthrough movie, suggested that the walking carpet ought to head back for Z-features, taking director William Dear (*Teen Agent*) along with him. The script began life as the premise for a proposed US TV sitcom, which duly got made after this had passed out of theatres, with Hall reprising his role inside the fur and Bruce Davison replacing Lithgow. And have you noticed how many Spielberg-backed movies have French villains? ★★ **KN**

HARRY AND TONTO (1974)

Starring: *Art Carnet (Harry Coombs), Ellen Burstyn (Shirley), Chief Dan George (Sam Two Feathers), Geraldine Fitzgerald (Jessie), Larry Hagman (Eddie)*
Director: *Paul Mazursky*
Screenwriter: *Paul Mazursky*
Unrated/115 mins./Drama/USA
Awards: *Academy Awards – Best Actor*

When his New York apartment block is demolished, 72-year-old widowed academic Harry Coombs puts his cat Tonto in a basket and decides to visit his three children on a journey to the West Coast.

Paul Mazursky spent several years trying to finance his first solo screenplay and amassed 14 rejections before Fox finally agreed a bargain budget. Realising he couldn't afford too many established stars, Mazursky turned for his lead to Art Carney, who had spent 25 years in television and was best known for playing Ed Norton opposite Jackie Gleason in the sitcom, *The Honeymooners*. The choice couldn't have been more felicitous, as Carney gave a touching exhibition of suppressed disappointment, calm acceptance and gradual understanding that earned him the Best Actor Oscar in his first major role.

The influence of *King Lear*, Vittorio De Sica's *Umberto D* and Yasujiro Ozu's *Tokyo Story* can be felt throughout the picture. But this is very much a portrait of its times, as Mazursky examines the socio-cultural state of America in its last days of pre-Watergate and Vietnam-defeat innocence. Everyone Harry encounters as he journeys to California is a type. But such is the skill of the writing and the cast that each episode has warmth that never becomes schmaltz and wisdom that's never sanctimonious.

Mazursky clearly sought to aim a blow at the intelligentsia by having Harry's retired professor come down from his ivory tower and confront reality on the road. But filial ingratitude, the fragmentation of traditional communities and the pace of modern life were also key themes. Yet, the film retains a gentle satirical wit, with grandson Josh Mostel's vow of silence and Harry's jailhouse meeting of minds with Sam Two Feathers – the Native American healer who fixes his shoulder in return for an electric blender – balancing the more fractious drama of Harry's reunion with Chicago bookselling daughter Shirley and his deeply moving last dance with old flame Jessie in the rest home. ★★★★ **DP**

HARRY POTTER AND THE CHAMBER OF SECRETS (2002)

Starring: *Daniel Radcliffe (Harry Potter), Rupert Grint (Ron Weasley), Emma Watson (Hermione Granger), Maggie Smith (Minerva McGonagall), Robbie Coltrane (Rubeus Hagrid), Richard Harris (Albus Dumbledore), Kenneth Branagh (Gilderoy Lockhart), John Cleese (Nearly Headless Nick), Tom Felton (Draco Malfoy), Toby Jones (Voice of Dobby, the House Elf)*
Director: *Chris Columbus*
Screenwriter: *Steve Kloves, based on the novel by J.K. Rowling*
PG/161 mins./Fantasy/Adventure/U.S./U.K./Germany

It's year two for Harry Potter at Hogwarts School of Witchcraft and Wizardry. When several of his fellow pupils turn up in a petrified state, suspicion at first falls on Harry. So can he – helped by his friends Ron and Hermione – uncover the mystery that lies at the heart of the Chamber of Secrets?

The assumption – and it's a fair one at that – is that everyone who sees this will have seen the first film. So there's no need to pack in as much explanation of how the wizard world works or about Harry's backstory – the scar, his parents, Voldemort, everything that sets him apart from the other pupils. *Chamber Of Secrets* treats all of this as presumed knowledge and even abandons Rowling's school calendar structure when the action moves swiftly to Hogwarts. Instead, the focus falls on the central mystery (minus some diverting red herrings) while breaking the flow with a few upgraded favourite scenes, including a breakneck Quiddich chase.

The teachers – even Alan Rickman and Robbie Coltrane, who as Snape and Hagrid provided much of the first film's fun – are relegated to the background, which places even more responsibility on the shoulders of young Daniel Radcliffe. No longer has he simply to gape in wonder at the magic around him: this time the kid's got to act and, during the final encounter with 'Tom Riddle', Harry's fierce loyalty and bravery finds a determined Radcliffe hitting all the right dramatic notes. Harry, as a character, is beginning to come of age; this movie nudges towards a darker good-versus-evil thread for later movies. Radcliffe, too, is making the move from boy to teenager. His voice has broken and, if it keeps deepening at the present rate, he'll be outrumbling Vin Diesel before they've even got to *Goblet Of Fire*.

Overall, *Chamber Of Secrets*' high points are funnier, scarier and more action-heavy than in the first movie. The effects also look more polished – no dodgy centaurs this time – and Dobby the house elf is an expressive little creation, even if he does induce that CG-inflicted disease, jarjaritis, during an early scene with Harry. On his second and probably final Potter flick, director Chris Columbus shows more visual confidence, and has become more daring with his swooping computer-assisted camera shots across landscapes and locations. But the film's length does remain a stumbling block – you could adapt *War And Peace* in a shorter running time – so perhaps only the most attentive children will remain spellbound for its entirety. ★★★★ **OR**

HARRY POTTER AND THE GOBLET OF FIRE (2005)

Starring: *Daniel Radcliffe (Harry Potter), Emma Watson (Hermione Granger), Rupert Grint (Ron Weasley), Jason Issacs (Lucius Malfoy), Robbie Coltrane (Rubeus Hagrid), Michael Gambon (Albus Dumbledore)*
Director: *Mike Newell*
Screenwriter: *Steven Kloves, based on the novel by J.K. Rowling*
12A/157 mins./Fantasy/Adventure/UK/USA

Awards: *BAFTA – Best Production Design, Empire Awards – Special Award for Outstanding Contribution to British Cinema*

When Hogwarts hosts the prestigious and dangerous Triwizard Tournament, the enchanted Goblet Of Fire inexplicably selects unqualified 14-year-old Harry as a competitor. Thus he has to face three terrifying tasks while a dark power gathers force against him. Even scarier, he has to get a date for the Yule Ball.

The fourth offering in the Harry Potter franchise sees The Boy Who Lived and his chums trying to get through another year at the increasingly dangerous Hogwarts School Of Witchcraft And Wizardry. This means, as ever, secrets and treachery within, hostilities with classmates and life-threatening magical sports days. New to the mix is the embarrassing reality of tortured adolescence, with sexual awakenings and brooding mood-swings exacerbated by the added distraction of glamorous foreign exchange students. Making quite the grand entrance are the chic girls of Beauxbatons Academy and the hunky boys of Durmstrang Institute. Welcome to Harry Potter And The Rampaging Hormones.

This is certainly not a movie for young children, however engaging its characters and comic touches. Teen angst and relationship problems are pretty boring if you're six. But it's not the burgeoning sexuality that's landed the picture its 12A certificate, rather its genuinely darker vein of fantasy horror. For the maturing Potter core audience this is well-developed, with teasing terrors and skin-crawling set-pieces as the dark Lord Voldemort rises again – as all dark lords must, it seems, DLs notoriously being even harder to kill totally dead than the nut-job in *Halloween*. (Quite why Lord V. is so preoccupied with plotting against the promising pipsqueak Harry is presumably something to be clarified for cinema audiences in the fullness of time.)

Mike Newell, as the first British director entrusted with a series entry, oversees plenty of spiffing special-effects action – the Quidditch World Cup final, a dragon fight, an underwater sequence and Gary Oldman's (all-too-brief) fiery apparition – but as one would expect, he does a good job with the more personal, realistic emotional content, bringing on the young leads' performances noticeably in the process. So it's a shame that he's less successful in handling the necessary novel-to-screen compression.

Even though Newell's adaptation runs to more than two-and-a-half hours, the book is such a doorstopper that screenwriter Steve Kloves had to ditch more material this time around. Harry's annual confinement with his ghastly Dursley relations and Hermione's house-elf-liberation campaign is gone. While he was at it, it's a pity he didn't also delete tabloid hackette Rita Skeeter – however much one likes Miranda Richardson – since she obviously functions as author J.K. Rowling's dig at celebrity-stalking gossips, adding nothing more than running-time the story doesn't need.

As it is, there's too much contrasting material with which to contend: the life-or-death challenges of the Triwizard competition are interspersed with a host of new characters and their sinister or serio-comic sub-plots, school lessons, the agenda of yet another eccentric new Defence Against The Dark Arts professor in Brendan Gleeson's fierce Mad-Eye Moody, Potter sidekick Ron's sulks, swotty Hermione's makeover and Harry's blushing attempts to ask a girl to a dance...

Consequently, the story editing goes through some distinctly choppy patches. It looks as if several scenes were filmed at greater length, surviving in quick snippets that are frequently unnecessary. The movie Newell set out to make – eccentric comedy-cum-Hitchcockian conspiracy – can only be glimpsed briefly, before that beast of a plot charges back into shot, demanding attention.

Thankfully, most of it is pulled together towards the end. It's no secret that Ralph Fiennes handles the long-awaited appearance of evil Voldemort himself, and thankfully his big scene is sensationally creepy, ensuring strong anticipation for frights to come. ★★★ **AE**

⓪ HARRY POTTER AND THE PHILOSOPHER'S STONE (HARRY POTTER AND THE SORCERER'S STONE) (2001)

Starring: *Daniel Radcliffe (Harry Potter), Rupert Grint (Ron Weasley), Emma Watson (Hermione Granger), Maggie Smith (Minerva McGonagall), Robbie Coltrane (Rubeus Hagrid), Richard Harris (Albus Dumbledore), John Cleese (Nearly Headless Nick), Tom Felton (Draco Malfoy), Warwick Davis (Professor Flitwick), Ian Hart (Professor Quirrel), Zoe Wanamaker (Madame Hooch)*
Director: *Chris Columbus*
Screenwriter: *Steven Kloves, based on the novel by J.K. Rowling*
PG/152 mins./Adventure/Fantasy/USA/UK

On his eleventh birthday, orphan Harry Potter discovers that he's a wizard, so off he goes to Hogwarts School to learn the ways of the wand. But it isn't all lessons and making friends: Harry must have a showdown with the evil Lord Voldemort.

Sometimes the best plan is to do things by the book. With over 100 million Harry Potter readers desperate to rush down cinema aisles to see their hero on the big screen for the first time, you can't blame Chris Columbus for sticking close to J.K. Rowling's novel. It's one thing to let your imagination loose with the words on the page; it's another to have those images backed up by a multi-million dollar Hollywood budget. And from the very first sight of an owl perched on the Privet Drive road sign to the closing shot of the Hogwarts Express pulling away from the station with the majestic school sitting high on the hills behind, we know that every golden galleon has been well spent.

That's why this faithful adaptation won't fail to win over the book's fans with its 'wow' factor. It thrives on audience recognition. John Williams' score swells at the key moments – Here's your first glimpse of Hogwarts! Isn't Diagon Alley crammed with Dickensian detail! – as Columbus pulls back curtain after curtain to reveal all of the avid readers' favourite bits. The stand-out sequence is the Gryffindor versus Slytherin Quidditch match, a fast-paced medieval Rollerball with broomsticks. It soars where The Phantom Menace's podrace stalled on the third lap.

Harry Potter And The Philosopher's Stone has one advantage over so many other blockbusters: it already knows that it's the first in a series, so it doesn't have to become a self-contained hit movie before its sequels can receive the green light. This means it deliberately takes its time setting up the characters and the scenario before, like the book, pulling in a quest-cum-whodunnit plot to provide a climax. This structure is fine for the initiated, but it might leave first-timers feeling a bit uncomfortable with the shape of the movie. And because it's more of a kids' film than the book was just a kids' book, the two-and-a-half hour running time is bound to provoke some cinema squirming from young viewers.

Tagline
Let the magic begin.

That said, Columbus ensures there's a bit of on-screen magic coming our way every couple of minutes, and not just in the shape of expensive effects. Near-perfect casting ensures character colour from the adult actors and allows the central trio of kids to prove that three heads are better than one (unless your name is Fluffy).

Coltrane as cuddly giant Hagrid and Grint as Harry's cheeky chum, Ron, steal some scenes, but it's Radcliffe who leads us through Harry's journey from open-jawed underdog to pint-sized hero. Sympathetic and strong, brave and believably ordinary, he becomes the audience's counterpart in this weird world of witches and wizards. ★★★★ **AM**

HARRY POTTER AND THE PRISONER OF AZKABAN (2004)

Starring: *Daniel Radcliffe (Harry Potter), Rupert Grint (Ron Weasley), Emma Watson (Hermione Granger), Maggie Smith (Minerva McGonagall), Robbie Coltrane (Rubeus Hagrid), Michael Gambon (Albus Dumbledore), Tom Felton (Draco Malfoy), Gary Oldman (Sirius Black), David Thewlis (Professor Remus Lupin), Timothy Spall (Peter Pettigrew), Paul Whitehouse (Sir Cadogan), Julie Christie (Madame Rosmerta), Robert Hardy (Cornelius Fudge), Richard Griffiths (Uncle Vernon), Pam Ferris (Aunt Marge)*
Director: *Alfonso Cuarón*
Screenwriter: *Steve Kloves, based on the book by J.K. Rowling*
PG/136 mins./Adventure/Fantasy/USA/UK

Now 13, Harry Potter and chums are back off to Hogwarts, only to find that a dangerous escaped prisoner is also heading back to school. Soon nasty prison guards called Dementors have taken up residence in the school grounds and Harry is warned that the prisoner is coming for him . . .

Were it not for the fact that he inflicted *Bicentennial Man* upon an unsuspecting public, it would be possible to feel some sympathy for Chris Columbus right now. A faithful servant of the material, Columbus cracked the brief, creating both Potter's world and a worldwide audience. He could, perhaps, have cut loose with *Secrets*, but one hit does not a franchise make, and he again opted for an artistic yardstick that merely measured how many pages could be faithfully recreated on screen before audience arses actually started to turn blue.

Now, with the Potter machine in unstoppable gear and even St. Rowling acknowledging that the later/longer books must be boned, Columbus might have finally started to enjoy himself. And yet, not only has he stepped aside, as producer he personally pushes through an exotic relief pitcher whose colourful CV virtually guarantees that every viewer will be aware of a fresh man at the mound and that every review will contain a variation on the following line: 'New director Cuarón injects much-needed visual flair and introduces a narrative daring that was noticeably lacking from "the Columbus era".'

Indeed, Cuarón so comprehensively re-imagines the Potter aesthetic that young fans are likely to wonder where all the colour has gone. From the moment the perfunctory Dursley scenes are invested with a beige-tinted suburban loathing straight out of Mike Leigh, it is clear that the magical kingdom has at last been rooted in our very own Muggle nation. Hogwarts, in particular, benefits enormously from a relocation to Scotland's Glen Coe.

Relying as much on wide-angle lenses as he does on computer-controlled tracking, Cuarón keeps the camera moving and the invention coming, unafraid to introduce ideas that Rowling has not personally authored. The entire piece is an absolute picture, with new cinematographer Michael Seresin working his own strange alchemy on Stuart Craig's miraculous sets.

Not that Cuarón has it all his own way. The young cast is still rather limited to good line-readings – they are not bad, exactly, but they are being asked to shoulder an increasingly heavy burden and the tantalising glimpses of the excellent Thewlis and Oldman amply demonstrate that expositional dialogue need not be entirely bereft of character.

Elsewhere, the all-plot-all-the-time novels remain curiously resistant to adaptation, and if house writer Kloves has mercifully abandoned the novel's three-term structure, he is yet to stumble across a recognisable three-act structure to put in its stead. As before, the third act still kind of happens along, and the middle-section is distinctly choppy, with a much more passive Potter coasting through several short scenes that will lose those who have foresworn the books. Luckily, when the ending (in parts one and two bungled by Columbus) finally arrives, it proves to be *Azkaban*'s ace.

Azkaban contains both the longest denouement and the most rousing finish of any of the books, and Cuarón wisely whips through the 'ah-hahs' so that the clever climax, complete with the series' best SFX, can enjoy its moment in the moonlight. Here, at last, Harry Potter And The Movie Adventure hauls itself up to the standards set by the brilliant books, and a middle-aged Mexican emerges as the story's unlikely hero. ★★★ **CK**

HARVEY (1950)

Starring: *James Stewart (Elwood P. Dowd), Josephine Hull (Veta Louise Simmons), Peggy Dow (Miss Kelly), Charles Drake (Dr Sanderson), Cecil Kellaway (Dr. Chumley)*
Director: *Henry Koster*
Screenwriters: *Mary Chase, Oscar Brodney, based on a play by Chase*
U/104 mins./Comedy/Fantasy/USA
Awards – *Academy Awards Best Supporting Actress (Josephine Hull)*

Elwood P. Dowd, a genial, wealthy, semi-alcoholic dreamer is always accompanied by his best friend, an invisible six-foot-three white rabbit called Harvey. Veta, Elwood's older sister, feels ostracised because of his obvious lunacy and considers having him committed.

Though this adaptation of Mary Chase's play has become such a pop culture icon that audiences get the joke about it in *Who Framed Roger Rabbit?* (set years before the play was written), Harvey is of interest mainly for preserving the stage performances of James Stewart and the Oscar-winning Josephine Hull. It's an 'eccentric family' comedy of escape into madness, with a melancholy streak, along the lines of such stage-to-film efforts as *You Can't Take It With You* and *Arsenic and Old Lace*, in which Stewart and Hull respectively had appeared, but director Henry Koster is no Frank Capra and the whimsy here too often turns leaden or hectic. The script relies on the creaking mechanics of the original, and the supporting players seem to have been doing their roles for too long and settled into complacency.

Nevertheless, the premise remains memorable and perpetually intriguing, with just enough hints that the 'pooka' (animal spirit) who pals around with Stewart's wide-eyed tippler might be more than his imagination to lend the farce a fantastical, even sometimes sinister, edge. The twist, of course, is that the outright loon seems not only happier but saner than the supposedly normal folks who dither about putting him away.

In the finale, a psychiatrist (Cecil Kellaway) who has come to share Elwood's vision of the world almost persuades Harvey to leave Elwood and move in with him and Veta is prompted by an anecdote about the character-sapping effects of anti-psychotics not to put her brother on a medication which will 'kill' his friend. ★★★ **KN**

THE HARVEY GIRLS (1946)

Starring: *Judy Garland (Susan Bradley), John Hodiak (Ned Trent), Ray Bolger (Chris Maule), Preston Foster (Judge Sam Purvis), Virginia O'Brien (Alma), Angela Lansbury (Em), Cyd Charisse (Deborah)*
Director: *George Sidney*
Screenwriters: *Edmund Beloin, Harry Crane, Nathaniel Curtis, James O'Hanlon, Samson Raphaelson based on the novel by Samuel Hopkins Adams*
U/102 mins./Musical/USA

Awards: *Academy Awards – Best Original Song ('On The Atchison, Topeka And The Santa Fe')*

Susan Bradley arrives in Sandrock, New Mexico, to wed her pen pal but ends up working in the newly established Harvey restaurant instead. But there's opposition to the travellers' rest from Judge Sam Purvis and saloon-owner Ned Trent, whose affections are jealously guarded by good-time gal, Em.

As the railroads spread across America, Fred Harvey made his fortune with a chain of restaurants which proudly claimed to have 'conquered the undeveloped territory with a beefsteak and a cup of coffee'. MGM bought the rights to Samuel Hopkins Adams's book about the Harvey houses as a dramatic vehicle for Lana Turner. However, Arthur Freed's right-hand man, Roger Edens, saw one of the New Haven tryouts for *Oklahoma!* in 1944 and, realising that the Western show was about to hit big, suggested turning the project into a Judy Garland musical.

However, Garland was less than enamoured with the idea, as she had set her heart on co-starring with Fred Astaire in *Yolanda And The Thief*, which was about to be directed by her new husband, Vincente Minnelli. But, convinced by Edens that Yolanda was merely a supporting role that might expose her dancing deficiencies, Garland signed up to what would become one of her few trouble-free productions.

Moreover, it provided one of her signature tunes. Written to cash in on the success of 'The Trolley Song' in *Meet Me in St Louis*, 'On the Atcheson, Topeka and the Santa Fe' was an old-fashioned showstopper and it earned Harry Warren and Johnny Mercer the Oscar for Best Song. Yet, ironically, both Mercer and Bing Crosby had bigger hits with it than Garland, whose bout of stage fright meant that Dinah Shore got to sing it at the Academy Awards ceremony.

Garland is radiant throughout this homespun morality tale. But she's admirably supported by Ray Bolger (who'd been her Scarecrow in *The Wizard of Oz*, 1939), the wisecracking Virginia O'Brien and the young Cyd Charisse (in what was her first speaking role). However, Angela Lansbury comes close to stealing the show as the catty floosie, Em. Indeed, she was so convincing that people abused her in the street for trying to lure John Hodiak from their Judy. ★★★ **DP**

⊚ THE HAUNTING (1963)

Starring: *Julie Harris (Eleanor 'Nell' Lance), Claire Bloom (Theodora), Richard Johnson (Dr. John Markway), Russ Tamblyn (Luke Sanderson), Fay Compton (Mrs. Sanderson), Lois Maxwell (Grace Markway), Valentine Dyall (Mr. Dudley)*
Director: *Robert Wise*
Screenwriter: *Nelson Gidding, based on the novel* The Haunting Of Hill House *by Shirley Jackson*
12/112 mins./Horror/USA/UK

In order to prove the existence of ghosts scientifically, Dr. John Markway takes a group of sceptics and mystics to spend the night in Hill House, a gloomy, labyrinthine mansion with a history of violence and insanity. The house, however, doesn't seem to welcome them.

Though it deserves its reputation as one of the most purely terrifying of all celluloid ghost stories, Robert Wise's 1963 film version of Shirley Jackson's 1959 novel *The Haunting Of Hill House* is actually a character study before it is a horror movie.

A lengthy, narrated prologue – a little like the preface to Hammer Films' version of *The Hound Of The Baskervilles* – establishes the evil history of a New England mansion built by mad patriarch Hugh Grain. Hill House has been the site of many tragedies over 80 years, but Jackson believes, and Wise suggests, the place isn't really haunted until Eleanor Vance moves in. Along with Theodora, a slinky psychic, and Luke (Tamblyn held over from Wise's *West Side Story*), who expects to inherit Hill House one day, Eleanor has been recruited by the suave-but-cranky parapsychologist Dr. Markway for a study project in the supernatural. Like Jack Nicholson in *The Shining* (1981), Eleanor is at once terrorised and seduced by the house and, at the end, becomes its resident ghost. She is included in Markway's experimental party because of a Carrie-like adolescent burst of telekinesis, which bombarded her childhood home with pebbles – an event which she still hotly denies.

Every one of the manifestations that torment the intruders throughout the film are, in fact, just side-effects of Eleanor's sustained psychic assault on herself. This is underlined by the opening and closing statement that 'Whatever walked there, walked alone', which affirms that poor Nell, dead on the grounds, is the only ghost that has ever haunted Hill House. Wise, though known in the 60s for big-budget musicals (*West Side Story*, *The Sound Of Music*) and remembered for distinguished science fiction films – (*The Day The Earth Stood Still*, *The Andromeda Strain*, *Star Trek: The Motion Picture* – began his directorial career under the aegis of Val Lewton's RKO horror unit in the 1940s, taking over the troubled production of *Curse Of The Cat People* in mid-shoot and helming the horrific Boris Karloff vehicle *The Body Snatcher*.

The Haunting, meanwhile, is in the Lewton tradition: a scary movie that makes a virtue of keeping any ghosts off-screen. The most unsettling moment is almost a radio-play gimmick, as Eleanor holds hands with Theo in the dark for comfort – the lights go on, and she realises Theo was on the other side of the room all the time ('Whose hand was I holding ?'). As with Lewton's best films, it's not true that *The Haunting* uses no special effects.

The door that seems to breathe, suggesting a vast monstrosity beyond, is justifiably famous, but also nerve-racking is the rickety spiral staircase that seems to go up forever and threatens to collapse every time it is used. Wise even gets a scare from shifting the light-source to cast face-shaped shadows on the wallpaper. *The Haunting* is yet another film ill-served by pan and scan television prints: Wise brilliantly uses black-and-white widescreen to strand his characters in odd-shaped rooms or corridors, making the watcher's eye skitter frantically over the letterbox screen to catch every ingeniously rendered detail.

Julie Harris, who specialised in playing exactly the type of neurotic spinster Jackson often wrote about, is especially good at revealing the stubborn strengths that lie within the timid Eleanor and make her, in the end, a danger both to other people and herself. She plays extremely well with the secondary characters, all of whom are slightly caricatured, representing Eleanor's fantasy of real people rather than the people themselves. Johnson's Markway (Montague in the book) is a well-spoken boffin, a little smug and rather too cavalier about this expedition into the dark. Bloom's Theo, in a black bodystocking and amulet, makes for a glamorous wish-fulfilment figure of independent womanhood, her sexual ambiguity (Eleanor calls her 'unnatural' – which is as near to being a lesbian as a movie character could get in 1963) frees her from the heartbreaking crush Eleanor develops on the (married) doctor. And Tamblyn's Luke is a happy-go-lucky rich kid, quick with the wisecracks and unsaddled with the family guilts that have tied Eleanor to her recently-dead mother and mean-spirited little sister.

The house itself, along with its hatchet-faced custodians, is equally 'unnatural', a giant nightmare playground that fulfils the sheltered Eleanor's desire for adventure and romance, even if it ultimately means she has to die to take up permanent residence in its echoing, gothic halls. Jackson and Wise set out to create the ultimate ghost story in their respective media, but *The Haunting Of Hill House* and *The Haunting* proved so successful that the story's influence has been felt down the years in numerous subsequent books and films.

Richard Matheson's *Hell House* – filmed as *The Legend Of Hell House* – is a conscious variation on the scientists-investigate-a-big-old-haunted-house theme, while the Stephen King and legendary Stanley Kubrick versions of *The Shining* also venture into Jackson's gothic 'badplace'. As for Hill House's darkest, most terrible secret – well, we had better not talk about the 1999 Jan De Bont remake. ★★★★★ **KN**

➂ THE HAUNTING (1999)

Starring: *Lili Taylor (Eleanor 'Nell' Vance), Liam Neeson (Dr. David Marrow), Catherine Zeta-Jones (Theo), Owen Wilson (Luke Sanderson), Bruce Dern (Mr. Dudley), Todd Field (Todd Hackett), Virginia Madsen (Jane)*
Director: *Jan de Bont*
Screenwriter: *David Self, based on the novel* The Haunting of Hill House *by Shirley Jackson*
12/113 mins./Horror/Thriller/Mystery/USA

In a 'psychological experiment' David Marrow plants three guinea pigs in a scary house and feeds them a series of clues that create a frightening narrative. However, this 'experiment' gets out of hand when the clues are no longer fiction and the ghost story spirals out of control.

There are lots of really scary things about *The Haunting*. Unfortunately none of them pertain to what you actually experience during the movie. What is really terrifying about this second big-screen adaptation of Shirley Jackson's *The Haunting Of Hill House* is the harsh light it throws on the old movies vs new movies debate. Whereas Robert Wise's 1963 version is a perfectly executed exercise in subtle, hinted-at horrors, Jan De Bont's 1999 incarnation is a crass, overstuffed, woefully inept demonstration of things that go rum in the night.

The plot device employed to get a group of disparate stereotypes to stay in a big old scary house is that psychologist David Marrow is conducting an experiment into the nature of group fear under the guise of an investigation into insomnia. Taking on board three guinea pigs – sensitive Eleanor, cosmopolitan bisexual artist Theo and cynical chancer Luke – Marrow starts spinning out a backstory and suggesting clues to create a fiction in the minds of his subjects. Wouldn't ya know that events supersede his scaremongering tactics and, oh, the risible rest is just too awful to contemplate.

Everything about the movie is overcooked – every door creaks, every curtain billows big time – creating a pantomime milieu rather than anything that could be genuinely unnerving. So intent is De Bont to make the house a player in the story that he wastes oceans of screen time on it: we are frequently treated to interminable shots of characters wandering around empty, overly designed corridors accompanied by leftover 'little girl moaning' sound effects from *Poltergeist*. The desired effect is menacing portent. The net result is audience rigor mortis.

If you're looking for plusses, the exterior of Hill House is magnificent, De Bont occasionally throws in an energising camera move, and it's nice to see Bruce Dern as a crazy caretaker. Cynics might derive glee from Zeta-Jones' misjudged moments or the unintentionally funny dialogue – the housekeeper's overstated invocation of doom ('There's not a town for at least ten miles') is priceless. Yet however you dress it up, laughs where there should be frights is patently piss poor. ★ **IF**

➂ HAWK THE SLAYER (1980)

Starring: *John Terry (Hawk), Jack Palance (Voltan), Bernard Bresslaw (Gort), Ray Charleson (Crow), Peter O'Farrell (Baldin), William Morgan Sheppard (Ranulf), Cheryl Campbell (Sister Monica), Annette Crosbie (Abbess), Roy Kinnear (Inn keeper)*
Director: *Terry Marcel*
Screenwriters: *Terry Marcel, Harry Robertson*
PG/90 mins./Fantasy/UK

After his father is slain at the hands of his twisted brother Voltan, the heroic Hawk sets out for revenge, especially as he is also responsible for the death of Hawk's fiancée. Teamed up with an elf, a dwarf and a giant, Hawk endeavours to stop Voltan's evil and rescue a kidnapped abbess in the process.

In these post-*Lord Of The Rings* days, it is easy to be dismissive of the rudimentary attempts to cipher Tolkien's gothic stylings onto the cinema screen that became a post-*Star Wars* preoccupation in the early 80s. Silly medieval odes to the fantastical on a budget that would have trouble hiring a tea party magician like *The Beastmaster*, *The Sword And The Sorcerer* and *Krull*. Out of this era, propped up by pre-pubescent boys obsessed with D&D, *Hawk The Slayer* stands as almost emblematic. It takes a heavily rose-tinted place in many hearts, even though it is entirely dreadful: wooden of script, shoddy of special effect and flamboyantly hammy of acting. Jack Palance as leery menace Voltan unfathomably grabs a breath between every utterance – asthma inhalers were obviously in short supply in this muddled world of ancient magic, mystical creatures and vulnerable nuns.

Terry Marcel, who'd worked as a second unit director on extraneous Pink Panther movies, in the strained hopes of covering up the threadbare sets and silly-string effects, takes to using a lot of slow motion or sped-up film. Any time pudgy elf Crow (a pointy-eared Ray Charleson, just like Orlando Bloom except for the grace, dexterity, dreamy good looks, even the acting skill) looses an arrow, the film blurs into high speed, like the chase scenes from Benny Hill.

Our intrepid cross-cultural team is made up of Hawk (John Terry, who can now be found in *Lost*), Peter O'Farrell's tall dwarf, Bernard Bresslaw's short giant and Crow the hyperactive elf. They are off to confront wheezy Voltan, and deal with the nun-napping, with the help of a nearby witch (Patricia Quinn) who provides magic mist and teleportation (whatever the effects boys can run to) in a world too damp and autumnal to inspire. There is a mulchy, depressing atmosphere that seeps into every frame.

But its woeful direction, appalling acting and really daft synth score all pale into insignificance compared to its dunderheaded self-importance. Not a joke is uttered across this contemptible universe, that's if you ignore the fact the whole thing is a joke. ★ **IN**

➂ HEAR MY SONG (1991)

Starring: *Ned Beatty (Josef Locke), Adrian Dunbar (Micky O'Neill), Shirley Ann Field (Cathleen Doyle), Tara Fitzgerald (Nancy Doyle), William Hootkins (Mr. X), Harold Berens (Benny Rose), David McCallum (Jim Abbott)*
Director: *Peter Chelsom*
Screenwriters: *Peter Chelsom, Adrian Dunbar, based on a story by Chelsom*
15/113 mins./Comedy/Drama/Romance/U.K./Ireland

Nightclub owner Micky goes in search of a missing Irish tenor to win back the respect of his girlfriend and his regular customers after being duped by an imitator.

Tough customers with an allergy to whimsy should probably steer clear of this fanciful, fresh, charmingly funny film. Everyone else, arm yourselves with a box of chocolates, a tissue or two and be prepared to be delighted. Just when we were convinced Film Four and British Screen didn't know a joke if it bit them, along comes writer/director Peter Chelsom – making his feature debut with a real out-of-left-field zinger – inveigling some of their dosh to disprove the theory.

The inspiration for this dotty piece came from the true and curious tale of tenor Josef Locke, 'Mr Blackpool' to his ardent post-War fans, whose disappearance – one step ahead of Inland Revenue – in the 50s was followed by the appearance of a singer billed as Mr. X who successfully passed himself off for a time as Joe Locke.

Set in the present, *Song* centres nicely on a sweet-talking, energetic entrepreneur and dreamer, Micky O'Neill (Dunbar, also Chelsom's co-writer). O'Neill runs an old-fashioned nightclub in Liverpool that is going to the wall when he books Mr. X (William Hootkins in a witty charade that owes as much to Orson Welles as it does to Locke). The deception discovered by a wronged woman and the copper obsessed for 30 years with nabbing the real Locke, Mickey sets off on a quest through Ireland to find Joe Locke, save his club, reclaim his scornful fiancée and redeem himself.

What ensues teeters dangerously on the edge of corn and cliché – naturally all the Irish rusticals are pixilated comedians – but Chelsom keeps everything lightly dancing along to a magnificently sentimental tuneful climax. Completely disarming and absolutely delicious. ★★★★ **AE**

HEARTS OF DARKNESS: A FILMMAKER'S APOCALYPSE (1991)

Starring: *as themselves, Sam Bottoms, Marlon Brando, Eleanor Coppola, Francis Ford Coppola, Sofia Coppola, Robert De Niro, Robert Duvall, Laurence Fishburne, Harrison Ford, George Lucas, John Milius, Martin Sheen*
Directors: *Fax Bahr, George Hickenlooper*
Screenwriters: *Fax Bahr, George Hickenlooper*
15/96 mins./Documentary/USA

A documentary about the troubled making of *Apocalypse Now*.

This combines footage shot on the set by Francis Coppola's wife Eleanor (who cunningly omitted to tell her husband precisely when he was being recorded, resulting in marvellous candid comments) and interviews with dazed survivors like Martin Sheen, Robert Duvall, Frederic Forrest, Sam Bottoms, Larry Fishburne (all of fourteen when he signed on for 'Mr Clean') and Dennis Hopper (who seems immensely sober in comparison with his wigged-out performance in the film).

A funny and horrifying portrait of bumbling genius at work, the film features unforgettable footage of Sheen drunkenly improvising his way through an on-set nervous breakdown and heart attack, though sadly nothing of Harvey Keitel, originally cast in Sheen's role and expensively fired well into filming. Also, we see Coppola throw a tantrum during the shooting of his 'Ride of the Valkyries' sequence, because President Marcos takes away the helicopters he has lent to the film to go and fight the rebels.

And, in painfully hilarious fashion, scads of footage of Marlon Brando's mumbled and improvised soliloquies, shot while Coppola tried desperately to think of an ending (one take ends when Brando swallows a fly). As a reminder of the film's origins as the archetypal movie-brat project, there is a wonderful give-and-take between the film's original writer (John Milius) and director (George Lucas) as the effusive Milius expresses his original idea that the film should have been shot on location in Vietnam during the war and the reserved Lucas explains that he was the one who would have wound up being shot at while Milius surfed the Mekong.

A revealing portrait of the human cost of a real masterpiece and a bizarrely comic chronicle of Coppola's family life (watch for little Sofia), this is essential viewing. ★★★★ **KN**

HEAT (1995)

Starring: *Al Pacino (Vincent Hannah), Robert De Niro (Neil McCauley), Val Kilmer (Chris Shiherlis), Jon Voigt (Nate), Tom Sizemore (Michael Cheritto), Diane Venora (Justine), Amy Brenneman (Eady), Ashley Judd (Charlene), Wes Studi (Casals), Natalie Portman (Lauren Portman)*
Director: *Michael Mann*
Screenwriter: *Michael Mann*
15/160 mins./Crime/Drama/USA

Neil McCauley is after one last big score before he retires but he is being hunted by a lawman who is as driven as Neil himself.

Your eyes are not deceiving you. This slick, highly charged crime thriller is creamed with the first ever on-screen pairing of uberthesps De Niro and Pacino (they never shared the screen in *Godfather II*). A tantalising prospect in itself. That Michael Mann's film is an extraordinarily intelligent, stylish, violent, realistic study of moral decay and human nature in the City Of Angels, makes it doubly important. Heat proves one thing absolute. If you put great actors in a great script with a great visionary director in control, then you get a great movie. It's as simple as that.

Mann, as writer, has concocted a duel. On one side the cop, Vincent Hannah, the dogged hunter prone to bursts of unwieldy emotion, possessing a sixth sense at second-guessing his prey. His foe, the robber, is Neil McCauley, icy cool, rational, brilliant, psychotic head of a gang of heistkings equipped with automatic weapons and never-say-die obsessions. The battleground is an LA shorn of glamour. This is a moody, expansive cityscape, shot in earthy pastels, a twilight world of twisted morals, crumbling relationships, and dying dreams. Compared to your average studio movie it could be the surface of the moon. The film's sense of environment is peerless.

As Hannah and his crew of besuited cops close in, McCauley and his crew – an impressively edgy Kilmer, and reliable class from Tom Sizemore – plan the big score, taking a downtown bank under the very eyes of police surveillance. What lifts this beyond being yet another crime thriller, is Mann's dedication to creating inner-life for all the characters. The film flits between a maze of credibly defunct relationships: Pacino in an imploding marriage (to Diane Verona), De Niro falling for the quiet Amy Brenneman, Kilmer's volatile marriage to Ashley Judd ... these characters have dimension. There is a genuine sense of loss for those who die, and understanding for those who strive.

Mann, who induced mood aplenty with *Manhunter* and visceral action with *Last Of The Mohicans*, here amalgamates his fetishes. *Heat* spills sobriety of feeling before (enhanced by the sleek synthesised score) erupting in moments of nerve-jangling action. The bank job, true to form, goes haywire, resulting in a ferocious, thumpingly loud gun battle more Beirut CNN-style.

Pacino and De Niro are shapeshifters extraordinaire, and they strike admirably different courses through the film (De Niro's vulnerable mastermind is the winner by a hand) and although they only meet twice in the film, the scenes are crucial and hair-tinglingly charged. And the huge support cast – including a transformed Jon Voigt – fill the overabundance of subplots with shape and colour. There is too much going on, for too long, but by the end everything slots neatly into place, and the parting shot carries a cool poignancy that hovers in the mind for days.

Heat packs more into one cop movie than the entire genre output of the last five years. It is a big film with big themes, and if it never quite makes the profundity it so hungrily seeks, it still goes straight to the head of the list of Oscar front-runners and essential viewing. You've rarely had it so good. ★★★★★ **IN**

HEATHERS (1989)

Starring: *Winona Ryder (Veronica Sawyer), Christian Slater (Jason 'J.D.' Dean), Shannen Doherty (Heather Duke), Lisanne Falk (Heather McNamara), Kim Walker (Heather Chandler)*
Director: *Michael Lehmann*
Screenwriter: *Daniel Walters*
18/102 mins./Comedy/Crime/Drama/USA

A girl who half-heartedly tries to be part of the 'in crowd' of her school meets a rebel who teaches her a more devious way to play social politics.

The notion of the intelligent teen comedy is, to many people, a. rather perverse contradiction in terms. Certainly even the most fervent admirer of John Hughes' movies would be hard pressed to find anything resembling a 'message' behind them (and, in fact, when he tries with the infamous letter at the end of *The Breakfast Club* giggles of derision were a common reaction). Indeed, the 'animal comedy' sub-genre spawned by *Porky's* and *Animal House* was hardly renowned for its dangerous intellectualism. But, amid the lightweight fluff and the hardcore gross-out of the golden age of the teen movies were two or three that dared to push the adolescent envelope and endeared themselves to a generation, partly because of the nostalgia that tinged anything that we watched in the slum cinemas of the early 80s, but more importantly because of their totally unique and utterly delightful capacity to genuinely appal adults. A quality that had for the most part been reserved by pop music as a territory all on its own.

Surprisingly enough it was Christian Slater who changed all that. In a shock development utterly unconnected to his bigshot casting director mother Mary Jo Slater, Christian had been 'discovered' (presumably in his room) in TV soap *Ryan's Hope* in 1985, and in 1986 made his mainstream film debut by shedding his kecks in the service of *The Name Of The Rose*. By 1990 he was triumphantly essaying the role of anarchic teen DJ Happy Harry Hard On in *Pump Up The Volume*, a minor clarion call to American youth that not only set parents' teeth on edge by wholeheartedly advocating illegal radio stations, student protest and excessive masturbation, but seemed to have at its heart a genuine glint of teenage rebellion. Essentially, though, Happy Harry was simply a variation on the character of JD he had established in *Heathers*. The initials were no accident. For a brief, odd moment Slater would look like shaping up to be his generation's James Dean. Strange days, indeed.

Heathers is a teen comedy as if made by David Lynch. The surrealistic tone is set in the opening credits when we see a croquet match, shot in dizzying day-glo colours that has a human head for its peg. It's a weirdness that permeates the film reaching its zenith in JD's bizarre relationship with his demolitions man father, who refers to his son as dad and vice versa and appears to have at some point blown up his mother.

But it's Daniel Waters' screenplay that really ratchets *Heathers* up into being something special. Not only did it invent the self-aware, sophisticated style of adolescent dialogue that Kevin Williamson would lift wholesale for *Scream* and *Dawson's Creek* but it had a central theme of teen suicide, usually treated with po-faced concern by anxious adults. Indeed, one of the movie's comedic highlights is Miss Fleming, a hippie dippy teacher for whom the mounting student body count is manna from heaven as she organises communal outpourings of faux grief and passes the suicide notes around class ('Are we going to be tested on this?' one teen wonders). 'Before a teenager decides to kill himself, there are a few things he needs to know. After all, this is a decision that effects all of us. And there's only one chance to get it right,' she solemnly pronounces.

In fact, it's this gleeful recognition of adult insincerity that gives the film its giddily vicious power. Fathers of school jocks set up to die as if they were involved in a homosexual suicide pact wail, 'I love my dead gay son' over the coffin prompting JD's sour remark: 'How do you think he'd react to a son that had a limp wrist with a pulse?' Principals announce that they'd 'be willing to go half a day for a cheerleader' when deciding on an appropriate period of mourning for yet another apparent suicide.

While Winona is perfectly serviceable as Veronica, the engine of the film is Slater, whose patented hormonal Jack Nicholson routine (though Slater claims that the mannerisms are in fact based on his dad) elevated him briefly to the ranks of the effortlessly cool (though it's probably a part he'd be unlikely to want to reprise today, despite Lehmann's plans for a *Heathers II*. Post-Columbine, firing guns in school cafeterias is a distinct no-no – and yes that's a trenchcoat he's wearing).

Tragically *Heathers* loses the courage of its nasty convictions in the last half hour of the film and begins to pull its punches. Any movie that promises an exploding school and a Jim Jones-style mass suicide should really deliver, and the denouement in which only Slater blows himself up can't help but feel like a disappointment. Still, for the most part *Heathers* is as bitter and dangerous as a cup full of liquid Draino. ★★★★ **AS**

HEAVEN & EARTH (1993)

Starring: *Le Ly (Hiep Thi Le), Tommy Lee Jones (Steve Butler), Haing S. Ngor (Papa), Bussaro Sanruck (Le Ly, age 5), Joan Chen (Mama)*
Director: *Oliver Stone*
Screenwriter: *Oliver Stone, based on the books* When Heaven and Earth Changed Places *by Le Ly Hayslip, Jay Wurts and* Child of War, Woman of Peace *by Le Ly Hayslip and James Hayslip*
15/140 mins./Action/Biography/Drama/War/France/USA

Awards: *Golden Globes – Best Original Score*

The long and harrowing tale of Phung Le Ly, a young Vietnamese girl caught up in the war.

Stone's earlier Vietnam-themed movies, *Platoon* and *Born On The Fourth Of July*, were generally admired, but there was a cavil that they represented entirely the viewpoint of an American trespasser in the South East Asian situation, focusing on the torment and agony of members of the US military to the exclusion of the far more appalling sufferings of the indigenous Vietnamese. Furthermore, all Stone's films, from *Salvador* to *JFK*, focus on obsessive, driven, hurting men and relegate women to the sidelines. In *Heaven & Earth*, based on the autobiographies of a Vietnamese woman, Stone redresses the balance, but in doing so makes arguably his worst film.

In a storyline that straggles the years, Stone follows Phung Le Ly from a happy peasant childhood through the destruction of her village by the French, indoctrination of her brothers by the Vietcong, torture by Americans, rape by the VC, servitude in Saigon, seduction by her master, unmarried motherhood, a tiny spot of prostitution, emigration as the wife of a GI, suburban alienation as her husband cracks up, and a return to the old country to be reunited with her equally long-suffering mother. The problem is that Stone is not as close to this pain as he was to that of his other heroes, and so Le Ly's ordeal is less moving cinematically than the comparatively trivial unhappiness of a rich loser like Jim Morrison.

Hiep Thi Lei is remarkable, but Stone conceives of the idyll she has lost in typical happy peasant terms, with Charlie Chan English dialogue and pastoral visions of pretty rice paddies. There is a perceptible rush of authenticity when Tommy Lee Jones, a more typical Stone protagonist, turns up halfway through and self-destructs despite Le Ly's love, providing all the film's best scenes. Depicting Americans in Vietnam as mainly horny aggressors and in California as tasteless gluttons, this tries for an outsider's feel, but it's still an American's film, and all the bursts of Stone's cinematic verve cannot get inside the mind of its heroine. ★★ **KN**

HEAVEN CAN WAIT (1943)

Starring: *Gene Tierney (Martha), Don Ameche (Henry Van Cleeve), Charles Coburn (Hugo Van Cleeve), Marjorie Main (Mrs Strabel), Laird Cregar (His Excellency)*
Director: *Ernst Lubitsch*
Screenwriter: *Samson Raphaelson based on the play* Birthdays *by Ladislaus Bus-Fekete)*
U/112 mins./Comedy/USA

Unconvinced that his credentials fit him for Hell, the Devil asks Kansas lothario Henry Van Cleeve to recount his womanising adventures, with particular reference to his relationship with the love of his life, Martha Strabel.

Newly arrived at Fox after two decades at Paramount and frustrated in bids to film *A Self-Made Cinderella* and *Margin for Error*, Ernst Lubitsch and longtime writing partner Samuel Raphaelson set about revising Leslie Bus-Fekete's 1934 play, *Birthday*. Himself going through a reasonably amicable divorce during preproduction, Lubitsch had a sharper than usual insight into gender politics and there's clearly something of himself in Henry Van Cleeve. Indeed, this would explain his dual intent of depicting a man who is always ahead of his time, while exploring how quickly recent memory becomes the distant past.

But this is anything but a regretful veteran's lament. Lubitsch wrote the part with Fredric March and Rex Harrison in mind and was disappointed when studio boss Darryl F. Zanuck insisted on casting Don Ameche to bring some commercial appeal to a character he felt would be wholly resistible to respectable audiences. However, Lubitsch came to admire the subtlety of Ameche's genial roguery and he was even eventually pleased with Gene Tierney's patient loyalty (although his determination to rein in her tendency to emotional excess caused initial friction). Indeed, there isn't a bad performance here, with the supporting turns of indulgent grandfather Charles Coburn, prosaic cousin Allyn Joslyn and nouveau riche grotesques Eugene Pallette and Marjorie Main among the standouts.

Yet this is always Lubitsch's picture. His famous 'Touch' is in evidence everywhere, but most notably in the scenes in which Henry learns that he's just bribed a showgirl that his son no longer cares for, in which Martha delivers her charming speech about realising Henry would no longer stray because he'd developed a tummy, and in which the couple dance a last waltz on their 25th anniversary. But even more impressive are Lubitsch's restrained use of Technicolor and period trapping, the narrative control that permits flashbacks within flashbacks, and the measured pacing that not only conveyed the mood of a bygone era, but which also encapsulated a classical style of Hollywood filmmaking that was soon to disappear forever as realism intruded upon the postwar world. ★★★★ **DP**

HEAVEN'S GATE (1980)

Starring: *Kris Kristofferson (James Averill), Christopher Walken (Nathan D. Champion), John Hurt (Billy Irvine), Sam Waterston (Frank Canton), Brad Dourif (Mr. Eggleston), Isabelle Huppert (Ella Watson), Jeff Bridges (John. H. Bridges), Joseph Cotton (The Reverend Doctor)*
Director: *Michael Cimino*
Screenwriter: *Michael Cimino*
18/219 mins./Drama/USA

A brutal piece of American history sees a Wyoming sheriff, James Averill, attempt to stave off a bloody clash between immigrant farmers and wealthy cattle interests. All the while he is involved in his personal drama with gun-for-hire Nathan Champion, as they both love the same woman.

Setting aside its reputation as an artistically indulgent studio-wrecker (which it pretty much is) Michael Cimino's infamous anti-Western is a striking if long-winded piece of lyrical history-making. It is not without some irony that the film is a portrayal of the Johnson County Wars, concerning the clash between money-hungry cattle wranglers and the hopes for pure living of the immigrant farmers (how much of a metaphor for the death of 70s filmmaking inspiration do you need?). And bleak symbolism apart, Cimino had certainly designed his story as a grandiose reflection of the ballooning power of contemporary corporate America. Crushed idealism hangs over the film like a cloud. Mainly, as it turns out, the director's own.

The film itself, variously cut to ribbons but now restored on DVD to its desired three and a half hours, is gorgeous, tranquil, and terribly slow, with shades of Terrence Mallick's floaty dreams. For much of the endless running time, the narrative remains wispy and indistinct as Cimino searches for the melancholy vagueness of life. It has the looks of a Western, but the naturalism of Euro-art. There is no doubting the stunning creativity at work, including strong performances from unshowy talents like Kris Kristofferson, Isabelle Huppert and John Hurt, but it also frustrates with its languid disregard for story. Cimino lacks Mallick's ability to ignite images with meaning, here they remain just eloquent images, stark and beautiful like the spinning wonder of the roller-skating rink, but overpriced sideshows in a little story.

The final eruption of violence, when the cattle-baron's private army push to eradicate the lowly farmers carries the chilling edge of tragedy, but it is an emotion not fully won. This an extraordinary piece of fateful art, but its imperfections are as loud as its reputation. ★★★ **IN**

HEAVENLY CREATURES (1994)

Starring: *Melanie Lynskey (Pauline Parker), Kate Winslet (Juliet Hulme), Sarah Peirse (Honora Parker), Diana Kent (Hilda Hulme), Clive Merrison (Henry Hulme)*
Director: *Peter Jackson*
Screenwriters: *Fran Walsh, Peter Jackson*
18/98 mins./Drama/New Zealand

Awards: *Empire Awards – Best British Actress*

Based on true events from 1950's New Zealand, where Pauline Parker and Juliet Hulme met as schoolgirls and instantly became best friends. They created a fantasy world together, gradually shutting out the real world and, when Parker's mother attempted to separate them, they murdered her.

Kate Winslet received all the praise for her striking performance in this true story of a pair of fantasist girls who kill the mother of one of the two, but in hindsight it's now more noticeable as the film that marked Peter Jackson as a director capable of more than gleefully daft horror.

Jackson holds the film in an almost permanent dreamlike state so that the girls' plotting of their horrible crime seems like just another part of the fantasy world they create to distract themselves, making the final scenes all the more shocking. The effects are impressive, and a fine example of style not overwhelming substance. While most true murder stories are relegated to movie-of-the-week fodder, this never wastes a moment in justifying its big-screen presence. ★★★★ **OR**

HEAVY METAL (1981)

Starring: *the voices of: Don Francks (Grimaldi), Richard Romanus (Harry Canyon), Al Waxman (Rudnick), John Candy (Den), Jackie Burrows (Katherine Wells), Eugene Levy (Captain Sternn)*
Directors: *Gerald Potterton, Jimmy T. Murakami*
Screenwriter: *Len Blum*
15/86 mins./Animation/Canada

An anthology of adult-orientated animated sci-fi stories linked by a glowing green orb called the Loc-Nar, the representation of ultimate evil. The tales it tells involve a cynical cab driver rescuing a girl from mobsters in New York; a nerd who is transported into the fantasy world of Neverwhere where he is transformed into a muscular stud; a wicked space captain on trial; a WWII bomber crew transformed into zombies; a Pentagon secretary abducted by randy aliens; and a final tale where the horrible Loc-Nar transforms a peaceful people into a rabid hoard of killers.

While undoubtedly rooted in a pubescent male fantasy of gigantic space-age breasts, aroused robots and limb-lopping ultraviolence, this animated portmanteau has become a cult film in a genuine sense. It even rivals the *Rocky Horror Picture Show* on the midnight circuit, a sleazy, sexist brilliantly made adventure movie that says more about the nature of comic books than a brigade of camp-clad X, Y or Z-men.

Its origins lie, suitably enough, in the 'adult' comic book *Heavy Metal*, a trippy fusion of wank-fantasy and geek-fest, a sexually liberated Dungeons And Dragons picture book whipped up with oodles of gore. And rather than circumventing the sheer political incorrectness of its wobbly teenage projections, the film embraces them wholesale. To the shuddering beats of the self-same named style of music, a procession of junky, giggly tales of varied science-fictional parts proceeds. What makes the difference, and allows the film a definite place in the pantheon of animation, is the fact that the stories are, Amazonian virtues aside, well-written, stunningly drawn and, often, very funny.

Indeed, such later sci-fi films as *Total Recall*, *The Matrix*, and most transparently *The Fifth Element* have all borrowed heavily from its fertile store of ideas. That it is a cartoon that takes kids right out of the equation is the best recommendation of all. ★★★★ **IN**

HEDWIG AND THE ANGRY INCH (2001)

Starring: *John Cameron Mitchell (Hedwig), Michael Pitt (Tommy Gnosis), Miriam Shor (Yitzhak). Stephen Trask (Skszp), Theodore Liscinski (Jacek), Rob Campbell (Krysztof)*
Director: *John Cameron Mitchell*
Screenwriter: *John Cameron Mitchell, adapted from the play by Mitchell and Stephen Trask*
15/91 mins./Musical/Comedy/Drama/USA

Hedwig is an East German who has a botched sex-change operation to be able to marry an Amerian GI. She finds herself stranded in a Kansas trailer park and ends up touring seafood restaurants with her rock band where she meets up with the young lad who stole all her tunes.

Writer/director/star John Cameron Mitchell opens up his impressive stage show, which was basically a nightclub act-cum-monologue, into something like a narrative film, with an inevitable toning-down of the effect. Hedwig is an East German gay guy who suffers a botched sex-change (the 'angry inch' is his/her 'Barbie Doll crotch') to marry a GI, only to find herself stranded in a Kansas trailer park as the Wall comes down.

She teams up with a nerd to form a band, only to see him burst big as a superstar who won't credit her for writing the songs. Despite dodgy animated scenes, Hedwig remains an astonishing creation, and the good lines remain sharp – asked, with reference to 'I Will Always Love You' if love really does last forever, she snaps, 'I don't know, but this song does.' ★★★★ **KN**

HEIMAT (1984)

Starring: *Marita Breuer (Maria), Will Burger (Matthias), Gertrud Bredel (Katharina), Rudiger Weigang (Eduard), Karin Rasenack (Lucie), Dieter Schaad (Paul)*
Director: *Edgar Reitz*
Screenwriters: *Edgar Reitz, Peter Steinbach*
15/923 mins./Drama/West Germany

Beginning and ending in the Rhineland village of Schabbach, this multi-episodic saga follows the fortunes of Maria Simon's three sons – Anton, Ernst and Hermann – between the end of the Great War and the Millennium.

Despite being hailed by some as a sophisticated soap opera, Edgar Reitz has always insisted that his magisterial Heimat trilogy owes most to the novels of Dickens and Proust.

Heimat concentrated on Maria Simon, a hausfrau in the Rhineland village of Schabbach, whose three sons were shaped by the rise and fall of Nazism.

Yet, while the focus lingered on one family, Reitz also showed how ordinary Germans responded to the socio-political events for which the victorious Allies later insisted they took responsibility. Thus, we're asked to empathise with the loser who joins the Party to acquire a semblance of civic status, as well as the mother who sees her husband and sons depart from the simple values that she had always cherished.

Although it provoked some angry domestic responses for its perceived romanticising of a traumatic era, *Heimat* was lauded by international critics and became a must-see TV series around the world.

Running 1,538 minutes, *Die Zweite Heimat* (1992) became the longest feature film in screen history. Its 13 episodes introduced us to 71 principal characters, whose freewheeling interaction touched on many of the key social, political and cultural issues that helped define the 1960s. But, despite its spectacular scale, this chronicle of country boy Hermann Simon's turbulent decade in the big city has the intimacy of a book, in which each chapter explored a facet of a Cold War Germany still coming to terms with its Fascist past.

There are clearly autobiographical elements in Reitz's scenario. But everyone can recognise snapshots from their own youth in the diverse storylines, which are played with authentic conviction by a splendid ensemble, led by Henry Arnold, as the impressionable Hermann, and Salome Kammer, as his elusive Muse, Clarissa.

The triptych reached its climax with *Heimat 3* (2005), a six-part masterpiece that brought the influence of America, Russia and East Germany to bear on the insular Rhineland region of the Hunsrück.

The way in which Reitz contrasted the tempestuous on-off relationship between Arnold's conflicted composer and Kammer's avant-garde chanteuse with the tensions that followed the reunification of Germany was masterly, not only for the assuredness of Reitz's storytelling, but also for his command of the complex politico-cultural details that made the action so engrossing and authentic. He also handled the impressive supporting cast with supreme delicacy. It was a fitting climax to a monumental achievement and will long remain a cinematic landmark. ★★★★★ **DP**

THE HEIRESS (1949)

Starring: *Olivia de Havilland (Catherine Sloper), Montgomery Clift (Morris Townsend) Ralph Richardson (Dr. Austin Sloper), Miriam Hopkins (Lavinia Penniman)*
Director: *William Wyler*
Screenwriters: *Ruth Goetz, Augustus Goetz, based on their play and the novel* Washington Square *by Henry James*
U/115 mins./Drama/USA

Awards: *Academy Awards – Best Actress, Best Art Direction-Set Decoration, Best Costume Design, Best Score*

New York in the 1850s and Catherine Sloper is so keen to escape the loveless protection of her doctor father, Austin, and her aunt, Lavinia Penniman, that she fails to realise that earnest younger suitor Morris Townsend is a gold-digger.

Ruth and Augustus Goetz always resented the fact that everyone but them drew praise for this adaptation of Henry James's *Washington Square*. Yet, they devised the emotionally crackling finale that many considered the movie's masterstroke when they brought the book to Broadway in 1947. Indeed, it was the power of the play that convinced Olivia de Havilland that this study of a put-upon woman's passage from innocence to bitter experience was the logical follow-up to *To Each His Own* and *The Snake Pit*, which had confirmed her rapid transition from Warners contract star to serious actress.

She wisely selected William Wyler as her director, as even de Havilland perhaps suspected that she would not have been able to switch from trusting despair to calculated cruelty without his guidance. Moreover, she would certainly not have survived the on-set tensions without his support, as neither Ralph Richardson nor Montgomery Clift held her talent in high regard.

Richardson had already played Dr. Sloper in the West End opposite Peggy Ashcroft, while Clift had been cast for his subtlety after Wyler dropped the idea of reteaming de Havilland with Errol Flynn and decided to muddy Townsend's motives for courting Catherine. But Wyler was thenceforth forced both to protect de Havilland from Clift's sneering disregard for her Hollywoodised approach to acting and to prevent Richardson from stealing scenes at will through his genius for eye-catching pieces of improvised business.

However, the fierce cast rivalries ultimately served to intensify the level of performance and while Clift occasionally slipped into modern Method mode, the standard of acting is extraordinarily high for a studio picture. De Havilland was perhaps fortunate to win her second Academy Award in such a mediocre year. But the manner in which she conveys her shifting personality through the gradual icing over of her eyes suggests that she is now wrongly overlooked as an actress of some quality. ★★★★ **DP**

THE HELICOPTER SPIES (1968)

Starring: *Robert Vaughn (Napoleon Solo), David McCallum (Illya Kuryakin), Carol Lynley (Annie), John Dehner (Dr. Kharmusi), John Carradine (Third-Way Priest), Julie London (Laurie Sebastian)*
Director: *Boris Sagal*
Screenwriter: *Dean Hargrove*
PG/90 mins./Action/Drama/Thriller/Crime/Comedy/USA

Napoleon Solo and Illya Kuryakin, the Men From U.N.C.L.E., enlist safe-cracker Luther Sebastian to help steal the thermal prism unit used by a mad genius in his death ray device. However, Sebastian keeps the prism to use in his own death ray.

During the Bond-inspired superspy boom of the 1960s, *The Man From U.N.C.L.E.* TV franchise – which was also semi-created by Ian Fleming, insofar as he made up a few of the character names – was huge. There was a spin-off TV series, *The Girl From U.N.C.L.E.*, best-selling paperback books and as much merchandise (triangular badges) as the 007 films managed. 'The Vulcan Affair', the pilot episode, was released to cinemas, with added 'steamy scenes', as 'To Trap a Spy', and a clutch of subsequent two-part TV stories were spliced together into a run of popular, likeable, far-fetched adventures in which a few grainy stock shots, Hollywood standing sets and California highways are passed off as globe-trotting locations.

We especially recommend this entry, which was shown on TV as 'The Prince of Darkness Affair': besides the usual U.N.C.L.E. virtues of supercool hero performances from Vaughn and McCallum (and M-like Leo G. Carroll), trademark gadgets like the pen-radio ('Open Channel D') and an unbeatable flute-based jazz theme from Jerry Goldsmith, *The Helicopter Spies* has a wild plotline about two competing bad-guy super-organisations, guest villainy from twitchy Bradford Dillman and smug John Dehner, and a wonderful, immobile John Carradine performance as a guru who hasn't said anything to his evil cult in years but is supposed to bring about the apocalypse when he does speak (at the end, he shrugs and dies).

Other U.N.C.L.E. adventures worth seeking out: *One Spy Too Many*, *The Spy in the Green Hat*, *The Karate Killers*, *The Spy With My Face*. ★★★ **KN**

HELL DRIVERS (1957)

Starring: *Stanley Baker (Tom Yately), Peggy Cummins (Lucy), Patrick McGoohan (Red), Herbert Lom (Gino Rossi), William Hartnell (Cartley), Wildfrid Lawson (Ed), Sid James (Dusty), Jill Ireland (Jill), Alfie Bass (Tinker), Gordon Jackson (Scottie), David McCallum (Jimmy Yately)*
Director: *Cy Endfield*
Screenwriters: *C. Raker Endfield, John Kruse*
PG/108 mins./Drama/UK

Ex-convict Tom Yately takes a dodgy job driving loads of gravel through winding British roads, and realises that sneaky boss Cartley has rigged a scam with the brutal foreman Red, which inevitably leads to human wastage.

Perhaps because it was directed by Cy Endfield, a blacklisted American exile, *Hell Drivers* is a rare British crime film with the blazing excitement and working-class grit of the best American hardboiled thrillers. A powerhouse cast of hard men, paid by the load delivered rather than the hours worked, bomb along dangerous country roads, brawl over fish and chips, try to beat the maniacal Red's record number of runs and crash to their deaths in the quarry. The sorely-underrated Baker was Britain's own Robert Mitchum, a hardboiled hero who could play sensitive without losing his battered authority, and he has a terrific punch-up with the hulking McGoohan, who plays up the Irish accent and lumbers about dangerously in a navvy coat.

Endfield gets on screen an unfamiliar, wholly credible milieu of pull-in cafes, village dances, works huts, rooming houses, backstreet newsagents and desolate quarries. Besides its authentic feel and action scenes, it boasts a once-in-a-lifetime cast of British film and TV greats: how many other movies have an ensemble which includes the original Dr Who (Hartnell), the first James Bond (Sean Connery), the Prisoner (McGoohan), a Man From *U.N.C.L.E.* (David McCallum), a Professional (Gordon Jackson), Clouseau's boss (Herbert Lom), plus Alfie Bass, the excellent Peggy Cummins (of the cult items *Gun Crazy* and *Night of the Demon*), the inimitably boozy Wilfrid Lawson, Jill Ireland and Sid James? Lom overdoes it somewhat as the sentimental Italian obviously doomed to become a plot sacrifice, but the rest of the hairy-knuckled blokes are spot on, and it winds up with an exciting race to the death between overloaded gravel trucks. ★★★★ **KN**

HELL'S ANGELS (1930)

Starring: *Ben Lyon (Monte Routledge), James Hall (Roy Routledge), Jean Harlow (Helen), John Darrow (Karl Armstedt), Lucien Prival (Baron Von Kranz)*
Directors: *Howard Hughes, Edmund Goulding*
Screenwriters: *Harry Behn, Howard Estabrook, Joseph Moncure March, based on a story by Marshall Neilan and March*
18/119 mins./Drama/USA

Two contrasting brothers both enlist in the RAF when WWI breaks out, but when Monte, the louche womaniser, seduces his upright brother Roy's girlfriend Helen, it threatens to sever their bond. It takes a near-suicide bombing mission for both men to prove something to themselves and to each other.

Another film whose fabled making of – where millionaire director Howard Hughes sought the ultimate movie experience by spending unheard of millions (resulting in a huge loss) on his own private airforce to film the dogfights (three pilots died in its making), with the risk-addicted director nearly killing himself in the process in an air-crash – fails to live up to its own fanfare. While the airbound photography is often breathtaking, the earthbound melodrama of two vividly different brothers squabbling over Jean Harlow's loose virtue is horribly dated and deathly dull.

It's best to view the overlong film in the context of what it achieved at the time. An early sequence of a doomed Zeppelin on a bombing raid over London is truly spectacular as crewmen leap to their fate through the billowing clouds. And despite the ridiculous stereotyping of Germans (as sadistic fops) and English (as stalwart rods) alike – not to forget its wholesale misogyny – their plane-to-plane fights are wildly authentic as in all but live ammunition they were. And its dibs and dabs of colourisation show adventure if not success.

However, many of the film's trite limitations cannot be put down to the period, an era where melodrama was natural, when you consider that the penetrative and powerful *All Quiet On The Western Front* was to beat it at the Oscars. Howard Hughes would drift into genuine aviation, leaving Hollywood to others' excesses. ★★ **IN**

◑ HELLBOY (2004)

Starring: *Ron Pearlman (Hellboy), John Hurt (Professor Trevor 'Broom' Bruttenholm), Selma Blair (Liz Sherman), Rupert Evans (John Myers), Karel Roden (Grigori Rasputin), Jeffrey Tambor (Dr. Tom Manning)*
Director: *Guillermo del Toro*
Screenwriter: *Guillermo del Toro, from a screen story by del Toro and Peter Briggs, based on the Dark Horse comic books by Mike Mignola*
12A/120 mins./Fantasy/Action/Horror/USA

In 1945, a Nazi secret society summons a demon, but the ritual is disrupted and the creature taken by Professor Bruttenholm. Now Hellboy, the star employee of the US Bureau For Paranormal Research And Defence, must stop evil monk Rasputin, who wants to immolate the world.

Hellboy might not have the name-recognition factor of Spider-man or Batman, but Guillermo del Toro brings the audience swiftly up to speed on artist-writer Mike Mignola's comic book anti-hero.

First, he treats us to an atmospheric World War II prologue. Then we meet the present-day Hellboy: a hulking action guy with red skin, sawn-off horns, a stone right hand and teenage jock attitude, coping with ickily-tentacled threats to the fabric of reality while nurturing a crush on a fellow agent, troubled pyrokinetic ('I hate the term "firestarter" ') Liz Sherman.

There are many characters and situations to introduce – also on hand is sensitive fish-man Abe Sapien (voiced by Frasier's David Hyde Pierce) and del Toro brings in a new BPRD agent, developing a romantic triangle by having him warm to Liz. This thread is easily the flimsiest, but so much else is going on that it doesn't get in the way.

Del Toro turned down opportunities to make this with a bigger budget in return for putting a star in Hellboy's giant boots, but he was right to hold out for Ron Pearlman, who's more used to jobbing as a character actor. Thanks to his gruff, blue-collar charisma, a character who could easily have been just a big, scarlet special effect works like gangbusters.

Meanwhile, Blair and Hurt (as the hero's adoptive pop) provide calming influences, but the best supporting turn comes from the always-welcome Jeffrey 'Hey now!' Tambor, as the smarmy bureaucrat boss.

Del Toro's already been down the comic-adaptation route in *Blade II* (which now looks like a practice run), but Mignola's series is far more congenial material for cinematic treatment, with its blocky stone-and-iron architecture translating wonderfully to the screen. It's just a shame the promised reign of giant evil squid gods is too nebulous a threat to play as well as an old-fashioned fist-fest.

As usual, a human-shaped foe (here, Kroenen – a near-immortal Nazi assassin in stylised gas-mask, with a wind-up key in his heart and dust in his veins) is more interestingly hateful than the pile of CGI tentacles brought on for one last bout after the show is really over. ★★★ **KN**

◑ HELLO, DOLLY! (1969)

Starring: *Barbra Streisand (Dolly Levi), Walter Matthau (Horace Vandergelder), Michael Crawford (Cornellius Hack), Louis Armstrong (Orchestra Leader), Tommy Tune (Ambrose Kemper)*
Director: *Gene Kelly*
Screenwriter: *Ernest Lehman, based on the play* The Matchmaker *by Thornton Wilder*
U/129 mins./Musical/USA

Awards: *Academy Awards – Best Art Direction-Set Decoration, Best Musical Score, Best Sound*

Widowed New York matchmaker Dolly Levi is deflected from her purpose when she falls for wealthy, grouchy merchant, Horace Vandergelder.

Considering he had already brought *The King and I, West Side Story* and *The Sound of Music* so successfully to the screen, writer-producer Ernest Lehman could have had few excuses for making such a hash of this adaptation of Jerry Herman and Michael Stewart's 1964 musical revision of Thornton Wilder's 1954 comedy, *The Matchmaker* (which had itself been reworked from Wilder's 1938 show, *The Merchant of Yonkers*).

The irony is that Lehman's decision to replace the Tony-winning Carol Channing had nothing to do with her suitability for the role: he'd simply disliked her performance in *Thoroughly Modern Millie* and couldn't bear the thought of watching her over 146 minutes. So, having rejected such experienced stars as Ginger Rogers and Betty Grable (who'd both played Dolly on tour) and more commercial possibilities like Elizabeth Taylor and Julie Andrews, Lehman took Mike Nichols's advice and cast Barbra Streisand, who had yet to begin work on *Funny Girl*.

At just 26, Streisand had her own doubts about her ability to play the ebullient widow and her wayward performance (in which she came across variously as Fanny Brice, Mae West and Marilyn Monroe) owed much to director Gene Kelly's preoccupation with the $24 million picture's considerable technical challenges. However, she wasn't helped much either by co-star Walter Matthau (who took exception to her and cheerfully watched her struggle) or equally inexperienced supports like Michael Crawford. Indeed, even Louis Armstrong couldn't resist competing with her in their showstopping duet.

The Oscar-winning 15-acre New York sets were truly splendid and Irene Sharaff's costumes and Harry Stradling's photography were equally stylish. But Kelly had always steered clear of this kind of cosy Americana and his direction often seemed to be striking against the nostalgic tone. But, even when numbers like 'Before the Parade Passes' were impressively staged, the problem of Streisand's age recurred, as she simply lacked the maturity to give the song its due poignancy. ★★★ **DP**

◑ HELLRAISER (1987)

Starring: *Andrew Robinson (Larry Cotton), Clare Higgins (Julia Cotton), Ashley Laurence (Kirsty Swanson), Sean Chapman (Frank Cotton), Oliver Smith (Frank the Monster)*
Director: *Clive Barker*
Screenwriter: *Clive Barker, based on his novel*
18/90 mins./Horror/UK

A man finds he is given more than he bargains for when he solves the puzzle of the Lament Configuration – a doorway to hell.

Stephen King, the world's most prolific author, once proved that not only does he write round the clock, he also has time to read, borrowing *Rolling Stone* writer Jon Landau's Bruce Springsteen quote when he said, 'I have seen the future of horror, and his name is Clive Barker.'

High praise indeed from the grandmaster, who had paid close attention to the writings of the native Liverpudlian. Barker moved to London in his early 20s and rapidly established himself in theatre-land, where his love of the bizarre, fantastical and theatrical found voice in such works as *Frankenstein In Love, The History Of The Devil* and the wonderfully titled *The Secret Life Of Cartoons*. He expanded his dark visions in short fiction, establishing himself as the new voice of British horror with such books as *The Damnation Game* and *The Books Of Blood* compilations. An early short story, Rawhead Rex, and a screenplay, Transmutations, found their way to the screen (Barker penned both scripts) much to the disappointment of the author. With those past experiences in mind, in 1987 he resolved to take control of the cinematic treatment of his work and reinvented himself as a film director for the purposes of adapting his novella *The Hellhound Heart*, filmed and released as *Hellraiser*.

It was at once a riposte to a genre dominated by American slasher franchises and the best British horror movie since the house of Hammer shut its doors. A revitalisation of the British horror movie? A paean to S&M sex? Or a cruel attack on the profound but unexpected success of the Rubik's

Cube? *Hellraiser* was all this. And more. Here was a film that dared to equate sensuality with fear, that cast its 'villains' as beautiful victims, who were described as 'demons to some, angels to others'.

Indeed, the film's most pivotal image – and in many ways its most successful element – was the creation of a new screen monster. From Dracula to Frankenstein to the dead-eyed Michael Myers, the image of the horror movie has always been one that leant itself to icon-status, the Munch-inspired *Scream* mask being the most recent example. Yet these key images are hard to find – witness the countless schlock-worthy entries in the horror-movie canon that inspire nothing more than casual interest. With the Cenobites – and Doug Bradley's Pinhead in particular – Barker created a unique horror-movie presence.

'They're like sado-masochists from beyond the grave,' Barker once said of the Cenobites. (In fact, Barker has joked that at one point he wanted to call the film 'Sado-Masochists From Beyond The Grave' adding that '*Hellraiser* turned out to be far weirder than I expected.') Pinhead was revealed (in *Hellhound: Hellraiser II*) to be Captain Eliot Spenser, a World War II veteran who had discovered a devilish box known as the Lament Configuration and found in it his own portal into Hell. By detailing his character in the manner he did, Barker made him instantly accessible to his audience, using the 'war is hell' metaphor in its most literal sense.

'I think what the monsters in movies have to say for themselves is every bit as interesting as what the human beings have to say,' Barker once stated. 'That's why in stalk'n'slash films I feel that half the story is missing. These creatures simply become, in a very boring way, abstractions of evil. Evil is never abstracted. I want to hear the Devil speak. I like the idea that a point of view can be made by the dark side.' In 1986, drawing on his background in theatre, Clive Barker took a paltry sum of money and made a low-budget movie, largely in a house in Dollis Hill. ('Low-budget moviemaking is fringe theatre, except you can actually get the audience numbers that I always wanted us to get.')

His ambition was to maintain control of his work. 'I always knew *Hellraiser* was going to be raw,' he said. 'It's a slightly misshapen baby – but it's mine.' And to think, when its American distributor didn't like the title it was almost renamed 'What A Woman Will Do For A Good Fuck.' Go figure. ★★★★ **BM**

HELLZAPOPPIN' (1941)

Starring: *Ole Olsen (Ole), Chic Johnson (Chic), Robert Paige (Jeff Hunter), Jane Frazee (Kitty Rand), Lewis Howard (Woody Tyler), Martha Raye (Betty Johnson)*
Director: *H.C. Potter*
Screenwriters: *Nat Perrin, Warren Wilson, based on the play by Nat Perrin*
U/84 mins./Comedy/USA

A romantic triangle involving showbiz-loving playboy Jeff Hunter, Kitty Rand and Woody Tyler is consistently disrupted by Ole and Chic and their eccentric acquaintances.

Between September 1938 and December 1941, *Hellzapoppin'* racked up 1404 live performances, becoming one of only three shows to play more than 500 times on Broadway during the entire 1930s. However, as the caption accompanying Universal's adaptation reads, 'Any resemblance between *Hellzapoppin'* and a motion picture are coincidental'. No wonder Richard Laine's director is given the line, 'This is Hollywood, we change everything here. We've got to!'

One of the strengths of Nat Perrin's stage show was that it was constantly being revised to reflect news stories and changing tastes. But, movie audiences were nowhere near as sophisticated as their theatrical counterparts and the Breen Office was determined that it should stay that way. Consequently, nearly all of the original's sharper material was removed by Perrin and Warren Wilson and it was replaced with the kind of romantic subplot that had been foisted on the Marx Brothers, along with a glut of songs and speciality turns to give the action a revue feel and the punters a sense of value for money.

Olsen and Johnson thus became bit players in their own picture, as H.C. Potter gave the screen over to Martha Raye for Don Raye and Gene De Paul tunes like 'Watch the Birdie' and to Slim Galliard and Slam Stewart for an impromptu Lindy Hop (choreographed by Frankie Manning) that cashed in on the dance's current vogue.

However, the film remains a cult favourite thanks to its madcap comedy. Some of the wisecracking has lost its zing. But many of the gags are wholly cinematic and remain as fresh and funny as ever. The parody of *Citizen Kane* (which had been released earlier in the year) is particularly slick. But the scenes involving the talking animals, projectionist Shemp Howard speaking directly to the audience, the interruption of a romantic number to tell Stinky Miller to leave the auditorium, and Olsen and Johnson's bout of top-and-tail invisiblity are equally amusing. ★★★ **DP**

HELP! (1965)

Starring: *John Lennon (John), Paul McCartney (Paul), Ringo Starr (Ringo), George Harrison (George), Leo McKern (Clang), Eleanor Bron (Ahme), Victor Spinetti (Foot), Roy Kinnear (Algernon)*
Director: *Richard Lester*
Screenwriters: *Marc Behm, Charles Wood, based on a story by Wood*
U/92 mins./Musical/Comedy/UK

John, George and Paul try to keep Ringo out of the clutches of Kaili cultist Clang and mad scientist Professor Foot, who are after the powerful sacrificial ring that has become stuck on the drummer's finger.

On their 1964 fan-club Christmas record, The Beatles sounded upbeat about the prospect of filming a follow-up to *A Hard Day's Night*. They had used their clout to secure location shoots in Austria and the Bahamas and Richard Lester had agreed to work in colour. However, John Lennon's antipathy had prompted screenwriter Alun Owen's dismissal and the storyline of what was then called Eight Arms to Hold You had been through a tortuous process.

Bored with Beatlemania, the band had insisted on an escapist approach and Lester and Joseph McGrath's original idea had been for Ringo to be pursued by a hitman, who was also a master of disguise. But when it was discovered that Philippe De Broca was doing something similar with *Up to His Ears*, Marc Behm was hired to concoct a chase scenario, which was Beatlified by Charles Wood (who had scripted Lester's Swinging Sixties comedy, *The Knack*).

Although they still played variations on themselves, the Fabs were very different from the foursome who had cheekily ad-libbed their way through their docudramatic debut. Indeed, John, Paul and George spent much of the production doped up and Lester implied they were 'passengers' in their own vehicle, who left Ringo to do the real acting alongside Leo McKern, Victor Spinetti and Eleanor Bron.

Yet, *Help!* is far from the mediocrity some critics have suggested. Lester's passion for silent slapstick frequently came to the fore, most notably during the 'Ticket to Ride' sequence, which he edited to the track's rhythm from spontaneous tomfoolery in the Alpine snow. There's also plenty of offbeat wit that drew comparisons with the Marx Brothers and The Goons, while the action is strewn with James Bond pastiches (mostly from *Goldfinger*) that reinforced the picture's conscious sense of cool.

Moreover, *Help!* was infinitely more musically mature than its predecessor, with Lennon's title track and 'You've Got to Hide Your Love Away' revealing a Dylan-influenced introspection that betrayed the group's growing disillusion with being loveable Mop Tops. ★★★ **DP**

HENRY AND JUNE (1990)

Starring: *Fred Ward (Henry Miller), Uma Thurman (June Miller), Maria de Medeiros (Anais Nin), Richard E. Grant (Hugo), Kevin Spacey (Osborn)*
Director: *Philip Kaufman*
Screenwriters: *Philip Kaufman, Rose Kaufman, based on the diaries of Anais Nin*
18/136 mins./Drama/Erotic/USA

In an adaptation of the autobiographical tale by Anais Nin, budding author Henry Miller taps away at his typewriter in 30s Paris, while torn between wife June and his raging passion for Anais.

Great writers, according to Philip Kaufman here, are able to pause at any time from their great works, have a quick bonk, then return to the typewriter or pen, rested and ready for another chapter or two. Featuring even more flesh per frame than Kaufman's earlier erotic adventure, *The Unbearable Lightness Of Being*, this story of the tempestuous relationship between Henry and June Miller and Anais Nin is set in 1931, amid the libertine chic of Paris, and is stuffed with Miller's circus and vaudeville friends.

Ward plays Henry Miller like Fred Flintstone, Maria De Medeiros is rather touching as Nin the feminist diarist, always looking for something, always ending up in bed with someone, while Uma Thurman as June Miller determinedly doesn't take her clothes off despite the libidinous advances of most of Henry's friends.

The whole thing has a horrid fascination but it's ultimately an arid message, rather like saying too much sex and booze screws you up. At its best between the sheets, this is a reminder that authors are always far less interesting in the flesh – even when there's lots of it – than on the printed page. ★★ **RB**

HENRY FOOL (1997)

Starring: *Thomas Jay Ryan (Henry Fool), James Urganiak (Simon Grim), Parker Posey (Fay Grim), Maria Porter (Mary), James Saito (Mr. Deng), Kevin Corrigan (Warren), Liam Aiken (Ned)*
Director: *Hal Hartley*
Screenwriter: *Hal Hartley (uncredited)*
18/137 mins./Comedy/Drama/USA

A garbage collector and his sister's quiet lives are disturbed when they take in lodger Henry Fool, who's ostensibly finishing his memoirs.

For his sixth feature, American indie hero Hal Hartley has pulled off a neat trick. He has turned out a film that is the same as his impressive back catalogue – quirky talk-driven curiosities about people living on the fringes of society – yet somehow different, managing to imbue his usual obsessions with the freshness and vitality of a first-time director.

The action centres on a withdrawn garbage collector Simon Grim (Urbaniak), his depressed mother (Maria Porter) and chain-smoking, nymphomaniac sister Fay (Posey). Their uneventful existence is disrupted by the arrival of Henry Fool (Ryan), a homespun intellectual-cum-egomaniac who takes up residence in the Grim family basement. Working on his memoirs, Fool encourages Simon to put his thoughts into poetry to help overcome his shyness: the upshot is Simon's pornographic poetry sees him lauded as a cutting-edge wordsmith whereas the neglected Fool turns his attentions to seducing Simon's mom and sis.

All the usual Hartley trademarks – oblique observations, zero degree humour, the experimentation with storytelling conventions – are thrown into the mix but what distinguishes *Henry Fool* from his previous movies is the skewed satire about the 'real' world (everything from publishing to politics), a dash of (literal) toilet humour and a touching demeanour toward its characters' flaws and aspirations. Ryan is intimidating as Henry, at once forceful yet pitiable, and Posey lends layers of decency and complexity to her potentially one-note sex bomb. But the film finds its real centre in Urbaniak, his quiet demeanour growing gradually affective as the film progresses.

The film is a tad too long and the second half fails to deliver on the promise of the first but Hartley's confident handling of the broad canvas is deft and controlled. It may not bring him to a wider audience but this emerges as one of Hartley's most interesting, accessible and enjoyable efforts to date. ★★★★ **IF**

HENRY V (1944)

Starring: *Laurence Olivier (King Henry V), Robert Newton (Ancient Pistol), Leslie Banks (Chorus), Renee Asherson (Princess Katherine), Esmond Knight (Fluellen)*
Directors: *Laurence Olivier, Reginald Beck*
Screenwriters: *Alan Dent, Laurence Olivier, based on the play by William Shakespeare*
U/127 mins/Drama/UK

Awards: *Academy Awards – Honorary Award (Laurence Olivier)*

King Henry V of England leads his troops to victory over the French at Agincourt in 1415 and seeks to consolidate his imperial position by courting the Princess Katherine.

Laurence Olivier had become convinced that Shakespeare belonged firmly on the stage during his participation in Paul Czinner's 1936 adaptation of *As You Like It*. However, having played Henry V in a radio broadcast in 1942, he had been persuaded of the patriotic potential of a film version by Filippo Del Giudice, the founder of the Two Cities company.

So, when William Wyler, Carol Reed and Terence Young all declined his invitation, Olivier agreed to make his directorial debut, although he wisely secured the services of editor Reginald Beck as his assistant. He also hired theatre critic Alan Dent to help him tailor the play for the screen and called on numerous stage pals to enhance the picture's artistic legitimacy. However, he was denied the services of his wife, Vivien Leigh (as Katherine), as Hollywood producer David O. Selznick (who held her contract) felt the role was too small for a star of her magnitude.

The ingenious framing device, which commenced the action on the stage of the Globe Theatre in Shakespearean London, had been conceived by Anthony Asquith (who had directed Olivier in *Moscow Nights*, 1935, and *The Demi-Paradise*, 1943) and it set the tone for the film's blend of artifice and actuality, which was consciously designed to capture the imagination of audiences who had probably never seen the Bard before. Paul Sheriff and Carmen Dillon's theatrical sets and painted backdrops exploited the atmospheric beauty of the Technicolor stock and made the outdoor Agincourt sequences (filmed in Enniskerry with Irish soldiers) seem all the more expansive and thrilling. However, such perfectionism pushed the budget up to £475,000 (a staggering sum for a wartime project) and Rank had to step in to keep the production afloat.

Driven by William Walton's rousing score, the film was a transatlantic success and earned Olivier a special Oscar in 1946. Despite occasionally indulging the star's tendency to melodramatics, it remains an impressive achievement and makes for fascinating comparisons with Kenneth Branagh's 1989 version. ★★★★ **DP**

HENRY V (1989)

Starring: *Derek Jacobi (Chorus), Kenneth Branagh (Henry V), Simon Sheperd (Gloucester), James Larkin (Bedford), Brian Blessed (Exeter), Emma Thompson (Katherine)*
Director: *Kenneth Branagh*
Screenwriter: *Kenneth Branagh, based on the play by William Shakespeare*
PG/131 mins./History/Drama/UK

Awards: *Academy Awards – Best Costume Design, BAFTA – Best Director*

Britain's young king still carries his reputation from his wild days as an irresponsible prince. After an insulting rebuttal, he marches an army of

Hairless Heroes — TOP10

	Character	Actor, Film
1	Master Li Mu Bai	Chow Yun Fat, *Crouching Tiger, Hidden Dragon*
2	Professor X	Patrick Stewart, *X-Men*
3	Morpheus	Laurence Fishburne, *The Matrix*
4	Chris	Yul Brynner, *The Magnificent Seven*
5	THX 1138	Robert Duvall, *THX-1138*
6	Evey Hammond	Natalie Portman, *V For Vendetta*
7	Wong Fei-Hung	Jet Li, *Once Upon A Time In China*
8	James Cole	Bruce Willis, *Twelve Monkeys*
9	Xander Cage	Vin Diesel, *xXx*
10	Ilia	Persis Khambatta, *Star Trek The Motion Picture*

inferior numbers into France, which becomes a journey of both personal and collective self-doubt, from which the English emerge to meet their opponents on the field of Agincourt.

Kenneth Branagh's bold decision to open his career as a film director with *Henry V* was brought into even sharper focus by the death of Laurence Olivier just two months prior to its release. Olivier also made his directorial debut with it in 1944, and his performance as Henry – perhaps like his Hamlet, and certainly like his Richard III – is regarded as pretty close to definitive. So it wasn't only the Bard that the 28-year-old Branagh is taking on here; 'twas also the stuff of film legend.

A tall order then – comparisons could hardly be more invidious. But Branagh has grasped the nettle, and it's a relief as much as a pleasure to see him emerge with credit, both as a director and performer. This is despite, rather than because of, a strange conviction he outlines in the production notes. Olivier's film was made in the heat of World War II, and it's impossible not to see part of it as an exercise in propaganda. Branagh, however, was apparently convinced that 'here was a play to be reclaimed from jingoism'. How can this be, when national fervour is its dominant note and the play is one of Shakespeare's most patriotic works? It's like attempting to 'reclaim' the New Testament from Christianity.

At any rate, what happens up on screen patently contradicts Branagh's avowed intention. He plays Henry as a noble warrior king (there's no other way to play it), believing in the justice of his claim to the throne of France and rousing the yeomen of England to follow him. He is also a man keenly aware of his past, and we are reminded, through flashbacks, of his days as a 'madcap prince' when he sought the company of knaves and low-lifes – Falstaff (a brief cameo by Robbie Coltrane) foremost among them. The latter is now dead, and Henry has since attained a stern maturity, to the point where he refuses clemency to Bardolph, a thief – and erstwhile friend – sentenced to hang. Yet there's still a touching hint of vulnerability behind the regal armour; when the Governor of Harfleur capitulates before Henry's threats of slaughter, Branagh, instead of strutting like a turkey cock, simply heaves a sigh of relief.

Derek Jacobi's prologue drifts in and out of frame, setting an appropriately dignified tone for the epic scenes about to unfold. Branagh has opened out the play from its stagebound origins to encompass what might easily pass for 'the vasty fields of France' and the Agincourt sequences are handled admirably – a melee of blood, mud and steel. The long tracking shot which closes the battle, accompanied by the Non Nobis anthem is a spectacular coup.

The only thing which threatens to puncture the film's august atmosphere is, oddly enough, its cast. You keep spotting great British Character Actors until it becomes a distraction – there's Judi Dench, there's Brian Blessed, and Ian Holm. Geraldine McEwan, isn't that Paul Scofield? and so on. A cast so full of stars begins to smack of Christmas panto, particularly with the likes of Richard Briers as the raddled Bardolph.

Branagh's *Henry V* must, however, be counted a success – it might never be as famous as Olivier's, but it should carry considerable clout for years to come. ★★★★★ **AQ**

HENRY: PORTRAIT OF A SERIAL KILLER (1986)

Starring: *Michael Rooker (Henry), Tom Towles (Otis), Tracy Arnold (Becky), Ray Atherton (Fence), David Katz (Henry's Boo)*
Director: *John McNaughton*
Screenwriter: *Richard Fire*
18/83 mins./Crime/Horror/USA

Henry, a serial killer, shares an apartment with Otis. When Otis' sister comes to stay both sides of his personality start to come out.

As every magazine and Sunday supplement will tell you serial killers are The Big Thing right now, and Henry, portrayed by Michael Rooker with brilliant restraint, truth and power, could well prove the last instalment for some time to come. This is sicko territory with a vengeance, and all the more so for the absolute and cold detachment of its tone.

Henry is an ordinary blue-collar Joe, strong, silent and not unattractive. He is also an ex-con who drifts from city to city, because he's a psychopathic killer with enough animal cunning to cover his tracks. Henry is lodging with his old prison buddy Otis when Otis' sister Becky turns up to stay and forges a close relationship with the killer, which, in an ending of chillingly banal horror, proves her undoing. Meanwhile, the repulsive Otis becomes privy to Henry's dark secret and a willing partner in murder. This plot development destroys credibility because it is at total odds with the essence of the serial killer's solitary nature. It also allows the film to move into areas of sexual sickness that are almost intolerable to watch (the audience walk-out rate is exceptionally high).

John McNaughton, inspired by the true case of Henry Lee Lucas, who claimed to have murdered over 300 women, offers a masterly evocation of smalltown low-life and psychopathic sadism. A spare and authentic screenplay unfolds in an almost documentary-like environment, there are no histrionics and the acting is of the highest order, but the film shocks and disturbs as much for its morally questionable purpose as in its ugly subject. This is no cops 'n' robbers movie: there is no retribution or confrontation, no illumination and little explanation. Henry and Otis just are, and the dispassionate depiction of their activities includes a slow and graphic rape and murder of a woman in front of her husband and a video camera, with Henry watching Otis on screen while we see both.

The very brilliance with which this movie is made emphasises the question, what is it for? The stars are strictly for technical excellence. ★★★★ **JB**

HERBIE: FULLY LOADED (2005)

Starring: *Lindsay Lohan (Maggie Peyton), Michael Keaton (Ray Peyton Sr.), Matt Dillon (Trip Murphy), Breckin Meyer (Ray Peyton Jr.), Justin Long (Kevin), Cheryl Hines (Sally)*
Director: *Angela Robinson*
Screenwriters: *Thomas Lennon, Ben Garant, Alfred Gough, Miles Millar, based on a story by Lennon, Garant and Mark Perez and characters by Gordon Burford*
U/101 mins./Comedy/Family/USA

Maggie longs to be a racing driver like her dad and brother, but isn't allowed near the track. Instead, her dad buys her Herbie, a Volkswagen Beetle with a mind of its own. Together with mechanic Kevin, Maggie and Herbie become a racing force to be reckoned with . . .

HERBIE RIDES AGAIN

Burdened with a title horribly reminiscent of the *Charlie's Angels* sequel, this Herbie movie is no car-crash for the franchise – but thanks to charisma-free performances from most of its human cast, it's a close call.

It starts promisingly with a headline montage showing Herbie's past glories, descent into ignominy and arrival on the scrap heap. Rescued by Lindsay Lohan in the film's best scene, Herbie takes his new owner racing against arrogant NASCAR champion Trip Murphy. Then things roll downhill. There's the early success, the training montage, pride, failure and soul-searching before ... well, no prizes for guessing how it ends.

This strict adherence to formula is wearing for anyone over ten, but worse is Lohan, who displays none of her Mean Girls' feistiness, flouncing and pouting and out-acted at every turn by the car's subtle CGI and animatronic flourishes. Perhaps the rumoured digital reduction of Lohan's two main talents (this being a family film, after all) affected her charm. ★★ **H O'H**

⊙ HERBIE RIDES AGAIN (1974)

Starring: *Helen Hayes (Mrs. Steinmetz), Ken Berry (Willoughby Whitfield), Stefanie Powers (Nicole Harris), John McIntire (Mr. Judson), Keenan Wynn (Alonzo Hawk)*
Director: *Robert Stevenson*
Screenwriter: *Bill Walsh, based on a story by Gordon Burford*
U/88 mins./Comedy/Family/Adventure/USA

Alonzo Hawk wants to tear down the home of sweet little old lady Mrs Steinmetz and erect San Francisco's tallest skyscraper. Fortunately, Mrs Steinmetz's nephew owns Herbie, the thinking Volkswagen.

This pleasant, forgettable sequel to *The Love Bug*, one of Disney's biggest live-action hits of the 1960s, is made on the template of all Uncle Walt's fantasy comedies back to *The Absent-Minded Professor*.

Since the Disney Corporation has a reputation for rapaciousness which makes McDonald's look like an organic soya collective, it's ironic that Keenan Wynn's snarling Alonzo P. Hawk – who'd previously given Fred MacMurray a hard time in *The Absent-Minded Professor* and *Son of Flubber* – is the ultimate capitalist villain, who longs to demolish the Colosseum ('think of the shopping centre and parking lot I could put there') and is tormented by a King Kong-inspired nightmare in which he is a giant atop the Empire State Building attacked by miniature flying Volkswagens.

Dean Jones sits out the sequel (Hayes explains Herbie is upset because he has gone on the Grand-Prix circuit and is being unfaithful with other European cars) and the blander Ken Berry does little as a token human hero.

A post-*Girl From U.N.C.L.E.*, pre-*Hart to Hart* Stefanie Powers is winning in a fetching red beret and matching miniskirt, though her role consists mainly of hitting people with lobsters and surprisingly semi-orgasmic oohs and ahhs as Herbie performs his stunts.

In addition to the living car, the film features a superannuated sentient streetcar and a sentimental jukebox, while the human cast tends to old-timers like John McIntire, Helen Hayes, Huntz Hall and Liam Dunn.

Herbie rode again and again, in *Herbie Goes to Monte Carlo*, *Herbie Goes Bananas*, a 1997 TV movie remake of *The Love Bug* and the 2005 comeback *Herbie: Fully Loaded*. ★★★ **KN**

⊙ HERCULES (1997)

Starring: *the voices of: Tate Donovan (Adult Hercules), Joshua Keaton (Young Hercules), Roger Bart (Young Hercules – singing voice), Danny DeVito (Philoctetes), James Woods (Hades), Charlton Heston (Narrator)*
Directors: *Ron Clements, John Musker*
Screenwriters: *John Musker, Ron Clements, Bob Shaw, Donald McEnery, Irene Mecchi, Barry Johnson (story supervisor)*
U/80 mins./Family/Animated/Musical/USA

Son of the Gods, Hercules, is kidnapped from heaven and brought up as a mortal, but his super-strength soon causes his fame to spread.

The more they re-promote the back catalogue, the easier it becomes to draw a line between Old Disney and New Disney. Stick on *The Aristocats*; then watch *The Hunchback Of Notre Dame* – they're both set in Paris, it's fair – each is beautifully drawn and contains virtually the same horse, yet one is charming, simplistic and compulsive, the other noisy, intellectual and relentless. *Hercules*, Disney's 35th full-length animated feature, falls in with the latter.

A Greek myth from the *Aladdin/Little Mermaid* crew, it charts the to-hell-and-back odyssey of the heroic son of Zeus, kidnapped by minions of Underworld boss Hades (a show-stealing Woods), and – after a bungled attempt to rub him out – stranded on earth as a mere mortal. In order to climb the stairway back to heaven, he must become a true hero, assisted by cloven-hoofed Philoctetes or 'Phil', cleverly styled on a down-at-heel Hollywood boxing trainer. Throw in Pegasus, mythical beasts aplenty, and a poisoned-chalice heroine Megara ('Meg'), and you have steroid-pumped good and intense, Satanic evil. With a soul-singing Greek chorus to boot.

Disney have always delighted in jazzy adaptation, and now, they've 'done' Greek mythology. But while the sources of the other films were – to the kiddy viewer – immaterial, a full enjoyment of Hercules requires a basic understanding of classical studies for its gags about Narcissus, Achilles, Nymphs, etc. Technically, the drawings are springy and delightful (the hand of British nib-punisher Gerald Scarfe looming loose and large), and the songs are fulsome and camp, if again hard to follow if you're under ten – which hints at the film's basic flaw: it works too hard for the grown-ups. Hercules is first and foremost a parent-pleaser, which is a fundamental distortion of the Disney ethic. ★★★ **AC**

⊙ HERE COMES MR JORDAN (1941)

Starring: *Robert Montgomery (Joe Pendleton), Evelyn Keyes (Bette Logan), Claude Rains (Mr. Jordan), Rita Johnson (Julia Farnsworth), Edward Everett Horton (Messenger No.7013)*
Director: *Alexander Hall*
Screenwriters: *Sidney Buchman, Seton I. Miller based on the play* Heaven Can Wait *by Harry Segall*
U/93 mins./Fantasy/USA

Awards: *Academy Awards – Best Original Screenplay, Best Original Story*

Boxer Joe Pendleton is transported to heaven before his time following a plane crash. So, celestial soul checker Mr Jordan assigns him the body of a murdered millionaire and he promptly falls in love with Bette Logan, one of the many people his alter ego had mistreated.

Columbia chief Harry Cohn had grave doubts about this adaptation of Harry Segall's minor stage play. Always under pressure from his Wall Street backers to run a tight ship, he preferred to reserve his more lavish budgets for the studio's only genuine star, Rita Hayworth. However, he was persuaded to splash out on some costly celestial sets and to hire Robert Montgomery from MGM by co-scenarist Sidney Buchman, who convinced Cohn that he had a surer appreciation of public taste than a bunch of bankers. Ultimately, Cohn was rewarded for his courage, as the picture scooped seven Oscar nominations – with Segall winning for Best Original Story and Buchman and Seton I. Miller for Adapted Screenplay.

With Pendleton inhabiting three different bodies in the course of 93 minutes, this was quite an intricate storyline for a Hollywood comedy. But Alexander Hall (an unsung journeyman whose credits included Shirley Temple's *Little Miss Marker*) kept the action briskly accessible, even where Death was involved. However, he couldn't prevent the romantic subplot from becoming saccharine and contrived and occasionally allowed Montgomery to lay on the durable geniality a little too thickly.

But he coaxed exceptional performances from a splendid supporting cast, with Edward Everett Horton bumbling to amusing effect as Messenger No.7013 and Rita Farnsworth and John Emery oozing malevolence as the millionaire's scheming wife and his smooth-operating secretary. There's even a touch of quiet menace about Claude Rains's celestial civil servant, who clearly resents having his meticulous system disrupted by angelic incompetence and human emotion. But the most likeable performance comes from James Gleason, as boxing coach Max Corkle, and, six years later, he turned in an equally affable variation on the role opposite Cary Grant in *The Bishop's Wife*.

Never one to waste a hit, Cohn recycled some of the movie's ideas for the 1947 Rita Hayworth vehicle, *Down to Earth*, in which Gleason and Everett Horton reprised their roles, while Roland Culver stepped in as Mr Jordan. However, the picture would eventually be remade as the likeable *Heaven Can Wait* by Warren Beatty in 1978. ★★★★ **DP**

HERO (YING XIONG) (2002)

Starring: *Jet Li (Nameless), Tony Leung Chiu Wai (Broken Sword), Maggie Cheung (Flying Snow), Ziyi Zhang (Moon), Daoming Chen (King of Qin), Donnie Yen (Sky)*
Director: *Yimou Zhang*
Screenwriters: *Li Feng, Wang Bin, based on a story by Zhang Zhen Yan, Li Feng, Wang Bin*
12A/99 mins./Action/Martial Arts/Historical/Hong Kong/China

In third century BC China, a nameless assassin – or rather, an assassin called Nameless – visits a warlord to describe how he's killed three of the tyrant's most terrifying enemies. But the truth may not be as he says . . .

The comparisons are inevitable, so let's get them out of the way. Hero is a better film than *Crouching Tiger, Hidden Dragon*. Ang Lee's sword-centred melodrama was, for most, their first taste of wushu – a Chinese film and fiction genre which loosely translates as 'heroic warrior' – and it certainly delivered on the lyrical action front.

But there was always, for some at least, a slight inauthenticity to it; it felt like a faithful imitation of something much greater. It was like watching a competent remake when you hadn't seen the original.

Hero, though, is the real deal. Zhang Yimou, who has emerged as one of the East's most visually adventurous directors, and cinematographer Christopher Doyle have between them raised Joel Silver's famous action bar too high for Hollywood's current reach. Indeed, it's an irony that a helmer of the Fifth Generation (a school of directors defined by their exposure both to Western movies and new filmmaking technologies) should now have pushed the craft of action way beyond anything that commercially-driven Western cinema has so far delivered.

The comparison of fighting with dance is such a hoary old reviewer's standby that it's almost embarrassing to dust it off; but it's impossible not to think of ballet as Yimou's camera tracks his characters through their airborne slaughter, with bodies hanging against the sky in graceful, perfect compositions. The fights form a consummately sustained crescendo: a contest in a rain-drenched chess arena, daringly conducted mostly in the protagonists' minds, is followed by a frantic battle in an autumnal forest in which the blood-red duellists swoop among an orange blizzard of falling leaves, before Yimou abruptly switches the colour palette to greens and blues as the pair of assassins dance a pas de deux above the glassy waters of a placid lake.

But the visual invention doesn't stop at the mano-a-mano rucking. Doyle – a cinematographic genius who gratifyingly prefers to do most of his work while, as legend has it, moderately pissed – points his camera at hissing swarms of arrows which turn the sky black; a deathly game of hide-and-seek is acted out between apparently endless sheets of billowing green silk; and a scene in a library involves . . . Well, no description could do it justice. You've seen a lot, but you've never seen anything like this.

After all that, though, there's a slight but persistent niggle. Namely the plot. Despite a surprising – to Western minds at least – subtext in which the security and unifying force of totalitarianism is valued above putative democracy and individual freedom, *Hero*'s central story is as flimsy and soggy as damp rice-paper. An attempt to bolster the simplistic machinations with a multitude of perspectives feels a little forced and even dishonest.

Nameless (an impressively impassive Jet Li) tells his story to the Quin warlord who simply rejects it and makes another one up. While this conceit provides a swift excuse for another astonishing action sequence, you have to wonder exactly what right he has to do so, not actually having been there.

But maybe stories work differently in third century BC China, and this is not a film about plot anyhow. It's one about movement and colour and music. And rarely in any country's cinema will you see a film so wondrously charged with all three. ★★★★★ **WL**

HIDDEN (CACHE) (2005)

Starring: *Daniel Auteuil (Georges Laurent), Juliette Binoche (Anne Laurent), Maurice Benichou (Majid), Annie Girardot (Georges's Mom), Bernard Le Coq (Georges's Editor-in-Chief)*
Director: *Michael Haneke*
Screenplay: *Michael Haneke*
15/117 mins./Drama/Thriller/France/Austria/Germany/Italy

A TV book show host seems to have the perfect marriage. But cracks appear when he decides to act alone after he and his publisher wife begin receiving videotapes from a stalker who seems to know a great deal about their lives . . .

Nothing is ever as it seems in a Michael Haneke film. So disquiet sets in immediately when we're presented with a lingering, static shot of the house in which complacent bourgeois Daniel Auteuil and Juliette Binoche are raising their tweenage son. Sure enough, the image proves to be a surveillance tape, designed to alert Auteuil that the price for his idyllic existence is about to be exacted.

By creating sufficient suspicion of the culprit in Auteuil's mind, the film forces us to confront our own attitudes to the post-colonial world and the extent to which we are culpable for the actions of our governments. Yet this slow-burning study in forgotten guilt and suppressed prejudice also works as an intriguing thriller that keeps us as much in the dark as the increasingly apprehensive Binoche, whose dismay at Auteuil's revelations contrasts with the trusting sympathy of his bedridden mother, Annie Girardot.

Although slightly underemployed, Binoche produces a sensitive display of bemusement and betrayed trust. But Auteuil's affronted arrogance and latent malevolence are even more impressive, confirming his sheer cinematic class. ★★★★ **DP**

THE HIDDEN FORTRESS (KAKUSHI-TORIDE NO SAN-AKUNIN) (1958)

Starring: *Toshiro Mifune (General Rokurota Makabe), Misa Uehara (Princess Yuki), Kamatari Shimura (Matakishi), Taskashi Shimura (The Old General), Susumu Fujita (General Hyoe Tadokoro)*
Director: *Akira Kurosawa*
Screenwriters: *Ryuzo Kikushima, Hideo Oguni, Shinobu Hashimoto, Akira Kurosawa*
PG./137 mins./Action/Adventure/Japan

Having lost everything in a civil war, a 16th century feudal princess calls on one of her generals, whose force comprises two captured bumpkins, to escort her and a consignment of gold to safety across enemy territory.

This is a picture with one heck of a heritage. It belongs to the chambara style of swordplay movies that were almost ten a penny in 1950s Japan. But this is anything but generic filmmaking.

Although it's an original story, its structure and music are classic Noh, while its thematic roots lie in the Kabuki play *Kanjincho*. There are echoes of Fritz Lang's *Metropolis* in the slave revolt and Olivier's *Henry V* in the overall spirit of patriotic fervour. Yet *Hidden Fortress* also clearly demonstrates the director's love of John Ford Westerns, as this is basically a cavalry escort oater. All that's missing is Monument Valley, but the gnarled forest is a more than adequate stand-in.

It's also tempting to see the influence of the Hollywood epic on the proceedings, despite the fact the film opens with such an intimate distillation of the essence of civil war, as the bickering farmers long for reconciliation only after they've been taken into slavery. But pleasingly, there's none of Hollywood's blatant space-filling in Kurosawa's compositions.

The film's influence on swordplay actioners across the Orient is clear, with philosophical codas between the fight sequences. But there's also a touch of the Bollywood masala about it, with the fire festival resembling a lavish production number. Moreover, the debt owed by such recent films as *Asoka* is plainly evident. Yet its most significant spin-off is *Star Wars*. A princess and a warrior crossing enemy territory? Tin-plate the farmers and you're there. ★★★★ **DP**

HIDEOUS KINKY (1998)

Starring: *Kate Winslet (Julia), Said Taghmaoui (Bilal), Bella Riza (Bea), Carrie Mullan (Lucy), Pierre Clementi (Santoni), Abigail Cruttenden (Charlotte)*
Director: *Gillies MacKinnon*
Screenwriter: *Billy MacKinnon, based on the novel by Esther Freud*
15/98 mins./Drama/UK/France/Morocco

A mother decides to take her two young daughters to Morocco in search of adventure.

The popular appeal of Kate Winslet boosted the claims for attention of another beautifully observed work from Gillies MacKinnon, a slight but sweet adaptation of Esther Freud's semi-autobiographical novel. Liberated from the waist-clinching gowns and tragic, watery ordeals of her previous four films, a glowing Winslet is delightful, presenting a warm, amusing, touchingly vulnerable and untogether but admirably brave character.

In Marrakech in 1972, scatty hippie Julia, wreathed in a cloud of hashish smoke and draped in fetching Pre-Raphaelite kasbah tat, has fled a disappointing relationship and sad cold London, dragging her two little girls along on her quest for spiritual enlightenment and domestic freedom. Raising her two young daughters, six-year-old Lucy and eight-year-old Bea on a constant diet of ideals and oranges, however, doesn't appear in any child-rearing manuals and Julia becomes ever more torn between her desire for self-actualisation and the ties of responsibility. The children take whatever comes with aplomb and droll word games (the source of the film's title), although Bea is stubbornly sensible and English middle class, demanding a school uniform and longing for the prerequisites of the normal life she has left behind.

Poverty, the elusiveness of the imagined mystical fulfilment, cat fights with the exotic prostitute neighbours, disenchantment and a string of disasters make for a funny, sad and anxious odyssey in a slender, anecdotal tale. Julia's relationship with a charming Arab rogue, Bilal, adds sexual heat, charisma and, vitally, some dramatic backbone as his own story of woes and his increasingly dangerous efforts to help Julia and her daughters balances the girlish dynamic.

The two child actors are real finds – enchanting, eccentric and natural, a good match for Winslet who barely looks old enough to have given birth to them. Director MacKinnon nicely delineates the relationships and personalities while evoking a rich and fascinating atmosphere from the sumptuous and colourfully seedy backdrops of Morocco and a trippy 70s soundtrack that includes Love, Jefferson Airplane and Richie Havens. Culture clashes have seldom been more appealing. ★★★ **AE**

HIGH AND LOW (TENGOKU TO JIGOKU) (1963)

Starring: *Toshiro Mifune (Kingo Gondo), Tatsuya Bakadai (Inspector Tokura), Kyoko Kagawa (Reiko, Gondo's Wife), Tatsuya Mihashi (Kawanishi)*
Director: *Akira Kurosawa*
Screenwriters: *Akira Kurosawa, Hideo Oguni, Ryuzo Kikushima, Eijiro Hisaita based on the novel* King's Ransom *by Ed McBain*
12/142 mins./Thriller/Japan

Gondo uses the money saved to take over his shoe company to ransom his chauffeur's kidnapped son. However, the cops are soon on the trail of the culprit, Takeuchi, a heroin-dealing intern who insists on seeing Gondo before his execution.

Dante's *Divine Comedy* was a key influence on Akira Kurosawa's adaptation of Ed McBain's pulp thriller, *King's Ransom*. The Japanese title translated as Heaven and Hell and Kurosawa consciously used the film's structure and setting to reinforce the psychological and socio-economic links between the story's principal protagonists.

The initial segment was staged in Toshiro Mifune's luxurious house on a rock overlooking Yokohama, while the police pursuit of Tsutomu Yamazaki took place in the city below before finally descending into the labyrinthine alleyways of Chinatown. However, Kurosawa reinforced the contrast between the locations by varying his shooting style, passing from the long takes (with time shown as passing through a trio of wipes) employed inside Mifune's premises to the jerky movements of the tense train journey and thence to the abrupt, staccato sequences in which the detectives search for clues and finally apprehend their suspect.

Yet, Kurosawa wasn't simply shifting visual styles for atmospheric reasons. He also sought to challenge the audience by posing it an emotional moral dilemma before confronting it with the intellectual intrigue of a methodical police procedural.

However, he was also keen to utilise the comparisons between high and low, illusion and reality to suggest that, despite finding themselves on opposite sides of the law, Gondo and Takeuchi were surprisingly similar. This emphasis on deceptive appearance explains the constant references to cameras, binoculars, mirrors, spectacles, sunglasses and eyes, which culminates in the merger of the pair on the prison glass to show that all men are essentially equal and the only thing that really separates them are the choices they make in the depths of a crisis.

Superbly played by Mifune and Yamazaki and photographed with great virtuosity by Choichi Nakai and Takao Saito, this may not be one of Kurosawa's best-known features, but it's certainly among his most cinematic and satisfying. ★★★★ **DP**

HIGH ANXIETY (1977)

Starring: *Mel Brooks (Doctor Richard H. Thorndyke), Madeline Kahn (Victoria Brisbane), Cloris Leachman (Nurse Charlotte Diesel), Harvey Korman (Doctor Charles Montague)*
Director: *Mel Brooks*
Screenwriters: *Mel Brooks, Ron Clark, Rudy De Luca, Barry Levinson*
15/94 mins./Comedy/USA

After the previous head doctor is found dead, new recruit Doctor Richard H. Thorndyke arrives at the Psychoneurotic Institute for the Very, VERY Nervous, to find himself framed for murder. In order to clear his good name he must first overcome is own mental disorder – a bad case of 'high anxiety'.

Mel Brooks aims his comedic crosshairs at the copious body and body of work of one Alfred Hitchcock, a subject of limited possibilities, and you can feel the keenness of old, the rowdy but dead-on spoofery of *The Producers* or *Young Frankenstein*, slipping away from him. Hitch is a tough subject, his films rest on the verge of hysteria already, often being outright funny, hence the jags and jibes of Brooks' throw-it-all-out-there approach come across less astute – how do you parody material born on the borderline of satire? Much of this procession of garbled movie references cancels itself out.

And given the limited range of possible targets (the Western, for *Blazing Saddles*, was sprawling enough to offer multitudes of punchlines) the flabby script sinks into the predictable with failed riffs on the Psycho shower scene, *Vertigo* and *North By Northwest*. There are laughs, mainly due to the talent of the cast of Brooks regulars who once again traverse the absurd contours of his mania without cracking: Madeline Kahn and Cloris Leachman, following inspired work in *Young Frankenstein*, maintain that shrill perspicacity, offering a shrug to the audience. An inspired gag involving an embarrassed camera prowling into the wrong bedroom reminds you that when he clicks Brooks really clicks, but the hit rate is poor.

As with all great spoofers, you can feel the love the director has for Hitchcock, the thoroughness of his jokes vouches for that and the entire plot is loosely based on *Spellbound*. Perhaps he was too devoted, the film lacks daring, it's soft, Hitch would have sneered at such weakness. **★★ IN**

HIGH FIDELITY (2000)

Starring: *John Cusack (Rob), Iben Hjejle (Laura), Todd Louiso (Dick), Jack Black (Barry), Lisa Bonet (Marie De Salle), Catherine Zeta-Jones (Charlie), Joan Cusack (Liz), Tim Robbins (Ian), Chris Rehman (Vince), Bruce Springsteen (Himself)*
Director: *Stephen Frears*
Screenwriters: *D.V. Devincentis, Steve Pink, John Cusack, Scott Rosenberg, based on the novel by Nick Hornby*
15/107 mins./Comedy/USA

After a slow-to-commit record shop owner is dumped by his girlfriend, he goes in search of the five women who previously broke his heart.

It sounded like a duff idea on paper. Uprooting Nick Hornby's decidedly Brit 'n' blokey world-view to the throb of Chicago was riddled with the potential for disaster in the transatlantic crossing, with all the subtleties and textures blanded out. However, against the odds, director Frears and co. have fashioned a funny, involving smart meditation on the prattle of the sexes by retaining most of the incident and attitude of the novel and adding a broader, more accessible feel.

Attempting to capture the freewheeling approach of the book (the infamous 'top five ...' lists and all), Frears' heavy dependence on direct-to-camera addresses and voiceover jars initially – there are few actual meaty scenes to get your teeth into – denying emotional involvement. But, with Cusack's eminent likeability acting as a conduit, you eventually slide into the film's rhythms and get drawn into Rob's world. Little actually happens – Rob has a fling with rootsy singer Marie DeSalle, seeks emotional rescue from The Boss himself, Bruce Springsteen – but the patchwork plotting builds an insightful collage of emotional dreads, doubts and joys that plays to the head rather than the heart.

If this is decidedly Cusack's show, starting at hangdog desperation then expertly descending towards frenzy, the gallery of supporting characters still have enough room to make their mark – step forward a flamboyant Catherine Zeta-Jones and a needy Lili Taylor as Gordon's exes. Moreover, if slightly more 'pantomime' than the rest of the movie, Tim Robbins' cameo role as a Zen-obsessed love rival to Cusack ranks as a real crowdpleaser.

Away from the love stuff, High Fidelity is probably the best film about the joys of retail since *Clerks* hit our screens in 1994; very good on the muso conversations born out of boredom – musically the film neatly finds the American equivalents of Hornby's UK musical lexicon – the threeway dissing and compiling of tastes sparkles. Louiso is a funny, passive presence as the shy Dick, but it is Jack Black's sarcastic, aggressive Barry who practically steals the movie, the perfect antidote to John Cusack's navel gazing. **★★★★ IF**

HIGH HEELS (TACONES LEJANOS) (1991)

Starring: *Victoria Abril (Rebecca), Marisa Paredes (Becky del Paramo), Miguel Bose (Judge Dominguez), Anna Lizaran (Margarita), Mayrata O'Wisiedo (Judge's Mother)*
Director: *Pedro Almodovar*
Screenwriter: *Pedro Almodovar*
18/112 mins./Drama/Spain/France

A girl's mother returns after 15 years to find her daughter has married one of the mother's old boyfriends.

High Heels starts off in camp fashion with a title sequence straight out of the mid-60s Monty Berman school, promising lots more japes in Swinging Madrid.

Instead, however, we get a mother-daughter murder melodrama even more far-fetched than the Joan Crawford classic, *Mildred Pierce*, on which this would appear to be loosely based.

Almodovar, in his double role of writer-director, intensifies this clash of styles and audience preconceptions by locating a just-about naturalistic dissection of family tensions within a milieu which Joe Orton would relish, all lawmen in drag, transvestite bars, and lots of singing.

That the film works at all – and an unqualified triumph it ain't – is down mostly to his star Victoria Abril, who, with total plausibility, handles all the seemingly impossible curve-balls her director throws her way, including one outlandish yet weirdly realistic sex scene, a confession to murder both tragic and hilarious. **★★★ MS**

HIGH NOON (1952)

Starring: *Gary Cooper (Will Kane), Grace Kelly (Amy Kane), Thomas Mitchell (Jonas Henderson), Lloyd Bridges (Harvey Pell), Katy Jurado (Helen Ramierez), Lon Chaney Jr. (Martin Howe)*
Director: *Fred Zinnemann*
Screenwriter: *Carl Foreman, based on the story* Tin Star *by John W. Cunningham*
U/85 mins./Western/USA

Awards: *Academy Awards – Best Actor, Best Editing, Best Original Song, Best Drama/Comedy Score, Golden Globes – Best Black and White Cinematography, Best Drama Actor, Best Score, Best Supporting Actress (Kary Jurado)*

A retiring lawman about to leave town with his new bride seeks allies among the fearful townspeople when an outlaw he put in prison returns with his gang to take revenge.

High Noon is plainly About Something – as you can tell from the opening credits. Men like producer Stanley Kramer (*Inherit the Wind*, director Fred Zinnemann (*From Here to Eternity* and writer Carl Foreman (*Champion*) were strangers in the sagebrush, but had ambitions to make Academy Award-type pictures, movies that tried to deliver some sort of content along with the shoot 'em up stuff.

Gary Cooper, the top-billed star, was a familiar cowboy face with a Western drawl to match, but he was in his third decade as a revered movie star, a little elderly for the rough stuff and with acting chops to spare. The innovation of *High Noon* is that it's significant, but not big. Its understated but unforgettable opening – three bad men (Lee Van Cleef, Robert Wilkie, Sheb 'Flying Purple People Eater' Wooley) at the station, waiting around on a Sunday morning while Tex Hitter's ballad explains the plot – prefaces a movie that takes place almost in real time, from mid-morning to just after midday, and never strays far from the main street of the Western township of Hadleyville.

In the 1940s and 50s, high-stakes Westerns were inclined to the epic, with Technicolor mesas and deserts and hordes of cowboy and Indian extras, but *High Noon* could be a TV script. Its style is like that character-and-suspense-based drama which would evolve when American television was broadcast live from New York. The simmering resentment of sidelined Deputy Pell that his soon-to-be-ex boss, retiring Marshal Will Kane, didn't get him appointed the new law in town pays off with a fistfight at the halfway point, but otherwise the film is all about suspense rather than action. Guns aren't drawn in anger until the last five minutes, when the streets are clear for one of the best gun fights in the movies.

The plot nugget is that just as Kane has married Amy and handed in his star, Hadleyville learns that Frank Miller, the villain who used to run the place, has been pardoned by, 'them Northern politicians'. Miller is due in on the noon train to keep his promise to gun down the man who sent him to prison. Kane takes back the badge, but is shocked to learn no-one will stand by him: some of the townsfolk have gone soft since the wild days ended, others yearn for the lawlessness Miller will bring back, some resent Kane for real or imagined slights, others try to tell him it's not worth getting killed for people who won't stand up for themselves, and his new wife is a Quaker prepared to forsake him.

Cooper, in agony from a bad back during shooting, is remarkable, conveying the inner pain of a man who learns that his earlier heroism no longer counts. In effect, *High Noon* is a sequel to an unmade earlier film about the town-taming he-man and the baddie he bested. Many films based on the legend of Wyatt Earp – *Law and Order*, *Dodge City*, *Frontier Marshal*, *My Darling Clementine* – had told this story of the bringing of civilisation to the wilderness. Hadleyville is the neatest, most domesticated town in Western movies, complete with nice white church, opera house (Mazeppa is playing), trains that run on time and folks who can hardly remember, 'when it wasn't safe for a respectable woman to walk in daylight'. The film shows the happy endings of earlier Westerns were sham: the savage outlaws can come back at any time, and the extras who benefited from law and order decide they'd rather be kicked around by Miller than shot dead. This enraged Howard Hawks and John Wayne, who responded with *Rio Bravo*, in which a Marshal turns down offers of help because he's being paid to do a job and doesn't want innocents killed.

Tagline
The story of a man who was too proud to run.

Wayne was proud of getting the blacklisted Foreman kicked out of America in revenge for the 'un-American' gesture that ends *High Noon*, though when the Duke was handing Cooper a Best Actor Oscar he said he wished someone would write him a Western part as good as Will Kane. Many commentaries on *High Noon* have assumed that it's making a statement about the bullying tactics of Senator Joe McCarthy, which exposed a wide streak of gutlessness in many Hollywoodites. However, it's possible McCarthy might have seen the film as an endorsement – identifying with Cooper, a real-life supporter, and thinking of the townsfolk as the fellow travellers and liberals whining about his crusade against creeping subversives like Frank Miller.

The film pays off with four bad men deservedly dead, the Marshal (and his now gun-toting wife) still standing, the townsfolk hanging their heads in embarrassed shame, and (as in *Dirty Harry*, 1971) the badge tossed in the dirt. ★★★★ **KN**

HIGH PLAINS DRIFTER (1973)

Starring: *Clint Eastwood (The Stranger), Verna Bloom (Sarah Belding), Marianna Hill (Callie Travers), Mitch Ryan (Dave Drake), Jack Ging (Morgan Allen)*
Director: *Clint Eastwood*
Screenwriters: *Ernest Tidyman, Dean Riesner*
18/105 mins./Western/USA

A lone gunfighter, of no known name or origin, drifts into the frontier town of Lago. At first the townsfolk are fearful, trying to rid themselves of him, but when a band of outlaws hot for revenge are sighted, it is to this strange man they turn for help.

Having learned his craft at the right hand of Sergio Leone, Eastwood's first Western unsurprisingly owes much to the grandiose mythical stylings of the Spaghetti tradition. The ingredients could well have been carried on from some further adventure between the taciturn actor and the flamboyant Italian director: a cowboy, grizzled and uncommunicative, arrives in town unwilling to share his name; despite his amoral attitude he will come to assist the town in its fight against some no-good outlaws. Yet, as the film begins its unethical march, the differences in outlook and style between the two men as directors become swiftly apparent.

High Plains Drifter has none of Leone's exuberance, it is terse, shadowy, and gothic, as much a ghost story as anything else. The townsfolk, unusually self-serving and cowardly, did nothing to stop the death by whipping of their former marshal, and Eastwood's presence pointedly suggests this is his vengeful spirit returned from the grave; which makes good sense of his rather ethereal character (an idea revisited in *Pale Rider*). Of course, it was the sadistic outlaws who were responsible for the murder, so they're pretty much for it as well despite being framed by the locals. There's nary a drop of innocence hereabouts.

What the film does so eloquently, with a towering menace, is carry on Leone's work in dismantling the Western myth. The clear-cut morality of tradition finds no grip in this hardened, sunbaked hellhole – little wonder, upon seeing the film, John Wayne wrote Eastwood an indignant letter for violating, 'the spirit of the West'. He, of all people, would never grasp that that was exactly the point. Eastwood was absorbing the Vietnam era bitterness that suffused his country and injecting it into their most beloved ideal.

Up until the salutary nostalgia of *Unforgiven*, he never found another role shaped so precisely to the grim aspect of his features, there is nothing that will surprise anyone here, but it fits the dark rigour of the film's intentions. The landscape, so necessary a facet of the genre, crystallises Leone's operatic grandeur into an arid emptiness, the back end of nowhere set off by a beautiful blue lake like the promise of salvation. ★★★★ **IN**

HIGH SIERRA (1941)

Starring: *Ida Lupin (Marie Garson), Humphrey Bogart (Roy Earle), Alan Curtis (Baby Kozak), Arthur Kennedy (Red Hattery), Joan Leslie (Velma)*
Director: *Raoul Walsh*
Screenwriters: *John Huston, W.R. Burnett, based on Burnett's novel*
PG/100 mins./Crime/USA

Roy 'Mad Dog' Earle is sprung from jail by a political fixer and teamed with an inexperienced crew to pull a hotel heist. Earle uses the money to finance an operation for a teenage girl but finds romance with a tougher chick. The authorities pursue the hood into the mountains, where he makes a last stand.

Directed by Raoul Walsh, scripted by John Huston from W.R. Burnett's novel, *High Sierra* is the last of a gangster cycle inspired by the exploits of John Dillinger, Bonnie and Clyde and other Depression-era stick-up artists. Bogart, shining in his first lead role, is made up to look older than his years, stressing that this type of gangster is becoming as outmoded as the Western outlaws they have supplanted.

Though a few Cagney movies, particularly *Angels With Dirty Faces* and *The Roaring Twenties* (in which Bogart plays secondary hoods who get shot), had presented gangster heroes redeemed by self-sacrificing death, *High Sierra* is among the first films in which a criminal is presented as admirable because he is a professional – good at his job, and impatient with the loose cannon tearaways (Arthur Kennedy, Cornel Wilde) he has to work with. Earle has a Cagney-like streak of respect for decency, financing an operation to fix the crooked ankle of an innocent girl (Joan Leslie), but this doesn't turn out well: in a marvellously uncomfortable scene, the cured Leslie becomes a selfish, brittle tart with a thirty-year-old, slick-moustached divorcee boyfriend. Regular folks may have enviable security, but aren't worthy of respect. Earle forms relationships only with Pard, a dog who turns out to be a jinx (the thug-and-his-dog sentimentality is undercut because Pard finally gets Earle killed), and 'taxi dancer' Marie (Ida Lupino, top-billed), 'who has more nerve than most men'. ★★★★ **KN**

HIGH SOCIETY (1956)

Starring: *Bing Crosby (C.K. Dexter-Haven), Grace Kelly (Tracy Lord), Frank Sinatra (Mike Connor), Celeste Holm (Liz Imbrie), John Lund (George Kittredge), Louis Armstrong (Himself)*
Director: *Charles Walters*
Screenwriter: *John Patrick, based on the play* The Philadelphia Story *by Philip Barry*
U/107 mins./Musical/Comedy/USA

The ex-husband of rich and beautiful socialite Tracey Lord tries to win her back on the eve of her wedding to another man.

As a remake of *The Philadelphia Story*, *High Society* has problems. Bing Crosby and Grace Kelly are wonderful, but look more like father and daughter than a divorced couple; and plodder Charles Walters isn't up to George Cukor when it comes to mixing the sweet and tart ingredients of a great screwball comedy.

But, chances are you won't care because, as a Cole Porter musical, *High Society* is nigh-unbeatable. It matches Bing with Frank Sinatra in 'Well, Did You Evah', establishes what everyone in 1956 would think of as 'our song' in Crosby's 'True Love', allows Celeste Holm a shot at immortality duetting with Frankie on 'Who Wants To Be A Millionaire?' and hauls in Louis Armstrong to act as singing Greek chorus on the title song 'Now You Has Jazz'. It's sensational. ★★★★ **CK**

HIGHLANDER (1986)

Starring: *Christopher Lambert (Connor 'The Highlander' MacLeod/Russell Edwin Nash), Roxanne Hart (Brenda J. Wyatt), Clancy Brown (Victor Kruger/The Kurgan), Sean Connery (Juan Sanchez Villa-Lobos Ramirez), Celia Imrie (Kate MacLeod)*
Director: *Russell Mulcahy*
Screenwriters: *Gregory Wilden, Peter Bellwood, Larry Ferguson, based on a story by Gregory Widen*
15/116 mins./Action/Fantasy/USA/UK

Connor MacLeod is one of a dwindling society of immortal human beings who are killing each other off on the grounds that the last survivor will attain great power. Over the centuries, Connor is tutored by another immortal, Ramirez, and battles a villain, the Kurgan.

Immortal Scotsman Lambert, with a French accent, is tutored in the ways of living forever and chopping off heads by equally immortal Egyptian Sean Connery, with a Spanish costume and a Scots accent, in Russell Mulcahy's daft swashbuckling fantasy.

Living the life of a retiring antiques dealer in the present day, Lambert is pursued by Clancy Brown, a bad guy immortal who used to be a barbarian warrior and is now a leather-clad punk thug. In the meantime, he flashes back to his earlier life, when Connery was around to brighten up the scenery and he first discovered the pain of staying young while all your friends grow old and die (or have their heads chopped off).

Despite a script that makes about as much sense as a Japanese cartoon, this is great fun as it hops across history between war-torn Scotland and modern New York, with Brown doing his best to decapitate all the good guys and Lambert broodingly trying to save the world.

Stunning visuals from video clipmeister Mulcahy, a hilariously camp score by Queen (even weirder than their Flash Gordon work), lots of overdirected sword fights with bizarre lightning effects and plentiful head-severing, this guarantees an hour and a half of amazement leavened with just enough humour to let it get away with plot holes you could get the Isle of Skye through. Though the apt slogan was 'There Can Be Only One', sequels and TV spin-offs were unwisely attempted and continue to this day. ★★★ **KN**

HIGHLANDER II: THE QUICKENING (1991)

Starring: *Sean Connery (Juan Sanchez Villa-Lobos Ramirez), Virginia Madsen (Louise Marcus), Christopher Lambert (Connor MacLeod), Michael Ironside (Gen. Katana), John C. McGinley (David Blake)*
Director: *Russell Mulcahy*
Screenwriter: *Peter Bellwood, based on a story by Brian Clemens, William N. Panzer and characters by Gregory Widen*
15/91 mins./Action/Sci-fi/France/UK/Argentina

In Argentina in 2024, ex-immortal Connor MacLeod rejuvenates in order to battle General Katana, dictator of the immortals' home planet Zeist.

A totally incoherent sequel to the imaginative but not exactly perfect original, scripted by a post-*Avengers* Brian Clemens who tries to rewrite the premise of *Highlander* by demonstrating that the Earthly immortal head-choppers we came to know and love last time are in fact aliens transplanted from a planet with one of the silliest-sounding names in the cosmos since *The Brain From Planet Arous*.

Michael Ironside plays a would-be dictator of the universe who can only summon two evil followers to back him up in his scheme to lop off Lambert's head, Sean Connery is dragged back from death at great expense for a bare-faced cameo, and Virginia Madsen wonders what the hell she's got into as the bewildered heroine.

With a plot that swallows itself and a series of confusing story premises (including MacLeod's big gadget to fix the ozone layer), this prompts director Russell Mulcahy, who graduated from promising to has-been without passing through success, to tired visual fireworks.

It's a mystery of movie-star charisma that Connery has been appearing in films as bad as this for decades (*The Avengers*, *A Good Man in Africa*, *Just Cause*, *First Knight*, *League of Extraordinary Gentlemen*) without becoming as big a laughing stock as Michael Winner.

Further *Highlander* sequels and spin-offs are more sensible, if bland and unremarkable: Lambert duels Mario Van Peebles in *Highlander III: The Sorcerer*, and teams up with Adrian Paul of the TV spin-off in *Highlander: Endgame*, with Paul taking over for *Highlander: The Source*. Also cluttering up the rental racks are *Highlander: The Gathering* (with a Lambert cameo) and *Highlander: Reunion*, which are mock features manufactured from stuck-together TV episodes. ★ **KN**

⦿ THE HILLS HAVE EYES (1977)

Starring: *Susan Lanier (Brenda Carter), Robert Houston (Bobby Carter), Virginia Vincent (Ethel Carter), Russ Grieve (Bob Carter), Dee Wallace Stone (Lynne Wood)*
Director: *Wes Craven*
Screenwriter: *Wes Craven*
18/89 mins./Horror/Thriller/USA

A family going to California accidentally goes through an Air Testing range closed to the public. They crash in a desert and find themselves stalked by a group of mysterious people as they try to find a way back to civilisation.

Anyone who experienced the shattering impact of Craven's early movies probably feels the director of the first and last *Elm Street* movies and the *Scream* franchise (not to mention *Music Of The Heart*) has become a somewhat sedate, avuncular figure. Freddy and *Scream*'s Ghostface are pantomime monsters, comfortably removed from our lives; Krug and Company, the villains of *Last House*, and Papa Jupe's brood, the cannibals in The Hills, are not so fast with the wisecracks. They go for all-out savagery in ways a contractually-mandated R rating just won't allow.

Last House is a gore movie remake of Ingmar Bergman's *The Virgin Spring*, but *The Hills Have Eyes* has no truck with art. Craven's script was inspired by Sawney Beane, a mythical/legendary Scottish cannibal whose clan preyed on unwary visitors to his highland domain, and the original draft was set after a cataclysmic breakdown of society. However, *Hills* is really a mutant Western with the wagon train of pioneers replaced by an Ohio family in a trailer, and attacking Indians transformed into a brood of inbred mutants sired by the monstrous, split-faced Papa Jupiter (Whitworth). They dress like a combination of Indian warriors, Ben Gunn and the hillbillies from *Deliverance*.

Most horror movies are about claustrophobia (even the *The Texas Chain Saw Massacre* is mostly set inside an old dark house) but this uses the wide-open desert spaces of an old nuclear testing range, where camouflaged creatures blend with the rocks and the broken-down trailer is a dot in a vast and hostile landscape. Like the 70s films of George Romero, Larry Cohen and Tobe Hooper, *Hills* is torn between Vietnam/Watergate-era cynicism and a commitment to being gruesome that owes much to the much-banned EC comics of the 1950s (Tales From The Crypt, The Vault Of Horror). As in *Last House On The Left* and *The Texas Chain Saw Massacre*, a family of whitebread Americans is set against a parallel clan of grotesques who torture, slaughter and consume the innocents. The city folks are a Brady Bunch of good-looking, bland blondes in pastel clothes. The most recognisable is Dee Wallace (*The Howling*, *E.T.*) as a young mum in yellow flares, while husband Martin Speer bears a disturbing resemblance to Sonny Bono.

The degenerates are barely seen in the first hour of the film, and are all the more horrible for it. Tall, bald, crag-faced Michael Berryman (a veteran of *One Flew Over The Cuckoo's Nest*), is poster-boy Pluto, but he's comic relief next to his brothers Mercury (Arthur King) and Mars (Lance Gordon). As in *Last House* and *Deliverance*, the message is that the middle classes, because they have more to lose, are capable of more extreme violence than the have-not outcasts. 'A typical American family', read the original poster, 'they didn't want to kill, but they didn't want to die.' Horrible atrocities are inflicted on the Carters (Big Bob is crucified, burned and decapitated) and Jupe's boys threaten to gut, cook and eat the stolen baby. But in the end, it's the savagery of the good guys that shocks, especially when Barbie and Ken teens Brenda and Bobby use their mother's dead body as bait to trap Jupiter, and the family's dog Beast avenges the murder of his mate Beauty by dispatching two of Jupiter's boys.

Tagline
The lucky ones died first...

Decades on *The Hills Have Eyes* no longer seems quite as breathlessly swift as it did. But it retains an air of low-budget reality: no costume designer with an eye for fashion-house product placement came up with the gear the Carters wear, and the interiors of both the trailer and Jupiter's cave are cluttered with the authentic detritus of messy lives. Like most great splatter movies, it's less violent than you remember – the curl of smoke rising from Big Bob's dead mouth and the jagged bone Beast exposes in Pluto's ankle are exceptions – but it always hits the unease button. These days, Craven looks back at his early films and wonders where the anger came from. ★★★★ **KN**

⦿ THE HILLS HAVE EYES (2006)

Starring: *Aaron Stanford (Doug), Ted Levine (Big Bob), Kathleen Quinlan (Ethel), Vinessa Shaw (Lynn), Emilie de Ravin (Brenda), Dan Byrd (Bobby), Desmond Askew (Big Brain)*
Director: *Alexandre Aja*
Screenwriters: *Alexandre Aja, Gregory Levasseur, based on the 1977 screenplay by Wes Craven*
18/107 mins./Horror/USA

Suburban family the Carters — Mom, Pop, their son, daughters, son-in-law, baby granddaughter and two dogs — are travelling through the Nevada desert to San Diego when they fall foul of a psychopathic family of cannibals, mutated by long-ago US military atomic tests on their home town. As the tagline says, the lucky ones die first . . .

When Alexandre Aja first submitted his remake of Wes Craven's 1977 grot-horror to US censors for classification, it was so violent, so gory, so outré – that's French for 'out there' – that it came back with the dreaded, box-office-death NC-17 rating. Yet, about 40 minutes in, you may be wondering what all the fuss was about. Apart from a brutal but brief pre-credits killing spree, Aja (whose French debut *Switchblade Romance* was fairly drenched in claret) has been remarkably restrained, allowing us time to get to know our heroes and, through creeping camerawork and a pseudo-John Carpenter score, establishing a feeling of scuttling, paranoid dread.

Slow burns, though, tend to be followed by loud bangs, and that's what we have as Aja orchestrates the sequence that got the MPAA's knickers in a twist: the mutants' assault on the Carters' trailer. It's a gruelling, blistering 15-minute ordeal that starts with the immolation of one character, ends with the death-by-gunshot of two more, and in between slots in some horrifying sexual degradation. Events play out in much the same way as they did in the original, but Aja cranks up the tension and the viscera. The sequence is not only unmatched by the rest of the movie, but places *The Hills Have Eyes* firmly in the new so-called 'horror porn' movement, along with the works of Park Chan-wook and Eli Roth's *Hostel* (with which this shares several characteristics).

Although Aja half-heartedly bungs in a few jump moments and, more gallingly, some old-as-the-hills-have-eyes clichés (Craven, who produced, must have had his back turned), his movie isn't out-and-out scary. That's the point of horror porn, where the emphasis is instead placed on suffering, on a downbeat mood and on pushing the boundaries of screen violence. In that sense, Aja's remake succeeds, especially in a bloodsoaked climax as the human survivors hit back at their unspeakable tormentors.

But for those who hailed the French helmer as the best thing to hit horror since sliced teenagers, *The Hills Have Eyes* has to count as a step backwards. The best of the recent rash of 70s horror remakes was Zack Snyder's *Dawn Of The Dead*, which reconceptualised the original as an action flick. Aja's movie isn't so bold, treading contentedly along in the 77 version's bloody footprints while adding nothing substantial apart from a rather heavy-handed post-9/11 subtext. It's a shame, because this match-up of horror's old master and young pretender really should have led to something great. ★★★ **CH**

THE HIRED HAND (1971)

Starring: *Peter Fonda, Warren Oates, Vern Bloom, Severn Darden*
Director: *Peter Fonda*
Screenwriter: *Alan Sharp*
12/92 mins./Drama/USA

The simple story of drifter Harry, who, following years in the Wild West wilderness with partner Arch, tries to reconnect with his estranged wife.

Peter Fonda's dated but fascinating 1971 directorial debut is an undiscovered treat. Made in that post-*Easy Rider*/pre-*Star Wars* golden age of Hollywood, the film is shot through with the languid pace, realistic characters and rejection of convention that marked out the early 70s. Lyrically lensed by Altman cinematographer Vilmos Zsigmond, it is a film marinated in melancholy.

Although it moves inexorably towards violence as Harry's past catches up with him, the gunfights are swift, brutal and believable, never descending into the realms of Peckinpah excess. And, if for no other reason, this is a glorious excuse to take in the genius of Warren Oates. ★★★★ **IF**

HIROSHIMA, MON AMOUR (1959)

Starring *Emmanuelle Riva (She), Eiji Okada (He), Stella Dassas (Mother), Pierre Barbaud (Father), Bernard Fresson (German Soldier)*
Director: *Alain Resnais*
Screenwriter: *Marguerite Duras*
PG/88 mins./Drama/France/Japan

A French actress in Hiroshima to make a film about peace has an affair with a married Japanese architect that reawakens memories of her romance in wartime Nevers with a German soldier.

In 1957, Alain Resnais was approached by some Franco-Japanese producers to make a film exploring life in Hiroshima since the dropping of the atomic bomb in August 1945. Unwilling to repeat the formula employed in his Holocaust masterpiece, *Night and Fog*, Resnais asked novelist Marguerite Duras to collaborate on a piece in which the 'atomic agony' was a facet of the action rather than its fulcrum. What resulted was the first truly modernist feature. But while its release in 1959 coincided with the launch of auteur cinema, this was very much a collaborative effort, with Sacha Vierny and Michio Takahashi's location photography being intricately linked by Henri Colpi's editorial team and sensitively complemented by Giovanni Fusco and Georges Delerue's contrasting musical contributions.

This is a film about memory, experience and representation. But rather than tackle their themes in a traditionally linear manner, Resnais and Duras borrowed the Proustian idea of involuntary association to create what Resnais called 'a sort of poem in which the images would act as counterpoint to the text'. Thus, Emmanuelle Riva is able to recall her past via a subliminal flash cut between the hands of her sleeping Japanese lover and his dying German counterpart and similar instances of metaphoric logic dictate that her recollections continue to intrude upon her present for the remainder of her stay.

In order to achieve this temporal and spatial dislocation, Resnais had to devise a new film grammar and the viewer has to concentrate throughout to make the links between events in occupied France and liberated Japan. Thus, he juxtaposed scenes of her post-collaborationist suffering with the tragedies that befell Hiroshima and Nagasaki and, in the process, he succeeded in questioning both the nature of narrative truth and the reliability of remembrance. In this regard, his use of clips from Hideo Sekigawa's dramatic reconstruction Hiroshima are particularly contentious, as, rather than urging us to learn from the lessons of history, Resnais seems to be suggesting that the only way in which humanity can cope with the atrocities it has perpetrated and endured is continuously to forget. ★★★★★ **DP**

Alain Resnais (born 1922)

Who he is: Major French director, more properly of the Second Wave than the New Wave.
Hallmarks: Tinkering with chronology; listlessly wealthy characters; enigmatic and circular conversations; formal beauty.
If you see one movie, see: *Last Year At Marienbad* (1961)

HIS GIRL FRIDAY (1940)

Starring: *Cary Grant (Walter Burns), Rosalind Russell (Hildy Johnson), Ralph Bellamy (Bruce Baldwin), Gene Lockhart (Sheriff Hartwell), Helen Mack (Mollie Malloy)*
Director: *Howard Hawks*
Screenwriter: *Charles Lederer, based on the play by Ben Hecht, Charles MacArthur*
U/92 mins./Comedy/USA

A newspaper editor uses every trick in the book to keep his ace reporter ex-wife from remarrying.

The normal rate of dialogue delivery in a movie has been estimated at 90 words per minute. In *His Girl Friday*, the exquisite verbal sparring between Gary Grant and Rosalind Russell has been clocked at 240 wpm. To coin a sporting analogy, that's like Patrick Rafter and Andre Agassi playing a rally so fast the crowd can't even see the ball. This isn't merely snappy, it's hypersonic. People can get hurt talking that fast. 'He looks like that actor fellah,' says Grant at one point, describing his ex-wife's fiancé. 'Ralph Bellamy!' The cast is three pages down the line before you remember that Ralph Bellamy plays Grant's ex-wife's fiancé.

The movie is an adaptation of Ben Hecht and Charles MacArthur's Broadway hit *The Front Page*, first filmed by Lewis Milestone in 1931 and later, with a surprising dearth of charm, by Billy Wilder in 1974. It opens in the newsroom of *The Chicago Morning Post* where Hildy Johnson, star reporter and ex-wife of editor-in-chief Walter Burns, has dropped by to deliver a message. Burns is involved in a frenetic telephone conversation. He, we learn, in a matter seconds, is a man who is used to getting his own way. Right now he is not getting it. *The Post* has been campaigning for the reprieve of convicted murderer Earl Williams and it's obvious that the Governor is refusing to play ball. Williams is due to hang the following day.

Enter Hildy with more bad news. Tomorrow she's getting married to mild-mannered insurance salesman Bruce Baldwin and is giving up the newspaper business for good. On the spot Burns launches into a campaign of breathtaking off-the-cuff audacity to get the woman he loves back into his life and back on the company payroll. In this scene and the one that follows it (the famous restaurant scene) Grant is unstoppable, a whirlwind conglomeration of every great role he ever played. It's hard to imagine an actress other than Russell who would not have been blown clear off the screen.

Hildy has left Bruce stranded on the wrong side of the newsroom's No Admittance rail telling him she'll be 'back in ten minutes.' But as soon as she crosses that boundary we know she's back where she belongs. And from the opening burst of rapid-fire repartee with Burns, it's abundantly clear that she will never get on the train with poor plodding Bruce. She puts up a good fight though, proving herself the only worthy adversary in Burns' orbit. But it's all foreplay. Walter deploys every ounce of steamroller charm at his disposal, manipulating the situation with the lightning fast cunning of a born shyster. Baiting the hook with the Williams case (he knows deep down she's got ink in her veins) and running rings round the hapless Bruce he gradually reels Hildy in.

Hawks was a great admirer of Hecht and MacArthur's play (Hecht collaborated with Hawks many times), and of Milestone's film. It was Hawks, not writer Charles Lederer who came up with the idea of making Hildy Johnson a woman. In the original the character is a man. He left the backbone of the plot intact (Walter Burns' scheme to keep his reporter on the team, while orchestrating the release of a wrongly accused murderer), but with his unfailing eye for character, Hawks put a dazzlingly fresh shine on the old chestnut. It is the knockdown drag-out romance that sprinkles *His Girl Friday* with magic.

Grant and Russell dominate proceedings to such an extent, however, it appears as if Hawks could hardly be bothered with anything else. Not renowned for throwing the camera around at the best of times, here he nails it to the studio floor and leaves it running. The sets are overtly stagey too. The newsroom, which should be a tumult of cynical bustle, awash with boot-nosed hacks chomping stogies and barking copy out of the unoccupied corners of their mouths, is determinedly flat and sparsely populated. But by the same token, Hawks' legendarily unobtrusive direction here achieves its apotheosis. Everything in the movie is in thrall to Grant and Russell. The cuts are crisp and decisive and the static camera faithfully documents every spellbinding syllable.

Hawks has been credited with inventing the overlapping dialogue that accentuates the film's dizzying pace. He purloined it from a 1932 Frank Capra movie, *American Madness*. His spin was to add ancillary words to the beginning and end of sentences so that even though it sounds as if Grant and Russell are jabbering away simultaneously, the gags register on an almost subliminal level.

Ultimately, though, it was Hawks' willingness to sit back and let his lead actors'genius for comic timing carry the day that imbues *His Girl Friday* with its inexhaustible energy. Sixty years on it still makes *When Harry Met Sally* look like *Waiting For Godot*. In mime ★★★★★ **SB**

A HISTORY OF VIOLENCE (2005)

Starring: *Viggo Mortensen (Tom Stall), Maria Bello (Edie Stall), Ed Harris (Carl Fogerty), William Hurt (Richie Cusack), Ashton Holmes (Jack Stall)*
Director: *David Cronenberg*
Screenwriter: *Josh Olson, based on the graphic novel by John Wagner and Vince Locke*
18/96 mins./Drama/Thriller/USA

Small-town restaurant owner Tom Stall becomes a local hero when he shoots and kills two hoodlums. But soon after Carl Fogaty arrives in town convinced that Tom is a violent gangster with debts to pay back in Philly. Meanwhile the violence begins to engulf the family.

Even David Cronenberg fans will have to admit that the director's output has been variable of late. After the *Daily Mail* fomented brouhaha over *Crash* he seemed to find it difficult to find a project that fully engaged him. *Existenz* had the odd nice idea but the slightly mildewed feeling of grandad discovering there was somewhere called virtual reality a decade after everyone else had moved on, while many found *Spider* maddeningly abstruse. *A History Of Violence* is a confident return to form and his most accessible film since *The Fly*, delivering what is in essence a comic-book fable heavily influenced by Westerns, but sneaking the familiar Cronenbergian themes in through the back door.

On the surface *History* bears more than a passing resemblance to *Straw Dogs* in its tale of Tom Stall, an apparently peaceful man forced to take action when he and his family are threatened first by a pair of psycho hillbillies and then by a set of hoods from Philly headed up by Ed Harris.

Cronenberg doesn't do much to disguise the story's genesis as a graphic novel, painting the characters and locals in broad pop-cinema strokes that sometimes sit (deliberately) uneasily with the sudden, explosive violence and leaving the audience uncomfortable about how to react – when the movie screened in Cannes an audience laugh provoked one irritated viewer to yell 'Stop laughing you fucking piece of shit critics and take this film seriously!'

The fact is you can, and are probably meant to do both as lurking underneath the plot mechanics and gory set pieces (surprisingly well wrought from a director whose ideas are often superior to his technical skills) are Cronenberg's usual concerns: violence is seen as a contagion, arriving like a virus uninvited into the family's lives, slowly infecting each of them: Stall's son winds up putting a school bully in hospital, the couple's sex life mutates from the eroticism of an early sex scene to something darker and more sadistic in a subsequent one. Meanwhile, like Seth Brundle in *The Fly* or Max Renn in *Videodrome*, Tom Stall is a man caught in the midst of a horrifying metamorphosis that he is powerless to control – from family man to professional killer.

Cronenberg's film quietly challenges your reactions to the violence as you enjoy it and its enigmatic, haunting final scene is as much about its audience as about the characters on screen. ★★★★ **AS**

THE HITCHER (1986)

Starring: *C. Thomas Howell (Jim Halsey), Rutger Hauer (John Ryder), Jennifer Jason Leigh (Nash), Jeffrey DeMunn (Captain Esteridge), John M. Jackson (Sergeant Starr). Billy Green Bush (Trooper Donner)*
Director: *Robert Harmon*
Screenwriter: *Eric Red*
18/97 mins./Thriller/USA

While transporting a car across the desert, Jim Halsey finds himself stalked by a relentless serial killer and framed for his very murders. With both cops and the killer on his tail, only a lonely truck-stop waitress believes his innocence. And only they can finally stop the killings.

A highly effective little serial killer thriller set on the lonely highways of the mid-West and featuring the icy stare of Rutger Hauer, the best Hannibal Lecter that never was. With this low budget hybrid of horror and action, the skill is in generating a taut atmosphere, and the endless plains of Middle America so shorn from civilisation make for the ideal breeding ground for motiveless murder. Robert Harmon utilises such emptiness to fine effect, there is just nowhere to run to, and his film has a relentless nastiness that propels it into apparent realms of the supernatural even as it stays resolutely earthbound.

Despite its rigid and efficient script – boy picks up lunatic hitchhiker and starts a cat and mouse game where the trail of bodies could lead to either of them – Harmon delivers it with the singsong feel of a dark fairytale in which Hauer is the bogeyman of myth and the tracks of New Mexico become the inversion of Freud's nightmare forest: glaringly bright but equally as unwelcoming. The sheer indestructibility of Hauer's killer happily reminds you of James Cameron's stark *Terminator* and slasher-gem *Halloween*, two films which effectively blurred genre boundaries.

Yet, it's also to its credit that the film never oversteps its purposes. There are no flamboyant ripples of gothic dialogue for the bad guy, his evil is born in remorseless action, and the transformation of Jim from a genial nobody into a reflection of the killer himself (in order to stop him) has the vital resonance of survival. You could read the film as a rather violent rites-of-passage. What it's not is a film of superheroics or mastermind detection being doggedly primal and upfront. A duel, also reminiscent of Spielberg's highway horror movie, where the killer is simply waiting for his opponent to be worthy enough to stop him. ★★★★ **IN**

HITCH (2005)

Starring: *Will Smith (Alex 'Hitch' Hitchens), Eva Mendes (Sara), Kevin James (Albert), Amber Valletta (Allegra Cole), Julie Ann Emery (Casey)*
Director: *Andy Tennant*
Screenwriter: *Kevin Bisch*
12/118 mins./Comedy/Romance/USA

A professional matchmaker's programme is threatened by a female journalist who plans on publishing an exposé on his methods.

So synonymous is Will Smith with the summer blockbuster that to see him stray out of the balmier months without his steely action face seems like trespass. He should be holed up somewhere building his prodigious biceps and practising ways of shouting 'sonofabitch'. Yet here he's laying down the guns and giving his goofier side a workout, one which has not been seen in full force since the first *Men In Black*, and it begs the question of why he doesn't indulge in action-free comedy more often.

While certainly not Smith at his best, this has him at his funniest in quite some time, sending up his slick persona as a usually unflappable smoothy who loses all poise when he tries to put his own dating advice into practice with Mendes' ballsy journalist. His ability to maintain a shiver of cool in the face of the ridiculous is a skill unmatched by any other Hollywood actor and makes him constantly watchable even when the material, as is often the case here, requires a little more polish.

It helps that he's ably supported by the extended cast. Sara is no stereotypical fiery latina, thanks to Mendes playing her as equally sexy and silly, happy to pratfall as the role demands. She's not as skilled as Smith comedically but certainly puts herself among the higher end of the current (fairly thin) crop of laugh-drawing leading ladies. Best, though, is the rotund love-loser Albert, played by US TV star Kevin James, of the underrated sitcom *King Of Queens*.

His propensity to do exactly the wrong thing in his wooing of ridiculously out-of-his-league company boss Allegra (supermodel Amber Valletta) produces moments of broad comedy tinged with pathos and contain far more heart than the clashing of equals in the Smith/Mendes match-up. It's a shame this B-list relationship is also relegated to B-list status in terms of screen time. Hitch won't likely become a highlightable entry on the CVs of any of the actors, given that, for all its cast-generated sparkle, it is resolutely middle of the road, but as disposable comedy that elicits far more giggles than groans, this delivers everything expected of it with cheerful likeability. ★★★ **OR**

THE HITCHIKER'S GUIDE TO THE GALAXY (2005)

Starring: *Martin Freeman (Arthur Dent), Mos Def (Ford Prefect), Zooey Deschanel (Trillain), Sam Rockwell (Zaphod Beeblebrox), Stephen Fry (Narrator/The Guide)*
Director: *Garth Jennings*
Screenwriters: *Douglas Adams, Karey Kirkpatrick, based on the book by Adams*
PG/109 mins./Sci-fi/Comedy/USA/UK

Arthur Dent's home is about to be destroyed to make way for a bypass. Not just his house, mind, but his planet, too. Our planet. You know. Earth. Luckily, his best friend, Ford, reveals himself to be an alien contributor to bestselling intergalactic book – *A Hitchhiker's Guide to the Galaxy*, and whisks Arthur off on a space-based adventure.

DON'T PANIC, fervent Douglas Adamites. This movie adaptation of the TV adaptation of the novelisation of the radio series is about as faithful as you can get. Yes, it's been tweaked and twizzled, with a romance inserted here, a new character plopped down there, but everything you love about *The Hitchhiker's Guide To The Galaxy* remains intact – not to mention reinvigorated by its big-screen reincarnation.

Over the years, the cinematic *Hitchhiker*'s has almost been an Ivan Reitman movie, a Jay Roach movie and a Spike Jonze gig, but debut director Garth Jennings, one half of the duo Hammer & Tongs, proves to be a savvy choice. Like many Hollywood tyros, this born-and-bred Brit is a former commercials/music-vid megaphoner, but with his CV bolding up the likes of Blur's 'Coffee And TV' (you know, that oft-copied one with little milk-carton man) and those Johnny Vegas/Monkey ads, it's clear he's going to be more Jonze than McG, with a sense of humour to match the source material.

While Terry Gilliam's *Brazil* and Luc Besson's *The Fifth Element* are obvious influences, Jennings consciously avoids turning Adams' idiosyncratic, philosophically tongue-in-cheek cosmos into a slick, CG-caressed mega-verse, instead maintaining that view of what's Out There as being pretty much the same as what's Down Here. Only bigger. And infinitely more daft, packed with the kind of alien races that invented underarm deodorant before the wheel, or whose poetry is so bad they use it as a form of torture. Jennings even subverts that sci-fi visual staple, the epic reveal. His Earth-surface-to-outer-orbit pull-back, which unveils the immensity of the planet-trashing Vogon fleet, isn't some portentous, graceful reverse-glide – it's a winking series of jump-cuts. When George Lucas sees that, he'll choke on his pan-galactic gargleblaster.

It's happy, it's scrappy, it embraces the aesthetic of lo-fi Brit TV sci-fi (including, yes, the BBC's *Hitchhiker*'s telly series, referenced here in several cameos and tributes) while rarely looking like it's being unintentionally cut-rate. In one scene, we see the main cast transformed into Clangers-style knitted dolls. In another, a queue of bureaucratically trammelled extra-terrestrials are shamelessly presented like *Doctor Who* rejects. Meanwhile, the Guide itself (silkily voiced by Stephen Fry) hasn't been transmogrified into some shimmering, holo-device; it's still a book-sized slab which illustrates its advice using kitschy 2-D animations. Occasionally, when this cheap, cheerful feel infects the editing, it does veer into messiness, and one or two gags become lost in the mix. But what the hell – that's what repeat viewings are for.

There's no faulting the cast. Martin Freeman (aka Tim from *The Office*) is an inspired choice for the bleary Arthur, as perpetually rumpled as his character's never-divested dressing gown, a perfectly mundane everyman struggling to comprehend both the immensity and the stupidity of the universe beyond. He's also capable of dealing with the (added) romantic element with Trillian (a luminous Zooey Deschanel) without allowing a flicker of schmaltz into the film. Mos Def retains all of Ford Prefect's aloof nerdiness while affirming his own impeccable comic timing, Alan Rickman's nasal grumbles are spot-on for manically depressed robot Marvin, and if Sam Rockwell's hyperactive, self-kidnapping galactic president Zaphod Beeblebrox is annoying, that's because Zaphod's an inherently irritating creation anyway.

As we said, those hardcore Hitchhikers out there have little to worry about. Although they should be warned that the movie's faithfulness means all its best jokes will be very familiar. For them, it's more a case of basking comfortably in the nostalgia than laughing out loud. But if you're new to all this, and have no idea about the significance of towels, or what a whale and a bowl of petunias have in common, then, boy, are you in for a treat ... ★★★ **DJ**

⊙ THE HOLE (2001)

Starring: *Thora Birch (Liz Dunn), Desmond Harrington (Mike Steel), Laurence Fox (Geoff Bingham), Keira Knightley (Frances 'Frankie' Almond Smith), Embeth Davidtz (Dr. Philippa Horwood), Gemma Craven (Mrs. Dunn)*
Director: *Nick Hamm*
Screenwriters: *Ben Court, Caroline Ip, based on the novel* After The Hole *by Guy Burt*
18/102 mins./Crime/Drama/Horror/UK

Deeply traumatised after two weeks of being trapped in a remote underground bunker with three classmates, Liz blames fellow student Martin for their imprisonment. He, however, paints a different picture.

Having made his mark with *Martha Meet Frank, Daniel And Laurence*, Hamm trod far murkier waters for his sophomore directorial effort, an adaptation of Guy Burt's novel *After The Hole*, which is about as far removed from fluffy rom-com territory as it's possible to get.

Pitched somewhere between *The Blair Witch Project* and *The Famous Five*, *The Hole* offers enough moments of duplicity, character degeneration and, of course, shock twists, to suggest it really wants to be the next *Shallow Grave*. And indeed, it boasts striking similarities – for example, the way in which it places its dislikeable protagonists in an extraordinary situation – but ultimately it lacks the necessary cleverness to really succeed. Holding things together is Liz (Thora Birch, replete with near-perfect plummy accent) who, having escaped from the hellish 'hole' of the title (actually a disused World War II bomb shelter), relates the whole sorry story to concerned counsellor Davidtz. A misfit at her private school, Liz is infatuated with classroom heart-throb Mike and left with only her creepy computer nerd buddy, Martin, to confide in, unaware that he, in fact, fancies her. According to Liz, it is Martin who imprisoned them in the bunker.

With the first half given over to Liz's sanitised tale, the latter part of the film takes on a darker note as Martin tells the cops his side of the story. And here's where the film loses momentum and veers dangerously towards standard thriller cliché territory, throwing in some horribly graphic moments (uncontrollable vomit, maggot-ridden toilets) and spiralling towards an all-too-obvious outcome.

What's more, the actual impetus behind the foursome's sojourn down the hole (it's a hiding place to escape the dreaded geography field trip) is unconvincing, given that the amount of generally permissive behaviour that takes place above ground suggests they could think of far more imaginative ways to escape trampling over the fells. ★★★ **CW**

⊙ HOLES (2003)

Starring: *Sigourney Weaver (Warden Walker), Jon Voight (Marion 'Mr. Sir' Sevillo), Rim Blake Nelson (Dr. Pendanski), Shia LaBeouf (Caveman), Khleo Thomas (Hector 'Zero' Zeroni)*
Director: *Andrew Davis*
Screenwriter: *Louis Sachar, based on his novel*
PG/117 mins./Family/Drama/Comedy/USA

After being wrongly convicted of stealing a pair of trainers, palindromic Stanley Yelnats is sent to Camp Green Lake, a godforsaken work camp in the middle of nowhere where the inmates are forced to dig mysterious holes every day. If Stanley can discover the secret of the holes, it will change his luck for good.

Louis Sachar's compelling children's classic is about as Disney as Freddy Krueger. It's got murder, racism, facial disfigurement and killer lizards.

Tightly plotted, it's a multi-layered, interlinking story that spans history to reveal Stanley's own heritage and the secret behind the holes. It races from Latvia's lush greenness to the pock-marked Camp Green Lake (hint: there's no lake and no green).

Disney's first success is re-creating the novel's environments so convincingly – the set design is superb and without gloss. The other plus is in the casting.

Rising star Shia LaBeouf (*Charlie's Angels 2, Project Greenlight*) might not be the fat boy of the book, but his attitude is right and he's far from the usual clean-cut hero.

The rest of the cast is filled out equally well, from Patricia Arquette as the Frontier school marm-turned-bank robber to Henry Winkler as Stanley's dad. The downside is the pop soundtrack – pure marketing department – and having the sentiment turned up to full volume at the end. ★★★ **EC**

⊙ HOLLOW MAN (2000)

Starring: *Elisabeth Shue (Linda McKay), Kevin Bacon (Sebastian Caine), Josh Brolin (Matthew Kensington), Kim Dickens (Sarah Kennedy)*
Director: *Paul Verhoeven*
Screenwriter: *Andrew W. Marlowe, based on a story by Marlowe and Gary Scott Thomson*
18/112 mins./Horror/Sci-fi/Thriller/USA/Germany

Scientist Sebastian Cane makes himself invisible and takes advantage of the situation to conduct a series of pranks. But then the 'pranks' turn nasty . . .

From Plato's musings to H.G. Wells, from Claude Raines to David McCallum pulling on his face for 70s TV, the consequences of turning a bloke transparent has long been a potent theme. Now with Paul Verhoeven's giddy hands at the helm, it's pretty obvious the latest venture into invisibility will be a little less tragic self-destruction and a little more internal organs.

There are familiar ingredients: a latex mask to give the semblance of form, and loads of closing doors and echoing footfalls, but the effects, naturally, are leagues ahead of the old floating pencil and mysterious footprint routines.

Verhoeven typically goes for the flamboyantly bloodthirsty – Caine transforms layer by biological layer, and there is playful delight in conjuring various methods of making him semi-visible again: he passes through smoke, he is plunged underwater, caked in blood and blasted with steam. It's a triumph of exploring the ways in which invisibility can be made manifest on the big screen, and one of the few times in recent CGI-baked movies that effects seem to service, rather than overblow, the story.

Occasionally – especially in the third act – the film reverts to formula, concluding in a violent, pick 'em off showdown. Shue and Brolin (as his straight-laced cohorts) chew earnestly on the cheesy dialogue and work the physical stuff pretty well. Bacon pushes extraordinarily hard as Caine, managing to evoke the flipped psyche even when there is only the trace of him on the screen. Sadly, any opportunities for satire are seldom taken up – containing most of the action inside the dark, metallic corridors of the lab limits the chance for Verhoeven's staple Americana piss-take. This remains, though, a juicy Verhoeven show: zero subtlety, but 100 per cent, full-on, vulgar showmanship.

As entertainment it's totally transparent, but trashily dazzling. ★★★★ **IN**

⊙ HOLLOW REED (1996)

Starring: *Sam Bould (Oliver Wyatt), Martin Donovan (Martyn Wyatt), Ian Hart (Tom Dixon), Joely Richardson (Hannah Wyatt), Jason Flemyng (Frank Donally)*
Director: *Angela Pope*
Screenwriter: *Paula Milne, based on a story by Neville Bolt*
15/104 mins./Drama/UK/Germany/Spain

A father, who left his wife for another man, tries to gain custody of his son when he discovers the wife's new lover is abusing the boy.

Despite an indecipherably trendy moniker leading, at first sight, into yet another worthy-but-dull British film ramming issues down our throat from somewhere in 'ordinary' England, this small, focused almost-thriller is a real find. Its subject matter – criss-crossing homosexuality, child abuse, divorce and violence – isn't exactly chockful of belly laughs, but without getting all stewed up with PC-ness, this manages both arthouse maturity and multiplex gutsiness with aplomb.

The opening salvo is a shocker. A pair of eight-year-old feet careering through undergrowth to the sound of panicked, grunting breaths. Oliver Wyatt arrives at his father's home streaked in blood, with a thin bullyboy story. What emerges is a Chinese puzzle of emotional prickliness. Donovan is the father who left his wife when he fell for another man. The shattered Richardson, with custody of their only son, turns to slick Jason Flemying, a control freak who, scared by his own sorry childhood, beats the child in secret. Bould, mightily (and understandably) confused says nothing of his plight to anyone. As Donovan realises the truth to which the bitter Richardson has blinded herself, he tries in vain – and against the sour prejudice of British justice – to regain custody to protect his son.

Acted with thorough conviction by all – Bould, so wantonly loveable it's almost cheating, is outstanding – and unfussily directed by Pope, the film is tellingly located in the middle-classhood of Bath. There are no laborious working class Loachisms here. By keeping you on tenterhooks through its twists and turns of prejudice and counter-prejudice and the horrors of abuse, it prises open issues of parenthood, custody, culpability and just what people can do when they are in pain.

Triteness rears its ugly head as Donovan finally takes matters into his own hands, but this is powerful stuff – a film where everybody is some kind of victim, and the biggest loser is the most innocent of them all. Charge up the tear ducts, they're going for a rough ride. ★★★★ **IN**

◎ HOME ALONE (1990)

Starring: *Macaulay Culkin (Kevin), Joe Pesci (Harry), Daniel Stern (Marv), John Heard (Peter), Catherine O'Hara (Kate), John Candy (Gus Polinski)*
Director: *Chris Columbus*
Screenwriters: *John Hughes*
PG/103 mins./Comedy/Crime/Family/USA

Misunderstood youngest sibling Kevin McAllister wishes his family would just disappear. But when they forget him in the rush to catch a plane to Paris he finds himself Home Alone with two bumbling cat burglars ready to loot his parent's expensive house.

Who could have predicted that a modest comedy about an eight-year old left alone in a big house would become the then third biggest film of all time, almost equalling the success of *ET* and *Star Wars*?

When *Home Alone* was first released, Macaulay Culkin was virtually unknown with only a role alongside John Candy in *Uncle Buck* to his credit, while director Chris Columbus just had the minor box-office comedy *Adventures In Babysitting* decorating his c.v.

So what made *Home Alone* so successful? There have been a succession of movies with cute kids doing adorable and not-so-adorable things ever since Shirley Temple danced across the screen in the 30s – but this one isn't just about a pesky child accidentally left behind when his family go to Paris for Christmas.

There is also the tale of his mom's odyssey to try and return home while up against the kind of odds Steve Martin suffered in *Planes, Trains And Automobiles*, plus Kevin's own problems, a mysterious old man and the dynamic duo of Harry and Marv who are making a few hilarious attempts to rob the family home.

It is while Kevin is defending his house against the comically inept intruders that the film really comes into its own, with Culkin tossing one-liners at the screen while throwing obstacles in the path of a manic Joe Pesci. Two sequels, the second without Culkin, followed. ★★★★ **PT**

◎ HOMICIDE (1991)

Starring: *Joe Mantegna (Bobby Gold), William H. Macy (Tim Sullivan), Vincent Guastaferro (Lt. Senna), J.J. Johnston (Jilly Curran), Jack Wallace (Frank)*
Director: *David Mamet*
Screenwriter: *David Mamet*
15/102 mins./Drama/Crime/USA

A Jewish cop investigates a drug cartel and uncovers an anti-semitic plot.

Playwright/screenwriter/director David Mamet's third feature assumes the guise of a cop thriller to present his favourite player, Joe Mantegna, in an absorbing character study of an outsider compelled to belong somewhere.

Within the context of another 'normal' day in a big city homicide squad, Mantegna's tough, respected Bobby Gold is a lone Jewish cop who regards his partners and his job as family and heritage. Irish, Hispanic or Black, their loyalties are to each other as they contend with crazies, killers and manoeuvring politicians. In his theatrical, almost stylised swirls around the police precinct, Mamet peppers this set-up with a rhythmic cross-fire of punchy one-liners, oaths, insults and philosophising; 'Don't you want to understand the nature of evil?' offers a murderer; 'No,' answers Bobby, 'because then I wouldn't be able to do my job.'

Just doing his job Bobby is then reluctantly sidetracked on a routine case of an elderly Jewish shopkeeper killed in a mean little robbery. Only things may or may not be what they seem and Bobby finds himself on a journey of self-discovery when a series of clues and strange events lead to an anti-Jewish conspiracy and a counter gang of Zionist vigilantes. Violent and appalling consequences loom when his need to confront who and what he is tests his loyalties.

Littered with McGuffins, menace and solid performances from Mamet regulars, *Homicide* is seldom less than intriguing as a crime thriller and mystery, complete with a shockingly mundane explanation for some of the things the audience has understood through Bobby's eyes. As a psychological drama, it's a sophisticated, gripping piece that unusually leaves you wanting to go on past its unsettling conclusion. ★★★★ **AE**

◎ UN HOMME ET UNE FEMME (1966)

Starring: *Anouk Aimée (Anne Gauthier), Jean-Louis Trintignant (Jean-Louis Duroc), Pierre Barouh (Pierre Gauthier). Valerie Lagrange (Valerie Duroc)*
Director: *Claude Lelouch*
Screenwriters: *Pierre Uytterhoeven, Claude Lelouch (uncredited)*
PG/102 mins./Drama/France

Awards: *Academy Awards – Best Foreign Language Film, Best Original Screenplay, BAFTA – Best Foreign Actress (Anouk Aimée)*

Racing driver Jean-Louis Duroc meets script girl Anne Gauthier while dropping off their children at school in Deauville. They drift towards a romance, but the widowed pair can't escape the memory of their deceased partners and they separate.

With two of his first five features being resounding box-office failures, another being so badly cut by the censors that it was unshowable and another still simply being abandoned on its completion, Claude Lelouch can be forgiven for taking so many easy options with *Un Homme et une Femme*. In many ways, he deserved his commercial success, as he shrewdly identified a gap in the market – a subtitled film which didn't intimidate those reared on mainstream mediocrity. But the critics castigated him all the way to the bank. He may have landed the Palme d'Or at Cannes and the Oscar for Best Foreign Film, but as far as the nouvelle vague bible, Cahiers du Cinéma, was concerned the movie didn't contain 'a centimetre of celluloid' worth screening.

Ironically, this is very much a work in the auteur tradition, as not only did Lelouch produce and direct the picture, but he also photographed and co-edited it and jointly penned the Oscar-winning screenplay with Pierre Uytterhoeven (from his own story). Indeed, Lelouch did such a good job of imposing his own personality on proceedings that Jean-Louis Trintignant and Anouk Aimée simply had to turn up and look photogenic (although Trintignant did have to handle a couple of interior monologues) against the glamorous backdrops.

However, in his earnestness to replicate the energetic camerawork and editorial audacity of his contemporaries, Lelouch too often came across as an homagist rather than an artist with a singular vision. His close-ups were calculating to the point of winsomeness, while his modish celebration of such chic careers as cinema and motor racing produced images more suitable for a commercial than a feature. He later protested that the story questioned this sort of cultural transience by insisting that the film was about the legacy that the dead leave in the hearts of the living. But the majority of people who flocked to see it in the mid-60s were much more interested in its glossy romanticism and Francis Lai's catchy score.

A best-forgotten sequel, *Un Homme et une Femme: Vingt Ans Déja*, emerged to much derision in 1986. ★★★ **DP**

⊙ HONEST (2000)

Starring: *Peter Facinelli (Daniel Wheaton), Nicole Appleton (Gerry), Natalie Appleton (Mandy), Melanie Blatt (Jo), James Cosmo (Tommy Chase), Rick Warden (Baz), Annette Badland (Rose), Corin Redgrave (Duggie Ord)*
Director: *David A. Stewart*
Screenwriters: *Dick Clement, Ian La Frenais, David A. Stewart, Karen Lee Street*
18/110 mins./Comedy/Crime/UK

Three East-End sisters support their family through a life of crime.

Set in the late 60s amid the rise of Flower Power, class A's and ineffectual student revolution, *Honest* is predominantly a love story with a touch of Mike Leigh-esque social drama. The pet project of the hairy Eurythmic for many years, it was only when he heard that the girls from All Saints were looking to make a film that *Honest* came out of development hell; All Saints minus one – Shaznay – that is, making it less a 'pop star movie' and more a movie which happens to feature pop stars in leading roles.

That said, the film hasn't got a whole lot else going for it. Although loosely based on Stewart's life, the story could have taken place in any period, the bad wigs and bad clothes little more than a cheap visual ploy. Equally, an acid trip scene goes for the obvious: naked people, swirling colours and distorted camera work, 'the gag' wearing thin after a few seconds. Most cringe-making is the spectacle of the gals dressed as guys.

Apart from that, the girls don't put in a bad showing. Nicole is competent as the eldest sister who falls for Daniel, an Oxford undergrad who just happens to be a critic on 'radical' publication *Zero* (another slightly dodgy diversion). Natalie is the tough one, an angry, gun-toting, justice-seeking tart, who shags greasy bikers, punishes the wife batterer next door and trades oral sex for weapons. But it's Melanie who shines, as innocent Jo. She has less to do than the others but makes the most of her screen time. None look like pop stars – they pass as poor, East End girls, and the family relationships are nicely handled.

Although the film is a colourful pop-art flick, it's savage in parts, with elements of graphic violence. The publicised nudity fits the storyline but still seems gratuitous, because those bearing their breasts are so well known. Yet at the core is a surprisingly sweet story of heroines trying to make the best of a bad situation. It just doesn't gel. Given a more experienced team, it could have been so much more. ★★ **AS**

⊙ HONEYMOON IN VEGAS (1992)

Starring: *James Caan (Tommy Korman), Nicolas Cage (Jack Singer), Sarah Jessica Parker (Betsy/Donna), Pat Morita (Mahi Mahi), Anne Bancroft (Bea Singer)*
Director: *Andrew Bergman*
Screenwriter: *Andrew Bergman*
15/96 mins./Comedy/Romance/Thriller/USA

Private dick Nicolas Cage loses fiancée Sarah Jessica Parker in a rigged poker game to card shark James Caan and goes through heaven and (comic) hell and a fair few Elvis' to win her back.

When a film opens with a cartoon credit sequence, you know you're in for either a wasted evening or a good comedy, and, make no mistake, this is a very good comedy indeed, a dynamite throwback to those 40s screwball numbers.

The plot is wonderfully straightforward. Dopey Jack Singer promises his possessive mother on her deathbed that he'll never marry. All well and good, until long-suffering Betsy (a pre-*Sex And The City* Parker) forces his hand, Jack capitulates, and the pair jet off to Las Vegas for a snap wedding.

And it's here where the fun and games begin. Kingpin card shark Tommy Korman spots Betsy in the hotel lobby, pegs her as a dead ringer for his departed missus and decides he's going to get his paws on her. He cajoles gullible Jack into a rigged poker game and before you know it, the twerp has gambled away the use of his bride-to-be for the weekend – just for company you understand, this isn't that sort of film. As Tommy whips Betsy off for a romantic tryst at his private Hawaiian estate, Jack hares off in pursuit to win his gal back.

Cage is superb as one of life's losers, combating the perils of commercial transport – airline schedules, queues and dodgy taxi drivers – as he zips between Vegas and Honolulu, and Parker tones down her familiar kooky act as the weary Betsy. Yet the biggest laughs are drawn from the constant references to Elvis, with impersonators lurking everywhere and even a troupe of flying Elvises (Yukon Chapter) on hand for a rousing climax. What's more, in complete absence of sex or swearing, this is a film that, with minimum fuss, simply gets on with the comedy. ★★★★ **JD**

⊙ THE HONEYMOON KILLERS (1969)

Starring: *Shirley Stoler (Martha Beck), Tony Lo Bianco (Ray Fernandez), Mary Jane Higby (Janet Fay), Doris Roberts (Bunny), Kip McArdle (Delphine Downing)*
Director: *Leonard Kastle*
Screenwriter: *Leonard Kastle*
18/115 mins./Crime/USA

Hefty nurse Martha Beck and her low-rent gigolo lover Raymond Fernandez take up serial murder for profit and passion, luring middle-aged women into marriage through lonely hearts ads, then killing them and raiding their savings.

Though preproduced by Martin Scorsese, who left the project after arguments with the producers, this wound up being written and directed by Leonard Kastle, who thus earned his place among the cinema's great one-hit wonder filmmakers. Based on a genuine crime case history from the late 1940s, it is filmed in the candid camera style of a Frederick Wiseman documentary, as intense scenes (the couple's frightening love play, escalating arguments that pay off with awkward killings, Beck's arguments with her appalling mother) unfold with a fly-on-the-wall blankness that shows off quite extraordinary acting from the leads and their cameo victims.

A rare film in which genuine romantic love does not excuse the central couple's amoral behaviour, this could almost be the anti-Bonnie and Clyde as it deglamorises thrill-killing for petty profit after decades of movies that have made outlawry glamorous. Stoler's truly monstrous Martha, who looks like a humourlessly malevolent Roseanne Barr, may not be sympathetic, but she is at least understandable (the actress scored several decades of bit-parts as lesbian prison guards and grotesque brothel madames on the strength of this terrifying performance). The washed-out black and white photography and sometimes scratchy soundtrack (the score is sampled from Mahler) have a (deliberately?) amateurish feel, which adds to the film's chilling memorability.

Arturo Ripstein's Mexican film *Deep Crimson*, based on the same true-life crimes, is a de facto remake, but takes a more stylised, conventional approach to the material. Todd Robinson's *Lonely Hearts*, with Salma Hayek and Jared Leto, is a third version of the sordid story. ★★★★ **KN**

HOOK (1991)

Starring: *Dustin Hoffman (Captain James Hook), Robin Williams (Peter Banning/Peter Pan), Julia Roberts (Tinkerbell), Bob Hoskins (Smee), Maggie Smith (Granny Wendy Darling), Caroline Goodall (Moira Banning), Charlie Kosmo (Jack Banning), Amber Scott (Maggie Banning), Phil Collins (Inspector Good)*
Director: *Steven Spielberg*
Screenwriters: *Jim V. Hart, Malia Scotch Marmo, from a story by Hart and Nick Castle, adapted from the original stage play and books by Sir James M. Barrie*
U/144 mins./Fantasy/Adventure/USA

When Capt. Hook kidnaps his children, an adult Peter Pan must return to Neverland and reclaim his youthful spirit in order to challenge his old enemy.

Mention *Hook* these days and you'll probably get a sniffy response. Perhaps the suggestion that this ambitious update of J.M. Barrie's smug, floaty little git hero is a rare Spielberg dud. Few may even go so far as to offer the sort of merciless kicking that the film suffered after its original theatrical release. Rubbish, boring, too long, too dull, came the reaction. It's all hook, and no real substance, guffawed several imaginative hacks. But did the film really deserve such critical and, relatively speaking, commercial scorn?

Well, *Hook* is certainly not without flaw, nor even a satisfactory watch. But the majority of the mud-slinging nay-sayers are missing the point. Or, at the very least, missing the bigger picture. Spielberg always had a Peter Pan movie in him, and this – rather than bad planning or poor performance – is the source of *Hook*'s problems: when that kernel of creativity finally emerged, clouded by a long-gestation and endless embellishment, it struggled to retain a sense of childlike wonder while relaying life lessons gathered along the way. A lot to ask.

And was the broad, colourful, heavily-spun yarn that resulted really just about Spielberg himself, as is commonly claimed, or is there a more sly and complicated agenda? A cautionary tale for his friends, warning against losing touch with the child within and the children without? A sideways dig at colleagues in the industry so fixated by the business, they've forgotten the importance of the show? All defensible but debatable interpretations – the answers remain unclear.

Unfortunately, such lack of clarity is evident at surface level too: just who is this movie for? Spielberg's revamped premise seems targeted at the junior market: Pan has soured into neglectful, vertigo-stricken Yank Peter Banning, unaware of his past and (ho ho) now a pirate in the cutthroat world of corporate mergers and acquisitions. Enter sleaziest sleaze of the Seven Seas, Captain James Hook for a spot of domestic vandalism and kidnapping, and later pint-sized pixie Tinkerbell, who leads the sceptical Peter back to Neverland, where he must remember how to fly, to fight, to crow, to do funny voices again.

But if it's a kids' movie the momentum's all wrong: whatever the demands of story set-up, half an hour to crank into gear is just too long, and when it looks like sneery, wit-strewn confrontation 'twixt the old rivals is finally in the offing, Peter is thrown into enforced Lost Boys rehab. And for adults, while Spielberg's themes of family, belonging and parent–child relations are strongly portrayed (Williams and Caroline Goodall depicting familial strain particularly well), the movie holds two giant dips into juvenile slapstick. Although the Hoffman/Hoskins odd couple routine as Hook and Smee (spiced up at Hoffman's request) is pitched older, should beardy Bob really be allowed to barrel about yelling 'Flock off' in a U cert.? And should Peter's slagging match with Rufio really include the insults 'mother-lover' and 'near-sighted gynaecologist?'

The film's other significant stumbling block is self-indulgence. At the time, Spielberg was firmly ensconced at Fantasy Central. *Hook* sits within an escapist quartet – *Indiana Jones And The Last Crusade*, *Always* and *Jurassic Park* – and with the director playing away from the bankable Indy brand, the ante was seriously upped. Along with the budget. Spielberg seemed intent on creating a spectacle behind the camera as well as in front of it, constructing colossal, elaborate sets on costly soundstages rather than employing CGI, as he would two years later. It was almost as if he had something to prove – a mark of the sort of resources he was capable of galvanising. And the production's theme park feel was hardly dispelled by numerous visits of assorted celeb chums for guided tours of Neverland.

But amid all this flexing of moviemaking muscle, there's possible evidence of uncertainty as well. Spielberg's use of established box office guarantors Williams, Hoffman and Roberts was uncharacteristic and pricey, especially as the latter amounts to little more than an extended cameo. And what the hell's Phil Collins doing in there?: 'It is entirely probable that this whole thing is some kind of ridiculous prank ...' Well, quite. Subtract one star automatically.

There are, of course, some performing gems too – the moppets capable and endearing; Hoskins' supplying bawdy comic relief, Gwyneth Paltrow in a micro cameo as the young Wendy, and Dame Maggie Smith priceless as Wrinkly Wendy. And though it's not Spielberg's most cogent, successful or entertaining offering, it's still a fascinatingly layered movie, with richly crafted set-pieces alongside a deftly-captured sense of the intimate, and the aforementioned flaws actually adding to the interest. Like it or loathe it, *Hook* is simply too big in too many senses to dismiss as mere excess and aberration, and – the theme park aspect duly noted – would lead inexorably to one place: dinosaur mayhem. ★★ **DB**

HOOP DREAMS (1994)

Starring: *as themselves: William Gates, Arthur Agee, Emma Gates – William's mother, Curtis Gates – William's brother, Sheila Agee – Arthur's mother, Arthur 'Bo' Agee – Arthur's father, Earl Smith – talent scout, Gene Pingatore – High school basketball coach*
Director: *Steve James*
Screenwriters: *Steve James, Frederick Marx*
12/171 mins./Documentary/Sport/USA

A film following the lives of two African American boys who struggle to become college basketball players on the road to going professional.

In American Cinema, baseball is always associated with nostalgia and fondly-imagined virtues of family and country, but more recent basketball films are about a divided, desperate American present. Easily outclassing the fiction films is this extraordinarily compelling near three-hour documentary, which follows a pair of black kids from Chicago's Cabrini Green housing project through four years of high school, examining the assumption that their basketball talent is a chance to get out of the ghetto and into college.

Both Gates and Agee are spotted as 14-year-olds by a recruiting man who arranges basketball scholarships for them at an up-scale school. Both struggle, Gates with injuries and Agee with low academic achievement, but continue to shine on the court. With exceptional skill at distinguishing drama from the raw footage of fly-on-the-wall shooting, James hits on a real irony: Agee's presence peps up his no-hope team into a winning streak while Gates is troubled by doubts and a 'good but not great' career.

Though there is plenty of hoop action, the film focuses on the various pressures on the heroes (and heroes they become) from families, schools, coaches, friends, sponsors, college recruiters and hangers-on. Confident enough to leave plenty to implication – both kids are fathers by the time they leave high school and Agee has a friend who seems to be leading him into a life of crime – this is the best type of documentary, giving an intensely personal story you can't help but become involved in, and also raising fundamental issues about America in the 90s. ★★★★ **KN**

ⓓ HORSE FEATHERS (1932)

Starring: *Groucho Marx (Professor Wagstaff), Harpo Marx (Harpo), Chico Marx (Chico), Zeppo Marx (Zeppo), Thelma Todd (Connie Bailey)*
Director: *Norman Z. McLeod*
Screenwriters: *Bert Kalmar, Harry Ruby, S.J. Perelman, Will B. Johnstone*
U/70 mins./Comedy/USA

Quincy Adams Wagstaff becomes President of Huxley College, where his son, Wagstaff Jr., is studying and pursuing Connie Bailey, the college widow. In order to beat rivals Darwin at American Football, they kidnap Baravelli and Pinky instead of a couple of star players, but all turns out well on the day of the big game.

Despite once conceding that his style was 'as quiet as a mouse pissing on a blotter', Norman Z. McLeod was the Marx Brothers most comedically intuitive and speed sensitive director. Following his success on *Monkey Business*, he reunited with the madcap quartet for this gleefully anarchic romp that makes less sense, but grows ever funnier, with each viewing.

Despite McLeod's genial guidance, life behind the scenes often proved as chaotic as it appeared on screen. Chico spent much of the shoot gambling with the stagehands before multiple injuries sustained in a car crash caused production to be closed down for 10 weeks. Groucho devoted himself to pursuing Thelma Todd, while the easily distractable Harpo once left the set in a bid to persuade a young Shirley Temple's parents to let him adopt her for $50,000.

Once they had been corralled on to the soundstage, the Marxes proceeded to drive screenwriter S.J. Perelman crazy with their insistence on ad-libbing around his carefully concocted wisecracks and sophisticated literary lampoons. Co-writers Bert Kalmar and Harry Ruby were more relaxed, however, especially as their songs 'Whatever It Is, I'm Against It' and 'Everyone Says I Love You' were among the picture's highlights.

Harpo had some inspired moments of silent pantomime, involving a coat full of crockery and a roaring fire, while he teamed with Chico to cause havoc in a classroom. But the revelation was Groucho's byplay with Thelma Todd (who had also featured in *Monkey Business*). Far less passive a stooge than Margaret Dumont, she gave as good as she got, especially during the scene on the lake (intended to parody the drowning sequence in Theodore Dreiser's novel, *An American Tragedy*) in which she tried to dupe Groucho into revealing his secret football plays.

However, the episode almost ended in catastrophe, as Groucho thought the non-swimming Todd's cries for help were a gag and he rowed away, leaving her to be rescued by a sextet of plucky technicians. ★★★★ **DP**

ⓓ HORSEMAN ON THE ROOF (LE HUSSARD SUR LE TOIT) (1995)

Starring: *Juliette Binoche (Pauline de Theus), Olivier Martinez (Angelo Pardi), Pierre Arditi (Monsieur Peyrolle), Francois Cluzet (The Doctor)*
Director: *Jean-Paul Rappeneau*
Screenwriters: *Jean-Claude Carriere, Nina Companeez, Jean-Paul Rappeaneau, based on the novel by Jean Giono*
15/135 mins./Adventure/Drama/Romance/France

In a time of war and disease, a young officer gallantly tries to help a young woman find her husband.

Six years after the magnificent, award-laden *Cyrano De Bergerac*, Jean-Paul Rappeneau again turned his attention to classical literature, this time with Jean Giono's sprawling tale of love amid 19th century France's cholera epidemic.

Although the film lacks the romantic grandeur of Depardieu's crowning moment, it is an expertly paced tale of love and denial played against a chaotic, relentlessly morbid background.

The plot revolves around Angelo, an idealistic young Italian officer on the run from Austrian agents. Seeking refuge in Provence, he discovers that the normally idyllic region has been ravaged by the rapacious spread of cholera, and has descended into anarchy and mob rule. After a chance encounter with Pauline, an aristocratic young woman determined to find her husband, the two flee together and gradually fall in love. Rappeneau has restructured and thankfully abandoned much of Giono's rambling, cadaverous story, placing greater emphasis on the emotionally charged and seemingly hopeless relationship between Pauline and Angelo. As with Cyrano, the director has stinted nothing and has produced a sweeping and visually sumptuous epic.

Admittedly, there are moments of ludicrous hyperbole – the frenzied mob riots and endless encounters with decaying corpses are often as risible as they are disturbing – but they are tempered with enough visually arresting moments and touches of humour to avoid ridicule. And it is the luminous Binoche rather than the over-zealous Martinez who lends genuine depth and intelligence to proceedings. This is still, though, a wonderfully romantic film, arrestingly told and spectacularly realised. ★★★★ **KMc**

ⓓ HOSTEL (2005)

Starring: *Jay Hernandez (Paxton), Derek Richardson (Josh), Eythor Gudjonsson (Oli), Barbara Nedljakova (Natalya), Jan Kaderbkova (Svetlana)*
Director: *Eli Roth*
Screenwiter: *Eli Roth*
18/95 mins./Horror/USA

Tempted by a stranger on a Eurotrain, travellers Paxton, Josh and Oli wander off the backpack map and book in to a hostel boasting a roster of European ladies. What sounds like heaven fires into hell, as sinister forces propel our trio into a world of pain . . .

Not to cause any reader distress, but if you've seen *Audition*, all it takes is one simple word to retrigger the nausea: ankles. So, in anticipation of anybody going to see *Hostel* and rereading this review, here's one for the memories: yolky eye. Crossing your stomach yet?

Eli Roth's (*Cabin Fever*) new movie is a 'squirmer', one of a growing crowd of sado-horrors à la *Saw* where audiences are sausage-machined through a series of unimaginably ghastly scenarios and come out the other side feeling like they've been riding the ghost train on a dentist's chair. This isn't jumpy-scary pulp. This is extreme test-your-nerve pulp. But it's still pulp, and deeply proud of it.

The 'Tarantino Presents' tag is more than bluster. QT had script input and, once the film gets into gear, the central set-piece feels like Bring Out The Gimp: The European Remix. Still, there's another, less fortunate comparison: *From Dusk Till Dawn*. *Hostel*'s a movie of two halves, and one of them doesn't measure up.

Having ragged the fear glands with a creepy tile-washing credit sequence, the mood flattens into a bland fratboy travelogue, complete with routine hash-and-hooker scrapes. Do we really care whether sensitive Josh pops his load with the Amsterdam dominatrix? No, but it does buy us some tits for the trailer. Exposition. Endurance. Fine line. Get to the room with the mucky tiles.

Happily, it delivers on its threat. For all his throwback genre licks

(*Hostel*, bizarrely, has its very own Igor), Roth's strongest game is playing on primal fears, and he's a merciless button-pusher. Entering *Hostel*'s snuff-world is a bit like reliving a running-from-something nightmare with an enchanting twist: somebody's cut your legs off. You might not feel that deeply for the characters, but you definitely feel their pain. There may also be regrets about eating those nachos early on.

Hostel's gristle is pretty explicit, but then, in this genre, gratuitous is what you pay for. Cut it, and a key part of Roth's hell goes with it. In fact, you could even argue this is splatter with conscience, the stupid-but-chilling revelation offering a bitter vision of how the world looks at a post-Guantanamo – and how it looks back. It's this souring aftertaste that lasts longest. Actually, that's a lie. It's the yolky eye bit. ★★★ **SC**

HOT SHOTS! (1991)

Starring: *Charlie Sheen (Lt. Topper Harley), Cary Elwes (Lt. Kent Gregory), Valeria Golino (Ramanda Thompson), Lloyd Bridges (Adm. Thomas 'Tug' Benson), Jon Cryer (Jim 'Wash Out' Pfaffenbach), William O'Leary (Pete 'Dead Meat' Thompson), Kristy Swanson (Kowalski)*
Director: *Jim Abrahams*
Screenwriters: *Jim Abrahams, Pat Proft*
PG/84 mins./Action/Comedy/War/Romance/USA

Topper Harley is a brilliant jet pilot asked back into the forces for a special mission that requires him to lead a team to raid a nuclear plant.

Applying the *Naked Gun* spoof treatment to *Top Gun*, this has Charlie Sheen as a traumatised but brilliant pilot, with Lloyd Bridges filling in for Leslie Nielsen in the now-familiar straight-faced bumbling idiot role. Given that this is the first whacky comedy to come out of the Gulf War it's a shame the whole enterprise isn't a lot more tasteless, but the half-funny goings-on give the impression that the script has been tailored not to offend a military machine on the point of massive war, perhaps at the expense of unpatriotic laughs. That said, it's a pleasant enough time-waster, and doesn't drag on too long.

If you're a fan of the *Naked Gun* series, then this is for you. With cheap jokes at the expense of many a great movie and so much slapstick humour that the film could be silent and still quietly amuse. While not very demanding the actors perform well and Sheen proves to be very adept at playing the handsome but dim Topper. ★★ **WT**

HOT SHOTS PART DEUX (1993)

Starring: *Charlie Sheen (Lt. Topper Harley), Valeria Golino (Ramanda Thompson), Lloyd Bridges (President Thomas 'Tug' Benson), Rowan Atkinson (Dexter Hayman)*
Director: *Jim Abrahams*
Screenwriters: *Jim Abrahams, Pat Proft*
PG/86 mins./Action/Comedy/War/USA

Topper Harley is sent in to save some hostages from dreaded Middle Eastern bad guys but on the mission he bumps into the girl that got away...

As one who found *Hot Shots!* a threadbare *Top Gun* spoof, this reviewer is tickled to see *Airplane!* and *Naked Gun* collaborator Jim Abrahams back on zany form with this much funnier sequel in which Sheen's Topper Harley is recalled to action with pumped-up muscles, shaved chest and headband for a Rambo leg pull.

His mission: to 'save the men who went in to get the men who went in to get the men' following a failed hostage rescue 'somewhere in the Middle East'. His commander-in-chief: US President Tug Benson, even more gaga than Reaganbush. Also on hand is Richard Crenna to reprise his hostage colonel in Rambo Whichever.

Naturally Abrahams and co-jokester Pat Proft are not content just to send up the Stallone action man cycle and plunder everything from *The Wizard Of Oz* to *Star Wars*, *T2*, *Basic Instinct*, *No Way Out* and *Robin Hood; Prince Of Thieves*. In one scene alone – a flashback to happier times and a romantic dinner for two in an Italian restaurant – there are nods to *The Godfather*, *Casablanca* and *Lady And The Tramp*, emphasising that the best laughs are reliant on the complicity of a knowing audience.

And as always with Abrahams, what's glimpsed going on in the background is often as funny as what's notionally happening immediately in front of the camera – just check out those saffron-robed monks while Topper is being recruited from his monastery retreat. Best bit – an *Apocalypse Now* gag guaranteed to bring the house down. Shamelessly artless, silly beyond absurd and truly juvenile ★★★ **AE**

HOTEL RWANDA (2004)

Starring: *Don Cheadle (Paul Rusesabagina), Sophie Okonedo (Tatiana Rusesabagina), Nick Nolte (Colonel Oliver), Mbutho 'Kid' Sithole (Head Chef), Rosie Motene (Receptionist)*
Director: *Terry George*
Screenwriters: *Keir Pearson, Terry George*
12A/121 mins./Drama/History/USA/UK/Italy/South Africa

Kigali, Rwanda, 1994. When the Hutu president is killed by Tutsi rebels, Hutu extremists take to the streets with machetes, slaughtering every Tutsi they see. Meanwhile, Paul Rusesabagina finds the four-star hotel he manages turned into an impromptu refugee camp. Only his quick thinking can keep its 1,200 inhabitants alive.

Sometimes it's a line of dialogue that stays with you. Others, it's a kick-ass set-piece. With Terry George's *Hotel Rwanda*, it's a single, heart-crushing image: that of prim hotel manager Paul Rusesabagina, wearing a spotless suit, his tie perfectly knotted, straight-backed and clutching an umbrella for his leaving guests as the rain pelts down around them. But these guests aren't merely checking out after a relaxing few weeks in Kigali.

They're non-nationals fleeing Paul's country, part of a total foreign withdrawal as Rwanda insanely tears itself apart, leaving Paul, his family and his employees virtually defenceless at the hands of the genocidal, machete-wielding Hutu militia. These people represent Paul's doom. Yet he still shelters them from the rain. Okay, so the symbolism's rather obvious, and it does imply a heavy-handedness on George's part, to which he resorts more overtly elsewhere in the film. But heavy-handedness is frankly forgiveable with this subject matter: in a few months, almost a million people were slaughtered in Rwanda.

This is one of the most intense acts of genocide in human history – and it happened only a decade ago, while most of us in the West, catching the odd news report, dismissed it as 'just a bunch of Africans killing each other again' before flipping channels.

Besides, who cares about overdone orchestral blasts or signpost-waving lines of dialogue when such raw, naked, painful humanity is displayed by Don Cheadle in the central role? The actor transforms from suave schmoozer of generals and militia leaders, to protective family man, to a reluctant saviour who's forever struggling to maintain his fragile composure, all the while sidestepping every histrionic outburst you'd expect.

At his side is fellow Oscar nominee Sophie Okonedo, similarly impressive as his distraught wife Tatiana, while bigger names – Joaquin Phoenix, Nick Nolte – effortlessly energise the smaller roles.

Watching *Hotel Rwanda* is a deeply humbling experience, and for all the uplift of Paul's Schindler-like achievement, you still feel acute guilt and rage at the fact that the West barely lifted a finger to help the people of a nation that, economically at least, had little to offer us in return. As Nolte's deflated U.N. colonel tells Paul in one scene, 'You're not even niggers. You're Africans.' ★★★★ **DJ**

⊙ THE HOUND OF THE BASKERVILLES (1939)

Starring: *Richard Greene (Sir Henry Baskerville), Basil Rathbone (Sherlock Holmes), Wendy Barrie (Beryl Stapleton), Nigel Bruce (Dr. Watson), Lionel Atwill (James Mortimer, MD), Ralph Forbes (Sir Hugo Baskerville)*
Director: *Sidney Lanfield,*
Screenwriter: *Ernest Pascal, based on the story by Sir Arthur Conan Doyle*
PG/80 mins./Crime/Mystery/USA

Sherlock Holmes and Dr. Watson are hired to protect Sir Henry Baskerville, who has just inherited an estate on Dartmoor and is supposedly threatened by a ghostly dog which has persecuted his family.

One of the finest adaptations of the often-filmed Arthur Conan Doyle novel, this was the first Holmes movie made at such a remove from original publication it was felt necessary to fix it firmly in the Victorian era, with hansom cabs, stiff collars, false whiskers and a Universal horror-look Dartmoor complete with Stonehenge-like ruins and plentiful studio fog. The script streamlines the tale to the extent of losing the explanations of a couple of clues and a rejigging of priorities in the cast-list (Greene's Sir Henry is billed above Rathbone's Holmes!) is reflected by the insertion of well-written and -played but essentially time-out-from-the-good-stuff love scenes between the Baskerville heir and a suspect's sister (Barrie).

However, more fun is had from the legend of wicked Sir Hugo, Rathbone and Bruce beginning their multi-film partnership with brisk banter, a spooky mid-point séance, a startling but brief mention of the detective's drug habit ('Watson, the needle!'), Rathbone's regular disguise act (doing the only authentic West Country accent in the film) as a whiskery comic pedlar on the moors (it's nice that Watson notices his limp changes legs), and an array of fine Hollywood hams (Lionel Atwill, John Carradine) doing their best to seem more suspicious than the innocent-faced fellow obviously behind the crimes.

It falls just short of classic status and is especially hurried at the climax, with a bland assurance that the diabolical villain who seems to be escaping to plot again will doubtless be apprehended by one of several unseen policemen secreted about the moor rather than the exciting action scene which would seem to be required. ★★★★ **KN**

⊙ THE HOUND OF THE BASKERVILLES (1959)

Starring: *Peter Cushing (Sherlock Holmes), André Morell (Dr. Watson), Christopher Lee (Sir Henry Baskerville), Marla Landi (Cecile Stapleton), David Oxley (Sir Hugo Baskerville), John Le Mesurier (Barrymore)*
Director: *Terence Fisher*
Screenwriter: *Peter Bryan based on the novel by Arthur Conan Doyle*
PG/87 mins./Crime/Mystery/UK

Sherlock Holmes and Dr Watson are hired to protect Sir Henry Baskerville, who has just inherited an estate on Dartmoor and is supposedly threatened by a ghostly dog that has persecuted his family.

Having reinvented British horror in 1957 with *The Curse of Frankenstein*, Hammer Films swiftly had house director Terence Fisher and new-minted stars Peter Cushing and Christopher Lee knock out versions of *Dracula*, *The Mummy* and Sir Arthur Conan Doyle's spookiest Sherlock Holmes tale.

Like other early Hammer horrors, *Hound* is a splendidly full-blooded period melodrama, richly-produced (it was the first Holmes movie in colour), gorgeously-costumed and incisively acted by a top-flight British cast. Peter Cushing's brisk, twinkling Holmes (less fussy than in his later television takes on the role) and André Morell's non-befuddled, resourceful Watson broke from the readings of the roles Basil Rathbone and Nigel Bruce had established twenty years earlier, opening the way for later revisions and reimaginings of the great detective and his sidekick.

Lee would seem to be stuck with the stooge role as the imperilled Sir Henry, paralysed with fear as a tarantula crawls up his arm, but actually gets more screen time and more emotional range than in his higher-profile monster roles.

Hammer litter the supporting cast with wonderful British eccentrics like Miles Malleson as a dotty Bishop, John le Mesurier as the sinister butler of Baskerville Hall and Francis de Wolfe as a glowering suspect, while finding room for the studio's traditional smouldering continental cleavage in the person of barefoot Dartmoor girl Marla Landi.

Purists might object to the script's deviation from the novel – Hammer even dare to change the identity of the ultimate villain – but *Hound* has been done so many times that this version has an intriguing capacity to surprise. ★★★★ **KN**

⊙ THE HOUR OF THE FURNACES (1968)

Directors: *Octavio Getino, Fernando E. Solanas, Santiago Alvarez*
Screenwriters: *Octavio Getino, Fernando E. Solanas*
Unrated/260 mins./Documentary/Argentina

This epic experimental documentary sought to educate and agitate through its revision of Argentinian history and its avowal of active measures to dismantle a system established by imperialists, oligarchs and crooks.

Fernando E. Solanas and Octavio Getino began assembling archive footage and conducting interviews for this landmark documentary in 1965. By the time they were finished, the military had seized power in Argentina and the outlawed film could only be screened in mobile units sponsored by the Grupo Cine Liberación, which later disseminated Solanas and Getino's celebrated manifesto, 'Towards a Third Cinema', which called for the emergence of a militant cinema dedicated to promoting the political causes neglected by filmmakers in the First (Hollywood) and Second (Auteur) traditions.

Running for some 260 minutes, the action comprised of newsreels, testimonies, dramatic reconstructions, filmic citations and photographic stills, which were given greater avant-garde intensity by the linking use of captions, pop graphics, freeze frames and montages. It was divided into three sections. The opening cine-essay, 'Neocolonialism and Violence', declared that Argentinian history had been corrupted and proceeded to posit the true story by juxtaposing images of class exploitation and social injustice. This paved the way for 'Act for Liberation' – which used talking heads to reclaim Peronism as a positive force and called for the triumph of socialist nationalism – and 'Violence and Liberation', which attacked the concept of peaceful co-existence and demanded revolutionary change.

Bearing the influence of Dziga-Vertov, Eisenstein, Joris Ivens, Glauber Rocha, Santiago Alvarez and Jean-Luc Godard, this wasn't a film to sit down and contemplate. It demanded active participation, as it consciously bombarded the senses to provoke reactions on an emotional and intellectual level. Solanas's advertising background was readily evident in the way that message and image were manipulated to shape opinion and spark debate. Indeed, Parts II and III contained natural breaks to allow those attending the illegal screenings to air their views and discuss future strategies.

Seen today, the film seems clumsy and naive in places, as propaganda seeps into the polemic. But its editorial power and audacity remain undiminished and it still packs an emotive punch. ★★★★ **DP**

Ⓓ THE HOURS AND TIMES (1991)

Starring: *David Angus (Brian Epstein), Ian Hart (John Lennon), Stephanie Pack (Marianne), Robin McDonald (Quinnones), Sergio Moreno (Miguel), Unity Grimwood (Mother)*
Director: *Christopher Münch*
Screenwriter: *Christopher Münch*
18/55 mins./Drama/USA

In April 1963, The Beatles's manager, Brian Epstein takes John Lennon to Barcelona in the hope of seducing him.

According to some music historians, John Lennon was the main reason that Brian Epstein left the security of his NEMS record shop in Liverpool's Whitechapel and offered to manage The Beatles. Rumours have long abounded about the exact nature of the relationship between the gay, Jewish bourgeois and the macho, lower-middle-class rebel and Christopher Münch's monochrome study explores the mutual fascination that existed between them with sensitivity and insight.

Set in April 1963, just before the craziness of Beatlemania changed both their lives, the film fantasises about the four-day trip to Barcelona that followed an exhausting tour.

No one will ever know what occurred at the Avenida Palace. But Münch's scenario relies more on character appreciation than salacious speculation and, consequently, what emerges is a compelling portrait of cultural, sexual, temperamental and intellectual opposites who were inextricably bound by curiosity, affection and respect, with Epstein's actions being coloured by self-loathing lust and Lennon's by insecure cruelty. Indeed, the latter's blend of cockiness and confusion even colours his contact with women, as Lennon is both teasing and doting on the phone to his wife Cynthia and aggressive and affable to Marianne, the air hostess whose Little Richard record intrigues him more than her availability.

As in *Backbeat*, Ian Hart admirably captures the petulant nihilism that Lennon used as a defence mechanism. Moreover, he adroitly suggests the emotional scarring (caused by the deaths of his mother, Julia, and best friend Stuart Sutcliffe) that made Lennon simultaneously angry and magnetic and, thus, so attractive to his manager. But David Angus is equally impressive, although his performance had greater latitude as Epstein had a much lower public profile. Despite his physical dissimilarity, he nonetheless nails the avuncular attitude that Epstein adopted towards the Fabs and suggests that for all his supposed sophistication and nous, he was already slipping out of his depth, both professionally and personally. ★★★ **DP**

Ⓓ THE HOURS (2002)

Starring: *Nicole Kidman (Virgina Woolf), Julianne Moore (Laura Brown), Meryl Streep (Clarissa Vaughan), Stephen Dillane (Leonard Woolf), Miranda Richardson (Mrs. Vanessa 'Nessa' Bell), John C. Reilly (Richie Brown), Toni Collette (Kitty Barlowe), Ed Harris (Richard Brown), Jeff Daniels (Louis Waters), Claire Danes (Julia Vaughan)*
Director: *Stephen Daldry*
Screenwriter: *David Hare, based on the novel by Michael Cunningham*
12A/114 mins./Drama/USA
Awards: *Academy Awards – Best Actress, BAFTA – Anthony Asquith Award for Film Music, Best Actress, Golden Globes – Best Drama, Best Actress*

In 1923, Virgina Woolf is fighting mental illness and writer's block, as she struggles with her latest novel, *Mrs. Dalloway*. The book will later play a role in the lives of two other women: repressed 50s housewife Laura Brown and modern-day socialite Clarissa Vaughan.

After his stint in theatre, *The Hours* comes at an important point in Stephen Daldry's career. Given carte blanche after the success of *Billy Elliot*, his next movie brought him the pick of Hollywood's A-list and the power to make an affecting film that could never get made without serious muscle – or never on this budget, at least.

And Billy Elliot was no fluke: Daldry is a deft, imaginative director who appreciates his new medium. It is certainly easy to see why his seamless blending of three apparently unrelated stories made *The Hours* a critical darling, with serious Oscar buzz.

As befits his background, Daldry handles the leads beautifully, drawing strong, understated performances from all three. This much we've come to expect from Moore and Streep, although both are diminished slightly by the proximity of similar works: Moore's housewife is an echo of her superb starring role in *Far From Heaven*, while Streep seems a little safe compared to her appearance in the surreal *Adaptation*. Kidman, though, is thoroughly amazing as the tormented Woolf. Hidden beneath plain make-up and a prosthetic nose, the trappings of her tabloid stardom all but disappear, leaving only the persuasive portrayal of a complex woman by a terrific actress.

But there is a downside, and it comes from the material: Michael Cunningham's novel. After setting up three very different time zones, the film comes down to earth in modern-day Manhattan amid an alienating, middle-class lit-pack. Here, the clichés of boho cinema come to the fore – Streep as the bookish but energetic lesbian single mother, Ed Harris as a brilliant but troubled poet crippled by Aids, Jeff Daniels as his fey, cavalier ex-lover.

And so, what started as a thoughtful exploration of a day in the life of three very different women becomes yet another showboating actors' workshop, full of tears, soul-searching and confessional speeches. Compared to all this, Kidman's dignified minor keys seem very special indeed. ★★★ **DW**

Ⓓ HOUSE (1986)

Starring: *William Katt (Roger Cobb), George Wendt (Harold Gorton), Richard Moll (Big Ben), Key Lenz (Sandy), Mary Stavin (Tanya), Michael Ensign (Chet Parker)*
Director: *Steve Miner*
Screenwriter: *Ethan Wiley, based on a story by Fred Dekker*
15/93 mins./Comedy/Horror/USA

Novelist Roger Cobb – haunted by Vietnam trauma, his young son's mysterious disappearance and a recent divorce – moves into the creepy old house where his aunt has just been mysteriously hanged. Naturally, he is attacked by supernatural creatures.

Producer Sean Cunningham and director Steve Miner forsook the *Friday the 13th* franchise for this formulaic horror. It poaches a few plot-points from other films (notably *Poltergeist*), then throws in goofily scarifying monsters, endearingly inappropriate pop music ('You're No Good'), contrived shock sequence, a central performance from William Katt that deserves a more substantial film to back it up, and a reassuring but ultimately self-defeating lightness of tone which means the kids don't have to take the horror seriously.

With George Wendt of *Cheers* handling deadpan comic relief as an unflappable neighbour, the movie gets down to the business of shouting 'boo!' every few minutes. Monsters lunge out of closets, gardening tools fly dangerously around on their own, a bloated toad woman impersonates the hero's ex-wife (Kay Lenz) and refuses to stop pestering him even after she's been dismembered, and the missing kid cries out for help from a limbo beyond the bathroom cabinet.

Richard Moll turns up as a fearsome monster from Vietnam – a grumbling, lumbering seven-foot zombie GI – and the script touches on interesting elements like the hero's war guilt and family troubles, but *House* cops out like too many 80s horror movies by sending itself up all the time.

It spawned a minor franchise: *House II: The Second Story* has a memorable title and one great gag sequence with another *Cheers* regular (John Ratzenberger) but is otherwise dreadful; *House III* is a grimmer cop-vs-ghostly-serial-killer picture (with Lance Henriksen and Brion James) that came out in the UK as *The Horror Show*; and *House IV: The Repossession* brings back and kills off Katt. ★★ **KN**

⊙ HOUSE OF THE FLYING DAGGERS (SHI MIAN MAI FU) (2004)

Starring: *Zhang Ziyi (Mei), Takeshi Kaneshiro (Jin), Andy Lau, billed as Andy Lau Tak Wah (Leo), Song Dandan (Madam Yee)*
Director: *Yimou Zhang*
Screenwriters: *Li Feng, Wang Bin, Yimou Zang based on a story by Zhang Li Feng and Wang Bin,*
15/119 mins./Martial Arts/Action/Romance/China/Hong Kong

It's 859AD, and China's fading Tang Dynasty is locked in conflict with rebel groups, primarily the mysterious House Of Flying Daggers. Tang captains Leo and Jin are charged with capturing the House's new leader, and suspect that a young dancer at the Peony Pavilion, blind girl Mei, may be their key to success...

It's amazing what you can do with bamboo. You can use it to make furniture, turn your garden into something Alan Titchmarsh would be proud of, or feed pandas. Plus, it tastes great in a stir-fry and, if you're a filmmaker working in the wushu genre, it's an almost obligatory component of any good action scene.

Ang Lee was the first to set Western jaws sagging with a bamboo-forest fight sequence (in *Crouching Tiger, Hidden Dragon*), but Zhang Yimou, the second Chinese filmmaker to successfully export wushu to our multiplexes, with *Hero*, trumps even Lee's anti-gravity cane-clash in his *Hero* follow-up, *House Of Flying Daggers*. Clearly concerned that his last movie's fight sequences, while astonishing, neglected the versatile plant, he's gone all-out here, sending an entire army into a forest, leaping from shoot to shoot, and even getting his combatants to slice off segments of cane and hurl them through the air as deadly weapons. Like we said, it's amazing what you can do with bamboo.

Impressive use of panda-feed aside, anyone who's seen *Hero* and *Crouching Tiger* will be on very familiar territory with *Flying Daggers*. It stars Ziyi Zhang – the actress formerly known as Zhang Ziyi – while the story involves intense romance, tangled yet gossamer-delicate webs of deception and tearjerking tragedy. Once again, Zhang Yimou reveals a great eye for lush locations, from the opulent interiors of the Peony Pavilion, to a shimmering, emerald-green lily pond, to expansive, undulating, golden fields.

And the fighting is once more beautiful, balletic and so meticulously executed it almost makes you want to cry, whether you're watching blind dancer Mei twirl a blade using her unfeasibly long, billowing silk sleeves in the applause-worthy 'Echo Game' scene, or heroic charmer Jin take down multiple opponents with some nifty bow-and-arrow action.

This is a far more intimate movie than *Hero*, less concerned with grand designs, more with personal portraits; Zhang Yimou is even bold enough at one point to show us the beginning of a huge, decisive battle, then ignore it completely to zoom in on the bitter love story that throbs at the film's centre and the far tinier conflict that it precipitates. This isn't entirely a bad move, especially when it all revolves around yet another pristine performance from Ziyi Zhang, an actress so dedicated she spent a month with a blind girl by way of preparation.

Yet, while narrowing his focus, Zhang allows repetition to creep in, batting his protagonists back and forth between the same few (admittedly gorgeous) locations without *Hero*'s neat narrative-trick excuse for doing the same. The various twists and revelations are also laid on too thick and packed in too tightly towards the end, weighing down the final act and matting out the glittering promise of the first hour.

For this reason, *Flying Daggers* stands as marginally inferior to *Hero*. But only marginally. And besides, that's not really the comparison we should be thinking about. The fact remains that, in the past year, Zhang Yimou – a director whose output was once strictly Soho-arthouse fare – has not once, but twice delivered an action movie that outdoes most of the CG-slathered, budget-heavy slam-bangers hurled out of Hollywood. And for that alone Zhang should be proud, while we – not to mention the world's bamboo growers – should be grateful. ★★★★ **WL**

⊙ HOUSE OF GAMES (1987)

Starring: *Lindsay Crouse (Dr. Margaret Ford), Joe Mantegna (Mike), Mike Nussbaum (Joey), Lilia Skala (Dr. Littauer), J.T. Walsh (Businessman)*
Director: *David Mamet*
Screenwriter: *David Mamet*
15/102 mins./Crime/USA

Psychiatrist Margaret Ford's attempt to study a working con-artist, Mike, causes her descent into a barely penetrable web of con and counter-con.

The film work of David Mamet has always divided audiences, with some spectators thoroughly irritated by the labyrinthine plotting, staccato dialogue and lack of obvious cinematic 'flourish'. Indeed, the films are often dismissed as stage plays somewhat unimaginatively transferred to the big screen.

House Of Games, the writer's directorial debut, contains all the ingredients that annoy his critics. The dialogue is arch, the acting style self-conscious, and Mamet revels in his usual enthusiastically inventive use of barrack-room language ('Where am I from? The United States Of Kiss My Ass').

It's a story that resembles an extended game of Find The Lady, with Mamet as street-corner huckster. Time after time he seems to reveal to the audience what's actually going on, only to turn the card and hornswoggle us out of the truth yet again.

As to Mamet's often criticised, restrained style, the debut director may not be in the Scorsese stakes when it comes to flamboyant editing or bravura tracking shots, but he, along with cinematographer Juan Ruiz Anchia, creates a thickly atmospheric cityscape complete with steam-hissing streets, dingy smoke-filled gambling dens and isolated pools of light around which the predators gather to stalk their prey.

The playful plot machinations and presence of a statuesque blonde with a gun make comparisons to Hitchcock inevitable and, like The Master's better films, *House Of Games* has a darker, more ambiguous chord resonating ominously beneath the exhilaratingly rapid pile-up of plot switcheroos.

At its core, the film contains a devastating demolition of the notion of trust, with Mike revealing to Margaret that she is as corrupt and potentially criminal as he is – only he has the decency to be honest about it. The movie's terminal shot, a mysterious little final sting, tantalisingly implies that Margaret might have always been something much worse than her con-man subject ever was. ★★★★ **AS**

⊙ HOUSE OF WAX (1953)

Starring: *Vincent Price (Prof. Henry Jarrod), Frank Lovejoy (Lt. Tom Brennan), Phyllis Kirk (Sue Allen), Carolyn Jones (Cathy Gray), Charles Brosnan, billed as Charles Buchinsky (Igor)*
Director: *Andre De Toth*
Screenwriter: *Crane Wilbur, based on a play by Charles Welden*
PG/90 mins./Horror/USA

A sculptor of wax figures for a museum is horrified when his partner wants to torch it for insurance. They fight and the sculptor is accidentally

knocked out in the scuffle and left to 'perish' among the flames. He resurfaces many years later for the launch of his own wax museum but the opening coincides with the sudden disappearance of some dead bodies from the city morgue.

'He makes his blood-curdling brothers, Herr Frankenstein and Mr. Hyde, seem like friendly folk,' wrote the Hollywood Reporter of Professor Jarrod, the hideously scarred, murderous sculptor in this remake of Michael Curtiz's 1933 shocker, *The Mystery Of The Wax Museum*. 'He' was Vincent Price, who was returning to horror for the first time since headlining The *Invisible Man Returns* – although he had contributed a vocal cameo, as the same character, to *Abbott And Costello Meet Frankenstein* in 1948.

Weary of essaying sneaky villains, Price was keen to alter his image. Critically, in the same week producer Bryan Foy contacted him about *House Of Wax*, he was also offered a pivotal role in the original Broadway production of *We're No Angels*, which later became a successful screen vehicle for Humphrey Bogart. Opting for the more lucrative Warners' contract, Price took his first steps towards becoming a horror icon. However, it's not the fact that it transformed the fortunes of a journeyman actor that makes this film so memorable. More significantly it was shot in 3D by Andre De Toth, a man whose perception of three-dimensional imagery was nullified by his having only one eye.

Part of Hollywood's increasingly desperate search to lure punters away from their newly acquired television sets, the short-lived 'depthie' boom had been launched by Arch Oboler's *Bwana Devil* in 1952. But rather than trot out another novelty movie, De Toth (who had written a learned article extolling the process in 1946) distanced himself from the predictable flaming arrows, pouncing lions and bouncing boulders by shooting a feature that was 'third-dimensional' rather than simply 3D. Consequently, the effect was sparingly used throughout – the street hawker playing with his paddle ball, the can-can dancers strutting their lacey stuff – and was all the more effective for it.

However, opportunistic mogul Jack L. Warner was not prepared to undersell the gimmick and proudly announced that this Natural Vision spectacle would not only be the first 3D picture to be produced by a major Hollywood studio, but would also be the first to be released in WarnerPhonic stereo. Costing a mere $680,000, *House Of Wax* was scripted by Crane Wilbur, a one-time matinee idol who had enjoyed fleeting fame as the rescuer of Pearl White from the railway tracks in the seminal silent serial *The Perils Of Pauline*. Subsequently, he had earned a crust writing and directing low-budget movies along Poverty Row.

A sublime sculptor and genial sophisticate, Henry Jarrod is feted by both the intelligentsia and the aristocracy. But when his grasping partner torches their museum for the insurance money, he crawls from the wreckage with his face disfigured and his artistic refinement corrupted into an embittered lust for the macabre. Thus, having fashioned himself a face-saving mask, he re-opens the gallery as a Chamber Of Horrors. But instead of being handcrafted models, his exhibits are murdered dopplegangers of his lost 'children', who have been dipped in wax and arranged in grotesque tableaux – thus, in death, becoming eerily lifelike.

Ultimately, Jarrod's quest for perfection proves his undoing, as his obsessive plan to cast the spirited Sue Allen as his new Marie Antoinette goes awry. Having made such a chilling job of Jarrod's cloaked pursuit of Allen through the foggy city streets, De Toth possibly missed a trick in revealing the extent of his monstrosity before she pulls away his mask during their do-or-die struggle.

The shoot proved an arduous one for Price. As the 3D technique required two cameras to be running simultaneously, he had to perform many of his own stunts, and the collapse of a balcony during the conflagration scene almost ended in disaster after it caught fire and nearly crushed him.

But the major source of discomfort was the make-up. Modelled on actual burns cases by George and Gordon Bau, the various layers of rubber and pure alcohol took three hours both to apply and remove. While encased, Price was forced to subsist on liquids and once fainted from oxygen deprivation. Yet the irritation caused by lingering skin rashes was somewhat eased by the film's critical and commercial success. A young Charles Bronson (still billed under his real name, Buchinsky) and Carolyn Jones (who would later play Morticia in TV's *The Addams Family*) also benefited from their involvement. A sequel, *The Man Of Wax*, was abandoned following copyright wrangles, leaving the irrepressible De Toth to embark on a 3D Western, *The Stranger Wore A Gun* (1953).

As for Price, he was condemned until recently to playing sympathetic horror heavies, driven by grief or unrequited love to commit acts of sadistic, and often blackly comic, barbarism. ★★★★ **DP**

⑮ HOUSE OF WAX (2005)

Starring: *Elisha Cuthbert (Carly Jones), Chad Michael Murray (Nick Jones), Brian Van Holt (Bo/Vincent), Paris Hilton (Paige Edwards), Jared Padalecki (Wade)*
Director: *Jaume Collet-Serra*
Screenwriters: *Chad Hayes, Carey Hayes, based on a story by Charles Belden*
15/113 mins./Horror/USA

Awards: *Razzie Awards – Worst Supporting Actress (Paris Hilton)*

A group of teenagers on the way across state are diverted towards a deserted town. Circumstances see them split up, and eventually they are drawn towards the mysterious wax museum at the top of the hill...

Audiences will watch this for two reasons – either they want to see Paris Hilton in her undies, or they want to see her horribly killed. But if you're hoping for something like the 1953 Vincent Price version, this remake is an unwelcome shock. The plot has devolved into the broken-down car/creepy house set-up of a thousand horrors, and the irritating teen heroes barely qualify as stock characters, only hastily sketched before the slaughter begins. Worse, the pathos of Price's madman has been entirely lost, except for a half-hearted attempt at empathy in the final reel.

Tagline
Prey.
Slay.
Display.

While the violence is nasty enough to provide some good scares, it's all as nonsensical as the idea of a house literally made of wax – which, in an attempt at wit, the film also provides. Horrific, but not in a good way. ★★ **HO'H**

⑱ HOUSE ON HAUNTED HILL (1999)

Starring: *Geoffrey Rush (Stephen H. Price), Famke Janssen (Evelyn Stockard-Price), Taye Diggs (Eddie Baker), Peter Gallagher (Donald W. Blackburn, M.D), Ali Larter (Sara Wolfe)*
Director: *William Malone*
Screenwriter: *Dick Beebe, based on a story by Robb White*
18/93 mins./Horror/Thriller/USA

A park developer offers a reward of $1 million to a group of strangers – if they can spend the night in a supposedly haunted house.

In this remake of William Castle's 1958 frightener, inflation has turned Vincent Price's ten grand into a cool million: the prize – proffered by barking billionaire Steven Price – for lasting one night in the HOHH. Only in this game, there's no phoning a friend (because all the lines have been cut) and 50/50 amounts to significantly better survival odds than any of the cast can expect.

Castle's original was a campy schlock-horror, packing as many chuckles as chills, and, likewise, the tone here is set by an opening title's sequence of elongated and initially comical screams, which grow more disturbing as they gather volume. Such an unsettling combo extends into early scene-setting, as theme-park owner Price puts the visiting news crew through a heart-stopping roller coaster experience and subsequently lifts the lid on his dysfunctional, love-hate relationship with lascivious wife Evelyn. And alongside Janssen's dark, red-lipped turn-on, there's enough clean-cut sex appeal amongst the other party guests to suggest that things may go hump, as well as bump, in the night. Diggs is all pumping heroic muscle, Gallagher takes the suave, doctorly approach, while Ali Larter pitches blonde glamour alongside the even more tawdry Bridgette Wilson.

However, the film gradually loses its edge. The Vannacutt Psychiatric Institute for the Criminally Insane is a superbly designed monolithic montrosity, but once inside, producers Joel Silver and Robert Zemeckis seem too keen to up the ante further, for having wrought a twisted, deeply unpleasant mood, the movie finds itself back on a formulaic track of shocks and scarefest staples. The finale, in fact, boils dangerously close to that of Jan de Bont's *The Haunting*, and as anyone in Hollywood's horror fraternity will tell you, affinity with that disaster area is something to really be afraid of.

Frequently effective and played with suitably off-kilter spirit, if only this had retained the courage of its early convictions, we could be looking at an exceptional – rather than just serviceable – blood-curdler. ★★★ **DB**

HOW GREEN WAS MY VALLEY (1941)

Starring: *Walter Pidgeon (Mr Gryffydd), Maureen O'Hara (Angharad), Donald Crisp (Mr. Morgan), Anna Lee (Bronwyn), Roddy McDowall (Huw Morgan)*
Director: *John Ford*
Screenwriter: *Phillip Dunne based on the novel by Richard Llewellyn*
U/118 mins./Drama/USA

Awards: *Academy Awards – Best Picture, Best Director, Best Supporting Actor, Best Cinematography, Best Black and White Art Direction-Interior Decoration*

Caught between the influence of his miner father, Morgan, and newly arrived preacher, Gryffydd, Welsh adolescent Huw witnesses the breakdown of his family and community.

Following *The Grapes of Wrath* and *Tobacco Road*, this adaptation of Richard Llewellyn's novel completes John Ford's social-consciousness trilogy, in which the decline of a single family reflected that of an entire community in the face of wider economic forces. It was originally planned as a four-hour Technicolor epic as Fox sought its own *Gone With the Wind*. However, the outbreak of the Second World War prevented location shooting in the Rhondda Valley and, after director William Wyler's departure, producer Darryl F. Zanuck settled for the construction of an authentic Welsh mining set in the San Fernando Valley (which took 150 builders six months to complete to Richard Day and Nathan Juran's specifications, pushing the film's budget to $1,250,000).

Zanuck initially planned to have Tyrone Power play the older Huw. But Ford insisted on retaining Roddy McDowall throughout (although Irving Pichel provides the older voice-over), as he was keen to show the decline and depopulation of the valley through his eyes and not as a series of incontrovertible facts.

Thus, the composition of each frame, the camera angle and even the lighting was designed to approximate Huw's presence and emotions. It was a brilliant bid to recreate the 'I' of the novel in filmic terms. However, many critics misunderstood Ford's motives and accused him of the reactionary sentimentality that he exhibited towards many of his other Celtic characters. But, rather than championing the stagnant values held by old man Morgan, Ford is actually denouncing his resistance to progress and castigating Huw for lacking the courage of his brothers' convictions. Indeed, by presenting events from Huw's naively tainted perspective, Ford implicates him in the tragedies and betrayals that education, unionism and religion might have prevented.

The performances are powerful throughout and Arthur Miller's deep-focus photography is exceptional. But did Ford really deserve to become the first director to win consecutive Oscars, especially when the competition included Orson Welles and John Huston for *Citizen Kane* and *The Maltese Falcon* respectively? ★★★★ **DP**

John Ford (1895–1973)

Who he was: Hollywood's populist poet
Hallmarks: Westerns; war films; big American subjects; Irish sentiment; brawling male buddies; regret at lost ideals; horsemen against the horizon; feisty but exasperated womenfolk; horde of Injuns; redeemable drunks
If you see one Movie, See: Stagecoach (1939)

HOW TO MAKE AN AMERICAN QUILT (1995)

Starring: *Winona Ryder (Finn Dodd), Anne Bancroft (Glady Joe Cleary), Ellen Burstyn (Hy Dodd), Kate Nelligan (Constance Saunders), Alfre Woodard (Marianna), Kate Capshaw (Sally, Finn's Mother), Adam Baldwin (Finn's Father), Dermot Mulroney (Sam), Maya Angelou (Anna)*
Director: *Jocelyn Moorhouse*
Screenwriter: *Jane Anderson, based on the novel by Whitney Otto*
15/109 mins./Drama/Romance/USA

A student reconsiders her life while spending the summer with her grandmother and her quilting circle.

Graduate student Finn retreats for the summer to the country home where her grandmother and great-aunt suppress a long-running, eccentric feud and make traditional patchwork quilts with a group of friends. The sewing circle includes celebrated authoress/poet Maya Angelou as their former maid, the artistic matriarch to whom they now all defer, Alfre Woodard as her sophisticated daughter, Jean Simmons and Kate Nelligan.

While Finn dithers over marital commitment to her would-be fiancé and labours over her thesis on womens' handicrafts, the ladies undertake a bridal quilt, pouring out the stories of their youths, family histories and loves as they stitch, the individual patches they create symbolising their life experiences. Their tales are enacted by a major collection of actresses from *Little Women*'s Claire Danes and Samantha Mathis, to venerable Esther Rolle. And when she isn't being diverted by a devastatingly sexy neighbour, Finn learns some useful and moving tips about women's eternal quest for love and fulfilment.

The weight given to some of these interweaving stories and denied others makes for an occasionally uneven but colourful and busy overall design. Many a man will run a mile to sit this one out in a pub, but with much gentler female bonding on offer, this proves to be a perfect candidate for a matinée with mother. ★★★ **AE**

HOWARD THE DUCK (1986)

Starring: *Lea Thompson (Beverly Switzler), Jeffrey Jones (Dr. Walter Jenning), Tim Robbins (Phil Blumburtt), Paul Guilfoyle (Lieutenant Welker), As Howard the Duck: Ed Gale, Chip Zien, Timothy M. Rose, Steve Sleap, Peter Baird, Mary Wells, Lisa Sturz, Jordan Prentic*
Director: *Willard Huyck*
Screenwriters: *Willard Huyck, Gloria Katz, based on the comic books by Steve Gerber*
PG/110 mins./Action/Comedy/Sci-fi/USA

Awards: *Razzies – Worst new star (The six guys and gals in the duck suit), Worst Pictures, Worst Screenplay, Worst Visual Effects*

Howard, a swinging bachelor on a world where ducks have evolved into the dominant species, is transported across the stars to Cleveland, Ohio.

He gets friendly with a rock 'n' roll chick and has to battle a scientist who is transforming into a Dark Overlord.

Before *Blade*, *Spider-Man* and the *X-Men* became blockbuster franchises, the highest-profile Marvel Comics movie was this George Lucas-backed commercial disaster – released in the UK as *Howard ... A New Breed of Hero* in a vain attempt to de-emphasise (indeed conceal) the lead character's duckiness.

Though Lucas has a reputation as a visionary when it comes to new special effects techniques, he badly misjudged here. If the film had taken the Roger Rabbit route of making its hero a toon interacting with a live-action world, *Howard the Duck* might have been the blockbuster he was hoping for. As it is, the film is stuck with, basically, a midget in a duck suit, snarkily voiced by Chip Zien.

Once you get past that, and an uncharacteristically boring performance from Tim Robbins in the Dean Jones whacky inventor role, the film isn't as bad as its reputation.

Howard – originally a supporting character in the Man-Thing comic who spun off his own, distinctively 1970s humour series – mellows somewhat in his transfer from panel to screen, though his relationship to Thompson gets perilously close to bestiality. Nevertheless, *Howard the Duck* manages to be two or three types of fun: as a crazy comedy, it has some good risqué/sick jokes to go along with its messy slapstick and bland rock music; as a monster movie, it has an outstanding performance from Jeffrey Jones as a scientist-cum-monster and an astonishingly repulsive Dark Overlord of the Universe shows up for the exciting climax. You still won't believe the duck ... ★★ **KN**

HOWARDS END (1992)

Starring: *Anthony Hopkins (Henry Wilcox), Emma Thompson (Margaret Schlegel), Vanessa Redgrave (Ruth Wilcox), Helena Bonham Carter (Helen Schlegel), Samuel West (Leonard Bast), Prunella Scales (Aunt Juley), Joseph Bennett (Paul Wilcox), Adrian Ross-Magenty (Tibby Schlegel), Jo Kendall (Annie), James Wilby (Charles Wilcox)*
Director: *James Ivory*
Screenwriter: *Ruth Prawer Jhabvala, based on the novel by E.M. Forster*
PG/140 mins./Drama/UK

Awards: *Academy Awards – Best Actress, Best Art Direction/Set Decoration, Best Adapted Screenplay, BAFTA – Best Actress, Best Film, Golden Globes – Best Drama Actress*

A family matriarch writes a note bequeathing her house to two sisters she has recently met. When she dies, her family destroy the note – but then her widowed husband becomes attracted to the older sister ...

For the last E.M. Forster novel that remained to be filmed, the reliable firm of Merchant, Ivory and Jhabvala engage a cast that is perfection in a very handsome, intelligent, witty piece.

Helena Bonham Carter and Emma Thompson are Forster's Schlegel sisters: educated, progressive thinking, middle-class gels who do kind deeds and have stimulating discussions at the tea table. An embarrassing romantic mini-drama has estranged them from the wealthy Wilcox family, but Vanessa Redgrave's ethereal Mrs. W. renews the acquaintance and takes to Thompson's Margaret so warmly she leaves her the cosy little rural retreat of Howards End. Pompous pater Anthony Hopkins is too mean to unhand the land but falls for high-spirited Margaret.

Meanwhile, Bonham Carter's Helen nobly interferes in the affairs of a poor young bank clerk desperate to better himself, entangling the three social strata of the principals in an intricate and sharp game of love, property and pride.

Thompson, in particular, is wonderful, and if all the young men look alike they are their types to a T. Events move with an astonishing and graceful rapidity in this perfectly delightful film. ★★★★ **AE**

HOWL'S MOVING CASTLE (HAURU NO UGOKO SHIRO) (2004)

Starring: *the voices of: Chieko Baisho (Sofi), Takuya Kimura (Hauru), Akihiro Miwa (Arehchi no Majo), Tatsuya Gashuin (Karushifa)/English version: Christian Bale (Howl), Jane Alan (Honey), Lauren Bacall (Witch of the Waste), Billy Crystal (Calcifer), Blythe Danner (Madam Suliman), Emily Mortimer (Young Sophie), Sofie Grabol (Sophie)*
Director: *Hayao Miyazaki*
Screenwriter: *Hayao Miyazaki, based on the novel by Diana Wynne Jones*
U/119 mins./Animation/Adventure/Japan

In a fairy-tale world between Harry Potter and Jules Verne, dowdy Sophie leads a dull existence in her family hat-shop. Then she meets Howl, a wizard who looks like a pop star, and the Witch Of The Waste, who turns her into a crone. And that's only the start ...

A few years ago, the standard perception of Japanese animé was of strange, noisy cartoons that made no sense. Animé fans would always respond in the same way: they'd point to the delightful and brilliant early films of Hayao Miyazaki, such as *My Neighbour Totoro* and *Kiki's Delivery Service*, with their thoroughly simple, lucid storytelling. Then Miyazaki's *Spirited Away* won an Oscar and suddenly everyone was a fan – despite complaints that his movies weren't so clear any more.

The irony is, now we've had a Miyazaki film in multiplexes, excellently dubbed by an A-list cast (with a subtitled version simultaneously released for purists), the director's abandoned clarity altogether. To most viewers, *Howl's Moving Castle* will prompt the same response that Lewis Carroll's Alice had to the Jabberwocky poem: 'It seems very pretty but it's rather hard to understand.' That didn't worry Japanese audiences, who made *Howl* a monster hit, but Western viewers may have less patience.

Fortunately, *Howl* is as much of a hand-drawn treat as *Spirited Away*, chock-full of numinous sunsets, fabulous organic machinery and gratuitously delightful touches. The Gilliamesque walking castle of the title is a star, stomping over hills like a misshapen dragon, but so is the wheezing little dog that pops up midway. Western viewers may find the European landscapes (based on Alsace) less exotic than the oriental bathhouse in *Spirited Away*, but a Freudian dream-cave where the heroine unearths Howl's true nature is as gorgeous an image as any in fantasy cinema, giving evocative power to an oblique love story.

On the downside, it's hard to tell if Miyazaki is playing silly buggers with expectations or has given up on plot altogether while heavily reworking this book by the fiendishly clever British kid's writer Diana Wynne Jones. The demonic war glimpsed throughout is little more than window-dressing (even though Miyazaki saw air-raids as a child and war-on-terror allegories are there for the taking), while the underlying parallels are with Peter Pan (a flying hero with arrested development) and *Eternal Sunshine Of The Spotless Mind* (a relationship turned into an out-of-synch odyssey). An outrageous cop-out ending sees castle and plot collapse in a way that may please avant-gardists, but it'll infuriate mainstream viewers who've been patiently waiting for things to come together. ★★★ **AO**

THE HOWLING (1981)

Starring: *Dee Wallace Stone, billed as Dee Wallace (Karen White), Patrick Macnee (Dr. George Waggner), John Carradine (Erle Kenton), Slim Pickins (Sam Newfield),*
Director: *Joe Dante*
Screenwriters: *John Sayles, Terence H. Winkless, based on the novel by Gary Brandner*
18/91 mins./Horror/Thriller/USA

Karen White, goes on a retreat after a traumatic incident with a serial killer. But is she really safe? And what should she fear more: regaining her memory or the creepy residents of 'The Colony'?

Right. First off, let's settle a debate that has raged among aficionados for nearly 20 years. Yes, Rick Baker won the Oscar a year down the line for his *American Werewolf In London* FX. And, yes, they are staggering. But it is Rob Bottin's work here (with inflatable air bags under a latex 'skin' and a pioneering 'hydraulic snout') that is – and ever shall be – the pinnacle of mutation effects. Amen.

And while, in certain respects, the films bear comparison, in others they couldn't be more different. Dante and old buddy John Landis tread similar ground, but they do so at opposing extremes. There may be plenty of dark humour in *The Howling* (the epilogue's 'burger shot', a character reading a book by Thomas Wolfe, clips of *The Wolf Man* and a *Little Red Riding Hood* cartoon playing in the background), but Dante scores by playing it straight: gritty, bleak and haunting right up to a climax that delivers in provocative and quite spectacular fashion. Given a green light after the success of Universal's Dracula remake the year before, not only was this the first in the 80s wave of like-minded creature features – *Wolfen* (1981), *The Company Of Wolves* and *Silver Bullet* – but it did for the lycanthropy subgenre what *Fright Night* did for vampires in 1985, cemented the ripple Dante caused with *Piranha* in 1978 and established itself as the finest, most terrifying film of its kind.

Opening with a credit sequence montage, in which wired-up television anchorwoman Karen White visits a seedy porn joint to act as bait for cannibalistic serial killer Eddie The Mangier, Dante immediately sets out his stall. Crackly, distorted voice-over (which is actually snippets of dialogue from some of the film's later scenes) is played over TV static, the neon-lit city streets stand in stark contrast to the later desolate country setting, and the pair's taut confrontation – in a claustrophobic booth – is illuminated by the flicker of a projector, culminating in an eerie sense of disorientation. Thematically it's ingenious; stylistically it's awesome. But it is when we move into the country (when Karen visits The Colony in a bid to overcome the psychological after-effects of her ordeal) that the atmosphere is calibrated up a notch or two. Repeated howls and rustlings resonate incessantly from deep within the woods, the camera becomes more frantic, more sinister and whispered tones suffuse the soundtrack: by comparison, Burkittsville seems quite the ideal spot for a picnic.

This, of course, is all foreplay. Dante probing and stimulating his audience into fevered anticipation, biding his time before unleashing the full extent of the horror. Good job then that the climax is well worth the wait. And if the film's most iconic moment (a classic of the genre) is still the sex/mate scene between Bill and Marsha, as they make the beast with two backs by bonfire-light, the film maintains the perfect balance between horror and eroticism (the legendary 'hot tub' sequence was cut from the final version to ensure it stayed that way). Trademark Dante, there is also, of course, a plethora of in-jokes to revel in. Dick Miller (as Walter Paisley, his character from Roger Gorman's *A Bucket Of Blood* in 1959) makes his standard cameo, as do Gorman himself (the man who gave Dante his big break: directing *Hollywood Boulevard* for his New World Pictures in 1975), Forrest J. Ackerman (the editor of *Famous Monsters Of Filmland*) and screenwriter John Sayles (who was in the midst of writing *Alligator* at the time).

And ten of the principal characters' names are those of real-life werewolf movie directors, reflecting this one's enduring passion for the classics – see also *Matinee*, his personal ode to bug movies in general and William Castle in particular. Ultimately, though, what elevates *The Howling* so far above its contemporaries is its uniform quality. The direction, effects, editing and script (by Sayles and Terence H. Winkless, who went on to direct the vastly underrated *The Nest* in 1988) are seamless. Likewise, the supporting cast (including trusty character players Slim Pickens, Kevin McCarthy and John Carradine) are outstanding in a field so often plagued by mediocrity.

Seminal 80s scream queen Wallace, too, whips up the perfect blend of vulnerability and sass, enlivening an already witty script and lending genuine pathos to the killer finale.

Even if its reputation has been slightly tarnished by no less than six, incrementally execrable, sequels, the original *Howling* stands alone. A low-key, lower-budget (and how wisely that paltry $2 million was spent) homage of the highest order. ★★★★ **MD**

HUDSON HAWK (1991)

Starring: *Bruce Willis (Eddie 'Hudson Hawk' Hawkins), Danny Aiello (Tommy Five-Tone), Andie MacDowell (Anna Baragli), James Coburn (George Kaplan), Richard E. Grant (Darwin Mayflower), Sandra Bernhard (Minerva Mayflower), David Caruso (Kit Kat)*
Director: *Michael Lehmann*
Screenwriters: *Steven E. de Souz, Daniel Waters, based on a story by Bruce Willis, Robert Kraft*
15/100 mins./Action/Adventure/Comedy/USA

A retired cat burglar is persuaded to come out of retirement for one last robbery spree.

Already known to have gone well over its budget while on location in Budapest and Rome, Hudson Hawk reached our screens with the added burden of having been slaughtered by US critics who likened it to famous big budget turkeys like *Raise The Titanic* and *Ishtar*. True, the film has its flaws (like an over-the-top Wicked Witch performance from Sandra Bernhard), but the positives outweigh the negatives, with Bruce Willis at his wisecracking best in the title role.

Hudson Hawk is a master cat burglar, released after 10 years in Sing Sing, who decides to go straight and run the bar he jointly owns with his best buddy Tommy. But, if his wish had come true there wouldn't be much of a movie, so it's not long before he's blackmailed by evil twosome Darwin and Minerva Mayflower into stealing the model of a horse made by Leonardo da Vinci. What he doesn't know is that the pair don't want the horse for its historical value, but for a crystal which, when connected with two others, will make da Vinci's legendary 'Gold Machine' turn lead into – hey! – gold.

After a few complicated plot twists involving James Coburn as a CIA agent who also wants the crystals and Andie MacDowell who may be working for him, the Mayflowers or someone entirely different, Hawk finds himself transported to Rome to steal another da Vinci objet d'art from The Vatican. It's all a bit like *In Like Flint* but with the advantage of the Willis-Aiello double-act; a nice touch is when the pair – neither of whom wear watches – time their burglaries to the length of a song, both singing 'Swinging On A Star' to themselves (backed up by a full orchestra) while they pick locks and dodge alarms.

What director Lehmann has made is essentially a multi-million dollar cult movie with great effects, a witty script and some good performances, but some of the eccentric (and occasionally slapstick) humour may not appeal to a mass audience. ★★ **JB**

THE HUDSUCKER PROXY (1994)

Starring: *Tim Robbins (Norville Barnes), Jennifer Jason Leigh (Amy Archer), Paul Newman (Sidney J. Mussburger), Charles Durning (Waring Hudsucker), John Mahoney (Chief)*
Director: *Joel Coen*
Screenwriters: *Ethan Coen, Joel Coen, Sam Raimi*
PG/115 mins./Comedy/Drama/USA

Just as Norville Barns lands a dull job in the mailroom of the Hudsucker corporation, the firm's founder is taking a suicide leap from the top floor. In order to take control of the business, the board must force shares to decrease in value rapidly, so they put Norville in charge.

Here, collaborating with uberproducer Joel Silver and co-writer Sam Raimi, the Coens go for an archetypally populist story but tell it in an arcane style that won't disappoint their fans but will prove hard to take for many.

Evoking the Hollywood urban fairytales of Howard Hawks or Frank Capra, this is set in a magical New York in 1959 where Norville Barnes arrives to take a job in the mailroom of the monolithic Hudsucker Industries just as the firm's founder takes a suicide leap from the top floor. Executive Mussberger reasons that the board can only take control of the company if they make the stock plummet until they can afford to buy it, so he recruits the mooncalf Norville as the company's new president. A hard-bitten lady journo (Leigh, doing a neat Katharine Hepburn-cum-Rosalind Russell turn) exposes Norville, feels guilty about it and then falls for him, and the empty-headed genius' stupid idea turns out to be the hula hoop, whose instant success sends Hudsucker stock rising and prompts Mussberger to extreme dirty trickery.

The Silver influence can be seen in the sheer scale of the production, reflected in the amazing architecture of the Hudsucker Building, which is half-Metropolis and half-Gotham City with a giant clock that relates to the inner workings of the universe. While the story and the characters are perfect pastiche, making them hard to be involved with, human warmth is imported by the sheer joy of the directorial flourishes. Always a master of the set-piece, Joel Coen stages a remarkable montage illustrating the snowballing of the 50s hoop craze. He also pulls off a wonderful side-trip into fantasy as Durning's angelic ghost shows up in the finale to influence the outcome of the plot.

The dark vision of *Blood Simple* or *Barton Fink* is mellowed slightly by the comic by-play and the oddly innocent, though corruptible, romantic leads. Like all Coen films, this has a human character who represents a demonic force (the Devil here is a little man who scrapes dead execs' names off their office doors), but it tries for balance by including an angelic time-keeper who helps restore the order of the universe. While not to everyone's tastes, this is without doubt one of the most exhilarating films on the Coen's CV. ★★★★ **KN**

⊙ HULK (2003)

Starring: *Eric Bana (Bruce Banner), Jennifer Connelly (Betty Ross), Sam Elliott (Ross), Josh Lucas (Talbot), Nick Nolte (Father), Paul Kersey (Young David Banner), Cara Buono (Edith Banner), Todd Tesen (Young Ross), Kevin O. Rankin (Harper), Celia Weston (Mrs. Krensler), Mike Erwin (Teenage Bruce Banner)*
Director: *Ang Lee*
Screenwriters: *John Turman, Michael France, James Schamus, based on a story by Schamus and Marvel characters created by Stan Lee and Jack Kirby*
12A/138 mins./Action/Sci-fi/USA

Genetic scientist Bruce Banner gets an unwelcome dose of gamma rays and begins to suffer violent mood swings. Very violent mood swings that capture the attention of some dodgy military geezers...

In what is probably the most hotly anticipated adaptation of a 'graphic novel' since the last one, director Ang Lee sets out his stall from the first frame.

In a bravura statement of intent, he whips through the expositional opening passages, wherein crazed genetic scientist Dr David Banner realises he has passed his self-mutilated genes on to his baby son Bruce and an unspeakably traumatic domestic disturbance ensues. Using every trick in the Exhibitionist Director's Handbook, Lee pushes his Avid to the point where you want to scream, 'Leave that poor digital editing suite alone!'

A combination of antic split-screen, wipes, cut-outs, overlays, match shots, collages, freeze-frame and artificial crash-zooms energetically mimic the dynamics of comic-book art. At certain points, he even pans between individually framed panels of action as if the camera is scanning a page. The ploy becomes slightly intrusive as the film progresses, but it sets the tone brilliantly, as does a mise en scène that ranges from full realism to slightly off-whack to outright surreal, with some disquietingly vivid dreamscapes thrown in.

What is so effective about this is that it nullifies the material's inherent absurdities by tackling them on their own turf. Just as Tim Burton's *Batman* did, albeit more literally, it creates a universe uncannily close to our own, but one in which plausibility becomes irrelevant. It also allows the film to explore some surprisingly dark psychological corners without fear of looking ridiculous.

That's further helped by a cast of actors skilful enough to deliver comic-book dialogue as if they mean it. Bana is perfect as the remote, damaged Bruce Banner, a sensitive, intelligent man who has a beast within him so terrible he daren't unleash it, but who gets off on the release whenever he does. Connelly – with her vast, soulful eyes, in which tears brim and spill over precisely on cue – invests an invariably thankless role with poignant grace, while Sam Elliott and Nick Nolte have fun seeing who can growl the best. It's a tribute to whatever hard living Nolte has been doing lately that he actually wins.

All of this would come to naught, of course, if the Big Green Man came over like Jar Jar Binks on steroids. Thankfully he does not (although he does look a bit like Brendan Fraser). We might look back on him in five years' time and cringe – hell, we might look back on him in six months and cringe – but for now, Hulk is the benchmark for a fully integrated CGI character. Glimpsed out of context in the trailers, he had us worried.

In Lee's artfully created environment, he works a treat, and the fact that he doesn't look quite real only adds to the larger-than-life effect. Whatever he's doing – smashing whole buildings to atoms, pummelling le merde out of a mutant French poodle, twirling tanks around like an Olympic hammer thrower or biting off the business end of a Stinger missile and spitting it back at the helicopter that fired it – he's absolutely the star of the show, a rampaging force of nature, an indestructible pea-green id.

There's an occasional iffy moment but, for the most part, Lee is careful to keep *Hulk* a blur of furious motion, which is what we came for anyway. There are some more subtle touches too, visual echoes of 50s sci-fi and sly references to *Frankenstein*, *American Werewolf* and, of course, *King Kong*.

The ending is over-ambitious and the film drags occasionally when Hulk isn't centre stage. But overall, this is outstanding entertainment. The only real disappointment is that we never find out where Banner gets his infinitely expandable purple boxers. Perhaps we should just be grateful that he does. ★★★★ **KN**

⊙ THE HUNCHBACK OF NOTRE DAME (1939)

Starring: *Charles Laughton (The Hunchback), Cedric Hardwicke (Frollo), Thomas Mitchell (Clopin), Maureen O'Hara (Esmeralda), Edmond O'Brien (Gringoire)*
Director: *William Dieterle*
Screenwriters: *Sonya Levien, Bruno Frank, based on* Notre-Dame de Paris *by Victor Hugo*
PG/115 mins./Drama/Horror/USA

A small act of kindness persuades the harangued bell-ringer Quasimodo to protect Esmeralda, when the gypsy girl takes sanctuary in the medieval Parisian cathedral of Notre Dame after she's accused of killing her lover by the hypocritical Count Frollo.

Charles Laughton always took great pride in having 'discovered' Maureen O'Hara (who had debuted opposite him in Alfred Hitchcock's *Jamaica Inn*) and there's a genuine affinity between them in RKO's adaptation of Victor Hugo's 1831 novel. The beauty and the beast story had twice been filmed as *Esmeralda* (1905 and 1922) before Wallace Worsley released his lavish silent 1923 version of *The Hunchback of Notre Dame*, which featured a tour de force performance from the 'Man of a Thousand Faces', Lon Chaney.

However, Laughton very much made the part of Quasimodo his own and it remained one of his personal favourites (if only because, for once, he didn't have to diet or wear a corset). Wearing make-up created by George and R. Gordon Bau, he exuded a humanity and humility that belied his grotesque appearance and, moreover, brought a surprising agility to the role – which was all the more impressive as he was saddled with a wire-framed, foam-filled hump, which was deeply uncomfortable to wear at the height of the Californian summer.

The shoot was tinged with melancholy, however, as war broke out between Britain and Germany on the day that William Dieterle filmed the sequence in which Quasimodo rings the tower bells. Laughton's disappointed rage is readily evident (as he recognised the poignancy of the moment, as the bells in his homeland would be silenced for the duration of the conflict) and he continued the peal long after the take was over. Indeed, Dieterle (who was a German emigré) intended the film to highlight the evils of authoritarianism and the Expressionist elements in Van Nest Polglase's sets and Joseph H. August's cinematography were consciously designed to evoke the dark psychology of German cinema in the immediate pre-Nazi era.

Costing around $2 million, this was one of the most expensive pictures that RKO ever made. But it was money well spent, as the judicious blend of medieval morality, Gothic melodrama and political allegory (which is occasionally leavened with sly humour) has lost little of its affecting power. ★★★★★ **DP**

THE HUNCHBACK OF NOTRE DAME (1996)

Starring: *the voices of: Tom Hulce (Quasimodo), Demi Moore (Esmeralda), Tony Jay (Frollo), Kevin Kline (Phoebus), Jason Alexander (Hugo), Mary Wickes (Laverne), David Ogden Stiers (Archdeacon), Heidi Mollenhauer (Esmeralda's singing voice)*
Directors: *Gary Trousdale, Kirk Wise*
Screenwriters: *Irene Mecchi, Jonathan Roberts, Bob Tzudiker, Noni White, based on a story by Tab Hunter and the novel* Notre-Dame de Paris *by Victor Hugo*
U/91 mins./Animation/Family/USA

Hunchbacked bell-ringer Quasimodo befriends the beautiful Esmeralda, but his adoptive father Frollo tries to corrupt their friendship.

Mischievous bunch, the Disney decision-makers. Having got historical sticklers' collective goats with the clap-trap that was *Pocahontas*, what do they do? Have a crack at a great literary classic, and for good measure make it French. Truly a case of Up Yours, Delors – we shall kidnap the delicate maiden that is your cultural heritage and do with her what we will. You have to admire their front.

Actually – although there are, of course, many liberties taken with Victor Hugo's story of the orphaned bell-ringer, Quasimodo, befriended by the beautiful Esmeralda – this is relatively free of the gag-inducing, moral-majority-pleasing, family values guff that blights many Disney movies. Preoccupied with tolerance and acceptance, its heart is definitely in the right place, with the only wrong note being the rewritten ending: who ends up with whom is a lesson in Disney's view of the natural order of things.

Disney films can be sliced up quite nicely into their component parts – Baddies, Goodies, Songs, Babe Factor, Laughs, Fascism, and Quality Of Funny Little Joke Characters. Split like this, *Hunchback* does quite well. The baddie Frollo (Quasimodo's adoptive dad) is a complete bastard, transmogrified into a government official from Hugo's corrupt archdeacon, and well worth five stars. Kevin Kline's war hero Phoebus is a self-deprecating man of the people, and Quasimodo is a goody of charm and valour. Five stars. The songs are rubbish – one star. Esmeralda, voiced by and bearing a resemblance to Demi Moore, is enough to reduce grown men to tears. If you thought Princess Jasmine was a comely coquette and Pocahontas, frankly, very attractive, Esmeralda will make you question your sanity. Eight stars.

There are, however, not enough laughs in this movie – the whole thing is tinged with a darkness and religious symbolism that sits ill with the film's supposed childish nature. Two stars. The Fascist tendencies of so much Disney output is largely missing. Four stars. As for the Funny Little Joke Characters, they're not up there with, say, Timon and Pumbaa, but the Gargoyles have sufficient charm to pull through. Three stars. All of which adds up to a solid, enjoyable, beautifully animated Disney movie, but one not quite out of the top drawer. ★★★★ **PT**

THE HUNGER (1983)

Starring: *Catherine Deneuve (Miriam Blaylock), David Bowie (John), Susan Sarandon (Sarah Roberts), Cliff De Young (Tom Haver), Beth Ehlers (Alice Cavender), Dan Hedaya (Lt Allegrazza)*
Director: *Tony Scott*
Screenwriters: *James Costigan, Ivan Davis, Michael Thomas, based on the novel by Whitley Strieber*
18/100 mins./Horror/USA

Blood-drinking immortal Miriam Blaylock realises her husband of the last few centuries is about to age rapidly, and targets longevity specialist Sarah as a replacement.

While it doesn't quite refute the oft-proposed theory that any film would be improved by the addition of a gratuitous lesbian sex scene, *The Hunger* remains a baffling, obscure effort – too arty to work as a horror film, too pretty-pretty to be a character drama.

Tony Scott's first mainstream directorial credit, it's the tonyscottiest vampire movie ever made, suffocating the horror with perfume commercial style. Catherine Deneuve and David Bowie are sharply-dressed predators who drift around New York showing off their ankh switchblades and perfect cheekbones as they slaughter and suck off disposable nightclubbers between fluttering pigeons, swirling smoke, billowing curtains, elegant artefacts and screeching monkeys.

As Scott pauses to admire the tasteful decor with which these killers surround themselves, the score ranges hiply between gloomrock (Bauhaus's 'Bela Lugosi's Dead', inevitably) and erotic opera (the Flower Duet from 'Lakme'). The plot, from a novel by famous alien abductee Whitley Strieber (which is poorly written but you'll need to read if you want a hope of following the story), is shored up with bits (especially the ending) borrowed from the much better (and sexier) *Daughters of Darkness*.

Dick Smith contributes excellent make-up effects which produce a horde of inexplicable zombies for a finale which goes beyond incomprehensibility into realms of the abstract guaranteed to have you howling for the screenwriter's blood. Despite arch affectations, it's kind of fun, memorable for its chicly absurd lesbian scene between elegant Deneuve and an unashamed Susan Sarandon and a classic bit of medical paranoia as Bowie, told to sit in the waiting room until the doctor can see him, ages two hundred years. ★★ **KN**

THE HUNT FOR RED OCTOBER (1990)

Starring: *Sean Connery (Captain Marko Ramius), Alec Baldwin (Jack Ryan), Scott Glenn (Commander Bart Mancuso), Sam Neill (Captain 2nd Rank Vasily Borodin), James Earl Jones (Admiral James Greer), Joss Ackland (Ambassador Andrei Lysenko)*
Director: *John McTiernan*
Screenwriters: *Larry Ferguson, Donald Stewart, based on the book by Tom Clancy*
PG/134 mins./Thriller/USA

Awards: *Academy Awards – Best Sound Effects Editing*

It is the mid-80s, and legendary Soviet skipper Captain Ramius, commander of the newest submarine in the Soviet fleet, the *Red October*, has snuck away from his masters and declared his intention to defect. While the American government suspect a trap, it is up to CIA agent Jack Ryan to work out whether they are facing friend or foe.

The first, and most successful, screen adaptation of Tom Clancy's fat and complicated Cold War techno-thrillers, which, nautical accuracy apart, makes for a robust Hollywood action movie. There is something almost nostalgic about its fizz of Cold War paranoia, and resolute stance that accents and realism can be damned in the face of broad star power and ILM's best special effects. There are even rare flashes of inspiration amongst such all round solidness, the sly segue from the 'Soviet' cast speaking subtitled Russian into audience-friendly English is a terrific piece of movie cheating.

John McTiernan, Hollywood's go-to man for the stiff-bricked formula of mature action movies, does a fine job spinning copious subplots out of what is a straightforward storyline. That Jack Ryan has to convince his superiors of his hunch that Ramius is for real, before they blow him out of the water as the irked Sovs have demanded. There's treachery in the pinging confines of the *Red October* and equal amounts of skulduggery Stateside, although the film strains to drum up some action for its hero to excel in. Alec Baldwin, who would foolishly relinquish the role of Jack Ryan to Harrison Ford, tempers down the snap and snarl of his personality, and comes across stalwart but dull. Connery is much more fun, despite his inescapable burr, and there is a cool mystery that underpins Ramius, in what his secret motive for betraying his communist brethren might be.

The underwater scenes bubble away authentically, but we're not exactly talking about the clammy verité of *Das Boot*. This is your basic well-mounted suspenseful epic, finely decked, muscular and gloriously nonsensical. ★★★ **IN**

⊙ HUSBANDS AND WIVES (1992)

Starring: *Woody Allen (Gabe Roth), Mia Farrow (Judy Roth), Judy Davis (Sally), Juliette Lewis (Rain), Liam Neeson (Michael), Sydney Pollack (Jack), Lysette Anthony (Sam)*
Director: *Woody Allen*
Screenwriter: *Woody Allen*
15/107 mins./Comedy/Drama/USA

Awards: *BAFTA – Best Original Screenplay*

When married couple Sally and Jack declare that they're going their separate ways, it forces their friends Gabe and Judy to reconsider their own relationship.

Rush-released at the time with typical Hollywoodian sensitivity to capitalise on the unfolding drama of Woody Allen and Mia Farrow's break-up, this black comedy of urban manners positively brims with poignant on-screen exchanges. Centred on the familiar Allen square-dance around two couples and shot self-consciously as a documentary, the film is a triumph both as art and propaganda, confirming Allen's skill as a comic director while attempting to acquit him of the charges of philandering he faced in real life.

Woody is Gabe Roth, an English literature lecturer and novelist, whose marriage to Judy (Farrow) is drawing to a close, though neither is quite ready to admit it. The catalyst comes when their best friends – Jack and Sally – break up, opening the Roths' own can of worms and sparking much angst and to-camera soul-searching about the nature of romantic love and passion in marriage. Asked by Judy whether he fancies the 'young girls' in his English class, Allen fences beautifully: 'Let me tell you, they don't want to know an old man,' but when Raine, a precocious 20-year-old who writes essays entitled 'Oral Sex In The Age Of Deconstruction', tells Roth she loves his new novel they quickly become platonically entwined.

'Do you ever hide things from me?' asks Judy. 'No, do you?' Allen lies. Incredibly, the real-life resonance of lines like these (admittedly dulled over time) doesn't so much kill the humour as make it all the more delicious, with Allen once again drawing fine performances from his supporting cast, particularly Davis as a frigid-neurotic, and Liam Neeson as Michael, her earthy stand-in lover. Cast again in her *Cape Fear* Lolita role – but this time more seducer than seduced – Lewis is also completely believable. The same cannot be said for Allen who, while allowing Farrow to get in some minor digs, emerges as the more sympathetic and honourable character.

Allen has long warned his fans against reading too much into his movies, but this time it can only be to his advantage. As a film *Husbands And Wives* is probably Allen's best effort since *Hannah And Her Sisters*, but as a kind of docudrama it may well be remembered as his least honest. ★★★★ **MH**

⊙ HUSTLE AND FLOW (2005)

Starring: *Terrence Howard (DJay), Anthony Anderson (Key), Taryn Manning (Nola), Taraji P. Henson (Shug), DJ Qualls (Shelby), Ludacris (Skinny Black)*
Director: *Craig Brewer*
Screenwriter: *Craig Brewer*
15/116 mins./Drama/Music/USA

Awards: *Academy Awards – Best Original Song*

While Skinny Black enjoys life as a platinum-selling artist, his former rap peer DJay works the Memphis streets as a small-time pimp. But a chance meeting with old friend Key, coupled with the news that Skinny is coming to town, convinces DJay that he might have one last shot at the big time …

Hustle and Flow flaunts all the features of an unwashed indie wannabe. It has a novice filmmaker at the helm, an anti-hero protagonist at the centre and is coloured by just enough chauvinism to create a whiff of controversy. The obligatory Sundance award completes the look. And yet, what appears to be a rap *Requiem For A Dream* actually plays like a pimp *Pretty Woman* – a feelgood fairy-tale with a big musical heart. In another life, *Hustle and Flow* might even have taken flight as a vehicle for that most dubious of double threats – Hilary Duff.

The effect is so striking it can only be deliberate. Writer-director Craig Brewer opens with Terrence Howard's charismatic DJay in soliloquy, outlining his brand of sexist Darwinism to jailbait rainmaker Nola, but the subsequent mean-street scenes lack the necessary mean streak to convince you that DJay can walk the walk as well as talk the talk. For all his bravado, DJay is a big pussycat, sheltering pregnant prostitute Shug long after she stopped bringing home the green.

But as soon as Howard steps up to the mic, the movie crackles to life. Any drama that places the creative act under scrutiny must have confidence in its material, and Brewer is sitting on platinum. It matters not if you enter the theatre thinking 'crunk' – the peculiar flavour of Southern hip-hop cooked up here – must be a misprint; to watch these rousing anthems take shape is genuinely thrilling.

Where Eminem picked his way through the dramatic moments in *8 Mile* before exploding on stage, the adventure here is to watch Howard, a rap novice, grow in stature until he's spitting out flows like a pro. The 33-year-old former supporting player seizes his once-in-a-lifetime opportunity, turning in a performance that manages to be cocksure one moment, vulnerable the next. DJay's nice-guy makeover borders on the trite, but so effective are the musical passages that Howard heads off to the climactic showdown with Skinny Black carrying the hopes of the entire audience along with his demo tape. The long-awaited tête-à-tête doesn't disappoint either, a nail-biting set-piece that leaves DJay's fate in the balance right through a coda that is far too tidy, but still enormously satisfying. ★★★★ **CK**

Most Expensive Move Memorabilia — TOP 10

1. Ruby slippers ... *Wizard of Oz* ... $666,000
2. Marlon Brando's script ... *The Godfather* ... $312,000
3. Clark Gable's script ... *Gone With The Wind* ... $244,500
4. Rosebud sled ... *Citizen Kane* ... $233,500
5. Aston Martin DB5 ... *Goldeneye* ... £157,750
6. Tony Monero's white suit ... *Saturday Night Fever* ... $145,000
7. Oddjob's bowler hat ... *Goldfinger* ... £62,000
8. Charlie Chaplin's cane ... *Modern Times* ... £47,800
9. Indy's whip ... *Indiana Jones trilogy* ... £27,600
10. Marilyn Monroe's 'Shimmy' dress ... *Some Like It Hot* ... £19,800

THE HUSTLER (1961)

Starring: *Paul Newman ('Fast' Eddie Felson), Jackie Gleason (Minnesota Fats), Piper Laurie (Sarah Packard), George C. Scott (Bert Gordon), Myron McCormick (Charlie Burns)*
Director: *Robert Rossen*
Screenwriters: *Sidney Carroll, Robert Rossen, based on the novel by Walter Tevis*
15/134 mins./Drama/Romance/Sport/USA

Awards: *Academy Awards – Best Black and White Art Direction/Set Decoration, Best Black and White Cinematography, BAFTA – Best Film, Best Foreign Actor*

Fast Eddie Felson, a hot young player, turns up at Ames' Pool Hall in Chicago, thinking he's ready to take on the legendary champion Minnesota Fats.

Adapted from the brilliant novel by Walter Tevis, who also wrote *The Man Who Fell to Earth*, this is perhaps the best-ever games-playing movie.

Despite the fragile excellence of Piper Laurie as the crippled alcoholic with whom the hero shacks up after his first humiliation at the cue of the Fat Man, audiences tend to resent time spent away from the table action as the hero suffers enough to develop the character he needs to back up his stick skills.

Like Tevis, director Robert Rossen isn't as much interested in the ins and outs of pool as in the way the game focuses the characters of the players. Early in his career, Newman was always best when cast, as here, as a shallow heel who gets his come-uppance (caught hustling in a bar, he has his hands broken by angry punters). Newman's showy Method performance is perfectly offset by the underplayed mastery demonstrated by TV legend Gleason (*The Honeymooners*) as the dignified Minnesota Fats and George C. Scott as the horrifically calculating gambler who sets Fast Eddie up for a final contest in a way that remains shocking decades later.

Rossen makes outstanding use of black and white widescreen cinematography (by veteran Eugen Schufftan), perhaps the best possible medium for filming shabby pool halls, Greyhound bus stations and smoke-filled gambling joints.

In the 1980s, Tevis wrote a sequel, *The Color of Money*, which was filmed – very loosely – by Martin Scorsese, with Newman reprising the Fast Eddie role and Tom Cruise strutting as the new hotshot. Another Scorsese connection is that Jake LaMotta, of *Raging Bull* fame, has a cameo as a bartender. ★★★★★ **KN**

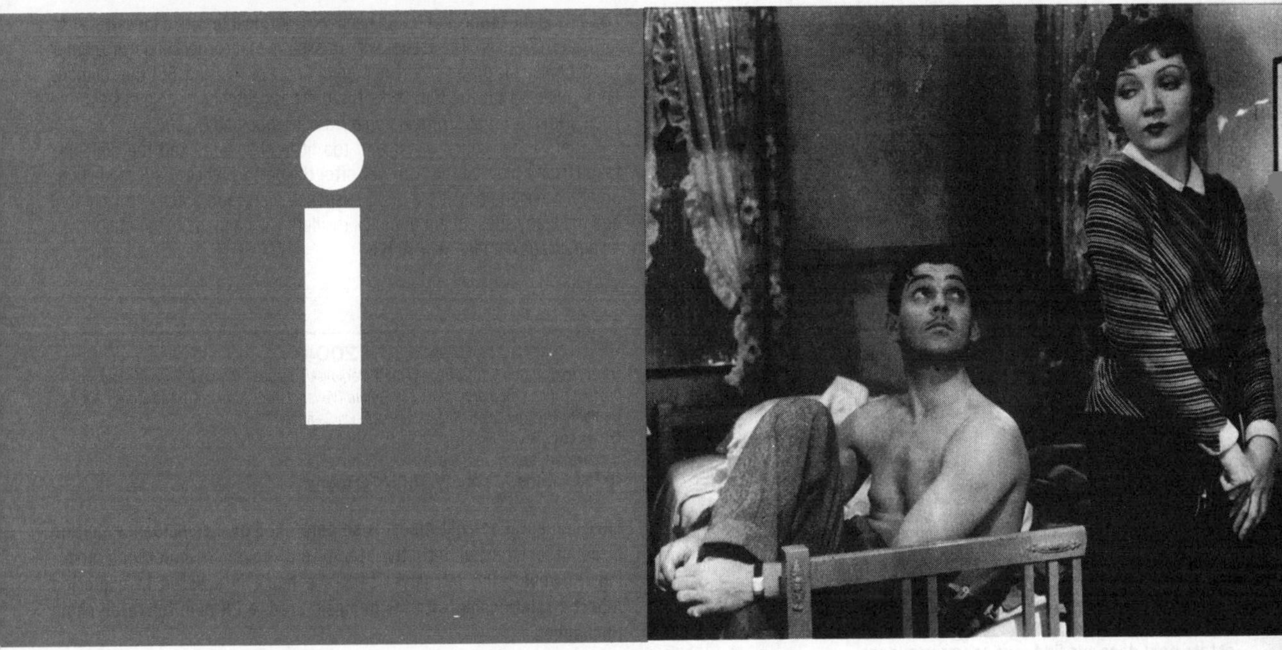

⦿ I AM A FUGITIVE FROM A CHAIN GANG (1932)

Starring: *Paul Muni (James Allen), Glenda Farrell (Marie Woods), Helen Vinson (Helen), Preston Foster (Pete), Allen Jenkins (Barney Sykes), Edward Ellis (Bomber Wells)*
Director: *Mervyn LeRoy*
Screenwriters: *Howard J. Green, Brown Holmes, Sheridan Gibney, based on the autobiography* I Am a Fugitive From A Georgia Chain Gang *by Robert E. Burns*
PG/93 mins./Crime/USA

James Allen is arrested after a minor robbery and sentenced to ten years in a brutal labour camp. He escapes and becomes a respectable citizen, but his vindictive wife informs on him and he finds himself back on the chain gang.

The most powerful of Warner Brothers' early 1930s 'social problem' films, this indictment of organised cruelty remains potent, hard-hitting melodrama. Adapted from the autobiography of escapee Robert E. Burns, it skates about some specifics, never naming the state which claps the hero into grand guignol prison camps (the book was called *I Am a Fugitive From a Georgia Chain Gang*) but is eye-openingly frank for a film of its vintage.

Besides the suffering convicts, who have to ask permission to wipe sweat out of their eyes while swinging sledgehammers and are whipped with a leather strap for 'pulling a faint' in the field, the movie features a sequence in a small-town brothel run by familiar character actor Allen ('Officer Dibble') Jenkins and a wry, sexy, touching scene as Allen, freshly broken out of jail and wrung out with paranoia and exhaustion, at first resists the gentle approaches of the hooker (Noel Francis) who has been told to make him happy.

Mervyn LeRoy, fresh from *Little Caesar*, stages classic set-pieces which turn on Muni's harrowing, understated performance: as when Allen's smug preacher brother tells him that the state has broken its promise to give him a pardon if he returned voluntarily to jail or the shadowed punchline as the fugitive Allen appears briefly like a haggard ghost to his society girlfriend (Helen Vinson). 'How do you live?' 'I steal!'

Val Kilmer plays Burns in a 1987 TV remake, *The Man who Broke 1,000 Chains* – but the film's influence can be seen in a run of pictures including *Sullivan's Travels*, *Cool Hand Luke* and *O Brother Where Art Thou?* ★★★★ **KN**

⦿ I AM CURIOUS – YELLOW (JAG ÄR NYFIKEN – EN FILM I GULT) (1967)

Starring: *Lena Nyman (Anna Lena Lisabet Nyman), Vilgot Sjöman (Vilgot Sjöman), Börje Ahlstedt (Börje), Peter Lindgren (Lena's Father), Chris Wahlstrom (Rune's Woman)*
Director: *Vilgot Sjöman*
Screenwriter: *Vilgot Sjöman*
18/121 mins./Docu-drama/Sweden

In between conducting interviews with celebrities and ordinary citizens on the state of the world, Lena makes love around Stockholm with her boyfriend, Börje.

Vilgot Sjöman was no stranger to controversy before the release of this notorious study of 1960s attitudes. He had discussed homosexuality, bestiality and rape in *491* before considering incest in the period drama, *My Sister, My Love*. However, this curious blend of agit-prop and pseudo-porn became a cause célèbre when it was seized by US Customs and Barney Rossett and Grove Press went all the way to the Supreme Court to secure its release, just as they had done with such novels as Henry Miller's *Tropic of Cancer* and D.H. Lawrence's *Lady Chatterley's Lover*.

The film went on to earn $15 million and remained the highest-grossing foreign film in the States for the next 25 years. It certainly divided the critics, with the New York Times branding it a 'genuinely vile and disgusting Swedish Meatball'. But Sjöman himself preferred to call it 'a polemic kaleidoscope. A mixture of reportage, imagination, demagogy. Made from the platform of the dissatisfied left.'

The inclusion of such serious figures as Martin Luther King, cabinet minister Olaf Palme and the Russian poet Yevgenii Yevtushenko gave the discussions a certain legitimacy. But in seeking people's opinions on everything from the Church and State to Franco and Vietnam and sex and violence, Lena Nyman made such an aggressive interrogator that few provided coherent, let alone intelligent answers. Indeed, we learn more about her than the mindset of the nation, as she comes to embody radicalism, politico-sexual liberation and the potential for change.

Sjöman shot 400,000 hours of footage in all and he followed *Yellow* with *I Am Curious* – Blue (1968), with the titles referring to the colours of the Swedish flag. However, the second film was somewhat overshadowed by the fuss caused by its predecessor. Yet, they offer fascinating contrasts when seen together, with the former's search for a father figure and the rejection of a male lover finding echo in the latter's pursuit of a maternal influence and the dismissal of Lena's lesbian friend, Sonja (Sonja Lindgren). **★★★ DP**

I CAPTURE THE CASTLE (2003)

Starring: *Cassandra Mortmain (Romola Garai), Rose Byrne (Rose Mortmain), Bill Nighy (James Mortmain), Tara Fitzgerald (Topaz Mortmain), Marc Blucas (Neil Cotton), Henry Thomas (Simon Cotton), Henry Cavill (Stephen Colley)*
Director: *Tim Fywell*
Screenwriter: *Heidi Thomas, based on the novel by Dodie Smith*
PG/113 mins./Drama/Romance/UK

Seventeen-year-old Cassandra lives with her eccentric family in a crumbling castle in 1930s Suffolk. Two handsome young brothers inherit the estate next door and first love seems imminent.

Luckily for the girls, they're not just wealthy, but handsome too. But fans of the Dodie Smith novel – a touchstone for a certain generation – may wonder why these would-be prince charmings are so bland.

It's warmly performed against luscious English scenery but despite a break-out performance by Romola Garai, never more than pleasantly pleasing. **★★★ JB**

I CONFESS (1953)

Starring: *Montgomery Clift (Fr. Logan), Anne Baxter (Ruth Grandfort), Karl Malden (Inspector Larne), Brian Aherne (Willy Robertson), Roger Dann (Pierre Grandfort)*
Director: *Alfred Hitchcock*
Screenwriters: *George Tabori, William Archibald, based on the play by Paul Anthelme*
PG/95 mins./Thriller/USA

Father Logan, a Quebec priest, takes confession from a murderer. He is tormented not only by the sanctity of the confession, his priestly vow never to reveal what he has heard in the confessional, but by the cops, and the killer begins to arrange things so that it seems the priest himself is the guilty party.

Made in 1953, in the awkward period between his glossy black and white 1940s romantic thrillers and coldly-coloured psychological masterpieces, *I Confess* has never been ranked among Alfred Hitchcock's best. The director himself, uncomfortable with star Clift, was dismissive and subsequent career studies have been hard-put to elevate its reputation.

Nevertheless, minor Hitchcock is usually more interesting than major anyone else – and there are a lot of fascinating angles and aspects. The sternly Catholic and fiendishly plot-happy Hitch picked this project because of what would now be called the 'high concept', which is so strong that it's surprising more elaborate remakes haven't been forthcoming.

Clift, a specialist in agonised male beauty, is better than Hitch thought, his own complex sexuality giving an edge to the character's clerical agony, not only in the crime plot but in his near-relationship with a lovestruck ex-girlfriend (Francis). The scenes with Hasse's meekly cruel killer, who comes to recognise his power over the man of God, are riveting. But the religious angle means that the film lacks the deftness Hitchcock displays even in such grim stories as *Strangers on a Train*, *Vertigo* and *Psycho*.

There is too much angst and too little suspense. And the dialogue, taken from a play, blathers on well after the performances have made their points. Nevertheless, it's a good suspense piece and stacks up very well against many subsequent gimmick thrillers – it's a muddle, but at least it's an ambitious muddle. **★★★ KN**

I HEART HUCKABEES (2004)

Starring: *Jason Schwartman (Albert Markovski), Isabelle Huppert (Caterine Vauban), Dustin Hoffman (Bernard Jaffe), Lily Tomlin (Vivian Jaffe), Jude Law (Brad Stand), Mark Wahlberg (Tommy Corn), Naomi Watts (Dawn Campbell)*
Director: *David O'Russell*
Screenwriters: *Jeff Baena, David O'Russell*
15/106 mins./Comedy/U.S./Germany

Environmental activist Albert is so perplexed by a coincidence that he hires an 'existential detective' team to discover its underlying meaning. However, the intrusive 'tecs are more interested in exploring Albert's relationship with his nemesis Brad, a PR man for retail chain Huckabees . . .

Two key questions throb at the centre of David O'Russell's first outing since 99 Gulf War actioner *Three Kings*. Firstly, the big one: what's the meaning of life? And secondly, the even bigger one: how the hell did he convince Fox to greenlight a bizarre, nebulous comedy which involves – among other things – bad poetry, quantum theory, a 9/11-frazzled fireman, Shania Twain eating chicken salad and an intellectual conflict between Eastern philosophical notions of universal interconnectedness and the more nihilistic musings of Sartre?

Of course, the first question can't really be answered, even if Russell makes a fair fist of it. As for the second, well, it seems that a good script can count for a lot, even if it's impossible to pitch in fewer than 50 words. It can attract a great cast, too, Russell's game ensemble savouring lines like, 'There is no remainder in the mathematics of reality,' and, 'I don't see this as therapy; it's just that I'm proactive and these people are action-oriented . . .'

Tagline
An existential comedy.

It's not for everyone, that's for sure. You could easily see it as a movie that's as much about nothing as it is about everything, and its meandering plot is little more than a collage of whimsical skits, allowing tangential events to become central while pushing seemingly important events out of the foreground. It's also arguable that what *I Heart Huckabees* really lacks is, ironically, heart, its characters mere vehicles for Russell's existential explorations.

But as a highbrow farce it quirks perfectly, kind of like a smaller, less melodramatic *Magnolia* with more laughs, and the cast is energetic and effective enough to generate warmth towards their sketchy roles. Wahlberg is particularly entertaining as the SUV-hating fireman who insists on riding his bike to emergency calls, while Hoffman has a twinkly, impish appeal as the therapist-cum-detective who teaches Albert how to deconstruct reality.

Russell also has some neat visual tricks up his sleeve, snipping squares out of the fabric of reality and floating them around the screen, and presenting Albert's subconscious conjurings as freakish cardboard cut-out animations. Even if you lose track of what precisely the film's trying to say, at least its smart style – not to mention some great physical comedy – will see you through. **★★★★ AS**

I KNOW WHAT YOU DID LAST SUMMER (1997)

Starring: *Jennifer Love Hewitt (Julie James), Sarah Michelle Gellar (Helen Shivers), Ryan Phillippe (Barry William Cox), Freddie Prinze Jr. (Ray Bronson), Anne Heche (Melissa 'Missy' Egan), Johnny Galecki (Max Neurick)*
Director: *Jim Gillespie*
Screenwriter: *Kevin Williamson, based on the novel by Lois Duncan*
15/100 mins./Horror/Mystery/Thriller/USA

Driving home from the beach, some friends accidentally run over a fisherman. They leave him for dead. But a year later it seems he may not be dead after all . . .

As the opening aerial shot sweeps into a gloomy coastline towards a solitary figure brooding above a long, rocky drop, it soon becomes clear that last summer didn't involve sun, sea and a number nine double-decker bus.

Having continued the end-of-school celebrations with some shenanigans on the beach, four chums are driving home along the darkened clifftop road when the BMW crumple zone is severely tested by an unidentified object. Further inspection produces a bloodied welly. And then the prostrate figure from whence it came. As tempers, adrenaline and fear run high, the decision is taken to ditch the body.

A year on and wracked with guilt, Julie wants nothing to do with her former mates until a spooky note bearing only the titular words turns up. Then things start turning sinister. Barry is mowed down by his own car, Helen has her hair chopped on the eve of her beauty queen parade, and something altogether more unpleasant winds up in Julie's boot.

With anniversaries, coastal setting, untimely deaths, and the town forever shrouded in foreboding meteorology, echoes of John Carpenter's *The Fog* ring out, and *Scream* scriptwriter Kevin Williamson's follow-up looks like another winner. The biggest disappointment then, is when it abandons its own neatly constructed premise far too early, and much of the fearful uncertainty drains away. There are, however, some cracking shocks, first time director Gillespie drawing a decent jump factor from his young cast (all good, especially Hewitt) and, at the time, it helped prove that nouveau horror was alive and kicking hard. ★★★ **DB**

I KNOW WHERE I'M GOING (1945)

Starring: *Roger Livesey (Torquil MacNeil), Wendy Hiller (Joan Webster), Pamela Brown (Catriona Potts), Nancy Price (Mrs Crozier), Finaly Currie (Ruairidh Mhor), John Laurie (John Campbell)*
Directors: *Michael Powell, Emeric Pressburger*
Screenwriters: *Michael Powell, Emeric Pressburger*
U/91 mins/Romance-Comedy/UK

Against the wishes of her bank manager father, headstrong Joan Webster journeys to the Hebridean island of Kiloran to marry Sir Robert Bellinger, a wealthy middle-aged industrialist whom she does not love. A storm forces her to take refuge on the nearby island of Mull, where she begins to fall for young naval officer Torquil MacNeil.

Predating the elaborate Technicolor fantasies like *The Red Shoes*, *Black Narcissus* and *A Matter Of Life And Death*, *I Know Where I'm Going* might well be the unheralded ace in the Powell and Pressburger pack. Conceived after the relative commercial failure of *A Canterbury Tale*, *I Know Where I'm Going* was the third instalment in Powell's Scottish island tryptich – along with *Edge Of The World* and *Spy In Black* – and served up an enchanting mixture of comedy, fantasy, Scottish folklore, flights of fantasy and lovely locations. Hiller and Livesey make for appealing attractive leads, Hiller not afraid to let Joan become insufferable during her journey toward enlightenment and Livesey a wise, calm, gentle presence. The ensemble is filled out with Powell and Pressburger's great eye for idiosyncratic character actors, including the bizarre bird-like Pamela Brown, Captain C.W. R. Knight as the island's falconer and John Laurie, better known as Pte Frazier in *Dad's Army*. Also keep 'em peeled for a pre-teen Petula Clark.

Arguably, Powell And Pressburger's most personal film to that point, *IKWIG* continued their departure from the dominant mode of British cinematic realism. The movie opens with a patently fake train climbing through a mythical Scottish highlands and the mood of magical realism pervades every frame – particularly in a dream sequence in which Joan imagines she is marrying a giant corporation. Powell also has a stunning, almost spiritual feel for the landscape. Erwin Hiller's beautiful cinematography delivers some indelible images, such as a duvet of black mist swirling across the sea.

Yet all this beguiling beauty is at the service of the film's central thesis as Joan's material ambitions are revealed to be petty by both the majesty of nature and the warmth of a small-island mentality. 'They're not poor,' says MacNeil about Mull's inhabitants, 'they just don't have any money.' There is an enticing simplicity in that line that is redolent of the whole film. Powell and Pressburger's seductive argument is that the world is a wondrous place full of sublime pleasures if you keep yourself open to its magic and mysteries. As such, it is a perfect film to fall in love to and with. ★★★★ **IF**

I MARRIED A MONSTER FROM OUTER SPACE (1958)

Starring: *Tom Tryon (Bill Farrell), Gloria Talbott (Marge), Peter Baldwin (Officer Frank Swanson), Robert Ivers (Harry Phillips), Chuck Wassil (Ted), Ty Hardin (Mac Brody)*
Director: *Gene Fowler*
Screenwriter: *Louis Vittes*
U/78 mins/Sci-fi/USA

Bill Farrell is waylaid and replaced by an alien who assumes his form and turns up at his wedding. Marge, Bill's new bride, begins to suspect her husband isn't the man he used to be. A small group of shapeshifting aliens are on Earth to mate with human women and renew their species.

This has a classic tabloid headline title, but is a quieter, creepier picture than its lurid poster suggests. It's mostly a portrait of a severely troubled marriage, with Gloria Talbott wondering why her blankly handsome husband (Tom Tryon, deliberately playing a stiff) no longer responds to her, even as the alien duplicate tries to overcome unexpected emotions he has picked up along with human form. It plays the Invasion of the Body Snatchers game as aliens take over a town, by replacing the Sheriff, the telephone operator and other authority figures, but is unusually interested in the *problems* the aliens have on Earth.

An amusing, almost-melancholy sub-plot finds the disappointed replacement husbands, none of whom are having any luck impregnating Earth women, sneaking out of their homes to commiserate in a bar, though they show themselves up as inhuman by not touching their drinks. Director Gene Fowler Jr., who made the similarly-titled *I Was A Teenage Werewolf*, has a knack for staging noirish, unsettling scenes – the biggest scare in the movie is a simple, unexpected bit of business as Tryon is staring out of the window at a storm when a lightning-strike shocks him into briefly showing his true (remarkably alien) form before recovering his crewcut all-American composure. Despite their perfidies (which include killing cats and a puppy), the aliens eventually seem surprisingly sympathetic, which gives the final attack by the townsfolk on their flying saucer something of a lynch mob feel. ★★★ **KN**

⊙ I ROBOT (2004)

Starring: *Will Smith (Detective Del Spooner), Bridget Moynahan (Susan Calvin), Alan Tudyk (Sonny), James Cromwell (Dr. Alfred Lanning), Bruce Greenwood (Lawrence Robertson)*
Director: *Alex Proyas*
Screenwriters: *Jeff Vinta, Akiva Goldsman, from a screen story by Jeff Vintar suggested by Issac Asimov's book*
12A/110 mins./Sci-fi/Crime/USA

In 2035, robots are commonplace – governed by three laws that prevent them from harming humans. But then robophobic cop Del Spooner is called to investigate the death of a robotics professor, which seems to have been caused by one of his creations.

From the early 1940s to his death in 1992, Isaac Asimov turned out a series of stories set in a future where robots were a part of everyday life, their conduct governed by his famous Three Laws Of Robotics – the first of which insists 'a robot may not injure a human being or, through inaction, allow a human being to come to harm'. Well aware that real-life robots are designed to inflict harm on human beings, Asimov concentrated on exercises in intellectual hair-splitting whereby the laws are circumvented in order to provide a plot.

Taking a title from Asimov's first robot collection, this movie uses the author's boffin Dr. Susan Calvin as heroine and cops some wrinkles from various vintage science-fiction stories while using a critique of the imaginary robotics industry to score points off all-too-real computer combines.

It's mostly an original conspiracy screenplay, dumping the 'three laws' angle at mid-point to deliver a more film-friendly melodrama leading to a mass uprising of red-hearted robots and some large-scale mecha-carnage. Alex Proyas tones down the Gothic-noir look of his spikier earlier features, *The Crow* and *Dark City*, opting for that smooth, silvery, slightly overcast urban future seen in recent Spielberg pictures (*A.I.*, *Minority Report*), with gadgets in every frame and human mess still very much in evidence.

It's hard not to feel that this has been assembled rather than created, but like a good robot it does the job it was designed for. Will Smith, although operating in slightly more sombre mood than usual, is too early-2000s a figure to be a credible future cop, though his Spooner is depicted as a nostalgic who prefers a good old-fashioned remote control to a voice-activated CD player and wakes himself up with a blast of Stevie Wonder.

His backstory, which shows why he hates robots yet also keeps prodding the audience about an ingrained connection with them, is Screenwriting 101 Driven Cop, and his Willsmithian wisecracks feel like a late-in-the-day rewrite to fit the vehicle to the star. But a running joke about Spooner's insistence that Calvin rephrase her plot explanations in language he can understand usefully grounds the picture for anyone who wants to cut to the chase.

The real star, though, is Sonny (Alan Tudyk, transformed by CGI), the sensitive robot programmed to dream and accused of the murder of his human father. This plot thread is tipped in from a book by Eando Binder, a less-well-known sci-fi writer, which has confusingly also been called *I, Robot*. With an expressive face that looks like a semi-transparent Richard E. Grant deathmask and the patented HAL 9000 cool, inquiring voice, Sonny is a marvellous creation, all the more so for refusing to go the A.I.-Pinocchio route and aspiring to explore his own highly-evolved robot identity rather than whine about not being a real boy.

Asimov began to write his stories in reaction to the 1930s cliché of the robot who rebels Frankenstein-style against his maker – but Proyas and company eventually embrace this for an ending that provides plenty of satisfying twists and turns. It's a creaky, ancient premise, but nevertheless stirring, helped by Proyas' whirligig direction, soaring almost nauseatingly around his set-pieces in an apparent effort to resurrect the summer movie 'rollercoaster ride' cliché.

The effects only add to the thrill as serried ranks of evil robots swarm up a building, pile onto a speeding car or slaughter the previous generations of helpful drones. If not quite the best blockbuster of 2004 – though it's a worthy contender – it certainly doesn't fail on effort. ★★★★ **AS**

⊙ I SHOT ANDY WARHOL (1996)

Starring: *Lili Taylor (Valerie Jean Solanas), Jared Harris (Andy Warhol), Martha Plimpton (Stevie), Lothaire Bluteau (Maurice Girodias), Anna Levine, as Anna Thompson (Iris), Tahnee Welch (Viva)*
Director: *Mary Harron*
Screenwriters: *Mary Harron, Daniel Minahan, with additional material by Jeremiah Newton*
18/103 mins./Biography/Crime/Drama/UK/USA

Based on the true story of Valerie Solanas who was a 60s radical preaching hatred toward men in her 'Scum' manifesto. She wrote a screenplay for a film that she wanted Andy Warhol to produce, but when he refused, she shot him.

Although her film bears his name and hangs upon his presence, this true life debut by Mary Harron is not about the peroxide blond late 60s pop guru but a woman, Valerie Solanas, who crossed his path and ultimately came within inches of assassinating him.

Other than being a determined but lousy shot, Solanas' main claim to fame was that she was the founder and sole member of SCUM – the Society for Cutting Up Men – and the author of The SCUM Manifesto. Cheaply printed copies of this radical feminist document she used to hawk on the New York streets (a dollar to men, 50 cents or less to women) in between attaching herself to Warhol's art studio/workshop The Factory and trying to secure a proper publishing deal for her work.

Initially, she is warmly received by Warhol and appears in one of his films – *I, A Man* – but gradually her persistence and general demeanour leaves everyone at The Factory wishing her gone. Taylor portrays this edgier side to Solanas' character superbly, veering between apparent insanity and intellectual genius. 'I'm not a lunatic, I'm a revolutionary' she insists, but the audience is left to wonder, albeit sympathetically.

With Taylor in such stunning form, Harron is free to concentrate on telling the story and to conjure the atmosphere of the period. Both she achieves quite magnificently. The silver-walled and screen-print-festooned Factory looks brilliant, the crash pads sordid and the costumes just perfect. Add to this a sassy soundtrack and a strong supporting cast portraying the Factory 'superstars' and *I Shot Andy Warhol* adds up to something far more a fascinating time capsule than mere docudrama. ★★★★ **NJ**

⊙ I SPIT ON YOUR GRAVE (1978)

Starring: *Camille Keaton (Jennifer Hill), Eron Tabor (Johnny), Richard Pace (Matthew), Anthony Nichols (Stanley), Gunter Kleeman (Andy)*
Director: *Meir Zarchi*
Screenwriter: *Meir Zarchi*
18/100 mins/Horror/USA

New Yorker Jennifer Hill goes to rural Connecticut to write a novel, and is gang-raped by four local degenerates. Surviving, she sets out to seduce and murder each of her abusers.

One of the most infamous of the so-called 'video nasties', this remains more controversial than interesting. Director Meir Zarchi, inspired by the personal experience of coming to the aid of a rape victim, claims he intended a sincere, harrowing indictment of the violation of women. The bluntly-shot, awkwardly-staged 45-minute rape is certainly not pleasant or arousing viewing (which isn't to say the film doesn't have some fans who are drawn to it for this scene) but the wish-fulfilment fantasy second half gets away from any pretence of realism, offering Dr Phibes-like set-pieces in which the blank-faced Camille Keaton wreaks apt, contrived revenge on the glowering dimwit villains (hanged, castrated, axed). Wes Craven's *Last House on the Left* and Abel Ferrara's *Ms. 45* cover similar ground, but are much better films: all *I Spit on Your Grave* has to distinguish it in this company is far less credible psychology (seriously, what are any of these characters thinking?), wildly variable performances (from zombie inexpression to pantomime eye-rolling) and (most of all) a tendency to believe that merely showing something on screen for longer than most other films would makes it more effective. Though Zarchi stages one or two moments effectively (the bathtub emasculation is a 'high point'), whole stretches are just thrown together – with too many plot turns that depend on all the people on screen acting like complete idiots, like the rapist who swims up to the heroine's boat and presses himself against the propellor ostensibly begging for mercy but actually so he'll be in position to be killed when she revs up the outboard motor. ★ **KN**

I WAS A MALE WAR BRIDE (1949)

Starring: *Cary Grant (Henri Rochard), Ann Sheridan (Lt. Catherine Gates), Marion Marshall (Lt. Kitty Lawrence), Randy Stuart (Lt. Eloise Billings), William Neff (Capt. Jack Ramsey)*
Director: *Howard Hawks*
Screenwriters: *Charles Lederer, Leonard Spigelglass, Hagar Wide*
U/105 mins./Comedy/USA

A bureaucratic SNAFU means that French Army captain Henri Rochard has to pose as a woman to return Stateside to his new WAC bride, Catherine Gates.

It was a case of diminishing returns where Howard Hawks, Cary Grant and comedy were concerned, with *His Girl Friday*, this tepid postwar farce and the laboured *Monkey Business* successively failing to match the screwball genius of *Bringing Up Baby*. However, Grant himself wouldn't have agreed, insisting that this was 'the best comedy I've ever done'.

Curiously, this far-fetched tale was based on fact, as Belgian nurse Henri Rochard had such a trying time attempting to leave Europe with his American bride that he related his experiences in the story 'I Was an Alien Spouse of Female Military Personnel En Route to the United States Under Public Law 271 of the Congress'.

Grant was initially to be teamed with Ava Gardner, but Hawks insisted on pairing him with Ann Sheridan, whose strong personality and confidence with comedy had earned her the nickname 'the Oomph Girl'. He took less trouble over the casting of her roommate, however, by selecting his then-mistress, Marion Marshall. Grant and Sheridan never really hit it off. But it's surprising that the film is as enjoyable as it is, considering the crises that befell its production. With Hollywood costs rising steeply, Fox opted to make the picture in Germany and Britain to release some of the monies frozen during the war. However, the shoot was dogged by poor health. Hawks suffered from an all-over rash, while Sheridan's pleurisy developed into pneumonia and Grant's hepatitis was complicated by jaundice (around 15 weeks were lost, as Grant recuperated and regained the 30lbs he had lost during his illness).

He returned to give a courageous performance, although his refusal to attempt a French accent somewhat undermines his characterisation. However, Hawks's decision to play the drag scenes for macho laughs pays off, as Grant is much funnier enduring the discomfort of the WAC uniform than he could ever have been attempting the feminine mannerisms that he had originally spent hours practising. ★★★ **DP**

I WAS A TEENAGE WEREWOLF (1957)

Starring: *Michael Landon (Tony Rivers), Yvonne Lime (Arlene Logan), Whit Bissell (Dr. Alfred Brandon), Tony Marshall (Jimmy), Dawn Richard Theres (Theresa), Barney Phillips (Det. Sgt. Donovan), Ken Miller (Vic)*
Director: *Gene Fowler Jr.*
Screenwriter: *Ralph Thornton*
15/75 mins./Horror/USA

Hot-headed Tony Rivers, a misunderstood juvenile delinquent, volunteers for a course of hypnotherapy conducted by mad scientist Dr. Brandon, and periodically transforms into a monster who terrorises the high school.

Quite apart from its modest but genuine virtues as an exploitation picture, this boasts one of the greatest titles in the cinema – a tabloid confessional exclamation which has been endlessly imitated, parodied and referenced down through the decades (star Landon appeared in an episode of the mild TV show *Highway to Heaven* called 'I Was a Middle-Aged Werewolf'). Besides the title, this has gone down in pop-culture history because it's a clever little film, rising above the limitations of its intermittently ridiculous script thanks to effective direction from Gene Fowler Jr. (who also made the soundalike *I Married A Monster From Outer Space*) and unusually committed performances. 'I don't like to hear the subject of a world-shaking experiment referred to as a "victim",' snarls mad scientist Bissell, who – under the influence of the then-topical Bridey Murphy case – attempts to solve Landon's social problems by regressing him to an earlier evolutionary stage. An unfortunate side effect is that he turns into a greasy-haired, repulsively-fanged werewolf when he hears the school bell.

Typical of a cliché scene pepped up by Fowler's touch is the werewolf's attack on a leotard-clad gymnast, where the creature is first seen from the point of view of the victim, upside-down. Bissell may look like a buttoned-down 1950s type, but he's just as mad as Karloff or Lugosi ever were, relishing the choice dialogue which enlivens the otherwise staider follow-up *I Was A Teenage Frankenstein*. Landon's dilemma as a Dean-age troublemaker whose uncontrollable hormones give him the worst ever case of unsightly facial hair and bad skin condition, makes the film a surprisingly perfect metaphor for miserable adolescence. ★★★ **KN**

I'M ALL RIGHT, JACK (1959)

Starring: *Ian Carmichael (Stanley Windrush), Peter Sellers (Fred Kite), Terry Thomas (Maj. Hitchcock), Richard Attenborough (Sydney de Vere Cox), Dennis Price (Bertram Tracepurcel), Margaret Rutherford (Aunt Dolly), Irene Handl (Mrs Kite)*
Director: *John Boulting*
Screenwriters: *John Boulting, Alan Hackney and Frank Harvey*
U/105 mins./Comedy/UK
Awards: *Bafta – Best British Actor (Peter Sellers), Best British Screenplay*

Keen to swing a crooked deal, Bertram Tracepurcel and his sidekick Sidney de Vere Cox persuade Major Hitchcock, the personnel officer at an armaments factory, to hire Tracepurcel's nephew, Stanley Windrush, in the knowledge that his incompetence will persuade shop steward Fred Kite to call a ruinous strike.

In the age of Kitchen Sink realism, Ian Carmichael's toff twit and Peter Sellers's leftist clot made something of a refreshing change from all the Angry Young Men who were then dominating the British stage and screen. Nevertheless, there's still plenty of socio-political bite in the Boulting brothers' adaptation of Alan Hackney's novel, *Private Life*. Indeed, no one gets off lightly, as the government, big business, the old-boy network, the trades unions and the media all come in for a kicking in this enduringly popular satire.

It's essentially a sequel to *Private's Progress*, in which Uncle Bertie and Coxie had nearly duped Stanley into helping them smuggle stolen artefacts across wartime Europe. But while the original cast were all in favour of a reunion, Peter Sellers (who had just starred in the Boultings' *Carlton-Browne of the F.O.*) took more persuading.

Accustomed to the lunacy of *The Goon Show*, Sellers simply didn't think the role of Fred Kite was funny enough and he initially returned the script. However, John Boulting persuaded him to make a screen test and Sellers spent weeks watching archive footage of labour leaders to grasp their proletarian pomposity before acquiring Kite's ill-fitting suit, cropped haircut and Hitleresque moustache. Even then he wasn't convinced he had found his character, but a standing ovation from the test crew persuaded him otherwise.

Kite's comic militancy might have seemed a little one-note had it not been for the inspired contrast of his rulebook martinet with the ineffectual chauvinist who is hen-pecked at home by his wife and daughter (Irene Handl and Liz Fraser). Indeed, it's this blend of belligerent indignation and emasculated irrelevance that made Kite such an irresistible character and earned Sellers his BAFTA.

The ensemble playing is equally impressive, however, with the underrated Carmichael selflessly boosting everyone from John Le Mesurier's time-and-motion man to his amiably snooty aunt, Margaret Rutherford. Sadly, he would never quite be as effective again. ★★★★★ **DP**

ICE AGE (2002)

Starring: *the voices of: Ray Romano (Manfred), John Leguizamo (Sid), Denis Leary (Diego), Goran Visnjic (Soto), Jack Black (Zeke), Tara Strong (Roshan/Start), Cedric the Entertainer (Rhino), Stephen Root (Rhino/Start), Diedrich Bader (Saber-Tooth Tiger), Alan Tudyk (Saber-Tooth Tiger/Dodo/Freaky Mammal)*
Director: *Lori Forte*
Screenwriters: *Michael Berg, Michael J. Wilson, Peter Ackerman, based on a story by Michael J. Wilson*
U/81 mins./Animated/Comedy/Family/USA

Misanthropic woolly mammoth Manny, lazy sloth Sid and wise-ass sabre-toothed tiger Diego embark on a trek to reunite abandoned human infant Roshan with his nomadic family.

Sharing a similar plot mechanic to *Monsters, Inc.* – goofy creatures discover themselves through caring for an abandoned infant – *Ice Age* is a likeable, fast-paced, computer-generated opus that opts for good gags and enjoyable action instead of sappy moralising and Phil Collins songs.

Tagline
Sub-zero heroes.

Sidestepping the attention to detail of Pixar, there is an intentional 'cartoon' quality to the character animation and backdrops. The comedy here covers all the bases, from the broad to the sly – in this world, creatures speak, human's can't.

While the journey throws up the requisite thrills and spills, *Ice Age*'s real strength lies in sharply defined relationship dynamics and likeable characters that are worth rooting for. Best of all is Romano's world-weary yet big-hearted mammoth – cold on the outside, warm on the inside. Just like the film itself. ★★★★ **IF**

ICE AGE 2: THE MELTDOWN (2006)

Starring: *the voices of: Ray Romano (Manny), John Leguizamo (Sid), Denis Leary (Diego), Seann William Scott (Crash), Queen Latifah (Ellie)*
Director: *Carlos Saldanha*
Screenwriters: *Gerry Swallow, Peter Gaulke, Jim Hecht*
U/90 mins./Animation/Family/USA

When it becomes apparent the Ice Age is coming to an end, prehistoric pals Sid, Manny and Diego leave their home and head for a safer place – but the journey is fraught with danger from predatory animals, new creatures and the new environment caused by the ice melting. Meanwhile, Scrat is still in search of acorns . . .

The original *Ice Age* was a very pleasant surprise, a computer-animated film which gave the likes of Pixar and DreamWorks a run for their money – so a sequel was pretty much inevitable. As with the original, the animation here is superb, with director Carlos Saldanha wasting no opportunity to fill the screen with cute creatures, broad landscapes and some stunning underwater shots.

This time around, however, it's all let down by a badly patched-together plot – our central trio simply catapult from one perilous situation to another, resulting in a string of hit and miss set-pieces rather than a cohesive story.

It's charming enough, though, and there's plenty of laughs, mainly thanks to the reappearance of hapless, bulge-eyed squirrel-rat-thing Scrat, whose ongoing quest for acorns is this time stretched across the entire film with increasingly hilarious results. ★★★ **CW**

ICE COLD IN ALEX (1958)

Starring: *John Mills (Captain Anson), Sylvia Sims (Sister Diana Murdoch), Anthony Quayle (Captain Van Der Poel), Harry Andrews (MSM Tom Pugh)*
Director: *J. Lee Thompson*
Screenwriters: *Christopher Landon, T.J. Morrison, based on the novel by Landon*
PG/124 mins./War/UK

An ambulance crew, cut off from its unit, must cross the arduous plains of the Sahara to reach the safety of Alexandria. Along the way they pick up a strange South African, and slowly secrets rise to the surface.

More a study of the endurance of British manners in the face of terrible hardships than a war movie. For all its desert backdrops, the physical strains of hulking an ambulance across the slipping sands, this is a rather theatrical piece. Based on Christopher Landon's novel, who also wrote the body of the script, his notion was to watch how characters unravel, or not, especially British ones under terrible extremes. Each of his stock set of characters will come to expose their souls, dally in mild but not too overbearing forms of madness, and rise a better person for it, as driven by John Mills' Captain's dream of reaching an ice-cold beer in Alex – since purloined, to the film's detriment, for advertising.

Inevitably, being so defined by the seesaw between talky nationalistic debates and the hard graft of desert survival – a sequence where they physically wind the ambulance up a steep incline only for it to tumble back, has a powerful Sisyphean torment – the film becomes predictable and rather stagy. A strong subplot involving the presence of a German spy in their midst, not exactly presented as a mystery but effective nonetheless, adds variation, but there is no escaping the overall stiffness in the filmmaking.

It takes a great set of performances, as unflaggingly British as John Bull and whelk stalls, but there is psychological enquiry in Anson's incipient alcoholism, Pugh's ingrained bigotry and the more sympathetic portrayal of the German cause in Quayle's eloquent performance, to lift it. Thus, it is a story of recovery, of ordinary men reaching their lowest ebb and seeing it through. There is cliché in that, especially with its doubty, old-fashioned manner, but value as well. ★★★ **IN**

ICE STATION ZEBRA (1968)

Starring: *Rock Hudson (Commander James Ferraday), Ernest Borgnine (Boris Vaclav), Patrick McGoohan (David Jones), Jim Brown (Captain Leslie Anders)*
Director: *John Sturges*
Screenwriters: *Harry Julian Fink, Douglas Hayes, W.R. Burnett based on the novel by Alistair MacLean*
U/148 mins./Acton/Thriller/USA

A US submarine crew, including a British civilian, a friendly Russian, and a platoon of marines, are given sudden orders to head to the Arctic Circle

and rescue the crew of the weather station Zebra. But danger and betrayal will await Commander Ferraday in the frozen wastes.

Yet another spin on one of Alistair MacLean's military potboilers, here taking a decidedly literal fix on the perilous tipping points of the Cold War, with a muddle of a plot, second rate performances and tons of fake snow. MacLean's stories tend to rest on preposterously complex set-ups, just take the ball of wool that unravels into *Where Eagles Dare*. To draw pleasure from his indecipherable ruses, the action needs to be spectacular and the actors able to knit some heroic charge out of old rope. Neither of which happens in this lumpen, cheesy plod through twisty-turny anti-commie dramatics. The Americans are racing the Russians to the remote, frozen outpost, but it feels about as cold as Somerset. Excuse us, but shouldn't there be clouds of breath coming out of the actors' mouths?

There's certainly plenty of surface, with the icy desert of the North Pole, the gleaming steel hides of the submarine, to the impermeable plains of Rock Hudson's handsome veneer. The film couldn't be more inert, as it desperately tries to drum up some shivery Cold War brinkmanship. The plot, or at least the surface of the plot, has the two superpowers duel over some secret satellite footage, but it increasingly doesn't seem to be about having a storyline rather than an intense mood. There's much in the way of wooden speechifying, especially by Patrick McGoohan, as a British spy, with the idea of giving it an intelligent thrust, but in the end, like most of MacLean's one-dimensional fiction, it's really just a hunt for the Red Octoberists amongst the named cast. ★★ **IN**

⓪ THE ICE STORM (1997)

Starring: *Sigourney Weaver (Janey Carver), Kevin Kline (Ben Hood), Joan Allen (Elena Hood), Christina Ricci (Wendy Hood), Elijah Wood (Mikey Carver), Adam Hann-Byrd (Sandy Carver), Tobey Maguire (Paul Hood), Katie Holmes (Libbets Casey)*
Director: *Ang Lee*
Screenwriter: *James Schamus, based on the novel by Rick Moody*
15/113 mins./Drama/USA

Awards: *BAFTA – Best Supporting Actress (Sigourney Weaver)*

A vision of an emotionally drained, dysfunctional suburban American family hopelessly mired in Vietnam and the Watergate scandal and ineffectually coping with wife-swapping and barbiturates.

With his fifth feature film in five years, Ang Lee seemed incapable of making a less than outstanding movie. Following his winning Taiwanese Father Knows Best trilogy – *Pushing Hands*, *The Wedding Banquet*, *Eat Drink Man Woman* – and his scrumptious journey in Jane Austen's *Sense And Sensibility*, he again explores a family's heartbeat and cross-generational conflict. But the time period and geography are something else again. This is an almost cringe-makingly detailed trip through middle-class confusion in 1970s Connecticut, beautifully adapted from Rick Moody's highly-regarded novel by Lee's regular producer James Schamus.

Kevin Kline is Ben Hood, the father who is trying but doesn't have a clue, like all around him in an America that has broken morally and spiritually adrift. His carefully coiffed wife Elena looks like a Stepford robot but is getting itchy for some liberated self-realisation. His neighbour Janey is the swinger next door who makes her waterbed freely available to him while denying him any warmth that may lurk beneath her cold, brittle indifference.

Simultaneously, Ben and Elena's teenaged son, en route from prep school for the Thanksgiving holiday, is having a Holden Caulfield weekend and pubescent daughter is playing 'I'll show you mine if you show me yours' with the anxious, oddball boys next door.

Lee's vision confirms the 70s as the most excruciating style decade of the century, the totally tragic duds emblematic of the mass inability to get a grip.

The film scores insights both in sharply observed social satire and poignantly universal details of sexual longing in the interwoven tales of parental mid-life crises and teen angst. But Lee's most impressive achievement is his almost imperceptible shift from sex farce to achingly funny youth drama to profound tragedy and despair as the approaching winter freeze of the title mirrors the family's emotional chill and the devastation it brings. The dazzling ensemble perfectly captures every nuance in one of the finest acting showcases you could hope for. ★★★★ **AE**

⓪ THE IDIOTS (IDIOTERNE) (1998)

Starring: *Jen Albinus (Stoffer), Bodil Jorgensen (Karen), Knud Tomer Jorgensen (Axel), Anne-Grethe Bjarup Riis (Katrine), Troels Lyby (Henrik), Nikolaj Lie Kaas (Jeppe)*
Director: *Lars von Trier*
Screenwriters: *Lars von Trier*
18/115 mins./Comedy/Drama/Denmark/France/Italy/Netherlands/Germany

We follow a group of intelligent, middle-class people who, for reasons never quite explained, have got together in a commune and taken to the practice of 'spazzing' – pretending in public to be mentally handicapped.

Coming off the international success of *Breaking The Waves* and *The Kingdom*, Lars von Trier could have made a slick, expensive picture but has opted for a low-budget, mostly-improvised comedy-drama that sets out to look exactly like a fly-on-the-wall docusoap. It follows a group of intelligent, middle-class people who, for reasons never quite explained, have got together in a commune and taken to pretending in public to be mentally handicapped.

In the opening scene, which is so disorienting you need a few minutes to catch up, a woman is patronised in a restaurant because she admits she can't afford some of the choicer items on the menu then falls in with the spazzers. Only after taking an impulsive car trip with them does she realise that they are faking. Slowly, she joins in and we get to visit the suburban mansion where the group gathers. We get fragmentary glimpses of their regular pranks, complicated interrelationships, parties and arguments, interspersed with talking-head interviews in which the protagonists seem as puzzled as anyone else by what they have got into.

Dogme '95

What is it: A manifesto presented at the Odéon Théâtre de l'Europe in Paris, laying down a back-to-basics set of rules for filmmaking.

Hallmarks: Edgy, handheld camera; improvised-seeming dialogue; use of real locations and natural light; all music sourced onscreen; no special effects or fantastical elements; no genre films; contemporary setting – these edicts are known in Dogme terms as the Vow of Chastity.

Key figures: Lars von Trier, Thomas Vinterberg, Søren Kragh-Jacobsen.

If you see one movie, see: *Festen* (*The Celebration*, 1998)

The film is full of funny, disturbing, even suspenseful scenes including a party that degenerates into a joyous but still unsettling gang-bang destined to be a real talking point. The thesis seems to be that you really are what you pretend to be, as the characters' inner idiots reflect deeper, sometimes disturbing truths, and those who are most into the game come across as genuinely damaged or dangerous. Its deliberately shambolic storyline is far more plausible than any Hollywood whacky-com and although some will find the jerky, shot-on-the-run style off-putting, this is real cinema: original, affecting, shattering. ★★★★★ **KN**

IF ... (1968)

Starring: *Malcolm McDowell (Mick Travers), David Wood (Johnny), Richard Warwick (Wallace), Christine Noonan (the Girl), Rupert Webster (Bobby Philips), Robert Swann (Rowntree), Hugh Thomas (Denson), Arthur Lowe (Mr. Kemp, Housemaster)*
Director: *Lindsay Anderson*
Screenwriter: *David Sherwin, based on a script by Sherwin, John Howlett, entitled* The Crusaders
18/110 mins./Drama/UK

Amid the sadism and repression of an English public school, three friends, flitting between reality and fantasies of sex and revolution, plot to disrupt Speech Day with an act of incredible violence.

When it was released in 1968, Lindsay Anderson's bellow of righteous outrage was described as 'a hand grenade' of a movie. Some critics and many politicians were made thoroughly queasy at its apparent message of total, uncompromising revolution. The fact that, across the Channel, the student population was busy building the barricades can't have helped.

And while a quarter of a century may have withered its agitprop politics somewhat, the mischievous spirit of anarchy that typified the best of Anderson's work still dazzles.

Shot in both colour and black-and-white – not for any artistic reason, but because the cash-strapped director ran out of the more pricey colour stock – *If ...* is a gleeful acid-attack on the kind of public school of which Anderson himself was a product, as well as a metaphorical demolition job on the stultifying mores of English society.

A documentary filmmaker by training, Anderson effortlessly blurs the line between the genuine surrealism of public school life and the stylised fantasy sequences that express the sexual and social repression that constantly threatens to explode.

It's a fascinating structure which leaves you unsure as to whether the fantastically violent final reel is for real or an extension of the schoolboy anarchist's (a fabulously swaggering McDowell) fervid imagination.

Whichever, it's a deliciously subversive piece of filmmaking which drips with wit and venom. And with the British film industry today churning out too many knock-off gangster movies and puke-inducing rom-coms, *If ...* is both exhilarating and depressing. It shows us what British movies could be like if only Anderson were still around to put a rocket up them. ★★★★★ **AS**

IGBY GOES DOWN (2002)

Starring: *Kieran Culkin (Jason 'Igby' Slocumb, Jr.), Claire Danes (Sookie Sapperstein), Jeff Goldblum (D.H. Banes), Jared Harris (Russel), Amanda Peet (Rachel), Ryan Phillippe (Oliver 'Ollie' Slocumb), Bill Pullman (Jason Slocumb), Susan Sarandon (Mimi Slocumb), Rory Culkin (10-year-old Igby)*
Director: *Burr Steers*
Screenwriter: *Burr Steers*
15/97 mins./Comedy/Drama/USA

The youngest scion of an old money Manhattan clan, 17-year-old Igby hates his yuppie brother, is estranged from his schizophrenic father, bemused by his crass godfather and loathes his self-absorbed mother.

At first glance, the plot of *Igby* – rebellious teenager flunks out of prep school, romances older women – is enough to make Ken Loach fans stage a protest.

But *Igby* works. For a number of reasons.

First: debut writer-director Burr Steers, until now best known as the 'Flock Of Seagulls' who gets shot by Jules in *Pulp Fiction*, is the nephew of both Gore Vidal and Jackie Onassis, and therefore knows the milieu inside out.

More importantly, Steers has no obvious axe to grind, and sketches all his characters with an even hand. They may not be likeable exactly, but they are both compelling and convincing.

Second: Steers has had so many lucky breaks with his supporting cast, it's difficult to know where to start. Those reliable old-stagers, Goldblum and Sarandon, have enormous fun as the filthy rich – and plain filthy – godfather and eccentric matriarch respectively.

As for Amanda Peet and Ryan Phillippe, well, anyone who has seen ... ooh, anything they've ever done ... will appreciate how revelatory they both are here.

Peet's craven mistress and Phillippe's stern Young Republican are textbook examples of how due diligence can transform slim stereotypes into telling thumbnails.

Lastly, Danes provides the kind of kookie-cool heartbreaker not seen round these parts since Winona Ryder paid for her hats.

Third: in the mostly undistinguished line of celluloid Holden Caulfields, Kieran Culkin's Igby comes closest to capturing the indomitable spirit of J.D. Salinger's original rebel.

You may want to hate the privileged, precocious brat but, in Culkin's hands, Igby is simply too playful – and too painful – to allow such a knee-jerk response. Think Ferris Bueller's *Year Off* and you will start to appreciate *Igby*'s unique appeal. ★★★★ **EH**

IKIRU (LIVING) (1952)

Starring: *Takashi Shimura (Kanji Watanabe), Nobuo Kaneko (Mitsuo Watanabe), Kyoko Seki (Kazue Watanabe), Miki Odagiri (Toyo), Kamatari Fujiwara (Ono), Makoto Koburi (Kiichi Watanabe)*
Director: *Akira Kurosawa*
Screenwriters: *Akira Kurosawa, Hideo Oguni*
PG/141 mins./Drama/Japan

Kanji Watanabe, a government bureaucrat, learns that he has stomach cancer and will die within six months. He binges on drink and has a desperate relationship with a lively young girl – then finds a purpose in a petition from housewives to convert a stretch of wasteland into a children's playground.

This quiet, touching film is a counterpart to Akira Kurosawa's great period epics of the 1950s, observing modern-day life with humane, intensely moving care. Bald, frog-faced Takashi Shimura, the leader of the Seven Samurai, gives a magnificent performance as the repressed, downtrodden clerk who reacts credibly to terrifying medical news by staying off work, getting drunk and hanging around with a slightly-spooked younger woman just to be near her vitality.

Only after these attempts to avoid reality have petered out does he decide to spend the rest of his life usefully, creating a children's playground. In a structural move as daring as the multiple viewpoints of *Rashomon*, the film leaps from the hero's decision to devote himself to the project to his wake, at which his colleagues talk about his effort – depicted in flashback vignettes – in various ways, trying to minimise his achievement, take credit for it, breastbeating over failing to appreciate the dead man and vowing in a hollow way to follow his inspiration.

It has a specific meaning in the context of modern Japan, questioning the values that drive the Japanese to work so hard, but it is also universal

Movie Bars, Clubs and Restaurants — TOP 10

1	Rick's Café Americain	*Casablanca*
2	Club Obi-Wan	*Indiana Jones and the Temple Of Doom*
3	McCool's	*One Night At McCool's*
4	The Titty Twister	*From Dusk Till Dawn*
5	Cantina	*Star Wars Episode IV: A New Hope*
6	Coyote Ugly	*Coyote Ugly*
7	Café Mozart	*The Third Man*
8	The Green Man	*The Wicker Man*
9	Café Eighties	*Back to the Future Part II*
10	The Whistle Stop Café	*Fried Green Tomatoes At The Whistle Stop Café*

in its examination of what is genuinely important in life. A Hollywood version of this story would be an endurance test, but this is the subtle work of a master, paying off unforgettably with the understated image of the old man sitting on the swing in his newly-finished playground, death settling on him in the form of a light snow. ★★★★★ **KN**

Akira Kurosawa (1910–1998)

Who he was: Japan's most celebrated director, famously mixing the heritage and tradition of his homeland with the action and spectacle of a John Ford Western. Hollywood has borrowed equally as much from him.

Hallmarks: Big battle sequences; formal filmmaking style; deep humanism.

If you see one film, see: *Seven Samurai* (1954)

IMITATION OF LIFE (1959)

Starring: *Lana Turner (Lora Meredith), John Gavin (Steve Archer), Sandra Dee (Susie, Aged 16), Dan O'Herhiliy (David Edwards), Susan Kohner (Sarah Jane, Aged 18), Robert Alda (Allen Loomis), Juanita Moore (Annie Johnson), Mahallia Jackson (Herself)*
Director: *Douglas Sirk*
Screenwriters: *Eleanore Griffin, Allan Scott, based on the novel by Fannie Hurst*
U/123 mins/Drama/USA

A melodrama following the intertwining lives of struggling actress Lora Meredith and her black penniless maid Annie Johnson. As Lora becomes a stranger in her own home in her pursuit of stardom, Annie undergoes the trauma of being rejected by her lighter-skinned daughter Sarah Jane on racial grounds.

Using the same source material – the novel by Fannie Hurst – and title as an equally entertaining 1934 John M. Stahl melodrama starring Claudette Colbert and Louise Beavers, this five-star women's picture gets the edge via the ersatz style and masterful manipulation of German émigré director Douglas Sirk. In a pitch-perfect parody of herself, Lana Turner exudes cold, strong-willed independence but the acting plaudits go to Moore and Kohner who invests Sarah Jane with an edgy sexual energy – in a standout scene Turner and Kohner go at it hell for leather, both piling on the malice and bitterness with delicious relish.

Yet for all the camp and pantomime on display, this is a consummate display of populist weepie-making. Cinematographer Russell Metty colour codes the character's surroundings to match their overblown emotions. Production designer Alexander Golitzen finds nifty contrasts between the small dingy apartment the characters inhabit in the first half and the nouveau riche mansion they occupy in the second. And Frank Skinner's score dials back the mushiness to poignantly underscore the emotions rather than hammer home the schmaltz.

Sirk displays his usual array of alienation techniques – placing objects between the actors and the characters to deny us identification, finding unusual angles rather than eye-level – to encourage us to look objectively at the characters and their choices. It's a sophisticated approach and one that bizarrely makes for a more moving experience. It proved to be Sirk's final feature, was a huge box-office smash and remains both superior soap opera and one of the director's finest films. ★★★★★ **IF**

THE IMPORTANCE OF BEING EARNEST (1952)

Starring: *Michael Redgrave (Jack Worthing), Michael Denison (Algernon Moncrieff), Edith Evans (Lady Bracknell), Joan Greenwood (Gwendolen Fairfax), Dorothy Tutin (Cecily Cardew), Margaret Rutherford (Miss Prism), Miles Malleson (Canon Chasuble)*
Director: *Anthony Asquith*
Screenwriter: *Anthony Asquith, based on the play by Oscar Wilde*
U/95 mins./Comedy/UK

Jack has always gone under the name of Ernest, feeling it helps make his lowly origins sound respectable. But when he proposes to Gwendolen both his future wife and her mother want to know more about his upbringing – and his name...

For many Edith Evans is the definitive Lady Bracknell. Her intonation of 'a handbag' echoed across the land, long after the film's 1952 release.

Anthony Asquith's lush Technicolor version makes no apologies for its stage origins, and keeps the sets simple while letting Oscar Wilde's deliciously knowing dialogue carry the show. It's helped by the effortless charm of the male leads. Michael Wilding, in particular – a British star whose box-office power has been unmatched to this day, even by the likes of Hugh Grant – is note perfect as the scheming, yet charming Ernest, while Greenwood and Tutin are sweetly adorable. This thoroughly British cast is rounded out by the grande-dame of daffy female character roles – Margaret Rutherford as a forgetful nurse, who in any other film would run the risk of stealing the movie.

But that is Ms Evans' job – and anyone who can't even feel the touch of a smile as she gears up for her big moment by rounding out the word 'found' into five syllables, is better off wallowing in some Ken Loach instead. ★★★★ **EC**

THE IMPORTANCE OF BEING EARNEST (2002)

Starring: *Rupert Everett (Algy), Colin Firth (Jack), Frances O'Connor (Gwendolen), Reese Witherspoon (Cecily), Judi Dench (Lady Bracknell), Tom Wilkinson (Dr. Chasuble), Anna Massey (Miss Prism), Edward Fox (Lane)*
Director: *Oliver Parker*
Screenwriter: *Oliver Parker, based on the play by Oscar Wilde*
U/97 mins./Comedy/France/UK/US

Jack has two identities. In the country, he is the well-meaning guardian of Cecily. In town, where he goes under the name of Ernest, he is the friend of Algy and an utter scoundrel. But when he proposes to Gwendolen, her mother asks him for his true credentials.

Anthony Asquith's 1952 film of Oscar Wilde's most popular play is widely regarded as the definitive version against which all others should be judged. So it's a brave man who takes on the task of creating a modern version to rival that – and an even braver one who does so under the banner of Ealing Studios.

This is the first film to come out of the much-loved British institution since 1959; so when the weight of expectation falls heavily on Oliver Parker (who tackled Wilde two years previously on *An Ideal Husband* with moderate success), you've got to hope that he has very broad shoulders.

Parker adds original material to the text, taking sole screenwriting credit and confounding the traditionalists' expectations with character interpretations that would have surprised even Wilde.

From the opening sequence of Algy fleeing his creditors, Parker makes it clear that his opening up of the play is going to include some of the baser aspects of British society in the 1890s. Lovers visit tattoo parlours, the country reverend ventures in for some saucy painting of his lost love, and Algy and Jack cavort in music halls. All of which provides a very good backdrop, but such distractions do somewhat deaden the beauty of the dialogue.

Visually, it's interesting enough to see Algy arrive in the country by balloon or to see Cecily's visions of everyone as medieval paintings (to say nothing of Firth and Everett's spontaneous burst of song), but if it's at the expense of Wilde's wit, it does seem like screen time wasted.

The humour is still there but the edge has gone, despite excellent casting. Firth and Everett, in particular, seem naturals for their parts, while Dench's deliciously understated Lady Bracknell is a joy. ★★★ **EC**

⊙ IN AMERICA (2002)

Starring: *Samantha Morton (Sarah), Paddy Considine (Johnny), Djimon Hounsou (Mateo), Sarah Bolger (Christy), Emma Bolger (Ariel), Ciaran Cronin (Frankie)*
Director: *Jim Sheridan*
Screenwriters: *Jim Sheridan, Naomi Sheridan, Kirsten Sheridan*
15/103 mins./Drama/Ireland/U.K.

Ten-year-old Christy moves to America with her family after the death of her brother, Frankie. They start their new life in a run-down New York apartment block, populated by 'junkies and prostitutes', and soon meet a mysterious painter, Mateo, whose friendship will change their lives.

Often it's hard to see why films like this are so hyped at festivals, but Sheridan's semi-autobiographical tale is an exception.

Loosely based on his experiences of moving to America to set up the Irish Arts Theatre, the masterstroke here is to tell the story from his daughters' viewpoint (both of whom helped with the screenplay). What could have been a self-indulgent exercise becomes a deep exploration of grief in the younger generation, made more poignant by the astounding quality of the two real-life sisters cast in these roles. Sarah Bolger, in particular, has a maturity and depth not seen in a young actor since Haley Joel Osment in *The Sixth Sense*.

Of course, this child's view does add a sentimental tone to the script, and there are scenes involving loner artist Mateo's growing affection for the family which could have the less saccharine-inclined reaching for the vomit bags. While Djimon Hounsou isn't bad, his role is the one jarring note in the film.

Paddy Considine emerges as a real presence as the roguish father, while Samantha Morton's ethereal nature perfectly suits a mother torn between grieving for her son and rejoining her remaining family.

The original title for the film was *East Of Harlem*, so it's no surprise that the other most obvious presence is the New York slums. The movie is effused with affection for this area, and what could have been a depressing setting transforms into a fairy-tale backdrop as the seasons change. Snow falls into comforting blankets and heat seems to condense, steam-like, on the screen.

It's these touches to Sheridan's most personal work that lend it a poetic quality and make it a fitting film for him to dedicate to his brother Frankie, who died from a brain tumour aged just ten. ★★★★ **EC**

⊙ IN BED WITH MADONNA (MADONNA: TRUTH OR DARE) (1991)

Starring: *as themselves: Madonna, Pedro Almodovar, Antonio Banderas, Warren Beatty, Sandra Bernhard, Christopher Ciccone, Martin Ciccone, Silvio Ciccone*
Director: *Alek Keshishian*
18/114 mins./Documentary/Music/USA

Documentary following singer Madonna on her 1990 tour.

Twack! The sound of Madonna's precious little neck being jerked back into its proper alignment is horribly amplified around the auditorium, a quite sickening noise immediately employed as the natural bridge into one of the live performances culled from the 1990 Blonde Ambition world tour. As an opening gambit, this distinctly unsettling device works wonderfully well. Nothing, it is immediately apparent, is too personal here to escape the gaze of Alek Keshishian's intrusive eye. Everything, osteopathy and all, is to be paraded for public consumption.

Between this opening sequence and the end of this extraordinary documentary some two hours later, the 26-year-old Keshishian goes behind the scenes of the biggest tour yet undertaken by the biggest pop star in the world, revealing a 32-year-old-woman at turns endearing, obnoxious, erotic, charmless, but never ever dull. Whether or not this is even remotely close to whatever the private Madonna Louise Ciccone may or may not be is, of course, impossible to answer. As a portrait of what it must be like to be this famous in these times, however, *In Bed With Madonna* is an absolute treat.

There is, not surprisingly, no shortage of incidents here likely to offend – the stimulated oral sex with an Evian bottle the most obvious shocker on display. The same game of Truth of Dare – the film's original release – also provides the rare spectacle of two men obviously enjoying a tongue sandwich for a good 15 seconds, while the genuinely tasteless inclusion of a visit to Madonna's mother's grave and the genuinely touching visit of a childhood friend and Madonna's subsequent brusque treatment of her invitation to become a godparent suggests that she has no shame.

The sheer enjoyment encapsulated in most of the things she does, however, comes across loud and clear, from flirting outrageously at a party thrown by Pedro Almodovar to coming over all coy while stuck in bed with a procession of her beloved dancers, and while there is certainly the occasional whinge of complaint of boredom, the overriding impression is that here is a huge star who enjoys being just that. Others may regret their involvement – Kevin Costner for one, will think twice before donning his Mr. Insincere mask again for a backstage visit – but for Madonna herself this entire project seems like the ultimate showing-off and thus the ultimate turn-on for all concerned. The most revealing pop documentary since *Don't Look Back* and the funniest since *This Is Spinal Tap*. Neat. ★★★★ **BMc**

⊙ IN HER SHOES (2005)

Starring: *Cameron Diaz (Maggie Feller), Toni Collette (Rose Feller), Shirley MacClaine (Ella Hirsch) Candice Azzara (Sydelle Feller), Anson Mount (Todd), Richard Burgi (Jim Danvers), Brooke Smith (Amy)*
Director: *Curtis Hanson*
Screenwriter: *Susannah Grant, based on the novel by Jennifer Weiner*
12A/130 mins./Drama/Comedy/USA

Sisters Rose and Maggie Feller couldn't be more different. Rose is a shy city lawyer; Maggie a gorgeous, good-time gal hopping from bed to bed, job to job. When Maggie betrays Rose's trust, the siblings part company

– only to find each other again (and themselves) via a grandmother they thought was dead.

Jennifer Weiner's sophomore novel, *In Her Shoes*, proved a huge hit on its publication in 2003, yet another addition to the post-Bridget chick-lit phenomenon. It was without doubt one of the classier examples; still, its very definitely womanly concerns – relationships, career crises, and yes, shoes – perhaps make it an unlikely choice for Curtis Hanson, whose previous three films – *8 Mile*, *Wonder Boys* and *L. A. Confidential* – have the distinct tang of testosterone about them.

Yet Hanson has never shied away from surprises, and to dismiss his earlier work as boys' stuff is to ignore the sensitivity to universal human quirks and weaknesses that is present in many of his films.

And so to this – a simple tale of sibling rivalry and inter-familial heartbreak and secrets. The central characters could have been gross stereotypes, Rose the frumpy but clever girl who loves shoes because at least they'll always fit; Maggie the va-va-voom blonde flitting from one man to the next and filching said shoes because at least she has occasions on which to wear them. Yet Weiner is blessed with the talent to create compelling, very real people from the dullest of clichés, something she shares with screenwriter Susannah Grant (*Erin Brockovich*) and Hanson himself, his male perspective bringing grittier notes to a story arc that could (and occasionally does) veer dangerously close to unabashed schmaltz.

They are helped in no small measure by Collette and Diaz, the former giving a typically intelligent, understated performance, while the latter finds hidden depths in a character who could easily have remained an unpleasant, one-dimensional brat. After Maggie commits an act of unspeakably hurtful betrayal and the sisters separate, Hanson pointedly splits the action between Rose's slate-grey, icy Philadelphia cityscape and Maggie's candy-coloured Florida bolthole, all palm trees and sunshine. But sunshine casts shadows, and it's in these scenes that Maggie faces up to her insecurities, loneliness and selfishness, giving the film its breadth and humanity.

Taking his time over 130 minutes, Hanson isn't afraid to pay tribute to the significance of human emotions, however apparently small, and the subtleties of evolving, maturing relationships. As such, while on the surface very much a girls' film, this ruefully honest picture has something to say to everyone. ★★★★ **LB**

IN LIKE FLINT (1967)

Starring: *James Coburn (Derek Flint), Lee J. Cobb (Lloyd C. Cramden), Jean Hale (Lisa), Andrew Duggan (President Trent), Anna Lee (Elisabeth)*
Director: *Gordon Douglas*
Screenwriter: *Hal Fimberg*
PG/114 mins./Comedy/Spy/USA

The second of superspy Derek Flint's adventures has him discover the President has been replaced by a clone, and it could be down to a nefarious gang of haughty women who are plotting to take over the world by brainwashing people in their beauty salons.

Long before *Austin Powers* parodied the 60s spy formula with all its Bondian pomp and glamour, James Coburn took the helm in a series of silly and splendid espionage romps based around the bone-dry spy Derek Flint. This was his second case (following 1965's *Our Man Flint*) which manages the not-inconsiderable achievement of being camper, hammier and more fantastically ludicrous than its predecessor. If it comes right down to it, and it does, this is a film about a gang of imperious female spa owners plotting to put a puppet regime in the White House eventually to take over the world. It could happen . . .

If 007 pretended not to notice how unrealistic his universe was, Flint revels in his own absurdity. Not exactly played for laughs, rather than accepting no one is going to take you seriously, especially when you have Derek Flint (James Coburn, so taciturn he might as well be walled in) joining the Russian ballet or dressing up like Fidel Castro or having lessons to speak dolphin. While Bond delivered the gags, Flint much of the time seems to be the butt of them. Which, interestingly, gives the film a genial grace, with so little tension it just seems to waft pleasantly past.

Gordon Douglas coats the whole thing in a nutty sixties veneer of primary colours and horrible modernist designs of the *Batman* television series, it is vile and garish but fits with its winning sub sci-fi book exuberance. And while it seems there is a loose parody of the battle of the sexes at work, in these awkwardly Stepford-alike minxes who brainwash their fellow sisters with hairdryers, don't worry devilish Derek ends up in orbit with two lovely female Russian cosmonauts and loads of time to kill. ★★★ **IN**

IN THE BEDROOM (2001)

Starring: *Tom Wilkinson (Matt Fowler), Sissy Spacek (Ruth Fowler), Nick Stahl (Frank Fowler), Marisa Tomei (Natalie Strout), William Mapother (Richard Strout), William Wise (Willis Grinnel), Celia Weston (Katie Grinnel), Karen Allen (Marla Keyes)*
Director: *Todd Field*
Screenwriters: *Rob Festinger, Todd Field*
15/131 mins./Drama/USA

Awards: *Golden Globes – Best Actress*

Life is good for the Fowler family. Matt is a successful doctor in small-town Maine, Ruth a teacher, and their son Frank is set for university. Just one problem: Frank's frowned-upon relationship with older, single parent, Natalie . . .

If only all debuts were this good. Low-key, but emotionally devastating, former actor Todd Field's first movie is a superbly crafted examination of family rifts, grief and the lengths to which one will go to appease a guilty conscience. It's also a scathing critique of the US legal system.

Admittedly this isn't laugh-a-minute stuff, but the performances alone are worth it. Spacek has the more obvious Oscar bait, as an embittered and tearful mother; but it's Wilkinson who quietly steals the plaudits, as a father consumed by his inner demons.

Yet the real revelation here is Field. As the film moves from family drama to sombre vigilante thriller without missing a beat, he exhibits a faultless control of tone. Two other deft touches mark him out as a major talent: an early, almost imperceptible camera shudder, filled with suggestions of impending violence; and a gunshot that packs more power into one bang than a thousand mindless thrillers. ★★★★ **CH**

IN THE BLEAK MIDWINTER (1995)

Starring: *Michael Maloney (Joe Harper), Richard Briers (Henry Wakefield), Hetta Charnley (Molly), Joan Collins (Margaretta D'Arcy), Julia Sawalha (Ophelia), Jennifer Saunders (Nancy Crawford)*
Director: *Kenneth Branagh*
Screenwriter: *Kenneth Branagh*
15/94 mins./Comedy/Drama/UK

An actor puts on a production of Hamlet in a church hall, hoping to attract a big-name casting agent.

Content to remain behind the camera in two roles as writer and director, Branagh sensibly downscaled *Frankenstein*'s excess with a small, idiosyncratic, black-and-white comedy of desperate thespians, clearly inspired by the Mickey Rooney/Judy Garland 'Hey, let's put the show on right here!' genre.

Against the advice of his agent, pretentious and unemployed actor Joe mounts a DIY production of Shakespeare's *Hamlet* in a disused village church at Christmas, hoping to make it a showcase vehicle for brilliance, and one to which he can lure London critics. The only company he can muster is a third-rate assortment of eccentrics, inebriates and no-hopers who include the scatty ingénue Nina/Ophelia, camp Terry/transvestite Gertrude, a peevishly politically correct Tom/Laertes (Nick Farrell) and grizzled, grumbling old trouper Henry/Claudius (Richard Briers). Needless to say, all does not go well, with the increasingly frenzied and broke Joe, who is directing and playing the Prince of Denmark, worn out by the spats, guilty secrets, failures and foibles of his troublesome, talent-challenged ensemble.

Branagh's soursweet screenplay is a rather odd mixture of malice towards and adoration of luvviedom, with sentiment and affection winning out as the cast pull together to reap miracles. The roles are an invitation to go OTT and the familiar cast oblige with ripe turns that get funnier as they go. Theatre buffs will especially appreciate the backstage jests and despite what one suspects is bound to be limited appeal, this is, in its sly, enthusiastic sending up of actorly angst, Branagh's most pleasing work to date. **★★★★ AE**

IN THE COMPANY OF MEN (1997)

Starring: *Aaron Eckhart (Chad), Stacy Edwards (Christine), Matt Malloy (Howard), Emily Cline (Suzanne), Jason Dixie (Keith)*
Director: *Neil LaBute*
Screenwriter: *Neil LaBute*
18/93 mins./Drama/Black Comedy/USA

Two men try to seduce and then dump a deaf girl — just for the fun of it.

Something of a transatlantic talking point due to its unflinchingly cruel treatment of women, LaBute's ultra-cheap ($25,000) debut is, in fact, a crafty concoction far removed from the realms of misogyny. Its storyline (two blokes exploit innocent woman for kicks) may be shocking but it never portrays said protagonists in a favourable light, and boasts a heroine far stronger than most. And despite the total lack of violence or graphic images, the mental torture is just as extreme.

Two white-collar employees at a nameless, antiseptic corporation – handsome, manipulative Chad and speccy, snivelly Howard – are understandably unhappy with their respective lots: both of their girlfriends have ditched them, and they have been passed over for promotion.

While lamenting their woes en route to a business engagement, Chad cooks up a plot – for the pair simultaneously to date the first vulnerable woman they meet on the trip and swear undying love, only to dash the victim's hopes in a manner that'll have her 'reaching for the sleeping pills'. The target of their twisted game turns out to be beautiful, sweet-natured but deaf secretary Christine (Edwards, playing hearing-impaired with real conviction). Something, somewhere, is destined not to succeed.

Christine's readiness to double-date the scheming twosome doesn't fully convince (it's hard to believe she would be date-deprived even with her handicap), while the all-talk format, flitting mainly between bedrooms, boardrooms and men's rooms, may prove wearing for some. Nevertheless this is compelling, memorable stuff, offering a glimpse of male bonding at its most dangerous along with three splendid central performances, especially Eckhart, whose personable manner and penchant for ritual humiliation (of both sexes, no less) make Chad as charming as he is utterly reprehensible. **★★★★ CW**

IN THE CUT (2003)

Starring: *Meg Ryan (Frannie), Mark Ruffalo (Det. James Malloy), Jennifer Jason Leigh (Pauline), Nick Damici (Det. Richard Rodriguez), Kevin Bacon (John Graham)*
Director: *Jane Campion*
Screenwriters: *Jane Campion, Susanna Moore, based on Moore's novel*
18/113 mins./Thriller/USA/Australia

English teacher Frannie Avery becomes obsessed with the detective investigating a brutal murder outside her apartment. Together they embark on a passionate, sexual relationship that begins to dominate her thoughts. Meanwhile, the murderer continues on his killing spree.

There's a time in every actress' career when, if she wants to be taken seriously, she has to get her kit off.

Look what it did for Nicole Kidman: she bared all on stage in *The Blue Room* and hasn't looked back. Ironic, then, that Meg Ryan's breakthrough naked role here was originally intended for Kidman.

Kidman retains a producer credit, but, for the first scenes, you'd swear she was on screen – Ryan's transformation is distinctly Nic-like. But that would be doing a disservice to Ryan. She makes a heroine whose howling stupidity could make her unsympathetic. Instead you want to follow her to the darkest places, and Campion is prepared to take you there.

Romantic images are subverted, the sex scenes are graphic and desperate. It's less grim than Susanna Moore's original novella, but the foreshadowing that all is not right is in everything, from the music to the dialogue.

But while technically brilliant, ultimately it's too voyeuristic and cold to recommend without reservations. **★★★ EC**

IN THE HEAT OF THE NIGHT (1967)

Starring: *Sidney Poitier (Detective Virgil Tibbs), Rod Steiger (Police Chief Bill Gillespie), Warren Oates (Officer Sam Wood), Lee Grant (Leslie Colbert), Larry Gates (Eric Endicott)*
Director: *Norman Jewison*
Screenwriter: *Stirling Silliphant*
PG/109 mins./Drama USA
Awards: *Academy Awards – Best Picture, Best Actor (Rod Steiger); Best Editing, Best Writing, Best Screenplay; BAFTA – Best Foreign Actor (Rod Steiger), UN Award (Norman Jewison)*

A black Philadelphian detective, Virgil Tibbs, comes home to visit his mother in the Deep South. When a rich white local is murdered, Tibbs is first arrested, being black, then offered, by his own boss, to help in the investigation. Thus begins a very tense relationship with the bigoted local police chief Bill Gillespie.

A landmark film, justly rewarded by the Oscars, principally about race relations in America – it was made at the height of the Civil Rights movement – that made Sydney Poitier a star and gave Rod Steiger his greatest role. The framework is a whodunit, but the story hinges on the see-sawing power games between this seething Southerner, whose bigotry courses through him like an instinct, and this intellectual black man who has excelled in the very job he has.

Poitier excels with the put-upon pride of a man insulted, but clever enough to grasp why it has happened: 'They call me MR. TIBBS!' he famously cries out to assert an identity beyond the colour of his skin. But the towering work is Steiger's, his is the harder role, he must make this vile, uneducated creature a human being, one coming to terms with his biggest nightmare: a black cop, who is demonstrably better at the job than he is. He wants to accuse him, but worse, he knows he needs him to crack the case, and worse still he is coming to respect him. That a young Norman Jewison soaks the film in humidity adds a sense of the very atmosphere closing in around them.

The plot itself does suffer in the face of the rich characters and their fierce interaction, but it is a major film, driving at the heart of America's own deficiencies. Significantly, Poitier didn't even get a nomination. ★★★★★ **IN**

IN THE LINE OF FIRE (1993)

Starring: *Clint Eastwood (Secret Service Agent Frank Horrigan), John Malkovich (Mitch Leary), Rene Russo (Lilly Raines), Dylan McDermott (Al D'Andrea), Gary Cole (Bill Watts)*
Director: *Wolfgang Petersen*
Screenwriter: *Jeff Maguire*
15/123 mins./Thriller/USA

Veteran Secret Service Agent Frank Horrigan is haunted by his failure to prevent the assassination of President John F. Kennedy. When another potential assassin Mitch Leary comes on the horizon, Frank throws himself back into Presidential protection, determined not to let another President die.

Essentially an old-fashioned two-hander, Petersen's pacey thriller traces the cat-and-mouse game acted out between veteran Secret Service Agent Frank Horrigan and would-be Presidential assassin Malkovich. Frank, a man who has literally seen it all before, is haunted by the memory of the day he failed to save JFK, a memory gleefully stamped upon by the genuinely frightening Malkovich. Together, Eastwood and Malkovich make up the best double-act to come our way for some time, the former's innate decency fighting it out every step of the way against the latter's reptilian scheming for the ultimate prize of the life of the US President.

What separates *In The Line Of Fire* from the rest of the bog-standard good-guy/bad-guy set-up is the clear implication throughout that these two sworn enemies have more in common than they may think, namely a desperate sense of a country gone horribly wrong, a country that has sold them both down the river. Petersen makes sure it's a theme never too far from the surface, but really kicks it home with one astonishing scene where Malkovich finally loses his previous deep cool and explodes down the phone at his quarry's apparent lack of respect.

The other thing that Petersen, director of *Das Boot*, has going for him is the presence of two of Hollywood's classier acts, with Malkovich in particular turning in an outstanding performance, easily his best since *Dangerous Liaisons* and one that confirms him to the hall of screen-baddie fame. Clint, meanwhile, is just very Clint, clearly relishing the freedom of having to simply play himself, and displaying a refreshing sixty-something twinkle in his eye whenever the action switches to the always watchable Rene Russo. ★★★★★ **BMc**

IN THE MOOD FOR LOVE (FA YEUNG NIN WA) (2000)

Starring: *Tony Leung Ciu Wai (Chow Mo-wan), Maggie Cheung (Su Li-zhen Chan), Ping Lam Siu (Ah Ping), Tung Cho 'Joe' Cheung (Cheun Tung Joe), Rebcca Pan (Mrs. Suen)*
Director: *Kar Wai Wong*
Screenwriter: *Kar Wai Wong*
PG/97 mins./Drama/Romance/Hong Kong/France/Thailand

Awards: *Cannes Film Festival – Best Actor*

A newspaper editor and his secretary move into the same apartment block. When they both discover that their partners are having affairs, they are drawn together – first in solace, but then with deepening emotion.

Hong Kong auteur Wai here opts for more traditional tactics in tracing the hesitant love affair between cuckolded neighbours, Maggie Cheung and Tony Leung (who won Best Actor at Cannes for his performance).

Wai recreates the 60s ambience with the same accumulation of small details that made his earlier *Days Of Being Wild* so authentic. But, like that film, form takes precedence over content. Similarly, the action shifts location towards the end, giving the impression that a much altered screenplay had received one last tweak.

Creating credible characters out of almost nothing, the performances are masterly, and the photography beautiful. It's a genuinely romantic romance and makes for sublime cinema. ★★★★ **DP**

IN THE NAME OF THE FATHER (1993)

Starring: *Daniel Day-Lewis (Gerry Conlon), Emma Thompson (Gareth Peirce), Pete Postelthwaite (Guiseppe Conlon), John Lynch (Paul Hill), Mark Sheppard (Paddy Armstrong), Beatie Edney (Carole Richardson)*
Director: *Jim Sheridan*
Screenwriters: *Terry George, Jim Sheridan, based on the book* Proved Innocent *by Gerry Conlon*
15/127 mins./Drama/Biography/Ireland/UK/USA

The story of Gerry Conlon, wrongly convicted with the 'Guildford Four' for bombing a pub in 1974. The police also rounded on Conlon's family and went on to send his father to prison as well.

The reunion for the winning director-star team of *My Left Foot* is another story of a real-life Irishman whose sufferings afford Daniel Day-Lewis the chance to crawl into the skin of a sympathetic character. Throwing a post-Oscar Emma Thompson into the mix suggests a project that could easily collapse under its own worthiness, but in fact this film is a considerable achievement. Aside from daring to tackle still-controversial material in a fair-minded but righteously wrathful manner, it manages to make gripping a story still headline-worthy enough to be familiar to most British (and Irish) audiences.

In 1974, the IRA bombed a soldiers' pub in Guildford, and the British police somehow seized on petty crook Gerard Conlon and three of his mates as the culprits, then spread the net wider and gained convictions against practically the whole Conlon family, notably Gerry's fiercely moralist father Guiseppe, who died in prison. A solicitor got interested in the case and discovered that the police withheld evidence which would have freed Conlon, and the 'Guildford Four' fought through to a successful appeal.

Like *My Left Foot*, this is so sure of itself that it doesn't mind depicting its hero as less than a perfect martyr: we first see him in the midst of a terrifically directed IRA-army skirmish in Belfast, filching the lead off a roof, while his alibi for the night of the bombing is an opportunist robbery of a whore's flat. The length of the film allows Conlon to go through a series of changes, even shunning the tragic 70s clothes and hairstyles for a sharper look as he goes from fringe hippie to despair to determination.

Establishing early a vividly horrid vision of the grubby 70s drop-out culture, the film potently conveys the reality of what the Conlons missed in prison as styles and trends come and go almost subliminally in the background while they endure the monotony of jail life. With the real IRA represented by a maniac who uses a home-made flamethrower on a prison guard, *In The Name Of The Father* avoids getting into Republican politics, though it indicts the behaviour of the police and (by implication) successive governments in the conduct of this particular case. The heart of the film is the relationship between Gerry and Guiseppe, as the father and son finally settle their lifelong arguments when unjustly imprisoned together. ★★★★ **KN**

⦿ IN THIS WORLD (2002)

Starring: *Jamal Udin Torabi (Jamal), Enayatullah (Enayat), Wakeel Khan (Enayat's Uncle), Nabil Elouahabi (Yusik), Hiddayatullah (Enayat's brother)*
Director: *Michael Winterbottom*
Screenwriter: *Tony Grisoni*
15/86 mins./Drama/UK
Awards: *BAFTA – Best Foreign Language Film*

Two refugees travel from the Pakistan/Afghan border, through Western Pakistan to Iran, Turkey, Italy and France, seeking asylum in Britain.

Michael Winterbottom's pertinent statement on asylum seekers, the political hot potato du jour, takes us right to the heart of the matter. It is presented as fiction, but the lines with documentary are blurred so much that you are never sure if what you are watching is actual or a construction.

Tony Grisoni's script is a distillation of first-hand accounts of refugees' journeys, and the non-actors in the lead roles had their journey 'organised' by the filmmakers, who captured their spontaneous reactions to suggested situations. These are effective tactics that heighten the emotional resonance of the gripping stories, and the use of DV technology also helps the cause.

It is shocking to read of people so desperate to get to this country that they hide in boxes or cling to the bottom of lorries. Winterbottom's intrepid camera takes us inside those boxes and under those axles. ★★★★★ **ND**

⦿ IN WHICH WE SERVE (1942)

Starring: *Noel Coward (Capt. Kinross), John Mills (Shorty Blake), Bernard Miles (Walter Hardy), Celia Johnson (Alix Kinross), Kay Walsh (Freda Lewis), Joyce Carey (Keith Hardy), Michael Wilding (Flags)*
Directors: *Noel Coward, David Lean*
Screenwriter: *Noel Coward*
U/115 mins./Drama/War/UK

As they cling to the wreckage of HMS *Torrin* during the Battle of Crete, Captain Kinross, Chief Petty Officer Walter Hardy and Ordinary Seaman Shorty Blake think back to better times in Blighty.

Commissioned by Anthony Havelock-Allan and Filippo Del Giudice to make a war film on a subject of his choosing, Noel Coward selected a naval story based on the exploits of Lord Louis Mountbatten aboard HMS *Kelly*. In addition to writing the screenplay, Coward also agreed to star. However, he recognised his cinematic inexperience and invited seasoned editor David Lean to act as his co-director. It proved to be a wise decision, as it was Lean's contribution (which was largely overlooked by contemporary critics) that has made this stiff-lipped flagwaver so durable.

Coward's initial script ran long. So, he devised the idea of flashing back from the scene of HMS *Torrin*'s sinking to salvage his more emotive Home Front sequences and emphasise both the human side of conflict and the aspects of everyday life that were so worth fighting for.

However, the producers were keen to make the picture even more inclusive and Havelock-Allan and cinematographer Ronald Neame compiled the semi-documentary opening (narrated by Leslie Howard) in which the ship is built, fitted and launched to acknowledge the efforts of those working in vital war industries. Moreover, this approach bound the film into the tradition of items like *Target For Tonight*, which sought to boost morale with a restrained approximation of reality rather than through the gung-ho antics that Hollywood had already started to embrace.

Very much a man of the theatre, Coward gave a somewhat stagy display of jaunty heroism (particularly during his clipped Dunkirk speech, which was delivered before a watching Royal Family). However, old hands like John Mills and Bernard Miles, along with such newcomers as Richard Attenborough and Michael Wilding, achieved a more credible sense of classless patriotism that was reinforced during the scenes ashore by Celia Johnson and Kay Walsh.

Coward received a special Oscar citation for his efforts after the feature doubled its $1 million outlay at the US box office. But, his assistant and ensemble have since been recognised as its real heroes. ★★★★ **DP**

⦿ THE INCREDIBLE SHRINKING MAN (1957)

Starring: *Grant Williams (Scott Carey), Randy Stuart (Louise Carey), April Kent (Clarice), Paul Langton (Charles Carey), Raymond Bailey (Doctor Thomas Silver)*
Director: *Jack Arnold*
Screenwriter: *Richard Matheson, based on his own novel*
PG/114 mins./Sci-fi/USA

Exposed to a strange possibly radioactive mist, Scott Carey begins to shrink to the size of an insect. Confounding doctors and evading his own cat, he must finally contend with the perils of being locked in his own basement.

A classic of 50s sci-fi paranoia, determinedly of the mind that dabbling with radioactivity is sure to be the end of us all, sees exposure to a contaminated mist shrink an average Joe to the size of a thimble. What gives Jack Arnold's adaptation of Richard Matheson's famous novel such a neat kick, is the fact that besides his immediate dilemma, Grant William's tiny hero never leaves his own home. Such everyday comforts as his own pet cat, climbing off a kitchen table, and the dusty confines of a basement, are transformed into a terrifying vertiginous world fraught with peril. A confrontation with a 'giant' spider, impressively realised, as are all the effects, for its day, has become one of the iconic images of the entire era.

Arnold's great skill is in keeping the camera's viewpoint that of his protagonist; the essential thrill is to envisage what it would be like to be 'this' high. And, with the assistance of Matheson's fiction, attempt to ground the plot in a scientific plausibility. Not that it could happen, just that it sounds like it could. Doctors decide he is shrinking care of an 'anti-cancerous' condition, and manage to arrest the damage before he completely disappears. By working the bitterness Grant Williams feels in becoming a 'little man', having to live in a doll's house, there is a cute subtext in the maintenance of masculinity. When finally abandoned, and thought dead, he must be man, no matter what height, and trawl for food and fend off predators. And in keeping with its serious mood, things end on something of a downer. ★★★★ **IN**

⦿ THE INCREDIBLES (2004)

Starring: *the voices of: Craig T.Nelson (Mr. Incredible), Holly Hunter (Elastigirl), Samuel L. Jackson (Frozone), Jason Lee (Syndrome)*
Director: *Brad Bird*
Screenwriter: *Brad Bird*
U/115 mins./Animation/Comedy/Family/USA
Awards: *Academy Awards – Best Sound Editing, Best Animated Feature Film, BAFTA – Best Film, Children's Award*

When Mr. Incredible, aka Bob Parr, catches a jumper who doesn't want to be saved, he opens the door to a wave of legal compensations that puts all superheroes out of business and into a relocation programme. Years later, Bob and Helen – formerly Elastigirl – are trying raise a 'normal' family when they receive a mysterious call for help.

Writer-director Brad Bird had been shopping his cartoon riff on comic books around Hollywood for nigh on ten years. During that decade, a digital revolution has sucked the lead from the pencils of traditional animators. Bird, who earned his stripes as a key member of *The Simpsons*' creative team and gave *The Iron Giant* a defiantly lo-fi sheen in 1999, may once have intended to hand-draw his superhero family, but it's no surprise that, once the 3D-CG era dawned, the director was himself drawn to Pixar Studios.

If it ain't broke, so they say, don't fix it, and – with five home runs from five at the only thing Pixar has broken so far is the bank. And yet, *Finding Nemo* proved to be the company's biggest box office whale so far, it was also apparent that the Pixar formula was now perhaps picked clean. Like *A Bug's Life* and *Monsters, Inc.* before it, *Nemo*'s design was drafted straight from John Lasseter's *Toy Story* blueprint – mismatched buddies, colourful supporting cast, road movie, yada, yada, yada. Bird, however, is the first outsider to be welcomed into the Pixar family, and he has parlayed the creative freedom afforded him to deliver something altogether different: part domestic sitcom with human characters and adult concerns, part costume caper with breathless action sequences and production design ripped from Bond boffin Ken Adam's most fevered dreams.

Most superhero movies employ a number of costume changes, but *The Incredibles* features just one of note. Following a bit of historical business to explain the crimefighter relocation programme, the first half keeps the suits – and the powers – firmly in the closet, as our humbled hero fights corporate tyranny as an insurance clerk by day and mines cheap thrills by listening to the police scanner at night. Only when Bob is lured out of retirement and into danger do he and the family call upon a celebrated fashion designer – voiced by Brad Bird himself in full 'dahling' mode, and an unmistakable highlight – to provide the obligatory threads.

The little black masks subsequently remain on, but for adults it is the earlier interplay between Bob and Helen that'll likely linger longest. Unlike, say, *Shrek*, Bird never scatter-guns gags at the screen or short-changes character for a joke. He has a smattering of bulletproof set-pieces to lean upon – look out for the bit with capes – but mostly the gags are organic, generated by the story rather than offered in place of one. In fact, the oddly melancholy first half is closer in tone to superior suburban indie comedies like *Office Space* or *The Good Girl* than anything Pixar has so far produced.

The younger demographic will doubtless be relieved when the evil mastermind is unmasked and the Incredible kids finally get in on the action, but the relentless – and overcooked – final reel inevitably leaves less room for character grace notes. And while the action is expertly tooled, those critics of CGI who feel cartoony FX can diminish the sense of jeopardy in live-action movies are hardly likely to be sweating bullets over the fates of drawings. Indeed, it's perhaps a shame it's taken Bird's movie a decade to reach the screen, as the recent glut of live-action superhero feats has inevitably stolen some of the thunder from his cartoon marvels.

Still, even if *The Incredibles* is just an arranged marriage between superhero romp and classic sitcom, this hybrid has enough highlights for everybody to guarantee Pixar another critical and commercial hit. Looks like 2004 has given birth to a new superhero franchise after all. ★★★★
OR

ⓘ INDECENT PROPOSAL (1993)

Starring: *Robert Redford (John Gage), Demi Moore (Diana Murphy), Woody Harrelson (David Murphy), Seymour Cassel (Mr. Shackleford), Oliver Platt (Jeremy), Billy Bob Thornton (Day Tripper)*
Director: *Adrian Lyne*
Screenwriter: *Amy Holden Jones, based on the novel by Jack Engelhard*
15/112 mins./Drama/USA

A billionaire offers a recently unemployed architect one million dollars to sleep with his wife.

Demi loves Woody. Woody loves Demi. The dog loves them both, and all is well in their comfy Californian lives until, in a spectacularly 90s-style plot development, the recession strikes and they get booted from their gainful employment as an architect (him) and estate agent (her). So, it's – rather unwisely – off to Las Vegas to try and raise the readies to fulfil that dream of a self-designed pad on the beach, or at least to keep body and soul together till the boom years return.

Just 15 minutes into *Indecent Proposal*, and things are not looking good. There have been unintentional chuckles courtesy of a silly flashback to school days (Demi's grin revealing a gobful of dental braces, Woody with a rug from hell); there have been the obligatory 'steamy' sex scenes – lots of shots of a tanned Demi in little white knickers – to illustrate just how much they damn well fancy each other, and there has been much gnashing of teeth as the horrors of unemployment dawn.

Once our billionaire gambler comes on to the scene with his 'indecent proposal' (one million dollars for a night with Demi), however, things brighten up considerably, with the complex emotions on display being handled with remarkable aplomb. Forget the carping that the hunksome Redford would never, in reality, have to pay for a woman. This is all about power and he plays the game brilliantly, driving a wedge between the lovebirds as they decide to go for the deal ('It's just my body, it's not my heart, it's not my mind') and then watch their supposedly invincible marriage buckle under the strain. Indeed, it is in this mid-section that the cast, director Adrian Lyne and screenwriter Amy Holden Jones conspire to present some seriously interesting emotional shenanigans, with what happened that night remaining a mystery to both the audience and hubby, and the subsequent jealousies and power struggles ringing entirely true.

Redford, as you'd expect, is brilliant as the scheming-yet-strangely-vulnerable rich git (and one cannot help but ponder that as a millionaire divorcee living on his own in Utah, Redford must have unusual insights into this character), Moore is beautiful enough to carry off the central plot point, and even Harrelson displays something other than his usually dim berk persona by successfully playing a sensitive thinking type in little round glasses.

Sadly, of course, the quality control doesn't last, with the tension gradually slipping away until we find ourselves, in the final, risible scene, back in unintentional chuckle territory. At times ridiculously corny, often strangely compelling, and never less than entertaining, this may lose its bottle towards the end, but at least it had some bottle to start with. ★★★
PT

ⓘ INDEPENDENCE DAY (1996)

Starring: *Will Smith (Captain Steve Hiller), Bill Pullman (President Thomas J. Whitmore), Jeff Goldblum (David Levinson), Mary McDonnell (Marilyn Whitmore), Judd Hirsch (Julius Levinson), Randy Quaid (Russell Casse)*
Director: *Roland Emmerich*
Screenwriters: *Roland Emmerich, Dean Devlin*
112/146 mins./Sci-fi/Thriller/Action/USA

Awards: *Academy Awards – Best Effects/Visual Effects*

When powerful aliens launch an all-out invasion against the human race, only a small band of American survivors can save the day.

Whatever one feels about the actual movie, only the dullest dog would deny *Independence Day* – or, as it is also known by its tidier tag, *ID4* – had one of the most bitchin' promo trailers ever spliced together. It raised the bar for teasers as audiences roared approval and salivated at the hors d'ouevre of the White House being disintegrated. As a result, when the film opened in North America it played around the clock to packed houses, crossing the magic $100 million mark in the first weekend.

Despite pooh-poohs that it's silly, hokey, sentimental and formulaic – well, yeah, but shamelessly, knowingly so – plenty of bang for your buck was delivered exactly as advertised. One day the people of the world collectively gawp at the arrival of a fleet of titanic flying saucers hovering over capital cities and scenic landmarks. Once again we learn that we are not alone in the universe. And, naturally, rather quickly we wish that we were as the mystery armada sets about incinerating city centres, famous architecture, traffic jams, brave pilots and comic supporting actors. Anyone who ever got a kick out of commie paranoia 50s B-movies, or monsters from space flicks, will have a ball with *ID4*. Also catered to are devotees of those 70s disaster movies structured to accommodate the romantic problems, redemption mini-dramas and destruction of large ensembles in preposterous, preferably fiery, set-pieces.

Director Roland Emmerich and his producer-writer partner Dean Devlin, coming off the surprise success of *Stargate*, took things the perfectly-timed step further, bringing the bad-ass aliens and the big production design home to planet Earth. The gusto with which Emmerich and Devlin stirred corn, clichés and conventions of pop culture into the spectacle of its year is really quite endearing and hilariously, excitingly entertaining. *ID4* cheerfully rips off H.G. Wells' *War Of The Worlds*, Kenneth Johnson's 1980s TV space invasion opera *V*, and every tentacled thingie pic ever made.

Throughout there are specific homages made to *The Day The Earth Stood Still* and Kubrick's duo of *Dr. Strangelove* and *2001: A Space Odyssey*. Other audience-friendly elements include R.E.M. ('It's The End Of The World As We Know It', of course), references to *The X-Files* and the Roswell Incident, and a multi-ethnic cast representing a stereotypical cross-section of American society, from US President Thomas Whitmore (Bill 'Let's nuke the bastards!' Pullman) to alcoholic 'Nam vet and trailer park denizen Russell Casse (Randy 'Hello, boys ... I'm ba-aaack!' Quaid). A favourite is the teen wolf who attempts to capitalise on the situation – imminent annihilation – by putting the make on Russ's daughter: 'This could be our last night on earth. You don't want to die a virgin do you?'

ID4 owes much of its charm to the exuberant presence of Will Smith as studly Marine flyboy Capt. Steve Hiller, who longs to be an astronaut and can't wait to get up there and kick some alien butt, which he does with wonderfully matter-of-fact 'That's what I call a close encounter' aplomb. The Designated Everyman is Jeff Goldblum's David Levinson, who saves civilisation from stinky telepathic techno-locusts with his laptop. *ID4* enshrines the great and greatly absurd action clichés of our time. 1) Heroes always escape an engulfing fireball by inches. Air Force One squeaks out of the DC inferno; Steve and David burst out of the exploding mother ship in the repaired Roswell craft. 2) In a crisis, class barriers fall. Steve's stripper squeeze rescues and bonds with the critically injured, high-toned First Lady; crop-duster Russ and the President become comrades-in-arms. 3) The pet is imperilled. Jasmine and winsome child escape a firewall, but pooch Boomer is a goner. No, by golly, a split-second from cremation the plucky retriever miraculously bounds to safety. Yay! 4) Isn't America great? Yankee cock-a-doodle can-do spirit brings the grateful world to its feet in an 'I'd Like To Buy The World A Coke' kind of moment. African youngsters scamper across the hillside and turban-sporting types reach for the sky, jubilant at the sight of flying saucer wreckage.

The checklist of required incidents, characters, quips, stunts and property destruction is worked through with almost none of the butch cynicism or irony that marks other B-sensibility blockbusters of the period. ★★★★ **KN**

Movie Trivia: Independence Day

The opening song was going to be 'Everybody Wants To Rule The World', but Emmerich preferred R.E.M's 'It's The End of The World As We Know It (And I feel fine)'. In one scene, one of Goldblum's colleagues makes a reference to *The X-Files*. In the X-Files movie, Mulder takes a leak on an *Independence Day* poster. The White House sets were originally built for *The American President*.

THE INDIAN IN THE CUPBOARD (1995)

Starring: *Hal Scardino (Omri), Litefoot (Little Bear), Lindsay Crouse (Jane), Richard Jenkins (Victor), Rishi Bhat (Patrick), Steve Coogan (Tommy Atkins)*
Director: *Frank Oz*
Screenwriter: *Melissa Mathison, based on the novel by Lynne Reid Banks*
PG/92 mins./Family/Adventure/Fantasy/USA

Omri receives numerous presents for his birthday, the apparently least interesting of which are a battered cupboard and a plastic Indian. However, when Omri locks his Indian in the cupboard, he comes to life in the shape of Little Bear.

Former Muppet man Frank Oz sets himself the difficult task of coming up with a modern children's classic. As *The Secret Garden* and *Black Beauty* proved, in a market dominated by Disney animation, this is not an easy thing to achieve, and, despite a heavy emphasis on low-key hi-tech effects, this sadly misses the mark.

For his ninth birthday, gawky Omri receives a number of gifts, the least interesting of which appears to be a battered up old cupboard from his brother, and a three-inch high plastic Indian from his best friend Patrick. But when Omri locks his Indian in the cupboard amazing things begin to happen, as he wakes up the next morning to find the Indian has come to life in the form of the slightly confused Little Bear (Native American rapper Litefoot). Adding a plastic cowboy to the mix, Omri now finds he has the ultimate history lesson accessory, while, inevitably, learning the value of friendship, responsibility and magic cupboard proprietorship.

Adapted from Lynne Reid Banks' novel – itself originally a bedtime story told to her son Omri – Oz's movie benefits greatly from the casting of the young Scardino who brings a distinct freshness to the role with his unconventional looks that diverts a good deal of the film's saccharine potential. David Keith makes a spirited shrunken cowboy and Steve Coogan does a fun turn as a one-time plastic World War I medic.

Where the film disappoints most is in the visuals that should, of course, be the movie's strong point. Mixing a host of outsize props and sets with advanced blue screen work means that our three-inch heroes convincingly interact with their normal size counterparts. But it also results in half the screen being out of focus at any one time, something that eventually becomes an overwhelming irritant. Oz's movie is well intentioned if a touch too heavy on the PC side of things, but ultimately proves just too uninspired. ★★ **BM**

INDIANA JONES AND THE LAST CRUSADE (1989)

Starring: *Harrison Ford (Indiana Jones), Sean Connery (Professor Henry Jones), Denholm Elliott (Dr. Marcus Brody), Alison Doody (Dr. Elsa Schneider), River Phoenix (Young Indy)*
Director: *Steven Spielberg*
Screenwriter: *Jeffrey Boam, from a story by George Lucas, Menno Meyjes, characters created by George Lucas, Philip Kaufman*
PG/112 mins./Action/Adventure/USA
Awards: *Academy Awards – Best Sound Effects Editing*

Renowned archaeologist Indiana Jones teams up with his father to try and find the Holy Grail. Once again, the Nazis are after the same prize, and try to foil Indiana's plans.

If Steven Spielberg had followed his heart, *Indiana Jones And The Last Crusade* might never have happened. In 1988, he was heavily involved in preproduction on *Rain Man*, when George Lucas reminded him of a gentleman's agreement to make the then-untitled Indy 3. Disappointed and slightly resentful, Spielberg nevertheless set to work, rejecting several scenarios for the return of the whip-wielding hero, including an outlandish Chris Columbus idea (which saw Indy battle an African Monkey King, at one point chasing a truck while riding a rhinoceros) before settling on the quest for the Holy Grail. In the end, it all worked out nicely – *Rain Man* won Oscars for Dustin Hoffman and Barry Levinson, to whom Spielberg passed on his copious *Rain Man* notes; while the Holy Trinity of Spielberg, Lucas and Ford all enjoyed a much-needed hit, in the wake of critical and commercial disappointments (*Empire Of The Sun, Willow*, and *Frantic* respectively).

Spielberg, smarting after yet another Oscar snub, (*Empire* was nominated for six Oscars, winning none; ironically, *Crusade* bagged one Oscar, for Best Sound Effects Editing), saw *Crusade* as 'consciously regressing', representing a critic-proof chance to show that he could still peddle popcorn. Ultimately, he succeeded, producing a movie which stands out like a sore thumb from his middling output of the late-80s to early 90s, and which, while not quite matching *Raiders*, serves as a fitting end to the Indy trilogy.

Perhaps low on confidence and anxious for a hit, Spielberg approached the material with caution (plotwise, it hugs tight to the *Raiders* formula, rejecting the darkness of *Temple Of Doom*; while, visually, it's the least-inspired of the trilogy, offering very few indelible images or Spielbergian trademarks). But it may well be the most entertaining of the series, with its playful tone established in the River Phoenix-starring, Indy-demystifying prologue – which, sadly, also paved the way for *The Young Indiana Jones Chronicles* – and reaching its apotheosis with the arrival of Sean Connery as Indy's dad, Henry Jones.

Thematically, the relationship between Ford's stoic hero and Connery's bookish father addresses one of Spielberg's major preoccupations: paternal absenteeism, although the unusually reconciliatory tone perhaps reflects his own ascension to fatherhood, and his concerns over his marriage to Amy Irving, then divorce courts-bound. Jones Snr. may have been a Lucas invention, but Spielberg uses him to invest *Crusade* with an emotional core lacking in its rollercoaster precursors, as the Grail finally becomes less important to Indy than his father. Quite frankly, as Spielberg himself postulated, only James Bond could play Indiana Jones' dad, and Connery's Henry contrasts superbly with the thorny Indy – courtesy of punched-up dialogue by Tom Stoppard – reducing him often to the level of chastened son, a truly amusing development. In fact, *Crusade* is comfortably the funniest Indy, incorporating several superb set pieces (the delightful 'No ticket' scene is spoofed adroitly in Kevin Smith's *Dogma*), but it's the interplay between Ford and Connery – totally believable, despite a mere 12-year age gap – that makes *Crusade* such a joy.

Humour aside, Spielberg elicits another cool, iconic performance from Ford – witness Indy taking out three Nazis with one bullet – who never loses sight of Indy's human side, while he stages the action sequences quite beautifully. It's a relief in this era of Indy rip-offs like *The Mummy Returns* and *Tomb Raider*, to see classically-composed action sequences where the camera doesn't suffer from Tourettes, and where the most important element isn't found on a PC hard drive. And if it's hard to reconcile the Spielberg of *Schindler's List* with the comic-book depiction of Nazis in this pre-WWII epic, imagine this as the Spielberg of his youth, delighting in blowing Nazis to high heaven. After Schindler's, Spielberg remarked that *Crusade*'s portrayal of Nazis embarrassed him – in fact, this is a sly and barbed condemnation of those 'goose-stepping morons'.

Tagline

Have the adventure of your life keeping up with the Joneses.

Crusade ends as perfectly as any film trilogy could, with our four heroes – Sallah, Marcus Brody, Henry Jones and, as we've just discovered, Henry Jones Jr. – riding off into the sunset, to John Williams' triumphant *Raiders* march. It's enough to bring a tear to the eye – that *Crusade* was intended as Indy: The Final Chapter is incontrovertible (Ford even told journalists at a 1989 press conference to 'read my lips: Bye-bye Indiana'). But when a movie makes $494m worldwide (holding its own against Tim Burton's *Batman*), bye-bye is a meaningless soundbite, and not every Crusade is the Last. Once the Big Three clear their multi-million dollar schedules, Indy 4 may be made. But it would be a shame to taint *Last Crusade* with a fourth episode, loaded down with untenable expectations. The Grail immortalised Indy; best keep him that way. ★★★★ **CH**

INDIANA JONES AND THE TEMPLE OF DOOM (1984)

Starring: *Harrison Ford (Indiana Jones), Kate Capshaw (Wilhelmina 'Willie' Scott), Jonathan Ke Quan (Short Round), Amrish Puri (Mola Ram), Roshan Seth (Chattar Lal)*
Director: *Steven Spielberg*
Screenwriters: *Willard Huyck, Gloria Katz, based on a story by George Lucas*
PG/112 mins./Action/Adventure/USA

Awards: *Academy Awards – Best Visual Effects, BAFTA – Best Visual Effects*

After arriving in India, Indiana Jones is asked by a desperate village to find a mystical stone. He agrees, and stumbles upon a secret cult plotting a terrible plan in the catacombs of an ancient palace.

The heart. Everyone remembers the bit with the heart. So it's only fair that affairs of it is where we'll begin.

The early 80s saw Steven Spielberg in something of a spin. Having split from Amy Irving after a fateful trip to Japan in 1980 (thus also nixing the plans for her to co-star in *Raiders*), three years later the pair ran into each other again at Los Angeles airport. He was en route to location scout *Temple Of Doom*, and was single again after a brief dalliance with Barbra Streisand. She had just returned from the sunny climbs of TV-movie *The Far Pavilions* and was looking particularly stunning ... Seconds out, Round 2.

But then, of course, there was Kate Capshaw. A struggling actress, she may not have been the girl that Spielberg and producing partner Kathleen Kennedy had been expecting for audition (there was a mix-up of publicity photographs), but she nevertheless wowed him as the prospective Willie Scott, Indiana Jones' future paramour for the sequel/prequel. Fine, so they didn't marry until October 1991, but the seeds (of the emotional variety, anyway) had surely been sown.

Throw into the mix the very public charges of 'conspiracy to illegally employ children' then being aimed at *Twilight Zone: The Movie* (perhaps it's little wonder that *Temple Of Doom* should focus on enslaved children) and one thing is clear: in the build-up to the second outing for the fedora-clad archaeologist, Steven Spielberg was riding something of a personal rollercoaster. Or, if you'd prefer, a mine cart without any brakes. Initially cooked up by Spielberg, George Lucas and Lucas' *American Graffiti* (1973) cohorts Willard Huyck and Gloria Katz, over a single week of script meetings at Lucas' Northern California pad, the first draft of *Temple Of Doom* was complete some six weeks later. Approximately 4000 storyboards would soon follow, rendering this possibly the most preplanned movie in Spielberg's canon. And while the director would later enlist John Milius for a swift dialogue polish, one thing was immediately apparent: Dr. Jones was in for a very dark time indeed.

And although its original title was eventually deemed too bleak for a family-orientated summer blockbuster (The Temple Of Death became instead merely one of Doom), Spielberg and co.'s early decision to inject a pervading strain of cartoon violence very much lived on. The result was the introduction of the PG-13 rating in the US (*Gremlins* is also cited as a contributory movie) and numerous public retractions from the director. Even if he did later go on record to observe that, 'The picture is not called The Temple Of Roses, it's called The Temple Of Doom.'

Indeed, its grottiness is just one of *Temple's* greatest fortes. A frenetic, ghoulish, fantastical romp straight from the stuff of childhood dreams – and not nightmares, as was originally decried – this is Spielberg at his most freewheeling. A fact apparent from an opening sequence in which Capshaw warbles a rendition of Cole Porter's 'Anything Goes' (in Cantonese), and in doing so perfectly sums up the film's no-holds-barred ethos. Monkey brains and impromptu open heart surgery? Well, you were warned.

There are, however, occasional downsides. Indy's chief adversary, Mola Ram, is underwritten to the point of insignificance, and compare Willie to *Raiders'* Marion and she comes off as a shrinking violet. Likewise, the claims of racist stereotyping that peppered the production (much was shot in Sri Lanka after the Indian government, concerned by what they felt to be a xenophobic script, refused permission to shoot) still carry some weight, and too often the wonderment of the original is replaced by gung-ho action. In fact, if reintroducing certain sequences intended for *Raiders*, but scrapped for budgetary reasons (the mine carts, the life raft from a plane), certainly raises the bar in the adrenaline stakes, there is an argument that a proportion of character-based exposition in turn falls by the wayside.

Naturally, this is but minor carping. Adhering to a similar dramatic arc to Lucas' Star Wars trilogy, *Temple Of Doom* is easily the most enticingly sinister. It features the most sizzling chemistry of the three – with Ford even managing to appear game despite the ruptured disc he suffered after performing many of his own stunts – and, courtesy of Indy and Short Round, generally hilarious repartee.

Most significantly, though, *Temple Of Doom*'s box-office success both justified MCA's $3.6 million thank you for *E.T.* – the Amblin Headquarters – and re-established Spielberg as King Of The Blockbusters, after the *Twilight Zone* debacle. It was a title he certainly needed to reclaim before embarking on his artistically commendable, but commercially unlikely, double bill of *The Colour Purple* and *Empire Of The Sun*. And one which maybe best sums up his enduring work ethic: Fortune and glory, kids. Fortune and glory. ★★★★ **MD**

The Movie Brats

Who they were: Emerging in the early 70s, the first group of American film directors to learn film as film. Practically invented the modern blockbuster.

Hallmarks: Technically proficient (renowned for use of storyboards, special effects and sound design); often revisited favourite childhood genres; canny use of marketing and merchandising; beards and baseball caps.

Key Figures: Francis Ford Coppola, George Lucas, Steven Spielberg, Brian De Palma, John Milius, Martin Scorsese.

If you see one film, see: *Star Wars* (Lucas, 1977)

INFERNO (1980)

Starring: *Leigh McCloskey (Mark Elliot), Irene Miracle (Rosa Elliot), Eleonora Giorgu (Sara), Sacha Pitoeff (Kazanian), Alida Valli (Carol), Veronica (Lazar)*
Director: *Dario Argento*
Screenwriter: *Dario Argento*
18/107 mins/Horror/Italy

Poet Rosa learns from a rare book that the New York apartment building she lives in may also be inhabited by one of three demonic goddesses, the Mother of Darkness. When she is killed, her brother takes over her investigation.

A semi-sequel to *Suspiria*, this is Dario Argento's baroque horror masterpiece. The earlier film's witch queen is retroactively identified as Mater Suspiriorum (the Mother of Sighs), sister to the Rome-dwelling Mater Lachrymarum (the Mother of Tears) – a pouting, cat-stroking beauty (Anna Pieroni) who has yet to have her own film – and New York's Mater Tenebrarum (the Mother of Darkness). Defiantly refusing to make narrative sense, *Inferno* has a succession of unfortunate mortals becoming intrigued with the mysteries of the Three Mothers, then meeting bad ends in sequences staged with all the imaginative flair of dance routines in a Vincente Minnelli musical: a girl (Miracle) exploring a flooded basement has a brush with a floating corpse, an old man (Pitoeff) is attacked by rats in Central Park while drowning cats during a lunar eclipse and a demonic hot dog vendor intervenes. Keith Emerson rescores snatches of Verdi for a pounding prog-rock soundtrack, while Argento dwells on the elaborate art deco art direction, the primary-coloured lighting scheme, tiny details and clues which establish the mysteries of the haunted house, ultra close-ups of cut fingers and dropped keys and flash-inserts of animals eating each other. Everyone is blankly beautiful or interestingly gnarled, but that's about it as far as characterisation goes – though the house of darkness turns out to be packed with barely-sketched sub-plots about nasty people doing horrid things to one another and deservedly suffering for it. It starts off with a climax and builds to a plateau of surrealist delirium that, one way or another, will have you shrieking. ★★★★★ **KN**

THE IN-LAWS (1979)

Starring: *Peter Falk (Vincent J. Ricardo), Alan Arkin (Sheldon S. Kornpett), Richard Libertini (General Garcia), Nancy Dussault (Carol Kornpett), Penny Peyser (Barbara Kornpett)*
Director: *Arthur Hiller*
Screenwriter: *Andrew Bergman*
PG/98 mins./Comedy/USA

A crazy CIA agent and a repressed dentist are brought together when their son and daughter are about to marry.

Recently – and rather pointlessly – remade as a modern comedy starring Michael Douglas and Albert Brooks, this original romp features Peter Falk and Alan Arkin as a crazy CIA agent and repressed dentist respectively.

The two are brought together when their son and daughter are about to marry, Falk's madcap agent wasting no time in involving his future in-law in a dangerous operation to do with stolen Treasury engravings and drawing the hapless Arkin into deeper and deeper trouble.

This is light, broad comedy through and through, with Falk and Arkin inviting plenty of smirks but few belly laughs. Writer Andrew Bergman went on to provide more laughs with his *Blazing Saddles* script – and those of the ironic kind for *Striptease*. ★★★ **ASm**

THE IN-LAWS (2003)

Starring: *Michael Douglas (Steve Tobias), Albert Brooks (Jerry Peyser), Robin Tunney (Angela Harris), Ryan Reynolds (Mark Tobias), Candice Bergen (Judy Tobias), Davd Suchet (Jean-Pierre Thibodoux)*
Director: *Andrew Fleming*
Screenwriters: *Nat Mauldin, Ed Solomon, based on the 1979 film by Andrew Bergman*
12/93 mins./Comedy/USA

Uptight Chicago podiatrist Jerry's meticulous arrangements for his daughter's wedding unravel when the groom's devil-may-care father, Steve, arrives.

You can just imagine the pitch for this modestly agreeable remake of Arthur Hiller's zanier 1979 rib-tickler.

Odd couple comedies that team an ageing Oscar-winning actor who wants to do a comedy with a comedian who will play the foil are perennially popular (*Anger Management*, *Analyse That*); spy spoofs and weddings gone awry always float; nobody will remember the original movie anyway; blah blah blah ...

Bergman's screenplay has been retooled by Nat Mauldin (*Doctor Doolittle*) and Ed Solomon (*Men In Black*, *Charlie's Angels*), with the best stuff left out, presumably so that Michael Douglas can play a rogueish superspy without being made to look silly and without mussing his hair. Speaking of which, what's up with that blond do?

For this reason, they apparently couldn't decide at first whether they were doing a comedy or a comic thriller. The film opens with a familiar 'espionage in Prague' prologue which establishes that Steve is leading a dangerous double life – thus blowing the potential for the audience to think he might just be nuts when he embroils mild-mannered, phobia-ridden square Jerry in his colourful fantasy adventure.

The welcome entrance of David 'Poirot' Suchet hamming it up as a camp Euro-villain (who doesn't torture his victims since he's discovered meditation; now he lets them run before he shoots them) clears things up in the genre-defining department. Candice Bergen as the embittered ex-wife who detests Steve, but gets excited remembering what great sex they had, is also a hoot but underused. Which leaves director Fleming to paper over the missteps and mundane dips with a couple of very cute CG and digital imaging enhanced action scenes. ★★★ **RW**

⑬ INNERSPACE (1987)

Starring: *Dennis Quaid (Lieutenant Tuck Pendleton), Martin Short (Jack Putter), Meg Ryan (Lydia Maxwell), Kevin McCarthy (Victor Eugene Scrimshaw)*
Director: *Joe Dante*
Screenwriters: *Chrip Proser, Jeffrey Boam*
PG/120 mins./Sci-fi/Comedy/USA

Awards: *Academy Awards – Best Visual Effects*

About to be injected into a rabbit during a top-secret miniaturisation experiment, American pilot Tuck Pendleton, inside a ship, inside a syringe, is stolen by rival scientists and accidentally injected into Jack Putter a hypochondriac supermarket assistant. With his oxygen running out, Tuck must convince Jack that, firstly, he is not possessed, and secondly, to help rescue him.

A rich, sugary pudding made up of familiar ingredients: the miniaturisation concept of *Fantastic Voyage*, the herky-jerky slapstick of *All Of Me*, the easy-grin of Dennis Quaid coupled with the kooky charm of Meg Ryan. It's about as broad-beamed a movie as you can get, but that's not necessarily to its detriment. Once you get over its brazen marketability, there's a bright pastiche of entertaining impulses going on here: light sci-fi, silly comedy, the pop and crackle of a mid-order thriller.

Away from the juicy special effects used to portray Martin Short's inner workings (which, strangely, while likely far more accurate, lack the day-glo pop glitz of the *Fantastic Voyage*'s 60s variation of the theme) the film genuinely works as a raucous comedy. Joe Dante realising you could never truly take shrinking seriously as a sci-fi proposition, allows it to relax into a frothy comedy, and Martin Short, with his array of twitchy tic and hoots, splendidly keeps stupidity front and centre. The idea of Quaid's ship connecting with its host's cerebral cortex to allow communication, fuels a hilarious rush of possession gags. Both his fraught neurotic putz and Quaid's washed up cowboy, ripe with the star's infectious self-possession, are stereotypes on order, but the film's whole lack of ambition has been turned to its own good.

Dante's film doesn't outstay its welcome, never overreaches its high concept nor forces us to dally in sentiment or any kind of genuine emotion. It's flat-packed Hollywood, but once upright surely stays that way. ★★★★ **IN**

⑮ INSIDE MAN (2006)

Starring: *Denzel Washington (Detective Keith Frazier), Clive Owen (Dalton Russell), Jodie Foster (Madeliene White), Christopher Plummer (Arthur Case), Willem Dafoe (Captain John Darius), Chiwetel Ejiofor (Detective Bill Mitchell)*
Director: *Spike Lee*
Screenwriter: *Russell Gewirtz*
15/129 mins./Thriller/USA

When well-organised robbers, led by the highly intelligent Dalton Russell, take hostages in a Manhattan bank, NYPD detectives Frazier and Mitchell are assigned. It's not long before the bank's owner surfaces with ruthless playmaker Madeliene White to do his bidding.

Spike Lee has come a long, long way in the last two decades. His 19 feature films encompass no-budget indies (*She's Gotta Have It*), an epic biopic (*Malcolm X*) and even a musical (*School Daze*), and he remains one of America's most audacious, ferociously independent filmmakers.

In these respects, the slick, commercial *Inside Man* is barely recognisable as a Spike Lee picture, but that's not to say it doesn't measure up; au contraire, it's a marvellous, carefully honed thriller that hurtles smoothly along at the pace of a bullet train. If *Do The Right Thing*, with its jarring blocks of colour, was his Picasso, then this is his Da Vinci: carefully planned and crafted in sharp detail.

It's also the safest film he's ever made – a pure genre flick, deftly taking inspiration from great heist films. Like its protagonist, it almost never deviates from a well-laid plan; Lee has considered everything, and his first contingency is a staggeringly classy ensemble cast. Denzel Washington (in their fourth collaboration) makes a stock character – a charmer prone to rash mistakes – into a rich, believably flawed one. It's as if Lee has requested the Washington of blockbusters past, and retrofitted him with nuances from their earlier work together. Chiwetel Ejiofor, meanwhile, offers fine support as his partner – watching he and Washington riffing together in a series of flashforwards, as they grill potential suspects, is a particular treat.

There are those who accuse Clive Owen of being one-note, but they'd have to admit it's a bloody good one, and nobody could do it better. Once again he exhibits that trademark steely control, achieving an air of calculation and potential menace even when he's behind dark glasses and a mask.

As for Jodie Foster, well, she's having a field day as one of the best unscrupulous bitches we've seen on the big screen since Linda Fiorentino said yes to *The Last Seduction*. Foster's Madeliene White is an interesting new take on the shady, backroom dealmaker. In the movies that inspire *Inside Man*, this character would be a shady lizard of a man operating from an ancient, smoke-filled office; Ms. White is a designer-outfitted Machiavellian machine with luxury office space who openly wheels, deals, wines and dines with the Mayor of New York City.

It's a pity, then, that Russell Gewirtz's script isn't quite as smart as his characters or cast. Owen's Russell forewarns us to pay attention (because he 'chooses his words carefully, and only says things once' – a line which Lee unfortunately chooses to use twice), but there's not much that will get past anyone who's concentrating. At one point the whole game is nearly given away by a single shot. Thankfully, though, neither that nor a correct guess will spoil the fun, because Gerwitz at least ensures there's some wonderfully original elements to the plan. In the tradition of the genre, by the time Denzel has put the pieces together, you may find yourself struggling with muddy motivations and fresh doubts, but this just adds to the entertainment value – after all, you have to have something to talk about over a post-movie beverage ... ★★★★ **ST**

◑ THE INSIDER (1999)

Starring: *Al Pacino (Lowell Bergman), Russell Crowe (Dr. Jeffrey Wigand), Christopher Plummer (Mike Wallace), Diane Venora (Liane Wigand), Phillip Baker Hall (Don Hewitt)*
Director: *Michael Mann*
Screenwriters: *Eric Roth, Michael Mann, based on the article The Man Who Knew Too Much by Marie Brenner*
15/151 mins./Drama/Biography/USA

Lowell Bergman, CBS reporter, pursues the ex-head researcher of a tobacco company who is willing to provide evidence that the big companies knew about the addictive nature of tobacco long before they admitted it.

Michael Mann could not exactly be described as a prolific director. The thing is though, that while sedate in the delivery, they're usually worth the wait. From the weird, utterly underrated Nazi horror flick *The Keep*, through the original, and best Hannibal Lecter vehicle, *Manhunter*, right up to *Heat*, which famously placed Pacino and De Niro on screen together for the first time, Mann quietly established himself as one of the most talented directors working in America. And with *The Insider*, a brilliant, nailbiter of a true-story conspiracy thriller which bears comparison with *All The President's Men* and *JFK*, he's delivered his best so far.

Based on a magazine article, *The Insider* follows the (disputedly true) story of Jeffrey Wigand (Crowe, through make-up that ages him 20 years), head of a tobacco company's Research And Development department, who discovers that the fag companies have for years not only known that nicotine was addictive (cue fat lawyers rubbing their hands sensing multi-billion dollar lawsuits), but worse, they've been farting around with the formula to make it even more so (cue fat lawyers calling for fresh biros as they add the zeroes). After being persuaded to give a TV interview by producer Lowell Bergman, Wigand discovers that smoking is deeply bad for your health, even if you've never lit a gasper in your life. Harassment, death-threats, a possible prison sentence and a collapsed marriage are a few of the ordeals that Wigand is put through – all, it would appear, to no avail when squabbling at CBS's *60 Minutes* news programme leads them to ditch the programme, much to Bergman's horror.

Mann's film is a devastating picture of corporate America at its most venal and corrupt, and at its heart are a pair of powerhouse performances: Pacino is at his finest, chewing the scenery with a corking series of his trademark slow-burn rants, but it's Crowe who is the soul of the film, as a man trapped by forces too massive for him to fully comprehend. Delivering an ambiguous performance, (we're never too sure what his motives are; money is at one point mentioned), which deftly avoids the cliché of the helpless victim and occasionally gives in to self-pity, Crowe manages to give what could be an overwhelmingly complex film a deeply human centre. Mann's direction is as assured as ever, his script (co-written with Eric Roth) skilfully delivers complex information without causing mental indigestion, his pacing is superb (two and a half hours plus feels like half the time) and of course, given that it's by the man who invented *Miami Vice*, it looks gorgeous. ★★★★ **AS**

◑ INSOMNIA (1997)

Starring: *Stellan Skarsgard (Jonas Engstrom), Sverre Anker Ousdal (Erik Vik), Bjorn Floberg (Jon Holt), Gisken Armand (Hilde Hagen)*
Director: *Erik Skjoldbjaerg*
Screenwriters: *Eric Skjoldbjaerg, Nikolaj Frobenius*
15/92 mins./Crime/Thriller/Norway

Two Norwegian homicide detectives investigate the murder of a teenage girl, in the land where the sun never sleeps . . .

With *Insomnia*, Skjoldbjaerg forays into that burgeoning genre – the existential thriller – in which atmosphere and angst replace car chases and cliffhangers.

Unlike the dark and claustrophobic *Se7en*, for example, the director has pulled off something of a coup here, pitching characters and plot into the stark, semi-permanent daylight of northern Norway, the land of the midnight sun. Film noir rarely comes any brighter than this.

When homicide detectives Engstrom (Skarsgard, fresh – or rather thawed – from *Good Will Hunting* and *Ronin*) and Vik are called to investigate the murder of a teenage girl (clinically dispatched and shampooed to remove all evidence, during the opening credits), resulting in an ambush to catch the killer that goes horribly wrong when Engstrom's gung-ho antics result in his accidentally offing his partner. Placing the blame on the suspect Jon Holt, a creepy crime novelist, but also caught up in his tacit double-bind, Engstrom suffers guilty, increasingly sleepless nights, descending into madness and depravity by degrees. By halfway, he's positively satanic, molesting minors and displaying an unhealthy interest in Alsatian intestines in futile attempts to stave his conscience.

Skjoldbjaerg crafts a chilly, cerebral, determinedly downbeat thriller with an almost lazy sense of menace, while Skarsgard's central performance is a masterclass in understatement, stalking through the snow like a latter-day Lee Marvin, his eyes two proverbial pissholes in a snow-covered cliff. Insomnia ought not to be sampled last thing at night, but those willing to risk it will be subjected to a finer quality of nightmare. ★★★ **EH**

◑ INSOMNIA (2002)

Starring: *Al Pacino (Detective Will Dormer), Martin Donavan (Detective Hap Eckhart), Robin Williams (Walter Finch), Hilary Swank (Detective Ellie Burr)*
Director: *Christopher Nolan*
Screenwriters: *Hillary Seitz, based on the 1997 film by Nikolaj Frobenius, Erik Skjodbjaerg*
15/113 mins./Crime/Thriller/USA

Veteran LAPD detective Will Dormer and his partner Hap Eckhart travel to a remote town in Alaska to help the local cops investigate the murder of a teenage girl. But when a fog-bound bust goes fatally wrong, Dormer's guilt, coupled with the region's perpetual sunlight, gives him sleepless nights.

How do you follow a one-of-a-kind cult classic like *Memento*? In Christopher Nolan's case, you move onwards and upwards.

On the surface, *Insomnia* looks like a standard Hollywood cop thriller – an American remake of a European original with A-list stars and a bigger budget. But, in Nolan's hands, it becomes a psychologically dense, inverted film noir (a film blanc, perhaps) that keeps the audience enthralled to the last.

Like *Memento*, *Insomnia* is all the more effective for streaming its plot through the unreliable mind of its main character. As Pacino's face visibly sags through lack of sleep, Will Dormer's ability to carry out his job objectively becomes less and less likely. This isn't a whodunit – the killer is revealed early on. And unlike *Murder By Numbers*, for example, it's not simply a case of watching the cop get the bad guy.

Because Dormer compromises himself by covering up a fatal error, his relationship with the killer and his gung-ho attitude to the Internal Affairs investigation hanging over his head become questionable. 'That's my job – I assign guilt,' he says bullishly at one point. This end-justifies-the-means mentality threatens to cloud not only his judgement, but also our trust in him as the film's hero.

Just like the cracks of sunlight breaking through the blinds in Dormer's hotel room, the flaws in his personality steadily creep out from beneath the surface. And so while we're enjoying the cop movie thrills on a basic level, Nolan, Pacino and scriptwriter Hillary Seitz offer us something much meatier in terms of an anti-hero character study.

That's not to say that *Insomnia* can't be enjoyed as a cracking story cranked up by a couple of tense scenes. Williams is cleverly used as Dormer's nemesis, a crime novelist who believes he can control the murder investigation as if it were one of his fictions. Their relationship hangs on a delicate balance, depending on which one has more incriminating evidence on the other. It's not quite a Lecter–Starling match, but it's head and shoulders above what we're normally offered in a crime thriller.

The film opens with the two city cops flying over a topographical wasteland, before landing in a town untainted by street smarts and internal politics. Before it ends, Dormer's years of experience will be held under a harsh light and an Alaskan sun that refuses to set.

Nolan, however, has nothing to fear from wider exposure. He has stepped up onto a bigger stage, where audiences are less forgiving than in the independent arena. But *Insomnia* is one of the best American films of the year, and a rare Hollywood movie that does justice to an excellent European original. ★★★★ **JB**

INSPECTOR GADGET (1999)

Starring: *Matthew Broderick (Inspector Gadget), Rupert Everett (Dr. Claw), Joely Fisher (Dr. Brenda Bradford), Michelle Trachtenberg (Penny), Andy Dick (Kramer)*
Director: *David Kellogg*
Screenwriters: *Kerry Ehrin, Zak Penn, based on a story by Dana Olsen, Kerry Ehrin and characters by Andy Heyward, Jean Chaolpin, Bruno Bianchi*
U/75 mins./Family/Adventure/Comedy/USA

A security guard on the point of death, is rebuilt using gadgets. Now an Inspector, he must take on his nemesis Claw.

Back in the mid-1980s, Children's ITV meant *Inspector Gadget*. Backed with the catchiest theme tune, a built-in catchphrase ('Go, Go Gadget ...') and a broad gaudy style, this Gallic tea-time pleaser made a hero of an inept, trenchcoated baddie-buster – half Clouseau, half Swiss army knife – who sought justice through a self-contained gizmo for every occasion. Always on the lookout for such a surefire premise, Disney has writ Gadget real, the effect emerging as scattershot but fun.

After an opening five minutes of barnstorming slapstick, the film sets up its premise well as security guard John Brown (Broderick in genial 'gee-whizz' mode) is turned into Gadget by scientist Brenda Bradford after he is severely wounded attempting to save her father's life. Yet, once Gadget is operational, the script is artless in exploiting the man-machine's capabilities – Rupert Everett curiously underplays his nemesis, the nefarious Claw, who (surprisingly) wants to take over the world – throwing in an evil Gadget doppelgänger (providing the film's best moments), an unfunny talking Gadgetmobile (providing the film's worst), an undercooked love story and some broad mugging that makes *The Three Stooges* look nuanced.

However, there's a likeable feel to the whole endeavour. Director Kellogg, originally a commercials whizz, throws everything in with gusto and occasionally conjures up great visuals that capture the show's look. Yet, he has little feel for how to mix the concoction: material squarely aimed at kids vies with in-jokery – everything from *Last Of The Mohicans* and *Godzilla* to the cartoon show's origins is plundered – in a slipshod fashion that never really gels. If the TV show was just a series of set pieces designed to show off its hero's capabilities, then this gets it down pat. But, over the extended running time of a full-length feature, something more coherent and engaging would not have gone amiss. ★★ **IF**

INTACTO (2001)

Starring: *Max von Sydow (Samuel), Leonardo Sbaraglia (Tomas), Eusebio Poncela (Federico), Monica Lopez (Sara), Antonio Dechent (Alejandro)*
Director: *Juan Carlos Fresnadillo*
Screenwriters: *Juan Carlos Fresnadillo, Andres M. Koppel*
15/104 mins./Thriller/Spain

Plane-crash survivor Tomas is tutored by Federico in the underground world of supernaturally fortuitous people who can absorb the luck of ordinary folk and then gamble with it. Federico sees Tomas as a challenger to holocaust survivor Samuel, long-reigning luckiest man in the world.

In the talking point scene of *Intacto* – as sure to be imitated by macho idiots as the stabbing-round-the-hand game of *Knife In The Water* or the bare-knuckles bouts of *Fight Club* – supposedly lucky contestants are blindfolded with their hands taped behind their backs, then made to run at top speed through dense forest, losers painfully eliminating themselves by smacking headlong into trees.

What impresses is not so much the cinematic verve, though it's shot with unfussy proficiency, but the idea.

The big draw of this Spanish film is that it is among the rarest of beasts, a truly original premise satisfyingly thought through.

It opens with a disorientating shot of a casino nestled in a desert mountain range that could be on the moon (it's actually Tenerife). From there, it plunges straight into a world whose rules we have to pick up as we go along, as the lucky draw fortune from ordinary folk with vampire-like hugs, then stake photographs of people and objects when they gamble.

Debuting writer-director Juan Carlos Fresnadillo displays amazing confidence as he takes an approach that suggests a less gimmick-addicted M. Night Shyamalan, always making emotional sense of the fantastical.

Considering the wild premise, the film is remarkably unflashy, rooting its supernatural kinks in credible, affecting human drama.

Max von Sydow, playing in English among Spanish-speakers, is the God of Chance – like most of the 'lucky' people we meet, he's someone who has survived a disaster so traumatic he can take no pleasure in his good fortune. With grave melancholy and a polythene carpet cover, he takes on challengers in a long-shot game of Russian roulette, with five bullets to one empty chamber.

Even tiny details – like the sand-coloured suits von Sydow and his opponents wear for their ritual matches – are given resonance in a monologue about Samuel's wartime origins, which is among the best screen work this great actor has ever done. ★★★★ **AM**

INTERMISSION (2003)

Starring: *Colin Farrell (Lehiff), Shirley Henderson (Sally), Kelly MacDonald (Deirdre), Colm Meaney (Det. Jerry Lynch), Cillian Murphy (John)*
Director: *John Crowley*
Screenwriter: *Mark O'Rowe*
18/101 mins./Crime/Drama/Comedy/Ireland/UK

A group of Dubliners – from a would-be reality TV star cop, to a lonely girl with a facial hair problem – find their lives interweaving when John's ex, Deirdre, starts living with a married bank manager who becomes the victim of a kidnapping.

There's a palpable sense of frustration and longing in director John Crowley's debut feature, emotions shared by all of his characters. It's when they try a short cut to happiness that they become unstuck.

Deirdre thinks a bank manager will give her the stability she needs; John hopes crime will gain him revenge and riches; and Noeleen (Deirdre O'Kane) tries to fill the void left by her husband by grabbing the nearest available young man.

Sounds depressing? Maybe – but this film's lively dialogue, bursts of brash Irish wit and hopeful conclusion help the medicine go down.

Several cast members shine: Farrell is pitch-perfect as a rough petty criminal, looking more at home in a grubby 80s jumper than a Hollywood star has a right to, while Meaney puts in a credible performance and Henderson's typically vulnerable turn hits the spot. Macdonald is less inspiring, however, and, despite his talent, Murphy struggles to fully convince as a hopeless supermarket employee. ★★★ **LB**

INTERNAL AFFAIRS (1990)

Starring: *Richard Gere (Dennis Peck), Andy Garcia (Raymond Avilla), Laurie Metcalf (Amy Wallace), Nancy Travis (Kathleen Avilla), Richard Bradford (Grieb)*
Director: *Mike Figgis*
Screenwriter: *Henry Bean*
18/109 mins./Crime/Thriller/USA

Dennis Peck is a cop with more serious vices than using the siren to get home a bit quicker. He defrauds, he does drugs, and he's being investigated by idealistic young Ray Avilla of the Internal Affairs Division.

Richard Gere's dubious taste in role selection comes even further into question with this relentlessly sordid thriller. Gere plays bent cop Dennis Peck, a thoroughly bad hat whose activities range way beyond the familiar drugs thefts and payoffs to vicious adulteries, multiple murder and very complicated fraud. His partner in crime is a drug-addicted wife-beater, his adversary Internal Affairs Division investigator Ray Avilla.

British director Mike Figgis and debuting screenwriter Henry Bean have loaded the sleazy proceedings with arty pretensions and psychological clichés – good-guy Avilla and baddie Peck mirror traits in each other; Avilla's bewildered wife is terrorised in the cat-and-mouse game between the men, evil is implicitly sexy.

Lesser irritants add up to overwhelming distastefulness. For one, these street cops are improbably married to women from another world – an art gallery hot shot, a high-powered banking executive – yet all the women look and behave like cheap hookers, save Avilla's sour IAD partner. She's supposed to be a lesbian, so she's homely as a mud fence.

Lacking everything it claims to investigate, this is a waste of a fairly strong cast. ★ **AE**

THE INTERPRETER (2005)

Starring: *Nicole Kidman (Silvia Broome), Sean Penn (Tobin Keller), Catherine Keener (Dot Woods), Jesper Christensen (Nils Lud), Yvan Attal (Philippe)*
Director: *Sydney Pollack*
Screenwriters: *Charles Randolph, Scott Frank, Steven Zaillian, based on a story by Martin Stellman, Brian Ward*
12A/128 mins./Drama/Thriller/UK/USA/France

After UN interpreter Silvia Broome overhears a plot to assassinate an African leader – the leader of her home country, in fact – the US Secret Service is brought in to investigate, in the shape of hard-bitten agent Tobin Keller. Of course, all is not what it seems.

Among the glut of freewheeling hyper-thrillers that dare not take a breather in case we all doze off, it's encouraging to see a wily old master like Sydney Pollack putting the emphasis back on the noble art of chinwagging. This is a dense, intricate story that demands your attention, so no flagging or fiddling about in your Revels or you'll most likely lose the plot. There's an old-fashioned sturdiness to *The Interpreter*'s dedication to meaty, thinky message-making, even if the film is finally overburdened by its good intentions.

The marriage of politics and suspense came to the fore during the 70s, the pervading Nixonian paranoia and the wound of Vietnam feeding into Hollywood thrillers, and it's difficult not to read a similar, if subtler, resonance with today's global climate here. Pollack gives serious time to Silvia's world-view; this smart, shaky lady values the purity of diplomacy over violence, she repeatedly insists that the UN matters, and Bush, the subtext hisses, should take note. It also dwells on African dissonance, a history of mass culls and fallen idealism in the fictional state of Matoba, and keeps tabs on the current vogue for ethnic tribulation.

Penn and Kidman are set up as a duel – he crushed by personal demons, she nervously protecting her own secrets – that slowly thaws into a quasi-romance. These two consummate talents thrive in the long, dialogue-driven scenes, even if there isn't enough about their characters to really stretch either. Kidman, whose alabaster complexion speaks less of an African upbringing than being kept locked in an attic her whole life, nimbly adopts the regional accent and fraught expressions of the put-upon heroine. Penn skilfully does his shredded-machismo bit, big on wobbling chins and glowering stares. They do, by contrast, make a fine match.

Pollack's calm, controlled hand is evident throughout. When required to quicken the pulse he ably cross-cuts between multiple viewpoints, giving the film a nervous jangle. Through the middle-third he gets to finally have some fun, adding a magnificent, if slightly nonsensical, bomb-on-a-bus crisis (the best scene). How ironic that *The Interpreter* should be at its most assured when cutting loose and clichéd ... It's also good to see New York – as in the real New York, not the make-do streets of Toronto or Montreal. Abundant use is made of the city, emphasising its, well, New Yorkiness, to give *The Interpreter* an authentic tone, a brownstone haven away from the dust storms of Matoba. And you can't fault the debut of the interior of the real UN building in movies (even Hitchcock was famously refused permission to shoot there). The camera seeks out the frayed lines and drab 50s décor of its hallowed halls and corridors like an in-built metaphor for the institution's struggle for relevance.

Where the film snags is in melding both its thriller framework and political philosophy. Too often the writers' mechanics become visible: credulity-yanking devices to get us from A to B and that all-important speechifying. While stretching plausibility is all part of the genre, Pollack's movie never quite snaps back into shape. In this time of taut, all-encompassing security, the Secret Service's inability to shut down such a threatening situation just smacks of gross incompetence. ★★★ **IN**

INTERVIEW WITH THE VAMPIRE: THE VAMPIRE CHRONICLES (1994)

Starring: *Tom Cruise (Lestat de Lioncourt), Brad Pitt (Louis de Pointe du Lac), Kirsten Dunst (Claudia), Stephen Rea (Santiago), Antonio Banderas (Armand), Christian Slater (Daniel Malloy)*
Director: *Neil Jordan*
Screenwriter: *Anne Rice, from her novel*
18/122 mins./Drama/Horror/USA
Awards: *BAFTA – Best Cinematography, Best Production Design, Razzie Awards – Worst Screen Couple (Tom Cruise/Brad Pitt)*

A vampire named Lestat takes a liking to Louis, a recent widower, and offers him the chance to become a vampire.

What a fuss. When, after a full 17 years in development hell, Anne Rice's bestselling novel *Interview With The Vampire* finally made it to casting, its eccentric author threw a very public hissy fit. She was happy with director Neil Jordan, who had done lavish, wonders with *The Company Of Wolves*, she didn't murmur over pretty Brad Pitt as the woeful Louis, but when it came to her beloved vampire Lestat in the shape of beaming flyboy Tom Cruise she went ballistic. 'He is no more my vampire Lestat than Edward G. Robinson is Rhett Butler,' she ranted. But to no avail.

Jordan remained unmoved and over a troubled five-month shoot (original interviewer River Phoenix tragically died and Christian Slater stepped in) took *Interview* to the screen. And, famously, when Anne Rice finally saw the movie she, very publicly, recanted. Cruise, she decided, was brilliant. Mind you, apologies were not forthcoming.

Written in 1976, shortly after Rice's five-year-old daughter had died of leukaemia (which fuelled the book's lament) and published to rapturous reviews, *Interview* was a vampire novel with a difference. It was concerned with the life of vampires rather than the deleterious effect they may have on mortals. A rambling, erotic story of bloodsuckers freed from mortality but tied to the dark night, it spawned a series of sequels and prequels (collectively the Vampire Chronicles) centred on the flamboyant, bitchy, aristocratic carnality of Lestat, villain and patriarch of the saga.

Hence its format is less linear than episodic – we traverse 200 years under the cover of night – biting at the significant moments in the grim half-life of Louis de Pointe du Lac and his turbulent relationship with Lestat and the film's eeriest character little Claudia. She, the companion Lestat creates for his tormented protégé, is trapped forever in the body of a 12-year-old, and as she develops mentally and sexually her desires transform into a homicidal rage. A disconcerting feature in a small girl.

Louis (played with stilted misery by an out-of-sorts Pitt, who hated every minute of it) is a vampire clinging desperately to his humanity, resisting Lestat's all-embracing attitude toward the necessary evils of their eternal existence. Killing is what they do, what they are. It is their only fulfilment and the only thing that brings them peace of mind (Louis prefers to pick off rats for blood). The film, as is common in vampire movies of recent years, is obsessed with detailing the lives and rituals of the night-dwellers. As with *Near Dark* (1987), the clutter of religious artifacts and garlic cloves have no effect. Louis has to contend with the fact he can never see another sunrise, or the true blue of the Mediterranean. When he and Claudia finally escape the clutches of Lestat, they head to Europe. Here we see the true scope of vampire society when they happen upon a troupe of bitter, corrupted vampires at the Theatre Des Vampires in Paris, all of them guided by the ancient cynicism of Armand.

Rice's material and Jordan's fairly faithful take on it seethes with metaphorical significance. Its homoeroticism is unavoidable (despite rumours that Cruise demanded it to be toned down). The relationships between Louis and Lestat and then, more overtly, Armand, are rife with erotic undercurrents. It all, of course, registers as a reference to Aids, but Jordan always saw the movie in broader terms – a study of loneliness and the search for companionship and meaning, something universal.

Of just as much interest is the movie's lavish decor. With no detail unstinted on, it is draped in magnificent period detail (by Dante Ferreti) and shot with a mix of sickly and shadowy gloom (by Philippe Rousselot), lit by the glittering flicker of candlelight. Their work is stunningly atmospheric, especially in the Paris sequences, creating the impression of decadence long soured and a pervading aura of decay. The ultimate price of their vampiric immortality is that which Lestat rails against the most – insignificance. As flawed as the rhythms of Jordan's movie sometimes are, he has created a unique horror experience: the existential vampire movie. ★★★★ **IN**

⦾ INTO THE BLUE (2005)

Starring: *Paul Walker (Jared), Jessica Alba (Sam), Scott Caan (Bryce), Ashley Scott (Amanda), Josh Brolin (Bates)*
Director: *John Stockwell*
Screenwriter: *Matt Johnson*
15/110 mins./Action/Crime/USA

While searching for a fabled wreck, deep-sea treasure hunter Jared discovers a downed plane with a hoard of cocaine. With the drug-runners on his trail, he must decide what to do with this very modern treasure.

It's a rare but comforting truth that a certain breed of film's strength lies in its lack of ambition, its disregard for plausibility and its dedication to the purity of formula. *Into The Blue* will linger in your memory no longer than the beat of an eyelash, but is a B-grade joy as deep-tanned and sun-kissed as a Club Tropics promo.

Thus we get Alba's golden bod barely muzzled by her designer bikini as she portrays the morally-inclined love interest of Walker's diving fanatic, whose bronzed pecs are, frankly, giving a much better performance than he is. They discover the drug haul, fret a bit, then discover a mythical pirate wreck and fret some more as to whether to come clean but give away the sacred salvage rights. Naturally, Scott Caan plays his loose-hinged best mate who forces the issue by trying to offload the coke. Enter drug dealers, screen left. Enter ravenous sharks, screen right. Yeesh!

Give director John Stockwell his due – *Into The Blue*'s gloriously silly, boasts crystal-clear underwater photography and musters a tidy bit of tension at the end. Any movie that features a school of coked-up sharks is not taking itself too seriously – and those locations are to die for. ★★★ **IN**

⦾ INTOLERABLE CRUELTY (2003)

Starring: *George Clooney (Miles Massey), Catherine Zeta-Jones (Marylin Rexroth), Geoffrey Rush (Donovan Donaly), Cedric the Entertainer (Gus Petch), Edward Herrman (Rex Rexroth), Billy Bob Thornton (Howard D. Doyle)*
Director: *Joel Coen*
Screenwriters: *Robert Ramsey, Matthew Stone, Ethan Coen, Joel Coen, from a story by Ramsey, Stone, John Romano*
12/95 mins./Comedy/Romance/USA

Miles Massey, a successful LA divorce lawyer, first meets gold-digger Marilyn Rexroth when he is hired by her millionaire husband to crush her crippling divorce suit. Though sparks fly, Massey trounces her in court. But that's not the last he will see of the one-woman bank account hoover . . .

Unabashedly commercial, crowd-tickling stuff, this dazzling screwball comedy – following proudly in the footsteps of Preston Sturges, Howard Hawks and Billy Wilder – stars George Clooney at his most charming and Catherine Zeta-Jones doing what she does best (however little that is) in an immediately accessible story about avarice, divorce and love, in that order.

Tight as a drum, glamorous and exquisitely funny, this one should earn them enough cash to make five more offbeat minor masterpieces like *The Man Who Wasn't There* – and the Coens deserve that as much as we do.

While the leads are every bit as charismatic as you'd expect, with Clooney on 'Dapper Dan Man' form as the Cary Grant-esque Massey and Zeta-Jones showing an admirable facility for old-school quickfire patter, the movie is peppered in typical Coen style with top-notch turns from character actors and cameos from striking bit-part players with freakish physiognomies.

Think about the 'funny lookin' scene from *Fargo* and multiply it to the nth degree: there's a surly blue-collar waitress who bristles at a snooty request for a green salad ('What other fuckin' colour is it gonna be?'), an asthmatic gangster called Wheezy Joe and an effeminate, poodle-carrying baron whose courtroom testimony must surely be one of the funniest scenes committed to film. Ever.

In fact, there's so much musicality in the lightning-quick dialogue, you'd almost think you were watching a song-and-dance number from the golden age of MGM. Key to the action is shady private eye Gus Petch (played by the improbably named Cedric the Entertainer), whose catchphrase 'I'm gonna nail yo' ass' runs through the film like a leitmotif and finally provides the payoff.

And, like a musical, the film counterpoints major notes with subtle tones, providing broad laughs with its almost slapstick routines, while at the same time satirising the modern concept of love and the horrible commercialisation of the marriage industry – from the garish kitsch of a Vegas wedding chapel to the mercenary combat of the divorce court.

For longstanding Coen fans, the only disappointment might be that it's not as visually flashy as we're used to, but one suspects this was a noble sacrifice to avoid frightening off mainstream viewers.

But watching this film, and seeing such a superb script brought to life, one can only wonder why no other star-driven romcoms made today – pay attention, Jim Carrey – are so finely tuned, smart, sophisticated and memorable.

If the masses don't take to this, there's no hope for any of us. After all, how can you not love a movie that has a lawyer objecting on the grounds of 'poetry recitation', a wealthy fish trader who's so powerful he is tuna, or that features a magazine called *Living Without Intestines*? ★★★★ **DW**

⊙ INTOLERANCE (1916)

Starring: *Mae Marsh (The Dear One), Robert Harron (The Boy), F.A. Turner (The Girl's Father), Sam De Grasse (Arthur Jenkins), Vera Lewis (Mary T. Jenkins), Howard Gaye (Christ/Cardinal Lorraine), Lillie Langdon (Mary), Olga Grey (Mary Magdalene)*
Director: *D.W. Griffith*
Screenwriters: *D.W. Griffith, Anita Loos, Frank E. Woods*
PG/163 mins./Drama/USA

Four intercut stories link an exploited worker's wrongful death sentence, the Crucifixion of Jesus Christ, the massacre of the Huguenots during the reign of Charles IX of France and the fall of Babylon to Cyrus the Persian after Prince Belshazzar controversially adds Ishtar to the city's pantheon of gods.

D.W. Griffith was completing *The Birth of a Nation* when he began work on 'The Mother and the Law', which would form the modern segment of this remarkable experiment. Capitalising on the 1914 Ludlow massacre, it was intended as an indictment of commercial exploitation and the hypocritical philanthropy of John D. Rockefeller. However, the furore caused by his Civil War epic lured Griffith into an attempt to surpass his achievement and the recent success of Meyerbeer's *Les Huguenots* at New York's Metropolitan Opera inspired him to add the events of 1572 to his design. But it was only when he was accused of racial bigotry towards the end of 1915 that Griffith's wounded sense of righteousness prompted the inclusion of the Babylonian and biblical storylines to demonstrate how truth had been crushed by intemperence and injustice throughout history.

Costing $386,000 and originally released in four identifying tints, *Intolerance* was as accomplished as it was ambitious. Drawing on every technique at his disposal, Griffith brought a new scope and scale to cinema, particularly through his lavish recreation of Babylon in 539BC. But it was the film's structure that proved its triumph and its undoing. Soviet montagists like Eisenstein and Pudovkin applauded the collision of images that Griffith achieved, as he arranged shots by metre and perspective to produce parallel sequences of unheralded rhetorical power and rhythmic precision. But, while they were able to appreciate the majesty of set-pieces like Belshazzar's feast and the modern romance between the Dear One (Mae Marsh) and the Boy (Robert Harron), audiences lacked the sophistication to comprehend these juxtapositions and the film's commercial failure saddled Griffith with monumental debts.

Critical opinion of *Intolerance*'s worth has been divided for nearly a century, with Griffith variously being hailed as a visionary and a Victorian middlebrow with a predilection for kitsch and old-fashioned morality. But the French director René Clair pretty much had it right when he declared: 'It combines extraordinary lyric passages, realism, and psychological detail, with nonsense, vulgarity, and painful sentimentality.' Yet, whatever its glories and flaws, it remains a landmark in filmic art and entertainment. ★★★★★ **DP**

⊙ INVASION OF THE BODY SNATCHERS (1956)

Starring: *Kevin McCarthy (Dr. Miles J. Bennell), Dana Wynter (Becky Driscoll), Larry Gates (Dr. Dan Kauffman), King Donovan (Jack Belicec)*
Director: *Don Siegel*
Screenwriters: *Daniel Mainwaring, Richard Collins*
PG/80 mins/Sci-fi USA

A small-town doctor comes to believe that his fellow citizens are being replaced with identical alien impostors; some kind of invasion is underway.

This excellent piece of sci-fi paranoia, based on Jack Finney's novel, can read most commonly as an allusion to the threat of communism turning everyone into lefty drones, or, alternatively, as an anti-McCarthy tale about the crushing of individual choice. The beauty of Don Siegel's fraught, pacy thriller, a kind of sci-fi noir, is that it functions perfectly either way. Or, it seems, as a play on both.

It is the most famed of the spate of 50s sci-fi allegories, and is a cut above most of the nervy tales of mutant insects and invaders because it is so unshowy – the alien presence is in the vacant eyes of loved ones, the subtle dehumanising of the cast into 'pod people' Siegel, as ever rough-edged and machismo, is clearly taken with this smart screenplay's many levels, and deliberately lets this film run from terror to melodrama to comedy. As screenwriters were being blacklisted, he went for the jugular of American paranoia. As Kevin McCarthy and Dana Wynter, both hitting a shrill exaggeration in performance, dash about avoiding assimilation while no one listens, Siegel's isn't a work of paranoia; it's a sarcastic attack upon it. How easily it might fit into today's America.

Yet, the concept still works as a finely conceived horror-thriller, and with its atmospheric black-and-white photography, needling score and telling little Americana setting, it is far more than just a subtext. Such that it has worked with two solid remakes in the 70s and the 90s. ★★★★★ **IN**

⊙ INVASION OF THE BODY SNATCHERS (1978)

Starring: *Donald Sutherland (Matthew Bennell), Brooke Adams (Elizabeth Driscoll), Jeff Goldblum (Jack Belicec), Veronica Cartwright (Nancy Belicec), Leonard Nimoy (Dr. David Kibner)*
Director: *Philip Kaufman*
Screenwriter: *W.D. Richter, from the novel by Jack Finney*
15/110 mins./Horror/Sci-fi/USA

Spores from outer space fall in San Francisco where they hatch flowers, which are then taken home by people. City health department chemist Elizabeth Driscoll confides in her colleague Matthew Bennell that her boyfriend seems to have changed. Bennell soon encounters similar reports . . .

Jack Finney's quietly creepy novel *The Body Snatchers*, serialised not in some wild sci-fi pulp but the relatively cosy *Colliers Magazine*, evidently struck a real chord with its tale of an America infiltrated and taken over by vegetable people from outer space who look and act just like the ordinary folks they've replaced, but can only fake emotional responses.

Don Siegel swiftly filmed the book as *Invasion Of The Body Snatchers* (1956), a black-and-white nightmare classic, and the property has been remade by producer Robert H. Solo in excellent updated versions tailored for subsequent decades, Philip Kaufman's *Invasion Of The Body Snatchers* (1978) and Abel Ferrara's *Body Snatchers* (1993).

You can tell how America itself is changing by the settings each film uses to represent the most vulnerable, typically American location for their creepy invasions: a small town in the 50s, a big city in the 70s, an army base in the 90s. If the 1956 film is informed by the paranoia of the McCarthy Era, with the pod people representing either commie infiltrators or right-wing witch-hunters, Kaufman's movie asks 'Where have all the flowers gone?' in depicting a San Francisco ten years on from the Summer Of Love, where the fragile hopes of the counterculture have been squashed (Veronica Cartwright and Jeff Goldblum are the leftover hippies, reduced to managing a health spa) and everyone is withdrawing into their own little isolation cells even before the alien seeds drift to Earth.

Cinematographer Michael Chapman had come from making New York look like Hell for Martin Scorsese in *Taxi Driver* and has a real eye for the telling detail that – like the rat-turd found in the soup at a fancy French restaurant by health inspector Matthew Bennell (Donald Sutherland) in his introductory scene – suggests something deeply wrong. Even before the story starts, the credits play out over effects shots of strange germinations and off-centre vignettes (Robert Duvall in an uncredited cameo as a priest on a swing) that clue us in to the invasion long before Bennell catches on.

The 1978 *Invasion* is not merely a remake of the 1956 film, though it reuses some character names and plot twists, but an upgrade (the Tom and Ellis Burman effects are especially striking) and, even, a sequel. After encountering a sinister cab driver played by Don Siegel himself, Bennell and his neurotic love-interest Elizabeth (wide-mouthed Brooke Adams, who never had the career she deserved) run into a screaming, unshaven lunatic played by Kevin McCarthy, hero of the 1956 original, who is still ranting at the top of his voice, continuing the terrifying speech he delivered to an uncaring world during the climax of the earlier film, 'They're taking over ... You're next!'

Kaufman and screenwriter W.D. Richter – who also did the Frank Langella *Dracula* and the oddball *Adventures Of Buckaroo Banzai* – don't tell their story in the straight-ahead fashion of Don Siegel. They allow a pattern to build up after disjointed scenes that have Bennell running into people who are convinced that people they know have been replaced with duplicates – Elizabeth takes a while to catch on, because her boyfriend (Art Hindle) was such a stiff even before he was podded. Bits of vital exposition are delivered as background chatter Altman-style or themes expressed through odd footnotes like the irrational (and therefore un-podlike) dislike that exists between drop-out poet Jack Belicec (Goldblum) and smooth pop psychiatrist David Kibner (Leonard Nimoy, faking warmth like a true alien). The characters catch on when it's too late, and the film turns into a terrific chase-action adventure, with the destruction of a pod greenhouse as a finale (a scene from the book Siegel didn't use). The downbeat punchline finds everyone transformed but waiflike Nancy (Cartwright) and the whole city going about its usual business in an eerie quiet interrupted only by the memorably ghastly open-mouthed pod yell (reprised by Ferrara for his version) a duplicate Bennell uses to accuse the last human in San Francisco and maybe the world.

Like Don Siegel, Philip Kaufman was not associated with science fiction, which means that he has few of the bad habits that come with genre filmmaking and occasionally has the smarts to make a hoary trick work. There's one great shock-horror moment as a human-headed dog (a mutant pod fusing a banjo player and his pet) trots into frame, and the scenes with unformed aliens hatching out of their seed-pods or the duplicated humans crumbling to dust are flesh-creepy in a way many subsequent effects bonanza horrors are not.

Tagline
The seed is planted ... terror grows.

Also a key player is sound-man Ben Burtt (who had just worked on *Star Wars*): the 1978 *Body Snatchers* has one of the subtlest, most layered soundtracks in science fiction cinema, incorporating a very unusual score by Denny Zeitlin and a great many almost subliminal noises and tics that add up to a genuinely unearthly feel.

Finney's original premise is good enough to stand a topically-skewed remake every 15 years – not to mention funky new spin-offs like *The Faculty* – but connoisseurs of 70s cinema will recognise this as among the most intelligent, most frightening American science fiction films of that decade.

★★★★ KN

THE INVISIBLE MAN (1933)

Starring: *Claude Rains (The Invisible One/Jack Griffin), Gloria Stuart (Flora Cranley), William Harrigan (Dr. Arthur Kemp), Henry Travers (Dr. Cranley), Una O'Connor (Jenny Hall),*
Director: *James Whale*
Screenwriter: *R.C. Sheriff, based on the novel by H.G. Wells*
PG/68 mins./Sci-fi/Horror/USA

A scientist turns himself invisible. However, the formula slowly drives him insane, causing him to terrorise the countryside as an invisible killer.

In 1933, the term 'science fiction' was barely in use – it was a development of the unwieldy 'scientifiction' coined by pulp magazine founder Hugo Gernsback – but there was a recognised tradition of 'scientific romance', which took in the great novels of H.G. Wells along with the likes of Conan Doyle's *The Lost World* and many another forgotten Victorian or Edwardian tales. James Whale – of *Gods And Monsters* fame – became a superstar director at Universal Pictures on the strength of the 1931 *Frankenstein*, which made a star of Boris Karloff.

Back then, the boundaries between genres were more fluid, and Whale's Frankenstein follow-ups took off in unexpected ways: emphasising the grotesque comedy and spooky theatrics in *The Old Dark House* (1932), and picking up on the laboratory shenanigans in *The Invisible Man*, a suitably spirited adaptation of Wells' ripping novel. In common with *Frankenstein*, *The Invisible Man* is vague about when it is set: the costumes are a mix of 1930s modern (*Titanic* star Gloria Stewart wears a selection of fetching hats) and Victorian/Dickensian fusty for villagers and policemen. Dudley-born Whale imported writer R.C. Sheriff, author of *Journey's End*, to throw out early drafts that have the invisible man mixed up in the Russian Revolution. The supporting cast is crammed with the British eccentrics Whale loved: screeching Una O'Connor as the termagant landlady, E.E. Clive as the moustachioed village constable ('I can't arrest a bloomin' shirt'), and Forrester Harvey as O'Connor's henpecked husband.

When Karloff, having done two star roles for Whale with no dialogue, baulked at a third in which he would talk a lot but be almost totally unseen, Whale again looked to the English acting community for an unknown. He came up with Brixton-born Claude Rains, who was thought too short to have movie potential, but had a terrific voice: velvety with a sly twist, perfect for those wonderful mad scientist speeches: 'We'll begin with a reign of terror, a few murders here and there. Murders of great men, murders of little men, just to show we make no distinction.' Rains, whose expressive gestures are also vital to his performance, recognised it as a career-making opportunity, a whole film that builds up to the revelation of his face, visible only in death. Like Karloff, Rains benefited greatly from Whale's boost and became one of Hollywood's most valuable players, in everything from *The Adventures Of Robin Hood* (as Bad King John) to *Casablanca* ('Round up the usual suspects').

Unusually for 1933, *The Invisible Man* starts in the middle of the story. During a tremendous storm, Jack Griffin takes a room at the pub in the village of Iping. Bundled up in coat, hat and gloves, the stranger's head is swathed in bandages. He sports goggle-like dark glasses and a visibly cardboard nose. The villagers are put out by Griffin's tendency to rant and the unknown experiments he performs in his room, and break in to confront him, whereupon he removes all his coverings (the gay Whale must have enjoyed sneaking the first male striptease past the censor) to reveal his invisibility. What special effects genius John P. Fulton accomplished with 1930s technology was certainly on a par with anything in 1992's Chevy Chase vehicle *Memoirs Of An Invisible Man*.

But Whale also added attitude: Griffin uses his invisibility larkishly – pedalling off on a stolen bicycle singing 'Here we go gathering nuts in May' – but he also has a mean streak that will transform him into a murderer. Griffin gets in touch with his old colleague Kemp and fiancée Flora, then explains how his experiments with a drug called monocaine have turned him invisible. In the novel, the psychological effect of being unseen leads Griffin into madness, but the film simplifies this into an unbalancing side-effect of monocaine. Flora tries to reason with Griffin but Kemp is appalled and betrays him to the police, whereupon the Invisible Man goes on a solitary rampage (killing off the weasley Kemp) and is tracked by mobs.

Griffin is wounded and the police follow a trail of blood and shoeprints (a notable blooper – the prints should be bare feet) to a farm. Griffin is captured and dies in hospital, musing in a last lucid moment, 'I meddled in things that man must leave alone' – an anti-science attitude entirely typical of the genre and still prevalent in the likes of *Jurassic Park*. Among future meddlers, of course, were Universal Pictures, never known to let a franchise lie. In 1940, Griffin's brother turned up to render Vincent Price transparent in *The Invisible Man Returns*. Jon Hall took over as new Griffins in the wartime *Invisible Agent* and *The Invisible Man's Revenge*, and Universal reused the premise for laughs in *The Invisible Woman* and the inevitable *Abbott And Costello Meet The Invisible Man*. There was also a television series in 1975 starring David McCallum. ★★★★★ **KN**

◎ THE IPCRESS FILE (1965)

Starring: *Michael Caine (Harry Palmer), Nigel Green (Major Dalby), Guy Coleman (Colonel Ross), Sue Lloyd (Jean Courtney), Gordon Jackson (Carswell)*
Director: *Sidney J. Furie*
Screenwriters: *Bill Canaway, James Doran, from the novel by Len Deighton*
PG/102 mins./Thriller/UK

Awards: *BAFTA – Best British Art Direction, Best British Cinematography (Colour), Best British Film*

A number of leading Western scientists have been kidnapped only to reappear a fews days later. Unfortunately, each scientist has been brain washed and is now completely useless. The British send their agent, Harry Palmer, to investigate.

In the 60s the secret agent emerged as premier screen hero, cold warrior and sex symbol. No one could touch Sean Connery's James Bond – until Michael Caine's Harry Palmer. Palmer was the creation of novelist Len Deighton, whose *Ipcress File* was adapted into the first and best of the Palmer thrillers during the goldrush of filmmakers seeking to mine lucrative spy caper franchises. (*Funeral In Berlin* and Ken Russell's fun *Billion Dollar Brain* followed in 1966 and 1967.)

Bowing in the same year Bond was saving the world from total destruction in *Thunderball*, bespectacled Harry, more modestly engaged in slowing the brain drain of British scientists, immediately endeared himself to average blokes. Harry Palmer is forever enshrined as the credible everyman alternative to Bond. In conception and in Caine's performance he was a fantasy figure for guys who wear glasses, people living in anonymous flats, driving unglamorous, functional cars and shopping for groceries after work. You can relate to Harry Palmer. He's capable and crafty. He's sexy. And he can cook.

Bond's fabulous world is one of exotic locations, babes, stupendous stunts, ingenious gadgets and gizmos. It is rich with explosively lavish underground lairs of megalomaniacal masterminds with whom 007 contends when he isn't between the sheets, behind the wheel of an Aston Martin or BMW, in a casino or relaxing with a vodka martini. Palmer's world is surveillance shifts in a grotty attic, furtive shenanigans in British Rail stations, the rendezvous on park benches, an HQ disguised as a domestic employment bureau, and a villains' lair in a disused warehouse. Harry drinks whiskey, plays the horses, is issued the keys to a boring blue Zodiac that doesn't do anything except go, and he is the first swinging London bachelor to be seen grinding his own coffee.

One witty touch hinting at the fact that Harry may have read an Ian Fleming Bond novel or two with relish is his picking a woman's charm bracelet and his gun out of the bed before he leaves for work. What they have in common – in addition to John Barry musical scores accompanying their adventures – is a studied unemotional mien, the ability to focus coolly under pressure, and an insolent disregard for going by the book or kowtowing to bureaucratic superiors. Bond has the suave insolence of an Old Etonian. Palmer's is the sturdy insolence of a Cockney squaddie.

An army sergeant assigned to a decidedly unglamorous corner of British Intelligence, Palmer is taken off surveillance and sent to a humble covert Home Office department to aid the search for a snatched physicist precisely because his qualities as an 'insubordinate bastard' are called for. He's also a handy disposable replacement for a murdered agent and when – having crossed paths fatefully with the CIA, cracked a dastardly foreign brainwashing, amnesia-inducing plot and exposed a traitor – he later reproaches his boss with, 'I might have been killed or driven stark raving mad.' He's briskly reminded, 'That's what you're paid for.' The risks of being killed or driven mad might be preferable to Palmer than the avalanche of paperwork and codespeak in this spy game. Amusing repeated references to the B107 (Palmer's career record), triplicate TI 04s, LIOls, a TX82, a 3H, a CC1 – even a park bench is designated T108 – are sufficient motivation to drive him out of the office run by a Fag Ash Lil secretary called Alice. The seasoning of dry humour plays nicely against the subdued but tense cat-and-mouse action: a silent combat with the bald heavily code-named 'House Martin' seen through the glass of a call box; a car park hostage exchange and confrontation; the assassination of Gordon Jackson's Jock after borrowing Harry's car.

These scenarios make the exciting, brutally in-your-face climax of Palmer's abduction and torture the more startling, Palmer enduring through his sheer bloody-mindedness and self-inflicted pain. Director Sidney J. Furie excelled himself pacing Palmer's adventure and got his ticket to Hollywood, where he was thereafter a moderately successful workhorse but never topped *The Ipcress File*. Caine, *Zulu* under his belt and *Alfie* ahead, is the cheeky working-class but aspirational bright-spark hero par excellence, captured at the exact moment he became a star. ★★★★★ **AE**

◎ IRIS (2001)

Starring: *Judi Dench (Iris Murdoch), Jim Broadbent (John Bayley), Kate Winslet (Young Iris Murdoch), Hugh Bonneville (Young John Bayley)*
Director: *Richard Eyre*
Screenwriters: *Richard Eyre, Charles Wood, based on the books* Iris: A Memoir *and* Elegy for Iris *by John Bayley*
15/86 mins./Biography/Drama/USA/UK

Awards: *Academy Awards – Best Supporting Actor, BAFTA – Best Actress, Golden Globes – Best Supporting Actor*

A biopic of Iris Murdoch focusing on her relationship with husband John Bayley. The story flashes back and forth between the pair's early romance and his attempts to nurse her through Alzheimer's later in life.

There's a lot to admire about Richard Eyre's biopic of renowned author Dame Iris Murdoch, chiefly that it boasts some of the best performances to grace a cinema screen in recent months. It also has the kind of charm and elegance seen all too rarely in contemporary British productions. But for all its class, there's no escaping the fact that this actually tells you very little about how Murdoch came to be one of the foremost female authors of the 20th Century.

As a depiction of her relationship with her husband it works well, displaying the deep love the pair had for one another. But those curious about other aspects of Murdoch's life will be left wanting.

It's certainly easy viewing. Eyre hits upon the clever directorial trick of intertwining the past and present, so that both Winslet and Dench appear throughout the film, and the emotional wrench of watching Murdoch lose her faculties to Alzheimer's Disease is tempered with the light relief of Murdoch and Bayley's courtship.

All the leads are terrific – Winslet makes a fine feisty foil to Bonneville's nervous, stammering Bayley – but the showier work is left to their older counterparts.

To make almost no mention of Murdoch's books, however, seems to be a wasted opportunity. By making only brief references to her love of words and philosophy, the film offers us no reason why we should have any more sympathy for Murdoch's plight than for that of millions of other gifted, intelligent people who fall prey to this debilitating disease every year. Given it works so well in other areas, it's a shame to find it lacking. ★★★★ **CW**

IRMA LA DOUCE (1963)

Starring: *Jack Lemmon (Nestor), Shirley MacLaine (Irma La Douce), Lou Jacobi (Moustache), Bruce Yarnell (Hippolyte), Herschel Bernardi (Inspector LeFevre), Hope Holiday (Lolita)*
Director: *Billy Wilder*
Screenwriter: *Billy Wilder, I.A.L. Diamond, based on the play by Alexandre Breffort.*
15/147 mins./Comedy/USA

Ex-cop Nestor Patou becomes so besotted with Parisian prostitute Irma La Douce that he becomes her pimp and then poses as English aristocrat Lord X to prevent her from meeting any other clients.

Billy Wilder was drawn to Alexandre Breffort's stage farce by the challenge of depicting a man who is jealous of himself. Stripping away the songs that had been added for the Broadway musicalisation, Wilder and co-scenarist I.A.L. Diamond concocted a bawdy tale of smut and deceit, in which good intentions wind up being tainted by their environment. It proved to be Wilder's biggest hit of the 1960s, but he later conceded that it should have remained a play.

Wilder never forgave himself for breaking his golden rule of having Americans play foreigners with a native accent. However, he only had himself to blame as he rejected Brigitte Bardot's overtures to play the tart with the heart and, having fallen out with Marilyn Monroe and thought better of Elizabeth Taylor, he cast Shirley MacLaine in the title role for a reunion with Jack Lemmon, her co-star in *The Apartment*.

Unfortunately, the pair failed to recapture the chemistry they has generated in that infinitely more innocent study in sexual infatuation. This has much to do with the storyline itself, as Lemmon is forced to spend much of the action in disguise and he struggles to emulate the comic ease of Tony Curtis's caricaturisation of a millionaire in *Some Like It Hot*. Indeed, his reliance on movie gags for Lord X's mannerisms becomes an irritation and sits uneasily with the abrasive innuendo that comes to dominate Nestor and Irma's relationship.

Lemmon and MacLaine visited a Parisian hooker named Marguerite to prepare for their roles (and she reportedly kept slipping away to service her regulars), but the only sense of realism comes from Alexandre Trauner's typically atmospheric sets for Rue de Casanova and the Les Halles meat market (how subtle), where Nestor works to finance Lord X's nocturnal philanthropy.

Irma La Douce is a much better film than its reputation suggests. But its best joke lay in getting so much overt vulgarity past the Production Code censors. ★★★ **DP**

THE IRON GIANT (1999)

Starring: *the voices of: Jennifer Aniston (Annie Hughes), Harry Connick Jr. (Dean McCoppin), Vin Diesel (The Iron Giant), James Gammon (Marv Loach/Floyd Turbeaux/General Sudokoff)*
Director: *Brad Bird*
Screenwriters: *Tim McCanlies, Andy Brent Forrester, from a story by Brad Bird, based on the novel by Ted Hughes*
U/83 mins./Sci-fi/Adventure/Family/USA
Awards: *BAFTA – Children's Award for Best Film*

In 1957 youngster Hogarth Hughes finds a visitor from space in the form of a giant iron man. He rescues him and hides him in a junkyard, but the Iron Man has been constructed as a weapon, and instead of giving him a chance to transcend his role, government agent Kent provokes him into the violence he hates.

In 1957, with Sputnik in orbit and America in a panic over the communist threat, youngster Hogarth Hughes stumbles over a newly-arrived visitor from space – a towering robot with a dented dome that has given it amnesia. After rescuing the wonderful being from electrocution at a power plant, Hogarth hides it in a junkyard run by sculptor Dean McCoppin while paranoid Government agent Kent Mansley searches for the creature that has been taking sizable bites out of cars and other metal structures. Realising that it has been constructed as a weapon, the giant decides that it doesn't want to be a gun, but when Kent calls in the army and even summons a nuclear strike, defence mechanisms switch on and a tragic outcome looks likely.

After the scrappy, opportunistic *Space Jam*, this second fully-animated feature from Warner Bros is a delightful surprise. Based on a children's story (*The Iron Man*) by the late Ted Hughes, this plays an interesting riff on the magical friend theme so common in American film and deserves points for its unfashionable commitment to pacifism. For a cartoon, it boasts a very sophisticated depiction of the 50s – a glimpse of a 'duck and cover' atomic survival instruction film in school, a warmly affectionate depiction of the espresso-chugging hipster Dean and his abstract sculpture projects, and Kent's right-wing nutcase militarism. After so many Japanese cartoons in which robot warriors blast anything that moves while their young pals cheer them on, it's refreshing that this hinges on the wish of the giant not to be a weapon.

Of course, the big attraction is the iron giant itself. At one stage, it transforms into a scary alien being with *War Of The Worlds* heat-rays and impressive zapping capability, but it is mostly a lovably old-fashioned, clanking 'bot with a big chin and the square shoulders of a 50s fridge. Animation auteur Bird, a veteran of *The Simpsons* and *King Of The Hill*, makes this a fully-realised character which should delight any kid. ★★★★ **KN**

IRREVERSIBLE (2002)

Starring: *Monica Belluci (Alex), Vincent Cassel (Marcus), Albert Dupontel (Pierre), Jo Prestia (Le Tenia), Philippe Nahon (Philippe)*
Director: *Gaspar Noé*
Screenwriter: *Gaspar Noé*
18/93 mins./Drama/Thriller/France

Following the self-set rule 'Time destroys everything', we are taken through a harrowing, gruesome night in the the lives of Alex, Marcus and Pierre, played in episodic reverse order.

'Time heals all wounds,' goes the old phrase. 'Time destroys everything,' counters an on-screen caption in *Irreversible*. But this is by no means an exercise in shock-value nihilism or gratuitous violence against women: two-thirds of the running time takes place after the controversial rape scene.

Noé's intention is to mourn the beautiful thing that has been destroyed, not to glorify its destruction.

That's why his bold narrative structure – telling a rape-and-revenge story backwards – isn't a cinematic gimmick. He is literally undoing a crime to make a profound social and artistic statement about evolution.

As in *2001: A Space Odyssey*, the film progresses from an animalistic orgy of violence to an embryo's serene spirituality; here, from a noisy nightclub hell to a peaceful outdoor heaven. Its self-conscious structure and unflinching portrayal of rape and murder are designed to make us think and feel at the same time. That's not a definition of entertainment, but it is a definition of meaningful, provocative art. ★★★★★ **AM**

ISLAND OF DR. MOREAU (1996)

Starring: *David Thewlis (Edward Douglas), Fairuza Balk (Aissa), Ron Perlman (Sayer of the Law), Marlon Brando (Dr. Moreau), Val Kilmer (Montgomery)*
Director: *John Frankenheimer*
Screenwriters: *Richard Stanley, Ron Hutchinson, based on the novel by H.G. Wells*
12/91 mins./Horror/Sci-fi/USA
Awards: *Razzie Awards – Worst Supporting Actor (Marlon Brando)*

After being rescued and brought to an island, a man discovers that its inhabitants are experimental animals being turned into strange looking humans, all of it the work of a visionary doctor.

The third official adaptation of H.G. Wells's novel arrived with a troubled history. Kilmer, after initially agreeing to star, sidestepped into a supporting role, and was replaced by Rob Morrow. Then, after only four days' shooting, the film's original director Richard Stanley (who had toiled away on the project for more than four years) was fired, Morrow walked, the script was rewritten and Thewlis drafted in to replace the *Northern Exposure* star. The resultant movie is, understandably, something of a mess, as deformed and half-realised as any of the beast-men hybrids it features.

The sole survivor of a plane wreck in the south seas, UN lawyer Edward Douglas is picked up by a schooner on which Montgomery, a vet, is travelling to the island where the Nobel Prize-winning recluse Dr. Moreau has spent more than 17 years working on his 'experiments'. Persuaded by Montgomery that he would be safer on the island than continuing on with the ship's crew, Douglas soon comes to rue his decision as its inhabitants turn out to be beast-men genetically created by Moreau.

Despite Brando's sad decline into embarrassing cameos, there is still an inherent excitement to any film featuring the great man. But any hope you may have held out for another captivating performance is soon dashed. When we first see him he's caked in white make-up, and speaking with a weird British lisp that makes him sound like Robert Morley. Later he turns up wearing an ice bucket on his head, and performs a piano duet with a monster midget. The one good thing to come out of this mess is it provided Mike Myers the inspiration for Mini-me in *Austin Powers*.

Frankenheimer (veteran director of *The Manchurian Candidate* among others) tries to keep things rolling along, but the incoherent script, like many of the characters, swiftly descends into madness, as Montgomery reveals himself to be as insane as the doc, sitting around, smoking dope, taking potshots at the creatures. Meanwhile, Moreau's monsters begin to question their maker and strike back, and there's a subtext to be had involving the nature of God and creation, but it's better left alone. Frankenheimer has the gall to have Kilmer white himself up and do a parody (voice and all) of Brando, yet this is, ultimately, at the root of the film's problem: it's campy when it really should have been scary. ★★ **MS**

ISLAND OF LOST SOULS (1933)

Starring: *Charles Laughton (Dr. Moreau), Bela Lugosi (Sayer of the Law), Richard Arlen (Edward Parker), Leila Hyams (Ruth Walker), Kathleen Burke (Lota, the Panther Woman)*
Director: *Erle C. Kenton*
Screenwriters: *Philip Wylie, Waldemar Young, based on the novel* The Island of Dr Moreau *by H.G. Wells*
12/67 mins./Sci-fi/Horror/USA

Ed Parker is shipwrecked on an island ruled by mad scientist Dr. Moreau, who has raised animals to semi-human shape and intelligence in the laboratory. Moreau plots to mate Parker with his finest work, Lota the Panther Woman.

This adaptation of H.G. Wells's *The Island of Dr Moreau*, outrageously gruesome for 1932, was banned by the British Censors for decades.

Chubby Charles Laughton, with an obscene fleck of goatee and a voluminous ice-cream suit, is a magnificent, whip-wielding sadist and all-round pervert who transforms animals into near-men in the way a small boy might cut the legs off a fly.

Made during the first great Hollywood horror boom, this combines the mad science of *Frankenstein* (as Moreau wields a scalpel in a laboratory his creations call 'the House of Pain') and the surreal jungle island adventuring of *King Kong* (with a horde of barely glimpsed monstrosities gathering in the undergrowth) and throws in value-for-money sleaze in the shapely person of Kathleen Burke (who won a national contest for the role) as the claw-nailed, sarong-clad Panther Woman.

There are conventional pith-helmet melodramatics from staid hero Richard Arlen, who unaccountably isn't that keen on mating with the Panther Woman, but Arthur Hohl is fine as Moreau's drunken, self-hating assistant and Bela Lugosi intones Wells's ominous laws of the beast-people ('Not to go on all fours, are we not men?') from behind a faceful of bristles. Incidentally, this is the source of the oft-quoted (and parodied) line 'the natives are restless tonight.'

Remade officially twice (with Burt Lancaster and Marlon Brando as Moreau) and often imitated, this exercise in surreal dementia has never been matched – especially in the horrid finish as hairy hands smash glass to pick up the medical implements that are used by the rebel beasts to 'operate' on their mad master. ★★★★ **KN**

THE ISLAND (2005)

Starring: *Ewan McGregor (Lincoln Six Echo/Tom Lincoln), Scarlett Johansson (Jordan Two Delta/Sarah Jordan), Djimon Hounsou (Albert Laurent), Sean Bean (Merrick), Steve Buscemi (McCord), Michael Clarke Duncan (Starkweather)*
Director: *Michael Bay*
Screenwriters: *Caspian Tredwell-Owen, Alex Kurtzman, Roberto Orci, based on a story by Tredwell-Owen*
12A/136 mins./Sci-fi/Thriller/USA

Lincoln Six Echo is beginning to question his utopian home, where every movement is strictly controlled and everyone is desperate to be sent to The Island, the final paradise in the apparently destroyed outside world. But sensing something is up Lincoln escapes with fellow inmate Jordan and discovers that not only is their world a lie, so is the nature of their existence.

You know what you're getting with a Michael Bay movie. It's gonna be loud, it's gonna be glossy and there's gonna be a whole lot of collateral damage. You should also know exactly what you're not getting. Bugger nuance, screw subtlety, just crank up that wind machine and throw in another helicopter. By these rules, *The Island* may be the most Michael Bay movie anyone will ever make.

Possessing more complex ideas than any of Bay's shiny, vacuous back catalogue, this does at least have something approaching intellectual ambition. The idea of a rigid self-contained society controlled by barely seen powers is hardly new (Bay's vision of sinister confinement predictably looks like the kind of spa frequented by wheatgrass-chugging Los Angelinos, all granite surfaces and an absence of door handles) but with the addition of cloning and its ethics, it is at least timely. Bay being Bay, he doesn't really delve much into the psychology of discovering that you're a human facsimile or that nothing you remember is real. There are hints of it: born into physical adulthood, the clones learn at the rate of newborns, questioning their surroundings as they get older. But such internal troubles lose out to the external and are too often brushed away, with Johansson pouting prettily or McGregor furrowing his heavily tanned brow before running away from whatever's exploding nearby.

It's often difficult to judge, in fact, whether the leads (a brave assemblage of arty talent for such mindlessness) are being fittingly blank and confused or simply not very good; until, that is, McGregor, playing an argument with his own genetic twin, shows an impressive subtlety undemanded by the movie. Of course, to complain about Bay lacking depth is like whinging that Oliver Stone is a bit political. Pure spectacle and luxurious visuals are what he does best, and Bay vigorously empties his bag of tricks all over the screen. Shoot-outs, wildly incendiary car chases, sweaty twilit sex ... all are pulled off with an expensive bravura that few other directors can top. If you've come for the action – and, really, what on earth else were you coming for? – your buck will certainly buy you many a bang. Hopefully loud enough bangs to drown out some of the lacklustre nonsense around them. ★★★ **OR**

IT CAME FROM OUTER SPACE (1953)

Starring: *Richard Carlson (John Putnam), Barbara Rush (Ellen Fields), Charles Drake (Sheriff Matt Warren), Russell Johnson (George), Kathleen Hughes (Jane)*
Director: *Jack Arnold*
Screenwriter: *Harry Essex, based on the story* The Meteor *by Ray Bradbury*
PG/80 mins./Sci-fi/USA

Awards: *Golden Globes – Most Promising Female Newcomer (Barbara Rush)*

An alien ship crashes in the Arizona desert, and crew take on human form while trying to make repairs. A local scientist can't get the local authorities to believe him when he reports the alien presence, and his girlfriend is replaced by a shapeshifting alien.

Originally in 3-D, this archetypal 1953 sci-fi film opens with a blazing meteor zooming out of the screen to crash into the desert and then spins an eerie, unusual science fiction story (a screen original by Ray Bradbury, hence a few stretches of 'poetic' voice-over) about a saucerload of 'xenomorphs' stranded in the Arizona desert. The one-eyed, tentacled, fog-shrouded things from another world are barely glimpsed, but the film makes extensive, precedent-setting use of a later creature feature cliché – the distorted subjective camera looming over screaming humans to convey the monster's point of view.

Unlike most 1950s flying saucer films, the script is somewhat sympathetic to the aliens, who mainly aren't a threat to anyone and (like E.T.) just want to go home, even if they have to co-opt the form of local bipeds to get their ship repaired. Entertainingly, one of the crew turns out to be a psycho who memorably impersonates the heroine, swanning about the edge of a crater in a chic evening dress while wielding a mean raygun. It has the tinny domestic scenes and off-the-peg performances typical of early '50s s-f, but director Jack Arnold – who would continue in the genre with remarkable films like *The Creature From the Black Lagoon* and *The Incredible Shrinking Man* – does wonderful things with the natural eeriness of the desert setting. Bizarrely, there was an *It Came From Outer Space 2* in 1996, though that turned out to be a TV movie remake rather than an actual *It Came Back From Outer Space* sequel. ★★★ **KN**

IT CONQUERED THE WORLD (1956)

Starring: *Peter Graves (Dr. Paul Nelson), Beverly Garland (Claire Anderson), Lee Van Cleef (Dr. Tom Anderson), Sally Fraser (Joan Nelson)*
Director: *Roger Corman*
Screenwriter: *Charles B. Griffith*
No certificate/71 mins./Sci-fi/Horror/USA

A scientist, Tom Anderson, paying attention to radio signals from space invites a Venusian who promises to help him create a utopian world but actually plans to conquer the Earth.

The wildest of Roger Corman's 50s rubber monster features (with only *Attack of the Crab Monsters* offering real competition) features a squat, snarling Venusian monster who resembles a giant turnip with teeth whose invasion is abetted by bat-like devices which enslave sundry human tools. 'It' beams down to Earth via radio waves and hides in a murky cave where the weird creature is kept in the shadows, and causes worldwide panic by shutting off all power a la *The Day the Earth Stood Still*, though we only get to see what's going on in the small town near the cave.

Staunch Peter Graves is the earnest hero scientist, swarthy Lee Van Cleef the misguided villain scientist and gutsy Beverly Garland the gutsy girl who goes after 'It' with her handbag. Despite the ludicrous menace, it has some very eerie moments, and the script notably refuses to go along with the clichés of the form, killing off the wrong characters – when Graves's wife welcomes him home in cheery 1950s sitcom fashion, she tosses a mind-controlling bat at him and is shot dead – and allowing for a heroic act of self-sacrifice on the baddy's part ('I invited you to this planet and you made it a charnel house!').

Corman, an engineer, reasoned that the inhabitant of a high-gravity planet like Venus would be squat and powerful, but Garland gave the Paul Blaisdell-created creature a solid kick on the set that convinced the producer-director that in all future films he would make the monster taller than the leading lady. ★★★ **KN**

IT HAPPENED ONE NIGHT (1934)

Starring: *Claudette Colbert (Ellie Andrews), Clark Gable (Peter Warne), Roscoe Kams (Oscar Shapeley), Henry Wadworth (Drunk Boy), Claire McDowell (Mother), Walter Connolly (Alexander Andrews)*
Director: *Frank Capra*
Screenwriter: *Robert Riskin based on the story 'Night Bus' by Samuel Hopkins Adams*
U/105 mins./Comedy/USA

Awards: *Academy Awards – Best Picture, Best Director, Best Actor, Best Actress, Best Adapted Screenplay*

Journalist Peter Warne recognises runaway heiress Ellie Andrews en route from Miami to New York and agrees to help her make her assignation with gold-digging playboy King Westley in return for the exclusive rights to her story.

Had anyone tried to produce a movie about the making of *It Happened One Night*, no one would have believed it. Things started off reasonably enough, with Robert Riskin turning Samuel Hopkins Adams's magazine story, 'Night Bus', into a screenplay. But the fanciful began to set in when MGM's Louis B. Mayer offered Columbia chief, Harry Cohn, Clark Gable in compensation for Robert Montgomery's refusal to play the gruffly genial journalist. However, this was no mere act of inter-mogul philanthropy, as Mayer had grown tired of Gable's pay demands and insistence on selecting his own roles. So, he agreed to loan out his fastest-rising star because he considered him 'a bad boy and I'd like to spank him'.

Less than amused by his demotion to Poverty Row, Gable reported for his first meeting with director Frank Capra fighting drunk and racially abusive. However, he eventually accepted his punishment and came to recognise the quality of the script in preproduction. Myrna Loy, Miriam Hopkins, Constance Bennett and Margaret Sullivan, however, failed to share his enthusiasm and they all nixed the project before Claudette Colbert signed up because she had four weeks to spare before her Christmas vacation in Sun Valley. That said, she had little faith in Capra, who had directed her debut, *For the Love of Mike*, and its failure had temporarily harmed her prospects.

But even though the lure of $50,000 (double her usual salary) assuaged her doubts, she arrived on set intent on playing the prima donna. She refused point blank to disrobe for the famous 'Walls of Jericho' sequence (in which the sight of Gable's bare torso sent vest sales plummeting) and only agreed to reveal her thigh for the hitch-hiking gag when Capra threatened to use a stand-in with better legs. Consequently, she told friends, 'I've just finished the worst picture in the world.'

Yet, in spite of the frictions, the film became the first to land the Big Five awards at the Oscars. But, more importantly, this fresh, fast and funny farce ushered in the screwball comedy, which remains its lasting legacy. ★★★★★ **DP**

⑫ IT'S A MAD MAD MAD MAD WORLD (1963)

Starring: *Spencer Tracy (Captain C.G. Culpepper), Milton Berle (J. Russell Finch), Sid Caesar (Melville Crump), Buddy Hackett (Benjy Benjamin), Ethel Merman (Mrs. Merman), Mickey Rooney (Ding 'Dingy' Bell)*
Director: *Stanley Kramer*
Screenwriters: *William Rose, Tania Rose*
18/115 mins./Comedy/USA

When a recently released thief careers off a cliff, a group of nearby drivers are on hand to hear his final words – revealing where $350,000 of stolen money is buried. So begins a madcap race across the desert to get to the hidden loot, transforming ordinary people into greedy maniacs capable of any trick to win.

The film, something of an acquired taste, that took the screwball comedy formula and upped the mania to warp factor ten. Cast with a just about everyone of those comedians you recognise but can't quite place, but kind of love all the same, the sheer momentum and rapid-fire gag count makes for an endurable three hours (did the cast's contract's demand a set screen time?). It's way too wacko for its own good, but for sheer zest and the presence of two incomparable, if highly contrasting talents – Spencer Tracy and Terry-Thomas – you can forgive its many sins.

Stanley Kramer, who barely keeps a grip on his overlapping storylines, the various cars teeming with deranged passengers, constructs a loose parable on the corrupting power of greed, although the $350,000 cache feels a bit sparse by today's standards. However, he was not a natural comedy director, allowing the nuttiness to ramble, and too many of the scenes to descend into an infuriating chaos with the talented cast just bellowing at one other. It is in the wild stuntwork and fraught action, dangling its precious stars over various precipitous drops, that you can thrill to its mania.

There is also no doubting the seminal effect the film has had, virtually inventing the 'madcap' style – screwball and then some – with everything from *The Cannonball Run* to *Rat Race* touched by its senseless delirium. Not a grand legacy, admittedly. Oh, and its four 'mads' in the title if you need to remember. A fifth would have been too much to bear. ★★★ **IN**

⑫ IT'S A WONDERFUL LIFE (1946)

Starring: *James Stewart (George Bailey), Donna Reed (Mary Hatch Bailey), Lionel Barrymore (Mr. Potter), Thomas Mitchell (Uncle Billy), Henry Travers (Clarence), Belulah Bondi (Ma Bailey)*
Director: *Frank Capra*
Screenwriters: *Frances Goodrich, Albert Hackett, Frank Capra, based on the story 'The Greatest Gift' by Philip Van Doren Stern*
U/130 mins./Fantasy/Drama/USA
Awards: *Golden Globes – Best Director*

It's Christmas and George Bailey is at the end of his tether feeling that taking his life is the only option. Then he is given a chance to see what would become of his beloved small town without him.

If there's one film synonymous with Christmas, it's Frank Capra's 1946 fantasy drama *It's A Wonderful Life*. Yet its top seasonal status is hardly the result of any instant success. The ultimate cult comeback movie, it was coolly received upon its release and lost more than $500,000, then was all but forgotten for more than 20 years. But after repeated TV showings during the Christmases of the 70s, it rocketed to the top of the list of favourite family viewing and is still paid affectionate homage throughout popular culture, from recurring references in other movies, to Sesame Street Muppets named after Bert the cop and Ernie the cabbie, to both a band and literary website named Zuzu's Petals. That it should be the best-loved of Christmas fables is a story as full of ironies as the picture itself. But it is endearingly appropriate, since the idea for the film came from a Christmas card – of sorts.

Up in heaven, a chorus of prayers for help are heard coming from the small town of Bedford Falls. So a despairing man named George Bailey is prevented from committing suicide by the intervention of a funny little old fellow named Clarence Oddbody, 'Angel, Second-Class'. The angel shows him what others' lives would have been like, and what their town would have been like, if, as he wished, he had never been born. George has an epiphany, cries, 'I want to live again!' and is restored to his family and friends who toast him as 'the richest man in town'. And a tinkling bell on the Baileys' Christmas tree tells George that Clarence's successful mission has won him his wings . . .

Historian and novelist Philip Van Doren Stern was in a contemplative mood one morning while shaving, and was struck with the idea for a story about a suicidal man confronted by his guardian angel, who shows him the difference he's made to people's lives. After having it rejected by several magazines, he added the seasonal setting, printed 200 copies as 24-page booklets titled 'The Greatest Gift', and sent them as Christmas 'cards'. One recipient was his agent, who sent it to the studios. At Cary Grant's urging, RKO bought the film rights and hired Dalton Trumbo to adapt it. Trumbo, never credited, became the first of nine screenwriters who contributed. His script was supposedly too political, too dark and too sophisticated, but it was he who wrote the immortal line: 'Every time a bell rings, an angel gets its wings.'

Meanwhile, Capra was vainly trying to re-establish himself as a major player in Hollywood. The first studio director to claim the accolade of having his name come first in the credits – hence calling his autobiography *The Name Above The Title* – and the winner of three directing Oscars, Capra had a string of hits throughout the 30s. We've come to know his comedy-dramas of Ordinary Joes versus The System as defining a style and tone so recognisable it's been adjectivised into 'Capra-esque'. His inimitable trilogy of satirical social-conscience comedies – *Mr. Deeds Goes To Town* (1936), *Mr. Smith Goes To Washington* (1939) and *Meet John Doe* (1941) established the warm mythos which idealises small-town values, scorns big-city cynicism and celebrates the goodness of common people.

The pictures all affirm democracy while expressing disillusionment with its failings, raising up messianic innocents to denounce the corruption of politicians, journalists and lawyers (Mr. Deeds says of one attorney, 'Even his hands are oily'). Deeds and Smith were hits. The bleaker Doe was not. And with the world at war, Capra decided to set aside social criticism for the uncontroversial patriotism of his Why We Fight series for the US Army.

But when the war was over, Capra was yesterday's man, and being Capra-esque was out of vogue. Egotistical, embittered, cynical and used to autonomy, Capra went independent, founding Liberty Pictures. (And he wasn't the only one suffering post-War angst. Returned bomber pilot

TOP10 Oscar Travesties

1 *Citizen Kane* missed out on Best Picture to *How Green Was My Valley.*

2 **Marisa Tomei won Best Supporting Actress – over Joan Plowright, Vanessa Redgrave, Miranda Richardson and Judy Davis.**

3 *Raging Bull* lost Best Picture to *Ordinary People*

4 ***Kramer Vs. Kramer*** **beat** ***Apocalypse Now*** **to Best Picture**

5 *Forrest Gump* beat both *Pulp Fiction* and *The Shawshank Redemption* to Best Picture.

6 **Humphrey Bogart lost out on Best Actor for** ***Casablanca*** **to Paul Lukas for** ***Watch on the Rhine***

7 *An American In Paris* beat *A Place in the Sun* and *A Streetcar Named Desire* – while *The African Queen* wasn't even nominated.

8 **Roberto Benigni won Best Actor for** ***Life Is Beautiful*** **over Nick Nolte, Tom Hanks, Edward Norton and Ian McKellen.**

9 *The Lord of the Rings: the Fellowship of the Ring* missed out on Best Costume to *Gosford Park. The Two Towers* didn't even get a Costume nomination.

10 **Sound mixer Kevin O'Connell has been nominated by his peers 18 times for films like** ***Spider-Man, Top Gun*** **and** ***Memoirs of a Geisha*** **but has never won.**

Jimmy Stewart was haunted by his experiences, no longer in demand and thinking of giving up acting altogether – until he had his own epiphany when Capra persuaded him to play George Bailey, and Lionel Barrymore, cast as Bailey's ruthless nemesis, the banker Mr. Potter, gave him a pep talk about what a valuable contribution to society an actor can make. Feeling an affinity with its darker aspects, Capra bought *It's A Wonderful Life* from RKO, hired his own writers and financed the production at the Bank Of America.

His old friend and rival William Wyler scored a triumphant comeback with *The Best Years Of Our Lives* (1946), which began filming the same day as *It's A Wonderful Life* and completely overshadowed it by perfectly capturing the country's mood. It was not until Capra's oeuvre was rediscovered in the 70s, as a lapsed copyright bargain package for TV syndication, that his message movies were embraced again by audiences for their charm and traditional values.

Oddly, even liberal fans persist in not acknowledging that Capra's films are full of the contradictions (some say hypocrisy) that marked his complex, conflicted personality and politics. A conservative Republican, Capra fancied himself one of the wealthy and powerful elite while boasting a populism that engaged Depression-era audiences. And he begrudged credit to his most valuable collaborators, particularly those known for being to the left politically, and unhesitatingly distanced himself from them when they all came under sinister, Red-scare scrutiny.

These contradictions are encapsulated in his work. In *Mr. Deeds Goes To Town*, hard-nosed reporter Jean Arthur mocks naive poet Gary Cooper, who inherits a fortune and is beset by grasping city slickers. His decision to give it all away sees him in a court battle to determine his sanity, but goodness, empathy and love win out. It was released to acclaim in the USSR, retitled *Grip Of The Dollar*. In *Mr. Smith Goes To Washington*, hard-nosed secretary Jean Arthur mocks naive new Senator James Stewart, who is framed for misconduct by a corrupt political machine but goodness, democracy and love win out. In *Meet John Doe*, hard-nosed reporter Barbara Stanwyck invents a fictitious Everyman and hires naive Coop to impersonate him. The national movement his folksy philosophy inspires is manipulated by a fascist, but goodness, the little man and love win out.

It's A Wonderful Life stands out, though, by going darker at points, yet better balancing that with the twinkly light. Despite the film being loved as an uplifting fable, many don't see that Capra's small-town Americana was a reactionary illusion, idealising a disturbingly cosy way of life that never was. George's nightmarish odyssey through Pottersville and a community that doesn't know him – what the filmmakers dubbed 'the unborn sequence' – is strikingly noir cinema, gloomy and disillusioned. And the events leading up to George's suicide bid bring out his selfish, abusive side – realistically the inevitable explosion of a man whose personal dreams and ambitions have been continually suppressed and thwarted by the needs and demands of others.

The true magic of the film is that Capra's undeniably vital creative genius, with the help of his perfect cast, pulls its conflicts and mood swings together, through comedy, sentimentality and despair, into a supremely entertaining homily on simple goodness, forever treasured for the cheer of its insistence that 'no man is alone who has friends ...' ★★★★★ **AE**

Movie Trivia: It's a Wonderful Life

The raven in the film, called Jimmy, appears in all of Frank Capra's films. The TV company that co-produced 80s TV drama Thirtysomething was called Bedford Falls Productions, after George Bailey's (James Stewart) home town.

IT'S ALIVE! (1974)

Starring: *John P. Ryan (Frank Davies), Sharon Farrell (Leonore Davies), Andrew Dugan (The Professor), Guy Stockwell (Clayton), James Dixon (Lt. Perkins), Michael Ansara (The Captain), Robert Emhardt (The Executive)*
Director: *Larry Cohen*
Screenwriters: *Larry Cohen*
18/90 mins./Horror/USA

Frank Davies takes his wife into hospital to have their second child. The baby, a super-strong fanged mutant, slaughters the delivery team and escapes. The Los Angeles authorities track the creature, while the shattered parents try to come to terms with their situation.

'There's only one thing wrong with the Davies baby,' read the posters, 'It's Alive!' The best mutant killer baby movie ever made, Larry Cohen's horror thriller is at once a great suspense/monster film and a darkly comic soap opera about strained parent-child relationships.

Taking its title from Colin Clive's declaration in *Frankenstein*, the film plays havoc with traditional ideas about an infant's place in society as 'the Davies baby' rampages through a darkened kindergarten or bloodily slaughters the milkman.

It winds up, like the 1950s giant ant epic *Them!*, in the Los Angeles storm drains as hordes of gun-toting cops round on the barely glimpsed, Rick Baker-created baby monster.

Writer-director Cohen's strong suit is combining outrageous science fiction ideas with credible, unconventional character scenes. Perennial supporting thug John P. Ryan has a rare lead role as the bewildered Mr. Davies, a public-relations man who loses his job because he has fathered a monster, and superbly plays an unusual arc from revulsion to near-devotion. With an eerie Bernard Herrmann score, one great joke scare involving a soft toy that falls into frame at the worst possible moment and good supporting work from character actors Andrew Duggan, James Dixon, Guy Stockwell and Michael Ansara. Cohen has made two sequels, both with their own interesting angles: *It Lives Again*, in which Ryan leads a pressure group for the parents of monsters, and *It's Alive III: Island of the Alive*, in which Michael Moriarty has a reunion with his grown-up monster son. ★★★★ **KN**

THE ITALIAN JOB (1969)

Starring: *Michael Caine (Charlie Croker), Noel Coward (Mr. Bridger), Benny Hill (Professor Simon Peach), Raf Vallone (Altabani), Tony Beckley ('Camp' Freddy), Rossano Brazzi (Roger Beckerman)*
Director: *Peter Collinson*
Screenwriter: *Troy Kennedy Martin*
PG/95 mins./Action/Comedy/Crime/UK/USA

Comic caper movie about a plan to steal a gold shipment from the streets of Turin by creating a traffic jam.

Blame the Great Train Robbers. On August 8, 1963, 15 armed men led by Bruce Reynolds held up the Glasgow-London postal train to the tune of £2,600,000. The job was breathtakingly audacious, making use of detailed technical knowledge and the skills of an unknown insider. The only downside was that the train's engineer was left severely injured. And the fact that the robbers so bungled the aftermath of the job that 12 of them were behind bars within weeks. Even so, the Train Robbers won a good deal of public sympathy, and it's this romanticised image of the dashing crook which underpins Michael Caine's portrayal of Charlie Croker in *The Italian Job*.

Apart from Caine's wonderfully breezy central character – blond, quite beautiful, flitting from high society to low villainy – *The Italian Job* is certainly the high watermark of British camp, with Troy Kennedy Martin's script composed of equal parts innuendo and waspish one-liners. One of the dandy highwaymen is even named Camp Freddie (a suitably elegant Tony Beckley, who also appears in *Get Carter*), whose asides include, 'Now, Butch Harry, tell us about Fulham.' For the role of crime boss Bridger, who controls his miniature British Empire from a prison cell, director Peter Collinson called upon his former patron, venerable theatrical queen Noel Coward. Despite his failing health, Coward is a triumph as the royalty-obsessed kingpin, delivering lines like, 'Camp Freddie, everybody in the world is bent!' with undisguised glee.

The other big name in the cast is Benny Hill, playing computer boffin and fancier of 'big women' Professor Peach with the mastery of seaside postcard smut that was to make him the world's favourite TV comic.

When Croker assembles the 16-man (and one woman) team for the titular job (knocking off a load of gold bullion in Turin), it becomes clear that this is a cross-section of British society finding themselves obliged to work together for the first time since the war. From the cockney spivs to the 'chinless wonder' drivers, everyone in New Britain is on the make. And, as dark references to the nation's balance of payments suggest, they'd better get their skates on, because the good times aren't going to last forever.

The team's preparations are meticulous but typically ham-fisted. 'You're only supposed to blow the bloody doors off!' yells Charlie when a hapless stooge employs a Krakatoa-like amount of dynamite. 'Apart from knocking over a few old dears with their carrycots,' Camp Freddie reports to Bridger, 'I think we can manage it.'

But the Mafia are on to them, confronting the Brits near the Italian border with a menacing show of strength. Croker responds with one of the most chilling speeches in the history of British cinema: 'There are a quarter of a million Italians in Britain, and they'll be made to suffer. Every restaurant, cafe, ice cream parlour, gambling den and nightclub in London, Liverpool and Glasgow will be smashed. Mr. Bridger will drive them into the sea.' But in spite of the glancing similarity to the right-wing rhetoric of Enoch Powell's late-60s 'Rivers Of Blood' rant, Charlie Croker is no racist, as the presence of black team member Big William attests. This is strictly business.

The Turin traffic jam, robbery and ensuing getaway are what people remember most warmly about *The Italian Job*. Such was the film crew's level of co-operation from the Turin police – having been given carte blanche by Fiat boss and 'King of Turin' Giovanni Agnelli – that they actually caused a real traffic jam. 'We simply went out with 50 cars and blocked up the streets,' recalls Second Unit Director Philip Wrestler. 'If they'd seen the camera we'd have been lynched.'

With the robbery itself, things momentarily turn serious. As the Brits give the guards a brutal beating and blow up a water cannon-equipped armoured car, there is an explosion of violence – succinct, controlled and nasty. But the escape of the bullion-loaded red, white and blue minis is pure fun. Master stunt driver Remy Julienne and cohorts turned the chase through Turin's subways, rooftops and sewers (the latter actually filmed near Coventry) into a lesson in getting unglamorous cars to do the impossible. Today, after *Mad Max 2* (1981) and the like, it all seems politely within the speed limit. In fact, as a 1999 Channel 4 programme showed, the cars were going much faster and performing stunts far more dangerous than is apparent on screen.

As the chase reaches its climax, the film rises to a series of crescendos. Bridger takes his bow while the massed prison ranks chant 'Eng-land!', Quincy Jones' theme music goes completely bonkers, and a cockney choir bellows Don Black's frankly insane, 'This is the self-preservation society' lyric as the minis board the speeding coach at 70 miles per hour.

Typically, the Brits make the mistake of celebrating too soon, ignoring Croker's orders to, 'leave the beer'. A dangerously ebullient Big William takes a bend too fast, and we're left with the famous cliff-hanging ending. Literally. As the wayward bullion slides towards the end of the seesawing coach with Croker crawling after it, the tension is incredible – all the more so for being totally unexpected. 'Hang on a minute, lads,' he murmurs. 'I've got a great idea. Er. Er . . .' As a metaphor for England at the dawn of the 70s, *The Italian Job* is a hard one to top. ★★★★★ **PR**

Movie Trivia: The Italian Job

Michael Caine and the film's composer Quincy Jones were born in the same hour of the same day of the same year, on 14 March 1933. The Italian Job Rally, an annual event raising money for charity, encourages owners of Minis to join a ten-day trawl through rural Italy.

THE ITALIAN JOB (2003)

Starring: *Mark Wahlberg (Charlie Croker), Charlize Theron (Stella Bridger), Donald Sutherland (John Bridger), Jason Statham (Handsome Rob), Seth Green (Lyle), Mos Def (Left Ear), Edward Norton (Steve)*
Director: *F. Gary Gray*
Screenwriters: *Donna Powers, Wayne Powers, based on the 1969 film by Troy Kennedy Martin*
12/105 mins./Action/Crime/Thriller/USA

A gang of thieves are double-crossed and left for dead by crew member Steve after pulling a gold heist in Venice. With grim determination, our anti-heroes head to LA and concoct an elaborate plan to relieve Steve of his ill-gotten gains – a plan involving a fleet of Mini Coopers . . .

Kudos to F. Gary Gray for stripping out most of the parts that made the original so memorable (no cliffhanger here), and instead fine-tuning his version so it resembles Steven Soderbergh's *Ocean's Eleven* more than its progenitor. Sadly, this doesn't quite possess *Ocean's* pizzazz, despite a decent script and performances.

Wahlberg, who has failed to convince as Charlton Heston and Cary Grant surrogates in *Planet Of The Apes* and *The Truth About Charlie*, is much more comfortable stepping into Michael Caine's size 10s (although he still needs to go to leading man charm school, and fast), while a slumming Norton is suitably slimy.

But, aptly for a heist flick, it's Wahlberg's eclectic gang – Green, Statham and Mos Def – who walk off with the picture, working wonders with their paper-thin stereotypes (the computer nerd, the rugged Brit, the token black) to keep the laughs coming.

Character, schmaracter. We're here for the Minis, one of the few elements to make the jump through the decades. It takes around 80 minutes of glossy foreplay (including an ingenious opening heist which takes place in Venice, for no reason other than to justify the title), before the souped-up Coopers are finally unleashed in a glorious chase through LA traffic, sidewalks and subways, before Wahlberg's Mini confrontation with Norton's helicopter. It certainly raises the movie's pulse, but ultimately it's hard to imagine this gluing us all to the goggle box on Bank Holiday Mondays in 2020. ★★★ **CH**

IVAN'S CHILDHOOD (IVANOVO DETSTVO) (1962)

Starring: *Nikolai Burlyavev (Ivan), Vealentin Zubkov (Capt. Kholin), Yevgheni Zharikov (Lt. Gaitsev), Stepan Krylov (Capt. Katasonych), Nikolai Grinko (Col. Gryaznov), Raush (Ivan's Mother)*
Director: *Andrei Tarkovsky*
Screenplay: *Vladimir Bogomolov, Mikhail Papava*
PG/94 mins./War/USS

Twelve-year-old Ivan, orphaned in war, insists on staying in the front lines as a valued scout, resisting the attempts of officers to pack him off to school.

Andrei Tarkovsky's debut feature is an oblique, poetic, monochrome war film, very Russian in its melancholia and humanism, implicitly patriotic if only because the barely seen Nazis are the ones committing all the atrocities, and memorable for its expressionist, *Night of the Hunter* swampland feel. Tarkovsky throws in magical dream memories of motherhood, playing on the beach and sunshine, but Ivan's waking war is all dark shadows, cringing underground or in trenches and people retreating into nervy quiet, leaving without saying goodbye, as afraid of making human connections as losing people.

There's no on-screen action, though the final mission is a suspenseful affair in a marsh, as officers try to retrieve the bodies of scouts killed and put on display while under fire. Tarkovsky has a knack for memorable bits of business: the showoff officer straddling a trench while hugging a reticent nurse whose legs dangle over the abyss, the recaptured records office with the air full of ash from burned papers, Ivan's displays of stubborn mood, a graffito begging for revenge illuminated by a torchlight-circle. The insertion of newsreel footage of Goebbels' dead daughters and other Nazis in defeat towards the end is jarring, but perhaps needed for the quiet final kick, which goes beyond the particularity of this story to convey the tragedy of a whole generation killed off before we catch Ivan in a flashback beach idyll which might also be some sort of afterlife. ★★★★ **KN**

◎ IVAN THE TERRIBLE. PART I (IVAN GROZNI) (1945)

Starring: *Nikolai Cherkassov (Czar Ivan IV – Ivan The Terrible), Ludmilla Tselikovskaya (Anastassia Romanova – the Czarina), Serafima Birman (Euphrosyne Strairzky – The Czar's Aunt), Pavel Kadochnikov (Vladimir Staritsky – Her Son), Mikhail Nazvanov (Prince Andrew Kurbsky)*
Director: *Sergei Eisenstein*
Screenwriter: *Sergei Eisenstein*
PG/96 mins./History/Drama/USSR

Ivan IV overcomes the loss of his wife Anastasia to unite Russia and confound the plans of his aunt, Efrosinia Staritskaya to usurp the throne for her simpleton son, Vladimir.

Prevented from making a trilogy about life in the Central Asian desert, a film about Spain and a history of the Red Army, Sergei Eisenstein returned to the theatre in 1939. But, while directing a production of Wagner's *Die Walküre* for the Bolshoi, he hit upon the concept of synaesthesia and this form of sensory domino effect became his artistic impetus for *Ivan the Terrible*.

He began work on the screenplay in early 1941, but the threat of a Nazi invasion prompted the relocation of Mosfilm to Alma Ata in Kazakhstan and it was here that he completed the task of bending fact into myth. Shooting began during a heatwave in the summer of 1943 and proceeded in strict accordance with the storyboards that also inspired Sergei Prokofiev's score. His longtime cinematographer, Eduard Tissé, was confined to the exteriors, while Andrei Moskvin lit Isaac Shpinel's sumptuous sets and also filmed the director's sole colour sequence, which utilised Agfa stock confiscated from the Germans.

Eisenstein returned to Moscow in the autumn of 1944 to begin shaping his footage. Abandoning montage in favour of functional editing, he focused on the mise-en-scène, in which the angular and highly expressive attitudes struck by the cast (which the outstanding Nikolai Cherkassov considered demeaning) were as crucial to his audiovisual strategy as the stylised décor.

But while *Part One* was awarded the Stalin Prize, it was accused of operatic formalism by some Soviet critics (particularly during the stunning Uspensky Cathedral sequence) and denounced as an apologia for Stalin's tyranny by many abroad. However, *Part Two* was censured by the Kremlin for the 'misrepresentation of historical facts' and was withheld until 1958. Worse still, the four completed reels of *Part Three* were destroyed. But the surviving epic remains one of the boldest and most exciting experiments conducted within the restraints of Socialist Realism. ★★★★★ **DP**

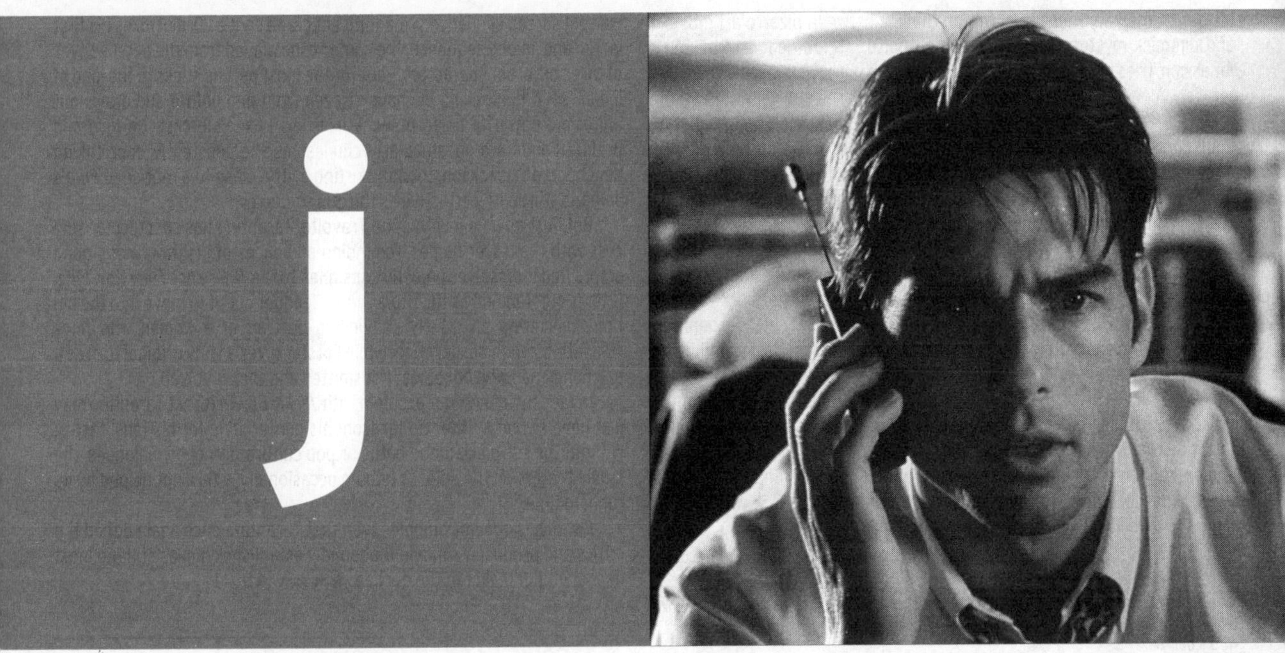

JACKASS: THE MOVIE (2002)

Starring: *as themselves: Johnny Knoxville, Bam Margera, Steve-O, Chris Pontius, Ryan Dunn, Jason Acuna, Preston Lacy, Dave England*
Director: *Jeff Tremaine*
Screenwriters: *Jeff Tremaine, Spike Jonze, Johnny Knoxville*
18/87 mins./Comedy/USA

Awards: *Razzie Awards – Most Flatulent Teen-Targeted Movie*

A feature-length version of the hit MTV show in which a group of extreme sports-loving funsters expose themselves to dangerous and deranged physical stunts.

Society's death knell? Performance art taken to its most logical, post-modern conclusion? Or a bunch of fearless stoners arsing (sometimes literally) around and getting paid for it? Whatever your opinion of *Jackass*, the big-screen expansion – it's not really a movie, by any strict, nor loose, definition of the word – practically demands your attention.

There's no cinematic merit here, but there's a certain surreal invention behind some of the more outlandish skits – all hail he who conceived the Bungee Wedgee! – and once you pluck up the courage to peer through your fingers, this is painful and painfully funny.

And with an interesting anti-authoritarian streak a mile wide (lead Jackass Knoxville takes tremendous delight in pissing off golfers with a well-timed klaxon), this is pure punk rock film. ★★★★ **CH**

THE JACKET (2005)

Starring: *Adrien Brody (Jack Starks), Keira Knightley (Jackie Price), Kris Kristofferson (Dr. Thomas Becker), Jennifer Jason Leigh (Dr. Beth Lorenson), Kelly Lynch (Jean Price), Daniel Craig (Rudy Mackenzie)*
Director: *John Maybury*
Screenwriter: *Massy Tadjedin, based on a story by Tom Bleecker, Marc Rocco*
15/103 mins./Thriller/USA/Germany

A military veteran returns to his native Vermont suffering from bouts of amnesia. When he is accused of murder and lands in an asylum, a well-meaning doctor puts him on a heavy course of experimental drugs, restrains him in a jacket-like device, and locks him away in a body-drawer in a morgue. The process allows him to see into the future, and his own death.

After striking, semi-underground works with titles like *Premonition Of Absurd Perversion In Sexual Personae, Part I* and *Remembrance Of Things Fast: True Stories, Visual Lies*, director John Maybury made a near-mainstream debut with *Love Is The Devil*, an intense biopic of Francis Bacon. However, according to Matthew Sweet's book *Shepperton Babylon*, Maybury once laid hands on Richard Curtis and said the *Love Actually* writer-director had 'ruined British cinema for people like me'. While *The Jacket*, which arrives seven years after Maybury's 'man to watch' notices for *Love Is The Devil*, was partially shot in Scotland and brings Daniel Craig back in a supporting role, it does its best not to seem in the slightest bit British, even if it does strive to avoid the straight genre tactics that would normally qualify it as full-on Hollywood product.

Still, this sort of head-scratching mystery-horror-thriller-psycho-drama has become surprisingly commonplace recently, as if a former generation's ideas of weirdness have become everyday. It grabs attention with a Gulf War sequence in which Adrien Brody's soldier is shot in the head and declared dead, which opens the possibility that the rest of the film consists of his dying fantasies or brain-damaged delusions. Then, while hitch-hiking in snowy Vermont, Brody meets a drunk driver and a girl who might grow up to be Keira Knightley, before taking a lift from Brad Renfro, who impulsively kills a cop and frames him.

Again, thanks to that Tyler Durden vibe, it could be that what we see isn't what's actually happened, raising the possibility that the bulk of the film is about someone fantasising that he's fantasising. That way lies madness, and Brody is duly committed to an asylum where his therapists are played by Kris Kristofferson and Jennifer Jason Leigh, bringing much-needed character weight to thinly written roles.

Brody has done near-solipsistic craziness often, in both *The Pianist* and *The Village*, for instance (will he do a movie called *The Something* next?), but his nervy intensity keeps this walking the line between bizarro art movie and gimmick mystery. Knightley, getting out of period gear and talking American, tries to broaden her range and is arguably well-cast as a character who might well be imagined by the hero – but she has very much the token anorexic angel role. Kristofferson, Leigh, Craig (as a secondary madman) and even tiny bits from Lynch and Renfro fit far better into this game of ambiguities, alternating scary and pathetic while doling out clues.

As often happens when folk with artier ambitions dip a toe in genre, Maybury labours long to reinvent the wheel, the evocation of his earlier output suggesting he'd rather be making something square that doesn't roll so much. Eventually, you realise that *The Jacket*, as interesting as it is, doesn't know how overworked its basic ideas have become, since it's as locked in its own head as its protagonist, blithely unaware that the cineplex is crowded with the muttering, stumbling, time-twisting, paradox-jumbling likes of *Donnie Darko* and *The Butterfly Effect*. This even has the frosty New England look of a Stephen King knock-off, not to mention that old plot gambit about struggling with the present to avert a foreseen unhappy ending. Can it be that Maybury's cultural parameters remain set by Francis Bacon and experimental art cinema and don't stretch to the SciFi Channel, which runs stories like this every week on the *Dead Zone* TV series? ★★★ **KN**

JACKIE BROWN (1997)

Starring: *Pam Grier (Jackie Brown), Samuel L. Jackson (Ordell Robbie), Robert Forster (Max Cherry), Bridget Fonda (Melanie Ralston), Michael Keaton (Ray Nicolette), Robert De Niro (Louis Gara)*
Director: *Quentin Tarantino*
Screenwriter: *Quentin Tarantino, based on the novel by Elmore Leonard*
15/147 mins./Crime/Drama/USA

An air hostess, pressurised into an entrapment scam after being caught smuggling illegal cash, decides to use the situation to her own advantage.

It is, as any cineaste worth his nachos knows, second films that are meant to be the tricky ones. With *Reservoir Dogs* Tarantino gave the 90s movie world its blistering wake-up call. With *Pulp Fiction* he effortlessly refuted the naysayers who dismissed his decade-defining debut as a flash in the pan. Tarantino became the hottest directorial property in Hollywood. And then came a couple of wilderness years. Underwhelming attempts at acting (*Destiny Turns On The Radio, Desperado*) were followed by his quarter of *Four Rooms*, directing a script which looked like it had been written by someone else, but wasn't. The naysayers got a second shot and Tarantino had to prove himself to the movie world all over again.

With *Jackie Brown* he does exactly that, refusing merely to re-rehearse the hip irony of his first two movies and delivering a much more thoughtful, generally less frantic, adaptation of the pulpish Elmore Leonard novel *Rum Punch*.

Jackie Brown is a middle-aged air hostess who, to supplement her meagre wage, couriers the odd consignment of cash for her gun-smuggling friend Ordell. Unfortunately, she gets lifted on one of these runs and is faced with an unpleasant choice: shop her boss – who has a distressing habit of bundling traitors into the boots of cars before casually plugging them; or spend some time in the big house. She, along with her bail bondsman and romantic admirer, hatches a scam to play both ends against the middle – snatching the next dispatch of loot without doing the 'bird' while simultaneously grassing her former employer to Michael Keaton's frenetic cop.

Tarantino's masterstroke has been to anticipate the backlash that could have greeted his third feature. Eschewing many of his 'trademarks', he doggedly gets down to the business of storytelling. Sure, there are flashes of the young buck who shook modern filmmaking to its foundations – a split screen sequence, a magnificent crane shot as Ordell nixes his first victim and, in one sequence, the same scene played from the perspectives of three different characters – but for the most part he sticks to the kind of linear, solid filmmaking we haven't seen from him before and draws out uniformly powerful performances from his ensemble cast. De Niro and Bridget Fonda are spectacularly clueless as the constantly dope-toking henchpersons, Jackson, though skirting a little close to a reprise of *Pulp*'s Jules, is still scarily effective as the gun smuggler.

But, just as he did with John Travolta, Tarantino has spectacular success with the lesser names, reminding audiences of just how many good actors find themselves unjustly consigned to the Where Are They Now? file. Grier is outstanding as the titular minor leaguer about to move into the big time, delivering an utterly convincing portrait of a woman who finds strength through desperation; while Forster gives a truly original turn as a bail bondsman who becomes first smitten and then involved.

In fact, the only slight problem with *Jackie Brown* is that Tarantino may just have swung a little too far from his earlier style for his fans' tastes. Without the set-piece blood baths or pop culture-drenched dialogues, the movie teeters on the edge of tedium occasionally, a flaw not helped by its running time.

But this is a minor quibble given that Tarantino once again defied the critics and produced a movie that solidly establishes him as still the most important filmmaker of the decade. ★★★★ **AS**

JACOB'S LADDER (1990)

Starring: *Tim Robbins (Jacob Singer), Elizabeth Pena (Jezebel), Dannny Aiello (Louis), Jason Alexander (Geary), Patricia Kalember (Sarah), Eriq La Salle (Frank), Ving Rhames (George)*
Director: *Adrian Lyne*
Screenwriter: *Bruce Joel Rubin*
18/115 mins./Horror/USA

Postal-worker Jacob Singer, a Vietnam vet, thinks he is going postal. He is being besieged by weird visions, flashbacks to his former marriage, his dead son and the agonies of Vietnam. As his grip on sanity slowly slips, a figure from his past turns up with a shocking explanation.

People tend to react to this strange film in one of two ways depending on their sensibility. It could speak to you as a profound meditation on death, a dense, dark, stylish fever-dream that hovers close to a horror movie (the battery of demonic doctors and entrail-strewn hospitals sees to that) and a paranoid governmental thriller, but whose elusive maudlin meanings will finally harken to the surrealistic chambers of David Lynch, Nicolas Roeg or Luis Buñuel. Alternatively, it could be interpreted as a somnambulistic smudge of pretension, whose slippery plotting allows its poseur of a director (*Fatal Attraction*'s flash dude Adrian Lyne) to fill the frame with whatever takes his fancy because the catch-all conclusion lets him off any narrative hooks.

From this angle it wavers between both interpretations: fake art with powerful undercurrents. It's also a bit of chore to get through, as Tim Robbins, who can really switch on the dour if he wants, endures all the pop-eyed dementia Lyne can throw at him. Screenwriter Bruce Joel Rubin, who has fixated on death throughout his career (*Ghost, My Life, Deep Impact*), and drawing from Ambrose Bierce's extraordinary metaphysical Civil War story, *An Occurrence At Owl Creek*, endeavours to conjure seething rhythms of religious fervour where existence starts to fragment. That he uses some sub-Oliver Stone prattling involving chemical testing in 'Nam to glue his dissonance together rather undermines the elliptical power of his intentions. While Lyne seems to care about nothing more than festooning the film with shocking imagery and warped editing, and tempting us with Macaulay Culkin as an angelic presence (how history has undermined that one).

And yet, for all its anything-goes devilry, the film sticks with you. The images do strike a terrifying chord, the feverish answer driving you back through the dizzy paths of the movie to assemble its purpose. It achieves a lot less than it intends to, but how many commercial films contemplate the physical transition into death? Although, exactly how many want to? ★★★ **IN**

JAGGED EDGE (1985)

Starring: *Glenn Close (Teddy Barnes), Maria Mayenzet (Page Forrester), Jeff Bridges (Jack Forrester), Peter Coyote (Thomas Krasny), Lance Henriksen (Frank Martin), Leigh Taylor-Young (Virgina Howell)*
Director: *Richard Marquand*
Screenwriter: *Joe Eszterhas*
18/104 mins./Crime/Thriller/USA

A female lawyer is gradually seduced by her new client, a newspaper publisher who is in court for murdering his own wife. This leads to Close testing her own judgment as well as endangering her job and of course, her life.

If, as seems to be the general consensus, Joe Eszterhas has only ever had one decent script in him then *Jagged Edge* is it. Or, to be a little more charitable to the old yeti (although after *Showgirls* he hardly deserves it), this slick, slithery little thriller is at least the blueprint for his subsequent forays into the realm of high-style crime drama with a twist – of which 1992's *Basic Instinct* stands as the most obvious, and most obviously derivative, example.

All the Eszterhas trademarks are out in force – murder, money, obsession, sex and dangerous romance – but in this case, seven years before Sharon Stone proved she was a natural blonde, the lurching plot can still tighten a sphincter or two and the red herrings are served on ice.

Glenn Close, excellent in a break-out role, plays disenchanted lawyer Teddy Barnes who is persuaded to renounce her vow never to practise criminal law again when newspaper editor Jack Forrester is accused of murdering his wife (from whom he has inherited the family publishing business) and finds himself in need of a hot-shot defence team.

Several things serve to sway Teddy's decision. First of all, the case presents an opportunity to exact high-profile revenge on her ex-boss, reptilian District Attorney Thomas Krasny, who poisoned her faith in the justice system four years earlier by withholding evidence in the trial of an innocent black youth, Henry Stiles, who later committed suicide in prison. Krasny, campaigning for political office, is out to nail Forrester from the off. The chance to ease an aching conscience over her unwitting involvement in Stiles' death is also a powerful draw. Plus she is irresistibly attracted to Forrester. The trouble is, Teddy is never able to fully decide whether Forrester is innocent or guilty – and neither are we. And this is why the film works so well.

Like most Eszterhas scripts, if you put *Jagged Edge* under too powerful a critical lens the cracks begin to show. Here, a couple of the plot twists are short on subtlety and the all-important diversionary scapegoat – a stud-muffin tennis pro – slots in rather too neatly. But because the characters are so well drawn – and well played – it never appears as anything less than a ruthlessly efficient nerve-shredder that binds you in an ecstasy of suspense until the very last frame. We don't notice we're siding irrationally with Teddy throughout the nail-biting courtroom scenes and the simmering show-downs with Krasny, because not only is Coyote such a convincingly arrogant shitheel ('He had a charge sheet as long as my dick,' he sneers at Close when she confronts him over Stiles) but Bridges is the perfect counterweight – tortured, enigmatic, charming. And always, always plausible.

The fulcrum, though, is Close, who manages to convince us that she is far too intelligent and savvy to ever embark on a major case simply to crush her former mentor, or to fall for a manipulative, cold-blooded killer just because he rides horses and has great hair.

Even so, she is plagued by doubt no matter how deep her relationship with Forrester runs, and this leads to some of the most effective moments in the film. The scene where she tentatively taps out a message on the ancient typewriter which – literally – holds the key to Forrester's guilt or innocence is a moment of brilliantly sustained agony.

Although it sports the trappings of a modern adult thriller – sex, violence, cuss words et al – *Jagged Edge* (the title, incidentally, refers to the murder weapon: a jag-bladed hunting knife) has a curious, and curiously effective, old-fashioned feel. The clearest indication that the film bowls along with its head in the 80s but its heart in the 40s is Robert Loggia as private investigator Sam Ransom. Sporting trench coat and snap-brim hat, Loggia growls foul-mouthed street smarts out of the corner of his mouth and maintains a healthy cynicism over Teddy's involvement with Forrester. Yet the affection between the two is one of the most memorable aspects of the film. 'Did your mother ever wash your mouth out with soap and water?' she asks, a prim eyebrow raised at a particularly colourful outburst. 'Yeah,' he drawls. 'But it didn't do any fuckin' good.' Loggia received a Best Supporting Actor Oscar nomination.

Jagged Edge also alerted audiences to Bridges. Having languished for decades near the top of the Tinseltown second division he finally proved that he not only possessed leading man charisma but that he was also an enormously talented actor. No further evidence is required than the sequence where, at Close's bidding, he returns to the beach house where his wife was killed to retrace the steps he took on the night he discovered the body. His sobbing, hysterical breakdown when he reaches her bedroom is utterly, chillingly convincing. Later we realise just how chilling this episode is – is he really a distraught husband reliving a nightmare, or a calculating killer revisiting the scene of his own grisly crime? At this point, Teddy thinks she knows. And so do we. ★★★★ **SB**

JAMES AND THE GIANT PEACH (1996)

Starring: *Paul Terry (James), Joanna Lumley (Aunt Spiker), Miriam Margolyes (Aunt Sponge/The Glowworm), Peter Postlethwaite (Old Man), the voices of: Simon Callow (Grasshopper), Richard Dreyfuss (Centipede), Jane Leeves (Ladybug), Susan Sarandon (Spider), David Thewlis (Earthworm)*
Director: *Henry Selick*
Screenwriters: *Steven Bloom, Jonathan Roberts, Karey Kirkpatrick, based on the book by Roald Dahl*
U/85 mins./Family/Adventure/USA

A boy, brought up in poverty by two cruel aunts, is given some mysterious beans that help him grow a giant peach that will change his life forever.

On paper it looks like the perfect warped marriage – Roald Dahl's darkly funny story of an orphaned boy escaping the random cruelties of his wicked aunts neatly teamed with the cartoon-Gothic visual imagination of team Burton (executive producer Tim Burton, director Selick) and FX designer Pete Kozachik – collaborators on the triumphantly subversive *The Nightmare Before Christmas*.

For those impoverished enough to be unfamiliar with one of the finest children's stories ever penned, James is a happy kid with two perfect parents, a perfect life and the promise of an upcoming trip to New York. Until, in a brilliantly capricious spanner-in-the-works moment, his folks are unexpectedly devoured by a giant rhinoceros and he's shipped off to live with his two pantomimic evil aunts – in this case the gruesomely toothsome duo of Miriam Margolyes and Joanna Lumley – who discharge their new-found parental duties by working the grieving lad almost to death, feeding him rotting fish heads and generally mucking about. All until, via some magical malarkey courtesy of Pete Postlethwaite, a mysterious giant peach puts in an appearance. James crawls inside, is accosted by a bevy of eccentric insects, and embarks on an airborne adventure as the big peach wings its way by seagull power towards the Big Apple.

Seamlessly blending live action, stop-motion animation and state-of-the-art digital jiggery-pokery, Selick delivers a visually splendid movie, with the opening live action sequence's stylised storybook sets almost rivalling *The Wizard Of Oz*. Animation's post-*Toy Story* hipness has attracted an eclectic range of vocal talents, with Callow's aristocratic grasshopper bagging all the best lines, Susan Sarandon as a Garboesque spider, and David Thewlis putting his Manc nasality to good use as the misery-prone earthworm.

With only a couple of Randy Newman's musical numbers diving tragically across the schmaltz barrier and an irritating reference to the insect characters as 'bugs' to sour the experience, James delivers enough gasps of pleasure and shrieks of terror. Just, as they say, peachy. ★★★★ **AS**

JAMÓN JAMÓN (1992)

Starring: *Stefania Sandrelli (Le madre puta), Anna Galiena (La puta madre), Juan Diego (El padre), Penélope Cruz (La hija de puta), Javier Bardem (El chrizo)*
Director: *Bigas Luna*
Screenwriters: *Cuca Canals, Bigas luna, Quim Monzo*
18/95 mins./Comedy/Spain

After his girlfriend Sylvia falls pregnant, José Luis, executive at his parents' underwear factory, promises to marry her. However, as she is merely a lower-class shop-floor worker, his mother hires would-be underwear model and would-be bullfighter Raul to seduce her.

If Pedro Almodóvar is the satirical genius of Spanish cinema, Bigas Luna is his bawdier, sillier cousin. His films, dotty, sexy melodramas dominated by the prowess of Latin manhood, what would have happened if the *Carry On* movies had just gone on with the process of shagging, are silly, guilty pleasures whose European credentials can hide a multitude of titillating fun. They are camp, sexually liberated fables almost designed to show how staid we Brits are, and this one is easily his best.

The title translates as Ham Ham, so you can see where Bigas is coming from so-to-speak. As in the parallels between vast hides of smoked pork, and the carnal offerings of Raul the lug (played with masterful emptiness by Javier Bardem. This is after all a town that proudly manufactures underwear and cures hams. Raul is merely a pawn in the farcical games of Conchita, mother of company princeling José (the pretty-pretty Molla), who is betrothed to Silvia, which really irks mean mama because she is the daughter of the town whore. With us? Actually, there's no need to worry, it's just an excuse for a bubble of sex and manners, proudly bawdy and energetic. Luna is the kind of director who shoots touching love scenes beneath the wavering testicles of a giant bull billboard. Everybody seems to jump into the sack with everyone else. It's that kind of town.

Sardonic and visually alive, Luna is all recklessness but with subtle purpose. Amongst his sprawl of vibrating buttocks and slabs of wobbly ham, he is puncturing the repressive devices of class. Stripped to our underwear everyone is driven by the same impulses. ★★★★ **IN**

JARHEAD (2005)

Starring: *Jake Gyllenhaal (Anthony Swofford), Scott MacDonald (D.I. Fitch), Peter Sarsgaard (Troy), Jamie Foxx (Staff Sgt. Sykes), Lo Ming (Bored Gunny), Lucas Black (Kruger)*
Director: *Sam Mendes*
Screenwriter: *William Broyles Jr., based on the book by Anthony Swofford*
15/123 mins./Drama/War/USA

It's 1990. Twenty-year-old US Marine Anthony Swofford is sent to the Saudi Arabian desert as Saddam has invaded Kuwait and Uncle Sam has promised to do something about it. 'Swoff' is part of the 'elite' STA (Surveillance and Target Acquisition) platoon: one-shot, one-kill sniping experts. He wants to see action. But all he can see is sand . . .

War movies? What are they good for? Absolutely nothing, argues Anthony Swofford in the autobiographical *Jarhead*, his 'Marine's Chronicle Of The Gulf War And Other Battles'. More accurately, Swofford has bad news for any filmmakers green enough to believe they are ever selling an anti-war message. As far as a Marine, a true 'jarhead', is concerned, it's all 'war porn', designed to get the trigger-finger twitching and the dick hard.

Swofford's disturbing recollection of his Vietnam video nights is the basis for one of the most effective scenes in Sam Mendes' movie version. With orders shipping them out to the Gulf expected any minute, gung-ho Marines (including the excellent Jake Gyllenhaal as Swofford) pass the time with a rowdy screening of *Apocalypse Now*, humming along to Wagner and hollering, 'Get some!' as the Hueys hunt down Charlie. The message here is clear – any previous message was lost on these boys long ago.

By rights, then, *Jarhead* the movie can expect record-breaking bookings at army bases worldwide. It's a technical marvel: Mendes, working with new cinematographer and regular Coen brothers' collaborator Roger Deakins, peppers the screen with visuals to stir the loins of any red-blooded male. War has rarely looked so real, or so ravishing. Meanwhile the screenplay, written by Vietnam veteran William Broyles Jr., takes as its sole subject the soldier – and it is a soldier most modern Marines would recognise. The members of Swoff's platoon are not glorified, nor are they ridiculed. *Jarhead* simply illustrates how modern warfare, in all its hi-tech, remote-kill cruelty, has made the skilled soldier mostly redundant. As an exercise in delivering the sense of what it was like to be a Marine, all dressed up and nobody to kill, in the Arabian Desert in 1990-91, it cannot be faulted.

And yet, is that enough? Let's say it again: war movies – what are they good for? A platoon of raw recruits might be expected to bark one answer; an Oscar-winning director, however, should surely believe in the power of his chosen medium. If Mendes does believe that war movies can serve a purpose, his own timely addition to the genre does not demonstrate the necessary ambition. Jarhead clocks in at two hours – can you imagine Oliver Stone making a war movie one third shorter than Peter Jackson's *King Kong*? Then again, can you envisage Oliver Stone wanting to make a movie about the first Gulf War and resisting attempts to read it as an indictment on our current misadventure?

The running time does leave an awful lot of good source material on the table and fans of Swofford's memoir will bemoan many of the cuts. However, extra ammunition would be of little use unless Mendes was ultimately willing to fix upon a target. As memoirist, Swofford is under no obligation to draw his fractured narrative together, but a movie adaptation cannot live on entertaining sequences alone. Us civilians endure the Half Metal Jacket training and all that heel-kicking in the desert in the expectation that it will lead to something; that the epiphanies, violent or otherwise, will follow. They do not.

In his book, Swofford makes it clear that he lusted for action since youth. In the movie he comes across as an enigmatic voyeur whose motivations are rarely made clear, a curious alteration that robs us of any sense of growing disillusionment. Like its hero, Mendes' film remains frustratingly distant, its characters unfocused, its purpose unclear, so that even as the indelible images sear onto your eyeballs and the emotional jabs knock you sideways, the mind is rarely completely engaged. In the end, *Jarhead* is less than the sum of its parts because of its admirable refusal to pick sides. ★★★ **CK**

③ JASON AND THE ARGONAUTS (1963)

Starring: *Todd Armstrong (Jason), Nancy Kovack (Medea), Gary Raymond (Acastus), Laurence Naismith (Argos), Niall MacGinnis (Zeus), Michael Gwynn (Hermes), Douglas Wilmer (Pelias), Honor Blackman (Hera)*
Director: *Don Chaffey*
Screenwriters: *Beverley Cross, Jan Read*
U/104 mins./Fantasy/UK

To regain his rightful place on the throne of Thessaly, Jason must cross perilous seas to the land of Colchis to retrieve the fabled Golden Fleece. Along the way Jason and his crew of legendary heroes must contend with harpies, crashing rocks, a giant bronze colossus, a multi-headed hydra and an army of skeleton warriors.

It may surprise you to find that Ray Harryhausen did not, officially, direct this, the film for which he is most venerated. To be fair, he was in charge of those sequences for which it is best remembered – the staggering stop-motion battles between actors and model creatures resplendently carved from legend. Don Chaffey was in charge of the real-life bit that is big and cheesy and forgettable. It takes a skeleton army, with those stiff jointed moves like an aged drunk at closing time, to lift a B-movie like this into the pantheon.

Indeed, it is easy to see how this has become the ne plus ultra of the Harryhausen canon. This is the point where he perfected the intricate devices of stop-motion, plucking an appropriate quest-story out of Greek myth with its attendant menagerie of beasties. Here is the many-headed hydra who upon losing a head simply grows another. Here is a giant bronze statue named Talos, irritated by an arrogant Hercules (Nigel Green), who storms their ship, the *Argonaut*. And here is the fabled clash with those skeletons. Each amazing for how much personality Harryhausen instils into their model faces furious with intent.

Back in the human half of the movie, the range of British and American hunks all basted to a vaguely Hellenic tan, are suitably gruff if rather stiff. Then, this is not a film watched for its acute study of humanity, nor for its meta-textual meaning, although Honor Blackman has a deal of fun as the goddess Hera playing the Olympian angle as she flowers unsubtle hints on her dumbfounded hero, and there is a sly discussion of the overweening self-regard of fame. In the end, though, it's a straight-up creature-feature, a classic of the breed, that will resist repeat viewing till the Harpies come home. ★★★★ **IN**

③ JASON X (2001)

Starring: *Kane Hodder (Jason Voorhees/Uber-Jason), Lexa Doig (Rowan), Chuck Campbell (Tsunaron), Lisa Ryder (Kay-Em 14), Jonathan Potts (Professor Lowe), Peter Mensah (Sgt. Brodski), Melyssa Ade (Janessa)*
Director: *James Issack*
Screenwriter: *Todd Framer, from characters by Victor Miller*
15/87 mins./Horror/Sci-fi/USA

2455 AD, the cryo-frozen Jason is transported off-world by a scientific/military research team. When Jason expert Rowan revives from her own cryo-sleep, she warns that the human killing machine is liable to get loose . . .

If you do something ten times, you're likely to get it right in the end. Nine years on from the last direct-to-video *Friday The 13th* sequel, the franchise is here revived by a film that manages to be better than the previous nine entries put together.

Set in a post-Armageddon future where belly-revealing tops are still in fashion, *Jason X* cleverly sends up the conventions of both the original stalker cycle and the post-*Aliens*, space-grunts-go-up-against-a-monster movie.

Deprived of his machete for a while, Jason comes up with some inventive new deaths, including real showstoppers like a sink of freezing liquid and a giant drill-bit ('He's screwed!').

The few survivors and many victims – beginning with an apt cameo from David Cronenberg – are comic-book characters, but all have neat bits of business, making this a unique F13 in which you actually cheer the good guys. ★★★★ **KN**

⑤ JAWS (1975)

Starring: *Roy Scheider (Police Chief Martin Brody), Robert Shaw (Quint), Richard Dreyfuss (Matt Hooper), Lorraine Gray (Ellen Brody), Murray Hamilton (Mayor Larry Vaughn), Carl Gottlieb (Ben Meadows)*
Director: *Steven Spielberg*
Screenplay: *Peter Benchley, Carl Gottlieb, Howard Sackler, from the novel by Benchley*
PG/118 mins./Adventure/Thriller/USA

Awards: *Academy Awards – Best Film Editing, Best Original Score, Best Sound, BAFTA – Anthony Asquith Award for music, Golden Globes – Best Score*

The peaceful community of Amity island is being terrorised by a man-eating shark. Sheriff Brody, with friends Hooper and Quint decide to go after the shark and kill it.

'No'. There's a word Steven Spielberg probably hasn't heard in a while. Back in 1974, though, it was a different story. Back in 1974, Steven Spielberg had yet to make *Jaws*. He'd seen the galley proofs of Peter Benchley's bestseller on producer David Brown's desk. 'What's this about?' he remembers thinking, 'a porno dentist?' Not quite. But although the transcript could hardly be described as high art, Spielberg was sold.

Having recently moved to Malibu, where he had taken to staring out to sea for hours at a time, the concept tapped into his psyche. As he himself says, 'I read it and felt that I had been attacked. It terrified me, and I wanted to strike back.' Zanuck and Brown turned him down nonetheless. Only when their first choice, Dick Richards (who had caused concern by continually referring to 'the whale'), wavered did they call Spielberg back.

And although by this stage he had convinced himself the project wasn't for him, legend has it that on arriving at the producers' office to find them wearing the Jaws sweatshirts he'd had commissioned after that first fateful read (to convince them he was the man for the job) he rescinded. 'We shamed him,' Zanuck said, 'into staying on.' Whatever its genesis, *Jaws* was Spielberg's breakthrough. The first summer blockbuster, it was also the first to ever break the $100 million mark (worldwide it exceeded five times that) and single-handedly caused a downturn in the package holiday trade. 'For years he just scared us,' commented his sister Anne after an early screening. 'Now he gets to scare the masses.'

And didn't he just? The head popping out of the boat (reshot from a different angle when preview audiences didn't jump enough), the moment the shark's head comes bursting through the surface, the first attack, by an unseen predator – our primal fears are tweaked incessantly. This last factor, the unseen element, is crucial. For despite a 27-year-old Spielberg publicly asserting that, 'I watch hundreds of old movies but I haven't learned that much from them,' there was undoubtedly one lesson he took on board. And where better to study than the school of Alfred Hitchcock?

'A bomb is under the the table, and it explodes: that is surprise,' the auteur famously observed. 'A bomb is under the table, but it does not explode, that is suspense'.

Spielberg's decision to follow suit, not unleashing his demon for over an hour – although there is the argument that endless technical difficulties with Bruce (the nickname, based on that of his attorney, he gave Robert Mattey's mechanical sharks) one, two and three contributed to the process – pays off handsomely.

Some say, however, that *Jaws* is essentially *Duel 2*. Certainly there are similarities (mirrored by Spielberg employing the same dinosaur sound effect for the deaths of truck then shark), but this later work thrives in the defter touches that pepper its perfect three-act chronology. The famous reverse zoom; Brody looking through the shark book; the confrontation between him and Mrs Kintner; the use of fences on land, in comparison with empty horizons at sea, to convey our protagonists' isolation; the use of the colour yellow (the lilo, the barrels, the torch) and the primary visual stimulus, to suggest impending danger.

If the cast also gels seamlessly, such harmony didn't come without a struggle. Zanuck wanted Charlton Heston as Brody ('What?' shrieked Spielberg. 'Moses? You want Moses? Everybody'll know he'll win!') and Sterling Hayden as Quint. Spielberg's ideal for the role was Lee Marvin, and thought Jon Voight spot-on for Hooper. Benchley meanwhile (who, it has to be said, had been awkward throughout, having seen his three original drafts radically rewritten), frankly, wanted shooting for his egotistical dream troika of Robert Redford, Paul Newman and Steve McQueen.

And if the equally problematic Dreyfuss, who complained constantly that he'd, 'rather watch this movie than shoot it,' took some convincing, it's unthinkable that the final result – including cameos from Spielberg (the voice on Quint's radio) and Benchley (a reporter), as well as sublime turns from Gary and Hamilton in support – could have been any more masterful. Add to that the timeless script, by Howard Sackler, Carl Gottlieb and John Milius (said to be largely responsible for the Indianapolis monologue, though Shaw's input is acknowledged); John Williams' score (even though Spielberg laughed on first hearing it), and the equation is complete.

An equation all the more impressive considering that both bigger budgets and time frames were needed in the wake of a disastrous shoot, nicknamed 'Flaws' by its crew, in Martha's Vineyard.

Zanuck and Brown's suggestion of, 'We'll get a trained one!' hardly helped solve the shark issues, Gottlieb and Spielberg were nearly killed in seafaring accidents and a sinking Orca had expensive consequences, despite the director's reputed order to: 'Fuck the actors! Save the sound department!' Rendering Spielberg's vow on wrapping what arguably remains his finest moment, perhaps not altogether surprising. 'My next picture will be on dry land,' he said solemnly. 'There won't even be a bathroom scene.' ★★★★★ **MD**

Movie Trivia: Jaws

Spielberg himself cameos as the person introducing Ellen Brody on Quint's radio. Brody's dog is in fact played by Spielberg's very own pooch, Elmer. In the summer that *Jaws* came out, ice-cream manufacturers created flavours dubbed Sharkolate, Finnila and Jawberry.

JAWS 2 (1978)

Starring: *Roy Scheider (Police Chief Martin Brody), Lorraine Gary (Ellen Brody), Murray Hamilton (Mayor Larry Vaughn)*
Director: *Jeannot Szwarc*
Screenwriters: *Carl Gottlieb, Howard Sackler*
PG/116 mins./Adventure/Thriller/USA

Four years after ridding the waters of Amity of a Great White, Police Chief Brody is confronted with the possibility of another shark attack. Again he is ignored by the townsfolk, and unbeknownst to him his kids have taken off on a boating trip that will prove Brody terrifyingly right.

While the need for a sequel to *Jaws* is highly debatable, what should have been a gross aberration, making a fast buck all round, turns out a passable B-flick replica of the great white original. Getting Roy Scheider back was a boon, he lends what is ostensibly a perfunctory rerun of Spielberg's moves, the softly-softly build to the confrontation of the big finale, a solid sense of cohering to the same universe as before. His gritty extension of the character allows us to believe in this trashy hokum.

Tagline
Just when you thought it was safe to go back in the water.

Under the risk of stating the gaspingly obvious, Jeannot Szwarc is no Steven Spielberg. He has no feel for pace, no gift for invention, no eye for the subtle details of human interaction. He requires Scheider, with help from fellow returnee Lorraine Gary, to land the drama of Brody's paranoia and eventual firing only, at a terrible cost, to be proven right. Again. Naturally, this requires him to take matters into his own hands, and overcome his swell of phobias to rescue the kids.

Here's where things descend into something cheaply obvious. The teens on a boating trip being molested by a ravenous monster, something more akin to the rise of the slasher movie than the forbidding man versus nature themes of Spielberg's making. It is not an ineffective approach, Szwarc plays the jumps dead on, and by the time Brody and shark face off, the film has mustered enough tension for you to care. And they come up with a terrific method for nailing this latest hunk of cartilaginous menace. Subsequent sequels three and four sunk into the preposterous, the former aided by the gimmickry of 3-D, the latter by Michael Caine. ★★★ **IN**

JAY AND SILENT BOB STRIKE BACK (2001)

Starring: *Jason Mewes (Jay), Kevin Smith (Silent Bob), Ben Affleck (Holden McNeil/Himself), Matt Damon (Will Hunting/Matt Damon), Chris Rock (Chaka), Shannon Elizabeth (Justice the Jewel Thief)*
Director: *Kevin Smith*
Screenwriter: *Kevin Smith*
18/100 mins./Comedy/USA

When New Jersey stoners Jay and Silent Bob discover the internet, they discover not only that a film is being made of their lives, but that reaction to this news has provoked a slew of insults directed at them. So they head for LA to disrupt the making of the movie.

Jay and Silent Bob have been weaving their way through Kevin Smith's slack movie tapestry, from the early inspired days of *Clerks*. In many ways in these films, they were among the funniest things on offer, blending a touching Tom 'n' Huck naivety with language that could peel paint.

The trouble is, Smith seems to have difficulty leaving the herbally-charged duo behind him. This, he says, is an attempt at closure – specifically a whole movie just for them, after which they will presumably retire to the great convenience store in the sky. But, as the internet dweebs presciently ask in the story, can these two support an entire movie?

The answer is ... sometimes. *Strike Back* is an infuriatingly patchy experience, with moments of inspired foulness. Jay's rant in support of the 'Coalition for the Liberation of Itinerant Tree-dwellers' (work it out for yourself) is a highlight, as is Chris Rock's angry, black film director ('They stole *Sesame Street* from me – I was going to call it Niggas With Puppets!').

But the gag hit/miss ratio is really only about 50/50 and the rambling, freewheeling plot is virtually non-existent at points. In the end, it's a kind of stoner Road To ... movie, with considerably more references to bitch-slapping than was usual in the Hope/Crosby franchise.

Regulars from the previous movies pop in and out of the less-than-weighty narrative. Matt Damon and Ben Affleck stand out, seen here on the 'set' of *Good Will Hunting 2*, bitching about their careers ('That'll be your next movie about a gay, golfing serial killer who rides a horse?' Affleck snaps. 'Two words: Reindeer Games,' Damon retorts). But there are also whole expanses of mirthless celluloid, and, even after an extended *Star Wars* skit and a cameo by Mark Hamill (Carrie Fisher pops up earlier on), Smith appears to have absolutely no idea how to end it. ★★★ **OR**

⦾ JEAN DE FLORETTE (1986)

Starring: *Yves Montand (César Soubeyran/La Papel), Gérard Depardieu (Jean de Florette/Cadoret), Daniel Auteuil (Ugolin Souberyan/'Galignette'), Elisabeth Depardieu (Aimee Cadoret)*
Director: *Claude Berri*
Screenwriter: *Pierre Grunstein, based on the novel by Marcel Pagnol*
PG/122 mins./Drama/France
Awards: *BAFTA – Best Film, Best Adapted Screenplay, Best Supporting Actor (Daniel Auteil), Best Cinematography*

When hunchback Jean de Florette arrives in 1920s Provence from the city, peasant farmer César Soubeyran and his simple nephew, Ugolin, deprive his property of water so that they can drive him away and acquire the land for a pittance.

Claude Berri spent six years trying to acquire the rights to Marcel Pagnol's 1962 *Water in the Hills* dualogy. Inspired by Pagnol's own 1952 feature, *Manon des Sources*, the story chronicled the destruction of an educated outsider by avaricious provincials, who meet their match in his free-spirited daughter. Berri raised much of the $18 million budget required for *Jean de Florette* and *Manon des Sources* himself and reaped a handsome profit when the films became box-office smashes around the world.

There were many French critics, however, who denounced his heritage approach and accused Berri of returning to the literate style of filmmaking that had been branded 'cinéma du papa' by François Truffaut and the young guns of the influential journal, *Cahiers du Cinéma*.

There's no question that Bruno Nuytten's Provençal landscapes tend towards the pictorialist. But Berri was always careful to integrate the characters within their environment, to emphasise both Jean's isolation outside the private paradise that eventually betrays him and César and Ugolin's grimy identification with the soil they're prepared to lose their souls to obtain.

Berri and Gérard Brach prided themselves on the fidelity of their adaptation. However, there's little of the realism that Alexander Korda, Marc Allégret and Pagnol himself invested in his magisterial Marseilles trilogy (*Marius*, 1931; *Fanny*, 1932; *César*, 1936). Yet, the cast manage to rise above the rustic chic of Bernard Vazet and Marcel Laude's designs and the emotive cues of Jean-Claude Petit's score, with Gérard Depardieu literally throwing himself into the role of the hunchback reduced to becoming a beast of burden to carry the water on which his idyll depends. But his flamboyant turn gains additional power from the response of his neighbours in Les Bastides Blanches, as Yves Montand and Daniel Auteuil expertly alternate between faux concern and calculated cruelty with a conviction that casts a chill over the sun-parched vistas. ★★★ **DP**

⦾ JEANNE DIELMAN, 23 QUAI DU COMMERCE, 1080 BRUXELLES (1976)

Starring: *Delphine Seyrig (Jeanne Dielman), Jan Decorte (Sylvain Dielman), Chantal Akerman (Neighbour P. Henri Storck, 1st Caller), Jacques Doniol-Valcroze (2nd Caller), Yves Bical (3rd Caller)*
Director: *Chantal Akerman*
Screenwriter: *Chantal Akerman*
Unrated/201 mins./Drama/France/Belgium

Belgian widow Jeanne Dielman devotes her mornings to her meticulous domestic routines and her afternoons to prostitution. However, one day, her schedule slips out of sync and she kills the client who causes her to orgasm.

Chantal Akerman was just 25 when she began making this avant-garde masterpiece. Abandoning her original screenplay, she completed the 200-minute film in just five weeks at a cost of $120,000. She worked with an all-woman crew and later confessed to finding this an unsatisfying experience, although cinematographer Babette Mangolte became a regular collaborator and her unobtrusive observational style gives the audacious imagery its power and compulsion.

The storyline of this disquieting study of alienated monotony, suppressed emotion and social marginalisation is deceptively simple. Widow Jeanne Dielman devotes her mornings to running errands and performing chores around her meticulously maintained Brussels home. The camera maintains a discreet distance as it records her activities with unblinking fascination and refuses to pry as she services her daily gentleman caller. However, it resumes its vigil as she bathes and prepares the evening meal for her teenage son, Sylvain.

But, her routine doesn't run quite as smoothly on the second day and by the third, editor Patricia Canino has begun to shorten the sequences to convey Jeanne's growing distraction as she wakes too early, finds shops closed and her coffee stale, and fails to stop her neighbour's baby from crying. However, none of this prepares us for the shocking conclusion, in which Jeanne stabs her client with a pair of scissors to punish him for bringing her to orgasm.

The film contains little dialogue and no narratorial justification. Yet, the sounds of domesticity provide an ominous soundtrack to Delphine Seyrig's supremely judged depiction of ordered ennui and eroding detachment, in which her manner of inhabiting space matters more than her conduct of activity (e.g. her seeming decapitation as she answers the door and her laceration by shafts of light as she rides in the lift).

Dedicated to Akerman's mother and designed to secure respect for the housewife's vocation, this is a mesmerising piece of rhythmical filmmaking that's as courageously experimental as anything produced in the history of the avant garde. ★★★★ **DP**

⦾ JEEPERS CREEPERS (2001)

Starring: *Gina Philips (Trisha Jenner), Justin Long (Darius Jenner), Jonathan Breck (The Creeper/Bald Cop), Patricia Belcher (Jezeller Gay Hartman), Eileen Brennan (The Cat Lady), Brandon Smith (Sgt. David Tubbs)*
Director: *Victor Salva*
Screenwriter: *Victor Salva*
15/86 mins./Horror/USA

Whilst driving through rural America on their way home from college, siblings Darius and Trisha spot suspicious goings-on from the driver of a old van. They investigate but wind up in mortal danger.

While driving through a rural American nowhere en route home for the vacation, college student siblings Darius and Trisha happen to glimpse the driver of a filthy old van dumping person-shaped, red-stained, white bundles into a hole.

After some credible arguments, they investigate, but wind up on the death-list of a killer who turns out to be a lot more monstrous than he at first seems. Check the clues: a licence plate that promises cannibalism (BEAT1NGU), his scarecrow wardrobe and his nasty need to take a little something from one of the kids.

Victor Salva's solidly creepy, 70s-style horror film has decent characterisations and a gloomy atmosphere that cuts deeper than most teens-in-terror flicks. ★★★★ **MD**

⦾ THE JERK (1979)

Starring: *Steve Martin (Navin Johnson), Bernadette Peters (Marie Kimble Johnson), Catlin Adams (Patty Bernstein), Mabel King (Mother), Richard Ward (Father)*
Director: *Carl Reiner*
Screenwriters: *Steve Martin, Carl Gottlieb, Michael Elias*
15/89 mins./Comedy/USA

Navin Johnson, raised as a 'poor black child' by his adoptive family, is eager to make his way in the world – which he does through the unlikeliest of circumstances.

Born the son of poor black sharecroppers, Navin Johnson sets off to seek his fortune in the big wide world. Initially he doesn't get further than the end of the fence, but eventually he finds employment at a gas station, becomes the target for a crazed psycho-killer (the splendid M. Emmet Walsh), finds out about his 'special purpose' from a female circus daredevil motorbike rider, realises true love with Bernadette Peters, and finds fame and fortune through his brilliant invention, the Optigrab.

Tagline
A rags to riches to rags story.

Loud and ludicrous, The Jerk is a strong contender for the funniest film of all time. Steve Martin gives a star-making physical comedy performance as the naive hero and purists justifiably wish there were a lot more 'Navin' and a lot less smoothed-out Martin in his later film performances. ★★★★★ **CW**

JERRY MAGUIRE (1996)

Starring: *Tom Cruise (Jerry Maguire), Cuba Gooding Jr. (Rod Tidwell), Renee Zellweger (Dorothy Boyd), Kelly Preston (Avery Bishop), Jerry O'Connell (Frank Cushman)*
Director: *Cameron Crowe*
Screenwriter: *Cameron Crowe*
15/133 mins./Comedy/Drama/Romance/Sport/USA

Awards: *Academy Awards – Best Supporting Actor, Empire Awards – Cameron Crowe, Golden Globes – Best Musical/Comedy Actor*

A high-profile sports agent loses his job after writing a manifesto about how work should have a more human approach. All that's left for him is one client – a second-rate footballer – and the secretary who agreed to leave the company with him.

If you don't walk out of Jerry Maguire with a goofy grin the size of Alaska plastered across your face, check your pulse – you're probably dead. Director Cameron Crowe has written and directed a deft, funny, shamelessly upbeat romantic comedy.

Jerry is a sports agent on the brink of breakdown. He's rich, successful, and has a sex life that would serve as a dictionary definition of 'rampant'. Yet he's not happy. He looks around and sees a business plunging towards cynicism; a world where a kid can't ask a sports star to do so much as sign a baseball card without endorsement deals and counter-deals hurtling to the fore. So, in one long lonely night of the soul, he hammers out a 'mission statement' demanding a more human approach, delivers it to his colleagues and is summarily given the order of the boot.

With only one desultory client left, Rod Tidwell (played with screwballish energy by Gooding Jnr.), a second-rate footballer with a surfeit of energy off the field but precious little on it, Maguire decides to go it alone, failing to persuade any of his colleagues to accompany him apart from lovestruck single parent from accounts Dorothy Boyd (the excellent Zellweger). Things don't run smoothly (natch) for the isolated couple: Maguire is screwed by both ex-colleagues and clients, and although he is attracted enough to his partner and her sprog to smooch, shag and finally wed, the marriage is in trouble within weeks with the outside world's cynicism and Jerry's escalating emotional crisis leaching in and poisoning the familial nest.

That this doesn't degenerate into an experience akin to being hit full in the face by the Tate & Lyle express is a testament both to Crowe's (director of *Say Anything* and *Singles*) script and direction plus a new maturity and confidence in Cruise's performance. Crowe takes a desiccated and predictable genre and invests it with a delightfully off-beam sensibility. Scenes never go quite as you expect. Take the opening montage in which a boxer-shorted Cruise narrates his plunge into pathological pessimism while simultaneously undercutting the schmaltz by admitting that this is all a bit 'touchy-feely'.

And then there's Cruise himself. Not satisfied to deliver the kind of by-the-numbers winsome romantic lead that a few years ago he'd probably have been satisfied with, here he fleshes Jerry's struggle with a developing disgust for the world to the point where it's finally possible to forget that this was the man who made *Cocktail* and *Days Of Thunder*.

Added to the soufflé are sterling supporting performances from Bonnie Hunt as Dorothy's concerned, cynical sister, plus a tousle-haired kid who'll have anyone leaning towards broodiness, repapering the box-room and spending a fortune down Mothercare. In the end *Jerry Maguire* is that rare beast: a movie that reminds you why you like movies in the first place. Be nice to yourself. Go see. ★★★★★ **AS**

JERSEY GIRL (2004)

Starring: *Ben Affleck (Ollie Trinke), Jennifer Lopez (Gertrude Steiney), George Carlin (Bart Trinke), Liv Tyler (Maya), Rachel Castro (Gertie)*
Director: *Kevin Smith*
Screenwriter: *Kevin Smith*
12A/102 mins./Comedy/Drama/USA

Ollie, a Manhattan workaholic publicist at the top of his game, marries the love of his life. But when she dies in childbirth Ollie finds himself a single father unable to cope with a job and a child.

Poor old Kevin Smith. Through no fault of his own, this film was saddled with anti-hype as Gigli 2, thanks to the presence of the now defunct Bennifer brand. It's entirely unwarranted, as although *Jersey Girl* rarely rises above gentle entertainment, it never deserves the venomous scorn that greeted that particular stinker.

Lopez is dispatched early on after a likeable cameo, leaving Affleck with a considerably younger leading lady. Castro, a convincing little J.Lette, keeps her confidence the right side of precocious and sparks convincing chemistry with Affleck, who tempers Ollie's arrogance with a dash of humility.

As a director, Smith is at times slightly overreaching in the dramatic stakes, almost abandoning comedy and grasping a little too enthusiastically at the heartstrings, which in turn leaves the more ribald gags hanging in midair. A frank speech about masturbation by love interest Maya might have been a hoot in *Chasing Amy* or *Clerks*, but feels misplaced here.

But full credit to the man for extending himself with more adult material, and to Affleck too for puncturing his own cocksure persona. In a clutch of affecting emotional moments there's a hint that Silent Bob may have a stronger voice than expected. ★★★ **OR**

JESUS CHRIST SUPERSTAR (1973)

Starring: *Ted Neeley (Jesus Christ), Carl Anderson (Judas Iscariot), Yvonne Elliman (Mary Magdalene), Barry Dennen (Pontius Pilate), Josh Mostel (King Herod), Paul Thomas (Peter), Pi Douglas (Apostle), Richard Orbach (John)*
Director: *Norman Jewison*
Screenwriters: *Norman Jewison, Melvyn Bragg, based on the book of the musical play by Tim Rice*
PG/108 mins./Musical/USA

Convinced that Jesus Christ is straying off message, Judas Iscariot betrays him to the Jewish authorities and he's crucified on the orders of the Roman governor, Pontius Pilate.

It always seems odd to see the name of Melvyn Bragg among the credits for this adaptation of Tim Rice and Andrew Lloyd Webber's rock musical. Why would the champion of artistic excellence have agreed to co-script this trivialised opening out of an enduring stage classic?

It's easy to see why director and co-scenarist Norman Jewison would have jumped at the chance to shoot the picture in the Holy Land. But, while Douglas Slocombe's photography is undeniably handsome, Jewison makes too little use of such significant locations. There's no sense of a place being revisited by momentous events and, consequently, the performances are diminished by their disconnection from the setting. Ironically, David Greene would exploit the New York landscape much more effectively in his grimly vibrant take on John-Michael Tebelak and Stephen Schwartz's hippy opera *Godspell*, which was released in the same year.

Accusations of anti-Semitism greeted the film's depiction of the Jews as the instigators of Christ's Passion. But there was even more wailing and gnashing of teeth over the casting of a black Judas. Yet, Carl Anderson gives easily the picture's strongest performance and rather than playing Iscariot as an opportunist traitor, he essays a devoted fan, who sees the potential dangers of celebrity and laments the fact that Jesus is beginning to believe his own press.

The greater problem lies with Ted Neely, who is woefully miscast in the title role that was originated on stage by Deep Purple's Ian Gillain. He certainly makes a gentle Jesus, particularly alongside Yvonne Elliman's Mary Magdalene. But his falsetto lacks the power to convey the righteous indignation needed for the Temple sequence and the lonely agony of Gethsemane.

Curiously, the soundtrack album stands up quite well. But the film looks very much an artefact of its time and it's difficult to see how it grossed $20 million on the back of largely lukewarm reviews. ★★ **DP**

THE JEWEL OF THE NILE (1985)

Starring: *Michael Douglas (Jack Colton), Kathleen Turner (Joan Wilder), Danny DeVito (Ralph), Spiros Focas (Omar), Avner Eisenberg (Jewel)*
Director: *Lewis Teague*
Screenwriters: *Mark Rosenthal, Lawrence Konner*
PG/106 mins./Adventure/USA

Jack Colton and Joan Wilder are getting bored with the easy life, drifting around the oceans on their yacht. Things soon rev up when Joan is invited to Egypt to write a local dictator's biography, where she is abducted, amid stories of another fabled jewel. Jack is soon in hot pursuit along with Ralph their irksome foe of before.

An energetic but uninspired sequel to *Romancing The Stone*, itself a sexy reworking of the *Indiana Jones* formula. Minus Robert Zemeckis' confident directorial hand, the adventures of adrenaline-junkie couple Jack and Joan comes across lightheaded and silly. Part of the problem lies in the fact Michael Douglas and Kathleen Turner are already a couple at the start of the movie thus removing the exciting if inevitable movie-trait of the lead pair becoming involved. You can see how hard the new screenwriters and makeweight director Lewis Teague are trying to reconcoct the former – splitting up the pair for much of the film, spinning the grab-the-ruby designs of the original on their head to have the 'jewel' of the title be a local mystic – but it seems to fall flat, and ends up with gags about DeVito riding a camel.

The action again manages to fuse both slapstick and peril to reasonable effect (especially a high-speed reworking of that old train routine) with Douglas, Turner and DeVito proving, again, a likeable set of movie stars. But this wildly careering adventure feels forced where Zemeckis' romp felt sweaty and real, its handle on the Middle Eastern people trite and foolish, where the *Stone*'s South American jungle felt strange and threatening. You can even boil it down to the theme song, Eddie Grant gave the first movie a revved up reggae rip-snorter, whereas here Ocean just delivers an insipid closer. It's pleasantly watchable as many weak movies can be, but the lack of a third adventure speaks volumes of an exhausted idea. ★★ **IN**

JEZEBEL (1938)

Starring: *Bette Davis (Julie Morrison), Henry Fonda (Preston Dillard), George Brent (Buck Cantrell), Margaret Lindsay (Amy Bradford Dillard), Fay Bainter (Aunt Belle Massey), Richard Cromwell (Ted Dillard)*
Director: *William Wyler*
Screenwriters: *Clements Ripley, Albert Finkel, John Huston, Robert Buckner based on the play by Owen Davis, Sr.*
U/104 mins./Drama/USA
Awards: *Academy Awards – Best Actress, Best Supporting Actress (Fay Bainter), Venice – Special Recommendation (William Wyler)*

New Orleans, 1852, and Preston Dillard breaks his engagement with Julie Morrison after she wears a red dress to a society ball. When he returns, three years later, he is married to Amy and Julie persuades Buck Cantrell to fight a duel for her honour.

Owen Davis's 1933 play closed after just 32 performances on Broadway. Yet, it became a pet project for Bette Davis after Jack Warner relinquished the rights to *Gone With the Wind* (1939) and David O. Selznick refused the casting of Davis and Errol Flynn. Consequently, she and Warner became determined to get their study of Southern chivalry, social propriety and noble sacrifice into cinemas before Selznick's much-vaunted adaptation of Margaret Mitchell's epic.

Davis was less than amused by the hiring of William Wyler from Goldwyn, as his insistence on repeated retakes didn't suit her diva approach to perfectionism. However, she soon fell in love with him and accepted his criticisms about the modulation of her performance, with the dual consequence that she not only gained a greater appreciation of screen craft, but she also won her second and last Best Actress award (although she would be nominated a further eight times).

Wyler's relationship with Henry Fonda was less straightforward, however. In addition to reckoning him miscast in the role of the social snob who is unable to handle a firebrand of Davis's calibre, Wyler resented the fact that Fonda had married his ex-wife, Margaret Sullavan (with whom he had considered making *Jezebel* in 1934). However, rumours of an on-set feud were exaggerated, as Fonda was merely irked by Wyler's sedate progress, as he had to be in New York before the picture wrapped for the birth of his first child, Jane.

The excellent Davis and Fay Bainter's Oscar-winning turns give the picture spirit. But its class comes from Ernest Haller's gliding camerawork, Richard Haas's evocative décor, Orry-Kelly's opulent costumes and Max Steiner's typically plush waltz score. However, Wyler failed to rectify the script's climactic improbabilities, even after John Huston was drafted in to humanise the melodramatics involved in Julie's insistence on nursing Preston through an outbreak of deadly yellow jack. ★★★★ **DP**

JFK (1991)

Starring: *Kevin Costner (Jim Garrison), Sissy Spacek (Liz Garrison), Joe Pesci (David Ferrie), Tommy Lee Jones (Clay Shaw), Gary Oldman (Lee Harvey Oswald)*
Director: *Oliver Stone*
Screenwriters: *Oliver Stone, Zachary Sklar, from the books* On The Trail Of The Assassins *by Jim Garrison and* The Plot That Killed Kennedy *by Jim Marrs*
15/189 mins./History/Drama/USA
Awards: *Academy Awards – Best Cinematography, Best Editing, BAFTA – Best Editing, Best Sound, Empire – Movie Masterpiece Awards, Golden Globes – Best Director*

New Orleans DA, Jim Garrison, discovers that the facts of the JFK assassination case just don't seem to add up . . .

Many Americans believe that truth about the assassination of John F. Kennedy has never been revealed. Former New Orleans District Attorney, Jim Garrison, one of the most extreme debunkers of the Warren

Commission's conclusion that Lee Harvey Oswald acted alone, spun his own theory which involved the CIA, anti-Castro Cubans, Lyndon Banes Johnson, and New Orleans businessman Clay Shaw – who was acquitted after Garrison brought him to trial.

JFK, Stone's film, based on books by Garrison and Jim Marrs, is dense with exposition. For three hours, Costner as Garrison spews out facts and pseudo-facts at a prodigious rate against a frantic visual mix of newsreel footage, recreated events, flashbacks and fiction, as he tries to prove that the United States government is engaged in a massive cover-up. Only the most attentive viewer will be able to keep it all straight. As history the film is bogus; as entertainment, it is intermittently riveting, thanks to generally excellent performances and Stone's visceral directorial energy, although interest flags during Costner's long courtroom summation.

Whatever one believes about the assassination, Garrison's continued good health is the best argument against his particular theory. If the conspiracy was, as the movie claims, so widespread that even minor participants met mysterious ends, why was he allowed to continue his investigation?

Stone, who co-wrote the film with Zachary Sklar, Garrison's editor, never answers this; his alleged purpose is merely to prod people into questioning the official position on the issue. However, Stone presents his version as the absolute truth – complete with recitations that read as fact – and Garrison as a maligned hero. Still, if conspiracy theories are your cup of tea – or if you just like a good yarn – *JFK* will satisfy and entertain. ★★★★★ **TS**

⦿ JIMMY HOLLYWOOD (1994)

Starring: *Joe Pesci (Jimmy Alto), Christian Slater (William), Victoria Abril (Lorraine de la Pena), Jason Beghe (Detective), John Cothran Jr. (Detective)*
Director: *Barry Levinson*
Screenwriter: *Barry Levinson*
15/104 mins./Crime/Comedy/Drama/USA

Jimmy Alto, an actor wannabe, becomes a vigilante crime-fighter, aided by his sidekick William. Jimmy's vigilante alter ego soon becomes a media wonder – but Jimmy remains a total unknown and his long-suffering girlfriend Lorraine is getting fed up with the whole situation.

Hollywood lore decrees any director (Levinson, for instance) who follows an expensive also-ran (think *Bugsy*) with a high-profile flop (say, *Toys*) and a personal picture that can only scrape a direct-to-video release outside America (e.g. *Jimmy Hollywood*) had better latch onto a sure-fire hit for his next film (namely *Disclosure*). Just as Levinson's stock is about to rise from the inevitable smash of the *Disclosure* money machine, this MIA effort creeps out to please the completists and mildly irritate anyone else who happens to rent it.

This is the sort of subject that ought to be a low-budget picture with an unknown cast and a street-level attitude. As made by an out-of-form A-list director and recognisable actors, it's too hectoring and obvious to get away with it. Pesci, with a mop that goes beyond even his *JFK* rug, is hustler Jimmy Alto who has come to Hollywood to make it as an actor. He's drawing sackloads of rejections and hanging around with confused street kid William when the theft of his car radio sends him on a vigilante spree. Suddenly, as videos of his anti-crime announcements get airplay, he becomes the celebrity he has always wanted to be, albeit in the invented character of 'Jericho'.

The American obsession with celebrity and crime is starting to feel like old-hat and Jimmy Hollywood had the misfortune to arrive in the same season as a batch of much hipper movies (*Natural Born Killers* and *S.F.W.* included) with the same idea. Pesci rants to his usual standard, though Levinson makes him beg for sympathy in a way Scorsese would scorn, while Slater underplays bewilderingly in the stooge role.

In the end, this fails because it's hard to think of anyone as a loser if his girlfriend is played by Victoria Abril, just as it's hard to be moved by the pathetic whinings of a nobody who keeps promising to thank people in his Oscar acceptance speech when said nobody is played by an actual Academy Award winner. ★★ **KN**

⦿ JIMMY NEUTRON: BOY GENIUS (2001)

Starring: *the voices of: Debi Derryberry (Jimmy Neutron), Patrick Stewart (King Goobot), Martin Short (Ooblar), Andrea Martin (Miss Fowl)*
Director: *John A. Davis*
Screenwriters: *John A. Davis, Steve Oedekerk, David N. Weisss, J. David Stern*
U/79 mins./Family/Adventure/Animation/USA

Jimmy Neutron is a child inventor whose communication device causes evil aliens to abduct all the parents in town. The local children must unite under Jimmy's command and soar into space to save them.

It may not be *Monsters, Inc.*, but this animated, Oscar-nominated comedy still manages to bridge the gap between kids' and adults' viewing to pleasing effect.

Well-observed characters – from kind-hearted parents to cartoon-obsessed kids – form the basis of the humour, and a high joke frequency holds the attention where the plot fails to do so.

Strong animation and nifty visual ideas also compensate for the rather basic set-up (the story and screenplay are co-written by *Ace Ventura 2* director, Steve Oedekerk), while the children's conversion of fairground rides into space ships is particularly enjoyable. Fun. ★★★ **ASm**

⦿ JOE VERSUS THE VOLCANO (1990)

Starring: *Tom Hanks (Joe Banks), Meg Ryan (DeDe/Angelica Graynamore/Patricia Graynamore), Lloyd Bridges (Samuel Harvey Graynamore), Robert Stack (Doctor Ellison), Dan Hedaya (Mr. Frank Waturi)*
Director: *John Patrick Stanley*
Screenwriter: *John Patrick Stanley*
PG/102 mins./Comedy/USA

Diagnosed with a terminal illness, Joe Banks accepts the strange offer of the chance to live like a king on the island of Waponi Woo before casting himself into the volcano as a sacrifice to appease the gods. On the way to the island a series of encounters start to hint that life, whatever there is of it, maybe worth living.

An overcooked romcom from the writer of *Moonstruck*, that marks the first pairing of Tom Hanks and Meg Ryan, but whose semi-surreal plot is more like Terry Gilliam for wimps. Joe is stuck in a dead-end job, going nowhere, he's dead long before the doctor diagnoses him with a fatal 'brain cloud'. Imagine Kafka's K as played by the loveable everybodying of Tom Hanks, it's not a good fit. His offer to live-it-up before casting himself magma-wards is a shaky premise to serve him signifying this movie's inability to find an even tone for itself. Fable, black comedy, pastiche, screwball, doe-eyed romcom, it touches base with them all, jerking about, unsettled and rhythm-less.

Certainly, Tom Hanks is easy to like, that's seared into his genes, but having Meg

Tagline
A story of love, lava and burning desire.

Ryan traverse three idiosyncratic roles, only one particularly kooky, is a failed gimmick. She's another emblem of the films failings – it is bursting with ideas and enthusiasm, but few of them are good and it is indifferently put together. Things that suggest they might be funny, just aren't: Dan Hedaya as Joe's boss who manages to be both a sleazebag and uptight; the goofy islanders, into orangeade; the jibs and jabs of Homeric fable to lend it an aura of mystery.

Essentially the problem is cowardice. While director John Patrick Stanley breaks the mould for romcoms, any comedy ostensibly taking death as its subject must be bold enough to stand up and admit it. Joe and his dance with the volcano should be black not yellow. ★★ **IN**

JOHNNY ENGLISH (2003)

Starring: *Rowan Atkinson (Johnny English), Natalie Imbruglia (Lorna Campbell), Ben Miller (Bough), John Malkovich (Pascal Sauvage)*
Director: *Peter Howitt*
Screenwriters: *Neal Purvis, Robert Wade, William Davies*
PG/88 mins./Comedy/Adventure/UK

Bumbling secret agent Johnny English foils a plot to steal the Crown Jewels cooked up by dastardly French businessman Pascal Sauvage, who wants to be King Of England.

It sounds like a recipe for disaster – a British spy spoof that goes straight for the lowest common denominator. Surely the *Austin Powers* films do that kind of thing better?

Well, the good news is that Johnny English, while hardly groundbreaking stuff, is at least as entertaining as anything Mike Myers' time-travelling crimefighter has done recently, reminding us just how talented Rowan Atkinson really is.

There's little here that you'll not have seen before: a convoluted plot, over-exaggerated French accents (mainly from a wonderfully hammy Malkovich), Imbruglia providing pretty set-dressing, and an array of pratfalls, sight gags and bodily fluid jokes.

But the set-pieces are mostly genuinely funny (an impressive car chase sequence is a particular gut-buster). The whole thing zips along at a fair old pace, it doesn't outstay its welcome and cleverly avoids any unpleasant xenophobia by poking as much fun at the British as it does the French. ★★★ **OR**

JOHNNY GUITAR (1954)

Starring: *Joan Crawford (Vienna), Sterling Hayden (Johnny 'Guitar' Logan), Mercedes McCambridge (Emma Small), Scott Brady (Dancin' Kid), Ward Bond (John McIvers), Ben Cooper (Turkey Ralston), Ernest Borgnine (Bart Lonergan)*
Director: *Nicholas Ray*
Screenwriter: *Phillip Yordan based on the novel by Ray Chanslor*
15/110 mins./Western/USA

Vienna runs a saloon outside a town run by the spiteful Emma and summons gunslinger Johnny Logan, who poses as pacifist 'Johnny Guitar', for protection as Emma and her allies work up a feud with outlaw the Dancin' Kid which will overflow into a full-scale shooting war.

A truly demented Western, with vividly colourful settings and an almost operatic intensity of emotional and physical violence.

The saloon where much of the action takes place is hewn out of a mountanside and boasts an interior wall of jagged red rock, which – along with several clouds of red dust – gives the whole proceeding an infernal tinge, while characters are symbolically clad in devil-black or angel-white.

Many of the genre's rules are broken: big confrontation scenes take place indoors and are framed like stage tableaux, the suggestively named and fetishistically outfitted cowboys Johnny Guitar and the Dancin' Kid are the sex symbols (though both Hayden and Brady are well into battered middle age), and strong-willed women (Crawford, McCambridge, both unique creatures with their gargoyle-like snarls and Expressionist body language) take leading roles as the antagonists who square off in gunfights, lead or face down lynch mobs and are driven to slaughter by their lusts.

Deliberately artificial-looking and heavy on high-flown dialogue, this has a certain subversive aspect for the 1950s as leftist director Nicholas Ray casts Ward Bond, a real-life McCarthyite, as the bigoted head of the lynch mob (as an inside joke, Bond got a lot of similar roles while the blacklist was in force), but it is most cherishable for its wonderfully overwrought performances (note John Carradine as the broom-pusher who finally gets noticed in his death scene, Royal Dano as a consumptive outlaw and Ernest Borgnine as one of his patented cowboy brutes) and bizarre musical stretches. ★★★★★ **KN**

JOHNNY MNEMONIC (1995)

Starring: *Keanu Reeves (Johnny Mnemonic), Dina Meyer (Jane), Ice-T (J-Bone), Takeshi Kitano (Takahshi), Dennis Akiyama (Shinji), Dolph Lungren (Street Preacher), Henry Rollins (Spider)*
Director: *Robert Longo*
Screenwriter: *William Gibson, based on his short story*
15/92 mins./Sci-fi/Action/USA

A 21st Century messenger finds himself in trouble, thanks to the top secret information he carries in a chip in his brain.

The future sucks. At least that's the case with this, the first of visionary cyberpunk author William Gibson's stories (a short taken from the Burning Chrome collection) to get the celluloid treatment.

An Armani-clad Reeves is Johnny, a man with space in his head to rent (this actor does himself no favours!), and so the perfect vessel for the transportation of illegal data. Having downloaded key memory space, Johnny wants his childhood back, and to get it he's going to have to make one more run. But the material he is currently transporting is hot stuff. The Yakuza are after it, the mysterious, and seriously demented Street Preacher is after it, and if they don't chop it off first, Johnny's head is about to seriously crash, forever. Now, if only he could remember where he put that download access code ...

All the elements of Gibson's work are here: the lateral, tunnel-like visions of a virtual reality – although, these computer effects look timid and outdated compared to the whizz thrills the likes of Cameron and Spielberg are currently wielding – the dark corporation-ruled world of the future, more hackers than you can throw a plate of chips at, even the techno-wired, ultra-genius dolphin puts in an appearance (as does everyone from Udo Kier to Ice-T to Henry Rollins).

What's missing is any sense of this movie being directed. Video artist Robert Longo may show some affinity for the material's technology, but he can't hold an action sequence together to save his life. The film plods along with no sense of pace, character or importance of event, and is utterly devoid of suspense. Reeves cut an impassioned hunk in *Speed*, here he's back to the arch-woodenness which has constantly beset his career, and it is only the overacting Lundgren who makes any impression. Gibson's future-world may be a cold one, but it should never be seen as a dull one. ★ **BM**

⊕ THE JOLSON STORY (1946)

Starring: *Larry Parks (Al Jolson), Evelyn Keyes (Julie Benson), William Demarest (Steve Martin), Bill Goodwin (Tom Baron), Ludwig Donath (Cantor Yoelson)*
Director: *Alfred E. Green*
Screenwriter: *Stephen Longstreet, Harry Chandlee, Andrew Solt*
U/128 mins./Musical/USA
Awards: *Academy Awards – Best Score (Musical), Best Sound Recording*

Defying his cantor father, Asa Yoelson enters showbusiness and becomes 'The World's Greatest Entertainer'. But, for all his success, Al Jolson's marriage to dancer Julie Benson is soon on the rocks.

Stephen Longstreet's screenplay for this landmark biopic owes more to *The Jazz Singer* than Al Jolson's real life. But this was never meant to be a warts'n'all portrait and Jolson's legendary egotism is airbrushed out to be replaced by an infectious geniality that made Julie Benson's decision to break up with him all the more agonising.

Yet, she is a construct character whose invention was necessitated by musical star Ruby Keeler's refusal to co-operate with a project that made such a mockery of her unhappy marriage. William Demarest's loyal sidekick, Steve Martin, is also a fiction, as was Tamara Shayne's mother (as the real Mrs Yoelson has died when Asa was a boy). However, their presence masks the absence of Jolson's other two wives and his adopted children.

Columbia boss and longtime fan, Harry Cohn splashed out on this impressive production, which packs in Jolson's greatest hits amongst the inaccuracies and untruths. The 60-year-old singer himself was desperate to take the title role and James Cagney was considered, in light of his Oscar-winning turn as vaudeville contemporary George M. Cohan in *Yankee Doodle Dandy* (1941). But producer Sidney Skolsky cast the little-known Larry Parks instead, although he wisely requested Jolson's assistance in capturing his mugging mannerisms and insisted on Joly providing the soundtrack, which was superbly arranged by Morris Stoloff.

Despite their physical dissimilarity, Jolson clearly approved of the choice and consented to a scene in *Jolson Sings Again* (1949), in which Parks meets himself during the biopic-making sequence. Even more divorced from fact than its predecessor (which grossed over $7.6 million and became the seventh most successful picture of the decade), the sequel became mired in the melancholia Jolson endured after the declamatory theatrics that made him a Broadway legend were replaced by the more relaxed crooning style. The overt patriotism of the wartime troop shows also ratcheted up the sentiment quotient, which was further glutinised by Jolson's romance with nurse Ellen Clark (Barbara Hale) – an à clef alias for Erle Galbraith. However, the dualogy still makes for magnificent entertainment. ★★★★ **DP**

⊕ JOSIE AND THE PUSSYCATS (2001)

Starring: *Rachael Leigh Cook (Josie McCoy), Tara Reid (Melody Valentine), Rosario Dawson (Valerie Brown), Alan Cumming (Wyatt Frame), Parker Posey (Fiona)*
Directors: *Harry Elfont, Deborah Kaplan*
Screenwriters: *Deborah Kaplan, Harry Elfont, based on characters by Richard H. Goldwater, Dan DeCarlo, John L. Goldwater*
PG/94 mins./Comedy/Music/USA

Girl band Josie And The Pussycats quickly become the next big thing. But they soon discover there is a sinister side to their new-found fame.

The similarities between the plot of *Josie And The Pussycats* and an episode that appeared around the same time of *The Simpsons* – in which Bart and buddies became boy band superstars – are, at first glance, startlingly apparent.

And that's not all *Josie* has in common with TV's foremost family. A 21st century update of the 1970s comic book, this is the cleverest 70s throwback to hit the screen since *The Brady Bunch Movie* – and its smart brand of veiled satire suggests that its appeal deserves to stretch far beyond the teen market at which it initially seems to be aimed.

From the moment when boy band DuJour break into a saucy number entitled, er,' Backdoor Lover', it's clear what sort of territory we're in. When friction between the pretty-boy quintet leads to their 'mysterious' disappearance, record company exec Wyatt (a splendidly oily Cumming) is ordered by his scheming boss, Fiona, to find a new bunch of wannabe musicians to manipulate – and after he stumbles upon Josie and co., they quickly become the next big thing. But it's only when they begin to question the rapidity of their rise to the top that Wyatt and Fiona's motives become all too clear.

Essentially, this pokes non-stop fun at the cult of celebrity, and the transience of a music scene where 15 minutes of fame is positively generous. But aside from its underlying message, this offers rapid-fire wit, some rockin' tunes and a sweet and feisty central trio.

The endless onslaught of product placement does become cloying after a while, and there is one forced final twist too many – but the end result is so much fun you'll forgive it its flaws. ★★★ **LB**

⊕ JOUR DE FÊTE (1949)

Starring: *Jacques Tati (François), Guy Decombie (Roger), Paul Frankeur (Marcel), Santa Reill (Roger's Wife), Maine Vallee (Jeanette)*
Director: *Jacques Tati*
Screenwriters: *Jacques Tati, Rene Wheeler, Henri Marquet*
U/90 mins./Comedy/France

During the Bastille Day celebrations in a sleepy French village, François the postman sees a film about the speed and efficiency of the US postal system and sets out to modernise his bicycle service.

Jacques Tati spent the latter part of the Second World War voluntarily exiled in the village of Sainte-Sévère-sur-Indre. He returned in 1947 to make his directorial debut with *L'École des Facteurs*, the hilarious short which provided the inspiration for his first feature.

Tati planned to produce France's first colour picture by shooting in Thomson-Color. However, he was warned that this experimental process was unstable and, so, he wisely opted to make a monochrome record as back-up.

The story of the lab's failure to process the Thomson stock is now part of film lore. But Tati's editor daughter, Sophie Tatischeff, and cinematographer François Ede used cutting-edge technology to develop the negative and, between 1987-94, they painstakingly pieced together Sophie's interpretation of her father's original intention. Her major amendment was the removal of the young painter who Tati had added when he re-edited and re-mixed Jour de Fête in 1964. Indeed, he had never been wholly pleased with the film and had revised it following a less than auspicious Parisian premiere.

However, there's an irony that modern techniques should have been used to create this approximation of Tati's design, as the clash between tradition and progress is one of the comedy's key themes. Indeed, Tati's mock homage to American efficiency could now be viewed as an advanced warning of the perils of globalisation, as he clearly felt caught between gratitude to the nation that had liberated France and resentment at the cultural cost being exacted by the economic aid provided by the Marshall Plan.

Establishing Tati's twin penchants for the comic counterbalance of sound and image and for allowing gags to unfold in their own time and space, this remains a wonderfully fresh and funny film. Tati's own performance as the ungainly but dauntlessly bouyant postman is a masterclass in silent pantomime. But the juxtaposition of this slapstick poetry with the precisely detailed pastoral idyll gives this unceasing delight an aching nostalgia to match its frantic energy. ★★★★ DP

JOURNEY TO THE CENTER OF THE EARTH (1959)

Starring: *Pat Boone (Alec McEwen), James Mason (Professor Oliver Lindenbrook), Arlene Dahl (Mrs. Carla Goetaborg), Diane Baker (Jenny)*
Director: *Henry Levin*
Screenwriters: *Charles Brackett, Walter Reisch, based on the novel by Jules Verne*
U/132 mins./Sci-fi/USA

An intrepid professor leads a party of explorers toward the centre of the Earth, a journey of wonder and terror that will lead to confrontations with prehistoric creatures and a lost world beneath their very feet.

An excellent science fiction fable from the Verne-adaptation school of wonder over paranoia, plain storytelling over satire.

You don't become entranced by this whimsical fable of adventurers discovering an incredible world below the surface, complete with lost cities, prehistoric creature, and an underground ocean, for any clever-clever commentary, but for the transporting power of old-fashioned fantasy. It's what use to be deemed a 'family adventure' but that sounds too detrimental now.

While deviating from the original Verne text considerably, Henry Levin's tale still carries that spirit of credible connection. It wants us to believe in its science. Having the redoubtable tone of James Mason helps, he's the brainiac geologist Lindenbrook at the head of the mission who with shades of Scott's race to the South Pole, finds his best friend Goetaborg has ploughed on ahead of him alone. Lindenbrook, sensibly with a sturdy team behind – including crooner Pat Boone as young hero sort Alec McEwen and a fetching goose – also discovers traces of another explorer who may have ventured this way centuries before. There's a small murder plot, and a cool spike of scientific rivalry, but the film is essentially an underground picaresque through a series of vivid sets stunningly lit to give the effect of the vast and subterranean.

It has dated a fair bit, but it's a film that takes its far-fetchedness seriously, and delivers a thrilling adventure that is untrammelled by cheese, melodrama or ludicrous tribes of extras shabbily dressed as bird-beings or lizard men. ★★★★ IN

JUBILEE (1977)

Starring: *Jenny Runacre (Queen Elizabeth I/Bod), Neil Campbell (Crabs), Toyah Wilcox (Mad), Jordan (Amyl Nitrate), Hermine Demoriane (Chaos), Ian Charleson (Angel), Adam Ant (Kid)*
Director: *Derek Jarman*
Screenwriter: *Derek Jarman*
18/100 mins./Drama/UK

A time-travelling Queen Elizabeth I visits an anarchic future London. Her lookalike, Bod, leads a group of rebellious drop-outs at war with the forces of repression.

The closest a British film could come to the John Waters of *Pink Flamingoes*, Derek Jarman's *Jubilee* combines a safety-pin and barbed wire vision of 1977 London in ruins (all burning prams and castrated policemen), a meditation on English mysticism guided by the immensely regal Jenny Runacre and a wild 'n' crazy account of the rampages of a gang of personality punk psychos. There are surprisingly lyrical stretches (the only songs sung all the way through are 'Jerusalem' and 'My Love is Like a Red Red Rose') and, though future pop stars Toyah Wilcox and Adam Ant are embarassingly amateurish as rebel street angels, some of the one-note maniacal performances, especially Lex Luthor lookalike Orlando as mad media tycoon Borgia Ginz, are relishable. Among the people you've forgotten are in it are Ian Charleson of *Chariots Of Fire*, celebrity shop assistant Jordan (as narrator Amyl Nitrate), Richard O'Brien and Little Nell of *The Rocky Horror Picture Show*, the Lindsay Kemp Dance Troupe and Adolf Hitler of World War II. Even as the haircuts and music have receded into cultural history, its acid-look vision of the worst of England remains horribly sound. The soundtrack features Adam and the Ants ('Deutscher Girls'), Wayne County and the Electric Chairs ('Paranoia Paradise'), Chelsea ('Right to Work'), Suzi Pinns (a thrash punk 'Rule Britannia' best appreciated by those with the aural range of a fox terrier), Siouxie and the Banshees ('Love in a Void'), Amilcar ('Wargasm in Pornotopia'), the Slits and Brian Eno ('Slow Water', 'Dover Beach'). In the 21st Century, the creative team are either dead or doing pantomime – which is so appropriate irony doesn't even come into it. ★★★ KN

Derek Jarman (1942–1994)

Who he was: Scourge of the British film establishment. Experimentalist who started as Ken Russell's production designer, marked out by his social critique and homosexuality. Famously kept garden at Dungeness.
Hallmarks: Super 8; punk sensibility; male nudity; classical art and philosophy
If you see one film, see: *Jubilee* (1977)

JUDE (1996)

Starring: *Christopher Eccleston (Jude Fawley), Kate Winslet (Sue Bridehead), Liam Cunningham (Phillotson), Arabella (Rachel Griffiths), June Whitfield (Aunt Drusilla)*
Director: *Michael Winterbottom*
Screenwriter: *Hossein Amini, based on the novel by Thomas Hardy*
15/117 mins./Drama/UK

A stonemason's pursuit of a better intellectual life and his free-spirited cousin is hampered by tragedy.

Thomas Hardy's eleventh and bleakest novel, *Jude The Obscure*, was so harshly received by critics and public alike that he never wrote another. Turning it into a piece of cinema is therefore hardly without risk. Winterbottom's film, then, is a brave, powerful, far from comfortable and distinctly English affair that bears all the hallmarks of a labour of love rather than an example of intellectual folly.

Jude tells the tale of a 19th Century stonemason who attempts to rise above his rural roots and earn a place at the university of Christminster where he plans to emulate his old schoolmaster and childhood hero Phillotson. Jude's plans are interrupted by a short marriage to a pig farmer's daughter Arabella but on separation he moves to Christminster to resume his studies. But then he meets and falls in love with his cousin Sue Bridehead and his life goes downhill. After Jude has persuaded Phillotson to give Sue a job, she falls in love with the older man – and Jude loses her and the hope of a university place when Christminster rejects him. Then, as he and Sue remain in touch, he tells her of Arabella and in a fit of anger she rejects him and marries Phillotson. But love conquers all, and so Jude and Sue reunite to face all the prejudices and pressures of their world, fighting to keep the flickering flame of happiness alight.

Those expecting a happy ending are in for a horrible, heart-rending shock. Those expecting a grim, unrelenting siphon of human suffering are less likely to be disappointed – not even the sterling turn by June Whitfield as Jude's Aunt Drusilla can inject any light relief. But the film's success lies in the two leads. Winslet gives an impressively mature portrayal of a woman strong enough to flout society's rules, seemingly revelling in the chance to strip herself (literally at one point) of all glamour and rely only on the power of her performance.

And yet for all her post *Titanic* pulling power, it is the shoulders of Eccleston that bear the millstone weight of *Jude*. To that task he is more than equal, his performance shining through all the misery like a beacon on a stormy night. It seems he was *born* to play Hardy's quasibiographical Jude, empathising with is fiercely determined and independent character as perhaps only an actor as single-minded as he could do. ★★★★ **NJ**

JUDGE DREDD (1995)

Starring: *Sylvester Stallone (Judge Joseph Dredd), Armand Assante (Rico), Rob Schneider (Herman Ferguson), Jurgen Prochnow (Judge Griffin), Max von Sydow (Chief Justice Fargo), Diane Lane (Judge Hershey)*
Director: *Danny Cannon*
Screenwriters: *William Wisher, Steven E. de Souza, from a story by Michael DeLuca and characters by John Wagner, Carlos Ezquerra*
15/91 mins./Sci-fi/Action/USA

In a future densely populated world, law is maintained by super-cops called Judges, who can dole out justice on the spot. The most famous of these is Judge Dredd . . .

Sly Stallone's foray into futuristic law enforcement isn't the witty adventure *Demolition Man* was. But, based on the celebrated ripple-jawed character from cult UK comic book *2000AD*, it still makes entertaining sci-fi action for fans craving more blood and guts than the younger-pitched super-hero flicks.

It's the 22nd Century and in an enclave called Mega City One surrounded by the devastated 'Cursed Earth', social order is in the hands of Judges, a force with the authority of police officer, judge, jury and executioner rolled into one, who zoom around in spiffy uniforms with great gadgets protecting the Haves from the understandably agitated Have Nots.

Living legend Judge 'I Am The Law' Dredd (a leaner, appropriately severe, helmet-offing Stallone) is tough, uncompromising and, frankly, a fascist – at least until he's framed by the even more extreme Judge Fargo (Jurgen Prochnow). Conspiracy, naturally, is afoot, in a genetic mutation fiddle that yields the line 'Send in the clones!' and a power snatch scenario in which renegade Rico (Assante) obliges as Sociopath Of The Week. Diane Lane looks good in leather and Saturday Night Live alumnus Rob Schneider provides a cowardly comic sidekick for sinew-shredding Dredd.

Tagline

In the future, one man is the law.

Aside from Stallone's occasional twinkle – delivering Dredd's limited repertoire of kick-ass catch phrases – it's the production design and special effects that engage. Evidently admirers of *Blade Runner* and *Star Wars* (catch Max von Sydow's Obi-Wan-ish manifestation), the visuals veer startlingly from stunning to laughably ropey (an aerial chase set-piece when one presumes the budget imploded). But Cannon's rough-around-the-edges direction doesn't betray Dredd's comic strip origins, and this is reasonable fun in the brute-as-hero line. ★★★ **AE**

JULES ET JIM (1962)

Starring: *Jeanne Moreau (Catherine), Oskar Werner (Jules), Henri Serre (Jim), Marie Dubois (Therese), Vanna Urbino (Gilberte)*
Director: *François Truffaut*
Screenwriter: *François Truffaut, Jean Grunault, based on the novel by Henri-Pierre Roché*
15/110 mins./Drama/France

Reserved Mitteleuropean entomologist Jules forges a 30-year friendship with Jim, a French writer with a passion for life and beauty. However, their Bohemian lifestyle is disrupted by the intrusion of the recklessly spontaneous Catherine.

As a critic, François Truffaut had railed against the reverentially literate form of filmmaking that he had branded the 'Tradition of Quality'. However, he was accused by some of his contemporaries of retreating into the cinematic past by adapting Henri-Pierre Roché's 1955 novel, *Jules et Jim*. But, rather than betraying the nouvelle vague, this glorious drama was a summation of its ideas and strategies.

Avoiding the pictorial approach of heritage lyricism, Truffaut perfectly evoked the changing tone of France between La Belle Epoche and the rise of Fascism by using photographs, paintings, books, plays, lantern shows and old films. But rather than appearing self-conscious, these nostalgic images were linked through such resolutely modern tactics as swish pans, freeze-frames, superimpositions and jump cuts.

Similarly, Truffaut remained faithful to the spirit of the book, but re-ordered certain episodes and re-apportioned some of the dialogue. Consequently, he was able brilliantly to shorthand Jules and Jim's growing cameraderie and the latter's attempts to introduce his diffident friend to the joys of love.

Moreover, Truffaut shifted the emphasis away from the pursuit of artistic beauty that had prompted the pair's trip to Greece and on to Catherine's impact upon their seemingly indivisible bond. He was deeply indebted here to the effervescence of Jeanne Moreau, whose modernity, spontaneity and capricious switches between affection and cruelty so wholly seduce these Bohemian devotees of classicism and the intellect.

There's no question that the narrative tends towards melodrama once Jim has failed to heed Jules's warning and jeopardises their friendship by instigating the ménage that will drive them apart. Yet, Truffaut deftly delineates the transience of their happiness through his symbolic contrast between indoor and outdoor locations, and daytime and nocturnal incidents. Moreover, he never loses sight of the trio's essential humanity, which allies this masterpiece with the cinema of Truffaut's role model, Jean Renoir. ★★★★★ **DP**

Nouvelle Vague

What is it: Literally 'New Wave'. A band of French film critics turned filmmakers who attacked the old guard of staid French directors and forged their own highly personal sense of cinema.
Hallmarks: Jazzy freewheeling style (freeze-frames, jump cutting); constant movie referencing; loose narrative structure; playing with genre iconography; ambiguous endings.
Key figures: Jean-Luc Godard, François Truffaut, Eric Rohmer, Jacques Rivette, Claude Chabrol
If you see one film, see: *Tirez Sur Le Pianiste* /Shoot The Pianist (Truffaut, 1960)

JULIET OF THE SPIRITS (GIULIETTA DEGLI SPIRITI) (1965)

Giulletta Masina (Juliet), Alba Cancellieri (Juliet as a child), Maria Pisu (Giorgio), Caterina Boratto (Juliet's Mother), Luisa Della Noce (Adele)
Director: *Federico Fellini*
Screenwriters: *Federico Fellini, Tullio Pinelli, Ennio Flaiano, Brunello Rondi, based on a story by Fellini and Pinelli*
18/148 mins/Drama/France/Italy/West Germany

Juliet feels neglected by her busy husband Giorgio and suspects he is having an affair. She seems to be assailed by phantoms unleashed by her dabbling in spiritualism.

For his first film in colour, Federico Fellini cast his wife and once-frequent star Giulietta Masina in a story everyone assumed was an unflattering portrait of their marriage, simultaneously paying homage to Masina by giving her a terrific star role and demeaning her by surrounding her with a carnival of magical or eccentric characters who are all more interesting than her. Masina, still recognisably the waif of *La Strada* and *Notte di Cabiria* but uncomfortable in a bourgeois role, is twisted by fantasies (happy and frightening) about her ordinary marriage and hung up on memories of odd childhood incidents (a characteristic Fellini touch is a neurosis about being burned as a martyr while taking part in a religious school pageant). There are strange interludes as Juliet wanders next door to hang out with a neighbour (Sandra Milo) who lives an impossibly glamorous and faintly ridiculous Bond girl lifestyle, and the drabber aspects of the heroine's life are illuminated by exhilarating flashes of the fantastic. As is suggested by a separate card in the opening credits which says the film could not have been made without Bri-Nylon, it's an attempt at creating a wholly artificial world, with production and costume design by Piero Gherardi which really cuts loose with Milo's outfits and hats, not to mention her sex-fantasy treehouse and bedroom with mirrored ceiling and a seashell-shaped chute for post-coital slides into a private swimming pool. In the finale, the phantasms crowd into Juliet's home, along with her odd circle of friends, and Fellini stages startling tableaux around figures like the fifteen-foot tall scowling patriarch with a fake red beard. ★★★ **KN**

JUMANJI (1995)

Starring: *Robin Williams (Alan Parrish), Jonathan Hyde (Samuel Alan Parrish/Hunter Van Pelt), Kirsten Dunst (Judy Shepherd), Bradley Pierce (Peter Shepherd), Bonnie Hunt (Sarah Whittle), Bebe Neuwirth (Aunt Nora Shepherd)*
Director: *Joe Johnson*
Screenwriters: *Jonathan Hensleigh, Greg Taylor, Jim Strain, from a screen story by Taylor, Strain and Chris Van Allsburg, based on a book by Van Allsburg*
PG/99 mins/Family/Adventure/USA

Two children discover a board game and accidentally release a wild man and a host of rampaging beasts.

Though entertaining, Jumanji – adapted from an idiosyncratic children's book by Chris Van Allsburg – feels more like a package than a movie: Jurassic Park-style CGI effects, *Gremlins*-style childhood traumas, *Honey I Shrunk the Kids*-style Joe Johnston direction and Robin Williams-style Robin Williams. On a scene-by-scene basis, it is mostly great fun but suffers from a contrived script which repetitively drags characters back to the eponymous magical board game for another effect-producing throw of the dice.

The story opens in 1869 with some kids burying the magical game Jumanji but without explaining who made it or what it's for, as if that stuff were being left for the sequel, then flashes to 1969 where the thing is rediscovered by mixed-up rich kid Alan and a few turns unleash African bats into New Hampshire and send Alan off to jungle hell. A quarter of a century later, the film finally starts proper as orphans Kirsten Dunst and Bradley Pierce restart the game and unleash the grown up Alan along with a collection of flora and fauna that run riot through the town, causing chaos.

The CGI creeping vines, capering monkeys, attacking alligators, fluttering bats, hungry lions and stampeding hordes are genuinely amazing: as hyperreal and odd looking as Van Allsburg's original illustrations. For once, the strange look of CGI is turned to its advantage as the jungle animals are supposed to be fantastical. A major trick is missed, however, by having the sole human to emerge from Jumanji to be a regular actor rather than an effect. This undermines the weirdness and allows Jonathan Hyde – who does a Captain Hook-like double as Alan's tyrannical father and a gun-toting white hunter – to overact shamelessly through too many slapstick stunts.

There is quite a lot going on in the film, which disguises the thinness of the central idea (African chaos erupts from board game at every turn). Williams' Tarzan act is a reprise of his Peter Pan and the less-than-stellar supporting cast – with the exception of the excellent Hann-Byrd and an amusing Bonnie Hunt as Williams' neurotic old girlfriend – just gape in amazement or consternation as the effects boys run rampant. ★★★ **AC**

THE JUNGLE BOOK (1967)

Starring: *the voices of: Phil Harris (Baloo), Sebastian Cabot (Bagheera), Louis Prima (King Louie), George Sanders (Shere Khan), Sterling Holloway (Kaa), J.Pat O'Malley (Col. Hathi the Elephant), Bruce Reitherman (Mowgli the Man Cub)*
Director: *Wolfgang Reitherman*
Screenwriters: *Larry Clemmons, Ralph Wright, Ken Anderson, Vance Gerry, based on the Mowgli stories in* The Jungle Book *by Rudyard Kipling*
U/78 mins./Animation/Family/Adventure/USA

An animated adaptation of Rudyard Kipling's famous tale of a lost human child raised by a pack of wolves, who is helped by a clever panther and a easygoing bear, and hindered by a hungry tiger and the power-crazed king of the monkeys, to return to his own kind.

You could use Disney's canon of animated tales as a fair barometer of the changing times and styles they were made in. The ornate, lovely classics such as *Snow White* and *Pinocchio* are steeped in the simpler, morally defined glow of the 30s and 40s, by the groovy end of the 60s *The Jungle Book* cuts loose from its Kipling origins for a jazzy, bopping nuthouse of a flick. It's a favourite more for its giddy humour and belting songs, than the teeming prettiness of the animations. It's arguable that the film, for all its joy, hardly does Kipling's anthropomorphised fable that much justice.

Kipling is the framework for this jumble, not to say jungle, of loud characters who cross diminutive Mowgli's path, and a clutch of amongst the best Disney songs ever written. It's just a road movie with great pipes. There's no forgetting the magic of Louis Prima's ribald rendition of 'King Of The Swingers' (loosely tugging at Louis Armstrong's legendary style), a manic flurry of a routine that borders on the edgy, or, indeed, Phil Davis' easy daydream 'Bear Necessities' (catchy as measles).

The characters too, care of Kipling and the actor-animator combos, bubble delightfully to life. Sebastian Cabot's world-weary Bagheera, the dignified black panther, is wonderfully exasperated, and whoever decided George Sanders would make a good Shere Khan, the dreaded tiger burning bright, deserves a medal of some sort. Seductive and wicked, he has become one of cinema's greatest villains, his words so honeyed they almost seem to drip from the cavern of his jaws. That the accents veer from the Cockney to Manhattan is of little concern, nor Mowgli's miraculous ability to converse with animals. This was the first animated movie to be made following Walt's death, and you can feel the slackening of storytelling detail. ★★★★ **IN**

JUNGLE FEVER (1991)

Starring: *Wesley Snipes (Flipper Purify), Annabella Sciorra (Angie Tucci), Spike Lee (Cyrus), Ossie Davis (Doctor Purify), Ruby Dee (Lucinda Purify), Samuel L. Jackson (Gator Purify), John Turturro (Paulie Carbone), Halle Berry (Vivian)*
Director: *Spike Lee*
Screenwriter: *Spike Lee*
18/132 mins./Drama/USA

Awards: *Cannes Film Festival – Best Supporting Actor (Samuel L. Jackson), Prize Of The Ecunemical Jury – Special Mention (Spike Lee)*

A story of the racial taboos that boil to the surface when successful black architect Flipper Purify enters into an affair with his white office assistant Angie. An event that ultimately echoes across every level of the social spectrum.

Spike Lee, at the height of his storming of the political barricades, investigates the repercussions of an interracial romance and, inevitably, society itself. And, despite its irkingly familiar sense of rubbing our faces in its righteous indignation, it's keen eyed and acutely acted like many of Lee's early movies. You also have to respect his dedication to overturning the gangsta clichés of new black cinema (of which he was meant to be a pioneer) – Snipes' Flipper is a buppie, sharp suited and successful, but, as the film investigates, does this also make him a man cut adrift from his own roots? Or, indeed, cutting himself adrift?

Such a challenging relationship story increases the view of Lee – although he understandably despises labels – as a less funny, but as socially aware and ambitious a filmmaker as Woody Allen, a fellow New Yorker determinedly adult in his style and subject. The subtlety of the observation is remarkable, draping the film in the cruel irony of real life – see how Angie's friends support her affair but are disgusted all the same; elsewhere racist Italians still slaver after a beautiful black girl. Racism, and its attendant hypocrisy, coats everything in modern life according to Lee, and, although it tends to feel too much like clamour, and trades in as many clichés as realistic characters (Flipper's white bosses look like sneery stereotyping), the point is effectively made.

It's typically visually vibrant, cutting a cool cross section of the racially defined districts of New York (note how geography also divides people by race and class), and set to some great music. But Lee's universe remains resolutely negative, he sees a world on the edge of chaos, inner cities about to explode. Maybe he's right, and that is what finally makes it a depressing experience. ★★★★ **IN**

⑮ JU-ON THE GRUDGE (2003)

Starring: *Megumi Okina (Rika Nishina), Misaki Ito (Hitomi Tokunaga), Misa Uehara (Izumi Toyama), Yui Ichikawa (Chiharu), Kanji Tsuda (Katsuya Tokunaga)*
Director: *Takashi Shimizu*
Screenwriter: *Takashi Shimizu*
15/92 mins./Horror/Japan

Rika, a social worker, is sent to a house where a murder was once committed, and finds an old lady apparently abandoned by her family. She also encounters two melancholy but dangerous ghost children, Kayako and her brother (Ozeki), who proceed to persecute a loosely connected string of folks.

The third film (but first theatrical release) in a saga that had already managed two straight-to-video instalments, explaining how the melancholy but malicious Kayako became a ghost and worked up a bad case of anger, Takeshi Shimizu's *Ju-On: The Grudge* became a breakthrough Japanese hit, carrying Shimizu on to a fourth entry confusingly titled *The Grudge 2* and an Americanised remake with Sarah Michelle Gellar that also counts as a fifth film in the ongoing saga.

Because the haunting is passed along like a dose of the flu, the film skips *La Ronde*-style (or at least in the Amicus anthology tradition) from one episode to the next (darting back and forth in time), as the ghost children pick on a social worker, a cop, a schoolgirl and others.

Not only does the random curse aspect echo the *Ring* films but many other elements (a lank-haired teenage girl ghost, obviously) follow that influential cycle.

Expect a Freddy vs Jason-type Sadako vs Kayako team-up sequel somewhere down the line. Shimizu obviously saw how effective the ghost-crawling-from-the-TV scene in *Ring* was, since *The Grudge* is constructed entirely around similarly ingenious bone-freezing scares as genuinely terrifying spooks appear under the sheets, crawl crablike down stairs, perch on beds, or otherwise go 'boo!'

As a film, it is at once too much a part of an overarching story and divided into too many episodes, to be all of a piece, but as a sustained collection of scare moments it's a winner. ★★★ **KN**

⑮ JURASSIC PARK (1993)

Starring: *Sam Neill (Dr. Alan Grant), Laura Dern (Dr. Ellie Sattler), Jeff Goldblum (Dr. Ian Malcolm), Bob Peck (Robert Muldoon), Richard Attenborough (John Hammond), Samuel L. Jackson (Arnold)*
Director: *Steven Spielberg*
Screenwriters: *Michael Crichton, David Koepp, from the novel by Crichton*

Awards: *Academy Awards – Best Sound Effects Editing, Best Visual Effects Editing, Best Sound, BAFTA – Best Special Effects*

Scientists clone dinosaurs to populate a theme park that suffers a major security breakdown and releases the dinosaurs.

Spring, 1993. Steven Spielberg has hired a hotel in Krakow, Poland so that he can keep his family around him throughout the emotionally draining *Schindler's List* shoot. Every day the director returns exhausted, troubled, empty. And yet, for two hours, three nights a week, Spielberg retires to his private room, where a satellite dish is receiving a scrambled signal from ILM in San Francisco.

It is here, within spitting distance of the concentration camp, that Spielberg completes post-production on a colourful adventure he wrapped less than four months ago among the very different flora and fauna of Kahuii, Hawaii. It is here that Steven Spielberg finishes *Jurassic Park*. No wonder 1993 has been called Spielberg's miracle year.

Obsessed with dinosaurs since childhood, Spielberg had been nursing *Jurassic Park* for some time (Spielberg found himself embroiled in a bidding war for Michael Crichton's novel despite the fact he had privately been promised the film rights before publication). However, in 1992, Spielberg had been intending to make *Schindler's Ark* his next project but having convinced MCA president Sid Sheinberg to gamble on a three hour, black and white holocaust movie, Spielberg was happy to abide by Sheinberg's solitary condition: he had to make *Jurassic Park* first.

To catch the end of the Polish winter, Spielberg was then forced to rush through the shooting schedule for *Jurassic Park*. Coming off the back of *Hook* – a movie that ran 40 days over its 76 day schedule – this may not have been a bad thing. Certainly Spielberg admitted to, 'walking away from a lot of takes', but despite tropical storm Iniki's cameo, the movie came in on budget and ahead of schedule. And if some of the human performances bear the imprint of a hurried hand – the film is riddled with mumbled line readings – Spielberg's apparently greater sympathy with the dinosaurs inspired technical achievement on a scale that represented an entire visual revolution. In their early script meetings author Crichton was unsurprisingly anxious to know how Spielberg was planning to tackle the technical challenge of the dinosaurs. Spielberg however, wanted to talk about dinosaur character. Taking Alan Grant's line that dinosaurs' closest living relatives were birds, Spielberg based a lot of velociraptor movement on his study of the chicken and geese who occupied the back yard of his beach house. He also brought to bear lessons learned on his previous creature feature: not *Jaws*, but *E.T.* Behavioural movement, breathing, pupil dilation: Spielberg wanted to capture the detail which suggests a living, thinking organism rather than a mere monster.

Eventually, all of this detail would end up on screen: the T-Rex eyes blinking in the flashlight, the velociraptor breath snorting against the kitchen door port-hole, the odd, nodding head movement of the poisonous dilophosaurus. However, during those early meetings, whenever Crichton asked Spielberg how he was going to achieve this detail, the director simply shrugged.

Serial Killer Nicknames — TOP 10

	Nickname	Actor, Film
1	Hannibal the Cannibal	Anthony Hopkins, *The Silence of the Lambs*
2	Cyrus the Virus	John Malkovich, *Con Air*
3	John Doe	Kevin Spacey, *Seven*
4	M	Peter Lorre, *M*
5	Chucky	Brad Dourif, *Child's Play*
6	Buffalo Bill	Ted Levine, *The Silence of the Lambs*
7	The Tooth Fairy / Red Dragon	Tom Noonan / Ralph Fiennes, *Manhunter / Red Dragon*
8	The Shape	Nick Castle, *Halloween*
9	Serial Mom	Kathleen Turner, *Serial Mom*
10	Diamond Dog	Ving Rhames, *Con Air*

'Prove it.' Those were the two words Spielberg said to ILM's Dennis Muren, when Muren suggested that CGI could capture, 'full motion' dinosaurs in daylight. The story then goes that the first time stop-motion expert Phil Tippet was shown the test footage he mumbled, 'I am extinct.' (A line Spielberg eventually gave to Ian Malcolm in the movie.) The first shot of the grazing bracheosaur; the sweeping herd of gallimimuses; the reappearance of the heroic T-Rex for a climax that Spielberg reworked after ILM's success; these are shots that would not, could not have appeared without CGI. Spielberg would have thought of something sure enough, but the full-scale, straight ahead wonder that wowed the world would have been severely truncated.

And the world was wowed.

Reunited with Universal – the studio behind *Jaws* and *E.T.* – who were themselves coming off a poor run, John Hammond's struggle to build Jurassic Park had some pertinent echoes. 'In a way,' Spielberg said at the time, '*Jurassic Park* tells the story of any studio head having a bad year who needs a hit.' Sheinberg need not have worried. Somewhere north of $120 million would have been respectable, but in a summer where JP's main competition was Arnie's mega-flop *The Last Action Hero* the movie took less than four months to beat the previous all-time record of $701 million set by *E.T.* Soon enough the critics were not reviewing the film but the box office. No wonder Spielberg was heard to moan: 'Part of me is afraid I will be remembered for the money my films have made, rather than the films themselves.'

Of course, on the one hand, Spielberg could not complain. *Jurassic Park* was always a purpose-built thrill ride, 'a roller coaster' to quote the director. Lacking the heart to rank with his greatest achievements *Jurassic Park* instead represents the apotheosis of his crowd-pleasing craft. 'I just opened the tool box,' Spielberg said, 'and took every tool I've ever used in my entire career.'

Besides, Spielberg need not have worried. He was about to reveal *Schindler's List*. ★★★★ **CK**

Movie Trivia: Jurassic Park

Jurassic Park became the first mainstream film in the UK to be dubbed into Hindi. Sean Connery was offered the role of Hammond but turned it down. For two shots in the movie, raptors are played by men in suits. The pilot who airlifts the crew to safety after Hurricane Iniki is the same pilot who rescues Indy in the opening sequence of *Raiders of the Lost Ark*.

JURASSIC PARK III (2001)

Starring: *Sam Neill (Dr. Alan Grant), William H. Macy (Paul Kirby), Téa Leoni (Amanda Kirby), Alessandro Nivola (Billy Brennan), Laura Dern (Dr. Ellie Sattler)*
Director: *Joe Johnston*
Screenwriters: *Peter Buchman, Alexander Payne, Jim Taylor, from characters created by Michael Crichton*
PG/88 mins./Action/Adventure/USA

Eight years after escaping the dinosaur rampage on Isla Nublar, palaeontologist Alan Grant is shanghaied to abandoned breeding site Isla Sorna by the Kirbys, on a desperate search for their son. When their plane crashes, the 'rescue party' learn that Grant's controversial theory of velociraptor intelligence is correct, as they become the prey . . .

Man, this is how *Big Brother* or *Survivor* ought to be. Collect a group of annoying people, strand 'em in a genetically-engineered theme park where it's all gone ka-ka, and see who gets out alive. Now that's entertainment. 'No force on Earth or in heaven could get me back on that island!' Obviously begging to be filed under Famous Last Words, this is the sensibly fervent vow of scholarly dino supremo, Alan Grant. Mysteriously, he has allowed a cameoing Laura Dern (as Ellie, his erstwhile sweetie in the original *Jurassic Park*) to marry someone else and breed dinosaur enthusiasts of her own.

Just as *JP* opened with a sudden chomp, and *The Lost World* flaunted a frightful child-in-jeopardy prologue, chapter three opens with a scare for which you are warned to get a good grip on your ice cream or it'll be in your lap. Fourteen-year-old Eric (played with aplomb by Trevor Morgan) is enjoying a turista paraglide billed as The Dino-Soar over Isla Sorna when . . . Well, you can guess. Cut to Grant expounding his hypothesis that 'raptors were highly intelligent and socially organised to a skeptical audience too amused to fund his dig. Enter the Kirbys, a wealthy couple claiming a yen to fly over Isla Sorna with the world's foremost dinosaur expert for a peek at grazing herds. Before you can say 'bribery', Grant has packed his toothbrush and protégé.

Of course, they break the plane! How else could they get trapped? Of course, they lose the only mobile phone! How else could they get cut off from the rest of the world? Halfway in, hearts sink as it looks probable that Téa Leoni's abrasive Amanda will manage to defy death, condemning us to endure her for another 45 minutes. 'It's a bad idea to do that,' Grant cautions when she leaps out of the plane, effectively acting as a blonde dinner bell for every spectacular carnivore of 'saur ILM can throw at us; of these Mesozoic monsters, the 'raptors lack their expected bite, the much-mooted spinosaurus fails to usurp the T-rex as Godfather of the dinosaur, so it is left to the pteranodons to provide the novelty factor, be it eerily emerging from mists or feeding the heroes to their infant offspring.

The welcome return of Sam Neill and William H. Macy's recruitment bring a degree of class unwarranted by a script suited to Jean-Claude Van Damme. The boy, who behaves like the love child of Tarzan and Sheena, gathering *T-Rex* urine and the junk Jeff Goldblum left behind, is an attractive child-friendly element, while Nivola's Billy thickens the plot by blatantly being up to something.

Director Johnston gives his outing the look of a dark, claustrophobic jungle adventure, but he's a reliable hack who brings more enthusiasm than inspiration to the task, giving it a comfy, family-oriented predictability and minimal gruesomeness in the action set-pieces – which come thick and fast enough to satisfy lovers of the chase. ★★★ **AE**

ⓞ JUST FRIENDS (2005)

Starring: *Ryan Reynolds (Chris Brander), Amy Smart (Jamie Palamino), Anna Faris (Samantha James), Chris Klein (Dusty), Julie Hagerty (Chris's Mom)*
Director: *Roger Kumble*
Screenwriter: *Adam 'Tex' Davis*
12A/96 mins/Comedy/Romance/USA

Chris and Jamie were best friends in high school, but the fat and nerdy Chris' crush on Jamie went unrequited. Ten years on, he's a buff music executive, back in town at Christmas with a spoiled star in tow – but can he get out of the friend zone and into Jamie's heart?

Don't be deceived. Though afflicted with an unfunny trailer and direction from the guy who made appalling sex comedy *The Sweetest Thing*, this is largely stink-free. About two seconds in, as a fat-suited Ryan Reynolds under a ginger wig sings along to Boyz II Men's 'I Swear', your face splits in a stupid grin that lasts, largely uninterrupted, for the next 90 minutes.

Reynolds is making a habit of winning audiences over despite themselves: this is, after all, the man who made *Van Wilder: Party Liaison* watchable. He plays on that winning charmer routine here, slipping in a dollop of nerdishness as the newly babelicious Chris.

Anna Faris provides the Beast to his Beauty as a wannabe rock star, proving again that she's better in over-the-top supporting roles than in any number of Scary Movies, and there's a great, all-too-brief cameo from *Airplane!*'s Julie Hagerty as Chris's anxious mother. If there's a weak link, it's Amy Smart, who's simply too bland to convince. A few of the set-pieces also fall flat – our hero's tussle with kids on ice is little more than an unwanted slapstick interlude, while his feud with love rival Dusty eats up more running time than it should. Thankfully, though, Reynolds manages to pull the material up to his level rather than being drawn down by it. ★★★ **HO'H**

ⓞ JUST LIKE HEAVEN (2005)

Starring: *Reese Witherspoon (Elizabeth Masterson), Mark Ruffalo (David Abbot), Donal Logue (Jack Houriskey), Jon Heder (Darryl)*
Director: *Mark Waters*
Screenwriters: *Peter Tolan, Leslie Dixon, based on the novel* If Only It Were True *by Marc Levy*
PG/95 mins./Comedy/Romance/USA

David gets more than he bargained for when he rents a swish San Francisco apartment – it comes complete with a ghost only he can see, former tenant Elizabeth. She's not about to leave, either, as Elizabeth's convinced she's not actually dead yet, so she enlists a reluctant David's help to find out what happened to her.

Leave all logical reasoning at the cinema door and any cynicism at home and you'll no doubt enjoy this 21st-century comedy twist on *Ghost*. Headlined by America's sweetheart, Reese Witherspoon – who gets to display all the over-achieving, snippy mannerisms she's perfected in movies like *Sweet Home Alabama* and *Election* – it's basically the story of a workaholic who finally gets a life when, erm, she's not actually living anymore.

Yes, it seems in today's busy work-first, social-life-later society, the only way Elizabeth can find true love is by having a head-on collision with a truck, then haunting the depressed tenant (Ruffalo) now living in her apartment until he falls for her. Which is all very predictable – and stuffed, of course, with just about every romcom convention: the sceptical but supportive best friend (Donal Logue) with all the best lines; the quirky spiritualist (Napoleon Dynamite's Jon Heder) as the only one who believes David; the misunderstandings involving a voluptuous neighbour; and various other confusions that would be cleared up in two minutes if the protagonists just sat down and had a proper conversation with each other. But there are some surprises here – just as love is finally on the way, director Mark Waters goes somewhere surprisingly darker, creating a final hurdle that our lovebirds must overcome on the road to happiness.

While it doesn't entirely work – there are annoying little inconsistencies such as Elizabeth being ghostly enough to walk through walls and furniture, yet seemingly full enough of body to sit in a car – Waters moves things along at such a sprightly pace you almost don't have time to notice (and, thankfully, he doesn't pack the film with sappy bits, either), while the San Francisco locations, glistening in the sunlight, add to the fairy-tale feel.

Most enjoyable of all, though, is the fun chemistry between the likeable Witherspoon and brooding 'serious' actor Mark Ruffalo (who looks a lot more comfortable here than he did in *13 Going On 30*). It's their on-screen rapport and sweet romance that make this cute affair worth watching. ★★★ **JB**

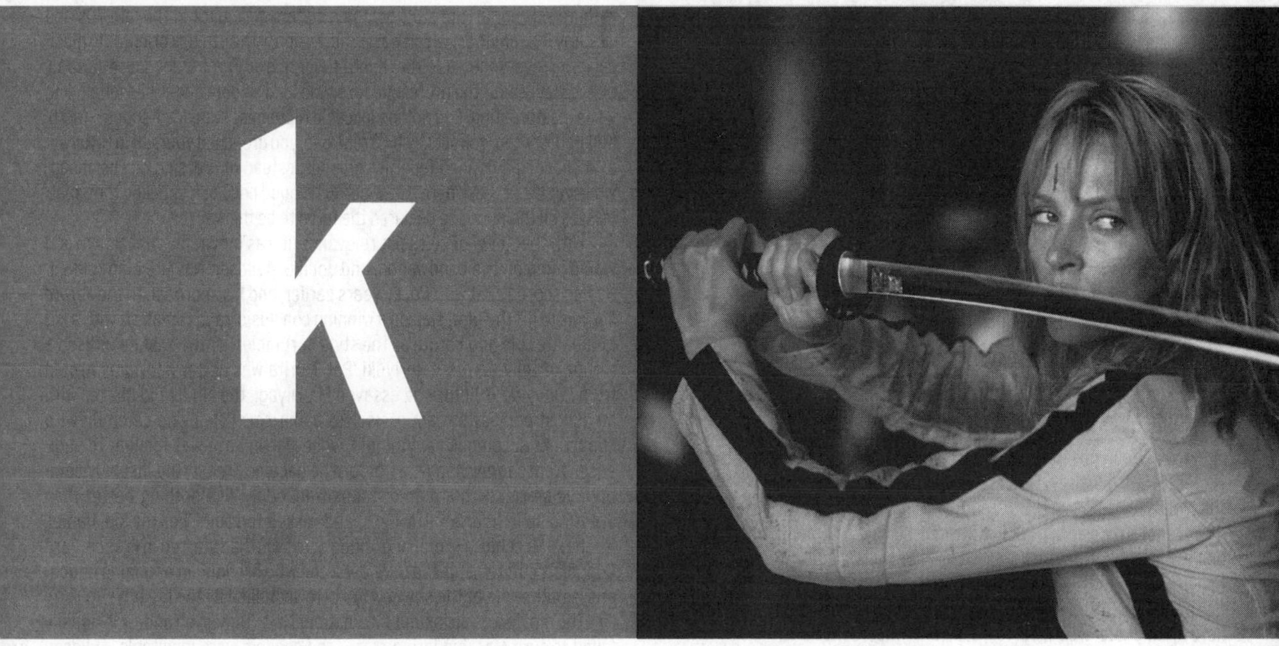

⦾ KAFKA (1991)

Starring: *Jeremy Irons (Kafka), Theresa Russell (Gabriela), Joel Grey (Burgel), Ian Holm (Doctor Murnau), Jeroen Krabbe (Bizzlebek), Alec Guinness (The Chief Clerk)*
Director: *Steven Soderbergh*
Screenwriter: *Lem Dobbs*
15/94 mins./Drama/Thriller/USA/France

Kafka is an insurance clerk in Prague who becomes embroiled in a secret organisation after his best friend and co-worker is murdered. As he gets closer to the group he realises that the conspiracies he has been writing about at night are worryingly close to the truth.

Steven Soderbergh's *Kafka* is the most famous modern example of the dreaded Second Film Syndrome. The follow-up to the director's internationally acclaimed *sex, lies, and videotape*, it was judged a pretentious failure and only received a UK release three years after production.

Actually, the film's terrible reputation is almost an advantage: while Soderbergh's debut was impossibly over-hyped, and, inevitably, disappointing, this comes on surprisingly strong and will, for many, be more satisfying. By day, a character called Kafka toils in a Prague insurance office, saving his mind for the nights when he struggles to be a writer. When his only friend at the office is mysteriously murdered by a lobotomised zombie, Kafka is drawn into a conspiracy world alarmingly like the one he imagines. There is something suspect in films about authors which suggest they didn't have to go to the trouble of exerting creative talent since their lives provided them with all their material.

Here, however, the game is played in such exaggerated terms that it's forgivable: this in no way tries to be a biographical drama of an adaptation of a specific Kafka work, and, while it has comically horrid officials and such 'Kafkaesque' concepts as the trial and the castle, is more a straightforward horror movie than a literary conceit. Irons wanders bemusingly through body-snatching, as the script drops names like Murnau and Orlac to evoke German Expressionist cinema of the 20s, but the on-location black-and-white gothic of Prague and studied period details are more reminiscent of the Hammer Horrors of the late 50s. It even has a sequence shot in odd-looking colour and a parade of distinguished actors as jovially sinister suspects ★★★★ **KN**

⦾ KAGEMUSHA (1980)

Starring: *Tatsuya Nakadai (Shingen Takeda/Kagemusha), Tsutomu Yamazaki (Nobukadu Takeda), Kenichi Hagiwara (Katsuyori Takeda), Kota Yui (Takemaru)*
Director: *Akira Kurosawa*
Screenwriters: *Massato Ide, Akira Kurosawa*
PG/179 mins./History/Drama/Japan/USA

Awards: *BAFTA – Best Director, Best Costume Design*

In the midst of a 16th-century civil war between three rival clans, a powerful warlord is mortally wounded. Terrified of the repercussions, his clan decides to place a lowly thief, who uncannily resembles him, in his guise. As the years pass this downtrodden no-mark Kagemusha becomes possessed with the spirit of the dead warrior.

Fallen on hard times, care of fashion and local indifference, it took the intervention of Francis Coppola and George Lucas to assist the once mighty Akira Kurosawa to get this epic return to the Samurai traditions that made him great before the cameras. We should be thankful they persevered, this masterful quasi-Shakespearean morality tale of an urchin placed as a surrogate king allowed colour to flood through the black-and-white splendour of old and, alongside *Ran*, marks the fabulous, near-divine, return to form of one of cinema's true greats.

Even at 70, Kurosawa reveals such calm control over the vastness of his vision. The film squalls with hoards of Samurai horseman, battlefields oceans of colour-coded warriors, and is extraordinary to behold. Again, the legion fans of Kurosawa's work are left to wonder if he has full control over the heavens themselves, as a rainbow clashes against the soot-dark skies as a warning of battle. History and nature are intertwined, lowly man slaves to forces beyond our meagre ken. Kurosawa was certainly not letting age or depression dim his ardour for the big-screen effect.

Yet, his brilliant small stuff is also here. Tatsuya Nakadai's flamboyant journey into Kagemusha's tragedy reveals that, although saved from a death sentence and placed in this miraculously noble position, he may still have got the rough end of the stick. Overcome with the spirit of the dead warlord, he descends into drink and, finally, insanity – the responsibilities of greatness can be as destructive as penury. *Ran*, his last great masterpiece, was to follow, and while its range and confidence surpass *Kagemusha*'s florid exemplar, it's not by much. ★★★★ **IN**

⓪ KALIFORNIA (1993)

Starring: *Brad Pitt (Early Grayce), Juliette Lewis (Adele Corners), David Duchovny (Brian Kessler), Michelle Forbest (Carrie Laughlin), Kathy Larson (Teenage Girls), David Milford (Driver)*
Director: *Dominic Sena*
Screenwriter: *Tim Metcalfe, from a story by Metcalfe and Stephen Levy*
18/113 mins./Crime/Drama/USA

A journalist and his photographer girlfriend are driving from Tennessee to California to research a book about serial killers but find their travelling companions offer them an insight that is a little too close for comfort.

The American obsession with serial killers and all they stand for – perverse individualism, suicidal nihilism, the general cult of celebrity weirdness – is a good subject for a hard, critical, intelligent movie. Unfortunately, *Kalifornia* isn't it. Structured as a picaresque road movie, it borrows heavily from Terrence Malick's *Badlands*, but, whereas the crazy couple in that movie were placed as the victims of the prevailing cultural myths (of romantic abjection and psychotic heroism), the crazy couple here are monsters, carnival turns, actorly impersonations.

Pitt and Lewis are barely credible as Early and Adele, the white trash holidaymakers from hell, and so it is left to Duchovny and Forbes to carry the movie as their sponsors-turned-prisoners, Brian and Carrie (get the funky De Palma reference?). The movie's premise is interesting enough. Brian is a broken-down writer planning to drive from Tennessee to California to research a coffee-table book about serial killers; Carrie decides to accompany him as photographer. To reduce the cost of the trip, they advertise for travelling companions and end up with Early and Adele, and it is from the point that the two couples meet that the movie loses its grip. The ironies click into place just a little too neatly as Brian and Carrie come to experience at first hand the terrors they wanted to report upon, while the fantasy romance between Early and Adele begins to disintegrate under the pressure of class friction.

Former pop promo director Sena knows how to give a glossy sheen to the blank surfaces and rough edges of roadside America, but the results look cheap and shoddy rather than seductively challenging. The main problem is that, unlike Brian and Carrie, Early and Adele are never granted any degree of self-consciousness, and are merely grotesque cyphers, who, in a final piece of symbolic manipulation, drift towards a showdown in a nuclear test zone. Blame it on the Bomb? What kind of message is that? ★★★ **SBe**

⓪ THE KARATE KID (1984)

Starring: *Ralph Macchio (Daniel LaRusso), Noriyuki 'Pat' Morita (Mr. Kesuke Miyagi), Elisabeth Shue (Ali Mills), Martin Kove (John Kreese), Randee Heller (Lucille LaRusso), William Zabka (Johnny Lawrence), Ron Thomas (Bobby), Rob Garrison (Tommy), Chad McQueen (Dutch), Tony O'Dell (Jimmy)*
Director: *John G. Avildsen*
Screenwriter: *Robert Mark Kamen*
12/126 mins/Drama/USA

Having moved from New Jersey to California, likeable teen Danny LaRusso doesn't fit in with his new surroundings and finds himself being bullied by kids from the local karate school. Salvation comes in the form of Mr Miyagi, a handyman-cum-janitor-cum Yoda, who agrees to mentor the youngster in both martial arts and life.

There was some rum stuff going on culture-wise back in the late 70s and early 80s, amongst which was an obsession with all things oriental. In musical terms, everyone was either Kung Fu Fighting or 'Turning Japanese' (a song, by the way, about the grotesque faces the lead singer caught himself pulling while masturbating, and not inexplicable Nipponese transformations – fact!). Ken Hom shifted wok sets by the truckload, you drenched yourself in Hi Karate aftershave and donned faux silk kimonos instead of dressing gowns; meanwhile yuppies everywhere threw perfectly good beds out, chucked their mattresses on the floor and declared the futon to be the way forward.

With that level of zeitgeist relevance, it was inevitable that Hollywood would jump on the bandwagon, and John G. Avildsen was the man to do it. He had scored a hit with *Rocky* years earlier, and his approach to the *Karate Kid* was to lift the plot, slap on a winning conclusion and remake it with a kid in the title role and karate as the style of rumble. For the cast he utilised a troupe of telly actors – Noriyuki 'Pat' Morita was better known as Arnold from *Happy Days* before he assayed Mr. Miyagi, the kindly old geezer with an almost endless stream of useless aphorisms ('Man who catch fly with chopsticks accomplish anything!'), while Martin Kove was familiar to audiences from *Cagney And Lacey* before he became Kreese, the insanely competitive sensei with a dojo of thugs who, oddly, like nothing better than dressing up in figure-flattering spandex skeleton suits. For the kid, Daniel, he chose Macchio, a promising young actor who had starred in Francis Ford Coppola's cult teen hit *The Outsiders*, and who brought an engaging gaucheness to the role of the shy new kid in town bullied by the big boys.

The movie was an instant international hit – though strangely it signally failed to turn Macchio into a star – and sequels were inevitable. Avildsen proved to be a director of the, 'If it ain't broke, don't fix it' school, and for *Part II* brought back his entire cast and located the action in the land of the rising sun. He also proved to be one who disliked waste; the whole of the opening credits consists of edited highlights from the first film, and even the apparently new sequences in the shower and car park were shot for the original and dropped, thus the first ten minutes of the sequel cost the studio precisely nothing. Though more sluggish than the original, the popularity of the characters ensured box-office success, aided by a hit soundtrack which included Peter Cetera's Oscar-nominated song, 'Glory of Love'.

The third instalment again began immediately after the predecessor, though in fact was shot three years later, leading to the unnerving appearance of Macchio gaining at least 30 lb and some height on the plane trip back from Okinawa. Predictably it was more insipid than the second. After this, while John G. Avildsen moved on, along with writer Robert Michael Kamen, to do exactly the same for Steven Dorff's career with the dismal boxing/apartheid flick *The Power Of One*, an ill-advised attempt to revive the franchise was made in 1994 with *The Next Karate Kid* – who turned out, surprisingly enough, to be future Oscar-winner Hillary Swank. It was, of course, an utter disaster. ★★★★ **AS**

⓪ THE KEEP (1983)

Starring: *Scott Glenn (Glaeken Trismegestus), Alberta Watson (Eva Cuza), Jurgen Prochnow (Captain Klaus Woermann), Robert Prosky (Father Fonescu), Gabriel Byrne (Major Kaempffer), Ian McKellan (Dr. Theodore Cuza)*
Director: *Michael Mann*
Screenwriter: *Michael Mann, from the novel by F. Paul Wilson*
18/91 mins./Horror/USA

Romania, 1942, a detachment of the German Army is sent to guard a mysterious Romanian citadel located on a strategic mountain pass. When soldiers begin to be mysteriously murdered, the SS arrives to investigate who – or what – is to blame.

After the success of his debut film *Thief* (1981) director Michael Mann decided that he wanted to surprise people by going in an entirely different direction. He certainly did that, a thematic swerve hasn't been quite as unexpected since *Spinal Tap*'s famed 'new direction'. And it managed to alarm and appal many of the critics who had hailed him only two years before. *The Keep* is Mann's only horror movie (if you don't count *Manhunter*) and was pretty much universally slated on its very limited release. It re-emerged briefly on video and now occasionally crops up in one of several versions on satellite. It remains Mann's least successful film. But, in fact, although it is afflicted with ropey dialogue and what, even for the time, are occasionally unimpressive special effects, it has an intriguing premise and a habit of lingering in the mind long after the superficial flaws have been forgotten.

Based on the first of a sextet of horror novels by F. Paul Wilson (who was unimpressed enough with Mann's movie to later write *Cuts*, a short story in which a writer puts a voodoo curse on a film director who mangles his work), *The Keep* has a battalion of German soldiers arriving in a small village in the Carpathian Mountains to occupy an ancient fortress. Within days the hapless soldiers have released an ancient force of some kind which occupies itself by regularly reducing Fritz to cinders. Enter both the SS, who import Dr. Theodore Cuza, an aged Jewish academic, from a concentration camp to try and sort out what exactly they've let loose, and a strange bloke with glowing eyes who is making his way from Greece to The Alps for some kind of supernatural showdown. Dr. Cuza is finally confronted by the monster (who unfortunately looks like a papier mache mask with a red light-bulb inside and who is named in the end credits as Molasar) who announces that he 'can smell death'. Cuza explains the Nazi concentration camps to him and, in the line that makes clear that Molasar is a Golem (see below) he bellows 'They're killing our people?' In return for carrying a talisman, which Molasar claims to be the source of his power, out of *The Keep* and thus liberating it, it promises to eliminate the Nazis while curing Cuza of his terminal disease as a kind of loyalty bonus.

The Keep is a real love-it/want-to-burn-the-negative kind of movie. For some the heady stew of trademark Michael Mann visuals (slow mo, lense-flare, billowing dry ice), occasionally impenetrable plot structure plus the ubiquitous Tangerine Dream's synth score is an intolerable reminder of the decade that taste forgot. And it is certainly a film with 'mid-80s' stamped all over it (Young One Rick Mayall even has a bit part as a German soldier who is visible, unfortunately, only in the widescreen version). But if you forgive the occasional excesses Mann's movie emerges as a unique, intelligent film which matches effective and haunting design to an original and subtle theme. *The Keep* itself, a giant looming edifice (the work of production designer John Box) nods towards German Expressionism while the small Romanian village at its foot is equally stylised with a gothic, fairy-tale feel as churches and houses hug the looming rocky outcrops (in fact, the exteriors for the movie were shot in an abandoned Welsh slate mine). But it's the theme that really marks Mann's film out. The story draws heavily on the ancient Jewish legend of The Golem, a clay man brought to life without a soul who has a habit of turning on his creators (the story has been filmed a number of times notably, and ironically, in the German *Der Golem* (1913) and its sequels). And it's in that theme, of the corruption inherent in empty power unleashed, that *The Keep* finds its strength.

The only sympathetic German soldier, Voermann, in a rant that will lead to his execution, declares that what is occurring in The Keep is the same as what has occurred in Germany. That the uncontrolled lust for power has 'unleashed the foulness in all men's minds' and thus the evil manifest in the form of the Nazis and Hitler himself. But Mann's movie matches this with the Jewish academic conjuring up the Golem in order to obliterate his oppressors. He is equally bedazzled by raw power and becomes corrupt, unable to see that once released Molasar will do pretty much what it wants to. Everyone, good or bad it seems, is capable of being corrupted. ★★★★ **AS**

KELLY'S HEROES (1970)

Starring: *Clint Eastwood (Private Kelly), Telly Savalas (Sergeant Big Joe), Don Rickles (Staff Sergeant Crapgame), Carroll O'Connor (Major General Colt), Donald Sutherland (Sergeant Oddball), Gavin MacLeod (Moriarty)*
Director: *Brian G. Hutton*
Screenwriter: *Troy Kennedy-Martin*
PG/144 mins./War/USA

After a captured German colonel discloses the whereabouts of a shipment of Nazi gold, former lieutenant Kelly hatches a plan to steal over into enemy territory. With his gang of misfits, and three Sherman tanks, a deeply unpatriotic mission sets forth.

A curious fusion of men-on-a-mission and caper flick, this late 60s war movie is arguably much more about Vietnam than it is the WWII setting it nominally dwells inside.

The tone is slightly whimsical and amoral, with its ragged gang of hoodlums out for themselves hardly the sturdy warriors of celluloid history. Greed is their motivation, the ideals of war can go hang. And Oddball, Donald Sutherland's oafish, vacant tank commander, is pure anachronism, a dopehead flower-child afloat twenty years before he should even exist. Brian G. Hutton is treating the plains of war and their grand cinematic representation with a swallow of disgust – why the hell shouldn't these grab-bag weirdos chase the loot? – but his accusations feel contemporary. Hey, isn't that the American Dream they are screwing with?

Cynical, goofy, dry and a little wayward, this is the kind of film where the characters go by silly nametags like Crapgame, Oddball, and Big Joe. It's instilled with the bite and bark of Bilko's capitalist fervour, and has a fun line in cool, snappy dialogue, although never intending to be quite so broadly a comedy. After all, Eastwood is still doing his desert creek delivery as the so-called hero. The action is flashy and intermittent, deliberately wallowing in a mire of revisionist grot, churned up vistas of European mud. Time has made it a more intuitive and caustic film, than its daft reputation might suggest. ★★★★ **IN**

THE KENTUCKY FRIED MOVIE (1977)

Starring: *Marilyn Joi (Cleopatra Schwatrz), Saul Kahan (Schwartz), David Zucker (Man), Marcy Goldman (Housewife)*
Director: *John Landis*
Screenwriters: *Jim Abrahams, David Zucker, Jerry Zucker*
18/90 mins./Comedy/USA

A network of interconnecting skits modelled on the modern sprawl of American television. Thus we get spoof news programmes, spy films, mob films, kung-fu epics, commercials, porn movies and a whole load of blaxploitation.

A rushed, puerile scattershot of sketches satirising American TV habits, that also manages that irritating trick of being occasionally funny too (in a scattershot and puerile way). Hence, *The Kentucky Fried Movie*, with its wobbly bosoms and un-PC hectoring, tends to feature heavily in pubescent boys rites-of-passage movies. Although John Landis directed it, the talents that emerged from its goonish, never-that-biting examination of American consumer foibles, are the writers, the two Zucker brothers and Jim Abrahams, collectively ZAZ who went on to make one of the funniest films of all time in *Airplane!*. They were still warming up here.

Their idea was to take the sketch comedy format, so successfully housed on television, and apply it to the movies, with the added postmodern gesture of making it about television. It's a splurge of mock-ups from dippy kung-fu movie parodies (A Fistful Of Yen is the centre piece running to a whole half hour) to the exceedingly low-slung sexploitation of Catholic Schoolgirls In Trouble that manages the crafty trick of being both a spoof and a cheeky bit of soft porn. The jokes hit as much as they miss, although ZAZ never have the energy or skill to truly fix on their target: it's really just about schoolboy tittering. As mock oil company Argon declares in their public service segment, 'We're extracting 2.5 billion barrels of crude oil each day from teenagers' faces.' They knew their target audience zits and all. ★★★ **IN**

KES (1969)

Starring: *David Bradley (Billy Casper), Freddie Fletcher (Jud Casper), Lynne Perrie (Mrs Casper), Colin Welland (Mr. Farthing), Brian Glover (Mr. Sugden)*
Director: *Ken Loach*
Screenwriters: *Ken Loach, Tony Garnett, Barry Hines, from the novel* A Kestrel For A Knave *by Barry Hines*
PG/106 mins./Drama/UK

Awards: *BAFTA – Most Promising Newcomer (David Bradley), Best Supporting Actor (Colin Welland)*

A boy from the rough end of town, endlessly bullied at school, finds solace in looking after a baby kestrel.

Based on Barry Hines' novel *A Kestrel For A Knave*, this was the film that marked Ken Loach's big-screen debut in 1969. Building upon his reputation for grittily realistic TV plays, Loach pushed kitchen-sink drama one stage further into quasi-documentary: 15-year-old Barnsley schoolboy Billy Casper finds release from the struggles of underachieving school days and a poor, fatherless family, by catching and training a baby kestrel.

Having no experience, Bradley can't help but be natural, winning viewers' hearts from the first scene when bullying big brother Jud makes him late for his paper round by nicking his bike. Billy steals, daydreams and is useless in class, but remains one of the screen's most loveable rogues – even before the beautiful scenes of him with his kestrel on the moor. Perfectly pitching the screenplay's sensitively woven story and natural ear for dialogue – the film's original US distributor thought Polish more discernible – Loach's low-key take is just the right side of sentimental.

The film is peppered with astonishing debuts from mostly non-professionals. Best of all is ex-wrestler Glover as the vaguely sadistic sports master, who almost steals the film during the farcical football match. Look out, too, for Lynne Perrie (who went on to infamy as Ivy Tilsley in *Coronation Street*) as Billy's brassy mum. Unforgettable when it first appeared over 30 years ago, *Kes* remains something of a landmark. ★★★★ **AM**

KEY LARGO (1948)

Starring *Humphrey Bogart (Frank McCloud), Edward G. Robinson (Johnny Rocco), Lauren Bacall (Nora Temple), Lionel Barrymore (James Temple), Claire Trevor (Gaye Dawn)*
Director: *John Huston*
Screenwriters: *Maxwell Anderson, Richard Brooks, John Huston*
PG/100 mins./Crime/USA

Awards: *Academy Awards – Best Supporting Actress (Claire Trevor)*

While visiting a run-down hotel in the Florida Keys, run by a widow of an old war buddy and her crippled father-in-law, Frank McCloud slowly decides to take on local gangster Johnny Rocco and his gang, who have taken over the hotel. Slowly, surely, Frank waits for his moment.

Amongst the films of the famed Bogart – Bacall period from the late forties, that vivid, sublimely erotic set of quasi-noirs that have all become classics, *Key Largo* is relatively the least impressive (emphasis on the 'relatively') and familiar. This is because it is far less concerned with the frothy interplay between the two magnetic stars, being more concerned with the man-to-man confrontation between Bogart's familiar rasping loner, an ex-GI, and Edward G. Robinson's salty lowlife gangster. It is less sexy than *The Big Sleep* or *To Have And Have Not*, but a more heady thriller built around a crackling conflict.

Based on a Broadway flop written by Maxwell Anderson, John Huston updated the story to a post-war America, a land battle-toughened and awash with illicit opportunity. It is a fork in the road for the nascent superpower marked by the slimy opportunism of Rocco or the tough deep-seated moralism of McCloud. Bacall, naturally, plays his love interest, but she is less of a sparky rival, and their relationship has none of the electricity of before.

Huston, though, is at home with the material, coating the lurid throes of his tale in the sweaty atmosphere of the high tropics, under the impending menace of a hurricane. There's great work with a storm-lashed hotel where the family are held hostage. It feels more formulaic than its fellow entries in the Bogart canon, but with its redoubtable performances and tightly-structured storytelling remains just as gripping. ★★★★ **IN**

THE KID (1921)

Starring: *Charles Chaplin (Tramp), Jackie Coogan (The Kid), Baby Hathaway (The Kid as a baby), Edna Purviance (Mother), Carl Miller (Artist), Tom Wilson (Policeman)*
Direction: *Charles Chaplin*
Screenwriter: *Charles Chaplin*
U/68 mins./Comedy/USA

Desperate, Edna leaves her child in a limo with a note – she's going to kill herself. Charlie rescues the child and cares for it, but five years later Edna has become a famous opera singer and she demands the child be returned to her.

After his Tramp persona had appeared in numerous short films since 1914, Chaplin's 1921 classic was his first feature and the first film in which he appeared as writer, director and star. It also marked a departure from all-out slapstick and towards moments of drama and social realism – aspects that became increasingly emphasized in Chaplin's later work.

Focusing on the relationship between the Tramp and an abandoned boy, it includes some wonderful comic sequences, yet is slightly marred by Chaplin's heavy-handed sentimentality. Chaplin is, of course, hilarious, but it's Coogan's cherubic charm that makes this so special. ★★★★ **ND**

THE KID STAYS IN THE PICTURE (2002)

Starring: *as themselves: Robert Evans (Narrator), Eddie Albert, William Castle, Francis Ford Coppola, Catherine Deneuve, Josh Evans, Errol Flynn, Ava Gardner, Ernest Hemingway, Henry Kissinger, Jack Nicholson, Tyrone Power*
Directors: *Nanette Burstein, Brett Morgan*
Screenwriters: *Brett Morgen, adapted from the book by Robert Evans*
15/89 mins./Documentary/Biography/USA

The rise, dramatic fall and rise again of legendary actor-turned-Hollywood producer, Robert Evans, is told in a documentary based on Evans' autobiography, and is narrated by the man himself.

Producer Robert Evans' life story is so extraordinary that even a Hollywood scriptwriter couldn't make it up. Spotted swimming in the Beverly Hills Hotel pool in 1956, he was, with no previous acting experience, signed up as a movie star.

Then he tried his hand at producing, making such classics as *The Godfather*, *Rosemary's Baby*, *Love Story* and *Chinatown*.

Friend to Warren Beatty and Jack Nicholson, and lover to Ava Gardner, Ali McGraw, Grace Kelly and many others, Evans is one of Hollywood's true characters whose story works so well because it has the fall (McGraw left him for Steve McQueen, and he was busted for cocaine use), as well as the rise.

To illustrate such a tale, the directors use a collage of clips, headlines and animated photos so that even still pictures seem like moving ones. Meanwhile Evans' distinctive voice punctuates each image with the occasionally fanciful but always riveting tale of his life. ★★★★ **CK**

KIDS (1995)

Starring: *Leo Fitzpatrick (Telly), Justin Pierce (Casper), Chloe Sevigny (Jennie), Sarah Henderson (Girl), Rosario Dawson (Ruby)*
Director: *Larry Clark*
Screenwriter: *Harmony Korine, from a story by Larry Clark, Jim Lewis*
18/90 mins./Drama/USA

A teenage Casanova, who enjoys deflowering young girls, is in for a shock when one of his former conquests tries to confront him.

For the last few decades there has been a definite series of conventions with regard to adolescent sexual encounters in coming-of-age movies. You know the score. A quick snog here. The odd fumble there. It is a rose-tinted view which somehow suggests a teenage innocence that seems reassuring if not strictly accurate.

To say that Larry Clark's debut does not adhere to such a tradition is like suggesting that Mike Tyson might be capable of giving someone a nasty clip. A loose semi-documentary about New York's teen youth, Clark's highly controversial debut feature tells the story of 24 hours in the life of pubescent layabout Telly who, in the film's opening shot, we discover playing tonsil hockey with his latest sexual conquest. Telly, it turns out, likes his girlfriends even younger than he is ('Virgins ... I love them! No diseases!') and between bouts of shoplifting and dope-smoking tries to woo as many as possible. In a parallel story we also find out that Jenny, one of Telly's previous underage one-night stands, is not only HIV positive but could only have contracted the disease from him.

That the end product is an experience can hardly be denied. Whether it is an experience that anyone would wish to endure on a Saturday night, though, is another question altogether. Indeed, while in one sense the film can be taken as an apocalyptic warning about modern-day latchkey kids there is little doubt that ex-photographer Clark's lingering camerawork frequently suggests something more creepy altogether. Perhaps there are just some stories that need to be told within the confines of a real documentary. Or not at all. ★★★ **CC**

KIDS IN THE HALL: BRAIN CANDY (1996)

Starring: *Dave Foley (Marv/Psychiatrist/New Guy/Raymond Hurdicure), Bruce McCulloch (Alice/Cisco/Grivo/Worm pill scientist/Cop #2/Cancer Boy/White-trash man), Kevin McDonald (Dr. Chris Cooper/Doreen/Chris's Dad/Lacey), Mark McKinney (Simon/Don Roritor/Cabbie/Gunther/Cop #1/Nina Bedford/Melanie/Drill sergeant/White-trash woman), Scott Thompson (Baxter/Mrs. Hurdicure/Wally Terzinsky/Malek/Big Stummies scientist/The Queen/Raj/Clempto)*
Director: *Kelly Malkin*
Screenwriters: *Norm Hiscock, Bruce McCulloch, Mark McKinney, Kevin McDonald, Scott Thompson*
15/84 mins./Comedy/Canada/USA

A researcher invents a mind-altering drug — and gradually the world comes under its thrall.

For the uninitiated, the first big-screen outing for the all-boy Canadian comedy quintet, whose Pythonesque exploits were once to be found lurking around Channel 4 in the small hours, may prove to be something of a tedious affair – but those familiar with their brand of stinging satire are in for a treat.

Set in a slightly skewed modern-day America, the film charts the misadventures of mousy pharmaceuticals researcher Chris Cooper as he invents a mind-altering drug and the resulting corporate shenanigans as a corrupt drugs firm gets the whole world hooked on it.

Essentially a series of sketches linked by a gossamer plot, this boasts about the same hit/miss ratio as the telly series, with the odd sketch plummeting into nil-laugh hell, but these are more than counterbalanced by moments of comic genius – specifically 'cancer boy' (a wickedly sick parody of the media's morbid fascination with cute terminal kids), a gag worth the entrance price alone, an indicator of the current of black social satire that the five have bolstered their buffoonery with.

The star of the show is Thompson, with creations such as repressed Wally Terzinsky and Mrs. Hurdicure, a matronly aunt sent into a coma by the replaying of her only happy memory undercutting the laughs with genuine warmth.

Not to everyone's tastes then, but, for fans of the show – big, big laughs. ★★★★ **AS**

KILL BILL: VOL 1 (2003)

Starring: *Uma Thurman (The Bride), Lucy Liu (O-Ren Ishii), Vivica A. Fox (Vernita Green), Daryl Hannah (Elle Driver), David Carradine (Bill), Michael Madsen (Budd)*
Director: *Quentin Tarantino*
Screenwriter: *Quentin Tarantino, from the character The Bride created by Tarantino and Uma Thurman*
18/106 mins./Action/Crime/Drama/USA
Awards: *Empire Awards – Best Actress, Best Director*

Gunned down on her wedding day by her former colleagues, an assassin wakes from a coma four years later intent on revenge. She makes a 'death list': number five is Bill, but first there are some old workmates to see ...

As a pitched battle between two assassins destroys a suburban home in Pasadena, in much the same way as drug overdoses and gun deals have invaded living rooms before now, you might be forgiven for thinking we are squarely in Tarantino territory. Ah, if only.

With a sly visual wit – watch out for the arrival of a school bus – and trademark banter, this is the most confident scene in the entire movie.

The rest is a curate's egg. Chapters two to four include an origin story told entirely in animé, a largely subtitled sojourn to a sword-maker which aspires to the gruff humour of Kurosawa's samurai classics but falls short, and a flashback to The Bride's escape from hospital which is pure pitch-black comedy.

Tagline
Here comes the Bride.

The final chapter, meanwhile, is a climax so bloody that – at least for western audiences – much of it takes place in black and white. If, as rumoured, both parts of *Kill Bill* were shot for two-thirds of the SFX budget on *The Matrix* sequels, Tarantino has succeeded in making the Wachowski brothers look very, very silly indeed.

Compared to Q.T.'s slice 'em, dice 'em deli, the much-hyped Neo versus 100 Agent Smiths showdown appears unforgivably gutless and soulless. Moral guardians may be outraged but, after a build that most audiences will find slow, it is the bloody geysers Tarantino uncorks here that will have them reaching for the replay button.

There is much to admire, not least a performance from Uma Thurman as steely as the plate in her character's head and a knowing soundtrack that effortlessly smears the boundaries between east and west.

The loss of limbs may feature highly, but the most notable missing appendage belongs to Tarantino himself. At times, the writer-director seems to be working with one hand – his writing hand – tied behind his back.

Perhaps he was so fed up of having quotable dialogue thrown back at him that he decided to write a movie without a single memorable line. Or perhaps, after being lauded as an Oscar-winning writer, he wanted to prove himself as an action director.

Kudos to Q.T. – painting like an old master (even John Woo will piss his pants!) first time out is an astonishing achievement, but most people will still miss the signature flourishes of his trusty 'write hand'. ★★★★ **CK**

KILL BILL: VOL 2

Starring: *Uma Thurman (Beatrix Kiddo/The Bride/Black Mamba), David Carradine (Bill/Snake Charmer), Lucy Liu (O-Ren Ishii/Cottonmouth), Vivica A. Fox (Vernita Green/Copperhead), Chia Hui Liu, as Gordon Liu (Pai Mei), Michael Madsen (Budd), Daryl Hannah (Elle Driver/California Mountain Snake)*
Director: *Quentin Tarantino*
Screenwriter: *Quentin Tarantino, from the character The Bride created by Tarantino and Uma Thurman*
18/136 mins./Action/Crime/Drama/USA

With Vernita Green and O-Ren Ishii already consigned to chopsocky hell, the Bride turns her deadly attention to the last three members on her deathlist – psycho Budd, one-eyed Elle Driver and ultimate nemesis and cause of all the carnage, Carradine's Bill.

Quite who suggested what to whom and when in that shadowy screening room, Quentin Tarantino and Harvey Weinstein must now look back on their July 2003 crisis summit with mixed emotions. It was, after all, the moment they made the brave, ground-breaking, ultimately detrimental decision to turn QT's 88-minute rampage of revenge into a four-hour, box office-accosting double bill. The moment they turned one five-star movie into two slightly chubby ones with the sum total of eight.

Make no mistake, *Vol. 1* was possibly the most invigorating, best directed, shot back-to-back action adventure in a while. (Ironically, what with it being part one of two, as opposed to The Return Of The King's final chapter, at least it knew how to end.) And it's not that *Vol. 2* is not a good movie in itself, more that that's its biggest disappointment – it's good, not great. Solid, not spectacular.

Sure, it's rammed with terrific ingredients – the screen fading to black as The Bride's coffin is nailed shut, her slapstick catfight with Hannah's bitchy Elle Driver, Carradine's enigmatic Bill, a lovingly retro, hilarious homage of a kung fu training sequence – but what work as individual vignettes occasionally slot together with a flat-pack shonkiness, jagged joins disrupting the veneer. And considering that this is all drafted by the same hand as the seamless *Pulp Fiction*, that's not just surprising – it's staggering.

Had it come courtesy of almost any other director working today, *Kill Bill Vol. 2* would most likely earn a further star. Unfortunately for QT, past glories demand he be measured by a tougher yardstick – the arrival of 'a new Tarantino' brings with it an unparalleled anticipation, a thirst that this time he never quite manages to quench.

Kill Bill's deficiencies are never more keenly noticeable than in its script. A script, let's not forget, knocked out by an Oscar-winning screenwriter. Yes, *Vol. 2* heralds a welcome return to the 'Tarantino dialogue' *Vol. 1* sorely missed, not least in a somewhat key character's perfectly judged and wonderfully executed final line. But from its pedestrian chapel intro – a lacklustre toe-dip back into the fray that promised so much but teaches us nothing we didn't already know, and that also features a virtual non-event of a Samuel L. Jackson cameo – the plot never once throws us a curveball. So telegraphed are the twists and turns on The Bride's final leg that there is sadly no mystery as to what will happen next. For once, Tarantino has no aces up his sleeve.

Whether or not *Kill Bill* would have been entirely successful as one movie will, of course, forever remain a tantalising puzzle. What's certain, though, is that it would have been more satisfying than the two resulting halves, two poorly structured pieces that simply don't fit together at all. Just reflect on that ending: an intimate affair that would have provided perfect bathos in the immediate aftermath of the House Of Blue Leaves fight sequence, a sweet comedown after the hyperkinetic high of Uma slashing her way through the Crazy 88. As it is, it's an aloof conclusion, an unclimactic climax to a stand-alone film. Having waited so long (six years!) and invested so much time (four hours!) and money (two tubs of popcorn!) in the experience, you know what? It turns out it was only a movie, after all. ★★★★ **MD**

THE KILLER (DIE XUE SHUANG XIONG) (1989)

Starring: *Chow Yun Fat (Ah Jong), Danny Lee (Insp. Li Ying/Little Eagle), Sally Yeh (Jennie), Fong Chu (Fung Sei), Kenneth Tsang (Sgt. Randy Chung)*
Director: *John Woo*
Screenwriter: *John Woo*
18/106 mins./Action/Crime/Hong Kong

When a kind-hearted assassin accidentally blinds a singer during a nightclub hit, he decides to perform one last job to pay for an operation to restore her sight.

Gunfire. Bullets thudding into human flesh. Dead bodies hitting the ground. This is what it sounds like when the doves fly.

John Woo's trademark style reached its zenith in *The Killer*, with its ying-yang relationship between a good-hearted hit man and an anti-authority cop. But underneath the Miami Vice tailoring, it's as much a doomed romance as a shoot-'em-up.

The best moments belong to the blind Jennie (at the time Sally Yeh was a huge pop star in Hong Kong), who provides some much needed light relief – serving tea oblivious to the guns on display and dodging bullets during battles with grace.

Early versions of this film were badly dubbed and edited, particularly in the US, which made nonsense of the plot and made the action sequences laughable. They also mistranslated the lead character's name as 'Jeff'. So avoid any copies of the film without the correct character names or you're in for an entirely different experience! ★★★★★ **MS**

KILLER'S KISS (1955)

Starring: *Frank Silvera (Vincent Rapallo), Jamie Smith (Davy Gordon), Irene Kane (Gloria Price), Jerry Jarret (Albert, the Fight Manager)*
Director: *Stanley Kubrick*
Screenwriters: *Stanley Kubrick, Howard Sackler, based on a story by Kubrick*
12/67 mins./Thriller/USA

Davy, a boxer, saves Gloria, a nightclub dancer, from a mugging. The couple start a relationship, which excites the jealousy of Gloria's menacing employer, Vince. Vince kidnaps Gloria, and Davy sets out to rescue her.

Stanley Kubrick's first feature film was *Fear and Desire*, an allegorical war movie he was so dissatisfied with that he managed to get it suppressed. *Killer's Kiss*, his second feature, is an exercise in film noir fairy-tale which shows just how powerful a filmmaker Kubrick was right out of the gate.

Followers of his later career will note the appearance of themes and images that recurred (a final axe-fight in a warehouse full of disembodied mannequin parts would not be out of place in *The Shining*), but this is also notably unlike later Kubrick films in its use of authentic New York locations (which extends to cinéma-vérité-look on-the-streets footage worlds away from the every-detail-controlled-in-the-studio films of the later years), an original story penned by the director and a 67-minute running time.

The plot is a tiny anecdote about a washed-up boxer, a dance-hall dame and a slimy hood, and one crowded weekend of brutality and romance. There's a sense of a young director playing games: the boxing match (a definite influence on *Raging Bull*) is all low-angle close-ups and subjective shots with plenty of thump and dazzle, and the traditional Expressionist look of noir is exaggerated with many a tricky shot or doomy plot twist.

The three unfamiliar leads are all excellent as small-timers struggling with big passions, and there is already a potent use of raucous source music and subtle sound design to augment the stark, haunted black-and-white imagery. Matthew Chapman's film *Strangers Kiss* is based on the making of this movie, with Peter Coyote as 'Stanley'. ★★★ **KN**

THE KILLING (1956)

Starring: *Sterling Hayden (Johnny Clay), Coleen Gray (Fay), Vince Edwards (Val Cannon), Jay C. Flippen (Marvin Unger), Elisha Cook Jr. (George Peatty), Marie Windsor (Sherry Peatty)*
Director: *Stanley Kubrick*
Screenwriters: *Jim Thompson, Stanley Kubrick, from the novel by Lionel White*
PG/80 mins./Crime/Drama/USA

After getting out of prison, Johnny Clay masterminds a complex race-track heist, but his scheme is complicated by the intervention of the wife of a teller in on the scheme, the boyfriend of the wife, airport regulations, and a small dog.

One of the great themes of the crime movie is the perfect heist that goes wrong. In classic Hollywood, the inevitable downbeat conclusion was mandated by censorship requirements that crime not be seen to pay.

However, when Stanley Kubrick set out in 1955 to film Lionel White's neat little novel *Clean Break*, the perfect heist was doomed to fall apart as much because of the director's bleak world-view as any kowtowing to public morality.

In Kubrick's world, there is no such thing as a perfect plan or a perfect machine – fallible human beings will always drop the ball at the vital moment, and the better-timed and planned a venture is the more likely a small diversion from the outline is to lead to catastrophe. Just as fail-safe systems designed to prevent an accidental nuclear war in *Dr. Strangelove* or the meticulous programming that puts a computer in charge of the Jupiter mission in *2001: A Space Odyssey* wind up turning on themselves leading to ironic tragedy, the race-track robbery of *The Killing* is pulled off almost flawlessly, but collapses because of human elements and impossible-to-foresee twists of fate (the moral being, never buy a cheap suitcase). In *The Killing*, someone dies because he throws away a lucky horseshoe then bursts a tyre by backing his getaway car over it.

With a stentorian, god-like narrator to identify precise times and places, *The Killing* unfolds in a daring structural jigsaw puzzle. A style that must have made a great impression on Quentin Tarantino, who has never quite been able to repeat the trick Kubrick manages of doubling back and skipping forth in time while darting around a central location to give a full picture of a complex situation. We begin at a Los Angeles race track as, 'The hundred thousand dollar Lansdowne Stakes' is about to be run, with the hotly-fancied favourite Red Lightning almost a dead cert. Around the track several people are strangely disinterested in the big race: strong-arm man Johnny Clay, tipsy customer Marvin Unger, meek cashier George Peatty, Officer Dibble soundalike cop Randy Kennan and bartender Mike O'Reilly. With two outside men – sniper Nikki Arane and intellectual wrestler Maurice – to stage diversions by shooting Red Lightning in the home stretch and occupying all the security guards in a barroom brawl, the mob have plotted how to slip past the guards, grab two million in untraceable cash and (vitally) get the loot off the site.

The heist is a perfectly-judged suspense sequence, but the flashbacks and -forwards let us in on the sad realities of the crooks' lives and hint at their dooms. Meek runt George has a trampy, vampy wife Sherry, who cajoles her way into the scam but sets Clay's crew up to be robbed of their takings by her thug boyfriend Val and his partner (Joe Turkel, later the bartender of *The Shining* and *Blade Runner*'s genius Tyrell). Johnny is a pro with a devoted girl and firm relationships with fellow pros Nikki (the grinning Carey is an unforgettable presence) and Maurice, but he finances this scheme by taking advantage of the discreetly homosexual Unger. By delicately rebuffing Unger's pre-robbery suggestion that the two of them go away together, 'and let the world take a couple of turns,' Johnny breaks his heart and turns him into a fatally loose cannon.

Kubrick was always great with actors: notice how much more Hayden does here with apparently less to go on than in the similar *The Asphalt Jungle* (1950), and the way familiar film gangland types like Cook, Windsor, Sawyer and Flippen manage to cram lifetimes of aching disappointment into a few intense yet understated scenes (the dialogue is by hard-boiled novelist Jim Thompson).

The fraying of the gang's solidarity and Sherry's power play leaves most of them dead on dirty floors. Great moments: Cook gunning down his wife's lover with a cry of, 'The jerk's right here'; Windsor's dying words, 'Just a bad joke with no punchline'.

Johnny comes to grief at the airport, where an official won't let him tote an oversized suitcase full of cash as hand baggage ('Sir, those are our flight regulations, which are designed for your comfort and safety'). A yapping dog causes a spill which pays off in an image as archetypally comic-tragic-awesome as the mushroom cloud of *Dr. Strangelove*, the hideously frozen Jack of *The Shining*, the luminous Star Child of *2001* and the Mickey Mouse Club of *Full Metal Jacket* – two million dollars in loose bills whipped into a whirlwind by aeroplane engines. ★★★★★ **KN**

KILLING FIELDS (1984)

Starring: *Sam Waterston (Sydney Schanberg), Haing S. Ngor (Dith Pran), John Malkovich (Alan 'Al' Rockoff), Julian Sands (Jon Swain), Craig T. Nelson (Major Reeves)*
Director: *Roland Joffe*
Screenwriter: *Bruce Robinson*
15/135 mins./Drama/History/War/UK

Awards: *Academy Awards – Best Supporting Actor (Haing S. Ngor), Best Cinematography, Best Editing, BAFTA – Best Actor (Haing S. Ngor), Best Cinematography, Best Editing, Best Film, Best Production Design/Art Direction, Best Adapted Screenplay, Best Sound, Outstanding Newcomer (Haing S. Ngor), Golden Globes – Best Supporting Actor (Haing S. Ngor)*

American reporter Sydney Schanberg, and his Cambodian guide Dith Pran make it their personal mission to bring news of the wanton killing of Khmer Rouge to the world at large.

Remarkably it's been some time since Roland Joffe made his seminal picture (and sadly has never regained the form), but the years have not dulled its searing power. As much as Oliver Stone has cracked open the fetid shell of Vietnam, Joffe penetrates the horror of Cambodia – when Pol Pot's three-year reign of terror in the late 1970s resulted in the slaughter of 3 million people – through the true relationship between American reporter Sydney Schanberg, and his Cambodian guide Dith Pran (the Oscar winning Haing S. Ngor, a Cambodian doctor and former refugee himself, who was tragically shot in an American gangland killing in the 1990s).

Their personal endeavours to bring news of the wanton killing of Khmer Rouge to the world at large, are depicted with brilliant, mind-numbing clarity, by Joffe's roving camera. The scene where Pran, having escaped his evil captors, awakes in a field of rotting corpses sticks with you for life.

A mighty accomplishment. ★★★★★ **IN**

ⓒ THE KILLING OF A CHINESE BOOKIE (1976)

Starring: *Ben Gazzara (Cosmo Vitelli), Timothy Agoglia Carey (Flo), Seymour Cassel (Mort Weil), Robert Phillips (Phil), Morgan Woodward (John), Soto Joe Hugh (Chinese Bookie)*
Director: *John Cassavetes*
Screenwriters: *John Cassavetes*
15/108 mins./Drama/USA

Cosmo Vittelli, manager of a sparkly but seedy Los Angeles strip club, is duped by mobster Mort Weil into running up a gambling debt he can only pay off by assassinating a criminal rival.

John Cassavetes's showbiz gangster movie (from an idea originally outlined with Martin Scorsese) is a semi-improvised, self-confessedly rambling character study which comes off oddly like *Broadway Danny Rose* with more guns. It's a deliberately-paced, loose study of character and milieu, liable to drive folks raised on 1980s gangland movies to frustration, but astoundingly rich in its detail and with a distinctive, faded-glory look that gives it a dream-like fascination. Like its committed hero, the film is surprisingly able to work up desperate enthusiasm for the third-rate Crazy Horse West club, investing speciality stripteasers (including Russ Meyer veteran Haji) with a compelling erotic sadness, letting Meade Roberts (as neurotic stand-up 'Mr Sophistication') do affectingly pathetic renditions of 'I Can't Give You Anything But Love, Baby' and 'Imagination' and establishing a touching sense of a nurturing community among g-strings and watered drinks.

Barely ecaping from the scene of the crime, after it has turned out that the supposed 'Chinese bookie' is not another lowlife but a well-protected mastermind, Cosmo is pursued by an eccentric killer played by the unforgettably grinning Timothy Agoglia Carey (of *The Killing*), and has to talk his way out of another shoot-out. The emotional climax comes after the gangland gunplay as a gutshot Gazzara returns to the club, where he delivers a pep talk to his exotic dancers and neurotic comedian Roberts.

In perhaps his best performance for Cassavetes, Gazzara gives a marvellously unshowy performance, inhabiting his role with a host of tiny, telling gestures. Released at 135 and 108 minutes, the shorter version is the director's preferred cut. ★★★★ **KN**

John Cassavetes (1929–1989)

Who he is: Hollywood character actor (*The Dirty Dozen, Rosemary's Baby*) but better known as the godfather of American independent cinema.
Hallmarks: Intensely personal films detailing the minutiae of relationships; a home-movie feel; hand-held camera and long takes, allowing actors to do their thing; interiors and a lack of sunlight.
If you see one movie, see: *A Woman Under the Influence* (1974)

ⓒ KIND HEARTS AND CORONETS (1949)

Starring: *Dennis Price (Duke Louis Mazzini/Mazzini Sr.), Valerie Hobson (Edith D'Ascoyne), Joan Greenwood (Sibella Holland), Alec Guinness (Duke Etherel/The Banker/Rev. Lord Henry/General Lord Rufus/Admiral Horatio/Young Henry/Lady Agatha/Lord Ascoyne)*
Director: *Robert Hamer*
Screenwriters: *Robert Hamer, John Dighton, based on the novel by Roy Horniman*
U/101 mins./Comedy/USA

Louis Mazzini's mother is abandoned by her aristocratic family D'Ascoyne. As an adult, Louis decides to avenges his mother, by becoming the next Duke of the family, by disposing of every family member who stands in his way.

It's hard to imagine a film about a conniving mass murderer being granted a U certificate, but the venerable Baling Films managed just that with this blackly comic gem. Taking a Tennyson quote as its title ('Kind hearts are more than coronets/And simple faith than Norman blood'), *Kind Hearts* gently undermines the notions of nobility and inherited privilege. The dapper, genteel yet impoverished Louis Mazzini, secures what he sees as his rightful position as the Duke Of Chalfont, by cold-bloodedly, and often hilariously, murdering the eight relations that stand in his way. Dennis Price cuts a fine figure as the murderous Louis, but if *Kind Hearts* is remembered and justly celebrated for anything, then it is for the tour de force of one man, Alec Guinness.

Director Robert Hamer took the then unprecedented step of securing Guinness – already established as a major British actor and renowned for his chameleon like versatility – to play the entire D'Ascoyne family, young and old, male and female. Guinness clearly relished the opportunity, fine tuning eight variations on the same family theme, from the delightfully doddery old Reverend to the young, puckish, slightly pickled Henry. Some of these roles were extended turns, some registered as mere cameos: the Admiral who goes down with his ship, and Guinness's drag turn as Agatha D'Ascoyne, a suffragette whose decision to leaflet London from a hot air balloon takes a fatal turn as Louis practices his marksmanship with a bow and arrow. 'I shot an arrow in the air, she came to earth in Berkeley Square.'

Agatha's initial ascent in the balloon – filmed in a field next door to Pinewood Studios – caused a few worries for Guinness. Concerned about the possibility of anything going wrong, he asked the producers if he was well insured. They told him he was, for the sum of £10,000, which Guinness promptly declared to be too small a sum. 'I decided it wasn't nearly enough and informed them I wouldn't get up more than 15 feet unless they raised the insurance to £50,000.' They refused, pointing out that Guinness had a rather well-qualified Belgian balloonist hidden in the basket with him. Guinness wouldn't budge and went no higher than the few feet he agreed – when the balloon takes off into full flight it is in fact the Belgian balloonist wearing Agatha's dress and wig. Guinness had the last laugh when a high wind pulled the balloon off course – the famed Belgian balloonist was found 50 miles away where he had to pitch into a river.

Much of the success of *Kind Hearts* must also be attributed to director Robert Hamer. Described by Guinness as a man, 'who looked and sounded like an endearing but scornful frog,' Hamer here moulds a kind of *Henry Portrait Of A Serial Killer* filtered through the whimsy of Baling. It is his sure touch (as director and co-writer) that makes this essentially morbid material as comically macabre, yet also acceptable and entertaining. He sets out his table right from the off, with the arrival of the hangman at the jail, housing the soon-to-be-executed – albeit for the wrong crime – Louis Mazzini. As Louis decides to write his arrogant confession (the voice-over for the movie), the hangman blithely discusses the nature of his business ('Some of them tend to be very hysterical. No sense of consideration.') while deciding how he should address his intended victim, settling on 'Your grace'. This is after all a comedy of geniality, despite the venality of the man in question.

Hamer ups the stakes as we flash back, greeting the young Louis ('In those days I never had any trouble with the sixth commandment') and mixing absurdity with the blackness (his father died at childbirth, his mother gets hit by a tram). Worst of all is the fact that Louis has to bury her in a hideous suburban cemetery. It is in this delicate balancing act between bad taste and bad manners, that *Kind Hearts And Coronets* is probably one of the few movies that can sell the death of twin babies by diphtheria as a comic moment. As a movie it remains a jewel in the crown of the finest comedy production line Britain ever saw. Baling would continue from strength to strength after this but, with the exception of *The Ladykillers*, it would never dabble in such splendidly dark material again. And it stands as Alec Guinness' finest series of comic screen moments. ★★★★★ **BMc**

A KIND OF LOVING (1962)

Starring: *Alan Bates (Voc Brown), June Ritchie (Ingrid Rothwell), Thora Hird (Mrs. Rothwell), Bert Palmer (Mr. Brown), Gwen Nelson (Mrs. Brown), James Bolam (Jeff)*
Director: *John Schlesinger*
Screenwriters: *Willis Hall, Keith Waterhouse, based on the novel by Stan Barstow*
15/112 mins./Drama/UK
Awards: *Berlin – The Golden Bear*

Northern draughtsman Vic Brown flirts with typist Ingrid Rothwell until he finally seduces her. However, he's forced to marry her when she becomes pregnant, but draws the line at living with her shrewish mother.

Following in the wake of several successful Kitchen Sink dramas, John Schlesinger's feature debut was overlooked by many critics who had yet to be convinced of Alan Bates's star quality in *The Entertainer* and *Whistle Down the Wind*. Moreover, moviegoers were less than enticed by the prospect of witnessing what was, to many of them, the everyday reality of being either ensnared in a loveless marriage or forced to live with disapproving in-laws until they found their financial feet.

Consequently, this adaptation of Stan Barstow's novel only found an audience after it won the Golden Bear at the Berlin Film Festival. Recognising that this wasn't just another portrait of an angry young man or a resolute study in northern miserabilism, viewers came to appreciate the sour wit of Willis Hall and Keith Waterhouse's screenplay and the compassion of the direction.

Having established his social realist credentials with the 1961 documentary, *Terminus*, Schlesinger was able to locate his characters within their industrial environment without reducing them to caricatures. He allowed Thora Hird to play Mrs Rothwell as a shrill, petty bourgeois termagent. But for all his arrogant self-obsession and her unemancipated consumerism, Bates and Ritchie are essentially decent people struggling to come to terms with the social, moral and economic temptations arising from their changing times.

Indeed, this is a compelling snapshot of Britain before the Sixties began to swing. Football matches and brass bands may still be the opiates of the urban masses, but television is clearly beginning to alter people's opinions and expectations through its dramas and insights into how the other half lived. Thus, this is as much a film about the decline of traditional communities in the face of growing individualism as it is about whether Vic and Ingrid will find the kind of loving they seek by striking out alone. ★★★★ **DP**

KINDERGARTEN COP (1990)

Starring: *Arnold Schwarzenegger (Det. John Kimble), Penelope Ann Miller (Joyce Palmieri/Rachel Crisp), Pamela Reed (Det. Phoebe O'Hara), Linda Hunt (Miss Schlowski), Cathy Moriarty (Sylvester's Mother)*
Director: *Ivan Reitman*
Screenwriters: *Murray Salem, Herschel Weingrod, Timothy Harris, based on a story by Salem*
15/106 mins./Comedy/Action/USA

An undercover cop must pose as a Kindergarten teacher to protect a young boy.

Taking time out on the action-man front between *Total Recall* and *Terminator 2*, Big Arnie now followed up his commercial success in the very bland *Twins* (yes, believe it or not, *Twins* was a hit) by re-teaming with director Ivan Reitman for another soft-centred comedy thriller.

This time around he is John Kimble, an Austrian somehow working as a hard-nut for the Los Angeles Police Department, who transfers out of his macho man surroundings into a kiddie movie suburbia when he has to go undercover as a kindergarten teacher. Although the first and last thirds are a densely plotted blend of humour and thrills, *Kindergarten Cop* sags desperately in the middle.

The initial joke of facing the man mountain from *The Terminator* with the one obstacle he can't possibly overcome – a classroom full of six-year-olds – fades almost instantly as the Macaulay Culkin-wannabe tykes proudly trot out in succession their personalised cute mannerisms and Arnie miraculously but expectedly turns from gruff kid-hater to dewy-eyed super-teacher in the space of an aerobics montage.

With a heart of purest mush, *Kindergarten Cop* still manages to be generally entertaining, even for folk with an aversion to Aryan body builders or perky pre-teenagers, while some of the jokes are a reminder that Reitman was once a promising comic talent, and the thriller stuff benefits from a stronger-than-usual set of villains and a nicely-judged sidekick performance from Pamela Reed as Schwarzenegger's gourmet colleague. ★★★ **KN**

k

THE KING AND I (1956)

Starring: *Deborah Kerr (Anna Leonowens), Yul Brynner (King Mongkut of Siam), Rita Moreno (Tuptim), Martin Benson (Kralahome), Rex Thompson (Louis Leonowens), Terry Saunders (Lady Thiang)*
Director: *Walter Lang*
Screenwriter: *Ernest Lehman, from the musical by Oscar Hammerstein and Richard Rogers, based on the book* Anna And The King Of Siam *by Margaret Landon*
U/127 mins./Musical/USA

Awards: *Academy Awards – Best Actor, Best Art Direction/Set Decoration, Best Color Costumes, Best Musical Score, Best Sound Recording, Golden Globes – Best Musical/Comedy, Best Actress*

An English school teacher arrives in Siam to teach the King's children, but soon finds their father's education an even greater challenge.

After storming Broadway in the 1950s, this hit musical transferred to the screen complete with its star – Yul Brynner – and with a leading lady, Deborah Kerr, who he'd personally recommended.

Based on the memoirs of Anna Leonowens, who was a governess and teacher in the court of Siam during the 19th Century, the film may play fast and loose with the truth (even Leonowens' writing was somewhat liberal with the facts) but thanks to the wonderful Rogers and Hammerstein score, some sumptuous looking set-pieces and the sexual energy between Kerr and Brynner it crackles with life.

Like many leading ladies – Audrey Hepburn and Natalie Wood included – Kerr had her singing dubbed by Marni Nixon, but the joins don't show, with stand-out songs such as 'Getting To Know You' and 'Whistle A Happy Tune'. It also represents a change in tone in the musicals of the times (such as *South Pacific*), which in their own way started to be more political – here there are debates on women's rights and slavery.

But it's the sharp-tongued exchanges between Brynner and Kerr that are worth coming back for, time and again. ★★★★ **EC**

KING ARTHUR (2004)

Starring: *Clive Owen (Arthur), Ioan Gruffudd (Lancelot), Keira Knightley (Guinevere), Madds Mikkelsen (Tristan), Joel Edgerton (Gawain), Hugh Dancy (Galahad), Ray Winstone (Bors)*
Director: *Antoine Fucqua*
Screenwriter: *David Franzoni*
12A/125 mins/Drama/History/War/USA

Set as the Roman Empire departs Britannia, Arthur is a local commander, his knights a band of enlisted Sarmatian mercenaries, Guinevere, a Woad princess, and Camelot is replaced by Hadrian's Wall. Meanwhile, the Saxons spoil the party by invading.

In a wordy pre-film caption, it is made clear we are about to witness King Arthur minus the frills. This is an epic based on the recorded fact that there was a bona fide Arthur, as in Lucius Artorius Castus, who may have been the germ from which local legends blossomed into fanciful myth. Shed your preconceptions for the sharp tang of truth: there's no love triangle, no preordained destiny, no Holy Grail ... and no magic. A questionable policy when it comes to the eager froth of summer moviemaking – it's like taking the Merry Men out of Robin Hood.

So, the names may be familiar but the setting and storyline are as bleak as a soggy Glastonbury. Arthur and his boys, hungry for retirement, get bogged down in one final mission – its relevance hastily abandoned – and happen upon an imprisoned Guinevere. With the pillaging Saxons bearing down on her tribe, she uses her wiles to entice Arthur into doing the decent thing by clobbering some incoming crusties.

Rather than lacking a story, the film seems to be struggling to keep 27 of them in the air at once. Half-Roman, half-proto Brit, Arthur is a mess of motives: is it honour, religion, patriotism, doubt, love, revenge or a dedication to free will that drives his struggle? Clive Owen, impressive to look at but limply unheroic, struggles with reams of exposition and a very silly helmet. We're supposed to believe his magnetic leadership has fuelled a localised PR frenzy.

Knightley, too, seems exhausted by the lead-weighted dialogue and thin romance. However, she perks up when dolled in war-paint and, with very little on, romps into battle to such vivid effect you wonder why she bothered to enlist the dour Arthur in the first place.

His seven-strong band is efficiently established, helpfully demarcated, despite infestations of facial fuzz, by weapon of choice, age, personality, fighting style and level of grumpiness. Ray Winstone bellows to much-needed comedic effect as the barrel-chested Bors, Dane Mads Mikkelsen spins non-regulation *Kill Bill* poses as Tristan, while the stand-out is Ioan Gruffudd's headstrong Lancelot.

He has the only genuine charisma on show, and in one variation of the plot could be regarded as the protagonist, but the turmoil of the man is another empty promise.

What becomes swiftly obvious is that Fuqua is more tickled by paying homage to *Seven Samurai* than refitting Excalibur's plush medieval romance to a mud-caked Dark Age.

Which is no bad thing in itself – if you're gonna pilfer, pilfer big – and if he'd concentrated solely on such a mission the movie could have harnessed some genuine dramatic thrust. No such luck. It's been scattered to the four winds of marketing, lavishing unwieldy screen time on Knightley's good looks at the expense of the leathery knights, and dashing hopes of flying giblets realism for an all-encompassing demographic.

Somewhere in the murk there's a decent movie just out of reach. Fuqua favours a rich, earthy look of airborne sods, pea-soupers and dizzying blizzards, peaking with a terrifically inventive clash on a frozen lake. Atmosphere spills from all directions, but to what purpose when the action is slashed to ribbons and the characters hobnailed by the script's indecision?

Nothing aligns, nothing builds, and before you know it we're hip-deep in the big showdown – a freewheeling frenzy of choreographed combat that neglects to find much space for the cast. And, by band-of-brothers movie lore, not nearly enough of the good knights buy it. ★★ **IN**

◎ KING KONG (1933)

Starring: *Fay Wray (Ann Darrow), Robert Armstrong (Carl Denham), Bruce Cabot (John 'Jack' Driscoll), Frank Reicher (Captain Englehorn)*
Directors: *Merian C. Cooper, Ernest B. Schoedsack*
Screenwriters: *James Creelman, Ruth Rose, from an idea by Merian Cooper*
PG/100 mins./Action/Adventure/USA

An expedition exploring a remote island capture a gigantic ape and bring him back to New York for exhibition. A beautiful actress who accompanies them is menaced when the monster's love for her causes him to break out.

King Kong is a brilliantly structured adventure movie. The first 40 minutes are all set-up, as wildlife documentary filmmaker Carl Denham sets sail for the South Seas in search of a rumoured fabulous beast, taking along apple-filching Depression waif Ann Darrow because exhibitors have told him his movies won't make any money unless there's a love interest.

Staging a screen test for Ann, Denham dresses her as a fairytale princess ('The beauty and the beast costume') and coaches her in screaming at nothing (a skill required of all who play opposite special-effects creatures). 'What does he really expect her to see?' remarks a crewman.

The Venture drops anchor off Skull Island, the natives of which live in the shadow of a massive wall. In the wall are a pair of huge doors obviously designed to keep something out. Periodically they sacrifice maidens to the deity ('Kong') that lives on the other side of the fortification. The voyage to Skull Island has been fraught with expectation, as everyone speculates on the dangers or romantic possibilities of the trip. But when the natives kidnap Ann and tether her to a sacrificial altar beyond the giant doors, *King Kong* stops promising and starts delivering. The second hour of the film, set on two savage islands (the other is Manhattan) is non-stop action. Out of the jungle comes Kong, a giant gorilla who carries Ann off to his lair.

When Denham and Driscoll, plus a crew of disposable sailors, set out to rescue Ann, they come across a whole ecosystem of prehistoric creatures, all of which (paleontological accuracy be damned) want to eat them. The reptiles also want to eat the blonde, but Kong, who is constantly fighting off rivals, is intrigued. In a 30s racist touch, it's taken as read he was unimpressed by the black girls sacrificed to him over the years and, in a scene censored for years but thankfully restored, peels off her clothes and sniffs his fingers. The ape may be a monster, but he's also an innocent in love. Chief technician Willis O'Brien gives Kong childlike human mannerisms: playing with the corpses of defeated enemies as if wondering where the life has gone, and chewing furiously on any passing human who doesn't meet his standards of beauty.

Carl and Jack rescue Ann and Kong is disabled with gas bombs. In a simple cut he is brought to New York and exhibited on Broadway as The Eighth Wonder Of The World. An elegantly-dressed crowd pay top dollar for the show, which ends abruptly when popping flashbulbs enrage Kong, who thinks the press are out to hurt Ann. He breaks loose, and goes on the rampage. Instead of dinosaurs, he rages against New York's mechanical beasts (a subway train, a flock of biplanes) and scales skyscrapers with Ann again in his huge paw. Atop the Empire State Building, then the tallest building in the world, he makes a defiant last stand as buzzing planes strafe him – the lead crew is played by producer-directors Cooper and Schoedsack. Mortally wounded, he plunges to the street, where Denham delivers his epitaph, 'It wasn't the airplanes, it was beauty killed the beast.'

Cooper, Schoedsack and O'Brien made *The Son Of Kong* in 1933 and the semi-remake *Mighty Joe Young* in 1949; Kong (rather, a Sumo wrestler in a ratty ape suit) featured in a couple of Japanese monster movies: *King Kong Vs Godzilla* (1962) and *The Revenge of King Kong* (1967). Then Dino de Laurentiis invited ridicule by remaking the original in 1976. He even turned out a laughable sequel *King Kong Lives* (1986), in which Kong gets a simian love interest his own size (which is severely missing the point). None of these pretenders count.

King Kong is an animated miniature imbued with character by a craftsman. He is not a man in a suit, just as Godzilla is a man in a suit and not a CGI creation. When Dino killed Kong atop the World Trade Center it was, as someone said, like Cecil B. DeMille crucifying Christ on a Star Of David.

The focusing on Kong's feelings for Ann gives the spectacle backbone, making it far more satisfying than busy updates like *Jurassic Park* (where the effects are stars but not characters). In the finale, *King Kong* delivers an image of supreme surrealism (a giant gorilla atop a skyscraper, buzzed by warplanes, clutching a blonde) that may be the greatest single image contributed by the movies to popular culture. ★★★★★ **KN**

KING KONG (1976)

Starring: *Jeff Bridges (Jack Prescott), Charles Grodin (Fred Wilson), Jessica Lange (Dwan), John Randolph (Captain Ross), Rene Auberjonois (Roy Bagley)*
Director: *John Guillermin*
Screenwriter: *Lorenzo Semple Jr. from the 1933 film*
PG/129 mins./Action/Adventure/USA

Awards: *Golden Globes – Best Female Debut (Jessica Lange)*

A 1970s update of the original *King Kong*, this time an anthropologist and a struggling actress stumble on Kong . . .

'I could see myself when I was 80 years old,' said Jeff Bridges to Bruce Behrenberg, the on-set diarist for Dino De Laurentiis' 1976 *Kong* remake, 'looking at a batch of stills from this picture and knowing I'd had something to do with what will surely be a landmark film in the history of Hollywood.' Given that he was speaking towards the end of a shoot that had fiasco written all over it from the get-go, it's hard to believe that Bridges was not either taking the piss or, at the very least, laying on the irony with a shovel.

At that point, even the irrepressible De Laurentiis must have had an inkling of what posterity had in store. Today, the '76 version of King Kong is regarded as a bloated carcass in the elephants' graveyard of 70s spectacle cinema, grossing just $80 million worldwide off a budget of $24 million. Updated to address the decade's fuel crisis, it had Bridges as Jack Prescott, a shaggy anthropologist, Jessica Lange as Dwan, a struggling actress, and most bizarrely of all, a showdown not atop the Empire State Building but on the World Trade Center, with Kong assailed by choppers and flamethrowers.

To publicise the film, and aping Carl Denham, the original's master showman, De Laurentiis took Kong on the road, drumming up column inches like an old-time huckster. The centrepiece of his travelling tent show, which played to audiences across America, was a 40-foot mechanical gorilla designed by the legendary Carlo Rambaldi. Trumpeted as a technological marvel, the acme of movie FX, rendering *Jaws*' Bruce The Shark a mere bathtub toy, it was a fantastic automaton that would put the original's primitive stop-motion animations to shame.

But Rambaldi's robo-monkey was about as convincing as the Energizer Bunny so it was fortunate De Laurentiis had had the foresight to commission make-up artist Rick Baker to create a stand-in gorilla suit.

So, although the producers fell cravenly shy of admitting it, the Kong we see for over 90 per cent of the movie is Baker in a monkey suit – one, moreover, that bore no resemblance whatsoever to its mechanical counterpart. The bally-hooed special effects, on which the film was sold, amounted to a glorified Hallowe'en costume at which Merian C. Cooper, Ernest Schoedsack and Willis O'Brien would have howled with derision back when synchronised sound was still regarded as pretty darn nifty.

Amazingly, that did not stop *King Kong* picking up an Oscar for Special Visual Effects, causing stop-motion animator Jim Danforth to resign from the Academy in protest. 'I went to great lengths to point out,' he commented, 'that Rick Baker was not in any way, in my opinion, to be considered "a special visual effect".'

'I don't think our version matched the original by any means,' understates Bridges. 'But I can look back on it now and laugh. And I'll tell you what I laugh about – that damn monkey.' ★★ **SB**

KING KONG (2005)

Starring: *Naomi Watts (Ann Darrow), Jack Black (Carl Denham), Adrien Brody (Jack Driscoll), Colin Hanks (Preston), Andy Serkis (Kong/Lumpy)*
Director: *Peter Jackson*
Screenwriters: *Fran Walsh, Philippa Boyens, Peter Jackson, based on a story by Merian C. Cooper, Edgar Wallace*
12A/187 mins./Action/Adventure/New Zealand/USA

Awards: *Academy Awards – Best Sound, Best Editing, Best Visual Effects, BAFTA – Best Visual Effects, Empire – Best Film*

Maverick filmmaker Carl Denham is determined to shoot his latest adventure flick on a mysterious, unexplored island, despite the fact his bosses want to close the picture down and his leading lady's walked. With the authorities on his tail, he convinces Ann Darrow to join him aboard the *Venture* – a ship which takes the actress to that very island to meet her giant-gorilla-shaped destiny . . .

There are many reasons why directors attempt remakes, but 'I wanna 'cos it's my favourite movie ever' shouldn't really rank as the most encouraging. Spielberg sensed contemporary relevance in his update of *The War Of The Worlds*. Soderbergh saw vast room for improvement with *Ocean's Eleven*. And numerous others have, quite simply, thought a new take on an old story would guarantee big bucks. No doubt Universal had the latter in mind when finally greenlighting this latest reworking of the 1933 monster classic, but, as is well-documented, that wasn't the key driving impulse. No, Peter Jackson just wanted to emulate the film that lit his first fires of inspiration and repay that creative ignition with a fitting tribute.

Pre-*Lord Of The Rings*, this sounded like pure folly, especially as the last *Kong* (John Guillermin's '76 monstrosity) was such a flop. No wonder Jackson struggled to get it rolling in '96, regardless of the fact that remakes of *Godzilla* and *Mighty Joe Young* were already crowding out the marketplace. Of course, after *Rings*, Jackson could have suggested remaking *Plan 9 From Outer Space* and been showered with greenbacks. Still wouldn't have made it a great idea. Yet his wanting to remake *Kong*, even if cinema quite frankly doesn't need another *Kong*, turns out to be this movie's greatest strength.

Like Sam Raimi, Jackson is a filmmaker who lets his inner fanboy guide him rather than blind him. Indeed, Jackson's avidity is so tangible – in his insertion of winking in-jokes, in his choreography of the action sequences and, most importantly, in his detailed realisation of the great, battle-scarred ape himself – it allows us to easily forgive the few flaws the movie does have.

Such as? Well, why, for example, spend so long in the first act detailing middle-rung characters like *Venture* crewman Jimmy (Jamie Bell) and Captain Englehorn (Thomas Kretschmann) if you're just going to drop them out of the story come the climactic New York rampage? It seems an odd choice to pad the script in one area, pushing our arrival at Skull Island back to the end of the first hour, then keep it lean in another. And on the technical side, the occasional CG shot looks unfinished; an ambitious brontosaurus stampede, for instance, doesn't quite gel its madly scrambling human element with its dino-participants to form a believable whole.

Fortunately, Jackson spends so much time knocking your socks off that you won't really feel like scratching your head. (Besides, there's a level of criticism you just can't go to, unless you want to start questioning Ann's Wolverine-like ability to resist skeletal fractures, while accepting the existence of a 25-foot-tall gorilla.) His horror sensibility serves the story well, as does his dark sense of humour – watch Denham mourn his ruined celluloid like his companions mourning their dead friends. He also teases fine performances out of his ensemble, Jack Black deserving a special mention for making Denham so appealingly reprehensible.

The overlong Skull Island section, meanwhile, might be an indulgent action binge but it still out-Spielbergs Spielberg at his most Jurassic: icky giant bugs elicit schoolgirl squeals, while Kong's T-Rex tussle causes fanboys to shriek with delight. Even the monster-free sequences will cause mandibles to slacken, such as the *Venture*'s attempts to navigate the island's rock-spike coast, or the Kong-summoning ritual, disturbingly portrayed as an ecstatic religious experience for the island's wretched, hissing natives.

As for the King himself, the special-effects Oscar speaks for itself. In fact, if the Academy weren't so damn conservative, Andy Serkis (who provided the motion-captured moves) would have been up for an acting gong, too. Kong represents the next evolutionary step up from Gollum in Weta's peerless splicing of performance and VFX. While the biplane-swatting and skyscraper-clambering undoubtedly impress, it's in his facial performance and interaction with Ann (Watts, in a knock-out turn) that he truly astonishes, not least because at all times he remains vigilantly unanthropomorphised – and yet still invites sufficient emotional involvement for you to blub come the Empire State showdown. It's as a romance that the '05 *King Kong* outdoes the original hands-down, with some wonderful interludes tautening the couple's bond to such a degree that its ultimate snapping is painful. ★★★★★ **DJ**

THE KING OF COMEDY (1983)

Starring: *Robert De Niro (Rupert Pupkin), Jerry Lewis (Jerry Langford), Diahnne Abbott (Rita Keane), Sandra Bernhard (Masha), Shelley Hack (Cathy Long), Ed Herlihy (Himself)*
Director: *Martin Scorsese*
Screenwriter: *Paul D. Zimmerman*
PG/109 mins./Comedy/Drama/Crime/USA
Awards: *BAFTA – Best Original Screenplay*

Rupert Pupkin, a showbiz wannabe, and Masha, an obsessive fan, kidnap talk show star Jerry Langford. Rupert threatens to kill Jerry unless the network let him be the guest host of his show.

Is it better to be king for a night than schmuck for a lifetime? Compared with the caterpillar-moustached, PeeWee-suited Rupert Pupkin, such Martin Scorsese-Robert De Niro creations as Johnny Boy, Travis Bickle and Jake LaMotta seem almost normal. They express their inadequacies through simple violence rather than submerge their identities completely into media fantasy, and are perversely icons of cool in their psychopathy.

Pupkin is just a real freak, a film protagonist you feel embarrassed for rather than identify with – as he practises celebrity patter on a fake set in the basement (with cardboard photo-standees as guests) while harangued by his unseen mother, or tries to impress a girl (Diahnne Abbott) he barely knows by taking her to a TV superstar's country estate for an uninvited weekend party and is seen off by the not-amused big shot.

Tagline
It's no laughing matter.

Big-lipped, striding Sandra Bernhard is almost equally strange as an aggressively scary, devoted fan who tapes her idol to a swivel chair so she can force him to model the cardigan she has knitted for him.

Scorsese reins in his usual kinetic camera style and colourful palette for chilly TV movie directness and steely bluetones, crawling inside Pupkin's diseased mind to an uncomfortable degree, giving you the choice of accepting the ambiguously happy ending as the truth or another fantasy.

A near-perfect script by Paul D. Zimmerman, remarkably acted down to the bit players, this is such an uncomfortable watch that it has still not been recognised as the major classic it is. It's among the first and sharpest of a wave of films dealing with stalking, celebrity and mass-media culture. ★★★★★ **KN**

KING OF KINGS (1961)

Starring: *Jeffrey Hunter (Jesus Christ), Siobhan McKenna (Mary), Hurd Hatfield (Pontius Pilate), Ron Randell (Lucius, the Centurion), Viveca Lindfors (Claudia), Rita Gam (Herodias), Carmen Sevilla (Mary Magdalene), Brigid Bazlen (Salome), Harry Guardino (Barrabas), Rip Torn (Judas)*
Director: *Nicholas Ray*
Screenwriter: *Philip Yordan*
U/168 mins./Religion/Drama/USA

Having failed to persuade Jesus Christ to join the cause of the anti-imperialist brigand, Barabbas, Judas Iscariot delivers him to the Jewish authorities for Crucifixion.

Forced by the code of Do Nots and Be Carefuls that regulated silent Hollywood, Cecil B. DeMille devised the tactic of depicting decadence in all its sinful glory as a pretext to punishing the wicked and rewarding the penitent and good. Consequently, no other life of Christ contains such overt sensuality as his 1927 effort, *The King of Kings*, which opened with Jacqueline Logan's scantily clad Mary Magdalene making the acquaintance of H.B. Warner's Jesus when she came to lure her lover Judas (Joseph Schildkraut) back to bed. Moreover, there's certainly nothing to compare with the sequence in which the Seven Deadly Sins were slowly purged from her body in a series of superimpositions.

Nicholas Ray's *King of Kings* is wrongly listed in some sources as a remake of DeMille's morality play. But Warner and Jeffrey Hunter's portrayals of Christ make for a fascinating contrast. The silent saviour was both virile and compassionate and wholly in touch with both his humanity and divinity. Hunter, however, seems as conflicted as Hamlet by his optimum course of action. Stripping the story of all but one miracle (which is a restoration of sight that recalls the 1927 version), Philip Yordan's screenplay moulds Jesus into another of Ray's rebels without a cause, who isn't sure whether his role is to lead his people in the manner that Judas suggests or to guide them to a more lasting form of liberation. Thus, he seems to be testing out his teachings rather than preaching with authority.

Made at a cost of $8 million and filmed with a cast of thousands in 70mm Technicolor on 396 sets, the picture has the epic feel of Samuel Bronston's earlier epics, *The Fall of the Roman Empire* and *El Cid*. But, despite the piercing eyes that made him something of a pin-up, Hunter cut a resoundingly anti-heroic figure, whose seemingly pointless death enraged Christian watchdogs who denounced the movie for its historical and theological inaccuracies. ★★★ **DP**

THE KING OF MARVIN GARDENS (1972)

Starring: *Jack Nicholson (David Staebler), Bruce Dern (Jason Staebler), Ellen Burstyn (Sally), Julia Anne Robinson (Jessica), Scatman Crothers (Lewis)*
Director: *Bob Rafelson*
Screenwriters: *Jacob Brackman, Bob Rafelson based on a story by Brackman and Rafelson*
18/103 mins./Crime/Drama/USA

Radio monologist David Staebler is called to Atlantic City by his brother Jason, who wants him to come in on an island real estate deal. David is drawn into the world of his brother, who is involved with 'middle-aged kewpie doll' Sally and her waif stepdaughter, but senses that things will soon fall apart.

Director Bob Rafelson and star Jack Nicholson reunited after the seminal *Five Easy Pieces* on this still-underrated 1972 classic.

As he would in *About Schmidt*, Nicholson shows his range by keeping his eyebrows steady and playing an interior-directed, repressed character, allowing the superb Bruce Dern to be the dangerous, charismatic, always-talking wild man, only tentatively emerging from his shell to join the role-playing games constantly indulged in by Dern and his two-girl harem.

The plot is oblique, with the hero never quite fathoming what the deal is between his brother and a genially sinister local gangster (Scatman Crothers). There is so much focus on the Staeblers' island dream of creating a resort called 'Staebleravia' that the finish comes out of left field, as the brothers are so wrapped up in each other's troubles they fail to notice just how cracked and dangerous nearly-cast-aside, gun-waving mistress Ellen Burstyn (in career-best work) is becoming.

Rafelson turns out-of-season Atlantic City into an eerie, depopulated locale, inhabited by hoods, hustlers and lost souls. Robinson, who never made another film, is one of the great lost faces of the 1970s, a hippie chick alternative Miss World who shows more grit than her outwardly with-it stepmother. Jacob Brackman's script gives Nicholson several set-piece to-camera talks, memorably an opening talk about his grandfather, and awards bit-part gangster Charles LaVine a quotable speech about the difference between 'a dirty double-crosser and a dirty trouble-causer'. ★★★★ **KN**

KING OF NEW YORK (1990)

Starring: *Christopher Walken (Frank White), David Caruso (Dennis Gilley), Laurence Fishburne (Jimmy Jump), Victor Argo (Roy Bishop), Wesley Snipes (Thomas Flanigan)*
Director: *Abel Ferrara*
Screenwriter: *Nicholas St. John*
18/99 mins./Drama/Crime/USA

After his release from prison a drug lord tries to leave a better mark on society but the dice is loaded against him from the start.

Abel Ferrara, what a positive outlook on life he has. Here, in one of his more upbeat numbers, he tackles the New York gangster scene, kills his entire principal cast and decides that there's pretty much zip that that is good in this sin-soaked world. It is probably his most accessible work, featuring a cast to die for (so to speak) - Christopher Walken, Laurence Fishburne (then Larry), David Caruso (pre-*NYPD* and *CSI Miami* fame), Wesley Snipes (pre-Blade), Victor Argo - and thrums with its director's street-evil nastiness and themes of moral redemption.

Walken is Frank White – a New York gang leader recently released from the clink, back on old turf with a quest to make a name for himself. The movie's enticing notion is his search for morality as he wipes out rival factions – with the able assistance of his gang of wiseacre black psychopaths and various corrupt members of the legal trade – and dreams of donating his gains to ailing hospitals, like some self-obessed Robin Hood. In his way stand the cops and the Irish American lunatic fringe chomping at the bit to go vigilante and fill White with their righteous bullets. The moral control for all this violence is an understated Bishop (a superb Argo), the detective in charge with a dodgy ticker determined to do things by the book.

Filmed in Ferrera's trademark neon lit underworld style, the movie bounces full-impact violence, riveting performances (Fishburne is wild as Jimmy Jump, White's fruitcake jive talkin' henchman) and cool, ethereal cityscapes to magnificently foreboding effect.

The message is ultimately simplistic – good and bad are indivisible – but Frank White's worldview speech delivered with all of Walken's hulking coldness lands a chilling punch. And for Ferrera this is happy-go-lucky. ★★★★ **IN**

KING OF THE HILL (1993)

Starring: *Jesse Bradford (Aaron Kurlander), Jeroen Krabbe (Mr. Erich Kurlander), Lisa Eichhorn (Mrs. Kurlander), Karen Allen (Miss Mathey), Spalding Gray (Mr. Mungo), Elizabeth McGovern (Lydia)*
Director: *Steven Soderbergh*
Screenwriter: *Steven Soderbergh, based on the novel by A.E. Hotchner*
PG/90 mins./Drama/USA

The story of a young boy's life as he has to look after himself during The Great Depression after his family have all gone their separate ways. It's not long before he meets the various salubrious characters who live in his block of flats.

After the career misstep of *Kafka*, his grimly problematic follow-up to *sex lies and videotape*, writer-director Steven Soderbergh's third feature was an exquisitely crafted and richly detailed adaptation of A.E. Hotchner's memoirs about growing up in St. Louis during the depths of the Depression, chronicling the coming-of-age of Aaron Kurlander, a quick-witted, resourceful and imaginative 12-year-old plunged into a progressively dark odyssey of survival.

The Kurlander clan live in the Empire hotel, where everything – people, situations and emotions – is ephemeral and transitory. Aaron's kid brother Sullivan is shipped off to live with relatives, warmhearted but sickly Mrs. Kurlander is sequestered away in a sanatorium, and luckless father dumps his ill-fated wickless candle scheme to sell watches door-to-door in another state, leaving Aaron to fend for himself in a series of beautifully rendered episodes which bring him face-to-face with all the humour and tragedy of life.

The period trappings are faultless, the acting superb, with the batty down-and-outs inhabiting the Empire – including Spalding Gray as a former moneybags turned boozer and Elizabeth McGovern as his hard-hearted prostitute companion – especially memorable. It is Bradford, however, who stands out. Whether giving lyrical speeches about Charles Lindbergh to his classmates or weaving fantastical tales to conceal his impoverished circumstances, he gives one of the best and most natural performances by a young actor in recent memory, while Soderbergh shows himself to be a truly remarkable filmmaker, filling every frame, no matter how nightmarish Aaron's predicament, with rapt wonder. ★★★★ **MM**

KING SOLOMON'S MINES (1950)

Starring: *Debora Kerr (Elizabeth Curtis), Stewart Granger (Allan Quartermain), Richard Carlson (John Goode), Hugo Haas (Van Brun), Lowell Gilmore (Eric Masters), Kimursi (Khiva)*
Directors: *Compton Bennett, Andrew Marton*
Screenwriter: *Helen Deutsch based on the novel by H. Rider Haggard*
PG/103 mins./Adventure/USA

Awards: *Academy Awards – Best Cinematography (Robert Surtees), Best Film Editing (Ralph E. Winters)*

H. Rider Haggard's epic story of famous African guide Allan Quartermain, who in helping search for Elizabeth Curtis's missing husband, happens upon the trail to the fabled lost diamond mines of King Solomon.

Feel that Technicolor, soak up those authentic African vistas, thrill to the traditions of grand adventure, and gawp in awe at the vast plains of Stewart Granger's manly chest. Long in tooth, perhaps, but this seasoned jamboree of flat-packed heroics and stunning locations comes easy on the eyes and brain. Shot across the plains of Kenya, Uganda and what was then the Belgian Congo, in 1950 the lengthy scenes of native wildlife and strange tribes was truly exotic; audiences were plunging into the dark heart of a continent alongside the fairly expressionless leads.

There's little deviation from Haggard's roomy travelogue, the film fits a road movie format as the heroes trek across the Veldt on the trail of fabulous riches. There is next to no psychological depth in this rangy adventuring, Deborah Kerr is rather whiney as the forlorn wife slowly falling for the dashing Granger (chosen after Errol Flynn became unavailable). And as the hero Granger is perfect: self-assured, snobby, jabbing with a dry, exasperated wit of the seen-it-all brigade. He's a distant prototype for Indiana

Jones, although rather irony deficient. Both stars were contending with 140 degree heat, and probably dysentery.

Surprisingly, for its time, the film treats the locals with a degree of respect. Exiled King Umbopa, carved with the image of a snake across his torso, is given wonderful authority by the statuesque Siriaque. His fight to regain his throne one of this sturdy epic's more vibrant subplots. **★★★ IN**

⓪ KINGDOM OF HEAVEN (2005)

Starring: *Orlando Bloom (Balian), Liam Neeson (Godfrey), David Thewlis (Hospitaller), Jeremy Irons (Tiberias), Edward Norton (King Baldwin), Sibylla (Eva Green)*
Director: *Ridley Scott*
Screenwriter: *William Monahan*
15/145 mins./190 mins (director's cut)/War/History/ Spain/Germany

Jerusalem, The late 12th century. The Christians occupy the city as the capital of their young crusader state; the Islamic Saracens want it back. As the teetering truce between them finally falters and war begins, a young knight named Balian, striving to hold onto to his principals, steps into the breach. He finds it is a struggle that will test everything he stands for.

You can trust the impeccable Sir Ridley Scott to arrive at the movies well dressed. A director who soaks up scenes draped in layer upon layer of lavish period detail, you imagine hordes of tireless assistants nagging Oxbridge professors to glean what heraldic badge or Eastern variety of eyeliner was all the rage in 1186. Just as he did so thoroughly with *1492* and *Gladiator*, and even his industrious future-gazing in *Alien* and *Blade Runner*, Scott makes sure *Kingdom Of Heaven* revels in a near microscopic level of scenic finery. No doubt, Bloom's beard length can assuredly be accounted for in 12th-century grooming guides. What's missing from this epic, so professionally clad, is meaning. Scott shows things but fails to interpret why they are happening. Motivations, historical context, any resonance with the modern world's tribulations are avoided in a strangely bare-boned edit that feels far too short. Two hours plus is plenty for many genres but the historical epic needs to be unbound, to fill lonely Sunday afternoons with its plethora of characters and moral debates. Kingdom Of Heaven is in such a big hurry, within half an hour we've had murdered priests, burning villages, skirmishes, fever, death, a shipwreck and one of those notable scenes where an enemy prince is spared to return the favour at a later date (*El Cid*, anyone?).

What we don't get is an idea of what's driving Balian. The film contradicts his every move; he seems both a traditionalist and a moderniser, this innocent blacksmith who has stumbled into the big picture of history. With nary a training montage and barely a slurp of backstory, he's transformed from a fledgling knight into a brilliant military tactician, not to mention the first man to devise digging a well in a desert country that had been populated for more than two thousand years. The film may look real – impressively so – but it never feels it.

Hence it fails to stir the blood. Every speech has only the gradient of grand importance, only bland echoes of virtuous lore. Even the carnality of medieval war comes across as neutered spectacle. It's a re-imagining of crusader battlecraft aided and abetted, in this post-*Rings* era, by the multitudinous armies that can be dreamt up on a desktop computer and spilled out over a shimmering desert horizon. Scott's restless camera adores creeping over sand dunes to take in the sprawl of 20,000 sweaty warriors like recently disturbed termites. Size, though, isn't everything. Such magic has worn thin with overuse.

The viper-like cutting between teeming siege towers doused in burning oil and the visceral clang of close-quarter fighting has a bludgeoning power, but the brutality comes soft-packed and, bar a few ostentatious splashes, relatively bloodless. Where is *Gladiator*'s thunder, *Black Hawk Down*'s chaos? Bloom is determinedly okay, with steely eyes and a laconic mood that doesn't test the mettle of his diction too hard, and he's alongside the kind of reliable pros who can strike an appropriate chord: Neeson, Irons, Thewlis, and an uncredited Ed Norton, superb as Baldwin, the Leper King hidden behind a silver mask. The romance, with Eva Green's Princess Sybilla, looks promising, but is cut short by further lurches of nonsensical plotting. And given the benign treatment of the Islamic foe – Gassan Massoud's Saladin is a wise, likeable sort of conqueror – it's left to the snarly Marton Csokas and bloodthirsty Templar Brendan Gleeson, to take on the task of being plain bad. With such pantomime morality, the film ultimately has nothing to say, keeping its pleasures assiduously superficial. **★★★ IN**

⓪ KINGPIN (1996)

Starring: *Woody Harrelson (Roy Munson), Randy Quaid (Ishmael Boorg), Vanessa Angel (Claudia), Bill Murray (Ernie McCracken), Chris Elliott (The Gambler)*
Directors: *Bobby Farrelly, Peter Farrelly*
Screenwriters: *Barry Fanaro, Mort Nathan*
12/108 mins./Comedy/Sport/USA

A former pro ten-pin bowler discovers a new talent in the Amish community and decides to coach him for the championship.

Having been separated from his bowling arm by a disgruntled mob after a con trick backfires, ten-pin pro Roy Munson stumbles across Amish bowling whiz Ishmael at his local bowling alley, takes the pudding-bowl protégé under his wing and heads for Reno and the national bowling championship to settle a score with sleazy title holder Ernie McCracken the man responsible for Munson's single-handed state.

As daft humour goes, *Kingpin* isn't in the same ballpark as the directors' debut *Dumb And Dumber*, and its everything-but-the-kitchen-sink approach to its genre – with parody, sight gags et al. – makes for a muddled picture. But the jokes succeed often enough, while the bowling is covered to great effect in a showdown between Harrelson and Murray, whose strutting poseur steals the show.

By being as subtle as the proverbial brick, the directors have come up with a film that manages to offend just about everybody; and given that the level of humour rarely rises above silly haircuts, bodily fluids and how Harrelson can best utilise his rubber hand, those seeking a discerning evening's entertainment should pass. But as a barrel of easy, unsophisticated laughs, *Kingpin* delivers in spades. **★★★ CW**

⓪ KINGS OF THE ROAD (1976)

Starring: *Rudolf Vogler (Bruno), Hanns Zischler (Robert), Lisa Kreuzer (Cashier), Rudolf Schuendler (Robert's Father), Marquad Bohm (Man Who Lost His Wife)*
Director: *Wim Wenders*
Screenwriter: *Wim Wenders*
18/176 mins./Drama/West Germany

Awards: *Cannes Film Festival – FIPRESCI prize*

When woman-troubled linguistics expert Robert Lander's motorised suicide bid in the River Elbe fails miserably, projection engineer Bruno Winter accepts him as a six-day travelling companion, as he services small-town cinemas along West Germany's border with the East.

Concluding the trilogy started with *Alice in the Cities* and *The Wrong Movement*, this is the heir of such road movies as *Easy Rider* and *Two-Lane Blacktop*, as its characters make as much psychological and spiritual progress as they do territorial. However, in embracing such a quintessentially American genre, Wim Wenders found himself trapped between his themes and his style. Indeed, such is his reliance on references to US culture that it becomes impossible to gauge Wenders' precise stance.

A key idea is his lament for the declining German film industry, whose miring between pulp and porn is movingly depicted by the state of the delapidated venues the twosome visit along the Zonenrandgebiet. But Robby Müller's sharply etched monochrome imagery owed more to the Depression photographs of Walker Evans than any Germanic art precedent. Similarly, the use of rock'n'roll on the soundtrack and the throwaway citations of such ephemera as posters, clothing and junk food all emphasised the fact that the Federal Republic had become a Cold War colony of the States in the same way that the Democratic regime across the border was in thrall to Moscow.

Yet, while he pays tribute to such Hollywood features as Nicholas Ray's *The Lusty Men*, Wenders also reveals his debts to Yasujiro Ozu and the French New Wave. The length and pacing of *Kings of the Road* was as much designed to demarcate it from the mainstream as the depiction of everyday events that other filmmakers eliminated through ellipsis. But by keeping conversation to a minimum and eschewing reaction shots in favour of detaching long shots, Wenders forces us to identify with the unlikely buddies and their relationship to the passing landscape, which virtually becomes a character in itself (something that Wenders hoped would happen, as he shot chronologically and Vogler and Fischler improvised spontaneous responses to the locations along a strictly prescribed route).

The film ends on a vaguely optimistic note. But even then, Wenders suggests that Robert and Bruno have only recognised the need for change rather than identified the means to exact it. ★★★★ **DP**

KINGS ROW (1942)

Starring: *Ann Sheridan (Randy Monoghan), Robert Cummings (Parris Mitchell), Ronald Reagan (Drake McHugh), Betty Field (Cassandra Tower), Charles Coburn (Dr. Henry Gordon), Claude Rains (Dr. Alexander Tower), Judith Anderson (Mrs Harriet Gordon)*
Director: *Sam Wood*
Screenwriter: *Casey Robinson, based on the novel by Henry Bellamann*
Producer: *David Lewis*
PG/127 mins./Drama/USA

Reckless playboy Drake McHugh gets his comeuppance at the hands of small-town doctor Henry Gordon for dallying with the affections of his daughter, Louise Gordon.

A fascinating acting contrast between a trio of Hitchcock alumni lies at the heart of this no-holds melodrama. Hitch cast Robert Cummings twice – in *Saboteur* and *Dial M for Murder* – despite thinking him one the blandest A-listers in Hollywood. He's certainly out of his depth here, as Parris Mitchell, the turn-of-the-century small-townie whose study of psychiatry under Claude Rains's Dr. Alexander Tower prompts him to drift off into misty-eyed eulogies to Freud that reflected cinema's then-obsession with the sins of the subconscious. Rains (who would excel in *Notorious*) cuts much more of an intellectual dash than his milquetoasted protégeé and his clinical interest in the specimens resident in *Kings Row* is amusing for all the right reasons.

However, they're both upstaged by the imperious Judith Anderson, who draws on all the malevolent menace she summoned in *Rebecca* for her performance as Harriet Gordon. Indeed, with her starched crinolins and even more inflexible Victorian values, she could be Mrs Danvers' kin. Her disdainful attitude towards Ronald Reagan's gadabout is particularly severe and her response to his motoring accident is almost as relishable as the famous sequence in which Drake McHugh wakes to discover his legs have been amputated and delivers the immortal line, 'Where's the rest of me?' (which Reagan later used as the title of his autobiography).

Although it seems tame (and occasionally risible) today, this adaptation of Henry Bellamann's novel was considered a hot property back in 1942 and moral guardian Joseph Breen wrote to Warners to declare that 'To attempt to translate such a story to the screen, even though it be rewritten to conform to the provisions of the Production Code is, in our judgment, a very questionable undertaking from the standpoint of the good and welfare of this industry.' However, screenwriter Casey Robinson was instructed by producer David Lewis to tone down the references to incest, homosexuality and euthanasia and concentrate instead on the more wholesome gossip, insanity, fornication, class hatred, suicide and murder.

What resulted was the prototype soap opera. So now you know who to blame. ★★★ **DP**

KINKY BOOTS (2005)

Starring: *Joel Edgerton (Charlie Price), Chiwetel Ejiofor (Lola/Simon), Linda Bassett (Melanie), Kellie Bright (Jeannie), Nick Frost (Don)*
Director: *Julian Jarrold*
Screenwriters: *Geoff Deane, Tim Firth*
12A/107 mins./Drama/Comedy/USA/UK

After inheriting his father's ailing shoe factory, Charlie meets a London transvestite, Lola, who inspires him to make glamorous boots for cross-dressing men. But Lola is met with some hostility in the Northampton factory – will the staff accept her and make the new range a success?

Following a path well-trodden by the likes of *The Full Monty*, *Kinky Boots* depends upon financial strife to elicit out-of-character enterprise from its protagonists. And of course it's always useful to have a helping of sauce on the side: in this case, sexy tranny footwear. It's an immediately engaging set-up and, like *Calendar Girls*, is boosted by its 'true story' basis.

Amusing culture clashes emerge as Lola teeters into the old-fashioned shoe factory to challenge the preconceptions of the workers, especially comically macho Don (*Shaun Of The Dead*'s Nick Frost). But while Ejiofor strikes the right note as the flamboyant-yet-fragile transvestite, Joel Edgerton proves almost too good at being mild-mannered Charlie, failing to convince as a romantic hero.

Attempts to draw parallels between the pair's parental problems appear contrived, too; this is stronger on good-natured humour than character and plot. While the London drag-club scenes bring colour and comedy, later factory sequences suffer through self-conscious plotting. So while *Kinky Boots* is a pleasant comedy, it's not a contender for the 'next Brit hit' crown. ★★★ **ASm**

KINSEY (2004)

Starring: *Liam Neeson (Alfred Kinsey), Laura Linney (Clara McMillen), Chris O'Donnell (Wardell Pomeroy), Peter Sarsgaard (Clyde Martin), Timothy Hutton (Paul Gebhard), John Lithgow (Alfred Seguine Kinsey)*
Director: *Bill Condon*
Screenwriter: *Bill Condon*
15/118 mins./Drama/History/USA/Germany

After suffering a repressed upbringing and a disastrous first night of marriage, biologist Alfred Kinsey determines to set America free from its hang-ups by producing the first scientific study of human sexual behaviour.

As some poet once put it, 'Let's talk about sex, baby'. Or rather, if it's any time before the publication of Alfred Kinsey's *Sexual Behaviour In The Human Male* in 1948, 'Let's absolutely not do that. Ever.'

These days, it's difficult to imagine the kind of impact that the good doctor's 804-page slab of meticulously compiled rudie-data had on swathes of Americans, who were under the impression that either they were the only person who did the things they did, or that doing the things that they wanted to do would send them straight to hospital, prison and Hell. In that order.

A biologist by profession, Kinsey attempted to investigate humanity's sexual behaviour in exactly the same dispassionate way he had examined gall wasps. He'd collected a million of those, so for his report he interviewed thousands of Americans about their sex histories, asking them the kinds of questions that would normally get you a smack in the mush. The result was a book that both titillated and shocked, but that blew open the debate on what America was getting up to in the sack. But the man at the centre of the brouhaha remained something of an enigma. What were his motives? Was he an impassive scientist or a proselytiser for an early version of free love? Or was he only justifying his own unorthodox sexual identity?

With *Gods And Monsters*, director Bill Condon demonstrated he was adept at delicately teasing out the contradictions of complex characters – in that case *Frankenstein* director James Whale – while leaving just enough unexplained. He pulls off the same feat with the same gentle dexterity here.

Tagline
Let's talk about sex.

Liam Neeson, as good as he has ever been, delivers a picture of an obsessional scientist who, while certainly dedicated to truth, could also be interpreted as using his research both to work out his own sexual nature (he finally placed himself as a three on his infamous straight/gay table, where one is the straightest and six the gayest) as well as to fashion a hammer out of his reams of stats with which to smash the repressive society represented by his bigoted, priggish father.

The supporting cast is universally impressive: there's something deliciously savoury about casting Frank-N-Furter himself (Tim Curry) as a prudish 'hygiene' lecturer; Laura Linney is convincing as the kind of unconventional wife who could put up with her husband's obsession while Lithgow, as Alfred's father, at first appears to be essaying a slightly less nuanced version of the sexually repressed killjoy preacher he played in *Footloose* (here is a man who believes that the world went to Hell in a haycart with the invention of the zip-fastener) before transforming his character into something much more moving. But it's Peter Sarsgaard, easily the most promising discovery of the decade so far, who really shines as assistant researcher and sexual adventurist Clyde Martin, a man who manages to seduce both Kinsey and his wife and who indicates that, desirable or not, a genie has definitely been let out of the bottle.

Critics will say that Condon is unduly lenient on Kinsey. His alleged scientific failings are all but glossed over, there's the odd minor stylistic misstep – Kinsey's marriage lectures are uncomfortably reminiscent of the sex education sketch in Monty Python's *Meaning Of Life*, and there's one too many cheap sniggers at the cutesy sexual ignorance of rural rubes. But, in a year when biopics were criticised for either being constipated with detail (*Alexander*) or frustratingly inconclusive (*The Aviator*), this is almost as good as the genre gets. ★★★★ **AS**

KISS KISS BANG BANG (2005)

Starring: *Robert Downey Jr. (Harry Lockhart), Val Kilmer (Gay Perry), Michelle Monaghan (Harmony Faith Lane), Corbin Vernsen (Harlan Dexter)*
Director: *Shane Black*
Screenwriter: *Shane Black, based on the novel* Bodies Are Where You Find Them *by Brett Halliday*
15/103 mins./Action/ThrillerUSA

Awards: *Empire Awards – Best Thriller*

Harry Lockhart is a petty thief turned accidental actor (don't ask) being shown the ropes by real private eye Gay Perry, who happens to be gay. Then he meets his childhood sweetheart, Harmony, a failing actress working the party scene. And then the bodies start turning up. In Harry's shower, for starters …

That this film is called *Kiss Kiss, Bang Bang* is a big hint. It's a snarky in-joke, a gleeful signpost to exactly where this energetic and blackly comic return to the fold for screenwriter Shane Black (who directs for the first time) is headed. For not only does it reference the working title of 007's fourth adventure *Thunderball*, it is the name of legendary critic Pauline Kael's second collected work, a label penned to deride the thrill-seeking shallowness she felt had irrevocably poisoned cinema. Which is where Mr. Black comes in. His murder-mystery-noir-farce (it's kind of a first) is, at heart, a deconstruction of both Kael's complaint and Bond's sexy, trigger-happy delirium. Can you make a movie undeniably shallow, base, violent (and incomprehensible), yet invest it with satirical cunning and knowingness, energised by brilliantly barbed screenwriting? Yes, it transpires, you can.

Black, who burned out at the close of the 80s, has taken the formula he helped cement – *Lethal Weapon, The Last Boy Scout* et al – turned it on its head and slammed it into the sidewalk. Out of the bloody remains, he's assembled a manically askew take on pulp fiction. The story is partly based on a Brett Halliday novel and keeps tabs on its own fictional dime-store scribe Johnny Gossamer, whose novels eerily echo the gumshoe smog of the plot. Or is it the other way around? It's a traditional beat lurching through a lurid, contemporary world. The LA scene, the director's old turf, is smeared across the screen and junked by Harry's motor-mouthed comebacks, fed by Black's caustic attack on his own industry. Check out the Native American Joe Pesci.

No holds are barred. We're talking the kind of meta-lunacy where the narrator – a testy Harry – can spool the film backwards to rerun to a forgotten detail, admit an evident cheapness, or even have the lead pair bid farewell to the audience.

At times it strains its own conceptual arrogance, shaving scarily close to the blather of *Last Action Hero* (which Black had a hand in). The plot itself is so jet-propelled it's impossible to follow. You're not really meant to, but it is a policy that opts for hip gesture over genuine drama, not so distant from Tarantino's movie-movie world where emotion is denied a visa. The violence is bloody but nonchalant – Harry variously loses a finger, acts as a local punch-bag and has his balls electrocuted, and the idea is to laugh.

That it doesn't cave in beneath the weight of its own chaotic, po-mo posturing is down to the charming, not to say disarming, delivery from three fabulous lead performances and Black's deft hardwiring of genre conventions with outrageously funny booby traps.

There are moments here that rival *Pulp Fiction*'s iconic dementia for permanence: Harry urinating over a dead body, Harry dangling from a coffin that is dangling from a freeway bridge, Harry's ill-considered variation on Russian roulette. Downey Jr., his face a blueprint for partying way too hard, gives this intrepid loser a restless vitality; he's our man, but an idiot all the same. Monaghan's leggy Harmony is all contradiction, a sweetheart femme fatale and a brainy-bimbo nerve-ball. And the inspired Kilmer, preened and put-upon, actually manages to camp things down. He and Harry are the oddest of odd couples: 'It's not good cop/bad cop,' snarls Perry at another upended cliché, 'this is fag and New Yorker – you're in a whole lot of trouble.' Get the drift? ★★★★ **IN**

KISS ME KATE (1953)

Starring: *Kathryn Grayson (Lilli Vanessi/Katherine), Howard Keel (Fred Graham/Petruchio), Ann Miller (Lois Lane/Bianca), Tommy Rall (Bill Calhoun/Lucentio), Bob Fosse (Hortensio), Ron Randell (Cole Porter)*
Director: *George Sidney*
Screenwriters: *Dorothy Kingsley, based on the play by Cole Porter, Sam Spewack, Bella Spewack, from the play* The Taming Of The Shrew *by William Shakespeare*
U/109 mins./Musical/Comedy/USA

Musical stars Fred Graham and Lily Vanessi were once married, but have been through an acrimonious divorce. They are reunited by Cole Porter for a musical version of Shakespeare's *The Taming of the Shrew*, and find it hard to keep their private lives separate from the roles they are playing.

If you get the chance, see this in a revival cinema where you can appreciate the eye-popping 1950s 3-D effects (not to mention 'miraculous stereophonic sound') as showgirls high-kick at the camera and the squabbling romantic leads constantly find excuses to throw things at the audience.

It's a brash, brassy, colourful filming of Cole Porter's Broadway musical travesty of *The Taming of the Shrew*, offering Howard Keel (at his very loudest) and Kathryn Grayson opportunities to chew the scenery and belt out the numbers as a bitchily feuding theatrical couple whose private life gets mixed up with their stage show.

The play-within-a-film stuff is clever for the time, though there's lowbrow comedy from dimwitted gangsters to take the edge off the high-toned artiness. It has some of Porter's wittiest, most intricate patter lyrics ('Brush Up Your Shakespeare', 'I Hate Men') but also unleashes wow-'em-in-the-stalls show-stoppers when the impossibly long-legged Ann Miller throws herself into 'Too Darn Hot', Keel laments 'Where is the Life That Late I Led?' and the entire company tears into 'Wunderbar', 'Always True to You Darlin in My Fashion' and 'From This Moment On'. Among the hard-worked supporting singers and dancers are Keenan Wynn ('give her one out of Coriolanus'), Bobby Van, the very limber Carol Haney and choreographers Hermes Pan and Bob Fosse. Director George Sidney acts more like a ringmaster than a visionary: but all the disparate elements – kitsch, class, camp and Shakespeare – hold together to deliver unbeatable entertainment.
★★★★ KN

⊙ KISS ME, STUPID (1964)

Starring: *Dean Martin (Dino), Kim Novak (Polly the Pistol/Zelda), Ray Walston (Orville J. Spooner), Felicia Farr (Zelda 'Lambchop' Spooner), Cliff Osmond (Barney)*
Director: *Billy Wilder*
Screenwriter: *Billy Wilder, I.A.L. Diamon, based on the play* L'Ora della Fantasia *by Anna Bonacci*
PG/125 mins./Comedy/USA

Vegas crooner Dino is ambushed in Climax, Nevada, by wannabe songwriters Orville J. Spooner and Barney Millsap, who pass off local hooker Polly the Pistol as Spooner's wife in the hope of seducing the singer into buying a few ditties.

Critics and the Catholic Legion of Decency had a field day over this shameless sex comedy. But had these people not seen *The Seven Year Itch*, *The Apartment* and *Irma La Douce*?

Billy Wilder had been steadily building up to this assault on the Production Code in order to expose the real morality of Kennedy-era America that was so teasingly alluded to in the coyly suggestive romps that Doris Day was making for Universal. Indeed, she might have been a shrewder choice than Kim Novak, who threw everything but talent at the part of the nasally congested, clumsily erotic Polly the Pistol, although the role really needed the kind of sensual vulnerability that only Marilyn Monroe possessed.

Wilder was frustrated by casting problems throughout this withering satire on bourgeois mores and the balance of marital power. Although he secured Jack Lemmon's wife, Felicia Farr, for Zelda, a scheduling conflict meant that he had to plump for Peter Sellers as the amorally scheming piano teacher. But then, four weeks into shooting, Sellers suffered a series of massive heart attacks and Wilder had to bring in Ray Walston, who was so keen to play against the image created in TV's *My Favorite Martian* that he overdid the cruelty towards both Zelda and Polly and earned the film its misogynist reputation.

Some of the gags fall flat and others seem unnecessarily provocative. But there's much to enjoy in this bold adaptation of Anna Bonacci's play.

Like Gloria Swanson before him, in *Sunset Blvd*, Dean Martin heroically lampoons his Rat Pack persona as the bibulous, womanising crooner, while Farr was never better than as the housewife who teams with the whore to turn the tables on her chauvinist husband. Alexander Trauner's sets were a triumph of tawdry backwater kitsch, while Gene Kelly supposedly produced the off-the-cuff choreography for 'Silvia' while visiting the set. However, the film's true glory are the excruciating songs, which were penned by George and Ira Gershwin (who provided the new lyrics) when they were first starting out. **★★★ DP**

k

⊙ KISS THE GIRLS (1997)

Starring: *Morgan Freeman (Dr. Alex Cross), Ashley Judd (Dr. Kate McTiernan), Cary Elwes (Det. Nick Ruskin), Alex McArthur (Det. Davey Sikes), Tony Goldwyn (Dr. William 'Will' Randolph)*
Director: *Gary Fleder*
Screenwriter: *David Klass, based on the novel by James Patterson*
18/110 mins./Mystery/Thriller/USA

Police detective Dr. Alex Cross is short of leads for his latest serial killer case, but help is at hand when he teams up with the only surviving victim Kate Mctiernan.

Bouncing around as Luke Perry's barking spouse 'Pam Anderson' in *Normal Life* is probably not what you want to be remembered for. But by the time of this 1997 release, Ashley Judd had paid her dues as 'the blonde wife' (*Heat*/*A Time To Kill*) or worse, simply the sibling of Country And Western star Wynnona, and here nets the sort of leading role that Brad Pitt must have hankered after for so long too.

Dr. Alex Cross has carved a much admired career as an intuitive but detached police detective specialising in forensic evidence and criminal psychology. And just when he's looking forward to spending his autumnal years with feet up, slippers on, watching his best-selling scribblings bolster an ever-swelling bank account, someone goes and swipes his niece.

Well, not just someone, in fact, but very probably a serial killer going by the name of Casanova, who's killed two and is suspected of abducting several others, fates unknown. One of his victims, however – plucky young medic Kate McTiernan (Judd) – has taken a walk into the jaws of hell and managed, by the skin of her teeth during a headlong flight through woods and a white water ravine, to escape. Being the case's only lead, she's suddenly forcing calm, methodical loner Cross into a partnership and a race against time, all beset by hitherto unknown emotional involvement.

Echoes of *The Silence Of The Lambs* ring strong, of course, simply due to common subject matter. But what made that such a classic was its conviction of performance and such conviction is here, too – in spades. His stoic, reliable self, Freeman brings depth and serious tone to the movie and just about manages to depart from *Se7en*'s Lt. William Somerset, while Judd displays a capable compassion and more than enough presence to lead a film.

There's solid support from Elwes, Brian Cox and Alex McArthur as local cops suspicious of external investigators, and it's a subtle balance from director Fleder – who debuted with *Things To Do In Denver When You're Dead* – drawing the audience into emotional involvement with his characters, while weaving in the shock and twist demanded by the genre.
★★★ DB

◎ KNIFE IN THE WATER (NOZ W WODZIE) (1962)

Starring: *Leon Niemczyk (Andrzej), Jolanta Umecka (Christine), Zygmunt Malanowicz (The Young Man)*
Director: *Roman Polanksi*
Screenwriter: *Roman Polanksi, Jerzy Skolimowski, Jakub Goldberg*
PG/94 mins/Drama/Thriller/Poland

On holiday in the North of Poland, an arrogant, young-middle-aged sports journalist Andrzej and his much younger, cooler wife Christine pick up a teenage hitch-hiker and take him along on their sailing boat as they travel through lake country. Tensions, conflicts and attractions simmer among the threesome, with a violent outcome seemingly inevitable.

Having attracted international attention in the early 60s with cruelly absurdist short films (*Two Men and a Wardrobe, The Fat and the Lean*) about isolated characters clashing as they struggle through empty landscapes, Polanski's first feature elaborates on the theme but with added depth of characterisation. Indeed Knife in the Water is so well-written and acted you don't notice until very late how artificial and stylised the whole set-up is.

The three characters obsessively flirt with each other and play one-upmanship games: pick-up-sticks, knife-throwing, tale-telling, that macho knife-between-the-fingers stunt seen in Aliens, yachtsmanship. These days, it's likely this story would be resolved by the revelation that one or more of the characters is a serial killer, but back in 1962 Polanski was sure enough of his effects to have the up-front action consist of apparently trivial conversations and contests with all the deep, disturbing character stuff going on below the waterline.

With then-modish and still-effective hand-held black and white photography of ominously calm countryside accompanied by an eerily burbling jazz score from Krysztof Komeda and excellent underplaying (Polanski, deemed not handsome enough to play the teenager himself, dubbed Malanowicz) from all three principles, this remains as fresh and rich as it did on its first release.

You can see the seeds of much of Polanski's later work here, in the only feature he has made in Polish; though he has made deeper, more ambitious movies he has never directed another piece as perfect as this miniature.
★★★★ **KN**

◎ A KNIGHT'S TALE (2001)

Starring: *Heath Ledger (Sir William Thatcher), Rufus Sewell (Count Adhemar of Anjou), Shannyn Sossamon (Lady Jocelyn), Paul Bettany (Geoffrey Chaucer), Laura Fraser (Kate the Farrier), Alan Tudyk (Wat Falhurst), Mark Addy (Roland), James Purefoy (Prince Edward)*
Director: *Brian Helgeland*
Screenwriter: *Brian Helgeland*
PG/126 mins./Action/Adventure/Comedy/USA

Heath Ledger plays the lowly medieval squire turned celebrity knight who enters a jousting tournament with the hope of besting Rufus Sewell's dastardly knight and winning the hand of Shannyn Sossamon's damsel.

Anarchic anachronism appears to be the order of the day, with this, LA Confidential screenwriter Brian Helgeland's latest directorial effort – complete with medieval jousts set to Queen's We Will Rock you, Mexican waves and Nike armour.

Plotwise we're in Rocky territory. William Thatcher is the kid from the wrong side of the tracks – in this case he's light on the aristocratic lineage front – who decides the thing to do is to fight his way out of the ghetto (well, 14th century rural France) with nothing but a big stick and a dream, while big bad knight Count Adhemar suspects there's something rum going on. From then on we embark on the standard series of battles towards the Grand Finale, in a somewhat ropily CGI'd ancient London.

There's plenty of enjoyable enough stuff here. Bettany is the standout as Chaucer, an inveterate gambler who spends much of the film stark-bollock naked – having lost his clothes – and who pens WWF-style opening rants for his man. Plus, the jousting sequences are suitably violent. But Helgeland's direction is a bit unsure and while Ledger, here borrowing his received English accent from Russell Crowe in Gladiator, is perfectly acceptable, he's less impressive than the supporting cast. In the end, *A Knight's Tale* doesn't so much rock you, as sway you gently.
★★★ **AS**

◎ KOLYA (1996)

Starring: *Zdenek Sverak (Louka), Andrei Chalimon (Kolja), Libuse Safrankova (Klara), Ondrej Vetchy (Broz), Stella Zazvorkova (Maminka)*
Director: *Jan Sverak*
Screenwriter: *Zdenek Sverak, from a story by Pavel Taussig*
12/100 mins./Drama/Czech Republic/UK/France
Awards: *Academy Awards – Best Foreign Language Film, Golden Globes – Best Foreign Language Film*

Franta Louka is a concert cellist, dropped from his orchestra and left to play at funerals. In order to make money he marries a Russian woman, who wants Czech immigration papers. She quickly jumps the country, heading to Germany, leaving her 5-year-old son with her mother. When the child's grandmother dies, he is sent to live with his stepfather Franta. It's a situation they both have to come to terms with.

The film that won the Oscar for best foreign language film in 1997, is a gem. Forced by the need for cash into a green-card style marriage with a Russian woman, Czech cellist Louka (Zdjenak Sverak, who also wrote the screenplay) suddenly finds himself sole guardian of the five-year-old son, Kolya, of a wife who has fled to Germany to be with her lover.

With politics a firm background and basis for the story (though never dominating), the story neatly juxtaposes the situation of the once-welcome Russians being ejected from Czechoslovakia with the growing bond between Czech bachelor and abandoned Russian boy. ★★★★★ **GM**

◎ KOYAANISQATSI (1982)

Director: *Godfrey Reggio*
Screenwriters: *Ron Fricke, Michael Hoenig, Alton Walpole, Godfrey Reggio*
U/84 mins./Documentary/USA

A visual chart of the world's development from the natural to the man-made.

There is no doubt that, for many among the public, a Stanley knife-'nads interface would be a more attractive proposition than sitting through *Koyannisqatsi*. Produced in 1983 under the auspices of 'Francis Ford Coppola Presents'... banner – back in the days when the Italian American had the clout to get any old arse released – Reggio's lengthy plotless poem is rightly caught the intelligentsia imagination, becoming influential on three counts. It catapulted the minimalist mood music of Philip Glass out of avant garde classical circles into wider avant garde circles; it reinvigorated the dying art of time-lapse photography leaving the door open for untold pop promos and commercials to jump on the speeded-up pictures band-

Movie Animals TOP 10

1	Babe	A pig	Babe
2	Toto	A dog	The Wizard of Oz
3	Baby	A leopard	Bringing Up Baby
4	Clyde	A chimp	Every Which Way But Loose
5	Charlotte	A spider	Charlotte's Web
6	Kes	A kestrel	Kes
7	Moby dick	A white whale	Moby Dick
8	Elsa	A lion	Born Free
9	Gertrude	A duck	Journey to the Centre Of The World
10	Zoltan	A vampire dog	Zoltan, Hound of Dracula

wagon; and it also, through its dreamy imagery and ability to provoke contentious codswallop, became the stoner's screen nivarna.

From a current perspective, however, Reggio's labour of love looks like the electrifying piece of pure filmmaking it always was. Taking its cue (and title) from the Hopi Indian word meaning 'a state of life that calls for another way of living,' Reggio builds up a flow of images starting with a barnstorming aerial photography of wilderness, clouds and crashing waves before moving on to the intrusion of machinery, culminating in urban chaos, depicting the movie's trademark footage of vastly accelerated people and freeways.

The points being made here do not reek with profundity: nature has its own order, humans have buggered it up big time. But his argument is seductively played out: the images delight at every turn yet it is the hypnotic ebb and flow of visuals that makes *Koyaanisqatsi* such compulsive viewing. It became obvious very quickly that Glass' score, a stunning mixture of slow, choral repetitive bits and fast orchestral repetitive bits, was being created in league with the picture assemblage and, as such, it is difficult to recall a film that employs movie/music synergy to such thrilling ends. ★★★★ **IF**

K-PAX (2001)

Starring: *Kevin Spacey (Prot), Jeff Bridges (Dr. Mark Powell), Mary McCormack (Rachel Powell), Alfre Woodard (Dr. Claudia Villars), David Patrick Kelly (Howie)*
Director: *Iain Softley*
Screenwriter: *Charles Leavitt, from the novel by Gene Brewer*
12/120 mins./Drama/Sci-fi/USA

Mystery man Prot is detained in a psychiatric hospital where Dr. Powell is fascinated by his claim to be on a mission from K-PAX, a planet 1,000 light years from Earth. While the doctors dispute his treatment, Prot has an electrifying effect on his fellow patients.

The trouble with delusions is that they can be so much more attractive than the truth. The insoluble problem in British director Iain Softley's intriguing and whimsical drama is that the fantasy is a lot more compelling than the reality.

As in Don Juan De Marco, we get an appealing oddball who is incarcerated, and a psychiatrist who, enchanted by his case, is drawn into his fully-realised, fantastical account of his life.

We have the caring doctor – opposed to drugging his patient while he gets to know him and investigates his story – versus the detached, practical doctor who doesn't want any nonsense. What we don't get is a crowd-pleasing resolution.

Romance doesn't entirely surrender to reason, but what begins with every appearance of a comic, sci-fi mystery becomes something more tricky and tragic. The revelation on which it turns is dramatic, but will be about as welcome to some people as food poisoning in the middle of a tasty meal.

Spacey does smart work as a disconcertingly composed, decidedly Christ-like enigma, who is utterly faithful to his conviction. For example, he eats unpeeled bananas whole with every sign of enjoyment. He's certainly the most supercilious and self-contained cinematic mental patient that we can remember – and evidently cine-literate, too, reassuring his shrink that, 'I'm not going to leap out of your chest.'

Prot is entertainingly articulate, and the sessions where he astounds astrophysicists with his galactic knowledge are delightful. He is, however, a tad low on fizz while he's slipping around the corridors of the psych ward, bringing hope and magical awakenings to the troubled minds of the usual nicely eccentric *One Flew Over The Cuckoo's Nest* assortment of nuts.

But it is Bridges, good as always, who becomes the more interesting – in what really amounts to a two-hander – as the man doing the questioning and coming to wish he hadn't looked so hard for logical explanations and truth. In a sense, as the analyst, he's doing the flip sides of Fearless and, of course, Starman.

It's a pity the doc's home life is so ho-hum, with McCormack given nothing to do as his wife but comment on his workaholism. No wonder he wants to believe in stranger possibilities.

Softley (director of *Backbeat*, *Hackers* and *The Wings Of The Dove*) and his two stars disdain the easy temptations of sentiment in the story, maintaining a thoughtful tone. They almost persuade us that this is as deep as it's trying (a little too hard) to be. ★★★ **AE**

KRULL (1983)

Starring: *Ken Marshall (Prince Colwyn), Lysette Anthony (Princess Lyssa), Freddie Jones (Ynyr), Francesca Annis (Lyssa), Alun Armstrong (Torquil), Bernard Bresslaw (Rell the Cyclops), Liam Neeson (Kegan)*
Director: *Peter Yates*
Screenwriter: *Stanford Sherman*
PG/117 mins./Fantasy/UK

The plans of two hostile nations to unite to fight the Slayers, and invading force from space, are wrecked when those evil beings crash the wedding of Princess Lyssa and Prince Colwyn and kidnap the bride to be. Colwyn then puts together a party of disparate talents and heads for the Slayer's mysterious black fortress t rescue Lyssa.

Another in the battalion of early 80s low-budget fantasy adventures clogged up with easily recognisable Equity members, bland but rugged heroes and special effects that may have satisfied young boys at the time but have become frail and silly with age. The plot is a pleasantly junked up variation on the Joseph Campbell-*Star Wars* quest formula, where rash hero Ken Marshall (where for art he?) is tutored by wise old-hand Freddie Jones (sounds familiar) who helps him retrieve a special weapon (oh, call the lawyers), the Glaive, capable of destroying the Beast (who really should have a silly name).

What this will require, as anyone who has taken in any of these dozy, rusty, but watchable fabulations of the era – *Hawk The Slayer, Dragonslayer, Beastmaster, Poundstretcher* – is a procession through some muddy Welsh locations, recruiting various oddbods to the cause, which must according to a local by-law include ex-*Carry On* lug Bernard Bresslaw as a giant (here known as Rell the Cyclops in case you didn't notice the single great eyeball in his forehead). There are some imaginative concoctions in Stanford Sherman's script, including Francesca Annis as an ancient witch trapped in the heart of a web and the presence of a doppelganger in the crew, but the film falters horribly in its final confrontation with the Beast which the effects team will prove ill-equipped to deal with. All too derivative, but mildly distracting, Peter Yates doesn't lend it much of a polish. Down the road Ridley Scott was carving the ornate, gothic world of Legend, but whether friend or foe of such potty, overbearing fantasy as this, it remains a markedly better attempt than Yor: The Hunter From The Future. ★★ **IN**

ⓓ KUNDUN (1997)

Starring: *Tenzin Thuthob Tsarong (Adult Dalai Lama), Gyurme Tethong (Dalai Lama, aged 12), Tulky Jamyang Kunga (Dalai Lama, Age 5), Tencho Gyalpo (Mother), Tsewang Migyur Khangsar (Father)*
Director: *Martin Scorsese*
Screenwriter: *Melissa Mathison*
12/128 mins./Biography/Drama/USA

A two-year-old boy is declared by monks to be the new Dalai Lama and taken away to be trained and, later, take up the post of Buddhist monk leader.

You have to marvel at Martin Scorsese's balls-out bravery; forsaking his well trod mean streets for mountains, he broached the childhood of the 14th Dalai Lama, peppered the cast with non-professional actors, then lensed the proceedings in an experimental, unconventional style.

Beginning in 1937, *Kundun* (which translates as 'Oceans Of Wisdom') opens on a two-year-old boy who, when discovered by a group of monks on a rural Tibetan farm, is deemed to be the new Dalai Lama – the latest reincarnation of the Buddha Of Compassion. From here, the film chronicles the boy's training as a religious leader, a role increasingly overshadowed by the spectre of communist China encroaching on Tibetan frontiers. Thus, the man of peace is forced to negotiate with the arbiters of violence, including Chairman Mao – to retain the political and spiritual autonomy of his homeland.

Even if *Kundun* lacks the commitment and penetration set by his own high standards, much of Scorsese's stock-in-trade is still present; impeccable performances (Tsarong as the 18-year-old Lama effortlessly embodying sedate wisdom), the evocation of private milieus, and a fascination with rite and ritual. Indeed, Scorsese's documentary style accumulation of exotic detail occasionally serves to distance rather than illuminate the sacred world. Yet, particularly in the final passage from Tibet, *Kundun* soars with directorial virtuosity: eschewing the talkiness and grandiose stodginess of the standard historical biopic, the movie is propelled via Philip Glass's exhilarating score and a stream of richly textured powerful images that mesmerise with their haunting beauty. The net result is difficult and demanding viewing yet strangely thrilling. ★★★★ **IF**

ⓓ KUNG FU HUSTLE (2004)

Starring: *Stephen Chow (Sing), Xiaogang Feng (Crocodile Gan Boss), Chi Chung Lam (Bone), Kwok Kuen Chan (Brother Sum), Zhi Hua Dong (Donut)*
Director: *Stephen Chow*
Screenwriters: *Tsang Kan Cheong, Stephen Chow, Xin Huo, Chan Man Keung*
15/95 mins./Action/Comedy/China/Hong Kong

China, the 1940s. Blundering into rickety ghetto Pig Sty Ally, smalltime bandit Sing attempts to blackmail the locals by posing as a member of the feared Axe Gang. When the villagers click and the Axe Gang pitch up, Sing is caught in between a raging turf battle that reveals some unexpected martial artistry from the locals . . .

Ever since *Crouching Tiger*, when dumb chopsocky went martial arthouse, the good old-fashioned fisticuff has turned into an acceptable and polite form of entertainment. Artful. Epic. Balletic. Often preoccupied with bamboo. Still, if the likes of *House Of Hero Tigers* are now dinner party banter, here, at last, is one for the pub. We are, after all, talking about a movie that dubs pinball noises over its fight scenes. Balletic? It's like a bull on rollerblades.

Kung Fu Hustle has already become something of a phenomenon in Asia, punching up box-office records across the continent. That this is largely down to one man, the agonisingly multi-talented Stephen Chow, is nothing short of heroic. Writer, director, producer and star, on-screen he's the heir apparent to Jackie Chan, while behind the camera he's a hyperactive stylist, an Oriental Sam Raimi. It's heartening to see that he's also a bit of a lunatic. If *Hero* was stupidly beautiful, this is beautifully stupid.

Chow cut his teeth on the criminally underseen *Shaolin Soccer*, which, along with being on-the-money dumb, used inventive CGI to liven up the superhuman footie. In the bigger budget *Hustle*, Chow's allowed to run riot with his preposterous visions. It's a Spaghetti Western via *Enter The Dragon* and *Tom And Jerry*, where screams are like earthquakes and foot chases are clocked at Roadrunner speed. Hollywood would never allow such state of the art absurdity. It'd probably steer clear of the gallows humour, too. If the slapstick intentions are *Tex Avery*, the oofing punchline's more often *Evil Dead*. But that's the perverse buzz of *Kung Fu Hustle*. It's like watching a blockbuster beamed from another planet.

For all its thundering effects and flickbook edits, it is, at heart, rabidly retro, recalling the lunacy of *Chinese Ghost Story* and the knuckle-basics of the Shaw brothers: that is, minimum plot, maximum rumble. The elaborate, copious fight scenes, choreographed by *The Matrix*'s Yuen Wo Ping, often beggar belief. If you don't have weird peanut dreams after watching the two old, blind assassins thrash their trowly fingernails over the strings of a homicidal harp, you were probably watching with your eyes closed. Subtle it ain't and God is it loud – half the time it's like having your head trapped between a pair of cymbals – but, really, it's one giant kick in the nuts for Hollywood. ★★★★ **SC**

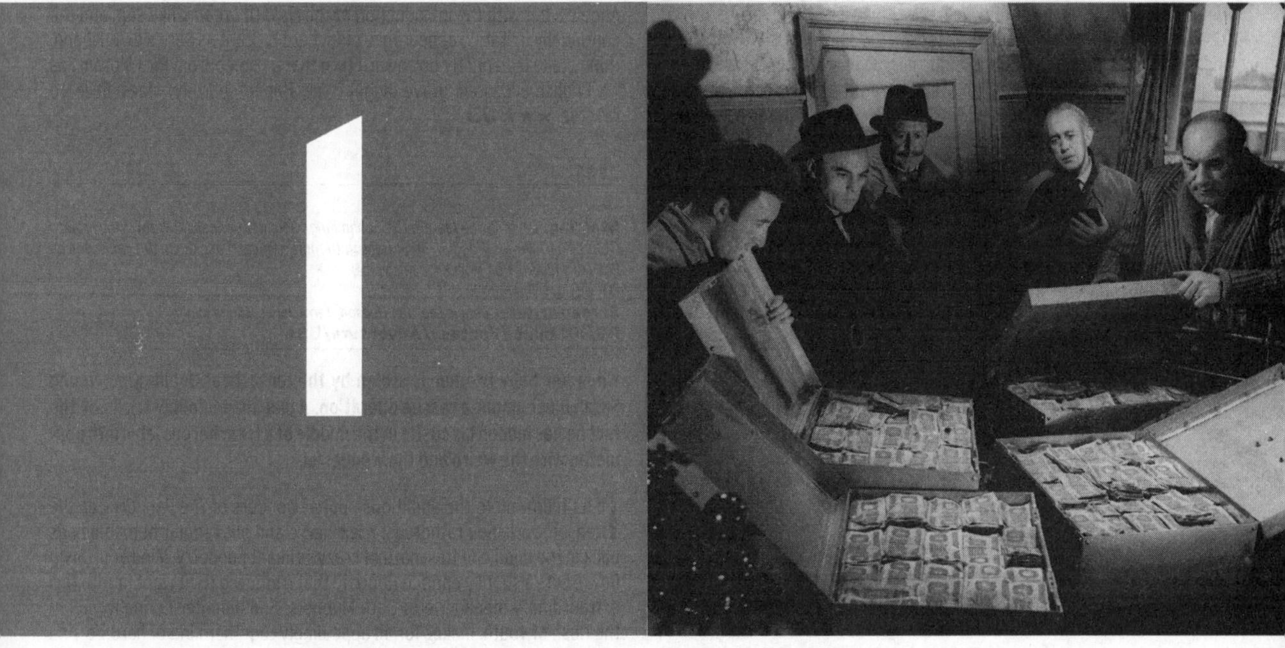

⦿ L.A. CONFIDENTIAL (1997)

Starring: *Kevin Spacey (Det. Sgt. Jack Vincennes), Russell Crowe (Officer Wendell 'Bud' White), Guy Pearce (Det. Lt. Edmund Jennings 'Ed' Exley), James Cromwell (Capt. Dudley Liam Smith), Kim Basinger (Lynn Bracken), Danny DeVito (Sid Hudgens)*
Director: *Curtis Hanson*
Screenwriters: *Curtis Hanson, Brian Helgeland, from the novel by James Ellroy*
18/132 mins./Crime/Drama/Mystery/USA

Awards: *Academy Awards – Best Supporting Actress, Best Adapted Screenplay. BAFTA – Best Editing, Best Sound, Empire Awards – Best Actor, Golden Globes – Best Supporting Actress*

A shooting at an all-night diner is investigated by three LA policemen in their own unique ways.

One of the great joys for any reader delving into James Ellroy's unofficially labelled 'LA Quartet', was not only discovering the only truly epic work in modern crime fiction, but revelling in the author's use of language. By the third of these novels – *LA Confidential* – Ellroy had reduced both dialogue and exposition down to an instantly accessible, visceral staccato beat. By the fourth – *White Jazz* – he'd practically given up on sentences altogether, but still managed to drag you head first into these tales of personal morality and municipal growth.

The great irony is the fact that Ellroy's unique literary style stemmed not from some great predetermined ambition to deconstruct the language of Chandler et al, but from the fact that when he delivered the manuscript for *LA Confidential*, he was 100 pages over length. Rather than pick away at his incredibly intricate plotting that mixed fucked-up fictional archetypes with even more fucked-up non-fictional figures from LA's shady history, he decided to deconstruct his sentences. The plot remained the same, who needs the odd adverb here and there? Given that the resultant text, hugely acclaimed on its publication in 1990, still clocked in just south of 500 pages, could any filmmaker even begin to attempt to do it justice?

By the mid-1990s, Curtis Hanson had established himself as a decent enough journeyman director who had delivered three variations on the middle-class/yuppie invasion movie – *Bad Influence*, *The Hand That Rocks The Cradle* and *The River Wild*. Yet somehow, alongside screenwriter Brian Helgeland, Hanson found the means to take Ellroy's noir world of underclass LA to the big screen.

More than anything of course, Ellroy's quartet owed a debt to Chinatown. Both look at the evolution of the city through a kaleidoscope of social types, essentially detailing how Los Angeles came into being at the expense of the ethnic working classes, and how crime in the ghetto became a matter of economic growth contributed to as much by the upper classes as those trapped by the cycle of poverty and crime. The story of LA is the story of a city of angels who have literally fallen. Hanson intuitively knew this.

'I've always wanted to deal with a city that has a manufactured image in the first place, an image that was sent out over the airwaves to get everybody to come there, as in the main title sequence,' he said. 'The truth of that image was literally being destroyed to make way for all the people that were coming there looking for it. It was being bulldozed into oblivion. It's without a doubt my most personal movie.'

Hanson took Ellroy's three-pronged approach, using the LAPD as a backdrop to explore the nature of personal versus societal morality. Thus, we see three crime fighters, each with their own agenda – Bud White, a violent brute of a man, driven to avenge the violence he saw perpetrated on his own mother by protecting every damaged woman he comes into contact with; Ed Exley, abused in subtler, more understated ways by the legacy of his father, to the point where the morality he clings to seems to have no home within himself; and finally Jack Vincennes. Ellroy himself best summed up Spacey's portrayal of this character: 'It's some of the best self-loathing I've ever seen on screen.' Hanson's film is a complex dive into Ellroy's world, replete with fine performances from the Oscar-winning Kim Basinger as Veronica Lake-a-like Lynn Bracken, and the estimably slimy

Danny DeVito as the reporter for whom everything is, 'Off the record, on the QT and very hush-hush.' Dante Spinotti's evocation of 1950s LA – by night and by day – is a delight, and Jerry Goldsmith delivers what is probably his best score since, well, *Chinatown*. It took seven drafts of the screenplay before Hanson showed it to Ellroy. The author had some initial misgivings, and for any Ellroy purist there are things wrong with the movie – Exley should never be played as a hero (despite fine work from Pearce), he's too morally ambivalent for that, and the villain shouldn't die at the end – evil always survives, especially when it's presented in such an obsequious form. But Hollywood has a need for black and white, while pulp fiction finds its metier in the grey and the dark, and one can accept these things. After all, Ellroy does: 'Hanson proved me wrong on a couple of things. When I read the script, I thought the shoot-out (the adrenaline-packed finale) was preposterous. And you know what? In the movie it's preposterous. Two guys holed up in a room where they kill 15 guys – it's bullshit. But you know what? It's inspired bullshit.' ★★★★★ **BM**

Movie Trivia: L.A. Confidential

Captain Dudley Smith, James Cromwell's character, doesn't die in the novel and returns in Ellroy's *White Jazz. Hush-Hush* magazine, the scandal sheet published by Danny DeVito's character, is based on the real-life *Confidential* magazine. *L.A. Confidential* was going to be made into a TV series starring Kiefer Sutherland as Jack Vincennes, but the project never lifted off.

LA STORY (1991)

Starring: *Steve Martin (Harris K. Telemacher), Victoria Tennant (Sara McDowel), Richard E. Grant (Roland Mackey), Marilu Henner (Trudi), Sarah Jessica Parker (SanDeE*), Kevin Pollak (Frank Swan)*
Director: *Mick Jackson*
Screenwriter: *Steve Martin*
15/90 mins./Comedy/Romance/USA

Harris Telemacher is a weather presenter for an LA TV station. Striving to achieve fulfilment, he finds a helping hand from the last source he expected: the city of Los Angeles itself.

It comes as no surprise that Steve Martin, who has acted in the past opposite such items as a brain and a series of vintage film clips, should decide here to co-star alongside an entire city, in this instance Los Angeles (hence the name).

What is a surprise is that despite Martin's reteaming with writer Daniel Melnick, this film has only half the wit and romance of their last collaboration, *Roxanne*. Martin is Harris Telemacher, a TV weatherman in a city where the temperature rarely drops below 72°F, thus allowing him to pre-tape his broadcasts.

His life is filled with Beverly Hills clichés – his girlfriend Trudi spends her time shopping and endlessly doing lunch while he drives everywhere, even to his next-door neighbour's house – until he falls in love with English journalist Sara.

The path of love is not smooth, however, and Harris finds himself with three women instead of one – Trudi, Sara and young Valley Girl Sandee (Parker). To complicate things further, he is fired from his job and discovers an electronic freeway sign that sends him – and him alone – cryptic messages.

It all starts well enough as a satire of the madness that is life in Los Angeles, but with the introduction of the *Field Of Dreams*-like sign and the continually irritating appearance of Richard E. Grant as Sara's ex-husband, things take a distinctly downward turn that a cameo from Rick Moranis as an English-accented grave-digger (cue Hamlet parody) does little to reverse. ★★★ **JB**

LABYRINTH (1986)

Starring: *David Bowie (Jareth the Goblin King), Jennifer Connelly (Sarah), Toby Froud (Toby), Shari Wesier (Hoggle), Brian Henson (Hoggle's voice), Dave Goelz (Didymus' voice), Rob Mills (Ludo), Ron Mueck (Ludo's voice)*
Director: *Jim Henson*
Screenwriters: *Dennis Lee, Jim Henson, Terry Jones, Elaine May*
PG/101 mins./Fantasy/Adventure/USA

When her baby brother is stolen by the fantastical Goblin King, young Sarah must mount a rescue operation. A plan made doubly tricky by the fact he has hidden his castle in the middle of a treacherous labyrinth populated with the weird and the wonderful.

In its follow up to the ambitious puppet wonders of *The Dark Crystal*, the Henson workshop rather lost their nerve and put regular human beings back in the middle of this maze of crazy-brilliant puppetry. Mind you, David Bowie cuts a spooky enough figure in that fright wig to fit right in with this extraordinary menagerie of Goth Muppets. And Jennifer Connelly, still in the flush of youth, makes for an appealingly together kind of heroine. And yet, this is a lesser adventure than *Crystal*, never quite as fully transporting for all its fine execution.

Broadly speaking, it's *Alice In Wonderland* made less trippy by its quest format, but still a picaresque through the heady world of Henson's making. The Labyrinth itself, referencing Escher's dizzying optical illusions, is a very literal nightmare world. The film is playing a distinctly Freudian game – after all, Sarah is plunging into puberty – that all of it might be going on in her dreams. A similar idea to that expounded in L. Frank Baum's world of Oz, that her companions on this journey are merely living versions of her most reassuring bedroom toys. When she departs the land, she is finally departing childhood.

Quite a clever notion to thread into a kid's adventure, and you have to admire Henson's reach, but he gets caught a little aimless, many of the encounters come to nothing, while the addition of Terry Jones to spruce up the scriptwriting team adds a strain of Pythonesque whimsy that feels awkwardly superimposed. Yet, Henson's handsome gifts of giving his exotic puppets the spark of life and personality is an unsung form of genius that remains sorely missed. ★★★ **IN**

LACOMBE LUCIEN (1974)

Starring: *Pierre Blaise (Lucien), Aurore Clément (France), Holger Lowenadler (Albert Horn), Thérèse Gieshe (Bella Horn), Stéphane Bouy (Jean Bernard)*
Director: *Louis Malle*
Screenwriter: *Louis Malle*
12/137 mins./Drama/USA/France

Awards: *BAFTA – Best Film*

Rejected by the Resistance, Provençal teenager Lucien Lacombe joins the Gestapo, only to see the error of his ways when he falls for France, the daughter of Jewish tailor, Albert Horn.

Having shocked polite society with his study of incest, *Le Souffle au Coeur*, Louis Malle might have been advised to keep a lower profile with his next picture. However, he opted to explore the nature of collaboration and for his setting he chose rural France during the Second World War – having thought better of focusing on either the right-wing workers paid by the Mexican government to disrupt student demonstrations in the late 1960s or the lower classes who abetted the French during the Algerian War.

However, even though he was aware of the sensitivity of his subject, Malle could never have anticipated the storm of protest that greeted this compelling character drama and persuaded him to spend the next 13 years working in North America. It was very much to his credit, therefore, that he chose the Occupation as the scene for his homecoming film, *Au Revoir, Les Enfants* (1987).

The main reason for *Lacombe, Lucien's* unpopularity was Malle's refusal to take sides at a time when Vichy's scars were still acutely painful. By limiting Lucien's education and making him the product of a broken home (his mother had taken a lover while his father was in a German camp), Malle presents him as a victim of his times rather than the incarnation of wickedness. Indeed, Malle's preoccupation is with the banality of evil and the part that chance plays in shaping human and historical destiny and not with the ideology or opportunism that prompted so many to betray their country. Moreover, he implies an elitism about the Maquis that causes it to reject the dullard teenager's services and suggests that a desire for affirmation rather than any political conviction turned Lucien into an accidental collaborator.

Consequently, there's a Renoiresque feel to Malle's contention that everyone has reasons for their actions and, thus, Lucien's capricious revenge on the Resistance finds echo in Horn's defiant gesture of surrender, as he ends his interminable confinement by dining in a restaurant filled with Nazi officers. ★★★★ **DP**

LADY AND THE TRAMP (1955)

Starring: *the voices of: Peggy Lee (Darling/Si/Am/Peg), Barbara Luddy (Lady), Larry Roberts (Tramp), Bill Thompson (Jock/Bulldog), Bill Baucom (Trusty), Stan Freberg (Beaver), Verna Felton (Aunt Sarah)*
Screenwriters: *Erdman Penner, Joe Rinaldi, Ralph Wright, Do DaGradi, Joe Grant, based on the novel by Ward Greene*
PG/103 mins./Animation/Adventure/Romance/Family/USA

The famous tale of the pampered uptown cocker spaniel Lady who meets charming scamp Tramp, a local mongrel. After Lady's owners bring an unforeseen addition to the household, she joins Tramp on the open road only for trouble to ensue.

Another classic, i.e. living-Walt, era animated fable. This one doing the reverse switch – setting itself in the real, then contemporary world with the fantasy of anthropomorphising its cast of canines into chatty human counterparts (see also: *Dumbo*, *The Jungle Book* or *Brother Bear* for variations on the theme). And while never touching the ornate loveliness of the true greats, is as sweet a piece of Disney pie as you could ask for. Especially, as this is one of the very few that is directly a romance.

Tagline
She's from the leash and license set ... he's footloose and collar free!

That is between rapscallion mutt Tramp, a true charmer with a voice as velvety as the painted skies, and Lady, a proper pedigree spaniel with big doe eyes giving her a rather vacant look. There is an amusing cross-class element, he's hardly up to her standards, but best not to think of the flea issues. It floats along easily enough, including a dreamy spaghetti scene that everyone remembers – ooh, they're both chewing on the same piece of pasta.

The songs are smoothly crafted, although only the slippery delights of the Siamese Cat Song is truly memorable. It's these two snobby furballs who get Tramp dumped in the pound to add just that shiver of thrill, and a wonderful array of fellow dogs to plot a breakout. Shy of magnificent, it's rather slight, but hard to fault. ★★★★ **IN**

THE LADY EVE (1941)

Starring: *Barbara Stanwyck (Jean Harrington), Henry Fonda (Charles Pike), Charles Coburn ('Colonel' Harrington), Eugene Pallette (Horace Pike), William Demarest (Muggsy), Eric Blore (Sir Alfred McGlennan Keith)*
Director: *Preston Sturges*
Screenwriter: *Preston Sturges, based on the story* The Faithful Heart *by Monckton Hoffe*
U/93 mins./Comedy/Romance/USA

Charles Pike has been in the jungle and, suspecting his desire of female company, is targeted by conwoman Jean Harrington. Jean falls genuinely in love, but when Charles finds out who and what she is he refuses her attentions. So, she sets about breaking his heart under the guise of Lady Eve Sidwich.

After a year up the Amazon 'without seeing a white woman', ale heir and keen ophiologist (look it up) Charles Pike is targeted by con woman Jean Harrington and her card-sharp father as prime sucker material. Jean actually falls for the naive mug, but when he finds out she's a crook the shipboard romance fizzles. To get revenge, Jean reinvents herself as an English debutante, 'Lady Eve Sidwich', and shows up at the Pike estate intent on breaking a heart. You can probably guess the end, but not the path which is taken to get there – the left-field kinks are all part of the fun.

Writer-director Preston Sturges was a rare Hollywood man whose comedy hits were popular successes but also prized and praised by high-toned critics (and, not least, peers like Orson Welles and Billy Wilder). He was as at home sending up the snobbish absurdities of the wealthy-but-vulgar Pikes as he was with the cheerfully crafty world of down-to-earth slobs. Not everything in *The Lady Eve* is as frothy as it might be – Fonda's repeated pratfalls become uncomfortable rather than funny, but never go as far into the comedy of agony as Cary Grant in his screwball roles – but it's still a wonderful picture, set (despite a good Hitler joke) in a world of silly heirs and sharp-eyed dolls as remote from reality and yet wholly credible as that of P. G. Wodehouse.

The bit about being away from 'white women' sounds like conventional 1940s racism, but is actually a sly joke on Fonda's blinkered asexuality – the jungle is draped with native lovelies he's ignored but who have made an impression on his bodyguard. Among the funniest moments is Stanwyck's commentary on the parade of flirts and gold-diggers trying to get the rich boob's attention, but her performance makes this more than just the funny tale of a woman pursuing an idiot. Her Jean/Eve is every bit as devastating, in midriff-bare evening gowns, as her murderess in *Double Indemnity*, and still charms and fascinates. ★★★★★ **KN**

THE LADY FROM SHANGHAI (1948)

Starring: *Rita Hayworth (Elsa Bannister), Orson Welles (Michael O'Hara), Everett Sloane (Arthur Bannister), Erskine Sanford (Judge), Gus Schilling (Goldie), Carl Frank (District Attorney), Lou Merrill (Jake), Evelyn Ellis (Bessie)*
Director: *Orson Welles*
Screenwriter: *Orson Welles, based on the novel by Raymond Sherwood King*
PG/87 mins./Crime/USA

Irish sailor Michael O'Hara saves Elsa Bannister from muggers and earns the gratitude of her older lawyer husband, Arthur. However, by making the acquaintance of Bannister's crooked business partner, George Grisby, O'Hara soon finds himself sinking into ever-deeper waters.

'I'll give $1,000 to anyone who can explain the story to me,' Harry Cohn ranted, as he emerged from screening the rough cut of Orson Welles's adaptation of Raymond Sherwood King's pulp thriller, *If I Die Before I Wake*.

The Columbia chief had been persuaded to produce the picture when

Welles promised him a masterpiece while calling to request $50,000 to recover the impounded costumes for his touring musical version of *Around the World in 80 Days*. But, in fact, Welles had feigned excitement over the first book that had caught his eye from the payphone and he had only reluctantly agreed to the casting of Rita Hayworth (over Barbara Laage), as he knew she would try to use the project to patch their failing marriage. Cohn similarly had misgivings over the decision to cut Hayworth's trademark red hair into a blonde feather bob. But greater problems were to lie ahead.

Filming on Errol Flynn's yacht off Acapulco went well, despite the inevitable Wellesian delays. But he had induced Rudolph Maté into shooting several uncredited sequences that reinforced the power of the visuals, in which the fore- and backgrounds teemed with compelling detail that were captured in intricate deep-focus. Reflective surfaces abounded (most notably in the aquarium and the famous Hall of Mirrors), while the Chinese exoticism of San Francisco's Union Square contrasted tellingly with the Elsa's guile and O'Hara's exploitability.

But Welles was prevented from editing the footage and loathed the soundtrack built around Hayworth's song, 'Please Don't Kiss Me'. Nevertheless, Viola Lawrence's first cut still ran for 155 minutes, until preview responses prompted Cohn to reduce it to 87 and withhold the picture for two years lest it damaged Hayworth's Love Goddess image.

When it was finally released, as a supporting feature, this classic noir in the *Double Indemnity* mould made few ripples. But its narrative and visual complexity eventually established it among Welles's most challengingly satisfying outings. ★★★★ **DP**

LADY IN THE LAKE (1947)

Starring: *Robert Montgomery (Philip Marlowe), Lloyd Nolan (Lt. DeGamont), Audrey Totter (Adrienne Fromsett), Tom Tully (Capt. Kane), Leon Ames (Derace Kingsby)*
Director: *Robert Montgomery*
Screenwriter: *Steve Fisher, based on the novel by Raymond Chandler*
PG/105 mins./Mystery/USA

LA private eye Phillip Marlowe is hired to find the runaway wife of magazine publisher Derace Kingsby. A female corpse turns up in a California lake near Kingsby's holiday cabin, but is identified as Muriel Chess, wife of the caretaker, rather than Crystal Kingsby. Marlowe digs further, and finds that the situation is even more complicated than it appears.

Like *The Thief*, the silent (rather, dialogue-free) film made in 1952 and *Scent of Mystery*, the first (and only) feature in Smell-o-Vision, this stands as a monument to the inadvisability of saddling an entire film with a technically interesting but ultimately pointless gimmick.

Most adaptations of Raymond Chandler's Marlowe novels try to adapt the author's distinctive voice with a first-person narration, but Robert Montgomery – who stars as 'Phillip' Marlowe and directs – shoots the entire film through a subjective camera, effectively casting the audience as the private eye, warning us to pay attention to clues and not trust any of the suspects. Though a few moments – when Marlowe is punched in the face by a thug or kissed by Audrey Totter – work well in the 'lion in your lap' manner favoured by 3-D movies, the trick soon wears thin, prompting audiences to recall that people do not see the world in black and white with elegant panning camera movements and a lush music track.

If you get past the tricksiness, this is a fine adaptation of the novel – though uncredited, Chandler worked on the script, the only time he tried to adapt one of his books for the screen, and is responsible for the in-jokes about the pulp magazine business – with Totter especially good in shoulderpads as the tart heroine and familiar grouch Lloyd Nolan excellent as the desperate, crooked cop in the case. ★★★ **KN**

THE LADY VANISHES (1938)

Starring: *Margaret Lockwood (Iris Henderson), Michael Redgrave (Gilbert Redman), Paul Lukas (Dr. Hertz), Dame May Whitty (Miss Froy), Cecil Parker (Eric Todhunter)*
Director: *Alfred Hitchcock*
Screenwriters: *Alma Reville, Sidney Gilliat, Frank Launder based on the novel* The Wheel Spins *by Ethel Lina White*
U/97 mins./Mystery/Romance/Comedy/UK

When the seemingly harmless Miss Froy disappears on a transcontinental train, Iris Henderson enlists the help of her fellow English passengers, including dilettante musicologist Gilbert Redman to confound the schemes of Dr. Hertz and his sinister accomplices.

Train thrillers were all the rage in the 1930s. Agatha Christie published *Murder on the Orient Express* in 1934, while Ethel Lina White's play, *The Wheel Spins*, had opened in the West End two years later. The latter's screen adaptation was written by Frank Launder and Sidney Gilliatt, who were no strangers to trainbound mysteries themselves, having penned *Seven Sinners* in 1936. Indeed, the two most memorable characters in this enduringly enjoyable Hitchcock classic, Charters and Caldicott, were inspired by Gordon Harker's golf nut in *Rome Express* and the voluble corset salesman that Robert Donat encountered en route to Scotland in Hitch's *The 39 Steps*.

As he would later prove with *Lifeboat*, *Rope* and *Rear Window*, Hitchcock was the master of confined spaces and he makes splendid use of the train's compartments and corridors to emphasise the audacious ingenuity of Dr. Hertz's kidnap plot.

However, it's the dialogue and characterisation that make *The Lady Vanishes* so mischievously gratifying. Countless lines crackle with wit and insinuation, whether it's adulterous politician Eric Todhunter (Parker) trying to sustain a modicum of propriety with his mistress Margaret (Travers) or Gilbert discussing his parentage and his relationship with the German woman who pays his rent.

But much of the humour centres on Charters and Caldicott, who were brilliantly played (as they would be in several subsequent features) by Basil Radford and Naunton Wayne, neither of whom were particularly known for their comic prowess. However, they don't just provide light relief. They also confound Hitler's view of the British as Woosteresque buffoons and someone at the Reich's Chancellory should have noted how they not only did their bit in the shoot-out, but also enabled Mrs Froy to slip away undetected and helped drive the train to safety.

Released to coincide with the Munich Crisis, the film proved a major success on both sides of the Atlantic and was key in securing Hitchcock an invitation to work in Hollywood. ★★★★ **DP**

LADYBIRD, LADYBIRD (1994)

Starring: *Crissy Rock (Maggie Conlan), Vladimir Vega (Jorge), Sandie Lavelle (Mairhead), Mauricio Venegas (Adrian), Ray Winston (Simon)*
Director: *Ken Loach*
Screenwriter: *Rona Munro*
18/97 mins./Drama/UK

Ken Loach docu-drama about a British woman's fight with Social Services over the care of her children.

In Europe, Ken Loach has a reputation as one of the UK's leading filmmakers, whereas in Blighty he is still sometimes seen as a jumped-up TV director. *Ladybird Ladybird* completed the loose trilogy of politically aware social dramas begun by *Riff Raff* and *Raining Stones*: more domestic in its scope than those earlier films but sharing their raw, in-your-face aesthetic, it tells the story of Maggie, a blowsy mother of four young lads who attempts to retain a measure of dignity in her dealings with the social services.

Explicitly harking back to Loach's celebrated family drama *Cathy Come Home*, this is apparently based on a true story. Sympathetically scripted by *Casualty* regular Rona Munro, it makes a point of presenting Maggie neither as a victim nor a case history, but as a woman trying to make the best of life on a low income. Out at the pub one night she meets a Latin-American refugee, Jorge, and shacks up with him. Flashbacks tell the painful details of her past – domestic violence, nicotine addiction, the taking of her children into care – while the future is shaped by a punitive social services department which refuses to believe Maggie has changed and literally cradle-snatches the two children she and Jorge have together.

Despite a brave and honest performance from professional newcomer Crissy Rock, this is not as accomplished as Loach's previous two films. The blistering black comedy has gone, replaced by a humour which is gentler and more rounded. The film is also unbalanced, with Jorge barely sketched as a character, while his problems with the immigration department take second place to Maggie's own. Compensating for this, however, is Munro's fine ear for dialogue, with the film working best in those scenes where the precision-tooled language of officialdom is used to crush Maggie's blueberry outbursts. ★★★ **SBe**

⓪ LADYHAWKE (1985)

Starring: *Matthew Broderick (Phillipe Gaston), Rutger Hauer (Captain Etienne Navarre), Michelle Pfieffer (Isabeau d'Anjou), Leo McKern (Faehr Imperius), John Wood (Bishop of Aquilla), Alfred Molina (Cezar)*
Director: *Richard Donner*
Screenwriters: *Edward Kharma, Michael Thomas, Tom Mankiewicz, David Webb Peoples*
PG/121 mins./Fantasy/Adventure/USA

Having escaped from the dreaded dungeons of Aquilla, petty thief Phillipe The Mouse falls in with a strange captain and his hawk. It turns out this noble knight is the victim of a curse that he will spend the night as a wolf while his true love, the Lady Isabeau, must spend the day as that hawk. But unknowingly this lowly criminal may have presented them with the chance to finally break the curse.

An elegant, hugely romantic fairy-tale with an exceptionally good cast and a sturdy Hollywood director, strange then that this gothic fable tends to be forgotten. Here is the kind of elaborate, gothic tragedy that fuels Germanic operas and Heavy Metal ballads – the lovers who can remain together but forever be apart. Richard Donner makes some wise choices with the material, letting the magical elements fade into the background of a murky medieval realism, the fact of the curse more important than how it works. His European locations tang with real life, and are only gently spotted with glimmers of mysticism. We are not talking about the juvenile tang of swords and sorcery, Donner is after rapture not thunder, tellingly keeping his eye on the two lovers' great adversity.

The director also manages to avoid sentimentality by viewing the story through the eyes of the sprightly, jabbering Matthew Broderick, a self-serving scamp induced to break back into a dungeon he was far happier breaking out of. A young Michelle Pfieffer makes an ideal romantic ideal – it is the lascivious desires she inspires in local but decidedly non-conformist bishop (John Wood) that is the source of the trouble to begin with. Leo McKern also turns up to give a sweetly comedic performance as a monk on the side of good (the Church don't come out of this too well). Only Rutger Hauer seems less at ease with the straight heroic role, his smile always bordering close to a sneer, he is too layered with threat to sweep ladies off ready heels. He is not cut from the heroic mould.

It's fairly predictable and small-scale (the special effects are kept to a bare minimum and still landed an Oscar nomination) but in its vivid setting and compelling story is a quiet gem. ★★★★ **IN**

⓪ THE LADYKILLERS (1955)

Starring: *Alec Guinness (Professor Marcus), Cecil Parker (Claude), Herbert Lom (Louis), Peter Sellers (Harry), Danny Green (One-Round), Katie Johnson (The Old Lady), Jack Warner (The Superintendent)*
Director: *Alexander Mackendrick*
Screenwriter: *William Rose*
PG/97 mins./Comedy/Crime/UK
Awards: *BAFTA – Best British Actor (Katie Johnson), Best British Screenplay*

A gang of rather eccentric thieves rent a room in a rail-side house owned by the sweetest old lady. Yet, as they plot to rob the nearby mail train, it will be this diminutive old dear who will prove their undoing.

Deemed one of the high-water marks in that high-tide of British filmmaking, the Ealing Comedies, this comedy manages the paradoxical brilliance of being, in equal measures, quaintly endearing and horrific. There's something indelibly British in that – menace opposed by the fortitude of good manners.

Alexander Mackendrick, one of the more unsung of Britain's great directing talents, adores this mix of ideas and plays the contrast beautifully, just on the cusp of absurdity, the sun-struck streets of London's King Cross painted as an almost village-like fantasy land. Into this pantomime set looms Alec Guinness, his mouth overcrowded with oversized molars, his face a-twitch with violent tics, the master criminal setting up home at twee little Katie Johnson's lopsided house. The house, built on an unnatural tilt, is a metaphor for the confrontation that will follow between Guinness and his gang of goons, masquerading as classical musicians, and the smallest, sweetest, dottiest landlady in all of London town. The joke being the criminal fraternity – admittedly of pretty low calibre in this chapter – are actually the underdogs.

One of the few Ealings to be made in colour, although you seem to remember it in black and white, this is more straightforwardly a comedy than its more socially aware counterparts, but Mackendrick, with American screenwriter William Rose, has a keenness for the twisted paths of black humour. Each of the lugs will come a cropper (including youthful turns from Peter Sellers and Herbert Lom), often quite violently, and their bodies will be tipped onto the coal trains figuratively steaming all the way to Hell. The Coen Brothers came a cropper themselves trying to reconfigure its sly Britishness, still encamped in a postwar austerity, to the banks of the Mississippi, proving just how entwined in the local fabric these films were. ★★★★ **IN**

⓪ THE LADYKILLERS (2004)

Starring: *Tom Hanks (Professor G.H. Dorr), Irma P. Hall (Marva Munson), Marlon Wayans (Gawain MacSam), J.K. Simmons (Garth Pancake), Tzi Ma (The General)*
Directors: *Ethan Coen, Joel Coen*
Screenwriters: *Ethan Coen, Joel Coen, from the 1955 film by William Rose*
15/103 mins./Comedy/Crime/USA

Plotting to tunnel into a river-boat casino's dockside vault, a gang of criminals, disguised as purveyors of religious music, fall foul of their gospel-clutching landlady, Marva Munson.

What was up with the Coens? Were they sick? Were they bored? Had their jazzy jiggery-pokery of antique genres been caught frozen in the headlights of the mainstream? Is it that lumpy industry bureaucracy has gone and forced them to share the director's credit? We all knew how it worked: Joel was director, Ethan was producer, the films entirely a double-act. No need to meddle.

Whatever the ailment, this sleight-of-hand – a chancy remake of Alexander Mackendrick's delicious 1955 Ealing comedy of sinister charm and murderous intent – arrives strangely off-kilter and lethargic, stuffed with forced jollity and broad mishap. Racial epithets and bowel gags from the makers of *Miller's Crossing*? Say it ain't so.

Of course, even a less-than-spec Coen movie is a good deal better than the aimless, guileless pap cranked out by mere mortals. So there's no need for panic, with some rich, tasty flesh still to be found on *The Ladykillers*' bones.

The relocation of the plot from a dank, post-War King's Cross to a Mississippi wayside conjures an edgy timelessness as the brothers underpin the contemporary setting with an archaic tinge of Southern Gothic. In place of the fogbound railway tracks we have the river itself, where from a gargoyle-lipped bridge-top the film's accumulating corpses are deposited on rubbish-totting barges, surely carting those perfidious sinners off to Hell.

Tom Hanks' Professor Goldthwait Higginson Dorr PhD, leader of this enterprise, has slithered straight out of the pages of a Mark Twain novel, flush with a fey gentlemanly delicacy, mud-brown fangs and a magician's sprig of a beard. How the superstar rises to the challenge of souring his milky persona, locating whispers of the devil in every dab of his handkerchief and gust of Southern loquaciousness.

The Coens lavish all their pranksters' delight in knotty word-play on the Professor's elitist etiquette, as he spouts Edgar Allan Poe verse at whim and, between vile spasms of gurgling laughter, transforms simple sentences into arcane volleys of sibilant prattle: 'We must have waffles,' he demands at one particular note of crisis. 'We must have waffles, forthwith!' When he plies the term 'rococo', it's as if Forrest Gump has been possessed by the spirits of Hannibal Lecter and Stuart Hall. To be direct, he is exquisite. Surely even the ghost of Alec Guinness, who added a vampiric splendour to the role in 1955, would doff his shadowy brim.

As Hanks thrills to the task, his directors seem to flounder. Replacing Katie Johnson's twee, tea-supping angel with the bosomy, black might of God-fearing Irma P. Hall doesn't work. Independently she's a voluminous presence, railing against the 'hippity-hop' of troublesome youth and eyeing the Professor's wheedling with an air of distaste, but the joke is lost.

She's obviously a match for this inept band of misfits – a suitably eccentric gang made up of flat-footed walking gags dubbed Pancake, The General and Lump, and filled by no-name actors straining at the bit. When has a Coen cast ever needed to strain? Marlon Wayans, as the 'hippity-hop' inside man, just jerks and cusses as irritatingly as he does everywhere else.

Oh, for a Goodman, a Turturro or a Buscemi to second-fiddle Hanks' mastery. For when he plots and prevaricates you want to cheer with honest delight – it is only then that the film truly works its wicked ways. ★★★ **IN**

LAGAAN (2001)

Starring: *Aamir Khan (Bhuvan), Gracy Singh (Gauri), Rachel Shelley (Elizabeth Russell), Paul Blackthorne (Captain Andrew Russell), Suhasini Mulay (Yahodamai), Kulbhushan Kharbanda (Rajah Puran Singh)*
Director: *Ashutosh Gowariker*
Screenwriters: *Kumar Dave, Sanjay Dayma, Ashutosh Gowariker, K.P. Saxena*
PG/224 mins./Musical/India

Awards: *Academy Awards – Best Foreign Language Film*

During a terrible drought, a crippled Indian village beg to be exempt from the heavy taxes of their British rulers in order to feed themselves. But the cruel British ruler, instead, challenges them to a game of this mysterious imported sport cricket. If they win, no tax, if they lose, it is doubled. Thus the young hero Bhuvanmust assemble a team, cutting across all castes, and train them in a sport they will prove to have a natural aptitude for.

An outstanding and fully accessible piece of Indian filmmaking that manages, over its near four-hour running time, to combine the colourful trappings of its nature – singing! dancing! melodrama! ribbons! – with the classic Hollywood sports formula. Think Rocky goes Hindi with cricket, and if that sounds crazy it shouldn't, Ashutosh Gowariker's film is truly beguiling and very stirring.

Lagaan is a folktale writ large and paradoxically Westernised while still being about the constraints of colonialism. This is a film that dwells in an arch-world of archetypes – the snidely British captain (Paul Blackthorne) has a moustache fully available for the twiddling – and wound ever tighter by its allusions to Spaghetti Westerns and the meaty glories of Kurosawa. There are training montages, last-minute reprieves, downtrodden fools who will have their day and a come-uppance for the British swine so sweet you have to suppress a cheer. Yet, with its cultural origins still intact, the film remains bracingly foreign and magical, loudly commenting on the ailments of colonial tax (known as 'lagaan'), religion, class and cross-cultural romance (English rose Elizabeth Russell will fall for dashing hero Aamir Khan).

Awhirl with colour and magnificence – it is beautifully shot – and long but never stretched, this is a film that will contradict every prejudice you might have against that most elusive of worlds – Indian cinema. It isn't subtle, it doesn't want to be, but a better entryway into the alien complexities and designs of Bollywood, or, for that matter, the dizzying rules of cricket (it even stops to clearly explain the vagaries of spin bowling) you will not find. ★★★★★ **IN**

LAKE PLACID (1999)

Starring: *Bill Pullman (Jack Wells), Bridget Fonda (Kelly Scott), Oliver Platt (Hector Cyr), Brendan Gleeson (Sheriff Hank Keough), Betty White (Mrs. Delores Bickerman)*
Director: *Steve Miner*
Screenwriter: *David E. Kelley*
15/58 mins./Comedy/Horror/USA

A fussy, mosquito-phobic New York paleontologist is sent to investigate what looks like a dinosaur tooth found after a fatal attack on a diver at Black Lake. Joining forces with a smooth game warden and a grouchy sheriff, they go in search of the 'dinosaur'.

Humour was a key dramatic strength of *Jaws*, from the drunken fishermen on the jetty to the verbal sparring between Hooper and Quint. With this in mind, Hollywood's latest post-modern take on the old-fashioned monster movie is not so novel – nor is it as difficult to take seriously. *Lake Placid*, a modest summer hit in the States, is easily summarised as The Big Crocodile Movie, but a more informative shorthand might be Eating Ally McBeal, since TV script supremo David E. Kelley has taken the easy, knowing, urban wit of his hit show and transplanted it to the picturesque sticks of Maine.

The 'dinosaur' turns out to be a 30-foot crocodile that's swum all the way from Asia. This we know thanks to the expertise of eccentric mythology professor Hector Cyr, who is immediately at odds with Gleeson's hick. 'How do you know?', asks the sheriff. 'They conceal information like that in books,' comes Cyr's barbed reply. In another priceless exchange, Cyr finds a human toe and asks, 'Is this the man that was killed?' The sheriff examines it, poker-faced: 'He seemed taller.'

So, it's part ecologically-themed oversize-beast thriller, part culture-clash comedy. The reptile itself (combined model/CGI showmanship from *Jurassic Park*'s Stan Winston) is magnificent – its jaw-dropping full-screen reveal, after much *Jaws*-like underwater point-of-view build-up, involves the consumption of a grizzly bear! But it's the easy, underplayed performances and the slick dialogue that make this more than a rural cat-and-mouse (or croc-and-cow, since a heifer gets used as bait). But it's not a spoof, and that's crucial. You can enjoy *Placid* as a straightforward camping-holiday nightmare, or as a sly, ironic take on the same. It works deliciously as both. ★★★★ **AC**

LANCELOT DU LAC (LE GRAAL) (1974)

Starring: *Luc Simon (Lancelot), Laura Duke Condominas (Queen Guinevere), Humbert Balsan (Gawain), Vladimir Antolek-Oresek (King Arthur), Patrick Bernard (Modrick), Arthur De Montalambert (Lionel)*
Director: *Robert Bresson*
Screenwriter: *Robert Bresson*
PG/80 mins./History/Drama/France

In Camelot, Sir Lancelot, haunted by his failure to find the Holy Grail, is torn between religion, duty and lust. Queen Guinevere, a neurotic flirt who keeps trying to get around the vows Lancelot has made to God that he not become her lover. King Arthur, harried by in-fighting among his knights, is drawn slowly into a civil war which will destroy his country.

Of all cinema's undoubted geniuses, Robert Bresson may well be the least-known outside purely cineaste circles. His films display an aesthetic rigour which often focus on insoluble spiritual crises to such an extent that he makes Ingmar Bergman seem like Mel Brooks. Having established a reputation with films that use contemporary or near-contemporary settings, Bresson turned in 1974 to Europe's great romantic-spiritual myth and turned out an unexpectedly lavish Arthurian drama, albeit taking an approach vastly different from the conventional heroic epic.

Paying attention to religious impulses that are all but incomprehensible to the modern mind, Bresson conjures up a God-bothered Middle Ages that is harrowing but not, it must be said, terribly exciting. By an unfortunate coincidence which can't help but provoke giggles, Bresson's take on Arthuriana is surprisingly close to that of the contemporary *Monty Python and the Holy Grail*, as knights struggle inside clanking armour and gout Peckinpah-ish gore when wounded. Typical of Bresson is the way all the vital sword-fights are filmed with the camera fixed at knee-level so we only see the bloodied ground and the legs of the duelling knights.

It's short enough not to be tedious though its depiction of the past as an alien world makes it hard to get involved with. Perhaps more approachable than Bresson's truly great films, this makes a fine 'shallow end' introduction to one of the movies' great minds. ★★★ **KN**

LAND AND FREEDOM (1995)

Starring: *Ian Hart (David Carr), Rosana Pastor (Blanca), Iciar Bollain (Maite), Tom Gilroy (Lawrence), Marc Martinez (Juan Vidal), Frederic Pierrot (Bernard Goujon)*
Director: *Ken Loach*
Screenwriter: *Jim Allen*
15/109 mins./Drama/UK/Germany/Spain/Italy

In the midst of the Spanish Civil War, a young unemployed communist believer joins up to fight the fascists. Drifting between factions, surviving injury, David Carr comes to examine his own motivations and the war around him.

If anything, this is grit and grime specialist Ken Loach's most epic film. Now, this should be qualified: Loach's film still occupies a docu-credible stance in his depiction of the daily toil of the Spanish Civil War in 1936 and the dreams, failings and ultimate nobility of the lowly man, but in enjoining the crags of conflict and history, and on foreign soil to boot, he gains a relatively exotic note compared to the scouring pads of say *Ladybird Ladybird* or *Raining Stones*. There are even battle scenes of sorts, between more than two people, and with guns.

Loach is engaging with the way epochal events such as this impact upon ordinary people and vice versa. David Carr (played with typical conviction by the too often underrated Ian Hart) is a downtrodden idealist, who rather than mulch about, take up arms in a noble struggle. But, with Loach's candid camera, this is not a tale of heroics but just that, a struggle. The point being made is how this struggle would come to define a man considered to have lived a normal life; the story is told in flashback from a secret store of letters discovered by his family. With its willingness to pause for a political deliberation over coffee and cigarettes, the film has a slow, real-time feel as it drifts through the multi-national ranks of the fighting bands, with David finding love, with the staunch Blanca (Rosana Pastor), and much in the way of soul searching.

Hard-edged, of course, but more eloquent and poetic than usual, this is Loach gazing toward the horizon rather than glaring at the cold streets of the downcast. ★★★★ **IN**

THE LAND BEFORE TIME (1988)

Starring: *the voices of: Gabriel Damon (Littlefoot), Candace Hutson (Cera), Judith Barsi (Ducky), Will Ryan (Petrie), Pat Hingle (Narrator/Rooter), Helen Shaver (Littlefoot's Mother), Burke Byrnes (Daddy Topps), Bill Erwin (Grandfather)*
Director: *Don Bluth*
Screenwriter: *Stu Kreiger*
U/70 mins./Animation/Family/USA

Separated from their families, a troupe of baby dinosaurs set out on a perilous journey to get back together with their elders. Littlefoot, who has been orphaned, emerges as the leader of the group.

Littlefoot the Long-Neck (brontosaurus), Cera the Three-Horn (triceratops), Petrie the Flyer (pterodactyl) slog through a sanitised prehistory with no mention of flesh-eating dinosaurs, extinction-producing meteorites, ice ages or mammals. Luckily, there's a tyrannosaurus rex in the film, but he doesn't get enough screen time compared to the lead characters, who look like aborted muppet fetuses and speak with those American kiddie accents that make you wish they'd fossilise at once and spare us the homilies to ghastly American family virtues.

The Land Before Time is a Lucas-Spielberg production, directed by Don Bluth, who was setting out on a career-long quest to smooth away the edge that made his first film, *The Secret of NIMH*, interesting. The screenplay is non-stop squidgy pap like 'there are some things you see with your eyes, others you see with your heart', and there's a sneaky reactionary edge to its anthropomorphism whereby the nuclear family is seen as the only way to live even among giant saurians and interracial harmony can be expressed by a brontosaurus being allowed to play with a triceratops.

It lasts only just over an hour, especially if you walk out before the awful Diana Ross song over the end credits, but that's still not short enough.

It might prove entertaining only if, like its heroes, you have a brain the size of a walnut. It has so far yielded ten sequels, from *The Great Valley Adventure* to *Invasion of the Tinysauruses*, several tapes of *Land Before Time* 'Singalong Songs' and a TV series – not to mention inspiring everything from *Barney the Dinosaur* to the CGI epic *Dinosaur*. ★ **KN**

LAND OF THE DEAD (2005)

Starring: *Simon Baker (Riley), John Leguizamo (Cholo), Dennis Hopper (Kaufman), Asia Argento (Slack), Robert Joy (Charlie)*
Director: *George A. Romero*
Screenwriter: *George A. Romero*
15/93 mins./97 mins (director's cut)/Action/Horror/Canada/France/USA

Fourth instalment of Romero's zombie series. Society has managed to regroup from the zombification of the Earth somewhat, and part of the population are now living in a small sealed-off city section of what used to be Detroit. Riley is a man who goes into the outside world and gets supplies for people to live on. One day he and his team notice a zombie who has become primatively self-aware.

In 2004, with the remake of *Dawn Of The Dead* and the parody *Shaun Of The Dead* in theatres, Empire ran a memo to Hollywood suggesting some of the profits should be used to finance an original from the still-active though ridiculously underemployed writer-director George A. Romero. After all, Romero did essentially invent the modern horror film with *Night Of The Living Dead* in 1968 and followed up with the equally challenging *Dawn Of The Dead* and *Day Of The Dead*. Either someone up there reads us or so obvious an idea could not be resisted: Universal greenlit a 'fourth part of the trilogy', raising Romero's fans' hopes and expectations so high that by comparison *The Phantom Menace* might as well have been *Air Bud 2*.

Of course, some things have changed: after the extreme splatter of Peter Jackson's *Braindead*, the radical DV stylings of *28 Days Later* ..., game-derived tosh like *Resident Evil* and more direct-to-video zombie dodos than the mind can stand, does anyone, even Romero, have anything fresh to say about the living dead? *Land* certainly has an old-fashioned feel, but still represents a make-over for Pittsburgh's independent son, who this time heads up to Canada for oppressive locations (including impressive zombie-plagued city streets), while contractually obliged to secure a US R-rating that theoretically curbs the necessary excesses of the unrated *Dawn* and *Day*.

Rest assured, liver-lovers, there's plenty of grue here. A scene involving a belly-piercing is sure to evoke winces, though not on a par with, say, the helicopter skull-slicing of *Dawn*. Plus, like the earlier films, this dissects present-day America in cartoonish but vivid terms through angry confrontations between the Man (ironically played by Dennis Hopper) and a range of rebels, from whitebread hero Simon Baker through tattooed wild child Asia Argento and ambitious wannabe John Leguizamo, to the latest of Romero's capable African-American heroes (Eugene Clark), here the nearly-smart leader of a shuffling, implacable zombie army. It's good to see Romero can still match blood and guts with heart and brains. ★★★★ **KN**

LANTANA (2001)

Starring: *Anthony LaPaglia (Det. Leon Zat), Rachael Blake (Jane 'Janie' O'May), Kerry Armstrong (Sonja Zat), Jon Bennett (Steve Valdez), Melissa Martinez (Lisa)*
Director: *Ray Lawrence*
Screenwriter: *Andrew Bovell, from his play*
15/111 mins./Thriller/Australia/Germany

Australian police detective Leon Zat investigates the disappearance of a woman, while trying to sort out his tangled love life. Meanwhile, his wife confides in a psychiatrist, who is herself convinced that her own husband may be having an affair.

Like Robert Altman's best movies, this drama/thriller is an aching examination of modern relationships concerning a handful of people who seem to have no connection at the beginning of the film, but whose lives and relationships somehow ultimately connect.

What brings them together is the catalystic disappearance of a woman, as investigated by cop Leon Zat. Unusually for a central character, Leon isn't very likeable and he's bang in the middle of a mid-life crisis that has caused him to cheat on his wife and become unnecessarily violent towards anyone who crosses his path (including an unfortunate jogger he smashes into).

LaPaglia (an Australian, although we are used to seeing him playing Italian-Americans in movies like *Summer Of Sam*, or Daphne's drunken English brother in *Frasier*) is superb as Zat. He's supported by an impressive cast, but it's his raw, uncompromising performance that makes this a terrific, must-see one-off. ★★★★ **JB**

LARA CROFT: TOMB RAIDER (2001)

Starring: *Angelina Jolie (Lara Croft), Jon Voigt (Lord Richard Croft), Iain Glen (Manfred Powell), Noah Taylor (Bryce), Daniel Craig (Alex West), Chris Barrie (Hillary)*
Director: *Simon West*
Screenwriters: *Patrick Massett, John Zinman, based on a story by Sara B. Cooper, Mike Werb, Michael Colleary, adapted by Simon West*
12/100 mins./Action/Adventure/USA/Germany/UK/Japan

Intrepid archaeologist Lara Croft discovers a mythical clock, bequeathed to her by her father, which, when reunited with the broken and scattered pieces of a magical artefact, has the power to control time. Croft ventures to Cambodia with guns blazing.

Jolie was born to play Croft, as surely as Bob Hoskins' destiny was pixel-lated plumber Mario Mario. And Jolie doesn't just look the part – although months of training have given her a whipcord physique and she sports perhaps the most strikingly engineered bosom since Jane Russell – she acquits herself well in the furious fight scenes and frantic action set-pieces.

Unfortunately, kick-ass brawling skills and hooters like a dead heat in a Zeppelin race do not a good movie make. Even when the MacGuffin is discovered, it takes a while to get into gear. And with a leather-clad Jolie roaring around London on a motorbike, stopping off at vividly imagined auction rooms and raffishly bedecked law offices, the impression is that we're in for *The Avengers* all over again. It's not that bad, of course.

Back at the ranch, Lara is surprised by a cadre of baddies. What follows – a blazing gun battle with the protagonists pinging around the vast chamber – is as good a piece of action cinema as you'll see this summer. But the film plateaus out and the eye candy soon becomes predictable.

Exotic locations – Cambodia, Venice, Iceland – are present and correct, and there's a half-hearted stab at romance between Jolie and Daniel Craig's rival adventurer, who may be a bad guy (and, then again, may not), and who may have a history with Lara (and, then again, may not).

Conspicuous by its absence is a narrative spark bright enough to engross you. Neither, save Lara, is there anyone to give a damn about. It's glaringly obvious from the outset that insipid villain Glen is no match for Lara, and this skews the adversarial dynamic and renders the traditional cheering and booing – surely a staple of the genre – rather redundant. ★★ **SB**

LARA CROFT: TOMB RAIDER THE CRADLE OF LIFE (2003)

Starring: *Angelina Jolie (Lara Croft), Gerard Butler (Terry Sheridan), Ciaran Hinds (Jonathan Reiss), Chris Barrie (Hillary), Noah Taylor (Bryce), Djimon Hounsou (Kosa)*
Director: *Jan de Bont*
Screenwriter: *Dean Georgaris, based on a story by Steven E. de Souza, James V. Hart*
12/112 mins./Action/Adventure/USA/UK/Germany/Japan

A mystic globe found in an Alexandrine temple contains instructions to the hiding place of Pandora's Box, which bio-weapons dealer Reiss wants to let loose on the world. World-travelling archaeologist and adventuress Lara Croft is on hand to save the day.

As you might expect of a film with three titles run together – let's just call it *Tomb Raider 2*, shall we? – this sequel suffers from fatally fuzzy thinking. Everything wrong with the first film is still not fixed, though replacing Simon West with Jan De Bont means slightly better-paced action sequences – one freefall dive from a Hong Kong skyscraper is worthy of 007, if only Roger Moore.

Angelina Jolie perfects her English posh bird accent, and she looks spectacular in a grey wetsuit. Otherwise, Lara Croft remains a pixel-thin hybrid of James Bond, Indiana Jones and Modesty Blaise, whose only character trait is a petulant snottiness that sits ill with last-reel idealism. Her entrance involves jet-skiing past a boat and splashing understandably resentful employees, who get killed a few minutes later and are promptly forgotten.

In the games, the joystick jockey is supposed to be tempted to guide Lara to an undignified come-uppance as often as he gets her through perils – but a smug heroine you half-want to see splattered over the landscape isn't a workable movie notion. She's also notably useless as an archaeologist: never turning up at a site without breaking dozens of irreplaceable artefacts in ill-defined grudge-fights.

The plot repeats the original's mistake: we hop around the globe (Greece, China, Hong Kong, Africa) in search of a mystic trinket that can destroy the world, but, in defiance of traditional scriptwriting rules, it's the villain (glowering Ciaran Hinds) who's on a quest. The climactic struggle – which includes a reversal that ought to be devastating but falls flat – is a limp tussle in CGI-monster-plagued caves. ★★ **KN**

LASSIE COME HOME (1943)

Starring: *Roddy McDowall (Joe Carraclough), Elizabeth Taylor (Priscilla), Donald Crisp (Sam Carraclough), Dame May Whitty (Dally Fadden), Nigel Bruce (Duke of Rudding), Elsa Lanchester (Mrs. Helen Carraclough)*
Director: *Fred M. Wilcox*
Screenwriter: *Hugh Butler, based on the novel by Eric Knight*
U/89 mins./Family/Adventure/USA

When Joe's family fall on hard times his dog, Lassie, a beautiful Collie, is sold to a Duke who takes Lassie to live hundreds of miles away. But the dog decides to make the long journey back to Joe . . .

The first of the Lassie films, inspired by Eric Knight's newspaper short story that later became a novel, was something of a phenomenon. A low-budget film, packed with character actors, it was only expected to do modest business at the box office. Instead it made stars of its juvenile leads, Taylor and McDowall (who also formed a life-long friendship) and the dog itself earned a star on Hollywood's walk of fame, becoming a major celebrity.

Now it's easy to see how this winning formula of a boy's love for his dog – equally reciprocated by the canine – struck a cord with wartime audiences across the globe. And although in later incarnations – several film sequels and television series – the dog's ability to communicate the most complex information became laughable – here the situation is much simpler and more believable. The dog simply tracks his way home, having various colourful adventures along the way, while the moppets fret photogenically for his safe return.

Every Lassie, except that of the most recent 2005 film, is descended from the star here – a one-year-old male collie called Pal, bought for $10 by dog trainer Rudd Weatherwax and put out to stud following the film so his line would be assured. Just as well since, following the film's release, the demand for collies quadrupled overnight. At least their fur would be thick enough to drown the inevitable tears that well up on repeat viewings of the final scenes, as once more the faithful dog limps forward to greet his master at school. ★★ **EC**

THE LAST ACTION HERO (1993)

Starring: *Arnold Schwarzenegger (Jack Slater/himself), F. Murray Abraham (John Practice), Austin O'Brien (Danny Madigan), Art Carney (Nick), Charles Dance (Benedict)*
Director: *John McTiernan*
Screenwriters: *Shane Black, David Arnott, based on a story by Zak Penn, Adam Leff*
15/125 mins./Action/Adventure/Comedy/USA

Agog poppet Danny is zapped into his hero Jack Slater's latest blastathon thanks to a golden ticket.

Snakeskin boots clomp down upon the sidewalk. The hero unclamps the stogy from his mouth and snarls 'You want to be a farmer? Here's a couple of acres!' before kicking an adversary in the balls.

Yes, Big Arnold, the Macho Man, is back . . . Except he's not, for what we are seeing here is a movie within a movie. Arnold is 'Jack Slater', star of firepower-fuelled action flicks, and an 11-year-old boy, Danny, is watching his idol (in 'Jack Slater IV') on the screen. Now, Danny has a magic cinema ticket and this whisks him off into film-land and the backseat of Jack's car right in the middle of a noisy chase sequence.

Such is the conceit of *Last Action Hero*: 'real' character joins 'fictional' character up on screen, 'fictional' character joins 'real' character in 'real' world. And just look at the difference. On film, 'Jack Slater' can punch through glass and plummet from tall buildings and do himself no injury; in the 'real' world, he discovers, these things hurt. In the 'real' world, the 'bad guys' sometimes win. Yes, sad to say, this is a film striving for a 'moral' of a 'hey-kids-don't-try-this-action-stuff-at-home/hey-kids-don't-take-this-action-stuff-too-seriously' nature.

Be careful out there, soft Arnold is cooing. There again, *Last Action Hero* is a film that wants to have its candy and eat it, too: for while it sends up action movies, its many lavish blowing-up scenes and its display of 'splendid' weaponry are as glossy and numbing as anything you're likely to get in a genuine 'actioner'. Having said all that, there are some not unamusing moments here. Like when Jack Slater's life is saved by a cartoon cat called Whiskers who works at the same fictional police precinct.

Or like when Danny, having to watch Olivier's *Hamlet* in English class, daydreams that it's 'Jack Slater' who is the Prince – 'Claudius. You killed my father. Big mistake. To be or not to be? Not to be' (Cue enormous explosion of Elsinore). Or like when Danny, attempting to convince 'Jack' that he's living in a movie, takes him into a video shop only to come across a display for *Terminator 2* starring Sylvester Stallone.

The 'plot'? Oh, a load of hokum about Charles Dance (obligatory English psychopath bad person) who's trying to kill everybody. That doesn't matter: the joke's the thing. And there's many a cameo personage on hand – Sharon Stone in that dress, Tina Turner, Little Richard, Arnie's real-life wife Maria Shriver (who almost steals the film by telling the 'real' Arnie how ridiculous he is) – to show that they think it's all quite funny, too. 'How would you feel if you just found out someone had made you up?' says 'Slater' in bewilderment. Oh, Arnold, you are a card. ★★★ **TH**

THE LAST BOY SCOUT (1991)

Starring: *Bruce Willis (Joe Hallenbeck), Damon Wayne (Damon Dix), Chelsea Field (Sarah Hallenbeck), Halle Berry (Cory)*
Director: *Tony Scott*
Screenwriter: *Shane Black, from a story by Black and Greg Hicks*
18/105 mins./Action/Thriller/USA

Ex-secret agent-turned-private eye Joe Hallenbeck, takes a case protecting an exotic dancer named Cory. But when she is murdered, he teams up with Cory's boyfriend, ex-football player Jimmy Dix, to investigate her death.

Take the following ingredients: a million-dollar script from *Lethal Weapon* screenwriter Shane Black, the wisecracking talents of Bruce Willis, a plot that takes second place to the action, and enough bullets-through-heads, punch-ups and exploding cars to fill three movies, and what you end up with is a concoction by the name of *The Last Boy Scout*, which proved a surprise hit, especially considering the performance of both Willis' (*Hudson Hawk*) and director Tony Scott's (*Days Of Thunder, Revenge*) previous outings.

What little plot there is centres around ex-secret agent-turned-private eye Joe Hallenbeck, who takes a case protecting an exotic dancer named Cory, only to see her shot to pieces in a gangland-style hit. Saddled with Cory's boyfriend, ex-football player Jimmy Dix, as a sidekick, the two begin to investigate her death, leading them to discover corruption in the world of football and politics.

It's very similar to Shane Black's previous scripts, but the action and the fast and funny one-liners almost make the film a five-star, must-see movie in the vein of *Lethal Weapon* and *Die Hard*. Wayans and especially Willis expertly deliver the lines even in the most unpromising situations – even when he discovers his best friend has been ruffling the sheets with his wife, he manages a comeback with 'So, Mike, you just slipped on the floor and accidentally put your dick in my wife?'.

The women don't come off as well, with Dix showing little remorse for his late girlfriend, Hallenbeck's daughter portrayed as a foul-mouthed teenager, and the only other female cast members being strippers, but this is a movie for the boys who like watching men being real men – cursing, shooting and fighting – and anyone who likes this kind of wham-bam entertainment will certainly get more than their money's worth. ★★★★ **JB**

THE LAST DAYS OF DISCO (1998)

Starring: *Chloe Sevigny (Alice Kinnon), Kate Beckinsale (Charlotte Pingress), Chris Eigeman (Des McGrath), Mackenzie Astin (Jimmy Steinway)*
Director: *Whit Stillman*
Screenwriter: *Whit Stillman*
15/108 mins./Comedy/Drama/USA

Charlotte and Alice shrug off their drab, daytime incarnations of office juniors to become night-time disco divas – immersed in the life of the hippest nightclubs in town.

It's the very early 80s, and the disco era is struggling to survive, but that doesn't deter the world-beatingly bitchy Charlotte and her put-upon, socially inept best pal Alice from their nocturnal activities. Underpaid juniors in a New York publishing office by day, at night they are transformed into sequined disco dollies, hanging out under the glitterball with the assortment of old college chums, upwardly mobile types and scuzzballs who populate their favourite club.

Those familiar with Stillman will recognise his leisurely, cerebral brand of filmmaking, his strong characterisation and sparky screen chatter coming across as effectively as in his previous two outings. In fact, there's a pervading sense of déjà vu here, as Beckinsale, Sevigny and their eclectic, intellectual dancefloor companions – bisexual bouncer, 'dancing ad man' Jimmy, cartoon-fixated lawyer Tom, upstanding D.A. Josh, and unlikely love interest Dan – grapple with romance, flat-sharing, pregnancy, venereal disease and frugging to a selection of toe-tapping beats over the course of two hugely entertaining hours.

Despite its occasionally complicated plot and over-intrusive support cast (with this many characters vying for attention, proceedings become a bit cluttered at times), *Disco* works best as a compendium of delightful, beautifully acted set-pieces – Alice's attempt to come to terms with her virginity loss is touchingly comic, while a brilliantly funny group dissection of the canine values displayed by *Lady And The Tramp* ranks among the most inspired moments.

By choosing well-rounded, likeable characters (even the mean-spirited Charlotte, played by Beckinsale with an impeccable transatlantic twang), an excellent script and lesser-known sounds of disco (not an Abba tune in sight), Stillman has created an affectionate, original and highly memorable tribute to a bygone age. ★★★★ **CW**

THE LAST EMPEROR (1987)

Starring: *John Lone (Pu Yi, adult), Joan Chen (Wan Jung), Peter O'Toole (Reginald Johnston), Ryocheng Ying (The Govenor), Victor Wong (Chen Pao Shen)*
Director: *Bernardo Bertolucci*
Screenwriters: *Mark Peploe, Bernardo Bertolucci, from the autobiography* From Emperor to Citizen: The Autobiography of Asisin-Gioro Pu Yi *by Henry Pu-yi*
15/209 mins./Drama/Biography/Italy/China/UK
Awards: *Academy Awards – Best Art Direction/Set Decoration, Best Cinematography, Best Costume, Best Director, Best Editing, Best Original Score, Best Picture. Best Sound, Best Adapted Screenplay, BAFTA – Best Costume, Best Film, Best Make-up, Golden Globes – Best Director, Best Drama, Best Original Score, Best Screenplay*

Three years after Pu Yi is crowned Emperor, China is declared a republic but within the Forbidden City life remains the same until a new tutor from England arrives . . .

In 1908, three-year-old Pu Yi is crowned Emperor of China. Three years later, China is declared a republic but within the walls of the Forbidden City life sticks to its traditional routine until the arrival of a sympathetic and inspiring new tutor from England brings knowledge from the outside world, opening the boy's mind to the possibilities of change. His first attempts are met with disaster and he is forced to leave his home and begin a journey of decadence and decline, encountering sycophancy, betrayal, imprisonment and, briefly, inner peace.

As the disenchanted (adult) emperor who believes in his God-given right to rule, Lone exudes arrogance and vulnerability as he is manipulated by the politicians, then forced to confront his own responsibilities and shortfalls. Chen's Empress is more tragic; initially charming and supportive, she declines into opium addiction as she loses faith and influence when her husband gets involved with the Japanese.

Bertolucci was given unprecedented access to the Forbidden City and other parts of China, successfully capturing the beauty of palaces which are at once claustrophobic and isolating. The small screen doesn't quite do justice to the rich visuals but with an incredible story and fine performances, it is still a compulsive and moving epic. ★★★★ **GM**

LAST EXIT TO BROOKLYN (1989)

Starring: *Stephen Lang (Harry Black), Jennifer Jason Leigh (Tralala), Burt Young (Big Joe), Peter Dobson (Vinnie), Stephen Badwin (Sal)*
Director: *Uli Edel*
Screenwriter: *Desmond Nakano, based on the book by Hubert Selby Jr.*
18/98 mins./Drama/Crime/West Germany/USA/UK

A gallery of Brooklyn's finest and filthiest undergo change (a hooker falls in love with her clients, a union boss discovers he's gay) against an imposing backdrop of union corruption, violence and neon lighting.

Over a quarter of a century after it became the subject of a celebrated court case centring on the meaning of the term 'a tendency to deprave and corrupt', Hubert Selby Jnr.'s American classic reaches the screen imbued, despite its all-American cast and locations, with a profoundly European sensibility. Producer Bernd Eichinger (*The Name Of The Rose*, *The Never-Ending Story*) first worked with Edel on *Christiane F*, a tale of heroin addiction and youthful despair set in Berlin and best known for its David Bowie score and inordinate length. Scarcely surprisingly, their interpretation of Selby's vernacular sleaze presents the low-life of 1952 Brooklyn as an exercise in stylised American-retro costume and mannerism. It looks like the first X-rated Levi's commercial; all quiffs, jeans, Big Suits and reverent recreations of the kind of Edward Hopper neon-diner grunge the commercial-makers dote on.

Collapsing Selby's half-dozen vignettes into a single sustained narrative, *Last Exit* becomes an ensemble piece with uniformly powerful performances: Jennifer Jason Leigh heists the entire movie as Tralala, the neighbourhood tramp, though Stephen Long's corrupt closet-case union boss and Alexis Arquette's tormented drag queen run her close. Ricki Lake – the delightful star of John Waters' *Hairspray* – has a nice cameo which requires her to do little except cry, smile and be pregnant. The script uses great wodges of Selby's original dialogue but his narrative style can't be reproduced cinematically, which reduces chunks of the movie to post-Scorsese scenes of Italian-Americans in their underwear yelling at each other, which is no longer a novelty.

So, *Last Exit To Brooklyn* again proves that great novels do not necessarily make great movies. (Paradoxically, mediocre novels fare better, probably because there is less to compete with. What price Coppola's *Godfather* against Puzo's or De Palma's *Carrie* against King's?)

Impressively staged, powerfully performed and exquisitely designed, *Last Exit To Brooklyn* attempts to compensate with sheer style what it lacks in content. It comes closer to succeeding than one might have feared; in an era dominated by schlock – and cowardly schlock at that – this is no mean feat. ★★★ **CSM**

THE LAST HOUSE ON THE LEFT (KRUG AND COMPANY) (1972)

Starring: *David Hess (Krug), Kucy Grantham (Phyllis),Sandra Cassel (Mari Collingwood), Marc Sheffler (Junior), Jeramie Rain (Sadie), Fred Lincoln (Weasel)*
Director: *Wes Craven*
Screenwriter: *Wes Craven*
18/91 mins/Horror/USA

Two teenagers (Sandra Cassel, Lucy Grantham) are abducted, abused and killed by a quartet of psychopaths led by the sadistic Krug Stillo (David Hess). One girl survives long enough to tell her respectable parents, who set out to get revenge on the lowlifes.

Rough, crude and horribly convincing, this micro-budgeted, cine-vérité-look, hard-to-watch exploitation picture is a contemporary-set remake of Ingmar Bergman's *The Virgin Spring*. It founded the horror careers of director Wes Craven (*The Hills Have Eyes*) and producer Sean Cunningham (*Friday the 13th*), but neither would do anything quite as grittily upsetting as this ever again. A subplot about bumbling deputies who don't turn up at the main plot in time to do anything but look appalled is a waste of footage which also seriously damages the escalating mood, but otherwise *Last House* is a remarkably-assured debut feature. The unbelievably depraved villains are broadly-played, but the initially grotesque comic effect turns horribly serious as atrocities escalate. The daily grind of Krug (hulking David Hess) and his sidekicks (weaselly Fred Lincoln, psycho-bitch Jeramie Rain and gutless junkie Marc Sheffler) stretches to every crime imaginable from bursting a child's balloon through dangerous driving, cheating on a drug deal and gang-rape to murder by disembowelling. However, the point comes in the final act, where a victim's parents even the score by slaughtering the villains in equally dreadful ways, including the cinema's first chainsaw massacre. Later imitations, like the odious *I Spit On Your Grave*, dwell on the upsetting rape/torture to allow an audience to get off on a *Death Wish*-style vengeance spree, but Craven (like Sam Peckinpah in *Straw Dogs*) shows there's something disturbing about the willingness of normal folks to wreak a violent revenge that does as much damage to their own ideal home and their minds as it does to the guilty parties. ★★★★ **KN**

LAST MAN STANDING (1996)

Starring: *Bruce Willis (John Smith), Bruce Dern (Sheriff Ed Galt), William Sanderson (Joe Monday), Christopher Walken (Hickey), David Patrick Kelly (Doyle)*
Director: *Walter Hill*
Screenwriter: *Walter Hill, based on a story by Ryuzo Kikushima, Akira Kurosawa*
18/96 mins./Western/USA

Drifter John Smith arrives in Jericho, a town dominated by the uneasy truce between a low-grade Mafioso outfit and a local Irish group. With both gangs embroiled in the lucrative bootleg trade Smith seizes the chance to exploit the situation.

Long the acknowledged master of style over content, Walter Hill returned to something akin to form with this ear-shattering bootleg drama adapted, with typical looseness, from Akira Kurosawa's *Yojimbo* (inspiration for Sergio Leone's *A Fistful Of Dollars*).

The story, such as it is, has an almost catatonically laid-back Willis wafting into Jericho, and acting as an amoral catalyst – within five minutes of arriving he's blasted one gang's lead henchman into the hereafter in the first of a relentless bloody cavalcade of claret-drenched shoot-outs.

Recruited first by one gang, and then defecting to the other, he creams both for all available cash while avoiding the stylishly psychotic attentions of Hickey (Christopher Walken, yet again lurching just too close to caricature for comfort). Finally, the law turns up and declares that if, when it returns, there is more than one gang running the show, by the time it's finished, there'll be none.

Hill turns in a typically polished actioner which boasts a couple of inventive visual twists – crashing the gangster and Western genres into each other to generate pleasingly weird moments such as tumbleweed rolling through a set-up for a gangster shoot-out. But plot is shovelled in whenever he's run out of squibs via the last resort of the desperate screenwriter – a moody voice-over from Willis.

There's also a shrieking two dimensionality to almost all the supporting performances with the exception of William Sanderson as bar-owner Joe who has, in the final sequence, the best line of the movie. ★★★ **AS**

THE LAST METRO (LE DERNIER METRO) (1980)

Starring: *Catherine Deneuve (Marion Steiner), Gérard Depardieu (Bernard Granger), Jean Poiret (Jean Louis Cottins), Heinz Bennent (Lucas Steiner), Andrea Ferreol (Arlette Guillaume)*
Director: *François Truffaut*
Screenwriter: *François Truffaut, Suzanne Schiffman, Jean-Claude Grunberg, based on the story Truffaut, Schiffmann*
PG/133 mins./Drama/France

With her Jewish husband, Lucas, hiding in the basement of his Parisian theatre, Marion Steiner hires Bernard Granger to head a misfit cast in her bid to mount a new production that will keep the venue afloat during the Nazi Occupation.

Budgetary constraint had mitigated against a wartime setting for François Truffaut's childhood memoir, *Les Quatre Cent Coups* and he had subsequently felt disinclined to make an Occupation drama following the release of Marcel Ophüls's documentary, *The Sorrow and the Pity*. So, he embarked on this tale of a Parisian theatre troupe in the wake of Louis Malle's *Lacombe, Lucien*, Costa-Gavras's *Section Spéciale* and Joseph Losey's *Mr Klein* and intended it to form the central segment of a 'performance' trilogy comprising *Day for Night* and *L'Agence Magic*, which was left unrealised on his death in 1980.

In fact, this was much more of a backstage than a war story. Marion and Lucas's plight is clearly prompted by the defeat of 1940, as is Bernard's association with the Maquis and Nadine (Sabine Haudepin)'s fraternising with German soldiers to further her career. But anti-semitism, censorship, black marketeering and collaboration are reduced to period givens that matter as little as ideology or communality in a world centred on individualism. Many critics attacked Truffaut for painting such a naively nostalgic portrait of this shameful time, but he conceded that he relied more on recollection than research and this personal juvenility coloured the film's tone.

Consequently, Truffaut rooted the action in his amateur enthusiasm for the stage – although many of the incidents were inspired by the experiences of such film folk as designer Alexandre Trauner, composer Joseph Kosma and actors Louis Jourdan and Jean-Pierre Aumont. Daxiat (Jean-Louis Richard), the fascistic critic, was based on Alain Laubreaux, whom Jean Marais had once punched for mocking a Cocteau play, although there's an element of Cahiers autobiography in his bitter rejection by the very artists whose approval he craves.

Designed as a showcase for Catherine Deneuve, *The Last Metro* swept the Césars and some suggested that its popular success lay in its rehabilitation of a contentious era without opening too many wounds. However, its secret derived more from Truffaut's adherence to Jean Renoir's humanist credo, that no matter what their actions, everyone has their reasons. **★★★★ DP**

THE LAST OF SHEILA (1973)

Starring: *Richard Benjamin (Tom), Dyan Cannon (Christine), James Coburn (Clinton Green), Joan Hackett (Lee), James Mason (Philip), Ian McShane (Anthony), Raquel Welch (Alice), Yvonne Romain (Sheila Green)*
Director: *Herbert Ross*
Screenwriters: *Anthony Perkins, Stephen Sondheim*
PG/120 mins./Crime/Mystery/Thriller/USA

Millionaire Clinton Green invites six friends to a party on his luxury yacht, named after his late wife Sheila. Green arranges a complicated murder mystery game that is also designed to reveal his guests' nastiest secrets – but when he is murdered, the guests have to become real sleuths.

Here's a terrific script – written by talented amateurs, as it happens – turned into an okay movie by merely professional direction from Herbert Ross. The actor Anthony Perkins and lyricist Stephen Sondheim loved murder mysteries, bitchy showbiz/high society gossip and elaborate party games – so they concocted this ingeniously intricate murder mystery set on a millionaire's yacht, with an array of amusingly nasty suspects squirming during a complicated guessing game that gets sidetracked by the host's murder.

The party includes washed-up screenwriter/toady Richard Benjamin, his brittle wife Joan Hackett (the only one with honest feelings), trash-mouthed agent Dyan Cannon ('Get me a glass of water and a couple of lesbians'), suavely perverse director James Mason, hirsute gigolo Ian McShane and dynamite dim-bulb starlet Raquel Welch. Along with an outrageous Coburn, who does one scene in drag, the entire cast enjoy themselves as thoroughly nasty, but entertaining people, and clawing verbally at each other as a genuinely ingenious, Agatha Christie-level set of clues (hint: 'the last of Sheila' is 'A') shuffle together to provide a satisfying puzzle.

Perkins said later that he wanted it to be as bizarre and incomprehensible as *Lady From Shanghai*, but Ross worked too hard at making the story clear to the rubes. It remains an underrated pleasure, a rare original film mystery (most whodunits are adapted from novels – which means your target audience already knows the solution) with dialogue as precisely turned as one of Norman Bates's twitches or Sweeney Todd's razor-rhymes. **★★★★ KN**

LAST OF THE MOHICANS (1992)

Starring: *Daniel Day-Lewis (Hawkeye), Madeleine Stowe (Cora Munro), Russell Means (Chingachgook), Eric Schweig (Uncas), Jodhi May (Alice Munro), Steven Waddington (Maj. Duncan Heyward), Wes Studi (Magua)*
Director: *Michael Mann*
Screenwriters: *Michael Mann, Christopher Crowe, adapted by John L.Balderston, Paul Perez, Daniel Moore, from the 1936 screenplay by Philip Dunne and the novel by James Fenimore Cooper*
15/107 mins/Action/Romance/War/USA

Awards: *Academy Awards – Best Sound, BAFTA – Best Cinematography, Best Make Up*

In 18th century North America during the French and Indian War, a white man adopted by the last members of a dying tribe called the Mohicans unwittingly becomes the protector of the two daughters of a British colonel, who have been targeted by Magua, a sadistic and vengeful Huron warrior who has dedicated his life to destroying the girls' father for a past injustice.

Michael Mann's earliest movie memory is of seeing Randolph Scott in *The Last Of The Mohicans* made in 1936. Its whole-hearted sense of pioneering Americana really tickled Mann Jr. Indeed, so much so that he returned to the oft-told story (12 times and counting), determined to breathe new life into the old dog. With a script (written by both Mann and Christopher Crowe) based in part on Philip Dunne's 1936 screenplay as well as the stodgy old tome by James Fenimore Cooper, *The Last Of The Mohicans* is a stirring, wonderful film encompassing an old-time splendour in storytelling boasting grand principles of heroism and character and loads of thunderous action.

Hawkeye, a settler adopted into the Mohawk tribe as an orphaned child, is a hunter-warrior ecophile, educated and refined with British sensibilities (hence he speaks perfect English) but harbouring a purist sense of the wild. Characterised by his extraordinary 18th century muzzle-loading rifle and unerring aim, he is wise enough to see through the transparent treachery of the British, yet is irresistibly drawn to the refined eloquence of Cora Munro, the daughter of a Scottish general who falls under his protection. As much as this is a story about colonial warfare and hand-to-hand combat with rapacious Indians over a rugged wilderness, there is a stirring love affair at its centre which through all its fierce romanticism never comes across as anything but authentic. There is nothing silly or sentimental about the attraction both Cora finds in the striking Hawkeye, and he in the beautiful, self-reliant heroine.

Reclusive and pathologically self-contained, Day-Lewis was never going to be an easy catch for a good old-fashioned yarn featuring much in the way of running around North Carolinan forests in moccasins, a raven mane flowing fetchingly in the summer wind. But catch him Mann did. Perhaps Day-Lewis recognised in the obsessive director (a Zen adept), a soul akin to his own – the commitment is absolute or not at all. And in a kind of double-top Method fest both director and star camped out in the Alabama wilderness, cutting firewood with authentic tomahawks, learning to survive native-style while sleeping under the stars. Day-Lewis, under the calming eye of Mann, literally transformed into Hawkeye.

'Daniel would carry his gun around all the time,' claimed Stowe, somewhat bemused by the boys' antics. 'When he went to lunch he'd have that gun with him, when he went to the bathroom he'd have that gun with him. He's sort of not of this world, Daniel.'

That is not to say that this is Hawkeye's show alone. Stowe does her finest work to date as the strong-willed, impulsive and entirely alluring Cora – making a mockery of the claim Mann cannot handle strong female roles. And for every hero you need a villain. Magua, a Huron, is a mesmerising, scowl-faced nightmare, motivated by a thirst for vengeance against the Munro family. Wes Studi fills him with bitter pride and grim resolve.

Casting Russell Means as Mohican Chingachook carries with it a real credibility. Means is a renowned Native American activist for the American Indian Movement: he famously occupied both Mount Rushmore and Wounded Knee in the early 70s and castigated both *Dances With Wolves* (1990) and *Thunderheart* (1992) for their fatuous depiction of the Native American plight. His acceptance of the role adds a knowing endorsement to Mann's delivery of tribal conflict in the burgeoning Americas.

It is this attention to detail that sets *The Last Of The Mohicans* apart. Each and every native was meticulously decked out in historically accurate make-up; the guns, the costumes, the language and the entire life-pattern of the leading man were the genuine article. Most spectacular is Fort William Henry, a monolithic wooden edifice, battered, bruised and finally smashed under a French siege, that was built from scratch to original specifications. The ensuing battle a graphic essay on the 18th century blitzkrieg.

Shot with an eye-boggling beauty by Dante Spinotti (after Doug Milsome was 'let go'), the film substitutes North Carolina's Burke County in the Blue Ridge mountains for the Northern New York State of Fenimore-Cooper's books. America seems primal under his lens, an untamed wilderness into which modernity is forcing its own strain of corruption. Hawkeye straddles both zones: he is a man inducted into the native fellowship with the earth but a champion of the pioneers (his true kin). Mann also incorporates a subtext that looks toward impending rebellion – the British are an oppressive, legalistic force; the idealistic farmers are seen making signals for independence and self-rule. ★ **IN**

THE LAST PICTURE SHOW (1971)

Starring: *Timothy Bottoms (Sonny Crawford), Jeff Bridges (Duane Jackson), Cybill Shepherd (Jacy Farrow), Ben Johnson (Sam the Lion), Cloris Leachman (Ruth Popper), Ellen Burstyn (Lois Farrow), Sam Bottoms (Billy)*
Director: *Peter Bogdanovich*
Screenwriter: *Peter Bogdanovich, Larry McMurtry based on the novel by McMurtry*
15/118 mins./Drama/USA

Awards: *Academy Awards – Best Supporting Actor (Ben Johnson), Best Supporting Actress (Cloris Leachman), BAFTA – Best Screenplay, Best Supporting Actor (Ben Johnson), Best Supporting Actress (Cloris Leachman), Golden Globes – Best Supporting Actor*

In the early 1950s teenagers in the dried-up Texas town of Anarene lament the closing of the local movie house after the passing of local hero, Sam.

Based on the novel by Larry McMurtry this is a more-bitter-than-bittersweet drama of growing up and winding down. Shot unusually in black and white while the rest of Hollywood was going psychedelic for 1971, it's an interesting contrast with the rock 'n' roll nostalgia of *American Graffiti*, visiting a recent past already nostalgic for a heroic Western era and discovering that whatever was wonderful was already gone by the time of these teenagers.

Introspective Timothy Bottoms and outgoing Jeff Bridges are best friends, stalwarts of the school's losing football team, and Cybill Shepherd the blonde teen queen who innocently spreads chaos everywhere, ditching longtime boyfriend Bridges to run with a richer, faster set, stealing Bottoms away from older married woman Cloris Leachman, and prompting a vicious falling-out between the fast friends. As the kids run around heedless, the town's older generation remember their own wilder days and wonder how they came to be so unhappy: Ben Johnson, in Academy Award-winning form, as the wise old cowboy who runs the movie house and pool hall, muses about his long-ago affair with Shepherd's feisty mother (Ellen Burstyn).

In essence, it's a soap, but director Peter Bogdanovich plays it as a John Ford-style 'closing of the frontier' Western, with ugly-beautiful images of a West that has swapped cattle for oil but failed to strike it rich, layering in evocative snatches of Hank Williams among the whistling winds and the whining locals. It perhaps has one tragedy too many in its last act, but delivers a signature line of wistful regret, 'nothing's been right since Sam the Lion died'.

The director and cast reunited in 1990 to film McMurtry's more farcical sequel *Texasville*. ★★★★ **KN**

THE LAST RESORT (2000)

Starring: *Dina Korzun (Tanya), Artyom Strelnikov (Artyom), Paddy Considine (Alfie), Steve Perry (Les), Perry Benson (Immigration Officer)*
Director: *Pawel Pawlikowski*
Screenwriter: *Rowan Joffe, Pawel Pawlikowski*
15/73 mins./Drama/UK

A Russian immigrant is detained at a holding centre when she arrives in Britain with her son. As she tries to build a life for herself, she is constantly exploited.

The British tradition for social realism is alive and well in documentarist Pawel Pawlikowski's follow-up to *The Stranger*. An angry indictment of current attitudes to political asylum, yet laced with humour and humanity, it is short, sharp and unerringly to the point.

Detained at Stansted, when her British fiancé fails to show, Tanya and her son Artiom are sent to a soulless holding centre, where her only hope of avoiding deportation to Moscow lies either with an internet porn baron or the manager of an amusement arcade.

With Ryszard Lenczewski's photography managing to lens bleak beauty, this is a sobering portrait of a self-satisfied nation, where protestations of melting-pot liberalism amount to little more than soundbites. ★★★★ **PP**

THE LAST SEDUCTION (1994)

Starring: *Linda Fiorentino (Bridget Gregory), Bill Pullman (Clay Gregory), Peter Berg (Mike Swale), JT Walsh (Frank Griffith), Bill Nunn (Harlan)*
Director: *John Dahl*
Screenwriter: *Steve Barancik*
18/105 mins./Thriller/USA

Bridget goads husband Clay into stealing pharmaceutical drugs only to make off with the loot they've made. Then she meets Mike and drags him into her complex web but Clay has sent a detective to find her...

This is one of those thrillers (like *Blood Simple*) that keeps coming up with genuinely surprising plot twists. Under the credits, we meet Bridget, a hard-as-nails New York bitch, and Clay, the gutless intern husband she has bullied into stealing and selling a cache of pharmaceutical drugs. Clay celebrates with a touch of spouse abuse, whereupon Bridget takes the cash and runs out on him, going to ground in a small-town where she plans on sitting out the time till her shifty lawyer gets her a divorce. In a bar she picks up Mike, an amiably dumb small-town failure whom she exploits for quick sex and then ensnares in her plan to be rid of all her personal ties. Clay has hired a private eye and is on Bridget's trail, but she sees ways she can get away with the cash and return to her beloved city.

Dahl did good work on the small-scale noirs *Kill Me Again* and *Red Rock West*, but this (which benefits from a superb screenplay) is his best movie to date. Fiorentino's Bridget, introduced in a spectacularly cynical sequence as she works as a whip-cracking slave driver for a telephone sales company, is an authentically wonderful monster. She is funny when demonstrating her direct perfidy, but also makes marvellous little turns out of her various sob stories and deceptions.

It's not just a star turn, however, since Berg and Pullman are also perfectly cast, bringing different brands of male inadequacy to the roles of Bridget's fall guys. There are strange sex scenes, sustained stretches of quotably cynical dialogue and an ending you'll be hard put not to find funny even if you're ashamed of it. ★★★★ **KN**

THE LAST SUPPER (1995)

Starring: *Cameron Diaz (Jude), Ron Eldark (Pete), Annabeth Gish (Paulie), Jonathan Penner (Marc), Courtney V. Vance (Luke), Bill Paxton (Zachary Cody)*
Director: *Stacy Title*
Screenwriter: *Dan Rosen*
15/87 mins./Comedy/Drama/Crime/USA

A group of liberals have an unknown guest round for dinner, and in disgust at their conversation he pulls out a knife. So, they stab him to death. Having rather enjoyed that, they invite round more and more people with whom they disagree and as the body count rises, their vegetable patch flourishes.

This entertaining, thoughtful black comedy might be seen as an American answer to *Shallow Grave*, since it focuses on a group of self-satisfied young people sharing accommodation, whose chance encounter with a criminal prompts them to descend into madness and confront their own violent impulses.

A houseful of grad students invite to dinner a truck driver who has given one of them a lift, only to be disturbed by his near-fascist opinions and thinly restrained violence. When he pulls a knife on them and accuses them of talking rather than defending their principles, he is stabbed to death and buried in the vegetable garden, inspiring the housemates to invite more right-wingers over for a friendly debate followed by murder. The garden fills up, the group squabbles over methods, a sheriff pokes around the disappearances and a far right talk show pundit happens along in time for a final meal-cum-massacre.

Neatly scripted by Dan Rosen and capably directed by Title, this scores genuine but slightly glib laughs at the expense of its victims – nice cameos from, among others, Jason Alexander (a burger-munching eco-slob), Mark Harmon (an arch sexist and seducer) and Charles Durning (a homophobic priest). The film's strength lies in its characterisation of the lazy liberals turned non-stereotyped murderers, played by a clever mix of stars out for credibility and less familiar players taking advantage of showy roles.

It seems as if, like *Shallow Grave*, *The Last Supper* is going to have trouble coming up with an ending, but this pulls a fable-like punchline out of a fairy-tale storm and leaves you with a wicked chuckle. It may be too clever for immediate cultdom – it would make a great stage play, which means there's little showy film business – but it's one of those films you'll remember. ★★★★ **KN**

ⓓ LAST TANGO IN PARIS (L'ULTIMO TANGO A PARIGI) (1972)

Starring: *Marlon Brando (Paul), Maria Schneider (Jeanne), Jean-Pierre Leaud (Tom), Massimo Girotti (Marcel), Maria Michi (Rosa's Mother), Veronica Lazare (Rosa)*
Director: *Bernardo Bertolucci*
Screenwriter: *Bernardo Bertolucci*
18/129 mins./Drama/Erotic/France/Italy

While looking for an apartment, Jeanne, a young French woman, meets Paul, an older American widower, in an unfurnished flat where they have an intense sexual affair. The couple try to set boundaries for their relationship, not telling each other of their lives outside the flat.

Probably the last subtitled film to gain a widespread general circuit release in the United Kingdom, and enormously disappointing to mid-70s schoolchildren who sneaked in to see major humping, this schizoid arthouse picture is essentially downbeat miserablism with an acting masterclass from Marlon Brando thrown in.

Bernardo Bertolucci, off his Italian home turf, pays tribute to all of French cinema, from *L'Atalante* to the New Wave in the sub-plot about Jean-Pierre Leaud trying to make a movie, but most of the film is almost Cronenbergian body horror business with middle-aged gloomyguts Marlon Brando and that 1974's Euro-minx Maria Schneider having a heartless affair in an unfurnished apartment.

It gained notoriety for the explicit, frank sex scenes – which run the gamut of positions and variations, including the famous, butter-assisted buggery and the odder moment when the couple sit together naked as Schneider wonders if they can 'curm wizzout toucheeng'.

Brando, delivering perhaps his final, fully-committed Method performance, has a set-piece soliloquy over his wife's corpse that probably stands with 'I coulda been a contender' as his finest screen acting – though the quixotic wilfulness that overwhelmed his later career is already evident in free-associational declarations like 'I could dance forever ... oh, my haemorrhoids!' and 'I'm going to get you, bimbo!'

Still, strong dramatic stuff for audiences who like emotional nerves being scraped, and old enough to have a certain nostalgic appeal for those who can remember when women wore coats with feathery fur collars and Marlon Brando had a waistline. ★★★ **KN**

ⓓ THE LAST TEMPTATION OF CHRIST (1988)

Starring: *Willem Dafoe (Jesus Christ), Harvey Keitel (Judas Escariot), Barbara Hershey (Mary Magdalene), Harry Dean Stanton (Saul/Paul), David Bowie (Pontius Pilate) Verna Bloom (Mary, Mother Of Jesus)*
Director: *Martin Scorsese*
Screenwriters: *Paul Schrader, based on the novel by Nikos Kazantzakis*
18/164 mins/Drama/USA

Jesus struggles with his role as the Christ. On the cross, he has a vision of the regular life he might have led if he had refused his destiny.

The subject of heated controversy, this sincere, respectful film admits at the outset that it's a fiction (from the novel by Nikos Kazantzakis) rather than drawn from the Gospels. It makes a brave attempt to answer some of the problems raised by Jesus Christ as a historical, religious and dramatic character. Dafoe's Jesus is a self-torturing messiah, reluctant to tread his preordained path, attracted to the simple pains and joys of the ordinary life he can never lead, and never quite sure what it is God wants him to do. The film has a dusty, realistic look – Judea is a Third World desert of tattooed women and vicious Roman occupation troops – and doesn't skimp on violence. Not until Mel Gibson's more gruesome, less-protested *Passion of the Christ* was the crucifixion depicted as such a bloody, agonising business, and the film is complete with an epic load of ear-loppings, stabbings, mutilations, sacrifices and heart-rippings. As in most religious epics, there are longeurs – including an ineffectual cameo by David Bowie as a bored Pontius Pilate – but Dafoe and (particularly) Harvey Keitel as an unusually heroic, red-headed Judas keep kicking the movie back into gear. The finale Mary Whitehouse was so upset by is worth the wait, though not for an extremely tasteful sex scene as Jesus becomes the husband of Mary Magdalene. In an inversion of the premise of *It's a Wonderful Life*, Jesus has a vision of the world as it would be if he chose not to die on the cross: he can live to a ripe old age, but humanity is doomed. ★★★★ **KN**

ⓓ THE LAST WALTZ (1978)

Starring: *as themselves: Rick Danko, Levon Helm, Garth Hudson, Richard Manuel, Robbie Robertson*
Director: *Martin Scorsese*
U/111 mins./Documentary/Music/USA

The Band's final concert featuring an astounding guest-line up interspersed with interviews and anecdotes.

They were rock's ultimate 'musical melting pot', a group whose mystique and musicianship came from 16 years on the road, their legendary role as Bob Dylan's band, and a mythic repertoire that fused the rural and traditional with the urban and cutting edge.

So The Band's farewell concert at San Francisco's Winterland on Thanksgiving Day, 1976 – when they were joined in an exhaustingly thrilling performance by a staggering guest line-up of their influences, friends and admirers – became an end-of-an-era event.

As beautifully captured by director Martin Scorsese (and now restored for DVD in brilliant picture and sound), it is probably the greatest of concert films, and one which occupies an intriguing position in Scorsese's own body of work.

The songs in *The Last Waltz* – interspersed with interviews and anecdotes – represent a tapestry of 20th century music, from pure blues (giant Muddy Waters singing 'I'm A Man') to the Brill Building (Neil Diamond), the Brits (Eric Clapton), a Beatle (Ringo), a Stone (Ronnie Wood), cult heroes (Dr. John) and former employers (Hawkins and Dylan). Band favourites abound in the gig – 'The Night They Drove Old Dixie Down', 'Shape I'm In', 'Up On Cripple Creek'. But Scorsese memorably uses an MGM sound stage to highlight signature song 'The Weight' with gospel greats The Staples, country gem 'Evangeline' with Emmylou Harris, and the *Last Waltz* Theme, played on traditional instruments.

Visually, *The Last Waltz* was prepared meticulously, with storyboards and a script using song lyrics for camera and lighting cues. Production designer Boris Levens (*West Side Story, The Sound Of Music, New York, New York*) borrowed *La Traviata* trappings from the San Francisco Opera as a classy setting for musicians' musicians who were the antithesis of spectacle or flash.

Director of photography Michael Chapman (*Taxi Driver, Raging Bull*) bathed them in the warm glow of classic theatre lighting that is dramatic and timeless. The seven-man camera team included cinematographers Vilmos Zsigmond and Laszlo Kovacs, with just one hand-held camera discreetly on stage, capturing everything without intruding on the mood. ★★★★★ **AE**

LAST YEAR AT MARIENBAD (L'ANNEE DERNIERE A MARIENBAD) (1961)

Starring: *Delphine Seyrig (A/Woman), Giorgio Albertazzi (X/Stranger), Sacha Pitoeff (M. Escort/Husband), Françoise Berlin, Luce Garcia-Ville, Helena Kornel, Francois Spira, Karin Toeche-Mittler, Pierre Barbaud, Willhelm von Deek*
Director: *Alain Resnais*
Screenwriter: *Alain Robbe-Grillet*
U/94 mins./Drama/France/Italy

Awards: *Venice Film Festival – Golden Lion*

While holidaying at a spa with M, A is approached by X, who tries to convince her that they have a prior assignation, which they arranged at a similar resort the previous year.

Breaking with traditional conventions of screen narrative, this modernist masterpiece explores the interaction of time, memory and imagination. For many it's an infuriating experience whose intellectual obscurantism rapidly wears the patience. But for others, it's an intriguing treatise on art, romance, gender politics or myth, while others still see its exploitation of temporal and spatial relationships as a signifier of how little film's potential has been tapped.

Working from a screenplay written by nouveau roman pioneer, Alain Robbe-Grillet, Alain Resnais clearly sought to further the cinematic experiment begun with *Hiroshima, Mon Amour*. Consequently, he allows Jacques Saulnier's art direction and Giorgio Albertazzi's narration to set the scene and mood, while he guides Sacha Vierny's camera through the chateau's baroque corridors and manicured gardens in a bid to reproduce on celluloid the abstract process of thought.

Thus, Resnais is scarcely interested in diegetic logic or the questions thrown up by Albertazzi's recollections, inconsistencies and embellishments – hence his reliance on sequences whose content is repeated, distorted or contradicted without us ever learning whether the action is real or imagined or is taking place in the past, present or future. He is more concerned with achieving a cinematic texture in which the stylised locales, somnambulistic performances, classical tableaux and non-linear structuring provoke the same response in the viewer as the supposedly symbolic Greek statue does in the spa guests.

This blurring of subjective and objective reality explains the minimalism and studied artificiality of the film's composition and enactment. However, by consistently contrasting art and actuality, Resnais was also inviting the viewer to impose their own interpretation upon the scenario and, thus, become an active intellectual participant in its proceedings.

Last Year At Marienbad won the Golden Lion at Venice and proved to be a surprising commercial success. Its stream of consciousness technique has since been much imitated, but it remains a uniquely beautiful, challenging and mesmerising artwork. ★★★★★ **DP**

LAURA (1944)

Starring: *Gene Tierney (Laura Hunt), Dana Andrews (Mark McPherson), Clifton Webb (Waldo Lydecker), Vincent Price (Shelby Carpenter), Judith Anderson (Ann Treadwell)*
Director: *Otto Preminger*
Screenwriters: *Jay Dratler, Samuel Hoffenstein, Elizabeth Reinhardt, based on the novel by Vera Caspary*
U/88 mins./Mystery/USA

Awards: *Academy Awards – Best black and white cinematography*

Detective Mark McPherson investigates the shotgun-slaying of New Yorker Laura Hunt, protégée of waspish columnist Waldo Lydecker and fiancée of gigolo Shelby Carpenter. Mark becomes obsessed with the dead girl, who then turns up alive.

A sophisticated noir mystery from Otto Preminger, based on Vera Caspary's novel, this tackles the subject of romantic obsession as a grumpy cop falls in love with a murder victim who turns out to be not only still alive – the old shotgun-blast-that-destroys-the-dead-girl's-face gambit was invented here – but whose shaky alibi suddenly promotes her to the top of the suspect list.

In a classic sequence, David Raksin's haunting 'Laura' theme (later a huge hit) plays while Dana Andrews gets comfortable before Laura's portrait in her apartment and tries to think through his feelings for the corpse in the case, only to nod off in a chair and wake up to find the miraculously living Gene Tierney hovering over him. This necrophile streak makes the apparently hard-boiled regular joe into just as much a neurotic freak as Clifton Webb's unforgettably prissy, bitchy, snarky columnist (a conflation of Alexander Woolcott and Walter Winchell), Vincent Price's big grinning unmanly Southern gigolo or Judith Anderson's glamorous, desperate, worthless but wealthy aunt.

Like *The Maltese Falcon*, *Laura* is as much a comedy of manners as a thriller, emphasised by the use of fictional analogues for famous real people, the high-society feel of its New York of advertising agencies and fashion salons. It's every inch a Fox quality product, with top-of-the-line fashions (though you may disagree when Shelby purrs 'I approve of that hat'), set decoration, the full glamour treatment for the impossibly beautiful Tierney and an all-round swank feel that's a world away from the slums and alleys of the average trenchcoat picture. ★★★★★ **KN**

THE LAVENDER HILL MOB (1951)

Starring: *Alec Guinness (Henry Holland), Stanley Holloway (Alfred Pendlebury), Sid James (Lackery), Alfie Bass (Shorty Risher), Marjorie Fielding (Miss Evesham)*
Director: *Charles Crichton*
Screenwriter: *T.E.B. Clarke*
U/77 mins./Comedy/Crime/UK

Awards: *Academy Awards – Best Screenplay, BAFTA – Best British Film*

A meek bank clerk plans a theft from his own bank and recruits a gang to carry out the 'perfect' robbery.

By 1951, Baling had established a reputation for the comedies with which its name would eventually become synonymous. However, prompted by a combination of Britain's proud documentary heritage and the current fashion for Italian neo-realism, the studio also felt it had a responsibility to examine the contemporary social scene. But rather than focus on downbeat domestic dramas (which were too close to home for the majority of patrons in those grim post-war times), the front office opted to explore how economic adversity had driven so many youths and returning war heroes to crime and, increasingly, violent crime at that.

The decision was partly prompted by the success of *The Blue Lamp* (1950), in which Dirk Bogarde's terrified tearaway murdered PC Jack Warner (who would miraculously revive to spend 21 years playing the same character in the BBC's legendary series, *Dixon Of Dock Green*). Indeed, T.E.B. Clarke was working on a similarly gritty crime story for director Basil Dearden, when he got the idea for *The Lavender Hill Mob*.

Clearly uninspired by *Pool Of London*'s (1951) humdrum account of a doomed robbery, Clarke concocted the tale of the timid, but fastidious bank clerk who executes the perfect bullion heist and smuggles the gold out of the country in the form of seemingly worthless tourist trinkets.

Studio boss Michael Balcon was reportedly furious when Clarke suggested this new direction. But a cursory perusal of the treatment persuaded him to team Clarke with Charles Crichton, who had directed Ealing's first true 'comedy', *Hue And Cry*, in 1947. Eleven full drafts of the screenplay and four revised endings were submitted, but even then Crichton shaved 27 minutes off the original running time to bring it in at a compact 78 minutes. Keen to ensure the authenticity of his caper, Clarke consulted the Bank Of England on how best to breach its security and a specially-convened committee obligingly came up with the bare bones of Holland's ingenious plan.

'Dutch' Holland was played with deceptively innocuous self-assurance by Alec Guinness, who was returning to Ealing for the first time since his triumph in *Kind Hearts And Coronets* (1949). He would be joined in the gang by Stanley Holloway as Pendlebury, the proprietor of the souvenir company that would transform the ingots into Eiffel Towers, and Sid James and Alfie Bass as the Cockney scamps who would provide the gentlemanly outlaws with a little professional expertise.

While nowhere near as subversive as *Whisky Galore!* (1949), the film was still scathing in its depiction of the forces of law and order. Having demonstrated the technological and forensic armoury at the police's disposal, Clarke and Crichton delighted in debunking its efficacy. Rather than facilitate the pursuit of villains, in-car radios are shown to be vulnerable to sabotage and capable of causing utter chaos. Similarly, bobbies on the beat are resented as jolly fools, who either hone in with tall stories about top hats or are too preoccupied with singing 'Old Macdonald Had A Farm' to realise the suspects are under their very nose.

But it's not just the law that is subject to ridicule. Just as William Rose would later reveal he had lampooned Clement Attlee's government in *The Ladykillers* (1955), a case can be made for Clarke having taken a pop at them here, too. Like Attlee and his cabinet colleagues, Guinness and Holloway's characters are clearly a couple of rungs up the social ladder from James and Bass's working crooks. Thus, the blind faith the latter two place in their superiors to fence the loot in Paris and still return with their proceeds smacks of the confidence voters placed in Labour in 1945. But Alfie, Sid and the electorate were all betrayed by their implicitly trusted betters.

Crichton also found room for a dig at Britain's most famous cinematic export. As Guinness and Holloway hurtle down the steps of the Eiffel Tower in pursuit of a lift full of schoolgirls carrying their dodgy golden replicas, it's impossible not to be reminded of one of Alfred Hitchcock's famous landmark set-pieces. Indeed, the action becomes genuinely disquieting as Holloway's hat and coat float like a plunging figure from the twisting staircase, until Crichton deflates the incident by giving both men the giggles.

This enjoyment of their villainy is a key feature of the film's attitude towards morality. It's clear from the bookend sequences in South America that Guinness has been having a high old time (cavorting with a young Audrey Hepburn, no less). There's a trenchant satirical irony in the fact that his ill-gotten gains have helped him become a pillar of the ex-pat community. It's this willingness to seize on any route away from the all-pervading austerity of victory (vital also to 1949's *Passport To Pimlico*) and the disregard for authority that has ensured the Lavender Hill Mob's place in history.

★★★★ DP

THE LAWNMOWER MAN (1992)

Starring: *Jeff Fahey (Jobe Smith), Pierce Brosnan (Dr. Lawrence Angelo), Jenny Wright (Marnie Burke), Mark Bringleson (Sebastian Timms), Geoffrey Lewis (Terry McKeen)*
Director: *Brett Leonard*
Screenwriters: *Brett Leonard, Gimel Everett*
15/108 mins./Sci-fi/Thriller/USA

A ground-breaking scientist manages to invent a machine that can turn a mental patient into one of the cleverest people on Earth. But then the government try to improve it by adding an 'anger' chip that turns the participant into an A Grade killing machine.

Aptly for a film about a strange metamorphosis, this project had undergone several bizarre mutations on its way to the screen, not the least being that it started out as two seperate ideas – an adaptation of one of Stephen King's lesser-known short stories, and a science fiction exploration of new-fangled Virtual Reality technology – that have coalesced together not quite seamlessly.

It was heavily touted as Stephen King's *The Lawnmower Man*, but almost nothing of the story had survived the scripting process and his name was removed following a lawsuit, although several plot elements from other King novels – specifically *Firestarter* – had been tipped into the brew, and the combination of mad science, small-town Americana, a paranoid's vision of corrupt government and the last-reel explosion to tie everything up is more in tune with King than many films closely taken from his works.

The Lawnmower Man has brooding scientist Angelo experiment on retarded gardener Jobe, raising him from drooling geek with frizzy perm to psychic superbrain with blow-dried bob by directly stimulating his brain (or something). While this resembles the plot of *Charly* – from Daniel F. Keyes's classic story 'Flowers for Algernon' – that film found enough emotional story material in the transformation of simpleton into genius, whereas this remembers that it's supposed to be a Stephen King movie, so in addition we get a subplot about an evil government agency that puts an aggression-stimulant factor into the process, hoping to create a high-tech killing machine.

Tagline
God made him simple. Science made him a god.

Since most of the first half hour of the film introduces extraneous characters against whom Jobe has a grudge, it's a fair bet that before you can say Carrie or Christine the augmented Jobe will be killing them off in bizarre, often lawnmower-oriented, ways. Not only do we get the regulation vengeance spree, which sets up a very neat effect whereby people are reduced to writhing bubbles, but Jobe comes over messianic and the finale has Angelo trying to prevent him from taking over the world.

Although patched together from loose ends, this works surprisingly well, with interesting and well-integrated visual effects, some nice humour and a few genuinely visionary touches. The trouble is that it has to boil itself down ridiculously for a finale, in which loner Brosnan sprouts an instant family just so he can have someone to hug after the laboratory has blown up. Nevertheless, well worth a look. **★★★ KN**

⊙ LAWRENCE OF ARABIA (1962)

Starring: *Peter O'Toole (T.E. Lawrence), Alec Guinness (Prince Feisal), Anthony Quinn (Auda abu Tayi), Jack Hawkins (General Lord Edmund Allenby), Omar Sharif (Sherif Ali), Jose Ferrer (Turkish Bey)*
Director: *David Lean*
Screenwriter: *Robert Bolt, from the book* Seven Pillars Of Wisdom *by T.E. Lawrence*
PG/209 mins./History/Adventure/Biography/UK

Awards: *Academy Awards – Best Art Direction/Set Decoration, Best Cinematography, Best Director, Best Film Editing, Best Original Score, Best Picture, Best Sound, BAFTA – Best British Actor, Best British Film, Best British Screenplay, Best Film, Golden Globes – Best Cinematography, Best Drama, Best Director, Best Supporting Actor (Omar Sharif), Most Promising Newcomer (Omar Sharif)*

T. E. Lawrence is a young maladjusted lieutenant in the British Army in North Africa during World War One. Unhappy with his current assignment colouring maps, he is ecstatic when he is offered a job as an observer in Arabia – but he plans to do more than observe . . .

David Lean's mythic blockbuster is both a stunning epic and a sensitive portrait of one of the greatest romantic legends of the 20th Century, 'poet, scholar, warrior, exhibitionist' T.E. Lawrence. Although the film opens on Lawrence's death, it eschews, 'the life' for its defining moment in history, the young Lawrence's role in the Arabian desert revolt of 1916-18 – as exaggerated by himself in *Seven Pillars Of Wisdom*, adapted by Robert Bolt and the uncredited Michael Wilson.

Lawrence's triumph – seven Oscars for Picture, Director, Cinematography, Score, Sound, Editing and Art Direction – and its enduring appeal are down to a combination of exhilarating, exotic adventure and an intensely personal, human story. Lawrence's tormented psyche and the political-cultural turmoil of the time and place are picked out against a spectacular, vast and timeless backdrop and absolutely thrilling action artistry. With several rival productions foiled over the years (including a mooted film version of Terence Rattigan's stage play in which Alec Guinness starred), two years of laborious preparation were followed by 14 dust-choked months of location shooting from May of 1961 in Jordan, Spain and Morocco.

This was longer than it took the real Lawrence, from lieutenant to colonel, to see the desert tribes unite under Prince Faisal and tip the balance for the Allies against the Turks in World War I. Guinness, too old for Lawrence by the time Lean got the go, played Faisal. Producer Sam Spiegel's choice for Lawrence was Marlon Brando. After Brando dropped out, 24-year-old Albert Finney (whose Lawrence screen tests in Arab costume are the most requested viewing item in Britain's National Film Archive) got the nod but said no, he didn't want to become a matinée idol just yet.

Lean happened to catch a caper called *The Day They Robbed The Bank Of England* and suddenly 28-year-old Peter O'Toole, the right age and with the same Irish heritage as Lawrence (though a good few inches taller than the diminutive T.E.), was on his gruelling way to glory on the back of a camel. When the film premiered Noel Coward famously quipped that if O'Toole had been any prettier the film would have had to be called Florence Of Arabia. He is pretty indeed, and the arresting image of his pale-blue eyes staring intensely under the white headdress is iconic. Inspired moments have the feel of classic silent film storytelling spiced with colour and sound effects of the most delicate technical invention, like the cut from Lawrence blowing out a match in Cairo to the desert. The last beat of his breath becomes a whisper over the sun rising red on the Sahara, the film poised in still purity before Maurice Jarre's sweeping musical theme swells up.

Action in *Lawrence* is not confined to battle sequences, railway explosions and whooping Arabs charging down sand dunes. Truly remarkable scenes empty the screen of extras and noise. In the most coolly audacious and entrancing of character introductions, cinematographer Freddie Young redefined the term 'long shot' with his miraculous mirage of a quavering dark speck on the white horizon slo-o-o-wly taking shape as camel and rider, finally revealing itself as the murderously proud Ali. They shot about nine minutes but Lean said he 'lost his nerve', cutting to under three. Another lulu: a man, Gasim, has slipped off his camel and is given up for dead. 'It is written.' Lawrence turns back, to the fury of the men convinced it is a futile, suicidal gesture. Lean cuts between Gasim's ordeal, the sun, burning from orange to a relentless, searing white, Lawrence, riding, riding, and the hero-worshipping boy Daud, keeping vigil. An empty horizon signifies expectation. Lawrence emerges with Gasim, to be greeted with amazement. Royally hailed El Aurens, he gasps 'Nothing is written' and passes out. It's eight minutes of genius.

In contrast, the taking of the Turkish stronghold of Aqaba is realised with breathtaking dispatch, most of it in one long panning shot, banners flying, horses and camels kicking up clouds of sand, surprised Turks overrun in a moment, riders pouring through white city to sapphire sea as the silent cannon, trained uselessly towards the ocean, squats above. Combat in *Lawrence* illustrates the concept of literate action. Imperious Faisal embodies courage, ambition and despair on horseback, wielding sword and ordering, 'Stand and fight' as his encampment is bombarded from the air, refusing to acknowledge his warriors with their fabled past are helpless against modern armaments.

The 'Noprisoners' bloodbath in which retreating Turks are hacked to death is practically discreet by today's 'standards ', but it has not lost its power to shock because the quivering, bloodied O'Toole's Lawrence has visibly snapped and the action is pictured as chaotic and ugly. We don't need dialogue exposition to understand why and how his boyish adventure has become an inglorious, masochistic madness from which, in self-disgust, he flees in search of reason and solitude, if not obscurity. ★★★★★ **AE**

Movie Trivia: Lawrence of Arabia

Albert Finney shot an elaborate screen test for the role of T.E. Lawrence, but he eventually turned it down. In nearly four hours of film, there isn't a single speaking part for a woman. The real T.E. Lawrence was a foot shorter than O'Toole and looked like Stan Laurel.

⊙ LAYER CAKE (2004)

Starring: *Daniel Craig (XXXX), Tom Hardy (Clarkie), Jamie Foreman (Duke), George Harris (Morty), Tamar Hassan (Terry), Colm Meaney (Gene), Kenneth Cranham (Jimmy Price), Sienna Miller (Tammy)*
Director: *Matthew Vaughn*
Screenwriter: *J.J. Connolly, based on the screenplay by J.J. Connolly*
15/105 mins./Thriller/Crime/UK

Awards: *BAFTA – Carl Foreman Award for Most Promising Newcomer (Matthew Vaughn), Empire Awards – Best British Director*

With a vast amount of money safely invested, a London cocaine peddler is preparing to leave England and start a new life. However, his gangland protector, Jimmy Price, has other plans . . .

When *Lock, Stock* producer Matthew Vaughn announced his directing debut, there were few cheers in the Empire office. Drugs? Check. Dodgy geezers? Check. London crime syndicate? Check. Whatever he cared to call it, Vaughn's *Layer Cake* sounded uncomfortably like it belonged to the worst of all genres: Yet Another British Gangster Movie.

But something didn't sit right. If that really were the case, what would an actor like Daniel Craig be doing in it? Since breaking out in 1998's *Love Is The Devil* as Francis Bacon's bit-of-rough lover, Craig has proven himself one of our most talented and versatile actors. And it's good to report that his faith in *Layer Cake* has paid off handsomely; under Vaughn's unfussy direction, Craig's nameless dealer is the focus of this often gripping film, an engaging and all-too-human presence after the cartoon archetypes of *Lock, Stock* and *Snatch*.

This is, above all, a movie about mood. Where sometime partner Guy Ritchie might dip into Scorsese's bag of tricks and crank up the volume, Vaughn looks to Michael Mann for inspiration. Lisa Gerrard's captivating score illustrates this thinking most explicitly, but it's perhaps more evident in the cinematography.

Looking out over the city and the square mile around its neon gherkin, Vaughn's directorial debut captures London's essence but doesn't Americanise it. This is the first time in a while that we've seen London as it is – an affluent European capital, not a concrete shrine to bad town planning.

The story, too, is less conventional than it might seem. At first glance, it's the classic one-last-heist scenario, but Craig's character is not drawn into the game by greed or anything so shallow. The reality is closer to Paul Schrader's *American Gigolo* or, more pertinently, *Light Sleeper*, both films in which the protagonist is swallowed up by a plot that unfolds around him, slowly and methodically blocking off the exits.

There are, of course, some flaws, and they mostly arrive at the end, as several storylines conclude one after another, undermining some of Craig's good work and posing more questions than answers. Still, this is a real surprise that stands head and shoulders above most other British gangster films. ★★★★ **DW**

ⓓ THE LEAGUE OF EXTRAORDINARY GENTLEMEN (2003)

Starring: *Sean Connery (Allan Quatermain), Naseeruddin Shah (Captain Nemo), Peta Wilson (Mina Harker), Tony Curran (Rodney Skinner – The Invisible Man), Stuart Townsend (Dorian Gray), Shane Wast (Tom Sawyer), Jason Flemyng (Jekyll/Hyde), Richard Roxburgh (M)*
Director: *Stephen Norrington*
Screenwriter: *James Robinson, based on the comic books by Alan Moore, Kevin O'Neill*
12/105 mins./Action/Adventure/Fantasy/US/Germany

It's 1899 and the British government asks retired adventurer Allan Quatermain to lead a group of 'extraordinary individuals'. Their task: to combat a technological terror campaign led by a mysterious madman, named 'The Fantom', intent on world war.

Of all the comic book properties eagerly purchased by studios following X-Men, Alan Moore's highly-acclaimed melding of Victorian adventure fiction and super-heroics was undoubtedly the most exciting. Teeming with inspired wit and invention, only a supreme effort could screw it up. 'Prepare For The Extraordinary' screamed the presumptuous trailer. You should indeed – albeit, crushingly, an extraordinary display of creative cowardice and mishandling.

The drive to concoct a period *X-Men* results in a depressingly clumsy action movie, one which treats the audience's intelligence with infuriating contempt.

The promising start – Quatermain (Connery's craggy charm on form) is lured from his colonial African home to London (hats off to Carol Spier's beautiful production design) to assemble the League – is quickly evaporated by the film's most damning trait: the assumption we know nothing of these characters. They are, of course, literary icons of many decades' cultural standing. The first hour comprises tediously detailed, ham-fisted character introductions via Robinson's painfully expositional dialogue – the actors flounder with characters free of depth, life or chemistry. Nemo merely provides the gadgets and martial artistry, the now-vampiric Mina Harker is wasted eye-candy, the new Invisible Man is an irritating Cockney spiv, and the Hulk-like Jekyll and Hyde moans and sweats between appearances as poor CG. Ironically, Tom Sawyer and Dorian Gray, who are not in the source comic, fare better. West's Sawyer has a good mentor/protegé schtick with Quatermain, while Townsend's Gray is undoubtedly the most fun role.

By the time the League actually does something, the film drowns in its own forced spectacle. Fight scenes are shoddily edited, ridiculous set-pieces fail to hide woeful effects and worse are the bewildering array of continuity errors. Anyone who has seen *Blade* knows that Norrington can direct slick action fare, but there's scant evidence here.

No matter how troubled the shoot was, the movie was shanghaied from the off, courtesy of Hollywood's dependence on market-defined 'success'.
★★ **DG**

ⓓ THE LEAGUE OF GENTLEMEN'S APOCALYPSE (2005)

Starring: *Mark Gatiss (Hilary Briss/Mickey Michaels/Matthew Chinnery/Himself/Sir Nicholas Sheet-Lightning), Steve Pemberton (Wolf Lipp/Himself/Tubbs Tattsyrup/Pauline Campbell-Jones/Barbara Dixon/Lemuel Blizzard), Reece Shearsmith (Edward Tattsyrup/Papa Lazarou/Geoff Tipps/Himself/Rev. Bernice Woodall/Father Silas Halfhearte/Red Devil), David Warner (Dr. Erasmus Pea)*
Director: *Steve Bendelack*
Screenwriters: *Jeremy Dyson, Mark Gatiss, Steve Pemberton, Reece Shearsmith*
15/91 mins./Comedy/UK/USA

Royston Vasey is facing destruction. On finding out that, in something called 'the real world', the writers of the TV series are planning to end the programme, three of its inhabitants cross over to persuade their creators to save the town.

Connoisseurs of the *League Of Gentlemen*'s exquisitely twisted universe will recall that the TV series began with a character from the 'real' world finding himself trapped among the grotesques of Royston Vasey. It's mildly appropriate, then, that the film should invert the situation and have characters from the nightmare parish erupt into our world.

It's anything but a new idea, already seen in the likes of *Pleasantville* and *The Brady Bunch Movie*. But, it has to be said, neither of those affected the device via the ominous fulfilling of an 'ancient prophecy' – namely, that 'a giraffe shall spunk up over a load of old biddies'.

The League's deft screenplay wisely benches the more well-known and hence slightly shopworn characters, though Tubbs and Edward, Pauline, Papa Lazarou et al all make appearances. Instead, pederast German teacher Herr Lipp, sinister butcher Hilary Briss (whose pies are 'all eyelids and bumholes, but nice') and angry ex-salesman Geoff Tipps take centre stage. Extra room for invention is via a third 'reality', the 17th century – the setting for the comedy the League have supposedly ditched Royston Vasey in favour of – in which a deliciously demented David Warner camps it up as a kind of magus able to conjure bad stop-motion at a few moments' notice.

But aside from the jokes, which are well up to scratch, there are incongruously affecting moments: the characters looking bewildered at a TV which reveals them to be comic inventions; Herr Lipp being coldly informed, 'You're nothing but a pun', and his desire, discovered while trying to pass himself off as his creator Steve Pemberton, to settle down with a wife and kids, all have a strange pathos.

They humanise the characters. It's a crafty strategy, as it addresses one of the film's major in-built problems. On television, the League were pretty much a working definition of 'cult viewing' and rather than widen their audience they progressively narrowed it; each season or special becoming less obviously funny and more disturbingly weird than the last. It's a sign of the League's success that, while Royston Vasey's welcome sign sinisterly promises that 'you'll never leave', these characters' final return home is oddly touching. ★★★★ **AS**

⊙ A LEAGUE OF THEIR OWN (1992)

Starring: *Tom Hanks (Jimmy Dugan), Geena Davis (Dottie Hinson), Madonna (Mar Mordabito), Lori Petty (Kit Keller), Jon Lovitz (Ernie Capadino), David Stragthairn (Ira Lowenstein)*
Director: *Penny Marshall*
Screenwriters: *Lowell Ganz, Babaloo Mandel, based on a story by Kim Wilson, Kelly Candaele*
PG/122 mins./Comedy/Drama/Sport/USA

In 1943 Major League Baseball has been decimated by call-ups to the armed services, leaving the ladies to take over America's national sport. One team stands out – that coached by drunken ex-player Jimmy Dugan.

A quick glance at the line-up suggests what one might expect from this comedy of baseball bonding bosom buddies. Re-teaming director Penny Marshall with *Big* star Tom Hanks, and with a screenplay by *City Slickers* and *Parenthood* writers Lowell Ganz and Babaloo Mandel, the agenda here is clearly along the lines of good-natured vignettes, smart one-liners and a healthy dose of heartstring tugging.

And, of course, it's not really about baseball at all, being in its way a kind of Pretty Slickers about sharing fellowship, jolly repartee and a few heartaches in the context of a liberating physical challenge. It's the tale of the formation of a women's professional league during World War II, when the armed forces picked the pro teams clean, and baseball's desperate bosses looked to the farms and factories for females who could play hard ball and flash their pins for the thrill-hungry fans.

Hanks, in another gem of a comic performance, is the drunken has-been with disgusting personal habits, reluctantly coaching the Rockford Peaches from a horizontal position until their abilities startle him into animation. Meanwhile, taking the field with robust assurance, is the perfectly peachy Geena Davis as farmer's wife and formidable batter Dottie. Madonna – not too stretched as team slut 'All The Way' Mae – is shown off in a jitterbug number, while more screen time is given to the sibling relationship between Davis's Dottie and Lori Petty as her overshadowed sister, the erratic pitcher Kit.

It's a mostly winning combination of sassy humour and sentiment, enlivened by some fun 'newsreel' recreations that catch the period flavour of a sport adopting showbiz tactics – flirty-skirted uniforms, cheesecake stunts and skin-scraping do-or-die game plays – to attract the crowds.

And, even more refreshingly, this doesn't always take the obvious route – apart from a few overly sombre moments, like the arrival of the inevitable War Office telegram in the locker room. The cast do passable impressions of useful athletes with few indiscreet long shots of actual play to shatter the illusion, and more often than not, to quote *Saturday Night Live* stalwart Jon Lovitz's odious scout Gappy, 'Ladies, it's been a thin slice of heaven.' ★★★★ **AE**

⊙ LEAVE HER TO HEAVEN (1945)

Starring: *Gene Tierney (Ellen Berent), Cornel Wilde (Richard Harland), Jeanne Crain (Ruth Berent), Vincent Price (Russell Quinton), Mary Philips (Mrs. Berent), Ray Collins (Glen Robie), Gene Lockhart (Dr. Saunders)*
Director: *John M. Stahl*
Screenwriter: *Jo Swerling, based on the novel by Ben Ames Williams*
U/110 mins./Drama/USA

Society beauty Ellen Berent ditches her politician fiancé, Russell Quinton, for writer Richard Harland, whose resemblance to her late father prompts her to remove anyone who might compete with her for his affections.

One of the unsung masters of the Hollywood melodrama, John M. Stahl was best known for the woman's pictures *Imitation of Life* and *Magnificent Obsession* when he made this classy adaptation of Ben Ames Williams's dime dreadful. Indeed, either could have served as alternative titles for this simmering study of debased passion and it's intriguing to note the extent to which Leon Shamroy's Oscar-winning use of Technicolor was reflected in Russell Metty's stylised imagery for Douglas Sirk's respective 1959 and 1954 remakes of the aforementioned.

The fascination of this unashamed melodrama lies in Gene Tierney's ability to shift from charming to harming without losing her allure. Indeed, the more wicked she becomes, the more beautiful she seems and this trait recurred in her finest noir outings, *Laura* and *Whirlpool*. Ellen Berent is the epitome of a femme fatale, whose male dupe is the cause of her crimes rather than their hapless perpetrator. Thus, it's possible to claim *Leave Her to Heaven* as the prototype non-monochrome noir, with its glorious use of light, landscape and a lustrous palette even categorising it as the first film couleur.

But while Tierney provides the irresistible centre of attention, her charisma is very much shaped by Stahl's sublime direction. Three times, he sets up false plot trails around potential ménages (with Vincent Price, Darryl Hickman's crippled brother and Jeanne Crain's decent sister) before bringing the focus back to Tierney's fixations. Moreover, he always employs motion to emphasise the energy she invests in her schemes – whether it's meeting Cornell Wilde on a train, seducing him in a swimming pool, scattering her father's ashes while on horseback or hurling herself downstairs to terminate an inconvenient pregnancy. Indeed, the only time she's wholly still, as she sits in the rowing boat, movement is chillingly implied by her impassive response to Hickman's drowning.

As a psychological study, this is preposterously simplistic. But as an example of slick studio entertainment, it ranks amongst the most intelligent and influential. ★★★★ **DP**

⊙ LEAVING LAS VEGAS (1995)

Starring: *Nicolas Cage (Ben Sanderson), Elisabeth Shue (Sera), Julian Sands (Yuri), Richard Lewis (Peter), Steven Weber (Marc Nussbaum)*
Director: *Mike Figgis*
Screenwriter: *Mike Figgis, based on the novel by John O'Brien*
18/111 mins./Drama/Romance/France/USA/UK

Awards: *Academy Awards – Best Actor, Golden Globes – Best Actor*

An alcoholic winds up in Las Vegas planning to drink himself to death but meets a beautiful call girl and falls in love.

The dire effects of alcoholism are brought horribly to life in this grim, darkly comic tale of dissipation and self-destruction in the world's capital of tack. From the opening shot of Nicolas Cage happily wheeling a shopping cart around a supermarket, piled with bottles of booze, this is clearly no *Honeymoon In Vegas*.

Cage is Ben Sanderson, an alcoholic screenwriter who goes to Vegas to drink himself to death, only to meet hooker Sera and unexpectedly fall in love.

Based on the semi-autobiographical novel by John O'Brien, an alcoholic who committed suicide shortly after the film rights were acquired, this is dark, disturbing, and exceptionally moving. Cage is utterly realistic, and sometimes hilarious, with his copious beverage guzzling, wired antics, and the inevitable DTs and blackouts. He is pure nihilism, his drinking has no motive, and even romance cannot save him.

It is Shue – in a stunningly sensitive performance as the working girl, even if she is too wholesome looking – who, having escaped the violent clutches of Russian pimp Yuri, tries to liberate them both.

Beautifully shot in Super 16mm, with a smoky, moody jazz score (written by the director), Figgis handles the interplay between the two main characters as deftly as he did in *The Browning Version*, creating a mood of dissonance with the world that most ordinary people in their cosy domestic lives never experience. ★★★★ **DB**

LEGALLY BLONDE (2001)

Starring: *Reese Witherspoon (Elle Woods), Luke Wilson (Emmett Richmond), Selma Blair (Vivian Kensington), Jennifer Coolidge (Paulette Bonafonte), Ali Larter (Brooke Taylor Windham)*
Director: *Robert Luketic*
Screenwriters: *Karen McCullah Lutz, Kirsten Smith, based on the novel by Amanda Brown*
12/92 mins./Comedy/USA

Pampered Beverly Hills blonde Elle Woods is dumped by her wealthy boyfriend, so she follows him to Harvard Law School in order to win him back. Everyone is surprised when she proves rather astute at legal matters.

A surprisingly successful 'sleeper' hit starring Reese Witherspoon that charged ahead of Julia Roberts and the rest of 'America's Sweethearts' brigade.

Legally Blonde is, essentially, a kind of sorority sister to *Clueless* – indeed, if there had been a follow-up to that film, in which Cher Horowitz opted for a career in law, it might have looked something like this.

Witherspoon's impressive performances and offbeat film choices have always attracted attention, but her stock skyrocketed on the strength of this outing.

The film looks to be in traditional territory when it kicks off, with Witherspoon's Elle every inch the stereotypically vapid Beverly Hills princess whose only ambition in life appears to be marriage to the similarly loaded Warner Huntington III (a splendidly arrogant Matthew Davis). When the romantic dinner at which she is convinced he will pop the question turns into a permanent termination of their relationship, our heartbroken heroine is forced to change tack and follow him to Harvard if she has any hope of winning him back.

This is where the action changes tack also, for rather than resorting to dumb humour or bawdy college comedy as Elle and her cute dog join the boringly conventional world of Harvard law, it shows her to be surprisingly resourceful. So, when the students become involved in the movie's inevitable big courtroom drama – the did-she-or-didn't-she? murder trial of a wealthy widow – there's no prizes for guessing who ends up arguing for the defence.

Essentially, it's Witherspoon's terrifically bubbly turn which holds proceedings together, but there's also some nice work from Wilson as the qualified lawyer who holds a candle for her. As Warner's fabulous bitchy new girlfriend, Blair eventually helps us to realise that, while it's probably better to be blonde, brunettes aren't so bad, after all.

Avoid the sequel *Legally Blonde: Red, White and Blue*, which takes Elle to Washington and looses all her charm. ★★★★ **CW**

LEGENDS OF THE FALL (1994)

Starring: *Brad Pitt (Tristan Ludlow), Anthony Hopkins (Colonel William Ludlow), Aidan Quinn (Alfred Ludlow), Julia Ormond (Susannah Fincannon Ludlow), Henry Thomas (Samuel Ludlow)*
Director: *Edward Zwick*
Screenwriters: *Susan Shilliday, Bill Wittliff, based on the novella by Jim Harrison*
15/133 mins./Drama/USA

Awards: *Academy Awards – Best Cinematography*

In the empty plains of Montana, shortly before, during, and after the First World War, three brothers compete for the love of one woman and the respect of their stern father. As the years pass, tragedy, heartbreak and finally death will test the bonds of blood that hold the family together.

This is exactly the kind of film that snags the best cinematography award at the Oscars, while being laughed out of court on grounds of arch-melodrama, overblown storytelling and some very silly native mysticism. It's a pretend epic that does wonders for the Montana tourist board, but very little for the dignity of its usually-dependable acting cast.

Director Edward Zwick is so satisfied he has hit the mother lode of American drama, a *Gone With The Wind* for boys, he can't see the gas for the wind blowing in Brad Pitt's lustrous hair.

All the way through its arduous running time, this is plastic masquerading as silver. In its squabbling brothers and overbearing father, it's trying to echo Shakespeare, but Pitt, doomed Henry Thomas, and Aidan Quinn are strapping stereotypes saddled with lumps of cheesy dialogue, as gorgeous and unreal as their National Geographic homestead. Poor Julia Ormond, supposedly the catalyst for all these inter-Ludlow travails, with her weepy eyes and yearning voice, seems far to fragile and wispy for these three rugged boyos to care a jot about. Indeed, not a whisker of the film feels like it looks. Off to war go the younger brothers, where it's muddy and terrible but merely a device for Pitt's free spirited middle bro to gain that essential lifelong burden of 'pain'. He expresses this torment by riding over the hill then fifteen minutes later (several years in narrative terms) riding back again followed by a heard of wild horses. Then as the local native witch doctory fellow expounds: 'He was a rock they broke themselves against.' Damn him, for his mystical subtext. He's like a song lyric in physical form.

In all, *Legends Of The Fall* is a grand bore, more laughable than stirring. So big everything becomes blurry and distant, so beautiful it could be an ad for male hair products. ★★ **IN**

LEMONY SNICKET'S A SERIES OF UNFORTUNATE EVENTS (2004)

Starring: *Jim Carrey (Count Olaf), Liam Aiken (Klaus), Emily Browning (Violet), Kara Hoffman (Sunny), Shelby Hoffman (Sunny), Jude Law (voice of Lemony Snicket)*
Director: *Brad Silberling*
Screenwriter: *Robert Gordon, based on the books by Daniel Handler*
PG/108 mins./Adventure/Comedy/Family/USA/Germany

When their parents are killed in a mysterious fire, the Baudelaire children – Violet, Klaus and baby Sunny – are sent to live with their nearest relative the villainous Count Olaf.

With no *Harry Potter* or *Lord Of The Rings* to bring fantastic seasonal cheer to multiplexes in 2004, the mantle of Big Christmas Film was passed to yet another adaptation of a kid-friendly book, namely the works of elusive author Lemony Snicket (actually San Franciscan scribe Daniel Handler).

This gloomy children's book series by Daniel Handler has been quietly gaining a worldwide following among both children and grown-ups, with 11 books (of a planned 13) having hit the shelves in the time it takes J.K. Rowling to sharpen her pencil. Brad Silberling's big-screen Snicket surpasses the early Potters, bolstered by a set of memorable performances and its atmospheric, Burtonesque visuals.

Silberling sets the tone early on, with a bizarrely brilliant opening sequence, and thanks to the ensuing blend of twisted comedy and tense set-pieces, offers much to enjoy thereafter. He's also smart and disciplined enough let the movie belong to its terrific child leads, rather than allowing it to become a runaway Jim Carrey vehicle. Not that Carrey's that restrained. As the vain, murderous and terrible-disguise-wearing Olaf, his performance will neither let down his fans or his detractors – it's guaranteed to delight and irritate in equal measures.

The film does suffer from a patchy, episodic script, though, which is a real shame given the florid style of the books. Scripter Robert Gordon shoehorns in the events of the first three novels, and it does make for an uneven tone. The sequences with Billy Connolly's Uncle Monty, while an important part of the saga on the page, do little to advance the action here, while Streep is so good as the neurotic Aunt Josephine you wish she had more to do. Other supporting players – including Luis Guzman and Jennifer Coolidge – are so underused you almost wonder why they bothered to sign on in the first place.

Still, Snicket-heads will naturally be thrilled to see their heroes recreated so deftly and vividly; the production design and costumes stay true to the spirit of the book and are impossible to fault. Those who have become accustomed to more epic Yuletide fare over the past few years may be harder to convince, but if you sit back, relax and just accept it for what it is – an enjoyable, escapist Gothic pantomime – you will go home happy. ★★★★ **CW**

LENNY (1974)

Starring: *Dustin Hoffman (Lenny Bruce), Valerie Perrine (Honey Bruce), Jan Miner (Sally Marr), Stanley Beck (Artie Silver), Frankie Beck (Artie Silver)*
Director: *Bob Fosse*
Screenwriter: *Julian Barry, from his play*
18/106 mins/Biography/Drama/USA

Awards: *BAFTA – Best Newcomer (Valerie Perrine)*

The life and times of anarchic comedian Lenny Bruce, a satirist and obsessed crusader who had the edge of a guillotine and broke every taboo of showbiz and polite society, freewheeling on race, sex, drugs and religion.

In the 'Genius or Madman' pantheon, they don't come more interesting and influential than the daring but tragic Lenny Bruce. Fosse's evocative film, adapted by Julian Barry from his play, commemorates Lenny as a champion of self-expression under the First Amendment, drawing heavily on authentic transcripts of his performances and court records from his numerous prosecutions across the country.

It's structured around dramatised interviews with Honey, his daughter, (powerfully played by voluptuous Valerie Perrine in a role of a lifetime), his mother and his agent, then intricately edited into a dramatic collage of incident until the discovery of Lenny's body, syringe in arm, on a bathroom floor.

Shot in smoky black and white, and suffused with period detail, Fosse's musical background comes to the fore during some of the extended night-club routines, where the legendary choreographer stages the stand-up as if Bruce is a master jazz musician, which, in a way, he was.

However, what the film and Dustin Hoffman's Oscar-nominated performance as Lenny don't convey fully – and it's pretty crucial – is that Lenny Bruce was – and still is – awfully, outrageously funny. At least, he was as he evolved from humorous teller of 'bits' into a brilliant improvisational comic, taking flight off whatever he'd just read or seen. He enjoyed a historic triumph – also recorded – at Carnegie Hall in 1961. Then began the relentless string of prosecutions for obscenity and drugs possession, some of these dubious and transparently harassment, that bankrupted him and turned him into a justifiably paranoid, pitiable spectacle, ranting tediously on stage when club owners dared to book him.

Lenny Bruce died, broke and facing imprisonment, in 1966, two months after his last gig with Frank Zappa and The Mothers Of Invention at San Francisco's premiere rock venue, The Fillmore West. Nevertheless, his legacy endures. Even people unaware of Lenny Bruce, or oblivious that he moved the goalposts in comedy improv. and social satire, are laughing at comedy inspired by comedy inspired by him. He was hounded to death for saying things that are less rude, crude and lewd – and a lot more intelligent – than what passes now for prime-time television. ★★★★ **AE**

LEON (1994)

Starring: *Jean Reno (Leon), Gary Oldman (Stansfield), Natalie Portman (Mathilda), Danny Aiello (Tony), Peter Appel (Malky)*
Director: *Luc Besson*
Screenwriter: *Luc Besson*
18/110 mins./Crime/Thriller/France/USA

A 12-year-old orphan girl is taken in by a ruthless assassin who – at her behest – trains her in the art of the hit man.

Luc Besson followed *Nikita* and *The Big Blue* with another of his outrageously plotted, highly improbable but throughly enjoyable tales, this time focusing on a milk-drinking, plant-tending, Gene Kelly-loving Sicillian hitman in New York who adopts a young orphan after her family is murdered.

Besson regular Jean Reno stars as the eponymous assassin whose ruthless efficiency will have you on tenterhooks for the first five minutes. Thereafter, the film changes tack and goes not for the jugular, but the heartstrings.

When the family of his 12-year-old neighbour Mathilda is killed by a shadowy bunch of characters led by a hammy Oldman, Leon finds himself as her surrogate father, teaching his young, precocious charge – at her insistence, mind you – how to load an automatic weapon or shoot politicans jogging in Central Park using a rifle with a telescopic sight, transforming her into a pre-pubescent version of Nikita. She, in return, teaches him to read and write and open up as a human being.

Driven by another electrifying score from Eric Serra, this features an astonishingly histrionic performance from Oldman, chomping drugs at every turn, and a touchingly affecting relationship between the stoic Reno and the quite extraordinary Louise Brooks-coiffured Portman in her first movie.

Despite its US setting, English dialogue and the presence of actors such as Gary Oldman and Danny Aiello, this is a fully fledged French arthouse film through and through, packed with incredible visuals, and featuring Besson's typical disregard for plot logic. There may well be something morally dubious about the idea of training a young girl in the ways of an assassin, but Besson manages to pull it all off with his typical flair and visual aplomb, instilling his narrative with an emotional centre hitherto lacking in his previous work. It's preposterous to be sure, but that's an essential part of its quality. ★★★★★ **MS**

THE LEOPARD (IL GATTOPARDO) (1963)

Starring: *Burt Lancaster (Prince Don Fabrizio Salina), Alain Delon (Tancredi), Claudia Cardinale (Angelica Sedara/Bertiana), Rina Morelli (Maria Stella), Paolo Stoppa (Don Calogero Sedara)*
Director: *Luchino Visconti*
Screenwriters: *Luchino Visconti, Suso Cecchi D'Amico, Pasquale Festa Campanile, Enrico Medioli, Massimo Franciosa, based on the novel* Il Gattopardo *by Giuseppe Tomasi di Lampedusa*
PG/161 mins./History/Drama/Italy

The 19th Century. As Garibaldi's army fights for the incorporation of Sicily into a united Italy, dignified landowner Prince Salina bows to the winds of change, encouraging a marriage between his nephew and the daughter of a nouveau riche businessman.

'Things must change a little, so they can stay the same,' decrees the dignified, almost mummified Prince, but in an alien Italian voice that sounds strange coming from the familiar gritted teeth of an iconic Burt Lancaster. Hailed as Luchino Visconti's masterpiece, this is a very personal film about the Sicilian aristocracy during a crucial period in the history of Italy (the 'Risorgimento'), but also a sumptuous, if chilly epic in which everything is shown in long- or medium-shots and strait-laced characters wander through huge, luxurious, fading rooms or discuss in the abstract the superficial political and cultural changes which il Principe trusts his own class will weather. It's a very deliberately paced three hours (the *Godfather* films take their leisurely tone from *Il Gattopardo*) and a great deal of what happens isn't exactly clear, but it has a magnificence that's undeniable.

Lancaster, grizzled but perfectly coiffeured, is the heart of the film and, it is suggested, his homeland, but Visconti's camera loves the cold beauty of il Principe's unprincipled, fit-to-survive nephew Tancredi (Delon) and, even more, the sheer presence of Claudia Cardinale. Fans of Spaghetti Westerns will find Mario Girotti (aka Terence Hill of the Trinity films) and Giuliano Gemma (of the Ringo films) in a very different mood, gussied up in handsome uniforms and propped up on the sidelines. Most of the last hour is devoted to a lavish ball, from magnificent entrances through to the final tidying-up, with the stately, sweating, fan-fluttering aristocrats on show for perhaps the last time and Lancaster joining Cardinale for an elegant dance. ★★★★ **KN**

LEPRECHAUN (1993)

Starring: *Warwick Davis (Leprechaun), Jennifer Aniston (Tory Reding), Ken Olandt (Nathan Murphy), Mark Holton (Ozzie), Robert Hy Gorman (Alex), Shay Duffin (Daniel O'Grady), John Sanderford (J.D. Reding), John Voldstad (Shop Owner)*
Director: *Mark Jones*
Screenwriter: *Mark Jones*
15/92 mins./Comedy/Horror/USA

An evil leprechaun travels from Ireland to California in search of his stolen pot of gold. After being locked in a cellar for ten years, he escapes and murders various people to get his treasure back.

The foundation of a franchise that – like the Critters, Wishmaster and Witchcraft films – has mostly bypassed theatrical release but found space on rental racks and cable television. It's in the history books as the film debut of Jennifer Aniston, who doesn't exactly show star potential as a typical dimbulb heroine who snarls dialogue like 'Nathan, that was no fucking bear!'

Warwick Davis, erstwhile Ewok and Willow, is under a rubbery make-up job, and dressed in buckled shoes and oversized hat. The mini-monster cracks wise or whimsical in a slippery Oirish accent ('try as they will, and try as they might, who steals me gold won't live through the night') as he pursues *Friday the 13th*-style characterless victims around a rural nowhere. It's fatally uncertain of its intent, veering between campy would-be comedy, with the leprechaun speeding in a kiddie car, and unpleasant sadism, as a lovable retarded man (Mark Holton) is gruesomely slashed about the face.

Writer-director Mark Jones invents his own mythology, advancing the ludicrous notion that leprechauns are as affected by four-leaf clover like vampires are by crucifixes. It's less distinctive than many similar quickies produced by Charles Band with miniature menaces (the Puppet Master films, *Demonic Toys*, *The Creeps*, etc). Jones tried the whole thing again in the unrelated *Rumpelstiltskin*, with Max Grodenchik in gnome make-up, but Davis returned in a string of follow-ups: *Leprechaun 2* (a 'Bride of Leprechaun' effort marketed in the UK as *One Wedding and Lots of Funerals*), *Leprechaun 3*, *Leprechaun 4: In Space*, *Leprechaun in the Hood* (with Ice-T and Coolio) and *Leprechaun: Back 2 Tha Hood*. ★ **KN**

LET HIM HAVE IT (1991)

Starring: *Christopher Eccleston (Derek Bentley), Tom Courtenay (William Bentley), Paul Reynolds (Chris Craig), Eileen Atkins (Lilian Bentley), Rebecca Eccleston (Iris, aged 10), Peter Eccleston (Derek, aged 8), Serena Scott Thomas (Stella)*
Director: *Peter Medak*
Screenwriters: *Neal Davis, Robert Wade*
15/115 mins./Crime/Drama/History/France/UK/Netherlands

In 1952, 19-year-old Derek Bentley and 16-year-old Chris Craig impulsively attempt to rob a warehouse. During the bungled robbery, Craig kills a policeman, but as a juvenile isn't prosecuted for murder whereas the slow-witted Bentley is hanged.

Originally set for Alex Cox, this project was taken over in pre-production by Peter Medak, who had just made *The Krays* and thus become a period crime expert. While it doesn't flounder as much as *Chicago Joe and the Showgirl* over a similar course, it does gently segue from overfamiliar reminiscence of times past – ration books, swing records, sharp hats, obsolete slang, *Blue Lamp*-style coppers – into an excruciatingly protracted final reel.

Part of the problem is that the points the film wants to make are so strong – the brisk, businesslike recreation of a 'humane' hanging at the end is shattering – that they really don't need to be underlined as heavily as they are.

From the outset, the shy and subnormal Derek is an embattled innocent whose family deserve sainthood, while his pal Craig is a junior Cagney whose background or psychology barely gets a look-in.

At the trial, Bentley's ambiguous statement 'let him have it' was taken as evidence that he encouraged the shooting of a policeman, though the defence claimed he was trying to convince Craig to surrender his gun. By the time the verdict comes in, the film has stacked the decks so heavily that you start to feel that something must have been left out or tidied up to make such a neat point. While a large and excellent cast – from Tom Courtenay and Eileen Atkins as the Bentley parents down to a tiny performance from Clive Revill as the hangman – do their best, they can't stop the film from seeming wildly overdone for its slender rewards. ★★ **KN**

LETHAL WEAPON (1987)

Starring: *Mel Gibson (Martin Riggs), Danny Glover (Roger Murtaugh), Gary Busey (Mr. Joshua), Mitch Ryan (General Peter McAllister)*
Director: *Richard Donner*
Screenwriter: *Shane Black*
18/112 mins./Action/Comedy/Crime/USA

Martin Riggs is crazy. He's also a police sergeant whose suicidal tendencies and disregard for life make him the ideal partner for easy going (by the book) cop Roger Murtaugh. Close to retirement, Murtaugh wants an easy life, but Riggs has other, more life-threatening, drug-ring busting ideas.

On the evidence of 80s movies, it seems the LAPD has found it impossible to partner just two like-minded cops. Every pairing adheres to the cliché that opposites (eventually) attract. And so it is with Murtaugh – the archetypal middle-class black boy-made-good cop who is looking forward to retirement and the obligatory seafaring yacht that that entails – and Riggs – who lost his wife in a car crash and is a certifiable psycho, shooting first and thinking much, much later.

Tagline
Two cops. Glover carries a weapon. Gibson is one.

The cross-generational, cross-cultural jokes work well, and it's hard not to feel for the convincingly geriatric Danny Glover. Gibson, too, wins us over in a tour de force of twitches, sniffs and trigger-happy enthusiasm.

While the script is sharp and the stunts are first class, the formula can't fail. The only question is, how many sequels can they extract from it? ★★★★ **AC**

③ LETHAL WEAPON 2 (1989)

Starring: *Mel Gibson (Martin Riggs), Danny Glover (Roger Murtaugh), Joe Pesci (Leo Getz), Joss Ackland (Arjen 'Aryan' Rudd), Patsy Kensit (Rika van den Haas)*
Director: *Richard Donner*
Screenwriter: *Jeffrey Boam, from a story by Shane Black, Warren Murphy, based on characters by Black*
18/112 mins./Action/Comedy/Crime/USA

The cop duo are on the trail of South African diplomats who are using their immunity to engage in criminal activities.

In America, *Licence to Kill* was unfortunate enough to open after *Lethal Weapon 2*, which knocked it right out of the water, Timothy Dalton's James Bond seeming cold and humourless next to the warm-blooded buddyhood of cops Mel Gibson and Danny Glover. They laugh, they cry, they are both near death several times, but we know these partners will never die; they're invulnerable. Murder and mayhem surround them, but it's stylised cartoon violence, Roadrunner-style.

Many viewers not seduced by Gibson and Glover's charms may find the jacked-up gleeful mayhem hard to tolerate; several critics have raised the spectre of the effects of these ultra-nasty movies on the general populace, but surely most moviegoers know the difference between gritty realism and stylised Hollywood action.

British-born director Richard Donner (of *Superman* fame) sets the tone from the first frame, jumping right into a raucous high-speed car chase that knocks the wind out of you. And he never lets up: the audience knows that every lull predicts another sequence of full-tilt excitement. Scripter Jeffrey Boam (who also wrote *Indiana Jones And The Last Crusade*) manages to keep the plot twisting and the audience on the edge of its seat, while at the same time deepening the two characters – we actually care what happens to these guys.

While the underrated Glover really helped carry the original picture, this time Gibson is given much more to do, and he delivers: he's funny, makes credible love to a fetching Patsy Kensit, deepens his friendship with Glover, and fills in some of the details of his past. The movie's villains are Hollywood's closest answer to contemporary fascists: South African functionaries using diplomatic immunity as a cover for serious drug running. The filmmakers give character actor Joe Pesci enough screen-time to create a money-laundering snitch under Gibson/Glover's guard who is both hilariously irritating and loveable. ★★★★ **AT**

③ LETHAL WEAPON 3 (1992)

Starring: *Mel Gibson (Martin Riggs), Danny Glover (Roger Murtaugh), Joe Pesci (Leo Getz), Rene Russo (Lorna Cole), Stuart Wilson (Jack Travis)*
Director: *Richard Donner*
Screenwriters: *Jeffrey Boam, Robert Mark Kamen, from a story by Boam and charcters by Shane Black*
15/115 mins./Action/Comedy/Crime/USA

Worn-down cop Murtaugh is counting down the days till he hangs up his badge, but he and madcap partner Riggs stumble across an arms racket run by ruthless ex-cop Jack Travis, who is providing LA street gangs with special cop-killer bullets.

Lethal Weapon 3 seems to be the perfect example of a successful formula film sequel, with each film in the *Lethal Weapon* saga making more money than the last, and boasting more explosions, more action, and – of course – more wisecracking Mel Gibson.

This, the somewhat plotless follow-up to 1989's *Lethal Weapon 2*, has Roger Murtaugh counting the days to his retirement, but, as ever, being dragged into various capers by his more reckless partner Riggs, leading to a literally explosive beginning that gets the pair demoted back on the beat (yes, Mel in uniform). It's not long before the pair are hot on the trail of some bad guys, however, and this time the baddies in question are dealing illegal arms with special armour-piercing, cop-killing bullets.

Throw in tough karate-kicking female sergeant Lorna Cole to team up with Riggs and Murtaugh – giving Riggs someone else to joke with and a love interest rolled into one – some explosions, expertly directed chase scenes, one-liners and a brief appearance by Leo Getz (the wonderful Pesci) for good measure, and what you get is a fun, if rather pointless continuation of the Gibson & Glover stand-up routine.

The movie's problem lies not in the performances – Gibson, Glover, Pesci and Russo are all excellent – but in the shallowness of the story, most noticeable when Pesci's character turns up for no reason at all.

Still, if you like fast food movies that you digest and then 10 minutes later forget what you had – or if a simple evening's entertainment is what you're after, this will certainly do the trick. ★★★ **JB**

③ LETHAL WEAPON 4 (1998)

Starring: *Mel Gibson (Martin Riggs), Danny Glover (Roger Murtaugh), Joe Pesci (Leo Getz), Rene Russo (Lorna Cole), Chris Rock (Lee Butters), Jet Li (Wah Sing Ku)*
Director: *Richard Donner*
Screenwriter: *Channing Gibson, based on a story by Jonathan Lemkin, Alfred Gough, Miles Millar, from characters by Shane Black*
15/120 mins./Action/Comedy/Crime/USA

Gibson and Glover are back as LA cop-couple Riggs and Murtaugh attempting to break a Chinese immigrant-smuggling ring.

Like the *Die Hard* franchise, *Lethal Weapon* demonstrates the law of escalating returns: each subsequent instalment has grossed more than the previous (Part *3* pulled in $300 million; *2* did around $220 million). Ergo, they'd be insane not to give it another whack.

If *4* has anything going for it, it's continuity. Gibson and Glover are back as LA cop-couple Riggs (reckless) and Murtaugh (careful), herein promoted to captains in order to keep them off the streets. Rene Russo returns as Riggs's squeeze Lorna (whose karate-kicking antics are cruelly reduced to waddling and doughnuts as she's now nine months pregnant), as does Pesci as Leo, whose squawking stooge role – essential to *2* and *3* – is expanded to private eye ('private eyesore,' cracks Riggs). Murtaugh's entire family is cast consistently with all three films, and the music is – yet again – by Michael Kamen, Eric Clapton and David Sanbourn. So far, so Lethal. In fact, watching Part *4* is more like switching on a favourite TV series than going to the pictures. All it lacks is a few commercial breaks. Disappointingly, it's also the worst: not bad, just not as good.

The series appears to be having a mid-life crisis ('We're not getting too old for this shit!' Riggs chants, doubtfully). While an honest development – commensurate with a long-running TV show's fourth season – the sore joints leave Murtaugh and Riggs reliant on verbal sparring rather than physical. Gibson and Glover's schtick is very entertaining, a relationship borne of experience, but they suddenly seem one step away from a pan-racial Matthau and Lemmon.

New blood, provided by Chris Rock as Murtaugh's new detective son-in-law and Jet Li, the now-obligatory Chinese action star, as a resilient Triad hitman, is welcome, but not sufficient to dispel the sinking feeling that we are gathered to watch the last in a once unmissable series. ★★★ **AS**

⓪ LETTER FROM AN UNKNOWN WOMAN (1948)

Starring: *Joan Fontaine (Lisa Berndle), Louis Jordan (Stefan Brand), Mady Christians (Frau Berndle), Marcel Journet (Johann Stauffer), John Good (Lt. Leopold von Kaltnegger), Leo B. Pessin (Stefan Jr.)*
Director: *Max Ophüls*
Screenwriter: *Howard Koch, based on the novel* Brief Einer Unbekannten *by Stefan Zweig*
U/86 mins./Drama/USA

On her deathbed in late-19th-century Vienna, Lisa Berndle writes to concert pianist Stefan Brand to remind him of the romance that has slipped his mind, yet which has prompted the duel he is to fight the following morning with her husband, Johann Stauffer.

No one would hire war emigré Max Ophüls during his first four years in Hollywood and when he was finally engaged for *Vendetta*, he was fired by envious producer, Howard Hughes. Consequently, he accepted the wholly unsuitable Restoration swashbuckler, *The Exile*, and made such a rousing job of it that John Houseman was persuaded to offer him this adaptation of Stefan Zweig's 1922 novella.

Collaborating with *Casablanca* (1942) co-scribe Howard Koch, Ophüls softened the storyline, so that rather than becoming a courtesan, Lisa marries a kindly older suitor, who mistakenly believes that she has again bedded the father of her lost child and, thus, demands satisfaction. However, the biggest alteration came during the denouement, as rather than being moved but unreminded by Lisa's letter, Stefan accepts the duel from a sense of purity and honour instead of sordid duty.

Reunited with Franz Planer, who had photographed *Liebelei*, Ophüls proceeded to execute a typically brilliant series of fluid camera moves, which took the viewer into the heart of the action. But he also made effective use of pan shots to follow the characters in a less intrusive manner and to locate them more significantly within Alexander Golitzen's majestic recreation of old Vienna's opera house, fairground, fashionable haunts and cosily cluttered domiciles. Indeed, it's tempting to see the influence of such fellow exiles as Ernst Lubitsch and Josef von Sternberg on Ophüls's elegant compositions, which would become ever-more impossibly exquisite after he returned to Europe.

Ophüls also coaxed a superb performance out of Joan Fontaine, who both draws on and plays against the waif-like innocence she exhibited in Alfred Hitchcock's *Rebecca* and *Suspicion*. Louis Jourdan also cuts a dash as the feckless musician who finds redemption in sacrifice.

But it's Ophüls's restraint and taste that make this so memorable. However, it was dismissed as lightweight schmaltz on its initial release and was only reappraised when Ophüls was hailed as an auteur during the 1950s. ★★★★ **DP**

⓪ LICENCE TO KILL (1989)

Starring: *Timothy Dalton (James Bond), Carey Lowell (Pam Bouvier), Robert Davi (Franz Sanchez), Talisa Soto (Lupe Lamora), Anthony Zerbe (Milton Krest)*
Director: *John Glen*
Screenwriters: *Michael G. Wilson, Richard Maibaum, based on characters by Ian Fleming*
15/126 mins./Action/Crime/Thriller/USA

James Bond, ignoring the pleas of M, Q, and every other letter at Her Majesty's Secret Service, seeks out greasy tyrant Franz Sanchez after he feeds Bond's mate to some killer sharks.

In the closing credits, betwixt cast and gaffers, we are cautioned: 'As tobacco products are used in this film, the producers wish to remind the audience of the Surgeon General's Warning: Smoking causes lung cancer, heart disease, emphysema and may complicate pregnancy.' Oh, dear, the fussbudget times we live in. Strangely, the producers do not see fit to add that falling out of aeroplanes, driving juggernauts over cliffs, swimming with killer sharks and shooting guns are quite dangerous pursuits, too. The 'snout' warning serves notice, however, that James Bond has been brought 'up to date' and the 60s fantasy figure – with his amoral, cynical approach to women and human life – has been remodelled to fit the caring, sharing 90s (or 1989, anyway). Even the villains have been watered down. No Jaws, no gloriously mad Gert Frobe as Goldfinger, no loony Donald Pleasence, just Robert Davi as Sanchez. If he didn't have an iguana on his shoulder and a very bad complexion, there would be nothing much to tell us that Sanchez is an evil person at all: compared with the villains of old, Sanchez is, well, quite normal and not a proper sadist. When he feeds Bond's old chum Felix to the sharks, Felix lives to tell the tale, and when he depressurises a turncoat, he doesn't even pull a wicked grin as his friend explodes. Useless, really.

Some of the 'style' of the 007 of old does, however, remain: there are corny, retrograde opening credits, there's the inevitable underwater frogman sequence ('directed and photographed by Ramon Bravo' – bravo!) where it's impossible to follow what on earth is going on and, of course, there's amiable secret service boffin Q (Desmond Llewelyn) who has, this time, invented some killer toothpaste (how, though, are you supposed to persuade an enemy to brush his teeth when you're attempting to do him in?). And there is Timothy Dalton who is really quite hopeless. Where Sean Connery was gruff, sardonic and oversexed and Roger Moore was sort of a ridiculous hoot, Dalton treats Bond as a serious acting role – Hamlet with a hand gun. He looks abashed delivering the J. Bond-styled one-liner chucklers – 'Looks like he came to a dead end,' he says stumbling upon a dead body. What a creep – embarrassed kissing the girls and thoroughly out of sorts when it comes to being violent with knife or gun. Dalton's last hurrah as Bond has strong moments, but it was about time for a change. ★★ **TH**

⓪ LIEBESTRAUM (1991)

Starring: *Kevin Anderson (Nick Kaminsky), Pamela Gidley (Jane Kessler), Kim Novak (Lillian Anderson Munnsen), Graham Beckel (Sheriff Pete Ricker)*
Director: *Mike Figgis*
Screenwriter: *Mike Figgis*
18/112 mins./Mystery/Thriller/USA

Architect Nick Kaminsky visits the dying mother who gave him up for adoption, and falls in with an old friend who is supervising the demolition of a long-abandoned department store. Nick is drawn to his friend's wife, and finds himself re-enacting a forty-year-old love triangle which ended in murder.

After making a flashy mid-Atlantic British crime flick (*Stormy Monday*) and an almost conventional Hollywood debut (*Internal Affairs*), British director Mike Figgis started seesawing between commercial (*Cold Creek Manor*) and bizarre (*The Loss of Sexual Innocence*) projects with this relentlessly drab and perverse mystery. Though obviously in the shadow of David Lynch, it's Figgis's first really interesting film and made a tentative step into darknesses he has subsequently explored with *Leaving Las Vegas* and *Timeline*. Kevin Anderson, an unfortunately bland central character, is drawn to the bedside of his dying mother (Kim Novak is cast, of course, for her Hitchcock associations) in a small town so strange it makes Twin Peaks seem like Ambridge. Creepy, unsettling scenes follow each other with little logic while characters sit back in the darkness and let things happen to them. It has as much rain and shadow as any melodrama of the 1940s and manages to be genuinely disturbing, though the lack of much in the way of an actual solution makes the puzzling last reels less satisfying than the mystifying opening.

Fictional Books in Movies — TOP 10

1. Swedish Maid Penis Enlarger Pumps And Me: This Sort of Thing Is My Bag, Baby, by Austin Powers (*Austin Powers: International Man of Mystery*)
2. Pinsky! Aka Women I would Like To Pork (*Throw Mama From The Train*)
3. Magical Me by Gilderoy Lockhart (*Harry Potter and the Chamber of Secrets*)
4. The Ravagers, The Return of Angelina and Romancing The Stone, all by Joan Wilder (*Romancing the Stone*)
5. The Hermann Goering Workout Book, by Hermann Goering (*Top Secret*)
6. Bare Ruined Choirs, by Barton Fink (*Barton Fink*)
7. A Match Made In Space, by George McFly (*Back to the Future*)
8. Misery's Return, by Paul Sheldon (*Misery*)
9. The Mystery of the Plantagenet Parakeet, by Andrew Wyke (*Sleuth*)
10. The Joy Of Impotence, by Dr Max J. Eggelhofer (*The Front Page*)

Nevertheless, it has a great many strong scenes and characters: a hair-raising nighttime drive with a drunken Sheriff (Graham Beckel), Bill Pullman acting ominously in one of his occasional detours into the sinister, a weirdly erotic performance from the severely-hairstyled Pamela Gidley (who deserved a much bigger career) and one remarkable sequence in which a long-shuttered 1930s department store is invaded like a tawdry art deco version of the mummy's tomb. ★★★ **KN**

ⓘ THE LIFE AND DEATH OF COLONEL BLIMP (1943)

Starring: *Roger Livesey (Clive Wynne-Candy), Deborah Kerr (Edith Hunter/Barbara Wynne/Johnny Cannon), Anton Walbrook (Theo Kretschmar-Schuldorff), Roland Culver (Col. Betteridge)*
Directors: *Michael Powell, Emeric Pressburger*
Screenwriters: *Michael Powell, Emeric Pressburger*
U/163 mins./Drama/War/UK

In WWII, Home Guard General Clive Wynne-Candy is humiliated by a young officer in an exercise, and remembers his career in the services. In Berlin during the Boer War, a duel for the honour of Britain leads him to make a lifelong friend of his 'enemy' Theo Kretschmar-Schuldorff.

Perhaps the greatest film ever made in Britain.

Michael Powell and Emeric Pressburger (who wrote, produced and directed) begin with a swing-scored sequence which shows brash, energetic, ruthless 1940s youth besting a complacent, blustering, comical relic of an earlier age ('war starts at midnight'), then takes extended flashbacks to show how a raffish young officer of the 1890s has turned into the living caricature of 1943.

The film was controversial because Prime Minister Winston Churchill took against the Blimp image of the British senior staff (Colonel Blimp was a cartoon character) and tried to hinder production. Now, it looks like an exquisite summation of the strengths as well as of the failings of the national character.

It also shows an uncommonly British sense of fair play, in the middle of a world war, to present a humane, sympathetic, anti-Nazi German not only as the hero's best friend but winning the girl (achingly lovely Deborah Kerr).

Over the course of three wars, Clive Candy's ideals take a battering from reality, and there's an undertone of sadness to his sacrifice of personal happiness on an altar of duty and decency. For all its intellectual content, this remains dazzling, delightful cinema: George Perinal's Technicolor photography is gorgeous, Powell and Pressburger's techniques startlingly modern (after elaborate preparations for the duel, the camera discreetly withdraws from the gymnasium for the fight itself), the dialogue an endless delight and the subtle, sad, heroic performances of Roger Livesey and Anton Walbrook fresher with every viewing. ★★★★★ **KN**

ⓘ THE LIFE AQUATIC ... WITH STEVE ZISSOU (2004)

Starring: *Bill Murray (Steve Zissou), Owen Wilson (Ned Plimpton), Cate Blanchett (Jane Winslett-Richardson), Anjelica Huston (Eleanor Zissou), Willem Dafoe (Klaus Daimler), Jeff Goldblum (Alistair Hennessey), Michael Gambon (Oseary Drakoulias), Noah Taylor (Vladimir Wolodarsky)*
Director: *Wes Anderson*
Screenwriters: *Wes Anderson, Noah Baumbach*
15/119 mins./Adventure/Comedy/Drama/USA

Having recently lost his closest friend to the jaws of a strange sea predator, oceanic adventurer-cum-filmmaker Steve Zissou sets out to find and kill the beast he's dubbed the 'jaguar shark'. Along the way, though, he has to deal with a prim Brit journalist, a man claiming to be his son, and impending financial ruin.

Just in case you hadn't noticed, that Wes Anderson's a bit of a quirkaholic. In the excellent *Rushmore*, we had the bizarrely violent school stage productions of The Max Fischer Players. Then, in *The Royal Tenenbaums*, there was the unnecessary but inspired inclusion of dalmatian mice scampering around the edges of all those elaborately dysfunctional family dramas. Anderson's dives into leftfield have always suggested self-indulgence, but have been well-executed enough to appeal rather than irritate – especially when beneath the artifice there's always throbbed a welcome ache of pathos, borne out by lovingly sketched characters.

Anderson's third flick is clearly closer to his heart than any of his previous movies, and features all his trademarks in garish Technicolor. His recognition of the comedic value of uniform – from *Bottle Rocket*'s boiler suits to *Tenenbaum*'s tight red tracksuits – here results in the hilarious 'Team Zissou' get-up: pastel-blue shirts, bright crimson woolly hats, Glock strapped to right thigh. His slavish attention to music results in an interesting mix of laidback acoustic cover versions and deliberately dated, analogue-electro flurries. His predilection for made-up animals like those spotty Tenenbaum rodents is realised via Henry Selick's exotic stop-motion sea-fauna creations. Plus, of course, his fascination with Jacques Cousteau, so apparent in *Rushmore* (a quote from the celebrated French sub-aquatic explorer is what spurs Max to campaign for a school aquarium), is elevated in this movie to raison d'être.

The Life Aquatic presents a parallel reality which straddles our world and another trapped in the late 60s, when Cousteau's international popularity was at its height. The technology invented and employed by Team Zissou is supposed to be cutting-edge, yet it displays a retro chunkiness which recalls early Bonds. Zissou's own movies, segmenting his various quests into hokily-titled chapters, feel like they were made decades ago; in fact, they're very deliberately reminiscent of TV series *The Undersea World Of Jacques Cousteau*, which charted the real diver's adventures.

Zissou, of course, isn't a real diver, and Anderson plays up the concept that, as Zissou's critics suspect, he might be a fraud, even possibly faking his friend's death to manufacture publicity for his latest quest – in search of a creature that doesn't even exist. The lines blur between the 'real' world as presented in Anderson's movie, and the 'fake' world shot by Zissou's crew within Anderson's movie. In one superb sequence, we're taken on a tour of Steve's ship *The Belafonte*, but rather than show it as a Steadicam whirl through hatches and cabins, we follow the characters as they walk around a very obvious cross-section set. Plus, of course, there's all those stop-motion critters, which, in this age of crisp CGI, can't look anywhere near realistic. The schtick being: how can Zissou be a fake if the entire world he inhabits is equally artificial?

Unfortunately, for all its comic, aesthetic astuteness, there's something very important missing from Anderson's latest that's always been there before: heart. There's a half-arsed attempt to jimmy in some romance between Blanchett's journo and Wilson's amiable Ned, while Ned's maybe-father/maybe-son relationship with Steve fails to stir up any feeling and climaxes with something of a dramatic gaffe. The artificiality encouraged by the helmer proves overwhelming, with the story's more serious elements either looking horribly out of place (such as when the Zissou ship is boarded by violent Indonesian pirates) or becoming so sapped of emotion they sink to the level of a cheap afternoon soap.

Even the ever-reliable Murray struggles. He's no doubt happy to be indulging Anderson, but all the while is seemingly unconvinced that Zissou could ever be a bona-fide, oxygen-inhaling human being. Consequently, neither are we. Yes, the wetsuits are snazzy, but when you tear into them like Steve's mythical jaguar shark, you won't find much meat within. **★★★★ SO'H**

⊙ LIFE IS BEAUTIFUL (LA VITA E BELLA) (1997)

Starring: *Roberto Benigni (Guido Orefice), Nicoletta Braschi (Dora), Giustino Durano (Eliseo Orefice), Lidia Alfonsi (Guicciardini), Sergio Bini Bustric (Ferruccio Papini)*
Director: *Roberto Benigni*
Screenwriters: *Vincenzo Cerami, Roberto Benigni*
PG/111 mins./Comedy/Romance/War/Italy
Awards: *Academy Awards – Best Actor, Best Foreign Language Film, Best Original Score, BAFTA – Best Actor*

A Jewish man has a wonderful romance with the help of his humour, but must use that same quality to protect his son in a Nazi death camp.

It's understandable that *Life Is Beautiful* attracted its fair share of controversy, publicity and opposition. After all, the nightmare of a Nazi concentration camp is hardly the stuff of high comedy. So it's all credit to Benigni that not only has he found some laughs but has crafted a genuinely remarkable film as powerful, moving, and capable of indelibly etching itself on the brain as *Schindler's List*.

The unnamed camp doesn't appear until the second half, leaving the first hour free to showcase the amazing physical comedy which has made Benigni a household name in his Italian homeland. Here, as Jewish waiter Guido, he divides his time between getting into scrapes with Fascists (as evinced in the dazzling opening sequence) and making fanciful attempts to woo teacher Dora (Braschi, Benigni's real-life missus).

Fast forward a few years and the couple, now married with a young son, are carted off to camp where, to shield the appalling reality from his child, Guido explains their new circumstances by saying they have joined a game to win a giant army tank.

It's all too easy to assume that Benigni has made a mockery of one of history's biggest tragedies. Yet *Life Is Beautiful* transcends such a quibble with its sheer inventiveness and energy, its emphasis placed firmly on the beautifully staged romance between Guido and Dora. Far from a heavy political tract, this is a bittersweet love story set against a turbulent backdrop, where true horrors are merely hinted at, as if trying to maintain the viewer's innocence as much as that of the impossibly cute child. **★★★★ CW**

⊙ LIFE IS SWEET (1990)

Starring: *Alison Steadman (Wendy), Jim Broadbent (Andy), Claire Skinner (Natalie), Jane Horrocks (Nicola), Stephen Rea (Patsy), Timothy Spall (Aubrey), David Thewlis (Nicola's lover)*
Director: *Mike Leigh*
Screenwriter: *Mike Leigh*
15/98 mins./Comedy/UK

The conflicts of a suburban family in an orbital town are played out as the twenty-something twins of a middle-aged couple push their parents to boiling point.

Wendy and Andy have twin daughters, named Natalie and Nicola. Natalie is not possessed of the most sparkling personality but she has all the down-to-earth qualities one would expect from a plumber. Nicola, by contrast, is unemployed, aggressive – and a complete pain in the butt. Their mother, for her sins, works part-time in a children's wear shop and takes children's dancing lessons on Saturday mornings. Her husband, a gullible sort, hates his job as a chef in a large company and longs to work for himself, which makes him an easy target for a devious drinking partner who persuades him to buy a clapped out mobile snack bar.

So the story unfolds. What follows is a mildly humorous attempt to tell an everyday tale of suburban folk with whom we are supposed to sympathise as they nag each other at every available opportunity. Mike Leigh's film lacks the razor sharp wit of his 1977 comedy *Abigail's Party*, although he hasn't lost his ability to find pathos in the most innocuous situations.

Despite a mediocre script, Alison Steadman puts in a sterling performance as the supporting wife and mother, and Jane Horrocks really steals the show as the highly strung, anorexic twin who twitches and fidgets her way throughout the mundane proceedings amidst a cloud of cigarette fumes. Her perverse sexual appetite, which involves a liberal dose of chocolate spread and a certain amount of bondage, will either make you laugh or squirm with embarrassment. Alternatively, it could have you reaching for a jar of peanut butter. **★★★ DN**

⊙ A LIFE LESS ORDINARY (1997)

Starring: *Ewan McGregor (Robert Lewis), Cameron Diaz (Celine Naville), Holly Hunter (O'Reilly), Delroy Lindo (Jackson), Dan Hedaya (Gabriel)*
Director: *Danny Boyle*
Screenwriter: *John Hodge*
15/99 mins./Drama/Romance/Crime/Fantasy/USA/UK
Awards: *Empire Awards – Best Actor*

A cleaning man in LA takes his boss's daughter hostage after being fired and replaced by a robot but finds she's far from the helpless rich girl he expected.

A *Life Less Ordinary* does have plenty going for it, scalpel-sharp direction, nicely judged performances, a believable chemistry between the leads. But crucially the spark, the sheer thrill and enthusiasm that ignited its predecessors, is noticeably absent. Even taken on its own terms, this makes for a lesser overall experience. In fact, it's apparent right from the curiously subdued outset (depicting a Capra-esque vision of the afterlife: a 60s police station decked out in dazzling white) that this is going to be a comfortable, rather than adrenaline-fuelled watch.

Having faced the charge from on-high that the world is caught in a plight of too much divorce and sorrow, and that true love these days frankly is just false, a pair of angels are despatched to earth by their celestial boss Angel Gabriel. They are given one chance to make good and bring love where it is least expected. If they fail, heaven won't have them back. The mismatched twosome they have to unite are Robert, a layabout Scots cleaner who has just been laid off in favour of a robot, dumped by his girlfriend and summarily evicted from his home, and Celine, his former boss's super-rich, spoilt daughter, who shoots apples off people's heads for fun.

In a last-ditch effort to get his own back on said former employer (a scenery-chewing Ian Holm), Robert – more by luck than judgement – kidnaps Celine, and the pair head cross-country. With the angels, now posing as hitmen, in hot pursuit, they proceed along the way botching bank robberies, bickering incessantly and, inevitably, falling for each other. As the action unfolds, the overall impression is that Boyle sets out to make a frothy, feel-good romantic yarn, something a little different from the trio's previous output, only to remember that heavy artillery, comical yet menacing bad guys and at least one moment of eye-watering agony (the faint of heart may care to avert their gaze during Ewan's moment in the dentist's chair) would add that all-important 'cool' edge and spice things up enormously.

The result is a surfeit of ideas which have great potential but little fruition, leaving the viewer a tad confused as to the true nature of the picture and in anticipation of a big twist that never comes. Your hat has to be taken off though, to the leads, McGregor doing hapless with ease to create his most sympathetic character to date, and Diaz the closest thing to luminous in the whole movie, who hold the film together during its slow patches, and are always watchable.

But in spite of its flaws, a handful of the scenes (McGregor's many failed attempts to make a threatening ransom demand being one of them) are spot-on in their combination of skewed humour and originality, and work just well enough to hold the attention throughout. ★★★ **CW**

THE LIFE OF EMILE ZOLA (1937)

Starring: *Paul Muni (Emile Zola), Gale Sondergaard (Lucie Dreyfus), Joseph Schildkraut (Capt. Albert Dreyfus), Gloria Holden (Alexandrine Zola)*
Director: *William Dieterle*
Screenwriters: *Norman Reilly Raine, Heinz Herald, Geza Herczeg based on the story by Heinz Herald and Geza Herczeg*
No certificate/123 mins./Drama/USA
Awards: *Academy Awards – Best Picture, Best Supporting Actor (Joseph Schildkraut), Best Screenplay (Norman Reilly Raine, Heinz Herald, Geza Herczeg)*

When army captain Alfred Dreyfus is accused of treason, novelist Emile Zola writes the courageous pamphlet 'J'Accuse' in his defence and risks the wrath of the military brass to expose the real culprit, Major Walsin-Esterhazy.

William Dieterle was Hollywood's master biographer. In addition to this life of the crusading French novelist, he also directed Paul Muni in *The Story of Louis Pasteur* and *Juarez*, as well as Edward G. Robinson in *Dr Erlich's Magic Bullet* and *A Dispatch from Reuters*. He was anything but a stickler for historical accuracy. But his evocation of a particular time and place was exemplary, while he always managed to capture the passion that drove his subject invariably to triumph over considerable odds.

Muni, on the other hand, was the prototype Method actor. He read Zola's complete works, researched the entire Dreyfus Affair and experimented with various make-up designs (with the peerless make-up artist Perc Westmore) before finding a look that best conveyed the writer's physique and psyche.

He was highly fortunate to land the role, however, as playwrights Heinz Herald and Geza Herczeg had originally brought the project to Ernst Lubitsch at Paramount and only his sense of artistic fair play had prompted him to sell it on to Warners, as he knew Muni was the only actor in Hollywood capable of essaying such a complex character. His perfectionism rubbed off on the rest of the cast and crew – who gave him a standing ovation after he pushed himself through repeated single takes of the famous six-minute trial speech. However, Muni was overlooked by the Academy, whose members curiously preferred Spencer Tracy's mannered turn in *Captains Courageous*.

Joseph Schildkraut did win Best Supporting Actor, though, for his moving portrayal of Dreyfus, whose Judaism is never openly referred to throughout the picture, although it is clearly implied – along with a condemnation of the Nazi treatment of the Jews in the exiled Dieterle's homeland.

The film was a considerable commercial success, unlike José Ferrer's redundant *I Accuse*, which boasted a Gore Vidal script and the director hamming it up as Dreyfus opposite Emlyn Williams's Zola. ★★★★ **DP**

THE LIFE OF OHARU (1952)

Starring: *Kinuyp Tanaka (Oharu), Tsukie Matsuura (Tomo), Ichiro Sugai (Shinzaemon), Toshiro Mifune (Katsunosuke), Toshiaki Konoe (Lord Harutaka Matsudaira)*
Director: *Kenji Mizoguchi*
Screenwriter: *Kenji Mizoguchi, Yoshikata Yoda, based on the novel* Koshuku Ichidai Onna *by Saikaku Ihara*
PG/148 mins./Drama/Japan
Awards: *Venice Film Festival – Silver Lion*

When her romance with lowly born Katsunosuke brings shame on her samurai father, Oharu becomes a concubine, a mother, a courtesan, a maid, a widow and a prostitute, as she's buffeted by the conventions and prejudices prevalent in Japan during the Tokugawa shogunate.

In 1950, after a five-year struggle, Kenji Mizoguchi quit Shochiku Studios for refusing to finance his proposed adaptation of Saikaku Ihara's 1686 picaresque novel, *Life of an Amorous Woman*. By the time he finally got to make it – allegedly as a riled response to the West's vaunting of Akira Kurosawa's *Rashomon* – he had completed three more studies of the subjugation of Japanese women, *A Picture of Madame Yuki*, *Miss Oyu* and *Lady Musashino*. Consistently reflecting his admiration for the sister who had raised him, these films demonstrated a unique insight into the female psyche and an unflinching appreciation of society's chauvinism.

Shot in a bombed-out park, where the schedule was dictated by the passing of trains, this is a remarkable blend of realism and melodrama, castigation and compassion. Oharu's endless round of disappointments, betrayals and abuses are flecked with moments of fleeting happiness to make her empathetic rather than pitiable and her strength and durability are subtly conveyed by the excellent Kinuyo Tanaka. But, the power of her performance also owes much to Mizoguchi's affecting camerawork, which uses long takes and long shots to keep a discreet distance from Oharu's sufferings, while also following the action to suggest a commiseration with her plight.

However, this isn't just a chronicle of female misfortune. Mizoguchi also exposes the carelessness and cruelty of the men in Oharu's life as a means of exploring the national character that brought about the militarist era that culminated in the Second World War. Thus, by using the conventions of the jidai-geki (or historical drama), he was able to denounce the patriarchal arrogance that saw Oharu sold into prostitution by her father, Shinzaemon (Ichiro Sugai), and exploited by the men who pester her at both the Shimabara house and the Buddhist convent.

The product of obsessive perfectionism (with the countless retakes driving the budget up to an unprecedented 46 million yen), the film did poor business in Japan. However, it helped secure Mizoguchi an international reputation when it shared the Silver Lion at Venice with John Ford's *The Quiet Man*. ★★★★★ **DP**

◎ LIFEBOAT (1944)

Starring: *Tallulah Bankhead (Connie Porter), William Bendix (Gus), Walter Slezak (The German), Mary Anderson (Alice), John Hodiak (Kovac), Henry Hull (Rittenhouse), Heather Angel (Mrs. Higgins), Hume Cronyn (Stanley Garrett)*
Director: *Alfred Hitchcock*
Screenwriter: *Jo Swerling, based on the story by John Steinbeck*
PG/96 mins./Drama/USA

When a merchant ship is torpedoed, survivors discover they are sharing their lifeboat with the captain of the U-boat which sank them. The group endure hardships and the Nazi plots to rendezvous with a German supply ship.

This 1944 picture is one of Alfred Hitchcock's 'experiments', an exercise in making a film on a single set (albeit a boat in the middle of a vast ocean). Taken from a screen treatment by John Steinbeck, it's a peculiar Allied propaganda movie – criticised at the time because its Nazi villain seems the strongest, most resourceful character among squabbling Brits and Americans – which lumps together a disaster movie-style cross-section of humanity and puts the screws on them.

Besides the Schubert-singing, water-hoarding, sneaky kraut (disturbingly battered and drowned by the angry survivors when the sweat on his brow reveals he's got a secret water stash), the boat contains an initially elegant columnist (Tallulah Bankhead) who prefers a mink coat to a lifejacket and calls everyone 'darling', a resentful stoker (John Hodiak) who spouts the communist party line, a cigar-chomping business tycoon (Henry Hull) who doggily admires the German, a jitterbug champion sailor (William Bendix) whose gangrenous leg has to be amputated and who goes mad from drinking salt water, a black ex-pickpocket steward (Canada Lee) who gets a different 'endearing' nickname from each passenger (Bankhead calls him 'Charcoal') and is surprised when Yankee Democrats in the boat give him a vote as to whether they should kill the German, a timid radio operator (Hume Cronyn) and a nurse (Merry Anderson) who canoodle in the bows, and a grief-stricken mother (Heather Angel) who throws herself over the side after her baby drowns. Hitch makes his cameo in a before-and-after weight loss ad seen in a soggy newspaper. Technically interesting, but also a strong, soapy melodrama. ★★★★ **KN**

◎ LIMBO (1999)

Starring: *Mary Elizabeth Mastrantonio (Donna De Angelo), David Strathairn (Jumpin' Joe Gastineau), Herminio Ramos (Ricky), Kris Kristofferson ('Smilin' Jack Johannson)*
Director: *John Sayles*
Screenwriter: *John Sayles*
15/121 mins./Drama/USA

Unconventional narrative about the interactions of a group of people in a small town in Alaska, each of whom guards a secret.

You know where you stand with John Sayles: watertight scriptwriting, real emphasis on character, vivid localities and a nonchalant ease in delivering smart stories without fuss. The man is like a top-of-the-range Volvo: reliablity with air conditioning and electric windows. Until now, that is – shockingly, *Limbo* is his first vehicle to stall in the driveway.

A strangely unengaging drama, the film is built around broken people reestablishing their lives in a forgotten corner of Alaska, before dramatic contrivance forces them into the titular state of purgatory. There's no doubting the solidness of the performances. David Strathairn does his polished internalised-bloke routine as the washed-up fisherman Joe Gastineau. Mary Elizabeth Mastrantonio beautifully delivers herself back from her own state of career limbo, as hopeless-at-relationships crooner Donna De Angelo, who is dragging her diffident daughter Noelle from pillar to post. They hook up. The film slips leisurely into mature love story mould.

But Sayles is seeking much more than the minutiae of ordinary people in a sophisticate's *Northern Exposure*; looking to deliver some dreadfully clever philosophical study of the forces of hiatus and indecision, the film stumbles by artless contrivance into its disaster movie second half. Utilising a mucked-up drug trade (involving Joe's goon of a brother, played by Casey Siemaszko) as a device, Joe, Donna and Noelle are stranded on a remote island with no food, warmth and only two pairs of shoes. Will they be rescued? Will Joe and Donna's bonding survive the travail? Will we ever find out? *Limbo*, you see, applies to the audience as much as the imperilled threesome.

You've got to admire a director willing to play silly-buggers with Hollywood conditioning, but his intentions this time are just too off-keel to work. ★★★ **IN**

◎ LIMELIGHT (1952)

Starring: *Charlie Chaplin (Calvero), Claire Bloom (Terry, a Ballet Dancer), Sydney Chaplin (Neville, a composer), Andre Eglevsky (Harlequin), Melissa Hayden (Columbine), Charles Chaplin Jr., Wheeler Dryden (Clowns), Buster Keaton (Piano Accompanist)*
Director: *Charles Chaplin*
Screenwriter: *Charles Chaplin*
U/145 mins./Drama/Comedy/USA

Awards: *Academy Awards – Best Score*

Calvero, a drunken music-hall has-been, saves ballerina Terry Ambrose from a suicide bid and regains his confidence in helping her find a new purpose. However, he becomes convinced that she's in love with a young composer, Neville, and dies of a broken heart while she dances before an adoring crowd.

Based on his unpublished novel, *Footlights*, this was Charles Chaplin's last great film. It may be melodramatic in places and Calvero's philosophising may often be more platitudinous than profound, but Chaplin's work had always combined slapstick and sentiment and he wisely resisted changing a winning formula.

Moreover, it saw him paired for the only time with his lone serious rival as a silent clown, Buster Keaton. However, he spent much of the running time playing opposite Claire Bloom, who was discovered at the end of an extensive search for a new star that included, among others, Anne Bancroft.

Many have seen Terry as the personification of Oona O'Neill, the 18-year-old daughter of playwright Eugene O'Neill, whose steadying marriage to the 54-year-old star in 1943 was the latest in a line of sexual and political scandals that convinced the FBI that Chaplin was an undesirable alien. However, the action abounds with similarly autobiographical references.

Named perhaps with his French nickname, Charlot, in mind, Calvero is an amalgam of Chaplin's own father and vaudevillians Frank Tunney and Leo Dryden, while the scenario is set in London in 1914, the year in which Chaplin first embarked for America. Moreover, his son, Sydney, plays his romantic rival and several other family members take cameos.

But, primarily, this was a valedictory summation of his own career, in what Chaplin was convinced would be his farewell feature. Calvero's passing out of vogue echoes Chaplin's own struggle to please critics and fans alike during the 1940s. But there's nothing defensive or self-pitying about his recollections of past glories. Indeed, this was a proud affirmation of his achievement and a confident avowal that pantomime would survive in other artforms, even if it was no longer considered cutting-edge comedy.

Having decided to premiere the picture back in Britain, Chaplin was denied re-entry to the States and the American Legion ensured that the film had only a limited US release. However, Chaplin won the Oscar for Best Score when *Limelight* finally opened in Los Angeles in 1972 and he returned to a hero's reception to collect his award. ★★★★ **DP**

THE LIMEY (1999)

Starring: *Terence Stamp (Wilson), Lesley Ann Warren (Elaine), Luis Guzman (Eduardo Roel), Barry Newman (Jim Avery), Joe Dallesandro (Uncle John)*
Director: *Steven Soderbergh*
Screenwriter: *Lem Dobbs*
18/85 mins./Crime/Drama/Thriller/USA

Wilson is an ageing Cockney gangster who arrives, blinking, in sunny Los Angeles to avenge his daughter's death. The trail leads – pretty much straightaway – to slimy record producer, Terry Valentine, and Wilson is soon meting out his East End brand of justice upon LA's badfolk.

After the irrepressibly hip Elmore Leonard adaptation *Out Of Sight*, it looked as if Steven Soderbergh had finally emerged from the wilderness, ten years after flashing his calling card (*sex, lies and videotape*).

It is testament to his apparent resolve to remain unfamous that a film as bemusing as *The Limey* should be his follow-up. Where *Out Of Sight* was sexy, intelligent and commercial, this is stilted, slight and, at best, truly bizarre.

Terence Stamp, whose presence in any film is categorically always a pleasure, never a chore, plays Wilson, an ageing Cockney gangster who arrives, blinking, in sunny Los Angeles to avenge his daughter's death. The trail leads – pretty much straightaway – to slimy record producer, Terry Valentine, and Wilson is soon meting out his East End brand of justice upon LA's badfolk.

The Limey is little more than a garden-variety fish-out-of-water yarn. It's like Lenny MacLean walked off the set of *Lock, Stock And Two Smoking Barrels* into the next Tarantino film: nice idea on paper, but an uneasy balance between brutal tension and outright comedy on screen.

Worse, it's unclear whether Stamp's outbursts are supposed to be funny or not, and in a script this leaden, you don't know who to trust. Wilson's dialogue bounces from anachronistic Americanism ('She wrote me' instead of 'She wrote to me'), to improbable rhyming slang, which then has to be translated for the Yanks – very tiresome.

The iconic casting of two 60s has-beens, plus cultish supporting turns from Barry Newman and Joe Dallesandro, almost generate the required knowing wink, but the result remains a thinly plotted, overstylised pantomime which runs out of juice as rapidly as a clockwork toy. ★★★★ **CC**

THE LION IN WINTER (1968)

Starring: *Peter O'Toole (Henry II), Katharine Hepburn (Eleanor Of Aquitaine), Anthony Hopkins (Richard), John Castle (Geoffery), Nigel Terry (John), Timothy Dalton (King Philip Of France), Jane Marrow (Alais)*
Director: *Anthony Harvey*
Screenwriter: *James Goldman*
PG/134 mins./History/Drama/UK

Awards: *Academy Awards – Best Actress in a Leading Role, Best Music, Best Screenplay; BAFTA – Best Actress, Best Music*

The conniving King Henry II decides to call a Christmas family reunion, with the secret intention of announcing a successor from his three sons all hungry for power. So, back to the fold, return his wife Queen Eleanor, who had been imprisoned, and the three petulant princes: Richard, Geoffery and John. Even King Philip of France is coming, who also has his eyes on the prize.

A rousing episode of historical melodrama, lit up by two really big performances from Katharine Hepburn and Peter O'Toole, and was followed with a handful of Oscars as due reward. It is also notable for the movie debuts of three theatrical actors as the irritable princes vying for their father's favour – Nigel Terry, John Castle and a fierce, young Anthony Hopkins. While stagy in its make-up – long, talky scenes tumbling with intrigue and deception – director Anthony Harvey creates a splendid medieval milieu of blazing fires, drinking mead from stone flagons and cold, hard stone, just on the cusp of realism.

It's a dark, forbidding setting for the various inter-family machinations that are to follow. O'Toole's King Henry II, all stridency and bellows, favours his youngest Nigel Terry's John (as in King John of Robin Hood notoriety). His wheedling, not-to-say needling wife, given vituperative fire by the brilliant Hepburn, favours her beloved eldest son Anthony Hopkins' Richard (as in King Richard the Lionheart). John Castle's nonchalant Prince Geoffery sits in the middle, the model of the lost middle-child syndrome. Indeed, this lot make for a stark Freudian model of family position.

It is the interplay, especially between Hepburn's authority and conniving, and O'Toole's volcanic spirit, twisting the story like serpent's coils, that makes it so compelling. Like Shakespeare in Hollywood language, grand, silly and rip-snorting. ★★★★ **IN**

THE LION KING (1994)

Starring: *the voices of: Jonathan Taylor Thomas (Young Simba), Matthew Broderick (Adult Simba), James Earl Jones (King Mufasa), James Earl Jones (King Mufasa), Jeremy Irons (Scar), Moira Kelly (Adult Nala), Ernie Sabella (Pumbaa), Nathan Lane (Timon), Robert Guillaume (Rafiki), Rowan Atkinson (Zazu), Whoopi Goldberg (Shenzi), Cheech Marin (Banzai)*
Directors: *Roger Allers, Rob Minkoff*
Screenwriters: *Irene Mecchi, Jonathan Roberts, Linda Woolverton, based on a story by Jim Capobianco, Lorna Cook, Thom Enriquez, Andy Gaskill, Francis Glebas, Ed Gombert, Kevin Harkey, Barry Johnson, Mark Kausler, Jorgen Klubien, Larry Leker, Rick Maki, Burny Mattinson, Joe Ranft, Chris Sanders, Tom Sito, Gary Trousdale, additional story material by J.T. Allen, George Scribner, Miguel Tejada-Flores, Jenny Tripp, Bob Tzudiker, Chris Vogler, Noni White, Kirk Wise*
U/84 mins./Animation/Musical/Adventure/USA

Awards: *Academy Awards – Best Original Score, Best Original Song, Golden Globes – Best Comedy/Musical, Best Original Score, Best Original Song*

On the African plains a lion, Simba, is born who is destined to be King. But his Uncle Scar has other ideas . . .

We must assume that *The Lion King* is the first Disney animation to contain a fart joke, albeit one aimed over the heads of the younger members of its audience and towards their Baby Boomer parents. There's also a moment when you could swear that our leonine lovers are about to make the two-backed beast, as they no doubt would if this were live action. Before long something similar will occur; the recent string of Disney animations have not become the biggest successes in movie history without understanding the importance of ensuring that parents don't come along reluctantly.

Here the computer animation that made *Aladdin* too frenetic and pleased with itself meets the vanished serenity of *The Jungle Book* and gets maximum spectacle out of Africa's landscape and livestock. The wildebeest stampede that kills the hero's father, thereby attracting much criticism in the US, looks like treated film footage rather than the work of human hand, and the drama throughout hits very hard indeed. The Elephants' Graveyard sequence in particular may well have very small children watching through their fingers, although they are never too far from laughing like drains at the antics of Timon the meerkat and Pumbaa the flatulent warthog. The sequence where the pair of them break into a Hawaiian dance to distract a whole bunch of hyenas is funny, big time.

The Lion King really scores on the soundtrack, with outstanding characterisations from Jeremy Irons as the evil Scar, wrapping threats round his tongue like long notes on a cello, Rowan Atkinson sardonic and pompous as the courtier bird Zazu and Whoopi Goldberg at the head of a trio of hyenas, 90s descendants of the crows in Dumbo. Elton John and Tim Rice's chart-topping music matches the movie gag for gag, sob for sob, African choirs swelling as the sun rises over the savannah and soupy lurve duets accompanying the canoodlings of the mating pair. This being 1994 you are never far away from the terrifying thwack of a synthesised bass drum, included as much because it's feasible as because it's appropriate. It's that kind of picture.

Two straight-to-video sequels followed – *The Lion King: Simba's Pride*, about his daughter (voiced by Neve Campbell), finding romance with Scar's son (voiced by James Marsden) and the inventive *The Lion King 3: Hakuna Matata*, in which Timon and Pumba tell the behind-the-scenes plot of the first film. ★★★★ **DH**

LITTLE BUDDHA (1993)

Starring: *Keanu Reeves (Siddhartha), Ruocheng Ying (Lama Norbu), Chris Issak (Dean Conrad), Bridget Fonda (Lisa Conrad), Alex Wiesendanger (Jesse Conrad)*
Director: *Bernardo Bertolucci*
Screenwriters: *Rudy Wurlitzer, Mark Peploe, based on a story by Bernardo Bertolucci*
PG/117 mins./Religion/Drama/France/UK/Liechtenstein

Monks begin to believe that Buddha will be reincarnated in a young child – and the quest to find him is intercut with flashbacks to the origins of the first Buddha.

In 1920, Hollywood biblical epics like Cecil B. DeMille's original *Ten Commandments* told modern-day stories of troubled souls finding comfort in religion, with the Scriptures dramatised in spectacular flashbacks to huge sets thronged with suffering and orgiastic extras.

Having long nurtured the idea of doing a film about Buddhism, Bertolucci here hits on exactly the same outmoded formula, tossing a Janet And John version of the early life of the Buddha into a plot about a blond Seattle school kid who just might be the reincarnation of a Major League lama. As in DeMille's day, this allows for a pleasing spectacle, but there's also a rather absurd attempt to wring great lessons out of the trivialities of post-recession America. The oddest aspect of the story is that Issak and Fonda, peculiarly cast as the spiritual kid's parents, are so unsuspicious about a bunch of bald-headed oriental strangers loitering around playgrounds in search of beautiful children. There is some token wrestling with the adjustment the kid would have to make to the lama life, but this issue is dropped in a silly plot development. Two other kids show up in Bhutan and Nepal who might also be the lama reborn and the film's head spiritual baldie has to decide which, or which combination, of the children will be elevated to semi-sainthood.

Despite the film's length and breadth, it never gets past the first hurdle of storytelling, emerging as even less gripping than the reincarnation drama *Audrey Rose*, which was slightly more credible in dramatising the reaction of parents after they're told that their precious child is merely someone else come back to life. In the flashbacks to the 6th Century, with Keanu Reeves doing a solemn job of the moral awakening of Prince Siddhartha (who, of course, became Buddha), Bertolucci falls back on his trusty *Last Emperor* mix of screen-filling spectacle and unfamiliar ethnicity. The pictures are pretty, but the characters talk as if they were reading lines out of fortune cookies. Reeves' Peter Sellers-esque Indian accent isn't much help and his Nautilus physique looks nothing like all the older Buddhas you've ever seen.

The story of Siddhartha has dramatic potential, but this reverential film makes little of it, ignoring any conflict between the Prince's duties and his spiritual leanings that arise when he deserts his family to become a filthy hermit for God. Long, solemn and humourless, this isn't going to win many converts to the cinema, let alone Buddhism. ★★ **KN**

LITTLE CAESAR (1931)

Starring: *Edward G. Robinson (Little Caesar), Douglas Fairbanks Jr. (Joe Massara), Glenda Farrell (Olfa Strassoff), William Collier Jr. (Tony Passa), Sidney Blackmer (Big Boy)*
Director: *Mervyn LeRoy*
Screenwriters: *Francis Edward Faragoh, based on the novel by W.R. Burnett*
PG/75 mins./Crime/Drama/USA

Rico joins Sam Ventori's gang. He replaces Sam as leader, pushes rival gang leader Arnie Lorch out of town, then goes after the job of next-higher-up – Pete Montana.

If Al Jolson's 'You ain't heard nothin' yet' in *The Jazz Singer* was the CGI water-tentacle in *The Abyss*, then the soundtrack of a Warner Brothers picture like *Little Caesar* was *Jurassic Park*. Audiences who had grown up with inter-titles, live piano music, and gesturing mimes were bowled over not only by the talk of the talkies but by the sound effects. Little Caesar has the rhythm of snarled urban street talk, the rat-tat-tat of tommy guns used in drive-by hits and the screech of getaway car tyres, as scenes blow up and over as fast as a child's tantrum. From the film, 1930s audiences learned slang phrases ('Make it snappy', 'Screw, mug', 'You said a mouthful') and criminal expressions ('torpedo', 'moll', 'cannon').

Based on a novel by W.R. Burnett (who also wrote *High Sierra* and *The Asphalt Jungle*), *Little Caesar* hit screens after a couple of successful talkie gangster movies (*Doorway To Hell*, *The Racket*) had appeared, but it was different. Producer Darryl F. Zanuck said: 'Every other underworld picture has had a thug with a little bit of good in ' him. He reforms before the fade-out. This guy is no good at all. It'll go over big.' Warners, the studio that had introduced the talkies, loved ripped-from-the-headlines stories and instructed directors like Mervyn LeRoy to make sure their movies really moved. Like most major gangster films, *Little Caesar* is roughly modelled on the plot of *Macbeth* – he gets ambitious, he gets violent, he rises to the top, he takes a huge fall, he dies in the gutter. *Little Caesar* rushes through this rise-and-fall in under 80 minutes.

But the film really went over big because of its star. Edward G. Robinson, born Emmanuel Goldenberg in Romania but raised in New York City, had played hoods before on stage and screen, and had established his acting chops in Shaw and Shakespeare. Invited to test for a supporting thug role, he held out for the lead and was cast over more conventionally handsome movie star types like Lew Ayres (*The Doorway to Hell* (1930)). Robinson's performance remains electric, dwarfing everyone else despite his small stature. Cesare Enrico Bandello – Rico, 'Little Caesar' – is the first great film gangster. A small-time heist-man, Rico comes to the Big City (unnamed, but plainly Chicago) and attaches himself to a second-string mob, rising through his willingness to break the criminal code and ruthless enough to gun down the city's crusading anti-crime commissioner.

'Sam,' Rico tells his soon-to-be-former boss, 'you can dish it out but it's getting so you can't take it no more. You're through.' As a new boss, he wipes out his rivals and wins the patronage of 'The Big Boy', a Capone-style political fixer. But he has one weakness, a surprisingly gay (for 1930) fixation on George Raft-like ex-gangster dancer Joe and can't rub the kid out when it's clear Joe is about to squeal to the cops. Rico falls to a skid row flophouse and dies because a canny Irish cop taunts him into a shoot-out.

It's a fully-realised performance and still imitated: Robinson's bullfrog features and strutting bantam walk, with the snarled catchphrases ('The bigger they come, the harder they fall') and repeated use of 'see' to emphasise threats or boasts, remains an archetype of the gangster. Rico starts out an uncouth hick but as he kills and robs his way to the top – the film is a bit vague about how he makes his money, with no mention of prohibition or protection racketry – he is transformed into a dandy in a derby hat, double-breasted waistcoat, pinstripes and camel-hair coat. Before meeting with the Big Boy in his lavish mansion (told a painting is worth $15,000, Rico muses 'Boy, those gold frames sure cost plenty of dough'), Rico gets into his first tuxedo and awkwardly admires himself in the mirror, at once a preening queen and a little boy dressed up.

Like the incestuous Tony of *Scarface* and the woman-beating Tom of *The Public Enemy*, Rico is sexually weird, making him a freak even among crooks. But Robinson sees a streak of pathos in his collapse, in Rico's desperate wish for class and respect rather than cold cash.

The last act is surprisingly moving. In the first great gangster death scene, the fatally wounded and disbelieving antihero breathes 'Mother of Mercy, is this the end of Rico?' as he dies in the shadow of a poster advertising the hit film of his former friend. ★★★★★ **KN**

THE LITTLE FOXES (1941)

Starring: *Bette Davis (Regina Hubbard Giddens), Herbert Marshall (Horace Giddens), Teresa Wright (Alexandra Giddens), Richard Carlson (David Hewitt)*
Director: *William Wyler*
Screenwriters: *Lillian Hellman, Arthur Kober, Dorothy Parker, Alan Campbell, based on the play by Hellman*
PG/115 mins./Drama/USA

Realising that she can profit from their nefarious schemes, Regina Giddens supports her brothers, Ben and Oscar Hubbard, in asking her husband, Horace for a loan to open a cotton mill.

Having already reworked Lillian Hellman's lesbian drama *The Children's Hour* into *These Three*, producer Samuel Goldwyn, director William Wyler and cinematographer Gregg Toland reunited on this seething domestic melodrama that was nominated for nine Academy Awards and won none.

Several of the cast reprised their roles from the Broadway production, but Bette Davis was hired to replace Tallulah Bankhead and she promptly fell out with Wyler over his suggestion that she injected some wit and charm into the malevolence that she wanted to play to the hilt. Indeed, such was the ferocity of their disagreement that Davis absented herself for 16 days and only returned amidst rumours of her imminent replacement by Miriam Hopkins or Katharine Hepburn.

Ultimately, Davis won the day as, despite Hellman's pleading, she proceeded (some would say ruinously) to duplicate Bankhead's performance. However, the strength of the ensemble prevented her from overbalancing the picture, which Wyler managed to steal in his own subtle way.

Although Dorothy Parker and her co-writers set some of the scenes outside the stultifying Southern residences, Wyler refused to open out the action too far. This was partly because he recognised that Regina was akin to a director herself and he wanted to retain a theatrical setting to emphasise her controlling nature. But, he was also aware of how the confined spaces heightened the tensions between the characters and he used the sombre décor within Stephen Goosson and Howard Bristol's ceilinged sets to increase the pressure-cooker sense of claustrophobia.

However, there was nothing stagy about the camerawork, which rivalled the deep-focus compositions that Toland achieved in his other 1941 masterclass, *Citizen Kane*. Indeed, there was a greater flexibility about Wyler's exploitation of field depth, most notably during the famous staircase sequence, in which he leaves the ailing Herbert Marshall in the indistinct background as he hones in on Davis's face as she listens mercilessly to her husband's distress. But the shot that earned the admiration of Sergei Eisenstein (who counted this among his favourite films) was the ingenious mirror image capturing the duplicity of the shaving Carl Benton and Dan Duryea. ★★★★ **DP**

LITTLE MAN TATE (1991)

Starring: *Jodie Foster (Dede Tate), Dianne Wiest (Jane Grierson), Adam Hann-Byrd (Fred Tate), Harry Connick Jr. (Eddie), David Hyde Pierce (Garth)*
Director: *Jodie Foster*
Screenwriter: *Scott Frank*
PG/95 mins./Drama/USA

The waitress mother of a 'genius' child attempts to protect him from the pressures his brilliance inevitably brings.

Jodie Foster's directorial debut is a nice little film, but what audience it's actually for is a poser. Families, perhaps, since the central character is a physically frail, mind-bogglingly brilliant seven-year-old who composes, solves physics problems, has an ulcer and wants more than anything 'someone to eat lunch with'. Foster is his single, tough cookie cocktail waitress mum, who dotes on the kid but doesn't want him to be a freak. Dianne Wiest is the child psychologist who turns prodigies into celebrities.

While both Foster as the sassy but nurturing mother and Wiest as the cold brain are excellent in their tug-of-war for the boy's allegiance, they present wildly exaggerated extremes if this is supposed to be addressing seriously the subject of gifted children. Still, it's sweet natured and gently humourous, particularly when the pipsqueak is packed off to university where, among other learning experiences he is befriended by campus cut-up and pool hustler Harry Connick Jr.

All those years observing on sets through her own unusual childhood were not wasted on Foster, who handles the child – unsurprisingly – with great sympathy, but also shows assurance with the film as a whole. ★★★ **AE**

THE LITTLE SHOP OF HORRORS (1960)

Starring: *Johnathan Haze (Seymour Krelboin), Jackie Joseph (Audrey), Mel Welles (Gravis Mushnick), Jack Nicholson (Wilbur Force)*
Director: *Roger Corman*
Screenwriter: *Charles B. Griffiths*
PG/70 mins./Comedy/Horror/USA

Seymour, a florist's minion, raises a plant that flourishes on human blood. He becomes a success, but his celebrity depends on his willingness to keep feeding the ever-hungrier Audrey Junior.

Scripted by Charles Griffith (who poached the idea from a John Collier short story 'Green Thoughts') and directed by Roger Corman, this ultra-cheapo film eventually inspired a hit Broadway musical and Frank Oz's megabudget remake starring Rick Moranis as Seymour and a never-better Ellen Greene as Audrey. Legendarily shot over a long weekend because it was raining and Corman couldn't play tennis, it's a disguised remake of his earlier *A Bucket of Blood*, even reusing the earlier film's distinctively cool jazz score by Fred Katz.

This time, a Faustian tale of success and greed in the highly unusual milieu of a skid-row florist shop. Jonathan Haze, whose Jerry Lewisisms are a bit thick, is the nerdy assistant who discovers a new plant which thrives on blood, and he is driven to placate the hungry and very vocal monster ('feeeed meee') with chunks of victims. It has a lot of strange Jewish humour (Haze is saving up to buy his mother an iron lung), a dead-on parody of the Dragnet TV show and a famous cameo from a young Jack Nicholson as Wilbur Force, a masochist who loves to visit his dentist ('no novocaine, it dulls the senses'), plus Mel Welles as the incomprehensible florist Gravis Mushnik, Dick Miller as a patron who eats flowers ('don't knock it till you try it') and Jackie Joseph as the sweet but dim blonde heroine. Even in a seventy-minute running time, it has its slow spots, but the oddball characters, strange plotting and weird morality are impressive.

Avoid the colorised (ugh) version. Besides Oz's musical – which drops the 'the' from the title – there was a strange 1973 porno remake *Please Don't Eat My Mother*. ★★★★ **KN**

LIVE AND LET DIE (1973)

Starring: *Roger Moore (James Bond), Yaphet Kotto (Kananga), Jane Seymour (Solitaire), Clifton James (Sheriff J.W. Pepper), Julius Harris (Tee Hee), Bernard Lee (M), Lois Maxwel (Miss Moneypenny)*
Director: *Guy Hamilton*
Screenwriter: *Tom Mankiewicz*
PG/121 mins./Spy/UK

After several British agents disappear, presumed dead, James Bond travels from New York to the Caribbean on the trail of a mysterious drug lord known as Mr. Big. His first port of call is the small island owned by Dr. Katanga, and home of the beautiful Tarot reader Solitaire.

After the debacle that was George Lazenby, and the hasty and expensive re-employment of Sean Connery for *Diamonds Are Forever*, this was a real test as to whether the franchise could ever cope with a new Bond. The pressure was on to get off to a flyer or Roger Moore, a handsome TV actor more debonair than versatile, would end up just as swiftly on the refuse pile and a new toupee would have to be ordered for the ageing Connery.

Putting Guy Hamilton back in the director's chair was a sound move, he had made *Goldfinger*, the most assured and dynamic of all 007 movies, and with a direct and fine-tuned script from old-hand Tom Mankiewicz, they did what they had to do – hit the ground running. This is good quality Bond, managing to reinterpret the classic moves – action, deduction, seduction – for a more modern idiom without breaking the mould. The film, with its rich Caribbean locations and crazy-spooky asides, manages to be more playful than before – Moore's chosen approach – without tipping into the painful parody of his later films. On one side we get the use of alligators as stepping stones and the pompous puffball of rootin' tootin' Sherriff Pepper, caught up in the thrilling boat chase. On the other, the genuine aura of threat through weird voodoo henchman Tee Hee, and the leaning toward – what's this? – realism in Mr. Big's plot to take over the drug trade from the Mafia.

Naturally, there's much of the regular Bondian kerfuffle – a stoney-faced M, an irascible Q, the gadgets and Jane Seymour as one of the more memorable lady-loves Solitaire – but delivered with a lighter touch. It can't quite muster an explosive third act to match previous jaunts, but Moore had got his feet under the table. ★★★★ **IN**

THE LIVING DAYLIGHTS (1987)

Starring: *Timothy Dalton (James Bond), Maryam d'Abo (Kara Milovy), Jeroen Krabbe (General Georgi Koskov), Joe Don Baker (Brad Whitaker), John Rhys-Davies (Gen. Leonid Pushkin), Art Malik (Kamran Shah), Andreas Wisnieswski (Necros), Desmond Llewelyn (Q), Robert Brown (M)*
Director: *John Glen*
Screenwriters: *Richard Maibaum, Michael G. Wilson, based on a story by Ian Fleming*
PG/130 mins./Spy/UK

James Bond refuses to kill sniper Kara Milovy while assisting in the defection of KGB General Koskov. Koskov plays a complex triple-cross involving an arms deal and Afghan heroin.

After the fizzle of the later Roger Moore Bonds, *The Living Daylights* brings in a new 007 in Timothy Dalton, who manages the Connery trick of seeming suave and tough at the same time, and tried to get away from the weak comedy in favour of proper international intrigue.

The sledging-in-a-cello case escape is a typical Moore stunt, and Dalton is visibly embarrassed by the punchline ('nothing to declare'), but the film offers a decent, fresh storyline as opposed to a warmed-over remake of *Dr No*. The plot nugget, Bond's refusal to kill a beautiful sniper, comes from the Fleming short story, and the major complication has to do with a bogus revival of Smiert Spionom aka SMERSH ('a Beria operation', snorts all-purpose foreigner John Rhys-Davies, here a Soviet General). Breaking with mad zillionaires and fantasy geopolitics, the film is set in a realworld 1987 where the USSR is riven with internal dissent and bogged down in Afghanistan. The series' first American master villain (Joe Don Baker's Brad Whittaker) is a flamboyant but credible international arms dealer, and Bond's most complicated opponent (Jeroen Krabbe's Koskov) is a jolly, treacherous, triple-dealing KGB man left alive at the end for a rematch which sadly never came.

With former second-unit director John Glen still in charge, it has more than enough set-pieces to keep in the action game: the assault of a killer milkman, a close-quarters fight in a rickety aeroplane with a bomb aboard, a one-on-one between Bond's old-fashioned Walther and Whittaker's array of high-tech gadgets.

A-ha's theme is, at least, better than Duran Duran's 'View To A Kill'. ★★★ **KN**

LIVING IN OBLIVION (1995)

Starring: *Steve Buscemi (Nick Reve), Catherine Keener (Nicole Springer), Dermot Mulroney (Wolf), Danielle von Zerneck (Wanda), James LeGros (Chad Palomino)*
Director: *Tom DiCillo*
Screenwriter: *Tom DiCillo*
15/86 mins./Comedy/Drama/USA

A film director struggles to get his movie made, dealing with a difficult star and budget restrictions.

Director Tom DiCillo knows the world of low-budget auteurism like the back of his clapperboard. His first film, *Johnny Suede*, received rave reviews and helped make Brad Pitt a star. Since then, however, the director has seen project after project crash on the rocks of Hollywood indifference. The result is *Living In Oblivion*: simultaneously a howl of rage against the restrictions of low-budget movie-making and a celebration of how, sometimes, things actually get done.

Split into three parts, the movie follows a luckless independent director as he attempts to get a series of shots in the can. First, technical problems plague an intimate scene. Then, the leading man flexes a few megastar muscles. And finally, while filming a dream sequence, Buscemi has to cope with both his whacko mum and a dwarf who refuses to be stereotyped as, well, a dwarf.

The movie is completely stolen by LeGros' womanising Hollywood egomaniac who insists on ad-libbing, altering the script and, in a perfect moment of cinematic in-jokery, informing Buscemi that the only reason he's doing the movie is because 'someone said you were tight with Tarantino'. Any similarities to Hollywood egomaniacs DiCillo may have worked with in the past is, presumably, entirely on purpose. ★★★★ **CC**

LOCAL HERO (1983)

Starring: *Burt Lancaster (Felix Happer), Peter Riegart (Mac), Fulton Mackay (Ben), Denis Lawson (Urquhart), Peter Capaldi (Oldson), Jenny Seagrove (Marina)*
Director: *Bill Forsyth*
Screenwriter: *Bill Forsyth*
PG/107 mins./Comedy/Drama/UK

Awards: *BAFTA – Best Director*

An American oil company sends a man to Scotland to buy up an entire village where they want to build a refinery. But things don't go as expected.

In retrospect, *Local Hero* seems the perfect melding of producer David Puttnam and writer-director Bill Forsyth's sensibilities. Combining the craftsmanship, commitment to issues (the raping of the environment by big business) and the prevailing sense of optimism of Puttnam's flicks

(*Chariots Of Fire*, *The Killing Fields*) with the idiosyncratic characterisation, wry observation and understated humour of Forsyth, *Local Hero* sees the collaboration coalesce into something near perfect.

Surprisingly, the impetus behind the Scottish-set movie did not start with Forsyth. Browsing through the newspaper, Puttnam's eye was caught by a story detailing negotiations for an oil development in a Scottish community. Puttnam presented the cutting to Forsyth – the producer had previously turned down *Gregory's Girl* – who was immediately hooked by the idea.

'In keeping with every other Scottish filmmaker, I thought there was a story to be made about the oil business,' Forsyth observed at the time. 'I saw it along the lines of a Scottish *Beverly Hillbillies*: what would happen to a small community when it suddenly became immensely rich? There was the germ of the idea and the story built itself from there.'

What Forsyth crafted from the idea is adroitly plotted, pleasingly sentimental and consistently surprising. Sent by crazed oil tycoon Felix Happer (Lancaster, gently satirising the blustering big business types that were his stock in trade) to buy a remote Scottish village so the company can drill for North Sea oil, hotshot exec MacIntyre, aided by bumbling local company rep Danny, enters into discussions with local lawyer-hotelier Gordon Urquhart. Rather than rejecting the move, the village embrace the get-rich-quick scheme while Mac comes under the spell of village life, bolstered by Happer's insistence that he keep an eye out for the Aurora Borealis that supposedly lights the Scottish night skies.

Although it is oft-stated that the film belongs to the tartan whimsy of *Brigadoon* and *Whisky Galore*, a more pertinent antecedent might be Powell and Pressburger's *I Know Where I'm Going* which predates *Hero*'s feel for landscape and sense of lilting Scottishness. Chris Menges' stunning cinematography finds beauty and wonder in equal measures, particularly in the moment in which a beach full of villagers follow a mysterious light in the sky which turns out to be Rapper's helicopter. That Mac's falling in love with rural life is so easy to swallow may have much to do with the location scouting – the beach was provided by the silver sands at Camusdarach with Pennan on the North East coast doubling as the village – but the luminous cinematography is an equally beguiling factor.

Around its main plot, *Local Hero* skilfully interweaves a number of subplots: Happer's psychiatrist trying to shake him out of his complacency by abusive phone calls; Danny's infatuation with oceanologist Marina who – typical of the film's magical realism – has a hint of mermaid which blossoms in the film's conclusion; the burgeoning friendship between Mac and Gordon, beautifully rendered by Reigert and Lawson, sees the two men imperceptibly swap personalities ('I'll be a good Gordon, Gordon'). Mac's business savvy is transformed by the laid back life and Gordon's easy-going nature is consumed by the dollar signs in his eyes. As both men fall in love with the same woman: Urquhart's wife – Forsyth, as in Gregory's Girl, juxtaposes feeble daydreaming men with sensible centred women and delights as the differences become apparent.

Moreover, containing a tighter, more complex and confidently told narrative than his previous flick, Forsyth still provides breathing space for the lovely vignettes and character moments that *Local Hero* solidified as his trademark. There are fantastic running gags (the mad, offscreen, motorcyclist who terrorises the roads, the continual coughing up of coinage so Mac can phone Houston from the nearby telephone box), crackerjack dialogue ('Are you sure there are two Is in dollar Gideon?' a passerby says to an old fisherman painting a boat. 'Yes, I know there're two gs in bugger off!') and delicious incidental detail (Urquhart's unmotivated dance atop his desk top). None of this comedy is forced, always organically emerging from the quirks of character and situation.

Topped off by Mark Knopfler's warm, triumphant theme (a standard now in TV sports montage spots), *Local Hero* left tracer elements throughout Forsyth's career. He directed Lancaster again as a business tycoon in a series of Foster's lager ads and Mac's character arc of a professional discovering a hollow in his life found a more full-blown exploration in Forsyth's next picture, *Comfort And Joy*. Away from Forsyth, *Local Hero* provided a template for US TV show *Northern Exposure*. A more unfortunate bi-product saw swarms of Americans flocking to the Pennan location hoping to experience something akin to Mac's life-affirming transformation. Canny yokels once again exploiting the Yankee dollar? What a great idea for a movie ... ★★★★ **IF**

⦿ LOCK STOCK AND TWO SMOKING BARRELS (1998)

Starring: *Jason Flemyng (Tom), Dexter Fletcher (Soap), Nick Moran (Eddie), Jason Statham (Bacon), Steven Mackintosh (Winston), Vinnie Jones (Big Chris)*
Director: *Guy Ritchie*
Screenwriter: *Guy Ritchie*
18/102 mins./Comedy/Crime/Thriller/UK

Awards: *BAFTA – Audience Award, Empire Awards – Best British Film, Best Debut*

A group of East End wide boys spend a frantic few days trying to raise half a million quid to pay a gambling debt or face the wrath of a local mobster.

Of all the recent attempts to put a Tarantinoid spin on the British gangster movie, this is the freshest and most successful. It is, at heart, an extended shaggy dog story, as is revealed by snippets of cockney narration that introduce minor characters or prod the plot along, but writer-director Guy Ritchie and his cast have enough freestyle energy and bizarro confidence to get away with it. Set entirely in a fantasy East End where women almost don't exist and shot through a drunken haze, it creates a world related to reality and to old crime movies but also self-contained and original.

The plot is a complex collision of several sets of crooked characters. Our heroes – Eddy, Tom, Soap and Bacon – are harmless wideboys who find themselves in a pickle when demon cardsharp Eddy loses a rigged three-card brag game with local mob boss/porn baron Hatchet Harry. The lads are required to hand over half-a-million quid by the end of the week or suffer the attentions of Harry's debt-collectors, a bald head-dunker called Barry The Baptist (bare knucks champ Lenny McLean) and the fearsome but paternal Big Chris (one-time football hard man Vinnie Jones).

The quartet overhear their nastier neighbours planning on robbing a group of public school dope cultivators and decide to rip-off the rip-off artists. Also mixed up in the escalating mess are an Afro-haired drugs czar, Eddy's bar-owning dad (Sting, but don't worry – he isn't in many scenes), middle-man Nick The Greek and an extremely unlucky traffic warden. *Lock Stock And Two Smoking Barrels* is too mixed-up to synopsise easily and too rickety to think about closely, but it gets plenty of laughs as it rushes from scene to scene. ★★★★ **KN**

⦿ THE LODGER (1927)

Starring: *Marie Ault (The Landlady – Mrs Bunting), Arthur Chesney (her Husband – Mr. Bunting), June (Daisy Bunting), Malcolm Keen (Joe Chandler), Ivor Novello (Jonathan Drew)*
Director: *Alfred Hitchcock*
Screenwriter: *Eliot Stannard, based on the novel and play by Marie Belloc Lowndes*
PG/101 mins./Crime/UK

With London grimly fascinated by the crimes of The Avenger, a serial killer who only murders blondes on Tuesdays, Daisy Bunting becomes obsessed with her parents' new lodger, much to the annoyance of her envious and maliciously suspicious policeman fiancé, Joe.

Subtitled 'A Story of the London Fog', this wonderfully evocative and melodramatic thriller was adapted from a 1913 novel by Marie Belloc

Lowndes. But, for all its British bustle and the allusions to Jack the Ripper, Alfred Hitchcock's first commercial success had more in common with a UFA than a Gainsborough production.

Having recently returned from making *The Pleasure Garden* and *The Mountain Eagle* (both 1926) in Munich, Hitch was keen to put into practice the Expressionist techniques he had picked up while watching F.W. Murnau directing *The Last Laugh*. The equation of the blacked-out windows of the van in the opening sequence with the vigilant eyes of the citizens and the voyeuristic gaze of the audience was typical of the Germanic influence, as was the dissolve through the ceiling to show Ivor Novello pacing above the inquisitorial Buntings. But, in fact, the brooding shadows and canted angles owed more to Fritz Lang's *Destiny* and *Dr Mabuse, the Gambler* than Murnau's psychological realism.

Whatever its source, producer Michael Balcon was acutely disturbed by this foreign stylisation and the Freudian suggestions that the lodger might be either homosexual or incestuously involved with his sister. So, he commissioned Soviet-influenced critic Ivor Montagu to take the curse off Hitchcock's amorality.

In addition to cutting down the number of captions from around 400 to 80 (and recasting them in a Gothic-Deco hybrid), Montagu also suggested some retakes, most notably for the climactic chase sequence. However, he agreed with the decision to ignore the book's guilty verdict (which was adopted by the 1932, 1944 and 1954 remakes; the latter being called *Man in the Attic*) and retain the air of ambiguous innocence that Hitchcock had concocted on being told that his preening matinee idol was not going to be allowed to play a killer.

Widely hailed as the finest British picture to date, this was Hitchcock's first study of a wronged man being judged by a hypocritical society. Moreover, it also contained his debut cameo appearance. But it was still very much the work of a hugely promising and highly ciné-literate beginner. ★★★ **DP**

LOGAN'S RUN (1976)

Starring: *Michael York (Logan 5), Richard Jordan (Francis 7), Jenny Agutter (Jessica 6), Farrah Fawcett (Holly 13), Michael Anderson Jr. (Doc), Peter Ustinov (The Old Man)*
Director: *Michael Anderson*
Screenwriter: *David Zelag Goodman, based on the novel by William F. Nolan and George Clayton Johnson*
PG/120 mins./Sci-fi/USA

In the year 2274, the planet is populated by content citizens living a life of total ease. However, in order to maintain the population balance, they must all die at 30, using enforcers, called Sandmen, to stop people making a run for it. When Sandman Logan is sent on a mission by his computer superiors to find the mythical Sanctuary, which runners are trying to reach, he comes to realise the system is corrupt.

Despite being set in a far-flung future, Michael Anderson's chirpy and appealing science fiction thriller can't escape its 70s origins. There is something in the future gazing of that era, all the glittery, monochrome sets and jumpsuits that defines contemporary obsessions rather than notions of future possibility. Hence, time has done it no favours, the details of its computer-run society quaint and silly in the aftermath of the internet. Yet, it still has spirit and energy, a compelling central idea and Jenny Agutter in a miniskirt. So what if the effects are clunky, this is memorable enough hokum.

After all, it's a long time since you would deem Michael York and the fragile-sexy Agutter as likeable leading actors. The idea of enforced suicide is cleverly draped in a pseudo-religion – a process of renewal marked by the crystals set in the palm of the hand – with some chilling overtones of the whacky religions currently on the go. And the gradual conversion of York's heroic Logan from smug believer to rebel, care of Agutter's stoic Jessica 6, certainly feels plausible. Once they're on the run, seeking out the fabled Sanctuary (which Logan has secretly been instructed to destroy), the film builds up a fair head of steam, plunging them through a series of dangerous encounters before they hit the great outdoors and confront old-man Ustinov as proof of a greater lifespan and the possibilities of family.

It's a dystopian fantasy, trilling with warnings about decadence, ageism, and allowing technology and science to run riot, done to a disco groove. Anderson fails to imbue it with darkness, real political thought, in his race to be zippy and sexy. The ideas are there, but they play second fiddle to York's well-to-do heroism and Agutter's lovely thighs. ★★★ **IN**

LOLA MONTÈS (1955)

Starring: *Martine Carol (Lola Montès), Peter Ustinov (Circus Monster), Anton Walbrook (Ludwig I, King Of Bavaria), Ivan Desny (Lt. James), Will Quadflieg (Franz Liszt), Oskar Werner (Student)*
Director: *Max Ophüls*
Screenwriters: *Max Ophüls, Jacques Natanson, Franz Geiger, Annette Wademant, based on the unpublished novel* La Vie Extraordinaire de Lola
PG/110 mins./Drama/West Germany

A ringmaster introduces his star turn, Lola Montès, whose eventful life is depicted as a series of flashbacks that centre in particular on her romantic dalliances with Franz Lizst and King Ludwig of Bavaria.

Max Ophüls was so dismayed by the ballyhoo attending the announcement of his first film in CinemaScope and Eastmancolor that he decided to subvert everyone's expectations. The prospect of seeing sex symbol Martine Carol playing a notorious 19th-century courtesan in an adaptation of Cécil Saint-Laurent's racy bestseller convinced the public they were in for a saucy romp. But when they saw Ophüls's 140-minute masterpiece, Parisian audiences rioted and Gamma Films cut the print to 110 and then 90 minutes and removed the flashbacks to impose a linear structure – to the dismay of Jean Cocteau, Jacques Tati, Roberto Rossellini and others who published a letter in *Le Figaro* urging filmgoers to see *Lola Montès* as an artistic landmark. Yet it still proved a commercial disaster.

Frustrated by the growing preoccupation with the private lives of the rich and famous, Ophüls launched an assault on celebrity and the peddlars of the prying gossip that dehumanised its victims. Thus, he inverted the taste and sophistication of his previous pictures to present a world of lurid decadence, in which Lola was reduced to a mere possession. Recalling the tragedies of Judy Garland and Diana Barrymore, he turned her life into a series of tawdry circus acts, in which her imperilment and objectification disrupted the easy pleasures of voyeurism.

Rarely had so visually sumptuous a film masked such intellectual disgust. Christian Matras's photography, Jean D'Eaubonne's sets, Georges Annenkov's costumes and Georges Auric's score were all superb and the galaxy of continental stars played their stylised parts to perfection. Ophüls's use of symbolic colour was almost as inspired as his gliding, swooping camerawork and his precise exploitation of the wide screen (which he tamed for close-ups using classic Von Sternbergian tactics).

Critics still debate whether Ophüls's audacious technical ingenuity atones for a lack of psychological depth. But, recognising that the tabloid mentality focuses on actions and appearances not human motives, he fashioned Lola as a beautiful object whose fascination lasted only as long as her lustre and this calculated swipe at public superficiality is now more pertinent than ever. ★★★★★ **DP**

LONE STAR (1996)

Starring: *Kris Kristofferson (Charlie Wade), Chris Cooper (Sheriff Sam Deeds), Matthew McConaughey (Buddy Deeds), Elizabeth Pena (Pilar Cruz), Frances McDormand (Bunny)*
Director: *John Sayles*
Screenwriter: *John Sayles*
15/129 mins./Drama/Mystery/Crime/USA

The mystery of a small-town sheriff's disappearance is resurrected 30 years later.

Almost uniquely among contemporary filmmakers, John Sayles has never directed a bad film. While most independent director-writers concentrate on refining their narrow fields of interest, essentially making the same film over and over, Sayles is astonishingly eclectic. His body of work is unified only by intelligence and commitment, ranging across genres, moods and scales.

In a terrific opening, a couple of off-duty soldiers fooling around in the desert near the border town of Frontera discover a human skull. Sheriff Sam Deeds is called in and guesses the long-dead man might have been Charlie Wade, an old-school lawman of the 'bullets and bribes' school who disappeared 30 years earlier, after an argument with Sam's dad, Buddy Deeds. Buddy, Sheriff before his son, is a legendary local whose stature is by no means an unmixed blessing to Sam as he tries to make his way in a changing town.

Also mixed up are Pilar, a Hispanic history teacher whose teenage romance with Sam was squelched by Buddy, and Mercedes, Pilar's powerful restaurant-running mother. Colonel Payne, C.O. of a soon-to-be-closed army base, has a tie-in through his father Otis, who runs an off-limits bar. As Sam asks questions and prompts conflicting flashback anecdotes, he comes to understand his own intricate family backstory – which includes a kicker of a last-act revelation – and its relationship with the evolving political and racial situation along the border.

Like the earlier *City Of Hope*, *Lone Star* demands the viewer's complete engagement with a huge cast and depends on the gradual release of plot information that makes connections between characters grow as the film progresses. Even one-scene characters are unforgettable, but Sayles really gets under the skin of his struggling-to-be-heroic leads, Sam and Pilar. ★★★★★ **KN**

THE LONELINESS OF THE LONG DISTANCE RUNNER (1962)

Starring: *Tom Courtenay (Colin Smith), Michael Redgrave (The Governor), Avis Bunnage (Mrs. Smith), Peter Madden (Mr. Smith), James Bolam (Mike), Julia Foster (Gladys)*
Director: *Tony Richardson*
Screenwriter: *Alan Sillitoe based on his story*
12/104 mins./Drama/UK

Awards: *BAFTA – Most Promising Newcomer (Tom Courtenay)*

Sent to the Ruxton Towers for robbing a bakery, Nottingham teenager Colin Smith thinks back on his dead-end life while training for the cross-country race against a nearby public school that is the over-riding pre-occupation of the borstal's governor.

Based on an Alan Sillitoe novella, this was less a study of an angry young man than of an alienated kid whose 'whatever' attitude contrasted sharply with the resentful socio-sexual consciousness of other Kitchen Sink anti-heroes. Colin Smith wasn't bright enough to understand what was wrong with the British class structure in the early 1960s. But he knew something wasn't right and he proceeded to kick against it in a childish, but undeniably effective manner.

As in the earlier Sillitoe adaptation, *Saturday Night and Sunday Morning*, the Nottingham backstreets are effectively used by Tony Richardson and cinematographer Walter Lassally. But, both the visual and the narrative style owe more to the nouvelle vague than what was becoming standard social realism. Consequently, this always feels more like a calculated work of agit-prop than an authentic proletarian drama. Nonetheless, the flash-backs are more than a contrivance, as the cross-cutting between Colin's past and present reinforces the political power of the parallel plotlines and confirms the hopelessness of his situation, as he's no better off with his own kind than he is with the patronising bourgeois Governor.

Richardson's self-conscious focus on the filmic quality of his story might have reduced Colin to a class cypher. But the debuting Tom Courtenay turns a resistible character into an unlikely rebel with a cause by adding a curt charm to Colin's nervous energy and eccentric non-conformism. There are certainly shades of Billy Fisher (whom the 24-year-old Courtenay had just played in the West End and would do again in John Schlesinger's film, *Billy Liar*) in Colin's confusion and unconventional recalcitrance. But it's more intriguing to compare his performance with that of David Bradley in Ken Loach's *Kes*.

Courtenay won a BAFTA for his work. But he was ably supported by Avis Bunnage, as the sluttish mother who bequeathed him his indomitable spirit, and Michael Redgrave as the complacent Governor, whose own inadequacies and class envy are so pitilessly exposed by that final glorious act of defiance. ★★★★ **DP**

THE LONG DAY CLOSES (1992)

Starring: *Marjorie Yates (Mother), Leigh McCormack (Bud), Anthony Watson (Kevin), Nicholas Lamont (John), Ayse Owens (Helen), Tina Malone (Edna)*
Director: *Terence Davies*
Screenwriter: *Terence Davies*
PG/81 mins./Drama/Biography/UK

Bud is a lonely 11-year-old boy in 1950s Liverpool. The film follows his doleful journey through everyday life, from his family, past his school and its bullies to his beloved cinema.

An autobiographical piece of delicate and meticulous filmmaking from British director Terence Davies, this revels in arty details – getting that shot of light falling onto a carpet just right – which, though undeniably affecting, show a typically British penchant for self-absorption.

Recreating the terraced box and cobbled street of his 50s youth in Liverpool, Davies patches together the gentle dramas of the everyday – neighbours paying a visit, a street party – as seen through the eyes of 11-year-old Bud, who stands in for the director. Bud is a solitary character who finds solace in the cinema, and Davies successfully weaves clips from classic films into the narrative.

Though Davies says this is a celebration of what were the best years of his life – he had a doting mum, nice sisters, and school was apparently okay – you'd hate to see what he'd produce if he were depressed, for the overall mood is heavy and glum. ★★★ **LB**

THE LONG GOOD FRIDAY (1980)

Starring: *Bob Hoskins (Harold Shand), Helen Mirren (Victoria), Dave King (Parky), Bryan Marshall (Harris), Derek Thompson (Jeff), Pierce Brosnan (First Irishman)*
Director: *John Mackenzie*
Screenwriter: *Barrie Keeffe*
18/109 mins./Crime/Drama/Thriller/UK

It's pretty rare that a little old gangster flick can upset whole governments, but in 1980 The Long Good Friday had Margaret Thatcher's gang of goons up in arms. There was the fact that, at the height of the Irish troubles, the IRA were portrayed as an invincible force whom even London's finest thugs couldn't defeat, and they were working outside the law. What

hope, it covertly pondered, did the British army have? It was hardly a message that the Tories would be particularly keen on being put about.

The ensuing brouhaha would delay the film's release by a year, but it did manage to distract the politicos from the fact that there was a much more damaging, gleefully insinuating edge to Barrie Keeffe's script. Harold Shand is pretty much the epitome of what many saw as Thatcherite values. He's a self made man, the 'boy from Putney' turned millionaire entrepreneur, an implacable patriot engaged in an ambitious property development which looks suspiciously like the jewel in her ironness' crown, Docklands. He's the ultimate Yuppie, greedy, nouveau riche tasteless (catch the flat) and corrupt – but he packs heat. Not at all bad for a film its director described as, 'Just a damned good gangster movie'.

Plotwise *TLGF* is pretty much a straightforward account of a South London turf war between Shand and his 'Corporation' and a group of unknown insurgents who take it upon themselves to launch their attack on the very day that he welcomes a group of American businessmen, intent on wooing them into investing in his dockside development. Shand's gay (reasonably adventurous for 1980) best mate is stabbed to death in an unfortunate swimming pool cruising incident; his Roller along with its driver are detonated (in a sequence that is possibly the finest example of the "unexpected car-bomb" cliche shot); explosive devices turn up in his casino; and they even have the temerity to reduce his favourite pub to rubble. After rounding up the usual suspects and, in one of the film's most memorable sequences, dangling them from meat-hooks, he discovers that the enemy are the IRA engaged in a revenge operation triggered by some unauthorised dealings.

Keeffe's script is a marvellously crafted piece of writing. Not only are there the expertly realised set pieces: the infamous meat-hook sequence; Razor's (aka The Human Spirograph, heavy P.H. Moriarty) torturing of Erroll the 'Brixton Ponce' and Harold's brutal stabbing of right hand thug Jeff (Derek Thompson, later to crop up as nurse Charlie in Casualty), but gangster dialogue doesn't come much saltier than Harold Shand's. There's the point at which he finds his best friend's body is to be transported to the abattoir in an ice-cream van. 'Well there's a lot of dignity in that,' he protests. 'Goin' out on a raspberry ripple!' There's his astute critique of La Cosa Nostra after they abandon his blood drenched business venture, 'The Mafia? I shit 'em!' Or there's his impeccable way with a threat, 'I'll have his carcass; dripping by midnight,' he hisses of an associate.

It's Hoskins' ability to leap deftly from Minder-style witticisms to steel-hearted promises of bloody retribution that is the powerhouse of the movie. 'His acting came straight ; from the gut with the brain slightly guiding it,' remembers Mackenzie. He's a complex, deeply human character, moving from toad-like pompous speechifying to bewilderment and rage as his empire collapses with remarkable ease from an actor who previously had only popped up in the likes of *Royal Flash* and *Zulu Dawn*, (plus adult literacy TV programme *On The Move*).

Hoskins' ballistic performance sometimes distracts audiences from the other acting strengths of the movie. Helen Mirren is superb as the devoted wife attempting to hold everything together and there's a rogue's gallery of classy supporting players including more than a few real-life London hoods. ('Not that I'd know,' one of them is reported to have informed Mackenzie, 'but you don't stab someone like that.') And for cameo spotters the real prize is not Pierce Brosnan (the IRA man with the gun at the end of the movie) but Dexter Fletcher – later himself to star in *Lock, Stock And Two Smoking Barrels* which revived the British gangster genre at the end of the 90s – as one of the kids outside the ponce's house.

But the icing on the cake is Hoskins' astounding, wordless performance in the movie's final shot as, bundled into a car he realises that he's taken on a foe far too powerful, and that whatever awaits is at least as bad as a meat-hook. Every emotion is visible from shock to a final, ambivalent expression that might be rueful acceptance. It's as good a performance as any in a gangster movie and why, in 1997, *Empire* voted *The Long Good Friday* best British movie ever made. And no *Lock Stock*, or anaemic imitation, is likely to change that. ★★★★★ **MD**

THE LONG KISS GOODNIGHT (1996)

Starring: *Geena Davis (Samantha Caine/Charly Baltimore), Samuel L. Jackson (Mitch Henessey), Yvonne Zima (Caitlin Caine), Craig Bierko (Timothy), Brian Cox (Dr. Nathan Waldman), David Morse (Luke/Daedalus)*
Director: *Renny Harlin*
Screenwriter: *Shane Black*
18/115 mins./Action/Thriller/USA

An amnesiac schoolteacher, who has flashbacks to a violent past, decides it's time to discover her former self when she is forced to stab an intruder.

After the dire *Cutthroat Island*, Geena Davis might have thought twice before working for her then hubby Harlin again, but this is a far more effective vehicle for them both, and has the advantage of a sharp and playful script by *Lethal Weapon* creator Shane Black.

Davis plays the frumpy Samantha Caine, an amnesiac schoolteacher and mother mired in suburbia. Unable to recall much beyond the present, Caine starts experiencing disturbing flashbacks that reveal a woman with a penchant for extreme violence. When she's forced to kill an intruder in the kitchen, she decides it's time to leave the burbs and try to discover exactly what sort of person she was before her memory loss. To help her, she recruits the superbly seedy Jackson, a bent cop turned private eye, and soon they're caught up in a classically paranoid government conspiracy being run by the gleefully evil Bierko and a slimy Patrick Malahide.

Shot against the freezing backdrop of an East Coast winter, much of the fun comes from the pairing of Davis and Jackson and the way Shane Black flips their roles – Jackson is the perfect sidekick, allowing Davis to show that she can be a convincing action heroine. Harlin too seems happier amid the ice and snow, skilfully setting up some spectacular sequences including a frantic confrontation at a train station and a suitably over-the-top finale at the US–Canadian border. Of course, it doesn't all work: there are too many 'meaningful' close-ups of cigarettes being lit and drinks downed, while the sound is so loud that it threatens to pop eardrums. But there's always the saving grace of Black's witty, high-speed screenplay, as well as the intriguing prospect of Davis presenting a serious challenge to the likes of Schwarzenegger and Stallone as a bona fide action star. ★★★★ **DE**

LOOK BACK IN ANGER (1959)

Starring: *Richard Burton (Jimmy Porter), Claire Bloom (Helena Charles), Mary Ure (Allison Porter), Edith Evans (Mrs Tanner), Gary Raymond (Cliff Lewis), Glen Bryan Shaw (Cpl. Redfern)*
Director: *Tony Richardson*
Screenwriters: *Nigel Kneale, John Osborne*
PG/115 mins./Drama/UK

Market stallholder Jimmy Porter takes out his frustrations at the restrictions and hypocrisies of postwar Britain on his docile wife, Allison, and her actress friend, Helena Charles, who is eventually seduced by his dangerous, righteous anger.

Written by John Osborne and directed for the Royal Court Theatre by Tony Richardson, *Look Back in Anger* shocked the British stage establishment when it opened in May 1956. Its fury, bitterness and coarse eloquence shattered the complacent classicism that held sway in the smugly middlebrow West End and riled the conservative press with its contention that there were 'no good, brave causes left'.

However, by the time that Nigel Kneale scripted this screen adaptation, much of the wind had been taken from its sails by the prior release of Jack Clayton's *Room at the Top*, which made Joe Lampton, rather than Jimmy Porter, the first 'angry young man' to reach suburbia and the inner-city backstreets. Both were misogynist predators who exploited women to disguise their own social inadequacy. But they became iconic figures for a generation unwilling to knuckle down to the realities of dwindling imperialism and welfare patronage.

Hired at the insistence of the backers (who included Warner Bros) to give this contentiously risky project a box-office safety net, Richard Burton turned in a typically titanic performance, as the cynic whose then subversive philosophising now sounds like so much wind and fury. But he is too old for the part and his style is too polished to convey Porter's self-pitying ennui and callous sexual arrogance. Consequently, he is less persuasive than his female co-stars – Mary Ure (who was reprising the role of the wife who can no longer distinguish between Jimmy's inarticulate love and his garrulous cruelty), Claire Bloom (who almost out-vamps Simone Signoret as the refined other woman) and Dame Edith Evans, who comes close to stealing the picture as Mrs Tanner, the Cockney mother of one of Jimmy's friends, who was invented for the film.

Richardson's Free Cinema background (films such as *Momma Don't Allow*, 1956) ensures that this is a cinematically credible exercise in social realism. But its dramatic tropes quickly became clichés and it's now hard to watch this important picture without some 50 years of subsequent parody continuously intruding. ★★★ **DP**

LOOKING FOR RICHARD (1996)

Starring: *as themselves: Al Pacino, Alec Baldwin, Kevin Spacey, Winona Ryder, Aidan Quinn, Estelle Parsons, Harris Yulin, Gordon MacDonald*
Director: *Al Pacino*
Screenwriters: *Al Pacino, Frederic Kimball (Narration), based on the play* The Tragedy Of Richard The Third *by William Shakespeare*
12/107 mins./Documentary/Drama/USA

Al Pacino's pet project sets out to express his conviction that the Bard is good for your health, through a graft of delivered scenes from *Richard III* (the case study) and documentary debate with both actors and members of the public.

Pacino's directorial debut leads you, the viewer, on an odyssey inside the hearts and minds of actors wrestling with *Richard III*: Shakespeare's infamous tale of powerlust, bloodlust, revenge and betrayal. The onscreen action tracks meetings and rehearsals, discussions and arguments, all interspersed with interviews (Gielgud, Jacobi, Branagh, Vanessa Redgrave, Kevin Kline et al) on the nature of the beasts of The Bard in general and Richard in particular.

As the film progresses, the cast's performance of the play comes to the fore but *Looking For Richard* is far more a journey than a destination. Actors are shown in and out of character, speaking their lines or directly to camera with insights and revelations such as, 'We're getting 40 dollars a day and all the donuts we can eat' (Baldwin).

Pacino – who spent years on this project as his hair changes testify – is uniformly hilarious whether rowing with his producer Michael Hadge or wandering around New York canvassing passers-by for opinions. He also visits London's New Globe (when under construction) and Straford-upon-Avon where, for reasons too bizarre to explain, he attracts the fire brigade to a listed monument.

In among all this jollity, the play is deconstructed, words translated, plots explained, and the whole demystified so that this will automatically become an English Lit. course staple. But it is so much more ... ★★★★ **IN**

LOONEY TOONS: BACK IN ACTION (2003)

Starring: *Brendan Fraser (D.J. Drake/Himself/Voice of Tasmanian Devil/She-Devil), Jenna Elfman (Kate), Steve Martin (Mr. Chairman), Timothy Dalton (Damien Drake), Heather Locklear (Dusty Tails), Joan Cusack (Mother)*
Director: *Joe Dante*
Screenwriter: *Larry Doyle*
PG/87 mins./Animated/Fantasy/Family/USA

Fired from Warner Bros on the same day, security guard D.J. Drake and comedy sidekick Daffy Duck are soon off around the globe rescuing the mysterious Blue Monkey Diamond from the chairman of the nefarious Acme Corporation.

Perhaps that lame pencil-it-in-for-now title is a marketing man's idea of a joke. After all, in a world awash with Bugs Bunny backpacks and Daffy Duck duvets, it's not as if the Looney Toons have ever exactly been away. However, having earned a hiatus from their more lucrative merchandising obligations, Bugs and co. belatedly return to more active duties under the stewardship of Joe Dante, a director whose experience with *Gremlins* should have schooled him in the necessary brand of mischief. And if the 'action' promised by the title ultimately – yet somehow inevitably – turns out to be a blind stumble through odd bits of *Who Framed Roger Rabbit* and *Spy Kids*, children of all ages will still sieve the plot debris for the comedy gold we really came looking for.

Luckily, for those happy to root around, *Back In Action* is occasionally inspired. Wily E. Coyote and Marvin The Martian both score laughs in tantalising cameos, while a gravity-defying car chase in the Looneyverse is much more daring than that one from *The Matrix Reloaded*. Best of all, an astonishing sequence in which Bugs, Daffy and Porky Pig leap from painting to painting in a breathless chase through the Louvre sufficiently demonstrates just how much life modern animation techniques can breathe into these timeless characters.

Viewed as individual shorts, none of the set-pieces completely misfires – even if the amusing stuff is often relegated to the fringes where Bugs and Daffy can be found bantering as of yore. Indeed, the only real bum note is struck by Steve Martin, who makes the fatal mistake of trying to compete with the cartoons. But Martin's mugging aside, the real problem here is not the component parts, but the lack of a decent engine to drive them anywhere. ★★★ **KN**

LORD OF THE RINGS (1978)

Starring: *the voices of: Christopher Guard (Frodo Baggins), William Squire (Gandalf), Michael Scholes (Samwise Gamgee), John Hurt (Aragorn), Simon Chandler (Meriadoc)*
Director: *Ralph Bakshi*
Screenwriter: *Chris Conkling, Peter S. Beagle, based on the novels* The Fellowship Of The Ring *and* The Two Towers *by J.R.R. Tolkien*
PG/132 mins./Animated/Fantasy/Adventure/USA

A group of hobbits are charged with carrying a magical ring into Mordor to be destroyed – knowing the Dark Lord will do everything in his power to stop them.

That Ralph Bakshi's ambitious but unfinished adaptation of Tolkien's tale has acquired a cult status is testimony to the quality of work the animator completed before the financial plug was pulled.

Bakshi's first innovation was to introduce live-action tracing and painting alongside traditional animation techniques. These lend the finished cartoon an unusual look, but one that largely succeeds in pitting our disparate Fellowship against a (genuine) phantom menace in the land of Mordor.

Echoing some of Tolkien's own drawing in the landscapes, each region is given its own distinctive feel through a broad use of colour. Narrative jumps sometimes make the plot hard to follow, and only half of the three books are covered. The enforced ending is rather hurried, but at least the closing battle makes for a fitting climax – smoky, demonic red and cold, stony blue.

It might seem a little crude in these days of CGI, but ultimately Bakshi succeeded in his most basic of tasks: a vivid imagining of Tolkien's timeless tale of Good and Evil. ★★★★ **AY**

THE LORD OF THE RINGS: FELLOWSHIP OF THE RING (2001)

Starring: *Elijah Wood (Frodo Baggins), Ian McKellan (Gandalf), Liv Tyler (Arwen), Viggo Mortensen (Aragorn), Sean Astin (Sam Gamgee), Cate Blanchett (Galadriel), Orlando Bloom (Legolas Greenleaf), Billy Boyd (Peregrin 'Pippin' Took), Ian Holm (Bilbo Baggins), Christopher Lee (Saruman), Dominic Monaghan (Merry), John Rhys-Davis (Gimli), Andy Serkis (Gollum), Hugh Weavering (Elrond), Sean Bean (Boromir)*
Director: *Peter Jackson*
Screenwriters: *Peter Jackson, Philippa Boyens, Fran Walsh, from the novel* The Fellowship Of The Rings *by J.R.R. Tolkien*
PG/171 mins./Fantasy/Adventure/New Zealand/USA

Awards: *Academy Awards – Best Cinematography, Best Visual Effects, Best Makeup, Best Original Score, BAFTA – Audience Award, Best Visual Effects, Best Film, Best Makeup/Hair, David Lean Award for Direction, Empire Awards – Best Actor, Best Debut, Best Film*

Young Hobbit Frodo Baggins becomes the unlikely and unwilling bearer of The One Ring of power, an instrument of unparalleled evil and along with his three Hobbit chums, the wizard Gandalf and a swordsman named Strider, they set out on an epic quest.

Brooking no argument, history should quickly regard Peter Jackson's *The Fellowship Of The Ring* as the first instalment of the best fantasy epic in motion picture history. This statement is worthy of investigation for several reasons.

Fellowship is indeed merely an opening salvo, and even after three hours you will be ravenous with anticipation for the further two parts of the trilogy. *Fellowship* is also unabashedly rooted in the fantasy genre. Not to be confused with the techno-cool of good science fiction, nor even the cutesy charm of family fare like Harry Potter, the territory of Tolkien is clearly marked by goo and goblins and gobbledegook. Persons with an aversion to lines such as, 'To the bridge of Khazad-dûm!' are as well to stay within the Shire-like comforts of home (their loss).

With those caveats in place, it bears repeating: fantasy does not come finer. There are electrifying moments – notably the computer-assisted swooping camera through Isengard as it transforms into a factory for evil – when Jackson's flight of fancy approaches the sublime as the romantic poets would understand it: inspiring awe.

Leaving aside the thorny issue of Tolkien die-hards and their inevitable gripes – 'What no Tom Bombadil?' – Jackson's screenplay (written in collaboration with Fran Walsh and Phillipa Boyens) is both bolder and more judicious than Steven Kloves' surprisingly timid retread of Harry Potter. In particular, rescuing the romance of Arwen and Aragorn from the footnotes and the elevation of Saruman to all-action bad guy actually has a corrective influence on Tolkien's often oblique and female-sparse source material.

There are problems, though. The three-hour running time is high on incident and low on discernible form. After successive detours to Elf habitats Rivendell (the watery home of Elrond) and Lothlórien (the forest home of the Lady Galadriel), the uninitiated might well ask why these crazy Elf kids can't just live together and spare us all this attenuated dramatic structure.

More importantly, the action clearly climaxes in the desperate flight from the Mines Of Moria, where the largely seamless SFX is showcased in the best possible light – total darkness – but the narrative demands a different, downbeat ending. Indeed, but for some fine emotional playing from Bean, Mortensen, Astin and Wood, the final fight might feel like a particularly brutal game of paintball in Bluebell Wood. But then, the real battles are yet to come ... ★★★★★ **CK**

Movie Trivia: The Lord of the Rings

The *Lord Of the Rings* trilogy shares the record for the longest ever shoot with *Apocalypse Now*: both took 274 days. The portraits of Bilbo's parents are actually of Peter Jackson and his wife and writing partner, Fran Walsh. Jackson also makes a cameo as a belching yokel outside The Prancing Pony Inn.

THE LORD OF THE RINGS: RETURN OF THE KING (2003)

Starring: *Elijah Wood (Frodo Baggins), Ian McKellan (Gandalf), Liv Tyler (Arwen), Viggo Mortensen (Aragorn), Sean Astin (Sam Gamgee), Cate Blanchett (Galadriel), Orlando Bloom (Legolas Greenleaf), Billy Boyd (Peregrin 'Pippin' Took), Ian Holm (Bilbo Baggins), Christopher Lee (Saruman), Dominic Monaghan (Merry), John Rhys-Davis (Gimli), Andy Serkis (Gollum), Hugh Weavering (Elrond), Bernard Hill (King Theoden), Miranda Otto (Eowyn of Rohan), David Wenham (Faramir)*
Director: *Peter Jackson*
Screenwriters: *Peter Jackson, Philippa Boyens, Fran Walsh, from the novel* The Fellowship Of The Rings *by J.R.R. Tolkien*
12/192 mins./Fantasy/Adventure/New Zealand/USA

Awards: *Academy Awards – Best Art Direction/Set Decoration, Best Costume, Best Director, Best Editing, Best Makeup, Best Original Score, Best Original Song, Best Picture, Best Sound, Best Visual Effects, Best Adapted Screenplay, BAFTA – Audience Award, Best Visual Effects, Best Cinematography, Best Film, Best Adapted Screenplay, Empire Awards – Best British Actor (Andy Serkis), Best Film, Scene of the Year, Golden Globes – Best Director, Best Drama, Best Original Score, Best Original Song*

The saga continues. Frodo and Sam edge closer to Mount Doom, but the deceitful Gollum plans to lead them into a trap and have the ring for himself. Meanwhile, the armies of Mordor are marching on the Gondorian city of Minas Tirith, where Gandalf finds Denethor, father of Boromir and Faramir, losing his sanity . . .

And so all good things come to an end. But now that Peter Jackson's epic has been unveiled in its entirety, what will be the lasting effects of his achievement?

Well, grand-scale fantasy filmmaking is back on the menu. Jackson has also proved that notions of risk and ambition needn't be confined to the low-budget, indie end of the spectrum; nor does California have an exclusive stranglehold on groundbreaking special effects.

And then there's the DVD factor. Just as *The Lord Of The Rings* was upping the stakes in theatres, so too was its DVD release pattern defining what can (and should) be done on disc for major movies.

In particular, the four-disc extended editions seem to have affected the director's thinking as to what he can get away with in his theatrical final cut. Hence the public grumbles from Christopher Lee about the non-appearance of Saruman in this final instalment. While it might have been fair to grant Lee a curtain call, Jackson quite rightly realises that it is Sauron, not Saruman, whose fiery eye encompasses all the narrative strands of the climax.

Return Of The King marks the first time in the series when Jackson's roots as a horror filmmaker creep through. As the orcs catapult severed Gondorian heads beyond the walls of Minas Tirith, flesh-rotted ghosts draw swords alongside Aragorn and giant spider Shelob stalks Frodo through dark, web-shrouded tunnels, the film pushes the boundaries of its 12A certificate.

And so it should, because the look and tone must necessarily grow darker as the Hobbits near Mount Doom and Mordor's evil hand grips Middle-earth ever tighter.

Character nuances have been crafted over an unprecedented ten hours-plus of cinematic storytelling: from Strider lurking in the shadowy corner to Aragorn rallying the troops; from Merry and Pippin as bumbling fools to stout-hearted, pint-sized warriors. Only Legolas and Gimli seem to have regressed (in screen time at least) to set-piece archer and comedy sidekick respectively. At least Andy Serkis is rewarded for his Gollum voice work with an early flashback that gets his face on screen, as well as warning us that, under the ring's power, Smeagol can be as murderous as Gollum.

Jackson has kept the momentum of the series rolling on and on through the traditionally 'difficult' middle part and 'weak' finale, delivering a climax to the story that's neater and more affecting than what Tolkien managed on the printed page. Some viewers might feel that the director sprinkles some cheese on his extended coda, adding at least one false ending too many (even if he does ignore the book's Scouring of The Shire).

But those who have walked beside these heroes every step of the way on such a long journey deserve the emotional pay-off as well as the action peaks, and they will be genuinely touched as the final credits roll. ★★★★★ **AM**

THE LORD OF THE RINGS: THE TWO TOWERS (2002)

Starring: *Elijah Wood (Frodo Baggins), Ian McKellan (Gandalf), Liv Tyler (Arwen), Viggo Mortensen (Aragorn), Sean Astin (Sam Gamgee), Cate Blanchett (Galadriel), Orlando Bloom (Legolas Greenleaf), Billy Boyd (Peregrin 'Pippin' Took), Ian Holm (Bilbo Baggins), Christopher Lee (Saruman), Dominic Monaghan (Merry), John Rhys-Davis (Gimli), Andy Serkis (Gollum), Hugh Weavering (Elrond)*
Director: *Peter Jackson*
Screenwriters: *Peter Jackson, Philippa Boyens, Fran Walsh, from the novel* The Fellowship Of The Rings *by J.R.R. Tolkien*
12/171 mins./Fantasy/Adventure/New Zealand/USA

Awards: *Academy Awards – Best Sound Editing, Best Visual Effects, BAFTA – Audience Award, Best Visual Effects, Best Costume, Empire Awards – Best Film*

The saga continues: Hobbits Frodo and Sam press on to Mordor in the company of the mysterious Gollum. Aragorn, Legolas and Gimli travel to the troubled Rohan, while Merry and Pippin discover a new ally in the shape of Treebeard the tree-shepherd.

Peter Jackson has always maintained that *The Two Towers* is 'the second act' of his epic undertaking, and perhaps the true greatness of the middle chapter will only be clear when viewed in context. As a stand-alone film, however, *The Two Towers* is not quite as good as *Fellowship*. (Nor, indeed, does it extend the universe or deepen the relationships in the manner of *The Empire Strikes Back*.) That it still merits the full five stars is merely an indication of how high the benchmark has been set.

Picking up pretty much where *Fellowship* left off, this is a considerably darker film, with Frodo falling further under the influence of the Ring (giving rise to some seriously spooky hallucinations), while Saruman wreaks even more havoc. There's also the first appearance of Saruman's spy, the sinister Wormtongue, and the complex Gollum, a brilliant combination of computer trickery and raspy vocals from Andy Serkis.

Other newcomers include Faramir, the understandably miffed brother of the recently deceased Boromir, and Éowyn, who spends much of her time casting winsome glances in the general direction of Aragorn. Eventually the plot complexities become more coherent, setting the action up for the forthcoming finale, *The Return Of The King*.

As we've come to expect, this is spectacular stuff – from an opening which sees Frodo troubled by dreams about the demise of Gandalf, through to the climactic Battle Of Helm's Deep, which is nothing short of breathtaking. But Jackson cleverly tempers the louder, brasher sequences with some heartstring-tugging moments – peasants despondent as they are forced to abandon their villages, Aragorn and Arwen's troubled relationship, and, of course, the return of Gandalf (Sir Ian McKellen, superb as ever), one of the film's most powerful, memorable images that may well leave Ring devotees a little misty-eyed.

However, those who still believe that the trilogy is beyond criticism may find their views challenged by *The Two Towers*. It's just as long as the first film, but gets the heroes no closer to a final victory. And, where the first movie developed its emotional tone from the brightness of The Shire to a darker climax, the sequel is more of a one-note affair, shadowy in both look and content.

This is particularly true of the Ringbearer's quest, which adds the not-insignificant Gollum to the party, but suffers more than the other story strands from the cross-cutting and finishes with a nearly identical pep talk from Sam to the tearful speech that climaxed *Fellowship*. Of course, given the nature of the material, and Jackson's desire to be faithful, this is all understandable. And by the time we all end up under siege at Helm's Deep, it's unlikely anyone will give a toss about narrative arcs: like Gollum, this is simply gob-smacking, mind-blowing, never-seen-before stuff. ★★★★★ **CW**

LORENZO'S OIL (1992)

Starring: *Nick Nolte (Augusto Odone), Susan Sarandon (Michaela Odone), Peter Ustinov (Professor Nikolais), Kathleen Wilhote (Deirdre Murphy), Gerry Bamman (Doctor Judalon), Maduka Steady (Omuori)*
Director: *George Miller*
Screenwriters: *George Miller, Nick Enright*
15/129 mins./Drama/USA

Aged 7, Lorenzo develops ALD, a fatal and degenerative disease. Not content with sitting and watching their son die, his parents Augusta and Michaela start to investigate the disease in the hope of finding a cure.

In this dramatic account of an extraordinary true story, director George Miller pursues unsentimental ends by laying bare the concepts of love, trust and faith, although it is not completely immune to Disease-Of-The-Week Syndrome, manifested in the viewer weeping despite resenting the blatant heartstring tugging that is going on here.

Heavy-hitting duo Nick Nolte (under the handicap of a painstaking Italian characterisation) and Susan Sarandon score heavily on the grief-and-rage-ometer as Augusto and Michaela Odone, whose son Lorenzo was diagnosed with an extremely rare and always fatal form of dystrophy, ALD, in 1984, when no treatment existed.

The devastated Odones, however, were not your average Joe and Betty next door, but highly educated take-charge people whose determination and medical detection – including putting themselves on crash science courses – would defy belief and invite sardonic hilarity but for the fact that their fanatical efforts did lead to the life-saving discovery now known as Lorenzo's Oil.

As co-written (with Nick Enright) and directed by Miller, who qualified as a doctor before birthing *Mad Max*, this is in part a gripping case of dogged intellectual sleuthing and in part a justifiable if unsubtle-bordering-on-the-satirical indictment of the medical establishment. It centres, though, on parental love approaching obsession, with the suffering of Lorenzo torturously depicted as the Odones refuse to give him up and the audience begins to ponder how much distress life is worth.

Compassionate but tough-minded, this emerges as a love story, and one which, for all its handsome visuals, elaborate shots and swelling music, is uncomfortable viewing with nothing cosy or compromised in the unflinching performances, particularly Sarandon's.

The only phoney note, ironically, comes from Miller's gaffe of enlisting retired Yorkshire biochemist Don Suddaby, extractor of the said oil, for a self-conscious appearance as himself. That aside, this is exhausting, intelligent and undeniably moving. ★★★★ **AE**

⊙ THE LOST BOYS (1987)

Starring: *Jason Patric (Michael Emerson), Corey Haim (Sam Emerson), Dianne West (Lucy Emerson), Kiefer Sutherland (David), Jami Getz (Star), Corey Feldman (Edgar Frog), Alex Winter (Marko)*
Director: *Joel Schumacher*
Screenwriters: *Jeffrey Boam, Janice Fischer, James Jeremias*
15/93 mins./Horror/Comedy/USA

Two boys move into an area populated by bikers and plagued by a series of bizarre deaths. Whilst shrugging off rumours about vampires, the older brother Mike begins to show signs of vampirism, so younger bro Sam enlists the help of two vampire hunters.

The Lost Boys' theme of dead things walking is more apt than anyone could have predicted. At the time a gallery of teenage pin-ups and promising talent, the film has now become a showcase for prematurely deceased careers.

That aside, Joel Schumacher's follow-up to *St. Elmo's Fire* stands as a genre landmark, one that bled new life into a mythos grown as old and musty as its undead protagonists. Not as nuanced or bold as Kathryn Bigelow's *Near Dark* (released the same year), what this brought to the table was style, sass and a sense of humour.

One of the first movies to successfully bridge the horror/comedy divide, this MTV-enhanced vamp outing dared to poke fun at its heritage, tempering the scares with some big laughs.

The third act is somewhat lazy but, taken as a whole, *The Lost Boys* remains a supremely watchable example of something the 80s did right. It also showcases Kiefer Sutherland in the most seductive and memorable role of his career, vampire leader David. ★★★★ **JD**

⊙ LOST HIGHWAY (1997)

Starring: *Bill Pullman (Fred Madison), Patricia Arquette (Renee Madison/Alice Wakefield), Balthazar Getty (Peter Raymond Dayton), Robert Blacke (Mystery Man), Natasha Gregson Wagner (Sheila)*
Director: *David Lynch*
Screenwriters: *David Lynch, Barry Gifford*
18/128 mins./Drama/Mystery/Thriller/USA

A man is taunted by increasingly disturbing videotapes that cause him to kill his wife, but when in jail for that crime, he becomes someone else and so begins an even more confusing life . . .

After a pulsating Bowie song – accompanied by a moronic cruise down a (presumably lost) highway, there is a disconcerting 20-minute overture. Pullman as Fred Madison puts in a splendidly foul-stenched performance opposite a high voltage Arquette (playing his wife Renee) – clad in the best wig and super sexy clothes since Uma T. in *Pulp Fiction*.

Things go pear-shaped when each morning, mysterious videos are left outside their house, the contents of which become more disturbing each day. Pullman starts hallucinating witchlike images of his wife. He kills her but doesn't remember doing it, is imprisoned, dies and comes back as car mechanic Pete Dayton who is working at a garage under the supervision of Arnie.

Meanwhile, Arquette returns as a blonde siren (called Alice Wakefield) who is stepping out with mob man Mr. Eddy. She has an affair with Dayton and in search of a fast buck tries to get him to commit murder. But will she double-cross and kill him? And so the dream becomes – as things are wont to do on Planet Lynch – a nightmare, signposted by the recurring presence of a Dracula-type Mystery Man who will try to destroy them all. There's also numerous other oddities including a cameo by visceral US rocker Marilyn Manson as a porn star. And much disturbance later, we're back for a laconic drive down the highway.

Confused? Oh well, go with it. Interested? You should be. ★★★★ **AM**

⊙ THE LOST HONOUR OF KATHARINA BLUM (DIE VERLOERENE EHRE DER KATHARINA BLUM) (1975)

Starring: *Angela Winkler (Katharina Blum), Mario Adorf (Beizemenne), Dieter Laser (Werner Toetgess), Heinz Bennent (Dr. Blorna), Hannelore Hoger (Trude Blorna)*
Director: *Volker Schlörndorff*
Screenwriters: *Volker Schlörndorff, Margarethe von Trotta, based on the novel by Heinrich Böll*
15/104 mins./Drama/West Germany

Unaware that Ludwig is an army deserter falsely suspected of terrorism, apolitical maid Katharina Blum wakes from a one-night stand to find herself in the middle of a police raid that will lead to her being villified as a fellow traveller by Police Komissar Beizmenne and journalist Werner Toetgess.

Following the emergence of the Red Army Faction in West Germany in the early 1970s, the right-wing tabloid press, led by Axel Springer at Bild-Zeitung, began a smear campaign designed to whip up the same Red-baiting hysteria that had paralysed America during the McCarthy witchhunts. The police responded by tapping phones, infiltrating protest groups and arresting suspects in raids that were often prompted by perfidious testimony.

Having been accused of harbouring fugitives, Heinrich Böll wrote the Nobel Prize-winning novel on which this film was based as a warning to the complacent German people that the authorities were resorting to fascist tactics to suppress essential liberties. Collaborating with Volker Schlöndorff and Margarethe von Trotta, Böll simplified the text's flashbacking structure to concentrate on the concept conveyed in its subtitle, 'How Violence Develops and Where It Can Lead'.

Thus, the married directors adopted a sinister visual style that relied heavily on the idea of surveillance, with Ludwig first being seen through the lense of a police camera and their sense of omnipresence reinforced by the frequent switches between colour and monochrome footage. Much of the action was also filmed through glass or similar barriers, which isolated the protagonists in general and Katharina in particular, as her space was continuously invaded by both the press and the police (and, thus, by implication, the public following her story in the papers and on the screen).

However, the characterisation was highly formulaic and Schlöndorff and Von Trotta left us little room for intellectual manoeuvre. Consequently, the international press were somewhat dismissive of the film's political and dramatic naiveté and its primary value now is as a snapshot of the national psyche at the height of the Baader-Meinhof crisis.

Yet, it was an esteemed popular success within the Federal Republic and it afforded New German Cinema its first commercial success. The pressures of its production took its toll on the co-directors' marriage, however, and Von Trotta struck out to build an uncompromising solo career. ★★★ **DP**

⊙ LOST HORIZON (1937)

Starring: *Ronald Colman (Robert Conway), Jane Wyatt (Sondra), Edward Everett Horton (Alexander P. Lovett), John Howard (George Conway), Thomas Mitchell (Henry Barnard)*
Director: *Frank Capra*
Screenwriters: *Robert Riskin, Sidney Buchman, based on the novel by Jame Hilton*
U/132 mins./Drama/USA

In the near-inaccessible Tibetan Valley of the Blue Moon, far from the ills of the world, is Shangri-La. Robert Conway is brought to the lamasery, to

take over as High Lama from the centuries-old priest who founded the community.

A magical 1930s best-seller by James Hilton (whose other filmed utopia was *Goodbye Mr Chips*) becomes a remarkably effective film by Frank Capra, who mainly abandons his usual social comedy for wistful romance and high adventure (Edward Everett Horton and Thomas Mitchell do get some kooky scenes). Escaping from a convincingly raucous Chinese uprising in 1935 (or a Japanese invasion in 1937, if you see the rejigged version re-released during WWII), a planeload of lost souls crash in the Himalayas and are escorted to a temperate valley in the snowy wastes where they find Shangri-La. Diplomat Ronald Colman, sporting a spiffy moustache, is impressed by the overpowering peace and harmony of the place, where people reputedly live hundreds of years, while everyone else – with the exception of Colman's cynical brother (John Howard) – discovers reasons not to return to the outside world.

A mammoth, difficult production, this has outdated, awkward stretches as the Lama and his Number One Sidekick (H.B. Warner) propose a sinister-sounding philosophy of polite pacifism, but its magical stretches, including a frankly sexy romance between Colman and Shangri-La girl Jane Wyatt (whose double has a nude swim scene), still play well. The memorable last reel finds Colman and Howard leaving the valley with a young girl (Margo) who reverts to her true old age away from the magic. At the end, against the odds, Colman struggles to return to the land 'on the other side of the mountain'. Remade in 1973 as a hideous musical. Shangri-La later inspired a girl group, a Kinks song and innumerable suburban house-names. ★★★★ KN

LOST IN AMERICA (1985)

Starring: *Albert Brooks (David Howard), Julie Hagerty (Linda Howard), Sylvia Farrel (Sylvia), Tina Kincaid (Model), Candy Ann Brown (David's Secretary), Maggie Roswell (Patty)*
Director: *Albert Brooks*
Screenwriters: *Albert Brooks, Monica Mcgowan Johnson*
15/91 mins./Comedy/USA

Upwardly-mobile ad man David Howard is just about to take possession of a new house, Cadillac and executive vice-presidency. When his wife accuses him of 'responsibility' and his boss tries to transfer him to New York, David decides to follow the example set by his favourite movie (*Easy Rider*) and drop out in search of America.

While Dennis Hopper and Peter Fonda had motorcycles filled with cocaine and cash, this amusing update/parody of *Easy Rider* finds Albert Brooks and Julie Hagerty setting out on their road movie trip in a mobile home stuffed with traveller's cheques, and sneering at a clod who gets *Easy Rider* mixed up with *Easy Money* ('Rodney Dangerfield – I like him'). However, even rebels with a hundred and fifty thousand dollars in cash find life on the road difficult, and the Howards soon learn that their dreams of great American freedom are sadly impractical and out of date.

Albert Brooks – who writes, directs and stars – is perhaps most familiar as one of life's nice-guy supporting actors, in the likes of *Broadcast News* and *Taxi Driver*, but his occasional all-round auteur films have the feel of a less egocentric, more open-minded, equally neurotic Woody Allen.

Cherishable, pointed and resolutely small-scale, *Lost in America* is probably Brooks's best film. The star is seen at his best when ranting in front of bewildered straight men like the fellow ad exec he upbraids with 'your song stunk, I hate your suit and I could hurt you!' or the Las Vegas casino manager he tries to brainwash into returning his wife's immense losings ('as the boldest experiment in advertising history, you give us our money back'). Julie Hagerty, the *Airplane!* stewardess, is fetchingly nervous as the hero's wife, and equally skilled at revealing the funny side of America's middle-class insecurities. ★★★★ KN

LOST IN LA MANCHA (2002)

Starring: *as themselves: Jeff Bridges (Narrator), Johnny Depp, Jean Rochefort, Terry Gilliam*
Directors: *Keith Fulton, Louis Pepe*
15/89 mins./Documentary/2002

Madrid, 2000: Terry Gilliam starts filming on *The Man Who Killed Don Quixote*, a pet project he has been working on since 1990. Despite major budgetary restrictions that allow him no margin for error, he must try to complete what is a seemingly jinxed production . . .

Having already made *The Hamster Factor And Other Tales Of Twelve Monkeys*, filmmakers Keith Fulton and Louis Pepe were enlisted by Terry Gilliam to chronicle the making of his newest film, *The Man Who Killed Don Quixote*.

However, due to the catastrophic bad luck which plagued the production, their film, *Lost In La Mancha*, ended up being the first 'un-making of' documentary about a film.

From the early pre-production stage onwards, Fulton and Pepe's unrestricted access to the set gives us a first-hand look at Gilliam's creative vision coming to fruition. But having sacrificed the financial safety of Hollywood for creative freedom, there is no studio money to keep the film alive when flash floods hit the set, damaging sets and equipment – and the actor playing Quixote, Jean Rochefort, becomes seriously ill.

The film's collapse is made all the more poignant considering the flashes of brilliance we have seen from the first rushes. ★★★★ JB

LOST IN SPACE (1998)

Starring: *William Hurt (Prof. John Robinson), Mimi Rogers (Dr. Maureen Robinson), Lacey Chabert (Penny Robinson), Heather Graham (Dr. Judy Robinson), Jack Johnson (Will Robinson), Gary Oldman (Dr. Zachary Smith)*
Director: *Stephen Hopkins*
Screenwriter: *Akiva Goldsman, based on a television series by Irwin Allen*
PG/124 mins./Action/Adventure/Sci-fi/USA

An American, space-age family get stranded en route to colonising a designated planet.

Pioneering legit efforts to colonise far-flung planet Alpha Prime, dogged, career-consumed Professor Robinson is set to haul spouse and sprogs across the stars. Shortly after disembarking however, the Robinsons' robot goes berserk at the behest of dastardly saboteur Dr. Zachary Smith, treating the ship like a rock band's hotel room and spinning it towards the sun. Out of options, they punch the hyperdrive, averting imminent fiery doom but leaving the family stranded somewhere in the galaxy, or – hey! – lost in space. And as this super-embellished onslaught ebbs, several complicating factors have been deftly sketched: the professor has intimacy issues with son Will, West fancies eldest daughter Judy, younger daughter Penny hates everyone, and Mrs. Robinson is a modern, sexy mum who cares deeply for her brood. Oh, and Smith is a bounder and a cad.

But sketches they sadly remain, due to the perennial danger forcing an endless parade of eye-poppers. It's true enough that among a seven-strong human ensemble, not all roles can be fully fleshed out – Oldman is good value and LeBlanc manages a nice, if standard, flirtation with Graham, but even Johnson's attempts to gain fatherly acceptance lack sufficient time to stick convincingly. And in this shortfall, the film loses its grand design, for though there's an obvious, admirable effort to supply character development and plot twists, the set-work and special effects – both stylish and stunning – tend to dominate. Praise is nevertheless due to the host of effects houses responsible for hideous space spiders, a ship ominously reminiscent of *Event Horizon* and countless other amazing visuals. And director Hopkins has at least produced a finished article that rips along, and while playing with a more nervy edge than the smiley 60s TV show, original cast members making cameo appearances makes for a clever nod to its origins – June Lockhart is upgraded to school principal and Mark Goddard, similarly promoted from major to general, browbeats LeBlanc as he rails against his 'baby-sitting' assignment. ★★★ **KN**

LOST IN TRANSLATION (2003)

Starring: *Scarlett Johansson (Charlotte), Bill Murray (Bob Harris), Giovanni Ribisi (John), Anna Faris (Kelly), Fumihiro Hayashi (Charlie)*
Director: *Sofia Coppola*
Screenwriter: *Sofia Coppola*
15/97 mins./Drama/Comedy/USA

Awards: *Academy Awards – Best Original Screenplay, BAFTA – Best Editing, Best Actor, Best Actress, Golden Globes – Best Musical/Comedy, Best Actor*

In Tokyo to shoot a whisky commercial, jaded movie star Bob Harris meets neglected wife Charlotte in a hotel. Bored with their lives and bemused by the city, they gradually fall for each other.

With cinemas dominated by underwhelming blockbusters and formulaic rom-coms, it's easy to become disillusioned with the state of the movies. Thank the almighty, then, for *Lost In Translation*, which will restore your faith in the power of the medium.

This is a film exploring themes of fidelity, disillusionment and commercialism, but one in which you're never far from a belly laugh or a delicate tug of the heartstrings. Sofia Coppola showed huge potential with her first feature, *The Virgin Suicides*, but her follow-up represents a leap into the A-list of young talent.

Ironically for a piece partly concerned with breakdowns in communication, Coppola and her cast convey complex ideas brilliantly. Neither the heart-stopping ecstasy of new love, nor the mind-numbing agony of jet lag, nor the inspirational, life-affirming qualities of pop music are easy to evoke on celluloid, but the film addresses these and every issue with an eloquent simplicity.

The writer-director is also smart enough to pepper her screenplay with comic set-pieces in which Bill Murray can cut loose. Photo shoots, TV sets, hospital waiting rooms, golf courses and hotel gyms serve as backdrops against which Murray displays his comic genius. These crowd-pleasing moments fuel the audience's affection for the character (even if they occasionally patronise his Japanese hosts), so we're deeply emotionally involved when, understandably, he begins to lose his heart to the delectable Johansson.

The growing romance is portrayed with delicate beauty, including a breathtaking moment in – of all the hackneyed, overused settings – a karaoke lounge. Murray croons Roxy Music's hit 'More Than This', his eyes meet Johansson's and, in a single take, with no heavy-handed close-ups, the electric connection between the two characters is made clear. Like lightning captured in a bottle, it will make the hairs on the back of your neck stand on end. ★★★★★ **RF**

THE LOST WEEKEND (1945)

Starring: *Ray Milland (Don Birnam), Jane Wyman (Helen St. James), Phillip Terry (Nick Birnam), Howard de Silva (Nat the Bartender), Doris Dowling (Gloria)*
Director: *Billy Wilder*
Screenwriters: *Charles Brackett, Billy Wilder, based on the novel by Charles L. Jackson*
PG/101 mins./Drama/Film-noir/USA

Awards: *Academy Awards – Best Actor, Best Director, Best Picture, Best Screenplay, Golden Globes – Best Drama, Best Actor, Best Director*

Don Birnam, a writer with a serious drink problem, is left to his own devices over a weekend by his girlfriend and brother and launches on a binge.

Ray Milland, usually a light leading man, gave his career-best work in Billy Wilder's then-daring drama of alcoholism. 'I'm not a drinker,' claims the protagonist, 'I'm a drunk!' Milland is charming enough to make it credible that people would stick by his character through endless disappointments, but has an unforgettable way of snarling with his fingers as he beckons bartender Howard da Silva to bend over and listen to another pointed anecdote.

Over the course of the film, one long weekend in New York, Birnam slides into the gutter, sponging off a bartender and a friendly streetwalker, desperately trying to pawn his typewriter to buy booze (it's Yom Kippur and all the pawnbrokers are shut), getting caught trying to lift a purse in a crowded bar, effectively robbing a liquour store by browbeating the clerk, spending a night in the locked alcoholic ward halfway between prison and hospital where snide attendant Frank Faylen (as close to gay as a film character could be in 1945) jeers that this is bound to be the first of many visits, then contemplating suicide before a tentative redemption.

The early stretches are light intoxication, with a typically Wilderian streak of dark comedy, but the film darkens and becomes nightmarish, with composer Miklos Rosza mixing in the science fiction sound of the theremin to convey distorted perception. It ends with a note of hope, and Birnam typing away at his novel, but the horrors are harrowing enough to suggest the hero will always have a bottle on a string outside his window and a bed waiting for him in the 'alkie ward'. ★★★★★ **KN**

THE LOST WORLD (1925)

Starring: *Bessie Love (Miss Paula White), Lewis Stone (Sir John Roxton), Wallace Beery (Prof. Challenger), Lloyd Hughes (Edward E. Malone), Alma Bennett (Gladys Hungerford), Arthur Hoyt (Prof. Summerlee), Margaret McWade (Mrs. Challenger)*
Director: *Harry O. Hoyt*
Screenwriter: *Marion Fairfax, based on the novel by Sir Arthur Conan Doyle.*
U/64 mins./Adventure/USA

Controversial Professor Challenger maintains that dinosaurs still exist on a plateau in South America. He leads an expedition up the Amazon, partly to find out what happened to another explorer whose daughter tags along, and proves his theories.

The first film version of Sir Arthur Conan Doyle's splendid novel of high adventure, and still the most-rewarding. It circulates in several cuts, most pruned of significant footage (a love triangle among the explorers almost disappears completely, and the 'comical' black servant Zambo loses a lot of embarrassing inter-title dialect), but the restored 93-minute version is highly recommended as an example of state-of-the-art special effects circa 1925. The explorers are a broad-strokes lot, though Beery enjoys exploding as the scrappy Professor Challenger, Lewis Stone is dignified as the big-game hunter and Love winning as the tagalong heroine written into Doyle's all-male drama.

The main attraction, however, is Willis H. O'Brien's pre-*King Kong* stop motion monster effects: here, his dinosaurs tear bloody chunks out of each other in their fights, a brontosaurus rampages through London (smashing the Blue Posts pub), a family of triceratopses see off a fiendish allosaurus ('the pest of prehistory'). The film cleverly includes some real nature footage early on, with the hunter lecturing the girl on the habits of sloths or miniature bears, subtly preparing us for similar tid-bits about the habits of extinct animals. The other interesting denizen of the *Lost World* is a fanged ape-man (Bull Montana), who acts like a precursor to Kong as he hinders the explorers' escape from the volcano-shattered plateau.

It was remade in 1960 with Claude Rains, Jill St John and iguanas with stuck-on fins and horns, and there have been TV versions with John Rhys-Davies, Patrick Bergin and Bob Hoskins; Michael Crichton had the cheek to lift Doyle's title for his sequel to *Jurassic Park*. ★★★ **KN**

THE LOST WORLD: JURASSIC PARK (1997)

Starring: *Jeff Goldblum (Dr. Ian Malcolm), Julianne Moore (Dr. Sarah Harding), Pete Postlethwaite (Roland Tembo), Richard Attenborough (John Hammond), Vince Vaughn (Nick Van Owen)*
Director: *Steven Spielberg*
Screenwriter: *David Koepp, based on the novel by Michael Crichton*
PG/129 mins./Action/Adventure/ USA

A research team is sent to the Jurassic Park Site B island to study the dinosaurs there but they face competition from another team of researchers with a different agenda.

There are few pressures on a director that can be equal to those facing a pre-*Lost World* Spielberg. Not only was he making a sequel to the then-highest grossing movie of all time, but his last film, the Oscar-winning *Schindler's List*, had been arguably his most critically acclaimed, and certainly his most serious work. To follow that with a people-munching monster screamer was both unusual and risky. But it was very Spielberg.

'I want to go back and forth from entertainment to socially conscious movies,' he'd said on his last day of shooting *Jurassic Park*, and by following *Schindler* with *The Lost World* (three years later), he couldn't have proved this statement better. Loosely based on Michael Crichton's *JP* 'successor' about a secret dino-populated Site B, *The Lost World: Jurassic Park* was always going to be a highly-anticipated release. As soon as news of a sequel was out, fans feverishly swapped rumours on the net, their enthusiasm fuelled by tales of on-set secrecy ('Ask any actor involved with *JP2* for some inside information and they'll tell you to get lost,' salivated magazine *Sci Fi Invasion*).

Critics were no less interested, but obviously more wary, perhaps torn between expecting a worthless copy-cat cash-in, or a sequel to rival the quality of *Indiana Jones And The Temple Of Doom*. They got neither. Firstly, *JP2* was a much darker, more brooding affair than its predecessor, in which good guys died and literal armies of bad men – not just the rogue few – marched around meddling with nature. This was not simply a rehashing of the same old formula. But despite going on to become the tenth highest grossing movie of all time, raking in $590 million, it had a mixed reception from both critics and public alike. It was accused of overusing CGI, of lacking suspense, and as being – horror of horrors – 'not very Spielberg.'

True, the feelgood factor so prevalent in Spielberg's earlier adventure movies was in relatively short supply. But his trademark absent-father-redeemed storyline was played out with both the dinosaur characters (protective parent seeks lost baby T-Rex) and the human ones (Ian Malcolm grows closer to his daughter and to girlfriend/mother figure Sarah Harding). Theme-wise it was certainly Spielberg, focusing on creatures out of their natural habitat (think *Jaws*, *E.T.* and *Close Encounters* as well as *Jurassic Park*). It also strongly reinforced his don't-mess-with-nature message. In this film, human interference brings the monster dangerously close to home, directly threatening the suburban family unit and by implication the viewers. Significantly, the T-Rex is brought back to the USA by what Nick (Vaughan) calls the 'cowboys': men who've violently intruded on (semi) natural territory. Which in a *Jurassic Park* movie, is the surest way to end up as dino dinner (second only to going to the toilet, it would seem).

As for lack of suspense, this was perhaps a comment better directed toward the arguably less involving plot, than to individual scenes. Take the scene when Sarah, Ian and Nick are hanging over the cliff edge in the jeep. When Sarah falls onto the pane of glass and realises it is all that lies between her and the empty, certain-death blackness below, the POV is incredible, focusing excruciatingly on the slowly cracking glass above the ravine. It is one of those accomplished Spielberg moments when despite our certainty that the character will survive, we are hanging on to her every move with intense concern.

The biggest, most inevitable problem for *The Lost World* was that the public had seen the dinosaurs before. Think of the fuss when *Jurassic Park* came out: it was the CGI dinosaurs everyone was excited about. In *Jurassic Park*, the characters' sense of awe when first encountering the creatures is palpable and incredibly effective, principally because it mirrors the audience's reaction. In *The Lost World*, not even different types of creature, a greater use of CGI or new, dino-virgin characters could match that initial marvel that awed an entire world.

Perhaps, the best way to view *The Lost World* is to not take it too seriously. After all, there are plenty of signs that it doesn't do so itself. Old B-movie tribute gags abound in its *King-Kong/Godzilla* ending. Ian Malcolm – who we first see here mid-yawn, echoing the roaring dinosaur's jaws – is an enjoyable wisecracker, quipping sardonically in even the most stressful situations. He serves as a useful summariser of the film, and a postmodern nod to its origins. 'Yeah, 'Ooh! Ahhh!' That's how this all starts,' he spits sarcastically to his wide-eyed colleagues when they first encounter the dinosaurs. 'Then there's the running, and the screaming.' And let's face it, as long as they weren't running screaming from the multiplexes, Spielberg could count himself as having done something right. Although, it is significant that Spielberg demurred the opportunity to go back a third time. *JP3* was handed over to Joe Johnson, with him as executive producer. ★★★★ **ASm**

LOUISIANA STORY (1948)

Starring: *Joseph Boudreaux (Alexander Napoleon Ulysses Latour), Lionel Le Blanc (His Father), E. Bienvenu (His Mother), Frank Hardy (The Driller), C.P. Guedry (The Boilerman)*
Director: *Robert J. Flaherty*
Screenwriters: *Robert J. Flaherty, Francis H. Flaherty*
U/78 mins./Docu-drama/USA
Awards: *BAFTA – Best Documentary*

Thirteen year-old Alexander Napoleon Ulysses Latour's capricious pursuit of an alligator in the bayou of Petite Anse is interrupted when he befriends a driller and his boilerman as they search the swamplands for oil.

In 1944, Robert Flaherty was invited by the Standard Oil Company to make a mainstream docudramatic movie about the dangers and difficulties involved in drilling for oil. Arriving in the Mississippi Delta, Flaherty saw a derrick being towed by a motor launch and was immediately inspired by the rough poetry of both the interloping industry and the backwater locales in which it was pursued.

Having recruited cameraman Richard Leacock (a future Direct Cinema pioneer) and editor Helen von Dongen, Flaherty chose his cast according to type from among the Cajun locals and prepared his locations on Avery Island. Standard came up with a budget of $175,000 and a contract that enabled Flaherty to keep the distribution rights with no obligation to refund any surplus costs (which was as well, as he went through another $83,000 as the shoot sprawled over 10 months).

Flaherty's personality is evident in every frame of a film that's as much about his own childhood as it is about an Arcadian kid's blithe acceptance of both the perils of the wilderness and the intrusion of industrialisation upon his idyll. It's also something of a summation of Flaherty's filmic fascination with the untamed nature that had also informed *Nanook Of The North*, *Moana* and *Man Of Aran*.

Yet, the power and poignancy of the action came as much through Von Dongen's adroit editing of footage that Flaherty had a habit of filming as the whim took him rather than with any preconceived design in mind. Thus, the sinister lyricism of the wetlands opening and the atmospheric potency of the nighttime drilling sequence are primarily Von Dongen's creation and their impact is heightened by the evocative beauty of Virgil Thomson's score, which became the first film music to win a Pulitzer Prize.

You only have to compare Joseph Boudreaux's performance with that of Enzo Stoiala in Vittorio De Sica's *Bicycle Thieves* (which was released the same year) to realise Flaherty's directorial limitations. But this prime example of American neo-realism confirms his genius for locating humanity within its environment and for making us care about both. ★★★★ **DP**

LOVE, ACTUALLY (2003)

Starring: *Bill Nighy (Billy Mack), Liam Neeson (Daniel), Emma Thompson (Karen), Kris Marshall (Colin Frissell), Martin Freeman (John), Joanna Page (Judy), Chiwetel Ejiofor (Peter), Andrew Lincoln (Mark), Kiera Knightley (Juliet), Hugh Grant (The Prime Minister), Martine McCutcheon (Natalie), Laura Linney (Sarah), Alan Rickman (Harry), Thomas Sangster (Sam)*
Director: *Richard Curtis*
Screenwriter: *Richard Curtis*

Awards: *BAFTA – Best Supporting Actor (Bill Nighy), Empire Awards – Best British Actress (Emma Thompson), Best British Film, Best Newcomer (Martine McCutcheon)*

In the weeks leading up to Christmas, the love lives of several people living in London intertwine . . .

After penning two of the biggest British films of recent years – *Four Weddings And A Funeral* and *Notting Hill* – it's only natural that Richard Curtis should expand his film career into direction. And there is plenty to like about his debut.

Grant, for example, makes for an endearing Prime Minister (even if he seems to spend more time trying to woo Martine McCutcheon than actually engaging in politics). Alan Rickman, Emma Thompson and Liam Neeson are a pleasure to watch, while Bill Nighy almost steals the entire film as a foul-mouthed, drug-addled rocker (his confrontation with a poster of Blue on an Ant-and-Dec-hosted TV show is a particular highlight).

Other comic highs see Grant indulging in one of the best bits of hallway dancing since *Risky Business*, and Firth virtually recreating his most famous Mr. Darcy moment by diving fully-clothed into a lake. And Curtis even throws in a few self-referential nods to his earlier work, including Nighy's character re-recording 'Love Is All Around' complete with cringe-worthy Yuletide theme.

However, this is a complex, densely-plotted affair, and in trying to tell the individual stories of so many people, you get the sense that Curtis has bitten off more than he can chew. He seems comfortable enough behind the camera – it's a well-made, good-looking film enlivened by frequent picture-postcard shots of London – but too many of the stories themselves are left wanting.

One, featuring Kris Marshall heading for Wisconsin, in search of rampant sex, goes nowhere, while a potentially interesting subplot involving Laura Linney's magazine worker and her mentally ill brother seems to be forgotten halfway through and ultimately is never resolved. While there's no denying Curtis's ambition, paring down some of the tales would have made the more interesting ones even stronger. The final reel also disappoints, combining a bunch of seen-it-all-before set-pieces with an unpleasantly manipulative finale.

The latter isn't helped by wildly over-the-top orchestral music that wouldn't sound out of place in an epic war movie, and a sense that the audience is being quite literally ordered to laugh and cry at key moments. Given that there is a really good film at the core of *Love Actually*, it's a pity that such aspects let it down.

Curtis is a rare talent (let us not forget he wrote *Blackadder*), and it would have been great to see him tackling something a little more challenging and different for his directorial debut. That said, it's a formula that works and, as crowd-pleasing mainstream Britcom goes, it's a relatively solid, if flawed, entry into the genre. ★★★ **CW**

LOVE AND DEATH (1975)

Starring: *Woody Allen (Boris Grushenko), Diane Keaton (Sonja), Georges Adet (Old Nehamkin), Frank Adu (Drill Sergeant), James Tolkan (Napoleon Bonaparte), Despo Diamaintidou (Mother Grushenko)*
Director: *Woody Allen*
Screenwriters: *Woody Allen, Mildred Cram, Donald Ogden Stewart*
PG/85 mins./Comedy/USA

Diminutive Russian peasant Boris is dragged, much against his better judgement, into the throes of history. With his none-too-committed lady-love Sonja by his side (some of the time) he is offered the opportunity to assassinate the great but not-so-tall invader Napoleon Bonaparte. However, his existential angst about the nature of love and death may get in the way.

One of Woody Allen's few excursions out of Manhattan, but definitely a fully paid-up member of the Early Funny Ones club, this magnificent, often anarchic pastiche of Russian literature's portentous habits with a side order in Bergmanesque death wallowing actually finds Allen at his silliest. Which also means it is extraordinarily clever silliness, with designs deliberately stolen from Chaplin, Keaton and the Marx Brothers. It is a film that explores comedy's infinite variety via the medium of the existential philosophy of those big Russian sagas slumped in history like sulking teenagers.

Slapstick, mime, and knockabout comedy spill about the chaotic story of a wimp intellectual having to play hero, alongside divine wordplay and clever-clever musing (catch the speech entirely made of Dostoyevsky book titles). Allen does his Allen thing, that fumbling if randy neurotic intellectual, only this time stuck out of time in rural Russia at the time of the Napoleonic invasion. In short, and it had to be, he's cross-the-road-to-have-a-gander hilarious. Diane Keaton is nearly better as the terrible love of Boris' idiotic life, who marries him as a last resort and keeps drifting into indecipherable philosophical spiel: 'To love is to suffer. To avoid suffering one must not love. But then one suffers from not loving . . .'

Fans of his caustic views on real relationships will find none of such honesty hereabouts, this is borderline spoof, but infinitely more informed than the work of Mel Brooks. You get Woody fired out of a cannon, and jokes so good you weep to be in possession of such divine wit: 'And so I walk through the valley of the shadow of death. Actually, make that, "I run through the valley of the shadow of death" – in order to get OUT of the valley of the shadow of death more quickly, you see.' ★★★★★ **IN**

LOVE AND DEATH ON LONG ISLAND (1998)

Starring: *John Hurt (Giles De'Ath), Jason Priestley (Ronnie Bostock), Fiona Loewi (Audrey), Sheila Hancock (Mrs. Barker), Harvey Atkin (Lou)*
Director: *Richard Kwietniowski*
Screenwriter: *Richard Kwietniowski, based on the novel by Gilbert Adair*
15/93 mins./Drama/UK/Canada

Awards: *BAFTA – Carl Foreman Award for Most Promising Newcomer (Richard Kwietniowski)*

A best-selling highbrow author becomes obsessed by a teen movie star.

After a sequence of much admired shorts, Kwietniowski made his feature film-debut with this bittersweet blend of *Death In Venice* and *Porky's*. Adapted from film critic Gilbert Adair's knowing novel, it takes a well-aimed

Actors Who Started As Waiters

1 Alec Baldwin
2 Barbra Streisand
3 Dustin Hoffman
4 Sandra Bullock
5 Meryl Streep
6 Gene Hackman
7 Robert Downey Jr.
8 Raquel Welch
9 Geena Davis
10 Antonio Banderas

swipe at the highbrows who all too readily dismiss popcorn pictures and the audiences for whom they're made.

Recently widowed Giles De'Ath is a best-selling author with little time for the modern world. But when a rain shower drives him to seek cinematic shelter, he wanders into a bawdy teenpic called *Hot Pants College II* and immediately becomes enamoured of its rising star, Ronnie Bostock.

Eventually, daydreams are not enough and De'Ath sets off for Long Island determined to declare his devotion to Bostock. Having gained the confidence of the actor's girlfriend Audrey, he persuades the actor that there is a Shakespearean quality to his work and suggests he is perfect for his own screenplay about a deaf-mute's search for love. Bostock is swept away by such intellectual overtures, but Audrey suspects ulterior motives.

Priestley sportingly parodies his pin-up image, as Bostock discovers the hidden depth of his thesping in such gleefully parodic pics as *Tex-Mex* and *Skid Marks*. But the film belongs to Hurt. Everything about his love-crushed fogey is authentic; the way he transforms his pristine study into a secret shrine to his idol; the slavish compilation of a scrapbook of teen mag clippings; the satisfaction of winning Mastermind with Ronnie as his specialist subject. It's a character to rank alongside his Quentin Crisp and John Merrick. ★★★★ **DP**

THE LOVE BUG (1968)

Starring: *Dean Jones (Jim Douglas), Michele Lee (Carole Bennett), David Tomlinson (Peter Thorndyke), Buddy Hackett (Tennessee Steinmetz), Joe Flynn (Havershaw), Benson Fong (Mr. Wu)*
Director: *Robert Stevenson*
Screenwriters: *Gordon Buford, Bill Walsh, Don DaGradi*
U/107 mins./Family/Adventure/USA

A Volkswagon Beetle who tends to make up his own mind, joins forces with race-car driver Jim Douglas, and despite the scrapes they get themselves into, it proves a wining combination.

Let's get over one thing straight away, this daft film, the first of many Herbie in-car-nations, requires you to buy into the idea of a VW Beetle that, well, is imbued with life. He putters along without a driver exposing a great deal of irascibility to things he doesn't like. Herbie's got an attitude. Upon reflection, he's quite sinister – is this speedy little motor possessed? We'll never know because the point of this chirpy, rather hippyish Disney movie of the late 60s is not to care. Herbie's like the anthropomorphised critters of Disney lore, but in four-wheeled form. We're meant to love the Bug for his mischievous spirit and cuteness. It's a tall order.

Glistening in that way all Disney franchises did at the time, a sun dappled Californian playground at one remove from reality, it has bland everyman Dean Jones as the hero and bland Michelle Lee as the love interest alongside chubby Buddy Hackett as the mechanic who tends to play fall-guy to the gags. Director Robert Stevenson had made *The Absent Minded Professor*, and doesn't stray too far from that formula of easy slapstick and the triumph of the little man (or car).

It's a thin premise but a popular one. People seemed to like the concept of applying human foibles to an inanimate object – we even get Herbie attempting suicide when he is superseded by a Lamborghini. Although, it really isn't very funny. ★★ **IN**

LOVE FINDS ANDY HARDY (1938)

Starring: *Mickey Rooney (Andy Hardy), Lewis Stone (Judge James K. Hardy), Fay Holden (Mrs. Emily Hardy), Cecilia Parker (Marian Hardy), Judy Garland (Betsy Booth), Lana Turner (Cynthia Potter), Ann Rutherford (Polly Benedict)*
Director: *George B. Seitz*
Screenwriter: *William Ludwig, based on the stories by Vivien R. Bretherton*
U/91 mins./Comedy/USA

All-American teenager Andy Hardy tries to juggle three girls at the same time – regular steady Polly Benedict, adoring girl-next-door Betsy Booth and blonde siren Cynthia Potter, whom he's squiring over Christmas for best pal Beezy in return for the cash he needs to get his jalopy back on the road.

This was the fourth in a 16-strong series of films produced by MGM between 1937–1958. It was launched with *A Family Affair*, which was adapted from an Aurania Rouverol play entitled *Skidding*. Lionel Barrymore played Judge Hardy and Spring Byington essayed his wife in this opening episode, but they were replaced by Lewis Stone and Fay Holden for the sequel, *You're Only Young Once*, and they remained in situ for the next eight years, alongside Mickey Rooney as Andy Hardy, Cecilia Parker as his older sister, Marian, and Sara Haden as their Aunt Milly (who was twice substituted by Betty Ross Clarke).

The focus shifted between the family members for the first three films. But by *Love Finds Andy Hardy*, it was clear that audiences were primarily interested in the misadventures of the Carvel high schooler with a talent for trouble and the sense to know that his dad could always be relied upon to extricate him from the tightest of corners – providing they had one of their obligatory man-to-man chats.

Forget James Dean in *Rebel Without a Cause*. Mickey Rooney was America's first screen teenager. Andy Hardy was more curious than non-conformist and mischief rather than malice tended to land him in hot water. His eye for beauty was usually the cause of his downfall and the studio shrewdly used the films to showcase several stars-in-the-making, including Judy Garland, Lana Turner, Esther Williams, Kathryn Grayson and Donna Reed. Yet, Andy always found his way back into the good books of his forgiving steady, Ann Rutherford.

The franchise was essentially an excuse to teach the nation's movie-mad juveniles some civics lessons – hence the award of a special Oscar in 1943 for 'its achievement in representing the American Way of Life' – and its blend of wholesome humour and folksy sentiment now seems highly patronising and archly conservative. But Mickey Rooney's ebullience ensures that the series retains its charm and still makes for entertaining viewing. ★★★ **DP**

LOVE'S LABOURS LOST (2000)

Starring: *Kenneth Branagh (Berowne), Alessandro Nivola (King Ferdinand of Navarre), Alicia Silverstone (The Princess of France), Matthew Lillard (Longaville), Adrian Lester (Dumaine), Timothy Spall (Don Armado), Nathan Land (Costard), Emily Mortimer (Katherine), Richard Briers (Nathaniel)*
Director: *Kenneth Branagh*
Screenwriter: *Kenneth Branagh, based on the play by William Shakespeare*

Shakespeare's obscure play is reimagined by Branagh. Set in 1939 – Gershwin and Cole Porter numbers provide a musical backdrop to a romantic tale.

As anyone who ever saw *Kiss Me Kate* will testify, setting Shakespeare to music is a formula as tried and tested as Kenneth Branagh filming the Bard's works in the first place. *Love's Labour's Lost*, his first attempt to bring Shakespeare to screen since 1996's splendid *Hamlet*, is one of the scribe's more obscure comedies, and boasts one of his flimsiest plots. Which is why bringing the setting up to 1939, and having the cast belt out Cole Porter and Gershwin numbers works so well, bringing substance to the story.

The plot structure follows the format of your average Shakespeare romantic comedy. In the romance corner – the boys, the King Of Navarre and his gang of mates, who have sworn off women for three years to concentrate on their studies are distracted by the arrival of the girls – the Princess of France and henchwomen. Meanwhile, in the comedy corner, Richard Briers dodders about as a local priest, Lane plays court jester and Timothy Spall almost steals the show with his heavily-accented rendition of 'I Get A Kick Out Of You'. And that's it, except it's punctuated with familiar tunes ('Cheek To Cheek', 'Fancy Free', 'Let's Face The Music And Dance' . . .), all impeccably and imaginatively choreographed.

There are pitfalls in mainly choosing talented actors over trained singers – those cast members who do have a background in musicals upstage everybody else whenever they get the spotlight (to wit: Lester's breathtaking dance solo in 'I've Got A Crush On You').

That said, there's no-one here who genuinely can't sing or dance, and the story is handled well, with largely great performances from the cast (McElhone and Timothy Spall are standouts, as, inevitably, is Branagh). Weak links aside (Silverstone's princess doesn't quite convince, and the straight-faced ending fails miserably), this potentially risky venture is a moderate success. Now howabout Girls Aloud Do Julius Caesar? ★★★ **EC**

LOVE ON THE RUN (L'AMOUR EN FUITE) (1979)

Starring: *Jean-Pierre Léaud (Antoine Doinel), Marie-France Pisier (Colette), Claude Jade (Christie), Dani Lilllane), Dorothea (Sabine), Rosy Varte (Colette's Mother)*
Director: *François Truffaut*
Screenwriter: *François Truffaut, Marie-France Pisier, Jean Aurel, Suzanne Schiffman*
PG/94 mins./Drama/Comedy/USA

While working on his autobiographical novel, Antoine Doinel divorces Christine, is briefly reunited with old flame Colette and finds new love with record store clerk, Sabine.

Having debuted in *Les Quatre Cents Coups*, Antoine Doinel made his final screen appearance in the fifth part of François Truffaut's compelling, but inconsistent cycle that also included the 'Antoine et Colette' episode in *L'Amour à Vingt Ans*, *Baisers Volés* and *Domicile Conjugale*.

Truffaut had always planned to use the footage left over from the previous pictures to complete the quintet as an homage to its star, Jean-Pierre Léaud, who had gone through a remarkable personal and professional journey during the series' 20-year span. But he didn't quite manage to integrate the old and the new quite as seamlessly as he would have hoped and many critics decried the fact that almost one-fifth of the running time was occupied with off-cuts. Indeed, some accused Truffaut of laziness, others of narcissism. But his graver failing was the tendency to over-complicate matters by incorporating material from outside the Doinel storyline.

The idea of using Antoine's novel as the justification for flashing back to past incidents was sound enough and Truffaut neatly challenged the reliability of memory by having Colette read the manuscript and question the accuracy of his facts. However, he missed the opportunity to exploit this encounter to explore the ellision between life and art – even though he alluded to his treatise on that theme, *Day for Night*, by showing Léaud with Dani (who had played the continuity girl) in clips from the original and scenes specially shot for *Love on the Run*.

This blurring of Truffaut and Doinel's pasts confusingly recurred during the sequence in which Antoine reconciled himself with his late mother, which drew on extracts from the non-Léaud features, *Une Belle Fille Comme Moi* and *L'Homme qui Aimait les Femmes*.

It's fascinating to see Doinel at 13, 19, 24, 28 and 33 in one film. But, while Truffaut recognised that this was a picture he had to make, he also regretted its production. 'He was like a cartoon,' he said later. 'In cartoons you don't get old. How can Mickey Mouse age? Antoine is like Mickey ... so I had to stop.' ★★★ **DP**

LUST FOR LIFE (1956)

Starring: *Kirk Douglas (Vincent van Gogh), Anthony Quinn (Paul Gaugin). James Donald (Theo Van Gogh), Pamela Brown (Christine), Everett Sloane (Dr. Gachet), Noel Purcell (Anton Mauve), Niall MacGinnis (Roulin)*
Director: *Vincente Minnelli*
Screenwriter: *Norman Corwin, based on the novel by Irving Stone*
PG/122 mins/Drama/USA
Awards: *Academy Awards – Best Supporting Actor (Anthony Quinn)*

The life of the tortured Dutch artist Vincent van Gogh, from his failed attempts at missionary work in Belgium, his miserable home life, his alienation of sponsor Anton Mauve and his on-off friendship with impressionist Paul Gaugin. In between there are some astonishing paintings.

Although perhaps best known for his grandiloquent musicals such as *An American In Paris*, *Gigi* and *The Band Wagon*, the majority of Vincente Minnelli's films were straight dramas and this exquisitely rendered biopic of Van Gogh's life is amongst his finest.

Taking some nine years to reach the screen after it was first optioned by MGM, Minnelli's adaptation of Irving Stone's hugely popular 'fictionalised biography' pulls off the nifty trick of being both an essay of a tragic life and a celebration of wayward genius. Minnelli is helped hugely in this respect by Kirk Douglas's towering performance. While the actor's dedication saw him learn to paint under the supervision of a French artist, what really sells the performance is Douglas's sensitivity and commitment to the extremes of the artist's emotions. It is a fiery, passionate piece of acting. Yet, in one of those all too familiar Oscar blunders, it was Anthony Quinn's supporting turn as Gaugin, the equally temperamental artist who attempts to befriend Van Gogh, that walked away with the bald statuette, remarkable for a turn that only lasts 8 minutes.

Yet unlike many modern biopics like *Ray* or *Walk The Line*, *Lust For Life* is not a film driven by performance alone. Minnelli uses the full extent of his filmmaking palette to replicate the master's vision on film – his crew also shot around 200 Van Gogh originals under special lighting conditions so as not to damage them – employing various lighting techniques and film stocks to appropriate the soft subtle tones of Van Gogh's artistry. It is a shame that a lot of this good work is undone by the studio's decision, enforced on Minnelli, to shoot the film in widescreen – a format that is completely at odds with the shape of Van Gogh's paintings. ★★★★ **IF**

ⓘ LUST IN THE DUST (1985)

Starring: *Tab Hunter (Abel Wood), Divine (Rosie Velez), Lainie Kazan (Marguerita Ventura), Geoffrey Lewis (Hardcase Williams), Henry Silva (Bernardo), Cesar Romero (Father Garcia)*
Director: *Paul Bartel*
Screenwriters: *Philip John Taylor*
15/84 mins./Comedy/Western/USA

To the sleepy border town of Chile Verde come various adventurers in search of a legendary fortune in gold: strong, soft-spoken, quick-on-the-draw stranger Abel Scott; fiery hispanic temptresses Rosie and Marguerita, who have halves of a treasure map tattooed on their bottoms; and 'Hardcase' Williams, the kind of varmint who only feels good while he's killing a priest.

'The legend of Chile Verde tells of men and women who became slaves to their passions. They paid the price here under the blistering, burning, blazing, scorching, roasting, toasting, baking, boiling, broiling, steaming, searing, sizzling, grilling, smoldering, very hot New Mexico sun. For there is a saying in these parts: those who lust in the dust shall die in the dust.'

This skit on 1950s Westerns has a few funny lines and funny pastiche performances from Tab Hunter as the kind of gritty Westerner Randolph Scott used to play and Geoffrey Lewis as 'garbage wrapped in a human skin'. However, the casting of female impersonator Glenn Milstead (Divine) and Lainie Kazan (who is practically a female female impersonator) as screeching senoritas gives director Paul Bartel an excuse to ditch the perverse-but-subtle wit which was his strong suit and indulge in crudely unamusing knockabout several notches on a gun-barrel lower than *Blazing Saddles* or even *Carry On Cowboy*.

Bartel was far less temperamentally suited than John Waters to getting the best out of Divine (Mary Woronov, his *Eating Raoul* muse, would have been much better). While the film fudges much of the foreground humour, it at least manages to get the background detail right – it actually looks like a Universal or Republic programmer from thirty years earlier – and the music score stretches to an authentically stupid showbiz frontier ballad called 'Tarnished Tumbleweed'. ★★ **KN**

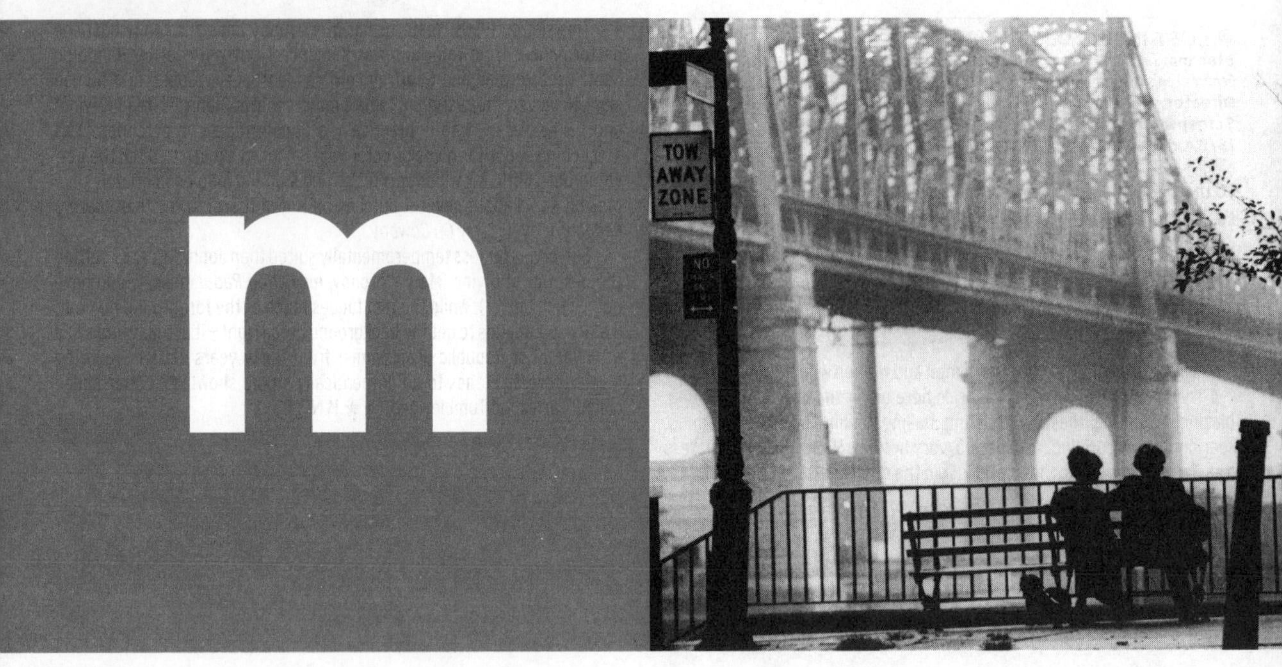

⑩ M (1931)

Starring: *Peter Lorre (Hans Beckert), Ellen Widman (Frau Beckmann), Inge Langut (Elsie Beckman), Otto Wernicke (Inspector Karl Lohmann), Theodor Loos (Inspector Groeber)*
Director: *Fritz Lang*
Screenwriters: *Thea von Harbou, Paul Falkenberg, Karl Vash, Adolf Jarsen, from an article by Ego Jacobson*
PG/110 mins./Crime/Drama/Germany

When the police in a German city are unable to catch a child-murderer, criminals join in the manhunt.

Having already created one of the screen's most sinister master criminals in Dr Mabuse, *The Gambler* (1922), Fritz Lang turned again to crime for his debut with sound. Originally, he planned to explore the impact of a series of poison pen letters on a tightly-knit community. But Lang and his screenwriter wife, Thea Von Harbou, were persuaded to change tack after reading about the exploits of Peter Kiirten, the serial killer known as the 'Monster of Diisseldorf'. Further inspired by the vigilante actions of the beggars' union in Bertolt Brecht and Kurt Weill's 1931 musical, *The Threepenny Opera*, the couple began studying the lurid press accounts of Kiirten's killings in order to gauge the public response to such heinous butchery. They also gained access to files at Scotland Yard and the Alexanderplatz police headquarters to discover how the law would pursue such a case, both from an investigative and forensic standpoint. Lang even visited asylums to interview and observe sex offenders to understand more clearly their motives, methods and madness.

Unable to make the picture for Germany's biggest studio, UFA, Lang signed to the less opulent Nero-Film, thus limiting the famously extravagant director to a six-week shoot between January and March of 1931. Fritz Arno Wagner, who had worked on such earlier Lang ventures as *Destiny* (1921) and *Spies* (1928), returned behind the camera to make ingenious use of brooding shadows and eerie low-key lighting, while Karl Vollbrecht who had helped create *Metropolis* (1927), teamed with Emil Hasler to design the sets. Unfazed by their limited resources, they transformed a disused zeppelin hangar into the office block where the murderer is finally cornered and a ramshackle schnapps factory into the location for the kangaroo court.

Ever the fabulist, Lang fashioned the myth that the manager of the hangar was a Nazi, who had threatened to prevent filming unless the original title, *Murderers Among Us*, was ditched – just in case anyone mistook it for a reference to Fuehrer-in-waiting Adolf Hitler and his hordes. Lang also claimed he packed the underworld jury with real-life criminals and fooled police readying to raid the set by tinkering with the schedule in order to spirit them to safety.

What's more reliable is his insistence that the film carried an anti-death penalty message. 'We force the one who throws the switch or pours the poison into the room to commit the same crime for which we kill another,' he declared. 'I don't think anybody has the right to kill anybody.'

This goes some way to explaining his decision to make Hans Beckert such a surprisingly sympathetic character. Beckert may have murdered eight children, but by casting Peter Lorre in the role, Lang ensured that he could never be portrayed simply as a depraved monster. Twice, Lang allows us to witness Hans' torment, as he ducks into a street cafe to conquer the goading voices in his head and then again at his 'trial' as he protests that other criminals act out of choice, whereas he has no control over his actions.

Despite the acclaim for his performance, Lorre never forgave Lang for his treatment on the set, particularly the need to throw him down some steps 12 times before he was satisfied with the take. Yet, Lang's sadism undoubtedly contributed to the haunted look of terror on Lorre's pudgy face as he confronts both his demons and his accusers. The performances of Gustaf Griindgens, as the sharply dressed underworld boss Schraenker, and Otto Wernicke, as the corpulent Chief Inspector Lohmann, were also superb. But, as ever, Lang was less interested in acting than visual effect.

Considering it was his first talkie, he was sparing with sound effects, although he did make chilling use of the killer's whistled motif, 'The House Of The Mountain King' from Grieg's *Peer Gynt* (which Lang performed himself, as no one else could get it so disturbingly off-key).

Instead, he concentrated on what amounted to silent set-pieces, most notably the opening montage segment in which little Elsie Beckmann is bought a balloon before being lured to her off-screen demise and the chase sequence that follows the chalked letter M being stamped upon Beckert's back by a member of the unholy alliance between the beggars and the underworld. Moreover, he also littered the action with close-ups of inert objects like documents, fingerprints, press cuttings, medical reports and scribbled notes to foreground the action's police procedural aspect.

With the public, press, police and politicians all blaming each other for the curse of Beckert's crimes, *M* presents a compelling portrait of a society on the verge of Nazi tyranny. But, viewed in the light of recent spates of anti-paedophile hysteria, it's clear that it retains a contemporary resonance that's as controversial as it's powerful. ★★★★★ **DP**

M*A*S*H (1970)

Starring: *Donald Sutherland (Hawkeye Pierce), Elliott Gould (Trapper John McIntyre), Tom Skerrit (Duke Forrest), Sally Kellerman (Hot Lips O'Houlihan), Robert Duvall (Frank Burns)*
Director: *Robert Altman*
Screenwriter: *Ring Lardner Jr, based on the novel by Richard Hooker*
15/110 mins./Comedy/War/Drama/USA

Awards: *Academy Awards – Best Adapted Screenplay, BAFTA – UN Award, Golden Globes – Best Musical/Comedy*

The staff of a Korean War field hospital use humour and hijinks to keep their sanity in the face of the horror of war.

While suicide may be painless – at least according to *MASH*'s theme song – the making of Robert Altman's Korean War-set comedy was anything but. Particularly contentious was the relationship between that of the improvisation-minded director and Elliott Gould who Altman informed one day at lunch had 'wasted his time' during a recently filmed scene.

'I started to shake,' the actor subsequently told Altman biographer Patrick McGilligan. 'I threw my tray up in the air, and I said, "From here on in, you tell me what the fuck it is you want me to do. You direct me. I'm not going to stick my neck out for you. You tell me what it is you fucking want, because I'm a craftsman. Don't tell me I'm wasting your fucking time." '

In fact, Altman, who at that stage in his career could only claim a couple of big screen credits, had not been anybody's first choice as director. 'Fifteen directors turned it down, maybe more,' says George Litto, the agent of *MASH* screenwriter Ring Lardner Jr, 'George Roy Hill turned it down. Bud Yorkin, who was then a hot director, turned it down. Every important director in Hollywood (including Stanley Kubrick and Sidney Lumet) turned the fucking project down. At first I couldn't believe it – except that the script was unconventional. Most of the time, pictures had a beginning, a middle and an end. MASH was a series of vignettes.'

This was not a problem, however, for Altman who, as subsequent films such as *Nashville*, *The Player* and *Short Cuts* would amply demonstrate, was more than capable of turning a multitude of apparently disparate story lines into a cohesive whole. Not that he was given a completely free rein, particularly in casting. To play one of the leads, for example Altman wanted Dan 'Hoss' Blocker whom he had directed in the TV show *Bonanza* (eventually the studio opted for the more obviously hip pairing of Gould and Donald Sutherland) while for the role of Hot Lips O'Houlihan he fought bitterly against the executives' choice of Sally Kellerman.

'There's a weakness in Altman, which is interesting,' the film's producer Ingo Preminger subsequently claimed. 'He loves unattractive people. Sally Kellerman is pretty, but not so pretty. But, for Altman, she was too beautiful. It's kind of an inferiority complex.'

Yet, for the most part, Altman was left alone by the studio, 20th Century Fox, which then had in production far more expensive ventures such as *Tora! Tora! Tora!*, *Patton*, and *Hello, Dolly!* The result was a freewheeling military satire in which martini-guzzling japester-docs Hawkeye Pierce, Trapper John and Duke Forrest repeatedly point up the insane situation that they find themselves in and make fun of anyone who declines to get with their decidedly anti-authoritarian programme. Notable targets include the priggish Maj. Frank Burns and Hot Lips O'Houlihan, whose sex session is broadcast over the medical camp's address system to the delight of all and sundry. The often chaotic nature of life during war, meanwhile, is more than reflected in Altman's idiosyncratic approach to dialogue recording which often means that it is quite hard to tell just who is speaking – a style that the director continues to use to this day, often with much less success.

While set in Korea the film was, of course, taken by many to be a savage indictment of the then ongoing Vietnam War and apparently the director had considered updating the original novel before dismissing the idea as too obvious. Despite costing a mere $3m the film rapidly became one of the top ten biggest box office successes of all-time and received five Academy Award nominations. It also ushered in an awesome purple patch for Altman who, in the next five years would make a trio of unarguable classics: *McCabe And Mrs Miller*, *Nashville* and his Philip Marlowe update *The Long Goodbye* which would reunite the director with Gould. But *MASH*'s real financial winner was not the director – he was paid a flat fee – but his son Michael who wrote the theme song's lyrics.

Initially Altman Jr asked for only a guitar in compensation but Ingo Preminger took him to the legal department and drew up a contract for the song which would not only be used in the hugely successful spin-off series but also would go on to top the UK charts in 1980. Thus, as Robert Altman was heard to complain on more than one occasion, his son made far more money from his most famous film than he ever did. ★★★★★ **CC**

MA NUIT CHEZ MAUD (MY NIGHT AT MAUD'S) (1969)

Starring: *Jean-Louis Trintignant (Jean-Louis), Francoise Fabian (Maud), Marie-Christine Barrault (Françoise), Antoine Vilaz (Vidal), Leonide Kogan (Concert Violinist), Anne Dubot (Blonde Friend)*
Director: *Eric Rohmer*
Screenwriter: *Eric Rohmer*
12/105 mins./Drama/France

Clermont-Ferrand in December and Catholic engineer Jean-Louis spots his ideal wife, Françoise, during Sunday mass. However, he's then introduced to divorced lawyer Maud by his philosophy professor pal, Vidal, and when they're snowed in together she attempts to test his moral resolve.

The third of Eric Rohmer's 'Six Moral Tales' is a typically teasing and intellectually intriguing study of human foible. Stylishly shot in monochrome by Nestor Almendros, it makes slyly effective use of both the provincial and yuletide settings to explore the friction between reason and religion and to question the biblical contention that man's greatest obstacle to eternal salvation is woman.

Jean-Louis sets himself up as a paragon in control of his appetites and opinions, as well as his destiny, and it's clear that he intends to allow nothing to deflect him from his righteous path. Moreover, he refuses to contemplate that the selection of a wife via certain rigid criteria might conspire against him because his faith will protect him against caprice. But a series of chance encounters begin to challenge his complacent convictions, even though the first – his sighting of the ideal Françoise across a

Americans Who Are Actually Canadian TOP 10

	Actor	Born in:
1	Michael J Fox	Alberta
2	James Cameron	Ontario
3	Leslie Nielsen	Regina
4	William Shatner	Montreal
5	Jim Carrey	Ontario
6	Donald Sutherland	St. John
7	Rick Moranis	Toronto
8	Martin Short	Hamilton
9	John Candy	Toronto
10	Ryan Reynolds	Vancouver

church – seems to confirm his belief that God is rewarding him for a life in which risk and morality have been balanced (albeit at the expense of passion and self-awareness). However, the unexpected reunion with Vidal subjects Jean-Louis to both his philosophical probing and Maud's secular sensuality.

Despite the force of Jean-Louis Trintignant's performance, our narrator is a weak hypocrite who uses his faith (which he maintains more out of habit than certitude) to justify his failings and inconsistent attitudes. His protestation of predestination as an excuse for past dalliances also exposes his cowardly refusal to take responsibility for his actions and both Vidal and Maud seek to make him confront the shallowness of his stance – he by citing Pascal and the logic of the mathematics that governs Jean-Louis's profession; she by arousing his physical and sexual appetites.

By shooting in black and white, Rohmer was able to emphasise the film's endless contrasts (most notably between the blonde Françoise and the brunette Maud and the purity of the sunlit snow and the allure of nocturnal temptation). But while this is a subtly cinematic work, it's the finely tuned dialogue that makes it so fascinating and amusing. ★★★★ **DP**

MAC AND ME (1988)

Starring: *Christine Ebersole (Janet), Jonathan Ward (Michael), Tina Caspary (Katrina Caspary), Lauren Stanley (Debbie), Jade Calegory (Eric), Vinnie Torrente (Mitford), Martin West (Wickett), Ivan J Rado (Zimmerman), Danny Cooksey (Jack Jr), Laura Waterbury (Linda), Jack Eiseman (Splatter Car Driver), Barbara Allyne-Bennett (Scientist)*
Director: *Stewart Rafill*
Screenwriters: *Stewart Rafill, Steve Feke*
PG/95 mins./Sci-fi USA

A cute alien with big glass eyes and a squeaky whistle is stranded on Earth and finds refuge with a lonely little boy (Calegory) and his family, who protect him when he is hunted down by the evil authorities.

This time out, the alien has a missing set of parents and a sister (yup, aliens have the nuclear family too), the little boy is crippled, and in the finale it is the human who dies and is resurrected by the alien rather than the other way around . . . but that's about all that distinguishes this – in terms of plot, at least – from its obvious inspiration, *E.T.: The Extra Terrestrial*. In terms of script, acting, action, special effects, music and everything else, this is overwhelmingly inferior to its model. MAC – an acronym for Mysterious Alien Creature – has a repertoire of facial movements and rod-puppet gimmicks, but is still resolutely a high-tech piece of hardware rather than a living creature.

The kids are well down to the standard of a Disney TV show, and the adults barely get a look-in. Investment in the film came from a couple of American fast-food and soft drinks concerns, hence the inordinate amount of product placement. You know you're in trouble when a film boasts a credit that reads 'and Ronald McDonald as Himself'. In one scene, the kids all boogie down to McDonald's for a big hip-hop party with Ronald himself in attendance, and the patrons and staff of the place help MAC escape from the bad guys. Also, a plot strand deals with MAC and his family's sole means of sustenance – yes, Coca-Cola! – and there are plenty of lingering shots of alien fingers grasping cans of coke as the sugary crap brings them back to life. Avoid. ★ **KN**

MACBETH (1948)

Starring: *Orson Welles (Macbeth), Jeanette Nolan (Lady Macbeth), Dan O'Herlihy (Macduff), Roddy McDowall (Malcolm), Edgar Barrier (Banquo), Alan Napier (A Holy Father)*
Director: *Orson Welles*
Screenwriter: *Orson Welles, adapted from the play by William Shakespeare*
PG/107 mins./Historical Drama/USA

Informed by three witches that he will become King of Scotland, warrior thane Macbeth prevaricates in pursuit of his ambitions and is driven to regicide and tyranny by his ruthless wife.

When Alexander Korda rejected his proposal for *Othello*, Orson Welles convinced Poverty Row outfit Republic Pictures to bankroll a production of *Macbeth* that he would road test on stage before filming for a mere $700,000 in 21 days.

In order to keep costs down, Welles shot in long, deep-focused takes with a trio of synchronised cameras and captured close-ups during the battle sequences by disguising cameramen using portable machines as combatants. He also decided to pre-record the soundtrack, so as not only to ensure a clarity of diction commensurate with Shakespeare, but also to enable his cameras to move freely without the risk of microphones intruding into the shot.

Even the design was conceived with economy in mind, as Welles and Fred Ritter devised roughly hewn, stony backdrops that were not only evocative, but also interchangeable. Moreover, their abstract texture also provided an anachronistic contrast with the smooth studio floors that reinforced the ethereality of action that Welles consciously staged as though it were occurring inside Macbeth's tormented mind.

Unable to persuade Tallulah Bankhead, Anne Baxter, Mercedes McCambridge or Agnes Moorehead to play Lady Macbeth, Welles cast Mercury radio star Jeanette Nolan (who had no prior stage or screen experience). Nolan's lack of conventional glamour intensified the callous cruelty of her character, but she wasn't always comfortable before the cameras and Welles effortlessly stole their scenes together.

But, he always intended himself to be the centre of attention – even during the banquet sequence when the astonished guests respond to his terrified tirades from a subjective perspective. Indeed, Welles came up with numerous equally innovative strategies, including interiorised soliloquies, drastic contrasts between high and low-level angles (which simultaneously recalled German Expressionism and Eisenstein's *Alexander Nevsky*, 1938) and the use of Vaseline on the filters for the depiction of Banquo's ghost.

However, a poor reception, in comparison with Laurence Olivier's *Hamlet*, prompted Republic to cut the picture from 107 to 80 minutes and to re-record 65% of the soundtrack (eliminating Welles's Scottish burr in the process). The film has since been restored and its atmospheric audacity is now readily evident. ★★★★ DP

◑ MACBETH (1971)

Starring: *Jon Finch (Macbeth), Francesca Annis (Lady Macbeth), Martin Shaw (Banquo), Nicholas Selby (Duncan), John Stride (Ross), Stephen Chase (Malcolm)*
Director: *Roman Polanski*
Screenwriters: *Roman Polanski, Kenneth Tynan, based on the play by William Shakespeare*
15/140 mins./ Drama/UK

Having already murdered King Duncan and his closest ally, Banquo, 11th-century Scottish usurper Macbeth becomes so steeped in tyranny that he fails to notice the effect their crimes are having on his scheming queen.

A lacerating pessimism rips through Roman Polanski's adaptation of the Scottish play. Made within two years of his pregnant wife Sharon Tate's murder by Charles Manson, it depicts a world without morality or hope, in which people act primarily from the basest of motives and, thus, even the most pitiful death is stripped of tragic import. Recalling both the brutality he had witnessed as a boy in wartime Poland and the pain of his senseless loss, the film was made all the more powerful by the dank realism of the locations and the restrained performances of leads whose youth and beauty somehow made their surrender to criminal instincts all the more shocking.

However, the fact that the picture had been produced by Playboy Enterprises (after Allied Artists and Universal withdrew) garnered most headlines on its initial release. Prudish critics were quick to accuse Hugh Hefner of foisting a nude sleepwalking sequence on Francesca Annis. But it had, in fact, been incorporated into Polanski and Kenneth Tynan's original screenplay and had prompted Tuesday Weld to reject the role of Lady Macbeth.

But while many were decrying this chastely symbolic depiction of a ruthless *femme fatale* being left utterly exposed by creeping remorse, others were denouncing the depiction of violent acts that ordinarily happened off stage. Yet, while others still could forgive the graphic goriness of the action, they attacked Polanski for melodramatising the Bard in attempting to equate events in 11th-century Scotland with those in their own times, when regimes around the world were being challenged by unscrupulously subversive forces.

Polanski was clearly still enduring a dark night of the soul when he made this Shakespearean palimpsest and he creates a hell on earth from the Welsh landscape that was made to look even more forbidding by the inclement weather that blighted the shoot and contributed to the delays that saw Hefner lose around $3.5 million on the project. However, the reputation of the film's coarse visual poetry continues to improve, as its place in Polanski's canon becomes more apparent. ★★★ DP

◑ THE MACHINIST (EL MAQUINISTA) (2004)

Starring: *Christian Bale (Trevor Reznik), Jennifer Jason Leigh (Stevie), Aitana Sanchez-Gijon (Marie), John Sharian (Ivan), Michael Ironside (Miller)*
Director: *Brad Anderson*
Screenwriter: *Scott Kosar*
15/102 mins./Thriller/USA

Emaciated metalworker Trevor Reznik is falling apart. He can't eat, he can't sleep and someone is playing Hangman on his fridge Post-It notes. And who's the big guy in the red sports car keeping tabs on him? Now, with a dead body on his hands, it's time for Trevor to face up to reality, whatever it is . . .

Given the current obsession with high-impact dieting, Christian Bale should think about marketing his own brand of weight-loss expertise. For this deep-set thriller, lurking somewhere in the hinterlands of the horror genre, the actor shed so many pounds he's barely intact. The almighty gulf between the full-pumped vision of *American Psycho* and this shocking skeletal shadow, just bones and sinew bound together by the translucent parchment of his skin, is enough to throw you into tailspin. What the hell is up with this guy?

The hideous imagery it references, that haunting footage of emaciated Holocaust survivors, all but threatens to tip Brad Anderson's brute nightmare completely out of whack. But give Bale his due – in a striking physical performance, he gives the film far more than xylophone ribs. The death mask is incidental – it's his mind where things are truly coming apart.

There's also the cold imagery to admire, a twilight of metallic hues and stark bathroom floors so drained of primary colour the film almost strays into a ghostly black and white. We're being presented with a conundrum. Why is this lowly, polite machine operator losing the plot? We're told he hasn't slept for a year, and, boy, it looks like it. He has passing sex with kindly hooker Jennifer Jason Leigh and, when we first glimpse him, he's rolling up a corpse in a carpet. Like a manic-depressive David Lynch, Anderson wants to freak us out, to rattle our own ribcages; we're only seeing the world through Reznik's eyes and they're not to be trusted.

Yet, for all the frozen wastes of his style, Anderson is not a subtle manager of mystery. With not-so-furtive symbolism, he has his sunken character reading Dostoyevsky's *The Idiot* to give us a little nudge. Add the presence of Polanski's *The Tenant*, *Fight Club*, *Memento* and Hitchcock's psychological leering, and Reznik isn't the only one suffering déjà vu. A few scenes into the gloom and you'll have à good idea what is generally up, if not the specifics, making the journey toward the eventual, inevitable twist fairly one-dimensional. It's a result so painfully logical it would make Lynch's hair stand on end. ★★★★ IN

Tagline
How do you wake up from a nightmare if you're not asleep?

◑ MAD CITY (1997)

Starring: *John Travolta (Sam Baily), Dustin Hoffman (Max Brackett), Mia Kirshner (Laurie Callahan), Alan Alda (Kevin Hollander), Blythe Danner (Mrs Banks)*
Director: *Costa-Gavras*
Screenwriters: *Tom Matthews, Eric Williams, from a story by Matthews*
12/110 mins./Crime/Drama/USA

A hostage crisis becomes a prime-time media event.

'We may be talking Oscars,' announced producer Arnold Kopelson of this absorbing hostage drama way back in 1996. Two years, a cluster of damning reviews and a disastrous US box office take later *Mad City* arrived on our shores with nothing. And yet we could have been talking Oscars because, for all its pitfalls, it tries desperately to expose the lies and hypocrisy used by the media to boost ratings. Too bad the film ends up pulling the same tricks.

The plot concerns a dim-witted security guard who, when fired from his post, gets his gun and takes hostage a group of children in the museum where he once worked. The police move in but the crisis snowballs when an ambitious TV reporter, hiding in the museum toilets, exploits the situation for his own airtime.

It's your basic *Dog Day Afternoon* hostage scenario (complete with absent-minded gunman) mixed with the media frenzy of *Ace In The Hole* and the ratings war of *Network*. *Mad City* comes into its own, though, when Travolta is being seduced by the newsflash suggestions of Hoffman, quite brilliant as the conscience-riddled reporter. As the blue-collar everyman,

Travolta is less convincing, though his wordless dialogue – nervous ticks, raging snorts and flapping hands – is mesmerising.

The movie's basic tenet – that the media covers its own side of the story – is well broadcast by director Costa-Gravas, clearly enjoying himself in the role of moral ringmaster. And the script, by ex-journo Tom Matthews, ripples with newsroom details and crisp one-liners from ruthless TV anchor Alan Alda, in his best role for years. ★★★ **JH**

MAD DOG AND GLORY (1993)

Starring: *Robert De Niro (Wayne 'Mad Dog' Dobie), Uma Thurman (Glory), Bill Murray (Frank Milo), David Caruso (Mike)*
Director: *John McNaughton*
Screenwriter: *Richard Price*
15/97 mins./Comedy/Drama/Crime/USA

The tale of a shy, lonely and kind-hearted forensics detective, Wayne Dobie – facetiously nicknamed Mad Dog – who saves the life of Chicago loanshark Frank Milo in a convenience store stick-up and as a thank-you gift receives the companionship of leggy Glory for a week.

Director McNaughton and writer Richard Price could have made this a romantic comedy, but clearly they had other ideas, serving notice with a violently ugly opening of a drug deal turned to murder – its casual suddenness a reminder of McNaughton's breakthrough *Henry: Portrait Of A Serial Killer* – and comely though Glory may be, her situation and sob story as an abused piece of property are not exactly crackling with comic potential.

The interesting relationships here are all male, between Mad Dog and his pugnacious partner Mike and, most fruitfully, the buddy notion stood on its head in the tremendous double act that is De Niro and Murray. In Milo, Murray is a knockout as a serio-comic heavy – slick, sardonic, unpredictable and blowing hot and cold to the off-balance Mad Dog.

What makes this uneasy viewing is the jumping from comedy to brutality, and from the progress of the love affair to the constant challenges to Mad Dog's 'manhood'. As a sensitive, gentle man, it seems he is unworthy of love until he can steel himself to beat the crap out of someone. Thus, despite some very funny moments, this is morally difficult to justify, while simultaneously sending up and celebrating macho bullshit. ★★★ **AE**

MAD MAX (1979)

Starring: *Mel Gibson (Max Rockatansky), Joanne Samuel (Jessie), Hugh Keays-Byrne (Toecutter), Steve Bisley (Jim Goose), Tim Burns (Johnny the Boy)*
Director: *George Miller*
Screenwriters: *George Miller, James McCausland, from a story by George Miller, Byron Kennedy*
18/88 mins./Sci-fi/Action/Australia

Australia. The future. Cop Max leaves the force because he's fed up with their inability to deal with corruption. He goes on vacation with his family; however, a group of evil bikers kill his best pal and Max goes seeking his revenge.

Director George Miller cast the unknown Mel Gibson in the lead in this low-budget Australian movie, and in doing so, set both himself – Miller went on to direct two more *Mad Max* films and *The Witches Of Eastwick* – and Gibson on the road to success.

For international release, the cast's strong accents were felt to be unintelligible outside Australasia so all the voices were dubbed. Now released with the original Strine accents, the film shows a very young, boyish Mel as cop Max Rockatansky, in some strange future, where the cops have high speed rocket cars to catch bad guys who have souped-up cars that go even faster.

After his best friend is maimed by a gang of bikers-from-hell, Max takes his family to a remote area, only to be pursued by the gang – leaving him ultimately to seek revenge.

The sequels showed what the star and director could do with a bigger budget but the lo-fi nature of the original is hard to beat. ★★★★ **KN**

MAD MAX 2 (1981)

Starring: *Mel Gibson (Max Rockatansky), Bruce Spence (The Gyro Captaiun), Vernon Wells (Wez), Mike Preston (Pappagallo), Virginia Hey (Warrior Woman)*
Director: *George Miller*
Screenwriters: *Terry Hayes, George Miller, Brian Hannant*
18/91 mins./Sci-fi/Action/Australia

A former police officer is now a lone wanderer, travelling through a devastated Australia after a nuclear war looking for the now-priceless fuel of petrol. He becomes the saviour of a small group of honest people running a remote oil refinery – and must protect them from a biker gang.

Cars, guns, petrol, leathers, desert, mohicans, and Max. According to George Miller – master purveyor of carmaggedon turned pioneer of talking pig movies – this is the extent of what you can expect to find after nuclear war has reduced society to rubble. These are also the magnificent contents of a sequel that betters its predecessor (the shoestring stuntfest/personal revenge movie that was *Mad Max*) addressing the post-apocalyptic scenario with a punk rock sensibility and creating a grungy future chic that propelled Mel Gibson to superstardom. And there was, of course, a further sequel, the inferior but interesting *Beyond Thunderdome* which made the mistake of diluting Max's darkness (concentrating on his journey back to himself).

Obsessed with his furious highspeed demolition derby, Miller structures a very linear plot in *Mad Max 2* – you could happily describe it as one long chase scene (but there is a little more than that). Since the events that turned Max Rockatansky, well, mad there has been a total global apocalypse leaving the world stark and empty and startling like the desert badlands of New South Wales. Here a bad gang (led by the towering, bemasked Lord Houmungus besieges a good gang, led by the idealistic naivete of Pappagallo who have an oil refinery and therefore the new gold: petrol.

Enter road warrior Max, hungry for fuel, who finally disposes of his studied indifference and comes to the aid of Pappagallo. The archetypes here are pretty obvious – this is the grand tradition of the Western transferred to a brutal new frontier. We have the loner, anti-hero Max steeped in mystique and ambivalence (Clint Eastwood reborn as Mel Gibson). We have the desolate outpost trying to establish moral order and community in a cruel, cold, unfeeling world. And we have the marauding natives: a leather clad, skinhead biker gang bent on destruction, using, instead of horses, the exotic panoply of ramshackle death machines and supercharged hotrods. Only the unreachable (anti)heroism of Max can save the homesteaders.

Miller's preoccupations beyond the noisy carnival of motorised destruction, lie in a musing on locating morality in a society deprived of civilisation. The conflict between men-as-they-should-be and men-as-they-are where the animal instinct has been amplified and social constraints are simply null-and-void. Max himself, played with lean menace by Gibson, remains a mystical figure, the desert wanderer, Shane, Dirty Harry and the Man With No Name squeezed into carnal leathers and a V8 Interceptor. An amoral, dehumanised force that is seeking a way back to some semblance of his former self.

Miller extends the topsy turvey schematics of his world further: the sole child in the movie, the *Feral Kid*, is a grunting, savage; Wez,

Houmungus' nutcase henchman, is unusually a homosexual, and the film has no trouble meting out violence to both men and women. Moral order has been laid waste.

Still, it is finally the whirlwind of mechanised combat that stamps the movie so indelibly on the collective memory. Utilising nought but raw stuntwork (not a whiff of CGI, remember) Miller catapults us through a riot of extravagant, ultra-violent car capers as Max attempts to break out with a tanker of priceless gasoline. Few films, even with all the available technology today, can match the turbulent edits and sheer visceral charge of Miller's elaborate choreography as it flings cast members across bonnets, into head-on collisions and under the wheels of fellow wacky racers (which could only have been done, in a filmmaking sense, for real). Consequently, *Mad Max 2* is almost as seminal a work of sci-fi as *Blade Runner* so many are the films that have been influenced by it – if not blatantly copied from it. *Waterworld* simply transferred the plotline to a flooded post-apocalypse and gave Max gills and a top rig. *Soldier* chucked him into outer space and an interplanetary dumping ground. *The Crow, Robocop* and *Demolition Man* all borrow unabashedly from Max's rich table. ★★★★★ **IN**

MAD MAX BEYOND THUNDERDOME (1985)

Starring: *Mel Gibson (Max Rockatansky), Tina Turner (Aunty Entity), Bruce Spence (Jedediah the Pilot), Adam Cockburn (Jedediah Jr), Helen Buday (Savannah Nix), Mark Spain (Mr Skyfish), Mark Kounnas (Gekko), Tom Jennings (Slake)*
Director: *George Miller*
Screenwriters: *George Miller, Terry Hayes*
15/107 mins./Sci-fi-action/Australia

In the middle of a post-apocalyptic desert sits Bartertown, a haven for scum and criminal held together by a frail rule of law. After his supplies are stolen the wandering Max seeks shelter there, and becomes embroiled in a power struggle. When he escapes with his life, just, back in the desert he discovers an oasis populated by children.

Although rather disdained for its shift away from the rugged nihilism of the first two *Mad Max* movies, this third, far more expensive, post-apocalyptic action adventure offers some cracking stunts, a more elaborate sense of the ruined world, and a more human side to Mel Gibson's stern antihero. It may not be as bracing as *Mad Max 2*, but George Miller, the series' guiding light, proves more assured than ever before.

It's a film distinctly sliced into three segments. First there is the arrival of Max into Bartertown to confront Tina Turner's haughty, self-appointed queen known as Aunty (ostensibly the villainess, but there is some sense to her endeavours to wrest civilisation from the desert) only to be condemned to battle in the Thunderdome. This, the film's most remembered sequence, has Max fight the ruling champion – a combo of simpleton hulk and brainy midget known as Master-Blaster – while suspended on an elastic harness from the vaults of a giant dome. He scrambles away to find a lost horizon of children, who think him a divine rescuer. A situation that will force him back, children in tow, for an appropriately motorised confrontation with the bandits of Bartertown. The action thrums away happily, the performances crackle, and the movie proves properly thought out top to tail, gathering up a mythic quality.

Indeed, Miller's vision of a future barely in tact, really takes on definition. Pigs are farmed for their methane gas, and beneath Bartertown is a literal shithole. The carnival of contraptions, including a ramshackle train left over from before the end, is dutifully whacky and lethal. It is a world fully occupied, a step into the beyond civilisation's fall into a wonder of ruin and making-do. And Gibson, grey templed and ever-taciturn, remains the rock on which it is all built. ★★★★ **IN**

MADAGASCAR (2005)

Starring: *the voices of: Ben Stiller (Alex), Chris Rock (Marty), David Schwimmer (Melman), Jada Pinkett Smith (Gloria), Sacha Baron Cohen (Julien), Cedric the Entertainer (Maurice)*
Directors: *Eric Darnell, Tom McGrath*
Screenwriters: *Mark Burton, Billy Frolick, Eric Darnell, Tom McGrath*
PG/86 mins./Animated/Family/Comedy/USA

Holed up in Central Park Zoo, pampered zebra Marty gets itchy hooves and decides to explore the Big Apple. When his buddies – vain lion Alex, straight-talking hippo Gloria and neurotic giraffe Melman – go after him, their rescue mission goes belly-up, seeing the four friends carted off to the untamed wilds of Africa.

There is something deliciously neat about the premise of taking institutionalised zoo animals and throwing them into their natural, wild habitat. But Eric Darnell (*Antz*) and Tom McGrath's (*The Ren And Stimpy Show*) film fails to fully mine the concept for comedic gold.

It is visually splendid, has a smattering of good set-pieces and gags and a likeable atmosphere, but it does not have the coherence nor the consistency to give anyone at Pixar a sleepless night.

Animation-wise, there is some gorgeous stuff here (the animals exploring New York at night), and the intention – to try and inject the sight gags and freeform visual lunacy of Chuck Jones and Tex Avery into the rigid realism of computer animation – is admirable. Yet while the characters' eyes pop, jaws drop and bodies twist and contort, what *Madagascar* won't commit to is the cruelty that made Avery and Jones so laugh-out-loud funny. What's left is a lot of broad gurning and slapstick, some of which hits, most of which does not.

As ever with feature-length animation, a lot of the pleasures can be found outside the main plot; there are a couple of beautifully orchestrated movie musical moments, particularly a jungle rave thrown by a tribe of techno-tastic lemurs ('I like to moove it, mooove it') whipped up by Baron Cohen's King Julien. There are also some memorable bit-part players: a pair of highbrow monkeys who want to join the New York literati and 'throw poo at Tom Wolfe' and, best of all, a squad of crack SWAT-team penguins who liven up proceedings every time things threaten to become tedious.

Yet where *Madagascar* falls down is in simple storytelling know-how. In the initial zoo sequences, the motivations and set-ups are clearly defined, but when the characters get shipwrecked, the plotting runs aground with them, grinding to a halt as the foursome argue for an eternity on a sun-kissed beach. While the characters are likeable riffs on the actor's recognisable personas – Schwimmer's giraffe is Ross Geller with a long neck – none of them are loveable, so the film fails to deliver the requisite uplift it is so patently striving for. ★★★ **IF**

MÄDCHEN IN UNIFORM (1931)

Starring: *Emila Unda (The Principal), Dorothea Wieck (Fraulein von Bernburg), Hedwig Schlicter (Fraulein von Kesten), Herta Thiele (Manuela von Meinhardie), Ellen Schwannecke (Ilse von Weshagen)*
Director: *Leontine Sagan*
Screenwriters: *Christa Winsloe, FD Andam, based on the play by Gestern Und Heute by Winsloe*
PG/110 mins./Drama/Germany

Miserably enduring life at a strict Prussian girls' school, Manuela von Meinhardie is coaxed out of her shell by kindly teacher Fraulein von Bernburg. However, while their burgeoning friendship enchants the other students, it arouses the ire of the Principal.

Adapted by Christa Winsloe from her own play, *Yesterday And Tomorrow*, this was one of the earliest lesbian dramas to reach a wide audience. Shot for 55,000 DM at the Potsdam military orphanage and Carl Fröhlich's

m

Templehof studio, it was also the first German feature to be produced on a co-operative basis. However, the planned profit share largely fell through, as the producers kept the bulk of the six million deutschmarks that the picture grossed around the world.

Winsloe's story had been based on her own schooldays and the real Manuela (who was still disabled from throwing herself down the stairs) attended the premiere. But, while Winsloe was on set throughout the shoot, Fröhlich's presence, as supervising director, seems to have been more significant, as Austrian stage actress Leontine Sagan was making her directorial debut. The extent of Fröhlich's input is unknown, but the film is full of inspired touches.

The accomplished opening montage efficiently established the tempo and tone of school life, while the use of light and shade recalled the Kammerspielfilme produced by the likes of F.W. Murnau in the mid-1920s. The insertion of occasional still vistas to suggest the ominous presence of the authoritarian male world beyond the Empress Augusta's boundaries was also highly effective.

Considering that Talkies were still in their infancy, the soundtrack is astonishingly sophisticated, with the metaphorical exploitation of sound being complemented by its use to heighten the tensions caused around the school as the girls whisper their gossip and eventually break out into chanting Manuela's name. But it was the superimposition of Hertha Thiele and Dorothea Wieck's faces that proved the most enduring psychological and sensual moment, with its influence stretching to Ingmar Bergman's *Persona* and beyond.

Indeed, the film inspired several imitations, including *Acht Mädels Im Boot* and *Anna Und Elisabeth*, which reunited Wieck and Thiele. However, they were all banned after the Nazis came to power, although *Mädchen* was initially reprieved by the addition of a pro-Party coda. A mediocre remake, directed by Géza von Radványi and starring Lilli Palmer and Romy Schneider, was released in 1958. ★★★★ **DP**

THE MADNESS OF KING GEORGE (1994)

Starring: *Nigel Hawthorne (George III), Helen Mirren (Queen Charlotte), Ian Holm (Dr Willis), Rupert Graves (Greville), Amanda Donohoe (Lady Pembroke)*
Director: *Nicholas Hytner*
Screenwriter: *Alan Bennett, based on his play*
PG/105 mins./Drama/History/UK

Awards: *Academy Awards – Best Art Direction-Set Direction, BAFTA – Alexander Korda Award for Best British Film, Best Make Up/Hair, Best Actor, Empire Awards – Best Actor*

When King George attacks a lady in waiting, he is shut away and declared insane. He goes through various humiliating 'treatments', none of which work. His son, the indolent Prince of Wales insists on taking the crown, and the PM tries to stop him whilst George attempts to gather his marbles.

Legend has it that George III once ordered hundreds of beef steaks to be buried in a field in the belief that, come spring, a nice herd of cows would sprout. Sadly, that piece of British history is absent from *The Madness Of King George*, but fans of idiot monarchs will find little else to complain about.

At the film's start, however, all is well as the King and 'Mrs King' rule the country happily enough with only that nasty business of losing that trifling little colony America blotting their regal copybook. Unfortunately, Hawthorne soon begins to act oddly and, after one assault on lady-in-waiting Amanda Donohoe too many, he is effectively shut away for his own good. Having been declared insane – although it would now appear he was suffering from the blood disorder porphyria – he is subsequently prescribed such contemporary 'cures' as skin-blistering, stool examination and, once the veritable Dr Willis comes on the scene, brutal restraint. Of course, none of this does much to improve his state of mind, and the perpetually indolent Prince Of Wales is soon demanding to be declared Regent. The remainder of the film traces the attempts of Prime Minister Pitt The Younger to thwart such a plan while Hawthorne painstakingly tries to regroup what is left of his marbles.

With only the occasional whiff of the film's theatrical roots coming through, this is an excellent debut from director Hytner who never lets Alan Bennett's script linger too long in either farce or tragedy. The real treat, though, is Hawthorne who, whether lecturing his family on regal responsibility or taking a dump in front of the PM, gives what is undoubtedly the performance of his career. Anyone, meanwhile, who doubts the relevance of such a tale to contemporary society might take note that porphyria is hereditary. ★★★★ **BM**

THE MAGDALENE SISTERS (2002)

Starring: *Anne-Marie Duff (Margaret), Nora-Jane Noone (Bernadette), Dorothy Duffy (Rose/Patricia), Geraldine McEwan (Sister Bridget)*
Director: *Peter Mullan*
Screenwriter: *Peter Mullan*
15/114 mins./Drama/UK/Ireland

Awards: *Venice Film Festival – Golden Lion*

In Ireland in 1964, three 'fallen' teenage girls – one unmarried mother, one raped by a cousin, one who simply flirted with boys – are sent to a Magdalene laundry run by the Catholic Church. Incarcerated under slave-like conditions in a harsh, morally hypocritical regime, escape isn't even an option.

Given the condemnations that poured from the Vatican when *The Magdalene Sisters* premiered (and went on to win top prize) at the Venice Film Festival, you'd think Peter Mullan was the Antichrist.

However, his second stab at directing (after *Orphans*) isn't a cynical attempt to kick the Catholic Church when it's reeling from contemporary scandals. This angry, emotionally manipulative but heartfelt film actually admires the faith of the girls locked away from the outside world. Mullan's target isn't religion: it's abuse of power, moral hypocrisy and sadistic authority. As such, the film has as much in common with the first half of *Full Metal Jacket* as *The Devils*.

The stark cinematography captures the oppressive mood of the Magdalene institution, while Mullan avoids the more stylish directorial flourishes of his debut and leaves the stage open for his ensemble cast to rise to the occasion. The performances are compelling, with Eileen Walsh a stand-out as Crispina. ★★★★ **ND**

THE MAGIC BOX (1951)

Starring: *Robert Donat (William Friese Greene), Margaret Johnston (Edith Friese Greene), Renee Asherson (Mrs Tagg), Richard Attenborough (Jack Carter), Robert Beatty (Lord Beaverbrook),*
Director: *John Boulting*
Screenwriter: *Eric Ambler, based on the book* Friese Greene, Close Up Of An Inventor *by Ray Allister*
U/118 mins./Drama/UK

Breaking both his photographic partnership with Arthur Collings and his marriages to Helena and Edith, William Friese-Greene sacrifices everything in a bid to produce a machine that will record and produce motion pictures.

Born in Bristol in 1855, William Friese-Greene began producing photographic images for John Rudge's magic lanterns in 1880. Despite their working in collaboration, he took sole credit for the Phantascope when he presented it to the London Photographic Society in 1886. Moreover, he gave no credit to engineer Mortimer Evans when, in 1889, he patented a sequence camera, which used unperforated paper film that moved through the mechanism at 4-5 frames per second. But, while the images it produced could be cut up and used for lantern presentation, they were never projected in a single continuous display and, thus, the claim on his tombstone that Friese-Greene was the inventor of 'commercial kinematography' is entirely false. He was credited with 79 patents, including a cigar lighter and an inkless printer. But his colour and 3-D film processes proved as impractical as his projector and he died with less than two shillings in his pocket at a film congress in 1921.

This, then, is the hero of this triumphalist biopic, which paid scant heed to fact as it sought to produce a fitting film to screen at the 1951 Festival of Britain. No one could blame the Boulting brothers or Eric Ambler, who based his screenplay on Ray Allister's book, Friese-Greene, *Close-Up Of An Inventor*, which purported to be an accurate account of his life and accomplishments. All they did was rearrange the events around two extended flashbacks to make them more dramatically satisfying – and they rousingly succeeded.

They also shrewdly cast Robert Donat in the leading role, who proceeded to turn Friese-Greene into a cousin of Mr Chipping and made him seem like a typically plucky British also-ran. Moreover, they surrounded him with a galaxy of co-stars to reinforce the celebratory nature of the project and imply that without Friese-Greene's indomitable ingenuity none of them would be where they were today. But the master stroke was the procurement of Laurence Olivier to play the night-beat copper whose suspicions that he had a crank on his hands were gloriously allayed by scenes of Hyde Park flickering dimly on a white sheet. ★★★★ **DP**

THE MAGNIFICENT AMBERSONS (1942)

Starring: *Joseph Cotten (Eugene Morgan), Dolores Costello (Isabel Amberson Minafer), Anne Baxter (Lucy Morgan), Tim Holt (George Amberson Minafer), Agnes Moorehead (Fanny Amberson), Ray Collins (Jack Amberson), Richard Bennett (Maj. Amberson), Erskine Sanford (Benson), J. Louis Johnson (Sam the Butler), Donald Dillaway (Wilbur Minafer)*
Directors: *Orson Welles, Freddie Fleck, Robert Wise*
Screenwriter: *Orson Welles, based on the novel by Booth Tarkington*
U/88 mins./Drama/USA

Spurned by Lucy Morgan, Indianapolis blue blood George Amberson Minafer denies her car manufacturing father, Eugene, permission to court his widowed mother, Isabel. However, the callous snobbery, inherent in his doomed family, eventually contributes to his downfall.

Following the box-office disappointment of *Citizen Kane* (1941), Orson Welles was informed by RKO that his next directorial assignment would have to be a commercial property. Unenthused by either Cyrano de Bergerac or a variation on the Landru theme and frustrated by a scheduling clash that confounded *The Pickwick Papers* with W.C. Fields, Welles plumped for Booth Tarkington's 1919 Pulitzer Prize-winning novel, which had previously been filmed as *Pampered Youth* and adapted for the radio under its original title by Welles himself in 1938.

Despite commitments to a radio series and his then-popular magic act, Welles wrote the screenplay in just nine days. Jettisoning much of Tarkington's Proustian detail and Victorian sentimentality, he shifted the emphasis away from the lost era and on to the moral values that disappeared with the coming of industrialisation.

Thus, he gave the story a new psychological depth and solemnity that was broodingly captured by Stanley Cortez's deep-focus chiaroscuro photography and conveyed with subtle intensity by the splendid ensemble. Promoted from B Westerns, Tim Holt held his own as the despicable scion, while Joseph Cotten exuded disappointed decency as Eugene Morgan and Welles contributed the knowingly mellifluous narration. But the standout performance was undoubtedly Agnes Moorehead's neurotic spinster aunt.

Deftly combining nostalgic screen grammar with innovative techniques, Welles's direction was also impeccable and such was his desire to accommodate RKO that he reduced his final cut by 17 minutes to 131 minutes before leaving for Brazil to shoot the aborted *It's All True*. By the time he returned, Ambersons ran for a mere 88 minutes and included a hospital finale directed by Freddie Flick and scored by Roy Webb in a style that bore no resemblance to Bernard Herrmann's glorious original.

What was left was clearly a bowdlerisation. But enough remained for the film eventually to be reclaimed as a lost masterpiece. However, few in Hollywood at the time were sorry to see Welles suffer his comeuppance alongside George Minafer, when *Ambersons* was released as the bottom half of a double bill with the Lupe Velez franchise farce, *Mexican Spitfire Sees A Ghost*. ★★★★ **DP**

THE MAGNIFICENT SEVEN (1960)

Starring: *Yul Brynner (Chris Adams), Eli Wallach (Calvera), Steve McQueen (Vin), Brad Dexter (Harry Luck), Charles Brosnan (Bernardo O'Reilly), Robert Vaughn (Lee), Horst Buchholz (Chico), James Coburn (Britt)*
Director: *John Sturges*
Screenwriters: *William Roberts, Walter Bernstein (uncredited), Walter Newman (uncredited)*
PG/127 mins./Western/USA

A bandit terrorises a small Mexican farming village each year. Several of the village elders send three of the farmers into the United States to search for gunmen to defend them. They end up with 7, each of whom comes for a different reason.

Few films are shown on TV more often than the big, all-star he-man action-adventures John Sturges made in the 1960s, *The Magnificent Seven* and *The Great Escape*. It's a standing joke that a rainy Bank Holiday can't slink by without a screening of one of them, although why programmers should so often reach for these particular cinematic six-shooters is easily understood. Both movies, although spectacular and expansive, play well on the small screen. Their fairly ordinary stories are told soap-style in overlapping sub-plots, each archetypal character arriving complete with a set of demons to overcome or character traits to show off. With Elmer Bernstein's memorable musical scores, inciting much whistling along from the sofa, the films rattle through lengthy running times and both deliver endings more satisfying than simple victory – the righteous are vindicated and too many good men are sent to their graves.

Akira Kurosawa's *Seven Samurai* was an attempt to combine the American western and Japanese swordplay movies, so it was a comparatively simple trick to retranslate the screenplay into a cowboy setting. However, it took a few years for this 'obvious' idea to take root. In the past, Hollywood had remade foreign films as star vehicles (*Intermezzo*, Ingrid Bergman's American debut, was a script she'd already played in Swedish) or exotic items (*Algiers*, based on *Pepe Le Moko*). There had been westerns with plots loosely appropriated from non-western sources (Howard Hawks's *Red River* is *Mutiny On The Bounty* in Stetsons), but *The Magnificent Seven* was the beginning of a trend to which we owe Sergio Leone's *A Fistful Of Dollars* (from Kurosawa's *Yojimbo* and, once science-fiction and thriller-action had replaced the oater as the primary Hollywood genre, the multi-remake-of-everything approach taken by *Star Wars* or the recycling of foreign hits like *Nikita* and *The Vanishing*.

The marauding bandits who prey on the isolated village are now sombrero-sporting Pancho Villa types, led by Eli Wallach (who gets a more substantial role than his barely seen equivalent in the Japanese film) with a first draft of his accent from *The Good, The Bad And The Ugly*. Instead of swift-sword samurai, the downtrodden villagers appeal to quick-gunmen.

When the naive villager suggests they approach a tough-looking scarred fellow, his wiser partner says they should instead look, 'for the man who gave him those scars.' As in the Kurosawa movie, the heroes are an unusual bunch of near-psychopaths, comic oddballs and mythic archetypes. The film was such a big hit that you now accept its eccentricities, but at the time bald Russian Yul Brynner (who seems to have been up for the job because he looks a bit like Takeshi Shimura in the original) was not an obvious choice for all-in-black gunslinger-with-integrity Chris. It was a role he would reprise in the first of a run of sequels (*Return Of The Seven*) and reference as a killer robot in *Westworld*, but you have to ask how someone with his accent and face got out West in the first place, let alone became such a western feature that he would be cast as an Indian (*Kings Of The Sun*) and a Mexican (*Pancho Villa*).

The rest of the seven were young, unfamiliar types with more TV experience than Hollywood clout: competing cool cats McQueen and James Coburn, solid presence (and another Russian) Charles Bronson, well-dressed but nerves-shot Robert Vaughn, combustible German Mexican Horst Buchholz and avaricious Brad Dexter. Dexter was best-known as Frank Sinatra's bodyguard, but the rest of the cast scored some sort of stardom.

Because he became arguably the biggest star in the posse, it's strange to look again at the film and find that McQueen takes the sidekick role, standing back to admire Brynner, while Coburn gets the part to kill for, as the ice-perfect knife-thrower who conies closest to being a samurai out west. They are a brawling, bothersome assortment and the mismatch of their personalities makes for weird entertainment: no one ever did more acting in a single film than Buchholz does here, in a vain effort to match Toshiro Mifune, but Bronson seems carved from rock (he gets stuck with the palling-about-with kids subplot).

Tagline
They were seven — and they fought like seven hundred!

Vaughn is a Method mannerist, quivering with neurosis as the others are gritting their teeth, and Dexter looks as if he was just happy they let him into the cast party. Rosenda Monteros wafts through in a peasant blouse but this is a boys' film. ★★★★★ **KN**

Movie Trivia: The Magnificent Seven

The film achieved such cult status that there was an entire episode of *Cheers* dedicated to watching it. Composer Elmer Bernstein also penned the score for *The Magnificent Seven Parody, Three Amigos*. *Superman*, *Star Wars* and Indy composer John Williams was a member of Bernstein's orchestra. Steve McQueen shot the film whilst on sick leave from his TV show *Wanted: Dead Or Alive*.

MAGNOLIA (1999)

Starring: *Julianne Moore (Linda Patridge), William H. Macy (Quiz Kid Donnie Smith), John C. Reilly (Jim Kurring), Tom Cruise (Frank T. J. Mackey), Philip Baker Hall (Jimmy Gator), Philip Seymour Hoffman (Phil Parma), Jason Robards (Earl Partridge)*
Director: *Paul Thomas Anderson*
Screenwriter: *Paul Thomas Anderson*
18/180 mins./Drama/USA

Awards: *Golden Globes – Best Supporting Actor (Tom Cruise)*

Interconnected characters struggle with love, death and desperation over a long day in Los Angeles culminating with a bizarre weather phenomenon.

Paul Thomas Anderson's debt to Robert Altman blatantly emerges with a scenario – interconnected characters struggle with love, death and desperation over a long day in Los Angeles that ends with a bizarre weather phenomenon – that could be pitched as *Short Cuts II*.

The tent poles of the story are bedridden TV producer Earl Partridge and quiz show host Jimmy Gator, both of whom have terminal cancer. Earl's dippy second wife Linda can't cope, but his devoted nurse Phil tracks down Earl's estranged son, Frank Mackey, who has made a fortune from terrifying seminars that teach men to be sexual predators. Jimmy, gamely trying to hold together one last show, also has an estranged child, cokehead Claudia, who is alternately grilled and chatted up by lonely cop Jim Kurring.

Also floating around are Stanley, a quiz kid rebelling against his image, and Donnie, his grown-up counterpart, whose adult life has been one big disappointment.

The more linear *Boogie Nights* didn't fumble much throughout a long running time, but this scattershot picture (it even has an anecdotal prologue) frankly sprawls. We are meant to compare and contrast the situations of the two dying men and their extended families (blink and you'll miss the connection between the two), but this sometimes feels like the same story being told twice with cutaways to the next vignette, just as the current one has got interesting.

Cruise, with a sharklike stance, gives a career-best performance as a total bastard (his course is called 'Seduce and Destroy') with quotable dialogue ('I'm judging you quietly', 'If those dogs come near me, I will drop-kick them'); and Reilly and Walters – valuable utility players who deserve to become superstars – make amazingly fresh and suspenseful the quietly moving business of two of life's losers edging painfully closer. ★★★★ **CK**

Movie Trivia: Magnolia

Over 7,900 frogs were created for the downpour scene. The numbers 8 and 2 are constantly mentioned throughout the film, such a such 'an 82 per cent chance of rain' and a gambler hoping for a two but getting an eight in blackjack. Exodus 8:2 is also referenced: 'And if thou refuse to let them go, I will smite all thy borders with frogs'.There is a picture of a flower on every wall of every living-room in the film.

MAGNUM FORCE (1973)

Starring: *Clint Eastwood (Inspector 'Dirty' Harry Callahan), Hal Holbrook (Lieutenant Neil Briggs), Mitch Ryan (Officer Charlie McCoy), David Soul (Officer John Davis), Tim Matheson (Officer Phil Sweet), Kip Niven (Officer Red Astrachan), Robert Ulrich (Officer Mike Grimes)*
Director: *Ted Post*
Screenwriters: *John Milius, Michael Cimino, based on characters created by Harry Julian Fink and R.M. Fink*
18/124 mins./Crime/USA

Idiosyncratic but effective San Francisco cop Dirty Harry Callahan is on the trail of a vigilante group that is taking out the city's undesirables. When he discovers there might actually be cops responsible, Harry has to go on the bounds of his own orders to bring them down.

A satisfying sequel to the immortal *Dirty Harry*, that still signalled the gradual slide from radical filmmaking into the stodgy maintenance of a franchise with further empty cases for the uncivil and amoral Harry

Non-Fictional Movie Acronyms

1 ILM – Industrial Light and Magic
2 AMPAS – Academy of Motion Picture Arts And Sciences
3 BBFC – British Board of Film Censors
4 DVD – Digital Versatile Disc
5 BAFTA – British Academy of Film And Television Arts
6 CAA – Creative Artists Agency
7 MGM – Metro Goldwyn Mayer
8 PAL – Phase Alteration Line
9 ACE – American Cinema Editors
10 RKO – Radio Keither Orpheum

Callahan. This lean thriller really feels the absence of Don Siegel, an expert in framing the excesses of movie violence in a stark, moral climate, but does maintain the gutsy 70s temper of its progenitor. Perma-sneered Eastwood glowers and growls as if the effort to spit out his lines is too much, and there is the basics of a moral dilemma in the comparison of Harry's loose approach to finesse of police work and the genuine vigilantism of his foes. It's message is about internal corruption rather than outward criminality that also echoes the recent tribulation of Nixon's foiled administration. When you realise that John Milius and Michael Cimino wrote the script, two arch-fretters at the borders of the establishment, things become a little clearer.

Yet when it is boiled down to some kind of neat essence, the dependence on the standard fabric of commercial policiers – shoot-outs, chase scenes, glib one-liners – tempers such aspirations to the meaningful. It plays to the feeble in the watcher where you just want to see the toughest sonofabitch on the 'Frisco force bring down the evil within, ironically represented by TV stalwarts David Soul and Robert Ulrich. Hal Holbrook – who had recently played Deep Throat – makes the usual moves as Callahan's boss but with some conviction.

Thus, as hard as the screenwriters try, the film never makes a telling point beyond just another classic Harry-ism: 'Nothing wrong with shooting, as long as the right people get shot.' ★★★ **IN**

THE MAJESTIC (2001)

Starring: *Jim Carrey (Peter Appelton), Martin Landau (Harry Trimble), Laurie Holden (Adele Stanton), David Ogden Stiers (Doc Stanton)*
Director: *Frank Darabont*
Screenwriter: *Michael Sloane*
PG/146 mins./Drama/Romance/USA

His life in ruins, blacklisted screenwriter Peter Appleton flees 1950s Los Angeles. Suffering amnesia when he arrives in the tiny town of Lawson, he is recognised and embraced as the local hero who never returned from the War.

In theory the story of a man finding his identity, purpose and moral values in smalltown America couldn't miss. The film and its star were considered Oscar contenders even before the cameras rolled. And then, people saw the movie.

The Majestic isn't bad, but so earnestly does the film wear its heart on its sleeve, and so tireless is its referencing of greater films, that many will find it syrupy and vexing. Its treatment of McCarthyism is crudely satirical and simplistic, too. But disappointed expectations always incite more sarcasm than pictures we always knew were going to be head-on crap.

This is a sweet, patriotic, romantic fable in which good, traditional Americana – neighbourliness, decency, the defence of freedoms – is upheld, along with nostalgia for the diner, dances under the stars, strolls down leafy streets, and picture palaces where hopes, dreams and everything important in life were affirmed by the movies showing.

This mood starts when ambitious screenwriter Peter Appleton – studio contract, flash convertible and blonde arm-candy all in place – scores a hit with pastiche B-adventure *Sand Pirates Of The Sahara*, and begins pitching his important opus, *Ashes To Ashes*, which he envisions as a work of 'pain, nobility, the human condition, truth – my *Grapes Of Wrath*!' just like the hero of Preston Sturges' *Sullivan's Travels*. A scene in which the shallow, acquiescent Peter witnesses his script being absurdly punched up by unseen execs (voiced by Matt Damon, Sydney Pollock, Carl and Rob Reiner) recalls *The Player*. But then Peter is investigated by the House Committee On Un-American Activities for flirting with Communists at college. Production of his film is suspended, and nobody wants to know him.

When traumatised Peter lands in the perfect mythic American town of Lawson, the redemption plot is assembled from *Hail The Conquering Hero*, *The Best Years Of Our Lives*, *The Return Of Martin Guerre*, *Random Harvest*, *Cinema Paradiso* and Frank Capra's greatest hits.

The depressed community, numbed by its heavy losses in World War II, wills itself to believe Peter is Luke Trimble, miraculously returned and pitching into the restoration of old man Trimble's derelict cinema as a communal act of faith and rebirth.

Ironically for a buff who does a swell Jimmy Stewart impression, Carrey is likeable in the kind of role synonymous with Stewart – but so carefully restrained he's flat, only releasing his twinkle in the inevitable *Mr Smith Goes To Washington* bit for a feel-good resolution. Now, we'd really like to turn him loose in *Sand Pirates Of The Sahara*. ★★★ **AE**

MAJOR BARBARA (1941)

Starring: *Wendy Hiller (Major Barbara Undershaft), Rex Harrison (Adolphus Cusins), Robert Morley (Andrew Undershaft), Emlyn Williams (Snobby Price), Robert Newton (Bill Walker), Sybil Thorndike (The General),*
Directors: *Gabriel Pascal, Harold French, David Lean*
Screenwriters: *Anatole De Grunwald, George Bernard Shaw, based on his own play.*
PG/121 mins./Comedy/UK

Quitting the Salvation Army after The General accepts a £50,000 donation from her munitions manufacturer father, Andrew Undershaft, Major Barbara is given a lesson in the social realities of capitalism by adoring Greek professor Adolphus Cusins.

Flushed by the success of Anthony Asquith and Leslie Howard's adaptation of *Pygmalion* (1938), George Bernard Shaw gave maverick Hungarian producer Gabriel Pascal a free hand in bringing his 1905 social comedy to the screen. Having excelled as Eliza Doolittle, Wendy Hiller was hired for the title role. But, more crucially, only editor David Lean was re-engaged from the principal crew. However, he was promoted to assistant director alongside Harold French and neither had the experience nor the standing to challenge the debuting Pascal's directorial decisions. Consequently, the sting was drawn from this contentious satire by a striving for prestige that resulted only in ponderous pacing and mannered thesping.

Indeed, such was Pascal's desire to produce a work of art that he commissioned Shaw to write new connecting sequences to give the film a

m

more contemporary feel. However, the Irish playwright refused to be hurried and the delay (along with the dual impact of the Battle of Britain and Pascal's own on-set hesitancy) helped double the 10-week shooting schedule.

But any hopes of recouping the additional costs at the box office were soon dashed as, despite respectful reviews, wartime audiences stayed away from a morality tale that suggested that the manufacture of weapons was of greater benefit to the working classes than faith, hope and charity. American viewers were even less impressed by the weighty philosophising, the denunciation of religious hypocrisy and the cynicism of Shaw's contention that poverty rather than wealth is the root of all evils and that hard cash would do more for the disadvantaged than soup and solace.

Hiller is suitably committed and then malleable as the converting heiress, while Robert Newton revels in the malignant ingratitude of slum-dwelling Cockney, Bill Walker. However, both Robert Morley (made-up to resemble Shaw) and Rex Harrison deliver rather fruity performances that owed little to life and much to the rarified traditions of the London stage. **★★★ DP**

MAJOR DUNDEE (1965)

Starring: *Charlton Heston (Maj. Amos Charles Dundee), Richard Harris (Capt. Benjamin Tyreen), Jim Hutton (Lt Graham), James Coburn (Samuel Potts), Michael Anderson Jr (Trooper Tim Ryan), Senta Berger (Theresa Gelto Santiago)*
Director: *Sam Peckinpah*
Screenwriters: *Harry Julian Fink, Oscar Saul and Sam Peckinpah, based on a story by Fink*
PG/123 mins./Western/USA

During the American Civil War, Major Dundee, commander of a remote stockade, leads a cavalry outfit of Union regulars, Confederate prisoners and disreputable civilians in pursuit of an Apache war party who have escaped to Mexico.

'Fall in Behind the Major.' Sam Peckinpah's first epic-scale Western was taken from him in post-production, severely re-edited and stuck with a music score he hated. In 2005, a longer version more in accord with his vision was assembled, and an entirely new score composed by Christopher Caliendo. Neither cut is in a league with Sam's greatest work, but both have so many wonderful things that they're worth watching.

One of the first Westerns made with Vietnam in mind, Dundee now seems to address the perennial problem of what the hell America thinks it's doing sending ill-prepared, internally-fractious military expeditions into third-world countries. Focused on catching a renegade Indian, Dundee still can't keep his own men – Confederate rebels, freed black men, horse-thieves, a lunatic artilleryman, one-armed half-Indian scout James Coburn and Irish Southern officer Richard Harris – in line, and there's a powerful stretch in which the granite-jawed, wide-shouldered Charlton Heston turns into a drunken derelict when cut off from his command.

In Mexico, the cavalry find a village of willing senoritas (including out-of-place Senta Berger) and oppressed peoples, but find themselves up against another, even stranger alien army – the French, who oppose the undisciplined Yankees with terrifying precision in a final battle at the Rio Grande.

Heston and Harris square off against each other, but the heart comes from Peckinpah's great supporting cast: Ben Johnson, Warren Oates, Slim Pickens, Dub Taylor, L.Q. Jones.

It makes amazing use of the wide screen, marshalling armies of men on horses against threatening landscapes, and the action scenes show stirrings of the genius that will deliver *The Wild Bunch*. **★★★ KN**

MAJOR LEAGUE (1989)

Starring: *Tom Berenger (Jake Taylor), Charlie Sheen (Rick 'Wild Thing' Vaughn), Corbin Bernsen (Roger Dorn), Margaret Whitton (Rachel Phelps), James Gammon (Lou Brown), Rene Russo (Lyn Wells)*
Director: *David S. Ward*
Screenwriter: *David S. Ward*
U/107 mins./Comedy/USA

In the efforts to move the Cleveland Indians to Florida, their owner Rachel Phelps puts together a ragtag team so they are definitely going to lose. But when this bunch get wind of the plan they decide the best action is to start winning.

A dumbed-down version of *Bull Durham* that still manages, through sheer doofus charm, to be a winning nonsense. It's the classic sports movie – loser team of oddballs unite to take the trophy and stick to the man (in this case woman, wicked club owner Margaret Whitton full of soap opera vim) – splayed out into a spoof. It's a strange cast to play a strange bunch of failed ball players – Tom Berenger is not known for his comic charm, Corbin Bernsen lavishes all his *LA Law* smarm, while Charlie Sheen as a wild card parolee has that mystified glint as if he really ought to know better. Somehow they glue into a funny whole, which is more down to the neatness and painful obviousness of David S. Ward's story.

The film has ambition and flouts it. There's s teasing swagger to the team of cranks flipping from loserville to the big hitters of the league, without waylaying us with too much sport, just plenty of locker room patter and the stirring mania of the Indian's home crowd. Little knowledge of baseball is required, when Charlie Sheen walks to the field to the rapturous chant of Wild Thing (his terrace nickname) its mass exuberance carries you all the way. Now one's looking for greatness, but it did serve up two sequels that had the effrontery to be awful. **★★★ IN**

MALCOLM X (1992)

Starring: *Denzel Washington (Malcolm X), Angela Bassett (Dr Betty Shabazz), Albert Hall (Baines), Al Freeman Jr (Elijah Muhammad), Delroy Lindo (West Indian Archie), Spike Lee (Shorty), Theresa Randle (Laura)*
Director: *Spike Lee*
Screenwriters: *Arnold Pearl, Spike Lee, from the* The Autobiography Of Malcolm X, *as told to Alex Haley*
15/193 mins./Drama/Biography/USA

The story of the life of Malcolm X, who was turned from a life of petty crime by his conversion to Islam and became an advocate of black power.

The movie that was supposed to cause such controversy in Middle America (even, if you will, to set cities a-burning) failed to do any such thing because director Spike Lee chose to tell the story of 'the angriest black man in America' with such surprising restraint.

In fact, at times the film seems in danger of collapsing into the tedium of History Lecture For Beginners. That it never quite does is testament to the immensely powerful performance of Denzel Washington. The film comes in two lengthy acts. Act One is the story of Malcolm Little, jaunty wide-boy from Boston who wears flash clothes and takes white women and gallivants in dance halls and does drugs and ends up in chokey. This section, directed with flash and panache, a jazz-styled, colourful 'romp' is, for want of a better term, the Entertainment.

Act Two, however, is the story of Malcolm X, the convert to the Nation of Islam who delivers harsh words to the white folk of America, a much more radical version of that nice Reverend King. This section, altogether more sombre as X casts away the gaudy togs and goes for grey hat and spectacles and dignified rage, is the Lesson.

Occasionally veering towards Made-For-TV- Biopic territory –

especially in the scenes of Malcolm's visit to Egypt (don't the camels and the Pyramids look nice?) and pilgrimage to Mecca – one is kept upon one's toes by some fire of oration and the growing tension between Elijah Muhammed, leader of the Nation of Islam (Freeman Jnr, splendidly spooky), and his driven protégé.

And while you know all along that Malcolm X is going to get shot to death, when it comes, it's still a shock. A pity, then, that Lee chooses to hammer home the Lesson by opening with footage of Rodney King's beating and closing with Nelson Mandela (who cannot act, alas) as a Soweto schoolmaster. Racism is a Bad Thing. Yes, I think we got that. ★★★ **TH**

MALENA (2000)

Starring: *Monica Bellucci (Malena Scordia), Giuseppe Sulfaro (Renato Amoroso), Luciano Federico (Renato's Father), Matilde Piana (Renato's Mother), Pietro Notrianni (Professor Bonsignore)*
Director: *Giuseppe Tornatore*
Screenwriter: *Giuseppe Tornatore, based on a story by Luciano Vincenzoni*
15/109 mins./Drama/Romance/Italy/USA

Malena is a statuesque beauty desired by the local menfolk in World War II Italy. Renato is a twelve-year-old boy who worships her from afar . . .

World War II is raging, but nowhere near as furiously as Renato's hormones each time he sees Malena, a statuesque beauty. Desired by the menfolk and despised by their women, Malena is left with little option than to exploit her allure to survive.

Despite an impressive debut by Sulfaro as the obsessed boy, this is Belluci's film, her haunting grace makes her a compelling object of a boy's adoration but her heartfelt rendition of a woman who is forced to move from widow to prostitute in order to survive is the film's emotional core.

Caught between glossy wish-fulfilment and hard-hitting realism, Tornatore, working well within his game here, doesn't always pull off the tricky transitions from whimsy to tragedy. But Ennio Morricone's score and Lajos Koltai's photography paper over some of the cracks, creating a beautiful, if not completely satisfying, work. ★★★ **DP**

MALLRATS (1995)

Starring: *Shannen Doherty (Rene Mosier), Jeremy London (T.S. Quint), Jason Lee (Brodie Bruce), Claire Forlani (Brandi Svenning), Ben Affleck (Shannon Hamilton), Joey Lauren Adams (Gwen Turner), Jason Mewes (Jay), Kevin Smith (Silent Bob)*
Director: *Kevin Smith*
Screenwriter: *Kevin Smith*
18/94 mins./Comedy/USA

Both dumped by their girlfriends, two best friends seek refuge in the local mall.

Director Kevin Smith made his previous mark on Generation X culture with the hilarious, inspired *Clerks*, which despite its black-and-white status and $27,000 price tag was one of the success stories of 1995. *Mallrats*, a sequel of sorts complete with throwbacks to certain characters and situations (but in colour and with 'studio picture' stamped all over it), proved the opposite, opening to comparative indifference in the US and bypassing UK screens completely. Which is a pity, for while the ensuing romp never quite achieves the majesty of its predecessor, it is far from disastrous.

Having been dumped by their respective girlfriends, slackers Brodie and TS seek sanctuary in the only place they see fit – the local mall. Once inside, they undergo a series of encounters that would shame even the most seasoned of shoppers, ranging from meeting Marvel comics creator Stan Lee, through to thoroughly annoying the chainstore suit who has spirited away Brodie's ex, culminating in their attempts to regain their loved ones by vandalising a live gameshow broadcast.

This is more a film of individually inspired moments rather than a constant barrel of laughs. While brilliant moments of irreverence and filth – one man's day-long struggle to make head or tail of a Magic Eye drawing; the return of *Clerks* dropouts Jay and Silent Bob; a cripplingly funny opening monologue – prevail, more often than not Smith relies on dim humour and downright stupidity as the comic book-obsessed loser protagonists slide giddily about the mall from one mishap to the next. And it loses its way in the final reel, resulting in a horribly cheesy finale.

Despite these shortcomings, though, proceedings benefit from a great deal of charm and appealing leads (Doherty, especially, displaying previously untapped talents) that carry it amiably to the finish line. Not a film for everybody, perhaps, but *Clerks* fans and those who prefer their dumb comedy infused with a little spice will not be disappointed. ★★★ **CW**

THE MALTESE FALCON (1941)

m

Starring: *Humphrey Bogart (Sam Spade), Mary Astor (Brigid O'Shaughnessy), Gladys George (Iva Archer), Peter Lorre (Joel Cairo), Barton MacLane (Det. Lt. Dundy)*
Director: *John Huston*
Screenwriter: *John Huston, based on the novel by Dashiell Hammett*
PG/96 mins./Film-noir/USA

Sam Spade, a private detective, gets involved in a murderous hunt for a valuable statuette.

As one of the two dizzying peaks of the private eye genre (although whether it is Everest to *The Big Sleep*'s K2 is open to debate), *The Maltese Falcon* is an unassailable triumph of script, casting, direction and editing. As an example of ensemble acting it takes some beating too. It put John Huston on the map as a writer-director – his debut in both disciplines – and finally furnished Bogart, who once joked bitterly that he's made a career out of playing George Raft's brother-in-law, with a showcase for his great talent and superhuman on-screen charisma. In the role of Sam Spade he stepped smartly off the B-movie treadmill that a spiteful Jack Warner, incensed at the actor's contractual grievances, had tied him to. And with *Casablanca* (1942), *The Big Sleep* (1946), The *Treasure Of The Sierra Madre* (1948) and *The African Queen* (1951) waiting in the wings this was a legend in the making. And Raft must have been killing himself. He had originally been offered the role but turned it down.

There's no doubt that Bogart, who appears in almost every scene, dominates the film. But he's surrounded by a cast of supporting players that any actor would die for – Mary Astor as the wide-eyed and deadly Brigid O'Shaughnessy (aka Ruth Wonderly), Peter Lorre as the effeminate, fastidious Joel Cairo; Sydney Greenstreet as the avuncular, yet sinister, fat man, Kasper Gutman. Even the minor roles are cast to perfection – Lee Patrick as Effie Perrne, Spade's secretary-factotum; Jerome Cowan as his partner Miles Archer; Ward Bond and Barton MacLane as a pair of lumbering flatfoots; Gladys George as Archer's widow; and Elisha Cooke Jr, brilliant as the teenage gunsel Wilmer. It's a fabulous, motley collection of characters. And superbly played though they are, credit for their creation must be given to Dashiell Hammett from whose novel the film was adapted.

A one-time operative for Pinkerton's Detective agency, Hammett based each one on somebody he had known in real life. Brigid O'Shaughnessy was based partly on his secretary, a Miss Peggy O'Toole, and partly on a woman who once employed him to fire her housekeeper. Joel Cairo's exotic real-life counterpart was a man Hammett picked up on a forgery charge in 1920. Wilmer, the boy gunman, was drawn from a baby-faced petty criminal known in Stockton, California, as 'The Midget Bandit'. Casper Gutman, Hammett once recalled, was based on, 'Someone suspected of being a German secret agent' whom he had shadowed in Washington while working for Pinkerton's.

It's widely held that Sam Spade was, to some extent, autobiographical. Hammett, though, was quick to deny the assertion. 'He's a dream man,' he remarked in 1934, 'in the sense that he is what most of the detectives I worked with would like to have been and what quite a few of them, in their cockier moments, thought they approached . . . A hard and shifty fellow, able to take care of himself in any situation, able to get the best of anybody he comes in contact with, whether criminal, innocent bystander or client. Writer William F. Nolan put it succinctly when he said, 'Samuel Spade is of course a direct extension of the author, a man caught up in an unstable universe of random violence who survives by following a rigid self-imposed code of honour.' Either way, Spade is both the template for every movie PI who followed – including Marlowe – and the epitome of Bogart's screen persona.

Critic Andrew Sarris, in a rare moment of idiocy, claimed that Huston's films, 'Owe more to casting coups than directorial acumen,' and disparaged Falcon as, 'An uncanny match up of Dashiell Hammett's literary characters with their visual doubles.' The former assertion is nonsense and the latter, since the book describes Spade as resembling a 'blonde Satan', demonstrably not true.

Huston's script owes a great deal to Hammett, but transposing the author's gripping prose to the screen was no picnic. After all it had been bodged before: in Roy Del Ruth's 1931 version and in William Dieterle's *Satan Met A Lady* (1936), which not even the presence of Bette Davis could salvage. In fact, it's cause for celebration that both the labyrinthine plot and Hammett's dialogue, which still quivers with racy innuendo, tough talk and pithy one-liners, survive intact. Virtually every scene is a classic, but a perennial favourite is the confrontation between Spade and Gutman where Spade calls the fat man's bluff, barking ultimatums at him and smashing his whiskey glass on the floor. Spade storms out of the room. As he walks towards the elevator, his face emerges from the shadow of his hat brim. He's grinning broadly, but when he looks down at his hands, they're shaking.

A succinct summary of the plot is a tall order – it's insanely complex, although unlike *The Big Sleep* it actually does make makes sense. But one of the ultimate joys of the movie is that its de rigueur web of intrigue, double-cross and murder, is spun by a fantastically imaginative device. And again, it's all due to Hammett's genius for merging fact with fiction. According to the film, the eponymous falcon was a present from the Order Of The Hospitallers of St. John Of Jerusalem to King Charles V of Spain. In 1530, Charles had bequeathed the island of Malta to the order and had asked in return for the annual payment of a bird of prey. The crusaders were so grateful that instead they sent a, 'Glorious golden falcon, encrusted from head to foot with the finest jewels in their coffers'. But the galleon carrying the prize was plundered and the falcon disappeared. Resurfacing at various intervals thereafter, the bird finally ends up in San Francisco where Gutman, Cairo and O'Shaughnessy are desperate to get their hands on it.

There actually was an arrangement made in 1530 whereby a Maltese bird of prey was presented to Charles V as rent on the island of Malta, but the payments were always living birds. Hammett though, invests his McGuffin with not only a whiff of history but also of romance, danger and mystery. The falcon fuels his characters' obsession in a way that mere money never could and the spell the falcon casts over everyone involved is what makes the whole movie tick. Not even the impenetrable Sam Spade, who delivers the last line before the fade, is immune. 'Heavy, what is it?' asks Detective Polhaus. 'The, uh, stuff that dreams are made of,' he replies. ★★★★★ **SB**

MAN BITES DOG (C'EST ARRIVE PRES DE CHEZ VOUS) (1992)

Starring: *Benoit Poelvoorde (Ben), Remy Belvaux (Reporter), Andre Bonzel (Cameraman), Jacqueline Poelvoorde-Pappaert (Ben's Mother)*
Directors: *Remy Belvaux, Andre Bonzel, Benoit Poelvoorde*
Screenwriters: *Remy Belvaux, Andre Bonzel, Benoit Poelvoorde, Vincent Tavier, based on an idea by Belvaux*
18/92 mins./Comedy/Crime/Drama/Belgium

A group of film students, doing a fly-on-the-wall doc on a serial killer, get drawn into his life of violence.

Arguably one of the most ferociously disturbing films ever made, this bleak, raw, uncompromising feature debut from three Belgian students is a sick, twisted, unbelievably depraved piece of work that haunts the consciousness long after the cinema lights have come up.

Pitched as a documentary chronicling the exploits of Benoit – a Belgian serial killer at work, rest and play in his provincial home town – made by a group of students, the film's gritty, grainy, black-and-white photography, hand-held camerawork and splattergun murders make for uncomfortable viewing.

A racist, sexist, opinionated thug, Benoit spouts off to the camera in between his homicidal handiwork, offering up his views on every conceivable subject, from the mundane to the murderous to the mechanics of weighing down a corpse. He even forks out the extra money to continue filming when the impoverished production runs short of cash. What succeeds initially as a searing, scabrous black comedy that questions the complicity of television in the portrayal of violence degenerates into a numbing series of increasingly shocking set-pieces as women, children and postmen are gunned down, suffocated and literally scared to death, culminating in a sickening gang-rape in which the entire film crew cease being observers and become participants. ★★★ **MS**

A MAN CALLED HORSE (1970)

Starring: *Richard Harris (Lord John Morgan), Judith Anderson (Buffalo Cow Head), Jean Gascon (Batise), Manu Tupou (Yellow Hand), Corinna Tsopei (Running Deer)*
Director: *Elliot Silverstein*
Screenwriter: *Jack De Witt*
15/114 mins./Western/USA

The story of Lord John Morgan, a mild-mannered aristocrat captured by the Sioux in 1825. Realising he has to adapt to survive, he endures torture and oppression, before earning their respect and acceptance as a member of the tribe.

Before *Dances With Wolves*, with its prettified view of the Sioux nation and comparatively gentle immersion of a white man as one of their number, there was *A Man Called Horse*, a harsh, visceral, so-very '70s treatment of a similar subject matter. In fact, this film is based on a TV script written in the 50s for the TV series *Wagon Train*, although that was far more sanitised again.

What lends Elliot Silverstein's version such power is a dedication to portraying Native American culture in a realistic manner. He even went to the lengths of hiring Clyde Dollar, a Sioux historian-archaeologist, to monitor their attempts to capture Sioux life and culture. The film, terse and unblinking, has a documentary's feel for historical clarity. Here were a people violent, primal, and often warlike but also loyal, intelligent and inspiring.

Richard Harris, with a script that for once constrains and utilises his chuck-it-all-out-there-and-screw-the-consequences approach to acting, endures no end of physical and spiritual torture as the formerly demure English lord. He is, quite literally, dragged through the mud, transformed

TOP10

Woody Allen Quotes Not By Woody Allen

1 **'I could never be a woman, cause I'd just stay home and play with my breasts all day.' (Harris, written by Steve Martin, *LA Story*)**

2 **'Go, and never darken my towels again.' (attributed to Groucho Marx as Rufus T. Firefly, *Duck Soup*)**

3 **'I cannot stand notes on my pillow. "We're all out of cornflakes, F.U." It took me three hours to figure out that F.U. was Felix Unger.' (Oscar, written by Neil Simon, *The Odd Couple*)**

4 **'You can't fight in here. This is the war room.' (President Muffley, written by Stanley Kubrick, Terry Southern and Peter George, *Dr Strangelove*)**

5 **'The London Underground is not a political movement!' (Wanda, written by John Cleese, *A Fish Called Wanda*)**

6 **'My name is Jim, but most people call me ... Jim.' (Wako Kid, written by Mel Brooks, *Blazing Saddles*)**

7 **'You fell victim to one of the classic blunders, the most famous of which is never get involved in a land war in Asia.' (Vizzini, written by William Goldman, *The Princess Bride*)**

8 **'Nobody does vegetables like me. I did an evening of vegetables on Broadway! I did an endive salad that knocked critics on their ass!' (Michael, written by Larry Gelbart, *Tootsie*)**

9 **'I am a musician and the monkey is a businessman. He doesn't tell me what to play, and I don't tell him what to do with his money.' (Blind Beggar, written by Frank Waldman and Blake Edwards, *The Return of the Pink Panther*)**

10 **'It's such a fine line between stupid and clever.' (David St. Hubbins, written by Christopher Guest, Michael McKean, Harry Shearer and Rob Reiner, *This Is Spinal Tap*)**

into a beast of burden and, in one unforgettable, eye-watering piece of hiding-the-joins realism, is lifted bodily by blades inserted in his skin for the Vow To The Sun ritual.

Learning from fellow captive Batise of the intricacies of this seemingly brutal people, the theme of the film emerges. How a man comes to understand his enemy as surely as a culture equal to his own. This is to such an extent that he eventually wins their trust, inevitably and rather tritely finds romance with the chief's daughter (Anderson), before fighting alongside them against their sworn enemy.

Very much a product of its time, the trippy editing, earthy rather than grandiose photography (the emphasis is constantly on the real, the believable) and lack of a sweeping score, not to say its candid violence, make it a far off cry from Costner's dandy epic. This is a far tougher parable about the clash of cultures. ★★★★ **IN**

A MAN ESCAPED (UN CONDAMNE A MORT S'EST ESCHAPPE) (1956)

Starring: *François Letterier (Lt Fontaine), Charles La Clainche (Francois Jost), Roland Monod (De Leiris the Pastor), Maurice Beerblock (Blanchet), Jacques Ertaud (Orsin), Roger Treherne (Terry), Jean-Paul Delhumeau (Hebrard)*
Director: *Robert Bresson*
Screenwriter: *Robert Bresson, based on articles by Andre Devigny*
U/102 mins./Drama/France

Sentenced to death by the Nazis for railway sabotage, Fontaine spends his days encouraging his fellow prisoners during their exercise periods and preparing his escape. However, his plans seem compromised when he is forced to share his cell with Jost, whose uniform comprises both French and German garments.

Inspired by André Devigny's account in *Le Figaro Littéraire* of his own escape from the notorious Montluc jail in Lyon, this is the first of Robert Bresson's three prison pictures and, like *Pickpocket* and *The Trial Of Joan Of Arc*, it is as much about Catholicism as it is crime and punishment – hence, the opening caption citing Jesus's words to Nicodemus, 'The wind bloweth where it listeth'.

However, this was followed by the statement, 'This is a true story. I have told it with no embellishments.' Bresson certainly insisted on complete authenticity and Devigny not only served as an adviser on the Montluc set, but he also loaned the director the ropes and hooks he had used in his escape. But this is, nevertheless, a film whose spiritual realism was controlled to the minutest detail.

Bresson's screenplay was confined to a series of elliptical episodes that reduced Sorbonne student François Leterrier to a model whose performance was wholly dictated by Bresson, to the extent that he almost played Fontaine himself via a primitive process of real-life motion capture. Yet the prisoner was virtually stripped of his personality, as his manual dexterity mattered more than any gesture or expression. He was, therefore, presented as an empty vessel for the will of the unseen power that guided his hand and this sense of divine intervention was reinforced by the arrival of Jost, as Fontaine initially considered killing him as a spy, only for him to prove crucial to the escape's success.

Making for fascinating contrast with both Jean Renoir 's POW picture *La Grande Illusion* and Jules Dassin's heist classic *Rififi*, this is a compellingly tense tale, even though we already know the outcome. Bresson's use of the claustrophobic setting and the alternately terrifying and tantalising sounds of incarceration and liberty is masterly. No wonder Jean-Luc Godard opined after seeing the film, that Bresson was 'to French cinema what Mozart is to German music and Dostoevsky is to Russian literature'. ★★★★★ **DP**

A MAN FOR ALL SEASONS (1966)

Starring: *Paul Scofield (Sir Thomas More), Leo McKern (Thomas Cromwell), Wendy Hiller (Alice More), Robert Shaw (King Henry VIII), Orson Welles (Cardinal Wolsey), Susannah York (Margaret More), Nigel Davenport (Duke Of Norfolk), John Hurt (Richard Rich)*
Director: *Fred Zinnemann*
Screenwriters: *Robert Bolt, Constance Willis, based on the play by Robert Bolt*
PG/120 mins./History/Biography/UK

Awards: *Academy Awards – Best Picture, Best Director, Best Actor (Scofield), Best Screenplay, Best Cinematography, Best Costume Design. BAFTA – Best Film, Best British Screenplay, Best British Actor (Scofield), Best British Cinematography, Best British Costumes, Best British Art Direction.*

Trying to gain the approval of the aristocracy, King Henry VIII runs up against the principles of his chancellor Sir Thomas More, who is willing to risk losing his head for treason rather than allow his king to corrupt all that he believes in.

A worthy if predictable sweep at the Academy Awards in 1967, Fred Zinnemann's highly polished costume drama manages the rarefied knack of being both highly intelligent and very accessible. Such complicated arcana as the Act of Succession and the recognition of Henry as the head of the English Church, a design that would see them break from Papal control, hardly lend themselves to the glossy operatics of populist film-making.

Screenwriter Robert Bolt, who had proven a dab hand at turning dense passages of history into ripe drama on David Lean's *Lawrence Of Arabia*, makes sure the film is not sunk in period protocol, seeing it, fundamentally, as a personal story. What does it take to stay true to yourself? What is the cost?

Scofield, who had made the role his own on stage, obliges again with a wonderfully eloquent and subtle performance – his stand is not necessarily a righteous one; the truth of the man is in his determination. As the King's displeasure with his former favourite's obdurate stance takes effect, More is plunged into penury, imprisoned and faces the real threat of losing his stubborn head. A fascinating point of order is that More makes no public statement as to the nature of his objections, which he felt would be used to condemn him. His treason, therefore, couldn't be proven, but corruption rather than truth will be his undoing.

The support cast seem to relish the chance for long, wordy scenes layered with double meaning: Shaw in the plum role of Henry, Leo McKern as his pawn Thomas Cromwell, and a stand-out, if brief, bit of showing-off from Orson Welles as Cardinal Wolsey.

All that Zinnemann need do is keep his camera in focus, but he goes much further than that with lavish production design and a real feel for the double-standards of royal pomp. Everything around More starts to appear dubious and untrustworthy. Even words themselves. ★★★★ **IN**

THE MAN IN THE IRON MASK (1939)

Starring: *Louis Hayward (King Louis XIV/Philippe Of Gascony), Joan Bennett (Princess Maria Theresa), Warren William (Philippe D'Artagnan), Jospeph Schildkraut (Nicholas Fouquet), Alan Hale (Porthos), Miles Mander (Aramis), Bert Roach (Athos)*
Director: *James Whale*
Screenwriter: *George Bruce, based on the novel by Alexander Dumas*
PG/110 mins./Adventure/USA

Based on the famous novel by Alexander Dumas, this tells of the wicked King Louis the XIV who keeps his identical twin hidden in an iron mask, deep within a dungeon, out of harm's way. When the fabled three musketeers learn of the plot, they unite with soon-to-be fourth member D'Artagnan to turn the tables.

James Whale lends his taste for the flamboyant, fed by his string of horror hits, to the classic tale of shadowy identities, royal wrong-doing and the correctional uses of the pointy end of a rapier with some aplomb. It's lavish, full of deep shadows and sweeping camerawork, playing the extravagances of Alexander Dumas' storytelling for all they are worth. There's no doubting the melodrama, or the thinness of its psychology, but it is bold and stirringly old-fashioned.

The pleasure of these musketeer fables is the intricacy of their plotting. Having one twin as a cruel king, and his brother as a potentially just one sets up a fairy-tale framework for the thriller to follow. Louis Hayward convincingly etches out the contrasting brethren, the manipulator on one side who eventually has his secret looky-likey stored in the basement of the Bastille with iron headgear to save any confusion. The swashbuckling trio of musketeers (always hearty and heroic), and hero D'Artagnan, are the only ones who knew of this double-trouble, having raised the good twin, and set about switching them the other way for the sake of France.

It rolls along with gusto and general silliness, never touching the heights of the Errol Flynn rousers, but thanks to its stylish director a natty stridency all its own, making it probably the best adaptation of the book there has been. ★★★★ **IN**

Ⓞ THE MAN IN THE MOON (1991)

Starring: *Sam Waterston (Matthew Trant), Tess Harper (Abigail Trant), Gail Strickland (Marie Foster), Reeese Witherspoon (Dani Trant), Jason London (Court Foster)*
Director: *Robert Mulligan*
Screenwriter: *Jenny Wingfield*
PG/99 mins./Drama/USA

In 1957, fourteen-year-old tomboy Dani Trant develops a crush on the farmboy next door only to lose him to her older sister.

This is one of those 'after that summer, nothing would ever be the same again' films. It opens with a pan down from a gorgeously glowing moon – photographed by an astronaut from an angle it is impossible to see from Earth, but never mind – to a picturesque Louisiana farmhouse.

A scratchy Elvis smooch number plays on the soundtrack as two young girls exchange cornpone profundities on the porch, and you know you're in for another coming-of-age movie in which the wistful longings of adolescents are examined against the soft-focus hard realities of life in a simpler bygone America, with the hard knocks sustained by the adults in the plot implicitly hanging over the futures of the bright-eyed kids.

Director Robert Mulligan, who made the enduring classic *To Kill A Mockingbird* and the forgotten hit *Summer Of '42*, specialised in wistful coming-of-age dramas, and this is a perfectly acceptable entry in the bittersweet nostalgic sub-genre, remembered mostly as Reese Witherspoon's debut feature.

The young players are all appealing, though Witherspoon already looks like the stand-out star character actress she would become, while Sam Waterston and Tess Harper, suffering showing in every line on their faces, struggle as the beleaguered farmer parents, perhaps equating the hard time they are having on the land with the way neither of their careers ever quite fulfilled their acting promise.

The trouble, of course, is that apart from occasional dramatic lurches that come out of nowhere, nothing much happens, resulting in a faint sprinkling of tedium beautifully photographed by Freddie Francis in his Straight Story mood, barely relieved by the occasional near-miscarriage or farm accident. ★★ **KN**

Ⓞ THE MAN IN THE WHITE SUIT (1951)

Starring: *Alec Guinness (Sidney Stratton), Joan Greenwood (Daphne Birnley), Cecil Parker (Alan Birnley), Michael Gough (Michael Gorland), Ernest Thesiger (Sir John Kierlaw)*
Director: *Alexander Mackendrick*
Screenwriters: *Roger MacDougall, John Dighton, Alexander Mackendrick, based on the play by MacDougall*
U/81 mins./Comedy/UK

Sidney Stratton, a humble inventor, develops a fabric that never gets dirty or wears out. This would seem to be a boon for mankind, but the established garment manufacturers don't see it that way; they try to suppress it.

Surprisingly few science fiction films care about actual science. Science is usually dismissed as the boring bit that has to be got out of the way before the monster shows up. In light of that Alexander Mackendrick's Ealing comedy is almost unique in considering the implications of an imaginary invention.

The script – by Roger MacDougall (who set the idea out in an unproduced play), John Dighton and Mackendrick – uses a wonderful laboratory breakthrough to raise questions about the application of science that in 1951 struck a chord with those worried about the proliferation of nuclear weapons (i.e. everyone) and today strikes even closer to home by envisioning the potentially disastrous effects of new technology on established manufacturing industries. It's also an unusual comedy in that it isn't especially concerned with being funny – the one scene of people laughing is as cruel as anything in cinema – but nevertheless pokes fun at sacred cows from all over the political spectrum, from pure scientific research through tool-downing shop stewards to monstrous capitalists.

Alec Guinness, at the height of his powers as Britain's most versatile character star, wears his own mild face for a change and gives a remarkable performance as Sidney Stratton, a single-minded but almost childlike chemist who has been fired from six textile mills for blowing the research budgets on an intricate H machine that seems only to produce droll sound effects (which were mixed with music and released as a single, 'The Man In The White Suit Samba') and explosions.

Like Stratton, Guinness hides in the background for the first half of the movie, noticed only by two contrasting women who fall for his reticent charm – brassy labour activist Bertha and the breathy Daphne, daughter of his blustering employer Birnley. If there were another actor in the lead role, the film might have had to rely on dreary dialogue sequences as Stratton explains why he is doing what he is doing and what he learns from it. Without seeming to pull any faces, Guinness makes it all too clear, even in the inevitable science gabble bit, which sounds unusually credible but is also an infallible comic highlight as Daphne, like us, tunes out before realising what she has been told.

Eventually, Stratton declares his mystery project is on the verge of delivering results – a 'long molecule' which makes a white thread from which can be woven clothes that will never get dirty or wear out. Birnley at first sees the enormous profit potential, and a prototype suit of dazzling (indeed luminous) white is manufactured. Then the unions and management realise that this means people will only ever buy one set of clothes and the whole industry – site of the original Luddite clashes between handloom weavers and the spinning jenny – will collapse. Stratton, unworldly enough not to have thought it through, has just enough savvy to realise that when a 'new contract' is put before him by super-tycoon Sir John Kerlaw (James Whale favourite Ernest Thesiger in a letter-perfect cameo of decrepit deviousness) it means the industry actually wants to suppress his irksome invention.

In an astonishingly frank sequence that wouldn't have been allowed in a Hollywood film back in prudish 1951, the corrupt industrial barons, including her callow fiance, prevail upon Daphne to seduce Sidney to win him over, and

m

the girl ups their price for her prostitution before making some impressive moves on the naive inventor. Joan Greenwood, possessor of the sexiest voice in the British cinema (qv. *Barbarella*), is encouraged when Stratton rejects her, and helps him escape by using his unbreakable thread to walk down a wall (the film ignores other applications of such amazing monofilaments, like the line used to slice Udo Kier into segments in *Johnny Mnemonic*).

A mob of capital and labour pursue the man in his shining white suit through the mill-town – where his landlady-cum-washerwoman accuses him of plotting to abolish her lifestyle – and a lynching is only averted when it turns out that there was a flaw in the process and the fabric becomes unstable, flaking away to nothing. Eventually the industry settles down and Birnley congratulates himself on weathering the crisis, just as Stratton perceives the mistake he has made and sets out to start all over again (an ending reprised by another scientist at the end of *The Quatermass Experiment*).

Mackendrick, who also made such blistering films as *The Ladykillers* and *Sweet Smell Of Success*, is invariably labelled a cynic, but *The Man In The White Suit* has a fairly complex attitude to its thorny subject matter. On the one hand, the hero is beset by small-minded, self-interested, venal characters who do everything to exploit him; but, on the other, he has proceeded blithely ahead on a dangerous (often explosive) course without thinking through the human impact of his theory (a voice unheard from is that of the consumer, whom neither management nor labour cared about in 1951). ★★★★★ **KN**

MAN OF ARAN (1934)

Starring: *Colman 'Tiger' King (A Man Of Aran), Maggie Dirrane (His Wife), Michael Dirrane (Mikeleen), Pat Mullin (Shark Hunter), Patch 'Red Beard' Ruadh (Shark Hunter), Patchen Faherty (Shark Hunter), Tommy O'Rourke (Shark Hunter)*
Director: *Robert J. Flaherty*
Screenwriter: *Robert J. Flaherty*
E/76 mins./Documentary/UK

Young Mikeleen spots a basking shark off the coast of the Isle of Aran and waits with his mother while his father spends two days on the treacherous Atlantic trying to capture the creature.

Robert Flaherty conceived the idea of a sea hunt in 1932 when he sighted a basking shark near his then-home on Achill Island, off the County Mayo coast. Undeterred by the fact that Irish fishermen hadn't caught sharks for oil for some 60 years, Flaherty had replica harpoons made and put his cast through an intensive training course. However, he arrived on Aran after the basking season had ended and had to secure a year's shooting extension from Michael Balcon at Gainsborough, who had provided him with cast-off film stock and a big enough budget to shoot in silence and construct a soundtrack in post-production.

Flaherty amassed 200,000 feet of film and frequently feuded with the Soviet-influenced John Goldman as it was edited down to a mere 7,000. However, the fascinating clash between Flaherty's predilection for natural mise-en-scène and Goldman's preference for montage was largely overlooked as the film provoked a fierce ethical and artistic debate about the nature of documentary film-making.

While some critics praised Flaherty's use of long lenses to record the intimidating majesty of the ocean, many more regretted his manipulation of fact. The fisherman's family were selected for their photogenicity, while the use of seaweed for potato planting was as anachronistic as the shark hunt. But it wasn't the romanticising of reality that they most objected to, but the failure to allude to such pressing issues as the islanders' exploitation by absentee landlords, the class conflict that existed on Aran and its relationship with the newly established Free State. Indeed, some accused Flaherty of producing a work of escapism whose patronising and reactionary attitudes to tradition and progress not only revealed his essential lack of humanity, but also abnegated the documentarist's duty to produce films with a social purpose.

Seen today, the action retains a heroic feel and it's not to admire Flaherty's eye for an image. But the compromised purity undoubtedly detracts from the picture's impact and it pales in comparison with the more astutely made *Louisiana Story*. ★★★ **DP**

MAN OF IRON (CZLOWIEK Z. MARMURU)

Starring: *Jerzy Radziwilowicz (Tomczyk), Krystyna Janda (Agnieska), Marian Opania (Winkiel), Wieslawa Kosmalska (Wieslawa Hulewicz), Irene Byrska (Wieslawa's Mother)*
Director: *Andrzej Wajda*
Screenwriter: *Aleksander Scibor-Rylski*
PG/140 mins./Drama/Poland

Sent to the Gdansk shipyard to monitor the involvement in the Solidarity union of Maciek Tomczyk, the son of a past labour hero, Winkiel, an alcoholic radio reporter who owes his job to a leading Party official after his failure to denounce the demonstrations of 1970, becomes increasingly sympathetic to the workers' demands.

In August 1980, Andrzej Wajda went to the Lenin Shipyard in Gdansk to film the workers whose strike had captured the imagination of the world. He was recognised at the gates by one of the guards who suggested that he should follow his 1977 political drama *Man Of Marble* with a feature about the foundation of the Solidarity trade union, called *Man Of Iron*. Having never previously been commissioned to make a picture by the people, Wajda rushed this loose sequel into production and spent much of the shoot reworking Aleksander Scibor-Rylski's screenplay, with Agnieszka Holland, to incorporate the latest events and ideas thrown up during discussions with the strikers and their supporters.

Wajda's aim was to shape events as much as record them. If *Marble* had been about the past, *Iron* would anticipate a future in which the masses – inspired by their political and religious convictions – had their say. However, Wajda was also keen to warn the populace about repeating the mistakes of the 1968 and 1970 uprisings, when the workers and students respectively failed to champion the others' cause. So, the action is packed with archive material, as well as contemporary scenes, whose authentic intensity was given additional resonance by cameos from Lech Walesa and Anna Walentynowicz, the activist whose reinstatement was Solidarity's key demand, alongside a fair wage.

Wajda also avoided the easy option of making Tomczyk (whose father had been titular Stakhanovite bricklayer in *Marble*) the hero and centred instead on Winkiel, whose conquest of both his alcoholism and his fear of the Party provided an easier model for ordinary citizens to follow. However, too few of his fellow Poles got to see *Man Of Iron* and there was a cruel irony in the fact that the tanks that Wajda requested from General Jaruzelski for the flashback sequences were used to impose martial law soon after the film was released – making its Palme d'Or triumph at Cannes seem rather hollow. ★★★★ **DP**

MAN OF MARBLE (1977)

Starring: *Jerzy Radziwiloicz (Mateusz Birkut/Maciej Tomcyk), Krystyna Janda (Agnieszka), Tadeusz Lomnicki (Jerzy Burski) Jacek Lomnicki (Young Burski), Michal Tarkowski (Wincenty Witek)*
Director: *Andrzej Wajda*
Screenwriter: *Aleksander Scibor-Rylski*
U/160 mins./Drama
Colour/ Black And White/Poland

In seeking materials for her diploma project, film student Agnieszka discovers the truth about Mateusez Birkut, 1950 Stakhanovite brick-layer who was

lionised in a propaganda film by Party-friendly director Jerzy Burski and then persecuted after an accident turns his thoughts to social justice.

Andrzej Wajda first tried to mount this exposé of socio-political attitudes in Stalinist Poland in 1963. However, the Script Assessment Commission refused to sanction the film for its negative depiction of the past, although the screenplay was published that August in the Warsaw weekly, *Kultura*. Thirteen years later, liberal culture minister Josef Tejchma passed the project for production and, even though every attempt was made by the Party to marginalise it, *Man Of Marble* became the cornerstone of the Cinema of Moral Anxiety that helped shape Polish political consciousness in the run-up to the foundation of the Solidarity trade union in 1980.

In many ways, this is a Polish *Citizen Kane*, as it opens with pastiche newsreel footage as Agnieszka begins her researches and is then structured around a series of flashbacks inspired by her interviews with key figures in Birkut's life.

Her first encounter with Jerzy Burski, who has clearly profited from his collaboration with the State, recalls Birkut's career as a shock worker at Nowa Huta, the new town created by the Communists as a symbol of the economic miracle they were sponsoring. This is the most satirical segment of the film, as it mocks Burski's tailoring of reality to make it look more impressive for the cameras. However, it ends with Birkut's hands being permanently damaged by a hot brick and Agnieszka's meetings with Witek – Birkut's workmate on the day of the 'accident', with whom he would later be jailed as an industrial spy – and Birkut's now-alcoholic wife, Hanka Tomcyzyk, are much more sombre and reflect the crushing of the Polish spirit in the 1950s and 60s.

Yet, Wajda ends on a more positive note by having Agnieszka (whom he modelled on emerging director Agnieszka Holland) befriend Birkut's son, Maciek (also Jerzy Radziwilowicz), who is a worker at the Gdansk shipyard, where the Solidarity campaign would begin three years later.

Very much a national epic, this is a complex portrait of misplaced idealism and betrayed trust and, although it's not an easy watch, it remains Wajda's most important work. ★★★★ **DP**

MAN ON FIRE (2004)

Starring: *Denzel Washington (Creasy), Dakota Fanning (Pita), Marc Anthony (Samuel), Radha Mitchell (Lisa), Christopher Walken (Rayburn)*
Director: *Tony Scott*
Screenwriter: *Brian Helgeland, based on the novel by A.J. Quinnell*
18/145 mins./Thriller/USA

In the kidnapping hotbed of Mexico City, ex-marine John Creasy is hired by industrialist Samuel Ramo to protect his family. When Ramos' young daughter Pita is snatched, Creasy sets forth on an unstoppable dervish of revenge.

At the heart of Tony Scott's rip-roaring rampage of revenge is an astonishing feat of cinematic alchemy. It's not the towering presence of Denzel Washington on tip-top blistering form. It's not the absorbing quality Scott manages to invest in the tired cliches of the kidnap genre (tapped phones, botched ransom drops etc.). It's not even the incendiary high style that starts at frame one and never lets up over the whole 146 minutes. No, it's the fact that, for the first time in any movie, Scott will make you bemoan the absence of Dakota Fanning, the loathsome little moppet from *Uptown Girls* and *The Cat In The Hat*.

On paper, we have a well-worn initial-mistrust-gives-over-to mutual-affection arc, but Washington's despair-tinged reserve and Fanning's astonishing naturalness give the relationship warmth and resonance. Fanning exudes more than enough charm and decency to make Creasy's renewal of faith completely believable.

What follows is like the finale of *Taxi Driver* played over 90 minutes. Sharing a 70s-style steeliness with screenwriter Helgeland's *Payback*, the movie sees Creasy hunting down Pita's kidnappers with the no-nonsense cruelty of a Lee Marvin or a Charles Bronson, lopping off digits or shoving explosives up a rectum like a Picasso of pain.

In one of his trademark little speeches, Christopher Walken, as Creasy's old military cohort, utters: 'Creasy's art is death. He's about to paint his masterpiece.' The same is almost true of the movie making you relish the gleeful celebration of mayhem and destruction.

It is a failing of the flick that, when the body count starts rising, the creases in Creasy are ironed out, the character taking on an indestructible Terminator-like superheroism. But Washington is too class an act to let Creasy drift into sub-Steven Seagalisms, and he is never less than completely compelling. As the action goes increasingly over the top, so does Scott's visual pyrotechnics. Probably setting a new world record for the number of different film stocks in one movie, Scott and hot-to-trot cinematographer Paul Cameron whip-pan and crash-zoom to new levels of excess, heightening both the teeming life of Mexico City and the anxiety around Pita's kidnapping. Best of all are the subtitles: rather than simply translating dialogue, they assault the viewer, conveying drama and emotion through aggressive graphic design. You've never seen any done like this before. ★★★★ **IF**

m

THE MAN WHO FELL TO EARTH (1976)

Starring: *David Bowie (Thomas Jerome Newton), Rip Torn (Nathan Bryce), Candy Clark (Mary-Lou), Buck Henry (Oliver Farnsworth), Bernie Casey (Peters), Jackson D. Kane (Professor Canutti)*
Director: *Nicholas Roeg*
Screenwriter: *Paul Mayersburg, from the novel by Walter Tevis*
18/133 mins./Sci-fi/Drama/UK

Thomas Jerome Newton, an alien from a dying desert world, comes to Earth and, using patents on advanced technology, accumulates a vast fortune to back his own space programme – but mysterious forces conspire against him, subverting the people who have come closest to the visitor.

Based on a novel by Walter Tevis, author of *The Hustler* and *The Color Of Money*, Nicolas Roeg's unconventional science fiction film is dazzling and evocative, deploying the full arsenal of cinematic technique to provide a skewed angle on a plot that unfolds like a mosaic.

David Bowie, a great actor so long as he isn't cast as a human being, is the alien with a British passport who appears in middle America and founds a major corporation to fund a doomed programme which is supposed to bring water to his drought-ridden homeworld.

Newton forges an alliance with a mild lawyer (Buck Henry, as perhaps the first non-freak gay character in the movies), has an intensely perverse affair with chambermaid Mary Lou who becomes his consort and is betrayed by Judas-like academic Nathan Bryce.

In the downbeat, melancholy third act, Newton is examined by bored scientists who aren't convinced that he's who he says he is, then abandons his mission to drink and stylish despair ('Mr Newton has had enough').

The fable-like story is embroidered with exhilarating timeslips, a background buzz of media imagery, deep-frozen still lives, sex scenes cut like musical numbers, acidic satire of American vulgarity and the wistful strangeness of a fedora-hatted alien crying into his gin.

Seen through the cat's eyes of an alien visitor, the film brilliantly presents contemporary America as a profoundly strange environment, using bizarre sound details and a remarkable collage soundtrack to celebrate the beauties, terrors and banalities of the world. ★★★★★ **KN**

◑ MAN ON THE MOON (1999)

Starring: *Jim Carrey (Andy Kaufman), Danny DeVito (George Shapiro), Courtney Love (Lynne Marguiles), Paul Giamatti (Bob Zmunda), Vincent Schiavelli (Maynard Smith)*
Director: *Milos Forman*
Screenwriters: *Scott Alexander, Larry Karaszewski*
15/113 mins./Biography/Comedy/Drama/USA
Awards: *Golden Globes – Best Comedy/Musical Actor*

The life of cult comedian Andy Kaufman – a man known for playing dark-edged practical jokes.

Although largely unheralded in this country, Andy Kaufman was a unique comic force. Part stand-up, part performance artist, part man-child, part borderline psychotic, Kaufman hugely influenced a generation of American comedians, among them Jim Carrey. He also had an effect on writers Alexander and Karaszewski, here completing their unofficial trilogy of oddball American biopics – *Ed Wood* and *The People Vs. Larry Flynt*.

To give a hint of the strange world of Andy Kaufman, Forman's film opens with a brilliantly surreal device – Carrey, as Kaufman, talking directly to the audience, explaining that the film you are about to see is rubbish, the best bit is the titles, so that's all you're going to see. Good night. He then stands there as the titles role for what seems like an impossibly long time – then the gag is broken and 'Andy' welcomes us into his world.

We leap between the notable and noted events – Kaufman's childhood job as a children's party entertainer and his desire to do the same act for adults, through to his TV success on *Saturday Night Live* and *Taxi*, his politically incorrect desire to wrestle women, and his possible descent into alter-ego madness with the creation of the truly obnoxious lounge singer Tony Clifton.

Naturally, such a film stands or falls on its central performance. At first, there is some doubt as to whether Carrey is up to the job. But slowly, almost imperceptibly, Carrey falls away and Kaufman comes to life before your eyes. It's a truly remarkable performance but it's a shame that the writers opt to play Kaufman as an overgrown innocent for the entire movie. Never examining what many feel was closer to madness than man-child. ★★★ **BM**

◑ THE MAN WHO KNEW TOO MUCH (1934)

Starring: *Leslie Banks (Bob Lawrence), Edna Best (Jill Lawrence), Peter Lorre (Abbott), Frank Vosper (Ramon Levine), Hugh Wakefield (Clive), Nova Pilbeam (Betty Lawrence)*
Director: *Alfred Hitchcok*
Screenwriters: *Edwin Greenwood, A.R. Rawlinson, Charles Bennett, D.B. Wyndham-Lewis, from a story by D.B. Wyndham-Lewis*
U/75 mins./Crime/Drama/UK

Bob Lawrence and his wife, Jill witness the murder of their friend, Louis Bernard, who has warned them of an imminent diplomatic assassination. To ensure the couple's silence, the conspirators kidnap their daughter. However, they have fatally underestimated the family's British pluck.

'Let's say the first version is the work of a talented amateur and the second was made by a professional.' Many have questioned the veracity of Alfred Hitchcock's throwaway line to François Truffaut about the relative merits of his 1934 British version of *The Man Who Knew Too Much* and its 1956 Hollywood remake. But whether the monochrome original or the Technicolor follow-up is superior is one of those debates whose very futility makes it all the more keenly argued. Suffice to say both survive cavernous holes in the plot and make expert use of their differing locations. But whereas one has Peter Lorre as a shifty spy, the other has Doris Day warbling the Oscar-winning ditty 'Que Sera Sera'.

Inspired by the 1911 Sidney Street Siege and, to a lesser degree, the Lindbergh baby killing, this was Hitchcock's return to suspense after his disastrous Terpsichorean diversion, *Waltzes From Vienna*. Rarely again would he stray from the realm of Macguffins, wronged innocents and delicious sleights of hand of which he eventually became the undisputed king.

Bob Lawrence and his crackshot wife, Jill are holidaying in Switzerland when their French friend, Louis Bernard is gunned down, warning them, with his dying breath, of an imminent diplomatic assassination. In order to ensure the couple's silence, the conspirators kidnap their daughter. However, Abbot and his comrades have fatally underestimated British pluck.

Leaving this superbly structured thriller with grisly humour, Hitchcock litters the action with cues to heighten the tension of the climactic sequences at the Royal Albert Hall and on the rooftops of an East End side street. He's abetted by a spirited cast, with Lorre (who was making his English-language debut) outstanding, whether delighting in his villainy or breaking down on the death of his accomplice. ★★★★ **DP**

◑ THE MAN WHO KNEW TOO MUCH (1956)

Starring: *James Stewart (Dr Ben McKenna), Doris Day (Jo McKenna), Brenda De Banzie (Lucy Drayton), Bernard Miles (Edward Drayton), Ralph Truman (Buchanan)*
Director: *Alfred Hitchcock*
Screenwriter: *John Michael Hayes, based on the story by Charles Bennett, D.B. Wyndham-Lewis*
PG/120 mins./Thriller/Drama/USA
Awards: *Academy Awards – Best Song (Whatever Will Be, Will Be – Que Sera, Sera)*

On holiday in Morocco, Ben McKenna witnesses the murder of a French secret agent who, with his dying breath, tells him about an assassination due to take place in London. The villains kidnap McKenna's son to keep him quiet but, along with his wife Jo, he tries to thwart the scheme.

The story of 'a single crash of cymbals and how it rocked the lives of an American family'. In 1935, Alfred Hitchcock directed a neat little British thriller that begins in the snows of Switzerland and ends up at the Albert Hall (where Peter Lorre is behind an assassination attempt).

In 1956, Hitch mounted an elaborate remake which lacks the original's crisp pace, but makes up for it with star value, sumptuous colour and sustained suspense.

The Moroccan sequence sets up James Stewart as the archetypal know-nothing American abroad, who can't get comfortable sat on a cushion in a restaurant and is perpetually on the point of setting off angry mobs with his ignorance of local customs – so it's a clever gag that he becomes the man who knows *too much*.

The action shifts to London, for an eerie red herring sequence set in a taxidermist's shop and some sinister business with an apparently benign parson (Bernard Miles) who is behind the villainy, while the unforgettably evil-looking Reggie Nadler (later the vampire in Tobe Hooper's *Salem's Lot*) lurks in readiness to fire the fatal shot covered by a cymbal crash.

Day, not immediately an obvious Hitchcock heroine, is surprisingly good, and the script deserves contrivance points for making several good excuses for her to perform a classic, Oscar-winning song ('Que Sera Sera').

The finale in the Albert Hall is an exact recreation of the 1935 film, with composer Bernard Herrmann on screen as the conductor. ★★★★ **KN**

THE MAN WHO WASN'T THERE (2001)

Starring: *Billy Bob Thornton (Ed Crane), Frances McDormand (Doris Crane), Michael Badalucco (Frank), Michael Badalucco (Frank), James Gandolfini (Dave 'Big Dave' Brewster), Katherine Borowitz (Ann Nirdlinger)*
Director: *Joel Coen*
Screenwriters: *Joel Coen, Ethan Coen*

Awards: *BAFTA – Best Cinematography*
15/116 mins./Comedy/Crime/Drama/USA

A small town in the late 1940s. Barber Ed, realising his wife Doris is having an affair, plots blackmail, but nothing goes according to plan and Doris is arrested for murder. Meanwhile, Ed is strangely interested in Birdy, a teenage pianist he believes could be a star.

The Coen brothers continue to riff off the styles of great American crime writers, following their Dashiell Hammett (*Miller's Crossing*) and Raymond Chandler (*The Big Lebowski*) films, with this variation on themes by James M. Cain.

Early film versions of Cain's *Double Indemnity* and *The Postman Always Rings Twice* streamlined his distinctive third acts, which seem like left-field sequels to the main stories. But here, the Cain homage carries through to *The Man Who Wasn't There*'s strange finale, with the hero collapsing as ironies unnoticed earlier spin round to trap him.

After the popular acceptance of the Coen style in such warm-ish movies as *The Big Lebowski* and *O Brother, Where Art Thou?*, this is a chilly film, in stark black and white, as if the brothers want to get back to their core audience.

Surrounded by motormouths, Ed – played by Thornton in a somehow disturbing toupee – keeps to himself. Sometimes he's distracted by tiny details or odd crusades, but usually he's uncommitted to any of his ambitions and unresentful of the worst that fate deals him. Ed refuses to take part in the story he is narrating or make any moral judgement at all, even on people who have done him enormous wrongs.

The Coens' trademark wry dialogue is present, with a literary love for the odd, everyday turn of phrase, and the terrific cast fit in perfectly with the style. Devotees note: a spinning hubcap/flying saucer serves the visual function here that in earlier Coen films was taken by a hat, a hula-hoop, a tumbleweed and a tin of pomade. ★★★★ **KN**

Movie Trivia: The Coen Brothers (born 1954 (Joel) and 1957 (Ethan))

Who they are: Hollywood's best-loved sibling director / writer / editor / producers. Makers of independent, beautifully crafted dramas and comedies marked by absurd and twisted humour and intricate wordplay and dialogue.

Hallmarks: Gangsters; the 1930s; black humour; genre-bending; touches of surrealism; witty and convoluted dialogue.

If you see one movie, see: *Fargo* (1996)

THE MAN WHO WOULD BE KING (1975)

Starring: *Sean Connery (Daniel Dravot), Michael Caine (Peachy Carnehan), Christopher Plummer (Rudyard Kipling), Saeed Jaffrey (Billy Fish)*
Director: *John Huston*
Screenwriters: *John Huston, Gladys Hill, based on the story by Rudyard Kipling*
PG/129 mins./ Adventure/USA

Two former soldiers wandering through colonial era India, end up the first white men in the mountainous county of Kafiristan where they are taken for Gods. But their decadent amoral purposes will bring about their ruin – a tale told to a young Rudyard Kipling on a shadowy train.

A grand old tale from the Kipling canon, rich with high adventure and stiff with moral value, told with verve and simplicity by another old campaigner John Huston. Huston had been dwelling on this grand buddy drama for years, first contemplating Clark Gable and Humphrey Bogart in the roles of the two soldiers confusing greedy opportunity with a kind of nirvana, he then thought of Richard Burton and Peter O'Toole, before fixing on Michael Caine and Sean Connery who make the most of shedding their stereotypes for a pair of scoundrels. It could be argued, that they give the best performances of their careers, a fact obscured by the film's unassuming devotion to story.

At first Dravot and Carnehan are merely scavengers who pass through all the intemperate ravages the Himalayas can throw at them to a sheltered valley with a hidden city with its hoard of succulent treasures. The story being a critique of imperialism, the two set themselves up as surrogate godheads and rulers after Daniel is struck by an arrow only to appear uninjured (it got stuck in his bandolier). Daniel is considered the reincarnation of Alexander the Great. Thus they scheme to gather up enough riches then hightail back to civilisation.

It is the drug of power that will undo their callous plan. Connery, with a sublime interpretation of human corruption, shows how subtly Dravot comes to believe in his own lie, as if he has taken on the form of story or myth. Carnehan remains pragmatic and itches to run from the scene, and the fates are about to turn on them. Huston revels in he opportunity for old-fashioned splendour, granting the film the sunset glow of *Lawrence Of Arabia* and the swashbuckling cadence worthy of the Errol Flynn days. It's the artful mix of Kipling's own writing, flights of fantasy with a political core. ★★★★ **IN**

MAN WITH A MOVIE CAMERA (CHELOVEK S KINO-APPARATOM) (1929)

Starring: *Mikhail Kaufman (Cameraman)*
Director: *Dziga Vertov*
Screenwriter: *Dziga Vertov*
Unrated/80 mins./Documentary/USSR

An experiment in montage, exploring everyday life and the workings of the cinema.

Though clearly intended as avant garde, this 1929 classic emerges out of a then-popular film genre, the impressionistic portrait of the collective life of the big city. We start with people waking, glimpse all human activity (marriage, divorce, birth, death, work, play, sport, sleep, drinking), get a lot of movement in public transport (the director, Dziga Vertov, and his brother, cameraman/star Mikhail Kaufman, fell out over the number of trams in the film) and see what could be taken as a hymn to the energy and bustle of the still-nascent Soviet Union.

But this isn't set in any particular place (it matches bits of Moscow, Odessa and Kiev) and is keen on playing with camera trickery – we get freeze frame, slow motion, fast motion, splitscreen, superimposition, animation, kinetic cutting and all manner of directorial hyperactivity.

As the title suggests, the medium is the star. Before the usual waking-up scene, which includes such unsoviet types as derelicts in the park, we begin in an empty cinema, with seats being lowered en masse and an audience assembling to watch this movie. The cameraman is sometimes framed like a giant bestraddling the city and sometimes shrunk so his image appears inside a glass of beer. Towards the end, the camera tripod even begins to move without human agency, and we end on a superimposition of a closing shutter and a closing human eye.

There are moments of everyday surrealism – chubby types covering themselves with mud at the beach (with some nudity) or being exercised in strange machines – and touches of near-cynical humour (a cut from a marrying couple to a divorcing one) that might well have ired the Stalinists about to come crashing down on the filmmakers, the masses observed and the vivacious mood of this picture. ★★★★ **KN**

THE MAN WITH THE GOLDEN ARM (1955)

Starring: *Frank Sinatra (Frankie Machine), Kim Novak (Molly), Eleanor Parker (Zosch Machine), Arnold Stang (SparrowO, Darren McGavin (Louie), Robert Strauss (Schwiefka)*
Director: *Otto Preminger*
Screenwriters: *Walter Newman, Lewis Meltzer, based on the novel by Nelson Algren*
15/119 mins./Drama/USA

Frankie Machine gets out of jail and falls back in with his petty criminal associates, dealing in an illegal poker game, getting hooked again on heroin and nagged by his crippled wife (Parker) to give up his dream of becoming a musician.

Controversial in the 1950s because director Otto Preminger challenged the prevailing industry censorship codes and presented drug addiction as a central theme, this remains a powerful, noir-tinged melodrama. With Elmer Bernstein's jazzy hit theme striking up whenever Sinatra is jonesing for a fix, drawn across the sleazy nighttime neighbourhood to score from the sharp-suited local pusher (McGavin), it presents a junkie world that differs from latterday dope operas only in that everyone on the street is white.

The hero's problem is not so much his 'golden arm' – as a mainliner, as well as a skilled card-dealer and a promising drummer – but the way all the lowlife losers around him, whether malicious like McGavin or the crook who runs the card-game (Robert Strauss), pretend-sympathetic Parker as the splendidly fake invalid/real hysteric wife (who even kills to keep him in line) or a genuine pal like a bespectacled, dog-kidnapping barfly (Arnold Stang, the voice of Top Cat), *want* Frankie to stay hooked, so their social lives and businesses can keep going. The harrowing 'cold turkey' scenes are reminiscent of Billy Wilder's treatment of booze withdrawal in *The Long Weekend*, which this often seems to be borrowing from, but Preminger's and Sinatra's best sequence is a three-day-long poker game which ruins Frankie's chance of a drumming job as he turns up at an audition with the jitters. Novak is good, if a touch too beautiful, as the bar girl who really cares for and helps Frankie, and the hard-won triumph at the end (when the tune goes away) is very moving. ★★★ **KN**

THE MAN WITH THE GOLDEN GUN (1974)

Starring: *Roger Moore (James Bond), Christopher Lee (Francisco Scaramanga), Britt Ekland (Mary Goodnight), Maud Adams (Andrea Anders), Herve Villechaize (Nick Nack), Clifton James (Sheriff J.W. Pepper), Richard Loo (Hai Fat)*
Director: *Guy Hamilton*
Screenwriters: *Richard Maibaum, Tom Mankiewicz, based on the novel by Ian Fleming*
PG/124 mins./Spy/UK-USA

This time round, secret agent James Bond 007 is on the trail of the Solex Agitator, a device that harnesses the sun's radiation. His job is made even more diffcult by top flight assassin Francisco Scaramanga, renowned for his gun made of gold, who has been paid $1 million to rub Bond out.

It was a marked feature of the early Roger Moore 007 flicks that, to avoid appearing anachronistic, they imported trace elements from the big hits of the period, be it *Shaft* (*Live And Let Die*), *Star Wars* (*Moonraker*) and *Raiders Of The Lost Ark* (*Octopussy*). Made at the height of Bruce Lee mania, *The Man With The Golden Gun*, Moore's second outing as Bond, transplants the atmosphere and kung fu licks of *Enter The Dragon* on the set in stone James Bond formula and delivers an entertaining 007 adventure, something that tonally, if not qualitatively, could happily sit within the Connery era.

Kicking off with that Bond rarity – a bad John Barry song belted out by Lulu – *Golden Gun* ticks all the boxes, some more squarely than others. As always there is some terrific action – on top of the kung fu, there is a terrific car chase that sees Bond's car corkscrew in mid-air jumping across a river and ends when Scaramanga's car turns into a plane – and Christopher Lee (actually Ian Fleming's cousin) imbues Scaramanga with a cold weirdness – this is a Bond villiain with interesting quirks (three nipples, he caresses women with his gun and a cardboard cut out of 007 for starters), who could easily be the pervy flipside of Bond himself. Also, amidst the bad innuendos, there is some genuine wit: 'Who'd pay a million dollars to kill me?' Bond asks M. 'Jealous husbands, outraged chefs, humiliated tailors – the list is endless.'

On the debit side, there is too much of an emphasis on knockabout comedy – the midget henchman Nick Nack (played by Harve 'The Plane! The Plane, boss!'Villechaize), the reprise of redneck cop JW Pepper from *Live And Let Die*, conveniently on holiday in the Orient – and the women are flimsy creations; Britt Ekland, as secret agent Mary Goodnight (a name that allows Moore the immortal line 'Goodnight, Goodnight') could simper for Sweden and Maude Adams,(who would later play a more fully developed Bond in Octopussy) is wasted in the potentially interesting role as Scaramanga's treacherous assistant.

Yet the real surprise revisting the movie is Moore. For all Moore's reputation for lightness of touch and suave urbanity, there are flashes of genuine brutality (not to mention misogyny) here. Watch him bitch slap Adams Andrea in order to get his own way. Next up for Moore was the gadget laden campery of *The Spy Who Loved Me* but, if he'd stuck closer to some of the spirit of *Golden Gun*, his tenure as Bond might have been coloured in a completely different, less cosy hue. ★★★ **IF**

THE MAN WITHOUT A FACE (1993)

Starring: *Mel Gibson (Justin McLeod), Nick Stahl (Charles E. 'Chuck' Norstadt), Margaret Witton (Catherine Palin), Gaby Hoffman (Megan), Fay Masterson (Gloria)*
Director: *Mel Gibson*
Screenwriter: *Malcolm MacRury, based on the novel by Isabelle Holland*
15/109 mins./Drama/USA

Chuck Norstadt is an unhappy 12-year-old, who dreams of going to boarding school and joining the military like his father, but he also needs his school grades to improve. He finds help in the form of local recluse, Justin McLeod, a former teacher whose face was horribly disfigured in a car accident.

The late lamented *Spy* magazine once ran a fine feature called Celebrity Refuseniks in which they examined the tendency of 90s stars to wish to be known for anything other than the talent that gained them their fame. Madonna wants to be an actress, Naomi Campbell wants to be a singer and Mel Gibson wants people to forget his outrageous good looks for a moment and take him seriously as an actor.

Not that Gibson isn't already a perfectly acceptable, enormously engaging screen presence, but that's apparently not quite enough, for here, in his directing debut, he turns up as a reclusive polymath, scarred Nikki Lauda-style by a terrible accident. This handicap is presumably meant to introduce the degree of difficulty that makes his performance all the more impressive. Instead it merely leaves you wondering why he bothered.

Had he not been both an A-list star and would-be director nobody would ever have suggested that this was a natural part for him to play. *The Man Without A Face* is essentially a rather dull two-hander, with Gibson's

Justin McLeod acting as tutor to alienated 12-year-old Chuck during a summer vacation in the late 60s, offering lots of opportunities for those scenes of showy book learning so beloved of all those actors who wish they'd got Robin Williams' part in *Dead Poets Society*.

Despite all the empirical evidence to the contrary, the confused 12-year-old who finds himself, via the dedication of a great teacher, the works of the Bard and a little male company, is one of those movie cliches that seems to have a life entirely of its own. ★★★★ **DHe**

Ⓓ THE MANCHURIAN CANDIDATE (1962)

Starring: *Frank Sinatra (Capt./Maj. Bennett Marco), Laurence Harvey (SFC. Raymond Shaw), Janet Leigh (Eugenie Rose Chaney), Angela Lansbury (Mrs Iselin), Henry Silva (Chunjin)*
Director: *John Frankenheimer*
Screenwriter: *George Axelrod, John Frankenheimer, based on the novel by Richard Conlon*
15/130 mins./Thriller/USA
Awards: *Golden Globes – Best Supporting Actress (Angela Lansbury)*

Raymond Shaw returns from Korea a decorated soldier, but his fellow servers can't remember him doing anything that warranted such reward. Strange psychological occurrences take place and Shaw begins to think he has been brainwashed and is a potential political threat.

The granddaddy of conspiracy thrillers, John Frankenheimer's nail-biting exercise in political paranoia felt ahead of its time upon its successful cinematic re-release in 1988. Christ knows what the impact was in the 60s. And now in the 21st century, available on DVD for the first time, *The Manchurian Candidate* still stands as one of the most intelligent and terrifying movies in Hollywood history.

Both a product of, and a commentary on, the Cold War, the central plot device of brain-washing may have dated, but the devastating final reel loses none of its power.

A career high for almost everyone involved (discounting Sinatra's singing), *The Manchurian Candidate* contains everything you could want from a movie, including celluloid's first ever karate fight. ★★★★★**CK**

Ⓓ THE MANCHURIAN CANDIDATE (2004)

Starring: *Denzel Washington (Ben Marco), Liev Schreiber (Raymond Shaw), Meryl Streep (Eleanor Shaw), Jon Voigt (Senator Thomas Jordan), Adam LeFevre (Congressman Healy)*
Director: *Jonathan Demme*
Screenwriters: *Daniel Pyne, Dean Georgaris, based on the 1962 screenplay by George Axelrod, novel by Richard Condom*
15/129 mins./Thriller/Drama/USA

Years after his patrol's ordeal in the Gulf War, Major Ben Marco has a recurring nightmare which casts disturbing light on his memory of those events, and especially an act of heroism by his comrade, Sergeant Raymond Shaw. Marco takes his fears to military superiors, but no one will listen and he's left uncomfortably witnessing Shaw's rise to power.

Remakes of celebrated films invite disaster. So it's exciting to see an apparently re-energised Jonathan Demme coming back at us with his best feature since *The Silence Of The Lambs*, a cracking conspiracy thriller that's well-cast, slyly satirical and – as a solid, glossy, contemporised remix of a classic – rings enough creepy changes to surprise.

The smart, gripping script has been reworked from both Richard Condon's Cold War novel, in which an American soldier was brainwashed to carry out assassinations via hypnotic suggestion, and scripter George Axelrod's sophisticated, faithful adaptation of the 1962 John Frankenheimer film starring Frank Sinatra, Laurence Harvey and Angela Lansbury (who stole the picture as Harvey's memorably monstrous mother although she was only three years older than him).

The original's plot drew on stories about the brainwashing of Korean War prisoners by the Chinese and the witch-hunting hysteria of the 50s, in which McCarthyites claimed that American government and society had been infiltrated by Communist subversives. That was in the good old days, of course, when an indictment of party-political machinations and extremism to left and right could be expressed in a nifty 'us versus the Commies' tale. Now that the Red Menace is old hat and zombification by hypnosis is cheesy, we have the compelling charge of undermining democracy levelled against a greedy globalist elite. This is coupled with the conceivable threat of a multinational corporation stealing minds and souls with a little neurosurgery and microchip implants.

This may not be as sexy or have as much clarity as antagonists who have ideologies – and we could wish the sinister, scheming suits of Manchurian Global (including an underused Dean Stockwell) and the Shaws' liberal opposition (represented by Voight's astoundingly naive senator) were fleshed out a tad more – but it's certainly worrying. The updating is also well-timed: it's set during a Presidential election campaign, and Schreiber's cold but pitiable Shaw is the inadequate scion of a powerful political dynasty, a puppet of his ruthless, ambitious mother (Streep, on wicked form) and the corporate interests with which she's chillingly allied.

The status of the women has been upgraded from the original: the mother's from pushy political wife to an influential senator, and romantic interest Rosie's from merely 'the girl' to more of a sidekick with an agenda. Jeffrey Wright, meanwhile, makes a haunting appearance as a shabby, seriously disturbed former comrade whose nightmares are so unnervingly similar to Marco's that the Major is driven to confront Shaw, who tantalisingly admits he remembers what happened to make him a decorated war hero, 'but I don't remember it happening'.

How sweet it is to see Schreiber with a long-overdue juicy part in a big picture. And as Marco, Washington, every inch the star, is swell as both a sober and true career soldier, and an obsessive whose night terrors are making him crazy – or not, as the case may be. Daniel Pyne and Dean Georgaris' updated script draws in elements reminiscent of *The Parallax View* and some of the best JFK assassination theories, while Demme so deftly stirs up both classic and modern anxieties with taut action and the hint of real-life parallels that you don't know where this is going, as the suspense builds to a finale of unbearable tension. ★★★★ **AE**

Ⓓ THE MANGLER (1995)

Starring: *Robert Englund (Bill Gartley), Ted Levine (Officer John Hunton), Daniel Matmor (Mark Jackson), Jeremy Crutchley (JJJ Pictureman), Vanessa Pike (Sherry Ouelette), Demetre Phillips (George Stanner), Lisa Morris (Lin Sue) Vera Blacker (Mrs Adele Frawley), Ashley Hayden (Annette Gillian)*
Director: *Tobe Hooper*
Screenwriters: *Tobe Hooper, Stephen Brooks, Harry Alan Towers, based on the short story by Stephen King*
18/106 mins./Horror/USA-Australia-South Africa

Bill Gartley, the owner of a Maine laundry, ensures the prosperity of the town by making regular sacrifices to a demon-possessed mangler, but a local cop gets suspicious.

It used to be said everything Stephen King ever put down on paper would wind up turned into a schlock movie or TV miniseries, including his laundry list. Adapted from an early short story King wrote after working (unhappily) in a laundry, *The Mangler* offers one of the dumbest premises ever spun into a serious horror movie. The big rolling, pressing and starching demon comes a long way after the possessed car of *Christine* or even the murderous trucks of *Maximum Overdrive* in the King machine-monster stakes; it's almost impressive when it justsits there evilly, clawing unwary souls into its clanking works to be messily mangled, but becomes ridiculous in the finale, when it gets loose from its moorings and stalks around an industrial hellhole, persecuting toupee-sporting cop Levine and his hippie exorcist sidekick.

Englund, as a crippled patriarch pithily described as 'a miserable piece of dogfuck', delivers one of his make-up-encrusted hambone ranting villain performances, and gets folded up like a sheet for his big death scene. Despite much repetitive gore (how many ways are there to show someone being caught in a mangle?) and grimily nasty art direction, this is too dreary to be a hoot, despite many clunker lines ('there's no such thing as external truth in theoretical parapsychology'). Yet another nail in the coffin of Tobe Hooper's once-promising career, it still managed to spin off sequels: the unrelated *The Mangler 2: Graduation Day*, which has Lance Henriksen attacked by a computer virus which turns him into a possessed cyborg, and the back-to-basics *The Mangler Reborn*, in which the original laundry machine is needlessly restored. ★★ **KN**

MANHATTAN (1979)

Starring: *Woody Allen (Isaac Davis), Diane Keaton (Mary Wilke), Michael Murphy (Yale), Mariel Hemingway (Tracy), Meryl Streep (Jill)*
Director: *Woody Allen*
Screenwriters: *Woody Allen, Marshall Brickman*
15/96 mins./Comedy/USA

Dissatisfied with his lot as a TV comedy writer and uncomfortable in his relationship with Tracy, a teenage drama student, Isaac Davis begins writing a novel and becomes besotted with Mary Wilke, a neurotic intellectual who's having an affair with his best friend, Yale.

When Woody Allen saw the rough cut of *Manhattan*, he asked producers Jack Rollins and Charles H. Joffe if United Artists would consider destroying every frame if he did his next film for them for free. However, thanks to editor Sandy Morse, this paean to his home town emerged as Allen's most effortlessly European feature.

Accompanied by George Gershwin's sublime *Rhapsody In Blue*, the shots of the fireworks over Central Park, of Brooklyn Bridge, the Empire State Building and dawn coming up over the skyscrapers may seen quintessentially New York – and some have even claimed the picture as an East Coast equivalent to Orson Welles's *The Lady From Shanghai* (1948). But this is, in fact, Allen's take on *La Dolce Vita* (1960), with Isaac discovering the empty decadence of the city's chattering classes in much the same way that Marcello realised the moral and intellectual bankruptcy of Rome's elite.

Filmed by Gordon Willis in Panavision on Technicolor stock that was printed in monochrome, this is not just Allen's most beautiful film. It's also the most personal. The absence of colour reflects Isaac's disillusion with both his career and the circle of friends with whom he has surrounded himself. They are all writers – Yale is working on a biography of Eugene O'Neill, Mary is a critic and columnist and his ex-wife, Jill, who left him for her lesbian lover, is writing a feminist tract on their marriage that he knows will lead to his socio-sexual humiliation. Moreover, their conversation is peppered with allusions to creative artists, from Strindberg and Kafka to Bergman, Fellini and Groucho Marx.

Yet, Isaac consistently denigrates the one person who offers him an escape from all this shallow pretension and he only realises Tracy's importance when he includes her in his charming litany of crucial pleasures. Typically, the critics chose to castigate Allen for choosing a 17-year-old blonde as his soulmate. But she symbolises the energy and excitement that Isaac had forgotten existed within Manhattan and her parting exhortion to have faith in people is the solution to his emotional and artistic crises. ★★★★★ **DP**

MANHATTAN MURDER MYSTERY (1993)

Starring: *Woody Allen (Larry Lipton), Diane Keaton (Carol Lipton), Jerry Adler (Paul House), Alan Alda (Ted), Anjelica Huston (Marcia Fox)*
Director: *Woody Allen*
Screenwriters: *Woody Allen, Marshall Brickman*
PG/103 mins./Comedy/Thriller/USA

Living in her New York apartment, a married woman watches the other residents and jumps to the conclusion that one of her fellow tenants has killed his wife. With persistence she manages to convince her cynical husband and even his friend as the three begin to make ludicrous assumptions. Or do they?

A remarkably carefree piece of work from a man majoring in real-life heavy turmoil at the time of its theatrical release, this now appears distinctly lightweight on the smaller screen. Indeed, set against the background of last summer's courtroom dramas, critics marvelled at the extent to which this latest Woodmeister snapshot was an angst-free zone.

Opening with a splendid rendition of Cole Porter's 'Happen To Like New York', the action – if action isn't a contradiction in terms for an Allen movie – centres upon comfortably married couple Larry and Carol, and their growing suspicions about the homicidal tendencies of the man next door. Spurred on by the always reliable Alan Alda as wannabe sleuth Ted, Carol quickly becomes obsessed with this particular Manhattan murder mystery (hence the name), gradually drawing her initially reluctant husband into the increasingly complicated plot.

For a good hour or so, this is more than passable video fare, but as time goes on the viewer is likely to be reaching for the remote in order to turn down the volume on Keaton. She and Allen, an odd enough couple at the best of times, eventually resort to simply shouting at each other at the same time, with the end result being that only the very best lines ('Claustrophobia and a dead body! It's a neurotic's jackpot round here!') escape from the mix, and what started as a typically dry Allenesque Upper East Side relationship ultimately descends into farce.

Still, Manhattan looks as good as ever, Alda is perfectly matched by the great Anjelica Huston and there are just enough one-liners to sustain a passing interest through to the classic cineaste climax. One of Allen's many therapists would no doubt make a lot of money explaining exactly why his client made such an apparently feelgood movie at a time when his life appeared to be collapsing around him. DVD viewers investing in a night in front of the telly are, however, more likely to feel a trifle short-changed. ★★★ **BMc**

MANHUNTER (1986)

Starring: *William L. Petersen (Will Graham), Brian Cox (Dr Hannibal Lecktor), Dennis Farina (Jack Crawford), Kim Greist (Molly Graham)*
Director: *Michael Mann*
Screenwriter: *Michael Mann, based on the novel by Thomas Harris*
18/119 mins./124 mins. (director's cut)/Thriller/USA

An FBI specialist tracks a serial killer who appears to select his victims at random.

'He has no sides, no boundaries, no past, no conscience. Just pure, unadulterated, evil, evil genius,' said Brian Cox of his most fearful incarnation to date - one Dr Hannibal 'The Cannibal' Lecktor. And although both the spelling of his name, and the man adopting the mantle were to be altered for Jonathan Demme's *The Silence Of The Lambs* five years later this is arguably the finer hour for cinema's most alluring psychopath (incidentally two of the original cast, support players Frankie Faison and Dan Butler, actually made the transition). In fact, despite appearing in a mere three scenes in Michael Mann's superlative chiller, he with the penchant for Italian plonk, dominates the running time, largely unseen but omnipresent, casting an incarcerated eye over external events very much under his control.

Unlike *Lambs*, *Manhunter* – initially titled *Red Dragon* after Thomas Harris' novel, but re-named when *Year Of The Dragon* (1985) flopped and Dino De Laurentiis decided to avoid a similar moniker – is an exercise in subtlety and nuance. Cox predates Anthony Hopkins' flamboyance with a cold, quietly sinister confidence. However, the serial killer he's enlisted to help track down The Tooth Fairy, represents the psychological opposite of *Lambs'* Buffalo Bill – calm, ordered, a follower of the 'savage mind' school of magic and mortality, and (chillingly) a more fully functioning member of society.

Likewise, the third spoke in the film's central troika of intelligent-but-flawed characters is FBI profiler Will Graham. Realised by Peterson, this character has an intensity bordering on the psychotic (as Lecktor so aptly taunts: 'The reason you caught me, Will, is we're just alike') and represents the theme of a hunter needing to achieve empathy for his quarry that Mann would re-explore in *Heat* (1995).

Here, in only his third feature, he is at his very best. An avid Zen enthusiast, Mann blends languid shots of stark horizons (again a nod to the relationship between mortal man and infinite nature) with his trademark aesthetics of 'neon angst', minimalist hues of colour, and modernist architecture. Those who at the time had hoped to draw parallels between this and his *Miami Vice* TV series were – aside, admittedly, from a couple of grey-flecked suits which would have done Crockett and Tubbs proud – missing the mark by a mile.

From the opening frame Mann grounds his audience squarely in the mindset of a psychopath (cue the tagline: 'Enter the mind of a serial killer ... you may never come back'), playing out a haunting pre-credit sequence from the POV of The Tooth Fairy's own Super 8 camcorder as he breaks into the house of his next victims. Combined with the stylised, bleak cinematography of twice Oscar-nominated – for *L.A. Confidential* (1997) and *The Insider* (1999) – Dante Spinotti, and a thrashing score that evokes a genuine sense of suppressed rage, it's the perfect introduction to a film imbued throughout with a sense of ominous inevitability.

For while *Manhunter*'s primary attack on the senses is a visual one, it's an underlying tone of foreboding and mental fragility that establishes its timeless quality. Indeed, Mann made a number of cuts to maintain the mood. Most notably in his portrayal of Francis Dollarhyde (The Tooth Fairy's real name) – a man obsessed by the surreal artwork of William Blake, just as Ted Bundy was with poetry – and his quest to transform himself into Blake's legendary depiction of the Red Dragon. Where early takes saw Dollarhyde's chest and back covered in a crimson dragon tattoo, Mann later felt this too obvious an indicator of his psychological disintegration, claiming it 'diminished the character', and re-shot the scenes sans body art. Similarly, he felt that early scenes of Lecktor's childhood, 'Slowed the action down too much,' a subplot examining the true depth of Graham's troubled psychosis 'confused things' and a sequence in which Molly pays her husband a conjugal visit detracted from his sense of isolation.

Comparatively, scenes between Dollarhyde and his blind muse Reba were expanded to fully convey their significance – she is his last (and rejected) chance at redemption before his personality becomes completely usurped by that of the dragon. The deliberate arrangement of his body, when he is finally put to rest by Graham, took on a new poignance, laid out in identikit fashion to the woman – not dragon – in Blake's painting. His merging with the mystical beast has failed. He is still a man.

And it is this final reel that perhaps best sums up *Manhunter*'s ultimate brilliance. In a decade where serial killer plotlines were ten-a-penny, their psychos simply masked degenerates and 'heroes' two-dimensional caricatures, here was a movie that dared to allow insight into a damaged psyche. Although it never entirely inspired sympathy it dared to help its audience try to partly understand, partly pity and partly even empathise with the plight of its reprehensible owner. ★★★★★ **MD**

Movie Trivia:
Michael Mann (born 1943)

Who he is: Film school graduate who came up through commercials and TV (*Miami Vice*) before becoming a film director. One of the most stylish and consistent filmmakers in America today.

Hallmarks: Dramatic, coloured lighting; use of pop and ambient music; criminals as heroes; scenes in front of wide horizon shots, usually involving water; scene where someone on a speakerphone asks 'Who am I talking to?'.

If you see one movie, see: *Heat* (1995)

MANIAC COP (1988)

Starring: *Tom Atkins (Frank McCrae), Bruce Campbell (Jack Forrest), Laurene Landon (Theresa Mallory), Richard Roundtree (Commissioner Pike), William Smith (Capt. Ripley)*
Director: *William Lustig*
Screenwriter: *Larry Cohen*
18/85 mins./Crime/Horror/USA

A killer dressed as a cop plagues New York, but only Lieutenant Frank McCrae believes the murderer is a real policeman. Meanwhile, patrolman Jack Forrest is being set up by the psycho to take the rap.

Directed by William Lustig, the man who gave you such objectionable trash as *Maniac* and *Vigilante*, this isn't entirely free of the kind of formula violence you'd expect from such worthies.

But it was written and produced by Larry Cohen, one of the most intriguing – if variable – creators in the low-budget exploitation field and bears many of his trademarks, including the weird police background of *Q* and *God Told Me To* and a few of his favourite bit players. The basic Halloween-style plot is complicated by the unusual milieu (almost everyone in the film is a cop) and Cohen works in a few almost subliminal bits about the attitudes of (and to) the police force.

The killer, who may be back from the dead, is more impressive when glimpsed as a shadowy figure in police blues than when his not-too-scarred face is actually seen, and the intriguing set-up the character is given – which includes a bizarre performance from former starlet Sheree North as the psycho's crippled girlfriend – doesn't really pay off when the time comes for car chases and slugfests. However, as straight, fast-paced, gutsy action movies go, this is a distinct cut above the rest.

Cohen's sense of humour is well served by an offbeat cast of quirky performers, from Atkins' trademarked fed-up look through heroine Laurene Landon's spunky determination to Campbell's amazing ability to take endless physical abuse.

The same writer-director team turned out two sequels, pitting a returning Z'Dar against swarthy Robert Davi: *Maniac Cop 2* and *Maniac Cop 3: Badge Of Silence*. ★★★ **KN**

ⓓ MANON DES SOURCES (MANON OF THE SPRING) SOUBEYRAN (1986)

Starring: *Yves Montand (César 'Le Papet' Soubeyran), Daniel Auteuil (Ugolin Soubeyran), Emmanuelle Béart (Manon Cadoret), Hyppolite Girardot (Bernard Oliver), Elisabeth Depardieu (Aimee Cadoret)*
Director: *Claude Berri*
Screenwriters: *Claude Berri, Gerard Brach, based on the novel by Marcel Pagnol*
PG/113 mins./Drama/France

Following her father's death, Manon Cadoret lives wild in the Provençal hills above the farm tended by César Soubeyran and his nephew Ugolin. When she accuses them of murdering Jean de Florette, the lovesick Ugolin hangs himself, leaving César to cope with the revelation that Jean was his long-lost son.

Although he was the villain of *Jean De Florette*, the first part of Claude Berri's sumptuously tragic adaptation of Marcel Pagnol's novel *The Water In The Hills*, César Soubeyran could always justify his hostility towards the outsider whose water he stole as a crime dictated by the need to uphold the tradition and continuity of the land. But, in the affecting conclusion of this stylish, if overly sentient sequel, Le Papet learns that he actually killed his own kin in prompting Jean's fatal accident and that he has been betrayed by the very notion of family that he held so dear.

However, Montand is more of a peripheral figure until this sobering revelation, as Berri has so much plot to deal with he doesn't always have time for the character study that made the first film so rich. Moreover, the loss of Gérard Depardieu's intense presence leaves a considerable hole and, despite her spirited performance as the vengeful nymph, Emmanuelle Béart is never quite able to fill it. She occasionally allows calculating loathing to vitiate her pastoral beauty. But Berri seems content to allow Manon to pout and flounce her way into poor Ugolin's heart and, consequently, her relationship with schoolteacher Bernard Olivier feels like a contrivance rather than the assurance of an optimistic future.

Daniel Auteuil, however, comes more to the fore and he deserved his César for Best Actor for the piteous manner in which his remorse is exploited as a weakness by Montand and then thrown back in his face by Béart (who was his off-screen partner at the time) when she realises his hopeless devotion to her. Indeed, his moral dignity provides the emotional core of a film that looks superb (thanks to Bruno Nuytten's lucent photography), but is too conscious of its heritage prestige to plumb its story's real human depths. ★★★ **DP**

ⓓ MAP OF THE HUMAN HEART (1993)

Starring: *Jason Scott Lee (Avik), Robert Joamie (Young Avik), Anne Parillaud (Albertine), Annie Galipeau (Young Albertine), Patrick Bergin (Walter Russell), Clotilde Courau (Rainee), John Cusack (The Mapmaker)*
Director: *Vincent Ward*
Screenwriter: *Louis Nowra, from a story by Vincent Ward*
15/104 mins./Drama/Romance/UK/Australia/Canada/France

Childhood friends, Avik and Albertine are separated by the arrival of WWII. Several years later, they happen to meet again in an Air Base where they have both been assigned and Avik realises he feels more than just friendship.

Vincent Ward's poignant vision of life and love in the uniquely charted world of Jason Scott Lee's half-Inuit hero, Avik, deserved greater things than it actually achieved on its theatrical release, when the sheer breadth and beauty of the tale could best be appreciated. Disappointingly, though perhaps inevitably, the film seems vastly diminished on its transfer to the small screen.

Plotting a life circumscribed by cultural confusion and unrequited love, the story sweeps the young Avik away from a bleak Arctic childhood when a visiting map-maker called Walter recognises the boy's tuberculosis and drops him off in Montreal for the cure, a horror show experience lightened only by the presence of Albertine, another abandoned outcast with whom Avik forms the lifetime bond at the very heart of Ward's film – a bond stretched by time, the perils of World War II, the loneliness of living life as a people apart, and the tears and hitches of fate's little surprises.

In retrospect, it seems extraordinary just how well Ward pulls off such an unlikely tale, contriving in its most unfeasible moment a reunion, years later, between the adult Avik and the lovely Albertine – he an RAF bomber flying raids on Germany, she working for the WRAP, analysing the very aerial photographs taken by his squadron – of such Casablanca-style proportions that a quote along the lines of, 'Of all the RAF stations in all the world, you had to walk into mine' wouldn't have gone amiss.

Carried along by the gloriously grand romance of the thing, the compelling central performance of Scott Lee, in particular, and the sort of all-embracing photography that makes you melt, such minor gripes seem trivial. In the end, however, where sweeping over the details of a lifetime with big, bold strokes seemed sufficient for the big screen, here on DVD they seem too broad and too shallow a device to really hold the imagination. ★★★ **PB**

ⓓ MARATHON MAN (1976)

Starring: *Dustin Hoffman (Thomas Babington 'Babe' Levy), Laurence Olivier (Christopher Hess/Szell)), Roy Scheider (Henry David Levy), William Devane (Peter Janeway), Marthe Keller (Elsa Opel), Fritz Weaver (Professor Biesenthal)*
Director: *John Schlesinger*
Screenwriter: *William Goldman, based on his own novel*
18/125 mins./Drama/USA

When Thomas Babington's secret agent brother is murdered before his eyes, he becomes embroiled in a plot involving smuggled diamonds and Nazi war criminal, former SS dentist Szell, the White Angel of Auschwitz.

The only movie to truly deliver the visceral power of a dental drill, John Schlesinger's taut, well-written if far-fetched and baffling thriller, is the film that gives you toothache in a good way. 'Is it safe?' Those words fire a Pavlovian shock of pain through the upper molars for anyone who has taken in the film, an empathic response to former Nazi Laurence Olivier drilling away inside Dustin Hoffman's innocent mouth, while asking that obscure question. He's after info, a clearance to sell his ill-gotten diamonds (stolen from Jews during the war), but Hoffman's luckless Babe has no idea what he's on about.

It's a moment of icy genius, a starburst of cinema's knee-jerk powers that almost overpowers all the knitted paranoia of the rest of the movie. William Goldman, a sharp, clean screenwriter, sprawls about in unusually complicated fashion – here is a tale of a CIA black ops organisation called The Division who have dipped dirty fingers on all sides, including housing former Nazis, and the clean brother of one doomed operative who doesn't possess the vital secret everyone thinks he does.

The title refers to Babe's compulsion to run, something that will end up serving him in good stead. Hoffman threw himself into the part with familiar zeal, you half expect he required Olivier to actually drill his teeth. Oliver's immortal response to the Method madness going on – 'Why not try acting? It's much easier' – harkens from this very shoot, although there is the air of the apocryphal about the story. The ease with which Olivier transforms into this chilling refuge from the swollen evil of the past grants the

Clockwork Orange Slang

1 Yarbles - testicles
2 Droog – friend
3 Prestoopniks – criminal
4 Doobiedoob – okay
5 In-out-in-out – sexual intercourse
6 Appy polly loggies – Apologies
7 Gulliver – head
8 Millicent – policeman
9 Pretty polly – money
10 Tashtook – handkerchief

film a resonance beyond its basic trappings. In real terms, there is nothing more than the motorised scheming of Goldman's script and John Schlesinger's up-close style going on, but his actors give its stretched ideas a seriousness and shock value, beyond putting your teeth on edge. ★★★★ IN

MARCH OF THE PENGUINS (LA MARCHE DE L'EMPEREUR) (2005)

Starring: *Morgan Freeman (Narrator)*
Director: *Luc Jacquet*
Screenwriter: *Jordan Roberts, based on an earlier screenplay by Luc Jacquet, Michel Fessler, story by Jacquet*
U/85 mins./Documentary/France
Awards: *Academy Awards – Best Documentary*

Shot over 13 months in Antarctica, this nature documentary follows the efforts of a colony of Emperor penguins to reproduce during the coldest months of the year, and despite the dangers posed by the weather and the predatory seals and petrels that prey on the birds and their chicks.

In the US, *March Of The Penguins* was hailed as a box-office triumph, the first nature film to succeed as mainstream entertainment. But like *Fahrenheit 9/11*, the only higher-grossing documentary in history, this isn't a documentary in the traditional sense, boasting a stronger story than many features. In an amazing account of life against the odds, thousands of penguins make the trek inland from their summer feeding-grounds to mate (largely off-screen – this is a U, after all) and lay their eggs. This epic quest for survival – eat your heart out, *Lord Of The Rings* – takes place amid the harshest weather on Earth, and it happens every year.

Sadly, apparently lacking confidence in the strength of their icy images and waddling stars, the filmmakers feel the need to use Morgan Freeman's voiceover to emphasise what devoted families these penguins make. This despite the fact that they mate for only a season at a time, that the chicks may never see their parents again once weaned, and that – hello! – they've got bird brains.

All too often, intriguing little details are ignored as the film struggles to anthropomorphise its stars. This sort of sloppy thinking makes *March* an occasionally frustrating experience for those brought up on Attenborough documentaries, which always successfully combined entertainment and scientific rigour. At least we can be grateful that the original French version, which dubbed the penguins with voices of their own, won't make it to this country.

That's not to say that the movie is totally uninformative, nor that anyone should be concerned that it's been adopted by creationists thrilled that it doesn't discuss evolution. But given that director Luc Jacquet and his crew spent more than a year shooting every aspect of these birds' lives, producing some of the most beautiful images of the Antarctic ever committed to celluloid, while using special cameras to capture underwater images (a little grainy compared to the rest of the movie, but when you're in a drysuit in sub-zero temperatures, that's probably the least of your worries), you wish they'd spent a little time feeding us some information to accompany the pictures. As it is, this docu-drama sometimes feels sanitised and toothless. ★★★ H O'H

MARIA FULL OF GRACE (2004)

Starring: *Catalina Sandino Moreno (Maria Alvarez), Virgina Ariza (Juana), Yenny Paola Vega (Blanca). Guilied Lopez (Lucy Diaz)*
Director: *Joshua Marston*
Screenwriter: *Joshua Marston*
15/101 mins./Drama/ USA/Colombia

Feisty, independent, pregnant 17-year-old Maria is tempted to become a drug mule, smuggling heroin from Colombia to New York for $5,000 to change her life. What she doesn't foresee, though, is a terrifying journey from which there's no going back.

The winner of some big festival gongs (including joint Best Actress with Charlize Theron at Berlin for Moreno), this first feature from another promising product of New York University's film programme is not for anyone with a sensitive gag reflex.

Joshua Marston provides a harrowing depiction of drug- muling for dummies. The raw, revolting, dangerous details of such an undertaking are graphic, from Maria, with retching difficulty, swallowing 62 balls of condom-coated heroin to their yukky recovery.

Initially, it's that old, sad story: the poor girl lured by a charming guy into a criminal nightmare. Needless to say, the simple plan goes awry almost from the moment Maria, her tagalong best friend Blanca and her experienced 'tutor' Lucy take off, triggering a violent, gory crisis and a decidedly desperate series of events in its aftermath.

But what Maria's full of is chutzpah, her youthful folly compensated for by her jungle-catlike instincts for self-preservation. As a result, Marston ends up encouraging us not to judge Maria, but celebrate her as a canny, fearless spirit taking control of her life – which does somewhat reduce the story to being all about her courage, with no objective reflection on morality. ★★★ AE

THE MARK OF ZORRO (1940)

Starring: *Tyrone Power (Don Diego Vega/Zorro), Linda Darnell (Lolita Quintero), Basil Rathbone (Captain Esteban Pasquale), Gale Sondergaard (Inez Quintero)*
Director: *Rouben Mamoulian*
Screenwriters: *John Tainton Foote, Garrett Fort, Bess Meredyth, from the novel* The Curse Of Capistrano *by Johnston McCulley*
U/89 mins./Action/Adventure/USA

In the 1820s, aristocrat Diego de la Vega returns to his native California to find the peasants oppressed by a tyrannical overseer Captain Esteban Pasquale. Don Diego puts on a black mask and cape and moonlights as the outlaw hero El Zorro.

This lavish, exciting action film was 20th Century Fox's attempt to build up the impossibly handsome Tyrone Power as a swashbuckling hero in competition with Warner Brothers' Errol Flynn. Though a remake of a property (Johnston McCulley's novel *The Curse Of Capistrano*) that had done for Douglas Fairbanks (the original screen swashbuckler) in 1920 and would be dusted off for many more film and television versions, *The Mark Of Zorro* is so closely patterned on *The Adventures Of Robin Hood* that the lovely Linda Darnell often seems to be reciting leftover Olivia De Havilland lines. Moreover, several Robin Hood support players are held over to do their old acts – Eugene Pallette as a Tuck-like Friar transplanted to Old California and (especially) Basil Rathbone as the deadly, sword-wielding antagonist.

Power is as handsome and athletic as Flynn, posing as a hankie-swishing fop in the Hacienda of Los Angeles by day, then spending his nights as a dashing defender of peons against the tyrannical tax collectors of the corrupt Alcalde, carving a Z at the sites of his various exploits to boost his heroic rep. Power cuts a handsome figure and handles dialogue as sharply as his blade, while Rathbone slyly satirises himself as the thoroughly rotten villain. Director Rouben Mamoulian plays up the costume romance for the first hour, allowing for the snogging collision of the superb profiles of Power and Darnell, holding back on the action until the finale, which offers one of the cinema's best-ever duels as Power and Rathbone match épées to the death. ★★★ **KN**

MARNIE (1964)

Starring: *Tippi Hedren (Marnie Edgar), Sean Connery (Mark Rutland), Diane Baker (Lil Mainwaring), Martin Gabel (Sidney Strutt), Louise Latham (Bernice Edgar)*
Director: *Alfred Hitchcock*
Screenwriter: *Jay Presson Allen, based on the novel by Winston Graham*
15/130 mins./Thriller/Mystery/Romance/USA

Playboy Mark Rutland realises Marnie is a kleptomaniac who specialises in stealing from her employers. He blackmails her into marriage, intent on curing her frigidity and criminal nature.

Alfred Hitchcock intended *Marnie* as a vehicle for Grace Kelly, but wound up casting Tippi Hedren, his discovery of *The Birds*.

The glacial Kelly might have made an interesting Marnie – Hitch was obviously turned on by the idea of having the Princess raped by James Bond – but Hedren gives the performance of her career, playing an uncomfortable visit to a mother who dotes on a Marnie-substitute little girl but is nervous of her real daughter ('Why don't you love *me*, Mama?') and the traumatic mercy-killing of her injured horse with such brilliance it's an injustice she wasn't even nominated for the Best Actress Oscar that went that year to Julie Andrews as Mary Poppins.

The first act is a cool study of a professional serial thief who juggles identities and hair colours as she takes jobs in a series of conservative firms and wins enough trust to walk away with substantial sums of money, allowing for a Hitch set-piece robbery complicated by a hard-of-hearing cleaning lady.

The second half is a strange crossbreed of sadistic love story and psychological drama. 'One might call *Marnie* a sex mystery, that is if you used such terms,' claims Hitch in his typically deceptive trailer.

Sean Connery finally got to show that he was more than 007 as the publisher-playboy with an interest in taming dangerous animals who tries, for his own perverse motives, to get to the bottom of the childhood trauma that has made Marnie frigid (a semi-rape honeymoon experience doesn't help), terrified of thunderstorms, a compulsive shapeshifter and thief and a nervous wreck at the sight of the colour red. ★★★★ **KN**

THE MARRIAGE OF MARIA BRAUN (DIE EHE DER MARIA BRAUN) (1978)

Starring: *Hanna Schygulla (Maria Braun), Klaus Lowitch (Hermann Braun), Ivan Desey (Oswald), Gottfried John (Will), Gisela Uhlen (Mother)*
Director: *Rainer Werner Fassbinder*
Screenwriters: *Peter Märtheseimer, Pea Fröhlich, Rainer Werner Fassbinder*
15/120 mins./Drama/West Germany

Maria spends a day with Hermann Braun after their marriage, but the Second World War, a murder and her affair with textiles tycoon Oswald conspire to keep them apart for a decade, by which time the spark of passion has died.

This is the first part in a trilogy of films about women surviving the tribulations of West German life under the postwar leadership of Konrad Adenauer. Rainer Werner Fassbinder originally conceived the project for Romy Schneider in the mid-1970s, but, as in the film itself, delays took the gloss off this dream pairing and Fassbinder cast Hanna Schygulla, who only accepted the role on the proviso that Maria Braun was less docile and exploited than her character in their previous collaboration, *Effi Briest* (1974).

The picture proved to be Fassbinder's last with cinematographer Michael Ballhaus and the imagery is nowhere near as complex as in their earlier teamings. However, the new screenwriting combination of Peter Märthesheimer and Pea Fröhlich – who would also script *Lola* and *Veronica Voss* – gave Fassbinder a new thematic impetus that enabled him to subvert the dramatic emphases placed in Hollywood woman's pictures by the likes of his frequent inspiration Douglas Sirk.

Despite her many mistakes, Maria is an unusually sympathetic Fassbinder character. But he avoided easy empathy by having Schygulla play her with such a lack of emotion that we are forced to examine her circumstances to gain an understanding of her actions. Thus, we see the often overlooked impact of the war on ordinary civilians, the false promises made by their American liberators and the struggle to recover a sense of self-worth during the so-called economic miracle. Hence, we realise that the idyllic marriage to which Maria pins her hopes is as much an illusion as that of her friend, Betti.

It's ironic that the workaholic Maria so closely resembles Fassbinder himself, even though his headlong existence couldn't have contrasted more with her constant postponement of real life. Indeed, they even share an ambiguous early death. The screenplay had Maria killing herself and Hermann in a car crash. But, Fassbinder left us to wonder whether the gas explosion was an accident or a suicide prompted by the contents of Oswald's will. ★★★★ **DP**

MARRIED TO THE MOB (1989)

Starring: *Michelle Pfeiffer (Angela de Marco), Matthew Modine (Mike Downey), Alec Baldwin (Frank de Marco), Mercedes Ruehl (Connie Russo), Joan Cusack (Rose)*
Director: *Jonathan Demme*
Screenwriters: *Barry Strugatz, Mark R. Burns*
15/104 mins./Crime/Comedy/Romance/USA

Angela de Marco, kind-hearted and long-suffering wife of mob hitman 'Cucumber' Frank de Marco. Fed up with living in a house furnished entirely with items that have fallen off the back of the nearest lorry, she offs and ups to the nearest tenement in the Lower East Side.

Married To The Mob is a comedy. It's important to get this straight right at the start, otherwise there'll be that terribly embarassing situation where you don't know whether to laugh or not when the fat bloke gets stiffed in the opening few minutes. Do.

Jonathan Demme's follow-up to *Swimming To Cambodia* is a typically entertaining diversion from the man who seems to be quite happy working with Melanie Griffiths one minute (*Something Wild*) and directing a Fine Young Cannibals video the next. Here is Michelle Pfeiffer, Dean Stockwell and a thoroughly entertaining tale of modern-day mafia, now out of little Italy and settled in suburb New Jersey.

Pfeiffer is Angela de Marco, kind-hearted and long-suffering wife of mob hitman 'Cucumber' Frank de Marco. Fed up with living in a house furnished entirely with items that have fallen off the back of the nearest lorry, she offs and ups to the nearest tenement in the Lower East Side, accurately described by Don Tony 'The Tiger' Russo as a 'real shithole'.

Stockwell, hopelessly smitten, follows her there, as does plucky but dim-witted cop Mike Downey, who goes undercover as a handyman, thus creating bags of opportunities for mistaken identities, badly timed entrances and general farce. It would be no surprise at all if the vicar was to arrive with his pants around his ankles. ★★★ **BMc**

MARS ATTACKS! (1996)

Starring: *Jack Nicholson (President James Dale/Art Land), Glenn Close (First Lady Marsha Dale), Annette Bening (Barbara Land), Pierce Brosnan (Prof. Donald Kessler), Danny DeVito (Rude Gambler), Martin Short (Press Secretary Jerry Ross), Sarah Jessica Parker (Nathalie Lake), Michael J. Fox (Jason Stone), Lukas Haas (Richie Norrish), Natalie Portman (Taffy Dale), Tom Jones (Himself)*
Director: *Tim Burton*
Screenwriters: *Jonathan Gems, from the trading card series by Len Brown, Woody Gelman, Wally Wood, Bob Powell, Norman Saunders*
12/101 mins./Sci-fi/Satire/USA

The Earth is invaded by Martians with irresistible weapons and a cruel sense of humour

Closer in its scattergun approach to *Beetlejuice* than his two blockbusting *Batmans*, this is by turns inspired, lumbering, visionary, infuriatingly wasteful and truly astonishing, so while it certainly doesn't always work, the overall effect is one of delirious mayhem, Burton-style.

Burton and British screenwriter Jonathan Gems (with uncredited assistance from *Ed Wood* writers Scott Alexander and Larry Karaszewski) have crafted a loving parody of 50s science fiction cinema, with its creaky flying saucers, bug-eyed aliens, and global annihilation, by way of cynical 90s sensibilities. The story, as you'd probably expect, is secondary to the effects. But what effects, as Burton fully exploits his CGI invaders; green, bulbous-brained, skull-visaged little buggers gleefully out for a bit of interplanetary argy bargy.

After a very slow first 30 minutes in which the film threatens to keel over and die, the action kicks into hyperdrive when the Martians land in the Nevada desert and, with a 'We come in peace' declaration, whip out their laserguns and incinerate the gathered masses. It's a thrilling scene, both horrifying and humorous, which aptly sets the tone for what follows.

As the attack turns global, the military proves ineffectual, and it takes the efforts of a heroic band of disparate individuals to save mankind as we know it. And while the method with which they defeat the Martians is no less hokey than ID4's, it's certainly a lot more fun. The heavyweight cast (Nicholson in dual roles as US President and a sleazy Vegas tycoon, Close as the First Lady, Pierce Brosnan as a pipe-smoking scientist, Bening as the latter's clippie-hippie wife, Michael J. Fox and Sarah Jessica Parker as rival TV reporters, Tom Jones as himself) pitch themselves firmly in the camp marked, well, 'camp', and act up for all they're worth, but are ultimately undone by the too slight script. ★★★★ **MS**

Tagline
Nice planet. We'll take it.

MARTHA, MEET FRANK, DANIEL AND LAURENCE (1997)

Starring: *Monica Potter (Martha), Rufus Sewell (Frank), Tom Hollander (Daniel), Joseph Fiennes (Laurence), Ray Winstone (Pedersen)*
Director: *Nick Hamm*
Screenwriter: *Peter Morgan*
15/88 mins./Comedy/Romance/UK

Record company hotshot Daniel returns from a US business trip and falls for emigrating American girl Martha after a chance meeting at Minneapolis airport. But it seems his friends have fallen for her too . . .

Hey, it's a small world and London is only part of it so anything is possible. Besides, watching Peter Morgan's screenplay unfold everything is wonderful. Brilliantly plotted, deconstructed and timeshifted in the style of, say, *Pulp Fiction*, Hamm views three emotionally charged days from the differing angles of each of the titular protagonists built from the flashback perspective of practising psychiatrist Ray Winstone (an excellent and unlikely cameo).

The deadpan comedy is frequently laugh-out-loud funny with Sewell and Fiennes taking to it like ducks to water after their more serious roots. Hollander is unusually likeable, too, as the potentially irksome yuppie. But at the core of everything is newcomer Potter (previously glimpsed briefly as Nicolas Cage's wife in *Con Air*),bouncing elfishly from pillar to post, streetwise but confused, loved and loveable, and glowing like Julia Roberts circa *Steel Magnolias*.

Fun, feelgood and fast-moving – this is everything you wanted from a Brit romantic comedy (but were afraid to ask). ★★★ **NJ**

MARY REILLY (1996)

Starring: *Julia Roberts (Mary Reilly), John Malkovich (Dr Henry Jerkyll/Mr Edward Hyde), George Cole (Mr Poole, the Butler), Michale Gambon (Mary's Father), Glenn Close (Mrs Farraday)*
Director: *Stephen Frears*
Screenwriter: *Christopher Hampton, based on the novel by Valerie Martin*
15/103 mins./Drama/Horror/USA

A housemaid falls in love with Dr Jekyll and his darkly mysterious counterpart, Mr Hyde.

Every so often a film comes along that people are determined to hate. This was practically disowned by its studio after disputes with the director, and victim of unanimously contemptuous reviews and an indecently hasty exit from theatres. And yet there's a lot to admire. Valerie Martin's original novel is a daring, brilliant and thoughtful embroidery on Robert Louis Stevenson's *The Strange Case Of Dr Jekyll And Mr Hyde*, freshening up the story by presenting it through the eyes of a maidservant in the Jekyll household. Its stroke of genius, employed cleverly in the film, is that everyone knows the solution to the mystery, but you can see how Mary could never possibly guess (that Dr Jekyll is Mr Hyde).

You spend the whole film knowing what the characters are thinking (very subtle direction sets up complex relationships) but also where they are wrong, and how tragic the consequences might be.

The down side is that neither lead performer quite works. Julia Roberts is physically right, and the reining-in of her usual big grin and big hair to suggest how downtrodden Mary has been is very moving, but her Irish always sounds strangled, especially when sharing scenes with Bronagh Gallagher. And John Malkovich's prissy, Canadian-sounding Jekyll and leering, nasal Hyde are also somewhat hit-and-miss readings of great roles.

What tips the scales in Mary Reilly's favour is that, in an era when *Bram Stoker's Dracula*, *Interview With The Vampire* and *Mary Shelley's Frankenstein* desperately try to sell themselves as romantic melodramas or literary adaptations, this isn't afraid to be a horror movie. The characters have more depth than Hammer would allow, but there are genuinely shocking moments (Hyde's appearance in Mary's bed, his trampling of a child, a hand grasping an ankle) and the dismal gloom of Jekyll's house, with its neglected courtyard and clanking chain-supported bridges, affords an atmosphere of real dread. ★★★ **KN**

MARY SHELLEY'S FRANKENSTEIN (1994)

Starring: *Robert De Niro (the Creature), Kenneth Branagh (Victor Frankenstein), Tom Hulce (Henry Clerval), Helena Bonham Carter (Elizabeth), Aidan Quinn (Captain Robert Walton), Ian Holm (Baron Frankenstein)*
Director: *Kenneth Branagh*
Screenwriters: *Steph Lady, Frank Darabont, based on the novel by Mary Shelley*
15/123 mins./Horror/UK-USA-Japan

Mary Shelley's classic story of man playing God, as obsessed scientist Victor Frankenstein injects life into a body assembled from odds and ends of various corpses. However, when his creature escapes, he realises tampering with nature is not a good idea.

After his florid re-telling of the Dracula story, Francis Ford Coppola produced this version of that other gothic perennial, Frankenstein, handing over the directorial reins to Kenneth Branagh who foolishly opted to shoulder the burdens of the book's literary status rather than just play it as a hammy house of horror. The resulting film, mummified by its own worthiness, manages to be both leaden and melodramatic.

The script, which *Shawshank* scribe Frank Darabont had a hand in, traces Shelley's paths oh-so faithfully and gets itself in a right pickle. We start on the vestiges of the North Pole, where a spent Victor Frankenstein (Branagh, as unbound as his entire movie) is rescued and recounts his story to a ship's captain. This immediately presents the two ailments that will floor the adaptation. Firstly, this rigorous, tiresome devotion to the multifarious layers of the original story. Did we need this framing device? Do we need to chart Victor's Geneva childhood and student years? The film is stuffy and crowded, with none of the clean lines of good horror. Then there is the evident staginess of the polar scene, it looks horribly false, and signals Branagh's misguided idea to chart a course tight to artifice. Coppola's *Dracula* – hardly a great – revelled in a Hammer-like flamboyance. This wooden texture is at odds with the film's realistic approach. By the time we make it to the lab, where Branagh will swing the camera about like a loony, and the film is collapsing. Perhaps, he realised and his only remedy was to fill the celluloid with surges of energy.

Robert De Niro, layered in prosthetics more mouldy than terrifying, although laudably distant from the clichéd bolts and boots look of Boris Karlof's, mumbles and moans, wallowing in his psychological trauma. But he prevents connection, coming across neither tragic nor monstrous, just a bit gross. All but tripping over the lumps of subtext liberally strewn about, it takes an age to reach the bloody finale that will bring the whole sorry mess to an end. A tragedy of a misbegotten creation, let loose by his misguided creator. And a film about Frankenstein's monster. ★★ **IN**

THE MASK OF FU MANCHU (1932)

Starring: *Boris Karloff (Dr Fu Manchu), Lewis Stone (Nayland Smith), Karen Morley (Sheila), Charles Starrett (Terrence Granville), Myrna Loy (Fah Lo See)*
Director: *Charles Brabin, King Vidor*
Screenwriters: *Irene Kuhn, Edgar Allan Woolf, John Willard, based on a story by Sax Rohmer*
Unrated/72 mins./Horror/USA

Evil genius Dr Fu Manchu schemes to get hold of the recently discovered sword and mask of Genghis Khan, artefacts which will enable him to assume command of an Asiatic horde and conquer the Western world. Stalwart British hero Nayland Smith sets out to stop him.

Sax Rohmer's oriental master fiend, 'the yellow peril incarnate', made his screen debut in the silent era and had been rehashed several times – notably in a series of three very early talkies starring Warner Oland – by the time MGM mounted this lavish pulp adventure as a vehicle for the reigning superstar bogey man, Boris Karloff. A troubled production, with credited director Charles Brabin replacing King Vidor in mid-shoot, it suffered so many rewrites and rethinks that the plot, not exactly sensible in the first place, gets lost amid a procession of bizarre, perverse incident.

Even in 1932, Fu Manchu was camp and Karloff slyly sends up the super-villain, lisping politely to various captives as he describes the tortures he intends to inflict on them, promising his Asiatic followers an apocalypse in which they can kill all the white men and take their women.

A svelte, slinky Myrna Loy is outrageous as Fu Manchu's equally strange daughter, who either has a brain seizure or the world's best orgasm while watching the shirtless hero get whipped.

As Nayland Smith of Scotland Yard, a perpetually angry Lewis Stone is so given to spitting 'you yellow monster' at Asian people it's hard not to feel Fu Manchu has a point about the unworthiness of the caucasian race.

In the 1960s, Christopher Lee wore the long moustaches in the excellent *Face Of Fu Manchu* and four increasingly shoddy sequels. The Devil Doctor has been out of the movies since the disastrous Peter Sellers comedy *The Fiendish Plot Of Fu Manchu*. ★★★ **KN**

THE MASK (1994)

Starring: *Jim Carrey (Stanley Ipkiss), Cameron Diaz (Tina Carlyle), Peter Riegert (Lt. Mitch Kellaway), Peter Greene (Dorian Tyrell), Amy Yasbeck (Peggy Bryant)*
Director: *Chuck Russell*
Screenwriter: *Mike Werb, based on a story by Michael Fallon, Mark Verheiden*
PG/97 mins./Comedy/USA

A bank clerk without much success with women comes in to possession of a mysterious mask that transforms him into a sexually charged extrovert.

From the late 1930s through to the late 1980s, there were only two major companies in the superhero comic business: *DC* (who had Superman and Batman) and *Marvel* (Spider-Man and the X-Men). Thanks to the longstanding dissatisfaction with the titans' labour relations, 80s' writers and artists became attracted to the proliferation of independent companies like Dark Horse and Image, and new hero franchises – funkier or darker than the majors would allow – established themselves.

While the later *Batman* films were being Schumachered stupid, Tim Burton failed to get a Superman movie together and *Marvel* (pre-X-Men) always came a cropper (an unreleased Fantastic Four film, *Howard The Duck*). The new kids were savvier about multi-media, which heralded the arrival of the films, animated TV shows, memorabilia, computer games, action figures and lunchboxes of the 90s spun-off from *The Crow*, *Tank Girl*, *Mystery Men*, *Spawn*, *Barb Wire* and *The Mask*.

All of these, like the more serious *Unbreakable* and the long-in-development *Watchmen*, are comic book concepts that trade on the history of the medium, spinning variants on longstanding themes and ideas. *The Mask* was created by Dark Horse toppers Mike Richardson and Randy Stanley in 1982, although he wasn't drawn (by artist Jim Smith) until 1985, didn't get a regular series (by Mark Badger) until 1987 and didn't appear in the stories that inspired the film (by John Arcudi and Doug Mahnke) until 1989.

Originally, the character owed something to a bunch of *DC* characters, with attitudes and style copied from Batman's archenemy the Joker. In the story collections 'The Mask' and 'The Mask Returns', we follow several characters who don the mask and run riot, more often causing anarchic mayhem than pursuing vigilante justice (Stanley Ipkiss, hero of the film, gets killed off and the chief mask-wearer is Lieutenant Kellaway, the cop played by Peter Riegert).

The film was tailored for Jim Carrey. Hot off TV's *In Living Color* and the first *Ace Ventura* movie, Carrey was hitting his stride as a comedy superstar and stopped off at mini-major New Line on the way to the big studios. Thus, the script is more about Stanley Ipkiss (a walking definition of 'nice guys finish last'), than the mask itself, which apparently embodies the spirit of mischeivous Norse god Loki. Watching *The Mask* again a decade on, it's hard not to get impatient with the time spent on Stanley's loser ways and single-guy relationship with his dog. The real business of the movie is what happens when he pulls on the mask and becomes a zoot-suited shapeshifter, riffing manically on Tex Avery's lecherous Wolf and Chuck Jones' Pepe le Pew, and stealing the odd gag from *Bugs Bunny*.

Although it's a 90s' artefact in many ways, the film has a weird visual and musical integrity in its 40s Latin look and style, just as Burton's *Batman* was rooted in noir and Expressionism. The tangled plot might get tiresome, as villain Dorian tries to take over the rackets of fictional Edge City, and the one clever plot switch (that gangster's moll Cameron Diaz really is better for the hero than Lois Lane-like reporter Amy Yasbeck) is disappointingly glib, but the film sparkles when Carrey puts on the mask – then-startling CGI gags come thick and fast and rhumba rhythms cut loose.

Copping a speech almost verbatim from the original comic, the enmasked Stanley muses, 'With these powers, I could be a superhero, fight crime, work for world peace. But first . . .' He then avenges himself on the cowboy garage that is bleeding him for work done on his crippled car, assaulting a pair of mechanics with car parts. In the comic, the mechanics die and the Mask proceeds to humiliate his old school teacher and cut a bloody swath through Stanley's enemies, suggesting he's less a nice guy than an embittered loser. In the movie, the mechanics live on to become a crude sight gag and Stanley, though he robs his own bank and is sought by the police, really does become a superhero, rescuing the girl from the gangsters and leading the cops to the villains.

He also, in another bit of plotting which will be instantly rethought if New Line and Carrey ever agree on a sequel deal, gives up the Mask, realising it's the inner nice guy that Cameron Diaz actually goes for. Yeah, right.
★★★ KN

⓪ THE MASK OF ZORRO (1998)

Starring: *Antonio Banderas (Alejandro Murrieta/Zorro), Anthony Hopkins (Zorro/Don Diego de la Vega), Stuart Wilson (Don Rafael Montero), Catherine Zeta-Jones (Elena)*
Director: *Martin Campbell*
Screenwriters: *John Eskow, Ted Elliott, Terry Rossio, from a story by Randall Jahnson, from characters created by Johnston McCulley*
PG/131 mins./Action/Adventure/USA

There's a mother lode of revenge to get straight – not only the sorrow of Hopkins' Zorro Senior, but Banderas' Zorro Junior is intent on catching up with evil henchman Colonel Love for lopping off his brother's head.

Playing to the flamboyant tune of a topmark Bond movie, albeit set in a late 19th century Mexican - held California, Martin Campbell's spirited rendition of the Latino Robin Hood is a splendidly straightforward adventure movie – dedicated to delivering the richest in action, humour and hot-blooded romance, while being well aware that in a comic book world of dashing heroics, silliness is a privilege not a complaint. And no manner of undiluted Welsh accents, achingly old-hat slapstick routines (come in comedy horse, your time is up) and vastly implausible swordplay can nullify the enjoyment levels of this treasurable nonsense.

Impeccably cast, Banderas is one of the few gorgeous leading men willing to temper their straight-up heroic stuff with a twinkle of self-deprecation, pulling off as many laughs as gasps at his flashing blade. He is the new Zorro, tutored to duelling perfection and gentlemanliness by Hopkins' old Zorro – recently absconded from his 20-year imprisonment by his long-standing nemesis Don Rafael. That swine also kidnapped his baby daughter to bring her up as his own. And she, naturally enough, has grown up to be ravishing beauty Elena (played with spicy vigour by a ravishing Zeta-Jones) getting all hot round the heaving bosom for this new masked hero romping around the luxurious Californian villas to bedevil the wicked plans of the sneering Rafael and his coterie of greedy Dons.

There's a mother lode of revenge to get straight – not only the sorrow of Hopkins' Zorro Senior, but Banderas' Zorro Junior is intent on catching up with evil henchman Colonel Love for lopping off his brother's head. There's also a dastardly Rafael plot to buy California from the Mexican overlords with their own gold which needs to be scuppered – the drama crescendos to an Indiana Jones styled gold mine peopled with reams of innocent children. Plus a daughter to reclaim and a purring beauty to be won over be it by delectable tango, illicit confession or smouldering glance.

Essentially, though, *Zorro* concerns itself with fabulous sword-fighting (and slashing big 'Zs' in the woodwork), rip-roarious stunts (including a spectacularly OTT horse chase that errs more on the level of horseplay) and a sparkling interplay between the leads (who all seem to be having a whale of a time). Banderas and Hopkins gel nonchalantly, igniting humour and passion off the master-pupil rote; Hopkins with Zeta-Jones adds a poignant note to the boysiness of it all; but it is the Banderas/Zeta-Jones inveiglement that really sizzles – in the film's raunchiest sequence they mock-duel with flirtatious glee, stealing kisses and removing clothing with well-placed swishes of the rapier. And with the sun glistening over tumbleweed deserts and appropriately-bedecked cantinas and ranchos, director Campbell (who instilled such gusto into *GoldenEye*) invests it all with a fine sense of the theatrical and keen storytelling skill, sweeping events without fuss from one great set-piece to the next.

Inevitably, none of this has any pretensions to profundity and its upfront style adds nothing to the textbook of filmmaking technique excepting perhaps the matchless stuntwork. Campbell also has a tough time cramming all the complicated ins and outs of the plot into a sensible running time – when the grandstand, all-action finale finally arrives it seems long overdue. *The Mask Of Zorro*, however, is attempting nothing greater than the purest escapism that will play right across the board, tongue tickling lightly in its cheek, eyes glinting with a jovial sparkle. Its sheer good nature is infectious. **★★★★ IN**

Movie Trivia: The Mask of Zorro

Robert Rodriguez was originally anticipated to direct but producers Columbia were deterred by his super-violent pitch for the movie. It was Steven Spielberg's idea for Zorro to redirect the firing squads' guns to their leader with his whip in the first action scene. Although Zorro is historically Spanish, Antonio Banderas is the first Spanish - born actor to actually play him — even though in this movie, ironically, Zorro is a Mexican.

ⓓ THE MASQUE OF THE RED DEATH (1964)

Starring: *Vincent Price (Prince Prospero), Hazel Court (Juliana), Jane Asher (Francesca), David Weston (Gino), Nigel Green (Ludovico, Francesca's father)*
Director: *Roger Corman*
Screenwriters: *Charles Beaumont, R. Wright Campbell, from the stories by Edgar Allan Poe*
15/84 mins./Horror/UK/USA

In mediaeval Italy, Prince Prospero invites his aristocratic friends to a lavish ball at his impregnable palace. He abducts a peasant girl who interests him, which spurs her father and lover to attempt a rescue.

The first of Roger Corman's Vincent Price-Edgar Allan Poe widescreen gothics to be made in Britain, *Masque* breaks with the comedy that had been stressed in *The Raven* to deliver a remarkable entertainment which is as much a homage to Ingmar Bergman's *The Seventh Seal* as an adaptation of Poe's baroque fable.

There's a youth-appeal sub-plot about the innocent abducted girl (Asher, looking very maidenly) and her revolutionary love interest (the 60s were already stirring against decadent aristos like Prospero) but the emphasis is on the corrupt luxury of a doomed ancient regime who throw a party while the plague ravages the countryside.

Price twitching his moustache with elegant, weary cynicism as the diabolist prince whose misdeeds are always designed to teach a lesson and savouring dialogue so ripe it's on the point of rotting. He also arches an eyebrow at lesser villains who miss the philosophical point of wickedness and display naked self-interest that earns them brutal deaths: Patrick Magee is dressed as an ape and burned alive by a dwarf jester (an import from Poe's story 'Hop-Frog') while Hazel Court brands her swanny cleavage in tribute to Satan before being murdered by a swooping falcon.

Finally, Death itself invades his ball and spreads the contagion in a beautifully choreographed dance of contagion.

Cinematographer Nicolas Roeg is encouraged to add his own flourishes, including long tracks through a succession of differently coloured rooms (an image from the story) while even the shock effects have a daring sensuality. ★★★ **KN**

ⓓ MASTER AND COMMANDER: THE FAR SIDE OF THE WORLD (2003)

Starring: *Russell Crowe (Capt. Jack Aubrey), Paul Bettany (Dr Stephen Maturin), James D'Arcy (1st Lt Tom Pullings), Edward Woodall (2nd Lt William Mowett), Chris Larkin (Capt. Howard)*
Director: *Peter Weir*
Screenwriter: *Peter Weir, John Collee, from the novels* Master And Commander *and* The Far Side Of The World *by Patrick O'Brian*
12/138 mins./Adventure/History/War/USA

Awards: *Academy Awards – Best Cinematography, Best Sound Editing, BAFTA – Best Costume, Best Production Design*

1805, and the HMS *Surprise*, a British frigate captained by Jack Aubrey, is charged with making sure that the Napoleonic Wars do not spread into exotic waters.

Weir, inspired by the obsessively detailed prose of author Patrick O' Brian, has employed Fox's considerable bounty and even greater human effort in the pursuit of total realism. This is not simply a matter of a retrofitted period vessel or some CG waves. In the best possible sense, *Master And Commander* is all at sea. Save for a brief sojourn on the alien landscapes of the Galapagos Islands, the picture does not touch ground. The sense of isolation that Weir has explored in various forms throughout his distinguished career – think of Truman's town in a bubble or the single sex school parties of *Dead Poet's Society* and *Picnic At Hanging Rock* – finds perhaps its fullest expression here, an entire floating world with not a woman to be found for a thousand miles.

And to master this miniature city, Weir has engaged the services of the most commanding actor in Hollywood: Russell Crowe. O'Brian's first choice for Captain Jack was apparently Charlton Heston, and you would have to cast your net that far back to find an actor who could challenge Crowe in this kind of form. And even then, Heston was never this nuanced, rarely this contained. Authenticity is therefore assured from the moment Crowe steps on deck; but during the double-checking of every little item, the filmmakers seem to have neglected to check if the maximum amount of fun had been packed into the capacious hold. The first attack on the HMS *Surprise* is arguably the most exhilarating twenty minutes in a 21st-century action film. Compared to the insubstantial illusions of CGI, the crack and splinter of wood torn apart by metal is enormously satisfying. Thereafter, however, the movie drifts a bit with Jack's obsession with besting *The Archeron* precipitating a rather straightforward chase.

The soggy middle section plays like a National Geographic travelogue: boat when cold, boat when hot, boat when wet again. The final sortie does scoop up all the plot strands, but the expected reversals and betrayals that might have raised the dramatic stakes or deepened the emotional ones simply do not come.

This largely linear journey is not without rough waters. The character of Maturin (a colourful yet grounded Bettany) is on board to ask stupid questions on our behalf but, in general, precious little quarter is given to land-lubbers, with authentic dialogue launched into the wind and forever lost. Imagine watching a period Robert Altman drama in a storm, and you can grasp the nature of the problem.

If it's not quite fun enough, *Master And Commander* is perhaps not quite rich enough either. Crowe's Jack is a complex soul, but unless you're a commissioned officer in the Royal Navy, his situation simply does not speak to the modern condition. While Crowe's indelible Maximus was father to a murdered son who would have his revenge in this life or the next, Captain Jack's motivation remains remote, an Ahab whose enemy is given no more shading than your average white whale. ★★★ **WL**

ⓓ MATA HARI (1931)

Starring: *Greta Garbo (Mata Hari), Ramon Novarro (Lt Alexis Rosanoff), Lionel Barrymore (Gen. Serge Shubin), Lewis Stone (Andriani), C. Henry Gordon (Dubois), Karen Morley (Carlotta)*
Director: *George Fitzmaurice*
Screenwriters: *Benjamin Glazer, Leo Birinski, Doris Anderson, Gilbert Emery*
PG/91 mins./Spy/USA

Caught between the ruthless World War I ambitions of Russian general Shubin and her German handler Andriani, exotic dancer-cum-spy Mata Hari falls for pilot Alexis Rosanoff and sacrifices herself to protect his honour.

Greta Garbo's 18th feature is now regarded as one of her weakest. Yet, on its original release, it caused more than a minor ripple, as the Swedish superstar not only performed a sensuous dance, but also turned off the lights on two torrid love scenes with Latin lothario, Ramon Novarro.

Very much the rival of Garbo's favourite co-star, John Gilbert, Novarro had made his name by alternating between silent adventures like *The Prisoner Of Zenda* and *Ben-Hur* and such exotic romances as *The Arab* and *The Student Prince* in Old Heidelberg. However, like Gilbert, he was one of MGM's fading stars and he needed this film to be a success following a series of undistinguished Talkies. But, while he conveys a suitable sense of dashing heroism, Novarro lacks the swagger to hold his own against Garbo, who compensated for her own miscasting by turning on the mysterious allure that was the secret of her off-screen persona.

Dressed in a spiked turban and a highly revealing gown, she looked distinctly uncomfortable during her opening exotic gyrations, especially when she has to wrap herself around a giant statue of Shiva. But, she was much more at home suffering the exquisite agonies of sacrificing herself for love in a manner more akin to Camille than the real Margaret Zella MacLeod, the Dutch dancer who had become the most notorious female participant in the First World War.

Indeed, Garbo's best scenes have her alternating between caprice and vulnerability, as she negotiates with competing spy masters Lionel Barrymore and Lewis Stone. In his fifth and penultimate collaboration with Garbo, the latter (who had previously crossed swords with Novarro in the swashbuckler, *Scaramouche*) gives a splendidly callous performance that stands in stark contrast to his turns as Mickey Rooney's indulgently sage father in the Andy Hardy series. ★★★ **DP**

MATADOR (1986)

Starring: *Assumpta Serna (Maria), Anthonio Banderas (Angel), Nacho Martinez (Diego), Eva Cobo (Eva), Julieta Serrano (Berta), Chus Lampreave (Pilar)*
Director: *Pedro Almodovar*
Screenwriters: *Pedro Almodovar, Jesus Ferrero, from a story by Pedro Almodovar*
18/101 mins./Drama/Thriller/Spain

Two serial killers – a bullfight-obsessed lady lawyer, who has taken to seducing young torreros and murdering them on the point of orgasm with a precise thrust of a dagger hairpin, and a retired matador who now kills only disposable girls – stalk each other, inevitably falling into a violently fetishist relationship.

Pedro Almodovar's labyrinthine tale of erotic horror opens provocatively by dramatising every censor's worst nightmare as the retired bullfighter masturbates while watching a video which comprises gory highlights from Mario Bava's *Blood And Black Lace* and Jesus Franco's *Bloody Moon*, then is inspired to go out and commit real-life murders.

While the major maniacs execute a dance-like ritual of courtship and atrocity, an apprentice matador tries to get over his homosexual inclinations by asserting his violent masculinity, though an attempted rape goes awry when he uses the wrong implement on his penknife (a bottle-opener) instead of a knife to threaten his prospective victim and he just winds up muddying the waters of the police investigation by confessing to both strings of murders.

Eventually, in a climax inspired by *Duel In The Sun*, Serna and Martinez execute each other during a sexual clinch – and all the other interested parties fail to intervene because they are distracted by an eclipse.

The most extreme of Almodovar's 'early, kinky films', this tribute to the chic slasher movies of Bava and Dario Argento is colourful and unreal enough to be less offensive than it sounds, with some of the most beautiful people seen on screen in the 1980s (Serna's strong profile is especially striking). It's a screamingly funny, intriguing meditation on sex and violence, delving sacrilegiously into the Almodovarish underpinnings of that arch Spanish ritual, the bullfight, in which beautiful young men in tight and frilly clothes elegantly gore animals to death. ★★★★ **KN**

THE MATADOR (2005)

Starring: *Pierce Brosnan (Julian Noble), Greg Kinnear (Danny Wright), Hope Davis (Carolyn 'Bean' Wright), Adam Scott (Phil Garrison), Portia Dawson (Genevive)*
Director: *Richard Shepard*
Screenwriter: *Richard Shepard*
15/96 mins./Crime/Drama/Comedy/USA/Germany/Ireland

Freelance hit man Julian Noble is past his best. He can still kill with efficient impunity, but there's a great hollow at the centre of his life – human contact. When he meets travelling salesman Danny Wright, an ordinary Joe down on his luck, a strange bond forms between them, somewhere between friendship and manipulation.

He's dabbed his toenails purple, told some snoopy kid where to get off and detonated a bomb under a Porsche, but it's the moment when Pierce Brosnan's fraying hit man, lubricated with Mexican beer, strolls through a hotel lobby that seals the deal. Not an unusual event, you might surmise. Many a Bond film has seen the actor swaggering through the world's most polished foyers in bespoke threads. But never before has the 007-that-was done so sporting only a pair of unfortunate black Speedos, Village People facial hair and ankle-high winklepickers, his knobbly white knees and growing paunch there for all to take in and hoot at. This is an acting showcase determined to explode preconceptions, to dismantle an ordered past and reveal its star as an able-bodied and fully game comedian.

Not that Richard Shepard's talky, loose-limbed movie is exactly a comedy. It's a wiry, energetic, genre-cracking serving of pulp fiction, spiced with the jalapeno-kicks of Tarantino and Rodriguez and dedicated to the quirks and calamities of its characters. The writer-director is entranced by the curious dynamic, the unpredictable qualities of human connection, between this lairy, odd-jobbing assassin and Greg Kinnear's uptight violet. As Brosnan cuts loose, leering, lying, and spilling about on the wrong side of best behaviour, Kinnear skilfully reels it all in, a mild-mannered dope lured way out of his comfort zone.

There is just the scent of threat to Noble's intent, a slight Tom Ripley-ish warp to the encounter that staggers among the heated, grumbling streets of Mexico City. By the time Noble crashes Wright's American home and draws his guileless wife (an ever-excellent Hope Davis) into his strident breakdown, you await the nasty shudder. No dice. Shepard concludes with a rather flat note, sapping the hilarious sprawl of their adventure of its creepy thrill, like a great gig that neglects the obligatory encore. Even so, all that's gone before still brings the movie close enough to that great intangible – cool. ★★★★ **IN**

MATCH POINT (2005)

Starring: *Jonathan Rhys Meyers (Chris Wilton), Scarlett Johansson (Nola Rice), Emily Mortimer (Chloe Hewett Wilton), Matthew Goode (Tom Hewett), Brian Cox (Alec Hewett)*
Director: *Woody Allen*
Screenwriter: *Woody Allen*
12A/124 mins./Drama/Romance/Thriller/UK/USA/Luxembourg

One-time tennis pro Chris is working as a coach when he meets wealthy posh bird Chloe. After they marry he embarks on an affair with his brother-in-law's fiancée, Nola, forming a love triangle that has violent consequences.

In a recent interview, Woody Allen, who turns 70 this year, remarked that, 'All that crap they tell you about getting joy and having a kind of wisdom in your golden years – it's all tripe.' But if the advancing years have given Allen nothing in the way of wisdom, they have equipped him with a newly stoked fury at the randomness of life. *Match Point* is a pleasingly sour shaggy-dog tale about how almost no one ever gets what they deserve, that plays like an episode of *Tales Of The Unexpected* directed by, well, Woody Allen.

The most obvious departure for Allen is the relocation from his beloved Manhattan to London, or at least, the more photogenic bits of London. (For the most part he manages to avoid the tendency to travelogue that most directors face when filming off familiar turf, so thankfully there are few red double-deckers or shots of Piccadilly Circus with the caption 'London', though characters do have an unnerving tendency to ostentatiously announce the chic locations for their rendezvous – 'Let's meet at the Tate Modern!') But there are other distinctly un-Woodyish elements: a sex scene that's certainly one of the most graphic he's ever filmed, together with some genuinely shocking violence. But its key distinction is the air of fatalistic irony that pervades this tart tale of hubris denied. (A biographical musing: would Woody have made this treatise on the essential unfairness of the universe before he was denied access to his children by a New York court?)

Both Scarlett Johansson and Jonathan Rhys-Meyers are well cast as the pillow-lipped love-birds, the former playing tennis coach and social climber Chris with just a tinge of Ripley-style ambivalence, and there's solid support from, among others, Brian Cox as the blissfully unaware paterfamilias, the actor here exercising his legal right to be in everything.

For fans of 'the earlier funny ones', it's worth pointing out that *Match Point* is certainly not a comedy in the conventional sense, but it is a recitation of the great cosmic joke: justice and fairness have nothing to do with where you end up – it's all about the breaks. Our good fortune is that with *Melinda And Melinda* and now *Match Point*, Allen seems, after nearly half-a-dozen disappointments, finally to be back on track. ★★★★ **IN**

MATCHSTICK MEN (2003)

Starring: *Nicholas Cage (Roy Waller), Sam Rockwell (Frank Mercer), Alison Lohman (Angela), Bruce Altman (Dr Klein), Bruce McGill (Chuck Frechette)*
Director: *Ridley Scott*
Screenwriters: *Ted Griffin, Nicholas Griffin, from the novel by Eric Garcia*
12/111 mins./Comedy/Drama/Crime/USA

Roy and Frank are a mismatched duo of low-level con men. But their dysfunctional partnership and Roy's teetering sanity face an even bigger challenge in the shape of Roy's 14-year-old daughter.

After the bullish brunt of making *Gladiator*, *Hannibal* and *Black Hawk Down* in quick succession, you can see why Ridley Scott's curiosity was piqued by this relatively low-wattage study of fragmenting lives, set against a bleached-out Los Angeles only a cab ride from the studio. Just five characters, a wash of small-time criminality and an emphasis on matters of the heart. Broadly speaking, it is a comedy.

The script's loose-limbed dialogue and teasingly back-to-front ethics – Roy, a con man, is dedicated to playing the moral guardian to his zesty daughter – make for ripe, complex set-ups. The plot only flirts with the wacky, elaborate grifts, being more concerned with paying off on its emotional trickery to bring the father-daughter bonding to fragrant life.

Most of this is down to the magical Miss Lohman. Sloughing away the designer jailbait brathood of vacuum-packed stars such as Hilary Duff and Amanda Bynes, Lohman inhabits a bright, tomboyish 14-year-old, flip-flopping between hair-trigger tears and the most beguiling movie smile since Natalie Portman in her heyday. Amazing to think that at the time Lohman was 24.

Cage's rattling cage is nothing new, but his vibrant pick 'n' mix of tics and stutters lacks the testy impact of Nicholson's recent compulsions. It's his exhaustive attempts at parenthood that reveal the man. Meanwhile, Rockwell purrs out his slick dialogue, a sub-role to the main drama, but one thick with humour.

Understandably and encouragingly, none of this feels like a Ridley Scott movie. Restrained in style and paced to the slow, midday thrum of a swollen summer, you might as well be strolling the sidewalks of one of Barry Levinson's family talkathons.

Scott's artistry is working in a subtler mode, editing to the jerky, awkward beats of Roy's mania, filling the frame with lurid, troubling POV shots that give the audience the uncomfortable sensation of having developed their own mental shudders. Ironically, it is one of the healthiest choices the director has made in years. ★★★★ **IN**

MATEWAN (1987)

Starring: *Chris Cooper (Joe Kenahan), Will Oldham (Danny Radnor), Jace Alexander (Hillard), Ken Jenkins (Sephus Purcell), Bob Gunton (CF Lively), Gary McCreery (Ludie), Kevin Tighe (Hickey), Gordon Clapp (Griggs), Mary McDonnell (Elma Radnor), James Earl Jones ('Few Clothes" Johnson)*
Director: *John Sayles*
Screenwriter: *John Sayles*
15/132 mins./Drama/USA

In a company-owned coal-mining town in West Virginia in 1920, off-the-boat Italians and donwtrodden Alabama blacks are brought in to replace the striking local work force. Joe Kenehan, a labour organiser, tries to bring the new workers into the union, while the company's hired thugs try to force a shoot-out.

With authentic folk songs, incidental details and period locations, writer-director John Sayles' *Matewan* is almost a socialist Western. The wandering hero drops off the train like Spencer Tracy in *Bad Day At Black Rock* to stir up the small town, and the individualist Sheriff straps on his guns like Gary Cooper in *High Noon* for the big showdown. And, like both those avowedly left-wing films, it tends to depict 'the people' as feckless bigots who can be manipulated for good by the hero and evil by the corporate villains.

The film sort of trails off after its big action scene, never quite following through the story of the incident, which was historically the first shot in a major series of union-company wars in the South, and leaving many of its dramatic conflicts unresolved.

Along the way, however, it has gutsy characterisations, a performance of heroic stature from Cooper, effective regional humour, distinctive backwoods score, the haunting visuals of cinematographer Haskell Wexler, and plenty of useful rabble-rousing.

It's a big story, but told through small moments – the ethnic mix of the strikers producing new sounds as musicians play together, menace over the dinner table as the company's killers leer at a landlady who has thrown in with the union – rather than expansive action scenes. It refuses to cop out by having its pacifist, communist hero strap on a gun for the finish, and is also balanced in its depiction of the inherent racism and conservatism of the 20s unions. ★★★★ **KN**

MATILDA (1996)

Starring: *Mara Wilson (Matilda Wormwood), Danny DeVito (Harry Wormwood/Narrator), Rhea Perlman (Zinnia Wormwood), Embeth Davidtz (Miss Jennifer 'Jenny' Honey), Pam Ferris (Agatha Trunchbull)*
Director: *Danny DeVito*
Screenwriters: *Nicholas Kazan, Robin Swicord, based on the book by Roald Dahl*
PG/94 mins./Adventure/Comedy/Family/USA

A girl discovers she has a special gift that may just help her get the better of her bullying parents and evil school headmistress . . .

Matilda is a blackly comic, delightfully off-the-wall picture that both kids and adults will lap up. The titular Matilda is the child genius born into a family of no-hopers, headed by crooked car salesman pop and flirtatious, white trash mom. Left to her own devices from an early age, Matilda is soon digesting the entire contents of the local library, discovering latent telekinetic powers and whipping up culinary masterpieces in the kitchen even though she has to stand on a chair to reach the work surfaces.

Her folks, on the other hand, are less convinced of their daughter's talents and pack her off to Crunchem Hall, a nightmarish school headed by the sadistic Miss Trunchbull. It's here that Matilda's abilities really come to the fore, her brain power attracting the attention of sickly sweet schoolmarm-with-secret Miss Honey, and her object-flinging tendencies exacting horrible payback on the headmistress from hell.

Clueless Speak

1 Baldwin – An attractive guy
2 Monet – attractive only from a distance
3 Surfing the crimson wave – having a period
4 Hymenally challenged – a virgin
5 Betty – An attractive girl
6 Barney – Unattractive guy
7 Audi – Goodbye
8 Smoked out – stoned
9 Loadie – drug user
10 Dope – smart, cool

In the wrong hands, this could have been an overblown mess, but thankfully there's taut, clever direction at work here, DeVito weaving hilariously twisted set-pieces (a nail-gnawing trek through the Trunchbull residence, a cake-scoffing marathon guaranteed to make even chocoholics lay down their Mars bars) and scrupulous attention to detail around this fantastical whimsy of a story.

In fact, this is exactly how you would expect a jaunt into Dahl's work to look – all kitsch chintzy furniture skewed overhead camera angles making everybody look enormous of bonce and gaudily-attired, larger than life characters. DeVito and Perlman excel, Ferris is a menacing hoot, but the real lynchpin here is the endearing Wilson proving after *Miracle On 34th Street* that she was one of the few child actors who really could deliver the goods. ★★★ **CW**

MATINEE (1993)

Starring: *John Goodman (Lawrence Woolsey), Cathy Moriarty (Ruth Corday/Carole), Simon Fenton (Gene Loomis), Omri Katz (Stan)*
Director: *Joe Dante*
Screenwriter: *Charlie S. Haas, based on a story by Haas, Jerico*
PG/99 mins./Comedy/Drama/Sci-fi/USA

A boy growing up in a small town learns lessons in showmanship from an outrageous independent film producer.

A beguilingly evocative tribute to independent producer, gimmick genius and showman supreme William Castle and 50s atomic-frightmares such as *Them!* and *The Blob*, Joe Dante's film centres on the arrival of schlockmeister Lawrence Woolsey in Key West, Florida, on the eve of the Cuban missile crisis in October 1962 to preview his new movie, *Mant (Half Man, Half Ant, All Terror!)* to the town's Saturday afternoon movie crowd.

The perfect time, Woolsey concludes, to open a new horror movie with the entire country poised on a nuclear knife edge. As played by Goodman, Woolsey is determined to lift himself out of life-long financial insecurity with one massive hit, arriving in town with Moriarty, his leading lady, girlfriend and ever-sarcastic, ever-reluctant accomplice.

Hooking up with horror movie fan Gene, whose father is on one of the US ships blockading Soviet-armed Cuba just 90 miles away, he schools him in the finer and not so finer points of his craft (such as rigging the seats with buzzers to administer electric shocks to his audience) while the islanders, to varying degrees, crack up around them.

Scripted by Charlie Haas and featuring appearances by Dante regulars Dick Miller, Bob Picardo, Kevin McCarthy and Belinda Balski, plus John Sayles (who wrote Dante's *Piranha* and *The Howling*) as a blacklisted cynic posing as a religious fanatic, this is likely to appeal to 50s horror movie anoraks and nostalgia freaks, though the pastiche black-and-white *Mant* footage and spoof trailers should tickle even those unaware of what they're meant to be parodying.

Dante has always ellicited fine performances from children, and here he pulls off a bunch more in the shape of Fenton, Katz and jailbait vixen Kellie Martin. By choosing to focus on their exploits instead of Goodman's gregarious huckster, however, he forfeits a valuable fourth star. ★★★ **MS**

THE MATRIX (1999)

Starring: *Keanu Reeves (Neo), Laurence Fishburne (Morpheus), Carrie-Anne Moss (Trinity), Hugo Weaving (Agent Smith), Gloria Foster (Oracle)*
Directors: *Andy Wachowski, Larry Wachowski*
Screenwriters: *Andy Wachowski, Larry Wachowski*
15/136 mins./Action/Sci-fi/USA

Awards: *Academy Awards – Best Editing, Best Sound Effects Editing, Best Visual Effects Edting, Best Sound, BAFTA – Best Special Visual Effects, Best Sound, Empire Awards – Best Debut (Carrie-Anne Moss)*

Hacker Neo is sought out to save the world. In so doing he discovers that his consciousness is part of a Matrix that keeps human bodies redundant and occupies their minds with a false reality. Is he 'The One' to save humanity from destruction?

Get this: what if all we know as reality was, in fact, virtual reality? Reality itself is a ravaged dystopia run by technocrat Artificial Intelligence where humankind vegetates in billions of gloop-filled tanks – mere battery packs for the machineworld – being fed this late 90s VR (known as The Matrix – you with us here?) through an ugly great cable stuck in the back of our heads. And what if there was a group of quasi-spiritual rebels infiltrating The Matrix with the sole purpose of crashing the ruddy great mainframe and rescuing humans from their unknown purgatory? And, hey, what if Keanu Reeves was their Messiah?

What sounds like some web freak's wet dream is, in fact, a dazzlingly nifty slice of sci-fi cool. The Wachowski Brothers (Andy and Larry – last seen dabbling in kinky lesbian noir with the excellent *Bound*) pulling off something like a million masterstrokes all at once. Taking the imprimatur of the video game, they meld the grungy noir of *Blade Runner*, the hyperkinetic energies of chopsocky, John Woo hardware and grandiose spiritual overtones into William Gibson's cyberpunk ethos to produce a new aesthetic for the millennium powered to the thudding beat of techno. And it is just incredible fun. The key is the technique of 'flo-mo', a process born from Japanese animation, whereby an object in motion is seemingly frozen while the camera miraculously spins around it as if time and gravity are on hold. It grants the action (including some killer kung fu which Reeves and crew spent months perfecting) liberty to take on surreal visual highs. Superhuman feats permissible, of course, in the context of VR as the rebels download Herculean 'talents' to fuel their subterfuge. Meanwhile, the audience can only gawp longingly, with its jaws thunking to the cinema floor in unison, as the heroes wrapped in skintight leather, sleek shades and designer cheekbones, spin up walls, leap from high rises and slip through streams of bullets in silken slo-mo. *Tron* this ain't.

Immediately reigniting the moribund cyberpunk genre (the kids can't get enough Stateside), this thrust Reeves from his imploding career back to *Speed* highs (and laying to rest the hideous ghost of *Johnny Mnemonic*) and stole much more of *Star Wars'* thunder than was thought humanly possible. For all its loony plot, *The Matrix* is fabulous.

Sure, the expert Fishburne is depended upon to expound the lion's share of the script as seer-like rebel leader Morpheus. Reeves, stunning in his new-cast slenderness, as Thomas 'Neo' Anderson, the hacker turned hope for all mankind (care of some ill-defined mystical calling) is asked little more than perpetual befuddlement. Like Speed, though, this movie plays on his iconic looks rather than his oak-like emoting. There's a major find, too, in the irresistible Carrie-Anne Moss, a majestically wrought combination of steely no-shit intelligence and rock-chick vivaciousness as fellow tripper Trinity. And Weaving, cast against type, neutralises his Aussie tones to a freaky deadpan, the head of the MiB-styled defence system set against the Goth invaders.

And sure, three minutes of post-movie deliberation and all this state-of-the-art cyberdevilry is reduced to the purest gobbledygook. That, though, is not the point. *The Matrix* is about pure experience. From head to tail, the deliciously inventive Wachowskis (watch them skyrocket) have delivered the syntax for a new kind of movie: technically mind-blowing, style merged perfectly with content and just so damn cool. ★★★★ **AS**

Movie Trivia: The Matrix

Will Smith was initially offered the role of Neo but refused. Leonardo DiCaprio was also considered. When Neo rubs his nose with his thumb before taking on Morpheus in combat training, he is actually alluding to a famous pre-fight habit of Bruce Lee. The helicopter scene almost caused filming to be cancelled as they had inadvertently infringed restricted Sydney airspace. All the intersections mentioned in the film are actually real junctions in the Wachowskis' home city, Chicago.

THE MATRIX RELOADED (2003)

Starring: *Keanu Reeves (Neo), Laurence Fishburne (Morpheus), Carrie-Anne Moss (Trinity), Hugo Weaving (Agent Smith), Gloria Foster (Oracle), Monica Bellucci (Persephone), Jada Pinkett Smith (Niobe)*
Directors: *Andy Wachowski, Larry Wachowski*
Screenwriters: *Andy Wachowski, Larry Wachowski*
15/138 mins./Action/Sci-fi/USA

With Zion under threat from an army of robot sentinels, Morpheus disobeys orders to defend the last human city so that Neo might await word from the missing Oracle. Neo needs to know many things, not least, why does he keep dreaming about his lover Trinity.

The Matrix was a stealth fighter, a secret weapon that utterly outfoxed its jumbo-sized near-contemporary, *The Phantom Menace*. *The Matrix Reloaded*, the first part of an epic single sequel, thunders into town minus that critical element of surprise. Indeed, trailing close behind *Reloaded* is the creeping suspicion that the torpedo is now bloated to the point where it has become everything it was once designed to detonate ...

If the only outstanding issues with *The Matrix Reloaded* were that it was too cumbersome to be cool, too obvious to be sexy; if all it failed to live up to was the attendant hype, then we could simply scoff at the non-believers. But, truth be told, *Reloaded* labours in places, and once or twice the juggernaut actually comes close to stalling. Overwritten exposition, often pretentious rather than profound, weighs heavily on a plot that is actually resoundingly linear. (No Cypher-style twist, here.) Underwritten new characters, meanwhile, distract attention from the core group. True obsessives might dedicate internet shrines to the wisdom of The Oracle or the architecture of the Matrix, but the rest of us will doubtless lament the fact that Neo's struggle with superpowers cannot possibly resonate as deeply as his first tumble down the rabbit hole. Not least because, by the credits roll, his journey has barely begun.

There's more: the disorienting Zion-set opening barely feels like a sequel to *The Matrix* at all, so keen are the Wachowskis to explore their underground city. The rather rushed climax is also confusing, with the episode where Niobe infiltrates the power-station so fleeting you might think it was little more than a set-up for a computer game. Oh, it is. The middle hour, however, is the Matrix to the max, and it rocks like a mutha.

Once Neo seeks the Oracle, *Reloaded* lurches into action and it quickly generates unstoppable momentum. It is not as sleek anymore perhaps, but it is a hulking brute that grips you by the throat and shakes you out of your seat. Where once there was a sly, Sergio Leone-influenced showdown between Agent Smith and Neo, now there is the 'Burly Brawl', a truly lethal combination of special effects and stunt work that unleashes 100 Agent Smiths on an amped-up Neo. (Total photo-realism? Not quite yet. But this is far too much fun to quibble.)

Add the Burly Brawl to a dazzling freeway free-for-all, throw in the Merovignian chateau sword-clash and a half dozen other bits of hand-to-hand business, and you have more than enough five-star thrills for mandatory repeat viewings. Praise for another quantum leap in action should be split between the Wachowskis, Yuen Wo-Ping's wire-team, John Gaeta's effects wizards and a thousand others, but let's not forget the four principal actors. Reeves et al were convincing enough in *The Matrix*, but the second time around, with the benefit of continuous training, they all kick serious, serious, grade-A ass. And there is absolutely nothing wrong with that. ★★★ **CK**

THE MATRIX REVOLUTIONS (2003)

Starring: *Keanu Reeves (Neo), Laurence Fishburne (Morpheus), Carrie-Anne Moss (Trinity), Hugo Weaving (Agent Smith), Gloria Foster (Oracle)*
Directors: *Andy Wachowski, Larry Wachowski*
Screenwriters: *Andy Wachowski, Larry Wachowski*
15/123 mins./Action/Sci-fi/USA

Neo is in a coma, caught between the Matrix and the Machine World, while in Zion, the human inhabitants await the onslaught of the Sentinel Army. Agent Smith's replicative powers are growing, the Oracle is still avoiding the key questions and the only thing we're sure of is that 'the war ends tonight' it'll be salvation or destruction before bedtime.

And so the *The Matrix* comes to an end. Truthfully, though, it should have ended in 1999, when the groundbreaking original proved to be the right film in the right place at the right time. Tapping into the cultural zeitgeist and Y2K fears about the power of machines over mankind, *The Matrix* not only revitalised slo-mo action sequences with its 'bullet-time' style, it had a political relevance that already seems dated in a 21st century world dominated by a war against terror, not technology.

The Matrix Reloaded, for all its faults, did try to up the ante, both in its creation of a wider Matrix myth and its budget-heavy effects. *Revolutions*, however, is content to follow in its wake, the final couple of hours of a four-and-a-half hour slab to which the original movie, in the makers' minds, is but a pre-title sequence. Granted, there's less philosophical babble and more emphasis on action in *Revolutions*, but the Wachowskis, having backed themselves into pseud's corner, can only deliver with a formula where spectacle and pretentiousness follow on from each other in steady succession. Gut thrills and intellectual stimulation are never integrated as one.

Revolutions' sustained action set-piece – the Sentinels' attack on Zion – is undeniably exciting, but it sure doesn't feel like an episode from a close sequel to the original *Matrix*. For a start, Zion was off-screen for the entire first movie. Secondly – and dramatically more importantly – this centrepiece relegates the main characters to, at best, mere bystanders. Neo and Trinity are off on a mission of their own. Morpheus – now dressed in what looks like a burgundy Benetton jumper rather than an outfit consistent with his standing as the coolest dude on (or under) the planet – takes a literal backseat to Niobe's driving. Instead, the key players are the Kid, whose backstory is apparent only to those dedicated enough to watch *The Animatrix* cartoons, and Mifune, whose on-screen impact is unfortunately as brief as it is memorable.

That such a primary scene is completely filled with secondary characters isn't just disappointing – it's damaging, because it draws attention away from the protagonists' climactic acts. Basically, this is the bit you remember, more than Neo's vital conversation with the *Wizard Of Oz*-like face of the machines or his up-in-the-air fisticuffs with Smith (a fight whose sfx impact has dwindled following *Reloaded*'s Burly Brawl).

Some viewers will indeed be completely satisfied, their questions answered, as the final credits roll, but they're the ones who have done their homework. Without filling in plot gaps by watching *The Animatrix* or playing derided computer game *Enter The Matrix*, a sense of confusion reigns. And those who are confused can't emotionally engage with the characters, thus rendering any amount of sacrifices and love themes null and void. In the original film, the casual viewer could relate to a slave race of pod people and their need to be freed, but the Wachowskis seem to have moved the goalposts as the story has progressed, sidelining what began as a focal point of the plot.

In other words, few box-office-storming blockbusters have been aimed so consciously at such a narrow and precise cult audience. The Year Of *The Matrix* will be remembered as an indulgence for fans, while the original movie will be affectionately held as a separate entity by a bigger crowd, much as the original *Star Wars* trilogy hasn't really been tainted by divisions over Episodes I and II. ★★ **OR**

A MATTER OF LIFE AND DEATH (1946)

Starring: *David Niven (Squadron Leader Peter D. Carter), Kim Hunter (June), Robert Coote (Flying Officer Bob Trubshawe), Roger Livesey (Dr Reeves), Richard Attenborough (An English Pilot)*
Director: *Michael Powell, Emeric Pressburger*
Screenwriters: *Michael Powell, Emeric Pressburger*
U/99 mins./Fantasy/Romance/Comedy/UK

An airman who fails to survive a warime crash finds himself so besotted with the American air controller who was trying to guide him in safely that he is reluctant to head off to heaven.

Powell and Pressburger's 1946 fable was harshly received by critics on its original release, despite making its debut as the first Royal Command Film performance. But time has served this unusual Brit flick well, so much that it now attracts a loyal and loving audience.

It's very much a film of its time and yet the themes are universal. Released while the world was still reeling from conflict on an unprecedented scale, this focuses on the human effect of that war.

Niven is the British airman who survives what should have been a fatal crash. In the next few hours he falls in love with the American air controller who was trying to talk him home to safety. Understandably, he proves reluctant to head on up to heaven when an 'angel' arrives to collect him.

Simple technical tricks help create a magical half world. In Heaven, and on the stairway that takes souls upwards, all is black and white, while earth blazes into glorious Technicolor (which is duly noted in an 'in joke' made by Goring). Actors freeze when celestial messengers appear, most dramatically in one sequence mid-table-tennis game. Most impressive is the vast celestial court, populated by thousands of spectators.

It's a story with humour and heart, a genuine classic that rewards with repeat viewings. And always the question remains: is what unfolds in the story something real or a product of the battling airman's imagination. ★★★★★ **EC**

MAVERICK (1994)

Starring: *Mel Gibson (Bret Maverick), Jodie Foster (Annabelle Bransford), James Garner (Zane Cooper), Graham Greene (Joseph), Alfred Molina (Angel), James Coburn (Commodore Lewis)*
Director: *Richard Donner*
Screenwriter: *William Goldman, from the TV series by Roy Huggins*
PG/121 mins./Comedy/Western/USA

A gambling cowboy is determined to enter a huge poker tournament but the only problem is he is short of the $3,000 stake needed to take part. So with the help of his rabble of friends, he sets about collecting all his debts . . .

This big-screen return of a well-loved Golden Age Of TV series trawls deeper than the baby boom demographics addressed by mid-60s retro-items such as *The Addams Family*, *The Flintstones* and *The Fugitive*. *Maverick* began in 1957 and ran until 1962, though original star James Garner left in 1960, which means audiences for the movie remake are unlikely to have more than a folk memory of the unconventional Western series, which set out to undercut the upright heroes of the era by following a cowardly con-man who was less interested in law and order than profit and loss.

Richard Donner and screenwriter William Goldman have wisely chosen to treat their inspiration with a great deal of respect. While Mel Gibson takes over the lead role of Bret Maverick, the film calls Garner back to play a part which very cleverly expands one of his roles on the forgotten show. Gibson, who has an unnerving tendency to seem less roguish than sneaky, acquits himself well enough to earn approving nods from Garner, though it's hard not to think that in his day Garner would have done better work in most of Mad Mel's leads.

The film opens with Maverick in a tricky situation, then ropes in a posse of supporting characters (flighty gambling belle Foster, man of integrity Marshal Garner, scurvy poker demon Alfred Molina) and gets round to a plot involving a massive cards tournament held on a riverboat by James Coburn. It seems like a simple traipse from exciting incident to hair's breadth escape (there are funny variations on traditional Western action scenes from *Stagecoach* to *A Man Called Horse*), but towards the end things get trickier with a series of twists entirely in tune with the snake oil charm of the series.

After the intense dramatics and revisionary grit of *Dances With Wolves* and *Unforgiven*, it was a relief to see a Western get back to the fun and spectacle of the genre, and Donner relishes the screen-filling landscapes. This even has Graham Greene doing a sly send-up of *Dances With Wolves* as a pragmatic Indian offering authentic native American holiday packages for loony Russian aristo Paul L. Smith.

One of the incidental pleasures of the movie is the canny casting: practically every bar room or card table face is familiar from years of TV and film Westerns, and the big game finale allows cameos from the likes of Doug McClure (Trampas from *The Virginian*) and Henry Darrow (Manolito from *The High Chaparral*). Fans of more recent vintage get nice joke appearances from a couple of unbilled stars who have worked with Donner and Gibson, and it's even a nostalgic delight to see the usually strait-laced Foster playing the sort of comic vamp part she last took in *Bugsy Malone*. Good solid fun. ★★★ **KN**

MCCABE AND MRS MILLER (1971)

Starring: *Warren Beatty (John McCabe), Julie Christie (Constance Miller), Rene Auberjonois (Sheehan), William Devane (The Lawyer), John Schuck (Smalley)*
Director: *Robert Altman*
Screenwriters: *Robert Altman, Brian McKay, from the novel by Edmund Naughton*
15/115 mins./Drama/Western/USA

A quick-drawing poker player single-handedly takes over a town's prospects and sets up a profitable brothel. Then a brainy-Brit of a whore enters his world and they go into business, leading to trouble with the townsfolk.

Robert Altman's fourth movie is perhaps his most perfect film, an expert and elegant deconstruction of American cinemaís primary myth – the Western – and a fitting elegy for the once noble genre fully two decades before *Unforgiven*.

Hot off *M*A*S*H*, the 45-year-old overnight success seized upon the rather shop-worn elements – the charismatic stranger, the tart with the heart, the lawless pioneer town – at the centre of Edmund Naughtonís simplistic source novel and fashioned something entirely new.

From the opening credits, when Warren Beatty's bowler-hatted hero slops through rain and mud to the fledgling settlement of Presbyterian Church, it is clear that we are far from the dustbowl vistas of Monument Valley. We are, in fact, north rather than west, the final frontier for the true American adventurer.

Filming on location just outside Vancouver, Altman decided to shoot in sequence, allowing his handcrafted timber town to grow in lockstep with the story, with a costumed crew becoming part of the community. The result is a uniquely organic production design, captured with all the detail of wood grain by Vilmos Zsigmond's 'daguerreotype' photography.

If Altman's approach represents a revolution, it is of a quiet, unassuming sort. Save for the whistling of arctic winds and the occasional acoustic lament from Leonard Cohen, there is no score. And the era's golden couple, Beatty and Julie Christie, both shed all vanity before inhabiting the title roles.

Indeed, newcomers hoping for fireworks may struggle to see what all the fuss is about; but just as trying to catch every line of Altman's signature overlapping dialogue is missing the point, it would be a mistake to strain too hard for sounds of greatness. ★★★★★ **CK**

ME AND YOU AND EVERYONE WE KNOW (2005)

Starring: *John Hawkes (Richard Swersey), Miranda July (Christine Jesperson), Miles Thompson (Peter Swersey), Brandon Ratcliff (Robby Swersey), CarlieWesterman (Sylvie)*
Director: *Miranda July*
Screenwriter: *Miranda July*
15/91 mins./Drama/Comedy/USA/UK
Awards: *Cannes Film Festival – Camera D'Or*

The worlds of newly single shoe salesman Richard and lonely artist Christine collide when she walks into his shop. Meanwhile, his sons are also learning about intimacy – the former via an internet chat room, the latter courtesy of two local Lolitas.

Writer/director/star Miranda July has created a beguiling treat with her debut feature, deservedly the winner of the Camera D'Or at 2005's Cannes Festival. It would be easy to saddle her film with the usual 'indie' adjectives ('offbeat', 'quirky', 'kooky'), but its freshness and honesty defy such lazy characterisation.

As struggling artist Christine, July's clear faith in the redemptive qualities of romantic love is deeply seductive. Meanwhile, her object of desire, Richard, is a man so frustrated by life's banal disappointments that he sets fire to his hand in front of his two young sons just to make something happen.

Around this central pair are a coterie of damaged adults and confused kids – so far, so miserable, but far from it; the script is shot through with a vicious wit that lays bare the innate ridiculousness of human beings, while taking pity on our childlike vulnerabilites. With moments that will bug you for days (a teenage blow-job contest, 'back and forth poop . . .'), July's tender, original movie is a wonderfully uplifting experience. ★★★★ **LB**

ME, MYSELF AND IRENE (2000)

Starring: *Jim Carrey (Charlie Bates/Hank Evans), Renée Zellweger (Irene P. Waters), Chris Cooper (Lieutenant Gerke), Robert Forster (Colonel Partington)*
Directors: *Bobby Farrelly, Peter Farrelly*
Screenwriters: *Peter Farrelly, Mike Cerrone, Bobby Farrelly*
15/116 mins./Comedy/USA

A mild-mannered cop's crazed alter ego comes to the surface after a series of bizarre events.

Just as *Kingpin* and *There's Something About Mary* relied on their crudeness for effect, so the latest Farrelly brothers' effort plumbs the depths of bodily unpleasantness for its laughs. This time around, however, the masters of mirth have come seriously unstuck. Irene's box office in the States – where it wheezed to the $80 million mark, less than half of Mary's takings – reflects the fact.

In reality, this should be a magic formula, one which reunites Carrey with his *Dumb And Dumber* brethren, sits back and watches the coffers swell. And indeed, for the first 20 minutes or so you get everything you've paid for, as hapless Carrey's life crumbles about his ears, his wife fathering black triplets as a result of her affair with a midget chauffeur, the locals treating him as a laughing stock, and little girls squealing expletives at him. His foul-mouthed, boorish alter-ego is obviously simmering below the surface and, on initial appearance, raises the requisite laughs.

However, Carrey's satanic mugging soon wears down to just occasional flashes of inspiration, and while Zellweger tries hard, she lacks genuine presence. Ultimately, *Irene* lacks the heart and sweetness that made *Mary* and *Dumb And Dumber* so appealing, in spite of their obsession with urine-drinking and 'hair gel'. Here, we see Carrey defecate on a neighbour's lawn, push children into ponds and fight with himself in a way that Steve Martin did much better 16 years previously in *All Of Me*.

But as the humour becomes increasingly desperate, so too does the movie, abandoning all notion of a decent story in its quest to out-gross its peers. ★★ **CW**

MEAN CREEK (2004)

Starring: *Rory Culkin (Sam Merric), Ryan Kelley (Clyde), Scott Mechlowicz (Marty), Trevor Morgan (Rocky Merric), Josh Peck (George Tooney), Carly Schroeder (Millie)*
Director: *Jacob Aaron Estes*
Screenwriter: *Jacob Aaron Estes*
15/90 mins./Adventure/Crime/Drama/USA

Having been beaten up by school bully George, Sam plots with his older brother to get revenge by inviting the boy on a birthday trip down the river. Once they get in that boat, there's no going back . . .

Mean Creek could teach *Ocean's Twelve* a lesson or two about how to handle an ensemble piece. Every one of the central characters is beautifully written and given such a fascinating backstory that the film could easily splinter off into six separate movies. The fact that they're all children only makes the level of detail even more impressive. Showing immense technical skill and emotional understanding, writer-director Jacob Aaron Estes switches our sympathies from character to character like a game of pass the parcel. At the centre are our mixed feelings about bully George.

He's incredibly rude – but that has something to do with his learning disabilities. His ongoing video diary emphasises his loneliness – but, boy, is he irritating at close quarters.

Estes enriches the plot by refusing to present each character's emotional dilemmas in black-and-white terms. Any sense of justice over a schoolyard beating stops being clear-cut when notions of conscience and guilt come into play. Equally ambiguous is the role of adults in this child's world – *Mean Creek* is a place where parents are noticeably absent, and the very mention of them only brings pain. ★★★★ **AM**

MEAN GIRLS (2004)

Starring: *Lindsay Lohan (Cady Heron), Rachel McAdams (Regina George), Tina Fey (Sharon Norbury), Lacey Chabert (Gretchen Wieners), Amanda Seyfried (Karen Smith)*
Director: *Mark Waters*
Screenwriter: *Tina Fey, based on the non-fiction book* Queen Bees and Wannabes: Helping Your Daughter Survive Cliques, Gossip, Boyfriends and Other Realities of Adolesence *by Rosalind Wiseman*
12A/97 mins./Comedy/Drama/USA

After years of being home-schooled, Cady Heron goes to high school for the first time and quickly becomes a part of the most powerful clique in her year, The Plastics — led by prize bitch Regina. However, matters are complicated when Cady falls for Regina.

Cementing her reputation as one of the busiest young actresses around, uber-teen Lindsay Lohan returned to the screen just weeks after starring in *Confessions Of A Teenage Drama Queen*, with this better-than-average high school romp.

Pitched somewhere between *Heathers* and *Clueless*, it may contain all the usual cliches of the teen movie – overwrought party scenes, awkward adolescent romance and the pressures of fitting in at school – but the sharp script (from *Saturday Night Live* alumni Tina Fey – who also takes the role of maths teacher here) renders it far funnier and edgier than many of its peers.

Lohan is appealing and likeable and there's equal fun to be had watching rising star McAdams as the splendidly evil Regina, Tim Meadows as the perpetually bemused school principal and Amanda Seyfried as a pathologically dim Plastic. ★★★★ **CW**

THE MEAN MACHINE (THE LONGEST YARD) (1974)

Starring: *Burt Reynolds (Paul Crewe), Eddie Albert (Warden Hazen), Ed Lauter (Captain Knauer), Michael Conrad (Nate Scarboro), John Steadman (Pop)*
Director: *Robert Aldrich*
Screenwriter: *Tracey Keenan Wynn, from a story by Albert S. Ruddy*
15/121 mins./Comedy/Drama/Sport/USA
Awards: *Golden Globes – Best Musical/Comedy*

A former pro-quarterback is tasked with training a team of cons to take on the prison guards, knowing the guards will use it as an excuse to 'accidentally' injure as many of his team as possible.

Released as *The Longest Yard* in the States – and recently re-made as a ropey Adam Sandler vehicle with Burt Reynolds cameoing – this is probably the most brutal sports movie set outside the boxing ring.

In the first 15 minutes floundering ex-footballer Paul beats up his girlfriend, steals a car – which he destroys – before pummelling some cops and ending up behind bars. Mr Nice Guy he ain't.

But before the end of the film you'll be rooting for him and his team of rapists, murderers and career criminals as they take on a team of the most corrupt guards imaginable.

What laughs there are are of the blackest kind and the match itself – taking over a third of the running-time – is completely compelling, thanks in no small part to half the cast being former college players, including Reynolds himself who regularly took the field for Florida State. ★★★★ **EC**

THE MEAN MACHINE (2001)

Starring: *Vinnie Jones (Danny Meehan), David Kelly (Doc), David Hemmings (Governor), Ralph Brown (Burton), Vas Blackwood (Massive)*
Director: *Barry Skolnick*
Screenwriters: *Barry Fletcher, Chris Baker, Andrew Day, from the 1974 film by Tracy Keenan Wynn, from a story by Albert S. Ruddy*
15/95 mins./Comedy/Drama/Sport/USA/UK

After disgraced ex-England football captain, Danny 'Mean Machine' Meehan, is sent to prison for assaulting a police officer, he quickly finds that, on the inside, his name counts for nothing. But then he takes control of a cons versus guards football match . . .

Football. It's a funny old game, apparently – full of unbelievable comebacks and last-minute reprieves. Not unlike Vinnie Jones' movie career. After his truly awful turn in *Swordfish*, it seemed that whatever acting talent the lovable lug possessed had well and truly evaporated. Not so. In this enjoyable remake of the 1974 Robert Aldrich American football movie, Jones may be no Burt Reynolds (it's all his own hair, for one thing), but in giving the film a likeable, commanding central presence, he's banged in a 30-yard, extra-time winner.

With Guy Ritchie warming the bench as 'supervising' producer, first-time director Barry Skolnick dons the sheepskin coat and, after an overly gimmicky opening, settles down to create a movie of two halves.

The first is a gritty portrayal of British prison life. This bit leaves no cliche unturned, from the characters – the wily old lag, the fixer, the corrupt governor (a superb performance from David Hemmings' elephantine eyebrows, hovering four feet above his head) – to events (Meehan's first night in solitary, the shiv attack in the showers). It's much the weaker section, although it does allow the excellent supporting cast, including old Ska Films stalwarts Statham and Blackwood, to establish their scene-stealing credentials.

It's in the second half – the football half – where *Mean Machine* really shifts into gear, abandoning all pretence of seriousness. Footie and film have always been unhappy bedfellows, but the boy Skolnick sure can shoot the beautiful game, assisted by the Jones stamp of authenticity.

Its admittedly not saying much, but the climactic 30-minute showdown between guards and cons could be the greatest celluloid soccer game ever – tough, realistic and hilarious. And if *Mean Machine* can't quite match Aldrich's acerbic ferocity, this should be entertaining enough, even if you don't know shit from Ginola. ★★★ **CH**

MEAN STREETS (1973)

Starring: *Robert De Niro (John 'Johnny Boy' Civello), Harvey Keitel (Charlie Cappa), David Proval (Tony DeVienazo), Amy Robinson (Teresa Ronchelli), Richard Romanus (Michael Longo)*
Director: *Martin Scorsese*
Screenwriters: *Martin Scorsese, Mardik Martin, based on a story by Scorsese*
18/107 mins./Drama/Crime/USA

Scorsese's breakout film follows the exploits of small time hood Charlie and his guilt-inspired caretaking of friend and local nutter Johnny Boy.

Originally titled *Season Of The Witch*, *Mean Streets* grew out of an abandoned script that Scorsese revitalised (on the orders of John Cassavetes) into a laboured religious allegory populated with picaresque local characters from his old Lower East Side stomping grounds. He showed it to his girlfriend, Sandy Weintraub, who offered more sage advice: tone down the God-bothering angst and put in more tales from the 'hood.

Mean Streets, the story of Charlie, a small-time wiseguy tortured by Catholic guilt, his loose-cannon best friend Johnny Boy and their coterie of cronies, was written by Scorsese and Mardik Martin cruising the streets of Little Italy in Martin's battered Valiant. Soaking up the familiar pageant with fresh eyes, they captured the flavour of Little Italy, spicing the narrative with incidents drawn from Scorsese's rich store of anecdotes.

It's safe to say that the chief pleasure to be had from revisiting *Mean Streets* is De Niro's performance. A whirlwind of random violence and casual mayhem, Johnny Boy is a perfect study of suicidal recklessness, a species of heedless maniac who, you never doubt, would cheerfully treat welching on debts to the local shylocks as if it were some kind of extreme sport. De Niro, improvising without a net and free from the introspective brooding that marks his later roles (the good ones, at any rate), invests him with equal parts menace and irresistible charm. That takes nothing away from Keitel, of course. He shoulders the film manfully, but as the vessel for Scorsese's religious musings, when they cross the line from heavy to heavy-handed, it's him with whom you lose patience.

Much of it has a rough, documentary feel and yet, like some hellish bordello, its diabolical glow bathing everyone and everything in shades of carnal red, the symbolism is stunning, infinitely more effective than Keitel sticking his hand in the nearest flaming object every time a stripper shakes her goods in his direction.

Scorsese's Little Italy has long gone. Its three small blocks of the Lower East Side, bounded by Elizabeth Street, Mott Street and Mulberry Street, are now a grotesque tourist trap, a theme park of chi-chi coffee shops and overpriced trattorias. Even the bullet holes in the window of Umberto's Clam House, a memento of mob boss Crazy Joe Gallo's last supper, have disappeared. *Mean Streets* takes you back to the days before it got respectable. More importantly, it takes you back to the days before Scorsese got respectable, too. ★★★★★ **SB**

⦿ MEDITERRANEO (1991)

Starring: *Diego Abatantuono (Nicola Lorusso), Claudio Bigagli (Raffaele Montini), Giuseppe Cederna (Antonio Farina), Claudio Bisio (Corrado Noventa)*
Director: *Gabriele Salvatores*
Screenwriter: *Enzo Monteleone*
15/96 mins./Comedy/War/Italy
Awards: *Academy Awards – Best Foreign Language Film*

During World War II, a group of Italian troops are marooned on an Aegean island and fall under the spell of the inhabitants.

Mediterraneo is an ironic, gently amusing charmer, even though its familiar anti-war elements jostle clumsily with its not entirely persuasive case for running away from real life's disappointments.

When a ragtag Italian troop of eight men and a donkey, sent to capture and occupy a remote Aegean isle in 1941, is cut off from Axis authority and all communication for the duration of the war, the hapless conquerors fall under the spell of the enchanting Greek inhabitants. Sex, drugs and bazouki music enhance their liberating idyll, with each of the eight misfits finding something he needs from the obligingly colourful, generous, wise or flagrantly uninhibited islanders.

The gentle lieutenant is put to work restoring the church frescoes, the peasant boys find a frolicsome shepherdess, the frustrated professional soldier discovers political philosophy and a flair for folk dancing, and there is even a perennial escapee, whose bordering-on-tragic antics seem at cross-purposes with the general conviviality.

At its least the film is a splendid advert for Greek island tourism, and even when director Gabriele Salvatores and writer Vincenzo Monteleone's ambitious hippy notions become muddled, there is a nicely wry and bittersweet tone. The affable ensemble playing is pleasing, too, if one can forgive some low-Continental buffoonery, with Diego Abatantuono most effective as the brutish sergeant in transition from thwarted combatant to politicised carer.

And based on a real story, it's less unlikely a parable than one might imagine. ★★★ **AE**

⦿ MEET JOE BLACK (1998)

Starring: *Brad Pitt (Joe Black), Anthony Hopkins (William Parrish), Claire Forlani (Susan Parrish), Jake Weber (Drew), Marcia Gay Harden (Allison Parrish)*
Director: *Martin Brest*
Screenwriters: *Ron Osborn, Jeff Reno, Kevin Wade, Bo Goldman, from the film* Death Takes A Holiday *by Alberto Casella*
12/172 mins./Fantasy/Romance/Drama/USA

Death takes a human form so he can experience life, but then he falls in love . . .

Tipping its good looking head to a brace of current Hollywood vogues – remaking a classic (of sorts) and clocking in almost at a swollen three hours – Martin Brest's puffball metaphysical daydream endeavours for big themes but only delivers pleasant whimsy. The much trimmer (78 minutes) 1934 film *Death Takes A Holiday* is the progenitor, suggesting the curious premise of Death (i.e. the Grim Reaper) taking on human form to dally among humankind for a while. In the original his motive was to discover why he is feared so much, here there seems no more to his arrival than boredom, a chance to sample the delights that a full quota of senses allows him and to hit upon the nearest babe.

Playing the great mortician is a beach blond Brad Pitt, who strains to give him an outlandish Rainman shtick, all clockwork twitches, clucking speech and an attractive wide-eyed vulnerability. He's nabbed the body of a recently deceased lawyer replete with those looks (clever Death) and chosen the ailing billionaire Bill Parrish as his guide on Earth. Then in virtual slow motion, amid a slew of soft-lit New York finery (he's also savvy enough to sample humanity in the comfort zone of the *Masters Of The Universe*), Death takes his holiday. It's a familiar fish-out-of-water spiel – experiencing peanut butter, table manners, corporate wrangles and 'true love' wrapped in a perpetual veil of incredulity – but brimful of comic value. However, we are in post-*Titanic* times and the main matter is a doomed romance. Death, temporarily rechristened Joe Black, falls for Parrish's supine doctor daughter Susan (the gaga Forlani) – she digging his oddball honesty, he swept away in a giddy schoolboy daze. It's tenderly done stuff, all the while nagged by those poignant (un)realities, but achingly long-winded and disguising what ultimately amounts to a peculiarly upmarket spin on necrophilia in an orange-hued soft focus.

The film becomes so obsessed with the heavy-lidded stares of its pretty leads that it completely squanders Hopkins. As beautifully crisp and effortless as ever, he charges events with the true nobility of a soul readying himself for death. The script, though, marginalises his character. When accompanying his illustrious co-star Pitt shines, punctuating his quirky wonderment with flashes of icy darkness if Parrish dares to question the whole deal. Joe Black revealing his true colours.

Meet Joe Black finally cheats on its complications, slipping uncomfortably between the supernatural question marks and any deeper emotional tangles to deliver no more profound a message than to grab life while we can. The reality of all this posturing is simply an overblown romance fused to a far more invigorating comedy of manners, revealing in its leading man a surprising knack for comic timing. At half its length it would have been twice the movie. ★★★ **IN**

⊙ MEET JOHN DOE (1941)

Starring: *Gary Cooper ('John Doe'/Long John Willoughby), Barbara Stanwyck (Ann Mitchell), Edward Arnold (D.B. Norton), Walter Brennan (Colonel), James Gleason (Henry Connell), Spring Byington (Mrs Mitchell), Gene Lockhart (Mayor Lovett), Rod La Rocqua (Ted Sheldon), Irving Bacon (Beany), Regis Toomey (Bert Hansen)*
Director: *Frank Capra*
Screenwriter: *Robert Riskin, based on a story 'The Life And Death Of John Doe' by Robert Presnell, Richard Connell*
U/135 mins./Drama/USA

Newspaper columnist Ann Mitchell invents a letter from 'John Doe', announcing his intent to commit suicide as a protest against injustice. Doe becomes so popular Ann has to find a hobo to play the role. A 'John Doe movement' forms and the newspaper's publisher tries to misuse it to become President.

When he quit Harry Cohn's Columbia, for whom he had made *Mr Deeds Goes To Town* and *Mr Smith Goes To Washington*, Frank Capra – along with regular screenwriter Robert Riskin – tried to play it safe with a third film in an unofficial trilogy about everymen who fall in with America's power-brokers, are exploited and finally turn the tables. This expensive independent production, backed by Warners but with total control invested in Capra, is less satisfactory than the earlier films the director had to fight with Cohn to make, often rambling on where a crass producer would have cut and frankly stuck for an ending.

It's still a fascinating work – though in 1941, it must have been squashed by thematic comparisons with *Citizen Kane* (which also technically outclassed it) and the rapid progress of news from Europe which rendered its Depression-era politics sorely out of date. The marvellous Stanwyck, taking the 'Jean Arthur' role, is sweet, hardboiled, lovestruck, cynical and guilty all at once as the news hen who whips up the storm, and Cooper perhaps overdoes the aw-shucksisms as the harmonica-playing baseball-pitching man of the people – while usually reliable supporting players Walter Brennan (as another hobo) and James Gleason (a cigar-chomping editor) get stuck with the worst patches of the script. However, Edward Arnold is outstanding in quietly evil mode as the businessman who wants to be America's Mussolini, marshalling a private army of motorcycle-riding stormtroopers and orchestrating a vast political rally in the rain that goes horribly awry. ★★★ **KN**

⊙ MEET THE FEEBLES (1989)

Starring the voices of: *Donna Akersten (Samantha the Cat), Stuart Devenie (Sebastian/Dr Quack/Daisy the Cow), Mark Hadlow (Heidi, Barry the Bulldog), Brian Sergent (Wynyard the Frog), Peter Vere-Jones (Bletch/Arfur the Worm)*
Director: *Peter Jackson*
Screenwriters: *Peter Jackson, Danny Mulheron, Stephen Sinclair, Fran Walsh*
18/94 mins./Comedy-horror/NZ

Minutes until call time on *The Fabulous Feebles Variety Hour*, Heidi the Hippo finds out her no-good husband Bletch the Walrus is cheating on her, but that's the least of the cast's problems. Try drug addiction, extortion, potential murder and a rabbit with AIDS.

Long before he became a household genius with the various glories of *The Lord Of The Rings* trilogy, a young, more subversively minded Peter Jackson tried his hand at puppetry. Although, dispel any thoughts of the whacky if wholesome fluff of the Muppets, these threadbare puppets (known as Feebles) are wrecked celebrities on the downward curve of celebrity. This is less satire than borderline anarchy, intent on outrage, capturing Jackson's sneaky desire to shake down social propriety via the medium of badly made felt puppets.

The litany of wrecks has its own sense of wonder. Harry the Hare is afflicted with an STD; cheating Bletch the Walrus runs an XXX video service on the side; Trevor the Rat, a true slimeball, deals drugs; Wynard the Frog, suffering 'Nam flashbacks, is a heroin addict; while singer-songwriter Sebastian the Fox latest tune is entitled Sodomy. As you can tell, we're a long way from both *Seasame Street* and Middle-earth, but the rank obscenity that will adorn their show, carries all of Jackson's skill at creating worlds and then gleefully stripping them bare.

It is very offbeam, even for early-period, gross-out Jackson (*Bad Taste*, *Brain Dead* et al) a cuckoo's nest of bad taste – a style exacerbated by situating the jokes amongst furry critters drawn from the safety zone of kids TV. There is meaning beyond the bodily fluids and rampant alcoholism of these D-list fur-lebrities, the director, ahead of his time, is dismantling the objectification of celebrity. Even so, its derangement has nothing on the puppet-worlds of reality TV. ★★★ **IN**

Movie Trivia:
Peter Jackson (born 1961)

Who he is: New Zealand's biggest export. Twisted early films, followed by mainstream success with the global smash-hits that were *The Lord Of The Rings* trilogy. Director most likely to become the next Spielberg.

Hallmarks: Attention to detail; storytelling skill; wry humour; ability to inject pathos into fantasy; impactful effects even on a small budget; seemingly boundless imagination; passion for filmmaking.

If you see one movie, see: *The Lord Of The Rings: The Fellowship Of The Ring* (2001)

⊙ MEET THE FOCKERS (2004)

Starring: *Robert De Niro (Jack Byrnes), Ben Stiller (Greg Focker), Dustin Hoffman (Bernie Focker), Barbra Streisand (Mrs Focker), Blythe Danner (Dina Byrnes), Teri Polo (Pam Byrnes), Own Wilson (Kevin Rawley)*
Director: *Jay Roach*
Screenwriters: *Jim Herzfeld, John Hamburg, based on a story by Herzfeld and Mark Hyman, characters by Greg Glienna, Mary Ruth Clarke*
12A/115 mins./Comedy/USA

Having met his fiancée's parents in *Meet the Parents*, the perennially unlucky Greg Focker introduces her family to his parents. How will ex-CIA man Jack Byrnes cope with the bumbling Mr Focker and his sex therapist wife?

They say you can't choose your family, but Jay Roach has done a superb job in picking his *familias horribilis* for this follow up to 2000's surprise smash, *Meet The Parents*. With De Niro already in place as the surly, paranoid father-of-fiancée, the mix is enriched with the dream team of Hoffman and Streisand as Greg's all-too-easygoing mom 'n' pop. Laden with Oscars, its hard to imagine a more able team. So it's an immense shame that their collective talents are squandered on what amounts to a disappointing retread.

Despite that little teasing comment from De Niro about meeting Greg's folks, *Meet The Parents* didn't particularly call out for a sequel, finishing with family tensions resolved. So in order to build any kind of momentum for a follow up, the screenwriters have to pick apart the conclusion of *Parents*, so that De Niro and Stiller end up at odds once again, this time with

De Niro suspecting Greg of hiding a secret past. But whereas in the first, comedy was derived from Stiller being the lone voice of reason in a surreal household, this pitches De Niro as the fish out of water. It's a concept which fails to illicit laughs, given that his character is an unlikeable self-important bigot who only works when torturing others, rather than being subjected to it himself.

With its broad concept, *Fockers* lives or dies by its set-pieces and disappointingly there's nothing in this to rival anything from its older sibling. Ripe comedy situations are raised in the script – Streisand's sex therapy classes for seniors, Hoffman and De Niro's opposing politics, a party with the extended Focker family – yet none is exploited to its full potential. The party, particularly, could have been an excuse for knowing cameos from a few members of the Stiller Frat Pack, but instead a couple of the Focker family are merely namechecked in an embarrassingly lame gag.

A few laughs are salvaged due to the sheer quality of the talent present. Hoffman enlivens his role by playing it as a cheeky schoolboy trapped in an elderly man's body, while Streisand keeps her potential caricature on the right side of bawdy, happy not to steal the limelight. It's Stiller and De Niro who sadly come off worst, doing their best with half-hearted gags yet being upstaged by a foul-mouthed baby ... ★★ **H O'H**

Ⓓ MEET THE PARENTS (2000)

Starring: *Robert De Niro (Jack Byrnes), Ben Stiller (Greg Focker), Blythe Danner (Dina Byrnes), Teri Polo (Pam Byrnes), Own Wilson (Kevin Rawley)*
Director: *Jay Roach*
Screenwriters: *Jim Herzfeld, John Hamburg, based on a story by Herzfeld and Mark Hyman and the 1992 screenplay by Greg Glienna, Mary Ruth Clarke*
12/108 mins./Comedy/USA

On the verge of proposing to his lovely girlfriend Pam, Greg Focker is faced with one final hurdle: meeting her parents. And when it transpires that daddy, Jack Byrnes, is a retired CIA spycatcher masquerading as a florist, the weekend from hell commences.

Great comedy is built around shared recognition. No matter how ludicrous the antics on screen become, there's something in there that really makes you itch because you've been there too. And there isn't a hopeful romantic the world over who hasn't experienced the trauma of meeting the parents. About this universal premise has been woven one of the year's most deliciously funny movies.

Stiller is a master of the put-upon dweeb, and lumbered with the surname Focker (now that's funny writing!) and the less-than-manly vocation of nursing, he might as well have 'victim' tattooed on his forehead. And there's nothing Jack hates more than weakness.

De Niro's beautifully controlled performance as a militaristic control freak out to terrify all potential suitors is the comic heart of the movie. Melding the obvious self-parody of *Analyse This* (1999) with the intuitive sense of reality he brings to his straight roles, his delivery is lethal. Who better than the former *Raging Bull* (1980) to stare balefully at the pathetic Greg, as he hooks him up to an antique polygraph machine he just happens to keep in his office?

Roach, having already proven himself as one of Hollywood's keenest comedy directors with the *Austin Powers* movies, handles it all with the steady fervour of great farce. Jokes build from a distance, with hints of catastrophe waiting to happen (a sewage tank, Jack's mother's ashes, flammable garden ornaments), and when the punchlines explode, they lift the seemingly predictable outcome to torturous unforeseen extremes. Quite literally the world collapses around Greg as he flounders to make good on the agony he's unwittingly wrought. And even as events resolve themselves in a rather flat love matters' patter, there is still a gem of a last laugh to finish it all off.

With current comedy obsessed with oh-so-clever ironic gestures and tricksy pastiche, *Meet The Parents'* dedication to consistent, straightforward belly laughs is totally refreshing. ★★★★ **IN**

Ⓓ MELINDA AND MELINDA (2004)

Starring: *Radha Mitchell (Melinda), Jonny Lee Miller (Lee), Chloe Sevigny (Laurel), Will Ferrell (Hobie), Amanda Peet (Susan)*
Director: *Woody Allen*
Screenwriter: *Woody Allen*
12A/100 mins./Comedy/Drama/USA

Over dinner in a New York eaterie, two writers discuss an anecdote that embodies the possibility for both tragedy and comedy. Centred on a single character, Melinda, two interpretations of the same anecdote are employed.

The film begins with the most explicit amplification of the dynamic that has consumed Allen's creativity – the pull between tragedy and comedy. *Melinda And Melinda* tackles these seemingly polar opposites head on, combining the straight-up laughs of 'The Early, Funny Stuff' with the gravitas of 'The Later, Serious Works', creating Allen's funniest, most affecting movie for some time.

Part of the thrill here is that, in many ways, *Melinda And Melinda* is a melting pot of Allen's best work, touching base in particular with *Manhattan*, *Broadway Danny Rose* and *Hannah And Her Sisters*. But if *M&M* negotiates typical Woody territory – the vagaries of romance, breakdowns in communication ('Of course we communicate, but can we not talk about it?'), identity and intimacy – it does it with a sharpness that's been absent in the *Deconstructing Harry/Anything Else* era.

The ace in the hole is the dual storytelling device. In the tragedy strand, a highly strung Melinda bundles into the life of an old friend and her alcoholic actor husband (Jonny Lee Miller, the film's weak link) and gets involved with composer Ellis Moonsong, who in turn forms a bond with Sevigny. In the comedy take, a free-spirited Melinda bundles into the life of neighbour/filmmaker Susan and her husband Hobie, the latter becoming besotted with Melinda. The comedy syringes Allen's Chekovian tendencies while the 'tragedy' grounds the broader elements, lending the movie a unique, compassionate tang. This may all sound overly gimmicky, but it isn't. As both director and screenwriter, Allen doesn't allow the stories to interact and mirror each other in slavishly programmatic ways. Instead, the events and motifs of one story (including a genie-like lamp) are judiciously placed and spread out to trigger knowing recognition in the other. Also, working for the first time with cinematographer Vilmos Zsigmond, Allen wisely avoids giving each story a distinct look, further underlining the duality of tragedy and comedy.

From Sevigny and Peet down to the smaller roles (such as Vinessa Shaw as a man-eating Republican), Allen confirms his place among America's best directors of women. In particular, he draws out a terrific turn from Radha Mitchell. The contrast from the neurotic Melinda to the open, carefree Melinda couldn't be more beautifully judged; it's the kind of performance that would get awards recognition at any other time of the year.

Joining the list of wannabe Woodys such as John Cusack (*Bullets Over Broadway*), Kenneth Branagh (*Celebrity*) and Jason Biggs (*Anything Else*), Will Ferrell swaps Anchorman nuttiness for affability as Allen's stock-in-trade nebbish hero, this time an actor who plays every character with a limp. In the tragedy take, meanwhile, Ejiofor's big-hearted composer lends a warm centre as the tale unfurls. 'Life is messy,' he observes, as the emotional strands becomes more and more knotted. But *Melinda And Melinda* makes it perfectly clear why it's always worth unravelling life's tangles. ★★★★ **IF**

⓪ MEMENTO (2000)

Starring: *Guy Pearce (Leonard), Carrie-Anne Moss (Natalie), Joe Pantoliano (Teddy Gammell), Mark Boone Junior (Burt), Russ Fega (Waiter)*
Director: *Christopher Nolan*
Screenwriter: *Christopher Nolan, based on the short story 'Memeto Mori' by Jonathan Nolan*
15/108 mins./Mystery/Thriller/USA

Former insurance investigator Leonard has short-term memory loss. He can't remember anything or anyone from only moments before. He knows who he is, and can remember everything up to the attack that killed his wife and left him in this condition but everything else is a haze . . .

For once you don't have to worry about giving away the ending, since this story starts there, with protagonist Leonard killing a man, and takes us backwards, scene by scene, to the beginning. Or rather, it's a beginning of a particular sequence of events. Although Harold Pinter did this in *Betrayal*, this is still something special, imaginative, and challenging, Christopher Nolan's exploration of memory and time toying with narrative and structure.

Reversed scenes overlap slightly so we know where we are, and there is crucial exposition stylishly conveyed, in black-and-white links of Leonard getting his bearings, revising his mementos and recalling the past as the story gathers momentum and takes both chilling and laugh-out-loud turns.

It's based on a short story by Nolan's brother, Jonathan, and the sneaky boys get the audience to enjoy speculating on questions about reality, the workings of the mind, self-awareness, identity and time, all within the context of a compelling murder mystery.

The actors do a great job messing with perceptions, with both Moss' enigmatic femme and Pantoliano's impatient sidekick – new to Leonard every time he encounters them – swinging from friend to foe and back again. Pearce is remarkably good, holding this together with an intent blankness across which flicker bewilderment, frustration, despair and fury.

Just try to remember that everything we think we know about Leonard – perceived from his clothes, his car, his cash, his compulsion, and his moral certainty – is as reliable as everything we think we know about ourselves. ★★★★ **AE**

⓪ MEMOIRS OF A GEISHA (2005)

Starring: *Ziyi Zhang (Chiyo/Sayuri), Ken Watanabe (The Chairman), Koji Yakusho (Nobu), Pumpkin (Youki Kudoh), Li Gong (Hatsumomo), Kaori Momoi (Mother)*
Director: *Rob Marshall*
Screenwriter: *Robin Swincord, based on the book by Arthur Golden*
12A/145 mins./Drama/Romance/USA

Awards: *Academy Awards – Best Art Direction, Best Cinematography, Best Costume, BAFTA – Anthony Asquith Award for Music, Best Cinematography, Best Costume, Golden Globes – Best Score*

Sayuri remembers how she was sold into servitude and misery as a child, trained and moulded by her mentor Mameha into a celebrated geisha, and sustained against both her rival Hatsumomo's treachery and the vicissitudes of war by her love for a man she could not have.

Among the 1,001 things we learn in Rob Marshall's vividly instructive movie is that 'geisha' actually means artist, these select women having been schooled in music, dance and witty conversation. Not to mention negotiating cobblestone streets in eight-inch platform shoes without tripping over their exquisite kimonos. But they still emerge from this fastidious picture as elegant sex slaves, personalities and desires ruthlessly suppressed.

Arthur Golden's phenomenal bestseller of life and longing in a geisha house at the end of a golden era (the 1930s) was inevitably destined for a high-toned screen adaptation, and Steven Spielberg was long set to direct before competing projects took him off. So the assignment went to Marshall, hot off *Chicago* and benefitting from a big-time production (from a picture-perfect geisha district constructed in California to Yo-Yo Ma cello solos). Meanwhile, chick-lit screenwriter Swicord negotiates the contemplative text by providing Sayuri with a sorrowful narration to chronicle women behaving badly to one other.

If geishas used to be the supermodels of Japan, Zhang's head-turning Sayuri is Giselle, Yeoh's cool, ultra-professional Mameha is Tyra and Gong's fragile, volatile diva Hatsumomo is Naomi. There's a definite catwalk-cum-*Chicago* sequence when Sayuri performs a strangely avant-garde dance number at the auction for her virginity – white-faced, spotlit, hair-tossing. All the actresses are wonderful, including mercenary house 'Mother' Kaori Momoi and young Suzuka Ohgo as Chiyo, turned into Sayuri after a *Little Orphan Annie* childhood with just one happy memory (being treated to an ice by Watanabe's kindly bon vivant) to inspire lifelong devotion and keep hope alive.

But is it just us, or is anyone else bothered by casting Chinese actresses – extremely gorgeous and accomplished though they most certainly are – as iconic Japanese women? Like there's no difference. (Rumour has it *Lost*'s Yunjin Kim turned down a role because she is, hello, Korean.) It's sooo Hollywood, as if no one will notice or care. Gorgeous and accomplished Japanese actresses must be spitting nails.

As for the life-changing intrusion of the Second World War, blink and you'll miss it. It's a carefully apolitical inclusion there solely to explain the arrival of gum-chewing Yanks who have trouble grasping Japanese culture. Ironically. ★★★ **AE**

⓪ MEMORIES OF UNDERDEVELOPMENT (MEMORIAS DEL SUBDESARROLLO) (1968)

Starring: *Sergio Carmona Mendoyo (Sergio Corrieri), Daisy Granados (Elena), Eslinda Nunez (Noemi), Omar Valdes (Pablo), Rene de la Cruz (Elena's Brother)*
Director: *Tomas Gutiérrez Alea*
Screenwriter: *Tomas Gutierrez Alea, based on the novel by Edmundo Desnoes*
18/97 mins./Drama/Cuba

Having seen his family go into exile, Cuban bourgeois Sergio begins keeping a diary and takes himself a teenage working-class mistress, Elena, as he seeks to avoid coming to terms with the realities of Castro's Revolution.

Tomas Gutiérrez Alea's fifth film was adapted from a 1962 novel by Edmundo Desnoes. As with many of Alea's features, it centred on a character out of step with his times and raised issues that suggested that the 1959 Revolution was still very much a work in progress. However, by raising the dilemma of whether Sergio should remain solitary or express solidarity with his compatriots, Alea gave the picture a dialectical power that was absent from more prosaic pieces of state-sponsored propaganda.

This is one of the most challenging political films ever made. Alea isn't content with presenting both sides of the argument, he also adopts a complex narrative structure that approximates Sergio's subjectivity, while simultaneously implying the more objective communality of his Havana neighbours.

The use of documentary footage and other archival material chronicles events between the exodus that followed the 1961 Bay of Pigs crisis and the ensuing year's missile stand-off between Kennedy and Khrushchev. However, Alea frequently presents these images from Sergio's perspective and, thus, emphasises his status as an outsider who lacks the courage to follow his family into exile, while retaining the arrogance of his class – hence his continuing to reside in a comfortable apartment while living off the profits of his property and his attempt to exploit Elena, in much the same way that America had sought to colonise Cuba.

Moreover, Alea exposes Sergio's intellectual superficiality by demonstrating how his Western attitudes and affectations distance him from the true Cuban character and it's Sergio's underdevelopment as both a citizen and a human being, as much as the state of the nation in the aftermath of the Batista regime, that provides the film's focus.

Memories bears the influence of neo-realism (which Alea had experienced at first hand in the 1950s), the dialectical Marxism of the Soviet montagists and the filmic audacity of the nouvelle vague. But it also typifies Alea's belief that cinema had a duty to criticise society, as unless its failings were explored they could never be rectified. ★★★★ **DP**

MEMPHIS BELLE (1990)

Starring: *Matthew Modine (Capt. Dennis Dearborn), John Lithgow (Colonel Bruce Derringer), Eric Stoltz (Danny Daly), Sean Astin (Richard 'Rascal' Moore), Harry Connick Jr (Clay Busby), Tate Donovan (Phil Rosenthal), DB Sweeney (Phil Rosenthal), Billy Zane (Val Kozlowski), Jane Horrocks (Faith)*
Director: *Michael Caton-Jones*
Screenwriter: *Monte Merrick*
PG/107 mins./War/Drama/UK

During the Second World War the crew of an American B-17 bomber prepare to fly their final mission over Germany.

Michael Caton-Jones' hymn to WWII heroics dramatises an American B-17 Bomber crew, who after surviving twenty-four flights are assigned on one final mission over Germany before they can all go home.

Based on the real-life combat missions of the Flying Fortress The Memphis Belle, which featured in an Anglo-American documentary in 1943, this provided something for everyone – gung-ho action, fit young men in uniform (the cast provided plentiful poster fodder at the time) and a touch of nostalgia. Some of the footage shot for the documentary is incorporated into this film to give it a touch of realism.

On the ground, the paper thin characterisations do little to grab but things really take off during the drama filled sortie, complete with stirring shots of the aircraft in flight, numerous thrills and spills and a strong sense of camaraderie evoked by the likeable cast. Harry Connick Jr's crooning is even shoe-horned into the plot, but stealing the show is Billy Zane as a medic who isn't quite what he seems.

The film was cut slightly on video release to tone down the language. ★★★ **WT**

MEN IN BLACK (1997)

Starring: *Tommy Lee Jones (Agent K), Will Smith (Agent J), Linda Fiorentino (Agent L), Vincent D'Onofrio (Edgar), Rip Torn (Chief Zed)*
Director: *Barry Sonnenfeld*
Screenwriter: *Ed Solomon, based on the comic book by Lowell Cunningham*
PG/93 mins./Comedy/Sci-fi/Action/USA

Awards – *Academy Awards – Best Makeup, Empire Awards – Best Film*

Two men who keep an eye on aliens in New York City must try to save the world after the aliens threaten to blow it up.

Comedy and Sci-fi have never been happy bedfellows. Han Solo may have been a dab hand at a passing quip and E.T. could gurgle on cue, but on the whole, sci-fi has always taken itself a bit seriously (there's hardly a slew of choice rib-ticklers in the frosty dystopias of *Blade Runner* or *Alien*). It takes the bona fide black comic arts of *Addams Family*-helmer Sonnenfeld, and a quite miraculously fabulous teaming of Tommy Lee Jones with Will Smith to buck the trend.

It's more of a complete reversal, this alien-bashing B-movie comedy is the rock'n'roll cinema experience of the summer. It's sci-fi and it's funny. Really funny. Based on a little-seen *Malibu* comic, the theme is a trippy twist on McCarthy paranoia as an ultra-secret government agency; jet-black suits, impenetrable Ray-Bans as standard (hence Men In Black) round up the illegal aliens hanging around Planet Earth. Aliens as in bug-eyed, slime-dolloping visitors from outer space. In this case with the joyous help of the creature-cooking talents of Rick Baker, they come flippered, polypoid, micro-sized, dog-shaped, and, particularly in the cranky form of a giant interplanetary cockroach with a bad attitude, bent for much of the film into Vincent D'Onofrio's human cossie.

But as showy as the 'visitors' are (and D'Onofno's gross big-bug getting riled whenever humans splat his insect buddies is inspired ugliness) the film rests on the actors and their crackling dialogue.

Yes, this is a big budget event movie not relying on its effects. It's the unexpected chemistry between seen-it-all Agent K (Jones) and whipper-snapping new recruit Agent J (Smith, clearly cast for all the Will Smith 'vibe' he can muster) that makes *MIB* sing. Trailing the malevolent roach, through a bemused New York, their cool doesn't slip for a moment and a groovy buddy-buddy double act of wise-cracking, deadpannery and big gunned science-friction soars.

Sonnenfeld keeps it all bubbling along with a vibrant, comic book buzz. Which at times does grate, he could pause for some better exposition, perhaps try his hand at developing the characters beyond the snappy 60s TV spy-cool riff and give all the weird concoctions a chance to breathe (how rare it is to cite a film for being too short). And it doesn't even pretend to have depth. But with the added bonuses of Rip Torn as a Mr Waverly-esque commander (Agent Z, resident at the alien-popping techno headquarters-cum-immigration control), the dead sexy Linda Fiorentino dragged into the chase, Danny Elfman's hip tunes and the best hardware of any movie, anytime, anywhere, there are no excuses for *MIB* avoidance. ★★★★ **IN**

Tagline
Protecting the Earth from the scum of the universe.

Movie Trivia: Men In Black

Danny DeVito, Sly Stallone, George Lucas and Steven Spielberg all play 'known aliens' in the movie. Linda Fiorentino won her part in a poker game with director Barry Sonnenfeld — but refused to do any nude scenes. Will Smith was convinced to star as J by his wife, Jada Pinkett Smith, after the role had already been turned down by David Schwimmer and Chris O'Donnell.

MEN IN BLACK II (2002)

Starring: *Tommy Lee Jones (Agent K), Will Smith (Agent J), Lara Flynn Boyle (Serleena), Rosario Dawson (Laura), Tony Shaulhoub (Jeebs)*
Director: *Barry Sonnenfeld*
Screenwriters: *Robert Gordon, Barry Fanola, from a story by Gordon, based on the comic book characters by Lowell Cunningham*
PG/93 mins./Comedy/Sci-fi/Action/USA

Jay is now MiB's top agent monitoring alien activity on Earth. But when an old menace, Serleena, returns in search of the hidden Light of Zartha, the Earth's very existence is threatened.

So *Malibu Comics'* finest, the boys in black, are came after a five-year absence. It doesn't seem as if they've been away so long. On the one

TOP10 Movie Power Ballads

1 My Heart Will Go On
Culprit: *Celine Dion*
Film: *Titanic*
Sample lyric: *Neaaaaaaaaaaaar, faaaaaaaaaar, whereeeeeever you are, you are here in my heart and my heart will go onnnnnn and onnnnn . . .*

2 Everything I Do (I Do It For You)
Culprit: *Bryan Adams*
Film: *Robin Hood: Prince of Thieves*
Sample lyric: *There's no love, like your love / And no other could give more love / There's no way, and there's nothing / All the time, all the way.*

3 I Will Always Love You
Culprit: *Whitney Houston*
Film: *The Bodyguard*
Sample lyric: *IiiiiiiiiiiiIIiiiiiii will always love yoooooo00000uuuu*

4 Take My Breath Away
Culprit: *Berlin*
Film: *Top Gun*
Sample lyric: *Through the hourglass I saw you / Each time you slipped away / When the mirror crashed I called you, and turned to hear you say / If only for today / I am unafraid*

5 Show Me Heaven
Culprit: *Moira McKee*
Film: *Days Of Thunder*
Sample lyric: *Hold my hand, don't let me fall / You've such amazing grace / I never felt this waaaaaaay.*

6 I Believe I Can Fly
Culprit: *R. Kelly*
Film: *Space Jam*
Sample lyric: *I used to think that I could not go on / And life was nothing but an awful song / But now I know the meaning of true love*

7 I Don't Want To Miss A Thing
Culprit: *Aerosmith*
Film: *Armageddon*
Sample lyric: *Cause even when I dream of you / The sweetest dream will never do / I'd still miss you baby*

8 (I've Had) The Time Of My Life
Culprit: *Jennifer Warnes and Bill Medley*
Film: *Dirty Dancing*
Sample lyric: *With my body and soul, I want you more than you'll ever know / So we'll just let it go / Don't be afraid, to lose controoooooolIllll.*

9 How Do I Live
Culprit: *Trisha Yearwood*
Film: *Con Air*
Sample lyric: *You're my world, my heart, my soul / If you ever leave / Baby you would take away everything good in my life.*

10 Love Is All Around
Culprit: *Wet Wet Wet*
Film: *Four Weddings And A Funeral*
Sample lyric: *I feel it in my fingers / I feel it in my toes / Your love is all around me / And so the feeling grows*

hand, that's a tribute. They were – and are – such sarcastically engaging characters that only a dour party pooper could seriously object to stepping out with them.

They're still looking mighty fine as they go about their business defending the galaxy from alien SFX supremo Rick Baker's ooky, many-tentacled, many-toothed thingies (being humanoid-centric is not a charge that can be levelled at this latex-dependent, wondrously visualised sci-fi franchise).

On the other hand, the decidedly sketchy script is what you'd expect from a more rushed job. It's as if all those other films Smith and Jones have made in the meantime – and the threatened Hollywood strikes that postponed production further – had not given the undeniably clever Sonnenfeld enough time to develop anything more than a bizarre combination of wit, encores of japes from the original film, and some faintly desperate silliness.

Perhaps that is asking too much. As sequels go, this is never less than cute; although we do find it slightly embarrassing that Frank the Pug (promoted from his previous diplomatic status to Jay's latest partner) sitting in the car singing – oh, you've guessed – 'Who Let The Dogs Out?' should make us giggle quite so much as it does.

This is not to suggest there aren't some superbly ridiculous and wickedly twisted jests: a 600-foot subway-swallowing worm named Jeffrey; the return of the large-living 'Worm Guys'; Kay's working environment at the U.S. Post Office. And when our men follow the cryptic trail of clues Kay left for himself, in case he forgot where he put the Light Of Zartha, there's a quite fantastic, sensationally funny find in a train station locker.

It also ends on a brilliant sight gag that's as philosophically unnerving as the original film's punchline. Jones and Smith (and the always welcome Rip Torn as unflappable Zed) are naturally the most fun. As for the rest, Flynn Boyle disproves the Duchess Of Windsor's infamous dictate that you can never be too thin, but gives suitably camp seductive villainy to her monster in the borrowed form of a lingerie model.

Head-sprouting Jeebs, the talking dog and the chain-smoking, martini-swilling Worm Guys do their things (again). But the tentative romance between lonely Jay and waitress-witness Laura is a non-starter; not surprising, really, given the hectic under-90-minutes-including-the-lengthy-credits remit, during which the rather more pressing matters of foiling Serleena's MIB HQ hostage siege and saving the Earth unfurl. ★★★ **CW**

MEN WITH GUNS (1997)

Starring: *Federico Luppi (Dr Fuentes), Damian Delgado (Domingo), Dan Rivera Gonzalez (Conejo), Tania Cruz (Graciela), Damian Alcazar (Padre Portillo), Mandy Patinkin (Andrew)*
Director: *John Sayles*
Screenwriter: *John Sayles*
15/127 mins./Drama/USA

A doctor travels through his native unspecified South American country slowly realising the extent of the political atrocities rife in his land.

With the possible exception of the Coen brothers, John Sayles is the most consistently interesting indie filmmaker in America today. His latest is a challenging political drama shot entirely in Spanish. Though failing to scale the pinnacles reached by 1996's *Lone Star*, it is nonetheless an absorbing, thoughtful and thoroughly rewarding watch.

Inspired by Francisco Goldman's novel *The Long Night Of The White Chickens*, this centres on Humberto Fuentes, a distinguished, idealistic doctor who decides to travel through an unnamed South American country to hook up with former students working in impoverished villages. During his road trip, Fuentes encounters an assortment of characters – a young boy, a gaudy American tourist, a soldier-turned-terrorist and a defrocked priest – and witnesses the government-sanctioned atrocities that have ruined the heart of his country. Gradually, Fuentes' naivete is transformed into political awareness.

Densely textured and always engaging, the film touches base with many recurrent Sayles ideas; the (impossible) search for truth, the fluid relationship between past and present and the importance of myth and storytelling. Moreover, the film is shot through with the director's compassionate humanism – two political terrorists discussing the merits of various ice creams far outstrips Tarantino in the trivial conversation stakes – finding a warm, distinguished centre in Luppi's increasingly disillusioned doctor.

Occasionally the story meanders and the non-specific locale blunts the political pointedness. Yet Sayles creates a yarn that is involving and genuinely surprising. In a movie world in which plots, characters and conclusions are spottable from frame one, such an offbeam intelligent approach provides a refreshing antidote. ★★★★ **IF**

MENACE II SOCIETY (1993)

Starring: *Jada Pinkett (Ronnis), Tyrin Turner (Caine), Larenz Tate (O-Dog), Charles R. Dutton (Mr Butler), Bill Duke (Detective), Samuel L. Jackson (Tat Lawon)*
Directors: *Albert Hughes, Allen Hughes*
Screenwriters: *Albert Hughes, Allen Hughes, from their story*
18/97 mins./Crime/Drama/USA

A young street hustlers tries, and fails, to get away from life in the ghetto.

Following *True Romance* and *Bad Lieutenant*, this is the third in what is fast becoming a regular series of movies back from the dead – films which were not granted a video certificate because they topped some ambiguous violence quota, but were then given one once the furore died down. In many ways *Menace* is the most unfair recipient of such treatment since the Hughes brothers are here slamming home a candidly anti-violence message, depicting the daily trigger-happy run-ins of South Central L.A. in all their senseless, shocking desperation. Tumbling late into the ghetto genre, this supreme example of the type is a cut above the rest care of its visceral pseudo-documentary style and passion for its subject.

The central character is Caine, young, unsure of where his head lies, caught between the need to make a better life for himself and remaining loyal to the often lethal street life of, as the script puts it, 'America's nightmare: young, black and doesn't give a fuck'. With sharp in-yer-face episodes of this bang-bang philosophy – in a jaw-dropping opening sequence Caine and his psychotic buddy Dog are caught on a security camera blasting a shopkeeper foolish enough to complain – the film studies the tragic way in which the patterns of violence are mirrored from generation to generation. Here black children are taught to hold a gun before they can ride a bike. So realistic and focused is the Hughes' direction that it is not inconceivable that their camera has merely shifted downtown to sample the daily toil. The acting is like a whiplash, hard and gritty, yet, especially with Turner's floundering Caine, touching upon a fierce emotional core while the soundtrack blares out the requisite raps to the stomach-pounding beat of gunfire.

Granted, the expletive-spilling dialogue is often utterly incomprehensible and the episodic structure makes the film feel uneven, but the Hughes pack more punch into their raw 97 minutes than a catalogue of Spike Lee or John Singleton movies. ★★★★ **IN**

⓯ MEPHISTO (1981)

Starring: *Klaus Maria Brandauer (Hendrick Hoefgen), Krystana Janda (Barbara Bruckner), Idiko Bansagi (Nicoletta von Niebuhr), Karin Boyd (Juliette Martens), Rolf Hoppe (The General)*
Director: *Istvan Szabo*
Screenwriters: *Istvan Szabo, Peter Dobai, based on the novel by Klaus Mann*
15/144 mins./Drama/West Germany

Awards: *Academy Awards – Best Foreign Language Film*

Refusing to follow his family into exile, actor Hendrik Hoefgen remains in his fascist homeland and, through the patronage of The General, he secures unprecedented prestige until he finally realises the nature of the pact he has made with the evil regime.

Mephisto is based on a 1936 *roman à clef* by Klaus Mann, whose brother-in-law (and rumoured lover), Gustaf Gründgens had accepted the patronage of Luftwaffe chief Hermann Göring to become one of the most celebrated stage and screen actors in Nazi Germany. Gründgens (who is best known for playing the underworld kingpin in Fritz Lang's *M*, 1931) was later exonerated by the Allies and allowed to resume his career in both the Federal and Democratic republics and, ironically, he even played Faust in a 1960 production.

His Mephistophelean plight formed the first part of Istvan Szabo's Central European trilogy, which was completed by *Colonel Redl* and *Hanussen*. However, Szabo has also subsequently explored the nature of artistic collusion in *Taking Sides*, which considered the case of Hitler's favourite conductor, Leon Furtwängler.

Thanks to cinematographer Lajos Koltai and art director Jozsef Romvari, Szabo brilliantly recreates the decadent worlds of the cinema/theatre and the inner-circle of the ruling elite in the Weimar and Nazi periods. But the film's morality is a little too easy, as it remains on the side of the angels in setting up Hendrik Hoefgen for his fall. Moreover, Klaus Maria Brandauer is restricted to a surface characterisation that never allows us to see whether Hoefgen has genuine talent (which Gründgens most certainly did) or whether he is simply a complacent pawn in a propagandist game. Consequently, his consistent melodramatics rob his assisting in black mistress Juliette Martens (Karin Boyd)'s escape of any heroism and his final realisation of his folly of truly affecting pathos.

This is mainly due to the fact that Szabo sought to make Hoefgen an everyman, whose weakness could recur in anyone with a taste for flattery and the limelight. However, it also owed something to the fact that *Mephisto* was an international co-production and the need for some accessible universality deprived the film of its specificity of focus and compromised its integrity. Despite (or perhaps because of) this concession, it still won the Academy Award for Best Foreign Film. **★★★ DP**

⓯ THE MESSENGER: THE STORY OF JOAN OF ARC (1999)

Starring: *Milla Jovovich (Joan of Arc), Dustin Hoffman (The Conscience), Faye Dunaway (Yolande D'Aragon), John Malkovich (Charles VII), Vincent Cassel (Gilles de Rais)*
Director: *Luc Besson*
Screenwriters: *Luc Besson, Andrew Birkin*
15/160 mins./Drama/History/France

From the cradle to the flames – the turbulent life and times of a 15th century heroine turned heroic.

High on bombast, low on subtlety, Luc Besson's character study of the iconic French saviour/nutter (delete where applicable) was never going to be an exercise in nuance and profundity. So why the American press ran it so ragged remains somewhat of a mystery; for while it does have some misjudged moments and – quelle surprise – a lack of genuine substance, it is glorious, intoxicating, intermittently powerful fun. Besson perfectly invokes the 15th-century world, then explores it with all the flair and eye candy he last reserved for a futuristic New York.

The film traces Joan's ascendancy from peasant girl (supposedly infused with 'His' will), to leading the French army into battle at Orleans, to subsequently being put on trial for heresy and sorcery, but Jovovich struggles to find the requisite depth. While she more than cuts it as a short-haired banshee battling the (stereotypically oafish) British, she never looks believable portraying a character wrestling with the responsibility of undertaking God's bidding, coming across more like a petulant school kid than a tortured soul. As if to counterbalance her inexperience, Besson rounds the cast out with heavyweights: the eminently regal Malkovich as the Dauphin, who abuses Joan's loyalty for political gain; an under-used Faye Dunaway as a scheming royal; and a black-clad Hoffman, who is used to bold effect as Joan's conscience.

But, as ever, the real star of a Luc Besson film is Besson himself. Alternating stunningly surreal images – the opening scenes of Joan's early village life have a dream-like quality that kidnaps the breath – with the visceral virtuosity and exhilaration of the war scenes, the French master is on great form. His creativity particularly extends to weaponry, which never skimps on the gore or invention: witness fantastic moments of soldiers being felled like skittles by giant cement balls rolled down olde worlde chutes. If the final burning at the stake setpiece feels rushed and small scale, it doesn't matter. *Messenger* may be cartoonlike, it may opt for crudity over complexity, but, at its best, it is moviemaking on the grandest scale. And, in times of dialogue dominated storytelling that is surely something to be truly cherished. ★★★ **IF**

⓯ METALLICA: SOME KIND OF MONSTER (2004)

Starring: *as themselves: James Hetfield, Lars Ulrich, Kirk Hammett, Bob Rock*
Directors: *Joe Berlinger, Bruce Sinofsky*
15/141 mins./Music/Documentary/USA

The world's most successful heavy metal band is in crisis. The bassist has resigned, the lead singer's battling alcohol, the drummer's despised by the fans and, amid bitter in-fighting, they reconvene for a new album . . .

The captivating sight of Madonna slobbishly supping soup while chatting subserviently to her father in 1991's warts 'n' all documentary *In Bed With Madonna* showed that, despite elevating celebrities to godlike status, we have rapacious curiosity for their apparent normality. Well, *In Bed With* . . . seems transparently stage-managed compared to this bullshit-free glimpse of a world-class rock act facing implosion.

Ostensibly chronicling the making of the *St. Anger* album, there's little music on hand. Instead, a fractured 'family' faces, via therapy, every embarrassing detail in order to rebuild itself, while this group of middle-aged men struggle to maintain their firebrand ideologies.

We witness bassist Jason Newsted's departure, singer Hetfield's unannounced 11-month sojourn into rehab, the PR disaster of drummer Ulrich's war with Napster . . .

Frankly, the band doesn't come off well. Hetfield's a control freak, Ulrich's a hypocrite and guitarist Hammett is pathetically non-confrontational. Yet the doc isn't a hatchet job, rather encouraging sympathy by capturing plenty of heart-breaking sadness. **★★★★ WL**

m

METROPOLIS (1927)

Starring: *Alfred Abel (Johhan Fredersen), Gustav Frohlich (Freder Fredersen), Brigitte Helm (Maria/The Machine Man/Death/The Seven Deadly Sins), Fritz Rasp (Slim), Theodor Loos (Josaphat/Joseph)*
Director: *Fritz Lang*
Screenwriters: *Fritz Lang, Thea von Harbou, from von Harbou's novel*
PG/210 mins. (premiere version)/119 mins. (DVD release)/Sci-fi/Fantasy/Germany

The son of the Master Of Metropolis falls for an angelic social worker, while a metal-armed mad scientist creates a gleaming, seductive, female robot to infiltrate the revolutionary movement.

At once the *2001* and *Heaven's Gate* of 1926, this sci-fi epic gave generations a fixed vision of the future and came close to bankrupting its studio. Vast skyscrapers full of Jazz-Age decadents tower above an underground hell of workers strapped to torture machines.

The son of the Master Of Metropolis falls for an angelic social worker, while a metal-armed mad scientist creates a gleaming, seductive, female robot to infiltrate the revolutionary movement.

It has some silly-even-for-the-silents performances and a plot that nearly collapses along with the city. But many sequences, characters and images are indelible: the shuffling slaves changing shift, the electrical creation of the robotrix, the hero strapped to a giant clock, Rudolf Klein-Rogge's Frankenstein of the future, Brigitte Helm's mechanical *femme fatale* driving men mad with lust or leading a riot. Still overwhelming, particularly in the restored print. ★★★ **KN**

METROPOLITAN (1990)

Starring: *Edward Clements (Tom Townsend), Carolyn Farina (Audrey Rouget), Christopher Eigeman (Nick Smith), Taylor Nichols (Charlie Black)*
Director: *Walt Stillman*
Screenwriter: *Walt Stillman*
15/94 mins./Comedy/Drama/USA

Observational drama of the tribal customs of teenaged Manhattan socialites as they party, court, philosophise and lament the decline of their class through one Christmas holiday season.

This small, gentle first feature written and directed by a New York journalist and book editor, Whit Stillman (later giving us *The Last Days Of Disco*), shows off his literary background to good effect while demonstrating sound cinematic instincts. Using a young, semi-professional cast, Stillman observes this group of young New York socialites with affection and wit.

Tom is the impoverished-but-genteel type who postures as a socialist but is welcomed by the self-styled 'UHBs' (urban haute-bour-geoise) to alleviate their shortage of suitable males. The heroine is Audrey, whose love of Jane Austen is amusingly reflected in the various relationships played out in Manhattan living rooms and dinner dances.

All of the set are nicely drawn, from Nick, the charming, manipulative leader of the group to the rake and the wordly girl who has turned the head of the hero. It's a pity that the more astringent social comedy gives way in the second half to the somewhat forced romantic nonsense of rescuing the hero from the cad. ★★★★ **AE**

THE MEXICAN (2001)

Starring: *Brad Pitt (Jerry Welbach), Julia Roberts (Samantha), James Gandolfini (Leroy), Bob Balaban (Bernie Nayman), Gene Hackman (Arnold Margolese)*
Director: *Gore Verbinski*
Screenwriter: *J.H. Wyman*
15/118 mins./Comedy/Drama/USA

Working off a debt to low-rent mobsters, mishap-prone Jerry is dispatched to Mexico to recover a beautiful but cursed pistol. This is the final straw for his long-suffering girlfriend Samantha, who leaves him and heads for Vegas, but when Jerry's task becomes ever more complicated, the mob decide to take out some insurance and send notorious hit man Leroy to kidnap Samantha.

There's an old Hollywood adage: never work with animals or movie stars. After extracting a remarkable performance out of a trained rodent in *Mouse Hunt*, sophomore director Gore Verbinski continues to make life difficult by saddling his $15 million indie film with not one, but two marquee players: Julia Roberts and Brad Pitt.

As a small movie, full of ideas, boasting a surfeit of plot and an ambitious mis-match of genres, *The Mexican* would be worthy of the attention it would doubtless have failed to attract. Cast Janeane Garofalo and Steve Zahn and you've got a cult favourite, maybe. However, as it stands, with both Roberts and Pitt to be applauded for swallowing a big salary cut for material they believed in, the stakes are higher and the critical angle changes.

During their rare scenes together, Pitt and Roberts never let the audience forget they are movie stars, not slumming exactly, but certainly with full licence to indulge themselves. Thus we are treated to unusually mannered performing, any chemistry frittered away on facial tics and hissy fits.

Both are better when apart. Pitt manfully shoulders most of the movie's more pointless quirks – hey, it's Brad on a donkey! – but likeable loser Jerry remains charming and oafish when squirming with the heavies who have him by the balls.

Better yet is the Gandolfini-Roberts story thread. The former, who knows how to hold a camera without mugging, brings out the very best in Roberts; rather than compete with him she is a perfectly sweet foil, slowly teasing out the hidden depths in the hit man who has kidnapped her. Indeed, for all the pre-release Brad and Julia hype, it is Gandolfini, in his first major movie role since his Emmy-winning performance as Tony Soprano, who deserves all the plaudits. Unlike Pitt and Roberts, you never once see him acting.

Strangely, in a film about a mis-firing pistol, Gandolfini is the lone straight shooter, and whenever he is on screen Verbinski calls off the hunt for laughs and lets the drama develop naturally.

The Mexican would love to be *Out Of Sight*, but where Soderbergh's hip thriller was pure jazz, effortless and fluid, too often this dissolves into dissonant percussion: in equal parts slack and forced. That's not to say there's not a lot of good stuff here, but you have to excavate harder than one would like. Somewhere inside this bloated star vehicle is an off-beat road movie trying to get out. ★★★ **DHu**

MI VIDA LOCA (1993)

Starring: *Angel Aviles (Sad Girl), Seidy Lopez (Mousie), Jacob Vargas (Ernesto), Devine (Devine), Monica Lutton (Chucky), Christina Solis (Baby Doll)*
Director: *Allison Anders*
Screenwriter: *Allison Anders*
15/92 mins./Drama/USA/UK

Mousie and Sad Girl are childhood friends from a poor Hispanic neighborhood. But they become enemies when Mousie's boyfriend impregnates Sad Girl.

Set in L.A.'s Echo Park district, this focuses on a group of teenage Hispanic girls forced to look out for themselves and their babies because their menfolk tend to be dead, crippled or in prison by the time they are old enough to shave. Anders, director of *Gas Food Lodging*, has tried for a Latino-flavoured, girl-centric *Boyz N The Hood*, working up a script from anecdotes from real gang girls and casting genuine hood hangers in the background. Out front, an unfamiliar, mostly engaging cast sport elaborate make-up and very big hair.

The film is constructed from various strands: two friends are set at odds when they both have babies by the same man; a slightly older girl comes out of prison and tries to live a more responsible life, only to be shocked by the death or deterioration of her contemporaries; a studious girl has her heart broken by a ladies' man and is supported by her friends; while another tries to learn drug dealing, only to be irritated by the ineptitude of the boys she works with. Despite all this plot, the characters mostly hang out and talk, toughing out their problems and hugging.

Structured more like a documentary than a fiction film, this never quite convinces. The actresses are all excellent, but look somewhere between rock video girls and John Waters' extras: the real gang members in the cast are three stone heavier and wear more make-up than the pretty principles. And it all winds up with a hackneyed death-of-an-innocent contrivance that underlines how bad things are. ★★ **KN**

MICHAEL COLLINS (1996)

Starring: *Liam Neeson (Michale Collins), Aidan Quinn (Harry Boland), Julia Roberts (Kitty Kiernan), Stephen Rea (Ned Broy), Alan Rickman (Eamon de Valera), Ian Hart (Joe O'Reilly)*
Director: *Neil Jordan*
Screenwriter: *Neil Jordan*
15/126 mins./Biography/Drama/USA/UK

Set in the 20s. A street terrorist becomes a powerful political leader in this biopic of Irish renegade Michael Collins.

Neil Jordan's mature, passionate biography of the tragic Irish revolutionary takes a considered, intelligent stance, depicting a man as much dedicated to peace as he was to, what he considered, necessary bloodshed. This is a film set in a specific historical context and its relation to the modern 'Troubles' is just that, historical.

Indeed, at the inevitably downbeat close – it is no giveaway to reveal that Collins was eventually felled by his own people as he strove to lay aside the bullet – there is a definite sense that if the man had lived, the shape of Ireland and the purposes of (perhaps, even the existence of) the modern IRA would be entirely different.

Jordan chooses to tell Collins' own story, in the main the crucial turbulent four years from 1918 to 1922, in a filleted, snapshot fashion with fact healthily spruced up with fiction (you know, faction). A largely seamless stream of vignettes that charts his progression from street terrorism to political leadership to assassination, with room (albeit somewhat thinly established) for a spot of romance to humanise the guy. This makes for less lyrical storytelling à la David Lean (although Jordan occasionally, and successfully, indulges in a bit of sweep) than powerhouse thriller – this is certainly not a 20s Oirish *Braveheart*. Writer Jordan's decision to concentrate on the literally explosive elements over talkie politics gives the film real momentum.

With his so-called 'invisible army' and right-hand man (and later turncoat) Harry Boland, Collins ran a chilling campaign against the British forces, murdering police officials – open warfare was never going to oust the occupying forces – with able assistance from his inside contact Broy. Meanwhile, his leader (and later foe), future Irish president Eamon de Valera kept up the public front with kudos gathering trips to America and frequent passive sojourns at Lincoln jail. How much of this holds up to historical scrutiny is up to the pedantic among us to nit-pick over, what is certain is that it makes for great cinema. There are moments here of absolute mastery: Jordan turns cross-cutting (normally the refuge of the floundering director) into an art form with a series of shock killings punctuated with a conscience-tortured Collins clutching his love Kitty Kiernan through the lonely night. His own death is magnificently framed with the lush pastures of county Cork and a lilting Gaelic air.

Where Michael Collins does stumble is in Neeson's lack of charisma. His supporting cast are, to a man, magnificent (top marks: Rea, Rickman, Ian Hart and, especially, Quinn), Roberts' accent may waver (bringing back shivers of *Mary Reilly* recall) but her understated acting is a revelation. This, however, only serves to further reduce the strength of Neeson. He holds the camera well, but never once do you swallow him as the inspiration of an enslaved nation. Like Schindler before there is a strange blankness to his acting. You're often left considering what a Day-Lewis or an Irons could have made of it and what a film that could have been. ★★★★ **IN**

MICKEY BLUE EYES (1999)

Starring: *Hugh Grant (Michael Felgate), James Caan (Frank Vitale), Jeanne Tripplehorn (Gina Vitale), James Fox (Philip Cromwell)*
Director: *Kelly Makin*
Screenwriters: *Mark Lawrence, Adam Scheinmann, Robert Kuhn*
15/98 mins./Comedy/USA/UK/

A young woman hides the secret of her family's mob connections from her straight auctioneer boyfriend.

Returning to the New York locale of Extreme Measures, Grant swaps scalpel for gavel as Michael Felgate who, in between fielding bids for distinguished auction house Cromwells, is summoning up the courage to propose to schoolteacher Gina Vitale. Who freaks. Not because she's unwilling, but because – unknown to Michael – her 'family' isn't exactly your common or garden variety, with dad Frank a prominent member of the Graziosi crime organisation. Still, blood's thicker than water, especially when it's spreading slowly across the floor.

From this swiftly worked premise spins an escalating comic farce, handled well for the most part by fledgling feature director Makin. As Michael's vow to remain unsullied falters with a reluctant favour for Uncle Vito, Grant enjoys a couple of showcase set pieces, the standout being a scene in which he creates the fictional titular gangster to impress two rival heavies.

An excellent Caan offers more than cliche or caricature as Frank – who's father first, mobster second – and with Tripplehorn a delightful watch too (on any level), the trio succeed in the key task of making you care about their predicament. So the comedy becomes engaging, not just a series of pratfalls, while also tempered as too knockabout or frivolous by Young's menacing turn as the Graziosi boss. ★★★ **DB**

MICROCOSMOS: LE PEOPLE DE L'HERBE (1996)

Starring: *Jacques Perrin (Narrator, French version), Kristin Scott Thomas (Narrator, English version)*
Directors: *Claude Nuridsany, Marie Perennou*
Screenwriters: *Claude Nuridsany, Marie Perennou*
U/73 mins./Documentary/France/Switzerland/Italy

A documentary of insect life in meadows and ponds, using incredible close-ups, slow motion, and time-lapse photography.

It's a rare film that can boast a cast of thousands, none of whom can speak or act. But this everyday chronicle of life, sex and death can do just that.

It follows a day in the life of a French meadow: a thistle bursting into flower; a bee hovering over a clutch of poppies; an ant tickling aphids who produce a drink in return, bees collecting nectar, ladybugs eating mites, snails mating, spiders wrapping their catch, a scarab beetle relentlessly pushing its ball of dung uphill, endless lines of caterpillars, an underwater spider creating an air bubble to live in, and a mosquito hatching.

Though a film of exquisite beauty, there is a sense that it might have been more. Nevertheless, even with its sparcity of incidental music (long periods pass in relative silence) rarely have so many remarkable and eminently watchable scenes been crammed into just 73 minutes. ★★★★ **NJ**

⊙ MIDNIGHT COWBOY (1969)

Starring: *Dustin Hoffman (Enrico Salvatore 'Ratso' Rizzo), Jon Voigt (Joe Buck), Sylvia Miles (Cass), John McGiver (Mr O' Daniel), Brenda Vaccaro (Shirley)*
Director: *John Schlesinger*
Screenwriter: *Walso Salt, from a novel by James Leo Herlihy*
18/108 mins./Drama/USA

Awards – *Academy Awards – Best Director, Best Picture, Best Adapted Screenplay, BAFTA – Best Actor, Best Direction, Best Film, Best Editing, Best Promising Newcomer (Jon Voigt), Best Screenplay, Golden Globes – Most Promising Newcomer (Jon Voigt)*

Texan Joe Buck comes to New York to make his fortune as a gigolo and falls in with lowlife 'Ratso' Rizzo, who offers to be his manager. The pair come to depend on each other, and Joe determines to get the ailing Ratso out of the city for his health.

A rare Best Picture Academy Award winner which stands the test of time, *Midnight Cowboy* scored additional Oscars for Best Adapted Script (Waldo Salt from the novel by James Leo Herlihy) and Director (John Schlesinger), plus strong contention in the Best Actor stakes from nominees Jon Voigt and Dustin Hoffman. The stars cancelled out each other's votes, ironically to make way for John Wayne's *True Grit* comeback.

The Duke's sacred name, and indeed the entire tradition of Western masculinity, is tarnished in the script – way ahead of *Brokeback* – when Hoffman's whiny Ratso tells Voigt's buckskin-fringed innocent that only homosexuals go for the cowboy act – whereupon the midnight cowboy snaps and shouts 'John Wayne! Are you tryin' to tell me he's a fag!'

British director Schlesinger takes an outsider's view of America in 1969, presenting cinema-verite on-the-streets Big Apple grunge footage with an overlay of acid trippiness in the wild partying as he puts on the mainstream cinema screen the sort of lives that had hitherto only been seen in Andy Warhol's underground films.

Several Warhol Factory acolytes (Ultra Violet, Viva, Paul Morrissey, International Velvet) cameo in the happening scenes, but Andy himself was laid up after the assassination attempt and missed out on the gig.

The film is rooted in reality by its excellent, deeply felt performances, with a heartbreaking finish on a Miami-bound bus the odd Laurel and Hardy partnership between hayseed stud and crippled comes to a sad end. The hit song was Harry Nilsson's 'Everybody's Talkin' at Me'. ★★★★ **KN**

⊙ MIDNIGHT IN THE GARDEN OF GOOD AND EVIL (1997)

Starring: *John Cusack (John Kelso), Kevin Spacey (James 'Jim' Williams), Jack Thompson (Sonny Seiler), Irma P. Hall (Minerva), Jude Law (Billy Carl Hanson)*
Director: *Clint Eastwood*
Screenwriter: *John Lee Hancock, based on the book by John Berendt*
15/148 mins./Crime/Drama/USA

Courtroom drama, small town expose and witchcraft-infected magicking in an archetypal southern community.

Based on John Berendt's best selling true-life tome, *Midnight* is a mildly engaging hotchpotch of disparate ideas but a far cry from Eastwood's best.

The action centres on Savannah, Georgia, an archetypal Southern community redolent with customs and mores belonging to a bygone age. Into this time-warped setting comes John Kelso, a young New York hack sent by *Town And Country* magazine to cover the prestigious Christmas party of Jim Williams, antiques collector and distinguished citizen.

Yet the post-party status quo is disrupted as Williams is arrested for the murder of his clandestine live-in lover Billy Hanson (Law, once again called upon to embody 'volatile youth').

With a murder trial in his lap, Kelso is drawn into both the anachronistic milieu – 'It's *Gone With The Wind* on mescalin' – and the veracity of Williams' self-defence plea, deciding to stay on in Savannah to help investigate the case.

Rejecting the powerhouse drive of a Grisham-style trial movie, Eastwood and screenscribe John Hancock overlay the 'will Williams walk free?' dynamic with a mosaic depiction of the townsfolk. This approach results in sprawling, languid storytelling that spends far too long wallowing in the minutiae of Savannah's social strata. To compound the wayward structure, Eastwood's direction lacks the fizz to enliven the proceedings.

Between the excesses there are pleasures to be had. Eastwood elicits a plethora of good performances – Spacey neatly adds to his pantheon of cultivated, slimy slicksters, Cusack lends his customary insouciant cool yet both are upstaged by The Lady Chablis as sassy transvestite Chablis Deveau who guides Kelso through the Savannah underworld. ★★★ **IF**

⊙ MIDNIGHT RUN (1988)

Starring: *Robert De Niro (Jack Walsh), Charles Grodin (Jonathan Mardukas), Yaphet Kotto (FBI Agent Alonzo Mosely), John Ashton (Marvin Dorfler), Dennis Farina (Jimmy Serrano)*
Director: *Martin Brest*
Screenwriter: *George Gallo*
18/121 mins./Comedy/Thriller/USA

A bounty hunter tries to bring in an embezzler, despite attempts by rivals, gangsters and the FBI to stop him.

In this fast-paced action-comedy, bounty hunter Robert De Niro and bounty Charles Grodin generate sparkling chemistry while on the run from the usual array of mobsters, FBI agents and competing bounty hunters. The mismatched pair manage to bring a freshness to a familiar story and De Niro flexes his comedy chops in practice for the comedy successes he was going to have ten years later.

Grodin is especially good, whinging on about smoking while taking an indignant moral high ground as a kind of latter-day Robin Hood.

Director Martin Brest comfortably folds in the standard car chases and shoot-outs with deliciously handled comedy that oozes with quick-fired wit.

An expert reworking of the tried and tested odd-couple-shackled-together routine. ★★★★ **IN**

⊙ A MIDSUMMER NIGHT'S SEX COMEDY (1982)

Starring: *Woody Allen (Andrew), Mia Farrow (Ariel), José Ferrer (Leopold), Julie Hagerty (Dulcy), Tony Roberts (Maxwell), Mary Steenburgen (Adrian)*
Director: *Woody Allen*
Screenwriter: *Woody Allen*
15/88 mins./Comedy/USA

The amorous temperature rises when pompous professor Leopold Sturges and his younger fiancée, Ariel Weymouth come to stay with his cousin Adrian Hobbes, her amateur inventor husband, Andrew, and his best friend, Dr Maxwell Jordan and his free-spirited nurse Dulcy.

The imminence of a Directors' Guild strike in the summer of 1981 prompted Jack Rollins and Charles H. Joffe to rush this period confection into production. Buoyed by the experience of *Zelig* (which was now in its extensive post-production) and the freshness of his relationship with Mia Farrow, Woody Allen wrote the screenplay in just three weeks.

Although Allen always denied the similarity, it's hard to resist comparisons with both Ingmar Bergman's *Smiles Of A Summer Night* and *A Little Night Music*, the Stephen Sondheim musical Bergman inspired. However, the luminosity of Gordon Willis's photography also recalls Jean Renoir's rural delight, Une *Partie De Compagne*.

Allen insisted *Smiles* was his least favourite Bergman film and, unfortunately, this is one of his own least persuasive pictures. Even in the mouths of turn-of-the-century intellectuals, the very modern conversation rings hollow too often and, despite Mendelssohn on the soundtrack, the atmosphere stubbornly refuses to become whimsical.

Part of the problem lies in Allen's own inability to tailor his standard delivery style to a flightier than usual character. But, more damaging is the suspicion that he doesn't really believe in his material. It may have been written in the throes of passion, but, for all its midsummer madness, the script regularly casts doubt on the wisdom of falling in love and succumbing to the foolish fancies that it invariably compels normally rational people to pursue. Moreover, Allen betrays a nagging doubt that his own personal and professional idyll will last and this fatalism introduces a faintly cynical note that curdles the action's exuberance and romantic idealism.

José Ferrer (who was mischievously cast for his inveterate grandiloquence) and Tony Roberts are much more convincing, as the pompous urban bourgeois seduced by their return to nature, while Mia Farrow's fragile beauty perfectly captures the ethereality of the film's fleeting wit. But Mary Steenburgen and Julie Haggerty are perhaps most amusing, as the mirror opposites afflicted by guilt-racked frigidity and gleeful promiscuity. **★★★ DP**

MIFUNE (MIFUNES SIDSTE SANG) (1999)

Starring: *Anders W. Berthelsen (Kresten), Jesper Asholt (Rud), Iben Hjejle (Liva Psilander), Sofie Grabol (Claire), Emil Tarding (Bjarke Psilander)*
Directors: *Anders Thomas Jensen, Soren Kragh-Jacobsen*
15/101 mins./Romance/Comedy/Drama/Sweden/Denmark

A newly wed couple return to the husband's family farm after the death of his father. Buried secrets are soon revealed.

Rules are there to be broken and for this third outing under the Dogma 95 banner, director Kragh-Jacobsen has embraced the sacred vow of cinematic chastity with anything but monastic rigour.

But Kragh-Jacobsen's study in deceit would probably have looked like this even if he hadn't followed, however loosely, Dogma's naturalistic principles.

It begins with the wedding of yuppie couple Kresten and Claire. Just as they have consummated the marriage (in the most vigorous comic fashion), he receives word that his father has died – which comes as a shock to new wife, since Kresten said he was an orphan.

Returning to the family farm, he decides against putting defenceless brother Rud, in a home and hires a housekeeper, Liva. But Liva has been economical with the truth about her own past: she is a hooker on the run from her pimp.

There's an inevitability about the resolution, and the sub-plots involving Liva's son and Kresten's envious neighbour are clumsily integrated. But this gently humorous romcom, which won the Jury Prize at Berlin, has an unobtrusive intelligence. **★★★ DP**

MIGHTY APHRODITE (1995)

Starring: *Woody Allen (Lenny), F. Murray Abraham (Leader), Helena Bonham Carter (Amanda), Claire Bloom (Amanda's Mother), Olympia Dukakis (Jocasta), Mira Sovino (Linda Ash)*
Director: *Woody Allen*
Screenwriter: *Woody Allen*
15/95 mins./Comedy/USA

Awards – *Academy Awards – Best Supporting Actress (Mira Sovino), Golden Globes – Best Supporting Actress (Mira Sovino)*

A yuppie sports writer becomes overwhelmed by the desire to discover the identity of his adopted daughter's natural parents.

After *Manhattan Murder Mystery* and *Bullets Over Broadway* the lightening up of Woody Allen continues apace. This contains everything we have come to expect from the feverish director: the woes of modern relationships, an awkward clash of ages between Allen and his leading ladies, the Big Apple aglow in the camera's eye and those one-liners to die for, all delivered with the emphasis on good comedy rather than pounding commentary.

The formula twist is to pen this one as pseudo-Greek tragedy – events are punctuated with cut-aways to a Macedonian mount where a troupe of thespians in full costume, led by F. Murray Abraham, narrate the ongoing story in wiseguy New York blather.

The plot proper has yuppie couple Lenny and Amanda adopting a child who grows up healthy, intelligent and happy. Naturally, Allen's neurotic sports writer flips, becoming overwhelmed with the desire to discover who the child's natural parents are. As irony would have it, the mother turns out to be Sorvino's loveable, dim-witted hooker Linda who squawks like Minnie Mouse with laryngitis – the father could be one of many. Struck with paternal concern, Lenny takes it upon himself to act as fairy godfather to the swell-hearted girl undone by life, misguidedly setting her up with lugheaded boxer Kevin.

Allen is, undoubtedly, one of the most astute and intelligent filmmakers about and, as ever, this brims with satisfying witticism ('I don't have an Achilles heel, I have an Achilles body,' he whimpers when confronted with Linda's musclebound pimp) and telling observation. And in the twittering, busty Sorvino, Allen has coaxed a golden performance of humour and humanity. **★★★ IN**

THE MIGHTY DUCKS (1992)

Starring: *Emilio Estevez (Gordon Bombay), Joss Ackland (Hans), Lane Smith (Coach Jack Reilly), Heidi Kling (Casey Conway), Josef Sommer (Mr Gerald Ducksworth), Joshua Jackson (Charlie Conway)*
Director: *Stephen Herek*
Screenwriter: *Steven Brill*
PG/100 mins. /Comedy/USA

A big-time lawyer, and former (failed) child ice hockey star, Gordon Bombay is ordered by a court to coach a team of young misfits at that very same sport. Initially reluctant, he will come to bond with the kids and face up to the ghosts of the past.

The Bad News Bears as done with ice hockey and far less wit, this is the cosy family movie, dumb and stirring in that way every sports-movie ends up being, that invented a genuine hockey team called The Mighty Ducks. That, though, is another story, the one here does everything by rote and with the minimum of personality – there is no sense that the film ever exists in any world but the bloated consumerist Planet Disney (feel the merchandising).

Emilio Estevez's truculent yuppie is a kid-hater (tick), forced by community service to work with kids (tick), and slowly their quirky-cute-honest ways will bring him round to stir him into being a real coach (tick). Although, we mustn't forget that wining isn't everything, it's all about feeling good about yourself or somesuch flatulent platitude for kids of every disposition.

Estevez works hard but is too bland an actor to define his personality against the gaggle of brats, themselves the usual blather of geeks, norms, blacks and a fat one who will go in goal. To show just how safe the formula has become since the caustic styles of *The Bad News Bears'* ribald seventies, where Walter Matthau's slothful coach was an alcoholic pool-cleaner, Estevez's clean-cut equivalent is a workaholic lawyer. Elsewhere the same old tricks work as they always do, building up a minor feelgood surge for the big final (enough to fuel several terrible sequels) but there's no escaping this hollow enterprise is more duck than mighty. ★★ **IN**

⓪ MIGHTY JOE YOUNG (1949)

Starring: *Terry Moore (Jill Young), Robert Armstrong (Max O'Hara), Ben Johnson (Gregg Ford), Frank McHugh (Press Agent), Douglas Fowley (Jones)*
Director: *Ernest B. Schoedsack*
Screenwriter: *Ruth Rose, based on a story by Merian C. Cooper*
U/93 mins./Fantasy/Adventure/USA

African-raised Jill Young is best friends with Joe, a giant gorilla. Promoter Max O'Hara brings Jill and Joe to Los Angeles to headline his new nightclub – but Joe, abused by patrons, goes on the rampage.

Seventeen years after producer Merian C. Cooper, director Ernest B. Schoedsack and special effects man Willis H. O'Brien created *King Kong*, the team reunited for this kiddie matinee reprise.

Even Robert Armstrong, Kong's discoverer, returns in an equivalent, even broader role – and the storyline is almost exactly the same, as a giant gorilla is brought to 'civilisation' and driven to a destructive rage. However, the savagery and horror are missing, and this is closer in feel to *My Friend Flicka* than *Beauty And The Beast*.

The winning Terry Moore is a big sister to 'Mr Joseph Young of Africa', a genial gorilla – no one in the movie even mentions that there might be something unusual about a sixteen-foot-tall ape – who performs with her in a memorably weird nightclub act (holding her above his head as she plays 'Beautiful Dreamer' on a grand piano), only becomes destructive when troublemakers get him drunk and finally redeems himself by rescuing orphans from a fire. O'Brien worked with newcomer Ray Harryhausen, who would become the leading monster-animator of the next generation, in bringing Joe to life: he's a smoother character than Kong, with a lot of heart, but he's a pretender rather than a king.

Fresh-faced Ben Johnson makes his screen debut as a cowboy in *Africa* – the film was co-produced by John Ford, and a few other familiar faces from his stock company get tossed about by the gorilla. Remade likably in 1998 by Ron Underwood with Charlize Theron, Bill Paxton and a lot of CGI pixels who still aren't as alive as the furry, manipulated puppet from the original. ★★★★ **KN**

⓪ MIGHTY JOE YOUNG (1998)

Starring: *Charlize Theron (Jill Young), Bill Paxton (Gregg O'Hara), Rade Servedzija (Strasser), Peter Firth (Garth), David Paymer (Harry Ruben), Regina King (Cecily Banks), Naveen Andrews (Pindi)*
Director: *Ron Underwood*
Screenwriters: *Mark Rosenthal, Lawrence Konner, from the 1948 film*
PG/114 mins./Family/Fantasy/Thriller/Adventure/USA

A giant gorilla is uprooted from the African jungle to urban America.

A shameless attempt to repeat the success of *King Kong. Mighty Joe Young* scaled down the size of the primate, made him more friendly than fearsome and upped the comedy and sentiment to differ from Kong's marauding magnificence. This Disney effort to modernise Joe with colour, cutting edge technology and Charlize Theron in a singlet has produced a likeable, well-crafted eco-action movie which inexplicably failed to find a respectably sized audience Stateside.

Both orphaned as youngsters by violent poachers, conservationist Jill Young and her 15-foot simian charge Joe live in a blissful isolation on a beautiful African mountain. Their idyll is broken by well-meaning zoologist Gregg O'Hara, chasing the local legend of a mythical beast.

It is here where the movie really takes flight; O'Hara pursuing Joe through the verdant terrain and his subsequent befriending of the ape is exhilarating, pushing the limits of photo-realistic CGI animals to unsurpassed levels. Indeed, it is much to the credit of the visual effects supremos (and actors) that Joe is a character you can care about and root for, a rarity among digitally booted creations.

Underwood's direction is always slick – the opening gorilla massacre is savage and intense – but once the action moves to LA (O'Hara convinces Jill that Joe would be safe from poachers in an urban conservation park), the movie loses both urgency and spirit. Scenes depicting Joe adapting to his new, cramped environment and the wrangling over his future become protracted, losing the film's momentum. Following kidnap by evil animal marketeers (Sherbedgia and Firth), Joe's inevitable tour of LA landmarks – climbing Mann's Chinese Theatre, hanging on the Hollywood sign, niftily evading pursuing helicopters – is enjoyable yet never really delivers on the previous promise. Moreover, the fairground-set finale ends on a note of manipulative heartstring yanking that is, frankly, cheating. ★★★ **IF**

⓪ MIGHTY MORPHIN POWER RANGERS: THE MOVIE (1995)

Starring: *Karan Ashley (Aisha Campbell/The Yellow Ranger), Johnny Yong Bosch (Adam Park/The Black Ranger), Steve Cardenas (Rocky DeSantos/The Red Ranger), Jason David Frank (Tommy Oliver/The White Ranger), Amy Jo Johnson (Kimberly Hart/The Pink Ranger), David Yost (Billy Cranston/The Blue Ranger), Paul Schrier (Bulk), Jason Narvy (Skull), Paul Freeman (Ivan Ooze)*
Director: *Brian Spicer*
Screenwriters: *Arne Olsen, based on a story by Olsen, John Kamps*
PG/95 mins./Action/Adventure/Fantasy/USA

Six teenage superheroes battle the evil Ooze.

An unexpected but huge hit, the *Mighty Morphin Power Rangers* TV series consists of action sequences from Japanese superhero shows spliced into new footage featuring the alter egos of the spandex-costumed Power Rangers, who undergo their own morphing from Japanese into American high-school kids. A worldwide sensation, with attendant action figures and computer games, the Power Rangers made it to the big screen in a more elaborate, if no less childish, scenario.

There are imaginative moments – a fight with an animated dinosaur skeleton, the zombie parent horde, the metal insect monster rampage – but the interchangeable, asexual, multi-ethnic heroes (top-billed Karan Ashley is an addition to the regular cast, and has a bit of rivalry with veteran Ranger Amy Jo Johnson) and the pantomime villainy ('I am Lord Zedd, sworn enemy of all that is good and decent') swiftly becomes wearisome. It all winds up with the children of Angel Grove trying to prevent their hypnotised parents from committing a lemming-like mass suicide.

The Rangers, whose 'zords' (animal totem robot fighting vehicles) have meshed into a giant robot warrior (a 'mega-zord') to go one on one with Ivan in outer space, using a foul move to shove him into the path of a comet. There is a lot of flashy editing and pounding music, with the Rangers chanting their totemic animals to summon their powers and a great deal of fairly feeble humour. Before the craze petered out, there was a sequel, *Turbo*. ★★ **KN**

A MIGHTY WIND (2003)

Starring: *Bob Balaban (Jonathan Steinbloom), Ed Begley Jr (Lars Olfen), Jennifer Coolidge (Amber Cole), Christopher Guest (Alan Barrows), John Michael Higgins (Terry Bohner)*
Director: *Christopher Guest*
Screenwriters: *Christopher Guest, Eugene Levy*
12/88 mins./Satire/Comedy/USA

In tribute to recently deceased folk music promoter Irving Steinbloom, his children stage a concert, bringing together a parade of musical eccentrics.

Having done mock-docs on community theatre (*Waiting For Guffman*) and dog breeding (*Best In Show*), Christopher Guest here harks back to his work with regulars Michael McKean and Harry Shearer on *This Is Spinal Tap*, as he takes a gently satirical look at the absurdities of the folk music business.

Guest's films basically involve roping in all of his friends to do schtick, but they're all amazing talents and deliver spot-on performances: Bob Balaban as the nervously clueless heir determinedly putting together the concert, Fred Willard as a busted sit-com star-cum-manager still chuckling over old catchphrases ('Hey, wha' happen?'), Paul Dooley as the surviving original Main Streeter whose microphone isn't even plugged in.

As in *Tap*, the songs are just exaggerated and double entendre-laden enough to be funny but remain convincingly ghastly. And the weird relationship between still-fractured Eugene Levy and settled-down Catherine O'Hara provides a genuine plot spine for all the routines. ★★★★ **WL**

THE MIGHTY (1998)

Starring: *Sharon Stone (Gwen Dillon), Harry Dean Stanton (Grim), Gena Rowlands (Gram), Kieran Culkin (Kevin Dillon), Gillian Anderson (Loretta Lee), Eldon Henson (Maxwell Kane)*
Director: *Peter Chelsom*
Screenwriter: *Charles Leavitt, based on the novel by Rodman Philbrick*
PG/96 mins./Comedy/Drama/USA

Max is a seemingly semi-literate oaf who's been held back in junior high for several years. Then his new neighbour, bright Kevin is assigned as his reading tutor and the pair strike up a unique friendship.

Although a film about a boy with a terminal disease bonding with a big lummox and pretending they are Knights Of The Round Table sounds suspiciously like 'family entertainment', don't be fooled because this is captivating drama.

Max is a giant, lumbering oaf who's been held back in junior high for several years. He seems a simpleton and a coward; raised by his grandparents, Gram and Grim, he's near-illiterate, near-mute and constantly taunted. Then his new neighbour, bright Kevin, a tiny, disabled, sarcastic wise guy bullied as 'Freak', is assigned as his reading tutor. A mutual passion for Arthurian legend impels the boys to embark on a series of 'quests', serio-comic adventures in which friendship and imagination empower the duo to vanquish wrong-doers. The giant carries the crippled boy piggyback everywhere, Max the legs and Kevin the brain becoming known as one heroic entity, Freak The Mighty.

If this sounds sickly, it isn't, but a funny, uplifting adaptation of an award-winning book. Distinctive British director Chelsom (*Hear My Song, Funny Bones*) infuses the film with a look of magical realism, so that the boys' perceptions have the style of mythic fantasy adventure. But he keeps the story true to life and grounded in the everyday reality of its working-class Cincinnati setting, through many moods, while disease-of-the-week cliches are dodged with rare sensitivity.

The adult cast get top billing and good roles (Gillian Anderson does a hilariously blowsy turn as a drunken slattern the boys innocently dub The Lady Of Essex). But it's the accomplished, very demanding star performances of Culkin (15) and Henson (20) that most genuinely move and charm in a movie you won't be embarrassed to weep in. ★★★ **AE**

MILDRED PIERCE (1945)

Starring: *Joan Crawford (Mildred Pierce Beragon), Jack Carson (Wally Fay), Zachary Scott (Monte Beragon), Eve Arden (Ida Corwin), Ann Blyth (Veda Pierce Forrester)*
Director: *Michael Curtiz*
Screenwriter: *Ranald MacDougall, from the novel by James M. Cain*
PG/106 mins./Film-noir/USA
Awards – *Academy Awards – Best Actress*

Gunshots crack and a dying man gasps, 'Mildred!' In a classic of mother love and murder, Mildred toils her way from waitress to restaurateur to fulfill her spoiled daughter Veda's demands.

People forget that *Mildred Pierce*, celebrated as a definitive 40s women's picture of maternal suffering and a seething domestic soap opera, is an adaptation of a breathtakingly perverse and misogynous novel by James M. Cain, a major influence on noir and explorer of the unhealthy mind.

After Bette Davis and Barbara Stanwyck turned it down, it was tailored at Warner Bros into a stunning comeback for Crawford, two years after MGM cut her loose as 'box office poison'.

Mildred's clinging devotion to her rotten Veda is sick. It drives her from happy homemaker to heartbroken entrepreneur in an upwardly mobile, morally bankrupt, spiral of obsession and greed, and ultimately sends her into a police station to confess to the murder of her second husband, the cad and wastrel Monte, with whom Veda has been carrying on.

Like most of Cain's protagonists, Mildred narrates. Fur-coated, she takes us, mesmerised, through major flashback sequences that depict her life in the kitchen, a parade of useless men and Veda's maturation into a viper.

Mildred Pierce won Crawford the Oscar she desperately coveted and still endures as her most popular picture. While the film launched her on a new phase as an icon of pulp torment, it is distinct from the rest because it is superbly nasty noir that plays havoc with the era's American ideals of women, home, mom and her apple pie.

Elsewhere, Blyth, only 17, earned one of the film's six Academy Award nominations (Best Picture among them), and is sneeringly sensational as the contemptuous teen *femme fatale*. Curtiz's masterly deployment of actors and technical elements (including a grade A supporting cast, cinematographer Ernest Haller's expressive shifts from sunny suburbia to shadowy nightmare and Max Steiner's score) is intoxicating. ★★★★★ **AE**

MILLER'S CROSSING (1990)

Starring: *Gabriel Byrne (Tom Regan), Marcia Gay Harden (Verna), John Turturro (Bernie Bernbaum), Jon Polito (Johnny Caspar), Albert Finney (Leo)*
Director: *Joel Coen*
Screenwriters: *Joel Coen, Ethan Coen*
18/110 mins./Crime/Drama/USA

Tom Reagan, an advisor to a Prohibition-era crime boss, tries to keep the peace between warring mobs but gets caught in divided loyalties.

Gabriel Byrne was trying to get into character. That of Tom Reagan, the hard-bitten, punch bag anti-hero of *Miller's Crossing*. So, he turned to

Hitchcock Cameos — TOP 10

1 Man in 'Reduco' weight-loss programme ad – *Lifeboat*
2 Man coming out of pet shop with two terriers – *The Birds*
3 Man carrying horn case – *Vertigo*
4 Man drinking champagne – *Notorious*
5 Man in cowboy hat outside office – *Psycho*
6 Man who misses bus – *North By Northwest*
7 Man holding baby in Copenhagen hotel lobby – *Torn Curtain*
8 Man whose profile is part of neon sign – *Rope*
9 Man introducing film (playing himself! And talking!) – *The Wrong Man*
10 Man at school reunion dinner (in photo) – *Dial M For Murder*

his director, Joel Coen, with an enquiry: 'What's the significance of the hat? I need to know.' Joel turned to Ethan Coen, never more than a beat away, 'Ethan, Gabe wants to know what the significance of the hat is.' Ethan paused for a moment, 'Yeah, it is significant.' Then he walked off.

Miller's Crossing is about a man chasing a hat, a significant hat. It is unswervingly the finest movie in the considerable Coen canon. Drenched in film lore (as always), designed with a sumptuous detail that extends the mood beyond reality into a meta-'movie' reality, it is shot with masterful elegance (by Barry Sonnenfeld) and performed, unusually for the brothers' work, with as much subtlety as caricature. And it has this script sent from God. A hyper-charged, multi-layered, whirligig of gangster lingo and idiom hatched from the noir pages of Dashiell Hammett by way of Raymond Chandler. This is as much a film about language and communication – with a pastiche phraseology unique and self-contained – as Tommy guns and gambling. The Coens are lovingly deconstructing another genre with a detail and care that constantly reveals new insights on every visit.

Their theme is friendship (brotherhood, almost) and a quest for integrity in a world morally devoid. And there you have your hat, although the Coens will have none of it – 'I don't think you need to read the movie that way to make sense of it.' As far as Tom's concerned it's everything he is, it's his identity and our laconic hero is the only moral order we can cling to in this sea of corruption, betrayal and bone-headed plays.

With due homage to the labyrinthine pulp that inspired them, the Coen boys tie the plot in a ridiculously complex knot of distinctive yet archetypal characters, nefarious double deals and constant betrayal. Second tier gangland boss Johnny Caspar wants to rub out Bernie Bernbaum because he suspects he's revealing his fixed fights (he is). City overlord Leo won't bend because he's sweet on Bernie's sister Verna. Leo's confidant and adviser Tom can smell trouble, he knows Caspar's got big ambitions and that Verna's playing Leo for a sap (anyway he's been bedding her on the quiet). So Tom defects to Caspar (but not really) while Caspar's right-hand man Eddie Dane (J. E. Freeman) remains suspicious (rightly). Dane, though, is sweet on Mink (Steve Buscemi) who's sweet with Bernie and any second now the whole damned city (unnamed, but filmed in New Orleans) is going to explode into a gang war with Tom at the centre of the maelstrom.

Complex as it is, events are driven by the verbal pyrotechnics (Tom and Verna's delicious sparring is comparable to anything betwixt Bogart and Bacall: Verna: 'Shouldn't you be doing your job?' Tom: 'Intimidating helpless women is my job.' Verna: 'Then go find one, and intimidate her.'

There are also thrilling set-pieces – the sequence where Leo turns the tables on potential assassins, filling one with enough Tommy gun lead to make him dance like a crazed marionette while Danny Boy lilts from his gramophone, is simply genius. The violence, frequent as it is, gyrates from the cartoonish (Tom's incessant stream of bruiseless beatings) to sharp bursts of bloody brutality (Dane has his face smashed in with a coal shovel). The film never commits itself to realism, existing in a heightened milieu ruled only by the laws of movies.

The casting is inch perfect. Finney makes the charismatic Leo his own, despite having stepped in at the last possible moment when original choice Sterling Hayden died. Harden, atypically attractive with voluminously mad Dorothy Parker hair, is all twitchy sexuality and pout. While the regular Coen troupe weave their rabbit-mouthed magic (Turturro, Buscemi, Polito – look out, too, for cameos from Sam Raimi and Frances McDormand) as a bunch of slickly attired, self-serving double-crossers. Tom is the converse, his motives are loyalty and friendship – even trust on some deeply buried level, only his method is betrayal. A sack of bitter wisecracks, fuelled by sour bourbon and ever-present smokes, he plays all ends against the middle with rubs of Bogart in his sharp tongue and street loner persona. It's Byrne's finest moment, although he struggled with it – those damned elusive brothers. Tom paradoxically gives the movie heart. Fluttering evasively around the edges of *Miller's Crossing* is a twisted form of devotion, even love.

By the end, bodies have been strewn across town with Shakespearian abandon: Caspar is dead, Bernie is dead, Mink is dead, Eddie Dane is dead and Leo has won and got the girl and his city back. It was a smart play, there's no escaping that. As for Tom? Tom winds up with nothing. Nothing except his hat. And that is significant. ★★★★ **IN**

MILLION DOLLAR BABY (2004)

Starring: *Clint Eastwood (Frankie Dunn), Hilary Swank (Maggie Fitzgerald), Morgan Freeman (Eddie Scrap-Iron Dupris), Jay Baruchel (Danger Barch)*
Director: *Clint Eastwood*
Screenwriter: *Paul Haggis, based on the stories by F.X. Toole*
12A/132 mins./Drama/Sports/USA

Awards: *Academy Awards – Best Director, Best Picture, Best Supporting Actor, Best Actress, Golden Globes – Best Director, Best Drama Actress*

Gym owner Frankie Dunn is a rotten Catholic and an over-cautious boxing manager who's never enjoyed a title shot. Maggie Fitzgerald is an untrained 31-year-old of pure white-trash stock. They have nothing in common, but if one-eyed ex-pro Eddie has anything to do with it, they will have . . .

Without so much as a decent shower break following *Mystic River*'s victory lap, Clint Eastwood rejoined the awards fray touting another heavyweight contender. Were it simply a thumping two in a swift one-two, *Million Dollar Baby* would have been impressive enough, but as a rueful rumination on sin and absolution, Eastwood's new *Baby* boldly measured up against the director's undisputed champion: *Unforgiven*.

Put together on the fly, with little pedigree to speak of, *Million Dollar Baby* is the movie equivalent of a no-hoper handed a title bout. The source material is a short story from a debut collection by 69-year-old fight insider F. X. Toole. The adaptation is the first produced screenplay by Paul Haggis, a decorated TV writer best known for creating offbeat Mountie comedy *Due South*. And Eastwood himself stepped in at short notice, moving his *Mystic River* crew onto the project with virtually no prep time.

In what is essentially an odd-couple drama charting the well-worn contours of seasoned trainer and spunky protégé, Morgan Freeman's salty sidekick is elevated to a third leading part principally to provide a semblance of narrative control. His intermittent voiceover, meanwhile, dispenses homilies that might make *Shawshank*'s Red blush. However, Eastwood employs the space cleared by Dupris to explore character in ways that standard Hollywood-movie time simply would not countenance. And *Million Dollar Baby*'s dancing is not entirely in vain. All the bobbing and weaving is clearly intended to put the audience off-balance, blinding seasoned pros to the sucker punch that Eastwood has been cocking all along. Even if you do see it coming – and it's best not to look – *Baby*'s final blow should still floor you, a shot to the gut that will wring tears from the toughest guy in the gym.

With the easy confidence only a true vet can possess, Eastwood tells his story at his own unhurried pace, in his own unadorned style. Ably supported by his usual backroom staff, notably DoP Tom Stern, Eastwood's striking framing has the muscular simplicity and directness of Ernest Hemingway's prose; the twist in this tale is that the embodiment of American manliness is a girl from hillbilly country. ★★★★ **CK**

Movie Trivia: Clint Eastwood (born 1930)

Who he is: The only A-list action star to become an A-list director. Multiple Oscar-winner. Traditional storyteller with an eye for drama.

Hallmarks: Reinvention of traditional genres; subverting of stereotypes; austere and minimalist directing style; interest in aging and death; appearances as an actor.

If you see one movie, see: *Unforgiven* (1992)

MILLIONS (2004)

Starring: *Alexander Nathan Etel (Damian), Lewis Owen McGibbon (Anthony), James Nesbitt (Ronnie), Daisy Donovan (Dorothy), Alun Armstrong (St Peter)*
Director: *Danny Boyle*
Screenwriter: *Frank Cottrell Boyce*
12A/98 mins./Comedy/Crime/Drama/Family/UK/USA

After their mother's death, nine-year-old Damian and seven-year-old Anthony move house, but the kids' adjustment is interrupted when they find a duffel bag containing a quarter of a million pounds.

Danny Boyle's career has been a distinctly up-and-down affair. In the early 90s, with *Shallow Grave* and *Trainspotting*, he was hailed as (yet another) 'saviour of the British film industry'. But since then there's been a series of less triumphant outings: *A Life Less Ordinary* was an over-egged attempt at romantic comedy (which brought to mind Francis Ford Coppola's similarly top-heavy *One From The Heart*); *The Beach* was misconceived and miscast, while *Alien Love Triangle* continues to be sat on by Harvey Weinstein; a fate barely worth contemplating.

But the one thing it hasn't been is predictable. With *Millions* he rings the changes again, moving from the gooey nihilism of *28 Days Later* to a shamelessly heartwarming family pic. In doing so, he delivers his most unalloyed success since *Trainspotting*.

Millions, like all kid-powered movies, stands or falls in the first place on the performances of its child actors, and Alex Etel and Lewis McGibbon both delight. McGibbon plays a moderately cynical nine-year-old whose expertise in emotional manipulation is typified by his wail of, 'Our mam's dead!' in order to appropriate chocolate biscuits from relatives, while Etel – a ridiculously, utterly unselfconsciously sweet-natured child – dazzles as Damian, a boy whose essential goodness leads him to use the money to help the poor, a group he at one point identifies as a bunch of crusties whom he treats to a feast in Pizza Hut.

Frank Cottrell Boyce's deft screenplay manages to undercut the risky levels of religiosity with sparkily surreal wit – saints pop by to sit in Damian's cardboard castle for a smoke and to shoot the breeze – while Boyle banishes the Children's Film Foundation feel that this could have had with his usual sophistication: a heist sequence which crosscuts between a train robbery and the same events acted out by a group of ten-year-olds with Tonka Toys is a standout, while the opening titles have the boys' new house springing up in real-time around them. ★★★★ **AS**

MILLIONS LIKE US (1943)

Starring: *Patricia Roc (Celia Crowson), Gordon Jackson (Fred Blake), Anne Crawford (Jennifer Knowles), Basil Radford (Charters), Naunton Wayne (Caldicott), Moore Marriott (Jim Crowson), Eric Portman (Charlie Forbes), Joy Shelton (Phyllis Crowson),*
Directors: *Sidney Gilliat, Frank Launder*
Screenwriters: *Sidney Gilliat, Frank Launder*
U/103 mins./Drama/UK

With her father Jim in the Home Guard and sister Phyllis in the WAAF, Celia Crowson begins work at an aircraft components factory with some reluctance. But she soon strikes up friendships with colleagues Gwen Price and Jennifer Knowles and new RAF recruit, Fred Blake.

No doubt stung by Hollywood's depiction of life on the British home front in *Mrs Miniver*, Frank Launder and Sidney Gilliat concocted this working-class riposte, which emphasised both the crucial importance of communal action to confounding the enemy and the random nature of both service and sacrifice.

There are no heroes here, just ordinary people, of all ages and backgrounds, doing their bit for the war effort – and not always with much conviction or enthusiasm. Anne Crawford's uppity city girl may not like her work at an aircraft components factory miles from the nearest town, but she makes the most of her lot (even though a flirtation with boss Eric Portman rather than a sense of patriotism prompts her to revise her priorities). Similarly, Patricia Roc conquers her disappointment at not being able to follow gregarious sister Joy Shelton into the WAAF. Indeed, such is her commitment to the cause that she even shrugs and joins in a morale-boosting song with her new family of co-workers on realising that she will have plenty of time to mourn her young RAF husband, Gordon Jackson, once the war has been won.

But Launder and Gilliat don't just concentrate on the emotional aspects of the conflict. They also stud the action with the everyday shortages and inconveniences that would have been familiar to audiences across the country, with the shots of barbed wire and landmines along the coast being a particularly sobering reminder of just how flimsy Britain's defences were and how much life in a traditional place of enjoyment and escapism had changed.

That said, there are occasional moments of light relief and the most amusing are provided by Basil Radford and Naunton Wayne as Charters and Caldicott, whom the co-directors had reunited after their thriller stints in Alfred Hitchcock's *The Lady Vanishes* and Carol Reed's *Night Train To Munich* (1940), which they had scripted. ★★★★ **DP**

MIMIC (1997)

Starring: *Mira Sorvino (Dr Susan Tyler), Jeremy Northam (Dr Peter Mann), Josh Brolin (Josh Maslow), Giancarlo Gianni (Manny), F Murray Abraham (Dr Yates)*
Director: *Guillermo Del Toro*
Screenwriters: *Matthew Robbins, Guillermo Del Toro*
15/101 mins./Sci-fi/Horror/USA

Three years ago entomologist Dr Susan Tyler genetically created an insect to kill cockroaches carrying a virulent disease, now the insects are out to destroy their only predator, mankind!

Spliced together from the murky preoccupations of horror flicks and B-movie histrionics (*Aliens*, *Them*, *The Relic*, Crichton's tampering with nature bugbear, etc.) Mexican director Guillermo Del Toro, who conjured up the curio-vampire Gothism of *Cronos*, has created a serviceable bugs-in-the-sewers routine.

Although Del Toro's deeper ponderings on the morality of science get overshadowed by state-of-the-art gloopy nastiness in the dank tunnelscape of NY underground, the set-up is a chiller, as a freak plague attacks the children of Manhattan threatening to wipe out a generation. Enter sexy insect boffin Sorvino who sources the carriers to the city's cockroach population, genetically engineers a sly anti-roach roach (the Judas breed) and saves the day. Jump-cut to now, and something big, ugly and vaguely humanoid is prowling the underground, preying on ignorant commuters.

Squelch, squelch. It doesn't take Einstein to fathom that what previously was a cure has leapfrogged up the evolutionary highway and man is facing a seriously big bug problem. Re-enter scientist Sorvino, tortured by a Frankenstein syndrome, and disease-monitor hubby, sourcing the problem to some disused sub-subway and coming face-to-face with flying cockroaches the size of telephone boxes and a mask-like capacity to 'mimic' humans.

Blood, screams, and CGI roaches chowing down on the supporting cast the net result, ensuring B-movie style pleasures with B-movie limitations. The script actually is not bad, the minimal science-as-doubled-edged-sword deliberations quite considered. There's even an occasional hint of satire; as jaded transport cop Dutton enters some slimy annexe of the hive, he bursts forth the familiar rejoinder: 'This is some weird shit!' only for Del Toro's crafty camera to peel back to reveal just that; weird shit all over the walls.

Sorvino is fine, getting smothered in gunk and grunting through some sub-Ripley energetics, but Brit Northam finds the NY twang a fiercer opponent than the psychopathic creepies. It all descends, inevitably, into preposterousness, contrivance and eventually bare-faced silliness. ★★★ **IN**

MINORITY REPORT (2002)

Starring: *Tom Cruise (Chief John Anderton), Colin Farrell (Danny Witwer), Samantha Morton (Agatha), Max von Sydow (Director Lamar Burgess)*
Director: *Steven Spielberg*
Screenwriters: *Scott Frank, Jon Cohen, from a short story by Philip K. Dick*
12/139 mins./Sci-fi/Thriller/USA

Awards – *Empire Awards – Best Actor, Best British Actress, Best Director*

The year is 2054, and the murder rate in Washington D.C. is zero, thanks to information supplied to the authorities by a trio of pre-cognitives. But then Pre-Crime unit chief John Anderton becomes the subject of a massive manhunt . . .

The best scene in *Minority Report* involves a major character gruesomely trading one set of eyeballs for another. It is a deliciously dark joke upon which to rest the action, for *Minority Report* is a movie concerned with new ways of seeing. As such, it gives fresh impetus to a growing suspicion about the world's most successful director: Steven Spielberg himself has traded eyeballs.

From the murderous visions of the pre-cognitive trio, to the retina scans personalising your shopping experience in Orwellian fashion, *Minority Report* is saturated with metaphors for seeing. But look closer, and each new metaphor also functions as a commentary on the hazards of movie direction itself.

Watching Cruise's cop, Anderton, conduct the Pre-Cog output, sorting through complex future images with expert waves of gloved hands, is how you would like to believe Steven Spielberg directs – musically, masterfully. But Spielberg, long removed from brash youth, understands that ultimately all such confidence is misplaced.

A little later, Anderton's own skill betrays him when he zeroes in on his own face perpetrating a future murder. Images in *Minority Report* are unreliable, subject to interference and editing. The gritty cinematography, once again provided by Janusz Kaminski, has the flavour of faded family photos and recurring dreams. You cannot quite trust it, yet the locations seem horribly familiar.

Do not, then, be hoodwinked by the film's atavistic 'Everybody Runs' tagline; clearly the marketing people at Fox would like the *Jurassic Park* audience to believe this is a breathless action spectacle. It's not.

Minority Report is a hybrid film noir, pitched in moral twilight and steeped in shadow. There may be no blue in the bleached sky, but this is not a standard-issue dystopian future. Nor is it a satirical cartoon in the Paul Verhoeven tradition. Indeed, Spielberg, that most apolitical of directors, could be the first visionary to fashion a near-future that feels distinctly ours – organic, market-driven and teeming with as much danger as promise.

The film noir structure is adhered to until the bitter end, even if the luxurious running time lacks the adamantine precision of the films Spielberg would most like to imitate: *The Maltese Falcon*, *The Big Sleep*. The denouement, during which the detective unmasks the villain, is classic noir. The action, let it be noted, ran out an hour ago. ★★★★ **IF**

Movie Trivia: Minority Report

One time Cruise directors Cameron Crowe (*Jerry Maguire*) and Paul Thomas Anderson (*Magnolia*) appear as commuters on a train. Cruise had only completed filming *Vanilla Sky* a few days prior to commencing work on *Minority Report*. One of the unused concepts from the think tank was a 'smart toilet' which analyses your, er… deposits and adjusts your diet accordingly.

THE MIRACLE OF MORGAN'S CREEK (1944)

Starring: *Eddie Bracken (Norval Jones), Betty Hutton (Trudy Kockenlocker), Diana Lynn (Emmy Kockenlocker), William Demarest (Officer Kockenlocker), Brian Donlevy (Governor McGinty), Akim Tamiroff (The Boss), Porter Hall (Justice Of The Peace)*
Director: *Preston Sturges*
Screenwriter: *Preston Sturges*
PG/99 mins./Comedy/USA

When small-town good-time gal Trudy Kockenlocker gets pregnant after a wartime fling with an unknown soldier, her bank clerk boyfriend, Norval Jones, agrees to marry her. However, all manner of ensuing misunderstandings force Norval to flee the law and only the arrival of sextuplets saves the day.

Preston Sturges created history in 1945, when his screenplays for both *The Miracle Of Morgan's Creek* and *Hail The Conquering Hero* earned Oscar nominations. However, what was even more noteworthy was the fact that he slipped two such joyously amoral and anti-heroic comedies past both Hollywood and Washington's moral guardians in wartime.

Sturges had first conceived the idea of a parody of the Virgin Birth in 1937. But he revised it five years later to satisfy the adoring Betty Hutton's desire to star in one of his pictures and his own determination to exact revenge on Paramount producer Buddy DeSylva for interfering in and then delaying *The Great Moment*. Sturges knew that the Breen Office would object to the sexual aspects of his story and thoroughly expected the War Department Pictorial Board to take exception to his depiction of US soldiers as promiscuous lugs. But, although they took their time in passing the screenplay – causing Sturges to start shooting without a finished script – they made surprisingly few recommendations and seemed genuinely amused by the entire caustic scenario.

Uncertain where his plotline would take him, Sturges worked unusually slowly and overshot both schedule and budget. He wasn't helped by Eddie Bracken's bid to steal every scene he shared with Hutton to pay back the studio for encouraging her to upstage him in the past. But, Sturges eventually coaxed splendid performances out of each, with Bracken coming up with much of his own timidity business and Hutton doing anything required to get a laugh. Moreover, he was well served, as ever, by the old pros he insisted on casting in minor roles, who looked as though they had wandered in from real life for the duration of their scenes.

The Catholic Legion of Decency presented some eleventh-hour hurdles, but this fizzingly written and superbly directed assault on heartland morality and the very values that America's forces were fighting for was a runaway success. Moreover, its audacious blend of screwball, slapstick, smut and sophistication confirmed Sturges's burgeoning reputation as a bona fide comic genius and it remains scabrously funny 60 years on. ★★★★ **DP**

MIRROR (1974)

Starring: *Margarita Terekhova (Mother/Natalya), Phillip Yankovsky (Aleksei, aged 5), Larisa Tarkovskaya (Nadezha), Ignat Danilltsev (Aleksei), Oleg Yankovskt (Father), Innokenti Smoktunovsky (Narrator), Arsenii Tarkovsky (Narrator – poetry)*
Director: *Andrei Tarkovsky*
Screenwriters: *Andei Tarkovsky, A. Misharin*
U/102 mins./Drama/USSR

The life of Aleksei, an abandoned son who became an absentee father – and whose mother strongly resembles his wife – is chronicled through a series of dreams, flashbacks and newsreel clips.

Inspired by a recurring dream of the house in which he was born, Andrei Tarkovsky's fourth feature began its life in 1964, as a proposed novella about childhood. However, by the time he and Alexander Misharin completed the script for *Confession* in 1968, the emphasis had shifted away from youth and on to motherhood. When Mosfilm rejected the project, Tarkovsky reworked the material into the short story, 'A White Day', which was published in 1970 and prompted producer-director Grigori Chukhrai to commission a screenplay.

Aware that this was his most personal picture and sensing that it would also be his most artistically significant, Tarkovsky found the film very difficult to make. He constantly revised the text during the protracted shooting process and then produced 20 different edits, with Ludmilla Feiginova. But while he was eventually satisfied with his work, the authorities were not. Thus, branded an 'artistic failure', *Mirror* was released with no fanfare in 1975 and its subsequent international acclaim proved something of an embarrassment for Goskino.

Divided into three main timeframes – the 1930s, the Second World War and the present – the film used alternating colour and monochrome sequences to convey a series of memories and dreams whose poignancy and lyricism was intensified by the verse and classical music on the soundtrack. Even newsreels of historical events like the Spanish Civil War and the Cultural Revolution and such Soviet landmarks as the 1934 balloon record attempt and Chkalov's 1937 flight over the North Pole were employed to bind the historical and the personal in this spellbinding life of a mind.

However, Tarkovsky doesn't always make it clear whose visions we are sharing and whose voice his poet father Arsenii is supposed to represent. Consequently, this has always been considered a difficult watch. Regardless of its dense intellectual and autobiographical content, however, *Mirror* can still be appreciated as an attempt to capture the human soul and to show that, for all our diverse individual experiences, we still have much in common on an emotional and spiritual level. ★★★★ **DP**

THE MIRROR HAS TWO FACES (1996)

Starring: *Barbra Streisand (Rose Morgan), Jeff Bridges (Gregory Larkin), Lauren Bacall (Hannah Morgan), George Segal (Henry Fine), Mimi Rogers (Claire), Pierce Brosnan (Alex)*
Director: *Barbra Streisand*
Screenwriters: *Richard LaGravenese, Andre Cayatte, Gerard Oury, from the screenplay Le Miroir A Deux Faces*
15/121 mins./Comedy/Romance/USA
Awards: *Golden Globes – Best Supporting Actress*

A New York has intellectual a makeover to revive her marriage with unexpected results.

Barbra Streisand plays a dowdy New York Jewish intellectual who gets a makeover and ends up as a permed Babs Streisand who looks like she just stepped out of a drag queen revue. Jeff Bridges – woefully miscast in ways that he probably still can't fathom – adjusts his spectacles and thinks of better days as he gamely falls for our heroine.

Rose thinks that she can spice up her marriage with some make-up and diet but little knowing that the platonic lack of passion is exactly what her emotionally stunted fellow University professor husband wants.

Richard LaGravanese's screenplay does make some sharp observations, while the Oscar-nominated Lauren Bacall excels as Babs' domineering mom, but Streisand the über-star (plus director) dominates the movie to its detriment. ★★ **BM**

MISERY (1990)

Starring: *James Caan (Paul Sheldon), Kathy Bates (Annie Wilkes), Richard Farnsworth (Sheriff Buster), Frances Sternhagen (Virginia McCain), Lauren Bacall (Marcia Sindell)*
Director: *Rob Reiner*
Screenwriter: *William Goldman, from the novel by Stephen King*
18/107 mins./Thriller/USA
Awards: *Academy Awards – Best Actress, Golden Globes – Best Actress*

Bed-ridden author James Caan is tortured by cock-a-doody number one fan Kathy Bates, in a taut and often blackly comic watershed moment for Stephen King adaptations.

It is clearly Rob Reiner's mission in life to prove that he can handle any kind of movie with equal aplomb – so far we've had comedy (*This Is Spinal Tap*), fantasy (*The Princess Bride*) and a lurve story (*When Harry Met Sally*). And with *Misery* came thriller.

Paul Sheldon is a best-selling novelist, fed up with his massively popular pot-boilers and their heroine Misery Chastain, and eager to create some Art. On his way to his publishers from his mountain hideaway, manuscript on board, he crashes, and is rescued by Annie Wilkes (the deservedly Oscar-winning Bates), the novelist's 'number one fan', and a nurse to boot.

All seems well until Annie suddenly clicks that Misery is a goner, and she ever-so-slowly loses the few marbles God gave her, victimising Sheldon mentally and physically for killing her beloved heroine, and forcing him to bring her back to life by plonking him in front of a typewriter and demanding that he write a Lazarus-style instalment to the series.

Veteran screenwriter William Goldman expertly creates a vivid sense of reality from the situation – a bit of a first, this, for a Stephen King adaptation – and the two leads complement each other brilliantly, with Caan back on form, and Bates creating in Annie Wilkes one of the screen's more memorable fruit-cakes. ★★★★ **PT**

⊙ THE MISFITS (1961)

Starring: *Clark Gable (Gay Langland), Marilyn Monroe (Roslyn Taber), Montgomery Clift (Pearce Howland), Thelma Ritter (Isabelle Steers), Eli Wallach (Guido)*
Director: *John Huston*
Screenwriter: *Arthur Miller*
PG/124 mins./Drama/Romance/Western

Roslyn, in Reno to get a divorce, meets a crowd of cowboys and falls for top-hand Gay. When she discovers that they are catching wild horses to be turned into pet-food, Roslyn tries to thwart their round-up.

The final film credit for Marilyn Monroe, Clark Gable and Montgomery Clift, this is aptly the story of a collection of deadbeats who get together in the Nevada desert and demonstrate that the old myths of the movies, as represented by the Western, have reached a sorry state.

Glamour girl Monroe is Out West not as a pioneer or even a showgirl but has come here for a quickie divorce, while battered modern cowboys Gable and Clift, assisted by tarnished flyboy Eli Wallach, are heading for a last round-up, which turns out not to be a romantic ranch venture but sordid butchery.

Scripted by Arthur Miller and directed with dusty brilliance by John Huston, this is one of the best contemporary-set Westerns, malformed only by Monroe's glory-hogging – she nagged hubby Miller into cutting scenes that made sense of Wallach's character for fear she was being upstaged – and redeemed by its acute vision of a degraded frontier.

The script makes acting demands of Monroe which she's not quite up to, but her performance is nevertheless poignant and affecting, especially when she shuts up and just looks at the state of things, while Gable and Clift similarly play on their own legends – the ageing but still-virile King of the Movies and the wounded, beautiful cowboy martyr who contrasts Gable's leathery toughness with vulnerable machismo.

These hard-riding rodeo boys here are not out for guts and glory, just rounding up stray horses for petfood, and Gable and Clift go out on high notes, embodying their own contradictory screen legends as heroes who must lose in the end. ★★★★ **KN**

⊙ MISHIMA: A LIFE IN FOUR CHAPTERS (1985)

Starring: *Ken Ogata (Yukio Mishima), Masayuki Shionoya (Morita), Junkichi Orimoto (General Mashita), Naoko Otani (Mother), Go Riju (Mishima, Age 18-19), Masato Aizawa (Mishima, Age 9-14)*
Director: *Paul Schrader*
Screenwriters: *Leonard Schrader, Paul Schrader, Chieko Schrader, from various works by Yukio Mishima*
15/115 mins./Biography/Drama/USA

In 1970, Yukio Mishima – the Japanese novelist, movie star, political conservative and s-m-inclined gay icon – leads members of the Shield Society, his private army of pro-Emperor traditionalists, in a suicidal assault on an army camp. Flashback episodes reveal his early life, while scenes from three of his novels are colourfully dramatised.

A *Citizen Kane*-style attempt to come to grips with the public and private faces of a real-life character, this finally reflects as much upon the neuroses and drives of its creator as its subject.

The reason writer-director Paul Schrader takes such an innovative, unusual approach to the biopic is that Mishima's heirs placed restrictions on what he could and couldn't show, insisting that various sides of his character (his masochism, homosexuality and right-wing politics) be shown obliquely, expressed mostly in chapters from his more autobiographical novels, which are staged in stylised, Noh-like fashion. The various strands of the film are woven into a pattern that not only delves deep into the fascinating personality of Mishima but does much to illuminate the strange drives which throb throughout Schrader's own work.

Schrader's obsessive-puritanical philosophising is at its purest here, as he channels his usual concerns into a meditation on Yukio's Mishima tussles with love, death, honour and the spirit. Few directors could have made a film about Mishima without descending to sensationalism, but Schrader shows a sensitivity to the man and his moods which makes for affecting cinema. Ravishingly shot, in three distinct styles, with a hauntingly brilliant Philip Glass score.

Ogata gives an excellent central performance, investing Mishima with a sense of humour and an often-endearing charm that makes him more than just a significant freak – even when he is lecturing bewildered troops avout the need to revive the samurai ideal and making his last point by ritually disembowelling himself. ★★★★ **KN**

⊙ MISS CONGENIALITY (2000)

Starring: *Sandra Bullock (Gracie Hart), Michael Caine (Victor Melling), Benjamin Bratt (Eric Matthews), Candice Bergen (Kathy Morningside), Ernie Hudson (FBI Asst. Director Harry McDonald), William Shatner (Stan Fields)*
Director: *Donald Petrie*
Screenwriters: *Marc Lawrence, Katie Ford*
12/105 mins./Action/Comedy/Romance/USA

A bomber is targeting the Miss America beauty pageant and Agent Matthews selects tomboy Fed Gracie Hart to go undercover as a contestant. First, however, Gracie must be shown the ropes by disgraced pageant expert, Victor Melling.

Over in America, this slight comedy restored some of Sandra Bullock's box office lustre. A genuine crowdpleaser boasting a charming star turn, *Miss Congeniality* is indeed difficult to dislike, but hey, sometimes it's worth the effort.

Much more believable as a beauty queen than a scruffy, ill-mannered Fed, Bullock snorts sweetly and falls off high heels very well. Which is just about enough to carry the first 30 minutes. After that it would be nice if the script gave her something else to do.

There are some incidental pleasures away from the leading lady: the screenplay mines broad comedy from the all-American crassness of beauty contests – although the film won't criticise them too far; the banter between Bullock's bumbling cop chums is amusing; and the growing rapport between Bullock and Caine's gay makeover expert is nicely, if programmatically, played out. Moreover, it's good to see Candice Bergen and William Shatner shine as fading pageant hosts. That said, there is a completely inconsequential feel to the whole exercise.

There are too many storylines, too many characters, too much sentiment: *Miss Congeniality* is a prime example of moviemaking by committee, a disease which kills comedy in particular. Each teeny character has their own little arc, each identifiable audience demographic is pandered to with a story beat here, or a cameo there. Baloney.

Do we care whether the shy contestant who befriends Bullock comes out of her shell? Do we care if Caine's character restores his pride and prestige? Do we even care if Bullock and Bratt get together?

No matter. This is not a complicated story – it's about a tom boy Fed who shaves her legs in order to go undercover at a beauty pageant, gets into a few scrapes, falls over a lot. And whenever director Petrie remembers this fact and points the camera at his engaging star (who earned a Golden Globe nomination for her performance), his film is good, easy-on-the-brain fun.

The sequel, *Miss Congeniality: Armed And Fabulous* (2005) ditched the romantic sub-plot and teamed Bullock with Regina King for a mis-matched buddy movie, which memorably involved them posing as drag queens. ★★★ **WT**

⊙ MISSION: IMPOSSIBLE (1996)

Starring: *Tom Cruise (Ethan Hunt), Jon Voigt (Jim Phelps), Emmanuelle Béart (Claire Phelps), Jean Reno (Franz Krieger), Ving Rhames (Luther Stickell), Kristin Scott Thomas (Sarah Davies), Vanessa Redgrave (Max)*
Director: *Brian De Palma*
Screenwriters: *David Koepp, Robert Towne, from a story by Koepp and Steven Zaillian, television series by Bruce Geller*
PG/105 mins./Action/Spy/Thriller/USA

A spider's web of stolen computer disks, moles, mayhem, double-crosses and murder.

It begins as it means to go on: with a bang. A fuse is lit and the credits literally explode in a rapid-fire barrage of images and music.

A revisitation of the famous 60s TV series with that impossibly cool theme tune and a cachet of catchy catchphrases ('This tape will self destruct ...' etc), this treats its inspiration with just the right amount of respect, while at the same time managing to reinvent the premise of a group of undercover agents, working in what is now the Cold War-less 90s. The plot is a contortionist's delight: a spider's web of stolen computer disks, moles, mayhem, double-crosses and murder that begins in Prague with Cruise's Ethan Hunt and his Impossible Missions Force (including Béart, Emilio Estevez and Kristin Scott-Thomas), under the direction of Jim Phelps (Voight in the Peter Graves role), called in to intercept a traitor and a disk containing the identities of every Western spy in Europe. When the mission goes awry and his team is annihilated, Cruise suspects he's been set up, only to find himself accused of being the mole. As Washington, London and finally the Channel Tunnel all go by in a blur, the rest of the film is taken up with Cruise, aided by Béart, all lips and tits, out to prove his innocence.

There are, of course, gadgets galore, Cruise peeling off various cool disguises, and that piece of music at regular intervals. De Palma, undisputed master of the set-piece, pulls out all the f-stops this time around, with edgy camera angles and a series of extended tension-building nerve-jangling sequences – including one in a white-walled vault resembling something out of *2001*, where Cruise is suspended on wires above a touch-sensitive floor.

At a little under two hours this fair zips by, but when the script, by David Koepp and Robert Towne, moves from action to plotting and concerns itself with upping the levels of paranoia, you'll be left scratching your head trying to decipher the twists within twists within twists. ★★★★ **MS**

⊙ MISSION: IMPOSSIBLE II (M:I-2) (2000)

Starring: *Tom Cruise (Ethan Hunt), Dougray Scott (Sean Ambrose), Thandie Newton (Nyah Nordoff-Hall), Ving Rhames (Luther Stickell), Richard Roxburgh (Hugh Stamp)*
Director: *John Woo*
Screenwriter: *Robert Towne, from a story by Ronald D. Moore, Brannon Braga, TV series created by Bruce Geller*
15/118 mins./Action/Spy/Thriller/USA

A special agent comes up against his defected partner and now evil nemesis.

Well, well, Mr Woo, we meet again. And this time around your mission – should, of course, you choose to accept it – is to deliver the sequel to a film directed by a (pre-blip) Brian De Palma, that boasted an eclectic cast, was based on a seminal 60s TV series and swooped $422 million at the world-wide box office. Quite a proposition, certainly. But then, this – to paraphrase the film's best line – isn't mission 'a little tricky', after all.

Although the result isn't exactly *Mission: Impossible*, either. Gone are the myriad characters, gloriously convoluted plot contortions and congealing mood of taut paranoia. Gone, too, is an actual team to speak of (Polson pootles about in a helicopter and Rhames does little more than tap aimlessly on his laptop), and criminally absent are gadgets of any real invention.

What we're left with is Hunt ... He's up against defected Agent Ambrose – *GoldenEye*'s 006 springing strangely to mind – while Exotic Love Interest With The Daft Name, Nyah flips from aloof *femme fatale* to infatuated girlie in a preposterously short space of time. So, it's James Bond then. A fluid, kinetic, visually impressive one admittedly, but Bond all the same.

And it starts – rather aptly, as it turns out – with more of a whimper than a bang, as a pre-credit mid-air heist (complete with prerequisite mountain-top collision cliché) culminates in the theft of both the crucial deadly virus and its only antidote. And so, enter he of the $taggering pay cheque (just maybe – and get this for depth – he's in fact the metaphorical cure and Scott the nasty bug) to save the day, grab the girl and look cool in sunglasses.

This, you see, is Tom Cruise's show. From scaling cliff faces to abseiling into confined spaces (simply lifting its predecessor's finest hour), he looks nothing short of spectacular; flowing locks, chiselled jaw, toned muscles and glistening brow, all captured in mouthwatering slo-mo and longing, brooding close-up. Again and again.

Which inevitably throws into question who was really wearing the trousers. For, as much as he has never been one to underplay his leading men, it's an over-indulgence that smacks of the excessive, even for John Woo. Couple that with two Woo unknowns – a nigh-on tortuous mid-section (dragging on for close to an hour) of dreary plot exposition and a climax that shoots its bolt far too prematurely – and the answer seems fairly clear ... ★★★ **MD**

⊙ MISSION: IMPOSSIBLE III (2006)

Starring: *Tom Cruise (Ethan Hunt), Ving Rhames (Luther Stickell), Keri Russell (Lindsey), Philip Seymour Hoffman (Owen Davian), Laurence Fishburne (Brassel), Billy Crudup (John Musgrave), Simon Pegg (Benji Dunn), Michelle Monaghan (Julia), Jonathan Rhys Meyers (Declan), Maggie Q (Zhen)*
Director: *J.J.Abrams*
Screenwriters: *Alex Kurtzman, Roberto Orci, J.J.Abrams, based on the televison series by Bruce Geller*
12A/125 mins./Action/Adventure/USA

Ethan Hunt, retired from active duty and recently engaged to the lovely Julia, returns to action when an IMF agent he trained is captured. But when Hunt's attempts to snare evil arms dealer Owen Davian goes violently wrong, events spiral back towards the innocent Julia, who suffers under the illusion her fiancé works in transport.

Tom Cruise is no mug. When he picked JJ Abrams to cover his back for another sally through his Big Franchise, he was knowingly hiring pop-culture's golden child. Abrams' hip TV jinks have stirred global water-cooler conflabs tracking the fathomless trails of his twin peaks: *Alias* and *Lost*. For his part, Abrams wanted to accomplish two things with his turn as Missionary. First, make it a personal story, to find what lurks behind the glacial features of Ethan Hunt, the superspy guy who would rather hang off tall buildings than confess his feelings. Second, to regain something of the tag-team trickery and camp nuttiness of Bruce Webber's original TV series. Something Abrams has proved adept at, given *Alias* was built out of *Mission: Impossible*'s knotty conventions.

The news is halfway good. While the personal touch struggles to be anything more than conventional, try a sequence in which the four-strong IMF team (count in Ving Rhames, an adorable Maggie Q, and Jonathan Rhys Meyers) infiltrates the Vatican. Here is Abrams' magpie devotion fully in gear: devious, silly, perfectly syncopated with crispy-clean edits, and featuring an orange Lamborghini blown to little orangey bits and Cruise in a cassock. Once you've drawn breath, and that immortal theme music begins its pulsating rush, you get the urge to applaud. *Mission 3* is leaps, bounds and base-jumps ahead of the turgid *Mission 2*, even a trick or two ahead of the convoluted original – but it's still not entirely the film you want it to be.

What we have with this ultra-expensive, thick-sheened superstar-vehicle is cracking sequences in a ragged whole; a movie crowded with ideas, a geek's trilling delight in envisioning gadgetry (love the brain bombs) and impossible situations (love the 'fulcruming' off a Shanghai skyscraper), that keeps writing itself into corners. While Abrams brilliantly explains exactly how those feature-perfect masks are carried off, to shunt a muddled Hunt from crisis to crisis a mobile phone must conveniently ring with the plot on the other end. On the build *Mission 3* is urgent and addictive, but when closing the deal it's contrived and predictable.

For instance, a chilling Philip Seymour Hoffman skirts the temptation to ham up nerveless villain Owen Davian, a global purveyor of techno-terror, but fades from importance when Abrams starts a rather obvious game of traitor-in-our-midst. The glassy romance, that touchy-feely bit, is made sweet by Michelle Monaghan, but requires lumbering scenes of Cruise, straining at his emotional range, getting all heated and unprofessional in order to save his lady. The increasingly fraught and dishevelled Hunt, forever front and centre, remains about as clandestine as Krusty the Clown. Wouldn't it be great to have a *Mission: Impossible* where no one has to go rogue and they, like, outwit the badguys?

Given all the violence meted out to women, it's no wonder Abrams has been dubbed the new Hitchcock. He's got a fair few of the fatman's magic licks as well. There's a classic macguffin called the Rabbit's Foot that could be the 'anti-God' – a hilariously lightheaded bit of conspiracy making, about a compound that will bring about the end of mankind, delivered by a pleasingly nerdy Simon Pegg. Hitch, though, would have realised such dark-dizzy fun doesn't need embellishing. ★★★ **IN**

THE MISSION (1986)

Starring: *Robert De Niro (Rodrigo Mendoza), Jeremy Irons (Father Gabriel), Ray McAnally (Altamirano), Aidan Quinn (Felipe Mendoza), Cherie Lunghi (Carlotta)*
Director: *Roland Joffe*
Screenwriter: *Robert Bolt*
PG/126 mins./Drama/War/UK

Awards: *Academy Awards – Best Cinematography, BAFTA – Best Supporting Actor (Ray McAnally), Best Editing, Best Score, Golden Globes – Best Score, Best Screenplay*

The period tale of a priest, a warrior and a tribe striving to support a mission in the face of political upheaval in South America.

Unsurprisingly, following the wealth of plaudits and awards that were heaped upon Roland Joffe's more documentarian passion play, *The Killing Fields*, he was keen to continue with such grandiose social scope. Producer David Puttnam (obviously with one eye on re-inventing the legacy of David Lean's epic productions of the 60s) married his director with Lean's former scriptwriter, Robert Bolt, to shape this tale of a priest, a warrior and a tribe striving to support a mission in the face of political upheaval.

Bolt's script cleaved to one of his familiar themes: the idea that the bigger picture will always smother the innocent. Add to this the struggle for redemption, the contradictions of faith and the dubious nature of progress – then shoot it on location in Colombia and Argentina, using genuine native tribes as the luminous Guarani. No one could accuse these filmmakers of lacking courage.

Lacking the centrality of Lean's work, Joffe and Bolt spread the story between three divided characters – a shadow-dance of the Holy Trinity. The most primal and colourful of these is Robert De Niro's Mendoza, the mercenary and slave-trader who murders his own brother in a fit of jealous pique. A man driven by powerful, redolent emotions, he suffers a Sisyphean penance, spectacularly and repeatedly hoisting the weight of his past, in the shape of his bundled armour and weaponry, up the cliff-face.

Accepted by tribe and Jesuit order, his is less a battle with faith than the furies of the real world, where the capacity for love and compassion can co-exist with the impulse for violence. De Niro, in a signal of the rigid, internalised characters of his later career and working with a script of limited words and no great attempt to align accents, cunningly reduced Mendoza to a man of physical expression.

Father Gabriel is a more elusive character to define. He starts as a saint and finishes as a martyr, giving Mass as Spanish soldiers annihilate his flock. Yet there is an arc for Jeremy Irons' emotionally contained priest. Faced with his own sense of betrayal, he too refuses to leave the mission, defying the orders of the Church.

Many read the film as an attack on the hypocrisy of a Catholic Church transformed into a political body, manoeuvring its own relevance in the face of a modernising Europe. But there is more subtlety to it than that. The film optimistically contests that the true Church actually resides in the individual priest or missionary, rather than the destructive bureaucratic bodies of the Papacy.

It is the brilliant Irish actor Ray McAnally's Bishop Altamirano – ostensibly the narrator and third lead, sent to judge and condemn the missions – who gives the clearest picture of the folly of man. He understands that survival depends on going with the flow, but suffers that it would have been better had neither slave-trader nor priest ever ventured in the jungle.

Upon release, many attacked the film for being cold-blooded and, true, there is a guardedness to Joffe's vision; he steeps his film in a historical leanness, where the beauty of the Colombian jungle is as stark and ruthless as the conquistadors.

Shooting in the dense, soiled tones of the real rainforest, gifted cinematographer Chris Menges opts for an overcast quality, drenching the humid drama in downpours of rain, caking everything in lank mud. The whole film has a swollen, sickly look to it – pestilence is in the air. For the filmmakers alike, the stylisation took an uncomfortable reality; with the exception of the indomitable De Niro, cast and crew were assailed by amoebic dysentery throughout the shoot.

Nothing is prettified to make the film more palatable, not even the emotional currents. Unlike David Lean, Joffe seems opposed to grandstanding, flatly refusing to wear his heart on his public school sleeve – an admirable restraint that may have contributed to the film's box office flop. ★★★★ **IN**

MISSISSIPI BURNING (1988)

Starring: *Gene Hackman (Agent Rupert Anderson), Willem Dafoe (Agent Alan Ward), Frances McDormand (Mrs Pell), Brad Dourif (Deputy Clinton Pell), R. Lee Ermey (Mayor Tilman)*
Director: *Alan Parker*
Screenwriter: *Chris Gerolmo*
18/121 mins./Crime/Drama/Historical/USA

Awards: *Academy Awards – Best Cinematography, BAFTA – Best Cinematography, Best Editing, Best Sound*

When three young civil rights activists are murdered by the Ku Klux Klan in Mississippi the largest FBI manhunt in history is sparked off.

Mississippi, 1964: two young white civil rights activists and a black colleague are driving along a country road when they notice a car dangerously close behind. Suddenly the car rams into them to stop at the side of the road. A fat white face appears at the side window and the young driver nervously asks him what's happening. Thirty seconds later the three youths are dead, murdered by the local Ku Klux Klan. Such was essentially the fate of the James Chaney, Mickey Schwener and Andy Goodman in

Neshoba County, Mississippi 1964. Their deaths sparked off the biggest manhunt in FBI history and led to the conviction of seven Klan members, including the deputy sheriff of Neshoba County. The affair has been repeatedly documented in various books and now it forms the core of Alan Parker's *Mississippi Burning*. And it's Parker's film that has sparked the controversy that probably explains why its fistful of Oscar nominations weren't turned into awards.

The main charge against Parker is that he twists the facts of the case to suit his own story and in doing so rewrites history of the early civil rights movement as yet another tale of Whitey to the rescue. Certainly, the film is littered with examples of fact giving way to fiction and the main focus of the movie is not the fight for equality but the fiery relationship between FBI agents Anderson and Wilson, with a romantic interest thrown in for good measure. It's hardly surprising that one American critic has accused Parker of behaving as if 'my talent is more important than your reality'. Setting aside *Mississippi Burning*: The Debate, *Mississippi Burning*: The Film hurtles along at a gripping pace. The South brought vividly to life with blazing churches, Klan crosses, dusty barbershops and segregated washrooms.

The white folk are podgy, ugly and slack-jawed, the blacks lean, handsome and with 300 years of suffering in their eyes. Hackman is marvellous as Anderson, charming the deputy sheriff's wife one minute, grabbing a local thug by the balls the next and applying himself with relish to threats like 'I'm going to get so far up your nose you're going to feel my boots on your chin.' (One feels like Popeye Doyle would have appreciated that one.) Dafoe offers a useful performance as his partner, the buttoned-down liberal from the North who genuinely can't understand the pitch of Mississippi's race hatred. ★★★★ **BMc**

MISTER ROBERTS (1955)

Starring: *Henry Fonda (Lt. Doug Roberts), James Cagney (Captain), Jack Lemmon (Ens. Frank Thurlowe Pulver), William Powell (Doc), Ward Bond (C.P.O. Dowdy), Betsy Palmer (Lt. Ann Girard), Phillip Carey (Mannion), Nick Adams (Reber), Harry Carey Jr (Stefanowski), Ken Curtis (Dolan)*
Directors: *John Ford, Mervyn LeRoy*
Screenwriters: *Joshua Logan, Frank S Nugent, based on the play by Logan and Thomas Heggen and the novel by Heggen*
U/123 mins./Comedy-Drama/USA

When not keeping scheming ensign Frank Thurlowe Pulver out of trouble, Lieutenant Doug Roberts attempts to mediate between the crew of the USS *Reluctant* and their captain, who resolutely refuses to engage in wartime action. But only the ship's doctor appreciates the pressure he's under.

Henry Fonda spent seven years as Mister Roberts. In all, he gave over 1000 performances on Broadway and some 600 more on tour. However, he was 50 by the time Warner Bros. came to adapt Thomas Heggen and Joshua Logan's play (making him 20 years too old for the role) and concerns were expressed that the camera would expose the years that could be disguised on stage. William Holden refused the part, insisting that it belonged to Fonda. But Marlon Brando had no such scruples and accepted, only for John Ford to threaten to quit unless Fonda was cast.

Unfortunately, this act of magnanimity was to backfire on both men, as Warners demanded a broadening of the humour and Ford and Fonda soon fell out over this roughhouse approach. Moreover, Fonda resented Ford's attempts to rework his interpretation of a role that had become second nature and, refusing to recognise the different demands of stage and screen, he confronted the director and was socked on the jaw for his trouble. Although Ford apologised, the rift with his favoured Man of Principle never healed and it was, perhaps, a mercy that the regretful drinking bout which poisoned the on-set atmosphere induced a gallbladder rupture that caused 'Pappy' to be replaced by Mervyn Le Roy, who consented to a shared credit, but refused to acknowledge the fact that Joshua Logan was brought in to reshoot a couple of crucial sequences.

Much had changed in Hollywood since Fonda had last starred in a movie. Consequently, his performance retained a stubborn theatricality, which occasionally sat uncomfortably alongside James Cagney and William Powell's old school restraint and Jack Lemmon's new kid bravura. Roberts's courage, decency and integrity remained affecting. But Fonda's familiarity with the character deprived Roberts of life and he was overlooked completely by the Academy, while Lemmon won Best Supporting Actor. It was the final frustration in a dream project that had turned into something of a nightmare. ★★★ **DP**

MOBY DICK (1956)

Starring: *Gregory Peck (Captain Ahab), Richard Basehart (Ishmael), Leo Genn (Starbuck), James Robertson Justice (Captain Boomer), Harry Andrews (Stubb), Orson Welles (Father Mapple)*
Director: *John Huston*
Screenwriters: *Ray Bradbury, John Huston, based on the novel by Herman Melville*
PG/115 mins./Drama-Adventure/USA

A young seaman recounts the tale of his first voyage, with the dreaded peg-legged Captain Ahab whose obsessive search for the white whale Moby Dick, who took his limb, will reap disaster.

What brave soul would ever attempt to adapt this treasure, widely considered the Great American Novel, rippling with subtext and laborious with detail? Why, John Huston, of course, that erstwhile Ahab of American directing. Sadly, it proves even beyond his grand designs, and the voluminous tide of Herman Melville's great, creaking ship of a book are reduced to a colourful odyssey of man striving against the forces of nature in the shape of a white whale. Casting Gregory Peck as the immortal Ahab was a brave decision, but one so synonymous with the genteel humanity of Atticus Finch could never truly ferment the venom of this crusading vision of blind obsession. It's a good effort, but he embodies the film's weakness, always a shadow of something far greater.

Filleted from the 600 pages by sci-fi author Ray Bradbury and Huston himself, the script does, at least, keep the first person narrative – Richard Basehart plays the callow youth through whose eyes we look, and gets to spout the most famous opening line in literary history: 'Call me Ishmael.' He, for those who have read the book (or pretended to) will hook up with enigmatic harpoonist Queequeg, who will play guardian as they set sail on the legendary whaler *The Pequod*. Meanwhile, Huston works hard to invest what is fast becoming a sturdy enough adventure tale with some of the book's religious foreboding and grand metaphors (Moby Dick is America!). A booming Orson Welles turns up for a cameo as a mordant preacher seeing the men off to battle with the ocean, and many of Ahab's Biblical cant is kept intact from the novel. But the authenticity of the seafaring and the magnificent modelwork finally diminish any opportunity for greater meaning. The film takes flight as a grand chase movie, and leaves its ambition in its wake. ★★★ **IN**

MODERN TIMES (1936)

Starring: *Charles Chaplin (A Factory Worker), Paulette Goddard (A Gamin), Henry Bergman (Café Proprietor), Tiny Sandford (Big Bill), Chester Conklin (Mechanic)*
Director: *Charles Chaplin*
Screenwriter: *Charles Chaplin*
U/87 mins./Comedy/USA

An assembly line worker is alienated by progress but struggles to get another job.

It's presumed that Chaplin's key target in his swan song to the silent era, *Modern Times*, was the impact of the Depression and the dehumanising nature of industry. But it's as easy to see it as an attack on Hollywood's transformation into a film factory, which suppressed individual inspiration in favour of bankable movies for the masses.

Another myth worth dispelling is that it was a political statement reflecting Chaplin's radical views. This notion has arisen from references to such Soviet classics as Pudovkin's *Mother* (the scene in which Charlie picks up the red flag and finds himself at the head of a workers' demonstration) and the fictitious claims of Kremlin film chief Boris Shumyatsky that he persuaded Chaplin to append an anti-capitalist finale. The film's banning by the Fascists in Germany and Italy, and Chaplin's hounding by the House Un-American Activities Committee further fanned the flames of Communist collusion.

But *Modern Times* was nothing more than another instance of the Little Tramp taking on the system, as he had done throughout his career. Indeed, it has more in common with the liberal parables that Frank Capra was producing in the same period than with Stalinist agitprop. Equally, the scenes in which Charlie and Conklin get stuck in the machinery are as much a lampoon of Constructivist montage sequences like those in Eisenstein's *Old And New* than an endorsement of Stalin's Five-Year Plan, which was even more brutally exploitative than any fat cat enterprise in the West.

Chaplin clearly resented the way mechanised society had turned individuals into drones, and vented his disgust in the hilarious episodes with the conveyor belt and the automatic feeding machine. But he was also prepared to accept that labour was a means to an end, hence Charlie's scramble to secure a job at the re-opened factory to help the gamin realise her twee and shamelessly bourgeois dream of a cosy cottage.

This is an ambitious, accomplished and frequently uproarious comedy. The exuberant energy of Charlie's manic bolt-twisting at the factory, his hallucinatory heroics during the prison riot (prompted by someone slipping 'joy powder' into a salt cellar), and his blindfold rollerskating balletics were remarkable for a 45-year-old who had been largely inactive for four years. Moreover, they proved that pantomime still had a place – even in an age of wisecracks and screwball. ★★★★★ **DP**

THE MODERNS (1988)

Starring: *Keith Carradine (Nick Hart), Linda Fiorentino (Rachel Stone). John Lone (Bertram Stone), Wallace Shawn (Oiseau), Genevieve Bujold (Libby Valentin), Geraldine Chaplin (Nathalie de Ville)*
Director: *Alan Rudolph*
Screenwriters: *Alan Rudolph, John Bradshaw*
15/126 mins./Drama/History/USA

Nick Hart is an expatriate living in Paris and a struggling artist. When a rich patroness offers him money to forge some paintings, his eyes light up. A similar goggling effect is had when he falls (again) for his estranged wife, Rachel.

Director Alan Rudolph launched his career with *Welcome To L.A.*, a gentle satire of Southern California with an obvious debt to Robert Altman. During the 80s, Altman went into exile while Rudolph and his regular troupe of actors continued to turn out offbeat ensemble pictures that buck the blockbuster trend. Rudolph's quirkiness and charm often go hand in hand with a pretentiousness that is largely missing from this winsome look at Americans in the Paris of 1926.

The Moderns' cast of characters includes a drunken Ernest Hemingway who is constantly pontificating, a bullish Gertrude Stein, and Nick Hart, a struggling American painter surviving on booze and caricatures that decorate the gossip column of his friend Oiseau. Enter Hart's estranged wife Rachel and her new husband Bertram Stone who has come to Paris to collect art. The two men fall out over Rachel while Hart is commissioned by the corrupt Nathalie de Ville to forge three modern masterworks in order to dupe her husband.

Rudolph's gentle satire plays around with notions of trust and originality in both art and life while gently mocking his characters. Chaplin is a notable monster. Carradine is all stares and cheekbones and Fiorentino is simply stunning. While the film pokes fun at cafe society, American materialism and modernist circles, the battle between Hart and the acquisitive Stone is played out against a Paris that is constantly fading back into the black-and-white of old photographs. Rudolph has always moved between detachment and self-conscious symbolism but the script and the milieu of *The Moderns* give his congenital playfulness a charm and an emotional force that it often lacks. ★★★★ **MC**

MONA LISA (1986)

Starring: *Bob Hoskins (George), Cathy Tyson (Simone), Michael Caine (Mortwell), Robbie Coltrane (Thomas), Clarke Peters (Anderson), Kate Hardie (Cathy)*
Director: *Neil Jordan*
Screenwriters: *Neil Jordan, David Leland*
18/104 mins./Drama/UK Awards – BAFTA – Best Actor

Down on his luck after a spell in the clink, petty gangster George takes up a lowly job driving around an expensive call girl, Simone. As he slowly falls in love with her, he becomes protector as she connives against local criminal kingpin Mortwell.

Neil Jordan's intelligent and taut fusion of gangster thriller, love story and exploration of class, race, even sexuality, in the heat of Thatcher's Britain, offers a fascinating inversion of the spit and valour of Bob Hoskins' previous home-grown mob-classic *The Long Good Friday*. Here Hoskins' George is everything Harold Shand is not: downtrodden, sapped of life, but with a heart beating still. Shand was in over his balding head, George knows he is getting deeper and deeper, aware it could be both his downfall and salvation.

His problem and his inspiration, in Neil Jordan's seamy, shadowy London holding boom-time at bay, is rangy black prostitute Simone (the striking Cathy Tyson). She has her own mission, to prise an underage hooker from the grip of her pimp, but it's causing ripples all the way up to slimeball boss Mortwell (Caine turning his cockney edges to famously black purpose). Theirs is a doomed romance on so many levels, but you can see George coming back to life, if not fully connecting with it, and that is the film's journey. Hoskins is so powerful, so rendingly alive, he, with Jordan's subtle guidance, lifts this delicate film from socially aware thriller into a Scorsese-like parable on exploitation, greed and the various dangerous guises of desire. The world Jordan envisions is desperate, but Hoskins's human heart offers a lovely thread of hope. ★★★★ **IN**

THE MONEY PIT (1986)

Starring: *Tom Hanks (Walter Fielding Jr), Shelley Long (Anna Crowley Beissart), Alexander Godunov (Max Biessart), Maureen Stapleton (Estelle), Joe Mantegna (Art Shirk), Philip Bosco (Curly)*
Director: *Richard Benjamin*
Screenwriter: *David Giler*
PG/91 mins./Comedy/USA

Luckless couple Walter and Anna are conned into buying a 'bargain priced' mansion, only to find it fall to pieces as soon as they move in. The race is on to get it renovated before it completely collapses.

A stretched Tom Hanks comedy, built with the sole purpose of literal cinematic wreckage – the gradual collapse of a house played as extended slapstick routine. It doesn't work, there's nothing but dust in the air and plaster on the floor, with Hanks and Shelley Long straining to turn desperation into punchlines. There isn't really a point here, just a juvenile love of destruction, the symbolic piano crashing to the floor ad infinitum.

There are those, assuredly, who might relate to home renovation tribulations and builders shaking their sorry heads, while snickering to themselves as they estimate, 'two weeks,' on repairs. But funny, how? Yet, that is the purpose of director Richard Benjamin, with Steven Spielberg also putting his name to the duff project as some extraneous producer, who never finds anything in the characters, their hopes and dreams dashed by their situation, beyond physical collapse. Hanks and Shelley deliver little charm, and little brain, making it hard to sympathise.

You have to congratulate the art director and his team for their imploding household, the final crash of the huge staircase has a disaster-movie-like flourish to it. There is genuine invention in the mishap, chains of events that grow inexorably bigger in their destructive power. But it is a masterclass in ruin, working on too many levels. ★★ **IN**

MONKEY BUSINESS (1952)

Starring: *Cary Grant (Dr Barnaby Fulton), Ginger Rogers (Mrs Edwina Fulton), Charles Coburn (Oliver Oxley), Marylin Monroe (Lois Laurel)*
Director: *Howard Hawks*
Screenwriters: *Harry Segall, Ben Hecht, Charles Lederer, I.A.L. Diamond*
PG/97 mins. /Comedy/USA

Scientist Dr Branaby Fulton, busy creating a formula for eternal youth, is caught between the homely charms of his wife and the full-throttle curves of his boss's secretary. When one of his test-chimps mixes the potion with the lab's water supply, Fulton begins to act like a teen. When his wife samples it, things get even worse.

A lesser known, and lesser accomplished, pairing of director Howard Hawks and superstar Cary Grant, which also features a small role for Marylin Monroe, but is so contrived and silly time has left it behind. Grant, akin to his superb dotty doctor in *Bringing Up Baby*, once again slides his charm into a nebbish academic, but Hawks' screwballing valour is off kilter and the actor sorely misses the prize sparring of Katharine Hepburn, leaving him out of sorts. The film aims for sweet rather than biting, lazily concocted around stupid notions about miraculous chemical formulas. It's high concept, whose comic potential is lost in a blather of established stars (Grant, Ginger Rogers and Monroe) trying to play teenage.

There might lie the disconnect for most. Hawks' notions of teen behaviour – Grant escapes from the lab to grab a new haircut and buy a sports car and natty threads, Rogers drags him to the honeymoon suite to re-enflame lost ardour – are strictly one-dimensional. The film is all antics and no commentary, beyond the stale reasoning that life shouldn't lose its sparkle with age. The three stars retain their immortal glimmer, that long-lost dash of personality that was the foundation stone for movies back then, but Hawks was having a rare but distinct off day. ★★ **IN**

MONSIEUR HULOT'S HOLIDAY (1953)

Starring: *Jacques Tati (Monsieur Hulot), Nathalie Pascaud (Martine), Micheline Rolla (The Aunt), Louis Perrault (Fred), Andre Dubois (Commandant)*
Director: *Jacques Tati*
Screenwriters: *Jacques Tati, Henri Marquet, Pierre Aubert, Jacques Lagrange*
U/85 mins./Comedy/France

While holidaying in the tiny Breton resort of Saint-Marc-sur-Mer, the courteous, affable and hugely accident-prone Monsieur Hulot so devotes himself to enjoyment that he barely notices the comic chaos that follows in his wake.

Jacques Tati was the heir of silent clowns like Max Linder, Charlie Chaplin and Buster Keaton, as he saw comedy primarily as a visual medium. However, his films were infinitely more democratic, as anyone or anything within the frame could potentially be amusing. Thus, while Hulot was the notional hero of this glorious seaside farce, it was very much an ensemble piece.

The action was filmed in Brittany in 1951. At its heart was Monsieur Hulot, a quixotic everyman whose angular posture and apologetic flounce belied his genius for the inadvertent chaos that impacted upon himself and his fellow guests. He plays his gramophone too loudly, disrupts card games, creates drafts and almost causes someone to drown. But, he also plunges into the sea while helpfully carrying suitcases and gets dragged along the beach by a runaway horse. Yet, the only thing that gets hurt is pride, as there's nothing malicious about Tati's precise pantomime.

Every gag was timed to perfection, whether it was the boat bobbing on the tide as Hulot attempted to paint it, his manic exploits at tennis and ping-pong or his frustrations with a wonky picture and a pesky rug. Much of the slapstick business recalled Tati's music-hall act. But he also launched a satirical assault on the modern world, as various modes of transport conspired to confound the hapless holidaymakers.

Yet, despite the stage origins of his physical technique, Tati's directorial tactics were wholly cinematic. In the absence of dialogue, sound took on a key comic role, with the audio and the visual frequently conniving at duping the audience into expecting pay-offs that never arrived in the anticipated form. Moreover, Tati also kept his camera at a distance to allow viewers to discover the gags in their own time. Indeed, it was an almost Hitchcockian approach to humour, as Tati built up the comic suspense.

But *Hulot*'s greatest achievement was its liberating contravention of the rules of screen storytelling, which had an incalculable impact on the nouvelle vague. Consequently, this is much more than an assemblage of comic cuts. It's a masterclass in filmic innovation. ★★★★★ **DP**

MONSTER'S BALL (2001)

Starring: *Billy Bob Thornton (Hank Grotowski), Halle Berry (Leticia Musgrove), Taylor Simpson (Lucille), Gabrielle Witcher (Betty), Heath Ledger (Sonny Grotowski)*
Director: *Marc Forster*
Screenwriters: *Milo Addica, Will Rokos*
15/111 mins./Drama/Romance/USA

Awards: *Academy Awards – Best Actress*

Corrections Officer Hank Grotowski heads the prison squad, which includes his troubled son, supervising the execution of Lawrence Musgrove. But after tragic events, Grotowski finds himself drawn towards Musgrove's emotionally drained wife Leticia . . .

Way to go, Halle! On one of the too-rare occasions Berry has had an opportunity to show what she can really do, she seizes her role as an exhausted woman at the end of her rope with such naked desperation and need that it's hard to watch – and harder to forget. Billy Bob Thornton certainly should also have been in the Oscar stakes, as he is riveting as a man of few words who initially seems unforgivably cold and harsh, but subtly and miraculously evokes understanding and pity.

Reduced to barest basics, this is a prison drama/romance, but it's about many things, all of them to do with compassion, humanity and the need for love. Fathers and sons are a major theme. Widower Hank is the son of an irredeemably selfish, nasty, racist, retired prison guard (Boyle playing the spectacularly horrid old Buck). Hank's sensitive, unloved son (Ledger's effective Sonny) is a third generation prison guard, bullied into the bitter family inheritance and rituals of small, mean, dusty lives.

They are imprisoned as surely as the cop killer sitting on Death Row.The condemned man, Musgrove (Combs doing a smart and impressive volte-face from his cool comedic role in *Made*), also has a browbeaten son. The bashful, ungainly boy has inherited his father's artistic talent and has eaten himself into obesity on the junk food and chocolate bars that are his only comfort.

As the sole woman to feature (besides a matter-of-fact prostitute who gets both Sonny and Hank's brisk, boorish custom), Berry's weary waitress Leticia is a bravely unflinching portrait of a woman so crushed, she's a drunk, abusive mother, with a palpably agonising need to feel something, anything.

Hank and Leticia would be no computer's dating match in a million years. However, the weight of cares and catastrophe on both of them is what makes it possible that these two, when their paths collide, could so touchingly, vulnerably, and tentatively, try to find their way back to life together.

As is so often the case with émigré directors, German-born, Swiss-raised, N.Y.U. graduate Forster brings an alert eye for specific detail and mood to the American scene. The heavy, stultifying atmosphere of the poor, rural, Southern setting dominates everything. Written by two struggling actors who showed remarkable tenacity and integrity by holding out through six frustrating years of negotiations with studios anxious to soften the script, this is a very adult, very humane drama. ★★★★ **AE**

MONSTERS, INC. (2001)

Starring: *the voices of: John Goodman (James P. 'Sulley' Sullivan), Billy Crystal (Mike Wazowski), Mary Gibbs (Boo), Steve Buscemi (Randall Boggs), James Coburn (Henry J. Waternoose III), Jennifer Tilly (Celia)*
Director: *Peter Docter*
Screenwriters: *Andrew Stanton, Daniel Gerson, from a story by Peter Docter, Jill Culton, Jeff Pidgeon, Ralph Eggleston*
U/88 mins./Animation/Comedy/Family/USA

Awards: *Academy Awards – Best Song, BAFTA – Childrens' Award (Best Film)*

Sulley and Mike are the number one 'scare team' at Monsters, Inc. — they jump out of closets to frighten kids and collect the scare energy which powers Monstropolis. However, when a (highly toxic) little girl gets trapped in Monstropolis their lives start to change.

If traditional animation enjoyed a tricky 12 months in 2001, then 3-D computer animation – *Final Fantasy* apart – was on a roll, as shown by this scooping the inaugural Best Animated Feature Oscar.

In some ways Monsters, Inc. – co-directed by Pete Docter, David Silverman and Lee Unkrich, with Pixar guru John Lasseter serving as executive producer – is everything we've come to expect from the Disney/Pixar axis.

It has a delicious premise, sumptuous animation and a mouth-watering voice cast. And yet this is a very different beast from Lasseter's *Toy Story* movies. Where *Toy Story* was knowing and occasionally arch, this is wide-eyed and innocent. (It is telling that the human child featured here is an impossibly cute two-year-old, compared to the *Toy Story* kids who were just starting to put away childish things.)

The familiar Pixar themes of childhood worlds of imagination are revisited but, unlike *Toy Story*, this is not an examination of the various threats posed to ephemeral pleasures. Instead, it is a joyful celebration of the power (literally, the power, as screams are the raw fuel of Monstropolis) of make-believe.

Sulley and Mike – brilliantly improvised by John Goodman and Billy Crystal – are bickering buddies in the Eric and Ernie mould. Funny, loveable and, above all, inseparable. This makes them a team in a way that Woody and Buzz were not. Woody and Buzz represented polar points of view and generated a genuine thematic tension that adults could grasp. Mike and Sulley are a more straightforward double-act. And, despite the monster menagerie on show, Mike and Sulley lack the fully realised supporting characters – the something-for-everyone approach – that so ably assisted Woody and Buzz.

On the plus side, technical leaps have definitely been made since *Toy Story*, and Sulley in particular is the most vivid and textured CGI character yet created.

Similarly, the climactic scramble through a labyrinth of closet doors – each one containing another world – is a breathless action-comedy set-piece that's several leagues ahead of the airport chase in *Toy Story 2*. And although *Monsters, Inc.* deserves to be seen on the big screen, arguably the definitive viewing experience will have to wait until DVD; only then will you begin to process the volume of fabulous sight gags tucked away in every corner of the beautifully detailed backgrounds. In other words, a treat for the eyeball. ★★★★ **CW**

Movie Trivia: Monsters, Inc.

Star Wars II: Attack Of The Clones made its trailer debut at this film. Many fans paid admission and then left after the teaser. Bill Murray was actually auditioned and chosen to be the voice of Sulley, but was un-contactable when he was called to be offered the part. Sulley's fur has over 2,320,413 CGI hairs. Old Disneyland posters adorn the walls of the children's bedrooms.

MONTY PYTHON AND THE HOLY GRAIL (1975)

Starring: *Graham Chapman (King Arthur/Voice of God/Middle Head/Hiccoughing Guard), John Cleese (Second Swallow-Savvy Guard/The Black Knight/Peasant 3/Sir Lancelot, the Brave/Taunting French Guard/Tim the Enchanter), Eric Idle (Dead Collector/Peasant 1/Sir Robin the Not-Quite-So-Brave-as-Sir Launcelot/First Swamp Castle Guard/Concorde/Roger the Shrubber/Brother Maynard), Terry Gilliam (Patsy/Green Knight/Old Man from scene 24 (Bridgekeeper)/Sir Bors/Animator/Gorilla Hand), Terry Jones (Dennis's Mother/Sir Bedevere/Left Head/Voice of Cartoon Scribe/Prince Herbert), Michael Palin (First Swallow-Savvy Guard/Dennis/Peasant 2/Right Head/Sir Galahad the Pure/Narrator/King of Swamp Castle/Brother Maynard's Brother/Leader of The Knights who say NI!), Connie Booth (Witch)*
Directors: *Terry Gilliam, Terry Jones*
Screenwriters: *Graham Chapman, John Cleese, Eric Idle, Terry Gilliam, Terry Jones, Michael Palin*
15/91 mins./Comedy/UK

King Arthur and his knights embark on a low-budget search for the Grail, encountering many very silly obstacles.

By the spring of 1974 Monty Python was on the verge of collapse. The cult comic group, with their surreal brand of humour, had been together for five years, three TV series and one tour and the cracks were beginning to show. John Cleese had decided amicably to take no part in a proposed fourth series while other members were also discussing solo projects.

Looking for one last hurrah which might succeed where the earlier, *And Now For Something Completely Different* had failed in cracking the American market, the group found inspiration in Arthurian legend. They forged a comedy which delighted in subverting the epic tradition, parodied contemporary society and delivered numerous timeless scenes and characters of laugh-out-loud silliness. Shrubberies were demanded, hamster insults traded, relative wing velocities of European and African swallows debated and a generation of engineering students were never again found wanting for conversational material.

Terrys Gilliam and Jones, longtime critics of Python's visual shortcomings, appointed themselves directors. The Arthurian subject matter was

Scripts By Actors TOP10

1 Sylvester Stallone – Rocky
2 Emma Thompson – Sense And Sensibility
3 Matt Damon and Ben Affleck – Good Will Hunting
4 Owen Wilson -Rushmore
5 Billy Bob Thornton – Switchblade
6 Carrie Fisher – Postcards From The Edge
7 Julian Fellowes – Gosford Park
8 Anthony Hopkins (with Steven Sondheim) – The Last Of Sheila
9 Jack Nicholson – The Trip
10 Alec Guiness – The Horse's Mouth

decided upon, although initially the film was going to be shot in both mediaeval and modern times with the knights buying the Grail from Harrods and Galahad being a solicitor in Surrey.

Shelving the modern component, they set about raising funds. Python's popularity with the rock fraternity ensured them several high-profile backers with Pink Floyd, Led Zeppelin and Elton John all happy to invest and thereby siphon some money from the Exchequer's punishing 90 per cent tax rate. Michael White, who would go on to produce *The Rocky Horror Picture Show*, put together a modest budget of around £229,000.

Just how modest this budget was soon became evident, necessitating drastic, but inspired, modifications to the original script. Discovering that real horses would take their shooting well beyond the five weeks allowed, the group hit on the idea of using coconuts instead. But such invention did not prevent it from being a highly arduous shoot.

Locations for a variety of castles were scouted in Scotland, but only two weeks before filming began, permission to use them was withdrawn, forcing the privately owned Doune Castle to become the main backdrop. On the first day of shooting, the camera broke down and it was swiftly followed by the lead actor. Graham Chapman, always a keen imbiber and a firm friend of another famous non-teetotaller, The Who drummer Keith Moon, was now regularly consuming two bottles of gin a day. He resolved to give up drinking on the first day of shooting. However, as Gilliam struggled to shoot close-ups for the Bridge Of Death scene, Chapman experienced a violent bout of DTs and was shaking so badly that costume designer, Hazel Pethig couldn't get his gloves off. He resolved to fall off the wagon forthwith.

To make matters worse, the novel idea of co-directors was not working smoothly. Jones and Gilliam argued incessantly with matters often only being resolved by Gilliam backing down and then coming back late at night to re-cut things his way. The one point on which the two directors did agree, however, was that this would be a mediaeval epic that accurately reflected the period's filth; think Ordure Of The Garter. Unfortunately, this obsession with dirt, combined with Gilliam's precise direction and the cast's inexperience at hitting their marks, served to make both directors unpopular with their fellow Pythons. Factor in an unseasonably cold and wet Scottish May, the indignities of working with the rotting carcass of a dead sheep and production problems which meant that rushes could not be seen on a daily basis, and after ten days the cast were close to mutiny.

Fortunately, Graham Chapman, by now firmly back on the booze, came to the rescue with a morale-boosting round of drinks and a traditional sing-song which staved off disaster.

The following day, the rushes arrived and it was clear that, despite all the difficulties, they were doing great work. Even Cleese, always the most likely to resent the tedium of shooting, rallied. Bonzo Dog Doo Dah Band member and unofficial seventh Python Neil Innes, who was brought in to write songs and find rhymes for Camelot, recalls whiling away time with Cleese defining the verb 'to sheep worry' with the future Basil Fawlty formulating an impeccable future perfect, 'I am about to have been sheep worried.'

Despite some disastrous early screenings, the film proved a huge success after opening in London on 3 April 1975, helping to break the Pythons in America and making them rich men. The group had forsaken a salary for points, a wise decision as to this day a one per cent stake brings in an annual income of £60,000. The film proved popular in places as far afield as Russia and Graceland, where Elvis ordered his own print and watched it five times.

The success of Holy Grail revitalised the group, inspiring them to complete a fourth series and team up for further big screen outings in *Life Of Brian* and *The Meaning Of Life*. It also gave Terry Gilliam his distinctive modus operandi for his highly accomplished directorial career. 'You plan everything carefully,' revealed the Python animator recently. 'Secretly hoping that things will go wrong.' ★★★★★ **JN**

Movie Trivia: Monty Python and the Holy Grail

Pink Floyd, Led Zeppelin and Elton John all helped to bankroll this film. Many scenes were filmed in a well-known London park. Michael Palin plays 10 different characters in the film. The photograph of God is actually famous 1800s cricketer W.G. Grace.

MONTY PYTHON'S LIFE OF BRIAN (1979)

Starring: *Graham Chapman (Wise Man #2/Brian Cohen/Biggus Dickus), John Cleese (Wise Man #1/Reg/Jewish Official/Centurion/Deadly Dirk/Arthur), Terry Gilliam (Man Even Further Forward/Revolutionary/Jailer/Blood & Thunder Prophet/Frank/Audience Member/Crucifee), Eric Idle (Mr Cheeky/Stan (Loretta)/Harry the Haggler/Culprit Woman/Warris/Intensely Dull Youth/Jailer's Assistant/Otto/Lead Singer Crucifee), Terry Jones (Mandy Cohen/Colin/Simon the Holy Man/Bob Hoskins/Saintly Passer-by/Alarmed Crucifixion Assistant), Michael Palin (Wise Man #3/Mr Big Nose/Francis/Mrs A/Ex-Leper/Announcer/Ben/Pontius Pilate/Boring Prophet/Eddie/Shoe Follower/Nisus Wettus)*
Director: *Terry Jones*
Screenwriters: *Graham Chapman, John Cleese, Eric Idle, Terry Gilliam, Terry Jones, Michael Palin*
15/94 mins./Comedy/UK

Brian is born on the original Christmas, in the stable next door to Jesus. He spends his life being mistaken for a messiah.

The jokes come tinned-custard thick and speeding-bullet fast, but it's not the volume of gags that sets the film apart – it's their variety and quality. *The Naked Gun* and *Airplane!* may boast similar joke counts, but the Zucker brothers can't compete with the Pythons in terms of stylistic eclecticism: they're as comfortable with slapstick as they are with satire, and equally at home with crass comedy or class comedy.

The competitive spirit among the writing/performing team acts as a kind of ruthless quality control, making each sequence simultaneously economical and incident-packed. For a team often, and at times rightly, accused of self-indulgence, it's pleasingly ironic that their finest hour-and-a-half should be so perfectly structured, with not a second of screen time wasted.

The idea of an ex-leper still begging on the streets of Jerusalem, for example, is amusing enough in itself, but the scene doesn't rest on its comedic laurels. Instead, Michael Palin presents a fully rounded, wholly annoying individual, whose tanned skin and perpetual motion hilariously contrast with the doleful, pathetic image of his pre-miracle self conjured up in the viewer's mind's eye.

With an adult rating guaranteed by the film's outwardly controversial subject matter, *Life Of Brian* also represented the team's first opportunity to use the foul language denied them in their TV incarnation. The result is some of the finest, *Withnail*-class comedy swearing available: Palin's outraged would-be pilgrim – 'I mean it, you call me Big Nose once more, I'll take you to the fucking cleaners' – or an exasperated Brian rounding on his ever-growing band of disciples – 'Alright, I am the Messiah, now will you all fuck off?' Pure class. ★★★★★ **RF**

MONTY PYTHON'S THE MEANING OF LIFE (1983)

Starring: *Graham Chapman (various), John Cleese (various), Terry Gilliam (various), Eric Idle (various), Terry Jones (various), Michael Palin (various)*
Directors: *Terry Gilliam, Terry Jones*
Screenwriter: *Graham Chapman, John Cleese, Terry Gilliam, Eric Idle, Terry Jones, Michael Palin*
18/107 mins./Comedy/UK

A portmanteau of sketches and mini-films all based around a study of the meaning of life. Religion, death, sex, contraception and accountancy all find their place.

The last hurrah from the Monty Python team is seen as a lesser accomplishment than *Life Of Brian* and *Holy Grail*, too piecemeal and unfocused, but it possesses some of their most iconic musings and inspired madness. Terry Gilliam, for one, was up to his usual excesses launching the film with a fifteen-minute story within the story, complete with all his operatic surrealism, involving accountants as literal pirates whose very office blocks lift anchor. He was also spending all the money, to least effect. Once the film begins proper, it flits from skit to ragged skit, rash with vulgarity if short on the nimbleness of their great TV days.

Taste is sensibly abandoned, and when they hit they really strike a chord. John Cleese as a prissy public school master teaching sex to his bored pupils by shagging his wife in class; the one-sided kids versus teachers rugby match; exploding fatty Mr Creosote (Jones), and Death making an unforeseen appearance at an awfully nice dinner party. And there's no discounting the musical inspiration of the epic number 'Every Sperm Is Scared', glinting with anti-Catholic edges. And as usual Gilliam punctuates the collection with his wild animations. There are plenty of jokes that miss and the film could have done with some judicious trimming, but there is just an air of reckless self-satisfaction (especially with that opening salvo), and their collective mania is sorely missed. ★★★ **IN**

MOONRAKER (1979)

Starring: *Roger Moore (James Bond), Lois Chiles (Dr Holly Goodhead), Michael Lonsdale (Hugo Drax), Richard Kiel (Jaws), Bernard Lee (M), Lois Maxwell (Miss Moneypenny)*
Director: *Lewis Gilbert*
Screenwriter: *Christopher Wood, based on the novel by Ian Fleming*
PG/126 mins./ Spy/UK

007 investigates the theft of a space shuttle, following the trail to madman Hugo Drax who plots to destroy the Earth and start the human race again in space.

The point where the Moore era lost complete touch with its Fleming-Connery origins and took flight into the preposterous. Still, there are some glorious pleasures here, the film is playful, energetic and memorable, even if it has no intention to do more than meet easy expectations and make glib references to the happenstance fashions of the day (space shuttles, computer gizmos et al).

Moore is still on the right side of the paunch, and spends the entire film, which has been pitched to the ironic glaze of his acting anyhow, eyebrow cocked and smirk in place. Strange, how lovable this routine seems in hindsight, something bizarrely precious as if better acting would have ruined the film's potty poise. Lois Chiles, meanwhile, is one of those Bond girls pitched as brainy, she is a rocket scientist no less, but suffers the ignominy (or genius) of being named Holly Goodhead (come on, that is good writing). While Michael Lonsdale is a better villain than you remember.

Ultimately, the joys of *Moonraker*, lie in its set-pieces not its plotting (plant seeds to destroy mankind?), and this one of the Bonds possesses more than its fair share: the cable car leaps at the Sugar Loaf mountain in Rio; the gondola on wheels in Venice; the motorboat in the Amazon. Inspired stuff, and a testament to the imagination, if not the realism, the series still boasted. It is too far-fetched – who could buy that space station stuff even for a Moore movie? – but it's worth enduring any amount of ludicrousness for Q's immortal punchline: 'I think, he's attempting re-entry sir!' ★★★ **IN**

THE MOTHMAN PROPHECIES (2001)

Starring: *Richard Gere (John Klein), Laura Linney (Connie Parker), Will Patton (Gordon Smallwood), Lucinda Jenney (Denise Smallwood), Debra Messing (Mary Klein), Alan Bates (Dr Alexander Leek)*
Director: *Mark Pellington*
Screenwriter: *Richard Hatem, from the non-fiction book by John A. Keel*
12/113 mins./Sci-fi/Thriller/USA

Two years after his wife scrawled pictures of a moth-like creature while dying of a brain tumour, reporter John Klein finds himself in a small American town, unable to explain how he got there. He investigates a rash of Mothman sightings and becomes convinced that a disaster is about to strike.

Until now, Mothman has been a lesser-known member of the cryptozoology Hall Of Fame, eclipsed by Bigfoot, the Loch Ness Monster and the anal-probing alien greys.

John Keel's book, recounting his 1967 experiences with the phenomenon, has been around since 1975, but Mothman hasn't even managed a guest shot on *The X-Files* until this star vehicle. It may be that the mythology is just too nebulous – the apparition seems related to the Irish banshee, showing up to foretell tragedy – to make a film subject. This movie certainly deploys a lot of unrelated spook stuff (as puzzling as it is creepy) before turning to more conventional suspense-disaster material for a Mothman-free, satisfying finish.

Following 1999's *Arlington Road*, this is the second Mark Pellington film in a row to concern a professional widower, hung up on his wife's mysterious death, who sees a vast web of shadow conspiracy and becomes a prophet of doom.

However, Gere delivers a very different reading to Jeff Bridges' obvious nut. Sleek and grey in a coat that gives him his very own moth-look, Gere's sincerity and intelligence sells the Fortean bizarre far more than Alan Bates' unfortunate cameo in the traditional, discredited, mad professor role. John Klein is a rare paranoid who knows how others are likely to react to his story, and always advances cautiously as he makes the connections.

The film offers a sustained deployment of weirdness connected by mood and imagery, including buzzing phone messages from something which calls itself 'Idris Gold' and ambiguous sightings of the Mothman. There's even a Lynchian thing going on in which a farmer mysteriously claims Klein has visited him three nights in a row as he shows up for his first visit. ★★★ **KN**

⦿ MOULIN ROUGE! (2001)

Starring: *Nicole Kidman (Satine), Ewan McGregor (Christian), John Leguizamo (Toulouse-Lautrec), Jim Broadbent (Harold Zidler), Richard Roxburgh (The Duke)*
Director: *Baz Luhrmann*
Screenwriters: *Baz Luhrmann, Craig Pearce*
12/127 mins./Drama/Musical/Romance/Australia/USA

Awards: *Academy Awards – Best Art Direction-Set Decoration, Best Costume, BAFTA – Anthony Asquith Award for Film Music, Best Supporting Actor (Jim Broadbent), Best Sound, Empire Awards – Best Actress, Best British Actor, Best Director*

Paris, 1899, and romantic poet Christian starts hanging out at the notorious Moulin Rouge. On first glimpsing the club's star, Satine, he falls madly in love, and she returns his feelings. But with her health deteriorating and a jealous Duke set on separating the pair, can their ardour overcome the forces that threaten to destroy them?

A glorified (literally) arthouse musical, but a delightfully quirky, irresistibly intoxicating one at that. Elaborating the self-consciously artificial 'Red Curtain' technique that he developed in his first two films, Luhrmann has created a natural successor to the hyper-kinetic *Romeo And Juliet*, upping the ante in just about every way and making even that seem muted in comparison.

Drawing from influences as diverse as Bollywood to grand opera, the result is a gaudy, opulent, invigorating spectacle that, while committing to celluloid some of the kitschest moments in 'mainstream' film history, never loses sight of its muse – as Peter Cetera (sadly not one of the artists reworked on the soundtrack) might say, the glory of love.

Shakespearean in its structure and emotional simplicity, the plot – while confusing for the first half hour – sees idealistic poet Christian and courtesan Satine battle the slings and arrows of outrageous fortune in the pursuit of their passionate, secret love. Around, above, beneath them revolves a cacaphony of dancing girls, freaks, dastardly villains and slippery characters, Absinthed up to the eyeballs and camping it up for all they're worth.

Amongst all this decadence, it's all credit to Luhrmann – and especially his two leads – that Satine and Christian's affair remains so convincing. Kidman and McGregor have that rare thing, real chemistry, and each gives a superb, profoundly moving performance. Supporting characters are perhaps less rounded – John Leguizamo's Toulouse-Lautrec is amusing but doesn't really do much, Richard Roxburgh's evil Duke is somewhat one-dimensional but these quibbles are minor and do nothing to spoil the experience.

And, of course, gluing it all together are the songs, gloriously revamped classics and contemporary pop songs from Rodgers and Hammerstein to Lennon and McCartney, by way of Elton John, Dolly Parton and David Bowie. What could have gone so embarrassingly wrong in fact turns out to be Luhrmann's true triumph – thankfully Ewan and Nicole CAN sing – highlights including a po-faced Jim Broadbent rendition of 'Like A Virgin', and a bravado 'Diamonds Are A Girl's Best Friend'. And watch out for a charming cameo from a rather special guest. ★★★★★ **LB**

Movie Trivia: Moulin Rouge

Kylie Minogue's Green Fairy 'roar' was actually dubbed over by the Prince of Darkness Ozzy Osbourne. Coca Cola was used to make the floor sticky in the 'Like a Virgin' sequence so the actors wouldn't slip. Nicole Kidman's necklace was the most expensive piece of jewellery ever made for film, worth about £700,000. Texas singer Sharleen Spiteri was in the running for the part of Satine.

⦿ MONSOON WEDDING (2002)

Starring: *Naseeruddin Shah (Lalit Verma), Lillete Dubey (Pimmi Verma), Shefali Shetty (Ria Verma), Vijay Raaz (Parabatlal Kanhaiyalal P.K. Dubey), Tilotama Shome (Alice)*
Director: *Mira Nair*
Screenwriter: *Sabrina Dhawan*
15/114 mins./Comedy/Drama/Romance/India/France/Italy/Germany

The Verma family gather in New Delhi for the arranged marriage of Delhi native Aditia and Texan engineer Hemant. As the wedding (and the monsoon season) approaches, five love stories are played out across the generations revealing cultures clash and family secrets to devastating effect.

When this film scooped the Golden Lion Award at Venice, it was greeted with surprise and consternation. Surely this low budget love song to India wasn't batting its weight with the more prestigious work of the world's great and good? But *Monsoon Wedding* is that rare film with enough 'arty' pretensions to satisfy the high-brow critics and enough old-fashioned storytelling to appeal to the widest audience.

Nair's track record – including an Oscar nomination for her debut feature, *Salaam Bombay*! – promised great things. *Monsoon Wedding* delivers in the best possible sense.

Many directors struggle with balancing stories of multiple casts, but Nair manages to switch between them with exactly the right pacing. No couple is off-screen long enough to be missed and no character outstays their welcome. In fact, all are so real, to admit their acting talents would be to break the spell.

Even in scenes where everyone is present, the technique of filming with hand-held camera allows you to switch effortlessly between faces, and every important facial expression and revealing reaction is there. Sometimes these are played out as repeated frames, capturing another's viewpoint in momentary flashes – the second that they fall in love, the instant they notice something new in the family.

Bollywood influences are apparent. Bright colours, soaring music and exuberant dancing represent the traditions of the Punjabi culture. But scratch the surface and there's much more. Key characters, such as the incoming Australians and Americans, are our guides as they discover their traditional expectations are confounded by knowledge of affairs, failing businesses and very modern views. ★★★★ **EC**

⦿ MORVERN CALLAR (2002)

Starring: *Samantha Morton (Morvern Callar), Kathleen McDermott (Lanna), Linda McGuire (Vanessa), Ruby Milton (Couris Jean), Colly Wells (Susan), Dan Cadan (Dazzer)*
Director: *Lynne Ramsay*
Screenwriters: *Liana Dognini, Lynne Ramsay, from the novel by Alan Warner*
15/93 mins./Drama/UK/Canada

Awards: *BAFTA, Scotland – Best Actress*

After finding her novelist boyfriend has committed suicide over Christmas, shop worker Morvern Callar cleans up the mess, empties his bank account, puts her name to his finished novel and tells everyone he has left her . . .

Very few movies have understood, or captured, the transporting power of music as completely as Lynne Ramsay's second feature, *Morvern Callar*.

When the titular heroine plugs into her Walkman, permanently playing the compilation tape prepared by her recently deceased boyfriend, the dead-end supermarket she toils in daily is transformed into a magic carpet ride.

Later, an inhospitable desert will be remade as a gorgeous foreign vista.The equipment emphasis – always a personal stereo, never a public performance – can hardly be a coincidence for, like her remarkable debut, *Ratcatcher*, Scottish filmmaker Lynne Ramsay weaves a fragile fantasy here; a fundamentally private experience that one imagines would be endangered by overexposure to harsh critical light.

The film's grammar is visual rather than verbal, emotional rather than intellectual, and depending on how beguiled you become by Alwin Kuchler's striking photography, the resulting picture is either suffused with a dream-like logic or hamstrung by elementary plotting. The effect may be less contemporary than Ramsay imagines but, like all the best pop songs, the lyrics are not meant to make sense.

In capturing the freshness so obviously fundamental to her art, Ramsay is again well served by non-professional actors. Her keen eye is most evident in the casting of unknown Kathleen McDermott as Morvern's best friend Lanna, a good time girl more fully and humanely realised than a job lot of Mike Leigh stereotypes.

However, it is Samantha Morton as Morvern who glues the picture together. Her pale moon face and liquid blue eyes have already been employed as a tabula rasa by Woody Allen and Steven Spielberg, but it is Morvern – as immediate as she is elusive, as earthy as she is ethereal – that provides the actress with a signature role. ★★★★ **AM**

ⓓ THE MOST DANGEROUS GAME (THE HOUNDS OF ZAROFF) (1932)

Starring: *Joel McCrea (Rober 'Bob' Rainsford), Fay Ray (Eve Trowbridge), Leslie Banks (Count Zaroff), Robert Armstrong (Martin Trowbridge), Nobel Johnson (Ivan)*
Directors: *Irving Pichel, Ernest B. Schoedsack*
Screenwriter: *James Ashmore Creelman, based on a story by Richard Connell*
12/63 mins./Adventure/Thriller/USA

Shipwrecked on a remote island, big game hunter Robert Rainsford encounters Count Zaroff, an aristocrat who has become bored with pursuing animals and now only tracks 'the most dangerous game', human beings.

Based on a much-anthologised short story by Richard Connell, this is one of the classic 'high concept' action movies. Ernest B. Schoedsack (co-directing with Irving Pichel) made this simultaneously with *King Kong*, using the jungle sets and keeping heroine Fay Wray and comic relief Robert Armstrong busy while the Kong unit were doing special effects miniature shots.

British actor Leslie Banks is marvellous as the mad Russian Count Zaroff, welcoming shipwrecked guests to a gothic pile in the middle of the tropical undergrowth, where he keeps the mounted heads of previous victims in a private trophy chamber. Fingering the tusk-scar on his forehead and holding a cigarette with a distinctively weird spiderfingered hold, Zaroff expounds bizarre, philosophical dialogue about the joys of hunting men and (it's strongly implied) raping women.

After the first-reel set-up, the film consists of one lengthy, nightmarish action-chase sequence, with a wild-eyed Banks striding through the undergrowth brandishing his favoured hunting tool (a Tartar war-bow) and letting his famously voracious hounds off the leash, while the macho McCrea and the fetchingly distressed Wray improvise death-traps as they try to survive till dawn.

It was remade officially by Robert Wise as *A Game Of Death* in 1945, with a then-topical Nazi villain and plenty of footage from the original, and has been done over and over again ever since (*Run For The Sun, The Man With The Golden Gun, Hard Target, Slave Girls From Beyond Infinity, Surviving The Game*); almost every action/adventure TV series from *Fantasy Island* to *Hart To Hart* does a 'most dangerous game' episode. ★★★★ **KN**

ⓓ MOTHER INDIA (1957)

Starring: *Nargis (Radha), Sunil Dutt (Birju), Rajendra Kumar (Ramu), Raaj Kumar (Shamu), Kanhaiyalal (Sukhilala)*
Director: *Mehboob Khan*
Screenwriters: *Wajahat Mirza, S. Ali Raza*
U/159 mins./Drama/Musical/India

Radha, an old peasant woman, remembers her long life in a small Indian village. Her lavish wedding is the beginning of her troubles, since her mother-in-law places the family in debt to the village usurer to pay for it, thus reducing successive generations to poverty.

An archetype of the 'suffering peasant' school of cinema, this Bollywood spectacular from 1957 manages to cram in in four generations of disaster in its two hours and forty minutes (with songs).

While Satyajit Ray was echoing Italian neo-realism in his contemporary dramas, Mehboob Khan goes here for big Hollywood-style soap in the manner of the Ingrid Bergman film *The Good Earth*. Nargis agonises ever more beautifully as the plot odds are piled against her: her handsome husband loses his arms in an accident and wanders off rather than remain a burden, a flood devastates the village and kills two of her babies in one night, one of her sons grows up to be a resentful rebel and eventually a bandit, that moneylender keeps pestering her with lecherous offers, the tearaway son assaults his family and the whole village as he tries to get to the moneylender and the hayricks are fired (a spectacular bit) to get at him.

The finale finds the son returning on the day the moneylender's daughter is to be married, intent on kidnapping the bride – he kills the villain, but his own mother sides with the village and shoots him dead as he goes for the girl, which leads to more wailing and corpse-hugging. It's a broad, melodramatic film, with tiny fantasy touches (a glimpse of the Indian rope trick), surrounding its indomitable heroine with various feckless folks whose every action piles on the misery.

Hailed as India's answer to *Gone With The Wind*, it is memorable for its rich, warm, gorgeous Technicolor look. ★★★ **KN**

ⓓ MR AND MRS SMITH (1941)

Starring: *Carole Lombard (Ann Krausheimer Smith), Robert Montgomery (David Smith), Gene Raymond (Jefferson Custer), Jack Carson (Chuck Benson), Phillip Merivale (Ashley Custer), Lucile Watson (Mrs. Custer)*
Director: *Alfred Hitchcock*
Screenwriter: *Norman Krasna*
U/95 mins/Comedy/USA

Manhattan lawyer David Smith discovers that he was never legally married to his tempestuous wife, Ann, because their Idaho licence was invalid in Nevada at the time of their wedding.

Humour had always been a key component of Alfred Hitchcock's cinema. In 1928, he'd directed the romantic comedy, *Champagne*, and even his darkest pictures were punctuated by macabre wit, for if a thriller was constantly played at fever pitch the audience would rapidly become emotionally shattered and incapable of responding to the intense psychological manipulation at which the Master of Suspense excelled.

However, he agreed to do this screwball romp as much to accommodate his leading lady, Carole Lombard, as from any conscious desire to explore new avenues. Hitch was still a relative newcomer in Hollywood and, conscious of the fate of such vaunted Euro-exiles as Fritz Lang, Jean Renoir and Max Ophüls, whose refusal to play studio politics had severely curtailed their careers, he reasoned that making a picture with Mrs Clark Gable could do him no harm.

Admittedly, the comedy might have gained more momentum had Cary Grant been available to play David Smith. But Robert Montgomery, who was about to snare a second Oscar nomination for *Here Comes Mr Jordan* was no comic novice. However, there's no denying that Hitchcock's farce lacked the fizz of Leo McCarey's *The Awful Truth* – the Cary Grant-Irene Dunne vehicle which shares several plot similarities with *Mr & Mrs Smith*, right down to its bouts of feigned drunkenness and its mountain chalet denouement. But it still takes a pop at Hays Code respectability by revealing that the Smiths have been living in sin for several years.

Moreover, there are also occasional moments to savour, including Lombard's recurring threat to finish off Montgomery while he shaves with a cutthroat razor and the bleak Italian restaurant sequence, in which the food is so bad that the cat won't eat it, yet it still entices the gaggle of urchins who mournfully watch the uptown swells turning up their noses. ★★★ **DP**

MR AND MRS SMITH (2005)

Starring: *Brad Pitt (John Smith), Angelina Jolie (Jane Smith), Vince Vaughn (Eddie), Adam Brody (Benjamin Danz), Kerry Washington (Jasmine)*
Director: *Doug Liman*
Screenwriter: *Simon Kinberg*
15/120 mins./Action/Comedy/Romance/USA

John and Jane Smith are the perfect couple: rich, stylish, ridiculously good-looking. But all is not as it seems. Jane's not a systems analyst and John doesn't work in construction. Unbeknown to each other, they're both international assassins.

The premise of a couple of oblivious contract killers whose marriage suffers a body blow when their next hit turns out to be each other is hardly a new one. It was, of course, the basis for John Huston's 1985 Mob flick *Prizzi's Honor*. But where that was a demure black comedy with all the kinetic energy of a chess game, *Mr & Mrs Smith* is a speedfreaks' pinball tournament.

Flushed with the success of *The Bourne Identity* and still cashing cult-cred cheques on *Swingers*, Liman brings every ounce of acid wit and furious style at his disposal to this party. The caustic tone is set in a title sequence that finds the Smiths squirming their way through a marriage guidance session, a scene you can imagine Jennifer Aniston finding rather less amusing than the rest of us.

Things hot up on the home front, however, when they bodge coinciding missions to rub out the same mark and their respective agencies assign them to eliminate the competition. Frantic cat-and-mousing ensues. As do oodles of gunplay, outlandish gadgetry and murderously barbed dinner-table quips, darkly mirroring the what's-wrong-with-this-picture? vision of American domesticity beloved of 60s TV shows like *Bewitched*, with an outwardly perfect couple circling each other over the pot roast (likewise Brad stashing his arms cache in their suspiciously pristine toolshed; Jolie in her spotless, state-of-the-art electric oven).

As you'd expect from a director who effortlessly flipped from the stylish humour of *Swingers* and *Go* to the gritty spy thrills of *Bourne*, the physical duelling's as deftly handled as the verbal, while he keeps the two inextricably intertwined. One spectacularly staged gunfight deteriorates into a drag-out brawl of quite astonishing ferocity. Naturally, as undiscovered tribes in the Peruvian jungle could have told them, this is simply foreplay to an epic shag, from which they emerge, drowsy and satiated, amid the symbolic wreckage of their model home.

Okay, so it's rather ridiculous, and it all goes a bit nuts come the end, but the perfectly formulated chemistry between Pitt and Jolie is sparkling cyanide throughout. Aside from being arguably the two most indecently attractive people on the planet, both achieve the perfect balance of self-deprecation and sexual dynamite, never taking anything too seriously. Pitt's at the top of his goofy-cool-guy's-guy game, and it's an unalloyed joy to finally see Jolie land a role worthy of her mettle. She's funny, sexy as all get-out and kicks ass with a shameless glee that would make Lara Croft blush (it's hard to believe that the more icy Nicole Kidman was originally signed up for the role). Vince Vaughn, essaying yet another delusional dim-wit as Pitt's boss, is just the icing on a cake that's almost entirely icing to begin with. Gloriously amoral, grown-up fun. ★★★★ **SB**

MR BLANDINGS BUILDS HIS DREAM HOUSE (1948)

Starring: *Cary Grant (Jim Blandings), Myrna Loy (Muriel Blandings), Melvyn Douglas (Bill Cole), Reginald Denny (Simms), Sharyn Moffet (Joan Blandings), Corinne Marshall (Betsy Blandings)*
Director: *H.C. Potter*
Screenwriters: *Norman Panama, Melvyn Frank, based on the novel by Eric Hodgins*
U/94 mins./Comedy/USA

Disillusioned with the daily grind in Manhattan, Jim and Muriel Blandings decide to build a model home in the Connecticut countryside. However, its construction lurches from one crisis to another.

The United States had experienced housing crises both during the Second World War and its immediate aftermath. Thus, with countless Americans moving out of the inner cities and into the suburbs, Eric Hodgins's satirical novel had struck a chord with the harassed, but upwardly mobile populace. So, RKO couldn't really fail with this adaptation, especially after David O. Selznick persuaded Cary Grant and Myrna Loy to reunite for the third time, following *Wings In The Dark* and *The Bachelor And The Bobby-Soxer*.

Yet, for all its polish, time has not been kind to this genial box-office hit. The repetition of its domestic travails in endless sitcoms makes the humour seem flatly familiar, while Grant and Loy's byplay with black maid Gussie (Louise Beavers) and the mostly immigrant tradesmen now seems complacently patronising.

The performances are, nevertheless, wholly engaging. Trading on her image as the perfect housewife, Loy revels in the opportunity to chide Grant and her baffling discussion of the colour scheme is delightful. But, while she prevents him from stealing every scene, her role was very much subordinated to Grant's fraught family man. Melvyn Douglas, however, was less willing to play second banana and he refused to co-star unless writer-producers Norman Panama and Melvin Frank made lawyer Bill Cole a touch more cynical and cheekier in his flirtings with Loy.

Selznick hoped to persuade Grant and Loy to form a comic partnership that could rival Spencer Tracy and Katharine Hepburn. But Loy, who had just made the last of her *Thin Man* mysteries with William Powell, was reluctant to become part of another team and, so, when the film transferred to radio in 1949, Grant had to co-star with then-wife Betsy Drake, who had an occasional hand in the scripts.

Richard Benjamin attempted to update the story to the yuppie era in *The Money Pit*. But, despite Tom Hanks's best efforts, the results were decidedly mediocre. ★★★ **DP**

MR DEEDS (2002)

Starring: *Adam Sandler (Longfellow Deeds), Winona Ryder (Babe Bennett/Pam Dawson), John Turturro (Emilio Lopez), Allen Covert (Marty), Peter Gallagher (Chuck Cedar)*
Director: *Steven Brill*
Screenwriter: *Tim Herlihy, based on the 1936 film by Robert Riskin and the short story 'Opera Hat' by Clarence Budington Kelland*
12A/96 mins./Comedy/Romance/USA

In this remake of Frank Capra's *Mr Deeds Goes To Town*, a simple guy from backwater USA finds himself the richest man in America overnight when he comes into a $40 billion inheritance. But can he hold onto it?

MR DEEDS GOES TO TOWN

Blasphemer! How could Adam Sandler, of all people, remake Capra? Well, shoddily, as it happens. Either way, Capra fans shouldn't get their knickers in a twist, because *Mr Deeds* bears little relation to the Gary Cooper classic – which, last time we checked, didn't have a scene in which a butler drives a poker through the eponymous hero's frost-bitten foot. Welcome to Sandlerworld.

Britain has never bought into Sandler, writing him off as an obnoxious, slapstick-obsessed lout. But in his better films – *The Wedding Singer*, *Happy Gilmore* – he aptly exploits the comic potential of rage. That, however, is Sandler at his best. At his worst, he can be leaden and uninteresting, and, sadly, that's the Adam Sandler who steps up to the plate here.

Mr Deeds is intermittently very funny, mainly thanks to the supporting cast – including The Adam Sandler Travelling Repertory Company stalwarts Buscemi (whose 'I love the Beach Boys' line is a prime contender for funniest line of the movie, contextually of course), Turturro (the best thing in the movie by a country mile as Deeds' Spanish butler), Allen Covert and Rob Schneider – who work tirelessly for laughs.

But Sandler is on autopilot, his outbursts of rage kept to a minimum. There's no disguising that *Mr Deeds* is a mere exercise in restoring Sandler's box office appeal, following the failure of *Little Nicky* (which, for all its faults, had ten times the verve on display here). And, though this worked in the US ($125 million at the box office), Sandler still looks shackled and distinctly uncomfortable as a romantic lead.

At least he's playing in a completely different league to Ryder, who sabotages any planned 'Winona steals the show' reviews with an astonishingly awful performance. She seems convinced that she's in an Oscar-class weepie, blubbing her heart out every five minutes. ★★ **JO**

MR DEEDS GOES TO TOWN (1936)

Starring: *Gary Cooper (Longfellow Deeds), Jean Arthur (Babe Bennet), George Bancroft (MacWade), Lionel Stander (Cornellius Cobb), Douglas Dumbrille (John Cedar), Raymond Walburn (Walter)*
Director: *Frank Capra*
Screenwriter: *Robert Riskin, based on the story by Clarence Budington Kelland*
U/115 mins./Comedy/USA
Awards: *Academy Awards – Best Director (Frank Capra)*

Despite falling in love with him, New York reporter Babe Bennett produces a series of mocking articles when hick Longfellow Deeds comes to the city to collect his $20 million inheritance. But when his act of generosity to the dispossessed lands him in court, she finally rallies to his cause.

Frank Capra was so convinced that Gary Cooper alone could headline Robert Riskin's adaptation of Clarence Budington Kelland's *Saturday Evening Post* story 'Opera Hat' that he persuaded Columbia chief Harry Cohn to delay shooting for six months (at a cost to the studio of $100,000) to accommodate Coop's schedule. While waiting, he stumbled across Jean Arthur in a B Western and cast her as the sob sister who befriends Mr Deeds while making him a sap in print. Despite being a veteran of 70 movies, this was the 27-year-old Arthur's first A-list lead and she was so nervous that she invariably vomited before takes and ran off set crying after them.

However, she turned in the archetypical Capra performance, as the sassy counterbalance to the guileless hero, and later reunited with the director for *You Can't Take It With You* and *Mr Smith Goes To Washington*. Cooper would also return for *Meet John Doe*, by which time this type of goodwill fantasy had become known as Capra-corn for its sentimental solution of socially implacable problems. Indeed, some critics complained that Deeds would have been a better film had the tuba-playing, verse-writing reserve fireman from Mandrake Falls lost his suit against the grasping lawyers to deny the audience an easy association with his Everyman affability and force them to recognise their own complicity in the capitalist conspiracy that he sought to resist.

The Oscar-nominated Cooper wisely avoided playing Deeds as a rube and, consequently, his dismay at the greed and self-centredness of city life seemed as genuine as his distress on discovering Babe's cynical duplicity. Indeed, the sequence in which he cries behind the pillar confirms the now-underrated Cooper as one of cinema's most gifted actors. However, his naturalism was no match for the scene-stealing brilliance of Margaret McWade and Margaret Seddon, as the twittering Faulkner sisters, whose whispering in the witness box and insistence that everyone, bar them, had been 'pixilated' was simply wonderful.

Capra won a second Oscar for this provocative dramedy, which was remade as the execrable Adam Sandler vehicle, *Mr Deeds*, in 2002. ★★★★ **DP**

MR HOLLAND'S OPUS (1995)

Starring: *Richard Dreyfuss (Glenn Holland), Glenne Headly (Iris Holland), Jay Thomas (Bill Meister), Olympia Dukakis (Principal Helen Jacobs), William H. Macy (Vice Principal Gene Wolters)*
Director: *Stephen Herek*
Screenwriter: *Patrick Sheane Duncan*
PG/143 mins./Drama/USA

A musician who reluctantly takes a teaching job in a Californian high school in the 60s for some temporary financial security (so he can compose important music) finds himself still teaching there 30 years later.

After his lengthy languishment in the anonymity career hell of Disney comedies and moribund thrillers, it's good to see Richard Dreyfuss' stock rise with a ripe dramatic performance. Understandably Oscar-nominated, he plays all the notes in his likeable role, as empathetic, delightful and touching as a modern-day, baton-wielding, wisecracking Mr Chips.

Glenn Holland is a musician who reluctantly takes a teaching job in a Californian high school in the 60s for some temporary financial security so he can compose important music. Life being what it is, however, fatherhood and a mortgage defer the dream and Mr Holland is still teaching 30 years down the line.

In that time he has progressed exuberantly from a frustrated bore to Mr Popularity after finding a way to communicate his passion for music from Bach to The Beatles (cue toe-tapping sampler soundtrack). Whether wrestling with a cacophonic school orchestra or exhorting a gawky gang into a marching band, Mr Holland inspires his kids to find their own abilities and enthusiasms. In case you haven't guessed, the students, you see, are Mr Holland's great work, though he doesn't realise it until the retirement watch is past due and we're montaged through numerous crises, concerts in the gym and era-spanning clips from news bulletins.

Patrick Sheane Duncan's syrup-coated script can't resist throwing every travail known to middle-class man at Mr Holland and his long-suffering wife, and director Herek is surer handling the laughs and fun than the elevated corn quotient. ★★★ **AE**

MR JONES (1993)

Starring: *Richard Gere (Mr Jones), Lena Olin (Dr Elizabeth 'Libbie' Bowen), Anne Bancroft (Dr Catherine Holland), Tom Irwin (Dr Patrick Shaye), Delroy Lindo (Howard)*
Director: *Mike Figgis*
Screenwriters: *Eric Roth, Michael Cristofer, based on a story by Roth*
15/114 mins./Drama/Romance/USA

A relationship develops between a manic-depressive, Mr Jones, and the female doctor who takes more than a professional interest in his treatment.

It's easy to see why Richard Gere agreed to this: if it had turned out halfway decent, the star would be guaranteed at least an Academy Award nomination for taking one of those Oscar potential roles that involve simulating the symptoms of a flamboyant medical condition.

Jones talks his way into a construction job, by convincing an unbilled Bill Pullman that he's a top-flight roofing person. Then he goes hyper and tries to fly, whereupon he's dragged off, for the first of many times, to the institution where unhappy therapist Libby Bowen diagnoses him as a manic depressive.

For a while the film trundles along, overly impressed by Gere's showoffy performance. It then turns into a ridiculous melodrama when Olin, following every other shrink in the movies, gets unethically involved with her charge.

This is a catalogue of psycho movie cliches, with Olin's Swedish-accented, repressed analyst a throwback to Ingrid Bergman in *Spellbound*. Gere buzzes around helping people and making friends when he's not risking his life and borrowing riffs from Matthew Modine in Birdy and Jack Nicholson in *Cuckoo's Nest*, emerging as another movie maniac who does a better job of treating his fellow crazies than the uptight, drug-dispensing doctors. ★★ **KN**

MR SATURDAY NIGHT (1992)

Starring: *Billy Crystal (Buddy Young, Jr), David Paymer (Stan), Julie Warner (Elaine), Helen Hunt (Annie Wells), Mary Mara (Susan)*
Director: *Billy Crystal*
Screenwriters: *Billy Crystal, Lowell Banz, Bablaoo Mandel*
15/114 mins./Comedy/Drama/USA

A vaudeville tradition comic finds a new lease of life playing to retirement homes.

For his directorial debut Billy Crystal takes on a subject about which he knows just about everything – stand-up comedy.

The Mr Saturday Night of the title is the fictitious Buddy Young Jnr, whose rollercoaster career and colossal failure as a human being are explored over the course of more than 50 years, from family parlour cut-up to geriatric wiseguy. In portraying Buddy, Crystal reinvents himself as a deeply unpleasant and completely self-absorbed applause junkie, a character he originated ten years ago, essayed on TV's *Saturday Night Live* and has regularly revisited in the decade since.

As such, he knows Buddy – a credible composite of a generation of American comic monsters – as well as he knows himself. Crystal is also able to invest Buddy with his own considerable career's worth of successful shtick, airing his best and funniest gags like the Dances With Jews routine which opens the movie, but the trouble is that Buddy, while undeniably a laugh a minute, is such an ungenerous, mean-spirited man to spend over 50 years with.

Between wowing them in 40s burlesque and making them wet their pants in 90s retirement homes in Florida, Buddy neglects and alienates his 'loved' ones, is just beastly to his long-suffering brother and cruelly ridicules everyone in sight. In his zeal to prove his worth as an Actor, Crystal spends too much of the film in old age make-up, encased so heavily in latex as to recall his cameo as the out-of-work wizard in *The Princess Bride*.

Clumsily flashing back and forth 'twixt juvenilia and near-senility also strikes against the viewer warming to a life in which belated reconciliations and reparations feature with embarrassing predictability. For all its flaws, however, the painful mirth, the parody (Buddy following The Beatles on The Ed Sullivan Show), and some useful casting assets (Ron Silver, Jerry Lewis as himself) nudge it just across the Laugh Till You Cry borderline. ★★★ **AE**

MR SMITH GOES TO WASHINGTON

Starring: *Jean Arthur (Saunders), James Stewart (Jefferson Smith), Claude Rains (Sen. Joseph Paine), Edward Arnold (Jim Taylor), Guy Kibbee (Gov. Hubert Hopper), Thomas Mitchell (Diz Moore), Eugene Pallette (Chick McGann)*
Director: *Frank Capra*
Screenwriter: *Sidney Buchman, based on the novel* The Gentleman From Montana *by Lewis R. Foster*
U/125 mins./Comedy/USA
Awards: *Academy Awards – Best Original Story*

Media magnate Jim Taylor, Governor Hubert Hopper and Senator Joseph Paine persuade Boy Ranger leader Jefferson Smith to stand for the Senate and seek to exploit his naivete for their own gain. However, much to the delight of his disillusioned secretary, Saunders, he stands up to be counted.

'No one else can balance the ups and downs of wistful sentiment and corny humour the way Capra can,' Pauline Kael ended her review of this political classic, 'but if anyone else should learn to, kill him.' Her cynicism is admirable. But she didn't live to see the devaluation of democracy that left neo-con America in desperate need of its own Mr Smith. Indeed, some 70 years after its release, this Washington morality tale is more prescient and pertinent than ever.

A touch of the story's spirit was evident in its genesis, when Rouben Mamoulian rejected Columbia chief Harry Cohn's offer of $75,000 for the rights to Lewis R. Foster's story and sold them for the cost price of $1,500 providing he could direct the long-cherished boxing drama, *Golden Boy*. Ironically, this once-prestigious project has since been largely forgotten as the reputation of Frank Capra's filibustering epic has grown.

However, many have accused Capra of sentimental populism in allowing James Stewart's gauche patsy to expose Claude Rains's suave villainy under the benevolent eye of Harry Carey's Vice-President and the adoring gaze of Jean Arthur's rejuvenated secretary. But this was a bleak indictment of a system that people were still in the habit of trusting implicitly and it would have been fascinating to see the reactions of the D.C. dignitaries who attended its gala premiere.

Cast for the hesitant naivete that distinguished him from Gary Cooper's folksy decency, Stewart's passage from idealism to harsh-won wisdom was not only credible, but also deeply moving, as he made superb use of both his beanpole vulnerability and his stuttering, initially poorly pitched delivery style to win over the sceptics in both the body and gallery of the meticulously recreated Senate Chamber.

But while the performances were universally outstanding, Capra bombarded viewers with provocative ideas that came as thick and fast as the instances of printed and verbal communication that he intimated were the making and the marring of modern governance in warning Americans to be on their own guard, for Mr Smiths were as rare as Paines, Taylors and Hoppers were plentiful and pernicious. ★★★★★ **DP**

MR VAMPIRE (JIANGSHI XIANSHENG) (1985)

Starring: *Lam Ching-Ying (Master Gau), Chin Sin-Hou (Chou), Ricky Hui (Man Choi), Billy Lau (Wai), Moon Lee (Ting-Ting), Pauline Wong (Jade)*
Director: *Ricky Lau*
Screenwriters: *Ricky Lau, Chuek-Hon Szeto, Barry Wong, Ying Wong*
15/93 mins./Comedy/Horror/USA

Master Gau, a priest/exorcist/undertaker, copes with a vampire who is preying on his living family, while dealing with the troubles of his foolish apprentices. Chou is in love with a ghost and Man Choi has been bitten by the vampire.

This lively Chinese horror movie pits knockabout comedians with martial arts skills against an oriental version of the Hammer-style vampire in a flavourful mix of Eastern and Western, comic and horrific, sophisticated action and pleasant naivete.

The chief menace is a Mandarin-robed, bloodsucking corpse with long blue nails, progressively mangled features and a distinctive arms-out hopping gait, while the ghost girl of the subplot is a winsome miss who sometimes has a mangled ruin with a popped eyeball for a face and can detach her head as a spike-haired cannonball.

It deploys an impressive range of Daoist techniques for coping with the supernatural: a mystically-charged cat's cradle which seems electrified to the undead; a scattering of sticky rice (a duplicitous merchant mixes in ordinary rice and compromises the spell); prayer parchments or blood-smears stuck to the foreheads of vampires to immobilise them; a crucifix-sword made out of coins; and old-fashioned kung fu moves used by the heroic, one-eyebrowed priest to batter vampires through very breakable furniture.

While it showcases serious occult lore and gruesome horror, it's essentially a comedy lark, with a Clouseau-like jealous police inspector getting in the way because the heroine (Moon Lee) prefers goofy, temporarily-fanged Hui and monsters who are as ludicrous as they are fearsome.

A huge hit in the Far East, this spun off a number of sequels, remakes, imitations and rip-offs, typecasting the supple Lam Ching-Ying (also the film's fight choreographer) in Van Helsing-type roles and inspiring the more export-friendly, romantic *Chinese Ghost Story* franchise. ★★★★ **KN**

MRS BROWN (1997)

Starring: *Judi Dench (Queen Victoria), Billy Connolly (John Brown), Geoffrey Palmer (Henry Ponsonby), Antony Sher (Prime Minister Benjamin Disraeli)*
Director: *John Madden*
Screenwriter: *Jeremy Brock*
PG/103 mins./Drama/History/Romance/UK/Ireland/USA
Awards: *BAFTA – Best Costume, Best Actress, Golden Globes – Best Actress*

Queen Victoria is deeply depressed after the death of her husband. Her servant Brown adores her, and through caress and admiration brings her back to life. However, their relationship creates a scandalous situation that puts the monarchy on the brink of crisis . . .

It's becoming increasingly apparent that the stand-up microphone is a surprisingly useful tool with which to prise open a backdoor into the movies. So it should have been no surprise to see Billy Connolly tackle a leading role as Queen Vic's horse-wrangling Highlander in a film that's a good deal more gutsy and compelling than you'd think.

Period cossies, historical story and earthy British production do not always make for scintillating entertainment. But this is a different matter altogether. It's more than two years since Prince Albert popped off, but Dench's starchy monarch is still in the depths of depression and unmoved by public obligations. In the desperate hope that a breath of fresh air may dispel her gloom and thereby quell republican ambition, John Brown is summoned from Balmoral with the Queen's nag.

What follows, however, is the last thing her staid Private Secretary had in mind, as the Scot develops a close and exclusive relationship with HRH, and clamours for Royal abolition are replaced by rumours of a scandalous affair. Which the film sees fit to neither confirm nor deny, and in striking this delicate balance, makes its impact.

Leading a host of strong, mature performances – other notables being Palmer and Anthony Sher's oily Disraeli – Connolly's brusque, straight-talking, stern loyalty and beardy compassion gradually wears down tangible walls of grief around Dench's incredibly convincing (and Oscar-nominated) Victoria, and before you know it, you're caught up in a difficult but touching friendship, and enjoying a history lesson more than you ever thought possible. ★★★★ **DB**

MRS MINIVER (1942)

Starring: *Greer Garson (Mrs Kay Miniver), Walter Pidgeon (Clem Miniver), Teresa Wright (Carol Beldon), Dame May Whitty (Lady Beldon), Henry Travers (Mr Ballard), Reginald Owen (Foley), Richard Ney (Vin Miniver)*
Director: *William Wyler*
Screenwriters: *Arthur Wimperis, George Froeschel, James Hilton, Claudine West,* based on the novel by Jan Struther
U/134 mins./Drama/USA
Awards: *Academy Awards – Best Picture, Best Director, Best Actress, Best Supporting Actress (Teresa Wright), Best Writing, Best Cinematography, Black And White*

Housewife Kay Miniver and her architect husband, Clement, survive the Home Front travails on the Second World War, while their Oxford-educated son, Vincent, falls for Carol, the granddaughter of rose-growing toff, Lady Beldon.

Greer Garson hadn't wanted to make this homage to British pluck, after it was rejected by Norma Shearer. She not only felt too young to play a fortysomething housewife, but she was also on the verge of breaking her MGM contract to return home to do voluntary work. However, she ended up landing both the Oscar for Best Actress (famously making a 6-minute acceptance speech) and a husband, as she married co-star Richard Ney (who was 10 years her junior).

German exile William Wyler, on the other hand, had been so keen to make this adaptation of Jan Struthers's morale-boosting stories from *The Times* that he was prepared to take on both Louis B. Mayer and the Isolationists in Washington (who believed that Hollywood was part of a Jewish conspiracy to coerce America into war with the Third Reich). But all attempts to tone down the story's anti-Nazi elements were abandoned after Pearl Harbor occurred just before shooting began.

Yet, this is not an overtly propagandist picture. Garson's capture of wounded Luftwaffe pilot Helmut Dantine and Walter Pidgeon's participation in the Dunkirk rescue were a touch fanciful for the residents of the once-quiet village of Belham. But the depiction of the air raid and the myriad inconveniences of everyday life were credible enough. Indeed, Wyler even had a gentle dig at the British class system by having May Whitty's blue blood challenged in the rose-growing contest by stationmaster Henry Travers and allowing Richard Ney to spout some fashionable Oxbridge notions of social equality.

But Wyler's pride in the picture's authenticity was dented when he came to Britain to make war documentaries and realised how much he had romanticised the whole Home Front experience. Yet, Churchill deemed the film 'propaganda worth a hundred battleships' and Franklin D. Roosevelt had vicar Henry Wilcoxon's rousing sermon (which he had written with Wyler on the night before shooting and performed in one take) broadcast on Voice of America radio and translated for a leaflet drop across Occupied Europe. Moreover, its unprecedented blanket release across the States made it the biggest box-office hit of the 1940s. ★★★★ **DP**

MRS PARKER AND THE VICIOUS CIRCLE (1994)

Starring: *Jennifer Jason Leigh (Dorothy Parker), Campbell Scott (Robert Benchley), Matthew Broderick (Charles MacArthur), Peter Gallagher (Alan Campbell), Jennifer Beals (Gertrude Benchley), Andrew McCarthy (Eddie Parker)*
Director: *Alan Rudolph*
Screenwriters: *Alan Rudolph, Randy Sue Coburn*
15/119 mins./Drama/Biography/USA

In New York in the 1920s, a snapping pack of intellectuals and artists gather at a round table in the Algonquin Hotel. Writer Dorothy Parker neglects her abusive husband in favour of humorist Robert Benchley and grinds through Hollywood drudgery to drunken obsolesence.

Alan Rudolph here returns to his favourite form, the ensemble movie, with a waspish historical document that stands as an American companion piece to his Paris-set *The Moderns*.

Jennifer Jason Leigh does a remarkable job of evoking Dorothy Parker's long, agonising decline through to the 1960s, but the bulk of the film is set back in the 'colourful' 20s as Parker tastes love and regret while the jazz age blares and prohibition gin flows. Flitting through are once-substantial, now-forgotten figures like playwrights Charles MacArthur and Robert Sherwood (Nick Cassavetes), crackerbarrel philosopher Will Rogers (Keith Carradine), novelist Edna Ferber (Lili Taylor), capon critic Alexander Woolcott (Tom McGowan) and silent comic Harpo Marx (J.M. Henry), who get to be amusingly malevolent as a reminder of how nasty these people could be before nostalgia tamed them. Ostensibly the story of a bunch of self-pitying slobs who happened to hit on the occasional funny line, this is a consistently entertaining anthology of everybody's best jokes and anecdotes (emerging from an unsatisfactory grope in the bushes, Parker tells her unsuccessful lover 'don't worry, I never review rehearsals').

With an arch affectation of Parker's unusual accent that goes beyond impersonation, Leigh exposes the real pain which lies behind Dorothy's morbid jokiness: her delivery of Parker's famous poem about suicide is a perfect dissection of the open wounds that drove her humour and her reaction to the news of Benchley's death is among the most moving scenes in 1990s cinema.

Try to spot Gwyneth Paltrow, Peter Benchley, Heather Graham, Stanley Tucci, Cyndi Lauper, Tom Robbins and Jon Favreau. ★★★★ **KN**

⑩ MRS HENDERSON PRESENTS (2005)

Starring: *Judi Dench (Laura Henderson), Bob Hoskins (Vivian Van Damm), Will Young (Bertie), Kelly Reilly (Maureen), Thelma Barlow (Lady Conway), Christopher Guest (Lord Cromer)*
Director: *Stephen Frears*
Screenwriter: *Martin Sherman*
12A/103 mins./Comedy/Drama/UK

Awards: *Empire Awards – Best Newcomer (Kelly Reilly)*

In the 1930s, a wealthy widow buys a run-down London theatre and opens her own risqué revue show, with the help of a talented manager. But when World War II breaks out, the theatre comes under threat.

Judi Dench has cultivated a certain type of character over the last few years – the grande dame with an edge of daring. This patented mix of imperious dignity and girlish whimsy serves her well as Mrs Henderson, the society widow-turned-vaudeville theatre owner and founder of London's first nude revue. The character is potentially a fascinating one, but the story around her doesn't allow Dench to completely stretch her wings. Her relationship with theatre manager Vivian Van Damm is well written, but their interplay feels a little too artful to be heartfelt and is sometimes lost amid a welter of subplots. Chief among those is the story of their leading (naked) lady, Maureen, who steals every scene she's in.

Reilly gets less screen time than she deserves, instead giving way to brief appearances by Will Young (in a glorified cameo) and Bob Hoskins' willy. Yet the intriguing subject matter and good performances mean it's still a diverting look at a time when Soho nude shows were still, basically, good, clean fun. ★★★ **H O'H**

⑩ MUCH ADO ABOUT NOTHING (1993)

Starring: *Kenneth Branagh (Benedick), Emma Thompson (Beatrice), Richard Briers (Signor Lenoato), Keanu Reeves (Don John), Kate Beckinsale (Hero), Robert Sean Leonard (Claudio), Denzel Washington (Don Pedro), Michael Keaton (Dogberry)*
Director: *Kenneth Branagh*
Screenwriter: *Kenneth Branagh, based on the play by William Shakespeare*
PG/111 mins./Comedy/Romance/UK/USA

Back from war Benedick and Claudio are looking for romance. But can Benedick be reconciled with the prickly Beatrice?And will the course of true love run smooth for Claudio and Hero?

Critics of Kenneth Branagh eager to see the boy wonder fall on his face had to wait just a little bit longer (until the disaster that was *Mary Shelley's Frankenstein*) as his fourth feature, and second Shakespearean screen adaptation, revealed itself as a delightful bit of fun and a starry crowd-pleaser.

Much Ado is arguably Shakespeare's wittiest comedy, dealing as it does with the feigned antipathy of its talkative, bantering protagonists, confirmed bachelor Benedick and spirited Beatrice, whose real love for each other is joyfully exposed by the ingenious match-making of their cronies.

Around and between these two, a hectic whirl of courting, conniving and clowning takes place as Don Pedro, Prince of Aragon (Washington dandy down to his leather trousers) energetically promotes his comrades' happiness; his jealous bastard brother Don John (Reeves permanently a'glowering) broods and plots; wan young drip Claudio falls in and out and back in lurve; and the famously inarticulate local constable Dogberry (a very funny, quirky Keaton twinned with stooge Ben Elton) bumbles upon the truth behind a despicable deed that threatens to undo all.

Branagh has deposited his production on a lovely Tuscan estate where the delicious repartee and romping unfold as a suitably sunny summer idyll, with ideas borrowed as much from Hollywood adventures as from theatrical tradition, from the gallants' arrival galloping into shot like something from *The Magnificent Seven*, to the lovestruck Benedick stomping about in a fountain like Genes Kelly or Wilder.

Emma T. reaffirms her brilliance as an actress who can declaim 'Hey nonny nonny' without appearing even the teensiest bit inane, and if occasionally the full-blooded cast (which includes Branagh's theatre colleagues Richard Briers, Brian Blessed, Imelda Staunton and then ingenue Kate Beckinsale) threaten to run riot, the quieter episodes of love declared, sinister scheming or near-tragedy mercifully cool their jets.

Be assured that any previous acquaintance with the play is unnecessary, since Branagh's forte in Shakespeare is, of course, to emphasise the sense, and he has done so here with charming playfulness and an exuberant ensemble. The result is wonderfully unrestrained, romantic and funny. ★★★★ **AE**

⑩ MULAN (1998)

Starring: *the voices of: Ming-Na (Mulan), Eddie Murphy (Mushu), Lea Salonga (Mulan, singing), BD Wong (Shang), Donny Osmond (Shang, singing)*
Directors: *Barry Cook, Tony Bancroft*
Screenwriters: *Rita Hsiao, Christopher Sanders, Philip Lazebnik, Raymond Singer, Eugenia Bostwick-Singer, from a story by Robert D. San Souci*
U/87 mins./Animated/Family/Musical/USA

A Chinese girl disguises herself as a boy, to take her father's place in battle and so maintain the family's honour.

Jettisoning the saccharine cutesiness, in-jokery and overt merchandising opportunities of recent Disney outings, *Mulan* serves up the sort of classic entertainment the Magic Kingdom was built on: stunning animation, sharply defined characters, a smattering of catchy tunes all seamlessly woven into a simple, powerfully told yarn. Ironically, by harking back to its semi-serious dramatic roots, the studio's 36th feature length cartoon may suggest the future for its animated output.

Based on traditional Chinese legend, *Mulan* sees the eponymous teen rebel, unable to fulfil servile wifely duties, attempt to save familial blushes by dressing as a man and becoming a war hero in the battle against the Hun. Aided by obligatory (and completely superfluous) comic sidekicks – a cricket and a jive talkin' dragon (Murphy, desperately aspiring to Robin Williams' Aladdin genie) – our plucky heroine hooks up with the motley ranks of the Imperial Garrison: cue basic army training (including likeable comedy song 'I'll Make A Man Out Of You'), Mulan's attraction to dashing Captain Shang and some stunningly staged skirmishes with the bad guys – all the while Mulan trying to keep her female identity secret.

While brimming over with 90s concerns – raising issues of female empowerment, women in the military, cross-dressing – *Mulan* rarely loses sight of its timeless folklore quality. Ancient China is beautifully evoked and the film throws up compelling dramatic beats – the opening attack on the Great Wall Of China, Mulan donning her father's armour, the final showdown – that linger long in the memory. Best of all, though, is a Hun stampede down the slopes of a snowy mountain, fantastically energised by swooping camera work, that rivals the great David Lean in its exhilarating, epic sweep.

The four songs, if not instantly memorable, are pleasant, well-staged diversions that embellish rather than intrude on the storytelling. Among the strongest heroines in Walt's cartoon canon, Mulan's engaging mixture of vulnerability and derring-do becomes incredibly easy to root for and, in Hun leader Shan-Yu, Disney have created their scariest villain for years. Add the contagious sense of adventure, light sprinkling of humour and a genuinely uplifting resolution and *Mulan* emerges as an unadulterated treat. ★★★ **IF**

MULTIPLICITY (1996)

Starring: *Michael Keaton (Doug Kinney), Andie MacDowell (Laura Kinney), Zack Duhame (Zack Kinney), Katie Schlossberg (Jennifer Kinnnery)*
Director: *Harold Ramis*
Screenwriters: *Chris Miller, Mary Hale, Lowell Ganz, Babaloo Mandel, from a short story by Chris Miller*
12/112 mins./Sci-fi/Comedy/USA

A man who never has enough time for the things he wants to do is offered the opportunity to have himself duplicated.

At first glance, *Multiplicity* would appear to be almost a carbon copy of the classic hit comedy *Groundhog Day*, complete with director Harold Ramis, star Andie MacDowell and a concept high enough to bring on a vertiginous bout. However, instead of Bill Murray living the same day over and over again, this time Michael Keaton is called upon to be the same person over and over again, with less successful but still enormously agreeable, results.

Keaton is Doug Kinney, a construction foreman who, with both a huge building contract to take care of, and a loving wife, Laura to appease, is suffering from a lack of hours in the day, until he meets a revolutionary doctor who offers to clone him. Doug number two promptly appears, and for a while things are just peachy – his new-found lookalike handles the business while the original plays house-husband. But things get really interesting, when Doug number three appears, followed soon after by a hopelesly retarded number four to add to the growing air of confusion.

The one – or four – man show that ensues, may reduce all the peripheral characters, including MacDowell, to the level of set dressing, but provides a marvellous tour de force for Keaton, with each of his individual clones cleverly given its own personality and managing to co-exist without any confusion as to which is which.

Occasionally the impression is given that this could have been perhaps a tad more frenetic, with much of the hilarity confined to a series of seamlessly crafted set-pieces that allow Keaton to high-five himself, quarrel with himself, and become repeatedly exasperated with you-know-who. And the whole thing stops short of delivering any potential dark undercurrents in its quest for the ultimate in feelgood conclusions. However, by the time all three clones have succeeded in bedding MacDowell, it becomes clear that *Multiplicity* scores so highly on the entertainment scale that any attempt to provide anything deeper is really unnecessary. ★★★★ **CW**

MULHOLLAND DR. (2001)

Starring: *Naomi Watts (Betty Elms/Diane Selwyn), Laura Harring (Rita), Ann Miller (Catherine 'Coco' Lenoix/Adam's Mother), Dan Hedaya (Vincenzo Castigliane), Justin Theroux (Adam Kesher)*
Director: *David Lynch*
Screenwriter: *David Lynch*
15/148 mins./Drama/Mystery/Thriller/France/USA
Awards: *BAFTA – Best Editing*

A beautiful woman suffers amnesia after surviving a car crash on L.A.'s Mulholland Drive. Hiding in an empty apartment, she meets an aspiring actress; as they attempt to unearth her identity, they fall in love. Or do they? Well, kind of. But, in fact, not.

For some, *The Straight Story* was evidence that David Lynch was at last emerging from the twisted obsessions of his oeuvre thus far. The director's elegiac ode to one man and his lawn tractor embraced some of the more established conventions of cinema – a linear narrative structure being chief among them.

For others, the film was a moribund dalliance with the mainstream that was unforgivably lacking in Lynchian trademarks – dwarves, weird sex and the realm of nightmares that teems beneath society's veneer of normality. Those in the latter camp should rejoice, then, because in *Mulholland Drive*, David Lynch gets Lynchian with a vengeance.

Linear narrative is, of course, conspicuous by its absence, but in its place Lynch orchestrates a liquid, undulating dreamscape that is at once beautiful, heartrending, madly confusing and, quite honestly, awe-inspiring in its daring and execution.

Set in a hyper-noir L.A., enveloped in night the colour and texture of a bruise, the film pulsates with disquiet. And with the waving, anemone strands of its storylines, Lynch weaves a tapestry of unease.

Occasionally sequences descend into bizarre farce or climax with the horror that they appear to promise. But more often events proceed with mounting, unaccountable menace. One of the most disturbing scenes, almost unbearably portentous, involves Naomi Watts simply making a cup of coffee.

At a point where the plot seems poised on the brink of resolution, the film suddenly folds in on itself, literally disappearing into a black hole from which it reappears more contrary than ever. That this is, in fact, the twist that binds the threads together probably won't occur to you until long after the credits roll. But then, this isn't a film to be followed in the traditional sense; it's one to let wash over you, one to wallow in. ★★★★ **SB**

THE MUMMY (1932)

Starring: *Boris Karloff (Imhotep/Ardeth Bey), Zita Johann (Helen Grosvenor/Princess Ankh-es-en-Amon), David Manners (Frank Whemple), Arthur Byron (Sir Joseph Whemple), Edward Van Sloan (Doctor Muller)*
Director: *Karl Freund*
Screenwriter: *John L. Balderston, from the story 'Cagliostro' by Nina Wilcox Putnam, Richard Shayer*
15/72 mins./Horror/USA

In 1921 a field expedition in Egypt discovers the mummy of ancient Egyptian prince Imhotep and accidentally bring him back to life.

Long before the discovery of Tutankhamen's tomb in 1922, filmmakers had been plundering the rich potential of ancient Egypt. Typically, Georges

TOP10

Arnie Kiss-Off Lines

1 'Don't disturb my friend – he's dead tired!' – after killing a man on a plane – *Commando*

2 **'Consider that a divorce!' – Shooting his wife (Sharon Stone) – *Total Recall***

3 'Hasta la vista, baby!' – Shooting the T-1000 (Robert Patrick) – *Terminator 2: Judgment Day*

4 **'Stick around!' – Impales a baddie with a stake – *Predator***

5 'He was a pain the neck!' – Garrottes a 'stalker' – *The Running Man*

6 **'To be or not to be? Not to be.' – Playing Hamlet – *The Last Action Hero***

7 'You're fired!' – Firing a missile at a baddie – *True Lies*

8 **'You're luggage!' – To a dead crocodile – *Eraser***

9 'I'm afraid my condition has left me cold to your pleas of mercy.' – Mr Freeze to a cop – *Batman & Robin*

10 **'You are terminated!' – On killing the T-X – *Terminator 3: Rise Of The Machines***

Melies showed the way with *Robbing Cleopatra's Tomb*, which was followed by *The Mummy Of King Rameses* and Ernst Lubitsch's *Eyes Of The Mummy*. Yet, by the end of the silent era, Hollywood deemed mummified monsters fit only for comedies like *Mummy Love*.

Indeed, even this classic template for what is, arguably, horror cinema's least successful sub-genre only adopted an Egyptian theme as something of an afterthought. Fresh from photographing *The Murders In The Rue Morgue*, Karl Freund was asked by Universal to rework the Dracula formula in his directorial debut. Initially, he intended to spin a yarn of longevity and black magic entitled *Cagliostro*. But Nina Wilcox Putnam's muddled story was completely revamped by John L. Balderston, another debutante who had earned a reputation for adapting literary horror for the stage.

Balderston had been a reporter on Howard Carter's expedition to the Valley Of The Kings, which had just concluded its decade-long excavation. However, King Tut wasn't the only inspiration for the screenplay. Elements of Dracula are clearly evident in the determination of an undead monster to possess the soul of an English rose, while Balderston's simultaneous involvement in a treatment of H. Rider Haggard's novel *She* also coloured his thinking. Indeed, the whole enterprise had something of a rehashed feel about it. Sets and props were recycled from *Dracula*, while David Manners was hired to reprise the part of the anguished beau and Edward Van Sloan was cast as a Van Helsing-style troubleshooter.

Even Jack Pierce was summoned to provide Boris Karloff with makeup to match that of Frankenstein. Much criticism has been levelled at the film for its lack of terror. Certainly Karloff is less menacing in a suit and fez than he is swathed in dust-encrusted bandages. Surviving scripts suggest that the inspired camera movements and subtle edits were Balderston's. But Freund's mark on both the look and tone of the action is indelible. As the cameraman on F. W. Murnau's *The Last Laugh* (1924), he had pioneered the concept of the subjective view, while his work on Paul Wegener's *The Golem* (1915) and Fritz Lang's *Metropolis* (1927) steeped him in the Expressionist tradition that dominated German filmmaking in the 1920s.

What's more, he had helped introduce Expressionism to Hollywood while behind the camera on Tod Browning's *Dracula* (1931). The Depression was biting deep by 1932 and it's no coincidence that the shambling figures of the bread queues should have found expression in the mesmerised souls of *The Mummy*. But shock and social comment were not the story's prime motives. Undying love (which would inspire many a Vincent Price picture and Coppola's *Dracula* (1993) prompt Imhotep's crimes in both the ancient and modern worlds. Thus, the moments of horror are muted. When Norton's incantation revives Imhotep, we see his slowly opening eyes, his arms across his chest, a hand reaching for the scroll and a straggle of loose bandages as he takes his leave of the stricken archaeologist, now a raving wreck after what he has witnessed.

Similarly, the flashback to Imhotep's incarceration is handled with great skill, with Karloff's wild eyes alone conveying the horror of his embalming. Indeed, as in *Frankenstein* (1931), Karloff's ability to communicate through his makeup is vital to establishing his character; even in human form, it's clearly pain and not incarnate evil that dictates his actions. Four indifferent Universal sequels followed before Hammer, inevitably, assumed the mantle, peaking with *Blood From The Mummy's Tomb* in 1971. Most recently, Stephen Sommers took a highly lucrative Indiana Jones-style approach in the 1999 blockbuster *The Mummy*. ★★★★ **DP**

THE MUMMY (1999)

Starring: *Brendan Fraser (Richard 'Rick' O'Connell), Rachel Weisz (Evelyn Carnahan), John Hannah (Jonathan Carnahan), Arnold Vosloo (High Priest Imhotep)*
Director: *Stephen Sommers*
Screenwriter: *Stephen Sommers, from a story by Lloyd Fonvielle, Stephen Sommers, Kevin Jarre*
12/119 mins./Action/Adventure/Horror/USA

Ex-Foreign Legionnaire Rick O'Connell teams up with Egyptologist Evelyn and her brother Jonathan to prevent a revived Mummy from destroying the world.

Scorned by critics, but loved by audiences, Universal's remake of its own 1930s classic is actually a lot of fun, its blend of low-rent Indiana Jones-style antics, impressive special effects and inevitably chaste romance scoring high in the risible escapist nonsense department.

Brendan Fraser is the likeable chiselled hero, a Foreign Legion deserter who has to swash and buckle his way through 1920s Egypt when a misguided treasure hunt actually re-awakens an ancient, heavily bandaged and rather unpleasant priest (hey, they actually mummified these people for a reason, you know).

The script is as dumb as they come, relying on the inevitable square-jawed heroics and vaguely distasteful middle-eastern stereotypes for effect, John Hannah is trapped in a thanklessly one-dimensional role, while Rachel Weisz's virginal heroine really doesn't exist for any purposes other than sexual awakening and human sacrifice. However, if you can forgive it its glaring faults and focus on the F/X department's field day, which ranges from morphing evil Egyptian priest types out of sand, to covering pointless extras in rivers of genuinely spine-tingling creepie-crawlies, there's a great evening's entertainment to be had. ★★★ **CW**

Movie Trivia: The Mummy

Brendan Fraser collapsed on set because his noose was too tight. Imhotep was named so in a tribute to the man of the same name believed to have developed the pyramids. It took 14 hours to apply Patricia Velasquez' body paint, which protected her dignity entirely but for a loincloth and some jewellery.

THE MUMMY RETURNS (2001)

Starring: *Brendan Fraser (Richard 'Rick' O'Connell), Rachel Weisz (Evelyn Carnahan), John Hannah (Jonathan Carnahan), Arnold Vosloo (High Priest Imhotep), The Rock (Scorpion King)*
Director: *Stephen Sommers*
Screenwriter: *Stephen Sommers*
12/124 mins./Action/Adventure/Horror/USA

Eight years after Imhotep was first reincarnated, he is once again brought to life and embarks upon a quest for immortality and world domination, this time by trying to overcome another recently resurrected evil force, The Scorpion King. The only people who can stop him? Rick and Evelyn O'Connell, now married and living in London with their eight-year-old son, Alex.

As we all know, the law of averages dictates that sequels shouldn't be as good as their predecessors, and this attempt to franchise 1999's highly enjoyable, and surprisingly profitable, caper, is no exception. *The Mummy Returns* (are two further efforts entitled *The Mummy Forever* and *The Mummy And Robin* set to follow, one wonders?) was a blockbuster waiting to happen, but for all its slick proficiency and brilliant special effects, it's hard to locate in the over-complicated story any of the innocent, tongue-in-cheek charm that made the first film so enjoyable. This is sequel-making by numbers, where the zealous attempts to outdo the predecessor, (one all-poweful baddy last time – hey! – let's have two this time!) loses sight of the finer points.

That's not to say that the second instalment is a lost cause; as escapist, noisy (and indeed the thrills are on an ear-splitting level here) popcorn entertainment, it certainly delivers. The plot, however, gets thoroughly messy, as our heroes fuss over whether or not it's really wise to open ancient Egyptian chests covered in cobwebs, and their resourceful child has to live with the consequences of putting on an antique bracelet which allows him to take a speeded-up virtual tour of ancient Egypt. Meanwhile, Fraser and Weisz find themselves involved with Imhotep and his band of undead followers, in such a convoluted way that they are forced to once again save the world from his grasp. You can guess the rest. Also caught up in all this is Hannah, reprising his toff in peril role to even more annoying effect, Velasquez as the kind of character you know was just included to get reincarnated and challenge Weisz to some nifty, post-*Crouching Tiger* catfights, and wrestler The Rock, whose triumphantly overblown billing as 'The Scorpion King' achieves little except to thoroughly disappoint his legion of tiny fans when they discover how little he is actually on screen.

Despite some neat set-pieces (highlights including a fast and furious man vs. mummy battle on a double-decker bus, and some seriously vicious pygmy mummies in the desert), the action takes too long and sags noticeably in the middle when stilted dialogue takes over from the special effects that are, unsurprisingly, the movie's real star. By the time the final reel happens along we're in familiar territory, with the CGI wizardry the audience will have paid to see unleashed in awesome, truly spectacular fashion. As crustaceans run riot and huge armies swarm the desert like marauding bugs, plot complications cease to become important and the action takes centre stage. If the rest of the movie had been so straightforward they'd have been on to a winner. ★★★ **CH**

⑩ MUNICH (2005)

Starring: *Eric Bana (Avner), Daniel Craig (Steve), Ciarán Hinds (Carl), Mathieu Kassovitz (Robert), Geoffrey Rush (Ephraim)*
Director: *Steven Spielberg*
Screenwriters: *Tony Kushner, Eric Roth, based on the book* Vengeance: The True Story Of An Israeli Counter-Terrorist Team *by George Jonas*
15/164 mins./Drama/History/Thriller/USA

After eleven Israeli athletes are murdered by a Palestinian terror group at the 1972 Munich Olympics, a hit squad is instigated by Israel's secret service agency to track down those thought to have organised the atrocity. But alongside their achievements, the team will come to question the morality and effectiveness of their fateful mission.

Munich is Steven Spielberg's most difficult film. It arrived inflamed by controversy (some consider it driven by dubious facts, although it claims only to be 'inspired by real events'). It is morally ambiguous and purposefully divorced from the thrill-seeking flamboyance of the director's glory-glory days. It is clear, lean and startlingly intelligent, with a brute hardness, unshrinking in the face of terrible events. It may confound people, irk them, because it's so resolutely uncompromised, offering no easy answers while revealing the edgy, focused humanity of 70s hard-hitters like Lumet's *Serpico* or Coppola's *The Conversation* – yet with a captivating style very much its own. So, when we say difficult, that's difficult in a very good way.

In genre terms it exists somewhere off-centre of an espionage thriller, as Avner (played with striking emotional engagement by Eric Bana) and his team methodically set up and execute their hits against stark European cityscapes of shabby, neon-smeared apartment blocks. Their work couldn't appear less glamorous. Aided by Tony Kushner's supple script (Eric Roth is officially credited for an earlier draft), which manages a dry, gallows humour amid the unravelling of souls, Spielberg contrasts the icy mechanics of, say, booby-trapping a Parisian telephone with the excruciating aftershock of close-range assassination.

Alongside the energy and tension of their covert action, each member of the team, from Daniel Craig's fiery getaway driver to Ciarán Hinds' meticulous clean-up man, finds their certainty undone. As their own keepers grow distant, they hang on to the tragic events of Munich itself, adroitly edited in from archive footage, to keep their conviction alive.

All the film's constituent parts bear this hallmark of reality. Even those Black Septemberists, the perpetrators of definable evil at the Olympic Village, are exposed as merely young men heightened on fear and adrenaline. In an entirely fictional scene, Spielberg implants an improbable but gripping encounter between Avner and a Palestinian counterpart who bleakly reports the film's themes of home and identity. That Avner, spent and bitter, ends up an exile is an ironic reflection of the film's central conflict: nationhood versus humanity.

Reinforcing this humane doctrine, Avner cooks lavish meals for his team and much of Kushner's erudite discourse is conveyed at the dinner table as they chew over their shadowy purpose. And in one tumultuous sequence Spielberg crosscuts between Avner having passionate sex with his wife, reconnecting with simple, honest hungers, and the dreaded outcome of the Munich tragedy.

Former Bond villain Michael Lonsdale does a swift, scene-stealing spin as a Gallic wheeler-dealer called Papa, who trades in information and explosives for profit. Under the dark spell of paranoia – watch how Spielberg never lets a scene settle, always allowing a flickering of light or movement within the frame – the team start to believe Papa could be selling them out. Meanwhile, a confrontation with another assassin, a personal vengeance within the greater political one of their objective, will surely go down as the director's coldest moment.

In a key shot, as Avner and his case officer Ephraim (a barking, steel-hard Geoffrey Rush) stroll along a Brooklyn river front, the Twin Towers stand boldly behind them. The message is hard to miss: this film could not be more relevant. ★★★★★ **IN**

⑩ THE MUPPET CHRISTMAS CAROL (1992)

Starring: *Michael Caine (Ebenezer Scrooge), David Goelz (Gonzo and various voices), Steve Whitmire (Kermit and various voices), Jerry Nelson (various voices), Frank Oz (Miss Piggy and various voices)*
Director: *Brian Henson*
Screenwriter: *Jerry Juhl, based on the novel by Charles Dickens*
U/85 mins./Musical/UK/USA

Charles Dickens famous story of a crotchety old stinge faced with his own past, present and future one snowy Christmas Eve, as retold through the medium of the Muppets.

For their brief return to form in the early 90s, the Muppets, led by the late Jim Henson's son Brian, elected to mine various familiar works of English literature to good effect (they subsequently tackled *Treasure Island* also). With the help of skilful screenwriting from Jerry Juhl, the important strains of the classic Dickens story remain intact, while the film takes on all those jaunty, faintly postmodern Muppet attributes (there is much direct to audience dialogue).

Having it narrated by the brilliant Gonzo (as Charles Dickens!) and winning newcomer Rizzo the Rat, a wisecracking rodent who keeps dropping off ledges, is the key. They give a ribald commentary to the ensuing Christmassy nonsense, deflating any sentiment, maintaining that sense that the Muppets have got this world entirely sussed.

Credit also to Michael Caine, who keeps a straight not-to-say mealy expression throughout, as Scrooge. It's the first rule, but surely a tough one – never actually recognise you're in a Muppet movie. He does it with aplomb. The songs are forgettable, Kermit (Bob Cratchit, natch) and Miss Piggy's ongoing relationship spats are a little tiresome, but checking off your favourite fuzzballs while keeping tabs on a great old story makes for an easy formula. And Waldorf and Statler as the Marley brothers is inspired. ★★★ **IN**

MUPPETS FROM SPACE (1999)

Starring: *the voices of: Dave Goelz (Gonzo/Dr Bunsen Honeydew/Waldorf/The Bird Man/Swedish Chef/Zoot), Steve Whitmire (Kermit the Frog/Rizzo the Rat/Beaker/Cosmic Fish #1/Bean Bunny/Beach Hippie) (voice) Bill Barretta (epe the Prawn/Bobo as Rentro/Johnny Fiama/Bubba the Rat/Cosmic Fish #2/Dr. Teeth/Rowlf), Jerry Nelson (Robin/Statler/Ubergonzo/Floyd), Frank Oz (Miss Piggy/Fozzie Bear/Animal/Sam the Eagle/Swedish Chef)*
Director: *Tim Hill*
Screenwriters: *Jerry Juhl, Joey Mazzarino, Ken Kaufman*
U/85 mins./Sci-fi/Comedy/Family/Adventure/USA/UK

The muppets head into space to help Gonzo find his place in the Universe.

While it would take a hard-hearted person to dislike a Muppet movie, it's fair to say that this most familiar and comforting of all movie franchises has been a tad lacklustre of late. So it's a relief to discover that *Muppets From Space* is the best Muppet movie for some time, adding film references a-plenty, dark, edgy comedy and even a touch of post-modernism to the usual all-singing, all-dancing ridiculousness.

This time around, the wafer-thin plot sticks Gonzo in the limelight, our blue hero troubled by his strange dreams and even stranger lack of past. When he starts getting mysterious messages from random food items, he becomes convinced that he is not of this earth.

Muppets From Space cheerily acknowledges that at least part of its audience will be made up of people who grew up watching the show two decades ago, as opposed to merely their children, and in that respect delivers on both levels.

There's a lot to keep the kids quiet, too – the opening musical number is a masterpiece of comic timing and the one-liners are frequently funny. Human cast this time around includes Andie MacDowell, F. Murray Abraham, Rob Schneider and Ray Liotta but the Muppets remain the stars. ★★★ **CW**

MURDER BY DEATH (1976)

Starring: *Truman Capote (Lionel Twain), James Coco (Inspector Milo Perrier), Peter Falk (Sam Diamond), Alec Guinness (Jamesir Bensonmum), Elsa Lanchester (Miss Jessica Marbles), David Niven (Dick Charleston), Peter Sellers (Inspector Sidney Wang), Maggie Smith (Mrs Dora Charleston), James Cromwell (Marcel)*
Director: *Robert Moore*
Screenwriter: *Neil Simon*
PG/94 mins./Comedy/Mystery/USA

Eccentric tycoon Lionel Twain invites a group of premier sleuths to his mansion and offers a million dollar prize to the detective who solves the mystery of a murder which is scheduled at midnight.

Most all-star comedy spoofs from the 1970s, especially the ones which feature a lot of big names in 'funny disguises', are dreadful – but this Neil Simon-scripted pastiche of an array of much-loved detective characters is surprisingly charming, with more good, smart lines to the page than any of the competition and a top-flight cast.

Truman Capote, in his only major acting role, is thoroughly strange, but everyone else is perfect – with Alec Guinness dryly presiding as a supposedly blind butler who remains unflappable while the house is swarming with deadly scorpions or death traps and convincingly mouths absolutely idiotic statements like 'she murdered herself in her sleep, sir'. David Niven and Maggie Smith are Dick and Dora Charleston, take-offs on Nick and Nora Charles of *The Thin Man*; Peter Sellers is the Charlie Chan-like Inspector Sidney Wang, who is criticised for being unable to use proper grammar in his aphorisms; Peter Falk is priceless as the hardboiled Bogart-like Sam Diamond, partnered by a game gal Friday (Eileen Brennan); James Coco is prissy as the Hercule Poirot knock-off Milo Perrier, a gourmet whose lanky slapstick butler is played by a young James Cromwell; and Elsa Lanchester pokes fun at Miss Marple as Jessie Marbles, whose nursemaid (Estelle Winwood) is more enfeebled than she is.

The plot is deliberately absurd, with a last-reel set of revelations that never make sense, and more unmaskings and improbable theories than any five Agatha Christies thrown together. It was successful enough to merit a sort-of sequel, also scripted by Simon, with Falk in a trenchcoat again as *The Cheap Detective*. ★★★★ **KN**

MURDER BY DECREE (1979)

Starring: *Christopher Plummer (Sherlock Holmes), James Mason (Dr John H. Watson), David Hemmings (Inspector Foxborough), Susan Clark (Mary Kelly), Anthony Quayle (Sir Charles Warren), John Gielgud (Lord Salisbury), Frank Finlay (Inspector Lestrade), Donald Sutherland (Robert Lees), Genevieve Bujold (Annie Crook)*
Director: *Bob Clark*
Screenwriter: *John Hopkins, based on the book by Elwyn Jones, John Lloyd, characters by Arthur Conan Doyle*
15/124 mins./Mystery/UK/Canada

In 1888, Sherlock Holmes and Dr Watson are called to investigate the Jack the Ripper murders, and uncover a conspiracy that extends from the gutters of Whitechapel to 'the highest in the land'.

The Hughes Brothers' *From Hell* is a de facto remake of this 1979 Sherlock Holmes movie, which proposes exactly the same far-fetched, later-discredited 'solution' to the mystery of Jack the Ripper – involving a Masonic conspiracy, the Queen's own surgeon and a hit-list of East End harlots who have their throats cut to conceal a Royal scandal.

This more obviously fictional earlier draft is the better bet, with a well-constructed screenplay from John Hopkins and a very fine Holmes and Watson teaming from Christopher Plummer and James Mason.

Mason makes a lot out of a tiny little scene about eating peas and provides a human centre for a fairly cynical tale, while Plummer is a more impassioned Sherlock than usual, dryly sorting through clues but appalled by the truths he uncovers and even, at one point, moved to tears. It has the expected Ripper business of prowling through foggy alleyways and riotous behaviour in Whitechapel gin-mills, but ventures into unusual areas with a series of guest star turns from David Hemmings as a Scotland Yard inspector who turns out to be a radical out to use the killings to inspire a revolution, Donald Sutherland as an enormously-whiskered psychic who claims to have an insight into the case, John Gielgud as the smug Prime Minister who decides to institute a Watergate-style cover-up to maintain public order and (especially) Genevieve Bujold as a former Royal mistress unjustly confined in an insane asylum. Director Bob Clark had a big hit with *Porky's*, but was also behind some interesting horror films, including *Children Shouldn't Play With Dead Things* and *Dead Of Night* (aka *Deathdream*). ★★★★ **KN**

MURDER ON THE ORIENT EXPRESS (1974)

Starring: *Albert Finney (Hercule Poirot), Lauren Bacall (Harriet Hubbard), Ingrid Bergman (Greta Ohlsson), Sean Connery (Colonel Arbuthnot), John Gielgud (Mr Beddoes), Martin Balsam (Signor Bianchii), Vanessa Redgrave (Mary Debenham), Anthony Perkins (Hector Willard MacQueen)*
Director: *Sidney Lumet*
Screenwriters: *Paul Dehn, Anthony Shaffer, based on the novel by Agatha Christie*
PG/128 mins./Mystery/UK-USA

Awards: *Academy Awards – Best Supporting Actress (Ingrid Bergman); BAFTA – Best Supporting Actor (John Gielgud), Best Supporting Actress (Ingrid Bergman); Best Music*

When the Orient Express is trapped by snow and a body turns up brutally stabbed, it is up to fellow passenger, the legendary Belgian detective Hercule Poirot to investigate. A case that becomes ever more intriguing when it seems all the passengers have a connection to the victim.

To paraphrase Comic Book Guy from *The Simpsons*, this is the: Best . . . Agatha . . . Christie . . . Adaptation . . . Ever. Sidney Lumet, a director who tends to the hardboiled, finds something terse and edgy in the convolutions of its plot, invites Albert Finney to make Hercule Poirot quite unlikeable, and still maintains that musty period mystique with which the queen of whodunits bewitched millions. He also manages to do the aged guest list thing (and, fading careers apart, this is some cast list) without sinking into the cheesy excesses of the Peter Ustinov era.

What is so redolent between the finery of the wood panelled Orient Express and the moody, high quality performances on show (Ingrid Bergman would pick up an Oscar for her show) is how devious Christie's thinking actually was. Unless you've previously encountered the plot, it takes a sharp mind to reveal its dark recesses, and there remains a delicious thrill to Poirot/Finney's deftly delivered final explanation. It is, inevitably, too busy to be a classic, each of those plush names bustling for attention, and no matter how good the performer you can't escape Christie's leisurely approach to characterisation – simple concoctions of quirk, guilt and red herring. But Lumet is having loads of credible fun with the formula, keeping up a genuine sense of claustrophobia in this isolated railway car surrounded by crisp white snow. ★★★★ **IN**

MURDERBALL (2005)

Starring: *as themselves: Joe Bishop, Keith Cavill, Andy Cohn, Scott Hogsett, Christopher Igoe, Bob Lujano, Kevin Orr, Joe Soares*
Director: *Henry Alex Rubin, Dana Adam Shapiro*
15/85 mins./Documentary/Sport/USA

Murderball – or quad rugby as it is more delicately, officially known – involves teams of quadriplegic men in souped-up wheelchairs ramming the hell out of each other on a basketball court. This documentary follows the US and Canada as they prepare for Athens 2004, appraising disabled life in frank style.

With alarming disregard for their remaining functioning limbs, wheelchair-bound quadriplegics smash into each other at high velocity in the opening of this kinetic documentary about a little-known sport and the men who play it.

Propelled with the drive of a sports flick, *Murderball* largely focuses on the bitter rivalry of two men: the US quad-rugby team's current star player, and his predecessor now coaching arch-rivals Canada. But the real fascination lies in the eye-opening examination of life in a chair. As the film strips away the layers of delicacy with which the able-bodied treat the disabled (even the practicalities of sex are discussed at length), a mirror is held up to our preconceptions about the physically impaired. Yet perhaps the most amazing discovery is that despite their traumatic external transformations, these guys seem unchanged internally: they were flag-waving, all-American, ultra-competitive jocks before, and they remain so after.

There are faults in construction, with fascinating strands never fully explored. But no structural failures can dampen the impact of witnessing the spirit and joie de vivre of these people to whom disability is their making, not breaking. When the credits roll, one's own petty concerns don't quite have the same ring. ★★★★ **S O'H**

MURIEL'S WEDDING (1994)

Starring: *Toni Colette (Muriel Heslop), Bill Hunter (Bill Heslop), Rachel Griffiths (Rhonda), Jeanie Drynan (Betty Heslop), Matt Day (Brice)*
Director: *P. J. Hogan*
Screenwriter: *P.J. Hogan*
15/101 mins./Comedy/Romance/Australia

Muriel finds life in Porpoise Spit, Australia, dull and spends her days alone in her room listening to Abba music and dreaming of her wedding day . . .

Australian filmmakers have a knack for feelgood comedy – witness such surprise sleepers as *Crocodile Dundee* and *Strictly Ballroom*. This latest addition to the crop, however, dares to be different, introducing social drama into an otherwise featherlight, adorably sweet tale of self-discovery, and although it doesn't quite gel, director Hogan at least deserves praise for trying.

Muriel Heslop is a frumpy, plump 22-year-old who lives for her ABBA collection and fantasies of a huge white wedding. The problem is, though her home town of Porpoise Spit is no nuptial haven, her family have hopeless written in their genes, and her beautiful, bitchy gang of so-called friends have a habit of sending her self-esteem straight down the pan.

Taking matters into her own hands, she hooks up with old school chum Rhonda and runs away to Sydney in an attempt to turn those bridal pipe dreams into a reality and make something of her otherwise mundane life. Needless to say, things don't go exactly to plan, and the twosome go through a collection of beautifully observed comic set-pieces before a series of tragic occurrences threaten to destroy Muriel's new-found freedom for good.

For the most part this works a treat, layered with crisp comic moments skilfully delivered by its largely unknown cast. Unfortunately, the frequent dramatic flashes eventually give way to a catalogue of events so depressing they sit rather uncomfortably alongside the film's ripe, wacky Aussie feel. ★★★★ **CW**

MUSIC BOX (1989)

Starring: *Jessica Lange (Ann Talbot), Armin Mueller-Stahl (Mike Laszlo), Frederic Forrest (Jack Burke), Donald Moffat (Harry Talbot), Lukas Haas (Mikey Talbot)*
Director: *Costa-Gavras*
Screenwriter: *Joe Eszterhas*
15/120 mins./Drama/USA

Ann Talbot is a successful lawyer who takes it upon herself to defend her father against preposterous claims that he was a Nazi war criminal during the war. But is daddy as innocent as his little girl at first assumes?

Following on from their contentiously received *Betrayed*, Costa-Gavras and screenwriter Joe Eszterhas here re-examine love, loyalties and betrayal to considerably sharper effect. Lange is the American Dream lawyer daughter of a good father, elderly immigrant Mike Laszlo (the first-rate Mueller-Stahl). Suddenly, unbelievably, he is accused of war crimes during the Nazi occupation of his native Hungary and his outraged daughter undertakes the old man's defence herself.

It proves an emotional trek, from furious indignation to fearful doubt as the evidence mounts against him and she is gradually forced to wonder just who this man she knows only as her father really is. The courtroom scenes effectively build the growing did-he-didn't-he tension, with the alleged atrocities skilfully if painfully evoked through the testimony of various witnesses rather than through the customary flashback scenes. Oscar-nominated Lange is quite superb throughout, conveying the tough criminal lawyer still capable of shocking below-the-belt tactics while also a daughter shaken to her core, all delivered with remarkable authority and a complete absence of histrionics. If the side is let down at all, as it occasionally is by an overblown score, some artificially imposed Dramatic Atmosphere and a fuzzy conspiracy sub-plot, this is still a must-see performance. ★★★★ **AE**

ⓓ THE MUSIC MAN (1962)

Starring: *Robert Preston (Harold Hill), Shirley Jones (Marian Paroo), Buddy Hackett (Marcellus Washburn), Hermione Gingold (Eulalie Mackechnie Shinn), Paul Ford (Mayor George Shinn)*
Director: *Morton DaCosta*
Screenwriter: *Marion Harsgrove, based on the book by Meredith Willson, Franklin Lacey*
U/151 mins./Musical/Family/Romance/USA
Awards: *Academy Awards – Best Score, Golden Globes – Best Musical*

River City, Iowa, 1912. Professor Harold Hill, a con man, persuades the townsfolk that they desperately need a boys' band – then sells them the instruments and uniforms. The librarian Marian sees through the scam, but he works hard to win her over.

If you've never seen *The Music Man*, you won't understand 'Marge vs the Monorail', the Simpsons episode which remakes, homages and parodies this exuberant widescreen version of Meredith Willson's Broadway smash-hit musical.

Robert Preston, in the role of his career, is the fast-talking hustler Harold Hill, whose best cons are delivered in rhythmic spiel that's kind of like a 1912 rap act (especially in his ranted diatribe against the alleged evil influence of the game of pool, 'Trouble'). Shirley Jones, looking lovely in pastel costumes, is the stereotypical old maid librarian who melts when she sees that being wholeheartedly rooked has turned her small-minded neighbours into much nicer people and even cheered up her depressed little brother (red-top moppet Ron Howard, billed as 'Ronny'). The breakout hit songs are the brassy '76 Trombones' and the romantic belter 'Til There Was You', but Willson's entire score is a delight, with intricate, imaginative lyrics (extra points for rhyming 'carrion' with 'Marian the Librarian' and working a joke about Nathaniel Hawthorne's *The Scarlet Letter* into 'The Sadder But Wise Girl For Me'). Director Morton DaCosta, in one of his too-few film credits, is a holdover from the stage version and recreates theatrical effects, often in breezy open-air settings, highlighting the emotions with lighting tricks and filling the entire Technirama frame with choreographed action. There are polished comic gems from Paul Ford (Colonel Hall from *Bilko*) and Hermione Gingold as the Mayor and his mad wife, and Buddy Hackett gets one exhausting, meaningless number ('Shi-Pupi'). Two and a half hours of delight. ★★★★ **DP**

ⓓ THE MUSIC OF CHANCE (1993)

Starring: *James Spader (Jack Pozzi), Mandy Patinkin (Jim Nashe), M.Emmet Walsh (Calvin Murks), Charles Durning (Bill Flower), Joel Grey (Willy Stone), Samantha Mathis (Tiffany), Chris Penn (Floyd)*
Director: *Philip Haas*
Screenwriters: *Belinda Haas, Philip Haas, based on the novel by Paul Auster*
15/94 mins./Drama/USA

In a faithful rendering of the Paul Auster novel, Jim, a former fireman is drifting across America, living off an inheritance. On the road he meets professional gambler Jack, who convinces him to back him in a poker game with two wealthy old men. When he unexpectedly loses, the men are forced to work off their debts by building an enormous wall.

When it comes to intriguing cinematic subjects, two blokes building a wall in someone's back garden hardly has its hand straining to get round your throat. Yet, so deftly staged and wonderfully acted is this adaptation of Paul Auster's deeply weird and, one would have thought, unfilmable novel about the paying off of a gambling debt, that it never lets up for an instant.

The story concerns James Nashe and Jack Pozzi – a drifter and a grifter – thrown together when Nashe, motoring along a road to nowhere, living off the remnants of a small inheritance, picks up battered Pozzi, a professional gambler, who proceeds to bend his ear with the tale of a 'sure thing' – a poker game against two gullible old millionaires with money to burn.

In a rash act of benevolence Nashe backs Pozzi to the tune of $10,000 and soon the pair are at the Pennsylvanian mansion of their Laurel and Hardy-ish opponents, the plan going horribly wrong as the odd couple – freshly tutored by a Vegas card sharp – not only take Pozzi to the cleaners but also win everything Nashe owns.

And this is where it all gets rather odd with the losers having to comply with the old men's rather bizarre predestinarian philosophy about the order of life and 'rediscover their goodness through hard work' by becoming sort of de facto slaves, holed up in a caravan and forced to build, in Sisyphus fashion, a seemingly pointless wall in the grounds of the residence.

Various interesting characters shuffle on and off this canvas – including Samantha Mathis' hooker and podgy bully boy Chris Penn (who else?) – while the proceedings are overseen by curmudgeonly taskmaster Calvin, but it is the performances of the lead players that elevates this to something quite extraordinary. Buoyed with a sense of purpose the lynchpin Patinkin, for whom the wall becomes a source of *Bridge On The River Kwai*-like pride, is a model of patience and honour, while Spader is outstanding as the spivvy greaseball Jack, good company but lacking the will-power of his companion even as their destiny lies ever more at the mercy of their sinister captors. ★★★★ **JD**

ⓓ MY BEST FRIEND'S WEDDING (1997)

Starring: *Julia Roberts (Julianne Potter), Dermot Mulroney (Michael O'Neal), Cameron Diaz (Kimberly Wallace), Rupert Everett (George Downes)*
Director: *P.J. Hogan*
Screenwriter: *Ronald Bass*
12/105 mins./Comedy/Romance/USA

Sports writer Julianne Potter has made a pact with her best friend Michael O'Neal that if neither has found true love by the age of 28 they will marry each other – which suits her just fine, but then he announces his engagement . . .

Australian director P.J. Hogan may well be in serious danger of being pigeonholed into forever filming marriages, if the subject matter of his follow-up to *Muriel's Wedding* is anything to go by. More importantly, though, this patchy but oh-so-cute confection provided Julia Roberts with yet another comeback. And the fact that this was the summer smash in the States, trouncing such big-budget fare as *Speed 2*, is hardly surprising as this is Roberts at her most crowd-pleasing – all Titian curls and big smiles, feisty yet vulnerable and loveable at the same time.

The set-up is one of love triangular dimensions with Roberts sports writer intent on nuptial sabotage. She had made a pact with her best friend Michael O'Neal that if neither had found true love by the age of 28 they would marry each other – which suits her just fine, having always adored him from afar. But just a few weeks shy of the significant birthday, he calls to tell her he is engaged to heiress Kimmy Wallace and the wedding is to be that weekend. Having recovered from the shock, and confided in gay pal

George, Julianne heads for the celebrations with just one aim in mind: nuptial sabotage . . .

It doesn't prove easy. For Kimmy, far from being the sort of other woman whose downfall the audience would relish, is beautiful, wealthy and – here's the catch – sweet-natured. What's more, Michael is so genuinely in love with her that every attempt by Julianne to split the couple up falls flat at every level.

While Hogan's new spin on an old theme is cleverer than most (Roberts becomes the unlikely villain, and the eventual outcome is not the one you might expect), it proves detrimental to the comedy, and all too frequently the film is bogged down in lengthy stretches of soul-searching and sentiment.

Diaz exudes sweetness and dignity, but the real revelation here is Everett, whose sidekick (far more interesting than Mulroney's thankless, cardboard cut-out of a hero) is a true original, camp, razor-witted and so mirth-inducing re-shoots extended his screen time. ★★★ **CW**

MY BIG FAT GREEK WEDDING (2002)

Starring: *Nia Vardalos (Toula Portokalos), Michael Constantine (Gus Portokalos), John Corbett (Ian Miller), Laine Kazan (Maria Portokalos)*
Director: *Joel Zwick*
Screenwriter: *Nia Vardalos*
PG/91 mins./Comedy/Romance/USA/Canada

A young Greek woman falls in love with a non-Greek and struggles to get her family to accept him while she comes to terms with her heritage and cultural identity.

By casting *Sex And The City*'s John Corbett (Carrie's ex-fiancee Aidan) as the romantic interest, *My Big Fat Greek Wedding* calls in its core audience loud and clear: young women with an eye for sharp comedy and a weakness for slush.

As such, this film serves them pretty well. It's the semi-autobiographical story of frumpy, Greek, 30-year-old Toula (played by the writer, Nia Vardalos – spotted doing stand up by Mr & Mrs Tom Hanks who helped get the film made), who has a makeover and lands Ian. Cue the wedding, and that's about it.

But despite a weak plot, the film boasts superb comic timing – the first hour, establishing the gender politics of the Greek family, delivers line after line of sharp, dark humour. Anyone from a Greek background will laugh loudest, but there's enough universality in the close-knit-family comedy to appeal across the board. ★★★ **CW**

MY COUSIN VINNY (1992)

Starring: *Joe Pesci (Vincent Gambini), Ralph Macchio (Billy Gambini), Marisa Tomei (Mona Lisa Vito), Mitchell Whitfield (Stan Rothenstein), Fred Gwynne (Judge Chamberlain Haller)*
Director: *Jonathan Lynn*
Screenwriter: *Dale Launer*
15/114 mins./Comedy/USA
Awards: *Academy Awards – Best Supporting Actress*

Dim-witted Billy and Stan confess to a murder after thinking they're owning up to accidental theft. When they seem set for the electric chair, Billy's wisecracking lawyer cousin shows up to get them off the hook.

As proven by *Nothing But Trouble* and *Doc Hollywood*, it's never a good idea to drive through rural America and irritate local lawmen. It is especially not a good idea, as a couple of students – Macchio and Whitfield – find out, to be picked up for murdering a store clerk and then confess to the crime under the impression that you're owning up to the accidental shoplifting of a can of tunafish.

However, Macchio has a cousin who is a lawyer, and no sooner has he made his one phone call than Vinny is turning up, with his microskirted Brooklynite girlfriend, the kind of woman who says 'axe' when she means 'ask'. Vinny is instantly irritating the crusty old judge due to hear the case by strutting into the courtroom in a black leather medallion-man outfit and demonstrating absolutely no legal finesse whatsoever. As the kids get lined up for the chair, Vinny, who has been practising for six whole weeks, has to learn elementary courtroom procedures from a reference book.

Directed by Jonathan 'Yes Minister' Lynn with flavourless competence, this has obviously been crafted as an excuse to give superstar supporting actor Pesci a rare lead role after his showings in *Goodfellas* and *JFK*, which means that he does the usual heavy-to-hero trick of mixing a little sentiment in with the obnoxious wisecracks.

The plot premise is every bit as ridiculous as you'd expect, with Vinny instantly turning overnight from moronic schlub to Perry Mason, springing surprise witnesses, puncturing testimony and finally cracking the case with a bit of expert advice from his girlfriend, who is fortuitously a walking mine of information on classic cars. Pesci is funnier than his material, and Marisa Tomei, after paying her dues with bits in *Oscar* and *The Flamingo Kid*, walks off with the whole film with her sexy whine and outrageous big city girl outfits, as if a creature from a Troma movie had landed in an episode of *Barnaby Jones*. ★★★ **KN**

Tagline
A comedy of trial and error.

MY DARLING CLEMENTINE (1946)

Starring: *Henry Fonda (Wyatt Earp), Linda Darnell (Chihuahua), Victor Mature (Dr John 'Doc' Holliday), Cathy Downs (Clementine Carter), Walter Brennan (Old Man Clanton)*
Director: *John Ford*
Screenwriters: *Samuel G. Engel, Winston Miller, based on the screen story by Sam Hellman, book* Wyatt Earp, Frontier Marshall *by Stuart N. Lake*
U/97 mins./Western/USA

A Western retelling the tale of the shoot-out at the OK Corral.

First released in 1946, this lyrically titled Western was only John Ford's second foray into the genre after the seminal *Stagecoach*, but it already bears all the characteristics which were to give his films their distinctive hallmark; stunning cinematography, incredible action sequences and the struggle of a noble hero in a hostile world, all played out against the epic vistas of Utah's Monument Valley.

The plot revolves around the legendary Wyatt Earp, a man who refuses to carry a gun yet is hellbent on avenging his brother's death at the hands of local outlaws, the Clanton brothers. Initially suspicious of the consumptive Doc Holliday, the two gradually form an uneasy but mutually respectful friendship, which survives even when Wyatt falls for Doc's beloved Clementine. After mistakenly arresting Doc for his brother's murder, Earp and Holliday set off for the Clanton ranch.

Nearly 50 years after it was first seen, there's little doubt that this is Ford – and the Western – at its very best. This is by no means a bloodfest of the Peckinpah variety, and with its frequent paroxysms of sexism and racism, it may at first glance seem irrelevant for a modern audience. But in terms of sheer scale and grandeur this is almost impossible to beat. Fonda is magnificent and his friendship with the depressive, alcohol sodden Doc is touching without descending into the ludicrous male bonding of most buddy movies. ★★★★★ **JMc**

MY FAIR LADY (1964)

Starring: *Audrey Hepburn (Eliza Doolittle), Rex Harrison (Professor Henry Higgins), Stanely Holloway (Alfred P. Doolittle), Wilfred Hyde-White (Colonel Hugh Pickering), Jeremy Brett (Freddy Eynsford-Hill)*
Director: *Geroge Cukor*
Screenwriters: *Alan Jay Lerner, from the musical play by Alan Jay Lerner, Frederick Lowe, from the play Pygmalion by George Bernard Shaw*
U/171 mins./Musical/Romance/USA

Awards: *Academy Awards – Best Actor, Best Colour Art Direction-Set Decoration, Best Cinematography, Best Costume, Best Score, Best Picture. Best Sound, BAFTA – Best Film, Golden Globes – Best Musical/Comedy, Best Musical/Comedy Actor, Best Director*

A misogynistic and snobbish phonetics professor agrees to a wager that he can take a flower girl and make her presentable in high society.

Wonderfully stylish, wittily scripted (using much of George Bernard Shaw's *Pygmalion* source material) and immaculately cast.

Audrey Hepburn's Cinderella transformation from Cockney guttersnipe to gloriously Cecil Beaton-clad belle of the ball, at the hands of voice coach Rex Harrison, remains a timeless, captivating classic.

A Broadway hits of its day, Lerner & Lowe's musical transferred to the big screen with the leading man who'd made the role of Higgins his own. Although Hepburn's casting in the lead, rather than the stage show's star Julie Andrews, caused consternation at the time and probably robbed her of the Oscar that went to Andrews for Mary Poppins – emotionally she is note perfect. Her singing was less so and was dubbed by Marnie Noxon, against her will – but extras on DVDs doing the rounds in which her original song track is heard suggest she had quite a passable voice.

The only small quibble would be the running time, which seems to spin the plot out to tortuous lengths long after the obstacles to the protagonists' romance have disappeared. Look out for future Sherlock Holmes Jeremy Brett in what now seems like an unlikely role as the love-struck Freddy. ★★★★ **EC**

MY FAVOURITE BLONDE (1942)

Starring: *Bob Hope (Larry Haines), Madeleine Carroll (Karen Bentley), Gale Sondergaard (Mme Stephanie Runick), George Zucco (Dr Hugo Streger), Lionel Royce (Karl), Walter Kingsford (Dr Faber)*
Director: *Sidney Lanfield*
Screenwriters: *Don Hartman, Frank Butler, based on a story by Melvin Frank and Norman Panama*
PG/78 mins./Comedy/USA

Spy Karen Bentley uses burlesque hack Larry Haines and his performing penguins to smuggle plans for a top secret bomber past Nazi agents Dr Hugo Streger and Madame Stephanie Runick.

Madeleine Carroll enjoyed making this Hitchcock spoof much less than Bob Hope. She had agreed to star because the comic had been singing her praises on his radio show and she realised that working with one of Hollywood's hottest properties would do much to boost a career that hadn't quite fulfilled the expectations generated by *The 39 Steps*. But, despite being supposedly happily married, Hope was more than just a fan and she spent much of the shoot deflecting his clumsy advances and keeping boyfriend Sterling Hayden from seeking a confrontation. Hope was reportedly furious when he discovered Carroll's secret marriage, but Sidney Lanfield pointed out how much his crush had benefited Larry and Karen's chemistry and so Hope remained curtly professional for the remainder of the production.

Things were no less tense with George Zucco, who had teamed with Hope and Gale Sondergaard on *The Cat And The Canary* and had deeply resented his scene-stealing antics. But he, too, retained his dignity and turned in a typically acerbic display of villainy, although he's upstaged by Sondergaard (who made four Hope vehicles in all), whose take on Mrs Danvers from *Rebecca* was one of the film's highlights. Furthermore, Hope's concerns about Lanfield's tyrannical reputation proved unfounded and the pair reunited on a further four occasions, although this was to be their biggest commercial success.

This had much to do with the eccentricities of the screwball plot and the surfeit of slick one-liners. However, there's so much backstory to establish that the pace takes time to pick up and the penguins provide most of the early laughs. But, once he realises he's in danger and cowardice replaces cockiness, Hope hits his stride and his impersonation of a renowned psychologist and reaction to Carroll's lapse into baby talk are as amusing as the cack-handed escape from the hotel room.

The crowd-pleasing moment, however, was *Road* movie co-star Bing Crosby's cameo as a truck driver and the pair would continue to guest in each other's pictures throughout the 1940s. ★★★ **DP**

MY FAVOURITE WIFE (1940)

Starring: *Irene Dunne (Ellen Arden), Cary Grant (Nick Arden), Randolph Scott (Stephen Burkett), Gail Patrick (Bianca), Ann Shoemaker (Ma), Scotty Beckett (Tim Arden), Mary Lou Harrington (Chinch Arden)*
Director: *Garson Kanin*
Screenwriters: *Sam Spewack, Bella Spewack, based on a story by Leo McCarey, Sam Spewack and Bella Spewack*
U/85 mins./Comedy/USA

Seven years after his wife Ellen was presumed lost at sea, Nick Arden marries Bianca, only to discover on their honeymoon that Ellen not only survived, but also spent her time on an idyllic desert island with handsome bachelor Stephen Burkett.

Alfred, Lord Tennyson's poem, 'Enoch Arden', has been the basis of six films. Yet it's hard to imagine that the same source inspired both D.W. Griffith's eponymous 1911 melodrama and this delightful screwball comedy. Intially tailored as a vehicle for the in-demand Jean Arthur, this inversion of the tale of a returning castaway passed to Irene Dunne, who was supposed to reunite with the star and director of *The Awful Truth*. But a car crash forced Leo McCarey to pass the reins to screenwriter and occasional director Garson Kanin, whose task was greatly facilitated by Dunne's instinctive chemistry with Cary Grant.

Dunne is one of the Golden Age's least appreciated stars. She was a fine singer (Jerome Kern entrusted her with some of his best tunes) and a superb actress, whose ability to play comedy and drama with equal restraint are admirably showcased in a storyline that has her reuniting with the kids she thought she'd lost forever and attempting to pass off an unprepossessing shoe salesman as her desert island companion to prevent Grant from discovering that she's been shacked up with hunk, Randolph Scott (whose mid-1930s stint as Grant's roommate had prompted a Hollywood whispering campaign that they were, in fact, lovers). Indeed, her easy style perfectly complemented Grant's eccentric naturalism and the passion between them is evident from their first (re)meeting.

However, such is the emphasis on Grant and Dunne that it's easy to overlook the contributions of both Scott and Gail Patrick. Parodying Ralph Bellamy's trademark 'other man' tropes, Scott (who had teamed with Dunne on the 1935 Fred'n'Ginger musical, *Roberta*) demonstrates the awkward finesse that made him so convincing in psychological Westerns, while Patrick plays the neurotic second wife with an exasperated excess that should have had casting directors beating down her door.

In 1962, the Arden plot was reworked as *Something's Got To Give* for Marilyn Monroe. But she was fired from what would prove to be her final picture and the project passed to Doris Day, as *Move Over Darling* (1963). ★★★★ **DP**

⦿ MY GIRL (1991)

Starring: *Anna Chlumsky (Vada Sultenfuss), Macaulay Culkin (Thomas J. Sennett), Jamie Lee Curtis (Shelly DeVoto), Dan Aykroyd (Harry Sultenfuss), Richard Masur (Phil Sultenfuss)*
Director: *Howard Zieff*
Screenwriter: *Laurice Elehwany*
PG/102 mins./Drama/USA

Early teen Vada Sultenfuss is obsessesd with death. Little wonder, her mother died when she was small, her dad runs a funeral parlour, and her best mate, Thomas J. is allergic to everything. And now his father has hired a new make-up artist and looks to be falling in love.

A sweetly unassuming teen flick about a young girl's quirky coming of age. Set a million miles from the brash Clueless-Mean Girl's high school hierarchies, the aim here is a small-town charm (as in 70s Pennsylvania), with just a hint of quasi-Lynchian weirdness – death hangs about this small girl, from the ghost of her dead mother, to the funeral parlour run by her pop (a jovial Aykroyd), through to the tragedy that steers the later half of the movie. That nothing much really happens adds a further scent of reality. We're investigating the lyrical side of puberty, as it were.

Anna Chlumsky, never too movie-cute, has pluck to spare as Vada, even subduing that little weevil Macaulay Culkin to just goofy grin and his best performance. Their friendship feels fresh, wafting to the soft rhythms of a sunny childhood. Tragedy naturally strikes, we've got to have some personal growth for Vada, a tribulation doubled when she is faced with a rival for her father's easy affections in Jamie Lee Curtis. But the slow shuffle to which Howard Zieff times his movie never breaks, allowing a quietly moving truth to emerge from its low horizons. A lesser sequel appeared later, sending Vada off to Los Angeles to find boys, but lacked the easy grace here. ★★★★ **IN**

⦿ MY LIFE (1993)

Starring: *Michael Keaton (Bob Jones), Nicole Kidman (Gail Jones), Bradley Whitford (Paul), Queen Latifah (Theresa), Michael Constantine (Bill)*
Director: *Bruce Joel Rubin*
Screenwriter: *Bruce Joel Rubin*
15/112 mins./Drama/USA

Bob is a wealthy, successful PR executive, with a beautiful wife Gail, who is pregnant with her first child. When Bob is given just a few months to live, he is forced to reevaluate his whole life's efforts and starts to make videos for his unborn son.

Ghost writer Bruce Joel Rubin's first film as director is a relentlessly manipulative, shallow exercise in which Michael Keaton is first-rate as Bob, a successful, wisecracking PR executive no one particularly cares for, and a man seething with lifelong resentments towards his parents and brother.

Struck down with terminal cancer, he makes videotapes of his life, a legacy of paternal tips and heart-to-hearts for his soon-to-be-born son. In the course of committing himself to videotape Bob discovers that he doesn't really know himself at all, and that his life has been meaningless. Thus he, and we, with the help of his ever-serene wife soothing his fevered brow and his Chinese homeopath dispensing life wisdom with herbal teas, embark on a journey of self-discovery and spiritual healing.

Fortunately, Bob has wealth to ease his passage into the light, cover the cost of flights to family reconciliations and employ a private nurse in the lovely home where his unfulfilled wishes can be gratified while he gets in touch with his feelings and lets go of his fear. Rubin's philosophy of life and death, peculiar but charming in *Ghost*, complex and nightmarish in *Jacob's Ladder* (both of which he wrote) is further expounded here in all its crankiness, a blend of psychedelic bad dreams, wishes on stars and metaphysical hooey by way of a Californian religion combining Chinese fortune cookies and bad acid trips.

His direction is tidy and the humorous face of the film is pleasing enough, with Bob demonstrating on camera to his child a variety of things a fella ought to know – how to cook spaghetti, how to shave, how to impress girls with one's musical taste, how to enter a room like Cary Grant – but Rubin loses points particularly over his endless gooey shots of the newborn baby. ★★ **AE**

⦿ MY LITTLE CHICKADEE (1940)

Starring: *W.C. Fields (Cuthbert J. Twillie), Mae West (Flower Belle Lee), Joseph Calleia (Jeff Badger), Dick Foran (Wayne Carter), Margaret Hamilton (Mrs Gideon), George Moran (Clarence), Si Jenks (Deputy)*
Director: *Edward F. Cline*
Screenwriters: *Mae West, W.C. Fields*
PG/83 mins./Comedy/Western/USA

Having met on a stagecoach, Flower Belle Lee and Cuthbert J. Twillie pose as a married couple to gain entry into Greasewood City, where Twillie is appointed sheriff by Jeff Badger, the local bigwig who is really the notorious gold thief, the Masked Bandit.

Mae West was touting a screenplay about Catherine the Great when she signed up for this lively comedy Western with W.C. Fields. The pair had once had adjacent dressing-rooms on the Paramount lot, but had always believed their comic styles too different to allow a worthwhile collaboration. However, Universal's offer was too tempting for stars deemed past their best and they embarked on producing a screenplay that has become unjustly notorious for their supposed bids to hog the limelight.

Each claimed more than their share of credit for the script. Fields contended that the core came from his idea 'December and Mae', which underwent numerous revisions before becoming a lampoon on the ignorance of American film audiences. West, however, insisted that she had written the scenario and left gaps for Fields to insert his own dialogue and comic business. Yet, producer Lester Cowan, whom Fields came to detest, further averred that the picture owed its genesis to Ferenc Molnár's play, *The Guardsman*.

Whatever its origins, the screenplay was typically mangled by Production Code chief, Joseph Breen, who removed countless instances of mild cheekiness and reduced West's 'Willie of the Valley' from being a bawdy torch song to a harmless ditty. Yet, the film retained plenty of choice moments, such as Fields spending his wedding night with a goat and cheating his way through a card game, while West ably demonstrated both her sharp-shooting and seduction techniques.

However, Fields gets much the best of the comedy, as he was just as funny with props as he could be exchanging quips. But the frontier setting left too little room for the kind of acute social and sexual satire that was West's speciality and she spent more of her time driving the serviceably flimsy plot than lacing it with innuendo.

Fields and West gel well in their scenes together, but don't overlook the practised support playing of Donald Meek (as a gambler impersonating a preacher) and Margaret Hamilton, as the town busybody. ★★★ **DP**

⦿ MY NAME IS JOE (1998)

Starring: *Peter Mullan (Joe Kavanagh), Louise Goodall (Sarah Downie), David McKay (Liam), Anne-Marie Kennedy (Sabine), David Hayman (McGowan), Gary Lewis (Shanks)*
Director: *Ken Loach*
Screenwriter: *Paul Laverty*
15/105 mins./Drama/Comedy/Spain/Italy/France/UK/Germany
Awards: *Empire Awards – Best Actor*

Unemployed former alcoholic Joe starts an unlikely romance with community health worker Sarah, but their relationship starts to falter when they both take very different approaches to helping drug addict Liam.

In *My Name Is Joe*, Ken Loach works very near the top of his form, his angrily unblinkered vision of life at the rough end of modern Britain tempered with humanity, humour and a storyline that could almost come from a classic screwball romantic comedy. Joe Kavanagh, a Glaswegian hard man with a quick-draw temper but a basically sweet disposition, has got sober after years of alcoholism, pulling himself back from the brink because he has realised how violent he can be when he drinks.

Coach to a ragged-arse local league football team, Joe's life is transformed, for better and worse, when he meets and slips into a relationship with Sarah, a health visitor. Given that Joe is one of the unemployed (he gets in trouble for papering her walls) and Sarah is a social worker, their romance is, in Loach terms, akin to a farmgirl falling for a cowboy in a range war Western. Still, the feuding couple find common cause in the problems of druggie Liam, one of Joe's players who has run a debt to the local druglord-cum-minicab tycoon McGowan.

The conventions of the reformed alkie picture require the ex-drinker to struggle with his addiction manfully for most of the running time then have a dramatic relapse, only to be jolted into sobriety by tragedy. One of Loach's great strengths as a filmmaker is that he isn't embarrassed to tell this familiar story, empowered by the realisation that the heart is in the details: this couple, this drinker, this team, this city.

Mullan's Joe is a commanding presence, showing strength and decency even when sucked into Liam's criminal morass – but also frightening in a drunk scene which relies on verbal rather than physical violence. The star performance is surrounded by good work, especially from the appealingly open Goodall. ★★★★ **KN**

MYSTERIOUS SKIN (2005)

Starring: *Brady Corbet (Brian), Joseph Gordon-Levitt (Neil), Elisabeth Shue (Mrs McCormick), Bill Sage (Coach)*
Director: *Gregg Araki*
Screenwriter: *Gregg Araki, based on the novel by Scott Heim*
18/99 mins./Drama/Mystery/USA

Shy, troubled, 18-year-old Brian Lackey is plagued by nightmares and believes he may have been the victim of an alien abduction as a boy. His need for closure brings him in contact with promiscuous gay teenage hustler Neil McCormick.

Gregg Araki rose to prominence during the early 90s New Queer Cinema with the nihilistic road movie *The Living End*, which followed Todd Haynes' *Poison* and Tom Kalin's *Swoon* in reinventing the perception and participation of gay men in film. Haynes matured and Kalin faded, while Araki made a clutch of angry but cliched movies – *Totally Fucked Up*, *The Doom Generation*, *Nowhere* – whose tired themes had threatened to make him the oldest and saddest angry young man on the block.

At 45, Araki has returned with a lyrical and moving adaptation of Scott Heim's hard-edged novel. Though it deals with gay issues and characters, this isn't strictly a gay film, and will only be termed so by dint of its graphic scenes of male nudity and eye-poppingly uncomfortable twist. Broad-minded audiences will find plenty to admire in the cast. Corbet emerges as an actor of sensitivity and depth, but it's Gordon-Levitt who steals every scene as the damaged, destructive but ultimately sympathetic rent boy.

A change for the better for Araki, but still too early to plan any retrospectives. ★★★ **DW**

MYSTERY MEN (1999)

Starring: *Hank Azari (The Blue Raja), Janeane Garofolo (The Bowler), William H. Macy (The Shoveler), Ben Stiller (Mr Furious), Paul Reubens (The Spleen), Greg Kinnear (Captain Amazing)*
Director: *Kinka Usher*
Screenwriter: *Neil Cuthbert, from the comic book by Bob Burden*
PG/116 mins./Comedy/Action/Adventure/USA

A group of frankly crap superheroes attempt to rescue kidnapped real super-hero, Captain Amazing, in this stupidly entertaining comedy.

Conjuring up fond recollections of a game often played on improv telly show *Whose Line Is It Anyway* (in which the contestants pretend to be crap superheroes, funnily enough), this Dark Horse-inspired comic book adaptation – complete with one of the year's best ensemble casts – gleefully lampoons the activities of Batman, Superman and any other bloke who ever donned tights to save the world. And if its everything-but-the-kitchen-sink approach does sometimes fall flat, its one-joke concept still manages to just about sustain the running time.

The setting, fictional metropolis Champion City, is kept a crime-free zone thanks to Captain Amazing, the flamboyant superhero who has put most of the city's villains behind bars and whose own fame extends to the boundaries of Pepsi sponsorship (he even has his own publicist). Enter Casanova Frankenstein, whose world domination plans kick off with kidnapping the Captain, and suddenly Champion City's future is in the hands of a bunch of superhero wannabes.

This is a slim conceit and would certainly have benefitted from half an hour's judicious pruning. And the plethora of characters means some inevitably suffer, in particular Lena Olin (as Rush's sidekick) and Claire Forlani (supplying romantic interest), who end up in brief, largely thankless, roles. That said, it's far more fun than most of the recent superhero efforts, lovely to look at (the backdrops of Champion City are stunning), there's a great sub-plot involving the group's Karate Kid-style mentor, and the script offers astute and witty one-liners.

It's these that really give the film its edge, veering from post-modern banter (notably a scene in which Macy and Stiller argue over Captain Amazing's true identity) and downright daftness, through to a final reel which throws in a few unexpected surprises, not all of them pleasant. *Mystery Men* tanked in the States, where its irony and subversiveness flew straight over the heads of summer audiences. The more cynical British market ensured it attained a small cult success. ★★★ **AS**

MYSTERY TRAIN (1989)

Starring: *Masatoshi Nagase (Jim), Youki Kudoh (Mitsuko), Screamin' Jay Hawkins (Night Clerk), Cinque Lee (Bellboy), Joe Strummer (Johnny), Steve Buscemi (Charlie)*
Director: *Jim Jarmusch*
Screenwriter: *Jim Jarmusch*
15/105 mins./Comedy/Drama/1989

Three stories unfold over one night in Memphis, Tennessee, involving lost souls who, for one reason or another, find themselves staying in a run-down fleabag hotel.

Sharing setting, mood and the ghost of Elvis Presley, this Jim Jarmusch film essentially offers a three-bite selection of mini-movies, one great and the others pretty damn good. 'Far From Yokohama' is about Japanese teenagers (Masatoshi Nagase, Youki Kudoh) who visit Memphis to assess the roots of rock 'n' roll only to find a nearly abandoned wasteland that looks like Yokohama with 60% of the buildings taken away.

Jarmusch perfectly captures the subtle disappointments of all holi-

Cameos By Stars In Remakes/Spin-Offs Of Their Hits

1 James Garner – *Maverick*
2 Charlton Heston – *Planet Of The Apes* (2001)
3 Faye Dunaway – *The Thomas Crown Affair* (1999)
4 Christopher Reeve – *Smallville*
5 Robert Mitchum, Gregory Peck, Martin Balsam – *Cape Fear* (1991)
6 Richard Roundtree – *Shaft*
7 Tom Savini, Ken Fore – *Dawn Of The Dead* (2004)
8 Krik Alyn (the serial Superman), Noel Neill (the TV Lois Lane) – *Superman: The Movie*
9 Michael Caine – *Get Carter*
10 Angie Dickinson – *Ocean's Eleven*

days, and draws marvellously subtle, charming performances from the Japanese actors. Nothing much happens to the engaging, disaffected tourists, but this episode makes a stronger impression than the more densely plotted follow-ups.

'Ghosts' is about a stranded (Nicoletta Braschi) stopping over in the city with her recently deceased husband's coffin, waiting for a connecting flight to Rome. She meets a weird guy (Tom Noonan) who tries to hit on her with a patently absurd story about picking up Elvis' ghost hitch-hiking. Later, in the hotel, the ghost really does turn up briefly to be puzzled, feeling that he's got the wrong room.

And in 'Lost in Space', Steve Buscemi and Joe Strummer drift around town and wind up in the worst room in the hotel, after committing a stupid liquor store hold-up, discussing the merits of the old TV show.

The film is much more than its spaced-out stories suggest it should be, with an affecting vision of a city that lives with its disappointments. Marvellously acted by a hand-picked cast, with understated use of an original John Lurie score (and Elvis' throwaway recording of 'Blue Moon') and excellent camerawork from ace Robby Müller, this more than exceeds its modest ambitions. ★★★★ **KN**

MYSTERY, ALASKA (1991)

Starring: *Russell Crowe (John Biebe), Hank Azaria (Charles Danner), Mary McCormack (Donna Bebe), Burt Reynolds (Judge Walter Burns), Colm Meaney (Mayor Scott Pitcher), Lolita Davidovich (Mary Jane Pitcher)*
Director: *Jay Roach*
Screenwriters: *David E. Kelley, Sean O'Byrne*
15/113 mins./Sports/Drama/USA

A no-good team of hockey players try to shape up so they can represent their hometown of Mystery, in Alaska, with pride, when a cruicial game is televised.

This never gained a cinema release in the UK, despite the presence of (then) rising star Russell Crowe and that's partly because it's less a Crowe movie than an ensemble piece – packed with the some of the best character actors in the business whose chemistry suggests they were having as good a time off-screen as on, but whose box office power wasn't enough to open the film.

It also has to be said that 'ice hockey' isn't quite as big in these cold-but-generally-unfrozen shores as it is in say, Canada. And it's no surprise to see some of that country's bigger stars and hockey fans – like Mike Myers – cameoing here.

For them this is probably the ultimate sports movie. For the lesser or non-fans, this is essentially *The Mighty Ducks* for adults – and there's no shame in that. ★★★ **EC**

MYSTIC RIVER (2003)

Starring: *Sean Penn (Jimmy Markum), Tim Robbins (Dave Boyle), Kevin Bacon (Sean Devine), Laurence Fishburne (Sgt Whitey Powers), Marcia Gay Harden (Celeste Boyle)*
Director: *Clint Eastwood*
Screenwriter: *Brian Helgeland, based on the novel by Dennis Lehane*
15/132 mins./Drama/Crime/Mystery/USA

Awards: *Academy Awards – Best Actor, Best Supporting Actor (Tim Robbins), Golden Globes – Best Actor, Best Supporting Actor (Tim Robbins)*

Driven apart by a childhood trauma, three men meet again when Jimmy's daughter is murdered, cop Sean investigates and loner Dave emerges as a likely suspect. Soon an air of vigilantism begins to poison their Boston neighbourhood.

Mystic River's apology for vigilante action is certainly disturbing, as any notion of guilt is quickly washed away in a rather unconvincing coda. But fans of the director will also breathe a sigh of relief that, after the disappointments of *Blood Work*, *Space Cowboys* and *True Crime*, this marks a genuine return to form.

Two things make Eastwood's task easier for him: a superb cast and a cracking source novel. Dennis Lehane's book is one of the very best thrillers of recent years, richer in Boston detail and closer in character study than anything Eastwood manages to bring to the screen.

That said, Brian Helgeland does redeem himself somewhat after his lacklustre adaptation of Michael Connelly's page-turner *Blood Work*. The screenwriter seems to understand the ageing director's desire to sacrifice plot pacing for loose, character-based meandering, and so places key points of information and discovery at appropriate intervals in order to keep even the most casual viewer hooked from the first frame.

He's faithful enough to Lehane's original material to also ensure that this story of a lingering human evil, capable of destroying lives in both past and present, retains a degree of moral complexity.

Eastwood takes a break from duties in front of the camera, leaving the stage free for Penn, Robbins and Bacon to strut their stuff. Penn delivers another multi-layered performance as a man in whom rage, grief and honour suffer a head-on collision, while Bacon sheds his psycho baggage as a cop caught in a compromising position.

Robbins, with the toughest role, is worst served by Helgeland's script, which cuts much-needed background from the book. We should find more sympathy for his character, as fate snaps its man-trap jaws around him, but even Robbins' best efforts can't quite fill in the gaps. Dave is supposed to be living proof of the way in which child molestation infects the victim and, by degrees, those closest to him; but by reducing his impact and this theme in the movie, a more routine and far less powerful whodunnit structure emerges in its place.

Nevertheless, the combined efforts of all three actors add psychological weight to the revenge-driven murder mystery. Despite secondary status, the women in the cast also strengthen the show, particularly Marcia Gay Harden's heartbreaking turn as a woman caught between love and disgust as she fears her husband's troubled past has mutated him into a killer. ★★★★ **AS**

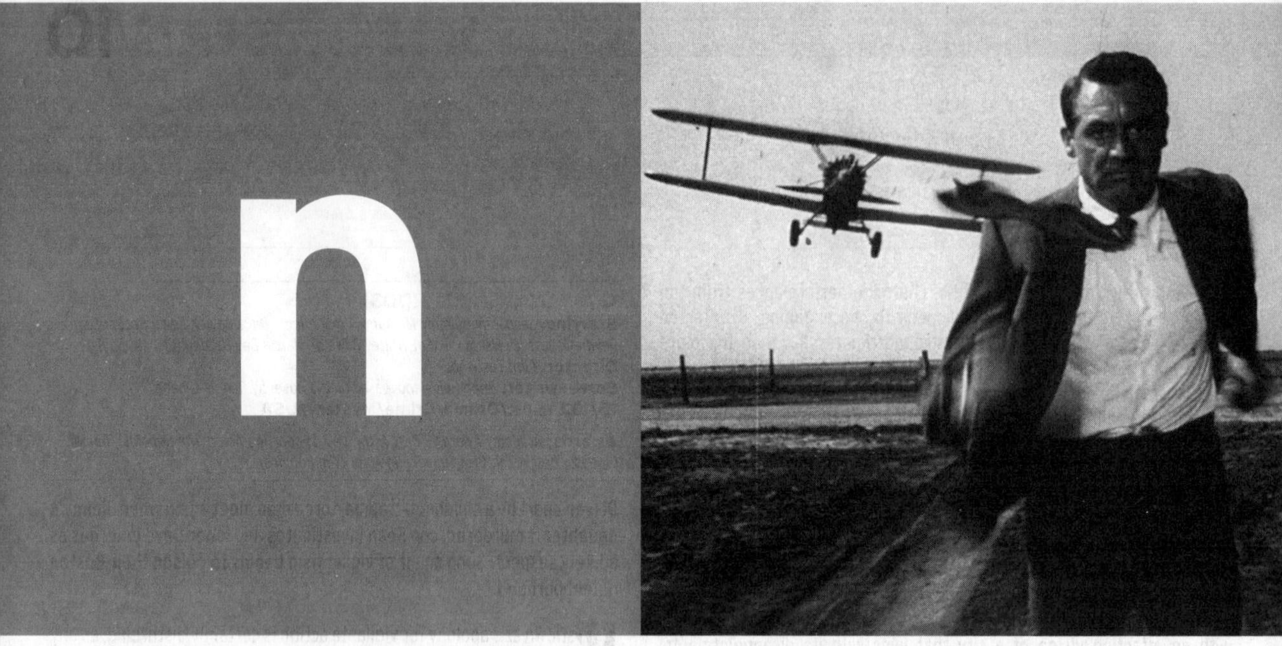

NADJA (1994)

Starring: *Elina Lowensohn (Nadja), Peter Fonda (Dracula/Dr Van Helsing), Martin Donovan (Jim), Suzy Amis (Cassandra), Edgar (Jared Harris)*
Director: *Michael Almereyda*
Screenwriter: *Michael Almereyda*
15/88 mins./Horror/USA

In contemporary New York, Jim has to bail out his uncle, Doctor Van Helsing, who has just staked 'Count Arminius Voivode Ceaucescu Dracula'. Meanwhile, Dracula's children try to make their own way in the world: Edgar flirts with humanity but Nadja becomes more committed to vampirism.

Vampire movies are amazingly salable, which sometimes tempts filmmakers into wilful obscurity and zombie mannerisms on the assumption that just so long as there's toothsome sex and a Dracula cameo an audience will turn up and suffer.

Michael Almereyda's follow-up to *Another Girl, Another Planet*, produced by David Lynch (who has a cameo morgue attendant role), is shot in luminously gorgeous black and white, with grainy PixelVision inserts that serve to disguise the shortcomings of the director's approach whenever he forsakes atmosphere for action.

The plot elements are mostly lifted from the 1936 *Dracula's Daughter*, but the sense of artfilm familiarity is reinforced by an excursion to a Castle Dracula borrowed from Tarkovsky's *Stalker* or one of Guy Maddin's tinted charades. Like its heroine, the film is a lovely blank, mesmerising but also sleep-inducing.

Moments of much-needed life come from Peter Fonda as an old hippie Dr Van Helsing, comparing his ancient enemy (played in snippets by Fonda or found footage of Bela Lugosi) to the Vegas-period Elvis, 'drugged, confused, surrounded by zombies, just going through the motions. The magic was gone.'

The performances are variable, with good work from Karl Geary as a winsome Irish Renfield but only glazed, beautiful somnolence from model Lowensohn in the title role.

Not without interest for committed fang fans, but less satisfying than even an average Hammer horror. Almereyda did much better by the genre in a (slightly) more conventional Irish-set 'mummy' movie with Harris and Christopher Walken, *The Eternal*. ★★ **KN**

NAKED (1993)

Starring: *David Thewlis (Johnny), Lesley Sharp (Louise Clancy), Katrin Cartlidge (Sophie, Louise's Roommate), Greg Cruttwell (Jeremy G. Smart), Claire Skinner (Sandra),*
Director: *Mike Leigh*
Screenwriter: *Mike Leigh*
18/125 mins./Drama/Comedy/UK

Fleeing Manchester after a particularly vicious sex attack, Johnny visits London, staying with his ex-girlfriend, and sleeping with one of her flatmates. He leaves soon after and walks around London, talking to strangers, while his ex-girlfriend's landlord visits his property and abuses his tenants.

Having fled Manchester after a violent sexual incident, Johnny – a crusty whose ragged 'tache and unwashed hair are not a grunge fashion statement but a way of filth – turns up at the London flat of an embittered and puzzled ex-girlfriend and has a one-night stand with her stringy, stoned, unemployed flatmate. After verbally (and borderline physically) abusing both girls the next morning, Johnny stalks out and pinballs around a succession of no-hopers.

When some strangers give him the beating he's been asking for all along, he crawls back to Sharp and Cartlidge only to find they've been invaded by their yuppie, rapist landlord. Then the girls' third flat-sharer comes back from Zimbabwe and finds no one has done the washing-up for three months and everyone needs help.

Mike Leigh sees a Britain everybody knows exists but would rather not think about, and this is a nightmare journey, at once horrific and funny, through a twilight London of the excluded and the rejected. Johnny, bitter, stupid, articulate, unpleasant and heart-breaking, is in no sense a hero, but absolutely symptomatic of the era which has produced him and which he hates enough to pour poison over at every opportunity. While one or two scenes ramble on longer than is either interesting or comfortable and the portable-phone-wielding monster landlord doesn't have the resonance of the rest of the deadbeat characters, this is a masterpiece of dark humour and horribly accurate observation.

If America's nightmare self-image is *Bad Lieutenant*, this is the British answer: just as driven, visionary and self-destructive but not needing an excess of drugs or blood to showcase human horrors. Brilliantly acted, especially by Thewlis, and free of the TV look that has sometimes cramped Leigh's style in the past. ★★★★ **KN**

THE NAKED AND THE DEAD (1958)

Starring: *Aldo Ray (Sergeant Sam Croft), Cliff Robertson (Lieutenant Robert Hearn), Raymond Massey (Gen. Cummings), Lili St Cyr (Lily), Barbara Nichols (Mildred)*
Director: *Raoul Walsh*
Screenwriters: *Denis Sanders, Terry Sanders, from the novel by Norman Mailer*
PG/130 mins./Drama/War/USA

The Pacific, WWII. Lt Hearn, a young idealist who leads from the front, General Cummings, a calmly insane exponent of 'power morality', and our anti-hero, Sergeant Sam Croft, try and fail to get along in close quarters.

Some kind of hero: Aldo Ray's Sgt Croft spits beer into bar girls' faces, opens bottles with his teeth, shoots defenceless prisoners and keeps the gold he's ripped out of their mouths in a little bag around his neck. The strange thing is though, this isn't Vietnam – it's World War II and this is a movie made not in the 80s, but in the 50s.

Of course, as everyone has pointed out, this surprisingly vicious adaptation is a massive simplification of Norman Mailer's thick, complex and often very pretentious work. All the 'fugging' foul language is gone, the ending is completely unrecognisable and none of the characters are presented with any real depth. Aldo Ray, with his hulking frame, close-cropped bullet head and rasping voice, is born to the role of Croft and, watching the film after *Platoon*, he can be seen as a recognisable ancestor of that film's Sgt Barnes (the heavily scarred Tom Berenger character). Cliff Robertson (later to play no less than John F. Kennedy in *PT109*) brings a keen sense of college-boy integrity to his portrayal of Hearn, and Massey too, as the General, strikes a telling chord, this time of ice-cold, technocratic mania.

Confidently crafted by action-movie veteran Walsh (*They Died With Their Boots On, White Heat*), graced with a superbly ironic score from Bernard Herrmann (*Psycho, Taxi Driver*) and with its attractive jungle exteriors filmed in (of all places) Panama, *The Naked And The Dead* is in several respects one of the key stages in the development of the American war movie. The sense of a gulf between officers and men is possibly even stronger than in such acknowledged 50s classics as *From Here To Eternity* or *Paths Of Glory*, while the instinctive brutality of Croft anticipates the continuing Vietnam movie cycle of atrocities (from *Apocalypse Now* to *Casualties Of War* and everything in between) by a good 20 years. Accept that this isn't the book, and also the direly optimistic last ten minutes, and you've got solid, visceral entertainment with a reputation that should be a lot higher than it already is. ★★★★ **TT**

THE NAKED GUN: FROM THE FILES OF POLICE SQUAD! (1988)

Starring: *Leslie Nielsen (Lt Frank Drebin), Priscilla Presley (Jane Spencer), Ricardo Montalban (Vincent Ludwig), George Kennedy (Capt. Ed Hocken), O. J. Simpson (Det. Nordberg)*
Director: *David Zucker*
Screenwriters: *Jim Abrahams, David Zucker, Jerry Zucker, Pat Proft, based on the television series by Abrahams, Zucker, Zucker*
15/81 mins./Comedy/USA

Captain Frank Drebin of the Los Angeles police is put in charge of security for the forthcoming visit of the Queen of England. Meanwhile, scheming mastermind Vincent Ludwig plans to use his hypnotised slaves to murder the monarch, and has sicced his attractive assistant Jane on Drebin to keep tabs on his activities.

This is a spin-off of *Police Squad!*, a spoof cop show which managed only a handful of episodes before being judged too sophisticated for American television and cancelled; the film was a huge hit, and inspired two sequels.

Director David Zucker, who co-wrote with Jim Abrahams and Jerry Zucker, hops over dud gags, tasteless spots and repetition, and mainly delivers crass, likeable comedy. Typical gag: a cop (O.J. Simpson) who's been riddled with bullets gets upset because he's stumbled against a just painted door and ruined his coat.

Having been a stand-out supporting stooge in the same team's *Airplane!*, Leslie Nielsen, once condemned to guest star parts in TV movies, siezed the opportunity to play a comic lead and turned his career around. He is at his funniest when most ludicrously deadpan, uttering supremely stupid statements – as a fireworks factory spectacularly explodes, he tells a crowd of gawkers 'go home, there's nothing to see'.

Also priceless are love scenes between Nielsen and Priscilla Presley, notably a carefree romantic montage scored to a Herman's Hermits hit during which they gaily laugh as they come out of a cinema showing Platoon.

The jokes keep coming thick and fast, with as many side-details as in the packed panels of *MAD* magazine, and the film only drops the ball during an extended baseball match finale which fails to top the general hilarity of the build-up. ★★★★ **KN**

THE NAKED GUN 2½: THE SMELL OF FEAR (1991)

Starring: *Leslie Nielsen (Lt Frank Drebin), Priscilla Presley (Jane Spencer), George Kennedy (Capt. Ed Hocken), O. J. Simpson (Det. Nordberg)*
Director: *David Zucker*
Screenwriters: *David Zucker, Pat Proft, based on the television series by Jim Abrahams, David Zucker, Jerry Zucker*
15/81 mins./Comedy/USA

Lieutenant Frank Drebin discovers his estranged girlfriend is involved with Quentin Hapsburg, an energy lobbyist who wants to suppress a breakthrough in solar power.

A by-the-book sequel to the crowd-pleasing comedy. This time, something vaguely resembling a plot (involving environmental issues and Drebin's interrupted love affair) takes place behind the jokes and the director's ego has inflated so much by the success of his last movie (*Ghost*) that he gives himself an 'un film de David Zucker' credit and parodies the pottery-and-snogging highlight on the assumption that simply recreating the sequence with Nielsen and Priscilla Presley is funny enough to warrant a whole five minutes' screen time.

One of the miracles of *The Naked Gun* was that it preserved exactly the mix of clever and crass and stupid and inspired that made the television series *Police Squad!* such a marvel, but the material doesn't quite gel in this third go-round. Whether accidentally assaulting Barbara Bush at the White House, unwittingly torturing the captive he's supposed to be rescuing, misinterpreting everything said to him, or brooding in a bar that caters exclusively to lovelorn losers, Nielsen makes the material work.

And he's ably backed up by George Kennedy, who has mastered the art of reacting hilariously to otherwise serious statements, and O.J. Simpson, who is around for whenever the filmmakers run out of verbal gags and decde to get laughs by hideously abusing one of the cast. However, the one-time joke casting of Presley sticks the picture with a dead weight at the centre, and the jokes this time round are a little less clever, a little less thick on the ground and a little less surprising. Though there's a belly laugh every five minutes or so, there's still a sense that Drebin should retire after this case. ★★ **KN**

Tagline
From the brother of the director of *Ghost*.

THE NAKED GUN 33⅓: THE FINAL INSULT (1994)

Starring: *Leslie Nielsen (Lt Frank Drebin), Priscilla Presley (Jane Spencer), George Kennedy (Capt. Ed Hocken), O. J. Simpson (Det. Nordberg), Anna Nicole Smith (Tanya), Ellen Greene (Louise)*
Director: *Peter Segal*
Screenwriters: *David Zucker, Pat Proft, Robert LoCash, based on the television series by Jim Abrahams, David Zucker, Jerry Zucker*
12/83 mins./Comedy/USA

Lieutenant Frank Drebin is recalled from retirement to infiltrate a terrorist cell run by Rocco, who plans to outrage America by blowing up the Academy Awards.

In *Empire*'s original review of *The Naked Gun 2½*, we suggested 'Drebin should retire after this case'. Someone in Hollywood obviously took note: in this second sequel, Drebin retires. What we actually meant was that the *Naked Gun* formula was wearing thin and it was highly unlikely that all concerned could get away with it a third time.

The *Naked Gun 33⅓* proves us right. After a reasonably amusing skit on the operatic, baby-imperilling shoot-out of *The Untouchables*, this is the usual collection of gags unburdened by its notional plot – it doesn't so much satirise the James Cagney classic *White Heat* as steal the story outright.

The regular cast return, trailing now overfamiliar running jokes, but director David Zucker has retired to become a producer and new boy Peter Segal doesn't quite have the knack.

At a hasty 83 minutes, the film gabbles through its few good jokes and stamps on its many bad ones. A sure sign of deterioration is the reliance on bathroom material (an endless sperm bank scene) not to mention the premature arrival of the climactic Oscars parody which drags on for a full half-hour, with Nielsen stumblingly humiliating Raquel Welch and then, as if the point weren't made, Pia Zadora.

Even Nielsen's straight face seems to crack and whole sub-plots (a half-hearted skit on *Thelma and Louise* with a wasted Ellen Greene) show the signs of having been mercilessly cut at the decree of an unsmiling preview audience.

As films which end with scenes of Zadora making a spectacle of herself at Oscar night go, this is less funny than *The Lucky Lady*. We'll be unambiguous this time: don't make another one. ★★ **KN**

THE NAKED KISS (1964)

Starring: *Constance Towers (Kelly), Anthony Eisley (Griff), Michael Dante (Grant), Virginia Grey (Candy), Patsy Kelly (Mac), Betty Brosnan (Miss Josephine)*
Director: *Samuel Fuller*
Screenwriter: *Samuel Fuller*
18/86 mins./Drama/USA

Call girl Kelly turns her life around working with handicapped children and becomes engaged to a small town's leading citizen. Discovering that her fiancé is a child molester, she kills him – whereupon her past is exposed and she is arrested for the murder.

Following the pulp noir *Shock Corridor*, Sam Fuller produced, wrote and directed this even more extreme effort, which tackles subjects (prostitution, paedophilia) rarely discussed in 1964, affords the underrated Constance Towers one of the most unusual leading lady roles in the cinema and is so committed to the bizarre it often strays into camp.

In the opening scene, hooker Kelly turns on her pimp, battering him so brutally her wig comes off and we see he has shaved her head – later, disgusted by her perfect fiancé's kink, she bludgeons him with a telephone receiver.

Here, prostitution is conducted in tawdry euphemisms, with women presented as tempting commodities that are still bad for you: Kelly claims to be a sales rep for 'Angel Foam Champagne' and the skeletal local madame Candy, whose joint is festooned with signs guaranteeing 'indescribable pleasure', offers girls ('the Bon-Bons') named after types of sweet. When reformed, Kelly becomes a weird saint – bitch-slapping Candy to save a naive student nurse (Marie Devereux, a familiar pin-up girl from Hammer horrors like *Stranglers of Bombay*) from life as a Bon-Bon, even performing a skewed Julie Andrews-style song with the accompaniment of a multi-racial choir of crippled children.

It's the sort of film which inspired ironists like Russ Meyer, John Waters and Quentin Tarantino, but – for all its oddly funny moments – it's a blazingly serious melodrama with non-stop tough talk, fabulous lighting (Dante's perversion is conveyed entirely by shadows on his face) and bursts of violent action all the more shocking for being perpetrated by the heroine. ★★★★ **KN**

NAKED LUNCH (1991)

Starring: *Peter Weller (William Lee), Judy Davis (Joan Frost/Joan Lee), Ian Holm (Tom Frost), Julian Sands (Yves Cloquet), Roy Scheider (Dr Benway)*
Director: *David Cronenberg*
Screenwriter: *David Cronenberg, from the novel by William S. Burroughs*
18/110 mins./Fantasy/Drama/UK./Canada

William Lee is a pest exterminator addicted to his own chemicals, but when a stunt with a pistol goes wrong he escapes to a strange, exotic city called Interzone.

Between *Shivers* in 1975 and *Dead Ringers* in 1988, David Cronenberg was peerless in the world of horror, a revolutionary thinker who transformed the genre without seeming to work within it. His extraordinary vision set him apart from his still slasher-flick-fixated rivals, so when it was announced that he was tackling William S. Burroughs' scabrous, heroin-drenched 1959 cult novel, fans of both expected a masterpiece.

Sadly, it wasn't. Though he used the technique to greater effect in *Crash* (1996), Cronenberg's attempt to meld his style with an established writer didn't exactly pan out.

Strangers to Burroughs' writing will be all at sea with a story that sees Weller – as Burroughs' alter-ego William Lee – escape to an exotic city called Interzone when a stunt with a pistol goes wrong. Posing as a secret agent, Lee meets 'mugwumps', takes orders from his insect typewriter and infiltrates the seedy ex-pat community.

Anyone who's read Ted Morgan's Burroughs' biog *Literary Outlaw*, however, will simply see veiled scenes from that book linking together the novel's best monologues. That in itself may be Burroughsian, but Cronenberg and Burroughs don't fuse in other ways; for the most part this is a reductive and messy riff on the novel's exploration of addiction as a control system, with the morally dubious (and not entirely true) conclusion that Burroughs only became a writer by killing his wife. ★★★ **DW**

THE NAKED SPUR (1953)

Starring: *James Stewart (Howard Kemp), Robert Ryan (Ben Vandergroat), Janet Leigh (Lina Patch), Ralph Meeker (Roy Anderson), Millard Mitchell (Jesse Tate)*
Director: *Anthony Mann*
Screenwriters: *Sam Rolfe, Harold Jack Bloom*
Unrated/91 mins./Western/USA

Bounty hunter Howard Kemp captures outlaw Ben Vandergroat. A small posse have to take Vandergroat through wild country – and the captive tries to turn the other travellers against Kemp.

The best of an outstanding run of Westerns (*Winchester 73*, *The Man From Laramie*, *Bend of the River*, etc) starring a middle-aged, interestingly neurotic James Stewart and directed by Anthony Mann before he became an epic specialist with *El Cid*.

It's a tight, driven story about seriously wounded characters, with heroes and villains whose psychological troubles are writ large on the rugged, dangerous, cinegenic landscape through which they take a difficult journey.

The backstory is that Stewart's character signed his ranch over to a feckless fiancée when he set off for the Civil War and came back to find she'd sold the spread and lit out. This dispossession drives him into the profession of bounty hunter – in the decade before Clint Eastwood and Sergio Leone, just about the lowest acceptable pursuit for a Western hero. The 'dead or alive' price on Robert Ryan will be enough to buy back the family property, but the outlaw's allies – including wild child Janet Leigh in the tightest jeans ever seen in a Western – and the mountains ensure Stewart doesn't have an easy time of collecting the reward on the talkative, charming, dangerous villain ('Choosin' a way to die? What's the difference? Choosin' a way to live. That's the hard part').

A masterpiece that's too easy to take for granted (it's a perfectly told *small* story), *The Naked Spur* is an exciting action picture that packs a powerful emotional punch, climaxing in a classic fight in a rushing mountain river that resolves the plot and prompts one of Stewart's great neurotic breakdown-catharsis scenes as he hauls the valuable corpse out of the water but acts as if he's killed himself. ★★★★ **KN**

THE NAME OF THE ROSE (1986)

Starring: *Sean Connery (William of Baskerville), Christian Slater (Adso of Melk), Helmt Qualtinger (Remigio de Varagine), Elya Baskin (Severinus), Michael Lonsdale (The Abbott), William Hickey (Ubertino da Casale)*
Director: *Jean-Jacques Annaud*
Screenwriters: *Andrew Berkin, Gerard Brach, Howard Franklin, Alain Godard, Jean-Jacques Annaud, based on the novel by Umberto Eco*
15/130 mins./Drama/France-Italy-West Germany

Awards: *BAFTA – Best Actor (Sean Connery), Best Make-up*

At an isolated 14th-century Benedictine abbey a series of terrifying murders has sent the collected monks into a frenzy, believing that the Devil may be among them. It is up to William of Baskerville, a freethinking visiting Franciscan, to find the rational solution.

The first thing to consider with Jean-Jacques Annaud's frothy and memorable adaptation of Umberto Eco's wonderful medieval thriller, is how he found so many willing grotesques blessed with fine acting talents to populate his movie. The procession of cantankerous monks is like the order of *The Hills Have Eyes*, a bunch of baldy freaks assailed by the icy air and pummeling medieval deprivation. Their hilltop home is a stone outcrop of holy hell allowing the story to drip with an intense near-horror movie mood of impending doom. Finding naked monks in vats of blood helps with the general pessimism.

In one of the roles that came to reinvent Connery as an excellent character actor and not just the man-who-was-Bond, William of Baskerville is a revelation, a transfixing mix of intellect and wit, possessed of the kind of irreligious thinking that would eventually bring about the Renaissance. Part of the purpose of both Eco and the host of screenwriters Annaud employed to unearth a workable script from the novel's dense detail, is to expose the conflict between religion and rationalism. Indeed, as if they didn't need any more bad news, the Inquisition is soon to pay a call and start burning fetching kitchen maids as witches.

Seen through the eyes of a perplexed Christian Slater, as William's innocent apprentice, the plot unravels as an agonising tease, its various secrets torturously nudged into the cold light as the monk corpses pile up. Annaud is also sly enough to keep the grip of belief front and centre, keenly creating one of the most original whodunnits of recent years out of one of those so-called "unfilmmable" books. ★★★★ **IN**

NANNY MCPHEE (2005)

Starring: *Emma Thompson (Nanny McPhee), Colin Firth (Mr Brown), Kelly Macdonald (Evangeline), Thomas Sangster (Simon), Eliza Bennett (Tora)*
Director: *Kirk Jones*
Screenwriter: *Emma Thompson, based on the books by Christianna Brand*
U/97 mins./Family/Adventure/Comedy/USA/UK

Numerous governesses have fled widower Mr Brown's house after being terrorised by his seven children. They're even more mischievous than usual when they discover Dad is going to remarry – unaware his rich aunt will stop helping the family if he doesn't – but then the mysterious Nanny McPhee arrives at the door...

For her first screenplay since 1995's Oscar-winning *Sense And Sensibility*, Emma Thompson has adapted a little-known children's book and, with the help of *Waking Ned* director Kirk Jones, delivers a wickedly fun family adventure.

Based on the *Nurse Matilda* series of books printed in the 1960s, *Nanny McPhee* has an old-fashioned feel mixed with some 21st century trickery as the warty, severe, black-gowned nanny slowly reveals that there may be more to her child-rearing skills than meets the eye (Thompson is clearly having a ball as the magical old maid).

The rest of the cast – kitted out in vibrantly coloured semi-Victorian garb (it's not set in a specific time or place but most closely resembles a bizarro panto-land) – keep the tone fun, from Imelda Staunton's bonkers cook to Colin Firth's befuddled dad and Celia Imrie's hideous Mrs Quickly, while the kids (led by *Love Actually*'s Thomas Sangster) are cute without being sickly. Of course, it's Thompson's show throughout, thanks to her superb interpretation of McPhee as Mary Poppins meets TV's Supernanny with a bit of Anne Robinson mixed in. ★★★★ **JB**

⦾ NANOOK OF THE NORTH (1922)

Starring: *Nanook (Allalariallak), Nyla (Nanook's Wife), Cunayou (Nanook's Wife), Allee (Nanook's Son), Allegoo (Nanook's Son)*
Director: *Robert J. Flaherty*
Screenwriter: *Robert J. Flaherty*
U/79 mins/Documentary/USA-France

Inuits from the Ungava region of Hudson's Bay, Nanook, his wife Nyla and their infant son survive the Arctic wilderness by adhering to traditional methods of ice fishing, igloo building, and walrus, fox and seal hunting.

Robert Flaherty first started shooting film on two trips to the Belcher Islands in the 1910s, during which he conceived the idea of making a 'scenic' about an Eskimo's daily life. However, it wasn't until 1920 that fur trapper Thierry Mallet provided funding for the year-long expedition.

Armed with two Akely cameras, whose gyro-motion tripods permitted smooth panning and tilting, Flaherty began shooting with a walrus hunt and screened the footage (which he developed in a homemade lab) for the Inuits to ensure they became active partners in his project. Indeed, by the time Flaherty left the peninsula, some of the locals had begun working as his technicians, one even fixing a broken stills camera.

However, Flaherty's relationship with his subject didn't impress some of those who first saw the feature in 1922. The fact that he had dressed Nanook and his family in long-discarded clothing and filmed them inside a bigger than usual igloo (a decision necessitated solely by technical demands) prompted some to denounce the picture as a phony and the criticism was even more hostile when a sound version was released in 1947.

Flaherty may not yet have been the most accomplished filmmaker and the edit achieved with Charles Gelb might have been confusing in places. But his creative treatment of reality chimed in entirely with John Grierson's concept of documentary cinema and Sergei Eisenstein considered *Nanook* to be the single biggest influence on the Soviet film revolution, on account of its pioneering reliance on the content and juxtaposition of images to forge an idea rather than the linear linkage of narrative events.

Flaherty consciously selected his cast and suggested episodes to convey the harshness of Nanook's struggle with his forbidding environment. But rather than breaking the rules of the still-undefined documentary tradition, Flaherty worked according to the principles of Inuit art, by which the spirit of an artefact emerges during its creation and not as the result of some preconceived design. Consequently, this remains a remarkable piece of filmmaking and humanist anthropology, whose influence recurs in the likes of *The Story of the Weeping Camel* (2003). ★★★★ **DP**

⦾ NAPOLEON (1927)

Starring: *Albert Dieudonne (Napoleon Bonaparte), Vladimir Roudenko (Napoleon Bonaparte as a child), Edmond Van Daele (Maximilien Robespierre), Alexandre Koubitzky (Danton), Antonin Artuad (Marat), Abel gance (Louis Saint-Just), Gina Manes (Josephine de Beauharnais), Suzanne Bianchettie (Marie-Antoinette)*
Director: *Abel Gance*
Screenwriter: *Abel Gance*
E/330 mins/Historical Drama/France-West Germany-USSR

Raised on Corsica and trained at the Brienne military academy, Napoleon Bonaparte rides out the vissicitudes of the French Revolution, marries Josephine de Beauharnais and reinforces his burgeoning reputation as a warrior by quelling a Parisian riot and leading a triumphal army into Italy.

Having followed his Impressionist masterpiece, *La Roue*, with slapstick genius Max Linder's last French film, *Au Secours!*, Abel Gance began researching what he envisaged would be a six-part biography of Napoleon Bonaparte. Accepting French, German and Russian coin (in a vague pan-European riposte to the growing dominance of Hollywood), Gance and his vast cast and crew worked from January 1925 to August 1926 on footage that took him and the scandalously overlooked Marguerite Beaugé seven months to assemble.

However, neither the four-hour premiere print nor the six-hour official cut were seen by more than a handful of audiences, as few venues could accommodate Napoléon *vu par* Abel Gance's unique technical demands and, moreover, the advent of Talkies seriously undercut its novelty value.

Many critics have denounced the epic's political naivety, barnstorming melodramatics, cheap sentimentality and clumsy attempts at humour. Some even accused it of encouraging dictatorial fascism. But, for all its bombastic patriotism and unquestioning hagiography, this is still an exceptional work of art.

Gance's use of subjective camera was almost recklessly ambitious in its bid to give the spectator the most visceral viewing sensation, while his skill in blending and multiplying images (one superimposition contained 16 separate shots, while the Brienne pillow fight divides the screen into nine segments) was unprecedented. The metaphorical intercutting of Bonaparte's sea crossing with tempestuous events in the Convention was also highly sophisticated and the picture would have included colour and 3-D interludes had Gance not decided against them as an unnecessary distraction. However, it did boast three Polyvision sequences, in which the screen became a giant triptych for the Bal des Victimes, the Italian triumph and the presentation of a hand-tinted Tricoloeur.

Much has been made by prudish academics of Francis Ford Coppola and Kevin Brownlow bowdlerising Gance's vision by screening restorations. But while they may not exactly replicate Gance's intentions, they are infinitely preferable to the director's own 1934 sound version and his 1971 compilation, *Bonaparte et la Revolution*. Indeed, Brownlow's second edit, again with a score by Carl Davis, represents a magnificent archival achievement and an unforgettable cinematic experience. ★★★★★ **DP**

⦾ NARC (2001)

Starring: *Ray Liotta (Lt Henry Oak), Jason Patric (Nick Tellis), Chi McBride (Capt. Cheevers), Busta Rhymes (Darnell 'Big D Love' Beery), Anne Openshaw (Katherine Calvess), John Oritz (Octavio Ruiz)*
Director: *Joe Carnahan*
Screenwriter: *Joe Carnahan*
18/100 mins./Thriller/USA

Persuaded back into active service by his superiors, Nick Tellis finds himself walking the same dangerous streets that almost got him killed when he was an undercover narcotics cop. Now he's investigating the murder of a fellow officer – but is his volatile new partner, Lt Henry Oak, entirely on the level?

Maybe it's the woollen hat and the handlebar moustache. Maybe it's the hefty good-cop-bad-cop pairing. Or maybe it's the split screen sequence. Whatever it is, there's something about *Narc* that's reminiscent of classic 70s cop movies such as *Serpico* and *The French Connection*. And if director Joe Carnahan doesn't quite match the output of that golden age, it's not for lack of effort on his or his cast's part.

Carnahan – whose directorial debut *Blood, Guts, Bullets And Octane* represented the worst of the American indies' infatuation with Tarantino posturing – has come of age with a movie that bristles with energy, from its stand-out, hand-held opening chase to its brutal, bloody denouement.

The film's visual hallmark is more *Se7en* than *Dirty Harry*, but this isn't

Die Hard Rip Offs

TOP10

1. *Die Hard* on a bus – *Speed*
2. *Die Hard* on a plane – *Air Force One, Executive Decision*
3. *Die Hard* up a mountain – *Cliffhanger*
4. *Die Hard* on a boat – *Under Siege*
5. *Die Hard* in a decommissioned prison – *The Rock*
6. *Die Hard* in a traffic jam – *Gridlock*
7. *Die Hard* in a military school – *Toy Soldiers*
8. *Die Hard* on a train – *Derailed*
9. *Die Hard* in outer space – *Assault on Dome 4*
10. *Die Hard* at a bioweapons lab – *Deadly Outbreak*

all about surface sheen. Carnahan's independent sensibilities go further than that, digging deep into the minds of his characters.

He takes undercover-cop clichés – tearful wife, black captain, mismatched partners – and uses them as psychological tools. What is it that drives these men to lay their lives on the line, day in, day out? *Narc* might not have all the answers but, unlike so many films in the same narrative ballpark, at least it has the audacity to ask the questions.

To this end, the director is helped in no small part by his leading men. Patric very probably has the harder of the two roles; the troubled, introspective Tellis is caught between loving duty to his wife and consuming empathy for the dead undercover cop. Note that it's not bullying from above, but a snatched glance at a scan photograph of the deceased's unborn child that convinces him to take the case.

That said, it's Liotta – Oak by name, oak by stature – who dominates the film with the best performance of his career. Quick to anger but with a smothered sensitivity, this character's essential ambiguity keeps the plot ticking over. ★★★★ **AE**

THE NARROW MARGIN (1952)

Starring: *Charlex McGraw (Walter Brown), Marie Windsor (Mrs Neil), Jacqueline White (Ann Sinclair), Gordon Gebert (Tommy Sinclair)*
Director: *Richard Fleischer*
Screenwriter: *Earl Frenton, from a story by Martin Goldsmith, Jack Leonard*
PG/71 mins./Crime/Drama/USA

Incorruptible cop has to escort a trashy floozy on a night train from Chicago to Los Angeles, supposedly to give evidence against the mob, but the underworld sends killers to silence the witness before she can talk.

The Narrow Margin is an archetypal 'sleeper'. Though it was made by an ambitious young director on the way up to bigger budgets and benefits from strong, if inexpensive leading actors (Charles McGraw, who seems carved out of granite, and Marie Windsor, who does cheap, shrewish and sexy like no other B-picture broad), the film rose above programmer status thanks to what would later be called a 'high concept'.

A couple who dislike each other have to take a train journey, with potential enemies on all sides – and their relationship changes. There's a twist near the end which rewrites the basic premise (and perhaps sidelines the most interesting character), but the reason this clicks is the claustrophobic train setting, with a soundtrack composed of artfully deployed railway noises, brutal fights in cramped compartments, sinister or overly friendly passengers who could either be hit men or allies, a carful of killers keeping pace with the locomotive, and staging that always emphasises the confines of space as if the camera had to squeeze in with the characters. Window reflections are crucial in many compositions; the hero even uses one to fire accurately through a door at the climax.

The simplistic characterisations are like something from a 1950s crime comic (especially unfortunate is a bratty kid you wish would stop a bullet), but its plot and pace are relentless and the casting of (mostly unfamiliar) supporting characters is always on the nail. It's just seventy minutes of suspense, but all the better for it – as demonstrated by the larger-scale, less-effective 1990 remake. ★★★ **KN**

NASHVILLE (1975)

Starring: *David Arkin (Norman), Barbara Baxley (Lady Pearl), Ned Beatty (Delbert Reese), Karen Black (Connie White), Ronee Blakley (Barbara Jean)*
Director: *Robert Altman*
Screenwriter: *Joan Tewkesbury*
15/160 mins./Drama/Politics/Music/USA

Awards: *Academy Awards – Best Song ('I'm Easy'); BAFTA – Best Soundtrack; Golden Globes – Best Song ('I'm Easy')*

In Nashville, a diverse group of people converge at a concert held in support of politician Hal Phillip Walker. The rally is aborted when a crazed fan attempts to assassinate a singing star.

Robert Altman's masterpiece brings 24 characters together in the capital city of country music, and has them interact directly and obliquely throughout a week in which an unseen politician launches a presidential campaign on a plainly meaningless platform ('does Christmas smell like oranges to you?'). As multi-faceted a mix of personal, political, satiric and scary as *Citizen Kane*, this yields more treasures with each viewing, and has catchy, often very funny songs to boot.

Memorable moments: Gwen Welles as the tragically untalented singer forced to do a strip-tease at a fund-raising dinner, Henry Gibson as a patriotic clown who sings 'We Must Be Doing Something Right to Last Two Hundred Years', studly Keith Carradine circulating among the entire female cast (he won an Oscar for his self-penned song 'I'm Easy'), Ronee Blakely's on-stage nervous breakdown as she puts off singing by recounting lengthy personal anecdotes, Shelley Duvall's spaced-out looks as a deeply weird drop-out girl, Geraldine Chaplin's ghastly monologues as 'Opal from the BBC' and Barbara Harris heroically leading a final chorus of the great apathy anthem 'It Don't Worry Me', Jeff Goldblum cruising through on a custom tricycle.

Scripted by Joan Tewkesbury, this also benefits greatly from Altman's semi-improv approach, with tiny bits of business, throwaway looks and non sequitur lines that seem to have been just caught or overheard but which add up to a mosaic portrait of America.

Also with: Scott Glenn, Lily Tomlin, Ned Beatty, Michael Murphy, Allen Garfield and (as themselves) Elliott Gould and Julie Christie. You'd swear Hal Phillip Walker got elected in '76 and has been in the White House ever since. ★★★★★ **KN**

NATIONAL LAMPOON'S ANIMAL HOUSE (1978)

Starring: *John Belushi (John 'Bluto' Blutarsky), Tim Matheson (Eric 'Otter' Stratton), John Vernon Dean (Vernon Wormer), Verna Bloom (Marion Wormer), Tom Hulce (Larry 'Pinto' Kroger)*
Director: *John Landis*
Screenwriters: *Harold Ramis, Douglas Kenney, Chris Miller*
15/108 mins./Comedy/USA

At a 1962 college, Dean Vernon Wormer is determined to expel the Delta House Fraternity, but those roughhousers have other plans for him.

At the time, *Animal House* was the most successful comedy ever, proving that belly laughs could be just as good for box office as rubber sharks and space opera. And yet, just as *Jaws* and *Star Wars* paved the way for legions of lame-brained, effects-driven blockbusters, so too did *Animal House* give birth to a veritable universe of appallingly unfunny movies, most of them starring Steve Guttenberg. Perhaps even more significantly, the movie marked a symbolic demise of the radicalism that had gripped America in the 60s and 70s. According to one critic, *Animal House* 'heralded the return of rampant conservatism to US campuses'.

Certainly, *Animal House* is a guilty pleasure. Although it's the ultimate teenage boy movie (or was until the arrival of *American Pie* 20 years later), to anyone with a modicum of social responsibility it's all a bit horrific. Indeed, the anarchic antics – beer blasts, food fights, toga parties – tend to leave grown-ups feeling sorry for whichever poor unseen minimum wage slaves are left to clear up all the mess.

The action takes place in 1962, mere months before the assassination of President Kennedy is due to bequeath the US an extraordinary decade of national self-examination, political turmoil and war, both internal and external. Coincidentally, this is also the year that *A Clockwork Orange* was published – albeit not yet in America – and, in common with that classic tome of unruly youth, *Animal House* isn't a particularly pretty or encouraging portrait of young manhood but, like a wild party veering dangerously out of control, it's a hell of a lot of fun.

Some scant knowledge of the bizarre nature of stateside further education is perhaps necessary for an enhanced appreciation of *Animal House*. When you attend a US university (or 'school' as they insist on terming it), you enter into a degrading scramble to gain admittance to the best fraternities: student clubs, some of which are powerful enough to strongly influence your future life and career. The girls, meanwhile, have their sororities, but they don't feature much here.

In the movie, Omega House are the elite of the student body at Faber College, set in an obscure all-American backwater town. Arrogant, white and upper class, they are manifest destiny at its nastiest – militantly square, scarily conservative and, naturally, sexually repressed. Led by the slimy Greg Marmalard and the blatantly fascist Neidermeyer (a superbly psychopathic Mark Metcalf), Omega House are the future ruling elite of the good old US of A. Over at Delta House, meanwhile, things are rather different. Rejected by Omega as 'a wimp and a blimp', new boys Larry Kroger (future *Amadeus* Oscar-winner Hulce) and Kent Dorfman (career tubby Stephen Furst) fall in with the rag-tag bag of non-conformists, led by Eric 'Otter' Stratton and epitomised by the vulgar vitality of one-offs like D-Day (the superbly-moustached Bruce McGill) and John 'Bluto' Blutarsk.

Director Landis uses this simple premise as the launch-pad for a fusillade of comic set-pieces. Bluto avoids a beating from Neidermeyer's thugs (including a young Kevin Bacon) by causing a food-fight in the canteen; Neidermeyer's beloved horse is abducted and secreted in Dean Wormer's office, where it promptly suffers a fatal heart attack; virginal Larry, agonising over whether he should have his way with a comatose cutie, is harangued by miniature angel and devil advocates (when he elects to do the decent thing and take her home, the outraged imp hisses, 'You homo!').

Hectored by Cesare Danova's Mafioso town mayor, the malevolent Dean Wormer resolves to have the Delta mob thrown off-campus. 'Get Neidermeyer onto it,' he orders Marmalard. 'He's a sneaky little shit, just like you, right?' The Delta boys face up to their threatened expulsion as you'd expect – spying on the girls' dorms (Bluto); making out with a dead fiancee's roomie (Otter), and smoking pot with the disillusioned Professor Jennings (played by an anachronistically haired Sutherland). When they finally do get expelled, Bluto and co. decide to go out in style. In what proves to be a demented parody of the Kennedy assassination, they sabotage the college's annual parade through Faber with predictably chaotic results.

With the collegiate setting's suitably sprawling cast, virtually all the speaking parts amount to little more than glorified cameos. Only the innocent Hulce, the lovably hapless Furst and the sensible, long-suffering Katy (Karen Allen's memorable portrayal of the kind of modern woman poised to out-evolve these Neanderthal males in the 60s) are anything like sympathetic. But John Belushi's performance – and remember, he died a drug-addled wreck a mere three years later – is one of wonderfully vital physical comedy. Whether he's crushing beer cans on his forehead, blithely smashing a folk singer's guitar into matchwood, or nonchalantly pissing on Kent and Larry's shoes, Bluto is the movie's enduring magic ingredient. And that includes the toga. ★★★★ **PR**

NATIONAL LAMPOON'S VAN WILDER (2002)

Starring: *Ryan Reynolds (Van Wilder), Tara Reid (Gwen Pearson), Tim Matheson (Vance Wilder Snr), Kal Penn*
Director: *Walt Becker*
Screenwriters: *Brent Goldberg, David Wagner*
15/94 mins./Comedy/USA

A swaggering, popular student by the name of Van Wilder spends his time throwing parties and generally promoting the cause of hedonism rather than actually graduating. When his father finally pulls the plug on his tuition, he decides to turn his organisational talents to the task of making some money.

A rather pointless attempt by the *National Lampoon* team to revisit former glories of the beloved frathouse mania of *Animal House*. Tim Matheson, one of the Delta-House's former luminaries, even turns up as a stuffy father. However, it becomes increasingly clear no matter how cocksure and charming is Ryan Reynolds as the titular party liaison he has none of that film's counter-culture bluster or the borderline insanity of John Belushi. This is a bland revisit that lacked the confidence to go out with the *National Lampoon* prefix in the USA.

Having Tara Reid as a prim student journalist is a bizarre thought, defined as a makeweight dumb blonde, here she's the love interest who will shake Wilder out of his groove. She's visiting to do a profile on this eternal student, to find, shock, he has no depth at all. But that's just window dressing, the rest is gratuitous nudity, semen gags, and big toothy grins as if it is all just a bit juvenile fun. It is. ★★ **IN**

NATIONAL TREASURE (2004)

Starring: *Nicolas Cage (Ben Gates), Diane Kruger (Abigail Chase), Justin Bartha (Riley Poole), Sean Bean (Ian Howe), Jon Voigt (Patrick Gates), Harvey Keitel (Sadusky), Christopher Plummer (John Adams Gates)*
Director: *Jon Turteltaub*
Screenwriters: *Jim Kouf, Cormac Wibberley, Marianne Wibberley, based on a story by Jim Kouf, Oren Aviv, Charles Segars*
PG/131 mins./Action/Adventure/USA

Benjamin Gates has devoted his life to finding the untold historical riches hidden by the Knights Templar. Learning that vital clues to the loot's

whereabouts are encrypted on the back of the Declaration Of Independence, Gates nicks the artefact ...

Being the first flick to draw on the fervour for *Da Vinci Code*-style ancient-history detective stories and the second Bruckheimer production (after *Pirates Of The Caribbean*) to deliver a PG booty trawl, *National Treasure* feels like a compromise. Caught uncomfortably between a kiddie adventure and a grown-up conspiracy thriller, it lacks the thrills for the latter and the smarts for the former, delivering a hokey, only vaguely fun romp.

Surprisingly for a Bruckheimer biggie, the action, ranging from a by-numbers van chase to a desultory climax involving a collapsing staircase in a New York catacomb, defines run of the mill. Even worse, while *National Treasure* shows little flair for spectacle, it shows less for yarnspinning. The whole plot – and this is nothing but plot – is packed with unfocused motivations and sluggish, hamfisted exposition, while the absurd clues that propel the story are so impenetrable that you expect Nic Cage to encounter Ted Rodgers and Dusty Bin at any moment.

The whole tale is populated by colourless characters, be it Sean Bean's one-note Brit villian, Jon Voight as Gates' estranged father (all very *Last Crusade*) and Harvey Keitel who pulls his detective from the drawer marked 'GRIMLY DOGGED COP'. As for Cage, the role of an obsessive treasure hunter would seem perfect for his brand of manic energy and eccentricity, but instead he proffers sub-Harrison Fordian determination, clearly caring little for a very undercooked character.

It isn't all bad, though. Despite respectively playing sidekicks named Abigail Eye Candy and Rollie Thick Person Who Acts As A Surrogate For A Confused Audience (they might as well be), Diane Kruger shows more spark than she did in the 162 minutes of *Troy* and Justin Bartha is an affable presence, his character the obvious recipient of a probable dialogue polish that punched up the humour quotient.

Plus, however absurd it gets, the treasure hunt mechanic tugs on your curiosity, the set-piece to steal the Declaration Of Independence is engaging and it's tough not to root for a gang of heroes who survive on their ingenuity and passion for history rather than the internet and brute force. There's just something likeable about *National Treasure*'s loopy inanity compared to *The Da Vinci Code*'s inate dullness. **★★ CH**

NATURAL BORN KILLERS (1994)

Starring: *Woody Harrelson (Mickey Knox), Juliette Lewis (Mallory Knox), Robert Downey Jr (Wayne Gale), Tommy Lee Jones (Dwight McClusky), Tom Sizemore (Jack Scagnetti)*
Director: *Oliver Stone*
Screenwriters: *David Veloz, Richard Rutowski, Oliver Stone, from a story by Quentin Tarantino*
18/114 mins./Crime/Drama/USA

Two victims of traumatised childhoods become lovers and psychopathic serial murderers irresponsibly glorified by the mass media.

Beset by controversy which delayed its release, Oliver Stone's *NBK* is an assault from start to finish. For the first hour, Stone looks like he's trying to equal the kill-count of his entire Vietnam trilogy, as deranged mass murderers Mickey and Mallory shoot, stab or drown just about everyone.

Eventually, the white-trash lovers are imprisoned where Harrelson's appearance on exploitative TV crime show *American Maniacs* provokes a riot which, in turn, allows the pair to escape.

Where *NBK* succeeds is in being the kind of risk-taking, all-out audio-visual experience that comes along all too rarely, with Stone constructing a frighteningly recognisable vision of America that would have the Founding Fathers weeping into their beards.

There are various versions of this in circulation though. Back in 1994, British censors granted Oliver Stone's murder-spree shocker an uncut 18 certificate for cinema release, while their American equivalent demanded 150 cuts. But previously available UK video and DVD versions were cut, while an unrated Region One disc has been available for years. So how much gore you see will depend on the version. **★★★★ AM**

Movie Trivia: Natural Born Killers

Mickey's mental instability is represented by the colour green (key lime pie, neon sign) just before he launches into violence. The riot sequence was shot in a real prison with real inmates, some of whom were inside for murder. Juliette Lewis actually broke Tom Sizemore's nose when she smashed his face against the wall. The film had over 2,500 cuts. Most movies would have less than a third of that.

n

THE NAVIGATOR: A MEDIAEVAL ODYSSEY (1988)

Starring: *Bruce Lyons (Connor), Hamish McFarlane (Griffin), Noel Appleby (Ulf), Marshall Napier (Searle), Chris Haywood (Anro)*
Director: *Vincent Ward*
Screenwriter: *Vincent Ward*
PG/87 mins./Fantasy/Adventure/Australia/New Zealand

In 1348, the Black Death creeps towards a Cumbrian mining village. Griffin, a visionary, dreams that disaster can be averted if a party of menfolk dig a tunnel to the other side of the world and put up a crucifix on a cathedral in 'God's City'. However, 'the other side of the world' turns out to be New Zealand in the 1980s.

Director Vincent Ward's gritty fantasy refuses to play the Hollywood time-twisting game of *Time After Time* or *Back to the Future*, depicting the grainily coloured present not as an excuse for jokes but as a world of dangerous wonders as physical and threatening as those of the monochrome Middle Ages. It makes much of the peril of crossing a road with demonic-seeming traffic whizzing in both directions, and is so firmly locked into a mediaeval worldview that its heroes never realise they've travelled in time.

In one unforgettable sequence, the Cumbrians are boating across the harbour (with a stolen horse aboard) when a nuclear submarine surfaces close by like Moby Dick, confirming that there are dragons and leviathans in the world. In another, the visionary who may be dreaming this whole thing is drawn to a bank of TV screens broadcasting a surrealist documentary on AIDS, reminding us that the modern era isn't without plagues.

The Navigator irritates some with its vague ending (hinging on a prophetic dream which means death for someone) and occasional overuse of blustering peasant mannerisms (one of the miners is a double for Pfc. Doberman from *Sergeant Bilko*), but is prized by others for its resolutely unusual approach. Essentially, it's a mediaeval movie: with Chaucerian characterisations, an illuminated visual style and a clear-eyed mysticism straight out of the 14th Century. Short on traditional action, but long on extraordinary moments. **★★★★★ KN**

⦿ NEAR DARK (1987)

Starring: *Adrian Pasdar (Caleb Colton), Jenny Wright (Mae), Lance Henriksen (Jesse), Bill Paxton (Severen), Jenette Goldstein (Diamondback)*
Director: *Kathryn Bigelow*
Screenwriters: *Eric Red, Kathryn Bigelow*
18/90 mins./Horror/USA

A mid-western farm boy reluctantly becomes a member of the undead when a girl he meets turns out to be part of a band of southern vampires who roam the highways in stolen cars. Part of his initiation includes a bloody assault on a hick bar.

The word 'vampire' is never mentioned in *Near Dark*. Yet, in the dustbowl gravities of its Oklahoma setting a van full of night-crawlers set to gorging on local blood. The touch of sunlight will chargrill them instantly, but they have no aversion to garlic or crosses and display no propensity for turning into flying mammals.

Released in the summer of 1987, *Near Dark* went head-to-head with the more brashly comic *The Lost Boys* and, in box office terms at least, took a heavy beating. Yet it was the superior movie by far. Its mix of edgy romanticism (the film is also a love story) and haunting melancholy makes it, as an immediate proposition, less accessible but far more memorable. These are vampires of a postmodern world in which belief has faded to the point where the paraphernalia of myth and religion are no longer effective. Bigelow, echoing the games the Coen brothers play, reconstructs genre conventions from the inside out. These are humanised monsters, almost likeable. Our first meeting with them is innocently romantic: Mae confusing blood lust withsexual desire when she is hit on by Caleb. They are depicted intight-knit family unity, Henriksen's Jesse and Jenette Goldstein's Diamondback are surrogate parents to the band. But their hermetic existence is a bleak one. We are never asked to sympathise, but we do empathise. Perhaps we even envy them. Still, their actions are quite despicable (having completely lost touch with the humans they once were). Paxton's overbearing, scene-stealing brute Severen devises new and vile ways to siphon the red stuff from his victims. In an idea nicked squarely from vampire doyenne Anne Rice (the same motif appears in *Interview With The Vampire*), the brat of the pack Ishmael has been preserved forever in a child's body while his mind and desires have grown older.

No excuses are made for the characters' behaviour: their nighttime existence as forever drifting outsiders (this is also a road movie) has driven them to the point where they have only mutual dependence to rely on. But neither are their victims innocent. No swooning virgins these, but oafish hicks and rednecks clamouring to die. The kernel of the plot is simple. Listless farmboy Caleb romances an itinerant girl who, instead of making out, takes a bite and drinks from his jugular. As his transformation to bloodsucker gathers pace, he is reluctantly taken into the fold of her nomadic vampire clan. Meanwhile his father fights to get him back and save his soul. The central metaphor here is hardly an original one – vampirism as drug addiction: the hostile, insular community, the dependence upon night, the cold turkey/transfusion link (an idea that stems from Bram Stoker himself, in *Dracula* he called it 'blood letting').

The ability to 'cure' vampires in *Near Dark* introduces an unusual factor to the genre, the chance for an immortal to return to humanity. Both Mae and Caleb find salvation, but in the process lose something immense and are forever tainted by the experience. Artist-turned-director Bigelow – a consummate blender of action staples and stylistic overtures (*Blue Steel* (1989), *Strange Days* (1995), the pumped up machismo piss-take of *Point Break* (1991)) – understood the key to the affair was atmosphere, and she drenches the film in it. Tumbleweed America bled dry, a world of ashen light and endless horizons, with the familiar woozy moods of Tangerine Dream in the background. Bigelow worked closely with cinematographer Adam Greenberg to invest the night scenes with a seductive warmth to suggest the allure of vampirism. The violence, when it happens, comes in brutal, imaginative bursts. There are some tangy visual licks – the sun barbecuing an agonised Paxton (utilising tubes of compressed smoking tobacco stuck under prosthetics); bullets punching through walls to let in laser beams of deadly sunlight.

A sequence where Paxton squeezes a redneck's head like an ugly great pimple had to be excised, however, to appease the censors. But the violence, laced with jaunty wit ('I hate it when they ain't shaved,' moans Severen of a hirsute kill), is seen as the truth of their existence rather than simply a sadistic impulse, never is it premeditated. This predilection for reinventing the vampire theme has struck something of a chord: *The Addiction*, *From Dusk Till Dawn* and *The Wisdom Of Crocodiles* all refit the classic motifs. None, though, have had quite the startling, unnerving effect of *Near Dark*. ★★★★ **IN**

Tagline
Pray for daylight.

⦿ THE NEGOTIATOR (1998)

Starring: Samuel L. Jackson (Danny Roman), Kevin Spacey (Chris Sabian), David Morse (Commander Adam Beck), Ron Rifkin (Commander Grant Frost), J.T. Walsh (Terence Neibaum), Paul Giamatti (Rudy Simmons)
Director: F. Gary Gray
Screenwriters: James DeMonaco, Kevin Fox
15/133 mins./Action/Drama/USA

Chicago set police procedural in which a hostage and a negotiator switch sides.

The police negotiator is a gift-wrapped Hollywood role for actors keen to demonstrate their running, jumping and reading skills. This film boasts not one but two: the street-tough Danny Roman and more cerebral Chris Sabian.

Archetypal good cop Roman has been framed for the murder of his partner amid an unfolding police insurance scam. Smelling a rat in Internal Affairs and about to indicted, he turns the tables and takes an officeful of hostages, including oily investigator Neibaum. With their best persuader now on the other side of the loudhailer, the Chicago P.D. enlists smooth operator Sabian, who, we learn, once talked a hostage-taker down for 54 hours. At this point, the film becomes a tense two-hander, negotiator negotiating with negotiator while on the ground itchy-triggered officer Beck begs to send his troops in and put an end to all the yakking.

For a film sold on the tantalisingly offbeat blend of its two stars, Jackson and Spacey spend precious little screentime together – they're mostly on the blower. In effect, it's Jackson's show. Much of the brow mopping arises from his relationship with the hostages and the escalating danger of his one-man stand. It's an action film in which the likelihood of action is as gripping as the engagement itself: plenty of false alarms, the flashing blue light of police build-up, and some handsome if predictable negotiatory bluffs – credit 27-year-old director Gray for keeping us hooked on possibility for two hours plus.

Jackson handles himself well and Spacey's apparently effortless grace is a welcome counterpoint. But a talky film like this demands a knockout denouement, and it's an anticlimax heavy with convenience. Just when we could've use some more action ... more chit-chat. ★★★ **AC**

THE NET (1995)

Starring: *Sandra Bullock (Angela Bennett), Jeremy Northam (Jack Devlin), Dennis Miller (Dr Alan Champion), Diane Baker (Mrs Bennett)*
Director: *Irwin Winkler*
Screenwriters: *John Brancato, Micahel Ferris*
12/114 mins./Action/Crime/Drama/USA

Forced to go on the run by cyber-criminals, she tries to clear her name and expose the baddies in the process

To say *The Net* takes some swallowing rather understates the issue. For starters, this fraught computer thriller, cooked up around the all-new information super-highway, asks us to accept that lovely, feisty Sandra Bullock is a reclusive computer nerd who shuns folks in favour of a desktop crammed with hardware. And, after she happens upon a nonsense plot of computer-fraud-world-domination hijinks with one click of the mouse too many, the poor lass finds her identity erased from all computer records, a crisis conveniently aided by the fact she has no friends, and her only living relation, her mum, has Alzheimer's and can't recall her name.

Yet arch contrivance is the lifeblood of the Hollywood potboiler and this is competent, eminently watchable stuff with some sneaky takes on computer paranoia and Bullock proving a chip off the Julia Roberts woman-in-peril block. The bad guys, when not fiddling with her pixelated existence, take on three dimensions in the form of the slippery – and yes! – British heavy Jeremy Northam, who stalks his prey through deserted Los Angeles streets by beaming into her mobile phone frequencies. And she, predictably, is completely on her own, as the police, hospitals, FBI – all wired to the Net – are told that she is the criminal. It's classic Hitchcock, reglossed with the big theme of the 90s – the Internet.

Winkler, whose direction is too meandering to really thrill, is best on the localised fear; this is a real wake-up call to the deficiencies and dehumanisation of a computer-run society. But the big conspiracy theory is sketchy at best, and Northam's smarmy killer is too obvious to give the film the required lift away from the techno buzz of the computer screen. Bullock has done, and will do, better work. *The Net* entertains but is unlikely to hang around on the cerebral hard disk for too long. ★★★ **IN**

NETWORK (1976)

Starring: *Faye Dunaway (Diana Christensen), William Holden (Max Schumacher), Peter Finch (Howard Beale), Robert Duvall (Frank Hackett), Ned Beatty (Arthur Jensen)*
Director: *Sidney Lumet*
Screenwriter: *Paddy Chayefsky*
15/116 mins./Drama/USA

Awards: *Academy Awards – Best Actor (Peter Finch), Best Actress, Best Supporting Role, Best Original Screenplay, BAFTA – Best Actor (Peter Finch), Golden Globes – Best Director, Best Actor (Peter Finch), Best Actress, Best Screenplay*

When TV news anchor Howard Beale is told that he is to be fired, he declares on-air that he will commit suicide on television, whereupon his ratings soar. Though he doesn't kill himself, he becomes a star as 'the mad prophet of the airwaves'.

Peter Finch won a posthumous Best Actor Oscar for his supporting role in this intense and insane nightmare satire on television, which can hardly have pleased William Holden, who actually plays the lead, especially since co-stars Faye Dunaway and Beatrice Straight copped Best Actress and Best Supporting Actress gongs. However, Finch is memorable as the increasingly demented Howard Beale, who gets to deliver a lot of pertinent, cynical editorial material ('when the twelfth largest company in the world controls the most awesome goddamn propaganda force in the whole godless world, who knows what shit will be peddled for truth?') as he spins further and further out of control, believing that God has spoken to him ('why me?' 'Because you're on television, dummy').

Beale's see-sawing ratings prompt a war of cynical one-upmanship between ruthless execs Dunaway and Robert Duvall while an appalled, tired man of integrity (Holden) looks sadly on and a megalomaniac tycoon (Ned Beatty) urges Beale to become even more insane but also (an ultimate sin) a ratings turn-off. Paddy Chayefsky's gutsy screenplay introduced the catch-phrase 'I'm mad as hell and I'm not going to take it any more' and savages the industry in which he had come to prominence, and Sidney Lumet directs on the knife-edge between comedy and horror, stranding his outstanding cast in soulless sets.

Obscene verbal wit pours out of everyone and it winds up with a horrible apotheosis, in a ratings-grabbing live assassination. Decades on, after Jerry Springer, Oprah Winfrey, the News Bunny and 'reality television', this seems more like docu-drama than satire. ★★★★ **KN**

NEVER BEEN KISSED (1999)

Starring: *Drew Barrymore (Josie Geller), David Arquette (Rob Geller), Michael Vartan (Sam Coulson), Molly Shannon (Anita), John C. Reilly (Gus), Leelee Sobieski (Aldys)*
Director: *Raja Gosnell*
Screenwriters: *Abby Kohn, Marc Siverstein, Jenny Bicks*
12/107 mins./Romance/Comedy/USA

A newspaper reporter is forced to relive her awkward past when she goes undercover at a high school.

Never Been Kissed is a peachy teen comedy that may be formulaic right down to its high school prom shenanigans but nonetheless wins you over with its eternally perky nature. The ace up its sleeve is Drew Barrymore giving the kind of performance that could liven up even the most humdrum of light comedies.

Barrymore is Josie Geller, the former Billy No-Mates of her high school (we see her lank-haired, brace-wearing former self in cringeworthy flashbacks). Now an anally grammatical, somewhat dowdy 25-year-old copy editor, she is eager to turn reporter, something which happens quite by chance when she is sent off on an undercover investigation of high school culture. In order to fulfil the brief, Josie has to disguise herself as a student, enrol in the local school and get with the in crowd.

When her initial attempts – a frankly ill-judged makeover and use of apparently cool lingo – fall flat, her brain-free brother, who just happened to be the most popular person in school, steps in to help out. And then there's the small matter of Josie's new English teacher, who finds himself on morally dodgy territory when mutual attraction rears its head.

Barrymore is remarkable here, given that she is essentially required to play three roles: the buck-toothed high schooler, the grown-up cool girl and an awkward, shy 25-year-old. She's ably backed by a host of quirky supports – the increasingly underrated Reilly as her stressed editor, Shannon's lascivious colleague and Sobieski's class misfit – while Vartan is clearly a leading man in the making.

And while the film itself doesn't offer up anything that hasn't been seen a million times before, it is endearing stuff, punctuated by some genuinely hysterical moments (the coleslaw-eating sequence has to be seen to be believed) in between the inevitable schmaltz. But if you can suspend disbelief long enough to assume that Barrymore could pass for 17, then such quibbles are minor by comparison. ★★★ **CW**

⊙ NEVER SAY NEVER AGAIN (1983)

Starring: *Sean Connery (James Bond), Klaus Maria Brandauer (Maximilian Largo), Max Von Sydow (Ernst Stavro Blofeld), Barbara Carrera (Fatima Blush), Kim Basinger (Domino Petachi), Alec McCowen (Q), Edward Fox (M), Rowan Atkinson (Nigel Small-Fawcett)*
Director: *Irvin Kershner*
Screenwriter: *Lorenzo Semple Jr, based on a story by Kevin McClory, Jack Whittingham, Ian Fleming*
PG/128 mins./Spy/Adventure/UK

SPECTRE operative Largo steals two missiles with atomic warheads, and implements a massive international extortion scheme. Secret agent James Bond stumbles into the plot while recuperating at a health farm. Along with Domino, who wants revenge on Largo since the death of her brother, Bond sets out to thwart the villain.

Because of a rights quirk, dating back to a collaboration between Ian Fleming and screenwriter-producer Kevin McClory on an outline which became the novel and film *Thunderball*, Sean Connery was able to return to the role of James Bond outside the aegis of the official Cubby Broccoli series then starring Roger Moore just so long as he starred in a de facto remake of *Thunderball*. It has a certain insouciance, as demonstrated when Alec McCowen's Q greets the returning star with 'Good to see you, Mr Bond. Things have been awfully dull around here. I hope we're going to see some gratuitous sex and violence.'

However, a toupeed, somewhat thick-middled secret agent seems more like an imitation of the ageing Moore series than gutsier counter-programming, and most of the fun of the picture comes from trimmings – Brandauer's nuke-napping villain literally slobbering over a shrinking Kim Basinger, Max Von Sydow making a wry cameo appearance as the cat-stroking Blofeld ('We have accomplished two of the functions that the name SPECTRE embodies: terror and extortion. If our demands are not met within seven days, we shall ruthlessly apply the third: revenge!') and, especially, Barbara Carrera striding about in 80s boots and trousers as the murderous Fatima Blush.

Irvin Kerschner, hot after *The Empire Strikes Back*, efficiently assembles the action scenes and the intrigue, but the more modish aspects – an electrified two-player video game – now look rather hokey. Also, a Bond movie without that jangling guitar theme just seems *wrong* somehow. ★★★ **KN**

⊙ THE NEVERENDING STORY (1984)

Starring: *Barret Oliver (Bastian Bux), Noah Hathaway (Atreyu), Tami Stronach (Childlike Empress), Deep Roy (Teeny Weeny), Patricia Hayes (Urgl)*
Director: *Wolfgang Petersen*
Screenwriters: *Wolfgang Petersen, Herman Weigel, Robert Easton, based on the book by Michael Ende*
U/104 mins./Fantasy/West Germany/USA

A young boy escapes from his regular bullies by diving into a bookshop. There the shopkeeper introduces him to an ancient storybook which he suspects is dangerous, and sure enough as Bastian begins to read he is magically transported to the land of Fantasia, a world in need of a hero.

A rigorous enough, if rather dated, version of a best-selling German fantasy fable, whose imprecise arcana involves such vague propositions as the blight of 'Nothingness' and the power of 'faith'. A rather hippish quality, that alludes to the possibility it might all be a dream. Kids tend to want this kind of thing to be certain of its own imagination. As Bastian (a bland Barret Oliver) reads is it into his bully-tormented mind we are journeying or into some extra-dimension ruled by juvenile royalty?

The structure, borrowed from such classics as *Alice In Wonderland* and *Peter Pan*, is the story within a story, the framing reality around a fairy-tale. The exotic denizens of the pointedly named Fantasia are a Muppet-styled crew of stone giants, white furred dragon-dogs and a cute little fellow who rides a giant, speedy snail, which favour cuddly over convincing.

Wolfgang Petersen, usually such a fierce director, isn't at home here, he keeps it trippy and loose, plenty of dream images, when to make this kind of thing work you need conviction. For all the art direction, it's drifty and limp compared to say *Labyrinth*, which follows a similar notion. Tots will like its triumph of the little-man overture, and those swooping flights atop the floppy dragon, but older kids will miss the ironclad muscle we might have expected from the director of *Das Boot* doing *Das Dwarf*. Two ignominious sequels followed, but alas the Nothingess was still thwarted. ★★ **IN**

⊙ NEW JACK CITY (1991)

Starring: *Wesley Snipes (Nino Brown), Ice-T (Scotty Appleton), Allen Payne (Gee Money), Marion Van Peebles (Stone), Michael Michelle (Selina), Chris Rock (Pookie)*
Director: *Mario Van Peebles*
Screenwriters: *Thomas Lee Wright, Barry Michael Cooper*
18/101 mins./Crime/USA

A New York gangster Nino, who calls his outfit Cash Money, gets big selling crack. But try as he might cop Scotty Appleton can't bring him down, a mission that has a personal agenda as Nino murdered Scotty's mother.

A brash, unconvincing crime thriller that can claim to have launched the hip-hop styled movie, and given Wesley Snipes a chance to be outrageous. It looks hackneyed and feels overwrought in hindsight, but at the time its kinetic edits, blurring like some drug trip, and violent immediacy were groundbreaking. Van Peebles, who would drift to the sidelines of cinema when he shouldn't have, was intent on transforming the black exploitation movie into an intense exposure of late 80s Harlem drug culture. But his approach was too of-the-moment and self-satisfied to be nuanced or telling, the boombox vernacular, thick with colloquial guttertalk, feels forced and showy rather than truthful.

Snipes, however, is having a ball. His Nino is is living the black, street-crime version of the yuppie dream. He's Don Corleone mixed with Richard Pryor, dressed in immaculate blue suits, and spouting mock philosophies on brotherhood. His foes in this hectic cops and robbers vibe, Scotty and Nick (played with that lazy snicker by Ice-T (good choice) and lonely Caucasian muddle by Judd Nelson), spar and break the rules – as we've got a new kind of mobster, so we have a new breed of cop, sour and naked of ideals.

It bounces, hyperbolic with its empty magnificence, to the thump of early hip-hop beats (another aged factor). With none of the racial politicking of Spike Lee or the social awareness of John Singleton, it can only turn into a personal vengeance story, Nino's downfall as inevitable and preposterous as some horror-movie freakzoid. It remains seminal, but for all its energy is a vacant lot. ★★ **IN**

⊙ A NEW LEAF (1971)

Starring: *Walter Matthau (Henry Graham), Elaine May (Henrietta Lowell), Jack Weston (Andrew McPherson), George Rose (Harold Henry, Graham's Butler), William Redfield (Beckett)*
Director: *Elaine May*
Screenwriter: *Elaine May, based on the short story 'The Green Heart' by Jack Ritchie*
U/102 mins/Comedy/USA

Faced with financial ruin, Henry Graham takes his butler Harold Henry's advice to marry money and descends upon naive heiress Henrietta Lowell with the dual intention of marriage and murder.

Based on Jack Ritchie's short story, 'The Green Heart', Elaine May's directorial debut was so compromised by the studio that it's funny almost in spite of itself. May's original version came in at 180 minutes and included a bogus marriage, blackmail, two murders and a fantasy sequence, in which Henrietta envisions herself as an irresistible femme fatale. However, Paramount chief Robert Evans ordered a second cut that so enraged May that she threatened to have her name removed from the credits. Typically, Walter Matthau claimed to prefer the bowdlerisation, as it bore a less obvious resemblance to the Jack Lemmon vehicle, *How to Murder Your Wife*, which also featured an unwanted bride and a calculating valet.

The missing 78 minutes remain a tantalising prospect. But this is still a wonderful character study that harks back to the screwball era, while retaining the bleak cynicism of Nixonian America. It's also something of a musical curio, as its score was imported wholesale from the 1967 black farce, *Oh Dad, Poor Dad, Mama's Hung You in the Closet and I'm Feeling So Sad*.

Matthau is superb as the playboy who has frittered away his father's estate and marries May's myopic socialite in the hope of bumping her off during her annual botany trip to the mountains. The contrast between the tetchy charm Henry turns on to seduce Henrietta and the barely concealed disdain with which he deals with her scheming lawyer Andrew McPherson and grasping housekeeper Mrs McTaggart (Doris Roberts) is effortlessly amusing. But it's his response to Henrietta's endless muddles and infantile clumsiness that gives the film both its edge and its affectionate undertone.

Best known then for her satirical cabaret teaming with Mike Nichols, May is an absolute delight as the harmlessly hopeless heiress, whose quirky character traits are infinitely more amusing than her crassly schematic wardrobe. However, her disastrous display at the haute tea party and her inability to don a nightgown on her wedding night are masterclasses in gauche pantomime and the comedy of embarrassment. **★★★★ DP**

NEW NIGHTMARE (1994)

Starring: *Heather Langenkamp (Herself/Nancy Thompson), Robert Englund (Himself/Freddy Krueger), Miko Hughes (Dylan Porter), Wes Craven (Himself), John Saxon (Himself/Lt Donald Thompson), Robert Shaye (Himself)*
Director: *Wes Craven*
Screenwriter: *Wes Craven*
15/112 mins./Horror/USA

Freddy Krueger, upset that he was killed off in the last *Nightmare on Elm Street* movie, attempts to murder his creators and actors from his previous films.

Given the promise of the title of *Freddy's Dead: The Final Nightmare*, you're entitled to feel a mite cheated by the existence of this follow-up. It should, by all rights, be called *A Nightmare On Elm Street Part 7: We Lied*. However, with series creator Craven back at the helm, this is a long way from the formula cheap thrills of the last five sequels. And quite how they contrive to bring back the definitively dead Freddy is radically original, stretching the concept of 'sequel' in ways hardly the norm for a multiplex movie.

Set in the 'real' world of Hollywood rather than on Craven's mythical Elm Street, the story follows actress Langenkamp – playing herself – star of the original *Elm Street* movie a decade ago. Things have become fraught, she is being pestered by a prank caller with Freddy's voice, troubled by bad dreams about the fiend and worried sick about the strange behaviour of her son (Miko Hughes). Meanwhile, New Line, the film company which actually made this movie, are wooing her to star in a fresh Freddy film, currently being written by Craven.

The play on fantasy and reality is teasingly clever, featuring both Craven, acting his big scene with a wonderfully surpressed chuckle, and a terrific self-parody from Englund, in the double role of himself and a streamlined, nastier Freddy. This new *Nightmare* is one of the strongest straight horror films of the decade, and even though the dreamworld finale may be a little familiar, the picture has a genuine creepiness that goes deeper than one-off shocks. **★★★★ KN**

THE NEW WORLD (2005)

Starring: *Colin Farrell (Captain John Smith), Christopher Plummer (Captain Christopher Newport), Christian Bale (John Rolfe), August Schellenberg (Powhatan), Wes Studi (Opechancanough), Q'Orianka Kilcher (Pocahontas)*
Director: *Terrence Malick*
Screenwriter: *Terrence Malick*
12A/135 mins./150 mins. (UK cut)/Drama/Biography/Adventure/USA

Virginia, 1607. As the English establish a settlement in Jamestown, disgraced soldier of fortune John Smith leads an expedition to establish trade with the Native Americans. Smith is captured by a tribe but released by the chief to his favourite daughter Pocahontas in order to gain insight into the outsider's intentions.

Where there were some 21 years between Terrence Malick's second (*Days Of Heaven*) and third (*The Thin Red Line*) films, there has been only a breezy seven years between the third and this one. But Malickites who may have feared that he rushed off any old tripe in such a short space of time can rest assured – his reinvigoration of the Pocahontas myth is the director working near the peak of his powers. Far too daring to trouble the Academy, far too niche to worry about opening weekends, *The New World* finds poetry in emotion (and vice versa) and once again reminds us that movies are far too rich to be the domain of the storytellers only.

From frame one, you know you're deep in Malick country. The film begins with a virtually dialogue-free, ten-minute sequence. To the strains of James Horner in minimalist, near-Philip Glass mode, the arrival of three English ships docking on the James River becomes a joyous set-piece of discovery and wonder. As the Europeans subsequently battle the Native Americans during the creation of the Jamestown settlement, Malick tempers the love story, action sequences and cuts of tribal life with his favourite concerns – a couple at odds with societal constraints, the primitive versus the modern, the purity of nature versus human hubris.

What could be a dry history lesson is turned into something unique and quietly heartfelt. Yet what really dazzles about *The New World* is that it is like looking at life through different eyes. In other hands, Smith and Pocahontas' initial courtship as they prance through fields could have been Pastoral Romance 101 (remember *Attack Of The Clones*?), but Malick makes it both sweet and affecting, conveying how the couple come alive to each other and their surroundings through images alone. Despite being Malick's most straightforward narrative since *Badlands* – the joyous courtship gives way to a downbeat study of loss, as Pocahontas believes Smith to be dead and is integrated into life with the white settlers who incongruously name her Rebecca – he still imbues the rituals and rhythms of 17th century life with a visual/aural lyricism that reaches places CGI can't touch. As perhaps befits a stranger in a strange land, Farrell spends much of the movie looking befuddled and bewildered. Christian Bale, who turns up in a touching, tender final third as an aristocrat who takes Pocahontas back to England, underplays to a tee, letting his innate decency eke out under a lifetime of restraint. But, performance-wise, the movie belongs to 15-year-old newcomer Kilcher, who bursts with energy and curiousity early on, her innocence giving way to a touching study of grief as her world crumbles around her. It's fresh, instinctive and – in a just world – an award-winning performance.

Yet take note: *The New World* will most certainly not appeal to everyone. The pace is so slow, it would have to pull over to let a funeral go by. There are competing voiceover narrations, unclear character motivations and untold pauses for breath; Malick revels in repetitions of images of burbling water, birds taking off, burbling water, swaying grass, burbling water ... But if you give yourself over to Malick's sensibility and his feel for cultures colliding, this feels less like indulgence and more like an absorbing, sumptuous and ultimately moving luxury. ★★★★ **IF**

NEW YORK, NEW YORK (1977)

Starring: *Robert De Niro (Jimmy Doyle), Liza Minnelli (Francine Evans), Lionel Stander (Tony Harwell), Mary Kay Place (Bernice), George Memmoli (Nicky), Murray Moston (Horace Morris), Barry Primus (Paul Wilson), Georgie Auld (Frankie Harte), Dick Miller (Palm Club Owner)*
Director: *Martin Scorsese*
Screenwriters: *Earl Mac Rauch, Mardik Martin, based on a story by Rauch*
PG/155 mins./Musical/USA

After meeting on VJ Day, sax player Jimmy Doyle and singer Francine Evans embark on a tumultuous relationship. However, Evans rise to stardom, combined with Doyle's lean years, leads to much professional and personal jealousy.

Martin Scorsese's criminally neglected tribute to the heyday of the MGM musical has aged astonishingly well. Following his 70s hat-trick of *Mean Streets*, *Alice Doesn't Live Here Anymore* and *Taxi Driver*, it was the director's first critical and commercial flop. But as per usual, Scorsese was ahead of his time, incorporating freeform East Coast film acting with the opulent fakery of the classic studio production, complete with giant sets, musical numbers and a cast of thousands. It's also the movie that gave Sinatra and the Big Apple its signature tune, the title song astonishingly overlooked in the Best Song Oscar category.

In a brilliant set-piece of riotous colour and music, it begins on VJ Day in 1945, when smooth-talking sax player Jimmy Doyle (method man De Niro obviously learned to play sax for the role) and demobbed singer Francine embark on a relationship that's made entirely unworkable by their different ambitions. Jimmy is a cool-headed jazz guy, motivated by talent and the need to be the best; to him, Francine is a sell-out, and her slow rise from singer to movie star fuels his jealousy and pent-up rage.

Stylistically, this was enough to confuse audiences back in '77, but today, having paved the way for self-reflexive melodramas by Todd Haynes, Gus Van Sant and Lars Von Trier, Scorsese's experiment with irony simply seems bold and sophisticated. More troubling for some will be the film's elegant arc into bathos, eschewing a big finish for something poignant, quiet and arguably more true to the spirit of the enterprise. In light of *The Aviator*'s success, maybe it's time this masterpiece was re-evaluated, albeit as the reissued 1981 version, which restored the stunning, multi-faceted Happy Endings musical montage sequence. Though he reined its excesses and inventions for future movies, *New York, New York* is more than a fascinating misfire, it's a rare and telling glimpse into a legendary filmmaker's fiercely guarded soul. ★★★★ **DW**

NEW YORK STORIES (1989)

Starring: *Woody Allen (Sheldon), Mae Questel (Mother), Mia Farrow (Lisa). Nick Nolte (Lionel Dobie), Rosanna Arquette (Paulette), Heather McComb (Zoe), Talia Shire (Charlotte), Steve Buscemi (Gregory Stark)*
Directors: *Woody Allen (Oedipus Wrecks), Francis Ford Coppola (Life Without Zoe), Martin Scorsese (Life Lessons)*
Screenwriters: *Richard Price (Life Lessons), Woody Allen (Oedipus Wrecks), Francis Ford Coppola & Sofia Coppola (Life Without Zoe)*
15/119 mins./Comedy/Drama/USA

Three stories related only by their dependence on and depiction through New York: an ageing painter falls for his young assistant (directed by Scorsese), a rich girl lounges in her hotel room (directed by Coppola), and a son faces up to his Jewish-American demons (directed by Allen).

On paper *New York Stories* sounds like a dream. Woody Allen invites his pals Martin Scorsese and Francis Coppola to contribute a segment each as part of a triptych, the only proviso being that the stories are set in New York. This is merely the cinematic equivalent of limiting Dickens to London, since all three directors have in their time shaped our cinema-fed conceptions of the Big Apple. Coppola's evocation of Little Italy and the wealthier reaches of Long Island in the *Godfather* films, Scorsese's *Mean Streets*, *Taxi Driver* and *After Hours*, and nearly all the Allen films – especially the romantic paean *Manhattan* – are as much the chronicle of a city as the gangsters, psychos and artists who people it.

Yet with these directors, it's often a question of form. The 80s were rather mixed for all three, though Scorsese managed at least one masterpiece with *Raging Bull* and almost triggered a religious war with *The Last Temptation Of Christ*. His contribution, *Life Lessons*, is a meditation on obsessional love and artistic inspiration, and it's a brilliant piece of work. Nick Nolte plays a celebrated painter, hounded by his agent over a forthcoming exhibition and hooked on his (much younger) personal assistant, Paulette, herself a fledgling artist. Nolte dominates the screen with his bearish physique and brooding demeanour – he's tortured by Paulette's rejection of him, but that's also what drives him to create his big, bold canvases. We are watching the end of an affair, and though both behave appallingly to each other, you can't help feeling a strange affection for them. Nolte has come through by the end, and we're left to ponder whether he'll make all the same mistakes again. An old story, perhaps, but superbly acted and directed with the sort of imaginative verve we see all too rarely in Scorsese these days.

It's a pity that Coppola's film is in the middle panel, since that means you can't walk out without missing the third – although at least at home you can spin through it. Simply put, it's a tedious, tasteless fiasco. Co-written with his daughter Sofia (showing none of her later potential), *Life Without Zoe* concerns a 12-year-old kid who lives a life of opulent ease in a swanky New York hotel, hanging out with a bunch of similarly moneyed, Chanel-clad brats. You get the idea we're meant to find them irresistible, but we don't. The story – or part of it – is a sliver of nonsense about the reunion of Zoe's beautiful, brilliant parents; the rest plays like a sick hymn to materialism, and it adds up to an all-time low for Coppola. Some of us still remember when he used to be a great director.

Oedipus Wrecks will be regarded by many as Woody Allen's return to form after his lugubrious Bergmanesque *September* and *Another Woman*. It's a madcap fantasy that revives the Jewish mother/son schtick to winning effect: we've seen it before, but it still charms. Completists will recall the 'magician's box' trick from one of his *New Yorker* short stories, The Kugelmass Episode, and if it's not quite as manically funny this time, it still affords the priceless shot of Woody smiling onscreen. Allen & Scorsese's stories: ★★★★ Coppola's story: ★ **AQ**

⓪ DIE NIBELUNGEN (1924)

Starring: *Gertrud Arnold (Kroenign Ure), Margarete Schön (Kriemhild), Hanna Ralph (Brumhild), Paul Richter (Siegrfried), Theodor Loos (Koenig Gunther), Hagen Tronje (Hans Adalbert von Schlettow), Etzel (Rudolf Klein-Rogge)*
Director: *Fritz Lang*
Screenwriters: *Fritz Lang, Thea Von Harbou*
E/144 mins./Fantasy/West Germany

Part I: Siegfried – Having vanquished a dragon and the dwarf king, the seemingly invincible Siegfried marries Kriemhild, the sister of Gunthe, the Burgundian king who is aided by his brother-in-law in the pursuit of Icelandic warrior queen, Brunhild. However, Siegfried is undone by a combination of sexual duplicity and court intrigue.

Part II: Kriemhild's Revenge – Siegfried's killer, Hagen Tronje steals his treasure. So, Kriemhild marries Etzel, King of the Huns in order to wreak vengeance on her treacherous uncle and his unscrupulous kinsmen.

Fritz Lang spent two years in pre-production and a further nine months filming this remarkable two-part epic. His new wife, Thea von Harbou, primarily based her screenplay on the fabled medieval verse saga, although she also drew on Wagner's *Ring Cycle* and Friedrich Hebbel's 19th-century play, *Die Nibelungen*, in which she had once starred.

But this was less a literary enterprise than a demonstration of German cinematic might. Keen to brandish its prowess after the merger with Decla-Bioscop made it the biggest film studio outside Hollywood, UFA encouraged Lang and set designers Otto Hunte, Karl Vollbrecht and Erich Kettelhut to indulge their imaginations and, inspired by artists like Wilhelm von Kaulbach, Caspar David Friedrich and Arnold Böcklin, they created an imposingly mythical neverland that epitomised the project's self-conscious grandeur.

But while the art direction and the picture's sheer ambition were praised by many critics, others accused Lang of stressing the monumental over the human. Indeed, later scholars, including Siegfried Kracauer, suggested that the film's architecture had influenced Albert Speer's design of the Nuremburg Rallies and Leni Riefenstahl's notorious documentary, *Triumph of the Will*. However, many non-fascists espoused poetic patriotism and while Lang admitted that his intention had been to restore German pride after the Great War, he was not responsible for the Nazis championing *Siegfried* (rather than its sequel, which depicted Aryans succumbing to Asians) or the release of a propagandist sound version, complete with a Wagnerian score.

Ironically, *Die Nibelungen* disappointed at the domestic box office, with audiences finding the complex narrative confusing and the pacing ponderous. The meticulously choreographed acting certainly tends to the grandiloquent. But Margarete Schön persuasively passed from being lovesick to hate-fuelled in a display of duality that anticipated Maria and the Robot's in *Metropolis*. Moreover, the dragon slaying and the 45-minute battle with the Huns were impressive set pieces, with the latter being handled with laudable formal and rhythmic precision. Consequently, this remains a silent landmark, whose technical ingenuity and fantastical scope finds echo in *The Lord of the Rings* trilogy. ★★★★ **DP**

⓪ NICHOLAS AND ALEXANDRA (1971)

Starring: *Michael Jayston (Nicholas II), Janet Suzman (Alexandra), Roderic Noble (Alexis), Ania Marson (Olga), Lynne Frederick (Tatiana), Candace Glendenning (Marie), Fiona Fullerton (Anastasia), Rasputin (Tom Baker), Lenin (Michael Bryant)*
Director: *Franklin S. Schaffner*
Screenwriters: *James Goldman, Edward Bond, based on a book by Robert K. Massie*
PG/183 mins./Historical Drama/UK
Awards: *Academy Awards – Best Art Direction-Set Decoration, Best Costume*

Tsar Nicholas II of Russia is so devoted to his capricious wife Alexandra that he allows her to sway the conduct of domestic and foreign policy, with the result that both Rasputin and Lenin are able to exploit their weakness and incongruity.

Having respectively won Oscars for *Lawrence of Arabia* and *Patton*, producer Sam Spiegel and director Franklin J. Schaffner were no strangers to historical epics. Yet, they got the tone of this lavish biopic of the last Tsar so wrong that a fascinating subject was reduced to costumed soap opera. Working from the bestseller by Robert K. Massie, screenwriters James Goldman and Edward Bond not only tried to pack too much detail into 183 minutes, but they also saddled the cast with reams of magniloquent dialogue that veered from the trite to the mawkish and bombastic.

However, the film's greatest fault was its bid to turn an inept ruler and his headstrong wife into tragic victims of domestic strife and the machinations of ruthless opportunists. Nicky and Alex are presented as a devoted couple who would have enjoyed an idyllic existence if they hadn't been burdened with the responsibilities of power and the strain of coping with a haemophiliac son.

But such an approach ridiculously diminishes the role they played in the deaths of millions of their subjects between 1894 and 1917 and the splendid BBC series *Fall of Eagles* came much closer to capturing Nicholas's Hamlet-like genius for indecision and the prejudicial snobbery of his German spouse, whose insistence on this weak man ruling as an autocrat consigned his fond family to their doom.

Michael Jayston and Janet Suzman struggle to cut through the script's deferential attitude to create credible characters, while the complex agendas of Tom Baker's Rasputin, Michael Bryant's Lenin and Brian Cox's Trotsky are depreciated into accessible clichés. The film deservedly won Oscars for its costumes and the ingenious art direction that Russified the Spanish and Yugoslav locations. But the wilful focus on a sentimentalised love story rather than the reign's momentous political and military events makes this a dull record of a compelling period. ★★★ **DP**

⓪ NICKLEODEON (1976)

Starring: *Ryan O'Neal (Leo Harrigan), Burt Reynolds (Buck Greenway), Tatum O'Neal (Alice Forsyte), Brian Keith (H.H. Cobb), Stella Stevens (Marty Reeves), John Ritter (Franklin Frank), Jane Hitchcock (Kathleen Cooke), Jack Perkins (Michael Gilhooley), Brion James (Bailiff)*
Director: *Peter Bogdanovich*
Screenwriters: *Peter Bogdanovich, W.D. Richter*
U/121 mins./Comedy/USA-UK

Failed lawyer Leo Harrigan becomes a director in the pioneering days of early American cinema, specialising in slapstick comedies featuring stunt man Buck Greenway and short-sighted gamine Kathleen Cooke.

Having lost a reported $6 million on *At Long Last Love*, his shambolic attempt at reviving the movie musical, Peter Bogdanovich contributed $500,000 of his own money to this fond, often fact-based, but deeply flawed tribute to the chaotic and occasionally violent world of filmmaking in Hollywood's infancy. The heroic efforts of America's independent producers to resist the monopolising tyranny of the Motion Picture Patents Company between 1908-17 should have made for compelling viewing. But Bogdanovich allows nostalgia to cloud his vision and, consequently, he devotes too much time to the mechanics of early movie making and not enough to his potentially engaging characters.

A respected critic before he turned director, Bogdanovich clearly knew his stuff and he not only captured something of the dangers involved in staying one step ahead of the MPPC's hired goons, but he also the celebrated the exhilarating nature of making pictures on the hoof, as inspiration and finances allowed. However, he singularly failed to rise to the challenge of paying homage to the likes of Mack Sennett, as his slapstick pastiches simply weren't funny – a fact that is doubly puzzling considering that not only was Bogdanovich such a keen student of the medium, but his knockabout passages in *What's Up, Doc?* had been so accomplished.

Irving Cummings had covered some of the same territory in *Hollywood Cavalcade* (1939), in which Don Ameche had played the pioneer whose ambitions were eventually thwarted by the advent of Talkies. But while Bogdanovich invested his film with considerably more affection than Cummings had mustered, he only had Burt Reynolds, Brian Keith and John Ritter at his disposal, instead of Al Jolson, Buster Keaton and Rin Tin Tin, Jr. Moreover, he succumbed to the same clichés and stereotypes, right down to Ryan O'Neal's wannabe realising the game is up at the premiere of *The Birth of a Nation*, while Ameche saw the writing on the wall at a screening of *The Jazz Singer*.

This is a well-meaning and often diverting picture. But it lacks focus and soul. ★★★ **DP**

NIGHT AND FOG (NUIT ET BROUILLARD) (1955)

Starring: *Reinhard Heydrich (Himself), Heinrich Himmler (Himself), Adolf Hitler (Himself), Julius Streacher (Himself), Michel Bouquet (Recitant/Narrator)*
Director: *Alain Resnais*
Screenwriter: *Jean Cayrol*
15/32 mins./Documentary/France

A devastating brief analysis of the Holocaust that seeks to identify exactly who perished in the concentration camps and who was responsible for the execution of such heinous crimes.

François Truffaut considered this 33-minute documentary to be the greatest film ever made. Yet, neither director Alain Resnais nor writer Jean Cayrol was particularly keen to work on it.

Inspired by a 1954 exhibition at the Institut Pédagogique National, producer Anatole Dauman asked Resnais to direct a study of the Holocaust. But Resnais was reluctant to express opinions on an event he had not witnessed at first hand and agreed only if Cayrol scripted the commentary. However, the novelist, who had survived Mauthausen and recorded his feelings in the 1946 volume *Poèmes de la Nuit et du Brouillard*, had no desire to revisit painful memories and was only persuaded to accept the commission by Chris Marker, who had collaborated with Resnais on his anti-colonial study of ethnic art, *Les Statues Meurent Aussi*.

The juxtaposition of colour images of the deserted environs of Auschwitz and Maïdenek with monochrome stills and newsreel footage gives the film a chilling immediacy, while also suggesting Resnais's perennial themes of memory and the difficulty of recollection. Abetted by Cayrol's commentary (voiced with a disconcerting lack of emotion by Michel Bouquet) and Hanns Eisler's sombre score, Resnais's prowling camera forces the viewer to look at what now seem unremarkable places and contemplate how easily they could become sites of mass extermination. The contrast between these stark realities and the stylised recreations of Hollywood-ised versions could not be more marked.

Yet some critics were less than impressed by Resnais's decision to impose an artistic aesthetic on such harrowing material. Others lamented the failure to count the 300,000 murdered gays and lesbians among the other ethnic, religious and political groupings who perished alongside the Jews, while others still dismissed the film's conclusion that such atrocities have always happened and will continue to do so unless we exercises constant vigilance as a feeble lesson to draw from such unprecedented barbarism.

But while *Night and Fog* all too evidently reflected the failings of imperfect humanity, it remains a powerful and profoundly moving memoir to the dead. Moreover, it encouraged others to explore the Shoah in greater depth. ★★★★ **DP**

A NIGHT AT THE OPERA (1935)

Starring: *Groucho Marx (Otis B. Driftwood), Chico Marx (Fiorello), Harpo Marx (Tomasso), Kitty Carlisle (Rosa Castaldi), Allan Jones (Roccardo Baroni), Walter Woolf King (Rodolfo Lassparri), Sig Rumann (Herman Gottlieb) Margaret Dumont (Mrs Claypool)*
Director: *Sam Wood*
Screenwriters: *George S. Kaufman, Morrie Ryskind, Al Boasberg, Bert Kalmar, Harry Ruby, based on a story by James Kevin McGuinnes*
U/90 mins./Comedy/USA

Promoter Otis B. Driftwood tries to persuade wannabe socialite Mrs Claypool to invest in Herman Gottlieb's opera company, whose arrogant star, Rodolfo Lassparri incurs the wrath of singing lovers Riccardo Baroni and Lassparri's dresser and Baroni's agent, Tomasso and Fiorello.

The Marx Brothers's sixth film was a double departure. It was not only their first picture without Zeppo, but it was also marked their debut at MGM, after they had been released by Paramount following the commercial disappointment of *Duck Soup*. Producer Irving G. Thalberg had initially irked Groucho, Chico and Harpo by telling them that their pacifist romp had been a stinker. But, he won them over by promising them improved production values and a musical comedy format that would provide a more logical basis for their inspired lunacy.

In addition to enlisting Allan Jones and Kitty Carlisle as the singing juveniles, Thalberg also suggested that the Marxes tested their best sketches before live audiences to hone the material and fine-tune the timing by gauging the amount of laughter each joke received. Happy to return to their vaudeville roots, the Brothers soon realised that this technique gave them a greater say over their material and they were able to bring in veteran gagman Al Boasberg to burnish material submitted by regular scribes George S. Kaufman and Morrie Ryskind.

Ironically, the stateroom skit (which is now regarded as one of the trio's finest five minutes) was nearly cut because of audience indifference. However, it provided the ideal opening balance to the climactic destruction of Rodolfo's production of Verdi's *Il Trovatore*, which rivals any chaos wrought by Messrs Laurel and Hardy.

Yet there are quieter moments of delirious verbal dexterity, such as Groucho's attempt to persuade Margaret Dumont to part with her millions and his ripping discussion with Chico of the inconvenient contract (complete with its sanity clause). Moreover, the musical interludes are also apposite and charming, particularly Chico and Harpo's rendition of 'Cosi-Cosa'.

Purists always rank the Paramount pictures over those made at MGM. But, while this may not be the funniest Marx movie, it's undoubtedly the most polished. ★★★★ **DP**

NIGHT MAIL (1936)

Starring: *John Grierson (Commentary), Stuart Legg (Commentary)*
Directors: *Harry Watt, Basil Wright*
Screenwriter: *W.H. Auden*
U/25 mins./Documentary/UK

An insight into the work undertaken by Post Office employees on the overnight mail special between London and Scotland.

John Grierson not only coined the term 'documentary' to describe a film attempting the creative treatment of reality, but he was also the father of the British Documentary Movement, whose influence continues to be felt in UK pictures today. His primary aim was to focus on everyday activities that audiences could readily identify with and, thus, he sought to improve community accord by giving each class grouping an insight into their neighbours' contribution to the general good.

However, Grierson was also an artist whose funding invariably came from state or commercial sponsorship. Consequently, he had to inform and persuade, as well as entertain, and this GPO Film Unit short was designed to reassure the public that not only was their mail safe within the vast network that transported it from postboxes and counters to the doorstep, but also that the government was doing a decent job in keeping such a complex system working efficiently.

Grierson began the project by asking a number of writers to contribute pieces on journeys between Euston and Edinburgh and then dispatched Harry Watt and cameramen Chick Fowle and Jonah Jones to record images that best conjured up their observations. But, despite the naturalistic sequences of the postmen bantering as they worked and the clipped commentary explaining procedures and disseminating statistics, Grierson decided that the film lacked a human touch and he commissioned W.H. Auden to compose verses identifying both those who had sent and those who would receive the various letters and packages being sorted on the night mail.

Collaborating with editor R.Q. McNaughton, sound supervisor Alberto Cavalcanti and co-director Basil Wright, Auden wrote to suit the visual rhythms and dozens of suggestions were discarded before the lines were finally spoken by Stuart Legg and Grierson himself to Benjamin Britten's rousing score. The result was a masterpiece of cinematic lyricism, whose evocative atmosphere has been further enhanced by the passing of steam. ★★★★★ **DP**

NIGHT OF THE COMET (1984)

Starring: *Catherine Mary Stewart (Regina), Robert Beltran (Hector), Kelli Maroney (Samantha), Geoffrey Lewis (Carter)*
Director: *Thom Eberhardt*
Screenwriter: *Thom Eberhardt*
15/94 mins./Sci-fi/USA

A passing comet wipes out almost all of humanity. Valley girls Regina and Samantha survive the apocalypse and hook up with a Chicano truck driver, then cope with deformed zombies and mad scientists.

An enjoyable throwback to 1950s science fiction, which has gained a nostalgic glow of its own for encapsulating 1980s archetypes: the big-hair teenage heroines see the end of the world as a great excuse to hit the mall for a shopping spree to the tune of 'Girls Just Want to Have Fun'.

After a plot device filched from *The Day of the Triffids* gets rid of all the spoilsports in the world (ie: parents), a few red filters and some ferocious but tacky zombies turn the streets and suburbs of Los Angeles into an alien landcsape. It falls into the movie buff in-joke genre beloved of John Landis and Joe Dante, with a heroine who survives the wiping out of humanity because her boyfriend is locked inside a cinema pirating a print of *It Came From Outer Space* and finds room in the cast for Roger Corman/Andy Warhol icon Mary Woronov as a suicidal femme fatale who brings a touch of melancholy to the film. In the villainy department, the film is well served by eyeballs-akimbo Geoffrey Lewis as an evil scientist who wants to exterminate the survivors.

Its mix of black humour and horror is exemplified by a sequence with a pair of mutating nurses chattering about how much they like working with children as they prepare to asphyxiate a couple of kids whose blood they want to drain – which sets up a darkly gruesome punchline, 'gone to see Santa Claus'.

Director Thom Eberhardt seemed to be a coming name, but after the Sherlock Holmes parody *Without A Clue* slipped to TV movies and series episodes. ★★★ **KN**

NIGHT OF THE DEMON (1957)

Starring: *Dana Andrews (Dr John Holden), Peggy Cummins (Joanna Harrington), Niall MacGinnis (Dr Julian Karswell), Maurice Denham (Professor Henry Harrington)*
Director: *Jacques Tourneur*
Screenwriters: *Charles Bennett, Hal E. Chester, based on the story* Casting The Runes *by M.R. James*
Unrated/95 mins./Horror/USA

Dr John Holden ventures to London to attend a paranormal psychology symposium with the intention to expose devil cult leader, Julian Karswell but ends up with an invitation to stay at his estate instead.

Legend has it that the prop man working on Jacques Tourneur's *Night Of The Demon* was one day asked to produce 'two sets of runic symbols'. Some time later he returned clutching an orchestral cymbal in each hand. 'We didn't have any runic,' the prop man explained. 'Will brass do?'

Would that this piece of cinematic apocrypha were true because Tourneur had precious little else to smile about while making what is recognised as one of the great supernatural horror movies of all time.

Tourneur had made his name with films like *Cat People* (1942) and *The Leopard Man* (1943) which, while undoubtedly horror vehicles, concentrated on psychological subtlety rather than special effects. In a Jacques Tourneur movie, more often than not, it is what you don't see that sends shivers down your spine rather than what you do. It was an approach that he fully intended to continue on *Night Of The Demon*. But the film's producer, Hal E. Chester, had other ideas.

'Hal was a real little schmuck,' Dana Andrews would later recall. 'He would come up and start telling Jacques how to direct the picture. Jacques would say, "Now, now, Hal" and try to be nice. But I just said, "Look, you little son-of-a-bitch, you want me to walk off the picture? I didn't come all the way over here to have the producer tell me what he thinks about directing the picture. Let the director direct the picture!" ' Most of the arguments revolved around the depiction of the titular demon itself. Tourneur would later claim that he didn't want to show the demon at all, preferring to imply its presence through the use of smoke. Certainly it seems that, at the very most, he intended to show this mythical beast only at the end of the film. But Chester insisted that the demon not only appear at the end but, much to Tourneur's dismay, at the beginning as well.

He also featured it heavily in the film's advertising material, which rather diminished what little shock value this less-than-terrifying vision possessed in the first place. Thankfully, Tourneur's talent was such that the rest remained a remorselessly nerve shredding ride as Holden slowly begins to realise that he is caught in a trap which he knows cannot logically exist, but which he must nevertheless escape. In this the director was more than ably assisted by legendary designer Ken Adam – later to find fame with his sets for *Dr Strangelove* and the Bond movies – whose work is so spooky it pretty much counts as a character in its own right.

Although dismissed as 'melodramatic' by *Film Daily* when released, Tourneur's movie rapidly gained a cult following and, in 1967, *Cahiers du Cinema* devoted a page and a half to praising his work.

What the film would have been like without Chester's intervention will, alas, never be known. Most people agree that the demon should never have been seen, although certainly *Night Of The Demon*'s writer, Charles Bennett, for one, never forgave the producer's ruinous meddling.

'I had to sit by while Chester made the biggest balls-up of a good script that I have ever seen,' he claimed years afterwards, adding that the appearance of the demon, 'took a major movie down to the level of crap. If Chester walked up my driveway now I'd shoot him dead.' ★★★★ **CC**

THE NIGHT OF THE HUNTER (1955)

Starring: *Robert Mitchum (Harry Powell), Shelley Winters (Willa Harper), Lillian Gish (Rachel Cooper), James Gleason (Birdie Steptoe), Evelyn Varden (Icey Spoon), Peter Graves (Ben Harper)*
Director: *Charles Laughton*
Screenwriter: *James Agee, from the novel by Davis Grubb*
12/93 mins./Drama/Thriller/USA

A sinister crook posing as a preacher pursues two children for the secret they are privy to of the location of a cache of money.

Film critics have a lot to answer for. Or at least they did in 1955 when Charles Laughton's masterpiece *The Night Of The Hunter* hit cinema screens. 'A horrible yarn ... a repulsive picture,' carped the *Daily Mirror*. 'Too often the effect is funny rather than frightening,' pronounced *The Times*; 'It should have been a sinister film, but mainly it was grin-ister,' the *Evening Standard* inexplicably declared. Ho ho. Frankly, you wonder if they were watching the same movie because, once all these geriatric buffoons were safely ensconced in seaside retirement homes for distressed film-folk, decent film pundits have recognised the true majesty of Laughton's achievement.

'One of the most frightening movies ever made,' said Pauline Kael and even the terminally bad-tempered Leslie Halliwell admitted, 'There are splendidly imaginative moments.' But by then the damage was done.

The howls of derision from the critics coupled with the financial road accident the movie became meant Laughton would never direct again. It's not exaggerating to say that this is one of cinema's greatest tragedies because *The Night Of The Hunter* is one of the finest movies ever made in any genre. If it doesn't transcend genre entirely.

It is almost impossible to categorise. There are elements of the horror movie, particularly since Laughton shoots portions of the film in the shadow-drenched German Expressionist style of *The Cabinet Of Dr Caligari* (1919) (though, typically of this film's uniqueness, some sequences are shot entirely naturalistically). Towards the end it heads towards a kind of sentimental Christmas melodrama reminiscent of Capra, and there are even elements of broad comedy.

But it is a crime movie in the sense that the plot revolves around two separate crimes, the first when Ben Harper, father of incalculably cute kiddiewinks John and Pearl, lifts a load of cash and hides it in Pearl's ragdoll before being hanged and the second when 'preacher' Harry Powell (Mitchum, in the finest performance of his career) arrives, having met the condemned man in jail, intending to hornswoggle the widow into marrying him and retrieve the loot. 'Lord you sure knowed what you was doing when you put me in this cell at this very time,' he obsequiously intones. 'A man with ten thousand dollars somewhere, and a widow in the makin'!'

Laughton's direction, together with Stanley Cortez's cinematography, is a feast of delights rivalling Welles' *Citizen Kane* in his expansive use of technical innovations. There are ambitious helicopter shots, deep focus, cutaway sets, underwater photography (a stunning, almost surreal image of a corpse sitting in a car at the bottom of the river, hair streaming in amongst the river weed) as well as incredible use of light and shadow.

A scene in which little Johnny tells his sister a bedtime story only to have the silhouette of the behatted preacher loom over him is one of the most terrifying since Max Schreck's hand crawled up the wall in *Nosferatu* (1922). But it is the children's trip down the river as they escape from Powell after he has murdered their mother, undoubtedly one of the most effortlessly lyrical, enchanting sequences in cinema, which sticks in the mind the longest.

Frogs, rabbits and even spiders look on protect even, as the fairy-tale-like drift down the river continues until the idyll is broken as they wake in a hayloft and hear the tones of Powell's singing, endlessly pursuing them. 'Don't he ever sleep ... ?' the boy bleakly wonders.

But if the machinery of the movie is impressive, it is Robert Mitchum that is at its incredible dramatic core. Preacher Harry Powell is one of cinema's greatest villains; the archetypal evil stepfather that only a child can see through.

From one of the first moments we meet him, sitting bolt upright at a strip show ('There are things you do hate Lord,' he hisses. 'Perfumed smellin' things, key things, things with curly hair ...') we know we're in the presence of a perfectly realised psychopathic misogynist. This is a man who shows a five-year-old girl the knife he has just cut her mother's throat with; who celebrates his wedding night by berating his newly betrothed. It's a picture of utter, simpering mendacity driven by Mitchum's delicious performance. There's been nothing like it on screen before or since (though Robert De Niro obviously drew on it for his Max Cady in Martin Scorsese's *Cape Fear* (1991) who, ironically, Mitchum played in the original).

And that might be why the movie failed so dismally on its first release. This is a film with a pessimistic message about wolves in priests' clothing and in a country where the likes of Jimmy Swaggart, Jerry Falwell and their spiritually fraudulent friends continue to milk the credulous population for money, no wonder this was a movie that didn't play well. ★★★★★ **AS**

NIGHT OF THE LIVING DEAD (1968)

Starring: *Judith O'Dea (Barbara), Russell Streiner (Johnny), Duane Jones (Ben), Karl Hardman (Harry Cooper), Keith Wayne (Tom)*
Director: *George A. Romero*
Screenwriter: *John A. Russo, from a story by George A. Romero*
18/95 mins./Horror/USA

A returning space probe seeds the atmosphere with radiation, and the recently dead revive as flesh-eating ghouls. Ben and Barbara seek refuge from the monsters in a farmhouse.

Made in 1968 on a hand-to-mouth budget by enthusiasts in Pittsburgh, this suitably grungy off-Hollywood production became one of the most influential horror movies ever made.

George A. Romero's film has had official sequels (*Dawn of the Dead*, *Day of the Dead*, *Land of the Dead*), remakes (one in 3-D), parodies (*Return of the Living Dead*, *Shaun of the Dead*), rip-offs (*Living Dead at the Manchester Morgue*) and several horribly mutilated re-releases with useless extra footage, new soundtracks or colorisation. It changed the face of the horror film, setting a precedent for the work of directors like Tobe Hooper, Wes Craven, John Carpenter and David Cronenberg in the 1970s.

In fact, it's such an important movie that it runs the risk of disappointing first-time viewers who've seen all the later films that copied its licks – part of its strength is that it's not a glossy, predictable Hollywood horror and so it has a grainy, semi-amateur, black and white look which gives it a dread sense of conviction. The shambling dead besiege a group of squabbling wannabe survivors in an isolated farmhouse, eating the entrails of those too inept to see them off with a bullet to the brain.

Many of its plot strands were unprecedented: a heroine who reacts credibly to an appalling situation by becoming a useless catatonic, a black hero who finally has less to fear from the zombies than from the ghoul-hunting posse combing the countryside as if on a Vietnam search and destroy mission, news bulletins that include expert advice ('kill the brain and you kill the ghoul') from the men on the ground, a relentlessly pessimistic ending. ★★★★★ **KN**

THE NIGHT PORTER (IL PORTIERE DI NOTTE) (1974)

Starring: *Dirk Bogarde (Maximilian Theo Aldorfer), Charlotte Rampling (Lucia Atherton), Philippe Leroy (Klaus), Gabriele Ferzetti (Hans)*
Director: *Liliana Cavani*
Screenwriter: *Liliana Cavani, based on a story by Barbara Alberti, Italo Moscati, Amedeo Pagani*
18/122 mins./Drama/Romance/Italy/USA

In 1957, Lucia recognises Max, the night porter in a Vienna hotel, as the Nazi officer who became her lover and protector when she was in a concentration camp. She is drawn back into a semi-sadomasochist relationship.

While the kinkier scenes of this once-controversial Liliana Cavani sadoromance, most of which involve broken glass and/or Nazi uniform, exert an undeniable prurient fascination, *The Night Porter* suffers from a storyline as rambling and illogical as the behaviour of its peculiar characters. The heat between the stars comes in glum scenes of sex and humiliation, but the actual line story turns on a sensitive Nazi's attempts to protect his aristocratic Jewish mistress, first from the regular murderers in the death camp and then from a shadowy undercover organisation of war criminals who see her as a dangerous witness who needs to be eliminated.

It has an interesting, sombre look, while Bogarde and Rampling work hard to make the psychology seem a lot less silly than it is, and a compelling erotic/horrific/tasteless scene retelling the story of Salome in fascist terms, but the movie is too protracted and pompous to get away with its extremely dubious *Last Tango in Paris*-style sexual politics. Like Luchino Visconti's *The Damned* (also with Italy's favourite British Nazi, Bogarde) and Tinto Brass's *Salon Kitty* – not to mention video favourites *SS Experiment Camp*, *Deported Women of the SS Special Section* and *Red Nights of the Gestapo* – this represents a peculiar 1960s-70s blip of Italian films which are both repulsed by and enamoured with the iconography and the atrocities of Italy's wartime Axis ally.

Rampling, the only actress ever cast as a concentration camp victim who didn't have to diet for the role, posed for a memorable poster, coyly topless in elbow-length gloves and an SS officer's hat. ★★ **KN**

A NIGHT TO REMEMBER (1958)

Starring: Kenneth More (Second Officer Charles Herbert Lightoller), Ronald Allen (Mr. Clarke), Robert Ayres (Maj. Arthur Peuchen), Honor Blackman (Mrs Liz Lucas)
Director: Roy Ward Baker
Screenwriter: Eric Ambler, based on the book by Walter Lord
PG/123 mins./Drama/Biography/USA
Awards: *Golden Globes – Best English-Language Foreign Film*

Largely accurate account of the sinking of the ill-fated ocean liner, with Second Officer Kenneth More as the figure linking everyone on board.

This sober account of the sinking of the *Titantic* was only recently unearthed, having previously been forgotten in favour of Jean Negulesco's *Titanic* (1953), starring Clifton Webb and Barbara Stanwyck. (Not forgetting Herbert Selpin's best-forgotten Nazi version of 1943.) Neither the first nor the most successful *Titanic* movie, *A Night to Remember*, based on the bestseller by Walter Lord, is still the best of the lot.

A crisply starched Kenneth More may lack DiCaprio's sexy glare, but proves a far more effective focal character, as the man from whose perspective the drama is seen. Baker's movie is also more inventive technically than Cameron's, and braver too, in that Kenneth More is only nominally the star – it's the story that matters. ★★★★★ **AC**

NIGHT WATCH (NOCHNOY DOZOR) (2004)

Starring: *Konstantin Khabensky (Anton Gorodetsky), Vladimir Menshov (Geser), Mariya Poroshina (Svetlana), Galina Tyunina (Olga), Yuri Kutsenko (Ignat), Aleksei Chadov (Kostya)*
Director: *Timur Bekmambetov*
Screenwriters: *Timur Bekmambetov, Laeta Kalogridis, based on the novel by Sergei Lukyanenko*
15/114 mins./Action/Fantasy/Horror/Russia

For the past millennium, the eternally battling forces of light and darkness have kept an uneasy truce. Opposing undercover agencies – the Night Watch and Day Watch – have been set up to ensure it remains unbroken. But the conflict could soon be reaching its Armageddon as a prophecy involving the arrival of a 'Great One' threatens to be fulfilled.

With its good-versus-evil theming, messianic prophecy plotline and lineup of the usual supernatural suspects (vampires, witches, changelings), *Night Watch* isn't, on the surface at least, the most original of fantasy-horrors. We've seen the clandestine clash of immortals before, while no script can get away with references to a 'Great One' these days without summoning up images of Keanu Reeves calmly halting bullets with a waft of his palm. Yet, though all its ingredients may appear stale, *Night Watch* cooks them up in such a smart way that the end product tangs of originality.

The twist is, this Russian box-office phenomenon is a movie less about a supernatural war than a supernatural cold war. With Light and Dark so evenly matched, the only logical outcome is total mutual annihilation, so their respective leaders call off their apocalyptic royal rumble in the first five minutes. This puts the conflict on a psychological level; the story's more about volition and manipulation than kung fu and gunfire, centring on beleaguered everyman Anton, a human whose belatedly discovered psychic talents hurl him into the middle of both sides' plottings.

The simplistic concept mutates into a surprisingly complex story, introducing a whole host of enticing characters, many of whom shift offstage only a few scenes later. It is important to view *Night Watch* as Part One of a trilogy, otherwise those loosely hanging plot strands will leave you feeling like you've watched an elaborate TV show pilot rather than a movie.

'Elaborate' being the key word – director Timur Bekmambetov, who's namechecked the likes of Tarantino, the Wachowskis and Ridley Scott (plus he's clearly a *Buffy* fan), ensures virtually every sequence is festooned with idiosyncrasies. At one point, a twitchy, spider-legged doll skitters across the floor; at another, a customised flashlight is used to maim a vampire. Even the subtitles join in, Bekmambetov seamlessly weaving them into the action, sometimes having them whisp onto and off the screen in smoky italics, sometimes blasting them out in capitals. His work, to risk an obvious word, is spellbinding – and the sequel, *Day Watch*, should ensure a cult in the making. ★★★★ **DJ**

THE NIGHTMARE BEFORE CHRISTMAS (1993)

Starring the voices of: *Danny Elfman (singing Jack Skellington and others), Chris Sarandon (speaking Jack Skellington), Catherine O'Hara (Sally), William Hickey (Dr Finkelstein)*
Director: *Henry Selick*
Screenwriters: *Tim Burton, Michael McDowell, Caroline Thompson*
PG/76 mins./Animation/USA

Bored with his lot Jack Skellington, the pumpkin king of Halloween Town, decides to take over Christmas Town, kidnapping Santa Claus and giving Xmas a Halloweeny make-over.

Everything we have come expect from the variable Goth-hued imagination of Tim Burton as presented in stop-motion form: thus it squeals with visual delight, strewn with loveable-morbid creations, ornate Danny Elfman compositions and has a story that runs out of juice halfway through. We are lazily encouraged to just sit back and soak up the rickety gleam of its grotesquery of inspiration – dashing Jack himself is a xylophone-boned, pin-stripped lounge singer-type, his dog, Zero, has a ghostly glowing nose, while his great love Sally is a rag doll who can wilfully unthread limbs – and ignore the deficiencies in its storytelling.

It's the schizophrenia of Burton, although the main duties of directing slow-slow process of stop-animation went to Henry Sellick, he's less a Brother Grimm than an Edward Munch. Energy and art abound everywhere, especially in the glorious whirligigging dance scenes, except in the momentum of tale-telling. The characters are cool but limited, just more Gothic filaments for this black gown knitted for kiddiewinks with death obsessions. There's plenty of smart referencing: German expressionism to Cure videos, but it lacks the warmth, and social detail of Nick Park's *Claymation*. Park's worlds are reflections of reality, Burton/Sellick's is a lawless sprawl of dreams. ★★★ **IN**

Movie Trivia:
Tim Burton (born 1958)

Who he is: Former animator turned blockbuster Gothic stylist. Crazy-haired designer of quirky fantasies and twisted nightmares.

Hallmarks: Gothic design; Johnny Depp; Danny Elfman scores; scary-looking but good-hearted characters; outcast heroes; quirky, curvy worlds; bright colours against a dark background.

If you see one movie, see: *Edward Scissorhands* (1990)

◎ 1900 (1976)

Starring: *Robert De Niro (Alfredo Berlinghieri), Gérard Depardieu (Olmo Dalco), Dominique Sanda (Ada),Francesca Bertini (Sister Desolata), Stefania Sandrelli (Anita Foschi), Donald Sutherland (Attila), Laura Betti (Regina)*
Director: *Bernardo Bertolucci*
Screenwriters: *Franco Arcalli, Bernardo Bertolucci, Giuseppe Bertolucci*
18/247 mins/Drama/Italy-France-West Germany

Landowner's son Alfredo Berlinghieri and peasant pal Olmo Dalco grow apart when the former drifts into the fascist complicity that wrecks his marriage to Ada, while the latter romances socialist schoolteacher Anita Foschi, with whom he challenges the tyranny of estate foreman Attila and Alfredo's embittered cousin, Regina.

Bernardo Bertolucci devised *1900* to rival Luchino Visconti's *The Leopard* as the Italian national epic. Filmed over 10 months in the Emilia-Romagna countryside around Parma, it boasted a stellar international cast and was then the most expensive picture produced on the peninsula. However, Paramount insisted on reducing its original 320-minute running time to 247 minutes and the film was invariably shown in two parts, making it something of an endurance test for critics and audiences alike. Consequently, it met with a mixed reception on its initial release and only later developed a cult following that reinforced those isolated insistences that it was an instant classic.

In many ways, it was a companion piece to Bertolucci's *Before The Revolution*, as for all the Marxist triumphalism of its postwar sequences, Bertolucci was fully aware that he was anticipating rather than celebrating the final demise of the padrone, who managed to survive the fall of Fascism, just as Alfredo escaped the punishment meted out to Attila.

Thus, Bertolucci indulged himself in a little political theorising in the second half of the action, which lacked the dramatic drive of the opening segment, as it followed the fates of Alfredo and Olmo from their birth on 27 January 1901 (the day Verdi died), through the agrarian riots of 1908, the Great War, the rise of Fascism, the victory of the Partisans and the collapse of the Salo Republic.

As ever with Bertolucci, the story bears autobiographical traces, with Alfredo and Olmo striking some as a 'divided hero' whose contrasting traits represented the director's own conflicted opinions – hence his tendency to romanticise the peasant experience (with Vittorio Storaro's photography in the prewar phases owing much to the 19th-century Macchiaiuoli school of rural painting), while neglecting to condemn Alfredo for the complacency that enabled Fascism to take root.

But while he clearly admired Gérard Depardieu's feisty decency, Bertolucci was also so begrudgingly drawn to Robert De Niro's mannered passivity that he almost allowed this unusually ineffective performance to undermine the entire picture. Fortunately, its scope, scale and ambition ensured that it emerged as a flawed masterpiece. ★★★★ **DP**

◎ 1941 (1979)

Starring: *Dan Aykroyd (Sergeant Tree), Ned Beatty (Ward Douglas), John Belushi (Wild Bill Kelso), Lorraine Gray (Joan Douglas), Murrah Hamilton (Claude), Christopher Lee (Von Kleinschmidt)*
Director: *Steven Spielberg*
Screenwriters: *Robert Zemeckis, Bob Gale, from a story by Robert Zemeckis, Bob Gale, John Milius*
PG/113 mins./Comedy/USA

Shortly after the attack on Pearl Harbor, a Japanese submarine surfaces off the coast of California intent on striking at Los Angeles. Panic spreads among Americans who aren't yet fully prepared for World War II.

Steven Spielberg's greatest flop is one of those odd movies that seems more interesting years later than his many successes.

Coming off the blockbusting of *Jaws* (horror) and *Close Encounters* (science fiction), Spielberg felt obligated to tackle comedy and the war film on a similar scale. It has wonderfully timed slapstick weirdness, a once-in-a-lifetime cast (John Belushi, Dan Aykroyd, Nancy Allen, John Candy, Ned Beatty, Christopher Lee, Toshiro Mifune, Warren Oates, Slim Pickens, Mickey Rourke, Tim Matheson), a streak of insanity that shows another side of the American Excessive who is Steven Spielberg, plus a touching moment of calm and innocence amidst the chaos as Robert Stack's stone-faced general is discovered in the middle of a riot, quietly crying during an emotional highlight of *Dumbo*.

A script which John Wayne rejected in disgust as anti-American, *1941* attacks America's self-image as 'the greatest country in the world' by depicting Los Angelenos as complacent goons who don't need international enemies because they're so insanely intent on destroying each other ('that's one thing I don't want to see, Americans fighting Americans!') and even their beloved Christmas-decorated streets.

What Richard Dreyfuss does to his living room in *Close Encounters of the Third Kind*, the entire cast of *1941* do to the Greater Los Angeles area, so enthused are they with the idea of war that they have one before the enemy even shows up.

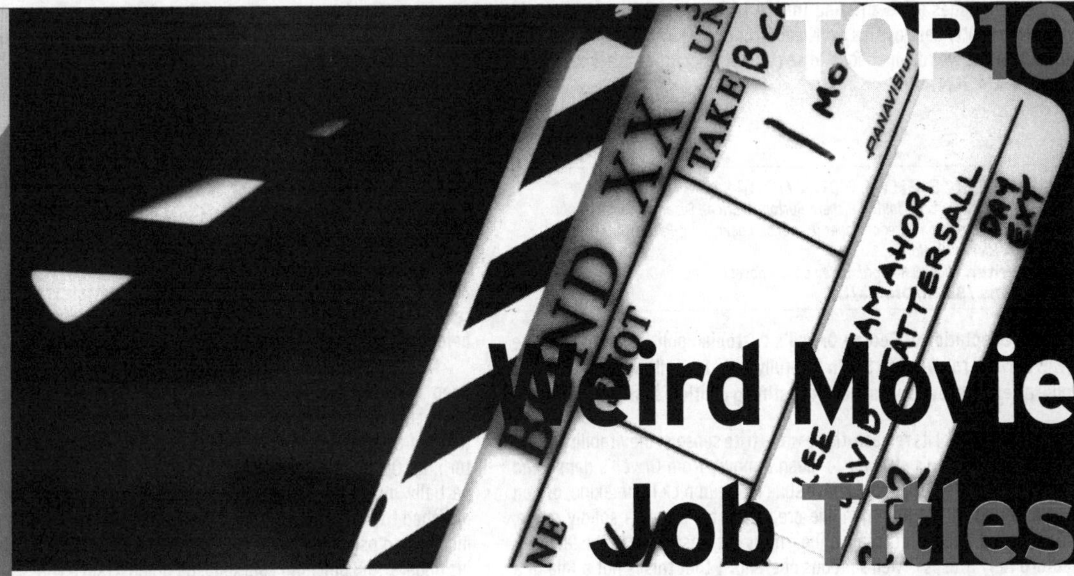

1 **Gaffer – The chief electrician on a film set, responsible for supplying, placing, lighting and maintaining the lights.**

2 **Best Boy – The assistant to the gaffer.**

3 **Boom Operator – The sound technician who operates the telescopic pole (aka the boom) with the microphone attached.**

4 **Foley Artist – A sound-effects artist who creates sounds that are recorded to match the images onscreen (e.g. footsteps on gravel). Named after sound effects pioneer Jack Foley.**

5 **Greensmen – The people responsible for the real and artificial trees and plants on set.**

6 **Grip – A stagehand responsible for many things: transporting and setting up equipment, props, the camera etc.**

7 **Dolly Grip – Stagehand who pushes the camera dolly (i.e. the trolley that the camera may be on).**

8 **Key Grip – The individual in charge of the grips.**

9 **Swing Gang – The team that sets up and dismantles a set for filming.**

10 **Craft Services – The team responsible for providing food and drink for the cast and crew.**

It's sometimes more amazing than it is funny, but the sequence in which Ned Beatty destroys his own beachfront home in order to fire a huge gun out to sea weirdly manages to say something either cracked or profound. ★★★ **KN**

NINETEEN EIGHTY-FOUR (1984)

Cast: *John Hurt (Winston Smith), Richard Burton (O'Brien), Suzanna Hamilton (Julia) Cyril Cusack (Charrington), Gregor Fisher (Parsons), Roger Lloyd-Pack (Waiter)*
Director: *Michael Radford*
Screenwriter: *Michael Radford, based on the novel by George Orwell*
15/113 mins./Sci-fi/Drama/UK

A timely adaptation of George Orwell's dystopian political satire, where lowly bureaucrat Winston Smith fatefully falls for fellow party member Julia, a secret subversive against the stifling political system.

Given the year of its release, there was a trite sense of inevitability about Michael Radford's attempt to glean a movie from Orwell's dense and moody classic. Yet, what could have sunk into gimmick filmmaking, driven by marketing rather than genuine creativity, turns out a solidly made, sternly acted, and faithful realisation. This is not least down to the fact that Radford fully grasps Orwell's modus operandi – that this is not a tale of a dreaded future at all, but a caustic parable of the writer's present (the late 40s). Thus, the year of its release is merely incidental, this is a movie set in a dystopian future-world yet chained to a bleak past somewhere on the vestiges of the Cold War.

This dichotomy is most apparent in Roger Deakins' murky, desaturated photography and the intricate, decayed production design. There is a junkyard decrepitude that infects the entire film, a forerunner of Gilliam's more esoteric *Brazil* (itself heavily influenced by the novel). You're confronted with a film occluded in misery, which makes it an endurance test but a rewarding journey all the same.

Orwell's dire sci-fi language – his indelible 'newspeak', 'thoughtcrime' and 'Big Brother' – sounds its warning bells as strikingly as when the novel was first published. The prophetic writer was demanding humanity be watchful of totalitarianism, be it fascism or communism, and in his dread post-Apocalyptic police state, watched over by the omnipresent Big Brother, sex has been banned, emotion ruled out, leaving the populous 'unpersoned' drones in a dark system.

As we trace Winston (Hurt, as ever, a master of the victimised) and Julia (Suzanna Hamilton)'s rebellion, their sex crimes, and his inexorable road to the dreaded door marked 101, Orwell's premonitions have gained a greater prescience still. He, and Radford, expose a society drugged on junk television and porn into submission. While Smith's task of 'rewriting' history and channelling propaganda bears all the hallmarks of endless political spin-doctoring. Remind you of anywhere?

Indeed, the only thing that truly hooks the film to the 80s, and hence dates it, is the steely synth score from the Eurhythmics, whose lumbering theme song ('Sex Crime') blurts out over the closing credits, cheapening those glowering visuals to the naff template of a pop video. ★★★ **IN**

A NIGHTMARE ON ELM STREET (1984)

Starring: *John Saxon (Lt Thompson), Ronee Blakley (Marge Thompson), Heather Langenkamp (Nancy Thompson), Amanda Wyss (Tina Gray), Jsu Garcia (Rod Lane), Johnny Depp (Glen Lantz), Charles Flesicher (Dr King), Joseph Whipp (Sgt Parker), Robert Englund (Freddy Krueger)*
Director: *Wes Craven*
Screenwriter: *Wes Craven*
18/91 mins./Horror/USA

Nancy and her friends are having violent nightmares that all feature one common element, a disfigured serial killer with a glove made of razors on his right hand. When one of the group is murdered in their sleep, Nancy realises that she must stay awake and try to uncover the truth behind this phantasmic killer Freddy Krueger.

There's a longstanding theory that dictates that if you dream you die, you actually do die, hence you always wake up at the critical moment. Subscribers to this theory believe it has something to do with inherent, subconscious defence mechanisms which prevent you succumbing to the reaper simply because your chosen midnight snack is cheese on toast. And anyone who dismisses it as a whiskery old wives' tale is still probably quite relieved to wake with a start after dreaming they are falling from a great height rather than having their scepticism put to the test.

No matter what your position, it's a notion that preys uncomfortably on deep-seated fears. A fact that obviously intrigued Craven, who exploits it to spine-chilling effect in this celebrated mid-80s shocker. Yet being something of a ghoul, Craven's premise is more specific and rather more disturbing. On Elm Street, if you dream you get slashed to ribbons by a partially incinerated psycho with a fistful of razor-sharp metal talons attached to his fingers, you really do get slashed to ribbons by a partially incinerated psycho with a fistful of razor-sharp metal talons attached to his fingers. And pinching yourself isn't going to save you.

A Nightmare On Elm Street was a shot in the arm for the fading teen slasher flick, one that Craven would once again rejuvenate with 1996's *Scream*. True to form, it centres on a group of hormonally charged American high-schoolers (among them big-screen debutante Johnny Depp who, spookily, starred in Tim Burton's *Edward Scissorhands* four years later) whose dreams are being infiltrated by a dead child-killer who is intent on bumping them off in extremely grisly fashion. First to go is Wyss who buys it in one of the most memorable instances of post-coital slaughter ever devised.

Craven cuts between Wyss's desperate dream-state struggle with the blade-handed maniac and her boyfriend (Corri), watching in horror as blood-spurting gashes appear on her body and an unseen force slams her against the ceiling. This is only topped by Depp's big scene in which, during an ill-advised nap, two disembodied arms burst through his mattress and pull him screaming into the void. As he disappears, a mighty geyser of blood erupts from the gaping hole in his bed. The Freudian implications of this do not, quite frankly, bear thinking about.

Apart from Depp, the rest of Elm Street's young cast have been largely forgotten. But in Freddy Krueger, played by the diminutive, moon-faced Englund, Craven created an enduring horror icon. With his peeling face, striped jersey and hideous killer mitt, Freddy has taken his rightful place alongside *Texas Chain Saw Massacre*'s Leatherface and the hockey-masked Jason Voorhees in cinema's celebrated chamber of horrors.

Moreover, he has the power to manipulate his environment, a domain in which his victims are at their most vulnerable. The dread of this will not be lost on anyone who has suffered a recurring nightmare or – worst of all – has ever woken in a sweat from one hellish sojourn in the land of nod only to realise they have stepped into another. On the downside, the denouement where Langenkamp lures Freddy into the real world, finally defeating him by the simple expedient of calling him 'shit' and turning her back, is something of a let down. Still, she does set him on fire first and there is an absolutely mental shock ending to savour. And if the riotous 80s fashions are occasionally the scariest thing on the screen (Depp's crop-top and jogging pant ensemble is particularly nerve-racking) there is more than enough here to ensure a sleepless night or two – Freddy bursting through the mirror while Langenkamp tries to persuade her reflection that it's all 'just a dream'; Wyss in an opaque, blood-smeared bodybag, appearing wraithlike in the classroom as Langenkamp drifts off to sleep; and the eerily prophetic children's song which opens and closes the movie.

And if that isn't enough to put ice in your veins, try this: Craven based the whole thing on a true story. The film stemmed from a series of articles in an LA paper about a group of Southeast Asian kids, all from the same neighbourhood, who died mysteriously in their sleep after a string of vivid nightmares. They probably weren't massacred by a stiletto-fingered sicko in a rugby shirt. But even so, the next time you find yourself back at school with no trousers on and the most frightening thing you've got to contend with is an A level physics exam you haven't revised for, count yourself lucky. ★★★★★ **SB**

A NIGHTMARE ON ELM STREET, PART 2: FREDDY'S REVENGE (1985)

Starring: *Mark Patton (Jesse Walsh), Robert Englund (Freddy Krueger), Kim Myers (Lisa Webber), Robert Rusler (Ron Grady), Clu Gulager (Mr Walsh), Hope Lange (Mrs Walsh)*
Director: *Jack Sholder*
Screenwriter: *David Chaskin, from a character by Wes Craven*
18/81 mins./Horror/USA

Jesse Walsh, the new kid on Elm Street, is troubled by dreams of ghost-murderer Freddy Krueger, who is scheming to get back into the real world through Jesse's body.

This hastily produced sequel ignores the dreamstalking premise that had made *A Nightmare on Elm Street* successful and reverts to the overfamiliar possession story.

There are clichés a-plenty, from the slow, low tracking shot past the ominously illuminated house that marks it out as 'a bad place' to the ludicrous finale in which the heroine defeats the monster by repeatedly and bathetically declaring her love for the drippy hero.

Robert Englund's Freddy begins his sad transformation from most fearsome bogeyman of the 1980s into a wisecracking goon, too often stepping out of the shadows to deliver punchlines while clacking his fingerknives.

Director Jack Sholder (*The Hidden*) delivers a lot of would-be scary idiocies: an exploding budgie (!), sports equipment with a mind of its own, human-headed dogs and (as was common in the 80s) the monster emerging from the rubbery ruins of its host's flesh.

Clu Gulager and Hope Lange have the thankless roles of the stupid parents who keep denying that there's anything wrong – and, in a strange kind of way, the film seems to be an allegory for Jesse's sexual confusion, as he repeatedly turns away from the willing girl to get close to half-naked guys (including the monster).

Lest the movie be accused of sensitivity, it also has the bullying gay gym teacher (Marshall Bell) tied up naked in the showers and whipped by possessed hoses.

The subsequent sequels, starting with *A Nightmare on Elm Street, Part 3: Dream Warriors*, ignored this film and went back to Wes Craven's playbook, though that didn't stop the series running out of steam by Part Five or Six ... ★ **KN**

A NIGHTMARE ON ELM STREET, PART 3: DREAM WARRIORS (1987)

Starring: *Heather Langenkamp (Nancy Thompson), Patricia Arquette (Kristen Parker), Laurence Fishburne, as Larry Fishburne (Max), Robert Englund (Freddy Krueger)*
Director: *Chuck Russell*
Screenwriters: *Wes Craven, Bruce Wagner, Chuck Russell, Frank Darabont, from a story by Wes Craven, Bruce Wagner, from characters by Wes Craven*
18/92 mins./Horror/USA

Nancy Thompson, last survivor of Elm Street, is now a psychiatrist whose patients are being stalked in their dreams by her old enemy, Freddy Krueger. When the kids start dying, Nancy resolves to confront Freddy.

After the misstep of *A Nightmare on Elm Street, Part 2: Freddy's Revenge*, New Line resolved to make a better sequel, calling in series creator Wes Craven (with *Wild Palms* writer Bruce Wagner) to craft a more elaborate storyline (and set-piece bad dreams), casting more interesting up-and-comers as Freddy fodder (Patricia Arquette, Laurence Fishburne) and giving director Chuck Russell (*The Mask*) something like an effects budget.

Heather Langenkamp, an appealing high school lead in the original, is miscast here as the world's only teenage psychiatrist, and a white streak in her hair doesn't help her get away with it. She's also jostled on all sides by better actors trying to take the film away, which means that the central plot thread tends to get lost.

However, the film delivers amazing scenes in spades, bringing to life the sort of bizarre images which used to be found only on comic book covers: a boy's veins are pulled from his limbs and used as strings to puppet-master him towards death, an antique tap grabs a girl's hand and sprouts Freddy's razornails, a victim is literally tongue-tied, a TV talkshow host (Dick Cavett) turns into Freddy and slashes guest Zsa Zsa Gabor ('who gives a fuck what you think, Zsa Zsa'), Freddy's bones rise from the grave as a Harryhausen-style skeleton and duel with cop John Saxon and shrink Craig Wasson in the scrapyard where he was dumped.

It's always a pleasure to see obnoxious American teenagers slaughtered like dogs, but it's especially nice to see them wiped out in such surreally imaginative ways. ★★★ **KN**

A NIGHTMARE ON ELM STREET 4: THE DREAM MASTER (1988)

Starring: *Robert Englund (Freddy Krueger), Lisa Wilcox (Alice), Rodney Eastman (Joey), Danny Hassel (Danny), Andras Jones (Rick), Tuesday Knight (Kristen Parker)*
Director: *Renny Harlin*
Screenwriters: *Brian Helgeland, Scott Pierce, from a story by William Kotzwinkle, Brian Helgeland, from a character by Wes Craven*
18/88 mins./Horror//USA

Freddy Krueger is brought back from Hell when a demon dog pisses on his bones. He kills the last surviving Elm Street kids, before homing in on Kristen, whose ability to draw others into her dreams gives him an opportunity to seek new victims.

Billed sixth in *A Nightmare on Elm Street*, Robert Englund's Freddy Krueger climbed the ladder of stardom and here won before-the-title status.

The pizza-faced monster followed the great Universal horror creations – the Mummy, Dracula, the Wolf Man – by getting heavily into merchandising – a TV anthology show (*Freddy's Nightmares*), books, models, dolls, gloves, masks, posters, etc. Some expressed concern that a child murderer should become such a cult hero, but Freddy only really broke through into the mainstream by neglecting his roots.

Like a punk rocker who becomes a big star in an MOR band, Freddy stopped being a perverse, sleazy character and became a walking joke who kills victims with a James Bond-ish wisecrack and opts for surreal Struwwelpeter touches like matching the method of death to the victim's single character note.

In this fourth film, directed by Renny Harlin before he became a blockbuster guy, impressive effects are undone by silliness. A girl's transformation into a giant cockroach – more Cronenbergian than Kafkaesque, of course – involves squirm-inducing modelwork and an imposing insectoid monster, but the laughable performance of the bimbette actress, who flaps her extended arms like a mildly upset cheerleader, scuppers the sequence.

With a plot that ties up loose ends from earlier films and introduces yet another generation of disposable young people ('Did you ever look at our town's history – it's not exactly a safe place to be a teenager?' says the nominal hero), this feels as if it's just marking time between resurrections. ★★ **KN**

A NIGHTMARE ON ELM STREET: THE DREAM CHILD (1989)

Starring: *Robert Englund (Freddy Krueger), Lisa Wilcox (Alice Johnson), Danny Hassel (Dan), Kelly Jo Minter (Yvonne), Erika Anderson (Greta), Joe Seely (Mark)*
Director: *Stephen Hopkins*
Screenwriter: *Leslie Bohem, from a story by John Skip, Craig Spector, Leslie Bohem, from a character by Wes Craven*

Pregnant teenager Alice worries that her unborn child is in danger of being possessed by murdering ghost Freddy Krueger, who wants to get back to the real world.

As if embarrassed by how many *Nightmare on Elm Street* films they had cranked out since Wes Craven's 1984 original, New Line Pictures omitted a numeral from the title format of this fifth film.

Even as the films get more impressive visually, the scripts make less and less sense – resulting in efforts as incoherent, flashy and uninteresting as *The Dream Child*.

There are the usual imaginative effects/dream scenes (Freddy as a motorbike engulfing a speeding teen, Freddy as a comic book superhero cutting apart a paper man) and the dumb humour which got out of hand last time round is slightly toned down, but the story still advances through disorienting lapses and leaps, another uninteresting selection of teenagers are brought on and killed off without making the slightest impression, and bits and pieces of the earlier films are rehashed in an attempt to keep up the continuity.

Director Stephen Hopkins, another dues-paying craftsman with bland s-f/blockbuster credits in his future (*Lost in Space*), does an astonishing job of getting the film to look good, especially in the dark and dripping dream scenes, making unsettling use of such typical genre images and the broken and bleeding doll, the womb-like tunnel of dreams and the scuttling, *It's Alive*-style Freddy baby monster. But this overdrive style is constantly hobbled by a storyline which never does anything but mark time between the open ending of *A Nightmare on Elm Street 4* and the bland beginning of the sixth film, *Freddy's Dead: The Final Nightmare*. ★★ **KN**

NIKITA (1990)

Starring: *Anne Parillaud (Nikita), Marc Dunet (Rico), Patrick Fontana (Coyotte), Alain Lathiere (Zap), Laura Cheron (La Punk), Bob (Tcheky Karyo)*
Director: *Luc Besson*
Screenwriter: *Luc Besson*
15/115 mins./Action/France-Italy

A drug-addicted petty criminal named Nikita is captured while trying to commit a robbery, and sent to be trained as a government assassin. As she begins her new life, she still feels the call of her old self.

The film that brought snazzy French director Luc Besson to prominence, and for some ruined his career as he began to get the idea he was some kind of Eurocratic blockbuster maker (although he did still have *Leon* to come). Not that that means Nikita is all that bad, it's like a movie made out of marble, ultra-slick and disco-lit, with big boom explosions and wild flourishes of action – neatly set off by having its punkette James Bond figure dash about in stilettos.

Sensuality was always Besson's thing, he loves surfaces, the ergonomic fit of his images into some cool holding pattern of an idea – here the espionage thriller done as rehabilitation. Anne Parillaud (the ex-Mrs Besson) is her own marble surface, skinny, beautiful and impenetrable. Her transformation from hoodlum into assassin, is like *My Fair Lady* with high explosives and no songs. Tcheky Karyo, with his gouged Euro-looks, is the Henry Higgins figure who must transform her into a government puppet. Quelling her anger, or, better, redirecting it.

Beyond that, there is little more. It has an arch-dynamism to match the neon chic of its looks, but no depth. Besson chooses close-fitting suits, incendiary attitude and perfectly lit cheekbones, over any psychology, even pop psychology. ★★★ **IN**

NIL BY MOUTH (1997)

Starring: *Ray Winstone (Ray), Kathy Burke (Valerie), Charlie Creed-Miles (Billy), Laila Morse (Janet), Edna Dore (Kath)*
Director: *Gary Oldman*
Screenwriter: *Gary Oldman*
18/128 mins./Drama/UK

Awards: *BAFTA – Alexander Korda Award for Best British Film, Best Original Screenplay;* Empire Awards *– Best Debut (Gary Oldman)*

A mock docu-drama portrayal of the violent and squalid underbelly of working class life in South London.

Oldman's vaguely autobiographical directorial debut is hard. As nails. And to watch. As awful yet compelling as a motorway pile-up, it will make an audience feel like voyeurs before its relentless and intensely unpleasant scenes of drug/alcohol/physical abuse, misogyny and social deprivation. Stop reading now if you thought this was some glossy hospital drama.

Nil By Mouth exposes in grainy Super 16 the violent and squalid underbelly of working class life in South London. It begins with a close-up of Raymond, ordering a round in a smoky club. All seems unremarkable until he delivers the drinks. Then in a torrent of bad language that makes *Boyz N The Hood* and *Twin Town* sound like *Teletubbies*, Oldman has Raymond confront those he has kept waiting – including Mark his partner in crime, his wife Valerie, her mother Janet and Valerie's smackhead younger brother Billy – the extended dysfunctional family from hell. Brutally, Raymond reinforces his dominance, denigrates the women and establishes a template for the film.

As settings switch between a high-rise flat, the streets and all-night shops, the brutish dialogue continues, spraying c-words like machine gun bullets, gradually shifting into the story of Billy who, after being attacked by Raymond steals from the family to finance his habit, then in a horribly poignant scene injects himself while his mother looks on in both concern and revulsion. But worse is to come in the final third as the women come to the fore and the pregnant Valerie is beaten by her drunken husband.

Long before that truly shocking moment, you may hate Raymond enough to want him off the screen. All nervous laughter at the swearing has long since been replaced by a craving for release that Oldman does not grant – either with a momentarily repentant Raymond's explanations or the sickeningly feelbad 'happy' ending. Burke and Winstone dominate but there are awesome performances from the entire cast as Oldman paints an unforgettable picture as realistic and stylish as Scorsese's *Mean Streets*. In it, men are trapped in a nauseating downward spiral and only women exhibit any humanity or love, as shown by their pathetic capacity for forgiveness. It will stun and numb in equal measure, proof unrequested that it can be grim down south. Approach with extreme caution. ★★★★ **NJ**

NINE QUEENS (NUEVE REINAS) (2000)

Starring: *Gaston Pauls (Juan), Ricardo Darin (Marcos), Leticia Bredice (Valeria), Tomas Fonzi (Federico)*
Director: *Fabian Bielinsky*
Screenwriter: *Fabian Bielinsky*
15/114 mins./Crime/Mystery/Drama/Argentina

After rescuing him from a botched con trick, experienced grifter Marcos takes small-time operator Juan under his wing for a day. Together, they get involved in a scam involving the sale of some rare stamps (the nine queens of the title). But who's scammin who?

Marking the debut of Argentinian writer-director Fabien Bielinsky, *Nine Queens* belongs to a rich tradition of films about con artists that includes Peter Bogdanovich's brilliant *Paper Moon*, Stephen Frears' *The Grifters* and pretty much every movie David Mamet has ever made.

Bielinsky apparently got his break after he won a screenplay competition – he was given funding for the movie, and the result is a brilliantly written film that cleverly manages to out-Mamet Mamet.

The film is set in present-day Buenos Aires, but it could be anywhere, as the action mostly takes place in hotels, restaurants, cafes and convenience stores. Bielinsky sets the tone of the film right from the opening scene, with Juan's small-time con-artist getting greedy by trying to pull the same 'change' trick on successive cashiers in the same store, and Marcos' older, wiser grifter stepping in to rescue him by posing as a policeman.

From then on, the script delights in piling on the twists so that the audience is never sure whom to trust and is immediately suspicious of each new character and their motives. Indeed, much of the pleasure of the film is derived from the fact that, time and time again, just as you think you've figured it out, something happens that forces you to completely re-think your theory. And, sure enough, the film keeps you guessing right up until the end.

Bielinsky cleverly ensures that neither angel-faced Juan nor the vaguely saturnine Marcos are entirely likeable characters (Marcos in particular isn't above pimping out his own sister in order to clinch a deal), though both Gaston Pauls and Ricardo Darin give immensely charismatic and assured performances.

There's also good support from Leticia Bredice as Marcos' embittered sister (who has her own reasons for getting involved with the latest scam), and Ignasi Abadal as a particularly sleazy stamp-collector. ★★★★ **AM**

9 SONGS (2004)

Starring: *Kieran O'Brien (Matt), Margo Stilley (Lisa), as themselves: Super Furry Animals, Primal Scream, Franz Ferdinand*
Director: *Michael Winterbottom*
Screenwriter: *Michael Winterbottom*
18/71 mins./Drama/Music/Romance/UK

After Matt meets Lisa at a rock concert, they embark on a torrid affair. Their interaction is almost entirely through increasingly adventurous and troubled sexual encounters, interspersed with trips to see bands playing at the Brixton Academy.

Michael Winterbottom's controversial two-hander sets out to show a relationship by focusing on the couple's sexual exploits. While clearly intended as experimental cinema rather than entertainment, it unfortunately fails badly, due to Winterbottom's choices.

Because what we see onscreen is unsimulated sex (including penetration and a money shot), he had to cast relatively unknown and, let's face it, less accomplished lead actors than he's used to. As a result, the performances are poor – made worse by the fact that the director encouraged former *Grange Hill* alum O'Brien (what would Mr Bronson say?) and American actress Stilley to improvise their dialogue. The only thing more embarrassing than the unflinchingly graphic sex is the interaction between these unlikeable characters ('Do I look like a boy?' Lisa coos in one scene; 'Yeah. That's why I like ya,' replies Matt).

The drab dialogue and groin-grinding scenes leave us so unaffected that Winterbottom proves, intentionally or not, that such intimacy only leads to banal revelations. It's left to the musical interludes to provide the few moments of interest and emotional honesty in the entire film. The fact that Winterbottom's previous work has been so impressive only makes this hollow exercise more disappointing. ★★ **ND**

NINOTCHKA (1939)

Starring: *Greta Garbo (Ninotchka), Melvyn Douglas (Count Leon Dolga), Ina Claire (Grand Duchess Swana), Sig Rumann (Michael Ironoff), Felix Bressart (Buljanoff), Alexander Granach (Kopalski)*
Director: *Ernst Lubitsch*
Screenwriters: *Charles Brackett, Billy Wilder, Walter Reisch, based on a story by Melchior Lengyel*
U/110 mins./Comedy/USA

Assistant Soviet commissar Ninotchka arrives in Paris to see why Buljanoff, Ironoff and Kopalski are taking so long to sell Grand Duchess Swana's confiscated jewellery, only to be corrupted by Count Leon Dolga and the frivolous pleasures of capitalism.

Directed by Ernst Lubitsch and co-scripted by Billy Wilder, this enduring delight stands at the crossroads of American screen comedy. Studded with instances of the 'Lubitsch Touch' and imbued with the screwball spirit, it contains significant traces of the acerbic satire that would become Wilder's trademark in the less innocent postwar world.

Yet, what most people remember about *Ninotchka* is the advertising slogan, 'Garbo Laughs!', which consciously echoed the 'Garbo Talks!' tag that boosted her sound debut, *Anna Christie*, just nine years earlier. She would only make one more picture, another comedy with Melvyn Douglas. But while it also suggested that the great diva was a deft comedienne, the writing and direction of *Two-Faced Woman* left a lot to be desired.

Despite her misgivings, Garbo was always set to headline this romantic comedy of political manners. However, William Powell and Cary Grant were originally considered as her co-star and Lubitsch only consented to direct after George Cukor decamped to *Gone With the Wind* and MGM agreed to make *The Shop Around the Corner* as part of the deal.

Disliking Gottfried Reinhardt and S.N. Behrman's screenplay (in which Buljanoff, Ironoff and Kopalski were played straight), Lubitsch commissioned a rewrite from Wilder, Charles Brackett and Walter Reisch, although he also made major uncredited contributions. Yet for all the sparkling wit, some of the Bolshevik-Capitalist gags feel forced and the storyline droops after Leon follows Ninotchka back to Moscow.

However, Lubitsch's major concern was Garbo, whose insecurities were exacerbated by the demands of deadpan clowning. She was particularly nervous about the drunk scene, which she considered highly vulgar. Reports vary as to the nature of their relationship. But Lubitsch managed to relax Garbo to the extent that she was not only very funny, but also more feminine than in any role bar Camille and it's the fact that she comes across as a woman and not an icon that makes this performance so memorable.

Cole Porter musicalised the story as *Silk Stockings*, which was filmed with Fred Astaire and Cyd Charisse in 1957. ★★★★ **DP**

THE NINTH CONFIGURATION (1980)

Starring: *Stacy Keach (Colonel Hudson Kane), Scott Wilson (Captain Billy Cutshaw), Jason Miller (Lieutenant Reno), Ed Flanders (Colonel Fell)*
Director: *William Peter Blatty*
Screenwriter: *William Peter Blatty, from the novel* Twinkle, Twinkle, Killer Kane *by William Peter Blatty*
15/113 mins./Thriller/USA

Psychiatrist Kane is sent to a mysterious lunatic asylum in an old castle where he is to analyse whether American soldiers sent home from Vietnam are genuine lunatics or fakes. There he finds Captain Cutshaw, an astronaut, who denies the existence of God on the grounds that evil exists.

1980's *The Ninth Configuration*, *Exorcist* author Blatty's directorial debut, is a beguiling, occasionally terrifying, and emotionally moving gem.

Essentially bolting a debate on the existence of God (and thus continuing the essential theme of *The Exorcist*) to a surrealistic thriller, *Configuration* has psychiatrist Kane sent to a mysterious lunatic asylum in an old castle where he is to analyse whether American soldiers sent home from Vietnam are genuine lunatics or fakes. There he finds Captain Cutshaw, an astronaut who aborted his moonshot at the last minute and who denies the existence of God on the grounds that evil exists. Kane declares that the existence of selfless good proves the existence of God and is challenged to produce a single example of which he has personal experience.

If all this sounds a tad on the heavy side that's because it is, and Blatty does himself few favours in the opening 45 minutes, moving what plot there is at a snail's pace. But the drama, when it arrives, is blistering with a truly shocking plot reversal as well as some inspired surreal imagery – the opening title sequence in which a huge moon wheels into view behind the silhouette of an Apollo spacecraft is probably one of the oddest, most inexplicably frightening shots put on film while a shot of a crucifix on the lunar surface nods expertly towards *2001: A Space Odyssey*. There are flaws, Keach's zombified performance may steer a little too close to comatose and the whole may irritate depending on your tolerance for protracted debate and Roman Catholic angst. But allowing that, *The Ninth Configuration* is still a fascinating film. ★★★★ **AS**

THE NINTH GATE (1999)

Starring: *Johnny Depp (Dean Corso), Frank Langella (Boris Balkan), Lena Olin (Liana Telfer), Emmanuelle Seigner (The Girl), Barbara Jefford (Baroness Kessler)*
Director: *Roman Polanski*
Screenwriters: *John Brownjohn, Enrique Urbizu, Roman Polanski, based on the novel by Arturo Perez-Reverte*
15/127 mins./Thriller/Horror/France/Spain/USA

Dean Corso, a shady New York book dealer, is hired by smooth millionaire Boris Balkan to authenticate a volume allegedly written in collaboration with the Devil. While tracking copies of the book in Portugal, Spain and France, Corso comes across a succession of eccentric and/or sinister types.

Based on Arturo Perez-Reverte's Spanish novel *El Club Dumas* (with all references to Alexander Dumas deleted), this bibliophile mystery-horror item finds Roman Polanski returning to the demonic concerns of his classic *Rosemary's Baby* at a more melodramatic level, with a tone pitched somewhere between *The Omen* and *The Name Of The Rose*.

Dean Corso a shady New York book dealer, is hired by smooth millionaire Boris Balkan to authenticate a volume allegedly written in collaboration with the Devil. While tracking copies of the *Book Of Nine Doors Of The Kingdom Of Shadows* in Portugal, Spain and France, Corso comes across a succession of eccentric and/or sinister types – black widow Satanist Liana Telfer and a pair of book-owners played by veterans of different types of Euro-horror, Jesus Franco collaborator Jack Taylor and Hammer Films baroness Barbara Jefford.

Dogging the glum, short-sighted hero is a mysterious green-eyed girl who displays the occasional supernatural power (elegant balletic flights) and helps him survive the contest between Balkan and Liana, which climaxes at a Satanic house party rather less impressive than the one in *Eyes Wide Shut*, but surprisingly similar to the Kubrickian orgy in that Polanski can't have seen it before he filmed his robes-and-chanting session.

This is a mystery whose set-up is far more intriguing than its muddled solution. Polanski and a fine cast of slightly off-centre players make much of the early ominousness, and well-chosen locations are imbued with a certain creepiness. But the last act falls apart. In an out-of-the-way chateau, Balkan goes through the ritual supposed to open the fabled Ninth Gate, and the film definitively shows itself rather better at promising than delivering. ★★★ **DH**

NIXON (1995)

Starring: *Anthony Hopkins (Richard M. Nixon), Joan Allen (Pat Nixon), Powers Boothe (Alexander Haig), Ed Harris (E. Howard Hunt), Bob Hoskins (J. Edgar Hoover)*
Director: *Oliver Stone*
Screenwriters: *Stephen J. Rivele, Christopher Wilkinson, Oliver Stone*
15/182 mins./Drama/Biography/USA

A biographical story of former US president Richard Milhouse Nixon, from his days as a young boy to his eventual presidency that ended in shame.

Reviled, despised and shunned by the public and media alike, a misunderstood genius who struggled to fulfil personal dreams against the odds, a man who always saw the bigger picture and struggled against the might of the system ... You've got to feel for Oliver Stone. He makes the most penetrating, unyielding studio films around, and everybody gets up on their high horse and shouts about historical veracity, botty crunching running times and interminably complex plotting.

Yes, *Nixon* is way too long. Yes, it assumes too much knowledge of the most controversial term of office in America's presidential history. Perhaps it massages known facts into a more colourful order. But it is also a tour de force of mighty acting that skilfully entwines intrigue and tension into a swirling world of political scheming, paranoia and self-destruction, and paints a moving picture of a man undone by self-loathing and misguided idealism. Nixon plays out like a Shakespearean tragedy – *Macbeth* as performed by the White House administration of the early 70s.

With Stone's arsenal of camera trickery at work, the film commences with Watergate – although it never really explains what the crucial scandal was all about – the linchpin for the abridged bio of Richard Nixon complete with Freudian childhood trauma, mucho conspiracy (spot Larry Hagman's Texan oilman out for JFK assassination), superlative talkfests in the Oval office and the eventual fall from grace as Watergate bursts forth. There is so much meat here sometimes it is hard to swallow.

Hopkins is simply magnificent, recognisably Nixonian but not a bald-faced imitation, tapping the psychological torment of the man (Nixon, Stone demands, was not a monster, just a flawed human) and visibly similar without an ounce of prosthetic. Then there's Joan Allen's poignant Pat Nixon, and an array of those actors who

Tagline
He changed the world, but lost a nation.

always deliver: Harris, Woods, J.T. Walsh, Powers Boothe and Mary Steenburgen.

Oliver Stone makes movies like hammer blows to the head, that leave you physically drained but totally nourished. Weighty? Nixon has its own gravitational pull. ★★★★ **IN**

⓪ NOBODY'S FOOL (1994)

Starring: *Paul Newman (Sully Sullivan), Jessica Tandy (Miss Beryl Peoples), Bruce Willis (Carl Roebuck), Melanie Griffith (Toby Roebuck), Dylan Walsh (Peter Sullivan)*
Director: *Robert Benton*
Screenwriter: *Robert Benton, based on the novel by Richard Russo*
15/110 mins./Drama/USA

Sully is a rascally ne'er-do-well approaching retirement age. While he is pressing a worker's compensation suit for a bad knee, he secretly works for his nemesis, Carl, and flirts with Carl's young wife Toby.

It's fair to say that not much happens in Robert Benton's first directorial outing since the disastrous *Billy Bathgate*. Indeed, those seeking their Friday night kicks from a short sharp burst of action would be advised to look elsewhere. Everybody else, however, should ready their purses for this mesmerising, magical portrait of smalltown America, dominated by a performance from Paul Newman so outstanding it must surely make him front-runner to hoist the Best Actor statuette come Oscar night.

Newman is Donald 'Sully' Sullivan, a 60-year-old construction worker who has somehow managed to side-step life, especially now that a building site accident has left him with a crook knee, rendering him virtually unemployable. Having walked out on his family and baby son years ago, his life now revolves around his God-fearing landlady Miss Beryl, his boss (an uncredited Bruce Willis) whom he holds responsible for his incapacity, and his boss's wife with whom he is conducting a strangely asexual affair. Until his now grown-up son and docile grandson appear on the scene, giving Sully the opportunity to put the past behind him and let that huge, golden heart of his out of its cage.

While the entire cast are to be commended, this is ultimately Newman's film. The actor is so utterly convincing as the cynical, time-worn Sully that he literally becomes him, bringing an unseen but oh-so perceptible layer of warmth and a surprising amount of wry humour to the role and turning what could have been a routine character piece into a riveting examination of shattered dreams, human failings and the basic need for love.

Unfortunately co-star, the glowing Tandy, in one of her last film roles, seems underused, continually being handed potentially interesting sub-plots which fizzle away to nothing. That aside, *Nobody's Fool* is an unprecedented treat, populated with charming, believable characters and a parting shot so beautiful even the hardest of hearts will melt helplessly at its sight. ★★★★ **CW**

⓪ NOISES OFF (1992)

Starring: *Carol Burnett (Dotty Otley/Mrs Clackett), Michael Caine (Lloyd Fellowes), Denholm Elliott (Selsdon Mowbray), Julie Hagerty (Poppy Taylor), Julie Hagerty (Poppy Taylor), Marilu Henner (Belinda Blair), Mark Linn-Baker (Tim Allgood), Christopher Reeve (Frederick Dallas), John Ritter (Garry Lejeune)*
Director: *Peter Bogdanovich*
Screenwriter: *Marty Kaplan, based on the play by Michael Frayn*
12/103 mins./Comedy/USA

Stumbling along Broadway on the opening night of *Nothing On*, a British farce he has just directed, a drunken Lloyd Fellowes remembers three disastrous pre-premiere performances of the play's first act, a cack-handed technical rehearsal and two increasingly horrible out-of-town try-outs.

Obviously, this film of Michael Frayn's clever stage play is highly theatrical, and the adaptors have to wrestle mightily to transfer its conceits to the screen, the upshot being that all the split-second timing and running around as on-stage and back-stage farces intersect falls a touch flat. It's like watching a magic act on television, and knowing that the conjurer can have 28 takes to pull off a trick properly.

However, that cavil aside, there's a great deal to like, including the opportunity of savouring Michael Caine ('None of us will get out of here alive; they've got big pictures of us in the lobby!') and Denholm Elliott ('Am I on ... I thought I heard my voice') being very funny, and the uncannily brilliant job Michael Frayn, a very funny writer, has done in imitating the style of Ray Cooney, who isn't, in producing a farce so authentically ghastly that you'd swear it ran in the West End for twelve years.

Throughout, the heroic director has had to deal with ego-driven performers, complicated sexual by-play among the cast, various actors' neurotic tics, a recalcitrant set and props, the alleged drunken senility of a grand old character actor (Elliott) and the essential duffness of the text. Bogdanovich, who was still crawling back on his hands and knees with sackcloth and ashes all over him after his career implosion of the late 70s, does as good a job as anyone could with the material, and some of the performers – especially Christopher Reeve and John Ritter – nobly trash their images. ★★★ **KN**

⓪ NORTH (1994)

Starring: *Elijah Wood (North), Jason Alexander (North's Dad), Julia Louise-Dreyfus (North's Momo), Bruce Willis (Narrator/Easter Bunny), Jon Lovita (Arthur Belt)*
Director: *Rob Reiner*
Screenwriter: *Alan Zweibel, Andrew Scheinman*
PG/87 mins./Kids/USA

Fed up with the lack of attention he gets from his folks, young North takes them to court. A ruling is passed that if he doesn't find replacement parents within two months, he must return to his original family. So, he sets off on a journey to sample an eclectic bunch of could-be moms and dads.

The seemingly untouchable Rob Reiner fell off his perch with this oddball comedy, vaguely satirising the, then, penchant for celebrity kids to divorce their parents. It's a strange concept – the search for a better upbringing – too quirky to be genuinely funny, too disorganised to be genuinely sweet, too edgy to sit comfortably.

What are we meant to make of North's adventure in search of replacement parents? It runs distressingly close to abandonment issues, as if trying to glean laughs from borderline abuse. Reiner obviously sees it as a slyly weighted fairy-tale, which he doesn't seem to have the imagination for – his skills are for needling adult foibles (*This Is Spinal Tap*, *When Harry Met Sally*). Still, off a baby-face Frodo sets on his quest (Elijah Wood was a bright-beamed young actor, with a sweet glow of goodness), a road movie of parenting mishap.

A host of middling celebrity cameos (Dan Aykroyd, Kathy Bates, Graham Greene etc.) are the try-out moms and dads for North, geographically spread from Texas to silly Eskimo sets. And Bruce Willis both narrates and crops up in Jiminy Cricket fashion to add advice to the increasingly forlorn North. Anyway, the final message rings dull: that put-upon kids should just get on with it. However, the only advice we should take from its rambling platitudes is that a clueless moral fable need not be heeded. ★★ **IN**

⊙ NORTH BY NORTHWEST (1959)

Starring: *Cary Grant (Roger O. Thornhill), Eva Marie Saint (Eve Kendall), James Mason (Phillip Vandamm), Jessie Royce Landis (Clara Thornhill), Leo G. Carroll (The Professor)*
Director: *Alfred Hitchcock*
Screenwriter: *Ernest Lehman*
PG/136 mins./Thriller/USA

Middle-aged Madison Avenue advertising executive Roger O. Thornhill is mistaken for a government agent by a gang of spies. He gets involved in a series of misadventures and is pursued across the States by both the spies and the government whilst being helped by a beautiful blonde.

Recovering from the psychological rigours of *Vertigo*, Alfred Hitchcock was intent on making entertainment. As he had tried, unsuccessfully, to secure the rights to Graham Greene's *Our Man In Havana*, his mind was evidently on a movie about a non-existent character – the personification, in fact, of the Macguffin, which links *North By Northwest* to its neighbours in the Hitchcock cannon, *Vertigo* and *Psycho*.

Although the screenplay was based on an original story, it's easy to see the influence of Sapper's Bulldog Drummond adventure *The Final Count* and *John Macnab*, which was written by John Buchan, whose *The 39 Steps* indirectly provided the 'pursued innocent' premise. Writer Ernest Lehman called it, 'The Hitchcock picture to end all Hitchcock pictures', although the director himself labelled it, 'A fantasy of the absurd'. Either way, it was a project with which Hitch was very much at ease – he even took time off in mid-shoot to direct two episodes ('Poison' and 'Banquo's Ghost') for his TV series, *Alfred Hitchcock Presents*. Mistaken for a spy and then forced to extricate himself from an international conspiracy, Roger Thornhill is the most resourceful of all Hitchcock's Everyman heroes. James Stewart was under the impression he'd landed the assignment. But just as John Ford was careful to shuffle John Wayne and Henry Fonda between 'action' and 'conscience' roles, so Hitchcock alternated Stewart and Cary Grant. In the event, it's hard to see anyone else capturing Thornhill's glib heroism with such effortlessly suave precision.

Thornhill is an egotistical chauvinist, totally in control of his (admittedly superficial) world (and is, thus, a potent symbol for America at the height of the Cold War). He's such a hollow man that he even admits his middle initial, 'O', stands for nothing. Yet, though he ends up having to clear his name, uncover a conspiracy and save his lady love, his heroism lies in the fact that he survives everything his adversary, Phillip Vandamm, can throw at him. In other words, he's something of an accidental hero. But once he knows what his objectives are, he snaps back into the cocky, committed and highly effective man of action he appears as in the opening sequence.

He's also a man who comes to know himself through his experiences. Initially, he's a self-centred, carefree bachelor. Yet, as he waits in the vast emptiness of the prairie for a mysterious stranger who will never come, he realises the sum worth of his status and wealth – a speck on a landscape that can be swatted from above at any moment. One of the most memorable set-pieces in cinema history, the cornfield sequence is almost seven minutes of non-stop action, with the only sound being that of the plane's engine. It's also one of the most Heath Robinson-esque murder attempts ever filmed. Forget the contraptions contrived by Bond villains. This is an assassination bid made in the middle of nowhere by the unseen pilot of a crop-duster plane. It's an act of almost surreal folly on Vandamm's behalf, which is reinforced by the Godot-like non-appearance of Thornhill's contact.

It's ironic that Vandamm is a much more refined and cultured man than Thornhill, with an appreciation of art and a knack for simple kindness that earns him the devotion of his covertly homosexual henchman, Leonard and the respect of his double-agent mistress, Eve Kendall. But his greatest failing is that he's a man unswervingly dedicated to chaos and treachery. Thornhill may be an alienated urbanite, but from the moment he leaves New York and returns to the soil (literally, as he hits the deck at the crossroads), he begins to rediscover his soul, ending his pilgrimage at that shrine to the natural American order, Mount Rushmore.

Compare this to the protagonist in *Saboteur* (to which *North By Northwest* bears many similarities), in which the hero winds up on the head of the Statue of Liberty. Even Saul Bass' credits reflect this journey of self-rediscovery. With so much of the focus falling on Thornhill, it's easy to overlook the less obvious heroism exhibited by Eve Kendall. Suppressing her true identity beneath the ice maiden exterior, she effectively has a dual personality, which not only recalls Kim Novak's character in *Vertigo*, but also Ingrid Bergman's in *Notorious*, in which Cary Grant also had to rescue his paramour from the clutches of a man to whom she'd given her body in the cause of national security. ★★★★★
DP

Movie Trivia: North By Northwest

Rather than pay to shoot in a forest, Hitchcock planted 100 pine trees at MGM studios. Thornhill is nearly always shot on the left side of the screen. James Stewart, despite his enthusiasm, was refused the role of Thornhill because he looked too old.

⊙ NORTH SEA HIJACK (1979)

Starring: *Roger Moore (Rufus Excalibur Ffolkes), James Mason (Admiral Sir Francis Brinsden), Anthony Perkins (Lou Kramer), Michael Parks (Harold Schulman), George Baker (Fletcher), Jack Watson (Captain Olafsen)*
Director: *Andrew V. McLaglen*
Screenwriter: *Jack Davies*
PG/99 mins./Action/UK

When a terrorist hijacks an offshore drilling platform in the North Sea, rather than meet his demands, wealthy adventurer Rufus Ffolkes leads a crack team of commandos to stop them.

A thoroughly daft but beguiling adventure yarn that crosses the sturdy, old-fashioned gung-ho of Alistair MacLean with a proto-*Die Hard* concept. Anyway, how can one not love a film where the hero is named Rufus Excalibur Ffolkes? OK ... But it does star James Bond, Captain Nemo and Norman Bates as a terrorist, and embodies a brief bit of bluster in the late 70s when the British film industry decided it could try its hand at action movies. On a budget, mind.

It's all a bit tinny by anyone's, let alone Hollywood's standards, and it's hard to feel huge amounts of peril for a threatened oil rig, but there is enough tension, as well as wit, to carry it though as the wry nonsense it is. Giving its heroes and villains quirks (as opposed to depth) grants it a comic-book lightness and degree of self-awareness: Ffolkes just loves cats and wears stripy woolly hats but is still tough as a weathered hide. And the very tame action sequences are, at least, offset by some top notch posh accents. ★★★ **IN**

NOSTALGIA (NOSTALGHIA) (1983)

Starring: *Oleg Yankovsky (Andrei Gorchakov), Domiziani Giordano (Eugenia), Patrizia Terreno (Maria), Erland Josephson (Domenico), Delia Boccardo (Domenico's 'Wife). Milena Vukotic (Civil Servant)*
Director: *Andrei Tarkovsky*
Screenwriter: *Andrei Tarkovsky*
15/120 mins/Drama/USSR/Italy

In Italy to research the life of an exiled Russian composer, poet Gortchakov dreams of his distant wife Maria, exasperates his smitten translator Eugenia and befriends Domenico, an eccentric activist who sets him a redemptive task.

Andrei Tarkovsky began contemplating this sombre drama while shooting the TV documentary, *Tempo di Viaggio*, in 1976. Initially, the focus was to fall on the man who had incarcerated his family for 40 years for fear of the Apocalypse. However, the musicologist storyline began to develop in collaboration with veteran Italian scenarist Tonino Guerra, who had perfected the art of depicting strong women and urban alienation with Michelangelo Antonioni. What emerged was one of Tarkovsky's simplest narratives, which was characterised by a haunting stillness that was reinforced by the settings, all of which were found locations, including St Catherine's Pool, where the candle sequence that Krzysztof Kieslowski declared a cinematic miracle was shot in one nine-minute take.

Problems with the budget and the Kremlin delayed shooting until March 1982, while illness and travel restrictions respectively prevented Anatoly Solonitsyn and Alexander Kaidonovsky from taking the role that went to Oleg Yankovsky, who embodied the film's themes with an affectingly melancholic inertia that was born out of homesickness and a longing to start afresh. By coming to accept Eugenia's determination to live for today and Domenico's fearful faith, Gorchakov unified the dualities that dominated the action – Russia/Italy, past/present, sanity/madness, belief/doubt and poetry/music – along with the dreams and flashbacks, which were filmed in monochrome and sepia to detach them from the scholar's colour reality.

On viewing the final print, Tarkovsky was surprised to discover *Nostalgia*'s unmediated gloom. However, Gorchakov's situation very much reflected his own, for not long after completing the project he learned that he would no longer be allowed to work in the Soviet Union and, consequently, he announced his defection to the West. Yet, Tarkovsky also shared Domenico's views about humanity's slow destruction of the planet and this increasing divergence from nature would inform his final feature, *The Sacrifice*.

Nostalgia was attacked by many critics for attempting to disguise its lack of depth with a surfeit of beauty. However, it has since been seen as an agonising study of loneliness and confusion by an artist in the process of being disowned by his homeland. ★★★★ **DP**

⊙ NOSFERATU, A SYMPHONY OF HORRORS (1922)

Starring: *Max Schreck (Count Orlok, Nosferatu), Alexander Granach (Knock, an estate agent), Gustav von Wangenheim (Hutter, his employee), Greta Schroeder (Ellen, his wife)*
Director: *Friedrich W. Murnau*
Screenwriter: *Henrik Galeen, from the novel* Dracula *by Bram Stoker*
PG/79 mins./Horror/Germany

Count Orlok's move to Bremen coincides with a number of deaths in the area and his absence with an estate agent's wife begins to have sinister undertones.

In 1921, director F.W. Murnau founded the company Praha-Film with a view to producing a series of occult films. Murnau was a better director than he was a businessman however, and the only film released by Praha before it went bust was *Nosferatu*. Originally Murnau had planned a straightforward adaptation of Bram Stoker's *Dracula*, but was prevented by Stoker's estate from obtaining the rights.

Unperturbed, and rather naively it must be said, he attempted to circumvent the ruling by changing the names of the principal characters and re-jigging certain plot points and settings – Dracula became Count Orlok, Jonathan Harker became Hutter and Van Helsing became Professor Bulwer; Orlok stalks the Gothic streets of Bremen rather than Victorian London. Confusingly, in later prints of the film where the original titles cards have been translated, the character's names appear as their Stoker counterparts. Still, Murnau's ploy fooled no one, least of all Stoker's widow who, impoverished by her husband's death and entirely dependent on revenue from his work, sued Praha for copyright infringement.

Unluckily for her, by the time the British Society Of Authors had filed suit on her behalf, Murnau's reckless spending, much of it on publicity for *Nosferatu*, had sent his fledgling studio into receivership: and thus the coffers were bare. But Florence Stoker was a tenacious old bird. She pursued the case relentlessly and in July 1925 a German court ordered all prints of the film to be destroyed.

Thankfully, several negatives survived and despite Stoker's best efforts to impede its wider distribution (she did prevent the London premiere in 1925), her cause was finally lost when the film reached America in 1929.

Although the film met with a respectable response from both public and critics on its release, *Nosferatu* was not widely acclaimed until well after World War II. Even then its rediscovery came after the belated critical praise heaped on Murnau's more accessible works, particularly *Sunrise*. By then, of course, surviving prints of the film were in a parlous state and it's now almost impossible to gauge how it would have looked to a contemporary audience. Not an unusual state of affairs by any means but, strangely, *Nosferatu* has suffered less from the ravages of time than most films of its age. Its opaque, ghostly appearance enhances its dream-like quality and the themes of corruption and decay are mirrored in the decomposing stock itself.

Serendipitous disintegration aside, *Nosferatu* remains a fascinating relic and one that can still raise a shiver even 80 years after it was made. Murnau was a disciple of flamboyant theatrical legend Max Reinhardt, and learn much about set design and composition from the master. He was also influenced to a degree by the Expressionist movement (scriptwriter Henrik Galeen had worked on seminal Expressionist films *The Cabinet Of Dr Caligari* and *Der Golem*, but it is a common mistake to label *Nosferatu* a work of pure Expressionism; Murnau's aesthetic was far more complex than that.

To begin with, he took the unprecedented step of shooting most of the film on location and, in essence, it's the juxtaposition of realism and Expressionism (most evident in the interiors of Orlok's castle) that give the film its hypnotic visual power. Murnau's experiences as a fighter pilot during World War I also had a profound effect on his technique as a film director. Throughout his career he strove to give the camera movement, allowing it to glide unhampered through scenes, like a plane travelling in three dimensions through the landscape, rather than to record the action from a fixed position. Primitive, unwieldy equipment confounded his grandest ambitions, but even so there is an implication in *Nosferatu* that untold horrors lurk beyond the focus of the camera.

Elsewhere, Murnau employs techniques like stop motion, fast motion, sophisticated cross-cutting and, in one truly arresting scene, Hutter's spectral carriage ride to Orlok's lair, negative imaging to orchestrate his macabre symphony. His insertion of documentary footage and written material – journals, log books, and newspaper cuttings – was revolutionary

Real Films Used In Other Films

TOP10

1 *Snow White and the Seven Dwarves* IN *Gremlins*
2 *The Sorrow and the Pity* IN *Annie Hall*
3 *The Evil Dead* IN *Donnie Darko*
4 *An Affair To Remember* IN *Sleepless In Seattle*
5 *Sleepless in Seattle* IN *How To Lose A Guy In Ten Days*
6 *Goldfinger* IN *Catch Me If You Can*
7 *Casablanca* IN *Play It Again, Sam*
8 *The Wizard of Oz* IN *Sky Captain and The World Of Tomorrow*
9 *The Shining* IN *Twister*
10 *Problem Child* IN *Cape Fear*

for a silent film and echoes of it can be seen in Bunuel's *L'Age d'Or* (1930). Although the plot is broadly based on Dracula, in one respect at least La Stoker's case seems to have been built on somewhat shaky ground. Count Orlok bears as much relation to the seductive, charismatic aristocrat of her husband's novel as the Wolf Man does to Deputy Dawg. In the title role Max Schreck, an obscure character actor whose surname means 'fright' in German, cuts a genuinely repulsive figure.

With skeletal features, deathly pallor and talon-like fingernails he is the antithesis of the vampire as sensual sexual predator. He moves in staccato, jerky movements, quick and furtive like a rodent. The name Nosferatu comes from the old Slavic word for 'plague bringer' and tumbling hordes of rats follow in his wake. Schreck contributes an extraordinary performance. He never fully escaped from Orlok's shadow and audiences found him so chillingly realistic, rumours circulated that he was, in fact, a real vampire. Sadly he wasn't. He was as human as Murnau who, after relocating to Hollywood, perished in a car crash at the age of 43. 'Men must die. Nosferatu does not die!' proclaimed the original publicity for the film. We can only hope it's the truth. ★★★★★ **SB**

NOTORIOUS (1946)

Starring: *Cary Grant (Devlin), Ingrid Bergman (Alicia Huberman), Claude Rains (Alexander Sebastian), Louis Calhern (Paul Prescott), Mme Konstantin (Mme Sebastian) Reinhold Schunzel (Dr Anderson), Moroni Olsen (Walter Beardsley)*
Director: *Alfred Hitchcock*
Screenwriters: *Ben Hecht*
U/101 mins./Thriller/USA

Government agent T.R. Devlin falls for socialite Alicia Huberman when he is detailed to ascertain whether she shares her treacherous father's Nazi views. Thus, he is horrified when she agrees to seduce Fascist industrialist Alexander Sebastian to discover what he is plotting at his Rio chemical plant.

Although it was loosely based on John Taintor Foote's 1921 *Saturday Evening Post* story, 'The Song of the Dragon' – which inspired the 1927 Dorothy Mackaill silent, *Convoy* – *Notorious* also bore a strong resemblance to John Buchan's 1919 novel, *Mr Steadfast*, in which Richard Hannay (the hero of *The 39 Steps*) reluctantly consented to girlfriend Mary Lamington risking her life for the Allied cause.

But, regardless of its source, producer David O. Selznick was never convinced of the plotline's credibility and he bombarded Alfred Hitchcock and screenwriter Ben Hecht with memos suggesting revisions. He persuaded them to change the McGuffin from a secret Nazi army to uranium ore – unaware that their discussion of atomic science with Dr Robert Andrew Millikan led the FBI to tail Hitch and Hecht for the duration of the shoot – but eventually decided to sell the project to RKO in 1944 for $800,000 and a 50% share of the profits.

Technically, this is one of Hitchcock's most accomplished pictures, with the sequence in which Ted Tetzlaff's camera cranes over the heads of the guests at the Sebastians' party to close in on the key in Ingrid Bergman's hand being a masterstroke. Yet it was also one of his most audacious outings, with the three-minute kiss between Bergman and Cary Grant somehow making it past the Hays Code prudes.

However, the narrative's amorality has since perplexed critics, who have complained about Devlin's puritanical devotion to duty, which causes him to suppress his feelings for Alicia until it's nearly too late. But, such a chauvinistically romantic approach ignores the fact that Alicia's destiny was, until Madame Sebastian begins poisoning her, in her own hands, as she had undertaken the assignment to demonstrate her disdain for her father's political views and to prove to herself that she was more than a playgirl of ill repute. Moreover, it also underestimates Hitchcock's genius for drama, as by investing Sebastian with refinement and charm, Claude Rains turns him into a disconcertingly decent villain, who allows Devlin to ride to Alicia's rescue, even though he knows the consequences will prove fatal to himself. ★★★★★ **DP**

LA NOTTE (1961)

Starring: *Marcello Mastroianni (Giovanni Pontano), Jeanne Moreau (Lidia), Monica Vitti (Valentina Gherardini), Bernhard Wicki (Tommaso Garani), Rosy Mazzacurati (Rosy), Maria Pia Luzi (Patient), Guido A. Marsan (Fanti)*
Director: *Michelangelo Antonioni*
Screenwriters: *Michelangelo Antonioni, Ennio Flaiano, Tonino Guerra*
18/121 mins./Drama/Italy/France

Novelist Giovanni Pontano and his wife Lidia visit his dying editor, Tommaso, at the start of an indolent day, which culminates in them contemplating infidelity with strangers Valentina Gherardini and Roberto before making passionless, outdoor love at dawn.

This is the central segment of Michelangelo Antonioni's 'alienation' trilogy that also comprises *L'Avventura* and *L'Eclisse*. Once again, the inability to communicate in a dehumanising society is the pivotal theme and Antonioni moves his characters with chilling precision around a city that's every bit as barren and hostile as *L'Avventura's* volcanic island.

Ostensibly, Lidia and Giovanni have an enviable lifestyle. They attend a book reception, patronise a trendy nightclub and receive an invitation to a wealthy industrialist's estate. But they don't enjoy anything and are so innured by habit and indifference that they manage to avoid adultery more through boredom than fidelity and only make love on the golf course out of mutual self-pity rather than any conviction that they can save their decaying 10-year marriage.

But, they're not alone. The film's sole sympathetic character is the dying Tommaso. But even the hospital visit is disrupted by a nymphomaniac (Puzi)'s bid to grab Giovanni, who only escapes thanks to the intervention of two callous nurses. This encounter finds ironic echo in Giovanni's dogged and pointless pursuit of Valentina at her father's mansion and his empty attempts at seduction are thrown back at him when he fails to recognise the love letter that Lidia reads to him before they screw without passion on the grass. This exposure of the emptiness of Giovanni's prose suggests his failure as a novelist, as while he is commercially successful, he no longer has anything worthwhile to say.

La Notte is every bit as technically accomplished as *L'Avventura*, with Gianni Di Venanzo's camera following the action with meticulous fluidity or spying through the rain-spotted car windows to record Lidia and Robert's wordless conversation. But it's never as dramatically satisfying, with its depiction of a bleak existence relying too heavily on the laboured symbolism of Lidia's walk through the redeveloped Milanese suburbs where she had once been content and the contrast between Valentina's vibrant attitude to life and art and Giovanni's flaccid ennui. This may have won the Golden Bear at Berlin, but it lacks the desperate humanity of its triptych companions. ★★★★ **DP**

LE NOTTI DI CABIRIA (1957)

Starring: *Giulietta Masina (Cabiria), Francois Perier (Oscar D'Onofrio), Amedeo Nazzari (Alberto Lazzari), Aldo Silvani (Hypnotist), Dorian Gray (Jessy), Franca Marzi (Wanda)*
Director: *Federico Fellini*
Screenwriters: *Ennio Flaiano, Tullio Pinelli, with additional dialogue by Pier Paolo Pasolini, based on an idea by Federico Fellini*
PG/110 mins./Drama/Italy/France
Awards: *Academy Awards – Best Foreign Language Film*

Fellini's muse (his wife Masina) plays a prostitute who provides the fulcrum for a set of mini-stories set on the ragged edges of Rome.

Fellini's 1957 movie that won the Best Foreign Language Film Oscar and was adapted as the Broadway musical *Sweet Charity* (itself filmed, with Shirley MacLaine). This is at once the last of Fellini's early, street-level, simple tales of marginal lives (*La Strada*, *I Vitelloni*) and the first of his more fantastical studies of big city absurdity (*La Dolce Vita*, *8 1/2*).

Like *La Strada*, *Cabiria* uses the star presence of il maestro's wife (Masina, whose billing is equal with his), casting her as a waif-like hooker. She is introduced on the banks of a river, just as her latest boyfriend has decided to push her in and run off with her purse. She is picked up by a famous film star and taken away to his palatial retreat, but kicked out unnoticed when the star's girlfriend returns.

She joins a procession to a hysterical religious ceremony which does little for her, but is struck by the example (in a scene originally cut on the insistence of the Church but restored in this re-released version) of a meek man who wanders the ragged edges of Rome dispensing charity.

The tone of these mini-stories varies from satirical farce through bitter satire to gentle melancholy, but Masina's fragility and Fellini's deft touch smooth over the transitions.

Fellini's genius was just starting to show, and such signature touches as the Nino Rota accordion score are well in evidence, but the film's heart is Masina, whose bursts of anger demonstrate a real sense of the desperation inherent in ageing cuteness. ★★★★ **KN**

NOTTING HILL (1999)

Starring: *Julia Roberts (Anna Scott), Hugh Grant (William Thacker), Richard McCabe (Tony), Rhys Ifans (Spike), James Dreyfus (Martin)*
Director: *Roger Michell*
Screenwriter: *Richard Curtis*
15/124 mins./Comedy/Romance/UK/USA
Awards: Empire Awards – *Best Britsh Actor, Best British Director, Best British Film*

A Portobello Road bookshop owner's life changes forever when a Hollywood film star walks into his life.

Notting Hill, while falling just short of the *Four Weddings* benchmark, still makes for solid, crowd-pleasing entertainment, with its delightful array of one-liners, quirky sidekicks and a central couple who fall in and out of love with alarming speed. As much an ode to the hip West London suburb as it is Cinderella-story romcom, Portobello Road should brace itself for an influx of the American tourists who will obviously lap up the landmarks on view.

Grant is William Thacker, owner of a vaguely unsuccessful travel book store, divorced, and living in his former marital home with a rodent-like half-breed called Spike (*Twin Town*'s Ifans on top, scene-stealing form). Life seems relatively normal until Anna Scott, the world's most famous film star, visits the shop – and falls for Thacker's foppish Brit charms. But the path of true love runs even less smooth than usual, given that it's littered with intrusive press photographers, unexpected film star boyfriends and, of course, the matter of the human hedgehog flatmate, whose actions may very well result in trouble. This is achingly familiar territory: aesthetically pleasing flats (how do these people afford them?), stiff-upper-lipped Brit humour, and a bunch of comedy mates to rally round our protagonist in times of need.

As wish fulfilment fantasy, *Notting Hill* is pretty hard to beat. And as romantic comedy, it stomps all over the anaemic efforts that have been populating screens of late. Grant has matured from a bumbling, pompous buffoon into the kind of leading man you actually end up rooting for. Roberts, meanwhile, is so radiant as the film star trying desperately to convince her new beau she's 'just a girl standing in front of a girl asking her to love him' that it's as if this was the role she was born to play.

If Curtis' sharply funny script has a flaw, it comes in trying to make a serious point about media intrusion and the boundaries of privacy. Although it's hard not to feel a pang of sympathy for Anna Scott when her every mistake, including one particularly embarrassing past revelation, is splashed across the tabloids, hearing her bleat about having to live a life of dieting and perfection (while earning $15 million a movie, poor thing) smacks of naivety on the part of a major Hollywood star – surely someone this famous would realise such attention comes with the territory?

Still, it doesn't detract from the feelgood element of the movie, the scintillating chemistry between Roberts and Grant, the refreshing lack of a Wet Wet Wet theme song, or some splendid set pieces. ★★★★ **IN**

Tagline
Can the most famous film star in the world fall for just an ordinary guy?

NOW, VOYAGER (1942)

Starring: *Bette Davis (Charlotte Vale), Paul Henreid (Jerry D. Durrance), Claude Rains (Dr Jaquith), Gladys Copper (Mrs Henry Windle Vale), Bonita Granville (June Vale), John Loder (Elliott Livingston), Ilka Chase (Lisa Vale)*
Director: *Irving Rapper*
Screenwriter: *Casey Robinson, based on the novel by Olive Higgins Prouty*
PG/117 mins./Drama/USA
Awards: *Academy Awards – Best Comedy/Drama Score*

Charlotte Vale is helped by Dr. Jaquith to break free from the repressive tyranny of her mother, Mrs. Henry Windle Vale and falls in doomed love with the unhappily married architect Jerry D. Durrance on a South American cruise. However, she finds contentment in helping his daughter, Tina, through her own crisis of confidence.

Taking its title from a line in Walt Whitman's poem, 'Leaves of Grass', this classic Warners melodrama was adapted from a novel by Olive Higgins Prouty, who had also written that durable potboiler, *Stella Dallas*. Producer Hal B. Wallis initially conceived the project as a vehicle for Irene Dunne and considered Norma Shearer and Ginger Rogers before alighting on Bette Davis.

On its release, the film was renowned for the sequence in which Paul Henreid lit two cigarettes and handed one to Davis, and her climactic line about not wishing for the moon when she had the stars. But the critics were less than respectful in their haste to consign it to the tearjerking margins of the woman's picture – territory that has since been reclaimed by genre scholars, who revealed how adroitly director Irving Rapper and screenwriter Casey Robinson exploited generic convention to produce a solid piece of studio art.

Rapper's direction is particularly effective for a Broadway exile who was still in his first year behind the camera after serving as a dialogue coach on a handful of William Dieterle pictures. Most notable are his use of expositionary conversations and close-ups of isolated body parts (mostly of her craft-working hands) to anticipate Charlotte's entrances at different times in her development and the employment of Max Steiner's Oscar-winning love theme to unite Charlotte and Jerry within the frame (such as during the Latin interlude and the dinner at which they have to suppress their emotions) and when they are apart, after he returns to his manipulative wife and she contemplates a future with Boston widower, Elliot Livingston.

Even a reliance on the old device of flickering pages to emphasise (and justify) the novelettish nature of the narrative pays off. As does the ingenious denouement, which archly remains within Production Code restrictions while giving Charlotte the love she craves and the chance to rectify her own spoilt youth, while also leaving her to enjoy her new-found independence. Few Hollywood pictures of the time played so fast and loose with filmic and moral tradition. ★★★★ **DP**

NURSE BETTY (2000)

Starring: *Morgan Freeman (Charlie), Renee Zellweger (Betty Sizemore), Chris Rock (Wesley), Greg Kinnear (Dr David Ravell/George McCord), Aaron Eckhart (Del Sizemore)*
Director: *Neil LaBute*
Screenwriters: *John C. Richards, James Flamberg, based on a story by Richards*
18/110 mins./Comedy/Thriller/Crime/USA

Awards: *Golden Globes – Best Comedy/Musical Actress*

After the murder of her husband, a woman becomes obsessed with a medical soap opera, believing its star doctor is the real thing – and the man for her.

One might get the distinct feeling that Neil LaBute – if you've watched his movies so far, that is – is not what expert psychoanalysts refer to as 'happy chicken'. His previous two films have been icy studies of either rampant misogyny – the fantastic *In The Company Of Men* – or full-blown misanthropy – the less successful *Your Friends & Neighbours* – so it's hardly surprising that for his third outing he should lighten up and choose a project with a more whimsical heart. Unfortunately, try as he might, he can't keep the movie entirely bile-free, and the result is a weirdly uneven, ultimately dissatisfying experience.

Nurse Betty's key strength is Zellweger. She is perfectly cast as the epitome of bewildered innocence who, catapulted into a 'fugue' – a psychological defence/reaction to the scalping and brutal murder of her slimeball hubby, played with trailer-park relish by LaBute regular Aaron Eckhart – heads off to propose to her favourite TV soap character, the unidimensional, Dr Kildare-lite Dr David Ravell: 'real' name George McCord (Kinnear, wheeling out the same deliberate cheesiness that he employed as Captain Amazing in 1999's *Mystery Men*). When she finally corners him, McCord interprets her refusal to address him by his real name as a Stanislavskian acting method, and offers her a job as the titular bedpan operative. Cue some mildly amusing misunderstandings and a burgeoning love affair.

But trouble, both for Betty and the movie, arrives when hit men Charlie and Wesley (Rock, as irritating as always) turn up, determined to off Betty.

In defter comedic hands – Tom DiCillo comes to mind – this could have been a leftfield little gem, but LaBute struggles somewhat with the light comedy. And there's also the small plot problem: since Betty is as mad as a bag of baboons, it's difficult to really sympathise with her. All of which leaves *Nurse Betty* in need of just a little first aid. ★★★ **AS**

THE NUTTY PROFESSOR (1963)

Starring: *Jerry Lewis (Professor Julius Kelp/Buddy Love/Baby Kelp), Stella Stevens (Stella Purdy), Del Moore (Dr Hamius R. Warfield), Kathleen Freeman (Millie Lemmon)*
Director: *Jerry Lewis*
Screenwriters: *Jerry Lewis, Bill Richmond*
PG/107 mins./Comedy/USA

To improve his social life, a nerdish professor drinks a potion that temporarily turns him into the handsome, but obnoxious, Buddy Love.

As Sergeant Bilko, Phil Silvers was given to flattering the pompous by declaring, 'In France, they'd build a statue to you.' Jerry Lewis, as the whole world is tired of hearing, is the test case of the insanity of the French. In Paris, intellectuals adore the spastic goon character Lewis played in film after film in the 1950s and 60s, taking seriously a performer (and writer-director) only appreciated in his homeland by children and lowbrows.

Actually, it's not hard to see why Lewis plays as well in France as Norman Wisdom in Albania. He has never been a witty-lines comedian, though he does universally translatable funny things with his voice, and his love of the human cartoon sight gag is quite close to the approach of France's own Jacques Tati. In Lewis films, nothing important is said but everything is shown. *The Nutty Professor* has cartoon jokes like Lewis stretching his arms to the floor by dropping a barbell, but he is also the master of the image that is just funny through very slight exaggeration, like the seat in the dean's office that is just too deep for comfort and seems to swallow Lewis when he sits in it.

A Jerry Lewis film festival would be an endurance test, for he has the traditional clown's failing of wanting to fall down sobbing on his knees and beg for love. The more control he gained over his films after the split with 50s partner Dean Martin, the more given he was to indulging in long periods of laugh-free tastelessness, climaxing in the legendary but unseen concentration camp comedy *The Day The Clown Cried* (1972) that more or less ended his auteur career. But Lewis has always been the most self-aware, self-critical of screen comedians – Chaplin or Stan Laurel wouldn't have accepted the roles in *The King Of Comedy* (1983) or *Funny Bones* (1995). There's a creepy sequence in *The Bellboy* (1960) where Lewis' sweet, mute title character runs into 'Jerry Lewis', taking a second role and playing himself as an obnoxious, sadistic bastard. And there's his one truly great movie, *The Nutty Professor*.

A skit on *Dr Jekyll And Mr Hyde*, this is a film that (as Eddie Murphy discovered) could only be made by someone who wasn't as secure in the affections of the audience as he had been in the previous decade. In 1963, it was read as a strange summation of the Martin-and-Lewis films, with infantile comic Lewis proving he didn't need a smooth straight man because he could play both roles, and the Mr Hyde figure of swinger 'Buddy Love' seen as a nasty caricature of Dino. Actually, Buddy plays more like Martin's Rat Pack padrone, Sinatra, but what Lewis was really doing was presenting his own showbizzy dark side, emerging from the cocoon of his child-pleasing but adult-irritating comic persona.

Americans familiar with Lewis' tireless but also self-serving host duties on the monumentally tasteless fund-raising telethons which make Red Nose Day seem like Remembrance Day, shiver to see in Buddy Love the beginnings of a Jerry Lewis they have come to dread. The Jekyll equivalent, Julius Kelp, is buck-toothed in an ironic nod to Fredric March's 1932 make-up as Mr Hyde, and speaks with that strangled Lewis whine that makes non-fans want to kill him. He elicits a near-masochistic series of humiliations as Kelp is picked on by the dean, football players, musclemen at a gym and his students, exciting the sympathy only of lovely blonde student Stella Purdy. Eddie Murphy's Buddy Love avenges wrongs done to his Sherman Klump, but Lewis' Buddy despises his alter ego and makes a play for Stella in such an unpleasant manner that he becomes just the worst of the series of bullies who have picked on Kelp.

From the wonderfully coloured Expressionist parody of the traditional Jekyll-And-Hyde transformation, in which Kelp turns into a series of ever-more grotesque Hyde types before becoming the 'swingingest' Buddy, through to Buddy's rise to power at the local happening place, The Purple Pit, *The Nutty Professor* is among the most uncomfortable of American comedies. Unlike Stevenson's Jekyll, Kelp learns his lesson, but not before he has had to accept that he has a monster inside him. The finale, in which Love untransforms into Kelp in front of the whole campus, is dead serious, and as devastating as Cliff Robertson's regression to imbecility in the last reel of *Charly* (1968). It takes a cynical series of gags, with Stella accepting the love of Kelp but keeping bottles of the swinger tonic on hand in case she needs the loving of Love, to take the edge off. ★★★★ **KN**

⊙ THE NUTTY PROFESSOR (1996)

Starring: *Eddie Murphy (Professor Sherman Klump/Buddy Love/Lance Perkins/Cletus 'Papa' Klump/Anna Pearl 'Mama' Jensen Klump/Ida Mae 'Granny' Jensen/Ernie Klump, Sr), Jada Pinkett Smith (Professor Carla Purty), James Coburn (Harlan Hartley), Larry Miller (Dean Richmond), Dave Chappelle (Reggie Warrington)*
Director: *Tom Shadyac*
Screenwriters: *David Sheffield, Barry W. Blaustein, Tom Shadyac, Steve Oedekerk, based on the 1963 motion picture by Jerry Lewis, Bill Richmond*
12/95 mins./Comedy/USA

Awards: *Academy Awards – Best Make-up; BAFTA – Best Make-up/Hair*

Obese college professor and biochemist Sherman Klump, manages to come up with a conconction that enables him to shed 300 pounds and all his inhibitions in 30 seconds.

It's Jim Carrey who's supposed to be the new Jerry Lewis. But this reworking (from *Ace Ventura*'s Shadyac) of Lewis' wildest comic favourite had Eddie Murphy giving his funniest performance (actually, make that seven performances) in over a decade. The lesson to be learned by him from this success is that letting other people do the writing, producing and directing frees him up to do what we'd justifiably forgotten he can do brilliantly – make us laugh.

In this wacky variant of *Dr Jekyll And Mr Hyde*, Murphy is the obese college professor and biochemist Sherman Klump, whose experiments enable him to shed 300 pounds and his inhibitions in 30 seconds. His streamlined persona is the flirtatious, fast-talking rascal Buddy Love, swaggeringly confident enough to woo a beauteous colleague and create havoc in Klump's life.

A lot of the humour is very naughty and brazenly crude – genital, lavatorial, and letting rip with so many fart gags a lit match could detonate the cinema – but offered with such cheerful abandon that only some of it strikes a bum note – as it were. Buddy Love is the Murphy we know: smarmy, saucy, irritating; Professor Klump is – even through the amazing padding and special effects morphing – the sweetest, most endearing character he's ever attempted. And whether Klump is being humiliated by his grotesque family (Murphy earning his salary playing his own mum, dad and gaga granny) or bashfully courting, his attempts to exercise and diet, his depressed binges on chocolate, and his heartache at ridicule are genuinely touching, huggy bits amid farcical frolics.

Shadyac and co. insists on squeezing in a suggestion of To Thine Own Self Be True platitudinising which is a little forced and whilst this doesn't really bear repeated viewing it works as a family film, especially if most of your family is a bunch of 13-year-old boys. Popular in Never Never Land then. ★★★ **AE**

⊙ NUTTY PROFESSOR II: THE KLUMPS (2000)

Starring: *Eddie Murphy (Professor Sherman Klump/Buddy Love/Cletus 'Papa' Klump/Young Cletus Klump/Anna Pearl 'Mama' Jensen Klump/Ida Mae 'Granny' Jensen/Ernie Klump, Sr./Lance Perkins), Janet Jackson (Professor Denise Gaines), Larry Miller (Dean Richmond), John Ales (Jason)*
Director: *Peter Segal*
Screenwriters: *Barry W. Blaustein, David Sheffield, Paul Weitz, Chris Weitz, based on a story by Steve Oedekerk, Barry W. Blaustein, David Sheffield*
12/106 mins./109 mins. (director's cut)/Comedy/USA

Sherman Klump, the overweight scientific genius, has finally found the love of his life in equally talented scientist, Denise. Trouble is, the other Love of his life – his demented alter-ego Buddy Love – is determined to make a reappearance...

For some, watching Eddie Murphy delight in his comedic abilities and re-ignite his career in the first *Nutty Professor* was akin to watching Muhammad Ali, circa 1974's 'Rumble In The Jungle'. By that analogy, *The Klumps* is a bit like watching Ali just a couple of years before he called it quits – occasionally still exciting to be around, but more often than not going through the motions, punching well below par.

There are numerous laughs to be had in *Nutty Professor II* – with Larry Miller's buggery by a giant hamster proving to be the unexpected highlight – but too often these laughs fall into two categories: self-indulgent, make-up-heavy turns from Murphy, and unexpected gross-out gags by the shovel-load, more than likely supplied by *American Pie* directors, the Weitz brothers. Murphy kindly leaves some of the bigger laughs to Miller. Still, when it hits, it's generally down to Murphy. With Sherman Klump, the comic once again opts not to play simple caricature, and finds a real depth hidden somewhere amongst the layers of blubber. Buddy Love is played at full tilt, aided and abetted by the fact that his genome has been crossed with that of a dog, allowing Murphy to go all out on the bestiality gags, and provide us with a unique game of 'catch'.

Jackson is suitably sweet as Klump's beloved, but the rest of the family are as sketchy as before – and while their on-screen intermingling (and Rick Baker's make-up) are even more dazzling than in their screen-stealing debut, Murphy and co. overplay the gag. Too often, the Klumps just ramble and rant, much of their arguing getting lost in frustrating asides and overlapping dialogue. It was a good gag originally – here, more often than not, it's a good effect. ★★ **BM**

⊙ O BROTHER, WHERE ART THOU? (2000)

Starring: *George Clooney (Ulysses Everett McGill), John Turturro (Pete), Tim Blake Nelson (Delmar O'Donnell), John Goodman (Big Dan Teague), Holly Hunter (Penny)*
Director: *Joel Coen*
Screenwriters: *Ethan Coen, Joel Coen, from the poem* The Odyssey *by Homer*
12/102 mins./Comedy/USA/UK/France

Awards: *Golden Globes – Best Musical/Comedy Actor*

The Coen brothers splice Homer's Odyssey with Preston Sturges and Depression era America and come up with a road movie-cum-screwball comedy.

Like most Coen movies, it isn't quite the way they used to make them, but is deeply in love not just with the films of the past, but all of popular culture, from product packaging (principally Dapper Dan hair pomade) through period pop music to modes of dress and politics. Though its down-home numbers are states away from the glamour of vintage Hollywood, this even manages to be the nearest thing to a real feelgood musical the movies have pulled off in years.

While earlier Coen movies pay homage to Dashiell Hammett (*Blood Simple*, 1983), William Faulkner (*Barton Fink*, 1991) and Raymond Chandler (The Big Lebowski, 1998), the touchstone here is short story-writer and fabulist Howard Waldrop (who has a character named after him). In his novel, *A Dozen Tough Jobs*, Waldrop retold the story of Hercules in the rural South in the 1920s. Here, the Coens use the Waldropian approach by replaying the story of Ulysses' long journey home from the Trojan Wars to Ithaca against the backdrop of Depression-era Mississippi.

Our heroes are: Ulysses Everett McGill, a fast-talking, fastidious wiseguy who says he's after treasure but really wants to get back together with his wife, Penny, and brood of daughters; Delmar, a slow-witted tag-along who wants to buy back the family farm from the bank; and Pete, a tearaway with ambitions to be a maitre d'. On their trail is a typical Coen demon villain, posse-leader Cooley, and in the background is an electoral contest between the genially corrupt incumbent governor, Pappy O'Daniel, and the reform-minded Homer Stokes. Along the way, they fall in with Tommy Johnson – a bluesman who has swapped his soul for musical talent, which leads the runaways into a profitable detour as a recording sensation – and manic depressive gunman George Nelson, who hates cows as much as cops.

Confidently cinematic in classical and modern terms, layered with subtleties but also a straight-ahead, crowd-pleasing comedy, with more witty lines and bits of visual imagination than a dozen regular movies, *O Brother* is where thou shouldst be. ★★★★★ **KN**

⊙ THE OBJECT OF MY AFFECTION (1998)

Starring: *Jennifer Aniston (Nina Borowski), Paul Rudd (George Hanson), John Pankow (Vince McBride), Alan Alda (Sidney Miller), Tim Daly (Dr. Robert Joley), Nigel Hawthorne (Rodney Fraser), Allison Janney (Constance Miller)*
Director: *Nicholas Hytner*
Screenwriter: *Wendy Wasserstein, from the novel by Stephen McCauley*
15/106 mins./Comedy/Romance/USA

Nina, life seems to going according to plan but then George, a cute gay schoolteacher, moves into her apartment and she finds herself falling for him.

Aniston is Nina, the kind of love-to-hate celluloid twentysomething with perfect job, wardrobe, partner and affluent social circle in tow. Enter George, a cute gay schoolteacher who takes the spare room in her apartment after splitting with his older boyfriend and the pair soon forge a boyfriend-girlfriend style relationship despite the lack of physical attraction and Nina's ever-present, irritating partner lurking in the background. The relationship takes a new turn, however, when she falls pregnant and decides she wants to be more than just George's buddy . . .

This unrequited love yarn may sound like a load of sentimental old claptrap, but Hytner carries it along rather nicely, relying on strong characterisation, subtle humour and winning performances to beef up the admittedly bland material – and thankfully never resorting to the show-tune-strumming loudly-frocked, gay stereotypes of yore.

Aniston, looking more like someone with a pillow stuffed up her top than a woman basking in gestation, turns in a curiously restrained performance, while the delightful Rudd is a leading man in the making. But it's the gallery of supporting players – Alda as a flashy book editor, Nigel Hawthorne as a lonely luvvy – who get the lion's share of the one-liners and steer the film away from saccharine territory. Unashamedly a chick-flick, but no less enjoyable for it. ★★★ **CW**

OCEAN'S 11 (1960)

Starring: *Frank Sinatra (Danny Ocean), Dean Martin (Sam Harmon), Sammy Davis Jr (Josh Howard), Peter Lawford (Jimmy Foster), Angie Dickinson (Beatrice Ocean)*
Director: *Lewis Milestone*
Screenwriters: *Harry Brown, Charles Lederer, based on a story by George Clayton Johnson, Jack Golden Russell*
PG/127 mins./Comedy/Crime/USA

A gang of World War II buddies – led by Danny Ocean – plan to rob five Las Vegas casinos in one night.

The Rat Pack! Broads! Mobsters! Gambling! And then they went to work! Leaving aside the superior Soderbergh version, the making of Lewis Milestone's 1960 Las Vegas heist caper would make a much more interesting movie than the knockabout comedy on offer here. Indeed, the double duties pulled by the principal cast during the shoot (playing two shows a night at The Sands) are evident in the sluggish pace, sleepy performances and narrative stitched together out of whatever scenes Sinatra showed up for.

Still, there are many incidental pleasures to be had, not least Sammy (cast as a garbage man, apparently because Sinatra was feeling spiteful) singing 'E-O-Eleven', Dean swinging the old Sahara lounge, Nelson Riddle's sizzling score and some neat hipster dialogue.

From smokes to suits, you get a real flavour of Las Vegas while it was still cool – all of it beautifully shot by the veteran cinematographer William Daniels. ★★★ **CK**

OCEAN'S ELEVEN (2001)

Starring: *George Clooney (Danny Ocean), Brad Pitt (Rusty Ryan), Julia Roberts (Tess Ocean), Matt Damon (Linus Caldwell), Andy Garcia (Terry Benedict), Don Cheadle (Basher Tarr)*
Director: *Steven Soderbergh*
Screenwriter: *Ted Griffin, from the 1960 film*
12/111 mins./Action/Crime/Comedy/USA

Fresh out of prison, Danny Ocean sets up a dream robbery, roping in ten other experts to help. His object: the vaults of the three biggest Las Vegas casinos. Along with a cool 150 million, he hopes to win back ex-wife Tess, who just happens to be dating a big casino owner. . .

Let's be honest. The original *Ocean's 11* wasn't a five-star movie. But it was certainly a memorable one. Vegas and the entire Rat Pack on screen for the first time made it an event picture. Soderbergh's film is just as much of an event and, more importantly, it has taken the essence of what was good about the first film and given it a new millennium polish, with a cast who don't buckle under the weight of expectation.

Bar a few in-jokes for the old school fans, no prior knowledge is necessary. This is entertainment of the effortless order. Soderbergh's pacing leaves scant room for fidgeting, and the story spills out frame by frame so that plots can twist just seconds faster than you can cotton on.

Clooney's generous headlining performance gives plenty of scope to showcase the rest of the talent, and no one here is lacking. Few directors have made their stars look as high-wattage. Garcia is just bad enough to want to destroy, and Roberts elusive enough to be the natural object of affection. Watch for the scene where she crosses the casino floor switching her allegiance from one man to another – that's a definite movie star scene. Damon relishes his role out of the limelight as the new kid on the block, while his same-age team-mates, Casey Affleck and Scott Caan, go for laughs.

Don Cheadle does a cockney accent to rival Dick Van Dyke, but somehow gets away with it, and Elliott Gould and Carl Reiner do some grade A scene-stealing without unbalancing the movie. Yet, special mention has to go to Brad Pitt. Loitering in the background, generally snacking, he delivers a quiet performance that suggests the hidden strengths beyond his pretty boy looks. This is one movie where wearing a suit well does him no harm at all.

But if your tastes are of a less superficial nature, there's Soderbergh's trademark cutting technique to hitch the movie up a notch, stunt work (particularly courtesy of grease-man Shaobo Qin) that can't be faked, and a heist that deserves the build-up.

This is a movie that plays to all demographics without feeling like a by-numbers production. To berate it for being shallow is to miss the point. This isn't the seamy Las Vegas, where the house always wins. It's a film that's as well-constructed and glamorously shiny as the monoliths that now dominate The Strip. The good guys are crooks? So what! If only all crooks were this nice. No guns, no gangster cliche swear-a-thon. This is a movie that plays to fantasies, and few do it with such relish. ★★★★★ **EC**

OCEAN'S TWELVE (2004)

Starring: *George Clooney (Danny Ocean), Brad Pitt (Rusty Ryan), Julia Roberts (Tess Ocean), Matt Damon (Linus Caldwell), Andy Garcia (Terry Benedict), Don Cheadle (Basher Tarr), Catherine Zeta-Jones (Isabel Lahiri)*
Director: *Steven Soderbergh*
Screenwriter: *George Nolfi, from characters by George Clayton Johnson, Jack Golden Russell*
12/125 mins./Action/Crime/Comedy/USA

Three years after their audacious Vegas heist, Danny Ocean's 11-strong crew are finally tracked down by fuming casino boss Terry Benedict. He gives them two weeks to pay him back with interest. So they whizz to Europe to pull off more heists in a bid to save their skins.

Ocean's Eleven is, without doubt, one of the best remakes ever made. The 1960 Rat-packed original never turned its star-wattage into onscreen brilliance, with its cast having a better time making it than anyone else had watching it. But Steven Soderbergh took the same premise and a similarly glitzy set of players, then produced a buff, disciplined little heist movie that glistened with effortless charm. So what about the sequel to the remake? A movie which, amazingly, reunites every player from the first – not to mention Lady CZJ and a few heavyweight cameos – and relocates them to sunny, glammy Euro-locales.

Unfortunately, it's horribly easy to argue that, returning talent aside, *Ocean's Twelve* has more in common with the original *Eleven* than the remade one. Perhaps that's too harsh. But it is riling to know that Pitt, Clooney, Roberts and co. had such a great time gallivanting around the Continent when what they've achieved fails to hit the heights of what went before. The script's largely to blame; where once there was sharpness there's now a lack of focus. *Eleven* concerned one elaborate heist, involving meticulous planning, deft employment of gadgetry, a few neat short cons and one ace long con, all played out to great effect. *Twelve* concerns two half-conceived heists and the process of pulling off either is unclear, while the cons involved simply don't work; the central one is a shameless cheat that'll leave any attentive audience-member exasperated come the final unveiling.

This doesn't matter so much given the movie manages to coast along on its cast's collective charm. Clooney and Pitt still amuse with Danny and Rusty's half-telepathic dialogues, while Damon's Linus is entertainingly awkward in his blundering attempts to develop his heisting leadership skills. But even so, the characters are somewhat lost – in more than one sense. Here, Clooney takes a back seat, and with that anchor aweigh, *Ocean's Twelve* bobs around aimlessly. Who's our hero here? Rusty? Linus? Zeta-Jones' determined thief-taker? It's never clear.

Furthermore, the cast's inherent starriness has this time been allowed to blind us to the characters. Everyone involved knows this. And they're not afraid to show it in a series of blatant in-jokes – some of which are hilarious, while others prove infuriating revealing the hollow Hollywood laugh-in beneath. As if in battle with the sparkling gloss spooned on by his cast, he keeps the look gritty and grainy, his partner in grime being David Holmes, whose original-score contributions are raw, fuzzy and Roy Budd-y. Soderbergh doesn't so much direct this movie as rescue it from itself. Actually, there's your answer to the question of who's the hero of *Ocean's Twelve*: Steven Soderbergh. ★★ **CK**

OCTOBER (1928)

Starring: *Nikandrof (Lenin), N. Popov (Kerensky), Boris Livanov (Minister)*
Directors: *Sergei Eisenstein, Grigori V. Alexandrov*
PG/99 mins./History/USSR

Though a provisional government headed by Alexander Kerensky has taken over from the Tsar, widespread injustices continue and Russia does not withdraw from the First World War. Organised by Lenin's Bolshevik party, the proletariat take control of the government.

Distributed internationally under the title of John Reed's best-selling eyewitness account of the Russian Revolution, *Ten Days That Shook the World*, this was produced in 1927 to commemorate the tenth anniversary of the October Revolution and the storming of the Winter Palace.

The film was directed and edited by Sergei Eisenstein as a silent, designed to be accompanied by a Dmitri Shostakovich score; Grigori Aleksandrov supervised the effecs track that turned it into a sound picture (if not a talkie).

It's less impressive than Eisenstein's earlier *Strike* and *Battleship Potemkin*, which deal with smaller, less-contested pieces of pre-Soviet history. Here, undeniable filmmaking genius is most compromised shaping material to suit state sponsors.

Because the official line was that the huge proletariat (rather than the tiny Bolshevik Party) were the victors of 1917, there's little individual characterisation. Lenin appears briefly to be hailed by a crowd and Stalin never shows up on screen; as ever, Eisenstein is better on 'villains', whether it be the well-dressed society ladies who stab a revolutionary to death with their parasols, or Kerensky broods amid leftover Romanov splendours (another 'Tsar Alexander?' asks the intertitle) and Trotsky (perversely, the most memorable character in the film) is always seen arguing for the wrong course of action.

Some sequences, shot on the sites of the actual events and with many of the original participants playing themselves, are still spectacular and many images (the huge statue hauled down by ropes, the corpse and dead horse stranded on a raised bridge) remain resonant well after the Soviet Union has gone the way of the Tsar. ★★★ **KN**

OCTOPUSSY (1983)

Starring: *Roger Moore (James Bond), Maud Adams (Octopussy), Louis Jordan (Kamal Khan), Steven Berkoff (General Orlov), Desmond Llewelyn (Q)*
Director: *John Glen*
Screenwriters: *George MacDonald Fraser, Richard Maibaum, Michael G. Wilson based on the novel by Ian Fleming*
PG/131 mins./Spy/UK-USA

After 009 is assassinated while carrying a rare Faberge egg, 007 is sent to investigate. He discovers a smuggling operation, that leads to a renegade Soviet general aiming to instigate World War III.

While this oft-forgotten Bond movie certainly suffers from an evidently ageing Roger Moore, a surfeit of daft postmoderny gags – former tennis ace Vijay Armitraj fighting off foes with a tennis racket; Bond quelling a tiger by shouting 'Sit!' just like dog-trainer Barbara Woodhouse – and a lack of focus for the villainy, there's still a good plot at work here. Bond is fully occupied tracking the origins of the Faberge Egg to Maud Adams' Octopussy (half villain, half Bond girl, great name) who is tied up with Kamal Kahn (slick Louis Jordan) and General Orlov (Steven Berkoff, yawn) who are plotting world domination or somesuch.

Tagline
James Bond's all-time high.

John Glenn has got it well-organised in its globe spanning (Berlin, India, the East German border country), building up a fair head of tension with all the familiar Bond ploys: disarming a ticking atomic bomb dressed in a clown suit, knife throwing twins, a scowling henchman with a kid of razor-edged Frisbee thing. The ending sags, with too much silly Q business, but makes up for it with an army of acrobatic babes in skin-tight Lycra. ★★★ **IN**

THE ODD COUPLE (1968)

Starring: *Jack Lemmon (Felix Ungar), Walter Matthau (Oscar Madison), John Fiedler (Vinnie), Herb Edelman (Murray), David Sheiner (Roy)*
Director: *Gene Saks*
Screenwriter: *Neil Simon, from his play*
PG/105 mins./Comedy/USA

Two friends try sharing an apartment, but their ideas of housekeeping and lifestyles are as different as night and day.

In *Marlowe*, an update of the Raymond Chandler novel *The Little Sister*, James Garner's sun-tanned private eye gets mixed up in a case which requires that he interview a prissy television exec.

The suspect is worried that the star of his hit sitcom is being blackmailed, but Marlowe is more puzzled by the industry slang and has to have the term 'sitcom' explained to him as 'situation comedy'. Clearly, we now know that a sitcom is a half-hour show with a laugh-track, but a good definition of what it actually means is the sort of thing Neil Simon (who started out writing for perhaps the greatest sitcom of all, *Sergeant Bilko*) does.

A New York live TV-and-theatre man, Simon writes funny, pointed dialogue you memorise and trot out in real life to suggest that you're wittier than you are ('Don't point that finger at me unless you intend to use it'), but he is the master of properties where the humour really does come from the

Actors Who Started As Extras

1 Clark Gable
2 Marilyn Monroe
3 Clint Eastwood
4 Michael Caine
5 Roger Moore
6 Robert Mitchum
7 Jean Harlow
8 Marlene Dietrich
9 Melanie Griffith
10 David Niven

situation. Having written a hit play and movie (*Barefoot In The Park*, 1967) about getting married, Simon followed through with one about divorce, but avoided the predictable marital screaming matches. Instead, he devised a set-up where, as in many sitcoms (cf: *Steptoe And Son*, *Dad's Army*, *Cheers*, *The Larry Sanders Show*, *Red Dwarf*, etc.) irreconcilable characters are trapped together, unsure whether they love or hate each other and locked in patterns of behaviour that are funny but also tragic. In the long opening sequence, fussy TV newswriter Felix, just booted out by a wife driven mad by his endless neatening, checks into a hotel to commit suicide (offered a room on the third floor, he asks 'Haven't you anything higher?'), then seeks refuge with his already divorced best friend, slobbish Oscar. The two share Oscar's apartment and grind up against one other, echoing the way they destroyed their marriages (they both semi-accidentally call each other by their ex-wives' names).

Though this is a widescreen, colourful film – with an irresistibly cool theme by Neal Hefti, creator of the 'Da-na-na-na-na-na Batman!' tune – it's almost all set in the spacious apartment. Director Saks merely referees the performances of a couple of pros, working together for the second time after Billy Wilder's *The Fortune Cookie*, in which they were also trapped together, when shyster lawyer Matthau forced Lemmon to pretend to be wheelchair-bound to make an insurance claim. Their partnership that would extend to Lemmon directing Matthau in *Kotch*, a couple of *Grumpy Old Men* pictures, two Wilder disappointments (*The Front Page*, *Buddy Buddy*) and, sadly, the last gasp of *The Odd Couple II*.

Matthau chews on Simon's dialogue ('Why doesn't he hear me? I know I'm talking. I hear my voice') as if it were aspirin, while Lemmon plays broader and more physically, clearing his ears with a 'fmah fmah' sound compared to a moose-call and twittering around in an apron. Despite Oscar habitually calling his menfriends 'pussycat', 'baby', 'darling' and 'dear' and Felix snaps at him for coming home late as the meatloaf he has prepared starts to frazzle, the joke is not that these two middle-aged men are gay but that their nonsexual relationship is falling apart exactly as their marriages did.

The third act brings on two English divorcees with names out of Oscar Wilde, Gwendolyn and Cecily, for a dinner party Oscar hopes will lead to a good time with 'the coo coo Pigeon sisters', but it's Felix who scores, crying about his broken marriage and impressing the women with his sensitivity. The women, described by the *Monthly Film Bulletin* as 'the kind of congenital English gigglers whom one often sees on buses but seldom on the screen', dress mod, but now seem like a rough draft for the kind of characters Mike Leigh would soon make his own. They went to the the real sitcom version, which ran from 1970 to 1975 with Tony Randall and Jack Klugman in the leads, and then again as *The New Odd Couple*, with black actors Ron Glass and Desmond Wilson.

Simon, Academy Award-nominated for the *Odd Couple* script, continued in the same vein, with a later play and film (*Chapter Two*, 1979) about remarriage. With Matthau, he created another grouchy male couple classic, *The Sunshine Boys*, but with Lemmon he followed the darker implications of the mid-life crisis. He made films that voiced the desperation of the 50s-style buttoned-down Felixes as they were swallowed by the chaos of the 60s and the cynicism of the 70s: *The Out-Of-Towners* and *The Prisoner Of Second Avenue*. The secret of great sitcom is knowing when to shut off the laugh track and feel the pain behind the gag lines. ★★★★★ **KN**

➂ ODD MAN OUT (1947)

Starring: *James Mason (Johnny McQueen), Robert Newton (Lukey), Kathleen Ryan (Kathleen), Robert Beatty (Dennis), William Hartnell (Barman), F.J. McCormick (Shell), Fay Compton (Rosie), Beryl Measor (Maudie)*
Director: *Carol Reed*
Screenwriters: *F.L. Green, R.C. Sheriff, based on the novel by F.L. Green*
PG/116 mins./Drama/UK

Six months after escaping from a Northern Irish prison, Johnny McQueen kills a man and is himself fatally wounded when a robbery to raise funds for The Organisation misfires and he spends the next eight hours evading capture and drawing closer to death.

Carol Reed's 15th feature was his first entirely personal project and the contrast with anything that had gone before immediately struck contemporary critics and audiences, who were somewhat taken aback by the fact that he had chosen to produce such an anti-heroic story about a divided part of the triumphant nation so soon after the Second World War. Belfast is never identified by name and Johnny McQueen's political allegiance is downplayed as much as possible. But few were in any doubt that Reed had made a sympathetic (not to say quasi-religious) character out of an IRA gunman, while demonising his neighbours on either side of the sectarian divide.

James Mason gives one of his finest performances as the outsider who doesn't seem to fit anywhere, yet whose name is on everyone's lips – whether it's kids recreating his bungled raid; the police on his tail; Fr Tom (W.G. Fay), the priest who is only interested in saving his soul; Pat and Nolan (Cyril Cusack and Dan O'Herlihy), the comrades who are desperate to locate him; Lukey, the artist desirous of capturing his death throes on canvas; Shell, the derelict who would sell him to the highest bidder, or the women who either offer Johnny solace (loyal sweetheart Kathleen Ryan and compassionate housewife Fay Compton) or betray him (tart without a heart, Beryl Measor).

Adapted by R.C. Sherriff and F.L. Green from the latter's novel, the story of a killer's desperate bid to avoid capture, despite knowing that he will die unless his wounds are treated, is as suspenseful as anything that Alfred Hitchcock produced during his British career. But, Robert Krasker's brooding monochrome photography (which anticipated the even more canted dislocations he would achieve in *The Third Man*) and Roger Furse and Ralph Binton's studio realist sets more readily recall the humane pessimism of such bleakly poetic Marcel Carné dramas as *Quai des Brumes* and *Le Jour Se Lève* in which Jean Gabin played tormented fugitives seeking refuge within Alexandre Trauner's atmospheric backstreet locales. ★★★★ DP

OH, MR PORTER! (1937)

Starring: *Will Hay (William Porter), Moore Marriott (Jeremiah Harbottle), Graham Moffat (Albert Brown), Sebastian Smith (Charles Trimbletow), Agnes Lachlan (Mrs. Trimbletow)*
Director: *Marcel Varnel*
Screenwriters: *J.O.C. Orton, Val Guest, Marriott Edgar, from a story by Frank Lauder*
U/80 mins./Comedy/UK

William Porter, an inept railway worker, is shunted off to a dead-end job in Buggleskelly, Northern Ireland, where several previous stationmasters have met a mysterious fate.

An always-welcome afternoon TV staple. Though he gets above-the-title billing, Will Hay was no more a solo comedian than Groucho Marx. This, one of his finest vehicles, finds him congenially teamed with sidekicks Moore Marriott and Graham Moffatt in one of the British cinema's greatest comedy gangs.

In a priceless opening, Hay, the latest in a long line of doomed souls, turns up at dilapidated Buggleskelly station with the presentation clock given him on departure from his last job only to find a row of similar, abandoned clocks on the mantlepiece, suggesting the dire fate of all the previous stationmasters.

Much delight comes in the interplay between Hay and Marriott, as single-toothed dotty old-timer Harbottle (asked when the next train is due, he says 'next train's gone'), and Moffatt, as chubby smart kid Albert.

The trio fail the most basic requirements of their railway jobs, but come up trumps in the *Scooby-Doo* stakes when investigating the ghost of One-Eyed Joe and his haunted mill and discover a branch line being used by cross-border gun-smugglers who are defeated in a spirited final chase.

There's some slapstick with an escape from the mill in a high wind and the last ride of the venerable locomotive Gladstone, but Hay works best with character comedy, pompously reprimanding his subordinates for dodges he proceeds to pull himself, reacting to every ominous line with a perfect double-take and blithely surviving the chaos his character causes wherever he goes.

Hay, Marriott and Moffatt reprised their acts in the similar, equally delightful *Ask a Policeman, Where's That Fire?*, *Convict 99* and *Old Bones of the River*. ★★★ KN

OH! WHAT A LOVELY WAR (1969)

Starring: *Ralph Richardson (Sir Edward Grey), Meriel Forbes (Lady Grey), Wensley Pithey (Archduke Franz Ferdinand), Ruth Kettlewell (Duchess Sophie), Ian Holm (President Poincare), John Gielgud (Count Berchtold), Kenneth More (Kaiser Willhelm II)*
Director: *Richard Attenborough*
Screenwriter: *Len Deighton, based on Joan Littlewood's stage production of Charles Chilton's play* The Long, Long Trail
PG/144 mins./Musical/UK
Awards: *BAFTA – Best Supporting Actor (Laurence Olivier), Best Art Direction, Best Cinematography, Best Costume Design, Best Sound Track*

The entire Smith family is wiped out in the trenches, while European royalty and the British military make an unholy mess of conducting the First World War.

Joan Littlewood's 1963 stage musical was based on Charles Chilton's radio play, *The Long, Long Trail*. Producer Brian Duffy and novelist Len Deighton (who was then on a cinematic roll with Michael Caine's Harry Palmer thrillers) acquired the rights and offered Richard Attenborough the opportunity to make his directorial debut. However, it proved to be an occasionally fractious shoot, which culminated in Deighton abandoning his writer-producer credit after falling out with the director over his approach.

Few British films had been as flamboyantly ambitious as this all-star vaudeville, although its pacifist sentiments had been anticipated by both Richard Lester's *How I Won the War* and Tony Richardson's *The Charge of the Light Brigade*. But, ultimately, too many stars spoilt the satire – even though Attenborough resisted the temptation to dot the action with cameoing thespians in the same way that Michael Anderson had done in *Around the World in 80 Days*.

Only Maggie Smith's raucous recruiting rendition at the fairground had the power to shock, as it showed the ease with which young men were shamed into fighting a war that only really benefited their imperialist-capitalist masters. There were several instances of bleakly surreal humour on the Western Front, but the top brass were made to look like pompous buffoons rather than dangerous incompetents, who wilfully sent millions to their deaths through their bludgeoningly inept tactics. Similarly, subtler digs, such as toffs Dirk Bogarde and Susannah York boycotting German wine for the duration, were lost amidst the novelty of seeing Olivier, Mills, Richardson, Gielgud and countless Redgraves warbling like turns at a village pantomime.

The closing aerial shot of the crosses studding the Flanders Fields is chilling in the extreme. It's just a pity that Attenborough lacked the imagination (as was later the case with *A Chorus Line*) to stage the 50 or so musical vignettes with the parodic panache that the material and the admirable costumes and sets deserved. ★★★ DP

LOS OLVIDADOS (1950)

Starring: *Alfonso Mejia (Pedro), Estela Inda (Pedro's Mother), Miguel Inclan (Don Carmelo), Roberto Cobo (El Jaibo), Alma Delia Fuentes (Meche), Francisco Jambrina (The Principal), Jesus Navarro (Julian's Father), Efrain Arauz (Cacarizo), Javier Amézuca (Julian)*
Director: *Luis Buñuel*
Screenwriter: *Luis Alcoriza, Luis Buñuel*
15/85 mins./Drama/Mexico

Escaped from a reformatory, El Jaibo returns to the Mexico City slums, where his taunting of blind beggar Don Carmelo earns him the fearful respect of street kid Pedro – until he seduces his mother, Marta, and Pedro betrays Jaibo to the cops for killing rival gang member, Julian.

Having spent 15 years in the cinematic wilderness, Luis Buñuel was afforded the opportunity to resume his directorial career by Mexican producer, Oscar Dancigers. Having released the ultra-cheap entertainments, *Gran Casino* and *El Gran Calavera*, Buñuel was considering adaptations of Maria Perez Galdos's *Doña Perfecta* and *Nazarin* when he agreed to make *Los Olvidados* (reportedly in response to Dancigers's request for a commercial children's film).

Basing the screenplay on reform school case studies and his own observations during a lengthy sojourn in the Mexico City shanties, Buñuel shot the film in 18 days for a mere 450,000 pesos. Taking neo-realism into unchartered surrealist territory, its study of lust, greed, vengeance and despair owed little to such romanticised visions of poverty as Vittorio De Sica's *Shoeshine* (1946). Indeed, Buñuel consciously corrupted the neo-realist ideal by casting experienced performers like Miguel Inclán, Estela Inda and Roberto Cobo in principal roles and was only dissuaded by Dancigers from inserting such provocatively anachronistic details as a 100-piece orchestra playing in the background while Jaibo killed Pedro.

The Mexican critics were appalled by the feature's unflinching depiction of what amounted to a medieval peasant enclave in the midst of their supposedly cosmopolitan city and denounced Buñuel for failing to alleviate the misery with some optimistic fantasy (as opposed to the unnerving slo-mo nightmare, in which Pedro endures the cruelty of both Marta and Jaibo). Dancigers was so intimidated by such negativity that he withdrew the picture after two days and it was only Buñuel's Best Director win at Cannes the following year that secured its reputation and rescued him from the obscurity into which he had lapsed since the release of the equally uncompromising documentary, *Las Hurdes*.

Although Gabriel Figueroa's meticulous imagery occasionally works against the lacerating content, this remains a potent exposé of the depravity into which humanity is lured when it loses hope. Refusing to judge and offering no easy solutions, Buñuel implied that the only way to conquer such base criminality was to start at the top. Consequently, this shattering indictment of social indifference is more relevant than ever. **★★★★★ DP**

➀ OKLAHOMA! (1955)

Starring: *Gordon MacRae (Curly McLain), Gloria Grahame (Ado Annie Carnes), Gene Nelson (Will Parker), Charlotte Greenwood (Aunt Eller Murphy), Shirley Jones (Laurey Williams)*
Director: *Fred Zinnemann*
Screenwriters: *Sonya Levien, William Ludwig, based on the plays* Oklahoma! *by Oscar Hammerstein,* Green Grow The Lilacs *by Lynn Riggs*
U/145 mins./Musical/Western/USA

Awards: *Academy Awards – Best Score, Best Sound Recording*

Cowboy Curly romances farm-girl Laurie, while resentful farmhand Jud seethes vengefully. Meanwhile, Oklahoma territory is on the point of being declared a state.

As a stage show, Rodgers and Hammerstein's *Oklahoma!*, which debuted in 1943, changed the whole form of the Broadway musical, which is perhaps why Hollywood deemed it important enough a film project to be given to Oscar-winning Fred Zinnemann.

The director, who had done a very different Western in *High Noon*, fusses too much over the famous ballet sequences, adding pretension touches to what ought to be a light, breezy affair, and isn't the man you'd go to for romantic charm or thigh-slapping rural comedy either. Despite recreation of the Agnes de Mille choreography and a bright, brassy widescreen Technicolor look, the visuals come off a poor second to the soundtrack. Leads Gordon McRae (in a role Hugh Jackman would reinvent on stage and in a 1999 TV movie) and Shirley Jones are attractive but colourless in talking scenes, but make up in vocal talent what they lack as actors and soar when given something worth singing.

It's one of the few musicals in which *every single number* is a hit – 'Oh What a Beautiful Morning', 'Surrey With a Fringe On Top,' 'The Farmer and the Cowman Should Be Friends', 'I'm Just a Girl Who Cain't Say No', 'Everything's Up to Date in Kansas City', 'Many a New Day', 'Pore Jud Is Dead', 'People Will Say We're In Love'.

Acting honours go to Rod Steiger, as the only miserable person in the whole of Oklahoma, and Gloria Grahame as that girl who cain't say no. **★★★★ KN**

OLIVER TWIST (1948)

Starring: *Robert Newton (Bill Sikes), Alec Guinness (Fagin), Kay Walsh (Nancy), Francis L. Sullivan (Mr Bumble), Henry Stephenson (Mr Brownlow), Mary Claire (Mrs Corney), John Howard Davies (Oliver Twist), Josephine Stuart (Oliver's Mother), Antony Newley (Artful Dodger)*
Director: *David Lean*
Screenwriters: *David Lean, Stanley Haynes, based on the novel by Charles Dickens*
U/105 mins./Drama/UK

Born in a workhouse, from which he is ejected for asking Mr Bumble for more gruel, Oliver Twist reneges on his apprenticeship to undertaker Mr Sowerby and runs away to London, where he falls in with street thieves Fagin, the Artful Dodger and the murderous Bill Sikes.

Such was the furore created by Alec Guinness's appearance as Fagin that the quality of David Lean's adaptation of Charles Dickens's second novel was somewhat overlooked. Despite the fact that he had drawn on both Cruikshank's original engravings and the author's cutting irony, Guinness's characterisation (complete with a hooked nose and lisping delivery) was deemed insensitively anti-Semitic with the Holocaust still agonisingly fresh in the memory. There were riots at the film's Berlin premiere and it was banned in America for two years, until a sanitised version was finally released. Indeed, the picture was only shown Stateside in its unexpurgated form in 1970, prompting some to suggest that Hollywood had finally wreaked its revenge on the British film industry for refusing to pass Frank Lloyd's 1922 take on the story, which had starred Lon Chaney as Fagin, lest it encouraged hooliganism.

Judiciously trimming the text to its essentials, Lean assembled an able cast around John Howard Davies (who would go on to produce *Monty Python's Flying Circus* and *Fawlty Towers*) and was particularly well served by Robert Newton as Sikes and Kay Walsh as his golden-hearted doxy, Nancy. Moreover, he evocatively recreated the shameful squalor of Victorian London, thanks to Guy Green's cinematography and John Bryan's oppressive sets, whose slums, back alleys and spartan interiors captured the grim realities of urban poverty with an unrivalled fidelity.

But, Lean seemed bent on surpassing his achievement with *Great Expectations*. Consequently, everything was a little more meticulous, literate and self-consciously stylised. He even took the liberty of inventing the entire six-minute opening sequence, in which Oliver's mother struggles across moorland during a storm to arrive at the workhouse in time for his birth. It was a spectacularly cinematic conceit, but it set a tone of expressionist melodrama that became more pronouced as the scene shifted to the capital.

However, when Lean does subjugate his ego to Dickens's genius, this becomes a powerful study of depravity, misery and cruelty, whose controversies (some have also suggested that Fagin has paedophilic tendencies) make it all the more compelling. **★★★★ DP**

➀ OLIVER! (1968)

Starring: *Ron Moody (Fagin), Mark Lester (Oliver Twist), Oliver Reed (Bill Sikes), Shani Wallis (Nancy), Jack Wild (The Artful Dodger)*
Director: *Carol Reed*
Screenwriters: *Lionel Bart, Vernon Harris, based on the stage play by Bart adapted from the novel by Charles Dickens*
PG/99 mins./Musical/UK

Awards: *Academy Awards – Best Picture, Best Director, Best Art Direction, Best Score, Best Sound*

Charles Dickens famous novel of a small boy, Oliver Twist, who escapes from a poorhouse to join a gang of pickpockets on the London streets as led by the conniving Fagin, adapted as a fully fledged musical.

Unforgettable songs, peerless source material, lovely art direction, and twinkling performances all round, yet it still beggars belief that this late 60s musical adaptation of *Oliver Twist* tiptoed away with the Best Picture Oscar. Talk about daylight robbery. While, this is a lovingly made family favourite, with Mark Lester the cleanest boy ever to grace a screen as Oliver himself, it is chirpy rather than important, chipper rather than valuable.

Much pleasure is to be had from the big numbers – 'Food, Glorious Food', 'Consider Yourself', et al – showy, street carnivals that spill about of the pantomimic rather than grim Victoriana. For the caustic, social bleakness of Dickens' disenchantment best to stick with the David Lean version (with no songs). This is slight, romantic repositioning of social commentary as glossy vaudeville hi-jinks with two outstanding performances – coursing with barely tamed violence Oliver Reed is the industry standard for Bill Sikes, and Ron Moody's tragi-wicked Fagin nabbed him a nomination. ★★★ **IN**

OLYMPIA (1938)

Director: *Leni Riefenstahl*
Screenwriter: *Leni Riefenstahl*
Unrated/111 mins./Documentary/West Germany

Divided into two parts — Festival of the People and Festival of Beauty — this epic record of the 1936 Berlin Olympic Games attempts to combine sporting reportage with a celebration of physical beauty and the spectacle involved in this uniquely unifying event.

It's still disputed exactly who commissioned Leni Riefenstahl to produce this account of the 1936 Olympiad or who provided the funding. The debate will also continue as to whether this is an exceptional documentary or a piece of pernicious propaganda. What's clear is that it would not be open to such conjecture had it been made by a Soviet icon like Eisenstein or, rather, had it not been made by the director of *Triumph Of The Will*.

If it's nothing else, *Olympia* is an object lesson in the making of a motion picture. In collaboration with production designer Walter Traut and cinematographers Walter Frentz and Hans Ertl, Riefenstahl spent months analysising film stock in varying lighting conditions and attending sports meets to ascertain the optimum angle, distance and exposure required to capture the aestheticism and athleticism of the different events.

Circumventing restrictions imposed by the International Olympic Committee, she made pioneering use of telephoto lenses and occasionally restaged action to secure the exact image she required (e.g. strapping Kinamo cameras to training marathon runners to gain a subjective insight into the race's gruelling nature). But Riefenstahl retained a fierce independence throughout the entire process, resisting in particular the envious snipes of Propaganda Minister, Joseph Goebbels.

Having worked tirelessly during the 16 days of competition, personally supervising the crews whenever possible, Riefenstahl spent the next 18 months editing the 1,300,000 feet of footage down to 18,000 feet. She also travelled to Greece to oversee Willy Zielke's prologue.

Dividing the two parts into 13 and 11 segments respectively, she gave the opening ceremony a mythical feel and turned the climactic diving sequence into a magisterial study of human poetry in motion. She also risked Nazi ire by emphasising the victories of African-Americans Jesse Owens and Ralph Metcalf, and regardless of the critical fraternity's mixed response, the IOC was suitably impressed by her homage to the Olympic spirit to make her an honoured guest at subsequent Games.

Inevitably reflecting the time and place of its making, this is a remarkable personal vision and it remains the finest example of documentary film art. ★★★★★ **DP**

THE OMEGA MAN (1971)

Starring: *Charlton Heston (Robert Neville), Anthony Zerbe (Matthias), Rosalind Cash (Lisa), Paul Koslo (Dutch)*
Director: *Boris Sagal*
Screenwriters: *John William Corrington, Joyce Hooper Corrington, based on the novel by Richard Matheson*
PG/98 mins./Sci-fi/USA

Having developed a vaccine too late, Robert Neville is the sole survivor of a biologically waged war. That is except for the deformed, vampiric night-creatures, desperate for Neville's death, the remaining representative of the scientific order that brought down mankind.

That startling what-if sci-fi proposition – the last man alive – is given atmospheric punch by novelist Richard Matheison (with *I Am Legend*), and adapting director TV veteran Boris Sagal. But the concept has a snag, once beyond the evocative stillness of a lone wolf in an empty city, where's the plot? The answer, here, is a disappointing variation on the zombie flick: the survivors (turns out Charlton Heston is not so lonely after all) face up to lurching hoards of albino killing machines made light averse by the bio-destruction.

The film does have some interesting undercurrents, especially with the presences of big social stickler Chuck – as anti counterculture. The zombie-vampires are referred to as 'The Family' a barely veiled reference to the murderous cult of Charles Manson. But the film has run out of petrol, its evocative, alien vision of the first half, Heston alone in the sprawling city, sputter into anarchic horror movie clichés, with a bleak ending just around the corner. ★★★ **IN**

OLDBOY (2003)

Starring: *Choi Min-ski (Dae-su Oh), Yu Ji-tae (Woo-jin Lee), Kang Hye-jeong (Mi-do), Dae-han Ji (No Joo-hwan), Dal-su Oh (Park Chelo-woong)*
Director: *Park Chan-wook*
Screenwriters: *Park Chan-wook, Hwang Jo-yun, Lim Chun-hyeong*
18/120 mins./Thriller/South Korea

One night, Dae-su is locked up in a mysterious prison — with no idea why. After 15 torturous years, he's suddenly released and given a mobile phone, a designer suit and a wallet full of cash …

No doubt about it, *OldBoy* is all about extremity. You want torture? Try getting your head around the idea of being in solitary for 15 years. Violence? Check out the one-take corridor brawl in which psychologically ravaged Dae-su takes on a score of goons … with a claw-hammer.

You want to know how far someone could go to wreak revenge? Well, we advise you to brave South Korean writer-director Park Chan-wook's helter-skelter descent into the dingiest pit of human behaviour, even if at times it is tough going and ludicriously unfeasible.

As *Empire* viewed a pre-BBFC-scrutinised cut of the movie, the infamous live-octopus-eating scene remained intact; this truly stomach-churning moment didn't make it into UK cinemas (although is on some DVD copies). But there's plenty else to shock even without it – and all done with such unabashed verve that you'll be as compelled as you are repulsed.

OldBoy recalls *Fincher* in its CG-assisted flourishes and doomy themes, and Tarantino with its sharp-suited, stylised bloodletting. But it's unlikely either of those guys would ever be allowed to push it as far as Park has with this. Like we said, the word is extreme … ★★★★ **DJ**

THE OMEN (1976)

Starring: *Gregory Peck (Robert Thorn), Lee Remick (Katherine Thorn), David Warner (Keith Jennings), Billie Whitelaw (Mrs Baylock), Harvey Stephnes (Damian), Patrick Troughton (Father Brennan)*
Director: *Richard Donner*
Screenwriter: *David Seltzer*
18/106 mins./Horror/USA

Awards: *Academy Awards – Best Original Score*

Gregory Peck is the ambassador to the United States whose wife has a stillborn child. Without her knowledge, he substitutes another baby as theirs. A few years go by, and then grisly deaths begin to happen. It turns out the child is the son of Satan and can only be killed with the seven daggers of Meggado.

As the recent eruption of fury towards paedophiles demonstrates, there is nothing more terrifying, particularly in the eyes of a parent, than the imperilling of a child. Both horror and sci-fi have exploited the vulnerability and innocence of children from the early days of cinema, perhaps most notably when Boris Karloff's monster tossed young Marilyn Harris into the lake in *Frankenstein*. But kids haven't always been defenceless victims. Take, for example, the alien infants in *Village Of The Damned* or the sinister schoolboys in *Unman, Wittering And Zigo*. Even Regan from *The Exorcist*, managed to be both sinned against and sinning.

Although the hysteria surrounding William Friedkin's film had finally died down, there was still a popular anxiety about demonic possession by the time *The Omen* was released. Indeed, its timing couldn't have been better – coming eight years after *Rosemary's Baby* (1968), it had a feel of 'What Satan Did Next'. But the driving force behind the production was, perhaps subconsciously, the desire of a parent to atone for what he perceived to be an unpardonable failing. In the summer of 1975, Gregory Peck's son, Jonathan, was found dead with a gun at his side. Holidaying in France at the time, Peck blamed himself for not being in California when his child needed him. The story of a father struggling to come to terms with his son's identity, therefore, had a certain cathartic appeal.

The project was already underway by the time Peck signed on. Indeed, it had originally been offered to Warner Bros., as a Charlton Heston vehicle. Heston passed after brief consideration. Developed from an idea by LA advertising executive Robert L. Munger, David Seltzer's script was inspired by a passage from the Book Of Revelation. When the Jews return to Zion And a comet rips the sky And the Holy Roman Empire rises Then you and I must die. From the eternal sea he rises Creating armies on either shore, Turning man against his brother 'Til man exists no more. Naturally, the Bible contains no such passage, but the 20th Century Fox publicity machine has to be applauded for attempting to give their film such feasible religious legitimacy.

Peck was unhappy with the idea that a man intelligent enough to be a US Ambassador would try to deceive his wife by substituting an orphaned baby for the one she had just miscarried. But director Richard Donner was less concerned, although he did try to shift the story emphasis away from the notion of the Antichrist and on to the suggestion that Robert Thorn might simply be suffering from a delusion. Moreover, everyone was rather amused by the knowing link between John F. Kennedy (the son of a onetime ambassador to Britain) and Satanism.

Having changed its title from *The Antichrist* to *The Birthmark*, the film seemed to fall victim to a sinister curse. Seltzer's plane to London was hit by lightning; Donner's hotel was bombed by the IRA; Peck cancelled a flight to Israel, only for the plane he'd chartered to crash, killing all onboard; and on day one of the shoot, the principal members of the crew survived a head-on car crash. The jinx appeared to persist well into post production, when special effects artist John Richardson was injured and his assistant killed in an accident on the set of *A Bridge Too Far*.

Predictably, the Vatican was less enthusiastic and, through its radio station, denounced the filmmakers for tackling such a serious theme 'for reasons and towards ends absolutely consumeristic and economical'. With a take of over $100m on a $2.8m budget (plus a further $6m for a lavish publicity campaign), Fox was laughing all the way to perdition. Jerry Goldsmith also had reason to smile as his score won an Oscar, although his 'Ave Satani' failed to convert its Best Song nomination.

Tagline
Good morning. You are one day closer to the end of the world. You have been warned.

The ballyhoo persuaded the studio to embark on a sequel. Although there was nothing to match Patrick Troughton's demise at the sharp end of a lightning rod, *Damien: Omen II* (1978) was quite a respectable follow-up, with the now teenage terror (played by Jonathan Scott-Taylor) dispatching various inquisitive types at his military academy. *The Final Conflict* (1981) was less accomplished, even though Sam Neill exuded mischievous malevolence as he duelled with monks bearing the Sacred Daggers Of Maggido. But the less said about the 1991 TV movie, *Omen IV: The Awakening* the better. ★★★★ **DP**

THE OMEN (2006)

Starring: *Liev Schreiber (Robert Thorn), Julia Stiles (Katherine Thorn), David Thewlis (Keith Jennings), Mia Farrow (Mrs. Baylock), Pete Postlethwaite (Father Brennan), Seamus Davey-Fitzpatrick (Damien), Michael Gambon (Bugenhagen)*
Director: *John Moore*
Screenwriter: *David Seltzer*
15/110 mins./Horror/USA

An American diplomat begins to suspect that something is wrong with his son, Damien, after a series of strange accidents takes place around him. He begins to suspect that Junior is actually the son of the devil, in this remake of the 1976 Richard Donner horror.

When Gus Van Sant was asked exactly what the point of making a shot for shot remake of a classic (in his case, Psycho) he responded, 'So nobody else has to.' Director John Moore obviously wasn't listening, because what he has managed to produce is the ultimate in pointless exercises, a remake that is neither much better nor much worse that the original.

Accordingly, when in Richard Donner's 1976 studio shocker Damien's nanny flings herself of the roof yelling, 'It's all for you Damien!' (surely a gift of Pokemon or Lego would have been more appropriate) we get a shot by shot retread of the scene in the 2006 version. Suspicious photographer Jennings discussed the American Ambassador's satanic son with him at a snow-flecked roadside cafe, so it is to a snow-flecked roadside cafe that David Thewlis and Liev Schreiber go in this redundant retread.

Moore has thrown in a little more gore and a few subliminal shocks – and there are a range of succulently hammy turns from the likes of Pete Postlethwaite and Mia Farrow (nodding to her starring role in the same era's *Rosemary's Baby*) but for the most part has followed the original screenplay with uncanny slavishness. Which makes it odd that Jerry Goldsmith's iconic score, which has forever associated screeching choirs with diabolical doings, is missing from the mix.

The overwhelming impression is of a lost opportunity, given that the current American administration's sinister attempts to infect politics with religion provide a contemporary backdrop even more fertile for this Mephistophelian melodrama than the post-Vietnam paranoia that boosted the original movie, though the final shot, of Damien holding the hand of the President - the back of whose head bears a passing resemblance to George Bush's - at least demonstrates that Moore and co. noticed the possibilities. ★★★ **AS**

⑩ OMEN III: THE FINAL CONFLICT (1980)

Starring: *Sam Neill (Damien thorn), Rossano Brazzi (DeCarlo), Don Gordon (Dean), Lis Harrow (Kate Reynolds), Barnaby Holm (Peter), Mason Adams (President)*
Director: *Graham Baker*
Screenwriter: *Andrew Birkin based on characters created by David Seltzer*
18/108 mins./Horror/USA

Now fully grown, and quite at home with his role as the Anti-Christ, Damien Thorn discovers that the Christ-child will soon be born in England. As he tries to track down the child, seven monks with sacred daggers forged to kill the Devil's child attempt to foil his plans.

Despite the fact a hopeless fourth instalment was made for TV, this was supposedly the last act in the Damien Thorn trilogy. Sam Neill plays the now fully-grown Anti-Christ, and with a stab of dark humour he is the head of a multinational megaconglomerate called Thorn Industries. The Prince of Darkness is a hit in business! How satirical. That's about as fun, or scary, or relevant, as this negligible horror movie gets.

The plot of the first two films were lean and telling – when people discover Damien's true nature, they die horrible and exotic deaths in the presence of the large, slavering black dog. *The Final Conflict* tries to keep the whole sticking-to-the-Bible style going, while pasting on some fatuous plotting about a squad of super-holy monks, who have knives that can rid of his eternal smarminess. The Christ turns up for his Second Coming in the form of a bright light, but let's not get ahead of ourselves.

Neill doesn't really take hold of the role – he is overly serious and uncharismatic. You really should have some fun when playing Satan's offspring. Since we've returned to England (after the American set *Omen II*) it looks grey and mundane, cloudy rather than apocalyptic, with none of the shadowy force that Richard Donner gave the original. Even the fanciful deaths are a let down, with the highlight a man who gets an iron in his face from his evil-consumed wife. Half the time it feels more like an *Omen* parody than a chance to give it a great send off. You've got to be a truly rotten filmmaker to make the second coming such an anticlimax. ★★ **IN**

⑮ OMEN IV: THE AWAKENING (1991)

Starring: *Faye Grant (Karen York), Michael Woods (Gene York), Michael Lerner (Earl Knight), Madison Mason (Dr Lou Hastings), Ann Hearn (Jo Thueson), Jim Byrnes (Noah), Don S. Davis (Jake Madison)*
Directors: *Jorge Montesi, Dominque Othenin-Girard*
Screenwriter: *Brian Taggert, from characters by David Seltzner*
15/97 mins./Horror/USA

Damien's prophecy is reborn in Delia who is adopted by a couple of attorneys Gene and Karen. When people around the mysterious little girl begin to die, Karen hires a private detective and discovers the awful truth about her adopted daughter.

Given that the last sequel to *The Omen* was called *The Final Conflict* and wound up with the Second Coming of Christ, you'd think it would be hard to come up with another instalment. However, that would underestimate severely Hollywood's power to flog a dead horse, as is demonstrated by this literally incredible attempt to get the series going again, produced for American television and given a theatrical release overseas in the hopes of ripping off people who don't realise they're being foisted off with a lousy old TV movie when they expect some of the big name guest stars, panavision gloom and spectacular decapitations of the earlier episodes.

Essentially a remake of *The Omen*, but cheaper, this has a politically ambitious couple (Grant, Woods) adopting a sinister little girl (Vieira) whose background is shrouded in mystery. The brat grows up creepy, and people around her tend to die in non-18 certificate freak accidents, which prompts Mummy into hiring a private eye to discover what we guessed in reel one, that the kid is the daughter of Anti-Christ Damien Thorn and intends to take over the family business in a new series of films.

This takes some major stretching of biblical prophecies to account for, but by the time the trendy priest is explaining that 'the Bible didn't mean to be sexist' and it turns out that the eight-year-old has been born pregnant with her equally evil twin brother, you'll be laughing too hard to care.

Among the conceits offered by the film are a New Age psychic fair that dissolves into chaos when the Anti-Christine calls round, a choir of Satanic carolsingers, a snake-worshipping revival meeting that goes wrong, and the usual throbbing black mass soundtrack. With two credited directors – like *Damien: Omen II*, funnily enough – and a notably less-than-lavish production, this mainly serves to remind you that, silly though they were, the earlier films were at least quality entertainment. ★ **KN**

Ⓟ ON GOLDEN POND (1981)

Starring: *Henry Fonda (Norman Thayer Jr), Katharine Hepburn (Ethel Thayer), Jane Fonda (Chelsea Thayer Wayne), Doug McKeon (Billy Ray), Dabney Coleman (Bill Ray)*
Director: *Mark Rydell*
Screenwriter: *Ernest Thompson*
PG/109 mins./Drama/USA

Awards: *Academy Awards – Best Actor, Best Actress, Best Screenplay. BAFTA – Best Actress*

Every summer elderly couple Norman and Ethel Thayer visit their cottage on Golden Pond, a large, beautiful lake. This summer, however, will be different. Their estranged daughter Chelsea is coming to visit, dropping off her soon-to-be stepson, who starts to develop a bond with her father that she always wanted.

For some it might have been just that bit too close to home, with Henry and Jane Fonda playing onscreen father and daughter whose difficult relations matched their own. For some it might be the emphasis on emotional release, a drift towards sentimentality in its tale of family attachments set amongst nesting loons and lovely sunrises. And for others it might be the octogenarian cast giving something of their last hurrah (it was to be Henry Fonda's final film) and thusly receiving those Oscars. *On Golden Pond* is a wrongly derided film, seen to embody all the dullness of something oh-so mature.

Actually, it is an extraordinary little piece about parents and marriages, involving the kind of naturalistic acting that resonates with the subtle details of life. That it also contains such a grand Hollywood legacy (two generations of Fonda and Katharine Hepburn) just adds a layer of accessibility to events. Through all its generational differences, the unspoken squabbles between a conservative father and a counterculture daughter who has flown through a marriage and lost her way, there runs this deep, disquieting pain that will finally have to be confronted between the real-life pair.

It is also a film about the ties that bind, a portrayal of the necessity of enduring relationships, Hepburn's simmering love for her grouch of a hubbie is so quietly sung it is worth watching for its moving refrain alone. OK, so it does cloy in places, but there is truth in its fractures and its seals, a soft-shimmering landscape of real people. ★★★★ **IN**

ON HER MAJESTY'S SECRET SERVICE (1969)

Starring: *George Lazenby (James Bond), Diana Rigg (Tracy Di Vicenzo), Telly Savalas (Ernst Stavro Blofeld), Gabrielle Ferzetti (Marc Ange Draco), Ilse Steppat (Irma Bunt), Lois Maxwell (Miss Moneypenny), George Baker (voice of Sir Hilary Bray), Bernard Lee (M)*
Director: *Peter Hunt*
Screenwriters: *Richard Maibaum, Simon Raven based on the novel by Ian Fleming*
PG/140 mins/Spy/UK/USA

Secret Agent James Bond 007 is once again on the trail of S.P.E.C.T.R.E. mastermind Ernst Stavro Blofeld, who plans to unleash a deadly virus on an unsuspecting world. Meantime, he falls in love.

Ask any 007 connoisseur that age old question about which is the best James Bond movie and the answer they are likely to give is this one, the sixth in the series and the one only to star the face of Fry's chocolate, Australian himbo George Lazenby in the signature role. For whatever Lazenby's limitations as an actor (rule of thumb, he's good at action, stilted at everything else), this is the Bond flick blessed with the best plot, a genuine sense of emotion and a spirit closest to Ian Fleming's novels that have seen it grow in critical/fan stature in the years since its release where it was greeted with outright derision.

Once the movie has reassured audiences with a clips package from the Connery era, highlighting treasured supporting characters and props, *On Her Majesty's Secret Service* does all that it can to break the traditions that were seen as defining Connery's tenure. Firstly, after a pre-credit fight on a beach, Lazenby turns to the camera and quips 'This never happened to the other fellow', the first time a Bond movie breaks the fourth wall. Then, out went the traditional brassy, brazen theme song and in came a rollicking John Barry instrumental that still sounds cool to this day (as counterbalance, the lovely, wistful Louis Armstrong ballad 'We Have All The Time In The World' gets an outing later).

Also *OHMSS* sees Bond rely much more on his wits than the usual plethora of Q dept wizardry. To infiltrate Blofeld's lair, Bond disguises himself as nitwit geneaologist Sir Hilary Bray (Lazenby dubbed in these scenes by George Baker) for some nicely comic moments. But the real big jump from previous Bonds to this one sees James Bond falling in love. Bond's romance with Tracy Di Vincenzo, the daughter of a European crime lord, forms a major part of the movie and is painted with surprising sensitivity. Giving the best performance by any actress in a Bond film, Diana Rigg (like Pussy Galore's Honor Blackman, an Avengers alumnus) is more than a match for 007 – in one scene she actually saves Bond's life – and gives her potentially embarrassing scenes with Lazenby a touching, tender quality. As a result, *OHMSS* has the most moving vignettes in the entire series; Bond wiping away Tracy's tears at her father's birthday party, their joyous wedding and the heartbreaking finale that sees Tracy gunned down in cold blood. Still shocking today, it's impossible to imagine a contemporary Bond film ending on such a downbeat note.

That said, it's not all doom and gloom. Series editor/2nd unit director turned main director Peter Hunt marshals the action (night-time skiing, a car chase through a stock car race, a helicopter attack on Blofeld's mountain hideaway) with ruthless efficiency and there is still the odd space for a throwaway gag: as a Blofeld goon is splattered in a snow plough, the viscera is greeted with a 'He's got guts.' But it's the changes in tone and pace that make this Bond so memorable – the only lingering doubt remains is how much better it might have been with a more natural, charismatic actor in the tux. ★★★★ **WT**

ON THE TOWN (1949)

Starring: *Gene Kelly (Gabey), Frank Sinatra (Chip), Jules Munshin (Ozzie), Betty Garrett (Brunhilde Esterhazy), Ann Miller (Claire Huddesen)*
Directors: *Stanley Donen, Gene Kelly*
Screenwriters: *Adolph Green, Betty Comden, Jerome Robbins, based on the play by Comden and Green*
PG/98 mins./Musical/USA

Awards: *Academy Awards – Best Score*

Three sailors hit New York city for one night before they ship out looking for a whole load of fun. They find much more than they bargained for.

The first time Gene Kelly, although working with Stanley Donen, got to choreograph and direct a movie is a magnificent old-time musical, bubbling with Leonard Bernstein tunes, with a little help from Roger Edens. Better still is the way Kelly absorbs such great songs into city filling dance numbers, mad and elegant and genius all at the same time. The resulting film is suffused with charm and thrill, pure therapy in a shuffle of deck shoes and sailor duds.

The plot is simple, which helps, just the tale told over one night of three jovial, and rather benign, sailors, Gabey (Gene Kelly), Chip (Frank Sinatra) and Ozzie (Jules Munshin), hitting the streets of the Big Apple on shore leave. Their excitement is nearly unbound, hence they keep breaking into song, especially as each will find their own love match (these guys are quick movers). Their landlubbing female matches are less memorable: pin-up glamour girl Vera-Ellen, spunky cabbie Berry Garrett and museum boffin Ann Miller, caught in the glare of their leading men.

Sinatra was never as much of a dancer as he was crooner, and he's shown up by the balletic grace of Kelly and the Broadway-honed licks of Munshin, but as a trio they sparkle, variations on their well-written personas (at least for the famous two) rather than developed characters. With songs like these, and sets lit up like theme parks, there was really no need for anything else. ★★★★ **IN**

ⓞ ONCE UPON A TIME IN AMERICA (1984)

Starring: *Robert De Niro (David 'Noodles' Aaronson), James Woods (Maximillian 'Max' Bercovicz), Elizabeth McGovern (Deborah Gelly), Tuesday Weld (Carol), Treat Williams (James Conway O'Donnell)*
Director: *Sergio Leone*
Screenwriters: *Leonardo Benvenuti, Piero De Bernardi, Enrico Medioli, Franco Arcalli, Franco Ferrini, Sergio Leone, based on the novel* The Hoods *by Harry Grey*
18/139 mins./229 mins. (director's cut)/Drama/Crime/Italy/USA

A former Prohibition-era Jewish gangster returns to Brooklyn over 30 years later, where he once again must confront the ghosts and regrets of his old life.

'I hope they burn the fucking negative!' James Woods raged about what had happened to Sergio Leone's *Once Upon A Time In America* in an anonymous editing suite in New York. 'Three weeks before the film is released, they have the assistant editor of *Police Academy* chop it to fucking ribbons! I mean, do you think I was suicidal? The film got fucking slaughtered by the critics, as well it should have. It was fucking dead in the water.'

It was the old, old story. Leone, the feted director of such modern classics as *The Fistful Of Dollars* trilogy had been contracted to deliver a film of not more than 165 minutes. Leone hadn't. He had probably never intended to. Instead, after extensive cutting, he delivered a final print of 229 minutes. If it had been released it would have been one of the longest films ever to hit American screens. But thanks to the attentions of Zach

TOP 10 Actors Turned Novelists

1 Carrie Fisher – *Postcards from the Edge*
2 Ethan Hawke – *The Hottest State*
3 Steve Martin – *Shopgirl*
4 Orson Welles – *Mr Arkadin*
5 Tony Curtis – *Kid Andrew Cody & Julie Sparrow*
6 Joan Collins – *Prime Time*
7 Julie Andrews – *The Last of the Really Great Whangdoodles*
8 Sophie Marceau – *Telling Lies*
9 Whoopi Goldberg – *Alice*
10 Pamela Anderson - *Star*

Staenberg, the *Police Academy* editor (who, for some audiences, redeemed himself 14 years later by editing *The Matrix*) the version that American audiences saw ran to just 144 minutes. 'It was such a stupid move,' mourned Woods. It was. The film tanked. And it was only when it was finally shown in its full three hour 49 minute cut that European critics recognised it for the enduring classic it now is.

All of which is somewhat ironic, because among its other many themes, *Once Upon* ... is a film about the inexorable passage of time. From the start of the movie Leone begins to manipulate it. We first meet Jewish gangster Noodles (De Niro) in an opium den (just one of the many fantastically evocative sets built in Rome); behind him a shadow play is dimly visible through the narcotic fug. But soon, in what's a regular occurrence in the movie, we flashback to the previous evening. We're in a 30s speakeasy where Noodles and his Jewish gangster gang are mourning the passing of prohibition and where he is about to betray his best friend, then back again to the early part of the century where we see the young rapscallions on the Lower East Side slowly moving more and more towards the life of organised crime that will ultimately destroy some of them. Then, in an audacious jump in time, we move forwards to 1968 where we find Noodles attempting to piece together his life, deciding whether to go to a mysterious party.

It's an incredible narrative achievement, indeed, the structure was so complex that, in the 15 years it took to bring the movie from inception to the screen, Leone had separate sets of writers working on the different sections (Norman Mailer's early screenplay having been dismissed as 'Mickey Mouse'). For many, the 'early years' are the most effective, combining astounding sets and location work (the sequences were filmed in Rome, Montreal and on location in New York, but the nine-month shoot also took the crew to Paris, Lake Como, and Miami) with excellent performances from the cast of mostly unknowns who play the junior hoodlums. It's the most obviously accessible and most narratively easygoing part of the movie as they lose their virginities, roll drunks for money and blackmail the local plod.

But it's the difficult, ambiguous elements of the movie that are the most satisfying. Ultimately *America* is much more than just a gangster picture. Certainly some of the familiar genre-trappings are floating about, rival gangs, money in suitcases, sudden vicious violence and corrupt police. And the betrayal of friends is a theme etched in most organised crime flicks. But it's at its deeper level that the film transcends genre and becomes something much more profound. It's a movie about the unreliability of memory; about ageing and guilt and indelible regret. Noodles lies on his cot in the opium den and tries to make some kind of sense of his life and actions. Three decades later he returns to finish that project. Or, as the pantomime phrase goes, does he? As Leone biographer Christopher Frayling points out, an intriguing reading of the film has Noodles never leaving 1933. The sequences set in 1968 have a strange symbolic quality to them, which may suggest they are opium-inspired dreams.

Either way you read it, it's a film that deliberately offers no real resolution, only a sense of melancholy and which leaves the audience, like Noodles, wondering, dazed, what it's all been about. ★★★★★ **AS**

Movie Trivia: Sergio Leone (1929–1989)

Who he is: Italian master of the Old West. Originator of the 'Spaghetti Western'. Maker of the hugely influential 'Dollars' trilogy, a panoramic trilogy about power and corruption in the New World.

Hallmarks: Black-and-white morality; high body counts; grotesque faces in extreme close-up; wide screens; corrida-style gunfights; craggy landscapes; long shots; absurd comedy.

If you see one movie, see: *Once Upon A Time in the West* (1968)

ONCE UPON A TIME IN MEXICO (2003)

Starring: *Antonio Banderas (El Mariachi), Salma Hayek (Carolina), Johnny Depp (Sands), Mickey Rourke (Billy Chambers), Eva Mendes (Ajedrez)*
Director: *Robert Rodriguez*
Screenwriter: *Robert Rodriguez, from his characters*
15/97 mins./Crime/Action/Adventure/USA

El Mariachi quits retirement to avenge the murder of his wife and daughter. He's then involved with an assassination attempt on the president, teams up with a bonkers CIA agent and a Latino pop star, and takes on a psychotic drug baron.

Rodriguez crash-bang-wallops his way back into more adult material with the third instalment in the Western saga he started with *El Mariachi* in 1992 and followed up with *Desperado* three years later.

Considering his overall trilogy arc – cracking low-budget original, bigger-budget remake, shambolic yet hugely entertaining final chapter – Rodriguez rather more mimics Sam Raimi's *Evil Dead* franchise than his Spaghetti hero's classic three-parter. Not exactly tragic, then, but nevertheless still something of a disappointment considering the kinetic razzmatazz of parts one and two.

Rodriguez certainly hasn't lost touch with his hyper-violent sensibilities, the stylistic melding of Peckinpah and Woo that so wowed us previously. Nor has he cast off his traditional shortcomings, the plot being once again secondary to the visuals. And as handy as his Hollywood buddies can be in delivering 'Hey, isn't that...?' cameos, in this instance he's hamstrung by the presence of so many – Rourke and Dafoe suffering most from an overload of familiar faces (Enrique Iglesias, for heaven's sake!) that sees them relegated to the sidelines. A shame, especially as Rourke gives comfortably the second-best performance on show. Top honours in that respect – a position he's starting to dominate – fall to

Depp, as he delivers a display of nutty characterisation that almost outshines his Keith-Richards-goes-boating Captain Jack Sparrow in *Pirates Of The Caribbean*.

His Agent Sands, in between dressing up in preposterously useless disguises and comparing the menu merits of whichever cruddy cafe he happens upon, is a source of constant chuckles, right down to his bonkers last half-hour.

Sadly for Banderas, Depp's domination leaves him more of an afterthought in a movie centred on his quest for vengeance. Through a series of flashbacks – one of which features the movie's finest set-piece, as he and Hayek scramble down the outside of a building whilst chained together – we see his pain. But as he gets lost in a meandering story, we lose empathy for his emotional journey.

Frankly, were it not for Depp explaining things to Eva Mendes' policewoman halfway through, no one would have the foggiest what's going on. But, hey, this is a Rodriguez flick, and his bloodstained fingerprints are all over it – from typical, Tarantino-type intro, as Cheech Marin narrates a tale of El's gunslinging bravado, through some deadpan dialogue ('Are you a Mexican, or a Mexican't?'), to neat visual wit and explosive action sequences that fudge reality and comic book fantasy into a single, surreal slice of pure illusion. ★★★ **OR**

⦿ ONCE UPON A TIME IN THE MIDLANDS (2002)

Starring: *Robert Carlyle (Jimmy), Rhys Ifans (Dek), Kathy Burke (Carol), Shirley Henderson (Shirley), Ricky Tomlinson (Charlie), Vanessa Feltz (Vanessa), Vic Reeves (Plonko the clown), Bob Mortimer (Kung fu clown), Shane Meadows (Bingo caller)*
Director: *Shane Meadows*
Screenwriters: *Shane Meadows, Paul Fraser*
15/100 mins./Drama/Comedy/UK

Watching Dek's failed marriage proposal to his ex, Shirley, on a daytime TV show, Glaswegian rogue Jimmy returns to claim the wife and daughter he left behind.

The last of Shane Meadows' 'Midlands trilogy' is a lighter, more upbeat affair than *TwentyFourSeven* and *A Room For Romeo Brass*. Replaying a classic Western scenario – a stranger comes to town with devastating consequences – in a Midlands suburb, Meadows has created his most plot-driven, easy-to-like, yet somehow disposable, flick to date.

The film will undoubtedly draw comparisons with the working-class parables of Ken Loach and Mike Leigh, but Meadows' sensibility is more joyous than that of the former and less sneering than that of the latter. It is easy to share his affection for his characters.

Meadows slyly alludes to the cowboy genre – a stand-off in the saloon, some Leone-esque compositions – without overwhelming the story. He also draws great performances from his cast. Ifans does some of his best film work to date, making Dek an engaging mixture of the clownish and heartfelt, while Henderson (Britain's most underrated actress) plays Shirley as sweet yet selfish, as she dithers between the two men. However, the acting honours are hijacked by young Finn Atkins who makes Marlene wise and real, never lapsing into cute kid tactics to ingratiate herself.

Surprisingly, Carlyle never really illuminates the delinquent Jimmy, and his subplot involving run-ins with Glaswegian outlaws adds an unwelcome false note to the proceedings.

Where *Midlands* really shines is in its smaller vignettes – Kathy Burke and Ricky Tomlinson provide trademark moments of salty comedy and pathos – but its central triangle fails to deliver the emotional punch the lovely trimmings deserve. ★★★★ **IF**

⦿ ONCE UPON A TIME IN THE WEST (C'ERA UNA VOLTA IL WEST) (1968)

Starring: *Henry Fonda (Frank), Claudia Cardinale (Jill McBain), Jason Robards (Cheyenne), Charles Brosnan (Harmonica), Frank Wolff (Brett McBain)*
Director: *Sergio Leone*
Screenwriters: *Sergio Leone, Sergio Donati, from a story by Sergio Leone, Dario Argento, Bernardo Bertolucci*
15/158 mins./Italy/Western/USA

Archetypal characters – the vengeful gunman, the outlaw, the villain, and the whore with a heart of gold – appear and do Western stuff, like kill each other in gunfights, turn each other in for rewards, climb on train roofs . . . You get the picture. It's a classic.

After the escalating grandiosity of the three Clint Eastwood/Man With No Name 'Dollars' Westerns, Sergio Leone went all out for scale in this monumental movie. It opens with a riff on *High Noon* as three expressive gunmen – Woody Strode, Jack Elam and Al Mulock – wait for a train, bothered by a drip of water and a buzzing fly, and Leone stretches out what ought to be dead screen time into an operatic crescendo of suspense (scored by the great Ennio Morricone) that pays off when a granite-faced Bronson, stepping into the Eastwood No-Name role as the vengeance-seeking Harmonica, arrives in a shimmering haze to face down the killers in a few brief, eventful seconds.

As much a meditation on the Western itself as it is an action movie rooted in American history, this casts an iconic Henry Fonda to trash his Wyatt Earp image as Frank, the blue-eyed killer who cheerfully slaughters an entire frontier family down to an angelic boy child but is well aware that his partnership with a crippled railroad tycoon is also an abandonment of his outlaw lifestyle and an admission that his times are over.

It's the most political of Leone's oat operas, indicting the corrupt railroad as it bulldozes across the landscape, displacing innocent people and hiring outlaw flunkeys to shift inconvenient settlers who won't unsettle easily. Rapaciously capitalist civilisation taints the wide open spaces, but the plot follows Bronson's obsessive quest to bring down Fonda, the sadist who hanged his brother, while widow Cardinale tries to fend off the railroad tycoons and bandido Robards just wants to be left in peace.

With its amazing widescreen compositions and epic running time, this Western truly wins points for length and width. ★★★★★ **KN**

⦿ ONE DAY IN SEPTEMBER (1999)

Starring: *as themselves: Michael Douglas (narrator), Ankie Spitzer, Jamal Al Gashey, Gerald Sermour, Alex Springer, Gad Zahari, Shumuel Lalkin*
Director: *Kevin Macdonald*
12/90 mins./Documentary/UK

Awards: *Academy Awards – Best Documentary*

Eyewitness accounts from the 1972 Munich Olympics that were interrupted by Palestinian terrorists taking Israeli athletes hostage.

Ten days into the 1972 Munich Olympics, eight members of the Palestinian Black September group stormed the Israeli team quarters and demanded the release of 236 political prisoners. Twenty-one hours later, eleven Israelis, five terrorists and one German policeman were dead. Awarded the Oscar for Best Documentary, Kevin Macdonald's film is a meticulously researched and revelation-packed insight.

Seamlessly inserted into archive footage, politicians, cops, relatives and reporters offer their recollections, but none is as revealing as Jamal Al Gashey, the terrorists' leader, in his first-ever interview. But what makes this jaw-slackening exposé of institutionalised incompetence so compelling is the understated disbelief with which Macdonald presents his damning evidence. ★★★★ DP

⦿ ONE FALSE MOVE (1992)

Starring: *Bill Paxton (Chief Dale 'Hurricane' Dixon), Cynda Williams (Lila 'Fantasia' Walker), Billy Bob Thornton (Ray Malcolm), Michael Beach (Wade 'Pluto' Franklin)*
Director: *Carl Franklin*
Screenwriters: *Billy Bob Thornton, Tom Epperson*
18/101 mins./Crime/Drama/USA

Ray, Fantasia and Pluto go on the run after a drugs robbery goes wrong.

Three desperadoes – ponytailed, coke-snorting redneck Ray (co-screenwriter Thornton), his mulatto girlfriend Fantasia, and bespectacled black pyscho Pluto – are on the run from Los Angeles following an underworld drugs heist that has left six people dead.

Heading for Star City, Arkansas, where both Ray and Fantasia have family, the fugitives are unaware that another unlikely trio – Star City's hick police chief 'Hurricane' Dixon and two streetwise LA cops – are lying in wait. Modelled on Fred Zinnemann's *High Noon*, this cracking modern day Western has a neo-noir realism that echoes the Coen brothers' *Blood Simple*.

First-time director Franklin, a former actor, proves himself remarkably adept behind the camera, wringing the plot for every bit of tension, then sitting back and letting his cast stew in it. Cutting back and forth between the criminals – increasingly desperate – and the cops, he insidiously unearths past secrets which link the two parties in a quite unexpected way, carefully balancing his first-rate cast with the cat and mouse game unfolding.

Williams' Fantasia is a classic loser, a tortured soul bound by the past, pathetically unable to escape the present. It's a riveting performance, one of many in this emotionally complex thriller. And if the finale, inevitably, is a bloody shoot-out, the underlying message, for once, is decidedly upbeat. ★★★★ MS

⦿ ONE FLEW OVER THE CUCKOO'S NEST (1975)

Starring: *Jack Nicholson (Randle Patrick McMurpy), Louise Fletcher (Nurse Mildred Ratched), William Redfield (Harding), Michael Berryman (Ellis), Danny DeVito (Martini), Christopher Lloyd (Taber), Brad Dourif (Billy Bibbet)*
Director: *Milos Forman*
Screenwriters: *Bo Goldman, Lawrence Hauben*
18/133 mins./Drama/USA

Awards: *Academy Awards – Best Actor, Best Actress, Best Director, Best Picture, Best Adapted Screenplay, BAFTA – Best Actor, Best Actress, Best Director, Best Film, Best Film Editing, Best Supporting Actor (Brad Dourif); Golden Globes – Best Male Debut (Brad Dourif), Best Director, Best Drama, Best Drama Actor, Best Drama Actress, Best Screenplay*

McMurphy is a free spirit placed in a mental home, but can his spirit survive the home's brutal regime?

Admittedly, Forman's *Cuckoo's Nest* is rather dishonest in dealing with mental illness, but the inmates are the guides to the alien world of the asylum – they need to engage the audience, which must feel their joy even more than it sees their pain.

As a result, the entire supporting cast was composed of unknowns to contrast with Nicholson's McMurphy, a swaggering bundle of braggadocio familiar to us all as both character and actor. Nicholson is one of the truly great actors, but he's also the greatest male sprite, the ideal capricious caperer to play opposite the inmates, not only to provide the catalyst for their partial recoveries, but also to reinforce their humour on screen. In the therapy sessions, the alchemy of McMurphy's sparking, quick-fire banter with Louise Fletcher's Nurse Ratched transforms the patients' twitches and tics into comedic gold as they react to the verbal frenzy, investing them with new meaning.

The most obvious example of the movie's sense of humour comes with, arguably, the most popular scene in the film, the fishing trip, the inmates' metaphorical two-fingered salute to Ratched and her hospital. As McMurphy introduces the patients to a sceptical shore man each patient reacts with the haughty expression of an academic boffin. As one critic noted: 'This has nothing to do with mental illness, but everything to do with comedy.'

For some, Kesey included, the scene didn't ring completely true, but it is key to Forman's movie. While he rejects an honest portrayal of the inmates' afflictions, he remains totally true to his film. The horror of McMurphy's environment, and the potential outcome, need to be relieved by moments drenched in levity, and the patients must allow the two main protagonists the space to conduct their duel. The only genuine insights into the causes of the patients' distress come with Chief Bromden's whispered words to McMurphy late at night and Billy Bibbit's crumbling tirade against Ratched before his tragic end. Indeed, Kesey was so irked by the adaptation of his novel that he launched a lawsuit against the filmmakers, but the fact remained that he couldn't provide a workable screenplay when asked – he'd performed one miracle in writing the book, he could not conjure another.

Hence it was Bo Goldman who finally brought Forman's vision alive and it held true to the Czech's bidding. The script was quick and punchy, flinging McMurphy straight onto the ward and channelling the humour and the horror into a string of memorable scenes. This story could not enjoy the luxuries of the novel – a movie couldn't recount the tale through the hallucinogenic visions of the Chief – and, to complicate matters, the production was working a full decade after the book's publication. Kesey's tome, railing against a hard-nosed administration, had caught the zeitgeist of the early 60s while by the film's release in 1975, people had different concerns. Consequently, in a bid to keep his theme relevant, Forman recalled his homeland and flicked through the tenets of Communism, until, in the calm face of Nurse Ratched, he found its apotheosis. Here was the devil with an angel's face, the force working vehemently for a misguided cause, imparting great suffering in the name of salvation. And here was Forman's greatest triumph.

Nurse Ratched had, for Kesey, grown as an embodiment of the Combine, a giant creature often described by an hallucinating Chief as an inhuman, electrical machine, all skittering wires and cracking circuits, her limbs and body frequently ballooning into monstrous proportions as she dispatched the orders of an ugly administration. True, he hints that the motivation behind the Combine's actions worked for the patients' benefit, yet the plainly drawn evil always lurks beneath the surface. In the face of Forman and Fletcher's Ratched, however, a *genuine* desire to do good shines forth, a misguided light paradoxically wrapping those she hopes to help in bewildering darkness. When Dr Spivey suggests that McMurphy be released from the hospital's care, her response, 'I believe we can help him, I really do', is laced with spine-chilling horror. She really *does* believe in her fallacious theories, and the only time she surrenders to spite is with Billy, after McMurphy's party has pushed her to breaking point.

Indeed this scene, in the aftermath of the party with Billy's death and McMurphy's retaliation, provides the dramatic crescendo, although the real horror is reserved for Ratched's response – not the manner of its execution, although that's grisly enough, but the final, dreaded confirmation of McMurphy's failure. This tragedy, the impotence of the sprite flailing against the overpowering conventions of his society, would inform much of Forman's later work, from *Amadeus* to *Man On The Moon*, a direct reflection of the director's own experience as the liberalisation of his country, the Prague Spring, crumpled under the heavy tracks of Soviet tanks.

The Chief's final decision is a victory of sorts, but it comes at a high price. That was the reality of Forman's experience, and given McMurphy's prone, neutered position, resigned to the empty environs of an oppressive world, Bromden had to steal the life of his friend, his brother. After all, he who does not steal steals from his family. And Forman knew that all too well. ★★★★★ **WL**

Movie Trivia: One Flew Over the Cuckoo's Nest

Many of the extras in the film were real mental patients. Marlon Brando and Gene Hackman were offered the part before Nicholson, and director Milos Forman had wanted Burt Reynolds to play McMurphy. It is rumoured that Nicholson actually went under ECT therapy for real when it was filmed. Kirk Douglas planned to star, but was too old by the time production began.

ONE FROM THE HEART (1982)

Starring: *Frederic Forrest (Hank), Teri Garr (Frannie), Raul Julia (Ray), Nastassja Kinski (Leila), Lainie Kazan (Maggie), Harry Dean Stanton (Moe)*
Director: *Francis Ford Coppola*
Screenwriters: *Armyan Bernstein, Francis Ford Coppola, based on a story by Bernstein*
15/102 mins./Musical/Romance/USA

Las Vegas. Frannie and Hank, who have been together for some years, have troubles in their relationship — each has a fling with a more glamorous partner, a singing waiter and a circus girl, but eventually get back together.

Like the *Godfather* saga and *Apocalypse Now*, this is among Francis Coppola's perpetual works-in-progress: each re-release seems to be a different cut, and there's a sense that Coppola has several more rethinks coming.

At once a stage-shot 'small' film and a technically innovative endeavour intended to establish American Zoetrope as an old-style Hollywood studio, it flopped on its 1982 release but its bittersweet charm has improved with age. An unconventional musical, it is structured around a superb Tom Waits song score (performed by Waits and Crystal Gayle, allegedly as Zeus and Hera) and has Gene Kelly-choreographed crowd scenes which aren't quite dance numbers. Cinematographer Vittorio Storaro and production designer Dean Tavoularis work movie magic by bringing to life a huge set which represents a sparkling vision of Las Vegas and the surrounding desert.

Teri Garr and Frederic Forrest, given the rare chance to carry a film, are sometimes downright annoying but always thoroughly human and believable. Against the glittery charms of Nastassja Kinski, caught on film during the years when she was literally the most desirable woman in the world, and the 'Rudolf Vaselino' good-humoured virility of Raul Julia, a mirage in a tuxedo and a powerhouse in the sack, the leads should be blown away — but they bring so much to the party that an audience can't help but invest hopes in their survival as a couple.

It's a melancholy, mature film, trying hard to argue that its down-to-earth lovers are not just settling for each other, and that the abandonment of romantic fantasy can lead to deeper romance. ★★★★ **KN**

Movie Trivia: Francis Ford Coppola (born 1939)

Who he is: Engine of the 1970s Second Golden Age of Hollywood. One of the 'movie brats' who defined the decade. Director of the *Godfather* trilogy.
Hallmarks: Epic productions; themes of immigration, family and political corruption; interest in the post-World War II American experience.
If you see one movie, see: *The Godfather* (1972)

ONE HOUR PHOTO (2002)

Starring: *Robin Williams (Sy Parrish), Connie Nielsen (Nina Yorkin), Michael Vartan (Will Yorkin), Dylan Smith (Jake Yorkin), Erin Daniels (Maya Burson)*
Director: *Mark Romanek*
Screenwriter: *Mark Romanek*
15/96 mins./Thriller/USA

Sy Parrish is the perfectionist head technician for a supermarket instant photo developer. But does his extra pride in the photographs of the picture-perfect Yorkin family and his clandestine meetings with young Jake betray a dark side?

Part Two of Robin Williams' rehabilitation (see *Insomnia* for further details) sees the furry comedian stray even further from the hapless creature of sentiment we had all grown to know and loathe (see *Patch Adams* for further details). But *One Hour Photo* is not merely Williams changing his look and staying in character: as lonely photo lab technician Sy Parrish, Williams really stretches his acting muscles, finding moments of vulnerable sweetness in a man who could come off as a one-dimensional weirdo.

Even when the material is a touch too literal, Williams' measured performance (yes, measured!) keeps enough emotion in check (yes, in check!) to leave an element of doubt in play. Sadly, anyone who has ever seen a lonely weirdo movie will still know exactly where this above average thriller is heading.

It had taken 15 years for writer-director Mark Romanek to follow up his debut movie, the 1986 cult fave, *Static*. An acclaimed video director, Romanek must have his reasons for the procrastination, but while this genre movie lacks the off-beat brilliance of *Static*, there's more than enough here to suggest that he should stick at this feature-making lark.

In particular, Romanek shows an immediate mastery of the basics of the stalker genre and cranks up a good atmosphere early on. He also manufactures a genuinely tense climax. *One Hour Photo* does, however, have a tendency to labour the point slightly, and fantasy sequences betray the fact that Romanek the writer has not given Romanek the director quite enough to work with.

This would not be so fatal a flaw if the narrative sprang a genuine surprise, but this is a suspense thriller on rails, linear when it should be elusive, predictable when it should keep you guessing. Williams, however, keeps the whole thing watchable. Romanek never once doubts the audience's intelligence. As much as you want to keep watching to see what develops, part of you wants to look away from images that will stay with you long after the film has run out. ★★★ **DHu**

ONE HUNDRED AND ONE DALMATIANS (1961)

Starring: *(the voices of) Rod Taylor (Pongo), Lisa Davis (Anita), Cate Bauer (Perdita), Ben Wright (Roger Radcliff), Frederick Worlock (Horace), J. Pat O' Malley (Jasper/Miscellaneous Dogs), Betty Lou Gerson (Cruella De Vil/Miss Birdwell)*
Directors: *Wolfgang Reitherman, Hamilton Luske, Clyde Geronimi*
Screenwriter: *Bill Peet, based on the book by Dodie Smith*
U/76 mins./Animated/Family/Adventure/USA

Evil Cruella De Vil plans to kidnap 99 puppies to make the perfect spotted fur coats, but the canine parents of one litter have other ideas . . .

Though some audiences might be more familiar with the live action version, this original Disney take on Dodie Smith's tale still sparks with jokes, swift action and one of the best villains of all time: Cruella De Vil, whose Machiavellian scheming and leering might frighten the very youngest of kiddies, but will delight everyone else.

The period details – it's set in 1952 England – add another layer of humour and, pleasingly for a Disney, the song count is low, thus sparing us the sight of a doggy chorus line. But what dogs they are – with seemingly every one of the ton-plus-one pooches imbued with a different personality, they're endlessly cute.

In fact, they're so doggone sweet that it's hard to believe that this was once one of Disney's most controversial movies – a scene in which the puppies suckle milk from cows udders was cut from some prints because the sight of teats was deemed offensive. In these much more enlightened times, we can finally see that this is one of the House of Mouse's finest efforts.

Dog lovers, in particular, will go ga-ga for this, but this remarkably fresh and funny period tale has all the ebullience and lovability of its titular characters. ★★★★ **EC**

101 DALMATIANS (1996)

Starring: *Glen Close (Cruella De Vil), Jeff Daniels (Roger), Joely Richardson (Anita), Joan Plowright (Nanny), Hugh Laurie (Jasper), Mark Williams (Horace), Tim McInnery (Alonzo, Cruella De Vil's Butler)*
Director: *Stephen Herek*
Screenwriters: *John Hughes, based on the novel by Dodie Smith*
U/103 mins./Family/Comedy/USA

When Pongo and Perdita's Dalmatian puppies are dognapped, the (mainly) British animal kingdom comes to their rescue.

It's doesn't take a genuis to join the dots in this movie and see they clearly spell hit. In case you've never seen the animated original, Disney's 1961 fave adapted from Dodie Smith's novel, Anita and Roger are brought together in a London park by their smitten, scene-stealing Dalmatians, Pongo and Perdita. There's a double wedding and the canines beat their people in producing offspring. But fashion designer Anita's former employer, flamboyantly fiendish Cruella de Vil (Close playing cartoonish villainy with fabulously dressed and two-tone relish), is *way* politically incorrect and craves to add a Dalmatian ensemble to her wardrobe of rare and endangered pelts. Perdita's fifteen pups are abducted and while the humans wring their hands helplessly, a countrywide network of animals bounds into action to save them.

At this point the hand of producer/screenwriter John Hughes becomes unmistakeable, with Cruella's nitwit henchmen (Hugh Laurie and Mark Williams) suffering a slapstick series of painful mishaps devised by ingenious critters (beasts of field plus raccoons, chipmunks and skunks which are not, as we recall, indigenous to these isles) who collectively perform the same amusing, mayhem-creating function as *Home Alone*'s Kevin.

The dawdling with the humans is ordinary; it's the animal action that provides the centrepiece. The true star of the show is a brilliantly trained (and animatronically doubled) Airedale terrier called Kipper, who does what a dog's gotta do to spring a total of 99 quivering puppies from a Colditz-like country manor.

Where the animated version wins paws down is in its creation of distinctive pup personalities – the chubby one, the wisecracker et al – the telling the story from the bow-wow's point of view. The live action version has its excitements, but since the animals don't speak, they don't attain Babe appeal, the pups necessarily limited to tumbling, being adorable or peeing cutely on cue.

Tagline
This Thanksgiving, the world's going to the dogs.

Director Herek, the *Bill And Ted* man, surprisingly shows a little too much restraint, failing to milk the full aaaahhhh potential in, say, an army of small Dalmatians fleeing across a picturesque snowscape, or the last-minute reappearance of limping hero Kipper and the believed-to-be-doomed litter runt Lucky.

Still, everyone gets what's coming to them, the production is large and lavish and the principal quadrapeds are relentlessly cuddlesome enough to make this, if not enchanting, then sufficiently chucklesome and likeable to have family audiences wagging their tales. ★★★ **AE**

102 DALMATIANS (2000)

Starring: *Glenn Close (Cruella De Vil), Ioan Gruffudd (Kevin Sheperd), Alice Evans (Chloe Simon), Gerard Depardieu (Jean-Pierre Le Pelt), Tim McInnerny (Alonzo, Cruella De Vil's Butler), Eric Idle (voice of Waddlesworth)*
Director: *Kevin Lima*
Screenwriters: *Kristen Buckley, Brian Regan, Bob Tzudiker, Noni White, based on characters created by Dodie Smith*
PG/100 mins./Family/Comedy/USA

A reformed Cruella De Vil is released from prison, but has she really changed her dog-napping ways?

Dalmatians were bred as coach dogs, and if they don't run 50 miles a day, they go a bit loopy. After the phenomenally successful live-action *101 Dalmatians* in 1996, hundreds of Dalmatian puppies were abandoned after being bought by people who mistakenly expected them to be as cute in real life as they were on screen.

This film therefore carries a 'dog is for life' message in its credits, but does far more to direct people away from Dalmatians by adding more misfit (and just as appealing) dogs of other breeds at the shelter, and making a hero out of the one Dalmatian who hasn't any spots, Oddball. Indeed, by the end, while you'll probably still be desperate for a dog, what kind and where from is likely to be less clear.

Ethics aside, this is great family entertainment. Right from the part-animated, part-live title credits, *102 Dalmatians* manages to balance child and adult appeal, holding everyone's attention until the finale. A dodgy moment comes in the form of a talking parrot that thinks it's a Rottweiler (voiced by Eric Idle), but even he becomes not only likeable but funny within the first half hour.

Gruffudd and Evans (who became a real-life couple after filming ended) are a lot less wet than *101*'s Jeff Daniels-Joely Richardson pairing, being both devastatingly attractive while playing their roles sweetly without being sickening – the highlight being a recreation of the spaghetti scene from *Lady And The Tramp*.

The script throws them plenty of smart lines, but not enough adult dialogue to alienate the kids. But the real genius here is Close – and her strenuous physical performance. Covered in all manner of gunk, she proves herself a wonderful slapstick comedienne, while still managing to embody pure evil. Breathtakingly stunning and totally brilliant in every scene, she is never afraid to be utterly humiliated. Set aside cynical mumblings about the size of her paypacket and it's obvious that the only reason such a respected actress would put herself through such horrors is if the film was worth it – thankfully – for kids and dog lovers – this is. ★★★ **EC**

ONE MILLION YEARS B.C. (1966)

Starring: *Raquel Welch (Loana), John Richardson (Tumak), Percy Herbert (Sakana), Robert Brown (Akhoba), Martine Beswick (Nupondi)*
Director: *Don Chaffey*
Screenwriters: *George Baker, Joseph Frickert, Michael Carreras, Mickell Novak*
PG/100 mins./Fantasy/UK

A caveman, Tumak, is banished from his tribe after a spat with the chief Akhoba. After wandering alone he stumbles across a coast dwelling and is nursed back to health by the lovely Loana. But with her betrothed getting jealous, so the pair make a run for it. Meanwhile, various dinosaurs reap havoc.

Only held in any regard because of Raquel Welch's fetching turn in a furry bra rather than even Ray Harryhausen's stop-motion dinosaurs and the nutty caveman politic of its plot (in fact, a remake of a 1940 Hal Roach movie). Other than that, it's a very silly film, whose idea of geological history is about as anachronistic as Welch's natty haircut – dinosaurs and man never crossed paths apart from in Jurassic Park. And once you've tossed your hand in with the fantasy league, is there really any need for the cast to grunt and pummel their chests in communication, as if that was the wholly authentic way to go?

Out of all the Harryhausen creature features, this one is the least attached to his legacy, although the pterodactyl sequence is pretty damn good for its time. There is something just a bit tame in only recreating dinosaurs, rather than say skeleton dinosaurs. The actors fair little better, subsumed into their grunts and facial hair. It's a tough gig considering the fabric of the story has to be conveyed with body language alone. Richardson manages some intensity, but Welch has one setting – come-hither let's get evolution going. Little wonder everyone is bashing everyone else with a rock over her.

It's notably Hammer's 100th film, no small achievement, but its pleasures are purely guilty ones: a laugh-out-loud, attempt to give prehistory a cinematic perspective. Although, it is much more fun than *Quest For Fire*. ★★ **IN**

ONE NIGHT AT MCCOOL'S (2001)

Starring: *Liv Tyler (Jewel Valentine), Matt Dillon (Randy), John Goodman (Detective Dehling), Paul Reiser (Carl Lumpke), Michael Douglas (Mr Burmeister)*
Director: *Harald Zwart*
Screenwriter: *Stan Seidel*
15/88 mins./Comedy/Crime/USA

Slacker Randy, smug Carl and lonely widower Detective Dehling all recount their fateful meetings on the same night, in the same bar, with dangerous beauty Jewel ...

Summarised with a straight face this is a primo film noir plot, but it's thrown into a tumbler with screwball complications and sex farce, resulting in a very cool, sly comedy thriller of one femme fatale and three chumps.

McCool's is the first film from Michael Douglas' new independent production company, Further Films, and he demonstrates his confidence in it with a generously supportive performance, looking unbelievably awful in toupee and sideburns. His Mr Burmeister is a sleazy hitman who hangs out in a bingo hall while half-listening to prospective client Randy's sorry tale of a tart in a red dress, a speedy seduction and the catalogue of disaster and home improvements that came with her. Jewel is Randy's bane and he wants her dead.

Meanwhile, Randy's cousin Carl tells his story – of the same woman, night and bar, but with an alternate, egocentric view of how things have gone down – to a psychiatrist who can barely conceal her contempt for his kinky delusions. Jewel is Carl's whore and he wants her in bed. And saddo cop Charlie Dehling, who first laid eyes on Jewel – and instantly invested her with the qualities of his dead wife – at the bar that night, bares his soul to a priest avid for juicy details. Jewel is Charlie's angel and he wants to get wed.

As the catalyst for all this male idiocy, Jewel is a con artist more impulsively than methodically exploiting her flagrant assets to get what she wants. And what she wants most is a humble enough dream, a home of her own, decorated to her frightful taste. Unfortunately for her kamikaze patsies, it's vital that Jewel's appropriated haven has all the mod cons – even if she has to tear such goodies from dead men while placating the troika of troublesome stooges.

All the men are good, Reiser delighting in a swinish reversal of his cuddly sitcom husband persona, and Dillon adeptly playing Randy as both the despairing victim of his hormones and the vicious brute Dehling wants to think he is.

Tyler does a tremendous job in what are essentially multiple roles (wittily signalled by costume alterations): Dehling's tremulous innocent who is pretty in pink, Carl's scantily clad slut, and Randy's passive-aggressive siren who shops, irons and does DIY between planning burglaries, shagging like a bunny and skipping over the bodies of redundant lovers. ★★★★ **AE**

ONE OF OUR DINOSAURS IS MISSING (1975)

Starring: *Derek Nimmo (Lord Edward Southmere), Peter Ustinov (Hnup Wan), Helen Hayes (Hettie), Clive Revill (Quon), Joan Sims (Emily)*
Director: *Robert Stevenson*
Screenwriter: *Bill Walsh, based on the novel by David Forrest*
U/100 mins./Family/UK/USA

With Chinese spies on his trail, debonair adventurer Lord Southmere hides the secret microfilm formula for the mysterious Lotus X in the bones of a brontosaurus at the National History Museum. When he is captured by the evil Hnup, it is up to his old nanny Hettie and her nanny buddies to find the formula. They proceed to steal the entire dinosaur skeleton.

An enthrallingly silly comedy-thriller from the Disney stable when kids movies didn't have to try too hard, and hence ended up all the better for their easy charm and lightness of touch. Here the, certainly, highly original concept is that a pair of gung-ho nannies (a formidable duo) get their hands on a brontosaurus skeleton perched on the back of a lorry (it's a long story) and hurtle about the London streets with a typically exuberant Peter Ustinov as the rather dubiously stereotyped Chinese villain Hnup giving chase. The clue is that there is a microfilm with valuable secrets sequestered somewhere in the bones.

The central joke, in fact, is not that a dinosaur is stalking the streets of a spurious 1950s London, but that some genteel English dears (the magnificently dotty Helen Hayes and *Carry On* stalwart Joan Sims) are taking on dastardly Chinese agents. A delightful set-up leaning towards the canny mismatch of Ealing's *The Ladykillers*. It's all as slight as a breeze, somewhere shy of fellow nanny-epics *The Sound Of Music* and *Bedknobs And Broomsticks*, but for what it lacks in ambition it makes up for in hearty spirit and unassuming wit. ★★★ IN

O

◎ ONG-BAK (2003)

Starring: *Tony Jaa (Ting), Petchtai Wongkamlao (Humlae/Dirty Balls/George), Pumwaree Yodkamol (Muay Lek), Suchao Pongwilai (Komtuan), Wannakit Sirioput (Don)*
Director: *Prachya Pinkaew*
Screenwriters: *Suphachai Sittiaumponpan, Suphachai Sithiamphan, from a story by Prachya Pinkaew, Panna Rittikrai*
18/105 mins./Martial Arts/Thriller/Thailand

All is peaceful in Ting's tiny Thai village. Until, that is, some nefarious no-gooders saw off the head of the Ong-Bak – the village's Buddha statue – and steal it away to sell to an evil businessman. It's up to martial-arts-master country boy Ting to save the day.

Martial arts fighting hurts. Stating the bleeding obvious? Well, yes, but most actors could be forgiven for forgetting this, what with their action caperings becoming so dependent on voguish, CG-assisted wire-work. It looks amazing but it just isn't real. And while there's nothing inherently wrong with that, it's good to see someone like *Ong-Bak* star/fight choreographer Tony Jaa spurning the cables, the VFX, the stunt doubles, even, and hurling himself into some astonishingly savage melees.

In terms of story, script and shooting style, it's undoubtedly B-grade. Attempts at inserting darker drama are ineptly handled, the lead girl character shrieks unbearably and we're lumbered with a standard-issue tubby comedy sidekick. Yet, when the fists are flying it's a balls-out joyride, boasting a level of pugilistic realism rarely seen on our big screens.

It's worth noting that this isn't, strictly speaking, a kung fu movie. The martial art practised here is Muay Thai, a style of kickboxing which we've not seen much on British screens due to the BBFC's previous dislike of crunching elbow- and knee-blows. Furthermore, the actors/stuntmen aren't afraid to be hit for real. In *Ong-Bak*, blows – often rendered in slo-mo and repeated from different angles – really connect.

This might all sound rather sad and boys-only, but it isn't. Between them, Jaa and director Prachya Pinkaew ensure every action scene thrums with applause-conjuring innovation. One chase comedically throws every clichéd obstacle Jaa's way – but not without some twists. Take the classic 'two men with pane of glass' schtick. Here, it's a sheet of double-glazing, with Jaa nimbly diving between the two panes, rather than smashing through just the one. Elsewhere we see Jaa (not a double, mind) leap through a ring of barbed wire, slide under a moving truck and deliver a flying knee-kick to someone's head while his leg is on fire. This guy's so full-on, he makes Jackie Chan look about as acrobatic as Charlie Chan.

Without doubt, Jaa's a star – a man very possibly worthy of the 'new Bruce Lee' tag. It's likely he'll go on to bigger, more American-flavoured things, and tone his act down in the process. Our advice? Catch him while he's fresh. ★★★★ **DJ**

◎ ONLY ANGELS HAVE WINGS (1939)

Starring: *Cary Grant (Geoff Carter), Jean Arthur (Bonnie Lee), Richard Barthlemess (Bat McPherson), Rita Hayworth (Judith McPherson), Thomas Mitchell (Kid Dabb), Noah Beery (Joe Souther)*
Director: *Howard Hawks*
Screenwriters: *William Rankin, Eleanore Griffith, Jules Furthman, based on a story by Howard Hawks*
U/121 mins./Drama/USA

Stopping off in Barranca en route from Valparaiso to Panama, chorus girl Bonnie Lee falls for American flyer Geoff Carter, who not only has to deal with the death of his best buddy, Joe Souther, but also the arrival at his Andean HQ of old flame Judy MacPherson, who has married disgraced pilot, Bat McPherson.

Expanded from Howard Hawks's story, 'Plane from Barranca', this is essentially a glorifed B movie that has somehow acquired a reputation for pulp artistry and technical virtuosity. Having been an aviator and plane designer before turning to movies, Hawks was returning to familiar ground that he had already explored in *The Air Circus*, *The Dawn Patrol* and *Ceiling Zero*. Screenwriter Jules Furthman had also been here before, having set a similar story onboard a Singapore-bound ship in China Seas. But this was the first time that Hawks had worked with Cary Grant on a non-comedy and he succeeded in bringing out a cynical romanticism, laced with bitter self-pity, that the star was never to rediscover elsewhere.

Only Hawks could have made such a thrilling adventure within such claustrophobic confines and he alone could have turned such a collection of clichés and caricatures into a riveting study of physical and psychological courage.

The air mail operation provided a typically Hawksian environment, in which real men went about their business with a passion and professionalism that got them through the perils of their reckless missions and the pain of isolation and loss. Emotions are mostly kept under wraps, but Hawks's fascination with macho decency and flawed heroism enabled Grant and his crew to mourn Noah Beery Jr, retain Thomas Mitchell as a team member despite his failing sight, and give Richard Barthelmess's coward a second chance, after he baled from a crash that killed his mechanic.

Barthelmess himself was being afforded another opportunity to prove that he still had the dash and charm that had made him a silent idol. But his is the only weak contribution from a sterling ensemble (that made light of the dime dreadful dialogue) and he never again landed a major lead. The film did, however, launch Rita Hayworth's career and also reinforced Jean Arthur's reputation for plucky loyalty.

But this was always Hawks's picture, with its celebration of stoic pragmatism and unflinching cameraderie epitomising his cinematic credo. But there's more humanity on display here than anywhere else in his canon.
★★★★ **DP**

◎ OPEN RANGE (2003)

Starring: *Robert Duvall (Boss Spearman), Kevin Costner (Charley Waite), Annette Bening (Sue Barlow), Michael Gambon (Denton Baxter)*
Director: *Kevin Costner*
Screenwriter: *Craig Storper, from the novel* The Open Range Men *by Lauran Paine*
12/133 mins./Western/USA

Driving cattle across the plains of America, Charlie Waite and Boss Spearman live a free existence in tune with nature. But violence intrudes into their lives when they come up against Baxter, the top man in a prairie town.

Kevin Costner is an easy man to knock. The blow-dried mullet he wore in *Robin Hood: Prince Of Thieves* and the windy pomposity he injected into *The Postman* certainly count against him. But it's the good Kevin who stands in front of and behind the camera in *Open Range*. The film is as complete a return to the traditional Western as fans of the horse opera could have hoped for.

Sure, there's more than a touch of Clint Eastwood's *Unforgiven* in its story of an essentially good man forced against his better nature to reawaken the violent spirit that lurks inside him. And the animosity between the farmer and the cowboy – here taken to an evil, lawless extreme by Michael Gambon – is as familiar a Western device as a six-shooter and a ten-gallon hat. But it's the very familiarity of these elements that makes *Open Range* such an unmissable event for those who love cinema in its most essential form.

TOP10

Straight to DVD/Video Films

1 *Say Anything* – Cameron Crowe's brilliant debut, starring a young John Cusack

2 *Cannibal: The Musical* – Trey Parker and Matt Stone's live-action classic

3 *Poison Ivy* – Drew Barrymore began her climb back to the A-list as a schoolgirl seductress

4 *The Prophecy* – Christopher Walken plays an evil angel

5 *Waking The Dead* – Indie stars Billy Crudup and Jennifer Connelly in a political drama

6 *The Puppet Masters* – Donald Sutherland vs. alien bodysnatchers

7 *The Keep* – Michael Mann directs Nazis vs. monsters

8 *Infested* – think *The Big Chill* with bug-ridden zombies

9 *Freeway* – Reese Witherspoon is a white trash Red Riding Hood; Keifer Sutherland is the Big Bad Wolf

10 *Night Rhythms* – the *Citizen Kane* of top-shelf erotic thrillers, apparently

The pace is slow – perhaps too slow for an audience weaned on gunplay inspired by cinema from the Far East rather than the Wild West – but Costner is a patient man, and he knows that good things come to those who wait. His direction is leisurely, but not loose. He takes time to set up the core relationship between his character, Charlie, and Boss Spearman so that a lifetime's worth of friendship can be seen to pass between them in a single look.

That father-son/teacher-pupil connection will fuel the action scenes that come later, when abstract notions of bravery and heroism are made more affecting for the audience because of the love and respect these two men have for each other. During the climax, Costner emphasises the toe-to-toe nature of the gunfight, as each shot hits like a heavyweight punch and roars like thunder.

As events escalate from a personal slight to physical violence, then on to murder and revenge, Costner concentrates the film's emotional content into small details which nevertheless take on huge significance for each character. For Charlie Waite and Boss Spearman, to be told that they are no longer allowed to roam the country is tantamount to taking away their sense of freedom.

They are fighting for their livelihood and, indeed, their lives. As part of this 'kill or be killed' scenario, Costner the actor introduces a keener, more credible undercurrent of darkness into his performance than we're accustomed to seeing. This is softened – but, again, with an emotionally credible approach – in Charlie's romance with doctor's sister Sue Barlow.

Even as the characters are being observed in close-up, the landscapes they populate are presented as epic backdrops. Given the traditional genre-centred thrust of the film, the red dust and wind-sculpted rock formations of John Ford's Monument Valley are conspicuous by their absence. Instead, it's lush green hills, flowers and sunsets that mark a fertile ground for this Western. At times, Costner's wide vistas almost stretch beyond the limits of the cinema screen. ★★★★ **IN**

ⓓ OPEN WATER (2003)

Starring: *Blanchard Ryan (Susan), Daniel Travis (Daniel), Saul Stein (Seth), Estelle Lau (Estelle), Michael E. Williamson (Davis)*
Director: *Chris Kentis*
Screenwriter: *Chris Kentis*
15/79 mins./Drama/Thriller/USA

Workaholic couple Susan and Daniel jet off to a tropical holiday spot for a well-earned week off. Keen on cramming in some scuba action they take a crowded boat out to a popular reef, 15 miles from shore. But a head-count error leaves them stranded.

With its small-change budget, FX-free execution, two-person crew and primal-fear-tapping concept, this invited comparisons with *The Blair Witch Project*. If you're desperate for a convenient, soundbitey boil-down, '*Blair Witch* meets *Jaws*' kind of does the job, but, despite *Open Water*'s merits, don't be hoodwinked into thinking it's the equal of either of those movies.

Unlike *Blair Witch*, Kentis' true-life thriller keeps the camera out of the characters' hands and firmly in 'impossible observer' mode, making its shaky, grainy look somewhat less appropriate – especially as Kentis and producer Laura Lau (both credited as cinematographers) are partial to inserting the kind of 'arty' close-up shots of dancing sunlight on rippling water you'd expect from Terrence Malick.

Plus, its admirable insistence on ultra-realism may prove off-putting for some: there's no getting away from the fact that Daniel and Susan are very average middle-class professional types. The unrushed set-up's tour of their little routines and numerous foibles, while brave and well-acted, does encourage fidgeting.

But it's not important to like the central couple, only to relate to their situation, and it's here that *Open Water* excels. Kentis pulls us in tight to his helpless, drifting protagonists, bobbing on the surface alongside them. Once the nightmare begins, we're only granted the occasional dip below; one particularly terrifying, second-long subaquatic glimpse reveals an ocean crammed with darting sharks, before returning us to a deceptively calm surface.

Tagline
Don't get left behind...

This aids the gradually ballooning sense of anxiety, the feeling of being insignificant when compared to nature's uncaring magnitude and the palpable fear of what's lurking in the murky depths beneath your dangling, very edible limbs. As it dawns on the couple that they've slipped several links down the food chain, you're right there with them. This isn't your average against-the-odds survival story.

Kentis and Lau keep things untinged by sentiment and are more concerned with churning your gut than making you punch the air. ★★★★
DJ

ⓓ OPEN YOUR EYES (ABRE LOS OJOS) 1997

Starring: *Eduardo Noriega (Csar), Penelope Cruz (Sofia), Chete Lera (Antonio), Fele Martinez (Pelayo), Najwa Nimri (Nuria)*
Director: *Alejandro Amenabar*
Screenwriters: *Alejandro Amenabar, Mateo Gil*
15/119 mins./Thriller/Mystery/USA

A wealthy playboy loses his physical beauty and his grip on reality following a car crash.

Having received seven Goya Awards for his debut, *Thesis*, twentysomething director Alejandro Amenabr was always going to be under pressure to produce a second feature of comparative quality. That he came up with a film of such visual and structural audacity confirms him as one of Spanish cinemas brightest new talents.

Csar has everything. Looks, wealth and a way with women. But, having flirted with Sofia at a party, he's given a lift home by his disgruntled ex, Nuria, who proceeds to speed over an incline. She is killed. But the hideously scarred Csar survives to be accused by his best friend, Pelayo, of murdering Sofia. Behind bars and behind an expressionless prosthetic mask, Csar explains his plight to Antonio, a psychiatrist, who slowly begins to unravel the terrifying truth about the mistaken identities, apparent betrayals and half-remembered memories that are tormenting Csar's mind.

Exploring everything from beauty to cryogenics and ingeniously combining such disparate genres as the thriller, melodrama, horror and sci-fi, this teasing treatise on the nature of dreams and reality demands total attention or it could easily lapse into an incomprehensible morass. However, whether referencing Hitchcocks *Vertigo* or *Franju's Eyes Without A Face*, Amenbar keeps such a tight rein on the scintillating temporal-perceptual shifts that only his hurried and rather trite resolution proves disappointing.

Considering he has to play Csar in three states of existence, Eduardo Noriega does remarkably well to convey the subtle psychological shifts that accompany each physical transformation. It's not surprising, therefore, that, having just emerged from a similarly nightmarish experience in *Eyes Wide Shut*, Tom Cruise remade the movie as *Vanilla Sky*. ★★★★ **DP**

⊙ THE OPPOSITE OF SEX (1998)

Starring: *Christina Ricci (Dedee Truitt), Martin Donovan (Bill Truitt), Lisa Kudrow (Lucia DeLury), Lyle Lovett (Sheriff Carl Tippett), Johnny Galecki (Jason Bock)*
Director: *Don Roos*
Screenwriter: *Don Roos*
18/105 mins./Comedy/Drama/USA

Dedee splits from her mother and then runs off with her gay half-brother's lover. She is then pursued across the country by a motley crew of neurotic if fundamentally decent characters.

Meet Christina Ricci as Dedee Truitt, a superbly original screen character who seems to combine the oddest aspects of Alicia Silverstone in *Clueless* and Linda Fiorentino in *The Last Seduction*. This sharp indie comedy follows a rather conventional sitcom format as a bunch of neurotic, lovelorn, witty, fundamentally decent characters are tossed together and sort each other out until a happy ending is achieved. The radical stroke is telling the whole thing from the point of view of a 16-year-old white trash sociopath who is constantly nasty to everyone and acidly amusing about them in her narration.

It opens with Dedee splitting from her mother – 'My mother was the sort of mother who always said she was her daughter's best friend. I thought: Great! Not only do I have a shitty mother, my best friend's a loser bitch' – and moving in with her sensitive gay half-brother Bill, whose lover she promptly seduces and runs off with, financed by money stolen from Bill. With his late lover's sister Lucia egging him on, Bill pursues the pair across country, irked because Dedee has stolen a dead man's ashes, and Sheriff Carl, who has a crush on Lucia, on their trail.

Director Roos realises he has created a winner in his central character and doesn't try too hard to be flashy in presenting her, though he gets amusing work from the befuddled Donovan and a whiny Kudrow. Ricci is a revelation, a convincing adolescent sexpot with a mile-wide mean streak that never cracks, engaging our interest with a succession of quotable put-downs and cynical sneers. With this performance, the former Wednesday Addams suggests she may be the first child star since Jodie Foster to graduate to grown-up stardom. ★★★★ **AC**

⊙ ORCA:THE KILLER WHALE (1977)

Starring: *Richard Harris (Captain Nolan), Charlotte Rampling (Rachel Bedford), Will Sampson (Umilak), Bo Derek (Annie), Keenan Wynn (Novak)*
Director: *Michael Anderson*
Screenwriters: *Sergio Donati, Luciano Vincenzoni, Robert Towne*
PG/92 mins./Horror/USA

After witnessing the killing of its mate and child, a male killer whale decides to get even, attacking the small fishing harbour where Captain Nolan, the man responsible, lives.

A cheap and tacky attempt by producer Dino De Laurentiis to cash on the phenomenon of *Jaws*, in which Richard Harris takes over crusty sea salt duties from Robert Shaw and Bo Derek gets her leg bitten off. There's a loose eco-message, attempting to add depth to its otherwise obvious copycatting, in which marine professor Charlotte Rampling teaches us all about how whales are good creatures and quite smart. Perhaps, smarter than even director Michael Anderson who, ostensibly, is delivering a blubbery slasher movie – Orca, driven mad, is on a killing spree and manages to burn the whole town down (clever whale).

There must be some irony in the fact Harris' old man of the sea (another of his tiresome 'shouty' performances) catches Great Whites to put in aquariums – man, that Quint was a wuss in comparison. It's all cod-profound – white man against nature, white man against women, white man against Inuits. Where does our great white hunter fit into the post-post whatever world? Not that anyone's questioning anything but those phoney looking icebergs. ★ **IN**

ORGAZMO (1997)

Starring: *Trey Parker (Joe Young), Dian Bachar (Ben Chapleski), Robin Lynne Raab (Lisa, Joe's fiancee), Michael Dean Jacobs (Maxx Orbison), Ron (Jeremy Clark)*
Director: *Trey Parker*
Screenwriter: *Trey Parker*
18/88 mins./Comedy/USA

Naive young Mormon Joe Young is recruited to act in porn movies.

While *South Park* flourishes, the live-action film career of co-creators Parker and Stone has been chequered. Their hugely underrated sporting spoof *BASEketball* bypassed cinemas here completely (although it deserved a theatrical run), while *Orgazmo* only arrived on the big screen in the UK after sinking beneath poor reviews (and the dreaded NC-17 rating) in the US. You can't help thinking that poor old Parker and Stone have been much maligned, for this bizarre sex comedy is far funnier and smarter than its American drubbing implies.

Parker stars as Joe Young, a Mormon whose attempts to spread the word door-to-door in LA lead him to the set of a porn movie. A string of coincidences see him being offered the lead role – namely, Orgazmo, a masked superhero who has lots of sex and offs villains with an earth-moving secret weapon.

Reluctantly, Joe, agrees, spurred on by the promise of a 'stunt cock' during his sex scenes, enough cash to pay for his wedding to fellow Mormon Lisa, and the fact that nobody will know it's him behind the mask – until the finished film becomes an unexpected smash.

Like *There's Something About Mary*, *Orgazmo* has a very sweet love story at its core, although it's more consistently entertaining, blending some outrageous moments with a surprising degree of restraint. And Parker's appealing screen presence is offset by the likes of Stone as the camera assistant who really gets into his work, and Bachar as his karate fixated, sex toy wielding co-star. ★★★ **CW**

⊙ ORLANDO (1992)

Starring: *Tilda Swinton (Orlando), Quentin Crisp (Queen Elizabeth I), Billy Zane (Shelmerdine), John Wood (Archduke Harry), Jimmy Sommerville (Falsetto/Angel)*
Director: *Sally Potter*
Screenwriter: *Sally Potter, based on the novel by Virginia Woolf*
PG/89 mins./Drama/Romance/UK/Russia/France/Italy/Netherlands
Awards: *BAFTA – Best Make-Up*

Orlando is a young nobleman who is given eternal youth by Elizabeth I, so that he can change between centuries (and sexes) to try and find a meaning in life and love.

Continually clearing its throat to utter something profound about sexuality, this never quite delivers the speech, though its failure to fully engage the mind is made up for by its captivation of the eye. A sumptuously shot stroll through the centuries, based on Virginia Woolf's novel of the same name, it has Orlando as a man born into Elizabethan England who lives forever and changes into a woman.

Packaging each period into a slight dramatic episode with its own theme – love, poetry, politics, society and so on – this whirl always has Swinton as a radiant stillness at the centre, with her classical English full moon of a face, gently fizzing charisma and wry asides to camera.

Yet she never convincingly plays Orlando the man, and it's here that the film really gets its knickers in a twist. In the most deliberately confusing moment, which nevertheless has an excruciating humour, Queen Elizabeth I takes a shine to Orlando, sending out a scramble of signals as a gay man plays an old woman flirting with a woman playing a young man.

As you would expect with Peter Greenaway collaborators on board, the design is lush and painterly, but though the look is outstanding, Potter offers slim pickings in the enlightenment department: Orlando reaches contentment when she stops trying to be something she or he isn't – which is fair enough, of course, but a message unworthy of the weight of work on display here. It is, however, arty but digestible, and considerably funnier and less pretentious than you could possibly have hoped. ★★★ **MT**

ORPHANS (1997)

Starring: *Douglas Henshall (Michael), Gary Lewis (Thomas), Rosemarie Stevenson (Sheila), Stephen McCole (John), Frank Gallagher (Tanga)*
Director: *Peter Mullan*
Screenwriter: *Peter Mullan*
18/97 mins./Comedy/Drama/UK

A black comedy-drama unfolds as four Scottish siblings wait to bury their mum.

After his blistering turn in Ken Loach's *My Name Is Joe*, Mullan moved to the other side of the lens, scripting and directing this triumphant first feature which recounts one long, darkly comic night of the soul as experienced by a clan about to bury their mother. What begins with the Catholic solemnity of a Terence Davies movie acquires a lopsided reality more akin to the work of Danny Boyle.

Eldest son Thomas gets the evening off to a bad start when his tribute song to the deceased sparks a brawl with a local thug that sees brother Michael being stabbed. In the aftermath of the fight, and against a gathering storm, each member of the family takes separate, almost allegorical, parts. Younger sibling John seeks out for vengeance; the bleeding Michael drifts aimlessly hoping to pass off his wound as a work injury. Thomas, meanwhile, throws himself into religious ritual, more concerned with mourning the dead than caring for his cerebral palsied sister Sheila who relies on strangers when her electric wheelchair conks out in an unlit backstreet.

Comic dramas rarely come blacker or more affecting than Mullan's and it is with a sureness befitting a seasoned veteran rather than a first timer that he is able to juxtapose the many incidental scenes of riotous hilarity and quiet pathos, never letting the gallows humour or the emotion run unchecked.

The uniformly excellent cast notwithstanding, what's also striking is the authenticity with which the director evokes the hues and sounds of the city; its expletive-strewn dialect and, as seen in a roadside knife fight of heart-pounding immediacy, its edgy air of danger. Grotesquely funny and desperately sad, a headbutt and a hymn, the film is something special. ★★★★ **CC**

ORPHEE (ORPHEUS) (1949)

Starring: *Jean Marais (Orpheus), Maria Casares (The Princess), Marie Dea (Eurydice), Francois Perier (Heurtebise), Juliette Greco (Aglanonice), Edouard Dermit (Cégeste)*
Director: *Jean Cocteau*
Screenwriter *Jean Cocteau based on the play by Jean Cocteau*
PG/112 mins./Fantasy/France

Having encountered a mysterious Princess on the death of his friend, Cegeste, Orpheus becomes so wrapped up in his poetry that it takes the Princess's angelic servant, Heurtebise, to persuade him to enter the Underworld to reclaim his dead wife, Eurydice, from her clutches.

Jean Cocteau's fascination with the poet's place in modern society had already informed *The Blood of a Poet* and he would conclude his lyrical trilogy with *The Testament of Orpheus* in 1959. But this central segment proved the summation of his lifetime obsession with the Greek god of creativity. Indeed, this enigmatic reworking of the myth of Orpheus and Eurydice could not have been improved upon – even had Marlene Dietrich or Greta Garbo accepted the challenge of playing the mysterious Princess, whose power over death seduces the hapless poet into descending into the Zone to find her.

Drawing on the classical legend that had inspired Cocteau's 1925 stage play, the story is wondrously intricate. Everything revolves around Cégeste's death at the hands of the Princess's motorcycling emissaries, as this not only causes Orpheus to be lured into the Zone, but it also introduces him (via Heurtebise's car radio) to the eccentric verses that enslave his imagination and cause him to neglect Eurydice, whose death strikes the doting Heurtebise as an injustice that demands the same vengeance that the Bacchanates mete out to Orpheus in mistaken retributon for Cégeste's demise.

But while it is a masterpiece of romantic storytelling and artistic analysis, this hymn to the poet's need to be reborn is also a superb technical achievement that invokes the spirit of the silent mesmerist, Georges Méliès, to create what Cocteau considered to be a mythical, supernatural detective thriller.

Conjuring up the Underworld in a bombed-out military academy at Saint-Cyr, Cocteau and effects artist Christian Bérard employed all manner of doubles, reflecting and transparent glasses, fake perspectives and ingenious tricks (e.g. using a vat of mercury to produce the impression of a rippling mirror) to blur the lines between fantasy and reality. Jean d'Eaubonne's sets, Nicholas Hayer's photography and Georges Auric's score are equally impeccable. But it's Cocteau's genius for the surreal, the supernatural and the sublime that makes this captivating film so magical – even though it's clearly rooted in a world still recovering from the ravages of war. ★★★★★ **DP**

OSMOSIS JONES (2001)

Starring: *Bill Murray (Frank Detorri), Chris Rock (Osmosis Jones), Laurence Fishburne (Thrax), David Hyde Pierce (Dix), Brandy Norwood (Leah), William Shatner (Mayor Phlegmming)*
Directors: *Bobby Farrelly, Peter Farrelly*
Screenwriter: *Marc Hyman*
PG/91 mins./Part-animated/Comedy/USA

When slobbish zoo worker Frank eats an infected egg, it's up to white blood cell Osmosis Jones, and cold relief tablet Drix, to save the city of Frank from destruction at the hands of evil virus, Thrax.

Remember the old *Beano* cartoon, The Numbskulls, about creatures controlling your body? Scary Orwellian implications aside, it was a great idea, and here it is, dusted off, and given a live action/animation makeover. Picture a David Cronenberg cartoon. With fart gags.

It's a lot funnier than that sounds. Kids, with their propensity for giggling at anything bodily functions-related, will have a field day. Meanwhile, adults are catered for by an extremely sharp script, stuffed with beautiful touches Mafia-like melanoma cells; a bureaucratic mayor; and top one-liners ('We'll go down to the haemorrhoids and get you a good lawyer').

It's billed as a Farrelly brothers movie, but Peter and Bobby's influence extends purely to the disappointing live-action segments. There are gross-out moments galore, but it seems like the Farrellys haven't got their hearts, or any other bodily organ, in it. Murray is suitably sleazy as the oafish Frank, but is as wasted here as he was in *Charlie's Angels*.

Thankfully, the animated side of things is inspired. Directors Kroon and Sito revel in the sheer scale of their human playground, unleashing a barrage of visual gags, many of which will escape detection until additional viewings. Their larger-than-life, retro-styled animation is reminiscent of an episode of *Duckman* with higher production values.

Voice-wise, Rock is unusually restrained as the sassy Jones, and Fishburne is memorably nasty as Thrax. But it's Hyde Pierce's prim, priggish, deadpan Drix – a cross between Buzz Lightyear and *Frasier*'s Niles – who steals the show. Dr *Empire*'s diagnosis? See *Osmosis Jones*. If sadness symptoms persist, see it again. It's a great work of body. ★★★ **OR**

OSSESSIONE (1942)

Starring: *Clara Calamai (Giovanna), Massimo Girotti (Gino), Juan De Landa (The Husband), Ella Marcuzzo (Lo Spagnuolo), Dhia Cristani (Anita), Vittorio Duse (The Lorry Driver)*
Director: *Luchino Visconti*
Screenwriters: *Mario Alicata, Antonio Pietrangeli, Gianni Puccini, Giuseppe De Santis, Luchino Visconti based on the novel* The Postman Always Rings Twice *by James M. Cain*
PG/112 mins./Drama/Italy

Drifter Gino begins an affair with Giovanna when he happens upon the truck-stop inn she runs with her older husband, Bragana. However, they become victims of their own murderous passion and, despite her pregnancy, they have already begun to drift apart by the time the police close in on them.

Luchino Visconti owed several debts to Jean Renoir. He not only gained his first on-set experience as the auteur's assistant on *Une Partie de Compagne* and *Les Bas-Fonds*, but he also got to help Carl Koch complete Renoir's abandoned adaptation of *Tosca*. Most significantly, however, Renoir gave him the copy of James M. Cain's *The Postman Always Rings Twice* that inspired Visconti's debut, which has since become acknowledged as the first neo-realist feature.

Having been prevented by Culture Minister Alessandro Pavolini from filming Giovanni Verga's short story, 'Granigna's Lover', and lacking the funds to adapt Hermann Melville's *Billy Budd*, Visconti translated Cain's seedy story to an Italian setting with the help of director Giuseppe De Santis and novelist Alberto Moravia. They ditched the book's first person perspective and introduced the ambiguous character of La Spagnola, the gay outsider whose relationship with Gino counterbalanced his unhappy passion with Giovanna. But, most crucially, they removed the original's hard-boiled cynicism and replaced it with an almost classical sense of tragedy, which saw fate playing the cruellest of tricks upon the lovers.

Some have seen *Ossessione* as an allegory of Italy's insane surrender to the bellicosity of Fascism. But the decision to make Bragana a fan of Verdi suggests that Visconti was more interested in operacising the action (as he would later do with *Senso* and *The Leopard*) – although he confined this grandiloquence to the melodrama by insisting on a resolutely realist mise-en-scène.

Visconti had Massimo Girotti and Clara Calamai adopt a naturalist acting style, which reduced their gestures and glances to a poetic minimalism that was reinforced by the atmospheric use of silence. Moreover, he also tended to film them in medium shots, which consistently located them within their environment, whether inside the inn or on the streets of Ferrara and Ancona. This uncompromising portrait of the Po provinces so enraged film critic Vittorio Mussolini that he declared the film to be unpatriotic. However, his father, Il Duce, permitted its release with minor cuts and it survived the war to become a cinematic milestone. ★★★★★ **DP**

THE OTHERS (2001)

Starring: *Nicole Kidman (Grace Stewart), Finnula Flanagan (Mrs Bertha Mills), Christopher Eccleston (Charles Stewart), Alakina Man (Anne Stewart), James Bentley (Nicholas Stewart), Eric Sykes (Mr Edmund Tuttle), Elaine Cassidy (Lydia)*
Director: *Alejandro Amenabar*
Screenwriter: *Alejandro Amenabar*
12/99 mins./Horror/Thriller/USA/Spain

Awards: Empire Awards – *Independent Spirit Award (Alejandro Amenabar)*

With World War II just over and her husband still away, Grace moves to a remote mansion in Jersey with her two children, both of whom have a dangerous allergy to sunlight. However, the arrival of a trio of servants brings with it a host of supernatural goings-on that threaten to seriously destabilise the family's closeted existence.

Fans of slasher horror – complete with spiralling body count, disfigured, wisecracking killer and hellishly sharp instruments of death – will find such things lacking in *The Others*.

The film marked the English language debut of Spanish writer-director, Alejandro Amenabar, already a Hollywood darling thanks to his previous effort, *Open Your Eyes* – which was remade as the Cameron Crowe/Tom Cruise collaboration, *Vanilla Sky*.

What you will get with *The Others*, however, are some of the creepiest, most atmospheric chills to permeate a cinema screen for years – for by choosing the unseen over the blatant, swapping graphic violence and gruesome murder for self-closing doors and self-playing pianos, and spilling not a single drop of blood along the way, Amenabar has created a haunting, imaginative shocker which is likely to rattle around in your brain for days after.

Kidman is superbly cast here, nailing the plummy English accent to perfection, as the repressed young woman who is forced to keep her photosensitive kids in a world where the curtains stay drawn.

It's the appearance of the new servants (including – yes!! – Eric Sykes) that serves as the catalyst for things to begin happening. And while you know that most of these are going to revolve around Kidman's desire to shield her children from the dangers of daylight and the peculiar list of rules she has imposed upon the household (permanently closed doors which suddenly develop a life of their own, forever-drawn curtains which mysteriously vanish overnight), that doesn't make them any less effective when they do.

While all of this might sound on paper like bog-standard haunted house theatrics (and anybody who saw *The Haunting* might well dread the thought of that), Amenabar's film is far cleverer.

The director's decision to opt for a slow ratcheting-up of tension is a wise one, given that it lends further credence to the scariest bits and instils a sense of dread and confusion in the audience during the film's quieter moments – the ones that serve to remind you that you never know exactly what's lurking round the next corner.

The small but strong cast display just the right level of creepiness, and the two child stars are a real find. Mann and Bentley do fall victim to the occasional bit of English whimsy, which makes the film feel rather too much like a BBC1 Sunday afternoon teatime drama, but for the most part they manage to be as unsettling as everybody else.

In a way, *The Others* finishes what *The Blair Witch Project* started – once again reminding us that unseen forces often make for the scariest, most memorable cinematic experiences. It's certainly true if this is anything to go by. ★★★★ **CW**

O

① OUR MAN FLINT (1966)

Starring: *James Coburn (Derek Flint), Lee J. Cobb (Cramden), Gila Golan (Gila), Edward Mulhare (Malcolm Rodney), Benson Fong (Dr Schneider)*
Director: *Daniel Mann*
Screenwriters: *Hal Fimberg, Ben Starr, from a story by Hal Fimberg*
PG/102 mins./Spy/Comedy/USA

A cartel of mad scientists set about murdering top espionage agents while plotting to take over the world with an earthquake-inducing machine. Playboy Derek Flint is commissioned by Chief Cramden to thwart the evil plot.

While James Bond was obviously the king of the international spy boom of the 1960s, there were many pretenders to the throne – Dean Martin's Matt Helm, the Men (and Girl) From U.N.C.L.E., Richard Johnson's Bulldog Drummond, television's Maxwell Smart. even *Neil* Connery as 007's alleged relative in *Operation Kid Brother*. The only super-agent who came close to Bond on the big screen was James Coburn's know-it-all Derek Flint, the man from ZOWIE (Zonal Organisation for World Intelligence and Espionage).

Flint is the sort of fellow who meditates by suspending his life functions for a three hours, fills his spare time by compiling a dictionary of dolphin language or teaching ballet in Russia, and lives in a chic, gadget-filled penthouse with four varied glamorous girlfriends. It doesn't pretend to be a serious thriller, though Coburn – the man who made silver hair and roll-neck pullovers into icons of cool – has some Bruce Lee-taught martial arts moves in acrobatic fight scenes which require him to toss stuntmen around the room.

The plot is the usual hokum and Edward Mulhare isn't really eccentric enough to compete in the villainy stakes, but Coburn is plainly enjoying himself so much, and the trimmings are so stylish, that it's impossible not to enjoy.

Jerry Goldsmith provides a jaunty, hummable score. Coburn and Cobb returned, in similarly lightweight style, in a sequel, *In Like Flint*, which took the super-agent into outer space a decade before Roger Moore got there in *Moonraker*. The character reappeared, played by Ray Danton, in *Dead on Target*, a 1976 TV pilot that didn't go anywhere. ★★★ **KN**

① OUR MAN IN HAVANA (1959)

Starring: *Burl Ives (Dr Hasselbacher), Alec Guinness (Jim Wormold), Maureen O'Hara (Beatrice Severn), Ernie Kovacs (Capt. Segura), Noel Coward (Hawthorne), Ralph Richardson ('C')*
Director: *Carol Reed*
Screenwriter: *Graham Greene, based on his own novel*
PG/111 mins./Comedy/UK

Cuban-based vacuum cleaner salesman James Wormold agrees to spy for British controller Hawthorne to finance his daughter Milly (Jo Morrow)'s social aspirations. However, his eccentric behaviour in compiling bogus reports arouses the suspicions of brutal police captain Segura, who has a courtly crush on Milly.

When Alberto Cavalcanti approached Graham Greene about making a film just after the Second World War, the novelist devised an outline about a vacuum cleaner salesman operating as a spy in the Estonian capital of Tallinn in 1938. The Brazilian-born director allegedly abandoned the project after being refused government permission to lampoon the Secret Service. However, Greene continued to develop the story, which had been inspired by his own wartime surveillance of Abwehr agents in Portugal, who had been paid per report and not according to results and, thus, submitted rumour as fact to boost their expenses.

Alfred Hitchcock was keen to purchase the rights to the resulting novel. But Greene had considered him an unnecessarily flamboyant director since his days as a critic, and, so he agreed to collaborate once more with Carol Reed – who had directed *The Fallen Idol* and *The Third Man* – and the pair wrote the screenplay in a Brighton hotel room before securing permission to shoot in Castro's Cuba.

Reed assembled a splendid cast and made atmospheric use of his Havana locations by reducing the light levels as Wormold's initially harmless deception came to have an increasingly sinister upshot.

However, in trying to translate a book about the act of invention as a comic thriller, Greene was forced to abandon the text's authorial parallels and, consequently, there simply wasn't enough going on to sustain the movie narrative. Wormold was too passive a character to generate much intrigue (although Alec Guinness had wanted to play him as a untidy, defeated soul rather than as a hapless non-entity) and he remained relatively unmoved by the machinations that he had set in motion.

Greene tried to blame the failing on Jo Morrow, whose tarty flirtations made Wormold's blind devotion seem pathetically foolish. But it was Reed who misjudged both the tone of the satire and the personality of the innocent abroad – something, ironically, that Hitchcock probably wouldn't have done. ★★★ **DP**

① OUT OF AFRICA (1985)

Starring: *Meryl Streep (Karen Blixen), Robert Redford (Denys Hatton), Klaus Maria Brandauer (Baron Hans Blixen), Michael Kitchen (Berkeley Cole), Malick Bowens (Farah)*
Director: *Sydney Pollack*
Screenwriter: *Kurt Luedtke based on* Out Of Africa *and other writings by Isak Dinesen,* Isak Dinesen: The Life Of A Storyteller *by Judith Thurman and* Silence Will Speak *by Errol Trzebinski*
PG/150 mins./Drama/USA

Awards: *Academy Awards – Best Picture, Best Director, Best Cinematography, Best Art Direction, Best Sound Best Screenplay; BAFTA – Best Cinematography, Best Adapted Screenplay, Best Sound*

The life and tribulations of the Danish Baroness Karen Blixen who ran a coffee plantation in Kenya and survived a bore of a husband, a drifty lover, schooling the natives, war and a bout of VD.

Interestingly, the role for which she is most famed, determined Baroness Blixen, did not grant Meryl Streep an Oscar. It just seems like it did, especially as Sydney Pollack's sturdy but turgid epic soaked up all the major Oscar categories apart from the acting categories.

So naturally, it's got plenty of glorious vistas, and the screenplays dutifully takes Blixen's memoirs at their word, but this is more *Thorn Birds* than *Lawrence Of Arabia*. It's got its effective barbs, what with all that Streep-strung heartache, but always fails to take shape against the landscape. After Redford's laconic hunter has dropped by with his sexy bi-plane, and washed his leading lady's hair, who then has to see off a lion and venereal disease, we're less swept away than spiritually absent.

There's a creeping ache in the umpteenth shot of the rolling Ngogo Hills, and the perfect twang of Streep's Danish accent, the film is so preened and self-satisfied. Blixen is not an inviting character, she's admirably dignified but remote. Redford is as rugged as the landscape, and as lumpy and distant. Actually, the best performance comes from Klaus Maria Brandauer who stomps in like a bear aiming to wake everybody up on set. ★★ **IN**

OUT OF SIGHT (1998)

Starring: *George Clooney (Jack Foley), Jennifer Lopez (Karen Sisco), Ving Rhames (Buddy Bragg), Don Cheadle (Maurice 'Snoopy' Miller), Dennis Farina (Marshall Sisco), Steve Zahn (Glenn Michaels)*
Director: *Steven Soderbergh*
Screenwriter: *Scott Frank, based on the novel by Elmore Leonard*
15/117 mins./Crime/Drama/Comedy/Romance/USA

An unlikely romance develops between a fast-talking but incompetent bank robber Jack Foley and sultry federal agent Karen Sisco.

It had to happen eventually. The George Clooney breakthrough. And, for that matter, the Steven Soderbergh comeback. *Out Of Sight*, another in the sterling canon of Elmore Leonard adaptations, is the proverbial double-whammy. Clooney has never looked so cool or acted with such silken-tongued charm, holding the screen with all the debonair magnetism of a late-breaking Cary Grant. Soderbergh, no longer swamped by the post-*sex lies and videotape* hoopla, has dispensed with his fringe existence and lent an intelligent lustre to the Leonard vibe, at once more weighty than *Get Shorty* and more thrilling than *Jackie Brown*, conjuring up a classy, jivey, beautifully laid-back, oh-so-sexy heist movie.

Using a tricksy and clever, but still subtle, multiple timeline structure – waltzing back and forth from the prison days to the present to the events that saw the luckless Foley nailed in the first place – Soderbergh establishes that Foley and partner Buddy Bragg are working their way up to a big shake-down, a 5 million diamond stash in the stately Chicago retreat of another former inmate, Richard Ripley. And while the trickily amoral romance gathers heat and Sisco frets with the knowledge that she really should be taking her foe down rather than to bed, a curious array of criminal parties (pothead Steve Zahn, Don Cheadle's psychotic mobster, Brooks' whiny fraudster, and a couple of cameo gems) stumble their way towards the diamonds and the inevitable shower of gunplay.

Displaying the sublime chemistry of an old-school double-act, Clooney and Lopez are electric, simply the sexiest cinema pas de deux for years. The groovy-funny script, capturing all the spin and idiom of Leonard's succulent prose, grants them the requisite feistiness before, in the luscious seduction sequence, dropping a few gears into a sensationally breathy sexual confrontation in a hotel bar. But Soderbergh doesn't blow all his class on the love angle. He dabbles in some pleasurably sicko twists on formula shoot-outs and a spread of story-centric stylistic flashes that mark the difference between real talent and overweening enthusiasm. And all the characters, rich and witty, interact with the cool insouciance and hilarity that are the benchmark of the modern crime caper.

There is something joyfully effortless about this movie. It doesn't move, it glides. Granted, its leisureliness may infuriate those who demand their films to be more pumped up and it is unmistakeably set within the overseen and morally suspect Leonard milieu of loveable crooks and their incompetent capers. But there is no getting away from the simplicity of its success – great script based on a good book, good actors working with great characters, a great director empowered to be great again. ★★★★ **IN**

Movie Trivia: Out of Sight

Samuel L. Jackson cameos as a prisoner at the end of the film, which he did free of charge. It took 2 days and 45 shoots to capture the trunk scene. The mug-shot of Foley that Karen sees is taken from Clooney's mug-shot as Gecko in *From Dusk Till Dawn*.

OUT OF THE PAST (1947)

Starring: *Robert Mitcheum (Jeff Bailey), Jane Greer (Kathie Moffat), Kirk Douglas (Whit Sterling), Rhonda Fleming (Meta Carson), Richrad Webb (Jim 'Jimmy'), Steve Brodie (Jack Risher)*
Director: *Jacques Tourneur*
Screenwriter: *Daniel Mainwaring, based on his novel* Build My Gallows High *written as Geoffrey Homes*
PG/97 mins./Film-noir/Thriller/USA

New York private eye Jeff is hired by gambler Whit to track down Kathie Moffett, who once shot and robbed him. Jeff tracks Kathie down, and they fall into an on-the-run affair that only disintegrates when he realises how rotten she really is.

'You're no good and neither am I,' coos fatale Greer to battered Mitchum, 'that's why we deserve each other.' Based on Daniel Mainwaring's wonderfully titled novel *Build My Gallows High* (remade badly by Taylor Hackford as *Against All Odds*), this opens with Mitchum lying low and pumping gas in nowheresville, only for a chance customer to drag him back into a plot tangle he has to explain in flashback.

If you've ever wondered what critics meant by film noir, this 1947 thriller stands as a working definition. It's all here: a crumpled 'tec in an immaculately grubby trenchcoat, a scheming woman whose lust for money and men never disturbs her immaculate coiffure, a smiling mobster villain (a young Douglas, literally leading with his chin), an intricate structure of flashbacks and intrigue and, most of all, a stylishly shadowed world of black and white lighting and murky motivations.

During World War II, a famous military training film about VD was withdrawn when love-starved service audiences said they wouldn't mind getting VD if it meant a chance to score with the glamour girl in the movie.

This is more or less a remake of that picture, with the startlingly beautiful Greer – who doesn't overplay the Dragon Lady mannerisms as Stanwyck or Crawford would – ensnaring a succession of men. As noirs go, it's surprisingly unclaustrophobic, as the plot goes from New York to San Francisco and Mexico to rural California, but that just emphasises the trap the characters are in. Directed with gothic flair by Jacques Tourneur. ★★★★★ **KN**

THE OUT-OF-TOWNERS (1999)

Starring: *Steve Martin (Henry Clark), Goldie Hawn (Nancy Clark), John Cleese (Mr. Mersault), Mark McKinney (Greg), Oliver Hudson (Alan)*
Director: *Sam Weisman*
Screenwriter: *Marc Lawrence, based on the 1970 screenplay by Neil Simon*
15/86 mins./Comedy/USA

Ohio ad exec Henry Clark is going through a standard mid-life crisis when a job interview in New York promises Henry and his wife the chance to escape their rut, but their trip to the big city is beset disaster.

This curiously old-fashioned remake of the 1970 Jack Lemmon/Sandy Dennis comedy veers more towards the Martin movies of late – in which he actually gets to act rather than do his wild and crazy thing.

Here – as Ohio ad exec Henry Clark – he's going through a standard mid-life crisis; his youngest kid has just left home, leaving him with only whiny, irritating wife and former business partner, Nancy, for company.

Meanwhile, his employers of 23 years have decided to let him go in favour of younger talent. A job interview in New York promises the pair the chance to escape their fiftysomething rut, but their trip to the big city is beset by the sort of disasters that only ever happen in dumb comedies like this.

They are mugged (by a Brit claiming to be Andrew Lloyd-Webber), chased by a really big dog, have sex in front of the mayor, get arrested and, in one arrestingly bizarre sequence, discover the (amazingly short-lived) effects of hallucinogens.

This bumps and grinds along pleasantly enough to its inevitably happy ending, with a smattering of nice moments – Martin's tussle with an airport vending machine provides some superb physical comedy, there's a nice set piece involving a horny Hollywood agent, and Cleese livens things up as an unsympathetic New York hotelier, a kind of portly, middle-aged Basil Fawlty.

However, the story takes some swallowing, expecting us to believe that an advertising executive of some repute could possibly find himself at odds with a big city or, indeed, that well-off Midwesterners (which they evidently are if their house is anything to go by) would behave so naively outside their natural habitat.

And Hawn's character, a stark reminder of what Meg Ryan is waiting to mature into, is so disarmingly brainless at times that it's hard to believe she ever held down a job in the first place.

In the end, it's perfectly watchable, but, as with *Housesitter*, you can't help thinking it should have been so much more. ★★ **CW**

OUTLAND (1981)

Starring: *Sean Connery (O'Niel), Peter Boyle (Sheppard), Frances Sternhagen (Lazarus), James Sikking (Monotone)*
Director: *Peter Hyams*
Screenwriter: *Peter Hyams*
15/109 mins./Sci-fi/USA

A police marshal for a mining colony on Jupiter's moon refuses to stand back when miners start dropping dead from a deadly narcotic, designed to make them more productive. With few allies, he hunts down the perpetrators.

Purposely a direct remake of the classic Gary Cooper Western *High Noon* in space, Peter Hyams, a journeyman's journeyman, does a decent job in creating a tense tough-guy thriller in a sci-fi environment. The effects have dated, dimming some of the icy atmosphere, but Connery gives one of most distinct performances as the rugged, moralistic marshal O'Niel, shorn of Bond's slick exterior he's a terse 70s-style reworking of Gary Cooper's noble warrior.

In truth, that applies to the movie as a whole, alongside *Alien*, this is the blue-collar grit and muscle sci-fi that harkens to the call of *The French Connection* more than *Star Wars*. While no Ridley Scott, Hyams is good at the style (he proved it again with *2010*), with great use of Steadicam to intensify chase scenes down tight corridors, and keeping as close to genuine physics as he can. Particularly memorable is a suicidal miner projecting himself into the vacuum of space and graphically exploding. Frances Sternhagen is no Grace Kelly but makes a good show as the doctor who proves his only ally, while Peter Boyle does a great shifty turn as the head of the bad corporation about to face the wrath of the righteous man. Good stuff. ★★★★ **IN**

THE OUTLAW (1943)

Starring: *Jack Beutel (Billy The Kid), Jane Russell (Rio), Thomas Mitchell (Pat Garrett), Walter Huston (Doc Holiday), Mimi Aguglia (Guadalupe), Joe Sawyer (Charley), Gene Rizzi (Stranger)*
Directors: *Howard Hughes, Howard Hawks*
Screenwriter: *Jules Furthmann*
U/126 mins/Western/USA

Despite the fact that he murdered her brother, Rio secretly marries Billy the Kid, but tensions grow between them and her former lover, Doc Holliday, as they're pursued through the desert by lawman Pat Garrett.

Having deeply resented Howard Hughes's constant interference during the making of *Scarface*, it was perhaps surprising that Howard Hawks signed up for this much-ballyhoo'd project. Doubtless, he reasoned that Jules Furthman (assisted by an uncredited Ben Hecht) would supply him with another serviceable study of tough men going about their business with rugged cameraderie, as he had done with *Only Angels Have Wings*. But Hughes made no secret of the fact that he wanted this to be a prestige production and he announced that he was going to unearth a couple of new stars to play Billy the Kid and Rio, in much the same way that David O. Selznick had drummed up publicity with his search for Scarlett O'Hara.

Hawks and cinematographer Lucien Ballard had filmed dozens of 16mm tests and Hughes had already selected his leads when they alighted upon dental assistant, Jane Russell. Hughes became so instantly obsessed with her voluptuous breasts that he had a loop made of her scene with Jack Beutel and decided to pair them in the picture. Indeed, such was his fixation that Hawks walked and the producer decided to direct for the first time since *Hell's Angels*.

Much has been made of the Hughes-designed cantilevered bra. But Russell insisted that she never wore it. However, she did allow her physique to be exploited by Hughes's fetishistic direction and in the countless cheesecake stills that he had produced to keep her in the public eye, after the Breen Office and then Hughes's wartime commitments delayed *The Outlaw*'s general release for five years (although it briefly opened in San Francisco in 1943 with the express purpose of scandalising the citizenry and generating more infamy from its hasty closure).

By eschewing traditional horse opera action in favour of character insight, Furthman's screenplay anticipated the concerns of the 1950s psychological Western. But Hughes's sordid objectification of Russell (which occasionally bordered on misogyny) dominated the ponderous proceedings and while it enjoyed a brief notoriety, the picture has since been consigned to the same erotic footnote as *Duel in the Sun*. ★★★ **DP**

THE OUTLAW JOSEY WALES (1976)

Starring: *Clint Eastwood (Josey Wales), Chief Dan George (Lone Watie), Sondra Locke (Laura Lee), Bill McKinney (Terill), John Vernon (Fletcher)*
Director: *Clint Eastwood*
Screenwriters: *Philip Kaufman, Sonia Chernus*
PG/135 mins./Western/USA

After his home is burned and his family murdered, formerly peaceful farmer Josey Wales joins a band of Confederate guerrillas, determined to get his revenge against those that hurt him. But no matter how dark his path, he cannot escape his own decency.

A strong prelude to the elegiac mastery of *Unforgiven*, this biting, intelligent, intense Western from Clint Eastwood, both as actor and, after he fell out with and fired writer-director Philip Kaufman, director, pitches the virtuous man against the corrupt government as if the Man With No Name possessed a soul. The journey of Josey Wales is from the disillusioned loner, striking out for empty territory, who becomes the father figure again, picking up a band of misfits along the way.

The film is set in the immediate aftermath of the Civil War, atrocity has struck the nation and death has become second hand (it allows the reading of the movie as post-Vietnam). The taciturn Eastwood, his face so set it might as well be stone, passing through a scoured landscape of drifting souls, an America scattered to the four winds. Yet, for all his coldness, Wales is a magnet for need, people attracted to some inescapable central humanity in the man. Here is where the film refuses the operatic, almost comic styles of Sergio Leone and Eastwood defines a style of his own – the man beneath the hat. He's ably assisted by some characterful turns from Chief Dan George as a genial old Indian, Paula Trueman as a grabby old grandma, and love interest Sondra Locke, rescued from rape – a regular motif of rescued-women found in all Eastwood's films.

As strange a territory as the movie encounters, it still holds to genre traditions. Hot on Wales' tail are bounty hunters, including the scowling John Vernon, giving the film its momentum, even if it is slender on outright action – the violence is abrupt, with a more shocking recoil. Josey Wales, and his film, are slowly drifting West as if venturing into myth, but this is a tale strong with the sour scent of disenchantment: 'We all died in that damn war,' a cowboy muses as he rides into the dusk. ★★★★ **IN**

Fictional Sports Teams In Film — TOP 10

	Team	Sport	Film
1	Average Joes	Dodgeball	*Dodgeball*
2	The Mighty Ducks	Ice hockey	*The Mighty Ducks*
3	The Bad News Bears	Baseball	*The Bad News Bears*
4	Miami Sharks	US football	*Any Given Sunday*
5	LA Riots	BASEketball	*BASEketball*
6	LA Stallions	US football	*The Last Action Hero*
7	Hickory High School Huskers	Basketball	*Hoosiers*
8	West Canaan Coyotes	US football	*Varsity Blues*
9	The Milwaukee Beers	BASEketball	*BASEketball*
10	GloboGym Purple Cobras	Dodgeball	*Dodgeball*

PADRE PADRONE (1977)

Starring: *Omero Antonutti (Elfisio, Gavino's Father), Saverio Marconi (Gavino), Marcella Michelangeli (Gavino's Mother), Fabrizio Forte (Gavino as a child), Marino Cenna (Servant/Shepherd), Stanko Molnar (Sebastiano), Nanni Moretti (Cesare)*
Directors: *Paolo Taviani, Vittorio Taviani*
Screenwriters: *Vittorio Taviani, Paolo Taviani, based on the book by Gavino Ledda*
18/114 mins./Drama/Italy

Awards: *Cannes Film Festival – Palme d'Or, International Critics Prize*

Denied an education by the Sardinian peasant father, Efisio, who insists that he tends the family's sheep, Gavino conquers his ignorance and insularity in the army and becomes a professor of linguistics, before returning to his homeland to write his autobiography.

Originally filmed on 16mm stock for Italian television, Paolo and Vittorio Taviani's adaptation of Gavino Ledda's 1974 autobiography became the first feature to win the Palme d'Or and the International Critics' Prize at the same Cannes Film Festival. There was much controversy over the Grand Prix victory and rumours spread that the jury's heated debates had hastened Roberto Rossellini's death. Considering that *Padre Padrone* challenged the tenets of neo-realism that Rossellini had done so much to establish in the 1940s, this was a deeply ironic coincidence whose generational significance echoed the father-son struggle at the heart of Ledda's story.

The Tavianis invariably challenged the conventions of the genre in which they were working and here they combined documentary and drama to subvert the ideological bombast of much Italian political cinema in the 1970s. By having Ledda appear as himself at the beginning and end of the film, they reinforced the grimly optimistic message that if he could triumph over illiteracy and insularity then anyone could. Yet, no attempt was made to sentimentalise Gavino's rite of passage or to demonise Efisio, as it was always apparent that the latter was as much a victim of the local culture and the wider socio-economic system as his son.

Thanks to the Mario Masini's alternation between lingering vistas and intense close-ups, the Tavianis achieved a heightened realism that went beyond the craggy beauty of Vittorio De Seta's *Bandits of Orgosolo*, which had also centred on the travails of a Sardinian shepherd.

But it was their use of sound, even more than imagery, that gave the action its authenticity and poignancy and the viewer quickly becomes as sensitive to the noises of nature as Gavino, who seemed to assimilate knowledge through sound, whether it was the wind, the breathing and bleating of his sheep, the melodic voice of the accordion or the Italian he was forced to learn because his dialect was outlawed at boot camp.

Rarely had the process of emancipation through enlightenment rather than rebellious disaffection been depicted with such raw emotional and cinematic honesty. ★★★★ **DP**

PAINT YOUR WAGON (1969)

Starring: *Lee Marvin (Ben Rumson), Clint Eastwood (Pardner), Jean Seberg (Elizabeth), Harve Presnell (Rotten Luck Willie), Ray Walston (Mad Jack Duncan)*
Director: *Joshua Logan*
Screenwriters: *Paddy Chayefsky, Alan Jay Lerner, adapted from the stage play by Lerner*
PG/164 mins./Musical/USA

A strange yet bountiful partnership forms between a gold prospector and a farmer in the untamed reaches of the Californian mountains. During the tenure of the pairing, they share a wife, hijack a stagecoach, kidnap a clutch of prostitutes and transform their mining claim into a going concern.

Lee Marvin and Clint Eastwood together in a Western sounds fine, but a musical Western? Mind you, Eastwood went on the star with an orang-utan, twice, so this is only his third maddest film. Although, it could be his dullest. Which was one thing no one would of expected of this madcap enterprise, born of a what-the-heck attitude from its macho stars – that it would struggle so hard to be fun.

The problem lies in that struggle, director Joshua Logan is working so furiously to establish the grand gusto of the big musical, he forgets his leading men basically can't sing, and that this in-joke could have lent it a chirpy irony. Thus we only endure Eastwood drifting between through the sunlit woods droning, 'I talk to the trees …' with some kind of choral backing (where were they hiding, in the bushes?) or Marvin growling out, 'I was born under a wandering star …' at a pitch so low it could cause stomach complaints. The film's score remains loud and manufactured at all times.

Such an overbearing mock-camp style hardly fits the down-home wilderness setting, either, nor its anachronistically bawdy sense of humour. The story focuses on the fellas threeway marriage with Jean Seberg (who can't sing either) as well as the clutch of silly adventures as their No Name Town is built from nothing but debauchery and sin (hey, this is America!). How this drones on (literally) for nigh on two and a half hours is beyond all comprehension. ★★ **IN**

THE PAJAMA GAME (1957)

Starring: *Doris Day (Katie 'Babe' Williams), John Raitt (Sid Sorokin), Carol Haney (Gladys Hotchkiss), Eddie Foy Jr (Vernon Hines), Reta Shaw (Mabel), Barbara Nichols (Poopsie), Thelma Pelish (Mae), Jack Straw (Prez)*
Directors: *George Abbott, Stanley Donen*
Screenwriters: *George Abbott, Richard Bissell, based on the Broadway musical by Bissell, Abbott and the novel* Seven And A Half Cents *by Bissell*
U/101 mins./Musical/USA

Trouble begins brewing at the Sleep Tite Pajama Factory when Katie 'Babe' Williams and her Grievance Committee demand a seven and a half per cent pay rise from new superintendent, Sid Sorokin. However, the feisty union rep's purpose is blunted when she falls for her adversary.

Lyricist Jerry Ross didn't see either of his Broadway hits with composer Richard Adler make it to the screen, as he died in 1955. However, the combination of co-directors George Abbott and Stanley Donen and choreographer Bob Fosse did him proud, as *The Pajama Game* and *Damn Yankees* were two of the freshest transfers that Hollywood produced as the movie musical slowly succumbed to the changing tastes of the rock era.

Abbott and Richard Bissell had adapted the latter's novel, *Seven and a Half Cents*, in 1954 and it became one of the decade's longest-running stage successes. But while the bulk of the score and the majority of the cast were retained for the Warner Bros' version, Janis Paige was deemed too great a box-office risk and she was replaced by Doris Day, who was coming to the end of her studio contract and would use her feisty display here to relaunch herself at Universal as everyone's favourite female combatant in producer Ross Hunter's comic battles of the sexes.

However, the most inspired decision was the hiring of Stanley Donen, as Abbott's co-director, as his experience on the likes of *On the Town* and *Seven Brides for Seven Brothers* enabled him to open out the stage numbers without losing their intimacy. Moreover, he also knew how to harness Harry Stradling's camera to Bob Fosse's choreography and the exuberance of outdoor numbers like 'Once-a-Year Day' contrasted splendidly with the eroticism of Carol Haney scintillating rendition of 'Steam Heat'. He even tinkered with the running speeds during 'Racing with the Clock', as the workers reduced their productivity to press their pay demands.

With Haney's 'Hernando's Hideaway', Eddie Foy, Jr's 'I'll Never Be Jealous Again' and Day's romantic duet with John Raitt, 'Hey There', also among the showstoppers, this is an endlessly enjoyable entertainment, whose effortless ease belies the exhausting efforts of some consummate professionals at the top of their game. ★★★★ **DP**

PAL JOEY (1957)

Starring: *Rita Hayworth (Vera Simpson), Frank Sinatra (Joey Evans), Kim Novak (Linda English), Barbara Nichols (Gladys), Bobby Sherwood (Ned Galvin), Hank Henry (Mike Miggins), Elizabeth Patterson (Mrs Casey), Robin Morse (Bartender)*
Director: *George Sidney*
Screenwriter: *Dorothy Kingsley, based on the New Yorker stories by John O'Hara, the musical play by O'Hara, Richard Rodgers, Lorenz Hart*
PG/111 mins./Musical/USA

Womanising singer Joey Evans is caught between love for demurre chorine Linda English and the prospect of his own nightclub being offered by onetime stripper now wealthy widow, Vera Simpson – providing he's unattached.

Broadway had been stunned in 1940 when Richard Rodgers and Lorenz Hart opened their adaptation of John O'Hara's epistolatory *New Yorker* stories, as such sordidly ironic material had never been musicalised before. Gene Kelly had swaggered through the production with the appealing arrogance that was to characterise even his most genial screen characters. But Columbia chief Harry Cohn couldn't afford MGM's asking price and he considered starring James Cagney or Cary Grant opposite Gloria Swanson, Grace Moore, Ethel Merman and Irene Dunne, before he shelved the project on account of its unsuitability for wartime entertainment. Marlon Brando and Mae West topped Cohn's 1950s wishlist, but he settled for Frank Sinatra, whose career he had helped salvage in *From Here to Eternity*. However, his casting of the female leads was more in keeping with the nasty tone of the storyline, as he paired Rita Hayworth with rising star Kim Novak to payback the fading Love Goddess for walking off *Joseph And His Bretheren*.

Although 10 of Rodgers and Hart's original songs were retained from the original show (alongside four interpolations), the demands of the Production Code meant that screenwriter Dorothy Kingsley had to heavily sanitise the narrative, with the result that an unregenerate heel became merely a flawed hero. Moreover, Sinatra's inclusion (which Kelly never forgave) meant that the emphasis shifted away from dance to song and he not only got to croon the likes of 'I Could Write a Book', but also belt out 'The Lady Is a Tramp' in the inimitable style he had recently developed with Capitol Records arranger, Nelson Riddle.

However, Novak and Hayworth were dubbed, respectively on 'My Funny Valentine' by Trudi Erwin and on 'Zip' and 'Bewitched, Bothered and Bewildered' by Jo Ann Garner. Hayworth (who was younger than Sinatra and resented having to play the older woman) often looks distant, as this was her studio swansong. But Novak was hopelessly miscast and her rigidity further devalued a project that could have done with remaining mothballed for another decade, so that its coarse cynicism could have been exposed in all its tawdry glory. ★★★ **DP**

THE PALM BEACH STORY (1942)

Starring: *Claudette Colbert (Gerry Jeffers), Joel McCRea (Tom Jeffers), Mary Astor (Princess Centimillia), Rudy Vallee (J.D. Hackensacker III), Sig Arno (Toto) Robert Warwick (Mr Hinch), Arthur Stuart Hull (Mr Osmond), Torbern Meyer (Dr Kluck)*
Director: *Preston Sturges*
Screenwriter: *Preston Sturges*
U/90 mins./Comedy/USA

Convinced she'd be more use to her impoverished inventor husband Tom if she divorced him and funded his exploits by marrying a millionaire, Gerry Jeffers heads for Florida and sets her sights on J.D. Hackensacker III, whose sister, Princess Centimillia, takes a shine to the pursuing Tom.

With the critics purring over *The Lady Eve* and *Sullivan's Travels* ready for release, Preston Sturges considered making another Veronica Lake comedy (eventually directed as *I Married a Witch* by René Clair) before embarking on a screenplay about ambition, greed and 'the aristocracy of beauty'. Once the Breen Office had rejected the title, *Is Marriage Necessary?*, the project was known as *Is That Bad?* during pre-production and its blend of screwball, satire and farce owed a debt to such French playwrights as Molière and Feydeau, whose *Le Mariage de Barillon* bore more than a passing similarity to Sturges's endlessly amusing round of musical partners.

However, a chance visit to the pictures prompted Sturges to rework his scenario, as Rudy Vallee's performance in the minor musical comedy *Time Out For Rhythm* inspired the creation of J.D. Hackensacker III and his man-mad sister, Princess Centimillia. Despite disliking her part intensely and finding Sturges an impossible director to please, Mary Astor excelled as the much-married vamp and together with Vallee comes close to stealing the film from nominal stars, Claudette Colbert and Joel McCrea. Indeed, it's their reaction to the revelation that Tom and Gerry are spouses not siblings that enables Sturges to get away with the wonderfully contrived denouement, in which the Jeffers summon up conveniently eligible identical twins.

Sturges studded the action with autobiographical references, none more amusing than Colbert's train-board encounter with the Ale and Quail Club, whose gleefully boorish antics culminated in their carriage being uncoupled and abandoned in the middle of nowhere. The rascally membership included such stalwart members of the Sturges stock company as William Demarest, Robert Grieg and Roscoe Ates and their typically polished comic contribution was matched by the unsung Franklin Pangborn, as the hotel manager, and Robert Dudley, as the splendidly named Wienie King.

Designed to provide wartime audiences with a madcap escape from the bad news emanating from the Pacific, this remains among Sturges's most consistently hilarious romps. ★★★★ **DP**

PALOOKAVILLE (1995)

Starring: *William Forsythe (Sid Dunleavy), Vincent Gallo (Russell Pataki), Adam Trese (Jerry), Gareth Williams (Ed the Cop), Lisa Gay Hamilton (Betty)*
Director: *Alan Taylor*
Screenwriter: *David Edpstein*
15/92 mins./Crime/Drama/USA

Unsuccessful crooks Sid, Russ and Jerry are on the point of giving up crime. A good deed, coming to the aid of a security van driver who is having a stroke, gives them an idea for a 'perfect' heist.

Drawn from stories by Italo Calvino, this comes on like yet another hard-boiled tale of desperate heist men who get deeper into trouble with every attempt to escape poverty, then reveals a distinctive, sweet sensibility.

It opens with an elaborate attempt to burglarise a jeweller's store which goes wrong because the crooks misread the plans and break into the bakery next door, further imperilling themselves when one is unable to resist the temptation to steal a doughnut.

Naturally, the heist that is carefully planned throughout the film goes awry, but the expected tragic outburst of violence never quite arrives and the story concludes with its heroes being apprehended by the police not for their failed crimes but for their successful heroism and hauled down to the police station to receive good citizenship awards for helping the stricken security guard.

A strength of the movie is that the cast would be capable of playing vicious hard men, suggesting a real danger that is ultimately avoided, with beefy William Forsythe in particular going against his typecasting as a monstrous thug (Al Capone on the TV revival of *The Untouchables*) to display a convincing sentimental streak as a dog-loving deadbeat.

The title, of course, refers to *On the Waterfront* – in which taking a dive offers boxer Marlon Brando 'a one-way ticket to Palookaville'.

It was the first of three American films to be modelled on the Italian neo-realist classic *Bog Deal on Madonna Street*, arriving well before Woody Allen's similarly pastry-obsessed *Small Time Crooks* and the *Madonna Street* remake *Welcome to Collinwood*. ★★★ **KN**

PANDORA'S BOX (1929)

Starring: *Louise Brooks (Lulu) Fritz Kortner (Dr Peter Schön), Francis Lederer (Alwa Schon), Carl Goetz (Schigolch), Krafft-Raschif (Rodrigo Quast), Alice Roberts (Countess Anna Geschwitz), Gustav Diessl (Jack the Ripper)*
Director: *G.W. Pabst*
Screenwriters: *Joseph Fleisler, G.W. Pabst, Ladislaus Vajda, based on the plays* Erdgeist *and* Die Büchse der Pandora *by Frank Wedekind*
Unrated/100 mins./Drama/West Germany

Having fled her Berlin trial for the murder of her husband, Dr. Peter Schön, Lulu absconds to London with his son Alwa and lesbian countess Anna Geschwitz, where she descends into prostitution and, on Christmas Eve, encounters Jack the Ripper.

Louise Brooks very nearly didn't land her most iconic role, as she only learned of G.W. Pabst's interest in her as Paramount was terminating her contract. He had seen her in Howard Hawks's *A Girl in Every Port*, but had received no reply to repeated requests to star her in his adaptation of anti-bourgeois dramatist Frank Wedekind's plays, *Erdgeist* and *Die Büchse der Pandora* (1902). Indeed, Pabst was on the point of casting Marlene Dietrich (whom he considered incapable of achieving Lulu's guilesss innocence) when Brooks arrived in Berlin.

With her bobbed hair and effortless sensuality, Brooks dominated the action and so shocked the Weimar censors with her amoral antics that not only were several captions rewritten – to suggest that Dr Schön was an adoptive father instead of a lover and that Countess Geschwitz was a confidante not a lesbian vamp – but the ending was also changed, so that Lulu was spared the Ripper's blade and was redeemed by the Salvation Army.

But for all its erotic insinuation and dramatic intensity, this is also a laudable technical achievement. Pabst deftly tailored the visual style to suit the narrative content, which was given additional diegetic and metaphorical significance by Joseph R. Fliesler's subtle cutting on movement. Thus, the Berlin sequences recall the studio realism that Pabst had devised for *The Joyless Street*, while the vibrant cabaret performance (which superbly conveyed the thrill of backstage tension) drew on the Impressionist techniques then current in French cinema. Finally, the scenes in the floating casino and on the forbidding London streets recalled the Expressionism that cinematographer Gunther Krampf had generated on F.W. Murnau's *Nosferatu*, while also anticipating Josef von Sternberg's habit of using shadow, smoke and décor to enclose space, in order to suggest how Lulu's fate was gradually closing in on her.

However, the film was accorded a mixed critical reception and Pabst was accused of betraying both Wedekind's prose and his own socio-political convictions by producing such a melodramatic potboiler. But its reputation has since been restored, thanks to Brooks's bestselling memoirs and Catherine Gaborit's painstaking reconstruction. ★★★★★ **DP**

PANIC ROOM (2002)

Starring: *Jodie Foster (Meg Altman), Forest Whitaker (Burnham), Dwight Yoakum (Raoul), Jared Leto (Junior), Kristen Stewart (Sarah Altman), Patrick Bauchau (Stephen Altman), Nicole Kidman (Stephen's girlfriend, on phone)*
Director: *David Fincher*
Screenwriter: *David Koepp*
15/107 mins./Thriller/USA

When a trio of intruders break into their vast Manhattan home, a newly divorced woman and her teenage daughter hide out in the 'panic room' – a specially equipped, sealed-off bunker designed for emergency refuge. But what the burglars want is hidden inside . . .

We all know by now to expect certain levels of stylishness from a David Fincher film, even when the movie's actual substance is a letdown. Style is evident right from *Panic Room*'s superb opening credits, which are laid out like signs and billboards across the rooftops of New York. This time around, however, he delivers something beyond mere superficial frills. *Panic Room* may be nowhere near as terrifying as *Seven* or have the impact of *Fight Club* – but with its uncomplicated premise, claustrophobic setting and fast-paced action (which kicks in almost from the start and never lets up), it still makes for one heck of a cinematic roller coaster.

It also marks a welcome return to the screen for Foster – stepping in at the last minute for an injured Nicole Kidman (listen out for her phone cameo) – as the beleaguered single mom attempting to start a new life away from her estranged hubby (Patrick Bauchau). Fincher sets the scene – mother and daughter view property, are introduced to concept of titular emergency bunker, move in, assess new station in life – within the first 15 minutes. He then confines the remainder of the action to the house itself, as a trio of bickering intruders break into the place and the women rapidly retreat to the panic room as their unwelcome visitors go in search of a hidden fortune. The ensuing cat-and-mouse game not only works because of Fincher's ability to ratchet up tension – the protracted build-up to Foster's discovery of the burglars is true edge-of-the-seat stuff – but because a streak of black humour in David Koepp's screenplay saves the film from ever becoming too intense. Witness Foster's attempts to communicate with the outside world via the soundproofed room, to a moment with a flame-thrower that might have come straight from the pages of a *Home Alone* script. Amazingly, there are even shades of Macaulay Culkin's finest hour here – to say nothing of the odd casual Joe Pesci reference – as Foster and Kristen Stewart resort to increasingly desperate methods to rid themselves of their interlopers.

Tagline

It was supposed to be the safest room in the house.

By using the house to its fullest effect, Fincher is also able to turn it into as much of an enemy as the film's human villains. He adds to the suspenseful atmosphere with extreme close-ups, bizarre camera angles and a tendency to move uneasily from one floor of the house to another, rather like the occupants.

Ultimately, though, the film truly stands out thanks to Foster's protagonist – a strong, independent and, above all, resourceful woman who takes matters into her own hands and belies any of the damsel-in-distress stereotypes that this material might have given rise to in the hands of a less capable filmmaker. Nor, however, is she some pumped-up action woman, rather a believable character struggling to cope with the extraordinary situation she has found herself in. Foster, of course, is terrific, but more importantly, her presence is likely to open up Fincher's work to the kind of wider female audience who may have found his previous films too violent or male-dominated for their liking. And, in a film industry where such roles are still few and far between, that's something to be applauded.

★★★★ CW

THE PAPER (1994)

Starring: *Michael Keaton (Henry Hackett), Robert Duvall (Bernie White), Glenn Close (Alicia Clark), Marisa Tomei (Martha Hackett), Randy Quaid (Michael McDougal)*
Director: *Ron Howard*
Screenwriters: *David Koepp, Stephen Koepp*
15/112 mins./Comedy-Drama/USA

The editor of a struggling New York tabloid is caught between a pregnant wife, a dreaded hatchet-woman, an offer to move to a better paid but duller job, and a top story.

Possibly Ron Howard's most underrated picture, this buzzy, noisy, sassily written, and nearly realistic satire on the world of tabloid newspapermen, possesses a smartly caustic edge rarely seen in his sturdy middlebrow moviemaking – it is located somewhere between *MASH* and *This Is Spinal Tap*. Rare in Hollywood, Howard paints the cause of workaholic editor Henry Hackett to get his paper out, to track down that killer story, as vaguely heroic. It's also one of those really well-cast films that celebrate the idea of ensemble as its disparate characters unify into a hilarious-dramatic whole. The inclusion of a cameo from Jason Robards, who won an Oscar for playing fabled *Washington Post* executive editor Ben Bradlee in *All The President's Men*, seals the deal.

The energy is what counts, keep it moving, like the fast-talking Howard Hawks comedies, except harder edged and more knowing. Henry is hunted by the magnificent Glenn Close's penny-pinching managing editor, a former reporter lost to the figures, and manipulated by old-paper man Robert Duvall, laden with prostate cancer and a Jurassic mentality. He's also avoiding getting to grips with impending fatherhood – Marisa Tomei smarts away at home, a newspaper hack herself, whose put the career on hold. Howard makes a crass but effective parallel between the furious birth of Hackett's child and the tumultuous birth of the daily paper. Especially as now Hackett's canny nose for a story has led him to two black kids wrongly accused of murdering white tourists.

There is some unevenness in balancing all these elements, but the characters thrive in the chaos, leading to a finale, that while cracking its authenticity, is outrageously neurotic and includes Close's immortal snarl: 'You are so fucking fired!' that's worth spending the entire film for alone.

★★★★ IN

PAPERHOUSE (1988)

Starring: *Charlotte Burke (Anna Madden), Elliott Spiers (Marc), Glenne Headly (Kate), Ben Cross (Dad), Gemma Jones (Dr Sarah Nicholas), Sarah Newbold (Karen)*
Director: *Bernard Rose*
Screenwriter: *Matthew Jacobs, from the novel* Marianne Dreams *by Catherine Storr*
15/88 mins./Fantasy/Horror/UK

Eleven-year-old Anna, bedridden with glandular fever, passes the time by making a drawing of a house, and – in her dreams – finds herself in the weird landscape she has created, along with a crippled boy. When Anna draws her father, she makes him look angry, and his dream-self becomes a threat to the children.

Based on Catherine Starr's classic novel *Marianne Dreams* (also done as a well-remembered TV series, *Escape into Night*), this junior *Nightmare on Elm Street* is one of the best horror movies ever made for a 'young adult' audience is also an unusually persuasive and affecting vision of British childhood.

Charlotte's Burke's Anna, initially as infuriating and feckless as all children can be, grows into a heroine of real maturity without having to suffer too many blatant rites-of-passage or getting into the artier, less accessible realms of *The Company of Wolves*.

The premise is cleverly worked out – as the heroine's shortcomings as an artist have dangerous repercussions in the gloomy fantasy world she has made up and moved in to.

First-time director Bernard Rose, who went on to *Candyman*, does a startlingly good job of capping the psychologically astute twinning of father and monster in presenting Ben Cross as a shadow-faced maniac, who shockingly comes after the children with a deadly hammer. Cannily, *Paperhouse* peaks as a fright film half an hour before the end, then switches into a suspenseful, melancholy mode that makes for a powerful, unashamedly emotional clifftop finale. It makes especially effective use of Gemma Jackson's dream designs, with objects like furniture or a bicycle built as the three-dimensional equivalent of a little girl's fumbled, crayon drawings. Despite a variable performance from Glenne Headly as Anna's mother, this is one of the all-round best British movies the 1980s. ★★★★ **KN**

PAPILLON (1973)

Starring: *Steve McQueen (Henri 'Papillion' Charriere), Dustin Hoffman (Louis Dega), Victor Joy (Indian chief), Don Gordon (Hjulot), Anthony Zerbe (Leper Colony Chief)*
Director: *Franklin J. Schaffner*
Screenwriters: *Dalton Trumbo, Lorenzo Semple Jr based on the novel by Henri Charriere*
15/150 mins./Drama/USA

The based on true story of Henri 'Papillion' Charriere, a petty criminal wrongly accused of murder and sentenced to the island penal colony off the shore of French Guiana, and his various attempts to escape.

Working firmly against his gritty-cool iconography, Steve McQueen shears off his blonde locks and paints his teeth a revolting grey colour to play the enigmatic Papillion, the butterfly man who repeatedly attempts to escape his cruel imprisonment from an island penal colony. It's one of those purely dramatic roles that stars hanker for all their careers, and never quite turn out the revelation they'd hoped for. Not that *Papillion* is a bad film, it's beautifully shot, horrifying in its grim pestilent setting, and the docu-candidness of its telling, and there's no doubting the determined performance from the leading man. But his co-star, Dustin Hoffman, as a bottle-spectacled counterfeiter, darts agitatedly about the screen, flirting with madness, always alive in the way McQueen is too enigmatic and haunted, spending much of his time squinting at the sun.

There is an interesting dimension in having once blacklisted screenwriter Dalton Trumbo adapt Charriere's biography, he even turns up in a swift cameo as a camp commandant. And while his script constantly reaches for poetic symbolism, director Franklin J. Schaffner wants to rub our faces in the gruelling hardships of what ostensibly he is portraying as Hell (it is after all dubbed 'Devil's Island' and is a leper colony). It's an exhausting experience, enduring such relentless and vivid cruelty, and the thwarted and repressed agonies of Papillon's various escape attempts.

The film is at its best in the leads' relationship, softly hinted as homoerotic, but more about mutual necessity. Hoffman's Louis Dega is a hunted man, even here in capture, a master-counterfeiter who still has money concealed about his very person, who needs protection. Papillion, in turn, will get the finance for his escapes. But overall the film has taken the notion of a prison sentence a little too literally. ★★★ **IN**

PARENTHOOD (1989)

Starring: *Steve Martin (Gil Buckman), Dianne Wiest (Helen Buckman Lampkin Bowman), Dennis Dugan (David Brodsky), Mary Steenburgen (Karen Buckman), Jason Robards (Frank Buckman), Rick Moranis (Nathan Huffner), Tom Hulce (Larry Buckman), Martha Plimpton (Julie Buckman-Lampkin Higgins), Keanu Reeves (Tod Higgins), Joaquin Phoenix, as Leaf Phoenix (Garry Buckman-Lampkin)*
Director: *Ron Howard*
Screenwriters: *Lowell Ganz, Babaloo Mandel, from a story by Ganz, Mandel and Ron Howard*
15/118 mins./Comedy/Drama/USA

An extended family tests the patience of its put-upon patriarch as he wonders if he really is a good father.

Ron Howard adds yet another gem to his resolutely commercial CV, in which Steve Martin gets to show off his acting talents in between the inevitable bouts of larking about and making balloon animals. This also marked the start of his typecasting as the troubled American father (see also *Father of The Bride*, *Cheaper by the Dozen*, ad nauseous sequels ...)

Keanu Reeves offers a reminder of his pre-*Speed* teen dude persona, Joaquin Phoenix is sweetly cute and a whole bunch of once-famous folk (including Mary Steenburgen and Rick Moranis) give performances that make you wonder why they aren't on screen more.

A funny and touching look at the joys of family life and let down only by a coda in which a bunch of pregnancies come full circle in the most appallingly slushy fashion. ★★★★ **CW**

PARENTS (1988)

Starring: *Randy Quaid (Nick Laemle), Mary Beth Hurt (Lily Laemle), Sandy Dennis (Millie Dew), Bryan Madorsky (Michael Laemie), Juno Mills-Cockell (Sheila Zellner)*
Director: *Bob Balaban*
Screenwriter: *Christopher Hawthorne*
18/78 mins./Horror/Comedy/USA

The 1950s. Young Michael Laemle suspects his perfect Eisenhower-era parents, Nick and Lily might well be cannibals. A child psychologist takes an interest.

A surprisingly perfect picture from first-time director Bob Balaban (previously best-known as a mild-mannered character actor), this makes unsettling use of kitsch 50s suburban décor (kidney-shaped coffee tables), creepy-comic performances and subversive ideas (the message is don't trust your parents).

The Laemle family seem utterly normal as Dad develops defoliants for the Toxico company while his adoring wife slaves over the cooker producing perfect meals, but their little boy can't stop wondering what goes into Mom's tasty meat dishes. The really scary idea isn't that parents might be cannibals but that grown-ups are alien creatures who have absolute power over children.

Two-parts *Eating Raoul* to one-part *The Stepfather*, *Parents* is a bizarrely nostalgic fable with a darkly gruesome centre in the scary, uptight ideal couple, perfectly played – in career-best turns – by Randy Quaid and Mary Beth Hurt. The film's most unnerving scene finds Hurt asked by a therapist if she can tell her something about her child. The immaculately coiffed housewife is completely unable to come up with anything beyond 'he's not a big eater'.

Young Bryan Madorsky doesn't quite click as the junior paranoid – although Juno Mills-Cockell is wonderful as his weird girlfriend who claims to be an alien – and the switch from warped sit-com to stabbing near the end is unsettling, but, for the most part, this is one of those films your warped friends bully you into seeing. The home stretch is particularly gruesome.

The score mixes 50s oddities ('The Flying Purple People Eater', Perez Prado) with eerie rhythms from David Lynch's regular composer Angelo Badalamenti, and the wicked jokes keep coming. Nearly a classic. ★★★★ **KN**

PARIS, TEXAS (1984)

Starring: *Harry Dean Stanton (Travis), Nastassja Kinski (Jane), Aurore Clement (Anne), Dean Stockwell (Walt), Hunter (Hunter Carson)*
Director: *Wim Wenders*
Screenwriters: *L.M. Kit Carson, Sam Shepard*
15/147 mins./Drama/France-West Germany

Awards: *BAFTA – Best Director*

A man with no recollection of his recent life is found by his brother. Slowly he begins to locate the memories of the life he led, and the fact he has walked out on his wife and child, and he embarks on a journey to reunite his family.

Thusly fabled for its hypnotic beauty and poise, a haunting European gaze across the lonely highways of Texas, Wim Wenders masterpiece is a road-movie of rare integrity, a film of landscapes both interior and to the limitless horizon. Credit also should go to screenwriter Sam Shepard, an actor and playwright who cuts straight to the psychological and philosophical drift of the feature, a film of elusive arty gestures offset against the very Americanness of its landscape, made ethereal and alien by Wender's luminous camera.

We learn so little of Travis (a perfectly cast Harry Dean Stanton) as a person, he is found mute and amnesiac in the Texan desert, seven years after walking out on his kin. The reason for his betrayal is the film's destination, but his enigma remains, an eternal drifter. Little time, or effort, is given to standard movie rules, the plot is secondary to the imagery, but Wenders is not aimless. He is studying the listless nature of America, a shifting world where it is impossible for humans to truly communicate. Face-to-face conversations are nearly absent from the film's long rumination, scored to the elegiac twang of Ry Cooder's guitar.

As Travis finally hones in on the tragedy of himself, having abducted his child and located his ex-wife Jane (the lovely Nastassja Kinski), it emerges as a study of grief and separation. Akin, in deep-seated ways to both *The Searchers* with its eternal quest, and *Taxi Driver* with its social dislocation, *Paris, Texas* is one of the great films about America, as directed by a German. ★★★★★ **IN**

PARIS TROUT (1991)

Starring: *Dennis Hopper (Paris Trout), Ed Harris (Harry Seagraves), Barbara Hershey (Hanna Trout), Ray Mckinnon (Carl Bonner), Tina Lifford (Mary Sayers)*
Director: *Stephen Gyllenhaal*
Screenwriter: *Peter Dexter, based on his own novel*
18/93 mins./Drama/USA

Paris Trout is not a popular man, this bigoted store-owner and loan-shark is constantly suing his fellow townsfolk and brutalises his young wife Hanna. He even shoots a 12-year-old black girl, figuring he'll get away with it. But things will spiral out of control when his lawyer Harry Seagraves begins an affair with Hanna.

A brute study of Deep Southern bigotry, adapted by Peter Dexter from his own novel, this sharply performed but pretty disgusting drama is to be praised for is unflinching approach, but those of weaker dispositions should turn away. Hopper seems to have made a career out of this vile breed of soulless American, Paris could well be the guileless brother of *Blue Velvet*'s Frank Booth, he is racist, abusive, and irredeemable, but a product of his world all the same. It's a cracking performance.

The film was, in fact, made for American TV, but deserved the cinema release it got here in the UK. Stephen Gyllenhaal (father of Jake and Maggie) paints an ironically quaint picket-fence nostalgia for his small-town, a happy face with a sour heart. Given the graphic content, including a vile scene of sexual abuse, the TV heritage is startling. This is a distinctly adult movie, steadily, if thinly (beyond the edges of the characters, the story runs a bit dry), encompassing American small-mindedness at its very worst and revealing what a destructive force it can become.

Alongside the crackling Hopper, Ed Harris and Barbara Hershey are as assured as ever in more sympathetic roles, creating that traditional love triangle that lies at the heart of so-much American literature. ★★★ **IN**

PARTING SHOTS (1998)

Starring: *Chris Rea (Harry Sterndale), Felicity Kendal (Jill Saunders), Bob Hoskins (Gerd Layton), Ben Kingsley (Renzo Locatelli), Joanna Lumley (Freda), Oliver Reed (Jamie Campbell-Stewart), Diana Rigg (Lisa), John Cleese (Maurice Walpole)*
Director: *Michael Winner*
Screenwriters: *Michael Winner, Nick Mead, from a story by Michael Winner*
12/98 mins./Comedy/UK

A photographer given six weeks to live decides to embark on a killing spree murdering all those who have wronged him.

Harry Sterndale has stomach cancer. With six weeks to live, he decides to kill everybody who has ever wronged him, from the unfaithful wife to the financier who ripped him off.

That's the plot, now let's get down to business: *Parting Shots* sucks on every conceivable level. Its technical ineptitude and dramatic impotence simply beggar belief. That performers as dignified as John Cleese and Ben Kingsley agreed to cameos (presumably as a favour to the bon viveur and sometime-director) merely adds to the film's opulent ruin.

Chris Rea – yes, the pop singer and motor car enthusiast – cannot act for toffee. To cast him in a lead role is suicide. Indeed, the whole venture has a whiff of *Springtime For Hitler* about it (perhaps Michael Winner was involved in some brandy-fuelled after-dinner wager) – Rea's bumbling, mumbling performance seems to drain the life out of everyone around him, as if they are killing time until the proper actor turns up. Even the extras in the crowd scenes are unconvincing.

If, let us suppose, you are kidnapped by terrorists and forced at gunpoint to watch this stultifyingly bad piece of cinema, you will be left open-jawed at the arrogance of it all. As you read this, there are British films that cannot find a distributor, young British directors and writers battling to get projects made – meanwhile, a restaurant critic who made *Death Wish* 25 years ago is allowed to foist a bloodless, unfunny comedy on the world. ★ **AC**

A PASSAGE TO INDIA (1984)

Starring: *Judy Davis (Adela Quested), Victor Banerjee (Dr Aziz H. Ahmed), Peggy Ashcroft (Mrs Moore), James Fox (Richard Fielding), Alec Guinness (Professor Godbhole)*
Director: *David Lean*
Screenwriters: *David Lean, based on the novel by E.M. Forster*
PG/163 mins./ Drama/UK
Awards: *Academy Awards – Best Supporting Actress (Peggy Ashcroft), Best Score; BAFTA – Best Actress (Peggy Ashcroft)*

Based on E.M. Forster's novel of 1924 British ex-pats in India, where skittish Adela Quested accuses a local doctor of raping her. As the case comes to court, racial tensions come to a boil, and her memory of the event becomes increasingly vague.

The return, after 13 self-imposed years of exile, of fabled director David Lean was everything we would have expected and, yet, a disappointment. Perhaps, it was the choice of material, a much more internalised story despite its glossy Raj setting, or the absence of Robert Bolt as screenwriter (it was he who put the fire in Lean's belly), but the film, for all Lean's innate elegance, is strangely remote and unmoving. It could easily have been a Merchant-Ivory film.

Lean notoriously battled with headstrong lead actress Judy Davis over his old-fashioned approach to female characters. She wanted to invest the complicated Adela with more dynamism, to give her variance some potency; Lean wanted her weak and confused. She emerges as neither. Where Lawrence was part-mad; Zhivago consumed by his own passion; Adela is a bit wet. He was also up to his old naive tricks by casting Alec

Guinness as the whimsical-wise Hindi sage Professor Godbhole – he is perfectly mild and beguiling, but you really can't get away with this in the mid-80s. Victor Banerjee proves energetic but hardly astounding as the innocent doctor at the hub of the film's racial crisis. It takes the stoic Peggy Ashcroft to give the film a heart, the immaculate Brit visiting her son, who peers distressed at the ensuring madness from the outside.

Lean is so good on a big canvas, his shots of elephant parades and the wild caves of the sunny picnic that would turn so sour, are typically vivid, but this is a film of manners, from a director who should be capturing the untamed sweeps of history. When the film is finally absorbed by the racial conflict, the strange court case that will impact on all the souls around – a top-notch range of British and Indian actors – it becomes laggardly, what energy there was seeping away, as if the camera was as afflicted by that airless courtroom as the characters. And no matter how stirring Maurice Jarre's slightly misjudged score or refined the literary adaptation, Lean's majesty had departed, those long years of isolation had told. ★★★ **IN**

PASSION FISH (1992)

Starring: *Mary McDonnell (May-Alice Culhane), Alfre Woodard (Chantelle), Lenore Banks (Nurse Quick), Vondie Curtis-Hall (Sugar LeDoux), David Strathairn (Rennie)*
Director: *John Sayles*
Screenwriter: *John Sayles*
15/134 mins./Drama/Romance/USA

Paralysed soap actress May-Alice returns home to rural America to convalesce but argues with each of her nurses until the arrival of Chantelle. Over time the two bond over life's differences, finding they have more in common than either expected.

Mary McDonnell received a deserved Oscar nomination for her bravura performance here as TV soap opera queen May-Alice, paralysed in a freak accident, returning to her remote Louisiana family home a bitter, boozing, self-proclaimed 'bitch on wheels'. Writer-director John Sayles' perceptive, frequently witty, always moving film is, however, considerably more than just a tale of coming to terms with paraplegia, and McDonnell is matched by a quietly superb Alfre Woodard in the less showy but equally affecting role of Chantelle, the latest in May-Alice's extraordinary line-up of nurse-companions, rehabilitating from an invisible but crippling life crisis of her own.

Solo, May-Alice goes through the stages familiar from male movies about disablement: denial, rage, humiliation and frustration, all met with tears and zinging wisecracks. Together, the two very different women wrestle with the power balance of their relationship, bond, contend with an intrusive procession of visitors (Angela Bassett among them as May-Alice's erstwhile soap co-star) in a string of funny and telling encounters, and succumb to the Cajun locals' infectious joie de vivre. What Sayles' *Return Of The Secacucus Seven* was for people turning 30, this is for people either facing the middle-age point of no return or trying to see beyond disappointments and lost hopes. Country cooking that almost sends its aroma off the screen, Zydeko music and irresistible male admirers (including marvellous Sayles veteran David Strathairn) provide a rich flavour of the place, and the title comes from a charming, Sayles-conceived "folk tale" that stresses that even the despairing can find something new to wish for. A heartening affirmation that the unplanned, unwanted surprises life throws at you can take you down a new path to somewhere worth going, this is accomplished with all Sayles' skills as a sharp, truthful storyteller. ★★★★ **AE**

THE PASSION OF JOAN OF ARC (1928)

Starring: *Renée Maria Falconetti (Jeanne D'Arc), Eugene Silvain (Bishop Pierre Cauchon), Andre Berley (Jean d'Estivet), Maurice Schutz (Nicolas Loyseleur), Antonin Artaud (Jean Massieu), Jean d'Y'd (Guillaume Evrard), Louis Ravet (Jean Beaupere)*
Director: *Carl Theodor Dreyer*
Screenwriters: *Joseph Delteil, Carl Theodor Dreyer*
PG/80 mins./Drama/France

Captured by the Burgundian allies of her English enemies, Joan of Arc is tried for heresy and witchcraft by Bishop Pierre Cauchon. Fearing for her life, she withdraws claims to have seen visions of St Michael, only to disavow her recantation and is burned at the stake on 30 May 1431.

Danish director Carl Theodor Dreyer supposedly chose this drama of a soul over biopics of Catherine de Medici and Marie Antoinette by drawing matchsticks. However, he soon became immersed in the material and spent months researching Joan of Arc's life before basing his screenplay – which compressed 29 sessions spread over three months into five in a single day – on Pierre Champion's 1921 version of the trial records.

Denied the opportunity to use sound, yet still armed with a budget of seven million francs, Dreyer commissioned art directors Hermann Warm and Jean Hugo to build a vast cement castle between Montrouge and Petit Clamart in the Parisian suburbs and hired an abandoned car plant at Billancourt to shoot his interiors. Ultimately, little of these imposing sets were seen, but Dreyer wanted his cast to experience an authentic medieval environment.

Lillian Gish was briefly considered for the title role before Dreyer saw Renée Falconetti in a boulevard comedy and was convinced that she had the ability to 'abstract from reality in order to reinforce its spiritual content'. He filmed her without make-up and reportedly treated her shabbily on set to elicit the right degree of persecuted suffering. But, whatever Dreyer's methods, her display of 'realised mysticism' clearly came from within and her sole screen appearance remains one of cinema's greatest.

Filming in strict chronological order, after extensive rehearsal, Dreyer often demanded countless retakes to capture precise emotions. Digging trenches to achieve low-angle perspectives, he had cinematographer Rudolph Maté shoot his typage cast with high-contrast lighting and in tight close-up to emphasise the expressions that best conveyed the unrelenting intensity of Joan's interrogation. However, this is far from the exercise in still photography that some have claimed, as Dreyer made subtle use of pans, tilts, subjective angles, cross-cutting and montage to place the viewer at the heart of Joan's ordeal, which was made all the more disconcerting by the absence of spatial certainty.

The Archbishop of Paris demanded numerous cuts. Yet, despite positive reviews, the film proved a commercial failure and Dreyer disowned all subsequent reconstructions of what remains a deeply moving masterpiece. ★★★★★ **DP**

THE PASSION OF CHRIST (2004)

Starring: *James Caviezel (Jesus), Maia Morgenstern (Mary), Hristo Jivkov (John), Francesco De Vito (Peter), Monica Bellucci (Magdalen)*
Director: *Mel Gibson*
Screenwriters: *Benedict Fitzgerald, Mel Gibson*
18/126 mins./Religion/Drama/USA

A coruscating passage through the last 12 hours of Jesus Christ's life on Earth, amalgamated from the biblical gospels of Matthew, Mark, Luke and John. In dramatic terms this takes Christ from Judas' betrayal in the Garden Of Gethsemane to his crucifixion and resurrection.

Stumbling into the light, having just endured Mel Gibson's two-hour pop-profound blitzkrieg on your senses, religious convictions (or lack of them) and prescribed interpretations of the events leading up to the crucifixion of Christ, first reactions race and ricochet like a pinball. You may feel anger, revulsion, even queasiness at the stinging stretch of bloody martyrdom; frustration at the film's obvious limitations or indelicate undertones; it may even leave a residue of religious contemplation, a return to questions and confusions that scarcely reach debate in our secular times. When was the last time a film managed any of that? There is no doubting the impact. A post-match lie-down in a darkened room comes highly recommended.

Ripping away years of indoctrinated Sunday School niceties, this is a film born less of Christ's message of love than a torrent of unfettered rage. Gibson's *Passion* is a downward spiralling journey into darkness and despair on an unprecedented scale. So, be warned, it will test your mettle – not least in its determination to have Aramaic and Latin as the spoken languages, leaving English captions to feed the lines. And amongst such vocal verisimilitude there is only the thinnest veneer of the gospels' eloquence, Christ's sanctified poetry to counter the cruelty into which he is delivered. Caviezel is almost mummified beneath layers of prosthetics, skin flayed red raw like an animal carcass, leaving him more symbol than character. The film functions more as a visual experience than an intellectual or emotional one, the actors almost throttled by the significance of their characters.

Meantime, no one will go into the movie immune to the peals of disgust hurled in Gibson's direction since he first declared his intentions – principally accusations of anti-Semitism and Catholic propaganda – and, even objectively, they are not entirely unfounded. For too much of the film there is an emphasis on the events as Jewish crime rather than any preordained sacrifice necessitated by scripture. There is also something half-deranged about its depiction of evil – deformed dwarves, mutilated children and storm clouds bloom daftly at the film's ropier fringes. Even Satan pops up as a hooded cue ball, part Sith, part Dr Evil.

For a film that is so determinedly putting its emphasis on the 'real', this is camp showmanship at its most redundant. Cinematographer Caleb Deschanel was charged with refining the religious depictions of baroque artist Caravaggio (striking works of morbid iconography) for the screen. It's a tough objective, and the film veers between moody, flame-lit arcana and a burnished, draining whitewash daylight sucked dry of scope; a docu-stark antidote to the dreamy twinkle of Cecil B. De Mille or Pier Pasolini's sculptured renditions.

And here lies undeniable power. This is the most brutal, vivid, sustained depiction of torture ever mounted. It shocks and stuns with unflinching clarity. If Gibson's sole purpose was to concoct a literalist depiction of gospel accounts, then he succeeds. The Bible may simply mention 'scourging', but here we watch in agonised minutiae the flagellation of Christ's torso, a passage of sickening physical degradation. Gibson is determined that the holy notion of the body and blood of Christ are given a very carnal context ★★★ **IN**

PASSPORT TO PIMLICO (1949)

Starring: *Stanley Holloway (Arthur Pemberton), Betty Warren (Connie Pemberton), Barbara Murray (Shirley Pemberton), Margaret Rutherford (Professor Hatton-Jones), Paul Dupois (Duke of Burgundy)*
Director: *Henry Cornelius*
Screenwriter: *T.E.B. Clarke*
PG/84 mins./Comedy/UK

After an unexploded bomb exposes a hidden treasure trove, the residents of post-war Pimlico find an ancient document that declares they are officially part of Burgundy in France. Thinking it could be a good earner, they declare independence from Britain, despite the best efforts of the British government to stop them.

Loveably dotty, while still smartly caustic (with a broad political message beneath its sly humour), this is the Ealing ethos at its very best. Indeed, with its communal hi-jinks, rich swathe of eccentric characters, and madly original plot it could be there most complete film. Who else would think up such a neat ploy as this tidy corner of London, populated with salt-of-the-Earth types, declaring themselves independent? It is a comedy about what is means to be British. Arguably, the subject of every single Ealing comedy, but never so piquantly observed as here.

This droll plot efficiently covers a lot of ground and a huge array of well-developed characters (stand out, as ever, is the peerless Margaret Rutherford as the exuberant professor who first spots the contractual clause), hanging on the idea that this wholesome patriotic community are willing enough to turn cheek to the rules if it means an end to rationing, stifling liquor laws, and the opportunity of making a few bob ('We always were English and we'll always be English,' demands one upstart resident. 'And it's just because we are English that we're sticking up for our right to be Burgundians!'). The British bureaucrats counter by cutting off the food supply.

Director Henry Cornelius, with T.E.B. Clarke's extraordinary script (Ealing's finest), is turning a satirical eye on our natural tendencies for bureaucracy and boorish nationalism, as well as good old British truculence, yet we still come out of it a stalwart bunch; the fervour of wartime patriotism not entirely dimmed by 1949. Special mention should also go to Lionel Banes' in situ photography capturing a post-war London, spread wide by bomb damage, rarely seen in the movies. ★★★★ **IN**

P

PAT AND MIKE (1952)

Starring: *Spencer Tracy (Mike Conovan), Katherine Hepburn (Pat Pemberton), Aldo Ray (David Hucko), William Ching (Collier Wield), Sammy White (Barney Grau), George Matthews (Spec Cauley)*
Director: *George Cukor*
Screenwriters: *Ruth Gordon, Garson Kanin*
U/95 mins./Romance-Comedy/USA

Sports promoter Mike Conovan is so impressed with PE teacher Pat Pemberton that he prises her away from her the jinxing influence of her college administrator fiancé, Collier Weld, and she begins to fulfil her sporting and romantic potential.

In *Woman Of The Year*, Katharine Hepburn marked her first screen teaming with Spencer Tracy by playing a character who detested sports. In what proved to be their seventh and last outing for MGM, she essayed a sporting goddess, whose tennis and golfing prowess matched her own. Screenwriters Ruth Gordon and Garson Kanin may have provided the duo with wittier material in *Adam's Rib*, but this is Tracy and Hepburn at their best, as their off-screen affection is more readily evident in their relaxed, precise performances.

Exploiting their friendship with the stars, Gordon and Kanin made choice use of Tracy's working-class Milwaukee chauvinism and Hepburn's patrician Bryn Mawr poise. But no attempt was made to stretch for laughs and this easiness was reflected in the loose structure, which concentrated more on banter than plot. Indeed, the picture is at its least convincing when it focuses on the subplot involving Tracy's crooked partners – although the role of Hank Tasling proved that Charles Buchinski (who would become better known as Charles Bronson) could do a nice line in Damon Runyon-like lowlife comedy. Aldo Ray was equally effective as a punch-drunk pug, but William Ching's controlling fiancé always feels like a contrivance designed to console producers and patrons who preferred their movies to contain a semblance of a story.

George Cukor, however, was clearly more interested in the aesthetics and athleticism of Hepburn's various activities. He films each event with an almost documentary realism that he reinforces by the inclusion of such contemporary sporting legends as Babe Didrikson Zaharias (whose own career clearly influenced the writers), Helen Dettweiler, Gussie Moran, Betty Hicks and Alice Marble. But Cukor shared the overall sense of informality, as he filmed the action with a combination of fluid tracks and pans that found echo in the overlapping dialogue on the soundtrack.

Sadly, Hepburn and Tracy were denied the opportunity to reprise such spontaneous comic elegance and Hollywood itself soon forgot the formula, as sex came to play an increasingly obvious part in gender comedy. ★★★★ **DP**

PATCH ADAMS (1998)

Starring: *Robin Williams (Hunter 'Patch' Adams), Daniel London (Truman Schiff), Monica Potter (Corinne Fisher), Philip Seymour Hoffman (Mitch Roman), Bob Gunton (Dean Walcott)*
Director: *Tom Shadyac*
Screenwriter: *Steve Oedekerk, from the book* Gesundheit, Good Health Is A Laughing Matter *by Hunter Doherty Adams, Maureen Mylander*
12/110 mins./Biography/Comedy/Drama/USA

Based on the true-life story of a doctor who advocated laughter as the best medicine.

After institutionalising himself with suicidal depression, the turning point for Hunter 'Patch' Adams is helping fellow inmate Rudy gun down an infestation of imaginary squirrels. He'd found a thread of connection. He'd helped another suffering soul. He'd discovered his calling. And so exit loony bin, enter med school.

The real-life Hunter Adams was a man intensely dedicated to his work, yet prepared to stretch slapstick to snapping point in pursuit of his ideology, and on that basis, there is surely no one more qualified than Williams to portray him. And dressed in shirts somehow louder than his own outsize character, the man delivers another memorable turn. Yes, the reins are allowed to slip for some showcase routines – and the finale is practically 'Oh doctor, my doctor' – but Williams is well supported here: London as Adams' nerdy but devoted comrade, Hoffman as his bitter, bookworm room-mate, as well as Gunton, Harve Presnell and Peter Coyote in smaller roles.

Connection as far as the film goes depends ultimately on whether you buy into its philosophy – and whether you're convinced that such a hairy old goat could woo Monica (*Martha, Meet* Uncle Tom Cobbley And All) Potter. So the prognosis is generally positive, though there may be a touch too much sugar in this motion picture panacea, which is, in places, shamelessly sentimental to an extraordinarily manipulative degree. ★★ **DB**

PATRIOT GAMES (1992)

Starring: *Harrison Ford (Jack Ryan), Anne Archer (Dr Caroline Ryan), Patrick Bergin (Kevin O'Donnell), Sean Bean (Sean Miller), Thora Birch (Sally Ryan)*
Director: *Phillip Noyce*
Screenwriters: *W. Peter Iliff, Donald Stewart, Steve Zaillian, from the novel by Tom Clancy*
15/111 mins./Thriller/USA

Retired CIA agent Jack Ryan is pressed back into action when he rescues the English minister to Northern Ireland from a terrorist bomb. He kills one of the perpetrators in the process incurring the wrath of the man's brother who pursues Ryan to the States swearing revenge on him and his family.

Harrison has for, an early 90s change, a decent haircut and is here doing what he does best – taking on a crowd of despicable baddies – in the slick second instalment of the adventures of Tom Clancy's Cold Warrior Jack Ryan.

This time out, Ryan's retired from the CIA to settle down in domestic-bliss style with sultry surgeon Anne Archer and their regulation Cute Child. Happily for the plot, they just happen to be on holiday in London, bumbling about Whitehall, in time for Ryan to foil a terrorist bid to snatch that ever-popular Royal HRH James Fox as one Lord Holmes, and henceforth the three Ryans are the object of a remorseless, irrational, trans-Atlantic revenge plot that builds up, in a really rather *Cape Fear* kind of way, to storm-tossed psycho-mayhem.

Certain aspects of this caper that will have been received with straight faces in Kansas don't pass muster here without provoking giggling fits. The rogue 'Oi Arrr Ay' folk, as presented by the balaclava-ed messieurs Bergin and Bean, are given to brooding in dingy cottages with a Clannad video on the telly or – step forward, Richard Harris – meeting in smoky pubs to the accompaniment of beedle-dee-deedle-dee music, while The Brits, from m'lud Fox to – yes! – *EastEnders'* Lofty, are bungling twits to a man. And in a particularly hilarious visual non sequitur, a lavishly made-up Archer (who we have been told is a doctor, but they know we don't believe them) engages in a not-highly relevant spot of gag-making eye surgery.

However the upside is huge. In one fascinating sequence a covert death-squad raid on a terrorist training camp 'somewhere in North Africa' is accomplished with chilling detachment, shown only on an infrared satellite monitor as Ryan (and the audience) observe with dismay the CIA/US Naval Intelligence types coolly providing sporting commentary, 'That's a kill!' and 'Target neutralised!'

Ultimately, of course, the moral and political issues – and any sense of the complexities of the situation in Northern Ireland – are merely batted around to thicken the 'man's gotta do what a man's gotta do' premise. Who better to do it in style, though, than Indiana Jones himself? ★★★ **AE**

THE PATRIOT (2000)

Starring: *Mel Gibson (Benjamin Martin), Heath Ledger (Gabriel Martin), Joely Richardson (Charlotte Selton), Jason Issacs (Col. William Tavington), Chris Cooper (Col. Harry Burwell)*
Director: *Roland Emmerich*
Screenwriter: *Robert Rodat*
15/165 mins./175 mins. (extended version)/Action/Drama/War/USA/Germany

Benjamin Martin is an ex-soldier and a family man at the start of the American Revolution who is haunted by his past military experiences and doesn't want anything to do with the conflict. When his son is arrested and condemned to hang he forced to get involved . . . and thus, a hero is formed . . .

Gibson is arguably the only person who could shoulder this project. Of the action A-list he is the one figure who carries the necessary threat, the physical strength and the oak-aged complexity to bring Benjamin Martin – family man and warrior both – to life. Even while the movie around him tends towards sweetness and light, Gibson stays deep and dark, brutal and bloody, wielding a tomahawk with a proficiency that would make Nathaniel Poe proud. His Martin has history, is history, you feel.

The only problem is, such is the sheer space that Gibson commands, pretty much everything else is squeezed off screen. All other characters are one-dimensional at best. There are cartoon baddies (sure to annoy *Daily Mail* readers on this side of the Atlantic), comic sidekicks and a gaggle of impossibly pretty children who seem to have stepped straight out of *Little House On The Prairie*. As for Richardson, her role requires her to do nothing more than tilt her head just right to catch the sunlight.

Gibson apart, this is not a picture of nuance or gesture. Over his 160 minutes, Emmerich paints the Revolution in broad strokes – John Williams' score alone has more bombast and sugar than even George Lucas would tolerate.

Critically, however, Emmerich does deliver the big stuff: the battles, the bloodshed, the tragedy. There is some rousing action here; sure, some of it is familiar – Michael Mann's *Last Of The Mohicans* springs to mind – but Emmerich orchestrates his mixture of historical re-enactors and CGI warriors to stunning effect. And there are also some undeniably powerful moments – Emmerich may be shamelessly manipulating the emotions, but so long as it's a successful manipulation, who really cares? That said, over the same 160 minutes there is plenty of opportunity for Emmerich and his screenwriter Robert (*Saving Private Ryan*) Rodat to hit some false notes. There's an uneccessary amount of flagwaving – often literally. Racial divisions between militia and slaves are glossed over, smoothed out and generally ignored. In fact, whenever Gibson is off screen, the story loses momentum, focus and credibility. Thankfully, our Mel is never gone for long. ★★★ **CK**

PATTY HEARST (1988)

Starring: *Natasha Richardson (Patricia Campbell Hearst), William Forsythe (Teko), Ving Rhames (Cinque), Frances Fisher (Yolanda), Jodi Long (Wendy Yoshimura)*
Director: *Paul Schrader*
Screenwriter: *Nicholas Kazan, from the autobiography* Every Secret Thing *by Patricia Campbell Hearst, Alvin Moscow*
18/103 mins./Biography/Drama/USA

Heiress Patricia Hearst is kidnapped by the Symbionese Liberation Army, a minor revolutionary group. Subjected to privations and sexual abuse, she seems to be converted to their cause.

Adapted from Hearst's own account of her abduction, imprisonment, decision to join her captors' fringe group, criminal career, capture and trial, Paul Schrader's film is in many ways impressive.

The opening sequence, with a blindfolded Patty locked in a closet and her kidnappers shown only as shadowy figures ranting at her in dark rooms, is oppressive enough to suggest why Patty does what she does when given the choice between 'going home' and joining up, and Natasha Richardson is excellent in the lead, playing the difficult central section – in which Patty at least seems to collaborate with the Symbionese Liberation Army in robbing a bank and going on the run – with forceful ambiguity.

Some of it is even funny/poignant as the middle-class drop-out white terrorists preen themselves on street credentials and try to become accepted as poor and black, and Ving Rhames is charismatic as the maniacal Cinque, the Manson-style black leader of this group of disaffected nuts.

There's a fascinating point to be made about the fragility of personal identity and the nerve Patty's conversion touched in the public ('what they want is equal justice for the rich'), and, from an 80s standpoint, a screamingly obvious one about the way Cinque preached the overthrow of fascism while espousing the most vicious form of sexism imaginable. However, to make sense, the film needs to be watched back to back with the documentary *Weather Underground* or Spike Lee's *Malcolm X* to remind you that the SLA were marginalised nuts within a larger, necessary revolt.

The film also makes an interesting double bill with the excellent documentary *Guerilla: The Taking of Patty Hearst.* ★★★ **KN**

PAULINE AT THE BEACH (PAULINE A LA PLAGE) (1983)

Starring: *Amanda Langlet (Pauline), Arielle Dombasle (Marion), Pascal Gregory (Pierre), Feodor Atkine (Henry), Simon de la Brosse (Sylvain), Rosette (Louisette)*
Director: *Eric Rohmer*
Screenwriter: *Eric Rohmer*
15/94 mins./Drama/France

Holidaying in Normandy with Marion, her older, divorced cousin, Pauline receives some confused lessons in love through their encounters with windsurfer Pierre, fortysomething lothario Henri, teenager Sylvain and seaside sweet seller, Luisette.

Eric Rohmer originally conceived the third in his 'Comedies and Proverbs' series as a project for Brigitte Bardot in the 1950s. However, it could also easily have slotted into 'Six Moral Tales', especially as some of its episodes were based on situations rejected for *Claire's Knee*. But while several critics identified a lack of intellectual depth in the pivotal ideas of careless talk and sexual hypocrisy, this still presents a typically wry insight into human foible. Indeed, its take on teenage disillusion with the games that adults play has rarely been bettered since.

Despite the lustrous summer imagery, this is one of Rohmer's more technically austere pictures. There is no music to guide the viewer's response to the constantly shifting action and the editing is almost perversely restrained, to the extent that the film contains almost half the usual number of shots. Camera movements are also at a premium and, according to cinematographer Nestor Almendros, the few that were permitted were mostly included on his advice to disrupt the steady, eye-level perspective that enabled Rohmer to view his characters from a discreet, detaching distance, as they sit and talk, in scenes that were more literate and pre-scripted than usual.

Rohmer also makes precise use of his Norman locations of Rennes, Granville and Mont St Michel to reinforce the realism of a slender storyline that otherwise has the feel of a classic French farce by the likes of Marivaux or Beaumarchais, in which the characters consistently enter at the most inconvenient moments or overhear revelations not intended for their ears. The use of parallels, doubles, repetitions and oppositions during the central segment, as Marion and Pauline establish their relationships with Henri and Sylvain, particularly recalls theatrical structuring and led some to accuse Rohmer of being old fashioned in his equation of modern youth with 18th-century aristocratic decadence.

Wittily ambiguous and sagely non-judgemental, this is a delicious treatise on the everyday narcissism and self-delusion involved in love and lust that becomes more acute and satisfying with each viewing. ★★★★ **DP**

PAYBACK (1998)

Starring: *Mel Gibson (Porter), Gregg Henry (Val), Maria Bello (Rosie), David Paymer (Stegman), Bill Duke (Detective Hicks), Deborah Kara Unger (Lynn)*
Director: *Brian Helgeland*
Screenwriters: *Brian Helgeland, Terry Hayes, from the novel* The Hunter *by Donald E. Westlake as Richard E. Stark*
18/96 mins./Action/Crime/Thriller/1998

A bad ass armed robber chases down a parade of low lives in a violent bid to get even and grab his share of the loot.

Characters in this mean and mean-spirited blast keep observing – with disbelief or awe – that Mad Mel Gibson's dogged, dirty antihero Porter is 'shit nuts'. He is definitely that, not to mention miraculously indestructible. Except that Porter, an armed robber whose ambitious partner Resnick and junkie wife double-crossed him and left him for dead, is absolutely the baddest ass Gibson has ever played – Porter makes Max Rockatansky and Martin Riggs look like cub scouts.

Before the opening credits have finished, the obstinately alive Porter has stolen (from victims including a beggar and a sympathetic waitress, that's how hard he is) the wherewithal for a suit, a gun and a plan. Like Lee Marvin in *Point Blank*, Porter has become an unstoppable force of nature with vengeance top of his agenda. But after a brief, rather unpleasant reunion with Mrs Porter, it emerges the money he stole from some Chinese gangsters has been appropriated by big time crime syndicate The Outfit.

He embarks on a bad-tempered, violent get-even mission, sparked with comic ironies and devilish reversals, in which he takes on and ploughs through bent cops, weasely racketeer Stegman, and a succession of seriously evil mobsters (notably William Devane, James Coburn and Kris Kristofferson). Porter's stop-at-nothing tactics include abduction, the odd explosion and enduring a spot of torture, with the masochistic Mel's tootsies meeting the wrong end of a sledgehammer.

Amazingly, you find yourself rooting for this heartless bad hat, although it's hard not to feel Porter's talents could have been more profitably engaged tyrannising a small country or, say, a Hollywood studio. Helgeland, who co-wrote *Conspiracy Theory* for Gibson and won an Oscar for co-adapting *LA Confidential*, makes a cocksure directorial debut, pounding along with cool brutality and a rugged retro style.

The obvious debt to John Boorman's *Point Blank* is in fact a debt to novelist Donald E. Westlake (writing under the pen name Richard Stark) whose book *The Hunter* was the common source. This is in no way a remake, however, taking a completely different tone and many different turns from Boorman's intense psychological revenge thriller. Gibson's Porter is uncompromising but flippant, a more detached cynic whose terse commentary suggests he is alive to the absurdity of his world. ★★★★ **AE**

⊙ THE PEACEMAKER (1990)

Starring: *George Clooney (Thomas Devoe), Nicole Kidman (Julia Kelly), Armin Mueller-Stahl (Dimitri Vertikoff), Marcel Iures (Dusan Gavrich)*
Director: *Mimi Leder*
Screenwriter: *Michael Schiffer, from an article by Leslie Cockburn, Andrew Cockburn*
15/118 mins./Action/Thriller/USA

A US Army colonel and a civilian woman supervising him must track down stolen Russian nuclear weapons before they're used by terrorists.

The basic notion of stolen nuclear weapons being chased through a crumbling, amoral Russia by a maverick intelligence officer, Tom Devoe and an uptight nuclear scientist, Dr Julia Kelly, aided by hi-tech military hardware and a passing political backstory, reeks of the charged Americanisms of Tom Clancy with more than a faint aroma of one 007.

Actually, it's based on an investigative article by journalists Andrew and Leslie Cockburn about the black marketeering of old Soviet warheads. In practice, the movie touches neither the solid gusto and know-how of the Jack Ryan movies, the self-referential charm and grand scale of the Bonds, nor does it crack any could-actually-happen shock value. Instead Leder charges along the linear script, which boils down to a high-paced chase from the Urals to Vienna to the Iranian borderland to New York City with the able assistance of satellite Peeping Tommery and Clooney's ability to divine his enemy's movements seemingly from thin air, delivering thrill and, indeed, spill at every juncture.

There's no doubting Leder's enthusiasm for the task, with the full repertoire of *ER's* spindizzy camerawork and cut and thrust edits used to maximum effect. Her efforts, though, resound with bombast. There is just so little to *The Peacemaker*. The big set pieces, excepting a stylishly Gothic train robbery sequence, reveal scant imagination, crunching cars, ticking bombs, and bouncing over New York City yellow cabs wielding a chunky revolver. Stunt graft as old as the Hollywood hills.

Clooney and Kidman's characters (and no one else, including the bad guys, really gets a look in), were poorly shaped on page and the actors fume and glare without eking out much chemistry or tangible charm. Michael Schiffer's script is arrogantly jingoistic; the former-Eastern bloc a morass of scurrilous ex-generals and ignorant peasantry, with only solid-jawed Americans able to tidy up the nuclear threatening mess. And the film has an edgy sadistic streak; each lead gets a brief weepy moment but that's about it for the human touch. Stuff the battalion of incinerated Russkies.

The straightforwardness of it all makes sure the running time careers by with attentions unspanned and those hardware-junking junkies out there will no doubt dig the pile-driven action. Kidman never really recovers from being frumpised by the horrific purply-brown dye job. Clooney, despite all, still cuts quite the heroic figure; but but it wasn't until *Out of Sight* that he realised his movie-star potential. ★★★ **IN**

⊙ PEARL HARBOR (2001)

Starring: *Ben Affleck (Capt. Rafe McCawley), Josh Hartnett (Capt. Danny Walker), Kate Beckinsale (Nurse Lt. Evelyn Johnson), Cuba Gooding Jr (Petty Officer Doris Miller), Jon Voight (President Franklin Delano Roosevelt)*
Director: *Michael Bay*
Screenwriter: *Randall Wallace*
12/183 mins./War/Drama/Romance/USA

Awards: *Academy Awards – Best Sound Effects Editing*

Best friends Rafe and Danny find themselves caught up in the violent chaos of both the Japanese bombing of Pearl Harbour and a love triangle with attractive nurse Evelyn.

'War,' as someone once trilled, 'what is it good for?' Well, bloody huge summer blockbusters, apparently. At least, that's what scourge of the arthouse crowd and best bud of the multiplex mob, Jerry Bruckheimer, was betting when he decided to plough $135 million of Disney's money into *Pearl Harbor*.

A risky proposition when you realise that it's not only a story about the invincible American military being caught with its pants down but has a cast, that while not by any means likely to turn up on *Strictly Come Dancing* in a hurry, are certainly no guarantee of financial success. The question, then, is, have Bruckheimer and his buddy Michael Bay (Armageddon) pulled it off?

The answer is that, as usual, the Bruckheimer brand has delivered an almost dead-cert hit. Whilst a bit on the anorexic side in the dramatic weight department, it's a natural born blockbuster that amply excuses its slightly soggy beginning and cut and shunt end with a centrepiece attack sequence that ratchets the action bar up dozens of notches and represents the final coming of age of CGI. Quite simply, you have never seen anything like it.

Story-wise best pal flying aces Affleck and Hartnett row over the affections of Kate Beckinsale, after she accidentally shags the latter when the former is supposed to have been shot down over Europe. It's a slightly soapy plot-line, not aided by Bay's determination to shoot everything by what appears to be a permanent sunset (and a pleasing sense of humour from Affleck vanishes far too quickly).

Bay's pre-war America looks like it emerged from a beer ad – little boys fly soapbox Sopwiths, while real-life biplanes zoom over amber waves of grain. But it's the bombing itself that was always what this movie was going to live and die on, and here Bay really delivers, from an astonishing first 'bomb's eye view' shot that sees the camera follow a falling munition through the decks of the USS *Arizona*. Then comes the perfectly timed detonation, using fantastically detailed long shots of hundreds of Japanese Zeroes buzzing around the exploding fleet.

It's an amazing, visceral experience. ILM's CGI is, for the first time, indistinguishable from reality. Torpedoes hiss under the thrashing feet of drowning soldiers, men are blown through upturned ship's propellers towards the camera, and fighters plough into each other. It's an astounding, nerve-shredding experience that leaves the mealy-mouthed whinings about flat-packed characterisation bobbing in the wreckage. ★★★ **AS**

Screen Cross-Dressers TOP 10

1. Tony Curtis – *Some Like It Hot*
2. Jack Lemon – *Some Like It Hot*
3. Jaye Davidson – *The Crying Game*
4. Dustin Hoffman – *Tootsie*
5. Gael Garcia Bernal – *Bad Education*
6. Hilary Swank – *Boys Don't Cry*
7. Terence Stamp – *Priscilla, Queen of the Desert*
8. Tim Curry – *The Rocky Horror Picture Show*
9. Patrick Swayze – *To Wong Foo, Thanks For Everything! Julie Newmar*
10. Alec Guiness – *Kind Hearts and Coronets*

LA PEAU DOUCE (SOFT SKIN) (1964)

Starring: *Jean Desailly (Pierre Lachenay), Francoise Dorleac (Nicol), Nelly Benedetti (Franca Lachenay), Daniel Ceccaldi (Clement), Laurence Badie (Ingrid), Sabine Haudepin (Sabine Lachenay), Philippe Dumat (Directeur cinema Reins)*
Director: *Francois Truffaut*
Screenwriters: *Francois Truffaut, Jean-Louis Richard*
PG/113 mins./Drama/France

Middle-aged literary critic Pierre Lachenay falls for air hostess Nicole Chomette on a flight to Lisbon. But although their affair never catches light, he is gunned down by his passionate wife, Franca, after she finds photographs of them together.

François Truffaut was so piqued by the intellectual romanticisation of the relationship at the centre of *Jules Et Jim* that he conceived this sordid *ménage* as a realist riposte. Basing his narrative on stories gleaned from the popular press, he inverted the central triangle by having a weak man at its apex and then concentrated on the parallel pairs that formed around him. By so doing, he turned a suburban melodrama into a Hitchcockian thriller, in which the eventual discovery of Pierre's misdemeanours was as inevitable as his violent demise was unexpected.

By keeping Pierre permanently on the move, Truffaut reinforced the impression that he was at the mercy of events that were bound to overtake him. The trip to the airport is structured like a chase sequence and it establishes the notion that everything affecting Pierre is dictated either by chance or coincidence. He only just makes the plane on which he meets Nicole, who just happens to be staying at the same hotel. Similarly, he fortuitously stumbles across the phone number that she left on a book of matches, in much the same way that Franca unfortunately comes upon the photographs of her husband with an ice cool blonde (right out of the Hitchcock mould). Caprice also ensures that his fate is sealed when he's prevented from reaching Franca by phone.

Truffaut clearly has little sympathy for Pierre, who is hopelessly inept outside the area of his academic expertise (although his study of Balzac has evidently taught him nothing of life). Nicole makes most of the running to initiate their affair, but Pierre fails to recognise that her casual compliance belies an unwillingness to commit that gradually manifests itself in frigidity. Similarly, he remains oblivious to Franca's domestic competence and suppressed passion and this combination of misplaced obsession and careless indifference has fatal consequences in a *crime passionel* that's scarcely worthy of the name.

Considered something of a misfire on its original release, this is one of Truffaut's bleakest and most cursive dissections of the bourgeois psyche.
★★★★ DP

PECKER (1998)

Starring: *Edward Furlong (Pecker), Christina Ricci (Shelley), Bess Armstrong (Dr Klompus), Mark Joy (Jimmy), Mary Kay Place (Joyce), Martha Plimpton (Tina), Mink Stole (Precinct Captain), Lili Taylor (Rorey), Patricia Hearst (Lynn Wentworth)*
Director: *John Waters*
Screenwriter: *John Waters*
15/86 mins./Satire/Comedy/USA

The wacky rags to riches tale of a young 'photographer' plucked from obscurity.

John Waters continues his colourful chronicles of blue collar Baltimore with a wacky tale of art and artlessness. And if you snigger at its naughty title, you'll know you're in the right movie.

Pecker, so named because he pecked at his food like a little bird when he was a kid, is a happy-go-lucky 18-year-old innocent who works in a diner but photographs his world with the camera his mother found in her junk shop. He snaps everything he likes including his girlfriend Shelley who runs a launderette and his bizarre family: grandmother Memama who listens to a talking Blessed Mother statue; elder sister Tina who works at a gay go-go bar; and younger sister Chrissy who's a hypermanic sugar junkie.

All's right with their world until a chic gallery owner discovers Pecker's pictures, and launches him on the New York art scene. He's the toast of the town for his photos of the 'culturally challenged' but fame and riches leave him and his clan hounded and humiliated. Pecker's artistic freedom is curtailed as well, causing him, in a society where it's downright un-American to reject celebrity, to take a startling stand.

Pecker, like its eponymous hero, is deceptively goofy and guileless. The characters are a daftly endearing bunch; their obsessions and aspirations are naive, their aesthetic trashy. But there's a sharp perception behind this lowlife fairy tale that art is whatever you think it is, wherever you see it.
★★★ AE

PEEPING TOM (1960)

Starring: *Carl Boehm (Mark Lewis), Moria Shearer (Vivian), Anna Massey (Helen Stephens), Maxine Audley (Mrs Stephens), Esmond Knight (Arthur Baden), Bartlett Mullins (Mr Peters), Shirley Anne Field (Diane Ashley)*
Director: *Michael Powell*
Screenwriter: *Leo Marks*
18/101 mins./Thriller/UK

Mark Lewis works as a focus puller by day, a girlie photographer in the evening and a serial killer after dark. Mark endlessly re-watches the films he takes of dying girls, while a neighbour gradually comes to understand the lifelong abuse that has perverted him.

At the time of its original release, this was so critically reviled that Michael Powell's career shuddered to a halt. Now it looks like one of the best British movies ever made. Not the least of Powell's 'crimes' was turning his back on the lush, 'quality' tradition of his work with Emeric Pressburger and getting his hands dirty in the then-exploding style of British horror film, working with a studio (Anglo-Amalgamated) that made Hammer Films seem respectable.

In the deliberately provocative scene, Powell even rewrites his own career by bringing in Moira Shearer, the exquisite dancer of *The Red Shoes*, and has her play a jazz-dancing tramp in slacks who gets stabbed up by the duffel-coated, mild-mannered killer. Similarly sacrilegious in British cinema terms is the casting of familiar face Miles Malleson, typecast for years as a dotty old vicar, as a leering pervert buying dirty postcards.

A first-rate psychological horror movie, it's also a brilliant examination of filmmaking itself, full of wicked jokes about *Sight and Sound*, Shirley Anne Field's shortcomings as an actress, the tyrannical tendency of all great directors (in home movies, Powell plays the sadistic psychologist father whose experiments drive Mark mad in the first place) and the dangers of film itself. Made before *Psycho*, it gives an insider's view of homicidal mania, and presents its madman as a sympathetic – but not admirable – character. Photographed in wonderfully garish Eastmancolour (harsh oranges and deep blues) with a score that alternates between jazz and gloom, this is at once sordid and classy. ★★★★★ **KN**

THE PELICAN BRIEF (1993)

Starring: *Julia Roberts (Darby Shaw), Denzel Washington (Gray Grantham), Sam Shepard (Professor Thomas Callahan), John Heard (FBI Agent Gavin Vereek)*
Director: *Alan J. Pakula*
Screenwriter: *Alan J. Pakula, based on a book by John Grisham*
12/141 mins./Drama/Thriller/USA

After two Supreme Court judges are assassinated, bright young law student Darby, comes up with a conspiracy theory that is worryingly accurate. Soon the government are after her and her mentor, Professor Thomas Callahan, breaking into houses and blowing up cars. Her only hope in exposing the truth and staying alive, lies in investigative reporter Gray Grantham.

The second of John Grisham's best-selling page-turners to reach the screen is satisfactorily ripping, gripping Friday night out stuff, with director Alan J. Pakula returning to his good old conspiracy thriller form. It also sees Julia Roberts squarely back in the star business, prettily watchable as sharp-witted law student Darby Shaw, whose speculative brief offering a fatefully bang-on-target theory on the who and why behind the mind-blowing assassination of two US Supreme Court Justices falls into the wrong hands and makes her the prey in a cross-country chase by the FBI, CIA and sundry freelance friends. Handicapped by some structural shakiness that keeps him off screen too often and for too long, Denzel Washington coolly does the manly support bit as Washington D.C. investigative reporter Gray Grantham who eventually hooks up with her to get his scoop. Like *The Firm*, this is a starry, big buck exercise in amateur sleuthing, law, corruption, sudden death, spooky surveillance and evasion of capture, very true to the book this time and extremely well cast (with Sam Shepard as Darby's boozehound law professor lover, John Heard as his FBI chum, Stanley Tucci as super-assassin Khamel, Tony Goldwyn as a power mad White House Chief of Staff, Robert Gulp as a doltish right wing US President to relish, and John Lithgow as Gray's editor).

Essentially glossy tosh with a way-out but sexily paranoiac promise, this has a few stand-out nail-biting set pieces (although the scariest revelation is John Heard's whale of a waistline!) and Julia is as bright as Jerry the Mouse at staying alive, though ever within reach of the cat's paw (the crucial lesson here: when you're on the run, don't pay with plastic). ★★★ **AE**

PELLE THE CONQUEROR (PELLE EROBREREN) (1987)

Starring: *Pelle Hvenegaard (Pelle), Max von Sydow (Lassefar), Erik Paaske (Forvalter/Foreman), Bjorn Granath (Eric), Astrid Villaume (Fru Konsgstrup)*
Director: *Bille August*
Screenwriters: *Bille August, Per Olov Enquist, Bjarne Reuter, based on the novel by Martin Anderson Nexo*
15/157 mins./Drama/Denmark/Sweden

Awards: *Academy Awards – Best Foreign Language Film; Golden Globes – Best Foreign Language Film*

Lasse and his young son emigrate from Sweden to Denmark in the early 1900s and wind up toiling on a remote, desolate farm.

An Academy Award winner for Best Foreign Language Film, this is an entry in the ever-popular arthouse cycle of Suffering Peasant movies.

No self-respecting Suffering Peasant runs for 78 minutes, and so this is a slow, steady two and a half hours of misery, alternating impressive cinema and bum-numbing tedium.

A girl is unjustly imprisoned for murdering her baby, new emigrants arrive frozen to death in a boat, a halfwit lets Pelle whip him with nettles for half a crown, the landowner seduces his wife's niece and drives her away, the landowner's wife cuts her husband's testicles off, Lasse thinks he'll have a cushy berth married to a widow but her husband returns alive, the halfwit runs away and joins the circus, the schoolmaster drops dead in class, and Pelle finally leaves through the snowy wastes to an indefinite future.

Max Von Sydow, long since established as the King of Screen Suffering thanks to Ingmar Bergman movies and roles as diverse as Jesus and *The Exorcist*, is a towering presence. The rest of the cast are mainly required to come on, suffer, and go away again, but do their jobs well.

Director Billie August and ace Scandinavian cameraman Per Holst make the film a visual treat, especially in scenes involving sea and winter – a ship looming out of the fog on the way to Denmark, a doomed rescue attempt, Pelle chased out onto the ice by his schoolfellows.

Unfortunately, slow pacing drags the whole thing out, and the relentlessly downbeat storyline ultimately goes over the top in piled-up wretchedness and tragedy to evoke giggles when you should be sobbing. Extremely worthy, but you'd be hard-pressed to enjoy it. ★★★ **KN**

THE PEOPLE UNDER THE STAIRS (1991)

Starring: *Brandon Adams ('Fool'), Everett McGill (Man), Wendy Robie (Woman), A.J. Langer (Alice), Ving Rhames (LeRoy), Sean Whalen (Roach)*
Director: *Wes Craven*
Screenwriter: *Wes Craven*
18/97 mins./Horror/USA

A young boy, Fool, is persuaded into burgling the house of his family's cruel landlord and discovers child abuse, incest and much more . . .

Wes Craven achieves more meaningful political commentary with this one brilliantly deceptive 'horror' movie than Oliver Stone does in his last four projects. McGill and Robie star as camouflaged Ronald and Nancy Reagan who live inside a spectacularly complex mansion of social horror, all funded by money swindled from the lower classes around them. There they physically abuse their 'daughter' to keep her in line, imprison and mutilate young white males who refuse to behave well, plus butcher blacks and all other minorities for cannibal cuisine.

Into this stunning symbolism comes teenage would-be burglar Adams, who courageously fights back against both 'Daddy' and 'Mommy' – pet names that the Reagans still use for each other to this day – in ways wonderously atypical for a teenager in any fright film.

Going against the rancid tradition of modern terror formulae, Craven immediately establishes empathy with the 'abnormal' folk, one intentional reason why his title is not *Mommy And Daddy Rule*. By the time he finally introduces those denziens in the basement, he builds not the expected fear but genuine emotional connection. Instead of snuff-style anticipation for the next victims to die, he invests all his support in the kids' fight to escape the house.

His shockingly sensitive portrayal of America's army of Have-Nots comes wrapped in enough whipcrack pacing and shrews set design to make even the staunchest Thatcherite swallow the medicine.

Anti-greed, anti-racist, and pro-feminist at the same time, this movie gem scores on levels few horror films ever have. At a time when the Reagan's spiritual son wanted four more years, Craven delivered one complicated sociopolitical exposé that would make Jonathan Swift and George Orwell spit up and cheer. ★★★★ **SCD**

ⓓ THE PEOPLE VS. LARRY FLYNT (1996)

Starring: *Woody Harrelson (Larry Flynt), Courtney Love (Althea Leasure), Edward Norton (Alan Isaacman), Bret Harrelson (Jimmy Flynt), Donna Hanover (Ruth Carter Stapleton)*
Director: *Milos Foreman*
Screenwriters: *Scott Alexander, Larry Karaszewski*
18/124 mins./Biography/Drama/USA

Awards: *Golden Globes – Best Director, Best Screenplay*

Biopic of Hustler publisher Larry Flynt, from his humble origins flogging moonshine to the rise of his publishing empire. En vonte, he is shot, paralysed, imprisoned and engaged in a running battle with moral majority preacher Jerry Falwell about his right to publish porn.

How you feel about *The People Vs. Larry Flynt* is going to depend a lot on how you feel about Larry Flynt himself. A hillbilly who rose from moonshine-brewing to running a strip club, Flynt got rich with *Hustler* magazine and became an American dissident while being prosecuted for various types of obscenity. The crux of this biopic is that defending the First Amendment Rights of the American Constitution (the bit about freedom of expression) means defending Flynt's right to publish sleazy porn and offend Moral Majority preacher Jerry Falwell.

Forman might have been attracted to the Larry Flynt story because he is well aware most countries would have Flynt quietly dropped in a canal rather than let him take his case to the Supreme Court. Working from a canny script by the *Ed Wood* team of Scott Alexander and Larry Karaszewski, Forman goes through Flynt's sleazeball career and lets the issues sneak up on the audience.

Woody Harrelson, a rare movie star who doesn't mind playing repulsive, is a powerhouse as Flynt – the real article cameos as a bigoted judge – modelling a range of hideous 70s leisure suits or offensive T-shirts. He goes through a bizarre religious phase, is crippled by a sniper's bullet, is medicated for years, sprouts green fur on his teeth and finally lets his lawyer plead a dignified case in defence of a libel suit brought by Falwell.

The other significant character is Althea, an ex-stripper who convinces Flynt that marriage doesn't mean giving up group sex but reacts to his crippling by becoming a heroin addict. Love, doing extremely well in her first star role, can't quite manage the jailbait scenes, but grows into the part marvellously, providing a quiet example of the downside of the '*Hustler* philosophy'.

The film finds it far easier to humanise and understand Flynt than Falwell, who is set up as a hypocritical creep with dodgy business associates and therefore never taken seriously.

In the end, this has a problem traveling: it's designed to provoke debate about the issues but, as as British censors constantly remind us, the UK doesn't have a constitution affording us the freedoms Flynt and Falwell are blessed with. ★★★★ **KN**

ⓓ A PERFECT MURDER (1998)

Starring: *Michael Douglas (Steven Taylor), Gwyneth Paltrow (Emily Bradford Taylor), Viggo Mortensen (David Shaw), David Suchet (Detective Mohamed Karaman), Sarita Choudhury (Raquel Martinez)*
Director: *Andrew Davis*
Screenwriter: *Patrick Smith Kelly, from the play* Dial M For Murder *by Frederick Knott*
15/102 mins./Mystery/Thriller/USA

Wealthy Steven Taylor is shocked to discover that his wife Emily is having an affair with artist David. Steven sets about planning the perfect murder of his wife.

Loosely adapted from Hitchcock's *Dial M For Murder* – generally considered to be among the more pedestrian outings from 'the master of suspense' – *A Perfect Murder* bolts the requisite 90s sheen onto the spouse-offing storyline, more often than not sacrificing substance at the altar of style. Yet, if it never actually hikes up the palm-sweating tension of the greatest potboilers, it delivers a solid, no frills, entertaining thriller.

At the heart of the movie lies a ménage à trois between shifty commodities trader Steven Taylor, his trophy wife Emily and her painter lover David. Learning of his spouse's passionate trysts, Taylor researches her beau's life and discovers the would-be bohemian is, in fact, a criminal with a history of fleecing wealthy women of their assets. However, rather than blow the whistle on the illicit affair, Taylor, with his own agenda, proposes a simple plan to the starving artist – kill Emily in return for $500,000.

In a terrifying and brutally handled set piece, the attempt on Emily's life goes horribly awry leaving the plot to plunge into a complex panoply of subterfuge, double-cross and blackmail. Sensibly, director Davis never tries to ape the Hitchcockian style. Yet while his direction is suitably slick and his storytelling taut, the staging is imbued with a colourless quality lacking the twisted imagination, macabre sense of humour and quirky sense of character that would have really brought the proceedings to life.

Still, there's loads to enjoy here: eschewing untold car chases and overwrought shock tactics, the film trades more in an intriguing battle of psychological cat-and-mousery, excellently orchestrating the shifting suspicion and tension between the protagonists. Douglas has a field day devising cover-ups in a flash, pulling evil faces and generally dallying with people's lives whereas Paltrow perfectly balances icy chic and fear-stricken vulnerability with a growing awareness of the machinations going on around her. ★★★ **IF**

ⓓ THE PERFECT STORM (2000)

Starring: *George Clooney (Capt. Billy Tyne), Mark Wahlberg (Bobby Shatford), Diane Lane (Christina 'Chris' Cotter), John C. Reilly (Dale 'Murph' Murphy), Karen Allen (Melissa Brown), Marry Elizabeth Mastrantonio (Linda Greenlaw)*
Director: *Wolfgang Petersen*
Screenwriter: *William D. Wittliff, based on the book by Sebastian Junger*
12/130 mins./Drama/Adventure/USA

Awards: *BAFTA – Best Visual Effects*

Captain Billy Tyne is a seafarer with a troubled past and something to prove and Bobby Shatford is the guy who just needs one big catch to stay ashore forever more with his love. When their fishing boat gets caught in the weather phenomena of a 'perfect storm' helicopters are sent to rescue them but can they make it in time?

Anyone who suffers from motion sickness would be well advised not to eat anything except a dose of Dramamine before taking in this roller coaster ride through a hurricane. Have you ever wondered, while contemplating your laundry spinning, what it would be like to be trapped in the rinse cycle? Well, now we know.

The pre-soak is close to an hour of setting up fishermen's culture, relationships and mood while running commentary from a TV weatherman helpfully explains the meteorological stuff as stormfronts head for collision on his computer screen and James Horner's score strikes ominous strains. You surely know the disaster drill.

Clooney (who looks like a Movie Star even in plaid flannel shirts) is the captain with a troubled past and something to prove. Wahlberg is the guy who just needs one big catch to stay ashore forever more with his love. She (Lane) presides fearfully over the local chapter of Women Who Wait. And in the port tavern a prophetic Old Salt says 'Ahrr, ahrr, I were there in '69. It were full o'fish and full o'weather.'

Screenwriter Wittliff, whose credits include *Lonesome Dove* and *Legends of the Fall*, upholds the romantic view of seafaring folk and the cast manfully play along, especially when required to say things like 'This is where we separate the men from the boys' without giggling.

Dramas filmed on water are notoriously problematic but Petersen, justly celebrated for *Das Boot*, is The Man. Once he puts out to sea this really starts rocking and he relentlessly builds up the claustrophobia and tension aboard the *Andrea Gail*, a foundering yacht, and an Air Force rescue chopper as the gasp-inducing wind and weather marvels mount to an almost unbearable series of aerial, roiling surface and underwater set pieces.

Oscar-winning cinematographer John Seale does a remarkable job in undoubtedly trying conditions while the special effects (supervised by *Armageddon*, *Twister* and *Speed* man John Frazier) are literally overwhelmingly effective. Even a wimpy spiritual revelation coda can't screw up the exciting, harrowing action. ★★★ **AE**

A PERFECT WORLD (1993)

Starring: *Kevin Costner (Robert 'Butch' Haynes), Clint Eastwood (Chief Red Garnett), Laura Dern (Sally Gerber), T. J. Lowther (Phillip 'Buzz' Perry), Keith Szarabajka (Terry Pugh)*
Director: *Clint Eastwood*
Screenwriter: *John Lee Hancock*
15/132 mins./Drama/USA

Having broken out of prison a murderer heads for Alaska, taking a young Jehovah's Witness hostage along the way. The two begin to bond and learn about each other's experiences as they try to outrun the Texas Ranger.

Even before the glorious triumph of *Unforgiven*, a palpable sense of expectation greeted any project directed by and starring Clint Eastwood. Add to the mix Kevin Costner, who with *Dances With Wolves* proved himself the one-time possible heir to Clint's actor-director throne, and it's doubly disappointing to report that *A Perfect World*, while not a total disaster by any means, squanders the talents of Eastwood and to a lesser extent Costner, as well as those of Dern, who appears, literally, to be along for the ride to counter-balance the prodigious amount of testosterone on display here. Equally perplexing is the question of just which audience the film is aimed at, being neither mainstream-friendly enough to satisfy those who lapped up Costner's do-goody turn in last year's *The Bodyguard*, nor those expecting another masterpiece from Eastwood in the wake of the Oscar-winning *Unforgiven*.

The problem herein is not that Costner is cast against acceptable type as a murderous con on the lam, but that John Lee Hancock's script – which offers half a dozen intriguing and potentially explosive possibilities, the majority of which come off as blanks under Clint's direction – allows the film to boil over in the heat of the midday sun, when, ideally, it needed to be left to simmer.

Set in a Texas still awaiting JFK's fateful visit, this is little more than a Western in 60s dress, with Costner's William 'Butch' Haynes breaking out of prison along with fellow convict Terry Pugh, and setting off on an ill-founded quest to Alaska, taking hostage a fatherless eight-year-old Jehovah's Witness called Phillip. Representing justice are Dern's state-appointed omni-nologist and Clint's grizzled Texas Ranger who set off in lukewarm pursuit, taking their manhunt to the backroads of Texas within the confines of a sleek silver caravan – their paths intersecting with Haynes only twice.

Indeed, with both Dern and Clint very much on the periphery, it's the relationship between Costner and the boy that is at the heart of the film. And despite a wobbly Texan twang, Costner equips himself more than admirably, his Haynes exhibiting a dangerous, potentially murderous unpredictability, but conversely a warmth and compassion in his dealings with children. While a hardened criminal, as a surrogate father to the boy his motives are grounded in morality – 'I've only ever killed two people,' he tells Phillip, 'one hurt my mamma, one hurt you.' Inevitably Haynes' affections are reciprocated by the boy, but unlike the back-story in which it transpires that it was Clint who recommended Haynes be sent to the juvenile detention centre where he learned the tricks of his criminal trade, the sentiments expressed ring true. ★★★ **MS**

PERFORMANCE (1970)

Starring: *James Fox (Chas Devlin), Mick Jagger (Turner), Anita Pallenberg (Pherber), Michele Breton (Lucy), Ann Sidney (Dana), Johnny Shannon (Harry Flowers)*
Directors: *Nicolas Roeg, Donald Cammell*
Screenwriter: *Donald Cammell*
18/101 mins./Drama/UK

Chas, fleeing a gangland feud, takes refuge in the London mansion of rock star Turner. While hiding out, Chas finds himself sucked into Turner's world of drugs and kinky sex.

'The only performance that makes it, that makes it all the way,' claims a strung-out but intense Mick Jagger, 'is the one that achieves madness. Am I right? Eh?'

The Siamese-twinned directorial debut of then-cinematographer Nicolas Roeg, who went on to great things in the later 1970s, and Donald Cammell, who made a few interesting films but never fulfilled his promise. Aptly, given that it's now impossible to watch the film without wondering which ideas or effects belong to which director, it's an exchange-of-personality piece about a Krayish wide boy and an agoraphobic pop star whose characters clash ('You're a comical little geezer,' Fox tells Jagger, 'you'll look funny when you're fifty') and merge. Confined in a swinging 60s version of the Old Dark House, attended by haggardly pixieish groupies and the striking Anita Pallenberg, Chas is sucked out of his tidy crime movie persona into an acid-tinged, exhilarating but terrifying freak-out of malleable personality, orgiastic behaviour and incredible coups de cinema.

One of those movies which puzzles on first aquaintaince but rewards repeated viewings, *Performance* has some of the psychedelic clutter expected of its era, plus an air of grotty sexual decadence, but its cinematic sensibilities were calculated to outlast its moment. Though it has the fashions, music and faces of '68, it is as fresh and disturbing now as it ever was, and moments – like the zoom through a bullet-hole into a brain – remain unmatchably astonishing. It now evokes nostalgia for flower-painted high times, but more pertinently for a commercial cinema willing to take chances like this. ★★★★ **KN**

PERSONA (1966)

Starring: *Bibi Andersson (Nurse Alma), Liv Ullmann (Actress Elizabet Vogler), Gunnar Bjornstrand (Mr. Vogler). Margareta Krook) (Dr Lakaren), Jorgen Lindstrom (The Boy)*
Director: *Ingmar Bergman*
Screenwriter: *Ingmar Bergman*
18/81 mins/Drama/Sweden

Actress Elisabet Vogler falls silent during a stage performance of *Elektra* and Dr Lakeren suggests that she spends some time in quiet recuperation by the sea. However, frustrated by her inability to induce her charge into speaking, Nurse Alma becomes increasingly loquacious and the women's personalities clash.

Inspired perhaps by Strindberg's play, *The Stronger*, Ingmar Bergman wrote the screenplay for this 'sonata for two instruments' to stave off boredom while in hospital with a virus. Discarding plans to call the picture *Cinematography*, he alighted on *Persona*, as it was the Greek word for 'mask'. However, it was also the name given by psychologist Carl Jung to the outer self that stood in opposition to the inner image or 'alma' and this premeditated nomenclature found further echo in the fact that Elisabet's surname recalled Albert Emanuel Vogler, the artist who sapped the energy of others for his artistic identity in *The Magician* (1958).

Bergman so blurred the line between reality and fantasy in this complex, but compelling drama that some have claimed that Alma and Elisabet are projections of a single character whose actual selfhood defies identification. Others have suggested that all of the events from Alma's falling asleep following her one-sided argument with Elisabet is a dream, in which she gains a greater insight into both her own and her patient's emotional status by journeying into her subconscious.

What makes these dramatic ambiguities all the more intriguing is the manner in which Bergman emphasises their innate filmicness. In addition to showing the leader numbers on screen before his opening montage depicting images of death, fear and humiliation, Bergman consistently draws the viewer's attention to the artificiality of the action by repeating passages of dialogue, briefly depicting himself and his crew in the process of recording a scene and halting the flow altogether by causing the celluloid to melt. Even the famous merging of Liv Ullmann and Bibi Andersson's faces into an iconic composite serves a dual purpose, while also subverting any conclusions that we may have drawn about the psychological source of the scenario and the emotional state of the protagonists.

Clearly reflecting Bergman's despondency at an increasingly turbulent world, this devastating treatise on mortal and intellectual impotence is also a technically audacious critique of the condition of cinema that rivals anything produced during the *nouvelle vague*, whose influence is evident in almost every frame. ★★★★★ **DP**

PET SEMATARY (1989)

Starring: *Fred Gwynne (Jud Crandall), Dale Midkoff (Louis Creed), Denise Crosby (Rachel Creed), Brad Greenquist (Victor Pascow), Michael Lombard (Irwin Goldman)*
Director: *Mary Lambert*
Screenwriter: *Stephen King, from his novel*
18/98 mins./Horror/USA

Despite initial doubts about the stories that a pet burial ground is actually a spawning arena for the undead, Louis Creed is forced to tackle the hell hole head on when his toddler is run over by a truck – perhaps he can grow to love the zombified version.

Of the 15-plus King-derived movies, only *Carrie*, *Stand By Me* and (debatably) *The Shining* are outstanding. It's also notable that no one is better at making bad or indifferent movies from the novels of Stephen King than Stephen King himself – he directed the video-only travesty *Maximum Overdrive* and scripted such losers as *Silver Bullet*, *Cat's Eye* and *Creepshow*. *Pet Sematary* is one of King's most personal and deeply affecting horror novels, replaying *The Monkey's Paw* on an epic scale in order to tackle the fear of death, parental anguish and other weighty topics. So why does it fall so flat?

One of the problems is that King usually writes about cliché subjects so well that you don't notice the hackneyed aspects of his books, and so when all the character detail, precise backgrounding and elaborate plot setting-up mechanisms are pruned away, all you get is a dumb TV movie with characters doing insanely stupid things to prolong the agony.

Tagline
A pet isn't just for life.

Here, our hero is told by an eccentric old neighbour that things buried in the Micmac graveyard beyond the pet cemetery come back to life as soulless monsters. This is demonstrated when a dead cat returns as a neon-eyed fiend. Midkiff is also told that human beings come back as violent zombies, and there's a brain-spattering ghost popping up at odd intervals warning him never to tamper with the forces of life and death. Predictably, he ignores the advice and when his toddling son is killed on the road, he robs his child's grave with a bathetic cry of 'I'm gonna bust you out, son' and heads off to get the kid back. In the book, with 300 pages of motivation, you can just about swallow the plot. But in the film this is impossible and you have to sit impatiently through scene after silly scene before the zombie attacks start. *Pet Sematary* has ambitions to be more than just another zombie flick, but it finally comes over as being more like a precis of its source novel than a proper adaptation of it. ★ **KN**

PETE KELLY'S BLUES (1955)

Starring: *Jack Webb (Pete Kelly), Janet Leigh (Ivy Conrad), Edmond O'Brien (Fran McCarg), Peggy Lee (Rose Hopkins), Andy Devine (George Tenell), Lee Marvin (Al Gannaway), Ella Fitzgerald (Maggie Jackson)*
Director: *Jack Webb*
Screenwriter: *Richard L. Breen*
PG/91 mins./Drama/USA

In 1927, New Orleans jazz band-leader Pete Kelly tries to stay free of the influence of bootlegger Fran McCarg, who wants a cut of the action and insists Kelly hire his untalented girlfriend as a singer.

This is one of the great unheralded classics of 1950s American cinema. It opens with a cornet falling off a hearse during a New Orleans funeral, then cuts to a post-WWI boxcar crap shoot where GI Pete Kelly wins the now-dented instrument, then cuts to the main story with Kelly as an established musician and that battered cornet as close to his heart as a cowboy's horse or a gangster's gun. Director-star Jack Webb, hot off the seminal *Dragnet* TV series, does several very unusual things: he treats jazz seriously (and fills the soundtrack with the authentic sounds of 1927 rather than re-orchestrating them to suit the tastes of 1955), depicts Prohibition-era gangsterism in a politically complex manner, and deals in a devastating manner with the psychological fall-out of creativity and criminality. All in the framework of a rattling good thriller with blazing musical turns from Oscar-nominated Peggy Lee ('The Rainbow Song') and Ella Fitzgerald ('Hard-Hearted Hannah').

The crux of the plot is that Kelly finds it impossible to retain his integrity when organised crime moves to take over all aspects of the night-club business along with the booze supply, while Edmond O'Brien's heavy is a serious version of the role he would send up unforgettably in another great 50s musical, *The Girl Can't Help It*. Lee, paradoxically cast as a gangster's moll who isn't a great singer, cracks up when she can't make it on stage, and has an affecting mad scene in a hellhole asylum. Watch out also for Lee Marvin as a trombone player and Janet Leigh as a predatory flapper. ★★★★ **KN**

PETE'S DRAGON (1977)

Starring: *Sean Marshall (Pete), Helen Reddy (Nora), Jim Dale (Dr Terminus), Mickey Rooney (Lampie), Red Buttons (Hoagy), Shelley Winters (Lena Gogan), Sean Marshall (Lena Gogan)*
Director: *Don Chaffey*
Screenwriters: S.S. Field, Seton I. Miller, Malcolm Marmorstein,
U/128 mins./Kids/USA

An orphan boy escapes from his nasty adoptive parents, with his secret friend, a dragon named Elliot, to live with a kindly lighthouse keeper. But an evil doctor has designs on the magical Elliot.

Another not very charming but harmless fusion of animation and good old real-life, a long way shy of *Mary Poppins*' sprightly fantasy. The problem is not in the conceit itself, after so many of its ilk, it becomes fairly easy to buy into some brightly coloured concoction hopping about (well, just about) amongst genuine people, it's how cartoon the real folk end up being.

The likes of Mickey Rooney, Helen Reddy and Jim Dale all act as if talking to senile grandparents, less hammy than downright patronising. The film seems to be pitched at shrieking level, as if that's the only timbre children can register. Sean Marshall as troubled orphan Pete, is just another of those beaming little clones that populated the Disney school throughout the 70s: as sweet as candyfloss, and about as palatable over the long-term.

The effects feel mixed, we after all live in the post *Roger Rabbit* universe, so as good as Pete tossing real apples into Elliot's goofy jaw might have been then it's no big deal now. Yet, the film is dedicated to playing its 'miracles' for all they are worth, showing off with ever more complicated slapstick routines working both with the bright green, faintly inebriated looking animated dragon (voiced with goofy hysteria by Charlie Callas) and an invisible version when adults are in view (cue: lumps under blankets and mysteriously upended tables). The songs, however, aren't worth mentioning. ★★ **IN**

PETER PAN (1953)

Starring the voices of: *Bobby Driscoll (Peter Pan), Kathryn Beaumont (Wendy Darling), Hans Conried (Captain Hook/Mr Darling), Bill Thompson (Mr Smee), Heather Angel (Mrs Darling)*
Directors: *Clyde Geronimi, Wilfred Jackson, Hamilton Luske*
Screenwriters: *Milt Bana, William Cottrell, Winston Hibler, Bill Peet, Erdman Penner, Joe Rinaldi, Ted Sears, Ralph Wright, based on the play by James Barrie*
U/76 mins./Kids/USA

The Disney version of J.M. Barrie's famous play, about the mischievous lost boy with the power of flight, Peter Pan, who takes Wendy Darling and her two brothers to Never-Never land where he pow-wows with Indians, battles pirates and flatly refuses to grow up.

To recall J.M. Barrie's adorable flight of fantasy for most is to immediately conjure up Walt Disney's lovingly animated adaptation with its starlight swirl past Big Ben, its lush and magical Never-Never land, and the formidable and wonderfully exasperated Captain Hook. It is a fully transporting fable that serves the play well, but in truth is divorced from the darker strains in Barrie's work.

Due to the effortless magnificence of the animation, it is easy to continually classify any of the 'toon films made while Walt was alive as automatically classic. And, indeed, the detail is astonishing, right down to the twinkles of fairy-dust that contrail behind irascible fairy Tinkerbell and remain a fixture on the Disney logo to this day. But when you consider that Barrie's play was about the perils of puberty, the strains put upon the parental-child bond, and the weight of responsibility that growing entails, none of which emerge from the geniality of Disney's approach, can only classify the film as limited.

Which feels mealy mouthed considering the catchy songs, all the energy and wit on show, and the presence of one of the most eloquent of all the great cartoon villains in Captain Hook, the most human figure on show. ★★★★ **IN**

PETER'S FRIENDS (1992)

Starring: *Hugh Laurie (Roger Charleston), Kenneth Branagh (Andrew Benson), Stephen Fry (Peter Moron), Alphosia Emmanuel (Sarah Johnson), Emma Thompson (Maggie Chester), Imelda Staunton (Mary Charleston), Phyllida Law (Vera), Rita Rudner (Carol Benson)*
Director: *Kenneth Branagh*
Screenwriters: *Rita Rudner, Martin Bergmann*
15/101mins./Drama/Comedy/UK

A Cambridge footlights revue troop reunite ten years after their success to spend New Year together.

Given those involved, *Peter's Friends* introduces itself as a love-it-or-shove-it state of affairs. Thankfully, appearances can be deceptive.

Ten years on from their final performance, six ex-members of a university comedy revue gather to celebrate New Year's Eve at an ancestral pile belonging to Peter. Although they're all successful – now comprising a jingles-writing couple, a costume designer, a publisher, a Hollywood screenwriter and Peter, Lord Melton – the intervening decade has, for highly individual reasons, left them emotional cripples. Thus, once the reunion euphoria is out of the way, frustrations, repressions and all manner of personal problems seep through.

So far so *Big Chill*, but what lifts the film is the strength of the script (by Rita Rudner), the characterisation and the playing. Everybody's bonkers, but accessibly so: the dry underplaying appreciates the situation's ludicrousness, and the screenplay never forgets that it is supposed to be funny. Nothing much happens, but not a minute is wasted, right from the squirm-worthy opening of the revue's last show to the highly unexpected conclusion.

Worth it by themselves are Tony Slattery's slobbish outsider; Laurie's grumpy ad man; Rudner's turn as Branagh's unbearably preening US sitcom star wife; and Fry's shambling young fogey who limits conversation to awkward Prince Charles-ish one-liners. ★★★ **LBr**

PEYTON PLACE (1957)

Starring: *Lana Turner (Constance MacKenzie), Hope Lange (Selena Cross), Lee Phillips (Michael Rossi), Lloyd Nolan (Dr Matthew Swain), Diane Varsi (Allison MaxKenzie), Arthur Kennedy (Lucas Cross), Russ Tamblyn (Norman Page), Terry Moore (Betty Anderson), Barry Coe (Rodney Harrington), David Nelson (Ted Carter)*
Director: *Mark Robson*
Screenwriter: *John Michael Hayes, based on the novel by Grace Metallious*
15/162 mins/Drama/USA

A chronicle of life before, during and after World War II in the picture-perfect New Hampshire town of Peyton Place, seen through the eyes of aspiring writer Allison Mackenzie, who lives with her overprotective single mother Constance, climaxing with a murder trial that brings out several nasty secrets.

Whenever Oscar season rolls around, it's worth remembering that back in 1957 this long, trashy, demure adaptation of Grace Metalious's longer, trashier dirty novel was taken seriously and thought to be a potential classic. After a sequel (*A Return to Peyton Place*), a long-running TV series and the co-opting of its basic plot structure by Stephen King for *Salem's Lot*, it's hard to see what steamed people up about this pastel-coloured soap in which nice people suffer nobly and the rotters all come to a bad end.

The plot weaves through the eponymous small town, taking in illegitimacy, drunkenness, incestuous rape ('when I say "child abuser", I mean it in the worst possible way'), prostitution, abortion, neurosis, frigidity, a murder trial and the scandal that sweet Allison has written a best-seller exposing the community's seamy secrets. Graduating to 'mother roles', Turner plays a queenly slut without changing her expression for fear of wrinkles, while a cast of starchy second-stringers (Hope Lange, Lee Philips, Lloyd Nolan, Russ Tamblyn, Terry Moore) revolve around her and only Arthur Kennedy, cast as the worst man in town (the drunken school janitor who rapes and impregnates his step-daughter then gets bludgeoned and buried in the woodpile), manages even a fraction of the ham needed to get by. Flatly directed by Mark Robson, who brings so much less to the material than Douglas Sirk did with equally silly stuff, this is utter tosh ... and yet, like the novel, it has a certain page-turning fascination and qualifies as a guilty pleasure. ★★★ **KN**

PHANTASM (1978)

Starring: *A. Michael Baldwin (Mike), Bill Thornbury (Jody Pearson), Angus Scrimm (Tall Man), Reggie Bannister (Reggie)*
Director: *Don Coscarelli*
Screenwriter: *Don Coscarelli*
18/84 mins./Horro/USA

Twelve year-old Mike tries to convince his older brother Jody that the Tall Man, a local undertaker, is a malign entity intent on enslaving the dead.

An incoherent but effective horror picture on the dreams-within-dreams theme, this wins points for the outrageousness of its premise: a small-town mausoleum is run by an extra-dimensional psychopath who has been killing people, shrinking their corpses into dwarf-sizes, stuffing them in barrels, and shipping them back to his red desert homeworld for revival as zombie labour.

It (deliberately?) makes no sense, but has more bizarre gimmicks to the minute than any other horror picture of 1979 – memorably, the flying chrome sphere that extrudes implements which bore into a victim's forehead and redistributes his entire blood supply through a spray-hole, but also the yellow-bleeding severed finger which transforms into a buzzing toy insect monster and the hordes of Jawa-like pointy-hooded zombie dwarves.

The skeletal Angus Scrimm is a memorable villain as the loping undertaker who turns to leer out of a Victorian photograph found in the attic (and has an alternate shape as Kathy Lester, 'the Lady in Lavender').

Michael Baldwin is an odd-looking 1970s kid hero – a twelve-year-old with a man-perm and a dirt-bike – but there's an unusual relationship between the sibling heroes, which is turned inside-out by the several twist endings.

Fans of imitable DIY weaponry will learn how to turn a hammer, a shotgun shell and a drawing pin into a real neat implement for escaping from a locked room. Director Don Coscarelli (*Bubba Ho-Tep*) had few resources to work with, and the film does have its listless aspects – but *Phantasm* proved memorable enough to inspire three lookalike sequels spaced out over the next two decades, all with Scrimm and the same support cast, plus added chrome ball action. ★★★ **KN**

THE PHANTOM OF THE OPERA (1925)

Starring: *Lon Chaney (Erik/The Phantom), Mary Philbin (Christine Daae), Norman Kerry (Raoul de Chagry), Snitz Edwards (Florine Papillon)*
Director: *Rupert Julian*
Screenwriters: *Raymond Schrock, Elliott J. Clawson, Tom Reed, Frank M. McCormack, from the novel* Le Fantome De L'Opera *by Gaston Leroux*
PG/90 mins./Horror/USA

A mysterious masked character who haunts the Paris Opera House seeks to protect and promote a young soprano. What are his motives and who is he?

They called Lon Chaney 'the man of a thousand faces', and one of his best was the skull-like monstrosity he devised for this silent classic.

The moment when young soprano Christine unmasks the shrivelled visage of her protector/ kidnapper has never lost its power to shock. Equally impressive is the Phantom's entrance during a masked ball.

There are two prints in circulation – one of which presents this scene in two-colour Technicolor with the Red Death costume making a bloody impact.

But it's Lon Chaney's magnetism and the overall impact of the suspense and reveal is still impressive. ★★★★ **AM**

THE PHANTOM OF THE OPERA (2004)

Starring: *Gerard Butler (The Phantom), Emmy Rossum (Christine), Patrick Wilson (Raoul), Miranda Richardson (Madame Giry), Minnie Driver (Carlotta)*
Director: *Joel Schumacher*
Screenwriters: *Andrew Lloyd Webber, Joel Schumacher, based on the stage musical by Andrew Lloyd Webber, novel* Le Fantome De L'Opera *by Gaston Leroux*
12/143 mins./Musical/Drama/USA/UK

Paris, 1870. A disfigured man lurks in the caverns beneath the Opera House, mooning over the new ingénue Christine. But she only has eyes for dashing Raoul, driving the Phantom into a jealous rage.

There have been numerous versions of Gaston Leroux's 1911 novel *The Phantom Of The Opera*, but none are more famous – or more successful – than Andrew Lloyd Webber's stage musical. The second-longest running musical in history (only Lloyd Webber's *Cats* had more durability), it debuted in London's West End in 1986, and has played to packed houses ever since.

It's a surprise, then, that it's taken this long for a movie adaptation of that version to appear. Fans of Lloyd Webber will no doubt think it was worth the wait, while the rest of us may wonder what took so long, since the end result, although entertaining and well-crafted, certainly isn't on the same breathtaking scale of, say, Alan Parker's epic *Evita*.

Instead Schumacher keeps things relatively simple and faithful to the stage show, offering few embellishments other than to frame the story with black-and-white scenes set in 1919, before flashing back to the main events in colour.

He hasn't employed big-name stars to detract from the production, either – young Christine is played by Emmy Rossum (Jake Gyllenhaal's girlfriend in *The Day After Tomorrow*) and her suitor Raoul is stage actor Patrick Wilson, while the Phantom himself is Gerard Butler (star of, ahem, *Tomb Raider 2*). More familiar are the supporting cast: Miranda Richardson (strangely the only cast member to use a French accent), ex-Brookie popster Jennifer Ellison (surprisingly good as Christine's best friend) and Minnie Driver, who's terrific as the opera diva whose tantrum thrusts young Christine in the spotlight.

With the notable exception of Butler, who struggles between manic and moody but never quite manages sympathetic, all the cast fit neatly into the grand, operatic surrounding, barely flinching as they deliver Lloyd Webber's dated 80s pop-opera songs while wafting through cemeteries of dry ice or candlelit corridors (at times it's as if Shumacher thinks he's making *The Lost Boys II*). For non-aficionados of the stage-musical maestro, those tunes will almost certainly block any enjoyment of this film; surely Sir Andrew could have drafted someone in to do away with the more pompous arrangements and give the songs a more timeless style. Which is unfortunate, since the story buried beneath them is a three-hankie corker. ★★★ **JB**

PHILADELPHIA (1993)

Starring: *Tom Hanks (Andrew Beckett), Denzel Washington (Joe Miller), Jason Robards (Charles Wheeler), Mary Steenburgen (Belinda Conine), Antonio Banderas (Miguel Alvarez)*
Director: *Jonathan Demme*
Screenwriter: *Ron Nyswaner*
12/120 mins./Drama/USA

Awards: *Academy Awards – Best Actor, Best Original Song ('Streets Of Philadelphia'); Golden Globes – Best Actor, Best Original Song ('Streets Of Philadelphia')*

Andrew Beckett a lawyer with a prestigious, conservative law firm, is fired after he develops AIDS, the company fearing he would be a health risk. Angry and wanting some justice before he dies, he hires a homophobic former adversary, to sue his firm for unfair dismissal.

The first major Hollywood film with a gay rights theme, this is, inevitably, determinedly mainstream. In its appeal to the emotions, its showy dramatic role for Hanks and its purposeful courtroom fireworks between Washington and pitiless opposing trial lawyer Mary Steenburgen, it is conservatively designed to provide a general audience with something tasteful to chew on.

Always good company, the personable Hanks dons convincing cosmetic lesions and bravely wastes away before our eyes as AIDS victim Andrew Beckett, a going-down-fighting lawyer who is determined to have his day in court, exposing the prejudices and discriminatory practices of the prestigious law firm that fired him. Washington has the thornier role as the homophobic attorney who reluctantly presses his former adversary's lawsuit, alive to the personal significance of the issue despite his butchly over-emphatic aversion to homosexuals.

Part courtroom drama, the narrative engages one's sympathies and slyly grips with a falsely laid trail of tension: will head of the firm Jason Robards be goaded into doing a Jack Nicholson on the stand? Will the firm associate, whose conscience is clearly bothering him, break down or come out? More surprisingly, given director Demme's satirical bent and his usual shunning of sentimentality, this is also, in part, reminiscent of a disease of the week TV movie with the attendant mush portions that implies, as Hanks is cheered on by a Too Good To Be True support system of devoted lover Miguel, indomitable mother and a Walton-like pack of kinfolk, supporting their relative to the teary end.

One suspects that those most personally and angrily concerned by the subject matter will be dissatisfied by the 'If Only' niceness on display and the timidity with which Andy's relationship with Miguel and his lifestyle is (barely) drawn. But that's another movie. This one comes down – quite successfully – to a touching demand for fraternity and justice, and is at its most powerful when Andrew, like a rape victim put on the defensive, is subjected to an appealing ordeal on the stand, an intrusion into privacy aimed to shame him as a 'deviant', and in its undeniably groundbreaking attempt to explore men's fearful and belligerent attitudes to their own sexuality ★★★ **AE**

THE PHILADELPHIA STORY (1940)

Starring: *Cary Grant (C.K.Dexter Haven), Katharine Hepburn (Tracy Lord), James Stewart (Macaulay Connor), Ruth Hussey (Elizabeth 'Liz' Imbrie), John Howard (George Kittredge)*
Director: *George Cukor*
Screenwriter: *David Ogden Stewart, based on the play by Philip Barry*
U/112 mins./Comedy/Romance/USA

Awards: *Academy Awards – Best Actor (James Stewart), Best Screenplay*

Tracy Lord, eligible daughter of a well-off Philadelphian family is due to marry an earnest nerdy type when her first husband returns with every intention of throwing a spanner in the works.

This delicious romantic comedy, first released in 1940, clearly has enough zip and drive to lick the cream of today's crop. Sure, it may not have the advantage of Technicolor, rude jokes or top production values but just one look at *The Philadelphia Story* and the message is: they really don't make 'em like this any more.

The magic formula is in the plotting: Tracy Lord, eligible daughter of a well-off Philadelphian family, is due to marry a blue-collar nerd when her previous husband Dexter Haven shows up at her door. Their animosity has previously been established by a delightful prologue in which she smashes his golf clubs and he pushes her in the face. Haven has returned to keep an eye on Tracy, but ends up instead stalking a new rival, Mike Connor, a hack for scandal rags *Dime* and *Spy* (read: real life mags *Time* and *Life*) who is covering the wedding. As the ceremony looms, Dexter stokes an old fire for Tracy while Mike stokes up a new one. By the end of the movie, everyone wants to stoke Tracy, such is the charm of Hepburn in one of her most perfect roles. Hepburn knew full well the potential for Tracy – and bought the rights to the play on which this is based as a vehicle to propel her away from the 'box office poison' label she'd been landed with after a string of duff movies. She recovered her career but it is Stewart, however, who walks away effortlessly with the picture (and an Oscar). Don't underestimate Cary Grant either, whose comic timing was never more perfectly showcased.

Director George Cukor, in his romantic element, proves just what a peerless entertainer he was. Grant may be just Grant – debonair, dashing and dry as sawdust – yet he perfectly dovetails with a cast which teeters on the cusp of perfection. *The PhiladepHia Story* boasts qualities other movies merely dream of: prestige wit and drop dead glamour. ★★★★★ **JH**

PHONE BOOTH (2002)

Starring: *Colin Farrell (Stu Shepard), Kiefer Sutherland (The Caller), Forest Whitaker (Captain Ed Ramey), Radha Mitchell (Kelly Shepard), Katie Holmes (Pamela McFadden)*
Director: *Joel Schumacher*
Screenwriter: *Larry Cohen*
15/77 mins./Thriller/USA

Trapped in a New York phone booth, slick-talking media consultant, Stu, is forced to come clean on his indiscretions by a sniper who threatens to shoot him if he hangs up. That's if the police don't misread the situation and riddle Stu with bullets.

Art imitates life. Life imitates art. And, in the meantime, the release of a movie like *Phone Booth* gets held up for months until a tide of particularly sensitive headlines recedes. Writer Larry Cohen and director Joel Schumacher surely thought that the only real-life raw nerves they'd touch with this tense but funny thriller would belong to the sleazebag publicists upon whom the main character is based. But that was before two men decided to take fatal pot shots at innocent American citizens, and the country froze in fear of 'The Washington Sniper'. The filmmakers' clever, low-budget scenario – one man trapped in a single location (in real time) by an unknown, gun-wielding adversary – suddenly became front page news.

That's not the only obstacle *Phone Booth* had to overcome. The role of the sniper was re-cast and re-shot (originally played by *ER*'s Ron Eldard). Leading men Jim Carrey and Will Smith backed out after having second thoughts about the insularity of the script. Director Michael Bay also passed. But maybe it's a karma thing, because luck is certainly turning in the movie's favour. Casting Colin Farrell (favoured by Schumacher after their collaboration on *Tigerland*) was a stroke of genius; he's far more credible in the cocky, motormouth charm department than any of the other names bandied about. Meanwhile, the release delay gave Farrell an additional six months to rise up the Hollywood ladder. In April 2003, he was hotter than he's ever been. Despite the *Tigerland* pedigree, on paper Schumacher doesn't look like the man for the job. No sooner did that boot camp drama help redeem his *Batman & Robin* sins than he delivered another empty dud in the shape of *Bad Company*. But the Schumacher of *Phone Booth* is more like the Schumacher of *Falling Down:* he spots the potential for social satire in the script, then manages to tease laughs and tension out of a ridiculous, life-or-death situation. Time flies while watching the movie, and not just because of its short running time. The concept is a corker and it continually ups the stakes as irate hookers, police marksmen and the protagonist's wife are dragged into the action. Visual breaks are provided by split screens that show either end of the phone conversations.

Meanwhile, the cast of fame-hungry characters – from a white rapper to Stu's poodle-like assistant to superficial Stu himself – are held up as empty vessels for all to see. It's to Farrell's credit that he's able to carry the audience along with him on Stu's moral journey. At first we're on the side of 'the caller' because we've seen what a manipulative asshole Stu is. OK, the confessions he's forced to make will ruin his career, but he is only reaping what he has sown. At this point, 'the caller' is little more than Jiminy Cricket with a high-powered precision rifle; but when he becomes a vigilante with a God complex, our loyalties swing towards Stu. It's all about degrees of evil. The real master at work here is B-movie king Larry Cohen. His script keeps the focus so lean and tight, it's barely out of breath by the time the credits roll. If there's one thing that runs through his work, it's his ability to take something innocent and fill it with a sense of threat – babies in *It's Alive!*, ice cream in *The Stuff*. Here Cohen transforms our thoughts about public phone booths – for who, after seeing this movie, won't think twice about answering a 'wrong number' as they pass by in the street. ★★★★ **AM**

ⓘ PI (1998)

Starring: *Sean Gullette (Maximillian Cohen), Mark Margolis (Sol Robeson), Ben Shenkman (Lenny Meyer), Pamela Hart (Marcy Dawson)*
Director: *Darren Aronofsky*
Screenwriter: *Darren Aronofsky, based on a story by Aronofsky, Sean Gullette, Eric Watson*
15/80 mins./Thriller/Sci-fi/USA

Maths prodigy Max Cohen notices a numeric pattern thrown up by the fluctuations of the stock market. With the 216 digit formula in his brain, Max is pursued by Wall Street manipulators who believe he can predict the financial future and Hassidic researchers who think he has hit upon the lost name of God.

This New York-shot ultra-low-budget indie combines something of the look and ambition of Abel Ferrara's *The Addiction* with the weird scientific rigour of early David Cronenberg. Even more hung up on its numbers than the similarly calculator-happy *Cube*, the film fully represents idiot savant Max's worldview, to the point when the audience can't fail to notice how many grids and spirals are worked into the movie: a Go board, the New York subway system, the exposed whorls of a human brain, computer chips, the Hebrew language, scribbled notes, even the Milky Way galaxy.

Naturally, given the famously non-recurring nature of the title number, no answer can possibly be forthcoming and we get rudely kicked out of Max's skull – during a hideous bit of DIY Black and Decker trephining – just before it all starts to make sense. Writer-director Darren Aronofsky, in a notable debut feature, suggests vast conspiracies just beyond comprehension, but limits the film to the viewpoint of the mad and maddening Max, depending heavily on the mannered performance of his lead performer.

Shot in grainy, high-contrast black and white with a lot of simple but effective optical and aural tricks to suggest the workings of his unusual mind, this is one of the most intimate movies of the 1990s. It can't fail to be absorbing but it also inevitably disappoints as the big breakthrough the script has been teasing us with is withheld in favour of a perhaps-chillingly ambiguous happy ending. ★★★ **KN**

ⓘ THE PIANIST (2002)

Starring: *Adrien Brody (Wladyslaw Szpilman), Thomas Kretschmann (Captain Wilm Hosenfeld), Frank Finlay (Father), Maureen Lipman (Mother), Emilia Fox (Dorota)*
Director: *Roman Polanski*
Screenwriter: *Ronald Harwood, from the book by Wladyslaw Szpilman*
15/142 mins./Biography/Drama/UK/France/Poland/Germany/UK

Awards: *Academy Awards – Best Actor, Best Director, Best Adapted Screenplay; BAFTA – Best Film, David Lean Award for Direction; Cannes Film Festival – Palme D'Or*

As the Nazis lay the groundwork for the Final Solution, concert pianist Wladyslaw Szpilman, a Polish Jew, evades imprisonment in the Warsaw ghetto and begins a precarious existence on the increasingly war-ravaged streets of Poland.

The critical consensus on Roman Polanski's intensely personal Holocaust drama is nigh on universal. Palme D'Or winner, best film at all the major European ceremonies including the BAFTAs, a trio of underdog victories at the Oscars for Polanski, Adrien Brody and screenwriter Ronald Harwood...

For all the august award bodies who seized upon *The Pianist* with giddy glee 'Important Director Tackles Big Subject Alert! ' it is, in fact, relatively easy to overlook the appeal of what is a disarmingly simple story, shot and structured with lucid transparency.

Concert pianist Wladyslaw Szpilman's true-life tale of survival against all odds lacks the broad sweep of, say, *Schlindler's List*, but benefits enormously from the intimacy and immediacy of an eyewitness account. (Two eyewitnesses in fact, as Polanski himself escaped the Krakow ghetto.)

Where Spielberg set out to capture a large canvas with both economy and elan, Polanski's movie is uncluttered by technique and remarkably singular in purpose – supporting characters come and go only as they passed through Szpilman's life.

Naturally, such fidelity to the source material does create its own set of problems. The near-silent third act – Szpilman alone in the ruins of the ghetto – plays like an extended anecdote, a shaggy dog survival story, so to speak.

It is certainly a remarkable yarn, and Brody weighs in with an astonishing physical performance – his gait, his gaze, his very bones aching with hunger – but it is hard to shake the feeling that history is taking place elsewhere. And because this is a survivor's story, *The Pianist* never quite generates the sheer terror of *Schlinder's List*, where death could seemingly visit any character, at any time.

There are other niggles if you look for them – pacing is stately to the point of slack in places, and the early scenes of domestic bliss have a very perfunctory feel. But the meat of the story, which covers the creation and

Films With The Largest Number of Extras

1 *Ghandi* (1982) – 294,560
2 *Kolberg* (1945) – 187,000
3 *Monster Wangmagwi* (1967) – 157,000
4 *War And Peace* (1968) – 120,000
5 *Ilya Muromets* (1956) – 106,000
6 *Dun Huang* (1988) – 100,000
7 *Razboiul Independentei* (1912) – 80,000
8 *Around the World in 80 Days* (1956) – 68,894
9 *Intolerance* (1956) – 60,000
10 *Dny Zrady* (1973) – 60,000

destruction of the Warsaw ghetto, is compelling stuff: equal parts absorbing adventure and stomach-churning tragedy.

And it is here, in the margins of Szpilman's story, where Polanski is – and any irony is duly noted – most comfortable, painstakingly recreating the almost incidental daily horrors that he himself lived through. The fact that the director never once caves into easy sentiment or cheap hectoring is almost as amazing as the story itself. ★★★★ **CK**

THE PIANO (1993)

Starring: *Holly Hunter (Ada McGrath), Harvey Keitel (George Baines), Sam Neill (Alisdair Stewart), Anna Paquin (Flora McGrath)*
Director: *Jane Campion*
Screenwriter: *Jane Campion*
15/181 mins./Drama/Romance/Australia/New Zealand/France

Awards: *Academy Awards – Best Actress, Best Supporting Actress, Best Original Screenplay; BAFTA – Best Actress, Best Costume, Best Production Design; Cannes Film Festival – Palme D'Or Golden Globes – Best Actress*

A mail-order bride, Ada, and her young daughter arrive on the shores of New Zealand with only a few possessions including a large piano. Her new husband leaves it on the beach but Baines, her husband's assistant, takes in the piano and asks for lessons in return, however they soon begin a passionate affair.

Splitting 1993's Palm D'Or honours with Chen Kaige's *Farewell My Concubine*, Jane Campion's fourth feature arrived on these shores a full five months after Cannes with 'chick movie' and 'arthouse' stamped all over it in big, bold letters, complete with an oddball period milieu (New Zealand during the very early days of European colonisation), daring casting (Holly Hunter as a mute Scottish mail-order bride; Harvey Keitel as a Scottish-or-is-it-Irish? settler-turned-honorary Maori) and bizarre subject matter (woman loves piano, woman loses piano, woman wins piano back with sexual favours). Don't let that scare you off, though. Precious as it sounds – and threatens to be at times – this is not just Merchant-Ivory with a Kiwi twist, but a strikingly unusual and arresting, sumptuous and transcendent parable of adultery and awakening passion featuring a knockout central performance from Cannes' Best Actress Holly Hunter.

Dumped on a bleak New Zealand beach front with her nine-year-old daughter Flora and her treasured piano, Ada, a fiercely expressive woman unable to articulate her emotions except in sign language through her daughter, but who reveals more with her eyes and piano-playing than words ever could, gets off to a rocky start with the husband she's never met, a stifling, sexually inhibited pioneer (Neill, hapless drip yet again) who refuses to haul her beloved baby grand up to his remote rainforest dwelling. It falls instead into the hands of instantly smitten landowner Baines (a profanity-free Keitel, cast against type as a sort of tattooed Valentino, but adeptly pulling it off), who strikes a deal with Ada to earn her piano back via piano lessons in his cabin. The lessons, however, are merely the cover for an elaborate and frankly handled courtship that evolves in progressively erotic stages from one-sided lust into a passionate affair. As the diminutive Ada switches her passion from the inanimate to the animate, disfigures her piano to send a message to her lover, is betrayed by her daughter and suffers brutal retribution at the hands of her humiliated husband, Campion's beautifully crafted tale unravels in perpetually muddy, rain-swept environs in bold, tactile strokes, with occasional flashes of humour and an almost otherworldly quality.

Delicate, sensitive and literate, this admittedly has a selective appeal, but you'd be hard-pressed to find a more serenely sensual or visually ethereal film. And, belatedly, Campion signs off with an unexpectedly uplifting twist, thumbing her nose at cinema's granite-bound lexicon of tragic, doomed heroines. ★★★★ **MM**

PICKPOCKET (1959)

Starring: *Martin Lassale (Michel), Marika Green (Jeanne), Pierre Leymarie (Jacques), Jean Pelegri (Police Inspector), Kassagi (Master Pickpocket), Pierre Etaix (Accomplice), Dolly Scal (Michel's Mother), Cesar Gattegno (Detective)*
Director: *Robert Bresson*
Screenwriter: *Robert Bresson, based on the novel* Crime And Punishment *by Feodor Dostoyevsky*
PG/75 mins./Crime/France

Ignoring his ailing mother and spurning the affection of her neighbour, Jeanne, and the benevolent advice of a police inspector, Michel devotes himself to the art of picking pockets, which he is taught by a master street thief.

Loosely inspired by Dostoevsky's *Crime and Punishment*, this was the second film in Robert Bresson's 'prison cycle' that also included *A Man Escaped* and *The Trial of Joan of Arc*. Originally entitled *Incertitude* and filmed on the streets of Paris at the same time as Jean-Luc Godard's *A Bout de Souffle*, this typically spartan drama fell foul of contemporary critics, some of whom decried its lack of psychological realism, while others accused Bresson of succumbing to elliptical self-indulgence. Yet Louis Malle described it as 'a film of lightning newness' and it has since been acclaimed as one of Bresson's masterworks. Indeed, Paul Schrader was so influenced by its visual and dramatic rigour that he shaped the ending of *American Gigolo* in its image.

Bresson again attained the austere authenticity that characterised all his pictures. He also insisted on precisely controlling the gestures and expressions of his non-professional performers and even reprised the voice-over tactic from *The Diary of a Country Priest* and *A Man Escaped*'s unflinching fascination with manual dexterity. In order to reinforce the latter's documentary feel, Bresson hired a genuine dipper, Kassagi, to teach Martin Lassalle the tricks of the trade, which he filmed in tight close-up to emphasise the impression that Michel was acquiring something that would fill the void at the centre of his existence rather than any baser material need.

But, for all the obvious criminality, this is very much a tale of redemption, in which Michel's transference of his obsession with theft to a love for Jeanne is couched in near-miraculous terms, with the constantly open door of

Michel's apartment signifying the free will that led him astray and the locked cell in which he finds salvation representing predestined divine intervention.

However, the film has also invited non-religious interpretations, with some seeing Michel's alliance with Jeanne as a deliverance from a repressed homosexuality that manifested itself in his fetishistic fixation with the techniques of pickpocketing, while others have identified an Oedipal bond between Michel and the mother whom he avoids for undisclosed reasons until she's on her death bed. ★★★★★ **DP**

PICNIC (1955)

Starring: *William Holden (Hal Carter), Rosalind Russell (Rosemary (Sydney), Kim Novak (Madge Owens), Betty Field (Flo Owens), Susan Strasberg (Millie Owens), Cliff Robertson (Alan), Arthur O'Connell (Howard Bevans), Verna Felton (Mrs Helen Potts), Reta Shaw (Linda Sue Breckenridge)*
Director: *Joshua Logan*
Screenwriter: *Daniel Taradash, based on the play by William Inge*
U/115 mins./Drama/USA

Awards: *Academy Awards – Best Art Direction-Set Decoration (Colour), Best Film Editing*

A drifter shows up in a Kansas town on Labor Day, hoping to touch up a rich college pal for a job and winds up at the town's picnic — where he stirs up the womenfolk, notably his friend's girl, her younger sister and 'old maid schoolteacher'.

Like *Bus Stop*, this was originally a Broadway play written by William Inge and directed by Joshua Logan; it's also another story in which a group of typical Middle American eccentrics (each with their very own sub-plot) are shaken up by an outsider and an obsessive love springs up between two ideal physical specimens (Holden's shirtless beefcake and Novak's small town teen queen are rather better matched than Marilyn Monroe and Don Murray), changing their lives and the lives of all the folks who revolve around them.

Logan opens things out more here, with a charming, funny, faintly sinister homage to all the ridiculous hijinx indulged in by this staid community on their one crazy day of the year, culminating in Novak's anointment as the 'Queen of Neewollah' and a lakeside dance that allows the stars to show off their natural but impressive moves.

It's a theatrical contrivance that everybody's life changes completely in the course of one day and night, with the requisite 1950s-style steamy lovemaking and macho fistfight scenes, and Inge's more poetic flights of dialogue haven't worn well, but this is nevertheless the sort of widescreen, pastel-coloured, sweet-and-sour entertainment that sparkles while the similar theatrical adaptations of later decades (e.g.: *Steel Magnolias*) have congealed into unwatchability.

The showiest support comes from Russell as a drunken spinster who clutches desperately at any passing man, but the best, most appealing performance comes from Strasberg as the bratty, smart, incipiently cute kid sister. ★★★ **KN**

PICNIC AT HANGING ROCK (1975)

Starring: *Rachel Roberts (Mrs Appleyard), Vivean Gray (Miss McCraw), Helen Morse (Mlle. De Poitiers), Kirsty Child (Miss Lumley), Tony Llewellyn-Jones (Tom), Jacki Weaver (Minnie)*
Director: *Peter Weir*
Screenwriter: *Cliff Green, based on the novel by Joan Lindsay*
PG/115 mins./Drama/Australia

Awards: *BAFTA – Best Cinematography*

The strange tale of three students and a teacher who clean disappear from a school picnic to Hanging Rock in Victoria, Australia on Valentine's Day in 1900. An event that leaves the 'survivors' traumatised.

A haunting and compelling oddity from Australian master Peter Weir, that doesn't fit easy categorisation; it is part mystery, part horror, an impressionist poem to lost innocence. Although since considered based on a true story, it is, in fact, merely an adaptation of Joan Lindsay's novel, but Russell Boyd's cinematography is so sumptuous and captivating it is little wonder watchers felt like they were stepping into some peculiar reality; his visionary camerawork keeps resting on plants, animals, hives of restless insects, the screen almost bursting with wildness. Weir's emphasis is on nature's alien quality, how these prim girls are set against unknowable forces.

That he also refuses to answer the questions the film presses upon us is a tactical risk, but it works because he is not setting it up as a straightforward narrative. He is playing with themes and images, and only elusively with a plot. The girls that remain behind become hysterical, unable to explain what became of their friends, and there is a strong allusion to the force of nature that also exists within their pubescent bodies, as if sexual awakening can have devastating outward results – an idea exemplified when the girls are spotted barefoot in the bush from afar by a stable boy and a young English aristocrat. From their point of view, they are both angels and sirens, and when the boys follow they find no trace of them. Meanwhile, their headmistress, played with stoic force by Rachel Roberts, is determined there is a rational explanation, but no answer will be forthcoming. It is a dreamlike journey with no resolution, just fragments and suggestions, leaving an almost painful sense of longing for these lost creatures. ★★★★★ **IN**

PIERROT LE FOU ((1965)

Starring: *Jean-Paul Belmondo (Ferdinand Griffon, 'Pierrot'), Anna Karina (Marianne Renoir), Dirk Sanders (Fred, Marianne's Brother), Raymond Devos (Man on the Pier), Graziella Galvani (Ferdinand's Wife)*
Director: *Jean-Luc Godard*
Screenwriter: *Jean-Luc Godard, based on the novel* Obsession *by Lionel White*
15/110 mins./Crime/France/Italy

Frustrated by his comfortably pointless existence in Paris, Ferdinand Griffon heads south with babysitter Marianne Renoir, who is mixed up with some gangsters. However, she quickly tires of his Provencal idyll and heads for the Riviera to find her 'brother', Fred, and the pursuing Pierrot becomes increasingly enmeshed in her double life.

Having freely adapted Lionel White's pulp novel, *Obsession*, Jean-Luc Godard considered casting pop star Sylvie Vartan and Richard Burton before plumping for then-wife Anna Karina and Jean-Paul Belmondo in what he claimed to be 'the story of the last romantic couple, the last descendants of La Nouvelle Heloise, Werther and Hermann and Dorothea'. Suggesting it was more of an essay than a movie, Godard made endless references to such artists as Velazquez, Renoir and Picasso, novelists and poets like Céline, Bernardin de Saint-Pierre, Rimbaud and Lorca, and filmmakers of the calibre of Sergei Eisenstein, Jean Renoir and Samuel Fuller, who even took a cameo to reinforce both the Hollywood maverick's contention that life was like a battlefield and Godard's self-fulfilling status as an outsider.

Embracing his reputation as the enfant terrible of the nouvelle vague, Godard abandoned the conventions of narrative cinema and adopted a loose picaresque format around which he could arrange subversive generic tropes, poetic digressions, political ideas and comic-book escapades. Consequently, he was able to achieve within the same anti-gangster picture a structural experiment, a confessional thriller, a treatise on cinema and a socio-cultural tract.

More than ever before, Godard employed Brechtian distancing devices to rouse the audience out of its complacent passivity, with the cast directly addressing the camera and an off-screen chorus commenting upon and occasionally anticipating action that was studded with quotations from literary sources and Ferdinand's diary, song interludes and disconcerting shifts in colour and style, such those as during the Parisian party, where the dialogue was taken from advertising copy for cars, deodorants and hairspray.

Yet, for all its cocky aggression, this is also a highly pessimistic picture, in which Ferdinand serves as Godard's alter ego, as he rails against consumerism, intellectual debasement, American imperialism, the breakdown of communication and the alienating mechanisation of urban living. But rather than merely extending the assault on modernity begun in *Alphaville*, Godard gives the first intimation of the political commitment that would come to dominate his work from 1966 onwards. ★★★★ **DP**

THE PICTURE OF DORIAN GRAY (1945)

Starring: *George Sanders (Lord Henry Wooton), Hurd Hatfield (Dorian Gray), Donna Reed (Gladys Hallward), Angela Lansbury (Sibyl Vane), Peter Lawford (David Stone), Lowell Gillmore (Basil Hallward)*
Director: *Albert Lewin*
Screenwriter: *Albert Lewin, from the novel* The Picture Of Dorian Gray *by Oscar Wilde*
Unrated/129 mins./Drama/Horror/USA

Awards: *Academy Awards- Best Black-and-White Cinematography; Golden Globes – Best Supporting Actress (Angela Lansbury)*

In the 1890s, Dorian Gray, a handsome youth, wishes his just-painted portrait would age in place of him. Mysteriously, his wish is granted – and he remains young, even as he becomes a dissolute libertine.

'If only it was the picture who was to grow old, and I remain young. There's nothing in the world I wouldn't give for that. Yes, I would give even my soul for it.' Oscar Wilde's classic novel has been filmed over and over since the silent days, often for television or in straight and gay porno movies – but this 1945 Hollywood movie is still the only big-budget mainstream adaptation.

Albert Lewin, a specialist in the tasteful but weird (*Pandora and the Flying Dutchman*), wrote and directed this classy production for Paramount, perhaps reining himself in a little too much in drawing a veil over what exactly Dorian does that's so evil (and unhealthy). It's a wonderfully cast picture, with Hurd Hatfield smoothly credible as both the lovely youth and the frozen villain, George Sanders (as Dorian's mentor Sir Henry) tossing off Wilde's lines ('forgive me for the intelligence of my argument – I'd forgotten that you were a Member of Parliament') as if they were written for him, and plump young Angela Lansbury heartbreaking as the music hall singer ('Goodbye Little Yellow Bird') who Dorian drives to suicide at the beginning of his long slide to depravity.

Lewin tidies up Wilde's plot a little, sometimes even improving on the book (the business with the girl makes much more sense here), but also bows occasionally to Hollywood convention, having even the cynical Sir Henry coming over religious at the climax. An arty touch is that the film is in luminous black and white, except for the picture – which is in glorious colour. ★★★★ **KN**

PILLOW TALK (1959)

Starring: *Rock Hudson (Brad Allen/Rex Stetson), Doris Day (Jan Morrow), Tony Randall (Jonathan Forbes), Thelma Ritter (Alma), Nick Adams (Tony Walters)*
Director: *Michael Gordon*
Screenwriters: *Stanley Shapiro, Maurice Richlin, from a story by Russell Rouse, Clarence Greene*
PG/98 mins./Romance/Comedy/USA
Awards: *Academy Awards – Best Original Screenplay*

A woman who shares a phone line with a neighbour she has never met – but despises on the basis of overheard conversations – is unknowingly wooed by him when he discovers her identity.

The first of three films that paired Rock Hudson and Doris Day – and made them a screen dream team – is the best of the lot. With tongue-permanently-in-cheek, this pastel-shaded, camper-than-camp, frothy comedy says the sharpest things about the essential differences between men and women while keeping the humour level turned up to high.

This was also one of the films that marked Day's transition from singer to actress. She does sing two songs here – the title song 'Pillow Talk' and 'Roly Poly' in one of the bar scenes – but her singing is incidental – it's the sass that she gave Hudson that kept the 1950s and 60s audiences coming back for more. And the manliness that Hudson displayed was so unimpeachable at the time, that the later revelations of his homosexuality, and diagnosis with AIDS, many years later really was a shocker to the women who had idolised him (maybe less so to the men who had done the same!).

There's also memorable support from Thelma Ritter and Tony Randall, and it was the latter who returned for the virtual re-make-cum-tribute *Down With Love*, starring Ewan McGregor and Renee Zellwegger. The existence of which is evidence that almost half a century later this film is still remembered very affectionately by the devoted. ★★★★ **EC**

PINK FLAMINGOS (1972)

Starring: *Divine (Divine/Babs Johnson), David Lochary (Raymond Marble), Mary Vivian Pearce (Cotton), Mink Stole (Connie Marble), Danny Mills (Crackers), Edith Massey (Edie), Channing Wilroy (Channing), Cookie Mueller (Cookie), Paul Swift (The Egg Man), Susan Walsh (Suzie), Linda Olgeirson (Linda)*
Director: *John Waters*
Screenwriter: *John Waters*
18/93 mins./Comedy/USA

Trailer trash Babs Johnson and upscale couple Raymond and Connie compete for the title of 'filthiest person in the world'. In the end, Babs wins by killing her rivals and eating a dog-turd.

John Waters' disposable masterpiece, made before he got anywhere near the mainstream likes of *Hairspray* and *Cry-Baby*, but after he had learned to work in colour and with synchronised sound. The storyline is essentially an excuse for a parade of the most nauseating offences ever committed to film: mock cannibalism, kidnapped girls being artificially inseminated so their babies can be sold to lesbian couples, gross transvestism, hardcore gay incest (Divine fellates her screen son), anal scat-singing, turkey-neck indecent exposure, a man raping a chicken (to death), a retarded grandmother in her underwear (Edy Massey) gorging herself on eggs, Divine hiding stolen meat in the crotch of her panties (and then serving it up for dinner) and plain old-fashioned sex and violence.

The money sequence comes in the finale, after the story is over and Babs has won the 'world's filthiest person title' as Divine succeeds in becoming the 'world's filthiest *actress*' by eating a dog-turd live on camera (the mutt has defecated in the same shot, just to prove the poo isn't fake). You can debate the rights and wrongs of the scene, but it's not something you'll see outside a *very* specialised undeground porno market. Despite its cheery, cheesy tone, which tends to render its atrocities less offensive, something makes *Pink Flamingos* hard to *like*. Perhaps its the relentlessly smug hip-ness, but probably it's the sub-home movie level production values and strident, hectoring, amateur acting.

Though he was an entry-level director, Waters's strength – as always – is in his witty, bizarrely moralist screenwriting. If nothing else, he's a unique voice. Beware heavily censored prints. Our rating is something of a compromise – *Pink Flamingos* rates higher or lower according to personal taste. ★★★ **KN**

THE PINK PANTHER (1963)

Starring: *David Niven (Sir Charles Lytton), Peter Sellers (Inspector Jacques Clouseau), Robert Wagner (George Lytton), Capucine (Simone Clouseau), Brenda De Banzie (Angela Dunning)*
Director: *Blake Edwards*
Screenwriters: *Maurice Richlin, Blake Edwards*
PG/113 mins./Comedy/USA

On the trail of the elusive jewel thief known only as 'The Phantom', bumbling French Inspector Closeau, ends up in Switzerland, in the company of the debonair Englishman Sir Charles Lytton, who should become his main suspect. For Closeau, however, the obvious will always remain elusive.

The first in the mixed array of *Pink Panther* movies was due to be a starring vehicle for David Niven, who does take top billing, but when director Blake Edwards started to witness what Peter Sellers was doing with a secondary character, creating a level of slapstick invention harkening to the skills of Chaplin and Keaton, the film, and subsequent sequels, became all about Clouseau. While the Pink Panther of the title is none of the characters at all, it was the diamond The Phantom was after.

What could have been a slick if forgettable caper movie, was transformed into an often hilarious, and giddily paced farce revolving around this extraordinary and supposedly off-the-cuff comic creation. The brilliance of Sellers' Clouseau is not simply in his physical ineptitude and slurring accent, but in his total lack of awareness that he is, in truth, an idiot. He is blind to everything, particularly his beautiful wife Simone's infidelities, and carries on adoring her all the same. This would become a running gag in the series – how, above all, Clouseau was a fool for love, although, with the emphasis on the fool bit.

There's a good bit of creeping around bedrooms in the middle of the night, but Sellers and Edwards never let it sag into anything bawdy, by the insanely hectic chase sequence, involving a thief in a gorilla suit and Clouseau in armour, the film has reached a rare height of visual complexity and confidence, jokes spinning everywhere, but never out of control. ★★★★ **IN**

THE PINK PANTHER (2006)

Starring: *Jean Reno (Gendarme Gilbert Ponton), Steve Martin (Inspector Jacques Clouseau), Beyonce Knowles (Xania), Kevin Kline (Chief Inspector Dreyfus), Emily Mortimer (Nicole)*
Director: *Shawn Levy*
Screenwriters: *Len Blum, Steve Martin*
PG/93 mins./Comedy/USA

A famous French soccer coach is murdered with a poison dart, and his priceless diamond ring, the Pink Panther, is stolen. On the case is the incompetent Inspector Clouseau – but only because Chief Inspector Dreyfus wants him to fail, so he can solve the case himself...

Expectations are strange things. Set them too high and anything disappoints; lower them enough and everything impresses. Seeing that the director/star team behind *Cheaper By The Dozen* were to flog the dead kitty that is the *Pink Panther* franchise, *Empire's* expectations flatlined. And so it is that we have a movie so much better than we expected that it's frustrating it didn't manage to be far better than it is.

What quickly becomes apparent is that Steve Martin is the ideal heir to Peter Sellers; after all, Clouseau is an arrogant idiot, the very persona Martin mastered back in his Wild And Crazy days. With Steve himself having contributed to the script, there are flashes of the Martin of old here; one scene, which sees Clouseau and sidekick Ponton (Jean Reno) in wallpaper-camouflage bodysuits, could have come straight out of *The Man With Two Brains*. Sadly, though, director Levy causes Martin to waste his comedic inheritance.

The original Panthers were no masterpieces, but they knew how to spin out a setpiece. Here we get a pummelling of one-note slapstick gags, some hit, most miss. Add a miscast Dreyfus (Kline can't play it straight enough) and a stifled yawn of a crime mystery, and you're left with a movie whose good moments only highlight the barely OKness of everything else. ★★ **DJ**

PINOCCHIO (1940)

Starring: the voices of (uncredited): *Cliff Edwards (Jiminy Cricket), Dickie Jones (Alexander/Pinocchio), Evelyn Venable (The Blue Fairy), Christian Rub (Geppetto)*
Directors: *Hamilton Luske, Ben Sharpsteen*
Screenwriters: *Aurelius Battaglia, William Cottrell, Otto Englander, Erdman Penner, Joseph Sabo, Ted Sears, Webb Smith, adapated from the novel* The Adventures Of Pinocchio *by Carlo Collodi*
U/88 mins./Family/Adventure/Animation/Musical/Fantasy/USA

Awards: *Academy Awards – Best Score, Best Song ('When You Wish Upon A Star')*

Woodcarver Gepetto makes a puppet who comes to life but wants to be a real boy. However, before the Blue Fairy will grant this wish, Pinocchio has to straighten out character flaws, like his predisposition to mendacity. Jiminy Cricket, an insect, is appointed as his conscience.

The Disney name became associated with squeaky-clean entertainment in the 1950s, but Walt's 1940 masterpiece makes no compromises in the name of family viewing. Richly animated throughout (few cartoons have such a physicality), Pinocchio also has a surprising earthiness and sensuality. The Blue Fairy is literally a vision of loveliness, and there are strange overtones to the affectionate but nervous relationship between Figaro the Cat and Cleo the goldfish (the sexiest anthromorphised animal in the cinema) and the famous, obviously phallic, nose-growing business. It also has the mercilessness of many fairy tales: Lampwick, the teenage beer drinker whose idea of a good time is breaking windows (in a theme park that seems like a dark premonition of Disneyworlds to come), is horrifically turned into a donkey and sold into the salt mines.

The puppet's road to humanity is littered with ordeals, finally the gigantic Monstro the Whale, one of the most convincingly huge villains in cartoons. The film has gorgeous background drawings, a collection of perfectly realised characters (the stooped and lonely Gepetto, the mountainous and mock-jovial villain Stromboli, the suave con man fox J. Worthington Foulfellow, the grotesquely sinister coachman who conveys victims to Pleasure Island) and the best-ever score for a Disney musical ('Give a Little Whistle', 'I've Got No Strings', 'When You Wish Upon A Star', 'Hi-Diddle-Dee-Dee') from composer Leigh Harline and lyricist Ned Washington. A true classic, capable of holding the interest through dozens of child-mandated viewings, with a sense of the wonders and terrors of the world outside its fairy-tale setting. ★★★★★ **KN**

Movie Trivia:
Walt Disney (1901–1966)

Who he was: Animator, producer and founder of the Walt Disney Company, Disney started off making animated shorts, and became the first to add sound and colour to cartoons before making the first animated feature, *Snow White and the Seven Dwarves* (1937).
Hallmarks: Cute, big-eyed animals; Mickey Mouse; happy endings; trilling songbirds; anti-Communism; true love triumphing over evil.
If you see one movie, see: *Bambi* (1942)

⦿ PIRANHA (1978)

Starring: *Bradford Dillman (Paul Grogan), Heather Menzies (Maggie McKeown), Kevin McCarthy (Dr Robert Hoak), Keenan Wynn (Jack)*
Director: *Joe Dante*
Screenwriter: *John Sayles, from a story by Richard Robinson, John Sayles*
18/90 mins./Horror/USA

Mutant piranha escape from a secret research station and head downriver towards a summer camp and a small town's lakeside tourist attraction. A gruff loner and a daffy private eye try to stop the monsters.

Joe Dante's first solo feature, scripted by John Sayles, is a textbook example of how to get the most out of a Roger Corman budget and a shoddy premise. The effects money extends to a couple of impressive mini-monsters and some nastily chewed corpses but is otherwise so meagre that few mutant fish get screen time and have to be represented by bloodily churning waters.

However, Dante and Sayles fill in between monster attacks, traditionally the dull stuff, with cynical dialogue, visual invention and amusing tributes to old-time movies. One reason Dante's films are so engaging, often despite their nastiness (this is a rare horror film in which children are mutilated and killed wholesale), is that he fills them with performers he clearly loves to see work.

Among the friendly faces are Kevin McCarthy and Barbara Steele ('fish genetics is a very small field') as mad scientists, Keenan Wynn as a garrulous old-timer who tells jokes to his dog, Paul Bartel as a comically tyranncal summer camp commandant always clamping down on signs of fun but who nevertheless has a moment of real heroism during the piranha attack and Dick Miller as the crass tycoon ('Ralph the Swimming Swine is a national institution') whose party is spoiled by a minion who discreetly coughs 'the piranha ... they're eating the guests, sir'.

Sayles is clearly laughing at America in his premise (the fish were bred to be used in Vietnam) and the finale (when all else fails, the hero releases pollution into the river on the grounds that it killed everything else). The low-grade sequel, known as *Piranha II: Flying Killers* or *Piranha, Part 2: The Spawning*, was the directorial debut of James Cameron. ★★★★ **KN**

⦿ PIRATES OF THE CARIBBEAN: THE CURSE OF THE BLACK PEARL (2003)

Starring: *Johnny Depp (Jack Sparrow), Geoffrey Rush (Barbossa), Orlanda Bloom (Will Turner), Keira Knightley (Elizabeth Swann), Jack Davenport (Norrington), Jonathan Pryce (Governor Weatherby Swann), Mackenzie Crook (Ragetti)*
Director: *Gore Verbinski*
Screenwriters: *Ted Elliott, Terry Rossio, from a story by Elliott, Rossio, Stuart Beattie, Jay Wolpert, from the Disney theme-park ride*
12/137 mins./Action/Adventure/Comey/USA

Awards: *BAFTA – Best Hair/Make Up; Empire Awards – Best Actor*

The only way the crew of the *Black Pearl* can lift the curse upon them is to return a golden Aztec coin to its treasure chest. But that coin is currently hanging around the lovely neck of British Governor's daughter, Elizabeth Swann . . .

Year after year, lazy poster quotes try to convince audiences that the latest blockbuster movie is 'a roller-coaster ride'. *Pirates Of The Caribbean* does, in actual fact, have its roots in a theme park attraction – a slow-moving boat trip past richly detailed tableaux of lusty buccaneers and skeletons who breathed their last grasping for forbidden treasure; not the most likely base material to turn into cinema gold. But producer Jerry Bruckheimer proves yet again that he's a big-screen alchemist where sheer entertainment is concerned.

Director Gore Verbinski steers his ship through choppy commercial waters by keeping the romance, adventure and comedy on an even keel. If there's the slightest niggle to be had, it's probably that the swashbuckling sequences don't really lay down a challenge to the Zorros or Robin Hoods. But such cares are swept aside by a rollicking tale of pirate lore, with cursed treasure, secret identities and enough acts of betrayal and loyalty to keep the final showdown as sparky as the firecrackers in Blackbeard's whiskers.

It's also very funny. *Shrek* writers Ted Elliott and Terry Rossio spice up the pirate genre as gamely as they did fairy tales; but on the comedy map it's Johnny Depp's inspired turn as Captain Jack Sparrow that really marks the spot. Depp, arguing that pirates were the rock stars of their day, models his entire performance on Keith Richards of the Rolling Stones: it's there in every slurred vowel and every drug-fried wiggle of the head. There's an endearing dignity to Sparrow's hunger for fame. 'You are, without doubt, the worst pirate I've heard of,' says one British officer. 'Yes,' replies Jack, 'but you have heard of me.' Gloriously over-the-top, this performance is pitched only as high as the film's fun factor itself. In terms of physical precision and verbal delivery, it's a masterclass in comedy acting.

Depp steals the show, but leaves some plunder for Orlando Bloom and Keira Knightley, surely the sexiest young couple in British cinema – nay, the world. Orlando plays it straight but gets the girl; and if you think Keira looks good in a dress, wait until you see her running around in redcoat and breeches.

Others clearly having a ball while gigging in the rigging include Geoffrey Rush with his panto Captain Hook routine, and CG-eyed pirate Mackenzie Crook (from *The Office*). Without a previous formula to adhere to or franchise to maintain (the spin-off ride exists already), *Pirates* revels in its freedom to do its own thing. That said, its adventure style is indebted to the likes of *Raiders Of The Lost Ark* and *The Mummy* in its mix of matinee action and horror that won't send the kids shrieking from the room.

The ghostly figures on the *Black Pearl* are cursed to sail the seas in a state between living and dead. When they step into full moonlight, their rotting flesh and bones become visible adding a delightful shiver to proceedings. Best of all, *Pirates* is a film that prides itself on lively detail and top-grade craftsmanship, but doesn't take itself too seriously. That's a lesson that nearly every one of its blockbuster rivals would do well to take on board. Audiences aren't cajoled into feeling that they should be having fun; they simply are having fun because the movie is too. ★★★★★ **AM**

⦿ THE PIT AND THE PENDULUM (1961)

Starring: *Vincent Price (Nicholas Medina), Barbara Steele (Elizabeth Barnard Medina), John Kerr (Francis Barnard), Luana Anders (Catherine Medina), Antony Carbone (Dr. Charles Leon)*
Director: *Roger Corman*
Screenwriter: *Richard Matheson, based on the story by Edgar Allan Poe*
15/76 mins./Horror/USA

Francis Barnard goes to Spain, when he hears his sister Elizabeth has died. Her husband Nicholas Medina, the son of a brutal torturer of the Spanish Inquisition, tells him she has died of a blood disease, but Francis finds this hard to believe.

In 1960, Roger Corman told AIP supremos Samuel Z. Arkoff and James H. Nicholson, for whom he had been making pictures like *Attack Of The Crab Monsters* (1957) and *Not Of This Earth* (1957), that he wanted to make Edgar Allan Poe's *The Fall Of The House Of Usher*. The producers responded negatively, saying that kids were forced to read Poe in school and so there was no way they'd pay to see his stuff in the movies.

But Corman knew what he was doing and put together a package with flamboyant star Vincent Price, who did so much acting that there was no need for anyone else in the cast to even try, and novelist-screenwriter Richard Matheson, whose credits stretch from *The Incredible Shrinking Man* (1957) to *Stir Of Echoes* (1999).

Hammer had just broken big with their Frankenstein and Dracula movies, and Corman saw the potential in period gothic. The Brits made movies for pokey provincial Rialtos and Coronets, while AIP were kings of the drive-in: Corman's Poe movies are in Panavision, a shape approximating that of a classic car windscreen. Key collaborators were cinematographer Floyd Crosby, a master of pre-psychedelic colour swirls, and art director Daniel Haller, who could stretch a budget to make crypts and castles seem vast on the big screen.

If you've only seen the Corman-Price-Poe movies panned and scanned on television, you've barely got an idea of how impressive they are.

The Fall Of The House Of Usher (1960) was a hit, and AIP wanted more, more, more. Corman handed Matheson Poe's classic tale 'The Pit And The Pendulum', which takes place entirely in darkness and has a situation rather than a plot (a nameless narrator suffers in the Spanish Inquisition). Matheson took a few leftover elements from his *House Of Usher* script (a young man comes to an accursed home to discover what has happened to a young woman who, it turns out, has been buried alive) and threw in a Diabolique-style it's-all-a-plot plot.

The dead wife turns out to be scheming in cahoots with her lover to drive poor old Vincent Price mad, then discovers that a mad Vincent Price isn't a very comfortable character to have around. Only in the finale does Matheson get round to dramatising Poe, and then by having the dim-bulb hero (Kerr) walk into the dungeon at the wrong time and be mistaken for someone else by the mad Price and strapped to a table in the pit under the slowly descending, sharpened crescent ('The razor edge of destiny'). It's a scene that crops up in other films – *Dr Goldfoot And The Bikini Machine* (1965) – and remains a classic, with the gears working and the blade whirring back and forth across the whole length of the screen as the camera is put in the position of victim.

Corman's *The Pit And The Pendulum* is, unusually, set in the 1540s, with the whole cast in ruffs and doublets, and revolves around a marriage of horror stars. Price, raising his moustaches as others raise their eyebrows, is mild-mannered Nicholas Medina, proprietor of a clifftop castle and heir to the madness of his torture-happy inquisitor father. The flamboyantly beautiful English actress Barbara Steele had just attained immortality as the vampire princess in Mario Bava's *Mask Of Satan* (1960). She has a few good moments as the pretend-ghost, emerging lank-haired from her tomb, but is hurried out of the way at the climax only to be left stranded and wild-eyed in an iron maiden as the cellars are sealed forever in the fade-out. The pair carry the picture virtually on their own, with John Kerr's hero a notable waste of space and Luana Anders a hard-faced pretty heroine. Price was a master of the grand gesture, and Corman gives him the room, whip-panning to huge facial close-ups for his entrances and letting him emote in a slyly camp, outrageously melodramatic, psychologically acute manner; that is to say, the exact equivalent of Poe's rapid, fevered prose.

The movie was another smash with the rock'n'roll generation, and the winning team stayed at bat, drawing in new players from the ranks of classic horror stars, with the portmanteau *Tales Of Terror* (1962 with Peter Lorre and Basil Rathbone), the comic *The Raven* (1963, with a young Jack Nicholson), the dour *The Premature Burial* (1962, Price-free, but with Ray Milland) and the Lovecraft-derived *The Haunted Palace* (1963). To cap off the series, they relocated to England and delivered their finest hours, *Masque Of The Red Death* (1964), which was gorgeously shot by a young Nicolas Roeg, and the ultimate mad-wife-back-from-the-dead necromance *The Tomb Of Ligeia* (1965). ★★★★ **KN**

PITCH BLACK (1999)

Starring: *Radha Mitchell (Fry), Vin Diesel (Riddick), Cole Hauser (Johns), Keith David (Iman), Lewis Fitz-Gerald (Paris), Claudia Black (Shazza)*
Director: *David Twohy*
Screenwriters: *Jim Wheat, Ken Wheat, David Twohy, from a story by Jim Wheat, Ken Wheat*
15/103 mins./Sci-fi/Action/Thriller/USA

The survivors of a spaceship wreck face internal danger and alien peril.

Low-budget this may be, but it's evident from the word go that writer/director Twohy has wrung every last drop from it – the opening crash sequence being an object lesson in how to manufacture shell-shocking, sci-fi thrills from tuppence-ha'penny: a fingernail-tearing, neck-wrenching ride into nose-dive terror, made all the more effective for its lack of warning and the unfamiliarity of the passengers – there's no comfy assurance that any of these people might make it to the second reel.

Indeed, casting an ensemble unburdened by former role recognition is one of *Pitch Black*'s primary strengths - forcing the viewer to take them at face value, this face value. So, Mitchell is sexy and stubborn as the pilot suddenly thrust into command, Hauser looks (and, at times, acts) like a young Tom Berenger, and David is solid as the faithful holy man. It's Diesel on show-stealing form, though: a voice growling like granite in a vice and his sheer, bulging presence perfect for the fearsome, serial-escapee, psycho convict.

And before you know it (provided you're so inclined), you're wrapped up in the race-against-time repair job hampered by the ongoing battle for basic survival and sanity in a blinding, hostile alien environment. On this front, Twohy (with director of photography, David Eggby) again scores by creating a stylish look for the piece. Bleached by the glare from the planet's three suns, there is perpetual daylight, although chronology is adhered to in a world without night by changing colours – the strongest star throwing a searing blue tinge, the other two combining for a burnished, day-long sunset effect. And though the script clangs alarmingly early on (a few one-liners are allowed to fall flat by poor delivery or poorer reaction), the movie seems to grow in confidence, with the odd flash of gore to keep the horror fans sated but the tension wisely cranked increasingly taut.

There's no time for stragglers as the film cracks on apace, trimmed of any and every extraneous linking scene. It's far more concerned, in fact, with bombarding its audience with artful visuals and brutal, thumbnail confrontation scenes than spoon-feeding unnecessary. ★★★★ **DB**

A PLACE IN THE SUN (1951)

Starring: *Montgomery Clift (George Eastman), Elizabeth Taylor (Angela Vickers), Shelley Winters (Alice Tripp), Anne Revere (Hannah Eastman), Keefe Brassele (Earl Eastman), Fred Clark (Bellows), Raymond Burr (Marlowe)*
Director: *George Stevens*
Screenwriters: *Michael Wilson, Harry Brown, based on the novel* An American Tragedy *by Theodore Dreisser and the play by Patrick Kearney*
PG/122 mins./Drama/USA
Awards: *Academy Awards – Best Director (George Stevens), Best Screenplay (Michael Wilson, Harry Brown), Best Cinematography, Black And White (William C. Mellor), Best Costume Design, Black And White (Edith Head), Best Film Editing (William Hornbeck), Best Music, Scoring Of A Dramatic Or Comedy Picture (Franx Waxman)*

Taking a job at his uncle's bathing-suit factory, social climber George Eastman becomes besotted with his cousin, Angela Vickers, and, when she returns his affection, he desperately tries to evade his responsibility to pregnant lover Alice Tripp, only to be charged with her murder in a boating accident.

Having confounded Sergei Eisenstein during his brief Hollywood sojourn and evaded the best efforts of Josef von Sternberg (in his otherwise admirably restrained 1931 adaptation), Theodore Dreiser's dourly realistic

1925 novel, *An American Romance*, was given a lustrous makeover by George Stevens in this Gothic soap opera. The film's political naivety was reinforced by William Mellor's glossy lighting of Hans Dreier's platitudinous sets, while its dramatic vulgarity was emphasised by Franz Waxman's bombastic score. Yet, somehow, this remains an imposing studio achievement, whose failings are largely subsumed by the director's doughty conviction and impossible beauty of its kissing cousins.

Stevens shifted the emphasis away from George Eastman's ruthless social ambition and downplayed his tawdry relationship with Alice in favour of his idealised romance with Angela. He was fortunate, therefore, that 18 year-old Elizabeth Taylor (who was initially unaware of his homosexuality) fell so hopelessly in love with Montgomery Clift that Stevens was able to capture the intensity of her emotion in scenes that were rewritten to exploit their mutual infatuation.

However, Stevens found Clift a difficult actor to work with, not least because he insisted on taking his motivation from drama coach Mira Rostova, who resisted all attempts to have her ejected from the set. His relations with Shelley Winters were often equally tempestuous. Initially, Stevens had refused to consider her for the role (even ignoring a letter from Norman Mailer), as she had become typecast in glamour roles. However, Winters had convinced him otherwise by showing up for a meeting without make-up and sporting a cheap hairstyle and even less fashionable clothing. But while Winters appreciated the opportunity to discover her character during extensive rehearsals, she eventually came to resent Stevens's hectoring direction and later regreted that her brassy portrayal had saddled her with another stereotype.

Stevens spent two years on *A Place in the Sun*, which landed six Academy Awards, including Best Director (although he also closely supervised William Hornbeck's editing) and he would repeat the feat with the even more grandiose *Giant* five years later. ★★★ **DP**

◑ PLAN 9 FROM OUTER SPACE (1959)

Starring: *Gregory Walcott (Jeff Trent), Mona McKinnon (Paula Trent), Duke Moore (Lt. Harper), Tom Keene (Col. Tom Edwards), Vampira (The Ghoul Woman), Bela Lugosi (The Ghoul Man), Tor Johnson (Police Inspector Clay), Lyle Talbot (Gen. Roberts), Dudley Manlove (Eros), John Breckinridge (The Ruler)*
Director: *Edward D. Wood Jr*
Screenwriter: *Edward D. Wood Jr*
PG/78 mins./Sci-fi/USA

Having failed to conquer the Earth with eight previous plans, aliens institute the dreaded plan nine. Eros and Tanna, the aliens in charge of the plan, resurrect the Ghoul Man, his wife and a policeman, then pit the zombies against a few cops and airline pilot hero Jeff Trent.

Thanks to several mocking books about terrible movies in general and director Ed Wood in particular, this has become generally accepted as the worst film ever made – though it is, in its own way, certainly no worse than, say, *Charlie's Angels: Full Throttle*, *The Care Bears Movie*, *Deep Throat* or *Top Gun*. Actually, it's not even the worst low-budget science fiction film of the 1950s – as a look at *The Astounding She Monster*, *The Incredible Petrified World* or *Phantom From 10,000 Leagues* will confirm.

The worst sin of these cheapies is that they are excruciatingly dull, but *Plan 9* is a rare low-budget turkey which manages to be consistently entertaining, thanks to Wood's distinctive ranting dialogue ('Wouldn't it be better to kill a few now than, with their meddling, permit them to destroy the entire universe?'), amazing narration from noted psychic Criswell ('Can *you* prove it *didn't* happen?'), camp performances (weedy alien villain Manlove keeps throwing hissy fits), wobbly graveyard sets, paper-plate flying saucers, a grotesquely ramshackle plot, talking-point weirdnesses like the use of home movie test footage of the late Bela Lugosi posing in a graveyard (then being doubled behind an upflung cape by a chiropractor for the rest of the film), acres of ill-used military stock footage, and the sheer bizarre presence of wasp-waisted Vampira and shambling hulk Tor Johnson as alien-influenced zombies. Even if you're fed up to the back teeth with bad movie faddists, this is worth seeing. ★ or ★★★★ **KN**

◑ PLANES, TRAINS AND AUTOMOBILES (1987)

Starring: *Steve Martin (Neal Page), John Candy (Del Griffith), Laila Robbins (Susan Page), Michael McKean (State Trooper), Kevin Bacon (Taxi Racer)*
Director: *John Hughes*
Screenwriter: *John Hughes*
PG/93 mins./Comedy/USA

Struggling the get home for Thanksgiving, Neal Page finds not only the snowy weather, but the very fates are allayed against him. His only companion on his quest is an oafish, overbearing shower curtain ring salesman Del Griffith, who will prove the biggest challenge of all.

When John Hughes finally set aside the pop-tribulations of 80s teens, and turned his eye to America's adults, he hit upon this sharp farce of the overworked, overstretched WASP male confronted with a world slipping out of his control. In its exaggeration, Neal Page's Sisyphean task of simply getting home for Thanksgiving, assailed as he is by Sod's, Murphy's and, for that matter, the actual Law, Hughes has created a very funny study of modern male neurosis. And who better to embody the fraying American family man who spends his life barely clinging on to the end of his tether, than Steve Martin?

In contrast, there is shower ring salesbody Del Griffith. He's all homey ease; life there's to be swallowed whole, then expressed in odorous burps. Where Neal fusses and frets, Del oozes, oblivious to the effect his bumptiousness has on others. Taking his shoes and socks off, he sighs, 'Boy, my dogs are barking today,' to Martin's icked-out Neal. He's the guy you least want to sit next to, played with the particular layering of the odious with the decent cove somewhere beneath a slobbery grin that made John Candy such a wonderful screen presence. At the heart of Neal's test, is that he will have to see the hollow in the middle of Del's life, he should realise his lot is so much better.

This is the unrefined moralism of John Hughes, a less subtle version of Frank Capra's universe, but he knows his comedy. The growing desperation Martin imbues into Neal's horror journey takes on an awful magnificence. As flights are re-routed, train engines burn-out and hire-cars prove non-existent (the swearing scene at the rental desk is a classic), and Del, well Del just keeps showing up, Hughes taps into that most modern of human torments – travelling. ★★★★ **IN**

◑ PLANET OF THE APES (1968)

Starring: *Charlton Heston (George Taylor), Roddy McDowall (Cornelius), Kim Hunter (Zira), Maurice Evans (Dr. Zaius), James Whitmore (President of the Assembly)*
Director: *Franklin J. Schaffner*
Screenwriters: *Michael Wilson, Rod Sterling, from the novel* La Planete Des Singes *by Pierre Boulle*
PG/107 mins./Sci-fi/Action/Adventure/USA
Awards: *Academy Awards – Honorary Award (John Chambers, for outstanding make-up achievment)*

In the year 3978 AD a spaceship with a crew of four crashes down on a distant planet which is inhabited by intelligent apes.

Three astronauts crash-land in the sea on a desolate, unwelcoming planet. They make their way to the rocky shore. One of them plants a sandcastle-sized American flag in the dust. Seeing this rather pathetic

TOP 10 Actors Who Aren't Singers Who Sing

1 Ewan McGregor and Nicole Kidman – *Moulin Rouge* (2001)
2 Joaquin Phoenix and Reese Witherspoon – *Walk The Line* (2005)
3 Michelle Pfeiffer – *The Fabulous Baker Boys* (1989)
4 Rosario Dawson – *Rent* (2006)
5 Sissy Spacek – *The Coal Miner's Daughter* (1980)
6 Audrey Hepburn – *Breakfast At Tiffany's* (1961)
7 Bruce Willis and Danny Aiello – *Hudson Hawk* (1991)
8 Michael J. Fox – *Back to the Future* (1985)
9 Val Kilmer – *The Doors* (1991)
10 Edward Norton – *Everyone Says I Love You* (1996)

sight, the cynic among them laughs – oh, how he laughs! George Taylor (Heston, for it is he), throws back his head and lets out a booming, sarcastic guffaw, which echoes eerily around the canyon in which the men find themselves, light years from home.

Planet Of The Apes is like that. Its visuals have become so imprinted on our minds, through sequels, spin-offs and straightforward repetition on TV, that we sometimes overlook its subtleties. When Taylor laughs at the Stars and Stripes, it crystallises the heart of the film. Here is a man with little time for mankind, and less time for worthless symbols of his so-called civilisation. A misanthrope in conquistador's clothing, he laughs in the face of his mission, now so obviously gone awry; he fully expects to perish on this godforsaken planet, and if he were the last representative of his species left alive, then good riddance. Extinction was too good for them.

It is Taylor's journey – and by that token, Heston's credible, athletic performance – that makes *Planet Of The Apes* so much more than a piece of rubber-mask sci-fi hokum: he begins the story hating himself and his fellow man; in the face of ape tyranny he learns to love himself (and his fetching mate, Nova); but he ends up on the beach, damning the human race all to hell, an ambassador now, but a very disappointed one.

We can admire John Chambers' pioneering simian make-up all we like (and there might never have been lunchboxes and *Marvel* comics and Saturday-morning cartoons without it) but *Planet Of The Apes'* abiding power as a movie rests squarely with the bloke who played Ben-Hur. Heston first encountered *Apes* in 1966, then just a pitch and a portfolio of preliminary drawings touted around by producer Arthur P. Jacobs, who'd acquired the rights to a French novel called *La Planete des Singes* by Pierre Boulle.

'The novel was singularly uncinematic,' recalls Heston in his autobiography. 'Still, I smelled a good film in it.' In this, Heston was apparently alone. But a year and half of blank faces and sealed cheque books later, Jacobs convinced Dick Zanuck at Fox to fund the picture once a few worries had been ironed out: 'What if the audience laughs at the make-up?' he asked, pertinently. In the event, Fox stumped up $50,000 just to develop the monkey faces. Prosthetic supremo Chambers did a miraculous job, and director Schaffner (later to win an Oscar for *Patton*) shot a test-scene between Heston and Edward G. Robinson playing orang-utan chief Dr Zaius. The studio loved it, and off they all went to Arizona to make sci-fi history – and $28m at the box office (except Robinson, who bailed due to a weak heart and aversion to latex).

Planet Of The Apes was a serious technical challenge, what with all those moulded rubber face-parts designed to move with the actors' features. 'You just have to over-act with your face, and it shows quite subtly on the make-up,' said Roddy McDowall, a man who went to his grave best-known for playing Cornelius in four of the five films, and Galen on TV. It was also a physically gruelling shoot, not least for the stripped, sprayed and hunted Heston ('Even rubber rocks hurt,' he complained), but the efforts by all concerned flesh out Boulle's political allegory with a conviction that ensured nobody was 'laughing at the make-up'.

There is humour in Rod Serling and Michael Wilson's script ('Human see, human do'), but the overriding effect is a terrifying one, from the visceral thrill of the gorilla troops on horseback, to the moment where 'Bright Eyes' (Taylor's cutesy nickname in captivity) speaks for the first time: 'Take your stinking paws off me, you damn dirty ape!'

The relentless cycle of sequels – which do, to their credit, form a time-bending circle – has had the effect of tainting the unique magic of the original film (in our collective memory, bits of *Beneath The Planet Of The Apes* and *Escape From* blur into the first), which is why sitting down and watching it again, in isolation, is so rewarding. It doesn't need a part two. Think of its powerful Statue Of Liberty denouement. As great movie endings go, it pisses on 'Nobody's Perfect!' ★★★★★ **AC**

PLANET OF THE APES (2001)

Starring: *Mark Wahlberg (Captain Leo Davidson), Tim Roth (General Thade), Helena Bonham Carter (Ari), Michael Clarke Duncan (Colonel Attar), Paul Giamatti (Limbo)*
Director: *Tim Burton*
Screenwriters: *William Broyles Jr, Lawrence Konner, Mark D. Rosenthal, from the novel* La Planete des Singes *by Pierre Boulle*
12/114 mins./Action/Sci-fi/USA

An electro-magnetic storm strands space station pilot Davidson far in the future on a planet ruled by simians who enslave humans. Attempting to escape with the help of human rights activist Ari, a chimpanzee, he becomes the reluctant leader of an uprising.

As every faintly cine-literate homo sapiens knows, Franklin J. Schaffner's 1968 sci-fi must-see *Planet Of The Apes* begat four sequels, two duff TV spin-offs and a 'Homerage' on *The Simpsons*. Tim Burton has dared a ri-damn-diculous revisitation which goes its own way with the premise of Pierre Boulle's 1963 novel, taking even more liberties than Michael Wilson and Rod 'Twilight Zone' Serling did, but pulls out Boulle's punchline for a shock ending that ain't all that after 101 genre trips to alternate realities.

Burton's renowned visual genius does not disappoint. His is a darkly imagined fairy tale realm, a fantastically primal habitation for make-up effects creator Rick Baker to go ape in, with distinctive gorillas, orang-utans and chimpanzees that outdo John Chambers' ground-breaking, Oscar-winning work in '68. ILM's FX, an army of digital dudes and spiffy stunt devisors also earn their bucks.

Too bad it's all in aid of a sketchy affair that tells us little about the simian society or the oppressed humans, as species or individuals. This tries awfully hard to be *Spartacus From Space*, but it's just not happening. Witness the questionable casting of Wahlberg, who fails to bring presence to a script that doesn't give him a lot to lean on. He should have reconsidered his 'no loincloth' stance, since hunkiness we can live with in the absence of authority.

As the necessary untamed beauty, Warren has all the emoting expertise of a Canadian synchronised swimmer (which she was). She's largely confined to pouting at action's edge while Bonham Carter gamely apes an ill-judged inter-species flirtation, but at least puts our minds at rest that no matter how badly human civilisation may degenerate, it appears collagen lip enhancement will survive. Roth steals the show, no problem, as a chimp Richard III.

This is at its best when it operates on its own adventure terms, but it can't resist referencing its iconic progenitor for – admittedly big – laughs. As for the in-jokes, there's no mistaking Chuck Heston even as a chimp in a rather fabulous cameo-homage, but keep an eye peeled for Linda Harrison ('68s pneumatic mute Nova and producer Zanuck's ex-wife) as 'Woman in Cart', and Rick Baker as 'Old Ape No. 2'. ★★★ **AE**

PLATOON (1986)

Starring: *Tom Berenger (Sgt Bob Barnes), Willem Dafoe (Sgt Elias Grodin), Charlie Sheen (Pvt. Chris Taylor), Forest Whitaker (Big Harold)*
Director: *Oliver Stone*
Screenwriter: *Oliver Stone*
15/114 mins./Action/Drama/War/USA

Awards: *Academy Awards – Best Director, Best Editing, Best Picture, Best Sound; BAFTA – Best Director, Best Editing; Golden Globes – Best Director, Best Drama, Best Supporting Actor (Tom Berenger)*

Two sergeants vie for a soldier's soul in the sordid battles of Vietnam.

The first wave took a long time to break. It pitched and broiled, swirling and swelling before finally it broke, unleashing a torrent that swept over the waiting landscape. It was the late 70s, and a tidal wave of Vietnam movies hit American cinemas – *Go Tell The Spartans*, *The Boys In Company C*, *The Deer Hunter*, *Coming Home* (all released in '78) and *Apocalypse Now* (released in '79). For the waiting nation, the waters were cleansing, washing away guilt rather than grime; it had taken America a decade since the war's outbreak to tackle Vietnam, and the string of movies did not seek to explain historical actions or chronicle events (as had the traditional World War II movie). Rather, these films sought to relate the hell of combat; to capture the anti-war fervour that altered the face of American politics and culture; to look at the post-war reality for the veteran; and to define the surreal, psychedelic experience that was peculiar to this conflict.

These five films defined the idiosyncratic nature of the Vietnam war movie, and while they prompted a flurry of reactionary, 'back to 'Nam' films – fostered by Conservative America and led by John Rambo (plus his M60, of course) – when a second wave of movies invaded cinemas during the mid-to-late 80s, they followed the same path. With this second wave came a squad of combat films; Oliver Stone's *Platoon* (1986) was on point, leading a company that comprised *Full Metal Jacket* and *Hamburger Hill* (all three arrived within nine months), while Brian De Palma's *Casualties Of War* brought up the rear in '89. As with their combat movie predecessors *Spartans* and *Company C*, all these stories presented a bleak, nihilistic, vision of man preparing for and fighting in war, and yet for Stone and De Palma, in particular, there was an even deeper, more esoteric remit.

For Stone, casting his vision of Vietnam from the two tours and four platoons in which he served, this internal struggle was externalised via the likes of Kevin Dillon's brutal Bunny, who lets his fear warp his mind, and most notably through the two sergeants, Tom Berenger's Barnes and Willem Defoe's Elias. Admittedly, Stone's screenplay seeks no subtlety in presenting the forces battling for PFC Taylor's soul as his idealism is gradually extinguished – Barnes vs Elias; cerebral vs visceral; life vs death – but it remains true to the director's passion for the epic. Barnes and Elias are like battling Titans cast from the Homeric world to wreak carnage in the jungle of Vietnam.

'Idealism in war is insane,' says Stone on his 'Ultimate Edition's' commentary, 'yet we love it in our war drama.' And, true to form, he sews the badge of the idealist onto Taylor's epaulettes, recounting a semi-autobiographical tale rife with observation; Stone's soldiers are like ghosts shifting through the landscape, revealing and concealing themes rather than being driven on by plot.

Platoon recounts the dehumanising nature of war with the incident in the village, recalling the real-life tragedy of My Lai. One thing is certain, as the waves broke across America, the nation saw how its young men drowned in the sea of horror that washed across the Vietnam War. By the time *Casualties* brought the 1980s' cycle to a close, what a nation couldn't conquer with napalm, it finally began to understand via the camera. ★★★★ **WL**

Movie Trivia: Platoon

Keanu Reeves was offered the role as Chris, but refused because the film was too violent. The trip to the Philippines to film was Johnny Depp's first time off American soil, aged 22.

PLAY IT AGAIN, SAM (1972)

Starring: *Woody Allen (Allan Felix), Diane Keaton (Linda Christie), Tony Roberts (Dick Christie), Jerry Lacy Humphrey Bogart), Susan Anspach (Nancy Felix), Jennifer Salt (Sharon), Mari Fletcher (Fantasy Sharon)*
Director: *Herbert Ross*
Screenwriter: *Woody Allen based on his own play*
15/85 mins./Comedy/USA

Despondent after being abandoned by his wife, Nancy, film critic Allan Felix takes the advice of his movie hero, Humphrey Bogart and reluctantly allows himself to be cheered up by his best friend Dick Christie, only to find himself falling for Dick's wife, Linda.

Woody Allen stumbled across his trademark screen persona in this engaging adaptation of the 1969 stage play that was inspired by his impending divorce from second wife, Louise Lasser. However, he would veer off into the future (*Sleeper*) and the Napoleonic past (*Love and Death*) before returning to this archetypical New York nebbish in *Annie Hall*. Ironically, an east coast union strike forced Herbert Ross to shoot the picture in San Francisco, but Allen Felix is essentially the template for Woody's Manhattan Man.

Perhaps just as significantly, the Broadway production also brought Allen into contact with Diane Keaton. He had only agreed to a casting call to appease producer David Merrick, but was instantly struck by the kooky Californian and began to rework the scenario to her advantage. Indeed, so intense was their personal and professional attraction that, part way through the 453-performance run, Keaton briefly moved into Allen's apartment, where he was in the process of reworking the screenplay for *Take the Money and Run*. However, he would also make *Bananas* before a deal could be struck to transfer *Sam* to the screen.

Woody was initially content for either Dustin Hoffman or Richard Benjamin to play Allan, as he still saw himself primarily as a comedian rather than a filmmaker. But the success of *Bananas* persuaded Paramount to stick with the original stage trio of Allen, Keaton and Tony Roberts – although this was to be the last time that Allen would allow another director to handle one of his screenplays.

Allen opened out the play by adding a couple of party and disco sequences and some self-lacerating reveries involving his ex-wife. However, the storyline retained its original three-act structure and this staginess is occasionally intrusive. But Allen was still able to imbue the action with a passion for cinema, not only through the memorabilia in Felix's apartment and Bogie's ethereal appearances, but also through the clips from *Casablanca* that reinforced the central celebration of movies as an escape from the pressures of daily life. ★★★★ **DP**

⦿ PLAY MISTY FOR ME (1971)

Starring: *Clint Eastwood (David 'Dave' Garver), Jessica Walter (Evelyn Draper), Donna Mills (Tobie Williams), John Larch (Sgt McCallum), Jack Ging (Frank Dewan), Irene Hervey (Madge Brenner)*
Director: *Clint Eastwood*
Screenwriters: *Jo Heims, Dean Riesner, based on a story by Heims*
18/97 mins./Thriller/USA

Late night disc jockey Dave Garver has a one-night stand with a fan, Evelyn Draper, while his girlfriend is out of town. When Evelyn wants to take the relationship further, Dave rejects her, whereupon she starts stalking and menacing him.

Clint Eastwood switched career horses with this thoughtful suspense film, not only making his debut as a director but also playing a role in direct contrast with his tough, laconic, sexless cowboy image.

Here, Eastwood's disc jockey is constantly purring suavely at his listeners, is a major lech who passes off his promiscuity by telling his official girlfriend he hasn't exactly been 'monk of the month' while she was away and – at the climax – takes the stereotypical 'menaced heroine' role as a scorned woman comes after him with a knife.

This 1971 movie, with paisley shirts and casual sex everywhere, makes a fascinating comparison with the 1980s blockbuster *Fatal Attraction*, which poached its basic idea from *Misty* but then botched it by missing out on the moral ambiguities and character depths that make it more than just an upmarket slasher. While Michael Douglas is bullied into infidelity, Eastwood is fully culpable; and whereas Glenn Close is depicted as a simple psychopath, the alarming Jessica Walter – whose career should have soared after this but didn't – is as vulnerable as she is frightening as the fan who constantly calls up the station with requests for Errol Garner's standard 'Misty' and eventually reaches into the cutlery drawer for a sharp solution to her neuroses. The final confrontation is edge-of-the-seat thriller stuff, with a painful bit of blade-grasping and melodramatic waves crashing at the foot of the cliff. Don Siegel, Eastwood's director on *Dirty Harry* and *Coogan's Bluff*, has a cameo as a bartender. ★★★★ **KN**

⦿ THE PLAYER (1992)

Starring: *Tim Robbins (Griffin Mill), Greta Scacchi (June Gudmundsdottir), Fred Ward (Walter Stuckel), Whoopi Goldberg (Det. Susan Avery), Peter Gallagher (Larry Levy)*
Director: *Robert Altman*
Screenwriter: *Michael Tolkin, based on his novel*
15/119 mins./Satire/Comedy/Thriller/USA

Awards: *BAFTA – Best Director, Best Adapted Screenplay; Golden Globes – Best Comedy/Musical, Best Actor*

High-flying studio exec Griffin Mill's career is on a slide. He's receiving postcard death threats, a feminist detective suspects him of murder and he needs to find a box office hit . . .

Few Hollywood satires have come close to matching the brilliance of *The Player*. Robert Altman's modern classic not only pokes fun at the moviemaking world, but also delivers a taut, skilfully crafted thriller – complete with 65 cameo appearances (Bruce Willis, Julia Roberts, Susan Sarandon, John Cusack, Anjelica Huston et al – all of whom appeared for nothing).

The film that really put Robbins' name on the map, he's superb here as beleaguered studio exec Griffin Mill, troubled with both a crumbling career and death threats from a mysterious screenwriter. After a slow build-up (which includes the terrific eight-minute, single-take opening shot), the fun really starts when Mill resorts to desperate measures to save both his career and his life, helped along by the crazed double act of Dean Stockwell and Grant, and Whoopi Goldberg's wackily eccentric cop. There's also the delicious delight of the realisation of the movie within a movie – *Habeas Corpus* – which, it is rumoured some moron film exec actually tried to option to in real life. Clearly he wasn't paying attention. ★★★★★ **CW**

⦿ PLAYTIME (1967)

Starring: *Jacques Tati (Monsieur Hulot), Barbar Dennek (Young Tourist), Rita Maiden (Mr. Schultz's Companion), Valerie Camile (Monsieur Luce's secretary)*
Director: *Jacques Tati*
Screenwriters: *Jacques Tati, Jacques Lagrange, Art Buchwald (English dialogue)*
U/114 mins./Comedy/France

The accident-prone M. Hulot visits a modern design show in Paris and then attends the opening of the ultra-chic Royal Crown restaurant.

In 1967, this 70mm masterpiece – which ran half an hour longer than the version that has survived – was disliked by audiences who missed the warmth and charm of *Les Vacances de M. Hulot*. Though it has precedents in the anti-mechanisation slapstick of Rene Clair's *A Nous la Liberte* and Charlie Chaplin's *Modern Times*, the vision of a science-fictionally modernist, dehumanised world of glass and chrome infected by chaos-spreading human beings feels like a demented crossbreed of Jerry Lewis's The Bellboy and Jean-Luc Godard's Alphaville.

Tati's tactic of relying on medium and long shots, observing the credible but comical behaviour of people struggling through a hostile man-made environment, keeps the audience at one remove from the action. In the opening sequence, set at Charles de Gaulle airport, a figure in hat and raincoat we take to be Hulot turns out to be someone else. The supposed star vanishes often into the crowd, mistaken for other people as other people are taken for him, getting centre screen only when he makes a particularly disastrous gesture. It uses the design show to present amusingly absurd inventions, like eyeglasses which can be raised to allow make-up application or a sound-suppressing door which slams silently (and frustrates an angry man who wants to make a point of slamming a door), but the film really starts cooking at the crowded, all-night restaurant opening where stylish architectural features and shoddy workmanship give the staff and patrons a busy, destructive time.

It's rarely belly-laugh funny, but rewards multiple viewings with its wealth of vivid background business, its fully realised modern world (a huge city set to rival *Blade Runner*) and a still-pertinent humanist attitude. ★★★★ **KN**

⦿ PLEASANTVILLE (1998)

Starring: *Tobey Maguire (David), Reese Witherspoon (Jennifer), William H. Macy (George Parker), Joan Allen (Betty Parker), Jeff Daniels (Mr Johnson)*
Director: *Gary Ross*
Screenwriter: *Gary Ross*
12/119 mins./Fantasy/Comedy/Drama/USA

Two '90s teenagers catapulted into a 50s sitcom world have a dramatic effect on their new surroundings.

Any plot involving people trapped inside a wholesome TV sitcom will inevitably invite comparisons to *The Truman Show*. However, the small-screen setting is where all similarity ends, for *Pleasantville*, while not quite scaling the outstanding heights of Truman Burbank's moment in the limelight, is smart and funny enough to be taken on its own terms.

Maguire and Witherspoon are David and Jen, the adolescents in question, poles apart despite being twins. She is a sluttish, chain-smoking flirt. He is a clean-cut borderline geek who fancies himself as world authority on

Pleasantville, a black-and-white 50s sitcom in which dinner is never late, toilets don't exist and marital beds are strictly single. The pair are forced to bond, however, when a new remote control zaps them into the telly right in the middle of a *Pleasantville* episode, and into the roles of squeaky-clean teens Bud and Mary Sue. Initially perturbed by their new-found 'pastiness', to say nothing of their saccharine sitcom parents (Allen and Macy), their 90s attitudes soon bring profound changes to the sleepy 'burb, gradually transforming the monochromatic residents into gloriously oversaturated Technicolor.

Director Gary Ross, whose screenplays for *Big* and *Dave* both won him Oscar nominations, makes a highly accomplished, beautiful-looking directorial debut. He also draws excellent performances from his entire cast, especially Allen, Macy, Daniels (as a diner owner/frustrated artist), and the late, lamented J.T. Walsh (as the town's bigoted mayor).

There are also many comic highlights (the near-perfect basketball team, Allen's pyrotechnic sexual awakening, a fire brigade trained only to rescue cats stuck up trees, the suggestion that back home the TV viewing public is watching every moment), that when the tone shifts towards the dramatic, and the town's elders begin denouncing the 'coloured' interlopers, it threatens to over-dramatise its own fantastic conceit. The lengthy, sentimental interlude which follows sits uneasily with the rest of the picture, but Ross' directorial control is so assured he manages to rein the action back in for a positively exhilarating finale. ★★★★ **CW**

THE PLEDGE (2001)

Starring: *Jack Nicholson (Jerry Black), Robin Wright Penn (Lori), Sam Shepard (Eric Pollack), Aaron Eckhart (Stan Krolak), Vanessa Redgrave (Annalis Hansen), Benicio Del Toro (Toby Jay Wadenah), Mickey Rourke (Jim Olstad), Harry Dean Stanton (Floyd Cage), Helen Mirren (Doctor)*
Director: *Sean Penn*
Screenwriters: *Jerzy Kromolowski, Mary Olson-Kromolowski, based on the novel* Das Versprechen *by Friedrich Durrenmatt*
15/118 mins./Drama/Thriller/USA

A child rape and murder obsesses retired cop Jerry Black, who is unable to let go of the case. When he makes a promise to track down the killer, his determination has unforeseen consequences.

Who would have thought that Sean Penn, the stoner in 1982's *Fast Times At Ridgemont High*, would turn out to be not only one of the most consistently interesting actors of his generation, but one of its more accomplished directors as well? It seems there's hope for Ryan Phillippe yet.

Slightly reminiscent of Paul Schrader's underrated *Affliction* (1997), *The Pledge* – Penn's third film as director – is a bleak, morally ambiguous yarn. It features a standout turn from Jack Nicholson (who also collaborated with Penn on 1995's *The Crossing Guard*), as a man whose obsession imperceptibly creeps up on him and finally poisons everything in his life to the point of madness. Sure, it isn't exactly feel-good fare, but then, not all movies can be *As Good As It Gets*.

Nicholson's Jerry Black begins as a movie cliché – the cop due for retirement who can't let go of a case, in this instance the brutal rape and murder of a little girl in the icy wastelands of Nevada – but he soon develops into something much more haunting and memorable.

A promise made to the dead girl's mother to catch the killer metastises into an overwhelming obsession, the roots of which remain mysterious. His move to an idyllic lakeside spot and meeting with battered wife Lori and her eight-year-old child seem to herald a new start, but instead signals another dreadful stage in his quest and a catastrophic willingness to do anything in his power to keep his promise.

Nicholson is on top form, delivering a subtly moving performance. His backstory, apart from a penchant for Scotch and a couple of failed marriages, is kept deliberately shallow – all that matters is the increasing danger of his determination. Penn's direction, while sometimes painfully slow, is nevertheless full of atmospheric moments, and Chris Menges' cinematography is coldly beautiful. ★★★★ **AS**

POCAHONTAS (1995)

Starring the voices of: *Irene Bedard (Pocahontas), Judy Kuhn (singing Pocahontas), Mel Gibson (John Smith), David Ogden-Stiers (Governor Ratcliffe), John Kassir (Meeko), Russell Means (Powhatan)*
Directors: *Mike Gabriel, Eric Goldberg*
Screenwriters: *Carl Binder, Chris Buck et al.*
U/81 mins./Animation/USA
Awards: *Academy Awards – Best Score, Best Original Song*

The story of Captain John Smith, who arrives in the New World, to fall in love with Pocahontas, the daughter of a tribal chief who has pledged her to their greatest warrior. The chief also suspects these new arrivals may not be a good thing.

The point where Disney's animated renaissance, after the back-to-back hits of *The Little Mermaid, Beauty And The Beast, Aladdin*, reaching a modern zenith with *The Lion King*, showed signs of flagging. By this, the 33rd of their animated fables, the formula seemed just that, formula – a famous tale, broad enough to capture unaware audiences (here the cross-cultural romance between Pocahontas and Captain Smith), lavish animation, some big, Broadway-style songs (thanks, here, to Alan Menken and Stephen Schwartz), and strait-laced characters backed up by a comedy sidekick or kicks (here, a funny raccoon, and a new addition, a wise tree).

The choices, however, lack inspiration – it's a good story, but the overtones are adult, it is, after all, a romance with racial issues. Which is a bit strong, for the necessary basic moral lesson. For all its fairy-tale beauty it lacks both literal magic and the anthropomorphised magic of talking lions. The humans are portrayed as overly elegant, and it reveals the strange way that the closer cartoons get towards our genuine shapes and sizes the less human they feel. Pocahontas, with the silky locks and curvy figure of a Californian beach babe, is like a supermodel in ink, just a bland stereotype. Disney was losing its ability to grip a child's (or adult's) imagination.

The story is clearly told, the effort is undeniable, but it doesn't stick with you like the classics. The songs barely register at all. That recent financial success was turning the yearly-animated output into a inflexible production line, and *Toy Story*'s revolution was waiting in the wings. ★★★ **IN**

POINT BLANK (1967)

Starring: *Lee Marvin (Walker), Angie Dickinson (Chris), Keenan Wynn (Yost), Carroll O'Connor (Brewster), Lloyd Bochner (Frederick Carter)*
Director: *John Boorman*
Screenwriters: *Alexander Jacobs, David Newhouse, Rafe Newhouse, based on the novel* The Hunter *by Donald E. Westlak, as Richard Stark*
18/85 mins./Action/Thriller/USA

Walker is betrayed by his wife and partner – and sets out on a deadly mission of revenge.

While 90s moviekids gush lyrical about the likes of Tarantino, Bryan Singer and Paul Thomas Anderson, back in 1967, during the 'headache' of Vietnam, an English filmmaker went to Hollywood only one-film-old and made one of the most stylised, amoral, violent exercises in cinematic showoffery of the era. Over 30 years later, John Boorman's Hollywood debut still hits like a knuckleduster to the eyeballs, one of the hardest movies of the century.

Based on Richard Stark's novel *The Hunter* this is a visceral stew of myth, pitch-black comedy, explosive action and staccato editing. Scuttling back and forth between real-time and flashback, Walker is the angel of death (both literal and symbolic) returning from the 'point blank' betrayal by his wife and partner. Revenge is order of the day, and with terrifying single-mindedness he exacts his punishment against the parched urban decay of LA. The subplot has a mysterious benefactor, Yost, guide Walker's murderous intent and quest for his stolen money through the heirachy of a criminal syndicate, simply dubbed the 'Organisation'. Walker, not a smile to be evinced from his stony face, is on an unshakeable mission both for reparation and his own humanity, ending on a note of pure ambiguity.

The film rests on two towering strengths. Marvin's formidable performance, his deadeye intractability a template for Eastwood's Harry Callahan, and Boorman's vivid transformation of LA into a Day-Glo hell of sleaze and desperation. If there is such a style as in-yer-face, it's this fierce mix of ultra-bold cinematography and inspired tricksiness, which forces its way inside your skull. ★★★★★ **IN**

POINT BREAK (1991)

Starring: *Patrick Swayze (Bodhi), Keanu Reeves (Johnny Utah), Gary Busey (Angelo Pappas), Lori Petty (Tyler Ann Endicott), John C. McGinley (Ben Harp)*
Director: *Kathryn Bigelow*
Screenwriter: *W. Peter Iliff, from a story by Iliff, Rick King*
18/122 mins./Action/Adventure/Sport/Thriller/USA

An FBI agent infiltrates a gang of surfers who are suspected of running a nice sideline in bank robberies.

Kathryn Bigelow, true to form, sets out her store from the opening sequence of *Point Break*. The title drifts across a shot of a gently rippling ocean surface before we move into crystal slo-mo shots of a lone surfer riding the Pacific waves to Mark Isham's portentous score. Intercut is Keanu Reeves in a rain-drenched T-shirt rolling around on an FBI shooting range, blowing the crap out of pop-up targets with a handgun that sounds like an anti-tank cannon in a Portaloo while our anonymous surfer performs graceful curls and dives as water washes across the screen. This, we discern, is going to be a film about violence, and violence is going to be extremely sexy.

It should be no surprise that *Point Break* was originally conceived as a project for that other proponent of the cinema du look Ridley Scott. Instead it went to Bigelow whose previous films had demonstrated an impressive visual style and a taste for balletic, explosive violence. Here, as in her vampire western *Near Dark*, two genres are crashed together: the surf movie and the heist-thriller.

Johnny Utah is the ex-star quarterback FBI agent gone undercover to bust The Ex Presidents, a band of marauding surfers who finance their summers catching waves worldwide by robbing banks. In order to do this he must infiltrate the secretive world of the surf dude, and as a consequence spend a fair amount of time in figure hugging wetsuits or the bed of his dudette tutor, Tyler. Things get gnarly however when her adrenaline-junkie pals, led by Bodhi, turn out to be the beach-bum hoods and Utah begins not only to understand, but also to yearn for their seductive, nomadic lifestyle.

Point Break rides the crest of its own ludicrous wave with loopy abandon, continually threatening to wipe-out but always just catching the curl at the last moment. The plot, such as it is, makes less sense than much of the dialogue ('Maaan, it jacks up, dropped down into the pit ... It's twenny-five straight down and maaan ... your balls are about this big' being one of the more coherent examples of screenwriter W. Peter Iliff's surf verbiage). But, like its studly young cast, Bigelow's direction is primarily something to look at – a collection of gleaming, sundrenched surfaces. Donald Peterman shoots the movie with the polished look of burnished chrome. Everything looks gorgeous, from the crashing, sapphire waves photographed through a headlight-illuminated beach football game, to a billow of orange dust past a roadside Harley. This is the California dream at the height of its potency.

It's not above poking fun at itself either. There's the playfulness of casting Reeves as a faux surf dude 'Why can't I just carry this thing and look dumb?' he enquires of his first surfboard. When a colleague takes the piss out of the whole plan by performing a frighteningly accurate Ted Logan impression, he simply looks on confused. (Not that the dumbness is always so deliberate: 'The fifty year storm ... what's that?' Reeves inquires at one point. Hmmm, it'll probably be a storm that comes every 50 years Keanu.) Or there's the fact that the clue that finally identifies them is a tanline on a surfer's arse caught while he mooned the CCTV – a fatal, ahem, crack in their plan.

But Bigelow gets serious when it comes to the octane quotient. She proffers stock action sequences, but in each case gives them enough of an off-beam twist so that the film becomes a building symphony of unique, inventive movement. There's spectacular surfing, of course, but the most striking scene is shot by moonlight (or rather an effective day-for-night filter). An incredibly tense stakeout ends with Reeves having seven bells beaten out of him by a completely naked, extremely upset, woman. A fast'n' furious car chase is followed by an even more effective, and extended, chase on foot – most directors would have staged the sequence the opposite way round. And then there are the utterly breathtaking skydiving sequences. Sure, it's all show for show's sake; you could crossfade from Reeves shaking his mane free of water in slo-mo to a sweating can of Schlitz on a bed of ice and you'd have a beer commercial. But you'd have the best-looking beer commercial ever.

Part of the uniqueness of *Point Break* is that it's one of a very few action movies directed by a woman. And, in a sense, it gives Bigelow licence to go further towards borderline laughable machismo than most male directors given that she always has the defence of a wry feminist piss-take of the whole testosterone-sodden genre. Or maybe she just likes a bloody good actioner. ★★★★ **AS**

POISON IVY (1992)

Starring: *Sara Gilbert (Sylvie Cooper), Drew Barrymore (Ivy), Tom Skerritt (Darryl Cooper), Cheryl Ladd (Georgie Cooper)*
Director: *Katt Shea*
Screenwriters: *Katt Shea, Andy Ruben, from a story by Melissa Goddard, Peter Morgan*
18/89 mins./Thriller/USA

Ivy is a flirtatious high school girl, who leaves her aunt to go and live in the enormous house of her wealthy but reclusive friend Sylvie. Soon Sylvie feels that she is being usurped and seeks to regain control.

Another home invasion psycho-drama with Drew Barrymore as Ivy, a pouting school slut with a short skirt and a stick-on thigh tattoo. Ivy hooks up with misfit rich kid Sara Gilbert (the neurotic daughter on *Roseanne*) and moves into her palatial house, charming her bedridden glamourpuss mom and making moist eyes at her stuffy dad.

At first, Gilbert comes to depend on her friend and sort of enjoys getting drunk and tattooed, but gradually she realises that Ivy appears intent on replacing her in the household and, supremely pissed-off, turns vigilante to get her life back. While most of these movies have gripping first halves taut with psychological drama and hidden menace then blow all the hatches with look-out-behind-you stab-athon climaxes, this remains ambiguous and intriguing even when the inevitable murders start.

Barrymore never becomes an outright monster, even when staging suicides and seducing older men, and the on-off relationship between her and the fantasising, mixed-up Gilbert suggests all kinds of odd things going on between the antagonists. Unlike all those other rich white homes, this family isn't perfect at the outset and Barrymore is as bewildered and terrorised by the irrational mood swings of the folks she is stuck with as they eventually are by her habit of resorting to violence to sort out her problems. ★★★ **KN**

POLICE ACADEMY (1984)

Starring: *Steve Guttenberg (Carey Mahoney), Kim Cattrall (Karen Thompson), G.W. Bailey (Thaddeus Harris), Bubba Smith (Moses Hightower), Donovan Scott (Leslie Barbara)*
Director: *Hugh Wilson*
Screenwriters: *Neal Israel, Pat Proft, Hugh Wilson, based on a story by Israel, Proft*
15/92 mins./Comedy/USA

Some young, inexperienced cops enter the Police Academy and cause some good-hearted high jinks. Hilarity ensues.

What we now know as the Police Academy Franchise™ actually came into being thanks, bizarrely, to *The Right Stuff* director Hugh Wilson, who become intrigued with the mine of stupidity that could be tapped by dumping a bunch of young, horny misfits into an institution together and seeing what happens.

Enter writer Neal Israel's assorted misfit police cadets – the one who makes all those funny noises, the REALLY BIG one, the psycho gun nut, the – oh, you know – supposedly recruited to the force by some wacky new law that's never quite explained, one clueless yet loveable chief, a psychotic drill sergeant and his buzz-cut goons, and a fitness trainer with the most gargantuan knockers you've ever seen, and it was game on.

'I remember I had a meeting with the studio,' says Wilson, 'and they basically told me, "What we've got here is a one-gag movie. But it's a damn good gag." ' Having found the perfect location – an abandoned psychiatric hospital (the irony!) in Toronto – the production began work in early 1983, eager to surf the crest of *Porky's* tidal wave of smutty slapstick.

As it turns out, it's by far the better movie, more evenly paced apart from one awkward incidence of racist Tourettes that probably remains Ron Atkinson's favourite line in a movie ever, but will not be repeated here, and consistently funny. The studio may have been constantly putting the pressure on to up the levels of nudity – hence the hastily added 'shower' and 'jugs around the bonfire' scenes of which Guttenberg is so enamoured – but for the most part, *Police Academy*'s sense of humour is naive and sweet, impossible to resist.

In part this is thanks to some cracking casting in support: human beat box Michael Winslow and Marion Ramsey's timid cadet (who had met Michael Jackson on Broadway the night before her audition, mimicked his squeaky voice in it and was given the part instantly) are particular standouts, while George Gaynes' Commandant Lassard inspires genuine affection – not least because at the time he was a classically trained actor who, as he stood there on the receiving end of the aforementioned podium blow job (from *The Devil In Miss Jones'* Georgina Spelvin, no less!), must have wondered what on Earth his career had come to.

But as infamous as that gag is – 'That one scene built my house', admits Wilson with a grin – it is unfair that the movie be remembered solely for it. There is, let us not forget: The Blue Oyster bar, the gay dance joint ripped off as recently as *American Pie 3*; the head up the horse's ass sequence (always guaranteed to bring the house down); the Podium Part Deux, and the shoe polish on the megaphone moment.

Revisit the last one especially. Not only was it introduced to the script by a crew member who had pulled the prank for real on Michael Winner (having suffered his insults for too long on a previous set), but Gaynes' reaction shot is simply priceless.

Hardly high art then, but *Police Academy* deserves far better than you looking down your nose at it. Just consider: with a huge (for its time) gross of $39 million, it was the seventh-biggest movie of 1984, just behind the likes of *Ghostbusters*, *Indiana Jones And The Temple Of Doom* and *Gremlins*. For a screwball, R-rated comedy in that esteemed company which then went on to repeat its box office domination the world over, that's a haul that commands your utmost respect. Not least when you compare it to that of its last and one can only hope final sequel, *Mission To Moscow*. Ready for it? $126,247.

It's a sad legacy for the *Friday The 13th* of the comedy genre. Sadder still that come part five, the sequels had got so bad that even Guttenberg couldn't take the humiliation any longer and bailed. That said, we can safely assume that none of them will go on to receive the prestigious Special Edition treatment that their elder, classier brother here does, which is something of a compensation.

As self-confessed fan and imitator, Bobby Farrelly, says: 'There are two movies without which I would not be doing whatever the fuck it is that I'm doing now, *Airplane* and *Police Academy*.' And whichever way you look at it, it's *Academy* that's got the better tits. And amen to that. ★★★★★ **MD**

POLICE ACADEMY 2: THEIR FIRST ASSIGNMENT (1985)

Starring: *Steve Guttenberg (Officer Carey Mahoney), Bubba Smith (Officer Moses Hightower), David Graf (Officer Eugene Tackleberry), Michael Winslow (Officer Larvell Jones), Bruce Mahler (Officer Douglas Fackler)*
Director: *Jerry Paris*
Screenwriters: *Neal Israel, Pat Proft, Barry W. Blaustein, David Sheffield*
12/97 mins./Comedy/USA

Having graduated from the police academy, Mahoney and his cronies, are issued with their first assignments as real cops. However, the city precinct they get landed with has a record crime rate, mainly due to the nutcase Zed and his gang. Meanwhile, the devious Mauser has his eye on Captain Lassard's post.

Not that they ever possessed much in the way of credibility, the second of the umpteen *Police Academy* comedies still had a good number of laughs, and we hadn't yet tired of the one-note routines of this inept squad of new recruits. It's juvenilia, straight-up goofballing, but there is a tittering innocence at work here that would wear out over another six sequels.

Thus, with its wafer thin plot of the gang fighting crime while saving their insensible Commandant Lassard (George Gaynes) from his rival, and butt of more than his fair share of the gags, Lt Mauser (Art Metrano), it goes through the motions exactly as it did before. And, just about, an equal hit rate on laughs (about fifty per cent). Mahoney (Steve Guttenberg) is smarmy and wise-talking; Hightower (Bubba Smith) is really, like, big; Michael Winslow's Jones does uncanny machine gun and car alarm impressions; while Marion Ramsey's Hook speaks really quietly and the late David Graf's Tackleberry is obsessed with armaments. It's doesn't sound much on paper, and doesn't do that much on screen, but the groups dumb togetherness grants a vacuous engagement.

And it did have a secret weapon in Bobcat Goldthwait's Zed, his was a brand new routine for the series (one that would also be worn out later) – a screeching voice that sounds like David Bowie suffering acute constipation. Sadly, for all of mankind, it turns out he's hilarious. Some things are hard to fathom. ★★★ **IN**

TOP10

James Bond Double Entendres

1 ***The World Is Not Enough***
Bond (snuggled up with Dr Christmas Jones in Istanbul): 'I thought Christmas only comes once a year.'

2 ***Diamonds Are Forever***
Bond (to Plenty O'Toole): 'Named after your father perhaps?'

3 ***Moonraker***
Minister of Defence (appalled at images of Bond and Dr Holly Goodhead in a clinch onscreen): 'My God! What's Bond doing?'
Q: 'I think he's attempting re-entry, sir.'

4 ***The Spy Who Loved Me***
M (as Bond is discovered in a clinch as his escape pod is pulled from the sea): 'Just what do you think you are doing?'
Bond: 'Just keeping the British end up, sir!'

5 ***Never Say Never Again***
Bond (about to go diving with Fatima): 'You appear tense.'
Fatima: 'You affect me, James.'
Bond: 'Oh, that's too bad. Going down, one should always be relaxed.'

6 ***Diamonds Are Forever***
Bond (to a bikini-clad woman aiming at gun at him): 'I'm afraid you caught me with more than my hands up.'

7 ***The Man With The Golden Gun***
Bond (aiming at a baddie in a compromised position): 'I'm now aiming precisely at your groin. So speak now, or forever hold your piece.'

8 ***GoldenEye***
Xenia Onatopp: 'You don't need the gun.'
Bond: 'Well, that depends on your definition of safe sex.'

9 ***Die Another Day***
Miranda Frost: 'I take it Mr Bond's been explaining his Big Bang theory?'
Jinx: 'Oh yeah. I think I got the thrust of it.'

10 ***Tomorrow Never Dies***
Moneypenny: 'You always were a cunning linguist, James.'

p

⦾ POLICE ACADEMY 3: BACK IN TRAINING

Starring: *Steve Guttenberg (Sgt Carey Mahoney), Bubba Smith (Moses Hightower), David Graf (Sgt Eugene Tackleberry), Michael Winslow (Sgt Larvell Jones), Marion Ramsey (Sgt Laverne Hooks), Leslie Easterbrook (Lt Debbie Callahan), Art Metrano (Cmdt Mauser)*
Director: *Jerry Paris*
Screenwriter: *Gene Quintano, based on characters created by Neal Isreal and Pat Proft*
PG/83 mins./Comedy/USA

When the governor declares that, due to public funding cutbacks, one of the city's two police academies will have to close, Commandants Lassard and Mauser begin to battle it out to win the governor's approval. Useless graduates Mahoney, Hightower et al return to Lassard's academy as instructors to help the cause.

Not so much a sequel, more a retread of the first film's 'glories', this is a slight improvement on *Their First Assignment*. Returning to the academy milieu of the original, *Back In Training* ups the gusto, tempers the bawdiness and – perhaps due to its constant referencing of the first flick – boasts more assurance this time round. Little of the new recruits get much screen time – the standout here is Brian Tochi's Asian exchange student Nogata, who falls for busty Lt Callaghan – and so it's left to the old hands to deliver familiar, if good-natured, schtick; Mahoney's ruse about waxing Mauser's eyebrows with duct tape, Jones makes funny sound effects with his mouth and the meek Hooks erupts with a 'Don't move, dirtbag!' Perhaps the most interesting addition here is the return of the first flick's bad guy Zed (Bobcat Goldthwaite) who, now enrolled as a cadet, has nerdy Mr Sweetchuck (his nemesis from the first flick) as his roomie. Be it badgering Sweetchuck for the loan of his soap or engaging in late night bongo sessions, Goldthwaite manages to make Zed's incessant droning funny.

There is a nice nod to the original when porn star Georgina Spelvin, who assisted Lassard from under the podium in the franchise's most memorable sequence, lures Proctor into stripping off, locks him out of her hotel room, resulting in the hapless cop stumbling into a never-ending tango contest at the gay watering hole The Blue Oyster. Efficiently marshalled by Jerry Paris (his last film, he died the same year), the film unsurprisingly never goes beyond Paris' sit-com roots and everything is delivered with a sledgehammer subtlety. But, looking at it with hindsight, considering the rest of the series, it now looks like something approaching a Golden Ages of *Police Academy*. ★★ **IF**

⦾ POLICE ACADEMY 4: CITIZENS ON PATROL (1987)

Starring: *Steve Guttenberg (Sgt Carey Mahoney), Bubba Smith (Moses Hightower), David Graf (Sgt Eugene Tackleberry), Michael Winslow (Sgt Larvell Jones), Tim Kazurinsky (Officer Sweetchuck), Sharon Stone (Claire Mattson), Marion Ramsey (Sgt Laverne Hooks), Leslie Easterbrook (Lt Debbie Callahan)*
Director: *Jim Drake*
Screenwriter: *Gene Quintano, based on characters created by Neal Isreal and Pat Proft*
PG/88 mins./Comedy/USA

Believing that the police force is overworked and understaffed, Commandant Lassard comes up with a hairbrained scheme to recruit civilians into the police with a programme called Citizens On Patrol. The Police Academy gang are chosen to train up the new lawmen.

Citizens On Patrol might well have been subtitled *When The Rot Set In*. In many respects, this is the end of an era as it marked the last appearance for series regulars Mahoney, Copeland, Zed and Sweetchuck (the latter did pop up in the ill-fated '97 TV spin off) and, without director Jerry Paris at the helm, it really feels like a franchise that has run out of steam, ideas and audience goodwill. Yet surprisingly, the film did well enough in international territories to see the franchise struggle on for three more entries.

Everybody does their requisite schtick – Tackleberry is militant, Callahan is big breasted, Hightower is, well, tall – but the only ones who emerge with anything approaching credit are Bailey's Capt. Harris who supplies a broad essay in comic exasperation as he plots against Lassard's plans and Goldthwaite-Kazurinsky's double act who instil a genuine strand of silliness into the lame pedestrian proceedings.

The film is of note for an early appearance of a pre *Basic Instinct* Sharon Stone who turns up as Mahoney's listless love interest – most of her scenes are in the deleted scenes section on the DVD, as does the groin sniffing police mutt Clarence – and for its sins, it is also the first film to unleash David Spade on the world. Yet things go from worse to Oh-My-God when the film delivers an action packed third act that takes in some bad skateboarding antics (interestingly enough, skateboard guru Tony Hawk was fired from the film's stunt team) and ends on a truly abysmal hot air balloon battle. There is more unintentional laughter here than in the rest of the sorry mess that proceeds it. ★ **IF**

⦾ POLICE ACADEMY 5: ASSIGNMENT MIAMI BEACH (1988)

Starring: *Bubba Smith (Moses Hightower), David Graf (Sgt Eugene Tackleberry), Michael Winslow (Sgt Larvell Jones), Leslie Easterbrook (Lt Debbie Callahan) Marion Ramsey (Sgt Laverne Hooks), Janet Jones (Kate), Lance Kinsey (Lt Proctor), Matt McCoy (Sgt Nick Lassard)*
Director: *Alan Myerson*
Screenwriter: *Stephen Curwick, based on characters created by Neal Isreal and Pat Proft*
PG/90 mins./Comedy/USA

Commandant Lassard and the Police Academy graduates travel to Miami for a Policeman Of The Year convention honouring Lassard. Lassard is kidnapped by a gang of diamond smugglers so the gang pull themselves away from the beach parties and set off in hot pursuit.

'Run for cover' ran the tagline for *Police Academy 3* and its hard not to take that advice when confronted with this dire mess of a sequel. Guttenberg had flown the nest (replaced here by the blander than bland Matt McCoy) and all the characters who were meant to be second fiddle comic relief were now pushed up front and centre. In an attempt to give the series new life, the franchise uprooted to sunny Miami but being away from the Academy confines makes the film feel more generic if that is possible. It also tried its hand at a more convoluted plot but you can just hear the gears grinding at every attempted set-up and gag. Lassard mistaking the smuggled diamonds in a camcorder as a retirement gift or believing that his kidnap is part of a planned police routine is the kind of laboured routine that wouldn't pass muster on an episode of *Last Of The Summer Wine*. Indeed, the whole second half of the flick bares more than a passing resemblance to the water bound kidnapping of *Police Academy 3*.

Director Myerson fails to inject any zip or fun into the proceedings and the only smile inducing moments involve Tackleberry's glee at playing with some heavy duty weaponry but it's not enough to sustain a whole movie. Tired, lamentable stuff. ★ **WT**

⦾ POLICE ACADEMY 6: CITY UNDER SIEGE (1989)

Starring: *Bubba Smith (Moses Hightower), David Graf (Sgt Eugene Tackleberry), Michael Winslow (Sgt Larvell Jones), Leslie Easterbrook (Lt Debbie Callahan) Marion Ramsey (Sgt Laverne Hooks), Janet Jones (Kate), Lance Kinsey (Lt Proctor), Matt McCoy (Sgt. Nick Lassard), Kenneth Mars (The Mayor)*
Director: *Peter Bonerz*
Screenwriter: *Stephen Curwick based on characters created by Neal Isreal and Pat Proft*
PG/84 mins./Comedy/USA

A crime wave hits the city forcing the local businesses into a panic and the the mayor to put the city on a state of red alert. It is up to the Police Academy grads to uncover the gang and increase the peace on the streets.

It is somehow fitting that someone with such a snigger-inducing surname as Bonerz should end up directing a *Police Academy* movie. It is also not surprising that this is funnier than almost anything contained within the body of the movie. A member of the cult comedy troupe The Committee, Bonerz finds some 'clever' spins on the tired material – at one point during a high speed, as the gang rapidly approach a fresh fruit cart, one of the characters shouts 'Look out for Gene and Roger's fruit stand!', a reference to film critics Siskel and Ebert – but this is really just a photocopy of elements from all the previous episodes.

Much of the story's groundwork is laid at the feat of Hightower, surely one of cinema's most one-dimensional characters, and the rest of the troupe play out their regular traits with little feeling for anything else – rarely has so much verbal or physical comedy been so obvious and ill conceived. Kenneth Mars plays it relatively straight as the mayor who turns out to be the criminal mastermind (it's obvious from frame one), the puppetmaster for three bumbling crooks who are as inept and unfunny as the cops.

If you were being generous, you might say that there is a nice feeling around a likeable ensemble going their familiar paces and that Michael Winslow's Jones' sound effects schtick, especially when he is doing his dubbed Bruce Lee routine, can raise a smile. But really, this is probably worse than you'd expect, even from a sequel to a sequel to a sequel to a sequel to a sequel. ★ **IF**

POLICE ACADEMY MISSION TO MOSCOW (1994)

Starring: *George Gaines (Cmdt Eric Lassard), Michael Winslow (Sgt Larvell Jones), David Graf (Sgt Eugene Tackleberry), Leslie Easterbrook (Lt Debbie Callahan) G.W. Bailey (Capt. Thaddeus Harris), Christopher Lee (Cmdt Alexandrei Nikolaivich Rakov), Ron Perlman (Konstantine Konali), Claire Forlani (Katrina)*
Director: *Alan Metter*
Screenwriters: *Randolph Davis, Michele S. Chodos, based on the characters Neal Israel and Pat Proft*
PG/83 mins./Comedy/USA

Russian gangster Constantine Konali is laundering money under the guise of a legitimate business, a video game called 'The Game'. To help bang Konali to rights, Commandant Rakov sends for the US help. Enter Lassard and his band of bumbling goons.

And so it came to pass. The point in the series where the numeral gets dropped off the title just to stop reminding people how tired and desperate things have become. An attempt to resurrect the franchise five years after *City Under Siege*, Number 7 in the series tried to uproot the same old characters, gags and situations, place them in a completely different environment – Russia – and hope the culture clash would spin comedy gold. Not surprisingly, it didn't.

Astonishingly, the sorry farrago of a script managed to attract the likes of Ron Perlman and Christopher Lee (who suffers the indignity of having to kiss Lassard) who ham about, presumably kept going by the pay cheque. Not only is there more plot this time to keep the comedy at bay, there is also a romantic strand involving cadet (Charlie Schlatter) and a Russian translator (a very young Claire Forlani) that seems to have wandered in from another movie. Elsewhere the surviving *Police Academy* gang (by now even Hooks and Hightower have left) are seeming sidelined; Lassard is dumped in the home of a Russian family in a saccharine sub-plot and left the rest of the movie to whither; Bailey's Captain Harris, devoid of a comedy lackey to spark off, is reduced to dressing up as a ballerina; and even Winslow's sound effects wise guy is given nothing to do.

After the awful *Mission To Moscow*, the franchise did spin off into a little seen TV series (there had previously been 2 cartoon series) and the Academy has remained shut ever since. Thank heavens for small mercies. ★ **IF**

POLICE STORY (GING CHAAT GOO SI) (1985)

Starring: *Jackie Chan (Chan Ka Kui), Brigitte Lin (Selina Fong), Maggie Cheung (May), Yuen Cho (Chu Tao), Bill Tung (Inpsector Wong)*
Director: *Jackie Chang*
Screenwriter: *Edward Tang*
15/95 mins./Martial Arts/Comedy/Thriller/Hong Kong

Sergeant Ka Kui Chan of the Hong Kong police is assigned to protect Salina, a potential witness against a major drug dealer, and finds himself in trouble with several factions of assassins, corrupt cops, honest cops who believe he's a killer and his girlfriend.

The main attraction of this comedy thriller is spectacular action, as the lithe Jackie Chan beats up the villain's hordes and survives enormous property damage in a shanty town prologue and a shopping mall climax.

A typical Hong Kong action film, it alternates the light-hearted with the brutal, as if random reels of *The Pink Panther* and *Dirty Harry* were shuffled together, with – for UK audiences – the added bizarre frill that 1985 Hong Kong had the same legal system as Britain and so the cops and lawyers involved in al manner of extreme behaviour wear familiar British-style bobby-on-the-beat uniforms and periwigs.

By 1985, Jackie Chan had made a reputation in more traditional, period-set martial arts films (*Drunken Master*, *Project A*) and failed in a first attempt to become an American-based movie star (*The Protector*, *The Big Brawl*). He achieved his biggest Far East success to date by starring in and directing this hybrid of his acrobatic style with the steroided Stallone-Schwarzenegger devastation then booming in Hollywood (the climax is modelled on the finish of *Commando*). Brigitte Lin and Maggie Cheung, action heroines in their own right, are given purely decorative roles here.

From his cameo appearances in the *Cannonball Run* films, Chan picked up the habit of running outtakes under the end credits, often showing him fouling up stunts deftly executed in the movie proper. A debatable number of sequels followed, depending on which export titles are applied to which films and, with the similarly toned US-made *Rush Hour* films, Chan finally became an international superstar. ★★★ **KN**

POLTERGEIST (1982)

Starring: *JoBeth Williams (Diane Freeling), Craig T. Nelson (Steve Freeling), Beatrice Straight (Dr Lesh), Dominque Dunne (Dana Freeling), Oliver Robins (Robbie Freeling), Heather O' Rourke (Carol Anne Freeling)*
Director: *Tobe Hooper*
Screenwriters: *Steven Spielberg, Michael Grais, Mark Victor, based on a story by Steven Spielberg*
15/109 mins./Thriller/USA
Awards: *BAFTA – Best Special Visual Effects*

While living in an average family house in a pleasant neighbourhood, the youngest daughter of the Freeling family, Carol Anne, seems to be connecting with the supernatural through a dead channel on the televison.

Horror fans – hardcore horror fans – don't rate *Poltergeist*. It lacks the gore of Argento,the intensity of Romero and the guts of Cronenberg to galvanise the Fangoria crowd. Yet the bloodlust of fanboys misses the point by a mile. A kind of scarefest starter pack for younger audiences – My First Horror Film – *Poltergeist* represents the finest example of cinema as fairground ghost train, a brilliantly orchestrated collection of jumps and jolts, childhood phobias that will scare you witless for its 114 minute duration but not trouble anyone over six once the house lights have come up.

Akin to many fairy tales, *Poltergeist* concerns itself with a child trying to find her way back to the comforts of home (see *The Wizard Of Oz* (1939)) yet plays out its yarn from the point of view of the adults. However, there is a more cynical encapsulation than the modern day fable; as spectres emanate from the TV set to kidnap blonde moppet Carol Anne (a captivating Heather O'Rourke, who Spielberg cast after spotting her dining in the MGM commissary), perhaps *Poltergeist* is best described as a black comedy about the dangers of kids catching too much tube. Even the afterlife looks like the blue flicker of late night TV.

Most of the attention surrounding the film on release was directed towards the question of authorship: while Tobe Hooper, the hand behind *The Texas Chain Saw Massacre* (1974) was nominally credited as director, *Poltergeist* (the word is German for 'noisy ghosts') had co-writer/executive producer Steven Spielberg's imprint indelibly stamped all over it: suburban milieu (check), roller-coaster plotting (check), deftly placed comic relief (check), a kidnapped child as a catalyst for the plot (check), light as a major player in the story, a source of both mystery and sanctity (check).

Spielberg created the storyboards, hired the cast, approved camera movements, and supervised the editing and visual effects. In fact, the only sequence that displays any hint of Hooper's sensibilities is the climax, in which a posse of rotting cadavers erupt from a muddy swimming pool – apparently, this is Spielberg's least favourite scene in the whole film. (After *Poltergeist* was released Spielberg, took out a full page ad in the trade papers, thanking Hooper for what he described as a 'unique, creative relationship'.)

If Spielberg's storyline owed much to *Twilight Zone* episode 'Little Girl Lost' (as well as being a twisted version of *Close Encounters*), the detail was ripped straight from the fabric of his life; the crack in the bedroom wall, the maniacal grinning doll, the ominous oak tree all have one foot in Spielberg's past. Unlike many haunted house flicks, *Poltergeist* locates its horrors in a warm, inviting environ, a haven of radio-controlled cars, *Star Wars* bedspreads, Sunday football and twee burial services for dead pets. The set-up is archetypal rather than stereotypical, tapping into collective childhood memories that brim with cognition.

The Freeling family (the moniker more than likely a reference to legendary animator Fritz Freleng) may be mere spectators to all the paranormal palaver, yet there are enough shades to make you care. Early on, the spectral activity is treated with the sense of playfulness – the room full of swirling playthings – and awe that Spielberg usually reserves for extraterrestrials. After the relatively benign beginning, however, the chill factor is ratcheted up as a panoply of shock tactics are unleashed at a breakneck pace – the ominous tree turns kidnapper; psychic investigator, played by Spielberg's assistant Marty Cassella, pulls the flesh from his own face (Spielberg, incidentally, supplied the hands); a demonic head erupts from the closet; Diane is thrown all over the walls and ceilings (a risqué notion of the ghost sexually assaulting Diane – ILM even created a rig that pulled Jobeth Williams' clothes off – was discarded). Oh yes, and then, the house implodes.

There are inconsistencies – why does a brand new house have the standard creaking door? – but the pace is so compelling that it is impossible to carp. Yet, for all the grand guignol on offer, the film is much more unnerving in its smaller moments: kitchen chairs rearrange themselves into illogical formations, a slab of steak inches its way across a kitchen surface and, it has to be said, Carol Anne's infamous 'They're here' far outstrips 'I see dead people' as dialogue to freeze the blood.

In the summer of 1982, *Poltergeist* was virtually buried alive by Spielberg's other suburban set fantasy, *E.T. The Extra Terrestrial*. ★★★★
IF

⑩ PORKY'S (1982)

Starring: *Dan Monahan (Pee Wee), Mark Herrier (Billy), Wyatt Knight (Tommy), Roger Wilson (Mickey), Cyril O'Reilly (Tim), Tony Ganios (Meat), Kaki Hunter (Wendy), Kim Cattrall (Honeywell)*
Director: Bob Clark
Screenwriter: Bob Clark
18/94 mins./Comedy/Canada

A group of Florida high scholars seek revenge on a nightclub owner and his sheriff brother.

The more distinguished Canadian film historians are no doubt apt to shudder violently when informed that, 20 years after its original release, *Porky's* is still the most successful Canadian film ever made. But then the venerable Canuck critics would do well to remember that, when you were 14, seeing a gargantuan female gym teacher doggedly playing tug of war with an anguished high-schooler's penis was the height of comedic sophistication, Woody Allen for adolescents. And as for 'has anyone seen Mike Hunt?' – quite frankly we cacked ourselves.

It is of course utterly impossible to defend *Porky's* as anything other than the lowest, knuckles-dragging-on-the-ground species of comedy; in evolutionary terms it hasn't discovered fire yet. But debut director Bob Clark's genius was to identify exactly what was funny to your average teenage boy (and it was a movie with a less than overwhelming female following) and provide it, lots of it. While a few years later John Hughes would add a touchy-feely dose of adolescent angst to the teen comedy genre, and with it court an audience broadly divided down the middle gender-wise, Clark's movie exuded an exuberant crudity aimed specifically at young boys.

It was an international smash-hit and fathered a stream of imitators along the lines of *Revenge Of The Nerds* (1984) and provided the impetus for the almost endless series of Israeli *Lemon Popsicle* flicks. And its influence endures to this day. When in the late 90s and early 00s cinema rediscovered the teen movie with the likes of *American Pie*, *Road Trip* and, tragically, *Dude, Where's My Car?*, it wasn't Hughes' deftly-observed comedy dramas which provided the nostalgic memories; and inspiration – it was the raucous raunchiness of *Porky's*. Essentially a series of juvenile pranks stitched together with the story of Pee Wee Morris' (a lusty and likeable Monahan) endlessly frustrated attempts to shed his virginity, *Porky's* is at heart a story about male friendship and the universal experience of hanging around in a gang. All the archetypes are present and correct; the local bigot, the slightly sophisticated older guys and in Pee Wee, the mildly embarrassing erotomaniac.

It's also a film that's not quite as straightforward as it might seem. *Road Trip* star Breckin Meyer may have felt, as he told *Empire*, that *Porky's* was 'A real, wow boobies, moment for me' but, in fact, it's the male anatomy that the movie's obsessed with. At the risk of indulging in a Tarantinoesque *Top Gun* deconstruction, *Porky's* is much more interested in knobs than it is in knockers. From Pee Wee's horrified observation that his morning hard-on appears to be shrinking through the infamous visit to Miss Cherry Forever and her pitiless assessment of their manhoods ('You'd better strap a board across his ass or he's liable to fall in,' she remarks of the hapless Pee Wee) to that girls' shower scene; it's a movie obsessed with male genitals with bloke nudity outstripping visible female flesh by a factor of at least two to one. Clark perceptively realised that younger male teenagers are at least as obsessed with their own bodies as they are with girls. Hordes of anxious adolescents recognised themselves in both Pee Wee's frustration and desperate sexual braggadocio.

It's also an unusual historical hybrid. The behaviour of the kids of Angel Beach would in fact be utterly intolerable by 1950s standards, leading if not to the electric chair, to reform school. But George Lucas had proved that audiences had an appetite for an airbrushed nostalgia with *American Graffiti* in 1973. Bob Clark takes the liberated sexual mores of the pre-AIDS 80s and rivets them to the social innocence of a fantasised 50s, which, in point of fact, probably never existed. It's a device which has many advantages, not least of avoiding the charge of crude sexism by implausibly painting the girls as being as up for it as the boys (during the cock-through-the-girls'-shower-sequence, for instance, the girls are portrayed as amused and delighted rather than shocked or threatened).

Clark even adds a couple of anti-bigotry subplots into the mix -Jewish student Brian Schwartz is taunted by a racist who calls him a 'kite'. 'It's "kike",' he coolly responds, 'you're too stupid to even be a good bigot.' And then there's the kids' war of attrition with redneck Porky, whose Confederate flag-bedecked roadhouse is triumphally destroyed. *Porky's* is a movie without a mean bone in its body; a movie that punishes intolerance and bigotry and rewards good humour, in Pee Wee's case with his final deflowering in the back of a school bus. And for a generation for whom it was a key video rental – two sequels failed to rekindle the magic – a part of our hearts, and indeed other vital organs will always belong to the testosterone drenched halls of Angel Beach High. ★★★★ **AS**

◎ THE PORTRAIT OF A LADY (1996)

Starring: *Nicole Kidman (Isabel Archer), John Malkovich (Gilbert Osmond), Barbara Hershey (Madame Serena Merle), Mary-Louise Parker (Henrietta Stackpole), Viggo Mortensen (Caspar Goodwood)*
Director: *Jane Campion*
Screenwriter: *Laura Jones based on the novel by Henry James*
12/142 mins./Drama/UK-USA

An American heiress, Isabel Archer, comes to Europe to discover herself. There she has to contend with various suitors including her sickly cousin, a fellow American Caspar Goodwood, and the cold, manipulator Gilbert Osmond, a collector of artistic objects.

Henry James, whose studied books on human nature don't necessarily square themselves with the visual needs of cinema, has the odious villain of his 1881 novel, *The Portrait Of A Lady*, Gilbert Osmond (played with typical archness by John Malkovich) symbolically a collector of arts. He likes the glistening surface, not human interiors. He might enjoy this movie, it's a surface as still as a statue, an artistic object frozen in its immaculate detail and deadened performances. A stultifying dull film, caught under the impression that art rests in some kind of noble repose, Henry James' novel is concerned with the forces that fracture such surfaces, Jane Campion's film is a porcelain cliché.

Nicole Kidman you would think well cast, her pale skin has the regal hue of an heiress, she is naturally elegant, a creature from a different era. But there is no role developed here – Isabel is as remote and icy as the Arctic, pained when is supposed to be free spirited. The film is stifling and airless, it feels like a painting come alive, and none of the actors can break its surface to breath, Even the reptilian cruelty of Malkovich is merely a damped down version of *Dangerous Liasions'* Valmont. It becomes indifferent as to how or when Isabel will escape his seductive, money-grabbing manipulations.

There is beauty, undoubtedly, in the meticulousness of the design and the shapely camerawork. But Campion can only see surfaces, unable to instill the fragility of Merchant and Ivory, or the splendour of David Lean. In the story's slow waftings, back and forth, of suitors and monies, as Isabel slowly discovers some kind of 'self', her greatest battle is against the watcher succumbing to such sullen rumination and nodding off. ★★ **IN**

◎ POSEIDON (2006)

Starring: *Kurt Russell (Robert Ramsey), Josh Lucas (Dylan Johns), Emmy Rossum (Jennifer Ramsey), Richard Dreyfuss (Richard Nelson), Jacinda Barrett (Maggie James), Freddy Rodriguez (Marco Valentin), Mike Vogel (Christian), Mia Maestro (Elena Gonzalez), Andre Braugher (Captain Michael Bradford)*
Director: *Wolfgang Petersen*
Screenwriter: *Mark Protosevich, based on the novel by Paul Gallico*
12A/98 mins/Disaster/USA

On New Year's Eve, luxury liner The Poseidon is up-ended by a giant rogue wave in the mid-Atlantic. On board, a mismatched group of survivors attempt to navigate their way to safety through the treacherous interior of the stricken ship. Not all of them make it . . .

Wolfgang Petersen opens his remake/reimagining/retread of 1972's The Poseidon Adventure – the prototypical disaster movie and still, perhaps, the best-loved example of the genre – with a stunning 360-degree aerial shot of the magnificent ocean liner gliding serenely through a millpond ocean as the sunset dapples the horizon with postcard perfection. This is classic and highly effective appetite-whetting; the calm before the storm. It is also, although you might not realise it at the time, a foretaste of the superb special effects that lie in store.

Being an unapologetic disaster flick of the old school, Poseidon possesses all the other salient features that go hand-in-hand with catastrophe, destruction and death. In the necessary but clumsy expository scenes, where we are introduced to the motley crew of survivors-to-be whose fortunes we will follow once it all goes pear-shaped, the meetings are a little too cute for comfort and the dialogue is cheesier than a bathful of nacho dip. But, thankfully, Petersen keeps these encounters brief, giving us only as much information as is required for us to give a toss whether they live or die. With a core group of ten characters to introduce, this is done with admirable economy. And, as is true throughout the movie, when the hokiness reaches crisis point you have to hand it to Petersen for embracing the clichés that are so integral to the disaster movie code.

Thus, fighting for survival as they forge their way up and out of the stricken ship, their number depleted at regular intervals as tradition demands, we have the stoic loner (Lucas), the suicidal gay man (Dreyfuss), the beautiful single mother with the tousle-headed kid (Barrett, Bennett), the taciturn concerned dad, ex-fireman and ex-mayor of New York (Russell), the star-crossed young lovers (Rossum, Vogel), the mysterious stowaway (Maestro) and the cocky young waiter (Rodriguez). It's as fine a collection of archetypes as you could wish for. And once the wave hits, there's little time for stirring speeches or sentimental guff. In this, Petersen shows that he means business by killing off one of the big names – horribly and shockingly in a scene that demonstrates the price of survival – almost immediately. From the moment the protagonists band together, deciding that their odds are better outside the sealed off ballroom where the other survivors wait in vain for the rescue helicopters, the action never lets up.

It's unlikely that Petersen's film will replace its Ronald Neame-directed predecessor in the public's affections. But in sticking closely to a tried-and-tested formula, peppering proceedings with world-class special effects, relentless, nerve-shredding action and characters we actually give a damn about, Poseidon is a more than worthy addition to the canon. ★★★★ **SB**

◎ THE POSEIDON ADVENTURE (1972)

Starring: *Gene Hackman (Rev. Frank Scott), Ernest Borgnine (Det. Lt Mike Rogo), Red Buttons (James Martin), Roddy McDowell (Acres), Shelley Winters (Belle Rosen), Carol Lynley (Nonnie Parry)*
Director: *Ronald Neame*
Screenwriter: *Wendell Mayes, Stirling Silliphant*
PG/117 mins./Disaster/USA
Awards: *Academy Awards – Best Song; BAFTA – Best Actor (Gene Hackman)*

When an aged ocean liner is hit by a tidal wave, and capsized so that it floats inverted in the sea, a band of disparate passengers, led by a Reverend Frank Scott, must work their way to the surface which technically is now the bottom.

Producer Irwin Allen's quest to find the ultimate disaster scenario through the 70s may have found his apotheosis in this wholly ridiculous but memorable action adventure through an upside world. The sets is where it's happening, built in various studio tanks, director Ronald Neame and his designers have built a topsy-turvy labyrinthine, gushing with ice-cold water, an endless procession of claustrophobic death-traps which test the mettle of this kooky-varied cast. And, of course, half the fun is playing spot-the-corpse. A game that works both on the ebbing celebrity of the actor and the nature of the character – former prostitutes, ancient swimming champions, and Jewish grandparents may get a chance to shine, but you don't rate their long-term prospects.

That it is delivered without any irony (something that afflicts the modern blockbuster) adds to the traditional quality of the piece. We are supposed to take their very redolent peril at face value, as well as the inevitable group conflict, and there is a lurch, no matter how predictably, as their number is gradually winnowed down to those who will make it. Hackman, tough and righteous, gives a certain gutsy humanity to the hero-figure (nice touch that he is a reverend) giving the film a bit more crunch and vitality than the bloated ranks of *Airport* movies and that singed skyscraper in *The Towering Inferno*. Repeat viewings have given it a familiar formulaic feel, but that is because the sight of Shelley Winters, cheeks puffed with air, that gold medal still around her neck after all these years, swimming through the wreckage, is something to cherish. ★★★★ **IN**

➂ POSTCARDS FROM THE EDGE (1990)

Starring: *Meryl Streep (Suzanne Vale), Shirley MacLaine (Doris Mann), Dennis Quaid (Jack Faulkner), Gene Hackman (Lowell), Richard Dreyfuss (Doctor Frankenthal)*
Director: *Mike Nichols*
Screenwriter: *Carrie Fisher*
15/101 mins/Drama/USA

With her drug addiction fast becoming out of control, actress Suzanne Vale is forced, as a condition of her continued studio employment, to move back in with her overbearing mother, a former actress and heavy boozer herself. Someone who has contributed to her very condition.

The not so thinly disguised attempt by actress turned novelist turned screenwriter Carrie Fisher to exorcise her own personal ghosts, we have is the 'fictional' account of her coke-snorting-rehab-shake-up days, afflicted, as she was, by her troublesome relations with her mother Debbie Reynolds. It's a real cloth that muffles some of the punch of both Fisher's own script, and Mike Nichols bustling but failed attempt to capture the fussiness and fawning of Hollywood itself. Bright and clichéd, the film does indeed resemble a postcard.

Meryl Streep and Shirley MacLaine, while bearing no resemblance to one another, work hard to create the necessary spiky mother-daughter relationship. It is here where the comedy-drama is trying to capture its drama element, but the film stays as a curio, all their jagged banter feels movie-like, a mockery, rather than tragic. Elsewhere, as we drop-in behind the scenes with various cameos and in-jokes, the film finds no direction or point to make. Isn't it terrible how fame can crush the individual, it whimpers, before delivering a horribly rigged slice of sentiment for its reconciliatory finale. By then, you realise, the film has no edge at all. ★★ **IN**

➂ IL POSTINO (1994)

Starring: *Philippe Noiret (Pablo Neruda), Massimo Troisi (Mario Ruoppolo), Maria Grazia Cucinotta (Beatrice Russo), Renato Scarpa (telegrapher)*
Director: *Michael Radford*
Screenwriter: *Anna Pavigano, Michael Radford, Massimo Troisi, Furio Scarpelli, Giacomo Scarpelli*
U/108 mins./Drama/France-Italy-Belgium

Awards: *Academy Awards – Best Score; BAFTA – Best Score, Best Foreign Language Film, David Lean Award for Directing*

On a small Italian island in the 1950s, the local postman, Mario, forms an unlikely friendship with an exiled Chilean poet, Pablo Neruda. When Mario reveals his secret passion for the beautiful Beatrice, Pablo reveals how to woo her through the beauty of poetry.

For a brief spell on its original cinema release, *Il Postino* became the foreign language film it was safe to watch. And so it became the hip little movie the chattering classes got all self-congratulatory about, missing the interesting point that it had an English director in Michael Radford, and for all its beguiling, wistful romance, remains a very uncomplicated, you could say simplistic, movie brimming with old-fashioned Hollywood-styled melodrama. Despite its burst of Oscar nominations, this daft heartbreaker's most sophisticated boast is that its principals are chatting in Italian.

Not that it should be painted as a bad film, it is lovely looking and very sweet, only a one-dimensionally limited one. The central philosophy is that even the most seemingly ordinary man, here Massimo Troisi's lanky, bumbling postie flitting about this sun-dappled island resting in the Aeolian sea, is extraordinary beneath his humble exterior. All very noble, except he only wants to utilise his newly discovered eloquence of person to woo the fittest girl in the vicinity. Although, to be fair, the eye-popping Maria Grazia Cucinotta is enough to have any man reaching for his *York Notes*.

Yet, there is an enchanting quality to the relationship developed between Ruoppolo and the old poet Neruda. Phillip Noiret especially gives an easy, touching performance of a great intellect's attempt to reduce his art to a seductive tool. It's a witty aside – that poetry's greatest power could be to get girls in bed. But the film isn't quite sharp enough to do much with such irony, it concentrates on Ruoppolo's dreamy, head-in-the-clouds idol worship of this perfect creature, a solid enough performance by Troisi given tragi-romantic overtones by his own death by heart attack on the last day of shooting. A sadness that grants the film more of a legacy than, perhaps, it really deserves. ★★★ **IN**

➂ THE POSTMAN (1997)

Starring: *Kevin Costner (The Postman), Will Patton (General Bethlehem), Larenz Tate (Ford Lincoln Mercury), Olivia Williams (Abby), James Russo (Idaho)*
Director: *Kevin Costner*
Screenwriters: *Eric Roth, Brian Helgeland based on the novel by David Brin*
15/177 mins./Sci-fi/USA

In the year 2013, after civilisation has been all-but destroyed by a global war, a drifter happens upon a skeleton in a postman's uniform. He first just takes it keep warm, but unwittingly he becomes a symbolic figure of hope for the survivors and leads the battle against the evil gang known as the Holnists.

Vilified, especially on the back of the similarly themed *Waterworld*, as a piece of tedious sci-fi junk, Kevin Costner's post-apocalyptic odyssey is in truth a Western, but at three hours it tried everyone's patience, and was held as laughable in its notion of a heroic postman. For most Americans, after a spate of killing sprees by disillusioned mail-workers, 'going postal' was at best a term of derision, at worst psychopathic breakdown. And yet, despite its, frankly, punishing length (it could lose an hour without anyone noticing what had been lost) this is not without its moments. You've got to look hard, mind.

Costner was also directing for the second time, and given his first go was the glorious *Dances With Wolves*, there were good reasons to be optimistic; David Brin's novel, on which the film is based, was also held in high regard amongst knowing geeks. But even the most gaga-Costner fanatic, or Brin reader, will have trouble figuring out the resulting fusion of *Mad Max*'s roving post-apocalyptic violence, murky religious sentiment (chief baddie Will Patton is named General Bethlehem), loose picaresque structure (Costner's enigmatic Postman drifts about on horseback having random encounters), and the dubiously divine virtues of getting the post (communication as the soul of civilisation, or something). As an example of the film's entire lack of definition, in one curious and utterly pointless scene a lion is spotted alone on the salt plains. What are we to make of this? Has the world gone so mad it has been taken over by non-indigenous predators? Had he escaped from a now defunct zoo? That the beast never figures is just indicative of the wispiness of Costner's intentions.

Sticking to what he knows best, he just plays it as a gassy Western, and in isolated jabs musters some stirring horse opera. Stephen Windon's sweeping cinematography also gives it an evocative cast, a telling idea of what America might be reduced to if unshackled from government. In one superb visual snap, Costner encounters a community who swing about in cable cars from the Hoover Dam (run for no discernible reason by a sage played by rock dude Tom Petty). It leaves the impression of a great setting in search of a workable plot, something that is just not covered by a Messianic postman. Even if he is played by Lieutenant Dunbar. ★★ **IN**

PREDATOR (1987)

Starring: *Arnold Schwarzenegger (Major Alan 'Dutch' Schaeffer), Carl Weathers (Major George Dillon), Elpidia Carrillo (Anna), Bill Duke (Sergeant 'Mac' Eliot), Kevin Peter Hall (Predator)*
Director: *John McTiernan*
Screenwriters: *Jim Thomas, John Thomas*
18/106 mins./Sci-fi/Action/Thriller/USA

Dutch Schaeffer is leading a team of commandos to rescue hostages being held by Central Americans but end up hunting an alien predator.

Released a year after James Cameron had matched hardcore space marines with acid-dripping endomorphs to superlative effect in *Aliens*, another action maestro (John McTiernan, who a year later would redefine the whole genre with *Die Hard*) played a similar, although contemporary, trick in the Central American jungle.

Classically 80s trunk-necked special ops commandos versus an alien with a chameleon cloaking device, green blood, a natty line in DIY surgery (ref: *The Terminator*) and infrared laser vision. Naturally, the only lunk in the group who can match the Predator's cunning is Schwarzenegger's Major Dutch Schaeffer. While the plot is structurally tight (the horror movie pick them off one-by-one format), McTiernan delights in the ritualisation of combat. The Predator is on a hunt, not for meat, but for prowess, competition, trophies (mainly human skulls and spinal cords). The soldiers are on a hunt (for missing hostages) equally enacting their own rituals of war and death – Bill Duke's Mac habitually shaving his hairless skull, Sonny Landham's Billy, the group scout, sniffs the air suspiciously, they all lavish attention upon the strict routines and orders of the mission. There is a comparison between two ugly species – tough guys against an alien being, not benign and bubble-eyed, not some technocratic invader, but a tribal, cruel race only marginally more technically advanced than themselves.

When the Predator finally meets his match in Schaeffer, he grants him a measure of respect (and the audience a measure of sicko gawping) by removing his helmet and revealing Stan Winston's fabulously hideous creaturework beneath (a snapping crablike jaw with dreadlocks and mottled lizard skin). In Stephen Hopkins' unfairly derided sequel the idea is taken a step further when a younger Predator (on some kind of initiation) loses to flabby Danny Glover and the alien hierarchy actually congratulates the cop by handing him a prize. The action is handled with all of the director's renowned prowess and delight in gunplay and hi-tech hardware. The jungle makes an impressive battleground, shot with an overpowering almost sickly sense of poisonous life, the impression is of something oppressive, threatening and boundless.

While frequent cuts to the Predator's heat-sensitive POV spookily build the unseen-creature tension and flashy moments of silly gore and deliberately laughable one-liners place the whole thing firmly in big budget B-movie territory. It's a monster flick for certain, but not without some metaphorical meaning. Beyond the obvious, even rather gratuitous, allusions to Vietnam – cocksure grunts getting their arse-kicked by an enemy using the jungle terrain to its own advantage – and a general cynicism towards American foreign policy (the very set-up has them fiddling about in Central American politics) there is a finely worked level of satire to Predator.

Satire of the 80s male machismo of which its leading man was the figurehead. Every member of the cast boasts biceps like coconuts, a kind of steroid-sodden brotherhood that makes even Schwarzenegger's exaggerated physique seem moderate. Laden with rugged dialogue, they are set up for a fall, ludicrous notions of manhood undone by a vagina-with-tusks which our 'ugly motherfucker' feminist alien fiend alludes to.

Schwarzenegger has to get back to caveman primal. This is a quintessential melding of 80s testosterone cinema and the central tenets of sci-fi instincts to overpower the foe. The whole movie teems with a sense of knowing parody. Ostensibly though this is a creature feature, pure and simple. Similar to the *Aliens* movies, it was the character of the alien that caught the imagination. Stan Winston works hard to generate the paradoxical primitive-yet-advanced persona (jungle warriors who fly spacecraft); it is the vivid array of technology coupled with the macho hunter ethic that separates this psycho prawn from endless other bug-flicks.

The Predator – played with hulking presence by Kevin Peter Hall – worked. Just don't mention *Alien Vs Predator*. ★★★★ **IN**

PREDATOR 2 (1990)

Starring: *Danny Glover (Lt. Mike Harrigan), Gary Busey (Peter Keys), Ruben Blades (Danny Archuleta), Maria Conchita Alonso (Leona Cantrell), Bill Paxton (Jerry Lambert)*
Director: *Stephen Hopkins*
Screenwriters: *Jim Thomas, John Thomas*
18/108 mins./Sci-fi/USA

In a sweltering near-future Los Angeles, being torn about by gang wars, a Predator arrives to test its mettle. As it picks off drug-dealers and innocents alike, tough-minded cop Mike Harrigan picks up his trail.

Given Arnold Schwarzenegger and director John McTiernan had declined to return, this sequel to their macho sci-fi rumble in the jungle is surprisingly good. Aussie director Stephen Hopkins, coupled with the original writers, sensibly relocates to an urban setting, a keenly thought out Los Angeles on the not-too-distant horizon cooked by global warming and abused by furious gang warfare. In other words it's ripe for the picking by a brand new Predator hoping to earn its Predator stripes.

There's invention too in pitching not a muscle-bound alpha-lug like Arnie against the creepy chameleon skull collector, but a grizzled old cop in the out-of-shape shape of Danny Glover, clearly too old for this shit. He'll have to use his street-smarts to defeat this unforeseen alien vigilante rather than brute testosterone. There's a cute sub-plot, harkening to *Robocop*'s postmodern fillips, that the lanky, dreadlocked space-warrior is accidentally helping the police clean up the streets of Jamaican drug lord King Willie's (Calvin Lockheart) equally dreadlocked foot soldiers. In fact, Schwarzenegger's tired one-liners are not missed at all.

Tagline
He's come to town – with a few days to kill.

There's plenty of gory action, as this younger more petulant Predator (still embodied by Kevin Peter Hall) also does his zappiest with Harrigan's hot-and-bothered team, including Ruben Blades, Maria Conchita Alonso and a splendidly smarmy Bill Paxton. And while it may lack a bit of refinement, for all its big-boned antic force, the characters do get a look in, and that *Alien* in-joke at the close is a beauty. ★★★★ **IN**

PRESUMED INNOCENT (1990)

Starring: *Harrison Ford (Rusty Sabich), Brian Dennehy (Raymond Horgan), Raul Julia (Sandy Stern), Bonnie Bedelia (Barbara Sabich), Greta Scacchi (Carolyn Polhemus)*
Director: *Alan J. Pakula*
Screenwriters: *Frank Pierson, Alan J. Pakula, based on the novel by Scott Turow*
15/127 mins./Mystery/USA

Deputy district attorney Rusty Sabich finds himself a murder suspect, when his lover his found with her head stoved in by a hammer. In the midst of a sea of internal politics, he finds himself short of friends, and when the case reaches court it is up to the flamboyant Sandy Stern to defend him. But, then, is he innocent?

A well-rigged whodunit based on the bestseller by Scott Turow, that pretends to investigate the various political manipulations that haunt your average district attorney's office (would it even lead to murder?) but is in truth about the wages of sin (that Harrison Ford's sturdy family man Rusty Sabich is doing some extracurricular bonding with Greta Scacchi's fast-tracked legal wannabe).

Ford is a good call as the stern Sabich, his attitude is like his haircut, cut to the temple. His innocence, deliciously, is never fully clear, but as he's played by Ford we can't help but presume him innocent, even if he has wronged his winsomely devoted wife Bonnie Bedelia. His boss, the evidently corrupt Raymond Horgan (played with smarmy leverage by the not-seen-enough Brian Dennehy) could be playing him a deuce, being fully stacked with his own political machinations and sexual indelicacies. The finger is soon pointing in every direction, but it ends up with Sabich in the dock, amid a flurry of fingerprints, sperm samples, carpet fibres and that elusive murder weapon.

The second half is some solid courtroom action, mainly because the great Raul Julia steps centre stage to lead the defence, while Fords gets to pout with internalised anguish, and Paul Winfield's inevitably stony-faced judge presides over the knotty case. Director Alan J. Pakula is a modern master of the broad-shouldered American thriller (he's responsible for *All The President's Men*, *Sophie's Choice* and *Klute*). Here he knows well enough it is well-dressed pulp, so works on the looming camerawork and long shadows, letting his actors push to the borders of melodrama while not allowing them to throw the game. He also does a good job bouncing proceedings back and forth through a myriad of flashbacks and sideshows. The denouement should be murky to all but lucky guessers and Hercule Poirot (indeed, Agatha would adore its crimes of passion disguising themselves as politics) and when it hits it signs off an expertly handled thriller with aplomb. ★★★★ **IN**

PRETTY WOMAN (1990)

Starring: *Richard Gere (Edward Lewis), Julia Roberts (Vivian Ward), Hector Elizondo (Barney Thompson), Laura San Giacomo (Kit De Luca), Jason Alexander (Philip Stuckey)*
Director: *Garry Marshall*
Screenwriter: *J.F. Lawton*
15/119 mins./125 mins. (director's cut)/Romance/Comedy/USA
Awards: Golden Globes – *Best Musical/Comedy Actress*

When corporate millionaire Edward Lewis loses yet another girlfriend, he's screwed. Bored of fortune-hunting females and faced with a week of social engagements, he finds that a business arrangement with cheery hooker Vivian might just work to his advantage.

The *Cinderella/Pygmalion* story is an old one, but never bettered in the years since Julia Roberts' smile, legs and hair charmed the pants off us. From the moment you see her climbing out of her apartment window to avoid her landlord, you know a superstar's arrived.

While Gere was arguably already a big star after *American Gigolo* and *An Officer And A Gentleman*, the film is a platform for Roberts. Fresh from her Oscar-nominated turn for *Steel Magnolias*, she shines in megawatts. Gere, on remarkably restrained form, is an attractive foil for her charms, a trend he's followed ever since. Roberts made some pretty shoddy choices – *Mary Reilly* anyone? – until she finally pulled it together and became box office gold, with the likes of *My Best Friend's Wedding* and *Notting Hill* sealing her A-list status. Gere, on the other hand, continued to show off his leading ladies while taking a relative back seat. Even in *Chicago*, where he *tap dances* for god's sake, his skills are wholly eclipsed by the vibrancy of his co-stars.

While by and large a fluff fest lifted by some superbly gleeful scenes – Vivian's revenge shopping spree on Rodeo Drive is 'hell yeah!' territory if ever there was – the film is littered with bitter reminders that, for Vivian, the dream is a long walk from her street corner. 'I want the fairy tale,' she says, but Edward wants to set her up as a mistress. Sharking his way through companies, Edward's no less of a hustler than Vivian; the only difference being that he gets called sir and wears good suits.

Still, it's not all grim up north Hollywood. The chemistry between Gere and Roberts is dazzling: witty, but never waspish, they dance rings round each other in a manner reminiscent of 50s screwball comedies, only with extra-strength condoms and polo instead of marriage. As Edward falls for Vivian, so do we all. By the time his limousine comes a-calling for that fairy tale ending, we want it as much for him as for her. ★★★★ **KB**

PRIDE AND PREJUDICE (2005)

Starring: *Keira Knightley (Elizabeth Bennet), Matthew Macfadyen (Mr Darcy), Rosamund Pike (Jane Bennet), Donald Sutherland (Mr Bennet), Brenda Blethyn (Mrs Bennet), Kelly Reilly (Caroline Bingley)*
Director: *Joe Wright*
Screenwriter: *Deborah Moggach, based on the novel by Jane Austen*
U/127 mins./Comedy/Drama/Romance/UK/France

Awards: *BAFTA – Carl Foreman Award for the Most Promising Newcomer (Joe Wright);* Empire Awards – *Best British Film, Best Newcomer (Kelly Reilly)*

Hearing their new neighbour is a wealthy young bachelor, Mrs Bennet goes overboard contriving a match for one of her five daughters. Amiable Bingley duly falls for beautiful Jane. Unhappily, his even more eligible chum Darcy disdains the Bennets, his growing attraction to spirited Elizabeth handicapped by her ghastly relatives, scandal and misunderstandings galore . . .

On behalf of the girlie contingent, we'd just like to say, 'Yay!' Sixty-five years since the last proper *Pride And Prejudice* played at a cinema near

Highest Grossing Films Of All Time — TOP 10

1. *Titanic* (1997) **$1.835 billion**
2. *The Lord of the Rings: The Return of the King* (2003) **$1.12 billion**
3. *Harry Potter and the Sorcerer's Stone* (2001) **$968.6 million**
4. *The Lord of the Rings: The Two Towers* (2002) **$921.6 million**
5. *Star Wars Episode I: The Phantom Menace* (1999) **$922.4 million**
6. *Jurassic Park* (1993) **$919.7 million**
7. *Harry Potter and the Goblet Of Fire* (2005) **$892.2 million**
8. *Shrek 2* (2004) **$880.9 million**
9. *Harry Potter and the Chamber of Secrets* (2005) **$866.3 million**
10. *Finding Nemo* (2003) **$865 million**

your great gran, seeing Jane Austen's most popular novel energetically refitted for the big screen after umpteen TV serials is a reminder that Austen created the basic romantic comedy formula we all know and love.

Take a heroine who's intelligent, good-humoured and loyal, but also judgemental, stubborn and a bit of a smarty-pants. Make the hero seemingly unavailable, beyond the heroine's reach in status, wealth, looks or eligibility. Give her embarrassing relatives, talkative friends, rich-bitch rivals and an unwanted suitor. Create a misunderstanding that keeps the leads apart but is quickly cleared up with an honest explanation or last-chance declaration of love. Voila, you have a Meg Ryan/Sandra Bullock/J.Lo movie. Not only have all these elements been used time and again in the rom-com genre, the source story itself has recently been lifted into the modern day for *Bridget Jones* and *Bride & Prejudice*. But this is the first straight adaptation for the big screen since the delicious 1940 version starring Greer Garson and Laurence Olivier. And very welcome it is, with a fresh, realistic approach, earthy settings and romantic suspense – and in Keira Knightley's superb Lizzy, a heroine for all time.

A rethink on characterisations goes back faithfully to Austen's social comedy. Blethyn's dippy Mrs Bennet is vulgar, but not the comic grotesque often depicted. She's funny and no one can accuse her of underplaying – you certainly feel the desperation of a woman with five daughters whose prospects are grim if they don't marry some money. Similarly, Tom Hollander's cousin-come-a-wooing, the self-righteous clergyman Mr. Collins, is a suitor no fun girl would want, but he's hardly contemptible. Since no English lit-flick is complete without Judi Dench, she obligingly terrorises as arrogant Lady Catherine de Bourgh. It's Knightley, though, who really stands out. She's delightful as Austen's best-loved character – the slender, clever figure who loves a laugh, such as when she sets eyes on Darcy's palatial pile and can't control her goggle-eyed mirth, realising it could have been hers. The emphasis is not on heaving cleavage but on wit and unstudied charm, and Elizabeth Bennet has more of those than any other heroine in the English language.

A few not-terribly-serious gripes: Matthew *'Spooks'* Macfadyen's Darcy is dishy, but his blushing sad-sack manner is at times more like Droopy The Dog than a Georgian grandee, while Simon Woods' Bingley is a tad too twittish to be sombre Darcy's buddy. And the ending looks lopped off (which it was after test-screenings nixed a fountain snog-a-thon). Yes, almost everyone knows how it goes, and not every Austen adaptation has to end with a wedding, but Jane-ites really shouldn't be deprived of one kissy shot.

Still, debut feature director Joe Wright should be applauded for delivering a vividly realised Austen adap – one which confirms Knightley has graduated from the Jackie Bisset of the 00s to this decade's Julie Christie.

★★★★ AE

Movie Trivia: Pride and Prejudice

Emma Thompson did an uncredited and unpaid rewrite on the script. At the start of the film, Elizabeth is reading a novel called *First Impressions* — Austen's initial title of *Pride And Prejudice*. The uniforms for the redcoats worn in the parade sequence were purloined from the TV series *Sharpe*.

PRIMARY (1960)

Starring (as themselves): *Robert Drew, Hubert H. Humphrey, Jacqueline Kennedy, John F. Kennedy*
Director: *Robert Drew*
Screenwriter: *Robert Drew*
Unrated/60 mins/Documentary/USA

A fly-on-the-wall documentary sketch of the Wisconsin primary that proved crucial to John F. Kennedy in his bid to secure the Democratic presidential nomination over Hubert Humphrey.

A former reporter on *Life* magazine, Robert Drew developed the technique of what he called Candid Camera while producing items for TV titans Ed Sullivan and Jack Paar. However, film history credits Canadians Michel Brault and Gilles Groulx's *Les Raquetteurs* (1959) with being the first conscious example of Direct Cinema, which found echo as Cinéma Vérité in Jean Rouch and Edgar Morin's *Chronique d'un Été* in 1962.

However, there's no doubting Drew's importance to the evolution of the documentary film. Eschewing the conventional tactics of voice-over narration, formal interviews and pieces to camera by an investigative reporter or celebrity presenter, Drew aspired to producing actualities that revealed 'the logic of drama' inherent in any given situation. Consequently, he pioneered the technique of shooting in long takes with direct sound in a bid not only to capture the energy and authenticity of an event, but also to seize the viewer's senses, as well as their intellect. In order to achieve this, he and Richard Leacock opted for new lightweight 16mm Auricon cameras and magnetic tape recorders, which were locked in sync.

For the week-long shoot of *Primary*, Drew operated as Leacock's sound recordist, while D.A. Pennebaker did the same for Albert Maysles, and their unprecedented all-areas access enabled them to catch the candidates in quieter moments, as well as in the hubbub of the convention circus. The American public had never before seen its political leaders in such uncompromising close-up and there's no question that the shot of JFK passing through empty corridors before striding on to the stage before an adoring crowd did as much as the iconic images of him with his wife Jackie to secure his eventual election and establish the myth of Camelot.

However, many have cited this landmark picture with undermining the cult of deference that surrounded US Establishment figures and unleashing the wave of protest movements that would transform the nation over the ensuing decade. It certainly forced politicians to reappraise their relationship with the media and Washington only succeeded in regaining control of the news agenda during the Bush administration. ★★★★ **DP**

PRIMARY COLORS (1998)

Starring: *John Travolta (Governor Jack Stanton), Emma Thompson (Susan Stanton), Billy Bob Thornton (Richard Jemmons), Kathy Bates (Libby Holden), Adrien Lester (Henry Burton)*
Director: *Mike Nichols*
Screenwriters: *Elaine May*
PG/143 mins./Drama/USA

Awards: *BAFTA – Best Adapted Screenplay*

The presidential campaign of likeable but dubious democratic candidate Jack Stanton, through all its backstage shenanigans, leads eventually to the exposure of an affair. As seen through the eyes of Henry Burton, an idealistic young campaign manager.

The book on which Mike Nichols well-intentioned but mediocre adaptation is based was originally published under the pseudonym Anonymous, and for a while it was the talk of Washington who this mystery writer might be. The reason for all the water-cooler gossip was that Anonymous' novel was a barely fictionalised account of Bill Clinton's 1992 campaign for the presidency. It later emerged that Anonymous was, in fact, Joe Klein, a *Newsweek* journalist who had accompanied Clinton's train-ride to the White House, but by then Clinton had moved on to greater scandals and it all seemed a bit passé. The same can be said by the time John Travolta's was working his big grin impersonation of Clinton's bonhomie and gravely voice, and Emma Thompson was plying her patent dignity-under-fire, with the added extra of a vein of hard driving ambition to Susan Stanton, sorry, Hillary Clinton.

For all Nichol's attempts to sharpen his satire for some very redolent blood-letting, his film is blunted by history moving on. For all the intelligent allegory Elaine May draws from the book, a very smart examination of America's electioneering, they still cotton-wool the 'truth' suggesting for all his roguish charm Stanton is a sincere soul (the book was never sure where his convictions lay). Thus Nichols film is cuddly rather than barbed. A sweet bit of mickey-taking of a naughty but loveable president rather than a cruel satire along the lines of *The Candidate* or *Wag The Dog*, or for that matter a stirring romcom like *The American President*.

Still, there is an ensemble of good names to do plenty of that sharp talking political banter that has made *West Wing* a big hit on telly, little of which registers as comprehensible but always feels authentic, like Kathy Bates and Billy Bob Thornton and Brit actor Adrien Lester doing a flawless American accent. ★★★ **IN**

PRIME CUT (1972)

Starring: *Lee Marvin (Nick Devlin), Gene Hackman (Mary Ann), Sissy Spacek (Poppy), Angel Tompkins (Clarabelle), Gregory Walcott (Weenie)*
Director: *Michael Ritchie*
Screenwriter: *Robert Dillon*
18/82 mins./Crime/Thriller/USA

Mary Ann, a Kansas City mob boss who ranches cattle and prostitutes, refuses to settle a debt owed to a Chicago crime syndicate. Hit-man Nick Devlin travels to the mid-west to teach Mary Ann a lesson.

In the striking opening sequence of *Prime Cut*, establishing the theme of human beings treated as agricultural products to be harvested, a slobbish hillbilly meat-packer (Gregory Walcott) in rural Kansas converts a mafia messenger into link sausages that are then posted to Chicago as a message to the mob.

Michael Ritchie, best known in the early 1970s for smart satires like *The Candidate* and *Smile*, *almost* disguises this bizarre, ultra-cool effort as an ordinary gangster movie. It has a cartoonish tone typified by the stereotyping of its opposing criminal factions – smart-suited, shotgun-wielding Irishmen from Chicago who look out of place in Kansas wheatfields vs dungaree-clad Waltons lookalikes with vicious pitchforks. Lee Marvin, as in *Point Blank*, is the brutal professional criminal blankly appalled by the over-the-top evil (and, worse, lack of business ethics) incarnated by Kansas City meat magnate Mary Ann, who tucks enthusiastically into plates of tripe ('guts') and harvests girls from orphanages who are hooked on heroin and kept in cattle pens for a livestock auction that leads to them being sold into slavery in a chain of brothels.

Sissy Spacek made her first bigscreen impression as Poppy, the girl Marvin rescues to get some leverage against the villains, and has a strange, waiflike presence – which pays off in a kicker that allows her to punch out an especially hateful baddie and free the next generation of orphan girls. Marvin's stone-blasted face and underplaying contrast well with Hackman's too-quick grin and line in corn-fed, self-justifying patter. Ritchie even delivers an impressive action sequence involving combine harvesters. ★★★★ **KN**

PRINCE OF DARKNESS (1987)

Starring: *Donald Pleasence (Priest), Jameson Parker (Brian), Victor Wong (Professor Black), Lisa Bount (Catherine), Dannie Dun (Walter)*
Director: *John Carpenter*
Screenwriter: *John Carpenter*
18/101 mins./Horror/USA

The Brotherhood of Sleep, an obscure Catholic sect, has guarded its terrible secret for centuries. When a priest learns that a huge, green-slime dripping cylinder in the basement of a Los Angeles church might contain an ultimate evil, he calls in a physicist and a truckload of instruments and experts.

After an unsatisfying sojourn in the Big Budget wilderness (*Starman*, *Christine*, etc.), John Carpenter returned to the quickie horror kingdom he used to own with *Prince of Darkness*.

A long, introductory sequence, scored with one of Carpenter's eerie synthesiser themes, shows that Carpenter is still one of the sharpest directors in the business as he gets the plot going, brings on all the (many) characters and establishes an air of menace with a series of brief snippets.

However, once the film gets into the haunted church, the storyline stumbles, suggesting that Carpenter has lost the scriptwriting and plotting skills that made *Assault on Precinct 13* and *Halloween* classics. It takes a lot to make what seems to be a large hippie lava-lamp into the embodiment of ultimate evil, and the artificial scare stuff built around this macguffin only works in fits and starts.

While the investigators get listless and squabble about what they're doing, a tribe of sinister street people led by Alice Cooper gather around the church, various creepy-crawlies get upto their creepy-crawling, and several of the scientists get squirted with green goo and come back to life as satanic zombies.

Prince of Darkness is a worthy attempt to play with the ideas introduced into the genre by Nigel Kneale (*Quatermass and the Pit*, *The Stone Tape*) and has more than a few clever touches, like bad dreams transmitted from the future, but it's just too complicated and diffuse to be really scary, and never really decides what it wants to do. ★★★ **KN**

THE PRINCE OF EGYPT (1998)

Starring: the voices of: *Val Kilmer (Moses/God), Ralph Fiennes (Rameses), Michelle Pfeiffer (Tzipporah), Sandra Bullock (Miriam), Jeff Goldblum (Aaron), Danny Glover (Jethro), Patrick Stewart (Pharaoh Seti I), Helen Mirren (The Queen), Steve Martin (Hotep), Martin Short (Huy)*
Directors: *Brenda Chapman, Steve Hickner, Simon Wells*
Screenwriter: *Philip LaZebnik*
U/98 mins./Animation/Family/Musical/Drama/USA
Awards: *Academy Awards – Best Original Song ('When You Believe')*

Hebrew Moses is adopted into an Egyptian family, but as he grows older he witnesses mistreatment of the Hebrew population that inspires him to lead an exodus, under God's guidance.

You have to admire the gall of DreamWorks. For their first foray into the realm of the cartoon feature, they have turned to the not-particularly merchandise-friendly biblical book of Exodus as their source material and Moses as their hero: no comedy ditties, loveable sidekicks or theatrical villains. Yet the gamble has paid off. In spades. *The Prince Of Egypt* is epic storytelling on the grandest scale. Big imagery, big themes, big emotions – all met head-on and accomplished triumphantly within a film that is in essence a live action movie – more precisely a Steven Spielberg live action movie – writ cartoon.

For those who never went to Sunday school, the tale begins with Moses as a toddler, cast into the Nile in a basket then rescued and taken into the court of Pharaoh Seti before realising his destiny to lead his people out of the pharoah's slavery. The movie finds a strong dynamic in the relationship between Moses and older brother Rameses – we first meet the two adolescents engaged in a stunning chariot race, the camera apparently struggling to keep up with their full throttle exploits – and the divergent paths they take: Rameses rising to become prince regent, and ultimately pharoah; Moses cast into the wilderness to become a humble shepherd. Yet the latter's mission to deliver the Hebrews to the Promised Land means one thing: the two brothers will ultimately have to confront each other.

With care and detail oozing from every frame, what isn't surprising is the sheer 'sod-off-Disney' epic quality of it all. The film is awash with stunning vistas, amazing architecture and astonishing set pieces that lower the jaw at regular intervals: a breathtaking sandstorm rushing towards Moses; the burning bush – represented here by a beautiful white glow and a Voice Of God you can actually take seriously; a nightmarish hallucination of the pharoah's slaughter cleverly played out in hieroglyphics, and most powerful of all, a scene where Moses unleashes the power of God – represented by spectral visions of white light skimming over Egyptian abodes – to kill the first born in every household is rendered in startling black and white, the lack of palette and haunting shrills adding shiver-inducing frissons.

Moreover, the film creates and explores dramatic beats that most live action movies strive and strain for: Moses turning the Nile the shade of blood red; Rameses laying out his dead son – beautifully lit by a solitary shaft of light – as Moses watches with silent remorse is testimony to the film's ability to add a skein of complexity to a potentially simplistic good brother/bad brother scenario.

Boasting the likes of Michelle Pfeiffer, Sandra Bullock, Danny Glover, Jeff Goldblum, Martin Short, the superstar ensemble of voices pulls off a neat trick – the identities of the thesps' vocal stylings are always apparent yet this doesn't preclude identification with character or pull you out of the drama. The songs by *Pocahontas'* composer Stephen Schwartz endeavour to add emotional colour rather than provide colourful sideshows – best of the bunch is 'Playing With The Big Boys Now' staged like a 1930s German Expressionist movie – while Hans Zimmer's score provides requisite biblical epic bluster. Indeed, by the time we reach the concluding mass exodus (boasting more extras than bullion could buy) and the parting of the Red Sea – a show of visionary spectacle that makes every hair stand to attention – Cecil B. De Mille's rendering is reduced to a storm in a tea cup. ★★★ **IF**

PRINCE OF THE CITY (1981)

Starring: *Treat Williams (Daniel Ciello), Jerry Orbach (Gus Levy), Richard Foronjy (Joe Marinaro), Don Billett (Bill Mayo), Kenny Marino (Dom Bando)*
Director: *Sidney Lumet*
Screenwriters: *Jay Presson Allen, Sidney Lumet, from the book by Robert Daley*
15/160 mins./Drama/Crime/Drama/USA

Corrupt New York cop Daniel Ciello is given the chance to escape prosecution for his dubious practices if he exposes other dodgy cops. But who can he trust?

Throughout Sidney Lumet's erratic, often brilliant, career he has achieved his greatest success with penetrating examinations of the American justice system. His courtroom dramas *Twelve Angry Men* (1957) and *The Verdict* (1982) are peerless examples of the genre, but it is the closed brotherhood of the police force and the corruption it appears to breed that has maintained a chokehold on his imagination. In the wake of 1973's *Serpico*, still his most famous venture into the territory, it's a theme he has returned to time and again. Apart from this early 80s offering, he trod similar ground with the generally solid *Q&A* in 1990 and the disappointing, if evocatively titled, *Night Falls On Manhattan* seven years later.

Excepting a bravura performance by Al Pacino in the title role, it is difficult to see why *Serpico* remains the most celebrated of Lumet's cop flicks. Up against this multi-layered, exhaustively detailed descent into the miasma of twisted loyalties, back stabbing, blackmail and deceit thrown up by an Internal Affairs probe of the NYPD, it's an uncharacteristically shallow little morality play. Even Pacino, in ludicrous tea cosy hats and drooping face fur, doesn't look too convincing these days. And even less so when pitted against Treat Williams as Danny Ciello, the gung-ho cop-turned-informer whose life is destroyed when the poisonous can of worms he conspires to prise open spills out around him.

In fact, the contrast between the characterisations of Frank Serpico and Danny Ciello mirrors the qualitative distance between the films themselves. Serpico is an honest cop out to bust corruption in his department; it's a straightforward white hat/black hat scenario. Ciello is infinitely more complicated. His decision to turn informer is not motivated solely by ethical convictions but more by a disastrous collusion of guilt, fear and an overarching lust for glory. Ciello is as crooked as every other blueshirt in the bureau, and if he does have a conscience it is one diluted by an instinct for self-preservation and a seriously warped hero complex. It's this dichotomy that leads him into the abyss.

Naively believing he can expose the dark side of the force without sacrificing his buddies he takes the Feds' shilling and goes undercover, stumbling on a narcotics scam that involves selling dope to police informers. Given the necessity of buying information this falls just inside the boundaries of acceptable practice. But, as Ciello soon learns, it's a system riddled with corruption, with cops hoovering up product before it reaches the street and falling over themselves to accept every bribe on offer.

Danny does his duty by the Feds and gives up the perpetrators. But in doing so, he breaks the trust that binds the force and is marked as a fink for life. And once he takes the plunge, and Lumet's intricate canvas broadens out, the boundaries between right and wrong becomes seriously blurred. On one hand the cops Danny turns have their hands in the till up to the elbows, heavily involved in drugs, bribery and corruption – they had it coming. On the other, they adhere to a strict code of honour (albeit honour among thieves) and they are fiercely loyal to their own – any one of them would have put his arm in the fire before ratting on a friend. Contrast that to the Feds who are busy putting the squeeze on Ciello: ruthless scum to a man they are a dyspeptic Inquisition in cheap suits and bad ties. And yet, with the whip being fiercely cracked over their narrow backs, what choice do they have but to force Ciello to give up everything he knows, betraying even his closest friends and family?

A pariah to his former colleagues, under siege by the Feds – at one point he is even threatened with prosecution over his own past transgressions – and with the Mob attempting to buy him off, Danny forges deeper and deeper into the moral maze, desperately searching his conscience for a way out. It's giving nothing away to report that he doesn't find one.

Prince Of The City is not simply Lumet's best cop movie by far, it's also, arguably, the best cop movie in the sub-genre's whole world-weary history. With its astonishing kaleidoscopic vision and compelling docu-drama feel it charts the murky territory where law enforcement and the underworld join hands with relentless clarity and a steely rejection of sentimentality. Lumet's supreme achievement is in maintaining absolute control over a narrative nest of vipers that constantly threatens to tie itself in knots. With its harsh, over-bright interiors, grainy New York locations and acres and acres of talk the film is at once sprawling and deeply oppressive.

That it was a commercial failure, however, is no surprise at all. It's a long, labyrinthine film that demands absolute attention. Even then it is hard to keep tabs on exactly what's going on. But like many 'difficult' films it rewards the effort tenfold, and it's doubtful whether a better performance was committed to celluloid in 1981 than Treat Williams' portrayal of the tortured Danny Ceillo. In a staggering feat of acting prowess. Williams essays a fundamentally good, yet deeply flawed, human being disintegrating under intolerable pressure with rare courage and intensity. He's surrounded by a formidable cast of supporting players, but he shoulders the bulk of the film's colossal weight nevertheless. Why this role did not propel Williams to the front rank of screen actors has been the subject of dark conjecture ever since.

Lumet might have lost his edge of late, but he's got a formidable body of work to rest on. How sad it is then to see Williams' great talent wasted on swill like *The Substitute IV* when he should, on this evidence, have been giving De Niro sleepless nights for the last two decades. ★★★★ **SB**

⦿ THE PRINCESS BRIDE (1987)

Starring: *Cary Elwes (Westley), Mandy Patinkin (Inigo Montoya), Robin Wright (Buttercup), Chris Sarandon (Prince Humperdinck), Christopher Guest (Count Tyrone Rugen), Wallace Shawn (Vizzini)*
Director: *Rob Reiner*
Screenwriters: *William Goldman, based on his own novel*
PG/98 mins./Comedy-Adventure/USA

As a grandfather tells a story to his disinterested but captive grandson, we are transported to the adventures of the beautiful Buttercup who is kidnapped by the dastardly Prince Humperdinck, and of Westley, her childhood beau, who has returned in the guise of hero Dread Pirate Roberts, and teams up with the great swordsman Inigo Montoya to go to Buttercup's rescue.

A warm and silly fairy tale, played with giddy delight by all concerned and directed with a rich vein of humour by Rob Reiner; a satire on fairy tales and fairy-telling as written with the consummate authority of William Goldman based on the flamboyantly knowing novel by, you got it, William Goldman; and a sly, sly attack on Hollywood's tendency to ignore the simple beauty of storytelling. *The Princess Bride* is all these things, a film all about the telling of tales: tall, short, moral – kind of – and whimsical. It is not to be trusted, only adored.

For a start the 'real' story exists in another story, the type where a weathered grandpop (Peter Falk) dislodges his flu-ridden grandson's antipathy to all but computer games, with the words, 'Once upon a time ...' Once we're upon a time, Reiner takes a tone somewhere between Grimm Brother and Zucker Brother allowing events to spill along without registering a smidge of genuine peril, coated as it is in an affectionate comic glaze. Sample, alone, the characters, redoubtable stereotypes just doing their time-honoured bit that bit more excitedly.

Tagline
She gets kidnapped. He gets killed. But it all ends up OK.

Cary Elwes, as the dashing hero, seems to have dug up Errol Flynn's swagger, adding a layer of insincerity as thick as a Swiss gateau. Then there's Robin Wright (now a Penn) as fair damsel in distress Buttercup, who seems to have drifted in from a sitcom. Or how about arch-swordsman Inigo, played by Mandy Patinkin, whose bouncy dash was stolen wholesale by Antonio Banderas for his Zorro? Everything is exaggerated, but with all of Goldman's postmodern twinkles and Reiner's clean-cut vision (rejecting the regulation mud-pile milieu of anything vaguely medieval) as he sends this merry bunch vaulting about the countryside with its clutter of icky beasts and oddballs, it should only be treasured. They even let Billy Crystal play a small wizardling called Miracle Max as a yabbering Yiddishe, flush from a more recognisable dimension. ★★★★★ **IN**

⦿ PRINCESS MONONOKE (MONONOKE-HIME) (1997)

Starring: the voices of: *Yoji Matsuda (Ashitaka), Yuriko Ishida (San), Yuko Tanaka (Eboshi-gozen), Sumi Shimamoto (Toki)/English version: Gillian Anderson (Moro), Billy Crudup (Ashitaka), Claire Danes (San), Minnie Driver (Lady Eboshi)*
Director: *Hayao Miyazaki*
Screenwriters: *Hayao Miyazaki/English version: Neil Gaiman*
PG/134 mins./Animation/Family/Adventure/Japan

Ashitaka, a young prince, is on a quest to discover how to break a curse on his right arm, which makes it a deadly weapon. He meets a host of strange and wonderful folk along the way, including the eco-warrior Princess Mononoke.

It cost $20 million to make, took $50 million in its first 12 days on domestic release, eventually grossed $157 million, and, in doing so, overtook *E.T.* to set an all-time Japanese box office record. It stars the vocal talents of a superb ensemble cast (see above). Its English dub was written by cult comic scribe, Neil Gaiman. And it's been described as one of the best animated films ever. Hell, Disney were so impressed, they bought the entire output of the studio that made it, Studio Ghibli, for worldwide distribution. And, chances are, you've never even heard of it.

Stuck in an international limbo since its Japanese release in 1997- a year which, on the strength of this, Takeshi Kitano's *Hana Bi* and Shohei Imamura's *Unagi*, was later dubbed 'The Year Of The Japanese Film Phoenix' – *Princess Mononoke* finally arrives on these shores minus a theatrical release and with rather less of a bang. And whatever the reasons for its delay – many anime quarters have suggested that Disney, having acquired the rights, then buried it so as not to impact on their own, similarly themed, *Mulan* – the result is certainly worth the wait.

A neat blend of environmentally friendly philosophy and action adventure, the plot centres on Ashitaka, a youthful prince forced into exile when a skirmish with a wild-boar-turned-vengeful-demon leaves his right arm scarred, possessed and capable of decapitating his foes with a single blow. Setting out to discover what has thrown nature so out of kilter, he comes upon an array of intriguing characters (Thornton's Jigo easily the most entertaining), before clashing with, and ultimately falling for, the titular princess – herself an eco-warrior.

Often breathtaking in its imagination and sheer scale, notable treats include monsters with writhing, snake-like skins, mythical animal gods and, best of all, tiny forest sprites which are at once eerily creepy and unashamedly cute. For audiences now accustomed to the CGI triumphs of *Shrek*, *Final Fantasy* and co., the animation itself is a refreshing return to the Japanese graphic artists of yore, whose influence has since been seen in everything from Herges Tintin to much of the early Manga stable. Gone is seamless, 3-D realism and back are fantastical imaginings and landscapes of startling scope. These have clearly benefited from Miyazaki's painstaking dedication (he personally corrected or redrew more than 80,000 of the film's 144,000 eels), and insistence that his art directors visit genuine, ancient forests to complete their master drawings.

As to whether *Princess Mononoke* will live up to its pitched tag of The Anime Movie Most Likely To Make The Crossover Between Cult And The Mainstream, however, the answer is ... perhaps not. Yes, this is a unique visual experience and, yes, some gushing notices in the US undoubtedly contributed to a respectable Stateside box office for what was essentially an arthouse release (again, those Disney burial murmurings abound).

But that said, all the anime sensibilities which have prevented a move into the mainstream in the past – a gripping, linear first third; a ponderous, philosophical second; and an often nonsensical 'demon god goes gaga' third – are all present and correct. A state of affairs which, at the very least, will delight the true, hard-core fan base. ★★★★ **MD**

THE PRIVATE FILES OF J. EDGAR HOOVER (1977)

Starring: *Broderick Crawford (J. Edgar Hoover), Jose Ferrer (Lionel McCoy), Michael Parks (Robert F. Kennedy), Rip Torn (Dwight Webb), Celeste Holm (Florence Hollister)*
Director: *Larry Cohen*
Screenwriter: *Larry Cohen*
Unrated/110 mins./Crime/Drama/USA

After the 1972 death of FBI Director J. Edgar Hoover, agent Dwight Webb recalls the G-man's career, from young manhood to old age, and his influence on American politics from the 1920s to the 1970s.

'I'll bug and burglarise who I please,' declares Hoover when Nixon aides ask to get in on the act for Watergate, 'but damned if I'll let anyone else do it.' Larry Cohen's radical revision of *The FBI Story* is a dissection of the life of a sexually stunted demagogue-cum-demigod whose career began with the birth of American anti-communism in the Palmer Raids of 1919 and extended through Prohibition, Dillinger, World War II, McCarthyism, bitter rivalry with Robert Kennedy (Michael Parks), assassinations, the Civil Rights movement and Vietnam.

Cohen's speculation that Hoover's long-time sidekick and rumoured gay lover Clyde Tolson (Dan Dailey) was the 'Deep Throat' who brought down the Nixon administration has been disproved, but this biopic – made before more extreme, far-fetched accusations (like transvestism) were levelled against Hoover – is usually credible in advancing scurrilous, backdoor speculations about modern history. It signals respect for the old-style Hollywood gangster shows with his exceptional casting of old-time faces (Jose Ferrer, Lloyd Nolan) and using a brassy Miklos Rosza score, but Crawford's Hoover is a semi-comic monster: drunkenly listening to the taped seduction of a political opponent, unintentionally horrifying a favourite waiter by revealing the extent of his knowledge of the man's private life or found asleep in his office by a tiptoeing Bobby Kennedy.

It's not a complete hatchet job, in that it grudgingly admires the 'top cop' for his bull-headed (profoundly undemocratic) refusal to follow orders from passing administrations of whatever political stripe, and presents unblinkered views of sainted figures like Franklin Roosevelt (Howard Da Silva) and Martin Luther King (Raymond St Jacques). ★★★★ **KN**

THE PRIVATE LIFE OF HENRY VIII (1933)

Starring: *Charles Laughton (Henry VIII), Robert Donat (Thomas Culpepper), Binnie Barnes (Katherine Howard), Elsa Lanchester (Anne Of Cleves), Merle Oberon (Anne Boleyn), Wendy Barrie (jane Seymour), Everley Gregg (Catherine Parr), Franklin Dyall (Thomas Cromwell)*
Director: *Alexander Korda*
Screenwriters: *Lajos Biro, Arthur Wimperis*
U/97 mins./Historical Drama/UK
Awards: *Academy Awards – Best Actor (Charles Laughton)*

More interested in sex and food than the affairs of state, Henry VIII marries six times, and having executed Anne Boleyn and Katherine Howard, been widowed by Jane Seymour and divorced Anne of Cleves, he settles into disappointed old age with Catherine Parr.

Alexander Korda always claimed that he got the idea for this costume romp on hearing a London cabby singing 'I'm 'Enery the Eighth I Am'. However, he more than likely noticed elsewhere the resemblance between the corpulent king and Charles Laughton and commissioned screenwriters Lajos Biro and Arthur Wimperis to fashion a bawdy drama out of the events of a tempestuous reign. However, the Reformation – along with such key protagonists as Katherine of Aragon, Cardinal Wolsey and Sir Thomas More – was deemed too dull for film fare and, instead, the action concentrated on Bluff King Hal's lusty appetites and intemperate humour.

Period pictures were considered box-office poison in the early sound era and Korda struggled to raise his £60,000 budget – whose penury makes cinematographer Georges Perinal's achievement in giving Vincent Korda's ingenious sets a modicum of courtly opulence all the more remarkable. Indeed, Laughton and his co-stars were asked to defer their fees until after premiere at New York's Radio City Music Hall. Ultimately, however, the movie scooped £500,000 worldwide and made history by securing the British cinema's first Academy Award. But, more significantly, its success enabled Korda to establish London Films as a major force in the UK film industry and ensconced the heritage picture as a keystone of indigenous production until the mid-1990s.

Moreover, Laughton's Best Actor triumph alerted Hollywood to the quality of British stage acting and a minor exodus followed, as the studios sought their own star thespians. Laughton himself would deliver more effective performances over the next 30 years. But even though his flamboyant portrait was decidedly mock-Tudor, his shifts from clumsy amorousness to betrayed fury and impenitent self-pity adroitly captured the popular conception of England's most colourful monarch. He was ably abetted by his screen spouses, who included his real-life consort, Elsa Lanchester, whose gloriously unglamorous turn as the Mare of Flanders provided the film's enduring highlight. ★★★ **DP**

THE PRIVATE LIFE OF SHERLOCK HOLMES (1970)

Starring: *Robert Stephens (Sherlock Holmes), Colin Blakely (Dr John H. Watson), Irene Handl (Mrs Hudson), Christopher Lee (Mycroft Holmes), Tamara Toumanova (Petrova)*
Director: *Billy Wilder*
Screenwriter: *Billy Wilder, I.A.L. Diamond, from the characters by Sir Arthur Conan Doyle*
PG/120 mins./Comedy/Mystery/USA

Dr Watson recounts the adventures he shared with Sherlock Holmes which he deemed too scandalous for publication in his lifetime, chiefly

Holmes's involvement with Gabrielle Valladon, a woman in distress who was also a spy scheming against the British government.

'We all have our occasional failures,' admits Billy Wilder's wry Sherlock Holmes. 'Fortunately, Dr Watson never writes about mine.' Wilder originally shot an epic-length Valentine to Victorian adventure, but the film was tragically taken from him and mutilated by the wholesale lopping of entire episodes, including 'The Case of the Upside-Down Room'.

What remains is so wonderful that those 1970 studio philistines should be sought out in retirement homes and cemetery plots and shouted at. A loving recreation of the world of Arthur Conan Doyle, this has a Holmes whose deductions and repartee are tossed off with a touch of Wilde and who constantly complains that Watson's accounts of his work have grossly misrepresented him ('he has saddled me with this improbable outfit which the public now expects me to wear!').

To Watson's fury and discomfort, Holmes even pretends to be gay in order to see off a ballerina who wants him to father her child ('Tchaikowsky is not an isolated case'), though we learn he is really a Wilderian cynical romantic, dangerously prone to be fooled by an amnesiac beauty fished out of the Thames.

The fiendish plot takes in bleached canaries, missing midgets, sinister Trappists, the Loch Ness Monster, and Queen Victoria. Also: sumptuous period settings, seductive Miklos Rosza score, and great character work from Irene Handl (a sarcastic Mrs Hudson) and Christopher Lee (pompous brother Mycroft).

A true evocation of the spirit of the *Strand Magazine*, this is the best Holmes movie ever made and sorely underrated in the Wilder canon. ★★★★ **KN**

THE PRIVATE LIVES OF ELIZABETH AND ESSEX (1939)

Starring: *Bette Davis (Queen Elizabeth I), Errol Flynn (Robert Devereux, Earl Of Essex), Olivia de Haviland (Lady Penelope Gray), Donald Crisp (Francis Bacon), Alan Hale (Hugh O'Neil, Earl Of Tyrone), Vincent Price (Sir Walter Raleigh)*
Director: *Michael Curtiz*
Screenwriters: *Norman Reilly Raine. Aeneas MacKenzie based on the play* Elizabeth the Queen *by Maxwell Anderson*
U/106 mins/History/Drama/USA

Ignoring the counsel of Francis Bacon and Lady Penelope Gray, Robert Devereux, Earl of Essex allows his vanity to clash with the pride of Queen Elizabeth, who reluctantly conquers her affection for him and has him executed on his return from an ill-fated expedition to Ireland.

Maxwell Anderson's play, *Elizabeth the Queen*, was written in blank verse that was deemed the epitome of cultured sophistication when delivered by those Broadway icons, Alfred Lunt and Lynn Fontanne. Always something of a snob, who considered herself several cuts above the lowbrow entertainment that Warners foistered upon her, Bette Davis reckoned this was the perfect vehicle for herself and Laurence Olivier and was, unsurprisingly, furious when Jack Warner insisted on teaming her with Errol Flynn, instead.

Davis deeply resented the fact that while she earned the studio kudos with her string of Oscar-nominated performances, Flynn's crowdpleasing knack of keeping the coffers filled made him the toast of the front office. However, Flynn was no better disposed towards Davis, especially as she seemed intent on acting him off the screen. Consequently, he demanded that the picture became known as *The Knight And The Lady* to reflect his commercial clout and it was only the hasty adoption of a compromise title that prevented Davis from quitting the project.

Caught in the middle of this battle of the egos was Olivia de Havilland, who was herself frustrated at having to play third fiddle after just completing her stint on *Gone With the Wind*. As a result, her indifference clashed with the scenery-gnawing antics of her co-stars and the atypical over-eagerness of such usually dependable character players as Henry Daniell and Henry Stephenson.

Clearly Michael Curtiz was ill at ease with an assignment that offered him little scope for action and his direction was as ponderous as Erich Korngold's score. However, he made the most of Orry-Kelly's opulent costumes and Anton Grot's deftly designed sets, whose contrasts between the oppressive décor of the court and the inviting intimacy of Wanstead were captured in artful Technicolor by his fellow Oscar nominee, Sol Polito.

Despite her unhappy experiences behind the scenes (which were far more dramatic than anything that appeared on camera), Davis enjoyed the imperious passion of the role and she played Elizabeth again in *The Virgin Queen* in 1955. ★★★ **DP**

THE PRODUCERS (1968)

Starring: *Zero Mostel (Max Bialystock), Gene Wilder (Leo Bloom), Kenneth Mars (Franz Liebkind), Estelle Winwood (Old Lady), Renee Taylor (Eva Braun)*
Director: *Mel Brooks*
Screenwriters: *Mel Brooks*
PG/84 mins./Comedy/USA

Awards: *Academy Awards – Best Original Screenplay*

Producers Max Bialystock and Leo Bloom aim to make money by producing a sure-fire flop.

Zany is the word for the comedy genre inhabited, for a time dominated, by funnyman writer-director-producer and sometime actor Mel Brooks. Brooks tickled, the masses and broke ground in brash, bad taste burlesques, with the compulsive lunacy of farting cowboys in Western spoof *Blazing Saddles* (1974), a tap dancing master and monster in *Young Frankenstein* (1974), and a birdshit attack in Hitchcock spoof *High Anxiety* (1977). But *The Producers*, his first feature, is his gem. It's less vulgar and much more dangerous than anything else in his oeuvre – which is why it was not comparably commercial on its release, although it did win Brooks kudos, a fan base and the Oscar for his screenplay.

It's a classic, far-fetched farce with a gasp-inducingly ironic notion: a New York showbiz Jew, however deviously, staging a celebration, however execrable, of Adolf Hitler.

The biggest (literally) joy of *The Producers* is the inimitable, incomparable Zero Mostel. A Broadway titan, he was just returning to the screen after his ordeal before the House Un-American Activities Committee and subsequent blacklisting blighted his career for years. In theatre history, Mostel is a multiple Tony-winning legend for work like his Tevye in *Fiddler On The Roof*. On film, Zero found immortality as *The Producers'* impresario Max Bialystock. Max was once king of Broadway, now reduced to a shabby subsistence romancing rich little old ladies 'stopping off at Max Bialystock's office to grab a last thrill on the way to the cemetery'. Mostel's loveable scoundrel Max, in mossy-looking velvet and wrapover hair, trumpeting like a bull elephant, is a masterpiece of extravagant desperation and irrepressibility.

His perfect foil is Gene Wilder, who had just made his film debut in a brief but eye-catching turn as the undertaker whimsically taken captive by Bonnie and Clyde. In the first of several great performances for Brooks, Wilder is uptight accountant Leo Bloom, a pale, wistful bundle of nerves who screams like a little girl and carries a scrap of his baby blanket for emotional security. Leo arrives to do Max's books, innocently observing that a dishonest man could make a fortune if he were certain a show would fail. Simply find the worst play in the world, raise a million dollars to produce it for a fraction of that, and when it quickly closes no one expects their money back.

Electrified, Max makes the fraud a reality, a show that must be an unmitigated disaster, for which he sells shares representing 25,000 per cent of any profits. The surefire flop is *Springtime For Hitler* – 'A gay romp with Adolf and Eva' – written by a demented, unrepentant Nazi. Max assembles a rotten director, a nightmare cast (Dick Shawn's hippy Lorenzo St DuBois or L.S.D. as Adolf, Renee Taylor as whining Eva Braun) and gleefully awaits the fastest closing in Broadway history. Unfortunately, unbelievably, the show is a smash. Although Brooks' background was in television, not theatre, he structured the film neatly like a play. (Indeed, in 2001 the piece reincarnated as a smash hit Broadway musical, for real.) Act One lays out the scheme, and sees Max beguiling Leo into partnering him. Max enchants the neurotic, hopeless Leo into having a dream, showing him New York as a world of 'thrills, adventure, romance' as viewed from the top of the Empire State Building.

This section climaxes with the magical night scene outside Lincoln Center, Leo having his epiphany – 'I want everything I've seen in the movies! I'll do it!' as the fountain gushes up in salute – and skipping around the fountain rim as Max, in bulking shadow against sparkling water, exults. Act Two is mounting the production, from schmoozing the insane German war veteran playwright Franz Liebkind and Max's flirtatious labours with backers, to the acquisition of a go-go dancing Swedish Barbie doll secretary, Ulla, and a casting call that draws Hitler impersonators of every size and shape. Act Three is opening night and its aftermath, culminating in an opening engagement at Leavenworth for Max's penitentiary opus, 'We're Prisoners Of Love'.

The film's beloved production number, 'Springtime For Hitler', gives new meaning to the term 'showstopper'. Brooks cuts between showgirls scantily clad in pretzels, beer foam and Valkyrie accessories, to the slack-jawed audience, from goose-stepping chorus girls and tap dancing Stormtroopers back to the audience frozen in shock, to an overhead Busby Berkeley-like shot of dancers in swastika formation. Brooks wrote the song himself: 'We're marching to a faster pace/Look out, here comes the master race'.

For a delicious cast of weirdos (like Estelle Winwood's tiny crone dubbed 'Hold Me Touch Me', with whom Max is forced to exhaust himself in such sex games as 'kitty and tomcat' and 'the innocent little milkmaid and the naughty stableboy') Brooks provides a stream of absurdities. Favourite moment: Max and Leo peep above the desk under which they are cowering from the maddened Franz, and as he puts his gun to his own head, croon 'Deutschland Uber Alles'. Outrageous delight. ★★★★★ **AE**

THE PRODUCERS: THE MOVIE MUSICAL (2005)

Starring: *Nathan Lane (Max Bialystock), Matthew Broderick (Leo Bloom), Uma Thurman (Ulla), Will Ferrell (Franz Liebkind)*
Director: *Susan Stroman*
Screenwriters: *Mel Brooks, Thomas Meehan, from the stage play by Mel Brooks, Thomas Meehan, and 1968 screenplay by Mel Brooks*
12A/134 mins./Musical/Comedy/USA

Failing Broadway producer Max Bialystock forms a devious plan after a visit from his nervous accountant Leo Bloom. Together they scheme to get rich by raising money for a guaranteed musical flop: *Springtime For Hitler*.

The Producers is a great stage show. Sadly, on screen it remains distinctly a stage show, and rarely comes close to being a great movie.

Where Mel Brooks succeeded with the Broadway production of his near flawless 1968 comedy was in realising that the stage and screen are very different things. In came even bawdier jokes and a selection of jaunty numbers that kept things running at breakneck speed. In the transformation back to a movie, Brooks and director Susan Stroman (who crafted the stage show) have often neglected to observe their own rules. Attempts to adapt the topped-out nature of the stage play and refine its comedy to the less forgiving rhythms of the cinema screen are minimal.

Stroman kicks the show off well, apparently aiming for MGM homage. It's colourful, brash and cheerfully proud of its own artifice. If she'd stuck to her guns the movie would have been infinitely more enjoyable, but with much of the action confined to Bialystock's office it starts to feel cramped and stagebound rather than enjoyably stagey. There's no question that Stroman knows how to choreograph a musical number ('I Wanna Be A Producer' builds cleverly on the stage version and 'Springtime for Hitler' remains a joy), but she's less confident with a camera. The dance sequences beg for a camera to dance with them, rather than watch statically from the audience.

The cast could never be accused of lack of gusto. Nathan Lane is brilliantly slimy as Bialystock; Broderick fares less well, inviting unfavourable comparisons with Gene Wilder and overdoing the facial expressions for the people in the cheap seats. The newcomers are inspired additions. Will Ferrell is everything you'd hope he'd be as a crazed Nazi, but it's Uma Thurman, slinking every curve she has as sexy secretary Ulla, who's the real surprise. Hoofing impressively and exhibiting a sturdy set of pipes, she peps up the movie whenever she's on screen.

Thanks to the bravura cast and the inherent quality of the little-changed script there are plenty of gentle laughs. With less faithfulness and a little more of the same bravery that messed with a classic movie and created a classic stageshow, this could have run and run. ★★★ **OR**

P

THE PROPHECY (1994)

Starring: *Christopher Walken (Angel Gabriel), Elias Koteas (Thomas Dagget), Eric Stoltz (Angel Simon), Virginia Madsen (Katherin), Amanda Plummer (Rachael), Viggo Mortensen (Lucifer)*
Director: *Gregory Widen*
Screenwriter: *Gregory Widen*
18/93 mins./Horror/USA

Gabriel, a rebel angel, is after the black soul of a human general. Simon, a loyal angel, hides the soul in a little girl. A cop, a schoolteacher and the Devil stand against him.

'I'm an angel. I kill first-borns while their mamas watch. I turn cities into salt. I even, when I feel like it, rip the souls from little girls, and from now until kingdom come, the only thing you can count on in your existence is never knowing why.' A dark version of *City of Angels*, this unusually theological horror movie has fascinating, provocative ideas and scenes: an autopsy on an eyeless hermaphrodite whose handwritten second century Bible has an extra chapter in Revelations, a tussle over the soul of a war criminal who could help a rebel angel defeat the hordes of Heaven, Gabriel's habit of keeping would-be suicides alive and wretched as minions, and the Devil being forced to help God because if Gabriel wins Hell will have competition.

Christopher Walken is at his crazed best, perching like a bird, flirting with children, and doing wry double-takes at the antics of 'talking monkeys'. He is well-matched in cameos from Eric Stoltz as a goody-goody angel and Viggo Mortensen as Lucifer ('sitting in that basement, sulking over your break-up with the Boss, you're nothing!'). It's a little too cheap to deliver on its apocalyptic promise, but the performances and the ideas are more than value for money. It founded a minor direct-to-video franchise – Walken is back, and delivers entertainment in more straitened circumstances, in *The Prophecy II* and *The Prophecy 3: The Ascent*, but is absent from the shot-back-to-back-in-Romania *The Propehcy: Forsaken* and *The Prophecy: Uprising*, which make do with Jason Scott Lee, Tony Todd and Kari Wuhrer. ★★★★ **KN**

⊙ THE PROPOSITION (2006)

Starring: *Guy Pearce (Charlie Burns), Emily Watson (Martha Stanley), Ray Winstone (Captain Stanley), John Hurt (Jellon Lamb), Richard Wilson (Mike Burns)*
Director: *John Hillcoat*
Screenwriter: *Nick Cave*
18/104 mins./Drama/Australia/UK

Late-19th century Australia, and Cpt. Stanley has captured the younger two siblings of the notorious Burns brothers. With them in custody he offers middle brother Charlie a deal: head into the outback to kill older brother Arthur, and the youngest won't be hanged.

What's that, Skippy? There's a turn-of-the-century outback town being terrorised by a vicious trio of bushrangers? They're rapin' and pillagin' and no one seems able to stop them? Well, Skip, better round up the younger two brothers and offer the middle one a pact: slaughter your older bro, or we'll string up your younger one. Skip? Where are you going, Skip . . . ?

Well, maybe that episode of *Skippy* never made it to air, but then, you should dump any other cutesy clichés about the Antipodes you might have in mind. Director John Hillcoat and screenwriter Nick Cave's film reveals an Australia you've never seen before: it's as tough and bloody a movie as you were likely to catch in 2006. It's also one of the best.

It's a Western in spirit, certainly, but don't expect the convenient moral certainties of the Hollywood classics. As drunken, dissolute bounty hunter Jellon Lamb (John Hurt, in a typically incendiary performance) declares, 'I came to this beleaguered land, and the God in me evaporated.' This is more Peckinpah than Hawkes, but it's Peckinpah stripped even of his characters' slimly comforting faith in loyalty and honour. These characters, the witnesses to the final shudder of Australia's bloody birthing pains, are scratching a living in unimaginable conditions – a kind of hard-bitten nihilism pervades the place.

At the film's centre are two men, each struggling to keep or regain their moral bearings among the bloody chaos. As Cpt. Stanley, Ray Winstone adroitly exploits his twin capacity for honest sentimentalism and sudden violence. At heart he's a decent man – his final aim is to civilise the apparently uncivilisable; but the violence he's willing to employ to do it threatens to explode out of control and destroy the idyll he's created for himself and his wife, whom he shields meticulously from the harsh realities of their lives – thus inviting a kind of terminal blowback.

As Charlie, Guy Pearce, who really has now proved himself to be the more versatile and subtle of the two Antipodean actors we first saw in *LA Confidential*, is taciturn and tantalisingly ambivalent as the man who has to choose between two brothers. Meanwhile, the under-used Danny Huston works hard with the most unforgiving role, that of the elder brother who essentially serves as a walking question mark: will Charlie sacrifice him to save his younger sibling or not?

Director John Hillcoat (who worked with screenwriter Nick Cave on the equally hard-bitten prison drama *Ghosts Of The Civil Dead*) handles the violence with explosive precision. There's no misplaced slo-mo romanticism here, just the shocking reality of sudden death and, in the film's gruelling flogging sequence, a kind of gleeful sadism. Together with his cinematographer Benoît Delhomme, he renders the outback a sweltering, dust-clogged, fly-blasted purgatory, while Nick Cave delivers a screenplay that, in its tortured morality, blood-drenched imagery and final ambivalence, calls to mind, of all films, *Taxi Driver*.

f there's a niggle at all, it's David Wenham's turn as Eden Fletcher: a disappointingly two-dimensional chinless wonder of a Brit town boss – an excuse for some casual Pommie-bashing via a character straight from central casting. It's one of the very few flaws in an otherwise thoroughly impressive film. ★★★★ **AS**

⊙ PROSPERO'S BOOKS (1991)

Starring: *John Gielgud (Prospero), Michael Clark (Caliban), Michel Blanc (Alonso), Erland Johnson (Gonzalo), Isabelle Pasco (Miranda), Tom Bell (Antonio)*
Director: *Peter Greenaway*
Screenwriter: *Peter Greenaway, based on the play* The Tempest *by William Shakespeare*
15/124 mins./Drama/France/Italy/Netherlands/UK/Japan

A dance orientated re-telling of William Shakespeare's *The Tempest*, in which the magician Prospero, exiled to a remote island, finds his plans for revenge curtailed when his daughter falls in love with the son of his chief enemy.

It's doubtful even old Willie himself could make head nor tale let alone detect the full scope of his final play, *The Tempest*, in this dense visual tapestry that the auteur Peter Greenaway, part artist, part mad inventor, has concocted out the famous work. It is tough to fully register it as a film at all, not in the traditional sense, as the narrative becomes subsumed by erotic dance, and video sideshows tracing rotting fruit and rotting bodies, every kind of bodily excretion, and symbols and suggestions tormenting us with their elusive meaning.

There probably isn't much meaning, beyond the suggestion that we really shouldn't be so stuck-up about Shakespeare, and a hippish glint in the lavish Mr Greenaway's eye as he spins such a web of trippy delights. On that level it works, a painting both surrealistic and hauntingly traditional, come alive as a thickly persuasive paradise, through the centre of which strides John Gielgud, his voice looped madly through a synthesizer, as the eloquent, weary Prospero, lost on this island with naught but his daughter Miranda, the lonely beast Caliban (played by famed ballet dancer Michael Clarke with eye-watering contortions), and his library of books on everything from cosmographies to pornography (do we need re-emphasise this isn't very faithful to the text?).

If it wasn't so lavish, such a divine symbolic world conjured from arcane texts and lost knowledge – and a kinky-minded director – one could see it as intellectualism run amuck. That feels unfair, but Greenaway unloosed is a fearsome thing to face. ★★★ **IN**

⊙ PSYCHO (1960)

Starring: *Norman Bates (Anthony Perkins), Janet Leigh (Marion Crane), Vera Miles (Lila Crane), John Gavin (Sam Loomis), John McIntre (Sheriff Chambers)*
Director: *Alfred Hitchcock*
Screenwriter: *Joseph Stefano, based on the novel by Joseph Stefano*
15/108 mins./Horror/Thriller/USA

Awards: *Golden Globes – Best Supporting Actress (Janet Leigh)*

Marion Crane goes on the run with $40,000 and holes up in a motel, run by the mysterious Norman Bates.

The Master Of Suspense delighted in startling and scaring audiences for over 30 years before Psycho, but never engaged in full on horror until this macabre riposte to the schlock frighteners of the late 50s. That it has been imitated often, never surpassed, is evidenced by 40 years of slasher flicks including its three variable (from so-so to stinkbomb) sequels, a TV movie spin-off and, especially, Gus Van Sant's 1998 re-make curio.

His version used the same screenplay, score, design and camera angles for a shot-by-shot near-replica which still fell dismally short. Hitchcock's *Psycho* macguffin, an object or plot element that occupies the audience's attention but which is ultimately irrelevant, is his most audacious exercise in misdirection. 'Psycho was designed first of all,' Hitch admitted, 'to lead an audience completely up the garden path.' Marion Crane is having a passionate affair with the heavily in debt Sam Loomis, and after a lunchtime tryst in a seedy hotel she impulsively runs away with the $40,000 she was supposed to bank for her employer.

Driving from Arizona to her lover in California she is overwhelmed by guilt and paranoia (thrillingly evoked by Bernard Herrmann's racing, staccato score and the conversations she imagines people having about her) until, exhausted, she pulls into the secluded Bates Motel just 15 miles short of her destination. For nearly a third of the film we have been carefully following the $40,000 as she moves it and removes it from her handbag, wraps it in paper and sets it on the nightstand. Forty-five minutes in, we realise that the film is not about the love story or the theft or the woman's flight. The $40,000 doesn't matter. It's a blind alley, the device that sends Marion Crane into the orbit of a boy and his mother. A pathological boy, with a telling hobby, a peephole, and personality to spare.

The basis for the film's Norman Bates (Anthony Perkins, a brilliant mix of sincerity, attractiveness and impenetrable insanity) was Robert Bloch's novel, itself based on the sicko case of a Wisconsin serial killer. In 1960 Alfred Hitchcock was the most famous film director in the world, his voice and rotund figure, unmistakeable from his television series *Alfred Hitchcock Presents* and his signature cameos (in *Psycho* he appears outside Marion's office). People went to see his films because they were his films, not for the stars, the plot, the production values or the scenery. Thus he was in a position to effect an abrupt change of pace from the popular, lavish romantic comedy-thriller *North By Northwest* he made the year before. Nevertheless Paramount were concerned about *Psycho* being too sleazy.

Unperturbed, Hitch saw it through on an extremely low budget, using many of the crew from his TV series. It cost just $800,000 dollars and took 30 days to shoot – seven of them spent on the justly celebrated, infamous shower scene. The scene, a tour de force of montage, illusion and shrieking violins, runs for less than two minutes and yet looms fearfully large in the collective memory. The film is in black and white because Hitch thought it would have been much too gory in colour. He regarded it as a wicked joke, a 'fairy tale of awfulness'. Much of the magic – which has eluded so many imitators – comes from Hitch's principle that less is more. The violence diminishes rather than escalates; our emotions, fears and expectations have been so roused that they become as much a part of the cinematic experience as what is actually on the screen. The detective Arbogast's trip up and down the stairs chez Bates, for example, is laden with our dread. We watch from a height that makes him small, exposed but distant. Only when the deed is done do we suddenly see his face filling the screen, emphasising his surprise and ours, despite our awareness of the menace.

The trailers for *Psycho* featured Hitch addressing the camera from the forecourt of the Bates Motel, taking us on a guided tour of Cabin 1, including the toilet, and impishly yanking back the shower curtain to reveal Vera Miles screaming. That was all audiences had to go on, and it was enough. More surprisingly, the secrets of what happens in that bathroom and the Gothic house on the hill above the motel were kept for a long time as critics and customers honoured Hitch's request not to reveal the shock twists. How long does a film's mystery remain now, when spoilers are on the internet before the picture's even made?

Anthony Perkins featured in several straight-to-video sequels in the the 1980s, and the whole film was pointlessly re-made, shot-for-shot by Gus Van Sant in 1998, with Vince Vaughn as Norman, Anne Heche as Marion and Viggo Mortensen and Julianne Moore in support. ★★★★★ **AE**

PSYCHO II (1983)

Starring: *Anthony Perkins (Norman Bates), Vera Miles (Lila Loomis), Meg Tilly (Mary), Robert Loggia (Dr Raymond), Dennis Franz (Toomey), Hugh Gillin (Sheriff Hunt)*
Director: *Richard Franklin*
Screenwriter: *Tom Holland, from characters by Robert Bloch*
18/113 mins./Horror/Thriller/USA

Norman Bates is released from an insane asylum, despite the protests of the sister of his most famous victim. Returning to his home, Norman worries that his mother has returned to torment him.

A two-decades-on sequel to a true classic might sound like a terrible idea, but *Psycho II* is a smart, blackly comic thriller.

Remembering that the original was as much mystery as shocker, screenwriter Tom Holland weaves a clever, surprising plot around Norman Bates. Here, the fragile, nearly sane Norman is besieged by insensitive clods like the manager (Dennis Franz, wonderfully crass) who has been getting the Bates Motel a bad reputation as 'an adult motel' and a callous plot by the vindictive Lilah (Vera Miles, returning to her old role) to drive him crazy again.

Meg Tilly is interestingly ambiguous as a waitress who befriends Norman, but turns out to be part of the plot against him – and unwittingly the cause of a last-reel disaster as she becomes one of several surrogate mothers to take up the wig, dress and knife.

The wittiest dark joke is that the entire world *wants* Norman to be mad, and 'normality' can only be restored if he's got a mummified mother in the window and is ready to kill again.

Director Richard Franklin stages 80s-style gore effects but seems more interested in character quirks.

Though two further sequels show some decline in quality, they're still interesting: *Psycho III*, directed by Perkins, finds Norman nearly entering a relationship with an equally screwed-up woman, a suicidal ex-nun (Diana Scarwid); and *Psycho IV: The Beginning*, directed for TV by Mick Garris from a script by *Psycho* screenwriter Joseph Stefano, delves into the backstory as Perkins recounts Norman's early life – with terrific work from Henry Thomas as young Norman and an unexpected Olivia Hussey as Mother. ★★★ **KN**

THE PUBLIC ENEMY (1931)

Starring: *James Cagney (Tom Powers), Jean Harlow (Gwen Allen), Edward Woods (Matt Doyle), Joan Blondell (Mamie), Beryl Mercer (Ma Powers), Donald Cook (Mike Powers), Mae Clarke (Kitty)*
Director: *William A. Wellman*
Screenwriters: *Kubec Glasmon, John Bright, Harvey Thew, from the story 'Beer And Blood' by John Bright, Kubec Glasmon*
PG/80 mins./Crime/Drama/USA

Chicago slum kid Tom Powers becomes a racketeer during Prohibition. After rising to wealth and success, he crosses a rival mob and is assassinated.

This archetypal Warner Brothers gangster film tries to get round criticism that the movies made heroes of hoods by opening with a caption that labels the protagonist a social problem and a bad example. However, James Cagney's strutting charisma – shifting his shoulders, flashing his grin, making friendly-aggressive mock-thump gestures to everyone and squaring up against his enemies – makes Tom Powers as appealing as much as he is menacing, even as the film works overtime to make him a psychopath (with a tendency to batter women – he famously shoves a grapefruit in Mae Clarke's face) as well as the product of slum deprivation.

Taking incidents from the short careers of Hymie Weiss and Louis Altieri (enemies of Al Capone), the movie is less grandiose than the competing *Little Caesar* and *Scarface* (which are about Capone) as Tom Powers, though he briefly gets a sharp suit and high-class dame Jean Harlow, remains a footsoldier in the bootleg booze business. A typical, torn-from-the-headlines moment has Tom combining honour and sadism by machine-gunning the frisky horse which has fatally thrown his gangland mentor. The finale doesn't even allow the law to prevail – Tom, who realises when gut-shot that he isn't invincible ('I ain't so tough'), is hauled out of a hospital bed by other crooks and his mummified corpse is propped up against his old mother's door to tumble in gruesomely when it's opened. William A. Wellman directs with a lot of discretion, often panning away from the violence and letting the soundtrack tell the tale – obviously, the talkies were made for machine gunfire, but there's also a creepy, ironic use of the song 'I'm Forever Blowing Bubbles' over the horrific finish. ★★★★ **KN**

◎ PULP FICTION (1994)

Starring: *Tim Roth (Pumpkin), Amanda Plummer (Honey Bunny), John Travolta (Vincent Vega), Samuel L. Jackson (Jules Winnfield), Bruce Willis (Butch Coolidge), Ving Rhames (Marsellus Wallace), Rosanna Arquette (Jody), Eric Stolz (Lance), Uma Thurman (Mia Wallace)*
Director: *Quentin Tarantino*
Screenwriters: *Quentin Tarantino, Roger Avery, from their stories*
18/154 mins./168 mins. (special adition)/Drama/Crime/USA

Awards: *Academy Awards – Best Original Screenplay; BAFTA – Best Supporting Actor (Samuel L. Jackson), Best Original Screenplay; Golden Globes – Best Screenplay*

The lives of two mob hit men, a boxer, a gangster's wife, and a pair of diner bandits intertwine in four tales of violence and redemption.

The least interesting thing about *Pulp Fiction* is what is in that bloody briefcase. Whether it is unlimited moolah, the soul of Crime Lord Marsellus Wallace or the gold lamé suit worn by Val Kilmer's Elvis in *True Romance* (1993) really misses the point of Tarantino's molotov cocktail of a picture. Making a mockery of the difficult-second-film cliché, Tarantino weaves a patchwork of crime film history into something shiny and new. Peppered with great moments eaten up by actors working at the top of their game (Travolta, Willis and Thurman have never been better, and the film created the aura of greatness that currently surrounds Jackson) *Pulp*'s witty writing, pop culture-surfing, gleeful amorality, cult tuneology and hyperkinetic energy has redefined the crime genre for the foreseeable future.

Drawing on the compendium format of *Black Mask* magazine and Mario Bava's Gothic flick *Black Sabbath* (1963) as well as the twisty-turny crime literature of Frederick Brown and Charles Willeford, Tarantino wrote *Pulp* on the European press push for *Reservoir Dogs* (1991) – hence Vincent Vega (Travolta)'s detailed knowledge of Amsterdam minutiae. As such, the film also boasts a European feel; both in specific incident – the day-in-the-life-of-a-hit-man strand acknowledges the influence of Jean-Pierre Melville's *Le Samourai* (1967) and the Vincent-Mia's twist has the same spirit as the impromptu dance in Jean-Luc Godard's crime flick *Bande A Part* (1964) – and in its rather intelligent sense of deconstructing Hollywood history.

Indeed, *Pulp Fiction* operates in the hinterland between reality and movie reality. Into a cadre of movie archetypes – the assassin, the mob boss, the gangster's moll, the boxer who throws a fight – Tarantino injects a reality check that is as funny as it is refreshing. Whereas most crime flicks would breeze over the rendezvous between Vincent and Mia, here we actually get to go on the date – polite chit-chat, awkward silences, bad dancing – before it spirals off into a drugged-up disaster. Just as *Dogs* is a heist film where you don't see the heist, *Pulp* is a boxer-takes-a-dive flick where you never see the bout, opting instead for conversations about muffins and *Deliverance*-style rape. Moreover, after Vincent and Jules take back Marsellus' briefcase, rather than cutting to a cop on their trail, we stay with them and revel in their banal banter as they dispose of a corpse (the genius of Keitel's Wolf in this effort is a moot point – how much intelligence does it take to clean a car, then throw a rug over the back seat?)

What startled about *Pulp* on release was its audacious story dynamics. It was originally planned as a straight anthology flick – Tarantino's decision to cross-reference the yarns mines even more dramatic gold (i.e. the hero can get killed halfway through). While none of the stories amount to much on their own – if you told *Pulp* in a linearity, it would start with Vincent and Jules arriving at Brett's apartment and end with Butch and Fabienne zooming off on Zed's chopper – in crisscrossing the exposition, Tarantino forges hooks of expectation and curiosity that pay off one by one in satisfying ways.

Through its tricksy plot structure, very few films capture such a rich sense of an interconnected crime community. Of course, this extends even beyond the parameters of the film itself to Tarantino's other movies – that Vincent Vega has a brother better known as Mr Blonde hints at a whole nexus of underworld activity – and to the whole crime genre itself. As Butch kills Maynard, Marsellus Wallace warns Zed he's going to get some henchman, 'To go to work with a pair of pliers and a blowtorch.' In *Charley Varrick* (1973), a character named Maynard warns a bank manager about the very same method of torture.

While all the plaudits may have gone to Tarantino's killer dialogue – it's appeared everywhere from parody *Plump Fiction* to the Fun Lovin' Criminals' hit 'Scooby Snacks' – *Pulp* is an equally stimulating visual experience. From the eyeful of Jackrabbit Slims to the magical square Mia draws to underline Vincent's geekiness to Andrzej Sekula's glossy, wide-angled image-crafting, the look of *Pulp* is equally as imaginative without ever calling attention to itself.

More protean than *Dogs*, more fun than *Jackie Brown*, *Pulp* is so perfectly wrought it makes you forgive the crimes against cinema that Tarantino has perpetrated with his acting. Three great movies for the price of one, the anaemic rip-offs that have followed have only served to sharpen its greatness. Besides, how could you not love a movie where a character called Antwan Rockamora is constantly referred to as Tony Rocky Horror? ★★★★★ **IF**

Movie Trivia: Pulp Fiction

The Big Kahuna Burger also features in other QT written flicks *Reservoir Dogs* and *From Dusk Till Dawn*. Tarantino wrote The Wolf character especially for Harvey Keitel, as he did also for Tim Roth and Amanda Plummers' Honey Bunny and Pumpkin. Vincent Vega (Travolta) is the brother of Vic Vega, Mr Blonde in *Reservoir Dogs*. The most popular word in *Pulp Fiction*? 'Fuck'. 271 times.

◎ PUMP UP THE VOLUME (1990)

Starring: *Christian Slater (Mark Hunter), Samantha Mathis (Nora Diniro), Andy Romano (Murdock), Keith Stuart Thayer (Luis Chavez), Cheryl Pollack (Paige Woodward), Lala Sloatman (Cheryl Biggs)*
Director: *Allan Moyle*
Screenwriter: *Allan Moyle*
15/105 mins./Drama/USA

A shy teenager finds it hard to communicate with his fellow high school pupils by day, transforms himself into the outrageous pirate radio DJ Hard Harry. As those various students tune in, he becomes a local hero, but tragedy will interrupt his triumph.

A stirring slice of pop-profound juvenilia given a cool heart by Christian Slater spouting screeds of fun-rebellious anti-establishment bile that gets a bunch of Gen X mopers all hot round their skateboard pads as played by a bunch of nowhere-soon teen actors. It should be dire, but is generally great fun because Allan Moyle avoids the temptation to apply heaps of

TOP 10 Highest Grossing Films In US Adjusted For Inflation

1	*Gone With The Wind* (1939)	$1.29 billion	6	*Titanic* (1997)	$821.4 million
2	*Star Wars* (1977)	$1.14 billion	7	*Jaws* (1975)	$819.7 million
3	*The Sound of Music* (1965)	$911.5 million	8	*Dr Zhivago* (1965)	$794.5 million
4	*E.T. The Extra-Terrestrial* (1982)	$907.8 million	9	*The Exorcist* (1973)	$707.6 million
5	*The Ten Commandments* (1956)	$838.4 million	10	*Snow White and the Seven Dwarfs* (1937)	$697.6 million

Heathers-bleak irony rather than give it a shrill but effective earnestness. You kind of feel, Happy Harry, Slater's midnight on-air identity, might have a point, at least until the credits roll.

Actually, there are various levels on which the film clicks into place. The monologues have a hip-stupid ferocity to them, and Slater launches into them like a boy possessed. Time may have told on Harry's dirty asides – 'Just look inside yourself and you'll see me waving up at you naked wearing only a cock ring' – which sound more camp than shocking by today's potty-mouthed standards, but his jabs of nihilism carry the same mock-philosophical cant that even beefed up *Fight Club*. The film also gels as a Cinderella story as shy-by-day, outrageous-by-night Harry finds a genuine lurve thang with hip cutie Samantha Mathis. And the strike of tragedy, a teen suicide misreading his angry blather, sends a caustic note of caution to shake up the film's finale. As the authorities close in to arrest the punk provocateur, Moyle allows the film to end on a surge a teen righteousness.

It's doubtful we should take any of its petty umbrage too seriously, but when it is delivered with such grave authority as this it's hard to resist the urge to take up arms to bring the establishment crashing down round its ears, by playing records really loudly and swearing at your parents. ★★★ **IN**

PUNCH DRUNK LOVE (2002)

Starring: *Adam Sandler (Barry Egan), Emily Watson (Lena Leonard), Philip Seymour Hoffman (Dean Trumbell), Luis Guzman (Lance)*
Director: *Paul Thomas Anderson*
Screenwriter: *Paul Thomas Anderson*
15/91 mins./Comedy/Drama/Romance/USA

Novelty toilet plunger manufacturer Barry's bland exterior masks permanent tension, exacerbated by the constant nagging of his seven sisters. When his tentative romance with gentle Lena is disrupted and he's menaced by a phone sex extortionist his life starts taking some unexpected turns.

Paul Thomas Anderson is such a genius that he has successfully created an anti-Adam Sandler movie that proves to be a highly defining moment for the actor. Sandler's socially inept Barry Egan is superficially a lot like the persona he always parades in his nitwit comedies: nice, innocent and burdened with anger management issues that make him fly off the handle in sudden outbursts of rage.

But this time he's a sad little man with many shades of darkness. He is so tightly buttoned-up, so lonely, so angry, so stressed and so close to despair that it occurs to us that he might do something really extreme and horrible.

Barry doesn't mass-murder his family although, given the earful he gets from his sisters, you wouldn't be the least bit surprised if he did. With his small business struggling and no one to love, he timidly treats himself to a spot of phone sex, only to be hounded in a nasty extortion racket masterminded by the deeply unpleasant Dean (Anderson-regular Hoffman getting in touch with his inner brute).

Sweet, offbeat Lena (Watson, relishing a calming character who is on an even keel) seems to like him for some reason, however. It's his unwavering determination to pursue her that gives Barry the resolve to use his head. His new-found love also prompts the mouse to roar. One of the joys of this film, although it is unlikely to impress Sandler fans who are wedded to the formulaic chucklesome shtick he turns out in *Mr Deeds* or *Little Nicky*, is that you really have no idea what's going to happen next.

It's also bright and perky-looking, in sharp contrast to its protagonist's stormy state of mind. Anderson's direction is simply captivating and exquisitely controlled, with a restless mood and no end of fascinating, beautifully-orchestrated oddness – like the baffling car crash that opens the film, our hero's acquisition of a harmonium, and Barry immersed in one of his ballistic mini-dramas at a pay phone when a parade passes by. ★★★★ **AE**

PURPLE RAIN (1984)

Starring: *Prince (The Kid), Apollonia Kotero (Apollonia), Morris Day (Morris), Olga Karlatos (Mother), Clarence Williams III (Father), Jerome Benton (Jerome)*
Director: *Albert Ragnoli*
Screenwriters: *William Blinn, Albert Magnoli*
15/111 mins./Musical/USA

Awards: *Academy Awards – Best Song*

A talented young singer, The Kid, on the cusp of big things, hits it off with a female singer, but neither path will run smoothly, as his own upbringing issues begin to cloud his judgement.

A fairly dappy and overlong attempt to turn Prince the then emergent rock-funk superstar into a movie star. It didn't work at all, but the soundtrack album became a classic. And that there is barely a plot worth speaking of is circumvented by the marketing spiel appealing to us that such a powerful tale is the result of it being semi-autobiographical, a trick that made hit movies out of everyone from Al Jolson to Eminem. Thus Prince, as The Kid, is a struggling but clearly brilliant musician-singer-sex bomb from Minneapolis, who wrestles with his troubles, including a bad old pop (Clarence Williams III), comes good through his musical expression to do a stonking gig for the big finale. That's pretty much it, and Albert Ragnoli sensibly keeps his camera pointed squarely at Prince and his luminous locks, clearly aware having a genuine icon in the middle of your movie is a real boon.

It's his crappy attempt to add a layer of psychology just ruins things. Most of us would be happy just to sit through a convoluted assemblage of videos and concert footage, which otherwise the film is, without the banal rot about an artist's self-destructive urges. We learned all about those when the diminutive funkster started drawing on his face and changed his name to a squiggle. Here given Prince isn't half the actor Eminem is (a strange sort of sentence for a film review) he just comes across as a petulant brat, rather than the symbolically tortured artist.

The music, however, is divine. From 'Let's Go Crazy' to 'When Doves Cry' it gifts the film a power it doesn't deserve in filmmaking terms, as the short-stuff with the licks from heaven, launches into a heart-stopping version of the title song, its hard to not join in. ★★ **IN**

THE PURPLE ROSE OF CAIRO (1985)

Starring: *Mia Farrow (Cecillia), Jeff Daniels (Tom Baxter/Gil Shepherd), Danny Aiello (Monk), Dianne Wiest (Emma), Van Johnson (Larry), Zoe Caldwell (The Countess)m John Wood (Jason), Milo O'Shea (Fr Donnelly), Deborah Rush (Rita)*
Director: *Woody Allen*
Screenwriter: *Woody Allen*
PG/84 mins./Comedy-Fantasy/USA

Cecilia seeks solace from her dead-end job and boorish husband Monk in the Jewel movie theatre. However, one matinee, Tom Baxter, a character in the RKO programmer *The Purple Rose of Cairo*, comes through the screen to sweep her away – much to the chagrin of the cast left behind on the screen and the actor who created him, Gil Shepherd.

Five years after depicting film fans as psychotic morons in *Stardust Memories*, Woody Allen sent them a bittersweet love letter in this fond, if slight memoir of his own lost days in the flickering darkness. Recapturing the simple pleasures that escapism could afford, he also lamented the extent to which films had ceased to matter as they had in the depths of the Depression and the shift from stardom to celebrity that had taken away so much of the romance of movies that were now packaged and sold like any other consumer product.

Allen staged the action in the Coney Island cinema he had frequented as a kid and the small town of Piermont, which still resembled oldtime New Jersey. However, in an ironic twist on the storyline, heavy snows hindered shooting and business premises were forced lay idle behind their film façades until the production wrapped.

Allen also had to pause after firing Michael Keaton just 10 days into the schedule, as he was (according to the press release) too contemporary for the dual role of Tom/Gil. Resisting Orion's suggestions that he or Kevin Kline assumed the part, Allen cast Jeff Daniels, although he proved to be much more persuasive as the celluloid figment out of his depth in coarse actuality than he was as the cynical star prepared to do anything to save his career.

Mia Farrow, however, was impeccable as the crushed spirit whose inability to distinguish between fantasy and reality had been diminished by her desperate psychological reliance on inaccessible icons enacting impossibly glamorous scenarios. But while Allen shrewdly eschewed nostalgia by making her environment as rundown as possible, he never quite solved the problem of blending Cecilia's whimsical adventures with the tragedy of her social situation. Thus, while the movie cast are amusingly able to slip out of character and resume being their egotistical selves and Tom/Gil are able to return to their familiar milieu, Cecilia is left only with Fred and Ginger in *Top Hat*, whose transient sophistication can never replace the dream that has passed forever. ★★★★ **DP**

Q (Q – THE WINGED SERPENT) (1982)

Starring: *Michael Moriarty (Jimmy Quinn), David Carradine (Det. Shepard), Candy Clark (Joan), Richard Roundtree (Sgt Powell), James Dixon (Lt Murray)*
Director: *Larry Cohen*
Screenwriter: *Larry Cohen*
15/92 mins./Fantasy/Horror/USA

Quetzalcoatl, an Aztec God, is resurrected by ritual in Manhattan. Jimmy Quinn, a petty crook, happens across the serpent's lair in the Chrysler Building and makes demands of the city before revealing the location.

This sprightly Larry Cohen monster movie literally starts where *King Kong* leaves off, with the decapitation of a horny windowcleaner on the Empire State Building, then wings its way across New York to the art deco splendours of the Chrysler Building, where a monster god prayed back into existence by a series of gruesome, skin-flaying human sacrifices has built a gory nest and laid a giant egg. 'It wouldn't be the first time in history that a monster was mistaken for a god,' says cop-on-the-case David Carradine (in one of his few suit-and-tie roles). 'I guess that's why I have to kill it – if you can kill it, it's not a god, just a good old-fashioned monster.'

Most giant, city-smashing monster movies have the same plot – the monster shows up, menaces the community, and the stalwart authorities rally round to defeat the beastie – but Cohen cannily relegates all the expected business to the background to concentrate instead on someone who'd be a minor, one-scene character in any other film, giving Michael Moriarty free rein to improvise as the petty hustler who happens across one vital piece of information and tries to bargain his way to a better life even as bodies are falling from the skies and feathered Aztec killer-priests are on the loose. Moriarty, partnered interestingly with Candy Clark as his bartender girlfriend, gives the sort of performance that'd earn awards nominations if it were in *Mean Streets* or *Midnight Cowboy* – making the valuable observation that even if there's a monster soaring through the skies, regular street-level lowlife carries on. The animated monster looks hand-made, but is still fun. ★★★★ **KN**

Q&A (1990)

Starring: *Nick Nolte (Captain Lt Mike Brennan), Timothy Hutton (Asst Dist Atty Al Francis Reilly), Armand Assante (Roberto 'Bobby Tex' Texador), Patrick O'Neal (Kevin Quinn), Lee Richardson (Leo Bloomenfeld)*
Director: *Sidney Lumet*
Screenwriters: *Sidney Lumet, based on the book by Edwin Torres*
18/132 mins./Crime/USA

In his attempts to help win a case against a corrupt police captain who has shot a Puerto Rican hood and then rigged the evidence to make it look like self-defence, a young, determined DA aims to get a crime boss to go on record, a crime boss who happens to have become a protector of his former lover.

After the excellent *Serpico* and *Prince Of The City*, this is the third in Sydney Lumet's unofficial trilogy of hard-nosed police procedurals set in his home city, that hotbed of tribal ferocity and corruption known as New York. And if you've already sampled the unvarnished moral tension of those films, that a good man is hard to find in a big city, and while *Q&A* amps up the brute intelligence, and the foul-tongue, it is a clumsier, more punishing film to the point where all the hard-hitting actually leaves you numb.

Yet, you can't help but applaud Lumet's determination to say something loud about the cultural mishmash of his city. This is a place slashed up into self-dependent racially defined tribes, testing the borders, pushing for territory: blacks, Puerto Ricans, Italians and the all-important Irish, who have the cop-shops sorted. That's where the plot comes in. Nick Nolte at his most thick-necked and threatening, is a cop with blood on his hands, and has stacked the evidence to make a brutal killing into justifiable homicide. Nolte's Captain Lt Brennan, spitting out racial epithets like a cornered cat, is a vicious, corrupt man who can't see the justice for the fog of bigotry he bullies through. He's also Irish, and the man against him, Assistant DA Reilly is too, so he's calling in the loyalty card. Timothy Hutton all fleshy idealism, is given the Q&A, the interrogation of Brennan, by his boss who might be looking for a quick fix. He's Lumet's great crusader, but a more diminished voice than Al Pacino's Serpico.

There is the usual guff about payoffs and fathers on the force, and following the corruption back to the source, which while ferociously delivered is pretty stale stuff. Armand Assante, a great actor seldom sung, crops up as a slick criminal (see the comparison – slick hood, brute cop) who might give Reilly what he needs, and bumps about in a subplot involving a former lover they share. It's very talky, or maybe that should be shouty, but is finally an old song just sung loudly again. ★★★ **IN**

QUADROPHENIA (1979)

Starring: *Phil Daniels (Jimmy Cooper), Leslie Ash (Steph), Philip Davis (Chalky), Mark Wingett (Dave), Sting (Ace Face), Ray Winstone (Kevin)*
Director: *Franc Roddam*
Screenwriters: *Dave Humphries, Franc Roddam, Martin Stellman, Pete Townshend*
18/120 mins./Drama/UK

In the London of 1965, Jimmy Cooper is a disillusioned youth, who finds some kind of purpose with his Mod gang, riding their Lambrettas and cruising for girls, especially Steph. But deep within him that feeling of dislocation is hard to shake.

An iconic ode to fallen youth of the Mod variety that has picked up a cult following mainly due to its hip imagery, its so-called grasp of the teen identity, and the fact it was based on an album by The Who, granting Pete Townshend a screenplay credit. There are some fine soap-operatics, and the rough-edged depiction of the period, the mid-60s with its fraught air of violence, feels pungently real. And Phil Daniels, in a role he has never quite shaken, is strangely charismatic (given he is supposed to represent the ordinary boy) as the scooter-riding anti-hero Jimmy.

Director Franc Roddam is caught between stools, he wants to depict an era he knew well, to give a documentary vibe of headiness and rebellion, building up to a Bank Holiday confrontation with the teddy boys heading for Brighton beach. Yet, he is also having to deal with Townshend's teen-death-dream thing – a mood piece full of stark symbolism and the much-debated significance of the downer ending. It is not a satisfying fit; the film is youthful and vague, gritty and quite weird.

Its reputation is better founded on the sharp, compelling recreation of the era, and there are some striking performances to go along with Daniel's tormented Jimmy: Leslie Ash is frail and beautiful as Steph, the girl who will force Jimmy to re-evaluate for the worse; Gary Shail, Philip Davis and Mark Wingnett froth and bubble with all the bloody-mindedness and energy of bad-youth as his Mod buddies; while Sting looks statuesque and icy without having to do much as Ace Face, a Mod fashion-icon, gang leader and Jimmy's hero. When he, also, proves to have a humble side to the cool sheen, Jimmy starts to see through the whole mystique of this tribal world. It's a haunting note, growing up is about losing your ideals. ★★★★ **IN**

LE QUAI DES BRUMES (PORT OF SHADOWS) (1938)

Starring: *Jean Gabin (Jean), Michele Morgan (Nelly), Michel Simon (Zabel), Pierre Brasseur (Lucien Laugardier), Robert Le Vigan (Michel Krauss), Jenny Burnay (Lucien's Friend), Marcel Peres (Chauffeur), Rene Genin (Doctor)*
Director: *Marcel Carné*
Screenwriter: *Jacques Prévert, based on the novel* Le Quai Des Brumes *by Pierre Mac Orlan*
PG/91 mins./Drama/France

Arriving in Le Havre from Tonkin, army deserter Jean hopes to jump a ship to Venezuela. But, despite being left the means to escape by suicidal painter, Michel, his fate is sealed when he becomes involved with Nelly and her murderous guardian Zabel and his gangster crony, Lucien.

In 1933, Marcel Carné published a critical essay entitled, 'When Will Cinema Descend into the Street?' Having made his name as a director with the realist drama *Jenny* (1936) and the eccentric comedy, *Drôle de Drame* (1937), he answered his own question with this brooding melodrama, which marked the first of his seven outings with the poet-cum-scenarist, Jacques Prévert.

He was to have filmed this adaptation of Pierre Mac Orlan's novel for producer Raoul Ploquin at UFA in Berlin, but propaganda chief Josef Goebbels deemed the story of an army deserter to be too decadent for the Reich. So, Carné returned to Paris, where the project received official sanction on the proviso that the word 'deserter' was never mentioned and that Jean Gabin treated his discarded uniform with suitable respect.

Updating the action from 1909 and transferring it from Montmartre to Le Havre, Prévert merged two of Mac Orlan's characters to produce Jean and changed Nelly from a prostitute who murders her pimp to a teenage waif at the mercy of her lustful godfather. But, more significantly, he invested the material with a philosophical gravitas and a sense of foreboding that was reinforced by both the coastal locations and Alexandre Trauner's atmospheric studio sets.

Indeed, the tone became so bleak that the suits at Ciné-Alliance tried to persuade Carné to fashion his story into a lighter, romantic tearjerker, while backer Gregor Rabinovitch urged Gabin to reconsider his participation in such a downbeat saga, in case it damaged his career. Clearly he had never seen Julien Duvivier's *La Bandèra* (which was also based on a Mac Orlan text) or *Pépé Le Moko* or Jean Renoir's *Les Bas-fonds*, as Gabin's tragic heroes were already becoming the screen barometer for France's dwindling sense of self-esteem.

But no one before had quite managed to imbue poetic realism with such an all-pervading air of fatalism. During the Occupation, Carné was accused of having preconditioned France to defeat by sapping their spirit with this hopeless vision. However, he was to summon up even more doomed melancholia in *Le Jour se Lève* in 1939. ★★★★★ **DP**

QUATERMASS AND THE PIT (1967)

Starring: *James Donald (Dr Matthew Roney), Andrew Keir (Professor Bernard Quartermass), Barbara Shelley (Judd), Julian Glover (Colonel Breen)*
Director: *Roy Ward Baker*
Screenwriter: *Nigel Kneale, from his television serial*
15/93 mins./Sci-fi/Thriller/UK

Workmen excavating the site of a new underground railway station unearth a mystery object which Professor Quatermass deduces is a five-million-year-old Martian spaceship. It turns out that the long-extinct Martians once meddled in human evolution, and their evil influence persists.

The third of Hammer's film adaptations of Nigel Kneale's BBC-TV *Quatermass* serials was made a decade on from *The Quatermass Experiment* and *Quatermass 2* – it's the best-scripted and acted of the three films (though still trims a lot of great material from the TV version), but its candy-coloured studio look is perhaps less effective than the black and white, location-based approach of the earlier movies.

That said, it's one of the best science fiction films of the 1960s, advancing some of the ideas soon to be used in *2001: A Space Odyssey* in a slightly more accessible form. It works as a puzzle-based mystery, with the bearded boffin (Andrew Kier), a mild-mannered paleontologist (James Donald) and a blimpish army officer (Julian Glover) arguing about the nature of the unidentified buried object discovered under London (the official story is that it's an unexploded Nazi bomb) and tracing historical ghost stories connected with the alien insects, finally coming to some disturbing conclusions about the nature of humanity.

The finale cuts loose with telekinetic action as a giant Martian Devil forms over London and atavistic impulses turn most of the city into insectile lynch mobs. Director Roy Ward Baker orchestrates the eerie business very well, and everyone works hard at making the mind-stretching business credible. It has one of the most effective, underplayed final shots in the movies – after the crisis has passed, Quatermass and an assistant (Barbara Shelley) slump against a wall, too exhausted to speak.

A rare intelligent science fiction movie with worthwhile ideas to go along with its creepy moments. ★★★★ **KN**

THE QUATERMASS EXPERIMENT (THE QUATERMASS XPERIMENT) (1955)

Starring: *Brian Donlevy (Professor Bernard Quatermass), Jack Warner (Inspector Lomax), Margia Dean (Judith Carroon), Richard Wordsworth (Victor Carroon), Thora Hird (Rosie)*
Director: *Val Guest*
Screenwriters: *Val Guest, Richard Landau, from the television serial by Nigel Kneale*
PG/78 mins./Sci-fi/Thriller/UK

An experimental man rocketship crashes back to Earth, and the surviving astronaut transforms into a giant creature which threatens all life on Earth. Professor Quatermass, head of the rocket programme, takes command of efforts to save the world.

Bernard Quatermass, author Nigel Kneale's British rocketry boffin and all-purpose defender of humankind against alien threat and government red tape, first appeared on BBC-TV in the 1953 serial which Hammer Films adapted into this tough, gritty science fiction thriller.

The original TV version (of which only two episodes survive) was more intellectual, but director Val Guest's film version has the advantage of effectively used London locations (backstreets, London Zoo, Westminster Abbey) and solid performances (even the thuggish Donlevy provides a *reading* of the Quatermass role and Wordsworth is outstanding as the man turning into a monster) while quite a lot of Kneale's well-thought-out story and script survives the streamlining into a more action-oriented medium. American science fiction monster movies were taking an increasingly juvenile approach at the time, but this plays to adults with its interesting vision of the political and emotional in-fighting that goes on around the space programme and then the Scotland Yard manhunt (led by reliable Jack Warner) for the monster. It's full of neat little character bits: the monster's encounter with a little girl (Jane Asher) playing in bombed-out rubble, the female drunk (Thora Hird) shocked to learn that the monster she's described to the police wasn't her imagination. More BBC-TV serials, *Quatermass II* and *Quatermass and the Pit*, followed, and were filmed by Hammer; a 1979 ITV effort was made simultaneously as a TV serial called *Quatermass* and a feature called *The Quatermass Conclusion*. In 2005, the BBC mounted an ambitious, live feature-length restaging of Kneale's original script for *The Quatermass Experiment*. ★★★★ **KN**

LES QUATRES CENTS COUPS (THE FOUR HUNDRED BLOWS) (1959)

Starring: *Jean Pierre Leaud (Antoine Doinel), Claire Maurier (Mme Doinel), Albert Remy (M.Doinel), Guy Decombie (Teacher), Patrick Aufay (Rene Bigey)*
Director: *Francois Truffaut*
Screenwriter: *Francois Truffaut*
PG/93 mins./Drama/France

Bored at school and betrayed by his mother Gilberte's adultery, Antoine Doinel is caught first in a lie and then in the act of returning a stolen typewriter and winds up in a reformatory. However, he escapes during a football match and heads to Normandy to see the sea, which he has always equated with freedom.

The Cannes Film Festival in 1956, and a young film critic for *Cahiers Du Cinema*, Francois Truffaut, is vociferously complaining that the rows of flowers running along the front of the auditorium are obscuring the view of the screen from the stalls. As a result, the organisers ban him from the world's premier festival. Three years later, and Truffaut returns as a filmmaker with *Les Quatres Cents Coups*. Watching the film from the privileged position of the balcony, he is struck by how beautiful the flowers are running along the bottom of the screen...

Indicative of the difference between those that do and those that *critique*, the 27-year-old Truffaut's change of heart must have been eased by the rapturous response afforded his feature film debut, including the Cannes Award for Best Director. As landmark films go, this is one unassuming masterpiece: intimate, accessible, funny, honest, fresh and heartbreaking.

Unlike, say *E.T.*, which locks you into a childlike point-of-view, or *Stand By Me*, which paints a patina of nostalgia on adolescent rites of passage, *The 400 Blows* is shot through with a matter-of-fact neutrality that borders on the documentary. *The 400 Blows* (the original title comes from the French phrase 'faire les quatres cents coups' meaning 'to raise hell') demolishes the barriers between autobiography and fiction, actor and character, performance and personality.

The character study follows 12-year-old Antoine Doinel (Jean-Pierre Leaud) – toyed with by his glam mother, patronised by his ineffectual stepfather, picked on by his teachers – descending into teen rebellion, resulting in a life of petty crime and juvenile incarceration. Around the narrative thrust Truffaut manages to weave some hilarious vignettes of school life (a pupil tearing out ink-stained pages of his book until there are none left), exhilarating digressions depicting Doinel's truancy, and a portrait of 50s Paris that teems with vitality, lending the film the unique quality of being at once light yet serious, both disciplined and free.

Part-rebel, part-slacker, part-innocent victim, Doinel is, without doubt, cinema's coolest kid. Truffaut discovered the 13-year-old Leaud after placing an ad in *Paris Soir*. Unlike modern cinematic searches for young leads which often encompass cattle-calls for kids, Truffaut only tested a few youngsters, finding one who resembled the director as a child and was preternaturally natural before the camera. Being interviewed by his social worker about his sexual experiences, Leaud's expression of surprise before finding his confidence is the perfect synthesis of character, script and actor.

Dotted around *Les Quatre Cent Coups* are references – some blatent, some subtle – to the central role movies played in Truffaut's existence. Tellingly, the only point when Antoine experiences any prolonged domestic happiness is following a family outing to see Jacques Rivette's *Paris Nous Appartient*. Later, during Antoine and his friend Rene's suspension from school, Doinel steals a film still of Monika from Bergman's *Summer With Monika*, itself a tale of young people on the run. Like his hero Hitchcock, Truffaut also makes a fleeting appearance, cameoing as Doinel wanders reeling after his amusement park escapades.

Despite its rep as the first stand of the nouvelle vague, *The 400 Blows* lacks the jazzy experimentation that the likes of Godard's *A Bout De Souffle* claimed for the movement. Instead, Truffaut lenses Doinel's life with a simple and lucid verisimilitude, punctured by flashes of lyrical eloquence: the lights of Paris at night glimpsed by a crying Doinel through the bars of a police van adds a poignancy to his plight.

Equally lyrical is the tracking shot that follows Doinel's escape from the detention centre. As he hobbles across the Seine estuary, the boy stops short of the lapping waves, walks parallel with the tide and turns to face the camera. The image freezes and the title 'FIN' appears. If the moment was a happy accident – 'I told him to look at the camera,' recalled Truffaut, 'like taking a bow in the theatre but he didn't look long enough so we froze the frame' – it remains the most effective use of freeze-frame in movie history. With Doinel's face full of bewilderment and uncertainty, it is a full stop on childhood before the sentence of adulthood begins.

In a run unique in any national cinema, Truffaut and Leaud collaborated on four more Doinel movies over the next 20 years, following young Antoine through the flushes of first love (*Antoine Et Collette*, from the international compilation film *Love At Twenty*), getting a job as a private detective then falling for a client's wife (*Stolen Kisses/Baisers Voles*), the pain of marital discord and infidelity (*Bed And Board/Domicile Conjugal*), and the aftermath of divorce (*Love On The Run/L'Amour En Fuite*). ★★★★★ **IF**

⦾ QUEEN CHRISTINA (1933)

Starring: *Greta Garbo (Queen Christina), John Gilbert (Don Antonio De La Prada), Ian Keith (Magnus), Lewis Stone (Chancellor Oxenstierna), Elizabeth Young (Ebba Sparre),C. Aubrey Smith (Aage), Reginald Owen (Prince Charles)*
Director: *Rouben Mamoulian*
Screenwriters: *H.M. Harwood, Salka Viertel, S.N. Berhman based on a story by Viertel and Margaret R. Levino*
U/97 mins./Historical Drama/USA

Resisting the efforts of her former lover, Magnus, to marry her off to the dashing Prince Charles, Queen Christina of Sweden falls for Spanish Ambassador Don Antonio De la Prada after a chance meeting and prepares to renounce the throne.

Greta Garbo was on sabbatical in Sweden when she first became interested in Queen Christina. Her companion Salka Viertel produced a screenplay that suitably romanticised her unsavoury personality and sanitised her sapphic proclivities and MGM agreed to Garbo's request that Rouben Mamoulian (who had just worked with Marlene Dietrich on *Song Of Songs*) should be her director and Laurence Olivier her co-star. However, she developed an inexplicable aversion to the British newcomer and, after Leslie Howard had declined the role of the Spanish Ambassador for fear of being upstaged, Garbo rejected Nils Asther, Bruce Cabot and Franchot Tone in preference to her one-time lover and most effective on-screen swain, John Gilbert.

Despite being incensed at having to rehire a man whose career he hoped he had sabotaged, Louis B. Mayer gave this austere historical the MGM prestige treatment. But it lost heavily on his $1,444,000 investment and there were fears that the Divine Garbo was losing her allure.

Yet, despite the sterility of the court intrigue, this critically acclaimed drama boasts one of Garbo's finest performances. She was delightfully mischievous in male disguise during her first meeting with Gilbert – who pulled faces at her off camera to elicit the spontaneous belly laugh that predated Ninotchka's more vaunted, but less convincing guffaw by six years – and she even allowed herself occasionally to be skittishly sensual.

Moreover, she was sublime in the film's two most celebrated sequences, in which she gathered her most cherished memory and then relived it to prevent the awfulness of reality from crashing in upon her. Mamoulian used a metronome to pace Garbo's movements as she drank in the details of the bedroom in which she had just discovered blissful happiness and she responded by caressing and gazing upon each object as though it were pricelessly precious. She then recalled them as she stood in the prow of the ship bound for Spain, although Mamoulian suggested that she maintained a neutral expression so that the audience could speculate about her bittersweet thoughts. Whatever, her motivation, Garbo never again appeared so captivatingly enigmatic or iconically beautiful. ★★★★★ **DP**

⦾ QUEEN KELLY (1929)

Starring: *Gloria Swanson (Kitty Kelly), Walter Byron (Prince Wolfram), Seena Owen (Queen Regina V), Sidney Bracey (Prince Wolfram's Lackey), Wilhelm von Brincken (Prince Wolfram's Adjutant), Tully Marshall (Jan Vryheid)*
Directors: *Erich Von Stroheim, Richard Boleslawski (uncredited)*
Screenwriters: *Erich Von Stroheim, Marion Ainslee*
PG/101 mins./Drama/USA

Driven from a Ruritanian kingdom by the decadent Queen Regina V for dallying with her fiancé, Prince Wolfram, Patricia Kelly is summoned to East Africa by an ailing aunt, who forces her to marry the syphilitic Jan Bloehm Vryheid and assume control of her sordid brothel.

This is a film whose backstory is better known than its narrative and which is more celebrated for its excerpted inclusion in Billy Wilder's *Sunset Blvd.* than for its various bowdlerised incarnations.

It started out as a vanity project for Gloria Swanson, who was keen to show a Hollywood increasingly obsessed with sound that she was still capable of silent greatness. Ignoring the warnings about the director's grandiloquence and profligacy, her producer-lover Joseph P. Kennedy commissioned Erich von Stroheim to develop an epic from his short story, 'The Swamp', that would enable the ageing Swanson to showcase her gifts for drama, comedy, passion and tragedy.

However, no one seemed to notice the blatant eroticism with which Von Stroheim had doused his screenplay and it was only when Swanson was asked to cup her hands to receive a mouthful of Tully Marshall's tobacco juice that she had the errant Austrian fired.

Renowned theatre director Richard Boleslawski was brought in to rescue the project, but Kennedy closed it down shortly afterwards and Swanson spent the next two years and $800,000 trying to salvage her reputation. In 1931, she sanctioned a version that culminated in Kelly's European suicide. But it only received a limited release and, although Von Stroheim cobbled together his own cut in the 1960s, 54 years were to pass before a reasonable approximation (complete with an epilogue comprising captions and production stills) was achieved.

Although Von Stroheim had realised only a third of his proposed 30 reels, he had filmed in sequence and, so, the Kronberg scenes survive pretty much as he had envisaged them. Apart from the obvious opulence, the footage was remarkable for the wealth of contrasting symbolism, as Von Stroheim used fairy-tale romance and ignoble reality, virility and impotence, bestiality and chastity, dressing and undressing to explore such themes as order and chaos, light and darkness, nature and artifice, and love and lust. His use of fire was particularly striking, although the vulgarity that underpinned his pompous sophistication was never far below the surface.

Maybe not a missing masterpiece, but this is definitely a cherishable curio. ★★★★ **DP**

⦾ QUEST FOR FIRE (1981)

Starring: *Everett McGill (Noah), Ron Perlman (Amoukar), Nicholas Kadi (Gaw), Raw Dawn Chong (Ika), Gary Schwartz (Rouka)*
Director: *Jean-Jacques Annaud*
Screenwriter: *Gerard Brach, based on the novel by JH Rosny Sr*
15/100 mins./Drama/France-Canada-USA

Awards: *Academy Awards – Best Make-Up; BAFTA – Best Make-Up*

A tale of three prehistoric warriors who embark on a quest to rediscover the flame their tribe has lost, braving mammoths, sabre-toothed tigers, and tribes of cannibals.

You've got to admire the effort put in to this attempt to recreate the realities of prehistoric living (a clue: it wasn't pretty); director Jean-Jacques Annaud even turned to linguist Anthony Burgess to create a genuine proto-language of grunts and burps just for the movie. We are supposed to marvel at man's emerging traits: communication, teamwork, civility (of a sort), but there is one inescapable problem with daring to go vérité with the land before time – whatever you do, it looks and, indeed, sounds, like a parody. And, no matter how hard you true to take it seriously, no dice.

In fact, for all its mud and blather, the savage landscapes captured from the Canadian and Scottish locations, you can't help missing the stop-motion dinosaurs chasing after Raquel Welch in *One Million Years BC*. Any half-bright schoolboy could tell you man and dinosaurs have never shared the same hunting grounds (65 million years separates the species) but it leaves a big fun-shaped hole. Thus the perils this trio of hairy, fur-clad actors (Everett McGill, Ron Perlman, Nicholas Kadi) earnestly ooga-booga-ing like its Shakespeare with mastodons, are left to face include such tame palaeontological difficulties as legging it from a sabre-toothed tiger, a tribe of argumentative apes (who could be relatives) and getting trodden on by woolly mammoths (elephants in disguise!). Any excitement is severely limited.

Annaud is fired by the idea of showing how mankind founded a primitive form of civilisation, and treats us to the rapid birth of art, industry (well, regular fire making) and, most radically, respect for women. Actually, there is something quite charming in the scenes where they discover comedy – one tribesman is hit on the head by a loose stone. It might be Annaud's most telling suggestion – that civilisation gained greatest ground through the powers of the belly laugh. ★★ IN

THE QUICK AND THE DEAD (1995)

Starring: *Sharon Stone (Ellen 'The Lady'), Gene Hackman (John Herod), Russell Crowe (Cort), Leonardo DiCarprio (Fee Herod 'The Kid')*
Director: *Sam Raimi*
Screenwriter: *Simon Moore*
15/103 mins./Western/USA

Ellen is a female gunslinger who rides into town to settle an old childhood score ...

Imagine, if you will, that Sharon Stone was a man. It would be totally acceptable for her (him) to attain world fame by starring in glossy popcorn action thrillers and baring her (his) chest; to harbour behind-the-camera aspirations; to be fit, fast and feisty. And if her latest movie was a daft, self-contained cartoon Western in which she (he) played a silent-but-deadly gunslinger, that would be dandy. As it is, she's a woman, and so making shallow hokum like this seems to bring Shazza little but scorn.

Shirt almost buttoned up, in classic Leone-Eastwood style, Stone rides, silently, dustily and moodily into the town of Redemption. She's Ellen, and she has a childhood score to settle. The town is holding its annual gunslinging contest (a strict local custom in which pistol-packers young and old, local and not, shoot to the death – it's very much a knock-out tournament). Ellen enters, keeps her motivation quiet, and works her way to the contest's nub. Redemption's despotic self-styled big cheese – he's the one with the only nice house on the street – Herod (Hackman, loving every minute of it), becomes fascinated with Ellen, and as the bullet-a-thon unfolds, gets sucked into conflict with both her and his own cocky young son (a sparky, unrealistic Leonardo DiCaprio). Meanwhile, preacherman Cort (an astonishingly handsome Crowe) is forced to conquer his own self-righteous pacifism.

Tagline
Think you're quick enough?

Raimi's chosen mode of direction is larger-than-life. Just as his infamous *Evil Deads* invited knowing sniggers, this ankle-deep story has a cheekful of tongue, providing opportunities galore for hammy, quick-draw melodrama and even some outrageous Bugs Bunny-style bullet holes (one with a shaft of light shining through it!). It's a perfect plateful of ham for Stone, a great movie decision: it's silly, it's surreal, it's shot full of holes – it's Clint Eastwood with all the macho posturing done by a woman. ★★★★ AC

THE QUIET AMERICAN (2002)

Starring: *Michael Caine (Thomas Fowler), Brendan Fraser (Alden Pyle), Do Thi Hai Yen (Phuong), Rade Serverdzija (Inspector Vigot)*
Director: *Phillip Noyce*
Screenwriters: *Christopher Hampton, Robert Schenkkan, from the novel by Graham Greene*
15/96 mins./Drama/War/USA/Germany

After the murder of 'quiet American' Alden Pyle in 1950s Saigon, British newspaper man Thomas Fowler reminisces on their friendship, their rivalry over Fowler's Vietnamese mistress, and the tension between them when Pyle's shadowy political connections come to the fore.

Sliver, *The Saint*, *The Bone Collector*, even with a couple of Jack Ryan hits to his credit (*Patriot Games*, *Clear And Present Danger*), Phillip Noyce's career in the 1990s wasn't exactly a shining beacon in the Hollywood wilderness. And yet in 2002 he delivered two very different, politically sensitive movies into UK cinemas in a single month.

While *Rabbit-Proof Fence* pricked the consciences of Noyce's fellow Australians by bringing a shameful episode in that country's history to light, *The Quiet American* raised questions about America's covert foreign policy in 1950s Vietnam.

The suggestion that the American government's meddling in Vietnamese politics – allegedly using the CIA to install a Washington-friendly military dictatorship – led indirectly to the Vietnam War was not likely to go down well across the Atlantic post-9/11. Hence Miramax's reluctance to give it more than a tiny US release in December to qualify it for Oscar consideration.

But Oscar nominations it richly earned, not least for Michael Caine, whose performance as an English reporter goaded out of his comfortable, opium-clouded, ex-pat lifestyle ranks among the very best of his career. Caine brings dry wit and tragic self-knowledge to his character, while Brendan Fraser, as the love-struck Pyle, trades on his charismatic screen presence.

Actually, for the majority of the movie, the focus falls more on the love triangle than any anti-American political dimension. However, as in Graham Greene's source novel, this story element itself captures a sense of history passing the empirical baton from Britain (the rumpled Fowler) to America (the clean-cut Pyle). Noyce's film restores several of the essential qualities of Greene's book that were ironed out of Joseph L. Mankiewicz's 1958 adaptation.

Most impressive is the manner in which the director evokes time and place, both in the locations settings and through the characters' attitudes to a young Vietnamese girl they both want to 'protect' (read: 'possess'). ★★★★ AE

THE QUIET MAN (1952)

Starring: *John Wayne (Sean Thornton), Maureen O'Hara (Mary Kate Danaher), Barry Fitzgerald (Michaeleen Flynn), Ward Bond (Fr Peter Lonergan), Victor McLaglen (Red. Will Danaher), Mildred Natwick (Mrs Sarah Tillane), Francis Ford (Dan Tobin)*
Director: *John Ford*
Screenwriters: *Frank S. Nugent, Richard Llewellyn, based on a story by Maurice Walsh*
U/129 mins./Romance-Comedy/USA

Awards: *Academy Awards – Best Director, Best Colour Cinematography*

Pittsburgh pugilist Sean Thornton returns to his Irish village of Innisfree and falls for strong-willed, flame-haired colleen Mary Kate Danaher, whose short-fused brother Red Will opposes the match and deeply resents widow Sarah Tillane selling a cottage he had coveted to 'a dirty Yank'.

John Ford had hoped to adapt Maurice Walsh's *Saturday Evening Post* story as an independent production in 1937 before funding problems

q

had frustrated his plans. So, he was determined to make an occasion of this 1951 shoot, after signing off the dispiriting war documentary, *This Is Korea*. Returning to the Connemara he had often visited as a boy, Ford indulged his nostalgic sense of homecoming by finding work for John Wayne's kids, Maureen O'Hara's siblings and Victor McLaglen's assistant director son, as well as his own offspring and brother, Francis, who was making the penultimate of his 29 appearances in Ford's films. Even brothers Barry Fitzgerald and Arthur Shields were reunited with old friends from the Abbey Theatre.

But while many critics lauded this as a charming slice of Oirish whimsy, *The Quiet Man* represented an inversion of the stark social message of *How Green Was My Valley*. There was certainly plenty of the manly bravura familiar from the barrack-room sequences in Ford's Cavalry pictures, and the fight between Wayne and McLaglen that thundered through the village remained among his best-remembered set pieces.

Yet, there was a real feel for the savage simplicity of life in the impecunious county and, while the troubles of the 1920s were downplayed, the tensions between the different social and religious groupings still simmered beneath the surface of Winton Hoch and Archie Stout's Oscar-winning Technicolor imagery.

Ford also exposed the hypocritical repression imposed by the Catholic Church. But he saved his special ire for Sean Thornton's barely suppressed brutishness that not only caused him to kill a man in the ring, but also inspired his chauvinist attitude towards Mary Kate. However, such boorishness was also intended to symbolise American insensitivity to local custom and practice, as it warmed to its self-appointed task of policing the world.

Faced with having to play stooge to a cast of natural born scene-stealers, Wayne always counted this display of emotional and cultural incivility among his toughest assignments. However, he was overlooked by the Academy, while Ford received his fourth and last Best Director award. ★★★★★ **DP**

THE QUILLER MEMORANDUM (1966)

Starring: *George Segal (Quiller), Alec Guinness (Pol), Max Von Sydow (Oktober), Senta Berger (Inge Lindt), George Sanders (Gibbs)*
Director: *Michael Anderson*
Screenwriter: *Harold Pinter, based on the novel by Adam Hall*
15/95 mins./Thriller/UK

Agent Quiller, sent into Cold War Berlin after two agents are murdered by Neo-Nazis, is captured by the sinister figure Oktober. He becomes caught in the middle of a set of mind games as each side tries to discover the whereabouts of the other's HQ.

In the wake of the twin successes of James Bond (spy as superhero) and Harry Palmer (spy as cockney hero), came Quiller a sort of fusion of them both, given a slightly neurotic American edge by George Segal. The character was created by novelist Elleston Trevor (writing as Adam Hall), who immersed him in a fairly realistic Cold War milieu of postwar Berlin split down the middle, and still echoing with the death rattle of the Reich. It is a place, suitably, of conspiracies within conspiracies, and playwright Harold Pinter's adaptation is so knotty it is nearly impossible to unravel. Although, the overarching story is of the rooting out of some old Nazis, in which the American agent Quiller ends up captured by their mysterious enemy.

Best, then, to sit back and let its rather trippy quality wash over you – it is much closer in tone to the Palmer movies than the Bond ones – and take pleasure in the shadowy espionage atmosphere and a typically severe performance from Max Von Sydow (as the menacing Oktober), a sternly British turn from Alec Guinness (as Quiller's spymaster) and George Sanders as a punctilious British diplomat. There is a delightful theme of all these Europeans getting to manipulate this brash, clumsy, ineffective American.

However, the film is limited by its structure. Dominated by intense interrogation scenes it slows to a crawl, while playing a frustrating game both with the sap Quiller and the audience in his various attempts to escape from Oktober turning out to be set-ups, further ploys to tease out precious info from their prisoner. It becomes hard to trust the narrative, and an already cloudy story becomes increasingly indistinct with too little action to carry it along. ★★★ **IN**

QUILLS (2000)

Starring: *Geoffrey Rush (The Marquis de Sade), Kate Winslet (Madelaine 'Maddy' LeClerc), Joaquin Phoenix (The Abbe du Coulmier), Michael Caine (Dr Royer-Collard), Billie Whitelaw (Madame LeClerc), Amelia Warner (Simone)*
Director: *Philip Kaufman*
Screenwriter: *Doug Wright, from his play*
18/118 mins./Drama/Romance/USA/Germany

A portrait of the notorious erotic writer's last days in Charenton asylum. The ever-active Marquis persuades an unwitting laundress to smuggle his works out of the asylum for publication with disastrous consequences.

After visualising erotic literature on screen in *Henry And June* and *The Unbearable Lightness Of Being*, director Kaufman turns his attention to the works of the Marquis De Sade, the erotic writer from which the term 'Sadism' justifiably takes its name.

Doug Wright adapts his own stage play, taking a fictional spin on the infamous writer and sexual deviant's final days in Charenton Asylum. The ever manipulative Marquis befriends a young laundress and persuades her to smuggle his final writings out of the asylum for publication. Not happy with this act of defiance, he also stirs up the other inmates to the point of inevitable destruction.

An intelligent study of voyeurism, eroticism, rebellion and censorship, the film is driven by a dark, stinging wit and passionate performances. ★★★★ **AM**

QUIZ SHOW (1994)

Starring: *John Turturro (Herbie Stempel), Rob Morrow (Dick Goodwin), Ralph Fiennes (Charles Van Doren), Paul Scofield (Mark Van Doren), David Paymer (Dan Enright)*
Director: *Robert Redford*
Screenwriter: *Paul Attanasio, based on the book by Richard N. Goodwin*
15/127 mins./Drama/History/USA

Awards: *BAFTA – Best Adapated Screenplay*

It is 1958 and the TV quiz *Twenty-One* can make stars of is winners. That is until it is exposed as being rigged, its contestants fall from grace and corruption and backstabbing pervades.

Many great true-life stories begin as trivia. In 1958, TV quizzes were so popular in America that contestants on a winning streak became celebrities. Charles Van Doren, a big winner on arch general knowledge tester *Twenty-One*, rose from an ill-paid teaching job to a potent-salaried spot as NBC's cultural commentator. Then out of the woodwork crawls Herbert Stempel, a less clean-cut former *Twenty-One* winner, alleging that contestants were given questions and answers in advance of the programme.

The Ivy League Van Doren finally owned up to the sham before a Congressional Oversight Committee, causing his own downfall and a minor purge in the industry that, of course, did not extend to the big-wigs and sponsors who, in truth, were the ones who ordered *Twenty-One* be rigged to swell those sacred ratings.

Quiz Show is undoubtedly Robert Redford's finest turn calling the shots to date. Having found this curious footnote to cultural history, and working from a first class script by Paul Attanasio, he has wrought a film that is weighty without being ponderous, full of acutely observed detail about the 50s and media issues that are still relevant, and hinges on a set of fascinating and marvellously played characters.

Tagline
Fifty million people watched, but no one saw a thing.

Stempel is a neurotic know-it-all whose abrasive personality and Jewish looks ('there's a face for radio') are far less telegenic than his smooth, handsome, modest successor. Van Doren, finely bred from a distinguished family led by a kindly overbearing poet patriarch, has his own problems. Redford cannily shows the need for recognition that nudges him into a Faustian bargain for wealth and fame, and the stirrings of conscience that prompt him eventually to collaborate, for far purer motives than the whining Stempel, with his own crucifixion.

As he did with Brad Pitt in *A River Runs Through It*, Redford builds a film around a role he might himself have played in his young sex symbol days if studios had let him flex his acting muscles. Fiennes, following his *Schindler's List* turn, is a rare gorgeous lead who can compete with a great character actor like Turturro, generating an intoxicating contrast between their characters and acting styles.

The middle ground is provided by Dick Goodwin, a lawyer with the Oversight Committee who carries on the investigation in hope of clearing out the crookedness of a whole industry only to see the hearings deteriorate into another witch hunt for minor sinners that serve to cover up the misdeeds of bosses played in marvellously slimy cameos by Allan Rich, as the NBC president, and Martin Scorsese as a Machiavellian sponsor. Barry Levinson, who might once have made the film, pops up in a deliciously sly moment as TV presenter Dave Garroway, while Christopher McDonald contributes a shark-like grin as Jack Berry, the host of *Twenty-One*, and David Paymer and Hank Azaria ooze half-ashamed smarm as the producers-cum-scam merchants.

Starting with something as preposterous as a rigged gameshow, *Quiz Show* tackles big American themes: the cult of celebrity, the demonic influence of big business, the hidden price of fame, the conflict between education and entertainment, the mushrooming power of the media and the simple lure of easy money. Rich and stimulating, this is also a film with character and real heart, distinguished by award-worthy performances, stunningly subtle direction and a streak of barbed wit. ★★★★★ **KN**

QUO VADIS (1951)

Starring: *Robert Taylor (Marcus Vinicius), Deborah Kerr (Lygia), Leo Genn (Petronius), Peter Ustinov (Nero), Patricia Laffan (Poppaea), Finlay Currie (Peter)*
Director: *Mervyn LeRoy*
Screenwriters: *S.H. Behrman, Sonya Levien, John Lee Mahin, based on the novel by Henryk Sienkiewicz*
PG/171 mins./History/Drama/USA

When General Marcus Vinicius returns to Rome from battle, he falls in love with Lygia, an adopted daughter of a fellow general, but effectively a hostage. When she is presented to him as a gift, he discovers she is in secret a Christian. When Emperor Nero decides all Christians must be thrown to the lions, it is up to Marcus to save Lygia and her family, and in so doing discover that Rome is in need of a soul.

A bold, blustering, afternoon gobbling mega-epic that set the template for that brew of postwar Classical renditions – very much pro-Christian and mounted with indomitable magnificence from the building blocks of purest melodrama. In concept it seems unbearable, but five minutes in and there's no going back, you're there for the long haul.

In its day, *Quo Vadis* was the biggest spectacle ever made (yes, even bigger if not better than *Gone With The Wind*) – the sets, the costumes, the cast of thousands, it was a marketeer's dream and they milked it for all it was worth (the trailers declared it to be most lavish screen spectacle ever!). So what if the performances drift between the hammy (Peter Ustinov's demented Emperor Nero) and the wooden (Robert Taylor's stoic General Vinicius), the history certainly dubious, and the stark Christian morality hard to swallow, feel that scope.

Mervyn Le Roy's endeavours are, as they boasted, spectacular: the fighting in the Coliseum devastating, the decadence of Nero's court succulently delivered, and that all important burning of Rome, as Ustinov's burbling Nero strums like a fruitcake on his fiddle, the dramatic climax. And the biblical touchstones are intriguing – saints Peter and Paul turn up to boost the Christian philosophy, while the conflict Vinicius faces between the offerings of love on one side and Roman decorum on the other reveals an attempt to define a context for the birth of Christianity. But, brainy sections aside, its great pleasure is the fact it is a soap opera in togas. Will Deborah Kerr's beautiful but devoted Lygia fall for the macho but proud Vinicius? Will Christianity win out over Rome's pagan hostility? Will the lions get dinner tonight? And will Nero lose the plot entirely? Pack a thermos of coffee and sandwiches, this will take a while.
★★★ **IN**

q

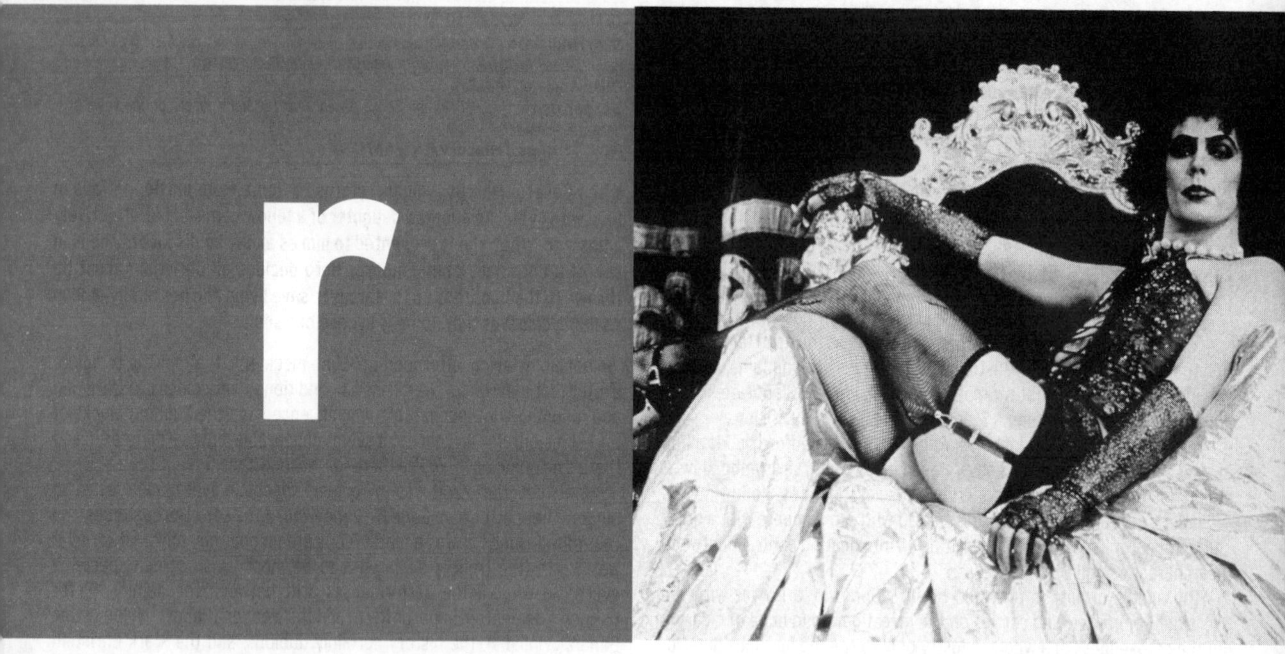

RABBIT PROOF FENCE (2002)

Starring: *Everlyn Sampi (Molly Craig), Tianna Sansbury (Daisy Kadibill), Laura Monaghan (Gracie Fields), David Gulpilil (Moodoo), Ningali Lawford (Maud)*
Director: *Phillip Noyce*
Screenwriter: *Christine Olsen, based on the book by Doris Pilkington*
PG/89 mins./Drama/History/Australia/UK

Australia in the 1930s: a law exists stating that 'half-caste' children must be separated from their Aborigine families. But when three young girls are snatched by the government and taken to an institution 1,500 miles away from home, they escape and begin the long walk home.

Phillip Noyce – best known for thrillers *Dead Calm*, *Patriot Games* and *The Bone Collector* – returns to his Australian roots for this captivating tale that could have ended up as a soppy Sunday-afternoon-on-Channel-Five film in the hands of another director.

Noyce, however, while obviously moved by the plight of these Aboriginal children, wisely decides not to wring every moment for maximum weepie effect. Instead he simply illustrates the true story with stunning locations and subtle performances that themselves are enough to break your heart by the end credits.

As the three girls make their way across the unrelenting countryside, using the wire fence that cross-sections Western Australia as a guide, the young actresses – all making movie debuts – relate the anguish, determination and fear of their characters with performances that would make any experienced, adult actor proud.

The real surprise, though, is Branagh. His character, A. O. Neville, the government's Chief Protector of the Aborigines, was the man responsible for taking 'half-caste' Aborginal children away from their parents to train as domestic servants and labourers (he believed that preventing children of mixed marriages from marrying Aborigines would eventually wipe out the Aboriginal race).

Neville could have been depicted as an evil caricature for easy effect, but instead Branagh gives him some humanity so that, while we hate his point of view and methods, he still comes across as a man (albeit a very misguided one) rather than a pantomime villain.

In the end, though, the achingly sad story really belongs to the girls, and especially to Everlyn Sampi, who plays Molly, the most determined of them all. And when Noyce shows us the real Molly and her sister, now both in their eighties and living on the land they were so desperate to return to, you realise the most inspirational movies don't have to have swirling music and Hollywood stars to bring a real tear to your eye. ★★★ **JB**

RADIO DAYS (1987)

Starring: *Woody Allen (Narrator), Seth Green (Little Joe), Julie Kavner (Mother), Michael Tucker (Father), Dianne Wiest (Aunt Bea), Josh Mostel) (Uncle Abe), Renee Lippin (Aunt Ceil), Sally White (Mia Farrow)*
Director: *Woody Allen*
Screenwriter: *Woody Allen*
PG/85 mins./Comedy/USA

As Little Joe and the extended family that lives with his parents rely on the radio to get them through the daily trials of life in Second World War Brooklyn, cigarette girl Sally White moves inexorably up the showbiz chain and becomes a celebrated gossip columnist.

Around a third of the material in this delightful domestic memoir was salvaged from *Annie Hall*, after rewrites shifted the emphasis away from Alvy Singer and his New York past. However, this is much more than an exercise in thrifty recycling.

Structurally, *Radio Days* was one of Woody Allen's most complex films, as around 150 characters (there were 220 before he began editing) populate the various storylines, subplots, flashbacks, cutaways and digressions. Indeed, the action has the feel of a novel, which is reinforced by Woody's voice-over narration. Yet, it is also highly cinematic, as Allen makes evocative use of the contrasting interiors of the radio station, the nightclubs and the crowded family home to create neighbouring worlds that collided only through the airwaves.

This is also one of Allen's least judgemental pictures, as he borrows Jean Renoir's forgiving humanism to allow everyone their reasons for actions that are more a product of an environment shaped by ethnicity, history, impecunity and the media than any baser motives. Indeed, Allen had hoped to introduce his characters in the manner Renoir had employed in *La Règle du Jeu*, but the complexity of the sequence eventually persuaded him to settle for an accompanying commentary.

Chance and coincidence similarly play their part in shaping destinies, most notably Sally's, although Allen intimates with the mirror shot that she might have made use of other oral talents than eloquence to secure her radio slot.

Naturally, the proceedings are bathed in rose-tinted nostalgia. But Allen could still highlight the transience of celebrity and the triviality of much of the radio output in exploring the extent to which the medium dominated people's lives. Fondly lampooning the quizzes, soaps, sportscasts, comedy hours, news bulletins and kids shows of the period, he showed how the grown-ups took ephemera like Roger and Irene's tittle-tattle as seriously as Joe treated the Masked Avenger and Biff Baxter. Moreover, he also highlighted the popularity of novelty tunes rather than the hits from the American Songbook that usually punctuated his soundtracks.

A rare box-office success Stateside, the film returned $16m on Orion's $6.4m outlay. ★★★★ **DP**

Movie Trivia:
Woody Allen (born 1935)

Who he is: The most prolific of the major modern filmmakers. Equally at home with comedies and tragedies, usually set among New York's (and lately London's) middle-class.

Hallmarks: New York's Upper East Side; angsty, intelligent, neurotic, death-obsessed central characters; references to Fellini, Bergman and the Marx Brothers; broad comedy and witty one-liners.

If you see one movie, see: *Annie Hall* (1978)

RADIOLAND MURDERS (1994)

Starring: *Brian Benben (Roger), Mary Stuart Masterson (Penny Henderson), Ned Beatty (General Whalen), George Burns (Milt Lackey)*
Director: *Mel Smith*
Screenwriters: *Willard Huyck, Gloria Katz, Jeff Reno, Ron Osbourne, based on a story by George Lucas*
PG/103 mins./Comedy/Thriller/USA

In 1939, the opening night of a radio station is troubled by a mystery voice who breaks into the programmes to utter ominous warnings, then kills off a selection of the station's employees. In addition, the broadcast is interrupted by mechanical mishaps, temperamental performers, unmoving sponsors and a police investigation.

George Lucas, who devised this story before turning it over to Willard and Gloria Huyck to work up into a script, must have an ambition to deliver his very own *1941* and this half-interesting period disaster is it, one-part hymn to a bygone medium (of the end of radio, it is mused 'that would be like killing the imagination'), to one-part misfired screwball comedy, to one-part transparent murder mystery (yes, it's who you think it is).

The on-the-air nostalgia was done better by Woody Allen in *Radio Days* and sadly the film never trusts this material, cutting away from perfect-pitch recreations of musical variety, adventure serial and comedy acts (Michael McKean does a neat Spike Jones) to unfunny scenes of characters running around shouting at each other. The cast is good: Ned Beatty, Brion James, Jeffrey Tambor, Corbin Bernsen as victims; Christopher Lloyd as the sound effects genius and Stephen Tobolowsky as an engineer embittered because no one is interested in his new television device; Bobcat Goldthwait and Peter MacNicol as harassed writers; Rosemary Clooney, Anita Morris (the girl with the va va voom voice) and Billy Barty as acts; Dylan Baker as a 30s-style dumb cop sidekick. Bo Hopkins and Candy Clark, Lucas-Huyck fixtures from *American Graffiti*, have bits as the parents of energetically annoying bellboy Scott Michael Campbell. The usually fine Mary Stuart Masterton and the acquired taste Brian Benben are strained and tiresome leads, with Benben dragged up as Carmen Miranda. Directed by Mel Smith, burying forever any possible Hollywood career. ★★ **KN**

RAGING BULL (1980)

Starring: *Robert De Niro (Jake La Motta), Cathy Moriarty (Vickie Thailer), Joe Pesci (Joey La Motta), Frank Vincent (Salvy Batts), Nicholas Colasanto (Tommy Como), Theresa Saldana (Lenore), Mario Gallo (Mario)*
Director: *Martin Scorsese*
Screenwriters: *Paul Schrader, Mardik Martin, based on the book by Jake LaMotta, Joseph Carter, Peter Savage*
18/129 mins./Drama/USA

Awards: *Academy Awards – Best Actor, Best Editing; BAFTA – Best Editing, Best Newcomer (Joe Pesci); Golden Globes – Best Actor*

A renowned portrait of middleweight champion Jake La Motta, whose ferocity in the ring is mirrored in his personal life. Caught in a spiral of self-destruction, he's physically abusive to his wife and brother and is reduced finally to a pathetic figure.

Let's not quibble, *Raging Bull* is everything it is cracked up to be. Those contrasting licks of docu-drab and dreamily inventive black-and-white cinematography, framed to perfection. Those virtuoso dimensions of character, boldly grim and depressing to the bitter end, reducing viewers to gibbering wrecks, slumped by the shocking depravity that can be touched by the human spirit. The chocolatey velvet of its blood – incidentally, all Jake LaMotta's – spurting, gushing and draining away like rainwater, where every vital droplet tells you something you probably didn't want to know. It is hard to adore *Raging Bull* like an *E.T.* or even a *GoodFellas*, but the angry voice of American cinema rang as clear and cold as the ringside bell back in 1980, when Martin Scorsese laid down a peerless imprint of what cinema could aspire to – art, truth and exhaustion.

What it's not is a film about boxing. For all the reams of paper poured out on the grandeur of the recreations of Jake LaMotta's most celebrated bouts, which strike the movie like a drumbeat, Martin Scorsese had no interest in strategy or prowess. When he came to research the sport, he visited a couple of fights where only two images stuck with him: the blood-soaked sponge wiped across the fighter's back, and the pendulous drops left smeared on the rope. Pugilism was mere context; Scorsese was sold on the heart of darkness. This is a film about man's capacity for self-destruction, where its protagonist lived his own metaphor.

While scholars and cineastes will harp on about Scorsese's indelible craft, this – even more so than *Taxi Driver* - is the collective work of the sacred triumvirate of the tiny Italian movie god, his earthly son Robert De Niro, and the holy spirit of screenwriter Paul Schrader (who reworked Mardik Martin's original script). In truth, it was De Niro's hunger that drove such an unsettling proposition to the screen. He nagged the director with

Directors Who Never Won A Competitive Oscar

1. Alfred Hitchcock (5 nominations)
2. Martin Scorsese (5 nominations)
3. Stanley Kubrick (4 nominations)
4. Howard Hawks (1 nomination)
5. Akira Kurosawa (0 nominations)
6. Charlie Chaplin (1 nomination)
7. Orson Welles (1 nomination)
8. Sidney Lumet (4 nominations)
9. David Lynch (3 nominations)
10. Robert Altman (5 nominations)

his well-thumbed copy of LaMotta's biography, *Raging Bull: My Story*, a book he had read while shooting *The Godfather Part II*. It must have appealed to his sense of the unbound: to expose his rigorous talent to the savagery not only of the boxing arena, but the consumptive demons that jabbed away inside LaMotta's battered skull.

But Scorsese demurred. He was dismissive of making a boxing film (*Rocky* had just been a massive hit), sceptical of the veracity of LaMotta's story and, more seriously, disillusioned by the failure of *New York, New York*. It was a bad time for the director, who was losing track of his muse amid a blizzard of cocaine and lithium, intent on partying himself into destruction. When he was rushed into hospital with massive internal bleeding, it looked like the gig might be up and a mighty talent would be lost, consumed by self-loathing. When De Niro visited him in hospital, the actor nudged him once more about this biopic of a boxer eaten alive by his own neuroses, who lashed out at all who loved him. Finally Scorsese saw something he could relate to – his own life. The movie was to prove the rebirth of a filmmaker.

With his mind cluttered with film lore, Scorsese would encourage references to the sub-genre of 50s boxing noir, such as *Body And Soul* (1947) and *Champion* (1949). Michael Chapman's lordly monochrome camerawork drew from the famous Weegee snapshots of 50s New York that enticed the director with their austere yet atmospheric power. However, Scorsese finally opted for black and white because it simply lasted longer and didn't suffer the sapping of hue that occurs with colour. From there he conjured two distinct flavours within the film. Outside the ring, in LaMotta's dense and explosive home life, the camera remains starkly still, allowing the drama to retain the unnerving veracity of real life. Here LaMotta fizzes like a lit fuse, the distinctions between canvas and kitchen violently blurred. More celebrated, despite occupying only ten minutes of the running time, are the bouts themselves, which are told in tightly edited snapshots of recorded events. Scorsese had no interest in the 'real' rope-a-dope thrill of Michael Mann's *Ali*; instead he created swelling dreamscapes, where the brute force of the sport is transposed into opera. The camera enters the ring like a dance partner, rendering the teeming violence as noble as the wife (and brother) beating is sickening and puerile. As the fragments of Pietro Mascagni's glorious *Cavalleria Rusticana* soothe the images, the flashbulbs of the cameras sparkle like shattering glass against the stinging lash of a whip. The film may have been a box-office flop, but those scenes have passed into movie iconography.

Let's not dwell on the much-lauded Method madness of De Niro. Yes, he actually entered real fights to confirm his boxing skills, and, indeed, he took two months to swell his belly and chops, care of Tuscan pasta and heaps of ice cream. Yet it is in the quiet of the man that the performance truly sings, revealing the loosening threads of self-control, the internal rupture.

When LaMotta is seen distinct from his demons, his collapse is all the more tragic. There were limits, however. Schrader was pushing harder than even De Niro was willing to go. His earlier script had LaMotta hopelessly attempting to masturbate in the prison cell; every time his juices rise, he pictures the face of a woman he has abused. It was 'softened' to De Niro punching the wall in uncontainable agony. Not to forget the extraordinary work of Joe Pesci, whose robotic tongue fires up Joey LaMotta, conscience and confidant to Jake and possibly the greatest piece of collateral damage wrought by the boxer's paranoid fury. And Cathy Moriarty who, aged just 17, ably depicted the mirror-conflict within second wife Vickie: between love and disgust.

Raging Bull prevails as a film about conflicts - most obviously, those within a man whose soul had become dependent on guilt and absolution. LaMotta was never floored by a punch, never counted out, withstanding wrecking-ball punishment; as his blood is sponged clear from the mess of swollen tissues where his face once was, there comes the blessed sense of relief. Scorsese and Schrader were turned on by the depths of his Catholic mother lode (it's the power that binds their boiling galaxy together): the ring as confessional, masochism as psychological need, psychosexual inadequacy fulminating away like a snorting bull. Little wonder that the studio, United Artists, was confounded by the film.

As hard as it might be for audiences to directly relate, they get an uncomfortable exposure to the netherworld of their own id taken to a devilish extremity. LaMotta repeatedly stares himself down in mirrors – an echo of Travis Bickle – eyeballing the crushed face of his greatest opponent. There are bigger conflicts still. *Raging Bull* was made at a time when the concentrated slab of commercialism was sweeping aside the brilliant opportunism of 70s American cinema. Scorsese could see and feel the strains around him, hence the film's unique tension between art and pleasure, spectacle and truth. As LaMotta pathetically intones to his louche, gutbucket of a face as the films slumps to its sorry close: 'So gimme a stage where this bull here can rage. And though I can fight, I'd much rather recite – that's entertainment.'

Hollywood was stirred by the thought, but gave the Oscars to *Ordinary People*. Ten years later, *Raging Bull* was voted the finest film of the 80s by the American Film Institute. As Scorsese instinctually knew, the film's power would never fade. ★★★★ **IN**

Movie Trivia:
Martin Scorsese (born 1942)

Who he is: Former seminarian from Little Italy. Often described as America's greatest living director. Even oftener overlooked come Oscar-time.
Hallmarks: Robert De Niro; gangsters; New York; graphic violence; Cathloicism, handheld camera shots, repulsive anti-heroes, his cameoing mother.
If you see one movie, see: *Goodfellas* (1990)

Movie Trivia: Raging Bull

Scorsese intentionally didn't mention to Joe Pesci that De Niro would attack him in the 'Did you fuck my wife?' scene for added shock value in his acting. Melted chocolate was used as blood for extra effect in the black and white fight sequences. Scorsese's father is one of the mafia mob intimidating the LaMotta brothers in the nightclub. The real Jake LaMotta said the film made him realise what a terrible person he had been.

RAIDERS OF THE LOST ARK (1981)

Starring: *Harrison Ford (Indiana Jones), Karen Allen (Marion Ravenwood), Paul Freeman (Dr Rene Belloq), John Rhys-Davies (Sallah), Denholm Elliott (Dr Marcus Brody), Alfred Molina (Staipo)*
Director: *Steven Spielberg*
Screenwriter; *Lawrence Kasdan, from a story by George Lucas, Philip Kaufman*
PG/110 mins./Action/Adventure/USA

Awards: *Academy Awards – Best Art Direction-Set Direction, Best Visual Effects, Best Film Editing, Best Sound; BAFTA – Best Production Design/Art Directon*

Renowned archeologist and expert in the occult, Dr Indiana Jones, is hired by the US Government to find the Ark of the Covenant, which is believed to still hold the ten commandments. Unfortunately, agents of Hitler are also after the Ark.

Tom Selleck was originally pencilled in to play Indiana Jones, don't you know. Of course you do. So, how about the fact that the name of the 'obtainer of rare antiquities', actually first belonged to George Lucas' dog? Oh, that too? And herein lies our problem – *Raiders Of The Lost Ark* is so adored, so worshipped, that it has been analysed to death.

In fact, even if it opened in the UK just one day after Charles and Di tied the knot, in the 'Where were you when?' stakes, some would say there's no contest. And, yes, there is a multitude of treasures to be unearthed. The *Star Wars*-inspired registration of Jock's plane (OB-CPO); the hieroglyphics of R2-D2 and C-3PO in the Well Of Souls; and cameos by ILM's Dennis Muren (as a Gestapo agent) and producer Frank Marshall (a Nazi pilot). More significant, though, is *Raiders'* resonance. Initially perceived as a $20.8 million spin on the Saturday matinee serials ('I made it as a B movie,' said Spielberg), it would go on to gross $363 million (Paramount's biggest ever earner until 1994's *Forrest Gump*).

It heralded a new dawn for the summer blockbuster; scooped four Oscars; elevated the dusty image of archaeology to the sexiest profession known to man and reinvigorated the hitherto lost art of whipping schoolmates' bare buttocks with rolled-up towels. 'Why'd it have to be snakes?' is Indy's lament, but it might easily have been Karen Allen's. Cast after Spielberg and Amy Irving had split up and Debra Winger passed, Allen had to endure an experience that made Tippi Hedren's in *The Birds* seem like a walk in the park. Spielberg elicited more convincing screams by throwing live snakes at her head. Legend has it that many of the reptilian extras were never recaptured and still live in the dark recesses of Elstree Studios.

But if the final result is one of the most exhilarating examples of action/adventure cinema – its pre-credit sequence, a glowing homage to ye olde Hollywoode, establishes a breakneck pace that can surely never be sustained, but is – this was not always on the cards. While the finished film arrived 11 days ahead of schedule, early on-set signals seemed ominous, with everyone bar the director taken ill on location in Tunisia. (It's rumoured that he avoided sickness by eating only the cans of Spaghetti-Os he'd packed.) It was precisely this unfortunate disposition which resulted in a diarrhoea-striken Ford's suggestion to 'Just shoot the fucker,' in the now mythical Indy vs. Arab guard face-off, but it was also the latest turn in a growing line of mishaps. 'Anything that promised serious injury or total disability, Harrison did,' said Spielberg of Ford's insistence on carrying out as many of his own stunts as possible. An insistence that very nearly had fatal consequences when the German Flying Wing fight sequence went awry. 'The crew's reaction was the normal one associated with having a film's star run over by an aeroplane when the movie is only half-completed,' said Ford in hindsight. 'I was a lot more careful after that.'

While Ford was perfect as the hell-for-leather, loveable rogue, the locations sumptuous, the special effects breathtaking and the cinematography dazzling, the real success of *Raiders'* lies in its conception. A product of the near-Holy trinity of Spielberg, George Lucas and Lawrence Kasdan, it is the collaboration that holds the key to the magic. Lucas' original brainchild (he pitched the idea to Spielberg in Hawaii, where he'd decamped to escape the critical mauling he feared awaited *Star Wars*), he provided the flair of the set pieces and the frenetic pacing. Add to that his harmonious working relationship with Spielberg – at one meeting Lucas snapped the wingtips off a model Flying Wing, reducing it from four to two engines and securing a reluctant compromise from Spielberg which saved some $250,000 – and his influence is clear.

Tagline
The return of the great adventure.

Kasdan, meanwhile, was the ideal choice as screenwriter. Fresh from co-writing duties on *The Empire Strikes Back* (1980), his screenplay was exceptional, lending essentially cartoon characters an extra dimension, whittling down an overlong script (scenes with a giant rolling gong and a mine-cart were cut and then re-employed for *Temple Of Doom* three years later) and easily covering for Lucas' Achilles heel with his timeless dialogue. Third and most significant in the triumvirate is, of course, Spielberg. His ability to capture a true sense of wonder oozes from every frame, from the opening Paramount mountain match shot, to tour-de-force finale. Indeed, although it was Philip Kaufman's suggestion that the quest should centre around the Ark of the Covenant, the Hebraic tradition suggesting the Arc has awesome mystical powers is a concept more likely to appeal to the Jewish Spielberg than the Methodist Lucas. ★★★★★ **MD**

THE RAILWAY CHILDREN (1970)

Starring: *Jenny Agutter (Bobbie Waterbury), Sally Thomset (Phyliis Waterbury), Gary F. Warren (Peter Waterbury), Bernard Cribbins (Albert Perks), Dinah Sheridan (Mrs Waterbury), William Mervyn (Old Gentleman)*
Director: *Lionel Jeffries*
Screenwriter: *Lionel Jeffries, based on the novel by E. Nesbit*
U/109 mins./Family/UK

E. Nesbit's beloved tale of three children shipped off to live in the country beside a railway line with their mother after their father is arrested on mysterious spying charges and they are left penniless. Yet, it proves the making of them, as they discover a way of helping their father from afar.

A comfortable, prettified adaptation of one of E. Nesbit's less showy books, i.e. it's free of fantasy elements but still set amongst the petticoats and tidy manners of Edwardian England. A charming if glassy setting that keeps the film a perennial Christmas favourite. The actor-comedian Lionel Jeffries stays behind the camera, gilding sensitive performances out of the three children – interestingly Jenny Agutter's serious Bobbie was two years younger than 'younger' sister Sally Thomset, and, soberingly, both would grow up to be sex symbols – and portraying the healing effect such an idyllic community can have on a troubled family.

The contrast between the Waterbury's well-heeled London life and the cottagey existence they are forced into following their father's calamity is, by today's notions of hardship, not quite the lurch it aims for. Yet, there is the sense of something undone – the children, especially Bobbie, have adulthood and responsibility thrust upon them as their mother sickens and life unravels. Their adventures along the railway sidings (not the best message to send out to watching kids) skids into heroics as they rescue a schoolboy who breaks his leg on the track, and eventually through an unlikely communication with an old man on a London bound train, find the solution to all their troubles – papa, free again!

It is all a bit a bit far-fetched and sentimental, but delivered with such calm grace by Jeffries with the assistance of cinematographer Arthur Ibbetson, the exaggerations don't seem to matter. It just looks the piece, an England, green and pleasant, a forgotten realm of pleasantries where total strangers turn into friends rather than threats, and stationmasters are loveable locals. Which, when you think about it, is a whole lot more fantastical than anything Harry Potter dabbles in. ★★★★ **IN**

RAIN MAN (1988)

Starring: *Dustin Hoffman (Raymond Babbitt), Tom Cruise (Charlie Babbitt), Valeria Golino (Susanna), Gerald R. Molen (Dr Bruner)*
Director: *Barry Levinson*
Screenwriters: *Ronald Bass, Barry Morrow, from a story by Morrow*
15/127 mins./Drama/Comedy/USA

Awards: *Academy Awards – Best Actor, Best Director, Best Picture, Best Original Screenplay; Golden Globes – Best Drama, Best Actor*

A man discovers he has an older, autistic brother who has inherited his father's fortune. He kidnaps him, intent on wangling the money for himself. But their road trip turns into a journey of self-discovery for older and younger brother alike.

It's sunset. Charlie Babbitt has kidnapped his autistic savant brother from a care home. They're stranded in the middle of the desert when suddenly they're surrounded by survivalists – brutal gang members out for the kill. Charlie grabs his gun. He knows they have no choice but to shoot their way out. He dons his Ray-Bans, the music kicks in...

If studio bosses had had their way, *Rain Man* would have been a different movie. They insisted this action sequence go in one of the rewrites to pick up the pace. But then, if *Rain Man*'s production schedule had gone at all according to plan it would have been a Marty Brest picture starring Bill Murray as the loveable retarded brother of uptight businessman Dustin Hoffman.

Just be thankful that studio bosses don't always get their way. *Rain Man*, the film that went on to win Oscars for Best Director, Best Picture, Best Actor and Best Original Screenplay, would not have been such a resounding success without the final unique grouping of talent.

The age gap between Hoffman and Murray as brothers may have been more believable, but despite Hoffman scooping the awards, Cruise is the one to watch. He makes the leap from film star to actor in this movie. Barely off screen for a moment, he has to go from being a nasty piece of work to someone that the audience can empathise with, while his co-star remains a wall of blank emotion and character tics. It's an ego-less performance that Cruise has rarely matched since.

Murray passed on the movie when he found out Hoffman was interested in playing the part intended for him. He knew it was the role that would get the plaudits, but as much as Murray has proved himself as a serious actor in recent years, there's no way he would have inhabited Raymond Babbitt the way Hoffman does. Hoffman spent a year working with autistic men and their families to understand their complex relationships. As a jobbing actor he'd worked in a psychiatric care home and he built on his experience from there, too.

Watching the extras on the DVD release allows you to glimpse the contemporaries on whom he based his performance. These were the men he thanked in his Academy Award acceptance speech, and one in particular is so close to Raymond in mannerisms and appearance it's hard to imagine the script wasn't written about him.

But the original script was slightly different. It was pitched by Barry Morrow, who'd previously written the Emmy-award-winning drama *Bill*, about a mentally retarded man who'd become a friend of Morrow's family. *Rain Man* was a further exploration of that relationship. The title was chosen by Morrow's children after they went through a book of names deciding which sounded most interesting when mispronounced. It was very nearly No-man (Norman).

United Artists almost didn't pick it up because Warners were working on what was rumoured to be a similar project – *Forrest Gump*. But then the 'Rain Man' in the original script was much closer to the Gump character: affectionate and always wanting to hug his cold brother. Hoffman was the one who pushed for the change to an autistic savant, who was the opposite in all respects. In fact, Hoffman's desire to make this crucial alteration and Marty Brest's reluctance to take it on board was one reason Brest parted company with the project.

The next director to sign up was Steven Spielberg. He brought in screenwriter Ron Bass to help him fine-tune the script and jetted off to Malibu with Cruise and Hoffman to work on the project. They all rented houses next to each other on the beach and spent the days swapping script notes and getting into the characters. This was a chance for Spielberg to fulfill the dream he'd had to work with Hoffman since seeing *The Graduate* in the 1960s. He wasn't going to screw it up. But he never got the chance to realise his ambition.

In September, George Lucas said he was good to go on the third instalment of *Raiders Of The Lost Ark*, and Spielberg knew he wouldn't have time to get *Rain Man* out and work with Lucas as promised. Regretfully he passed on *Rain Man*, breaking the news to the cast and Bass in person.

Rain Man was fast becoming the hot potato of Hollywood. Next to pick it up was Sydney Pollack. But his heart never seemed to be in it. He made the smart move of ditching the action sequence, but he wasn't keen on the whole idea of the road movie. 'I'd have made it if I could have stayed in New York,' he commented, half joking.

But there was one man who couldn't stop thinking about *Rain Man*. Pollack's friend Barry Levinson had borrowed the script from him. He was driving across the desert one evening, watching the windmills spinning on the horizon, and he turned to his wife and said, 'You know, this would make a perfect backdrop for that bit where Charlie is talking to his girlfriend.' 'You should make that movie,' she said. 'I can't,' he replied. 'Sydney Pollack's making the movie.'

Fate dictated otherwise. Seven weeks before shooting, Pollack passed it over to Levinson. With a writers' strike looming, shooting could not be delayed. They already had a great cinematographer in Australian John Seale, who was good at seeing something bigger in the vast American landscape – as his work on *Witness* and *Children Of A Lesser God* had proved.

A couple of other pieces were needed to complete the puzzle. Hans Zimmer, then little known, was brought in to give a Cuban/African feel to the soundtrack. It was his first Hollywood movie and he pitched in with the perfect score, his haunting theme giving the brothers' journey a mystical feel. And then there was the unusual casting choice of Valeria Golino as Cruise's girlfriend. The part had been written as WASPish, blonde. Choosing someone whose native language was not English was a neat narrative trick; at a stroke Cruise's character had a reason to explain all his actions and in the simplest of terms.

This was not a movie that needed forced emotion; it played better because it was understated, because the ending is oblique and because it rang true. This film changed how many people perceived the autistic; suddenly they weren't 'retards' to be shut away, but intriguing individuals. Few movies really do this. But *Rain Man* did something even rarer: it not only made the audience think, it made them happy. ★★★★★ **EC**

RAISE THE RED LANTERN (DA HONG DENGLONG GAOGAO GUA)

Starring: *Gong Li (Songlian), Ma Jingwu (Master Chen Zuogian), He Caiffel (Meishan), Cao Cuifeng (Zhuoyun), Jin Shuyuan (Yuru), Kong Lin (Yan'er), Ding Weimin (Mother Song), Cui Zhigang (Doctor Gao)*
Director: *Zhang Yimou*
Screenwriter: *Ni Zhen, based on the novel* Wives And Concubines *by Su Tong*
PG/125 mins./Drama/China/Hong Kong

In 1920s China, Songlian arrives at the isolated estate of Master Chen Zuoqian to become his fourth wife, behind Zhuoyun and Meishan, who compete fiercely for their husband's attention and the nightly privilege of a sensuous foot massage.

Adapted from Su Tong's 1989 novel, *Wives and Concubines*, this was the final part of Zhang Yimou's Confucian trilogy that opened with *Red Sorghum* and *Ju Dou*. Although the screenplay was passed by the censors and the finished film was allowed to garner acclaim and awards abroad, it was banned by Beijing for its subversive political content.

By setting the action in a *sanheyuan* (a traditional courtyard house that epitomised the Confucian ideal of self-sufficient harmony that the Communists had adopted), Zhang was implying that there was something rotten in the Chinese system and by having Songlian stress her academic credentials, he alluded to the students who had been the driving force behind the Pro-Democracy Movement. Similarly, by having Meishan's executioners deny her death, he was attacking the Party's defensive attitude to the Tiananmen Square Massacre.

Moreover, by filming mostly in long shot in lingering deep-focus takes, Zhang sought to suggest the isolation of the Chinese authorities and their entrenched positions regarding reform, while the consistent use of delimiting framing devices reinforced the overall sense of repression. However, this was also very much a film about both the historical and contemporary status of Chinese women. For all the delicate artistry of the décor and visuals, this is an uncompromising study of the part that women play in their own subjugation within a society that denigrates them from birth.

A former opera singer who still demands to be the centre of attention, Meishan deeply resented the arrival of a younger rival, just as Zhuoyun continued to harbour a grudge against her. However, rather than emulating the dignified withdrawal of First Wife, the trio resort to deception, disloyalty and perfidy to advance their cause, as Songlian pretends to be pregant, Meishan seeks solace in the local doctor and Zhuoyun exposes the affair that leads to her adversary's murder in a room beneath the rooftops on which she used to sing.

The entire ensemble, along with cinematographer Zhao Fei, excels throughout. But it's Zhang's aesthetic subtlety and Gong Li's spirited defiance that make this so compelling, moving and courageous. ★★★★ **DP**

RAISE THE TITANIC (1980)

Starring: *Jason Robards (Admiral James Sandecker), Richard Jordan (Dirk Pitt), David Selby (Dr Gene Seagram), Anne Archer (Dana Archiblad), Alec Guinness (John Bigalow)*
Director: *Jerry Jameson*
Screenwriters: *Eric Hughes, Adam Kennedy, based on the novel by Clive Cussler*
PG/115 mins./Drama/UK-USA

A group of American salvage experts, along with adventurer Dirk Pitt, discover that a rare mineral was being carried on the *Titanic* before it hit the iceberg. With the only other known deposits in the Soviet Union, and the US defence eagerly in need of it for a secret project, they devise a way of raising the old ship from its berth on the seabed.

It's easy to see why this adaptation of Clive Cussler's popular if dim-witted novel became a celebrated flop. Indeed, such was its expense, and paucity of the result, that producer Lord Grade was legendarily said to have commented on its failure: *Raise the Titanic*? It would have been cheaper to lower the Atlantic? Which, in turn, might have made a much better movie than this irredeemably daft and wooden action-thriller, optimistically aiming to turn Richard Jordan into the novel's action hero (later portrayed by Matthew Maconaughey in *Sahara*), that saw it end up $23 million in the red.

Time has not helped either. The film was made back when the whereabouts of the wreck was still unknown, but now science and James Cameron have seen to it that its proposals of a complete ship on the sea floor are nonsense – it split into two halves! But it isn't just its naivety that hamstrings it, the execution is so bland it makes even the ludicrous stretches of the plot seem airless and unexciting. To conjure suspense there is a baffling mess of a plot involving secret stashes of mineral in the hold of the famous ship, and various American government agents trying to get their hands on it. An espionage element that requires us to skirt back to the days of the Cold War to feels its urgency. When we finally get to the disaster movie in reverse section of the film, any potential thrill is lost in swathes of boring exposition and in undistinguished special effects (where did the money go?). It feels as tethered and limp as a TV movie,

So, what can you say for it? Well, John Barry as usual delivers a sturdy rather haunting score, Jason Robards is reliably stern as a retired admiral thrown into the midst of events, and the underwater photography is not half bad as the submersibles search the ocean floor for the fabled wreck. But, so po-faced and turgid is its delivery, it can't even muster the necessary silliness to be a guilty pleasure. ★ **IN**

RAISING ARIZONA (1997)

Starring: *Nicholas Cage (H.I. McDunnough), Holly Hunter (Edwina 'Ed' McDunnough), Trey Wilson (Nathan Arizona Huffhines, Sr), John Goodman (Gale Snoats), William Forsythe (Evelle Snoats)*
Director: *Joel Coen*
Screenwriters; *Ethan Coen, Joel Coen*
12/90 mins./Comedy/USA

When a childless couple of an ex-con and an ex-cop decide to help themselves to one of another family's quintuplets, their lives get more complicated than they anticipated.

Coen brothers' Rule No. 1: there are no rules. And *Raising Arizona*, possibly the most undervalued of their eclectic canon, is no exception. Is it all just a dream? Certainly our hero himself asks, 'Was it wishful thinking? Was I just fleeing reality, like I know I'm liable to do ?' Is it simply the product of one man's overactive imagination? The constant references to Ronald Reagan – someone well known for his inability to distinguish between fiction and reality – would seem to suggest so. Or maybe even a political satire, picking away at the American Dream of the yuppie 80s? As always with a Coen brothers' movie, *Raising Arizona* is all of these things and none of them. But, as always with a Coen brothers' movie, it remains a wonderfully surreal, hilarious joy. At face value, the plot centres around odd couple H.I., a bungling ex-con, and his wife Ed, the police line-up photographer who has taken his picture on more occasions than she can remember. On discovering that they're unable to have children, or – as H.I. 'You can just call me "Hi" ' puts it – that 'her insides were a rocky place where my seed could find no purchase', the perfectly cast pair decide the only sensible option is to steal someone else's. And having relieved a local crook/entrepreneur of one of his quintuplets (figuring him to be 'somewhat overloaded' in the infant department) along with the 'bible' that is *Dr Spock's Baby And Child Care*, they embark on an adventure of thrills, spills and beautifully pitched humour.

Throughout, however, the unlikely 'family unit' is plagued by adversity. All of which arguably stems from Hi's own subconscious. Most notable is Leonard Smalls, The Lone Biker Of The Apocalypse 'especially hard on the little things' who is Hi's sinister alter ego, a demon straight from the back of his tiny mind. The personification of Hi's fears, Smalls (a tribute to *Of Mice And Men*'s Lenny Smalls) is his direct opposite, similar only in the Woody Woodpecker tattoo they both share. Likewise, Gale and Evelle, Hi's escaped prison buddies, could represent his worries over the responsibilities of fatherhood. Their 'birth' scene in particular, as they emerge screaming from the mud, and their eventual return back to the 'womb' of the prison walls, reflecting Hi's wildly differing states of mind.

But as much as one can read a multitude of subtexts into what is only the Coens' second feature, whatever way you look at it, one thing's for sure: it's unashamed, frantic fun. Exploring a genre they've only since revisited with *The Big Lebowski* (although, look out for early signs of *O Brother*'s pomade fixation), they make the most of a sumptuous location (one that's *Fargo*'s geographical flipside), orchestrate a series of superb chases (the nappy sequence is truly timeless), and achieve a slapstick treat so charming that, more often than not, it feels as if it's from another era altogether. 'What's most appealing about not tying yourself down to particular period boundaries,' explained Ethan, 'is it somehow removes everything from reality.'

Then, of course, there's that sublime dialogue. 'And it seemed real,' dreams Hi. 'It seemed like us. And it seemed like ... Well, our home. If not Arizona, then a land, not too far away, where all parents are strong and wise and capable, and all children are happy and beloved ... I dunno, maybe it was Utah.' Or, 'There's right and there's right, and never the twain shall meet.' Or, 'Name's Smalls. Leonard Smalls. My friends call me Lenny ... Only I ain't got no friends.' Or ... Well, we could be here all day. In-jokes abound, with nods towards *Evil Dead* (which Joel edited for old buddy Sam Raimi), *The Shining*'s REDRUM reflection gimmick and even Larry Cohen's *It's Alive*. Carter Burwell's wonderful score zips at a breathtaking pace, while Barry Sonnenfeld's cinematography revels in Arizona's wide open landscapes. Oh, and those still harping endlessly on that Coen movies don't have a heart? What of Nathan Arizona Snr's climactic speech? And Hi's post-sunset 'That was beautiful'? Pah.

Positively anarchic in its influence on the 80s' trend towards family oriented movies (*Baby Boom*, *Three Men And A Baby*, *Look Who's Talking*), *Raising Arizona* refuses to be bound by generic convention. From prison movie to gangster, screwball comedy to Spaghetti Western, no stone is left unturned. Hell, even the apocalyptic likes of *Mad Max* get a look in. But whether it's turning stereotypes on their head, or simply reducing its audience to uncontrolled bouts of laughter (Evelle: 'Do these [balloons] blow into funny shapes and all?' Shopkeeper: 'Well, no. Unless round is funny'), it's a movie that is as effective today as it was two decades ago. And why not? As Joel himself puts it, it has all the essential elements of modern cinema: 'Babies, Harleys and explosives.' Who could ask for anything more? ★★★★★ **MD**

⓪ RAMBO III (1988)

Starring: *Sylvester Stallone (John Rambo), Richard Crenna (Colonel Trautman), Marc de Jonge (Colonel Zaysen), Kurtwood Smith (Griggs)*
Director: *Peter MacDonald*
Screenwriters: *Sylvester Stallone, Sheldon Lettich, from characters by David Morrell*
18/97 mins./Action/Drama/USA

John Rambo, living in a Buddhist monastery in Thailand, returns to action when Colonel Trautman is captured by the Soviets while supplying stinger missiles to the Afghan resistance. Rambo opts to go in on a one-man rescue mission to rescue his old commanding officer.

Though there's a dud stretch with Israeli actors in robes blathering on about the spirit of the Mujahideen and the vileness of the Russian occupation forces in Afghanistan, *Rambo III* offers the usual procession of fire-fights, shoot-outs, tortures, escapes, one-on-one conflicts, crashing helicopter gunships and minimal dialogue.

The sole stylistic frill is the use of tilted cameras for much of the action, presumably because the cinematographer was cringing out of the way of the explosions. The interesting quirks of David Morrell's original novel *First Blood* have been ironed out, and the script even tries to take back the entire premise by having Trautman claim he did not turn Rambo into a supersoldier but simply smoothed off the rough edges of a natural warrior king.

With Trautman an unquestioning patriot and Rambo a spaniel-eyed liberal, it's hard to believe these are the same characters we saw before. It doesn't have the comic book verve of *Rambo: First Blood, Part 2*, and too many sequences that should have been highpoints – the duel between Rambo and a huge Russian soldier, for instance – are fumbled by awkward editing. Stallone often resorts to camp self-parody as a writer and as an actor, and the film goes so far as to have a cavalry rescue climax.

With its busy but painless battles, flip wisecracks and globe-trotting locales, this is more like a Bond movie with its shirt off than a proper Rambo film, and is consequently a good deal less like mindless fun than it might have been. ★★ **KN**

⓪ RAMBO: FIRST BLOOD PART 2 (1985)

Starring: *Sylvester Stallone (John J. Rambo), Richard Crenna (Col. Samuel Trautman), Charles Napier (Marshall Murdock), Steven Berkoff (Lt Col Podvosky), Julia Nickson-Soul (Co Bao)*
Director: *George B. Cosmatos*
Screenwriters: *Kevin Jarre, Sylvestor Stallone, James Cameron, based on characters created by David Morrell*
15/94 mins./Action/USA

Pulled out of jail by his former commanding officer, John Rambo, is sent on a mission to go back in Vietnam and survey where American POWs are still being held captive. But incensed with their treatment Rambo teams up with a female freedom fighter to rescue them first hand.

While *First Blood*, this film's predecessor, can still be held up as a sharp thriller of dislocated souls in the heart of America, its sequel is a comic-book aberration whose pounding lack of political judgement has lent it a hilariously un-PC quality, and a fond place in people's heart it surely doesn't deserve. This is a film co-written by Sylvester Stallone and James Cameron, and is accordingly dementedly macho, a right-wing wetdream of righteous American annihilation, as this walking walnut with a noble heart, played with Stallone's particular stroke-victim clarity, returns to win the Vietnam war single-handedly. On that level it's a fascinating piece, an inflamed representation of how so many Americans cannot face up to their great historical failure.

As a film it's too easily mocked for its unironic transformation of the battered soul of John Rambo (Stallone's second righteous thicko after Rocky) into an indestructible superhero, who crudely burbles the film's cranky hypothesis: 'Do we get to win this time?' The action is equally crude and sado-masochistic – while there's plenty of scenes of Rambo mowing down cannon-fodder gooks, he also partakes in a gruelling torture scene. When the Russians turn up, led by indefatigable Soviet-for-hire Steven Berkoff, things have so slipped into some netherworld of hideous small-mindedness, the only response is gales of appropriate laughter.

Rambo asks a lot of us, it's a real test. Here is a film fully xenophobic, touting guileless version of military honour, but with Jack Cardiff's furtive camerawork and some excellent editing, it sucks you in to its disturbing heroic sweep. But that doesn't count as a recommendation. Reappraisal is not due. ★★ **IN**

ⓒ RAN (1985)

Starring: *Tatsuya Nakadai (Lord Hidetora Ichimonji), Akira Terao (Taro Takatora Ichimonji), Jinpachi Nezu (Jiro Masatora Ichimonji), Daisuke Ryu (Saburo Naotoro Ichimonji), Mieko Harada (Lady Kaede)*
Director: *Akira Kurosawa*
Screenwriters: *Akira Kurosawa, Hideo Oguni, Masato Ide, based on the play* King Lear *by William Shakespeare*
15/160 mins./History/Drama/Japan/France
Awards: *Academy Awards – Best Costume Design; BAFTA – Best Foreign Language Film, Best Make-up*

A Japanese warlord, coming to the end of his days, decides to divide his kingdom up between his three sons. But his youngest thinks him mad, and that his plan will lead to bloodshed, and soon enough the older brothers have taken up arms against one another.

The last great masterpiece from Akira Kurosawa returns the Japanese genius to the pages of Shakespeare, and as appropriate for a man in the autumn of his years it is *King Lear* he recreates with an epic but passionate tale of rival brothers and father's destructiveness wrong-headedness. Kurosawa had previously transported *Macbeth* into the turbulent battlefields of 16th century feudal Japan to powerful effect with *Throne Of Blood*, and here with the addition of full-blooded colour he again transforms the Bard's eloquence in a form of cinematic thunder, a spectacle for mind and heart.

What makes *Ran* impossible to forget, or avoid, is more than simply the dazzling battle scenes in which thousands of horsemen, colour-coded with individual flags, flooding valleys and woods; not just the bloody repercussions of violence from a battered warrior clutching his dismembered arm to a devious wife taking her own life and a cascade of blood spraying across a wall; nor, still, simply the vivid, ferocious performances that burst out of the hugeness to live and breathe with angry gasps (Tatsuya Nakada's fallen father's descent into madness strikes a deep despairing chord). No, it is the entirety of its achievement, the sheer monumental size of the production, both physically and in the strikes of its drama that seize you so tightly. The title translates as 'chaos' but its director who seems to have control of even the stormclouds he summons to accent the sweeps of his plot, is nothing but a master of control. While never quite as intimate as *Seven Samurai*, this remains a film born of rare greatness. ★★★★★ **IN**

ⓒ RANDOM HARVEST (1942)

Starring: *Ronald Colman (Charles Rainer), Greer Garson (Paula), Philip Dom (Dr Jonathan Benet), Susan Peters (Kitty), Reginald Owen ('Biffer'), Edmund Gwenn (Prime Minister), Henry Travers (Dr Sims), Margaret Wycherly (Mrs Deventer)*
Director: *Mervyn LeRoy*
Screenwriters: *Claudine West, George Froeschel, Arthur Wimperis, based on the novel by James Hilton*
U/125 mins./Drama/USA

Suffering from amnesia after the First World War, John Smith marries music-hall singer Paula Ridgeway and embarks on a writing career. However, in recovering his identity as wealthy Charles Renier after a car accident, he forgets the past few years and makes plans to marry the eligible Kitty Chilcet.

Ronald Colman and Greer Garson probably had very different opinions of James Hilton when they signed up for this adaptation of his sentimental 1940 novel. His classic school story, *Goodbye, Mr Chips*, had afforded Garson her screen debut and he had also contributed to the screenplay of *Mrs Miniver* that was shortly to being her an Academy Award. However, Colman's career had never quite recovered from the setback it received following the critical mauling accorded Frank Capra's inexorably naive take on Hilton's *Lost Horizon*.

However, neither could have had any complaints after Mervyn LeRoy's effortlessly smooth tearjerker boosted both of their careers. Garson is, if anything, more appealing than she was as Mrs Miniver, as she's not constrained by the need to be permanently in control of her emotions. The ever-mellifluent Colman is also genially effective, although the 51-year-old always feels a little too old for the role, even after he's been restored to his previous life, where Susan Peters provides a spark of modernity that ruptures the patronising patina of English pastoral perfection imposed by art directors Cedric Gibbons and Randall Duell.

Yet, while the production values may now seem cloyingly MGM, they gave American wartime audiences a greater sense of what they were fighting for at a time when they had still to come to terms with how conflict could impact upon the Home Front. Ever keen to ensure that only the purest message was purveyed, the Breen Office insisted on removing all mention of Smithy's first wife (to avoid any implications of bigamy) and suggested that it was made clear that he and Paula had not consummated their relationship before marriage.

Doubtless the lingering hint of illicit passion persuaded punters to part with $4.5 million at the US box-office. But, while it was nominated for seven Oscars, it failed to win any, as *Mrs Miniver* went home with six. ★★★ **DP**

ⓒ RASHOMON (1950)

Starring: *Toshiro Mifune (Tajomaru), Machiko Kyon (Masago), Massayuki Mori (Takehiro), Takeshi Shimura (Firewood Dealer), Minoru Chiaki (Priest). Kichijiro Ueda (Commoner), Fumiko Homma (Medium), Daisuke Kato (Policeman)*
Director: *Akira Kurosawa*
Screenwriters: *Shinobu Hashimoto, Akira Kurosawa, based on the short story 'Yabu no Naka' and the novel* Tash-Mon *by Ryunosuke Akutagawa*
12/90 mins./Drama/Japan
Awards: *Academy Awards – Honorary Award*

In the woods, the bandit Tajomaru rapes Masako and then murders her husband. At a trial, all three give self-serving accounts of the incident. Later, a woodcutter who has witnessed the crimes gives another, more objective view of what happened.

The film that woke up the world to Japanese cinema, this is a still-effective 'gimmick' melodrama about a rape-murder seen from four different viewpoints, each wildly different. The abused wife, the embittered husband and the lecherous bandit all get to tell their stories – the husband speaking through a medium – and all present themselves in the best light (as brave, noble, ferocious, self-sacrificing) while doing down the others (as cowardly, grasping, lecherous, hypocritical), but finally a bystander comes along and reveals that actually everyone involved is a moral and physical coward, reducing high tragedy to black slapstick as a duel we've seen as an epic struggle is re-presented as a knockabout between two men too terrified to fight properly with the final death caused by an accident rather than malice or skill.

There's a showboat performance from Toshiro Mifune as the swaggering yet hollow bandit desperate to live up to his reputation, but it's Akira Kurosawa's direction that commands the attention as he mood ranges from the savage to the wistful to the comic. Its cynical neatness perhaps lodges it a notch down from masterpiece level, but still outstanding.

It was adapted for American and British television in 1960 and 1961, with Anglo actors playing Japanese under the direction of Sidney Lumet and Rudolph Cartier, then remade as Martin Ritt's Western *The Outrage* in 1964 and the odd Bridget Fonda vehicle *Iron Maze* in 1991, and imitated so often as episodes of everything from *The Simpsons* to *The X-Files* that you can pitch something as 'a *Rashomon* story'. ★★★★ **KN**

RATCATCHER (1999)

Starring: *William Eadie (James), Tommy Flanagan (Da), Mandy Matthews (Ma), Michelle Stewart (Ellen), Lynne Ramsay Jr (Anne Marie), Leanne Mullen (Margaret Anne)*
Director: *Lynne Ramsay*
Screenwriter: *Lynne Ramsay*
15/89 mins./Drama/UK
Awards: *BAFTA – Carl Foreman Award for Most Promising Newcomer (Lynne Ramsay)*

A 12-year-old boy accidently contributes to the drowning of another. The boy retreats into himself, away from his desperate family and towards the gang of misfit teens that roam the grimy streets.

Set in the grotty tenements of 70s-era Glasgow during a protracted dustman's strike, Lynne Ramsay's powerful first feature relates the story of James, a lonely 12-year-old urchin forced deeper into his shell by his accidental part in the drowning of another boy.

As his secret festers inside like so much uncollected rubbish, he drifts away from his hard-drinking Da and put-upon Ma, becoming the runt of a gang of likely borstal candidates and striking up friendships with naive pal Kenny and affection-starved teen slut Margaret Anne. With his family waiting on a council transfer, James journeys to the fringes of the city, where a half-constructed paradise of golden fields and Barratt homes offers flickering hope for a better life, but the rat-infested streets and murky waters of the canal cast a dark spell on the troubled hero.

That you could write a thesis on the line of influence between Ramsay's feature and Ken Loach's *Kes*, via the respective trilogies of Bill Douglas and Terence Davies, does not detract from the fact that *Ratcatcher* is one of the finest British films about childhood in recent years.

The naturalistic ensemble acting of the young cast is something to behold, and although the picture is harder than a Glasgow kiss and often unflinchingly bleak, it is also studded with quirky humour and quietly inflected lyricism, the latter used so sparingly that each manifestation becomes a tiny epiphany.

Bare of sentimentalism, and oozing raw authenticity from every dirty pore – the children look old before their time, the adults as if they were never young – Ramsay evokes the strangeness of the everyday world, and through Eadie's melancholy eyes lets us experience the snuffed dream and waking nightmare of a tragic adolescence. ★★★★ **TL**

RAVENOUS (1991)

Starring: *Robert Carlyle (Colqhoun/Ives), Guy Pearce (Captain John Boyd), David Arquette (Cleaves), Jeremy Davies (Private Toffer), Jeffrey Jones (Colonel Hart)*
Director: *Anthonia Bird*
Screenwriter: *Ted Griffin*
18/96 mins./Horror/USA/UK

A bunch of stranded settlers eventually turn to the only food available – each other.

Based on a real incident in 1846 known as the Donner Pass Disaster, in which a group of pioneers heading for California became snowbound and survived by eating their dead companions, this is a stomach-churning take on the most potent of all celluloid taboos. Be warned: *Ravenous* might start out as a kind of macabre, frontier-set *Alive*, but a few neck-cricking plot twists take it to some very dark places, very quickly.

After an act of cowardice during the Mexican-American War, Captain John Boyd is banished to a desolate military outpost in the remote reaches of the Sierra Nevada mountains. Here he encounters a motley collection of military misfits under the despondent command of Colonel Hart.

One night, a half-starved Scot named Colquoun staggers into the camp. He claims to have escaped from a group of west-bound settlers who, on becoming snowbound, turned to cannibalism to survive. He also recounts the old Indian myth of Weendigo, which states that a man who eats the flesh of another steals that person's strength, his spirit and very essence. His hunger becomes insatiable and death is the only escape.

Perhaps unwisely, the company resolve to rescue the women and children who, Colquoun insists, are still alive, and the mysterious Scot leads them back to the cave where the atrocities took place. At this point, things take a turn for the seriously weird, to say nothing of the damn scary and the absolutely revolting. And it just keeps getting more bizarre, more sickeningly gory and more queasily comic right up to the totally demented finale. *Ravenous* is not like any film you've seen before. And if you've ever felt a bit funny in the butcher's, you'll never want to see anything like it again. ★★★ **SB**

RAY (2004)

Starring: *Jamie Foxx (Ray Charles), Kerry Washington (Della Bea Robinson), Regina King (Margie Hendricks), Clifton Powell (Jeff Brown)*
Director: *Taylor Hackford*
Screenwriter: *James L. White, from a story by White and Taylor Hackford*
15/152 mins./178 mins. (extended version)/Drama/Music/USA
Awards: *Academy Awards – Best Sound, Best Actor; BAFTA – Best Actor, Best Sound; Golden Globes – Best Actor*

In 1948, teenage musical genius Ray Charles Robinson (Foxx) sets off alone to join the jazz scene in Seattle. He then commences battle with the demons of childhood tragedy, disability, segregation and heroin addiction in a warts-and-all biopic that celebrates his life and legacy

Taylor Hackford's Ray Charles story – 15 years in the making, involving a tenacious, at times testy, collaboration with its subject – couldn't be more timely, coming out within months of Ray's much-mourned passing. His 50-odd-year career coincided with major cultural upheaval, and this depiction of his artistic evolution not only reflects the changing social landscape around him, but emphasises his significance as he graduated from the Chitlin Circuit to concert halls, fusing gospel with blues (an innovation denounced as blasphemous) and jazz with rock, breaking all barriers in his way.

It's a given that a musical biopic will find dramatic incident to namecheck and prompt big numbers. So a perky kid with a trumpet will mosey in announcing, 'I'm Quincy Jones.' And, with delicious inevitability, a heated lover's quarrel will segue into a rousing performance of 'Hit The Road Jack'. When the characters and songs are this strong, it's a pleasure anticipating the next cue. And there are some electrifying musical sequences, like the genesis of Ray's sensuous, driving anthem 'What'd I Say', or the angry departure of one backing singer/lover supplanted by another, interwoven with the chicks strutting their stuff on stage.

The structure is ambitious to exhaustion, focusing on the 'heroin years', taking Ray from 18 to around 40 and ending rather abruptly with the future as historical footnote. Ray's torrid love life spices up the grimmer aspect of growing addiction, drug bust and rehab. Flashbacks in brighter colours abound, covering the Depression-era childhood of loss, piano lessons, the onset of blindness and the tough love with which Mama Robinson shaped Ray's hard-headed approach to life. (The seemingly obligatory depiction of the child's brilliant ear for music and mimicry becoming more acute as his vision dims is, yes, a tad cute, but well-handled.)

Falling on the meaty, potential role of a lifetime like a ravenous lion, erstwhile comedian Jamie Foxx, so good in *Collateral*, is just wonderful as the eponymous star. His impersonation of Charles (who okayed him after they played piano together) is uncanny, and his empathy with Charles' sharp mind, artistry, self-absorption, suffering and survival mechanisms is complete, compelling and charismatic. ★★★★ **AE**

RAZORBACK (1984)

Starring: *Gregory Harrison (Carl Winters), Arkie Whiteley (Sarah Cameron), Bill Kerr (Jake Cullen), Chris Haywood Berry (Baker)*
Director: *Russell Mulcahy*
Screenwriter: *Everett DeRoche, from the novel by Peter Brennan*
18/90 mins./Horror/Australia

In the Australian outback, a pair of kangaroo-slaughtering psychopaths assault an American journalist who is then eaten by a giant pig. Her husband investigates, and finds himself allied with a vengeance-seeking farmerwho has lost his grandson to the razorback.

The best killer pig movie of all time. Director Russell Mulcahy's first feature is a scary, sleazy thriller – mixing the backwoods psychopathy of *The Texas Chain Saw Massacre* with the rampaging wildlife of *Jaws*.

Mulcahy, fresh from a batch of Duran Duran clips, backlights everything and litters the desert with bits of art direction, working hard to make every shot interesting – though some have wondered where the huge banks of lights in the night come from.

The film manages many stand alone, surreal images (a car stranded in a tree by a flash flood, a pigfaced nightmare wioman, the desert disgorging its dead) and dwells on a supremely disgusting image of the grotty side of Australia, which is still rather an uncomfortable watch. The tusky monster doesn't stand up to prolonged examination, but Mulcahy stages its attacks in shadowy, fragmentary scenes that amp up the terror, and Chris Haywood and David Argue are unforgettably repulsive as the giggling, roo-killing outback maniacs.

These guys are so degenerate that, after a hard night of torturing animals, abusing women and leaving victims to be eaten by the pig, they go home to a disused opal mine decorated with Barry Manilow posters. Bill Kerr, Tony Hancock's old sidekick on the wireless, plays an Aussie version of the Robert Shaw-in-*Jaws* character.

The climax takes place in a vile, filthy factory where kangaroos are turned into pet food, and battered hero Harrison confronts the big pig among dangling, clanking chains and hideous grinding, whirring blades. ★★★ **KN**

REACH FOR THE SKY (1956)

Starring: *Kenneth More (Douglas Bader), Muriel Pavlow (Thelma Bader), Lyndon Brook (Johnny Sanderson), Lee Patterson (Stan Turner), Alexander Knox (Mr Joyce), Dorothy Alison (Nurse Brace), Michael Warre (Harry Day), Sydney Tafler (Richard Desoutter)*
Director: *Lewis Gilbert*
Screenwriter: *Lewis Gilbert, based on the novel* The Story Of Douglas Bader *by Paul Brickhill*
U/135 mins./War/UK
Awards: *BAFTA – Best British Film*

Having lost both legs in a flying accident, Douglas Bader not only mastered his artificial limbs, but also rejoined the RAF to become a squadron leader during the Battle of Britain. Even when he's shot down over France, he refuses to quit and winds up in Colditz after numerous escape attempts.

The majority of 'now it can be told' war movies produced in Britain after the Second World War tended to espouse mass heroism. There were occasional tributes to such unique individuals as Odette Churchill (*Odette*, 1950) and M.E. Clifton-James (*I Was Monty's Double*), but celebrations of communal courage like *The Wooden Horse*, *The Dam Busters* and *The Battle of the River Plate* were supposed to have a more unifying effect on a populace still enduring the effects of postwar austerity.

However, Douglas Bader was no ordinary hero and *Reach for the Sky* lionised the larger-than-life personality, whose triumphs over adversity had been chronicled in Paul Brickhill's bestselling biography.

There were those who felt that Bader was an irascible, self-aggrandising bore, who had endangered the lives of his air crew in seeking to disprove the naysayers who claimed that he would never fly again after losing his legs in an accident that was largely the result of his own arrogance. But the producers countered such a negative impression by casting one of Britain's most popular stars as the indomitable flyer.

Kenneth More was so beloved by millions for his performances in *Genevieve* and *Doctor in the House* that Lewis Gilbert was convinced that his bonhomie would take the curse off Bader's egotism and make him seem more than ever like an ebullient patriot. Moreover, More was fresh off the back of winning the Best Actor prize at Venice for *The Deep Blue Sea*.

So, there's no question that More was shrewd casting and while his habit of overdoing the hail fellow cheeriness occasionally tended towards caricature, he not only carried the lengthy narrative, but also made Bader seem inspirational rather than reckless. However, his hectoring theatrics left little room for anyone else, whether they were flying chums or Muriel Pavlow, as the devoted nurse who became his indulgent wife.

Bader's fortitude has to be admired. Yet, while this biopic was reverentially made, its stiff upper-lipped glorification of combat meant that it was infinitely more propagandist than anything produced during the war itself. ★★★ **DP**

REALITY BITES (1994)

Starring: *Winona Ryder (Lelaina Pierce), Ethan Hawke (Troy Dyer), Janeane Garofalo (Vickie Miner), Steve Zahn (Sammy Gray), Ben Stiller (Michael Grates), Swoosie Kurtz (Charlane McGregor), Renee Zellweger (Tami)*
Director: *Ben Stiller*
Screenwriter: *Helen Childress*
12/94 mins./Comedy/Drama/USA

After graduating from film school, a young girl finds herself attracting the attention of two guys who couldn't be more different — a cynical, suited studio executive and a young, handsome, likeable slacker.

If the title is an observation that life in the real world hurts, it's reasonable. If it's meant to indicate little snippets of reality (as in sound bites), get a grip, guys! Billed as hip, 90s romantic comedy for an audience American trend analysts condescend to label Generation X, this is really the old, old love triangle tangle, dressed by Gap and styled by MTV, in which new university graduate, aspiring (inept, we'd call it) filmmaker and idealist Lelaine seeks meaningful employment along with her identity and is torn between sweet, older, well-dressed video exec Michael and hip, scornful, dishevelled and directionless Troy.

The most graceful note in Stiller's feature directorial debut is Ryder, winsome despite the contradictions in a character who is her class

TOP 10 Greatest Movie In-Jokes

1 *Indiana Jones and the Temple of Doom*
The opening scenes take place at Shanghai's Club Obi-Wan, in tribute to producer George Lucas. C3PO and R2D2 also appear in hieroglyphics in *Raiders of the Lost Ark*.

2 *THX-1138*
The title of George Lucas' first film is referenced in all the *Star Wars* films (except *Jedi*) as well as everything from *Swingers* to *Sesame Street* to *Sky Captain and the World of Tomorrow*.

3 *Toy Story*
There are loads of film in-jokes here, but perhaps the best is *Full Metal Jacket*'s R. Lee Emery voicing the bossy toy soldier.

4 *Back to the Future II*
Marty McFly arrives in 2015 to see a billboard for *Jaws 19*, directed by Max Spielberg (Steven's son) and cars taken straight from *The Last Starfighter* and *Bladerunner*.

5 *Maverick*
Danny Glover turns up to share a moment with his *Lethal Weapon* partner Gibson and utter the immortal catchphrase, 'I'm getting too old for this shit.'

6 *The Blues Brothers*
The phrase 'See you next Wednesday,' a throwaway line in *2001: A Space Odyssey*, is used to refer to a fictional film-within-a-film in at least six Landis films and his video for 'Thriller'.

7 *Gremlins*
A double bill at the local movie theatre lists *A Boy's Life* and *Watch The Skies* as the films showing – these were the working titles for producer Steven Spielberg's *E.T.* and *Close Encounters*.

8 *Enemy of the State*
Gene Hackman plays an ageing ex-CIA spook, but photos of him as a younger man were taken from *The Conversation*, where he played – you guessed it – a CIA spook.

9 *The Fog*
Director John Carpenter named half the characters in the film after his collaborators, including Nick Castle, Dan O'Bannon and Tommy Wallace.

10 *The X Files Movie*
At one point, in the background, you can see Agent Mulder urinate on a poster for *Independence Day*.

valedictorian but curiously inarticulate, questionably literate, and, for a bright, attractive 23-year-old, embarrassingly coy on dates. Around her is the now customary mixed bag of college buddies struggling with young adulthood: promiscuous clothing store manageress, inoffensive gay pal, and grungy Troy – all expert at the art of 'time-suckage' and diverted by pizza-fuelled quiz games or post-Boomer junk culture like the *Brady Bunch* or thrashing around to nostalgic tunes like The Knack's 'My Sharona'.

The nods to AIDS and the vacuity of the 90s TV and slacker sensibilities (frequently unintelligible to those who didn't receive their life-training in an American shopping mall) are merely decoration on what, unadorned, is about how youthful aspirations are compromised by the boring but true prognostications of parents on the theme 'After You've Been In The Real World A While . . .' ★★★ **AE**

RE-ANIMATOR (1985)

Staring: *Jeffrey Combs (Herbert West), Bruce Abbott (Dan Cain), Barbara Crampton (Megan Halsey), Robert Sampson (Dean Halsey), David Gale (Dr Carl Hill), Gerry Black (Mace), Peter Kent (Melvin, the re-animated)*
Director: *Stuart Gordon*
Screenwriters: *Dennis Paoli, William J. Norris, Stuart Gordon, from the story* Herbert West – Re-Animator *by H.P. Lovecraft*
18/83 mins./Comedy/Horror/USA

A medical student returns from Austria after working in regenerative experiments with a scientist who died under mysterious circumstances. He enrolls at Miskatonic University where he eventually enlists his roommate to help him continue experiments on re-animating the dead.

Stuart Gordon has never exactly been a stranger to controversy. Having already had obscenity charges levelled at him after a university production of *Peter Pan* (Tinkerbell was gay, Peter a hippy and the trip to Never Never Land was on LSD), his co-founding of Chicago's infamous Organic Theater soon followed. All before he'd even picked up a camera. No surprise, then, that his first foray into filmmaking can hardly be described as understated.

Based on H.P. Lovecraft's 1921-22 pulp series *Herbert West: Re-Animator* – which the author always actually looked down on – Gordon originally produced a half-hour television script shaped around the first two instalments, only for producer Brian Yuzna (who directed sequel *Bride Of Re-Animator* in 1990 and *Beyond Re-Animator* in 2003) to be so intrigued that he insisted on him adapting all six into a feature. And so, after Gordon spent weeks of research in morgues ('You never forget the smell, I can assure you') and forensic labs, the modern-day spin on the Frankenstein theme was born.

Shot in the same studios as *The Terminator* (1984), immediately after the sci-fi epic had wrapped, the two films actually have much in common. As well as sharing much of the same crew, *Re-Animator* features a cameo by Cameron's father (the hospital patient with a bandaged head), and boasts Arnie's body double, Peter Kent, as the first corpse to be revived (the similarity – both physically and in acting style – is uncanny, by the way). In fact, so excited was Kent about the project that Schwarzenegger himself requested a screening, and subsequently loved the film so much that he personally recommended Gordon as director for *Fortress* – which eventually starred Christopher Lambert when Arnie bailed.

Not surprisingly, when the finished version was shown to the ratings board, with a request for an R certificate, the result was a barely stifled guffaw. But, faced with the choice of making the necessary cuts, and being left with a 40-minute short, or risking financial calamity by opting for an unrated release, Gordon and Yuzna stood firm, unleashing their uncut masterpiece first at Cannes (where critics went wild) and then at the box office (where the audiences followed suit). Even in its present form, *Re-Animator* remains a splashy hark back to the glorious 80s love affair with all-things bloody – to the point that Gordon was convinced he'd used more fake blood than anyone else in the history of horror ... Until, that is, he compared notes with *Braindead*'s Peter Jackson.

Consider also a budget reputed to be barely over $1 million (very much in keeping with second producer Charles Band's school of penny-pinching filmmaking) and the effects are all the more impressive. Although the shoestring budget with which Bret Culpepper (the man behind *The Stuff* later the same year) had to work with resulted in a number of improvisations being made. Hamburger mince was sometimes used in place of latex, a lack of pubic prosthetics – used to cover up naked zombies' genitals – meant that Gesundheit's (the crew's nickname for the shotgun-wound-in-the-face member of the undead) penis had to be sprayed black to make it more discrete, and the neon 'life juice' was, in fact, flare fluid bought from a local hardware store.

But if there was one person who suffered most from the measly effects budget, it was David Gale. As Herbert West's enemy, Dr Hill, the actor had to be hit around the head with a 'rubber' shovel made from a cheap variant that had set far too hard, and was also forced to wear a hideous wig for the whole shoot to match the hair on his fake head (this was considerably cheaper than reproducing the colour of his real barnet). No wonder the film is now dedicated to his memory.

Tagline
Herbert West has a very good head on his shoulders – and another one in a dish on his desk.

Of course, no discussion of *Re-Animator* is complete without mentioning its infamous 'head' sequence (Barbara Crampton gets some from a severed one). But while, in creating 'The world's first visual pun', Gordon established himself as a hot new talent, others fared less favourably. Gale's wife stormed out of a screening, wailing 'David! How could you?' and Crampton (who landed the part when her predecessor's mother read the script and forbade her daughter from playing it) spent the next few years confiscating stacks of smutty stills from excitable fans at horror conventions.

This, after all, is the effect the film has had on audiences worldwide, infecting them with its canny combination of unashamed borrowing (look out for Polanski shots lifted straight from *Rosemary's Baby*, and a score that may well have had Bernard Herrmann turning in his grave), a simplistic storyline (a hypnotism subplot was eventually cut) and, yet, breathtaking originality. Not least one Jim Belushi, of Chicago, Illinois, who to this day occasionally rings the director in the early hours of the morning, simply to utter his favourite line: 'Wessst . . . You . . . Basstarrrd!' Hear, hear! ★★★★ **MD**

REAR WINDOW (1954)

Starring: *James Stewart (L.B. Jefferies), Grace Kelly (Lisa Carol Fremont), Wendall Corey (Det. Lt. Thomas J. Doyle), Thelma Ritter (Stella), Raymond Burr (Lars Thorwald)*
Director: *Alfred Hitchcock*
Screenwriter: *John Michael Hayes, based on the short story by Cornell Woolrich*
PG/107 mins./Thriller/USA

A wheelchair bound photographer spies on his neighbours from his apartment window and becomes convinced one of them has committed murder.

A news photographer, a restless man of action, is confined to his apartment and a wheelchair by a broken leg. He spends weeks looking out of his window at people who live in the apartments across the courtyard. Afraid of committing to his high-class girlfriend, he takes refuge in the petty lives of the semi-strangers who are his neighbours. The camera stays with the leading man inside his flat, and supporting characters appear only in long-shot, joys and miseries glimpsed and half-understood.

Sounds like an art movie, doesn't it?

Depending on the degree of wry comedy or domestic tragedy, it could be a delicate French comedy, an Italian neo-realist masterpiece or a despairing slice of Swedish miserabilism. All the hallmarks are there: a technical gimmick (staying on one set throughout), thematic complexity (a voyeur whose involvement in human stick figures is exactly that of a cinema audience), an unconventional mode of narrative (the hero and his few visitors discuss the stories they observe, like a chatty group at a hard-to-follow movie).

But one of the neighbours is a murderer. And the director is Alfred Hitchcock. The rotund Englishman was already well-established in America, but this was the first of a run of huge hits or true masterpieces that would last ten years. Having won long-sought independence from a contract with tyrannical producer David O. Selznick (the murderer of *Rear Window* is made up to look like Selznick), Hitch was declaring himself an auteur. Well before the craze for possessory credits, the title card boldly announces 'Alfred Hitchcock's *Rear Window*'. So it's a thriller, with big Hollywood stars.

In 1954 they didn't come bigger than James Stewart, a real-life ageing juvenile who had surprised fans by becoming an authentic war hero and showing real depth in *It's A Wonderful Life* (1946) and a run of outstanding Westerns. Grace Kelly, a few years away from transformation into a genuine princess, was so beautiful and blonde she could only be convincingly cast as a fashion model. *Rear Window* is a murder story with big stars from a famous studio director. All of which doesn't mean it's not an art movie.

The first third contains not a mention of crime, as L.B. 'Jeff' Jeffries grumbles at enforced confinement and tries to worm his way out of engagement to Lisa Fremont. She wants him to remain permanently crippled (as he sees it) by switching from photographing wars and disasters to a life of moneyed ease shooting fashion spreads. Stella (the marvellous Ritter), a sour but funny nurse, comes every day and gossips with Jeff about the neighbours as if they were keeping up to date with a soap opera.

All the characters around the courtyard keep Jeff thinking about love, sex and marriage. 'Miss Torso' jives in underwear and fends off wolfish young men while 'Miss Lonelyhearts' prepares romantic candlelight meals she eats alone. Newlyweds pull down the blinds and spend the whole film having sex. A middle-aged couple sleep on the fire escape because of the New York heatwave, their dog a substitute child. A songwriter struggles with a melody, getting drunk or elated as a hit ('Lisa') coalesces. And weary jewellery salesman Lars Thorwald is nagged by his shrew of a wife.

One night as Jeff dozes and watches, Thorwald struggles out with his sample case. The next morning, his wife is gone. In his apartment, Thorwald wraps used knives and saws for disposal. The dog digs at Thorwald's floral border, and Jeff notices some zinnias have shrunk. The dog is killed. Keen to switch the subject from marriage, Jeff tells Lisa he thinks Thorwald has murdered his wife and Stella fills in the gruesome details. Scenarist John Michael Hayes, like original author Cornell Woolrich, is a master of the horrid hint: the problem has been disposed of 'in sections', the deed would have had to be done in the bathroom, under the zinnias is buried something 'in a hatbox'.

It is a measure of Hitch's genius that the murder story doesn't completely take over. At a crucial point, Jeff and Lisa are distracted from snoopy sleuthing when Miss Lonelyhearts seems on the point of suicide only to be dissuaded by the songwriter's piano-playing. When Thorwald realises he is being watched and comes to Jeff's flat, he is not a fiend in human form but a pitiably trapped little man who has found no relief in escape from his intolerable marriage, who has no money to pay off a blackmailer, and is puzzled that anyone would care about him and what he has done.

Rear Window ends with all stories resolved: the song is finished, Miss Torso welcomes home her tubby soldier boyfriend, the couple have a new puppy, Miss Lonelyhearts is with the songwriter and Thorwald's apartment is being redecorated. But Hitchcock doesn't let up: Jeff now has two broken legs and is asleep in domesticity with Lisa, who still thinks of taming him; and the sex-happy honeymooners are starting the whole cycle again, the wife having turned into a nag. ★★★★★ **KN**

Movie Trivia: Alfred Hitchcock (1899–1980)

Who he is: Arguably the most influential filmmaker ever. Master of the thriller in a career that spanned over 50 years and every major technological innovation until digital effects.

Hallmarks: Hitchcock cameos; blonde heroines; cold, calculated plotting of impassioned stories; dazzling technique; twisted sexual subtexts.

If you see one movie, see: *Psycho* (1960)

REBECCA (1940)

Starring: *Laurence Olivier (Maxim De Winter) Joan Fontaine (Mrs De Winter). George Sanders (Jack Favell), Judith Anderson (Mrs, Danvers), Nigel Bruce (Major Giles Lacy), Reginald Denny (Frank Crawley), C. Aubrey Smith (Colonel Julyan), Gladys Cooper (Beatrice Lady), Leo G. Carroll (Dr Baker)*

Director: *Alfred Hitchcock*

Screenwriters: *Phillip MacDonald, Michael Hogan, based on the book by Daphne Du Maurier, adapted by Robert E. Sherwood and Joan Harrison*

PG/130 mins./Thriller/USA

Awards: *Academy Awards – Best Picture, Best Black And White Cinematography.*

A young woman marries Maxim De Winter, master of the huge estate of Manderley – then finds herself overshadowed by the memory of his beautiful first wife, who died in mysterious circumstances.

When *Rebecca* won the Best Picture Oscar for 1940, it was universally regarded as David O. Selznick's super-produced follow-up to *Gone With the Wind*. Now, we tend to think of it as Alfred Hitchcock's first American film, though the director tended to dismiss it as a work-for-hire project which he shot professionally without feeling able to make it his own. Adapted from Daphne du Maurier's best-seller, it's an important, entertaining film – but also an example of what happened to great material when put through the Hollywood mill.

Joan Fontaine and Laurence Olivier are enormously enjoyable as the trembling, unbelievably naive and gauche heroine and her overbearing, Gothic-romantic husband (his idea of a proposal is 'I'm asking you to marry me, you little fool'), but there are flamboyant, scene-stealing supporting performances from George Sanders as the caddish cousin who was Rebecca's lover ('I'd like to have your advice on how to live comfortably without working hard') and Judith Danvers as the crowlike, all-in-black sinister housekeeper Mrs Danvers ('You've moved her brush, haven't you?').

With its lavish production values, doom-haunted atmospherics and high-pitch emotionalism – reaching a peak as Mrs Danvers tries to drive the heroine to suicide – it's superb Gothic romance, until the last five minutes when censorship requirements dictate that Du Maurier's perfect original ending is replaced by an appallingly feeble revelation (that Rebecca fell over and hit her head) that comes close to ruining the whole story. The proper ending is used in British TV versions made in 1978 with Joanna David, Jeremy Brett and Anna Massey and 1997 with Emilia Fox (Joanna David's daughter), Charles Dance and Diana Rigg. ★★★★ **KN**

REBEL WITHOUT A CAUSE (1955)

Starring: *James Dean (Jim Stark), Natalie Wood (Judy), Sal Mineo (John 'Plato' Crawford), Dennis Hopper (Goon)*
Director: *Nicholas Ray*
Screenwriter: *Stewart Stern, based on a story by Nicholas Ray, adapted by Irving Shulman*
PG/106 mins./Drama/USA

Jim Stark, a troubled teenager, arrives at a new school, and gets into a feud with the local toughs, which leads to a 'chickie run' in which his rival is killed. With Judy, the dead boy's girlfriend, and Plato, an even more troubled kid, Jim hides out in an old mansion. But Plato has a gun.

The classic teenage angst movie, emblematic for successive generations, with James Dean sprawling in a widescreen gutter playing with a toy monkey, modelling a cool red bomber jacket, showing off a full range of Method acting tics, inarticulately expressing youthful misery at the unfairness of the world ('You're tearing me apart'). Dean is neurotic but innately decent, rejecting his unmanly father (Jim Backus, in a frilly apron) and shrewish mom (Ann Doran) and falling in with a fast-living teenage set (Corey Allen, Dennis Hopper, Nick Adams) who indulge in knife fights and drag-race to the death, then establishing a strange, utopian pseudo-family with maternal co-ed Natalie Wood and even more-mixed-up classmate Sal Mineo.

Dean was already dead by the time his greatest star vehicle hit screens, making him a posthumous idol and the chicken run – in which Dean's character escapes while his rival plunges to a fiery death – a chilling evocation of his fatal crash. Director Nicholas Ray originally intended an intense, earnest, black and white 'social problem' picture about juvenile delinquency, but the use of CinemaScope, vivid WarnerColor and a lush Leonard Rosenman score turns it into a melodrama of doomed youth and romantic agony. In the classic finish, the forces of adult repression come to bear and someone winds up a martyr as the Los Angeles police – in another horribly prophetic bit – gun down unarmed teenager Mineo at the planetarium. ★★★★★ **KN**

THE REBEL (1961)

Starring: *Tony Hancock (Anthony Hancock), George Sanders (Sir Charles Broward), Paul Massie (Paul), Margit Saad (Margot), Gregoire Aslan (Carrereas), Dennis Price (Jim Smith), Irene Handl (Mrs Crevate), John Le Mesurier (Office Manager), Liz Fraser (Waitress)*
Director: *Robert Day*
Screenwriters: *Tony Hancock, Ray Galton, Alan Simpson*
U/105 mins./Comedy/UK

Anthony Hancock quits his 9 to 5 job to become an artist in Paris, where he achieves overnight success and the patronage of art dealer Sir Charles Brewer by passing off the work of his disillusioned friend, Paul, as his own.

Tony Hancock always needed to be the centre of attention. Consequently, Kenneth Williams was unceremoniously dumped from the long-running radio show, *Hancock's Half Hour*, for getting bigger laughs and Sid James suffered much the same fate when he was dropped from the TV spin-off in 1960. However, for the time being, at least, Hancock still recognised his dependence upon writers Ray Galton and Alan Simpson and he retained them for this return to cinema, following his inauspicious debut in *Orders Are Orders* in 1954.

The Rebel marked the only time that Anthony Aloysious St John Hancock made it to the big screen, as he sought to escape from the persona of the 'cunning, high-powered mug' in subsequent outings. All the ignorance, arrogance, pomposity and juvenility that made Hancock a star were on view, as he swopped his bowler hat for a beret and launched himself upon Bohemia. But, the sitcomic Hancock had specialised in passive resistance rather than rebellion, as he sought to make a quick quid, buck the system or acquire some cheap kudos. Moreover, for all his aspirations, he rarely strayed far from Railway Cuttings, East Cheam and the best moments here are set in his familiar milieu, as he secures himself a seat on the commuter train and trades banter with his landlady (brilliantly played by the peerless Irene Handl) while working on his hideous sculpture, *Aphrodite at the Water Hole*.

However, once the scene shifts to Paris, the screenplay settles for too many easy shots at artistic clichés and caricatures and the parochial smugness of the Brits abroad. Hancock's attempts to hold his own in conversations about aesthetics recall the desperate bluffing of Will Hay, while the affectations he adopts on achieving success are amusingly true to form. But the excess of plot to shoehorn into the later stages meant that there was too little room for the kind of character comedy at which Hancock excelled.

In many ways, his next picture, *The Punch and Judy Man*, was more ambitious. But its monochrome bleakness failed to find an audience. ★★★ **DP**

RED DAWN (1984)

Starring: *Patrick Swayze (Jed Eckert), C. Thomas Howell (Robert Morris), Lea Thompson (Erica), Charlie Sheen (Matt Eckert), Jennifer Grey (Toni)*
Director: *John Milius*
Screenwriters: *John Milius, Kevin Reynolds, based on story by Reynolds*
15/109 mins./Action/Drama/USA

The USSR invades and occupies the USA. In Colorado, high-school kids become a guerilla resistance unit and give the occupation forces a fight.

Made at the height of the Reagan Era, with the then-monolithic Soviet Union tagged as 'the Evil Empire', *Red Dawn* is at once a mainstream shoot 'em up action picture and an ideologically demented exercise in American paranoia. It opens with a high school class being lectured about Mongol Hordes as Russian paratroops land on the playing field and set about gunning down innocents and taking over the town. Our junior heroes, mostly members of the loser local football team ('the Wolverines'), stock up on guns, snack food and toilet paper and head for the mountains to keep fighting.

It's pretty much a hard-bitten camp, with Harry Dean Stanton shouting 'avenge me' behind the wire at a drive-in turned into a 're-education centre', but the It Happened Here business of an unfamiliar, invaded backdrop (Alexander Nevsky at the local movie-house, Russian troops in McDonald's) still has a frisson. Weirdly, as in the *Rambo* movies, the wish-fulfilment fantasy is that Americans get to be underdog, freedom-loving rebel guerillas, whereas the other side are big bullies crushing the will of the people.

To John Milius's way of thinking, America *needs* to be attacked, invaded and overthrown for Americans to regain any sense of purpose – even if it means teenagers becoming mountain men and outright psychopaths. Though C. Thomas Howell does something almost subtle with the role of the youth who comes to enjoy summarily executing prisoners, other 80s teen icons (Patrick Swayze, Jennifer Grey, Charlie Sheen) just look glum and are upstaged by 'guest stars' Powers Boothe (downed pilot) and Ben Johnson (grandfatherly plot-explainer) or contrasted commies Ron O'Neal (sympathetic Cuban) and William Smith (nasty Russian). A guilty pleasure. ★★★ **KN**

THE RED DESERT (IL DESERTO ROSSO) (1964)

Starring: *Monica Vitti (Giuliana), Richard Harris (Corrado Zeller), Carlo Chionetti (Ugo), Xenia Valderi (Linda), Rita Renoir (Emillia), Aldo Grotti (Max), Valerio Baroleschi (Valerio), Giuliano Missirini (Workman)*
Director: *Michelangelo Antonioni*
Screenwriters: *Michelangelo Antonioni, Tonino Guerra*
15/116 mins./Drama/France-Italy

Recovering from the depression that prompted a suicide bid, Giuliana drifts into an affair with Corrado Zeller, an associate of her engineer husband Ugo, who is in Ravenna to recruit workers for an industrial enterprise in Patagonia.

Opinion is not only divided over the quality of Michelangelo Antonioni's first film after completing his celebrated 'alienation' trilogy' (*L'Avventura*, *L'Eclisse*, *La Notte*) but also over his precise intentions. Many critics were content to see the film – in which Monica Vitti gives a devastating display of brittle vulnerability – as a furtherance of Antonioni's preoccupation with the dehumanising nature of modern society, with some even suggesting that he no longer had anything original to say about the human condition. Most applauded his use of colour to emphasise the ugliness of industrial architecture and the shallowness of contemporary culture, while Marxists and Greens respectively averred that he was denouncing capitalism and the reckless destruction of the environment.

But, rather than presenting Giuliana as a victim of soulless technology, Antonioni claimed that her problems lay in her failure to acclimatise to a brave new world. Thus, he insisted that the oil refinery, power plant and radar installation possessed a beauty that matched Ravenna's Byzantine past and that his bold colour symbolism was intended to highlight the exciting modernity of progress.

There's no denying the brilliance of Antonioni's colour scheme, which was exploited for the same psychological purposes as the hostile Sicilian landscape in *L'Avventura*. His transformation of objects and vistas to conform to his emblematic design was also laudable, as was his astute shift from deep-focus photography to the utilisation of zoom lenses that flattened and distorted the image in the manner of abstract art. Even Giuliana's isolated island idyll was rendered in terms of a tawdry TV advertisement, complete with pseudo-Freudian overtones linking her neuroses with the onset of puberty (which invited comparisons with Hitchcock's approach in *Marnie*).

But it's difficult to reconcile such a stance with Antonioni's allusions to Dante's *Divine Comedy*. Not only does Corrado recall Ulysses in the epic poem, but Ravenna was also the model for the earthly paradise at the summit of Purgatory. It could be argued that Antonioni was positing Chiassi's industrial landscape as a new Eden, but the more obvious implication was that it represented a foretaste of Hell. ★★★★ **DP**

⦿ RED DRAGON (2002)

Starring: *Anthony Hopkins (Dr Hannibal Lecter), Edward Norton (Will Graham), Ralph Fiennes (Francis Dolarhyde), Harvey Keitel (Jack Crawford), Emily Watson (Reba), Mary-Louise Parker (Molly Graham), Philip Seymour Hoffman (Freddy Lounds)*
Director: *Brett Ratner*
Screenwriter: *Ted Tally, from the novel by Thomas Harris*
15/119 mins./Thriller/USA

Retired FBI Investigator Will Graham is lured back into action after a series of grisly murders undertaken by serial killer Francis Dolarhyde, aka The Tooth Fairy. To help crack the case, Graham enlists the help of Dr Hannibal Lecter . . .

Let's be honest, it didn't look very promising, did it? The auteur behind *The Family Man* and *Rush Hour 2* tackling the movie's favourite cannibal with the residue of the dreary Hannibal still ripe in the memory. But Brett Ratner's adaptation of Thomas Harris' 1981 prequel to *The Silence Of The Lambs* (already adapted by Michael Mann as *Manhunter*) delivers the goods with minimum fuss.

As if to atone for Ridley Scott's uninspired instalment, *Red Dragon* feels like a concerted effort to get back to the glory days of *Silence* and, to a large extent and against all the odds, Ratner pulls it off. It may not have *Manhunter*'s sense of style or interesting contours, but *Red Dragon* surpasses Mann's movie in its dogmatic desire to entertain.

Putting the cult of Lecter aside for a moment, *Red Dragon* works as a cracking detective story. Going the Christopher Columbus/Harry Potter route, Ratner, in tandem with *Silence* screenwriter Tally, has been remarkably faithful to Harris' tautly constructed mystery. He offers a well-tooled, workmanlike compendium of the book's greatest hits – the great scene in which Lecter's cell is searched for clues as to how he is contacting Dolarhyde, the horrific burning wheelchair set piece – that is the cinematic equivalent of a page-turner.

Where Ratner does deviate from the novel, it pays dividends: a pre-credits opener that pitches Lecter and Graham against each other, first mentally, then physically, is a fantastic curtain-raiser, satisfying our immediate appetite to see the good Doctor while setting up the Lecter-Graham mind-games to come.

Hopkins, who doesn't make much effort to convince us that the character is any younger, coasts through his scaremongering, conveying an astuteness and intelligence that was missing last time round. Although Lecter's comedy schtick is much better judged here – droll wit replacing grandstanding one-liners – and keeping Lecter in his cell is far more unnerving than him roaming freely, it is a shame that much of the menace from the monster in *Silence* has evaporated. At times bordering on the pantomimic, Lecter has turned into a Freddy Kruger for the *Friends* generation.

Elsewhere, Ratner has invested in quality casting and it shows. As Lecter's foil, Norton gives the movie a likeable, easy-to-root-for centre, nicely conveying a man masking his fear with a determination to do right. Be it scoffing a painting of William Blake's *Red Dragon* or torturing a snivelling journalist (nobody plays snivelling and enfeebled like Phillip Seymour Hoffman), Fiennes manages to take Dolarhyde to the extremes without ever making the character's evil laughable.

If not quite as shit-scary as Tom Noonan's incarnation from *Manhunter*, he also finds a real shift of gear in his tentative, affecting relationship with Reba (Watson, once again putting in good work), the blind woman who offers the killer a redemptive state of grace.

What ultimately stops *Red Dragon* from being truly great rather than merely good is the bog-standard quality in Ratner's direction. Everything is crisp, everything is proficient but nowhere does he generate the foreboding atmosphere or memorable image that really hits home: visually, the movie is a sitcom version of *Silence*, all flat lighting and bland set-ups, the infamous corridor approaching Lecter's cell having none of its previous power.

Indeed, the movie doesn't really deliver any real scares and nail-gnawing tension until a last reel denouement. But when the shocks do come, they work a treat. ★★★ **IF**

⦿ RED EYE (2005)

Starring: *Rachel McAdams (Lisa Reisert), Cillian Murphy (Jackson Rippner), Brian Cox (Joe Reisert), Jayma Mays (Cynthia)*
Director: *Wes Craven*
Screenwriter: *Carl Ellsworth, based on a story of Ellsworth, Dan Foos*
12A/85 mins./Thriller/USA

Aviophobic Lisa is pleased to find herself seated next to handsome stranger Jackson on a flight to Miami. Little does she know this is no chance encounter, and Jackson has sinister motives, involving the highest levels of government, in hooking up with the pretty hotel manager . . .

For his 20th feature, horror legend Wes Craven took a conscious decision to leave behind the genre which has served him so well over 30 years in favour of close relative the psychological thriller, in this case transferring the tribulation and terror from suburban, picket-fenced Middle America to the edgy context of the passenger jet.

It's a neat little concept, as hotel manageress Lisa Reisert (*Mean Girls'* McAdams) – not a fan of flying as it is – takes the red-eye home to Miami, only to discover that crashing is the least of her worries when she finds herself effectively taken hostage by fellow passenger Jackson, on a murderous mission of which she now finds herself an unwilling part. Tapping into and then exaggerating anxieties many of us share, Craven handles the first hour with aplomb (but no bomb), slowly building the set-up while having fun with the clichés (a young blonde child is seen boarding her first flight alone), before switching gear abruptly when Jackson proves in an instant to be far from the charming would-be suitor Lisa was hoping would distract her from the flight.

As they near Miami and Lisa's deathly dilemma becomes more desperate, Craven keeps the energy high, introducing vicious new twists at a breathless pace while increasing the claustrophobia with almost constant close-ups of the central pair (screenwriter Ellsworth cites *Phone Booth* as an influence). McAdams makes an engaging and admirably resourceful heroine, while a typically impressive Murphy proves he doesn't need a sack-cloth shroud and fear serum to scare – his ice-blue eyes, cold calm and sunken cheekbones making him an alluring yet deeply unnerving villain. Still, you can take the boy out of *Elm Street*, but as the last 20 minutes prove, it would seem you can't entirely take *Elm Street* out of the boy.

As the plane lands and the action transfers to Lisa's family home, Craven returns to the standard tropes of the genre he shaped, with little of the postmodern irony of *Scream* – after a (presumably unintentionally) comic injury, Murphy's Jackson even finds himself rasping, stumbling and demonically glaring like the best horror-movie monster. Although disappointing after the superior thriller of the first 70 minutes, the audience is by now having so much fun, and Craven knows this stuff so well, happily this makes for a far from fatal flaw. ★★★ **LB**

RED ROCK WEST (1992)

Starring: *Nicholas Cage (Michael Williams), Lara Flynn Boyle (Suzanne Brown), Dennis Hopper (Lyle), J.T. Walsh (Wayne Brown), Craig Reay (Jim)*
Director: *John Dahl*
Screenwriters: *John Dahl, Rick Dahl*
15/94 mins./Comedy/Thriller/Crime/USA

A drifter is mistaken for a hit man and hired to assassinate a bar owner's wife, then the real hired killer turns up . . .

Starring a trio of actors with more than a passing association with David Lynch, John Dahl's film takes the familiar Lynchian theme of smalltown America – Red Rock, Wyoming – and does the old trick of peeling back the veneer to reveal that all is not well beneath the dusty exterior.

Idling into town comes Michael, an out-of-work former Marine, meandering his way north in search of gainful employment. Pulling over for an innocent bevvy at the local bar, a classic case of mistaken identity occurs and, by virtue of his motor's Texas plates, shady bar proprietor Wayne assumes Michael to be the Lone Star hitman he hired to bump off his heiress wife.

With a $5,000 downpayment slapped into his grubby mitts and being, well, a bit strapped for cash, Michael goes along with the ruse, traipsing off to despatch the brains of Wayne's missus in a general westerly direction. Being a decent sort of bloke, he never really intends to go through with it, of course, but a further complication prevents him doing a speedy runner from Red Rock.

Thus, when the real hitman shows up, the fun and games begin, with everybody doublecrossing everybody else but with all of them out to nail Michael good and proper. Cage, Hollywood's favourite world-weary individual, slopes about with his usual downtrodden competence and J. T. Walsh, the supporting actor's supporting actor, is nicely chilling, but the real joy here is Hopper in a superbly psychotic turn as gunman Lyle, not a million miles away from, and probably related to, *Blue Velvet*'s Frank.

Unfortunately, Flynn Boyle doesn't cut the mustard as a scheming femme fatale, but there are enough cracking twists and a genuine feeling of suspense to notch this up as one of the superior 'noirs' of the early 90s. ★★★ **JD**

THE RED SHOES (1948)

Starring: *Anton Walbrook (Boris Lermontov), Moira Shearer (Victoria Paige), Marius Goring (Julian Craster), Leonide Massine (Grischa Ljubrov), Robert Helpmann (Ivan Boleslawsky), Albert Basserman (Sergei Ratov), Esmond Knight (Livy)*
Director: *Michael Powell, Emeric Pressburger*
Screenwriters: *Michael Powell, Emeric Pressburger, Keith Winter*
U/133 mins/Drama/UK

Awards: Academy Awards – *Best Score, Best Art Direction-Set Decoration*

Vicky Page, a promising ballerina, is compelled by her Diaghilev-like Svengali, Boris Lermontov, to choose between her career and composer, Julian Craster, who scored the 20-minute Red Shoes ballet that has made her a star. But having opted for love, Vicky finds the lure of ballet dancing too strong and she weakens, with terrible consequences.

At a time when filmmakers around the world were plumbing the depths of neo-realism or exposing social iniquity in monochrome problem pictures, Michael Powell and Emeric Pressburger were revelling in the Technicolored glamour of the theatre. Based on a story by Hans Christian Andersen and originally commissioned by Sir Alexander Korda for his then-wife Merle Oberon, this glorious (though some would say somewhat precious) picture brought a new refinement to the backstage musical.

While the tragic drama, intense performances and ravishing visuals have earned the film its reputation for exquisite artifice, the other technical credits are also hugely impressive. Robert Helpmann, who plays the company's leading dancer, Boleslawsky, also choreographed the ballet, while such superstars as Ludmilla Tchérina and Léonide Massine headlined the corps.

Former documentary composer Brian Easdale won an Oscar for a score that was performed by Sir Thomas Beecham and the Royal Philharmonic Orchestra. Additionally, production designer Hein Heckroth was similarly rewarded for his stylised sets. Yet, cinematographer Jack Cardiff was scandalously overlooked, despite the film's sumptuous imagery. Martin Scorsese apparently ranks this among his favourite films. And that should be good enough for the likes of us. ★★★★★ **WT**

RED SONJA (1985)

Starring: *Arnold Schwarzenegger (Kalidor), Brigitte Nielsen (Red Sonja), Sandahl Bergman (Queen Gedren), Paul L. Smith (Falkon), Ernie Reyes Jr (Prince Tarn)*
Director: *Richard Fleischer*
Screenwriters: *Clive Exton, George MacDonald Fraser, from a character by Robert E. Howard*
15/84 mins./Fantasy/Adventure/USA

Awards: *Razzie – Worst New Star (Brigitte Nielsen)*

Wicked Queen Gedran steals a talisman which will make her mistress of the world. Sonja, sister of the murdered talisman-keeper, joins with man of mystery Kalidorto overthrow the tyrant.

This spin-off from producer Dino de Laurentiis's *Conan the Barbarian* films returns to the Hyborean Era of barbarism and magic created by pulp author Robert E. Howard. However, the female warrior heroine was created not by Howard but by Roy Thomas, as a love interest in *Marvel* comics' Conan series.

Originally, Schwarzenegger was due to reprise his Conan role, but one of the many last-minute rethinks which blighted the production shifted him to the Conan-like role of 'Prince Kalidor' instead.

The idea of a strong-willed, strong-armed, flame-haired barbarian heroine who can hew her way through hordes of baddies is appealing, and there's serious chick-fight action in the finale as Brigitte Nielsen takes on Sandahl Bergman, but the film lacks the guts to make Sonja the Xena-like role model she ought to be. Whenever our heroine gets into any trouble, the mysterious superhunk Kalidor pops out of nowhere and comes to her rescue.

Finally, a ridiculous romance develops, complicated by the fact that Sonja won't sleep with any man who can't defeat her in a fair fight. 'Why is she fighting so hard?' asks an annoying tagalong prince (Ernie Reyes Jr) in the worst of the film's many cringe lines. 'She doesn't want to win.'

While the sets and matte paintings, beautifully photographed by Giuseppe Rotunno, create a marvellously evocative vision of Howard's mythological world, this is a laughably inept adventure peopled with awkward performers and afflicted with a ridiculous script. Director Richard Fleischer, held over from *Conan the Destroyer*, delivers far less heroic fantasy than in his mighty-thewed masterpiece *The Vikings*. ★ **KN**

⊙ REDS (1981)

Starring: *Warren Beatty (John 'Jack' Reed), Diane Keaton (Louise Bryant), Edward Herrmann (Max Eastman), Jack Nicholson (Eugene 'Gene' O'Neill), Paul Sorvino (Louis Fraina), M. Emmet Walsh (Speaker – Liberal Club), Maureen Stapleton (Emma Goldman)*
Director: *Warren Beatty*
Screenwriters: *Warren Beatty, Trevor Griffiths*
15/186 mins./Biography/Drama/USA

Awards: *Academy Awards – Best Supporting Actress (Maureen Stapleton), Best Cinematography, Best Director; BAFTA – Best Supporting Actor (Jack Nicholson), Best Supporting Actress (Maureen Stapleton); Golden Globes – Best Director*

A radical American journalist becomes involved with the Communist revolution in Russia and hopes to bring its spirit and idealism to the United States.

With such an impressive cast and epic sweep (mostly thanks to cinematographer Vittoriao Storaro doing what he's best at), it's hardly surprising that *Reds* was so critically acclaimed (Warren Beatty won one of the film's three Oscars for Best Director, and it was nominated for six more) on its theatrical release in 1981.

In retrospect, though, this slightly overlong (easily passing the three-hour mark) account of a US journalist's bid to bring communism back home to America seems occasionally just too ambitious – and worthy – for its own good. Still a memorable piece of cinema, though, with Beatty and Keaton in impressive form throughout as John Reed, the author of *Ten Days That Shook The World*, who inspired this film, and his on-off lover left-wing activist Brant.

Lookout, too, for Gene Hackman in an unbilled cameo role. ★★★★ **KN**

⊙ REGARDING HENRY (1991)

Starring: *Harrison Ford (Henry Turner), Annette Bening (Sarah Turner), Bill Nunn (Bradley), Mikki Allen (Rachel Turner), Donald Moffat (Charlie)*
Director: *Mike Nichols*
Screenwriter: *Jeffrey Abrams*
15/102 mins./Drama/USA

High-powered lawyer Harry struggles to find time for his family and after a late-night shooting he wakes up with no memory of them at all. With the support of his ever-loving wife and an inspirational nurse he sets out on the long road to recovery, which will uncover a terrible secret.

Regarding Henry has sufficient pedigree attached in the shape of director Nichols and its two stars to suggest this may be the most successful variation on the old tradition of turning bastards into loveable good guys. It isn't.

Everything starts well enough, with Ford back to attractive leading man status after the disaster that was his haircut in *Presumed Innocent* and coming over sufficiently nasty as the bigshot lawyer who just hasn't got any time for all that family and friends shit. Then, popping out for a packet of snouts late at night, that hopeless Mexican maid has forgotten to get them in for him again, he inadvertently stumbles across a routine hold-up and, in the best anti-smoking advertisement ever made, takes one in the brain.

Cue lengthy vegetable period, only enlivened by Spike Lee regular Bill Nunn as Bradley, the inevitably big black male nurse with more humanity in his dodgy knees than Harrison ever had back in those bad, if highly profitable, old days. Not surprisingly, the former yuppie scum sets out to atone for his previous mistakes, learns how to love his wife (a decidely ornamental Bening), daughter and pooch and realises that, hey! he might be poor but it's easier for a camel to enter etc. and, boy, this is the life, what?

From a director of such proven quality as Nichols, it's all remarkably clumsy, every development signposted way in advance, every hoary old device pulled out to signify the transformation taking place. More cloying than *Awakenings*, if that's possible.

Regarding Henry is ultimately just about bearable thanks to Ford's sheer presence and the occasional reminder, the first 20 minutes in particular, of what might and should have been. ★★ **BMc**

⊙ REGENERATION (1997)

Starring: *Jonathan Pryce (Capt. William Rivers), James Wilby (Siegfreid Sassoon), Jonny Lee Miller (Billy Prior), Stuart Bunce (Wilfred Owen), Tanya Allen (Sarah), Dougray Scott (Rupert Graves)*
Director: *Gillies MacKinnon*
Screenwriter: *Allan Scott, based on the novel by Pat Barker*
15/108 mins./Drama/War/UK/Canada

Based on Pat Barker's novel of the same name, *Regeneration* tells the story of soldiers of World War One sent to an asylum for emotional troubles.

Adapted from the first part of Pat Barker's World War I trilogy, Gillies Mackinnon's *Regeneration* focuses on the work of psychiatric pioneer Dr William Rivers and his attempts to heal the lives of a group of men, all of whom have been left emotionally devastated by the effects of the 1914–18 conflict.

Most notable among these is the poet Siegfried Sassoon, formerly a heroic soldier who is sent to Rivers' asylum after he reveals his plans to make a public protest against the war. As Rivers tries to convince him to change his plans, Sassoon starts to bring to the surface the doctor's own wounds and it becomes clear that the patients and the carers are all fighting the same war, all equally scarred by it.

Mackinnon's film is a worthy, often engrossing tale, delicately acted and beautifully shot. The sheer horror of trench warfare haven't been captured this vividly and emotionally since Kubrick's *Paths Of Glory*. The opening scene; an aerial view of a mud-filled battlefield covered with corpses, immediately sets the tone of the piece, while Michael Danna's score is mournfully moving. Sassoon is the kind of role Wilby can deliver in his sleep and here he's very good, bristling with upper-class righteous indignation.

Pryce, too, is on top form, with a well-judged portrayal of a man becoming unravelled by virtue of his trying to help others put their lives back together. Just as impressive is Miller's initially mute enlisted man, Private Billy Prior, struggling to prove his manhood, haunted by fear of his own cowardice.

The film works less well, however, in terms of focus. Miller's soldier's story is of equal import to that of the doctor and Sassoon, while the latter's formative relationship with fellow war poet and inmate Wilfred Owen is in there, too, struggling for screen time. ★★★★ **BM**

LA REGLE DU JEU (RULES OF THE GAME) (1939)

Starring: *Marcel Dalio (Robert de le Chesnaye), Nora Gregor (Christine de la Chesnaye), Rouland Toutain (André Jurieu), Jean Renoir (Octave), Mila Parely (Genevieve de Marrast), Paulette Dubost (Lisette), Gaston Modot (Schumacher), Julien Carette (Marceau), Odette Talazac (Charlotte de la Plante)*
Director: *Jean Renoir*
Screenwriter: *Jean Renoir*
PG/110 mins./Drama/France

The romantic entanglements of Robert de la Chesnaye and his wife Christine – who is pursued by both flying ace André Jurieu and his friend, Octave – are mirrored by her maid Lisette's ménage with gamekeeper husband Schumacher and Marceau, the poacher.

The only film that Jean Renoir made for his co-operative production company, Nouvelles Editions Françaises, turned out to be his last French project for 16 years. Inspired by De Musset's *Les Caprices de Marianne*, Marivaux's *Le Jeu d'Amour et du Hasard* and Beaumarchais's *Le Mariage de Figaro* and the music of Lully, Couperin and Rameau, *Fair Play* or *La Chasse en Sologne* (as the feature was originally to be called) was concocted to focus on people who 'lived to baroque rhythms'.

But casting alterations, the improvised nature of the shooting and the deteriorating world situation left Renoir uncertain whether he was making a comedy or a tragedy. In 1938, he declared that he was preparing 'a precise description of the bourgeoisie of our age. I want to show that for every game, there are rules. If you don't play according to them, you lose.' However, he later claimed that he wanted to depict a society 'dancing on the edge of a volcano'.

Critics applauded Renoir's use of deep focus to implicate all classes in the film's thesis that French society was approaching implosion. But, audiences despised its sentiments from the night of the premiere, when one man attempted to set light to the theatre that dared to show such unpatriotic filth. Just days before France declared war on Germany, the picture was banned by a Ministry of Foreign Affairs 'especially anxious to avoid representations of our country, our traditions, and our race that change its character, lie about it and deform it through the prism of an artistic individual who is often original but not always sound'.

It was presumed that only a handful of poor quality, bowdlerised prints survived the conflict. However, in 1956, 224 boxes of positives, negatives and sound mixes were discovered and a restored version (missing only Octave and André's brief musings on the morality of maidservants) was screened at the Venice Film Festival in 1959 – the year in which the nouvelle vague broke in France – and *La Règle du Jeu* has rightly been regarded as an indisputable masterpiece ever since. ★★★★★ **DP**

REIGN OF FIRE (2001)

Starring: *Christian Bale (Quinn Abercromby), Matthew McConaughey (Denton Van Zan), Izabella Scorupco (Alex Jensen), Gerard Butler (Dave Creedy), Scott James Moutter (Jared Wilke)*
Director: *Rob Bowman*
Screenwriters: *Gregg Chabot, Kevin Peterka, Matt Greenberg, from a story by Chabot, Peterka*
12/97 mins./Fantasy/Adventure/USA/UK/Ireland

A witness to the first ever modern-day dragon attack, Quinn leads a small community of survivors in the wastes of England. The whole world is at war with the fire-breathing, flying creatures.

The camera never lies, but you can't say the same about the poster. The buzz of anticipation that began with *Reign Of Fire*'s excellent trailer, leapt with an electric jolt the first time *Empire* spied the movie's promotional artwork.

Fire-breathing dragons! Battling with helicopters! Trashing Big Ben! Put the popcorn on order and block-book the front row, we're ready to witness the best scenes of world destruction this side of *Independence Day*. Or not, as the case turns out to be.

Instead of an apocalyptic special effects extravaganza, what we get is not one, but two scrapbook montages featuring newspaper clippings, *Time* magazine covers and archive documentary footage, as Christian Bale's Quinn recounts the years between the 2002 prologue and the 2020 meat of the movie.

Clearly the budget didn't stretch far enough to deliver on the poster's promise, and audience disappointment is inevitable. Bale, however, brings dramatic depth to his character, while McConaughey is a splendidly over-the-top, pumped-up, adrenaline freak.

Arriving on a tank turret with the gun sprouting phallically between his legs, Van Zan approaches this apocalypse as Kilgore, Chef and Kurtz rolled into one (note the dragon's napalm breath and Jimi Hendrix on the soundtrack).

What the film lacks in a full-on city attack, it makes up for with a satisfying final confrontation between the stars and the father of all dragons. But even then, the impact would have been greater if we had a better sense of the enemy – unlike *Jurassic Park*'s dinosaurs, the dragons here are a somewhat anonymous threat.

Likewise the rest of Quinn's near-medieval community, few of whom are developed beyond the status of extras, other than Gerard Butler's by-the-numbers sidekick. It says something when the highpoint of the film is when Butler and Bale re-enact *Star Wars* for the orphan kids. ★★★ **AM**

LA REINE MARGOT (1994)

Starring: *Isabelle Adjani (Margot), Daniel Auteuil (Henri de Navarre), Jean-Hugues Anglade (Charles IX), Vincent Perez (La Mole), Virna Lisi (Catherine de Medici)*
Director: *Patrice Chereau*
Screenwriters: *Patrice Chéreau, Daniéle Thompson, based on the novel by Alexander Dumas*
18/162 mins./Drama/Biography/Romance/France/Italy/Germany

France, 1572. In a bid to prevent civil war, Catherine de Medici, the power behind the throne of her son, Charles IX, marries her Catholic daughter, Marguerite de Valois, to Henri, the Protestant King of Navarre. However, Margot is more interested in her lover, Le Mole, than the affairs of state.

Screenwriter Danièle Thompson first interested Patrice Chéreau in Alexandre Dumas's historical novel in 1992. Although he had made films before – *L'Homme Blessé* had scandalised Cannes with its graphic depiction of gay sex – Chéreau was best known for his work in the theatre and opera. Consequently, most people expected a heritage picture along the lines of producer Claude Berri's Pagnol adaptations or his 1993 take on Zola's *Germinal*, especially after *La Reine Margot* landed the Special Jury Prize at Cannes, where Virna Lisi was also acclaimed Best Actress for her feral performance as Catherine de Medici.

However, audiences and critics alike were shocked by Chéreau's uncompromising delineation of both the barbarity of the Wars of Religion and the bestiality of life at Charles IX's court. Instead of historical opulence, they were treated to filthy costumes, unkempt hair and boorish manners, as well as an anachronistic approach to period detail and dialogue, and a boomingly modern score. Moreover, the action was drenched in blood, as Chéreau sought to swamp any romanticised notions of a period awash with crimes like the St Bartholomew's Massacre that stained the reputation of Royalist France. (There were those, however, who claimed that such carnage was a response to the civil wars then erupting across Eastern Europe following the collapse of Communism.)

Some pointed out that Isabelle Adjani was too old to play the teenage queen. But the majority of complaints concerned the complexity of the plot, which particularly taxed non-French viewers even though the action had been trimmed by 16 minutes and the opening credits had included a handy history lesson. However, even though the court intrigue took some following, this still worked as a Grand Guignolic soap opera, with Margot's relationships with her husband, lover and fiercely protective brother, the Duc of Anjou (Pascal Greggory), being as satisfyingly melodramatic as Catherine's pitiless villainy. Thus, while it may not have performed well at the box office, it has since exerted a considerable influence on the tone of historicals across the continent. ★★★ **DP**

THE REMAINS OF THE DAY (1993)

Starring: *Christopher Reeve (Lewis), Anthony Hopkins (Stevens), Emma Thompson (Miss Kenton), James Fox (Lord Darlington), Hugh Grant (Cardinale)*
Director: *James Ivory*
Screenwriter: *Ruth Prawer Jhabvala, based on the novel by Kazuo Ishiguro*
U/128 mins./Drama/Romance/History/UK/USA

A repressed English butler agrees for a free-thinking housekeeper to join the 1930s household where he works but is not prepared for the emotional effect her arrival will bring.

E.M. Forstered out, producer Ismail Merchant, director James Ivory and screenwriter Ruth Prawer Jhabvala (in her thirteenth Merchant-Ivory collaboration) have taken into their masterly hands Japanese-born Kazuo Ishiguro's Booker Prize-winning novel of duty, betrayal and loss and turned out another perfectly crafted, perfectly 'British' film.

Anthony Hopkins head the top-class home side as Stevens, the perfect butler and head of the vast household staff of Darlington Hall where, in the 1930s, his lordship James Fox's enthusiasm for order, tradition and stability takes a disquieting turn with his ominous penchant for all things Teutonic. Opening in the late 50s with a new American owner keen to restore the Darlington spread, the story unfolds as faithful Stevens reviews his lifetime of service, his own personal drama played out against hints of the treason and tragedy that will take place as war and sweeping social change touch all in Lord Darlington's domain.

Stevens, born to serve, is rigidly suppressed and dutiful, internalising – in a string of acutely observed, comic and painful incidents – all his most important personal experiences (of death, of love, of conviction) in the cause of serving his master. Thompson is Miss Kenton, the prickly but wistful young housekeeper at touching odds with the gentleman's gentleman who has never learned to express his own needs or serve his own interests.

Beautifully detailed, from the nuances of the domestic hierarchy to the events 'upstairs' which Stevens observes but can never venture to comment on, one scarcely need add, of course, that it looks splendid. Cleverly structured, this has all the obvious commercial appeal of an *Upstairs Downstairs* with Nazis while offering a more profound character study in its quiet If Only and What Might Have Been tragedy of a man who knows his place and keeps it, while losing himself. Though it is becoming redundant to describe Hopkins as brilliant, his performance here is so remarkable as to evoke wonder, and for that alone this film represents one of the distinguished achievements in the Merchant-Ivory catalogue. ★★★★ **AE**

RENT (2005)

Starring: *Taye Diggs (Benjamin Coffin III), Jesse L. Martin (Tom Collins), Wilson Jermaine Heredia (Angel Dumott Schunard), Anthony Rapp (Mark Cohen), Idina Menzel (Maureen Johnson), Tracie Thoms (Joanne Jefferson), Adam Pascal (Roger Davis), Rosario Dawson (Mimi Marquez)*
Director: *Chris Columbus*
Screenwriter: *Stephen Chbosky, based on the musical by Jonathan Larson*
12A/135 mins./Musical/Drama/USA

Struggling artists in New York's East Village unite against former friend-turned-yuppie landlord Benny. Philosopher Collins meets soulmate drag queen Angel, filmmaker Mark loses Maureen to another woman, and Roger falls for junkie dancer Mimi.

Cards on the table: rock operas pretty much suck except for *Tommy*, which knows it's mad. It's the sung dialogue between proper songs that does us in. In classical opera they get away with it – it's melodic, it rhymes, and it's preferably in a foreign language. But when a contemporary character tra-las, 'You promised you'd be cool!' or, 'Have you got a light?', the word that comes to mind is 'ick'.

Inspired by Puccini's *La Bohème* (impoverished Parisian artists with tuberculosis), this landmark Broadway musical (impoverished Manhattan artists with AIDS) won every award going, including multiple Tonys and the coveted Pulitzer Prize. Adding to its legend, *Rent*'s author, composer and lyricist, Jonathan Larson, died on the eve of previews, a loss that intensely bonded its cast as the tightly knit friends and lovers sharing poverty, passion, eviction, addiction, performance art, illness and a rent strike over the course of one year (the show opened in 1996 but is set firmly in 1989).

Most of that cast have been reunited for the film, most famously Diggs (whose role is unfortunately the briefest) and Martin (*Law & Order*'s Detective Green), with excellent new recruits Dawson as tragic Mimi and Thoms as lesbian lawyer Joanne. While this makes a *Rent* buff's heaven-sent souvenir of record (it's a rare chance, for example, to enjoy the supercharged vocalising of Diggs' wife Idina Menzel, a big star on Broadway), the downside is that the *Fame*-like vivacity – dancing atop tables and through traffic features – is a tad incongruous since the cast are nearly all closer to 40 than 18.

Columbus' direction and the adaptation from intimate grunge musical theatre to screen spectacle comes out a curate's egg: every time a set-piece number lifts proceedings – Dawson's sizzling 'Out Tonight', Martin's moving, gospel-flavoured lament at a funeral – the mood immediately crumbles with a toe-curling interlude.

By the time it reaches its big emotional climax, Mimi's laboured breathing invites giggles in the stalls. The production also suffers from '*Hair* syndrome'; it comes to the screen far too late to capitalise on its fame for originality and impact. Producers were unable to secure film finance for nearly a decade, during which time elements like the gay pride and AIDS support group themes have been, done and moved on. ★★ **AE**

REPO MAN (1994)

Starring: *Emilio Estervez (Otto), Harry Dean Stanton (Bud), Tracey Walter (Miller), Olivia Barash (Leila), Sy Richardson (Lite), Susan Barnes (Agent Rogersz)*
Director: *Alex Cox*
Screenwriter: *Alex Cox*
18/88 mins./Sci-fi/Thriller/USA

A young punk quits his job and is recruited as a trainee 'Repo Man' only to fall into their bizarre, paranoid, conspiracy theory driven world.

Alex Cox is no Orson Welles, and *Repo Man* is no *Citizen Kane*. Nevertheless, the directors do have something in common: after an attention-grabbing debut, neither of them quite managed to hit the same high mark again, despite offering up a string of interesting failures.

Cox, of course, is still on the go (and the moderately well-received *Revengers Tragedy* was a return to the spotlight), but it's *Repo Man* that continues to form the core of his reputation.

Its mix of alien conspiracy theories, car repo noir, consumer society satire and LA punk scene would be a rather self-conscious attempt at securing cult status were it not for the spot-on performances from Harry Dean Stanton and Emilio Estevez. ★★★★ **AM**

REPULSION (1965)

Starring: *Catherine Deneuve (Carole Ledoux), Ian Hendry (Michael), John Fraser (Colin), Yvonne Furneaux (Helene Ledoux), Patrick Wymark (Landlord), Roman Polanski (Spoons player)*
Director: *Roman Polanski*
Screenwriters: *Roman Polanski, Gerard Brach, David Stone*
18/100 mins./Thriller/Horror/UK

Carol Ledoux, a Belgian manicurist living in London, is left alone in a flat when her sister goes on holiday with her married lover and spends a week going mad.

Roman Polanski's first English-language film. It was conceived as an entry in the new-horror sub-genre that had been created (and named) by *Psycho*, but takes a different approach to terror. We only discover that Norman Bates is a psychpath at the end of Alfred Hitchcock's film, but Polanski locks us in with Carol from the first, forcing us to share her warped perceptions.

He films early 60s London with a foreigner's eye, as Carol flinches from aggressive workmen, pub bores or eccentrics and drifts off while her customers chatter away while she polishes their nails.

When Carol retreats to a cavernous Earls Court flat, Polanski terrifyingly depicts her hallucinations – clutching hands which reach through the walls – and parallels the decay of her mind with the rotting of a rabbit she intended to cook but has just left out on the sideboard. She always sees men as a threat, and eventually takes a knife to the guilty – her bullying landlord – and innocent – her nice would-be boyfriend – alike.

Hitchcock ends the film with a lecture on why Norman is mad, but Polanski just closes in on a family photograph to drop hints about the roots of the blonde angel's insanity.

Rather than making a mad person scary, the film terrifies by giving an audience a sense of what it's like to lose sanity. It's a film full of perfect little details, like the commingled look of appalled disgust and guilty fascination on Ian Hendry's face as he finds a butchered corpse in the bath – torn between looking away and looking closer. ★★★★★ **KN**

REQUIEM FOR A DREAM (2000)

Starring: *Ellen Burstyn (Sara Goldfarb), Jared Leto (Harry Goldfarb), Jennifer Connelly (Marion Silver), Marlon Wayans (Tyrone C. Love), Christopher McDonald (Tappy Tibbons)*
Director: *Darren Aronofsky*
Screenwriter: *Hubert Selby Jr Darren Aronofsky, based on the Selby Jr's novel*
18/96 mins./Drama/USA

Amongst the dilapidated tenement blocks of Coney Island, a mother and son descend separately into drug addiction.

The 'drug movie' has a less than distinguished history. *Reefer Madness* warned kiddies of the hellish dangers of marijuana way back in the 30s. By the 60s it was LSD, with *The Trip*, and in the 80s and 90s, cocaine attracted the horrified gaze of Hollywood with movies like *Bright Lights, Big City* – or at least it did when Hollywood managed to drag itself out of the toilet cubicle rubbing its nose.

Reproducing the technical flair he showed with his daring debut, 1998's *Pi*, Darren Aronofsky's adaptation of Hubert Selby Jr's novella has heroin as the subject substance, and Harry and girlfriend Marion who perform the requisite 'descent into drugs hell', treating the audience to the usual, ill-advised 'maybe we'll just try the merchandise ... ', through the inevitable spiral of rooting behind the sofa for cash to buy smack, and, in a real 'crowdpleaser' of a moment, shooting up into a gangrenous vein.

Then there's Mom who receives a telephone call inviting her on telly, and turns to diet pills to squeeze into a little red number she hasn't worn for years. She too embarks on a plot of catastrophic collapse, winding up confined in a local booby hatch.

While the 29-year-old certainly knows every visual technique in the book, he isn't helped by the source material – Selby's work is deeply dated – and Aronofsky's own script has inherited some of the more superficial elements. But the performances – especially by Connelly – pack real power and end result is utterly chilling. ★★★★ **WT**

Movie Trivia: Requiem For a Dream

Leto and Wayans were told to stay off sex and sugar for 30 days to better appreciate overwhelming cravings. Each character's last scene in the film shows them turning onto their right side and pulling their knees up to their chest. Director Aronofsky cameos as a visitor in Big Tim's gathering. Leto lost nearly 2 stone and socialised with heroin addicts to authenticate his part.

RESERVOIR DOGS (1992)

Starring: *Harvey Keitel (Mr White/Larry), Tim Roth (Mr Orange/Freddy), Michael Madsen (Mr Blonde/Vic Vega), Chris Penn (Nice Guy Eddie), Steve Buscemi (Mr Pink), Quentin Tarantino (Mr Brown)*
Director: *Quentin Tarantino*
Screenwriter: *Quentin Tarantino*
18/94 mins./Crime/Drama/USA

Five total strangers team up for the perfect crime. But something goes wrong. One of the men is the rat, an infiltrator working for the cops. But can they work out who?

Debuts are not meant to be like this. Debuts are either meant to be second spear-carrier minimalist or so cringingly inept that they find themselves in a side-splitting edition of *Before They Were Famous*. Debuts are not meant to capture all the plaudits at Sundance before storming to cult status around the world and igniting a forest fire of newsprint in an endless debate about the morality of screen violence. Few debuts – with the possible exceptions of The Clash's first album and The Marriage Feast at Cana – have been so widely admired. But above all, debuts in the crime genre are not meant to begin with an in-depth exposition of the lyrics to a Madonna

Stars Who Never Won A Competitive Oscar

1. Richard Burton (7 nominations)
2. Cary Grant (2 nominations)
3. Deborah Kerr (6 nominations)
4. Rosalind Russell (4 nominations)
5. Peter O'Toole (7 nominations)
6. Fred Astaire (1 nomination)
7. Tom Cruise (3 nominations)
8. Albert Finney (5 nominations)
9. Glenn Close (5 nominations)
10. Kirk Douglas (3 nominations)

song followed by a discussion on the ethics of paying gratuities and the problems experienced by women working on minimum wage.

With *Reservoir Dogs*, Quentin Tarantino started as he meant to go on. And what he meant to go on to be is evident from the opening shots of the movie: an auteur, no less. Simply to tell the story of a heist gone wrong would seem to have held little appeal to a writer as visually literate and soaked in film culture as Tarantino. It's almost as if he employs the flashback, 'answers first, questions later' narrative structure to give himself a challenge. What really interests him is finding opportunities for dialogue diversions. And so it's no accident that our introduction to the diamond heist via Tim Roth making a mess of the upholstery doesn't arrive until after Mr Brown's 'Like A Virgin' speech and Mr Pink's, 'world's smallest violin' paean to non-tipping.

It helped, of course, that although *Reservoir Dogs* was Tarantino's directorial debut, he had already written screenplays for *True Romance* (1993) and *Natural Born Killers* (1994). Not only did this enable him to hone his writing skills, but the flourishes necessary for auteur status were already coming together nicely. Aside from the-inclusion of the ubiquitous pop culture discussions ('Get Christie Love', 'The Night The Lights Went Out In Georgia') these would include a raft of self-referential allusions. Thus: Mr White's former partner, Alabama (see *True Romance*) Mr Blonde's real name, Toothpick Vic Vega (see *Pulp Fiction*'s Vincent), Blonde's unseen parole officer being called Scagnetti (a name Tarantino has worked into every one of his screenplays to date). Not to mention the cameo performance of which he's become so fond.

It's one thing, however, to aspire to be an auteur, quite another to achieve it. In *Reservoir Dogs*, Tarantino assembles a cast of more widely mixed ability than the average comprehensive Year Eight, ranging from the acknowledged master (Keitel), through the talented youngsters (Buscemi and Roth) to the fairly abject (Madsen and, ahem, himself), but still draws compulsive performances from all. Primarily, this is down to the virtues of that script, packed with zinging one-liners and meaty speeches of the kind every aspiring thesp would kill to give. Everyone (apart from Mr Blue – such a spare part he should have been sponsored by Lucas) enjoys their time in the sun.

It's not every debutante who has the cojones to aspire to auteur status and because of this (and the film's success) the Tarantino backlash arrived rapidly in the wake of the movie's acclaim. Similarities with Kubrick's *The Killing* and more pertinently Ringo Lam's *City On Fire* were pointed out. Others (*Empire* included) speculated long into the night over how Nice Guy Eddie met his demise. But most of the objections focused on the gratuitous ear-ectomy performed by Mr Blonde on the hapless cop, Marvin Nash (as played by Kirk Baltz who despite turning up in *Face/Off* and *Bulworth* has never since enjoyed such success when acting with his full complement of aural organs).

The aged chestnut that is The Screen Violence Debate does not need another outing here except to say that it was particularly ironic that Tarantino took flak for the realism of his violence. The one thing Michael Madsen's soft-shoe-shuffle-and-slash is not is realistic.

Indeed, and this is not a criticism of the film, there is very little in *Reservoir Dogs* that could by any stretch be termed realistic. The world of diamond heists and crooks may be real enough, but once it has been refracted through Tarantino's pop-cultural sensibility it emerges as darkly comic and extremely knowing. Do criminals discuss 70s cop shows en route to their jobs? Do old-timers like Mr Blue really have an opinion on Madonna? Would Mr Orange, having survived several gunshots, choose that particularly inopportune moment to confess all to Mr White? The answer to all three is probably 'No': something Quentin Tarantino understands implicitly and just one of the reasons why film is better than real life.

Reservoir Dogs also proves beyond reasonable doubt that Tarantino is a far better writer and director than he is an actor. If he's to achieve the status he clearly craves it will only be behind the camera. Fewer cameos in *Little Nicky*, please. More proper films. For Tarantino, it was time to get back to work. ★★★★★ **JN**

Movie Trivia:
Quentin Tarantino (born 1963)

Who he is: Film geek turned cinema hero. Video-store clerk who became a Hollywood revolutionary as writer and director. Reshaped 90s cinema in his own cinephile image.

Hallmarks: Chronological reshuffling; violence as comedy; pop-culture dialogue; homages to gangster, Western and kung fu movies; criminals as heroes; foot fetish; bold use of forgotten pop hits.

If you see one movie, see: *Pulp Fiction* (1994)

THE RETURN OF MARTIN GUERRE (LE RETOUR DE MARTIN GUERRE) (1992)

Starring: *Gérard Depardieu (Martin Guerre), Bernard-Pierre Donnadieu (Martin Guerre), Nathalie Baye (Bertrande de Rois), Roger Planchon (Jean de Coras), Maurice Jacquemont (Judge Rieux), Isabelle Sadoyan (Catherine Boere)*
Director: *Daniel Vigne*
Screenwriters: *Daniel Vigne, Jean-Claude Carrière*
15/111 mins./History/Drama/France

Nine years after he abandoned his adolescent bride, Bertrande de Rols, Martin Guerre returns to his village and, despite certain discrepancies in his story, is accepted on the strength of his wife's identification. However, passing troops and a one-legged stranger challenge his claims and Martin is put on trial.

The story of Martin Guerre was first recorded by a Toulouse magistrate during the reign of Francis I and it had been the subject of an essay by Montaigne, an operetta and several novels before it was brought to the screen by Daniel Vigne and Jean-Claude Carrière, Luis Buñuel's long-time collaborator, who had just finished working with Gérard Depardieu on

Danton. The actor has been known to rank this among his favourite roles, on account of its ambiguity. However, he was also doubtlessly amused by the rumour that he had pipped his *1900* co-star, Robert De Niro, to the project (supposedly opposite Meryl Streep for Martin Scorsese).

Depardieu certainly gave one of his most charismatic performances in this very modern parable on identity and the role of the individual in a conformist society, which often belied its 16th-century setting. However, this was also a powerful human drama, whose themes of love, trust, greed and deception appealed to audiences in Britain and the United States (after it curiously underwhelmed in France), where it not only landed Anne-Marie Marchand an Oscar nomination for her costumes, but it also prompted a remake, *Sommersby* (1993), which starred Richard Gere and Jodie Foster and transferred the action to the Civil War era.

However, for all its melodramatic fascination and persuasive period atmosphere, the film departed from fact in one crucial aspect – the role played by Bertrande in Martin's trial. Well aware that she would be eternally damned for fornicating with a man who was not her husband, the real Bertrande kept her counsel at the end of the case. However, by having Nathalie Baye deliver a speech to judge Maurice Jacquemont justifying her actions, Vigne and Carrière opted for an easy romanticism that robbed the narrative of any lingering intrigue. Moreover, such revelations also undermined Baye's otherwise sensitively enigmatic performance, whose watchful silences provided a subtle balance to Depardieu's dubious ebullience. **★★★ DP**

RETURN OF THE PINK PANTHER (1975)

Starring: *Peter Sellers (Inspector Jacques Clouseau), Christopher Plummer (Sir Charles Litton), Catherine Schell (Lady Claudine Litton), Herbert Lom (Chief Insp. Charles Dreyfuss), Burt Kwouk (Cato)*
Director: *Blake Edwards*
Screenwriters: *Blake Edwards, Frank Waldman*
U/113 mins./Comedy/UK

When the fabled diamond, The Pink Panther, is once again stolen by an expert thief, it falls to inept Inspector Clouseau to track down the guilty party whom he is convinced is The Phantom returned from his past.

While certainly a far lesser film than either *The Pink Panther* or *A Shot In The Dark*, this third venture for the dotty Clouseau, Seller's immortal doofus, has enough hilarious inspiration to mark it as one of the better ones once the series deteriorated into painful re-runs of outmoded slapstick. With the plot a basic reworking of the original film – Clouseau versus elusive upper-class thief – with a touch or two from Hitchcock's *To Catch A Thief*, Blake Edwards was hardly working on a creative high, resting assured that his leading man was still capable of sublime silliness.

Ostensibly, the film is just a collection of those great Clouseau moments interrupted by some fairly uninteresting plot-stuff with Christopher Plummer taking over from David Niven in the role of the gentleman thief who is, now, being taken off by an impostor. Out there amongst the comedy routines, costumes suddenly became a big deal – we get Sellers with a big fake nose, Sellers as a cranky fisherman, Sellers as midget artist Toulouse Lautrec slumping about on his knees while clutching a 'berm' (that is a bomb) with a lit fuse. There is far more of Clouseau's ongoing attempts to educate his Chinese manservant (Burt Kwouk) in the subtle art of self-defence, including the chopsockey crazy Cato brilliantly concealing himself inside a fridge. There is, of course, the ongoing conflict with his anal boss Dreyfuss (Herbert Lom) who will end up driven far beyond the limits of his sanity. And there is Sellers' near-Chaplin-like gift for slapstick as he wrestles with vacuum cleaners and disco dancing, and the surreal borders of his impenetrable accent – 'Do youuu aave a leesense for your minkey?'

Edwards doesn't interfere too much, just lifting the production from Gstaad in Switzerland to Morocco to the all-important French Riviera to grant it a glossy international sheen. And Henry Mancini's music remains as indelibly perfect as ever. **★★★ IN**

RETURN TO OZ (1985)

Starring: *Fairuza Balk (Dorothy), Nicol Williamson (Dr Worley/Nome King), Jean Marsh (Nurse Wilson/Mombi), Piper Laurie (Aunt Em), Matt Clark (Uncle Henry), Michael Sundin (Tik-Tok)*
Director: *Walter Murch*
Screenwriters: *Gill Dennis, Walter Murch, based on the book by L. Frank Baum*
PG/113 mins/Family/USA

With her guardians convinced she is mad, with all this talk of Oz, Dorothy is sent for some sinister psychiatric treatment, only to escape back to that fabled land. But Oz is in disarray, the Yellow Brick Road and the Emerald City in ruins. Teaming up with a talking chicken, a wind-up man and a pumpkinhead, she must confront the wicked Nome King and the witch Mombi to save the land she loves.

A long-distance sequel to the classic 1939 fantasy-musical, this evocative, well-mounted adventure ditches the songs, putting greater emphasis on the scarier elements of the Oz mythology created by L. Frank Baum, and hence cleaving closer to the books. Apart from names and character traits, there is nothing stylistically to attach the two films, Walter Murch (the famed editor of Francis Coppola) gives his film a harder, colder looking fantasy world – the film starts off with Dorothy (played much more as a child-figure by Fairuza Balk) escaping electro-shock therapy, not quite the fluff of her whirlwind departure back in '39.

When we arrive in Oz, there is none of the Technicolor gleam, this is a devastated world: the Yellow Brick Road is all but destroyed, the Emerald City in ruins. Murch flips the game the original played, by having Kansas rich and colourful, and this dying Oz desaturated and wan. Things are bad.

Dorothy, clutching the talking chicken Belinna, meets up with a new set of companions on her quest to right Oz's wrongs, after all The Tin Man, Scarecrow and Cowardly Lion have been inconveniently turned to stone. So we have Tik-Tok a wind-up man with onetime *Blue Peter* presenter Michael Sundin inside, Jack the Pumpkinhead, a lanky scarecrow-alike, to accompany her. Murch is also trusting to his special-effects to give him a more elaborate, dare-we-say realistic depiction of Oz, using a combination of puppetry, animatronics, and relatively ineffective claymation to bring to life the weird denizens, especially chief foe, the Nome King, a kind of talking rock face. The other enemy is Mombi the witch, played with waspish cunning by Jean Marsh, who in one quite terrifying sequence proves to be able to possess interchangeable heads.

It's enthralling as well as rambling, you do miss the songs, but there is clearly no place for them here. Best to see them as individual films with nothing in common apart from source material, one a classic, the other a strong enough picaresque amongst some decent fabulation. **★★★ IN**

REVERSAL OF FORTUNE (1990)

Starring: *Glenn Close (Sunny von Bulow/Narrator), Jeremy Irons (Claus von Bulow), Ron Silver (Professor Alan Dershowitz), Annabella Sciorra (Sarah), Fisher Stevens (David Marriott)*
Director: *Barbet Schroeder*
Screenwriter: *Nicholas Kazan, based on the book by Alan M. Dershowitz*
15/106 mins./Biography/Drama/USA
Awards: *Academy Awards – Best Actor; Golden Globes – Best Actor*

Based on the true story of American heiress, Sunny von Bulow, who collapsed in a coma on the bathroom floor of her opulent mansion in 1981. Was her husband Claus guilty of attempted murder, or not?

Based on Dershowitz's published account of the case, *Reversal Of Fortune* is, in one respect, infuriating; the only person in the world who actually knows whether or not he is guilty is Claus Von Bulow himself. This major reservation aside, Barbet Schroeder here delivers an intriguing and absorbing movie, reeking of class and quite packed with powerhouse performances.

From the opening credits over a continuous pan of Rhode Island mini-palaces, we immediately know we are in the world of the mega-rich and overprivileged. Borrowing from *Sunset Boulevard*, the screenplay has the comatose Sunny herself plunging us into the narrative from her hospital bed, with Glenn Close expertly revealing the sad mess of this tragic woman's life. Irons, meanwhile, using an initially disturbingly odd – but doubtless accurately researched – accent makes of Von Bulow an elegant and enigmatic figure, alternately beguiling and loathsome, while Silver's electrically charged, ambitious Jewish liberal proves conclusively that he has now graduated to major screen status.

The literate script manages some humour, and the supporting cast is uniformly excellent, from relative newcomer Annabella Sciorra, to veteran Broadway actress Uta Hagen in a rare screen appearance as Sunny's loyal housekeeper.

This is a movie rich in moral ambiguities and one which should thoroughly please voyeurs and detective story enthusiasts alike. ★★★★ **RK**

REVOLVER (2005)

Starring: *Jason Statham (Jake), Ray Liotta (Macha), Vincent Pastore (Zach), Andre Benjamin (Avi), Terence Maynard (French Paul)*
Director: *Guy Ritchie*
Screenwriter: *Guy Ritchie, adapted by Luc Besson*
15/115 mins./Drama/Crime/Drama/USA

Gambler Jake Green did seven years of solitary thanks to his dealings with short-fused gangster Dorothy Macha. Now he's out and wants pay-back. Just as well his cell happened to be situated between a pair of mysterious criminal superbrains – one a chess master, the other a master conman – who shared all their wisdom with him . . .

On the face of it – well, if you believe the movie posters, anyway – Guy Ritchie's returned to his comfort zone with *Revolver*, after a disastrous sojourn beyond very edge of credibility with 2002's *Swept Away* (winner of five Razzies). *Revolver*'s populated with the same breed of fast-talking, sharp-suited criminal that entertained so many of us in *Lock, Stock* and *Snatch*, the story hinges on gambles and cons and the violence is strong and stylish. Plus, of course, Ritchie's favourite leading man, Jason '*Transporter*' Statham is back, too, albeit with the kind of hair/'tache combo that makes him look like an extra in a Spaghetti Western.

Good news, no? Well ... The first warning sign comes with an opening quote from *Julius Caesar*. Followed by another from the *Fundamentals Of Chess*. Then another from a business guide. And then, just for good measure, a final one from Machiavelli. Some of which are repeated later in the movie, just in case you missed them first time around. He's been doing a lot of reading, that Guy Ritchie. Yup, he's certainly been filling his head with some very complex ideas, and has admitted even he found it tough to weave them all together and turn them into his *Revolver* script – a process that took him 18 months.

Problem is, he spectacularly fails to communicate exactly what those ideas are. It's all got something to do with the con as a game – one that also follows the rules of business – and the importance of knowing who your worst opponent/enemy is. Or understanding that your worst enemy is actually you. And convincing them/you that they're/you're not. Or really are. Or something.

It kicks off intriguingly enough with no doubt deliberate echoes of *The Usual Suspects* (via repeated references to a Keyser Soze-esque underworld phantom), introducing us to some fun, skewed characters, like André Benjamin's chess-dabbling loan shark and Mark Strong's stuttering, balding hitman. But it's not long before an overload of red herrings start stinking up a show already hindered by Statham's overused voiceover, Ritchie's tiresomely tricksy editing and Ray Liotta's seeming desire to shout himself to death. By the final act, all pretence at logic is shrugged off, *Revolver*'s plotline contorting itself into the cinematic equivalent of a scribble on a maze in a child's puzzle book. You'd do better to skip attempting this conundrum and stick with your Su Doku. ★★ **DJ**

RICHARD III (1955)

Starring: *Laurence Olivier (Richard III), Ralph Richardson (Duke Of Buckingham), Ralph Richardson (Duke Of Buckingham), Claire Bloom (The Lady Anne), Cedric Hardwicke (King Edward IV)*
Director: *Laurence Oliver*
Screenwriters: *Alan Dent, Laurence Olivier, Colley Cibber, David Garrick, from the play by William Shakespeare*
U/150 mins./History/Drama/UK
Awards: *BAFTA – Best British Actor, Best British Film, Best Film from any Source; Golden Globes – Best English-Language Foreign Film*

In 15th century England Richard Plantagenet plots to steal the crown and convince others of his rightful claim to be King of England. . .

Unfairly the least-regarded of Olivier's three Shakespeare films, this has a certain cardboardy feel in the sets and costumes, but enshrines one of Lord Larry's great stage performances as the crook-backed, putty-nosed, Beatle-wigged knave who wheedles, murders and snickers his way to the throne only to regret it.

An unabashed darstard redeemed only by his wit, Richard limps through the film enjoying himself, disposing of lesser theatrical knights Sir Ralph Richardson and Sir John Gielgud. Also on hand are Claire Bloom as an unwilling queen and a young Stanley Baker as a bluff, Welsh Henry Tudor.

It winds up with a pretty good Battle of Bosworth Field and Olivier following the famous 'my kingdom for a horse' business with one of the great twitchy, splattery, prolonged death scenes of the 1950s. ★★★★ **KN**

RICHARD III (1995)

Starring: *Ian McKellen (Richard II), Annette Bening (Queen Elizabeth), Jim Broadbent (Duke of Buckingham), Robert Downey Jr (Lord Rivers), Nigel Hawthorne (George, Duke of Clarence), Kristin Scott Thomas (Lady Anne)*
Director: *Richard Loncraine*
Screenwriters: *Richard Loncraine, Ian McKellen, based on the stage production by Richard Eyre of the play by William Shakespeare*
15/99mins./History/Drama/UK/USA
Awards: *BAFTA – Best Costume, Best Production Design*

The classic Shakespearean play about a murderously scheming king staged in an alternative fascist England setting.

Since *Richard III*, Shakespeare's classic dissection of power politics and evil's allure is, rather than history, an outrageous piece of Tudor propaganda, there really is no reason why it can't be removed from the 15th century. And so several years ago, Richard Eyre gave us an arresting, sharply written, intelligent interpretation of the play, starring Ian McKellen and staged with 1930s Fascist trappings at London's National Theatre.

That production was the inspiration for Richard Loncraine's daring, flashy film, for which he and the actor worked as screenwriters and in which McKellen authoritatively revisits one of the greatest roles in the English language.

Opening deliberately in the style of a *Die Hard* action yarn, this *Richard* introduces its bitter, twisted protagonist as the military genius victorious in a civil war that has rent a fictitious England in the 30s. His first sour soliloquy becomes a public toast at a victory ball; the court is composed of pinstriped gents, officers in black, and women in slinky satin.

Hawthorne's touching Duke Of Clarence is assassinated in a steaming bath; Richard's lady in red, Lady Anne, is a tortured dope fiend, and his nemeses the Rivers, Queen Elizabeth and her brother 'Earl' (Robert Downey Jnr, cheekily stealing scenes as a Panama-hatted sport) are American arrivistes.

This provocative stylisation serves the content well and emphasises the steamroller effect of evil, from one deviant's resentful power lust to a popular movement. McKellen, rejecting the comic temptations contemporary actors commonly snatch in the hunchback, conveys the sardonic, savage wit but plays the dark malice to the hilt. Everyone in the cast is a strong Somebody, from Queen Mother Maggie Smith to assassin Adrian Dunbar.

The only drawback of this 're-imagining' is that it is dispassionately cold in its sustained artifice, despite the splashy nods to modern cinemagoers' frames of reference – sex, violence, explosions – which do pep up the popular appeal without condescension or gutting the text. Largely this is a fascinating, cerebral exercise, one that is acutely interesting rather than emotionally involving, but absolutely a notable cinematic tackling of the Bard. ★★★★ **AE**

RIDE WITH THE DEVIL (1999)

Starring: *Skeet Ulrich (Jack Bull Chiles), Tobey Maguire (Jake Roedel), Jewel (Sue Lee Shelley), Jonathan Rhys Meyers (Pitt Mackerson), Jim Caviezel (Black John), Tom Wilkinson (Orton Brown)*
Director: *Ang Lee*
Screenwriter: *James Schamus, based on the novel* Woe To Live On *by Daniel Woodrell*
15/132 mins./Drama/Romance/War/USA

'Coming-of-age' film, as Tobey Maguire defies his father he joins up with the guerrilla gangs of the South (known as the Bushwhackers) with his best pal, Skeet Ulrich.

What's this? A Western? Surely Ang Lee, delicate maestro of the parlour-room conflict, is finally out of his depth.

Yet with *Ride With The Devil* (based on Daniel Woodrell's novel *Woe To Live On*), dripping with horse sweat and ragged, furious gunplay, Lee proves as adept at divining the mythology of America's birth pangs as he is at creating the worlds of Taiwanese social mores, Jane Austen's corset repression and 70s staypress familial agonies.

And while not as intense or talky as his back catalogue, *Ride* is every bit as groundbreaking and intelligent – just with less wife-swapping and more horses.

Shot with the kind of cinematography that loosens Oscar cabinets, and populated with a cast of less familiar hip young things, this is a masterwork, melding internal conflict with external drama and vivid, sprawling action pieces that the likes of Eastwood, Ford or even Peckinpah would tip their hats towards. Put oversimply, it follows the rites-of-passage of young Jake Roedel (the auspicious Maguire), who ignores his Unionist father and elects to follow his best friend Jack Bull Chiles and his own beliefs into the Confederacy – and a brutal war that will finally render any ideology pointless. Set (and accurately made) on the Missouri/Kansas border, a stunningly lush Brit-like landscape of farms and dense woodland, it is a long way from the military manoeuvres of the Greys and the Blues. Tapping into a Vietnam-esque war of attrition, the friends join a callous band of killers (including a beardy James Caviezel and a psychotic Jonathan Rhys-Meyers) and endure a conflict of guerrilla tactics and deception between the Southernist Bushwhackers and Yankee Jayhawkers, which allows Lee to try his hand at brutal shoot-outs and, in one huge opera of violence, re-enact a real-life mass slaughter, as a rag-tag Confederate army reduce the town of Lawrence, Kansas, to rubble.

This is also, of course, an Ang Lee movie – a grandiose Western concerned with human relationships. Jewel makes a polished and attractive debut as the love interest of both friends; far from a clichéd love triangle, her maddening attempts to woo a resolutely bachelor Jake are among the film's most touching moments.

Jeffrey Wright (who shone in 1996's *Basquiat*) is an even more complex character, a slave conversely fighting for the South and the cause of slavery, whose strange yet devoted friendship to Jake is a pivotal feature. James Schamus' politically astute script is at pains to consider the mindset of the Southern fighters, painting a realistic vision of men fighting for family and land, and not simply a bunch of racist Dixie baddies.

And even within this highly charged drama, Lee succeeds in adding humour to the range and colour of emotions he evokes from his material, slipping in the gentle laughs inherent in the absurdity of their situation. He even manages his trademark lavish mealtime motif.

Ride falls narrowly short of five-star glory, care of its occasional loss of narrative focus, and fails to truly get into the hearts and minds of some of the characters – chiefly Ulrich's frustratingly vague Jack Bull and Rhys-Meyers' overblown nutcase – but these are just irritants, not flaws. Ang Lee's sweeping romantic Civil War adventure clips the bar of masterpiece and remains a magisterial movie experience. ★★★★ **IN**

RIFIFI (DU RIFIFI CHEZ LES HOMMES) (1955)

Starring: *Jean Servais (Tony le Stephanois), Carl Mohner (Jo le Suedois), Robert Manuel (Mario Ferrati), Jules Dassin (Cesar le Milanais), Marie Sabouret (Mado les Grands Bras)*
Director: *Jules Dassin*
Screenwriters: *Jules Dassin, Rene Wheeler, Auguste Le Breton, from a novel by Auguste Le Breton*
12/117 mins./Crime/Film-noir/France

Tony Stephanois, just out of prison and angry at his girl Mado's infidelity, decides to join his pals Jo and Mario in an ambitious crime. With Italian safe expert Cesar, they meticulously plan the burglary of a large jewellery establishment. Not a word is spoken as the crime is carried out. And then things begin to go wrong . . .

Just as *Bullitt* is remembered for its definitive car chase even as the plot details fade in the mind, the 1955 French crime movie *Rififi* (originally entitled *Du Rififi Chez Les Hommes*) is universally recalled as the film with the long, wordless robbery sequence. This set piece takes up over a quarter of the running time of the movie, and has been imitated by heist pictures ever since.

A crew of efficient burglars force their way into an apartment over the Paris salon of Mappin & Webb jewellers, tie up the aged occupants, and hammer through the ceiling into the shop below – forced to chip away at the hole without using heavy equipment because a super-sensitive alarm system will be triggered by any major disturbance.

Later variations on this theme, like director Jules Dassin's glossier *Topkapi* or the *Mission: Impossible* films, deploy hi-tech equipment and feature robbers who are acrobats or secret agents with unbelievable skills, but Rififi is credibly craftsmanlike. The crew use an umbrella lowered through the initial hole to catch chunks of falling masonry and disable the alarm by filling it with foam from a fire extinguisher. Special tools are required to cut into the safe in which the jewels are kept, but so are off-cuts of wood and, at one perilous moment, the strong back of the team's youngest member.

The robbery, including a getaway under the noses of *les gendarmes*, lasts about 25 minutes and plays with only minimal sound effects and no background music. The crooks keep silent for the same reason that they wear gloves: just to be on the safe side. Having achieved this cinematic coup, Dassin can't resist capping it with a gag – the first line of dialogue to interrupt the wordlessness comes from a moll who barges into the room where the burglars are celebrating with, 'Sorry, I heard noises.'

Though his name makes him sound French, Jules Dassin was actually an American director. He made a name in Hollywood with the horrific prison movie *Brute Force* in 1947, then pioneered the documentary-style on-the-streets crime movie with *The Naked City*, the underrated *Thieves' Highway* and the masterly British-shot original of *Night And The City* in 1950. He skipped America ahead of a subpoena from the House Un-American Activities Committee, served because director Edward Dmytryk had named him as a card-carrying Communist and became an international filmmaker; eventually settled in Greece where he entered a personal and professional partnership with Melina Mercouri. In France in the mid-50s, Dassin hooked up with Auguste le Breton, a crime novelist famous for carrying a gun and acting like one of his characters, to develop a script based on le Breton's recent novel. It is ironic that Rififi is famous for a dialogue-free sequence, since le Breton was known for his command of underworld argot and all the characters in the film speak in a distinctive Franco-Italian crook patois. The title expression was so unfamiliar even to French audiences that a song had to be written in to explain it.

The actual plot is along the lines of the earlier *The Asphalt Jungle* and the later *The Killing*. Tony le Stephanois, a craggy burglar just out of jail after a five-year stretch, discovers his girl Mado has ditched him for dope-dealing pimp Pierre. His younger, married protégé Jo and genial, grinning Mario try to talk him into a smash and grab raid on the jewellers' window so Jo can buy toys for his young son and Mario can splash out on his bubbly floozy Ida. Tony is reluctant but commits if the raid can be stepped up into a real heist, with specialist Cesar the Milanese ('They say there's no safe that can resist Cesar and that there's no woman Cesar can resist') called in. Perlo Vita, who plays the lounge lizard-like Italian safe-cracker, is Dassin himself, stepping on screen under an assumed name to thumb his nose at the red-baiters back home. These are subtly different from the sort of hoods found in American crime movies: pipe-smoking, wine-drinking, sentimental, fatalist. Though suspenseful, the film has little of the melodrama of similar American movies, even after the robbery when things inevitably fall apart.

As in *The Asphalt Jungle* and *The Killing*, the problem isn't the cops but better-organised and nastier crooks. When word gets out that Tony's mob have scooped '240 millions *des bijoux*', Pierre tortures Cesar into talking, sets a razor-wielding junkie on Mario and Ida, and has Jo's son kidnapped. Tony, appalled that the criminal code he believes in no longer applies, regretfully but remorselessly murders the squealer Cesar ('I liked you, Macaroni, but you know the rules') and shoots his way into the derelict hideout where Tony's son is being held. However, though the kid is rescued, Jo is already on the way with the cash for the ransom and winds up dead too. Tony, lonely and gutshot, touches Jo's dead face with a tenderness he'd never show a woman (earlier, he beat up Mado) and empties his gun into Pierre, who is already dead in a grave. It ends, like many French crime films, with a shrug and the almost-unnoticed death (another wordless scene) of the protagonist. *Ça va.* ★★★★ **KN**

ⓓ THE RIGHT STUFF (1983)

Starring: *Sam Shepard (Chuck Yeager), Scott Glenn (Alan Shepard), Ed Harris (John Glenn), Dennis Quaid (Gordon Cooper), Fred Ward (Gus Grissom), Barbara Hershey (Glennis Yeager), Kim Stanley (Pancho Barnes), Veronica Cartwright (Betty Grissom), Pamela Reed (Trudy Cooper), Lance Henriksen (Wally Schirra)*
Director: *Philip Kaufman*
Screenwriter: *Philip Kaufman, from the book by Tom Wolfe*
15/184 mins./Drama/History/USA
Awards: *Academy Awards – Best Sound Effects Editing, Best Editing, Best Score, Best Sound*

In 1959, seven test pilots are recruited to serve in NASA's Mercury space programme of the 1960s. A media/scientific circus stirs around the astronauts, but little attention is paid to sub-stratospheric specialist Chuck Yeager, the pilot who broke the sound barrier.

Philip Kaufman's film of Tom Wolfe's non-fiction book about the Mercury programme is a stirring mix of patriotism, comedy, mythologising and satire.

A true American epic, with one of the best ensemble casts of the 1980s, opens in the late 1940s with the near-mythical, Gary Cooper-like Chuck Yeager showing that he has 'the right stuff' by 'pushing the outside of the envelope' in an experimental plane, contesting 'the demon' who lives in the air beyond the speed of Mach 1.

The tone here is elegiac-heroic, as wives cope with a vast death rate among their menfolk, and rookies make the blunder of asking what they have to do to get their pictures up behind the bar (that honour is always posthumous) and the horse-riding, gum-chewing, professionally modest Yeager epitomises the lone hero.

Then, to counter Soviet space successes, the government downplay Yeager-style rocket plane experiments and concentrate on putting men into space, recruiting characters who are initially the second-best to sit in the capsules ('spam in a can') while not entirely sure that monkeys couldn't do the job as well.

Here, comedy business dominates as the fallible, slightly stiff astronauts suffer through a near-farcical training programme – with Harry Shearer and Jeff Goldblum as lunatic recruiters – and heroism takes a back seat to politics and public relations. However, as the programme progresses, the astronauts gain their own stature, signified in that much-imitated shot of the men in pressure suits striding together down a corridor to face the unknown – which, as it happens, is a rowdy press conference.

It's a film that valorises small moments of integrity, like John Glenn's refusal to let Lyndon Johnson get publicity by bullying Glenn's nervous, stuttering wife into a TV appearance, as well as the life-or-death risks of leaving the Earth's atmosphere.

And, after the craze for spacemen had long since died out, the film rediscovered the magic of scientific achievement, delivering some of the most stirring, affecting sequences in modern Hollywood cinema. ★★★★★ **KN**

ⓓ THE RING (2002)

Starring: *Naomi Watts (Rachel Keller), Martin Henderson (Noah), David Dorfman (Aidan), Brian Cox (Richard Morgan), Jane Alexander (Dr Grasnik)*
Director: *Gore Verbinski*
Screenwriter: *Ehren Kruger, from the 1998 film*
15/110 mins./Horror/Thriller/USA

Investigating the urban myth of a videotape which kills you a week after watching it, journalist Rachel Keller makes the fatal mistake of taking a sneak peak herself.

Let's cut right to the chase: if you've seen the Japanese original, you can knock a star straight off the four below. Put simply, this isn't a patch on Hideo Nakata's sublime, low-budget, 1998 horror movie of the same name. Anyone, for instance, who has never looked at a TV in the same way since that freaky chick crawled out of the gogglebox will no doubt bemoan the update's poor CG replacement in its Identikit scene.

That said, in terms of the 'Hollywood remake', this is about as solid as the sub-genre gets. It's a wholly justifiable sleeper hit – an $11 million opening weekend in the States blossomed into an overall gross of $123 million – and marked a terrific follow up to *Mulholland Dr.* for future superstar Naomi Watts.

If the plot seems to veer near the ludicrous, then fear not; the odd thematic wobble apart, Verbinski's execution builds from a wonderfully tense, although undeniably *Scream*-inspired, pre-credit sequence towards a final reveal well worth the wait.

Watts is superb as the single mother forced to re-team with her ex, Henderson, to battle the ultimate in 'deadlines', and some of Kruger's tinkerings with the screenplay (the horse on the ferry sequence) zip things along nicely. Other bits, however (what the introduction of Brian Cox's character adds is anyone's guess) come across as lazy padding.

Actually, Kruger's task here must have been something of a tough gig. For starters, the fact remains that transferring a Japanese urban legend to modern-day Chicago often doesn't convince. Age-old mythology is, after all, more believable coming from the rich historical tapestry of The Land Of The Rising Sun than the land of peanut butter and Jell-o.

Similarly, sending his heroine on a quest that adds at least two unnecessary locations and four bit-parts to the fantastically lean Nakata version drags out a running time that threatens to spiral out of control. And, as for changing the ending, well, that's daft.

All this aside, Verbinski and co. had such a terrific template from which to work that it's little wonder the result is a traditional horror that shows recent pretenders to the throne – *My Little Eye*, *Deathwatch* – how it should be done.

Rick Baker's gruesome effects, primarily in the shape of the victims of the mysterious videotape – mouths agape in frozen shrieks of terror – are relegated to the sidelines, hinting (as opposed to sticking on a plate) at the horrors inherent in the killer VHS. And even though it's not unreasonable to assume that much of this was more to do with securing a PG-13 with the MPAA (15 certificate here) than any qualms of artistic integrity, either way the effect is a cracker: a squirm-inducing tale of bone-chilling suspense.

In fact, just when Watts' investigation has taken you so deep into the country you've forgotten all about the videotape, her adversary turns out to be one of cinema's most unrelenting, unreasonable, plain uncontrollable baddies ever. And if you thought *The Sixth Sense*'s twist was a doozy, then here's a comfortable silver medal in the shock stakes.

Besides, if Nakata has any bones about being ripped off, then he should bear in mind his forthcoming *Dark Water* – itself such an outrageously petrifying plagiarism of *Don't Look Now* that one can only hope Nicolas Roeg is currently swanning about in the Caribbean on the yacht bought with his royalties. ★★★★ **MD**

⓪ THE RING TWO (2005)

Starring: *Naomi Watts (Rachel Keller), Simon Baker (Max Rourke), David Dorfman (Aidan Keller), Elizabeth Perkins (Dr Emma Temple), Gary Cole (Martin Savide)*
Director: *Hideo Nakata*
Screenwriter: *Ehren Kruger, based on the 1998 film by Hiroshi Takashashi, novel Ringu by Kôji Suzuki*
15/110 mins/128 mins (unrated cut)/Horror/USA

Two years after escaping the video curse of Samara, Rachel Keller and her son Aidan have settled in a small town – but Samara returns, intent on possessing Aidan so Rachel will be the mother she never had. Rachel digs deeper into the ghost's origins to save her son.

If you've been following the *Ring* cycle since its origin as a Japanese novel, and have clocked every adaptation, remake and sequel hurled out since, then you'll want to see this, too. However, *The Ring Two* is not the best place to come aboard the Sadako (now Samara) Express Train To Terror: it's one of those sequels that not only assumes you've seen the previous film, but expects you to have watched it again on DVD the afternoon before you turn up at the cinema.

The expected unsettling prologue, in which a nervy teenage boy tries to get a reluctant girl to watch a copy of the deadly Samara video so he can dodge the curse by passing it on to her, doesn't exactly ease the newcomer in. Instead, it works a vein of creepy laughs for *Ring* regulars, as they realise what's going on while the not-quite-as-dimwitted-as-she-might-be girl is just spooked by the boy's eagerness to make her watch something unpleasant (why not tell her it's bootleg outtakes of Johnny Depp's nude scene from *Pirates Of The Caribbean* so she'll keep her eyes on the screen?). Spooky ghost-girl Samara (Kelly Stables, replacing Daveigh Chase), still lank-haired and dead after all these years, comes to town via the cassette. We pick up with Rachel (Naomi Watts, with tanglier hair) and Aidan (David Dorfman, taking more of the acting strain) as they try to live under the spectral child's radar.

Like the Kellers, you shouldn't get too attached to friendly new characters, since, as you'd expect from a mainstream American horror, they're probably doomed. In that the film exists for purely commercial reasons, don't expect too much originality or sense: screenwriter Ehren Kruger, whose job description rhymes with 'whack', throws the haunted cassette into a fire early on (who thought a burning VHS could look so nasty?) and simply goes for a different story with the same structure as *The Ring*; this time, the kid is not threatened with death but possession, which leads to 70s-TV-movie-style scenes in which the tot goes pale and looks angelically sinister (just like in that early Spielberg credit *Something Evil*). Cue our fetchingly distressed heroine being suspected of child abuse, then sleuthing her way back into Samara's troubled childhood.

The big twist on the production side is that, with *The Ring* director Gore Verbinski now out of the picture and originally announced helmer Noam Murro quitting over script differences, Hollywood has cleverly gone back to the source and hired Hideo Nakata – director not only of the Japanese *Ring*, but an entirely different *Ring 2* – to import his own brand of unease. Like Takashi Shimizu, who recently remade his movie *The Grudge* as a slick, Sam Raimi-produced Hollywood horror, Nakata knows the material best.

As the official Mr Ring, he works harder with the lead actors (especially Dorfman, who does a good 'evil child') and stages set-pieces that keep pulling you into the picture even as Kruger's story hits cruise control. The most memorable is an early attack on the Kellers' car by a malevolent and suicidal deer, but Nakata's fondness for water-based scares also pays dividends in several excellent bathroom and well-bottom scenes. ★★★ **KN**

⓪ THE RINGER (2006)

Starring: *Johnny Knoxville (Steve Barker), Leonard Flowers (Jimmy Washington), Brian Cox (Gary), Katherine Heigl (Lynn Sheridan)*
Director: *Barry W. Blaustein*
Screenwriter: *Ricky Blitt*
12A/94 mins./Comedy/USA

Saddled with a friend's massive medical bills, Steve Barker conspires to rig the Special Olympics by faking a disability so his gambler uncle can place bets on him to win. He faces the challenge not only of fooling his rivals, but of dethroning the current champion.

Finally, after such egregious swill as *Walking Tall* and *The Dukes Of Hazzard*, likeable yahoo Johnny Knoxville finds a vehicle worthy of his genial white-trash mettle. In this warm-hearted, minor comic treat – artfully disguised, in the best Farrelly tradition (they're producing), as splutter-inducing spazzploitation – Knoxville plays Steve Barker, an affable office drone who pretends to be 'retarded' (note quotation marks) to win the Special Olympics.

Which sounds, admittedly, like a gratuitous excuse for a chortle at the 'differently abled' folks' expense and for Knoxville to funny it up by acting like a 'spacker'. And, yes, it is. Sort of. True, Knoxville impersonates a 'spacker', but the solid supply of laughs comes at no one's expense.

Fully endorsed by the real-life Special Olympics, the film also stars a number of real-life disabled athletes who are obviously so used to being patronised and/or underestimated that they have developed a deliciously bone-dry sense of pre-emptive humour that's both disarming and hilarious. And to whom pussyfooting around in PC slippers would have been a disservice …

As with *Stuck On You*, this is proof that when the Farrellys are involved (even as mere producers), ribald yet humane comedy can be mined from the most potentially offensive sources. ★★★ **SB**

ⓓ RINGU (RING) (1998)

Starring: *Nanako Matsushima (Reiko Asakawa), Miki Nakatani (Mai Takano), Hiroyuki Sanada (Ryuji Takayam), Yuko Takeuchi (Tomoko Oishi), Hitomi Sato (Masami Kaurahashi)*
Director: *Hideo Nakata*
Screenwriter: *Hiroshi Takahashi, based on the novel by Kôji Suzuki*
15/96 mins./Horror/Japan

Investigating inexplicable deaths, reporter Reiko Asakawa watches a cursed videotape and realises that she is doomed to die in a week's time. With her ex-husband and child also under threat, Reiko investigates the origins of the curse.

A major box office hit in the Far East, spinning off many sequels and remakes (including Hollywood's *The Ring*), this subtly creepy ghost story is based on a popular teen-appeal novel by Kôji Suzuki – who brings the traditional Japanese ghost (a lank-haired, pale-faced girl) into a contemporary setting, and finds ways of squaring the old-fashioned supernatural with an increasingly complex modern world.

Influenced by Stephen King or *The Twilight Zone*, *Ringu* spins a plausible yarn about haunted gadgetry, but also uses the ghost story to tackle family failings. When the plot gets beyond psychic phenomena and terrifying apparitions, it's about broken families: the single mother heroine and the estranged father of her son collaborate to investigate the backstory of ghost girl Sadako, which turns out to involve another sundered marriage and an appalling act that *still* doesn't justify the random revenge the spirit takes on innocents.

In a messy, gruelling scene, Sadako's murdered body is found at the bottom of the now-covered well and the curse seems to be lifted, but the next day (on schedule) the ghost crawls out of a television set to bring about death by terror, incidentally introducing a new image to the roster of classic horror moments.

A restrained but cruel tale, *Ringu* approaches ridiculous subject matter with high seriousness and builds an effective atmosphere of quivering dread through committed performances and unsettling touches like the bizarrely arty curse video, the amplified telephone ring which signals the activation of the curse and the way that an invented mythology has permeated the world so that all the characters have heard of it. ★★★★ **KN**

ⓓ RIO BRAVO (1959)

Starring: *John Wayne (Sheriff John T. Chance), Dean Martin (Dude), Ricky Nelson (Colorado Ryan), Angie Dickinson (Feathers), Walter Brennan (Stumpy), Ward Bond (Pat Wheeler)*
Director: *Howard Hawks*
Screenwriters: *Jules Furthman, Leigh Brackett, based on a short story by B.H. Campbell*
PG/135 mins./Western/USA

Sheriff John T. Chance arrests a brutish murderer who happens to be the brother of a powerful cattle baron and has to defend his jail against a hundred guns.

Howard Hawks purportedly made this classic Western as an 'answer' to *High Noon*, arguing a true professional lawman wouldn't waste his time begging amateurs for help and would only go up against superior odds if he thought he could cheat his way to victory. Sheriff John Wayne assumes that he's being paid to the job himself, but eventually accepts help from reforming drunk Dean Martin, whiskery old coot Walter Brennan, cocky young gun Ricky Nelson and svelte gamblerette Angie Dickinson.

The epitome of confident machismo, Wayne is nevertheless piqued and undermined by Angie's leggy insolence, and constantly forced to show odd sides of his screen personality as Hawks puts him in semi-comic situations (he even has to kiss Brennan). A long, leisurely film, this even has room for a couple of impromptu musical numbers (including a once-in-a-lifetime trio of Rat Packer Dino, teen crooner Ricky and frog-voiced Brennan) and lots of loveplay, but crackles in its suspense sequences. Great moments: Martin sinking so low he'd fish a dollar out of a spittoon for drink, the wounded gunman dripping blood in the beer, the villains playing the Mexican death tune round the clock to fray the heroes' nerves, a dynamite-throwing hostage exchange at the finale, and Angie in a black body-stocking.

It owes a great deal to earlier Hawksian action adventures, *Only Angels Have Wings* and *To Have and Have Not*, and was itself essentially remade by Hawks and Wayne as the lazier but still loveable *El Dorado* and *Rio Lobo*. The film was also the model for John Carpenter's *Assault From Precinct 13*. ★★★★★ **KN**

ⓓ RISKY BUSINESS (1983)

Starring: *Tom Cruise (Joel Goodson), Rebecca De Mornay (Lana), Joe Pantoliano, Richard Masur (Rutherford), Bronson Pinchot (Barry), Curtis Armstrong (Miles)*
Director: *Paul Brickman*
Screenwriter: *Paul Brickman*
18/98 mins/Comedy/USA

When his folks are away Joel Goodson decides to hire a high-class call-girl named Lana. But when he also trashes his dad's Porsche, the only way he can afford to pay for the repairs is to go into business with Lana and her friends.

The film which shot Tom Cruise to fame, is a strangely affecting mix of frathouse hi-jinks and philosophical treatise. It's *Ferris Bueller* with an existential crisis. Very funny and very weird. Cruise's cocky whelp, cutting loose while his rich folks are out of town, is far too self-aware and troubled to be just a stock heroic hedonist from *National Lampoon*, despite being a raging hormone with big white underpants dancing to Old Time Rock And Roll by Bob Seers. 'It seems to me that if there were any logic to our language, trust would be a four letter word,' he considers in a quiet moment between bouts of big grinning. Director Paul Brickman is looking to examine the inner-workings of the preppy straight-A student with the world at his feet and the keys to his dad's Porsche. Although, we're not sure we want to get that deep with him.

His relationship with knowing hooker Lana (Rebecca De Mornay) seems to drift from rented shagging to therapy, even if the sex scene on the subway train, all flickering lights and soft rock, chains the film to the 80s. The film, however, is trying to have its cake and analyse it – to be juvenile and naughty as Joel schemes to fleece his mates by turning the family home into a brothel for the night, and then to Catch Some Rye as it debates such a rich kid's place in the universe. It's too big an ask.

Cruise, though, makes us care enough. He's never been a hugely versatile actor but he can knit his brow as if thoughts and worries are gathering up there, and for all the innuendo which is surprisingly fleshless, creates a credible character. A star was born. ★★★ **IN**

⊙ A RIVER RUNS THROUGH IT (1992)

Starring: *Craig Sheffer (Norman Maclean), Brad Pitt (Paul Maclean), Tom Skerrit (Rev. Maclean), Brenda Blethyn (Mrs Maclean), Emily Lloyd (Jessie Burns)*
Director: *Robert Redfrod*
Screenwriter: *Richard Friedenberg, based on a story by Norman Maclean*
PG/118 mins./Biography/Drama/USA

Awards: *Academy Awards – Best Cinematography*

Two sons of a Presbyterian minister maintain their relationship through a common love of fly-fishing, despite increasing personal differences.

Adapted from Norman Maclean's best-selling autobiographical novella of the same name, Robert Redford's first directorial outing since 1988's *The Milagro Beanfield War* is a ravishingly photographed, elegiac memoir of Maclean's younger brother Paul, and a rumination of the finer points of that most uncinematic of pastimes, fly-fishing.

Lyrical without begin trite, this captivates from the moment Redford's effortless voice-over slides and we flashback to the narrator's childhood in Montana at the turn of the century – a time untouched by war, and a place seemingly blessed. For the male members of the Maclean family – Presbyterian minister Tom Skerritt and his two young sons, Norman and Paul – there is one place where communication between them is possible, here on the Big Blackfoot River, where life, religion and art merge as one; as they cast their fishing lines into the water, a hithero untapped harmony descends upon them.

Years pass by in a blur of sepia-tinted photos, eventually settling in 1926 when Norman returns from college, wise in the ways of prose, but a man still in his father's shadow. Paul is the wild card of the pair, a consummate fly-fishing artist, a killer with the ladies, and a liability for the operators of the local gambling den when he runs up huge debts. In the role, Pitt showed the first inkling that he was more than a pretty face, turning in a layered performance that anchors the entire movie. It's a part Redford knows well – all bright-eyed brilliance and fatal inevitability – and 20 years ago he would have played it himself.

Consequently, Sheffer's Norman is less well defined, a stoic proposition lacking his sibling's pose, flair and looks, his character's relationship with Jessie the only one in the movie that fails to convince.

That aside this is an elegant if simply structure film, one crafted with a warmth and understanding reflective of the director enamoured of his subject matter – Redford courted Maclean for years to gain the rights to the book. And, despite being at least half an hour too long, there is much to be recommended – from Phillippe Rousselot's exquisite cinematography, with the stunning scenery of Montana as a backdrop, to Redford's assured direction, this is utterly alluring, and manages to make fly-fishing seem not just romantic, but thrilling. ★★★★ **MS**

⊙ RIVER'S EDGE (1986)

Starring: *Crispin Glover (Layne), Keanu Reeves (Matt), Ione Skye (Clarissa), Daniel Roebuck (Samson 'John' Tollet), Dennis Hopper (Feck)*
Director: *Tim Hunter*
Screenwriter: *Neal Jimenez*
18/99 mins./Drama/Crime/USA

Samson, a 17-year-old slob, murders a schoolfriend on impulse and leaves her body by the river, returning with his friends to boast of his handiwork. Layne wants to shelter the killer while Matt is more conscience-stricken.

A real shocker, based on an actual incident. The kids on a trek to see a corpse make it seem an anti-nostalgic *Stand By Me*, the film is also a refutation of John Hughes' then-dominant vision of teen life, showing how a group of no-hope kids without money, fast cars or rich parents were taking the 1980s.

This crowd are sunk into an apathy even murder can't shake up, borrow their idea of heroism from Chuck Norris movies and gradually succumb to the numbing emptiness of leftover lives. Dennis Hopper stands as a living embodiment of a failed generation as the aptly named old hippie Feck – who claims that in the 1960s 'I ate so much pussy my beard was like a glazed doughnut' – while then-new teen faces like Glover, Reeves and Ione Skye bizarrely look to him for guidance he can't give.

Glover, who is at least energetic, devises more and more complex and unworkable schemes to protect the murderer, who no longer seems that interested in protecting himself, while Joshua Miller Jr (the vampire kid from *Near Dark*) is amazingly creepy as a twelve-year-old psychopath who represents an even worse younger generation.

Moral without moralising, blackly comic without being tasteless, acutely tuned-in to the way kids talk and act and amazingly capable of compassion while it deals with a startlingly callous set of characters, this is an outstanding American movie.

Director Tim Hunter, who had written Jonathan Kaplan's similarly toned *Over the Edge*, seemed set to become a major talent, but has spent most of his subsequent career doing episodic television. ★★★★ **KN**

⊙ ROAD TO PERDITION (2002)

Starring: *Tom Hanks (Michael Sullivan), Paul Newman (John Rooney), Liam Aiken (Peter Sullivan), Jennifer Jason Leigh (Annie Sullivan), Daniel Craig (Connor Rooney), Jude Law (Harlen Maguire)*
Director: *Sam Mendes*
Screenwriter: *David Self, from the graphic novel by Max Allan Collins, Richard Piers, Rayner*
15/112 mins./Crime/Drama/USA

Awards: *Academy Awards – Best Cinematography; BAFTA – Best Cinematography, Best Production Design*

Following a messy murder, hit man Michael Sullivan is betrayed by the man he called father, formidable Irish hood John Rooney. Leaving behind a murdered family and with a killer on his tail, Sullivan goes on the run, hungry for revenge.

The year is 1931, and dapper immigrant mobsters are running an icy America with big guns and deadly honour codes. You know, the stuff of cinematic pearls since time immemorial, and the canvas on which Max Allan Collins and Richard Piers Rayner painted their graphic novel (posh comic book).

It's this emotional exploration of the gangster myth that Yank-fixated Brit Sam Mendes was drawn to after his blistering debut, *American Beauty*. 'Perdition' translates as 'damnation', and with wry whimsy is also the name of the elusive Midwest town planned as sanctuary for enforcer Michael Sullivan's young son, desperate to find love in his cold-blooded father.

This is a moody, pristine study of paternal woe, localised to an Illinois chapter of the mob run by Newman's ageing patriarch, a man tormented by a trigger-happy dolt of an heir, Connor (Craig, slimeballing with relish). His is the devilry that rips apart Sullivan's life, sending echoes up to Chicago, in the form of a slick Stanley Tucci as real-life Capone general, Frank Nitti. Gangsters are the ultimate dysfunctional family.

Chastely violent and sombre, the movie is a blood-rush of visual magnificence (take a bow, cinematographer Conrad L. Hall). However, it's at times weighed down by its own gravity, and perhaps too eager to touch its forelock to Mendes' forebears, Scorsese and Coppola, not to mention John Ford's scope and Michael Powell's lushness.

Comparisons with *The Godfather*, *The Untouchables* and *Miller's Crossing* will fly, but the true reference point here is *Unforgiven*. Sullivan's journey into a hell of his own making is pure William Munney. It falls short of Eastwood's classic, but not by very much.

Mendes conducts with a grace the material can't quite handle, and we do not hear clearly the earnest notes of the designated quest for salvation. Look, it's Hanks and Newman together! As crooks! Worry not, though, we've still got Jude Law as the real scumbag, a Weegee-styled hit man with stained molars and a porkpie hat, who shoots his victims with both gun and camera.

Hanks – hunkered down in a heavy skin with a threadbare moustache and the rigid posture of moral deep-freeze – works hard not to force things. Neither hero nor anti-hero, for the audience it proves too taxing to shake the notion that this is Forrest Gump doing his best Clint Eastwood. Amoral? Ambiguous? Evil? Too big a leap.

Newman, meanwhile, is electrifying. Coating Rooney in dead eyes and a soft smile, his conflation of the jovial grandfather with flints of absolute darkness is a performance that chimes with (and betters) Brandos Don Corleone. His is the crowning speech, power's inevitable corruption writ heavy across his soul: 'This is the life we chose ... And there is only one guarantee: none of us will see heaven.'

When he and Sullivan finally cross swords, Mendes pulls out a moment of transcendent cinema: a speechless sequence washed in the film's signature downpour, lit to throw Tommy guns and fedoras into stark silhouettes – you watch agape as simple celluloid transforms into poetry. Mendes has the eye, if not yet the ear, to be amongst the greats he honours so much. The luxury is that this is only film two. ★★★★ **IN**

ROAD TO SINGAPORE (1940)

Starring: *Bing Crosby (Joshua 'Josh' Mallon V), Dorothy Lamour (Mima), Bob Hope (Ace Lannigan), Charles Coburn (Joshua Mallon IV), Anthony Quinn (Caesar)*
Director: *Victor Schertzinger*
Screenwriters: *Frank Butler, Don Hartman, from a story by Harry Hervey*
U/81 mins./Musical/Comedy/USA

Josh, irresponsible son of a tycoon, flees an arranged marriage and sets up home with his best friend Ace in Singapore, where they compete for the affections of native girl Mima.

This pleasant 1940 comedy-drama hit on the successful double-act teaming of crooner Bing Crosby and patter comic Bob Hope, throwing in sarong-clad Dorothy Lamour for glamour and working through a trivial plot about fleeing responsibility for a South Seas idyll.

Anything that might be seen as content was dropped for *Road to Zanzibar* (1941), a follow-up in which Bing and Bob have different character names, but remain themselves – and Lamour is yanked in for some more pin-ups.

The series hit its stride with *Road to Morocco* (1943) and *Road to Utopia* (1946, set in Alaska), with running gags carried over from picture to picture (the 'patty-cake' routine), surreal gags (a talking camel, the Paramount mountain passing by in the background), vestigial plots with villains chasing vaudeville boys, comedy duets with knock-out silly lyrics ('like *Webster's Dictionary*, we're Morocco-bound'), studio backlot exotic settings and one of the odder, more painful comedy relationships in the movies as the purportedly charming, sympathetic Bing is forever on the point of selling dumb, greedy, lecherous Bob into slavery or allowing him to be sacrificed to an octopus god.

Road to Rio (1947) is a little tired; *Road to Bali* (1952) is in colour but otherwise unremarkable; and *Road to Hong Kong* (1962), which reduces Lamour to a cameo as herself and partners Bing and Bob with Joan Collins, failed to revive the series.

They manfully refrained from doing a *Carry On Columbus* reprise in their later years, though Hope cameoed in John Landis's homage to the series, *Spies Like Us*. Huge hits in their day, with a lot of topical gags that make no sense any more, these are still great afternoon TV fun. ★★★ **KN**

ROAD TRIP (2000)

Starring: *Breckin Meyer (Josh), Seann William Scott (E.L.), Amy Smart (Beth), Paulo Costanzo (Rubin), D.J. Qualls (Kyle), Rachel Blanchard (Tiffany)*
Director: *Todd Phillips*
Screenwriters: *Todd Phillips, Scot Armstrong*
15/93 mins./Comedy/USA

After mistakenly sending his girlfriend a videotape of himself having extra-relationship sex with a college student, Josh must travel cross-country from Ithaca to Austin before she gets it. He is joined in this quest by a lothario, a geek and a perpetual.

Ah, the college road trip. What japes! What memories! The visceral thrill of having to extricate yourself from endless one-way systems by sheer centrifugal force. The sound of the engine seizing up in a traffic jam on the M25. The sight of RAC operatives openly laughing at the smouldering hunk-of-junk that used to be your car.

OK, so Britain may not be the best place to hit the open road in between lectures. Over in America, though, they get to do these things properly. For one thing, Yanks have a damn sight more tarmac to trip on. And, for another, their students seem able to equip themselves with vehicles capable of travelling further than the nearest all-night garage. Finally, American females seem happy to videotape their one-night stands – thereby setting up a situation whereby the guy in question must travel halfway across the country to retrieve the accidentally mailed tape before his childhood sweetheart gets the opportunity to see her beau playing hide the salami with a stranger.

This, at least, is what happens in *Road Trip*. Although, in truth, the 'plot' is really an excuse for our hero, Josh, and his fellow passengers to engage in all manner of antics as they attempt to finance their 1,800-mile New York to Texas trip by donating sperm, cadge a bed at an all-black fraternity, or steal a bus from a school for the blind. Further un-PC weirdness emanates from the film's narrator – MTV's resident madman, Tom Green – who feels obliged to add a few tits to his tale whenever the mood takes him.

If all this sounds like The Farrelly Brothers Go To College, then you're pretty much on the money – although director Todd Phillips can claim his own gonzo pedigree, having made the documentary *Frat House*, which showed American college students behaving in a manner that makes the *Road Trip* characters look like saints.

He is also considerably helped by the film's excellent cast, particularly *American Pie*'s Scott who, having set the entire ball rolling by suggesting that Meyer sow his wild oats, attempts to make the poor bastard feel better by setting out a handy set of 'cheating rules': it's not cheating if you're in different area codes; if you're too wasted to remember it; if you're with two people at the same time because they cancel each other out, etc.

Naturally, of course, *American Pie* comparisons will be drawn. And, while it's a close run thing, this film is probably better, thanks to some increasingly knowing digs at the 80s movies it so lovingly mirrors. The result, then, deserves to reside somewhere in the same keg-and-vomit-strewn ball park of humour as *National Lampoon's Animal House*, while also featuring a character-building subtext about the importance of getting all that one can out of life – even if that involves letting a nurse stick her hand up your arse. ★★★ **CC**

Groucho Marx Character Names

1 Captain Jeffrey T. Spaulding - *Animal Crackers*, 1930
2 Professor Quincy Adams Wagstaff - *Horse Feathers*, 1932
3 Rufus T. Firefly - *Duck Soup*, 1933
4 Otis B. Driftwood - *A Night At The Opera*, 1935
5 Dr Hugo Z. Hackenbush - *A Day At The Races*, 1937
6 J. Cheever Loophole - *At The Circus*, 1939
7 S. Quentin Quale - *Go West*, 1940
8 Wolf J. Flywheel - *The Big Store*, 1941
9 Ronald Kornblow - *A Night At Casablanca*, 1946
10 Lionel Q. Devereux - *Copacabana*, 1947

THE ROARING TWENTIES (1939)

Starring: *James Cagney (Eddie Bartlett), Priscilla Lane (Jean Sherman/Hart), Humphrey Bogart (George Hally), Gladys George (Panama Smith), Jeffrey Lynn (Lloyd Hart)*
Director: *Raoul Walsh*
Screenwriter: *Jerry Wald, Richard Macaulay, Robert Roseen, based on the story 'The World Moves On'*
PG/101 mins./Crime/Drama/USA

After the First World War, Eddie Bartlett gets mixed up in the bootlegging racket and becomes an important mob figure. Ruined in the stock market crash, he takes up his gun again when he learns his vicious ex-partner intends to kill the crusading district attorney who has married the girl he idolised.

A 1939 Warner Bros super-production, summing up the Prohibition-era gangster movies they made earlier in the decade. We follow nice guy bootlegger Cagney from the trenches through the bathtub gin-fuelled 20s to the end of his gangland empire and his last hurrah in the early 30s.

Initially a naive doughboy, Cagney drifts into crime when he can't get his old job back and a speakeasy siren hires him as a bootlegger. The dark side of gangsterism is represented by Cagney's old war buddy partner Bogart, first seen shooting teenage Germans five minutes before the Armistice is declared.

Relishing one of his best early bad guy roles, the sharklike Bogart turns to crime not through social necessity but for the sadistic love of it, memorably taking the opportunity during a heist to murder his old sergeant (Joe Sawyer) when he finds the man working as a security guard. Using a stentorian narrator and extraordinary symbolic montage newsreels (staged by Don Siegel), director Raoul Walsh effortlessly weaves together social history, romantic comedy, gang warfare, rat-tat-tat tough guy dialogue, sharp suits, spaghetti house shoot-outs, speakeasy singalongs, nostalgia, wonderful Warners character players (Frank McHugh, Paul Kelly) and a great Cagney star performance.

In a redemptive finish Cagney guns down the cowardly Bogart and is himself shot, expiring in the snow on the steps of a church as George delivers his epitaph, 'He used to be a big shot.' ★★★★★ **KN**

THE ROBE (1953)

Starring: *Richard Burton (Marcellus Gallio), Jean Simmons (Diana), Victor Mature (Demitrius), Michael Rennie (Peter), Jay Robinson (Caligua), Dean Jagger (Justus)*
Director: *Henry Koster*
Screenwriters: *Albert Maltz, Philip Dunne, from the novel by Lloyd C. Douglas, adapted by Gina Kaus*
U/133 mins./Religion/Drama/USA

Awards: *Academy Awards – Best Art Direction-Set Decoration, Best Colour Costume; Golden Globes – Best Drama*

Banished from Rome, Roman officer Marcellus is put in charge of crucifying Jesus. Afterwards, he wins Christ's robe in a dice-game and comes to believe that the executed rabble-rouser was the Messiah.

Pompous schlock in CinemaScope, from the Lloyd C. Douglas novel few will have read these days, *The Robe* typifies the worst aspects of the Hollywood Christian epic: performances which are either stiff or demented, enormous pageantry and spectacle just stuck unmoving on the screen, appalling dialogue delivered by actors who know they're onto a loser ('Renounce your misguided allegiance to this dead Jew who dared to call himself a king!') and, worst of all, a stultifying religiosity that deadens even the camp enjoyment factor.

Richard Burton, looking handsome in a breastplate, is the noble Roman who bickers with heir-to-the-throne Caligula (Jay Robinson, dreadful but nearly fun) and is sent to the dead-end gig of Jerusalem just in time for Jesus to pass through the back of the wide frame on a donkey. The one tiny job Burton has to do before his pull with an old girlfriend who is pals with Emperor Tiberius (Ernest Thesiger) gets him a transfer is to supervise the Crucifixion. His Greek slave Demetrius (Victor Mature, en route to his own sequel – *Demetrius and the Gladiators*) has turned Christian after a midnight chat with a tormented Judas (an uncredited Michael Ansara), and knows no good will come of this – which turns out to be the case as the Roman is tormented by bad dreams and thunderstorms that, along with a sermon from Peter, convince him to convert to the new faith.

It has some minor swordfights, but little action – the ridiculous climax has Rich and Jean walking meekly away to be martyred by arrows as the music swells into huge hallelujahs. ★★ **KN**

ROBIN AND MARIAN (1976)

Starring: *Sean Connery (Robin Hood), Audrey Hepburn (Lady Marian), Robert Shaw (Sheriff Of Nottingham), Richard Harris (King Richard), Nicol Williamson (Little John), Denholm Elliot (Will Scarlett)*
Director: *Richard Lester*
Screenwriter: *Richard Goldman*
PG/106 mins./History/Drama/USA/UK

Returning from the Crusades an old man, Robin Hood finds his former hunting grounds a changed world. Marian has entered a nunnery, King Richard is dead, and the chances for high adventure passed. But when the Sheriff Of Nottingham starts playing up, it is up the elderly Robin to gather his Merry Men once more to the cause.

An eloquent if slow 'what if?' scenario that posits an ageing Robin Hood returning to Sherwood Forest after 20 years at the Crusades. Naturally, it is a very changed world, as he is a very changed man, and Richard Lester, with sterling and mature performances from Sean Connery and Audrey Hepburn, is making an intelligent point about what happens when you are no longer relevant. When the good fight has been won what would Robin Hood do with himself? A matter made especially confusing as, in his long absence, his legend has grown far so much more than the reality.

Robin's return also sends his fellow players in the dusty panoply of the past into something of a tizz. Marian (Hepburn) has joined a nunnery, smarting over Hood's abandonment 20 years earlier, but is having trouble resisting the urge to change her habit. Robert Shaw's Sheriff seems delighted that his old nemesis is back in town, and reinvigorates his dastardly dealings to stir something out of a game grown rusty with lack of use. There is an almost magnetic drift back into these prescribed roles, as if they depend on them. People are defined by their own stories – and the players in them. Are we only a product of our pasts?

It is also a film about ageing. Lester plays some obvious but funny tricks on the England's most fabled of pastoral iconography. Early on, Lester has Little John and Robin embark on a rescue mission, scaling a castle wall that would have been nothing to the sprightly Robin of all those youthful songs, but now with grey beards and thin hair, it leaves them panting and doubled over. The atmosphere is one of melancholy as Lester penetrates through the gauze of fantasy to find the human heart, and softly finds it beating. ★★★ **IN**

➂ ROBIN HOOD (1973)

Starring the voices of: *Brian Bedford (Robin Hood), Peter Ustinov (Prince John), Phil Harris (Little John), Terry-Thomas (Sir Hiss), Monica Evans (Maid Marian), Carole Shelley (Lady Kluck)*
Director: *Wolfgang Reitherman*
Screenwriter: *Ken Anderson, Larry Clemmons*
PG/106 mins./Animation/USA

The great fable of Robin Hood and his Merry Men, who rob from the rich to give to the poor, as told by Disney through the use of animals. Robin and Marion are foxes, Prince John is a lion who sucks his thumb, and the Sheriff is a snake.

While the greatness was somewhere behind them, by 1973 Disney were still capable of creating magic. After Uncle Walt departed to the real Magic Kingdom, his troops were always more confident when turning legends and fairy-tales in cute critters rather than sticking with human figures – hence this sprightly and funny take on Robin Hood is so much more appealing than the humanoid *Sword In The Stone*. It seemed to bring out the personality in them.

So, while this is hardly the most dazzling of animated features, it has that cut-corner feel that seemed to hold sway in the 70s (mainly because Disney were cutting corners), the characters spark to life, and the story remains as rock steady as ever. It's especially delightful to see, or maybe that is hear (one is a lion, the other a slippery snake), Peter Ustinov and Terry-Thomas spark up a comedy double act as a stroppy King John and a sycophantic Sheriff. They do wonders with only their voices, with Ustinov bumptious and spoilt and Thomas playing that magnificent wheedling tone that made him cinema's greatest cad. By comparison, Brian Bedford's foxy Robin comes across a bit bland.

It's going to surprise no one, the songs have nothing on *The Jungle Book* (the last true great), but as the archery contest (splitting the arrow!) succumbs to what seems to be an all-out American football match, the pleasures are all ours. ★★★★ **IN**

➂ ROBIN HOOD: PRINCE OF THIEVES (1991)

Starring: *Kevin Costner (Robin of Locksley), Morgan Freeman (Azeem), Morgan Freeman (Azeem), Mary Elizabeth Mastrantonio (Marian Dubois), Christian Slater (Will Scarlett), Alan Rickman (Sheriff Of Nottingham)*
Director: *Kevin Reynolds*
Screenwriters: *Pen Densham, John Watson, from a story by Pen Densham*
PG/148 mins./Action/Adventure/Romance/USA
Awards: *BAFTA – Best Supporting Actor (Alan Rickman)*

Peasant Robin musters an army of Merry Men to even out the Sherwood social strata, much to the annoyance of a cranky sheriff of Nottingham.

Some 82 years after making his motion picture debut, Robin Of Locksley, the ultimate good guy, the prototype for every non-pacifist righter of wrongs in Western culture, now returned to our screens in this $55 million, major-talent, somewhat 'loose' interpretation of the legend of the man in tights of green.

Fraught with problems, horribly rushed, and with six producers too many, this particular *Robin Hood* was never going to be a particularly slick affair and, depending on your own personal level of pedantry, the considerable technical, historical, geographical and linguistic gaffes deflect particularly on this side of the Atlantic.

That words such as turncoat, not invented for another 400 years, are inexplicably sprinkled about the generally turgid script may not be too great cause for alarm, along with the extraordinary selection of accents on offer – Californian, New York, Devon, cockney and Shakespearian English to name but a few.

When it comes to single scenes embracing the landscape of the Yorkshire Dales, highland moors and rolling middle-English countryside, however, patience is stretched a touch, finally snapping when 'Sherwood' Forest is seen for the first time as a distinctly 20th-century conifer plantation (only to transmogrify into a beautiful beech and oak affair when we get inside), while the various trees on display oscillate between full autumn-gold splendour and the bare-branched bleakness of winter and back again within a single fight scene.

With a $55 million budget, one does wonder at times like these if the filmmakers could not perhaps have spent a few bob and a little time to check these things. The story – give or take a few druids, a Moor (the excellent Freeman), some devil-worship and the notable absence of Prince John – is the same as ever. Landless nobleman Robin (Costner, frankly sleepwalking through his $7 million role) repairs to the forest to lead a bunch of outlaws (all good value) against the Sheriff of Nottingham, robs from rich gits in gold braid, poleaxes a few conical-hatted Normans, gives the poor the readies, and falls for the feisty-yet-chaste Marian (Mastrantonio, who we know can do a better English accent, because she did it in *Fools Of Fortune*).

As such, it's fun and frantic, although the wit – the use of the word 'fuck' being deemed hilarious – falls way short of an *Indy* or a *Terminator*, and nearly everything that happens has been done before, and better, in movies from *Beetlejuice* to *Die Hard*.

Things do liven up immensely, however, whenever Alan Rickman hits the screen. This man is obviously having a lot of fun here with his Sheriff, a diabolically petulant bastard, played with gleeful pantomime-esque camp, and backed up brilliantly by his sidekick, the deeply unpleasant Guy of Gisborne.

Indeed, between them, these two regularly save the whole thing from grinding to a dreary halt. *Robin Hood: Prince Of Thieves* still more than recouped its considerable outlay, drawing huge box office in the face of a considerable critical mauling. ★★★ **PT**

➂ ROBOCOP (1987)

Starring: *Peter Weller (Murphy/Robocop), Nancy Allen (Officer Anne Lewis), Dan O'Herlilhy (Old Man), Ronny Cox (Dick Jones), Kurtwood Smith (Clarence Boddicker)*
Director: *Paul Verhoeven*
Screenwriters: *Edward Neumeier, Michael Miner*
18/102 mins./Sci-fi/Action/Thriller/USA

In his first day patrolling Detroit, Officer Alex Murphy is killed by feared gang leader Clarence Boddicker. OCP scientists are able to use Murphy's remains to build a cybernetic soldier codenamed Robocop and so Robocop begins a one-man war on crime.

Although *Robocop* would be the film largely responsible for introducing English-speaking audiences to the mad, bad world of Paul Verhoeven, it was by no means his first brush with Hollywood. Five years before unleashing his half-man/half-cyborg law enforcer on an unsuspecting public, the Dutch director was in the frame to direct *Return Of The Jedi*. He had been recommended to George Lucas by Steven Spielberg who greatly enjoyed Verhoeven's WWII epic *Soldier Of Orange*. Legend has it that Spielberg subsequently withdrew his support after viewing *Spetters* – a film Verhoeven directed wearing biker leathers and which followed the adventures of three motocross champions, one of whom turns homosexual after being gang-raped. 'I suppose he was scared,' Verhoeven would later comment, 'that the Jedi would immediately start fucking.'

Of course, given the rumpy-pumpy-oriented shenanigans of subsequent Verhoeven vehicles such as *Basic Instinct* and *Showgirls* it is reasonable to suggest that Spielberg would have been justified in his fears. But, ironically, before *Robocop* it was generally thought that the director was not too shag-obsessed for a big studio blockbuster but too arty. Indeed, Verhoeven films such as Spetters and *Flesh + Blood* had become arthouse favourites around the world. Certainly they seemed to have little in common with a film like *Robocop* which, on paper at least, is just another sci-fi shoot 'em up and not even a particularly original one at that. Set in a near-future Detroit where police matters are controlled by the all-powerful OCP corporation the movie follows the travails of nice copper Alex Murphy who, after being blown to bits by a gang of crooks, is brought back to life as the titular man-machine. Robocop's arrival is met with dismay by his more fleshy colleagues while problems arise when he begins to hunt down Murphy's killers – a trail that leads all the way back to the corrupt corridors of OCP itself.

In short, the plot of *Robocop* is essentially similar to any number of superhero tales with a smattering of *Dirty Harry* and *Judge Dredd* thrown in for good measure. But, in the hands of Verhoeven, the film became – like his later *Starship Troopers* – a satirical critique of the totalitarianism which he had seen first hand as a child growing up in the Hague. Verhoeven was little more than a toddler when the Germans invaded the Netherlands and his earliest memories are of a life dominated by jackbooted soldiers. He witnessed people 'picking up pieces of pilots'. 'There were a lot of uniforms in the Hague,' Verhoeven has said of his childhood. 'Living in an occupied country dominated by an evil empire is something that's close to me. Being a child of the war my tolerance for violence is larger than normal.'

It was this love of mayhem combined with a biting comic attack on neo-fascist corporatism – most notably seen in the TV ads for products like the apocalyptic board game Nuke 'Em – which helped raise *Robocop* above the common sci-fi herd. Yet what really put the film ahead of the game was Verhoeven's technical expertise. The director was originally attracted to science fiction because he thought, being unfamiliar with American society, it would help his cause if he was allowed to re-imagine it. There is no doubt the genre suited his skills which had been developing since the late 60s when, during national service, Verhoeven made a propaganda film utilising helicopters, divers, an aircraft carrier and several divisions of marines.

Tagline
Part man. Part machine. All cop. The future of law enforcement.

Moreover, having ordered around half the Dutch navy, the director had few qualms going to battle with special effects wizard Rob Bottin – Verhoeven dismissed his early robot designs as 'crap' – or Peter Weller who conceded that 'It was the first time I was convinced I'd have a fist-fight with a director.' Yet, even Weller – who endured months of torture within the suit – would eventually concede that the result was more than worth the aggravation. ★★★★ **CC**

ROBOTS (2005)

Starring: the voices of: *Ewan McGregor (Rodney Copperbottom), Mel Brooks (Mr Big Weld), Robin Williams (Fender), Amanda Bynes (Piper), Greg Kinnear (Rachet), Drew Carey (Crank)*
Director: *Chris Wedge*
Screenwriters: *David Lindsay-Abaire, Lowell Ganz, Babaloo Mandel, from a story by Ron Mita, Jim McClain, David Lindsay-Abaire*
U/91 mins./Animated/Family/Comedy/USA

Smalltown robot and would-be inventor Rodney Copperbottom heads for Robot City in the hope of showing off his latest creation to businessman Mr Big Weld. But all is not well when he gets there, and he finds himself fighting against the evil machinations of some corrupt robot bosses.

Having scored a big hit with his computer-animated debut *Ice Age* (the film that proved it's not just Pixar and DreamWorks who can do this kind of thing), it's no wonder that expectations have been high for director Chris Wedge's follow-up.

And there's plenty to like about *Robots* – it's a gleaming, candy-coloured spectacle whose sweetly nostalgic theme gives rise to some very impressive visuals.
Unfortunately, while it all looks impressive, *Robots* is let down badly by a weak plot (which relies too heavily on the well-worn 'big city' theme, with bad-punning signs brimming in the background à la *Shrek 2* and *Shark Tale*), overly frantic action and characters who, while superficially endearing, are hard to truly warm to.

Part of the problem is Wedge's insistence on throwing as many ideas at the screen as he can – and while this does result in some great set pieces (Rodney's initial 'subway ride' into Robot City is a particular high point), it also feels as though there's just too much going on.

The second half, when Rodney hooks up with a motley crew of outdated robots and sets out to save the city from the bad guys, is a lot more fun – but given the slender running time, you can't help wishing it had kicked into gear much earlier. ★★★ **CW**

ROCCO AND HIS BROTHERS (ROCCO ET SES FRERES) (1960)

Starring: *Alain Delon (Rocco Parondi), Renato Salvatori (Simone) Parondi), Annie Girardot (Nadia), Katina Paxinou (Rosaria Parondi), Roger Hanin (Morini), Paolo Stoppa (Boxing Impressario)*
Director: *Luchino Visconti*
Screenwriter: *Luchino Visconti, Suso Cecchi D'Amico, Pasquale Festa Campanile, Massimo Franciosca, Enrico Medioli based on the novel The Bridge Of Ghisolfa by Giovanni Testori*
15/175 mins./Drama/France/Italy

Widow Rosaria Parondi quits the south for Milan with her five sons – Vincenzo, Simone, Rocco, Ciro and Luca. However, boxing siblings Simone and Rocco fall for the same local prostitute Nadia, whose murder breaks up the fractious family for good.

Such is the status of opulent works like *Senso*, *The Leopard* and *Death in Venice* that it's easy to forget that Luchino Visconti was among the founding fathers of neo-realism. The sensitivity to a place and its people, acquired while making his earliest features, *Ossessione* and *La Terra Trema*, was readily evident in this supremely evocative epic, as he made Milan seem both a city of elegance and despair.

Indeed, Visconti always regarded this film as a sequel to the latter study of Sicilian fishermen – even though its roots lay in such novels as Dostoevsky's *The Idiot* and Thomas Mann's *Joseph and His Bretheren*, as well as such Giovanni Testori stories as 'Il Ponte della Ghisolfa' – and it's easy to see Milan as a convenient backdrop for a classic southern clan feud.

However, Visconti was also keen to explore the stock responses of his varyingly macho characters to the problems of migration and he shrewdly contrasted traditional notions of honour and family loyalty with the individualism of modern urban life. Consequently, the city provided the same realist environment as Aci Trezza. Indeed, Visconti's sense of authenticity was so heightened that the council withheld permission to stage Nadia's murder in a popular tourist spot and then banned the film, despite the excision of 45 minutes by the state censor.

Notwithstanding the factuality of the setting, Visconti's genius for operatic melodrama was also to the fore. Alain Delon was perhaps a touch too saintly as Rocco, whose every action atoned for the feckless wickedness of Renato Salvatori, the brother who botches a boxing career, murders his mistress and takes up with a gay pimp. But Salvatori was superb, particularly in his dealings with the outstanding Annie Girardot, whom, ironically, he would marry in real life.

The themes that preoccupied Visconti throughout his career, societal transition, familial disintegration and basic humanity were all present here. But the veniality, violence and simmering sexual tension, which were considered highly controversial back in 1960, gave this monochrome masterpiece a rawness that was decidedly at odds with Visconti's undeserved reputation for decadence. ★★★★★ **DP**

① THE ROCK (1996)

Starring: *Sean Connery (John Patrick Mason), Nicolas Cage (Dr Stanley Goodspeed), Ed Harris (General Francis X. Hummel), John Spencer (FBI Director James Womack), David Morse (Major Tom Baxter)*
Screenwriters: *David Weisberg, Mark Rosner, Douglas S. Cook, from a story by Weisberg, Cook*
15/140 mins./Action/Thriller/USA

A disposal bomb expert is forced to team up with the only man ever to escape Alcatraz, now under maximum security for a mystery reason, to break into the Rock and thwart the evil plans of a disgruntled ex-army general.

Bad Boys. Armageddon. Pearl Harbor. When arguing with people who believe the Jerry Bruckheimer/Michael Bay collaboration is a cinematic axis of evil, that trio provides evidence that's hard to dispute. Yet just introduce *The Rock* into conversation and watch them founder.

Yes, it's got all the hallmarks of a standard B 'n' B production – it's loud and bombastic, it's crammed with orange filters and epilepsy-inducing editing, and it doesn't make a great deal of sense. But set against that is the fact that it's breathlessly exciting, as Nic Cage and Sean Connery break into Alcatraz to thwart Ed Harris' disgruntled general from bombing San Francisco with lethal nerve gas.

The superb action is choreographed with zing by Bay, before he mutated into Jim Cameron-lite. And the film has a real trump card in Harris' conflicted bad guy – it's a rare and intelligent move for a big budget studio venture to feature a villain with an agenda that's hard not to sympathise with.

Luckily he's matched by the quality of the heroes. While *The Rock* proved that Connery could still cut the mustard as an OAP action star, it was the making of Cage as action hero, his wild and wired approach gelling perfectly with Connery's gruff demeanour.

And when they're not shooting Alcatraz to bits, they're the funniest buddy-movie double-act in years. In short, *The Rock* has more pizzazz than an entire roomful of Dwayne Johnsons. ★★★★ **CH**

① THE ROCKETEER (1991)

Starring: *Bill Campbell (Cliff Secord), Jennifer Connelly (Jenny Blake), Alan Arkin (A. 'Peevy' Peabody), Timothy Dalton (Neville Sinclair)*
Director: *Joe Johnston*
Screenwriters: *Danny Bilson, Paul De Meo, based on a story by Bilson, De Meo, Dear, graphic novel by Dave Sevens*
PG/108 mins./Action/Adventure/USA

Stunt pilot Cliff discovers a rocket backpack that turns him into a flying hero, but Hollywood star Neville Sinclair is after the backpack too – and Cliff's budding movie-star girlfriend.

It's 1938 and daredevil stunt pilot Cliff Secord, an all-American boy with a rebellious cowlick and a chiselled chin, accidentally comes into possession of an experimental and dangerous rocket backpack that can make a man fly, designed by none other than Howard Hughes. Adding a helmet created by Cliff's crusty mentor, who recycles an art deco radio set, Cliff becomes the leather-jacketed rocketeer, a human rocket committed to Truth, Justice and the American way. Which is just as well, since Neville Sinclair, an Errol Flynn-style swashbuckling movie star who happens also to be the Number One Nazi Saboteur in Hollwood, also wants to get his hands on the rocket suit, and he has a gang of hoodlums, a Zeppelin full of stormtroopers and a lumbering monster – in the exact image of 40s B-picture monster Rondo Hatton – to help him, not to mention a line in smarmy chat-up he fully intends to apply to Cliff's bosomy but naive girlfriend.

Based on the retro-chic 1982 comic book, which was itself inspired by the 50s serial character Commander Cody (aka King Of The Rocketmen), this is a great action movie for all the family. Thanks to a script by Danny Bilson and Paul De Meo – veterans of the outstanding B-movie *Trancers* and TV's *The Flash* – and clean-lined direction by Johnston, fresh from *Honey I Shrunk The Kids*, *The Rocketeer* lacks the self-conciously hip tone that mars so many attempts to revive old-style thrills, last horridly in evidence in *Dick Tracy*.

Campbell may be just a touch dull as the hero, but certainly no duller than Buster Crabbe used to be, and he is here cleverly surrounded by performers who have been let in on the joke and don't feel the need to camp it up. Likewise, Dalton's villain is a very funny character, while never overbalancing the film to the hero's detriment.

With plentiful action, climaxing with some derring-do on a doomed dirigible and lots of snappy dialogue, *The Rocketeer* expertly captures the innocence and pep of 30s adventure movies. ★★★★ **KN**

① ROCKY (1976)

Starring: *Sylvester Stallone (Rocky Balboa), Talia Shire (Adrian), Burt Young (Paulie), Carl Weathers (Apollo Creed), Burgess Meredith (Mickey Goldmill)*
Director: *John G. Avildsen*
Screenwriter: *Sylvester Stallone*
PG/114 mins./Sports/Drama/USA
Awards: *Academy Awards – Best Director, Best Editing, Best Picture; Golden Globe – Best Drama*

In the Bicentennial Year, world heavyweight boxing champion Apollo Creed cynically offers a title shot to an unknown over-the-hill Philadelphia club fighter, Rocky Balboa. Though not taken seriously, Rocky puts up a fight.

The 1976 Best Picture Award-winner has the look of a contemporary on-the-streets movie like *Taxi Driver*, but the heart of a fairy-tale.

Unlike the sequels, *Rocky* is a rare American sports movie to realise there's more drama and emotional resonance in losing than winning. The unique finale – which would *not* be reprised – finds Rocky still standing at the end of the fight but losing narrowly on points, suggesting that for a no-hope underdog, taking the punishment and going the distance against the odds is more of a triumph than a conventional victory.

Stallone, then an unknown as an actor and a writer, crafts the script to his own strengths – mumbling, Brando-like sincerity combined with explosive physicality expressed in his use of a side of beef as a punch-bag or wintery jogs around Philly. Surprisingly little of the film is taken up with ring action, as we follow Rocky's awkward courtship of pet-store minion Adrian and uneasy relationship with her slobbish brother (Burt Young), while Burgess Meredith provides old pro licks as the curmudgeonly trainer and Weathers is showy as a Muhammad Ali-like stars-and-stripes blowhard.

Though it led to a slick, steroid-fuelled franchise, director John G. Avildsen gives this original a pleasing roughness, exemplified by the memorable funk/brass band score and the array of fidgety, credible method acting tics. For the record, the sequels cover a rematch with Creed (II), a bout with Mr T (III), a Cold War grudge match with Soviet champ Dolph Lundgren (IV), a street brawl with renegade protégé Tommy Morrison (V) and a geriatric comeback (Rocky Balboa). ★★★ **KN**

Movie Trivia: Rocky

The fight with Apollo Creed was shot from the final round back, gradually removing make-up as it regressed. Stallone's knuckles were permanently flattened from punching the animal carcasses. The film took Stallone just 3 days to write and under a month to shoot.

ROCKY II (1979)

Starring: *Sylvester Stallone (Rocky Balboa), Talia Shire (Adrian), Burt Young (Paulie), Carl Weathers (Apollo Creed), Burgess Meredith (Mickey Goldmill)*
Director: *Sylvester Stallone*
Screenwriter: *Sylvester Stallone*
PG/119 mins./Drama/USA

Looking to lead a peaceful life away from the boxing ring, Rocky Balboa finds himself down on his luck. So he accepts an offer of a rematch with his great rival Apollo Creed, against his wife Adrian's better judgement.

After the Oscar-wining glory of the original *Rocky* movie, Sylvester Stallone took it upon himself to be the champion of a set of ongoing, and increasingly demented sequels. With the first one, however, he was still concerned with keeping credibility to the fore, ostensibly remaking the first movie – the rise from the gutter to aspiring champion – with the added fillip of a victory rather than heroic defeat at the end.

Which means the film, written again by Stallone, has to contrive away to put Rocky, played again by Stallone, at the bottom of those symbolic steps. With often lurid levels of sentiment, we find our favourite monosyllabic pugilist hanging up his gloves as his wife, Adrian (the winsome Talia Shire), is now pregnant. Rocky also has a dodgy eye, and really shouldn't even be contemplating a return to the ring. But, hell, this is *Rocky II*, where else are we headed but the big showdown (albeit the same one) with Carl Weathers' sneery Apollo Creed?

Which means the second half of the film, directed with rougher, less engaging force by Stallone, will centre around the big man training his way back to fighting fitness with raspy Burgess Meredith geeing him along. There is inevitably a crude excitement in the underdog having his day, all those ticker-tape montages of the ursine Stallone's growing physique interrupted by the whingeing Adrian begging him to cease his foolish ideas (you occasionally get the ungentlemanly wish he would just deck her). By the punishing heft of the big fight, there is the clear hint that the series will soon plunge into an unpalatable patriotic fervour. For now, though, with its leathery texture of working class Philly-life it felt enough like reality, which counts for a lot. ★★★ **IN**

ROCKY III (1982)

Starring: *Sylvester Stallone (Rocky Balboa), Talia Shire (Adrian Balboa), Burt Young (Paulie), Carl Weathers (Apollo Creed), Burgess Meredith (Mickey Goldmill), Tony Burton (Duke), Mr T (Clubber Lang), Hulk Hogan (Thunderlips), Ian Fried (Rocky Jr), Al Silivani (Al)*
Director: *Sylvester Stallone*
Screenwriter: *Sylvester Stallone*
PG/99 mins./Drama/USA

After finally snatching the title from Apollo Creed, Rocky is enjoying life as the heavyweight champion of the world. But when he learns that his recent bouts have been fixed to give him an easy run, he must retrain and fight a formidable new opponent.

Abandoning the mildy gritty tone of the first two *Rocky* instalments, Part III is aimed more directly at a teen demographic. Everything's bigger, flashier and louder than before – not least the Italian Stallion's new nemesis, Clubber Lang, played in pantomine style by the inimitable Mr T. Lang is the burly thorn in Rocky's side, a hungry, vicious up-and-comer who takes advantage of our hero's newly pampered lifestyle to whup him in the opening act. Nowadays more acquainted with the inside of a sports car or a TV studio than the sweaty section of a gymnasium, Balboa takes the loss hard, and things get even rockier for Rocky when his beloved manager Mickey (Burgess Meredith) heads to the big locker room in the sky.

When it comes, Rocky's predictable rise back up to the top is melodramatic, slick and a huge crowdpleaser – when Carl Weathers' Apollo Creed steps forwards to offer his old enemy his hand and his expertise, you might just forget yourself and let out a whoop. And, just as Bill Conti's catchy music fuelled the franchise original, the whole thing is propelled along by Survivor's 'Eye Of The Tiger', a rock-synth monster created when Stallone failed to get clearance rights for Queen's 'Another One Bites The Dust'. The track couldn't be more perfect for this movie: silly, shallow and dated, but also undeniably fun. ★★★ **NDS**

ROCKY IV (1985)

Starring: *Sylvester Stallone (Rocky Balboa), Talia Shire (Adrian Balboa), Burt Young (Paulie), Carl Weathers (Apollo Creed), Brigitte Nielsen (Ludmilla), Tony Burton (Duke), Michael Pataki (Nicoli Koloff), Dolph Lundgren (Ivan Drago)*
Director: *Sylvester Stallone*
Screenwriter: *Sylvester Stallone*
PG/91 mins./Drama/USA

Rocky Balboa has wiped the floor with every heavyweight contender in America. But a new peril faces him, in the shape of Drago, a 261-pound Russian fighting machine whose ring technique is more primal and powerful than anything Rocky has yet encountered.

This is the one where the *Rocky* series threw in the towel on the credibility, even for this series of increasingly daft boxing fantasies. From numbers one to three (with one being a genuinely decent tale of sporting triumph) you still held onto the notion they were happening within a real universe. For some reason, Sylvester Stallone (who was now starring, writing, directing and not listening to good sense) decided it was high time that America's favourite unintelligible sports hero should fight the Cold War.

On closer inspection, the film seems to be more concerned with becoming some kind of homoerotic classic than a great nationalistic parable, the amount of time Stallone's camera lavishes on the bulging landscapes of his and the robotic Dolph Lundgren's bodies. The training sequence for Rocky, a staple of his micro-genre, tuned to the exhausting vibes of light rock and set in the Russian wilds (rather than good ol' Philly) involves him chopping wood and lifting trees so his biceps can reach the size of cannonballs and his veins stick out like grass snakes. It's enough to put you off the gym for life, if you hadn't otherwise.

The jingoism is blindingly awful, but by the time of the showdown, the film has descended into an unaware parody of itself. As Rocky enters the ring in his Stars'n'Stripes shorts, and the crowd of oppressed masses will soon change sides as, after taking his usual pounding, our man is inspired to fight back because he has the heart. Quite what this all means about the heart of America is hard to fathom, but maybe Sly was a highly prophetic soul as communism would end up losing on points anyway. Or as his laughable turd of a script has it: 'Russians are evil. Rocky will hurt them.' ★★ **IN**

⊙ ROCKY V (1990)

Starring: *Sylvester Stallone (Rocky Balboa), Talia Shire (Adrian Balboa), Burt Young (Paulie), Sage Stallone (Rocky Balboa), Burgess Meredith (Mickey Goldmill), Tommy Morrison (Tommy 'Machine' Gunn), Richard Gant (George Washington Duke), Tony Burton (Duke)*
Director: *John G. Avildsen*
Screenwriter: *Sylvester Stallone*
PG/104 mins./Drama/USA

Returning from his title bout in Russia, Rocky learns that he has lost most of his fortune due to an unscrupulous accountant. Even worse, a medical condition forces him to hang up his boxing gloves. When a hot new fighter asks Rocky to manage him things start looking up, but family problems and worse lie ahead.

Give Stallone his due – at least he tried something different. Like Rocky Balboa himself, his pet franchise succumbed increasingly to glamour and expensive thrills at the expense of credible drama, but with *Part V* the writer-star takes the Italian Stallion back to his raw beginnings on the poor, grimy streets of Philadelphia. It was a brave move that risked alienating young fans, as was depriving our brawny hero of a larger-than-life baddie to pummel in the final reel. Instead, Rocky is recast as a trainer, managing a hot new fighter with the absurd monicker of Tommy 'The Machine' Gunn.

Like most of this film, though, that storyline hasn't much chance of pleasing anyone, fan or not. However ludicrous Rocky's antics were in previous chapters, at least they were fun, with a cheesy montage and big fight guaranteed as part of the ticket price. Here, the seemingly invincible champ is brought way down to earth with brain damage and betrayal, and the magic is all but drained away. Even worse, the plot developments here are not only depressing but unbelievable. There's the spectral return of Burgess Meredith's Mickey – a scene which looks like a misplaced outtake from *Scrooged* – and a villainous boxing promoter who's a thinly disguised (and pretty lame) Don King parody. There's also a lot of feeble, mumbled banter from Balboa. And there's a focus on father-son/mentor-apprentice issues that makes almost every scene drag. This is the film that put the franchise in a coma – and the Rocky movie fans would rather forget. ★ **NDS**

⊙ ROCKY HORROR PICTURE SHOW (1975)

Starring: *Tim Curry (Dr Frank-N-Furter), Susan Sarandon (Janet Weiss), Barry Bostwick (Brad Majors), Richard O'Brien (Riff Raff), Patricia Quinn (Magnenta), Meat Loaf (Eddie)*
Director: *Jim Sharman*
Screenwriters: *Jim Sharman, Richard O'Brien, from the musical by O'Brien*
15/95 mins./Musical/Comedy/Horror/USA

A young couple get lost and stumble across a mad transvestite doctor from the planet Transsexual. He is in the midst of unveiling Rocky Horror, a humanoid creation who unfortunately spurns the doctor's advances, much to his annoyance . . .

Pretty much the grandaddy of all cult films, *The Rocky Horror Picture Show* became more of an interactive event than a stand- alone movie very soon after its release.

American college kids, gripped by a desire to leap into the 'don't dream it, be it' ethos of the mid 70s, got dragged up and generally horrified their parents, and, in doing so, transformed the movie into a hit, albeit a belated one.

Detached from the historical hoopla, you'd expect the film to be a bit on the time-withered side, but in fact it's stood the test of over a quarter of a century pretty well. The tunes are as loopily catchy as ever, Sharman's direction is zippy and the movie looks much bigger than the £1.5 million it cost.

But the powerhouse of the film is Tim Curry's cross-dressing alien, Frank N. Furter, who would never reach these kinds of gloriously demented heights again.

Simply a cult classic. See it once and laugh about it at dinner parties for the rest of your adult life. Or go along to the interactive viewings, dress up, and sing along. It's your call. ★★★★ **AS**

⊙ RODGER DODGER (2002)

Starring: *Campbell Scott (Roger Swanson), Jesse Eisenberg (Nick), Isabella Rossellini (Joyce), Elizabeth Berkley (Andrea), Jennifer Beals (Sophie)*
Director: *Dylan Kidd*
Screenwriter: *Dylan Kidd*
15/101 mins./Comedy/Drama/USA

Arrogant advertising copywriter Roger thinks he's capable of talking any woman into bed. But a night out on the tiles in Manhattan, teaching his 16-year-old nephew the rules of the game, reveals the flaws in Roger's worldview.

There's an obvious comparison to be made between Dylan Kidd's debut and Neil LaBute's *In The Company Of Men*: both feature cocky American office workers whose chat-up techniques and attitudes to women are misogynistic by anyone's definition.

But while LaBute's film is the more acidic of the two, Kidd is the more judgemental. Before the end, slick-talking Roger's career, family standing and sense of self-worth all come under attack.

The hand-held camerawork mirrors Roger's unsettled state, but this talk-heavy movie would be little more than a script on screen were it not for Scott's performance.

As a predator ruthlessly searching for vulnerability in his prey, Roger thinks himself a master of the universe. But as this uncle-nephew Faustian pact moves from penthouse to underground brothel, Scott chips away at Roger's obnoxious facade to reveal a man hell-bent on self-destruction. ★★★★ **AM**

⊙ ROLLERBALL (1975)

Starring: *James Caan (Jonathan E.), John Houseman (Bartholomew), Maud Adams (Ella), John Beck (Moonpie), Moses Gunn (Cletus), Ralph Richardson (Librarian)*
Director: *Norman Jewison*
Screenwriter: *William Harrison, based on his short story Roller Ball Murder*
15/119 mins./Action/Sci-fi/Sport/USA

Awards: *BAFTA – Best Art Direction*

The year is 2018 and Rollerball is the sport of the masses. Its star, Johnathan E., refuses to retire and in so doing challenges the corporations who now control the sport, and the world.

Set in a future where corporate giants rule the world, *Rollerball* depicts the battle of one man against the establishment. *Rollerball* was intended to be director Norman Jewison's big anti-violence statement, although it is easy to see how cinemagoers instead took it to be a celebration of an imaginary future-sport; the rollerball scenes are simply breathtaking, while the rest sinks without trace thanks to an over-wordy plot.

James Caan lends a farm boy innocence to the role of Jonathan E, the champion of the death sport that's worshipped by the inhabitants of this sanitised world, but who is becoming too popular for the establishment's liking.

Brilliant editing and some bone-crunching sound effects put you right in amongst the bloodthirsty crowd, and while the anti-capitalist message is a little heavy-handed at times, you can't beat this for adrenaline-pumping action.

A 2002 remake, directed by John McTiernan and starring Chris Klein, Jean Reno, LL Cool J and Rebecca Romijn, was high on flash and low on audience-gripping action. ★★★ **CC**

ROMAN HOLIDAY (1953)

Starring: *Gregory Peck (Joe Bradley), Audrey Hepburn (Princess Anne), Eddie Albert (Irving Radovich), Hartley Power (Mr Hennessy), Laura Solari (Hennessy's Secretary), Harcourt Williams (Ambassador), Margaret Rawlings (Countess Vereberg), Tullio Carminati (General Provno)*
Director: *William Wyler*
Screenwriters: *Ian McLellan Hunter, John Dighton based on a story by Dalton Trumbo*
U/119 mins./Romance-Comedy/USA

Awards: *Academy Awards – Best Actress, Best Screenplay, Best Costume Design, Black and White; BAFTA – Best British Actress*

Slipping away from her chaperons, Countess Vereberg and General Provno, Princess Anne goes on the lam in the Eternal City with American journalist Joe Bradley and photographer Irving Radovich. But true love prevents Joe from publishing his scoop.

A good deal of opportunistic pragmatism lay behind the production of this charming inversion of the Cinderella story. When Dalton Trumbo was blacklisted as part of the Hollywood Ten, Ian McLellan Hunter agreed to act as a front for his story idea, which was optioned by Frank Capra, who hoped to cast Cary Grant and Elizabeth Taylor in what amounted to a variation on his multi-Oscar-winning screwball, *It Happened One Night*. However, financial problems at his Liberty Films company forced him to sell the property to Paramount, where a combination of political timidity (on Capra's discovering Trumbo's involvement) and a tight budget prompted him to withdraw.

After George Stevens passed, the project was offered to William Wyler, who was not only glad to make his first comedy since the mid-1930s, but was also keen to work abroad in order to exploit a tax loophole. Paramount similarly saw the advantages of a runaway production (as it had assets frozen in Italy), while Gregory Peck, who had initially been reluctant to star opposite a newcomer, recognised the value of lightening his image. Even Audrey Hepburn – who had been chosen over Jean Simmons and Suzanne Cloutier, despite the fact that none of her seven European screen roles had amounted to much – realised this was her big chance to follow up her stage success in *Gigi*.

However, the cynicism and hard-nosed business sense that had shaped *Roman Holiday*'s genesis evaporated once shooting began. Wyler was as enchanted with Hepburn as he was with his glorious locations and, while he indulged his usual passion for retakes, he allowed more improvisation than usual and was rewarded with a film of such freewheeling spontaneity that it became one of Hollywood's biggest international hits of the decade. It also landed 10 Oscar nominations and became such a firm favourite of John F. Kennedy that he watched it as a pressure release at the height of the Cuban Missile Crisis and the Soviets capitulated the next day.

Witty, warm and beautifully filmed by Franz Planer and Henri Alekan, it remains an unabashed romantic delight, with Hepburn particularly luminescent. ★★★★ **DP**

ROMANCE (1998)

Starring: *Caroline Ducey (Marie), Sagamore Stevenin (Paul), Francois Berleand (Robert), Rocco Siffredi (Paolo)*
Director: *Catherine Breillat*
Screenwriters: *Catherine Breillat, Severine Siaut*
18/94 mins./Drama/France

Deeply in love but frustrated by her boyfriend's sexual inhibitions, a teacher turns to other sources to fulfil her mounting desires.

In copulating 251 times while shooting the recently released documentary, *Sex: The Annabel Chong Story*, its star claimed to have been driven by a radical need 'to project the power of female sexuality'. Jasmin St Claire (300) and Kimberley Houston (620) intimated much the same sentiment before embarking on their own attempts at the world gangbang record.

Fascinatingly, porn stars are permitted such fanciful justifications. But when a female French filmmaker depicts one or two acts of penetrative sex in an arthouse exploration of the relationship between emotion and physicality, the more self-righteous on the intellectual fringes of filmdom throw up their hands in disgust.

Marie is desperately in love. But, frustrated by the frigidity of her underendowed boyfriend Paul, she turns to an Italian stallion, an S&M maestro and a casual pick-up for her sexual fulfilment.

Partly inspired by Nagisa Oshima's *Ai No Corrida*, this audacious study of sex and sensibility also contains distinct echoes of Bertolucci's *Last Tango In Paris* and Luis Bueuel's *That Obscure Object Of Desire*. Director Breillat deserves credit for striding so boldly into what remains a largely male domain.

But while her visual approach is too detached to be erotic, her pronouncements are simply too predictable to be provocative. Only a disturbingly De Sadean brothel sequence and a live birth jolt the action out of its voyeuristic lethargy.

Breillat has certainly created a dangerously daring film. But whether she has succeeded in demolishing our preconditioned responses to lust and trust is another matter altogether. ★★★ **DP**

ROMANCING THE STONE (1984)

Starring: *Michael Douglas (Jack T. Colton), Kathleen Turner (Joan Wilder), Danny DeVito (Ralph), Zack Norman (Ira), Alfonso Arau (Juan)*
Director: *Robert Zemeckis*
Screenwriter: *Diane Thomas*
PG/100 mins./Action/Adventure/Comedy/Romance/USA

Awards: *Golden Globes – Best Comedy/Musical, Best Comedy/Musical Actress*

Joan Wilder, a writer of romantic novels, travels to South America to look for and rescue her kidnapped sister. She soon finds help in the form of the soldier of fortune Jack Colton.

A dizzy New York romance author dreams of action and adventure and an old-style rugged hero to whisk her away from her humdrum existence. As she delivers the latest of her books a mysterious treasure map turns up at her apartment, her sister is kidnapped and before she knows what's happening she's slap bang in the middle of the South American jungle, pursued by shady villains and accompanied by a reluctant, though distinctly rugged, Michael Douglas.

Cue action, adventure and, inevitably, romance. It's implausible, dementedly silly and lightweight – pure Hollywood fluff. But spinning top quality Hollywood fluff is no easy task, as the cinematically challenged Golan-Globus/Cannon Films would find the next year when they attempted to leap on the bandwagon with the truly dire *King Solomon's Mines*.

Critics, of course, dismiss the film as a cheap *Raiders* rip-off. It certainly has more than a few similarities: the relentless action and arch genre trappings, corrupt cops, exotic locales, ancient maps and lost gemstones. And given the success of Spielberg's blockbuster it was obvious in 1984 that the public was in the mood for innocent, adventure escapism. In fact, the two movies are very different, not least in tone. While Spielberg shied away from all but the briefest love interests for Indy, concerned no doubt that his audience of 12-year-old boys was more up for hectic heroism than soppy smooching, *Romancing The Stone* puts sexual chemistry at the heart of the movie along with the snappily directed action. Both elements are in evidence from the outset as in a brilliantly constructed credit sequence we see Joan Wilder both as she'd like to see herself – the feisty adventuress warding off black-hatted cowboys before being swept away by a shadowy stranger – and as she really is, a mousy novelist living alone in a tiny New York apartment with nothing but a cat and collection of booze miniatures.

Kathleen Turner is surprisingly effective as the introverted, shy scribe – especially surprising for audiences who had previously seen her as sex bomb Matty Walker in *Body Heat* three years earlier. She radiates charming nervousness while Douglas (who also produced) is the perfect foil for her initially timid, reluctant heroine. As pissed off exotic bird breeder Jack Colton, he's a distillation of every sweaty romantic hero from every pulp romance novel, but, initially at least, has none of the charm. 'They were Italian,' Wilder mourns as he hacks the heels off her shoes in the middle of the drenched Columbian jungle. 'Now they're practical,' he retorts. Inevitably the two begin to exchange 'glances' and embark on the Hollywood ritual of falling in love (a scene when they get to know one another while smoking dope in a crashed plane is a standout). It should all be sentimental, predictable and mawkish, but thanks to deft performances the potential for saccharine over-indulgence is avoided and there's a humanity and ease to the relationship.

But the main plaudits must go to director Zemeckis and screenwriter Diane Thomas. Spielberg himself had spotted Zemeckis as a like-minded director way back in 1978 when he executive produced the young director's debut *I Wanna Hold Your Hand*. They worked together on the ill-fated comedy *1941* and, post Romancing, on *Back To The Future* which was produced by Spielberg's Amblin Entertainment production company (Zemeckis would pay tribute to his mentor by naming the water taxi which carries Joan to her sister's kidnapper's lair The Orca, the name of the boat in *Jaws*).

The two share a populist sensibility and a flare for big screen action, but in *Romancing The Stone* Zemeckis demonstrates a capacity to realise the type of credible female characters that Spielberg has always struggled with. It shows an adroit, playful touch that, inexplicably, would be replaced with the crass, occasionally offensive, sentimentality of *Forrest Gump* and *Contact*. Tragically, Diane Thomas would never follow up her immensely promising scripting debut. A few months after *Romancing The Stone* was released to tremendous reviews and huge box office she was killed in a car accident. Mark Rosenthal and Lawrence Konner showed none of her lightness of touch in 1995's lacklustre cash-in sequel *The Jewel Of The Nile*. ★★★★ **AS**

◎ ROME, OPEN CITY (ROMA, CITTA APERTA) (1945)

Starring: *Anna Magnani (Pina), Giorgio Manfredi (Marcello Pagliero), Don Pietro (Aldo Fabrizi), Bergmann (Henry Feist), Ingrid (Giovanna Galletti), Maria (Maria Michi)*
Director: *Roberto Rossellini*
Screenwriters: *Serfio Amidei, Federico Fellini, from a story by Sergio Amidei, Alberto Consiglio*
15/97 mins./Drama/War/Italy

Needing to pass funds to his comrades, resistance leader Giorgio Manfredi enlists the help of lithographer Francesco, his pregnant fiancée Pina and Catholic priest Don Pietro, only for their plans to be betrayed to Nazi officer Bergmann's drug-dealing accomplice, Ingrid, by addict actress, Marina.

Few films have had as seismic an impact on world cinema as Roberto Rossellini's compelling, but unashamedly melodramatic account of the Italian underground's duel with the occupying Nazis. However, it wasn't the storyline that proved so influential, but the rough, newsreel-like visuals that brought a visceral immediacy and authenticity to the struggle of Fr Aldo Fabrizi's flawed, but courageous parishioners.

Financed by a politically committed old lady, Rossellini originally intended to make a pair of documentaries, about Don Pietro Morosini, who had been murdered by the Gestapo, and the part played by Rome's children in resisting the Germans. However, co-scenarists Federico Fellini and Sergio Amidei suggested combining the subjects into a single feature about the Eternal City's response to repression.

With Cinecittà out of action and electrical supplies unreliable, Rossellini decided to shoot on the streets in natural light on scavenged film stock. He also bolstered his cast with non-professionals. But the reliance on pathos, epitomised by Renzo Rossellini's manipulative score, disappointed advocates of pure neo-realism, while left-wingers lamented the quasi-religious sentiments of the finale, which seemingly equated defiance and optimism with the Catholic Church and not the Communist Party.

The film touched too many raw nerves to be accepted in Italy, where it was less successful than the second part of Rossellini's war trilogy, *Paisà* (1946). Written by six different writers, the episodes in this audaciously elliptical portmanteau followed the Allies from the 1943 Sicilian invasion to the Liberation. The action was pretty much improvised, yet Rossellini consistently linked his characters to their environment and managed to impart an individual imprint on vignettes designed to depict the war as a series of personal tragedies rather than an historico-military event.

The critics were less kind to *Germany, Year Zero* (1947), however, which was denounced by some as a naive apologia for the nation that had presented Hitler with his unprecedented mandate. Young Edward Moeschke's murder of his ailing father and subsequent suicide undeniably border on melodrama. But the sequence in which the Führer's recorded voice echoes around the bombed-out Berlin ruins has lost none of its terrifying power. ★★★★★ **AE**

◎ ROMEO AND JULIET (1968)

Starring: *Leonard Whiting (Romeo), Olivia Hussey (Juliet), John McEnery (Mercutio), Milo O' Shea (Friar Laurence), Pat Heywood (The Nurse), Robert Stephens (The Prince), Michael York (Tybalt)*
Director: *Franco Zeffirelli*
Screenwriters: *Franco Brusati, Masolino D'Amico, Franco Zeffirelli, adapted from the play by William Shakespeare*
PG/132 mins./Romance/Drama/UK/Italy
Awards: *Academy Awards – Best Cinematography, Best Costume Design; BAFTA – Best Costume Design; Golden Globes – Best English Language Foreign Film, Most Promising Newcomers (Olivia Hussey, Leonard Whiting)*

Two young lovers battle to love each other in Verona of old, their bickering families driving them to a tragic end.

Zeffirelli's absolutely ravishing version of The Bard's most popular piece packed in 1960s teens because he chose to cast two beautiful children – 15-year-old Olivia Hussey and 17-year-old Leonard Whiting – rather than experienced Shakespearians as the star-crossed lovers.

As a result, some of the poetry and power are lost (two of the most famous soliloquies were jettisoned), but the adolescent passions and grief are quite palpable.

The location work is breathtaking, with the duel between John McEnery's Mercutio and Michael York's Tybalt a thrilling set piece. Nino Rota's score is simply rapturous, and there were well-deserved Oscars for

Pasqualino De Santis' cinematography and Danilo Donati's costumes. ★★★ AE

⊙ ROMEO + JULIET (1996)

Starring: *Leonardo DiCaprio (Romeo), Claire Danes (Juliet), John Leguizamo (Tybalt), Harold Perrineau (Mercutio), Pete Postlethwaite (Father Laurence), Paul Sorvino (Fulgencio Capulet), Brian Dennehy (Ted Montague), Paul Rudd (Davis Paris), Vondie Curtis-Hall (Captain Prince)*
Director: *Baz Luhrmann*
Screenwriters: *Craig Pearce, Baz Luhrmann, based on the play by William Shakespeare*
12/120 mins./Drama/Romance/USA

Awards: *BAFTA – Anthony Asquith Award for Film Music, Best Production Design, Best Adapted Screenplay, David Lean Award for Direction*

Shakespeare's famous play is updated to the hip modern suburb of Verona still retaining its original dialogue.

A bare screen with a lone TV set in the middle. A brave opening for a movie. But this is a brave movie. The TV crackles into life and Shakespeare's introduction to *Romeo And Juliet* is recited as a modern day news broadcast. As the MTV-style editing kicks into gear, Baz Luhrmann takes the audience on a unique ride through one of the Bard's best-known texts, illuminating the story, occasionally subjugating the language but always delivering a vision that is bold, brassy, hugely inventive and accessible and, in a strange way, just right.

It was big a leap from an Antipodean dance hall with sequins to Shakespeare with guns, but one he appears more than accomplished enough to turn into something special. Just as *West Side Story* appropriated the source material to make the tale of young, tragic love contemporary in the early 60s, Luhrmann has contextualised the original text in the modern visual idiom. In short, Verona becomes Verona Beach, dude, and while a rapier is still a weapon, it's now the brand name of a particularly popular handgun.

This is a world in which Prince songs have become hymns sung by angelic choirs. To back up this modern reinterpretation, the director relies on two leads who regularly appropriate the epithets Best Actor/Actress Of His/Her Generation, and on the evidence here, these are titles most deserved.

DiCaprio brings his usual instinctive grace and gut-wrenching emotion to Romeo, a teenager beset by a first love doomed by a war between families, the Montagues and the Capulets, here recast as battling corporate bodies.

Meanwhile, anyone who saw Danes on TV's short-lived show *My So-Called Life* knew that here was a special talent. Her Juliet is young, yearning and genuinely moving, as close to a star-making performance as it is possible to get. ★★★★ **BM**

⊙ LA RONDE (1950)

Starring: *Anton Walbrook (Raconteur), Simone Signoret (Leocadie, the Prostitute), Serge Reggiani (Franz, the Soldier), Simone Simon (Marie, the Housemaid), Daniel Geelin (Alfred), Danielle Darrieux (Emma Breitkopf)*
Director: *Max Ophuls*
Screenwriters: *Jacques Natanson, Max Ophuls, from the play by Arthur Schnitzier*
PG/88 mins./Drama/France

Awards: *BAFTA – Best Film from any source*

An on-camera narrator observes a series of amorous encounters, in which lovers move on to other partners in a circle.

Arthur Schnitzler's play is so perfectly constructed it's a surprisingly hard adapt to the movies. Marcel Ophuls takes a daring approach by having Anton Walbrook as a ringmaster who even sings a song to keep the carousel turning. He strides into a stylised set representing Vienna in 1900, puts on period clothing, walks past film equipment and moves into a more 'realistic' but equally stagebound set, where he encounters the whore who starts and ends Schnitzler's round of liasions and seems to set the whole plot in motion like a clockwork toy.

Ophuls and Schnitzler are a natural match; here, with a French cast (Gerard Philippe, Simone Simon, Jean-Louis Barrault) as the Viennese characters, he manages the charm, cynicism and knowingness perfectly, never despising lecherous or self-deluded characters as the chain carries on with each participant playing different roles to play up to their current partners.

Much of Schnitzler's dialogue is retained, and played expertly – especially good is the momentary lapse (into impotence) of the young lover (Daniel Gelin) with the married woman (Danielle Darrieux), and the wife's wry exchange with her husband about his own wild youth and the dreadful sort of wives who take lovers.

Walbrook, a clear substitute for the director, carries off his role as deity and nobody perfectly, and the film's fussy period look explodes with touches of the fantastical to emphasise the artifice of it all. These people are, in one sense, tin toys, though there's also a great heart in the depiction of them all as foolish but somehow sympathetic, no matter how mean their behaviour might be, as this round is not only of seductions but punishments. ★★★★ **KN**

⊙ RONIN (1998)

Staring: *Robert De Niro (Sam), Jean Reno (Vincent), Natascha McElhone (Deirdre), Stellan Skarsgard (Gregor), Sean Bean (Sepnce), Jonathan Pryce (Seamus O'Rourke)*
Director: *John Frankenheimer*
Screenwriters: *J.D. Zeik, David Mamet as Richard Weisz, based on a story by Zeik*
15/116 mins./Action/Thriller/USA

A group of rogue outcasts are hired to steal a case from some ex-KGB spies. But one of them has his own agenda.

Essentially *Mission: Impossible* without the latex slap, John Frankenheimer's Parisian spy-heist is noticeably old-school and has a markedly more worthy international cast (although Reno has appeared in both franchises).

Ronin – meaning Samurai without a master – here refers to a group of rogue outcasts from all across the globe who are assembled by a woman desperate to get a case back from some ex-KGB spies about to sell it to the Russians. But once in possession of the case, one of the group seems to have an agenda of his own …

Despite solid performances from Robert De Niro and Jean Reno, though, the plot lacks enough dynamism to make *Ronin* memorable beyond the ace car chases, which are nothing short of spectacular. ★★★ **SR**

⊙ ROOM AT THE TOP (1959)

Starring: *Laurence Harvey (Joe Lampton), Simone Signoret (Alice Aisgill), Heather Sears (Susan Brown), Donald Wolfit, Ambrosine Phillpotts (Mrs Brown), Donald Houston (Charles Soames), Raymond Huntley (Mr Holyoake)*
Director: *Jack Clayon*
Screenwriter: *Neil Paterson, based on the novel by John Braine*
15/115 mins/Drama/UK

Awards: *Academy Awards – Best Actress, Best Adapted Screenplay; BAFTA – Best British Film, Best Film From Any Source, Best Foreign Actress*

Joe Lampton arrives in the thriving Yorkshire town of Warnley and sets out to elevate his social status by seducing wealthy industrialist's daughter Susan Brown. However, by the time of his shotgun wedding, he has fallen for Alice Aisgill, an unhappily married Frenchwoman, who is 10 years his senior and ruinously in love with him.

A ROOM FOR ROMEO BRASS

Although John Osborne's *Look Back in Anger* had already opened at the Royal Court Theatre, it was Jack Clayton's adaptation of John Braine's scathing portrait of northern working-class life that turned social realism into headline news. It was one thing for continental films to tackle such taboo topics as pre-marital sex and adultery. But no British film had previously discussed such adult situations in so caustic a vernacular, let alone depicted them with such casual frankness. For viewers reared on Ian Carmichael and Norman Wisdom, *Room at the Top* was a devastating discovery, made all the more thrillingly immediate by the fact that so much of the action related to their own everyday experience.

There had been cads in British movies before. But James Mason's sins had been committed in costume in Gainsborough period romps that consciously romanticised his roguery. Laurence Harvey, however, wore an ordinary suit and worked in the borough treasurer's department. Moreover, he was a former RAF POW. Yet, he was prepared to use his looks and charm to seduce his way to affluence and acceptability.

But while Joe Lampton was cynical and exploitative, he wasn't an archetypal 'angry young man'. He was proud of his roots: he just recognised their inconvenience to his aspiration. Moreover, despite Jack Clayton and Freddie Francis's evocative use of their Yorkshire locations, this wasn't exactly a 'kitchen sink' drama, either, as neither Heather Sears's naive daddy's girl nor Simone Signoret's coolly sensual outsider skivvied away in the inner-city backstreets.

However, Neil Paterson's acrid screenplay still scandalised the British Establishment and so appalled the Breen Office that it was denied a release certificate. Indeed, this did as much for the film's international reputation as its raft of awards, which eventually included a Best Actress Oscar for Signoret. Despite being on screen for a comparatively short time, she walks away with the picture and her sophisticated passion contrasts sharply with Harvey's poorly accented and occasionally awkward display of narcissistic chauvinism. ★★★★ **DP**

A ROOM FOR ROMEO BRASS (1999)

Starring: *Andrew Shim (Romeo Brass), Ben Marshall (Gavin 'Knock Knock' Woolley), Paddy Considine (Morell), Frank Harper (Joseph Brass), Julia Ford (Sandra Woolley), James Higgins (Bill Woolley), Vicky McClure (Ladine Brass), Shane Meadows (Fish and Chip Shop Man)*
Director: *Shane Meadows*
Screenwriters: *Paul Fraser, Shane Meadows*
15/86 mins./Drama/Comedy/UK

A teenage boy growing up on a Midlands council estate befriends an awkward loner, much to the chagrin of the boy's best friend.

The brilliant *TwentyFourSeven* was a commercial dud, despite critical approbation, film festival hype and a note-perfect marketing campaign. Why? Because it was in black and white? Because it didn't have Julia Roberts in it? What are we, a nation of total Philistines?

Don't fret. Still in his 20s, Shane Meadows has plenty of time to turn into a bums-on-seats filmmaker – for now, let us be grateful that someone in the British film industry has ambitions above and beyond sentimentalising the working class or chasing the American dollar (or both). For those who have also seen his earlier, amateur work, *Romeo Brass* is instantly recognisable as A Shane Meadows Film – for its setting (Nottingham estate), its story (simple, domestic, free of allegory) and its style (naturalistic, often hilarious but with a serious core). It centres on two 13-year-old boys, one black, one crippled, Romeo and Knocks, alienated from their families and drifting. They befriend a childlike man in a van, Morell (Considine, beguiling in his first professional acting role), and the film traces their doomed relationship.

There are, once again, shades of Ken Loach in the painful portraits of fractured family life; there is no join-the-dots abuse here, but Romeo's father (Frank Harper, emerging here as the new Ray Winstone) is estranged, and Knocks' dad is an emotion-shy couch potato. As writers, Meadows and childhood pal Paul Fraser share Mike Leigh's ear for heard dialogue, which, mixed with partly improvised performances, brings a reality to the proceedings that makes it both extra-warm and extra-disturbing when it all goes off at the end. ★★★★ **AC**

A ROOM WITH A VIEW (1985)

Starring: *Maggie Smith (Charlotte Bartlett), Helena Bonham Carter (Lucy Honeychurch), Denholm Elliot (Mr Emerson), Julian Sands (George Emerrson), Daniel Day-Lewis (Cecil Vyse), Simon Callow (Rev. Mr Beebe), Patrick Godfrey (Rev. Mr Eager)*
Director: *James Ivory*
Screenwriter: *Ruth Prawer Jhabvala, based on the novel by E.M. Forster*
PG/117 mins./Drama/UK

Awards: *Academy Awards – Best Art Direction, Best Costume Design, Best Adapted screenplay; BAFTA – Best Actress (Maggis Smith), Best Supporting Actress (Judi Dench), Best Film, Best Production Design*

Lucy Honeychurch, a passionate girl repressed by society and an loveless engagement, has her life thrown into turmoil when she meets George Emerson, a man of lesser social standing who with his father offers to change their Florence hotel rooms with her and her chaperone as their's has a view. When she returns to England and her fiancé, she finds she cannot forget him, especially when he moves in locally.

The most adorable of all the Merchant-Ivory productions, as it is the one that breaks through cleanest and truest to the heart while retaining all the porcelain grace and sumptuous art direction that is their wont, this adaptation of E.M. Forster's romantic novel is a high-class British classic. There was something liberating in the initial setting of Florence and its magnificent countryside, such that it injects their usual refined poise with genuine sexual undercurrents. Unforgettable images of heady beauty, these images are literary dreams painted with languid cinematography.

But the wit is what makes this film so much more alive than their other shapely but frozen adaptations. Ruth Prawer Jhabvala's biting script gives wings to both Forster's sweeping romance (when will stifled Lucy realise she has fallen for liberated George?) and his social satire. Once the film is grounded back in England, a comfy well-bred Surrey contrasted as a fussier, less elegant version of paradise than poetic Florence, James Ivory mines rich humour out of the crowd of characters that will come between the couple, and the various contrasts between the plain-speaking Emersons' and the Honeychurchs' starchy social circle.

Thus, for all its magnificent looks, it is a film of delightful performances. Familiar faces (and for one skinny dipping sequence, bottoms) breathing vital life into the succession of long-winded names: Maggie Smith, Judi Dench, Simon Callow, a lovely, understated Denholm Elliot, and Daniel Day Lewis injecting an air of wounded pride into the priggish Cecil, transforming a panto dupe into a decent man unable to connect. By comparison the leads, Helena Bonham Carter and Julian Sands, feel more like ciphers, but they have our hearts anyway. ★★★★★ **IN**

ROPE (1948)

Starring: *James Stewart (Rupert Cadell), John Dall (Shaw Brandon), Farley Granger (Phillip), Joan Chandler (Janet Walker), Cedrick Hardwicke (Mr David Kentley's Father), Constance Collier (Mrs Atwater), Edith Evanson (Mrs Wilson, The Governess)*
Director: *Alfred Hitchcock*
Screenwriter: *Arthur Laurents, Hume Cronyn, Ben Hecht, based on the play* Rope's End *by Patrick Hamilton*
PG/80 mins./Thriller/USA

Shaw Brandon and his roommate Phillip strangle their Harvard undergraduate friend, David, and hide his body in a trunk in the middle of their apartment. However, during the course of a single evening, their crime is eventually uncovered by their old, war-wounded prep school teacher, Rupert Cadell.

Always keen to set himself technical challenges, Alfred Hitchcock took more risks than usual in making *Rope*. It was not only his first film as producer-director for the Transatlantic Pictures company that he had founded with Sidney Bernstein, but it was also his first colour feature. Moreover, he proposed to shoot the action in real-time continuous takes, with direct sound, within a single studio set. Following 10 days of acting and camera rehearsals, he completed the assignment in 18 days for $1,500,000, with James Stewart's fee and the New York backdrop accounting for much of the expense.

Based on the infamous Chicago case of Leopold and Loeb, Patrick Hamilton's 1929 play, *Rope's End*, echoed the theme of corrupting arrogance that Hitch had just tackled in *The Paradine Case*, in which he had also used fluid camera movements to emphasise Alida Valli's inexorable ensnarement of Gregory Peck.

However, the Production Code forced him to downplay the killers' homosexuality, although it was frequently alluded to in Arthur Laurents's screenplay and reinforced by Brandon's interrupted piano renditions of the gay composer Francis Poulenc's 'Perpetual Movement No.1'. Hitchcock also toned down the play's comparison between Brandon and Philip's cold-blooded crime and Rupert's war record. However, the implication remained that the moral gap between the tutor and his onetime pupils was not as wide as events suggested it to be.

There was almost a stunt ingenuity about Joseph Valentine and William V. Skall's camerawork. But Hitchcock succeeded splendidly in using placement, distance and angle to approximate the psychological and intellectual impact of montage. His exploitation of the meticulously operated living skyline, with its spun-glass clouds and twinkling lights, was just as masterly, particularly as night set in and he treated himself to the mischievous sight gag of illuminating a sign saying 'Storage' over the trunk containing the corpse.

Ultimately, this was something of a self-indulgent exercise in style. It was certainly more clever than compelling, especially as the acting was occasionally somewhat theatrical. But *Rope* was as dark as anything that Hitchcock attempted before *Psycho* and, moreover, it was very daring for its time. ★★★★ **DP**

ⓓ ROSEMARY'S BABY (1968)

Starring: *Mia Farrow (Rosemary Woodhouse), John Cassavetes (Guy Woodhouse), Ruth Gordon (Minnie Castevet), Sidney Blackmer (Roman Castevet), Maurice Evans (Edward 'Hutch' Hutchins), Ralph Bellamy (Dr Abraham Sapirstein)*
Director: *Roman Polanski*
Screenwriter: *Roman Polanski, based on the novel by Ira Levin*
18/136 mins./Horror/USA

Awards: *Academy Awards – Best Supporting Actress (Ruth Gordon); Golden Globes – Best Supporting Actress (Ruth Gordon)*

Rosemary and Guy Woodhouse move into an apartment in a building with a bad reputation. They discover that their neighbours are a very friendly elderly couple named Roman and Minnie Castevet, but are they a little too friendly?

Talk about strange food cravings and hormonal crazies. Welcome to the most famously difficult pregnancy in movies. Surprisingly, this elegant treat was produced by William Castle, the shrewd and indefatigable schlockmeister whose gimmick-promoted oeuvre includes *Macabre* (1958) (for which Castle handed out Lloyds policies insuring moviegoers against death by fright), *The Tingler* (1959) (for which he had electric shock buzzers wired under some theatre seats) and *House On Haunted Hill* (1958) (at which skeletons flew over the audience's heads).

Rosemary's Baby was the ambitious and aesthetic highpoint of Castle's career. Thank God he didn't direct it. The property itself was a clear winner. Novelist Ira Levin's page-turner of witches on Manhattan's Upper West Side was a best-selling sensation, and his work has a creepy, compelling energy irresistible to filmmakers (*A Kiss Before Dying* (1956), *The Stepford Wives* (1975), *The Boys From Brazil* (1978)). But Polanski had an important reservation about Levin's novel. Polanski had seen too much real horror in his life – and this was before the Manson murders – to treat diabolism seriously. He added notes of fantasy and black comedy to a grim fairy-tale and emphasised its psychological undertones. His screenplay adaptation (Academy Award nominated) does stick to the story. Young newlyweds Rosemary and Guy Woodhouse, he a struggling actor, rent and prettily redecorate a gloomy but spectacular apartment in The Branford, an apartment building with an unpleasant history of cannibalism, witchcraft, infanticide and suicide. (The film was shot at the exclusive Dakota Building at 1 West 72nd Street, where the remarkable tenant roster has included Boris Karloff, Lauren Bacall and John Lennon, who was murdered outside.) They are befriended by aged, eccentric neighbours, the raucous Minnie and well-travelled Roman Castevet. During her longed-for pregnancy (after dreaming that she'd been raped by something monstrous), oddities, miseries and weirdness accrue before Rosemary realises the Castevets lead a witches' coven. She becomes convinced they want to sacrifice her baby to the Devil, and that her husband has agreed to help them in return for professional success.

The 'truth' is even worse than Rosemary's feverish imagination and mounting paranoia paints it, but Polanski, who so shockingly depicted a sexually repressed, solitary young woman going crazy in *Repulsion* (1965), keeps things as disturbingly unsettled and ambiguous as he can right up to the end. Rosemary doesn't work, she never sees friends or communicates with the large family she mentions, and she's married to a vain, selfish man – well, he's an actor – all of which reinforces her isolation. Her Catholic guilt and sexual repression are reflected in her dreams: surreal sequences in which John and Jackie Kennedy, nuns, and the Pope flit through erotic fantasies. When Rosemary and Guy actually have sex it isn't spontaneous or heated but studied and pre-arranged.

The film revolves around Farrow, who is in all but a very few shots. Polanski slyly exploits her mannered childishness. Even before she gets pregnant she wears shapeless little smocks and flat, little girl shoes. When she has her hair trendily cropped at Vidal Sassoon (one of the film's ubiquitous, precise notations of a cultural signpost for the year of the story, 1965-66) she is even more pathetically waifish. She is so unwomanly it seems odd that Cassavetes' Guy would be married to her, unless it is for her compliance. Easily led, Rosemary repeats parrot-fashion other characters' statements and allows herself to be utterly dominated. Polanski's first choice for Guy was Robert Redford, who turned it down. It would have been interesting to see Guy as a golden boy whose darkness and betrayal is not so evident and plausible as it is in Cassavetes' sardonic style.

The elderly folk around them are all highly-seasoned, savvy veteran actors. Seventy-two-year-old Ruth Gordon was a Broadway star more widely renowned as the screenwriter (with her husband Garson Kanin) of witty hits including *Adam's Rib*. Her pushy Minnie scores at every turn, with her syllable enhanced shrieks of 'preg-a-nant!' and 'ca-lumsy!', her outre dress sense, and her hausfrau mentality that makes her more concerned about the mark left in her hardwood floor by Rosemary's knife than she is about any threat from the distraught young woman.

That she could be the lynchpin of a satanic conspiracy is hilariously fantastic. Hers is an inspired performance, and it won her an Oscar. More soberly Sidney Blackmer and Ralph Bellamy provide nicely judged grandfatherly-but-

1 **'I believe in America.' (Bonasera, *The Godfather*)**

2 **'Saigon ... Shit. Still only in Saigon.' (Captain Willard, *Apocalypse Now*)**

3 **'Choose life.' (Renton, *Trainspotting*)**

4 **'All my life I wanted to be a gangster.' (Henry Hill, *Goodfellas*)**

5 **'My mother died of pneumonia when I was just a kid. My father had kept their wedding cake in the freezer for ten whole years. After the funeral he gave it to the yard man. He tried to act cheerful, but he could never be consoled by the little stranger he found in his house...' (Holly, *Badlands*)**

6 **'Fiddle-dee-dee. War, war, war.' (Scarlett O'Hara, *Gone With the Wind*)**

7 **'My name is Lester Burnham. I'm 42 years old. In less than a year, I'll be dead.' (Lester Burnham, *American Beauty*)**

8 **'Yes, this is Sunset Boulevard, Los Angeles, California. It's about five o'clock in the morning. That's the homicide squad, complete with detectives and newspaper men...' (the late Joe Gillis, *Sunset Boulevard*)**

9 **'Car 727. Car 727. Open door at the Watergate office building. Possible burglary.' (Police call, *All The President's Men*)**

10 **'What can you say about a twenty-five-year-old girl who died? That she was beautiful and brilliant? That she loved Mozart and Bach, the Beatles, and me?' (Oliver, *Love Story*)**

sinister figures to whom Rosemary fatefully defers. Maurice Evans, whose illustrious stage career has been overshadowed by his Dr Zaius in the *Planet Of The Apes* cycle, is the concerned, avuncular old friend Hutch, whose bequest to Rosemary, a book on witchcraft and the deathbed message 'The name is an anagram,' stir her to action for a nail-biting 30 minutes.

But even at the last minute you can't be sure she isn't crazy. Maybe they're all nuts. We never see what is in that black-draped cradle. It's that smile playing on Rosemary's lips, suggesting that her maternal instinct and the conspirators' hold on this vapid baby doll have prevailed, that provides the biggest chill. ★★★★ **AE**

THE ROYAL TENENBAUMS (2001)

Starring: *Gene Hackman (Royal Tenenbaum), Anjelica Huston (Etheline Tenenbaum), Gwyneth Paltrow (Margot Tenenbaum), Ben Stiller (Chas Tenenbaum), Luke Wilson (Richie Tenebaum), Owen Wilson (Eli Cash), Danny Glover (Henry Sherman), Bill Murray (Raleigh St Clair), Alec Baldwin (Narrator)*
Director: *Wes Anderson*
Screenwriters: *Wes Anderson, Owen Wilson*
15/105 mins./Comedy/Drama/USA

Awards: *Best Musical/Comedy Actor (Gene Hackman)*

The child prodigies of the Tenenbaum family — Chas, Margot and Richie — have fallen on hard times in adulthood, something they blame on their estranged father, Royal. However, when he announces that he has only weeks to live, the family is reunited for the first time in years.

For all its critical adoration, Wes Anderson's break through film, the quirky 1998 comedy *Rushmore*, was a genuine love-it-or-loathe-it experience. Chances are that if you fell into the latter category, *The Royal Tenenbaums* will have a similar effect – for this is yet another reminder that a trip into Wes' world is riddled with offbeat eccentricities, damaged, dysfunctional characters and the kind of weird, wonderful comedy that comes along all too rarely.

While not a film for everybody, there's no doubt that this is a dazzlingly original piece of work. It's a more accomplished film than *Rushmore*, sharing many similar themes and ideas while at the same time taking the comic complexities of its characters to new levels.

Hackman, who nabbed a Golden Globe for his performance as the curmudgeonly Royal Tenenbaum, is as good here as he's ever been. When we first meet him, we learn through a narrator that he is now living in a hotel, away from his family. His wife, Etheline, who is being romanced by colleague Henry- the closest thing this film has to a 'normal' character – wants nothing to do with him, and his children blame him entirely for their hang-ups.

One-time financial whizz kid Chas, recently widowed, protects his two sons in a fortress-like setting; Margot, an award-winning playwright, hasn't put pen to paper for seven years; and former tennis ace Richie is on a boat in the middle of nowhere.

Royal's desire to be accepted as a parent serves as the catalyst to reunite these lost souls, who gather at the family home on learning he is dying and come to terms with their losses and repressed feelings.

None of this sounds like material for a rip-roaring comedy, but Anderson and Wilson's smart screenplay relies more on small subtleties, obtuse one-liners and quirks by the dozen, while never insulting the intelligence of its audience. And the sight gags are superb – witness Richie mooching around in a headband, or Stiller dressing his sons in matching tracksuits exactly like the one he wears.

Tagline
Family isn't a word. It's a sentence.

It's a testament to Anderson's pulling power that he can attract such a good team of players with only his third film, suggesting that he may well go on to rival the likes of Paul Thomas Anderson in the ensemble cast stakes.

While not everybody has a great deal to do, the whole cast is fabulous and every character is memorable – from Bill Murray as Paltrow's kindly but rather dull hubby, to Owen Wilson's inspired turn as a drug-addled novelist, desperate to be a part of the Tenenbaum clan. However, the wackiness is undercut with an element of pure poignancy, making the film's slower moments almost heartbreaking and reminding us that sometimes human tragi-comedy can be the most effective of all. While this isn't a world you would have any wish to inhabit, it's one you do find hard to leave. Yet for all its sadness, Anderson still comes up with a final pay-off which will leave you chuckling long after the credits roll. ★★★★ **CW**

THE RUGRATS MOVIE (1998)

Starring: the voices of: *E. G. Daily (Tommy Pickles), Christine Pickles (Chuckie Finster), Kath Soucie (Philip Deville/Lillian Deville/Betty Deville), Melanie Chartoff (Didi Pickles/Minka), Iggy Pop (Newborn baby), Whoopi Goldberg (Ranger Margaret)*
Directors: *Norton Virgien, Igor Kovalyov*
Screenwriters: *J. David Stern, David N. Weiss, from characters by Arlene Klasky, Gabor Csupo, Paul Germain*
U/79 mins./Animated/Comedy/Adventure/Family/USA

When one of a group of toddler friends gains a brother, the toddlers decide to return the little tike to the hospital.

Those familiar with *The Rugrats* cartoon from Saturday morning TV will know its episodes are short, snappy purveyors of superb baby/toddler's eye-views of a grown-up world. So expansion of the witty format into an 80-minute plot might raise an eyebrow. After all, aren't rugrat attention spans as short as, well, Rugrats?

The inevitable concession is to remove the 'rats – the permanently nappied Tommy Pickles, his domineering cousin Angelica, his bespectacled friend Chuckie, his neighbours' twins Phil and Lil and dog Spike – from the Pickles suburban home and give them a big wide world adventure. The catalyst is the birth of Tommy's brother Dylan and our heroes' decision to return him to the 'hop-sickle' (the hospital to you) in order to restore normal life. Taking off in the Reptar Wagon, one of Tommy's dad's inventions, they end up lost in the forest at the mercy of escaped circus monkeys, the elements and a big bad wolf. While their families are searching for them (shadowed by TV news crews), Tommy learns to love his baby bro' and all The Rugrats learn life lessons.

Young 'uns will delight in the constant stream of nappy gags while for adults there's a number of film references – it opens like Baz Luhrmann's *Romeo And Juliet*, shifts into a superb *Raiders Of The Lost Ark* pastiche, and tips its hat to *The Fugitive* and *Bambi* – but it's unlikely this will draw in unaccompanied adult fans of the Saturday experience.

Nonetheless, it's well drawn and the chuckles come thick and fast. And any film which uses a bunch of rock stars (including Lenny Kravitz, Patti Smith and Iggy Pop) to sing a maternity ward musical set piece has got to be worth a look.

Two sequels followed, both as satisfying to the core audience. ★★★ **NJ**

THE RULES OF ATTRACTION (2002)

Starring: *James Van Der Beek (Sean Bateman), Shannyn Sossamon (Lauren Hynde), Ian Somerhalder (Paul Denton), Jessica Biel (Lara), Kip Pardue (Victor), Thomas Ian Nicholas (Mitchell), Kate Bosworth (Kelly), Fred Savage (Mark), Eric Stoltz (Mr Lance Lawson), Faye Dunaway (Mrs. Denton)*
Director: *Roger Avary*
Screenwriter: *Roger Avary, based on the novel by Bret Easton Ellis*

Campus drug dealer Sean thinks Lauren is sending him love letters, but she's saving her virginity for boyfriend Victor, who's visiting Europe. Bisexual Paul is drawn to Sean's dark side and once dated Lauren. Meanwhile, their fellow students prepare for the weekend's End Of The World Party . . .

r

RUN LOLA RUN (LOLA RENNT)

The prettier they are on the outside, the uglier they are on the inside. That's General Rule Of Thumb # 1 in the acerbic vision of Bret Easton Ellis. His depictions of spoilt rich kids filling the empty hours of their empty days with empty pursuits defined an American generation in seminal 80s novels *Less Than Zero* and *The Rules Of Attraction*.

It was a natural progression for these emotionally vacuous, callous, surface-obsessed characters to evolve into Patrick Bateman and his designer-label fantasy life in *American Psycho*. Here was Ellis' definitive statement on how boredom and self-loathing turned the world into a malicious, egocentric playground for the privileged.

Inner ugliness must be hereditary in the Bateman family, as Patrick's brother Sean is the main character in *The Rules Of Attraction*. The campus drug dealer at a New England arts college, Sean hasn't yet developed his sibling's talent for dismemberment and mutilation, but he's the master when it comes to laying waste to the emotions of the girls he sleeps with.

It's just as well that they're usually too stoned to notice or care. Daddy's favourites – both male and female – are gorgeous to behold, but they're already displaying a repulsive vicious streak that will no doubt take them far when they enter into their ready-made jobs in big business or go off to squander their trust funds.

Ellis' books have translated fairly well to the big screen. Perhaps the Brat Pack (Robert Downey Jr aside) were a little lightweight for Marek Kanievska's *Less Than Zero*, but Christian Bale and director Mary Harron perfectly captured the writer's spirit in their version of *American Psycho*. Here, however, Roger Avary tops them all, with a movie that's as stylistically bold as its content is unflinchingly honest.

If Avary's script input into *Pulp Fiction* was swept aside by Tarantino fever (as was his so-so directorial debut, *Killing Zoe*), then *The Rules Of Attraction* should at last give him the credit he deserves.

As he rewinds chunks of the action back to cross the story over to another character, he uses cinematic tricks that give the film a cooler-than-thou energy, but also underline the consequences of the characters' selfish behaviour.

These kids literally have no forward momentum, other than the fact that they're headed on a multiple collision course. The rewinds, split-screen sequence and speeded-up video diary of Victor's trip to Europe (a set piece as remarkable as any in *Pulp Fiction*) make for an extremely self-conscious film language, but no more so than Ellis' prose.

Both author and director relish a style that, like their characters, struts around like a peacock proudly drawing attention to itself. As Sean, James Van Der Beek ruthlessly undermines his *Dawson's Creek* image – almost the first time we see him he's in extreme close-up, his angry, red face straining during sex.

Perhaps Sossamon and Somerhalder's characters elicit more sympathy than most Ellis creations, but they are far from innocent. Avary is not trying to paper over harsh truths: an edgy mood of coked-up tension ripples through his campus parties, which aren't fun events but stalking grounds for couples on the lookout for loveless sex. Maybe early on, the director encourages us to laugh at the characters' pretensions. But when real pain enters into the fray, it hits the audience like a kick in the teeth.
★★★★ AM

◑ RUN LOLA RUN (LOLA RENNT) (1998)

Starring: *Franka Potente (Lola), Moritz Bleibtreu (Manni), Herbert Knaup (Vater), Nina Petri (Jutta Hansen), Armin Rohde (Herr Shcuster)*
Director: *Tom Tykwer*
Screenwriter: *Tom Tykwer*
15/80 mins./Crime/Drama/Romance/Germany

When Lola's boyfriend leaves 100,000 Deutschmarks of his drug running boss's money on the subway, Lola has twenty minutes to replace the money and get it to her lover before he is Krispy Kremed.

Foreign-language action pictures are all too rare, but *Run Lola Run*, with its portmanteau structure, frenetic pace and searing techno soundtrack, proves that the genre isn't just confined to Hollywood.

What's more, this stylish, hugely likeable bit of adrenaline-pumped Euro-nonsense should shatter the illusions of those convinced that all subtitled fare is musty, wordy and dull.

Scarlet-haired Berlin punk Lola is spurred into athletic action when her petty gangster boyfriend Manni calls her in desperation at 11.40 a.m.; he's just left the spoils of his latest drug deal (100,000 Deutschmarks) on the subway, and is liable to wind up as sandwich filling when his somewhat antisocial boss turns up at noon to claim the loot. Lola has just 20 minutes to replace the cash and race across town to rescue her soon-to-be-dead lover. And if she doesn't, he'll rob the nearby convenience store, an idea likely to land the pair in even bigger trouble.

Working with a pared-down script that focuses on non-stop action, Tykwer's movie tells the same story three different ways, giving a tricksy spin to what is essentially identical footage of our heroine pounding the pavement, and creating characters it's easy to care about. Even though they say little and reveal even less about themselves, you'll be willing them to succeed by the time the story enters its third incarnation.

Meanwhile, the gloomy, imposing Berlin backdrops are livened up enormously by animated sequences, flashy editing and some hugely effective gimmickry (the characters Lola encounters on her marathon meet different fates in every version of the tale, all of which are played out in snapshot form).

Combining the best elements of a mainstream blockbuster with low-budget European sensibilities, Tykwer has created breathlessly exhilarating cinema that will satisfy multiplex-goers as well as arthouse lovers – in other words, exactly the sort of movie that Britain ought to be making.
★★★★ CW

◑ THE RUNNING MAN (1987)

Starring: *Arnold Schwarzenegger (Ben Richards), Maria Conchita Alonso (Amber Mendez), Yaphet Kotto (William Laughlin), Jim Brown (Fireball), Jesse Ventura (Captain Freedom), Richard Dawson (Damon Killian)*
Director: *Paul Michael Glaser*
Screenwriter: *Steven E. de Souza, based on the short story by Stephen King*
PG/117 mins./Sci-fi/USA

In the near future, convicted criminals are forced to take part as bait in a hideous TV manhunt. When Ben Richards refuses to fire on a crowd of starving citizens, he is picked to go on the show, and must survive such hunters as Captain Freedom and Fireball before teaming up with some revolutionaries and fighting back.

Arnold Schwarzenegger may have been in his ascendancy in the late 80s, but this duff piece of dystopian sci-fi warbling, based very loosely on a Stephen King short story and optimistically aiming for satire, could well have been a piece straight-to-video trash if it wasn't for the hulking, monosyllabic presence of the big man. Strangely, time has given its preposterous ideas of capital punishment as reality TV a meniscus of relevance (in the face of recent obsessions with real-life consumed programming) but no amount of bitter humour can make-up for the shoddy production values, ham-fisted action, awful performances (and wackier casting) and over-reliance on Schwarzenegger tossing out turgid one liners when a scene inevitably flags.

Surprisingly, given how indifferent the script is, it was written by Steven E. de Souza who lent *Commando* an ironic glint, but here seems stranded, caught between the potential for caustic relevance (a future driven by TV consumption while downtrodden masses starve) and the necessity of crunching Arnie-action. There is some unctuous urgency in

Fictional Movie Acronyms And What They Stand For

1 CHUD - Cannibalistic Humanoid Underground Dwellers, or Contamination Hazard Urban Disposal
2 DARYL - Data Analyzing Robot Youth Lifeform
3 DOA - Dead On Arrival
4 FUBAR - Fucked Up Beyond All Recognition
5 IPCRESS - Induction of Psycho-neuroses by Conditioned Reflex with StresS
6 M*A*S*H* - Mobile Army Surgical Hospital
7 SFW - So Fucking What
8 S1mOne - Simulation One
9 SPECTRE - Special Executive for Counter Intelligence, Terror, Revenge and Extortion
10 TIE - Twin-Ion Engines (fighters, *Star Wars*)

Richard Dawson's take on the smarmy TV host who sends his victims off down a shoot to get running before the hulks in tights try to fry or chainsaw them to bits. Such lumpen foils as Jim Brown and Jesse Ventura (and a clutch of former pro-wrestlers) take on the job of annihilating the Lycra-clad Schwarzenegger but only manage to make him not the worst actor on show.

There is more madness awaiting the film as it desperately tries to pad out the telling but slight King story of an ordinary man caught in this television created nightmare – aged rockers Mick Fleetwood and Dweezel Zappa turn up as revolutionaries camped out in the backlot ruins of the show. Now Schwarzenegger, sounding words like depth charges with all the varied intonation of a bassoon, must take up the cause with pretty Maria Conchita Alonso, which amounts to little more than a splurge of tame explosions and lot of shooting, accompanied by those increasingly stale one-liners bouncing off the four walls. Director (and former Starsky) Paul Michael Glaser's dreaded futurescape amounts to a few chainlink fences and oil drums ready for the exploding, making *Blade Runner* seem, like, well *Blade Runner* (it's not even worth the comparison). However, with history's helpful hindsight, it transpires the greatest nonsense of all was the very idea of casting the Governor of California as a revolutionary: 'I'm not into politics, I'm into survival.' Yeah, whatever. ★★★★ **IN**

RUNNING ON EMPTY (1988)

Starring: *Christine Lahti (Annie Pope), River Phoenix (Danny Pope), Judd Hirsch (Arthur Pope), Jonas Abry (Harry Pope), Martha Plimpton (Lorna Phillips)*
Director: *Sidney Lumet*
Screenwriter: *Naomi Foner*
15/111 mins./Drama/USA
Awards: *Golden Globes – Best Screenplay*

The Popes have a reclusive life-on-the-lam existence since, in their radical student days, Mummy and Daddy blew up a napalm factory and having been fleeing the Feds ever since. Now their 17-year-old son, Danny is offered a prestigious music scholarship and they must deal with his participation in the world and the danger it may bring to their door.

What would it be like growing up 'underground' with parents who have been fugitives on the run from the law for 15 years? It's an unusual premise for a superior family drama from Sidney Lumet, a director renowned for making entertaining films with a social conscience: *Twelve Angry Men, Fail Safe, The Offence, Serpico, Network, The Verdict*. Having previously explored the 'sins' of dissident parents being visited on their children with the brave, ambitious, commercially disastrous *Daniel*, Lumet went for a more modest, accessible project on a related theme: 'Why do you have to carry the burden of someone else's life?'

Arthur and Annie Pope are good parents, concerned citizens and a likeable, cultured couple. They are also on the FBI's wanted list. As student radicals during the Vietnam War they bombed a laboratory manufacturing napalm, unintentionally maiming someone in the process, and went underground to keep their infant son, Danny. Now 17, Danny and his kid brother have been raised constantly on the move, trained to recognise pursuing agents, to change their names, hair colour and personal histories and to remain aloof from schoolmates for fear of betrayal. Necessarily tightly knit, the family is faced with its biggest crisis when the gifted Danny is offered a prestigious music scholarship. What every parent and child experiences is intensified here – if Danny leaves home and establishes an identity he will never see his family again.

Threaded in thriller-style are enough details to make the Popes' mysterious lifestyle plausible – how Arthur assumes new identities and jobs, how they get the boys into new schools, cloak and dagger assignations with a network of sympathisers. But the centre of the film is Danny, torn between parents, budding romance with Martha Plimpton (an uncanny lookalike of her father Keith Carradine) and a chance for a good life in the 'straight' world. Here River Phoenix, not yet 19 himself, enhanced his reputation as the very best of a young bunch with an attractive, sensitive performance that earned him an Oscar nomination. Christine Lahti is terrific as the mother suppressing her own losses and regrets; an angry, tearful scene in which she confronts her own father after 15 years of unforgiving silence is the most powerful in the film. Judd Hirsch allows his usual goody two-shoes persona to become progressively less sympathetic as the resentful outlaw losing his grip on the only thing he has, The Family.

Unfortunately, despite meticulous work from Lumet and the cast, *Running On Empty* cannot avoid sentimental clichés inherent in the situation. Like renegade Waltons, the Popes inevitably lapse into 'I love you, Dad' 'I love you too, son' type conversations so familiar in American melodrama and guaranteed to make the more stoic among us snicker rather than blub. That said, the progress of young love is less hackneyed than in most teen pics, the performances are outstanding and those interested in the fate of people who acted on their beliefs and have to cope with the consequences will get pleasure from a solid modern weepie. ★★★ **AE**

THE RUNNING, JUMPING AND STANDING STILL FILM (1959)

Starring: *Richard Lester (Painter), Peter Sellers (Photographer), Spike Milligan, Mario Frabrizi, David Lodge, Leo McKern, Graham Stark,*
Directors: *Richard Lester, Peter Sellers*
Screenwriters: *Richard Lester, Peter Sellers, Spike Milligan*
U/11 mins./Comedy/UK

A manic procession of surreal events, involving a charwoman who cleans a field with a scrubbing brush, a man who runs around a tree stump to play a phonograph record and a violinist who reads his score by telescope and has to mount a bicycle to turn the pages on his music stand.

Richard Lester had the happy knack of impressing important people. He began his career in live television in the United States, which he later claimed was the finest school ever invented for surrealism, as freak incidents like the appearance of a gaggle of periwigged 18th-century characters within a Nazi POW camp were always likely to happen.

Indeed, it was exactly this brand of eccentricity that Lester sought to bring to British television in 1956. Aping the crackpot comedy patented by *The Goons*, *The Dick Lester Show* was a largely ad-libbed affair that proved to be a spectacular failure. However, it so amused Peter Sellers that he invited Lester to direct a string of *Goon* spin-offs – *A Show Called Fred*, *Idiot's Weekly* and *Son of Fred* (all 1956) – that also convinced Spike Milligan that Lester was on their comic wavelength.

In between his *Goon* assignments, Lester began directing commercials, which not only taught him visual economy, but also gave him plenty of latitude for experimentation. And it was this preoccupation with the madcap, the avant-garde and the precise that manifested itself in this 11 minutes of mayhem.

Shot over two Sundays with Sellers's 16mm Bolex camera for just £70 (a fiver of which went on the hire of the field), *The Running, Jumping and Standing Still Film* was a homage to both classic slapstick clowning and the silent Impressionism that René Clair and Luis Buñuel had attempted in the late 1920s.

Sellers, Milligan, Leo McKern, David Lodge, Graham Stark and Mario Fabrizi threw themselves into a project (often literally) that was initially only devised as a kind of wacky home movie. However, it wound up landing an Oscar nomination and so impressing The Beatles that they insisted on Lester directing *A Hard Day's Night* (1964), whose 'Can't Buy Me Love' sequence reprised the delirious exuberance of this midget gem. ★★★★ **DP**

RUSH HOUR (1998)

Starring: *Jackie Chan (Chief Inspector Lee), Chris Tucker (Detective James Carter), Tom Wilkinson (Thomas Griffin), Chris Penn (Clive Cod), Elizabeth Pena (Tania Johnson)*
Director: *Brett Ratner*
Screenwriters: *Jim Kouf, Ross LaManna, based on a story by LaManna*
12/93 mins./Martial Arts/Action/Comedy/USA

When the Chinese consul's daughter is kidnapped he prefers to hire his old Hong Kong inspector, rather than rely on the FBI. The inspector teams up with an LAPD inspector, also sidelined, and the unlikely pair reluctantly go to work together.

Arriving on these shores with almost $130 million of US box office receipts in its pocket, *Rush Hour*'s attempts to resuscitate the buddy movie genre proved so profitable that a sequel was rushed into production. And if Chan and Tucker don't have quite the same box office pulling power here, this glossy blend of amiable comedy and beautifully choreographed action should still kept up suitable levels of interest.

The serviceable plot (for really it does just serve as a framework to showcase the manic energy of its leading men) has Chan, as Detective Inspector Lee, summoned from Hong Kong to LA by the Eastern city's US consul whose daughter has been kidnapped by Oriental crimelords. The FBI, however, far from keen to land in a diplomatic pickle if harm should befall the new arrival, employs the services of LAPD loose cannon James Carter to keep Lee as far away from the case as possible.

It's a scheme that swiftly hurtles out of control; Lee is determined to crack the case, while Carter, aggrieved with his apparent babysitting gig, has his own plans to rescue the kidnapped tyke. Forming the de rigueur initially reluctant partnership, the two decide to take matters into their own hands.

Despite its title, *Rush Hour* takes an uncomfortably long time to fully crank up, with much of the first half devoted to Tucker's love-it-or-hate-it sub-Eddie Murphy shtick. Given that his obviously huge talents are here given over to lame Michael Jackson impersonations and all the variants on ass-kicking related dialogue the script can muster, this soon begins to grate.

Luckily Chan, imbued with all the gleeful innocence of a tourist abroad for the first time, manages to save the day, actually tempering Tucker's hyperkinetic behaviour with some of his own as the pair attempt to overcome their cultural differences to save the day.

And here's where the movie really kicks in, because when Tucker is forced to stop whining and actually play off his new-found partner, he is far more likeable; and of course, this gives Chan a chance to break into the blistering, balletic brand of action that made his name. The set pieces that follow are masterly, as Chan sets about defeating the bad guys with snooker cues, bar stools and, in one vintage sequence, a set of priceless Ming vases he's desperate to keep intact.

In short, *Rush Hour* may be as brainless as they come, with its thankless support roles (Wilkinson as a British ambassador, Pena as an LAPD bomb disposal expert) ropey script, and entirely predictable outcome, but taken as an unfussy crowd-pleaser it amply delivers the goods. ★★★ **CW**

RUSH HOUR 2 (2001)

Starring: *Jackie Chan (Detective Inspector Lee), Chris Tucker (Detective James Cater), John Lone (Ricky Tan), Zhang Ziyi (Hu Li), Roselyn Sanchez (Agent Isabella Molina)*
Director: *Brett Ratner*
Screenwriter: *Jeff Nathanson, from the characters created by Ross LaManna*
12/86 mins./Martial Arts/Action/Comedy/12

A gang of deadly counterfeiters are causing havoc in Hong Kong, spoiling a nice vacation for local detective, Lee, and visiting American cop, Thomas Carter. The intrepid duo take the smugglers on, following them from HK to America, where things get complicated.

After the success of *Rush Hour*, this was commissioned faster than New Line could say 'cash cow'. And this certainly is second verse, same as the first (banter, fight, banter, fight), as our mismatched heroes – Chinese cop Chan, Yank cop Tucker – foil counterfeiters.

Taking in three locations – Hong Kong, LA, and Las Vegas – gives way to a slew of ever-so-slightly racist and sexist gags, replacing the original's sense of fun.

Tucker is less annoying than usual, but this is Chan's show. He really should be too old for this shit, but you can't help but admire the grace with which he takes on a small army armed with only a towel, and a wastebin.

Ratner squeezes in nice cameos from Jeremy Piven and – inexplicably – Don Cheadle, and villainess Zhang Ziyi kicks suitable arse. But really, any movie in which the outtakes are better than what goes before, is in trouble. ★★ **CH**

RUSHMORE (1998)

Starring: *Jason Schwartzman (Max Fischer), Bill Murray (Herman Blume), Olivia Williams (Rosemary Cross), Seymour Cassel (Bert Fischer), Brian Cox (Dr Nelson Guggenheim), Mason Gamble (Dirk Calloway), Luke Wilson (Dr Peter Flynn)*
Director: *Wes Anderson*
Screenwriters: *Wes Anderson, Owen Wilson*
15/93 mins./Comedy/Drama/USA

Max is king of extra-curricular activities but his school work is suffering. Enter the elementary school teacher that he falls in love with, and throw the fact that Max's industrialist friend is after her too into the mix, and you get a whole lot of complications.

Bypassing the theory that the 'awkward second film' can be a stumbling block (nobody saw their first, *Bottle Rocket*), the directing/writing team of Wes Anderson and Owen Wilson have created a movie as offbeat as you're likely to see all year.

In a summer stuffed with high school dilemma movies, *Rushmore* turns the genre on its head to tell the tale of Max Fischer (newcomer Schwartzman), a student at the exclusive Rushmore Academy. A demented cross between Ferris Bueller and Adrian Mole, Fischer's penchant for extra-curricular activities (he is president of everything from the Beekeepers Society to his own drama group) is having a disastrous effect on his academic prowess. However, his efforts to shape up go awry when he falls for teacher Rosemary, and worsen when she begins dating Herman Blume, a steel tycoon Max has befriended. Determined to win her back, the infatuated Fischer takes on Blume in a battle which becomes more adolescent at every turn.

Max Fischer is a unique creation, a smart aleck brat who, unlike the lily-livered high schoolers currently populating US teen movies and TV shows, might actually survive more than half an hour in the *Grange Hill* playground. But the impossibly talented Schwartzman is just the icing on a particularly appetising cake. The script is stuffed with fantastic, acerbic one-liners which hang teasingly around the brain for days, while Anderson keeps the tone fresh and vibrant, effortlessly blending wry poignancy and surprising warmth with startling high comedy (witness Fischer's drunken outburst and pop culture playwriting).

And the casting is perfection: Murray, as the businessman in mid-life crisis, has never been better, Williams more than makes up for being in *The Postman*, and colourful supports – notably Gamble as Fischer's best mate, and Stephen McCole as a foul-mouthed Scot – heighten the attention to detail; everybody, right down to the smallest of characters, is fully sketched. It may have brought in multiplex megabucks and its quirkiness will irritate the hell out of some but *Rushmore* certainly attracted a cult following. ★★★★ **CW**

⦿ RUSSIAN ARK (RUSSKU KOVCHEG) (2002)

Starring: *Sergey Dreiden (The Marquis). Maria Kuznetsova (Catherine The Great), Leonid Mozgovoy (The Spy), Mikhail Piotrovsky (Himself), David Giorgobiani (Orbeli), Maxim Sergerey (Peter The Great), Alexander Chaban (Boris Piotrovsky) Lev Yeliseyev (Himself), Oleg Khmelnitsky (Himself), Alla Osipenko (Herself)*
Director: *Alexander Sokurov*
Screenwriters: *Sergey Yevtushenko, Alexander Sukorov*
U/96 mins./History/Drama/Russia

Flitting through 33 rooms, occupied by over 2,000 costumed characters, this is an extraordinary moving tableau chronicling both momentous events and intimate incidents from Russian history from the pomp of Peter and Catherine the Great to the fall of the Tsars and the collapse of Communism.

It's not often that an arthouse film finds its way into the *Guinness Book of Records*. But in completing this sublime mastepiece of form and content in a single 96-minute take, Alexander Sokurov easily surpassed the 35 minutes it took Viva and Louis Waldon to make love in Andy Warhol's *Blue Movie*.

He cheated, of course, as Tilman Büttner's high-definition digital video camera wasn't hindered by the need to change reels every 10 minutes. But what was more important than the longevity of the take was the balletic ingenuity of the Steadicam movements, the sumptuous recreation of Russia's imperial and Soviet yesteryears, and the majestic use of the Hermitage Museum that once housed the Romanov dynasty.

Whether pursuing royals, eavesdropping on courtiers or perusing priceless paintings, this truly was poetry in motion. Yet Sokurov could speak only of his disappointment at not being allowed to use the 4,000 extras he had originally envisaged and his submission to the producers' insistence that his direct soundtrack was dubbed in a German studio. He even accused Büttner of making mistakes during the course of the two kilometres he walked during the shoot because he was essentially a technician and not an artist.

Yet, to less demanding eyes, the 'philharmonic cinematography' required to capture the endless stream of overlapping, flashbacking vignettes was not only intricately ingenious, but also evocative, exhilarating, mesmeric and deeply moving.

However, there were critics who, while applauding the logistical and choreographic precision involved, accused Sokurov of conducting a self-indulgent experiment that constantly kept the viewer at a distance from even the pivotal characters inhabiting what was essentially a pageant. It was also claimed that he had trivialised the theory of mise-en-scène espoused by André Bazin and employed in the pursuit of truth by such mentors as Robert Flaherty, Andrei Tarkovsky and Ingmar Bergman.

But such rigid academicism was as petty as Sokurov's own criticism of Tilman Büttner. Whatever its intellectual, dramatic or technical shortcomings, this was an exceptional cinematic achievement and, sometimes, that should simply be enough. ★★★★★ **DP**

⦿ RYAN'S DAUGHTER (1970)

Starrring: *Robert Mitcham (Charles Shaugnessy), Trevor Howard (Father Collins), Christopher Jones (Randolph Doryan), John Mills (Michael), Sarah Miles (Rosy Ryan), Leon McKern (Thomas Ryan)*
Director: *David Lean*
Screenwriter: *Robert Bolt*
PG/195 mins./Drama/UK

Awards: *Academy Awards – Best Supporting Actor (John Mills), Best Cinematography*

While in the thick of World War I, a young shell-shocked British officer comes to a small Irish town already seething with resentment towards the occupying forces. When local beauty Rosy Ryan, who has only recently married the schoolteacher, falls for this tormented soldier, a storm both figurative and literal will break across the entire village.

This is the film that brought the David Lean myth, that he was the grandest filmmaker in all the world, crashing down around his sizeable ears, as critics lambasted its overwrought, over-directed style, so suddenly out-of-fashion, and Lean took himself off into exile to lick his wounds and not return to the big screen for 13 long years. It was a terrible waste of talent, and *Ryan's Daughter* is hardly the great mishap it has been painted, but in Lean's overreaction lies the foundations of this film's failings – it is too keenly felt, lacking the subtlety and character of his previous work, with a director overwhelmed by an obsession towards perfection that robs him of his storytelling craft.

Part of the problem lies in its setting. The Irish revolution was never going to be as grand or showy as the Russian or Arabic versions, it was a shadowy affair, fraught with religious prejudice and secret plotting. It just didn't fit Lean's huge gestures. Of course, his slow-slow storyline looks the business, full of earthy tones and, as love blossoms, isolated moments of stunning sunlit beauty, but Lean's madness was striking deep into the production as he took off for South Africa for a perfect beach shot, and his style bulges pointlessly around the edges.

Robert Bolt's script, as always, has its share of emotional shards and pointed, purposeful characterisation. Sarah Miles, Christopher Jones, Leo

McKern and a strident Trevor Howard all deliver the goods, while John Mills picked up an Oscar for his transformation into town simpleton Michael (the innocent eyes viewing the mess man makes of himself). But Robert Mitchum as stoic schoolteacher Charles strained against both the accent and the confines of his character, he also wasn't getting on with Lean, and it becomes increasingly hard to fathom why the director ever cast him. It does end on a powerful note of tragedy and undoing that pertains to the way Ireland eventually found itself so divided, but this is more folly than triumph, though, at least, it's the kind only the greatest of directors can deliver. ★★★ **IN**

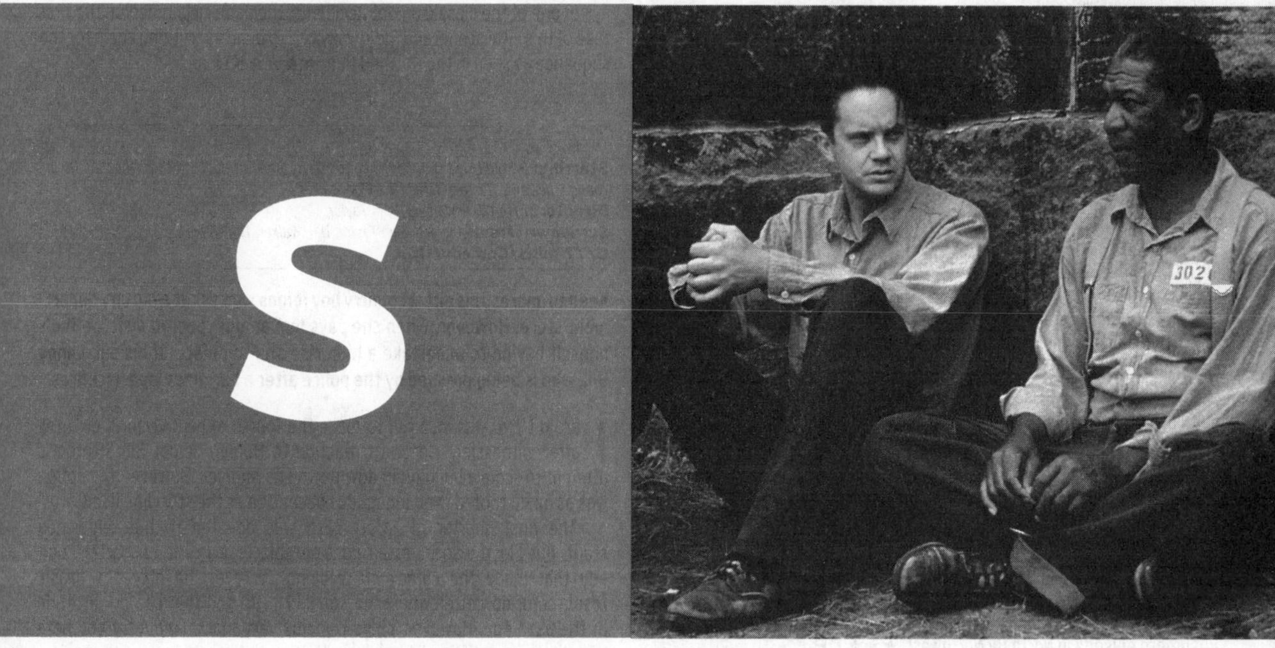

⓪ SABOTAGE (1936)

Starring: *Sylvia Sidney (Sylvia Verloc), John Loder (Ted Spencer), Oscar Homolka (Karl Verloc), Desmond Tester (Steve), Joyce Barbour (Renee), Matthew Boulton (Supt. Talbot, S.J. Warmington (Hollingshead)*
Director: *Alfred Hitchcock*
Screenwriters: *Charles Bennett, Ian Hay, Alma Reville, Helen Simpson, E.V.H. Emmett, based on the novel* The Secret Agent *by Joseph Conrad*
PG/76 mins./Thriller/UK

Posing as a greengrocer, Scotland Yard sergeant Ted Spencer keeps tabs on East End cinema owner Karl Verloc, who is suspected of being a saboteur. However, he becomes fond of Mrs. Verloc and protects her from retribution after she stabs her husband following the accidental death of her younger brother, Steve.

Having just rendered W. Somerset Maugham's *Ashenden* as *Secret Agent*, Alfred Hitchcock adapted Joseph Conrad's dense 1907 novel, *The Secret Agent*, as *Sabotage*. He never cared for the film, which was the last he produced for Michael Balcon at Gaumont-British, telling François Truffaut that he made too many mistakes in its execution. Yet, it remains an atmospheric London thriller, whose overarching sense of pessimism reflected a world that had inched closer to crisis by the Nazi remilitarisation of the Rhineland and the outbreak of the Spanish Civil War.

Hitch's greatest regret seems to have been his inability to persuade Alexander Korda to loan him Robert Donat to play Ted Spencer. He clearly had little faith in John Loder and rewrote scenes in a bid to disguise his shortcomings. However, many contemporary critics commended Loder's performance, along with Hitchcock's assured escalation of suspense through the aggregation of telling details. But others felt that he had laid on the psychology with a trowel at the expense of exciting action.

Hitchcock himself felt that he had wrongly encouraged the audience to side with Verloc by allowing Oscar Homolka (who was as capable of rotund geniality as Mitteleuropean menace) to appear the injured party, as Loder made his less than subtle play for Sylvia Sidney. Moreover, by having him plead with his bomb-making handler, the Professor (William Dewhurst), to avoid a loss of life, Verloc seemed to be even less directly culpable for Steve's death (especially as the boy dawdled on his errand to Piccadilly Station).

However, Hitchcock considered killing a kid to be an unforgivable error of judgement, which he compounded by having Sidney murder Homolka, in a dinner table sequence that never quite conveyed its accidental design. Yet it was superbly staged, as was the devastating preceding scene in which Winnie watched the Disney cartoon *Who Killed Cock Robin*? having just learned of Steve's demise. Less subtle, however, was the inclusion of the poster for Graham Cutts's farce, *Aren't Men Beasts*?, in the background, as Ted tried to persuade her to run away with him. ★★★ **DP**

⓪ SABOTEUR (1945)

Starring: *Priscilla Lane (Patricia Martin), Robert Cummings (Barry Kane), Otto Kruger (Charles Tobin), Alan Baxter (Freeman), Clem Bevans (Nelson), Norman Lloyd (Frank Fry), Alma Kruger (Mrs. Henrietta Sutton), Vaughan Glaser (Phillip Martin)*
Director: *Alfred Hitchcock*
Screenwriters: *Peter Viertel, Joan Harrison, Dorothy Parker, based on a story by Hitchcock*
PG/108 mins./Spy/USA

Engineer Barry Kane is falsely accused of an arson attack on a Californian aircraft factory that was committed by Frank Fry on behalf of Fifth Columnist, Charles Tobin. But, as Kane seeks to track down the perpetrators, reluctant accomplice Patricia Martin is far from convinced of his innocence.

America had been at war for a less than a month when Alfred Hitchcock embarked on this flagwaving variation on *The 39 Steps*. He was less than enamoured with his principals, having failed to land either Gary Cooper and Barbara Stanwyck or Henry Fonda and Gene Tierney. However, his biggest disappointment lay in losing Harry Carey as Tobin, as Carey's wife felt the role would damage his avuncular image.

But if Hitchcock was disgruntled with his actors, he was delighted to count the celebrated wit Dorothy Parker among a scriptwriting team that also included his longtime collaborator Joan Harrison and novelist Peter Viertel. Indeed, he considered Parker's disconcertingly comic sequence, in which Cumming and Lane hide out on a train among some bickering circus performers, among the film's highlights.

Much less successful, however, was the encounter between the handcuffed Cumming and the blind man who offers him sanctuary. Already embarrassingly reminiscent of a similar two-way involving Boris Karloff and O.P. Heggie in James Whale's *Bride of Frankenstein*, the scene was rendered almost unwatchable by the scenery-gnawing excesses of Vaughan Glaser.

Yet *Saboteur* also contains two memorable Hitchcock moments, each of which turned on one of his trademark themes – terror within the everyday. The first was the society ball, in which Cumming and Lane were surrounded by ordinary people in a public place, while simultaneously being menaced by Tobin's henchmen. The second was set in the cinema auditorium at the Radio City Music Hall and showed the audience continuing to roar with laughter at the action on screen, initially oblivious to the life and death struggle occurring within its midst.

The haunted expression of Norman Lloyd was key to this sequence, as it was to the climactic cliffhanger. Hitchcock later suggested that he had made a mistake in having Lloyd cling to the Statue of Liberty's torch rather than Cumming, as the viewer was less likely to be concerned about the fate of the traitor. However, he more than made amends with the Mount Rushmore episode in *North By Northwest*. ★★★ **DP**

◑ THE SACRIFICE (OFFRET) (1986)

Starring: *Erland Josephson (Alexander), Susan Fleetwood (Adelaide), Allan Edwall (Otto), Sven Wollter (Victor)*
Director: *Andrei Tarkovsky*
Screenwriter: *Andrei Tarkovsky*
PG/142 mins./Drama/France/Sweden

In World War III, a Swedish intellectual promises God he will destroy his entire life if the deity takes back the nuclear holocaust. He wakes up to find that the devastation was either all a nightmare or has indeed been revoked by divine intervention, and wonders what he should do about his promise.

Andrei Tarkovsky's last film, a Swedish-French co-production made while he was suffering from terminal cancer, features many of the Soviet exile's distinctive traits (inordinate length, long-held static shots, an enigmatic ending, a clear-eyed child who observes adult madnesses) but blends in with the works of his idol, Ingmar Bergman, by using actors (Josephson), settings, themes and technicians (cinematographer Sven Nykvist) associated with the Swede.

Bergman's *Shame* and *The Silence* are especially evoked in the confrontation of a withdrawn ascetic and a violent war, leading to the conclusion that even a tortured genius can only retreat so far from the world. The endless dinner tables and icy relationships also evoke Bergman's island-set psychodramas.

Reduced to the bare bones of its plot, *The Sacrifice* contrives to 'say' less about nuclear war than, say, Roger Corman's *The Day the World Ended*, and focuses instead on thorny spiritual issues.

Though it's not exactly an easy watch, several stretches are undeniably fascinating and resonant: the war itself is conveyed by characters moving sedately from window to window as unseen missiles buzz the house, monochrome flashes of a ravaged world encroach upon the hero's bleak but settled existence and the extraordinary one-take finale finds Josephson fulfilling his part of the bargain with God by burning down his house.

In one of the classic on-set accidents, the camera jammed on the first take of this vital scene, and Tarkovsky had to build everything again for the sequence as seen in the finished film. ★★★★**KN**

◑ SAFETY LAST! (1923)

Starring: *Harold Lloyd (The Boy), Mildred Davis (The Girl), Bill Strother (The Pal), Noah Young (The Law), Weston Clarke (The Floorwalker)*
Directors: *Fred C. Newmeyer, Sam Taylor*
Screenwriters: *Hal Roach, Sam Taylor, H.H. Walker, Tim Whelan*
U/77 mins/Comedy/USA

Keen to impress his girl, a country boy feigns success at a big city department store. However, when she pays him an unexpected visit, he finds himself having to undertake a high-rise stunt in place of his pal, Limpy Bill, who is being pursued by the police after a harmless jape backfires.

Harold Lloyd was inspired to make the fourth of his five thrill pictures after witnessing a crowd's reaction to Human Spider Bill Strother's attempt to scale a building in downtown Los Angeles. However, the action was as much rooted in an innocuous deception as the storyline itself.

The final quarter of *Safety Last!* was devoted to the celebrated stunt. But Lloyd also invested considerable care in the character comedy that made the climax so gripping. As ever, he played a brash, resourceful go-getter whose personality reflected the 'can do' attitude of the Jazz Age. However, Lloyd remains very much a country boy here and it's love and friendship rather than social or economic aggrandisement that prompts him to take on the ascent after Limpy Bill is distracted by the cops.

The case of mistaken identity that necessitates Lloyd's heroism was something of a contrivance. But none more so than the plethora of obstacles that made the climb so difficult. Pigeons, ropes, a mouse, a swinging window, a net, a flagpole, a weather vane, a painters' platform, a flash gun and a clock face all conspire to hinder Lloyd's progress and each incident inspires amused apprehension rather than the guffaws usually elicited by such silent pratfalls.

Lloyd always insisted that he performed his daredevil pantomime at the heights seen on the screen and so he did. But it was Bill Strother who appeared in the long shots, while Lloyd did the medium and close-up work on reconstructions that were precisely positioned on rooftops commensurate with the different stages of the climb. It was still a perilous enterprise, but Lloyd always had mattresses some 20 feet below him.

However, the authenticity of the stunt is largely immaterial. The illusion was all that mattered and directors Fred Newmeyer and Sam Taylor, along with their four cameramen, made supremely inventive (not to say ingenious) use of angle and space to pull this off spectacularly. Contemporary audiences were undeniably impressed and a feature that cost $120,963 raked in $1,588,545. ★★★★ **DP**

◑ SAHARA (2005)

Starring: *Penelope Cruz (Eva Rojas), Matthew McConaugher (Dirk Pitt), Steve Zahn (Al Giordino), William H. Macy (Admiral Jim Sandecker)*
Director: *Breck Eisner*
Screenwriters: *Thomas Dean Donnelly, Joshua Oppenheimer, John C. Richards, James V. Hart, based on the novel by Clive Cussler*
12/124 mins./Action/Adventure/UK/USA/Spain/Germany

Explorer Dirk Pitt is obsessed with finding a mysterious US Civil War ship, which he believes wound up somewhere in Africa. Upon finding a rare gold coin in Lagos, he knows he's close; but how does it tie in with a 'plague' epidemic threatening thousands of North Africans?

Short Hollywood Marriages

TOP10

1 5 months - Natasha Henstridge and Damian Chapa
2 4 months - Henry Fonda and Margaret Sullivan
3 8 weeks - Drew Barrymore and Jeremy Thomas
4 38 days - Ernest Borgnine and Ethel Merman
5 21 days - Wallace Beery and Gloria Swanson
6 13 days - Patty Duke and Michael Tell
7 8 days - Dennis Hopper and Michelle Phillips
8 5 days - Cher and Greg Allman
9 1 day - Jean Arthur and Julian Anker
10 6 hours - Rudolph Valentino and Jean Acker

Sand. Gets everywhere, doesn't it? In your hair, in your sarnie, down your pants ... Not to mention all those Hollywood action-adventure scripts. From *Lawrence Of Arabia* to *The Scorpion King* via *Raiders Of The Lost Ark*, the golden, gritty stuff has proven an ideal milieu for brash, tanned heroic-types with treasure to hunt, girls to save and stuff to blow up.

It was only a matter of time, then, before the stupidly named Dirk Pitt, hero of several pulpy novels by Clive Cussler, was given a cinematic excuse to romp around the dunes of West Africa. After all, what better use for the Third World's arid regions is there than as a playground for rugged Americans with little more in mind than salvage and carnage?

Places where corrupt military dictators (in this case, the barely convincing Lennie James) need to be foiled; where camel-thrashing tribal rebels need to be patronised; where feisty maidens (Penelope Cruz, just about keeping up) need romancing; and where the clueless natives need saving.

In case you hadn't guessed, Sahara ain't about to redefine the dune-adventure sub-genre. In fact, it's a bit rubbish, really. Breck Eisner (did Cussler give him his name, too?) directs with effective economy but little flair, the action sequences are been-there-exploded-that, while the plot is downright preposterous. But – and this is a big, hefty, ass-kicking but – it's all such tongue-vaguely-in-cheek fun you don't particularly care.

At the eye of this silly, swirling desert storm is the winning buddy act of McConaughey's Dirk and Steve Zahn's Al Giordino. Buff, browned, with a blinding ivory grin and twinkly baby-greens, McConaughey fills out Pitt's grubby khakis perfectly. Here's a guy you believe can have a solution to every life-threatening problem, who matches brawn with brains and who rarely breaks a sweat, even when the bullets are flying.

Zhan, meanwhile, is superb as the sidekick, forever exasperated by Pitt's impulsiveness, always ready to help him execute his get-out plans. As asinine as it all is, the two make sure every splutter is matched by a smile, every sneer by a cheer. At one crucial point, Al says to Dirk: 'I'll find the bomb, you get the girl.' And that pretty much sums up *Sahara*.
★★★ DJ

THE SAINT (1997)

Starring: *Val Kilmer (Simon Templar), Elisabeth Shue (Dr. Emma Russell), Rade Serbedzija (Ivan Tretiak), Valery Nikoleav (Ilya Tretiak)*
Director: *Phillip Noyce*
Screenwriters: *Jonathan Hensleigh, Wesley Strick, from a story by Jonathan Hensleigh, character by Leslie Charteris*
12/111 mins./Action/Thriller/USA

Simon Templar stays one step ahead of the law, outswindling gangsters, protecting the good guys and charming beautiful women all over the globe.

Despite jumping from the Batman bandwagon for the alluring potential of this bright new action-hero franchise, alternate identity and disguise remain the order of the day for Val Kilmer – albeit from the Mr. Potato Head school of stick-on specs, sidies and other assorted facial furniture – in the shoes of arch-thief Simon Templar. For many, *The Saint* will conjure images of a stick man lobbing his halo all over the shop, the honing of open-shirted eyebrow archage – which Roger Moore would employ to considerable effect upon subsequent recruitment by MI6 – and a sleek white Volvo sports. Or, for the less lengthy of tooth, perhaps the far cooler Jaguar XJS of Moore's successor, the equally suave but rather more bland Ian Ogilvy. But this is the latest addition to the Leslie Charteris canon: Kilmer's stab at the author's meddling, larcenous smoothie, under the guidance of *Patriot Games/Clear And Present Danger* director Philip Noyce.

Lurking behind costume, wig and various European accents, Templar's time is spent half-inching miscellaneous items and thwarting impossible security systems, and pricing such skills well into the six-figure bracket in the search of a retirement goal of 50 big ones. And that may finally be in sight with the fee from the Russian billionaire and would-be dictator Ivan Tretiak, who needs to jolly-up a revolting population caught in the deadly grip of a deep freeze and drastic fuel shortage. The solution in this near-future set world (tantalisingly heralded by the early caption 'Red Square, Moscow – tomorrow') appears to be some vague, chemical test-tubery called Cold Fusion, a sort of pocket-sized nuclear reactor, minus the fall-out hazard.

Tretiak commissions Templar to nick the formula from the visionary Dr. Emma Russell, and here's where things assume the outline of pear. Because she looks like Elisabeth Shue, and for the first time, Templar's coolly detached head is receiving stern argument from first his trousers, then his ribcage. All of which means the woman whose discovery could transform the global economy may also be the catalyst for his own personal redemption.

In their tricky blend of love story and international theft caper, Noyce and *Die Hard With A Vengeance* screenwriter Jonathan Hensleigh's decision to flesh out the Saint's childhood origins (which Charteris never touched in over 50 novels) carries an unfortunate side-effect. The need to race the plot from flashback explanation to Templar's light-fingered prowess in the Bondian infiltration of tightly defended Russkie buildings, before arriving at the emotional quandary of Dr. Russell, merely establishes the disjointed and episodic format which carries through the film in a staccato of (admittedly well-choreographed) scenes delivered at jarring speed.

Indeed, it seems that in every department, quality is hampered by shortfall. Serbedzija and Valery Nikolaev (as Tretiak's fiery son) both look the part, but dubious dialogue often reduces them to frothing Muscovite megalomaniacs; shooting in Red Square is impressive, but the bizarre tunnel underworld beneath the Kremlin tests even the most elastic credibility; and even Kilmer's plethora of disguises, while studied, inventive and amusing, have a whiff of pantomime about them. There's no lack of style or pace from Noyce, just the sense that it isn't quite gelling together.

Kilmer inevitably came under toothcomb scrutiny after the whole *The Island Of Dr. Moreau*/divorce/supermodel/divorce/downright stroppy bugger reportage of the time, but the truth is – like *The Ghost And The Darkness* – although questions may hang over the movie's storyline and basic construction, his strident, leading-man presence is beyond debate. ★★★ DB

⓪ SALÒ OR THE 120 DAYS OF SODOM (1975)

Starring: *Paolo Bonacelli (The Duke), Gigio Cataldi (The Bishop), Uberto Paulo Quintavalle (Chief Magistrate), Caterina Boratto (Signora Castelli), Helene Surgere (Signora Vaccari)*
Director: *Pier Paolo Pasolini, Sergio Citti, from the novel* Les 120 Journées de Sodome *by Madame de Sade*
18/111 mins./Politics/Drama/Italy/France

In the last days of World War II, a group of decadent aristocrats in Salò – the rump of Mussolini's fascist state – retreat to a castle with a crowd of beautiful young people for an orgy of torture.

One of those films anyone would be hard put to *like*, this transposes the Marquis de Sade's exercise in highly personal pornography to a specific Italian setting.

It's an atrocity staged with precision, mostly shot in theatrical tableaux, with a great deal of attention to the sparse, decaying, luxurious décor and speechifying from the four establishment figure libertines and the story-telling mature harlots whose reminiscences are supposed to inspire the company to re-enactments.

Aside from the libertines, none of the characters are individuated – despite arbitrary divisions into guards, 'fuckers', male and female victims and other sub-categories. It is literally impossible at a first viewing (who would want another?) to tell these people apart except that one has a moustache or another curly.

The nastiest wrinkle is that the handsome young folk abducted into the castle all become complicit with the atrocities – there's no difference between those who become the tormenting guards and those who become victims, and the final massacre is precipitated when victims try to get out of their fates by informing on other victims.

It's mercifully distanced. Realising that on film shit-eating is a bigger shocker than tongue-cutting or scalping, director Pier Paolo Pasolini stages the last, fatal round of atrocities through distancing views or mullioned windows (oddest but somehow truest moment – a libertine turning binoculars the wrong way round to make a hanging seem further away than it is).

A disturbing, necessary film – designed to provoke extreme reaction, but blankly impersonal as it tries to conceal the clues (which are there) as to Pasolini's own attitudes as they jibe or clash or exacerbate those of Sade. ★★★ KN

⓪ SALVADOR (1986)

Starring: *James Woods (Richard Boyle), James Belushi (Doctor Rock), Michael Murphy (Ambassador Thomas Kelly), John Savage (John Cassady), Elpidia Carrillo (Maria)*
Director: *Oliver Stone*
Screenwriters: *Oliver Stone, Rick Boyle*
18/116 mins./Biography/War/Thriller/USA

Richard Boyle, a slumming journalist, is sent to El Salvador to cover the political unrest and gets more involved than he would like...

A journalist, down on his luck in the US, drives to El Salvador to chronicle the events of the 1980 military dictatorship, including the assassination of Archbishop Oscar Romero. He forms an uneasy alliance with both guerrillas in the countryside who want him to get pictures out to the US press, and the right-wing military, who want him to bring them photographs of the rebels. Meanwhile he has to find a way of protecting his Salvadorian girlfriend and getting her out of the country.

Based on the real-life experiences of photojournalist (and co-scriptwriter) Richard Boyle, *Salvador* is a searing indictment of the right-wing death squads kept in power in Central America by CIA collusion.

James Woods gives a terrific, animated performance as the morally righteous but highly dislikeable journalist, while Jim Belushi, as his drug-addled companion, makes the perfect foil, offering a less righteous, plain man's view of events.

Hilarious and terrifying by turns, but always gripping, *Salvador* gave the first indication that, in Stone, Hollywood had a screenwriter who could make the transition to top-notch director with remarkable ease. ★★★★ WT

⓪ LE SAMOURAI (THE SAMURAI) (1967)

Starring: *Alain Delon (Jef Costello), François Perier (Inspector), Nathalie Delon (Jane Lagrange), Cathy Roseir (Valérie)*
Director: *Jean-Pierre Melville*
Screenwriter: *Jean-Pierre Melville, from the novel* The Ronin *by Joan McLeod*
PG/100 mins./Thriller/France/Italy

Assassin-for-hire Jeff Costello accidentally lets a witness live and is pursued by both the police and his ruthless employers.

Alain Delon, with a Buster Keaton stone-face and the coolest hat in French cinema, lives in a shabby flat with only a canary for company, killing with a professional fanaticism that borders on both saintliness and psychosis.

After executing the manager of a chrome-and-darkness nightclub, Costello makes a rare slip and is seen by Valérie, an enigmatic black jazz pianist. Delon's face never cracks but he falls to pieces inside and becomes obsessed with Valérie, whose refusal to identify him at a line-up suggests her own involvement in the web of crime.

At once a riveting thriler (influenced by Don Siegel's 1964 version of *The Killers*) and a nightmare of chic urban alienation, this 1967 production is the most ruthlessly effective of director Jean-Pierre Melville's reinterpretations of the dark world of Hollywood's gangster noir films of the 30s and 40s as a complex, 1970s style conspiracy thriller (cf: *The Parallax View*) embroils an anachronistic 1940s 'samurai' hit-man (cf: *This Gun for Hire*).

Lone killer, dogged cops and organised criminals act with Bond-like cruel efficiency, lending the film a haunting coldness, epitomised by Delon's bleakly anonymous lifestyle (if he actually spent the money he made he'd become so conspicuous he could never work again), that makes it more than just a first-rate chase picture.

Shot in steely tones, this has a monochrome look deliberately designed to evoke old movies: everything is colourless, even to the extent of using photocopies of banknotes or packages rather than realistic items. There are perfectly-staged suspense scenes (a quiet pursuit through the Metro) and the intricate conspiracy is ultimately unravelled, but this is memorable mainly for its hard-edged style and potent vision of zero-degree life in a limbo-like parallel world. Outstanding. ★★★★ KN

⓪ SAN FRANCISCO (1936)

Starring: *Clark Gable (Blackie Norton), Jeanette MacDonald (Mary Blake), Spencer Tracy (Father Tim Mullin), Jack Holt (Jack Burley), Ted Healy (Matt), Margaret Irving (Delia Bailey (Jessie Ralph) Maisie Burley Harold Huber (Babe)*
Directors: *W.S. Van Dyke, D.W. Griffith (uncredited)*
Screenwriters: *Anita Loos, Erich Von Stroheim, based on a story by Robert E. Hopkins*
U/115 mins/Disaster/USA
Awards: *Academy Awards – Best Sound Recording*

Father Tim Mullen despairs of his disreputable boyhood buddy Blackie Norton when he thwarts soprano Mary Blake's chances at the city opera house and attempts to turn her into a cheap chanteuse at his seedy Barbary Coast club. Then disaster, in the form of a tremendous earthquake, strikes.

Although *Wings* had been recognised for its engineering ingenuity at the inaugural Academy Awards, the visual effects fraternity was to remain overlooked until 1939. Thus, Arnold Gillespie and James Basevi were deprived of much-merited Oscars for their astonishing full-scale and miniature achievements on this period barnstormer. Douglas Shearer did win, however, for his atmospheric sound recording, which captured the vibrancy of Jeanette MacDonald's glorious soprano and the cacophony of the 1906 earthquake with equal fidelity.

But events behind the scenes were occasionally as seismic as those upon it, with Clark Gable being particularly hostile towards Jeanette MacDonald, even though she had persuaded MGM's Irving G. Thalberg to greenlight Anita Loos and Robert Hopkins's screenplay and insisted that she would only headline with the then King of Hollywood. Gable was better disposed towards Spencer Tracy, however, who earned the first of his nine Oscar nominations in what was essentially a supporting role that he accepted at the urging of director, 'One-Shot Woody' Van Dyke.

Yet, this was only fitting, considering the number of favours that Van Dyke extended to those who had helped him during his formative silent days. In addition to offering Erich von Stroheim the chance to write some additional dialogue, he also gave extra spots to such onetime icons as Flora Finch, King Baggott, Jean Acker, Naomi Childer and Rhea Mitchell. He also invited his mentor, D.W. Griffith, to direct a scene, although it's not known whether he supervised one of MacDonald's operatic numbers, a saloon fracas or the human aspects of the epic 20-minute quake sequence.

The intervening years may not have been kind to Gillespie and Basevi's SFX, but they were as impeccable as they were innovative. Moreover, they were more responsible for the picture's phenomenal commercial success than either the shamelessly melodramatic storyline (which were based on the antics of Barbary rogue Wilson Mizner) or the polished performances of Gable, Tracy and the scandalously underappreciated MacDonald, who proved what an effervescent presence she could be away from her inanimate regular co-star, Nelson Eddy. ★★★★ **DP**

◎ SANJURO (1962)

Starring: *Toshiro Mifune (Sanjuro Tsubaki), Tatsuya Nakadai (Hanbei Muroto), Keiju Kobayash (The Spy), Yuzo Kayama (Iori Izaka), Reiko Dan (Chidori), Yunosuke Ino (Mutsuta)*
Director: *Akira Kurosawa*
Screenwriters: *Riyuzo Kikushima, Akira Kurosawa, Hideo Oguni, based on the novel* Peaceful Days *by Shugoro Yamamoto*
PG/95 mins/Action/Japan

Wandering samurai Sanjuro agrees to help a band of nine inexperienced warriors expose the corruption and greed of Superintendant Muroto and the clan elders and delivers the abducted chamberlain, Mutsuta from their clutches.

Based on a story by Shugoro Yamamoto (whose novel would be the inspiration for Kurosawa's *Red Beard*), this splendid samurai satire was conceived before *Yojimbo* and was initially to focus on an itinerant whose quick wits atoned for his shortcomings with a sword. However, *Yojimbo*'s success persuaded Akira Kurosawa to rework the screenplay, which was originally to have been directed by Hiromichi Horikawa before the studio asked Kurosawa to take over.

It would prove to be one of his most enjoyable assignments and his fondness for the scenario shines through the numerous instances of ribald humour. Sanjuro's first meeting with the junior samurai is particularly amusing, as Kurosawa contrasts their prim Bushido eagerness with the older man's unkempt cynicism. With their gung-ho energy, virtuous enthusiasm and meticulous attire, Yuzo Kayama's comrades in arms are right out of the jidai-geki textbook and Kurosawa delights throughout in mocking generic convention – right down to exploiting such Kabuki clichés as the flowing stream as a means of conveying messages.

Yet, Kurosawa approached his trademark theme of illusion and reality with typical conviction, with even Sanjuro himself failing to heed his own advice of not judging by appearances by overlooking the unassuming sapience of the chamberlain's seemingly dotty wife (Takako Irie). Indeed, it's this recognition of her insight and his own arrogance that prompts him to deliver the surprisingly aggressive concluding speech, in which his indulgent attitude towards his idiotic protégés turns to despairing anger.

Mifune's showdown with Tatsuya Nakadai provides the film's action highlight, as the villain is cleaved through the heart with a single slash that unleashes a gush of gore that was actually carbonated chocolate sauce. The conquest of the superintendant's minions is equally pitiless. But Kurosawa mischievously undercuts the chambara savagery by inserting shots of Irie and her daughter, Reiko Dan, being enraptured by the beauty of the camelias (which had been used as the attack signal) floating gently by on the placid water. Such subtle mastery makes *Sanjuro* a cherishable treat. ★★★★ **DP**

◎ SANSHO THE BAILIFF (SANSHO DAIYUU) (1955)

Starring: *Yoshiaki Hanayagi (Zushio), Kyoko Kagawa (Anju), Kinuyo Tanaka (Tamaki), Eltaro Shindo (Sansho), Akitake Kono (Taro), Masao Shimizo (Masauji Taira)*
Director: *Kenji Mizoguchi*
Screenwriters: *Yahiro Fuji, Yoshikata Yoda, based on the story* Sansho Daiyuu *by Ogai Mori*
PG/125 mins/Drama/Japan

S

A decade after being sold to the merciless 11th-century bailiff Sansho, the corrupted Zushio recovers his governor father's sense of nobility and, after the selfless suicide of his sister Anju, he sets out to find his mother, Tamaki, who had been dispatched to a remote island brothel.

Based on the novel by Ogai Mori, which was itself inspired by a traditional Japanese folk tale, this is one of the few Kenji Mizoguchi films to centre on a male protagonist. However, Zushio's redemption owes much to the courage and sacrifice of the women around him – Namiji (Noriko Tachibana), the elderly slave who serves as his surrogate mother and whose cruel exile from Sansho's estate prompts the recollection of his father that renews his sense of decency; Anju, the sister who drowns herself so as not to hinder his mission; and Tamaki, the doting mother who never gives up hope that she will be delivered from her exploitation on Sado Island.

Water and fire are key to the imagery of this classic quest storyline. But, while the setting may be the 11th century, Mizoguchi explores the idea that humanity is debased without pity to consider the recent clash between liberal benevolence and totalitarian tyranny. Mizoguchi's humanism may have been less idealistic than in his first golden phase in the 1930s, but his loathing of subjugation and injustice was just as strong. However, it finds more eloquent expression in his later career, thanks to his mastery of technique.

Cinematographer Kazuo Miyagawa had pioneered the use of tracking and crane shots to duplicate the composition and mood of traditional Japanese painting in collaboration with the prolific, but little seen Hiroshi Inagaki. So, he was perfectly in tune with Mizoguchi's emphasis on the diagonal elements within the frame and his subtle use of camera movement and distance to keep the figures located within their symbolic environment. Whether following the characters to bind the viewer into the drama or retreating to a contemplative distance (which had been his preferred style in his earlier career), Mizoguchi sought to suggest both the realism of the action and its location within a wider world, a tactic that culminated in the concluding shot in which the camera accompanies Yoshiaki Hanayagi as he nears his reunion with the now blind Kinuyo Tanaka before pulling upwards to reveal the beachcomber gathering seaweed following the tidal wave. ★★★★★ **DP**

SANTA SANGRE (1989)

Starring: *Axel Jodorowsky (Fenix), Blanca Guerra (Concha), Guy Stockwell (Orgo), Thelma Tixou (Tatooed woman), Sabrina Dennison (Alma), Adan Jodorowsky (Young Fenix)*
Director: *Alexandro Jodroowsky*
Screenwriters: *Roberto Leoni, Claudia Argento, from a story by Roberto Leoni, Alexandro Jodorowsky*
18/118 mins./Horror/Drama/Italy/Mexico

In Mexico, madman Fenix, survivor of a traumatic circus childhood, apparently serves as the arms of his mother, whose own were torn off by her husband. Together, mother and son commit serial murders.

A 1989 comeback from Alexandro Jodorowsky, bizarro auteur of *El Topo* – who promptly went away again.

The provisional plot offers a succession of incredibly grotesque fantasies that reference and parody classic horror movies: a series of murders that set up a sad finale in which the Norman Bates-like protagonist's mother turns out to be a giant doll; the hero's attempt to escape by dressing up as Claude Rains's Invisible Man; a bout with a gargantuan female wrestler out of Mexican cinema history; a Lon Chaney-ish mime act in which Fenix acts as the arms of his armless, on-a-pedestal mother; business with uncontrollable knife-throwing hands from Mad Love; and amazing graveyard hallucinations that echo Brazil's Jose Mojica Marins (*Tonight I Will Eat Your Corpse*).

These horror film excesses are hardly more surreal (or potentially offensive) than the 'realistic' sequences which stress tatty, demented Mexican squalour with a wild streak: the funeral of a circus elephant who is flung into a ravine and torn apart by starving slum-dwellers, a field trip from the asylum where a party of Down's Syndrome kids are given cocaine by a pimp and take part in an orgy with a mountainous whore.

Though still concerned with degradation, violence and madness, Jodorowsky has mellowed enough to import a deal of humane feeling, allowing even the killer's awful parents a strange dignity, struggling against the tide of gore to find a strain of redemption.

In tone, it veers between Buñuel and *The Rocky Horror Show*, with bizarre set-pieces and outrageous ideas, blending high art and buckets of blood. ★★★★ **KN**

SATURDAY NIGHT AND SUNDAY MORNING (1960)

Starring: *Albert Finney (Arthur Seaton), Shirley Ann Field (Doreen Gretton), Rachel Roberts (Brenda), Hylda Baker (Aunt Ada), Norman Rossington (Bert), Bryan Pringle (Jack)*
Director: *Karel Reisz*
Screenwriter: *Alan Sillitoe, based on his novel*
PG/90 mins/Drama/UK

Awards: *BAFTA – Best British Film, Best British Actress (Rachel Roberts), Most Promosing Newcomer To Leading Film Roles (Albert Finney)*

Detesting his job as a lathe-operator, Nottingham rebel Arthur Seaton seeks solace in weekend boozing bouts, the pursuit of the chaste Doreen Gretton and the easy conquest of workmate Jack's bored wife, Brenda. That is, until the latter gets pregnant.

Czech-born Karel Reisz had established his reputation with the Free Cinema classics *Momma Don't Allow* (co-directed with Tony Richardson) and *We Are the Lambeth Boys* and his sense of place and the ability to locate drama within the everyday made this adaptation of Alan Sillitoe's novel one of the best entries in the kitchen sink canon. It's also the least dated, as Arthur Seaton's sour assertion, 'All I want is a good time. The rest is propaganda.', could also have been the mantra of Thatcherite Yuppidom and Blairite Laddism.

Such is the veracity of cinematographer Freddie Francis's industrial vistas that Nottingham almost becomes as potent a character as Seaton himself. But the factories and backstreets have none of the bluff charm that Albert Finney summoned for his surly anti-hero, whose impish disregard for authority took the curse off his cavalier attitude towards women.

But while such chauvinism would now be considered inexcusable, contemporary audiences could identify with Seaton's desperate bids to escape from the soul-destroying monotony of his job and his frustration at the social and sexual conventions that further restricted his options. Consequently, he was hailed as a true working-class icon in a way that neither Joe Lambton nor Jimmy Porter ever were, as instead of bourgeois pretentions he nursed a credibly simmering sense of resentment and resignation that dominated every waking hour until he finally recognised that life was more about responsibility than rebellion.

Some critics have accused the film of misogyny. Yet, in revealing the extent to which women had resumed their traditional subservience in postwar Britain, Reisz also suggested the emergence of a new independence by giving Brenda and Doreen a measure of control over their angry young man by respectively indulging and resisting his carnality. However, Reisz remains acutely aware of the fact that it's invariably the woman who pays the sexual consequences and the sequence in which the impotent Jack slaps the pregnant Brenda at the fairground (having been forced to ask his brother's squaddie mates to beat up Arthur) contrasts with Doreen's pragmatic acceptance of Seaton's churlish proposal of marriage. ★★★★ **DP**

SATURDAY NIGHT FEVER (1977)

Starring: *John Travolta (Tony Manero), Karen Lynn Gorney (Stephanie), Barry Miller (Bobby C.), Joseph Cali (Joey), Paul Pape (Double J.), Donna Pescow (Annette)*
Director: *John Badham*
Screenwriter: *Norman Wexler, based on the magazine article 'Tribal Rites of the New Saturday Night' by Nik Cohn*
18/118 mins./Music/Drama/USA

Tony's only escape from his small-town life is dancing at the disco. When he meets a girl who can match him on the dance floor, they get together hoping to win a prize that will change their lives.

Saturday Night Fever has become something of a joke – a kitsch touchstone for nostalgia TV and 70s club nights – but John Badham's film deserves better than that.

Away from the flashing lights of the discotheque, this is dark stuff, littered with racism, violence, date rape and salty dialogue ('If you're as good in bed as you are on the dancefloor, you must be one lousy fuck'). Lose the dancing, and you could be forgiven for thinking you were watching a Ken Loach movie.

At the heart of all this seediness is John Travolta's Tony. An angry young man in the tradition of 50s melodrama or 60s kitchen sink, he is nasty, dumb, insecure and utterly compelling. Badham shoots him like an icon from frame one – the legendary strut along the Brooklyn street, paint can in hand – so we're hooked on his charisma before he's revealed as a shop assistant in a neighbourhood hardware store.

Throughout the film, loser beats work in counterpoint with movie star moments: the smack on the head from his old man comes right after a sequence in which Tony styles his hair, clad only in skimpy black briefs and his own narcissism.

Travolta is mesmerising in every scene, carrying the film despite some woeful performances from the supporting cast. Naturally, his dancing is etched on the culture's collective consciousness, but it was the dramatic work which earned him an Oscar nomination (criminally, he lost out to Richard Dreyfuss' showy wiseass in *The Goodbye Girl*).

Perversely, it's the musical sequences that have failed to stand the test of time. Even if you ignore two decades' worth of parodies and pastiches, the heavily choreographed shapes J.T. and the rest throw verge on the ridiculous.

To borrow from a later Bee Gees hit, the fact that *Saturday Night Fever* is remembered only for the disco action is a real tragedy. ★★★★ **RF**

SATURN 3 (1980)

Starring: *Farrah Fawcett (Alex), Kirk Douglas (Adam), Harvey Keitel (Benson)*
Directors: *Stanley Donen, John Barry*
Screenwriters: *Martin Amis, John Barry*
15/88 mins./Sci-fi/UK/USA

Two humans, Adam and Alex, live on Saturn's third moon Titan with the helpful addition of a synthetic food-making factory. Then into their harmonious existence comes Benson, a murderer on the run from Earth, with a demented robot in tow called Hector.

A daft piece of sci-fi hokum renowned for its troubled shoot (original director, *Star Wars* designer John Barry, died two weeks in) and for the script being done by celebrated British author Martin Amis. The best you can say for its prattling about sexual politics and daft sci-fi foibles is that it musters a campy quality born of its crackpot contrivances, and there is an icky bit where Fawcett nearly loses her eyeball. What was clever-soul Amis thinking? Was it that he was young, and didn't know better? Although there is a delicious candidness to Benson's chat-up line: 'You've got a great body, can I use it?'

It starts off as a dumb love triangle, then the robot joins in (not something even the freakiest of fetishists are going to stomach). Character motivations, especially Keitel's evil Benson, remain foggy, giving the film no sense of why events are happening. Is this really a film about everyone wanting to shag Farrah Fawcett? In space. Who knows, the film, absent of logic, is not about to tell us. Then it turns into a chase movie, as the robot Hector, evidently a man in a suit, goes whacko.

Much is made of the hardware, as if they had aspirations to the Kubrickian warnings of technology run riot (not sure he had this in mind), but the effects are painfully clunky and it has Fawcett in a leading role. Douglas and Keitel just look embarrassed. As they should. ★ **IN**

SAVING PRIVATE RYAN (1998)

Starring: *Tom Hanks (Captain John H. Miller), Tom Sizemore (Sergeant Mike Horvath), Edward Burns (Pvt. Richard Reiben), Barry Pepper (Pvt. Daniel Jackson), Adam Goldberg (Pvt. Stanley Mellish), Vin Diesel (Pvt. Adrian Caparzo), Giovanni Ribisi (T-4 Medic Irwin Wade), Matt Damon (Pvt. James Francis Ryan)*
Director: *Steven Spielberg*
Screenwriter: *Robert Rodat*
15/162 mins./Drama/History/War/USA

Awards: *Academy Awards – Best Cinematography, Best Director, Best Sound Effects Editing, Best Film Editing, Best Sound, BAFTA – Best Sound, Best Special Effects, Empire Awards – Best Actor, Best Director, Golden Globes – Best Director, Best Drama*

A group of American soldiers are sent to France with one mission — to find and return the only surviving son of five sibling soldiers back home to his mom — safe.

Saving Private Ryan was not the first time Steven Spielberg turned his camera on a small unit of American infantrymen caught under heavy fire by German soldiers. Made by the filmmaker at aged 15, *Escape To Nowhere* recreated the US skirmishes with the Nazis in East Africa with 20 of his school friends, his mother driving a jeep and explosions created by a seesaw/flour combo. The only glitch was that the American army never fought in East Africa, only in North Africa.

Spielberg had originally envisaged Ryan as more of a Boy's Own adventure, until interviews with WWII vets gave him a sobering reality check. Inspired by the 50th anniversary of the D-Day landings, Robert Rodat's screenplay followed Captain John Miller (Hanks) and his unit on a PR mission to retrieve Private James Ryan (Damon) from the front line after his brothers have been killed in action. Ostensibly a men-on-a-mission movie, Spielberg sharpened the moral complications inherent in the premise – when is one life worth more than another? – and invested the film with a harsher, more realistic tone.

It was *The Shawshank Redemption's* Frank Darabont (undertaking script doctoring duties with Scott Frank) who suggested opening the sortie with the unit landing at Omaha Beach. The resulting battle, and the often overlooked concluding action to hold the bridge at Ramelle, are landmarks in action movie history. As a soldier searches for a severed arm or Miller drags a body along the beach to see the legs fall away, violence is stripped clean of both comic book exuberance and Peckinpah-esque lyricism. To create this unbridled ferocity initially meant upping the ante on the viscera front: to realise graphic shots of soldiers losing body parts, 20 amputee stuntmen were drafted in and fitted with detachable prosthetic limbs.

Played down on release so as to not suggest Ryan was an effects-fest, the input of Industrial Light + Magic is similarly vital: many of the bullet hits were digital, creating gut-curdling bloodshed without ever putting the actors at risk. Scenes left on the cutting room floor – the unit discovering burnt out tanks and charred corpses – suggest that Spielberg's ability to shock surpassed even his own expectations. But more importantly, it is the directorial arsenal that supplies the flash and thunder.

In previous Spielberg John Williams' music has been crucial in cranking up the excitement factor. Here it is eschewed completely from the battle set-pieces, the furious sound design delivering its own brand of shellshock: at vital points, as Miller surveys carnage, the sound is sucked down to a confused din locating us firmly inside his dazed and confused mindset. If others, particularly Oliver Stone, have previously captured combat in a documentary-styled dynamism, Spielberg pushed the envelope, encouraging cinematographer Janusz Kaminski to find new ways of seeing old horrors: the shutter was adjusted 90 degrees to create sharper, more realistic images, an Image Shaker to vibrate the camera, approximating the impact of explosions.

Gone are Spielberg's customary crane and dolly shots. Here the action is caught on the hop, completely at a grunt's eye view, locking the audience in the thick of the fighting. From *Gladiator* to *Three Kings*, *The Patriot* to *Enemy At The Gates*, *Ryan's* visuals have determined how cinematic conflict looks in the 21st century. If *Ryan* embodies the future of action movies, it also has one foot firmly in the past. In both generalities – the small band of fighting men banding together can be found in *A Walk In The Sun*, *They Were Expendable*, *Fixed Bayonets!*, *Castle Keep* – and specifics – the battle-weary Captain Miller is modelled on Lt. Walker (Robert Mitchum) in *The Story Of GI Joe*, Godfearing rifleman Private Jackson (Barry Pepper) is a haunted version of Gary Cooper's Sergeant York – the sortie to find Ryan is, in many ways, a catalogue of war movie staples and stock characterisations.

But the skill of the writing and the canny casting often subverts the stereotypes. Bookish Corporal Upham (Jeremy Davies) bumbles his way through the carnage and cliché dictates he will eventually prove his

S

worth as a soldier. When he finally acts, however, the result is far more horrific than heroic. There is time for tenderness – Wade rewriting the dead Caparzo's letter home so it is not stained by blood – and humanity which prevails in Miller's moving revelations about his peacetime life and his struggle to keep body and soul together. More than anything, *Saving Private Ryan* redefines the notion of courage away from the gung-ho deeds of movie bravery into something far simpler: staying on your feet and keeping your sanity untouched. ★★★★★ **IF**

SAW (2004)

Starring: *Leigh Whannell (Adam), Cary Elwes (Dr. Lawrence Gordon), Danny Glover (Det. David Tapp), Ken Leung (Det. Steven Sing), Dina Meyer (Kerry)*
Director: *James Wan*
Screenwriter: *Leigh Whannell, from a story by James Wan, Leigh Whannell*
18/102 mins./Horror/Thriller/USA

Two men wake up in a bathroom – with a corpse between them and no memory of how they got there...

A surgeon and a nobody wake up in a derelict bathroom, ankle-chained to pipes, with a corpse between them. They are the latest victims of 'Jigsaw', a tricky serial killer who plays games with victims, teaching them life lessons through torture. The doctor is ordered to find a way to kill the stranger within hours, or his wife and daughter will be executed.

Saw, ingeniously co-scripted by Whannell and debuting director James Wan, is styled like early David Fincher and boasts an intricate structure – complex flashbacks-within-flashbacks explain how the characters have come to this crisis – and a satisfying mystery to go with its ghastly claustrophobia.

It's a series of squirm-inducing moments, with a creepy puppeteer villain, and strong performances, which was enough of a gripper at cinemas to inspire sequels of diminishing returns – an attempt to turn 'Jigsaw' into the Freddie of the 00s. ★★★★ **KN**

SAY ANYTHING (1989)

Starring: *John Cusack (Lloyd Dobler), Ione Skye (Diane Court), John Mahoney (James Court), Lili Taylor (Corey Flood), Amy Brooks (D.C.)*
Director: *Cameron Crowe*
Screenwriter: *Cameron Crowe*
15/96 mins./Drama/Romance/Comedy/USA

Sporty high-school senior Lloyd is entranced by aloof protégée Diane, who is closely guarded by her dad. When she is offered the chance of a lifetime to study in England, she must decide on her affections as well as her future.

Say Anything never did manage a cinema airing, despite an extraordinary thumbs-up in America. The year of release a round-up of US critics' films of the year ranked it with *Henry V*, *Do The Right Thing*, *My Left Foot* and *Roger & Me*, but Fox insisted that cinema scheduling made a theatrical release impossible in the UK.

It's baffling, because *Simpsons* producer James L. Brooks and former teenage prodigy rock journalist with *Rolling Stone* turned *Fast Times At Ridgemont High* author Cameron Crowe, here making his debut as director, crafted a hugely enjoyable teen pic. It mixes pathos and repartee; and, for once, the plot's primary preoccupation isn't the pursuit of sex. Instead it adopts a refreshingly mature approach to a story we've seen many times before. Diana is pretty but prissy, a straight-A high school student, the kind of Daddy's Girl who plumps for Pa over Ma in divorce custody proceedings. Lloyd is the nonconformist offspring of a US Army Colonel who lives with his single-parent sister and practises Bruce Lee drop-kicks on his baby nephew. She has a prestigious biochemistry scholarship awaiting her in England, he retains aspirations of becoming a professional kickboxer.

A more incongruous pair you'd be pushed to match, but after agreeing to date number one, she falls for his charms. Daddy Court, understandably, feels somewhat alienated and indeed miffed at his beloved baby's sudden transfer of affections: cue much relationship questioning and strenuous soul-searching. So Diane dumps Lloyd, but just as soon as Pop's back as her main man, a tax investigation into his nursing home exposes him as a crook. The performances, in particular Cusack's, are solid, the angst painfully plausible and the humour very, very funny. There's no saccharine Happy Ending either – instead we get a remarkably satisfying one – and a true cinema moment in in Lloyd's Peter Gabriel serenade. Watch out too for an uncredited walk-on from Dan Castellenetta as Diane's teacher. ★★★★ **MS**

SCARFACE (1932)

Starring: *Paul Muni (Tony Camonte), Ann Dvorak (Cesca Camonte), Karen Morley (Poppy), Osgood Perkins (Johnny Lovo)*
Director: *Howard Hawks*
Screenwriters: *Ben Hecht, Seton I. Miller, John Lee Mahin, W.R. Burnett, Fred Pasley, from the novel* The Armitage Tale
PG/89 mins./Crime/Drama/USA

Gangster Tony Camonte rises in the Chicago rackets, mostly by murdering his bosses. Obsessively devoted to his sister, Camonte takes over the town – but a policeman vows to destroy his empire.

With the gangster film ground rules freshly established by *Little Caesar* and *The Public Enemy*, producer Howard Hughes, director Howard Hawks and writer Ben Hecht were able to play an operatic variation in this masterpiece.

The plot uses the familiar rise-and-fall-of-a-hood scenario, mixing incidental detail from the career of real-life scarface Al Capone (recreating actual events like the St Valentine's Day Massacre) with the history of the Borgia Family. It has the tabloid feel of earlier gangster films, but also a streak of extraordinarily black horror comedy: one hood is not inaptly played by Boris Karloff (he gets machine-gunned in a bowling alley) and Muni's Camonte comes across as a mix of Frederic March's Mr Hyde and the Jewish-Italian clowning of Chico Marx. Scarface is full of strange elements like the incestuous passion between Tony and his trampy sister (a Borgia touch) and the Xs that appear in the frame whenever anyone is killed ('crossed out') and was lurid and offbeat enough to excite even more censorious controversy than its predecessors, often accused of making heroes out of real-life criminal monsters.

The release was delayed until a few flat moralising scenes could be inserted – with a newspaperman and an honest Italian cop vilifying Camonte – and an excessive subtitle (*The Shame of a Nation*) added, along with George Raft's coin-tossing trick, more rat-tat-tat dialogue than any contemporary film, and a finale which has Camonte go down like Richard III (or King Kong), escaping from his steel-lined hide-out to be riddled with bullets under a Cook's Tours sign which reads 'The World is Yours'. ★★★★★ **KN**

SCARFACE (1983)

Starring: *Al Pacino (Tony Montana), Steven Bauer (Manny Ribera), Michelle Pfeiffer (Elvira Hancock), Mary Elizabeth Mastrantonio (Gina Montana), Robert Loggia (Frank Lopez), F. Murray Abraham (Omar Suzrez)*
Director: *Brian De Palma*
Screenwriter: *Oliver Stone*
18/170 mins./Crime/Drama/USA

Tony Montana is a Marielito freed from Castro's jails and sent to Florida along with the political prisoners taken in by the Carter administration. After a harrowing introduction to the US coke business he makes his way swiftly up the crime ladder, ruthlessly squashing anyone who dares to stand in his way, even bent cops.

From its first moments, *Scarface* is Al Pacino's movie. The opening shots of Tony Montana reveal that we're in the presence of a truly Mephistophelean character, and one of modern cinema's great performances. The gimlet eyes flash with demonic intensity. There's the ingratiating grin, the much-imitated accent ('I am a Yankee – like choo!') and the nervy, jerky movement that suggest a man liable to erupt into violence at any moment.

It's a delicious performance from an actor who knows he's on top form, and Pacino's swaggering arrogance bleeds into the character, juicing it up even further. Pacino would play Satan much later in *The Devil's Advocate*, but would never come as near to instantiating pure, snickering evil on screen again.

Scarface was received with almost universal disdain, as critics dismissed it as heartless satire, over-the-top Grand Guignol or just plain obscene. Needless to say, with De Palma's name on it and reviews like that it soon gained cult credibility, but the depressing adoption of the film as a ghetto classic by hip-hop stars and gangsta rappers shows how badly a film can be misunderstood.

Among the other things that *Scarface* undoubtedly is – contemporary epic, incest drama, cautionary tale of interior design run amok – it's a black-hearted satire on exactly the kind of garish, acquisitive, bling culture they personify.

From his vile shirt to the zebra-skin Cadillac, to the shots of him face down scarfing a mountain of cocaine like a truffle-hog, Montana, like many of the gold-drenched rappers who have eulogised him, is revealed as a tasteless idiot. If he has any insight at all, it's the creeping one that this endless consumption is unlikely to finally satisfy, rendering happiness an impossibility.

However, to have one's film dismissed by the critics as, among other things, inept satire and then to see it adopted as iconic by the kind of people it condemns is surely some kind of perverse validation. That sound you can hear on the breeze might well be an uncharacteristically cheerful De Palma, cackling. ★★★★★ **AG**

◑ THE SCARLETT EMPRESS (1934)

Starring: *Marlene Dietrich (Sophia Frederica), John Lodge (Count Alexei), Sam Jaffe (Grand Duke Peter), Louise Dresser (Empress Elizabeth), Maria Sieber (Sophia as a child), C. Aubrey Smith (Prince August), Ruthelma Stevens (Countess Elizabeth)*
Director: *Josef von Sternberg*
Screenwriter: *Manuel Komroff, based on the diary of Catherine the Great*
12/110 mins/Historical Drama/USA

German princess Sophie Friederike Auguste von Anhalt-Zerbst is renamed by the Empress Elizabeth prior to her marriage to Peter, the imbecilic heir to the throne. However, Catherine wastes no time in taking lovers and planning the coup that will give her supreme power over all the Russias.

Despite the existence of three silent features set during the same period, including Rudolph Valentino's *The Eagle*, and the imminent release of Paul Czinner's *Catherine the Great*, Josef von Sternberg embarked on this 'relentless excursion into style' to demonstrate both his own cinematic mastery and the screen majesty of Marlene Dietrich. Von Sternberg liked to insist that he had created an historical comedy that poked fun at the pomposity of Hollywood period pieces. But while the action was strewn with acerbic asides and sly innuendo (that somehow eluded the gaze of the guardians of the newly invigorated Production Code), this was very much a serious study of both the role of women in a patriarchal society and the politics of sex.

Yet, Dietrich had less to do here than in any of her previous five outings with her eccentric mentor. She looks ravishing, but she was so bound into the décor that little of her personality emerged. Despite the fact that art director Hans Dreier had designed Dmitri Buchowetski's *Peter the Great* (1922), Von Sternberg dictated the look of the film, personally commissioning Peter Ballbusch to produce the evocative statuery and Richard Kollorsz to paint the icons. He also influenced Travis Banton's costumes, including John Lodge's enormous fur coat and Dietrich's increasingly masculine attire, which reflected her realisation that she would have to suppress her femininity to rule in a manner that her courtiers would respect.

Von Sternberg's efforts were wholly overlooked by the Academy. But he received a more significant accolade when Sergei Eisenstein emulated his blend of palace, dacha and church for the regal interiors in *Ivan the Terrible* (1944).

Part of the reason for the film's muted reception was down to Paramount's own indifference. Angered by Von Sternberg's unsanctioned insertion of a crowd sequence from his own 1928 drama, *The Patriot*, production chief Ernst Lubitsch had taken exception to the picture and, exploiting its poor box-office and the Austrian's growing detachment from his Muse, he encouraged Dietrich to consider collaborating with other directors. Consequently, they only worked together once more, on *The Devil Is a Woman*. ★★★★ **DP**

◑ SCARLET STREET (1945)

Starring: *Edward G. Robinson (Christopher Cross), Joan Bennett (Katharine 'Kitty' March), Dan Duryea (Johnny Prince), Margaret Lindsay (Millie Ray), Jess Barker (David Janeway), Rosalind Ivan (Adele Cross)*
Director: *Fritz Lang*
Screenwriter: *Dudley Nichols, based on the play* La Chienne *by Andre Mouezy-Eon, adapted from the novel by Georges De La Fouchardiere*
PG/101 mins./Film Noir/USA

Chris Cross is a cashier duped into crime and murder by Kitty and her boyfriend, Johnny. Cross rescues Kitty, who then persuades him to sell his paintings under her name, with some chilling results.

Fresh from the success of *The Woman In The Window* (1944), Fritz Lang renewed his partnership with independent producer Walter Wanger and the exceptional Edward G. Robinson for a second noir classic.

Adapted from a novel by Georges de la Fouchardiere, this tale of desperate love and casual betrayal had already been filmed by Jean Renoir as *La Chienne* in 1931. But Lang brought to it not only an intuitive expressionism, but also a gnawing personal insight, for while he would never have depicted himself as such a weak character, the auteur trapped in the Studio System would not have missed the irony that Chris Cross is an artist whose vision has been snatched away from him and exhibited under another's name (in Lang's case, Universal).

Downtrodden bank clerk, timid husband and amateur artist Christopher Cross sees a thrilling way out of his humdrum existence when lazy-limbed Kitty March agrees to become his model. However, his idyll is shattered when he discovers she's been in league with petty con Johnny Prince all along.

Rarely has a noir victim fallen under a fatale's spell so willingly or broken free with such merciless violence. Played with consummate skill by Edward G. Robinson, Cross is initially made to seem an amiable sap. But gradually, Lang's contempt for his impotence emerges and there's no pity whatever in his decline and fall after he allows Johnny to take the rap for Kitty's ice-pick demise.

Revelling in their callous exploitation, Bennett and Duryea also turn in splendid performances. But this is very much the director's film, with Lang swathing the later scenes in increasingly sinister shadow to convey Cross's disgraced descent into a living hell. No wonder it remained one of his favourites. ★★★★ **DP**

SCARY MOVIE (2000)

Starring: *Carmen Electra (Drew Decker), Dave Sheridan (Doofy Gilmore), Anna Faris (Cindy Campbell), Jon Abrahams (Bobby Prinze), Regina Hall (Brenda Meeks), Marlon Wayans (Shorty Meeks)*
Director: *Keenan Ivory Wayans*
Screenwriters: *Shawn Wayans, Marlon Wayans, Buddy Johnson, Phil Beauman, Jason Friedberg, Aaron Seltzer*
18/88 mins./Horror/Comedy/USA

A group of teenagers are stalked by a serial killer because he knows what they did last Halloween. Can they outwit the masked slasher and survive?

Death by penis! Trimming pubic thatches with hedge cutters! Fountains of jissum! You can forget subtlety. And, while you're at it you'd be advised to ignore the many old internet rumours citing this as 'one of the best spoofs ever!' It isn't.

Spoofs, you see, are a mixed bunch – for every *Naked Gun*, there is always a 'Spy Hard', a fact of which the Wayans are well aware. The creators of *I'm Gonna Git You, Sucka* and *Don't Be A Menace To South Central While Drinking Your Juice In The Hood*, they've been here before.

Originally titled *Scream If You Know What I Did Last Halloween*, it comes as no surprise that their next natural step takes as its source Wes Craven's *Scream* – itself originally titled *Scary Movie*. A great idea on paper maybe, but this is actually the Wayans' fundamental mistake. Because in focusing so much on one, single film, the other, multitudinous references (as well as those in its working title, *The Blair Witch Project*, *The Sixth Sense* and, ignoring genre confines, *The Matrix* and *The Usual Suspects*, are just a few) tend to sit awkwardly. And, more importantly, what appears to have been overlooked is that *Scream*, too, was a spoof. More satire and certainly more intelligent, but a spoof all the same.

So where the majestic *Airplane* took the rise out of a series of disaster movies that had taken themselves far too seriously, *Scary Movie* (which only once tries to parody its source's parody – and fails) loses considerable impact by not having its necessary straight man. A Morecambe, if you like, without its Wise.

But even if the humour is perhaps too American (the US Budweiser ads are frequently referenced) to be universal and borders on the offensive with its latent homophobia, the set-pieces do tickle, with many a slapstick gem to be discovered – just about often enough to forgive some excruciatingly painful lapses in momentum.

The franchise is now on it's fourth sequel, with the *Airplane!* team, led by David Zucker, gradually taking over the reins and continuing high box office returns proving the movies are critic proof. ★★ **MD**

SCENES FROM A MALL (1991)

Starring: *Bette Midler (Deborah Fifer), Woody Allen (Nick Fifer), Bill Irwin (Mime), Daren Firestone (Sam), Rebecca Nickels (Jennifer)*
Director: *Paul Mazursky*
Screenwriters: *Roger L. Simon, Paul Mazursky*
15/89 mins./Comedy/USA

After 16 years of marriage, the Fifers are drifting around a shopping mall, when Nick Fifer confesses he has had affairs. Deborah Fifer immediately goes spare, demanding a divorce, and as they discuss the division of their spoils, it transpires she too has been unfaithful.

One of the few times Woody Allen stepped out of his own universe, to merely star in another filmmaker's movie. It's little wonder he tends to keep to his own devices, given how bland and unfunny this study of a fragmenting marriage turns out. Actually, director Paul Mazursky seems to be almost parodying Allen's tight and witty relationship dramedies, with this pointed tale of a smug, blathering couple, drifting zombie-like around that LA dead zone The Beverly Centre, or as Nick puts it in sub-Allenesque terms, 'Kafka in California'.

Allen's Nick is everything he has striven against, a sports lawyer layered in money, with an ever-trilling beeper and a ponytail for Manhattan's sake! And the comedian looks about as comfortable in the character as he would playing The Terminator. Better Midler, erroneously thinking she was stepping up to some prize piece of relationship satire, contains the volume, but seems at a loss with the film's lack of bite.

Mazursky is not quite sure what he's after. A study of a marriage encountering rough water while still anchored to a habit that is hard to break? Or is he smirking at modern Angelino foibles, all their consumerist shallowness? Both and neither is the answer. His empty film just lollops along beside this irritable, whingeing couple, its messages as stale as its comedy. ★★ **IN**

SCHINDLER'S LIST (1993)

Starring: *Liam Neeson (Oskar Schindler), Ben Kingsley (Itzhak Stern), Ralph Fiennes (Amon Goeth), Caroline Goodall (Emilie Schindler), Embeth Davidtz (Helen Hirsch)*
Director: *Steven Spielberg*
Screenwriter: *Steven Zallian, based on the book by Thomas Keneally*
15/195 mins./Drama/History/War/USA

Awards – *Best Art Direction-Set Decoration, Best Cinematography, Best Director, Best Film Editing, Best Original Score, Best Picture, Best Adapted Screenplay, BAFTA – Best Supporting Actor (Ralph Fiennes), Best Cinematography, Best Editing, Best Film, Best Score, Best Adapted Screenplay, David Lean Award for Direction, Golden Globes – Best Director, Best Drama, Best Screenplay*

Oskar Schindler uses Jews to start a factory in Poland during the war. As he becomes more aware of the concentration camp life that awaits them, he works to save those he can.

Box office supremo. Hollywood's baby boomer wunderkind. The finest architect of audience thrill since Hitchcock. All of these things were true of Steven Spielberg in 1993, yet there was the nagging sense that the Oscar-deprived director remained a pretender, a popcorn-maker of unrivalled talent but not the real thing. In an astonishing double-whammy, 1993 upheld all the suspicion, then undid it utterly. This was the year he remade dinosaurs and then on an unparalleled template envisioned the Holocaust. By 1994 Spielberg was presiding over the most successful picture of all time and, finally, his treasured Oscar.

Fourteen years previously, a well-regarded Australian writer strolled into a luggage shop to escape the LA heat. Thomas Keneally immediately struck up conversation with the shop owner, one Leopald Page, formerly Poldek Pfefferberg, a Schindlerjuden. There Page told him the story of Oskar Schindler, the German industrialist who had saved him and 1200 others from certain death in occupied Poland. Here was a Nazi who had not stood back. Keneally was so inspired he turned it into the Booker Prize winning novel *Schindler's Ark*. Spielberg, in turn, was transfixed by the story which awakened feelings of his own Jewish heritage and picked up the movie rights in 1982. Then he dallied, he wasn't ready, he hadn't matured enough. It took him ten years, as he put it, 'to develop his own consciousness about the Holocaust.'

Made without his trademark storyboarding, the whizz kid bravado put away, *Schindler's List* was shot from the gut, where all of his God-given skills as a filmmaker were distilled into something instinctual and fiercely emotional. The film was daringly – although it is hard, now, to consider it otherwise – shot in black and white, alternating between a documentarian-vibe of jarring hand-held confusion for the Jews and a sumptuous German Expressionism for the Nazis (we first meet Schindler in a nightclub shot with the back-lit beauty of a 30s movie star). Constructed around a brilliant script by Steve Zallian, the film meticulously threads the historical facts of Schindler saving the Jews by employing them in his enamel (and later armaments) factory with the story of a man discovering his conscience despite everything he is. On a more subtle, thematic level Zallian pits a battle for Schindler's soul between camp commandant Amon Goeth and Jewish accountant Itzhak Stern.

History has been massaged. Aspects were contracted for more direct storytelling (it actually took Schindler three weeks to retrieve his female Jewish workers from Auschwitz) but impressively Neeson's philandering entrepreneur is presented with an ambiguous lustre. He was a womanising profiteer, whose actions constantly contradict his instincts, not a cleancut hero. War transforms men, it made Schindler far more than he appeared. It did the same for the director.

Through its wrenching three hours, Spielberg takes an unblinking eye and steely humanity. In its most extraordinary moments, the film presents the Holocaust as a reality that defies understanding: nothing in Spielberg's career could prepare us (or him) for the numbing brutality of the 16-minute liquidation of the Krakow ghetto. The film charts a barrage of the unthinkable, summed up in the stunning image of the Nazis unearthing the mass graves and burning the corpses on a vast, hellish funeral pyre. Ash rains down on Krakow in a perverse mockery of snowfall and a German officer laughs with the unsettling intensity of the insane.

It is hard to explain the first reaction to watching *Schindler's List*, it is one of emotional exhaustion, of elation at artistic triumph, of eyes stung by tears of outrage and a strange sense of loss. The director you once knew like a favourite uncle had become something else. He had become important. And he was asking us to grow up with him.

The reviews were ecstatic. Exultant notices from critics whose expectations and doubts had been confounded. Twelve nominations and seven Oscars were the result from the fusty Academy. There was, inevitably, a backlash. The Zealot community decried the fact the Holocaust must remain beyond artistic interpretation, Claude Lanzmann – who made the nine-hour documentary *Shoah* – criticised him for shifting the focus away from the six million who perished. There was a wave of reactionism citing Spielberg's motivation as suspect: his sudden rediscovery of his Judaic roots, his yearnings to be taken seriously as a filmmaker. Yet, in the face of the movie, such judgements are hard to swallow.

The fact remains that regardless of what Spielberg was personally hoping to achieve, *Schindler's List* brought the history of the Holocaust back to public consciousness like nothing else (it is enormously telling that it was a smash hit in Germany). It was (and remains) irreducibly his masterpiece. The apprenticeship was over. The dreamer was born-again as a supreme artist. ★★★★★ **IN**

Movie Trivia:

Steven Spielberg (born 1946)

Who he is: Movie brat turned leader of American cinema. All-rounder with unparalleled commercial and critical success.

Hallmarks: Childlike wonder; World War II; aliens; ground-breaking effects; John Williams score; an oft-overlooked dark side; broken homes; everyman as hero.

If you see one movie, see: *E.T. The Extra-Terrestrial* (1982)

SCHOOL FOR SCOUNDRELS (1960)

Starring: *Ian Carmichael (Henry Palfrey), Terry Thomas (Raymond Delauney), Alistair Sim (Stephen Potter), Janette Scott (April Smith), Dennis Price (Dunstan Dorchester), Peter Jones (Dudley Dorchester), Edward Chapman (Gloatbridge), John Le Mesurier (Headwaiter), Irene Handl (Mrs. Stringer)*
Director: *Robert Hamer*
Screenwriters: *Hal E. Chester, Patricia Moyes, Peter Ustinov, based on the books* Theory And Practice-Gamesmanship, Same Some Notes On Lifemanship and One of upmanship *by Stephen Potter*
U/94 mins/Comedy/UK

Consistently humiliated in his dealings with the caddish Raymond Delauney, Henry Palfrey repairs to the College of Lifemanship to ask Stephen Potter how he can get the better of his nemesis and prevent him from seducing his beloved April Smith.

Terry Thomas is one of the unsung greats of British cinema. An inveterate scene-stealer, he also had the happy knack of upping the game of his co-stars. Ian Carmichael particularly benefited from their unofficial double act. But while their exchanges counted among the comic highlights of *Private's Progress, Lucky Jim, Brothers in Law, Happy Is the Bride* and *I'm All Right, Jack*, they were only once afforded a film of their own. *School for Scoundrels* may suffer from its sketch-like structure, but it still has a couple of classic set-pieces and is one of the more underrated satires of the post-Ealing era.

The storyline was inspired by a series of bestselling parodic self-help manuals by Stephen Potter – *Gamesmanship* (1947), *Lifemanship* (1950) and One-upmanship (1952). Although Patricia Moyes and producer Hal E. Chester were credited with the screenplay, it was predominantly written by Peter Ustinov and blacklisted HUAC exile, Frank Tarloff. It should have provided the perfect material for director Robert Hamer, who had triumphed with the similarly episodic *Kind Hearts and Coronets*. However, a lot of booze had flowed under Hamer's bridge since then and he was fired for lapsing back into alcoholism soon after shooting began (dying three years later without making another movie). Chester and the uncredited Cyril Frankel completed the project, but the lack of a single controlling hand significantly affected the outcome.

Sim was somewhat miscast as the self-assured cynic whose Yeovil courses in the likes of 'woomanship' and 'partymanship' give Carmichael's typically flaky twit some backbone. Similarly Carmichael looks uncomfortable as he strives to lure Janette Scott into bed. However, he's at his most amusing while being duped by crooked secondhand car dealers Dunstan and Dudley Dorchester (superbly played by Dennis Price and Peter Jones) and soundly thrashed in a tennis match punctuated by Delauney's insouciantly insincere commiseration of 'hard cheese' each time he loses a point. ★★★ **DP**

SCHOOL OF ROCK (2003)

Starring: *Jack Black (Dewey Finn), Joan Cusack (Principal Rosalie Mullins), Mike White (Ned Schneebly), Sarah Silverman (Patty Di Marco), Joey Gaydos, Jr. (Zack), Maryam Hassan (Tomika), Miranda Cosgrove (Summer), Kevin Clark (Freddy)*
Director: *Richard Linklater*
Screenwriter: *Mike White*
PG/104 mins./Comedy/Music/USA/Germany

Dewey has been kicked out of the latest in a long line of rock groups. In an attempt to earn money, he takes a teaching job intended for his flatmate. But what starts out as an excuse for paid slacking turns into something more . . .

This unashamed ode to the power of rock music was a sleeper hit in the States and confirmed what we at Empire have known for ages: that, given the right material, Jack Black is a bona fide movie star. 'Shallow Hal'

– Black's previous leading role, after his breakout turn in Stephen Frears' 'High Fidelity' was not the right material.

The School Of Rock, though, is a perfect fit, and the result is a feel-good hit. Be warned, though: if you think a little Jack Black goes a long way, then this isn't for you. For everyone else, Black gives one of the finest comic lead performances since Jim Carrey's early, funny period.

Screenwriter Mike White (who also co-stars as Black's roommate) penned the film specifically for Black, and it shows. The highly-strung Dewey Finn may be a watered-down version of the actor's anarchic Tenacious D persona, but Black's leering, grinning, gurning, sweating, wise-cracking turn is a comedic tour de force, augmented by an obvious passion for the subject.

Indie darlings Richard Linklater and White (who also wrote *The Good Girl* and *Chuck & Buck*) are savvy enough to know that *The School Of Rock* is a cross between, say, *Dead Poets Society* and *Sister Act*, and they whole-heartedly embrace formula conventions. Shy kid harbouring an amazing voice? Check. Selfish teacher learning to care for others? Check.

But they also inject these clichés with much-needed energy and humour, while gently subverting the formula and cloaking the film's exuberance in a muted, autumnal colour scheme, which manages to avoid gooey sentiment. In fact, what should be the film's key emotional moment (an unmasked Dewey's heartfelt plea for clemency from the kids' irate parents) rapidly becomes a very funny, if slightly dubious, paedophile gag.

But all the genre gymnastics wouldn't have mattered if the kids weren't alright. Luckily, they graduate with honours. Not only are they genuinely good musicians but, as actors, they show enough chutzpah to hold their own against Black. For Linklater to prise one good performance from a child actor is commendable. To get seven, without any hint of the Stepford Stage School, is a charming and winning surprise – much like the movie itself. ★★★★ **CH**

SCOOBY-DOO (2002)

Starring: *Freddie Prinze, Jr. (Fred), Sarah Michelle Gellar (Daphne), Matthew Lillard (Shaggy), Linda Cardellini (Velma), Rowan Atkinson (Emile Mondavarious), Isla Fisher (Mary Jane)*
Director: *Raja Gosnell*
Screenwriter: *James Gunn, based on a story by Craig Titley, James Gunn, characters by William Hanna, Joseph Barbera*
PG/82 mins./Mystery/Comedy/Adventure/USA

The world-famous Mystery Inc. disbands after internal pressures force them apart, but they are brought together again by the enigmatic theme park owner, Mondavarius, to solve the mystery of 'Spooky Island'.

Zoinks! Who let the dog out? The world has, apparently, been waiting for a live-action 'Scooby-Doo' film for 33 long years (that's 231 years for canines). And the good news is, it's finally here. The bad news is, it's directed by the guy who gave us *Big Momma's House* and stars Freddie Prinze Jr. And it's clearly not the Scooby-Doo we know and love.

Which is fair enough, because for 310 episodes (or seemingly one episode on a perpetual loop), the 'Scooby-Doo' we do know and love went something like this: Mystery Inc. – four humans and a talking dog – investigate a spooky haunting; find out said haunting was perpetrated by Old Man Smithers; end of mystery. And that does not a 90-minute movie make.

Tagline
Be afraid. Be kind of afraid.

So 'Scooby-Doo: The Movie' gets the conventional mystery-solving stuff out of the way immediately, with a gaudy, shoddily-staged opening sequence which raises the miserable spectre of Warner Bros farragoes past, like *The Avengers* and (shudder) *Batman & Robin*.

Luckily, it soon improves, branching out into a postmodern, Brady Bunch-esque reimagining, in which Fred is an arrogant egotist, Daphne turns into an ass-kicking Buffy-a-like and Velma is stifled by her spinster image. Only Shaggy and Scooby, the eternal innocents, are left untouched. It's tinkering which could have worked, had not the film been pitched squarely at the under-tens.

Anyone looking for sophistication from a movie which features a two minute-long farting contest between man and CG dog is going to be sorely disappointed. And what nods there are to the oldies aren't exactly subtle. Ever wondered why Shaggy and Scooby were so hungry? It's because they're druggies! But because they can't show drug use, here's Scooby snacks – in a baggie! And Shaggy's love interest is called Mary Jane! Oh, the wit! Oh, our aching ribs! Bring back the farting dog! Or not.

Because Scooby himself is the movie's trump card and chump card all in one. Although recognisably Scoob in deed, voice and mannerisms, the CG never really integrates convincingly. It's baffling to think why director Gosnell – who never uses light brushstrokes where a chuffing great roller would do – plumped for a cross between photo-realistic 3D and the old cartoon animation, when a traditional 2D Scoob would have worked perfectly within the context of a live-action cartoon.

Performance-wise, Prinze Jr. and Gellar are blandly acceptable. But it's fitting that, for a movie which champions the (under) dog, it's Lillard and Cardellini who take centre stage, with performances which channel their cartoon counterparts perfectly.

In fact, they deserve a lot better than the shoddy material – a couple of zingers aside – on display. Because frankly, any movie which 'boasts' a Pamela Anderson cameo probably belongs in the doghouse.

The sequel *Scooby-Doo 2: Monsters Unleashed* was a slight improvement, bringing back the best monsters from the TV series and adding guest stars Seth Green and Alicia Silverstone. ★★ **CH**

SCORPION KING (2002)

Starring: *The Rock (The Scorpion King), Michael Clarke Duncan (Balthazar), Steven Brand (Memnon), Kelly Hu (Cassandra), Bernard Hill (Philos)*
Director: *Chuck Russell*
Screenwriters: *Stephen Sommers, William Osbourne, David Hayter, from a story by Sommers, Johnathan Hales*
12/87 mins./Action/Adventure/Fantasy/USA/Germany

A fearsome horde laid waste the ancient world. Their leader, Memnon, slaughtered all who resisted him. One survivor, a warrior named Mathayus, would one day become the Scorpion King...

Spin-off movies are risky ventures – for every *Leon* there's an *Ewok Adventure*. And *Scorpion King*, Universal's off-shoot of the *Mummy* franchise, is perhaps riskier than most, since it takes a relatively minor character from *The Mummy Returns*, then strips him of the special effects which made those movies so enjoyable and him so memorable (though not for the best of reasons).

In that box office-guzzling sequel, WWF star and (eek!) bestselling author Dwayne 'The Rock' Johnson played a half-man, half-scorpion beast which turned up late but stole the show (even if director Stephen Sommers berated the efforts of ILM in this very magazine). Now, the future of one of Universal's most successful franchises has been put in the giant mitts of a professional wrestler and the uncertain hands of director Chuck Russell, whose last effort was *Bless The Child*.

Although the opening sequence, in which Mathayus rescues his brother from what look like aggrieved extras from *Xena: Warrior Princess*, bodes well, the rest of the film never matches it, despite eye candy in the shape of

The Man In The Suit TOP10

1 Alien, *Alien* - Boris Balejo
2 Gort, *The Day The Earth Stood Still* - Lock Martin
3 The Creature, *The Creature from the Black Lagoon* - Ricou Browning, Ben Chapman)
4 Godzilla, *Godzilla* - mainly Ken Satsuma
5 Predator, *Predator* - Kevin Peter Hall
6 Harry, *Harry and the Hendersons* - Kevin Peter Hall
7 Swamp Thing, *Swamp Thing* - Dick Durock
8 Moonwatcher, the head ape in *2001* - Dan Richter
9 Darth Vader, *Star Wars* saga - David Prowse, Bob Anderson, later Hayden Christensen
10 Chewbacca, *Star Wars* saga - Peter Mayhew

Hawaiian hottie Kelly Hu, and an impressive but under-used Michael Clarke Duncan. Perhaps this bit stands out because, rumour has it, Universal brought in Sommers to film something exciting.

Russell instead delivers a straightforward barbarian fight-fest with a fraction of the appeal of *The Mummy Returns* – and barely a scorpion or a special effect in sight. Besides, any movie too lazy to name a 'Comedic Sidekick' who has almost as many lines as the lead deserves universal scorn. ★★ **GH**

SCREAM (1996)

Starring: *Neve Campbell (Sidney Prescott), Courteney Cox (Gale Weathers), David Arquette (Deputy Dwight 'Dewey' Riley), Skeet Ulrich (Billy Loomis), Drew Barrymore (Casey Becker), Matthew Lillard (Stuart Macher), Jamie Kennedy (Randy Meeks), Rose McGowan (Tatum Riley), Henry Winkler (Principal Himbry), Wes Craven (Fred, the janitor)*
Director: *Wes Craven*
Screenwriter: *Kevin Williamson*
18/106 mins./Horror/Comedy/USA

A teenage girl becomes the target of a killer who has stalked and killed one of her classmates. A tabloid news reporter is determined to uncover the truth, insisting that the man who raped and killed the target's mother one year earlier is the same man who is terrorising her now.

The audacious, much-parodied prologue of Drew Barrymore's home alone Casey making chatty with a mystery caller, popping corn and being subjected to escalating torment lasts 12 tortuous minutes. It serves notice that this self-mocking teen slasher flick wears its gore with a difference.

Such a disreputable genre has invited spoofing – usually limp, crude and undistinguished – but not since 1981 's *An American Werewolf In London* had a full-blooded horror film delivered its bona fide frights along with a snappy sense of humour. Scream is a scary movie, but it is also a clever, witty, and stylishly adroit movie.

Wesley Earl Craven has had a major impact on horror films since, as a holder of a Master's degree in philosophy and a onetime humanities teacher, he turned his hand to the utterly repugnant with *Last House On The Left* in 1972. He got better (*The Hills Have Eyes*) and wildly successful at creating a perverse phenomenon of popular culture (*Nightmare On Elm Street*'s outrageous, razor-fingered Freddy Krueger). But his intentions have always been expressed in one prevailing theme: the subversion of the safe middle-class American ideal and its expectations of normality. His preoccupation is playing on the distinction between sanity and insanity, reality and dreams. By the late 80s his feel for the fantastique added on-screen discussion of mass media, violence and censorship, and led to his playing on the distinction between reality and screen dreams (hence the sophisticated film-within-a-film scenario and intellectual defence of horror films articulated in *Wes Craven's New Nightmare*).

It was a perfect meeting of minds when Craven filmed new boy Kevin Williamson's hip, flip script, stuffed with irony, in-jokes and knowing references drawn from an encyclopedic knowledge of the teen slasher genre. He went on to deconstruct it and affectionately send it up while giving it an ironic shot in the arm. The heroine of *Scream* is Sidney Prescott (Campbell, a pert brunette practised at giving good ingénue anguish in the TV melodrama *Party Of Five*, inheriting Jamie Lee Curtis's scream queen crown). In an isolated house (aren't they always?) on the outskirts of Northern California small town Woodsboro, Sid is left home alone (aren't they always?) to brood on her mother's supposedly solved murder exactly one year earlier, just when a senseless bloodbath gets underway. The stock company of characters include boyfriend Billy, confidante Tatum, class cut-ups Stu and Randy, and aw-shucks deputy Dwight 'Dewey' Riley. After the first double murder a media invasion brings in tabloid TV reporter Gale Weathers whose interest is summed up when she crows excitedly to her cameraman: 'An innocent man on Death Row, a killer still on the loose; Kenny, tell me I'm dreaming! If I'm right about this I could save a man's life! Do you know what that could do for my book sales?' Barely glimpsed (in a newscast) but neatly set up for the sequels that were already on the cards is Liev Schreiber's Cotton Weary, convicted of killing Sid's mom.

The characters in *Scream* certainly know their horror movies – enumerating the clichés, shocks and delights of *Halloween*, *Prom Night*, *Terror Train*, *Hellraiser* and the *Nightmare* cycle as well as more legit cinematic terror as *Frankenstein*, *Psycho*, *Carrie*, *The Silence Of The Lambs*, *The Bad Seed* and *The Exorcist*. The characters – better drawn and less naive than in routine cullings of a town's teens fare – also understand the conventions and dynamics of these pictures, and can't resist commenting on them with both ridicule and a kind of reverence throughout to draw parallels, predict behaviour and scorn red herrings. Not that all this awareness helps anyone elude the psychokiller. Craven himself, incidentally, gets half a name check in the referential roll call, Tatum (Rose McGowan, the busty blonde best friend who gets caught in the cat flap) cautioning Sidney 'You're starting to sound like some Wes Carpenter flick.' He also gets a cameo as the high school janitor, dressed in Freddy Krueger garb, who lurks in the hallway while the principal (an uncredited Henry Winkler) buys it in a time-honoured, expertly handled look-behind-you set-piece.

Randy, who works in a video store and reports 'a run in the Mass Murder section' springing from the killings, is, ironically, an archetypal horror buff and the obligatory virgin nerd. To him falls the celebrated dissertation on The Rules Of Horror Movies, rules to survive by, delivered in exasperation at the climactic party that takes place in a large and remote house (natch) where the parents are absent (natch) and where the body count will eventually tot up to seven completely dead and several of those essential not-dead-after-all and not-dead-yet rebounds. 'Number One: You can never have sex. Big no-no. Sex equals death. Number Two: You can never drink or do drugs ... Number Three: Never, ever, ever, under any circumstances, say "I'll be right back", 'cause you won't be back.'

Williamson became his own follow-up industry with credits including the *I Know What You Did Last Summer* films and Craven oversaw the successful expansion through sequel to trilogy. ★★★★ **AE**

⊙ SCREAM 2 (1997)

Starring: *David Arquette (Dwight 'Dewey' Riley), Neve Campbell (Sidney Prescott), Courteney Cox (Gale Weathers), Sarah Michelle Gellar (Casey 'Cici' Cooper), Jamie Kennedy (Randy Meeks), Laurie Metcalf (Debbie Salt), Jerry O'Connell (Derek Feldman), Jada Pinkett Smith (Maureen Evans)*
Director: *Wes Craven*
Screenwriter: *Kevin Williamson, based on his characters*
18/116 mins./Horror/Comedy/USA

Scream Queen Campbell shakes off the trauma of the first movie and goes to college, only to be followed by the masked slasher who now has a whole new social circle to terrorise.

Early in *Scream 2*, a class of film students discuss sequels, and movie geek Randy challenges his friends to name a sequel that improves on the original. Waving aside *Godfather 2* and *Aliens*, a lonely voice pipes up for *House 2: The Second Story*. It's clear that we're back in postmodern slasher territory.

When guest star Jada Pinkett is murdered in a cinema during a sneak preview of *Stab*, a convincingly cheesy based-on-fact horror flick about the murders seen in the first film, Randy reasons a copycat killer is putting on his own sequel and lists the rules: bigger body count, more elaborate death scenes, etc. The film, of course, proceeds to follow those rules, right down to the important, but unmentioned, one of not being quite as good as the first film (even though it is ten minutes longer) – which one would like to think was done deliberately.

The set-up is that heroine Sidney has almost got over the ghastliness of the first film and gone to college, pursued by most of the surviving characters – hanger-on Kennedy, crippled ex-deputy Arquette, rapacious newslady Cox and one-time fall guy Schreiber – and there attracting a brand new circle of soon-to-be-victims, red herrings, bystanders and psychopaths.

It would be unfair to reveal too many twists, but the windy plot allows Wes Craven to demonstrate again just how good he is at punching your scare buttons, employing sharp editing and a superb sound mix to make even the hokiest sudden-appearance-out-of-the-dark a moment guaranteed to spill your popcorn. Given an original idea, like the need to clamber over the unconscious murderer to escape a crashed car, he comes up with real tension and pays off with a proper shock.

Scream screenwriter Kevin Williamson, who has already added *I Know What You Did Last Summer* to his résumé, has returned and shows again a feel for the way movie-literate students talk, getting laughs from gags at the expense of *Top Gun* and Paul Verhoeven ('What's your favourite scary movie?' the killer asks one victim, only to be told, '*Showgirls*').

But *Scream 2* strains for a more all-encompassing theory of horror, paralleling a gimmicky screening of *Stab*, with an audience full of knife-wavers dressed as the *Scream* killer, with a performance of a Greek tragedy in which Campbell is similarly beset by masked figures.

There is a trainspottery charm to the ticking-off of all the obligatories: a sinister guest appearance from David Warner as a one-scene professor who works hard to make himself suspicious, Sarah Michelle Gellar's perky showing as the smart-mouthed blonde who gets on the killer's list by objecting to the whole idea of sequels, characters who are worried because their equivalents in the first film were gutted, the gathering of all the survivors on stage in the finale so their mutilations of each other take on the aspect of a student drama bloodbath.

In-joke fans will especially relish the extracts from *Stab*, in which – as she feared in the first film – Sidney is played by Tori Spelling. In *Stab*, key moments from *Scream* are done again with caricature cheap horror movie twitches that pile up on what were already essays in textbook genre-making.

Like most sequels, it's hamstrung because giving you what you liked last time doesn't take into account the fact that what you liked last time was surprising then but isn't any more. Arquette and Cox are allowed to develop their characters a bit, though the warming romance doesn't undercut his slightly suspect geniality or her rampant careerism too much.

If it has a real problem it's that all the good stuff piled into the film means that the heroine rather fades into the background until the literally stagey climax, with traumatised good girl Campbell too often required to play straight woman to masked people with knives or unmasked people with better lines. Still, that's sequels for you, and this is loads better than *House II: The Second Story*, not to mention *House III: The Horror Show* and *House IV: The Repossession*. ★★★★ **KN**

⊙ SCREAM 3 (2000)

Starring: *David Arquette (Dwight 'Dewey' Riley), Neve Campbell (Sidney Prescott), Courteney Cox (Gale Weathers), Patrick Dempsey (Det. Mark Kincaid), Parker Posey (Jennifer Jolie), Scott Foley (Roman Bridger), Emily Mortimer (Angelina Tyler)*
Director: *Wes Craven*
Screenwriter: *Ehren Kruger, based on characters by Kevin Williamson*
18/116 mins./Horror/Comedy/USA

All bets are off in this final instalment that sees Campbell hiding away as a therapist in the mountains, until she receives a phonecall informing her of the murders of the cast of *Stab 3*. With every body, there is a picture of her mother, prompting another whodunit . . .

One of the most memorable – not to mention memorably 'ironic' – moments in *Scream 2* occurs when a class of soon-to-be-chopped-liver students discuss whether film sequels can ever improve on the original. While the general consensus is that second instalments 'blow', there are just enough examples given of films that do actually better their cinematic predecessors to suggest that *Scream 2* itself might have a chance of joining them. Moreover, although this eventually proves to be not quite true, at least it isn't embarrassingly wide of the mark, either.

It comes as little surprise, however, that no one in Wes Craven's third *Scream* outing makes a similar case for second sequels. After all, this time around, the knife-centric action has moved from sleepy Woodsboro to Hollywood, where everyone knows that any film with a number above 2 in its title has a good chance of sucking so much that even passing vacuum cleaners stand around and applaud.

Not that *Scream 3* attempts to hide its chronological status. Chief irony-monger Kevin Williamson may have abandoned scriptwriting duties to concentrate on his directing 'career' – not so 'funny' now is it, Kev? – but replacement Ehren Kruger (no relation) is hardly a slouch when it comes to finding the inverted comma on his keypad.

As a result, during one of the film's ultra-rare action breaks, Campbell is treated to a posthumous video lecture from film nerd/comic relief/*Scream 2* victim Randy Meeks who informs her that, in the final part of a trilogy, all bets are off and that even the most entrenched of series characters can expect a visit from The Grim Reaper.

Plotwise – predictably – the now standard murder is just the start of the mayhem, and soon the rest of *Stab*'s cast of young good-looking actors are being slaughtered like, well, young good-looking actors in a schlock horror movie. It is a turn of events that attracts the attention of first tabloid hack Gale Weathers and then Sidney Prescott who, following the events of *Scream 2*, has secreted herself away as a counsellor in some remote backwoods.

And so the gore-soaked stage is set for fun frolics and fear with Arquette, Cox and Campbell once more dodging the attentions of our Munch-loving maniac, whoever he may be this time. Indeed, one of the strangely under-acknowledged aspects of the *Scream* series is that they owe every bit as much to the traditional Agatha Christie whodunit as they do the slasher genre.

Certainly, one of the original movie's most accomplished moves was the way it first made us suspect Skeet Ulrich, then utterly absolved him before turning everything on its head in the peerless final act. This time, though, the finger of suspicion is pointed at so many people that you begin to believe it's only a matter of time before Craven puts himself in the frame.

Moreover, even given the traditions of the genre, it is a little tiring to watch Campbell et al yet again abandon all common sense as they repeatedly split up to wander around darkened corridors on their own. Yet, while not half as scary as its predecessors, *Scream 3* does go some way to match their joke-quotient, thanks in large part to cameos from Kevin Smith creations 'Jay and Silent Bob', and, best of all, Carrie Fisher – the *Star Wars* gag is to be truly relished.

The result is a film that may have run out of ideas, but still has energy to spare. One can only hope, though, that Wes really does call it a day now. After all, even 'George' has trouble with those fourth episodes. ★★★ **CC**

SCROOGE (1951)

Starring: *Alastair Sim (Ebenezer Scrooge), Mervyn Johns (Bob Cratchit), Hermione Baddeley (Mrs. Cratchit), Michael Hordern (Jacob Marley), George Cole (Young Ebenezer Scrooge)*
Director: *Brian Desmond Hurst*
Screenwriter: *Noel Langley, adapated from the novel by Charles Dickens*
U/86 mins./Fantasy/Drama/UK

The miserly Scrooge refuses to help the poor at this festive time of year, and is visited by the ghosts of Christmasses past, present and future who will help him mend his ways.

Since its publication in 1843, Charles Dickens' *A Christmas Carol* has been adapted nine times for the big screen, running the casting gamut from Reginald Owen to Bill Murray to Kermit The Frog.

Brian Desmond Hurst's faithful adaptation is festive fare par excellence, and by far the best version committed to celluloid. Superbly shot in chiaroscuro for full ghoulish effect, it tells the tale of the miserly Scrooge's transformation after visitations from the Spirits of Christmasses Past, Present and Yet To Come.

Check your cynicism in at the door and you'll find a supporting cast of well-loved characters, including Bob Cratchit (an excellent Mervyn Johns) and Tiny Tim, and with a smattering of carols all adding to the atmosphere of good cheer.

The success of this interpretation, however, largely rests on the shoulders (and in the wonderfully doleful eyes) of Alastair Sim, whose wry performance gives us a fully three-dimensional Scrooge: a miserly yet pitiful character who extends beyond the normal caricature. When told that, 'At this time of year, it is more than usually desirable that we should make some slight provision for the poor and destitute', Sim's ironic delivery of, 'Why?' manages to invest humour into the most simple of one-liners, and sums up all that is great about his performance. While some of the other performances have dated, Sim's haunted Scrooge stands the test of time, even today eliciting sympathy and – you just can't help yourself – joy at his transformation. ★★★★ **MM**

THE SEA HAWK (1940)

Starring: *Errol Flynn (Capt. Geoffrey Thorpe), Brenda Marshall (Dona Maria Alvarez de Cordoba), Claude Rains (Don Jose Alvarez de Cordoba), Flora Robson (Queen Elizabeth 1), Alan Hale (Carl Pitt), Henry Daniell (Lord Wolfingham)*
Director: *Michael Curtiz*
Screenwriters: *Howard Koch, Seton I. Miller*
U/121 mins./Action/Adventure/Romance/USA

In the reign of Queen Elizabeth, privateer Geoffrey Thorpe preys on the galleons of Spain. The Spanish Ambassador and an English traitor conspire against Thorpe and other 'sea hawks', Britain's only naval defence, to have them out of the way so that the Spanish armada can attack.

The most elaborate of Warner Brothers' Errol Flynn swashbucklers, this casts the star as a happy-go-lucky (but patriotic) pirate in the service of a cheerful Good Queen Bess, defeating the humourless minions of Spain (Claude Rains, Henry Daniell) on the high seas and in swordfights.

It expresses wartime sentiments with jolly pirate singalongs ('Ho for the Shores of Dover'), speeches about Britain's indomitable navies and an explicit depiction of King Philip of Spain as a Hitler figure who cannot be appeased in his desire for world-conquest.

Flynn prevents it from becoming a simple propaganda film, swishing a mean cape as he drives his trusty blade into black hearts, slogging with his crew across the isthmus of Panama (in a sun-scorched sepia sequence) and shackled to an oar (with his shirt off) as a galley slave before fomenting a daring plan to take over the ship. Olivia de Havilland, perhaps sensing that the Queen would get all the best scenes with Flynn, passed on the heroine role, which is taken by the appreciably less winsome if still-lovely Brenda Marshall, and in any case there's not enough kissy stuff to compromise the energetic leaping about and rip-roaringly bloodthirsty sea battles.

Rains is underused, but Daniell is perfectly Rathbone-like as the scheming villain and the supporting cast is aces: Alan Hale, Donald Crisp, Una O'Connor.

It has some of the best sets, costumes and effects of any Hollywood spectacle, and an Erich Wolfgang Korngold score that is a triumph of old-time movie music. ★★★★★ **KN**

THE SEA INSIDE (MAR ADENTRO) (2005)

Starring: *Javier Bardem (Ramón Sampedro), Belén Rueda (Julia), Lola Dueñas (Rosa), Mabel Rivera (Manuela Sampedro), Celso Bugallo (Jose Sampedro)*
Director: *Alejandro Amenábar*
Screenwriters: *Alejandro Amenábar*
PG/123 mins./Drama/Biography/Spain/France/Italy

Awards – *Academy Awards – Best Foreign Language Film, Golden Globes – Best Foreign Language Film*

Quadriplegic Ramón campaigns for the right to assisted suicide, which sparks controversy in his own caring household and draws in lawyer Julia, herself suffering from a degenerative disease, and working woman Rosa, who tries to persuade him to live . . .

Alejandro Amenábar's first three features – *Tesis*, *Open Your Eyes* (remade as *Vanilla Sky*) and *The Others* – were all export-friendly genre fare. His fourth is a very different proposition, even if, in outline, it sounds like a Spanish retread of *Whose Life Is It Anyway*?, or even one of those issue-of-the-week TV movies that play on the Hallmark Channel.

Based on a true story, *The Sea Inside* is mercifully light on significant scenes in which the pros and cons of assisted suicide are debated, and only shifts into the courtroom for a black joke about the legal system that prompts one of the hero's many telling eye-roll moments. Early on, Ramón insists he's not speaking for all quadriplegics, and when his lawyer shyly confesses that she too would like to die, he even seems on the point of showering her with all the arguments he's suffered through.

Having broken his neck diving into the sea in 1968, Ramón has been living with his aged father, gruff brother, nurturing sister-in-law and surrogate-son nephew for 25 years. Any film about a housebound invalid has to cope with claustrophobia, and Amenábar relieves the dangerous cosiness of Ramón's upstairs world with stirring, literal flights of fantasy as the hero's imagination rushes over the countryside.

Javier Bardem, one of the most physical actors in Spain, is brilliantly cast as the bed-bound Ramón, body credibly limp and unmanageable, face subtly expressive. He delivers a tour de force without that begging-for-an-Oscar showboating that tends to come when stars play disabled. Though the hero is focused on his obsession with death, the film doesn't entirely go along with him, respecting his decision but showing the tangle of relationships around him with such emotion that the viewer might wonder how he can bear to leave so many people who love him in so many ways.

There is a sense of what Ramón has missed, as friends pop in with stories of the outside or other lives rush on in spurts, but Amenábar eventually closes in on the strong, strange women who come to dote on Ramón – each perhaps projecting a different fantasy of child, lover, non-threatening man or father. Bardem is matched by the excellent actresses Belén Rueda, Lola Dueñas and Mabel Rivera and, thanks to their contributions, the more intimate scenes are almost unbearably poignant. ★★★★ **KN**

SEA OF LOVE (1989)

Starring: *Al Pacino (Det. Frank Keller), Ellen Barkin (Helen Cruger), John Goodman (Det. Sherman), Michael Rooker (Terry), William Hickey (Frank Keller Sr.)*
Director: *Harold Becker*
Screenwriter: *Richard Price*
15/113 mins./Thriller/USA

While investigating a serial killer who picks their prey through the lonely hearts ads of a newspaper, Detective Frank Keller falls in love with one of his suspects. As the clues increasingly point toward her, it could be Frank's life is at risk.

Having returned to his theatrical roots for five years, Al Pacino returned fully refreshed for this tight thriller, let down only by the implausibility of its denouement. Detective Frank Keller is a good fit for Pacino, or it could just be how skilfully the actor moulds him into a genuine human being: he's a loner, trying to keep the bitterness at bay, hunkered down in his job, the only place his instincts can live. Imagine *Heat*'s Vincent Hanna after years on the sauce. In short, a great character.

Little wonder that the sexually vital but vulnerable suspect in this peculiar riff on standard serial-killer dynamics brings him so recklessly to life. Ellen Barkin's Helen Cruger is a true sex-bomb using her body like its driven by animal impulses alone. As a screen couple they steam away, giving the standard motion of this thriller a real vitality and predates the is-she-the-killer froth of *Basic Instinct* by a good four years.

Harold Becker, a hot-cold kind of director (*City Hall*, *Malice*), composes a really good script from Richard Price (central theme: loneliness; secondary theme: the perils of sex) into an edgy game. Will Frank's jovial partner John Goodman talk sense into him before the worst happens? Is she truly the killer? Can their relationship survive all this suspicion, anyway?

Like many of these either-or thrillers, it doesn't offer enough alternatives to the main debate, painting itself into a corner. So when things finally unravel, and the killer's fateful identity exposed, it is stage-managed and unsatisfying. But the journey there has been outstanding. ★★★★ **IN**

SEABISCUIT (2003)

Starring: *Tobey Maguire (Red Pollard), Jeff Bridges (Charles Howard), Chris Cooper (Tom Smith), Elizabeth Banks (Marcela Howard), William H. Macy ('Tick-Tock' McGlaughin)*
Director: *Gary Ross*
Screenwriter: *Gary Ross, based on the book by Laura Hillenbrand*
PG/134 mins./Drama/History/Sport/USA

Three broken men — bereaved millionaire Charles Howard, displaced cowboy Tom Smith and drifter Red Pollard — are brought together by a broken-down horse whose rescue, rehabilitation and racetrack heroics will mend their shattered lives.

During the 1930s a funny-looking little racehorse named 'Seabiscuit' became America's most unexpected idol, smashing records for speed, audience attendance and winnings in an amazing career that was avidly followed by millions of people who had two things in common. Mostly they were on their uppers, but they almost all had radios.

Laura Hillenbrand's non-fiction bestseller on the remarkable true story of 'Seabiscuit' and three men united in his cause – the owner, the trainer and the rider – is a tremendous read, and a recent documentary made by America's PBS confirmed that this tale comes ready-made with absolutely everything for a popular film: romance, tragedy, humour, triumph against the odds, athletic magnificence and, crucially, despairing people and a traumatised animal getting second chances in their lives.

For those whose reflex is to groan at the prospect of another film about Hope, Gary Ross's epic tapestry of hard-luck heroes, horse racing, the Great Depression and the power of an unquenchable spirit may be too much of a good thing. Inevitably, some of the finest points in Hillenbrand's book aren't here, but every speck of pathos, human drama, comic potential and equine suspense is magnified.

You are very aware that you are watching a superbly crafted Hollywood movie that pats real life into formula fit (Jeepers, do you think the limping 'biscuit will win that Last Big Race?), even though it comes with an educational strand.

This provides historical context, using archive stills and narration by historian David McCullough (whose voice, so familiar from major documentary series like Ken Burns' *The Civil War*, brings folkloric authenticity), highlighting the gulf between Haves and Have-nots and the rivalry between America's East Coast elitists and the upstart, self-made Westerners whose hopes 'Seabiscuit' carried along with undernourished jockey Red Pollard.

This is tip-top entertainment, though, with a great cast and racing sequences spectacularly conveying the power, excitement and terror amid 1,500 lb beasts threaded through the stampedes around a track by brave men who weigh less than supermodels. The kind of careful thought Ross gave to the visuals in *Pleasantville* is evident here, with horses trained foot-perfect for daring camera work, a feat made feasible by the key involvement of champion US jockeys. One of these, Racing Hall Of Famer Gary Stevens, playing Red's friend and rival George Woolf, cuts such a creditable figure in his silks, one would take him for an assured actor rather than a man who has won racing's Triple Crown events.

A gaunt and auburn-haired Maguire is terrific as the bedevilled, pugnacious poetry lover Pollard, and so is Bridges as the colourful car tycoon. Meanwhile, Cooper's terse Tom Smith suggests the mystic authority of a frontier horse whisperer with the slightest body language.

William H. Macy is a scream as the composite radio announcer whose hyperbolic racetrack reports are not only hilarious, but illustrate the impact of radio in creating a mass culture and how it was instrumental in making sporting events a nationwide obsession. Yes, and the crowd goes wild – precisely on cue. ★★★★ **AE**

THE SEARCHERS (1956)

Starring: *John Wayne (Ethan Edwards), Jeffrey Hunter (Martin Pawley), Vera Miles (Laurie Jorgensen), Ward Bond (Rev. Capt. Samuel Clayton), Natalie Wood (Debbie Edwards)*
Director: *John Ford*
Screenwriter: *Frank S. Nugent, based on the novel by Alan LeMay*
U/113 mins./Western/USA

Ethan Edwards, an ex-Confederate soldier, finds that his family has been massacred and his niece captured by the Comanches and vows to bring her back and kill every one of the indians who did this to him.

Producer Merian C. Cooper tried to rope in his old *King Kong* colleague David O. Selznick on *The Searchers*, but the *Gone With The Wind* mini-mogul sneered that he didn't think a John Wayne Western was important enough to bear the sacred Selznick logo. Over the last 30 years, in the 10-yearly *Sight & Sound* poll of world critics, *The Searchers* has risen from the 19th best film of all time to the fifth. *Gone With The Wind* (1939) isn't as well-liked as it once was, and none of Selznick's other 'important' pictures are remembered at all.

The Searchers is an in-depth character study of Indian-hating Ethan Edwards that is also a probing examination of just what it meant to be John 'Duke' Wayne. Rarely taken seriously as an actor, Wayne proved here, and in other films for Ford and Howard Hawks, that his often-ridiculed mannerisms of speech and walk could serve an unforgettable performance.

Adapted from a novel by Alan LeMay, much-improved in translation to the screen, the film opens with Ethan, a diehard who has been drifting into mercenary soldiering and outlawry since losing the Civil War, returning to the Texas farmstead of his brother Aaron. Ethan is idolised by Aaron's kids: daughters Lucy and Debbie and son Ben. It's also clear that he is in love with, and loved by, his sister-in-law Martha. Texas Ranger-cum-preacher Captain the Reverend Samuel Clayton turns up with a posse in pursuit of some varmints who have run off the cattle of neighbour Lars Jorgensen. Clayton remarks, 'I haven't seen you since the surrender – come to think of it, I didn't see you at the surrender.' 'I don't believe in surrenders,' replies Ethan. The posse includes one-eighth Cherokee Martin Pawley, orphaned in a massacre of settlers by the Comanche and raised in Aaron's family, whose dark skin offends the racist Ethan ('a fella might take you for a half-breed'). When the posse find Jorgensen's slaughtered cattle, Ethan knows the culprits are Comanche, luring the men of the region away so they can stage a 'murder raid'.

In a primal scene, famously restaged in *Star Wars*, Ethan returns to Aaron's farm and finds it burning, the two girls missing, and Martha raped and murdered. Presumably, Aaron and Ben are dead too, but Ethan barely notices – a suggestion that the lust for vengeance which permeates the rest of the film isn't as clear-cut as might be expected. In searching for Scar, the war chief who has planned the raid and kidnapped Debbie, Ethan recognises the savage as his secret self, acting out the suppressed desire to take Martha and sunder his brother's family. Ethan and Martin spend five years tracking Scar, trailing through desert and snow, and our expectations of good and evil, civilisation and savagery are in dispute. Martin accidentally barters for an Indian bride, Look, the sort of slapstick ethnic stooge who makes modern audiences cringe.

But there's nothing funny about the way she up and offs at the mention of Scar's name and turns up as a corpse at the site of another massacre, of Indian women and children by the US Cavalry (we learn Scar's sons have been killed by whites). As Martin becomes the hero of the film, we are forced to confront the possibility that John Wayne – Duke! – is the villain, a man so possessed by hatred of Indians that he plans not to rescue Debbie but shoot her dead because she has become the sexual property of the Comanche. The home stretch, shot like most of the film in and around Ford's beloved Monument Valley, is an emotional rollercoaster as the initial attack on the Edwards' home is mirrored by a joint Texas Ranger-US Cavalry action against Scar's camp. Ethan finds Martin has already killed his arch-enemy and has to content himself with scalping Scar.

He then fights his way past Martin and seems intent on killing Debbie. Instead, in one of the greatest moments in cinema, he picks her up in a desperate embrace. 'Let's go home, Debbie,' he croaks. Martin and sweetheart Laurie Jorgensen are together at last, Debbie is apparently adopted into the Jorgensen family and a new compound family of 'Texicans' are together. Only Ethan is left outside. Earlier, he had mutilated a Comanche corpse by shooting out his eyes: 'He can't enter the spirit lands and has to wander forever between the winds,' he says. In the end, he shares the Indian's fate, walking away from the camera into the desert as the closing door blots him out. ★★★★★ **KN**

Movie Trivia: The Searchers

Debbie Edwards' character was played by two sisters, Lana and Natalie Wood, aged 8 and 16. John Wayne often had to pick up Natalie Wood from school to take her to the set. Wayne also named his own son Ethan as a tribute to his character. His other son, Patrick, played young cavalry officer, Lieutenant Greenhill.

SEARCHING FOR BOBBY FISCHER (INNOCENT MOVES) (1993)

Starring: *Max Pomeranc (Josh Waitzkin), Joe Mantegna (Fred Waitzkin), Joan Allen (Bonnie Waitzkin), Ben Kingsley (Bruce Pandolfini), Laurence Fishburne (Vinnie)*
Director: *Steven Zaillian*
Screenwriter: *Steven Zaillian, based on the book by Fred Waitzkin*
PG/110 mins./Drama/Biography/USA

Although his dad expects him to play baseball, Josh wants to learn chess, so to show his support his father buys him lessons and is surprised when he shows a talent for the game.

Sports writer Fred Waitzkin expects his seven-year-old son Josh to be a Little League baseball star and is surprised when the kid wants to hang out in the park with the hustlers who play chess on the public boards. It gradually emerges that Josh is America's greatest potential master since Bobby Fischer, whose erratic career and periodic disappearances punctuate the film.

Fred hires Bruce Pandolfini to coach the kid to tournament level, and arguments rage about how best to treat the pre-teen genius. Meanwhile, a deadly rival emerges in Jonathan Poe, a monstrous child who has been raised to be a soulless chess ninja. In the finale, the kids face each other over the board and, with the crazed spectre of Fischer somewhere about, the film upholds the values of well-rounded normality over creepy weirdness, though the outcome of the final match includes an unexpected twist.

Released in the UK under the title *Innocent Moves*, Zaillian's first feature is funny, tense and demanding, with cerebral clashes to equal the physical bouts of Rocky. Pomeranc is a miraculous movie kid, expressive in his soulful looks at the board but never cute or forced. The rest of the cast are similarly perfect. Zaillian (screenwriter of *Awakenings*, *Jack the Bear* and *Schindler's List*) manages to get an incredible variety into its repetitive games, and surrounds the action with an uncringemaking family story. Forget your preconceptions and give this one a try. ★★★★ **KN**

SEBASTIANE (1976)

Starring: *Barney James (Severus), Neil Kennedy (Maximus), Leonardo Treviglio (Sebastian), Richard Warwick (Justin), Donald Dunham (Claudius), Ken Hicks (Adrian), Robert Medley (Emperor Diocletian)*
Directors: *Derek Jarman, Paul Humfress*
Screenwriters: *Derek Jarman, Paul Humfress, James Whaley*
18/90 mins./History/Drama/UK

303AD. Emperor Diocletian demotes his favourite guard Sebastian to ordinary soldier and despatches him to a backwater barracks because he suspects him of being a covert Christian. Eventually, Sebastian is martyred, and becomes a saint.

Shot entirely in sub-titled Latin, which makes it a strange precedent for Mel Gibson's *The Passion of the Christ*, *Sebastiane* is Derek Jarman's first work as a director (though he shared the job with the less well-known Paul Humfress). It's a strange combination of gay nudie movie, pocket-sized Ancient Roman epic and meditation upon the image of Saint Sebastian.

It opens with the Lindsay Kemp dance troupe romping around with huge fake phalluses to represent Ken Russell-style imperial decadence, then decamps to Tuscany where athletic youths in minimal thongs romp around the countryside, soaking themselves down between bouts of manly horseplay or sylvan frolic. It comes to a bad end as the lecherous but guilt-ridden commanding officer Severus fails to cop off with Sebastian and instead visits floggings and tortures upon his naked torso, finally ordering his men to riddle the future saint with arrows, thus securing him a place in cultural history.

The public schoolboy cleverness of scripting dialogue in Latin – a popular soldier's insult is represented by the Greek 'Oedipus' – works surprisingly well, with the cast reeling off profane Roman dialogue like passionate Italian declarations rather than marbled classical sentences. It suffers from the not-uncommon skinflick failing that the best-looking actor is given the largest role but delivers the weakest performance: Treviglio's Sebastian is a handsome cipher, far less interesting than the rest of the troubled, bullying, awkward or horny soldiers in the platoon. The countryside looks as good as the cast, and Brian Eno delivers an evocative, ambient-style score. ★★ **KN**

SECONDS (1966)

Starring: *Rock Hudson (Antiochus 'Tony' Wilson), Salome Jens (Nora Marcus), John Randolph (Arthur Hamilton), Will Geer (Old Man), Jeff Corey (Mr. Ruby), Richard Anderson (Dr. Innes)*
Director: *John Frankenheimer*
Screenwriter: *Lewis John Carlino, based on the novel by David Ely*
Unrated/107mins./Thriller/USA

A mysterious corporation offers to transform middle-aged businessman Arthur Hamilton into swinging bachelor Tony Wilson. When he tires of his 'reborn' life, he discovers that the corporation has a nasty side.

What's the most chilling last line in the cinema? How about 'cranial drill'? Followed by an unforgettable, uncomfortable sound effect.

Made in 1966 but astonishingly fresh and relevant three decades on, this mix of science fiction, horror and Kafkaesque satire (from a fine novel by David Ely) is the sort of film that you catch on late-night television and think you've dreamed.

The opening sequence (virtually remade by David Fincher in *The Game*) has sagging, middle-aged John Randolph going through secret agent-like business in noisy New York, as he is approached by an elusive corporation represented by hawkish execs (Jeff Corey), smooth surgeons (Richard Anderson) and a folksy founding father (Will Geer).

After a process whereby his death is faked, he undergoes radical medical procedures which turn him into a reasonable facsimile of Rock Hudson.

The 'reborn' is set up in California with a bohemian beachfront lifestyle, a slyly efficient manservant (Wesley Addy) and a neurotic goddess girlfriend (Salome Jens, who should have made more films). But, despite the pleasures of a proto-hippie bacchanalia, the Hudson creature isn't satisfied, only to find he can't reconnect with his old life (and wife) and that the company have an excruciating way of dealing with their failures.

Hudson gives a career-best performance, exploring the dichotomy between his public image as the handsome, carefree guy every tired failure wishes he were and his own inability to live that kind of 'normal' life.

After *The Manchurian Candidate*, this is John Frankenheimer's greatest film. Photographed in ravishing, surreal black and white by James Wong Howe, with a haunting Jerry Goldsmith score. ★★★★ **KN**

THE SECRET LIFE OF WALTER MITTY (1947)

Starring: *Danny Kaye (Walter Mitty), Virginia Mayo (Rosalind van Hoorn), Boris Karloff (Dr. Hugo Hollingshead), Fay Bainter (Mrs Mitty), Ann Rutherford (Gertrude Griswold), Thurston Hall (Bruce Pierce), Konstantin Shayne (Peter van Hoorn)*
Director: *Norman Z. McLeod*
Screenwriters: *Ken Englund, Everett Freeman, based on the story by James Thurber*
U/105 mins/Fantasy-Comedy.USA

Mild-mannered accountant Walter Mitty escapes from his humdrum existence and his mother's incessant nagging to a fantasy world where he performs acts of comic-book derring-do. However, he proves to be less of a hero when called upon to rescue Rosalind van Hoorn from the clutches of Dr Hugo Holingshead.

First published in 1939, James Thurber's short story about a hen-pecked milquetoast who seeks sanctuary from reality in delusions of B-movie heroism was such a popular success that a protracted bidding war was conducted for the screen rights. However, Thurber was so horrified when Samuel Goldwyn emerged victorious and announced the project as a vehicle for his leading star, Danny Kaye, that he offered the producer $10,000 not to make the movie.

Thurber even accepted script-doctoring work in a bid to salvage what he felt to be a calamitous bowdlerisation, which had turned Walter Mitty into a hapless bachelor who is constantly browbeaten by his domineering mother. However, he was forced to walk when he saw how little influence he was having on a scenario that seemed to be dictated more by the content of Sylvia Fine's songs than Walter's daydreams. Indeed, Fine (who was Kaye's wife) even suggested ditching a couple of reveries as they interfered with her score.

However, the fault lay squarely with Goldwyn and screenwriters Ken Englund and Everett Freeman, who not only botched the byplay between Walter and his mother, but also swamped the conceit with an actual adventure that was nowhere near as engaging as any of Mitty's imaginings.

Boris Karloff provided some typical menace, but Kaye had already played the accidental hero in *Up in Arms* and *The Kid from Brooklyn* and the gag was wearing a little thin. He was much more amusing impersonating bravado as the sea captain battling the storm, the Wild West gunslinger, the Mississippi riverboat gambler, the ultra-cool surgeon and the daring pilot. Even his diversion into the world of haute couture worked well, as did Fine's 'Anatole of France' song.

Drolly designed by George Jenkins and Perry Ferguson and filmed in bright phantasmic colours by Lee Garmes, this proved a confident, undemanding and lively slice of entertainment for postwar audiences subsisting on war movies, woman's pictures and films noir. However, a little Kaye can go a long way and he's now regarded in some quarters as an acquired taste, à la Jerry Lewis. ★★★ **DP**

SECRETARY (2001)

Starring: *James Spader (E. Edward Grey), Maggie Gyllenhaal (Lee Holloway), Jeremy Davies (Peter), Lesley Ann Warren (Joan Holloway), Stephen McHattie (Burt Holloway)*
Director: *Steven Shainberg*
Screenwriter: *Erin Cressida Wilson, from the short story by Mary Gaitskill*
18/106 mins./Drama/Comedy/Romance/USA

When Lee is released from a mental institution, her family worries about her upsetting tendency to harm herself. However, when she gets a job at a local law office, her life seems to take a turn for the better. But her boss, Mr. Grey, has an unorthodox attitude to 'work'.

Opening with one of the most arrestingly bizarre sequences in cinema – a woman with her head and hands cuffed in an outlandish S&M device drifts dreamily through an office performing the usual menial tasks of a legal secretary – Steven Shainberg's skewed love story is testament to the hoary observation that there really is someone out there for everyone.

In this case, the couple whose relationship we watch flower – and for whom we find ourselves rooting – don't engage with the usual romance movie clichés like mistaken signals, conflicting romantic entanglements or the inevitable 'failure to commit'. Instead there's the burgeoning realisation that their mutual love is best expressed through leather restraints and over-the-desk spanking sessions.

It's a daring idea, and one that could easily drift unintentionally into comedy or exploitation (and the crass tag line, 'Assume the position!', is a step too far in the latter direction). However, Shainberg's deft direction keeps the prurience to a minimum and gives the whole thing a slightly surreal quality.

Meanwhile, Erin Cressida Wilson's screenplay (adapted from Mary Gaitskill's short story) effortlessly charts the shifting power relationships between Gyllenhaal (who needs the couple's unorthodox sexual expression, and gives Spader permission to play out his fantasies) and Spader (whose guilt about what they are up to threatens to derail their oddly tender relationship).

Both Gyllenhaal and Spader (for whom charting the extremes of sexual expression seems to be something of a vocation – see *Crash, sex, lies, and videotape* etc.) are on top form, with Gyllenhaal particularly effective.

A sub-plot in the third act, in which Gyllenhaal becomes something of a cause célèbre and the focus of a media frenzy, is a misstep, deflecting our attention from the affectingly sketched relationship, and clodhoppingly attempting what is presumably meant to be some kind of social satire. But that apart, *Secretary* is a quirky and unexpectedly heartwarming treat. **★★★★ AS**

SECRETS & LIES (1996)

Starring: *Timothy Spall (Maurice Purley), Phyllis Logan (Monica Purley), Brenda Blethyn (Cynthia Rose Purley), Marianne Jean-Baptiste (Hortense Cumberbatch), Claire Rushbrook (Roxanne Purley), Lee Ross (Paul), Elizabeth Berrington (Jane)*
Director: *Mike Leigh*
Screenwriter: *Mike Leigh*
15/141 mins./Drama/UK

Awards – *BAFTA – Alexander Korda Award for Best British Film, Best Actress, Best Original Screenplay, Empire Awards – Best Actress, Golden Globes – Best Drama Actress*

Timothy Spall is in a tragically childless marriage, his sister is living a life of grime with her moody daughter, while Hortense, a young black woman, is searching for her birth mother. Gradually, long-kept family secrets are revealed as the characters learn to trust and help one another.

Many who saw Mike Leigh's previous film, *Naked*, would have stumbled out into the street in shock. With this, Leigh returns to the familiar hearth of bittersweet suburban comedy, *Life Is Sweet* and Timothy Spall. The result is hilarious, as touching a film as any Leigh has made.

This is the story of people who were once connected by birth but are currently, for a variety of reasons, estranged. Maurice is a decent, well-meaning portrait photographer who has worked hard to provide his fastidious wife Monica with a large, comfortable home. For all their gadgets and accoutrements, they badly want children.

In their upward climb, they have neglected Maurice's older sister Cynthia, a dowdy, pinched-faced worrier who is stuck in her cluttered terraced house with an outrageously moody 21-year-old daughter Roxanne (newcomer Claire Rushbrook).

As Maurice and Monica choose from a scintillating range of pre-cooked freezer fare, Cynthia and Roxanne spend their evenings smoking fags and scowling bitterly at their fate.

Meanwhile, oblivious to them all, an adopted young black woman, Hortense (the brilliant Marianne Jean-Baptiste), is scouring London for her real mother – who, she learns to her shock, is white. The convergence of these five characters is gradual, beset by hitches, red herrings and more questions than answers.

The last-reel pathos of *Life Is Sweet* is present here from the start; the cringe-inducing social gatherings – a Leigh speciality – are worthy of his hands-over-eyes classic *Bleak Moments*. Belly-laughs are frequent, as are some terrific running gags (Spall's 'relaxing' spiel to his customers; Roxanne's awesomely seedy boyfriend played to perfection by Lee Ross).

Flush with superb dialogue and interesting sub-plots, this uses every minute of its lengthy running time to surprise and to balance Blethyn's poignant, close-to-tears performance against those of the loveable Spall and the coolly troubled Logan. It is one of the most ambivalent and riveting comedy-dramas of recent times. **★★★★ DC**

SENSE AND SENSIBILITY (1995)

Starring: *Emma Thompson (Elinor Dashwood), Kate Winslet (Marianne Dashwood), Gemma Jones (Mrs. Dashwood), Hugh Grant (Edward Ferrars), Alan Rickman (Colonel Brandon), Greg Wise (John Willoughby)*
Director: *Ang Lee*
Screenwriter: *Emma Thompson, based on the novel by Jane Austen*
U/136 mins./Drama/USA/UK

Awards – *Academy Awards – Best Adapted Screenplay, BAFTA – Best Film, Best Actress, Best Supporting Actress, Golden Globes – Best Drama, Best Screenplay*

Two sisters, Elinor and Marianne, are deprived of their family home by greedy relations but try to make their way in society and find appropriate suitors who will improve their position.

Having just got over the Darcy hysteria created by the Beeb's *Pride And Prejudice*, the British nation had nary time to gird its collective loins before Austen mania took another bow, in the shape of the first big-screen adaptation of a Jane Austen novel for 50 years. *Sense And Sensibility*, however, is not simply hitching a lift on the coat-tails of a period drama fad. For star and, just as impressively, screenwriter Emma Thompson this has been a labour of love. She has spent five years adapting Jane Austen's first novel and the dedication has reaped rewards to shame even Auntie's seasoned hand.

For the uninitiated, the story tells of the fortunes of two sisters: the sensible Elinor and the romantic Marianne. Love, money and social position are the objects of interest in Regency England, and while Elinor pines for the shy but kind Edward (Grant at his most annoyingly depreciative), Marianne falls, literally, for the dashing but unsuitable Willoughby (Greg Wise, entering swooningly on horseback). Cue various ruptures, reunions, misunderstandings and impediments to true love.

In spite of the predictability of Austen's narrative, Thompson has done a dazzling job in bringing out the comedy of the work. The script bubbles with lovely comic vignettes, and there are some hilarious performances, particularly from Hugh Laurie as the rude monosyllabic Mr. Palmer and Elizabeth Spriggs as the obligatory plump panto-style matchmaker. Thompson leads with assurance as the responsible elder sister who bottles up her emotions for the sake of others, getting some plum emoting as heartbreak and joy drag out her feelings. Winslet, who spends a great deal of the plot passing out, struggles in the more experienced acting company, most notably a wonderfully subtle Alan Rickman as Marianne's faithful admirer, Colonel Brandon.

Taiwanese director Ang Lee (*Eat Drink Man Woman*) makes a surprising, but ultimately apt choice of director. This is no BBC bodice-ripper drama, nor is there a hint of the lush superficiality of Merchant Ivory. Rather the stormy, muted aspect of the English countryside, plain costumes, and wonderful interplay between the characters take centre stage – Lee is a proven realiser of human emotion. Americans, after the heady mix of *Pride And Prejudice* and *Persuasion*, are gluttons for all things British-in-tight-pantaloons, and Oscars glory was no surprise. And deservedly so, since *Sense And Sensibility* is a beautifully-crafted, witty, moving film likely to overcome even the stiffest Austen prejudice. ★★★★ **AE**

SERENITY (2005)

Starring: *Nathan Fillion (Mal), Gina Torres (Zoe Allen Washburne), Alan Tudyk (Wash), Morena Baccarin (Inara), Adam Baldwin (Jayne), Jewel Staite (Kaylee), Sean Maher (Dr. Simon Tam), Summer Glau (River), Chiwetel Ejiofor (The Operative), David Krumholtz (Mr. Universe)*
Director: *Joss Whedon*
Screenwriter: *Joss Whedon*
15/119 mins./Drama/Action/Sci-fi/USA

Mal Reynolds is captain of the spacecraft *Serenity*, home to a nomadic crew of mercenaries whose relative tranquillity has been disturbed by their taking on Dr. Simon Tam and his troubled sister, River. River is caught up in a conspiracy involving galactic superpower The Alliance, and they'll stop at nothing to get her back.

The multiplexes are already crammed with the fetid, mewling cinematic offspring of hit TV shows, so why on earth should anyone want to watch a spin-off of a series that failed to even make it through its first season?

Well, firstly: it's the feature film diverting debut of Buffy god Joss Whedon, a man with more pop-culture funnies than *Scream*'s Kevin Williamson. Secondly: everybody knows that these days truly great shows rarely make it beyond a debut run. Thirdly: it's a hell of a lot better than *The Dukes Of Hazzard*.

Genre obsessives will already be fully clued up on the seemingly doomed course of the good ship *Serenity*, which, in the US show *Firefly*, launched with great fanfare before being buffeted by network execs to such an extent that only the most dedicated viewer could find it on the schedules. But with its complex mix of Western, sci-fi, thriller and comedy, not to mention a sprawling cast and twisting back-stories that 14 episodes could barely touch on, it was Whedon's most ambitious project, and a show of such wit and originality that naturally it refused to die. Thus, through the power of the browncoat (read: *Firefly* nerd) and stellar sales on DVD, the lawless cast was given a reprieve and Whedon $40 million to resurrect his project.

All of which should send anybody disinclined to conventions and mint-condition collectables running from a darkened cinema for the sunshine of the outside world. Fear not; herein lies black comedy, spiky romance and action adventure – without an alien to be seen.

You could question Whedon's wisdom in making this his first foray into movie direction (he's previously been Oscar-nominated for co-scripting *Toy Story*), with its demands to satisfy both the faithful few and the indifferent masses. Screw this up and he's not only dashed the dreams of his die-hard following, but also called into question his big-budget future.

Thankfully, through pluck, talent and enormous imagination, Whedon's done it, cheerfully Frankensteining the smart mouth of *Buffy*, the dust of *Deadwood* and all the fun bits of *Star Wars*. Which, in some ways, is the movie's sole problem. *Serenity* exists on a plane somewhere between cinema and TV. For much of the running time it feels like an extended episode of the series, with televisual staging and a slow-reveal strategy that seems to be saving something for next week's show. A large lead cast (played wonderfully by the original TV actors, all stretching their comedy and action muscles with 'may never get the chance again' vigour) demands a great deal of screentime to draw in newcomers.

Whedon's economical with his exposition but, with the amount of story to be squeezed in, even a tiny lapse in concentration will leave some scratching their heads during a few of the plot twists.

Gloriously, though, around the halfway point *Serenity* blossoms, breaking free of its small-screen confines. Whedon lets loose a series of confident action sequences befitting any summer blockbuster, the cast step up to big-screen presence (all hail Nathan Fillion, the new Han Solo!), and the careful seeding of the characters and story bears the fruit of an ending in which nothing is certain, no clichéd outcome inevitable and no crew member safe from the jaws of death. ★★★★ **OR**

SERGEANT YORK (1941)

Starring: *Gary Cooper (Alvin C. York), Walter Brennan (Pastor Rosier Pile), Joan Leslie (Grace Williams), George Tobias (Michael T 'Pusher' Ross), Stanley Ridges (Maj. Buxton), Margaret Wycherly (Mother York)*
Director: *Howard Hawks*
Screenwriters: *Abem Frinkel, Harry Chandlee, Howard Koch, John Huston, based on* War Diary Of Sergeant York *by Sam K. Cowan,* Sergeant York and his People *by Cowan and* Sergeant York – Last of the Long Hunters *by Tom Skeyhill*
U/134 mins/War/USA
Awards: *Academy Awards – Best Actor, Best Film Editing*

Tennessee hillbilly Alvin C. York spends his life drinking and scrapping until a religious conversion transforms him into a hard-working farmer. However, his plea to be considered a conscientious objector is denied and, reasoning he's fighting for God and country, he becomes America's biggest hero of the First World War.

From the moment he saw Alvin York at the Armistice Day Parade in New York in 1919, producer Jesse Lasky was determined to make a biopic of the man who had led Company G, 328th Infantry of the 82nd (All-American) Division through the Meuse-Argonne offensive and single-handedly killed 20 and captured 132 Germans in a raid on a machine-gun emplacement. However, the Tennesseean was a reluctant hero, who had already turned down movie stardom to return to his mountain community, and he only consented after the outbreak of the Second World War.

York insisted on certain terms, however. In addition to his share of the profits going towards the founding of a Bible school, he wanted his wife, Gracie, to be played by a non-smoking actress (Joan Leslie was chosen, although Howard Hawks wanted Jane Russell), while he was to be portrayed by Gary Cooper. Coop was initially against the idea, but agreed after meeting York on his farm and hearing first-hand the pacifist's reasons for becoming a warrior.

Coop was keen for Hawks to direct, but he only landed the assignment after Warners failed to persuade Michael Curtiz, Henry Koster, Henry Hathaway, Victor Fleming and Norman Taurog. Yet this was a classic Hawksian subject, as York epitomised the kind of uncompromising individual that the director most admired – whether taking odd jobs to buy the parcel of bottom land, undergoing basic training or striding across No Man's Land. Moreover, the boot camp and trench sequences enabled Hawks to revisit his perennial theme of the cameraderie between professional men dedicated to their cause.

However, the majority of the action concerned York's Damascene conversion from feckless rebel to abstemious sodbuster and Hawks wisely eschewed John Ford's brand of roistering folksiness to make the Western Front sequences seem more like a philosophically justified sacrifice than mere gung-ho heroics.

Not all the critics agreed, however, and Isolationists decried the picture's obvious propagandist purpose. But it landed 11 Oscar nominations (although only Coop and editor William Holmes were successful) and became one of the most popular films of the war. ★★★★ **DP**

⊙ THE SERPENT AND THE RAINBOW (1987)

Starring: *Bill Pullman (Dennis Alan), Cathy Tyson (Dr. Marille Duchamp), Zakes Mokae (Dargent Peytraud), Paul Winfield (Lucien Celine)*
Director: *Wes Craven*
Screenwriters: *Richard Maxwell, A. R. Simoun, from the book by Wade Davis*
18/98 mins./Horror/USA

Scientist, Dennis Allan, finds more than he bargained for when researching a paralysing drug and its connection to the Zombie myth in the turbulent atmosphere of revolutionary Haiti.

Wes Craven enjoyed something of a return to form with this chilling – albeit bitty – take on ancient voodoo mythology. Given his *Elm Street* track record, it comes as no surprise that the film's strength lies in its increasingly surreal dream/hallucination sequences.

Ultimately though, the combination of some wayward casting (Bill Pullman fails to convince – even when having his scrotum nailed to a chair) and a 'shock' ending that can be seen coming from the 20 minute mark, take the sheen off what is otherwise solid horror hokum. ★★★ **MD**

⊙ SERPICO (1973)

Starring: *Al Pacino (Officer Frank Serpico), John Randolph (Chief Sidney Green), Jack Kehoe (Tom Keough), Biff McGuire (Capt. Insp. McClain), Barbara Eda-Young (Laurie)*
Director: *Sidney Lumet*
Screenwriters: *Waldo Salt, Norman Wexler, based on the book by Peter Mass*
18/124 mins./Crime/Drama/USA

Awards: *Golden Globes – Best Actor*

Frank Serpico is an honest cop in the NYPD who decides to take a stand against corruption.

In 1973,after the disenchanted, psychotic cops of *The French Connection* and *Dirty Harry*, Al Pacino's Frank Serpico came as a paradoxical change of pace. Despite his hairy hippie disguises and rebel attitudes, he was in fact a throwback to the *Dixon Of Dock Green/Dragnet* image of cop as paragon of personal integrity and social justice. Sidney Lumet's film, however, is the ultimate development of the all-cops-are-bent theme that understandably proliferated in the counterculture-dominated, post-Watergate 1970s.

The real Serpico was a New York 'tec whose contribution to fighting crime was not in action against the underworld, but in testifying against police corruption, thus making himself very unpopular with the rest of the boys in blue. Lumet opens with an edgy suspense sequence that winds up with the hero gunned down in the line of duty, and the suggestion that his own department has colluded with the mob to have him shot. He then adopts a straggling, biopic approach, flashing back through Serpico's career.

We see the hero develop from a naive rookie who refuses even to accept free meals from restaurateurs on his beat, through a period as a hot-dog undercover man, into his lonely crusade against the NYPD. Pacino interestingly makes Serpico a misfit, his inability to sustain relationships and semi-vigilante street tactics suggesting that sheer bloody-mindedness might have as much to do with his stand as idealism. Finally, the hero is an isolated, broken man who retires to Switzerland with his only faithful friend, an equally shaggy dog. It's no great victory, but it is great. ★★★★ **KN**

⊙ SEUL CONTRE TOUS (I STAND ALONE) (1998)

Starring: *Philippe Nahon (The Butcher), Blandine Lenoir (His Daughter, Cynthia), Frankie Pain (His Mistress), Martine Audrain (His Mother-in-Law), Olivier Doran (Narrator)*
Director: *Gaspar Noe*
Screenwriter: *Gaspar Noe*
18/93 mins./Drama/France

A disaffected man, just released from prison, descends into a cycle of violence.

Remember the fuss that greeted *Falling Down*? Well, the bile bubbling inside Michael Douglas's 'D-fens' is nothing compared to the seething rage that drives the unnamed hero of this brutal and terrifyingly credible film, which is not only a searing indictment of modern France, but also the grimmest black comedy in decades.

From the breathless opening montage to the ambiguously optimistic ending, this is a hugely manipulative feature, as first-time director Noe slowly compels you to identify with this jaundiced individual whose every thought and action fills you with repugnance. The son of a concentration camp victim, the butcher has spent his entire life going uphill. Released from prison for knifing the neighbour he assumed had assaulted his daughter, he pitches up in Lille, only to go on the run after battering his pregnant mistress. Humiliated in his search for work, he wanders the shabbiest streets of Paris with his sense of resentment and desperation gradually coming to the boil.

With its array of shocking images, crash zooms, soundtrack bangs and belligerent captioning, this stunning film gives you some idea of the thrill audiences must have felt as the young guns of the New Wave abandoned classical storytelling convention and showed how cinema might challenge and provoke.

Some will be put off by the flashy technique, while others will take offence at the stream of consciousness voice-over presenting the bitter thoughts of a simple man whose notion of morality and justice have been cobbled together from half-digested political tracts, bar-room maxims and twisted pieces of logic forged by frustration and poverty. But this is a film that demands you stick with it no matter what your response. ★★★★ **DP**

⊙ SE7EN (1995)

Starring: *Brad Pitt (Det. David Mills), Morgan Freeman (Det. Lt. William Somerset), Gwyneth Paltrow (Tracy Mills), Kevin Spacey (John Doe), R. Lee Ermey (Police Captain)*
Director: *David Fincher*
Screenwriter: *Andrew Kevin Walker*
18/126 mins./Drama/Thriller/Mystery/USA

Awards: *Empire – Best Actor (Morgan Freeman), Best Film*

Two cops go on the trail of a killer who slays his victims according to which of the seven deadly sins they have committed.

Se7en isn't just a movie, it's a mind fuck, a psychological trip through hell that leaves your head spinning, your heart pumping and your stomach crying out for the medicinal properties of a stiff whiskey, or five. Not since *The Exorcist* has there been a mainstream Hollywood studio movie as extraordinarily dark, bleak, intense, and as monumentally scary as this. From its sensory assaulting opening credits, through to its desolate and very shocking finale, *Se7en* goes for the gut, and like an insidious gnawing in the pit of your stomach, it never lets up. Be warned, this is not comfortable viewing.

In an anonymous US city in which it always rains and nobody seems to have bothered to pay their electricity bill, a serial killer is busy slaying his victims according to the seven deadly sins: gluttony, greed, sloth, envy, etc., leaving a sick procession of corpses, each one murdered in a way related to their own particular sin: a wealthy defence lawyer is force to cut off a pound of his own flesh (greed); an obese man is force fed until his stomach explodes (gluttony); a prostitute (lust) is ... well, best see for yourself. Assigned to the case are veteran cop William Somerset, a methodical, world-weary thinker and a week away from retirement after 34 years on the force, and his hot-headed young new partner David Mills, recently relocated, along with his wife, to this hellhole of a city, eager to make a name for himself. Try as they might they are always one step behind the murderer, but all too late his true motives are revealed to them.

Director David Fincher, who previously helmed the equally gloomy

Alien[3], creates an overwhelming sense of unease, presenting a world of irredeemable ugliness, a grim, melancholic, depressing, decaying society from which there is no escape. This movie even smells rank. But despite the gruesomeness of the crimes this is no slasher movie. In the same way that *Manhunter* relied on the psychological for its impact, so too does *Se7en*. The victims are never killed onscreen. Instead, we catch glimpses of the corpses at the crime scene, or in the morgue, or in the snatches of black-and-white police photographs that are flashed before us. Perhaps more disturbingly, you are mostly left to visualise in your mind the full extent of the killer's atrocities when they are discussed, matter-of-factly, by Pitt and Freeman.

As the cops move closer to their foe (whose identity is revealed late and by then it doesn't really matter anyway since it's fundamentally irrelevant) the movie shifts from thriller territory into the realms of horror, and it's here that Fincher and screenwriter Andrew Kevin Walker pull off their greatest coup, a piece of cinematic genius – the most downbeat ending imaginable. Ever. You come away reeling, emotionally and mentally, shaken and most definitely stirred, muttering to yourself that they couldn't possibly have done that. But they did. Oh boy, did they. For the ending alone, this is simply unmissable. ★★★★★ **MS**

SEVEN BRIDES FOR SEVEN BROTHERS (1954)

Starring: *Howard Keel (Adam Pontipee), Jane Powell (Milly), Jeff Richards (Benjamin Pontipee), Russ Tamblyn (Gideon Pontipee), Julie Newmar (Dorcas Gailen)*
Director: *Stanley Donen*
Screenwriters: *Albert Hackett, Frances Goodrich, Dorothy Kingsley, from the story* The Sobbin' Women *by Stephen Vincent Benet*
U/101 mins./Musical/Romance/USA

Awards: *Academy Awards – Best Musical Score*

Adam goes to town to get a wife and comes back with Milly. But then he talks his six brothers into kidnapping women to marry them too and Milly and the women concerned are less than impressed.

'Bless yore beautiful hide, wherever you may be.' Who, on hearing Howard Keel, burst into deep-voiced song, as he seeks out Jane Powell, can fail to feel similarly inspired? Yes, on the surface it seems quite sexist, but there's no doubt that whatever the menfolk's posturing, it's the women who are running this show and that's enough to condone a wagonload of inappropriate song lyrics, especially sing-a-long friendly ones like this.

Keel and Powell spar nicely off each other as the couple who inspire the rest of his brothers to take wives. He tries to pretend he's just married for practical reasons, she gradually civilises him – and the rest of the family – and he has to admit she was right all along. Of course, none of this comes easily and there's a barn dance that goes awry, an ill-advised mass-kidnapping and avalanche, exile to the mountains (for Keel) and exile from the house (for the rest of the men) to deal with before the women gradually lower their defences to allow true love to blossom.

MGM's infectiously, rabble-rousing musical bursts with life, colour and songs – the Barn Raising is a real show-stopper thanks to Michael Kidd's choreography, featuring male dancing at its most athletic (rather than the usual compliment of good-looking faces who could dance a little, four of the male cast were trained dancers and one a gymnast) while 'Sobbin' Women' is both catchy and as non-PC as any male – dominated pub conversation. 'June Bride' has a lot to answer for in terms of the wedding season and 'Spring, Spring, Spring' manages to wheel in lots of cute barnyard animals and establish the final romantic pairings.

The CinemaScope format is also a bonus, maximising the visual appeal of an immaculately styled Hollywood frontierland. ★★★★★ **EC**

Movie Trivia: MGM Musicals (1929 onwards)

What were they: Large-scale, extravagant, elaborate musicals made by MGM. Steered by songwriter/producer Arthur Freed. Heyday between 1928 and 1959.
Hallmarks: Busby Berkeley choreography; more stars than in the heavens; glorious Technicolor; chorus girls; wind machines; Judy Garland and Mickey Rooney deciding to 'do the show right here!'
If you see one movie, see: *Singin' in the Rain* (1952)

THE SEVEN PER CENT SOLUTION (1976)

Starring: *Alan Arkin (Dr. Sigmund Freud), Vanessa Redgrave (Lola Deveraux), Robert Duvall (Dr John H. Watson/Narrative), Nicol Williamson (Sherlock Holmes), Laurence Olivier (Professor James Moriarty), Joel Grey (Lowenstein), Samantha Eggar (Mary Morstan Watson)*
Director: *Herbert Ross*
Screenwriter: *Nicholas Meyer based on characters created by Sir Arthur Conan Doyle*
15/113 mins/Comedy/USA

Concerned by Sherlock Holmes's growing addiction to cocaine, Dr Watson persuades him to consult Sigmund Freud in Vienna and the pair unite to rescue psychology patient Lola Deveraux from kidnappers and Professor Moriarty from Holmes's misguided obsession.

Revisionist takes on Baker Street's most celebrated resident were all the rage in the early 1970s. But, whereas Billy Wilder's *The Private Life of Sherlock Holmes* and Gene Wilder's *The Adventures of Sherlock Holmes' Smarter Brother* were primarily lampoons, this was a serious attempt to get inside the mind of the brilliant, but troubled sleuth.

Having failed to persuade his psychologist father to write a book about Holmes and the appeal of mystery fiction, Nicholas Meyer took advantage of a screenwriters' strike to research Sir Arthur Conan Doyle's stories. He even met with the Baker Street Regulars fan club to discuss his ideas before publishing a bestselling novel, whose title referred to the 7% cocaine, 93% water solution with which Holmes frequently injected himself.

Conan Doyle's executors, Baskerville Investments Ltd., took some persuading to license the use of its flawed hero, but they finally consented, unlike Anna Freud, who was so opposed to the project that she insisted on being reinvented as a son for the screen version.

A splendid cast rose admirably to the script's challenges, with Robert Duvall's capable Watson contrasting sharply with Nigel Bruce's avuncular bumbler and Nicol Williamson intensifying the hint of latent menace that had informed Basil Rathbone's otherwise rigidly controlled interpretation. Laurence Olivier also cleverly traded on the malevolence he had generated in *Marathon Man* to turn in a mischievously misleading performance as Moriarty.

However, the star turns were production designer Ken Adam's London and Vienna sets, which avoided the usual period clichés to produce vibrant cities whose grandeur hid sinister secrets. The picture was also to have boasted a Bernard Herrmann score, but, having just finished work on *Taxi Driver*, he succumbed to his final illness and the estimable John Addison stepped in, with whodunit aficionado Stephen Sondheim contributing 'The Madame's Song'. ★★★ **DP**

10 Famous Last Lines

1 **'Well, nobody's perfect.' (*Osgood, Some Like It Hot*)**
2 **'This could be the beginning of a beautiful friendship.' (Rick, *Casablanca*)**
3 **'The greatest trick the devil ever pulled was convincing the world he didn't exist. And like that, he's gone.' (Verbal Kint, *The Usual Suspects*)**
4 **'Shut up and deal.' (Fran, *The Apartment*)**
5 **'After all, tomorrow is another day.' (Scarlett O'Hara, *Gone With The Wind*)**
6 **'Now, where was I?' (Leonard Shelby, *Memento*)**
7 **'I do wish we could chat longer, but I'm having an old friend for dinner.' (Hannibal Lecter, *The Silence of the Lambs*)**
8 **'Forget it Jake, it's Chinatown.' (Lawrence Walsh, *Chinatown*)**
9 **'Watch the skies, everywhere. Keep looking! Keep watching the skies!' (Ned 'Scotty' Scott, *The Thing From Another World*)**
10 **'Sure, I could have stayed in the past. I could have even been king. But in my own way, I am king. Hail to the king, baby' (Ash, *Army of Darkness*)**

S

⊙ SEVEN SAMURAI (SHICHININ NO SAMURAI) (1954)

Starring: *Takashi Shimura (Kambei Shimada), Toshiro Mifune (Kikuchiyo), Yoshio Inaba (Gorobei Katayama), Seiji Miyaguchi (Kyuzo), Minory Chiaki (Heihachi Hayashida), Daisuke Kato (Shichiroji)*
Director: *Akira Kurosawa*
Screenwriters: *Akira Kurosawa, Shinobu Hashimoto, Hideo Oguni*
PG/160 mins/206 mins (restored version)/Action/Drama/Japan

A veteran samurai, who has fallen on hard times, answers a village's request for protection from bandits. He gathers six other samurai to help him.

Any pub quiz clod can name the Magnificent Seven, even down to Brad Dexter. But only a true sensei of movie trivia can list all of the Seven Samurai – Takashi Shimura, Toshiro Mifune, Daisuke Kato, Yoshio Inaba, Seiji Miyaguchi, Minoru Chiaki and Isao Kimura.

Period-set tales of swordplay (chambara films) had been a staple of Japanese popular cinema since the silent era, holding the same place in the affections of the home audience that the Western did for Americans or the Boys' Own Adventure for the British. However, by the 1950s, with Japan's martial heritage tainted by the country's conduct during World War II and loss of face after the Allied victory, the form fell into a decline.

Until, that is, Akira Kurosawa stepped in. An established director who had earned an international reputation with Rashomon in 1950, Kurosawa was an admirer of the Hollywood method and saw in the chambara an opportunity to fashion a high adventure along the lines of John Ford's *Stagecoach* or George Stevens' *Gunga Din*. It is no surprise that *Seven Samurai* could so easily be remade as *The Magnificent Seven* (1960) – not to mention *Battle Beyond The Stars* (1980), *The Seven Magnificent Gladiators* (1983), *World Gone Wild* (1988) and *A Bug's Life* (1998) – because it draws so much of its plot and character from the Wild West.

The film opens with some swift plot groundwork. A farmer overhears a group of bandits agreeing to hold off a raid on a village because the peasants will not have had time to harvest their crops since the last attack. They vow, however, to return after the harvest. In despair, the villagers send emissaries to hire samurai to protect them. The swordsmen of the nearest town are mostly not interested in a venture that pays off only in rice, until – after a vignette modelled on the establishment of Wyatt Earp's heroism in Ford's *My Darling Clementine* involving the rescue of a child from a robber – Kambei takes the position of group leader, deciding from a description of the village that 40 bandits can be held off with a minimum of seven men.

Here, Kurosawa one-ups Hollywood. Before 1954, even the most epic American adventures featured a lone hero and a stooge posse, or at best two brawling buddies. But here Kurosawa invented the now-familiar device of a heroic leader assembling a team of specialists to meet a challenging task. At well over three hours, the movie has time to give each of the Samurai rich characterisation: Shichiroji is Kambei's long-term right-hand man; Kyuzo is the icy master swordsman; Gorobei signs up because he admires Kambei's heroism; Katsushiro is the youth who yearns to learn from the masters; Heihachi is the second-rate sword, welcomed because of his cheery disposition; and Kikuchiyo (a hyperactive, star-making role for Mifune) is the crazy amateur whose insane clown antics mark him as the wild card in this otherwise dignified, professional pack.

Set in the 16th century, when civil wars had reduced Japan to chaos, the film also speaks to the defeated people of 1954, who regarded the occupying Americans much as the peasants regard both the rapacious bandits and the martially-superpowered samurai. The early stretches, influenced by *High Noon*, show the farmers as gutless whiners who hide the womenfolk from their would-be protectors. A crunch comes when the samurai discover a cache of armour and weaponry looted from ronin (masterless samurai) who have been caught fleeing from losing battles and murdered by the farmers.

It is only when Kikuchiyo delivers a great speech about the way the samurai have treated the farmers ('You're the son of a farmer, aren't you?' Kambei observes) that the team really bond together and commit to the redemptive purpose of their mission, even if (inevitably) it means most of them will die. Also, by their example and with their training, they enable the farmers to stand up for themselves, recognising that it is the tillers of the soil who must always survive. In his staging of sword duels and mass battles, Kurosawa changed the way action scenes were shot.

Well before Sam Peckinpah hit on the device, he used tiny flashes of slow motion to emphasise moments within busy scenes – usually as wounded characters stagger to their deaths – and before Sergio Leone he recognised the importance of establishing the characters' places within the frame before the fighting starts. ★★★★★ **KN**

⊙ THE SEVEN YEAR ITCH (1955)

Starring: *Marilyn Monroe (The Girl), Tom Ewell (Richard Sherman), Evelyn Ketes (Helen Sherman), Sonny Tufts (Tom McKenzie), Robert Strauss (Kruhuik), Oscar Homolka (Dr. Brubaker), Marguerite Chapman (Miss Morris)*
Director: *Billy Wilder*
Screenwriter: *Billy Wilder, George Axelrod, based on the play be Axelrod*
PG/105 mins/Comedy/USA

With his wife Helen and son Tom away on vacation, New Yorker Richard Sherman flirts with the girl from the apartment upstairs, but despite his lusts and daydreams, he manages to remain true to his marriage vows.

Adapted by Billy Wilder and George Axelrod from the latter's hit Broadway play, this was essentially an extension of the opening sequence in Wilder's 1942 farce, *The Major and the Minor*, in which Robert Benchley's home alone husband orders a scalp massage and fantasises about the pulchritude of his masseuse. There was also more than a hint of *The Secret Life of Walter Mitty* about the reveries that punctuated this dated, sniggeringly smutty, but occasionally amusing romp.

However, Wilder shifted the emphasis firmly on to the The Girl to exploit Marilyn Monroe's innocent sensuality and her gift for breathless comedy, which was just as well as her co-star struggled throughout to convey a credible sense of guilty temptation, even though he had starred in the original stage production, opposite Vanessa Brown.

Recognising Tom Ewell's tendency towards theatricality, Wilder had attempted to cast Walter Matthau (whom he had tested with Gena Rowlands). But producer Charles K. Feldman nixed the idea and, as Wilder was on loan to Fox from Paramount, he had no bargaining power. He was similarly boxed into shooting in CinemaScope for the first time and didn't always make the most imaginative use of the additional space.

However, Wilder did coax a spirited performance out of Marilyn Monroe, whose 23rd film proved to be her most successful to date. The triumph came at a cost, however, as husband Joe Di Maggio was so dismayed by the filming of the legendary subway vent sequence that he walked off the set, leaving Marilyn to complete the shoot before a vast watching crowd. Unsurprisingly, the footage was heavily censored, with only the billowing dress being shown on screen, consigning the iconic full-length view to the publicity campaign.

Wilder was equally frustrated by his inability to conclude the picture with a shot of the family maid finding a hair clip in Ewell's bed. But the Breen Office clearly felt it had been sufficiently lenient in permitting innumerable references to adultery, the risqué *US Camera* magazine and the permanent hotness of a girl who keeps her underwear in the ice box. ★★★ **DP**

◑ THE SEVENTH SEAL (DET SJUNDE INSEGLET) (1957)

Starring: *Max Von Sydow (Antonius Blok), Gunnae Bjornstrand (Jons), Nils Poppe (Jof), Bibi Andersson (Mia), Bengt Ekerot (Death), Ake Fridell (Blacksmith Plog), Inga Gill (Lisa)*
Director: *Ingmar Bergman*
Screenwriter: *Ingmar Bergman, based on his play* Tramaining
15/105 mins./Drama/Sweden

Crusader knight Antonius Blok returns to 14th-century Sweden with his squire, Jons, seeking a purpose to assuage his religious doubt and finds it in challenging Death to a game of chess so that travelling players Jof and his wife, Mia, can escape from the ravages of the Plague.

Filmed over 35 days for a mere $150,000 and expanded from a sketch entitled Wood Painting that he had written for his Malmö drama students in 1954, this was Ingmar Bergman's first drama to exhibit the emergence of a mature, individual style. Its examination of God's absence from the world and the manner in which humanity had debased worship and indulged persecution linked it into a loose trilogy with *The Magician* and *The Virgin Spring*. However, this oratorio for doubting voices was also an allegory on Bergman's own religious crisis and his conviction that the world had become gripped by an evil that manifested itself in the form of the atom bomb, which he considered to be the 20th Century's equivalent to the Black Death.

Taking its title from the Book of Revelation, *The Seventh Seal* was a film of pairs and opposites. Jof and Mia were doubled by Plog the doltish blacksmith and his adulterous wife, Lisa (who sleeps with the troupe's third member, Skat), while the girl whom Jöns delivers from being raped found echo in the waif accused of witchcraft. Similarly, Raval the wicked seminarist and the flagellants together symbolised the unreformed religiosity that Bergman despised, while the sardonic Squire and the idealistic Knight represented contrasting sides of the director's own spiritual intellect.

The films's themes were also conveniently twinned – faith/atheism, life/death, light/darkness, innocence/corruption, hope/despair, love/lust, comedy/tragedy and crusading piety/clerical hypocrisy. Even some of the episodes were contrasted, including Jof's humiliation in the tavern and Blok's idyllic strawberries and milk picnic with Mia, whose purity recalls Jof's visions of the Blessed Virgin.

But the picture's iconic moments were the chess game and the Dance of Death (which have often since been lampooned, most notably in *Bill & Ted's Bogus Journey*, 1991 and *Love and Death*, 1975). However, the latter sequence owed much to luck, as Bergman shot it on location after noticing how dramatic the sky had become. The ray of light that alighted on Raval after his agonising forest death was similarly felicitous. Perhaps Bergman was not working in such godless isolation after all? ★★★★★ **DP**

◑ THE SEVENTH VOYAGE OF SINBAD (1958)

Starring: *Kerwin Matthews (Sinbad), Kathryn Grant (Princess Parisa), Richard Eyer (Baronni the Genie), Torin Thatcher (Sokurah the Magician), Alec Manggo (Caliph)*
Director: *Nathan Juran*
Screenwriters: *Ken Kolb, Ray Harryhausen*
U/88 mins./Fantasy/USA

When the illustrious Sinbad brings home a strange magician from a fabled island, trouble brews. This evil sorcerer, determined to return to the island and find the magic lamp he covets, shrinks the Calpih's daughter to the size of a pixie, and forces Sinbad to mount a voyage to save her. She is after all, his betrothed.

While his sixth and eight voyages have gone unrecorded, Sinbad, that dashing Arab adventurer and stop-motion's favourite son, had a whale of a time on his seventh. It's an early Ray Harryhausen carnival of monstrosities, but one of his most delightful, even if Kerwin Matthews' Sinbad looks bland compared to Patrick Wayne let alone the prancing, razzmatazz of Douglas Fairbanks Jr.

While the script dallies with some typical guff about Sinbad's commitment issues in marrying Kathryn Grant's Princess Paris – he's but a carefree sailor – there's not much required of these childish but enchanting fables: a quest for a magic potion, an evil sorcerer, a stern Caliph, a mystical land hosting a menagerie of creatures David Attenborough, so far, has missed, and idiot-proof character names (Sokurah the Magician, Baronni the Genie). Rather sporadically – there were budget and time pressures on the masterful Mr. Harryhausen and his Dynamation – we, and Sinbad of the pointy sword and flappy trousers, get up close and personal with a Cyclops, a skeleton, a dragon and a two-headed Roc, as well as a smart-mouthed genie. All terrifically designed and brought to life.

Interestingly, this was the first time the process was used on colour stock, and Harryhausen was worried the joins between real footage and creatures would be obvious. To be honest, the delineations are clear but somehow that lends to the overall charm. ★★★ **IN**

◑ SEX, THE ANNABEL CHONG STORY (1999)

Starring: as themselves: *Annabel Chong, John T. Bone, Ed Powers, Dr. Walter Williams, Charles Conn, Dick James, Monica Moran, Steve Austin*
Director: *Gough Lewis*
18/85 mins./Documentary/USA

Documentary about Annabel Chong, who in 1995, had sex with 251 men in 10 hours in front of cameras, as a kind of social experiment.

There have been a number of late 90s films in which graphic sex has been used as a symbol of female empowerment, among them Catherine Breillat's *Romance*. But while Grace Quek would have you believe that her porn star alter ego, Annabel Chong, is fighting the same cause, this furtive documentary suggests she is driven far more by self-loathing than the pursuit of female emancipation.

Annabel Chong was 22 when, in January 1995, she fornicated with 251 men in 10 hours before the handheld cameras of hardcore director John Bowen. She was deceived into believing that all the volunteers had taken AIDS tests and has yet to receive her full fee. However, she insists that the ego-boosting bonking, fleeting fame and aggressive advocacy of female sexuality were all worth dying for.

A convent-educated, bourgeois single child, Quek is a psycho-babbling mess of contradictions. Blagging post-feminist extroversion for all she's worth, the confused and insecure Quek allows herself to be filmed taking a blade to her forearm, waiting in a public clinic for HIV results and plucking up the courage to come clean to her unsuspecting folks.

The interviews, with Quek, her friends, family and pornographers, raise more questions than they answer. But still more troubling is the role of the British-born Lewis, who slept with Quek during the shoot. She may have put herself at his disposal, but he isn't entirely free of the exploitation charges his film levels against the porn barons. Nonetheless, this is still a wincingly compelling study of subversion, voyeurism and self-delusion. ★★★ **DP**

◑ SEX, LIES AND VIDEOTAPE (1989)

Starring: *James Spader (Graham Dalton), Andie MacDowell (Ann Bishop Mullany), Peter Gallagher (John Mullany), Laura San Giacomo (Cynthia Patrice Bishop)*
Director: *Steven Soderbergh*
Screenwriter: *Steven Soderbergh*
18/100 mins./Drama/USA

John betrays his wife, Ann, by sleeping with her sister, Cynthia. Things get even more complicated when old buddy Graham turns up to record all the repressed sexuality on his camcorder.

SEXY BEAST

Steven Soderbergh's *sex, lies and videotape* had a good buzz about it before anyone had even seen the movie. The title was so different and intriguing. Boasting the Palme d'Or (Best Film) and Best Actor awards from Cannes, this small, low-budget, independent first feature from the 26-year-old Soderbergh did indeed represent a remarkably original debut that is fresh, confident and, frankly, clever.

The marriage of neurotic middle-class princess Ann and her all-too-thrusting lawyer husband John is already in trouble, with him bonking her sister Cynthia while she's obsessing on world starvation and garbage disposal. Then old friend Graham hits town, dressed 'like an undertaker to the art world', intense, impotent and disturbingly honest. A passive observer whose sexual outlet is videotaping women discussing their sex lives, he unwittingly inspires the sisters-at-odds to review their relationships with lying scoundrel John. That candid confidences about masturbation, penises and orgasms should be combined with some acute social observation and tight plotting to offbeat but witty effect is in itself startling. Even more surprising is the good-natured perception with which the youthful Soderbergh as the screenwriter has drawn the women, guaranteed to draw squirms of amused recognition from female viewers. As director and editor he has elicited spontaneous, natural performances and exposed nerves with uncanny insight. ★★★★★ **AE**

◎ SEXY BEAST (2000)

Starring: *Ray Winstone (Gary 'Gal' Dove), Ben Kingsely (Don Logan), Ian McShane (Teddy Bass), Amanda Redman (Deedee Dove), James Fox (Harry)*
Director: *Jonathan Glazer*
Screenwriters: *Louis Mellis, David Scinto*
18/84 mins./Crime/Drama/USA

The Costa del Crime, Spain. Gary 'Gal' Dove is an ex-criminal whose blissful retirement with wife Deedee is rudely interrupted by the arrival of violent gang boss Don Logan, who is here to convince Gal to come back to London for one last bank job. Something unexpected and violent happens by the pool, but Gal ends up doing the job, risking all that he holds dear.

We don't need another British gangster flick. Fortunately, *Sexy Beast* isn't just another British gangster flick. Sure, it's got gangsters in it, swears like a stevedore, starts with an evocatively-chosen British hit from yesteryear ('Peaches' by The Stranglers) and radically casts Ray Winstone as a Cockney – but thanks to the toil of two individuals, *Sexy Beast* snaps the restraints of a knackered sub-genre and emerges a prize fighter.

The first of the two men who carry this handsome, brutal film aloft is debut director Jonathan Glazer, alumnus of ravishing TV ads (those surfing Guinness horses) and music (Blur, Radiohead). Tracing Ridley Scott's footsteps, he brings an unfettered visual imagination to bear on what is actually a rather straight story. Accustomed to making an impact in 60 seconds, Glazer sets the theme and place immediately. A sun-baked first act almost smells of burnt flesh, while later scenes confirm Glazer as a master showman as well as a keen stylist.

The second key figure is Ben Kingsely, who won a surprise Oscar nomination for this role and finally lays Gandhi to rest with a turn so Tarantinoesque, you will believe that Ray Winstone is shit-scared of him. After the high stakes of the Spanish set-up, the final-reel heist can only be a letdown – although the robbery does take place underwater! – but Winstone is so firmly established as our hero, the emotional momentum carries it.

Perhaps we should be poncey and say *Sexy Beast* is not about gangsters, it's about marriage and work. But it's about gangsters too. ★★★★ **AC**

◎ SHADOW OF A DOUBT (1943)

Starring: *Teresa Wright (Young Charlie), Joseph Cotten (Uncle Charlie), Macdonald Carey (Joseph Newton), Patricia Collinge (Emma Newton)*
Director: *Alfred Hitchcock*
Screenwriters: *Thornton Wilder, Sally Benson, Alma Reville, based on a story by Gordon McDonell*
PG/108 mins./Thriller/USA

Charlie adores her Uncle, whom she's named after, but on his latest visit she begins to suspect he may be a serial killer – and her knowledge could make her the next victim.

In the first scene a train enters the station, filling it with black smoke – and from the first it is clear that all is not right with Uncle Charlie. He might look alright and have a voice that charms, but he is the devil in disguise.

Hitchcock often said this was his favourite film – and certainly the one he found easiest to defend from his critics, in that it had the most plausible scenario. It's unusual in having a central villain who is almost the hero. Certainly he is hero worshipped by his niece, and yet she alone learns his true nature and ultimately (accidentally) causes his death. The townsfolk around are oblivious and talk of him throughout as a wonderful man, only a detective who has infiltrated the family household posing as a censor suspects otherwise, and this allows him to form a bond with the young Charlie and in the end he is the only other person who gets to find out what really happened and while he wins the girl, it's clear that her heart will always truly belong to her uncle.

The Merry Widow waltz is regularly repeated as a theme with sinister undercurrents since Uncle Charlie's speciality is offing rich widows. Images of whirling dancers reappear as the two Charlies get caught up in a dance towards an inevitable fate. Their close relationship is symbolised by near telepathy between them, the niece instinctively reading his thoughts and yet emotionally the uncle is the less devoted of the two, plotting her death in a detached way, and in some ways his death is seen as comeuppance for his lesser devotion.

This is certainly one of Hitchcock's most satisfying thrillers, mostly thanks to Wright and Cotten's believable relationship. It also has that aspect of life behind the white picket fence being not quite so rosy as it first appears, a theme David Lynch was later keen to exploit in films like *Blue Velvet*. While *Shadow Of A Doubt* is less extreme than that, there's still something not quite right about the love that bonds Charlie and her uncle, and the idea of the serial killer being the most attractive character in the movie was something that Hitchcock was to exploit later in *Psycho*. ★★★★ **EC**

◎ THE SHADOW (1994)

Starring: *Alec Baldwin (Lamont Cranston/The Shadow), John Lone (Shiwan Khan), Penelope Ann Miller (Margo Lane), Peter Boyle (Moe Shrevnitz), Ian McKellen (Reinhardt Lane), Tim Curry (Farley Claymore)*
Director: *Russell Mulcahy*
Screenwriter: *David Koepp, from the characters created by Walter Gibson*
12/102 mins./Action/Adventure/USA

In 30s New York City, the Shadow battles his nemesis, Shiwan Khan, who is building an atomic bomb.

Slinking onto the screens just after *The Mask* and *The Crow*, which are much hipper, and a few years after *Batman* and *Dick Tracy*, which were based on much more famous heroes, *The Shadow* was the latest masked avenger to be reincarnated as a big-budget live-action hero. A mysterious vigilante with the power to cloud minds to make himself seem invisible and who knew what evil lurks in the hearts of men, the Shadow was originally a 30s radio character (voiced by a young Orson Welles) and pulp magazine hero.

This lavish adventure opens with an 'origin' story set in the late 30s and starring opium lord Alec Baldwin who turns good under the tutelage of a mystic Tibetan guru and returns to New York. Posing as an idle playboy a là Bruce Wayne, Lamont Cranston fights crime while wearing a natty hat and a false beak, employing a network of agents to terrorise the mob. He still finds time to romance telepathic sweetie Margo Lane, whose crusty old scientist dad has just invented an atom bomb which is in danger of falling into the hands of Shiwan, the last descendent of Genghis Khan.

The film has a wonderful super-production look and Baldwin's Shadow breezes through via nifty 'invisible' effects, but the plot never really gels, and for an action fantasy is rather cold. It evokes the conventions and charms of 30s pulp fiction in rather more nostalgic mode than Quentin Tarantino, and is a pleasant, eye-pleasing movie, but, after Brandon Lee's zombie rock star and Jim Carrey's green-headed 'toon, the mysterious Baldwin seems somewhat grandfatherly and remote. ★★★ **JY**

◎ SHADOWLANDS (1993)

Starring: *Anthony Hopkins (Jack Lewis), Debra Winger (Joy Gresham), John Wood (Christopher Riley), Edward Hardwicke (Warnie Lewis), Joseph Mazzello (Douglas Gresham)*
Director: *Richard Attenborough*
Screenwriter: *William Nicholson, from his play*
U/125 mins./Romance/Biography/Drama/USA/UK

Awards: *BAFTA – Alexander Korda Award for Best British Film, Best Actor*

Based on the true story of Narnia author C.S. Lewis, known as Jack, who meets Joy, an American fan of his, while he is a professor at Oxford University. The two fall deeply in love, only for her to be diagnosed with cancer.

Anthony Hopkins and Debra Winger love and suffer to irresistibly sob-inducing effect in Richard Attenborough's handsome, moving, big-screen adaptation of William Nicholson's award-winning play, inspired by the late-blooming romance between the fiftysomething C.S. Lewis – devout Christian, professor of literature, logician and author of wise and witty books that included sci-fi and the Narnia classics for children – and American writer Joy Gresham.

For dramatic purposes, many of the facts, friendships and experiences of the real personalities are side-stepped: Lewis's comfortable affair with his housekeeper for instance, or that in reality Gresham had two sons, not the solitary, sad little soul touchingly played by young Joseph Mazzello from *Jurassic Park*. And yet, while the breadth of 'Jack' (as Lewis was known) and Joy's intellectual accomplishments is barely conveyed, the essence of their profound relationship is.

What began as correspondence was formalised as convenience, so that Joy could remain in Britain. Somewhere along the way, however, it found resolution as deep, fulfilling love. This provides an affecting spiritual journey for Hopkins' Jack from vague, dry academic, philosophising under the spires of Oxford, to the thrill of needing someone else, through to the agony of watching her die of cancer and carrying on when his insides have been torn out.

Attenborough takes his time getting to the heart of the matter, although the meandering among the ivory tower dwellers of Academe is not without pleasure in a musty Magdalen where the Fellows are a tweedy peevish bunch receiving the unconventional, foreign, feminine Mrs. Gresham and an inferior claret with the same unwelcoming moues.

It may sound like a terrible thing to observe, but this really gets good with Joy's diagnosis of incurable cancer and Jack's despairing crisis of faith. For all its sorrow, and the pain of loss that Jack comes to accept as the cost of needing another, this is a wonderfully affirmative tale of love as the richest and most liberatingly meaningful experience in a thinking man's life, and an extremely compelling testimonial to living in the now.

Winger's forthright and challenging Joy is a warm, disarming and sympathetic portrait of a romantic forcing open Lewis's shell. As for Hopkins, this is another fastidiously perfect characterisation, perhaps even topping his recent mesmerising performances. This time he gets to let rip and cry, and by heaven, when he does, it's a sorry individual who won't be crying with him. ★★★★ **AE**

◎ SHADOWS AND FOG (1992)

Starring: *Woody Allen (Kleinman), Mia Farrow (Irmy), John Malkovich (Clown), Madonna (Marie). David Ogden Stiers (Hacker)*
Director: *Woody Allen*
Screenwriter: *Woody Allen*
15/81 mins./Comedy/Drama/Mystery/USA

Local bookkeeper Kleinman is woken one night by his neighbours who enlist him in their vigilante group searching for the town strangler. While out searching, Kleinman meets Irmy, who has run away from the circus after catching her clown husband in the arms of Marie.

A strangler who casts a silhouette exactly like Max Schreck's Nosferatu stalks the fog-shrouded streets of an unspecified, central European-looking town in the 1920s as Woody Allen's Kleinman – another archetypically anxious and bewildered schlep – is rudely awakened and conscripted by a vigilante group hunting the serial killer.

Meanwhile, Mia Farrow's circus artiste Irmy walks out on her clown after catching him in flagrante with fellow trouper Madonna. Their paths inexorably cross as Kurt Weill music insistently plays amid a welter of visual and verbal references to German Expressionism, Bergman, Kafka and the existential mysteries of life.

Rendered in suitably moody, grainy black-and-white, this comic drama is by turns sly, witty and tiresome, a cinema buff's in-joke restating the familiar Allen preoccupations of man's inability to control events or to comprehend the nature of evil in an avalanche of homage gags and '100 Arty Cinematic Moments' recreations. A catastrophic failure at the US box office, this suffered from a delayed release in Britain, coming after the later and superior *Husbands And Wives*, though it does at least provide a diverting game of Spot The Allusion And The Star, notably Jodie Foster, Kathy Bates and Lily Tomlin. ★★★ **AE**

◎ SHADOWS OF OUR FORGOTTEN ANCESTORS (1964)

Starring: *Ivan Mikolajchuk (Ivan), Larisa Kadochnikova (Marichka), Tatyana Bestayeva (Palagna), Spartak Bagashvili (Yurko), Nikolai Grinko (Batag)*
Director: *Sergei Paradjanov*
Screenwriter: *Sergei Paradjanov, Ivan Chendej, based on the novella by Mikhaylo Kotsubinsky*
12/97 mins/Drama/Russia

Despite the feud between their fathers, Ivan and Marichka become lovers. However, she drowns during a temporary separation and, after a period of grief, he marries Palagna, whose treacherous carnality contrasts with the purity of the lost love, with whom he is eventually reunited in death.

Adapted from the Carpathian writer M. Kotsubinsky's novella, *Wild Horses of Fire*, Sergei Paradjanov's masterpiece won a raft of awards at international film festivals. Yet it was scarcely seen in his homeland, as much through studio hostility as official disapproval. However, the accusations of formalism and Ukrain'an nationalism stuck and, having had numer-

S

ous projects blocked, Paradjanov was arrested on bogus charges of gay rape, the spread of venereal disease and the trafficking of icons, and, although he was released in 1977, he never completed another film.

Perceptive critics have identified the indomitable spiritual dimension of this astonishing feature as the reason for its hostile reception. But the audacious technique, which was intended to convey both the ethereality of the tale and its allegorical discussion of the stages of existence, so confused the Soviet cinematic establishment that it presumed that the shadow cast by the past shrouded a seditious political message.

However, Paradjanov's sole purpose was to challenge conventional methods of screen storytelling and redefine the audience's relationship to the moving image. Thus, he deconstructed the very processes of narration and representation, so that every frame confounded the viewer's expectation and forced them to reappraise both the action itself and their approach to spectatorship.

In order to achieve this, he made flamboyant use of Yuri Ilyenko's camera, which seemed to plunge from the top of a tree, peer without distortion through a pool of water and elongate vistas through the use of 180° fish-eye lenses, whose wide angles disorientated as much as the minute-long 360° spin that blurred shapes and images into an abstraction that approximated the troubled world of the mythical storyline.

Sound and colour were similarly exploited. Lush orchestrations, discordant sounds, folk music, natural noises and religious chanting were all employed to reinforce the psychological significance of scenes that were designed according to a 'dramaturgy of colour' that passed from the white innocence of childhood and the green optimism of youth through moments of monochrome and sepia despair to the blazing shades of transient contentment, the autumnal hues of resignation and the reds and blues of oblivion. Pure genius. ★★★★★ **DP**

⓪ SHAFT (1971)

Starring: *Richard Roundtree (John Shaft), Moses Gunn (Bumpy Jones), Charles Cioffi (Vic Androzzi), Christopher St. John (Ben Burford), Gwenn Mitchell (Ellie Moore)*
Director: *Gordon Parks*
Screenwriters: *Ernest Tidyman, John D.F. Black, from the novel by Tidyman*
15/100 mins./Action/Crime/Drama/USA

Awards: *Academy Awards – Best Song ('Theme From Shaft'), Golden Globes – Best Song ('Theme From Shaft')*

A private eye is enlisted to find a Harlem racketeer's kidnapped daughter.

'Who's the black private dick that's a sex machine with all the chicks?' asks Isaac (Chef) Hayes in the Oscar-winning theme song; the answer, as is patently obvious from the title, is John Shaft, a dude with a generously-cut brown leather jacket and a slightly Afro-ed Burt Reynolds moustache seen wandering purposefully around New York under the jazzy opening credits. Shaft is Sam Superspade, a continent away from the Californian ironies of Dashiell Hammett and Raymond Chandler, and far closer to the broken-nose, gals 'n' guns approach of Mickey Spillane's Mike Hammer – as the song and character name suggests, he's a 'dick' not an 'eye'.

Though it launched the 'blaxploitation' genre, Shaft never really lives up to its soulful on-the-streets introduction, trotting out a trite plot about a black gangster's daughter who's kidnapped by the Mafia as part of a plan to take over the Harlem rackets. It also pays minor attention to the politics of the 70s by having the hero call in a black radical group to wage war on the honky mob. The material is dressed up with grimy locations, then-unfamiliar African-American slang and fashions, a few sub-Panther political footnotes and that million-selling soul score, but former model Richard Roundtree's Shaft (the creation of white writer Ernest Tidyman) is a humourless thug, using 'chicks' (of various races) as sexual Kleenex and whupping ass with monotonous regularity.

Veteran Charles Cioffi chews scenery in the role of 'The Man', an Italian-American swine who's such a venomous stereotype that even the nastiest black hoods look good next to him. Sequels, a duff remake (starring Samuel L. Jackson and Christian Bale) and a TV series followed, and Roundtree wound up in Seven; here's a chance to revisit the original. 'Can you dig it?' ★★★ **KN**

⓪ SHAKESPEARE IN LOVE (1998)

Starring: *Joseph Fiennes (Will Shakespeare), Gwyneth Paltrow (Viola De Lesseps), Judi Dench (Queen Elizabeth), Colin Firth (Lord Wessex), Simon Callow (Tilney), Geoffrey Rush (Philip Henslowe), Tom Wilkinson (Hugh Fennyman), Ben Affleck (Ned Alleyn), Rupert Everett (Marlowe – uncredited)*
Director: *John Madden*
Screenwriters: *Marc Norman, Tom Stoppard*
15/118 mins./History/Romance/Comedy/USA

Awards: *Academy Awards – Best Actress, Best Supporting Actress (Judi Dench), Best Costume, Best Score, Best Picture, Best Original Screenplay, BAFTA – Best Editing, Best Film, Best Supporting Actress (Judi Dench), Empire Awards – Best Actress, Golden Globes – Best Comedy/Musical, Best Comedy/Musical Actress, Best Screenplay*

The young William Shakespeare is facing writer's block until he meets his muse – a theatre-loving noblewoman named Viola.

Effortlessly fusing the slyly clever, the broadly comical and the hopelessly romantic, John Madden's follow-up to *Mrs. Brown* tinkers with history, art and the love-life of Britain's most celebrated playwright to delicious effect. Art imitates life, life imitates art, life takes art outside for a good kicking and art gives as good as he gets. This is postmodernism without the ponce, period drama without the pomposity.

In 1590, as the world of theatre struggles to gain respect, an egocentric Will Shakespeare hits the plague of writer's block, unable to realise his latest comedy *Romeo And Ethel The Pirate's Daughter* (you can see where we're coming from) without a new romantic muse. Amid a hasty and rather uneven first half-hour, a curious courtship begins between theatre-loving noblewoman Viola De Lesseps and the smitten Bard. Naturally, the path to true love will be fraught with mishap, social dudgeon and bad timing. This is, after all, Shakespeare.

Circling this problematical love story spin a catalogue of subplots. Stuck-up buffoon Lord Wessex buys Viola's hand in marriage. Rival theatre companies vie for Shakespeare's unfinished play, while he vies with arch-rival playwright Christopher Marlowe (an underused Rupert Everett). And the company of actors – shaped from the familiar mugs of British moviedom and members of *The Fast Show* – strain to pull the play into shape with all the spirited bluster of a show-must-go-on 40s-era Hollywood number.

The jocular script, imprinted with Stoppard's familiar gamesmanship, is a fabulous thing and under the assured care of Madden's direction grants the movie a delightful literary playfulness; Shakespeare and Viola's burgeoning romance deliberately reflecting that of Romeo and Juliet growing inside the head of the love-struck writer; numerous references to Shakespeare's other plays (try, at least, *Two Gentlemen Of Verona*, *Hamlet*, *Twelfth Night*, *The Tempest* and *Titus Andronicus*) dotting the action; the presence of Gothic playwright John Webster as a gore-hungry street urchin. There's even an attempt to resolve Marlowe's mysterious murder. There are various themes – sexual liberation, feminism, artistic freedom, the nobility of acting and the power of theatre – plus two duels, some arty sex, cross-dressing, and a genuine sense of Elizabethan life without endless schlopping about in mud and starving peasants.

More subtle still is a parody of Hollywood's many lunacies with pompous actors grabbing bogus percentages, an endless list of credits topping the flyers for the play, even a Thames boat-cabby who fancies himself as a writer.

But *Shakespeare In Love*'s clever-cleverness doesn't alienate; the lavish production, superlative array of supporting characters (in-joke Ben Affleck does a fabulous 16th century luvvie) and triumphant final third make it, surprisingly, the crowd-pleaser of the season. The central romance may not ring as true as that of Shakespeare's own work – while Fiennes has never been better, Paltrow (despite that Oscar win) frequently seems out of her depth – but this is a great success, bawdy, silly, handsome, brainy and energetic, which says more about that bloke from Stratford than any smarty-pants lecturer could hope for. ★★★★ **IN**

➂ SHALL WE DANCE? (1996)

Starring: *Koji Yakusho (Shohei Sugiyama), Tamiyo Kusakari (Mai Kishikawa), Naoto Takenaka (Tomio Aoki), Eriko Watanabe (Toyoko Takashashi), Yu Tokui (Tokichi Hattori), Yu Tokui (Tokichi Hattori)*
Director: *Masayuki Suo*
Screenwriter: *Masayuki Suo*
PG/114 mins./Comedy/Japan

Businessman Shohei becomes entranced by the vision of a ballroom dancing teacher he sees teaching in her studio from his train and signs up for classes. His dancing and mood improves and this worries his wife...

Finding comic and heart-warming mileage in the most unlikely milieu – the world of Japanese ballroom dancing – *Shall We Dance*? emerges as an unadulterated joy. Comparisons to *Strictly Ballroom* will be inevitable, but Suo's film revels less in the glitzy, sequinned tack and more in the transformational qualities of dance, resulting in a perfectly poised mixture of gentle humour and feelgood sentiment.

Teetering on the verge of a mid-life crisis, married businessman Shohei (a dignified, eminently likeable Yakusho) becomes fixated by a beautiful woman he glimpses at a dance studio window every night on his train journey home. Secretly enrolling in a beginners class to get close to his mystery woman – aloof instructor Mai – he gradually discovers a delight in dancing and transforms into a ballroom ace, ready to take on the national championship. Yet his dreams seem threatened as his wife, noticing his happier demeanour, believes he is having an affair and puts a detective on his tail.

While there are (intentional) laughs to be had from the cheesy incongruity of Japanese folk foxtrotting, Suo's sensibility is a generous, sympathetic one, never poking fun at the aspirations of Shohei and his oddball classmates – such as Tomio, Shohei's repressed co-office worker who, on the dance floor, turns into a fiery Latin love god, perfectly expressing the movie's funny but poignant tone.

Yet, the comedy is overlaid with an unashamedly old-fashioned romance: Shohei's journey from unhappy worker bee – the early scenes are cleverly sketched to show his mundane routine without ever themselves being boring – to rejuvenated free spirit is credible, actually earning the film's final emotional wallop. Irresistible. ★★★★ **IF**

➂ SHALL WE DANCE? (2004)

Starring: *Richard Gere (John Clark), Jennifer Lopez (Paulina), Susan Sarandon (Beverly Clark) Lisa Ann Walter (Bobbie) Stanley Tucci (Link)*
Director: *Peter Chelsom*
Screenwriter: *Audrey Wells, based on the 1997 film by Masayuki Suo*
12/106 mins./Romance/Comedy/USA

Beguiled by a face in the window of a dance studio, Chicago lawyer John Clark impulsively gets off the train and signs up for dance lessons. He's ashamed to tell his wife, who imagines he's having an affair and hires a detective to discover his secret.

The pleasant surprise in this Americanisation of Masayuki Suo's smashing global hit of 1996 is that it follows the storyline of the Japanese original quite closely. Contrary to the ad implications, this is not a romance between the Gere and Lopez characters, and the part of Lopez's heartbroken dance instructor has not been blown up to unbalance the ensemble and the film's essentially comedic nature. Though greeted with some derision in the US, it must stand a better chance here with its distinct *Strictly Come Dancing* appeal: celebrities with two left feet sweating through gruelling tango-foxtrot trials and trying not to trip over the sequins.

The heart of it is that something intangible is missing in 9-to-5-er John Clark's comfy life. Instead of getting his ya-yas out with a sports car, a call girl, gambling or fishing, he rediscovers his joie de vivre by releasing his inner Astaire. The Japanese Ordinary Joe was liberated by this, defying the rigid conformity of a society in which such dancing is viewed as shamelessly intimate. Writer Audrey Wells (*The Truth About Cats & Dogs*) has tried to get around that by making her hero loathe to let his wife know he's not 100 per cent happy. Only in America could that be postulated as shaming.

Two problems are insurmountable. Lopez can dance, but she comes with so much baggage you can't get over her being J.Lo. The other is that the taboo aspect is lost in translation – men in the West have nothing to fear from being known to enjoy a foot-shuffle. Gere's transformation is funny and charming, but it's never really believable that this man, with this life and this wife, would find his joy in ballroom dancing.

What works best is the fellowhip in Miss Mitzi's studio. Tucci, excruciatingly toupéed and spray-tanned, is wild as John's co-worker with his own closeted Latin dance addiction. John's disparate classmates, including The Station Agent's Bobby Cannavale, all have a story to tell and limbs to be tamed, and the surveillance 'tecs, *Sins Of The Father*'s Richard Jenkins and rapper Nick Cannon, acquire an amusingly critical appreciation for footwork. Director Peter Chelsom brings an affectionate eye and, at times, such as a flying-footed waltz, a distinctive bounce to the proceedings. ★★★ **AE**

➂ SHALLOW GRAVE (1994)

Starring: *Kerry Fox (Juliet Miller), Christopher Eccleston (David Stephens), Ewan McGregor (Alex Law), Ken Stott (Det. Inspector McCall), Keith Allen (Hugo)*
Director: *Danny Boyle*
Screenwriter: *John Hodge*
18/88 mins./Drama/Thriller/Comedy/UK

Awards: *BAFTA – Alexander Korda Award for Best British Film, Empire Awards – Best British Actor (Ewan McGregor), Best British Film, Best Director*

Three friends discover their new flatmate dead but loaded with cash. Internal wrangles ensue with grisly results.

Shallow Grave hit the screens like an electric shock. Here was a rave of a thriller, pounding with energy and pulsing with tension right through to its brutal twist ending. And although some decided it was Tarantinoesque and a British *Reservoir Dogs* – admittedly there is a common formula element of conspirators falling out and both memorably feature a vintage pop tune loudly as blood spreads on the floor – the cuts, pans, style flourishes and coolly sardonic tone are more Coens than Quentin.

The most exciting aspect of *Shallow Grave* is its acute Britishness and the unsentimental modernity of that characteristic. The collaborative triumvirate of writer John Hodge, producer Andrew McDonald and director Danny Boyle, all making their first feature film, successfully negotiated a sharp, smart, cracking thriller. There is scarcely a homage to Baling, a reference to the tough Brit thrillers of the 60s, a literary source or a cheeky Cockney in sight. The narrator, David, says, 'This could have been any city. They're all the same'. In some ways, yes. But there wouldn't be a parking

S

space in front of the building in Manhattan for suspicious vehicles to bring detectives (one of whom is John Hodge) straight to the door. In Paris the flatmates would fret more about the meaning of life. It is also precisely of its time, in its smarty-pants attitude, the cruel, mocking humour, the mean-spiritedness and the brash, uninhibited vitality. Three frankly obnoxious, alarmingly realistic flatmates – journalist Alex Law, doctor Juliet Miller and accountant David Stevens – seek a fourth. The self-satisfied trio subject a string of applicants to humiliating quizzings and dismiss one hapless candidate because, they taunt him, he lacks the 'presence, charisma, style and charm' they believe they ooze.

When the mysterious Hugo turns up claiming to be a novelist and demonstrates both a simpatico smugness and ample funds, he's invited in. He creeps in during the night, but when he fails to make an appearance the three friends break down his bedroom door to find his nude corpse artistically sprawled, a stash of drugs and, ta-da, a suitcase packed with cash. What to do? What to do? The most reasonable greedy course would be to stash the bundles of banknotes (interestingly never totalled for our benefit, inviting the self-reflection, 'How much money would it take for me to do what they do ?') in knicker drawers and the microwave before calling in the authorities. But the crime wouldn't be very interesting if this was about being reasonable. This is about the mounting distrust, jealousy, paranoia, fear and increasingly extreme, shocking, grotesque deeds that spring out of unreasonable greed.

Flattering the viewer, the film takes for granted that contemporary audiences are one step ahead of the 'dot every i' expositions and TV-mentality dialogues that plague too many British productions. Instead the principals have near-telepathic shorthand discussions, like chums do. They contemplate the cash. David: 'No.' Juliet: 'It's unfeasible.' David: 'You mean immoral.' Juliet: 'I know what I mean.' And so do we. Initially their only crime is inertia, but trust the crafty tabloid reporter (Alex's mind perfectly revealed by his succinct phone conversation at work: 'Y'see, what I need here is "PC Plod Saves Harry The Hamster From House Of Horror", y'know? ... Y'see no pets, no human angle.') to devise an unnecessarily complicated and gruesome scheme to keep the money. Hugo is mutilated beyond identification – by the short straw-drawing David – with the bulk of his bits left in a pit Alex is too lazy to dig deep.

Up to this point the film is firmly black comedy with wisecracks like Alex's protest to the suddenly squeamish Juliet, 'But Juliet, you're a doctor! You kill people every day!' (a line Hodge must have particularly enjoyed writing, since he is actually a doctor). It develops into something more chilling, more relentlessly unnerving – and certain to involve an apportioning of doom – when it turns on boring, diligent David being the only one of the three with any sense of moral dilemma, guilt or possible consequences. So he's the one who has to go spectacularly crazy. Alex and Juliet would happily slop champagne and buy toys for the rest of their lives without a twinge, but for the fatefully-charged arrival of the professional criminals (one of whom is Peter Mullan).

Insofar as it is needed we can take for granted their history from the grisly torture trail they take to the haven turned hell of a flat. The macabre disintegration that results is clever, cautionary and stimulating, even provoking, and as unreasonable as life. ★★★★ **AE**

◎ SHANE (1953)

Starring: *Alan Ladd (Shane), Jean Arthur (Marian Starrett), Van Heflin (Joe Starrett), Jack Palance, as Walter Jack Palance (Jack Wilson), Emile Meyer (Rufus Ryker)*
Director: *George Stevens*
Screenwriters: *A.B. Guthrie, Jr., Jack Sher, from the novel by Jack Schaefer*
PG/112 mins./Western/USA

Shane, a gunfighter weary of killing, finds refuge and peace with a homesteader family, but is drawn into a conflict between the small farmers and a big rancher who wants to drive them off their land. The cattle baron sends for another fast gun to even the odds.

So archetypal it feels as if it were the first Western ever made, this adaptation of a great novel by Jack Schaefer tells a familiar farmers-vs-cattlemen range war tale through the eyes of the youth (Brandon de Wilde) who idolises glamorous pistolero Shane ('Come back, Shane') while undervaluing his fallible, hard-working farmer father (Van Heflin). The buckskin-clad hero, like all-in-black demon villain Jack Palance – seems to have ridden out of a simpler, more morally clear-cut Western and stirs the cowed farmers into standing against the ruthless ranchers.

The film recognises the appeal of gunslinging matinée fantasy but finally sides ambiguously with sod-busting reality, awarding points to the practical men who have to get the crops in. Director George Stevens works hard on the beauties of the landscape (Shane is first seen framed perfectly between the horns of a startled deer) and makes a stump-pulling scene a lyrical hymn to hard work and male bonding, but the nasty, corrupt town is characterised by the expanse of mud into which unregenerate Confederate Elisha Cook Jr is blasted when goaded into a gunfight and gutshot by the sadistic Palance (his soft-spoken, menacing catch-phrase, always uttered as he's forced someone to fight, is 'prove it').

It's a tad overconscious of its attempt to be a classic, with Ladd's Roy Rogers woodenness not quite getting the depths of Schaefer's fallen hero, but all the supporting performances are excellent, especially Jean Arthur as a yearning farm-wife and Ben Johnson as a conscience-struck bully. ★★★★ **KN**

◎ SHANGHAI EXPRESS (1932)

Starring: *Marlene Dietrich (Shanghai Lily), Clive Brook (Capt. Donald 'Doc' Harvey), Anna May Wong (Hu Fei), Warner Oland (Henry Chang), Eugene Pallette (Sam Salt), Lawrence Grant (Rev. Carmichael), Louise Closser Hale (Mrs Haggerty)*
Director: *Joseph von Sternberg*
Screenwriter: *Jules Furthmann based on a story by Harry Hervey*
PG/82 mins/Drama/USA

Awards: *Academy Awards – Best Cinematography*

Shanghai Lily meets up with old flame Donald Harvey on a Chinese express, whose passengers all have secrets to hide, especially arrogant merchant Henry Chang, who is really a rebel warlord, whose men ambush the train in the hope of exchanging the hostages for some jailed comrades.

Having demythologised Marlene Dietrich in *Dishonored* and proved he could create effectively without her on *An American Tragedy*, Josef von Sternberg renewed his frustrated fixation with his Muse in this exotic melodrama, whose ingenuity and intrigue owed much to Jules Furthman's canny screenplay.

However, the narrative was never allowed to deflect attention from the atmospheric décor, which von Sternberg designed in collaboration with Hans Dreier. But, for once, Dietrich succeeded in holding her iconic own against her mentor's visual finesse and, consequently, this represents their most equitable achievement.

Dietrich is at her sultry best in her scenes with Clive Brook's British military medic, but she also shows spirit and backbone in her showdowns with Warner Oland's bandit. But her performance is exquisitely incorporated into the overall design by von Sternberg and Oscar-winning cinematographer Lee Garmes, who were collaborating for the fourth and last time.

As ever, von Sternberg surrounded Dietrich with feathers, drapery, smoke, shadows and shafts of light emanating from lanterns and through window blinds. But, he also turned calligraphy into a co-character and the action is littered with letters, notes, cables, signs, newspapers, magazines, documentation and ideograms, which not only helped establish the setting, but also suggested that the writing was on the wall for Lily and her fellow travellers.

But von Sternberg also used the cramped compartments, narrow corridors and crowded platforms to convey the sense of claustrophobia that found echo in the deadpan delivery style, which was designed to reflect the monotony of the long-distance journey. However, the pace picked up once the train slowed down and the false personas adopted by the opium dealer (Gustav von Seyffertitz), the cashiered soldier (Emile Chautard), the duplicitous gambler (Eugene Pallette) and the born-again prostitute (Anna May Wong) were exposed under Oland's callous interrogation.

Only Dietrich and Brook had nothing to hide and, thus, resisted his hectoring. But, even as he celebrated their enduring passion, Von Sternberg couldn't resist reminding his star of her debt to him by using a picture from her voluptuous past in Brook's watch to contrast with the sophistication he had helped fashion. ★★★★ **DP**

SHANGHAI KNIGHTS (2003)

Starring: *Jackie Chan (Chon Wang), Owen Wilson (Roy O'Bannon), Fann Wong (Chon Lin), Aaron Johnson (Charlie Chaplin), Aidan Gillen (Lord Nelson Rathbone), Donnie Yen (Wu Chow)*
Director: *David Dobkin*
Screenwriters: *Alfred Gough, Miles Millar, based on characters by Alfred Gough, Miles Millar*
12A/114 mins./Action/Comedy/USA/UK/Czech Republic

1887. Former outlaws Chon Wang and Roy O'Bannon are reunited after Wang's father is killed in China by Lord Rathbone, an English peer who is tenth in line to the British throne. With revenge in his heart, Wang travels with Roy to London to put a stop to Rathbone's dastardly ways – with his kid sister in tow.

Now here's a pleasant surprise: a sequel to a pleasant surprise that's even more pleasantly surprising than its predecessor.

When *Shanghai* Noon appeared in 2000, it was quickly lauded as Jackie Chan's finest American film – praise based on decent fight scenes and the offbeat central relationship between the stoic Chan and the extremely laid-back Owen Wilson.

Writers Alfred Gough and Miles Millar – who scripted the original – clearly recognise this, and so wisely eschew both the Western setting and anything resembling a coherent plot in order to focus on the two stars' strengths. Chan's American movies have generally been let down not only by the star's pidgin English (a situation addressed here by a simple solution: Chan punches, Wilson wisecracks) but by stodgy fight sequences marred by MTV editing.

Director David Dobkin, though, resists this urge and leaves Chan alone to craft some wonderfully innovative fight sequences – in a revolving door, a library, in the inner workings of Big Ben – which recall the very best of the star's Hong Kong work. Dobkin also leaves Wilson to his own devices and again he's a constant delight. His patented combo of romantic, optimistic, New Age-y, childlike awe and drawled, deadpan sarcasm is, of course, his usual schtick, but here refined to the nth degree. His chemistry with Chan is priceless; watching him confound Chan by saying, 'I love you, buddy' is worth an extra star in itself.

Which is just as well, for elsewhere Dobkin drops the ball. For example if, during a sublime scene where Chan wields an umbrella, you didn't realise that it's an homage to *Singin' In The Rain*, well, Dobkin helpfully plays the song for you. Elsewhere, he succumbs to obvious culture clash gags and oh-so-subtle references to British history (so our heroes encounter a young Charlie Chaplin and Jack the Ripper, and invent Sherlock Holmes along the way).

Quibbles aside, though, The Owen And Jackie Show is so charming that a potential third instalment is actually very appealing. Shanghai Brunch, anyone? ★★★ **CH**

SHANGHAI NOON (2000)

Starring: *Jackie Chan (Chon Wang), Owen Wilson (Roy O'Bannon), Lucy Lui (Princess Pei Pei), Brandon Merrill (Falling Leaves), Roger Yuan (Lo Fong)*
Director: *Tom Dey*
Screenwriters: *Miles Millar, Alfred Gough*
12/105 mins./Western/Action/Comedy/USA

An Imperial Guard is sent to America to rescue a Chinese princess and hooks up with a hobo cowboy along the way.

A no-frills, unpretentious mixture of cowboy clichés, martial arts licks, buddy-buddy movies and low comedy, *Shanghai Noon* is the kind of fun flick that will never generate tons of hype or expectation, but is all the more refreshing for it.

A showcase for Chan's martial arts dexterity and little-guy-against-the-world persona, this also benefits from a broad canvas, a gossamer touch from director Dey, oodles of filmic in-jokery (say Chan's character name Chon Wang very quickly) and a performance from Wilson that erases all memory of *The Haunting* and may catapult him to stardom.

While it appears on the surface to be a by-the-numbers romp through overused Western standards – there are neatly staged hold-ups, barroom brawls and hair's-breadth escapes from hanging – *Shanghai Noon* does possess enough quirks to lift it way beyond the average. Chiefly this lies in the relationship between Chan and Wilson which, if it follows all the rules of buddydom (mutual antagonism flourishing into respect), is decidedly more offbeam than, say, *Rush Hour* (1998).

Even if his stunt shenanigans are not as inspired as his best work, Chan turns in a performance of likeability, vulnerability and self-parody. Yet this is far and away Wilson's movie: with Chan clever and generous enough to allow his co-star time in the sun, Wilson's verbose, slightly anxious, introverted outlaw delivers a goofy winning turn through sheer off-kilter charm rather than anything inherent in the script. The chemistry between the two is a delight – a moment where they play a bizarro drinking game while sharing adjacent bathtubs holed up in a bordello is infectious – and gives Shanghai Noon a strangely moving centre in which to anchor its funny, exciting edges. ★★★★ **IF**

SHAUN OF THE DEAD (2004)

Starring: *Simon Pegg (Shaun), Kate Ashfield (Liz), Nick Frost (Ed), Lucy Davis (Dianne), Dylan Moran (David), Nicola Cunningham (Mary)*
Director: *Edgar Wright*
Screenwriters: *Simon Pegg, Edgar Wright*
15/99 mins./Comedy/Horror/UK/France

Awards: *Empire Awards – Best British Film*

Shaun, a North London loser, is a disappointment to his girlfriend, family, friends and flatmate. Only his mate Ed, an even bigger loser, looks up to him. Then flesh-eating zombies overrun the city and Shaun is forced to take responsibility for the survival of his corner of humanity . . .

Somewhere out there is a movie graveyard for the careers of British comedians – successful in home entertainment – who died a death trying to make an impact on the big screen. For every break-out Peter Sellers or John Cleese there are a dozen disappointments, as national institutions such as Morecambe and Wise, Smith and Jones, and . . . um, Cannon and Ball land with a thud.

In *Shaun Of The Dead*, director-writer Edgar Wright and star-writer Simon Pegg – plus many of their mates from the innovative Channel 4 sitcom *Spaced* – spin off a *Resident Evil* sketch wrapped-up inside five minutes in one episode into a whole feature.

This is a rare TV-to-film transfer that retains the things you liked on television but still comes on like a proper (if low-budget and shambolic) movie. A difference between American crazy comedy and the British variety is that Hollywood always puts out pretend losers as leads – in *Bruce Almighty*, for instance, we're supposed to accept Jim Carrey as a failure, though he has a job on television and is living with Jennifer Aniston; Pegg' s Shaun watches a lot of television and is living with a friend from college who hates the friend from primary school who's on a permanent visit.

The point is not to make you feel good, but to prompt laughs of horrified recognition that we really are like that. The basic joke is that Shaun stumbles zombie-like through his regular life, not paying attention to the Night Of The Living Dead crisis taking place in the background, but shapes up when society falls apart and, though still essentially useless, becomes the best chance his friends have to survive (most of them, it's fair to say, don't).

It's a workable premise and the early scenes, with unnoticed zombies on buses, working checkout tills or snogging in the street, are creepy-funny. But the film gets impatient (especially in two or three awkward 'serious' bits) and eventually winds up down the pub, with beer on the table, inappropriate music on an apparently malign jukebox and hordes of zombie flesh-eaters hammering at the doors as idiot Ed tries to cheer up his just-dumped mate with, 'It's not the end of the world.' ★★★★ **KN**

THE SHAWSHANK REDEMPTION (1994)

Starring: *Tim Robbins (Andy Dufresne), Morgan Freeman (Ellis Boyd 'Red' Redding), Bob Gunton (Warden Norton), William Sadler (Heywood)*
Director: *Frank Darabont*
Screenwriter: *Frank Darabont, from the short story* Rita Hayworth And Shawshank Redemption *by Stephen King*
15/136 mins./Drama/USA

A US Lawyer is sent to Shawshank prison for life and spends year protesting his innocence against the backdrop of a brutal regime.

This movie is based on a novella by Stephen King, but don't let that put you off. It's not a horror film, rather a thumpingly good ode to friendship, hope, wit, wiles and wisdom, brimming with crackling characters and topped with the most twisteroo of twists since *The Crying Game*. Found guilty of killing his unfaithful wife and her lover in a fit of passion, sullen accountant Andy Dufresne (Robbins, casting off his goofball image to display more layers than the proverbial onion) is shipped to the gothic wind-swept corridors of the Shawshank State Prison for life. It is here the movie gracefully unfolds. With a beautifully rounded script, writer/director Darabont conjures up a spellbinding personal odyssey stretching through the years from 1946 to 1967.

Tagline
Fear can hold you prisoner. Hope can set you free.

Dufresne, all the while protesting his innocence, slowly overcomes the hellfire tortures of the prison system – an unblinking range of beatings, rapings and abject humiliations – while managing to inspire his fellow inmates to lift their degraded horizons. Among them is Red (Freeman, in a matchless supporting role), the lifer who can, given time, provide virtually anything. And for reasons best known to himself, Dufresne requires 40s starlet Rita Hayworth, provisioned in poster form.

The mood swings rigorously through every emotion as the cranky, wiseguy and downright crazed array of criminals bare the brunt of the turbulent life within the doomy Shawshank catacomb. Then it gets really mean, gearing up for its injury-time shockers. Dufresne, a whiz with figures, is bullied into running the warden's petty accounting scams, giving him the chance to execute his and the film's final, greatest miracle.

If you're miserable enough to look for gripes then, yes, it does drift on too long and who needs prison buggery again? Yet the ending has such poetic completeness you're too busy contentedly chuckling to worry about sore behinds. This may have confounded American audiences – it flopped big-time on planet Yank and lost out in all its seven Oscar nominated categories – but it's been topping 'favourite film' polls ever since. Keep spreading the word. ★★★★★ **IN**

SHE DONE HIM WRONG (1933)

Starring: *Mae West (Lady Lou), Cary Grant (Capt. Cummings), Owen Moore (Chick Clark), Gilbert Roland (Serge Stanieff), Noah Beery Sr. (Gus Jordan), David Landau (Dan Flynn), Rafaella Ottiano (Russian Rita), Dewey Robinson (Spider Kane)*
Director: *Lowell Sherman*
Screenwriters: *Mae West, Harvey Thew, John Brights, based on the play* Diamond Lil *by Mae West*
PG/66 mins./Comedy/USA

Lady Lou runs a Bowery saloon for Gus Jordan, who also operates a counterfeiting and pickpocketing racket with accomplices Serge Stanieff and Russian Rita. However, the crooks are being watched by Cummings, a cop posing as a charity worker from the local mission, who also has his eye on Lou.

Having made her screen debut with a cameo in *Night After Night*, Mae West sought again to bring her controversial 1928 play Diamond Lil to the screen. However, Will H. Hays had already blocked one proposed adaptation in 1930 and he was more determined than ever to protect American audiences from such smut.

Realising that the treatment for Ruby Red that West had concocted with John Bright (who had confirmed his crime credentials with *The Public Enemy*, 1931) was only a shallow revision, Hays threatened to close the picture down and it took Paramount chief Adolph Zukor's personal intervention to salvage the project, minus its references to white slavery, the Salvation Army and the Brazilian origins of Gus's accomplices, lest they jeopardised good relations with a thriving movie market (which Soviet Russia was not).

Reluctantly accepting the Motion Picture Production Code ruling, West nevertheless succeeded in sidelining Bright (who wanted to emphasise the story's criminal aspects) after a Hays representative suggested that she concentrated more on the comedy than the melodrama. Thus, she completed the final drafts with Harvey Thew and got away with keeping the occasional celebrated line, including 'You can be had,' and 'Why don't you come up some time and see me?', both of which were delivered to a young Cary Grant.

West tried to take credit for discovering Grant, but he had already made several films, including Marlene Dietrich's *Blonde Venus*. However, the success of *She Done Him Wrong* – which earned over $3 million worldwide from a $200,000 budget – put him firmly on the road to stardom, having taught him the timing and sensitivity to strong female co-stars that would make him such a screwball natural.

But it was West who made all the headlines, with her voluptuous charm and unique delivery style turning her overnight into the Talkies' first female comedy star. She reunited with Grant on *I'm No Angel*, which reprised her trademark blend of self-assurance and self-abasement, both to celebrate and caricature her sensuality and convey her disdain for drooling males. But the 1934 Code effectively ended her screen career. ★★★★ DP

SHERLOCK, JR (1924)

Starring: *Buster Keaton (Sherlock Jr.)/Projectionist), Kathryn McGuire (The Girl), Joe Keaton (Her Father), Erwin Connelly (The Butler/Gandyman), Ward Crane (The Sheik/Villain)*
Director: *Buster Keaton*
Screenwriters: *Clyde Bruckman, Jean Havez, Joe Mitchell*
U/44 mins./Comedy/USA

Fake Films Within Films — TOP 10

1 *Habeas Corpus* - *The Player*
2 *Stab* - *Scream 2*
3 *The Duelling Cavalier* - *Singin' in the Rain*
4 *Gump Again* - *Cecil B. DeMented*
5 *Asses of Fire* - *South Park: Bigger, Longer & Uncut*
6 *TJ Hooker: The Movie* - *Charlie's Angels*
7 *Driving Over Miss Daisy* - *Stay Tuned*
8 *Hot Pants College II* - *Love and Death On Long Island*
9 *Holly Does Hollywood* - *Body Double*
10 *Teenage Werewolf Meets Teenage Frankenstein* - *How To Make A Monster*

Framed for the theft of a watch belonging to his beloved's father, a nickeleodeon projectionist dozes off and finds himself playing the detective in a mystery movie (*Hearts And Pearls*), whose triumph over the villain echoes the exposure of his real-life nemesis, The Sheik.

Buster Keaton's third and shortest feature ranks among his best. An ironic comment on social injustice, it's a deceptively serious study of fantasy and reality, life and art. But, most significantly, it's also a film about film that places so much stress on creativity and escapism that the dream sequence relegates the everyday to the margins.

The visual and clowning ingenuity required to execute such a sophisticated picture was matched by a technical assurance that was rare for a slapstick silent. Keaton's entry into the screen world of *Hearts And Pearls*, for instance, was a masterclass in comic montage that was not only perfectly timed, but also anticipated both the advances in editing usually associated with the Soviets and the surrealism achieved by such French Impressionists as Germaine Dulac and René Clair.

Indeed, not even the iconoclasts of the nouvelle vague attempted such a sustained assault on the conventions of screen storytelling, as Keaton did while passing from the prologue realms of Griffithian melodrama into a ciné-existence utterly devoid of linear logic and independent of standard spatial and temporal systems.

The cross-cutting between the house steps, garden, street, mountain ledge, jungle, desert, beach, snowbank and forest in this opening sequence is sublime and it's all framed within the nickelodeon proscenium, which Keaton proceeds to abandon as the projectionist acclimatises to his new surroundings and adopts the sleuthing persona he will require to find the loot.

However, in returning to a more typical narrative mode, Keaton has alerted us to the fact that anything might happen and it promptly does. The sequence in which Buster escapes with the pearls and dives into a box to escape in bonnet and crinolines was an old conjuror's trick, whose mechanics Keaton was prepared to reveal by filming it straight (albeit with the aid of some nifty set construction). But he withheld the secret of the stunning illusion that allowed him to leap through the chest of his valet and a locked barn door (which was achieved using dummies and trap doors) and, consequently, the effect remains more magical than anything since produced by CGI. ★★★★★ **DP**

SHINE (1996)

Starring: *Geoffrey Rush (Adult David), Armin Mueller-Stahl (Peter), Noah Taylor (Adolescent David), Lynn Redgrave (Gillian), John Gielgud (Cecil Parkes)*
Director: *Scott Hicks*
Screenwriter: *Jan Sardi, based on a story by Scott Hicks*
12/107 mins./Biography/Drama/Music/Australia/UK

Awards: *Academy Awards – Best Actor, BAFTA – Best Actor, Best Sound, Golden Globes – Best Drama Actor*

A brilliant pianist suffers a mental breakdown and doesn't perform in public for 20 years. Then a trip to a wine bar brings him into the limelight again . . .

At first glance, *Shine* doesn't exactly sound like a joyous experience – Nazi oppression, strained paternal relations and prolonged mental illness, all surrounded by some intense classical music should, by rights, make for a depressing evening's viewing. But, quite simply, it doesn't. For Hicks' biopic is a startlingly well-made tale of triumph over adversity, that makes for compelling, powerful viewing, leaving no emotional chain unyanked.

The subject matter in question is the acclaimed, but relatively unknown (at least in this country) Australian ivory-tinkler David Helfgott (brilliantly portrayed at various stages by the gawky Taylor and the far more normal-looking Rush). After showing prowess at an early age, he is mentally tortured through his teens by his concentration camp victim father, heads for the Royal College Of Music against Dad's wishes, has a nervous breakdown mastering some particularly tricky Rachmaninov, turns into a stuttering, muttering wreck, and spends the next 20 years in comparative obscurity, banned from having so much as a second's contact with anything resembling a piano. Until, that is, an incident in a local wine bar sparks off a comeback of John Travolta proportions.

With a supporting cast that includes Googie Withers, Lynn Redgrave and Sir John Gielgud as a crusty, cravat-sporting piano teacher, *Shine* reeks of class even before the opening credits have rolled, and Hicks doesn't disappoint. The acting is faultless, the classical soundtrack stirring even to those for whom music begins and ends with the Gallagher brothers, and the story is told with a warmth and humour that saves it from the self-pitying wallow it could so easily have become. Indeed, the protagonist veers between heart-rending sadness and touching eccentricity, coming over as an adorable innocent and giving rise to an ending far more uplifting than anybody had a right to expect. ★★★★★ **CW**

THE SHINING (1980)

Starring: *Jack Nicholson (Jack Torrance), Shelley Duval (Wendy Torrance), Danny Lloyd (Danny Torrance), Scatman Crothers (Dick Hallorann), Barry Nelson (Stuart Ullman)*
Director: *Stanley Kubrick*
Screenwriters: *Stanley Kubrick, Diane Johnson, from the novel by Stephen King*
18/114 mins./Horror/Thriller/USA

Jack Torrance becomes the caretaker of the Overlook Hotel up in the secluded mountains of Colorado and moves there with his family. Then his son starts seeing strange apparitions . . .

Stanley Kubrick was looking for his next project after *Barry Lyndon*. As his then secretary recalled, he was stationed in his office with a stack of recent books, opening them, starting to read, then tbwumpp! she would hear the sound of a paperback meeting the wall. The process went on for a while. Then, all of a sudden, there was silence. Kubrick had picked up a novel called *The Shining* by a young up-and-coming horror author by the name of Stephen King.

You can well imagine King's sense of validation at having such a director as this turn to his pulp morbidities for inspiration and Kubrick, the notorious obsessive, pestered the author with calls at unearthly hours to inquire whether he believed in God, or some other vital clue.

The relationship, however, was soon to fragment. King hated the film. Kubrick (with co-screenwriter Diane Johnson) filleted the novel, ditching its more formulaic horror elements in favour of a study in madness and ambiguous evil – that, of course, of father, drunk, caretaker, and wannabe novelist Jack Torrance (a defining role for Jack Nicholson). Kubrick, akin to his trippy treatment of the sci-fi genre, was elevating horror to a different plane, removing its camp wiggeries and bogeymen to infuriate and bedazzle with sinewy suggestion and sumptuous, awe-inspiring technique. Technically, there is no better film in the genre. Its chills are less direct (that is until Torrance finally throws off the shackles of sanity), rather something that creeps under the skin to unsettle and disturb. King though was having none of it, describing Kubrick's film as a 'big and beautiful car. Ultimately a piece of machinery with neither heart nor soul.' Foolishly the author also elected to remake the book faithfully as a TV mini series to derisory reaction.

In accordance with the Kubrick legend, the process of making the movie took meticulousness to staggering levels – Shelley Duvall was reputedly forced to do no less than 127 takes of one scene; Nicholson was force fed endless cheese sandwiches (which he loathes) to generate a sense of inner revulsion, and the recent invention of the Steadicam (by Garret Brown) fuelled Kubrick's obsessive quest for perfection. The result is gloriously precision-made. The use of sound especially (listen to the remarkable rhythm of silence then clatter set up by Danny pedalling his trike intermittently over carpet then wooden floor.) And that's not forgetting the procession of captivating images: a lift opening to spill gallons of blood in slow motion; a beautiful girl transformed into an old hag in Jack's arms; and, as a million posters now attest, Jack's leering face through the gaping axe wound in the door.

Alive with portent and symbolism, every frame of the film brims with Kubrick's genius for implying psychological purpose in setting: the hotel's tight, sinister labyrinth of corridors; its cold, sterile bathrooms; the lavish, illusionary ballroom. This was horror of the mind transposed to place (or, indeed, vice versa). The clarity of the photography and the weird perspectives constantly alluding to Torrance's twisted state of mind. The supernatural elements are more elusive than the depiction of his madness. The 'shining' itself – the title comes from the line 'We all shine on' in the John Lennon song 'Instant Karma' – is the uncanny ability to see dark visions of the truth (young Danny manifests the power through an imaginary alter-ego Tony). A power separate from yet entwined with the evil that dwells in the building (the whole family will come to experience it).

The Overlook, sacrilegiously built on an ancient Indian burial ground (a minor point for Kubrick and stolen by *Poltergeist*), is haunted by evil spirits. When Jack enters the sprawling ballroom, he is entering into the building's dark heart (possibly even Hell itself): 'Your credit's fine Mr Torrance.' It's unclear whether it is Torrance's growing insanity that invites this or The Overlook itself taking possession of his soul. Grady, the previous caretaker, a man driven to slaughter his family (the source of Danny's disturbing second sight of the blue-dressed sisters) is another of Torrance's visitation states – 'You have always been the caretaker,' Grady suggests menacingly. The evil may have always been there in Jack, The Overlook merely awakened it.

It's a question the whole film is posing: does the potential for evil reside in all men, just waiting to come to life? The final shot of Torrance trapped inside a photograph of the ballroom in 1921 hints at his destiny: he has become one with The Overlook – as he always was (death, you see, is never the end). The point, though, for the infuriatingly brilliant Kubrick was to always keep the answers out of reach. Indeed, he had a mantra he exhorted to all concerned (actors and journalists alike), it's a quote from H.P. Lovecraft: 'In all things that are mysterious – never explain.' ★★★★★ **IN**

THE SHIPPING NEWS (2001)

Starring: *Kevin Spacey (Quoyle), Julianne Moore (Wavey Prowse), Judi Dench (Agnis Hamm), Cate Blanchett (Petal), Pete Postlethwaite (Tert Card), Scott Glenn (Jack Buggit), Rhys Ifans (Beaufield Nutbeem)*
Director: *Lasse Hallstrom*
Screenwriter: *Robert Nelson Jacobs, based on the novel by E. Annie Proulx*
15/106 mins./Drama/Romance/USA

After a family tragedy, Quoyle heads to Newfoundland with his aunt and daughter. Taking a job with the local paper and beginning a tentative romance with a single mother, he slowly discovers his self-esteem.

After the early promise of *My Life As A Dog* and *What's Eating Gilbert Grape*, Lasse Hallstrom settled down as Miramax's in-house director of middle-brow literary adaptations. *The Cider House Rules* and *Chocolat* garnered the requisite number of Oscar nominations, although some fans of the books reckoned that their impact had been softened in the process.

E. Annie Proulx's Pulitzer Prize-winning novel is the next one on Hallstrom's library shelf. Although the character of Quoyle, as described in the book, cries out for Philip Seymour Hoffman, Kevin Spacey is excellent in the role. In the early scenes he makes Quoyle a piece of putty in other people's hands: a man whose life is shaped by those around him and who utterly lacks the desire or ability to act for himself. As the film progresses, he reveals to us Quoyle's strengthening from the inside out. In his eyes and the tiniest movements of his face, he charts the character's journey towards self-belief.

Needless to say, the rest of the cast are on equally strong form. Julianne Moore has an enigmatic allure as the solitary single mum, Judi Dench, as always, packs pages of emotional backstory into each individual line of dialogue, and Scott Glenn conveys the crusty eccentricity that would appear to be a genetic trait of all Newfoundlanders. It is only Pete Postlethwaite who fails to nail his character.

The ruggedly beautiful coastal landscapes are a gift for any director trying to give cinematic breadth to a novel, and Hallstrom does tap into the unique spirit of the place. However, the film's authenticity is unfortunately hindered by the fact that every single character requires their own dramatic revelation of a past tragedy; this, and Quoyle's recurrent drowning dream, underline the story's symbolism a bit too boldly. ★★★ **AM**

SHOAH (1985)

Starring: *Simon Srebnik (Himself), Michael Podchlebnik (Himself), Motke Zaidl (Himself), Hanna Zaidl (Herself), Jan Piwoski (Himself), Itzhak Dugin (Himself)*
Director: *Claude Lanzmann*
PG/566 mins./Documentary/France

Awards: *BAFTA – Flaherty Documentary Award*

Railway workers, bureaucrats, technicians, coerced labourers and civil bystanders from Germany, Poland and beyond recall the processes by which millions of Jews, gypsies, gays and other so-called subversives and undesirables were murdered by the Nazis as part of the Final Solution.

On its initial release, Claude Lanzmann's epic documentary was hailed as a monument to the victims of the Holocaust. Some doubts were cast about his hectoring interviewing technique and his resort to deception to secure on-the-record testimony from those who co-operated only on the guarantee of anonymity. But most felt that Lanzmann had a duty to expose the guilty in order to ascertain the truth about humanity's most heinous crime.

However, Lanzmann's reputation as a filmmaker has since been challenged and his objectivity called into question. Following the denunciation in some quarters of his third feature, *Tsahal*, as Zionist propaganda, the authenticity of some of Shoah's more emotive content was similarly disputed, with Treblinka barber Abraham Bomba's descriptions of the gas chambers coming under the closest scrutiny.

Lanzmann's most persistent critics revealed that he had set out to produce a standard documentary record of the Shoah (from the Hebrew word for 'chaos' or 'annihilation'), whose backers included the French and Israeli governments. However, the discrediting of much of the material he had chosen to use in 1979's *Faurisson Affair* prompted him to abandon found footage and primary documentation and rely solely on eye-witness accounts.

Consequently, no stock footage was used to set the scene or provide any historical verification and Lanzmann presented his subjects as living witnesses whose recollections were much more real and vivid than any grainy newsreel image.

The testimonies certainly made an impact and while some of them may now seem dubious (even allowing for the vagaries of memory), much of what is stated here can be corroborated by other sources. Lanzmann's use of repetition and circularity may strike some as manipulative, but it makes organisational sense and reaffirms the necessary warning that humanity has the awful habit of making the same mistakes over again.

But, regardless of whether Lanzmann's agenda or methodology can be queried, *Shoah* still contains some irrefutably powerful moments. None more so than the images of what remains of the camps in what is now tranquil countryside, which suggest that the landscape also remembers and still bears the scars of the crimes perpetrated upon it. Indeed, the screams that one witness recalls seem to hang silently over the chillingly eerie footage of greenery than now hides mass graves and terrible secrets that not even these eloquent (if occasionally unreliable) witnesses can reveal. **★★★★ DP**

SHOCK CORRIDOR (1963)

Starring: *Peter Breck (Johnny Barrett), Constance Towers (Cathy), Gene Evans (Boden), James Best (Stuart), Hari Rhodes (Trent), Paul Duboy (Dr. J.L. Menkin)*
Director: *Samuel Fuller*
Screenwriter: *Samuel Fuller*
15/101 mins./Drama/Mystery/USA

Journalist Johnny Barrett fakes madness in order to investigate a murder which has occurred in a mental hospital. One of three inmates can identify the killer, but they only have moments of lucidity. And Barrett's sanity is strained by life inside the asylum.

Writer-producer-director Sam Fuller's pulp masterpiece reduces its whodunit angle to a mantra – 'who killed Sloan in the kitchen' – and concentrates instead on institutionalised insanity.

From the first, the hero's carefully faked madness shades into the real thing – he has his stripper girlfriend pose as his sister, for whom he has incestuous, fetishist desires, but instantly loses focus on who she actually is, and becomes tormented by her dream image.

The enclosed world of the literally insane asylum is depicted in grand guignol terms: with Johnny constantly woken up by a too-friendly, bearded, massive opera singer who is just a more subtle sexual threat than the harpies who swoop upon him (in an incredible sequence) in 'the nympho ward'.

The potential witnesses all represent tabloid headline versions of America's ills: Stuart, a one-time brainwashed turncoat who went over to 'the commies in Korea' because his dirt-poor parents fed him 'bigotry for breakfast and prejudice for supper', imagines that he's a Dixie-playing Confederate General; Trent, cracked by persecution after being the only black student at a Southern university, thinks he's the leader of the Ku Klux Klan and whips other inmates up into a lynching frenzy; and Boden has gone mad working on moon rockets and nuclear weapons and mostly acts like a child.

In a unique suspense sequence, Boden has a spell of sanity but a temporarily mute Johnny, shattered by shock treatment, is unable to ask the question which will solve the case.

Stark, harsh and black and white, with bravura freak-outs. **★★★★★ KN**

SHOOT THE PIANO PLAYER (TIREZ SUR LE PIANISTE) (1960)

Starring: *Charles Aznavour (Charlie Kohler/Edouard Saroyan), Marie Dubois (Lena), Nicole Berger (Theresa), Michelle Mercier (Clarisse), Albert Remy (Chico Saroyan), Jacques Aslanian (Richard Saroyan), Richard Kanayan (Fido Saroyan)*
Director: *François Truffaut*
Screenwriters: *François Truffaut, Marcel Moussy, based on the novel* Down There *by David Goodis*
12/80 mins/Crime/France

Still stung by the treachery of his suicidal wife, Thérésa, one-time concert pianist Charlie Kohler hooks up with Lena, a waitress at the club where he now plays honky-tonk, only to become involved in the feud between his brothers, Richard and Chico, and bungling gangsters Momo and Ernest.

Adapted from David Goodis's pulp thriller, *Down There*, François Truffaut's second feature was closer in spirit to Jean-Luc Godard's *A Bout de Souffle* than his own *Les Quatre Cents Coups*. Essentially a pastiche of the Hollywood B movie, it adopted a maverick attitude towards melodrama and romance that was reinforced by an irresistible jokiness that rendered it an offbeat delight.

Truffaut later claimed that he had intended 'to make a film without a subject, to express all I wanted to say about glory, success, downfall, failure, women, and love by means of a detective story. It's a grab bag.'

But this was as much an act of revenge as homage, as Truffaut set up American noir only to gun it down, for while he had learned lessons from its generic conventions and shaped them to his own ends, other French filmmakers have assimilated them wholesale at the expense of both more individual and more cinematic modes of expression. Thus, Truffaut sought to subvert the imported staples and stereotypes by casting the unprepossessing Charles Aznavour in a role that would ordinarily have been played as a hero by a chiselled star. Similarly, he turned the villains into cartoonish palookas and consistently confounded the audience expectations generated by both the action and the soundtrack.

From the moment he interrupted a chase sequence with an irrelevant aside about a bypasser's marriage, Truffaut strove to put into practice the theories of *caméra stylo* and *les politiques des auteurs* that he had been espousing since his days as a critic at *Cahiers du Cinéma*. Consequently, he dotted the picture with references to the Marx Brothers, Roberto Rossellini's *Stromboli* and Alfred Hitchcock's *Dial M for Murder*. He also drew on the techniques of silent cinema, with the superimposition of impresario Lars Schmeel's head between Charlie (then still known as Edouard Saroyan) and Thérésa as they lay in bed recalling the camera trickery in Georges Méliès's *feéries*, while the iris triptych evoked Abel Gance's *Napoléon*.

However, the film's commercial disappointment inhibited Truffaut and he was never to be this exuberantly experimental again. **★★★★★ DP**

◑ SHOOTING DOGS (2006)

Starring: *John Hurt (Christopher), Hugh Dancy (Joe Connor), Dominque Horwitz (Capitaine Charles Delon), Louis Mahoney (Sibomana), Nicola Walker (Rachel)*
Director: *Michael Caton-Jones*
Screenwriter: *David Wolstencroft, based on a story by Richard Alwyn, David Belton*
15/115 mins./Biography/War/Drama

Kigali, Rwanda, 1994. When Hutu militias begin slaughtering thousands of Tutsi, many flee to the safety of a school – also a post for UN soldiers – run by Father Christopher. Also present is Joe Connor, a young Englishman straight out of college who's looking to 'make a difference'.

Among so many painful moments in Michael Caton-Jones' film, there is one that best sums up the atrocious state of affairs: a Tutsi man – the head of a family living in the school that has become a refugee camp – politely asks, with all the dignity he can muster, for the UN soldiers who are about to leave to shoot them; it will be quicker and less painful than being hacked to death by machetes. It's offered up without grandstanding, and it's typically, utterly heartbreaking.

Shooting Dogs shares common ground – at some points crossing over – with last year's *Hotel Rwanda* (comparisons will be as inevitable as they are obvious). But here, by telling the story primarily from the point of view of Father Christopher and Joe, the burden of white Western guilt is pressed upon us more specifically.

As the world-weary priest fast running out of faith, Hurt plays the type of role he might as well get trademarked, never missing a beat. He's ably supported by Dancy, Horwitz and newcomer Ashitey, but everyone in front of the camera owes a debt to David Wolstencroft's understated script, which has the feel of on-form Loach and only ever falters in its final scenes.

There's no way this story could ever have made a bad film, but a script that refuses sentimentality and fine acting elevate it just short of greatness. ★★★★ **ST**

◑ THE SHOOTIST (1976)

Starring: *John Wayne (John Bernard Books), Lauren Bacall (Bond Rogers), Ron Howard (Gillom Rogers), James Stewart (Dr. E. W. Hostetler), Richard Boone (Mike Sweeney)*
Director: *Don Siegel*
Screenwriters: *Scott Hale, Miles Hood Swarthout, based on the novel by Glendon Swarthout*
PG/100 mins./Western/USA

Carson City, 1901. Legendary gunfighter J.B. Books, diagnosed with terminal cancer, takes a room in the house of a widow and becomes a mentor to her young son.

John Wayne's last movie is a dignified, thoughtful Western, heartbreakingly close to the star's actual situation and cunning in its use of the star's screen persona (and brief clips from earlier movies) to fill in the background of the swaggering, Duke-like gunman John Bernard Books, who rides painfully into Carson City the week Queen Victoria dies. Based on a terrific novel by Glendon Swarthout, best-known for *Where the Boys Are*, and directed with autumnal tones and a sombre pace by Don Siegel, this proved after a succession of flabby vehicles (*The Train Robbers, Cahill – US Marshal* etc), that Wayne was still a powerful screen actor, and was one of the best of a cycle of 70s movies which served as obituaries for the Western itself. The exciting, poignant finish finds Books deciding to go out in a hail of bullets and glory rather than succumb to the slow agony of cancer, and arranging to meet his three would-be killers in a cavernously luxurious saloon for a last showdown. Guest stars James Stewart and Lauren Bacall are links to Wayne's cinematic past, while rival guns Richard Boone and Hugh O'Brian are significantly Western stars from the movies' old enemy, television. There's smart work also from Henry Morgan (as a nastily cheery US Marshal), John Carradine (in his umpteenth undertaker role) and Scatman Crothers (who gets to horse-trade with the Duke) as vultures gathering before the grave is filled. Ron Howard, well before his directing days, is the eager-eyed kid who idolises the gunman, but is dissuaded from a career of violence by witnessing the old man's bloody death. ★★★★ **KN**

◑ THE SHOP AROUND THE CORNER (1940)

Starring: *James Stewart (Alfred Kralik), Margaret Sullavan (Klara Novak), Frank Morgan (Hugo Matsuchek), Joseph Schildkraut (Ferencz Vadas), Sara Haden (Flora), Felix Bressart (Pirovitch)*
Director: *Ernst Lubitsch*
Screenwriter: *Samuel Raphaelson, based on the play* Parfumerie *by Nikolaus Laszlo*
U/97 mins./Romance-Comedy/USA

Klara Novak comes to work at Hugo Matuschek's Budapest clothing store unaware that trusted clerk Alfred Kralik, with whom he has struck up an immediate mutual antipathy, is the lonely hearts pen pal she has come to know as 'Dear Friend' during their secret romantic correspondence.

Fresh from completing *Ninotchka*, Ernst Lubitsch embarked on his second assignment for MGM, which was based on Nikolaus Laszlo's stage play, *Parfumerie*, to which he had owned the rights before selling them to Louis B. Mayer for $62,500.

Although he always claimed that Matuschek & Company was inspired by a shop that he fondly recalled in Budapest, there's little doubt that Lubitsch had his father Simon's Berlin outfitters in mind. Such personal inspiration was reinforced by exhaustive research to ensure that Matuschek's sold exactly what was then for sale back home. Even the $1.98 dress that Margaret Sullavan unearthed for her character had to be altered and bleached in the sun to conform to Lubitsch's precise vision of both the emporium and its employees. But such meticulous preparation enabled him to complete the shoot in just 27 days at a cost of $474,000.

With Europe already at war, this was an unashamedly nostalgic film about maintaining the status quo. The clerks tolerated the indecision and impoliteness of the customers for fear of alienating Mr Matuschek, who himself dreaded the discovery of his wife's long-suspected infidelity, lest it damage his reputation and authority. Even Alfred and Klara resist the temptation to meet their epistolary sweetheart, in case their romantic illusion was shattered by cruel reality.

However, life at its most melodramatic does intrude upon the idyll, with Matuschek firing Kralik in the mistaken belief that he is his wife's lover (when it is, in fact, the arrant Ferencz Vadas – who is played to ingratiating perfection by Joseph Schildkraut) and then attempting suicide. But such extremes enabled Lubitsch to establish a new idealised harmony, in which Kralik is promoted to manager and, thus, gains the confidence to declare his feelings for Klara.

But while the storyline was undoubtedly sweet, it was the sense of community – complete with its petty rivalries and sycophancies – and the need to remain employed at a time of economic uncertainty that made the film infinitely more charming than its descendants, *In the Good Old Summertime* and *You've Got Mail*. ★★★★ **DP**

◑ SHOPGIRL (2005)

Starring: *Steve Martin (Ray Porter), Claire Danes (Mirabelle Buttersfield), Jason Schwartzman (Jeremy Kraft), Bridgette Wilson (Lisa Cramer)*
Director: *Anand Tucker*
Screenwriter: *Steve Martin, from his novel*
15/104 mins./Drama/Romance/USA

A young woman, bored with her work, relationship and life, is swept off her feet by an older divorcee. Then she meets a young, disorganised but

attractive misfit. As the relationships progress, it doesn't get any easier to choose ...

Just as Bill Murray has set out to prove his worth as a credible actor, with the introspective likes of *Lost In Translation* and *Broken Flowers*, so Steve Martin has done the same. True, the former Wild And Crazy Guy has been experimenting with serious roles for longer (witness his terrific performance in *The Spanish Prisoner*, for example), but it's only with *Shopgirl* that the parallels between his career and Murray's become apparent.

In this uneven but charming comedy-drama (based on Martin's own novella) he plays the kind of eccentric, middle-aged loner we've become used to seeing Murray tackle lately – and in doing so he bags his best role in years. Not that, given his recent CV, that's too much of an achievement (*Cheaper By The Dozen*? *Bringing Down The House*? We rest our case), but it's still nice to see him do something a bit more challenging. In fact, the wild and crazy aspect of this three-hander is left to Jason Schwartzman, who almost steals the film from under the noses of his co-stars. As Jeremy, who loves, and then loses, Claire Danes' Mirabelle, he plays the kind of goofy but loveable weirdo you could almost imagine Martin portraying 20 or 30 years ago.

Yet while all three leads make this very watchable (Danes, too, excels as the title character), the film itself feels just too slight to maintain the more serious aspects of the storyline. A subplot involving one character suffering depression, for example, is glossed over so rapidly, and features the character making such a rapid recovery from an obviously serious condition, that you wonder why they bothered. And as beautifully shot as it is – at times looking like Hollywood's answer to *Amélie* – there's barely enough story to sustain a 104-minute running time, leaving director Anand Tucker to plug the gaps with just a few too many scenes of Danes sitting in the bath, drying her hair, shaving her legs (honestly, just how many moments of personal grooming can one film take?) or just generally looking a bit wistful.

It scores points for the great central performances, and for an offbeat script that's considerably sharper and funnier than your average rom-com; but you're left with the feeling that minus the padding this could have been a much better movie. ★★★ **CW**

A SHORT FILM ABOUT KILLING (1987)

Starring: *Miroslaw Baka (Jacek Lazar – The Murderer), Krzystof Globisz (Piotr Balicki – The Lawyer), Jan Tesarz (Waldemar Rekowski – The Taxi Driver), Zbigniew Zapasiewicz (Bar Examiner)*
Director: *Krzysztof Kieslowski*
Screenwriter: *Krzysztof Piesiewicz*
18/85 mins./Drama/Poland

Following a half-hearted bout of anti-social behaviour, Warsaw ne'er-do-well Jacek strangles ill-tempered taxi driver Waldemar in order to steal his cab and is executed despite the efforts of his idealistic lawyer, Piotr.

The fifth film in Krzysztof Kieslowski's *Dekalog* TV series, here expanded for cinema, was the only one to advocate a commandment rather than simply base a moral dilemma upon it. The price to be paid for ignoring the injunction 'Thou Shalt Not Kill' remained at the core of this feature-length variation, but Kieslowski was less interested here in crusading against capital punishment than in exploring the origins and manifestations of evil in late-Communist Poland.

A Short Film About Killing was more than a mere extension of the original story. The murder seemed random in *Dekalog 5*, in keeping with the fixation with chance and fate that informed much of Kieslowski's canon. But, Jacek now appeared to have a dual motive for his crime, as he was not only paying back Waldemar for flirting with his beloved Beata, but he was also out to steal his car in the hope of impressing the vegetable seller who usually treated him with disdain.

Indeed, this sense of alienation and its attendant absence of respect were key themes that Kieslowski reinforced by having Slawomir Idziak shoot the action through green filters that not only emphasised the contrast between light and darkness, but which also gave Warsaw and its environs a forbidding aspect that insinuated its pitiless cruelty.

There was certainly little humanity evident in either Jacek or Waldemar's behaviour prior to their meeting, with Jacek dropping stones onto passing cars and abusing the elderly, while Waldemar refuses to give a neighbour a lift and scares a man out walking his dogs. Yet neither deserved to die in such a callous manner – Waldemar struggling to escape a makeshift noose before being pulped with a rock as he pleaded for his life, and the terrified Jacek (whose actions were perhaps motivated by the loss of his younger sister in a tractor accident) at the hands of a chillingly dispassionate hangman.

Running for some seven and five minutes respectively, these are among the most harrowing deaths ever enacted on screen and they leave an indelible impression of emptiness and despair at the state of modern society. ★★★★ **DP**

A SHORT FILM ABOUT LOVE (1987)

Starring: *Olaf Lubsszenko (Tomek), Grazyna Szapolowska (Magda), Stefania Iwinska (Godmother), Piotr Machalica (Roman), Artur Barcis (Young Man)*
Director: *Krzysztof Kieslowski*
Screenwriter: *Krzysztof Piesiewicz*
18/86 mins./Drama/Poland

Warsaw teenager Tomek works as a part-time postman and milkman to get closer to Magda, the thirtysomething artist he spies upon with a telescope from his tenement flat. She agrees to a date, only for Tomek to slash his wrists after a disastrous evening and Magda comes to see him in a different light.

Although both *Dekalog 6* and this extended (and ultimately revised) version were inspired by the commandment 'Thou Shalt Not Commit Adultery', Krzysztof Kieslowski's theme was actually the sanctity of love and the difficulty of living up to its high ideals in a dehumanising society. It may have struck some as odd to base a treatise on courtly love on a fixated snoop and his sexually active neighbour. But, whereas in the teleplay the optical instruments were used to emphasise the gulf between Tomek and Magda's diametric worlds, in the feature edition they become means of contact and self-analysis that gradually bring about a possibly redemptive rapprochement.

Magda and Tomek are not just separated by age, gender and physical distance. She is creative, sensual and outwardly confident, while he is voyeuristic, obsessive and socially awkward. Moreover, she treats love as a transient escape from the boredom and disappointment of daily life, whereas he adheres to a naive romanticism that stands in contrast to the petty criminality that procured the offending telescope.

Yet, Tomek is a platonic Peeping Tom who chastely watches over Magda when she is at her loneliest (he turns away and indulges in agonising bouts of self-harm when she's entertaining her lovers). But, unlike a typical guardian angel, he actively interferes in her life in the hope that she will notice him. However, she also indirectly controls him, as he arranges his entire day around her movements so as not to miss a single glimpse. Moreover, as Tomek was orphaned at an early age, Magda also represents a surrogate mother, hence her recurring identification with milk.

The *Dekalog* story culminated in Tomek rejecting Magda's offer of friendship and abandoning his vigil. However, Grazyna Szapolowska

S

suggested that the feature should end on a more optimistic note and, so, she visits the flat and hears about Tomek's passion from his landlady before peering through the telescope to see herself weeping in her room as Tomek enters to console her. Some felt the shift erred towards sentimentality, but it turned this touching parable into a genuinely affecting, if still unconventional love story. ★★★★ **DP**

A SHOT IN THE DARK (1964)

Starring: *Peter Sellers (Jacques Clouseau), Elke Sommer (Maria Gambrelli), George Sanders (Benjamin Ballon), Herbert Lom (Charles Dreyfus), Tracey Reed (Dominque Ballon)*
Director: *Blake Edwards*
Screenwriters: *Blake Edwards, William Peter Blatty, from the plays* A Shot In The Dark *by Harry Kurnitz and* L'Idiote *by Marcel Achard*
PG/98 mins./Comedy/Mystery/USA

As murder follows murder, beautiful Maria is the obvious suspect; bumbling Inspector Clouseau drives his boss mad by seeing her as plainly innocent.

It was never supposed to be about that cartoon panther. In the first movie, the Pink Panther was the name of the diamond that gentleman cat burglars Robert Wagner and David Niven were desperate to get their mitts on. It wasn't until director Blake Edwards commissioned noted animation team DePatie-Freling to come up with a title design that the cartoon hero (aided and abetted by Henry Mancini's classic sax-led theme) took centre stage. The success of a kids' TV cartoon series in 1966 led to all subsequent Clouseau movies being branded by the Pink Panther, a fact that never made sense outside of marketing circles. (Think about it – Roberto Benigni starred as Clouseau's offspring in 1993's *Son Of The Pink Panther* – son of a diamond?) But in 1964, both Edwards and his star Peter Sellers weren't too interested in the cartoon, here they were in love with the buffoon, providing Sellers with the best outing for what was to become the defining character of his erratic, yet brilliant, career.

But it didn't start off that way. *L'Idiote* was a French farce written by Marcel Achard, adapted into the equally farcical play *A Shot In The Dark* by American Harry Kurnitz. Sellers was due to move into the piece straight after filming *The Pink Panther*, playing the role of a foolish magistrate; the other lead role was taken by Walter Matthau. But Sellers, fresh from stealing the show in *The Pink Panther*, was unhappy with the way the project was developing, and was threatening to leave. MGM brought in Edwards to placate him; Edwards took one look at the material and thought this could be a perfect vehicle for another adventure of Inspector Jacques Clouseau. Matthau was out, as was the original play. Things progressed so rapidly on *A Shot In The Dark*, that Edwards hadn't even finished work on *The Pink Panther* when he started. And this second outing for the bumbling French detective hit cinema screens only three months after the first, making *A Shot In The Dark* possibly the fastest released sequel in movie history.

To help him retool the screenplay, Edwards drafted in writer William Peter Blatty. 'We wrote the scripts very quickly, in just a few weeks,' recalls Blatty, later the author of *The Exorcist*. 'I not only wrote comedy then, I was a specialist in the wild farce off-the-wall kind of material.'

With *A Shot In The Dark* Edwards and Blatty created the Clouseau template that would run throughout the numerous sequels. Unlike in *The Pink Panther*, Clouseau was the real star here. He was no longer married as in the first film, but a bachelor always falling – often literally – for his leading lady. Herbert Lom was drafted in for the first of many appearances as Chief Inspector Dreyfus, Clouseau's boss, who would eventually become his chief nemesis, something that begins here when his attempt to blow up Clouseau with a 'beumb' results in the deaths of all those responsible for a series of murders. The final element the writers brought to the mix was Clouseau's manservant Kato (Burt Kwouk), always ready – as per Clouseau's instructions – to keep his employer on his toes by attacking him at the most inopportune moments.

The plot, as it is, is simple: beautiful maid Elke Sommer is accused of murder, Clouseau is the only one who thinks she is innocent and through his beautifully detailed incompetence he manages to prove this and end up with several bodies along the way. But plot was never the important thing in a Clouseau movie, what counts are the gags and this one has plenty. In particular it has more beautifully sustained and played sequences than any of the other films, especially the 70s sequels that often substituted fart gags for the humour and flair on display here. Fresh on the heels of his bravura turn(s) in *Dr. Strangelove*, Sellers knew he had found something special in Clouseau. In truth, he wouldn't find a part as good as this until his swansong *Being There* 15 years later (not counting his 1974 Parkinson appearance where he played a version of 'himself').

Check it out for the brilliantly sustained seduction scene in Clouseau's apartment (complete with 'beumb' and Kato-interruptus); admire it for the wonderfully ridiculous watch synchronising sequence with Sellers and Graham Stark; and witness the wit and comic elegance of the drawing room finale where Clouseau attempts to flush the killer into the open only to completely lose the plot when he finds out they all did it. Oh, and don't forget to look twice at the nudist camp attendant, billed as one 'Turk Thrust' (in actuality film director Bryan Forbes). ★★★★ **BM**

SHOWGIRLS (1995)

Starring: *Elizabeth Berkley (Nomi Malone), Kyle MacLachlan (Zack Carey), Gina Gershon (Cristal Connors), Glenn Plummer (James Smith), Robert Davi (Al Torrest)*
Director: *Paul Verhoeven*
Screenwriter: *Joe Eszterhas*
18/125 mins./Drama/USA

Awards: *Razzie Awards – Worst Actress, Worst Director, Worst New Star, Worst Original Song (Walk Into The Wind), Worst Picture, Worst Screen Couple (any combination of the cast), Worst Screnplay, Worst Picture of The Decade*

Nomi dreams of making it as a star dancer in Vegas, but she'll have to claw her way to the top.

There are two things you can rely on when you watch a cheap porn film: rotten acting and porn. Meanwhile, away from the top shelf, this venture into mainstream, mass-market titillation from the *Basic Instinct* team of director Paul Verhoeven and script-factory Joe Eszterhas has plenty of the former, but – despite appearances – very little of the other.

That it's a good, old-fashioned swiz has already become painfully apparent to those American moviegoers hoodwinked by its controversial (and courted) NC-17 rating, who voted with their backsides and refused to put any more of them on cinema seats for the sake of what Eszterhas maintains is a non-exploitative insight into the life of a Vegas 'lap-dancer'.

Nomi Malone (Berkley – you may have seen her in woeful US teen-com *Saved By The Bell*) begins life at the bottom, as a two-bit stripper, then works her way up to, well, the lap, as 'private dancer' at the Cheetah Club, until her big break arrives and she graduates to the chorus line of a major casino show, *Goddess*, where, still very much unhindered by clothing, she gyrates around a plastic volcano. Along the way to this personal epiphany, she juggles amorous shenanigans with club owner Zack (a ventriloquist's dummy-like McLachlan) and jobless songwriter James (played with near-zero conviction by Glenn Plummer).

It seems over-vigilant to give the plot so much space, since it is little more than a crutch for some admittedly very athletic dancing, and related bosom-jigglage. Dramatically limp (romantic hepcat Plummer plays Berkley a 'song he's written for her' and away she goes, slinking around to a tape as if she's only heard it about, ooh, 100 times) and about as genuinely arousing as intricately choreographed nude livestock, *Showgirls* would be offensive if it hadn't been hyped ('Leave your inhibitions at the door' winked the US publicity). But it was. ★ **AC**

SHREK (2001)

Starring: the voices of: *Mike Myers (Shrek/Blind Mouse), Eddie Murphy (Donkey), Cameron Diaz (Princess Fiona), John Lithgow (Lord Farquaad), Vincent Cassel (Monsieur Hood)*
Directors: *Andrew Adamson, Vicky Jenson*
Screenwriters: *Ted Elliott, Terry Rossio, Joe Stillman, Roger S.H. Schulman, based on the book by William Steig*
U/90 mins./Animation/Family/Comedy/Adventure/USA
Awards: *Academy Awards – Best Animated Feature, BAFTA – Best Adapted Screenplay*

When Shrek, an antisocial ogre, finds his swamp overrun with refugee fairy-tale characters, who are escaping from evil Farquaad's efforts to clean up his kingdom, he takes his beef to the midget despot himself. However, in return for the turfing out of his squatters, Shrek finds himself roped into the rescue of a cute princess from a dragon-guarded castle.

An ugly, big, green bloke and his smartarse donkey sidekick rescue a prissy princess from a lovelorn dragon for a self-obsessed lordling lacking in stature? And it's a clever-clever parody-type thing? An animated fairy-tale all about animated fairy-tales? Tee-hee, how postmodern. Yes, but it works a treat.

Ever since *Toy Story* shook the animation rafters, CGI's awe-inspiring intricacies have become a matter of course. So, naturally, the work in this inverted fairy-tale is a knock-out: humans with proper human faces, not bubble heads, actual furry fur and landscapes that hover delightfully between lush, 3-D, Oz-like backdrops and photo-realistic video game aesthetics. Yet it's not the dazzle factor that impresses so much with Shrek, as the directors' flare for storytelling on a sumptuous visual level, letting the script (based on William Steig's book) do the talking.

And it's one joyous miracle of a script (how is it that only animation writers seem able to do great comedy anymore?) doing the yakking. This is more than simply ex-Disney honcho Katzenberg taking sly potshots at his former employers; it's a full-scale parody of the Mousedom's chirpy ethic of old. *Snow White*, *Sleeping Beauty*, *Cinderella*, every Andersen/Grimm fantasy is caught in a fusillade of affectionate piss-take (Farquaad's rigid kingdom is a direct dig at Disneyland).

Like the Zucker spoof-principals, the film teems with incidental genius – we defy you not to bust a gut laughing at Farquaad's interrogation of the Gingerbread Man, or the untimely arrival of the Three Blind Mice at Shrek's hovel, or Robin Hood's posse Riverdancing. Don't panic, though, this doesn't begin to scratch the surface of the whirlwind of gags, hinting that repeat visits may be in order.

Shrek genuinely offers something for all ages: fart jokes for the tots, WWF-style bouts and *Matrix* skits for the teens, while Eddie Murphy's hysterical, jabbermouthed Donkey's stream of psychobabbled relationship talk – for defensive ogre and attitudinal princess – is hip for grown-ups. Murphy hasn't touched these comedy heights for years; his chorus of city-literate jive never allows the movie a flat moment.

There are weaknesses. Myers gives Shrek an inconclusive Scottish accent and seems strangely confined playing the straight guy. And when the story finally begins to wrap itself up, the counter-classic edge succumbs to predictable, sturdy, moral outcomes. Not to worry too much, though – the movie crashes out with a musical number boasting Donkey (with shades)'s soul-ribbed version of The Monkees' 'I'm A Believer'. Pinocchio this is not. ★★★★ **IN**

Movie Trivia: Shrek

Chris Farley was originally cast as Shrek before his death, and even recorded some dialogue. Over 1,000 fantasy and fairy-tale characters overrun Shrek's pond at the start of the film. None of the stars met during filming, they all recorded separately. Mike Myers modelled Shrek's voice on his mother's when she read him bedtime stories.

SHREK 2 (2004)

Starring: the voices of: *Mike Myers (Shrek/Blind Mouse), Eddie Murphy (Donkey), Cameron Diaz (Princess Fiona), Julie Andrews (Queen), John Cleese (King), Antonio Banderas (Puss In Boots)*
Directors: *Andrew Adamson, Kelly Asbury*
Screenwriters: *Andrew Adamson, J. David Stern, David N. Weiss, Joe Stillman, based on the book by William Steig*
U/92 mins./Animation/Family/Comedy/Adventure/USA

Newlyweds Shrek and Princess Fiona are greeted with horror in her parents' kingdom of Far Far Away. A furious Fairy Godmother demands that the king make good on his deal for her boy Prince Charming to wed the princess. Can love prevail against prejudice and magic potions?

In When Shrek Meets The Parents the question is simple: is it as resoundingly good as our first encounter with the loveable green giant, or is it even better? No and yes. In its execution of the tale of a determinedly anti-social ogre, Shrek was so disarmingly original that it astonished.

That dropped-jaw reaction is probably impossible to incite again, but clearly *Shrek 2* can't really lose. Already the monster hit of America's blockbuster season, it's utterly likeable and consistently, hugely funny. And yet we could wish it had taken some risks. The genius of *Shrek* was in its subversion of fairy-tales and its cheeky mickey-take of Disney's strictly sweet, clean magical kingdom. *Shrek 2* spoofs celebrity and the cult of beauty, but the satirical edge is so blunted it's as dangerous as a plastic picnic knife.

On arrival in Far Far Away (distinctly like Hollywood and its ritzy neighbours) we gather from the designer shops (the likes of Versarchery) and the mansions that this is where the rich and famous and power elite of the fairy-tale world reside. But sadly we don't encounter many of them or get a taste of the politics of the place. It's all carefully inoffensive in its cuteness, even in its few cheerful vulgarities. This popular-culture-plundering sequel is more a straight, if fractured, fairy-tale – one in which the Fairy Godmother is evil, the handsome prince is a vain jerk, and Pinocchio wears women's underwear – that doesn't get under characters' skins. All the plot worries about is whether Fiona and Shrek want to be themselves or want to be pretty, and whether Shrek can kick conniving in-law butt. Since he fought a dragon in the original movie, what's a hostile daddy and a hex or two? Once again the moral is that handsome is as handsome does, blah blah blah.

The opening honeymoon montage is like a pop promo, while Prince Charming (Rupert Everett's petulant tones amusingly at odds with his blond beach-god visage) swaggers into the dragon's castle to learn he's too late to claim the princess. This blow, and the subsequent royal summons, trigger the anti-ogre machinations.

Fortunately Donkey has insisted on coming along for the ride, since Eddie Murphy's comic riffing is still a highlight. Julie Andrews and John Cleese as Queen and King and Jennifer Saunders' Fairy Godmother are all fun, but things really take off with the enlistment in Team Shrek of Zorro-esque feline assassin Puss In Boots (over jealous Donkey's objections that he's the 'annoying talking animal').

El gato is BRILLIANT, in animation, in a running gag that brings the house down, and in the voice performance of Antonio Banderas. You've also got to love the hook-handed pirate pianist, voiced on separate numbers by Tom Waits and Nick Cave. In the Overegging The Pudding Department: while they were replacing American celeb voices (Larry King, Joan Rivers) with UK 'personalities' (Jonathan Ross, Kate Thornton) for our release, they might have done us a kindness and lost a lame retro pop tune or two.

Technically, Pacific Data Images/DreamWorks' upgrade to their facial animation system, their innovative lighting softwear breakthrough – the 'bounce shade' – and their DCC (Dynamic Crowd Character) program advance 3-D CGI artistry and photorealism beyond even Shrek and Pixar's gems.

Happily Ever After may not come in a bottle, but state-of-the-art wizardry apparently comes in a Hewlett Packard. And it remains hilarious throughout, with too many frantically funny film lampoons – *Raiders Of The Lost Ark, Spider-Man, LOTR, Ghostbusters, Flashdance,* Disney's catalogue – to take in at one viewing. So, a classic that wittily reflects the human condition? No. A Friday night laugh riot? Resoundingly, yes. ★★★★ **AE**

SIDEWAYS (2004)

Starring: *Paul Giamatti (Miles), Thomas Haden Church (Jack), Virginia Madsen (Maya), Sandra Oh (Stephanie), Marylouise Burke (Miles' Mother)*
Director: *Alexander Payne*
Screenwriters: *Alexander Payne, Jim Taylor, based on the novel by Rex Pickett*
15/123 mins./Drama/Comedy/USA
Awards: *Academy Awards – Best Adapted Screenplay, BAFTA – Best Adapted Screenplay, Golden Globes – Best Musical/Comedy, Best Screenplay*

Ageing voice-over actor Jack is finally tying the knot. To celebrate, his longtime friend Miles treats him to a stag week in the Californian vineyards, to teach him the ways of wine tasting. But Jack has different plans: he wants to get the morose Miles laid – and get his own end away while he's at it...

Fact: Alexander Payne is one of America's most exciting filmmakers. Not because he delivers slick, cobalt-tinged thrillers or CG-fuelled sci-fi swirlers, of course... In fact, his material is placed very deliberately at the other end of the spectacle spectrum. Payne is concerned with the mundane: his is a USA where Jack Nicholson travels the freeways not perched on the back of a Harley, but slumped at the wheel of a Winnebago.

He and co-writer Jim Taylor don't need to worry about being cool or spectacular, because, in the likes of *Election, About Schmidt* and now *Sideways,* they've mastered the most important element of storytelling: character. They're not concerned with heroes, just people: small people, bruised people, rumpled people – people like Miles (an Oscar-deserving Paul Giamatti), a depressed, divorced wannabe novelist, who has an encyclopedic knowledge of wine but can't even remember how old his mother is. Or people like Miles' crass buddy Jack, whose rugged good looks are starting to melt, and who uses this as an excuse to cram as much sex as possible into his final week of bachelorhood.

Making these people interesting is one thing; making them likeable is another, and Payne and Taylor achieve this not in spite of, but because of, their flaws. It's quite a feat – Miles and Jack don't so much get under your skin as climb inside your heart. One scene in particular strikes you hard: while clumsily, reluctantly attempting to seduce waitress and fellow vinophile Maya (an excellent, back-from-obscurity Virginia Madsen), Miles explains why he rates the Pinot grape above any other. Because it's thin-skinned, he says, temperamental, requiring patient nurturing ... He's oblivious to the fact he's really describing himself, but Maya isn't.

Payne and Taylor's script sings melodiously in every scene, their acuteness of observation perfectly servicing both the drama and the comedy (you'll giggle at Miles pretentiously holding his finger to his ear as he inhales a wine's aroma), while they're not afraid to occasionally force it broad and farcical, thereby supplying some hearty belly-laughs. It may suffer a slight second-act sag, but as with its characters, *Sideways'* flaws are no obstacle to loving it. ★★★★★ **DJ**

Movie Trivia: Sideways

George Clooney lobbied for the role of Jack but director Alexander Payne thought he was too big a star. Most of the wine used in the wine tasting scenes was non-alcoholic. The movie saw sales of Pinot Noir rise by 20% over the Christmas 2005/2006 period. A scene where Miles runs over his dog was cut as it was deemed to be too slapstick in tone.

THE SIEGE (1998)

Starring: *Denzel Washington (Anthony 'Hub' Hubbard), Annette Bening (Elise Kraft/Sharon Bridger), Bruce Willis (Major General William Devereaux), Tony Shalhoub (Agent Frank Haddad), Sami Couajila (Samir Nazhde)*
Director: *Edward Zwick*
Screenwriters: *Lawrence Wright, Menno Meyjes, Edward Zwick, from a story by Lawrence Wright*
15/111 mins./Action/Thriller/USA

Marital law is declared in New York City when terrorist attacks rain on the city following the abduction of a Muslim religious leader.

America is a country that until recently didn't know a great deal about terrorism. Before the World Trade Center and Oklahoma bombings, American soil was thought to be sacrosanct. That's certainly the way FBI agent Anthony 'Hub' Hubbard feels in Ed Zwick's clever, provocative thriller. Now Hubbard, and everyone else is facing up to the fact that a political Arab faction is out to take on New York City.

It begins with a hoax and very quickly escalates to an exploding bus and an attack on FBI headquarters. Hub and partner Frank Haddad are on the case, finding themselves in bed – metaphorically speaking – with CIA operative Elise Kraft. Proving itself singularly ill-equipped to deal with such a situation, the government orders the military in – in the form of no-nonsense, it-doesn't-matter-if-your-hair's-going-if-you're-in-the-army Bruce Willis as General William Devereaux. Soon, all Arab-Americans are interned in the local basketball stadium and the city that never sleeps is now not sleeping because of the racket all those tanks are making. With New York under martial law, Hubbard must find the bombers before they strike again.

The Siege, running with the extremely provocative tag line 'Freedom is history', managed to create all sorts of racial angst when it opened in America. The truth is that yes, the film does rely on your all-purpose rent-an-Arab villain, but Zwick and co. are at pains within the film itself to point out all sides of the situation, showing the injustice of the actions taken in the movie and putting everything correctly in context. And none of this obscures the fact that *The Siege* is a great urban thriller, a movie that understands the pulse of a city and its environs, that uses its locations to emphasise the tension and paranoia of its plot. It's helped, of course, by a superb cast: Washington is simply one of the best screen actors around and knows better than most how to command any scene he's in; Bening is less annoying than usual; and Willis, who always ups his game when he knows he's in good company, is superb. Best of all however is Tony Shalhoub, who's rapidly proving himself to be just about the most useful character actor in town.

The Siege may well be based on a huge 'what if?' premise, but it's smart, taut and knows exactly what the hell it's doing. And it does it well. ★★★★ **BM**

SIGNS (2002)

Starring: *Mel Gibson (Rev. Graham Hess), Joaquin Phoenix (Merrill Hess), Rory Culkin (Morgan Hess), Abigail Breslin (Bo Hess), Cherry Jones (Officer Paski), M. Night Shyamalan (Ray Reddy)*
Director: *M. Night Shyamalan*
Screenwriter: *M. Night Shyamalan*
12/102 mins./Drama/Mystery/Sci-fi/USA

Following the death of his wife, former man of the cloth Graham Hess lives on a farm with his two young children and younger brother. One morning, huge crop circles appear around the world – a 500-foot one shows up right outside the Hess house. Is it a prank? Or a sign of an alien invasion? Cue Hess embarking on a voyage of discovery.

Anyone harbouring lingering doubts about M. Night Shyamalan's towering talent will find them dispelled completely during the first hour of *Signs*. Hell, the opening credits alone channel genius: a Hitchcockian brew that Saul Bass could have concocted, complete with James Newton Howard's Bernard Herrmann tribute-theme. Sadly, great filmmakers do not a great film guarantee, and fans of *The Sixth Sense* and *Unbreakable* will have to wait a while longer for Shyamalan to move into the Spielberg-Hitchcock league which, just occasionally, appears to be his birthright.

Make no mistake, Shyamalan cuts beautifully, his camera movement is fluid yet never tentative, and his mise en scène is brilliantly composed. This is clearly a man who storyboards every shot. The results may be too hermetic for some tastes, too constructed, too cinematic even, but that is Shyamalan's singular style and it fits his slow-build storytelling like a glove.

As a director of actors, he again encourages subtle, sardonic performances, especially from the children. And to add to the control of tone which distinguished *The Sixth Sense* and *Unbreakable*, Shyamalan the writer now reveals an unexpected wit – *Signs* is very funny indeed.

With the exception of one piece of miscasting (himself), the first two-thirds of *Signs* feels like a five-star classic. And yet, even when the movie is succeeding brilliantly, you might start thinking, 'Where is this going? Can he pull this off?' But then you remind yourself, 'Hey, this is the director of *The Sixth Sense* – his speciality is endings. He can do this.'

Well, sorry to report that M. Night Shyamalan does not have the ending this time around. The story he ultimately wants to tell, the themes he wants to highlight – family and faith – do not tally with what the audience came to see. And after all the fantastic foreplay, the audience needs and deserves an orgasm. This was Steven Spielberg's ace with *Close Encounters Of The Third Kind*. But that spectacular ending, for obvious reasons, was off the table, so Shyamalan goes the other way – deep into small, emotional territory, which only serves to highlight the most contrived elements of his style.

In some ways, Shyamalan is a victim of his own success. Many movies tail off in the last act but are still judged to be triumphs. But Shyamalan does not structure his stories that way; all the meaning is locked up in that key, final reel.

And, in the final analysis, you don't need to be a movie critic or to know what mise en scène means, to conclude: 'Jeez, those alien guys were rubbish.' ★★★ **CK**

THE SILENCE OF THE LAMBS (1991)

Starring: *Jodie Foster (Clarice Starling), Anthony Hopkins (Dr. Hannibal Lecter), Scott Glenn (Jack Crawford), Anthony Heald (Dr. Fredreric Chilton), Ted Levine (Jame 'Buffalo Bill' Gumb), Kasi Lemmons (Ardelia Mapp)*
Director: *Jonathan Demme*
Screenwriter: *Ted Tally, based on the novel by Thomas Harris*
18/113 mins./Thriller/USA
Awards: *Academy Awards – Best Actor, Best Actress, Best Director, Best Picture, Best Adapted Screenplay, BAFTA – Best Actor, Best Actress, Golden Globes – Best Drama Actress*

Clarice Starling, a young FBI agent, is assigned to help find a missing woman, and save her from a psychopathic killer with the help of another killer.

Even if *The Silence Of The Lambs* were not the superb film it clearly is, it would still have given the world one of the great villains of cinema history. Or, to be more precise, it gave a second, but far more memorable, version of a great screen villain.

Warped psychiatric genius Hannibal Lecter (or Lektor as he was originally known) had already been portrayed by Brian Cox in 1986's *Manhunter*, Michael Mann's chilling adaptation of Thomas Harris's *Red Dragon*. Cox's Lektor – a detached, contemptuous psycho – certainly has his fans, but it's Hopkins who caught the public's imagination. It's easy to forget how few scenes he has in the film since each is so unforgettable. The first time we encounter him, in the dank bowels of the asylum, he manages to convey an aura of pure evil by doing nothing more than standing stock still in the middle of his arcane cell.

His posture is unnaturally precise, his gaze is disconcertingly steady and his prison overalls are fastidiously neat and slightly too tight. It's a collection of subliminally unnerving details that add up to a single overwhelming whole – this is one fucked up, dangerous loony; far more terrifying than the raving, pud-pulling Miggs who occupies the cell next door. It's this icy calm and the infallible logic of Lecter's self-justification that are so disturbing, and Hopkins plays it right to the hilt.

His scenes opposite Jodie Foster as rookie FBI investigator Clarice Starling are genuinely riveting. Kicking off with a few effortless mind games, he eventually recognises something he admires in the gauche, ambitious young woman. Thereafter, their relationship becomes a fascinating back-and-forth duel of teasing, trepidation and mutual need. It's a rewarding diversion for Lecter, but a perilous balancing act for Starling. And early on we're given a taste of the psychological havoc that Lecter's fearsome intellect can inflict when the mood takes him. When Miggs is disrespectful to Starling (he rasps, 'I can smell your cunt,' as she passes his cell and, later, flicks his ejaculate at her) Lecter talks him into committing suicide by swallowing his own tongue. It's entirely to Foster's credit that she holds her own during these exchanges; her vulnerability and terrier-like determination are a winning combination. But when Hopkins is pitched sitters like 'I ate his liver with some fava beans and a nice Chianti,' (plus fantastically revolting slurp), everyone else takes a back seat. That he also manages to elicit our sympathy is a remarkable achievement.

But it's not entirely Hopkins' show. This is also an excellent, taught thriller, directed with pace and style by Demme and boasting a first-rate screenplay by Ted Tally. The ever-dependable Foster gives one of her best performances as Starling and there's stoic support from Scott Glenn as her taciturn boss Jack Crawford and Anthony Heald as the sleazy psychiatrist Dr. Frederick Chilton.

Lambs also scores as a superb criminal procedure movie and even though we're introduced to sicko serial killer Buffalo Bill less than a third of the way in, the trail leading up to his capture is the equal of any whodunit. And from the severed head in the tank to the death's-head moth lodged in the murdered girl's throat and the explanation, furnished by Lecter, of why

S

Bill is flaying his victims, a sense of the macabre dominates the film. And if that were as far as things went, *The Silence Of The Lambs* would still be a way above average crime drama. But the icing on the cake is the premise that to catch a psychopath you have to be able to think like a psychopath.

It's a fascinating theme, one that dominates several of Harris's books including *Red Dragon*, and here it forms the basis for Clarice Starling's strange, and strangely touching, relationship with Lecter. To track Buffalo Bill, Clarice has to get inside Lecter's mind; the danger being, of course, that in return she must allow Lecter into hers. As an incentive to lure him into the fray Starling offers herself, permitting Lecter to analyse her in return for his guidance in the case. Lecter's enjoyment over probing Starling's dark secrets and deep anxieties is palpable, but this is far more than a game for him. In exchange for the cryptic snippets of information he gives out, Lecter makes small demands that, once they're met, will facilitate the escape plans that his quick mind has been preparing all along. Plus, of course, he develops deep feelings for Clarice.

What's at stake for her is her standing in the Bureau and the kidnapped daughter of a US Congresswoman who Buffalo Bill is fattening up for the kill. Demme also manages to cram in a couple of thrilling set pieces – Lecter's escape and the nerve-racking false ending when the Feds show up at the wrong house – classic quotes abound and among a clutch of fine performances Hopkins' Oscar-winning turn writes a new chapter in the book of movie monsters. Furthermore, not only is *Lambs* a key film of the 90s and one of the finest crime films ever, it's also the weirdest love story this side of *Harold And Maude*. ★★★★★ **SB**

Movie Trivia: Silence of the Lambs

Hopkins based the voice of Lecter on a cross between Truman Capote and Katharine Hepburn. There is a *Bon Appetit* magazine in Lecter's holding cell. Author Thomas Harris has never watched the movie for fear of it influencing his writing. Hopkins' screen time was the shortest ever to win a Best Actor Oscar, lasting only 16 minutes.

THE SILENCE (TYSTNADEN) (1963)

Starring: *Ingrid Thulin (Ester), Gunnel Lindblom (Anna), Birger Malmsten (The Bartender), Hakan Jahnberg (The Waiter), Jorgen Lindstrom (Johan)*
Director: *Ingmar Bergman*
Screenwriter: *Ingmar Bergman*
15/91 mins./Drama/Sweden

During an undefined international crisis, three Swedes – sisters Ester and Anna and ten-year-old Johan – are stranded in a vast hotel in the city of Timoka, in a foreign country where they don't speak the language.

One of the most enigmatic of Ingmar Bergman's outwardly cool, inwardly turbulent movies, this dispenses with background information about who the characters are and why they are in this apparently mythical country (are they refugees, or just having a particularly miserable holiday?) to concentrate on their emotional squirming, revelations about the nature of their relationships and the subtle chaos creeping around them.

There's a real eve-of-war, beginning-of-the-end feel that keys into the precise neuroses of 1963: with tanks massing in the streets, repressive measures being brought in by the authorities, and the spectre of nuclear holocaust looming.

But the real crack-up comes between the women – the glacial Ingrid Thulin, who has a semi-lesbian obsession with her sister and an acute distaste for heterosexuality ('Semen smells nasty to me. I've a very keen sense of smell and I stank like rotten fish when I was fertilised'), and the passionate Gunnel Lindblom, who needs straight sex with something approaching desperation.

The strangest part of the film is a sub plot which feels like *The Shining* in miniature as the young boy wanders around the hotel with his toy gun running into strange folks (at one point, he opens a door to find a room full of circus dwarves), but we keep coming back to the women agonising at each other.

It ends, as expected, with a death and the survivors blankly moving on to a hotter, though probably not safer country.

As usual, shot to monochrome perfection by Sven Nykvist. Bergman invented the Slavic-sounding language spoken by the background characters. ★★★★ **KN**

SILENT RUNNING (1972)

Starring: *Bruce Dern (Freeman Lowell), Cliff Potts (John Keenan), Ron Rifkin (Marty Barker), Jesse Vint (Andy Wolf)*
Director: *Douglas Trumbull*
Screenwriters: *Deric Washburn, Mike Cimino, Steve Bochco*
U/85 mins./Sci-fi/Drama/USA

Lowell Freeman looks after plants in giant space greenhouses. When orders from earth are received to destroy the greenhouses, Lowell can't go through with it, and cannot persuade his three colleagues to help him save the plants, so he makes other 'arrangements'.

The history of special effects technicians deciding to direct is not a particularly distinguished one. Chris Walas (*The Fly*) delivered the insipid *The Fly II*, Tom Savini (*Friday The 13th*) inexplicably remade horror classic *The Night Of The Living Dead*, while Joe Johnston (*Indiana Jones And The Temple Of Doom*) delivered ILM showreel *Jumanji*.

American movies of the 70s, the decade of Vietnam and Watergate, tend to have an angsty, anxious feel, and *Silent Running* is sci-fi's contribution to that uneasy national mood. Penned by Deric Washburne and the unlikely pairing of Michael Cimino (who would bring down UA with *Heaven's Gate*) and Steven Bochco (the creator of *Hill Street Blues*).

It's hardly groundbreaking sci-fi to hint that technological advances may have a downside. But in the main it is either alien invasion or nuclear war that devastate the Earth. *Silent Running* however voices the early popular inklings that unchecked technological development may destroy, or at least seriously compromise, the planet. Lowell, who recognises that Earth is less of a place because it lacks green spaces, is pretty much a voice in the wilderness. 'There's hardly any more disease, there's no more poverty, no-one's out of a job' one of the astronauts comments, bemused by his colleague's insistence that the planet is soporifically monotonous without its flora and fauna.

Given the fact that in the intervening three decades ecological issues have moved into mainstream politics it's difficult to believe that this was a genuinely radical position in 1972. It's this unusually strident, obvious, political stance that distinguishes *Silent Running* from the Commie infiltration fantasies of the 50s or the action-packed space operas that emerged at the end of the decade. Trumbull shot his debut for a paltry $1 million in a couple of abandoned aircraft hangers reducing his costs by minimising the cast and spending the bulk of the budget on the gracefully deployed effects instead. In order to reduce costs further he hired a group of inexperienced college kids to help him. One, John Dykstra, would pioneer the effects for *Star Wars*.

For the drones he employed four multiple amputees who operated the different robots at different times (it's worth noting that these squat, speechless robots predate R2D2 by five years). As a first movie it's a daring

Hitchcock Heroines

TOP10

1. Grace Kelly - *Rear Window, Dial M For Murder, To Catch A Thief*
2. Ingrid Bergman - *Notorious, Spellbound, Under Capricorn*
3. Tippi Hendren - *The Birds, Marnie*
4. Eva Marie Saint - *North By Northwest*
5. Janet Leigh - *Psycho*
6. Kim Novak - *Vertigo*
7. Madeleine Carroll - *The 39 Steps, Secret Agent*
8. Anny Ondra - *Blackmail, The Manxman*
9. Doris Day - *The Man Who Knew Too Much*
10. Barbara Leigh-Hunt - *Frenzy*

choice. For the bulk of the film Lowell has no one to talk to but his drones, which he names Huey and Dewey. Trumbull fills the time with a number of montage sequences which have Lowell wandering around the station in positively messianic robes munching on the garden's produce. Dern's performance, all wistful glances and pained sighs, keeps you watching (in fact Dern's at his worst when he's got other actors around him), but it's the conclusion that really gets the lachrymal ducts going. The final image, of the remaining drone tending a flower with a battered child's watering-can is the kind of bittersweet ending that focus-groups, test-screenings and nervy execs have made virtually extinct. ★★★★★ **AS**

SILVER CITY (2004)

Starring: *Chris Cooper (Dickie Pilager), Richard Dreyfuss) (Chuck Raven), Danny Huston (Danny O'Brien), Michael Murphy (Senator Judson Pilager), Kris Kristofferson (Wes Benteen), Daryl Hannah (Maddy Pilager), Thora Birch (Karen Cross)*
Director: *John Sayles*
Screenwriter: *John Sayles*
15/128 mins./Drama/Comedy/Mystery/USA

In Colorado, a senatorial candidate is embarrassed by a corpse that bobs up in a lake while he's shooting an environmental campaign ad. A fixer hires an ex-journalist to investigate, but the mystery has answers the politicians don't want publicised.

Another of John Sayles's snapshot-of-American-corruption pictures, using the conventions of the private eye movie to take a tour through a network of deep-rooted rottenness in public life, typified by a dim-bulb politico (Chris Cooper, in an unusual role) fronting for folksy, manipulative tycoons (Michael Murphy, Kris Kristofferson).

It's plain from early on that the sleuthing will lead back to the political masters, and a range of guilts link them all in typical Chandler style. Sayles takes advantage of film noir structure to stage scenes in which tarnished hero Danny Huston meets various characters to get information, which provides dramatic meat, editorial and informative content and the kind of spin on character the writer-director used to do when writing monster movies and gangster films for Roger Corman.

Tim Roth is an underground editor driven to the internet, Thora Birch a fledgling idealist journo, Miguel Ferrer a right-wing radio shock jock, Daryl Hannah the candidate's drop-out nymphomaniac sister, Mary Kay Place (significantly, the first *Big Chill* star ever to appear in a Sayles film) as an unusual corporate detective and David Clennon a hustler trying to turn a poisoned wasteland into a new community. Sayles deserves credit for remaining angry in G.W. Bush's America, and applying jump leads to tired radicalism even as there's a lingering despair about entrenched evils.

The punchline, slightly muffed by a poor process shot that sits ill with Haskell Wexler's cinematography, is a classic image – dead fish clogging up a lake, implying the land is so poisoned that the story will have to come out. ★★★ **KN**

SILVERADO (1985)

Starring: *Kevin Kline (Paden), Scott Glenn (Emmett), Kevin Costner (Jake) Danny Glover (Mal Johnson), John Cleese (Sherriff John T. Langston), Rosanna Arquette (Hannah), Brian Dennehy (Sherriff Cobb), Linda Hunt (Stella), Jeff Goldblum ('Slick' Calvin Stanhope), Jeff Fahey (Deputy Tyree)*
Director: *Lawrence Kasdan*
Screenwriter: *Lawrence Kasdan, Mark Kasdan*
132 mins./PG/Western/USA

In the old west, a misfit group of cowpokes – sturdy sharpshooter Emmett, his wayward younger brother Jake, gambler Paden and vengeful Mal looking for payback after his pa's murder – come together to right the wrongs that exist in the new town of Silverado.

With his scripts for *The Empire Strikes Back, Raiders Of The Lost Ark* and his directorial debut *Body Heat*, Lawrence Kasdan displayed a breathless skill at revitalising moribund genres and a genuine affection for movie lore. For his third movie as a director – his second, *The Big Chill*, practically invented its own genre, the yuppie nostalgia movie – he went back to that most traditional of American artforms, the Western, and pulled off exactly the same trick. Sophisticated and knowing about the rules of the cowboy picture yet shot full of carefree innocence and exuberance, *Silverado* is the kind of picture that makes you want to play cowboys the moment it is over.

Everything about the movie feels fresh – even the title *Silverado* feels shiny and new. Rather than casting grizzled he-men in the hero roles, Kasdan's selection of Kevin Kline, Scott Glenn, Danny Glover and, in his first Western, Kevin Costner could almost be called The Mild Bunch, etching a group of characters as vulnerable as they are courageous. It's a considered approach to casting that pays dividends; if you've only seen Costner's later, more stately Westerns, he is a revelation here, all easy charm and puppy dog enthusiasm. Beyond the lead foursome, Kasdan's cast has strength in-depth, filled out by great character actors like Dennehy (a boo-hiss villain), Goldblum (a tricksy gambler) and Arquette (a pioneer who strikes up a romantic subplot with Emmett – much of it was left on the cutting room floor).

Whereas many of the Westerns from the 70s try a revisionist take on the genre, *Silverado* offers a wholehearted embracing of Western traditions. This is a film unembarrased to see the good guys get caught in a box canyon, have its heroes bound by honour, to base a whole set-piece around a prison break and to end with a brilliantly staged shoot-out on dusty streets. But it also provides some memorable tweaks to the formula. John Cleese as a unreservedly British sheriff, Linda Hunt as a formidable if diminutive barkeep. Knitted together by Bruce Broughton's rousing Oscar-nominated score, full of nifty action licks, *Silverado* has all the energy of riding off with the wind in your hair on a brand new adventure. Why it failed to catch fire at the box office is a damn disgrace. ★★★★ **IF**

S1MØNE (2002)

Starring: *Al Pacino (Viktor Taransky), Catherine Keener (Elaine Christian), Pruitt Taylor Vince (Max Sayer), Jason Schwartzman (Milton), Winona Ryder (P.A.), Rachel Roberts (SImOne)*
Director: *Andrew Niccol*
Screenwriter: *Andrew Niccol*
PG/112 mins./Comedy/Sci-fi/Drama/USA

Down-and-out movie director Viktor Taransky makes a comeback when he is gifted the world's first synthespian, Simone. But soon he is trapped by his creation's success.

From CG stuntmen to a CG Yoda, synthespians are big business. Hence, Andrew Niccol's *Simone* couldn't be more timely – but the surprise here is that the normally preachy Niccol has discovered his funny bone, reworking the Frankenstein myth (creator destroyed by creation) into a broad comedy. But can *Simone* intentionally do what Jar Jar achieved by accident? Yes, but only in patches.

Niccol's chief problem is that the CG Simone, as moulded by Rachel Roberts and a team of sweaty FX wizards, just doesn't convince. She's beautiful enough to make computer geeks shower their splatter-proof screens, and at times is stunningly photorealistic. But it's asking a lot to believe she fools the world, despite Taransky's assertion: 'It's easier to make 100,000 believe than just one.'

But we're nitpicking. *Simone* is just a smoke screen for Niccol's real target: Hollywood, the only place where someone as fake as Simone would seem so real. From bitchy studio bosses to demanding starlets (personified by Winona Ryder's scheming bitch), and the Oscars (the best gag sees Simone give an acceptance speech from a Third World country, while war rages behind her), Niccol frequently hits home. He's brilliantly served by Pacino, who revels in the chance to play physical comedy. It's a wonderfully sustained performance, but with a human touch as Taransky gradually becomes overwhelmed by his creation. With this, *Insomnia* and *People I Know*, Pacino thankfully seems to have laid his shouty persona, Mr. Hoo-Hah, to rest.

It's a shame, though, that his talented supporting players (Jason Schwartzman, Jay Mohr, Catherine Keener) have nowt to do. And when faced with Niccol's patchy script, as replete with groaners as it is zingers, everyone is occasionally left stranded as gags disappear into thin air.

It looks good, though, and Niccol's got a great eye (witness Pacino dwarfed by a Simone billboard). But in trying to ally his favourite themes – the triumph of the human spirit over an oppressive system; criticism of the pursuit of bodily perfection – with such a broad approach, he overreaches himself. ★★★ **CH**

A SIMPLE PLAN (1998)

Starring: *Bill Paxton (Hank Mitchell), Bridget Fonda (Sarah Mitchell), Billy Bob Thornton (Jacob Mitchell), Gary Cole (Baxter), Brent Briscoe (Lou)*
Director: *Sam Raimi*
Screenwriter: *Scott B. Smith, based on his novel*
15/116 mins./Crime/Drama/Thriller/USA

Two brothers are driven to murder by the lure of stolen cash.

Scott B. Smith's debut novel – which he has adapted for the screen – bears a jacket recommendation from no less than Stephen King ('The best suspense novel of this year'), and it's easy to see why it tickled the great man's fancy. It may not deal in the supernatural but *A Simple Plan* bears many King parallels with its domestic tale of smalltown equilibrium shattered by an unexpected event. Of all King's stories, *A Simple Plan* most readily conjures *Misery*, largely because it's also set in the snowy Midwest, specifically Minnesota – in other words, *Fargo* country. That it compares favourably with both those films gives you a clue how good it is.

A simple story: the Mitchell brothers, Hank and Jacob, are thankfully nothing like their Albert Square namesakes – one is an unassuming, happily-married mill worker, the other a funny-looking simpleton and virgin ('We don't have one thing in common except maybe our last name'). When they stumble upon a crashed plane in the woods with Jacob's buddy Lou, their lives change forever, for inside is a duffel bag containing $4 million cash. The pilot is dead – his eyes forebodingly pecked out by crows – so the three conspire to keep the money until the snow thaws, and then share it out. In covering their tracks, Jacob makes a string of blunders and Hank's Lady Macbeth-like pregnant wife Sarah pushes him deeper and deeper into trouble, involving blackmail, lies and, you guessed it, murder.

Director Raimi apparently received coaching from his pals Joel and Ethan Coen about how best to work in snow, and it figures. *A Simple Plan* is more than just staged in wintertime, its narrative is deeply embedded in the unyielding drifts: the agonising wait until spring serves to hammer dissensions within the fraternal pact, and yet in masking the accidental conspirators' footprints, the weather also becomes an accomplice. Meanwhile, it gives Raimi a stunning, graphic backdrop against which to play his economical psychodrama; although characterised by acrobatic camerawork in the *Evil Dead* films and others, *A Simple Plan* sees the director maturing, and pulling off a remarkably impressive character piece. Which is where Paxton and Thornton come in: the former overcoming a previous blandness (and the fact that he resembles Jack Dee) with a powerful turn as the Minnesotan Macbeth, subtly countered by perhaps Thornton's most three-dimensional hick shtick to date.

As the kind-hearted, guilt-ridden dimwit, he becomes Hank's conscience ('Do you ever feel evil?'), and never plays the part for facile sympathy. Little wonder he was Golden Globe-nominated and honoured by the LA Film Critics Association for his role (and with those sticky-out teeth, too).

Although the simple plan itself spirals out of control and becomes complicated, this remains a simple, modest film: chilly, engrossing and human. Some of the novel's unpleasantness has been pruned for the screen and wisely so, allowing greater scope for the brothers' uneven relationship to develop (there's a touching scene in which Hank talks Jacob to sleep with soothing memories of their father and we realise that murder has actually brought them closer together). *Shallow Grave* will inevitably spring to mind, as will *The Treasure Of The Sierra Madre*, but the film's emphasis on setting, performance and Shakespearean symbolism put it on another shelf entirely. ★★★★ **AC**

SIN CITY (2005)

Starring: *Bruce Willis (John Hartigan), Clive Owen (Dwight McCarthy), Mickey Rourke (Marv), Jessica Alva (Nancy Callahan), Nick Stahl (Roark Jr./Yellow Bastard), Elijah Wood (Kevin), Carla Gugino (Lucille), Rosario Dawson (Gail), Benicio Del Toro (Jackie Boy)*
Directors: *Frank Miller, Robert Rodriguez*
Screenwriter: *Frank Miller, based on his graphic novels*
18/124 mins./147 mins. (director's cut)/Action/Crime/Drama/USA

Three hardboiled tales from Basin City, an American film noir community. Ex-con Marv avenges a murdered hooker, private eye Dwight helps a red light district stay independent from the Mob and disgraced cop Hartigan shields a dancer from a psychotic sadist.

Of all the comic-book adaptations that have ever been mounted, from *Flash Gordon* in 1936 to *The Fantastic Four* in 2005, this is liable to score highest in the 'fan satisfaction' category. No niggling here along the lines of 'Spider-Man shouldn't have organic web-shooters' or 'Batman's parents shouldn't be shot by the Joker'. This collaboration between two one-man bands, comic-book writer-artist Frank Miller and director-writer-editor-cinematographer-producer Robert Rodriguez, is as faithful to the source material as those cheapo 60s Marvel cartoons that panned over panels from the comics while voice-over artists read out the word balloons. Like most successful comics, *Sin City* created a recognisable concrete-but-unreal world. Miller mixed a stew of thugs in trenchcoats out of Chandler or Spillane, a spice of the 'bad girl art' that made paperback covers of the 1950s stand out from newsracks and a splash of the manga-ish stylised goriness which inspired movie buffs like Quentin Tarantino (who guest-directs one scene) have only recently discovered. The film exactly matches the look of the comic: stark black-and-white images, with the occasional shocking or beautiful splash of rich colour. Most modern noirs incline to the blacker side of monochrome, but Miller's scratchboard techniques, adapted superbly by Rodriguez, often get the most impact out of white – the blank round reflections of a killer's sunglasses, crosses of sticking-plaster on a much-wounded face, arterial gushes of milky blood.

The movie script also matches the original stories virtually word for word. The original mini-series was about Marv (perfectly incarnated here by comeback kid Mickey Rourke) an unstoppable but soft-hearted freak who avenges the murder of his sweetie-for-a-night by taking on a ghastly cannibal (a blank-faced, wordless, far-from-Frodo Elijah Wood). The film adapts this (later retitled The Hard Goodbye) and two of its follow-ups, The Big Fat Kill and That Yellow Bastard, seemingly unconcerned about the similarities between the plots and characters, confident that the seductive images and picturesque people will hold the interest. Lifting structure from *Pulp Fiction*, which is hardly in a position to complain if it's imitated, *Sin City* has top-and-tail scenes that frame the three episodes, which are told out of order.

Be warned, though – this is a working definition of a boys' film. Men are either wounded, sensitive mass murderers (good guys) or repulsive, sadistic mass murderers (bad guys). Women are either improbably beautiful whores (good girls) or improbably beautiful pole-dancers (very good girls). Any exceptions, like Carla Gugino as a male-fantasy lesbian, tend to get killed off – nastily.

The extreme stylisation takes the sting out of the pandering, though, in that the hallucinatory female characters tend to be exploiting male desire while living their own lives removed from others' ideas about them. Arguably, the male characters are even more of an insult to the sex; Rodriguez and Miller's once-in-a-lifetime cast of bruised, near-unrecognisable faces bring to life an array of tarnished heroes, each tougher than Mike Hammer on steroids, and appalling villains who'd be too deformed and demented even for Gotham City's Arkham Asylum. ★★★★ **KN**

SINBAD AND THE EYE OF THE TIGER (1977)

Starring: *Patrick Wayne (Sinbad), Taryn Power (Dione), Margaret Whiting (Zenobia), Jane Seymour (Princess Farah), Patrick Troughton (Melanthius)*
Director: *Sam Wanamaker*
Screenwriters: *Beverely Cross, Ray Harryhausen*
U/113 mins./Fantasy/USA

When an evil sorceress with an eye on the throne transforms the heir to the throne in a baboon, it is up to heroic Sinbad to mount a voyage to find the brilliant Melanthius, who may know of a cure.

A better-than-you-remember conclusion to Ray Harryhausen's trilogy of Sinbad adventures. The plot remains just a reworking of the satisfyingly dumb formula – Sinbad must travel to a remote location to fix a curse set by the film's villain (here Margaret Whiting's howlingly wicked Zenobia who, with a bit of magical mishap, ends up with a webbed foot). But as long as the cast are charismatic (Patrick Wayne, son of John, makes for a robust enough Sinbad) and Harryhausen is on his game (he is) you can sit back and let the stop-motion roll all the way to Hyperborea, the mystical and, inevitably, lost land in the far north surrounded by impenetrable fields of ice (and a giant walrus, naturally).

Patrick Troughton has fun as a hammy alchemist who determines, with a load of jabber about Aristotle, that to save the monkey-prince (one of Harrryhausen's finest stop-motions given how much interaction it has with the actors) they must stick him in a Hyperborean fountain when the elements are in alignment or something. It's more varied and epic in scale than its predecessors (good locations including an early call for familiar city-in-a-cliff Petra), and Harryhausen (who co-produces and conceived the storyline) delights in conjuring up a golden minotaur (the Minoton!), a gang of evil skeletons (Ray's party piece), giant wasps, a creepy troglodyte, and the ever-so slightly disappointing but all-important sabre-toothed tiger for the finale. And for boys who are just starting to lose interest in ancient curses and mythical beasties, Jane Seymour and Taryn Power managed to lose large proportions of their clothing along the way. ★★★ **IN**

THE SINGIN' DETECTIVE (2003)

Starring: *Robert Downey, Jr. (Dan Dark), Robin Wright Penn (Nicola/Nina/Blonde), Mel Gibson (Dr. Gibbon), Jeremy Northam (Mark Binney), Katie Holmes (Nurse Mills)*
Director: *Keith Gordon*
Screenwriter: *Dennis Potter, based on his television series*
15/108 mins./Musical/Drama/Mystery/USA

In the mid-80s, writer Dan Dark is admitted to hospital with a debilitating skin disease. A scathing misanthrope, he alienates his doctors, his nurses and his ex-wife – until treatment from the laid-back Dr. Gibbon unlocks a dark secret from the past.

Dennis Potter's 1986 musical mini-series was a milestone in British television, with Michael Gambon as the acid-tongued, psoriasis-riddled novelist whose inner demons have made both him and his life unbearable.

A Hollywood adaptation was inevitable, but Potter so hated the US remake of his previous hit, *Pennies From Heaven*, starring Steve Martin, that he insisted on writing his own script. He finished it shortly before his death in 1994. The script did the rounds of Hollywood before Mel Gibson stepped in to personally fund this stellar but surprisingly low-budget production. Directed by Keith Gordon, the result couldn't be more faithful – and that, to be blunt, is the problem. Not that you'd know it straight away, but the story is now set in the 80s, with rock 'n' roll interludes replacing the wartime singalongs of the TV original.

As the irascible Dark, disgraced golden boy Downey Jr. puts his heart and soul into a demanding tragi-comic role that he clearly hopes will remind Hollywood of his underrated, wide-ranging talents. And this is the film's chief – well, only – pleasure: a chance to root for an actor on the rebound. But where Gambon made the perfect misanthrope, Downey doesn't quite fit the role. Astonishingly, despite his drug-related crimes and misdemeanours, he actually seems too innocent to be so crabby and vile. Around him, the cast of characters drift in and out like the supporting players they are, sometimes in flashbacks to Dark's tortured childhood, sometimes in his jealous fantasies and sometimes in twisted scenes from his own cheap crime novels. The latter is where we find the film's strongest moments of light relief, with Adrien Brody on surprisingly funny form as one of two fictional hoods who burst out of Dark's books and come gunning for him.

Gibson's own appearance (against type) as the balding, good-hearted doctor gives the film a similar boost, but ultimately it's not enough to save a movie that never once catches fire – made with noble intentions but long after its time and place had gone. ★★ **DW**

⑤ SINGIN' IN THE RAIN (1952)

Starring: *Gene Kelly (Don Lockwood), Donald O'Connor (Cosmo Brown), Debbie Reynolds (Kathy Selden), Jean Hagen (Lina Lamont), Millard Mitchell (R.F. Simpson), Cyd Charisse (Dancer)*
Directors: *Stanley Donen, Gene Kelly*
Screenwriters: *Adolph Green, Betty Comden*
U/102 mins./Musical/Comedy/Romance/USA

Awards: *Golden Globes – Best Musical/Comedy Actor (Donald O'Connor)*

Don Lockwood is a bored star of the silent screen, but an accidental meeting with dancer Kathy Selden and the advent of talkies could change his life for the better.

Once asked how he was going to approach the song and dance centrepiece of *Singin' In The Rain*, Gene Kelly famously replied, 'It's going to be raining and I'm going to be singing. I'm going to have a glorious feeling and I'm going to be happy again.'

There is an enticing purity in Kelly's philosophy, a simplicity that courses through *Singin' In The Rain*. The most charming, infectiously exuberant and plain old entertaining film ever to feature on a Greatest Film Of All Time Top Ten (where it usually shares space with such grim-o-ramas as *Battleship Potemkin* and *The Seventh Seal*), the Gene Kelly-Stanley Donen-directed musical is an ode to joy: to the joy of moviemaking, the joy of friendship, the joy of rhyming Moses with roses and toes-es, the joy of falling in love and the joy of – as the man says – singin' and dancin' in the rain.

Centring on a trio of actors (Kelly, Debbie Reynolds and Donald O'Connor) who attempt to save a disastrous period drama by turning it into a musical, *Singin' In The Rain* was conceived as a vehicle for the musical output of songwriting duo Arthur Freed (lyrics) and Nacio Herb Brown (music).

Freed, who headed up the specialist musical unit at MGM, commissioned the screenwriting team of Betty Comden and Adolph Green to weave the tunes together. Struggling for six months to come up with a workable plotline, Comden and Green hit paydirt when they stumbled on the idea of locating the story in the Hollywood between the transition from silent movies to sound – exactly the period from which the Freed-Brown songs originate. As such, SITR's structure owes much to the framework of a typical Judy Garland-Mickey Rooney let's-do-the-show-right-here-in-the-barn musical, swapping a farmyard theatre for the sound stages of the fictional Monumental Pictures.

But where *Singin'* improves on the old-school musical is in its sophisticated deployment of the musical form. Rather than merely stringing its songs together by means of a play-within-a-play, Rain's tunes – be it the sunshiney 'Good Morning', the knockabout 'Make 'Em Laugh' (a shameless rip-off of Cole Porter's 'Be A Clown') or the wordplay of 'Moses Supposes' – are adroitly sutured into the story, utilised to underline and enhance plot points or underscore the characters' feelings and emotions at every turn. Nowhere is this approach more prevalent than in the film's title showstopper. Originally conceived as a number for the central trio, Kelly nabbed the sequence for himself to illustrate his character's creative rebirth and growing feelings for Reynolds' Kathy Selden.

To create the scene, a black tarpaulin was pulled over the backlot to block out the daylight, six holes were dug to create puddles and ink was added to backlit raindrops to make the precipitation visible on film. To create the mood, Kelly regressed into the mindset of a child splashing and jumping around in puddles. Referenced by everyone from Morecambe and Wise to Stanley Kubrick (*A Clockwork Orange* features a savage assault by Malcolm McDowell humming 'Singin'), the result is ten shots, five minutes of unadulterated movie magic. The only time that *Rain* awkwardly tacks on its musical pleasures is in the final Broadway Melody ballet, the climax of the film-within-a-film.

Seeking to top the finale of *An American In Paris*, Kelly insisted on perfection. As Debbie Reynolds (who was left physically and mentally exhausted by Kelly's hard taskmastering) could not cut it as a dancer, Kelly drafted in ballerina Cyd Charisse to pull off the complex pas de deux. Made of see-through silk, Charisse's costume originally failed to cover her pubic hair – following a rethink, costume designer Walter Plunkett quipped, 'Don't worry, fellas, we've got Cyd Charisse's crotch licked!' With aeroplane motors blowing Charisse's 50-foot scarf in time to the music, the sequence combines physical prowess and technical ingenuity to create the atmosphere of a half-remembered dream.

Yet, where *Rain* improves on most of its musical contemporaries is in the bits between the showstoppers. From the opening scene – where Kelly's Don Lockwood embellishes his rise to fame as the images show the truth in a witty demonstration of the film's obsession with artifice versus reality – to the hilarious attempts at sound recording with microphones hidden in a bush, the writing is crisp, clever, comedic, played to a tee by a clutch of great supporting performances. While O'Connor is pitch-perfect comic relief and Reynolds is well-nigh irresistible, the real performance on show is Jean Hagen's Lina Lamont, the silent movie diva ruined by her shrill tones. In the movie, the songbird Reynolds is co-opted into redubbing Hagen's high-pitched squeal. In reality, it was Hagen who lent her vocal stylings to Reynolds.

As well as its storytelling sophistication, *Singin' In The Rain* also appears ageless through its sky-high level of film literacy. Boasting more filmic references than a Quentin Tarantino scrapbook, *Rain* is chocker with Hollywood skits and spoofs (the opening premiere is a riff on *Show Girls Of Hollywood*, and that's just for starters), mounted with love and affection. With its network of allusion and pastiche, *Singin' In The Rain* is a postmodernist film before postmodernism was invented. *SITR*'s self-referencing is one of the major reasons why it still figures regularly in egghead critics' Top Ten polls, but it's not the whole story. A moderate success on its original release (it made $7.7 million on release), it was yanked out of cinemas to make room for *An American In Paris*, which had just romped home at the Oscars. *SITR* languished until the 70s, when interest was revived by its appearances on TV and a prominent place in the MGM musical compilation flick, *That's Entertainment*. This, coupled with the Movie Brat-ish fascination with movies about moviemaking, put *Singin'* back on the moviegoing map. That it is The Greatest Musical Ever Made has kept it there ever since.
★★★★★ **IF**

Movie Trivia: Singin' In The Rain

Gene Kelly had a 103 degree temperature shooting the title number. Howard Keel was originally considered for Kelly's role and the role of Cosmo was created with Oscar Levant in mind — it went to Donald O'Connor. Originally, Kathy was to sing 'You Are My Lucky Star' to a Billboard showing Lockwood's character. It was later transposed as a duet.

⑤ SINGLE WHITE FEMALE (1992)

Starring: *Bridget Fonda (Allison Jones), Jennifer Jason Leigh (Hedra Carlson), Steven Weber (Sam Rawson), Peter Friedman (Graham Knox)*
Director: *Barbet Schroeder*
Screenwriter: *Don Roos, from the novel* SWF Seeks Same *by John Lutz*
18/103 mins./Thriller/USA

Allie takes in a new flatmate, Hedy, but Hedy is soon revealed to more sinister than it first appeared.

If anyone loves a trend, it's Hollywood. Chasing hard on a pack started by early 90s smashes such as *Basic Instinct*, and *The Hand That Rocks The Table* et al, was *Single White Female*, providing conclusive proof (like it's needed) that Women From Hell were in back then. Barbet Schroeder followed up his vintage work on Reversal Of Fortune with this impassively calculated attempt to merge Hitchcockian thrills with Bergman-type mind games.

After booting out her philandering beau, twentysomething Allie (Fonda, occasionally convincing), cheery and confident but afraid of being alone, advertises for a flatmate, picking sweet, dowdy and dishevelled Hedy (Leigh, occasionally chilling) as her seemingly unthreatening ideal. Fashion design software expert Allie – who always manages to look fresh out of a Vogue fashion spread, and possesses a cavernous Upper West Side apartment, despite having just the one client in the Rolodex – and bookstore minion Hedy go through a honeymoon period of nicely observed sisterly bonding rituals, but when the clingy Hedy starts cloning herself after Allie, it's abundantly clear she's after more than just fashion tips.

Yet when repentant boyfriend Sam pops up again, the bitterly malevolent Hedy sets out to frame him as a killer of fluffy puppies and a faithless clod, with Schroeder lurching schizophrenically into yuppie nightmare mode as the besieged fashion-conscious yuppette races against time to get the wacko out of her life before she runs out of warm-blooded mammals to ice.

What Schroeder lacks in character development – both Fonda and Leigh battle valiantly to beef up their thinly written roles – he more than makes up for in mood and atmosphere, honing the creepy grandeur of the ominous, shadowy Manhattan apartment building with all the pinpoint perfection, filtered light and grainy texture of a man who knows his Roman Polanski. Although he laces it with several macabre and unsettling touches, the supremely talented Schroeder merely seems to be flexing his filmmaking muscles here, biding his time until he finds something he can really sink his teeth into. ★★★ **MM**

SINGLES (1992)

Starring: *Bridget Fonda (Janet Livermore), Campbell Scott (Steve Dunne), Kyra Sedgwick (Linda Powell), Matt Dillon (Cliff Poncier), Bill Pullman (Dr. Jeffrey Jamison), Eric Stoltz (Mime), Tim Burton (Video Director)*
Director: *Cameron Crowe*
Screenwriter: *Cameron Crowe*
15/95 mins./Romance/Comedy/USA

A group of young people, sharing an apartment block, fall in and out of love against the background of the 90s grunge scene.

It is set in Seattle; members of Pearl Jam and Alice In Chains loiter listlessly in the background; Matt Dillon sports a cascading, unkempt grunge-wig; writer-director Cameron Crowe's apprenticeship was as a writer for American rock bible *Rolling Stone*. In fact, all the signs suggested that *Singles* was to be a very swift, opportune cash-in on the phenomenon that is grunge.

Thankfully it is far better than that. There may be plenty of fashionable alienated noise playing quietly in the background, Dillon may front a band called Citizen Dick (theme song 'Touch Me – I'm Dick') and characters may occasionally fondle the odd record sleeve (not Nirvana), but despite the pun of the film's title, this is not a tediously contemporary film about music but rather a timeless one about love.

Crowe is smart enough to realise that whatever may be distinctive or new about the world of grunge, it is also just another subcultural vortex around which young people do the very same things – fall in love, fall out of love, and fool themselves about either state of affairs – as they did to 'Rock Around The Clock', punk, disco and Fleetwood Mac.

The film itself is not carried by Dillon but by Campbell Scott, Kyra Sedgwick and Bridget Fonda, their lines well-observed without being mannered and, for the most part, witty without being played for laughs. What actually happens – the action is based around the comings and goings in a complex of single apartments – could be conveyed in a couple of very flat sentences.

There are not even any of the obligatory suicides or drug overdoses usually wheeled in to provide pathos and melodrama during the final act of supposedly intimate American films about the young, and this steers the viewer towards no remarkable insights or simple conclusions. Instead it is crammed with the sort of mild, messy emotions that even the most cloth-eared grunge-o-phobe will find frustratingly familiar. ★★★★ **CHe**

SISTER ACT (1992)

Starring: *Whoopi Goldberg (Deloris Van Cartier), Maggie Smith (Mother Superior), Kathy Najimy (Sister Mary Patrick), Harvey Keitel (Vince LaRocca), Bill Nunn (Lt. Eddie Souther)*
Director: *Emile Ardolino*
Screenwriter: *Joseph Howard*
PG/96 mins./Comedy/USA

A nightclub singer hides out in a nunnery after witnessing a mob hit.

This is a film of such, if you must, 'high concept' that one simply needs to hear the 'pitch' to know everything that will inevitably unfold: Whoopi goes into a convent. Yep, that's it. And a thoroughly inane, inoffensive affair it is too – absurd, predictable but not actually inept, and completely dependent upon Whoopi playing it at full throttle.

She is Deloris, a third-rate nightclub chanteuse who has Big Hair and keeps company with club owner/hood Vince, the kind of guy who gives a girl a purple mink – and it's his wife's. Disenchantment rapidly turns to consternation after Deloris sees Vince rub out a squealer, whereupon she sensibly runs to the cops and nonsensically is stashed with the good sisters at St. Katherine's in a witness protection 'twist'.

Naturally, she drives humourless Mother Superior (Maggie Smith on one grim note) mad, and, naturally, the cute convent inmates comprise one fat, jolly nun, one daffy dear old nun, one timid novice, etc. Since this nunnery also boasts an impossibly bad choir, Deloris takes charge and turns the poor parish into a happening congregation, boogeying down to ditties like 'My Guy' re-addressed to the dude upstairs, though the forces of evil inevitably intrude for a no-surprises-here climax that is never quite as madcap as it would like to be. A rehash sequel is notable for the starring role taken by future Fugee Lauren Hill. ★★★ **AE**

16 BLOCKS (2006)

Starring *Bruce Willis (Jack Mosley), Mos Def (Eddie Bunker), David Morse (Frank Nugent), Jenna Stern (Diane Mosley), Casey Sander (Captain Gruber)*
Director *Richard Donner*
Screenwriter *Richard Wenk*
12A/102 mins./Drama/Crime/USA

Beaten-down, boozehound cop Jack Mosley experiences a moment of moral clarity – and some heavy gunfire – while escorting a no-mark prisoner across Manhattan for a curiously scrutinised court appearance.

There are a number of good things in director Richard Donner's taut, effective tale of a grizzled NYPD burn-out attempting to chaperone an annoying dweeb across the titular distance without either of them getting their heads blown off. First, in its well-sustained ticking-clock suspense and explosive yet restrained action sequences, *16 Blocks* provides clear evidence of a return to form for director Richard Donner, seemingly a spent force given most of his post-Lethal Weapon oeuvre.

Second is Willis who, gratifyingly, has grasped the fact that audiences will continue to tolerate ageing action stars only if they accept the ravages of time with good grace, embrace their newfound crustiness and realise that just because they're playing a 'character part' doesn't mean they can't still kick ass from time to time ... Just as long as they throw us a little Danny Glover-style 'I'm too old for this shit' self-deprecation along the way. Thus, with his game leg, crisis-point hairline, fried-egg eyes and dyspeptic conscience, Willis's turn is his most credible performance in years.

Third is a satisfying answer to the question of 'what the hell happened to David Morse?', that most dependably stable of supporting players who appeared to have taken a powder after 2001's crappy kidnap thriller *Proof Of Life* (not that anyone would blame him if he had). He's back with a vengeance here as the kind of menacingly soft-spoken career cop, cancerous with corruption, that no gritty policier worth its salt can live without.

Then there's rapper-turned-actor Mos Def proving his chops yet again by opting for a character interpretation that, initially, stirs uncomfortable memories of Adam Sandler in *Little Nicky* but which, against the odds, grows on us as inexorably as it does on Willis's worldweary curmudgeon – quite a feat, as anyone who saw *Little Nicky* will confirm.

All the above would most likely agree that this movie's appeal rests firmly on its not overreaching its grasp. You'd hardly call it a modest undertaking – another treat is the authentic Lower Manhattan locations, which don't come cheap – but it has a sense of proportion. Donner is content to execute a twist on the buddy-cop formula, rather than break his neck trying to reinvent it. And in that, *16 Blocks* goes the distance. ★★★ **SB**

◑ 633 SQUADRON (1964)

Cast: *Cliff Robertson (Wing Cmdr. Roy Grant), George Chakiris (Lt. Erik Bergman), Maria Perschy (Hilde Bergman), Harry Andrews (Air Vice-Marshal Davis), Donald Houston (Group Capt. Don Barrett)*
Director: *Walter Grauman*
Screenwriters: *James Clavell, Howard Koch, based on the novel by Frederick E. Smith*
PG/101 mins./War/Drama/UK/USA

At the height of WWII a squadron of Mosquito fighter-bombers is sent on a potentially fatal mission to bomb the loose cliff face above a Nazi arms factory in Norway. A direct hit would bring the whole rock face crashing down on the enemy's head.

The skill in making and, indeed, the guilty pleasure in watching such dumb but big-hearted wartime movies as this RAF adventure has become something of a lost art. Anything vaguely WWII must be leavened by realism in modern thinking. Which is a shame as Walter Grauman's loud, triumphalist crowd-pleaser still warms a sodden Sunday afternoon like a hot toddy. Not that the film possesses any greater merits than a stirring score (applause due to Ron Goodwin), a polished combo of aerial photography and model-work and a general well-worn gusto.

With a mind on the American box-office, it is the square-jawed Cliff Robertson who takes command of the otherwise British 633 boys (including Johnny Briggs, Coronation Street's Mike Baldwin), ready to knock 'em into shape during the extended training session. A sequence of dedicated cliché, especially as Harry Andrews does what he always does under such circumstances and bellows a lot about the needs of the mission.

Naturally, as there's plenty of empty time to pad between initial training and ultimate mission, the film idles along in some weak subplots. Robertson and Perschy's romance is so prepackaged it could have been copied down from the back of a cereal box. Meanwhile, the Norwegian freedom fighter, George Chakiris, who landed them the base's secret location to begin with, is captured by the Nazis and tortured to reveal the plan. Just in time to add that extra soupçon of peril for our pilots, who are so constant and heroic they determine to carry on all the same.

It doesn't give much away to reveal that last gasp heroics will be in order before those damned Nazis feel the sky fall in, but the sight of those glorious De Havilland Mosquitoes floating over the glassy water of the fjord can still stir the blood. ★★★ **IN**

◑ THE SIXTH SENSE (1999)

Starring: *Bruce Willis (Dr. Malcolm Crowe), Haley Joel Osment (Cole Sear), Toni Collette (Lynn Sear), Olivia Williams (Anna Crowe), Mischa Barton (Kyra Collins), Donnie Wahlberg (Vincent Grey)*
Director: *M. Night Shyamalan*
Screenwriter: *M. Night Shyamalan*
15/107 mins./Drama/Mystery/USA
Awards: *Empire Awards – Best Director*

Child psychiatrist Malcolm Crowe takes on a troubled boy named Cole Sear, who claims to see ghosts.

That *The Sixth Sense* became the phenomenon it did is perhaps less to do with its inherent qualities as a ghost story than the slyly worked 'shock' ending being traded off at dinner parties the world over.

Indeed, it drew countless back to the cinema for reappraisal, just to see how they were hoodwinked so easily. The real trick, however, was to deliver such an emotionally complex story in the guise of a horror movie. In fact, nothing in the film was ever what you expected. M. Night Shyamalan, an Indian-born but Philadelphia-grown director who stems from a family of doctors, has a rather morbid fascination with linking children, spirituality and the paranormal. His first film, the ineffective *Wide Awake* (1998), studies a young Catholic boy trying to prove the existence of God after his grandfather dies. In *The Sixth Sense*, his device is more poignant and direct, a ghost story about emotional loss and unresolved differences – in which a boy is the cipher to the needs of the recently departed. A traumatic experience at its mildest, so child psychologist (and, yes, recently deceased) Malcolm Crowe comes to his rescue and, in turn, his own.

As is oft the case, watching *The Sixth Sense* knowing that Willis is a ghost, opens the film up to a different perspective. A game of totting up all the pointers – most of which seem pretty blatant back to front – and just how skilled Shyamalan is at throwing us off the scent. The creative team devised a set of rules in which the film would operate while sustaining the shock of the denouement. Whenever the colour red appears it is a sign of something tainted by the dead; the steaming of breath in the presence of ghosts implys a strong negative emotional undercurrent (thus explaining why Willis's benign therapist doesn't elicit any); and the fact that Crowe can only add clothes to the look he was wearing the night he was killed.

Of course, this does not answer all questions: the fact that ghosts do not know they're ghosts would suggest a degree of personal confusion on their behalf – like why can I only talk to this pint-sized know all? Why do I not sleep or eat? Willis's expert performance, every inch of him understated, is vital in concealing the truth. He is soft and humane, suggesting psychological details with small gestures and an almost whispering tone (a skill only *12 Monkeys* has born witness to before). How could he possibly be thought of as dead? But all the evidence is there.

The film, for its first half at least, is terrifically chilling (once the ghosts have proven benign much of its scariness evaporates). With Osment's ability to project childlike vulnerability without mawkishness or smarm, events play to the heart of a very basic human instinct: protecting a child.

When the ghosts appear, they whisk past the camera, the temperature drops suddenly, filigree hand-prints appear on table tops, building to full scale revelations of seemingly normal apparitions – with the exception of their fatal wounds (a boy turns round to reveal that the back of his head has been blown off). Subtlety is the key throughout, not big ding-dong stingers but evocative trails and hints of the truth, most of them mapped out across

Osment's tormented face. Shyamalan's direction is the model of restraint – disquiet and stillness pervade while he expertly utilises sound to enhance the discomforting feeling of something indefinable being present (allowing the audience its own 'sixth sense').

The background noise is a symphony of hissing breaths, the score, by James Newton Howard, splices in sonorous markers – such as just discernible evil, snarling voices – to add dramatic impact. Visually the film is elegantly austere, *The Silence Of The Lambs* cinematographer Tak Fujimoto shoots in mute, autumnal browns and greys, evoking a funereal gloom cast over the European-style architecture of Philadelphia (ironically, the same setting as *12 Monkeys* – this city does Willis a lot of favours).

Osment – whose casting was pivotal – is a true discovery. He has to carry the heart of the movie as well as distract us from paying too much attention to Willis's, well, deadness. Especially in the moments of supposed peril (the boy is, in fact, never in serious jeopardy) that he faces alone, the young actor handles the fear and vulnerability of his predicament with an emotional force. One of the film's sweetest nuances is in the expertly realised relationship between Cole and his blue collar mother – he feels he cannot explain his predicament to her; in turn she cannot comprehend what is tormenting her son – emphasising Shyamalan's message of reconciliation. We must all just connect before it's too late. ★★★★★ **IN**

Movie Trivia: The Sixth Sense

This was Bruce Willis's second film where he is involved with a character called Cole who saw dead people — the first being *12 Monkeys*. It was only the fourth horror movie to ever receive a Best Picture Oscar nomination. Director Shyamalan cameos as Dr. Hill. The film was shot in sequence, which is unusual in filmmaking.

THE SKELETON KEY (2005)

Starring: *Kate Hudson (Caroline Ellis), Gena Rowlands (Violet Devereaux), John Hurt (Ben Devereaux), Peter Sarsgaard (Luke)*
Director: *Iain Softley*
Screenwriter: *Ehren Kruger*
15/104 mins./Horror/USA

Caring soul Caroline takes up a live-in nursing role with paralysed stroke victim Ben and his scowling wife in their weathered Louisiana mansion – a house that harbours more than its share of secrets.

Those who have sampled the sweaty etchings of William Faulkner or seen *Angel Heart* will be aware the sulky doldrums of the Deep South are thick with bad juju. Five minutes out of New Orleans and you're swamped in cataractous witches, severed chicken heads and the ululations of slave-song. Stranding yourself in a house on the cusp of the bayou, lorded over by two cracked old coots and minus air-conditioning, is positively foolhardy.

Yet, for the sake of this excitable horror-lite, that's just what the irresistibly cute Kate Hudson does. In a heartbeat, she's got on the wrong side of Gena Rowlands' moody matriarch (who may lack a right side) and discovered a secret stash of dusty hoodoo paraphernalia; ingredients for a terrible curse.

Director Iain Softley harkens to the call of the Southern Gothic with a treacly atmosphere and the twangy lament of authentic 'Louisicana', but he's too eager to leap into formula frightwigging. When the plot threatens to falter, 'weird locals' conveniently hand out exposition and advice. And what use is a subtext of belief versus pragmatism when supernatural activity is already on display? Still, the performances are strong (Rowlands has a ball) and the twist is a corker – an unexpectedly nasty outcome that casts an evil gleam over the preceding movie. ★★★ **IN**

SKY CAPTAIN AND THE WORLD OF TOMORROW (2005)

Starring: *Gwyneth Paltrow (Polly Perkins), Jude Law (Joe 'Sky Captain' Sullivan), Giovanni Ribisi (Dex), Michael Gambon (Editor Paley)*
Director: *Kerry Conran*
Screenwriter: *Kerry Conlan*
PG/106 mins./Action/Fantasy/Adventure/Sci-fi/USA

When 1930s New York finds itself besieged by giant robots, only one man can come to the rescue – flying ace Joe Sullivan, aka Sky Captain. Teaming up with his ex-flame, ace reporter Polly Perkins, he embarks on an adventure that will take him around the world – and possibly to the end of it.

Sky Captain starts as it means to go on – with the semi-destruction of Manhattan by giant flying robots. Later on, we meet giant underwater robots, giant mutated dinosaurs and the giant recreated head of Sir Laurence Olivier. It's that kind of movie – everything but the kitchen sink's thrown in. And even then, it would be a giant kitchen sink with laser cannons for taps.

It's director Kerry Conran's dream project, six years in the making, using actors shot on greenscreen and later composited into prerendered CG backgrounds that constitute a fusion of all his major influences, from 1930s and 40s serials, to the Superman cartoons of the Fleischer brothers and the cityscapes of Fritz Lang's *Metropolis*.

Sky Captain is unlike anything else you'll have seen – and spare a thought for the actors stranded against a green screen. Law is all stiff upper-lipped hero and Paltrow is sassy, sexy and all-action.

Internet fanboys have clutched it to their portly man-bosoms, but then, this is a movie precisely calibrated, by one of their own, to appeal to them. But, with a bit of an imagination, a wider audience could find it just as appealing. ★★★ **WT**

SLACKER (1991)

Starring: *Richard Linklater (Should Have Stayed At Bus Station), Rudy Basquez (Taxi Driver), Jean Caffeine (Roadkill), Jan Hockey (Jogger), Stephan Hockey (Running Late)*
Director: *Richard Linklater*
Screenwriter: *Richard Linklater*
15/96 mins./Comedy/Drama/USA

The lives of a Texan community as seen through individuals whose time on camera lasts only as long as is needed, until the next passer-by takes on the story.

A film that sharply divided audiences into two distinct groups: those who hailed it as a ground-breaking masterpiece, a perfect snapshot of a lost generation; and those who fell asleep, frustrated not only by its lack of anything approaching a plot but also by its refusal to let any of its myriad characters appear on screen for more than five minutes.

Opening with a young man (director Linklater) taking a taxi ride from the bus station in Austin, Texas, and rabbiting on about alternate realities, the film then latches on to a young man who calmly waits to be arrested after running down his mother in front of their house – the police summoned by Linklater. Then the cops are briefly the focus, then a young man walking from a coffee shop to his home, then a loon ranting about conspiracy theories, then some people whose flatmate has left, then a guy who wants to move into the empty room, and so on, with each character passing on to the next in a relay which straggles throughout the city.

No one ever reappears, but a portrait of the community is eventually

S

filled in via kind of cinematic pointillist dots, concentrating on footloose youths, more concerned with hanging out than getting on. Inevitably, the crazies stand out, but the heart of the film is in its collection of likeable drifters who just go along with the madness, hoping to get in free to a rock gig or thinking about doing something artistic. Seemingly improvised, but in fact fully scripted and tightly if unconventionally structured, this is about people you know but rarely get to see in the movies. One of a kind. **★★★★ KN**

SLEEPER (1973)

Starring: *Woody Allen (Miles Monroe), Diane Keaton (Luna Schlosser), John Beck (Erno Windt), Maya Small (Dr. Nero), Bartlett Robinson (Dr. Ona)*
Director: *Woody Allen*
Screenwriters: *Woody Allen, Marshall Brickman*
PG/83 mins./Comedy/Sci-fi/USA

A clarinet player who also runs a health food store is frozen and brought back in the future by anti-government radicals in order to assist them in their attempts to overthrow an oppressive government.

Woody Allen hit upon the idea of doing a science fiction spoof just after completing the What Happens During Ejaculation? episode of *Everything You Always Wanted To Know About Sex*. According to John Baxter's 1998 biography, Allen asked assistant director Fred Gallo about the logistics of building a futuristic town. A somewhat sceptical Gallo replied, 'There are four things to stay away from in movies – boats and water, animals, kids, and futurism.'

Thankfully, Allen ignored him. (And it's a good thing James Cameron didn't go to Fred Gallo for advice too.) *Sleeper* would mark the fulfilment of Allen's slapstick ambitions and, for many, it epitomises his 'early, funny films', crammed as it is with unforgettable sight gags and sly conceits. Mel Brooks' *Blazing Saddles* had set a new precedent for genre spoofs (though he was yet to really start churning them out), and Allen took the baton and ran with it, doing for sci-fi what Brooks would later do for horror and Hitchcock. Sci-fi, of course, was big again in the early 70s after the success of *Planet Of The Apes* and Kubrick's *2001* – and ripe for parody – but Allen and TV-grounded co-writer Marshall Brickman took a larger part of their inspiration from books like H.G. Wells' *When The Sleeper Wakes* and Huxley's *Brave New World*, and more esoteric movies such as *THX 1138* and *Alphaville*.

Like much of the most enjoyable science fiction, *Sleeper* is set on Earth but in the future, specifically 2173. Miles Monroe (Allen), owner of the Happy Carrot health food restaurant, has been cryogenically frozen for 200 years. In this particular future there is no sex (all men are impotent, all women are frigid, and orgasm must be achieved inside the Orgasmatron), robots act as domestic help, food is instant, and America is ruled by a dictator – in fact, a dictator's nose, which is all that's left of him after an assassination attempt. Monroe falls in love with revolutionary poet Luna (Diane Keaton) and woos her with his quaint 20th century notions and by playing jazz clarinet for her. Indeed, the ragtime jazz of the soundtrack represents Allen's love of a more innocent past – not the first or last time old-fashioned music provided a counterpoint to futuristic goings on (see also: The Blue Danube in *2001*, the jazz in *Star Wars'* cantina, and the subversive use of 'Singin' In The Rain' in *A Clockwork Orange*).

Sleeper makes some pertinent political points (Allen calls science an 'intellectual dead end', and predicts that, having overthrown the dictator, they will soon be overthrowing revolutionary leader Erno's nose) and throws in plenty of tart contemporary references: Richard Nixon, McDonalds, sportscaster Howard Cosell and Norman Mailer (who 'donated his ego to the Harvard Medical School'). However, the joy of the film almost 30 years later remains its set pieces.

One or two of them are among Allen's finest, and act as a worthy tribute to his comedy heroes such as Buster Keaton and Charlie Chaplin. While on the run, Monroe encounters a farm growing giant fruit and vegetables – GM foods v predicted by stand-up comic in 1970s! – and having peeled a ten-foot banana, he proceeds to enact the world's biggest slipping-on-a-banana-peel gag. Having disguised himself as a robot, Monroe is called upon to pass round the Orb at a dinner party, a 2173 replacement for dope, and because he is in fact human, he gets as high as the guests. (The fact that we know about Allen's dislike of drug-taking makes it all the more funny.) And the sequence simply involving him attempting to escape using a ladder that is too short has to be seen to be believed.

Ironically though, *Sleeper* is characterised by its stunts and pratfalls, as a filmmaker Allen found the technicalities of his most ambitious film a bore. United Artists only granted the film a measly $2 million budget and a 50-day shoot – thus, taking into account the rigours of its futuristic *set-up*, Allen was forced to shoot in his despised Los Angeles (partly on the old Selznick lot in Culver City, home of *Gone With The Wind*). On such a shoestring, it is worth applauding the work of both production designer Dale Hennesy and costume designer Joel Schumacher (yes, that one).

Allen attempted a string of complicated physical gags – the scene where he dangles from a building on computer tape took two days to complete, and no stunt double was used – and ended up complaining, 'This is a movie about wires.' **★★★★ AC**

SLEEPING WITH THE ENEMY (1991)

Starring: *Julia Roberts (Sara Waters/Laura Burney), Patrick Bergin (Martin Burney), Kevin Anderson (Ben Woodward), Elizabeth Lawrence (Chloe Williams)*
Director: *Joseph Ruben*
Screenwriter: *Ronald Bass, based on the novel by Nancy Price*
15/94 mins./Drama/Thriller

An abused wife fakes her death and runs away from her husband to start a new life. But will he track her down?

In a modernist hell-house on the beach, Laura, fragile and abused wife of a psychotic commodities dealer, plots to leave her monster hubby. He signals his thoroughgoing rottenness by putting Berlioz on the CD when they have sex, insisting his meals be served on time, making sure all the cans in the food cupboard are stacked tidily, and beating her up if the towels in the bathroom are out of place. Annoyed, Laura pretends not to be able to swim and fakes a drowning accident, whereupon she hightails it for the mid-West to start all over again with a new name, no identity, and a tentative relationship with the guy next door, a drama teacher who signals his thoroughgoing niceness by playing Dion and the Belmonts, taking her to funfairs, dressing her up in stage costumes and having a cuddly thirty-something beard. Naturally, the baddie catches on and sets about tracking our heroine down, with Bergin displaying an ever-more exaggerated clutch of madman twitches and mannerisms.

Joseph Ruben is best known for his masterly *The Stepfather*, another psycho-thriller about a husband whose demands on his family lead to ultra-violence, but, by comparison, the much starrier, much more elaborate *Sleeping With The Enemy* is a lightweight, silly film. Whereas Terry O'Quinn's stepfather was one of the subtlest, scariest and most intriguing villains in 80s cinema, Bergin's mad stockbroker – the 90s 'in' profession for psychotics, as demonstrated by *Blue Steel* – is just another slasher baddie. With all the things that made *The Stepfather* interesting trimmed away, you're left with an acceptable but dumb TV movie with a few moments of violence and Julia Roberts in designer peril, draped with frocks only the villain could afford to buy her and even, in one scene, demonstrating her versatility by dressing in drag.

When Bergin is stalking Roberts around a dark house, the film does rev up some suspense, throwing in those false alarm scares that get everyone jumping. However, frustratingly, it jumps on the band wagon of films like *Misery*, *Dead Calm* – by pulling that tired old *Halloween*-*Fatal Attraction* last-minute-return-from-the-dead-for-one-more-cheap-shock stunt, and the use of the device here, following hard on *Pacific Heights*, does nothing but confirm Jon Polito's advice to would-be murderers in *Miller's Crossing*, 'always put one in the brain'. ★★ **JY**

SLEEPLESS IN SEATTLE (1991)

Starring: *Tom Hanks (Sam Baldwin), Meg Ryan (Annie Reed), Bill Pullman (Walter), Ross Malinger (Jonah Baldwin), Rosie O'Donnell (Becky), Gaby Hoffman (Jessica), Rob Reiner (Jay), Rita Wilson (Suzy)*
Director: *Nora Ephron*
Screenwriters: *Nora Ephron, David S. Ward, Jeff Arch, from a story by Arch*
PG/100 mins./Comedy/Romance/USA

After being tricked by his son into going on a radio show, a widower is inundated with requests from lonely women wanting to meet him. Could one of them be Ms Right?

A hugely enjoyable romantic comedy, directed by the writer of *When Harry Met Sally*, this attacks both funny bone and tear-ducts with equal success. When recently widowed architect Sam Baldwin is conned into taking part in a late night Christmas Eve phone-in radio talk show by his young son Jonah, his on-air 'why-I-loved-my-wife' confession has heart-string tugging repercussions throughout the land as women all over America fall in love with the disembodied voice known only as 'Sleepless in Seattle'. These include lovelorn Baltimore journo Annie Reed who finds herself becoming increasingly obsessed by his description of his first meeting with his wife as 'magic' and fears that if she marries her sensible but sterile fiance Walter she will settle for 'satisfactory' rather than 'magical'.

As the offers of marriage flood in for 'Sleepless', Jonah takes it upon himself to play matchmaker and find himself a mother, and his dad a new wife from the thousands of applicants. Plucking from the burgeoning pile a letter purporting to be from Annie, who Jonah is convinced is the one, he hatches a scheme to introduce them, despite their living 3,000 miles apart.

Very much in the vein of *When Harry Met Sally*, this cannily uses clips from the 1957 Cary Grant vehicle *An Affair To Remember* to delightfully screwball effect, even going so far as to have Jonah arrange a meeting between Hanks and Ryan atop the Empire State Building on Valentine's Day. Conspiring to keep the star-crossed lovers apart for the majority of the film, Ephron's script is often uproariously funny (Hanks and buddy extolling the merits of *The Dirty Dozen* is especially memorable), while there is able support from O'Donnell and Rob Reiner as Annie's and Sam's best buddies respectively.

The soundtrack may be at times surprising (Jimmy Durante singing 'As Time Goes By'?), and at times too literal for its own good (do we really need 'In The Wee Small Hours Of The Morning' to tell us what we already know?), but Ryan looks good enough to eat, Hanks women will find hard to resist, and the kid is one of the most appealing on screen for years. Shamelessly slushy fluff it may well be, but you'd have to be hard-hearted indeed to watch this without feeling just that touch gooey inside. A real treat. ★★★★ **MS**

SLEEPY HOLLOW (1999)

Starring: *Johnny Depp (Constable Ichabod Crane), Christina Ricci (Katrina Anne Van Tassel), Miranda Richardson (Lady Mary Van Tassel), Michael Gambon (Baltus Van Tassel), Christopher Lee (Burgomaster), Christopher Walken (The Hessian Horseman)*
Director: *Tim Burton*
Screenwriter: *Andrew Kevin Walker, from a story by Kevin Yagher, Andrew Kevin Walker, from the story* The Legend Of Sleepy Hollow *by Washinton Irving*
15/94 mins./Fantasy/Horror/Mystery/USA

Awards: *Academy Awards – Best Art Direction-Set Decoration, BAFTA – Best Costume, Best Production Design*

In 1799 a New York City constable is sent to investigate a series of brutal murders in Sleepy Hollow.

In adapting *The Legend Of Sleepy Hollow* – formerly a classic short story by Washington Irving and a classic animated featurette by Walt Disney – arch visualist Tim Burton declared his desire to make a movie inspired by the classic horrors of Hammer. What? Fake sets, dry ice, big boobs and Christopher Lee?! Well, in Burton's sumptuous tale you get the cleavage. You even get Lee. You also get what is probably the most beautiful horror movie ever made. And a cracking piece of action cinema to boot.

In both the Irving and Disney version, Ichabod Crane was a scaredy-cat school teacher; here it's still late 1799, but he is a New York city police constable, a man ahead of his time in his belief in scientific evidence and forensics, at the dawn of a new century of enlightenment. Sent by his superior (a brief but telling cameo from Lee) to the quiet upstate town of Sleepy Hollow to investigate a series of brutal murders, Crane arrives, appropriately enough at Halloween, and quickly learns that all the victims were beheaded and their bonces never found.

Ensconced in the home of Sleepy Hollow's finest, Baltus Van Tassel, Constable Crane is told the story of the Hessian Horseman (a pointy-toothed Christopher Walken) – a former German mercenary who specialised in decapitating the locals during the War of American Independence. It is his ghost – the Headless Horseman – whom the locals believe is responsible for the killings. Crane believes nothing of the sort – until he finds himself face to, well, neck with the demonic being. In between fainting with fear, leering with desire at the Van Tassels' daughter Katrina and several more attacks from the headless one, Crane begins to uncover the true story behind the town's killer ...

Always a filmmaker with an eye for eccentric visual detail, with *Sleepy Hollow* Tim Burton has produced what could be his most lavish film yet. Taking his love of the cheesier Hammer movies of yore, Burton, along with production designer Rick Heinrichs and the luminescent camerawork of Emmanuel Lubezki, has created a beautifully dark world, rich in shadows and swirling mist, full of dread. Limiting his palette to dark hues and earth tones, Burton gets maximum impact from the one primary colour he allows himself – blood red. And boy, does it flow when the Headless Horseman is in town.

Cast wise, Burton is well met by his on-screen alter ego Depp, who delivers a finely nuanced and entertaining turn as Ichabod. Ricci is elegant and as mysterious as she needs to be, while Gambon and Richardson – particularly the latter – get their teeth into just about all of the fine scenery on display. Veterans like Michael Gough, Richard Griffiths and *Star Wars'* Emperor-in-the-making Ian McDiarmid flesh out the background in fine style, whilst Burton veteran Jeffrey Jones' wig reminds us that Burton has not lost his touch for humour. Indeed, there's much to laugh at in *Sleepy Hollow* – some might argue a touch too much.

Yes, there are faults – Depp's fainting becomes a tad wearisome and the climax ups the melodrama factor to about 11 – but what remains is a beautiful slice of fear. This is Tim Burton's world – we should be grateful just to spend a couple of hours in it. ★★★★ **BM**

SLEUTH (1972)

Starring: *Laurence Olivier (Andrew Wyke), Michael Caine (Milo Tindle), Alec Cawthorne (Inspector Doppler), John Matthews (Det. Sergeant Tarrant), Eve Channing (Marguerite Wyke), Teddy Martin (Police Constable Higgs)*
Director: *Joseph L. Mankiewicz*
Screenwriter: *Anthony Shaffer, based on his play*
15/138 mins./Mystery/Thriller/USA

Andrew Wyke invites Milo Tindle to his home. Milo has been having an affair with Andrew's wife, and Andrew claims he is now happy to give Milo permission to marry her but really he wants to trick and humiliate Milo.

S

When Anthony Shaffer's play *Sleuth* opened in the West End starring Anthony Quayle and Keith Baxter, Laurence Olivier came backstage after seeing it to huff at Quayle, 'What are you doing in a piece of piss like this?' Funnily enough, several years later when he was asked to take the part on screen that Quayle had made famous, when Quayle was unavailable, he couldn't accept fast enough.

But by then *Sleuth* was recognised as offering him a part of award-winning potential. Indeed, Olivier gained both Oscar and BAFTA noms for the role but this was the year of *Godfather*, and an intense two-handed thriller never stood a chance against a mob of quote-happy gangsters.

Caine was also Oscar nominated (in a role originally intended for Alan Bates), as the 'jumped up pantry boy' who doesn't know his place, so marvellously entangled with Olivier's landed, bitter husband. Both manage to keep this claustrophobic mystery ticking over, playing off each other as the plot twists and turns without becoming too 'actorly'. For it soon becomes clear that each party is plotting death or social destruction for the other and are equally matched in their nasty game.

Director Joseph L. Mankiewicz enjoys the technical trickeries of disguising his limited cast – famously the other players were made up names to make the audience believe that there were more actors present than it first appeared. The house in which the action takes place is marvellously creepy – seemingly packed with glassy-eyed mannequins and portraits, and when the two men don masks themselves it becomes even more disturbing. ★★★★ **EC**

⓪ SLIDING DOORS (1998)

Starring: *Gwyneth Paltrow (Helen Quilley), John Hannah (James Hammerton), John Lynch (Gerry), Jeanne Tripplehorn (Lydia)*
Director: *Peter Howitt*
Screenwriter: *Peter Howitt*
15/95 mins./Drama/Romance/Comedy/USA/UK

Awards: *Empire Awards – Best British Director*

The two lives of London PR Helen are played out simultaneously based on whether she catches a tube train – or not.

For his first outing as director former actor Howitt (a.k.a. Joey in *Bread*) took the hopelessly romantic notion that one right love is out there, fated somehow to cross your path. Then he plays a clever game of 'what if?' with it, juggling one set of characters through two alternate plot lines of love, unprotected sex, lies and destiny.

Paltrow (refined English accent down pat) is London-based PR gal Helen, who arrives at work one day to be told she's sacked. Meanwhile, her would-be novelist lover Jerry is keeping their bed warm having duplicitous rumpy with the absurdly bitchy Lydia. Homeward bound early, Helen catches the Tube (just getting through those sliding doors), meets the charming James and arrives to catch Jerry with Lydia, a chain of events precipitating major changes for the better in Helen's life. Perhaps.

A reversal of time (and footage) leads into a parallel scenario in which the sliding doors slam in her face, Helen misses the train, doesn't meet James, and arrives home later, after Jerry's concealed the evidence of infidelity. The deceived Helen thus carries on, out of the loop, with bounder Jerry.

Sound tricky? It is, and all a little too cutely so, the switches back and forth between realities ever more contrived and eventually tiresome, prompting giggles of relief as the storylines painfully draw towards a soap operatic convergence. Thankfully, one Helen changes her hairstyle early on, so we know which universe we're in as the same people are forever rubbing shoulders in the same watering holes or just missing each other in Howitt's precision-cut scheme and interchangeable settings. No wonder the two Helens begin experiencing the woozy, déjà vu confusion of a new arrival in The Twilight Zone.

Paltrow and Hannah, who have the advantage of playing characters that are kind, funny and giving, are lovely. Lynch and Tripplehorn are not. Okay, we're not supposed to like them, but too much acquaintance with their laboured ghastliness drags the film down. There's also one serious fallacy here: nobody ever met a decent catch on the London Underground. But this should go down a storm with folks who still cherish the hope that the solution to all their problems is just around the corner or in the next lift. ★★★ **NJ**

⓪ SLING BLADE (1996)

Starring: *Billy Bob Thornton (Karl Childers), Dwight Yoakam (Doyle Hargraves), J.T. Walsh (Charles Bushman), John Ritter (Vaughan Cunningham), Lucas Black (Frank Wheatley), Natalie Canerday (Linda Wheatley)*
Director: *Billy Bob Thornton*
Screenwriter: *Billy Bob Thornton, based on his play*
15/129 mins./Drama/USA

Awards: *Academy Awards – Best Adapted Screenplay*

A lifer, surprised to be out of prison after 25 years, tries to rebuild his life in the town where he grew up but fears his past violent streak may resurface.

Astonishing. Both to watch, and to think that the film that won Billy Bob Thornton the 1997 Best Adapted Screenplay Oscar, took over a year to get a UK release.

Thornton, making his directorial debut, also stars as Karl, a simple-minded man who, after an extreme upbringing by zealous parents, has spent 25 years in an Arkansas psychiatric asylum for killing his mother and her lover with the titular lethal weapon. Judged to have been incarcerated long enough to make him well again, Karl is released. Completely institutionalised, he'd rather stay – but go he must and, having nowhere else to go, returns to his small-town home. There he immediately befriends a young boy, Frank, who introduces Karl to his widowed mother Linda and, reluctantly, to her (no) good-ol'-boy partner Doyle. Although a man of few words, Karl is a gifted mechanic and finds work, with the help of the asylum's director, then gets offered lodgings with Frank and his ma. But at the house he finds great conflict in the shape of Doyle's cruel rages against himself, Frank and his mom, and even Vaughan, a gay man Linda works with and confides in.

Filmed in muted colours yet populated by dazzling characters, this is an ensemble piece oozing quality. Country star Yoakam and Black (best known as Caleb in TV's chilling *American Gothic*) are both stand-outs playing bad-to-the-bone and innocent youth respectively. Canerday brings great heart to the naively kind mom, and Ritter immense strength to the bashful and outcast homosexual.

Around this core spin a dizzying array of bit-parts including J.T. Walsh as Karl's creepy fellow inmate, Christy Ward as his would-be date, a troupe of real musos downplaying as Doyle's buddies in the worst band in the world plus cameos from Robert Duvall as his father and Jim Jarmusch as the paper-hatted Mr. Frostee Cream man.

In the eye of this menacing and frequently hilarious maelstrom is the pivotal and gobsmacking performance of Thornton himself – transformed into a stooped and grimacing cross between Charlie Chaplin and Private Pile, with a voice like Popeye – as a man whose inherent goodness (and love for French-fried 'taters) is balanced by the threat of extreme violence.

Behind the camera Thornton turns oddballs into heroes, behind the script he makes a very simple tale work on so many levels – as morality play, as black comedy, and hard-hitting social commentary. His screenplay will scare you. It will make you laugh and cry. And it will make you think long and hard about the last time you saw a movie this good. ★★★★★ **NJ**

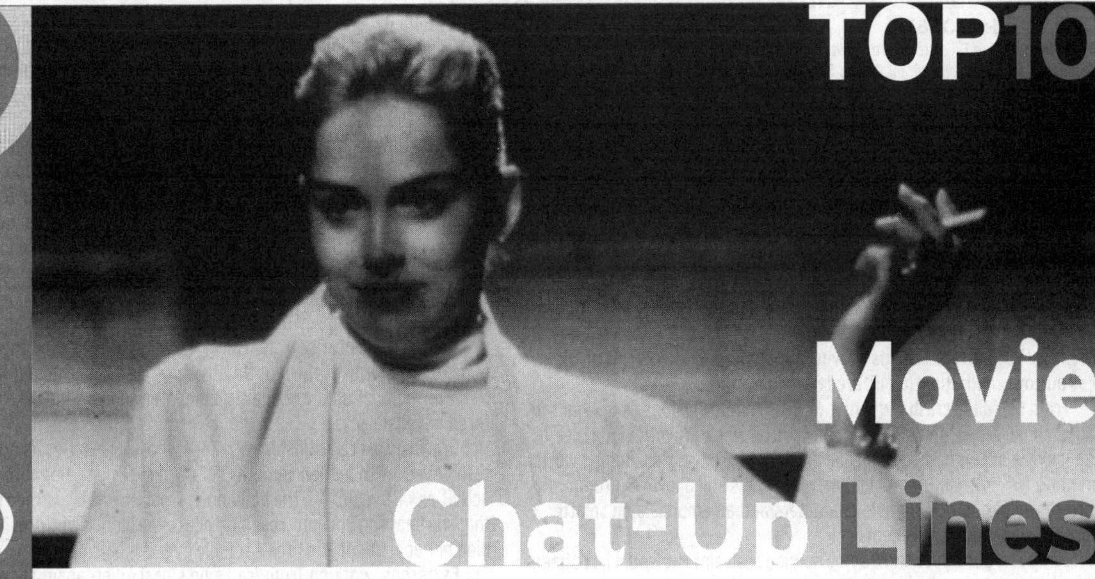

1 **'I've got a head for business and a body for sin.' (Tess McGill, *Working Girl*)**

2 **'I'm hung like a horse. Think about it.' (Mike Swale, *The Last Seduction*)**

3 **'You make me want to be a better man.' (Melvin Udall, *As Good As It Gets*)**

4 **'You're not too smart, are you? I like that in a man.' (Matty Walker, *Body Heat*)**

5 **'Do you want to dance? Or do you want to *dance*?' (Thomas Crown, *The Thomas Crown Affair*)**

6 **'How would you like to have a sexual experience so intense it could conceivably change your political views?' (Gibbs, *The Sure Thing*)**

7 **'Have you ever fucked on cocaine, Nick? It's nice.' (Catherine Tramell, *Basic Instinct*)**

8 **'I'm very important. I have many leather-bound books and my apartment smells of rich mahogany.' (Ron Burgundy, *Anchorman: The Legend Of Ron Burgundy*)**

9 **'You know how to whistle, don't you, Steve? You just put your lips together and blow.' (Slim, *To Have and Have Not*)**

10 **'I really feel, uh, in short, to recap it slightly in a clearer version, uh, the words of David Cassidy in fact, uh, while he was still with the Partridge family, I think I love you, and I-I just wondered by any chance you wouldn't like to... Um... No, no, no of course not... I'm an idiot, he's not... Excellent, excellent, fantastic, eh, I was gonna say lovely to see you, sorry to disturb... Better get on...' (Charles, *Four Weddings and a Funeral*)**

SLITHER (2006)

Starring: *Nathan Fillion (Bill Pardy), Elizabeth Banks (Starla Grant), Gregg Henry (Jack MacReady), Michael Rooker (Grant Grant), Don Thompson (Wally)*
Director: *James Gunn*
Screenwriter: *James Gunn*
15/96 mins./Horror/Comedy/USA

The slumbering Southern town of Wheelsy becomes the focal point of an alien invasion when an extraterrestrial parasite crashes to Earth and possesses the town bully. As the alien's spawn turns the townsfolk into zombies, chief of police Bill Pardy sets out to turn the tide.

Dawn Of The Dead remake scribe James Gunn returns to the zombie genre for his directorial debut. But where *Dawn* was the rejuvenation of a seminal 70s horror, *Slither* is a loving nod to the shoddy charms of countless bottom-shelf titles that littered 80s video stores.

From the initial crash sequence, we're under no illusions as to what's in store: slime, blood, phlegm and gore, splattered about with giddy glee as the movie wallows in the primordial muck of its DTV origins. But it's worth pointing out that, self-aware as it may be, this is still a low-rent romp with throwaway plot, stock B-movie characters and an emphasis on splatter – hardly a giant leap for the genre.

However, Gunn does show some needed restraint – it would have been easy to blow his budget on unwarranted post-production. Instead, the director uses CGI only to enhance the horrific mutations he's created, relying on acres of dripping, fleshy prosthetic to carry the monster's share of effects and making the horror all the more visceral (and faithful) for it.

Entrails and appendages make up only one part of *Slither*'s appeal, though. While Michael Rooker's shambling horde takes over the town and increasingly disgusting mutants go on the offensive (watch out for the killer deer!), Gunn underwrites the carnage with a parched sense of humour that provokes barking belly laughs to off-set the offal. A string of artfully delivered one-liners and deftly handled exchanges crackle through the script, the (quite intentional) comedy not only adding substance but hoisting *Slither* above its schlocky source material.

It's no surprise that the majority of laughs are ably captured by Fillion, showing off the knack for deadpan delivery previously tapped by Joss Whedon in *Serenity*. As Pardy, he fills out the role of an unlikely hero dealing with extraordinary events, bringing bumbling affability to a part that could so easily have been lost to square jaws, steely eyes and other clumsy stereotypes.

Tipping its hat at everything from the original *Puppet Masters* to bargain-bin trash like Ted Nicolaou's *TerrorVision*, *Slither* is a carefully crafted parody (the *Predator* nod in particular will bring a smile to your face). But this is the scalpel to the *Scary Movie* series' bludgeoning sledgehammer, skirting cheap imitation in favour of affectionate irreverence and managing to produce a genre hybrid that's far more than the sum of its pilfered parts. ★★★★ **JDY**

SLIVER (1993)

Starring: *Sharon Stone (Carly Norris), William Baldwin (Zeke Hawkins), Tom Berenger (Jack Landsford), Polly Walker (Vida Warren), Colleen Camp (Judy Marks), Martin Landau (Alex Parsons)*
Director: *Phillip Noyce*
Screenwriter: *Joe Eszterhas, based on the novel by Ira Levin*
18/103 mins./Erotic/Thriller/USA

Recently divorced Carly Norris moves into her new apartment in upstate New York. As Carly begins a steamy relationship with computer obsessed Zeke, she discovers that the building has seen a number of mysterious and gruesome deaths. What's more, she thinks she might be next.

Following its post-production furore – last minute reshoots, censorship wrangles over Baldwin's todger – *Sliver* emerged as a film sadly lacking in both sauce and thrills. Not a bad film exactly, just a clinical, inaccessible one, directed with impersonal efficiency by Phillip Noyce (*The Bone Collector, Dead Calm*).

The main problem lies with Joe Eszterhas's script, which reworks themes from his earlier efforts – *Basic Instinct, Jagged Edge*, et al. – as well as a good portion of Michael Powell's classic *Peeping Tom*, into an incoherent tale about voyeurism and murder that trades on our expectations but does little to fulfil them, rounded off by an ending which, altered following its disastrous US preview screenings, undermines all that's gone before.

Carly Norris, a newly divorced literary editor who takes an apartment in a Manhattan high-rise – the 'sliver' building of the title – the scene of a number of recent, mysterious deaths. Carly then finds herself flattered by the attentions of fellow residents: computer games whiz Zeke and embittered novelist Jack.

Drawn into a relationship with Zeke who, it transpires, is not only a hi-tech voyeur with hidden cameras set up in every apartment to record the activities within but also the building's owner, Norris is alarmed to discover that she bears an uncanny resemblance to the blonde who previously occupied her apartment and took a tumble over the balcony.

Eszterhas, working from Ira Levin's bestseller, again shows his 'gift' for dialogue – 'it's worse than anal intercourse' – trotting out another round of sexual clichés and murky intrigue, never once drawing back the psychological curtain to probe the protagonists' psyches and wasting the endless possibilities offered up by Zeke's prying pursuit. Stone, however, with much to prove after *Basic Instinct*, is an engagingly edgy heroine, better clothed than naked, but Baldwin's anonymous Zeke fails to convince as either a psycho, prince or pervert. Not awful, just dull. ★★ **MS**

SMALL CHANGE (L'ARGENT DE POCHE) (1976)

Starring: *Geory Desmouceaux (Patrick), Phillippe Goldman (Julien), Claudio Deluca (Mathieu Deluca), Frank Deluca (Franck), Richard Golfier (Richard), Laurent Devlaeminck (Laurent Riffle), Bruno Staab (Bruno Rouilliard)*
Director: *François Truffaut*
Screenwriters: *François Truffaut, Suzanne Schiffman*
PG/105 mins./Comedy/Drama/France

While their classmates get on with the everyday business of growing up, Patrick has to cope with a disabled father and an overwhelming desire to savour his first kiss, while Julien turns to petty crime as an escape from the brutality of life in his cramped shack of a home.

Throughout his career, François Truffaut had a habit of alternating consciously contrasting films and this episodic study of childhood couldn't have been more different from the period intensity of *L'Histoire d'Adèle H.* He had originally intended to explore classroom life without focusing on any particular characters. But, despite a determination to improvise as much as possible and recreate the free-wheeling spirit of *Day for Night*, the final film proved rather more conventional, as Patrick and Julien emerged as the centre of attention.

Moreover, Truffaut indulged himself by returning to themes that he had already explored in *Les Mistons, Les Quatre Cents Coups* and *The Wild Child*, most notably the notion that youth exists in a 'state of grace' and that while it's good for kids to develop a certain toughness, they will become irrevocably hardened unless they are cherished.

Autobiographical elements stipple the action, particularly where Patrick and Julien are concerned. Each is missing a parent (a recurring

Truffaut theme) and both find solace in literature and cinema (as Truffaut himself had done). But while Patrick seeks compensation for the neglect of his disabled father in both a surrogate mother and a tweenage crush, Julien's beatings at the hands of his mother and grandmother turn him into a loner, who (in the manner of Antoine Doinel) resorts to petty crime in order to survive.

Yet Julien's fate is very much the exception here, as the baby who falls from the window while chasing a kitten manages to land safely in a bush, while the girl left home alone makes impudent use of a megaphone both to expose her parents' cruelty and demand some supper. Indeed, Truffaut tended to rose-tint many of the vignettes in his bid to demonstrate the wit, resourcefulness, vulnerability and strength of youth. But if he's occasionally guilty of sentiment and whimsicality, he makes shrewd use of his Thiers locations and coaxes wonderfully natural performances from an adolescent cast that included his own daughters, Eva and Laura. ★★★★ **DP**

SMALL SOLDIERS (1998)

Starring: *Gregory Smith (Alan Abernathy), Kristen Dunst (Christy Fimple), Dennis Leary (Gil Mars), Tommy Lee Jones (Major Chip Hazard)*
Director: *Joe Dante*
Screenwriters: *Gavin Scott, Adam Rifkin, Ted Elliott, Terry Rossio*
PG/105 mins./Action/Sci-fi/Fantasy/Comedy/USA

A group of toy soldiers, programmed to kill, go on the rampage in a small town.

Small Soldiers falls awkwardly between the two main categories – too frightening for younger kids, too childish for adults. Nevertheless, there is still much to enjoy.

The setting is (surprise!) an idyllic looking small town, in this case Winslow, Ohio. There a teen delinquent takes delivery of a shipment of voice-activated Action Man-style toys – the army-fatigued Commandos and the gentle Gorgonites – to sell in his dad's plaything emporium. But unknown to Alan, the toys have been fitted with munitions chips – thanks to a spot of tampering on the part of toy company worker Larry Cross. Led by he-man Chip Hazard (voiced by Tommy Lee Jones), the Commandos (lent vocal power by the surviving cast members of the Dirty Dozen bar Charles Bronson) come to life, break out of their boxes and go in search of the Gorgonites.

The subsequent levels of damage caused by the shin-high plastic figures is staggering, especially when they target Alan, his would-be girlfriend Christy and their parents simply for the crime of apparently 'siding' with the Gorgonites (vocalised by the Spinal Tap cast) after Alan rescues their genial leader Archer.

Small Soldiers comes across as a toy shop, rather than pet shop, version of *Gremlins*, and one with a great premise rapidly drowned in a sea of computerised mayhem. The set pieces, while unnecessarily unpleasant at times (Christy is set upon by her own dolls in one spectacularly vicious scene) are hugely well staged. Stan Winston's grotesquely ugly animatronic figures fit seamlessly with the CGI and live action, no more so than in a finale which sees thousands of pint-sized militia men converging on the neighbourhood.

Dunst and Smith make for blandly appealing teen romantics but of the adults only a cameo from Denis Leary as a military magnate, and the late Phil Hartman (in his last role) as Christy's gadget-hungry dad raise much interest.

Yet for all its shortcomings, the end result is quite entertaining. It may be another blockbuster over-reliant on its special effects, but thanks to its excellent visuals and semblance of a story, *Small Soldiers* works considerably better than some. ★★★ **CW**

SMALL TIME CROOKS (2000)

Starring: *Woody Allen (Ray), Carolyn Saxon (Candy Salesperson), Tracey Ullman (Frenchy), Michael Rapaport (Denny), Tony Darrow (Tommy)*
Director: *Woody Allen*
Screenwriter: *Woody Allen*
PG/94 mins./Comedy/Crime/USA

Inveterate dreamer and bungling crook Lenny persuades wife Frenchy to front a cookie bake shop while his gang use the premises to tunnel into a bank. The robbery's a bust, but Frenchy's munchy morsels make their fortune. The new challenge is breaking into society with their cookie dough.

Unlike so many humorists who repeat themselves, there seems to be no end to Woody Allen's inspiration for unexpected and laugh-out-loud funniness, both visual and verbal.

This sweet, very light-hearted caper has a basic plot that couldn't really be much simpler: lowbrow losers come into money, crash high society, and wind up learning what they really value. The joy in their tale is in its goofy twists, marvellously sketched characters and wall-to-wall wisecracks (from the minute Lenny answers his wife's 'Who's there?' with 'It's the Pope. I've always wanted to see your apartment!' to the final parting shot).

Allen's character, ex-con Lenny, a dishwasher with delusions, is a complete hoot. Grant's charmer who ultimately proves to be a snake deftly teases his image of stammering adorability. But the genius element here is the women.

Ullman's Frenchy, former exotic dancer and manicurist, is a creature of breathtaking vulgarity but immense likeability, as she embarks on her spend spend spend spree, undertakes to improve herself by memorising the dictionary and engages Grant's smarmy Brit to teach her some culture and polish. Allen rightly revels in her performance, but for good measure rediscovers the awesome comic talent of May (who, before she became a director, was Mike Nichols' partner in a legendary satirical stand-up duo some 40 years ago) as the daffy, slow, somewhat literally minded poor relation who upstages them all.

Small Time Crooks has no pretensions to being anything other than a cute wheeze of an urban fairy-tale, with a 'be careful what you wish for' punchline. As such, it doesn't bother to concern itself with the Zeitgeist; it's simply cracking good fun. ★★★★ **AE**

SMILE (1975)

Starring: *Bruce Dern ('Big Bob' Freelander), Barbara Feldon (Brenda DiCarlo), Michael Kidd (Tommy French), Geoffrey Lewis (Wilson Shears), Doria Houston (Annette O'Toole), Melanie Griffith (Karen Love)*
Director: *Michael Ritchie*
Screenwriter: *Jerry Belson*
Unrated/112 mins./Comedy/USA

The California finals of the Young American Miss contest are held in Santa Rosa. Big Bob Freelander, chairman of the judges, has a trying week, and almost comes to question the values of the pageant.

One of the best 'unknown' movies of the 1970s. For a while, director Michael Ritchie was competing with Robert Altman in delivering multi-character satires of American institutions, though his later career (*The Golden Child*, *Fletch*) tended to obscure his earlier, quality work.

Smile touches some obvious bases later covered by *Drop Dead Gorgeous* (conniving and scheming contestants, lechery dressed up as patriotism, ghastly amateur 'talent' displays) but is more truthful, strange and unexpected, managing to be cynical and heartwarming at the same time. Bruce Dern, cast against his psycho image as an all-round booster for the pageant, is hilarious in many uncomfortable scenes; his finest acting hour might well be a sequence in which he takes his young son, caught snapping polaroids of

S

the girls in the changing rooms, to a psychiatrist, then starts squirming as he realises the shrink sees there's more wrong with him than the kid.

There are hilarious monsters among the contestants, especially Maria O'Brien as a Mexican-American who tries to seduce judges with guacamole dip and a fake accent, but Ritchie gives the girls points for at least being honestly ambitious, and a sweet relationship grows between uncertain Joan Prather and her more confident roommate (Annette O'Toole).

Watch also for: Barbara Feldon's embalmed den mother, Michael Kidd as the 'Hollywood choreographer' appalled at what he's doing, Geoffrey Lewis's double-crossing local businessman, Nicholas Pryor as the only man in town who thinks there's something wrong about dressing up in clan robes and kissing a dead chicken's ass, and a very fresh Melanie Griffith as the girl in the polaroid. ★★★★★ **KN**

SMILES OF A SUMMER NIGHT (SOMMARNATTENS LEENDE) (1955)

Starring: *Ulla Jacobsson (Anne Egerman), Eva Dahlbeck (Desiree Armfeldt), Margit Carlqvist (Charlotte Malcolm), Harriet Andersson (Petra The Maid), Gunner Bjornstrand (Fredrik Egerman), Jarl Kulle (Count Malcolm), Ake Fridell (Fid The Groom)*
Director: *Ingmar Bergman*
Screenwriter: *Ingmar Bergman*
PG/108 mins./Comedy/Sweden

Lawyer Fredrik Egerman and his virginal wife Anne attend a house party thrown by his ex-mistress Desiree Armfeldt, who is currently involved with Count Malcolm, whose wife, Charlotte, makes a play for Egerman, while Anne finds solace in his son, Henrik.

Ingmar Bergman produced his most successful screen comedy despite being weighed down by money troubles, stomach pains and a dwindling romance with Harriet Andersson. He later said that had he not made this picture his only other option would have been suicide. But such despair is scarcely evident in this charming period roundelay, which was filmed in 55 days during a heatwave and represented Bergman's most expensive film to date.

The consistently shifting action bore traces of Shakespeare's *A Midsummer Night's Dream*, the farces of Molière and Marivaux, Mozart's operas *The Marriage of Figaro* and *The Magic Flute*, and such films as Mauritz Stiller's *Erotikon* and Jean Renoir's *La Règle du Jeu*. Yet, Bergman still managed to explore such pet themes as the nature and longevity of love and the problem of identity, while the fluidity of his camerawork suggested a growing maturity and confidence that further manifested itself in the astute manner with which he used each coupling to comment on a particular aspect of love.

However, this was as much a satire on class as a romantic comedy. Indeed, its equation of status with lust (whether repressed or luxuriated in) echoed Luis Buñuel's views on the matter, especially where Egerman and Malcolm were concerned – with the latter being more concerned with putting his bourgeois rival in his place than in keeping his mistress.

Indeed, only Petra the maid and Frid the groom surrender fully to their passions, although as an actress (and therefore a social outsider) Desiree is also allowed to know what she wants and go after it. Charlotte also seems in tune with her physical needs, but she turns out to find sex as disgusting as the virginal Anne discovers it to be thrilling, albeit with her stepson, whose high romantic ideals and theological inclinations are gleefully surrendered to illicit passion.

With its beautiful baroque designs, sublime Gunnar Fischer photography and assured ensemble playing, this is an intricate, lyrical and surprisingly bawdy study of elegant carnality that deserves to rank among Bergman's finest achievements. ★★★★ **DP**

SMOKE (1995)

Starring: *Harvey Keitel (Augustus 'Auggie' Wren), Jared Harris (Jimmy Rose), William Kurt (Paul Benjamin, Novelist), Forest Whitaker (Cyrus Cole), Stockard Channing (Ruby McNutt)*
Director: *Wayne Wang*
Screenwriter: *Paul Auster, from his short story* Auggie Wren's Christmas Story
15/107 mins./Drama/USA

The story of a small community that congregates around a Brooklyn cigar shop.

'You might call it a hobby,' suggests Auggie, manager of the Brooklyn Cigar Co. corner shop. He refers not to his stogies, but to his daily photographic snapshots of Brooklyn life. Which nicely frames the whole concept of this film and the partner with which it was released – *Blue In The Face* – both written by Paul Auster, both directed by Wayne Wang and both conversation-driven ensemble pieces starring Keitel.

Smoke traces the interlocking lives of writer William Hurt (a character loosely based on Auster), Auggie's one-time lover Stockard Channing, teenage runaway Harold Perrineau Jr. and his estranged father Forest Whitaker – each one playing with a rotten hand dealt to them by a fluke twist off the deck of fate. The stories and characters are engrossing, the accents delicious and the slice-of-life action totally irresistible.

Smoke picked up a string of international awards including the Silver Bear, but perhaps the prestigious prize of all was the MTV Movie Award for Best Sandwich in a Movie, proving once and for all that a good Ham & Cheese on white can't be beaten. ★★★★★ **NJ**

SNATCH (2000)

Starring: *Jason Statham (Turkish), Brad Pitt (Mickey O'Neil), Dennis Farina (Abraham 'Cousin Avi' Denovitz), Robbie Gee (Vincent), Lennie James (Sol), Vinnie Jones (Bullet Tooth Tony), Benicio Del Toro (Franky Four Fingers), Mike Reid (Doug 'The Head' Denovitz), Jason Flemyng (Darren)*
Director: *Guy Ritchie*
Screenwriter: *Guy Ritchie*
18/102 mins./Comedy/Crime/Thriller/UK/USA

Awards: *Empire Awards – Best British Actor (Vinnie Jones), Best British Director*

Intertwining stories about a boxing match, a mob plot and a diamond heist.

Guy Ritchie is Quentin Tarantino. Young, visionary writer-director makes big splash with debut feature: a cheap, stylised crime caper that meshes snappy dialogue with excessive gun-play and a hip soundtrack. But what did Tarantino do after *Reservoir Dogs*? Did he greedily oversee a spin-off TV series that subtracted from the magic of his own film? No. And for the all-important follow-up, did he remake *Reservoir Dogs*? No. But that, in effect, is what Ritchie has done with *Snatch*. This should have been – but isn't – his *Pulp Fiction*.

Those who remain unmoved by *Lock, Stock And Two Smoking Barrels* usually write off its creator as all style, no soul. These people are mad – it is a magnificent piece of entertainment, and the legion of pale Brit-flick imitators that have come in its wake only serve to highlight its unique swagger. Ritchie is stylised: as a director he's unsurprisingly prone to every pop-video camera trick in the box, and as a writer he's almost pantomime. In terms of this heavily-stamped trademark style, *Snatch* is identical to *Lock, Stock*. Fair enough. But it's also identical in terms of plot, structure, subject, pace and setting. Four of the cast recur – Statham, Jones, Ford and, in cameo, Jason Flemyng – yet Ritchie has taken care to cast them in new roles. Why bother? *Snatch* would have been a more honest not-sequel if it had been the further adventures of Big Chris. Instead, Jones does the same scene-stealing schtick under a new name – including some self-referential door-slamming. Who are they trying to kid?

Sure, Ritchie's added Yardies, Jews, Americans and Gypsies to the pan-criminal mix, replaced cards with boxing and antique rifles with a diamond, but it's more like a remix than a remake, with Yanks Dennis Farina and Benicio Del Toro thrown in for cross-pond appeal.

That said, if you liked *Lock, Stock*, you'll like this. The turns are superb (and their uniformity is a credit to Ritchie's 'happy family' style of film-making); Statham makes an engaging lead; Alan Ford (who narrated *Lock, Stock* so perfectly) is *Long Good Friday* threatening and gets the script's best 'caant!'; while Pitt pitches his indecipherable 'pikey' just right, drawing on the physicality of *Fight Club*, the insanity of *Twelve Monkeys* and the dodgy accent of *The Devil's Own*. Plus, it's a treat to see *EastEnders*' Mike Reid off the Square, and Vinnie, of course, has become a draw in his own right.

So even though *Snatch* is almost actionably similar to *Lock, Stock*, for many that will be its selling point. ★★★ **AC**

SNEAKERS (1992)

Starring: *Robert Redford (Martin Bishop), Dan Aykroyd ('Mother'), Ben Kingsley (Cosmo), Sidney Poitier (Crease), Mary McDonnell (Liz), David Straithairn (Whistler), James Earl Jones (Bernard Abbott)*
Director: *Phil Alden Robinson*
Screenwriters: *Phil Alden Robinson, Lawrence Lasker, Walter F. Parkes*
15/120 mins./Comedy/Thriller/USA

A team of computer hackers go after a decoding device belonging to a Russian scientist.

Apart from seeing Robert Redford in a role similar to those he made his name by (cool charmer in hot water), the good news here is that *Sneakers* is among the cleverest caper comedy-thriller of the 90s. First conceived by Phil Alden, Robinson and *War Games* writers Lawrence Lasker and Walter F. Parkes as a high-tech *Dirty Dozen*, this emerges as a very neatly plotted blend of elaborate heist and twisting thriller, peppered with amusing gags and smart one-liners for its top class ensemble.

The scene is set in the late 60s, when a pair of young pioneer computer hackers play student activist pranks like switching Republican Party funds into a Black Panther account, after which one is nabbed in an FBI raid, and the other escapes and goes on the run, ending up twentysome years later as Robert Redford's Martin Bishop, still living under an assumed identity and heading a state-of-the-art security and surveillance team of marvellous oddballs – the Sneakers of the title.

Dan Aykroyd's gadget master 'Mother' is a hilariously paranoid 60s relic who attributes even earthquakes to political conspirators; Sidney Poitier's voice of reason is ex-CIA; the late River Phoenix is the punk computer genius; and David Strathairn is a standout as a blind audiotronics wizard dubbed 'Whistler'.

At a tidy pace the famous five are set up in an ingenious round of blackmail, theft, covert operations, murder and disorganised crime as they set about nicking a top secret decoding gizmo from a dissident Russian scientist. Add Mary McDonnell as Martin's ex-girlfriend roped in for Mata Hari shenanigans, a pony-tailed Ben Kingsley as a megalomaniac criminal mastermind and San Francisco locations that are actually fresh, and you have a scam that is enormously entertaining, quite gripping and a fun-filled Valentine to cyberpunks and computer hackers everywhere. ★★★★ **AE**

SNOW WHITE AND THE SEVEN DWARVES (1937)

Starring: the voices of (uncredited): *Adriana Caselotti (Snow White), Harry Stockwell (Prince), Lucille La Verne (Queen), Roy Atwell (Doc), Pinto Colvig (Grumpy), Eddie Collins (Dopey), Billy Gilbert (Happy), Scotty Mattraw (Bashful), Moroni Olsen (Magic Mirror)*
Director: *David Hand*
Screenwriters: *Ted Sears, Richard Creedon, Otto Englander, Dick Rickard, Earl Hurd, Merrill De Maris, Dorothy Ann Blank, Webb Smith*
U/81 mins./Animation/Family/Musical/Fantasy/USA

Awards: *Academy Awards – Honorary Award (Walt Disney)*

The beautiful Snow White lives with her stepmother the Queen, but when the Queen realises Snow White's beauty eclipses her own, she banishes Snow White to the woods to be killed. But Snow White runs away and finds refuge in a house belonging to seven dwarves.

In 1917 a fifteen-year-old newsboy attended a screening of the silent film *Snow White And The Seven Dwarves* starring Marguerite Clark. In 1939 that same newsboy picked up an Honorary Academy Award (and seven miniature ones) for pioneering a new entertainment field. Walt Disney's imagination, so inspired by that silent film, had grown to invent the first feature-length animated film and even today it stands up as a monument to ingenious storytelling and technical achievement.

Disney must have felt smug standing on that stage to accept an award for what, for the three years of the film's production, had been referred to as his 'folly'. But his idea of taking a familiar tale and making it come alive in a way not possible through traditionally live-action filming – and in colour too – turned out to be nothing short of genius. In his first animated feature he also managed to design a template for every future animated movie which few substantially veered from – an adorable heroine, a genuinely scary baddie, comic sidekicks, a smattering of memorable songs and a pacey story.

What is surprising is how scary the scary bits are – the run for the woods is still the stuff of nightmares, more powerfully realised through the unique multi-plane animation used. The songs – 'Whistle While You Work', 'Heigh-Ho', 'Some Day My Prince Will Come' – are just as hummable as they ever were and who hasn't wished that a forest full of woodland animals would come and do their housework?

Get hold of the special edition DVD if you can, the extras on the 'making of' are really illuminating and serve as a reminder that this isn't just one of the finest films ever made, but one of the most incredible pieces of cinema history too. ★★★★★ **EC**

Movie Trivia: Snow White And The Seven Dwarfs

So convinced were they that the movie would fail, Hollywood tagged the film as 'Disney's Folly'. It was the first film to have a separate soundtrack released. Other dwarf contenders for the final seven were Biggy, Dirty, Blabby, Jumpy, Nifty and Shifty. Pinto Colvig, who was the voice of Sleepy and Grumpy, is most well known for supplying the voice of Goofy.

SOCIETY (1989)

Starring: *Billy Warlock (Bill Whitney), Devlin Devasquez (Clarisa), Evan Richards (Milo), Ben Meyerson (Ted Ferguson), Charles Lucia (Jim), Connie Danese (Nan)*
Director: *Brian Yuzna*
Screenwriters: *Woody Keith, Rick Fry*
18/94 mins./Horror/USA

Bill, adopted son of a monied California family, discovers that his parents

and sister aren't entirely human, and that he is liable to be sacrificed in an appalling rite before he is out of his teens.

One of the most extraordinary horror films of the 1980s, this finds Brian Yuzna, producer of Stuart Gordon's *Re-Animator*, taking over the megaphone for an unclassifiable fable that, like John Carpenter's *They Live*, proposes that rich people are literally inhuman.

When his sister's boyfriend produces a tape recording of a bizarrely suggestive conversation intimating that her coming-out party turned into an incestuous orgy, young hero Billy Warlock tells the psychiatrist that he is feeling increasingly estranged from all those people who want him 'to make a contribution to society'.

In an almost indescribable extended finale, Bill crashes a social event and discovers the Los Angeles elite performing a bizarrely sexual ritual involving shape-shifting, plentiful slime, grotesque physical unions, po-faced pronouncements about the individual's responsibility to 'society', and torturous duels.

'The rich have always sucked off low-class shit like you,' his sister's boyfriend tells him, while the cigar-smoking, slime-covered Judge explains 'you're a different race from us, a different species, a different class … you have to be born into society.'

With a credit for 'surrealistic make-up effects' for a technician who calls himself Screaming Mad George, *Society* goes as far – and indeed further than you would think – as is possible for a BBFC-certificated movie. Flesh is twisted into surreal shapes and people are literally turned inside out, as the film segues from *The Graduate* into Gustave Doré, presenting ichorous horrors far more imaginative than the tame throat-slashings of Jason and company. Despite Warlock's callow haircut of a performance, this is a remarkable, unusual and challenging film that genuinely stretches the horror genre into new areas. And it's probably true. ★★★★ **KN**

◑ SOLARIS (1972)

Starring: *Natalya Bondarchuk (Hari), Donatas Banionis (Kris Kelvin), Juri Jarvet (Dr. Snaut), Vladislav Dvorzhetsky (Berton), Nikolai Grinko (Kelvin's Father), Anatoli Solonitsyn (Dr. Sarorius)*
Director: *Andrei Tarkovsky*
Screenwriters: *Fridrikh Gorenshtein, Andrei Tarkovsky, based on the novel by Stanislaw Lem*
PG/165mins./Drama/Sci-fi/Soviet Union

Cosmonaut Kris Kelvin is sent to a space station orbiting around the living planet Solaris, where Earthmen are visited by beings who take the form of absent loved ones. Kelvin is confronted by a creature which looks like his dead wife Hari.

Based on a novel by the Polish writer Stanislaw Lem and directed by Andrei Tarkovsky, *Solaris* was widely seen as a Soviet answer to *2001: A Space Odyssey*. Like the Kubrick-Clarke film, it has an enigmatic Earthbound prologue, follows a scientist to a space outpost affected by an alien intelligence, and concludes with an apparent return to Earth which actually finds the hero in a recreation of his home created by unknowable alien powers. There's even a direct reference: one of the cosmonauts who has come back alive from Solaris claims to have seen a giant infant floating in its sentient seas.

The film is less interested in rocketships and spacesuits than 2001, and goes against the prevailing clichés of Western science fiction by depicting – well before *Dark Star* or *Alien* – a space station which is a mess of exposed wires, hasty repair jobs and absent-mindedly strewn clutter, inhabited by stir-crazy neurotics who are no longer sure what reality is and dream only of being buried on Earth. Once the hero's dead wife manifests, it follows the reverse of the usual human-and-alien-duplicate relationship: at first, Kelvin treats Hari like a monster, tricking her into a probe he shoots into space, then he tries to use her to get through to the thinking planet itself, and finally he wonders whether being the physical form of his memories rather than the woman herself isn't still enough to love. Long and deliberately-paced (like 2001), it gets repetitive in its mid-section, but is full of stunning images and moments. The last shot is justly famous. ★★★★ **KN**

◑ SOLARIS (2002)

Starring: *George Clooney (Chris Kelvin), Natascha McElhone (Rheya), Viola Davis (Gordon), Jeremy Davis (Snow), Ulrich Tukur (Gibarian)*
Director: *Steven Soderbergh*
Screenwriter: *Steven Soderbergh, based on the novel by Stanislaw Lem*
12/94 mins./Drama/Romance/Sci-fi/USA

Psychologist Chris Kelvin is sent to a space station orbiting the planet Solaris. One crew member has committed suicide; the others are suffering from acute paranoia. Then Kelvin's dead wife, Rheya, appears in living form – the latest 'visitor' sent by Solaris to confront the humans' feelings of guilt and remorse.

A fast-cut trailer, a glossy poster, a big-spend marketing campaign … Hollywood has plenty of tricks up its sleeve to sell audiences something that isn't actually there. Such was the case in the US with *Solaris*. It's George Clooney. It's Steven Soderbergh, hot off the back-to-back successes of *Ocean's 11*, *Traffic* and *Erin Brockovich*.

But *Solaris* is really a slow, meditative psychodrama set on a space station. Sensing box-office disaster, 20th Century Fox decided to mis-sell the movie as a sci-fi love story. The crowds came but, understandably, left angry and confused. Positive word-of-mouth was zero. The film died.

Solaris also comes burdened with another weight of expectation, albeit from an entirely different direction. Based on a novel by Stanislaw Lem, an earlier version was made in 1972 by Russian director Andrei Tarkovsky. His is a ponderous piece of art cinema, much beloved by film masochists for whom no work can be too slow, no detail too painstaking. This critically obsessive audience isn't exactly going to warm to the idea of someone who used to be an incurable Casanova in a TV hospital soap soiling their original, much-loved masterpiece.

None of this does Soderbergh any favours. And so, quite correctly, he just went out and made the movie he wanted to make.

Solaris is a measured piece in a classic filmmaking style. The content of every shot is carefully constructed, while every cut is timed to the exact millisecond. Music is used sparingly, and at times only rainfall or machine noise quietly fills the soundtrack. This is how Soderbergh subtly sets the scene in order to ask big questions about life, love, predetermination, religion and free will.

Solaris is proper, grown-up science-fiction – an attempt to examine some of the major philosophical issues of the present day by setting them in a recognisable future. No lightsabers or alien wars here. Instead, the space station design is functionally minimalist, and the planet – cloudy blues and pinks threaded with darker veins and electrical lines – like a huge colour scan of a human brain. Soderbergh leaves room in the movie's running time to allow audiences to think and feel. It's not an all-out barrage on the senses, but rather a delicate study of human grief that really does encourage us to examine our place in the universe.

As such, it's surprisingly – but genuinely – moving, driven by stellar, understated performances from Clooney and McElhone. The film acknowledges the complexity of their marriage, of his feelings of guilt, of her return to 'life'. Clearly Rheya's reappearance is, emotionally, a double-edged sword – perhaps it can be more painful to regain the thing you've lost than to lose it in the first place.

As the film touches on imaginary childhood friends or the relationship between a being and its 'higher power' creator, it becomes psychologically, rather than narratively, compelling. This may not be the film everyone was expecting from Soderbergh and Clooney, but it's a major landmark in their ongoing collaboration. ★★★★ **DHu**

◑ SOLDIER (1998)

Starring: *Kurt Russell (Todd), Jason Scott Lee (Caine 607), Connie Nielson (Sandra), Gary Busey (Captain Church), Jason Issacs (Colonel Mekum), Sean Pertwee (Mace)*
Director: *Paul Anderson*
Screenwriter: *David Webb Peoples*
18/94 mins./Sci-fi/Action/Thriller/USA

A career soldier defends a band of low-lifes from the genetically-engineered troops who have replaced him in the army.

Kurt Russell occupies an unsatisfying position in the Hollywood firmament. A sort of hard Jeff Bridges, he is nobody's favourite actor of all-time, and yet has some solid work behind him (*Backdraft*, *Breakdown*, *The Thing*, *The Fox And The Hound*). However, agreeing to star in low-grade filler like *Soldier* does him no long-term favours. His one consolation is that so few people saw it in American cinemas and even fewer saw it in the straight-to-video release in the UK.

Ditching the bloke-next-door persona for a near-roboticised, near-mute combat übermensch some 40 years in the future, Russell gets to show off the fruits of his work-out regime – but not a lot else.

He is Todd 3465, a soldier trained from birth as part of the Adam Project to obey orders and kill without concession (in an opening montage, we she him shoot *through* a mother and baby to the enemy). But his crack platoon is replaced by genetically-engineered warriors and Todd is suddenly on the scrapheap – literally.

Exiled to a municipal dump planet, he is taken in by a band of tip-dwellers, and, in time, must defend them from an attack by the very soldiers who made him obsolete.

It's every Western you can think of, it's *Frankenstein*, it's *The Terminator*, it's rubbish. Impossible to care about a preprogrammed automaton (Todd calls everyone 'Sir!' and utters about seven lines in total), we are left instead to gasp at the hardware-reliant action, for which slow-motion must generate which slow-motion must generate all the portent. Pompous generals, indestructible foes, cute kids – all stereotypes are here – and Sean Pertwee (held over from director Anderson's previous sci-fi bomb *Event Horizon* in 1997) proves yet again that he is the crap one out of the Britpack. But you can't blame then newboy Pertwee for hopping aboard but when Mr. Russell was offered it, he should've Kurtly refused. ★ **AC**

◑ SOLDIER BLUE (1970)

Starring: *Candice Bergen (Kathy Maribel Lee), Peter Strauss (Honus Gent), Donald Pleasence (Isaac Q. Cumber), John Anderson (Col. Iverson), Jorge Rivero (Spotted Wolf), Dana Elcar (Capt. Battles)*
Director: *Ralph Nelson*
Screenwriter: *John Gay' based on the novel by Theodore V. Olsen*
PG/114 mins./Western/USA

A trooper and a white woman, who has been married to a Cheyenne chief, survive in the wilderness after an Indian attack on a Cavalry detachment. To their horror, a bigoted martinet leads a raid against an Indian village in which men, women and children are massacred.

A controversial film in 1970, this now looks hideously dated and is not often revived. It's an attempt at a counterculture Western, recreating historical atrocities in a manner obviously supposed to evoke then-current headlines about war crimes committed by American troops in Vietnam. For the most part, the plot involves a standard trek through the wilderness, with a mannered Bergen playing a white woman who has lived with the Indians as if the character were a drop-out flower child and Strauss overdoing the naïveté as the eventually sensitive young man who falls for her.

Donald Pleasence, with bizarre false teeth, pops up for comic villainy as 'Isaac Q. Cumber', who is selling guns to the Cheyenne, and the melodramatic tone set by this performance continues into the famously gory finale. This blood-soaked fifteen-minute sequence was entirely responsible for the film's notoriety, as a fanatical, absurd cavalry officer (marked as a square by his complaints about 'modern young people') orders his men to carry out a massacre which includes shooting, dismembering and raping women and children. As movie massacres go, it deploys lots of sliced-up dummies and ketchup but pales in comparison with the cinematic verve of the finale of *The Wild Bunch*.

The Vietnam parallel is done much better in Robert Aldrich's similarly-themed *Ulzana's Raid*, and director Ralph Nelson makes several bizarre misjudgments, notably a score which opens with a folkie moan from Buffy Sainte-Marie and then extends to jolly, easy listening tunes from the usually reliable Roy Budd. ★★ **KN**

◑ SOME CAME RUNNING (1958)

Starring: *Dave Hirsch (Frank Sinatra), Dean Martin (Bama Dillerf), Shirley MacLaine (Ginnie Moorhead), Martha Hyer (Gwen French), Arthur Kennedy (Frank Hirsh), Nancy Gates (Edith Barclay), Leora Davis (Agnes Hirsch), Betty Lou Kelm (Dawn Hirsch)*
Director: *Vincente Minnelli*
Screenwriters: *John Patrick, Arthur Sheekman, based on the novel by James Jones*
PG/137 mins./Drama/USA

Parkman, Illinois. Dave Hirsch, a would-be writer, returns home after World War II and gets mixed up with good-time girl Ginnie and higher-class dame Gwen.

Adapted from a steamy brick-sized novel by James Jones which was his peacetime follow-up to *From Here to Eternity*, this is one of the great 1950s soap operas. Frank Sinatra comes out of the army and struggles with his burning need to become a great novelist (as signalled by the Viking portable Hemingway packs in his kit-bag) while returning to a home town which has more scandals than Peyton Place, Twin Peaks and King's Row put together.

The coolly neurotic Sinatra rejects the values of his hypocritical, conventional brother in order to run around with low-class tramp-with-a-heart Shirley MacLaine. In a large and wonderful supporting cast, MacLaine and Kennedy are outstanding as the doomed free spirit and the stuffy alcoholic, while Dean Martin enjoys himself as Bama, the gambler who keeps his signature hat on even in the bath (until he takes it off at a climactic, tear-jerking funeral).

A lot of critical attention is paid to the contemporary melodramas of Douglas Sirk, but Vincente Minnelli, after a career in musicals, made even more overheated, highly-coloured, edge-of-camp masterpieces – see also *The Bad and the Beautiful*, *Tea and Sympathy*, *The Cobweb*, *Designing Woman*, *Home From the Hill* and *Two Weeks in Another Town*. Everything is played on an operatic scale, and Elmer Bernstein contributes one of the great whistle-friendly movie-movie scores. In a hilarious scene conveying the dawning of Sinatra's literary awareness, he shows a short story to good girl Martha Hyer, claiming he's been having trouble with the ending, only to have her comment 'don't you see, when the girl leaves him, that *is* your ending'. ★★★★ **KN**

◑ SOME LIKE IT HOT (1959)

Starring: *Marilyn Monroe (Sugar Kan Kowalczyk), Tony Curtis (Joe), Jack Lemmon (Jerry), George Raft (Spats Columbo), Joe E. Brown (Osgood Fielding III)*
Director: *Billy Wilder*
Screenwriters: *Billy Wilder, I.L. Diamond, from the film* Fanfares Of Love *by Robert Thoeren, Michael Logan*
U/121 mins./Comedy/Crime/Romance/Music/USA

Awards: *Academy Awards – Best Costume Design, BAFTA – Best Foreign Actor (Jack Lemmon), Golden Globes – Best Comedy, Best Comedy/Musical Actor (Jack Lemmon), Best Comedy/Musical Actress*

S

Chicago, 1929: two broke jazz musicians flee mobsters intent on silencing them. They cross-dress their way onto an all-female jazz band gig in Florida but both are hot for band singer Sugar Kane Kowalczyk, a wistful chanteuse with a weakness for sax players and bourbon . . .

This legendary comedy, which fizzes from start to finish with great situations, wisecracking banter, breakneck pace, vulgarity, wit and sensational performances, is hysterically funny every time, no matter how many times, you see it. It mixes roaring 20s crime picture elements, of bootleggers, Tommy guns and chorus girls doing the Charleston, with the screwball staples of false identities, naughty repartee and madcap pursuits.

The 50s top sex goddess at her most enchanting, Monroe's forlorn-funny turn, maddening though it was for her co-stars and director to capture (83 takes just for her to say 'Where's that bourbon?' with her back to the camera) is mythic. Dishy Curtis's off-screen self-consciousness in drag gives him an aloof control that is in superb contrast to uninhibited Lemmon, whose expressiveness is priceless. Clever set-ups sustain one gag after another (note the clues tossed off about the band manager's missing belongings before 'Josephine' uses them to transform into his Cary Grant impersonation 'Shell Oil Jr.' to seduce Sugar, or the comic tension built up before he realises he's still got his earrings on when he races to their rendezvous) and the parade of pay-offs are sublime.

Some Like It Hot was produced and directed by Billy Wilder and it was his second screenwriting collaboration with I.A.L Diamond. Wilder was inspired by a German film called *Fanfaren Der Liebe* (1951), in which two unemployed musicians join an all-girl band, take a train journey and go in for some quick-change romancing with the band's singer. All similarity ends there. Wilder didn't want his two heroes camp; they had to be heatedly heterosexual so that their escapade aboard the train, surrounded by tempting totty, was excruciating. Therefore they had to have a desperately good reason to masquerade as women. Running for their lives from ruthless killers – who they've seen slaughter seven people – provided ample motivation. While the gangsters' strand has its own good jokes – 'I was at Rigoletto,' alibis Spats. 'What's his last name? Where's he live?' demands the G-man – it's effectively played straight.

Lifelong tough guy George Raft's not sending himself up gives a delicious note of menace, as does Wilder's neat noir touch of shooting Raft's key entrances from the dandy footwear upward. The famous last line was written the night before shooting finished, by Diamond, who insisted over Wilder's doubt that it was funny because it's so unexpected – the last reaction the audience expects to Jerry's big revelation 'I'm a MAN!'. Osgood shrugs philosophically, 'Well, nobody's perfect.'

The other most fondly recalled moment is Daphne's engagement announcement. Lemmon, shaking his maracas in absurd ecstasy, is a masterpiece of comic timing, Wilder presciently insisting on joyous fits of gourd rattling to leave space for audience laughter between lines. He also overrode objections to filming in black and white, not only to enhance the period setting but, shrewdly, to mute the men's make-up. Their transformation is startlingly amusing, but imagined in Technicolor it would be way too grotesque.

Bizarrely, the very first preview audience to see the finished *Some Like It Hot* reacted catastrophically badly. In Pacific Palisades, 1200 people who had paid to see *Suddenly Last Summer* sat in stony silence, apparently proving industry mavens like David O. Selznick's dire predictions to Wilder about mixing murder, romantic comedy and cross-dressing: 'It will be a disaster'. The lone voice heard guffawing belonged to comedian Steve Allen, who could only theorise later that his fellow punters must have been horribly depressed by the Tennessee Williams drama. The second preview, in Westwood, drew the college crowd from nearby UCLA and was a spectacularly different story, one repeated happily ever after. 'They screamed,' remembered Jack Lemmon. 'They really went cuckoo.' Audiences are still howling at a laugh riot that broke several fundamental rules of film comedy (the story springs from a grisly mass murder, the script was only half-written when shooting commenced, and the picture runs two hours, to cite three big no-nos), but went on to be enshrined by the American Film Institute as the Best Comedy Of All Time. ★★★★★ **AE**

ⓓ SOMMERSAULT (2004)

Starring: *Abbie Cornish (Heidi), Sam Worthington (Joe), Lynette Curran (Irene), Nathaniel Dean (Stuart), Erik Thomson (Richard)*
Director: *Cate Shortland*
Screenwriter: *Cate Shortland*
15/106 mins./Drama/Australia

16-year-old Heidi runs away from home after being caught making out with her mother's boyfriend. She ends up in an off-season ski resort, seeking love from anyone who will give it to her and ensnaring a cattle-rancher who has his own problems.

The little film that came from Oz arrived on our shores weighed down with prizes – and expectation. Its record haul of 13 awards at the Australian equivalent of the Oscars (the AFIs) and a handful of other independent prizes suggested this was something very special. But while there's no denying that *Somersault* is different and visually impressive enough to make an impact, it's also so wrapped up in its own theory and imagery that it ends up as cold as the ski resort in which it is set.

It does makes for a welcome change from the brash, sun-baked comedies we've come to expect of Australia. The frosty palate of icy blues and whites suits its detached heroine, who strives for intimacy by indulging in a string of sexual encounters that skirt on the edge of danger. Newcomer Abbie Cornish is undeniably impressive and her preternatural sex appeal on full display, with her character's tendency to throw her mittens aside at even the briefest hint of a shag leaving her exposed in every way for much of the film.

But what's missing, apart from her clothes, is any sort of development for Heidi, while other characters (notably Sam Worthington's confused rancher) are only just beginning to start their personal journeys when the film finishes. ★★★ **EC**

ⓓ SOMMERSBY (1993)

Starring: *Richard Gere (John Robert 'Jack' Sommersby), Jodie Foster (Laurel Sommersby), Bill Pullman (Orin Meecham), James Earl Jones (Judge Barry Conrad Issacs)*
Director: *Jon Amiel*
Screenwriters: *Nicholas Meye, Sarah Kernochan, based on the film* The Return Of Martin Guerre, *based on the story by Nicholas Meyer, Anthony Shaffer*
12/114 mins./Drama/Romance/USA

When Laurel's husband returns from the Civil War he is so changed that she has doubts that it is really him. But she likes the improved version so much she decides not to blab. But some in the community feel otherwise . . .

Having served notice of his considerable storytelling skills with 1989's underrated *Queen Of Hearts*, British director Jon Amiel here made the huge jump into the Hollywood first division with this major studio production bringing together two of the very biggest stars in the firmament. And, in the main, it was a jump he successfully carried off.

An American remake and update of Daniel Vigne's 1982 French classic *The Return Of Martin Guerre*, this is the tale of Jack Sommersby, a bad old Southern boy who returns from the Civil War apparently reconstructed, reformed and, when it comes to the boudoir, considerably revitalised. Wife Laurel suspects that things may not be quite what they seem, but this guy's a lot more fun than the previous version and her lips remain firmly sealed, as do those of most of the other village folk. Unfortunately, the chief rival for Mrs. Sommersby's affections doesn't quite see it that way, kicking off a gradual process that will ultimately seal the fate of the two key players.

A genuinely romantic piece of work, *Sommersby* features two class performances from Gere and Foster, both managing to somehow convey the depth of their mutual longing without ever having to hang from the chandeliers to prove it. Gere, in particular, demonstrates a maturity and confident sense of what it is about him that works best, while Foster, through her overt primness, conjures up an effective sense of the barely suppressed passions of the period.

The key issues of identity, deception and betrayal, however, are never really tackled head-on by Amiel or his leads, with too many clues strewn along the way, and undue emphasis placed upon the development of the pleasantly diverting love affair that should, in reality, be kept taut and constantly challenged by the threat of potential exposure. Still, it all looks very nice in a 19th century sweet Virginia kind of way, and fans of Gere and Foster will find no shortage of moments to enjoy. Fans of *The Return Of Martin Guerre*, rightly fearing the liberal application of Hollywood soft soap, are best advised to rewind the original and keep their pleasant memories intact. ★★★ **BMc**

SONATINE (1993)

Starring: *Takeshi Kitano (Aniki Murakawa), Aya Kokumai (Miyuki), Tetsu Watanabe (Uechi), Masanobu Katsumua (Ryoji), Susumu Terjima (Ken)*
Director: *Takeshi Kitano*
Screenwriter: *Takeshi Kitano*
18/89 mins./Action/Crime/Drama/USA

A yakuza lieutenant is reassigned to Okinawa to help smooth over a local turf war.

Sonatine is a singularly unusual film – its premise being that to understand violence you must explore the moments of calm that punctuate it.

On the surface this is a gangster movie. Murakawa, a yakuza mob boss is sent to Okinawa to sort out the local in-fighting among the gangsters there. He is aware that this assignment may just be a ploy to take him away from his own turf – and soon has his suspicions confirmed – but holed up on a beach with the rest of his 'family' he returns to a more innocent state.

But there are ominous overtones to their games on the sand and, as things take a turn for the worse, Murakawa is left defending a beach hut trying to avenge his clansmen's blood.

Takeshi delivers a perfectly-measured performance as the man who wants out, but retains the strength to recognise that circumstances and obligations will never allow it.

Beautifully shot and sharply observed, with a hauntingly minimalist score, *Sonatine* is poignant and unforgettable. ★★★★ **JB**

SONS OF THE DESERT (1933)

Starring: *Stan Laurel (Stanley), Oliver Hardy (Oliver), Charley Chase (Charley Chase), Mae Busch (Mrs Lottie Chase Hardy), Dorothy Christy (Mrs. Betty Laurel), Lucien Littlefield (Dr. Horace Meddick)*
Director: *William A. Seiter*
Screenwriters: *Frank Craven, Byron Morgan, Jack Barty, William A. Seiter, Glenn Tryon, Eddie Welch*
U/68 mins./Comedy/USA

Desperate to attend a convention in Chicago, Stan Laurel and Oliver Hardy tell their wives, Betty and Lottie, that they're going on a sea voyage for Ollie's health. However, the ship they were supposed to be cruising on sinks. But grief soon turns to fury, when the wives see their husbands alive, well and having a fine old time on a newsreel.

Frustrated by the narrative variability of *Pardon Us* and *Pack Up Your Troubles*, Stan Laurel was determined to eschew slapstick set-pieces in order to produce a feature in which the humour was not only derived from situation and character, but which was also fully integrated into the storyline. Consequently, he hired new writing partners for this variation on the 1928 silent two-reeler, *We Faw Down*, which had supposedly been inspired by a piece of gossip that Oliver Hardy had heard from his laundress.

Frank Craven wrote the treatment while the duo was completing *Busy Bodies* and Stan then worked with Frank Terry on the dialogue and ex-comic Glenn Tryon on additional material, while Byron Morgan was polishing the continuity. But even more significant than the meticulous plotting was the contribution of director William A. Seiter, whose background lay in drama and light romance rather than clowning, and his sure sense of pace and flow ensured the kind of seamless scenario that Stan had envisaged.

Indeed, this is one of Laurel and Hardy's tightest pictures and it's hard to argue against the exclusion of sequences in which the pair first cause chaos during the parade by bicycling into a banner and then wind up in the hoosegow after a drunken fracas. Even the songs are all of the piece, with the Sons' anthem riffing on such standards as 'Give My Regards to Broadway' and 'Yankee Doodle Dandy', while 'Honolulu Baby' suggested that the picture was a parody of *Convention City*, especially as Ty Purvis (who had once been Betty Grable's dance partner) turned in such a mischievous impersonation of its crooner star, Dick Powell.

As ever, Mae Busch steals scenes as Ollie's firebrand wife and Dorothy Christy provides solid support in a role that she only landed four days into shooting when Patsy Kelly was held up on Bing Crosby's *Going Hollywood*. But not everybody enjoyed the experience, as Charley Chase resented having to play against genial type as Ollie's obnoxious brother-in-law, while *Variety* continued its vendetta against Laurel and Hardy by posting a negative review. ★★★★ **DP**

S

THE SORROW AND THE PITY (1969)

Starring: *Georges Bidault (Himself), Matthaus Belibinger (Himself), Charles Braun (Himself), Maurice Buckmaster (Himself), Emile Coulaudon (Himself), Emmanuel d'Astier de la Vigerie (Himself)*
Director: *Marcel Ophuls*
Screenwriters: *Marcel Ophuls, Andre Harris*
12A/260 mins./Documentary/France/Switzerland/West Germany

An epic chronicle of collaboration and resistance in the French provincial town of Clermont-Ferrand between the capitulation of 1940 and the Liberation of 1944, which also explores the part played by France in the Final Solution.

Originally produced for French television in 1969, Marcel Ophuls's landmark documentary finally went on release in a small cinema in Paris's Latin Quarter two years later. It was certainly a film with an agenda, as its producers, Andrew Harris and Alain de Sédouy, had actively supported the Soixante-Huitards during the May Days of 1968 and they were determined to expose the resistancialism that had amended history to place Charles de Gaulle and his Free French at the heart of underground activity against both the occupying Nazis and Henri Pétain's Vichy regime.

But, while its revelations still have a shocking power, *The Sorrow and the Pity's* enduring effectiveness owes much to Ophuls's mastery of his material.

Everything about this extraordinary account of France's wartime experience is arranged by meticulous contrast. The town of Clermont-Ferrand itself was chosen as it was both close to Vichy and served as the centre of Maquis activity in the Auvergne. Personal testimonies were juxtaposed with contemporary newsreels, while prominent politicians and everyday citizens were encouraged to ponder both local incidents and their wider national context.

Expert and unreliable witnesses alike were given equal opportunity to testify, as they had all been in the crowds that had witnessed the respective arrivals of Pétain in 1940 and de Gaulle four years later. Consequently, French and Germans, aristocrats and peasants, intellectuals and workers, diplomats and spies, democrats and fascists were all invited to contribute to this demolition of the war's clichés and stereotypes in order to reveal that the population which endured the Nazi tyranny could not be divided so easily into resistors and collaborators as even those who lived through this traumatic time would suppose or, indeed, prefer those who came after to believe.

Ophuls's use of archive footage was exemplary. But the indelible moments were provided by such dismayingly unrepentant figures as Wehrmacht captain Helmut Tachsend and Charlemagne Division veteran Christian de la Mazière, whose arrogance contrasted sharply with the unassuming recollections of British agent Denis Rake, Maquis chief and Buchenwald survivor Louis Grave, and Jewish historian Claude Lévy. One of documentary cinema's genuine masterpieces and a touchstone for Woody Allen fans – it is the film that obsesses Alvy Singer in Annie Hall. ★★★★★ **DP**

SOUND OF MUSIC (1965)

Starring: *Julie Andrews (Maria), Christopher Plummer (Captain Georg von Trapp), Peggy Wood (Mother Abbess), Anna Lee (Sister Margaretta), Eleanor Parker (Baroness Elsa Schraeder), Charmain Carr (Liesl von Trapp), Nicholas Hammond (Friedrich von Trapp), Heather Menzies (Louisa von Trapp), Duane Chase (Kurt von Trapp), Angela Cartwright (Brigitta von Trapp), Debbie Turner (Marta von Trapp), Kym Karath (Gretl von Trapp)*
Director: *Robert Wise*
Screenwriter: *Ernest Lehman, based on the book by Howard Lindsay, Russel Crouse*
U/174 mins./Muscial/Biography/Romance/War/USA

Awards: *Academy Awards – Best Director, Best Editing, Best Score, Best Picture, Best Sound, Golden Globes – Best Musical/Comedy, Best Musical/Comedy Actress*

You know the one where the singing nun escapes the convent to look after a gang of motherless children, falls in love with their father and helps them all avoid capture by the Nazis. Set in beautiful alpine countryside, and riddled with unforgettable tunes.

Oover forty years after Julie Andrews and her adopted brood of chirping little ones first charged down the streets of Salzburg chorusing in unison, Robert Wise's Oscar-laden classic is as popular as ever. For those unfamiliar with the story, Andrews is the free-spirited nun Maria who becomes governess to the seven uniform-sporting kids of the irascible Austrian Captain von Trapp. Maria soon puts paid to the children's regimented lifestyle by fashioning new clobber out of her bedroom curtains and discovering their untapped musical talents. She consequently wins the heart of her new employer, with only a last-minute Nazi intervention threatening to put the mockers on everything.

Sandwiched between the opening and closing mountainous landscapes is a cavalcade of superb set-pieces, picturesque scenery and Rodgers and Hammerstein musical numbers immediately recognisable even to that small segment of the population who have somehow managed to avoid the film.

While all-too-frequent TV appearances may have relegated this to ridicule status in some quarters, there can scarcely be a soul who doesn't complain of having something in their eye when Captain von Trapp regains an inkling of humanity and butts in on his extended family's rendition of the title track. The phrase 'they don't make them like they this any more' has rarely been so accurate. One of the greatest screen musicals ever. ★★★★★ **CW**

SOUTH PARK: BIGGER, LONGER, UNCUT (1999)

Starring: the voices of: *Trey Parker (Stan Marsh/Eric Cartman/Satan/Mr. Herbert Garrison/Phillip Niles Argyle/Randy Marsh/Tom (news reporter)/Midget in a bikini/Ticket taker/Canadian Ambassador/Bombardiers/Mr. Mackey/Army general/Ned Gerblanski/Additional voices), Matt Stone (Kyle Broflovski/Kenny McCormick/Saddam Hussein/Terrance Henry Stoot/Jimbo Kearn/Gerald Broflovski/Bill Gates/Additional voices), Mary Kay Bergman (Liane Cartman/Sheila Broflovski/Sharon Marsh/Wendy Testeberger/Clitoris/Additional voices), Issac Hayes (Chef)*
Director: *Trey Parker*
Screenwriters: *Trey Parker, Matt Stone, Pam Brady, from the television series* South Park
15/81 mins./Animated/Comedy/USA

Kyle's mom launches an anti-Canada campaign when she feels young Kyle is being corrupted by a Canadian TV show.

Although *South Park* the TV series has racked up nine series, many feel it has never reached the giddily brilliant heights of the first series and this film is a reminder of that time.

In its fun'n'filthy feature-length form, it offers flexibility for a string of gags guaranteed to offend almost every audience member at some point. And swearing. Lashings of it.

It's the latter that forms the basis of the plot, as Kyle, Stan, Cartman and Kenny, having been 'influenced' by the movie debut of flatulent Canadian comedy duo Terrence And Phillip, begin turning the air blue, much to the annoyance of their folks. Soon Kyle's mom launches an anti-Canada campaign which culminates in the arrest of the twosome on national TV and, subsequently, Canada going to war with its American cousins. Meanwhile Kenny, having suffered the inevitably painful death, finally gets his kit off.

Creators Parker and Stone use their clever plot to take prescient sideswipes at everything from censorship and parental control to internet porn and Jar Jar Binks, interlaced with a string of perky, hilarious musical numbers which could have come straight off the set of a Disney movie. Like the TV series, when it works (Cartman's anti-swearing V-chip implant, a fabulous ER send-up featuring the voice of George Clooney), it's outstanding stuff. However, like a lot of scatological humour, it suffers from a hit-and-miss quality; a subplot featuring Satan and Saddam Hussein as lovers is dragged out far too long, while the absence of key show characters (Jesus, Mr. Hankey, Pip the English kid, etc.) is sorely noticeable.

Like the creators' previous movie outings *BASEketball* and *Orgazmo*, *South Park* the movie will annoy and delight in equal measures, before vanishing from memory within seconds of the closing credits. As such it's best enjoyed late at night surrounded by a large group of show devotees. Preferably ones who know all the words to Kyle's 'Mom's A Bitch'. ★★★★ CW

SOUTHERN COMFORT (1981)

Starring: *Keith Carradine (Private Spencer), Powers Booth (Corporal Charles Hardin), Fred Ward (Corporal Lonnie Reece), Franklyn Seales (Private Simms), T.K. Carter (Private Tyrone Cribbs)*
Director: *Walter Hill*
Screenwriters: *Michael Kane, Walter Hill, David Giler*
18/99 mins./Drama/USA

While on training exercises in the Louisiana swampland, a squad of soldiers is attacked by local Cajun hunters after they take a few pot-shots at them for a joke. A situation that escalates into a life and death battle, as the soldiers bereft of live rounds of ammunition, try to survive in this alien landscape.

While Walter Hill has never been a director of much subtlety, this macho thriller stocked with hard-as-nails types like Powers Boothe, Keith Carradine, and Fred Ward, is pointedly alluding to Vietnam. It may be set in the sickly swamps of Louisiana, but the hidden menace that the

Highest Grossing Box Office Stars + Biggest Hit

1. **Tom Hanks: $3,104.9million (*Forrest Gump*)**
2. **Harrison Ford: $3,044.7million (*Star Wars*)**
3. **Eddie Murphy: $2,925.5million (*Shrek 2*)**
4. **Tom Cruise: $2,537.6million (*War of the Worlds*)**
5. **Bruce Willis: $2,165.5million (*The Sixth Sense*)**
6. **Robert DeNiro: $2,139.4million (*Meet the Fockers*)**
7. **Samuel L. Jackson: $2,098.5million (*Revenge of the Sith*)**
8. **Robin Williams: $2,094.4million (*Mrs. Doubtfire*)**
9. **Julia Roberts: $2,093.9million (*Ocean's Eleven*)**
10. **Mel Gibson: $2,022.2million (*Signs*)**

Cajun backwater stalkers represent, setting traps amongst the trees, have the ghostly menace of the Vietcong, the sullen atmosphere full of impending death.

This is a war movie, where the war is at one remove. It's also Hill's best movie – pulsating, terrifying, with a grip like steel. Following the culture clash dynamics of *Deliverance*, it has these 'civilised' soldiers replete with hi-tech weaponry up against the Hillbillies armed only with shotguns and guile. The reference again is direct, how American know-how and armaments were so useless in 'Nam.

The team of actors effectively reveal both terror under fire, and fragging group dynamics. The film even takes on the quality of a horror movie as the various soldiers of the nine-strong group are picked off one by one. It's a genre piece, cleverly avoiding the traps of genre. ★★★★ **IN**

SOYLENT GREEN (1973)

Starring: *Charlton Heston (Detective Robert Thorn), Leigh Taylor-Young (Shirl), Chuck Connors (Tab Fielding), Joseph Cotton (William R. Simonson), Brock Peters (Lt. Hatcher)*
Director: *Richard Fleischer*
Screenwriter: *Stanley R. Greenberg based on the novel by Harry Harrison*
15/97 mins./Sci-fi/USA

With the world overpopulated and food running scarce, a New York cop finds himself hunted by the authorities when he starts to suspect a miraculous new good stuff is not what it seems.

Often seen as the companion piece, if not the exact negative scenario, of *The Omega Man*, here we have Charlton Heston in a near-future assailed by overcrowding. Adapted from the Harry Harrison novel, and set in a not-so-outrageously envisioned 21st Century, this is an effective dystopian fable because it presents a world of potential crisis. The could-happen scope that Richard Fleischer assuredly brings the material gives it startling quality.

If our planet was too thick with people – the camera stays tight in on crowd scenes to give the idea of people physically pressing against each other – and food was running out, the rich would clamour for jars of jam, and the poor are given strange wonder foods by a disturbingly aloof government. It becomes a satire of planetary crisis, and also a play on cultural faddism. Soylent Green is the new wonder food stuff that will save humanity. Or at least the downtrodden desperate for handouts – there is a blackly comic aside in a boom in suicide services. This being a swollen world, every human ill is in abundance from crime to disease.

Big Chuck Heston, as forthright and one-dimensional as ever, is the stern cop who smells a rat in the factory-sized kitchen. There is good support from Edward G. Robinson in his final role, as the friend and researcher to Heston's Detective Thorn, who happens upon the secret to Soylent Green. There is that obvious 70s art direction, but Fleischer's green-tinged photography gives it an appropriately sickly look, and its relentlessly grim attitude still feels relevant. The year is 2022, replace food for oil, and you have something scarily prophetic depicted here. ★★★★ **IN**

SPACEBALLS (1987)

Starring: *Mel Brooks (President Skroob/Yogurt), Rick Moranis (Dark Helmet), Bill Pullman (Lone Starr), Daphne Zuniga (Princess Vespa), John Candy ('Barf'), George Wyner (Colonel Sandurz), Dick Van Patten (King Roland)*
Director: *Mel Brooks*
Screenwriters: *Mel Brooks, Thomas Meehan, Ronny Graham*
PG/96 mins./Comedy/USA

When Princess Vespa, daughter of King Roland, ruler of Druidia, is kidnapped by an evil race, The Spaceballs, space pirate Lone Starr is persuaded by Roland to lead a daring rescue mission.

At some point in movie history, the director who split our sides with superb spoofs *The Producers*, *Blazing Saddles* and *Young Frankenstein* became the schmuck who caused our lips to curl and arses to pucker with *Robin Hood: Men In Tights* and *Dracula: Dead And Loving It*. That quality-shedding metamorphosis could well have occurred during the production of *Spaceballs*, when Brooks settled his parody-seeking eye on sci-fi – mainly the big, fat, soft target that is the *Star Wars* saga, but also a collection of other obvious space-based targets like *Alien*, *Planet Of The Apes* and, er, *Transformers*.

Subtlety had never been Brooks' thing, but even blunt blows need to be well aimed, and while *Spaceballs* doesn't exactly miss its targets, it certainly bounces off them embarrassingly. It's not entirely without its charms – John Candy's half-man, half-dog Chewbacca-substitute Barf does get some good lines ('I'm my own best friend!'), and there's an occasional smile-raiser – like the opening, seemingly never-ending spaceship reveal. But even this is a bit of a cheeky lift from *Airplane!*, in which the same technique was used to convey the ludicrous complexity of a cockpit dashboard.

Elsewhere, the humour rarely rises above the level of school panto; you'd titter indulgently at characters like Barf the dog-man, Yogurt (Yoda? Yogurt? Do you see?) and Pizza The Hutt if you were watching a bunch of children doing a self-scribbled *Star Wars* pisstake, but this from the man who wrote *Springtime For Hitler*? Unforgiveable then, unforgiveable now. ★★ **DJ**

SPACECAMP (1986)

Starring: *Kate Capshaw (Andie Bergstrom), Lea Thompson (Kathryn Fairly), Kelly Preston (Tish Ambrosei), Larry B. Scott (Rudy Tyler), Leaf Phoenix (Max), Tate Donovan (Kevin Donaldson), Tom Skerritt (Cmdr Zavh Bergrstrom) Barry Primus (Brennan), Terry O'Quinn (Launch Director)*
Director: *Harry Winer*
Screenwriters: *Casey T. Mitchell and W.W. Wicket, based on a story by Patrick Bailey and Larry Williams*
PG/104 mins./Sci-fi/USA

A crowd of squabbling teenagers are mistakenly launched into orbit in the space shuttle, and have to become a real crew of astronauts in order to make it safely back to Earth.

In the mid-1980s, between the tentpoles of *WarGames* and *Back to the Future*, there was a weird trend for science nerd teen movies – cf: *Real Genius*, *The Manhattan Project*, *My Science Project*, *Weird Science*.

S

Despite its cast of 80s icons and Joaquin Phoenix back when he was still billed as Leaf, *SpaceCamp* is amongst the least memorable of the run. Unfortunately released in 1986 in the wake of the *Challenger* space shuttle disaster, this pro-NASA teen movie deservedly splashed down and sank without trace. The lead characters, all played by 80s teen faces, are a group of misfit kids who enrol in a summer training camp for wannabe astronauts: an all-American overachiever (Lea Thompson), a bimbo who isn't as stupid as she pretends (Kelly Preston), a cocky nerd who discovers responsibility (Tate Donovan), a stock black kid without a character trait (Larry B. Scott) and a truly annoying pre-teen brat who thinks he's Luke Skywalker (Phoenix). After foul-ups and comedy business with various training and testing mishaps, the kids are allowed to sit in a real space shuttle just to see what it's like, and get semi-accidentally blasted into outer space thanks to the intervention of Jinx the cute robot.

In the last act, the junior heroes show all their Right Stuff/Space Cowboys moves in order to return safely to their proud, nervous parents. With the annoying junior characters driving old pro instructors Tom Skerritt and Kate Capshaw to exasperation, this juggles predictable dumb comedy with embarrassing self-help homilies. In addition to its other demerits, it is saddled with surprisingly ropey special effects, with many a matte fringe on view. ★★ **KN**

SPANGLISH (2004)

Starring: *Adam Sandler (John Clasky), Téa Leoni (Deborah Clasky), Paz Vega (Flor Moreno), Cloris Leachman (Evelyn Wright), Shelbie Bruce (Cristina)*
Director: *James L. Brooks*
Screenwriter: *James L. Brooks*
12/131 mins./Drama/Comedy/USA

Despite not speaking a word of English, Latino housekeeper Flor uproots her daughter Cristina to LA and is hired by Deborah Clasky to run her opulent household. Worried about Deborah's influence over Cristina, Flor finds solace in Debs' husband John.

Taken individually, the movies which form the not-exactly-prolific output of James L. Brooks (in particular *Terms Of Endearment*, *Broadcast News* and *As Good As It Gets*) are object lessons in how to make smart, grown-up, awards-friendly entertainment. Taken as a whole, they form a coherent image of middle-class Americans, exposing their lives with compassion and intelligence. *Spanglish* is his first film in seven years, and while it doesn't quite reach vintage Brooks, it didn't deserve its Stateside critical drubbing, standing as a satisfying sample of his wordy, worldly wisdom.

Brooks' background is in legendary sitcom (*The Mary Tyler Moore Show*, *Rhoda*, *Taxi* and latterly *The Simpsons*), and *Spanglish*'s premise of a poor Mexican nanny taken in by a wealthy LA family smacks of a Fresh Princess Of Bel-Air 'high concept'. His storytelling achieves an engaging quality of being serious-yet-easygoing that gives the impression of a comedy, but *Spanglish* cares much more about humanity than humour, allowing both laughs and drama to emerge straight out of character rather than crowbarring in increasingly bathetic situations or contrived one-liners.

Brooks' strongest suit is the originality of his writing, finding fresh spins on stock rom-dram scenarios. Late on, John is confronted with the highpoint of Debs' neurosis and, rather than fall back on obvious histrionics or faux melodrama, Brooks takes the scene to a completely different place, as we see a man's world quietly disintegrate around him. Another potentially obvious scene – in which Flor and John, holed up in a darkened restaurant, begin to discuss the reality of their feelings for each other – captures the genuine thrill of romantic realisation but filters it through a touching tentativeness.

Brooks really knows how to draw the best out of his casts. In a role that's much more of a departure than *Punch-Drunk* Love, Sandler finds some of the likeable vulnerability of his characters in *The Wedding Singer* and *50 First Dates* but grounds it in something much more real, more soulful. Meanwhile, in what will undoubtedly be one of the more daring performances of the year, Téa Leoni goes full tilt as an unsympathetic, highly-strung wife, unintentionally hurting all around her – she's the kind of mother who buys clothes a size too small for her heavy-set kid. Cloris Leachman has a blast as Debs' booze-sodden, showtune-singing mother, and the two kids, Shelbie Bruce and Sarah Steele, ooze understated naturalism in every scene.

Yet the show belongs to Spanish actress Paz Vega, who finds quiet dignity in a mother trying to protect her daughter from the lure of LA. Flor's burgeoning relationship with John is sweet and sexy, all furtive glances and late-night conversations, and Vega shines in a touching, terrific Brooksian set-piece, in which a heated argument erupts between John and Flor, requiring her daughter to rapidly translate back and forth, unconsciously mimicking the gestures and attitudes of each adult.

It's not all plain sailing, though. While terrific with words, Brooks has never been big on images, the visual sense feeling obvious and monotone. Moreover, Hans Zimmer's Mexican-tinged score reinforces emotional beats that didn't need stating. Brooks may not unravel his tangle of themes – notions of femininity and masculinity, the dangers of assimilation, the difficulty of communication – but then, the mire and messiness of reality is where he loves to live and breathe. ★★★ **IF**

THE SPANISH PRISONER (1997)

Starring: *Campbell Scott (Joseph A. 'Joe' Ross), Steven Martin (Julian 'Jimmy' Dell), Rebecca Pidgeon (Susan Ricci), Ben Gazzara (Mr. Klein)*
Director: *David Mamet*
Screenwriter: *David Mamet*
PG/110 mins./Drama/Thriller/Mystery/USA

Joe has developed a process that could make his company fortune, but worries his company won't give him a fair share of the profits. So he enlists the help of a new friend as advisor . . .

David Mamet has really stumped us this time. This, his fifth film as writer-director, is one of his most mainstream, but it also happens to be his cleverest, craftiest and most conniving. In fact, *The Spanish Prisoner* is so smartarse the only way to fully appreciate this film is to watch it with an open mind. Simply because the more you know about the plot beforehand the less impressed you will be with the outcome.

As you would expect with Mamet, the entire movie is a huge confidence trick. Without spoiling things, company man Joe Ross has invented a 'Process', a secret formula which could make him an extremely wealthy man. He is eager to sell this 'Process' but a chance meeting with jet-setter Jimmy Dell (Martin, expertly cast against type) and the charms of his infatuated secretary Susan make him doubt the intentions of his colleagues. Mamet being Mamet, we never actually get to see the 'Process' even though the entire movie hangs on its existence. Obviously, somebody gets caught with their pants down but to say who will spoil a movie that comes dangerously close to brilliance.

Everybody is on the make, of course, pulling confidence tricks left, right and centre – but the greatest of all tricks is pulled by Mamet himself. The title, a reference to the world's oldest confidence bluff, is as much aimed at Scott's everyman character as at the gullibility of the audience. And being a complete hoodwink, the movie can only be savoured once. Otherwise loopholes will be found in the sharp script and sly direction. Don't talk to anyone about this film, steer clear of any more reviews. Just sit back and let the movie take you for a ride. ★★★★ **JH**

SPANKING THE MONKEY (1994)

Starring: *Jeremy Davies (Ray Aibelli), Alberta Watson (Susan Aibelli), Carla Gallo (Toni Peck), Benjamin Hendrickson (Tom Aibelli), Matthew Puckett (Nicky)*
Director: *David O. Russell*
Screenwriter: *David O. Russell*
18/95 mins./Drama/USA

A young medical student starts to develop a highly inappropriate relationship with his mother.

Mother-son relationships can be tricky things. Just ask Sigmund Freud. Or, for that matter, Norman Bates. Up until now, however, Hollywood has run scared of looking at the subject of incest in anything other than the most lurid manner. Not any longer. David O. Russell's impressive debut feature may be about many things, but there is no getting away from the fact that, two thirds of the way through, the central character gets it on with his mum in the most serious way imaginable.

Ray is a medical student who has to forego a prestigious summer internship after his mother breaks her leg. To make matters worse, dad has gone away on a sales trip, all Ray's old friends turn out to be sadistic small-town bastards and every time he retreats to the bathroom for a quick 'Sherman' the family dog howls the place down. Within this atmosphere mother and son are forced into ever closer physical and emotional proximity until, one drunken evening, Ray's daily massage of his mum's legs turns into something altogether different.

Naturally, given the subject matter, the film's tone tends towards the decidedly dark. Russell's success, however, is in creating a film that avoids being freaky or an exercise in titillation by employing a mixture of sympathetic writing and black, black comedy. The result is a thought-provoking movie. ★★★★ **CC**

SPARTACUS (1960)

Starring: *Kirk Douglas (Spartacus), Laurence Olivier (Marcus Licinius Crassus), Jean Simmons (Varinia), Charles Laughton (Sempronius Gracchus), Peter Ustinov (Lentulus Bariatus)*
Director: *Stanley Kubrick*
Screenwriter: *Dalton Trumbo, from the novel by Howard Fast*
PG/186 mins./History/War/Romance/USA

Awards: *Academy Awards – Best Supporting Actor (Peter Ustinov), Best Color Art Direction-Set Decoration, Best Color Cinematography, Best Color Costume Design, Golden Globes – Best Drama*

Spartacus, a Thracian slave, refuses to allow himself to become the animal the Roman civilisation would have him be. So he escapes, joined by more runaways, whose numbers swell to become a vast army.

The Thracian slave Spartacus, thought to have been a deserter from the Roman army, was sold to a school for gladiators at Capua but never got to the arena, leading a slave revolt in 73 BC and devastating Southern Italy with an army of former slaves and gladiators. He was defeated in battle in 71 BC by Marcus Crassus, probably dying on the field of combat rather than surviving (as in the movie) to be crucified. Crassus, with Pompey and Julius Caesar, formed the first Triumvirate of Rome, precursor to the Emperorship of the Caesars, but came to a bad end in 53 BC when he was himself killed in a war he had started.

In the film, Crassus remarks, 'This campaign is not done to kill Spartacus, it is to kill the legend of Spartacus.' The real rebel was a ruthless plunderer who had 300 captives put to death to avenge the killing of his best friend Crixus (the part played by John Ireland) and once, before a battle, crucified a captured Roman soldier in front of his own men to show them what would happen if they lost to the legions.

But the legend of Spartacus stands for resistance to tyranny. In the 20th century, a German socialist faction called themselves the Spartacists, and communist Howard Fast's *Spartacus* depicted the slave revolt in Marxist terms. Another blacklistee, Dalton Trumbo, hewed a screenplay from Fast's novel, relishing the scene in which Crassus delivers straight McCarthyist rhetoric ('The enemies of the state are known, arrests are in progress, the prisons begin to fill. In every city and province, lists of the disloyal have been compiled'). Trumbo stirred in incidents from Arthur Koestler's novel *The Gladiators*, which might have been a Yul Brynner movie if producer-star Kirk Douglas hadn't made sure his rival project was so much bigger.

Excepting a stint on Marlon Brando's *One-Eyed Jacks* (1961), which the star ended up directing himself, *Spartacus* was Stanley Kubrick's only film as a for-hire director. He was brought in when Douglas fell out with the original helmer, Anthony Mann – director of great Westerns in the 1950s, who shot the opening Libyan mine sequence – and never quite got up to speed on the picture. Still, many scenes and ideas in *Spartacus* are completely Kubrickian: he returned almost obsessively to brutal training regimes that turn men into machines in *A Clockwork Orange* (1971) and *Full Metal Jacket* (1987) and staged another huge historical battle in *Barry Lyndon* (1975). But the director is clearly much happier with Spartacus the Legend and the power struggle between Patrician Crassus and Plebean Gracchus than he is in scenes that try to show Spartacus the Man: pining for peace, loving his wife and palling around with his men.

The gladiator training sequence and its pay-off in the 'matched pairs' fight bests in 40 minutes the whole length of *Gladiator* (2000). We see the raw slaves drilled and pounded until they are perfect killing machines, with the unforgettable image of the trainer daubing Douglas's naked torso with different-coloured paints to illustrate the varieties of wounds ('always go for the quick kill.') The two duels, one seen only through the slats of the pen as Spartacus and Draba wait their turn, and one between sword and trident staged in the sandy arena, are both a backdrop to a bit of intrigue between Crassus and his dim supporter Glabrus, and a perverse distraction for ladies Helena and Claudia.

The women are more interested in how few clothes the well-muscled fighters are wearing than in their lives and deaths. In a neat bit of plotting, Crassus's casual insistence on a minor fight to the death triggers the revolt, started not by the defeated Spartacus but by the victorious Draba, who dies trying to attack the audience (Olivier sneers superbly as he stabs Strode in the neck, blood splashing his face). Too intent on scheming against Gracchus, Crassus doesn't even consider that the slaves could cause him any trouble.

Douglas was always great in movies that required suffering, and he often played roles that involved extreme mortification or even mutilation (no other Van Gogh hacked off his own ear with such conviction). Here he is at his best under the lash or up on the cross, almost relishing his own agony and burning with righteous fury. The irony is that even as a free man, Spartacus is a slave. He serves Crassus's interests by riling the people of Rome to the point where they are forced to call on his military genius, transforming him into a virtual dictator to save them from an enemy who only wants to go home.

Spartacus's merry rabble swarms across country to face a Roman army that, seen from a distance, resembles either a group of ants moving in perfect formation or living chessboard squares marching in order – an unbeatable, fascist machine. It's a breathtaking moment, which forces you to realise that Kubrick (before CGI) had to command extras as rigidly as Crassus runs Rome, and it takes Douglas's death on the cross to trump it. ★★★★★ **KN**

S

Movie Trivia:
Stanley Kubrick (1928–1999)

Who he is: Probably the most technically proficient filmmaker in cinema history. Former studio hired hand who became fiercely independent and controlling of his films. Slow worker.

Hallmarks: The colour red; multiple takes in obsessive pursuit of the perfect shots; meticulous design and preparation; scenes in hotels, lavatories and ballrooms.

If you see one movie, see: *2001: A Space Odyssey* (1968)

SPAWN (1997)

Starring: *Michael Jai White (Al Simmons/Spawn), John Leguizamo (Clown/Violator), Martin Sheen (Jason Wynn), Theresa Randle (Wanda Blake), Nicol Williamson (Cogliostro)*
Director: *Mark A.Z. Dippe*
Screenwriter: *Alan B. McElroy, from a story by Mark A.Z. Dippe, Alan B. McElroy, comic book by Todd McFarlane*
12/92 mins./Thriller/Fantasy/Action/Horror/USA

A mercenary is killed, but comes back from Hell as a reluctant soldier of the Devil.

Spawn is a movie aimed, apparently, at the kind of 15-year-old boys who don't get out much, unless to loiter vacantly in video arcades or by comic book racks. Indeed this particular toxic mutant avenger from Hell originates from the Image Comics series and is already a successfully merchandised 'superhero'. The entire film looks like a protracted video game.

By most of the standards usually applied, it certainly doesn't play like a film. From an incoherent screenplay and frequently unintelligible dialogue, a plot sketch just about emerges. Covert operative and assassin Al Simmons believes he's acting for truth, justice and The American Way. But the director of ultra-secret government agency A-6 Jason Wynn (Martin 'What am I doing in this?' Sheen) is in league with Satan and plans to destroy mankind with the ultimate biological weapon.

Jason and an evil spy babe kill Simmons, who goes to Hell, where the rest of us have been since the opening credits. The Devil renames the mutated Simmons 'Spawn' and makes him General of Hell's Army, in return letting him out to visit his beloved wife.

Back among the living, who shun him, poor old Spawn is torn between his commitments in Hell and doing the right thing while more preoccupied with jealousy over his widow becoming an item with his erstwhile best friend. Throughout all of this, Satan's right-hand fiend, Clown (an unrecognisable Leguizamo) bounces around being evil and eating pizza with maggots on it. And occasionally the mysterious Cogliostro (Nicol 'I've played Hamlet for God's sake' Williamson) appears wielding a sword and providing portentous voice-over that makes us none the wiser.

Only the creature formerly known as Al's yappy little dog Spaz recognises Spawn and remains a faithful friend. Ahhhhhhh!

First-time director Dippe has a CV boasting tip-top credits as a special effects whizz (*Terminator 2: Judgment Day*, *Jurassic Park*) and, with the Industrial Light And Magic team, he's devised scads of wizard FX and morphing that keep shifting spectacularly across the screen.

But he's clueless at telling a story. It's simply a parade of toys and tricks, without a jot of playfulness, knowing humour or campery to endear itself. ★ **AE**

SPECIES (1995)

Starring: *Natasha Henstridge (Sil), Michelle Williams (Young Sil), Ben Kingsley (Xavier Fitch), Michael Madsen (Preston Lennox), Alfred Molina (Dr. Stephen Arden), Forest Whitaker (Dan Smithson)*
Director: *Roger Donaldson*
Screenwriter: *Dennis Felman*
18/103 mins./Drama/Thriller/Sci-fi/USA

A female alien goes on the hunt for male humans to impregnate her – killing her lovers once they've served their usefulness.

Take one part *Invasion of the Body Snatchers*, one part *Alien*, one part *Basic Instinct*, one part of the Michael Crichton back-catalogue, and mix together with liberal helpings of hokum. The result is *Species*, a very silly sci-fi horror movie which, if not aiming to be a glossy B-movie, certainly ends up that way with a quota of snigger-inducing lines, a cheesy Earth-invasion plot and gloriously dumb entertainment value.

Gorgeous ex-model Henstridge is the babe with alien-coded DNA who escapes from her mad scientist creator, looking for the perfect mate with whom to populate the world with her H.R. Giger-designed nasties. This, naturally, involves Miss Henstridge removing her top at frequent intervals to entice healthy LA 'meat' to join her for some rumpy, before she finishes them off in gruesome style. Following in her blood-strewn wake is a select team of boffins, each with their particular expertise: Madsen is the muscle; a shrunken Alfred Molina is the Limey anthropologist; Marg Helgenberger is the microbiologist; and Forest Whitaker provides ESP talents which seem only to reflect the painfully obvious. All of them adopt the uniform expressiveness of plywood – a post-Schindler Kingsley is, hopefully, just cleaning the valves.

The result is cranky, unconvincing and, at times, out-loud laughable. The effects budget was clearly reserved for the *Aliens* rip-off climax with its all-too-brief burst of Giger-illuminated weirdness, and there is none of the other-worldly gloom of *Alien* among the neon-lit arid streets of downtown LA. Donaldson is unable to brew up serious chills; Henstridge is too cute and her alien manifestation (popping out during fits of pique or orgasm) a bizarre cross between scuttling spider and hood ornament.

Yet stupidity doesn't necessarily deliver boredom. There is an appealing vibrancy to this potty monster flick, clambering out of video hell to haunt the popcorn halls. If you're up for a giggle, it's an absolute scream. ★★ **IN**

SPEED (1994)

Starring: *Keanu Reeves (Officer Jack Traven), Dennis Hopper (Howard Payne), Sandra Bullock (Annie Porter), Jeff Daniels (Det. Harold 'Harry' Temple), Alan Ruck (Stephens)*
Director: *Jan De Bont*
Screenwriter: *Graham Yost*
15/111 mins./Action/Thriller/USA
Awards: *Academy Awards – Best Sound Effects Editing, Best Sound, BAFTA – Best Editing, Best Sound*

Bomber Payne sets a challenge for LAPD cop Traven: he places a bomb on a city bus which will arm itself when the bus reaches 50 mph, and which will explode if the bus drops below that speed or if any of the passengers try to escape.

In downtown LA a bus explodes in front of bomb-disposal cop Jack Traven. Shocked, he walks to a ringing pay-phone and picks the receiver up. 'Pop quiz hotshot,' a voice hisses, 'there's a bomb on a bus …' Meanwhile office worker Annie Porter boards the 2525, unaware of the drama about to unfold … The pitch, of course, is as good as it ever was. But had 20th

Century Fox gone with the original casting choices, who knows if *Speed* would have become the major action hit of the 90s.

But then again Fox had few hopes with the cast and key crew that they eventually wound up with. Graham Yost was an unknown screenwriter with a factual book about spy gadgetry and a few sitcom scripts behind him. Jan De Bont was better known as Joel Schumacher's cinematographer of choice (Flatliners). And Keanu Reeves, well wasn't he the guy from *Bill And Ted*? Great at the shambling surf-dude schtick, sure ... but playing an action hero? It's tempting to credit *Speed*'s success to Graham Yost's screenplay; the central conceit is certainly a classic. It should be. Much of the original idea was Akira Kurosawa's. Back in 1990 Yost, then a struggling writer of book jacket copy and entries for The Encyclopaedia Britannica had first heard of an unproduced Kurosawa screenplay about a train that had a bomb on board and couldn't stop from his father Elwy, who with his regular TV show was Canada's version of Barry Norman.

The screenplay was made by the infamous Golan/Globus Cannon partnership in 1985 and predictably transformed into a box-office disaster *Runaway Train*. Yost eventually went to see the film and realised that Dad had got it wrong, there was no bomb involved (in fact, his dad may have been remembering the 1975 Japanese movie *Bullet Train* and mixing it up with the similar Kurosawa script). 'I came out of the movie and thought it was pretty good,' he later remembered, 'but I thought it would have been better if there was a bomb that was going to blow up. Being physically able to stop but not being able to because something horrible would happen. And I thought it would work better on a bus. I pitched the idea to a friend and said the bus shouldn't go below 20 miles an hour. He said "Make it 50." ' *Speed* started to gather, well, momentum.

Tagline
Get ready for rush hour.

But if the problem that *Speed*'s screenplay sets is a compelling example of the high-concept hook, the casting of Reeves and Bullock is the classy chassis over the purring plot engine. 'Chemistry' is an overused word in movie circles, but this couple have the celluloid equivalent of Thomas Salter's Lab 7, the one with two tubes of magnesium ribbon. A fact attested to by *Speed 2: Cruise Control*'s disastrous failure, partly the result of a moronic script certainly, but Jason Patric, ruggedly good-looking as he was, just couldn't match Reeves's buzz-cut brio.

When Jack Traven first arrives he's the picture of gum-chewing action man heroics complete with all the cool optional accessories: neck mikes, outrageous firepower, combat pants, a ramp-leaping car and a slightly less good-looking buddy with whom to trade wiscrackery. You wind up feeling that there is quite possibly a switch behind his velvety noggin with which to operate the Eagle Eyes. Sandra Bullock avoids the traditional screaming imperilment traditionally required of women in action movies and, as a couple, they're as attractive as any in screen history.

And then there's the pace. *Die Hard* springs to mind, but even McTiernan's classic didn't leap into the action and salty Shane Black-esque one-liners (in fact, mostly penned by an uncredited Joss Whedon who did a comprehensive dialogue polish) as rapidly as De Bont's movie; he wastes no time at all. We meet our villain – Dennis Hopper as a psychotic action movie baddie, why didn't anyone think of that before – within a minute of the opening credits. Within seconds we've had a brutal head stabbing, a lift plunge, and Dennis Hopper laughing demonically.

Here, as with the rest of the film De Bont – with surgical precision – guts the movie of any extraneous material leaving only one gloriously extended action scene. For a movie so apparently self-assured it seems strange that *Speed* turned out to be an unrepeatable confluence of happy accidents.

Jan De Bont would reveal himself to be a directorial flash in the pan, delivering with *Speed 2: Cruise Control* the worst sequel to a genuine hit since John Boorman ordered up a mess of locusts and excreted *Exorcist II: The Heretic*. Graham Yost sans Japanese input would prove unable to pull off the same bravura screenplay fireworks, penning the relatively disappointing *Broken Arrow* (1996) and *Hard Rain* (1998) before producing the truly unbearable *Mission To Mars* (1999). Sandra Bullock would go on to the sappy likes of *Forces Of Nature*. But it did transform Reeves into a copper-bottomed superstar who would cement his rep as the key action performer of the decade by appearing in the next movie to utterly redefine the action and sci-fi genres simultaneously: *The Matrix*. ★★★★★ **AS**

Movie Trivia: Speed

Tom Hanks, Johnny Depp, Tom Cruise and Bruce Willis were all offered the lead before Reeves. The bus was initially intended to circle the LA Dodgers stadium car park but changed to LAX airport because they couldn't gain permission. The bridge jump sequence had to be taken twice because the first landing looked too smooth. And the bridge was always there – it was just digitally removed for the film.

ⓞ SPEED 2: CRUISE CONTROL (1997)

Starring: *Sandra Bullock (Annie), Jason Patric (Officer Alex Shaw), Willem Dafoe (John Geiger), Temuera Morrison (Juliano), Brian McCardie (Merced)*
Director: *Jan De Bont*
Screenwriters: *Randall McCormick, Jeff Nathanson, from a story by Jan De Bont, characters by Graham Yost*
PG/119 mins./Action/Thriller/USA

Awards: *Razzie Awards – Worst Remake or Sequel*

Former bus driver, Annie Porter, is on a cruise with new boyfriend, SWAT man Alex, hoping to relax. But when the ship is overtaken by diamond thieves she's called into action once again ...

How good was the original *Speed*? So good that the balsawood Keanu Reeves couldn't spoil it. Its runaway lift/bus/train axis was so brazen, it was impossible not to get carried along. The inevitable *Speed 2* docks with a dippy subtitle, a convenient pun characteristic of the entire movie, which isn't anything like bad – just likely to induce that sinking feeling before it starts.

It's wet. And not just in a maritime sense. Aboard the *Seabourn Legend*, a luxury liner messing about in the Caribbean, we find *Speed*'s Annie Porter, who's wisely dumped Keanu and is on a make-or-break romantic holiday with new beau Alex Shaw, an intrepid SWAT who risks his finely-chiselled life on a daily basis. After going steady for seven months, he plans to spring the engagement ring while at sea. Human interest in place (the diamond sparkler will remain, implausibly, in Patric's trouser pocket for the action's entire duration), the trouble is piped aboard in the form of Geiger, a disgruntled ex-employee of the line who devised its computer infrastructure, and plans to hijack the tub with one mad eye on some diamonds, the other on a psychotic industrial tribunal. By the way, he keeps leeches in his bath and talks to them.

Geiger infiltrates the system to trigger a bogus fire alarm in order to necessitate a passenger evacuation, and in the ensuing lifeboat confusion, Patric and Bullock opt to stay behind when he smells a rat who isn't leaving the sinking ship. As they grapple for control, the boat hurtles towards an oil tanker, various stragglers need rescuing, and the Speed bit begins.

The well-staged, evening-dress panic scenes are straight out of *The Poseidon Adventure*, which is no bad thing, even if one gag is a shameless

S

steal – survivors are forced to take off their clothes to plug a gas leak, and one woman refuses to disrobe because she hasn't got any underwear on. *Speed 2*'s continual nods to old movies like the aforementioned, *The Last Voyage* and *A Night To Remember* are balanced out only by *Speed* in-jokes – the dude who had his car nicked in the first film returns, only to have his speedboat acquisitioned; Bullock is almost hit by a speeding bus while on a driving test – and, curiously, a 'quote' from *Crimson Tide* about Kurt Jurgens' role in *The Enemy Below*.

The action, as you'd expect with *Speed* king Jan De Bont at the rudder, is coolly done – plenty of slippery ropes, thundering propellers, flooding corridors, tricky hatches, even a chainsaw – and anything the out-of-control liner rams into is a point in the momentum's favour. However, this particular runaway vehicle is moving at 18 knots (roughly 20 miles an hour!) and thus lacks the urgency of the big bus. Meanwhile, top-billed Sandra Bullock, formerly an accidental heroine, is insultingly sidelined here to boyfriend's little helper and hostage-in-waiting. Patric is the film's actual seabourn legend, and a watchable one, but the pair's gooey relationship sorely lacks *Speed*'s thrown-together dynamic.

Indeed, the entire shebang could've done with a dose of the first film's dark, nutty urgency; hell, the climactic crash is even played for knockabout comedy. *Speed 2* is a well-above-average armrest-gripper with little in it to upset the children excepting, perhaps, Dafoe's lengthy white teeth, and the fact that UB40 provide onboard cabaret. ★★ **AC**

SPELLBOUND (1945)

Starring: *Ingrid Bergman (Dr. Constance Peterson), Gregory Peck (John 'JB' Ballantine), Jean Acker (Matron), Donald Curtis (Harry), Rhonda Fleming (Mary Carmichael), John Emery (Dr. Fleurot), Leo G. Carroll (Dr Murchison)*
Director: *Alfred Hitchcock*
Screenwriters: *Ben Hecht, Angus Macphail, based on the novel* The House Of Dr Edwardes *by Francis Beeding (John Palmer, Hilary St. George Saunders)*
PG/111 mins/Thriller/USA

Awards: *Academy Awards – Best Drama/Comedy, Score*

John Ballantine arrives at the Green Manors mental insitution in Vermont under the impression that he is psychiatrist Dr. Edwardes. However, he gradually comes to remember his real identity and the event that prompted his bout of amnesia with the help of Dr. Constance Peterson, who learns to liberate her own repressed emotions in the process.

Having introduced some subtle Freudian symbolism into *Lifeboat*, Alfred Hitchcock was keen to go further and produce Hollywood's first feature about psychoanalysis. So, while he was in Britain shooting the wartime propaganda shorts Bon Voyage and Aventure Malgache, Angus MacPhail and Ben Hecht worked on this adaptation of the 1927 novel *The House of Dr Edwardes*, which was written by John Leslie Palmer and Hilary Aidan St. George Saunders under the more manageable name of Francis Beeding.

Hecht's screenplay was strewn with Freudian allusion, ranging from Ballantine's ownership of a single suitcase to the opening of doors on his first kiss with Constance (the last of which gave onto a radiant white light). But Hitchcock's visuals owed just as much to the Expressionist tendency he had acquired while working in Germany in the mid-1920s. His use of angle and shadow was particularly UFA-like, as was the inclusion of gambling motifs (with the inmates' card game replacing the script's original sequence in which they rehearsed William Congreve's 1700 comedy of marital manners, *The Way of the World*). However, the most obvious Expressionist connection, with Robert Wiene's *The Cabinet of Dr Caligari*, would only become apparent during the denouement.

Yet, for all its Germanic influences, the film's most famous sequence was produced by the Spanish surrealist Salvador Dali. Echoing both Dali's own distinctive paintings and his 1928 screen collaboration with Luis Buñuel, *Un Chien Andalou*, Ballantine's dream was originally filmed in four parts. But producer David O. Selznick removed a ballroom segment in which Constance turned into a statue as he was convinced that audiences would find it as baffling as he did. Ironically, such psycho-symbolism also eluded the Breen Office, which must have suspected what Hitch was up to and yet it passed several instances of phallic and castratory imagery.

However, no amount of intellectual ingenuity could turn Ingrid Bergman into a credible shrink and there's precious little spark between her and Gregory Peck. But Hitchcock had become hooked on his themes and he would return to them in *Vertigo*, *Psycho* and *Marnie*. ★★★ **DP**

SPELLBOUND (2002)

Starring: as themselves: *Harry Altman, Angela Arenivar, Ted Brigham, April DeGideo, Neil Kadakia, Nupur Lala, Emily Stagg, Ashley White*
Director: *Jeffrey Blitz*
U/92 mins./Documentary/USA

Eight American high school kids from different parts of the country compete for the 1999 National Spelling Bee – a nail-biting competition whose teen contestants train as rigorously as athletes.

Among the more unique aspects of Americana is the National Spelling Bee – an annual competition in which those who are no doubt picked last for basketball practice demonstrate their alternative talents by spelling words like 'Schadenfreude' and 'haemoglobin' live on television.

This documentary follows eight hopefuls from their home towns across the country to the national finals.

What emerges is a captivating picture of what it's like to be a teenager and 'different' in the USA. From the gawky farm boy whose parents sit on the porch bemused by their son's intelligence, to the daughter of Mexican immigrants whose father speaks no English at all, these kids are isolated by their 'smartness' and find some solace in the realisation that they're not alone.

There is the odd glitch: first-time documentarian Jeffrey Blitz follows too many kids in insufficient depth, and the structure of the film is disappointingly unimaginative. But, otherwise, this is a compelling, sometimes surprisingly emotionally involving film. ★★★★ **AS**

SPHERE (1998)

Starring: *Dustin Hoffman (Dr. Norman Goodman), Sharon Stone (Dr. Elizabeth 'Beth' Halperin), Samuel L. Jackson (Dr. Harry Adams), Peter Coyote (Captain Harold C. Barnes), Live Schreiber (Dr. Ted Fielding), Queen Latifah (Alice 'Teeny' Fletcher)*
Director: *Barry Levinson*
Screenwriter: *Stephen Hauser, Paul Attanasio, based on the novel by Michael Crichton, adapted by Kurt Wimmer*
12/134 mins./Sci-fi/Thriller/USA

An intrepid crew explore a spaceship that contains a golden sphere which will realise their darkest dreams.

Take a science-fiction best seller by überscribe Michael Crichton, throw in a heavyweight cast, float the project on a $100 million budget, entrust it to the skilled hands of Barry Levinson (*Diner*, *Rain Man*, *Bugsy*) and you have a project that generates no small degree of expectation. Especially given the substance – alien contact – still Hollywood's flavour du jour.

Comparisons will inevitably be drawn with James Cameron's 1989 thriller *The Abyss*, but the 'big idea' – a space odyssey that takes place underwater – can be copyrighted by Crichton, whose 1987 novel is followed here to the letter. Thus a posse of disparate scientists plumb the depths to investigate a massive spacecraft that has – judging by the coral encrusted upon it – been lodged at the bottom of the Pacific for around 300 years.

There's a psychologist, a biochemist, a mathematician and an astrophysicist – all cooped up in a claustrophobic underwater habitat and duly drilled by their military charge into a welcoming committee to greet the spacecraft's presumed crew of little green men. They, we learn, are still emitting some sort of signal from within.

All is not what it seems, however, and after a shock discovery about the nature of the craft on the ocean floor, the vibes are traced to a mysterious golden globe in the cargo hold which possesses the power to evoke killer jellyfish and mean little sea snakes, and to induce neurotic hallucinations in the humans. Hell, it even finds time to pop up on-line for a cyberchat with the folks from science central. And it is here, unfortunately, that the movie becomes slightly unstuck, for while the stage is set for an Alamo of isolated earthlings to face the awesome power 'out there', in the absence of a discernible antagonist, the film's attempted psychological drama becomes increasingly muddled.

It is not merely the characters who are left to wonder what the hell is going on. There's a baffling bombardment of ideas, including underwater eggs and an inexplicable power cut. And while one would normally divorce oneself from the source novel when appraising a film, Levinson doesn't allow that, following Crichton's novel too literally, dividing the film up episodically, each segment preceded by a flashed chapter heading. Indeed, on more than one occasion this tends toward anticlimax. That's not to say that *Sphere* is without its moments. There's some stewing tension between Hoffman and Stone (potential members of the Mile Low Club), and an inspired gag in which Hoffman, upon whose report the government based its alien and encounter strategy, confesses he merely ripped off Isaac Asimov and Rod Serling. However, it's a curious indictment when the best moments in a film of this magnitude come from characters sitting around and talking.

He may have pulled off a Crichton story before (in 1994's sexual harassment caper, *Disclosure*), but one suspects that Levinson's first foray into sci-fi may be his last. His arch political satire, *Wag The Dog*, shows where his sensibilities really lie. ★★★ **JD**

SPIDER (2002)

Starring: *Ralph Fiennes (Dennis 'Spider' Cleg), Miranda Richardson (Yvonne/Mrs. Cleg), Gabriel Byrne (Bill Cleg), Lynn Redgrave (Mrs. Wilkinson), John Neville (Terrence)*
Director: *David Cronenberg*
Screenwriter: *Patrick McGrath, based on his novel*
15/94 mins./Drama/Mystery/Canada/UK/Japan/France

After 20 years in a hospital for the mentally ill suffering from schizophrenia, Dennis 'Spider' Cleg is released to live in a boarding house for recovering mental patients on the outskirts of London. Returning to his childhood haunts, Spider starts to relive the events that led to his madness.

Spider is one of those truly baffling oddities: a film that has brilliance in it, yet almost does its best to hide it. Adapted from the acclaimed novel by Patrick McGrath, the film gives Ralph Fiennes' eponymous central character little to do other than wander around a haunted and desolate London, only muttering occasionally, re-enacting traumatic scenes from his childhood.

Having a central character whose role in the film is entirely passive makes for very difficult viewing, and while Fiennes' performance is impressive and committed, it is not one from which we can derive any pleasure.

The film, which director Cronenberg describes as a psychodrama influenced by Samuel Beckett, is as minimal and perplexing as anything the playwright himself produced. After the criticism of his last film, *eXistenZ*, as insubstantial fun, it's almost as if Cronenberg wanted to make a film that was its polar opposite. Fluffy and light this is not. ★★★ **ND**

SPIDER-MAN (2002)

Starring: *Tobey Maguire (Spider-Man/Peter Parker), Willem Dafoe (Green Goblin/Norman Osborn), Kirsten Dunst (Mary Jane Watson), James Franco (Harry Osborn), Cliff Robertson (Ben Parker), Rosemary Harris (May Parker), J.K. Simmons (J. Jonah Jameson)*
Director: *Sam Raimi*
Screenwriters: *David Koepp, from the Marvel comic books by Stan Lee, Steve Ditko*
12/116 mins./Fantasy/Action/Sci-fi/USA

Awards: *Empire Awards – Best Actress*

When a high school photographer is bitten by a genetically altered spider, he gains arachnid-esque powers and becomes a crime-fighter.

With a $100 million-plus budget and a comic book legend comes great responsibility, and Sam Raimi has not fumbled. A perfect melding of director and subject, this supremely entertaining take on the worldwide web-slinger pulls off the nifty trick of satisfying the fanboy geeks, the Raimi freaks, and the movie thrill-seeker in one sublime swoop.

What's great about *Spider-Man* is its ability to hold onto seemingly obsolete values – characters you can root for, plotting that makes sense – while still delivering maximum bang for the buck.

In a leisurely opening more reminiscent of *Superman* than anything by Simon West, Raimi sketches Peter Parker's geek credentials with telling character beats. Once the spider skills have been acquired – Maguire brings an endearing goofiness to his first attempts at web-slinging – the script (although lacking trademark Spidey one-liners) strikes a streamlined simplicity: it's Spidey vs. Green Goblin. No masterplans to freeze the city, just showdown after beautiful showdown.

Amid all the comic book action, however, Raimi preserves Spider-Man's (both character and movie) humanity. Maguire effortlessly makes the transition from alpha-nerd to action man with skill and aplomb; playing niftily on his indie film persona, he invests Peter with a winning warmth while remaining believable as someone uneasy in the confines of his own skin.

His relationship with small-town love Mary Jane (Dunst, appealing in a poorly-conceived role) is sweet and endearing, adding an emotional element missing from many blockbusters. Staying the right side of hammy, Dafoe is brooding with intensity as mad scientist Norman Osborn, and brimming with evil glee as his alter-ego, Green Goblin.

If occasionally a dodgy CGI shot slips through the net, the realisation of Spider-Man cavorting through a bustling metropolis, barely in control of his own trajectory, is a spandex ballet so exuberant and damn-right cool that it doesn't matter. Be it the sight of Spidey swinging round flagpoles or landing on balconies, exhilaration outstrips execution to make neck hairs stand to attention.

For all Spider-Man's reputation as the gaudy, sunny side of superherodom, Raimi manages to syringe some darkness into the mix. There's the genuinely unnerving moment when Norman, taunted by the Goblin's cackles, goes searching for the source, only to be confronted by his own face in the mirror.

Or the fantastic image of Parker's face glimpsed through the ripped Spider-Man's mask, capturing the warped duality of the character. And the final Spidey/Goblin showdown has a stylised brutality that's more punishing than any cert. 12 has the right to be.

Despite a below-par Danny Elfman score, Raimi's direction is marked by a craftsmanship that befits blockbuster prestige but still retains his unique sensibility. When the genetically-modified spider bites into Parker, the camera is total Raimi with its twists and spirals.

Even more impressive, an impressionistic montage depicting Parker dreaming up the Spidey suit and the *Matrix*-esque portrayal of his emerging spider-sense rank among cinema's greatest renderings of purely comic book conceits. Much like the movie itself. ★★★★ **IF**

S

Movie Trivia: Spider-Man

Tobey Maguire had never read a Spider-Man comic prior to making this film. John Malkovich and Nicolas Cage were offered the role of the Green Goblin. Spidey co-creator Stan Lee briefly appears as a man saving a child from falling debris in Times Square. In the same scene, an ad for Terminix is noticeable, a comic allusion to insect control.

SPIDER-MAN 2 (2004)

Starring: *Tobey Maguire (Spider-Man/Peter Parker), Kirsten Dunst (Mary Jane Watson), James Franco (Harry Osborn), Alfred Molina (Doc Ock/Dr. Otto Octavius), Rosemary Harris (May Parker), J.K. Simmons (J. Jonah Jameson)*
Director: *Sam Raimi*
Screenwriter: *Alvin Sargent, from a story by Alfred Gough, Miles Millar, Michael Chabon, from the Marvel comic books by Stan Lee, Steve Ditko*
PG/127 mins./Fantasy/Action/Sci-fi/USA

Awards: *Academy Awards – Best Visual Effects, Empire Awards – Best Director*

Two years on, and life's just got tougher for Peter Parker. He's having problems dealing with his feelings for Mary Jane, his editor at the Daily Bugle keeps firing him and his best mate Harry is desperate for vengeance against his crimefighting alter ego. All that and a new, unhinged technology-boosted bad guy appears on the scene: Dr Octopus . . .

'With great power,' goes the Spider-Man credo, 'comes great responsibility.' Well, for the primary-coloured webslinger's second multiplex swing shift, it's not 'great responsibility' he's had to contend with so much as great expectation. Sam Raimi's back at the helm with a promise to keep the first movie's balance of heart and high-flying action, while the original cast's return signals the fact that this is very much a character-powered 'part two' continuation, rather than a shallow, *Batman*ish excuse for some fresh, ham-scented villains to flounce about.

Thankfully, *Spider-Man 2* does undoubtedly pounce out of the top drawer as a most satisfying, spectacle-packed movie. Like its predecessor, it offers a strong story rather than a feeble excuse to connect set-pieces, now focusing on Peter Parker's struggle to balance his identities – the great responsibility versus all those smaller ones required to get by in everyday life – and suppress his not-so-unrequited love for Mary Jane. Given the amount of time Raimi spends dealing with this, rather than Spidey's mask-on antics, he does run the risk of losing our attention. But Maguire and Dunst are too accomplished to let us wander, keeping their scenes taut and tingling with sexual energy.

As for Raimi, it's clear he's been given more freedom on this instalment. When he's not stirring up the Parker angst or toying with his protagonist's lovelife, he indulges his own cheeky sense of humour. In one scene he allows a tuneless busker to trill the old *Spider-Man* TV cartoon theme-music (just one of so many compulsory winks to the sizeable fanboy contingent), in several others he requires Maguire – in beleagured, shoved-around-by-the-world mode – to perform some of the brutal pratfalling he was so fond of forcing on old buddy Bruce Campbell in the *Evil Dead* movies. Speaking of which, there's even one moment when he tests the classification boards with a stylish and unashamedly violent homage to his early splatterstick comedy-horrors: just substitute the floor-skimming unseen-evil POV for Doc Ock's tentacle-cam, a panicking surgeon for Ash and a chainsaw for a bonesaw, and you're there.

It helps, of course, that Raimi has some much-improved FX at his disposal, plus a more malleable bad guy to play with than the Green Goblin. Not to diss Willem Dafoe – as the pumped-up, brain-wronged Norman Osborn, he was perfect; but that stiff, Power Rangers-reject battle armour canned a great performance and constrained the action choreography. Despite his burliness, Alfred Molina's Doctor Octopus is a far more kinetic opponent for Spidey and their intense, frantic, very often vertical man-dances, with Ock's whirling, serpentine superlimbs stretching his foe's fighting talents to the limit, trounce any of the first movie's showdowns.

Beyond the battlezone, Molina shakes up just the right cocktail of brooding, storm-eyed menace and showy villainy, bringing necessary weight to a character who, at the end of the day, is a man possessed by a quartet of sinister robot snakes. It's just a shame that we don't, as an audience, get to spend a bit more time with him, and that personality-wise he's virtually a rushed carbon copy of the Goblin – you know: good scientist, experiment goes wrong, consumed by ambition, internal struggle . . .

In other ways, too, the sequel treads rather too closely to Part One. There's a moment when an astonished Peter plummets mid-jump, another involving a burning building and MJ gets wet again – while repeating her irked abductee act. But it's not so familiar it breeds contempt, and when something screams with this much quality, it seems churlish to criticise it for being more of the same. ★★★★ **DJ**

THE SPIDER'S STRATAGEM (STRATEGIA DEL RAGNO) (1970)

Starring: *Giullio Brogi (Athos Magnami), Alida Valli (Draifa), Pippo Campanini (Gaibazzi), Franco Giovanelli (Rasori), Tino Scotti (Costa)*
Director: *Bernardo Bertolucci*
Screenwriters: *Bernardo Bertolucci, Eduardo de Gregorio, Marilu Parolini, based on the story 'Theme Of The Traitor And Hero' by Jorge Luis Borges*
PG/100 mins./Drama/Italy

Thirty years after the assassination of anti-fascist leader Athos Magnani, his son, Athos Jr., returns to the small Italian town of Tara and is urged by his father's mistress, Draifa, to find out who was responsible for a crime that still remain a mystery.

Having forced his hero in *Partner* to confront his alter ego, Bernardo Bertolucci nigh-on simultaneously joined the Communist Party and entered psychoanalysis. A period of intense political and personal introspection followed and its ramifications can be detected in this masterly adaptation of the Argentinian writer Jorge Luis Borges's short story, 'Theme of the Traitor and the Hero', which was produced by the Italian television station, RAI.

Transposing the original setting from revolutionary Ireland to the provincial Italian town of Tara (whose name had links to both Ireland and *Gone With the Wind*), Bertolucci sought to show how the past repeated itself by staging a series of repetitions that were enacted by the same cast in the same roles, costumes and locations.

However, this was more than a mere dramaturgic gimmick, as *The Spider's Stratagem* is less a film about politics than a study of a father's imprint upon the psyche of his son. Thus, Freud triumphed over Marx in Bertolucci's approach and he even toned down the techniques borrowed from Jean-Luc Godard that had contributed to *Partner*'s misfiring.

However, Bertolucci still used Vittorio Storaro's mobile camera and the atmospheric Sabbioneta locations to suggest Athos Jr.'s fraught state of mind, as he revisited the places that had staged his father's own drama. Thus, he attends a performance of Verdi's *Rigoletto* in the same opera house where Athos Sr. had been murdered during the aria 'Maledizione' and flees the tavern when he had gone to plan the attempt on Mussolini's life.

Yet, even though he thinks he has come to understand his father's legacy, Athos Jr. is left unsure whether he was a coward or the architect of his own mythologising demise. All that's clear, as he waits on the train station and notices that the track has become overgrown, is that he is as trapped in the web that has been spun around Athos Sr.'s reputation as

Draifa (Alida Valli in a role echoing *The Third Man*) and the residents of a town that seems to have stood still since 1936. ★★★★★ **DP**

THE SPIRAL STAIRCASE (1946)

Starring: *Dorothy (Helen Capel), George Brent (Prof. Warren), Ethel Barrymore (Mrs. Warren), Kent Smith (Dr. Parry), Rhonda Fleming (Blanche), Gordon Oliver (Steve Warren), Elsa Lanchester (Mrs. Oates)*
Director: *Robert Siodmak*
Screenwriter: *Mel Dinelli, based on the novel* Some Must Watch *by Ethel Lina White*
PG/83 mins./Thriller/USA

Mute from childhood and increasingly unnerved by the activities of a serial killer who preys on women with physical imperfections, Helen Capel serves as a companion to bed ridden widow, Mrs. Warren, who despises her weak sons, a bookish scientist and a dissolute cad.

Based on Ethel Lina White's novel *Some Must Watch*, this was a throwback to the early days of Talkie horror when the Expressionist visuals imported from Germany were allied to the latest sound effects to produce what became known as the 'Old Dark House' thriller. Indeed, this was almost a case study in stock shock effects, with the whistling wind, creaking doors and gates and blowing curtains and candles to whip up the eerie atmosphere.

But director Robert Siodmak also made numerous references to cinema's silent past to reinforce Helen Capel's mute vulnerability (in a change from the book, where she was crippled but quite capable of speech). Thus, the trip to the nickelodeon was not only a quaint period detail (the first makeshift movie theatres had opened in 1905, the year before the film story takes place), but it also emphasised the limitations of non-verbal communication to anticipate Helen's imminent peril. The surfeit of mirrors and windows in the Warren mansion similarly recalled the German films of Fritz Lang, who was UFA's star director when Siodmak began his career, and whose use of mood and shadow was a key influence on the house horror style at Universal, where Siodmak had made the likes of *Son of Dracula*, *Phantom Lady* and *The Suspect* (all 1944) before moving to RKO.

However, some have claimed this chilling classic for film noir, on account of its use of brooding chiaroscuro and psychological dislocation. There's certainly plenty of then-chic Freudian allusion on display, with Helen having been dumb since a childhood trauma, while the sins of the sons owed much to the domineering nature of the now bed ridden matriarch. Moreover, audiences in 1946 would probably have recognised the link between the killer's motive and the newly exposed Nazi experiments in eugenics, which had been inspired by a similarly sinister detestation of non conformity.

Although Ethel Barrymore earned an Oscar nomination, the ensemble playing was uniformly excellent. But the star turns here were Albert S. D'Agostino's wondrously unsubtle sets and Nicholas Musuraca's prowling deep-focus photography, which kept viewers ever vigilant while leaving them in the dark. ★★★★ **DP**

THE SPIRIT OF ST. LOUIS (1957)

Starring: *James Stewart (Charles Augustus 'Slim' Lindbergh), Murray Hamilton (Bud Gurney), Bartlett Robinson (Benjamin Frank Mahoney), Marc Connelly (Father Hussman)*
Director: *Billy Wilder*
Screenwriters: *Billy Wilder, Wendell Mayes, Charles Lederer, from the autobiography by Charles A. Lingbergh*
U/129 mins./Drama/Biography/USA

Pioneering flyer Charles Lindbergh dreams of designing and piloting a plane across the Atlantic but faces his many obstacles in fulfilling that dream.

In 1927, the 25-year-old Charles Lindbergh, equipped with 451 gallons of gas, two canteens of water and four sandwiches, completed the first solo transatlantic flight in his plane *The Spirit of St Louis*. Over 100,000 people were there to greet him in Paris and he returned home to a New York ticker tape parade and was acclaimed a true American hero.

But by the time this film was released thirty years later, to a critical and box office drubbing, Lindbergh was seen as a more complicated character. He was a rich man and had married an Ambassador's daughter, but fame had led to their first son Charles being kidnapped and killed and before World War II Lindbergh was active in the Isolationist movement making a speech that identified three groups as unwisely advocating the war: 'the British, the Roosevelt Administration and the Jews'.

Is it any wonder this film had a negative reception? Added to the raw feelings the postwar public may have had about Lindbergh, was the casting of James Stewart (in a role James Dean had considered before his death) – a man of almost 50, twice as old as the flier.

Yet the best parts of this film are Stewart's monologues in the cockpit, articulating the internal workings of a man trying to keep himself awake (for thirty-three and a half hours), calculating out if he can technically stop flying long enough to scrape ice off the wings and picking a fly as a conversation partner. If Tom Hanks was modelling his *Cast Away* performance on anyone it was Stewart.

Wilder's picture is characteristically talky – if you want airplane action Howard Hughes is your man, Wilder was all about what made Lindbergh tick. So while it never quite captures the excitement of the flight, what this film does nail is the mental processes that made it possible and, as a slice of history, it's well worth it for that alone. ★★★ **EC**

THE SPIRIT OF THE BEEHIVE (EL ESPIRITU DE LA COLMENA) (1973)

Starring: *Ana Torrent (Ana), Isabel Telleria (Isabel), Fernando Fernan Gomez (Fernando), Teresa Gimpera (Teresa), Jose Villasante (the Monster), Lally Soldavilla (Milagros)*
Director: *Victor Erice*
Screenwriter: *Francisco J. Querejata, based on an idea by Erice, Angel Fernandez Santos*
PG/98 mins./Drama/Spain

Detached from her parents, Fernando and Teresa, seven-year-old Ana seeks solace from the deprivations of post-Civil War Spain in caring for the deserter who reminds her of the Monster she came to pity at the screening of James Whale's *Frankenstein*, which she attended with her older sister, Isabel.

With Ana Torrent's beguiling display of confused curiosity and trusting innocence recalling Brigitte Fossey's in René Clément's *Jeux Interdits*, Victor Erice's masterly discourse on juvenile psychology is an elliptical, lyrical exploration of myth, misunderstanding, deception and illusion that defies precise interpretation.

The action was sublimely photographed by Luis Cuadrado, who used long, static shots to convey the pace of life in Francisco Franco's new Spain and yellow filters to suggest the gloom that Ana and the nation would have to pierce to attain enlightenment. But this is a no mere political critique, as Erice eschewed overt allegiances in order to avoid the ire of Franco's famously sensitive censors. Instead, he concentrates on the three distinctive worlds that Ana comes to inhabit following her fateful encounter with Boris Karloff in James Whale's *Frankenstein*.

The first is the remote Castilian village, which has become a community of widows and casualties, despite evading the ravages of the Civil War. However, its poverty, despair, isolation and ennui are clearly attributed to the failure of Fascism and they also impinge upon the second world, inside the rundown farmhouse, where Ana's parents eke out an empty existence

 Child Stars Who Successfully Became Adult Stars 

1. Jodie Foster
2. Christian Bale
3. Elizabeth Taylor
4. Drew Barrymore
5. Kurt Russell
6. Mickey Rooney
7. Judy Garland
8. Elijah Wood
9. Kirsten Dunst
10. Joaquin Phoenix

with the few belongings they managed to salvage during their flight from a large estate. Teresa spends her days writing to a young lover who may be a POW, an exile in France or long dead and her preoccupations are mirrored by Fernando's obsession with his journal, his bees and his occasional, furtive visits to the nearby city.

However, the Sunday screening affords Ana an escape from this stifling confinement and she eagerly comes to equate the deserter with the helpless Creature, who so aroused her compassion that she accepts him as a surrogate father (hence giving him Fernando's treasured timepiece). Indeed, the two are so bound together in her mind that even when the deserter is arrested and shot, she takes comfort from discovering the ability to summon the Monster at will – even though his lack of memory, instinctive immorality and willingness to destroy what he does not understand identify him with the Caudillo. ★★★★★ **DP**

SPIRITED AWAY (SEN TO CHIHIRO NO KAMIKAKUSHI) (2001)

Starring: the voices of: *Rumi Hiragi (Chihiro/Sen), Miyu Irino (Yubaba/Zeniba), Takashi Naito (Chihiro's Father)/English version: Daveigh Chase (Chihiro/Sen), Michael Chiklis (Chihiro's Father)*
Director: *Hayao Miyazaki*
Screenwriter: *Hayao Miyazaki, based on his story, English version adapted by Cindy Davis Hewitt, Donald H. Hewitt, Linda Hoaglund, Jim Hubbert*
PG/124 mins./Animated/Fantasy/Adventure/Japan

Awards: *Academy Awards – Best Animated Feature*

With her parents transformed into pigs after straying into what seems to be an abandoned theme park, a spoilt ten-year-old girl takes a job in a bathhouse belonging to a wizened old crone and vows to deliver her family from its plight.

We're all used to the Hollywood ballyhoo that accompanies the release of a new cartoon. But, for once, the fuss is entirely justified (and not a merchandising opportunity in sight), as Hayao Miyazaki's masterpiece has already notched up the notable double of the Golden Bear at Berlin (which it shared with *Bloody Sunday*) and an Academy Award.

It also broke all Japanese box office records, becoming the first film to open in the States having already racked up $200 million. For the UK release, subtitled and dubbed options are available. Pixar's John Lasseter has handled dubbing duties with typical sensitivity and, thus, opened up this magical experience to young and old alike.

Owing as much to Eastern mythology as to the works of Lewis Carroll or Mervyn Peake, this is an epic with a decidedly personal touch. The plot is gloriously labyrinthine and, as in most Miyazaki films, the quest element is key. But it's subservient to the themes of self-discovery and the value of relationships and, consequently, the tone and scale of the action feels much closer to the little-seen *My Neighbour Totoro* than the overrated *Princess Mononoke*.

There are still numerous flights of fancy, however, as characters constantly shift shapes – Chihiro's parents turn into pigs, the evil Yubaba into a sinister bird, the timid No Face into a rampaging carnivore, Okutaresama the malodorous monster into a benign river spirit, and the kindly but mysterious Haku into a dragon. Then there's the spider-like boilerman, Kamaji, and his scurrying soot-ball assistants, who help Chihiro escape the forbidding bathhouse on a ghostly railway.

But what really fires the imagination is the beauty and ingenuity of the wonderland that lies at the end of a tunnel leading off from the quiet country road where Chihiro and her parents get lost. Moreover, the fact that Miyazaki and his team hand-draw the images before they're digitally coloured and animated gives them an artistry that has been woefully lacking from many recent American features. ★★★★★ **PP**

SPLASH (1984)

Starring: *Tom Hanks (Allen Bauer), Daryl Hannah (Madison), Eugene Levy (Walter Kornbluth), John Candy (Freddie Bauer), Dody Goodman (Mrs. Stimler), Shecky Greene (Mr. Buyrite), Richard B. Shull (Dr. Ross), Bobby DiCicco (Jerry)*
Director: *Ron Howard*
Screenwriters: *Bruce Jay Friedman, Lowell Ganz and Babaloo Mandel based on a story by Friedman and Brian Grazer*
PG/111 mins./Comedy USA

Boy meets mermaid. Boy leaves mermaid in sea. Mermaid tracks down boy in New York. Boy and mermaid fall in love. Boy and mermaid's happiness jeopardised by insane mermaid hunter.

In the days before he was an A-list Oscar-winning director, Ron Howard used to run a nice little sideline in small, perfectly honed comedies. This one starring Tom Hanks, another expert comedy practitioner, who went all serious, is a delight from beginning to end, a likeable, funny literal fish out of water fantasy that wins you over with its unpretentious warm heart.

The film that launched Disney's Touchstone production arm as the company had fears over the low-level nudity and adult humour, *Splash* milks its premise of an impossible love story (very popular after *E.T.*) mining all the familiar stranger in a strange land clichés (Madison learns about US culture through TV, she embarrases herself in a posh restaurant) for all they're worth. But Howard also finds some nice contrasts to the appealing love story; John Candy as Allen's boorish serial dater brother gives a salty texture to the proceedings and Eugene Levy's madcap scientist hellbent on exposing Madison as a fish-woman lends the film an edgy sense of slapstick. Howard is not afraid to commit to the potentially sillier aspects of the story, inviting the audience to participate. Elsewhere, he gives the underwater/fantasy sequences a beguiling magical quality that help to mitigate against the film's sitcom feel.

But the real reason *Splash* works is the spot-on playing of the central duo. Hannah's Madison (named after the Big Apple street corner) is charmingly innocent and naïve, proving along with *Blade Runner* that the actress feels far more comfortable playing non-humans. And Hanks is terrific as the fruit and veg seller whose listless life is transformed by an unexpected romance. Hanks can make a scene where he is just waiting for a lift funny yet doesn't shortchange on the emotional stuff too. He provides a touching centre to a sweet but never too cloying, terrifically entertaining confection. ★★★★ **IF**

SPY KIDS (2001)

Starring: *Antonio Banderas (Gregorio Cortez), Carla Gugino (Ingrid Cortez), Alexa Vega (Carmen Cortez), Daryl Sabara (Juni Cortez), Alan Cumming (Fegan Floop), Tony Shalhoub (Alexander Minion), Teri Hatcher (Ms. Gradenko)*
Director: *Robert Rodriguez*
Screenwriter: *Robert Rodriguez*
U/84 mins./Action/Adventure/Comedy/Family/USA

Carmen and Juni think they have the squarest parents around. Little do they know, they used to be two of the best spies in the biz. When their olds get kidnapped by TV kids' show host Floop, it's time for the siblings to save the day.

Robert Rodriguez has proved himself to be a fast-paced, tightly kinetic filmmaker with a knack for brevity. *El Mariachi* (1992) allegedly cost only $7,000 to make, and few of his films teeter past the 90-minute mark. Yet surprisingly – for a filmmaker who could give John Woo a serious run for his money in the cinematic gun play stakes – Rodriguez has unexpectedly found his true calling in making a kids' film.

Spy Kids is unashamedly brilliant, a fast and furious fusion of hip references, cute action, dynamic visuals and sheer delight. Rodriguez – here also acting as editor – opens strongly with a sustained bedtime story that sees mother Ingrid recount her fateful meeting with husband-to-be Gregorio and their subsequent wedding, hounded by choppers and Uzis. If God really is in the details, then Rodriguez seems to have a hotline to the deity, right down to the heart-shaped parachutes that conclude this bravura sequence.

Antonio Banderas – Rodriguez's screen alter-ego – is note perfect as the suaver-than-suave special agent, ably accompanied by Carla Gugino as his wife/fellow spy. Best of all, the kids – Vega and Sabara – are likeable and more than adequate, eschewing your typical Hollywood treacle.

Indeed, the film is so set on avoiding the sentimental traps that spoil so many kids' flicks that it even delivers its final moral directly to camera, with all the family posing as if for a snapshot, in a moment that is full of genuine wit as well as invention.

And just when you thought it couldn't get any better, an old Rodriguez buddy – we're not saying who! – shows up for the last few minutes in a hilarious cameo. ★★★★ **BM**

SPY KIDS 2: ISLAND OF LOST DREAMS (2002)

Starring: *Antonio Banderas (Gregorio Cortez), Carla Gugino (Ingrid Cortez), Alexa Vega (Carmen Cortez), Daryl Sabara (Juni Cortez), Steve Buscemi (Romero)*
Director: *Robert Rodriguez*
Screenwriter: *Robert Rodriguez*
U/96 mins./Action/Adventure/Comedy/Family/USA

When the Cortez clan are discredited by nasty secret agent counterparts, the kids journey to a mysterious island to retrieve an electronics-blocking ultra-weapon.

This comic wish-fulfilment fantasy is the proverbial treat for the whole family. Satirical touches (flying presidential Secret Service limos) and leg-pulls of espionage conventions abound, exemplified by teen spy Carmen's explanation of how she knows a particular object is what they seek: 'Because it's big and weird, and in the middle of the room.'

Rodriguez devises all the hectic stunts and ingenious gizmos a techie could want, from a robotic nose-picker to jet shoes. He also celebrates the wonder of the imagination, creating – in mad scientist Buscemi's genetic experiments and the skeletal army guarding a treasure – a beautifully executed, cute-scary homage to the wizardry of model animation pioneer Ray Harryhausen, who put the spectacular effects in spiffy Saturday adventures of yesteryear. ★★★★ **AE**

SPY KIDS 3-D: GAME OVER (2003)

Starring: *Antonio Banderas (Gregorio Cortez), Carla Gugino (Ingrid Cortez), Alexa Vega (Carmen Cortez), Daryl Sabara (Juni Cortez), Sylvester Stallone (Toymaker)*
Director: *Robert Rodriguez*
Screenwriter: *Robert Rodriguez*
U/84 mins./Action/Adventure/Comedy/Family/USA

Juni has to rescue his sister from a video game – but this time in 3-D.

This latest instalment of Rodriguez's hugely enjoyable franchise has the added spin of being almost entirely in 3-D as pint-sized secret agent Juni Cortez has to rescue his sister from a virtual reality video game that is also threatening to warp the minds of the planet's teenagers. Visually, it's a treat – Rodriguez makes the most of the multi-dimensional novelty to fling cars, knives and assorted other objects at the audience with impressive fervour – but it somehow lacks the sparkle and the wit that made the first two so much fun for kids and adults alike.

Sylvester Stallone hams things up thoroughly as the evil Toymaker, and there's a bunch of amusing celebrity cameos from the likes of George Clooney and Salma Hayek. But the film itself falls into the classic summer movie trap of selling itself on eye candy at the expense of everything else. ★★★ **CW**

THE SPY WHO CAME IN FROM THE COLD (1965)

Starring: *Richard Burton (Alex Leamas), Claire Bloom (Nan Perry), Oskar Werner (Fiedler), Peter Van Eyck (Hans Dieter-Mundt), Sam Wanamaker (Peters), George Voskovec (East German Defence Attorney), Rupert Davies (George Smiley), Cyril Cusack (Control), Michael Horden (Ashe), Robert Hardy (Carlton)*
Director: *Martin Ritt*
Screenwriters: *Paul Dehn, Guy Trosper, based on the novel by John Le Carré*
PG/112 mins./Spy/Thriller/UK

Awards: *BAFTA, Best British Film, Best Actor, Best Art Direction, Best British Cinematographer*

Disillusioned spy Alex Leamas returns from Berlin, desperate to 'come in from the cold' and leave espionage behind him. His masters agree on the condition he embarks on one last mission, going undercover as a defector. But he is merely a pawn in a much larger game.

No film has caught the graven inhumanity and hollow intellectual chess game of move and counter-move charted by John Le Carré's famous spy fiction better than Martin Ritt's masterful, if heavy, depiction of flawed idealism. Shot in a metallic monochrome that divorces the sleek sixties of their familiar vigour, he unveils an underworld of cool-headed old gents manipulating their foot-soldiers in gestures long since removed from notions of moral right and political hope. It is the very antithesis of 007's grandiose adventures: dour, talky, depressed, but fiercely intelligent, strikingly austere and beautifully acted.

Richard Burton, who ironically the author felt too glamorous to fill the sallow skin of his beaten hero, was always at his best when shrinking into harsh, human foibles than lending his sonorous voice to some murderously bloated epic. Leamas is emerging from a stupor, falling for shrewy librarian and proto-communist Claire Bloom, a man conflicted between what he represents and what he knows to be the truth – there is no right. As the plot stretches out, and we get to the centre of its labyrinth of betrayals and manipulations, the very concept of the enemy becomes blurred: 'Before, he was evil and my enemy; now, he is evil and my friend,' shrugs the desolate Leamas at another fateful twist.

It is hard work, cold and relentlessly negative, but there is such intricacy amongst the host of eloquent British character actors who float in and out of the mission, reliable, avuncular men in tweed suits gesturing with tea cups – Cyril Cusack, Robert Hardy, Michael Horden, and Rupert Davies who, all too briefly, gives life to the fabled George Smiley long before Alec Guinness turned him into an icon. And you can't help but admire Ritt's dedication to long, sinewy interrogations and scenes of wordy discourse; there is next to no action. The strange, ghostly antagonism of the Cold War never felt as real. ★★★★ **IN**

THE SPY WHO LOVED ME (1977)

Starring: *Roger Moore (James Bond), Barbara Bach (Major Anya Amasova), Curt Jurgens (Karl Stromberg), Richard Kiel (Jaws), Caroline Munro (Naomi), Walter Gotell (General Gogol), Geoffrey Keen (Minister Of Defence), Bernard Lee (M), Shane Rimmer (Capt. Carter), Bryan Marshall (Commander Talbot)*
Director: *Lewis Gilbert*
Screenwriters: *Christopher Wood, Richard Maibaum, based on the novel by Ian Fleming*
PG/125 mins./Spy/USA/UK

When a British and Russian nuclear sub go missing, secret agent James Bond teams up with his USSR counterpart Major Anya Amasova to find them. The investigation leads them to billionaire shipping magnate Karl Stromberg, who has a crackpot scheme to destroy life on the Earth's surface and create an undersea kingdom.

Roger Moore's third outing as Bond is undoubtedly his best. After the more streamlined secret agenting of *The Man With A Golden Gun*, Cubby Broccoli (here producing 007 for the first time without co-producer Harry Saltzman) decided to return to the outlandish approach of a *Goldfinger* or a *You Only Live Twice*. The result is a terrifically entertaining adventure that played all the Bond staples up to the hilt without straying too far into the territory of camp and cliché.

If you wanted to rate *The Spy Who Loved Me* on an imaginary 007 scorecard, it would score well on almost every Bondian discipline; the plot, basically a rerun of *You Only Live Twice* (also directed by Gilbert) with the bad guy stealing nuclear subs instead of spacecraft, covers a lot of exotic locations very quickly and keeps the surprises and climaxes coming; Ken Adam's sets, from Stromberg's underwater lair to the astonishing submarine pen (the first set built on the specially built 007 soundstage at Pinewood), are pure brilliance; Jaws, the 7ft assassin with metal teeth, is that rare thing in a Bond henchman – someone who is a real match for Bond; Barbara Bach is a Bond girl with guts (at least for the first two thirds) outwitting 007. And the action stuff is uniformly gripping, from the iconic opening ski chase that sees Bond ski off a mountainside only to be saved by a Union Jack parachute to a terrific Bond-Jaws fistfight among Egyptian ruins to a car chase that results in Bond's Lotus Esprit transforming into a submarine to a grandstanding finale in the submarine pen that sees kidnapped sailors join forces with 007 to battle it out with Stromberg's men. It even has a terrific song, 'Nobody Does It Better', that unusually centres on Bond rather than the villain.

If there are minus points, Curt Jurgens' Stromberg is a colourless Rent-a-Bond villain and some of the effects (considering it was made in the same year as *Star Wars*) are just laughable. But *Spy* is perhaps the one Bond flick in which Roger Moore's lighter approach feels right. His cocked eyebrow, his pitch-perfect delivery of terrible one-liners ('Do you know any other tunes?' as Anya grinds the gears while driving) sits right at home with Gilbert's jaunty tone. It may not be Fleming but it is terrific fun. ★★★★ **IF**

SPRING IN PARK LANE (1948)

Starring: *Anna Neagle (Judy Howard), Michael Wilding (Richard), Tom Walls (Uncle Joshua Howard), Peter Graves (Basil Maitland), Marjorie Fielding (Mildred Howard)*
Director: *Herbert Wilcox*
Screenwriter: *Nicholas Phipps, based on the play* Come Out Of The Kitchen *by A.E. Thomas, the book* Come Out Of The Kitchen *by Alice Duer Miller*
U/100 mins./Comedy/Romance/UK

When Richard is accused of losing the family fortune, he goes into hiding in the house of Judy Howard, but risks giving himself away when he falls for her.

Was London's Mayfair ever really this sparsely populated, blossom-tree lined and carefree? This candyfloss concocted romantic comedy certainly makes it look like the place of dreams, and to the postwar audience that flocked to see this film – and made it the most successful British movie *ever* in terms of ticket sales – it must have seemed nigh perfect. Yet this languishes unjustly forgotten by its country – rarely available on video, never on DVD and hardly ever on television.

But it's worth seeking out because while it might be fluff, it's highly enjoyable fluff. Anna Neagle was a phenomenon at the time, for twenty years the biggest box office star of her day. Groomed for stardom by husband/producer/director Herbert Wilcox, her pictures made the most of her limits as an actress and much of her appeal as the smart-talking, lady of the screen who could dance, sing, have a career and romance her men in a way that was believably within reach of her audience. Her pairing with the charming Michael Wilding, always an affably relaxed on-screen presence, was gold-dust, and they became the Brit equivalent of Fred and Ginger, albeit with less athletic dancing.

The plot is entirely predictable but the ahead-of-its-time script is full of surprises including a postmodern joke about Richard looking like Michael Wilding (one that was to be repeated a year later, except in reference to Anna Neagle, in the virtual rehash of this film *Maytime In Mayfair*). There's some nice digs at the British filmstars who've got too big for their boots (surely not referring to Wilding's future wife Elizabeth Taylor), especially in a scene where Richard is forced to wait upon moviestar Basil (regular Neagle/Wilcox supporting player Graves) and peppers his service with inappropriate comments. ★★★★ **EC**

STAGE BEAUTY (2004)

Starring: *Billy Crudup (Ned Kynaston), Claire Danes (Maria), Rupert Everett (King Charles II), Tom Wilkinson (Betterton), Richard Griffiths (Sir Charles Sedley), Ben Chaplin (George Villers), Hugh Bonneville (Samuel Pepys)*
Director: *Richard Eyre*
Screenwriter: *Jeffrey Hatcher, based on his play*
15/110 mins./Drama/USA/UK

Ned Kynaston is famous all over London for his female roles on the Restoration stage. But when the law banning women from acting is overturned, his career takes a sudden dive. What's worse is that his newest rival is actually his dresser, Maria . . .

When a successful stage play becomes a movie, one of two things tends to happen. Either it struggles and fails to break free of its theatrical straitjacket; or it evolves comfortably into big-screen form, its 'text' gaining multiple layers of meaning along the way. Jeffrey Hatcher's adaptation of his original play, *Compleat Female Stage Beauty*, is very much the latter – a film that, despite being about theatre itself, is remarkably cinematic and entirely unafraid to revel in the English language.

At the 1998 Academy Awards, Miramax muscle helped Gwyneth Paltrow blub her way to an Oscar as *Shakespeare In Love* edged out *Saving Private Ryan* and *Elizabeth*. There are similarities here – cross-dressing,

Shakespeare and in-the-wings shenanigans set in ye olde days – but *Stage Beauty* is the better movie by far.

Its historically accurate(ish) story of the last male actors to achieve stardom exclusively in female roles is the starting point for an exceptionally rich exploration of gender, ambition, sexuality, politics, ego and the true nature of acting. And anything Gwyneth can do, Billy can do better. Crudup (the thinking man's Johnny Depp?) climbs completely inside Ned to the extent that every step, every look, every flick of a limp wrist exists in a fluid boundary between masculine and feminine, neither wholly one nor the other, but undoubtedly containing something of both. It's a tremendously graceful physical performance that doesn't ignore the emotional and psychological repercussions on the character. Meanwhile Danes, so beautifully fragile in Baz Luhrmann's *Romeo + Juliet*, must have a thing for the period, because this is the best performance of her young career. Not only does she capture all of Maria's contradictions (particularly the mix of love, awe and annoyance with which she views Ned), but her transformation from 'bad' actress to breathtaking Desdemona is a little masterclass in itself.

One key sequence, in which Maria and Ned switch from one sexual position to the next, questioning who is the man and who is the woman, is not just thematically relevant – it is also, in their hands, one of the most intimate and erotic sex scenes in recent memory. ★★★★ **AM**

STAGE FRIGHT (1950)

Starring: *Jane Wyman (Eve Gill/Doris Tinsdale), Marlene Dietrich (Charlotte Inwood), Michael Wilding (Wilfrid O. Ordinary Smith), Richard Todd (Jonathan Cooper), Alistair Sim (Commodore Gill), Kay Walsh (Nellie Good), Sybil Thorndike (Mrs Gill)*
Director: *Alfred Hitchcock*
Screenwriters: *Whitfield Cook, Alma Reville, James Bridie and Ranald MacDougall, based on* Man Running *by Selwyn Jepson*
PG/111 mins./Thriller/UK

When chorus dancer Jonathan Cooper is accused of killing his mistress's husband, his drama student friend, Eve Gill poses as housemaid Doris Tinsdale to spy on actress Charlotte Inwood. However, her ruse is discovered by investigating detective, Wilfrid O. Smith, who has fallen in love with her.

Alfred Hitchcock had already explored the confluence of filmed life and theatrical artifice in *Murder!*. However, he found several new ways of making the contrast in this diverting, if never exactly thrilling adaptation of Selwyn Jepson's 1948 novel, *Man Running* (known in the *States as Outrun the Constable*), which had been partly based on the infamous 1920s Thompson-Bywaters murder case.

Indeed, in order to sustain his contention that everyone is an actor in their own drama, Hitch transformed Eve from a farm girl into a drama student (although this might also have been a fond allusion to the fact that his daughter, Patricia, was then at RADA). But rather than casting an ingénue, he opted for 35-year-old Jane Wyman, who had not only just won an Oscar for playing a deaf-mute in *Johnny Belinda*, but who also had the presence to hold her own against the scene-stealing Marlene Dietrich.

Both Eve and Charlotte are born performers. But, whereas Charlotte can treat her widows weeds as just another costume and can play grande dame or vulnerable victim with the same practised ease, Eve keeps forgetting she's in character and the sequence in which she is supposed to announce the doctor's arrival feels like something from a bad amateur dramatics production (which she ends up watching from the wings).

Hitchcock's insistence that the story's entire world was a stage even results in Smith, Cooper and Eve's father, Commodore Gill (an out of sorts Alastair Sim), playing roles in her melodramatic enterprise. But the implication of façade was also carried over into the depiction of postwar London, as it sought to maintain a stiff upper lip in the face of austerity and the dwindling of Empire. Thus, St Paul's dome towers over the rubbled city and the locals make the best of the rain threatening the garden party for war orphans.

However, few critics picked up on either the gleeful theatricality or the fact that the pacing was supposed to convey the uncertainty of a brave new Britain and *Stage Fright* has never really recovered from this initial indifference. ★★★ **DP**

STAGECOACH (1939)

Starring: *Claire Trevor (Dallas), John Wayne (The Ringo Kid), Andy Devine (Buck), John Carradine (Hatfield), Thomas Mitchell (Doc Boone)*
Director: *John Ford*
Screenwriter: *Dudley Nichols, based on the story* Stage To Lordsburg *by Ernest Haycox*
U/96 mins./Western/USA
Awards: *Academy Awards – Best Supporting Actor (Thomas Mitchell), Best Score*

A simple stagecoach trip is complicated by the fact that Indian Geronimo is on the warpath in the area. The passengers on the coach include a drunken doctor, a pregnant woman, a bank manager who has taken off with his client's money, and the famous outlaw Ringo Kid.

It's a matter of Hollywood legend that when the producers of the 1966 remake of John Ford's immaculate Western realised what a truly monstrous turkey they had on their hands, they rounded up and destroyed as many prints of the original as they could find. Ford's film only survives, apparently, because John Wayne had a personal copy locked away in his safe. In a way you can't blame them, the 1966 film is so appalling that desperate measures were called for. Then again it's hard to feel much sympathy for anyone who attempts to recut a perfect gem by casting Alex Cord (later a stalwart guest-star of *The Love Boat*), Ann-Margret, Mike Connors and Bing Crosby in place of John Wayne, Claire Trevor, John Carradine and Thomas Mitchell.

The producers of the 1986 made-for-TV debacle, which starred Johnny Cash, June Carter Cash, Waylon Jennings, Kris Kristofferson and Willie Nelson as Doc Holiday (the Apaches were played by members of the Charlie Daniels Band – just kidding!), were faced with an even greater dilemma. Their only hope lay in massacring not only prints of the original, but also anyone who was even dimly aware of its existence. If the dazzling brilliance of Ford's version of *Stagecoach* isn't immediately obvious, a glance at either of the above abominations should bring it into sharp focus.

All three films sport the same simple plot – an odd assortment of travellers journey from A to B and are beset by hostile Apaches en route – but it's a mark of Ford's genius that he transforms garden variety source material into a feast of characterisation, visual poetry and heart-pounding action. The screenplay, by Dudley Nichols, was based on the short story *Stage To Lordsburg* by Ernest Haycox. It also bears trace elements of Guy de Maupassant's *Boule de Suif*, and Ford further spiced things up by importing a few pungent souls from Bret Harte's dime novel classic *Outcasts Of Poker Flat* (which was itself the subject of four film adaptations). It proved a winning combination. Ford's first Western in 13 years (he took a hiatus after *Three Bad Men* in 1926), *Stagecoach* trumpeted the master's return by taking the conventions of the genre and spinning them on their ear.

Out went the indomitable lone hero, out went the clear-cut delineation of good and evil, out went the traditional pacing of action sequences and out went the 'riding into the sunset' ending. In their place, Ford substituted as strange a band of bedfellows as ever boarded

S

the Wells Fargo. He put his hero in handcuffs, ripped up the rulebook on romance, placed the climactic action scene two thirds of the way through the film and, in the finale, had Wayne drive off into a shimmering dawn, heeding not the call of the wild, but heading instead for a life of domestic bliss.

Wayne, as Johnny Ringo, the role that made him a superstar, is the closest thing to a traditional hero on offer. But Ford puts his cards on the table early. When we first meet Ringo he's just busted out of jail and is stranded in the desert with a dead horse. A cowboy hero without a mount was an act of subversion, as was placing him in the midst of the microcosmic society inside the stagecoach. When Wayne clambers aboard – he submits to arrest so he can hitch a ride to Lordsburg where he plans to kill the gunmen who murdered his family – the relationships between the passengers begin to percolate. And as the stage trundles through the spectacular landscape, heading ever closer to its date with Geronimo's marauding braves, their less-than-perfect lives are laid bare. It's in these scenes that Ford really messes with the stereotypes. The woman of virtue is actually a stone-cold snob; the boozy doc is a stand-up guy; the gambling man (Carradine – excellent) turns out to be a gentleman after all; the self-righteous banker is a thief. Moreover, the vengeful outlaw and the faded whore – routine Western coffin-fodder – are the tender heart of the film.

Featuring groundbreaking editing and camerawork, some of the most daring stunt riding ever filmed and – the icing on the cake – Yakima Canutt's unbelievably courageous fall under the galloping horses, it is still an incomparable piece of adrenaline-fuelled action cinema.

Even Ford realised he couldn't top it, deliberately playing down Ringo's tail-end shootout with the Plummer gang. Again, a significant break with tradition. It has been noted, of course, that had the Apaches really wanted to capture the stage, all they had to do was shoot the horses. This is a quite reasonable observation, and anyone who feels compelled to make it should be punched repeatedly in the face. ★★★★★ **SB**

STALAG 17 (1953)

Starring: *Wiliam Holden (Sefton), Don Taylor (Lt. Dunbar), Otto Preminger (Oberst von Scherbach), Robert Strauss ('Animal' Stosh), Harvey Lembeck (Harry), Richard Erdman (Hoffy), Peter Graves (Price), Neville Brand (Duke)*
Director: *Billy Wilder*
Screenwriters: *Billy Wilder, Edwin Blum, based on the play by Donald Bevan, Edmund Trczinski*
PG/120 mins./Comedy-/War/USA

Awards: *Academy Awards – Best Actor*

American POWs Price and Duke become convinced that there is a spy in Barracks Four when another escape attempt is thwarted by German commandant, Von Scherbach (Otto Preminger). However, unpopular wheeler-dealing loner J.J. Stratton refuses to play the patsy and exposes the traitor before embarking on his own bid for freedom.

Having walked out during the first act when he saw Donald Bevan and Edmund Trczinski's play on Broadway, William Holden initially rejected Billy Wilder's offer to star in this screen adaptation. But, such was his trust in the director who had resurrected his career with *Sunset Blvd.* that, after Kirk Douglas had turned it down, Holden took the expanded role of the self-serving Sefton and won himself an Oscar for his efforts.

Playing down the original's emphasis on jokey mystery, Wilder and Edwin Blum reshaped the material to introduce an element of film noir into its POW drama. Consequently, this became an incisive study of American mob mentality and the ease with which a party line can be disseminated. Made at the tail end of the HUAC investigation into Hollywood Communism, the action equated the sergeants in Barracks Four with the film folk who had swallowed Senator Joe McCarthy's line and acquiesced in the blacklisting of artists whose crime lay in being different from themselves and in having the courage to stand up for their convictions rather than follow the crowd (a trait common to the insular inhabitants of movies as different as Capra comedies and B Westerns).

Consequently, Sefton would rather take his chances with Dunbar, the bourgeois saboteur he neither likes nor trusts than accept the adulation of such knee-jerk patriots as Duke. Indeed, Wilder suggests that by living by his wits, Sefton has more in common with Oberst Von Scherbach and Schulz, the corruptible guard (Sig Rumann), than his fellow prisoners and, consequently, they are portrayed as anything but the comic-book Nazis that had populated so many wartime adventures. Indeed, if anything, Von Scherbach is the pragmatically brutal cousin of Von Rauffenstein in Jean Renoir's *La Grande Illusion*, who was also essayed by an Austrian director who was a more than capable actor, Erich von Stroheim.

Hollywood got its own back on Wilder, however, by bowdlerising his scathing scenario for the long-running sitcom, *Hogan's Heroes*. ★★★★ **DP**

STALKER (1979)

Starring: *Aleksandr Kajdanovsky (Stalker), Nikolai Grinko (Professor), Anatoli Solonitsyn (Writer), Alisha Friendlkh (Stalker's Wife), Natasha Abramova ('Monkey' – Stalker's daughter)*
Director: *Andrei Tarkovsky*
Screenwriters: *Boris Strugatsky, Arkady Strugatsky, based on their novel* Roadside Picnic
PG/161 mins./Sci-fi/USSR

Evading armed patrols, Stalker leads Professor and Writer across The Zone in order to find The Room, which supposedly has the power to grant heartfelt wishes.

The number three plays a curious role in the production of the first film in the apocalyptic triptych that would conclude with *Nostalgia* and *The Sacrifice*. Three characters pass through a landscape not wholly dissimilar to the three levels of Dante's *Divine Comedy* in a scenario that was devised by Andrei Tarkovsky in collaboration with Arkady and Boris Strugatsky, the authors of the source novel, *Roadside Picnic*.

Known during its production as The Wish Machine, *Stalker* went through three art directors (Tarkovsky himself and the uncredited Alexander Boym and Shavkat Abdusalamov) and three cinematographers (Georgy Rerberg, Leonid Kalashnikov and Alexander Knyazhinsky). It was also delayed three times each because of natural causes (an earthquake in Tajikistan, which forced the location to relocate to Estonia; Tarkovsky's heart attack in April 1978; and a relapse while editing in February 1979) and for technical reasons (the stock used for the first Estonian shoot proved faulty and all the footage was lost; Tarkovsky's equipment had to be replaced when it was found to be deficient; and a cash shortage prompted Tarkovsky to revise the screenplay, which then had to secure official sanction).

The soundtrack even contained three pieces of classical music (by Beethoven, Ravel and Wagner) and three poems, by Arseny Tarkovsky, Fyodor Tyuchev and Tarkovsky himself, paraphrasing the *Tao Te Ching*.

The film was even open to three interpretations – science-fiction dystopia; political allegory; and spiritual search. Tarkovsky certainly wished to express his concerns about the future of the planet and while it's implied that the Zone had been created by a meteorite, the intervention of careless humanity can't be discounted. Tarkovsky also transferred the novel's action from North America to a nameless wilderness that had all the hallmarks of a soulless Iron Curtain environment (indeed, some even claim that Tarkovsky anticipated the Chernobyl disaster here), while the trek to the Room could also represent Stalker's struggle to find faith, an act that recalled the Arthurian quests for the Grail.

Whatever its ultimate meaning, this is a complex, challenging work of rare beauty and power whose elusiveness is part of its fascination. ★★★★ **DP**

STAND BY ME (1986)

Starring: *Wil Wheaton (Gordie Lachance), River Phoenix (Chris Chambers), Corey Felman (Teddy Duchamp), Jerry O'Connell (Vern Tessio), Kiefer Sutherland (Ace Merrill)*
Director: *Rob Reiner*
Screenwriters: *Raynold Gideon, Bruce A. Evans, based on the novella* The Body *by Stephen King*
15/84 mins./Drama/USA

Four boys set off to find a dead body that's rumoured to have been found in the countryside nearby.

On a Stephen King adaptation scale of one to ten (where one would be *Graveyard Shift* and ten your *Shawshank*), this definitive short story turned feature film may never challenge the long-established frontrunners, such as *Carrie* and *The Shining*, but effortlessly takes up residence well into the top order.

Expanded from the horror guru's original (and semi-autobiographical) rites of passage fable, *The Body* (which itself was one of his four Different Seasons), the film version sees Richard Dreyfuss cameo as the grown man remembering – in flashback – the fateful summer of 1959, when he and three friends set out in search of a dead body, only to discover more about themselves than they initially bargained for.

But as well as the standard coming-of-age preoccupations, Raynold Gideon's moving, intelligent screenplay is peppered with canny pop culture cross-referencing, sweet (while thankfully never sickly) observation and slick dialogue, uniformly delivered by its cast with understated panache.

Indeed, it is the caliber of this fresh-faced quartet that ultimately gives the film its eternal charm – while the absorbing performance of a young Phoenix provides a truly poignant reminder of just what a talent was lost on that fateful pavement in 1993.

Reiner, too – who five years later would direct Kathy Bates to Oscar success in an adaptation of King's bestseller *Misery* – is on top form, imbuing proceedings with a beautiful symbiosis of airy nostalgia and the same high quality of wit that graced his glorious *This Is Spinal Tap* (this film's now legendary 'vomit scene' is just one of its timeless joys). Add to that an array of quite unforgettable moments (leeches have never, ever, possessed such a power to nauseate), showcased by an era-defining soundtrack and the result is an absorbing, touching examination of loss of innocence that despite occasionally drifting towards sappy, undeniably deserves its place in the heart of a generation. ★★★★ **MD**

Movie Trivia: Stand By Me

$2.37 is the amount of money the boys collectively pool, and a number also featured in other significant Stephen King flicks: Red's cell number is 237 in *The Shawshank Redemption*, as is the number of the haunted room in *The Shining*. All night-time scenes had to be shot in the studio due to child labour laws. Jerry O'Connell, then 11, was chuffed at being allowed to swear for his role.

STANDER (2003)

Starring: *Thomas Jane (Andre Stander), Ashley Taylor (Deventer), David O'Hara (Allan Heyl), Dexter Fletcher (Lee McCall), Deborah Kara Unger (Bekkie Stander)*
Director: *Bronwen Hughes*
Screenwriter: *Bima Stagg*
15/116 mins./Canada/Germany/South Africa/UK

South Africa, the 1970s. Andre Stander, a white police detective, asks to be excused from riot duty after shooting a black demonstrator. Alienated and guilt-ridden, he embarks on a bank-robbing spree. Caught by his former colleagues, he escapes from prison and forms an outlaw gang.

This needs its 'based on a true story' caption because otherwise you'd never believe it. It also means the film is obliged to depict the headline-grabbing incidents while just hinting at the stories behind the story. Thomas Jane's Andre Stander – a cop-turned-crook-turned folk hero – remains a mystery to the end. Is he deranged by the surrealism of a system that prosecutes him for robbery but not murder? Such a clever detective he feels compelled to outsmart his own colleagues? A doomed rebel on the run imitating the movie versions of Butch Cassidy and Clyde Barrow? A family man agonised by his estrangement from his wife and father? A privileged white Sahth Afrikaan boor who deserves a thorough beating from the township blacks he's taken shots at? A bit of a nut out for a good time and plenty of cash? A ruthless criminal genius who wants to make a quick buck and clear out for the States? All of the above? Different scenes take different tacks, as does a running commentary from the media, family and friends, the authorities and the man in the street.

Credit to Jane, fresh from the clear-cut action antics of *The Punisher* (a not dissimilar character in many ways), for letting the ambiguities stand while delivering a career-best performance (and accent). Stander executes heists with casual efficiency and near-suicidal daring – at one point, the gang deliberately rob the bank next door to the HQ of the police task force specifically charged with running them to ground – but Jane gets a lot out of moments of quiet, unfathomable reflection.

Director Bronwen Hughes, who made the Ben Affleck-Sandra Bullock rom-com *Forces Of Nature*, uses Stander's crime spree to depict a divided, dysfunctional society, showing sleek Johannesburg banks and shack-filled shanty towns through a sunny but sickly haze, as if moral pollution hangs in the air. After the smug liberal breast-beating of films like *Cry Freedom* and *A Dry White Season*, it's refreshing to see a film set in pre-Mandela South Africa that isn't just about the injustices of apartheid – though, in the end, the central thesis is that a country where 'a white man can get away with anything' makes Andre Stander inevitable. ★★★★ **KN**

STAR TREK II: THE WRATH OF KHAN (1982)

Starring: *William Shatner (Captain James T. Kirk), Leonard Nimoy (Captain Spock), DeForest Kelley (Dr. Leonard 'Bones' McCoy), James Doohan (Montgomery 'Scotty' Scott), Walter Koenig (Pavel Chekov), Nichelle Nichols (Cmdr. Uhura), George Takei (Hikaru Sulu), Kirstie Alley (Lt. Saavik), Ricardo Montalban (Khan Noonien Singh)*
Director: *Nicholas Meyer*
Screenwriter: *Jack B. Sowards, based on a story by Harve Bennett, Jack B. Sowards, TV series by Gene Roddenberry*
PG/111 mins./Sci-fi/Adventure/USA

It is the twenty-third century. Admiral James T. Kirk is feeling old; the prospect of accompanying his old ship the *Enterprise* – now a Starfleet Academy training ship – on a two-week cadet cruise is not making him feel any younger. But the training cruise becomes a deadly serious mission when Khan appears after years of exile – and holding the power of creation itself . . .

Although the slow, gabby, and, frankly, rather insipid *Star Trek: The Motion Picture* did the business, it was pretty lame to all but the most dedicated, particularly coming two years in the wake of *Star Wars*.

Nicholas Meyer, a successful novelist (*The Seven-Per-Cent Solution*) turned able director, understood that the interplay between the characters, back on familiar footing, was as important as the impressive FX. A sequel 15 years on to the classic Trek TV episode 'Space Seed', the very enjoyable hokum of *Wrath Of Khan* is energised by the return of a fabulous Ricardo Montalban as the exiled, genetically enhanced tyrant Khan, once ruler of an empire on Earth (round about now, actually) who was originally encountered in suspended animation on the vessel *Botany Bay* and revived in the 23rd Century.

Kahn has escaped the dead planet where he's been stranded, with his mitts on a starship, a cutthroat band of followers and an all-consuming obsession with exacting terrible revenge on the U.S.S. *Enterprise* gang – chiefly, of course, former captain James T. Kirk. Khan is exactly what's required for camp piratical space fun – a formidable foe who is charismatic, brainy, and ruthlessly fanatical. The necessity for a showdown takes on save-the-universe urgency when Khan snatches up a highly desirable gizmo – the Genesis Device, which reorganises energy into living matter – containing the power of creation or mass destruction. The Genesis Device is well named since it provokes dialogue that, in 1982, would have struck anyone with no taste for speculative science fiction as wincingly pretentious. Today it seems more apt as Kirk and cronies debate the potential for and consequences of science second-guessing God. The real heart of the story is, however, almost unique in the annals of screen sci-fi. It's about getting old.

The most elegiac of the big screen Treks, the adventure celebrates comradeship above all the other fundamentals and imperatives of the Trek ethos (like courage, curiosity and cultural imperialism). And it's a tale told with considerable warmth and humour, some spiffing explosions and a multiple-hanky act of self-sacrifice to round things off. At the beginning the once irrepressible Kirk's birthday (which one it is we aren't told, but the big five-o seems likely) brings on morose reflection. The former intergalactic babehound says 'Galloping around the cosmos is a game for the young,' considers the paths not taken (unaware that an old flame and his hitherto unknown, full-grown son are about to be sprung on him) and is passively resigned to an assignment commanding a computer console in place of his 'first, best destiny' – command of a starship.

Spock gives him an ancient copy of *A Tale Of Two Cities*. Bones gives him a pair of antique spectacles for his middle-age myopia, so he can read it, which comes in handy when he misquotes Sydney Carton in the eventual denouement. A simple training cruise for Starfleet cadets (including a debuting Kirstie Alley as Vulcan smarty-pants Saavik) is tiresomely routine and seems set to be Kirk's last mission. Then Khan rears his vengeful head – yippee! – forcing Kirk to boldly go once more.

The point is, he learns, there are still big challenges: 'I haven't faced death. I've cheated death. I've tricked my way out of death, and patted myself on the back for my ingenuity. I know nothing.' That understood, the adventure of life goes on, age, a crazed villain and a warp drive engine on the blink be damned. As is the case in the best of the classic Trek screen adventures (let's hear it for *IV* and *VI*, both co-written by Meyer), Jack B. Sowards's script is witty and literate, the crew are on top self-mocking form and there are neat references to Dickens and Melville. But *Wrath Of Khan* is capped by a daring shocker: killing a beloved character (or at least so fans believed until *Star Trek III*) to press home such weighty Trekian sentiments as 'The needs of the many outweigh the needs of the few, or the one.'

What haven't worn as well are the disastrous fashion statements: striped bell-bottom uniform trews tucked into boots and those absurd Santa Claus tunics. And then, of course, there's the trademark dodgy coiffures. Still, it's a far, far better thing they do than they have ever done when they can save civilisation as we know it even on a bad hair day. ★★★★ **AE**

STAR TREK III: THE SEARCH FOR SPOCK (1984)

Starring: *William Shatner (Captain James T. Kirk), Leonard Nimoy (Captain Spock), DeForest Kelley (Dr. Leonard "Bones" McCoy), James Doohan (Montgomery 'Scotty' Scott), Walter Koenig (Pavel Chekov), Nichelle Nichols (Cmdr. Uhura), George Takei (Hikaru Sulu), Christopher Lloyd (Kruge)*
Director: *Leonard Nimoy*
Screenwriters: *Harve Bennett, TV series by Gene Roddenberry*
PG/105 mins./Sci-fi/Adventure/USA

Kirk, Scotty, Bones, Sulu and all the Trekky regulars defy higher orders and take the *Enterprise* on a vigilante mission across space to resurrect their comrade, Spock. Alerted by the prospect of a scrumdown with an old enemy, the Klingons set out to intercept Kirk. But can anything stand in the way of our lycra-clab tubby hero . . . ?

Not quite as good as voyages II or IV, but light years ahead of I, Leonard 'Spock' Nimoy's directorial debut has Kirk and crew going AWOL with the *Enterprise* to chase after their fallen comrade. This is an atypically tragic Trek, with more than the usual poleaxed extras getting their share of pain here – including, most memorably, Kirk's son, who was introduced in *Star Trek II*.

Nimoy obviously relishes being behind the camera for a change, and being in the position to administer all kinds of intergalactic torment on his space buddies and envisage his own rebirth.

For Spock is not dead, as *Wrath of Khan* suggested, but alive and being regenerated on a new planet – Genesis – while his spirit inhabits the body of his own sparring partner, 'Bones' McCoy. So the crew warp off there to 'mind-meld' body and spirit back together and stir up some Klingon baddies on the way.

Don't worry if this makes little sense. Unlike most franchises Star Trek seems to soar when it borders on the ridiculous so the young Spock being rapidly aged through 'fal-tar-pan' on Vulcan and the O.A.P fight scenes (couch potato Kirk in action is a fine thing) are highlights. More traditionally spectacular were the development of the planet Genesis and – gasp – the destruction of the *Enterprise*! ★★★ **WT**

STAR TREK IV: THE VOYAGE HOME

Starring: *William Shatner (Admiral James T. Kirk), Leonard Nimoy (Captain Spock), DeForest Kelley (Dr Leonard 'Bones' McCoy), James Doohan (Scotty), George Takei (Sulu), Nichelle Nichols (Uhura), Jane Wyatt (Amanda), Catherine Hicks (Dr. Gillian Taylor)*
Director: *Leonard Nimoy*
Screenwriters: *Steve Meerson, Peter Krikes, Harve Bennett, Nicholas Meyer, based on a story by Nimoy and Bennett and characters by Gene Roddenberry*
PG/119 mins/Sci-fi/USA

After Earth is ravaged by an alien probe, Kirk, Spock et al travel back in time to the twentieth century to secure the one thing that can save humanity: a pair of humpback whales.

Of all ten films in the Star Trek canon, *The Voyage Home* stands as the only one to successfully break away from its genre roots and enjoy genuine mainstream appeal. Gone are the mind-melds, Klingons and spatial anomalies that have made up the franchise so far, replaced here by a surprisingly accessible and amusing fish-out-of-water comedy.

Immersing the crew of the *Enterprise* (sans the *Enterprise* itself, having been blown up in the previous film) in the popular culture of 80s San Francisco, The Voyage Home is light on story, relying on situational comedy to drive the action as Kirk and his team tackle the logistics of abducting two gargantuan marine mammals. Enter biologist-cum-love-interest Gillian Taylor (Hicks), who, along with Kirk and Spock, enjoys the bulk of screen time.

Comedic elements are surprisingly well-handled, both by the usually stoic cast and director Nimoy – who made this his last Trek film behind the camera before attempting full-on funny with *Three Men and a Baby*. From Spock's experimentation with expletives to Scotty's 'conversation' with an ageing PC computer, there are situational laughs for newcomers as well as knowing chuckles for the fans, though it leans more towards gently amusing than truly side-splitting.

The save the whales (literally) plot is undeniably preposterous and so far removed from the previous episodes that die-hard Trekkies could easily have condemned *The Voyage Home* as an unforgivable dumbing down of a pioneering sci-fi franchise. The change in tone works, though, and besides being oft-cited as the most cherished of all the Trek films, this is also highly enjoyable family fun. ★★★★ **JD**

STAR TREK V: THE FINAL FRONTIER (1989)

Starring: *William Shatner (Captain James T. Kirk), Leonard Nimoy (Captain Spock), DeForest Kelley (Dr. Leonard 'Bones' McCoy), James Doohan (Captain Montgomery 'Scotty' Scott), Walter Koenig (Comdr. Pavel Chekov), Nichelle Nichols (Cmdr. Uhura), George Takei (Captain Hikaru Sulu), David Warner (St. John Talbot), Laurence Luckinbill (Sybok)*
Director: *William Shatner*
Screenwriter: *David Loughery, based on a story by William Shatner, Harve Bennett, David Loughery, TV series by Gene Roddenberry*
PG/107 mins./Sci-fi/Adventure/USA

En route to the mystery of life and an audience with God himself, Captain Kirk runs riot, defying age, gravity and directorial subtlety.

There is something to be said for a film that lists among its technical credits a Klingon dialogue consultant. But much as it grieves a serious Trekkie to say it, *The Final Frontier* is the biggest disappointment since Spock blew his cool with that awful woman in 'The Cloudminders' episode. Following the unusual critical approbation of *Star Trek IV: The Voyage Home*, and no doubt envying Leonard Nimoy his successful transition to directing, William Shatner took over directorial duty for *The Final Frontier*. In that respect he has not embarrassed himself. In originating the story, however, he has.

The voyage is a Search for God, a quest for – uhoh! – Ultimate Knowledge. And for one terrible moment at the end of this Trek to the centre of the universe we are led to believe that Heaven is a purple desert and the big G looks like the Wizard of Oz. It is one of the script's few mercies that it is only someone pretending to be God.

In attempting to entertain and amuse, Shatner and his co-writers have, presumably unintentionally, crossed the frontier into self-parody when what every lover of the Star Trek ethos wants is sci-fi peril, a few thrills and a few chuckles met with honour, comradeship, courage and straight faces. The gentle satirical in-jokes of *The Voyage Home* were humorous; the broad japes laid on thick in *The Final Frontier* are not. The 'serious' bits are equally ill-judged, particularly a risible scene in which the three senior officers 'share their pain' in what resembles a spoof encounter group.

Even more alarming is the condition of the crew members. While the new *Enterprise* is recognisable, nice and shiny with lots more flashing panels, real Trekkies will feel genuine concern for the denizens of the bridge. Scotty and Uhura are now so grey and tubby, Bones and Sulu so wasted, there is every reason to fear someone will peg out before they reach the next Federation starbase.

On the plus side: well, the scenery looks fine. Spock clings to some dignity despite the awful buddy-buddy buffoonery he is roped into and the family secrets he has suddenly to reveal at this rather late stage of the game. Guest star David Warner has too little to do to mortify himself severely, and there are a few nice moments ('Excuse me, but if you're God what do you need my ship for?'). But a lot of fans will, sadly, echo McCoy's complaint: 'You really piss me off, Jim'. ★★ **AE**

STAR TREK VI: THE UNDISCOVERED COUNTRY (1991)

Starring: *William Shatner (Captain James T. Kirk), Leonard Nimoy (Captain Spock), DeForest Kelley (Dr. Leonard 'Bones' McCoy), James Doohan (Captain Montgomery 'Scotty' Scott), Walter Koenig (Comdr. Pavel Chekov), Nichelle Nichols (Cmdr. Uhura), George Takei (Captain Hikaru Sulu), Kim Cattrall (Lieutenant Valeris), Mark Lenard (Ambassador Sarek), Christopher Plummer (General Chang)*
Director: *Nicholas Meyer*
Screenwriters: *Nicholas Meyer, Denny Martin Flinn, from a story by Leonard Nimoy, Lawrence Konner, Mark Rosenthal, TV series by Gene Roddenberry*
PG/108 mins./Sci-fi/Adventure/USA

When the *Enterprise* crew discover that the Klingons are trying to trick the Federation into a bogus peace treaty, they undertake a mission to stop their arch enemies.

It comes as a joy and relief that the 25th Anniversary voyage of Captain Kirk and his crew is much better than the self-indulgent *Star Trek V*, matters having been taken out of William Shatner's hands. This time out the story is the brainchild of Leonard Nimoy and direction was entrusted to *Wrath Of Khan* helmer Nicholas Meyer. It's an honourable, rather clever and decidedly enjoyable addition to the canon, appropriately dedicated to the late *Star Trek* creator Gene Roddenberry.

True, the aged crew are only a hair's breadth short of doddering, from skeletal McCoy to ham-in-command Kirk, sporting what seems to be a dead tribble on his head and beginning to talk to himself. Their not-to-be-ignored length of tooth, however, is the basis for several gags, references to imminent retirement, and some quite neat links to *The Next Generation*. This mission plays on recent current affairs on Earth, with the Klingons-in-crisis mirroring Soviet disintegration and Kirk cast as the Cold Warrior required to revise the thinking of a lifetime. Throw in an ecological disaster, Kim Cattrall as Spock's Vulcan protégée, Christopher Plummer, unrecognisable and deliciously villainous as a one-eyed, Shakespeare-spouting Klingon and Iman as a beauteous mutant, stir them all up in an assassination conspiracy in space caper, add good special effects and some pleasing chuckles and voilà, it's a fun for Trekkers.

Serious buffs will dote on titbits added to the Lore, like Spock claiming Sherlock Holmes for an ancestor and the revelation that Klingons have lavender blood. Even those who can take or leave the whole business, however, might appreciate a swell slaughter in zero gravity or the knowing jokes like Kirk's cheerful observation 'Well, Spock, once again we've saved civilisation as we know it.' ★★★ **AE**

STAR TREK: FIRST CONTACT (1996)

Starring: *Patrick Stewart (Captain Jean-Luc Picard), Jonathan Frakes (Commander William Riker/Holodeck Musician), Brent Spiner (Lt. Commander Data), LeVar Burton (Lt. Commander/Dr. Beverly Crusher), Marina Sirtis (Commander Deanna Troi), Alfre Woodard (Lily Sloan)*
Director: *Jonathan Frakes*
Screenwriters: *Brannon Brega, Ronald D. Moore, based on a story by Rick Berman, Brannon Braga, Ronald D. Moore, television series by Gene Roddenberry*
12/106 mins./Sci-fi/Adventure/USA

Capt. Picard and his crew pursue the Borg back in time to stop them from preventing Earth from initiating first contact with alien life.

Just as they saw *The Wrath of Khan* rescue the Star Trek franchise from the deathly pomposity of the first movie, Trekkers will be looking to *First*

S

Contact to set the tone for the second phase of the series – *Generations* having had the benefit of the reassuring presence of William Shatner, and the novelty of seeing him offed.

Unfortunately, left alone on the big screen, distinctly thin characterisation and a plot that looks like a distended television episode, let the new crew down slightly but there are still enough classic moments to keep fans happy. *First Contact* finds Jean-Luc Picard aboard a new *Enterprise* heading off to do battle with the Borg, a rapacious cyber 'collective' intent on assimilating the human race into its 'hive', a process which involves slicing off limbs, drilling into eyeballs and generally mucking people about.

Having had his own brush with Borgification in the telly series, Picard is uncharacteristically vengeful. After plunging through a bargain basement optical effect, the crew finds itself on 21st century Earth, as Riker and Geordi – now sporting a dinky pair of electronic eyes – fight to ensure that man's first warp jaunt goes off without a hitch.

Debut big-screen director Frakes wisely saves his special effects budget for two key sequences – a battle with the Borg and a spacewalk on the hull of the *Enterprise*. Using these, a truly impressive opening shot and enough in-jokes and series references, he aims to distract Trekkers from the distinctly cheap-looking remainder. But what he loses is the cosy sense of family which the TV series drew upon, with most characters looking thin and lost on the big screen, and some (Dr. Crusher and Councillor Troy, in particular) almost totally ignored. And with a script that plunges right into the action, there's nowhere near enough time for those not familiar with the series to get to know and care about the characters.

The exceptions are Stewart as Picard, who gets his own scenery chewing big speech, and Brent Spiner as Pinocchio-esque android Data who has long had the most interesting role and for whom assimilation has its own attractions. However, with so many series showing simultaneously on televisions the world over, there's a sense that a movie is nothing all that special. Paramount execs may want to consider rationing their output a bit more rigorously if they're not going to overdose its audience. ★★★ **AS**

⊙ STAR TREK: GENERATIONS (1994)

Starring: *Patrick Stewart (Captain Jean-Luc Picard), Jonathan Frakes (Commander William Riker/Holodeck Musician), Brent Spiner (Lt. Commander Data), LeVar Burton (Lt. Commander/Dr. Beverly Crusher), Marina Sirtis (Commander Deanna Troi), William Shatner (Captain James T. Kirk), James Doohan (Captain Montgomery 'Scotty' Scott), Walter Koenig (Commander Pavel Chekov), Malcolm McDowell (Dr. Tolian Soran)*

Director: *David Carson*

Screenwriters: *Ronald D. Moore, Brannon Braga, from the story by Moore, Braga, Rick Berman, TV series by Gene Roddenberry*

PG/117 mins./Sci-fi/Adventure/USA

A time 'nexus' allows old and new *Star Trek* crews to unite to defeat a mad scientist.

The curse of the odd-numbered *Star Trek* films strikes again with this seventh cinematic mission materialising far short of the mark. This is a disappointment since it is an arena in which the torch of the world's favourite sci-fi saga is handed from the classic *Star Trek* crew to the Next Generation.

Erswhile *Enterprise* Captain James T. Kirk has an unfortunate encounter with a vocarious, planet-munching nexus – whatever *that* is – and disappears with a bang into a time-warp. Seventy-eight years late the *Next Generation*'s crew, led by Captain Jean-Luc Picard are going boldly aboard the 24th Century's *Enterprise* model 'D' when the nasty nexus reappears, to the evident and worrying delight of a mysterious mad scientist.

What is he up to? Well, nothing terribly comprehensible in a poorly paced screenplay that mistakes techno-babble for narrative, and is peppered with sporadic bouts of flashy action and lowbrow, cutesy humour that betrays the sophistication the *Next Generation* frequently attained in its seven TV years.

Stewart is the most accomplished actor from either series, but even this former RSC thesp is crippled by a script that has his well-established character behaving embarassingly atypically and pairs him with Kirk in a loop in the space-time continuum where Shatner is ludicrously indulged with unseemly action-man stunts.

Buffs of the original team will be disheartened by the absence of Spock while *Next Generation* fans will deplore how little their faves are given to do. Meanwhile, the uninitiated will be mystified by the many in-jokes and working out just who the hell all these sketchy subordinates are (such as Whoopi Goldberg's Guinan), since, as saving civilisation adventures go, this is shockingly low on sense or thrills. Mercifully, there are occasionally some sensational special effects.

Devoted Trekkers will have to see it to keep abreast of the ships' logs, but Saturday night at the flicks fun-seekers are apt to concur this one only fires on stun. ★★ **AE**

⊙ STAR TREK: INSURRECTION (1998)

Starring: *Patrick Stewart (Captain Jean-Luc Picard), Jonathan Frakes (Commander William Riker/Holodeck Musician), Brent Spiner (Lt. Commander Data), LeVar Burton (Lt. Commander/Dr. Beverly Crusher), Marina Sirtis (Commander Deanna Troi), F. Murray Abraham (Ad'har Ru'afo)*

Director: *Jonathan Frakes*

Screenwriter: *Michael Piller, based on a story by Rick Berman, Michael Piller, television series by Gene Roddenberry*

12/106 mins./Sci-fi/Adventure/USA

Captain Jean-Luc Picard races across intergalactic space when he hears that Data is causing problems on a peaceful planet. Once there he discovers the reason for Data's behaviour – and the planet's secret.

Like that other major sci-fi franchise bearing a stellar prefix, there's something about the hauntingly slow, brass section rendition of the theme's opening bars that brings neck hairs to attention and quickens the heart. Failing to deliver this potential has often nagged the feature-length forays of the good ship *Enterprise*, but it has boldly come a long way in two decades, and with Stewart and Frakes at the helm (associate producer and director respectively, alongside acting duties), Star Trekking has never seemed in safer hands.

In the nearest thing outer space has to an Amish community, the happy babble of contented, techno-free village life amid leafy nature is abruptly ruined by Commander Data, for mysterious reasons revealed much later, going berserk. And we're not talking comic-relief, more the phaser-drawn, shooting shit to bits. It soon becomes apparent – thanks mostly to Data's blasting – that the peaceful Ba'ku community is being observed by Admiral Dougherty and Ru'afo. Some two days away, Captain Jean-Luc Picard gratefully breaks a diplomatic function short to race to the scene just in time to prevent his android commander from being reduced to blobs of molten circuitry. Dougherty praises his intervention and the *Enterprise* is all set to depart, but we know something's up because shifty looks are starting to fly, and the ever-vigilant Picard begins to smell a rat. A spot of Sherlock-work reveals a plan to dupe the planet's 600-strong population onto a holodeck (that's a spaceship-cum-hologram for non-Trekkers) and off into space. And the reason becomes apparent as Picard learns of the planet's extraordinary rejuvenating properties, sees his crew begin acting in sprightly and vigorous manner, and realises that the rather lovely villager he's been eyeing up is about 900 years old.

Frakes may be suffering that common affliction of long-serving Federation officers, 'Shatner-belly', but his experience is now really telling, and this exceptionally well-crafted movie is paced and edited to perfection. *Star Trek* has always worked best when used as a canvas for mythical themes, and the elixir of life/desire for eternal youth is a classic.

Upon such a plot, Frakes embellishes with some romance, a flash of drama here, a dab of comedy there; perpetuating running gags, adding the odd novelty, and above all letting his cast have fun. So, under the planet's influence, Lieutenant Worf (Michael Dorn – seconded from *Deep Space Nine*) wrestles with sudden, adolescent cravings, Geordi La Forge sees a sunrise for the first time, while Counsellor Troi and Beverly Crusher comment that their boobs are firming up again. Picard bemoans lost youth, but pulls on a natty black leather jacket for some adventure, and enjoys a moonlit walk with the foxy Anij. Even Riker scrapes off the beard and finds time for hot-tub shenanigans with Troi, before getting bloodied and battered on a besieged *Enterprise* bridge, defiantly spitting, 'We're through running from these bastards!' (which is pure Kirk), and steering the starship by old-fashioned, joystick control.

Such fun is more than conveyed to the audience – an outrageous Gilbert and Sullivan singalong sequence is irresistible – and what's probably most praiseworthy is the movie's sheer feelgood factor that'll keep you buoyant for days. For devotees, this is a strong, sure-footed instalment; but those indifferent to the franchise (and the genre) should take note, this is a good deal more than just another sci-fi movie. ★★★★ **DB**

⊙ STAR TREK: NEMESIS (2002)

Starring: *Patrick Stewart (Captain Jean-Luc Picard), Jonathan Frakes (Commander William Riker/Holodeck Musician), Brent Spiner (Lt. Commander Data), LeVar Burton (Lt. Commander/Dr. Beverly Crusher), Marina Sirtis (Commander Deanna Troi), Tom Hardy (Praetor Shinzon), Ron Perlman (The Reman Viceroy), Kate Mulgrew (Admiral Janeway), Wil Weaton (Wesley Crusher)*
Director: *Stuart Baird*
Screenwriter: *John Logan, based on a story by Logan, Rick Berman, Brent Spiner, television series by Gene Roddenberry*
12/111 mins./Sci-fi/Adventure/USA

As the crew of the *Enterprise* split up — Riker and Deanna Troi are married and the former has a command of his own — the *Enterprise* is dispatched on a mission to Romulus to investigate the possibility of a peace treaty, only to encounter Picard's evil clone.

Rules are made to be broken, and it seems *Star Trek* – now one of film's most lucrative franchises – is no exception. For decades, fans have worked on the 'odd ones bad, even ones good' principle, and most of the time it's been reliable. But *Nemesis*, the tenth in the series and by all accounts the last to feature the complete *Next Generation* crew, flies in the face of convention, being a resolutely 'middling' entry.

Screenwriter John Logan provides little in the way of innovation, bolting the television series' familiar characters onto a couple of plot devices that might have been found in the bottom of Gene Roddenberry's wastepaper basket sometime during the late 60s.

First there's the promise of a Romulan peace treaty which – and we're really not revealing anything here – turns out to be phony. Then there's a riff on the 'split personality' plot perennial with Picard encountering a cloned version of himself (played with admirable lack of restraint by a scenery-masticating Tom Hardy), who has the somewhat predictable ambition of reducing the Earth to 'smithereens'.

All of which is all very well if a tad unimaginative, but *Nemesis*' real weakness is an unaccountable talkiness which results in the first half of the film moving with all the alacrity of a doped tribble. It's a flaw that's exacerbated by what appears to be the contractual demands of the cast to split the big scenes evenly.

Still, things start to pick up in the second half: Stuart Baird (veteran editor of *Superman* and director of *Executive Decision*) directs with a sure if uninspired hand, and there's a 'shock' ending that will give anyone who saw *Star Trek II: The Wrath Of Khan* a dose of déjà vu.

Perhaps *Trek*'s problem is that after ten movies over 23 years, the sense of 'event' that once greeted the early entries is now a distant memory. Nevertheless, for fans, *Nemesis* will be a welcome, if somewhat bittersweet, final return to familiar territory. ★★★ **AS**

⊙ STAR TREK: THE MOTION PICTURE (1979)

Starring: *William Shatner (Admiral James T. Kirk), Leonard Nimoy (Commander Spock), DeForest Kelley (Dr. Leonard 'Bones' McCoy), James Doohan (Cmdr. Montgomery Scott), George Takei (Lt. Cmdr. Hikaru Sulu), Majel Barrett (Dr. Christine Chapel), Walter Koenig (Lt. Pavel Chekov), Persis Khambatta (Lieutenant Ilia), Stephen Collins (Capt. Willard Decker)*
Director: *Robert Wise*
Screenwriter: *Harold Livingston*
U/132 mins/Sci-fi/USA

Admiral James T. Kirk returns to his old ship, the USS *Enterprise* and commands a mission to confront V'ger, a huge and threatening mechanical entity which has wiped out several Klingon vessels and is on a course for Earth.

Trekkies waited over a decade for their beloved franchise to reach the big screen, and then didn't much like the results – which director Robert Wise and special effects men Douglas Trumbull and John Dykstra modelled on the visionary, stately style of *2001: A Space Odyssey* rather than the soap-with-pulp approach of the original TV show (hence, the return to that format in *Star Trek II: The Wrath of Khan*). Tagged Star Trek: The Slow Motion Picture by many bored audiences, it is undeniably a bloated, pompous effort – which takes a lot of time to get the old TV gang (whose small-screen acting tics look very tired) back aboard the *Enterprise* and works hard to set up a couple of new characters (macho Shatner-lite Captain Stephen Collins, bald alien babe Persis Khambatta) who get summarily written out in the climax.

However, a second look reveals there are real virtues – the revelation of what V'ger actually is might be a groaner (especially since it had been done already on an old episode), but Dykstra delivers effects on a grander scale even than his *Star Wars* work. The climactic sequence in which the *Enterprise* is swallowed by the space cyber-leviathan and Spock floats out to communicate with the thing is the sort of astonishing vision it would have been impossible to do on television, even if fans would have preferred a phaser shoot 'em up. Jerry Goldsmith's epic score is also outstanding. Successful enough to warrant a run of sequel films and TV series – though most subsequent Trek tries to pretend that this didn't happen. ★★★ **KN**

⊙ STAR WARS EPISODE I: THE PHANTOM MENACE (1999)

Starring: *Liam Neeson (Qui-Gon Jinn), Ewan McGregor (Obi-Wan Kenobi), Natalie Portman (Queen Padme Naberrie Amidala), Jake Lloyd (Anakin Skywalker), Ian McDiarmid (Senator Palpatine/Darth Sidious), Pernilla August (Shmi Skywalker), Ahmed Best (Jar Jar Binks), Samuel L. Jackson (Mace Windu), Frank Oz (voice of Yoda), Ray Park (Darth Maul)*
Director: *George Lucas*
Screenwriters: *George Lucas, Jonathan Hales, based on a story by Lucas*
U/131 mins./Sci-fi/USA

Awards: Razzies – Worst Supporting Actor (Ahmed Best)

The peaceful planet of Naboo is under threat from the manipulating forces of evil at work in the Trade Federation of a galaxy far, far away. The Queen of Naboo, the powerful Jedi knights and a young boy with intimidating promise endeavour to defend justice and the forces of good.

Around the twenty-minute mark of Jon Shenk's miraculous documentary The Beginning about the making of *Episode I*, the true villain of *The Phantom Menace* makes a cameo appearance. You can glimpse the shadowy figure lurking in the background as Ewan McGregor gets his Padawan

S

buzz cut. His name is Jett Lucas, adopted son of George, and seasoned *Star Wars* apologists should take note of his most insidious characteristic – he is around the same age as Jake Lloyd's Anakin Skywalker.

A great many fluffed details derailed the most anticipated movie of all time, but the miscalculation that undermined the entire prequel enterprise was George Lucas's insistence that when we first meet the future Darth Vader he is a little boy who cries when he is separated from his mother. Lucas risked his legacy based on a father's simple conviction that bad things can happen to good people and a divorcee's guilt that children from single parent families are more vulnerable than most.

To make his point painfully obvious Lucas arranges the action of his first movie since his separation from Marcia Lucas in 1983 around the discovery of a miracle child by a doomed father figure and the eventual passing of this boy from his natural mother to an adoptive parent who is perhaps not yet mature enough to master the task alone. But to accommodate this one action Lucas is forced to postpone every other key event to a later movie – how could a nine-year-old participate in the Clone Wars? – and effectively botches up his starting position. It is a mistake from which the prequels never recover.

Things get off to a cold start with the much parodied credit crawl. Where *Episode IV* goes for the *in medias res* jugular – 'It is a time of civil war!' – problems in *Episode* I are not quite so pressing. Events are 'alarming' perhaps, there's certainly plenty of 'turmoil' and we all know 'taxation' is a thorny issue but the context is clear: like Anakin, this conflict still has some growing up to do. The menace is still phantom.

An inexcusably lazy establishing shot – the Jedi shuttle cruises past the camera – and lethargic opening sequence hardly help pick up the pace. In *A New Hope*'s famous opening salvo the bad guys fire first and ask questions later, in *The Phantom Menace* the Jedi are ushered into a meeting room while the semi-bad guys go into video conference with Darth Sidious about whether an invasion of Naboo is legal or not.

This arse-numbing inactivity recurs throughout *The Phantom Menace*: because the battles lines are not yet drawn and sides are still being taken there is always much explaining to be done, characters are forever having update meetings or being introduced to one another. The plot machinery lumbers through the gears, hampered further by the strange declarative dialogue and by an apparent disinterest in making these scenes visually interesting.

Critics complained that Lucas had got yet worse at writing for humans in the twenty-two years since *Star Wars*, in fact it is simply that, beyond Alec Guinness talking about the force, the plot of *A New Hope* requires no exposition – *The Phantom Menace* on the other hand is all explanation, much of it, like the midichlorians, unwanted and unnecessary. (To be fair, Lucas waited a generation before spoiling his enigmatic myth with background material, the Wachowski's jumped that particular shark in film two.)

And yet there is still much pleasure to be had watching our full-blown Jedi guides in action. Qui-Gon and Obi-Wan quickly discover that things are mercifully worse than the credit crawl predicted, a robot invasion force is being unpacked, Naboo is under actual threat. Sadly, we never actually see any of the massacres that are apparently taking place, instead we land somewhere that looks suspiciously like the woods near Leavesden and meet one of the galaxy's more annoying comedy sidekicks (although not as annoying as fans frantically searching for a scapegoat would have you believe). After all, this film has as its hero a small boy – it cannot visit the dark 12A places.

What Lucas later confessed was a 'jazz riff' of a plot wafts our heroes to the holy ground of Tatooine, all sense of urgency dissipated. In *A New Hope* Luke and Ben, heading the other way, are already too late: Alderaan is gone. From that moment it is a race against time (collapsed to provide greater unity) and a struggle just to stay alive. In *The Phantom Menace* our heroes are waylaid by a faulty engine. Hmm. The fate of the galaxy hangs in the balance and Qui-Gon prefers to gamble with a junk-yard dealer than twat him with his lightsabre.

Tatooine turns out to be a total bust. They leave Obi-Wan behind, Amidala pretends to be Padme for no good reason, Anakin whines a lot, there's some mumbo jumbo about a mystical birth and at absolutely no point does Han Solo turn up. Bastard. This is a section so flabby that even the electrifying pod race goes on for one lap too long.

But hell, we meet Vader Jr. and he says goodbye to his mother, which is the only essential action of the movie, so it's almost worth the trip.

Despite the unspeakable Yoda puppet, more endless politicking and some iffy CGI, the arrival on Coruscant and the subsequent battle of Naboo provide most of the lasting excuses for forgiving *The Phantom Menace*. At last there are new worlds to explore, new creatures to encounter and new wrinkles to the *Star Wars* myth. On Coruscant we are free to marvel at the work of Doug Chiang's design department – every bit the equal of the original trilogy. And during the saga's very best lightsabre battle John Williams adds another classic theme ('Duel Of The Fates') to his masterpiece. The final act is a mess of conflicting ideas and we are forced to root for a tweenage space pilot but you certainly can't fault it for pace.

Perhaps best of all, we have the death of Qui-Gon. Liam Neeson has manfully carried the action on his shoulders throughout (the subsequent prequels desperately miss him) and his final words – 'Obi-Wan, promise … Promise me you will train the boy' – provide the movie with its only real weight.

Lucas probably imagined that Anakin's goodbye would be the real heartbreaker but he couldn't write it and Jake Lloyd couldn't act it. The irony is, we don't need it. Given where he is destined to end up, Anakin doesn't need to be innocence personified when we meet him. Indeed, we are told that the kid is too old to be trained and that the Jedi council fear him, facts that are utterly lost on an audience who see only a bowl-headed brat.

And yet if only Lucas could have stopped thinking like a fearful father and acted more like the fearless myth-maker of old, there's a quick fix that would change everything. Imagine for a moment a street urchin orphaned by the Clone Wars, a scoundrel scamming to survive, already using the force without even realising it. Imagine a cocky fifteen-year-old robbing Qui-Gon, competing with Obi-Wan and flirting with Padme. Imagine, for a second, an Anakin invested with the spirit of a young Han Solo … ★★★
CK

⓪ STAR WARS EPISODE II: ATTACK OF THE CLONES (2002)

Starring: *Ewan McGregor (Obi-Wan Kenobi), Natalie Portman (Senator Padme Amidala), Hayden Christensen (Anakin Skywalker), Christopher Lee (Count Dooku/Darth Tyranus), Samuel L. Jackson (Mace Windu), Frank Oz (voice of Yoda), Ian McDiarmid (Supreme Chancellor Palpatine/Darth Sidious), Pernilla August (Shmi Skywalker), Temuera Morrison (Jango Fett), Daniel Logan (Boba Fett), Jimmy Smits (Bail Organa)*
Director: *George Lucas*
Screenwriters: *George Lucas, Jonathan Hales, based on a story by Lucas*
PG/132 mins./Sci-fi/USA

Awards: *Empire Awards – Scene Of The Year; Razzies – Worst Screenplay, Worst Supporting Actor (Hayden Christensen)*

Ten years after *The Phantom Menace*, the Galactic Republic is under threat from charismatic separatists, forcing Naboo Senator Padme Amidala to seek protection in the guise of Jedi Padawan Anakin Skywalker, while Obi-Wan Kenobi discovers a secret Clone Army …

The collective fever that characterised the countdown to *The Phantom Menace* had long since dissipated by the time the first sequel prequel rolled off the ILM production line. Casual spectators, once stung, had decamped en masse to the newly discovered Middle-Earth, leaving George Lucas with just the few million hardcore fans – true believers who, with all the apprehension of parents at a nativity play, willed their defrocked hero back towards respectability.

TOP10 Star Wars Double Entendres

1 **You came in that thing? You're braver than I thought – *Princess Leia, A New Hope***
2 **Aren't you a little short for a Stormtrooper? – *Princess Leia, A New Hope***
3 **I must've hit pretty close to the mark to get her all riled up like that, huh? – *Han Solo, The Empire Strikes Back***
4 **Into the garbage shoot, flyboy! – *Princess Leia, A New Hope***
5 **I thought that hairy beast would be the end of me – *C3PO, The Empire Strikes Back***
6 **Curse my metal body, I wasn't fast enough! – *C3PO, A New Hope***
7 **I don't think the Empire had Wookiees in mind when they designed her, Chewie – *Han Solo, Return Of The Jedi***
8 **At last we will reveal ourselves to the Jedi – *Darth Maul, The Phantom Menace***
9 **Master Kenobi, you disappoint me. Yoda holds you in such high esteem. Surely you can do better – *Count Dooku, Attack Of The Clones***
10 **Good relations with the Wookiees I have – *Yoda, Revenge Of The Sith***

S

There are certainly stretches in the patchy *Attack Of The Clones* when Lucas's flat-packed dialogue struggles to keep the hecklers quiet – Anakin's seduction of the former Queen has all the charm of a teenage lunge behind the bike-sheds and none of the feeling – but by the time climactic 'reel six' cranks into high gear the saga's reputation as the godfather of modern sci-fi spectacle is more or less restored. Indeed, when Yoda finally unsheathes his mini-sabre and kicks Sith ass the faithful can reliably be found standing on seats hollering as if the outcome was never in doubt. But, as the little Jedi might say, in doubt it was.

Where *Episode V* fairly zipped around the galaxy with all the breezy confidence of youth, unafraid to travel anywhere, even dark places, the second middle child of the saga is saddled with an altogether heavier burden from which it struggles to escape. *Empire* hits the ground running on ice planet Hoth, *Clones,* however, has a truly cold start to contend with, aware perhaps that the movie's most pressing task is to simply atone for the more egregious sins of *Episode I*. Thus, Jar Jar is quickly sidelined, the upgraded CGI Yoda gets a showcase and those damn Amidala-clones are killed off on page one. On Coruscant we also meet the grown-up 'Ani' – okay so he's a whiny teenager but that's still a vast improvement on the bowl-haired moppet the world was asked to root for in 1999.

Also more powerful than when last we met is Ewan McGregor's Obi-Wan, the Jedi who was simply wan in *Menace* is a much more forceful presence as a full-bearded Master, struggling manfully with the endless exposition and even landing the odd punchline.

As with *Empire*, the protagonists are separated for the second act: while Obi-Wan is busy uncovering the conspiracy of the Clones, Anakin and Padme turn into colourless clones of Han and Leia in the romance stakes. There are pleasures (Obi-Wan squares off against Jango Fett) and pitfalls (Anakin and Padme have a picnic) in roughly equal measure throughout this flabby middle act but as with *Episode I* mostly you get a sense of drama that is willed into being, a necessary bridge to *Episode III* that requires Lucas to traverse territory – romance, politics – he is simply not comfortable in.

Matters improve greatly in the final forty minutes: Christopher Lee's Count Dooku arrives to provide some much needed gravitas, C-3PO turns up to do his C-3PO thing and Padme puts on a skin-tight white leotard. Best of all, Lucas finally cuts loose. The classic trilogy bristled with seat-of-your-pants filmmaking, our heroes bouncing from cliffhanger to cliffhanger, and in the final section of *Episode II* – almost four hours into this prequel enterprise – Lucas at last cranks up to this Saturday morning serial pace: from the Tex Avery goofiness of the droid factory, to the Cecil B. DeMille grandeur of the gladiator arena, the action never lets up.

Also in the last reel we finally get to divine something of Lucas's grand design, with ironic pay-offs for the fans still paying close attention – it is the witless Jar Jar who makes the creation of a clone army possible and Yoda who first leads what will become Stormtroopers into battle. In its own way, the end of *Episode II* is every bit as dark as the famous end of *Episode V*.

Unsurprisingly, the least-anticipated movie of the saga suffered at the box office – *Episode IV* raked in more money at the US box office back in 1977 – and remains largely unloved by the fanbase for its emphasis on the central love story but despite no real improvement in dialogue or acting it functions perfectly well as an old-fashioned romantic epic, complete with stand-alone set-pieces, rich political intrigue and a painters' palette. Indeed, so indebted is Lucas to David O. Selznick here, ultimately he may have been better served abandoning his own trilogy structure and boiling both *Episodes I* and *II* down to a 3-hour *Gone With The Wind*-style classic – an approach that would have at least halved all that damn anticipation.

★★★ CK

③ STAR WARS EPISODE III: REVENGE OF THE SITH (2005)

Starring: *Ewan McGregor (Obi-Wan Kenobi), Natalie Portman (Senator Padme Amidala), Hayden Christensen (Anakin Skywalker), Christopher Lee (Count Dooku/Darth Tyranus), Samuel L. Jackson (Mace Windu), Frank Oz (voice of Yoda), Ian McDiarmid (Supreme Chancellor Palpatine/Darth Sidious), Anthony Daniels (C-3PO), Jimmy Smits (Bail Organa)*
Director: *George Lucas*
Screenwriter: *George Lucas*
12A/140 mins./Sci-fi/USA

Awards: *Empire Film Awards – Scene Of The Year, Best Sci-Film, Razzies – Worst Supporting Actor (Hayden Christensen)*

The Clone Wars are at last coming to an end but troubles are only just beginning for the Jedi order. The devious masterplan of Palpatine/Sidious needs but a new apprentice and young Anakin Skywalker, troubled by dreams of pain and loss, appears to fit the bill.

In perhaps the most blatant instance of a *Star Wars* character plugging a plot hole, at one point in *Return Of The Jedi*, Obi-Wan Kenobi brushes aside the lies he told Luke about Vader with this infamous equivocation, 'Many of the truths we cling to depend greatly on our own point of view.' So then, from a certain point of view, *Revenge Of The Sith*, simultaneously the middle and last *Star Wars* movie, is the best sequel, and the most pleasing surprise, in the entire saga.

In true Saturday morning serial fashion *Sith* begins with a chapter leftover from a previous adventure: the rescue of the Chancellor from General Grievous by Anakin, Obi-Wan and the saga's best sidekick: R2-D2. Fast, loose, inventive and within touching distance of funny, this is the spiritual sequel to the original escape from the Death Star, reloaded with full Jedi powers. Like a fragment from a lost civilisation, this episode hints at countless Clone Wars escapades that sadly exist only in the extended universe – still, at least we have that bit where Jar Jar falls over the explosive marbles captured on film.

The sequence ends with the saga's single most audacious shot since the Star Destroyer first passed overhead – the front half of Grievous's flagship *The Invisible Hand* screeching to a halt yards from camera – and it becomes clear that being faced with the thankless task of directly dovetailing into a timeless classic everybody from Lucas down has raised their game considerably. ILM finally seem to have finished the digital toolkit they've been toying with since the late nineties fashioning flora and fauna that has real weight and substance for the first time. There are 2,200 effects shots in *Sith* – more than *Menace* and *Clones* combined – and there's not a single specimen of bad compositing, which is more than can be said for 2006's SFX Oscar winner *King Kong*.

Also flawless is Gavin Bouquet's production design – indeed, *Sith*'s most unambiguous joy is watching Bouquet and Lucas retrofit their galaxy – often there seems to be no escape as the mismatched trilogies crunch together, but a deft aside or throwaway motif always gets us out of the compacter.

So far, so certain point of view – however *Sith* carries a far graver responsibility than the prequels it quickly outclasses. Lucas himself admitted that fully 60 percent of his original outline was slated for this bridging episode, which means that all the unanswered questions that made the prequels permissible in the first place are addressed here. In other words, *Sith* is it: this is where the myths get set in stone, Lucas can muck around on Naboo all he likes, but if he screws up the birth of Vader, big black 'ain't ever going to be the same.

And once *Sith* starts forging myth, fingers are burned. The shortcomings may be familiar by now but they rankle more than ever here. Just as it was becoming possible to tune out the constant clanking of Lucas's lumbering dialogue the words are invested with real import. And just as we were getting used to the declarative 30s-style line readings that Lucas alone finds an adequate substitute for acting, the drama is asked to support some really heavy shit. Many of the key components of the *Star Wars* legend – Vader's birth, Padme's death – are ultimately undone by dialogue that is ludicrous either in intent or execution.

Sometimes you simply think 'Noooo!'

Most damagingly, Anakin's conversion to the dark side is rushed through during a slack middle act where the chosen one bounces back and forth between Mace Windu and Palpatine like a confused teenager in a soap opera love triangle. The self-inflicted 20-20-60 story split that starved *Episodes I* and *II* of real incident, leaves Lucas with far too much ground to make up here: so far we've gathered that Anakin is arrogant, horny and has bad dreams – well, we all know it's just a short step from there to baby killer.

The delicious McDiarmid does his best to make the dark side sound seductive but unless you are steeped in Force lore (for the record, once Anakin cracks open the door, the flood-gates burst and it is near-impossible to resist) this critical moment utterly fails to convince.

Mercifully then, the *Star Wars* myth is so powerful, so pre-imagined by so many, that much of it requires no explanation bar our constant narrator: the peerless John Williams. The twin duels that bring the third act to a rousing close confirm *Sith* as not just the darkest but also the prettiest entry in the saga – the lava landscape of Mustafa, in particular, has obviously been bubbling in Lucas's imagination for nearly thirty years. (A few shots also benefit from having best pal Steven Spielberg play around with the 'pre-viz' animatic software.)

In the end then, it depends on your point of view. As a sequel to the prequels, *Sith* is more than anyone can reasonably have hoped for, a movie that made it okay to be a *Star Wars* fan again. However, a few fans will always cling to a different truth, to an alternative universe where at least one prequel was the equal of the original trilogy. And for those people, *Revenge Of The Sith*, the last chance to get it right, will always rate as the biggest disappointment of all.

From a certain point of view. ★★★★ **CK**

STAR WARS EPISODE IV: A NEW HOPE (1977)

Starring: *Mark Hamill (Luke Skywalker), Harrison Ford (Han Solo), Carrie Fisher (Princess Leia Organa), Peter Cushing (Grand Moff Tarkin), Alec Guinness (Ben Obi-Wan Kenobi), Anthony Daniels (C-3PO), Kenny Baker (R2-D2), Peter Mayhew (Chewbacca), David Prowse (Darth Vader), James Earl Jones (Darth Vader – voice)*

Director: *George Lucas*

Screenwriter: *George Lucas*

U/121 mins./125 mins. (special edition)/Action/Adventure/Fantasy/Sci-fi/USA

Awards: *Academy Awards – Best Art Direction-Set Decoration, Best Costume, Best Visual Effects, Best Film Editing, Best Score, Best Sound, BAFTA – Anthony Asquith Award for Film Music, Best Sound, Golden Globes – Best Score*

Princess Leia is held hostage by the evil Imperial forces in their effort to take over the Galactic Empire. Farmboy Luke Skywalker joins mysterious Ben Kenobi on a quest to save her . . .

It's tricky, but try to imagine a time before *Star Wars*. Close your eyes, concentrate hard, rewind those famous scrolling credits until there's just blackness. Good. Back in that dark, pre-enlightenment age, 20th Century Fox conducted some market research on their forthcoming sci-fi adventure.

Researchers armed only with a title and brief synopsis came back with some worrying results: only males under 25 expressed a desire to see a film called *Star Wars*. As a direct result of this research, *Star Wars* was deliberately packaged to attract older and female cinemagoers: the humans were pushed centre-stage and the film's epic, fairy-tale qualities were emphasised in the publicity material. When *Star Wars* came out in the summer of 1977 it had been focus-grouped, and to great effect – everybody went to see it.

By November, it had dethroned *Jaws* in the all-time box office charts, a position it held until *Independence Day*. Blimey, even the novelisation sold two million copies, and let's not get started on the merchandising. So what happened? After all, nobody's attributing *Star Wars'* epoch-making, culture-shifting success to a wily decision to put Princess Leia on the posters. The answer is timing.

The 1970s, Hollywood's second golden age, were characterised by baby-boomer film students making pictures personal and dark enough to reflect the political morass of post-Watergate, in-Vietnam America. Though *The Exorcist* and *Jaws* are credited with kicking down the doors of the Blockbuster Age, these were not family films. *Star Wars* was. George Lucas, feted after *American Graffiti* had made $55 million off a $1.2 million budget, started writing his moralistic space opera in 1973. He worked on the script for two and a half years in a back room containing a Wurlitzer jukebox and a portrait of Sergei Eisenstein, during which he could never remember how he spelt all those crazy names (Wookiee was different every time he wrote it). It's said that he based maverick Han Solo (bearded, originally) on his pal Francis Coppola and Darth Vader on Richard Nixon.

Influenced by Joseph Campbell's writings on the power of ancient mythology, Lucas created a cosmic Western, the 'black hats' replaced by Vader and the evil Empire, and the 'white hats' by farmboy Luke Skywalker (Solo was the equivalent of the drunken gunslinger). Lucas's movie brat mates thought he was nuts, and indeed, by the end of a tortuously difficult shoot at Elstree Studios, he very nearly was.

Meanwhile, in an old warehouse near Van Nuys airport, the newborn Industrial Light And Magic had spent $5 million of the $9.5 million budget and not produced a single usable effects shot in one year of working. Of course when they did, ILM redefined movie effects as sure as the finished film would redefine the experience of 'going to the pictures'. We all know why Lucas felt the need to digitally tidy up his original trilogy for the great, money-hoovering 1997 reissue, but it set a worrying precedent for *The Phantom Menace*, where too much technology smothered characterisation and story.

Star Wars' timeless appeal lies in its easily identified, universal archetypes – goodies to root for, baddies to boo, a princess to be rescued and so on – and if it is most obviously dated to the 70s by the special effects, so be it. We all love the stormtrooper banging his head! To remove that digitally would be a crime. Mark Hamill said he felt 'like a raisin in a giant fruit salad' when making *Star Wars*; 20 years later, Liam Neeson almost retired from screen acting after his experiences on *The Phantom Menace*. But George Lucas does not make actors' films – his interest is in the *Star Wars* myth, not the cult of some Hollywood star.

Isn't it ironic then, that *Star Wars* remains a rewatchable classic because of the characters and the performances behind them (especially Ford, Fisher, and James Earl Jones). Sure, you can snigger at R2-D2 trundling along the sand like a wheelie-bin, but his signature beeps and clucks are as essential to the personality and momentum of the film as the rousing John Williams score. Just as it's hard to remember what cinema was like before *Star Wars*, it's impossible to view the original film in isolation now. In 1977, it was not *Episode IV*, it was a self-contained pleasure that made it okay again to cheer at the screen. ★★★★★ **AC**

STAR WARS EPISODE V – THE EMPIRE STRIKES BACK (1980)

Starring: *Mark Hamill (Luke Skywalker), Harrison Ford (Han Solo), Carrie Fisher (Princess Leia Organa), Alec Guinness (Ben Obi-Wan Kenobi), Anthony Daniels (C-3PO), Kenny Baker (R2-D2), Peter Mayhew (Chewbacca), David Prowse (Darth Vader), James Earl Jones (Darth Vader – voice), Frank Oz (Yoda – voice), Jeremy Bulloch (Boba Fett), Billy Dee Williams (Lando Calrissian), Denis Lawson (Wedge)*

Director: *Irvin Kerhner*

Screenwriter: *Leigh Brackett, Lawrence Kasdan, based on a story by George Lucas*

U/124 mins./127 mins. (special edition)/Action/Adventure/Fantasy/Sci-fi/USA

Awards: *Academy Awards – Best Sound, BAFTA – Best Original Film Music*

S

STAR WARS EPISODE VI: RETURN OF THE JEDI

Luke, Han and Leia have now joined forces with the rebel army to defeat the Imperial forces. But then Luke gets a call to join a Jedi master – Yoda – on the planet Dagobah . . .

It's generally agreed that The *Empire Strikes Back* is the best film of George Lucas's initial trilogy (despite a latter-day shift toward the original's storytelling purity). Not a sequel as such, but the next part of a continuing story, *Empire* marks enormous progression both in terms of the mythos of the series and in the filmmaking quality itself.

No longer tethered by the need to establish this fabulous universe wrapped in the arcane mysticism of the Force, this is a film far more sophisticated, awe-inspiring and daring (what do you mean Han Solo stays frozen in carbonite?). The actors too, reassured this was not some tinpot sci-fi quickie, have settled comfortably into their characters. Which is a good thing given the nightmare wrought for them by writers Lucas, Lawrence Kasdan and Leigh Brackett. At once more graceful and melancholic than its predecessor, Kershner enhances the pensive mood of impending tragedy with an array of inhospitable worlds (we travel from the icescape of Hoth to the swamp of Dagobah to a sleek, sterile city in the clouds). Bespin, the Cloud City, the most awesome of any of the *Star Wars* arenas, is a beautiful exterior with a dark heart. The film culminates in a whirl of emotional intensity and the infernal machine of the carbon freezing chamber. With John Williams' breathtaking score and the dark red hellish lighting (the characters have arrived in Hell – this being the 'second day' of the trilogy), the whole feel is of a Wagnerian opera: dark and epic.

Then there is the devastating confrontation between Luke and Vader. Masterfully choreographed, their duel culminates on a thin gantry protruding out over the vast depths that are the hollow core of the Cloud City. Magnificently visualised, the dizzying vertiginous terror of the moment encapsulated Luke's disorientation and horror at Vader's revelation of paternalism. Significantly, Luke chooses death over the outstretched hand of the dark side and is eventually born again as a Jedi.

But Act 2 is never consumed by darkness. There is comedy: C-3PO is still fussily camp as the Shakespearean chorus; Solo cracks wiser than ever before and new entry Yoda's knack of getting straight-to-the-point via the syntactical equivalent of Spaghetti Junction ('No! Try not. Do . . . or do not. There is no try.') is pure delight. And effectswise it offers unforgettable, if sometimes impractical, marvels: the awesome AT-ATs marching on the rebel base on Hoth, whose lurching gait was modelled on elephants, or Solo piloting the Milennium Falcon straight into an asteroid field.

It is on a psychological level, though, where *Empire* really reaches beyond its brethren. On Dagobah, where Luke is tutored in Jedi philosophy by the rubbery icon-to-be Yoda, the notion of the Force turns from the simple good/bad divide of *Star Wars* into a sea of moral ambiguity. Luke must fight the urges of anger and emotion to find the true path (a factor which left much of *The Phantom Menace* so limp – the Jedi characters were by definition unexciting). In the film's (and probably the series') most complex sequence Luke descends into a metaphorical dream womb, a representation of his unacknowledged fears. Here, prophetically, he confronts Darth Vader and discovers his own face beneath the mask. This is dark stuff, way beyond funny robots and knights in space.

Empire slipped the insufficient *Return Of The Jedi* a hospital pass. There was too much to settle (the whole damn universe to be saved before tea), and we had been so exhilarated by *Empire* that teddy bears at war was inevitably trite. ★★★★★ **IN**

➂ STAR WARS EPISODE VI: RETURN OF THE JEDI (1983)

Starring: *Mark Hamill (Luke Skywalker), Harrison Ford (Han Solo), Carrie Fisher (Princess Leia Organa), Peter Cushing (Grand Moff Tarkin), Alec Guinness (Ben Obi-Wan Kenobi), Anthony Daniels (C-3PO), Kenny Baker (R2-D2), Peter Mayhew (Chewbacca), David Prowse (Darth Vader), James Earl Jones (Darth Vader – voice), Frank Oz (Yoda – voice), Jeremy Bulloch (Boba Fett), Billy Dee Williams (Lando Calrissian), Ian McDiamid (The Emperor)*
Director: *George Lucas*
Screenwriter: *George Lucas, Lawrence Kasdan, based on a story by George Lucas*
U/134 mins./135 mins. (special edition)/Action/Adventure/Fantasy/Sci-fi/USA
Awards: *BAFTA – Best Visual Effects*

The rebels must rescue Han Solo from Jabba the Hut, destroy the second Death Star and bring Darth Vader/Anakin Skywalker back to the light side . . . but it's OK because they have some teddy bears to help them.

Queen of spleen critic Pauline Kael called it 'an impersonal and rather junky piece of moviemaking' while the rest of the world clearly thought otherwise (and so did the Oscar Academy, who gave it five nominations and one gong – for best special visual effects). Certainly, Marquand's 1983 take comes across as peculiarly anodyne after the broad sweeps of darkness and disturbing drama of Irvin Kershner's *The Empire Strikes Back*, and many cast members recall this as their least favourite of the trilogy.

In this final episode (of the middle trilogy at least), the evil Empire has managed to claw back power and get a substantial way through construction of a new and even more powerful Death Star – although Darth Vader is not satisfied with progress and tries to chivy things along before the arrival of the awe-inspiring Emperor. Luke Skywalker has gone to Tattooine to rescue Han Solo from evil crimelord and giant lump-of-lard Jabba The Hut, before the rebels regroup to launch an attack on the Empire's Death Star Mark II. Business as usual.

Despatched to a forest on a neighbouring planet to close down a Death Star's shield before a Rebellion attack clincher, the heroes come across some cutesy Ewoks – who ruin this film for many purist Star Wars fans, but who nevertheless prove pivotal in destroying the Empire. Oh, and the romance between Solo and Princess Leia comes on strong.

Marquand was manifestly more interested in the furry creatures than he was in the Death Star, the battle in the sky or even the Emperor and extraordinary lackey Vader. That said the asthmatic one's inner conflict of will makes for stirring stuff, as does his son's emerging struggle with the dark side (styled on Kurosawa). The final dramatic redemption and defeat of evil is as satisfying to watch many years on as it was to the crowds of weenies ignoring the deeper conflicts.

The special effects are the best of the original trilogy – the six years between this and *Star Wars* allowed ILM to increase its talents tenfold and produced the coolest (speeder) bike chase in movies – and ironically benefits the most from Lucas's latterday overhaul. Probably the weakest in the original trilogy, but still a worthy finale to an epoch-defining franchise. ★★★ **CH**

➂ STARDUST MEMORIES (1980)

Starring: *Woody Allen (Sandy Bates), Charlotte Rampling (Dorrie), Jessica Harper (Daisy), Marie-Christine Barrault (Isobel), Tony Roberts (Tony), Daniel Stern (Actor), Amy Wright (Shelley)*
Director: *Woody Allen*
Screenwriter: *Woody Allen*
15/91 mins./Comedy/USA

Unable to think of a suitable ending for his new movie, Sandy Bates attends a weekend film seminar, where he seeks release from both the pressure and cheapness of celebrity, and memories of his former lover, Dorrie, in flings with his married French mistress, Isobel, and a violinist named Daisy.

Stung by a hostile article by novelist Joan Didion and the Academy's snub to *Interiors*, Woody Allen changed the tone of this treatise on creativity and celebrity so that an amusing soul-searching became a sour, disillusioned assault on the critical community and the movie-going public. Basing his living nightmare on Judith Crist's Tarrytown seminars, Allen launched a pitiless fusilade against gnomic academics, sycophantic columnists and fans in all their eager ignorance. But the people he was most scathing towards were the liggers who hoped to cash in on their encounters with the famous, by pushing a script, seeking charitable patronage or simply putting a high-profile notch on their bedpost.

Indeed, had Allen not met Mia Farrow during post-production and embarked upon a new romance, this might have been an even more pessimistic diatribe, as he resisted the temptation to kill off one character and decided to leave Sandy feeling vaguely positive about his relationship with Isobel, despite the mixed response accorded the movie that had near driven him to distraction.

Although it occasionally referenced Ingmar Bergman, *Stardust Memories* was very much Woody Allen's $8\frac{1}{2}$. Indeed, he even opened it with a train sequence that echoed the ending that Federico Fellini had discarded from his 1963 reverie on the torment of creative block. But while Sandy's angst recalled that of Fellini's alter ego, other incidents were clearly autobiographical. Dorrie, for instance, was modelled on Allen's ex-wife, Louise Lasser (who took an uncredited cameo, along with many other satirical victims), while Og the alien got to repeat the fans' favourite lament by asking Sandy why he no longer made movies like his 'early funny ones'.

But critics and audiences alike found Gordon Willis's wide-angled close-ups unnecessarily cruel and the edge imparted by new art director Santo Loquasto and editor Sandy Morse a touch too strident. Moreover, the murder of John Lennon shortly after the film went on release eerily mimicked Sandy's dream of dying at the hands of a demented devotee and added to the melancholic mood that has since hung over this frank, if ungallant confessional tirade. ★★★ **DP**

STARGATE (1994)

Starring: *Kurt Russell (Col. Jonathan 'Jack' O'Neil), James Spader (Dr. Daniel Jackson), Viveca Lindfors (Catherine Langford, Ph.D), Jaye Davidson (Ra), Djimon Hounsou (Horus)*
Director: *Roland Emmerich*
Screenwriters: *Dean Devlin, Roland Emmerich*
PG/115 mins./Fantasy/Action/Adventure/Sci-fi/USA/France

A group of soldiers and an Egyptologist travel to another planet using an ancient Egyptian artifact.

At first glance *Stargate*'s credentials don't exactly spell out must see: a $40 million action epic with a PG rating, no A-list stars and plot-line that sounds remarkably similar to *Chariots Of The Gods: The Movie*. It didn't rate too highly with the majority of American critics either who dismissed the movie as a 'no-brainer' and then had to sit back and gnash their teeth as it became a smash hit.

The action opens in a 1928 Egypt where what looks alarmingly like an enormous stone Polo mint is uncovered in the middle of the desert. Flash forward to the present and we learn that said confection is both of extra-terrestrial origin and can transport matter across the universe. Enter Egyptologist James Spader who first figures out how the thing works and then accompanies Kurt Russell and his team of indentikit grunts across the galaxy to some far-flung planet.

Predictably, things go wrong almost immediately, with sandstorms, unintelligible locals and the body-possessing alien sungod Ra spoiling a fine day's space-travel. The rest of the movie follows our heroes as they get the girl, defeat the baddie and drop lines such as 'Give my regards to King Tut, asshole!' without cracking up.

There's no doubt that this has been pieced together like a plagiarist's scrapbook with bits of *Star Wars*, *Raiders Of The Lost Ark* and even *The Man Who Would Be King* chucked in, and it's at least half an hour too long for its own good. However, both Russell and Spader are amiable enough as the mismatched explorers and the special effects are well up to scratch. Most importantly, there's a sense in which, while it may be ridiculously far-fetched, suspension of disbelief is just about possible as it swings along with a committed gusto rarely seen since the heyday of George Lucas.
★★★ **CC**

STARSHIP TROOPERS (1997)

Starring: *Casper Van Dien (Johnny Rico), Dina Meyer (Dizzy Flores), Denise Richards (Carmen Ibanez), Jake Busey (Private Ace Levy), Neil Patrick Harris (Colonel Carl Jenkins), Michael Ironside (Lt. Jean Rasczak)*
Director: *Paul Verhoeven*
Screenwriter: *Edward Neumeier, based on the book by Robert A. Heinlein*
18/129 mins./Sci-fi/Adventure/Action/USA

A space army wage war against a planet of giant bugs.

The novel *Starship Troopers* by Robert A. Heinlein was published in 1959. It won sci- fi's prestigious Hugo Award and promptly sailed into a maelstrom of controversy. An account of a young grunt's induction into a futuristic military and his subsequent glory as an officer, you can get the gist of where it's coming from by its dedication: 'To "sarge" Arthur George Smith – soldier, citizen, scientist – and to all sergeants anywhere who have laboured to make men out of boys.' reads the title page. Hmmmm. This will be a 'guy thing' then.

For the next 200-odd pages we're treated to a khaki-moistening militaristic wet-dream as Heinlein treats us to homespun philosophy ('it's just as foolish to hit an enemy city with an H Bomb as it would be to spank a baby with an axe,' – hey, for the sake of the kids let's all remember that), gratuitous violence and meticulously, not to say leeringly, described public floggings. It's an insane hymn to smooth-limbed, blue-eyed, firm-buttocked fascism and it would take a lunatic with suspicious political leanings and equally dubious taste to even think of making such a book into a multi-million dollar movie.

Enter Paul Verhoeven. Verhoeven had his eye on the material for some time and, as Hollywood legend goes, finally stumped up his own cash to make a short test reel to show wary execs. A futuristic soldier stands in the middle of the screen before being ripped limb from limb by a giant insect. After which the director himself walks into shot. 'Pleeeshe let me make Shtarship Troopersh!' he implores. Either the Dutchman's chutzpah or the state-of-the-art digital carnage did the trick and the studio, despite the road-accident that was *Showgirls*, Verhoeven's previous outing, coughed up.

Storywise the audience has nothing too complicated to worry about. Earth is at war with the suspiciously Celtic sounding 'bug' planet Klendathu and the world's youth, unlike the novel both male and female, are being exhorted to join up and kick insect abdomen. Rich kid Johnny Ricco (Van Dien, sporting a jaw that looks as if it has been drawn with a set-square) and high-school pals hit movie boot camp and all its attendant clichés: nasty drill instructors who routinely break their charges' arms, getting tattoos and – innovative this – engaging in horseplay in the mixed sex showers (a sequence which Verhoeven persuaded his pneumatic young cast was 'artistically essential' by himself stripping off to direct it). After that it's off to a bug planet for an hour or so's gratifyingly gooey mayhem as Verhoeven showcases some astounding tommy versus tarantula CG action.

Hordes of arachnids swarm across desert battlefields strewn with human bodyparts, giant beetles fart fire into space (only Verhoeven would attempt to get away with that) while the whole shebang is punc-

S

tuated with the same kind of faux newsreels which he used to such great effect in *Robocop*. Hate-faced children stamping on cockroaches while shouting 'Kill! Kill!'. ('They're doing their bit!' the cheesy voice-over proudly announces.) Cows get ripped to shreds in 'demonstrations' of terrifying bug power and criminals are tried, sentenced and executed in the same day, all channels, all nets. Do you want to know more?

Verhoeven's movie treads the line between satire and jingoism with almost mesmerising inconsistency, falling on either side at different points. On the one hand you can hardly take po-faced dialogue like 'Come on you apes! You wanna live forever?' or 'They sucked his brains out!' with anything other than a wry smile. And then there's 'Fort Cronkite' and a cameo by Paul 'Pee Wee' Reubens. On the other, the constant fetishising of weaponry, the camera's lavishing heroic glances at its, frankly, Ayrian cast and the reduction of the enemy to insects (hey, no guilt when you're fragging a fruit-fly) together with Verhoeven's previous dabblings with militaristic imagery in *Robocop* and *Total Recall* hint that the director may be slightly closer to out-and-out admiration than he would like to admit. As might be some of his audience.

Given the levels of hammery involved, it simply wouldn't have worked with good actors – or even competent ones for that matter. So Verhoeven simply chose pulchritudinous mobile mannequins and forced them to deliver some of the most vapid dialogue imaginable ('I'm from Buenos Aires, and I say kill 'em all!'). It is also, as a matter of record, the only film in which you get to see a soldier stabbed to death up the arse by a giant space dragonfly, and for that alone, must take its place in science fiction movie history. ★★★★ **AS**

Ⓓ STARSKY & HUTCH (2004)

Starring: *Ben Stiller (David Starsky), Owen Wilson (Ken 'Hutch' Hutchinson), Snoop Dogg (Huggy Bear), Fred Williamson (Captain Doby), Vince Vaughn (Reese Feldman), Juliette Lewis (Kitty), Jason Bateman (Kevin), Amy Smart (Holly), Carmen Electra (Staci)*
Director: *Todd Phillips*
Screenwriters: *John O'Briend, Todd Phillips, Scot Armstrong, based on a story by Stevie Long, John O'Brien, characters by William Blinn*
15/101 mins./Comedy/Crime/USA

Overly dedicated Detective David Starsky is forced to work with overly laid-back Ken 'Hutch' Hutchinson. A lead on a new type of undetectable cocaine takes them to the door of businessman and philanthropist Reese Feldman...

Starsky & Hutch the movie is, of course, a very bad idea. The TV show ran from 1975 to 1979, which would put any remaining fans in their late thirties, not exactly a marketing man's ideal movie audience. And, unlike some later variants on the buddy-buddy cop genre, *Starsky & Hutch* does not live on in syndication – it has dated too badly. But it is precisely this unflattering passage of time that makes *Starsky & Hutch* a perfect property for the kind of comedy retrofit that worked wonders for that other unlamented bunch, the Bradys.

Apart from a deadly accurate spoof of the opening titles, some spot-on casting and the obligatory car chase, *Starsky & Hutch* the movie does not do a rich trade in its TV progenitor.

The satire, such as it is, has a bigger target in mind: the 1970s. Unlike the show itself, the 70s do live on in syndication, an easy and obliging victim for good-natured ribbing. For those who lived through it, 1970s America was probably dominated by Watergate and Vietnam; but for those of us who experienced the decade second-hand, it looks like one long roller-disco of bad fashion and cheesy tunes. And *Starsky & Hutch* never knowingly passes up a cheap shot. From clunky technology to chunky knitwear, all the signature naffness of the decade is lovingly lampooned.

Director Todd Phillips does dig a little deeper in exploiting the gay undertones of practically all cop duos – the titular pair follow a classic love story arc, falling for each other, then falling out before making up again. And he strikes a particularly rich vein with the comic exposition of an interesting and rather arresting phenomenon: everything that was considered macho then is utterly camp now.

Old School director Phillips is admirably old school in his approach; in places the movie looks not unlike a failed pilot for the original series, and the endearingly ramshackle production extends to a plot held together with spit and goodwill. But nobody cares if cut-to-the-gag editing strips action and logic to the bone, just so long as the jokes are worth waiting for. And even if *Starsky & Hutch* is more consistently amusing than laugh-out-loud hilarious, the hit rate is always high.

Phillips' Old School alumni Vince Vaughn and Will Ferrell pitch up with a coupla oddballs and, as Huggy Bear, Snoop Dogg proves more than a one-line casting joke. But even when the Gran Torino screeches across screen, there's never any doubt that this is Wilson and Stiller's movie.

On their sixth outing together, the real-life friends finally get an equal share of the spotlight, and the result is the best buddy pairing in recent memory. In stark contrast to the look-at-me antics of many above-the-line comedians, Wilson and Stiller are as generous as they are evenly matched. Stiller is apparently still on a one-man quest to redefine the limits of shame, while every line drawled out the corner of Wilson's odd-shaped mouth qualifies as a genuine comic aside.

Despite the fact that neither Stiller nor Wilson receives a writing credit, the movie cleaves closer in spirit to the supremely silly *Zoolander* than anything else.

Goofy and easygoing, *Starsky & Hutch* is not exactly politically correct, but you'd be hard pushed to find a single mean frame. This is the kind of movie where cocaine is easily confused with Canderel. The kind of movie where the villain just wants to buy a pony for his daughter's Bat Mitzvah. The kind of movie where sexual threesomes are organised by Owen Wilson. In other words: sweet. ★★★★ **CK**

Ⓓ STATE OF GRACE (1990)

Starring: *Sean Penn (Terry Noonan), Ed Harris (Frankie Flannery), Gary Oldman (Jackie Flannery), Robin Wright Penn (Kathleen Flannery), John Turturro (Nick)*
Director: *Phil Joanou*
Screenwriter: *Dennis McIntyre*
18/134 mins./Drama/USA

After ten years away, Terry Noonan returns to his childhood neighbourhood in New York's Hells Kitchen, and meets up with his former pal Jackie, whose brother, Frankie, now runs the local chapter of the Irish mob. But as friendships are rediscovered, loyalties will be severely tested as Terry is actually an undercover cop.

If you're looking for a dour thriller, heavy-weighted with the Method mood of Sean Penn, the itchy wildness of Gary Oldman, and Ed Harris's reliable stoicism, made yearning and tribal with slabs of U2 on the soundtrack, here you go. A gangster movie on the tough-guy streets of Western Manhattan, which is really a Western in disguise, thick-headed and self-important but enjoyably pretentious.

The theme is of loyalty and family ties versus justice. Will Terry Noonan stick to his task of bringing down the Oirish mob from within, and thus breaking ties with former best pal Jackie and former flame Kathleen? Will treacherous Frankie catch on to the deception? How long before holy Irish blood is spilt on the paving stones of Hells Kitchen?

While Phil Joanou (who would keep with the Irish-thing directing the U2 movie, *Rattle And Hum*) seems to think he is making a tale of brotherhood strained, it's a blarney-fied nothing with silky-smooth slo-mo gunfights

Retired Oscar categories TOP 10

1. Best Assistant Director – 1934 to 1938
2. Comedy Direction – 1929 only
3. Best Dance Direction – 1936 to 1938
4. Best Title Writing – 1929 only†
5. Engineering Effects – 1929
6. Best Short Film (Colour) – 1937 to 1938
7. Best Short Film (Live Action – Two Reels) – 1937 to 1957
8. Short Film (Novelty) – 1933 to 1936
9. Best Story – 1929 to 1957
10. Unique and Artistic Production – 1929 only

†Awarded for titles that appeared between scenes to convey story in silent films.

and few jokes. But the atmosphere is taut, its smoky streets and ruptured neon is Michael Mann-lite, the actors doing some damn serious scowling. Forgiving its obvious faults and luminous shallowness, it's got grudging romantic allure. ★★★ **IN**

STATE OF SIEGE (ETAT DE SIEGE) (1972)

Starring: *Yves Montand (Phillip Michael Santore), Renato Salvatori (Capt. Lopez), O.E. Hasse (Carlos Ducas), Jacques Weber (Hugo), Jean-Luc Bideau (Este), Evangelline Peterson (Mrs. Santore), Maurice Teynac (Minister Of Internal Security)*
Director: *Constantin Costa-Gavras*
Screenwriters: *Franco Solinas, Constantin Costa-Gavras*
15/120 mins./Thriller/France/US/Italy/West Germany

Posing as a civil adviser, US counter-terrorist agent Philip Michael Santore is kidnapped by Latin American guerillas, who demand the release of political prisoners while trying to coerce Santore into revealing the true nature of his work. But when Captain Lopez's police close in, the guerillas are left with no option but to murder their hostage.

Having just completed *Z*, Constantin Costa-Gavras was working on *The Confession* when he became intrigued by the kidnap by Uruguayan Tupamaros guerillas of an American named Daniel A. Mitrone, who was described in successive editions of *Le Monde* as an official, a policeman and a diplomat. Following Mitrone's murder, Costa-Gavras and Franco Solinas (who had co-scripted Gillo Pontecorvo's *The Battle of Algiers*) went to Montevideo to research the case and unearthed documentation which proved that Mitrone – who was supposedly an expert in traffic control and communication – had been teaching counter-insurgency techniques, including torture, to the Uruguayan security forces.

Unsurprisingly, there was a storm of protest from Washington when the feature was released and the American Film Institute was denied permission to screen it. Yet in banning *Stage Of Siege* on account of its perceived anti-Americanism and justification of political assassination, the US authorities laid themselves open to the same accusations of abuse of power that had been levelled in the picture.

However, the ensuing furore about bias and the filmmaker's right to provoke intellectual debate rather obscured the fact that the socialists who had applauded *Z* and *State of Siege* had also denounced *The Confession* for the supposed anti-Communist attitudes that had been commended by the right-wingers. Thus, Costa-Gavras had successfully proved the contention posited in all three films that no single ideology had all the answers and that those that refused to brook the existence of alternative doctrines were the least laudable.

But while the controversy proved instructive, it somewhat disguised the film's shortcomings. Yves Montand impressed by playing Santore as an arrogant advocate of ruthless capitalism, but Costa-Gavras's resort to the same flashbacking technique he had employed on *Z* seemed as self-conscious as the punchy editorial style and Mikis Theodorakis's clamorous score. Yet, the director insisted that this commercial approach was the best way to ensure that a serious message reached the largest possible audience and his political trilogy certainly had a profound influence on Hollywood in the Watergate era, when it also began to examine the corruption and paranoia of US society. ★★★ **DP**

STATIC (1985)

Starring: *Keith Gordon (Ernie Blick), Amanda Plummer (Julia Purcell), Bob Gunton (Frank), Barton Heyman (Sheriff William Orling), Lily Knight (Patty), Jane Hoffman (Emily Southwick)*
Director: *Mark Romanek*
Screenwriters: *Mark Romanek, Keith Gordon*
15/93 mins./Drama/USA

Ernie Blick, an orphaned young man, works on an invention which will 'make people happy, not sad'. Encouraged by his punk musician best friend Julia, Ernie unveils his breakthrough, a television set which should enable viewers to 'see Heaven'.

A genuinely original film, co-scripted by director Mark Romanek (who waited a long time to deliver his second feature, *One Hour Photo*) and star Keith Gordon (on the point of becoming a director himself). Set in an Arizonan desert nowhere around Christmas, *Static* has a Lynch-like feel for small-town bizarre, as represented by the hero's odd day job of weeding defective crucifixes out of a production line for religious artefacts, which leads to him getting fired when it's discovered he has been collecting deformed Jesuses for use in his own artwork. You can tell how skewed from normality the picture is because Amanda Plummer, usually typecast as a loon, plays the anchor of sanity in this world.

Gordon and Plummer are particularly good as the not-quite romantic leads, substantiating their claim that they once felt like twins by matching each other tic for tic in a toned-down screwball relationship that is one of the cinema's rare attempts at depicting something as complicated as a friendship. The gradual revelation of just what it is that the hero is making in his workshop is well-handled, as is the disappointment that comes when most folk (and the audience) only see static on the monitor that should be a portal to Heaven. The film is bewildering, sometimes close to whimsical, but its wit, humanity and unique outlook stay in the mind.

It has a soundtrack mix of punk, New Wave British bands, Christmas kitsch and country and western, and a distinctively weird but naturalistic visual style to go with its fantastical but down-to-earth storyline. ★★★★ **KN**

THE STATION AGENT (2003)

Starring: *Peter Dinklage (Finbar McBride), Patricia Clarkson (Olivia Harris), Bobby Carnavale (Joe Oramas), Paul Benjamin (Henry Styles)*
Director: *Thomas McCarthy*
Screenwriter: *Thomas McCarthy*
15/85 mins./Comedy/Drama/USA
Awards: *BAFTA – Best Original Screenplay*

S

When his boss dies, diminutive model railway shop worker Fin McBride inherits a disused railway depot in a sleepy provincial town. Although he tries to ignore friendly overtures from the curious local community, Fin finds himself slowly drawn into their odd, tragicomic lives.

When it debuted at Sundance – the world's most right-on festival – we feared a politically correct study of the harsh plight of the vertically challenged in patriarchal America. But, almost magically, Tom McCarthy's sometimes hilarious, touching film is no such thing.

Drawing on all the requisite elements of modern US indie cinema (dreams, suburbia, isolation, Patricia Clarkson), *The Station Agent* is a small but sprawling comedy of manners that ignores the temptations of cheap melodrama to take us off the map to a place seldom visited by its peers.

A place, it must be said, where nothing much happens. But, like the community Fin finds when he moves into his new home, McCarthy's film is alive with personality and intrigue.

Sharply written and beautifully realised, these are characters with depth and feeling – oddballs, certainly, but warm and credible. There's Joe, the nosy Cuban hot dog man who runs a fast-food stall in the middle of nowhere. There's Emily, the pretty librarian in lumber with her deadbeat boyfriend. There's Cleo, the curious little schoolgirl who desperately wants Fin to help with her show-and-tell.

But most of all there's Olivia, the artist who harbours a fascination for Fin from the day she almost runs him over. The closest thing this film has to a love interest, Clarkson gives her best here: tough but vulnerable, teetering on breakdown but somehow reined in by her own survival instinct and distracted by the strange, steely pull of the surly Fin. Though it never reaches the surface, this muted love affair is one of the film's many charms, another avenue left tantalisingly mysterious.

It would be a tough job for any actor to command such a light and quixotic patchwork but, in the lead, Dinklage proves himself a subtle actor and gifted comedian. Indeed, the part was initially written for a normal-sized actor, and it's a measure of his talent that McCarthy had to tweak the script so little to suit him. Eschewing sentiment and never scared of size jokes, Dinklage's Fin McBride is a regal, rude and enigmatic presence, his cool only ruffled in a bittersweet scene in which his height makes him comically ineffective in a boy-girl fight.

Happily, this is more than just a showcase for a first-time writer-director or an acting workshop for his cast. It's *The Station Agent*'s meditation on the smaller things in life that make it such a big deal. ★★★★ **DW**

⓪ STEALTH (2005)

Starring: *Josh Lucas (Lt. Ben Gannon), Jessica Biel (Lt. Kara Wade), Jamie Foxx (Lt. Henry Purcell), Sam Shepard (Capt. George Cummings), Richard Roxburgh (Dr. Keith Orbit)*
Director: *Rob Cohen*
Screenwriter: *W.D. Richter*
12A/121 mins./Action/Thriller/USA

The prototype of an unmanned, artificially intelligent jet fighter goes kerflooey and, like a kamikaze HAL 900, sets out to single-handedly instigate World War III. Only a trio of elite US Navy pilots can save the day ...

Anyone familiar with Rob Cohen's oeuvre will be aware that subtlety is not his strong suit. Even so, the director of such cinematic mayhem as *The Fast And The Furious* and *xXx* blows his wad in spectacular fashion with this face-melting ode to fly-boy braggadocio and supercool killing machines.

Lending its title an air of supposedly unintentional irony, *Stealth* is an orgy of pyrotechnic overkill, fetishised military hardware and mind-boggling special effects, employed most ardently in scene after scene of aerial combat so dazzlingly kinetic they make *Top Gun* (to which this owes not only a debt of gratitude but dinner and a show) look like a day out with the Wright brothers.

The plot concerns a trio of elite and insufferably smug US Navy fighter pilots (Josh Lucas, Jessica Biel and Jamie Foxx) whose new wing-man is a robo-brained stealth fighter, or UCAV (Unmanned Combat Aerial Vehicle), named EDI (Extreme Deep Invader), the latest, and by a wide margin the sexiest, weapon yet in the war on terror.

It takes place at an unspecified time in the near future. And if you think it a little far-fetched to imagine the Pentagon spending billions of dollars on a new hypersonic jet fighter, an outmoded Cold War relic of no use whatsoever against an enemy who, we have recently been tragically reminded, doesn't exactly operate out in the open with hi-tech modern weaponry, think again. Cohen was inspired by the fact that the US military has unmanned planes in operation and is spending vast sums of money developing more sophisticated models (that military-industrial complex, don'tcha just love it?).

This would seem to raise all sorts of interesting questions. But while there is the odd moment of ethical introspection and even a greetings-card platitude or two on the moral implications of war itself (especially after EDI is struck by lightning and develops a predictably alarming mind of its own), the philosophical pondering neither distracts from the blowing shit up nor drowns out the subsonic crowing over America's ability to kick the world's ass.

On one level, *Stealth* is technically breathtaking, viscerally thrilling action cinema of the highest order. On another, it is slavering, state-of-the-art war porn. ★★ **SB**

⓪ STEAMBOAT BILL, JR (1928)

Starring: *Buster Keaton (William Canfield, Jr.), Tom McGuire (John James King), Ernest Torrence (William Canfield, Sr.), Tom Lewis (Tom Carter), Marion Byron (Marion King)*
Directors: *Charles Reisner, Buster Keaton (uncredited)*
Screenwriter: *Carl Harbaugh*
U/71 mins./Comedy/USA

Harvard fop Willie Canfield is disowned by his Mississippi boatman father, Bill, whose business is under fire from go-getting J.C. King, whose daughter, Kitty, is Willie's dream girl. But when a cyclone hits River Junction, the East Coast softie gets to prove his mettle.

Although everyone remembers this comic classic for its meticulously executed stunt gags, plenty of thought went into its themes, too. Buster Keaton's strained relationship with his father, Joe, clearly informed the Bill-Willie situation. But Keaton also used their contrasting stature and attitudes to examine the whole concept of American masculinity and this also tied in with the sense of resentful provincialism that informs Bill's disdain for the namby-pamby Easterner. Yet, despite the Freudian motifs, Keaton identified with the old-timer's fondness for his tub, the *Stonewall Jackson*, and uses its triumph over Tom Lewis's new-fangled steamer, *The King*, to challenge the US obsession with progress and its scorn for tradition.

It's ironic, therefore, that this should prove to be Keaton's last silent masterpiece, as the Talkies arrived during its production and he would never recapture past glories after he signed to MGM. Indeed, the influence on proceedings of supervisor Harry Brand was a foretaste of the loss of control that Keaton would subsequently experience. But it was Brand's idea to change the natural disaster striking River Junction from a deluge to a cyclone to avoid offending Mississippians who had just been through a series of ruinous floods. However, Keaton was initially less than impressed by the change, as he had to rethink all of his set-pieces and spend over $20,000 on new sets.

But the sight gags he devised ended up being among his best. The hospital bed being swept along the street and through the stable is splendid, but it was immediately bettered by the shocking sight of a two-storey house front collapsing onto Keaton, only for him to be standing in the tiny space left by an open window. His rooftop rescue of Marion Byron and the Ernest Torrence prison breakout were also superbly achieved, with the comedy of thrills retaining a sense of accidental heroism thanks to Keaton's pragmatic bewilderment. Director Charles Reisner persuaded Keaton to smile during the parson's climactic deliverance to anticipate his marital bliss, but test audiences howled their disapproval (as Keaton knew they would) and the myth of the Great Stone Face was preserved. ★★★★★ **DP**

⦿ STEEL MAGNOLIAS (1989)

Starring: *Sally Field (M'Lynn Eatenton), Dolly Parton (Truvy Jones), Shirley MacLaine (Ouiser Bourdreaux), Daryl Hannah (Annelle Dupuy Desoto), Olympia Dukakis (Clairee Belcher), Julia Roberts (Shelby Eatenton Latcherie), Sam Shepard (Spud Jones), Dylan McDermott (Jackson Latcherie)*
Director: *Herbert Ross*
Screenwriter: *Robert Harling, based on his play*
PG/113 mins./Drama/Comedy/Romance/USA

Awards: *Golden Globes – Best Supporting Actress (Golden Globes)*

A beauty parlour in Louisiana is the fulcrum around which the lives of the town's women revolve.

Robert Harling's original moving piece was written as a tribute to his own mother and sister and the manner in which they dealt with personal tragedy. His award-winning stage play was set entirely in the local hair salon, where the women came and went with the seasons, sharing their life stories, problems, gossip and griefs over shampoo and sets. Harling's and Ross's screen adaptation opens up the setting to take in town, neighbours, events from wedding to fete to funeral, and introduce the men in the women's lives.

While this arguably makes for a more interesting film visually, it has unquestionably weakened the force of words in the play, in which the good-natured flow of shriekingly funny lines gave way suddenly and shockingly to the poignant climax. It may be unfair to compare a film with its stage source, but the fact remains that the film, while retaining a great deal of both humour and pathos, is a less persuasive work and more obviously a vehicle for a starry ensemble.

The most notable element here is a sensational central performance from Sally Field. She of the perennially twee image has already proved that she can play doughty with the best of them with two Oscar-winning roles in *Norma Rae* and *Places In The Heart*, and here she dominates *Magnolias*, playing matron M'Lynn with heartbreaking conviction and assurance as she takes her from routine cares and irritations to grief and rage against fate.

Running her close seconds in support are Shirley MacLaine as the outrageous, unkempt battleaxe Ouiser and Olympia Dukakis, all elegance and wit as the wealthy widow Clairee, showing the youngsters how it's done. Less impressive are Daryl Hannah as dippy salon junior Annelle, labouring under the misapprehension that sporting funny glasses and stringy hair and tripping over kerbs constitute acting, and the much-vaunted Julia Roberts, whose playing makes M'Lynn's frail daughter Shelby appear abrasively wilful rather than courageous, undercutting the crisis that comes. Likeable Dolly Parton still isn't really an actress at all, but she is on safe ground as gutsy, good-hearted, hair-teasing Truvy, rejoicing in some hilarious one-liners and the opportunity to roll in the sack with Sam Shepard. The inclusion at all of the oft-discussed husbands, lovers and sons is half-hearted. Shepard blinks in and out to little effect and only Tom Skerritt as Fields' husband creates a real presence.

Director Herb Ross, returning to the territory he handled well in *The Turning Point* and *The Goodbye Girl*, knows how to orchestrate the tears and Fields serves him spectacularly in that department. A good film for the soft-hearted more than the paean to womanly strength that was its motive. ★★★ **AE**

⦿ STELLA DALLAS (1937)

Starring: *Barbara Stanwyck (Stella Martin Dallas), John Boles (Stephen Dallas), Anne Shirley (Laurel Dallas), Barbara O'Neill (Helen Morrison), Alan Hale (Ed Munn), Marjorie Main (Mrs. Martin), Edmund Elton (Mr. Marton), George Walcott (Charlie Martin)*
Director: *King Vidor*
Screenwriters: *Sarah Mason, Victor Heerman, based on the novel by Olive Higgins Prouty and the play by Harry Wagstaff Gribble, Gertrude Purcell*
U/104 mins/Drama/USA

Loathing life in a backwater mill town, brassy dame Stella Martin lures disinherited blue-blood Stephen Dallas into marriage. However, he can't forget Helen and moves away, leaving Stella to raise their daughter Laurel alone. But she eventually realises that her uncouth behaviour and friendship with drunken Ed Munn are jeopardising Laurel's social chances.

The story of a commonplace slattern who sacrifices everything for her child clearly struck a chord with American audiences. Not only was Olive Higgins Prouty's 1923 novel a bestseller, but the 1924 stage version and Henry King's 1925 screen adaptation were equally successful and inspired a long-running radio series, in which Ann Elstner took the title role. So, having produced a sound remake of another 1925 hit, *The Dark Angel*, producer Samuel Goldwyn decided to revive his biggest silent smash in 1937.

He considered some 40 actresses for the part of Stella, but director William Wyler's preferred candidate was Ruth Chatterton, who had just revived her career in *Dodsworth*. However, Wyler was delayed shooting *Jezebel* at Warners and his replacement, King Vidor, insisted on Barbara Stanwyck taking the part, even though Goldwyn thought she lacked sex appeal. He even put her through the humiliation of a screen test, but she and Anne Shirley were so affecting in the birthday party scene (in which they are snubbed by the invited guests on account of Stella's reputation) that he withdrew his objections.

However, it proved an uncomfortable shoot, with Vidor resenting Goldwyn's interference and Stanwyck and Shirley dismayed by the director's preference for camera movements over dramatic motivation. Consequently, Stanwyck based her performance on Belle Bennett's acclaimed silent interpretation and surprised many in Hollywood with the depth of emotion that she managed to summon. Both she and Shirley received Oscar nominations and the film proved a critical and commercial success. Moreover, it suggested that woman's pictures could be more than mere soaps and paved the way for the denser psychological melodramas of the postwar period.

In 1990, the well-cast Bette Midler headlined a lavish remake, only to receive a Razzie nomination as Worst Actress for her blowsy display in a misfire that exposed the Me Generation's callous attitude to Mother Love. ★★★★ **DP**

⦿ THE STEPFORD WIVES (1975)

Starring: *Katharine Ross (Joanna Eberhart), Paula Prentiss (Bobbie Markowe), Peter Masterson (Walter Eberhart), Nanette Newman (Carol Van Saint), Tina Louise (Charmaine Wimperis), Carol Rossen (Dr. Fancher), William Prince (Ike Mazzard), Carole Mallory (Kit Sundersen)*
Director: *Bryan Forbes*
Screenwriter: *William Goldman, based on the novel by Ira Levin*
15/115 mins./Sci-fi/USA

Joanna moves with her husband to the commuter community of Stepford, Connecticut, where the womenfolk are placidly subservient to their husbands. When her best friend transforms into a 'Stepford Wife', Joanna worries that the men of the town are in on a vast conspiracy.

Ira Levin's satirical horror novel, which follows the 'betrayed wife realises she is the target of a conspiracy' plot of his *Rosemary's Baby*, becomes an effective, paranoid thriller in this careful adaptation by screenwriter William Goldman and director Bryan Forbes. Goldman clashed with Forbes over the director's decision to cast his own wife, Nanette Newman, as the archetypal Stepford wife, arguing that the robot women should have looked like Playboy centerfolds – but Forbes made the right decision, in that Newman, who later made a run of housewife TV commercials in almost exactly the same persona, incarnates a subtler, creepier vision of some man's idea of a perfect woman. The vision of willowy housewives in pastel floral dresses and huge hats drifting mindlessly around a supermarket remains chillingly apt as a caricature of the subjugation of women, and the climax works up some real shrieks as heroine Katharine Ross is confronted by her false-chested, black-marble-eyed doppelganger. The Nicole Kidman remake plays Levin's story as outright comedy, but this cannily leavens its horror with wry humour (Paula Prentiss is especially funny, in both her incarnations) and gradually lets a smooth Disneyland mad scientist (Patrick O'Neal) reveal just what the men of Stepford have done to their real wives. Followed by TV sequels (*Revenge of the Stepford Wives*, *The Stepford Children* and *The Stepford Husbands*), plus a great many blatant imitations (*Disturbing Behavior*, *Zombie High*). Mary Stuart Masterson, daughter of co-star Peter, has an early role as one of Ross's children. ★★★★ **KN**

◑ THE STEPFORD WIVES (2004)

Starring: *Nicole Kidman (Joanna Eberhart Kresby), Matthew Broderick (Walter Kresby), Bette Midler (Roberta Markowitz), Glenn Close (Clarie Wellington), Christopher Walken (Mike Wellington)*
Director: *Frank Oz*
Screenwriter: *Paul Rudnik, from the novel by Ira Levin*
12A/93 mins./Comedy/Sci-fi/USA

After a career and nervous breakdown, uptight New York exec Joanna relocates with her weak-willed husband Walter to the picture-perfect community of Stepford – where the Men's Association is turning high-achieving wives into sexually compliant home-making robots. Will Walter let his wife be 'perfected'?

Bryan Forbes' 1974 film, scripted by William Goldman, spelled out what Ira Levin's novel implied – that the Stepford Wives are robot replacements. This remake acknowledges that even people who didn't see the first film know the solution to the mystery by letting us know early on that the women of Stepford are micro-chipped zombies – the exact zombification process is closer to the one seen in the TV movie *Revenge Of The Stepford Wives* – but it invents new surprises to string out the plot.

Whereas Levin and Forbes managed a creepy thriller with sharp satiric jabs, Frank Oz and screenwriter Paul Rudnick go for candy-coloured broad comedy. Katharine Ross's Joanna was a real woman whose replacement was felt as a tragedy, but Nicole Kidman's 'castrating Manhattan career bitch' is one caricature of womanhood threatened with transformation into another. The heroine's sidekicks are even more cartoonish – superslob authoress Bobbie, whose book about her mother was called *I Love You But Please Die*, and waspish architect Roger, who in these enlightened times also gets to be body-snatched into a 'gay Republican' Stepford Wife. Ruling the town are wonderfully iconic, bizarre turns from starched and smiling Glenn Close and blazer-clad patriarch Christopher Walken.

Rudnick teamed with Oz on *In And Out*, and also wrote the gay rom-com *Jeffrey* and *Addams Family Values*. This new *Stepford* is obviously his creation, with a constant patter of stinging lines and hilarious visions of a male fantasy world where the Men's Association parking lot is crowded with ostentatious sports cars and classic bikes and the women's book club discusses the use of pine-cones in Christmas decorations ('I could use pine-cones to write "Big Jew" in the snow on my lawn,' snaps Bobbie).

Though the new set-up theoretically deepens the story by depicting horrible women it might be a relief to swap for robots, this perhaps misses the pain, bewilderment and sadness the first film managed between laughs and scares. Oz fades out the perfect Forbes-Goldman ending, then delivers another act of reversals, cop-outs and cartoon justice. ★★ **KN**

◑ THE STING (1973)

Starring: *Paul Newman (Henry Gondorff/Shaw), Robert Redford (Johnny Hooker/Kelly), Robert Shaw (Doyle Lonnergan), Charles Durning (Lt. Wm. Snyder), Ray Watson (J.J. Singleton)*
Director: *George Roy Hill*
Screenwriter: *David S. Ward*
PG/129 mins./Crime/Drama/Comedy/USA

Awards: *Academy Awards – Best Art Direction-Set Decoration, Best Costume, Best Director, Best Editing, Best Score, Best Picture, Best Original Screenplay*

A young conman in 1930s Chicago teams up with an enthusiastic amateur to pull off the mother of all cons against a crime boss and revenge the death of his mentor.

Guy Ritchie may have become the crown prince of the comedy crime caper (although *Revolver* appears to have blasted that diadem from his noggin), but the real king remains George Roy Hill, the man who turned David Ward's slick and snappy script for *The Sting* into one of cinema's sassiest films. Hill and Ward structure the movie episodically, weaving together the myriad components of the con into such a beautifully layered web that the viewer is immediately snared, hooked as easily as bad-guy Lonnegan, and stung just as well (although without the fiscal pain, of course).

The Sting shows Hill as a genuine screen craftsman, blessed with an uncanny skill for economy of storytelling, rattling us from one scene to another, zipped along by Robert Redford's young buck, Johnny Hooker, and his wily old wag of a mentor, Henry Gondorff, (Paul Newman), both of whom are always one step ahead of the game ... and the viewer. Both men clearly revel in their roles, breathing sizzling charisma into their characters; these con men work against such nasty types that they're almost morality Robin Hoods, albeit with their fingers in the coin purse. And that those fingers tap to a now-iconic ragtime soundtrack (Marvin Hamlisch rearranging Scott Joplin) only adds to the feather-light comedy touch. ★★★★★ **WL**

◑ STIR CRAZY (1980)

Starring: *Gene Wilder (Skip Donahue), Richard Pryor (Harry Monroe), George Stanford Brown (Rory Schultebrand), JoBeth Williams (Meredith), Miguel Angel Suarez (Jesus Ramirez), Craig T. Nelson (Deputy Ward Wilson), Barry Corbin (Warden Walter Betty), Charles Weldon (Blade)*
Director: *Sidney Poitier*
Screenwriter: *Bruce Jay Friedman*
15/108 mins./Comedy/USA

After heading west to make their fortunes, playwright Skip Donahue and actor Harry Monroe get mistakenly accused of robbing a bank and are thrown in the clink for at least 30 years. When Harry turns out to be a genius at the warden's chosen sport of rodeo, an escape plot is hatched to coincide with an inter-prison rodeo competition.

After their scene-stealing pair-up in *Silver Streak*, it was a given that Gene Wilder and Richard Pryor would be given their own comedy to head up. The result, efficiently directed by Sidney Poitier, is a likeable buddy movie that never really lives up to the promise of its premise or players.

Things start well. Early scenes of Skip and Harry dressed as chickens (they are both mascots for a bank) are funny but never sacrifices the comedy for believable characters. The movie really hits its comedic stride when, pleading guilty in a plea bargain, the pair are sentenced to 125 years – Wilder's single, monosyllabic scream is a delight – and, in the film's iconic scene, the pair act streetwise, talking jive, as they walk into a holding cell.

Yet, once in prison, the gag rate begins to slow up. There are funny moments – particularly those involving Skip and Harry's encounters with sullen slaphead mass murderer Grossberger (Erland Van Lidth) – but the film gets bogged down in its own plotting. The whole hatching of an escape plan at a rodeo tournament and the inevitable lengthy rodeo set-piece offers little in the way of laughs and quickly becomes repetitious and tiresome. A subplot romance with Skip falling for his attorney's cousin (Williams) also hamstrings the comedy.

Still it is an enjoyable watch, has some standout moments and the chemistry between the upfront Wilder and the laidback Pryor is appealing. The pair tried to recreate *Stir Crazy*'s box office success with *See No Evil, Hear No Evil*, with a blind Pryor and deaf Wilder 'witnessing' a murder. Some people just don't know went to quit. ★★★ **WT**

STIR OF ECHOES (1999)

Starring: *Kevin Bacon (Tom Witzky), Kathryn Erbe (Maggie Witzky), Illeana Douglas (Lisa), Liza Weil (Debbie Kozac), Kevin Dunn (Frank McCarthy)*
Director: *David Koepp*
Screenwriter: *David Koepp, from the novel by Richard Matheson*
15/95 mins./Sci-fi/Thriller/USA

After being hypnotised by his sister-in-law Tom starts to see ghosts – and he believes they will help him find a murdered girl's body.

Overshadowed at the American box office by *The Sixth Sense*, which spins off from a similar premise, this quietly creepy adaptation of a Richard Matheson (*I Am Legend, What Dreams May Come, The Incredible Shrinking Man*) novel is worth checking out now that time has made it less obviously comparable to that blockbuster.

In an everyday Chicago neighbourhood, the supernatural creeps in at a party as telephone lineman Tom Witzky challenges his New Age-y sister-in-law Lisa to demonstrate her hypnotic power on him. When she has him under, she suggests he should be 'a little more open-minded', and he wakes to discover that this is literally true – his mind is open to messages from the dead with whom his Sixth Sense-style son Jake has always been in tune. The spectre impinging on their lives is a flitting girl, missing sister of the Witzkys' hysterical babysitter, and Tom becomes obsessed with the belief she is buried somewhere nearby.

As Tom gets into Close Encounters-style destruction of his garden and house in search of the corpse, his wife Maggie learns to be afraid not only of the ghosts who appear to her husband and son, but of human menaces who would rather a crime was buried and forgotten.

David Koepp, an A-list screenwriter (*Jurassic Park, Carlito's Way*), made a small directorial debut with *The Trigger Effect*, also about a homey neighbourhood made monstrous. Here, he does a neat job of adapting and updating Matheson's novel, and demonstrates a real flair with actors – the always-undervalued Bacon is on top form as an ordinary man on the point of cracking up, while Erbe is one of the best housewife heroines in recent memory.

There are neat camera tricks – the spook moves at a slightly different film speed to the living – and a couple of great bad dream moments, but the real skill Koepp shows is that he grounds the scary stuff in a believable reality and delivers a ghost story that doesn't lose its grip after the spirits have unambiguously been made manifest. The title sounds slightly pretentious, but a stir of echoes is exactly what the movie delivers. ★★★★ **KN**

STONED (2005)

Starring: *Leo Gregory (Brian Jones), Paddy Considine (Frank Thorogood), David Morrissey (Tom Keylock), Ben Whishaw (Keith Richards), Luke de Woolfson (Mick Jagger)*
Director: *Stephen Woolley*
Screenwriters: *Neal Purvis, Robert Wade*
15/102 mins./Drama/Biography/Music/UK

1969. On the verge of being sacked from The Rolling Stones by Jagger and Richards, band founder Brian Jones (Gregory) wallows in wine, women and self-pity in his English country mansion. Shortly thereafter, he's found dead in his swimming pool . . .

Having spent ten years developing *Stoned* (which originally bore the title The Wycked World Of Brian Jones), producer Stephen Woolley elected to direct what had become a labour of love. The script went through a series of rewrites, and the finished version, penned by James Bond scribes Neal Purvis and Robert Wade, interestingly takes the form less of a straight rock star biopic than an homage to trippy 60s cinema – most obviously *Performance*, in which Jagger starred (and reportedly modelled his burnt-out musician character on Jones).

Accordingly, *Stoned* features a good deal of nudity, much tricksy camerawork and a kaleidoscopic rock 'n' roll soundtrack, the latter employing modern covers of early Stones classics by the likes of The White Stripes. These retro stylings are used not just to evoke Jones' hedonistic lifestyle, but also to paint black, as it were, the butt-end of the 60s, when the hippy dream had turned sour.

It's all anchored by a spirited performance by Leo Gregory as Jones and a sultry one by Monet Mazur as girlfriend Anita Pallenberg, with Paddy Considine putting in a typically impressive turn as Frank Thorogood, the labourer secretly charged with keeping Jones on the straight and narrow. ★★★ **MF**

STOP MAKING SENSE (1984)

Starring: as themselves: *Bernie Worrell, Alex Weir, Steven Scales, Lynn Mabry, Ednah Holt, Tina Weymouth, Jerry Harrison, Chris Frantz, David Byrne*
Director: *Jonathan Demme*
Screenwriters: *Jonathan Demme, Talking Heads*
PG/88 mins./Documentary/Music/USA

The *Silence Of The Lambs* director captures Talking Heads in concert . . .

Boasting a sublime collaboration that few rockumentaries can muster, *Stop Making Sense* practically sparks with the synergy between filmmaker and subject.

Shot shortly after the release of their *Speaking In Tongues* LP, this 1984 concert movie catches Talking Heads at the peak of their powers with all the restraint and guile of a master filmmaker. From lead singer David Byrne's solo and gloriously edgy rendition of 'Psycho Killer' to the fully expanded nine-piece's barnstorming rendition of Al Green's 'Take Me To The River', this is a textbook example of how to put a great gig on celluloid.

Half of *SMS*'s genius is to throw out the clichéd rock movie rule book: out goes the MTV editing, backstage dramas, grainy black and white tour bus footage and cutaway shots to a rapturous audience. In their place are long takes and rhythmic, beautifully organised editing that invites involvement with the music, reveals the dynamics of a band who are really clicking together and showcases TH's nutty, imaginative staging to blinding effect. The gradual building up of the band as they enter one by one: Byrne's impromptu laps of the stage in 'Life During Wartime', the haunting low-lighting of 'What A Day That Was' – all have ample time to work their magic.

The other ace up the film's sleeve is, of course, the band itself. For all their off kilter, arty reputation, Talking Heads really know how to cut it up live, mixing quirky funk licks ('Burning Down The House', 'Girlfriend Is Better' and the seminal 'Once In A Lifetime') with aching, affecting 'ballads' ('Heaven', 'Naïve Melody') all shot through with consummate musicianship, tons of energy and Byrnes' warped worldview. Indeed, be it his rubbery dancing or his amazing outsized suit antics, Byrne emerges as a spellbinding frontman. This plus his bands' infectious enthusiasm and Demme's sleight of hand make this just about the best concert film ever made. ★★★★★ **IF**

Ⓓ LA STRADA (1954)

Starring: *Giuletta Masina (Gelsomina), Anthony Quinn (Zampano), Richard Basehart (Matto 'The Fool'), Aldo Silvani (Columbiana), Marcella Rovere (La Vedova), Livia Venturini (La Suorina)*
Director: *Federico Fellini*
Screenwriters: *Federico Fellini, Tullio Pinelli, Ennio Flaiano, based on a story by Federico Fellini and Tullio Pinelli*
PG/115 mins./Drama/Italy

Awards: *Academy Awards – Best Foreign Language Film*

Travelling strongman Zampano buys the simple waif Gelsomina from her impoverished mother and trains her to assist in his act. Despite his brutality, Gelsomina remains devoted to Zampano, even after Matto, a kindly clown and high-wire walker, takes a shine to her after they join a circus.

Federico Fellini's first draft of this affecting road movie centred on an itinerant clown and her overpowering mentor. Indeed, he even shot test footage in 1952 in the hope of finding a backer. But while he retained the Beauty and the Beast element, he and co-scenarist Tullio Pinelli shifted the emphasis so that Gelsomina became the devoted sidekick of the one-trick strongman whose brutality had contributed to her sister's death.

However, fellow writer Ennio Flaiano felt that the story was excruciatingly sentimental and he persuaded Fellini to tone down the tweer elements so that Gelsomina emerged as a Harry Langdon-Harpo Marx hybrid, who not only learns from everything that she sees, but who also builds up her part in the act as the excitement of showbusiness (albeit tawdry) and the enthusiasm of the crowds give her the timid confidence to express herself.

Yet she ultimately repents of her individualism and elects to abandon possible happiness with Matto the Fool to remain loyal to Zampano, only for him to abandon her as she sleeps on the street (waking to the sight of a riderless horse, which was a favourite Fellini symbol for isolation).

Her choice tied in with one of the film's key themes, that even the lowliest in society have a purpose. But Fellini was also keen to deviate from his neo-realist past and invest the action with a blend of lyrical fantasy and awed spirituality. Consequently, he linked Gelsomiana and Matto with the commedia dell'arte characters of Columbia and Arlecchino, while also giving The Fool a Messianic feel (that was reinforced by his first appearance in an angel-winged costume on a wire high above the town square following a religious procession) and Gelsomina a touch of St. Francis, through her affinity with nature and the helpless. Even Zampano was eventually touched by redemptive love when he broke down on hearing of Gelsomina's death.

The first in a trilogy of solitude that would conclude with *Il Bidone* and *Le Notti di Cabiria*, *La Strada* won the Academy Award for Best Foreign Film and finally established Fellini's international reputation. ★★★★★ **DP**

Ⓓ THE STRAIGHT STORY (1999)

Starring: *Richard Farnsworth (Alvin Straight), Sissy Spacek (Rosie 'Rose' Straight), Harry Dean Stanton (Lyle Straight), Everett McGill (Tom the John Deere Dealer)*
Director: *David Lynch*
Screenwriters: *John Roach, Mary Sweeney*
U/107 mins./Adventure/Biography/Drama/USA/France/UK

A man takes a cross-country journey to visit his estranged brother – on a lawnmower.

After the spiralling despair of his films, *Twin Peaks: Fire Walk With Me* and *Lost Highway* – 'underperformers' at the box office – David Lynch evidently cheered up. *The Straight Story*, perfectly titled on several levels, is an exercise in strange sweetness that wouldn't have shamed John Ford at his most elegiac. Indeed, the film several times relies on that Fordian staple, a cowboy slowly crossing the horizon against a gorgeous sunset. The difference is that this cowboy has a somewhat more unusual steed than most.

Declaring itself to be based on a true story, the film follows the journey of geriatric Alvin Straight, an ailing mid-westerner whose eyes are too dim to qualify him for a driving licence and whose hips are giving him gyp. When he learns his estranged brother has suffered a stroke 500 miles away, Alvin decides it's time to patch up a family feud and sets out to visit, attaching a cart of survival supplies to his sit-astride lawnmower. When the vehicle lets him down, he shoots it like a broken-legged horse, gets himself a tractor-mower and begins his quest proper.

This must be the slowest road movie ever made, which makes for a hilarious shot as cinematographer Freddie Francis pans up from the trundling Alvin to a magnificent sky and then pans down to show our hero has moved on only a few feet. Without shoving Waltons-like lessons down our throat, the film demonstrates that Alvin brings out the best in the people he meets. Earlier Lynch small towns, like Twin Peaks and the Lumberton of *Blue Velvet*, harbour psychopaths and monsters, but everyone along Alvin's route from 'Ioway' to Mississippi is as bedrock decent as he is, instinctively understanding the importance of his apparently absurd trip.

Richard Farnsworth has been a stuntman/bit player for decades, falling off horses and taking arrows in the back in dozens of blink-and-you'll-miss-him Westerns. Finally given a starring role in *The Grey Fox* over 15 years ago, he is still underrated even as a veteran, taking a few decent but hardly showstopping supporting roles (he was the Sheriff in 1990's *Misery*). Here, he finally gets to carry another film, doing an award-calibre job. That this isn't saccharine is almost entirely down to Farnsworth's resigned, frail presence, which never turns into that 'feistiness' Hollywood usually requires of old people.

Alvin constantly admits his life has not been perfect – at one point he shares a World War II anecdote that makes you think harder about his generation than all of *Saving Private Ryan*. We slowly gather he was once a wild drunk, but has grown out of his meanness – hence the need to make up that one last time with his brother and look at the stars. You probably wouldn't take this from anyone else, but Lynch's tribute to the human spirit in twilight leaves the likes of *Driving Miss Daisy* and *Grumpy Old Men* stranded on the verge while the mower moves inexorably on. ★★★★ **KN**

STRANGE DAYS (1995)

Starring: *Ralph Fiennes (Lenny Nero), Angela Bassett (Lornette 'Mace' Mason), Juliette Lewis (Faith Justin), Tom Sizemore (Max Peltier)*
Director: *Kathryn Bigelow*
Screenwriters: *James Cameron, Jay Cocks, from a story by Cameron*
18/139 mins./Sci-fi/Action/Thriller/USA

In an alternate reality, an ex-cop who runs a dealership in 'clips' – movies 'recorded' from people's memories and sold to buyers who want to experience the same thing – uncovers a murder.

Strange Days is no easy business. Set on the eve of the millennium, this futurephobe thriller is a daring, controversial freefall through violence, voyeurism, love, brain-frying technology and political hard sell. It's a difficult, depressing, listless vision given a dazzling, provocative whirl by one of Hollywood's most fascinating directors. Comfortable cinema it ain't.

Typical of Bigelow's work (*Point Break, Near Dark*) is the plot's comparative shakiness: it's a gumshoe flick of sorts imbued with political motivations – a Rodney King-style racial execution by frazzled cops; a burst of neon-coloured murder and sleaze that crosses into the path of ex-cop Lenny Nero's black market dealership in 'clips' – snippets of reality recorded on disk straight from the cerebellum. Into his slippery possession falls the potentially deadly clip of this powder-keg assassination.

The bigger concern of *Strange Days* is a no-holds-barred shot at our social ills: technology as drug, racial tension as epidemic, a self-obsessed world on the brink of self-destruct. And, of course, style. Ninety per cent shot at night, it has a vivacious atmosphere, part *Blade Runner*, part contemporary noir. A soulless netherworld finally enlivened by the story's rapturous culmination: a riotous street-filling, New Year's Eve party under a precipitation of confetti where Lenny finally uncovers the culprits. This is a film permanently on edge. It's itchy, paranoid, Oliver Stone seduced by the dark side of the Force.

Fiennes, as always, manages an extraordinary luminescence. Lenny is a shabby hollow of stained charisma, contradiction, broken heart and bruise (the plot gets written across his face in blood stains). Dysfunctional hustler as movie hero. Not since Dustin Hoffman in *Midnight Cowboy* has a dirtbag been so assured.

There are flaws. Tom Sizemore as Lenny's best friend is miscast and his role, the scabby, ebullient PI Max, never really fits. The role-reversing Mace (the excellent Basset) – Lenny's so much more capable partner – is never fully developed. Lewis's Faith, as Lenny's lost love, is a bombshell rock starlet, but hardly the picture of romantic ideals. And there are far too many bad guys.

Bigelow has, though, encapsulated a million paranoias under one guise, and her craft borders on the sublime. From the visceral plunges of the first-person mind clip sequences (including a terrifying, controversy-courting rape sequence) to the overwhelming finale this is a, literally, stunning event. Some directors can, thank God, still make you experience films.
★★★★ IN

STRANGE INVADERS (1983)

Starring: *Paul LeMat (Charles Bigelow), Nancy Allen (Betty Walker), Diana Scarwid (Margaret), Michael Lerner (Willie Collins), Louise Fletcher (Mrs. Benjamin), Wallace Shawn (Earl), Fiona Lewis (Waitress/Avon Lady), Kenneth Tobey (Arthur Newman), June Lockhart (Mrs Bigelow)*
Director: *Michael Laughlin*
Screenwriters: *Bill Condon, Michael Laughlin, based on a story by Condon, Laughlin and Walter Davis*
12/92 mins./Sci-fi/USA

Entomologist Charlie Bigelow traces his missing, estranged wife Margaret to an eerily perfect small town and learns that she is one of a party of aliens who have been stranded on Earth since 1958.

'Of all the worlds in all the galaxies ... why did they pick this one?' Opening with a prologue set in a decade when 'except for the communists and rock-and-roll, there was not much to fear', *Strange Invaders* has a clever basic joke: the aliens who identity-snatch the folks of Centerville in 1958 assume their disguises will be good for the duration of a twenty-five year mission, and are weirdly conspicuous in 1983 as they attempt to infiltrate the big city while driving finned cars, wearing spotted bow-ties and listening to doo-wop music.

Director Michael Laughlin and screenwriter partner Bill Condon (later director of *Gods And Monsters* and *Kinsey*) had made a good teen-zombie splatter film called *Dead Kids* (aka *Strange Behavior*) and reteamed for this more elaborate, sweeter-natured satire of every space alien visitor from *It Came From Outer Space* to *ET: The Extra-Terrestrial*. It has a lot of goofy charm but isn't too knowing to lose its sense of wonder and boasts some 1980s-style rubbery transformation effects as bug-eyed aliens peel off their human faces.

It's especially well cast, with genial Paul LeMat as a bug specialist who can't get used to the fact that his daughter is part-alien, Nancy Allen as a tabloid Lois Lane who has written so many fake alien abduction stories that she's bewildered by a real one, Fiona Lewis as an evil Avon Lady from Outer Space and Diana Scarwid as the mid-western Mom who is the only spacewoman on Earth to have moved with the times (though her 80s culottes and jade earrings now look more alien than compound eyes and antennae).
★★★★ KN

STRANGERS ON A TRAIN (1951)

Starring: *Farley Granger (Guy Haines), Ruth Roman (Anne Morton), Robert Walker (Bruno Anthony), Leo G. Carroll (Sen. Morton), Patricia Hitchcock (Barbara Morton)*
Director: *Alfred Hitchcock*
Screenwriters: *Raymond Chandler, Czenzi Ormonde, based on the novel by Patricia Highsmith, adapted by Whitfield Cook*
PG/96 mins./Thriller/USA

Psychotic mother's boy Bruno Anthony meets famous tennis professional Guy Haines on a train and comes up with a scheme whereby each should dispose of the unwanted female in the other's life.

Coming off the back of four flops, Alfred Hitchcock's yen for a hit prompted him to plump for this readily accessible thriller, in which an unhappily married man meets a sexually repressed psychotic, who suggests they carry out the perfect, undetectable murder by exchanging victims. In order to ensure a bargain price, Hitch anonymously secured the rights to Patricia Highsmith's novel, which he promptly proceeded to fillet with Whitfield Cook. Guy Haines was transformed from an architect to a tennis player with political aspirations and instead of standing trial for the murder of Bruno Anthony's father, he is given sufficient conscience to try and warn him. Furthermore, the slim volume of Plato, which Bruno uses to implicate his reluctant partner in crime, is changed to a lighter, inscribed to Guy from his mistress, Anne Morton.

Having failed to interest a number of leading writers, Hitchcock turned his treatment over to Raymond Chandler to work into a screenplay. However, there was instant antipathy between the two, with Hitch being particularly unhappy with the ending, in which a strait-jacketed Bruno is left writhing in an asylum cell. Ultimately, Chandler retained his credit. But much of the shooting script was actually written by the novice scenarist Czenzi Ormonde. Among her contributions was the merry-go-round finale, which was borrowed from Edmund Crispin's pulp novel, *The Moving Toyshop* (1946). A couple of other set-pieces were also slightly secondhand. The famous tennis gag, in which Bruno sits impassive amidst a crowd intently following a rally, had featured in the Somerset Maugham compendium picture, *Quartet* (1948), while the symbolic use of a barred gate to imply Guy's culpability for Bruno's crimes was lifted from Robert Siodmak's film noir, *The File OnThelma Jordan* (1949).

But, if the script could be fixed, the cast couldn't. While he was content with Robert Walker as Bruno, Hitchcock wanted William Holden for Guy and was disappointed to end up with Farley Granger, with whom he'd already had problems on *Rope* (1948). Furthermore, he found Ruth Roman cold and stiff as Anne, although he cheerfully cast his own daughter, Patricia, as her gauche sister, Barbara.

Pandering to popular expectation, Hitchcock produced a thriller to restore his status as the Master Of Suspense – even though there were gaping holes in the narrative's logic. But he was less concerned with why Guy failed to go to the police after his initial meeting with Bruno or after his wife Miriam's murder or before the death of Bruno's dad.

Instead, he was preoccupied with the thematic contrasts between light and dark, order and chaos, innocence and guilt.

Moreover, he was besotted with images depicting circles, doubles and traverses. Curvilinear imagery had already dominated such early Hitchcock outings as *The Ring* (1927). But here he litters the screen with round objects, whether it's the records in Miriam's shop, the abundance of clock and watch faces, Guy's racket and tennis balls or the balloon Bruno bursts before he murders Miriam beside the fairground carousel – during which he is hideously magnified (and doubled) in the lenses of her discarded glasses.

The double motif is pursued with equal rigour. There are two tennis matches, two scenes centred on a merry-go-round, two respectable, but domineering and distant, fathers and two assaulted women wearing glasses. There are two old maids fascinated by the mechanics of murder, two sets of private detectives and two rounds of double whiskeys. Even Hitchcock's cameo adhered to the idea: he carried a double-bass case, which he thought resembled his own physique.

Just as the surfeit of annular objects is supposed to convey the vicious circles from which both Guy and Bruno seek to extricate themselves, so the various pairs, in those Production Code days, suggest the homoerotic connection between the prospective killers. Similarly, the recurrent crisscross patterns also carry symbolic weight – from the shadowy bars that bedeck Bruno on the train and Guy's face on the Washington street to the decussating tennis rackets on Guy's lighter – for, even though he benefits from Miriam's demise, Guy still intends to double-cross Bruno by refusing to carry out his part of the bargain.

Guy may be our hero, but he is a thoroughly resistible character and, thus, seems set to do well in politics. Recalling the lethal charm of Uncle Charlie in *Shadow Of A Doubt* (1943) and anticipating the Oedipal derangement of Norman Bates in *Psycho* (1960), Bruno is far more engaging, making the death of Robert Walker (the year after, at 33) all the more tragic.

In conclusion, it's worth noting that the luncheon sequence, in which Bruno asserts that everyone is a potential killer, was excised from the original US print. But, then again, Anne and Guy's climactic train-board meeting with a star-struck clergyman was absent from the British version. ★★★★★ **DP**

STRAW DOGS (1971)

Starring: *Dustin Hoffman (David Sumner), Susan George (Amy Sumner), Peter Vaughan (Tom Hedden), Sally Thomsett (Janice Hedden)*
Director: *Sam Peckinpah*
Screenwriters: *David Zelag Goodman, Sam Peckinpah, from the novel* The Seige Of Trencher's Farm *by Gordon Williams*
18/116 mins./Drama/Thriller/UK

A mild-mannered mathematician and his Cornish-born wife move to her home town to start a quieter life but local resentment of them soon turns to violence.

Sam Peckinpah's 1971 opus is still a casualty of the BBFC's video-banning shenanigans, and heated controversy.

Based on the Gordon Williams novel *The Seige Of Trencher's Farm*, the less obvious title used here, from the Chinese Proverb; 'Heaven and Earth are not humane and regard people as straw dogs', does more to explain the attitude towards violence in the film. For it isn't the violence itself that caused this film's censorship – as those who defended it at the time pointed out far more sickening films were passed uncut – it is the *nature* of the violence.

It is also clear from the opening scenes that all is not well in the idyll in which quiet David and his scornful wife Amy have chosen to make their home. He is instantly despised for his nerdish status, while she openly flaunts her sexuality and goads the villagers in their treatment of him and lust for her. This culminates in the much discussed double rape scene, in which she is seen – at first – as a willing participant.

But it is not this rape that culminates in the final bloody showdown – David never learns of the incident – but their unknowing rescue and sheltering of the town simpleton, who has accidentally killed a young girl who has modelled her behaviour on Amy's. David is forced to defend their home and it is this last transformation of David, from benign male presence to gleeful despatcher of invaders, and, so, master of his domain, that is so shocking, partly as it suggests a sympathetic audience should endorse his actions as heroic.

George and Hoffman are both unforgettable here, but are by no means comfortable to watch, and Pekinpah's manipulative direction was seen by turns as misogynistic or highly insightful.

Today, it is as divisive as it ever was and, despite its technical brilliance, still harrowing viewing. ★★★★ **EC**

Movie Trivia: Sam Peckinpah (1925–1984)

Who was he: AKA Mad Sam. Bloodily reinvented the Western. Famed for his graphic approach to violence. Huge influence on today's action genres.
Hallmarks: Multiple cameras; dazzling montages of images; blood-soaked violence; extreme chauvinism; booze and drug-fuelled excesses.
If you see one movie, see: *The Wild Bunch* (1969)

A STREETCAR NAMED DESIRE (1951)

Starring: *Vivien Leigh (Blanche DuBois), Marlon Brando (Stanley Kowalski), Kim Hunter (Stella Kowalski), Karl Malden (Harold 'Mitch' Mitchell), Rudy Bond (Steve), Nick Dennis (Pablo Gonzales), Peg Hillias (Eunice)*
Director: *Elia Kazan*
Screenwriter: *Tennessee Williams, based on his own play, adaptation by Oscar Saul*
PG/122 mins./Drama/USA

Awards: *Academy Awards – Best Actress, Best Supporting Actor (Karl Malden), Best Supporting Actress (Kim Hunter), Best Art Direction-Set Decoration (Black & White), BAFTA – Best Actress*

Fragile neurotic Blanche DuBois visits her more practical sister Stella and thuggish, needling brother-in-law Stanley Kowalski. Blanche almost gets together with the lonely Mitch but Stanley sets out to destroy her.

In adapting Tennessee Williams's hit play from stage to screen, Elia Kazan was obliged to tweak the ending to suggest the brutish Stanley Kowalski is punished for abusing faded belle Blanche into catatonia by losing the love of his wife. However, director and writer fought to keep in the precedent-setting rape scene as Stanley mauls Blanche in front of a symbolically broken mirror and the bedroom tussle cuts to an orgasmic hose washing garbage off the street. In a wonderfully seedy New Orleans apartment quarter, at once an Expressionist set to delight the fantasist Williams and a realistic locale to appease Kazan's documentary streak, Marlon Brando has as much trouble as the Incredible Hulk keeping his tight shirts and sweaty vests untorn, while Vivien Leigh flutters mesmerisingly as Scarlett O'Hara gone battily to seed ('I don't want realism. I want magic! Yes, yes, magic. I try to give that to people. I do misrepresent things. I don't tell truths. I tell what ought to be truth.').

Made in 1951, when Brando could strip to the waist on screen and excite shivers of lust, this scooped three acting Oscars (for Leigh, Hunter and Karl Malden) but, surprisingly, not for Marlon (it was Bogart's year). The play is endlessly revived: it was redone for television in 1984 with Ann-Margret and Treat Williams and 1995 with Jessica Lange and Alec Baldwin; The Simpsons did a knockout parody featuring a tacky musical adaptation called *Streetcar*! ('Stella, Stella, you're treatin' me like hell-a!'), and André Previn really did turn the text into an opera, which was mounted for television in 1998. ★★★★ **KN**

◑ STREETS OF FIRE (1984)

Starring: *Michael Paré (Tom Cody), Diane Lane (Ellen Aim), Rick Moranis (Billy Fish), Amy Madigan (Amy McCoy), Willem Dafoe (Raven Shaddock), Deborah Van Valkenburgh (Reva Cody), Richard Lawson (Officer Ed Price), Rick Rossovich (Officer Cooley), Bill Paxton (Clyde)*
Director: *Walter Hill*
Screenwriters: *Larry Gross, Walter Hill*
15/93 mins./Action/Musical/USA

When singer Ellen Aim is kidnapped by Raven, leader of the Bombers, her ex-boyfriend, soldier of fortune Tom Cody, crosses town to rescue her.

Sub-titled 'a rock 'n' roll fable', Walter Hill's retro action movie musical goes beyond even the stylisation of his earlier youth gang fantasy *The Warriors* by combining the look of the 1950s with the sounds of the 1980s and creating an enclosed, urban fantasy playground for his usual macho games.

Too much of the music dated instantly, though Ry Cooder, Stevie Nicks and Jim Steinman contribute some fine sounds, augmented by a vintage Leiber & Stoller track in 'One Bad Stud'. However, it's a movie that's easy to like, with its comic book stylings (its world was an influence on Tim Burton's Gotham City) and strutting, iconic personalities. Michael Paré has diluted his image with too many straight-to-video pictures, but he has a Shane-like presence here, striding in a trenchcoat and clenching his jaw manfully, surrounded by live wires like Rick Moranis as the heroine's bespectacled, check-jacketed hustler manager, Amy Madigan (in a standout role) as the beer-drinking, tough-talking army chick who tags along and Willem Dafoe in PVC overalls as the shark-mouthed lunatic who leads the worst gang in the city.

Also down there in the cast are Bill Paxton as a bartender, punk rocker Lee Ving as a gang-banger, Robert Townsend (director of *Hollywood Shuffle*) and Mykelti Williamson as quiffed doo-woppers, early 80s squeaky-cutie Elizabeth Daily (later a Rugrat and a Powerpuff Girl) as 'Baby Doll' and Ed Begley Jr. as Ben Gunn (a character tipped in from *Treasure Island*). In 1984, it was too way out to connect with audiences, but a few years later – with MTV in the ascendant – other films were lining up to imitate its attitudes. ★★★ **KN**

◑ STRICTLY BALLROOM (1992)

Starring: *Paul Mercurio (Scott Hastings), Tara Morice (Fran), Bill Hunter (Barry Fife), Pat Thomson (Shirley Hastings), Peter Whiford (Les Kendall), Barry Otto (Doug Hastings)*
Director: *Baz Luhrmann*
Screenwriter: *Baz Luhrmann, Craig Pearce, from the screenplay by Baz Luhrmann, Andrew Bovell, from an idea by Luhrmann*
PG/90 mins./Romance/Comedy/Australia
Awards: *BAFTA – Best Costume, Best Score, Best Production Design*

Talented dancer Scott is struggling to make it to the Pan-Pacific Grand Prix, due in part to his refusal to adhere to the dance steps approved by his team. Step forward the only club member prepared to partner him: clumsy novice Fran.

The sleeper hit of the 1992 Cannes Film Festival where it received a 15-minute standing ovation, Baz Luhrmann's offbeat, vibrant and at times decidedly hilarious tale has justifiably been branded Dirty Dancing Down Under – but don't let that put you off.

When ballroom champ Scott Hastings outrages the dance fraternity by dancing his own steps rather than those laid down by the staid Federation, he finds himself partnerless three weeks before the most important event of his young life, the coveted Pan-Pacific Championships. Step forward frumpy Fran, the local dance club klutz, offering her services to an initially reluctant Scott who swiftly discovers that underneath her ugly duckling pimples and horn-rim specs there lies a whirlwind on the dancefloor with Spanish blood coursing through her veins and the Paso Doble down pat. So while Scott's domineering mother scampers round in search of a suitable replacement for her beloved son and Federation President Barry Fife endeavours to sabotage the renegade partnership, Fran's father covertly coaches the two hoofers in the finer points of the Flamenco.

What originally began life as a drama school production is conclusive proof of the enduring power of the fairy-tale – in this case Cinderella by way of David And Goliath. Snappily scripted, it has a brashness inherent in Aussie soaps and a charm all of its own, then-debutant director Luhrmann revealing a light, irreverent touch and mustering superior comedic performances from his largely unknown cast. Mercurio, with his floppy fringe and sequinned Matador jacket, is a real find, cutting a dash on the dancefloor to rival that of Swayze himself. ★★★★ **MS**

◑ STRIKE! (STACHKA) (1924)

Starring: *Grigori Alexandrov (Factory foreman), Aleksandr Antonov (Member of the strike committee), Yduif Glizer (Queen of Thieves), Mikhair Gomorov (Worker), I. Ivanov (Chief of Police)*
Director: *Sergei Eisenstein*
Screenwriters: *Sergei Eisenstein, Grigori Alexandrov, V. Peltniev, I. Kravtchunovsky*
12/86 mins./USSR/Politics/Drama

In pre-Revolutionary Russia, downtrodden factory workers come out on strike. The management call in cossacks, who brutally put down the strike.

Sergei Eisenstein's first feature is stronger overall than his better-known second film, *Battleship Potemkin*, and indeed arguably his best picture – he would refine his filmmaking techniques, but they had their most impact at the beginning, before the rest of the movies caught up with (and surpassed) his innovations. As suggested by the archetypal title (not to be confused with the much later Comic Strip Presents . . . episode), the movie presents propaganda as mythology: whereas *Potemkin* dramatises a well-known incident, this – though elements are inspired by several actual strikes from 1912 – has a more fable-like feel, without an apparent specific setting or date.

The masses are just that, noble faces but not really characters,

S

following an official edict discouraging veneration of any individual heroes of the revolution.

Eisenstein spends more time on the capitalist villains, who are presented as cartoonish grotesques: the overweight factory director in a top hat, with his hierarchy of gap-toothed, odd-looking minions, and a parade of police spies and agent provocateurs with animal nicknames ('the Owl', 'the Fox') who are intercut with nature footage and pull spaghetti-western-like faces to underline their double-dealing fiendishness.

It opens almost like a comedy, with capitalist buffoons who could make trouble for Charlie Chaplin or Buster Keaton, but it becomes grimmer and more rousing as it presents images of injustice and violence. The film climaxes with a sequence of slaughter that remains shocking, using abattoir footage of bloodily-killed animals to represent men murdered by rampaging horsemen – an approach evoked as late as the finale of *Apocalypse Now*.

The horrors resonate universally, and now look as much like an indictment of the Stalinist regime that backed the film as the Tsarist oppressors they had supplanted. ★★★★ **KN**

SUBWAY (1985)

Starring: *Isabelle Adjani (Helena), Christophe Lambert (Fred), Richard Bohringer (The Florist), Michel Galabru (Commssioner Gesberg), Jean-Hugues Anglade (The Roller), Jean Bouise (The Station Master), Jean-Pierre Bacri (Batman), Jean-Claude Lecas (Robun), Jean Reno (The Drummer)*
Director: *Luc Besson*
Screenwriters: *Luc Besson, Pierre Jolivet, Alain Le Henry, Marc Perrier, Sophie Schmidt*
15/104 mins./Crime/France

Fred, an amiable drifter, crashes a stolen car into the Paris Metro in order to escape mob hit men. He discovers a vast enclave of folks who live underground.

Luc Besson's first feature was the widescreen, black and white, wordless absurdist science fiction film *Le Dernier Combat* (*The Last Battle*). After that, he moved towards a slightly more conventional area with this romantic thriller – which retains the love of weird incidental characters and surreal detail, but also develops some of the action movie muscles that would emerge in Besson's later, more obviously commercial work.

Christopher Lambert's enigmatically-named Fred, in a dinner jacket and spikey punk hairdo, makes an intriguingly offbeat mooncalf hero, on the run from the heavies surrounding elegantly-coiffeured and cockatoo-plumed Isabelle Adjani. Among the interesting denizens of Besson's bande dessinée-style Paris underground are le rolleur (a skating pickpocket), le drummer (a busker-philanthropist whose rhythms drive the movie), Big Bill (a handcuff-breaking muscle-man) and the florist (a would-be blackmailer), while the Maigret-look rumpled cop in charge of policing the chaos is partnered by an ambitious gloryhog nicknamed Batman.

The plot is reduced to the broadest strokes (some stolen paper barely even qualify as a McGuffin), allowing Besson to explore the nooks and crannies of his extraordinary location (various Parisian authorities and vandals are to be complemented for their imaginative art direction and set decoration).

Stylish, if insubstantial, and with a lot of comic-adventurous flair, this wholly pleasurable jeu d'esprit plays less like an action movie than a virtuoso jazz ensemble improvisation, with various riffs and licks spun off as odd characters do their own pieces and then recede into the background. A film of wonderful small moments: Adjani descending a staircase in a flouncy dress, Lambert dooby-dooby-doing to himself as he smashes up his car. ★★★ **KN**

SUDDEN DEATH (1996)

Starring: *Jean-Claude Van Damme (Darren McCord), Powers Boothe (Joshua Foss), Raymond J. Barry (Vice-president), Whittni Wright (Emily McCord)*
Director: *Peter Hyams*
Screenwriter: *Gene Quintano, from a story by Karen Baldwin*
18/110 mins./Action/Thriller/USA

A fire officer at a hockey stadium has to prevent Powerse Boothe from detonating a bomb in the crowd.

Journeyman Peter Hyams claims in all apparent sincerity that *Sudden Death* is an action picture in the tradition of *Die Hard* – when any sneaking-in-underage 12-year-old can tell you that it's actually a blatant imitation of *Die Hard*. Nearly ten years after Bruce Willis first ripped his vest, his plot has been used by every action man in the business: from Steven Seagal (*Under Siege*), Wesley Snipes (*Passenger 57*) and Sylvester Stallone (*Cliffhanger*) to direct-to-video hopefuls such as Thomas Ian Griffith (*Crackerjack*).

Here it's Jean-Claude Van Damme's turn to play loose cannon, careering around offing baddies and thwarting criminal mastermind Powers Boothe's extortion scheme while the authorities are powerless. He also gets to show off his sensitive side by doing all his daring to prove to his kids that he's a hero.

The high concept has Boothe threaten not only to murder the US vice-president but an entire stadium-full of hockey fans during a championship play-off unless the government gives him lots of money.

Van Damme is a traumatised ex-fireman working as a safety marshal at Pittsburgh's picturesque Civic Arena (with a dome which opens up like the Tracey Island swimming pool), and Boothe, doing some English villain actor out of a job, is a sneery CIA agent who injects the requisite jokey nastiness. Hyams, whose CV might stand as a working definition of competence (*Capricorn One*, *2010*, *Outland*, *Timecop*), injects not a lot of originality into a flat script from Gene Quintano (of *Police Academy* sequels fame), but things simmer early when JC has a punch-up in the kitchen with a killer babe dressed as a penguin.

There's a wonderfully ridiculous contrivance whereby our hero not only saves the spectators but gets on the ice and plays in goal for the home team, making a crucial save. But this only edges out of two-star status in its vertiginous last 20 minutes, which feature an infallibly rousing succession of dangling from high-places fights. Tripe, but hard not to enjoy. ★★★ **IN**

SUDDENLY, LAST SUMMER (1959)

Starring: *Elizabeth Taylor (Catherine Holly), Katharine Hepburn (Mrs. Violet Venable), Montgomery Clift (Dr. Cukrowicz), Albert Dekker (Dr. Lawrence J. Hockstader), Mercedes McCambridge (Mrs. Grace Holly)*
Director: *Joseph L. Mankiewicz*
Screenwriter: *Gore Vidal, Tennessee Williams, from the play by Williams*
15/109 mins./Drama/UK
Awards: *Golden Globes – Best Drama Actress*

In 1937, millionairess Violet Venable, obsessed with her dead son Sebastian, offers brain surgeon Dr. Cukrowicz enough money to build a hospital if he will perform an unnecessary lobotomy on Sebastian's cousin Catherine to suppress the horrible truth about his death.

'The sun was like the great white bone of a giant beast that had caught on fire in the sky.' A one-act play by Tennessee Williams, expanded into a feature script by Gore Vidal, which makes for one of the most deliciously overripe writing combinations in film history.

Director Joseph L. Mankiewicz isn't quite up to a story that demands the kind of overwrought style Robert Aldrich (*Hush … Hush, Sweet Charlotte*) or Curtis Harrington (*Whoever Slew Auntie Roo?*) brought to similar mixes of high camp and gothic horror.

Taylor is marvellously martyred, wandering about the hellhole asylum provoking riots, the scarred Clift is ambiguously idealist as the decent man tempted to a terrible crime, and the magisterial Hepburn elegantly chews the scenery in little bites, descending from the heavens in her chairlift, rambling about the brilliance of her departed (and obviously cracked) genius poet son and scheming deviously to pull off a truly ghastly crime.

The mystery angle, which is revealed in a sunlit nightmare flashback, is a William S. Burroughs fantasy involving homosexuality, incest, sadism, class exploitation, nature red in tooth and claw and ancient rituals as it turns out the strutting, predatory Sebastian, who uses luscious Liz in a blinding white bathing suit to lure youths for his sexual purposes, was overwhelmed *and eaten* by a flock of beach boys!

It is naturally talky, with Vidal adding extra venom to already high camp horror, but with a hothouse pleasure in eloquence.

Remade for TV by Richard Eyre in 1993, with Maggie Smith, Rob Lowe and Natasha Richardson. ★★★★ **KN**

⦾ THE SUGARLAND EXPRESS (1974)

Starring: *Goldie Hawn (Lou Jean Poplin), Ben Johnson (Captain Harlin Tanner), Michael Sacks (Patrolman Maxwell Slide), William Atherton (Clovis Michael Poplin)*
Director: *Steven Spielberg*
Screenwriters: *Hal Barwood, Matthew Robbins, from a story by Steven Spielberg, Hal Barwood, Matthew Robbins*
PG/104 mins./Drama/Crime/USA

Lou Jean convinces her husband to escape from prison. They plan to kidnap their own child, who was placed with foster parents. The escape is partly successful, they take a hostage, who is a policeman and are pursued through Texas . . .

The Sugarland Express has never sat very comfortably in the Spielberg canon. It's always gratifying to go back to the source of a great career and to pinpoint the seeds of promise from which that greatness grew. The problem with Spielberg though, is knowing where to start. It's easy, for instance, to argue that *The Sugarland Express* was not his first feature. 1972's *Duel*, although made for TV, was released theatrically in Europe.

There is also a certain reluctance to accept *Sugarland* as the beginning of anything. *Duel*, in many respects, is a vastly superior film and makes for a far more arresting curtain-raiser to Spielberg's big-screen career. The seeds of greatness are obvious in *Duel*; they are not nearly so prominent in *Sugarland*.

It's a cop-out, of course. *The Sugarland Express* marked Spielberg's de facto debut as a feature film director, and should be treated accordingly. It's strange to think that in 1974 Spielberg, 28 at the time, was considered a leading light of the American New Wave. Or, at least, the tail end of what certain critics, with rapidly waning conviction, were touting as such. *Sugarland* was widely regarded as the aesthetic bedfellow of Scorsese's *Mean Streets*, George Lucas's *American Graffiti*, Robert Altman's *Thieves Like Us* and Terence Malick's *Badlands*, all of which were released during the same 12-month period. It was well received critically and undoubtedly smoothed Spielberg's transition from workaday TV director to fully fledged filmmaker. Even so, few people (save Pauline Kael) saw in it anything more than a glimmer of the phenomenal talent at work beneath its grainy, downbeat surface. Many commentators made the inevitable comparisons with Malick's *Badlands* – the theme of fugitive lovers is common to both – concluding that Spielberg's film was far less promising.

It's difficult to disagree. Based on a true story, *Sugarland* chronicles the exploits of a Springer-fodder, white trash Texas couple and their desperate attempt to wrestle their child from the clutches of social services. The film begins with Lou Jean Poplin bullying her docile husband Clovis into busting out of jail and joining her on a quest to kidnap the youngster from its foster parents. In the process they take Highway Patrolman Maxwell Slide hostage by mistake, and are pursued across the Texas plains by a train of patrol cars. A media frenzy erupts and the duo become minor folk heroes, cheered on by masses of well-wishers at the roadside.

It's a thoroughly competent film, the action is well choreographed and fine performances abound, notably from Hawn and Michael Sacks as the hapless prisoner who forms a bond of trust and friendship with his captors. But it's also a frustrating one in that it tells us almost nothing about where, artistically speaking, Spielberg was at the time. It's such a confoundedly timorous affair. Getting the audience rooting for the bad guys leans heavily on *Bonnie And Clyde* (1967) and the revved-up road movie format is a nod to both *Easy Rider* and *Badlands* – all highly credible reference points. Unfortunately, *Sugarland* bottles it. Lou Jean and Clovis aren't bad people, they're the victims of circumstance. Their crimes are committed in the course of a noble quest, their actions fuelled by the purest of motives. The cops run out of patience, but they're decent human beings. Johnson's avuncular chief of police comes across as particularly implausible, this is Texas after all.

It's as if Spielberg was being pulled in two directions at once: towards the rebel poetry of Altman, Scorsese and Malick on the one hand, and the allure of popular approval on the other. He never seems entirely comfortable with the material. And if it was a conflict of art versus commerce (or, perhaps more accurately, alt versus pop) then the film's commercial failure surely influenced his decision to opt emphatically for the latter in future endeavours.

There are certainly flashes of brilliance in *Sugarland*, most notably in Vilmos Zsigmond's dour cinematography. And, as with all Spielberg's movies, certain visual set-pieces linger in the memory. But for all that, it remains a steadfastly ordinary moment of transition: a skilful film, not an inspired one. The moral canvas is a pastel-hued blur – and whatever stance Spielberg has taken in the years since, you could never accuse him of ambiguity in that department. The shifts in tone, too (a prerequisite of any New Wave contender), are present and correct, but too often the lurches from comedy to drama, pathos to violence are jarring, and the final descent into tragedy is gratuitously harsh. Again, compared to the queasy menace that courses through *Badlands* it's maudlin and contrived.

Sugarland is, ultimately, both interesting for what it isn't – a celluloid Petri dish teeming with protean Spielbergisms – and for what it is – an unremarkable instance of a gifted director searching cautiously for his own voice. What is remarkable is that he found it barely a year later; unleashing a deafening roar with *Jaws*. ★★★ **SB**

S

⦾ SULLIVAN'S TRAVELS (1941)

Starring: *Joel McCrea (John L. Lloyd 'Sully' Sullivan), Veronica Lake (The Girl), Robert Warwick (Mr. Lebrand), William Demarest (Mr. Jones), Franklin Pangborn (Mr. Casalsis)*
Director: *Preston Sturges*
Screenwriter: *Preston Sturges*
PG/90 mins./Adventure/Comedy/Romance/USA

A director of escapist films goes on the road as a hobo to learn about Life . . . which gives him a rude awakening.

Sullivan's Travels is affectionately dedicated, 'To the memory of those who made us laugh: the motley mountebanks, the clowns, the buffoons, in all times and in all nations, whose efforts have lightened our burden a little.' It opens with a typical movie serial scene: two men having a roughhouse fight atop a speeding train, and then cuts in with an 'End' title. As in the same year's *Citizen Kane*, we are in a studio screening room, and enthusiastic young director John Lloyd Sullivan gets up and earnestly declaims, 'You see the symbolism of it? Capital and Labour destroying each other?' Sullivan is a successful Hollywood musical comedy man, whose films (*So Long Sarong*, *Ants In Your Plants Of 1939*, *Hey Hey In The Hayloft*) sound significantly crasser than the three tart satires that had made the name of writer-director Preston Sturges: *The Great McGinty* (1940), *Christmas In July* (1940) and *The Lady Eve* (1941). Having turned out lightweight hits, Sully now wants significance and hopes to make a film of a depressing novel, *O Brother, Where Art Thou* ?. Told by the studio heads (Warwick, Hall) that he knows nothing of the sufferings of the poor, the director gets himself a hobo costume from the wardrobe department and sets out to experience wretchedness first hand – with a studio-mandated silver trailer full of publicists, minions and servants trundling along behind. His first attempt to escape this overprotection involves hitching a ride with a 13-year-old with a souped-up go-kart-cum-hotrod, leading to a wild, silent comedy style. It's a strange sequence, like a cruel caricature of the kind of comedy Sullivan doesn't want to make any more, and you have to wonder how funny it was supposed to be.

The real charm comes in the central section, where Sullivan, having sent his entourage to Las Vegas, runs into a nameless girl, who has just given up on her attempt to get into pictures. They become a team, with the studio approving her as his companion in the hobo adventure, though there can be no romance because Sullivan has a wife arranged by his crooked business manager as a tax dodge. The frenetic pace slows down, and the gags are hung on a growing relationship played extremely well by the lunkish, good-natured, likeable but clueless McCrea and the wry, astonishingly beautiful, sceptical but not cynical Lake.

The meat of the movie is the last act, as Sullivan is thought dead through a mix-up and sent South, where he is sentenced to six years on a prison farm for attacking a railroad guard, now he experiences the sufferings of the really wretched, working all hours of the day shovelling sludge in a swamp when he's not doing punishment spells in 'the sweat box'. Here, Sturges gets a chance to make the real *O Brother Where Art Thou*?, though this venture into *I Am a Fugitive From a Chain Gang* (1932) territory is mostly set-up for the punchline. The only pleasure the convicts have is their occasional visit to 'the picture show' to watch Disney cartoons.

As he joins with the miserable of the Earth in howling at Pluto's attempt to get free of flypaper, Sully learns his lesson and, by making a bogus confession of his own murder, spirits himself back to a Hollywood happy ending (his wife has remarried, leaving the way clear with Lake). The studio, eager to exploit the sensational publicity, now want him to make *O Brother*, but he just wants to make people laugh, so we assume that *Ants In Your Plants Of 1941* gets a greenlight.

Some people thought Sturges was too smart for his own good. John Ford, who was in the middle of a run of big hit movies from serious novels and plays about poverty sneered at him as 'Pisston Sturges'. And his winning streak didn't last much longer – after *The Palm Beach Story* (1942), he sat out most of the war before coming back with brassier, cruder, less pleasing (though still intermittently hilarious) films like *The Miracle Of Morgan's Creek* (1944) and *Hail The Conquering Hero* (1944).

His films are populated by a stock company of prissy or hardboiled comic character actors and straddle the worlds of the inanely rich and the cynically crooked, but the best of them revolve around a certain earnest innocence best embodied by Joel McCrea. Sturges was never as lightweight as Sullivan, but he was also never pretentious (or courageous) enough to try to make *O Brother Where Art Thou*? in earnest. Ford, as great an entertainer as Sturges, was willing to take a chance on *The Grapes Of Wrath*, whose conclusion that the poor need to fight injustice is a bit more convincing than Sullivan's belief that they could do with a good cheering-up. ★★★★★ **KN**

Ⓓ THE SUM OF ALL FEARS (2002)

Starring: *Ben Affleck (Jack Ryan), Morgan Freeman (DCI William Cabot), James Cromwell (President Fowler), Liev Schreiber (John Clark), Bridget Moynahan (Dr. Cathy Muller), Alan Bates (Richard Dressler), Ciaran Hinds (President Nemerov)*
Director: *Phil Alden Robinson*
Screenwriters: *Paul Attanasio, Daniel Pyne, from the novel by Tom Clancy*
12/118 mins./Thriller/USA/Germany

An analyst Jack Ryan goes on the hunt to foil a group of terrorists who plan to detonate a bomb at the Superbowl.

Alarming, foreboding, perplexing . . . just why was Ben Affleck cast as the new Jack Ryan? At 30 years younger than previous Ryan incarnation Harrison Ford, Affleck's involvement in *The Sum Of All Fears* does nothing for an already inconsistent series that has seen four outings and three different leading men.

The solution? A script that sets the action in the present day while paradoxically placing Ryan at the beginning of his CIA career, and thus rather arrogantly disregards the previous three movies. Simple, yet not necessarily effective.

To be fair, Affleck is adequate enough, displaying the right mix of uncertainty and frustration as he searches for the source of a terrorist attack on Baltimore while nuclear war looms. However, despite the complexity of the crisis and the techno-thriller dialogue, the plot is under-written and overly hasty. ★★★★ **AM**

Ⓓ SUMMER HOLIDAY (1962)

Starring: *Cliff Richard (Don), Lauri Peters (Barbara), Melvyn Hayes (Cyril), Una Stubbs (Sandy), Teddy Green (Steve), Jeremy Bulloch (Edwin), Pamela Hart (Angie)*
Director: *Peter Yates*
Screenwriters: *Peter Myers, Ronald Cass*
U/103 mins./Musical/Comedy/UK

Four London Transport mechanics do up a Routemaster bus as a hotel on wheels, and take a tour of Europe, finding love and adventure along the way.

This British institution opens with black and white images of rainswept seasides and stay-at-home misery, then sends its lads and girls off to the Continent in a bright red bus, connecting with audiences who had shucked off miserablism and rationing and would be the first generation of young Brits who got a chance to go abroad without having to be in the army.

The plot is crowded but slight, with an ambisexual fillip as Cliff Richard winds up with a runaway starlet he seems to fall for while she's disguised as a 14-year-old boy (and to whom he sings a smug lecture on singleness, 'Bachelor Boy'). Cliff's pals – Melvyn Hayes, Jeremy (Boba Fett) Bulloch, Teddy Green – get palmed off with the girls – Una Stubbs, Pamela Hart and the other one – in a stranded group who never get to sing. The bus hauls through France (Ron Moody as a Marceau parody mime), Switzerland (a St. Bernard up a mountain), Austria (a waltz number), Yugoslavia (a near marriage and escape from gun-wielding peasants) and Greece (a whizz around Athens), while the heroine's mad stage mother (Madge Ryan) pretends she has been kidnapped for the publicity.

It marginalises and ridicules crass American showbiz characters while valorising homegrown talent like Cliff and the Shadows, but doesn't really give them much to do beyond rush through scenery. Director Peter Yates, later known for the more dangerous driving of *Bullitt*, makes a hash of the slapstick mime and the awful waltz, but cheery songs ('Summer Holiday', 'Put On Your Dancing Shoes') and a general air of amiability make it an infallible afternoon TV pick-me-up. ★★★ **KN**

Movie Stars' High School Yearbook Citations — TOP 10

1. Sylvester Stallone – Most Likely To End Up In The Electric Chair
2. Gillian Anderson – Most Likely To Go Bald and Most Likely To Be Arrested
3. Sandra Bullock – Most Likely To Brighten Your Day
4. Natalie Portman – Most Likely To Be A Guest On Jeopardy
5. Teri Hatcher – Most Likely To Become A Solid Gold Dancer
6. Meg Ryan – Cutest Girl in Class
7. Jimmy Fallon – Most Likely To Replace David Letterman
8. Heather Graham – Most Talented
9. Matthew McConaughey – Most Handsome
10. Dennis Hopper – Most Likely To Succeed

SUMMER OF SAM (1999)

Starring: *John Leguizamo (Vinny), Mira Sorvino (Dionna), Jennifer Esposito (Ruby), Adrien Brody (Richie), Michael Rispoli (Joe T), Bebe Neuwirth (Gloria)*
Director: *Spike Lee*
Screenwriters: *Victor Colicchio, Michael Imperioli, Spike Lee*
18/136 mins./Drama/USA

Trust and loyalty are strained when a New York neighbourhood is tested by a serial killer.

It's too easy to pigeon-hole Spike Lee as a black filmmaker, but this ambitious drama demonstrates that he is beyond doubt a New York filmmaker. Set during the long, hot summer of '77, this is not another true crime piece chronicling the crimes of a real-life psycho, but a portrait of the spiral of terror and chaos that radiates outwards from the murders of car-bound couples, committed by the self-titled 'Son of Sam'. We glimpse the madman in his hallucinatory hell, taking orders from a black dog, but the film is mostly concerned with a tangle of Italian-Americans in The Bronx.

As in *Do The Right Thing*, the plot puts a large number of characters in a pressure cooker and as petty grudges escalate, it seems that the neighbourhood will erupt. Hairdresser Vinny has trouble in his marriage to Dionna because he devotes so much time to infidelity that he can't perform sexually with her. His friend Ritchie gets heavily into punk (even adopting a hilarious Johnny Rotten accent) while working as a dancer in a gay club. Vinny is traumatised because he has only just missed becoming a Son of Sam victim himself, and his marital problems nudge him closer to a situation whereby he will betray his friend and precipitate ghastly violence. The cops and the Mob want the killings stopped, but boss Gazzara's decree that his soldiers look out for the maniac only makes things worse.

Like many recent US films, this is hung up on the styles of the 70s, but Lee goes for something between the black exploitation pictures of the period and the neon sizzle of David Lynch at his darkest. There are so many characters and threads that only a few get the full treatment. One scene, however, raises the kind of cheers usually reserved for couples getting together, as Dionna finally dumps Vinny, leaving him drugged-out and afraid.

It seems that Lee is saying that all New Yorkers are potential mass murderers, but the climax of the film is curiously less hard-hitting than it might have been. That said, it has some daring dramatic coups (the talking dog is a jaw-dropper) and enough verve to get through its lengthy running time. In short, an enormously energetic, flavourful film. ★★★★ **KN**

SUMMER WITH MONIKA (1953)

Starring: *Harriet Andersson (Monika), Lars Ekborg (Harry), Dagmar Ebbesen (Harry's Aunt), Ake Fridell (Monika's Father), Naemi Briese (Monika's Mother), Ake Gronberg (Harry's friend at work)*
Director: *Ingmar Bergman*
Screenwriter: *Ingmar Bergman, based on the novel by Per Anders Fogelström*
PG/96 mins./Drama/Sweden

Bored with life in the city, Monika and Harry spend an idyllic summer on a Swedish island, only for the dream to sour upon their return to reality, as a pregnant Monika abandons Harry for another lover.

According to Ingmar Bergman two chance meetings on the Stockholm streets proved key to the making of the film that finally brought him international recognition. In addition to offering Lars Ekborg the part of Harry on first sight, Bergman claimed to have begun work on the screenplay after novelist Per Anders Fogelström gave him a 10-word outline of his latest project. However, Svensk Filmindustri reader Allan Ekelund later recalled presenting Bergman with a finished copy of the book, as he knew that he had no original scenario in the pipeline.

Whatever its origins, this was a bold, shamelessly sunny picture whose nude swimming sequence so shocked members of the Svensk board that a number resigned rather than be associated with such filth.

Despite this executive discomfort, *Summer With Monika* turned out be be one of Bergman's happiest productions, with a cast and crew of around a dozen sharing the parish clerk's house for the two months of location shooting on the island of Ornö to the south of the capital. Even the discovery that the negative had been scratched did nothing to dampen Bergman's spirits, as the retakes gave him more time with 18-year-old Harriet Andersson, with whom he had begun an intense affair.

Indeed, Bergman's fixation with Andersson is evident in every frame, as he iconises her fresh good looks and unselfconscious physicality. Making sensual use of light on the water and the simple beauty of wild nature, Gunnar Fischer's photography not only captured her spirit, but also the very essence of summer in a way that only Nestor Almendros has since emulated in collaboration with Eric Rohmer.

But it was François Truffaut who first referenced the film by having Antoine Doinel steal pictures of Andersson in *Les Quatre Cents Coups* and both he and Godard borrowed the shot of her staring intently into the camera, as she realises the extent of her despair on returning to the city. The conclusion harked back to the bleak realism of Bergman's early studies of doomed love. But this was very much a step in a new direction. ★★★★ **DP**

A SUMMER'S TALE (CONTE D'ETE) (1996)

Starring: *Melvil Poupard (Gaspard), Amanda Langlet (Margot), Gwenaelle Simon (Solene), Aurelia Nolin (Lena), Aime Lefevre (The Newfoundlander)*
Director: *Eric Rohmer*
Screenwriter: *Eric Rohmer*
U/109 mins./Romance/Comedy/France

A young man must decide between three beautiful women.

The French director once again explores his obsession with the vagaries of love and characters who reveal themselves through endless chat. That it emerges more enjoyable than its predecessors is due mainly to a

S

teasing central ménage à quatre and an attractive cast in skimpy swimwear in Brittany locations.

The film follows musician Gaspard as he awaits the arrival of his girlfriend Lena at a seaside resort. He is chatted up by waitress Margot with whom he quickly establishes a close platonic relationship. Yet this friendship is put on the back burner when he meets self-confident and sultry Solene. Her predatory advances boost his ego and he looks set for the rest of his stay – until Lena turns up to reawaken old feelings. Paralysed by choice, Gaspard struggles to determine his true feelings and gradually boxes himself into conflicting plans with all three women.

If all this sounds farcical and contrived, it shouldn't. Without pretension, Rohmer unravels the emotional implications of the situation in a fresh, vivid manner, contrasting the liaisons to probe the nature of attraction and difficulty of commitment. Gaspard may annoy in his lack of decisiveness and the predicament does smack of male wish fulfilment but the action is always believable, often poignant and laced with amusing insights. Like much subtitled fare, it is leisurely and totally talk-driven. ★★★ **IF**

SUNRISE: A SONG OF TWO HUMANS (1927)

Starring: *George O'Brien (The Man), Janet Gaynor (The Wife), Margaret Livingston (The Woman From The City), Bodil Rosing (The Miad), J. Farrell McDonald (The Photographer), Ralph Sipperly (The Barber), Jane Winton (The Manicure Girl)*
Director: *F.W. Murnau*
Screenwriter: *Carl Mayer, based on the novella* Die Reise Nach Tilsit *by Hermann Sudermann*
U/95 mins./Drama/Germany

Awards: *Academy Awards – Best Picture (Unique And Artistic Production), Best Actress (Janet Gaynor), Best Cinematography*

In a lakeside village, 'the Man' is seduced away from his wife by the vampy 'Woman From the City'. He contemplates murder, but is overcome by conscience and reaffirms his love for his wife on a trip to the city, though their lives are imperilled by a storm that rises as the couple are on their way home.

In the first year of the Oscars, covering the 1927-28 season, the Academy handed out two separate but equal Best Picture statuettes: one to the big, brassy, popular middle-brow commercial movie which remains in the reference books (*Wings*), and the other to *Sunrise*, which was singled out for its 'artistic achievement'.

This practice was discontinued by crass producers – raising the question of what alternative Best Artistic Picture gongs ought to have been awarded since 1927. Directed by German genius F.W. Murnau (of *Nosferatu* and *The Last Laugh*) in his Hollywood debut, this silent art movie has a fairytale story which is less important than its performances, technical innovations and remarkable evocation of moods and passions. Janet Gaynor, who took home the Best Actress Oscar in 28, is extraordinarily delicate as the non-weepy heroine, while malleable O'Brien and slinkily seductive Livingston throw themselves into sustained mime excesses, memorably in a steamy, swamp-set adulterous clinch.

Abetted by the imaginative cinematography of Charles Rosher and Karl Struss, Murnau takes a story which wouldn't have been substantial enough for a Hollywood two-reeler shot in 1907 and spins it out into a remarkable, dreamlike symphony of moments and insights. Murnau was among the first foreign talents to fetch up in Hollywood and attempt to meld his own artistic sensibilities with the effects, art direction and technical expertise available only in the studio system – count the number of trick shots he works into the movie. ★★★★ **KN**

SUNSET (1988)

Starring: *Bruce Willis (Tom Mix), James Garner (Wyatt Earp), Malcolm McDowell (Alfie Alperin), Mariel Hemingway (Cheryl King), Kathleen Queenan (Nancy Shoemaker), Jennifer Edwards (Victoria Alperin), Patricia Hodge (Christina Alperin), Richard Bradford (Captain Blackworth), M. Emmet Walsh (Chief Marvin Dibner), Joe Dallesandro (Dutch Kiefer)*
Director: *Blake Edwards*
Screenplay: *Blake Edwards, based on a story by Rodney Amateau*
15/102 mins./Comedy/USA

Awards: *The Razzies – Best Director*

Hollywood, 1929. Cowboy star Tom Mix and old-time frontier marshal Wyatt Earp team up to solve a complicated murder case awash with floozies, blackmailers, gangsters and crooked cops and near-libellous depictions of historical figures.

Wyatt Earp and Tom Mix were a matched pair of frauds, considerably more interesting and considerably less endearing than the characters given them in this Blake Edwards comedy-mystery. Authenticity apart – and history is shamelessly ignored – *Sunset* has a terrific story idea and a potentially winning star combination, but comes out as a terrible movie.

Bruce Willis's Tom Mix is reduced to modelling outrageous Western outfits and playing sidekick, and James Garner's dignified Wyatt Earp – more in line with the heroic Henry Fonda portrayal from *My Darling Clementine* than his own, earlier, more sinister, interpretation of the character in *Hour of the Gun* – comes on like an ageing Jim Rockford, sleuthing through a case so complicated that *Chinatown* seems transparent but bereft of the snappy lines or bits of business he could turn to his advantage. If *Sunset* is at all watchable, it's down to Garner – one of the best, most consistently underrated light leading men in the movies – but the film keeps tripping up.

As usual in his later career (*That's Life, Blind Date, Skin Deep, Switch, A Fine Mess*), it's down to Edwards' astonishingly maladroit direction. This could profitably be played as light comedy adventure or a brooding, cynical, violent latterday film noir, but Edwards shoots off in all directions, cutting from badly staged slapstick to brutal violence with no regard for tone. The best thing in it is also the most subversive idea: Malcolm McDowell brilliantly plays Alfie Alperin, a comedian-cum-studio head modelled on Charlie Chaplin, as a smiling sadistic psychopath who commits slapstick killings. A major disappointment. ★★ **KN**

SUNSET BOULEVARD (SUNSET BLVD.) (1950)

Starring: *William Holden (Joe Gillis), Gloria Swanson (Norma Desmond), Erich von Stroheim (Max von Mayerling), Nancy Olson (Betty Schaefer), Fred Clark (Sheldrake)*
Director: *Billy Wilder*
Screenwriters: *Billy Wilder, Charles Brackett, D.M. Marshman, Jr., from the story* A Can Of Beans *by Charles Brackett, Billy Wilder*
PG/105 mins./Drama/USA

Awards: *Academy Awards – Best Black-and-White Art Direction-Set Decoration, Best Score, Best Screenplay, Golden Globes – Best Drama, Best Drama Actress, Best Director, Best Score*

Trapped by a faded silent movie star, screenwriter Joe is torn between a life of dead decadence and living desire.

Measured against any reasonable index, the 1950s were Billy Wilder's miracle decade. But perhaps the most extraordinary thing of all is that after *Sunset Boulevard* had gnawed the hand that feeds it down to a bloody stump, it is a wonder Hollywood ever let Wilder work again.

For their 17th and final screenplay collaboration, Charles Brackett and Billy Wilder began with a simple idea. 'We wanted to make a picture about a star who was passé,' explained the director.

Originally intended as a broad comedy with Mae West, the first choice for Norma Desmond, the faded silent movie goddess who lives an existence worthy of Miss Havisham in a decrepit pile on Sunset Boulevard, the screenplay developed into a cold-blooded satire that was at once more subtle and more savage.

The driving force towards darkness was always Wilder. Brackett, the Harvard Law School graduate and son of a New York senator, was the sophisticate, the voice of reason, the insider.

Often, it can take an outsider to launch an all-out attack on their adopted country, and for Wilder, a war orphan who had lost most of his family to Auschwitz, the adopted country was, of course, Hollywood.

Undisturbed in her dilapidated delirium, Norma Desmond would remain a harmless comic grotesque, a relic of old Hollywood; it is the young opportunist Joe Gillis that takes contemporary Hollywood, and the audience, to her door.

Brackett and Wilder had wanted to infuse the movie with a Hollywood insider's feel and had drafted in a number of real locations, including Schwab's Pharmacy, the legendary hangout where Lana Turner was discovered.

The most important single location, however, was Paramount itself, and after six straight pictures with the studio, including *Double Indemnity* and *The Lost Weekend*, Wilder was perhaps the only director able to ask for the keys. The famous gates, the sound stages, the rabbit warren of writers' offices, all of these form part of the backdrop for *Sunset Boulevard*.

It is a mark of the esteem in which Wilder was held that Paramount did not ask the director to disguise the studio. Or perhaps they had an inkling of how important this project might prove to be; during the daily round of rushes screenings, *Sunset Boulevard* became the hottest ticket on the lot.

It was Wilder's friend, director George Cukor, who suggested Gloria Swanson for Norma Desmond. Like Desmond, Swanson was an icon of the silent era who had worked with DeMille but been largely forgotten by modern audiences. Swanson delivered a bold, brazen performance, theatrical and yet precise, a study of ego that is remarkably devoid of vanity.

It had been almost ten years since Holden had made an early impact with *Golden Boy*, and his reputation had definitely lost its lustre, largely thanks to alcohol. In other words, there was no better choice for the hopelessly compromised Gillis.

The clash between old and new Hollywood is reinforced by the contrasting acting styles; Holden's minimal naturalism and Swanson's exaggerated expressionism is the context for the movie's most famous line: 'I am big,' Desmond tells Gillis; 'it's the pictures that got small'.

From Edith Head's baroque costumes to John F. Seitz's nightmarish noir photography, every aspect of *Sunset Boulevard* retains a formal beauty rarely attempted in a modern comedy, and yet the screenplay contains not one line that could be thought callow by 21st-century audiences.

The images of death that suffuse *Sunset Boulevard* are a clue to a worldview that was informed by the most profoundly disturbing event of any age, the Holocaust, and Wilder's natural defence mechanism, the mordant wit, has ensured that his movies have been embraced by our more cynical age. And yet, great art does not survive simply because it eschews easy sentiment.

Sunset Boulevard should stand for as long as Hollywood stands because of the simple reminder it posts for studio executives and humans alike: the emotions that are hardest won are the only ones worth keeping. ★★★★★ **CK**

Movie Trivia: Billy Wilder (1906–2002)

Who he is: Hollywood all-rounder. Refugee from World War II Europe who came to Hollywood to write and direct the sharpest, wittiest comedies and dramas of the century.

Hallmarks: Cynicism; satire; clipped, clever dialogue; romantic minimalism ('Shut up and deal'); equal ability across any genre.

If you see one movie, see: *Some Like It Hot* (1959)

THE SUNSHINE BOYS (1975)

Starring: *Walter Matthau (Willy Clark), George Burns (Al Lewis), Richard Benjamin (Ben Clark), Lee Meredith (Nurse In Sketch), Carol Arthur (Doris), Rosetta (Le Noire), F. Murray Abraham (Mechanic), Howard Hessemann (Commercial Director)*

Director: *Herbert Ross*

Screenwriter: *Neil Simon, based on his own play*

PG/111 mins./Comedy/USA

Awards: *Academy Awards – Best Supporting Actor (George Burns)*

New York agent Ben Clark lands his cantankerous Uncle Willy, a slot on a TV show tracing the history of comedy, on the proviso that he performs the famous Doctor Sketch with his ex-vaudeville partner, Al Lewis, who had taken his festering grudges with Willy into retirement some 12 years earlier.

Jack Albertson and Sam Levene took the parts of Clark and Lewis (who were supposedly modelled on the duo of Smith & Dale) when Neil Simon's comedy opened to rave reviews on Broadway. But, despite the fact that Albertson was one of only three actors to have landed the triple crown of an Oscar, an Emmy and a Tony, he was not considered big enough box-office for the movie version and Walter Matthau was drafted in to co-star with Jack Benny. However, the veteran comic succumbed to the illness that would eventually kill him and George Burns agreed to end a 36-year absence from the screen (having only narrated *The Solid Gold Cadillac*) as a favour to an old pal.

The gesture earned him an Oscar, although the ever-sentimental Academy doubtlessly took into account that Burns had himself been in virtual retirement since the death of his beloved wife, Gracie Allen, in 1964. However, he had always been at his best as part of a double act (albeit as the straight man) and he stole every scene as the embittered trouper who refuses to forgive or forget (despite the vagaries of a failing memory).

This was partly down to the fact that Herbert Ross encouraged the 54-year-old Walter Matthau to ham up the part of the 79-year-old kvetch, whose egotistical outbursts were too often delivered at the top of his voice. Nevertheless, the byplay between the pair fizzed with some of the writer's choicest one-liners.

But it was Simon's knowledge of and fondness for a bygone showbiz era that gave the story is authenticity and charm. He clearly empathised with the old-timers forced to audition for commercials or subsist on their memories and shared Ben's concern to do right by these forgotten favourites. But when Richard Benjamin (who is touchingly forebearing throughout) came to remake the film for television in 1995 with the horribly miscast Woody Allen and Peter Falk, he made the same mistake as Ross by playing up the comic peevishness of the dialogue rather than its furious, but deeply melancholic despair. ★★★ **DP**

⊙ SUNSHINE STATE (2002)

Starring: *Edie Falco (Marly Temple), Angela Bassett (Desiree Stokes Perry), Jane Alexander (Delia Temple), Ralph Waite (Furman Temple), Mary Steenburgen (Francine Pinkney), Timothy Hutton (Jack Meadows)*
Director: *John Sayles*
Screenwriter: *John Sayles*
15/134 mins./Drama/USA

As Delrona Beach celebrates 'Buccaneer Days', rival property developers arouse mixed emotions among townsfolk. Marly longs to sell her family's motel, while Desiree, back after 25 years, resists being drawn into the community's fight to preserve its ideals.

Indie emeritus John Sayles crosses the continent from his Alaskan-set *Limbo* for a more emotionally accessible comedy-drama on a Florida seaside, well off the Miami-Disney World itinerary.

From a teenage arsonist to a failed actress and a suicidal embezzler, the characters wrestle with their problems while battles ensue between property developers around a proposed resort. The most engaging element is the tentative romance between Falco's weary ex-mermaid and landscape architect Hutton, while most poignant is venerable Bill Cobbs, championing a once prosperous black community.

In an excellent ensemble (which includes Sayles regular Tom Wright as the local has-been hero and *NYPD Blue* duo James McDaniel and Gordon Clapp) Steenburgen is a scream as the harassed organiser trying to drum up tourism with tacky pirate shows and a man-eating alligator. The Sopranos' Falco is also terrific. ★★★ **AE**

⊙ SUPER MARIO BROS. (1993)

Starring: *Bob Hoskins (Mario Mario), Dennis Hopper (King Koopa), John Leguizamo (Luigi Mario), Samantha Mathis (Daisy), Fisher Stevens (Iggy)*
Directors: *Rocky Morton, Annabel Jankel*
Screenwriters: *Parker Bennett, Terry Runte, Ed Solomon, from the characters by Shigeru Miyamoto, Takashi Tezuka*
PG/99 mins./Fantasy/Adventure/USA

Two plumbers enter a parallel universe ruled by a dinosaur race to save a Princess.

The first film to be adapted from rather than into a Nintendo cartridge, *Super Mario Bros.* is a shrill, hectic and tiresome fantasy with little story, less excitement and no imaginable audience.

Millions of years ago, a meteor hits the Earth and causes time to fissure around the island of Manhattan, resulting in a cramped parallel universe where humanity has evolved from dinosaurs rather than apes. Lizard King Koopa runs the alternate city and has kidnapped fugitive Princess Daisy, an orphan who was raised from an egg by nuns in our world, and who has just caught the attention of Luigi Mario, younger brother and business partner of mustachioed plumber Mario Mario.

Hauled into the parallel world along with a shard of meteor that powers the plot, the Brothers set out to rescue her, blundering around a series of theme park rides trying to save the girl and depose the villain. What few good lines there are get snatched by Hopper who, partnered by the supposedly lizardy but notably mammalian Fiona Shaw, handles the villainy as if there were a real film to back him up rather than a melange of fungus-strewn, leftover *Batman* sets populated by shouting humans.

Occasionally, the special effects (a pet-size dinosaur, transformations, disintegrations) raise some interest, but there is never any sense that this is more than a technical showreel interspersed with *Three Stooges* cast-offs. Produced by Jake Eberts and Roland Joffe, usually so keen on Serious Quality Subjects, and directed by the husband-and-wife team who gave you lots of videos and *Max Headroom*, this poor imitation of a 90s blockbuster stumbles from the start and winds up flat in the dirt. Game over, man. ★★ **KN**

⊙ SUPERGIRL (1984)

Starring: *Faye Dunaway (Selena), Helen Slater (Kara/Supergirl/Linda Lee), Peter O'Toole (Zaltar), Mia Farrow (Alura), Brenda Vaccaro (Bianca), Peter Cook (Nigel), Simon Ward (Zor-El), Marc McClure (Jimmy Olsen), Hart Bochner (Ethan)*
Director: *Jeannot Szwarc*
Screenwriter: *David Odell*
PG/105 mins./Sci-fi/UK

When the power source of Argo City, home to survivors of Krypton, is lost, the leader Zaltar sends Kara Zor-El to Earth to retrieve it. Kara is the cousin of Kal-El, and just as he takes the names Clark Kent and Superman on Earth, she becomes Linda Lee and Supergirl.

A by-blow of the Christopher Reeve-starring *Superman* franchise, this wasn't much liked on its release as a two-hour-film and its reputation has hardly been elevated by the appearance of a 138-minute director's cut on DVD.

The chief culprit is a script that contrives to pile silliness upon idiocy in a manner outrageous even for a comic book movie. In an extra-dimensional crystal city where some survivors of blown-up Krypton still live, the likes of Peter O'Toole (effectively, in the Brando role) mouth absurd dialogue and Mia Farrow and Simon Ward put in earnest cameos as the heroine's parents.

The one thing the film does right is cast its lead – Helen Slater is just as perfect as the blue-eyed blonde Supergirl as Reeve was as her cousin, managing not to look silly in the cape, boots and miniskirt, projecting Amazonian strength and teen princess innocence, even managing to slyly send up her own heroic posing. What a shame, then, that S-girl's only big screen outing should find her pitted against diva-like witch Selena (top-billed Faye Dunaway) in what boils down to a cat-fight over the affections of a hunky but dull landscape gardener (Hart Bochner).

Marc McClure's Jimmy Olsen is the only cast hold-over from the main series, and there's too much from Brenda Vaccaro and Peter Cook as Dunaway's comedy sidekicks. Director Jeannot Szwarc gives it a big, expensive feel, and a satisfyingly huge monster shows up at the climax to battle the heroine, but it's a missed opportunity. ★★ **KN**

⊙ SUPERMAN II (1980)

Starring: *Gene Hackman (Lex Luthor), Christopher Reeve (Clark Kent/Superman), Ned Beatty (Otis), Jackie Cooper (Perry White), Sarah Douglas (Ursa), Margot Kidder (Lois Lane), Jack O'Halloran (Non), Valerie Perrine (Eve Teschmacher), Susannah York (Lara), Clifton James (Sherriff), E.G. Marshall (The President), Marc McClure (Jimmy Olsen), Terrence Stamp (General Zod)*
Director: *Richard Lester, Richard Donner (Uncredited),*
Screenwriters: *Mario Puzo, David Newman, Leslie Newman based on characters created by Jerry Siegel and Joe Shuster*
PG/127 mins./Fantasy/USA

This time round, Superman faces off against three villains – General Zod, Ursa, Non – from his home planet Krypton, while getting to grips with his growing attachment to Lois Lane.

Given the behind-the-scenes machinations that went on during the making of *Superman II* (with original director Richard Donner fired, having shot about 70 per cent of the script, to be replaced by Richard Lester), the end product should have been a barely coherent mess. Instead, somehow, *Superman II* is one of the most exciting comic book films ever made.

Sure, with hindsight you can see the joins, but somehow Lester's more freewheeling style meshed well with Donner's quest for reality and love for Americana, leading to a truly epic and entertaining tale in which

Christopher Reeve's peerless Superman is confronted with three Kryptonian adversaries (led by Terence Stamp's General Zod), each as powerful as he. Meanwhile, though, the film is also focused on the battle for Superman's heart, as Margot Kidder's intrepid Lois Lane tries to discern the truth about her colleague Clark Kent, who for some reason has never been seen in the same room as Superman...

Notably the first superhero movie to really show godlike beings going toe-to-toe (the fight between Superman and his enemies in the middle of Metropolis is a set-trashing triumph, with a refreshing emphasis on physical effects), where this sequel really succeeds is in aiming for, and hitting, the funnybone (Hackman's Lex Luthor takes something of a back seat, but makes up for it by getting all the best lines) and in upping the dramatic content from the first movie's relatively straightforward origin story.

In mining the always-engaging ménage à trois between Lois, Clark and Superman for dramatic mileage (Superman turns his back on true love for the benefit of mankind), this deserves its place in the classic comic book canon for showing that the Man Of Steel is just as human as the rest of us.

★★★★ **CH**

⓪ SUPERMAN III (1983)

Starring *Christopher Reeve (Superman/Clark Kent), Richard Pryor (Gus Gorman), Jackie Cooper (Perry White), Marc McClure (Jimmy Olsen), Annette O'Toole (Lana Lang), Annie Ross (Vera Webster), Pamela Stephenson (Lorelei Ambrosia), Robert Vaughn (Ross Webster), Margot Kidder (Lois Lane), Gavan O'Herlihy (Brad)*
Director: *Richard Lester*
Screenwriters: *David Newman, Leslie Newman, based on the characters created by Jerry Siegel and Joe Shuster*
PG/125 mins./Fantasy/UK/USA

Multimillionaire Ross Webster exploits likeable computer genius Gus Gorman to play havoc with the world markets. When this brings him into conflict with Superman, he tries to devise his own version of the Man Of Steel's Achilles heel – Kryptonite.

With Richard Lester solely at the helm, there is a much lighter, breezier tone to *Superman III*. Opening the movie with a well-orchestrated, extended piece of slapstick that could have been pilfered from one of his 60s comedies, Lester brings his own sense of the absurd across the entire proceedings. Occasionally, this works brilliantly – Superman straightening the Leaning Tower Of Pisa – but far too often the movie sacrifices the drama and sense of wonder that made the first two films so great. There is good action (as in a set-piece where Supeman battles his evil alter-ego the latter created by a synthetic piece of kryptonite) and Christopher Reeve commands the dual role with real authority, but there is a whimsicality here that doesn't fit right with the Superman mythos.

One of the most interesting facets about *Superman II*, Superman's increasingly complex relationship with Lois Lane, is jettisoned from the get-go (Margot Kidder, disgusted that Richard Donner was fired, makes her excuses and leaves), replaced by a likeable, if insubstantial, subplot about Clark Kent going back to his home town for a school reunion, facing up to the local boor Brad and wooing high school honey Lana Lang (O'Toole, who now has a role as Superman's mom in the TV series *Smallville*). Elsewhere, special guest star Richard Pryor, as bumbling computer whiz Gus Gorman, has some good moments but is an innocuous presence, bereft of his usual spark and edginess. Vaughn brings an understated class to his rent-a-villain and Annie Ross and Pamela Stephenson ham it up to the nines as his sidekicks But by the time the movie has moved into the third act, when many of these villains change side to help Superman, you know you are watching a franchise that's lost sight of its dramatic dynamics in favour of something much more safe and colourless. Still the worse was yet to come.

★★★ **WT**

⓪ SUPERMAN IV: THE QUEST FOR PEACE (1987)

Starring: *Christopher Reeve (Superman/Clark Kent), Gene Hackman (Lex Luthor), Jackie Cooper (Perry White), Marc McClure (Jimmy Olsen), Jon Cryer (Lenny), Sam Wanamaker (David Warfield), Mark Pillow (Nuclear Man), Mariel Hemingway (Lacy Warfield), Margot Kidder (Lois Lane)*
Director: *Sydney J. Furie*
Screenwriters: *Lawrence Konner, Mark Rosenthal, based on a story by Konner, Rosenthal and Christopher Reeve based on characters created by Joe Shuster and Jerry Siegel*
PG/90 mins/Fantasy/UK

After Superman rids the world of its nuclear arsenal, an even bigger threat is posed by Lex Luthor's latest attempts to extinguish the Man Of Steel – Nuclear Man!

From *Police Academy IV* to *Batman And Robin*, there is an unwritten law in Hollywood that the fourth instalment of any franchise must be awful, as if all the last dregs of creative energy to make a third movie have been used up and there is nothing left in the barrel. This rule applies to *A Quest For Peace*, a dreadful end to the mostly majestic *Superman* series of the 70s/80s, that takes everything you hold sacred about The Man Of Steel and flushes it down the toilet.

Based on a story idea by Christopher Reeve, who only returned to the role if the character became more socially relevant, *A Quest For Peace* sees Superman, spurred on by a schoolboy's letter, pull off the not insubstantial task of ridding the world of nuclear weapons by rounding them up in a big old net and lobbing them up at the sun. If this wasn't terrible enough, Lex Luthor (Hackman, woefully over the top), in cahoots with his surfer dude nephew Lenny, creates a new nemesis with the risible moniker Nuclear Man to battle Superman against a plethora of terrible backscreen projections.

Financed by the bargain bucket company Cannon, the budget was slashed by some $17 million just before shooting started and you can see the squeeze (not to mention the wires) in every frame. Set-pieces involving the destruction of The Great Wall Of China and Superman rescuing a runaway subway train fail to convince and the decision to shift the shoot from New York to the new town of Milton Keynes is like shooting *Apocalypse Now* on Hampstead Heath. The scenes involving Clark Kent, the heart of previous Superman flicks where Reeve is so self-assured at being awkward, feel tired and weary. Happily, good sense prevailed and this incarnation of the character came to a thundering halt. The sighs of relief were more, shall we say, Supersized. ★ **WT**

SUPERMAN RETURNS (2006)

Starring: *Brandon Routh (Superman/Clark Kent), Kate Bosworth (Lois Lane), Kevin Spacey (Lex Luthor), James Marsden (Richard White), Frank Langella (Perry White)*
Director: *Bryan Singer*
Screenwriters: *Michael Dougherty, Dan Harris, based on characters created by Jerry Siegel, Joe Shuster*
TBC/150 mins/Fantasy/Action/Adventure/Romance/USA

Superman returns from a five-year journey to Krypton to find paramour Lois Lane is now a mother who is about to be married. Meanwhile, Lex Luthor's lust for real estate threatens to kill billions ...

With the inspired appropriation of John Williams' majestic 1978 theme music raising acres of gooseflesh, Superman flies again, bringing mankind what Marlon Brando's Jor-El called 'the light to show the way'. Like the flag-waving hero of Richard Donner's Superman movies, the boy from Krypton comes bathed in nostalgia, reverence and oodles of religious symbolism. The result is that most beatific of superhero's most magnificent screen incarnation yet.

Bryan Singer is a besotted man, with a determination that Superman belongs to the movies. Amongst the visual razzmatazz, those dreamy effects and gilded edges, he references *Casablanca*, *Close Encounters*,

Citizen Kane and *Titanic*, films in the widest possible sense. If Steven Spielberg were to have made a *Superman* movie, it would surely have this sense of wonder, exaltation and romance.

The story loosely follows on from *Superman II*, with Lois Lane's memory of Superman's true identity wiped by a kiss, and Singer stays fully in touch with the heartache that murmurs beneath that iconic blue suit – the idea that our hero's divine nature acts as a barrier to love. Clark's unrequited love for Lois and her crush on Superman are the soul of the story, far more central, say, than the mind-blowing action sequences clamouring for your attention. This may confound those just looking for a regular can of fizzy action juice, but will taste like fine wine to the growing legion of Singer fans who admire his dedication to adding emotional weight to summer thrills. The news that Lois is the mother of a five year-old boy and engaged to newcomer Richard White sends the Man of Steel into meltdown, the unfolding emotional conflict steering the movie. While such sentimental concerns could become cloying, Singer, as with his X-Men, finds the perfect middle way to explore the conflicts within his characters.

Kate Bosworth brings an eager intensity to the star reporter; even though she lacks the world-weary wryness of Margot Kidder, she fully evokes Lane's conflict and tough exterior. But the real victory is Brandon Routh. The resemblance between Routh and Christopher Reeve is uncanny (when he first turns around as Clark Kent, you'd swear it was 1978) and, while proving every bit as wholesomely heroic, Routh even adds his own melancholic touch.

Singer has built a larger, worldwide arena here: Superman traverses the globe, not just the US, in his fight for 'truth and justice...' (references to the 'American way' are conspicuously absent), and consequently Spacey's eloquent Lex Luthor is a further-thinking and far crueller customer than Gene Hackman's. His diabolic and rather complicated master plan is inevitably fuelled by shards of that dreaded green kryptonite, while Parker Posey's moll makes delightfully dim-witted fun of his megalomania.

Such dastardly deeds do, naturally, furnish the movie with a series of breathtaking action sequences. While symbolically carrying the world on his shoulders, Superman literally carries continents across his broad back. More than that, though, Singer realises it isn't enough to believe a man can fly; these are flights of emotional expression, exhilarating in their sense of freedom set against rapturous skylines. Indeed, the film floats in a preposterous, magical America forever bathed in golden light. Singer has reinvigorated an American icon, with a film that sits happily in the upper tiers of Superman's grand pantheon. His Superman doesn't fly, he soars. ★★★★★ **IN**

SUPERMAN: THE MOVIE (1978)

Starring: *Christopher Reeve (Superman/Clark Kent), Margot Kidder (Lois Lane), Marlon Brando (Jor-El), Gene Hackman (Lex Luthor), Ned Beatty (Otis), Jackie Cooper (Perry White)*
Director: *Richard Donner*
Screenwriters: *Mario Puzo, David Newman, Leslie Newman, Robert Benton, based on a story by Mario Puzo, character created by Jerry Siegel, Joe Shuster*
PG/137 mins./Fantasy/Action/Adventure/Romance/USA

Awards: *BAFTA – Best Newcomer (Christopher Reeve)*

The planet Krypton is doomed. Only one man, Jor-El, knows it, and rockets his infant son to refuge on a distant world called Earth. As Jor-El's son grows to manhood, he learns he possesses super-powers he must hide from the ordinary mortals around him. And so, he disguises himself as Clark Kent, mild-mannered reporter.

There was a brief moment back in 1978 when, still giddy from the form-reinventing rush that was *Star Wars* the year before, we actually believed a man could fly. After all, there were all these posters saying just that: 'You'll believe a man can fly'.

That and the radiant 'S' symbol universal to all, told us all we needed to know, that we were in for something special. *Superman: The Movie* offered the potential of finally doing justice to one of the great action hero icons of the 20th century. And it went a fair way to delivering just that.

Having debuted in a 1938 edition of DC Action Comics, Superman rapidly established his hold over his adopted home planet through a series of comic books, cartoons, Saturday morning serials and a 1950s television show. By the time he reappeared on celluloid in 1978, you were hard-pressed to find a kid who didn't know that the man from Krypton was faster than a speeding bullet, could leap tall buildings in a single bound and most certainly wasn't a bird or a plane. And of course that, day to day, he was Clark Kent, mild-mannered *Daily Planet* reporter.

Everyone may have known what Superman was, but nobody had a clue who he was. The casting hunt for Alexander and Ilja Salkind's epic was the Annakin Skywalker casting call of its day. Every big name in Hollywood was linked to it at some point; notions of Clint Eastwood and Burt Reynolds may now seem ridiculous (add Ryan Neal to that list), but both Robert Redford and James Caan have confirmed that they passed on it. (A then untested Steven Spielberg was also in the running to direct, but the Salkinds decided to wait and see how well 'the fish movie' did.) Donner, then hot from *The Omen*, and the pervasive Salkinds, settled on the statuesque but relatively unknown Christopher Reeve, who proved to be perfect for the role, all muscles, X-ray vision and kiss curl when in costume, and an adept light comedian when playing his Clark Kent alter-ego. He bulked up in preproduction with Darth Vader himself, Dave Prowse.

The Salkinds wanted to make a bold statement with their *Superman*: this was a BIG film and, with Reeve a relative nobody, they needed some big stars. Both Marlon Brando and Gene Hackman were billed above the actor who played Superman, even though the once great Brando only appeared, as Superman's father, for the first few minutes of the film, launching his baby son Earthward-bound as Krypton goes supernova. A small role, but for it he was paid some $4 million, then one of the biggest fees ever, for essentially doing little more than wandering through a badly costumed prologue sporting the naffest rug this side of Bill Shatner. Hackman had the time of his life camping it up as Lex Luthor. (For those keeping trivia score, Lois's parents were played by Kirk Alyn and Noel Neill, who played Supes and Lois in a 40s serial.)

Four (credited) writers worked on *Superman*, including *The Godfather*'s Mario Puzo, with Tom Mankiewicz additionally billed as 'Creative Consultant', a title that implies he was the one who stitched it all together. Right from the off the Salkinds were determined to build a franchise, with the prologue briefly establishing Terence Stamp's General Zod and his villainous fellow Kryptonians, imprisoned by what appears to be two hula hoops on a perpetual motion jag. Their reappearance in *Part II* was inevitable, just as it was inevitable that these sequels would lessen the impact of this original. (And by part four, kill the franchise.)

As a young man, Clark Kent was powerless to do anything over Pa Kent's death; but with Lois he turns back time to suit his own needs, proving that the alien Kal-El is maybe a little human after all. As Lex Luthor says, 'There's a strong streak of good in you Superman. But then, nobody's perfect.' ★★★★ **BM**

Movie Trivia: Superman The Movie

The title role was also offered to Robert Redford, Clint Eastwood, James Caan and even Patrick Wayne, son of John. Lex Luthor had two henchmen in the original script, but it was cut to one (Otis) for the filming. Marlon Brando and Gene Hackman appeared first in trailers for the film as Reeve was then an unknown. Brando was paid nearly $4 million for his ten minutes on screen.

⓪ SUPER SIZE ME (2004)

Starring: (as themselves): *Morgan Spurlock, Alexandra Jamieson, Dr. Daryl Issacs, Dr. Lisa Ganjhu, Dr. David Stacher, Dr. Stephen Seigel, Dr. Lisa Young*
Director: *Morgan Spurlock*
Screenwriter: *Morgan Spurlock*
12/100 mins./Documentary/USA

After hearing of two girls suing McDonald's for their obesity and seeing the burger chain's subsequent denial of responsibility, documentary filmmaker Morgan Spurlock undergoes an experiment: for 30 days he will only eat and drink items from McDonalds.

Sit yourself down, stop eating that burger and pay attention, because this is going to come as a surprise: junk food is bad for you. Imagine. As revelations go, it's up there with the news that footballers cheat on their wives and politicians lie. But shocking his audience into dropping their McCoronary with cheese isn't the point of Morgan Spurlock's film.

It's a documentary without any particular sermons to preach or politics to hammer home; simply a visual representation of all the questions that go through anybody's mind when they chow down on the Golden Arches' finest. It's a hugely enjoyable descent into epic gluttony.

It's the thinking man's *Jackass*. *Super Size Me* works mainly thanks to the goofy watchability of Spurlock, a man who makes his way through a month living off nothing but the McDonald's menu with remarkably good humour, even when vomiting his experiment (on the second day!) out of his car window. He constructs his little seminar in such an anger-free, cheery-faced way that even the most revolting facts slide down with ease. When ordered by his doctors to stop his diet before his liver 'turns to pâté', he doesn't dwell indulgently on the situation, cutting to a shot of his flabby, greasy self miserably, but amusingly, tucking into another burger.

He has none of the righteous indignation of Michael Moore, letting the facts speak for themselves with little need to editorialise, making his viewer feel less beaten down by rhetoric than politely informed. That lack of passionate viewpoint does, however, mean that the important points sometimes get lost amongst the comedy. A section dealing with the proliferation of junk food in American schools feels a touch undercooked and out of pace with the rest of the doc's geniality.

Anyone familiar with Eric Schlosser's book *Fast Food* Nation will already have heard these horror stories and many more besides. But a book rarely has the immediate effectiveness of film, and for all his jollity, Spurlock has achieved something Schlosser only did in small part: he's got McDonald's running scared. How many salads do you remember seeing in Ronald's hangout before the release of this film?
★★★★ OR

⓪ THE SURE THING (1985)

Starring: *John Cusack (Walter 'Gib' Gibson), Daphne Zuniga (Alison Bradbury), Anthony Edwards (Lance), Tim Robbins (Gary Cooper), Lisa Jane Persky (Mary Ann Webster), Nicollette Sheridan (The Sure Thing)*
Director: *Rob Reiner*
Screenwriters: *Steven Bloom, Jonathan Roberts*
15/90 mins./Comedy/Romance/USA

A college boy hitches a lift across America on a quest for 'The Sure Thing' – a girl who won't spurn his sexual advances. But on route he hooks up with a girl from his class who begins to make him view his female ideal slightly differently.

So just what was it with the 80s and teen pics? Not since love found Andy Hardy in the late 1930s or AIP churned out the likes of *I Was A Teenage Werewolf* and *How To Make A Monster* during the 1950s did Hollywood get so enthusiastic about young people – and young middle-class white people at that. Maybe it was all the hairspray in the air.

During the 80s, of course, John Hughes was the godfather of adolescent celluloid, pulling off the almost impossible task of making a bunch of introspective stereotypes sympathetic in *The Breakfast Club* and delivering unto the world the echt cool pubescent Ferris Bueller (another triumph of dramatic sleight of hand: there he manages to make a likeable hero out of a kid whose one life tragedy is that he got a computer for his birthday instead of a car). Hughes had an almost mystical ability to channel the fragile emotional states of teenagers without patronising them or engaging in prurience or preachiness. But there were other directors working around the edges of the genre at least as interesting as Hughes. Allan Mel delivered the truly subversive *Pump Up The Volume* (one of the very few teen movies to end with an image of undefeated rebellion, Christian Slater punching the air as he's arrested for running a pirate radio station) while Michael Lehmann introduced the world to Slater's medium-rent Jack Nicholson impersonation in *Heathers*.

Often neglected among the adolescent flotsam, though, is this somewhat overlooked classic from Rob Reiner, who the previous year had left his impressive directorial calling card with *This Is Spinal Tap*. But while *Tap* was a sharply written and effortlessly knowing spoof, *The Sure Thing* was a less tightly wrought confection: at heart it's an irresistibly sweet-natured rom-com. Essentially a remake of Frank Capra's *It Happened One Night* (not the first time Reiner would indulge in a little unacknowledged pilfering – his 1989 hit *When Harry Met Sally* is a direct descendent of Woody Allen's *Annie Hall*) it has John Cusack (you've heard of him) in the Clark Gable role and Daphnie Zuniga essaying Claudette Colbert duties (she wound up in *Melrose Place*).

The pitch is neat enough. A mildly neurotic, very horny college freshman at an East Coast Ivy League University named Gib is promised by his best friend in California, Lance, that there is the almost mythical Sure Thing waiting for him there: this being a girl 'in her experimental phase' who is all but guaranteed to sleep with him. Unable to afford the air fare he hitches his way to Nirvana first with a very young Tim Robbins and his girlfriend – both enthusiastic devotees of showtunes – but then finds himself unexpectedly alone on his priapic odyssey with Alison, an uptight straight-A student on her way to meet her nerdy financé and distinctly unimpressed with her travelling companion's penchant for fried pork-rinds and the expert chugging of lager.

There is of course a delightfully satisfying predictability to the set-up: the moment they wind up on the road together you know that the Sure Thing is anything but and the nerdy boyfriend may as well pack his bags. Thus the film's interest relies on the two leads rather than any plot bombshells. The most obvious draw was Cusack himself who, having shown some obvious promise in two previous teen outings, *Class* and John Hughes's *Sixteen Candles*, nailed down forever the likeably excitable, verbose schtick he would build his subsequent career upon. Like a teenage Woody Allen he's the master of the nervy quip – but unlike Allen he was in some ineffable way intensely cool and he gave hope to the dweebs, geeks and nerds of the world that a quick wit would make up for a distinct absence of many obviously discernible physical attributes. He, however, looks back on these films with anything other than affection; 'I was a teen star – that's bad enough,' he's reported to have said when asked about his early years. And despite her lacklustre subsequent career Zuniga, who has the less showy role, also shines as the ice-maiden slowly thawed by Gib's unconventional charm.

Possibly the oddest thing about *The Sure Thing* is that for a movie nominally about sex there's virtually none of it on the screen. The two characters behave for the most part like the slightly cocksure but nervous adolescents that they are. Like the teen-slasher movie in which naughty behaviour by curious kiddiewinks is somewhat disproportionately punished by hockey mask-wearing maniacs, the typical teen flick is actually more conservative than your average Supreme Court nominee. The message is that sex should be accompanied by love and respect; the surprise being not, of course, that the studios would produce such morally and emotionally engaged stuff, but that young hormonal audiences would lap it up. When Gib and Alison finally arrive at their destination, both geographically and emotionally, the movie resolves itself with the kind of chaste, romantic kiss that would have had Louis B. Meyer – Andy Hardy's real paterfamilias – nodding in warm approval ... ★★★★ **AS**

⑩ SUSPIRA (1976)

Starring: *Jessica Harper (Susy Bannion), Joan Bennett (Madame Blanc), Alida Valli (Miss Tanner), Udo Kier (Frank), Flavio Bucci (Daniel)*
Director: *Dario Argento*
Screenwriters: *Dario Argento, Dario Nicolodi*
18/94 mins./Horror/Italy

An American at an exclusive German dancing academy notices her fellow students have an unfortunate habit of being murdered ...

Dario Argento, horror's Italian Stallion, put his bloodstained cards on the table right from *Suspira*'s gory get-go. In the middle of the night in a raging storm a young woman runs screaming through the woods, illuminated by lightning. After she arrives at a friend's apartment she peers though a window into the tumult only for an arm to smash through one window pane and, in a loving extended shot, suffocate her against the other. While her friend drums hysterically against the locked door the gloved hand repeatedly stabs the girl. In the next shot the stabbing continues, this time in full close-up as the fiend winds a rope around the shrieking victim's legs. And in the *pièce de résistance*, we cut to the friend running into the lobby of the apartment building looking for help. As she looks up towards a stained-glass ceiling, the victim's head crashes through it in a hail of glass shards followed by her body. We cut to the blood-drenched corpse suspended by the rope dripping blood onto the floor, finally Argento pans the camera to reveal his next horror. The falling glass has pinned the friend crucifix like, the largest sliver having split her face in half.

We are now 13 minutes into *Suspira*, and if the poster tagline – 'The only thing more terrifying than the first 80 minutes of *Suspira* ... is the last 10' – has any truth in it we're in for a deeply unnerving experience.

Argento, often called the Italian Hitchcock (it's a misnomer, the only things the two share are grandiose misogyny and a liking for sustained sequences) is arguably Italy's foremost horror director and *Suspira* is his finest movie to date. It's difficult to give a flavour of its unique, surreal, hyper-intense mood by simply describing it. It's not all that helpful to outline the plot, since there's very little of it, and what there is doesn't make much sense.

An American goes to a Frieberg dance academy, finds that people have a habit of vanishing or getting killed in unusual circumstances, discovers it's all down to an ancient coven of witches and burns the place to the ground. And there you have it.

But in fact the plot, such as it is, is just a device to link a series of gloriously realised set-pieces. Argento is a maestro of sustained horror sequences. In one, a blind man is suddenly set upon by his own guide-dog – the scene is shot audaciously in either extreme long shot (a kind of pigeon's eye view) or extreme close-ups of the hound tearing horribly realistic chunks out of the unfortunate man's neck. A young dancer is combing her hair at night only to find a maggot in it. And then another. As she looks up she discovers the whole ceiling is crawling with them and they begin to rain down on her. In one of the most gleefully sadistic sequences ever put on film a scantily clad co-ed tumbles into a barbed wire-filled pit. The camera looks on, unmoving, as she struggles, working herself deeper and deeper into the seemingly endless barbs. It's possibly the clearest expression of the director's embedded hatred of women, or at least his desire to see them tortured and mutilated. He remains unrepentant about it. 'A woman in peril is emotionally affecting,' he told *Empire* back in 1997. 'A man simply isn't.'

And then there's Argento's masterful use of deep primary colours – the sets are bathed in garish red and green light (he acquired 1950s Technicolor stock to get the effect) giving the whole film a hallucinatory intensity. The score, composed by Argento and performed by his frequent collaborators, rock band Goblin, sounds as though Hell's demons rented a studio and decided to jam. Screams, wailings, hissing steam and some kind of diabolical didgeridoo are punctuated with the occasional distorted shriek of 'Witch!'. It's enough to loosen the bowels on its own.

Argento, who started out in gialli (pulp thrillers) has never really delivered on the promise, in horror terms at least, he showed with *Suspira*. There was a disappointing sequel, *Inferno*, in 1980, which despite a couple of the trademark set-pieces failed to attain the demented heights of inspiration. *Creepers* (aka *Phenomena* (1984)) has B-movie stalwart Donald Pleasance battling 'moths' while *The Stendhal Syndrome* (1996) was simply a step too far even for Argento fans with a graphic rape sequence, particularly tasteless since its victim was played by Argento's daughter Asia. Still, in spite of these shortcomings, as an appetiser to the thoroughly bizarre world of Italian horror, *Suspira* is the perfect antipasto. ★★★★★ **AS**

⑩ S.W.A.T. (2003)

Starring: *Samuel L. Jackson (Sgt. Dan 'Hondo' Harrelson), Colin Farrell (Jim Street), Michelle Rodriguez (Chris Sanchez), LL Cool J (Deacon 'Deke' Kay), Josh Charles (T.J. McCabe)*
Director: *Clark Johnson*
Screenwriters: *David Ayer, David McKenna, based on a story by Ron Mita, Jim McClain, characters by Robert Hamner*
12A/117 mins./Action/Crime/USA

Unfairly disgraced cop Jim Street is given the chance to redeem himself by joining an elite S.W.A.T. unit, headed up by hard-ass veteran Hondo Harrelson. Their first assignment: to keep an international drug kingpin in custody after he has publicly offered a cash reward for his breakout.

Even when he's wasn't dropping his trousers for the amusement of his co-stars on the set of *Alexander*, Colin Farrell knew how to keep busy. *S.W.A.T.* marked his sixth big screen release of 2003 (after *Daredevil*, *The Recruit*, *Phone Booth*, *Veronica Guerin* and *Intermission*) – entire continents have less of a cinema presence than he does.

Needless to say, the quality of his choices has been inconsistent, although Farrell can usually be relied upon to bring a spark to the bonfire. That's also true of *S.W.A.T.*, which has its roots in a little-known TV series from the 1970s and, after a get-the-team-together opening salvo, settles down into a story that's virtually episode-length in scope and running time.

All of the character shading has to fall into that early section and, even then, only Farrell and Jackson are offered adequate screen space to develop the bare bones of their stereotypes (the good cop misunderstood by his fellow officers, the anti-authority veteran who gets results). Elsewhere, Michelle Rodriguez and LL Cool J are 'female cop' and 'family cop' respectively.

As Farrell drives Jackson around recruiting members for the team, the Irishman provides the older actor with his best verbal sparring partner since John Travolta in *Pulp Fiction*. It's a welcome comedy interlude sandwiched between action sequences, and we could have done with a bit more, especially when such frivolity is sidelined and the serious task of finding a plot takes over.

The style change at this halfway point is tangible. In comes Elliot Goldenthal's score; out goes the jukebox selection of loud songs (from Jimi Hendrix to Linkin Park) that helped create the rockin' good mood. No longer is the banter light and funny; now it's time to knuckle down with a scowl and judge who in the team can be trusted with your life. Formula is now the name of the game, although a steady diet of stunts and shootouts ensures that the audience is never bored. ★★★ **AM**

SWEENEY! (1976)

Starring: *John Thaw (Detective Inspector Regan), Dennis Waterman (Detective Sergeant Carter), Barry Foster (McQueen), Ian Bannen (Baker), Colin Welland (Chadwick), Diane Keen (Bianca), Brain Glover (Mac), Lynda Bellingham (Janice)*
Director: *David Wickes*
Screenwriter: *Ranald Graham, from the TV series by Ian Kennedy Martin*
18/92 mins./Crime/Drama/UK

Detectives Regan and Carter investigate a weaselly image consultant who uses blackmail and murder to manipulate the world oil price.

This TV spin-off pushes the envelope on what Euston Films had been allowed to do on TV – call girls Lynda Bellingham and Diane Keen both get nude scenes and a hit man (dressed as a constable or a traffic warden) cuts loose with then-unprecedented bursts of automatic machine-gun fire to mow down guest stars.

Playing up the slash fiction subtext, Regan is discovered in sidekick Carter's bed at the beginning, though Carter is shacked up on a sofa with an air hostess to reassure you of their heterosexuality.

A typical Sweeney-like foiling of a wages blag ('you're nicked!') prompts Regan to muse that the stunt man villains were only after what a crooked accountant can make in minutes of fiddling. This line of thought leads to a higher level conspiracy than the TV series was used to and 1970s concerns about corruption in the oil business.

There's a lot of on-location action with Thaw hauling Keen around the city, on and off buses, ahead of the gunmen – though after Regan has shagged the posh tart, she gets gunned down and he only looks mildly upset.

The ending is 70s cynical as the Establishment are set to let the baddie off but Regan ensures he is killed by his own hit men, leading to the unusual finish of Carter turning angrily on his superior ('they didn't kill him, you did!').

Among the familiar British faces: Colin Welland (killed by a window cleaner), Joe Melia, Brian Glover, Ian Bannen and Nadim Sawalha.

Sweeney 2, a sequel, is more like a padded TV episode with extra swearing, but it's still value for money. ★★★ **KN**

SWEENEY TODD OR THE DEMON BARBER OF FLEET STREET (1936)

Starring: *Tod Slaughter (Sweeney Todd), Eve Lister (Johanna), Bruce Seton (Mack), Davina Craig (Nan), D.J. Williams (Stephen Oakley)*
Director: *George King*
Screenwriters: *Frederick Hayward, H.F. Maltby, from the play by George Dibdin-Pitt*
Unrated/66 mins./Horror/UK

Sweeney Todd keeps a barbershop in Olde Times London, cutting the throats of customers who have pilferable fortunes about their persons and disposing of the bodies through mysterious means which involve the pie-shop next door to his premises in Fleet street.

The jug-eared, moon-faced Tod Slaughter is one of the forgotten marvels of British cinema. For decades, he toured the provinces with his tiny theatre company, booed and hissed by audiences as he incarnated a succession of mid-Victorian villains in penny dreadful melodramas. Most of his vehicles were turned into lower-than-low-budget films and remain astonishingly entertaining when chanced upon on late-night television.

Sweeney Todd affords him the chance to roll his eyes in one of his greatest roles – 'polishing off' lonely, wealthy customers by tipping his special chair so they fall into a basement where he can cut their throats, turning the corpses over to his confederate Mrs. Lovat (Stella Rho), who keeps the pie-shop next door, for disposal. The famous cannibal theme is played in a way that gets round the censors – the question of what happens to the corpses is raised several times, often as supporting customers are cheerfully tucking into tasty pies, but the film never solves the mystery, leaving audiences to leap to the obvious conclusion.

This fiendish Todd has a wonderfully archetypal death as fire breaks out in his shop and he plunges through his own trap-door to a suitably infernal fate.

Much of the fun of Slaughter's films comes from the sheer number of crimes the villain manages to commit in their brief running time – no other screen baddie was as lecherous, cowardly, hypocritical, sadistic, money-grubbing, vindictive and murderous as Slaughter. Also recommended: *Maria Marten, The Face at the Window, The Crimes of Stephen Hawke, Sexton Blake vs the Hooded Terror*. ★★★ **KN**

SWEET AND LOWDOWN (1999)

Starring: *Sean Penn (Emmet Ray), Samantha Morton (Hattie), Uma Thurman (Blance), Brian Markinson (Bill Shields), Anthony LaPaglia (Al Torrio)*
Director: *Woody Allen*
Screenwriter: *Woody Allen*
PG/91 mins./Comedy/Drama/Music/USA

A faux biography of jazz guitarist Emmet Ray, constructed through a string of outrageous gags, gigs and misbehavin'.

Woody Allen's most delightful film of the 90s – and he's made some real treats in that time – takes the form of an anecdotal 'biopic' which, in creating a fictional musician as its subject, celebrates music and all the maniacs who make it best through a string of outrageous gags, gigs and misbehaving.

Jazz guitarist Emmet Ray may not be real, but he is so painfully and hilariously truthful that he is in many ways every flamboyant, iconic tune peddler from Mozart to Madonna. Certainly he's an amalgam of any number of jazzers, and Penn – Oscar-nominated – captures the spirit just brilliantly. His Emmet is colourful, pathetic, self-obsessed, a feckless, reckless monster without even being aware of it; and crucially, if amazingly, endearing. He also presents a credible guitarist, faking his way through a cleverly used vintage songbook which includes gems by Duke Ellington and Emmet's idol, Django Reinhardt.

Also superb is Samantha Morton, whose speechless performance (which also brought her an Oscar nomination) as the waifish, adoring, mute little laundress who endures Emmet's abuse, is staggeringly expressive, touching and hits rib-tickling heights when Hattie gets a shot at the big screen in a silent movie. Uma Thurman is straight out of F. Scott Fitzgerald here, well-suited to the glamour of a madcap sophisticate toying with dangerous men.

The insertion of documentary-style interviews (with Allen himself and other jazz buffs) suggests that Emmet's self-inflicted chaos is running out of steam, but the device pays off when the narrators' conflicting accounts of an infamous 'Emmet and the gangster' incident set up three wildly different, marvellously choreographed versions of the anecdote. ★★★★ **AE**

⊙ SWEET CHARITY (1969)

Starring: *Shirley MacLaine (Charity Hope Valentine), Sammy Davis Jr. (Big Daddy), Ricardo Montalban (Vittorio Vitale), John McMartin (Oscar Lindquist), Chita Rivera (Nickie), Paula Kelly (Helene), Stubby Kaye (Herman), Dante D'Paulo (Charlie)*
Director: *Bob Fosse*
Screenwriter: *Peter Stone, based on the play by Neil Simon, Cy Coleman, Dorothy Fields, adapted from the screenplay Notti Di Cabiria by Federico Fellini, Tullio Ponelli, Ennio Flaiano*
PG/157 mins./Musical/USA

Ditched by her hoodlum boyfriend Charlie and spurned by slumming movie star Vittorio Vitale, Charity Hope Valentine finds unexpected happiness with insurance actuary Oscar Lindquist until he discovers that she's a hostess at the Fandango Ballroom and calls off their wedding.

Bob Fosse had given Shirley MacLaine her big break in the mid-1950s by promoting her to be Carol Haney's understudy in the Broadway version of *The Pajama Game*. So, when she learned that the head of Universal Studios, Lew Wasserman, was looking for a project to cash in on the musical boom following *The Sound of Music*, MacLaine suggested Neil Simon's adaptation of Federico Fellini's 1957 classic, *Le Notti di Cabiria*, which Fosse had steered through 608 performances in New York.

But while Wasserman was prepared to take a chance on Fosse directing his first feature, he insisted on Fosse's wife-star Gwen Verdon stepping down in favour of MacLaine, who was desperate to prove that she was capable of better things than *Can-Can* and *What a Way to Go!*. Having already lost the former to MacLaine, Verdon passed with good grace and agreed to coach her through the demanding dance routines. However, MacLaine lacked Verdon's technique and grace and she struggled to hold her own alongside Ballroom buddies Paula Kelly and Chita Rivera, although she was scarcely helped by Fosse's angulated postures, typically fussy business with props and his excessive use of zoom lenses and gimmicky camera moves that were intended to catch the viewer up in the kinetic energy of the choreography.

Cy Coleman and Dorothy Fields's score held up well, with 'Hey, Big Spender!' and 'If My Friends Could See Me Now' being the standouts, while Stubby Kaye's 'I Always Cry at Weddings' and Sammy Davis Jr.'s 'The Rhythm of Life' provided diverting asides. But time often hung heavy during the 157-minute running time, which was eventually trimmed after a disappointing roadshow release.

Many of the problems lay in MacLaine's performance, which was brassy and needy and utterly devoid of the vulnerable charm that had made Giulietta Masina's screen original both adorable and authentic. Moreover, falling between the vibrant realism of *West Side Story* and the period pizzazz of *Hello, Dolly!*, *Sweet Charity* also failed to capture the distinctive Big Apple atmosphere and it returned only $4 million on a $20 million outlay. ★★★ **DP**

⊙ THE SWEET HEREAFTER (1997)

Starring: *Ian Holm (Mitchell), Caerthan Banks (Zoe), Sarah Polley (Nicole), Tom McCamus (Sam), Gabrielle Rose (Dolores)*
Director: *Atom Egoyan*
Screenwriter: *Atom Egoyan, based on the novel by Russell Banks*
15/107 mins./Drama/Canada

The death of 14 school children in a bus accident has repercussions for the close-knit Canadian community in which they live and things only get worse when a lawyer arrives hoping to persuade the parents to sue those responsible.

This is a clear development of themes that Canada's third-weirdest auteur (after David Cronenberg and Guy Maddin) has been working in *The Adjustor* and *Exotica*.

The plot unfolds in several interleaved time periods, and a few dizzying revelations and connections might make you want to go back and see it again to confirm what you've been led to suspect. Lawyer Mitchell Stephens arrives in a small town in British Columbia. His aim is to get the parents of children killed in a schoolbus accident to retain him in suits against those responsible.

It is at once apparent that Stephens, suffering through his own parental trauma, is as much concerned with sorting out his own demons as stirring up those of the town. We flash back to the days before the accident, the gradual recovery afterwards and Stephens' flight north, learning more and more about the people involved in the knot of tragedy. The focus slowly shifts from the lawyer to Nicole, a wheelchair-bound teenage survivor of the disaster, as she comes to a decision about how best she can cope with her grief and guilt.

An evocative parallel with The Pied Piper underlines a more complex set of emotions than the cinema is usually keen on depicting. It's a tactfully acted film, beautifully shot in snowy widescreen, subtly scripted and directed with a rare touch. The subject is as painful as it is possible to imagine, but the treatment, while never preachy or affected, is humane, insightful and extremely moving. ★★★★★ **KN**

⊙ SWEET HOME ALABAMA (2002)

Starring: *Reese Witherspoon (Melanie Smooter), Josh Lucas (Jake Perry), Patrick Dempsey (Andrew Hennings), Candice Bergen (Mayor Kate Hennings), Mary Kay Place (Pearl Smooter)*
Director: *Andy Tennat*
Screenwriter: *C. Jay Cox, based on a story by Douglas J. Eboch*
12/104 mins./Comedy/Romance/USA

New York fashion designer Melanie Carmichael has the world at her feet – even the mayor's son has just proposed to her. But before she can tie the knot, Melanie must return to her Southern roots. And, back home in Alabama, there are more than a few skeletons in amongst the sweet potato pies.

Sweet Home Alabama raked in a record-breaking $35 million in its opening weekend, and judged on opening weekends, Reese is now officially bigger than Julia.The $20 million pay cheque is now in the post, but *Sweet Home Alabama* proves that she's worth every last cent.

Few actresses of Witherspoon's generation could so successfully grab hold of the darker currents beneath this slight fairy-tale's surface and pull it upstream against a tide of rom-com clichés. It's the dramatic aspects of this feel-good movie that set it apart. Before it settles down snugly into a formulaic final act, the film visits areas of character psychology where your typical Hollywood fluff fears to tread.

It starts off in make-believe mode, with cute and sparky Melanie wowing the New York fashion elite and indulging in romantic overload as the mayor's son, Andrew, proposes to her in Tiffany's, of all places. Then, with a nod to Witherspoon's previous box office clout, the story takes on a *Legally Blonde* form, as the snooty city sophisticate goes on a fish-out-of-water trip back to her small-town Southern roots.

All the comedy contrasts you'd expect are present and correct. But, as Melanie's checked-shirt past starts to show through the cracks of her designer-clad present, there's more on offer here than first meets the eye. Why exactly has Melanie reinvented herself? Why is she so ashamed of her loving family? Isn't she – now that we're scrutinising her more closely – rather selfish, rude and condescending? In other words, she's not the lightweight heroine who floats through other romantic comedies. And so, as both Melanie and the audience come to realise that the Manhattan world she has created for herself is indeed a fantasy land that's at odds with the person she really is, it takes an actress of Witherspoon's calibre to keep us on her side.

TOP 10 Movie Insults

1 **'Get your stinkin' paws off me, you damn dirty ape!' (Charlton Heston, *Planet of the Apes*)**

2 **'You are the lowest form of life on Earth. You are not even human, fucking beings. You are nothing but unorganized grabastic pieces of amphibian shit.' (Gunnery Sergeant Hartman, *Full Metal Jacket*)**

3 **'He needs a blow-job more than any white man in history.' (Adrian Cronauer about Sgt. Dickerson, *Good Morning Vietnam*)**

4 **'I fart in your general direction. Your mother was a hamster and your father smelled of elderberries.' (French knight, *Monty Python and the Holy Grail*)**

5 **'You're semi-evil. You're quasi-evil. You're the margarine of evil. You're the Diet Coke of evil, just one calorie, not evil enough.' (Dr Evil to Scott Evil, *Austin Powers 2: The Spy Who Shagged Me*)**

6 **'You're a strange, sad little man – you have my pity.' (Buzz Lightyear, *Toy Story*)**

7 **'Why, you stuck up, half-witted, scruffy-looking nerf-herder.' (Princess Leia, *The Empire Strikes Back*)**

8 **'You're dumb, you're ugly – that's the truth of you.' (Billy Bathgate, *Billy Bathgate*)**

9 **'You're a neo-Maxi zoom dweebie!' (John Bender, *The Breakfast Club*)**

10 **'What is your malfunction, you fat barrel of monkeyspunk?' (Officer Hadley, *The Shawshank Redemption*)**

S

That cute girl-next-door persona is just the bait: she really does have the dramatic ability to guide us through the character's less appealing points and towards a happy ending. On the way, unfortunately, we're forced to travel roads inhabited by Southern stereotypes, cheesy sob scenes and a couple of turnarounds (Dempsey's Andrew especially) that seem to be more plot-driven than character-credible. It's hardly a documentary, but you get the feeling that this particular homely Southern scene has had the more troubling bits airbrushed out. Where are the black faces? And would these good ol' boys really accept the unexpected 'outing' of one of their own quite so readily?

So, despite Witherspoon's best efforts (and those of a decent supporting cast, particularly Josh Lucas as her Southern beau and Ethan Embry as her abandoned best friend), there's not enough here to fulfil an across-the-boards crowd. Fans of the rom-com, however, should be ready to book their place at My Big Fat Redneck Wedding. ★★★ **AM**

THE SWEET SMELL OF SUCCESS (1957)

Starring: *Burt Lancaster (J.J. Hunsecker), Tony Curtis (Sidney Falco), Susan Harrison (Susan Hunsecker), Martin Milner (Steve Dallas), Sam Levene (Frank D'Angelo)*
Director: *Alexander Mackendrick*
Screenwriters: *Clifford Odets, Ernest Lehman, based on the novelette by Ernest Lehman*
PG/92 mins./Drama/USA

Broadway. All powerful journalist J.J. Hunsecker has cut press agent Sidney Falco out of his column after Sidney has failed to break up a relationship between J.J.'s beloved sister and a musician. Luckily, Sidney has a plan; a plan involving blackmail.

Drag a lungful of Alexander Mackendrick's 1957 hymn to Manhattan sleaze and you can almost taste the city. As J.J. Hunsecker, gossip columnist and proto-shock jock remarks: 'I love this dirty town'. The irony is that Mackendrick, the Scottish director of Ealing comedies *Whisky Galore* and *The Man In The White Suit* was actually a fish out of water, this career high marking his first American gig. And if Mackendrick's 1955 classic, *The Ladykillers*, had served notice that the director was capable of twisted satire, nothing could quite prepare the audience for this shock to the senses.

One of the darkest films ever to emerge from Hollywood, no modern mainstream movie could dare boast an ending as bleak or a subtext as sexually, socially and politically provocative as the one on display here. And this is a movie starring two reliable studio players: all-American Burt Lancaster and pretty boy Tony Curtis. Certainly the hucking and jiving publicist, Sidney Falco, would inspire Curtis to consistently break his straight studio image, and Lancaster's formidable J.J. Hunsecker would send him towards an Oscar for *Elmer Gantry*, but neither would ever be better than they are here.

The natural meeting point of Howard Hawks and Orson Welles, *Success* takes the scattershot patter of screwball comedy (the arsenic-laced screenplay comes courtesy of blacklisted playwright Clifford Odets and prolific screenwriter Ernest Lehman) and grafts it onto a stylised melodrama of moral turpitude. Stand back for some of the most pointed barbs in movie history. Sit up close for the delicious depth of James Wong Howe's photography and the fat, juicy jazz score by Elmer Bernstein. ★★★★★ **CK**

THE SWIMMER (1968)

Starring: *Burt Lancaster (Ned Merrill), Janet Landgard (Julie Ann Hooper), Janice Rule (Shirley Abbot), Tony Bickley (Donald Westerhazy), Marge Champion (Peggy Forsburgh), Nancy Cushman (Mrs. Halloran), Bill Fiore (Howie Hunsacker)*
Director: *Frank Perry*
Screenwriters: *Eleanor Perry, based on story by John Cheever*
PG/95 mins./Drama/USA

Connecticut. Ned Merrill drops into a friend's pool for a dip, then works out that he can swim home using his neighbour's pools. As he gets nearer his 'house on the hill', it becomes obvious that there's something seriously wrong with Ned's apparently ideal life.

An enigmatic, poetic, disturbing, interestingly pretentious 1968 fable from a John Cheever story, this has Burt Lancaster, naked but for Speedo trunks, 'swimming home' via a river of backyard pools, with spells of 'portage' through the woods in between. With each pool, he encounters different people from his past and the apparent perfection expected at the end of the swim seems more in doubt.

It's a memorable premise, and sets up a series of elliptical scenes which drop hints about the state of things without coming out and saying anything. Lancaster shows off his ageing physique and crawls inside his cracking-up character, playing off a series of friendly, hostile, naïve, lost, hard-bitten, cruel or kindly folks, who wrongly assume he's back on track after a collapse, are still upset with him after unspecified wrongs, react with muted concern as he talks about the way things used to be as if all was still well, turn viciously on him as a deadbeat or sympathise with his plight but can't do anything to help.

Standing around pools are the likes of Kim Hunter, Diana Muldaur, Joan Rivers (a *young* Joan Rivers!), Bernie Hamilton, Gower Champion and House Peters. Director Frank Perry – assisted by an uncredited Sydney Pollack, who stepped in to handle a scene between Ned and a former mistress (Janice Rule) inserted in order to add *some* explanation – finds sylvan beauties and suburban crassness along the way, leading to an oblique but powerful homecoming finish. Incidentally, *Falling Down* is what you'd get if you remade *The Swimmer* with guns and action scenes. ★★★★ **KN**

SWIMMING WITH SHARKS (1994)

Starring: *Kevin Spacey (Buddy Ackerman), Frank Whaley (Guy), Michelle Forbes (Dawn Lockard), Benicio Del Toro (Rex), T.E. Russell (Foster Kane)*
Director: *George Huang*
Screenwriter: *George Huang*
15/89 mins./Comedy/Drama/USA

A Hollywood studio vice president terrorises his lowly film school graduate assistant, only to find Guy's talent and an ingenious script place him is the position of humiliation all too familiar to his assistant.

This darkly funny blend of film industry foibles and office politics beggars the question: how much longer can Kevin Spacey get away with playing the bad guy? On the strength of this performance, as the kind of seething, temperamental, lecherous movie mogul any sane person would cross the street to avoid, let's hope it's for as long as he bloody well likes.

Spacey is Buddy Ackerman, the studio vice president and archetypal boss from hell. The object of his venom is Guy, a naïve film school graduate who lands the unenviable job of his assistant. On the surface his new employer is a likeable professional chap who charms the pants (literally) off every would-be actress who flits past his office door, but underneath it all Guy endures public humiliation, unreasonable demands and executive toys flying in the general direction of his head with gay abandon. That is until a spot of underhand one-upmanship involving a not unattractive producer, a brilliant script, and an equally inspired idea of Guy's causes him to crack, with the ensuing revenge far from sweet.

While comparisons with *The Player* are inevitable; the success of Huang's movie hinges more on its portrayal of the work ethic than anything else, although the setting does pave the way for some gleeful film industry parody ('Don't ever say that! He's just ... unavailable!' barks Spacey upon being informed by his minion that David Lean is, in fact, dead). However, it's the office-based scenes that provide the film's sharpest barbs. Where the film falters is in the revenge sequences. Whaley does a good job of portraying Guy as a hapless individual stretched to breaking point, but the treatment he metes out seems just a little too extreme, while the ambiguous ending dents the satisfaction. Nonetheless, this is a bold, enormously enjoyable effort, by turns both hilarious and disturbing. ★★★★ **CW**

SWINGERS (1996)

Starring: *Jon Favreau (Mike Peters), Vince Vaughn (Trent Walker), Ron Livingston (Rob), Patrick Van Horn (Sue), Alex Desert (Charles)*
Director: *Doug Liman*
Screenwriters: *Jon Favreau*
15/92 mins./Comedy/Drama/USA

Mike has recently relocated to Hollywood and his difficulties trying to find his way in the tough town, coupled with a break-up he just can't seem to get over, has prompted his couch-potato mates to leave their couches and potatoes behind for one special mission – to get Mike laid.

Just like *Clerks*, *Swingers* is a rough diamond where the occasional touch of poor lighting or shaky camera work genuinely adds to the charm. What carries it furthest, however, from a budget sheet not far above a decent wedding video to the realms of box office kerching!-dom is a script delivered like manna from the god of guffaws up in comedy heaven.

Said script was written by former stand-up comedian Favreau who also co-produced and stars as Mike, recently relocated to Hollywood from New York and trying forlornly to get work as a comic and get over a relationship that ended six months ago. It's hard to tell which he's making a bigger hash of, but as all his mates are struggling similarly to be actors, they all switch their focus to cheering him up by, er, trying to get him laid. First to try is Trent (Vaughn, who could talk the dinos in *The Lost World* into submission using half his lines from *Swingers*) on a road-trip to Vegas that exposes both of them as something less than highrollers, and Mike as an all but lost cause in the love life department. And so the action returns to Hollywood where 'swinger' friends Rob, a boy named Sue and Charles cruise the clubs and bars telling each other – in Trent's words – that they 'are so money' and trying it on with all the 'beautiful babies' they meet.

Given a budget that had stretched to big stars, designer suits and feng-shui'd apartments, this might have been a very different movie. But with a cast that consists of mainly (then) sitcom actors as pizza-eating, beer-drinking Ordinary Joes who play video hockey and drive 'piece of shit' cars, first-time feature director Liman has made a film as charming as it is hilarious. Add to that an answerphone sketch to die for, brilliant pastiches of both *Reservoir Dogs* and *GoodFellas* plus the worst version of 'Staying Alive' known to man and *Swingers* emerges as an unmissable Men Behaving Sadly for wannabe lovers everywhere. ★★★★ **NJ**

SYLVIA SCARLETT (1935)

Starring: *Katharine Hepburn (Sylvia Scarlett), Cary Grant (Jimmy Monkley), Brian Aherne (Michael Fane), Edmund Gwenn (Henry)*
Director: *George Cukor*
Screenwriters: *Gladys Unger, John Collier, Moertimer Offner, based on the novel by Compton MacKenzie*
U/95 mins./Comedy/USA

Sylvia Scarlett disguises herself as a man on fleeing France with her con man father, Henry. They hook up with rascal Jimmy Monkley on the ferry and embark on a series of adventures that culminate in her falling for preening artist, Michael Fane.

A cult favourite among gay and lesbian audiences, George Cukor's adaptation of Compton Mackenzie's picaresque novel was a critical and commercial disaster. Yet he retained an inordinate fondness for it, even though its failure persuaded him against undertaking anything as contentious and unconventional for another two decades. Moreover, Katharine Hepburn later considered the premiere among her triumphs, as she not only discovered a woman in a dead faint in the washroom whom she presumed had lost the will to live because of the film's badness, but when she and Cukor offered to make a picture for free in recompense, RKO producer Pandro S. Berman opined that he never wanted to work with either of them again.

Only Cary Grant emerged from the calamity with any credit and that was, ironically, because he had been playing Archie Leach rather than the Hollywood palimpsest that he had created for himself. The Cornish setting not only returned him to his West Country roots (albeit on Californian location), but he also got to parade the vaudeville skills that had earned him his passage across the Atlantic in 1920.

But while Grant revelled in the crafty duplicity that was later said to have been an inspiration for Harry Lime in *The Third Man*, Hepburn was declared 'box-office poison' for a cross-dressing display that confused and disconcerted in equal measures.

She invested the part of Sylvia/Sylvester with a Peter Pan puckishness that was wholly in keeping with both the fact that he was usually played by an actress in drag and with her own regard for J.M. Barrie (having already appeared in two adaptations of his works, *The Little Minister*, 1934 and *Quality Street*, 1935). But few were sure how to take either her blend of wit and melancholy or her attractiveness to both the maid who wanted to give Sylvester a moustache and a kiss and to Brian Aherne's narcissistic artist, who no longer finds him a fascinating subject once he knows that he's a she. Clearly, it was one thing to be a transvestite in Shakespeare, but in stylised reality ... ★★★ **DP**

SYMPATHY FOR MR VENGEANCE (2002)

Starring: *Song Kang-ho (Park Dong-jin), Shin Ha-kyn (Ryu), Bae Doo-na (Cha Yeong-mi), Lim Ji-eun (Ryu's sister)*
Director: *Park Chan-wook*
Screenwriters: *Lee Jae-sun, Lee Mu-yeong, Lee Yong-jong, Park Chan-wook*
18/121 mins./Action/Thriller/South Korea

Deaf mute Ryu kidnaps the young daughter of his ex-employer Park to finance a kidney operation for his sister. However, the sister commits suicide and the child accidentally drowns. The bereaved father sets out for revenge.

In this contemplative yet violent Korean thriller, the plot is constructed around the proposition that 'things get worse' as circumstances drive basically decent folk to ever-more ghastly acts.

The first half consists of appalling injustices, as the decent Ryu is ripped off by black market organ transplanters who take one of his kidneys but neglect to hand one over in return and dump him naked in the middle of nowhere. Then, the kidnap goes wrong and tycoon Park becomes as righteously vengeance-crazed as Ryu – the self-made engineer strips himself of his fortune and sets out to use electrical torture gadgets and police contacts to pursue Ryu, who is himself after the evil organleggers.

With twinned avengers on the loose, both justified yet culpable, the film inevitably winds up with more blood in the river as the antagonists finally face off, each recognising kinship with the other, and a previously-mythical-seeming terrorist group appear to avenge *another* incidental murder. Park Chan-wook's film has a rep for ultra-violence which is more down to its harsh worldview than actual gore (though severed Achilles tendons bleeding dry in the river are memorable).

Music Video Directors Turned Filmmakers

TOP 10

Best Video

1. **David Fincher (*Fight Club, Seven*) 'Janie's Got A Gun' (Aerosmith)**
2. **Spike Jonze (*Adaptation, Being John Malkovich*) 'Praise Me' (Fat Boy Slim)**
3. **Michel Gondry (*Eternal Sunshine of the Spotless Mind*) 'Human Behaviour' (Björk)**
4. **Lasse Hallstrom (*Chocolat, Cider House Rules*) 'Dancing Queen' (Abba)**
5. **Mark Romanek (*One Hour Photo*) 'Hurt' (Johnny Cash)**
6. **Mark Pellington (*Arlington Road*) 'Best Of You' (Foo Fighters)**
7. **Brett Ratner (*Red Dragon, X-Men: The Last Stand*) 'Beautiful Stranger' (Madonna)**
8. **F. Gary Gray (*The Italian Job, Be Cool*) 'Waterfalls' (TLC)**
9. **Jonathan Glazer (*Sexy Beast*) 'Radiohead' (Karma Police)**
10. **McG (*Charlie's Angels*) 'Walking On The Sun' (Smashmouth)**

A poised, mostly effective picture, it owes as much to Jean Renoir ('everybody has their reasons') as Takeshi Miike. The scenes with the little girl, a true innocent who plays with her kidnappers, have a warmth which belies the cruelty of the plot turns, while the Jacobean parade-of-corpses plot winds through characters who are all more righteous than the acts they commit. The first of Park Chan-wook's 'vengeance trilogy' followed by *Oldboy* and *Sympathy for Lady Vengeance*. ★★★ **KN**

SYRIANA (2005)

Starring: *George Clooney (Bob Barnes), Christopher Plummer (Dean Whiting), Chris Cooper (Jimmy Pope), Matt Damon (Bryan Woodman), Amanda Peet (Julie Woodman)*
Director: *Stephen Gaghan*
Screenwriter: *Stephen Gaghan, suggested by the book* See No Evil: The True Story of a Ground Soldier in the CIA's War on Terror *by Robert Baer)*
15/126 mins./Drama/Politics/Thriller/USA

Awards: *Academy Awards – Best Supporting Actor (George Clooney), Golden Globes – Best Supporting Actor (George Clooney)*

US access to dwindling Middle East oil resources is a multi-billion-dollar problem that affects everyone: financial brokers, CIA officers, corporate lawyers, and even poor Pakistani immigrants like Wasim Khan who travel to Saudi Arabia seeking work, and find only the teachings of radical Islam . . .

When Steven Soderbergh and George Clooney set up their Section 8 production company in 2000, they took as their benchmark American cinema from 1964 to 1976, specifically the comparatively overlooked output of studio stalwarts Sydney Pollack, Alan J. Pakula and Sidney Lumet. Mainstream movies like *All The President's Men, Three Days Of The Condor* and *Network* were assembled according to evergreen genre guidelines, and yet at the same time were daring liberal commentaries on Nixon's America, pictures that could not have emerged at any other time.

Until recently, Section 8's mission statement has been little more than a theoretical gold standard, the sort of lofty promise that allows two well-heeled insiders to dabble in offbeat fare like *Far From Heaven*. However, with the release of Stephen Gaghan's audacious *Syriana*, hard on the heels of Clooney's own stealth weapon *Good Night, And Good Luck*, it's become clear that the gold standard is no longer hypothetical. The world has shifted significantly in the last few years and it's no longer artistic ideals that America urgently requires, but idealistic artists.

Although *Syriana* shares DNA with the great 70s conspiracy thrillers and a common purpose with Clooney's companion picture *Good Night*, the movie it's most clearly patterned after is Steven Soderbergh's *Traffic*, which won Gaghan a Best Adapted Screenplay Oscar in 2001. Like the drug trade *Traffic* carefully picked apart, *Syriana* tackles a BIG subject – US reliance on foreign oil – by weaving together small stories. By entangling flawed individuals at every level of a complex network, each side of the debate is given a recognisable face.

Of the various faces on show, Clooney's beard-and-bloat disguise has unsurprisingly hogged the acting plaudits, but the actor puts in an unselfish producer's performance here; his low-key CIA veteran is visibly uncomfortable on centre stage. Indeed, each of the four main protagonists are unassuming bit-players who must tap hitherto unseen resources if they are to ever shape their destiny. Scenery-chewing is left to the distinguished supporting cast, notably the redoubtable trio of Christopher Plummer, Chris Cooper and William Hurt, plus two faces familiar from British TV – Mark Strong and Alexander Siddig, as a terrorist-for-hire and idealistic prince respectively.

As the story ranges over three continents and the faces multiply, there's much to admire and even more to absorb in every scene. However, the problem with this kind of narrative tapestry is that the audience is offered heaps of thread and asked to take on faith the grand design.

For much of the opening hour it remains hard to divine anything more than thematic tissue connecting the storylines, and many will pine for the narrative clarity Soderbergh's experience as editor and cinematographer brought to the superior *Traffic*.

Still, as soon as the various protagonists attempt to take charge of their own fate, the net suddenly draws tighter and the stories converge in both surprising and tragically predictable ways. As the movie accelerates into a breathless final act, salient details are left behind (none of the personal particulars amount to anything significant), and the narrative never quite justifies the roots-of-terror thread that is central to Gaghan's thesis, but by the time you can recall the forgotten faces the momentum is irresistible, the climax shattering. ★★★★ **CK**

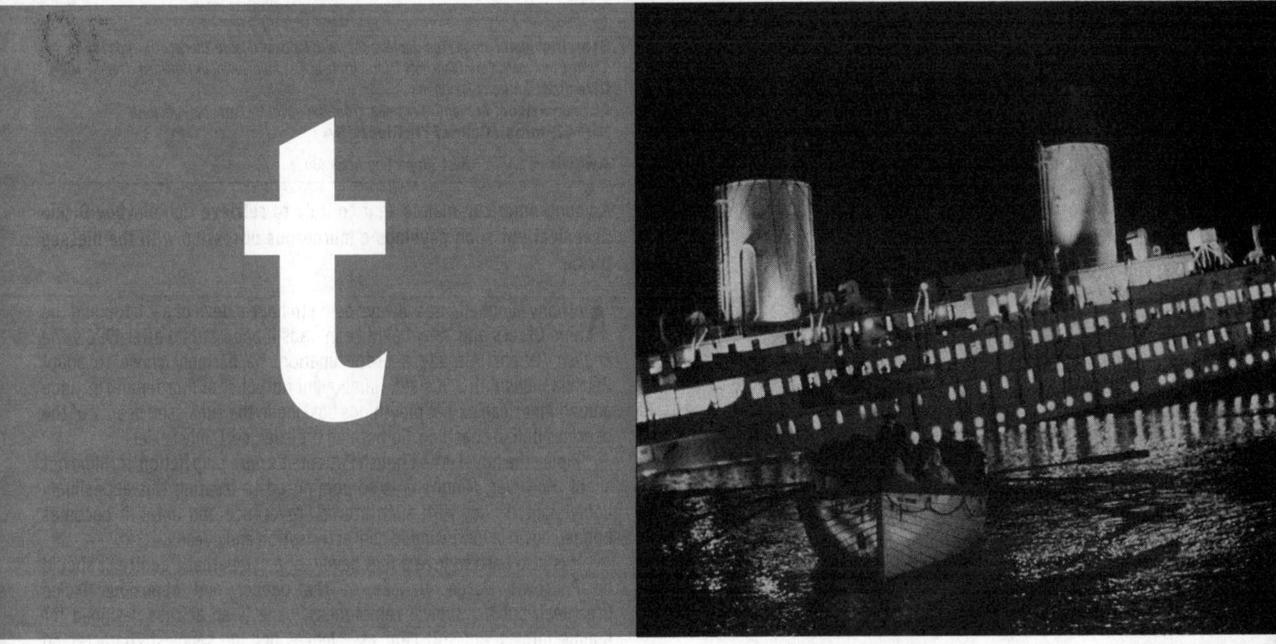

THE TAILOR OF PANAMA (2001)

Starring: *Pierce Brosnan (Andrew 'Andy' Osnard), Geoffrey Rush (Harold 'Harry' Pendel), Jamie Lee Curtis (Louisa Pendel), Catherine McCormack (Francesca Pendel), Daniel Radcliffe (Mark Pendel)*
Director: *John Boorman*
Screenwriters: *Andrew Davies, John le Carré, John Boorman, based on the novel by John le Carré*
15/105 mins./Spy/Drama/USA/Ireland

Corrupt spy Andrew Osnard is stationed in Panama to keep an eye on the political rumblings over the canal. There, he homes in on Harry Pendel, tailor to government officials and rebels alike, a big-hearted man with a dubious past of his own. Both begin to manipulate each other, creating a distortion that has repercussions right the way up to the wings of NATO.

Boorman, once a director of some note, is off the pace with this study of the insidious nature of the spying game. Taking one of the master (le Carré)'s more recent novels and working in the richly lurid setting of Central America with a couple of top-notch actors, could have presented him with strong possibilities. Yet the film, for all its earnestness, snaky comedy, and would-be intelligence, never manages any real fizz.

Amongst all the clandestine goings-on, Brosnan is the stand-out, comfortably subverting his Bond image to create an odious but alluring egotist, a devil always on the make. The opening shot has him standing in the familiar MI6 headquarters, but within a moment the loose attitude, looser neck tie and listless slouch tell you this man is light years from 007. Rush doggedly invests Pendel and his secrets with a nervy compassion, a man swamped by his own illusions.

In a bizarre effort to insert the book's internal dialogue, Harold Pinter keeps popping up as Pendel's ghostly conscience. The females, however, are mere sideshows: McCormack, as a stuck-up British diplomat, is simply a device to reveal Osnard's predatory skills, while Lee Curtis, as Pendel's devoted wife, feels underdeveloped as the moral centre of the film.

Boorman has tonal problems throughout, veering clumsily from quasi-comedy to thriller to an offbeam character study of fractured psyches (a theme typical of the author). It's hard to register just what the film is getting at.

Le Carré's books are just too involved and complex to translate satisfyingly to film – they fit the TV serial with aplomb – for squashing all the detail of character and plot into two hours makes for a muddled and inaccessible movie.

Action scenes are at a premium (just a bit of a chase at the close) and there's lots of tense dialogue, but not enough to explain the sudden shifts in behaviour. There's too much talent on show not to garner a few sturdy moments, hinting at what could have been, but you're too busy deciphering the muddle of a plot to soak them up. ★★ IN

TAKE THE MONEY AND RUN (1969)

Starring: *Woody Allen (Virgil Starkwell), Janet Margolin (Louise), Marcel Hillaire (Fritz), Jacqueline Hyde (Miss Blaire), Lonny Chapman (Jake), Jan Merlin (Al), James Anderson (Chain Gang Warden), Howard Storm (Fred) Mark Gordon (Vince)*
Director: *Woody Allen*
Screenwriters: *Woody Allen, Mickey Rose*
PG/85 mins./Comedy/Crime/USA

The life and crimes of Virgil Starkwell, a petty hoodlum who finds love with a laundress, Louise, in between botched blags and stints on a chain gang.

Following *Casino Royale*, United Artists offered Woody Allen the chance to make his directorial debut, providing he did it in Britain, in black and white and for $750,000. There was even talk of a collaboration with Jerry Lewis before Allen persuaded Charles H. Joffe and Jack Rollins to produce. Keen to avoid actorly ego and producotial interference, Allen turned the project into something of a one-man operation, although Mickey Rose co-wrote the screenplay, which was based on the *Naked City* type of TV show. But it was only after the picture wrapped that any problems became apparent.

Allen's preparation was reasonably thorough. Having screened a documentary on Eleanor Roosevelt to gauge the narrative and visual style of a newsreel, he studied such features as Mervyn LeRoy's *I Am A Fugitive From A Chain Gang*, Jean-Luc Godard's *Vivre Sa Vie*, Michelangelo Antonioni's Blow-Up and Bo Widerberg's *Elvira Madigan*. He also borrowed the escape episode from Stanley Kramer's *The Defiant Ones* and the blaze of bullets finale from *Bonnie And Clyde*, whose director, Arthur Penn, Allen consulted before production began.

Shooting also went smoothly enough. But test audiences found the picture wholly unfunny and Ralph Rosenblum was called in to do a similar salvage job to the one he had just performed on William Friedkin's *The Night They Raided Minsky's*. With Allen on tour with the stage version of *Play It Again, Sam*, Rosenblum had a freeish hand to reconstruct the essentially sketch-like material into a coherent casebook narrative and set-pieces like the 'gub' bank robbery and the cello playing in a marching band found their place alongside running gags like the smashing of Virgil's glasses. Rosenblum even suggested the use of New Orleans jazz on the soundtrack (which was supplemented by Marvin Hamlisch interludes), which became a staple of future Allen projects.

Yet still only two prints were struck and it took Vincent Canby's *New York Times* review to secure the film an audience. Even then, seven years were to elapse before the film turned a profit on its $1.53 million budget. **★★★ DP**

THE TAKING OF PELHAM ONE TWO THREE (1974)

Starring: *Walter Matthau (Lt. Garber), Robert Shaw (Blue), Martin Balsam (Green), Hector Elizondo (Grey), Earl Hindman (Brown), James Broderick (Denny Doyle), Dick O'Neil (Corell), Lee Wallace (the Mayor), Tom Pedi (Caz Dolowicz)*
Director: *Joseph Sargent*
Screenwriter: *Peter Stone based on the novel by John Godey*
15/104 mins./Crime/USA

A group of criminals take a New York subway train hostage and make a brutal demand: the city pay $1 million in ransom within one hour or they will begin killing the passengers for every minute they are late. It is up to veteran detective Lt. Garber to undertake the difficult negotiations.

The kind of gritty, relentless thriller that could only come from the 70s, Joseph Sargent's subway suspenser is a hardboiled treat. A culturally influential flick (Quentin Tarantino would later nick the criminals using colours as codenames gambit for *Reservoir Dogs*; the Beastie Boys reference it in the song 'Sure Shot'), it mixes traditional action licks, cat and mouse mindgames, political satire, male camaraderie and a decidedly Noo Yawk sensibility (all wrapped up in David Shire's terrific blaxploitation-esque score) into a genre movie, without ever foregoing respect for the audiences intelligences.

Based on John Godey's potboiler, Sargent plays out the premise of a subway hold up with a logical, ruthless efficiency, creating the set-up in crisp clean tones (as we meet Garber, he is giving a delegation from the Tokyo subway system a guided tour of the control centre, imparting lots of knowledge the audience will need later) and then wringing out the hostage crisis for every drop of tension. The core relationship of the film, between Shaw's cold-eyed crim and Matthau's wisecracking cop, is terrifically etched, especially considering it is conducted entirely over the radio. Shaw's Blue, a former Brit Army colonel and mercenary, is another one of the actor's gallery of terrific villains, coolly flicking through the pages of a puzzle book as he bargains with people's lives.

If the film has a weak spot, it is that the passengers – a pimp, a wise old man, a mother with 2 snotty kids – are too thinly drawn and stereotypical, too overtly designed to be a cross section of the general public. But this shouldn't detract from what is a terrific exercise in thriller making. **★★★★ WT**

THE TALENTED MR. RIPLEY (1999)

Starring: *Matt Damon (Tom Ripley), Gwyneth Paltrow (Marge Sherwood), Jude Law (Dickie Greenleaf), Cate Blanchett (Meredith Logue), Philip Seymour Hoffman (Freddie Miles)*
Director: *Anthony Minghella*
Screenwriter: *Anthony Minghella, from the novel by Patricia Highsmith*
15/142 mins./Crime/Thriller/USA

Awards – *BAFTA – Best Supporting Actor (Jude Law)*

A young American man is sent to Italy to retrieve rich playboy Dickie Greenleaf but soon develops a murderous obsession with the blessed Dickie.

Anthony Minghella was always going to have a devil of a job topping the nine Oscars and 'new David Lean' tags lobbed at him after 1996's *The English Patient*. Already a preoccupation, he daringly chose to adapt Patricia Highsmith's 50s-set, flamboyant potboiler of murder and intrigue among American ex-pat playthings basking in the sunkissed beauty of the peerless Italian coastline. Something breezier, certainly sexier.

Ripley the novel is no English Patient; it's pure pulp fiction, thrilling but slight. However, Minghella is so committed to treating this appealingly lightweight thriller with such literary reverence and detail it becomes bogged down in long-winded characterisation and over-plotting.

It is also hard to love a film devoid of a sympathetic centre. It should be Paltrow's Marge, fiancée of the dapper and obnoxious Dickie Greenleaf, but her typical remoteness – she is an actress designed for femme fatales, not soft centres – leaves her the sappiest character on show. Anyway, the script is far too wrapped up in Damon's Tom Ripley and his deception to notice her.

This bespectacled young man is the deeply unstable no-mark sent out to retrieve the errant wonder of Dickie for his weary father, and his immediate infatuation with the carefree jazz-fiend soon slips eerily into obsession, a fractured psyche consumed by its dark soul where murder will beget murder. It's a great performance, brave and complex, where Ripley's whispers of homosexuality are just one facet of the need to utterly possess this man he is so drawn to – Ripley, with his weird talent for mimicry, literally takes over his person. Jude Law delivers his doomed prey with deliciously vainglorious panache, where the hedonistic lure is as obvious as the inevitable abandonment; there are secret edges to his shiny shallowness. Quality stuff, but when the central character is a psychopath and his victims reprehensible brats, you get a film confused as to whether we should despise or root for his extraordinary madness. Amorality is fine and clever, but here it cuts all the graceful menace adrift.

Applying to it every inch of his luxuriant style (although the film is only intermittently beautiful), stuffing it to the gills with gorgeous talented young things (add Blanchett and Philip Seymour Hoffman delivering scene stealing cameos) and launching it into the heart of the around season revealed no small amount of Minghella self-confidence. And it did reap nominations aplenty. Ripley, though, thrills most as a fascinating, good-but-not-great study of the outsider who will go to extreme lengths to lose himself. Ironically, less ambition would have paid more attractive dividends. **★★★ IN**

TALES FROM THE CRYPT (1972)

Starring: *Joan Collins (Joanne Clayton), Peter Cushing (Arthur Edward Grimsdyke), Roy Dotrice (Charles Gregory), Richard Greene (Ralph Jason), Ian Hendry (Carl Maitland), Patrick Magee (George Carter), Barbara Murray (Enid Jason), Nigel Patrick (Maj. William Rogers), Robin Phillips (James Elliott), Ralph Richardson (The Crypt Keeper), Geoffrey Bayldon (The Crypt Guide)*
Director: *Freddie Francis*
Screenwriter: *Milton Subotsky based on the comic book stories* Tales From The Crypt *and* The Vault Of Horror *by Johnny Craig, Al Feldstein, William M. Gaines*
18/92 mins./Horror/UK-USA

Five tourists in an old abbey stray into a crypt, and encounter the Crypt Keeper – who reveals to each of them that they are damned souls by telling the gruesome tales of their deaths.

After the 1964 hit *Dr Terror's House Of Horrors*, Amicus Films – Hammer's major rival in the British horror business – specialised in anthology films on the model of *Dead Of Night*, often drawing on the stories of Robert Bloch (*Torture Garden*, *Asylum*, *The House That Dripped Blood*). Their biggest commercial success was this 1972 adaptation of the scurrilous, much-banned 1950s EC horror comics of the 1950s, directed with tact and style by Freddie Francis, led off by an amazing coup in the casting of Sir Ralph Richardson as the Crypt Keeper.

All five stories are winners, with memorably nasty highlights: 'All Through the House' is the one about a murderess (Joan Collins) being menaced on Christmas Eve by a homicidal maniac dressed as Santa Claus; 'Reflections of Death' has Ian Hendry staggering away from a car wreck in a lengthy subjective camera sequence that pays off with a predictable but chilling encounter with a mirror; 'Poetic Justice' is about the persecution of a lonely old man (Peter Cushing, acting above and beyond the call of duty) who gets to return as a hollow-eyed ghoul to get revenge; 'Wish You Were Here' is a gruesome variation on 'The Monkey's Paw' with Richard Greene, and 'Blind Alleys' pits the cruel new director of a home for the blind (Nigel Patrick) against an inmate (Patrick Magee) who stages an elaborately unpleasant come-uppance involving a narrow corridor lined with razor-blades and a starving alsatian. It has an effective, matter-of-fact style, with solid cameos from interesting guest stars and punch-lines that can still make you cringe. ★★★★ **KN**

THE TALES OF HOFFMANN (1951)

Starring: *Moira Shearer (Stella/Olympia), Ludmilla Tcherina (Giulietta), Anne Ayars (Antonia), Pamela Brown (Nicklaus), Leonide Massine (Spalanzani/Schlemil/Franz)*
Directors: *Michael Powell, Emeric Pressburger*
Screenwriters: *Michael Powell, Emeric Pressburger, Dennis Arundell, based on the stories by E.T.A. Hoffmann, libretto by Jules Barbier*
U/124 mins./Opera/UK

The poet Hoffmann tells three fantastical tales of doomed love to fellow carousers while waiting for the ballerina he loves in a tavern. Throughout the tales, Hoffmann is thwarted by an enemy who appears with many faces.

The best-ever filmed opera. The producer-director team of Emeric Pressburger and Michael Powell explore the fusion of musical, ballet and filmmaking magic in *The Red Shoes*, and go even further into artifice in this adaptation of Jacques Offenbach's opera, itself based on horror stories by E.T.A. Hoffmann.

The frame story, set in Nuremberg, has the poet (Rounseville) yearning for the latest incarnation of the magical woman he has pursued all his life. What undoes Hoffmann, in an irony the filmmakers must have relished, is his need to tell stories, which take so much out of him that when the ballerina (Moira Shearer) turns up for their post-performance date he is an exhausted drunk and she goes off under the cloak of the malign Lindorf (Helpmann).

The best story is the first, set in Paris, where Hoffmann dons magic spectacles and falls in love with the wind-up doll Olympia. Shearer, the star of *The Red Shoes*, gives an astonishing performance as the automaton, dancing inhumanly and finally coming to pieces.

A Venetian tale, which has the show's hit tune ('La Barcarole') has duels, deals with the Devil, stolen reflections and voluptuous courtesan Giulietta (Ludmilla Tcherina).

A Greek-set third act is a slight falling-off, though its climax, as an evil conductor makes soprano Antonia (Ann Ayers) sing herself to death is masterly. It uses special effects techniques Georges Méliès would have understood, but in ravishing Technicolor, with stylised sets and costumes, and amazingly physical performances mostly from dancers who mime to the perfect playback of opera singers. ★★★★★ **KN**

TALK RADIO (1988)

Starring: *Eric Bogosian (Barry), Ellen Greene (Ellen), Leslie Hope (Laura), John C. McGinley (Stu), Alec Baldwin (Dan)*
Director: *Oliver Stone*
Screenwriters: *Eric Bogosian, Oliver Stone, from the play by Eric Bogosian, Ted Savinar, from the non-fiction book* Talked to Death: the Life and Murder of Alan Berg *by Stephen Singular*
18/104 mins./Drama/USA

Barry Chaplain is a 'shock DJ' who begins to resent the aggressive public that have made his show a success.

Shot in a mere four weeks in the spring of 1988 and sandwiched between two epic consciences at war, *Wall Street* and *Born On The Fourth Of July*, *Talk Radio* proves that Oliver Stone can turn on a sixpence. Based on star and co-writer Eric Bogosian's stage play, the action is largely confined to the underlit studio of KGAB, a fictional Dallas radio station, where 'shock DJ' Barry Champlain has perfected the art of insulting his callers. Stone has opened the play out a little bit by using a couple of flashbacks, and by adding an understanding ex-wife for Champlain, but the film remains a claustrophobic affair that limits itself to a single weekend in Champlain's life and whose most powerful moments are Champlain's monologues.

Much of *Talk Radio's* plot and final resolution have been lifted from the autobiography of Denver talk-show host Alan Berg, yet while Stone's prescient feel for social issues has ensured that it remains confrontational, TV and radio have become only marginally interested in what should and should not be said on the air. While Champlain's lonely callers give voice to the stupid and psychotic underbelly of America, Stone concentrates on the unshaven chin and beady eye of Champlain, a dissenting conscience who has turned his opinions into entertainment and his verbal flair into a means of control.

Like Stone, Champlain prides himself on his rebel voice, and when he is offered national syndication for his show provided he tones down his attacks, he goes out of his way to offend his audience, his boss and his few friends. As the mood of the film darkens, the Jewish Champlain receives death threats from anti-Semitic listeners, yet even these enemies seem welcome as Champlain slowly realises that he is not so much a voice in the wilderness as a mere entertainer to be turned on and off with the flick of a switch.

Talk Radio is a riveting portrait of a complex man who's driven to communicate and yet is unable to love either his listeners or his intimates. Stone fans will liken Champlain to Richard Boyle in *Salvador*, and may be tempted to interpret its ambivalence towards entertainment in terms of the director's reaction to his adoption by Hollywood as its favourite rebel. Others will discover a fraught chamber piece that takes America's prejudices and Champlain's tortured personality and stares them right in the face. ★★★★ **MC**

TALK TO HER (HABLE CON ELLA) (2002)

Starring: *Javier Camara (Benigno Martin), Dario Graninetti (Marco Zuluaga), Leonor Watling (Alicia), Rosario Flores (Lydia Gonzalez)*
Director: *Pedro Almodóvar*
Screenwriter: *Pedro Almodóvar*
15/112 mins./Drama/Spain

Male nurse Benigno and a sentimental travel writer, Marco, form an unusual friendship due to the fact that their girlfriends are both in comas in the hospital. However, their relationship is tested when Benigno's 'relationship' proves to be a bit on the dodgy side.

Pedro Almodóvar says that, 'Women inspire me to write comedies and men, tragedies,' referring to this film as a 'testicular' story. Here, the women – usually larger than life and centre-stage in his films – are literally silenced, as both central female characters are in comas.

The script, however, makes excellent use of a free-flowing, flashback structure that allows us to get to know them, albeit through the eyes of the male narrators.

Accordingly, *Talk To Her (Hable Con Ella)* is a personal film exploring several of Almodóvar's favourite themes: story-telling, loneliness, friendship and the importance of communication in relationships.

Despite its potentially bleak subject matter, it's not without the Spanish director's trademark black humour, evident in its master-stroke – the addition of a saucy, silent film-within-the-film called *Shrinking Lover*, which here serves a subtly clever purpose. ★★★★ **MT**

Movie Trivia:

Pedro Almodóvar (born 1949)

Who he is: Spain's foremost auteur. A Spanish David Lynch with a mother complex. Leader of the Spanish cinema revival after the end of the Franco regime.

Hallmarks: Primary colours; women in starring or central roles; absurd humour; challenging of conservative sexual morals; transsexuals, transvestites and the Catholic Church.

If you see one movie, see: *Women On The Verge Of A Nervous Breakdown* (1988)

THE TALL GUY (1989)

Starring: *Jeff Goldblum (Dexter King), Rowan Atkinson (Ron Anderson), Emma Thompson (Kate Lemmon), Geraldine James (Carmen), Anna Massey (Mary), Kim Thomson (Cheryl)*
Director: *Mel Smith*
Screenwriter: *Richard Curtis*
15/88 mins./Comedy/Romance/UK

A lanky American plays stooge to an obnoxious comedian and rues his cheap, hayfever-ridden existence until a too-filthy-to-be-true nurse enters his life, bringing order, commitment and sex aplenty.

Clearly if you have one of your female characters exhorting your male lead to take the female lead and "shag her till her ears drop off", then Sophisticated Comedy instantly becomes Sex Romp. For if you strip away the odd *Comic Strip*-isms and the knowing references to contemporary Britain that are the stock in trade of TV graduates like director Mel Smith and writer Richard Curtis, then *The Tall Guy* is nothing if not a snappy, highly-polished two-hander of the kind that Gary Grant used to roll out in the 30s.

Thompson, brisk, classless, coquettish and just a little bit twee, leads the fumbling Goldblum by the nose and introduces him to her individual notion of sexual morality. She prefers to have sex first and thus avoid the tension and expense of ten pre-coital dinners. She reorganises his life, flings out his Madonna posters, bans his Superman pyjamas and helps him escape a life sentence with vicious Ron. And they do indeed shag each other's ears off in one delightful sequence among the knick-knacks and stray groceries of her flat.

But what she demands from him is absolute fidelity. When he blunders into a one-night stand with a fellow actor she takes it more seriously than we're used to seeing young women in the movies do. She leaves, he crumples and even his success in a West End musical version of *The Elephant Man* called 'Elephant!' doesn't heal his despair.

Mel Smith ably manages the narrative, moving between the not-quite glamorous West End, the shabby bohemian fringes of Hampstead, late-night walks on Primrose Hill and the hard-pressed hospital where Thompson works, taking pointed sideswipes at Andrew Lloyd Webber in particular and the acting profession in general.

Richard Curtis deserves great credit for having the nerve to write a serious love story while retaining the wit to make it sharp and knockabout. And London Weekend Television are to be congratulated on having the shrewdness to invest in what is a terrifically tube-friendly film rather than an awful TV movie. Goldblum and Atkinson did their careers no harm whatsoever but it's Thompson's performance – persuasive, intelligent, mannered but with a sexuality that crackles like clean sheets – that ignites the film. Brushing past the hapless Goldblum in the hospital corridor she excuses herself with one of *The Tall Guy's* many terrific lines: 'There's a man expecting my hand up his bottom and one doesn't like to disappoint the old folk.' Quite. ★★★★ **DH**

TAMPOPO (1986)

Starring: *Tsutomu Yamazaki (Goro), Nobuki Miiyamoto (Tampopo), Ken Watanabe (Gun), Koji Yakusho (Man In White Suit), Rikiya Yasuoka (Pisuken)*
Director: *Juzo Itami*
Screenwriter: *Juzo Itami*
18/114 mins./Comedy/Japan

On a mission to find the perfect noodle, Japanese trucker Goro alights upon the failing Lai Lai ramen shop in the outskirts of Tokyo and determines to turn its widowed fortysomething owner, Tampopo, into a mastercook.

Having acted in films as different as Nicholas Ray's *55 Days At Peking* and Koji Wakamatsu's *The Notorious Concubines*, Juzo Itami made his directorial debut with the gently subversive satire, *The Funeral*, in 1984. In collaboration with his wife, Nobuki Miiyamoto, he further lampooned Japanese society in *A Taxing Woman* and *A Taxing Woman Returns* before *Minbo* hit such a raw nerve within the yakuza community that many were convinced that Itami's mysterious death was a mob hit.

Tampopo (from the Japanese for dandelion) was the least socially corrosive of Itami's pictures and its inspired movie pastiches have made it an enduring cult favourite. But Tsutomo Yamazaki's quest was primarily intended to explore the extent to which Occidental influences had pervaded Japanese culture and to restore a little pride in fast-passing traditions.

Itami stuffed his 'noodle' Western with homages to the likes of *Shane* and the 'spaghetti' works of Sergio Leone, as well as such chambara classics as Akira Kurosawa's *Seven Samurai* and *Yojimbo*, which were, of course, recast as the Westerns *The Magnificent Seven* and *A Fistful Of Dollars*. Consequently, with his cowboy hat and long-horned truck, Yamazaki comes across as a hybrid of Alan Ladd, Clint Eastwood and Toshiro Mifune, who is as ready to rescue Miiyamoto from the bullies blighting her business as he is to sit at the feet of noodle master Ryutaro Otomo to learn the ancient rituals involved in the preparation and consumption of the perfect dish.

But Itami refused to be tied down by his central storyline and he peppered the action with delightful diversions, which reinforced his contention that food was a sacred part of Japanese life that should not be profaned by the junk products whose speedy convenience mattered more than their gastronomic quality and socio-cultural significance. He even found room for a movie parody here, too, with gangster Koji Yakusho's foodie romps with mistress Fukumi Kuroda designed to mock the fetishistic eroticism of Nagisa Oshima's *Ai No Corrida*. ★★★★ **DP**

Films with the most prolific use of the F-word

1. *Casino*...422 times
2. *Born On The Fourth Of July*...289 times
3. *The Big Lebowski*...281 times
4. *Pulp Fiction*...271 times
5. *Dead Presidents*...247 times
6. *The Boondock Saints*...246 times
7. *Goodfellas*...246 times
8. *Jay And Silent Bob Strike Back*...228 times
9. *Scarface*...218 times
10. *American History X*...205 times

N.B. *South Park: Bigger, Longer And Uncut* actually has the most instances of all swearing, with 399 in total. Only 146 of those were "Fuck".

TANGO AND CASH (1989)

Starring: *Sylvester Stallone (Raymond 'Ray' Tango), Kurt Russell (Gabriel 'Gabe' Cash), Teri Hatcher (Katherine 'Kiki' Tango), Jack Palance (Yves Perret), James Hong (Quan)*
Directors; *Andrei Konchalovsky, Albert Magnoli*
Screenwriter: *Randy Feldman*
15/98 mins./104 mins (original cut)/Action/Crime/Comedy/USA

Tango and Cash are two on-the-level cops who are framed by crimelord Jack Palance and forced to do time in a prison where most of the inmates are their lock-ups. A tight spot, out of which only hokey one-liners and greased biceps might find a way out of . . .

Reprising the near-farcical pitch of the *Lethal Weapon films, Tango and Cash* is another mismatched-cop-buddy-movie that throws smartly dressed, bespectacled Ray Tango together with the long-haired gung-ho Gabe Cash when the pair of them are framed for murder.

Sporting his much-touted 'new look', the normally monosyllabic Stallone, while not exactly crackling with wit, at least here displays a modest grasp of comic timing. The laughs, however, are far from subtle. Ever since *Dirty Harry* first advised the punk to make his day, these kind of movies have hinged on lippy one-liners and smart-assed exchanges, and *Tango and Cash* is no exception. You know the sort of thing: 'Who do you think you are Tango, Rambo?' 'Rambo's a pussy'. 'Where did you learn to drive?' 'From Stevie Wonder'. 'Is he telling the truth?' 'I don't know, but there's a puddle on the ground and it isn't raining'. And when they run out of original lines, they simply steal them from other movies. (Tango's question 'Did you bump uglies with my sister?' is one of Ed Harris' more memorable lines in *Sweet Dreams*.)

The plot is pure comic strip hokum: pitting the LAPD's finest, 'Tango and Cash', against arch-villain Jack Palance, who is fed up with the 'downtown clown and Beverly Hills yuppie' frequently busting his gun-running and drugs operations. Caught 'red-handed' (i.e. set-up) by the Feds with drugs, money, a dead body and a falsified tape-recording attesting their guilt, the pair are forced to accept an 18-month sentence in an open prison. Instead they find themselves inside a maximum security jail, half of whose inmates were incarcerated by – yes! – Tango and Cash.

Keeping the tension high as it thunders through prison drama, escape drama, and a race-against-the clock finale, this is a fairly enjoyable rollercoaster ride, with the accent firmly on sleek action sequences. Stallone and Russell work well together, and both get a chance to display their bulging biceps. Sly's are bigger and he still has that dropped-shoulder-no-neck look, so prized by bodybuilding enthusiasts.

Despite its unusual pedigree – Guber and Peters teamed up with Soviet-born director Konchalovsky, who worked with Tarkovsky before moving to the States and clocking up a mixed bag of screen credits – *Tango and Cash* is played strictly to formula. ★★★ **KMc**

TANK GIRL (1995)

Starring: *Lori Petty (Rebecca Buck/Tank Girl), Ice T (T-Saint), Malcolm McDowell (Kesslee), Naomi Watts (Jet Girl), Don Harvey (Sergeant Small)*
Director: *Rachel Talalay*
Screenwriter: *Tedi Sarafian, from the comic strip by Alan Martin, Jamie Hewlett*
15/99 mins./Sci-fi/Action/Comedy/USA

In a *Mad Max*-style futurescape, Tank Girl goes about sabotaging her arch-nemesis' plan to control the world's water supply by blowing lots of things to pieces.

Featuring the adventures of a lager-obsessed skinhead and her dozy kangaroo boyfriend, *Tank Girl* was, for the best part of a decade, second only to *Judge Dredd* as Britain's most popular comic strip. Unfortunately, the very things that made it such a cult success – violence, knob jokes, references to Keith Chegwin – are also the reasons why only an idiot would think it suitable material for the blockbuster treatment. If there's one thing that Hollywood's never been short of, however, it's people with more money than sense. And so we have *Tank Girl: The Movie* as a day-glo, slam-bang, loud soundtracked, $35m reality.

Set in a drought-stricken *Mad Max* futurescape – that can't seem to make up its mind whether it's Australia or, indeed, the US of A – the film stars Petty as the gun-crazed heroine and spends its first hour setting her up with motivation, in the form of slaughtered pals, imprisonment – all care of her nemesis, corporate psycho Kesslee (McDowell in suitably hammy, sneering form). She also takes possession of a large armoured vehicle, soups up its engines, gives it a psychedelic makeover, and picks up a sidekick in the shapely form of Jet Girl. Together the pair set about escaping from McDowell's grim gulag and undoing his plan to control the world's water supply.

Matters really get going when the pair meet up with The Rippers. Designed by special FX wizard Stan Winston and including Ice T among their number, this gang of human/kangaroo hybrids turn out to be the main reason to see the film as they bicker among themselves, tear apart the bad guys and play really awful sax solos.

The most infuriating thing about the movie, however, is how close director Rachel Talalay actually comes to the spirit of the comic. Some of the gags are suitably nasty, the film is interspersed with a series of cartoon panels by TG-creator Jamie Hewlett, and Petty herself gets as close to the sprit of the character as the film's ludicrous plot will allow. In particular, the movie's middle section features the kind of insane Busby Berkeley-style song and dance routine that only someone at least fairly near the *Tank Girl* ballpark could come up with.

Sadly, despite its various attributes and overall funky, MTV sensibilities, this never gets quite brutal or blockbusterish enough and the result is a movie both likely to offend the family and infuriate the aficionados in roughly equal amounts. ★★ **CC**

⊙ TARANTULA (1955)

Starring: *John Agar (Dr. Matt Hastings), Mara Corday (Stephanie Clayton), Leo G. Carroll (Professor Gerald Deemer), Nestor Paiva (Sherriff Jack Andrews), Ross Elliott (Joe Burch), Edwin Rand (Lt. John Nolan), Raymond Bailey (Prof. Townsend), Hank Patterson (Josh)*
Director: *Jack Arnold*
Screenwriters: *Robert M. Fresco and Martin Berkeley based on a story by Fresco and Arnold*
PG/80 mins./Sci-fi/USA

Professor Deemer synthesises a formula designed to increase the growth of livestock. Struck down with a deforming disease which is a side-effect of exposure to the formula, Deemer loses control of the experiment – and a spider grows to giant size.

One of the best creepy-crawly monster movies of the 1950s. It opens with a memorable nightmare image – a scientist with a hideously-malformed face staggering through the desert in his pajamas – and spends a great deal of time on a sub-plot about acromegaly, the pituitary disease which actually causes gigantism (as opposed to making things gigantic) and has been a topic of fascination in films from *The Monster Maker* to *Doomwatch* (the minor 1940s horror star Rondo Hatton suffered from the condition and was tastelessly billed as the only monster actor who didn't need makeup). Mild-mannered Leo G. Carroll is an unusually well-intentioned mad scientist, going the monster route as his features expand lopsidedly before the business with the giant spider kicks in. John Agar is the usual two-fisted small-town hero and Mara Corday makes a fetchingly imperilled lab assistant, though the monster is actually done in at the end by napalm dropped from a jet-fighter by a young Clint Eastwood, who plays his entire part with a pilot's mask over his lower face. Stills tend to make the monster look like a giant puppet, but that only appears in a few inserts – for the most part, the big tarantula is a genuine arachnid optically inserted into the landscape or rampaging across effective miniature sets. Director Jack Arnold was a monster specialist, whose major credits were *It Came From Outer Space*, *The Creature From The Black Lagoon* and *The Incredible Shrinking Man*; *Tarantula* – like *Monster On Campus* and *The Space Children* – is a step down from those lasting classics, but still great fun. ★ **KN**

⊙ TARZAN (1999)

Starring: the voices of: *Tony Goldwyn (Tarzan), Minnie Driver (Jane Porter), Glenn Close (Kala), Brian Blessed (Mr. Clayton), Nigel Hawthorne (Professor Archimedes), Lance Henriksen (Kerchak)*
Directors: *Chris Buck, Kevin Lima*
Screenwriters: *Tab Murphy, Bob Tzudiker, Noni White, Evelyn Gabai, Henry Mayo, David Reynolds, Jeffrey Stepakoff, Ned Teitelbaum, based on the novel Tarzan Of The Apes by Edgar Rice Burroughs*
U/84 mins./Animation/Adventure/Family/USA

Awards – *Academy Awards – Best Song ('You'll Be In My Heart'), Golden Globes – Best Song ('You'll Be In My Heart')*

An orphaned boy, in the African jungle, is brought up by gorillas. Then, as an adult, he meets his first humans and has to decide where his loyalties lie.

Tarzan marked a wonderful, triumphant return for Disney to something which is fundamental – glorious old-fashioned storytelling – and a step valiantly and successfully into a new visual lexicon. In the face of the onslaught of Pixar's expansive digital revolution, *Tarzan* fused the hip style of Japan's Anime graphics (big eyes, sharp features, kinetic action) with old-time Disney (the comedy elephant Tantor is pure *Jungle Book*) and a solid use of computer-aided whizzkiddery (Tarzan motors through the jungle by 'surfing' on tree branches in a dizzyingly cool kind of 3D video game manner).

The emphasis here is on trad storytelling made wondrous – and it works. Partly because the script is so sharp, and confident enough to treat the kids like adults (we have death, we have danger, we have sexual awakening), and partly because it dispenses with all the usual forms of irony to concentrate on such divine elements as romance, adventure and comedy.

Sticking faithfully to Burroughs' original *Tarzan Of The Apes* story, first published in 1912, the tale is a well furrowed one: a small child is left alone in the jungle after his shipwrecked parents are killed by a mean old leopard. Adopted by a forlorn female ape, Kala, Tarzan is raised as a gorilla before reaching puberty and hitting the requisite Disney identity crisis – 'Why am I bald?' Enter Jane stage left, along with her explorer pop Professor Archimedes Q. Porter and Clayton, a sinister big game hunter.

Love, danger, and issues of belonging all ensue in enthralling fashion. And if you're wondering, a sly dramatic device allows us to understand the gorillas' voices, while the non-jungle-savvy homo sapiens simply hear 'oooh ooohs'. Directors Lima and Buck are not simply willing to resort to the simple 'Oh, it's just a cartoon' defence for plot improbabilities.

The music, thank God, is all background. Some perfectly acceptable Phil Collins tunes – not, as it transpires, a contradiction in terms – are present to establish mood. The comedy sidekick comes unusually in female form (O'Donnell's gorilla chum Terk), and there's even some minor violence in amongst the fabulous set pieces; all in the service of the strong storyline (the smallest of tots may find it a bit much).

And while it may ultimately lack a quality baddie to match the level of a Shere Khan or *Lion King*'s Scar (although Clayton certainly has a sneery Captain Hook quality), it's as polished and entertaining an animated feature as you're likely to see. Walt would be proud. ★★★★ **IN**

⊙ TARZAN AND HIS MATE (1934)

Starring: *Johnny Weissmuller (Tarzan), Maureen O'Sullivan (Jane Parker), Neil Hamilton (Harry Holt), Paul Cavanagh (Martin Arlington), Forrester Harvey (Beamish), Nathan Curry (Saidi)*
Director: *Cedric Gibbons*
Screenwriter: *James Kevin McGuinness based on the novel by Edgar Rice Burroughs, adapted by Howard Emmett Rogers and Leon Gordon*
U/93 mins./Adventure/USA

White hunters visit the remote jungle home of Tarzan and Jane still hoping to loot the elephants' graveyard.

MGM's sequel to *Tarzan The Ape Man* is on a grander, richer scale, with a frenzy of the violent and sexual business which would soon be wiped off American screens by the coming of the Hays Code. Tarzan and Jane are clearly a couple – she calls herself his 'wife', without benefit of clergy but with much near-naked canoodling in scenes of extraordinary intimacy between lithe O'Sullivan and the muscular Weissmuller. The pair take a lengthy underwater swim, in which O'Sullivan's double appears nude, and are literally unable to keep their hands off each other – a relationship made all the more intriguing by the fact that Jane is Tarzan's surrogate mother as much as she is his lover, protecting this natural innocent from the corrupt ways of the world.

As usual, a safari from the outside world into this idyll means trouble, with a villain who leches after Jane and casually murders his own bearers in order to get to that fortune in ivory – among the most perfidious acts in the cinema comes when Tarzan refuses to lead him to the elephants' graveyard so he fatally wounds a nearby bigears and follows the limping beast's trail. Animals attack every five minutes or so, and are seen off by Tarzan – an exciting alligator fight would crop up in many subsequent sequels.

After this, the series got tamer, especially with the arrival of Boy in *Tarzan Finds A Son* and the Hays Code insisting O'Sullivan wear something more decent. O'Sullivan lasted as long as the fish-out-of-water *Tarzan's New York Adventure*, but Weissmuller stayed in the loincloth, shifting studios to RKO, to tackle Nazis, dinosaurs, Leopard Men and Amazons into the 1940s, then ceded the role to Lex Barker, Gordon Scott and others. ★★★ **KN**

TARZAN THE APE MAN (1932)

Starring: *Johnny Weissmuller (Tarzan), Neil Hamilton (Harry Holt), Maureen O'Sullivan (Jane Parker), C. Aubrey Smith (James Parker), Doris Lloyd (Mrs Cutten), Forrester Harvey (Beamish), Ivory Williams (Riano)*
Director: *W.S. Van Dyke*
Screenwriters: *Cyril Hume, Ivor Novello based on the novel by Edgar Rice Burroughs)*
PG/99 mins./Adventure/USA

Jane Parker joins her explorer father (Smith) in Africa and sets off on safari in search of the fabled elephants' graveyard. In the jungle, she is swept away by Tarzan, a white savage who lives with apes and has never seen a human woman.

Edgar Rice Burroughs' Lord Greystoke, aka Tarzan of the Apes, had been in silent pictures since the 1918 *Tarzan Of The Apes*, starring Elmo Lincoln, and there were competing early talkies – but this MGM production, starring Olympic swimmer Johnny Weissmuller as the lithe jungle man and Maureen O'Sullivan as Jane, kicked off the long-running series.

It takes character names from Burroughs, but ditches the backstory – this Tarzan just happens to be living with apes 'beyond the Mutia Escarpment' with no further explanation needed – and introduces a few elements (like Cheetah the chimp and the famous yell) which would become indelibly associated with the character. Incorporating African stock footage shot by director W.S. Van Dyke the year before on *Trader Horne*, it's a picture of its times – with explicit sensuality (really, Tarzan is naked throughout) and bloody violence that wouldn't have been possible after the censorship crackdown of 1934, and racist attitudes that now seem appalling (when a native bearer falls to his death, white hunter Neil Hamilton grumbles about losing the supplies that were in his pack – and later he lays about his 'boys' with a whip).

It comes to life in the jungle idyll with the boyish, doesn't-know-his-own-strength Tarzan and the initially resistant, eventually adoring Jane – Weissmuller and O'Sullivan are splendid, and she carries the scenes with monologue (by Ivor Novello, no less) as Tarzan remains mostly mute. Plus: charging elephants, a tribe of evil dwarves, a giant gorilla, a hippo attack, crocodiles, lions and a million pounds' worth of ivory. ★★★ **KN**

A TASTE OF HONEY (1961)

Starring: *Dora Bryan (Helen), Robert Stephens (Peter), Rita Tushingham (Jo), Murray Melvin (Geoffrey), Paul Danquah (Jimmy)*
Director: *Tony Richardson*
Screenwriters: *Tony Richardson, Shelagh Delaney, based on the play by Delaney*
12A/100 mins./Drama/UK

Awards – *BAFTA – Best British Actress (Dora Bryan), Best British Film, Best British Screenplay, Most Promising Newcomer (Rita Tushingham), Golden Globes – Most Promising Newcomer (Rita Tushingham)*

Frustrated by her mother Helen's preoccupation with her latest fling, Peter, Salford teenager Jo becomes pregnant after a brief romance with Jimmy, a black sailor on shoreleave, and she moves in with gay shoe salesman, Geoffrey.

Shelagh Delaney packed so many contentious issues into her Royal Court stage play that it could almost have been played as a parody of the kitchen sink style. Pre-marital promiscuity, cross-racial romance and homosexuality were just some of the tabloid topics she seized upon. But, by tightening the episodic structure and returning to his documentary roots, director and co-scenarist Tony Richardson was able to give the only 60s social realist drama with a female protagonist a human interest angle that was lacking from its more confrontational contemporaries.

Jo is much less angry than her male counterparts. But her lot is, in many ways, much tougher, as not only does her gender limit her employment prospects, but she is also expected to adhere to a stricter moral code, if only to avoid the stigma of an unwanted pregnancy. Moreover, in Helen, she has interfering in every aspect of her existence an example of what happens to those who do not abide by such bourgeois rules.

Reuniting with Walter Lassally, who had photographed the 1955 short, *Momma Don't Allow*, that he had made with Karel Reisz, Richardson set out to transfuse the Free Cinema spirit into a dramatic feature. Shooting exclusively on location – in Salford, Blackpool and a disused house on the Fulham Road that cost £20 a week to rent – he worked in whatever conditions he found on the day and, consequently, captured a sense of life being lived.

This was reinforced by the laudably naturalistic performances. The debuting Rita Tushingham handled wisecracks, insults and laments without ever seeming cocksure or mawkish, while Murray Melvin reprised his stage role with a dignified melancholy that contrasted strongly with Dirk Bogarde's showier display in the same year's *Victim*. But it was Dora Bryan's turn as the hard-drinking, self-serving Helen that most surprised 60s audiences used to seeing her in harmless comedy roles.

Despite its occasionally patronising tone, this proved a significant influence on the spit'n'sawdust soap opera and it remains a touching study of both vulnerable youth and a social order that's not as bygone as some would have us believe. ★★★★ **DP**

TAXI (1998)

Starring: *Samy Naceri (Daniel Morales), Frédéric Diefenthal (Emilien Coutant-Kerbalec), Marion Cotillard (Lilly Bertineau), Manuela Gourary (Camilly Coutant-Kerbalec), Emma Sjoberg (Petra), Bernard Farcy (Commissaire Gibert)*
Director: *Gérard Pirès*
Screenwriter: *Luc Besson*
15/86 mins./Action/Crime/Comedy/France

A taxi driver and partner-in-crime go on a clean-spree to thwart criminals everywhere and catch a couple of hearts while they're at it.

From the simplistic grandeur of *The Big Blue* to the plot-flawed, visual majesty of *The Fifth Element*, it's clear where Luc Besson stands on the style-over-substance debate. To wit, in *Taxi* – as writer-producer – he continues to explore banality with eye-catching panache.

Made in a reputed 30 days, this film equivalent of a 'holiday read' sees taxi driver Daniel and partner Emilien, become embroiled in catching a gang of bank robbers (uncannily similar to *Point Break*'s Ex-Presidents), while winning the hands of Lilly and Petra. Can they get the bad guys and the girls? Of course, but then, as we've seen with Besson before, it is not about where the characters are going – it's how they get there that counts. A breakneck credit sequence sets the high-speed tempo that never lets up over the film's disappointingly brief running time.

Likewise, the action sequences' slapstick cartoon realism contributes to a feel reminiscent of an early Jackie Chan vehicle. As well as the mania, a hint of particularly wry humour and some ill-fated bed-hopping shenanigans are added to give an eminently amusing and terrifically exciting end product. Ultimately, a combination of the storyline's lack of depth and the generally uninspired direction of Gérard Pirès is unlikely to win awards. Nonetheless, for a film that never tries to be anything but fun, such unashamed hedonism provides a hefty slice of entertainment at its most pure.

A two star American re-make starring Jimmy Fallon and Queen Latifa served as reminder of the original's superiority, as did a string of sequels. ★★★★ MD

TAXI DRIVER (1976)

Starring: *Robert De Niro (Travis Bickle), Cybill Shepherd (Betsy), Jodie Foster (Iris Steensman), Peter Boyle (Wizard), Harvey Keitel (Sport), Albert Brooks (Tom), Leonard Harris (Charles Palantine), Martin Scorsese (Passenger), Diahnne Abbott (Concession Girl)*
Director: *Martin Scorsese*
Screenwriter: *Paul Schrader*
18/112 mins./Drama/USA

Awards: *BAFTAs – Best Supporting Actress (Jodie Foster), Best Newcomer (Jodie Foster), Anthony Asquith Award For Film Music (Bernard Herrmann). Cannes Film Festival – Palme D'Or*

Vietnam vet Travis Bickle takes a job driving late-night cabs in New York. By day, he tries to win the affection of presidential campaign worker Betsy. By night, he glides around the city, growing increasingly disgusted by the low-lifes on the streets.

In *The Adventures Of Rocky And Bullwinkle*, Robert De Niro reprises his 'you talkin' to me?' speech – as much an impressionists' calling card as Brando's 'coulda been a contender' – as deadpan comedy, perhaps in an attempt to break free of the role which, thirty years on, still defines his screen persona. 'God's lonely man', Travis Bickle is one of a handful of truly iconic screen characters, a howling, wounded, dangerous male at odds with the world. His shoulder-patch displays the face of perhaps his greatest predecessor, King Kong, but Travis can also keep company with Welles' Kane, Bogart's Rick, Dean's Jim Stark or Spacey's Lester Burnham: sensitive enough to see something is wrong but not sure what to do about it, incapable of making a lasting connection with women they idealise, boiling with a violence which might tear them apart unless directed at someone else. Travis is also an ultimate American movie archetype from numberless Westerns and gangster movies – to quote a Randolph Scott title, the Man Behind the Gun.

A landmark film of the 70s, *Taxi Driver* is shaped by the overlapping sensibilities of director Martin Scorsese, who grew up in movie houses, and screenwriter Paul Schrader, whose parents kept him away from cinemas until his late teens. Scorsese loved John Ford, Howard Hawks and Michael Powell; Schrader wrote a book about Bresson and Dreyer. *Taxi Driver* is at once expansively Catholic and puritanically spare. In *Mean Streets*, where 'you pay for your sins on the street', redemption is possible, but *Taxi Driver* is shadowed by a Calvinist belief in predestination – the street and the hero's skull are hells that can't be escaped. Travis is hailed a hero after he saves twelve-and-a-half-year-old Iris from life as a sex slave, but we know he could as easily have used his trick guns to assassinate smooth, smug Senator Charles Palantine who has the unearned devotion of Travis' original fantasy object, campaign worker Betsy. Even as she is 'saved', Iris pleads for the life of a disgusting pimp, clearly (and sensibly) terrified of the man rescuing her. For Travis, there is no release – when he tries to shoot himself, his gun is empty.

Tagline
On every street in every city, there's a nobody who dreams of becoming a somebody.

Schrader had written an important article on film noir and *Taxi Driver* may well be the first noir made by folks who understood what the term meant. It was once a matter of debate whether it was possible to 'shoot noir in colour', but Scorsese found a way. The shimmering New York, with prowling yellow cabs and splatters of ketchup-red blood, is a neon-lit equivalent of those starkly monochrome urban nightmares of the 1940s and 50s. 'All the animals come out at night,' purrs Bickle, 'whores, skunk pussies, buggers, queens, fairies, dopers, junkies, sick, venal. Someday a real rain will come and wash all this scum off the streets.' Travis' voice-over, accompanied by Bernard Herrmann's old-school score, may be more profane than any of Philip Marlowe's, but the hardboiled, romantic, brutally idealistic tone derives from the private eye whose mean streets gave Scorsese's earlier film its title. Schrader's 'real rain' paraphrases a Chandler-Marlowe musing about Los Angeles' Santa Anna wind, itself a reference to Conan Doyle, who had Sherlock Holmes talk of 'an East wind coming'. As observant as Holmes or Marlowe – spotting the tiny pin which identifies a secret service agent and showing skewed insight into Betsy's relationship with a clueless co-worker (Albert Brooks) – Travis winds up closer to the vigilante sadism of Mickey Spillane's Mike Hammer, casting himself as a horseman in his own imagined Apocalypse.

Schrader and Scorsese patterned *Taxi Driver* on *The Searchers*, in which John Ford examines the stock figure of the never-give-up hero (as played by John Wayne) and finds he is spurred by racism and sexual inadequacy, as likely to murder his niece (Natalie Wood) for the 'crime' of being captured by the Comanche chief Scar as he is to rescue her. Travis Bickle is Ethan taken to greater extremes: he effectively masturbates with his guns as he dry-fires at his own reflection. Though surrounded by a world out of crime cinema, or even the horror film (the Lynchian dark corridor from which Iris' pimp crawls), Travis wants to be in a Western – he shaves his head like a Huron before setting out on his 'murder raid', and draws down on Sport (Harvey Keitel), a Scar-like hustler who wears Apache-style hippie hair and a cowboy hat. At the end of *The Searchers*, Ethan is overpowered by family feeling and takes the girl home, but is himself excluded from the reunion. The same thing happens to Travis, who has the handwritten, apologetic gratitude of Iris' father pinned to his wall with his other press cuttings, but is still sliding back into his cab, and swallowed not by a Fordian desert but by the neon shadows of the naked city. ★★★★★ KN

Movie Trivia: *Taxi Driver*

Screenwriter Paul Schrader paid tribute to his ninth grade girlfriend by naming Cybill Shepherd's character Betsy after her. Jodie Foster's older sister doubled for some of the young actress's lewder acts in the film. Travis' story is partially autobiographical. Schrader suffered a nervous breakdown when he moved to Los Angeles, and literally didn't speak to anybody for months.

TEAM AMERICA: WORLD POLICE (2004)

Starring: the voices of: *Trey Parker (Gary Johnston/Joe/Kim Jong Il/Hans Blix/Carson/Matt Damon/Drunk in Bar/Tim Robbins/Sean Penn/Michael Moore/Helen Hunt/Susan Sarandon/Others), Matt Stone (Chris/George Clooney/Danny Glover/Ethan Hawke/Matt Damon/Others), Kristen Miller (Lisa)*
Director: *Trey Parker*
Screenwriters: *Trey Parker, Matt Stone, Pam Brady*
15/98 mins./Satire/Comedy/Action/Puppet/USA

Awards – *Empire Awards – Best Comedy*

Actor Gary is recruited to replace a killed-in-action member of Team America, an anti-terrorist force. He soon finds himself facing his personal idol, Maurice LaMarche, whose coalition of anti-war Hollywoodites is unwittingly carrying out the evil schemes of North Korean dictator Kim-Jong Il.

The *Thunderbirds'* live-action adaptation missed the point so dispiritingly that there's a sense of justice served as *South Park* creators Trey Parker and Matt Stone use Gerry Anderson's Supermarionation methods with wit, affection and a surprising degree of background subtlety in this mock action movie-cum-political cartoon. That's matched, though, by plenty of upfront piss-everybody-off blatancy.

The main target is the Bruckheimer-Simpson style of big action blockbuster with covert gay content. There's a whole song about how the hero misses the heroine 'as much as Michael Bay missed the mark with *Pearl Harbor*', and the back stories everyone gives to explain their prejudices are spot-on – like the T.A. member who's hated actors ever since he was raped by the touring cast of *Cats*.

It opens with a demonstration of Bush II-era foreign policy, as the elite, patriotic Team America (theme tune: 'America, Fuck Yeah!') take out would-be bombers in Paris, incidentally destroying the Eiffel Tower, the Arc de Triomphe and the Louvre. Working out of a base hidden in Mount Rushmore, T.A. flies off to trouble spots, while dealing with its own soap operatic tangle about who 'has feelings' for who – which results in the hilarious puppet sex scene that caused a US ratings fuss. After a while, the film leaves off bashing the hawks to go on a tear about Hollywood liberals – with 'socialist weasel' Michael Moore depicted as a gross suicide bomber.

Despite good spot gags, *Team America* falters when it goes over old material: the treatment of the North Korean dictator isn't as sharp as that of Saddam in the *South Park* movie. The attacks on celebs flounder, in that too many targets (Janeane Garofalo? Helen Hunt?) are hauled on and blasted too quickly for satiric personalities to be established. And the *South Park* claim that all voices are impersonated '... poorly' rebounds, as some of the caricatures need to be labelled in order to be recognised – and still aren't especially amusing. It makes for a patchy comedy that's stronger as a genre-mocker than a political satire. But you have to love the use of unthreatening pussycats as 'deadly panthers' to menace the miniature heroes ... ★★★★ **KN**

TEEN WOLF (1985)

Starring: *Michael J. Fox (Scott Howard), James Hampton (Harold Howard), Susan Ursitti (Lisa 'Boof' Marconi), Jerry Levine (Rupert 'Stiles' Stilinski), Matt Adler (Lewis), Lorie Griffin (Pamela Wells), Jim MacKrell (Vice Principal Rusty Thorne), Mark Arnold (Mick McAlister), Jay Tarses (Coach Bobby Finstock), Mark Holton (Chubby)*
Director: *Rob Daniel*
Screenwriters: *Jeph Loeb, Matthew Weisman*
PG/91 mins./Comedy/USA

High school loser Scott Howard learns that, thanks to a family curse, he is due to turn into a werewolf. As a monster, he becomes a basketball star and the most popular kid in school.

This squeaky clean 1980s teen comedy will make anyone nostalgic for the era of *I Was A Teenage Werewolf*, where an adolescent cursed to turn into a monster realises he should prowl the gym after dark ripping out throats and menacing screaming girls.

After an admittedly funny sequence in which Fox's character 'goes through changes' in the bathroom and is told about the curse by his paunchy, bespectacled, equally lycanthropic Dad (Hampton), *Teen Wolf* is a typical fable about the high school pecking order, as nobody minds the star player on the basketball team is a monster and cheerleaders fawn all over him so long as he keeps winning. The finale would like to sell a message about being your own man, as the hero tries to score without turning into a werewolf to do it, but the actual message seems to be that it's better to be a normal mediocrity than a weirdo.

Teen Wolf is fairly painless, but its cuddly werewolf and uninspired use of all the cliches of the terrible teen movie prevent it from being much else. Fox, on the brink of stardom, is pretty good with undemanding material, but the few smart lines are lost amid the usual party hijinx and non-threatening tearaway stuff. In *Teen Wolf Too*, Jason Bateman turns up as the cousin of the by-then-too-expensive Fox and the sport is boxing rather than basketball. There was also an animated series which scored a video release as *The Cartoon Adventures Of Teen Wolf*. Only Hampton is in all three incarnations of the franchise. ★★ **KN**

TEENAGE MUTANT NINJA TURTLES (1990)

Starring: *Josh Pais (Raphael/Man In Cab), David Foreman (Leonardo/Gang Leader), Michelan Sisti (Michelangelo/Pizza Man), Leif Tilden (Donatello/Foot Messenger), Judith Hoag (April O'Neil), James Saito (Shredder)*
Director: *Steve Barron*
Screenwriters: *Todd W. Langen, Bobby Herbeck, based on a story by Herbeck, characters by Kevin Eastman, Peter Laird*
PG/87 mins./Fantasy/Adventure/USA

In the midst of a Fagin-style crimespree the Heroes In Halfshells' leader is kidnapped and they make it their ninja-mission to rescue him.

After so much headline coverage, could this turtle extravaganza possibly live up to such eager expectation? Happily, and a little surprisingly, the movie *Teenage Mutant Ninja Turtles* far exceeds it, largely because it's worlds removed from the kiddies' TV cartoon.

A clue that all is not what it might be is the word Ninja in the title. Struck out by the BBC (along with a fair amount of the TV series' original martial artistry) in favour of Hero, it's re-inserted here in a film that stays the course of Laird and Eastman's original comic while the amphibians themselves, vastly simplified by the animator, have been suitably reconstructed to resemble those first muscular, vaguely threatening drawings. And the biggest, most enjoyable difference of all is the foursome themselves. Devoid of the cartoon's gadgetry – flying cars and the like – they're afforded recognisable and very individual characters, thus providing through their interplay a platform for the snappy, bickering, fully grown-up humour the originators bestowed on their streetwise creations.

The story itself is mercifully simple. New York City is in the grip of Shredder's Fagin-style crime wave and the Turtles interrupt his progress by saving April O'Neil, a perpetually if impractically mini-skirted TV reporter, from a mugging. They do this more because they a) fancy her and b) like a good fight, rather from any deep-seated sense of right and wrong. After a quick spot of meditation and a crash course in moral fibre, the self-styled Heroes In Half Shells set out to rescue their kidnapped leader, during which we are treated to a deliberately hilarious flashback of how the Turtles became mutant, teenage and ninja, much chopsocky-type action, and love interest between said reporter and a bat-wielding vigilante called Casey Jones. Cleverly constructed as it all is – fights for the boys; a hunk for the girls; attitude for the teens; and sharp, satirical humour for adults (plus gratuitously generous flashes of O'Neill's thighs) – the end mix is so well blended as to never seem too cynical but merely a well-rounded, unpretentious, very funny, knockabout adventure. Truly a comic strip brought to life and, genuinely, fun for all the family. ★★★ **LB**

TEN (2002)

Starring: *Mania Akbari (Driver), Amin Maher*
Director: *Abbas Kiarostami*
Screenwriter: *Abbas Kiarostami*
12/92 mins./Drama-documentary/Iran

In between bickering with her wilful 8 year-old son, Amin, a well-dressed, self-aware Teheran divorcée offers lifts to various strangers, with whom she discusses the status of women in contemporary Iranian society.

Dispensing with a traditional film crew, Abbas Kiarostami wrote, directed, shot and edited this sequence of 10 vignettes, which provided a fascinating insight into gynocentric attitudes in post-millennial Iran. Recalling the simple immediacy of neo-realism, yet exploiting the latest digital technology, it confined the action to the inside of a car, much as The *Taste Of Cherry* had done. But whereas Homayoun Ershadi had circled the outskirts of Teheran in search of someone to assist in his suicide, chic divorcée Mania Akbari seems stuck in the city in a fate that many would consider worse than death.

Indeed, from its opening moments, in which 8 year-old Amin Maher indulges in the petulant chauvinism of a tirade against his mother and her independent lifestyle, the action serves to emphasise just how powerless Akbari and her various passengers are to change their lives.

Kiarostami had originally intended to centre the film on a psychiatrist who was forced to meet her patients in her car because her office was being redecorated. However, he decided to make Akbari's encounters with her feisty sister, the jilted spinster, the prostitute and the loney widow seem more casual by having her offer them lifts in busy traffic.

But this more accidental approach also made the discussion of such contentious topics as identity, gender, desire, repression and faith seem less like the confessional outpourings of women in need of professional help and more like the statements of individuals who were fully aware of themselves, their opinions and their status.

Yet, Kiarostami still had to resort to socially symbolic juxtapositions between sound and image to circumvent censorship. Thus, he alternated between shots of the speaker and the listener to challenge Islamic notions of how women are seen and heard. Similarly, he contrasted the way in which Akbari's sister sensually fanned herself by lifting her veil with the exposure of the spurned spinster's self-laceratingly severe haircut. Most tellingly of all, he kept hidden the faces of both the hooker and the devout old lady.

Audacious and ingenious, this masterpiece of cinematic humanism confirmed Kiarostami among the world's most important filmmakers. ★★★★★ **DP**

THE TEN COMMANDMENTS (1956)

Starring: *Charlton Heston (Moses), Yul Brynner (Rameses), John Carradine (Aaron), Olive Deering (Miriam), Anne Baxter (Nefretiri), Edward G. Robinson (Dathan), Debra Paget (Lilia)*
Director: *Cecil B. DeMiller*
Screenwriters: *Aeneas MacKenzie, Jesse Lasky, Jr., Jack Gariss, Fredric M. Frank, based on the novels* Pillar of Fire *by Rev. J.H. Ingraham,* On Eagle's Wing *by Rev. A.E. Southon,* Prince Of Egypt *by Dorothy Clark Wilson*
U/220 mins./Adventure/Drama/Religion/USA

Awards – *Academy Awards – Best Special Effects*

Left in the bulrushes by his Hebrew mother, raised by the Pharaoh's sister and disliked by his stepbrother Rameses, Moses becomes a warrior and possible future Pharaoh. However, his worldview changes when he discovers his real origins.

Cecil B. DeMille: the name is a kind of instant shorthand for Hollywood in all its brash vulgarity and meretricious splendour. Just as Hitchcock implied suspense and Lubitsch sophistication, DeMille stood for spectacle in an era when these were virtually the only three directors whose names meant anything to the general public.

DeMille crowned his services to the Cinema of Excess with his 1956 remake of *The Ten Commandments*. With its exteriors filmed on location in Egypt and at a total cost of $15 million, there's nothing at all modest about this movie. Listing 'The Cavalry Corps of the Egyptian Armed Forces' among its opening credits, introduced by DeMille in person in a strange Cold War prologue as a celebration of 'the birth of freedom' (his hint to communists: 'Are men the property of the State or are they free souls under God?') and with Charlton Heston not only playing the part of Moses but also, via some electronic reprocessing, providing the Voice of God, it's a truly monumental film. The story may be familiar, but DeMille rams it home as though he were telling it for the first time with his camera platform as a pulpit linked up by a direct line to the Deity.

It's very easy to snigger at *The Ten Commandments*' occasionally inane dialogue ('Oh, Moses, Moses, you stubborn, splendid, adorable fool!' is probably the worst excess) and oak panelled plotting, but what justifies the film is DeMille's gigantic self-confidence in taking on such a huge subject, reducing it to his typical formula and then triumphantly delivering the goods in terms of lavish spectacle and deeply chiselled morality. The various plagues visited on Egypt, the Exodus of over 12,000 extras, the pursuit by Pharaoh Brynner's chariots, the famous parting of the Red Sea, the Pagan revelries around the Golden Calf and Charlton finally taking his tablets are big, big sequences served up by DeMille in his supreme master showman manner.

The special effects and colour may now sometimes seem garish and lurid, but in terms of performance and sheer matinee-level entertainment, this holds up much better than most other religious epics. William Wyler's *Ben-Hur* and Stanley Kubrick's *Spartacus* are much superior films, but both their stories are smaller and even parochial by comparison with this. DeMille's lavish canvas may be vulgar, shallow and pompous (the director himself provides the scene-linking self-righteous commentary), but it would be impossible to imagine any other actors doing better than Heston and Brynner as Moses and the Pharaoh, nor any other director but DeMille powering the story forward with the kind of vain, simplistic arrogance that only an old-fashioned true believer could bring to it.

Somehow, despite all its obvious crassness, *The Ten Commandments* is a great film. A kind of celluloid Las Vegas, lighting up the desert sky with an overwhelming sense of its own importance, finally it's as fine a tribute to C. B.'s legendary large head as anyone could wish for. Biggest may not always be best, but sometimes just being the biggest is enough. And this is a big film. ★★★★ **TT**

10 THINGS I HATE ABOUT YOU (1999)

Starring: *Heath Ledger (Patrick 'Pat' Verona), Julia Stiles (Katarina 'Kat' Stratford), Joseph Gordon-Levitt (Cameron James), Larisa Oleynik (Bianca Stratford), David Krumholtz (Michael Eckman), Andrew Keegan (Joey Donner), Susan May Pratt (Mandella), Gabrielle Union (Chastity), Allison Janney (Ms. Perky)*
Director: *Gil Junger*
Screenwriters: *Karen McCullah Lutz, Kirsten Smith based on the play* The Taming Of The Shrew *by William Shakespeare*
12/98 mins./Comedy/Romance/USA

Teen rebel Patrick agrees to woo school bitch Kat for a bet, but soon finds himself genuinely attracted to her.

Just as *Clueless* modernised Jane Austen's *Emma*, so this bright 'n' breezy teen comedy turns to classic literature for its inspiration – the target this time being Shakespeare's *Taming Of The Shrew*.

Of course, the Bard's story of a man-despising lass whose mind is changed by a vaguely dangerous love interest has already been filmed as *Kiss Me Kate*, but giving it a bang-up-to-date setting in one of the hottest genres around is such a good idea you almost wonder why they didn't think of it earlier.

Taking cues from its source material (the setting is Padua High School, the family name Stratford), *10 Things* ... focuses on cute, affluent sisters Bianca (Oleynik) and Katarina (Stiles), the former as sweet and popular as the latter is mean-spirited and sulky. Their dad (the always watchable Larry Miller) has imposed a house rule that Bianca can't start dating until her older sis does – not the best news for besotted Cameron (Gordon-Levitt).

In order to win the saccharine sophomore, he plots to find someone willing to date Kat – the ideal candidate being loner-with-past Patrick Verona (Ledger, in his first Hollywood role) – and the inevitable sparks fly. It all takes a good 20 minutes to establish characters and plot, and flounders quite worryingly at first, with jokes that feel forced and uneasy. Once the romantic merry-go-round kicks in, though, things pick up considerably, with hugely likeable characters and spirited performances (Stiles is especially noteworthy as a rapidly softening queen bitch). And the incidental players (notably Miller's teen pregnancy-obsessed parent and Daryl Mitchell's jive-talkin' English teacher) bag most of the laugh-out-loud moments, suggesting this is one teen movie that isn't just for teens.

If it feels patchy, with some inexplicable plot developments (a guidance counsellor – *The West Wing's* Alison Janney – who vanishes after 15 minutes, a student whose obsession with Shakespeare is randomly and irrationally thrown in halfway through), *10 Things* ... still makes for a solid summer crowd-pleaser, with enough good-natured humour and wonderfully silly set pieces to carry itself through.

Oh, and Ledger's football field rendition of *Can't Take My Eyes Off of You* (possibly the best musical sequence in a teen movie since *Ferris Bueller's Day Off*) is worth the price of purchase alone.

Although already off to a winner thanks to its derivation from the finest source material around, this also succeeds in its modernisation, providing teen comedy that is somehow tried and true, but fresh all at the same time.
★★★★ CW

THE TENANT (LE LOCATAIRE) (1976)

Starring: *Roman Polanski (Trelkovsky), Isabelle Adjani (Stella), Melvyn Douglas (Monsieur Zy), Jo Van Fleet (Madame Dioz), Bernard Fresson (Scope), Lila Kedrova (Madame Gaderian), Claude Dauphin (Husband), Claude Pieplu (Neighbour), Rufus (George Badar)*
Director: *Roman Polanski*
Screenwriters: *Roman Polanski, Gerard Brach based on the novel by Roland Topor*
18/124 mins./Horror/France

Meek office worker Trelkovsky moves into an apartment to replace a previous tenant, Simone Choule, who apparently attempted suicide by jumping out of a window. Trelkovsky is either subtly bullied by his neighbours or succumbs to extreme paranoia, and gradually comes more and more to identify with Simone.

Based on a novel by Roland Topor (Renfield in Herzog's *Nosferatu*), this seems almost an anthology of Roman Polanski's favourite, oppressive themes – presenting a Paris apartment which is as threatening as the London digs of *Repulsion*, nasty neighbours who are as demonic as those in *Rosemary's Baby* and identity-switch games as humiliating as *Cul-De-Sac*.

A difference is that Polanski casts himself in the central role, constantly having to deny that he's a foreigner, suggesting this is an even more personal, painful film.

Trelkovsky suffers persecution from apparently everyone in sight: a cafe serves undrinkable chocolate he nevertheless drinks without complaint; a housewarming party for his patronising or bullying office colleagues excites complaints about his alleged noisiness that reach a humiliating height when he is blamed for the racket made by thieves ransacking his apartment while he's away; he nearly lands a gorgeous girl but shrinks away when he suspects she's in on the conspiracy; a busybody turns against him when he refuses to sign a petition to evict a neighbour but this lone heroic stand means that when the persecuted woman takes a shit on every other tenant's doormat he has to scoop up some excrement and put it outside his own flat so he won't be blamed. The final reel, which finds Polanski dressed as a woman and *twice* throwing himself out of a window, is among the most despairing in the cinema, and acutely painful to watch. **★★★★ KN**

TENEBRAE (TENEBRE) (1982)

Starring: *Anthony Franciosca (Peter Neal), Christian Borromeo (Gianni), Mirella D'Angelo (Tilde), Veronica Lario (Jane McKerrow), Ania Pieroni (Elsa Manni), Eva Robins (Girl On Beach), Carola Stagnaro (Detective Altieri), John Steiner (Christiano Berti)*
Director: *Dario Argento*
Screenwriter: *Dario Argento*
18/110 mins./Horror/Italy

Thriller writer Peter Neal comes to Rome to promote his latest novel, and finds that a razor-murderer apparently inspired by his work is at large, killing beautiful women.

Dario Argento made his name with stylish, cutting edge mysteries from *The Bird With The Crystal Plumage* to *Deep Red*, then changed style for the colourful, baroque supernatural horror films *Suspiria* and *Inferno*. In 1983, he got back into psycho-thriller mode for this elegant, nasty picture. *Tenebrae* tackles fascinating, perhaps-autobiographical subject matter as a creator of gruesome stories becomes implicated in the crimes of a fan who has taken his words too much to heart (the first victim has pages torn from the book shoved into her throat) but a typically contrived, triple-twist third act turns in on itself for the sake of shock and surprise.

Franciosa brings conviction and warmth to the central role, but the characters are mostly beautiful stick figures: Argento includes a journalist who, like the nagging critic in *8 1/2* points out the shortcomings of the script, and then slashes her to death. It's a playful, perverse, exhilarating piece of weird cinema: with the camera pursuing victims in lengthy tracking shots scored with pounding rock music (one victim asks someone offscreen to turn the music down), death scenes which play like collaborations between Antonioni and Peckinpah (a woman action-paints a white wall with blood after her hand is chopped off), coups de cinema like the character who bends over to reveal the axeman who has been standing behind him, and truly strange explain-the-killer's-motive flashbacks.

Despite the title, it's one of the most brightly-lit of all horror films, with bleached-out daytime scenes and disco-lit rainswept nights. In the English language release, heroine Daria Nicolodi is dubbed by Theresa Russell and cop Giuliano Gemma is man-of-a-thousand-voices David ('Parker' from *Thunderbirds*) Graham. **★★★ KN**

THE TERMINAL (2004)

Starring: *Tom Hanks (Viktor Navorski), Catherine Zeta-Jones (Amelia Warren), Stanley Tucci (Frank Dixon), Chi McBride (Mulroy), Diego Luna (Enrique Cruz)*
Director: *Steven Spielberg*
Screenwriters: *Sacha Gervasi, Jeff Nathanson, based on a story by Andrew Niccol, Sacha Gervasi*
12A/128 mins./Drama/Comedy/USA

Viktor Navorski lands at JFK airport, to find his homeland of Krakozhia has dissolved in a rebellion and his passport is no longer valid. Stranded in a bureaucratic no-man's land, he must live in the airport, unable to go home, unable to venture onto American soil ...

You may have got the wrong idea about *The Terminal*. You might be thinking it's another splashy romantic comedy with Tom Hanks back on home turf, goofing off in a funny accent and lifting those puppy-dogs in the direction of brittle, lovely Catherine Zeta-Jones. Well, Sleepless At Gate 67 it ain't.

For Steven Spielberg, in later career, is having a whale of a time mixing up his native crowdpleasing with a caustic independent spirit. Yes, *The Terminal* is funny, romantic and sentimental, but inside Spielberg's purpose-built airport lounge, an open-plan cathedral of endless flux, he's channelling both Capra and Kafka. This is a post-millennial fable about how the world really kinda sucks.

The plot itself is loose-limbed, a vague blend of quest (to get out of the damn airport), survival and romance. It makes you think of *Cast Away*, while the posters, with their lone journeyman Hanks, recall the sap and charm of *Forrest Gump*. Yet this graceful satire feels more in touch with *The Shawshank Redemption*, where the looming prison boasts its own sushi bars and Borders superstore, but is every bit as repressive.

Navorski must live by his wits or go under, and in the slow churn of Hanks' expert performance lies the movie's substance, a subtle process of unpeeling a goofball tourist, located somewhere between Charlie Chaplin and Andy Kaufman, to reveal a singular man of purpose: direct, noble, irrepressible, and so very un-American. It's a brilliant deception, forcing us to confront the rash judgment that all English-deficient travellers are basically idiots.

Less effective, though, is Navorski's role as romancer. Wearing his heart on the sleeve of a new Hugo Boss suit, he woos listless, man-troubled stewardess Zeta-Jones, who is drawn to his honesty, failing to register this curious person as anything more than a frequent flier. Half the world, it seems, is to some extent trapped in an airport.

Never Spielberg's forte, the romance unfortunately feels false, too removed from the movie's menacing undertow. So he sensibly keeps it sidelined from the ongoing duel with Tucci's brusque commandant. In a delicious performance, the vibrant actor underscores the required weaselling with an understanding that rules are necessary. Navorski, to his mind, represents chaos – a slipping cog in vital clockwork. In many ways, he's right.

The film also traverses a wonderful array of supporting players, immigrant workers caught on the fringes of life with whom Navorski finds communion. In one throwaway yet spellbinding sequence, Wes Anderson regular Kumar Pallana, as a perpetually agitated Indian cleaner, displays a sublime knack for plate-spinning and juggling hoops. It's a welcome burst of surreal indulgence, both hilarious and poignant, a new type of 'Spielberg moment'.

Away from the knots of dramedy, you can sit back and drink in the director's effortless class. His camera glides, feather-light, across this multi-storied shopping mall, keeping pace with the ebb and flow of passengers, Navorski the one static point of focus. There is a dazzling use of reflection, impossible shots in mirrors and glass panels; everything in the terminal is a reflection of the real America, a microcosm of the capitalist wonderland outside the doors.

And it's very evident that the last thing Navorski's chasing in the world – a bitter, unreliable place – is this dubious American Dream that comes wrapped in Cellophane, emblazoned with logos and wrung-dry by corporate red tape. Without giving anything away, the last line says it all: 'Take me home.' ★★★★ **IN**

➂ THE TERMINAL MAN (1974)

Starring: *George Segal (Harry Benson), Joan Hackett (Dr. Janet Ross), Richard Dysart (Dr. John Ellis), Donald Moffat (Dr. Arthur McPherson), Michael C. Gwynne (Dr. Robert Morris*
Director: *Mike Hodges*
Screenwriter: *Mike Hodges based on the novel by Michael Crichton*
PG/107 mins./Sci-Fi/USA

After a serious head injury computer scientist Harry Benson experiences terrifying and dangerous seizures. To control them, he embarks on some radical surgery having a microcomputer fitted into his head, but the results could become more drastic still.

Despite being based on a novel by that master of the broad commercial stroke Michael Crichton, this sci-fi thriller is millions of stylistic years away from *Jurassic Park* or *Sphere*. Indeed, this austere but intriguing piece about a form of brain surgery that goes hideously wrong, transforming an ordinary man into a Frankensteinian killer, is more a keen example of how the filmmaking flavours of the times (the early 70s) had spread across genres. This is a cold, pessimistic film, eschewing sci-fi's more flamboyant conventions, but not as un-Crichton as you would think. At the same time he was very much preoccupied with paranoid medical-themed adventures such as *The Andromeda Strain*, *Runaway* and his own directorial effort *Coma*.

Adopting the same approach he took to the gangster genre in *Get Carter*, Mike Hodges creates a slow, drawn-out style, strong on character, at times infuriating, but on the quiet quite powerful. Here we have a man already nervous of the technological world, fearful, possibly insane, in his belief people are being transformed into machines, who will become the fulfilment of his own paranoia. George Segal playing effectively his usual sunny disposition works hard as computer scientist Harry Benson (a job that is either an irony or a contradiction given the nature of his terrors) whose brain is seizing up on him, pushing him closer to the edge. So far, so clinical, with strong supporting performances from Richard Dysart and Joan Hackett.

From there the film shifts in polarity, moving into the vestiges of horror rather than sci-fi. After a gruelling surgery sequence, delivered with credibility-making exactitude, the computer inside Harry's head becomes the cause rather than cure of his homicidal mania. His synapses have become addicted to its bursts of electrical energy, sending him into deadly rages. While never needing to pick up the pace to conventional highs – it keeps its icy calm until the morbid close – the film becomes more a matter of hunt the tragic psycho, but in the hands of the divergent but gifted Hodges and Crichton, remains effectively unusual. ★★★ **IN**

➂ THE TERMINATOR (1984)

Starring: *Arnold Schwarzenegger (The Terminator), Linda Hamilton (Sarah Connor), Michael Biehn (Kyle Reese), Paul Winfield (Lt. Ed Traxler), Lance Henriksen (Det. Vukovich)*
Director: *James Cameron*
Screenwriters: *James Cameron, Gale Anne Hurd, William Wisher, Jr.*
18/102 mins./Action/Adventure/Sci-fi/Thriller/USA

A cyborg assassin called 'The Terminator' is sent back through time to 1984 to kill the seemingly innocent Sarah Connor – a woman whose unborn son will lead the human race to victory in a bitter future war with a race of machines.

When James Cameron started shopping around his *Terminator* script in the early 80s studio enthusiasm was, to put it mildly, muted. Why should it have been otherwise? Cameron, after all, was then a relatively unknown quantity whose first and only movie (*Piranha II: Flying Killers*) hardly ranked alongside *Citizen Kane* in the pantheon of great Hollywood debuts. Nor did the collective studio pulse quicken at the idea of D-list character actor Lance Henriksen playing the film's eponymous death machine.

Finally, Cameron decided that merely running through a bog standard pitch wasn't quite getting the message across and, before a meeting with the independent production company Hemdale, persuaded Henriksen that the executive responsible needed to be shown the power of what he intended. 'I went in decked out like The Terminator,' recalls the actor. 'With gold foil from a cigarette packet over my teeth and a cut on my head. I kicked the door open and the poor secretary just about swallowed her typewriter. I sat in the room with (the executive) and wouldn't talk to him. I just kept looking at him. After a few minutes of that he was ready to jump out the window.'

Hemdale agreed to back Cameron and, once Henriksen nobly stepped aside in favour of the then hot-ish Arnold Schwarzenegger, put up a sizeable chunk of the film's $6m budget. It proved to be an investment that would be paid back many times with *The Terminator* racking up a box office gross of around $60m. Indeed, Schwarzenegger's shades-sporting time-travelling cyborg would become nothing less than a cinematic icon as he laid waste to Los Angeles in an attempt to kill Linda Hamilton and hence irrevocably change the future to humanity's detriment.

Yet, even after being given the greenlight by Hemdale, there is no doubt that the fortunes of the film itself could have gone either way. Certainly, back in the mid-80s, having Arnold Schwarzenegger in your film was no guarantee of success. The Austrian Oak's previous movie, *Conan The Destroyer*, had performed disappointingly while his next, the Brigitte Nielsen-starring *Red Sonja*, would pretty much sink without trace. To mainstream cinemagoers Schwarzenegger was little more than a joke, a mumbling behemoth whose grasp of both acting and the English language appeared minimal at best. Moreover, *The Terminator*'s budget, while sizeable compared to *Piranha II*, appeared disastrously small given the amount of Stan Winston-assisted special effects that the director had in mind. Finally, there was the problem of how much of the film Cameron had half-inched from other sources. Certainly fans of Michael Crichton's *Westworld* couldn't help but notice the similarity between the Terminator and Yul Brynner's invincible robo-cowboy while the film's premise of a sentient all-controlling computer that would wage war against humanity was similar to a short story by sci-fi author Harlan Ellison.

'I loved the movie,' says Ellison. 'Was just blown away by it. I walked out of the cinema, went home and called my lawyer.' (Ellison would eventually receive a credit after threatening legal action.) Indeed, the fact that Cameron's film would become one of cinema history's headline-grabbers rather than a shoddy footnote is largely due to the obsessive, if not downright maniacal, determination of its director. A college dropout, the Canadian-born Cameron honed his technical skills, like so many others, at Roger Corman's New World company before graduating to fully-fledged director on *Piranha II*. Unfortunately the filmmaker fell out with the movie's Italian producer who informed Cameron that the dailies were 'shit' and locked him out of the editing room – forcing the director to break in at night and secretly splice together his own movie.

On *The Terminator*, Cameron decided, the movie would be done his way or not at all. And if that meant personally demonstrating stunts or even having to tell Schwarzenegger exactly where to put each of his limbs at any given time then so be it. 'Jim would say, "I want you to lay there Arnold," ' recalls Henriksen who played LA cop Sergeant Vukovich. ' "Then, when I tell you, I want you to start lifting up with your head. Then your shoulders. ' "Then I want you to sit up. Then I want you to look straight up." He had to give up any ego at all.'

Schwarzenegger threw himself into the part, enduring hours in the makeup chair and training in the use of guns so as to demonstrate a robotic lack of emotion despite the mayhem going on around him. It was a commitment, like that of the financiers, which would be handsomely rewarded. Linda Hamilton and Michael Biehn may have been the film's nominal heroes but it was Schwarzenegger who would indeed 'be back'. 'No matter what I did after that,' says Schwarzenegger, 'people always come up to me and ask, "When are you going to do another *Terminator*?" '

Cameron, meanwhile, would find himself back on the sequel treadmill for his next project, *Aliens* – although this time no one would have the nerve to lock him out of anywhere. ★★★★★ **BM**

Movie Trivia: *The Terminator*

Schwarzenegger, in probably his most famous role to date, utters a mere 16 lines in total ... At one point, O. J. Simpson was being considered for Arnie's role. The initial script was sold to director Cameron's then wife for $1. In the original script, the Terminator's immortal lines are 'I'll come back'. Schwarzenegger trained with guns for four weeks before filming, and earned a special mention in *Soldier of Fortune* magazine for his realistic handling skills.

TERMINATOR 2: JUDGMENT DAY (1991)

Starring: *Arnold Schwarznegger (The Terminator), Linda Hamilton (Sarah Connor), Edward Furlong (John Connor), Robert Patrick (T-1000)*
Director: *James Cameron*
Screenwriters: *James Cameron, William Wisher, Jr.*
15/145 mins./Action/Adventure/Sci-fi/Thriller/USA

Awards – *Academy Awards – Best Sound Effect Editing, Best Visual Effects, Best Makeup, Best Sound, BAFTA – Best Sound, Best Visual Effects*

Nearly 10 years have passed since Sarah Connor was targeted for termination by a cyborg from the future. Now her son, John, the future leader of the resistance, is the target for a newer, more deadly terminator. Once again, the resistance has managed to send a protector back to attempt to save John and his mother Sarah.

He said he'd be back, and true to his word, Arnie did indeed return seven years on from the seminal killer cyborg adventure that proved to be a breakthrough movie for both the actor, and the film's director, James Cameron.

When *The Terminator* first appeared, making the most of its meagre budget, it managed to reinvigorate the science fiction genre, made an icon out of Hollywood's favourite body builder and secured the career of the director who would one day make the most successful movie of all time in *Titanic*. For the second outing, both Arnie and Cameron knew that everything had to be bigger. And better. Having recently shown that he knew a thing or two about making sequels that outstrip their classic originals with *Aliens*, Cameron was more than up for the task of outdoing himself.

At first, though, the premise behind the sequel seemed like a huge mistake. This time out, Arnie's kickass 'borg was to be the good guy. Surely not! Was this some mistake? Or simply the decision of an actor now too big to risk playing a villain, even if it was the very villain that had turned him into one of the biggest stars in Hollywood? Instead of copping out however, Cameron delivered the stunning T-1000, a molten metal killing machine that, in its use of the emergent morphing technology – developed in part for Cameron's previous effort, *The Abyss* – radically raised the bar in terms of computer-generated special effects in movies.

When we left Sarah Connor in 1984, she was a woman reborn, a veritable Madonna, out to protect the Messiah she knew she carried inside. When we join her in *T2*, she has spent those intervening years haunted by the certain knowledge of mankind's imminent doom, and is now incarcerated in a mental institution; her ten year-old son John, is in care. The intervening years also appeared to have done a fair amount for Linda Hamilton, whose first shot in the movie is a close-up of her seriously pumped biceps. The actress spent several weeks before the movie working out and training in gunplay with a former Israeli commando. It paid off. Sarah Connor was effectively transformed into the perfect warrior queen, moving over the course of the movie from buff women-in-prison sensuality to full out *Guns And Ammo* chic.

And Hamilton wasn't the only one whose appearance Cameron was intent on making iconic. He takes an almost fetishistic delight in having a newly arrived naked Schwarzenegger walk into a tough biker bar and fight his way into the best leathers and onto the coolest hog in the place. When the Terminator walks in naked the music playing is all Dwight Yoakam hillbilly; when he walks out, all leather, shotgun and shades, it's 'Born To Be Bad' blaring out on the soundtrack. Cameron takes great delight initially in quashing the audience's expectations, not only keeping Schwarzenegger's actions deliberately ambiguous – is he good guy or bad guy? – but taking an early opportunity to allow the relatively diminutive Robert Patrick to trash him in their first fight. (He even manages to slip in a few sly gags – such as the T-1000 eyeing up a silver-headed mannequin in a department store window, and John's significant talents with video games presaging his later abilities as leader of the human rebels of the future.)

Porn Movie Puns

1. *Sleeping With Seattle*
2. *Edward Penishands*
3. *Jurassic Poke*
4. *Terms Of Endowment*
5. *The Sperminator*
6. *Thighs And Dolls*
7. *White Men Can't Hump*
8. *The Best Rears Of Our Lives*
9. *Driving Miss Daisy Crazy*
10. *Muffy The Vampire Layer*

Metal dominates Cameron's film – from the opening shot of a freeway jampacked with automobiles, to Stan Winston's remarkable prowling Exo-skeletons to the presence of Guns N' Roses on the soundtrack. Indeed, for much of the movie the predominant sound is the screeching of metal on metal as Cameron sets out to redefine that old action movie staple, the car chase. Here articulated lorries take on dirt bikes, helicopters tailgate vans, and everything is explosively levelled by Arnie's increasingly large arsenal.

Twins also unexpectedly feature in *T2* – the appearance of Don and Dan Stanton (best known for *Good Morning Vietnam*) allows the T-1000 to take on the appearance of the hospital guard, while Linda's Hamilton's twin sister, Leslie Hamilton Geanen, does the same for Sarah Connor later (Hamilton actually played the T-1000 version of herself in this shot, while her sister played the real Sarah.)

Originally Cameron ended on a happy note – Sarah 30 years later, sitting in a park much like the one she imagines being blown away at the beginning of the film – watching her grandchild play, her son John now a Senator. Wisely this was dropped in favour of a more ambiguous shot of a dark lonely road heading into a future now unknown. ★★★★★ **BM**

Movie Trivia: *Terminator 2: Judgment Day*

Arnie was paid at the time a record-breaking $15 million, working out at $21,429 per word. Most of Edward Furlong's dialogue had to be re-dubbed by the actor post-production, because his voice broke during filming. The dying screams of the T-1000 are actually performed by James Cameron, not Robert Patrick. KY Jelly was rubbed into Arnold Schwarzenegger's face during makeup to give him a more 'synthetic' look.

TERMINATOR 3: RISE OF THE MACHINES (2003)

Starring: *Arnold Schwarzenegger (Terminator), Nick Stahl (John Connor), Claire Danes (Kate Brewster), Kristanna Loken (T-X)*
Director: *Jonathan Mostow*
Screenwriters: *John Brancato, Michael Ferris, from a story by Brancato, Ferris, Redi Sarafian*
12/104 mins./Sci-fi/Action/Thriller/USA/Germany

T-X, a female terminatrix, stalks John Connor in contemporary Los Angeles. The future rebel leader is protected by a familiar T-101 model, whose mission is to keep Connor alive on the day when the Skynet system is due to launch its first attack on humanity.

James Cameron is gone, and Jonathan Mostow (*Breakdown*) is ringmastering the stuntwork. Sarah Connor is dead, signalling Linda Hamilton's departure, and leaving Nick Stahl's jittery John Connor and Claire Danes as his bewildered, predestined wife to shoulder the human side of things.

Schwarzenegger's admission that the sleek, blonde T-X is far superior to his T-101 because he is 'an obsolete model' has a certain extra-filmic poignancy given that the former box office champ has been on a slide since, well, *Terminator 2: Judgment Day*.

Also, the CGI that made the first *Terminator* sequel such a revelation a decade back can now be approximated by kids with home computers, suggesting this franchise might fall prey to its own nightmare vision and be rendered extinct through mushroom-growth technological progress. And yet, *T3* does what it does with machine-like efficiency.

Cameron's films were ground-breaking melds of action, effects and time-trickery – signature films of the 80s and the 90s, the ruthlessness of the first softened by the reworking of Arnie's cyborg killing machine as a good-guy protector of children in the second.

T3 can't punch in that league, and sometimes verges on parody of its earlier instalments – Schwarzenegger struts nude into a redneck bar to be mistaken for a stripper by a raucous hen night, then cops his familiar threads from a gay dancer (whose star-spangled shades are ditched in favour of something cooler.

Since audiences loved Arnie's gag lines, everything he says here has some double meaning or back-reference to spur a cheap laugh. Even the fearsome supermodel-look T-X inflates her breasts to impress a traffic cop before cutting loose with a succession of creepily flexible moves and morphs all the more effective for not being showstoppers like the liquid metal gags from T2.

Sarah Connor didn't prevent Judgment Day at the end of *T2*, she just put it off. Those following the convoluted timelines of the series – as mutable pasts, presents and futures are created and taken back between loud action scenes – will probably give up after five minutes and go with the ride.

Stahl, using junkie mannerisms that might be construed as a nasty joke at Edward Furlong's expense, and Danes, who essentially has the Sarah role from the first film, are an appealing anchor for the thin story, which is really an excuse for a succession of chases.

The T-X has a new gimmick – remote-controlling other machines – so there's a bravura bit as she commandeers a fleet of emergency vehicles to pursue a fleeing veterinarian ambulance while the T-101 doggedly rides to the rescue in a fire-truck. Later, at a military HQ, the first-generation clunky ancestors of the terminators are wheeled on to show the beginnings of the man-machine war that rages in the films' future.

For 90 minutes, all the intellect and most of the emotions of the earlier films are put on hold in favour of gunfire and excitement. But the last scenes spring a genuinely surprising, affecting finish that recalls the haunting mix of pessimism and determination at the end of *The Terminator* and – of course – leaves things opens for another re-run. ★★★ **KN**

⦿ TESIS (1996)

Starring: *Ana Torrent (Angela), Fele Martinez (Cherma), Eduardo Noriega (Bosco), Nieves Harranz (Sena), Rosa Campillo (Yolanda)*
Director: *Alejandro Amenabar*
Screenwriter: *Alejandro Amenabar*
18/118 mins./Thriller/Spain

A student researching a thesis on violence gets a taste of her subject matter thanks to another student.

The first horror thriller from Alejandro Amenabar casts Ana Torrent as a student researching a thesis on 'audio-visual violence and the family'. When one of her professors dies watching a snuff movie featuring a girl who disappeared from campus two years earlier, Torrent gets into a game of menace with a grad student.

A rawer film than *The Others*, which later made his name, when it was first released many interpreted it as a film that said as much about the state of Spanish cinema, as it did about violence – the purity of the experience of both being lost the further the audience is removed from the process.

Watched as a pure movie it is overly long, but the performances are all excellent and there's quite a bit of meaty unsettling drama. ★★★★ **KN**

⦿ THE TESTAMENT OF ORPHEUS (LE TESTAMENT D'ORPHEE) (1959)

Starring: *Jean Cocteau (Himself, The Poet), Edouard Dermithe (Cégeste), Jean-Pierre Léaud (The Schoolboy), Henri Crémieux (The Professor), Françoise Christophe (The Nurse), María Casares (The Princess), François Périer (Heurtebise)*
Director: *Jean Cocteau*
Screenwriter: *Jean Cocteau*
PG/79 mins./Drama/France

Emerging from the Underworld, an 18th-century poet is given a flower by Cégeste and, when he can only produce an image of himself when attempting to draw it, he is dispatched in search of the goddess Minerva.

This was not merely the concluding part of Jean Cocteau's Orphic trilogy: it was also the final cinematic statement of France's greatest poetic auteur. The 70 year-old polymath clearly revelled in every second of its production. As he would later write: 'The original sin of art is that it wanted to convince and to please, like flowers that grow in the hopes of ending up in a vase. I made this film without expecting anything other than the profound joy that I felt in making it.'

However, Cocteau clearly embarked on this highly personal enterprise because he still felt he had something to say – if only that cinema was still a demanding art-form despite the fact that technical progress had enabled it to be invaded by the uncouth vandals of the nouvelle vague. But even this sour dismissal seems more mischievous than disingenuous, as Cocteau had only been able to complete the film with the prize money that François Truffaut had won at Cannes for *Les Quatre Cents Coups* (1959).

Moreover, he was fully aware that the likes of Truffaut held him in high esteem and eagerly followed his heroic refusal to obey the rules of whatever medium he cared to indulge in. They also copied his penchant for littering his pictures with autobiographical detail and this portrait of the artist as an old man not only recalled Cocteau's creative struggles, but it also contained cameos by friends, lovers and former collaborators, including Picasso, the bullfighter Dominguin, Jean Marais, Maria Déa, Françoise Sagan, Roger Vadim, Brigitte Bardot, Jean-Pierre Léaud and Yul Brynner.

Cocteau also paid tribute to Salvador Dali by imbuing the imagery with a 'phoenixological' quality that seemed to renew its meaning on each viewing. There's certainly much to mesmerise in this 'active poem', which merged the rigorous illogicality of dreams with the realistic intrigues of the universe. But this charmingly self-guying reverie was largely ignored by a public that had moved on to Sartre, Camus and Godard, with some even seeing it as a smug self-tribute by an unrepentant narcissist rather than a priceless confessional odyssey. ★★★★ **DP**

⦿ THE TEXAS CHAINSAW MASSACRE (1974)

Starring: *Marilyn Burns (Sally), Allen Danziger (Jerry), Paul A. Partain (Franklin), William Vail (Kirk), Teri McMinn (Pam), Edwin Neal (Hitchhiker), Jim Siedow (Old Man), Gunnar Hansen (Leatherface)*
Director: *Tobe Hooper*
Screenwriters: *Kim Henkel, Tobe Hooper, from their story*
18/79 mins./Horror/USA

A group of teenagers unwisely enter a household of former abattoir workers.

The outright sensationalism of Tobe Hooper's regional horror masterpiece begins with its eye-grabbing, unforgettable title. It takes real guts to be so blatantly up-front. More guts, in fact than are spilled in the movie.

Nothing could possibly be as bloodily atrocious as title and poster ('Who will survive, and what will be left of them?') suggest that *The Texas Chainsaw Massacre* will be, so Hooper goes the other way. There are no close-ups of open wounds (a gore film trademark since H.G. Lewis' *Blood Feast* (1963), and all limb-lopping happens out of shot (though patrons who cover their eyes and just listen to buzzing and screaming might imagine things no non-snuff filmmaker could put on screen). Instead of the single mummy of *Psycho* (1960), which was also based on the real-life story of Wisconsin ghoul Ed Gein, Hooper has a whole houseful of human and animal remains artistically arranged to freak out the unwary visitor.

Rather than Alfred Hitchcock's delicate, suspenseful manipulation, Hooper follows the lead of fellow independents George A. Romero *(Night Of The Living Dead* (1968), and Wes Craven (*Last House On The Left* (1972), and feeds the audience through a mangle of unrelenting horror and violence. Once his film starts, it doesn't let up until the fade-out: other horror films are as frightening, but few are so utterly exhausting.

We begin deep, deep in the heart of Texas, where dead armadillos curl by the roadside and violated corpses are arranged like scarecrows. Unfriendly locals snarl in incomprehensible accents and the 70s economic downturn has scattered the landscape with abandoned farms and disused slaughterhouses. A group of vapid teenagers in a Scooby-Doo bus, with a whining cripple in place of the big dog, take a trip that ends when they unwisely enter an old, dark house. The apparent leading man, a real Freddy type, wanders down a filthy corridor towards a red room walled with animal trophies. Suddenly, without any Hitchcockian overhead shot to pre-empt the shattering shock, Leatherface – a squealing, obese goon in a tanned skin mask – appears from nowhere and smashes in the kid's head with a sledgehammer. Before you've had time really to register what you've just seen, the killer slams an unexpected, grating steel shutter across the corridor and, out of the audience's sight, finishes off the still-twitching boy.

Tagline
Who will survive and what will be left of them?

Leatherface slaughters three more teens in quick succession, using a meathook, the sledge, and a buzzing chainsaw. The fleeing Sally, Daphne in white flares, is repeatedly caught in brambles and bushes that the killer easily saws his way through. The girl winds up at the mercy of the down-home cannibal clan, a combination of the Addams Family and the inbred rednecks from *Deliverance* (1972). Out of work since the abattoir shut down, they keep to the old ways by treating passing strangers the way they used to treat beef cattle. The nameless degenerates (they become the Sawyers in the sequel) are a parody of the sitcom family, with the bread-winning, long-suffering garage proprietor as Pop, the bewigged, apron-wearing

Leatherface as Mom, and the rebellious, birthmarked, long-haired hitchhiker as teenage son. The house is a similarly overdone, degraded mirror of the ideal home. Impaled clocks hang from the eaves, an armchair has human arms, and a hen is cooped up in a canary cage. Sally is served up at a family meal, presented to the centenarian half-dead Granpaw ('The best killer of them all') to be killed. She survives, but only because the human corpse can barely hold the hammer he uses to smack her skull. This may be the most unpleasant scene in any 70s film. The family cackle and taunt like mad children while Sally screams and rolls her eyes in extreme close-up, certain that she won't live through the night. With an unlikely burst of superhuman strength, Sally breaks free and crashes through a window. On the main road, the hitchhiker is messily run over and Sally clambers into the back of a speeding pickup truck. She survives, but as a blood-covered, shrieking, probably insane wreck. We fade out on a long shot of the enraged Leatherface whirling his chainsaw in the air.

The film has outstanding sound effects, art direction and editing, and a clutch of effective, if necessarily, one-note performances. Unlike the notorious and comparable *I Spit On Your Grave* (1978), *Chainsaw* is not a complete turn-off. If Hooper and his collaborators do not make their subject palatable, they succeed in justifying their film with sick panache. With a surprising amount of intentional comedy, the film is an important precursor to the horror comic style of Wes Craven's *The Hills Have Eyes* (1978), Sam Raimi's *The Evil Dead* (1982) and Stuart Gordon's *Re-Animator* (1985). Hooper reprised the tone of Chainsaw in the demented *Death Trap* (1976) (the one where the crocodile eats the puppy) and in *The Texas Chainsaw Massacre 2* (1986), with Dennis Hopper and bolstered chainsaw. The franchise was resurrected for *Leatherface: Texas Chainsaw 3* (1990), with Viggo Mortensen, and for *Return Of The Texas Chainsaw Massacre* (1994), with Renée Zellweger and Matthew McConaughey. But TCSM is one of those 'there'll never be another' movies. ★★★★★ **KN**

Movie Trivia: *The Texas Chainsaw Massacre*

The deleted scenes on the DVD reveal that Leatherface likes to dress up for dinner by applying lipstick to his mask. One of the actors claimed his filming experience was more horrendous than the time he served in Vietnam, and threatened to kill Tobe Hooper if they ever crossed paths again.

TEXAS CHAINSAW MASSACRE (2003)

Starring: *Jessica Biel (Erin), Jonathan Tucker (Morgan), Erica Leerhsen (Pepper), Mike Vogel (Andy), Eric Balfour (Kemper), David Dorfman (Jedidah), R. Lee Ermey (Sheriff Hoyt), Andrew Bryniarski (Thomas Hewitt/Leatherface)*
Director: *Marcus Nispel*
Screenwriter: *Scott Kosar, from the film by Kim Henkel, Tobe Hooper*
18/94 mins./Horror/USA

Texas, 1973. Five teenagers pick up a traumatised girl on a lonely road. When she commits suicide in the back of their van, they try to alert the authorities but wind up at the mercy of the extended family of a local mass murderer.

Had The *Texas Chainsaw Massacre* – 2003 vintage – been perceived as competing against only *House Of 1000 Corpses* or *Cabin Fever*, it may have stood out as an above-average rural horror movie. However, as the first of a wave of pointless genre remakes (with *Dawn Of The Dead* due in cinemas soon), it's doomed to go up against Tobe Hooper's ferocious 1974 original and, in that league, simply can't quite cut it.

When writer Scott Kosar and director Marcus Nispel play variations on the original, almost setting this up as a sequel rather than a remake, the film is effective. The point of entry into horror is cannily contrived to be reminiscent of Hooper's opening, but spins off in a different direction.

The freaky hitchhiker turns out not to be a killer but a survivor (maybe the girl from the 74 film) who inconveniences her benefactors by blowing her brains out through the back window (a memorable shot tracks through the wound).

This gets the new kids, all credible 70s types, into an awkward mix of terror and embarrassment as they try to get locals even interested in the death. They run into a nightmare Texan sheriff (Ermey, still in *Full Metal Jacket* abuse mode) who takes an opportunity to grope the corpse and is casual about violent death, but goes into supercop overdrive at finding one joint-roach in the van's ashtray.

The film only turns conventional when it gets back to the old plot and starts replaying scenes. There's an attempt to rethink the premise as a franchise: while the new Leatherface has a larger group of weird relations, he's the only actual killer and the original's sitcom family arguments are missed, making this a freak show rather than a skewed State Of The Nation editorial.

The look, created by Hooper's cinematographer Daniel Pearl, and expert art direction is persuasively nasty ... but somehow that buzzing saw doesn't sound as scary as it used to. ★★★ **KN**

THAT OBSCURE OF DESIRE (CET OBSCUR OBJECT DU DESIR) (1977)

Starring: *Fernando Rey (Mathieu), Carole Bouquet (Conchita), Angela Molina (Conchita), Julien Bertheau (Judge), Milena Vukotic (Traveller), Andre Weber (Valet), Pierre Pieral (Psychologist)*
Director: *Luis Buñuel*
Screenwriters: *Luis Buñuel, Jean-Claude Carrière based on the novel* La Femme Et Le Pantin *by Pierre Louÿs*
15/100 mins./Drama/France-Spain

Respectable bourgeois widower Mathieu Faber falls for his new housemaid, Conchita and pursues her through a series of desperate entreaties and chance encounters in the hope that she will eventually surrender to his advances.

Luis Buñuel had a habit of announcing his retirement. But the onset of deafness and diabetes meant that many took the septuagenarian at his word after he completed the satirical triptych of *The Milky Way*, *The Discreet Charm of the Bourgeoisie* and *The Phantom of Liberty*. However, he was soon considering an adaptation of Huysman's *Là-Bas*, with Gérard Depardieu in a dual role. Yet, ironically, when he did finally embark on a new project (which he had a premonition that he wouldn't finish) it involved two performers playing the same character.

This stunt casting had not been his original intention, however. Buñuel had hoped that Isabelle Adjani would play Conchita, but she was unavailable, and he had started the shoot with Maria Schneider as the 'sensual, virginal, demonic little girl'. However, her drug problem and his disappointment with her lacklustre performance resulted in her early dismissal and the hiring of the other two actress that Buñuel had tested, Carole Bouquet and Angela Molina.

It was the perfect swansong motif for cinema's most enduring Surrealist – especially as the pair alternated at random rather than representing the different aspects of Conchita's devious nature – as it not only enabled him to challenge the reality of the screen image, but also to invest the action with a conceptual reality that was unique to cinema.

They were certainly following in august footsteps, as Geraldine Farrar, Conchita Montenegro, Marlene Dietrich and Brigitte Bardot had also headlined adaptations of Pierre Louÿs's short 1898 novel, *La Femme Et Le Pantin*.

But while Buñuel insisted that he had been wholly faithful to the text, he had actually chosen to reinterpret certain key elements. Thus, the two suitors were merged as Mathieu, while the Seville setting was abandoned in favour of a transcontinental odyssey that seemed to linked the whole of Europe with concepts that had fascinated Buñuel throughout his entire career – repression and the liberating power of desire; the mockery of taboos; the detestation of tyranny; the interchangeability of reality and dreams; the cruelty of fate; and the barbarism of love. Genius. ★★★★★ **DP**

THAT'S ENTERTAINMENT (1974)

Starring: *Fred Astaire (Himself), Bing Crosby (Himself), Gene Kelly (Himself), Peter Lawford (Himself), Liza Minnelli (Herself), Donald O'Connor (Himself), Debbie Reynolds (Herself), Mickey Rooney (Himself), Frank Sinatra (Himself), James Stewart (Himself), Elizabeth Taylor (Herself)*
Director: *Jack Haley, Jr*
Screenwriter: *Jack Haley, Jr*
U/134 mins./Musical/USA

A history of the MGM musical from *The Hollywood Revue* of 1929 to *Gigi*, with the clips being introduced by such luminaries as Gene Kelly, Fred Astaire, Frank Sinatra, James Stewart, Bing Crosby, Liza Minnelli and Elizabeth Taylor.

In October 1973, MGM stopped making movies. But while airline mogul Kirk Kerkorian began selling off the lot and the studio's most famous sets and props, he retained control of the film catalogue, which afforded Jack Haley, Jr. and his team unique access to the MGM musical's greatest hits. However, this was no mere an act of crassly commercial compilation. It was a work of archival preservation, as not only were old prints saved, but the sound was remastered to guarantee the optimum performance quality.

It was also a history lesson in what was and still is an essentially dormant genre. Thus, it was all the more regrettable that the writers chose to take such a patronisingly lofty view of the earliest Talkies, with their chubby chorines in virtually static lines and tinny tenors trying to stay within range of the primitive microphones, as some of the later excerpts were hardly the height of sophistication themselves.

The denial of musical activity elsewhere in Hollywood was equally foolish, as the suggestion that Fred Astaire and Busby Berkeley only really came into their own at MGM made the picture feel more like propaganda than a celebration of a uniquely American artform. Even Bing Crosby was forced to concentrate on the pair of pictures he made at the studio and he looks as uncomfortable reminiscing about someone else's memories as Frank Sinatra, Peter Lawford and James Stewart (unlike Elizabeth Taylor and Liza Minnelli, who ham up their parts shamelessly).

As you would expect, the selection concentrates on such icons as Astaire, Gene Kelly and Judy Garland. But the unexpected showstoppers featured the dazzling tapping of Eleanor Powell and the aqua-balletics of Esther Williams. There were also some charming surprises, such as James Stewart warbling through 'Easy to Love' in *Born to Dance* and Clark Gable strutting his way through 'Puttin' on the Ritz' in *Idiot's Delight*.

Having racked up over $12 million at the box-office, Haley sought to repeat the trick with *That's Entertainment, Part 2* (1976), *That's Dancing* (1985) and *That's Entertainment III* (1994), which featured several fascinating outtakes. ★★★★ **DP**

THEATRE OF BLOOD (1973)

Starring: *Vincent Price (Edward Lionheart), Diana Rigg (Edwina Lionheart), Ian Hendry (Peregrine Devlin), Harry Andrews (Trevor Dickman), Coral Browne (Miss Chloe Moon), Robert Coote (Oliver Larding), Jack Hawkins (Solomon Psaltery), Michael Hordern (George Maxwell), Arthur Lowe (Horace Sprout), Robert Morley (Meredith Merridew), Dennis Price (Hector Snipe)*
Director: *Douglas Hickox*
Screenwriter: *Anthony Greville-Bell based on ideas by Stanley Mann and John Kohn*
15/102 mins./Horror/UK

The members of the London Theatre Critics Circle are murdered in scenarios lifted from Shakespeare's plays by mad matinée idol Edward Lionheart who feels he should have been given a Best Actor award.

The crowning glory of Vincent Price's career as the screen's horror-comic bogeyman, this develops the 'body count' plotting of his *Dr. Phibes* pictures as he slaughters his way through an almost-embarrassingly distinguished supporting cast while tossing off Shakespearean soliloquies even Sir Donald Wolfit would have found overblown and doing a series of in-disguise 'turns'. Among the most priceless Price moments: got up in fab gear as gay hairdresser 'Butch', promising client Coral Browne 'ash with flame highlights' before setting fire to her head; in enormous false nose as Shylock carving chunks out of Harry Andrews, prompting Ian Hendry to muse 'it must be Lionheart, only he would have the temerity to rewrite Shakespeare'; dressed as Richard III, haranguing tippling critic Robert Coote for drunkenly falling asleep during one of his greatest performances and then dumping him headfirst in a barrel of wine; as a TV celebrity chef, forcing bouffant-haired fusspot Robert Morley to choke on his beloved poodles in a crime derived from *Titus Andronicus*.

Price is partnered wonderfully by the equally versatile Diana Rigg, who brings a moment of poignance to the fiery finish as the murderer's Cordelia-like daughter, and among the acting greats siezing a welcome opportunity to caricature hateful critics and be bloodily despatched are Arthur Lowe (severed head), Dennis Price, Michael Hordern (stabbed like Caesar) and Jack Hawkins (duped Othello-like into strangling wife Diana Dors). With Milo O'Shea and Eric Sykes (who gets a funny death) as the plodding plods, and 70s pin-up Madeline Smith as pompous, foulard-wearing hero Hendry's girl Friday. It's a key influence on later gimmick serial murder pictures like *Se7en*. ★★★★★ **KN**

THELMA AND LOUISE (1991)

Starring: *Susan Sarandon (Louise Elizabeth Sawyer), Geena Davis (Thelma Yvonne Dickinson), Harvey Keitel (Investigator Hal Slocumb), Michael Madsen (Jimmy Lennox), Brad Pitt (J.D.)*
Director: *Ridley Scott*
Screenwriter: *Callie Khouri*
15/129 mins./Drama/Adventure/USA

Awards – *Academy Awards – Best Original Screenplay, Golden Globes – Best Screenplay*

Two female friends set off on a fun road trip and end up as fugitives, after one shoots a man in self-defence.

Hailed by some critics as a feminist manifesto for the 90s, while Ridley Scott's *Thelma and Louise* falls short of fullblown masterpiece status this self-discovery-on-the-road movie really is a genuine must-see for Scott's breathless, epic realisation of a smart, funny script and bravura performances from its wonderful leading ladies.

This entertaining, giddy tale of two friends who become fugitives is a Big Deal, however, not because it is that original – screenwriter Callie Khouri couldn't have concocted this movie without *Butch Cassidy And The Sundance Kid* and William Goldman's much-copied pattern for an action adventure about comically wisecracking comrades – but because of the astonishing fact that this was the first big-budget Hollywood picture in which the pals are gals.

And what gals! When Geena Davis' bullied housewife Thelma and Susan Sarandon's worn waitress Louise sneak off for a quiet weekend break from their cares (synonymous with their men), a drunken, foul-mouthed, would-be rapist in the car park of an Arkansas honky-tonk sparks Louise's pent-up rage and memories of past abuses. One unthinking, split-second of violence later, and the sickened, terrified women are on the run across the

Southwest from a murder charge. That their route to freedom and fulfilment goes way over the top in a Bonnie And Bonnie scenario of escalating disaster and crime is less troublesome than it ought to be, thanks to Davis and Sarandon raising hell and cracking wise with wild, womanly, utterly captivating style.

For a change, the actors trailing in their wake get to be the ciphers: Thelma's repulsive husband, Louise's Peter Pan unable-to-commit fella, Plod of the FBI, the Nazi redneck cop, the lewd trucker, the seductive thief, with even Harvey Keitel's comprehending 'tec a tad paternalistic in his sympathy for the women. Few men-who-would-be-ideologically-sound will, however, dare to demur as angry women in audiences around them find their voices to cheer and scream thrilled encouragement at Thelma and Louise violently and hilariously taking charge.

One cannot but share these women's exultation as they answer 'the call of the wild', speeding along the highway in a convertible T-bird, chugging Wild Turkey, swapping delightful one-liners and harmonising with the radio. Scott and his British collaborators have created a visual sensation using stunning, desolate landscapes as a mythic backdrop for the women's daring odyssey. And the ultimate, significant difference that makes this buddy movie its very own heart-in-the-mouth job is that when Butch and Sundance went out they were holding guns; when Thelma and Louise are indelibly freeze-framed, pedal to the metal in their crazy act of defiance, they are holding hands. Way to go! ★★★★★ **AE**

Movie Trivia: Sir Ridley Scott (born 1937)

Who he is: One of the first commercials directors to turn to filmmaking. A master of the low-key as well as the blockbuster. Also a producer with his brother, and fellow director, Tony.

Hallmarks: Stunning visuals; lots of steam and smoke; tales of the alienated and outcast; strong female characters.

If you see one movie, see: *Blade Runner* (1982)

THEM! (1954)

Starring: *James Whitmore (Police Sgt. Ben Petersen), Edmund Gwenn (Dr. Harold Medford), Joan Weldon (Dr. Patricia 'Pat' Medford), James Arness (Robert Graham), Onslow Stevens (Brig. Gen Robert O'Brien), Sean McClory (Maj. Kibbee), Chris Drake (Trooper Ed Blackburn), Sandy Descher (The Ellinson Girl)*
Director: *Gordon Douglas*
Screenwriters: *Russell Hughes, Ted Sherdeman based on a story by George Worthing Yates*
PG/94 mins./Sci-fi/USA

Mysterious deaths in the New Mexico desert are traced to a colony of giant ants, the mutated descendants of insects affected by the first A-bomb test. The authorities rally against the threat, fumigating an underground lair but a giant queen ant, which could spawn new generations of monsters, escapes to Los Angeles.

An early entry in the 1950s creature feature cycle, *Them!* is the one about hordes of giant ants – played by large, impressively-detailed puppets with eerie accompanying sound effects. An exciting exercise in paranoid science fiction, it exhibits an interesting tension between cautious warning about irresponsible scientific tampering with the atom and a Cold War vision of the authorities taking on extraordinary powers to combat a threat to the country (note the civilian who has seen the monsters, left ranting in an insane asylum to prevent the true story leaking to the press). It opens as an eerie desert mystery, with cop James Whitmore investigating disappearances and deaths – a mobile-home and a general stores are crushed as if tanks have rolled over them, a shopkeeper is found dead of a huge injection of formic acid, quantities of sugar have been stolen (the film's sole straight-faced joke) and a catatonic little girl is shocked into shrieking 'them, them'. FBI agent James Arness takes charge and a plaster-cast of a strange imprint summons a father-and-daughter investigative team from the Department of Agriculture, cherubic Edmond Gwenn and smart-suited Joan Taylor, who are soon advising on the nation's serious bug problem. Law enforcement, military and scientific experts deduce the nature of the problem and take swift, decisive action to counterract the danger. Director Gordon Douglas stages several great monster-suspense scenes: a first encounter in a sandstorm, a venture into a poisoned nest, a glimpse of horror at sea, and the powerful finale in the Los Angeles storm drains. ★★★★ **KN**

THEOREM (1968)

Starring: *Silvana Mangano (Lucia, the mother), Terence Stamp (The Visitor), Massimo Girotti (Paolo, the father), Anne Wiazemsky (Odetta the daughter), Laura Betti (Emilia, the servant), Andres Jose Cruz Soublette (Pietro the Son), Ninetto Davoli (Messenger)*
Director: *Pier Paolo Pasolini*
Screenwriter: *Pier Paolo Pasolini*
15/98 mins./Drama/Italy

A charismatic stranger comes to stay with a bourgeois Italian family and transforms the lives of the father, mother, son, daughter and maid through a series of sexual encounters and enigmatic discussions.

Critics have fallen over themselves attempting to dissect this scathing spirito-political parable. They debated whether Terence Stamp's stranger was divine or demonic and whether the family was blessed or cursed by his intervention. Some saw the film as a typical 60s demand for liberation from the constraints of capitalist tyranny, while others thought it a blasphemous parody of the Messianic myth. The Church didn't know what to believe, with the International Catholic Film Office giving Pier Paolo Pasolini an award, while the Vatican denounced him. The Italian authorities were no less conflicted, as they sanctioned the film's release after Pasolini was acquitted of obscenity charges.

Even the Marxists complained that Pasolini had exhibited 'a certain compassion' for the detested middle-classes, even though the director had stated that 'the point of the film is roughly this: a member of the bourgeoisie, whatever he does, is always wrong'.

Pasolini had envisaged *Theorem* as a verse tragedy for the stage and had initially conceived the stranger as a kind of fertility god. But he eventually proclaimed him to be 'a generically ultra-terrestrial and metaphysical apparition', who could equally be the Devil or a mixture of God and Devil. However, his identity mattered less than the fact that he was 'authentic and unstoppable'. He's certainly that, as he forces the father to give away his business and head naked into the wilderness, drives the mother into a promiscuous search for his image, turns the son into a self-loathing artist, leaves the daughter in a catatonic trance and prompts the peasant maid to return to her roots and begin performing miracles.

Theorem clearly seems to adhere to Luis Buñuel's contention that spiritual growth and political consciousness are dependent on sexual freedom. But it's also faithful to its title in that it posits an answer to the question 'would a bourgeois household implode if it encountered a force from outside its experience?' Thus, this is a revision of the Edenic fable, with the family realising its shame as a serpentine tempter exposes the reality of its consumerist paradise and forces it to confront its true nature. ★★★★

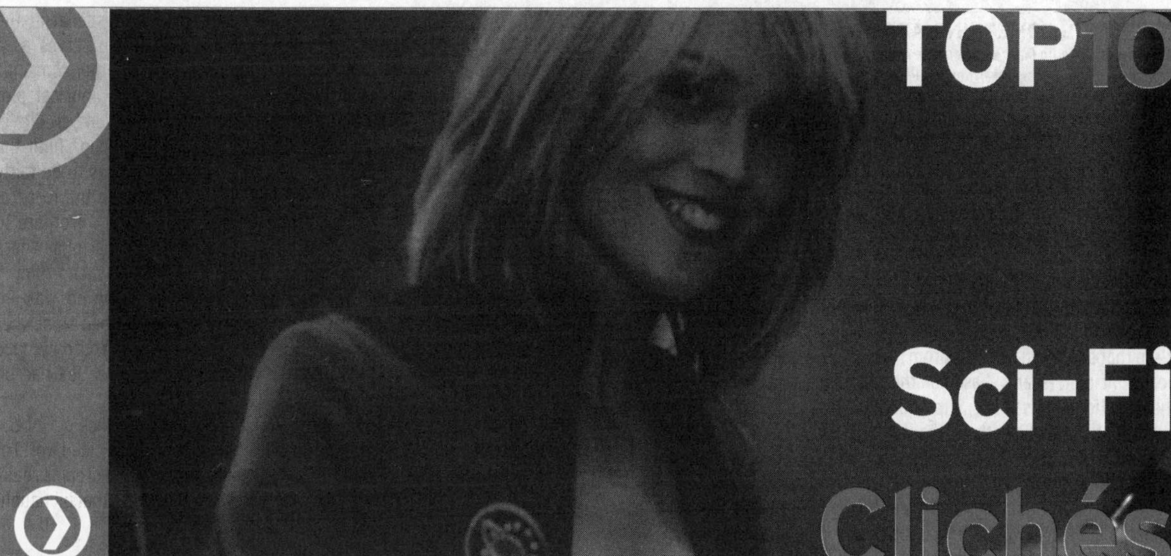

1 Every alien society has a sociology, value and belief system that are indistinguishable from those of feudal Japan.

2 Computers with voice synthesisers either use a sensuous female contralto, a threatening male baritone or a nasally tinny neutral voice.

3 Everyone in the post apocalypytic future dresses like a Heavy Metal bassist.

4 The less technologically advanced a culture, the more spiritually advanced it is.

5 All female scientists are good looking. All male scientists are average looking.

6 If a science fiction movie ends on a big surprise, more often than not the reveal is the barbaric society is really a post-apocalytic western society

7 A fighter pilot destroying an alien vessel must yell 'yeeee-haaaaa'.

8 When an astronaut arrives on an alien planet, there is always a tense moment when the first astronaut removes his helmet on a new planet to prove that the air is breathable.

9 All alien females, galaxy-wide, fancy Earth men.

10 If the ship sends out a landing party to an unfamiliar world, the guy you've never heard of on the team is a dead man.

⦾ THERE'S SOMETHING ABOUT MARY (1998)

Starring: *Cameron Diaz (Mary Jensen), Matt Dillon (Pat Healy), Ben Stiller (Ted Stroehmann), Lee Evans (Tucker/Norman Phipps)*
Directors: *Bobby Farrelly, Peter Farrelly*
Screenwriters: *Ed Decter, John J. Strauss, Peter Farrelly, Bobby Farrelly, based on a story by Ed Decter, John J. Strauss*
15/114 mins./Comedy/Romance/USA

A man gets a chance to meet up with his dream girl from high school, even though his date with her back then was a complete disaster.

The thing about the Farrelly brothers' humour, is that it really shouldn't be funny. We shouldn't be laughing at disabled people, dying dogs, or an unfortunate accident involving our hero, a zipper and his crown jewels. But it's in that scene, where Ted's prom night plans are foiled by the 'frank and beans' incident (scarily, based on the experience of a Farrelly friend) that the affectionately sadistic, improbably hilarious and decidedly incorrect humour of *There's Something About Mary* is set. Irresistibly. As the tagline so succinctly put it: 'Warning: The guys who did *Dumb And Dumber* and *Kingpin* bring you a love story.'

Writer-director siblings Peter and Bobby had already made 'Farrelly' something of a byword for gross-out guy comedies when they came across the *Mary* script from TV writers Ed Decter and John J. Strauss (*Boy Meets World*). Together, the four rewrote the script. Perhaps it was the commercial sensibility of the writers that helped give *Mary* wider appeal, perhaps the brothers had just grown up a bit – but there's no doubt that the collaboration resulted in wider appeal and more critical acclaim than previous Farrelly titterfests. Set pieces like the prom night saga have taken their place in modern comic history, working as more than just a series of unrelated gags. The building ridiculousness of this sequence works as a neat introduction to the film's premise: a well-meaning person unintentionally invites more and more chaos at every turn. Or more accurately, two people: both the blissfully ignorant Mary and the publicly humiliated Ted.

The choice to cast a comedian, Stiller – then best-known for his *Saturday Night Live* sketches and *The Ben Stiller Show* – against a Hollywood belle, Diaz, worked beautifully with the film's theme of opposites (awkwardness versus grace, lies versus honesty, basically, imperfection versus perfection). Mary is gorgeous, kind, clever, talented – hey boys, she even likes sport. She's admired by a series of increasingly flawed eccentrics (Stiller's geeky Ted, Dillon's goofy spy Pat, Evans' fraudulent disabled architect/pizza boy, Elliott's hive-ridden Dom/Woogie) and also by Warren's fellow 'retards', as PC-illiterate Pat calls them. Diaz gamely deadpans her wide-eyed way through this prom-queen-with-a-heart role, earning herself a rep for quirky fare (further confirmed by *Being John Malkovich*), as well as several awards. The Farrellys were so keen to cast her, they put back the film's start date to accommodate her schedule. 'Cameron is Mary,' asserts Peter. 'Like Mary, Cameron seems like the ultimate woman. Every guy on the set was crazy about her.' Peter's praise for Stiller is similarly high. 'I can think of no one other than Ben who could have played Ted. We really have to be behind Ted because the world dumps on him. Ben is one of the best comedic, reactive actors out there.'

The fact that the geek gets the girl – Mary chooses Ted over similarly 'perfect' jock Brett (real-life pro quarterback Brett Favre, a typical Farrelly casting) – makes this an unusually bloke-friendly romcom. To add to its unisex appeal (and hence much of its box-office success), it is at once both one of the most romantic gross-out comedies, and one of the most gross romantic comedies. Stiller has said that the talent of the salesmen-turned-directors lies in relaxing actors enough to do things they wouldn't normally do – and that when he saw the movie, he himself couldn't believe what he'd agreed to do.

That the audience shares this sense of shock and disbelief at the film's extremes certainly adds to its humour. But it also serves as a reminder that this is Only A Film – setting it apart from other romcoms in its relative emotional distance. The *Cat Ballou*-style musical plot updates from Farrelly regular Jonathan Richman and the end credits in which the entire cast sing along to 'Build Me Up, Buttercup,' fulfil the same purpose. That *There's Something About Mary* manages to be fairly light on emotion, yet distinctly memorable, is a tribute to the force of its comic structure. It wears its influences (from the Marx Brothers to *Porky's*) on its sleeve, but wraps them in a tight, original plot where every joke has a purpose as well as a punchline. Making such a film in 1998 also opened up the opportunity to exploit the knowing, post-PC humour that the MTV generation so embraced (later echoed somewhat less successfully in the Farrellys' *Me, Myself And Irene*). You only have to look at *American Pie* and *Road Trip* to see the influence it's had on the teen movie.

There's Something About Mary brought the gross-out flick out of the grubby toilet cubicle of frat boy lite, and into the shiny, blue-skied world of romantic comedy where goodness is (finally) rewarded and dreams really do come true. It's just that the Farrelly brothers' dreams are that bit naughtier than most. ★★★★ **ALs**

⦾ THEY DIED WITH THEIR BOOTS ON (1941)

Starring: *Errol Flynn (George Armstrong Custer), Olivia de Havilland (Elizabeth Bacon), Arthur Kennedy (Ned Sharp), Charley Grapewin (California Joe), Gene Lockhart (Samuel Bacon, Esq), Anthony Quinn (Crazy Horse)*
Director: *Raoul Walsh*
Screenwriters: *Wally Kline, Aeneas Mackenzie*
U/134 mins./Biography/Western/War/USA

Impetuous George Custer goes to West Point, becomes a hero in the Civil War, is appointed commander of the Seventh Cavalry in the West and rides to his death in a battle with the Sioux at Little Big Horn.

A lavish, guts-or-glory biopic of General George Custer, with Errol Flynn as the dashing braggart who turns up at West Point in a self-designed uniform modelled on that of Marshal Murat and impresses his superiors as 'the worst cadet we've seen since Ulysses S. Grant'.

It's an unusual epic: the first half is a knockabout comedy, even during the bloodiest battles of the Civil War, with a hero who is as absurd as he is daring; but it turns serious as Custer heads out West to take command of the rag-tag Seventh Cavalry, turning them into a crack outfit and riding to doom at Little Big Horn.

Flynn's slightly hollow, smirking, self-loving style is exactly right for the most wrong-headed of all American heroes, but this 1942 film bizarrely paints Custer as a friend to Indians (Anthony Quinn as Crazy Horse) and an enemy to politicians (scurvy Arthur Kennedy), blaming the Indian Wars on unethical businessman from 'back East' trespassing on tribal lands and then leaving the poor old cavalry to sort things out.

All lies, of course, but a triumph of classic era Hollywood filmmaking, with every scene built around some entertaining contrivance or eccentric guest star (Sydney Greenstreet as a general, Hattie McDaniel as a tealeaf-reading housekeeper, Charley Grapewin as a Western coot). Director Raoul Walsh stages thrilling big-scale battles to the tune of 'Garry Owen' but the talk scenes are fun too, with Olivia de Havilland as usual well-matched against Flynn as the General's long-suffering wife. The last stand is the definitive print-the-legend version. ★★★★ **KN**

⦾ THEY LIVE (1988)

Starring: *Roddy Piper (Nada), Keith David (Frank), Meg Foster (Holly Thompson), George 'Buck' Flower (Drifter), Peter Jason (Gilbert)*
Director: *John Carpenter*
Screenwriter: *John Carpenter, from the story* Eight O'Clock In The Morning *by Ray Nelson*
18/93 mins./Sci-fi/Thriller/USA

Homeless Nada finds a pair of dark glasses which enable him to see the world as it actually is – in black and white, covered in slogans which urge humans to conform and ruled by aliens who are in league with the rich. Naturally, he rebels.

One of John Carpenter's finest half-brilliant films. It's got some terrible old clichés and is too willing to fire off its guns all over the place, but for the most part it's a funny, exciting and pointed satire committed to saying some very pertinent things about America in the late 80s (and, indeed, any time). Even a ten-minute fight scene – totally gratuitous in story terms – has a valid ideological point to make about how poor people are too busy beating each other up to start the revolution.

The thuggish ex-wrestler Piper is a surprisingly likeable central figure, and the opening sequences – which benefit enormously from a downbeat, bluesy score from Carpenter and Alan Howarth – are an effective depiction of the seamy underside of the yuppie success ethic as the hero drifts from construction site to squatters' camp.

The science fiction aspects are deliberately arch: the 'real' world is exactly like a 50s paranoia movie – in black and white ('they colorised us!'), with retro-look flying saucers in the sky and corpse-faced aliens on the streets – and the invaders are equipped with an outrageously unlikely weakness out of the *Flash Gordon* serials to make a sort-of upbeat finale possible.

There are many priceless ideas, like the interplanetary teleport centre that's just as boring as any earthly airport and the low-tech mind-control devices on every lamppost. Nada's motto: 'I have come here to chew bubblegum and kick ass, and I'm all out of bubblegum!' ★★★★ **KN**

⦾ THEY WERE EXPENDABLE (1945)

Starring: *Robert Montgomery (Lt. John Brickley), John Wayne (Lt. 'Rusty' Ryan), Donna Reed (2nd Lt. Sandy Davys), Jack Holt (Gen. Martin)*
Director: *John Ford*
Screenwriter: *Frank Wead, from the book by William L. White*
U/135 mins./War/Drama/USA

As the Japanese invade the Philippines, Lt. John Brickley and Lt. Rusty Ryan try to convince the US Navy of the efficacy of small, manoeuverable torpedo boats against heavier craft.

One of John Ford's most personal movies (though star Robert Montgomery stepped in to direct some scenes when the Master fell ill), this is an account of the early, losing days of America's war in the Pacific. Based on the career of Lieutenants John Bulkely and Robert Kelly, the pioneer of torpedo boats represented here as Robert Montgomery's John Brickhill and John Wayne's Rusty Ryan, the film sets out to be a semi-documentary account of a very minor tactical turning point – the big victory, almost unnoticed in the last reel, is not against the Japanese but that the Navy finally listens to the heroes – but is actually a deeply romantic vision of the heroism of ordinary servicemen.

The war film has been called 'the male weepie', and this, more than any other film, bears that out. If you didn't understand why *The Dirty Dozen* makes Tom Hanks cry in *Sleepless In Seattle*, take a look at the understated, male emotion on view in the finale of *They Were Expendable* as two stragglers (Louis Jean Heydt, Leon Ames) get places on the last transport plane out before the Japanese overwhelm an island because the junior officers who are supposed to take the spots are delayed, but then get bumped when the kids turn up after all. Perhaps the finest Hollywood war film made during WWII. Instead of an end title, it quotes Douglas MacArthur's 'We Shall Return' – of course, by the time the film was out, the tide of war had turned, giving this study of a losing campaign and a humiliating retreat an elegiac, noble-but-doomed, sacrifice-in-the-short-term-for-the-good-of-all feel that's entirely Fordian. ★★★★ **KN**

⦾ THE THIEF OF BAGDAD (1940)

Starring: *Conrad Veidt (Jaffar), Sabu (Abu), June Duprez (Princess), John Justin (Ahmad), Rex Ingram (Genie), Miles Malleson (Sultan), Morton Selten (Old King), Mary Morris (Halima), Bruce Winston (Merchant), Hay Petrie (Astrologer), Adelaide Hall (Singer)*
Directors: *Tim Whelan, Ludwig Berger, Michael Powell*
Screenwriters: *Miles Malleson, Lajos Biro*
U/106 mins./Fantasy/UK-USA
Awards: *Academy Awards – Best Art Direction (Colour), Best Cinematography Colour), Best Special Effects*

The wicked Grand Vizier Jaffar tricks rightful heir Ahmad into becoming a blinded beggar and usurps the throne of Bagdad, intending to marry a Princess. Abu, a thief and friend to Ahmad, is turned into a dog, but still resolves to set things right.

The 1924 version of *The Thief of Bagdad* was co-written by its star, Douglas Fairbanks, and became hailed as one of the great all-action fantasy spectacles of the silent era. In 1940, producer Alexander Korda mounted a remake which, partly thanks to his own overlarge ambitions and partly thanks to the inconvenience of a world war, wound up being made on three continents, with three credited directors and at least one fix-up man (Zoltan Korda).

The miracle is that it's such a consistently wonderful piece of work, exuberant and magical as it patches together every element of the *Arabian Nights* fantasy sub-genre: a wicked and sorcerous usurper (Conrad Veidt, eyes blazing), a handsome dispossessed prince (John Justin), a winsome princess (June Duprez, gazing longingly into the harem pool for the reflection of her suitor), a gigantic blustering genie (Rex Ingram), a mechanical dancing girl who slips a dagger into the back of a bubbleheaded sultan (Miles Malleson, who also contributed to the script), adventure on the high seas and in the deserts, Sabu fliching everything that's not nailed down in an absurdly high-spirited performance in the title role, marble palaces, a giant spider lurking inside a giant copper statue, a flying horse, etc.

All in gorgeous, pastel Technicolor. It has been remade several times, with Steve Reeves in 1960 and Roddy McDowall in 1978 – and Disney's *Aladdin* cartoon is a complete steal, down to making characters look like those in the old film. ★★★★★ **KN**

⦾ THE THIN BLUE LINE (1988)

Starring: as themselves: *Randall Adams, David Harris, Gus Rose, Jackie Johnson, Marshall Trouchton, Dale Holt, Sam Kittrell, Hootie Nelson*
Director: *Errol Morris*
Screenwriter: *Errol Morris*
15/101 mins./Documentary/USA

Randal Adams, on Death Row after the fatal 1976 shooting of a Texas cop, protests his innocence, though it seems likely that the real killer was David Harris, the key prosecution witness.

Errol Morris originally intended a documentary about an American eccentric who ends up in this riveting film only by proxy – Dr. James Grigson, a psychiatrist who specialises in ruling that condemned murderers are sociopathic threats who should be sent to the chair. Grigson assesses these individuals by the degree of remorse shown, an approach which falls down when the subject is innocent of any crime, and naturally shows more anger than regret. The film consists of talking head interviews with many of the principles – excepting the DA who cited 'the thin blue line' of police protecting lawful folks from anarchy and the dead cop's partner who seems to have fouled up at the crime scene – intercut with stylised re-enactments that are as vague and shifting as memories, overlaid with Philip Glass's hypnotic score. Amazingly, everyone comes across as reasonable and is forthcoming on film – Harris, jailed for a later murder, seems an all-American boy even to the arresting officer who is only too aware of his crazy streak, while the judge who passed sentence reminisces about his FBI agent Dad's presence at the Dillinger shooting and seems genuinely satisfied with his conduct. The woman who did the most to finger a man she was unable to pick out of a line-up consoles herself with the fact that Adams was definitely identified by another witness, David Harris. There are hints that we aren't getting the whole story: the incendiary racial politics of the area are touched on but don't come into focus and everyone speaks in a roundabout way to avoid definite accusations (for legal reasons?). An important film. ★★★★ **KN**

THE THIN MAN (1934)

Starring: *William Powell (Nick Charles), Myrna Loy (Nora Charles), Maureen O'Sullivan (Dorothy Wynant), Nat Pendleton (Lt. John Guild), Minna Gombell (Mimi Wynant), Porter Hall (MacCauley), Henry Wadsworth (Tommy)*
Director: *W.S. Van Dyke II*
Screenwriter: *Albert Hackett, Frances Goodrich based on the novel by Dashiell Hammett*
U/93 mins./Mystery-Comedy/USA

Retired detective Nick Charles is content to live off his wife Nora's fortune, until the secretary of absconded scientist Clyde Wynant is murdered and they accept his daughter Dorothy's commission to track down the missing thin man.

Although Clark Gable was hailed King when Myra Loy was crowned Queen of Hollywood, she was always at her best when paired with the ever-charming William Powell. They made 14 features together, but the best six saw them playing the ultra-chic sleuths Nick and Nora Charles in the whodunits spun off from W.S. Van Dyke's 1934 adaptation of Dashiell Hammett's hard-boiled masterpiece, *The Thin Man*.

MGM chief Louis B. Mayer had planned to headline Laura La Plante (who was on the verge of retiring after failing to make the transition from silents), but 'One-Shot Woody' Van Dyke, who had directed Powell and Loy in *Manhattan Melodrama*, insisted on casting the 29 year-old, who was already a veteran of over 80 pictures. His instincts were sound, as the shoot was completed in 16 days (although some sources say 12, others 18) on a bargain budget and it went on to land four Oscar nominations. Not bad for what was essentially a programmer.

It was something of a misnomer, however, to brand the entire series after the victim in the first case. But somehow the moniker seemed to suit Powell's bibulous shamus, who was equally at home with sophisticated socialites and quick-fisted thugs. But he would have been just another B-movie troubleshooter without Loy's wisecracking sidekick, whose shrewd intuition and readiness with a martini made the Charleses seem the perfect American couple. And then there was Asta, the wire-haired terrier with a nose for clues, and Nick Jr., who became a fixture after *Another Thin Man* (1939).

The quality dipped slightly in the later entries, as Loy lost interest in the increasingly formulaic plotlines and the impossibly urbane banter (although Powell continued to revel in a role that he claimed came closest to his off-screen personality). But *After The Thin Man* (1936), *Shadow Of The Thin Man* (1941), *The Thin Man Goes Home* (1944) and *Song Of The Thin Man* (1947) remain utterly irresistible. ★★★★★ **DP**

THE THIN RED LINE (1998)

Starring: *Sean Penn (First Segeant Edward Welsh), Adrien Brody (Corporal Fife), James Caviezel (Private Witt), Ben Chaplin (Private Jack Bell), Nick Nolte (Lieutenant Colonel Gordon Tall), John C. Reilly (Sergeant Storm), John Travolta (Brigadier General Quintard), John Cusack (Captain John Gaff), Woody Harrelson (Sergeant Keck), George Clooney (Captain Charles Boche)*
Director: *Terrence Malick*
Screenwriter: *Terrence Malick*
15/163 mins./Action/Drama/War/USA

A group of GIs struggle to gain ground against the Japanese in Guadalcanal.

The Thin Red Line is something special. Really special. In truth, the choicest comparison to make is the dreamscape genius of Coppola's 'Nam epic *Apocalypse Now*, depicting as it does a vision of war as a state wholly divorced from reality and utterly wrong. Malick, whose sumptuous at-one-with-nature style was set way back with his revered duo *Badlands* and *Days Of Heaven*, effects a hyper-reality within the verdant jungles of Pacific island Guadalcanal where the US infantry strive to gain ground against the Japanese.

Setting aside the narrative textbook – while the action is linear (fundamentally the tactical taking of a ridge), characters have a habit of disappearing, plotlines are left hanging in the flak, and star names take tiny roles while the emotive-power pivots on unknowns – events are driven by ethereal voice-overs and images of mud-caked GIs struggling to come to terms with the possibility of imminent death. The focus is Charlie company, a brotherhood of men unified by being shit-scared, marked out by individual reactions to that fear. Sean Penn's enigmatic Sergeant Welsh embitters himself to the pointlessness of it all. Ben Chaplin's placid Private Bell pines for his wife, torturing himself with erotic daydreams in which to protect his fraying psyche. Nick Nolte's vitriolic Colonel Tall fights a paranoia of failure by driving men to their deaths while Elias Koteas' noble Captain Staros steadfastly refuses his orders. And, at the centre, is Private Witt (Jim Caviezel) whose Zen-like serenity offers the film's spiritual focus. In various ways, tragedy will visit them all.

John Toll's cinematography is second to none (if the Oscar goes elsewhere there is officially no justice in this world). Be it the divine camera floating miraculously across the hillsides and terrified troopers obscured by the long-grass or sensuously drifting through jungle foliage, every damn frame is a work of art. The action itself is charged and brutal, brilliantly edited, more often using the soldiers' silent faces to reflect the grim bloody aftermath rather than puddles of intestines.

It is long, very, very serious and neck-deep in tropical symbolism – war as a crime against nature, thankyouverymuch. But where other war-is-hell movies essentially depict the loss of innocence, Red Line goes degrees further. War, reckons big brain Malick, is about the loss of your soul. As one sullen soldier confesses to Penn's sergeant that he is no longer able to feel anything, Penn's whispered reply is cruelly dehumanised: 'That sounds like bliss.'

Some, of course, may dismiss the endless recourse to lush, languid shots of light cutting through leaves and dreamy images of native children as so much directorial bottom gazing, especially combined as it is with rambling poetic monologues. This, though, is a major work from a major artist, a lose-yourself-in epic that reaches beyond mere entertainment, thrill or shock (and it covers those bases with ease) to touch the profound. It is the glorious return of a long-lost talent, impossible to ignore, impossible to forget. ★★★★★ **IN**

ⓘ THE THING (1982)

Starring: *Kurt Russell (MacReady), Wilford Brimley (Dr. Blair), T.K. Carter (Nauls), David Clennon (Palmer), Keith Davids (Childs)*
Director: *John Carpenter*
Screenwriter: *Bill Lancaster, based on a story by John W. Campbell, Jr.*
18/103 mins./Horror/Sci-fi/Thriller/USA

An American scientific expedition to the Antarctic is interrupted by a group of seemingly mad Norwegians pursuing and shooting a dog. Only the dog survives the crash but the scientists soon wish they hadn't taken it in.

In 1982 a generation was entranced by a thing from another world. Kids of all ages thrilled as E.T. waddled through Elliot's back yard; chortled as he followed the trail of Reese's Pieces before sobbing helplessly and having to be carried out and placated with Maltesers at the bit where the little bugger fell in the river and turned grey. But there was another kind of alien movie playing on the screen next door. And it seemed to be very, very, different. You could tell. Because through the rubbish multiplex-not-invented-yet soundproofing, you could hear the screams.

John Carpenter's *The Thing* began its protean life as a short story by John W. Campbell entitled *Who Goes There*? published in *Astounding Science Fiction* magazine in 1938. It raised little interest then, being just another of the pulpish sci-fi yarns that filled the fantasy fiction mags of the time. But its star, a creature from outer space that could perfectly disguise itself as another human being, as your wife, husband or best friend, was perfectly suited to the burgeoning paranoia of the Cold War. Terror of reds-under-the-bed, that your neighbour could be one of them set an eerily prescient background for infiltration-themed sci-fi.

Producer Howard Hawks was sharp enough to recognise a zeitgeisty story when he saw one and *The Thing From Another World* was made in 1951. A well made but bog-standard monster movie, it caught John Carpenter's attention when he was five years old. Thirty-five years later and by now a Hawks devotee he nodded to the movie by having it play on a TV in his seminal slasher *Halloween*. But it was the short story that captivated him and he returned to the material for his, very different, remake.

The Thing breaks the rules from the get-go. A pre-credits sequence shows a futuristic saucer flaming in Earth's atmosphere, but we are in the distant past. The film will turn out to be intensely claustrophobic, yet the opening shot is of the wide open spaces of Antarctica. And for a monster movie, it shows the beast ridiculously early, in fact it is the first living thing we will see. Only we don't know that yet, because it is in the form of a cute dog ruthlessly hunted from a helicopter by unnamed bad guys. Half an hour later, when the audience (but no character) sees the dog's face peel open like a banana and issue oodles of gore-drenched tentacles, we will reverse our opinion and wish that the guy in the chopper had got a better shot on the dog.

Carpenter's film is about men in isolation and he peoples the Antarctic station with a cast of bored, bickering blokes comprising some of the finest ensemble actors around at the time (standouts are Richard Dysart, A. Wilford Brimley, Donald Moffat and the late Charles Hallahan) plus Kurt Russell, a criminally underused hero of the old, gruff school prevalent before all these pretty boys came along, as MacReady the reluctant, taciturn leader. One by one the men are relentlessly whittled down in a crimson haze of flying gore, disembodied limbs and helpless screams with the permanent paranoid question of which of them is still human hanging over them all.

Tagline
Man is the warmest place to hide.

But if the plot of *The Thing* is a compelling exercise in suspense, Rob Bottin's groundbreaking prosthetic makeup effects provide release, albeit for some a release of their lunch. The first time we see Bottin's (an obscenely precocious 23 year-old) handiwork it is inanimate on the surgeon's operating table. A distorted, screaming human face pokes out from a mess of insectoid leg and undifferentiated flesh and slime. It's a clever way of nodding to the forthcoming horrors. If this is the aftermath, we wonder, what the hell does this thing look like when it's in action? We find out, properly anyway, one hour and 12 minutes in.

There are a few sequences in films that transcend the movies they're part of and take on a life and reputation of their own: Robert De Niro's 'You talkin' to me' in *Taxi Driver* or the ape flinging the bone heavenwards in *2001*. When Copper pushes the defibrialator paddles against Norris' chest for the second time, his arms crashing through the flesh before being severed by a giant set of jaws (the figure who staggers backwards shrieking and armless is in fact an amputee double wearing a mask) we know we are in the presence of such a scene. And just as we think that things simply cannot get any more extreme his head slips off the table and sprouts legs.

In six words Palmer expresses the feelings of the slack-jawed audience: 'You've got to be fucking kidding'. It's a sequence that any ordinary film would have trouble recovering from. How do you provide an ending that will in any way live up that kind of excess? Brilliantly Carpenter and screenwriter Bill Lancaster go in entirely the opposite direction, continuing his rule breaking. There's no happy ending, and no tragic one. In fact there's no conventional ending at all, just two men, alone in the icy dark of Antarctica one, or both, of whom may not be all they appear. ★★★★★ **AS**

ⓘ THE THING FROM ANOTHER WORLD (1951)

Starring: *Margaret Sheridan (Nikki), Kenneth Tobey (Captain Patrick Hendry), Robert Cornthwaite (Dr. Carrington), Douglas Spencer (Scotty), James R. Young (Lt. Eddie Dykes), Dewey Martin (Crew Chief), Robert Nichols (Lt. Ken McPherson) William Self (Corporal Barnes), Eduard Franz (Dr. Stern), James Arness (The Thing)*
Director: *Christian Nyby III*
Screenwriter: *Charles Lederer based on the novella* Who Goes There? *By John W, Campbell Jr.*
12/87 mins./Sci-fi/USA

A flying saucer is discovered under Arctic ice, and the defrosted pilot – a vegetable creature with a taste for human blood – menaces an American outpost.

Template for hundreds of subsequent science fiction movies, this was Hollywood's first major stab at an invasion from space. Produced by Howard Hawks, often given more credit than director Christian Nyby for the film, it's based on the short story *Who Goes There*? by s-f writer John W. Campbell (more faithfully adapted by John Carpenter for the 1982 remake *The Thing*) and translates the conventions of the gothic horror film into the cold, grey functional 1950s. The Thing isn't a tragic creature, like most previous movie monsters, but a brutal, unreasoning threat – as played by big James Arness, it looks like the Frankenstein Monster in a boiler suit and has Dracula's lust for blood. It's an exciting, suspenseful, still-scary picture, which treats its monster as a problem that the diverse human characters – soldiers, scientists, a journalist – have to solve, and makes an unmistakable Cold War point in having the flying saucer detected by an early warning station which is there to guard against Soviet missiles and making a bearded scientist (Robert Cornthwaite) with a Russian-looking hat the only human who admires the unemotional, ravening invader. It's also very Hawksian in its sense of a male-bonding community led by a Duke Wayne-like hero (Kenneth Tobey), with a token laddish girl (Margaret Sheridan, as the first of many 1950s s-f heroines with a boy's name, Nikki) who banters and scraps with the best of the guys (she's the one who works out what to do with a vegetable, 'you cook it'). Classic moments: the ring of men outlining the saucer under the ice, a great hand-through-the-door shock, the Thing on fire running into the night, the 'keep watching the skies' closing speech. ★★★★★ **KN**

⊙ THINGS TO DO IN DENVER WHEN YOU'RE DEAD (1995)

Starring: *Andy Garcia (Jimmy 'The Saint' Tosnia), Christopher Lloyd (Pieces), William Forsythe (Franchise), Bill Nunn (Easy Wind), Treat Williams (Critical Bill), Jack Warden (Joe Heff), Steve Buscemi (Mister Shhh), Fairuza Balk (Lucinda), Garielle Anwar (Dagney), Christopher Walken (The Man with the Plan)*
Director: *Gary Fleder*
Screenwriter: *Scott Rosenberg*
18/110 mins./Crime/Drama/Romance/USA

Five different criminals face imminent death after botching a job quite badly.

The Tarantinofication of American Independent Cinema continued with this entry in the thriving quirky crime genre. *The Usual Suspects* proved it was possible to tackle a wittily scripted heist-gone-wrong and be more than just a *Reservoir Dogs*-alike. *Things To Do* etc. doesn't quite pull off the feat of rejigging these elements, but it does offer engaging character actors doing enjoyable schtick. It also tries, in the person of Garcia's soft-hearted ex-gangster (unsubtly named Jimmy The Saint), to bring a moral dimension to a genre which too often indulges in admiration for utter scum just because they talk so cool and point guns at each other with insouciance.

Jimmy is called back into the criminal life by his crippled boss The Man With A Plan (Walken at his most relishably venomous), and given the job of scaring off the new boyfriend of the ex-fiancée of Walken's simple-minded son and heir. Jimmy puts together a team of eccentric lowlifes: biker William Forsythe (who is to biker leathers what Helena Bonham Carter is to period frocks), leprous Christopher Lloyd (his fingers fall off), doomed Bill Nunn and, most entertainingly, crazed Treat Williams ('I am Godzilla, you were Japan'). Naturally, the sorry crew foul up, and Walken has to call in genre staple hitman Steve Buscemi to track them all down and do them in.

Alongside the fun crime stuff, which involves much sitting around a diner exchanging sparky repartee, Garcia has time to involve himself with contrasting women: the impossibly angelic Anwar and grunged-out hooker Fairuza Balk. Writer Scott Rosenberg follows the easy assemble instructions for Quentindom too closely and director Gary Fleder clearly enjoys the cynical comedy more than straining-for-significance relationship stuff. From now on, indie filmmakers would do well to think up another plot, but this one last time the heist-gone-wrong story clicks. ★★★★ **KN**

⊙ THE THIRD MAN (1949)

Starring: *Joseph Cotton (Holly Martins), Alida Valli (Anna Schmidt), Orson Welles (Harry Lime), Trevor Howard (Major Calloway), Bernard Lee (Sergeant Paine)*
Director: *Carol Reed*
Screenwriter: *Graham Greene, based on his story*
PG/99 mins./Film-Noir/UK

Awards – *Academy Awards – Best Black-and-White Cinematography, BAFTA – Best British Film*

Arriving in Vienna, Holly Martins learns that his friend Harry Lime, who has invited him, recently died in a car accident.

So captivated was Martin Scorsese by *The Third Man* that he wrote a treatise on it while in film school. But his idiot tutor landed him with a meagre B+: 'Forget it, it's just a thriller,' he sneered. Scorsese has since become one of the greatest directors in cinema history, his tutor, if he's still with us, is most likely still a tutor. *The Third Man* is not just a thriller.

Fifty-two years old, it is a living, thriving testament to that much-contested adage that old films did it so much better. Rife with vivid characterisation, startling plot developments and the cold, cruel cynicism (love is no paragon, it's a nuisance) that is the trademark of Graham Greene, *The Third Man* is a thing of true cinematic beauty.

Out of decayed post-war Vienna, twisted and fragmented into multinational zones, Carol Reed carves an expressionist wonderland of vast, looming shadows and weird, off-kilter camera angles – a world out of balance where moral order has gone the way of the endless sewers. Friendship, love and hope irrelevant ideals in the face of Harry Lime's Darwinistic philosophy. Where the search for truth is a double-edged sword.

It was Sir Alexander Korda who was first struck that this ambivalent, skeletal city would make a wonderful backdrop to a thriller. Having successfully spliced the disparate talents of novelist/screenwriter Greene and director Reed together on *The Fallen Idol*, he was keen to keep the partnership alive and approached them immediately. Meanwhile, in an effort to smooth the American release, Korda brought in fabled Hollywood producer David O. Selznick – forming a relationship that, while certainly bearing fruit, was based entirely on a series of fuming confrontations. Greene, meanwhile, delivered a script (the novella was written as its basis and only published subsequently) whose lean simplicty belied evocative undertones of a post-war Europe facing the birth of the Cold War. A story a million miles from the one-dimensional moralism of protagonist Holly Martins' forgettable Western novellettes.

Harry Lime is dead. A car accident, apparently: two people were seen to carry the body. But Martins, a two-bit novelist stumbling into Vienna at Lime's behest, is not so sure, especially when he hears of a 'third man' at the scene. And as the evidence builds that Lime, his best friend, was utterly corrupt, dealing in diluted quantites of black-market penicillin (a plot device Greene based on real events), it also becomes clear that the mysterious villain/friend may not be quite so deceased.

All these events hinge around the fabled entrance of Welles' Lime: the cat mews (actually symbolic of the smuggler – dwelling in the shadows, serving no-one but itself) and the shaft of light falls across his face as the zither score begins its forlorn twang. It's ironic that an actor so famed for the lovely bass rumble of his voice would be best remembered for a scene where he delivers only the childish smile of prankster finally caught out. But it is one of cinema's truly magical moments, and here the film spins about-heel from a murder mystery to a morality play where Martins wrestles with betrayal, love (for the vulnerable Anna, Harry's ex-lover) and Lime's ambivalently cruel motives – emphasised by his legendary Ferris Wheel speech: 'Nobody thinks in terms of human beings. Governments don't. Why should we?' Watch as his air of menace increases as the wheel rises, then eases back into silky charm again as the wheel descends.

Beyond Welles' glorious cameo (and he is on screen for merely five minutes), beyond Reed's (and cinematographer Robert Krasker's) visual invention, and beyond Greene's bitterly brilliant script, there is one other, distinct factor in this astonishing collaboration: Anton Karas and his zither. A paradoxical mix of the jaunty and melancholic, its frigid timbre encapsulates *The Third Man* alchemy and offers yet another dimension ('He'll have you in a dither with his zither,' rang the silly but really rather true claim on the trailer). It was to become a huge soundtrack hit in its own right and launch Karas – a jobbing musician whom Reed overheard in a Vienna bar one night – as a global star.

Voted the finest British film ever made by the BFI's poll of critics and filmmakers, what the *The Third Man* does right up to the desolation of its final shot (for a speechless three minutes Anna walks up to and straight past Martins' expectant loser) is confound convention. We believe we are in a straightforward murder story, but the truth is far trickier and more provocative. The setting is vivid and expansive, yet the film is as claustrophobic and paranoid as any noir thriller. None of the characters are easy to root for – they're all washed-up, cruelly amoral, rigidly legalistic or : simply lost to fallen ideals – yet their destinies are compulsive. It is a bleak, hard-nosed crime story that encompasses a ruined continent, sick and cynical from war. *The Third Man* finally endures because it offers a simple thing that so many modern films neglect: the power of story. ★★★★★ **IN**

⊙ THIRTEEN (2003)

Starring: *Holly Hunter (Melanie Freeland), Even Rachel Wood (Tracy Louise Freeland), Nikki Reed (Evie Zamora), Jeremy Sisto (Brady), Brady Corbet (Mason Freeland), Deborah Kara Unger (Brooke LaLaine)*
Director: *Catherine Hardwicke*
Screenwriters: *Catherine Hardwicke, Nikki Reed*
18/95 mins./Drama/USA

Nice girl Tracy is led by friend Evie into drinking, committing petty crimes and scaring her struggling mother Melanie with her downward spiral into teen hell.

This LA-set drama could have been entitled *Every Mother's Nightmare* or, possibly, *Cinematic Contraception*.

No one in their right mind would consider having a child – especially a girl – after seeing what a horrible, scheming, back-talking slut she could turn into, as Tracy does when she falls in with cool (and emotionally distressed) kid Evie.

What makes this movie more disturbing – if watching two 13 year-olds attempt to seduce a grown-up male neighbour isn't alarming enough – is that it was co-written by Nikki Reed, who was 13 when she put pen to paper, and 14 when she played the role of Evie.

The film is based on her own experiences (director Hardwicke was dating her dad and suggested she wrote down her teenage problems as a way of working through them), so no matter how many times you tell yourself that the things you're watching don't really happen, she's walking, talking, screeching evidence that it does. ★★★ **JB**

THIRTEEN DAYS (2000)

Starring: *Kevin Costner (Kenny O'Donnell), Bruce Greenwood (John F. Kennedy), Steven Culp (Robert F. Kennedy), Dylan Baker (Robert McNamara), Michael Fairman (Adai Stevenson)*
Director: *Roger Donaldson*
Screenwriter: *David Self, from the books* The Kennedy Tapes – Inside The White House During The Cuban Missile Crisis *by Ernest R. May,* During The Cuban Missile Crisis *by Philip D. Zeilikow*
12/139 mins./Drama/History/USA

Based on the extraordinary events of October 1962, we follow the brief period when the world teetered on the brink of World War III after Russian missiles were located in Cuba.

Okay, so the world is still here. Which means we pretty much know the outcome of *Thirteen Days*, a surging, intelligent, nerve-gripper of a thriller centred around the political intrigue and sphincter-clenching peril of the Cuban Missile Crisis. But that's certainly not a fault; this is a history lesson as taut and terrifying as any fictional movie plot.

Less histrionic and flashy than the canon of verbose Oliver Stone American epics, Donaldson directs with a meaty clarity, never bogging his film down in too much political machination but attributing his audience with the wherewithal to keep track of a highly complex situation. The body of the action is confined to anterooms of the White House and the Pentagon, as JFK and his two closest advisors (brother Bobby and Kenny O'Donnell) wrestle with the crisis – leaving it to brief but thrilling jet-rides over Cuba to remind us of the scope of the threat. The Russians remain an elusive, unseen opponent.

Hence, the film's heart-quickening urgency is left to a ream of heavyweight performances (there's not a dullard in the pack), razor-sharp editing and Self's vociferous script. Indeed, *Thirteen Days* seems constructed around startling scenes of truculent men in snappy suits shouting at one another. There is also a tasty paranoid edge, as the various military heads surreptitiously push for war, while O'Donnell starts to find himself excluded from the brothers' intimacy.

This is home turf for Costner (he made the fabulous *No Way Out* with Donaldson back in 1987); obviously passionate about the subject (he produces and even pondered directing), he gives a stately, effective performance as O'Donnell, who although central never quite seems the leading man. It is, however, Canadian actor Greenwood, as JFK, who shines brightest. Smart enough to avoid getting completely sucked into replicating those regal, Bostonian tics, he goes for the essence of Kennedy, presenting a rarely seen side of the man: the intelligence, integrity and sheer nerve to quite literally hold the fate of the world in his hands for 13 terrifying days. And Steven Culp delightfully plays the nervy, brainiac Bobby like a hunched terrier excitedly engaged in a deadly chess game.

There's the occasional lapse into cheap Americanisms we are presented with O'Donnell's homespun family as a symbol of freedom under fire – but surprisingly little flag-waving. What is most apparent is that this sophisticated tale of impending thermonuclear war stands as a powerful tribute to the conviction and humanity of Washington's finest. ★★★★ **IN**

⊙ THE 39 STEPS (1935)

Starring: *Madeleine Carroll (Pamela), Robert Donat (Richard Hannay), Lucie Mannheim (Miss Smith/Arabella), Godfrey Tearle (Prof. Jordan), Peggy Ashcroft (Margaret), John Laurie (John)*
Director: *Alfred Hitchcock*
Screenwriters: *Charles Bennett, Alma Reville, Ian Hay, based on the novel by John Buchan*
U/85 mins./Spy/Mystery/Thriller/Romance/UK

After stepping into a music hall at random, Richard Hannay finds himself mixed up with spies, a mystery woman and murder. On the run, he uses his wits to escape the police and is, literally, attached to a blonde with whom he shares the rest of his journey, filled with intriguing characters.

The ultimate testament to the genius of Sir Alfred Hitchcock is that he is still being egregiously ripped off left, right and centre. When you've seen 1935's *The 39 Steps* again, note all the bits and pieces Hitch casually makes up which you've seen in chase/ thriller/action films made in the last few years. Never mind Gus Van Sant's silkscreen *Psycho*, if you took all the Hitchcock bits away, *Enemy Of The State*, *Ransom* and *Snake Eyes* would simply collapse.

Like Bruckheimer-Simpson, Hitchcock instantly understood that plot means nothing as long as the hero keeps running. Richard Hannay, Buchan's macho hero incarnated as a tweedily decent chap, impulsively steps into a music hall and finds himself mixed up with spies when a mystery woman (Mannheim) begs him to take her to his hotel room and is murdered after passing on some clues. Sought by the police for the killing, Hannay heads for Scotland.

In a train carriage en route, he attempts to hide from the coppers by smooching a convenient blonde (Carroll). Uncharitably she gives him away and, after an escape, the pair have to yomp across the moors while handcuffed together. The thrills keep coming, as Hannay eludes the police and the villains through such ruses as stepping unprepared in front of a politi-

Actresses who were beauty queens — TOP 10

1. Michelle Yeoh ... Miss Malaysia 1983
2. Cybill Shepherd ... Miss Teenage Memphis 1966 and 1968
3. Zsa Zsa Gabor ... Miss Hungary 1936
4. Michelle Pfeiffer ... Miss Orange County 1976
5. Kelly Hu ... Miss Teen USA, Miss Hawaii Teen 1985
6. Sharon Stone...Saegertown's Spring Festival Queen, Miss Crawford County 1976
7. Halle Berry ... Miss Teen All American, Miss Ohio 1986
8. Raquel Welch ... Miss Fairest of the Fair, Miss Photogenic, Miss Contour, Miss Maid of California 1958
9. Eva Longoria ... Miss Corpus Christi 1998
10. Aishwarya Rai ... Miss World 1994

cal meeting to deliver a stirringly meaningless speech. But the director is also excited by the pervy touch of having hero and heroine cuffed together and playing up their sexual attraction and natural mutual suspicion. In the middle of the action, there's a starkly brilliant sequence as they shelter with a dour crofter (Laurie) and his wife (Ashcroft), and Hitch sketches in the bleakness and the unfulfilled yearning of the woman's life. It all winds up back at the music hall, with a little man called Mister Memory (Wylie Watson) and a mastermind (Tearle) short of a finger. After the curtain has fallen, you'll be happy for a week. ★★★★★ **KN**

THIS BOY'S LIFE (1993)

Starring: *Robert De Niro (Dwight Hansen), Ellen Barkin (Caroline Wolff Hansen), Leonardo DiCaprio (Tobias 'Toby' Wolff), Eliza Dushku (Pearl), Chris Cooper (Roy), Carla Guigino (Norma)*
Director: *Michael Caton-Jones*
Screenwriter: *Robert Getchell, based on the book by Tobias Wolff*
15/110 mins./Drama/USA

Caroline drifts from State to State and boyfriend to boyfriend, dragging her now teenage son along with her. Finally it seems she may have met the man of her dreams but it becomes apparent they were a little swift to judge.

The ubiquitous Robert De Niro rings the changes yet again in an emotionally high-pitched coming-of-age period drama adapted from the autobiography of award-winning American writer Tobias Wolff, whose troubled adolescence was exacerbated by a bullying stepfather.

Ellen Barkin is divorcee Caroline, a pretty, ever-optimistic woman whose way of resolving problems is to run from them, and who drags her understandably moody son Toby around the country on one feckless rainbow chase after another between liaisons with losers and abusers. Then, in Seattle in 1958, the apparently stable nerd Dwight enters their lives and overwhelms Caroline with comically gentlemanly wooing. But once ineffectual mother and incipient, juvenile deliquent Toby – a bright smart-ass who affects the greasy quiffed rebellious style of the day – are snared, Dwight's mean, sadistic, unpredictably cruel character is revealed with horrifying rapidity. And Barkin, whose Caroline sinks into weary acceptance, is then consigned to the role of cowed bystander, as man and youth engage in physical and psychological combat.

An exploration of what it is to be a man and how small men reinvent themselves as bigshots by tormenting the weak, this is full of powerful emoting and is painstakingly redolent of time, place and mood, right down to the eclectic soundtrack. But just as De Niro struggles – arresting, but a bit too much so – to find a balance between pained humour and the unbearable circumstances that prompted Toby's elaborate plan of escape to a new life, the film also struggles to find its tone. Despite its admirable strengths and the fact of it being a true story, there is somehow a failure to completely connect with the fierce boy, giving his unhappy and alienating youth an unfortunate air of unreality. ★★★ **AE**

THIS GUN FOR HIRE (1942)

Starring: *Veronica Lake (Ellen Graham), Robert Preston (Michael Crane), Laird Cregar (Willard Gates), Alan Ladd (Philip Raven), Tully Marshall (Alvin Brewster)*
Director: *Frank Tuttle*
Screenwriters: *Albert Maltz, W.R. Burnett, from the novel* A Gun For Sale *by Graham Greene*
15/80 mins./Crime/Drama/USA

Hit man Raven seeks revenge on Gates who has paid him off in stolen money. He falls in with Ellen, who has been called to testify against Gates in an investigation of his criminal activities.

This adaptation of Graham Greene's novel swaps seedy English boarding house atmospherics for Paramount's slightly decadent glamour. A typical Hollywoodisation is that Greene's assassin has a tell-tale harelip, whose plot purpose is taken by handsome Alan Ladd's kinky wrist (a remnant of the child abuse that has turned him into a neurotic who only loves cats).

There's an odd, early-in-the-war vision of Californian corruption in the shape of evil munitions millionaire Tully Marshall, as geriatric and feeble as Mr Burns, a prototype Bond villain who hopes to profit by selling poison gas to the enemy.

The wonderfully flabby, creepy Laird Cregar is a chorine-chasing, chocolate-gobbling coward who hires and betrays the hit man on the mastermind's orders and runs a cabaret club on the side so he can ogle the likes of Lake's singing conjurer.

Ladd, ill-set wrist hidden in a cavernous trenchcoat pocket, is the main draw and Raven is the ancestor of all the cool, morally neutral but somehow decent-when-pushed hit men who recur in later action cinema, especially from the Far East.

In 1942, Raven could only be as interesting as he is because Ladd, in his breakthrough role, didn't get top-billing. Honest cop Robert Preston is the supposed hero, but grimaces as if he knew from the start he had no chance of stealing this film.

Lake, reteamed with the equally diminutive Ladd in later thrillers, may be best remembered for her hairstyle, but is provides lazy-lidded, somehow unsettling glamour, speaking in a wry, sexy monotone, untouchable as men get shot all around her and she watches them die with mild interest. ★★★★ **KN**

THIS HAPPY BREED (1944)

Starring: *Robert Newton (Frank Gibbons), Celia Johnson (Ethel Gibbons), John Mills (Billy Mitchell), Kay Walsh (Queenie Gibbons), Stanley Holloway (Bob Mitchell), Amy Veness (Mrs. Flint), Alison Leggatt (Aunt Sylvia), Eileen Erskine (Vi)*
Director: *David Lean*
Screenwriters: *David Lean, Ronald Neame, Anthony Havelock-Allen based on the play by Noël Coward*
U/110 mins./Drama/UK

The life and times of the Gibbons family – father Frank, mother Ethel, their children Reg, Vi and Queenie, her mother and his sister, Sylvia – and their Clapham neighbours Bob and Billy Mitchell between 1919 and 1939.

Noël Coward had played Frank Gibbons when *This Happy Breed* opened at London's Haymarket Theatre in 1943. However, having been so impressed by David Lean while collaborating on *In Which We Serve* that he had conceded him artistic freedom in directing all future screen versions of his work, Coward had to accept being dropped from this adaptation of his own play, as Lean felt that his mannered style would undermine his attempt at studio realism. Yet Robert Newton (who was cast when Robert Donat declined) was scarcely more naturalistic, as he fought his inveterate inclination to overact, while Celia Johnson's south London accent was as unconvincing as John Mills' typically clipped tones were anachronistic.

Yet, this domestic saga – whose title came from John of Gaunt's speech in Shakespeare's *Richard II* – remains as affecting as it was in 1944, when audiences marvelled at the somewhat patronising effort to put their own daily experience on the screen.

In essence, it was a lower-class variation on Coward's earlier *Cavalcade* (which had won the Oscar for Best Picture in 1933) and similarly used landmark events like the British Empire Exhibition of 1924, the General Strike and the rise of Fascism to place the family chronicle within an historical context.

But this was no mere parade of passing time, as Lean used incidents in the wider world to impinge upon the attitudes and actions of the residents of Sycamore Road. Consequently, his situations were far more authentic than those presented in present day soap operas, which, for all their aspiration to social realism, are forced by the nature of their production to skirt contemporary references.

Despite confining much of the action to his interiors, Lean avoided overt theatricality. Indeed, he turned No.17 into the eighth member of the Gibbons family, using it to absorb the tragic news of Reg's car crash death and provide a nostalgic farewell after Frank and Ethel depart for their self-contained flat, in a manner that would be duplicated at the close of the classic TV drama, *Upstairs, Downstairs*, which owed its episodic, history-led domesticity to Coward's household scenarios. ★★★★ **DP**

③ THIS IS SPINAL TAP (1984)

Starring: *Rob Reiner (Marty DiBergi), Christopher Guest (Nigel Tufnel), Michael McKean (David St. Hubbins), Harry Shearer (Derek Smalls), R.J. Parnell (Mick Shrimpton), Bruno Kirby (Tommy Pischedda), Anjelica Huston (Designer), Billy Crystal (Mime)*
Director: *Rob Reiner*
Screenwriters: *Christopher Guest, Michael McKean, Harry Shearer, Rob Reiner*
15/79 mins./Comedy/Music/USA

Spinal Tap, the world's loudest band, is chronicled by hack documentarian Marti DiBergi on what proves to be a fateful tour.

When they first showed *This Is Spinal Tap* to the British press, the distributors handed out only biographical notes on the fictional band, complete with a lot of priceless detail not included in the film (like a list of all 37 people who had played with the band). Since its stars came out of US sitcoms (*All In The Family, Laverne And Shirley*) without much of a profile in the UK, it was disturbingly easy to accept the 'if you will, rockumentary' as genuine and Rob Reiner in his Scorsese beard and Spielberg hat as 'filmmaker Marty DiBergi'. There were mutterings around the screening room about why none of us had ever heard of this group, supposedly, 'one of England's loudest bands' and what the point was in making a film about such an obviously mediocre crowd of ageing heavy metallurgists. It wasn't until genial old Patrick Macnee showed up in a cameo as Sir Denis Eaton-Hogg, chairman of Polymer Records, that the penny finally dropped and we all realised we were watching a made-up documentary (if you will, mockumentary) of extraordinary brilliance, dancing on that 'fine line between stupid and clever'.

The greatest laugh-out-loud comedy of the 80s, *Spinal Tap* has turned out to be an amazingly influential film, without even taking into account a few *Tap* revival tours, videos and an appearance on *The Simpsons*. The Comic Strip crowd responded with the vastly inferior knock-off *Bad News* and the *Tap* feel informs *Still Crazy*, and even real rock biopics like Oliver Stone's *The Doors*. Movies that explicitly pay homage include the rap-themed *Fear Of A Black Hat* (1993) and Tim Robbins' paranoid political folkie satire *Bob Roberts* (1992).

Christopher Guest, the man born to be Nigel Tufnel, has directed *Waiting For Guffman* and *Best In Show* in more or less the same style, and mockumentary licks show up in everything from *Drop Dead Gorgeous* to *The Blair Witch Project*. So, not only is *Tap* funny but it was also cinematically innovative, taking elements from real rock documentaries (cf: *Don't Look Back, Let It Be, The Last Waltz*) and creating a new genre, a totally fresh way of telling familiar stories. Rob Reiner's career may have been up and down ever since, see-sawing between faceless Hollywood star vehicles (*A Few Good Men*) and oddball comedies (*North*), but this near-homemade film, an expansion of a 40-minute short and some *Saturday Night Live* appearances, marked him out as more than just another sitcom grad with residuals to spend.

Tap fans treasure favourite routines and lines: Derek Smalls trapped in a stage pod or setting off an airport metal detector with the foil-wrapped pickle in his underpants; the band getting lost backstage as they try to reach an eager audience ('Hello, Cleveland!'); the undersized Stonehenge triptych descending to be 'in danger of being crushed by a dwarf'; the blank looks of the band when confronted with their backlist of bad reviews or a radio DJ's classification of Spinal Tap as 'currently residing in the "Where Are They Now?" file'; the arguments over the offensive cover of the *Smell The Glove* album; Nigel's tour of his guitar and amp collection ('it's one louder'); 'You can't do heavy metal in Doubly'; 'It's called *Lick My Love Pump*'. And it's a collection of masterly cameos, from Fran Drescher as publicist Bobbi Flekman (her clones can still be found working in the business) to Bruno Kirby as the Sinatra-loving limo driver, with micro-bits from Billy Crystal and Dana Carvey as mime waiters ('Mime is money!'), Paul Benedict as a huffy gay hotel clerk, Anjelica Huston (name misspelled in the credits) as the monolith builder and Fred Willard – as the jovial air force officer who wants to get the concert over with.

However, it's a lot more than a collection of inspired gags. Copping the Yoko thread from *Let It Be* (1970), *This Is Spinal Tap* delivers a genuine plot as childhood friends David St. Hubbins and Nigel Tufnel fall out when David's girlfriend Jeanine Pettibone worms her way into the band as manager, displacing the long-suffering Ian Faith, who memorably characterises the dim girl as dressing 'like an Australian's nightmare'. It's an achievement that after an hour of jokes at the expense of the crassness and stupidity of Spinal Tap, with hideously accurate parodies of the strutting pretensions of the dinosaurs of rock ('Big Bottom,' 'Sex Farm'), the film can manage to wring some emotion out of the threat that the band will break up. McKean, whose London accent is letter-perfect, has a great acting moment as he becomes so angry and hurt at his friend's betrayal that he can hardly speak.

There's a happy ending, of course: Nigel makes an onstage comeback and Jeanine is put in her place, and the whole band – with a replacement drummer after poor old Mick spontaneously combusts – head for Japan and the inevitable comeback tour. ★★★★★ **KN**

Movie Trivia: *This is Spinal Tap*

The actors played all their own instruments in the film, and toured as a band after the film's release.

After the release of the film, director Rob Reiner was often approached by fans of the film commenting that maybe he should have picked a more famous band to follow. The statement that the band has had 37 members in all over the years means that 32 drummers have died or left inexplicably.

◎ THIS ISLAND EARTH (1955)

Starring: *Jeff Morrow (Exeter), Faith Domergue (Dr. Ruth Adams), Rex Reason (Dr. Cal Meachum), Lance Fuller (Brack), Russell Johnson (Steve Carlson), Douglas Spencer (The Monitor of Metalunia)*
Director: *Joseph M. Newman*
Screenwriters: *Franklin Coen, Edward G. O'Callaghan, from the novel* The Alien Machine *by Raymond F. Jones*
PG/82 mins./Sci-fi/USA

Weird events in the life of atomic scientist Cal Meacham culminate in an invitation from the strange-looking Exeter to work at a secret lab in Georgia, supposedly in the cause of world peace. Other scientists are already there, including the gorgeous Ruth Adams. They quickly discover there's more to Exeter than meets the eye. Is he benevolent? It may take an interstellar journey to find out ...

At 8pm on Sunday, 30 October, 1938, CBS presented *The War Of The Worlds*, as part of its Mercury Theatre On The Air series. The opening lines, of a show that was to cause nationwide panic and carve itself a niche in entertainment history, were delivered by the play's star and director, Orson Welles – 'We now know that in the early years of the 20th Century, this world was being watched closely by intelligences greater than man's and, yet, as mortal as his own.' Clearly these words lodged in the memory of Welles' assistant director that night, William Alland. Best known on screen for playing the investigative reporter in *Citizen Kane*, Alland had abandoned an unremarkable acting career to turn producer with the inexpert Gothic thriller, *The Black Castle*. Recognising that horror was a bankrupt genre, he moved into science fiction and enjoyed a modicum of success with *It Came From Outer Space* and the 3D classic *The Creature From The Black Lagoon* before acquiring the rights to Raymond Jones' novel, *This Island Earth*.

Alland would go on to produce such B-movie standards as *Revenge Of The Creature, The Deadly Mantis* and *The Colossus Of New York*. But never again would he chance upon such a fortuitous coincidence of topical theme, technical aplomb and thespian credibility. Nine years after President Truman ended World War II with an atomic assault on Japan, America put into commission the first controlled fission reactor. Instead of being a destructive menace, nuclear power was suddenly being hailed as the fuel of the future and a source for good, and it was this potential that underpinned the narrative logic of *This Island Earth*.

However, this was just about the only shred of science fact present in Joseph M. Newman's film. Much of the far-fetched fantasy came from the fevered brain of screenwriter Edward G. O'Callaghan, who was replaced for the later drafts by Franklin Cohen. O'Callaghan, for example, devised the idea that Dr. Cal Meachum (played by the ludicrously monikered Rex Reason) should be some sort of latterday alchemist, who could turn lead into uranium. He was also behind the concept of the versatile neutrino beams which not only had the power to pass through planets, but were also capable of destroying or transporting matter at will.

But, if the science was flawed, the gadgetry was unrivalled in its ingenuity and inconsequence. Take the interociter, which Meachum constructs from a myriad of mysterious components. A cubic cabinet with a triangular screen plonked on top, this was not merely a communication device, but also an intelligence test, via which Exeter (Jeff Morrow) invites Meachum to join him, along with other handpicked boffins, at a top-secret rural location.

No sooner has Meachum arrived, by neutrino-powered plane, than the interociter and its blueprints are destroyed. But, then, everything at Exeter's mansion seems to be disposable, including Dr. Steve Carlson. who is slaughtered shortly after serving his sole purpose of disseminating to Meachum and his colleague, Dr. Ruth Adams, the vital information that Metalunians have a habit of brainwashing those who cross them.

Naturally, the pair try to escape, only for their plane to be swept onboard Exeter's spaceship by another burst of neutrino waves. There they learn about Metalunia facing destruction at the hands of its hostile neighbour, Zahgon, unless a source of uranium can be found to replenish the planet's defensive force shields.

Already the film is heading off on its fourth different plotline and there are still plenty more to come, as the ship lands on the eerily barren planet, with its underground cities and hideous insectoid workforce. Unfortunately, Cal and Ruth spend so little time here that the glorious matte paintings, hand-drawn animations and full-scale models are gone before they can be savoured. Using the soon-to-be-outmoded three-strip Technicolor process, cinematographer Clifford Stine and his FX assistant, Stanley Horsley, created a place of desolate grandeur that has rarely been equalled in almost half a century. Its destruction, in a sequence directed by Jack Arnold, is almost heartbreaking.

Less imposing, although more fondly remembered, is the Mutant, which was detailed by Metaluna's tyrannical ruler, the Monitor, to prevent the earthlings from abandoning the planet to its fate. Reportedly costing $24,000, Eddie Parker's costume would have been little more than a reinforced rubber suit were it not for the genius of makeup maestro, Bud Westmore, who designed the fly-like head with its split, protruding brain matter (subsequently pilfered for the huge bonces of the Mighty Mekon and the aliens in *Mars Attacks!*).

There's an undoubted comicbook feel to *This Island Earth*. Yet, with its atypically benevolent view of extraterrestrial lifeforms and its pro-nuclear stance, it's unusual among 50s sci-fi features for its intelligence and allegorical relevance. However, what most sets it apart are its restless narrative and the imaginative beauty of its imagery. ★★★★ **DP**

◎ THIS SPORTING LIFE (1963)

Starring: *Richard Harris (Frank Machin), Rachel Roberts (Mrs. Hammond), Alan Badel (Weaver), William Hartnell (Johnson), Colin Blakely (Maurice Braithwaite) Vanda Godsell (Mrs. Weaver), Arthur Lowe (Slomer), Anne Cunningham (Judith)*
Director: *Lindsay Anderson*
Screenwriter: *David Storey based on his own novel*
15/129 mins./Sports-Drama/UK

Awards: *BAFTA – Best Actress (Rachel Roberts). Cannes Film Festival – Best Actor (Richard Harris)*

Yorkshire coal miner Frank Machin finds fame as an uncompromisingly combative rugby league player at a club controlled by rivals Weaver and Slomer. However, his boorish behaviour is nowhere near as effective off the field and he becomes increasingly frustrated by widow Margaret Hammond's resistance to his clumsy advances.

Lindsay Anderson was the first of the Free Cinema pioneers to taste success, winning an Oscar for the documentary short, *Thursday's Child*, in 1955. However, he was also the last to move into features and the 'grim oop north' phase of British film-making was coming to a close when he released this adaptation of David Storey's acclaimed novel.

Slower, longer and less forgiving than its predecessors, it failed to find an audience with a public then reveling in the first throes of Beatlemania and looking to invest its hopes in witty, well-groomed working-class heroes rather than self-obsessed angry young men.

The critics were more positive, however, with some even claiming this as the best picture that Britain had ever produced. But it now enjoys something of a mixed reputation, with those who applaud its actorly intensity, psychological power and auteurish integrity being countered by others who lament its impersonality, uncertain sense of place and self-conscious striving for significance.

If the nouvelle vague-inspired flashback opening now seems the most outdated aspect of the film, then Anderson's limp grasp of his sporting context is the least credible and not even Richard Harris' passion for rugby could disguise the over-deliberation of the action sequences, in which he exhibits the thuggish tendencies of the 'great ape' that he finally realises himself to be after Margaret's brain haemorrhage.

Indeed, the entire sporting scenario seems strained, as Anderson never fully resolves the issues involving either Johnson, the gay scout or the disdainfully exploitative Weaver and, thus, the club setting always feels like a contrivance designed to prove that macho men would be incapable of understanding or expressing their emotions whether they were in a dead-end job or feted as a titan.

The leads prove equally problematic as, while Harris won the Best Actor prize at Cannes and both he and Rachel Roberts landed Oscar nominations, it's always obvious that they're giving a performance. Moreover, because they were so well matched, it's hard to believe in the inarticulateness and immaturity that ultimately dooms their relationship. Yet such shortcomings only reinforce this flawed film's elemental fascination. ★★★★ **DP**

THE THOMAS CROWN AFFAIR (1999)

Starring: *Pierce Brosnan (Thomas Crown), Rene Russo (Catherine Olds Banning), Denis Leary (Det. Michael McCann), Ben Gazzara (Andrew Wallace)*
Director: *John McTiernan*
Screenwriters: *Leslie Dixon, Kurt Wimmer, based on a story by Alan R. Turstman*
15/108 mins./Romantic/Crime/Adventure/USA

Bounty Hunter Catherine Banning is sent to bring in Thomas Crown, but will their mutual attraction interfere with her work?

Die Hard director John McTiernan had his work cut out for him retooling and updating Norman Jewison's 1968 caper classic. After all, that movie had the iconic cool of Steve McQueen and came to define late 60s cinematic chic. It also had that haunting Oscar-winning number *The Windmills Of Your Mind*. Well, McTiernan's remake has the song and a good deal more to boot, including, in the well toned post-Bond Brosnan and sex on legs Russo, the hottest celluloid couple of the year.

Thomas Crown is a rich, self-made man from Glasgow(!) with millions to spare and no challenges left in life. He divides his time between high level deal-making and telling his shrink (Dunaway, the female lead from the original) just how empty and unsatisfying his life is. That is, until he takes up art theft on a grand scale – 'borrowing' a $100 million Monet from the local museum. Detective Michael McCann is soon on the trail of the thief, as is big-time insurance bounty hunter Catherine Banning, who very quickly sets her sights on Crown. In more ways than one. Thus begins an elaborate cat and mouse seduction, in which both hunter and the hunted find themselves on dangerous ground, with no one sure of where their feelings may lead them.

Such a situation of course stands or falls on the sexual chemistry between its leads – not a problem! Brosnan is all graceful elegance and smouldering charm, a confident, attractive man who even manages to push the presence of Bond out of the frame, while Russo is a veritable cat on heat, all smouldering sensuality, masking potential vulnerability. To say they heat the screen up is an understatement, landing them both in one of the most stylish and inventive sex scenes of recent memory.

While their passion is obvious, their real feelings are constantly unsure, lending the film a much-needed tension that plays right through to (almost) the last frame. As absorbed as he is with his characters, McTiernan is still able to provide a couple of dazzling set pieces – the sustained opening heist (involving a pun-intended Trojan horse) is a doozy, while the Magritte-inspired, music-fuelled denouement is, well, inspired.

The jazz-tinged soundtrack also lends the film a distinctly different tone, fuelled by the syncopated rhythms that run through it (though the inclusion of the full version of Noel Harrison's *Windmills* tune does almost overplay things). As smart, stylish, sophisticated and sexy as its leads. ★★★★ **BM**

¡THREE AMIGOS!

Starring: *Chevy Chase (Dusty Bottoms), Steve Martin (Lucky Day), Martin Short (Ned Nederlander), Patrice Martinez (Carmen), Phillip Gordon (Rodrigo), Michael Wren (Cowboy), Fred Asparagus (Bartender), Gene Hartline (Silent Movie Bandito), William B. Kaplan (Silent Movie Bandito), Sophie Lamour (Silent Movie Senorita), Alfonso Arau (El Guapo)*
Director: *John Landis*
Screenwriters: *Steve Martin, Lorne Michaels, Randy Newman*
PG/104 mins./Comedy/USA

Mexico, 1916. The village of Santa Poco, subject to repeated bandit attacks, appeals for help to the Three Amigos – Dusty Bottoms, Lucky Day, Ned Nederlander – swashbuckling stars of the silent screen. Just fired by the studio, the heroes travel South and try to take on the villain El Guapo.

In the 1980s, John Landis was perhaps the only director in Hollywood who understood the comic formula, neither high sophistication nor low slapstick, that worked in the 1940s and 50s for the 'Road to' films, Frank Tashlin or (at their best) Abbott and Costello and Martin and Lewis. This affectionate spoof of singing cowboy heroics has Martin, Chase and Short kitted out in embroidered Cisco Kid finery and *huge* sombreros as the blithely self-confident fakers who, naturally, are shocked to learn the vicious villain really would be happy to see them die like dogs.

Landis is willing to halt the flow of gags and one-liners in order to build a sustained comic set-piece, like the scene in which the Amigos prance idiotically in a tough bar while the cowering patrons, who think them merciless killers, are forced to join in the chorus of an asinine song. Also relishable are a campfire sing-song in a gloriously artificial set where the amigos are joined by a horde of animals, one-upmanship duologues between El Guapo and his dumb sidekick El Jefe (Tony Plana), Martin's speech about how everyone has to face up to 'their own El Guapo' ('For some, shyness might be their El Guapo. For others, a lack of education might be their El Guapo. For us, El Guapo is a big, dangerous man who wants to kill us'), and a completely stupid scene worthy of Danny Kaye in which the heroes have to get directions from the Singing Bush (Randy Newman) and the Invisible Swordsman. ★★★ **KN**

THE THREE BURIALS OF MELQUIADES ESTRADA (2006)

Starring: *Tommy Lee Jones (Pete Perkins), Barry Pepper (Mike Norton), Julio Cedillo (Melquiades Estrada), Dwight Yoakum (Belmont), January Jones (Lou Ann Norton)*
Director: *Tommy Lee Jones*
Screenwriter: *Guillermo Arriago*
15/121 mins./Crime/Drama/Western/USA/France

Boorish border patrol officer Mike Norton semi-accidentally shoots an illegal immigrant dead. Local law enforcement turns a blind eye, but the dead man's buddy has other ideas, forcing Norton on a bizarre pilgrimage to bury the body in Mexican soil.

There's something about border country that brings out the best in filmmakers. From *Touch Of Evil* to *The Wild Bunch*, from *Lone Star* to *Kill Bill*, directors at the height of their powers are drawn to the inherently dramatic, culture-clash-heavy location. Welles, Peckinpah, Sayles and Tarantino might make for illustrious company but, judging by this stunning film, Tommy Lee Jones deserves his place alongside them. Indeed, comparisons have been made with Peckinpah's *Bring Me The Head Of Alfredo Garcia*, but if anything, *The Three Burials Of Melquiades Estrada* is the more humane, emotionally engaging work.

As anyone familiar with the career of screenwriter Guillermo Arriaga (*Amores Perros*, *21 Grams*) would expect, the initial 'modern revenge

Western' premise is merely the framework for a subtle, involving exploration of friendship, loyalty, sex, death and forgiveness – all the good stuff. Arriaga's fragmented style allows the audience to experience Melquiades' (Julio Cedillo) life when he's already dead, flavouring the warmth and charm of his scenes alongside best pal Pete (Jones himself, marvellous) with an underlying sadness and sense of fate. Similarly, we know Officer Norton is a killer-to-be when we witness his callous attitude both to his wife and the 'wetbacks' he brutalises at every opportunity.

Great writing is, of course, a gift to actors, and every member of the cast excels. January Jones deserves special praise for making a neglected young woman credible despite her luminous good looks, while Barry Pepper outperforms every expectation you could have as the weak, mean Norton. A sex scene between the two manages to be heartbreaking, soulless and bleakly funny, as husband interrupts toenail-cutting to improve wife's self-esteem by bending her over the kitchen worktop for all of 30 seconds. It's behaviour like this which sees Norton dismissed as 'a sonofabitch beyond redemption'. However, it gradually becomes apparent that the film is as much about saving his soul as it is laying Melquiades' to rest.

Once Pete has abducted Norton and disinterred his late, lamented amigo, the movie becomes a meandering, picaresque series of mini-adventures involving rattlesnakes, hungry ants, vengeful healers, a rapidly disintegrating body and – perhaps most memorably – a blind hermit. Levon Helm, once of 70s rock legends The Band, delivers an impactful cameo as the visually challenged lonely old man, in a sequence which eloquently conveys the harsh realities of an isolated frontier existence.

Everything from craggy ravine to sterile, stifling trailer park is expertly framed by master cinematographer Chris Menges in a style which manages to be both subtle and breathtaking. With only a TV movie – 1995 Western *The Good Old Boys* – to his credit as director, it was a smart move on Jones' part to secure the services of the veteran in bringing his vision to the screen. The man who shot *The Killing Fields*, *Local Hero* and *The Mission* knows a thing or two about making landscape a character in itself.

You might expect the journey to be over once the bizarre trio reaches Melquiades' home town, but in fact when this occurs, audience and protagonists alike must take a leap of faith in order to see the story through to a satisfying conclusion. It's a bold gamble, but one which pays off handsomely and makes for a rich, rewarding experience. ★★★ **RF**

ⓓ THREE COLOURS BLUE (TROIS COULEURS: BLEU) (1993)

Starring: *Juliette Binoche (Julie Vignon), Benôit Régent (Olivier), Florence Pernel (Sandrine), Hélène Vincent (Journalist)*
Director: *Krzysztof Kieslowski*
Screenwriters: *Krzysztof Kielowski, Krzysztof Piesiewicz*
15/93 mins./Drama/Music/France/Swizerland/Poland

After the death of her husband and daughter in a car crash, Julie struggles to re-build her life . . .

On March 13, 1996, Krzysztof Kieslowski, documentarian, director and game-winning Scrabble score, kept a promise that his fervent if narrow band of acolytes had hoped he would one day break. Aged just 55, the life-long smoker succumbed to heart complications in Warsaw, Poland, thereby honouring his avowal that *Red*, the majesterial closing chapter of his commanding *Three Colours Trilogy*, would be his last film as a director.

The death of a director, at least a great, white, male European one, does not simply draw a curtain across his career – it seals the immediate area with yellow police tape so that the acknowledged experts can go about their business without fear of being disturbed. To the casual observer it can seem as if casual observers are no longer welcome – all at once, appreciating Kieslowski has become a serious pastime. This is, of course, bollocks.

The *Three Colours Trilogy* is neither forbidden nor forbidding. *Blue*, *White* and *Red* may be described in the current catalogue as works of art – a boring distinction, anyway – but these were just movies once, scrambling for punters' pounds and festival prizes with all the other hopefuls. Hell, *Red* even lost the 1994 Palme D'Or to an upstart called *Pulp Fiction*. (Admittedly, *Blue* did win The Golden Lion at Venice not nine months earlier, with *White* taking the Silver Bear at Berlin in-between, so the lad didn't do bad, exactly).

More to the point, watching movies should never be a chore, nor a rite of passage, imposing titles to be scratched off some fancy-pants list of must-see shibboleths. If great art endures, it doesn't follow that it requires enduring.

To Kieslowski novices, the *Trilogy*'s allure is hardly assisted by the standard three-line set-up, namely that the three colours reflect the French flag and each film examines the current status of one of the ideals of the French revolution: liberty, equality and fraternity. Wow – you can almost hear the essay question now: 'How does Kieslowski examine the ideals of the blah, blah, blah?' Well, here's the short answer – he doesn't. For a start, the rather forced framing device was suggested by co-writer Krzysztof Piesiewicz and, as with their earlier *Dekalog*, putatively based on the Ten Commandments, Kieslowski immediately abandons anything so schematic and predictable, settling instead on a more impressionistic approach: people not politics, emotions over ethics.

And so, to the first of the trilogy – the only one set in France. *Blue*'s liberty belle is Julie, who loses her husband, daughter and entire narrative thread when the family car fatally veers from its designated path. Julie, however, refuses to be unduly delayed by grief and immediately begins exploring the new avenues that have opened up to her quite out of the blue.

Understandably, she peeks down suicide's dead-end first before simply plumping for a new apartment in a new street in another part of town. And yet, Julie's attempts to keep things simple, to keep the past in the past, are frustrated at every turn. Life keeps dropping by unannounced to funny (just how do you kill baby rats in the closet?) and frightening (the mugging victim banging down doors in search of sanctuary) effect. Most of all, the music in her head – music that nominally belonged to her composer husband and bound them together – won't leave her alone, and in the trilogy's most famous effect the screen swoons blue as Zbigniew Preisner's rousing theme gatecrashes Julie's day.

If all this sounds rather solemn and grand, it doesn't play that way; rather it is spontaneous and urgent and hugs tightly to the halting rhythms of life as most of us experience them. Kieslowski narratives are constantly distracted by trivia – when the camera should properly record the car crash it is sidetracked by a boy with a wooden toy. Julie's consolations are likewise entirely commonplace – when she should, perhaps, be heeding a declaration of love she is captivated by the satisfying plop of sugar in a coffee cup.

Kieslowski's critics maintain that his universe is ultimately too designed, that upon closer inspection both catastrophe and coincidence bear the imprimatur of their Catholic creator. And yet, the point is not to divine final meaning, divine or otherwise. The point, as always, is to marvel at the fireworks – and if you cannot relish a master storyteller enjoying the hard-won command of his chosen craft, then you can only pray the higher powers send you a Valentine of your own. ★★★★ **CK**

Actors who lost/gained significant weight for roles

1. Vincent d'Onofrio...*Full Metal Jacket*...+70lb
2. Robert De Niro...*Raging Bull*...+60lb
3. Toni Collette...*Muriel's Wedding*...+40lb
4. George Clooney...*Syriana*...+35lb
5. Shelley Winters...+35lb...*The Poseidon Adventure*
6. Rénee Zellweger...*Bridget Jones's Diary*...+25lb
7. Johnny Depp...*Edward Scissorhands*...-25lb
8. Matt Damon...*Courage Under Fire*...-40lb
9. Tom Hanks...*Cast away*...-50lb
10. Christian Bale...*The Machinist*...-63lb

THREE COLOURS RED (TROIS COULEURS: ROUGE) (1994)

Starring: *Irène Jacob (Valentine Dussaut), Jean-Louis Trintignant (Le Juge), Frédérique Féder (Karin), Jean-Pierre Lorit (August Bruner)*
Director: *Krzysztof Kieslowski*
Screenwriters: *Krzysztof Kieslowski, Krzysztof Piesiewicz*
15/99 mins./Drama/France/Switzerland/Poland

A model, who lives alone, becomes intrigued by the life of a retired judge who, she discovers, eavesdrops on his neighbours phone calls.

The third and final part of the trilogy of films inspired by the symbolism of the French tricolour, *Red* is a fitting summation of Kieslowski's oeuvre (even before he failed to win the Palme D'Or at Cannes this year, he insisted he was retiring to Poland for good), as well as an adept recapitulation of the themes of the previous two films. Whereas *Blue* dealt with 'liberty' and white with 'equality' in bold strokes, *Red* manages to dissolve 'fraternity' into a motif always present in Kieslowski's films: the idea that we live in a fated universe.

Red begins with a misplaced telephone call and ends with a shipping disaster and plays skilfully with the idea of random contact at all points in between. Valentine is a solitary and restless model who lives in the same Swiss neighbourhood as an ambitious young lawyer. The pair cross each other's paths constantly, but never meet until they are thrown together by fate at the very end of the film.

The pivotal figure in all this is the retired judge Valentine meets after a street accident. Embittered, sorrowful and careless, he spends all his time eavesdropping on his neighbours. Slowly the old man and the young woman begin to straighten each other out, until everything falls into place and the climactic image of the film arrives with the force of a revelation. Exquisitely shot, superbly acted and deftly written, this is easily one of the best arthouse movies ever. ★★★★★ **SB**

THREE COLOURS WHITE (TROIS COULEURS: BLANC) (1994)

Starring: *Zbigniew Zamachowski (Karol Karol), Julie Delpy (Dominique), Janusz Gajos (Mikolaj), Jerzy Stuhr (Jurek)*
Director: *Krzysztof Kieslowski*
Screenwriters: *Krzysztof Kieslowski, Krzysztof Piesiewicz*
15/91 mins./Drama/France/Switzerland/Poland/UK

A down-on-his-luck Pole is reduced to busking on the Metro after divorcing his hairdresser wife. Then a fellow Pole rescues him. Second in the trilogy of Kieslowski's films about the three big ideas underpinning the French tricolour, this is by far the most playful and accessible of all his films to date. Loosely structured as a picaresque romantic odyssey with flashes of black comedy and glum pathos, it tracks the experiences of Polish fortune-hunter Karol as he is bounced around an allegorical European landscape of exile, betrayal and fear ruled only by the brute sanctions of the profit motive.

Karol starts off as a mutely timid hairdresser married to beautiful French model Dominique, but, unable to satisfy her, they divorce. Abandoned in Paris he is reduced to busking on the Metro. It is at this lowest point that he is rescued by fellow Pole Mikolaj, who smuggles him back to Warsaw. Once back in his home town, Karol's luck begins to turn and he soon sets himself up as a spiv trading commodities across the old East/West border.

Kieslowski plays all this for laughs, and the anti-capitalist satire which fuels Karol's rake's progress remains the most satisfying part of the film. Bubbling under the surface of the narrative, however, is the old obsession with symbolism and enforced moralising. Karol fakes his own death and lures Dominique to Krakow to attend the funeral, and it is at this point that he takes an ambiguous revenge. As the pair exchange a glance through barred windows at the end of the film, there has been a complete reversal in fortune between the two. Was it worth it? Has some form of 'equality' been established? Only the intensity of the look lets you know. ★★★★ **SBe**

THREE KINGS (1999)

Starring: *George Clooney (Maj. Archie Gates), Mark Wahlberg (Sfc. Troy Barlow), Ice Cube (Sgt. Chief Elgin), Spike Jonze (Pfc. Conrad Vig)*
Director: *David O'Russell*
Screenwriters: *John Ridley, David O'Russell*
15/114 mins./Drama/Adventure/Comedy/War/USA

Three Gulf War soldiers go on the trail of some hidden gold.

Until this film the Gulf War was deemed a little too close for comfort to get all 'Nam revisionist about. On hypocritical grounds of taste, this so-called 'media war' was considered out-of-bounds, apart from the odd sturdy thriller like 1996's *Courage Under Fire*. Adios to delicacy, because David O. Russell's battering ram of a war movie has bypassed the usual 15 years of telling-it-as-it-wasn't filmmaking to go straight for the historical jugular. Throwing caution to the desert wind, he tosses slices of Catch-22, Tarantino, Leone's Spaghetti Westerns, *M*A*S*H* and *Saving Private Ryan*'s verisimilitude into the movie blender to create a violent, blackly comic, ultra-cool, anti-war satire. A visual powerhouse, visceral rock-concert of a movie, *Three Kings* is limited only by a clumsy quest for moral redemption at its rather flaky close. It may upset (it's kind of meant to). It may disturb (yes, that too). It may treat good taste like a fungal growth. But it's one of the most wide-awake movies to trip out of Hollywood in many a moon. And it's got George Clooney in shades and army fatigues which is about as cinematic as you can get.

Covering the full variation of Hollywood machismo, a posse of Desert Storm troopers – combat veteran Archie Gates, earnest rookie Troy Barlow, toughguy Chief Elgin, brainless jabbermouth redneck Conrad Vig – turn radical opportunists having retrieved a treasure map, leading to stolen Kuwaiti bullion, out of the arse of an Iraqi prisoner. We're in post-surrender Iraq, so the plan is to 'officially' retrieve the gold from among the piles of materialist plunder in an enemy bunker and then leg it to safety. No fuss. No bullets. Inevitably, this has to go haywire – after all, we've got movie imperatives to fulfil here (heists never go according to plan). What pulls the highly-charged screenplay back from the precipice of predictability is the war-ravaged world the amoral foursome are suddenly exposed to.

In a blistering stand-off (another movie convention redefined), they are faced with the blind cruelty of the rag-tag Iraqi army shooting dead the wife of a suspected rebel leader. In a split second and by way of some dazzling visual pyrotechnics (the combat is shot like a whirligig, acid trip variation of *The Matrix*'s slick slo-mo), the ceasefire is cracked open and the boys are forced into a flux of moral dilemmas (helping the rebels, keeping the gold, getting captured, dodging a court martial, staying alive).

For sheer brio, only *Fight Club* has recently come close to the giddy fervour and exhaustive excitement generated by Russell's extremist ideas (including the graphically yucky truth about a bullet's internal damage) and inspired direction, as the film caustically dismantles American foreign policy (fiercely exposing just how the world views America) and the easy pigeon-holing of Iraqis as towel-head bad guys. The actors drum up some manic chemistry, with Clooney's drop-dead charisma and Jonze's dweeby pathos standing out as the film's wisdom and comedy respectively. The only slip is the final loss of nerve, dishing up a pat redemption entirely at odds with all the calculated cynicism – but it doesn't dent the effect. By turns hysterically funny and just plain hysterical, this is a compelling, shocking, razzmatazz event of a war movie cum Western cum heist thriller cum media satire ... Oh, see it yourself. ★★★★ **IN**

THREE MEN AND A BABY (1987)

Starring: *Tom Selleck (Peter Mitchell), Steve Guttenberg (Michael Kellem), Ted Danson (Jack Holden), Nancy Travis (Sylvia), Celeste Holm (Jack's Mother)*
Director: *Leonard Nimoy*
Screenwriters: *James Orr, Jim Cruickshank, from the film* Trois Hommes Et Un Couffin *by Coline Serreau*
PG/98 mins./Comedy/USA

When baby Mary is left on the doorstep of three bachelors, they are forced to look after it until the mother returns.

This remains the most successful US remake of a French film to date and it's not hard to see why. The three likeable leads (each thought of as potential break-out leading male stars at the time) play nicely off each other as men stranded with an infant and zero parenting skills between them.

Tom, the architect is the 'grown-up' of the family but still doesn't want to carry the can (or change a diaper), Michael is a cartoonist and ends up playing 'mom' most frequently, while Jack, the selfish ham actor who fathered the child, absents himself as much a possible. Together they share a palatial apartment and an enviable bachelor lifestyle which they begrudgingly yield as they form a bond with the baby.

An unnecessary and thoroughly nonsensical drug-smuggling sub-plot is retained from the French version, but the best moments are in the new fathers' attempts to entertain, feed and change the youngster – a lullaby, the constant bickering over who does what and their disparaging attitude towards each other. When one woman expresses surprise that Jack had a baby, Peter dryly replies, 'I realise such a concept tends to negate our belief in a benevolent God, but yes.'

When it was released on video this film became just as famous for reportedly capturing a ghost on film – in the background in the scene when Jack's mother comes to visit Mary. Sadly, the 'ghost' turned out to be a prop (a cardboard cut-out of Danson). Although in retrospect perhaps it was the ghost of Guttenberg's career which inexplicably petered out soon after this franchise. ★★★★ **EC**

THREE MEN AND A LITTLE LADY (1990)

Starring: *Tom Selleck (Peter Mitchell), Steve Guttenberg (Michael Kellem), Ted Danson (Jack Holden), Nancy Travis (Sylvia), Robin Weisman (Mary Bennington), Christopher Cazenove (Edward Hargreave), Sheila Hancock (Vera Bennington)*
Director: *Emile Ardolino*
Screenwriter: *Charlie Peters, based on a story by Sara Parriott, Josann McGibbon, from the film* Trois Hommes et un Couffin *by Coline Serreau*
PG/99 mins./Comedy/USA

Follow up to the 1987 film, which left the baby cared for by three 'fathers', little Mary now gets taken to the boys' baseball games and her fathers no longer sing her a lullaby – they now perform a rap song. Things seem fairly idyllic, until Sylvia, Mary's mother, announces that she wants to marry snotty English director Edward and move to England.

They're back! Well, Selleck, Guttenberg and Danson anyway, leaving original director Leonard Nimoy as the notable absentee from the 1987 line-up, replaced here by *Dirty Dancing* helmer Ardolino. And now, five years on, baby Mary has grown into an achingly cute little girl, being raised by her 'fathers' and her English mother Sylvia. This is all to the disgust of Sylvia's mother who views the whole set-up with distaste, calling true dad Jack 'the biological one', while studiously ignoring Peter and Michael.

Up to this point this sequel scores fairly high on the fun factor, but from the moment Guttenberg and Selleck arrive in England in search of Mary to the strains of 'Rule Britannia,' it's time to wheel in every worn out Brit-cliché in the book. Sure enough, there's the sex-starved English schoolmarm, the booze-sodden vicar, the forgetful doddery butler, and numerous shots of narrow country lanes and church steeples.

That said, this sequel has moments that are considerably funnier than the original, with the male leads excelling in their roles. ★★★ **JB**

THE THREE MUSKETEERS (1973)

Starring: *Michael York (D'Artagnan), Richard Chamberlain (Aramis), Oliver Reed (Athos), Frank Findlay (Porthos), Raquel Welch (Constance de Bonancieux), Christopher Lee (Rochefort), Charlton Heston (Cardinal Richelieu)*
Director: *Richard Lester*
Screenwriter: *George Macdonald Fraser based on the novel by Alexandre Dumas*
PG/105 mins./Adventure/USA/UK

Based upon the famous novel by Alexandre Dumas, this is the story of young, ambitious swordsman D'Artagnan, who riles then joins up with the King's fabled musketeers, Athos, Aramis and Porthos. Together they must foil a sinister plot against the crown by the scheming Cardinal Richelieu.

A rich, splendidly cast pantomime that while not following Dumas' colourful epic to the letter, at least does it a rambunctious form of justice. There are huge amounts of pleasure to be found in Richard Lester's simple, warm-hearted and clear-sighted storytelling – for all its sinewy twists and political conniving always makes abundant sense. Who cannot enjoy the roguish, busman's holiday performances of Oliver Reed, Frank Finlay and Richard Chamberlain as the ribald but determined trio of musketeers, aided by the effervescent heroics of Michael York, once the poster-boy for debonair English leading men? Nor indeed the hammy villainy of Charlton Heston and Christopher Lee? Now, there's a ripe pair of scoundrels.

Lester keeps the film, adapted with dedicated brio by novelist George Macdonald Fraser, buzzing between the demands of its involved plotting, dancing swordplay and cheerful slapstick. It is conventional stuff without doubt, but done with such a lightness and ease it tumbles through its bawdy range of sex, power, espionage, laughter and some quite creepy violence with nary a leather boot put wrong. Not that it is purely a boy's show, Raquel Welch and Faye Dunaway, both squeezed impressively into their dresses, mark a fine cross section of the moral spectrum on show in this feisty and authentic looking 18th century Paris.

As an interesting footnote, with the actors being aware and therefore no extra pay for their exertions, a sequel was being planned out of the extended shoot – the slightly darker but on-the-nose *The Four Musketeers*. Producer Ilya Salkind ended up successfully sued by the cast, in both cases they'd more than put the work in. ★★★★ **IN**

THE THREEPENNY OPERA (DIE DREIGROSCHENOPER) (1931)

Starring: *Rudolf Forster (Mackie Messer), Carola Neher (Polly), Reinhold Schunzel (Tiger-Brown), Fritz Rasp (Peachum), Valeska Gert (Mrs. Peachum), Lotte Lenya (Jenny)*
Director: *Georg Wilhelm Past*
Screenwriter: *Bertolt Brecht, inspired by* The Beggar's Opera, *adapted by Balazs. Lania, Vajda*

Mackie Messer, the most violent thief in London, marries Polly Peachum. His new father-in-law, king of the city's beggars, objects to the marriage and threatens to disrupt the coronation of a new queen unless Mackie is jailed and/or executed, which gives the chief of police, Mackie's best friend, a dilemma.

Bertolt Brecht and Kurt Weill were so alarmed at the 'betrayal' of the vision of their stage play by filmmaker G.W. Pabst in this film that they brought a lawsuit against the company. Oddly, this was more a matter of aesthetics than politics – they objected not to the (slight) dilution of the depiction of society as hypocritical and rapacious from top to bottom but to the abandoning of the musical play's bare sets in favour of an elaborate, semi-Expressionist warren representing Brecht and Weill's fantastically-imagined and very Germanic take on London.

Rudolf Forster's preening, sharklike 'Mack the Knife' – introduced loitering in the crowd as someone sings a theme song about his many crimes – isn't so much an outlaw hero as a naked representation of the callous, greedy, self-indulgent attitudes everyone else pretends not to have, and over the course of the story we see that bankers and policemen are just as bad as robbers and beggars.

Some of the crass humour wears well – when accused of seducing underage twins, Mackie tells his wife they said they were 'over thirty' and she snaps 'added together' – and much of the great Brecht-Weill songbook is warbled in deliberately croaky, strident style, with Lotte Lenya delivering an especially vicious version of 'The Black Freighter'. One of those early talkies made in two versions, this exists also as *L'Opéra de Quat'Sous*, a trimmer, lesser French language film made on the same sets with Albert Préjean as Mackie. ★★★ **KN**

THRONE OF BLOOD (KUMONOSU JO) (1957)

Toshiro Mifune (Taketori Washizu), Isuzu Yamada (Lady Asaji Washizu), Takashi Shimura (Noriyasu Odagura), Hiroshi Tachikawa (Kunimaru Tsuzuki)
Director: *Akira Kurosawa*
Screenwriters: *Shinobu Hashimoto, Ryuzo Kikushima, Akira Kurosawa, Hideo Oguni, based on the play Macbeth by William Shakespeare*
PG/104 mins./Drama/Japan

A samurai is told by a witch that he will assume the throne. However, only the vaunting ambition of his ruthless wife prompts him to act. But retaining power proves more problematic than winning it in a bloody way . . .

The most Western of all Japanese directors, Akira Kurosawa is rightly revered as one of the masters of the artform. Whether demonstrating the duplicity of the moving image in *Rashomon*, or the pitiless pageantry of war in *Kagemusha*, he managed to remain true to his cultural identity, while achieving a universality of emotion and theme.

In keeping with its source, this is one of Kurosawa's bleakest films. Swept along by events he is too weak to control, General Washizu is undone less by the corrupting promise of power than by his inability to fulfil his destiny. His wife and accomplice ultimately suffers a similar fate. But at least Lady Asaji has the self-possession to pursue her ambitions.

Although this is an adaptation of Shakespeare, several of Kurosawa's staging strategies derive from Noh theatre – among them the use of a chorus, the formalised movement of the characters, the mask-like makeup of the female figures and the precise union of story and style. Even the absence of close-ups approximates the audience's distance from the stage.

Yet it's also highly cinematic: shrouding shadows and translucent mists swirl round the wondrously atmospheric castle, while the wind and rain ceaselessly symbolise a world calamitously out of sorts. Moreover, it's a film studded with magnificent set-pieces – none more memorable than the invasion of Cobweb Castle by countless birds of ill omen, the relentless march of the forest and Washizu's hideous demise at the hands of merciless bow-men. ★★★★★ **DP**

THUNDERBALL (1965)

Starring: *Sean Connery (James Bond), Claudine Auger (Domino Derval), Adolfo Celi (Emilio Largo), Luciana Paluzzi (Fiona Volpe), Desmond Llewelyn (Q), Bernard Lee (M), Lois Maxwell (Miss Moneypenny)*
Director: *Terence Young*
Screenwriters: *Richard Maibaum, John Hopkins, from the story by Kevin Mclory, Jack Whittingham, Ian Fleming, from characters by Ian Fleming*
PG/125 mins./Spy/Adventure/UK

SPECTRE operative Largo steals two missiles with atomic warheads, and implements a massive international extortion scheme. Secret agent James Bond stumbles into the plot while recuperating at a health farm. Along with Domino, who wants revenge on Largo since the death of her brother, Bond sets out to thwart the villain.

The fourth 007 epic is perhaps a slight falling-off from the high watermark of *Goldfinger*. Though it's the entertaining combination as before, there's a sense that the story – devised by Fleming specifically for the movies rather than as a book – consists of bits of the earlier movies pumped up and stitched together (we're back in Jamaica, for instance), while the nuclear extortion premise is so standardised that it served for many other 1960s masterminds, down to Dr Evil. It ups the serial-like feel of the 1960s Bond series by bringing back the as-yet-unseen cat-stroking Blofeld (Anthony Dawson), head of SPECTRE, and establishing that the plots of Dr. No and *From Russia With Love* were only initial moves in a vast campaign of evil which would continue, with Blofeld out of the shadows, in the next three movies.

Connery is already seeming more bored than cool, an eyepatched Celi is just a smidgen less bizarre than previous Bond villains and the glamour girls (nice Claudine Auger, nasty Luciana Paluzzi) get little to do other than melt in 007's arms (which is where Paluzzi is when she gets shot dead).

It was the first Bond which really went overboard with watersports – featuring a mass attack of frogmen on a SPECTRE base (a very exciting scene, though Bond himself tends to get lost in the melée) and one of the series' wildest gadgets in the villain's breakaway yacht the Disco Volante. Through a rights quirk, remade as *Never Say Never Again*. ★★★ **KN**

THUNDERBIRDS (2004)

Starring: *Brady Corbet (Alan Tracy), Philip Wincester (Scott Tracy), Bill Paxton (Jeff Tracy), Sophia Myles (Lady Penelope), Ron Cook (Parker), Ben Kingsely (The Hood)*
Director: *Jonathan Frakes*
Screenwriters: *William Osbourne, Michael McCullers, based on a story by Peter Hewitt, William Osbourne, television series by Gerry Anderson, Sylvia Anderson*
PG/95 mins./Action/Adventure/Family/USA/UK

The Tracy family's International Rescue is infiltrated by slaphead telekinetic nutter The Hood, who is hellbent on utilising IR's state-of-the-art vehicles to rob the world's banks. With The Hood marooning the Tracy brothers in space, it is left to younger sibling Alan and pals to save the day.

Any live action incarnation of Gerry Anderson's legendary puppetathon had a difficult job to do. Simultaneously, it has to invoke wistful nostalgia in a generation raised on Supermarionation in the 60s, while providing smart, snappy entertainment for a hyperactive generation raised on Sunny D.

Without satisfying either remit, Jonathan Frakes' colourful, splashy moppet movie lands squarely on the side of youth, serving up a sub-rate *Spy Kids* that never nails the required light-yet-knowing tone.

What was great about the TV show – and what is largely absent here – was its penchant for peril and appetite for destruction. Frakes shifts the focus from actually rescuing people to The Hood's machinations, so that the characters you cared about (Scott, Virgil et al) are barely in it. Moreover, he also fumbles many of the show's signature moments: MIA is the network of slides and collapsible furniture that took the Tracys to their vehicles; the countdown to take off is so rushed that there is no sense of occasion when a Thunderbird soars into the sky. Frakes tries to have fun with the origins – at one point The Hood uses his powers to make Brains (an uncomfortable Edwards) walk like a puppet – but his clunky feel for the material never lets the joke land.

Messing with the mythos wouldn't be so heartbreaking if *Thunderbirds* was the rollicking kids adventure it clearly wants to be. Frakes fails to inspire spirit and chemistry in his young leads – early scenes sketching Alan as a wannabe Thunderbird are too on the nose to be affecting – with scenes of them outwitting The Hood's henchman (aka Shockingly Bad Minions) echoing the Children's Film Foundation at its worst.

The adult actors fare equally badly. Hamstrung by hamfisted exposition, it is hard to recall when Paxton has been so leaden, Kingsley snacks on, rather than chews, the scenery, and the remaining Tracy brothers are totally characterless and interchangeable.

Yet there are plus points. Myles peps up the proceedings as a sassy Lady Penelope, the animated title sequence is a fun homage and the sleek 60s retro design is terrific; the vehicles are subtly souped up while retaining everything you liked about them in the first place. It's just a shame that the rest of the movie couldn't pull off the same trick. ★★ **IF**

THUNDERBIRDS ARE GO (1966)

Starring: the voices of: *Sylvia Anderson (Lady Penelope Creighton-Ward), Ray Barret (John Tracy/The Hood), Alexander Davion (Space Captain Greg Martin), Peter Dyneley (Jeff Tracy), Christine Finn (Tin-Tin)*
Director: *David Land*
Screenwriters: *Gerry Anderson, Sylvia Anderson*
U/93 mins./Action/Adventure/Puppet/UK

International Rescue prevents several disasters connected with the Zero X program of manned Mars missions. Meanwhile, Alan Tracy of Thunderbird 3 feels that he is undervalued in the organisation.

The first big-screen spin-off from Gerry Anderson's much-loved puppet action series, this puts on screen the kind of action, effects and excitement (not to mention terrific toys) that would not become commonplace until after the *Star Wars* s-f boom of the 1970s.

The main story thread, which would be continued in the next Anderson TV series (*Captain Scarlet And The Mysterons*), is the Zero X space programme of manned expeditions to Mars; after one test launch ends in the disastrous loss of the ship thanks to the intervention of a bald master villain, International Rescue foil a further evil scheme to infiltrate the crew. However, the most impressive sequences are time-outs from the plot: a wonderfully silly 69s dream in which Alan Tracy goes on a date with posh Lady Penelope to the Swinging Star orbital night-spot, and is entertained by Cliff Richard Jr. and the Sons of the Shadows (their song includes the wonderfully silly line 'the man in the moon will jump on you if you don't love me no more'), and a creepy encounter with hostile Martian fire-spitting rock snakes.

Traditional Thunderbirds business comes into play in the suspenseful finale, as the Zero X suffers re-entry malfunction and International Rescue have to deploy their machines to rescue the crew – as was typical in the show, vastly expensive technology is abandoned in an instant (the Zero X crashlands in a small town) and human life is paramount.

The immediate sequel, *Thunderbird 6*, lacks this picture's sprawling scope, but has a better plot. Both are a great deal more fun than the contemptible live-action film from 2004. ★★★ **KN**

THX-1138 (1971)

Starring: *Robert Duvall (THX 1138), Donald Pleasence (SEN 5241), Don Pedro Colley (SRT), Maggie McOmie (LUH 3417), Ian Wolfe (PTO)*
Director: *George Lucas*
Screenwriter: *George Lucas, Walter Murch, based on a story and earlier screenplay by Lucas*
15/86 mins./Sci-fi/Drama/USA

THX-1138 is a nameless worker in a soulless urban society where laws are enforced by merciless androids. He breaks free from the state-required drug-stupor to recover from his nightmare world.

In a white-on-white future society, bald citizens are known by code numbers and toil in drugged stupour over meaningless tasks while chrome-faced robot policemen herd dissidents convicted of 'drug avoidance' into vast white limbo prisons.

THX is puzzled by the awakening of his emotions as he falls in love with his room-mate – who has altered his drug intake – and becomes a rebel. Notably adult in theme, structure and approach, its commercial failure doubtless motivated George Lucas's regression through adolescence (*American Graffiti*) to childhood (*Star Wars*) in his subsequent films.

Neglected on its initial release, this now stands as a classic science fiction movie and one of the most remarkable debuts of the 70s. ★★★★ **IF**

TIE ME UP, TIE ME DOWN (ATAME!) (1990)

Starring: *Victoria Abril (Marina Osorio), Antonio Banderas (Ricky), Loles Leon (Lola), Julieta Serrano (Alma), Maria Barranco (Medica)*
Director: *Pedro Almodóvar*
Screenwriters: *Pedro Almodóvar, Yuji Bernigola*
18/111 mins./Drama/Crime/Romance/Spain

Just released from a psychiatric hospital, Ricky determines to track down his favourite porn star and one-time lover Marina, with the ultimate aim of matrimony. Marina is not convinced, so Ricky imprisons her in a bid to convince her of his affections.

The pressure certainly shows in *Tie Me Up! Tie Me Down!* Things begin well enough: the camera is wielded with panache, the irreverence with bravado, and the décor, as ever with Almodóvar, is wild.

Recently released from a mental asylum with the good wishes and cash present from its female director ('for the hours of mad pleasure you gave me'), Ricky kidnaps former porno actress and junkie Marina and ties her up in his flat. Marina, as it happens, has been trying to keep clean and, moreover, go legit in 'a second-rate horror film' (in the words of its director, played by Francisco Rabal).

Our glimpses of the making of this less-than-masterpiece are far more easily endured than waiting out Marina's imprisonment, which stickily resembles the basic scenario of *The Collector*. For Ricky's idea is to keep Marina in bondage until she loves him; and this film proposes that if someone were to offer us true love, we'd have no choice but eventually to accept. Hence the movie's hearts-and-flowers finale. ★★★★ **LO'T**

TIGERLAND (2000)

Starring: *Colin Farrell (Pvt. Roland Bozz), Matthew Davis (Pvt. Jim Paxton), Clifton Collins, Jr. (Pvt. Miter), Tom Guiry (Pvt. Cantwell)*
Director: *Joel Schumacher*
Screenwriters: *Ross Klavan, Michael McGruther*
18/96 mins./Drama/War/USA

It's 1971 and America is heavily committed to the Vietnam War. During the final stages of training, draftees are sent to 'the second worst place on Earth', Tigerland, a recreation of the Vietnamese jungle in Louisiana. But one soldier is less than co-operative, and exploits loopholes in the system to get his colleagues out of the army.

For his detractors, the news that Joel Schumacher was in the midst of making a 'Nam movie was about as welcome as Michael Winner announcing a *Lawrence Of Arabia* re-make. 'Oh Christ,' they were heard to mutter of the *Lost Boys/Batman Forever/Flawless* director, 'it'll be *St. Elmo's Under Fire*, then.'

Not only was the subject matter hardly typical for him, but the movie was said to be heavily influenced by the stripped-down Dogme 95 shooting style, with his usual lush production design and polished cinematography abandoned in favour of grainy 16 mm, a cast of unknowns, a 28-day shoot and minimum external lighting and makeup. Things did not bode well. Yet what the naysayers were missing is that this kind of low-budget ensemble piece is what Schumacher has always been good at.

Despite being tarred with some of the excesses of the 80s, both *The Lost Boys* (1987) and *St. Elmo's Fire* (1985) featured young, talented casts of unknowns in 'bonding' situations, while in *Falling Down* (1992) he proved he could successfully tackle edgier, more provocative material. With *Tigerland* he draws on both strengths, to produce a beautifully crafted, brilliantly acted and gently moving film that only occasionally lapses into sentimentality.

Drawing more on boot-camp flicks like *Biloxi Blues* and the first half of Kubrick's *Full Metal Jacket* than *Platoon* or *Casualties Of War*, *Tigerland* presents a company of trainee soldiers resigned to their grim fate, until congenital rebel Bozz arrives, both giving hope to his fellow draftees with his knowledge of military law, and driving the American war machine spare with his misdirected talents.

Schumacher shows his familiar talent for rooting out new talent (in the effortlessly charismatic Farrell he has pretty much conjured up a ready-made superstar, while Shea Whigham is also a standout as uptight army-boy Wilson), while Matthew Libatique's cinematography (also utilised by Darren Aronofsky on *Pi* and *Requiem For A Dream*) is in gritty faux-documentary style, with colour drained out leaving only the dull, muddy greys and greens of boot camp.

But it's Klavan and McGruther's screenplay – based on Klavan's real-life experiences in the army – that's the movies' real strength, as it deftly negotiates the odd cliché (the sadistic NCO who's a coward at heart, the obligatory barracks assault together with a truly stupendous level of nudity) and heads for a poignant, understated ending in which yet another batch of America's finest head off to become very lost boys indeed. ★★★★ **AS**

TIME BANDITS (1981)

Starring: *Craig Warnock (Kevin), John Cleese (Robin Hood), Sean Connery (King Agememnon), Shelley Duvall (Dame Pansy), Katherine Helmond (Mrs. Ogre), Ian Holm (Napoleon), Michael Palin (Vincent)*
Director: *Terry Gilliam*
Screenwriters: *Terry Gilliam, Michael Palin*
PG/116 mins./Fantasy/UK

Much to young Kevin's surprise, his bedroom wardrobe contains a time hole, through which spill a gang of time-travelling dwarves with a map of the universe that they have elicited from The Supreme Being. So begins a journey for the young Kevin that will include dropping by Robin Hood's Sherwood Forest, ancient Greece, and the Fortress of Ultimate Darkness.

Arguably Terry Gilliam's most wholly satisfying film, this dazzling, dizzying fantasy is everything that makes the sublime if infuriating director so revered with added solidity. This could be down to the fact he aims the story squarely at kids, without abandoning those familiar strains of surrealism, humour and darkness that make him such a unique artistic proposition. Here, with its ordinary boy on extraordinary adventures theme, we are granted an accessible guide through his ineffable weird-verse in the wide-eyed but unmawkish Craig Warnock. Which means it also comes nearly clean of that potential for keep-it-in-the-club clever-funny smugness left over from the *Monty Python* days.

Without the need for too much logic (never Gilliam's strength) this is a picaresque tumble through time in the company of a half-dozen scamps given tremendous personality by Michael Rappaport and his crew as they bicker and badger their way along their bumbling quest. There's some good starry stuff thrown in: old mucker John Cleese does a memorable reworking of Robin Hood as an awfully decent, rugger-bugger buffoon, Sean Connery is striking, and manly as legend's King Agememnon, and Ian Holm's is a suitably gruff and stroppy Napoleon.

Yet, as we are voyaging through the extraordinary spaces of Gilliam's imagination, with some help from fellow-Python Michael Palin on the script (which counts for the sharp turns of wit), mere time travel is only half the adventure. There is also the idea we are penetrating a dream-universe inside bookish Kevin's head, an escape from his humdrum existence where he is all but ignored by his parents who are zoned out to television game shows and worship pointless gadgets. Thus the litter of toys across his bedroom floor come to form the emblems of his encounters (Greek warriors, Merry Men etc.). It allows Gilliam the freedom to drift into complete fantasy as the huddle of untrustworthy dwarves are tapped in the Fortress of Ultimate Darkness, where David Warner turns up as the Devil and Ralph Richardson makes for an entirely reasonable God. All part of an *Alice In Wonderland*, the one story he is forever remaking, skewed fittingly to the enduring Gothic spill of this curious director's untameable creativity. ★★★★★ **IN**

THE TIME MACHINE (1960)

Starring: *Rod Taylor (George), Alan Young (David Filby), Yvette Mimieux (Weena), Sebastian Cabot (Dr. Philip Hilyer), Tom Helmore (Anthony Bridewell), Whit Bissell (Walter Kemp), Doris Lloyd (Mrs. Watchett)*
Director: *George Pal*
Screenwriter: *David Duncan, based on the novel by H.G. Wells*
PG/103 mins./Sci-fi/USA

In 1899, George invents a time machine and travels to the far future, where he finds the descendants of humanity living in the ruins of London and intervenes to help a peaceful tribe fight off their brutal oppressors.

Producer-director George Pal – the science fiction specialist who had made the 1953 *War of the Worlds* – is guilty of reshaping H.G. Wells' thoughtful, ironic novel into an action movie, replacing the writer's concern with biological and social evolution with Cold War era fear of nuclear holocaust and converting the detached, despairing Time Traveller into a hairy-chested, two-fisted man of action played by Rod Taylor. He even implies that Taylor is supposed to be Wells himself, as everyone calls him George and his machine bears a plate which indicates that it was 'manufactured by H.G. Wells'. That said, this is one of those movies which is so

Most expensive movies ever made (adjusted for inflation) TOP10

1. *Cleopatra* (1963) ... $286,400,000
2. *Titanic* (1997) ... $247,000,000
3. *Waterworld* (1995) ... $229,000,000
4. *Terminator 3* (2003) ... $216,400,000
5. *Spider-man 2* (2004) ... $210,000,000
6. *King Kong* (2005) ... $207,000,000
7. *Wild Wild West* (1999) ... $203,400,000
8. *Speed 2: Cruise Control* (1997) ... $198,800,000
9. *The 13th Warrior* (1999) ... $190,700,000
10. *Troy* (2004) ... $184,300,000

appealing to children and adults that it deserves classic status on its own merits. On New Year's Eve 1899, a group of fussy Victorians gather in Taylor's chintzy, overstuffed parlour to hear him tell of his expedition to the future, where the world is divided between the surface-dwelling, childish, beautiful Eloi and the hideous, underground, cannibal Morlocks. Wells intended both factions to seem degenerate, the logical final evolution of the class system, but Pal has Taylor side with the Eloi and teach them to fight against the Morlocks. The time travel sequence remains a tour-de-force, with a shop window mannequin demonstrating a parade of fashions as the years fly by in seconds and stop-offs at several wars to demonstrate that nothing really changes, while the future is a wonderfully coloured landscape with properly gruesome monsters and a winning Eloi heroine in Yvette Mimieux. It may not be Wells, but it's always a New Year treat. **★★★★ KN**

A TIME TO KILL (1996)

Starring: *Matthew McConaughey (Jake Tyler Brigance), Sandra Bullock (Ellen Roark), Samuel L. Jackson (Carl Lee Hailey), Kevin Spacey (D.A. Rufus Buckley), Donald Sutherland (Lucien Wilbanks), Kiefer Sutherland (Freddie Lee Cobb)*
Director: *Joel Shumahcer*
Screenwriter: *Akiva Goldsman, based on the novel by John Grisham*
15/143 mins./Crime/Drama/Thriller/USA

A young lawyer must defend a black man guilty of killing the racist white trash who raped his daughter.

So enamoured was he with Joel Schumacher's solid if unremarkable handling of *The Client*, that one-time legal eagle turned author-of-the-moment John Grisham handed the director the reins to his precious debut novel. By far his best work, *A Time To Kill* carried semi-autobiographical overtones that the scribe (and, now indeed, producer) had, fearing the worst, been unwilling to fritter off onto the Hollywood production line.

It proved less a gift than a hot potato: a moral tightrope of a subject, casting antipathy between director and author (over who would play the lead) and a shoot in the inflammatory and sweltering atmosphere of a Mississippi summer haunted by the ghosts of movies past – *To Kill A Mockingbird* casts a long shadow. Yet bad karma has led to enriched moviegoing. This is easily the most thought-provoking and stimulating of the Grishamised movies.

Unknown beforehand but immediately a superstar in the offing, McConaughey is Jake Brigance, the local boy lawyer embroiled in a case that is more akin to a legal firebomb. After two redneck bullyboys brutally rape his black eight-year-old daughter and then slip through a hole in the law, impassioned father Jackson dispenses home-made justice by a lethal injection. Of lead. It is, of course, Brigance who elects to defend his vigilante actions and blow issues of justice wide open. Enter the Ku Klux Klan, led by the sneering lustre of Kiefer Sutherland, to stir up the locals, propping up the thriller elements with top quality nastiness. And enter hotshot law student Sandra Bullock to boil up some serious sexual chemistry and add right-on viewpoints.

The rest of the rangy cast reads like a talent devotee wish-list: Kevin Spacey smarming away as the egotistical prosecutor; Ashley Judd as the fretting wife; Donald Sutherland the drunken old-timer with sly advice; and Oliver Platt providing comic asides as a cynicism-sodden buddy lawyer. Even down on the third echelon the players are still hot: M. Emmet Walsh, Charles Dutton, Brenda Fricker.

Once it is assured McConaughey can do the business, whipping up sex appeal and camera hoggage like a thoroughbred, it is hard for Schumacher to mess up. An actual niggle is, ironically, talent overload: there are hints of too many cooks with scant opportunity to savour the likes of Sutherland, Platt and Spacey, even top-billed Bullock is only a support player. With all the acting bases covered – jail-bound Jackson, as taut as a piano string, is fantastic – and the stormy southern location squirming with sweaty confrontations, lynchings and racial tension, there comes the reliable bluster of the movie courtroom complete with stir-'em-up staples – rent-a-mob riots, objections, last-ditch evidence, wholesale implausibilites and Patrick McGoohan's sneery judge.

It's all very Grisham – swish courtroom antics by blue-eyed golden boy win day – but one balanced precariously on an ethical quagmire. What would you do if it were your daughter? Can vigilantism ever be acceptable? Schumacher is never quite smart enough to keep the debate neutral, and the unrestrained hero worship at the close leaves a nasty taste. But a rare thing is a courtroom thriller daring to venture into the grey areas of the law, and *A Time To Kill* is a prime slice of legal Americana. **★★★★ IN**

TIMECODE (2000)

Starring: *Salma Hayek (Rose), Jeanne Tripplehorn (Lauren Hathaway), Saffron Burrows (Emma), Holly Hunter (Renee Fishbine), Kyle MacLachlan (Bunny Drysdale), Stellan Skarsgård (Alex Green), Julian Sands (Quentin)*
Director: *Mike Figgis*
Screenwriter: *Mike Figgis*
15/89 mins./Comedy/Drama/USA

Four movie business-related stories unfold in real time simultaneously in four separate frames on screen.

Though those with long memories will remember *Wicked-Wicked* (1973), a thriller shot in 'Duo-Vision', as a precedent, this experiment for the digibeta age, consisting of four single takes shot simultaneously in one afternoon, audaciously tries to do something at once different and approachable. The takes each fill a quarter of the screen and run continuously, though the dialogue – improvised by the cast to a story template by Figgis – is mixed up and down to indicate which frame should hold the attention. Presumably, when it comes out on DVD, the viewer will be able to choose which segment he/she looks at or listens to.

As avant-garde items go, it's not offputting – if headachey in parts – with its attractive, talented cast and flashes of *Player*-like wit, though one imagines Figgis' pitch might have emphasised the cheapness and the number of babes in the cast.

Lesbian businesswoman Jeanne Tripplehorn is suspicious of her aspiring actress girlfriend Salma Hayek, whom she ferries to an audition in her limo while planting a bug in her bag, and Hayek actually has a liaison planned with laid-back producer Stellan Skarsgård, who is on the outs with his wife, the latter careening from shrink to coke (like several other characters) as she decides whether or not to leave him.

Meanwhile, Skarsgård's development team are waiting to take a pitch from an amusingly pretentious young filmmaker (agented by Kyle MacLachlan). All along, several earthquakes jolt cast and camera (but not background buildings or extras), and it's clear that only an act of violence will bring everything together. ★★★ **KN**

TIN CUP (1996)

Starring: *Kevin Costner (Roy 'Tin Cup' McAvoy), Rene Russo (Dr. Molly Griswold), Don Johnson (David Simms), Cheech Marin (Romeo Posar), Linda Hart (Doreen)*
Director: *Ron Shelton*
Screenwriters: *John Norville, Ron Shelton*
15/129 mins./Comedy/Drama/Romance/Sport/USA

A golf range owner tries to give the US Open a shot – but can he keep his infamous reckless streak under control?

Having survived the aquatic minefield that was *Waterworld* with his integrity more or less intact, Kevin Costner returned to a genre he's far more adept at, namely romantic comedy, reteaming with his *Bull Durham* writer/director Ron Shelton for a film that reconfirms his position as both modern cinema's finest romantic leading man and a gifted comedy actor to boot.

Costner stars as Roy 'Tin Cup' McAvoy, an ex-college golfing champion whose stubbornness and 'inner demons' hampered his natural ability to swing a club and consequently kept him off the professional touring circuit. Now on the (fair)way to being an alcoholic, Tin Cup trades on his former glories giving lessons on a run-down driving range in the middle of rural Texas.

But when the new pscyhiatrist in town, Molly (Russo, never better) turns up one evening for a lesson, he's immediately smitten. Disavowing all the waitresses and strippers that have become his romantic stock, he sets out to woo Molly, only to find that she is already the girlfriend of top pro David Simms (Johnson, remarkably slimy), Tin Cup's former golfing partner and now a bitter rival. And after Tin Cup's normal romantic technique fails to convince, he decides that only a grand gesture will do and sets out to win the US Open, with Molly working on his inner demons, and caddie/buddy Romeo his swing.

As much a film about golf as *Bull Durham* was about baseball, *Tin Cup* is a deliciously witty, profound, sly and erotically charged exploration of love, redemption and one man's quest for immortality.

A decidedly adult comedy, you could slice the sexual chemistry between Russo and Costner with a three iron; Johnson, meanwhile, makes a perfectly credible sleazoid; and Shelton (who co-penned the script with John Norville) keeps the humour straight down the middle and, just like *Bull Durham* before it, uses the rituals and metaphors of sport to relate the complexities of love and relationships. The performances throughout are spot on: Russo, so often thought of as mere decoration, shines, while Costner, after trouble with his stroke (pun most certainly intended), is once again on top of his game. Quite wonderful. ★★★★ **MS**

THE TINGLER (1959)

Starring: *Vincent Price (Dr. Warren Chapin), Judith Evelyn (Martha Higgins), Darryl Hickman (David Morris), Patricia Curtis (Isabel Stevens Chapin), Pamela Lincoln (Lucy Stevens), Phillip Coolidge (Oliver 'Ollie' Higgins)*
Director: *William Castle*
Screenwriter: *Robb White*
15/82 mins./Horror/USA

Dr. Warren Chapin theorises that extreme fear in humans creates a centipede-like parasite organism at the base of the spine which will kill the host unless dislodged by a scream. Believing this theory, cinema owner Ollie Higgins sets out to terrify his wife Martha, a mute who can't scream.

This gets listed in reference books solely because producer-director William Castle – the original for the showman played by John Goodman in *Matinee* – launched it in theatres with a bizarre gimmick, Percepto. At the point when the 'tingler' gets loose in a cinema, little motors under selected seats administered mild shocks to patrons. The ballyhoo is fairly crazy, but the film itself is even more insane, boasting the single whackiest premise of any horror film ever made (yes, whackier than the flying brains of *Fiend Without A Face* or the space helmeted gorilla in *Robot Monster*), delivered with a mostly straight face by the plummy Price (who even gets to take a bug-eyed acid trip). Given that its made-up biology could only seem logical to a child (at last, an explanation for the chills that run up and down your spine when you're afraid!), the film takes a weirdly, nastily adult approach with snarling, unpleasant characters who are perpetually plotting to do away with each other in horrible ways.

The most influential horror movie of the mid-1950s was *Les Diaboliques*, and a major set-piece here is a minu-rerun of the Clouzot classic, with haggard Judith Evelyn terrified by a series of stunts designed to awake her inner caterpillar monster – the black and white film briefly turns to colour in a bathroom where a hand rises out of a tubful of rich red blood. *House on Haunted Hill* and *13 Ghosts*, Castle's other horror hits, have been remade, but no one has dared disturb *The Tingler* again. ★★★★ **KN**

TITANIC (1997)

Starring: *Leonardo DiCaprio (Jack Dawson), Kate Winslet (Rose DeWitt Bukater), Billy Zane (Caledon 'Cal' Hockley), Kathy Bates (Molly Brown), Frances Fisher (Ruth DeWitt Bukater), Gloria Stuart (Old Rose), Bill Paxton (Brock Lovett)*
Director: *James Cameron*
Screenwriter: *James Cameron*
12/186 mins./Action/Drama/Romance/History/USA
Awards – *Academy Awards – Best Art Direction-Set Decoration, Best Cinematography, Best Costume, Best Director, Best Sound Effects Editing, Best Visual Effects, Best Editing, Best Score, Best Song ('My Heart Will Go On'), Best Picture, Best Sound, Empire Awards – Best British Actress, Best Film, Golden Globes – Best Director, Best Drama, Best Score.*

In his search for a blue diamond that was believed to have gone down with the Titanic, Brock Lovett discovers a sketch of a beautiful woman wearing the diamond on her neck. When the sketch appears on a news programme, an old lady steps forward, claiming to be the woman in the drawing. She then recounts her story of what took place on the ill-fated ship . . .

For your consideration: a couple of stories regarding directors, budgets and Hollywood executives. On the set of one of his productions, Alfred Hitchcock was confronted by a studio exec panicked by spiralling costs. 'What are you going to do about this?' he demanded of the director. Hitch turned to the upstart and said, 'I shall do whatever is necessary to make what, in the due course of time, you will come to refer to as our film.'

A good three decades later, on the set of one of his larger productions, James Cameron was approached by a similarly anxious suit who asked pretty much the same thing. Cameron turned to the upstart – and shouting 'shut the fuck up,' promptly attempted to asphyxiate him. Different reactions maybe, but to the same problem. Huge productions attract the attention of first the money men desperate to slash scenes, but shortly after that, the press. Knives are drawn, the dreaded words 'troubled production' raise their ugly heads and, when it comes to release time, the movie has to battle against a positive lynch-mob of hacks out baying for blood.

Had he had the decency to deliver the expected flop, to play to the critics' and industry-watchers' lust for a truckload of hubris dumped over a director playing fast and loose with hundreds of millions of dollars, then the reviews might have read differently.

Titanic wears its flaws as boldly as it does its abundant strengths. Sure, the dialogue is often nearer to teen soap than Merchant Ivory (leading *Beverly Hills 90210*er Jason Priestley to remark that the verbiage was so dire that, 'I half expected myself to walk through the door.') James Horner's score often lists towards faux Celtic parpings and all Billy Zane needs to complete his personification of silent-movie villainy is a top hat and a waxed moustache to twirl. But then, ironically, *Titanic* was never meant to be a 'deep' film. It is, however, like the ship itself, a bloody big one.

At heart Cameron is a kind of celluloid engineer; his films habitually act as showrooms for the latest technology (and thus his keen interest in the cutting-edge maritime engineering – witness the loving shots of the ship's engine room: no character ever goes there and the hugely expensive sequence was an obvious candidate for cutting, but Cameron just couldn't sacrifice the pounding pistons) and his screenplays are masterpieces of structure rather than style. Titanic is no exception, masterfully employing match-dissolves backwards and forward from the salvage operation to the sumptuously designed sets of the ship herself and thus engrossing an audience whose previous dramatic stamina had probably been 50-odd minutes of *Dawson's Creek*. Equally Cameron turns what could have been a major flaw (notwithstanding current educational standards, even the thickest teen is dimly aware that the ship sinks) into a strength, teasing the audience for over an hour and a half, and losing some in the romance, before the iceberg actually hits, and sacrificing no opportunity to ratchet up the sense of grim inevitability.

The casting of DiCaprio was visionary. At the time the studio had demanded Matthew McConaughey but Cameron, who had seen early cuts of *Romeo + Juliet*, shrewdly saw a matinee idol in the making, and resisted his star's attempts to deepen the character – Leo apparently at one point demanding a lisp or a limp or something to engage his acting gears. Cameron though realised that it wasn't Leo being anyone else that was going to have women swooning, it was Leo being Leo. And then there is the sinking ...

There simply is not, and never has been, any filmmaker who can direct prolonged dramatic action with such exuberant flair. Unlike his imitators, Cameron never loses sight of character in the midst of spectacle; thus a sustained action sequence of well over an hour doesn't even approach longueur. The traditional directors' nemesis, water, is literally putty in his hands. As in *The Abyss* (1989), he turns it into a living, almost breathing monster. It crashes through corridors, seeps through doorways, gushes up stairwells, and in one of the movie's best shots, trickles along the floor like the mildly inconvenient product of an overflowing bathtub. And the money shot, of Jack and Rose perched on the upended stern as passengers plunge into the boiling brine is as spectacular as anything in action cinema.

Titanic may have left many of the jaded critics unimpressed, but there's a fair chance that if, in a decade or so's time you ask the generation then producing, directing or hacking out reviews what turned them on to movies in the first place, more than a few will answer '*Titanic*.' And only a very few directors leave a legacy like that. ★★★★★ **AS**

TIME OF THE GYPSIES (1989)

Starring: *Davor Dujimovic (Perhan), Bora Todorovic (Ahmed), Ljubica Adzovic (Grandmother), Elvira Sali (Danira), Sinolicka Trpkova (Azra), Husnija Hasimovic (Merdzan)*
Director: *Emir Kusturica*
Screenwriters: *Emir Kusturica, Gordan Mihic*
15/142 mins./Drama/Yugoslavia
Awards: *Cannes Film Festival – Emir Kusturica*

When his sister, Ahmed, requires medical attention in Italy, Perhan leaves the Skopje Roma community to accompany her and soon becomes embroiled in the child smuggling activities of his charismatic neighbour, Ahmed.

This was the last entry in the trilogy of rites-of-passage pictures with which Emir Kusturica began his career. Following his collaborations with Muslim poet Abdulah Sidran on *Do You Remember Dolly Bell? and When Father Was Away On Business*, this was also Kusturica's first contemporary outing and its shift away from bleakly nostalgic satire established a trend for dividing critics along ethnic and political lines. Yet whether Kusturica was presenting life as he found it or reinforcing patronising stereotypes, it's impossible not to be swept along by the intoxicating combination of comedy and tragedy, fantasy and realism that has since become the Bosnian's trademark.

The child-smuggling storyline was inspired by a newspaper article. But the biggest influence on the film was Luis Buñuel's *Los Olvidados*, which made similar use of magic realism to capture the delirious desperation of poverty (although Kusturica also acknowledged a debt to John Ford). Life in the Skopje enclave is presented as every bit as vibrant, violent and vulgar as it was in Buñuel's Mexico City. But the wedding, the funeral and the St George's Day parade sequences suggest a joyous community spirit that is conveyed with unaffected vitality by Kusturica's impressive non-professional cast.

Yet, while the fluid opening shot depicts beggars, gamblers and supplicants hoping for easy answers, Perhan's meticulous preparation of limestone – as he seeks to impress his beloved Azra whose mother refuses to let them marry on account of his penury – makes his descent into exploitative crime all the more dispiriting. His devotion to his sister and his grandmother reinforce this sense of innocence being corrupted. But, while it's clear that he inherited his telekinetic powers from his faith-healing grandmother, it's also implied, by the brutish presence of his sleazy uncle, that criminal tendencies also run in the family.

Lyrical, elliptical, mesmerising and disconcerting, this is an exhilarating insight into the mysticism and pragmatism of Roma culture. But it's also a shocking indictment of a continent that ignores the perpetuation of the almost Dickensian abuse of youth. ★★★★ **DP**

TO BE OR NOT TO BE (1942)

Starring: *Carole Lombard (Maria Tura), Jack Benny (Joseph Tura), Robert Stack (Lt. Stanislav Sobinski), Felix Bressart (Greenberg), Lionel Atwill (Rawitch), Stanley Ridges (Prof. Alexander Siletsky), Sig Rumann (Col. Ehrhardt), Tom Dugan (Bronski)*
Director: *Ernst Lubitsch*
Screenwriter: *Edwin Justus Mayer, based on a story by Lubitsch and Melchior Lengyell*
U/99 mins./Comedy/USA

Egocentric ham actor Joseph Tura is persuaded to impersonate both Professor Alexander Siletsky and Gestapo officer Colonel Ehrhardt after exiled pilot Lt. Stanislav Sobinski enlists the help of Tura's vivacious wife Maria to prevent a plot to compromise the Polish underground.

Ernst Lubitsch had always abhorred jokes about blindness until he saw W.C. Fields' *It's a Gift* and that realisation that serious subjects could be funny underpinned this vituperative black comedy.

Sig Rumann's boast, 'So they call me Concentration Camp Ehrhardt?', must rank as the most subversive joke of the entire Second World War. Yet, it was closely followed by his earlier quip, 'What he did to Shakespeare, we are now doing to Poland', which so shocked some members of Lubitsch's cast and entourage that they suggested its removal. But the only dialogue that was cut from this courageous farce thriller was the question 'What could happen in a plane?', as the answer had been made all too chillingly clear by Carole Lombard's tragic death on a bond-selling rally less than a month after the picture wrapped.

Having prompted Charlie Chaplin to make The *Great Dictator*, producer Alexander Korda must take some credit for ensuring United Artists' backing for this contentious project. Lubitsch had originally considered making it a comeback vehicle for Maurice Chevalier and Miriam Hopkins, but his preference soon switched to Jack Benny and he dropped Hopkins after she began lobbying to have her role boosted. However, Carole Lombard was only cast in the face of opposition from her husband, Clark Gable, who not only objected to the screenplay, but who also (in true Tura fashion) disliked Lubitsch's habit of flirting with his wife.

However, it proved a happy production, despite Benny's occasional bouts of anxious inferiority and Miklos Rosza's refusal to compose the score. But a storm of protest greeted its release and Lubitsch was forced to defend his film against accusations of trivialising both Poland's plight and the German threat. Insisting that he had depicted Tura's troupe as resourceful and united in their reckless heroism, Lubitsch countered claims that his Nazis had been mere cartoon buffoons by stressing their potential for evil that had been established in the opening footage of a blitzed Warsaw.

But, like most satire on a supposedly taboo topic, this masterpiece could only be fully appreciated with the passage of time. Remade in 1983 by Alan Jonhnson starring Mel Brooks with a tenth of the wit. ★★★★★ **DP**

TO CATCH A THIEF (1955)

Starring: *Cary Grant (John Robie), Grace Kelly (Frances Stevens), Jessie Royce Landis (Jessie Stevens), John Williams (H.H. Hughson), Charles Vanel (Bertani)*
Director: *Alfred Hitchcock*
Screenwriter: *John Michael Hayes, based on the novel by David Dodge*
PG/106 mins./Thriller/Mystery/Romance/USA

Awards – *Academy Awards – Best Colour Cinematography*

An American thief retires to the Côte d'Azur but becomes chief suspect in a string of local robberies. Can he find the true villain and win the heart of the striking beauty Frances Stevens?

Despite favouring Grace Kelly among his leading ladies, Hitchcock was fairly dismissive of *To Catch A Thief* calling it 'a lightweight story which wasn't meant to be taken seriously.' In fact, for him, the highlight of the picture was achieving a more realistic colour for the night sky than the Technicolor blue so fashionable at the time.

But there's more than a 'dark slate blue' sky to enjoy here. Although *To Catch A Thief* has a fairly insubstantial plot, the audience are happily distracted from the mystery behind the cat-burglar's identity by the central Grant-Kelly romance. The frisson of their flirting always has an undercurrent of danger, particularly since it's subject to the manipulations of her character's mother, astutely played by Royce Landis, who grabs many of the best lines – 'I'm sorry I ever sent her to finishing school. I think they finished her there.'

There's some humourously literal inter-cutting of fireworks and passion (Hitchcock was a sucker for this – see also the kiss followed by a train going into a tunnel in *North By Northwest*) and for those wanting to spot Hitchcock's traditional cameo, keep an eye on the bus passengers ten minutes in.

The travelogue setting has other connotations now, in light of Grace Kelly's death in 1982. Although her son denies it, many claim that her fatal car accident happened on the very same Monaco road she is seen driving along here. Even if it's not true, it's a hard-hearted viewer who can watch that scene without feeling a tinge of regret for the glowing star who died too soon. ★★★ **EC**

TO DIE FOR (1995)

Starring: *Nicole Kidman (Suzanne Stone Maretto), Matt Dillon (Larry Maretto), Joaquin Phoenix (Jimmy Emmett), Casey Affleck (Russel Hines), Illeana Douglas (Janice Maretto), Alison Folland (Lydia Metz)*
Director: *Gus Van Sant*
Screenwriter: *Buck Henry, based on the book by Joyce Maynard*
15/102 mins./Drama/Comedy/USA

Awards – *Empire Awards – Best Actress, Golden Globes – Best Actress*

Suzanne Stone is an aspiring TV personality who will do anything to be in the spotlight – including enlisting three teenagers to kill her husband.

Acclaimed arthouse director Gus Van Sant regained some of the ground lost by the disastrous *Even Cowgirls Get The Blues* with this crafty, extremely well-timed black comedy on infamy and TV celebrity, based on the novel by Joyce Maynard and centered on a revelatory performance from Nicole Kidman as the pretty princess who is really the wicked witch.

Kidman plays Suzanne Maretto, a smalltown girl so obsessed with television and her craving for fame that she triumphs in what should be her downfall. The film opens with the media stampede when Suzanne is arrested for her husband's murder and via a series of monologues-to-camera Suzanne relates her story from the perspective of a pert, utterly confident, subtly moronic, cold-blooded fantasist.

The film also cuts to other characters to provide different vantage points, including those of the dead man's sister and a trio of braindead teenagers led by Joaquin Phoenix's randy loser Jimmy, seduced into getting rid of Suzanne's husband for her. Playing nifty tricks with time, lighting, design, and film stock (videotape segments were shot by Kidman in character), the narrative flows between their recollections and reconstructions, chronicling Suzanne's determined ascent to rinky-dink recognisability as the local cable-channel's inexpert weatherperson and the deterioration of her marriage to adoring, ordinary working stiff Larry.

The result is sharply pointed and cruelly funny (with a brilliant, killer punchline to the tale involving a cameo from David Cronenberg). The supporting players, notably Douglas and Dan Hedaya, excel, but above all this is Kidman's moment, her timing and feel for the irony of the character is scarily spot-on. ★★★★ **AE**

TO HAVE AND HAVE NOT (1944)

Starring: *Humphrey Bogart (Harry 'Steve' Morgan), Walter Brennan (Eddie), Lauren Bacall (Marie 'Slim' Browning), Dolores Moran (Helene De Bursac), Hoagy Carmichael (Cricket), Walter Molnar (Paul De Bursac), Sheldon Leonard (Lt Coyo), Marcel Dalio (Gerard)*
Director: *Howard Hawks*
Screenwriters: *Jules Furthmann, William Faulkner, based on the novel by Ernest Hemingway*
PG/100 mins./Drama/USA

American expatriate Harry Morgan makes a living on the French colonial island of Martinique by running fishing expeditions. But his cushy existence is transformed by wartime encounters with stranded twentysomething Marie Browning and resistance fighters, Paul de Bursac and his wife, Héleǹe.

t

Cinema snacks from around the world

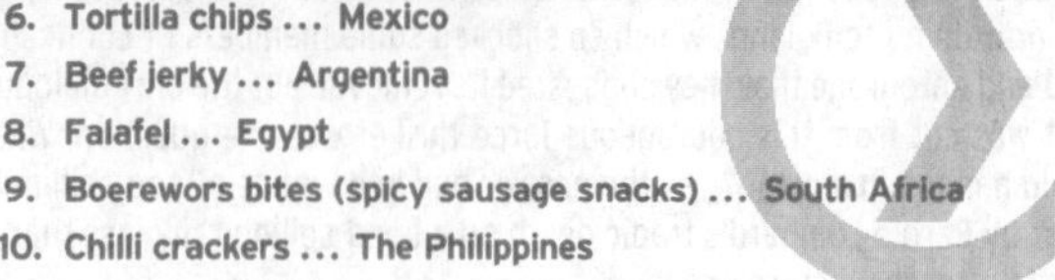

1. Fried leaf cutter ants ... Columbia
2. Roll-mop herring ... Iceland
3. Beetroot chips ... Latvia
4. Poppadoms ... Pakistan
5. Pickled gherkins ... Poland
6. Tortilla chips ... Mexico
7. Beef jerky ... Argentina
8. Falafel ... Egypt
9. Boerewors bites (spicy sausage snacks) ... South Africa
10. Chilli crackers ... The Philippines

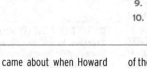

According to Hollywood legend, this film came about when Howard Hawks made a bet with Ernest Hemingway that he could make a good movie out of his worst novel. Although he won his wager, Hawks actually ditched most of *To Have And Have Not* and worked instead from a screenplay written by regular collaborator Jules Furthman and William Faulkner (making this the only studio picture to boast two Nobel laureates among its creatives).

Hemingway's scenario wasn't wasted, however, as its ending wound up in John Huston's *Key Largo*, its basic plotline serviced Michael Curtiz's *The Breaking Point* and 'One Trip Across', the short story from which it had been expanded, resurfaced in Don Siegel's *The Gun Runners*.

Indeed, Hawks' picture owed more to a brace of earlier Furthman projects – Josef von Sternberg's *Morocco* and Hawks' own *Only Angels Have Wings* – and *Casablanca*, which had recently reinvented Humphrey Bogart as a hard-bitten romantic. In fact, it could be said that Hawks' wife, Nancy, made more of an impact on the project than Hemingway, as 'Steve' and 'Slim' were not only the Hawks' pet names, but she had also spotted the teenage Lauren Bacall on the cover of *Harper's Bazaar* and suggested that she had star quality.

There's no question that the chemistry that developed off screen between Bogie and Bacall impinged upon their scenes together. But she also appears to advantage alongside fellow debutant Hoagy Carmichael, despite some complaining that Hawks slipped in too many numbers to disguise the paucity of his material. Indeed, her singing reinforces comparisons with Marlene Dietrich in *Morocco*, while Carmichael's saloon pianist recalls Dooley Wilson's Sam in *Casablanca*.

The dialogue crackles in true Warners fashion, while Hawks uses Bogart's partnership with rummy Walter Brennan to conduct his customary investigation into professional men seeing a tough job through to the end. But the war is too often reduced to a convenient backdrop (with the Free French connection again consciously evoking *Casablanca*) in what is essentially a terrifically entertaining exercise in studio escapism. ★★★★ **DP**

TO KILL A MOCKINGBIRD

Starring: *Gregory Peck (Atticus Finch), Mary Badham (Scout), Philip Alford (Jem), Robert Duvall (Boo Radley), John Megna (Dill), Brock Peters (Tom Robinson)*
Director: *Robert Mulligan*
Screenwriter: *Horton Foote, based on the novel by Harper Lee*
PG/123 mins./Drama/USA

Awards – *Academy Awards – Best Actor, Best Black-and-White Art Direction-Set Decoration, Best Adapted Screenplay, Golden Globes – Best Film in Promoting International Understanding, Best Drama Actor, Best Score*

Two children begin to learn the ways of the world – and America's south in particular – as their father, lawyer Atticus Finch, defends a black man accused of raping a white woman.

Harper Lee's legendary novel was carefully, and unfussily translated to screen by Robert Mulligan who intelligently shares the emphasis between the children (debutants Mary Badham and Philip Alford) – the core of the novel – with their lawyer father, played gracefully by Gregory Peck.

As the million readers are well aware, the crux of Lee's story surrounds Peck defending Negro Brock Peters on a charge of rape, but alongside the examination of racism the film also manages to encompass the themes of childhood, poverty, love and an unsentimental look at the Deep South of the past that make the book so rich a tale.

Lee based much of the story on her own small town observances and the model for her wildly imaginative story-telling companion Dill here was her lifelong friend Truman Capote. In this tale she proved she could match him nuance for nuance. What the film managed to convey so well was the atmosphere of the Deep South – the heat in the courtroom, the deep-rooted prejudices which can flip to violence when stirred and the small gestures that can make a difference.

Overriding it all is the heart-warming mystery of local bogey man Boo Radley. Peck gives a career-best turn, but true to the source, is understated enough to let the kids shine. And shine they do, lighting up a wise, thoroughbred movie with an irresistible streak of youth. Harper Lee could ask no more. ★★★★★ **AE**

TO LIVE AND DIE IN L.A. (1985)

Starring: *William L. Petersen (Richard Chance), Willem Dafoe (Eric 'Rick' Masters), John Pankow (John Vukovich), Debra Feuer (Bianca Torres), John Turturro (Carl Cody), Darianne Fluegel (Ruth Lanier), Dean Stockwell (Bob Grimes), Steve James (Jeff Rice), Robert Downey Sr. (Thomas Bateman)*
Director: *William Friedkin*
Screenwriters: *William Friedkin, Gerald Petievich based on a novel by Petievich*
18/116 mins./Thriller/USA

After the death of his partner, loose cannon Secret Service agent Chance teams with the more ethical Vukovich to bring in the killer, ambitious Masters.

If, near the start of a movie, one member of a two-man government team happens to mention he has only three more days to go before retirement, you can be sure that he's due to meet a bloody death before he gets his gold watch. Which, indeed, is what happens here.

For a while, *To Live And Die In L.A.* is a cross between *Miami Vice* on a particularly rough night and Anthony Mann's brilliant 1950 semi-documentary thriller *T-Man* as William Friedkin, in his best film credit since the 1970s, turns in a fascinating, rock-scored visual essay on the mechanics of forging currency while grizzle-haired hero Petersen goes outside the law to get revenge on the villain by beating up petty crooks, bullying judges, committing armed robbery, driving like a maniac and being rude to everyone in sight.

However, about half-way through, the director shifts into his *French Connection* gear and devotes *a full quarter* of the movie to a car chase around the Los Angeles freeways that may be the single most exciting action scene in 80s cinema but has damn-all to do with the plot. The film never recovers momentum after the drive-about, and winds down rather than resolves. The main problem is that the supposed good guys are all such reprehensible toads it's impossible to care whether they get to bring down Willem Dafoe's charismatic, polo-necked super-crook. The rhythm of the often-irritating rock score by Wang Chung and the mixture of gloss and tack in Robby Muller's cinematography make much of the film compulsive, but it is finally hard to like unless you're a fanatical devotee of cinematic car chases. ★★★ KN

TO WONG FOO, THANKS FOR EVERYTHING, JULIE NEWMAR (1995)

Starring: *Wesley Snipes (Noxeema Jackson), Patrick Swayze (Vida Boheme), John Leguizamo (Chi Chi Rodriguez), Stockard Channing (Carol Ann), Blythe Danner (Beatrice), Arliss Howard (Virgil)*
Director: *Beeban Kidron*
Screenwriter: *Douglas Carter*
PG/103 mins./Comedy/USA

Three drag queens cross the States to compete in a beauty competition, the two 'old timers' coaching the newcomer en route.

At first glance this appeared to be Hollywood's answer to the previous year's Antipodean sleeper *The Adventures Of Priscilla Queen Of The Desert*, with the added bonus of three established beefcake stars donning nail varnish, gaudy attire and camp manner. Except it's not a mudpack on the quirky original.

This lengthily titled tribute to the statuesque Catwoman actress (explained by her message scribbled on a photo to a Chinese restaurateur), may revel in its high-spirited feelgood factor but, even in treading the same terra firma as Terence Stamp and co., it evades much of the wit and insight which made *Priscilla* so enjoyable. Having jointly scooped the Drag Queen Of New York title (from previous holder RuPaul), Vida Boheme, and Noxeema Jackson win the opportunity to compete in the Drag Queen Of America contest in Hollywood. However, taking pity on drag wannabe and glaringly obvious bad loser, Chi Chi Rodriguez (Leguizamo, doing a shockingly accurate take on Rosie Perez), Vida takes the protégé under his/her wing, and the three set off on a cross-country trip to LA in a battered old convertible. And when the car gives up the ghost in a tiny backwater town, it doesn't take a genius to predict the outcome.

The underlying problem is the failure to introduce anything new and original to an already fading genre. Any opportunity to probe more deeply into the subject of cross-dressing is shrugged off at a moment's notice in favour of the more obvious avenues of campy quips, dumb stereotypes and eye-straining outfits, with more serious issues such as domestic violence and non-conformity chucked in hamfistedly as an attempt to add depth.

Swayze and Snipes do their best to wring some entertainment value out of the limited material, winning the audience over to a certain extent (Snipes bags all the best lines, while Swayze looks worryingly at home in his feminine guise). This little whimsy of a movie, however, is liable to hit home only with niche audiences, and those swayed by the novelty of seeing a bunch of action types slip into something a little more comfortable. ★★ CW

TOKOYO STORY (TOKYO MONOGATARI) (1953)

Starring: *Chishu Ryu (Shukishi Hirayama), Chieko Higashiyama (Tomi Hirayama), Setsuko Hara (Noriko), Haruko Sugimura (Shige Kaneko)*
Director: *Yasujiro Ozu*
Screenwriters: *Kogo Noda, Yasujiro Ozu*
U/129 mins./Drama/Japan

A retired Japanese couple travel to stay with their grown-up children, who are so busy with their own lives that they do not have time to show their parents around. Instead, it is left to their daughter-in-law to do the honours . . .

Yasujiro Ozu, who died in 1963, was one of the undisputed masters of world cinema, a quietly deceptive talent who insisted on a rigorously formal style and perfect compositions. Throughout his prolific career he frequently tackled universal human themes through his unforced examinations of Japanese middle-class family life – here making a study of the Japanese preoccupation with filial duty so deeply affecting that it's impossible to see the film without getting a deep urge to call your mother.

A retired schoolmaster and his loving wife travel from their seaside home of Onomichi to Tokyo, where they visit two of their four remaining children. While there are no arguments, it transpires that their doctor son and hairdresser daughter are too preoccupied to show them much of a good time. The paragon of virtue is their daughter-in-law, who remains true to the memory of a husband who disappeared in the war. While the blood children shuffle their parents around Hara is dutiful and loving, even at the expense of her own life.

A lengthy, leisurely film, sometimes delicately amusing but more often heartfelt and moving, this spotlights marvellous lifelike performances and a lack of overt emotion that is positively British in tone. In the last act, Ryu's children learn the truth of the old Japanese saying that you should serve your parents while they're alive because you can't do anything for them beyond the grave, though it's hard not to feel that the director's real feelings – Ozu never married and lived dutifully with his mother all her life – are with the dignified, tentatively proud parents. Your life can only be richer for seeing this. ★★★★★ KN

TOM JONES (1963)

Starring: *Albert Finney (Tom Jones), Susannah York (Sophie Western), Hugh Griffith (Squire Western), Edith Evans (Miss Western), Joan Greenwood (Lady Bellaston), Diane Cilento (Molly Seagrim), George Devine) (Squire Allworthy), David Tomlinson (Lord Fellamar), Joyce Redman (Mrs Walters/Jenny Jones), Blifil (David Warner)*
Director: *Tony Richardson*
Screenwriter: *John Osborne, based on the novel by Henry Fielding*
PG/131 mins./Comedy/UK

Awards: *Academy Awards – Best Picture, Best Director, Best Adapted screenplay. Best Score. BAFTAs – Best Film, Best British Film, Best British Screenplay. Venice – Volpi Cup, Best Actor (Albert Finney)*

Disgraced in the eyes of his patron, Squire Allworthy, by the machinations of his envious son, Blifil, and barred from marrying Squire Western's chaste daughter, Sophie, Tom Jones heads for London to make his fortune and has numerous saucy adventures along the way.

Tony Richardson became the first of the Free Cinema generation to tear himself away from the kitchen sink with this bawdy period romp, although there were those who claimed that he was actually returning to an even earlier form of social realism by adapting Henry Fielding's scurrilously satirical novel in the style of a William Hogarth painting.

Indeed, there was plenty to link Albert Finney's anti-heroic foundling with the womanising opportunists who had figured in the likes of *Room at the Top*, *Look Back In Anger* and *Saturday Night And Sunday Morning*. Moreover, the lampoon of the manners and mores of the 18th century had more than a little bearing on a society about to enter its own permissive phase and it's clear that the film's success at the Academy Awards in the same spring that The Beatles broke America helped to launch the international impression that the 60s really had begun to swing.

But the biggest influence on Richardson's approach to this picaresque pantomime was hardly homegrown, as from its opening prologue, in which silent mumming is complemented by parodic intertitles and a pastiche score, the spirit of the nouvelle vague is readily evident. It informs Walter Lassally's dislocating handheld photography which emphasises that this is a movie recreation of both the 1740s and the text, as well as in Richardson's use of stop-motion, freeze frames and direct addresses to the audience.

Yet, Ralph Brinton's production design and John McCorry's costumes were meticulously researched and bound the picture into the UK heritage tradition, although its lusty approach to eating scenes rendered it more akin to Alexander Korda's *The Private Life Of Henry VIII* than that other British Best Picture winner, Laurence Olivier's *Hamlet*.

The ensemble cast is mostly excellent, with Diane Cilento, Edith Evans and Joan Greenwood's deft cameos shaming heavier handed contributions by Hugh Griffith and David Tomlinson. But if Tom Jones now feels something of a product of its times, it still deserves credit for attempting something new – no matter how derivative. ★★★ **DP**

THE TOMB OF LIGEIA (1964)

Starring: *Vincent Price (Verden Fell), Elizabeth Shepherd (Lady Ligeia Fell/Lady Rowena Trevanion), John Westbrook (Christopher Gough), Richard Vernon (Dr. Vivian)*
Director: *Roger Corman*
Screenwriter: *Robert Towne, from the story* Ligeia *by Edgar Allan Poe*
12/81 mins./Horror/UK

Verden Fell brings his new bride Rowena to the ruined abbey where he lived with his first wife Ligeia. Rowena is persecuted by Ligeia's evil black cat, and worries that the dead woman is unwilling to let Verden go.

The last film in Roger Corman's early 1960s run of Edgar Allan Poe movies starring Vincent Price, this gets out of the studio-bound claustrophibia of the earlier entries and uses lovely English locations. Shifting the production from Hollywood to Shepperton also means that Price, who is here oddly cast as a supposedly handsome youth but sports the coolest pair of 1821 sunglasses (with sides!) seen in the movies, has to work harder not to be upstaged by a distinguished supporting cast of British thespians rather than the teenage pushovers he was used to.

Scripted by Robert Towne, this is a full-blooded gothic romance in the tempestuous manner, with high-flown dialogue just this side of camp ('not ten minutes ago I tried to kill a stray cat with a cabbage, and all but made love to the Lady Rowena. I succeeded in squashing the cabbage and badly frightening the lady. If only I could lay open my own brain as easily as I did that vegetable, what rot would be freed from its grey leaves?') and many opportunities for the fetching if skull-faced heroine to run about lavishly-appointed, cobwebbed corridors in her powder-blue nightie pursued by the villainess in the form of a malicious cat who would have spooked Poe himself.

Towards the end, it gets into truly transgressive material as we discover that Price has been spending his evenings in the embrace of Ligeia's stiff-armed corpse, but the finale is that old Corman-Poe standby, the out-of-control blaze that destroys an ancient pile in a matter of moments. ★★★★ **KN**

TOMBSTONE (1993)

Starring: *Kurt Russell (Wyatt Earp), Val Kilmer (Doc Holliday), Sam Elliott (Virgil Earp), Bill Paxton (Morgan Earp), Powers Boothe (Curly Bill Brocious)*
Director: *George P. Cosmatos*
Screenwriter: *Kevin Jarre*
15/124 mins./Action/Drama/Western/USA

Gunslinger Earp comes to Tombstone in search of a quiet life but is soon driven back to his guns by the local bad boys.

This flat, almost comatose Disney effort should be sent back to the kitchen on the grounds of being undercooked and bereft of flavour. In Cosmatos' retread of the classic Old West tale, good guys wear black, cowboys are villains and infamous Kansas 'law dog' Earp (Russell, unremarkable), awe-inspiring reputation preceding him, rolls into the dusty mining town of Tombstone with brothers Virgil and Morgan in tow, determined to make his fortune running a local gambling den and rebuffing all requests to don the sheriff's badge and disperse the vicious red-sashed cowboy gangs running rampant. 'I don't do that any more,' growls Earp, echoing *Unforgiven*, except of course he does, driven back into violent crime-busting by the all-round havoc-wreaking of nasties Johnny Ringo, Curly Bill and sundry other members of the Clanton and McLaury clans.

Quite apart from there being far too many characters to keep tabs on – Michael Rooker, Billy Zane, Jason Priestley and Charlton Heston all pop in and out – the acting is generally dodgy, the visuals curiously drab, the personal melodramas supremely dreary, and the romantic subplot useless, with token female Dana Delany's vaudeville actress merely rustling her skirts a lot. The only actor who redeems himself, and by default the film, is Kilmer, an absolute hoot as Earp's foppish tuberculosis-ridden best pal Doc Holliday. If this had been Doc's story, it might almost be worth shelling out for. Since it's not, go for the marginally better Costner version instead. ★★ **MM**

TOMORROW NEVER DIES (1997)

Starring: *Pierce Brosnan (James Bond), Jonathan Pryce (Elliot Carver), Michelle Yeoh (Wai Lin), Teri Hatcher (Paris Carver), Ricky Jay (Henry Gupta), Judi Dench (M), Desmond Llewelyn (Q), Samantha Bond (Miss Moneypenny), Colin Salmon (Charles Robinson), Geoffrey Palmer (Admiral Roebuck)*
Director: *Roger Spottiswoode*
Screenwriter: *Bruce Fierstein, from characters by Ian Fleming*
12/114 mins./Spy/Adventure/UK/USA

Bond has to team up with his Chinese counterpart to prevent a media mogul from taking over the world.

Carry On, the UK's only comparable long-running franchise, ran out of steam when history overtook it. This has never been a problem for the Bond series, which started out ahead of the century. Ever since *Dr. No*, they've been full of computers and microtechnology, and, give or take the odd outbreak of peace, the threat of World War III hasn't gone away in 35 years. So how do you update the series for the late 1990s? Easy. You dial 'M' for Murdoch and make your villain a media mogul.

In the 18th re-run of a most enduring formula, Elliot Carver, the head of Carver Media Global Network, plans to kick-start hostilities between Britain and China in order to land an exclusive scoop for his media empire, including a new satellite TV network and the tabloid *Tomorrow*. 'Words are the new weapons! Satellites the new artillery!' he rants, writing splash headlines mere seconds after his own stealth ship in the South China Sea has sunk a British warship. 'There is,' he chuckles insanely, 'no news like bad news.'

Enter Commander Bond, whose mission is to save the world from World War III in only 48 hours, with a multi-million budget and in travelogue locations: Hamburg, Saigon and the South China Seas (he's already done a 'terrorist's supermarket' high in the Russian mountains for the pre-credit sequence). Never mind New Labour, this is Old Bond: we first see him in bed with his language teacher as the script, by Bruce Fierstein, goes into innuendo overdrive ('I'm brushing up on a little Danish … I enjoy exploring a new tongue'). The scene is thus set for holiday brochure cat-and-mouse which, next to *Con Air* and the *Die Hards*, is medium octane but no less entertaining for it. And at least it dresses for dinner.

Carver lectures Bond that the public don't care what, when or where, just why. As far as Bond films go, it's simply a case of how. How will he get off that high building? How will he foil the henchmen with sledgehammers and get out of the underground car park? (Well, remember all the features of his new BMW 750 which Q went through at the start? It'll probably involve one or two of those). And so on.

After a ropey patch, Bond is categorically back. *Goldeneye* took $350 million and minted Pierce Brosnan as The Spy Whom We Loved. He looks tip-top in this (his hair withstands getting shaken and stirred) – less Connery, more Moore, with whom he shares a talent for dry delivery of post-mortem puns. If Pryce is a little subtle, Judi Dench's M compensates with a relish you could spread on toast. Fast, funny, very British and less militaristic than, say, *The Peacemaker*. On this evidence, we may be forced to say, Carry on, Bond. ★★★★ **AC**

TOO HOT TO HANDLE (THE MARRYING MAN) (1991)

Starring: *Kim Basinger (Vicki Anderson), Alec Baldwin (Charley Pearl), Robert Loggia (Lew Horner), Elisabeth Shue (Adele Horner), Armand Assante (Bugsy Siegel)*
Director: *Jerry Rees*
Screenwriter: *Neil Simon*
15/115 mins./Comedy/Drama/USA

Playboy Charley Pearl marries singer Vicki Anderson, but bickering drives them apart. Not that it stops them marrying again . . . and again . . .

Bugsy Siegel was a happening dead hood in the 90s, with three films about him being released, including this one with Armand Assante impersonating the famously vicious psychotic in this disastrous 'romantic comedy' – originally entitled *The Marrying Man* – set from 1948 to 1956. Bugsy here amuses himself by making a society playboy marry Siegal's girl, a trampy chanteuse, when he catches them practising the Latin vocabulary. In real life he would have air-conditioned their brains.

Subsequently, Bostonian Charley and Vegas Vicki separate and re-marry many times, ill-suited to live with each other but – gee, you guessed – unwilling to keep their hands, mouths and sundry bits off each other. As it has turned out, the much publicised off-screen doings of B and B were considerably more entertaining and, one must assume, more exciting than in this vulgar exercise, surely Neil Simon's lamest ever work – although perhaps prescient in that it predicted the couple's later love/hate relationship which led to an acrimonious divorce. What few chuckles there are come courtesy of Robert Loggia as the Hollywood studio chief father of Charley's twice-jilted fiancée, while Baldwin and Basinger's debatable comedic talents founder in the protracted, witless proceedings.

Basinger performs her many musical numbers on key, but her male admirers will be more impressed by her accompanying fondling of her own breasts and pelvis in a display of self-adoration that might make Madonna blush, most embarassingly during Cole Porter's *Let's Do It*. Let's not. ★ **AE**

TOOTSIE (1982)

Starring: *Dustin Hoffman (Michael Dorsey), Jessica Lange (Julie Nichols), Teri Garr (Sandy Lester), Dabney Coleman (Ron Carlisle), Charles Durning (Les Nichols), Bill Murray (Jeff Slater), Sydney Pollack (George Fields), George Gaynes (John Van Horn), Geena Davis (April Page)*
Director: *Sydney Pollack*
Screenwriters: *Larry Gelbart, Elaine May (uncredited), Murray Schisgal based on the story by Don McGuire and Gelbart*
15/116 mins/Comedy USA

Awards – *Academy Awards – Best Supporting Actress (Jessica Lange), BAFTA – Best Actor, Best Makeup*

Out of work actor Michael Dorsey attempts to improve his employment chances by creating a female alter-ego Dorothy Michaels. Landing a role on a daytime soap, Dorothy becomes a huge hit, forcing Michael to live a dual existence that plays havoc with his love life.

It's not just the cross-dressing element of *Tootsie* that reminds you of Billy Wilder's comedies. There is something old school and proper about this terrific Sydney Pollack-directed comedy where every element just clicks into place, creating an entertainment that just sparkles. Like the best of Wilder, *Tootsie* embraces a broad range of approaches – broad comedy, social satire, bittersweet romance, serious drama – and has the deftness to juggle such conflicting attitudes into a seamless whole.

Considering that there were so many writers on the project – Larry Gelbart once joked that he didn't meet the other writers until they were up on stage at awards ceremonies – it is to Pollack's credit that the piece feels so coherent and unified. As well as finding interesting angles on gender identity, the movie takes gentle swipes at dime a dozen soap operas, sexism within the entertainment industry and the ease with which America creates celebrities. It is also tremendously funny, building up absurdity upon absurdity but sill retaining a believable logic.

Apparently hellish to work with on set, Dustin Hoffman delivers the goods. Full of terrific energy and as likeable as he's ever been on screen, he finds some interesting angles on potentially hackneyed men-in-drag antics – as Dorothy takes on a life of her own, he gives Michael a real glee and curiousity about where his creation could go. If he doesn't make a completely believable woman, Hoffman does enough to get by according to the reality of the movie, his Southern accent and delightfully observed eccentricity making Dorothy an easy character to root for and so believe in.

Tootsie's secret weapon, however, is that, although it feels solely like a vehicle for Hoffman's fireworks, it is also a terrific ensemble piece; an Oscar winning Jessica Lange finds a real humanity to her put-upon soap star, Teri Garr is terrific as Dorsey's neurotic ex, Bill Murray steals scenes as the actor's flatmate ('Don't play hard to get,' he deadpans to Dorsey looking at Dorothy's frock), Charles Durning finds quiet, touching notes as Julie's father who falls for Dorothy and Pollack is terrific as Dorsey's exasperated agent. ★★★★ **WT**

TOP GUN (1986)

Starring: *Tom Cruise (Lt. Pete 'Maverick' Mitchell), Kelly McGillis (Charlotte 'Charlie' Blackwood), Anthony Edwards (Lt. Nick 'Goose' Bradshaw), Tim Robbins (Lt. Sam 'Merlin' Wells), Meg Ryan (Carole Bradshaw)*
Director: *Tony Scott*
Screenwriters: *Jim Cash, Jack Epps, Jr., based on an article 'Top Guns' in California Magazine by Ehud Yonay*
15/105 mins./Action/Drama/USA

Awards – *Academy Awards – Best Song ('Take My Breath Away'), Golden Globes – Best Song ('Take My Breath Away')*

A trainee pilot with a healthy disrespect for authority has something to prove to clear his father's name as a dangerously reckless non-team-player . . .

Some movies are best treated as cinematic souvenirs. Like tacky snow-globes brought back from school trips to Switzerland, or bronze Eiffel Towers with dangerously sharp edges that linger on mantelpieces the world over, worthless and unloved, until they catch someone's eye and remind them of the vanished age from which they came.

Top Gun is such a film. Defending it as a work of art would be either brave or reckless. As an historical artifact, though, it's peerless. Like it or not, if you want to know what pop-film was like in the mid-80s, there's no better example than this chrome-burnished, distilled-to-within-an-inch-of-its-life, high-gloss tale of testosterone-charged flyboys and their big, fast planes.

It was, of course, an outrageous hit, and *Top Gun* contains most of the pan-audience pleasing features that *An Officer And A Gentleman* (another Simpson / Bruckheimer film, and template for this one) had boasted: a military setting; exciting training sequences; good-looking male lead with a spiffy uniform; a love story; and a competitive element. The formula had worked before, and Simpson was betting it would work again.

Top Gun is not so much a movie in the conventional sense as an escalating series of masterfully crafted adverts: motorcycles, aircraft carriers, pectorals and planes all look as if they've been shot for a particularly luminous beer campaign (and while this style looks tired now, it was a revelation at the time). No wonder the American Navy not only provided millions of dollars' worth of hardware gratis, but also stationed recruiting officers outside suburban multiplexes to catch testosterone-addled adolescents still promisingly drenched in cinematic piss and vinegar.

For their leading man, Simpson and Bruckheimer had their eye on a promising kid called Tom Cruise. Cruise had been bubbling under as a potential breakthrough star with *Risky Business* and *All The Right Moves*. Having just finished filming the mildly troubled *Legend* – directed by Tony's brother – Cruise (hell, let's call him The Cruiser, this is the 80s) was nervous about *Top Gun*; even that early in his career he was smart enough to see that the movie had the potential to be, as he put it, 'just *Flashdance* in the sky'. But Simpson was determined, finally coughing up what would in retrospect be a very reasonable $1 million (Cruise's first) for the 24 year-old. And Simpson was also determined to get his money's worth. When an on-set military adviser pointed out that the majority of professional discourse in navy flight schools did not happen in locker rooms, nor with the flyers clad only in their underwear, Simpson was unimpressed. 'I have just paid a million dollars for that kid,' he impatiently announced, 'and I need to see some flesh.'

And so to the question, 'Is it any good?' Well, what can be said with certainty is that with some of the contemporary dreck sloshing around the multiplexes, 80s dreck doesn't look too bad. The flying sequences remain exciting, there is something approaching a story – even if it is emaciated – and, for good or ill, it inaugurated the Cruise grin, which still beams down from multiplex screens two decades later. Tat, certainly, then. But tat to be treasured. ★★★★ **AS**

TOP SECRET! (1984)

Starring: *Val Kilmer (Nick Rivers), Lucy Gutteridge (Hilary Flammond) Peter Cushing (Bookstore Proprietor), Jeremy Kemp (General Streck), Christopher Villiers (Nigel 'The Torch'), Warren Clarke (Colonel von Horst), Harry Ditson (Du Quois), Jim Carter (déjà vu), Eddie Tagoe (Chocolate Mousse), Omar Sharif (Agent Cedric)*
Directors: *Jim Abrahams, David Zucker, Jerry Zucker*
Screenwriters: *Jim Abrahams, David Zucker, Jerry Zucker, Martyn Burke*
15/90 mins./Comedy/UK-USA

Nick Rivers, an anachronistic rock 'n' roller, tours an even more anachronistic Nazi-run East Germany and gets caught up with Hilary Flammond, the beautiful daughter of an imprisoned scientist and a band of stalwart resistance fighters.

Made and apparently set in 1984, this effort from the David Zucker-Jim Abrahams-Jerry Zucker team blithely melds time-periods and features one of Val Kilmer's rare comic turns. As usual, the ZAZ team offer a live-action *MAD Magazine* movie satire, throwing in jokes so stupid as to seem almost surreal, an amazing range of cultural referents and a smattering of genuinely witty conceits.

Rather than home in on one film-form like the disaster movie as in *Airplane!* or the cop story as in *The Naked Gun*, this sends up two apparently unrelated genres, the pop performer vehicle – with Kilmer as a mutant crossbreed of Cliff and Elvis – and the World War II spy picture. This tactic sacrifices the vestiges of coherence found in their other, better-known films but is in itself so ridiculous it's hard not to warm up to it. For the most part, the three-handed direction is merely functional, but several inventive pastiche songs (during one tear-jerker, Kilmer has to be dissuaded from suicide by his backing group) allow for a subtler approach and some gags are so ancient ('I know a little German. He's sitting over there') you almost feel pestered into laughing.

Among the inevitable star cameos are Jeremy Kemp, a villain seen perusing the *Hermann Goering Work-Out Book*, Peter Cushing, whose scene is played entirely backwards (and who wears a bizarre, half-enlarged facial prosthetic for the sake of a magnifying glass gag), and Omar Sharif, as a trench-coated spy who keeps turning up in unlikely places. Never mind that a high percentage of jokes misfire, there'll be a funny one along in a minute. ★★★★ **KN**

TOPSY-TURVY (1999)

Starring: *Jim Broadbent (William Schwenck Gilbert), Allan Corduner (Sir Arthur Sullivan), Timothy Spall (Richard Temple), Lesley Manville (Lucy Gilbert), Ron Cook (Richard D'Oyly Carte)*
Director: *Mike Leigh*
Screenwriter: *Mike Leigh*
12/153 mins./Biography/Comedy/Drama/Music/UK/USA

Awards – *Academy Awards – Best Costume, Best Makeup, BAFTA – Best Makeup*

Composing and writing team Gilbert and Sullivan try to salvage their careers with a new comic opera – *The Mikado*.

While we're all overjoyed by the return to the big time of character-driven films with fresh, unpredictable stories, let us not forget that Mike Leigh has been making them for more than 25 years. The acknowledged master of contemporary tragi-comedy makes what seems like an uncharacteristic departure from his creative manor for a study of Gilbert and Sullivan during the year of collaboration on their comic opera *The Mikado* – and turns the musical biopic on its head for a hilarious, tender, intimately detailed and passionately humane panoply of life that is, quite simply, superb.

Following the mediocre reception accorded their *Princess Ida* in 1884, composer Sir Arthur Sullivan tells writer William Gilbert and impresario Richard D'Oyly Carte that he is breaking up their renowned partnership to write serious opera. But after a visit to a Japanese exhibition stokes Gilbert's fire, his romantic comedy of deception and disguise, peopled by Nanki-Poo, Yum-Yum, Pooh-Bah and the great and powerful Mikado, charms Sullivan back to the Savoy Theatre and production gets underway, to debut in 1885.

Superficially, that's all the plot. But it's almost none of the story, which flits gracefully through an inspired ensemble for wistful vignettes and whacky incidents, sad soliloquy and public gaiety, gathering impressions of artists and their creative demons, life on the stage and back of it.

Gilbert is its centre, and Broadbent's is a magnificent portrayal of a complex comic genius, gifted with wit but with a limited capacity to take joy from it. Besides him it's almost criminal to single out delicious performances, but newcomer Martin Savage as the company's drug-dependent comedian is a real discovery and little Shirley Henderson (then best known as Robert Carlyle's love interest in *Hamish Macbeth*) is a revelation as the alcoholic soprano (the actors do their own singing, by the way, with surprising excellence).

All life is here, with and without songs: Gilbert grappling with his latest gadget (a telephone!) and his eccentric family's disputes; D'Oyly Carte raising finance for a hotel he outrageously proposes shall have a bathroom for every bedroom (The Savoy!); bon vivant Sullivan enjoying R&R in a Parisian brothel; the hysterical dressing room double act of Timothy Spall and Kevin McKidd laced into corsets and swapping gossip, embodying the vanity, pretension and fragility of actors.

Leigh's observations of people's contradictions, tics, desires, pettiness and pain have never been sketched with more delicacy, drollery or deeply felt insight. It's a masterpiece. And the tunes are pretty good, too. ★★★★★ **AE**

TOP10 Horror Cliches

1 **Victims always run upstairs. Or into that sinister-looking house.**
2 **Unless the bad guy has been dismembered or shot in the head, he's not dead.**
3 **Girls with large breasts who don't take their tops off generally survive.**
4 **Small, quiet children (especially if of Japanese origin) are not to be trusted. If you see one, run.**
5 **Psychos and monsters can break down any door.**
6 **Any knife you pick up to defend yourself is likely to be used against you.**
7 **Anyone who drinks, has sex or says, 'I'll be right back' is dead meat (See *Scream*).**
8 **If you're scared by a cat / your best friend, you'll be killed just as you breathe a sigh of relief.**
9 **Something visible when you look in the mirror will not be there when you look around.**
10 **Any search plan which involves splitting up will inevitably lead to multiple deaths.**

TOTAL RECALL (1990)

Starring: *Arnold Schwarzenegger (Douglas Quaid/Hauser), Sharon Stone (Lori), Rachel Ticotin (Melina), Ronny Cox (Vilos Cohaagen), Michael Ironside (Richter)*
Director: *Paul Verhoeven*
Screenwriters: *Ronald Shusett, Dan O'Bannon, Gary Goldman, based on a screen story by Shusett, O'Bannon, Jon Povill, short story* We Can Remember It For You Wholesale *by Philip K. Dick*
18/108 mins./Sci-fi/Thriller/USA

Douglas Quaid is haunted by a recurring dream about a journey to Mars. He hopes to find out more about this dream and buys a holiday at Rekall Inc. where they sell implanted memories. But something goes wrong with the memory implantation and he remembers being a secret agent fighting against the evil Mars administrator Cohaagen.

Something that should be born in mind whenever exposing oneself to Paul Verhoeven's particular brand of sensationalist entertainment is that the man, by a conservative estimate, is as mad as a snake. In the late 80s, with a maturing arthouse reputation in his native Holland, he abruptly ditched all vestiges of highbrow aspiration and headed for Hollywood. He quickly established himself as a master of nosebleed sci-fi/action with *Robocop* in 1987 and has obviously not felt the urge to don a beret or smoke a Gauloise since.

A series of liberal-baiting blockbusters, including underrated thriller *Basic Instinct* and the awesome *Starship Troopers*, confirmed that, in spite of his stylistic volte-face, Verhoeven had retained his auteur's commitment to uncompromising vision. On the other hand, 1996's lap-dance epic *Showgirls* confirmed him as a borderline pornographer and a complete and utter fruitcake. *Total Recall* (1990) might be eclipsed by *Robocop*, but it's still a handy example of the Verhoeven modus operandi: crank the volume to 11, pile on the violence and invite the critics to go fuck themselves.

And if it does lack the satirical edge of his other sci-fi outings, it exhibits ample evidence of Verhoeven's queasy sense of humour and kaleidoscopic dystopian fantasies: violent, repressive and liberally splashed with hilarious surrealism. Adapted from the Philip K. Dick short story *We Can Remember It For You Wholesale*, *Total Recall* is what 1984 would have been if PlayStation 2 had figured as heavily in George Orwell's formative years as the playing fields of Eton. Arnold Schwarzenegger, in one of his last truly effective roles and still the right side of terminal self-parody, plays Doug Quaid an ordinary Earth-bound Joe who is plagued by disturbing dreams of Mars, a politically unstable off-world colony ruled by a corrupt dictator whose draconian control of the air supply is fuelling a revolution. Quaid's wife can't understand her husband's obsession with the hellish planet, nor why he is so keen to go there.

In an attempt to scratch his inexplicable itch, Quaid visits Rekall Inc. a memory implant service who promise him a virtual trip to Mars with all the trimmings. But during the implant procedure something goes disastrously wrong. Quaid discovers – or seems to, at least – that his entire memory has been erased and replaced with a manufactured version. His whole life is a pre-fabricated fantasy. The plot really kicks in when Quaid finds himself pursued by agents of the ubiquitous 'organisation' and his wife tries to kill him. Acting on a mysterious tip-off he locates a device, apparently hidden by himself before his memory was wiped, on which a recording of his previous self spills the beans – he was once in the employ of the organisation and stationed on Mars.

The right hand man of dictator Cohaagen he was a key element in the regime until he converted to the rebel cause. In retaliation, Cohaagen erased his mind and dumped him on Earth. Or did he? When Quaid journeys to Mars to unravel the mystery (disguised, it appears, as Claire Raynor with an exploding head), we begin to wonder whether this is, in fact, reality or simply the recreational memory implant he bought on Earth going into overdrive.

It's a clever and intriguing premise, the stuff of many of Dick's stories, including *Do Androids Dream Of Electric Sheep?*, and Verhoeven exploits it to the full – embroidering it with plenty of brutal violence and big bangs, naturally. The scene where a representative of Rekall Inc. turns up on Mars, with Quaid's wife in tow, to persuade him that he is dangerously lost inside his own head is painfully tense. A bead of sweat on the Rekall tech's forehead gives the game away and Quaid simply blows them away – 'Consida dat a divoors,' he quips after putting a bullet through Stone's skull. Vintage Arnie, vintage Verhoeven.

Things get a little formulaic after that, with Quaid throwing in his lot with the rebels to defeat Cohaagen, liberate the air supply and solve the riddle of the monolithic alien machines found in a vast cavern beneath the planet's surface. But there's at least one more major twist round the corner and the action keeps coming thick and fast. With a budget of $63m, *Total Recall* was, at the time, the most expensive movie ever made. That wouldn't buy you a Jennifer Anniston romcom these days and, to be honest, the film doesn't have quite the jaw-drop factor we've come to expect since the CGI revolution. That said, the blood-red mountains of Mars (actually Mexico) look splendid and there's some exceptional modelwork. ★★★★ **SB**

ⓘ TOUCH OF EVIL (1958)

Starring: *Charlton Heston (Ramon Miguel 'Mike' Vargas), Janet Leigh (Susan 'Susie' Vargas), Orson Welles (Police Captain Hank Quinlan), Oseoph Calleia (Police Sergeant Pete Menzies), Akim Tamiroff ('Uncle' Joe Grandi)*
Director: *Orson Welles*
Screenwriter: *Orson Welles, based on the novel by Whit Masterson*
12/95 mins./112 mins. (director's cut)/Film-noir/Thriller/USA

A Mexican government investigator and his young American wife put their honeymoon on hold in an American border town when they become embroiled in a frame-up planned by the town's chief investigator

For over 40 years critics and filmmakers from François Truffaut to Paul Schrader to Curtis Hanson (citing its influence on *LA Confidential*) have paid homage to the technical mastery and inspiration of Orson Welles' potent 50s noir. It's a lurid tale of corruption and conscience played out in the gaudy strip joints and cheap motel rooms of a sleazy border town, with honourable Mexican narcotics official Charlton Heston and bloated, degenerate American cop Welles at odds over a murder whose jurisdiction is in dispute. All the while Heston's bride, Janet Leigh, becomes a terrorised pawn in their battle of wills.

Heston arguably did the best day's work of his glamorous career when he used his A-list clout to strongarm Universal into hiring the Hollywood pariah Welles to direct the good versus evil melodrama. Initially producer Albert Zugsmith offered Welles the role of Hank Quinlan. Heston, a fan, misunderstood, assuming Welles would also direct. The reluctant Zugsmith was forced to agree when Heston rightly pointed out 'He's a pretty good director, you know'.

He was no mean screenwriter, either. Welles immediately threw out the script and wrote his own free adaptation of the source novel, *Badge Of Evil* by Whit Masterson. Thus began the transformation of a pulp fiction, a cheap little thriller, into great art. The film, shot at Universal Studios and in the nearby beach community of Venice, is steeped in the sinister atmosphere of desperate turista towns like those tamiliar noir dens of iniquity Tijuana, on the California border, and Juarez, a spit away from El Paso, Texas.

If for nothing else the film is remembered (and still imitated) for its remarkable single tracking shot opening, a dazzling, three minute set-up that sucks you into this neon-lit cesspool. The camera crane swoops through the busy night scene as Miguel 'Mike' Vargas and his pert blonde all-American bride Susie, slumming on honeymoon, stroll across into America in search of a chocolate ice cream soda. An unidentifiable man plants a bomb in a convertible, pedestrians scurry around, the driver's floozy companion complains at the checkpoint that she's 'Got this ticking noise in my head,' Vargas, Susie and the border patrol guard exchange enough small talk to establish their thumbnail back story, and ka-boom, the honeymoon is over. Welles' evil Hank Quinlan is the police chief from the American side of the border, who arrives to take control of the car bombing investigation and get in Vargas' face while Susie is waylaid and menaced by the drug-dealing gang Vargas has been working to shut down. Within minutes the cards have been dealt in a malevolent, deeply perverse game. To prevent Vargas from exposing him for the criminal he is, Quinlan will have the abducted and drugged Susie dumped (by a lesbian in leather and her reefer-maddened thugs!) in a squalid dive with a dead man.

Quinlan is one of the giant noir psychopaths of the screen, a bloated figure whose abuse of power has turned him into a spiritual and physical monstrosity (the already hefty Welles expanded with padding and false nose). 'You're a mess, honey!' exclaims Marlene Dietrich's enigmatic, fortune-telling, chilli-cooking whore, failing to recognise one-time regular Hank. This dark vision of dissolution is kin to *Citizen Kane*. The idea of Heston as a Mexican may be preposterous, but his performance is actually interesting, his confidence in a sophisticated role sufficient to prevent the satirical Welles from crushing him. Leigh is fine as the headstrong WASP saucepot, honing her 'trapped with a nutcase motel clerk' reactions with a twitching Dennis Weaver for her impending date with Norman Bates. The most affecting character is not abused Susie, however, but the tragic, belatedly ennobled figure of Quinlan's adoring lackey, Pete. Adding flavour are cameos from Mercedes McCambridge ('Thee fun ees chust begeening!') and *Kane* vets Joseph Gotten and Ray Collins.

Rivalling the opening are a series of bold, complex set-pieces which have given the film its reputation as noir's epitaph. Welles' theatrically exaggerated style elements achieve a hyper-realism with Russell Metty's sharp black-and-white cinematography and Henry Mancini's Latino/jazz/rock and roll score. Consider the interrogation of bombing suspect Sanchez. Cast and crew moving in a carefully rehearsed choreography, the claustrophobic apartment is crowded with characters, all presented from striking angles, in one single continuous take. The nightmarish end chase is a delirium of flamboyant visuals, experimental sound effects and pervasive doom.

Welles disliked the editing done by Universal and wrote a 58-page memo specifying his intentions. In 1998 a restoration meticulously done from these notes was released. Just a few minutes longer, its most apparent, satisfying alterations are the removal of credits over the famous opening sequence and more intricate cutting between Susie's motel ordeal and Vargas' disturbing journey with Quinlan. Whether the 'before' or 'after' version, it endures as a superbly kinky masterpiece of technique, imagination and audacity. ★★★★★ **AE**

TOUCHING THE VOID (2003)

Starring: *Brendan Mackey (Joe Simpson), Nicholas Aaron (Simon Yates), Ollie Ryall (Richard Hawking)*
Director: *Kevin Macdonald*
Screenwriter: *Joe Simpson*
15/101 mins./Drama/Documentary/USA/UK
Awards: BAFTA Awards – *Alexander Korda Award For Best British Film*

Two mountaineering buddies hit catastrophe when one breaks his leg near the top of a remote Peruvian mountain. The other tries to lower his partner to safety, but disaster strikes again when the injured party is dangled over a 150-foot ice cliff. Does the healthy climber allow himself to be dragged to his death, or cut the rope and send his doomed friend spiralling into the void?

Following several abortive attempts to transfer Joe Simpson's mountaineering bestseller to the screen (at one point Tom Cruise was attached to star), *Touching The Void* finally makes its appearance in docudrama format, with British Oscar-winner Kevin Macdonald (*One Day In September*) behind the camera.

It's not difficult to see why Hollywood screenwriters struggled with Simpson's story of disaster and endurance on Peru's forbidding Siula Grande peak. The protagonists barely speak to each other and, aside from two perilous falls, there's little in the way of traditional action.

However, Macdonald overcomes this headache by blending interviews with the survivors into his well-crafted reconstruction, and the result is as much an exploration of ethics and psychology as it is of uncommon human endurance.

Though it takes a while to empathise with these curiously detached characters, the internal tension of the climbing psyche ultimately proves as gripping as the physical horror suffered on the mountain. ★★★★ **EH**

TOWERING INFERNO (1974)

Starring: *Steve McQueen (Chief Michael O'Hallorhan), Paul Newman (Doug Roberts), William Holden (James Duncan), Faye Dunaway (Susan Franklin), Fred Astaire (Harlee Claiborne), Susan Blakely (Patty Simmons), Richard Chamberlain (Roger Simmons), O.J. Simpson (Harry Jernigan), Robert Vaughn (Dan Bigelow), Susan Flannery (Lorrie)*
Directors: *John Guillermin, Irwin Allen*
Screenwriter: *Stirling Silliphant, based on the novels* The Tower *by Richard Martin Stern,* The Glass Inferno *by Thomas N. Scortia, Frank M. Robinson*
15/165 mins./Drama/Action/Thriller/USA
Awards – *Academy Awards – Best Cinematography, Best Editing, Best Original Song ('We May Never Love Like This Again'), BAFTA Awards – Anthony Asquith Award for Music (John Williams), Best Supporting Actor (Fred Astaire), Golden Globes – Best Supporting Actor (Fred Astaire), Most Promsing Newcomer – Susan Flannery*

A brand new high-rise architectural wonder is hosting a big-deal society affair when a fire starts in an 81st floor store-room. The architect and the local fire chief are both livid at the dangerous construction short cuts they discover but saving the guests is more the task in hand . . .

'It's as though General Motors and Chrysler combined their respective brainpower and manpower and went Dutch treat on the bill to produce a new model automobile.'

Thus ran the statement issued by Warner Bros and 20th Century Fox in October 1973, announcing their historic union for one picture only. After the success of *The Poseidon Adventure*, Warner Bros had aced Fox in a $400,000 bid for rights to *The Tower*, a novel about a burning skyscraper. Fox paid $300,000 for *The Glass Inferno*, a similar fiery yarn. Producer Irwin Allen suggested a collaboration instead of a scrap, and the two behemoths split the costs down the middle, including the building of 57 sets, all of which would be burned down in the process. It paid off, of course. The film grossed $100 million worldwide (a lot of money in those days).

A few years ago, *Towering Inferno* was a museum piece: spectacular, successful, rubbish. But it stands today – after *Daylight*, *Volcano*, *Titanic*, *Hard Rain* – as the giant of a reassessed genre. *Poseidon* will always be the original and best, but there remains something irresistible about this film's expensive swagger, from the helicopter shot into San Francisco onwards.

Today's disaster movies today tend not to attract Hollywood's superleague; in the good old days, only the biggest names would do – McQueen and Newman (the Cruise and Hanks of the early 70s) as inscrutable fire chief and dependable architect. Holden, playing the mogul who built the tower, took a lower billing, but not without complaint ('It's a lousy script,' he complained to his agent).

There is something quaint about the fact that the actors did many of their own stunts (in the climactic flooding of the Promenade Room, which extinguishes the blaze, you can see the look of real terror in Fred Astaire's face), but McQueen takes the crown. He actually fought a real $80 million inferno during fire department research for the role, and was more concerned on set about his helmet ('I look like an idiot!' he complained). If the dialogue is cheesy ('Is it bad?' 'It's a fire – all fires are bad'), it's spoken in the face of some breathtaking set pieces. *Backdraft*'s homage in 1991 gave fire a malevolent life of its own; here, it simply looks out of control. A rare 70s film that doesn't look like a TV movie. ★★★★ **AC**

THE TOXIC AVENGER (1985)

Starring: *Andree Maranda (Sara), Mitchell Cohen (Toxic Avenger), Jennifer Baptist (Wanda), Mark Torgl (Melvin), Robert Pritchard (Slug)*
Directors: *Michael Herz, Samuel Weil*
Screenwriters: *Joe Ritter, Lloyd Kaufman, Gay Partington Terry, Stuart Strutin*
18/87 mins./110min./(director's cut)/Comedy/Horror/USA

A practical joke misfires and nerdy janitor Melvin gets stuffed into a vat of toxic waste while dressed in a ballerina outfit. He emerges mutated into a Swamp Thing/Hulk-style monster hero and romps around Tromaville, New Jersey, slaughtering grotesque villains and mooning over his blind true love.

The foundation stone of the Troma trash movie empire, this signals a slight shift of effort from the production of unfunny gross-out comedies (*Stuck on You*, *The First Turn-On*) to a distinctive genre mutation which gene-splices the fart-puke-boobs gaggery with extreme splatter, comic-book superheroics and embittered satiricial swipes at big business. The Troma style perhaps predates the anything-gross-for-a-laugh approach of the Farrelly Brothers (who also made a film called *Stuck on You*), but real seaminess between good-natured gags makes for a shifting tone that too often gets beyond the boundaries of *good* bad taste into merely tiresome unpleasantness.

You can gauge your likely appreciation of the film by whether you find any of these incidents actually funny: a) a guy in a tutu duped into kissing a sheep, b) a ten-year-old knocked off his bicycle and having his head crushed by laughing hit-and-run drivers, c) a girl masturbating over photographs of murdered children, d) an obese man having his insides pulled out, e) a middle-aged dwarf lady shoved into a spin-dryer, f) a guide dog shotgunned dead by a robber who then tries to rape its owner. If none of these raise a smile, buy something else.

Though the effects are gloopy, the filmmaking – which is down to Troma supremo Lloyd Kaufman – is strictly entry-level. 'Toxie' has returned in four sequels, and you get much the same bad taste in the mouth from the *Class of Nuke 'Em High* films, *Troma's War*, *Terror Firmer*, *Tromeo & Juliet*, Sgt *Kabukiman NYPD*, etc. ★ **KN**

Movie Trivia: Troma (established 1974)

What is it: Film production and distribution company, specialising in low-budget, independent, cult movies. Fine purveyors exploitation and shock-mongering. Hits include *Cannibal: The Musical* and *Blood Sucking Freaks*.

Hallmarks: Graphic violence, gore and nudity; overt sexuality; shocking imagery; B-movie titles and Z movie budgets; mysterious mainstream popularity.

If you see one movie, see: *The Toxic Avenger* (1984)

TOY STORY (1995)

Starring: the voices of: *Tom Hanks (Woody), Tim Allen (Buzz Lightyear), Don Rickles (Mr. Potato Head), Jim Varney (Slinky Dog), Wallace Shawn (Rex), John Ratzenberger (Hamm), Annie Potts (Bo Peep), John Morris (Anday), Erik von Detten (Sid), Laurie Metcalf (Andy's Mom), R. Lee Ermey (Sergeant)*
Director: *John Lasseter*
Screenwriters: *Joss Whedon, Andrew Stanton, Joel Cohen, Alec Sokolow, based on a story by John Lasseter, Pete Docter, Andrew Stanton, Joe Ranft*
PG/81 mins./Animation/Adventure/Comedy/Family/USA
Awards: Academy Awards – *Special Achievement Award (John Lasseter)*

A cowboy toy is profoundly threatened and jealous when a fancy spaceman toy supplants him as top toy in a boy's room.

About ten years before Junior decides to get a 'Hail Satan' forehead tattoo on the day the Vicar is coming round for tea or your little princess opts to neglect GCSE revision for an exciting new career as a mama with the local biker gang, the worst agony of parenthood is the kiddie movie.

Not only does the release of one of these suckers mean the money you saved for Grandpa's kidney machine is about to be earmarked for action figures, tie-in sweets, colouring books and video games, but you've also got to sit through something like *Pokemon 2000*, *The Tigger Movie* or *My Little Pony* in a cinema full of yard-apes who've dosed up on that breakfast cereal which fills the tykes with surplus energy they need to discharge by running around, screaming and kicking and biting. It would be enough to give you a headache, if the film – a colourful riot of eye-abusing animation – hadn't already done that.

The whole point of a craze like Pokemon – and the Power Rangers, Ninja Turtles, Transformers, The Care Bears and every other kid-craze all the way back to Tiger Tim And His Pals (ask a pensioner) – is to alienate adults, to create a cultural space that only an eight year-old can inhabit; in which you as a grown-up may have a degree in rocket science and be among the three best cello virtuosi of the age but you're clearly a moron if you can't tell the difference between Pikachu and Mewtwo, and beneath contempt should you get Pokemon mixed up with Digimon ('Daaaad, how could you embarrass me like that?'). Then there's *Toy Story*.

The reason that the United Nations should strike a special medal for John Lasseter of Pixar is that *Toy Story* is, at last, a real film 'for children of all ages'. In an age when children own videos of their favourite films and insist they be played every day for three straight years, even during funerals or the cup final telecast, *Toy Story* has been so intensely crafted that there are fresh jokes to appreciate every time. Some are amazingly subtle, like a slight camera jiggle to imitate a rough edit; in computer animation, it would be easier to have a perfect match shot but you need the flaw to interpret the visual information – watch it again, and be astonished at the creativity.

It's also – courtesy of the script involvement of Joss Whedon – the *Scream* of kiddie movies, a pointed reflection on the meaning of its genre. It deploys cutting edge technology in a film affirming the place of hand-stitched stuffed toys beside 'Made In Taiwan' plastic high-tech, and unifies parent and child by encouraging a post-film debate about how toys have changed since the old days.

Given that *Toy Story* was the first all-CGI animated feature, it's a miracle that it didn't turn out to be as plodding as *Dinosaur* – which spends so much time on the tech that it forgets to include the drama, the humour and the heart. Spinning off from the old idea of the playthings that come to life when the children aren't looking (there's a creepy Victorian music hall song called When 'The Dolls Dance After Dark' that appears in the film *The House In Nightmare Park* (1973), *Toy Story* has a genuine story in the rivalry between Sheriff Woody (Hanks), the old-fashioned stuffed cowboy doll, and Buzz Lightyear (Allen), a cartoon space-ranger that parodies the worst of kidblitz teevee. How a 1995 eight year-old has a toy from the 1950s is a question we shouldn't ask. Oddly, there's real bite in the film.

Woody, the ostensible hero, is a paranoid middle-management drone ('Staff meeting, everybody!') so jealous of his pole position in Andy's life that he's willing to murder the naively heroic Buzz (who initially refuses to believe he isn't a real space ranger). With a less supernaturally likeable voice performer than Allen, you probably wouldn't put up with him. And forget Sid the toy-torturer next door, it's Andy who's the monster, turning his toys into emotional wrecks by capriciously bestowing and witholding affection and never conscious of the agonies suffered under his feet.

Stunt voice casting is an art perfected by the corporate Disney cartoons of the 1990s, most successfully with Robin Williams in *Aladdin*, but see also Eddie Murphy in *Mulan*. *Toy Story* hauls in star names but also brilliantly-chosen character actors, and comes up with animated creations, unimaginable without their voices but not completely reliant on them for humour – you hear John (*Cheers*) Ratzenberger (Ham the piggy-bank), Wallace ('Inconceivable!') Shawn (Rex the pathetic T-Rex), R. Lee (*Full Metal Jacket*) Ermey (Sarge of the Bucket O'Soldiers) and Jim ('Ernest') Varney (Slinky) but they aren't making the faces move though you'd swear they were.

This is a film that realises kids can and do love crap toys – the dinosaur whose parts don't quite match, the soldiers with bent guns and plastic mould ridges – because imagination makes them live, and there's a lovely irony in that *Toy Story*'s merchandising means you can now buy lovingly-crafted versions of these creatures, right down to their deliberatley placed flaws.

And, miracle of miracles, Pixar managed to do it all over again with the inevitable but still magical *Toy Story* 2. ★★★★★ **KN**

Actors who play/sing in bands — TOP 10

1. Russell Crowe, Singer, 30 Odd Foot of Grunts*†
2. Kevin Bacon, Singer, The Bacon Brothers†
3. Jack Black, Singer/Guitarist, Tenacious D†
4. Keanu Reeves, Guitarist, Dogstar†
5. Johnny Depp, Guitarist, Tonto's Giant Nuts
6. Mark Wahlberg, Rapper, Marky Mark and the Funky Bunch*†
7. Jada Pinkett Smith, Singer, Wicked Wisdom†
8. Jeff Goldblum, Piano, Mildred Snitzer Orchestra
9. Jared Leto, Singer, Thirty Seconds to Mars
10. Woody Harrelson, Madly Moondog and the Three Kool Hats

*Have since left

†Have released material commercially

Movie Trivia: *Toy Story*

The carpet texture in the hallway of Sid's house is identical to that of the hotel in *The Shining*. Whenever a character blinks, both eyes do not blink together, but one at a time. Buzz's nemesis Zurg has 11 settings to his gun, a reference to *This Is Spinal Tap*'s 11-notch amplifier. Billy Crystal was first choice to play Buzz Lightyear.

TOY STORY 2 (1999)

Starring: the voices of: *Tom Hanks (Woody), Tim Allen (Buzz Lightyear), Don Rickles (Mr. Potato Head), Jim Varney (Slinky Dog), Wallace Shawn (Rex), John Ratzenberger (Hamm), Annie Potts (Bo Peep), John Morris (Andy), Laurie Metcalf (Andy's Mom), Joan Cusack (Jessie), Kelsey Grammer (Stinky Pete)*
Screenwriters: *Rita Hsiao, Andrew Stanton, Doug Chamberlain, Chris Webb, based on a story by John Lasseter, Pete Docter, Andrew Stanton, Ash Brannon*
U/92 mins./Animation/Adventure/Comedy/Family/USA
Awards – *Golden Globes – Best Comedy/Musical*

When Woody is kidnapped by a Toy trader the rest of the toys set out to rescue him.

Having made such a remarkable impact on the world of animation, swapping sentiment and dodgily-etched 2-D stereotypes for something distinctly more multi-dimensional – while creating the same sort of real-life demand for its screen playthings that it portrayed in the movie – it was inevitable that a sequel to *Toy Story* would appear at some point.

Originally envisioned, however, as one of the straight-to-video efforts that have proven so successful for Disney (to wit: *Aladdin* follow-up *The Return Of Jafar*, and *The Lion King* sequel *Simba's Pride*), the folks at Pixar sensibly decided this film was worthy of a big screen outing first. And right they are, for *Toy Story 2*, while lacking the immediacy of its predecessor and taking just a little too long to switch into high gear, is a highly superior sequel. In the States it zoomed its way to $150 million in just four weeks, kicking off with a not-to-be-sniffed-at $80 million opening weekend – proof, then, that this sort of thing may well come with a built-in audience, but at the same time, a little quality and thought goes a very long way.

This time around it's the summer after the original movie and Andy is heading off to cowboy camp, Woody in tow. Until, that is, Woody is incapacitated in a playroom accident and left on a neglected top shelf, along with a broken penguin, for repair. A further string of mishaps, mainly involving Woody's attempts to save the dusty bird from a yard sale in a brilliant rescue sequence, see him landing in the clutches of toy collector Al (of Al's Toy Barn fame), and finding out facts about his past life, involving a crap 50s black-and-white telly show, a bunch of new characters – cowgirl doll Jessie, boxed gold prospector Stinky Pete and mute pony Bullseye – and one of the biggest merchandising opportunities since, well, *Toy Story*. Meanwhile, Buzz and his pals set off to the toy store in order to bring Woody back to Andy's room, encountering a string of obstacles – from Tour Guide Barbie to a whole shelf of other Buzz Lightyears – along the way.

While Toy Story's plotline depended largely on Buzz Lightyear's refusal to believe in his action figure origins, this time around Lasseter ups the stakes; the underlying story strand, treated in one of the movies handful of songs, gets the toys pondering their fate once they become broken or outmoded, or their owner simply outgrows them. Knowing that the characters have only a limited lifespan lends proceedings a rather curious poignancy, although it doesn't detract from some quite sensational animation which, as it was first time around, is the major selling point. Here the detail is evident in everything from the amazing opening sequence, pitting Buzz against his arch nemesis, Emperor Zurg, through to the monolithic shelves of Al's Toy Barn. However, its the little touches – such as the thick dust layer adorning Woody's new shelf-top home – which stick in the mind longest.

Perhaps the most striking aspect of *Toy Story 2*, however, is the amount of care that has gone into creating a film which is every bit as impressive as its predecessor, rather than delivering something vastly inferior that can be sold on the strength of its characters. Lasseter and new arrival Brannon have skilfully woven their way around the lack of surprise element to create new characters that charm and convince, set-pieces galore – leading up to a finale every bit as breathtaking as its predecessor – and a whole range of new and original jokes, not least of which is a canny repetition of Buzz's space ranger delusions to hilarious effect. *Toy Story 2* doesn't quite knock *The Godfather II* from its best-sequel-of-all-time perch, but it still provides the kind of exhilarating cinema experience that leaves you gasping in admiration and actually wanting a third instalment. If only all sequels were this good. ★★★★★
CW

Movie Trivia: Pixar Studios (established 1986)

What is it? Originally a software company created by Lucasfilm, bought by Steve Jobs in 1986. gradually became a purveyor of high-quality computer animation. Leapt into feature films with *Toy Story* in 1996.
Hallmarks: Buddy movies; gorgeous and innovative animation; Randy Newman songs; sly nods to Hollywood history; meticulous storycrafting; sterling quality.
If you see one movie, see: *Toy Story* (1996)

⊙ TOYS (1992)

Starring: *Robin Williams (Leslie Zevo), Michael Gambon (Lt. General Zevo), Joan Cusack (Alsatia Zevo), Robin Wright Penn (Gwen Tyler), LL Cool J (Captain Patrick Zevo), Donald O'Connor (Kenneth Zevo)*
Director: *Barry Levinson*
Screenwriters: *Valerie Curtin, Barry Levinson*
PG/116 mins./Fantasy/Comedy/USA

An eccentric toymaker leaves his factory to his militaristic brother, much to the dismay of his children Alsatia and Leslie. When the General starts using the factory to produce weapons, Leslie and Alsatia realise they need to regain control.

'May joy and innocence prevail,' is the epitaph on a character's tomb in this fantastically bizarre fable which uses themes of madness, power, lust and war extravagantly played out in a toy factory to reiterate the message.

When jokester toy magnate Kenneth Zevo ('Make 'Em Laugh' man Donald O'Connor in a whacky cameo) expires, he leaves control of his happy kingdom to his redundant hawk US Army general brother rather than to his children Leslie and Alsatia who are, respectively, a flake and a fragile, child-like loon.

How the general runs the business, his evil intent, and Leslie's leap from clown to champion of sweetness and light make for a quirky, soppy narrative that is part Grimm, part Gilliam and part Kubrick. Devoid at times of both taste and sense, but at others madly endearing, this was written years ago by Levinson and his first wife Valerie Curtin and understandably shunned by pragmatic studios until stock in the firm of Levinson and Williams rose high enough to attract the necessarily hefty budget.

Necessary, because whatever one makes of this touchingly naive labour of love, it is a work that, visually, one would never have looked to Levinson for, an eye-popping, surreal dreamworld that is a constant delight to look at between Ferdinando Scarfiotti's brilliant production design and Albert Wolsky's witty costumes (both Oscar nominated). The Zevo mansion folds out of a hillside like a spread in a fairytale pop-up book; a music video the Zevo siblings make marries Magritte to MTV; the bright primary colours of the factory throw up astonishing and extremely weird jokes; and the climactic battle between the forces of good and evil – clockwork nursery toys and miniature weapons of destruction – is executed like a mechanical ballet envisioned in a nightmare.

And if the characters are grotesques – think *Dr. Strangelove* meets *Tom Thumb* in *Brazil* and you're approaching the ball park – Williams is at his most appealing here, squeezing in hilarious impersonations of Michael Williams and Mother Theresa, Cusack is extraordinary and L L Cool J as Gambon's son can also hold his head up for a usefully amusing turn. ★★★ **AE**

⊙ TRADING PLACES (1983)

Starring: *Dan Aykroyd (Louis Winthorpe III), Eddie Murphy (Billy Ray Valentine), Ralph Bellamy (Randolph Duke), Don Ameche (Mortimer Duke), Jamie Lee Curtis (Ophelia), Denholm Elliott (Coleman)*
Director: *John Landis*
Screenwriter: *Timothy Harris, Herschel Weingrod*
15/111 mins./Comedy/USA

Awards – *BAFTA – Best Supporting Actor (Denholm Elliott), Best Supporting Actress (Jamie Lee Curtis)*

A snobbish investor and a wily street con artist find their positions reversed as part of a bet by two callous millionaires.

Trading Places is, of course, *The Prince And The Pauper* meets *A Christmas Carol*, updated for the brash, morally-confused 1980s. At the same time, it attempts to say something about the society it depicts. But don't let that put you off. *Trading Places* is still a right good laugh. The social comment is laid on pretty thick right from the start, though. The movie opens with shots of vagrants huddled in doorways, juxtaposed with Coleman preparing his master's fresh orange juice and croissants (presumably this was considered the height of opulence in the early 80s). It may be a trifle heavy-handed in getting its message across, but *Trading Places* is still an innovative movie. Indeed, it pre-empts everything from *Wall Street* (1987) and *Working Girl* (1988) to *Pretty Woman* (1990), not to mention the 'yuppie nightmare' sub-genre that proliferated in the mid-80s with the likes of *After Hours* (1985) and *Something Wild* (1986). Even Tom Wolfe's literary masterpiece *The Bonfire Of The Vanities*, disastrously filmed by Brian De Palma in 1990, has a little of *Trading Places* in it.

The film marked the end of John Landis' ascendancy as the golden boy of US cinema. The death of actor Vic Morrow on the set of *The Twilight Zone* the same year was a tragic portent of two decades unmarred by anything approaching a decent movie. It was good news for Eddie Murphy, however, whose rise to superstardom was set in motion by his never-bettered performance here as street hustler Billy Ray Valentine. Perfectly at home histrionically vamping his way through a series of pratfalls and black stereotypes, when he is transformed into a career-driven buppie something remarkable happens, and Eddie Murphy begins to act. It's a pity his material has so rarely matched his talent since.

The movie's plot hinges on a simple bet. Outside Philadelphia's exclusive Heritage Club a sign reads 'With liberty and justice for all. Members only'. Within, tycoon Randolph Duke is convinced that a man is a product of his environment, while his brother Mortimer argues that success is down to breeding. When Billy Ray is wrongly accused of mugging their nephew, the priggish, aristocratic Louis Winthorpe, the brothers decide to have a wager, agreeing to elevate Billy Ray and decimate Winthorpe in the interests of social science.

Billy Ray is given Louis' apartment, his manservant Coleman and an over-the-top salary. Initially bemused and wary, he soon takes to his new life as though born to it. Simultaneously, Louis is drummed out of the Heritage Club on a trumped-up charge of theft, and lands in jail on a fabricated drugs charge. Meanwhile, Billy Ray is changing fast. Having thrown a wild party at his new home, the ex-hustler starts chiding the guests for dropping cigarette butts on his Persian rug and failing to make appropriate use of the coasters. Clad in ludicrous rags, Winthorpe is disappearing through the cracks in society, with only Jamie Lee Curtis' kind-hearted, level-headed hooker Ophelia (improbably, at 24 she has 40 grand in the bank) to help him.

'Why is someone deliberately trying to ruin my life?' he wails. All is not lost, however, especially when Curtis affords a teasing glimpse of what was famously considered the best body in all of Hollywood.

Under Ophelia's influence, Louis eventually starts to resemble a human being, while Billy Ray is disturbed by what he glimpses lurking in the murk at the top. In the obligatory executive washroom scene the Dukes chuckle over their omnipotence, but reveal their chilling heart. 'Do you really believe I would have a nigger run our family business?' Mortimer spits. 'Of course not,' the seemingly more liberal Randolph replies. 'Neither would I'. It's a moment that sends a clear signal that something is badly wrong with America – a pretty brave message for a comedy.

A despairing Louis overdoses, but Ophelia and Billy Ray save him, hooking up with the redoubtable Coleman to plan their next move. 'Coleman, I had the most absurd nightmare,' bleats Louis on waking. 'I was poor and no one liked me – and it was all because of this terrible, awful negro.' Cue a blood-freezing scream as his eyes fall on Billy Ray. The new allies resolve to foil the Dukes' plot to corner the orange juice market. Their plan involves a scene featuring James Belushi in a gorilla suit and Murphy decked out as an Exchange student from Cameroon. It's dumb, but it finally resolves itself with a killer punchline when the Dukes' villainous lackey Beeks ('I'll rip out your eyes and piss on your brain') gets royally rogered by a bona fide great ape.

The denouement takes place on Wall Street, with Louis back on fiery form. 'Think big, think positive,' he barks to Billy Ray. 'Never show any sign of weakness. Always go for the throat ... Let's kick some ass!' The Dukes are duly vanquished in the trading pit frenzy that ensues, and the hustler, the hooker, the butler and the toff repair to the Caribbean. As movie endings go, it's a decade-defining moment. Nice work if you can get it. ★★★★ **PR**

TRAFFIC (2000)

Starring: *Michael Douglas (Robert Wakefield), Benicio Del Toro (Javier Rodriguez), Don Cheadle (Montel Gordon), Luis Guzman (Ray Castro), Miguel Ferre (Eduardo Ruiz), Topher Grace (Seth Abrahms), Erika Christensen (Caroline Wakefield), Catherine Zeta-Jones (Helena Ayala), Albert Finney (Chief Of Staff)*
Director: *Steven Soderbergh*
Screenwriter: *Stephen Gaghan, from the miniseries* Traffik *by Simon Moore*
18/147 mins./Crime/Drama/Thriller/USA/Germany

Awards – *Best Supporting Actor (Benicio Del Toro), Best Director, Best Editing, Best Adapted Screenplay, BAFTA – Best Supporting Actor (Benicio Del Toro), Stephen Gaghan, Golden Globes – Best Supporting Actor (Benicio Del Toro), Best Screenplay*

In Tijuana, an honest cop struggles to survive in a country where the drug cartels own everybody. Meanwhile in San Diego, a society wife faces ruin when her millionaire husband is arrested as a suspected drug trafficker. And in Ohio, a conservative judge who is being groomed to sort out this complex scenario discovers his own daughter is a drug addict.

Watching *Traffic*, it's a while before you realise you're watching a movie made in America. We open on a car parked in the desert, suffused with sun-bleached light. Inside, two Spanish men talk in their native tongue about dreams. Then a plane lands overhead and the movement starts in the form of constant running, camera slung loose over a shoulder, which doesn't let up for two and a half hours. Welcome to Steven Soderbergh's 'run and gun' movie.

Not much in *Traffic*'s screenplay is entirely new – painstakingly researched and full of inside detail, certainly, but we have been here before (especially if you caught the original Channel 4 mini-series, *Traffik*, upon which Stephen Gaghan based his script). What elevates this company – drug dealers, corrupt cops, informants etc. – to a new plane is Soderbergh's storytelling skills. Just as his imaginative framing of a seduction reinvigorated the traditional love scene in 1998's *Out Of Sight*, Soderbergh works similar wonders with his largest canvas yet: two countries, three distinct storylines, well over 100 speaking parts. But what we are dealing with here is economy: Soderbergh's signature cutting, always to the chase, establishes a breathless rhythm which is more real than real. It's like a documentary with all the boring bits taken out.

Soderbergh describes *Traffic* as his $49 million Dogme movie, and certainly the hand-held style pushes the post-*Blair Witch* boundaries of mainstream moviemaking, but with the multiple storylines and delicately poised moral ambiguity, *Traffic* is closest in feel to a feature-length episode of *NYPD Blue* – indeed, it's no coincidence that Gaghan won an Emmy for his work on the revolutionary cop show. And the fact that Soderbergh, as his own cameraman and cinematographer, has employed natural light, doesn't make *Traffic* any less visually da ring. Pre- and post-production processes achieve a distinctive look for all three storylines: steely blues for the Beltway-bound Douglas; burnt yellows for the oppression of Del Tore's Mexico; bright colours and deep shade for the crumbling cocktail society of Zeta-Jones.

As for the cast themselves, newlyweds Douglas and Zeta-Jones are just fine in a uniformly excellent ensemble, Douglas especially finding real pain and pathos in an unshowy role; however, the ace in the pack here is Del Toro's Tijuana lawman, an honest guy caught in an impossible situation. Mumbling mostly in Spanish, Del Toro turns in a performance of such effortless and classic cool that they should spin him off into his own TV show.

If Gaghan's ambitious script is not perfect – there is a little hectoring at times, and some of the allegiance shifts in this treacherous world are not entirely convincing and sometimes hard to follow – Soderbergh's electrifying pace always keeps this huge project firmly on the rails, always moving, always running. ★★★★★ **CK**

TRAINING DAY (2001)

Starring: *Denzel Washington (Alonzo), Ethan Hawke (Jake), Scott Glenn (Roger), Tom Berenger (Stan Gursky), Harris Yulin (Doug Rosselli)*
Director: *Antoine Fuqua*
Screenwriter: *David Ayer*
18/117 mins./Crime/Drama/Thriller/USA/Australia

Awards – *Academy Awards – Best Actor*

Greenhorn L. A. cop Jake Hoyt hooks up with narcotics officer Alonzo Harris for a training day that will make or break him. Pass the test, he becomes a detective. Fail, it's back to traffic duty. But nothing prepares Jake for Alonzo, who is slowly revealed to be a corrupt cop.

Training Day could have so easily been bottom-shelf fodder. But thanks to Denzel Washington's fantastic against-type performance as the none-more-black anti-hero, Alonzo Harris, and – most surprisingly – the thoughtful and stylish direction of Antoine Fuqua, this in fact resembles nothing less than an urban *L. A. Confidential*.

It shares themes of corruption, betrayal and redemption with Curtis Hanson's classic, not to mention several tense set-pieces, including a drug 'bust' best viewed through the fingers. And all this from the director of *The Replacement Killers*. Who'd have thunk it?

One can only guess how the LAPD feels about this movie. For, Hoyt aside, every cop here is outrageously dirty, while it's the criminals that cling to an honourable set of values. And if Fuqua eventually shoehorns the complex moral debate into a traditional good vs. evil finale, it's still a damning indictment of the situation on L. A.'s streets, where the cops are so powerless they have to break the law to make a difference.

Performance-wise, Hawke fares well in a role that eventually transcends its repetitive nature. In fact, many of the film's dramatic flashpoints can be summed up in a single, one-size-fits-all exchange, which goes something like this: Washington: Do something bad. Hawke: No. Washington: Oh, go on. Hawke: (pause) Alright, then.

However, the film belongs to the swaggering Washington. Armed with dainty PC catchphrase 'my nigger' and wearing jewellery from Ali G 'R' Us, by the time you realise that Harris is up to no good on an almighty scale, your – and Hawke's – complicity is assured. ★★★★ **CH**

TRAINSPOTTING (1996)

Starring: *Ewan McGregor (Renton), Ewen Bremner (Spud), Jonny Lee Miller (Sick Boy), Kevin McKidd (Tommy), Kelly Macdonald (Diane), Peter Mullan (Swanney)*
Director: *Danny Boyle*
Screenwriter: *John Hodge, based on the novel by Irvine Welsh*
18/94 mins./Drama/Comedy/UK

Awards – *BAFTA – Best Adapted Screenplay, Empire Awards – Best British Actor, Best Britsh Director, Best British Film, Best Debut (Ewen Bremner)*

Renton is a Scottish youth with a problem ... a big, scary, dirty heroine problem and so have most of his friends. He wants to give up, but how?

Trainspotting doesn't glorify heroin. It glorifies youth. Youth at its worst, mostly, but youth trying to sort things as only youth can. Watch it again on DVD and it's still, in parts, hilariously funny. But whereas in the cinema peer pressure helped everyone laugh as the junkies got it all wrong, sitting on your own sofa, heroin looks more serious than ever. This doesn't spoil the film, but it destroys the idea that *Trainspotting* could ever glorify heroin. No way.

It begins with Renton giving up 'that shite' but falling at the first hurdle, right down the worst toilet in Scotland. Truly one of cinema's most disgusting sequences, and perfect to introduce the rollercoaster rush of an unforgettable first half hour. Rich, earthy dialogue gushes like a ruptured sewer, etching characters deeper than any laughter lines. Sick Boy mixes Connery's Bond with cod philosophy, Spud mixes dorky geekdom with the world's worst interview technique, while Begbie mixes psycho sensibilities with impressive dexterity using the wrong end of a pool cue. But these personalities, like the settings – bile green apartment walls, the blood red den of their dealer Mother Superior – are stylised and get a sudden and shocking reality injection straight after a catalogue of hilariously catastrophic sexual encounters.

The morning after, everything's changed. Renton's already classic rant against fresh air and the English can signal one thing only: a return to heroin, to crime and to hell. Director Boyle allows roughly two minutes before throwing the viewer into the pit, and it's a stunning turnaround. A baby dies, Spud goes to jail, Renton goes cold turkey – humiliated by his parents, tormented by ghosts and lectured, bizarrely, by Dale Winton about HIV.

Once again Renton gets his life back on the rails, but the nightmares of his past follow him even to London where he snatches despair from the very jaws of hope. Fittingly, he and his unwelcome flatmates Begbie and Sick Boy return briefly to their Edinburgh roots to bury another heroin statistic, before a coach trip back south for an amateurish, pathetic drug deal – selling rather than buying, for once, and for one last thrill. It all goes pear-shaped, naturally, and no one is surprised, because by now the message is sinking in: heroin is for losers. For useless, unreliable fuck-ups, But in the hands of Boyle and this fantastic cast, and with a stunning soundtrack, it is possible to receive that message in an unprecedented and unrivalled piece of entertainment. Something Britain can be proud of and Hollywood must be afraid of. If we Brits can make movies this good about subjects this horrific, what chance does Tinseltown have?

Choose life? Get a life – choose *Trainspotting*. ★★★★★ **NJ**

TRANCERS (1985)

Starring: *Tim Thomerson (Jack Deth), Helen Hunt (Leena), Michael Stefani (Martin Whistler), Art La Fleur (McNulty), Telma Hopkins (Ruthie Raines), Richard Herd (Chairman Spencer), Anne Seymour (Chairman Ashe), Miguel Fernandez (Officer Lopez), Biff Manard (Hap Ashby)*
Director: *Charles Band*
Screenwriters: *Danny Bilson, Paul De Meo*
15/76 mins./Sci-fi/USA

The consciousness of Jack Deth, a cop in 2247, is sent back in time to possess the body of his 1985 ancestor Phil Dethston in order to defeat an evil cult leader who has also taken this route and is murdering the ancestors of civic leaders who are therefore wiped out of existence.

Producer-director Charles Band is among the most prolific names in the low-budget B-picture and direct-to-video arena. Scripted by Danny Bilson and Paul De Meo, *Trancers* is his masterpiece and one of the liveliest, wittiest, cleverest cheapies ever made.

Hard-boiled Tim Thomerson is outstanding as future cop Jack Deth, who has a nice line in wry gruffness, partnered in the 20th Century by young Helen Hunt, as a rare heroine who acts sensibly when confronted by a rabid mind-controlled Santa Claus and still has the spunk to make jokes (claiming the villain has sent a threat via fortune cookie) in a crisis.

It contains a wide variety of smart comic book/s-f ideas, from the sunken city of Lost Angeles, the tough cop who has to inhabit the body of a ten-year-old girl on his visit to the past, a heroic streak displayed by a down-and-out baseball pitcher (Biff Manard) in saving the future, and credible, pithy, meaningless future slang ('dry hair is for squids'). Thomerson's Jack Deth returns in *Trancers II* and *Trancers III*, both with Helen Hunt loyally hanging on, and *Trancers 4: Jack of Swords* and *Trancers 5: Sudden Deth*, sillier fantasy stories shot in Romania. *Trancers 6* gets round Thomerson's absence by having Deth's consciousness wake up in the body of his daughter Jo Deth (Zette Sullivan). A better follow-up than the sequels is Bilson and De Meo's *Zone Troopers*, a WW II-set GIs-meet-aliens story with Thomerson as 'the Sarge' and *Trancers* veterans Manard and Art La Fleur in the platoon. ★★★★ KN

TRANSAMERICA (2005)

Starring: *Felicity Huffman (Bree Osbourne), Kevin Zegers (Toby), Fionnula Flanagan (Elizabeth), Elizabeth Pena (Margaret), Graham Greene (Calvin), Burt Young (Murray)*
Director: *Duncan Tucker*
Screenwriter: *Duncan Tucker*
15/103 mins./Drama/Comedy/USA

Awards – *Golden Globes – Best Drama Actress*

Pre-op transsexual Bree is on the brink of surgery when she finds out she has a hustler son she's never met. She travels cross-country to New York to bail him out of jail, and then they begin a long journey back to Los Angeles, with Bree struggling to keep all her secrets hidden.

It's easy to forget that, before she was a high-heeled and highlighted Desperate Housewife, Felicity Huffman had established herself as a respected indie actress. So it's not as much of a surprise to see her in a mildly grungy film playing a dowdy pre-op transsexual as it would be if it were, say, Eva Longoria dangling a prosthetic penis.

Initially Huffman's appearance is off-putting. Ears pushed out, face drooping towards her shoes, she resembles nothing so much as Stan Laurel attempting to blend in with the Women's Institute.

But so convincing is she that her appearance is soon secondary to a heartfelt performance told through awkward silence and frightened eyes that rightly won her a Golden Globe, and a place in 2006's Oscar final five.

Sadly the film around her is not quite as strong, taking very few unexpected turns and never entirely deciding on whether it wants to be a serious account of coming to terms with deeply felt insecurities or a slightly knockabout buddy-buddy comedy. On the occasions that the two elements gel, it succeeds in being both moving and funny, but its sense of confusion, while certainly fitting, will hamper it receiving much adulation beyond that directed at Huffman. ★★★ **OR**

THE TREASURE OF THE SIERRA MADRE (1948)

Starring: *Humphrey Bogart (Fred C. Dobbs), Walter Huston (Howard), Tim Holt (Curtin), Bruce Bennett (Cody), Barton Maclane (McCormick), Alfonso Bedoya (Gold Hat), Arturo Soto Rangel (Presidente)*
Director: *John Huston*
Screenwriter: *John Huston, based on the novel by Berwick Traven Torsvan*
PG/126 mins/Adventure/USA

Awards: *Academy Awards – Best Director, Best Supporting Actor (Walter Huston), Best Screenplay*

Tampico, 1925 and Fred C. Dobbs and Bob Curtin hook up with Klondike veteran Howard to go gold prospecting in Mexico's Sierra Madre mountains. However, a growing sense of greedy paranoia and the intrusion of covetous strangers Cody and Gold Hat drive the trio apart.

When John Huston first read B. Traven's novel in 1935, he reckoned that the role of Fred C. Dobbs was perfect for his actor father, Walter. However, he was then still only a screenwriter and twelve years were to pass before he finally persuaded Warner Bros. to let him adapt the most sobering study of malevolent avarice of since Erich von Stroheim's *Greed*.

However, Huston now felt that Dobbs was perfect for Humphrey Bogart, with whom he had made *Across the Pacific* and *Key Largo* since their first collaboration on the prototype noir, *The Maltese Falcon*. Huston, Sr. was reluctant to play an old timer, as he still saw himself as something of a matinee idol. But he was selfless enough to help boost his son's career and was rewarded for the brave decision to perform without his false teeth with a Best Supporting Oscar. Indeed, John Huston's double for his direction and screenplay meant that this was the only occasion on which a father and a son landed Academy Awards in the same year.

Jack Warner, however, was less than enthralled by the picture. He never understood why it couldn't have been made at the studio's Calabasos ranch and deeply resented the $3 million budget that Huston racked up on in the Mexican outpost of Jungapeo (making this the first Hollywood feature to be filmed exclusively on location since the war). Warner also disliked the idea of Bogart turning bad and dying for his sins, a view shared by an American public that had become accustomed to seeing him playing cynical romantics.

But Bogart delivers one of his most effective performances here and his failure to live up to his boast that wealth could never corrupt him is far more credible than his more-vaunted display as Captain Queeg in *The Caine Mutiny*. Walter Huston is also outstanding. But Huston, Jr. perhaps deserves most credit for coaxing such gritty turns out of those essentially B stalwarts Tim Holt, Bruce Bennett, Barton MacLane and Alfonso Bedoya, whom he plucked from a crowd to make his screen debut. ★★★★★ **DP**

Ⓞ THE TREE OF WOODEN CLOGS (L'ABERO DEGLI ZOCCOLI) (1978)

Starring: *Luigi Omaghi (Batist), Francesca Moriggi (Batistina), Omar Brignoli (Minek), Antonio Ferrari (Tuni), Teresa Brescianini (Widow Runk), Giuseppe Brignoli (Grandpa Anselmo), Carlo Rota (Peppino), Pasqualina Brolis (Teresina), Massimo Fratus (Pierino)*
Director: *Ermanno Olmi*
Screenwriter: *Ermanno Olmi*
12/185 mins./Drama/Italy
Awards – *BAFTA – Flaherty Documentary Award*

Five families living in a ramshackle house on an estate in 1890s Lombardy endure the vagaries of their harsh rural existence under the pitiless supervision of the padrone to whom they owe two-thirds of their produce.

Based on stories related by his grandmother, Ermanno Olmi's rural epic is one of the most neglected masterworks of the Italian cinema. Following in the neo-realist tradition, this deeply moving recreation of a bygone era employs a non-professional cast (speaking its own Bergomesque dialect) and a near-docudramatic shooting style. Through a meticulous accumulation of detail – that gives the film both its power and its heart – Olmi celebrates both the rugged regality of the changing landscape and the indomitability of the 19th-century Lombard peasantry, as they conduct their partnership with nature under the unforgiving gaze of their exploitative superiors.

Originally made for Italian television, *The Tree of Wooden Clogs* provides a more authentic insight into the lot of the tenant farmer than either Bernardo Bertolucci's *1900* or the Tavianis' *Padre Padrone*. Shooting in 'the light of the seasons' and without resort to artificial colours or psychological camera angles, Olmi captured the pace and flow of country life by basing events on recurrent rituals and the very humanity of characters who were just as likely grow tomatoes in secret or try to hide a gold coin in a horse's hoof as they were to chop down a tree to make the clogs that would enable a child to walk to the school that represents his only chance of bettering himself.

Yet, despite such efforts to deglamorise rural toil – through such unflinching incidents as the slaughter of the hogs – this remains a work of bucolic beauty whose images gleam with a perfection that only memory can inspire. Moreover, the contrast with the discontent that Lucia Pezzoli and Franco Pilenga witness during their honeymoon in Milan could not have been more telling, as though Olmi were lamenting the urban impatience that had come to replace rustic constancy during the rapid industrialisation of northern Italy.

Indeed, left-wing critics took Olmi to task for contriving a romanticised pastorale that was sustained by an unerring confidence in the benefits of faith. But the Cannes jury disagreed and awarded the film the Palme d'Or. ★★★★★ **DP**

Ⓞ TREMORS (1990)

Starring: *Kevin Bacon (Valentine McKee), Fred Ward (Earl Bassett), Finn Cater (Rhonda LeBeck), Michael Gross (Burt Gummer), Reba McEntire (Heather Gummer)*
Director: *Ron Underwood*
Screenwriters: *S.S. Wilson, Brent Maddock, based on a story by Wilson, Maddock, Ron Underwood*
15/96 mins./Action/Comedy/Horror/USA

Unsuspecting handymen Val and Earl pass though a sleepy, dusty town called Perfection, and end up being handier than they thought as they help rescue the inhabitants from a plague of giant underground worms who keep popping up and picking off the populace.

Americans in science fiction movies have, of course, always distrusted the desert, at least since those A-bomb tests in the 50s raised generation after generation of giant ants, revived dinosaurs, enormous spiders, alien pod people, killer shrews, giant gila monsters and ping-pong-ball-eyed mutants. Ron Underwood's first feature – produced by Gayle Anne Hurd of *Aliens* and *The Abyss* fame – is a clever, unfussy pastiche of this breed of 50s monster movie.

A folksy desert community is terrorised by man-eating, sand-burrowing worms which turn out to be merely the mouth-tentacles of much larger creatures. Fred Ward and Kevin Bacon are dim-witted cowboy handymen who discover the monsters and proceed to spend their time arguing about what they ought to be called or trying to think of a way of turning the creatures into a profitable business, while heroine Finn Carter is a seismologist who gets irritated when the locals expect her to be an instant expert on the life cycle of the monsters just because she is a scientist.

Broadly humorous in its opening stretches, which plays the *Jaws*-style rampage off against the antics of its New West characters, *Tremors* becomes more suspenseful as a small group of the monsters surround the town, forcing the handful of survivors up on to the roofs to think of various home-made methods of seeing them off. In one sequence, a comic survivalist couple expend an enormous amount of firepower to disable one of the monsters, prompting Bacon to remark 'I guess we don't get to make fun of Burt's lifestyle any more'.

The monsters are cleverly designed and utilised creations which make formidable villains, and the threads of humour make the whole B movie feel rather endearing. ★★★★ **KN**

THE TRIAL (LE PROCES) (1962)

Starring: *Anthony Perkins (Josef K), Arnoldo Foa (Inspector A), Jess Hagn (Second Assistant Inspector), Billy Kearns (First Assistant Inspector), Madeleine Robinson (Mrs Grubach), Jeanne Moreau (Marika Burstner), Maurice Teynac (Deputy Manager), Nayda Shore (Imrie), Suzanne Flon (Miss Pitl)*
Director: *Orson Welles*
Screenwriter: *Orson Welles, based on the novel by Franz Kafka*
PG/118 mins./Drama/France-Italy-West Germany-Yugoslavia

Clerk Joseph K is arrested by policemen who don't specify the charge against him. He tries to negotiate his way through an incomprehensible, threatening legal system … but is doomed.

In 1962, the Salkind Brothers, later known for *Superman*, offered Orson Welles the total artistic control he hadn't had in America since *Citizen Kane*, providing a) he adapted an out-of-copyright literary masterpiece and b) he made the film in Yugoslavia. Then the Yugoslav deal collapsed in mid-shooting, and Welles had to retreat to Paris, with almost no money, and complete the picture using locations in and around a disused, cavernous railway station. Far less respectful of Franz Kafka than the Harold Pinter/Kyle MacLachlen TV movie embalming of the same novel, this may be the best film Welles shot outside America, transforming the grim, concrete exteriors of Zagreb and the gothic corners of Paris into a haunted modern city seductive and menacing enough even to give Kafka the creeps. Anthony Perkins, quivering with twittery paranoia, is an ideal Josef K, collaborating with his persecutors as he is dragged through a nightmarish black and white world towards his bungled execution. Typical of Welles is the moment when K creeps through a doorway to what he assumes will be a secret meeting with a single power broker and finds himself in a huge room packed with hundreds of extras all staring accusingly at him, though there's an equally creepy later sequence in a rickety painter's studio besieged by smiling, menacing children. A parade of eccentric and cosmopolitan supporting players (Akim Tamiroff, Michel Lonsdale, Elsa Martinelli, Jeanne Moreau, Romy Schneider) pop up to bewilder Perkins, with Welles under one of his falser noses as another of the circus acts and providing the voices for at least ten characters. Overwhelmingly bleak, but exciting cinema. ★★★★ **KN**

THE TRIALS OF OSCAR WILDE (1960)

Starring: *Peter Finch (Oscar Wilde), Yvonne Mitchell (Constance Wilde), James Mason (Sir Edward Carson), Nigel Patrick (Sir Edward Clarke), Lionel Jeffries (John Douglas, the Marquis Of Queensberry), John Fraser (Lord Alfred 'Bosie' Douglas), Sonia Dresdel (Lady Wilde), Maxine Audley (Ada Leverson)*
Directors: *Irving Allen, Ken Hughes*
Screenwriter: *Ken Hughes, based on the play* The Stringed Lute *by John Furnell and the book* Oscar Wilde *by Montgomery Hyde*
X(15)/123 mins./Drama/UK

Awards: *BAFTA – Best British Actor (Peter Finch)*

In 1895, Oscar Wilde sues the Marquis of Queensberry for libel after he accuses the Irish playwright of committing the illegal act of sodomy with his son, Lord Alfred Douglas.

How often are two films on identical subjects released nigh-on simultaneously? But while the pair of 1960 pictures focusing on the trials of Oscar Wilde had much in common, they also made for fascinating comparison.

Filmed in monochrome by Hollywood exile Gregory Ratoff (who was directing what turned out to be his last feature), *Oscar Wilde* was based on a play by Leslie and Sewell Stokes and boasted a flamboyant display of fey bon mot-ery from Robert Morley. But, while he bore a passable physical resemblance to the Irish wit, Morley couldn't resist a preening look of satisfaction at the deliverance of each quip and it was, therefore, difficult to take seriously either his marriage to Phyllis Calvert or his passion for John Neville's Lord Alfred Douglas. However, such roly-poly assurance made his courtroom humiliation at the hands of Ralph Richardson's sneering Sir Edward Carson all the more affecting.

Peter Finch, in Ken Hughes' full-colour Super Technirama 70 widescreen version, on the other hand, looked nothing like Wilde and made no attempt at any kind of impersonation. Inspired by John Furnell's play *The Stringed Lute* and Montgomery Hyde's eponymous biography, Finch created an urbane, but tormented individual who took the art of comedy as seriously as he took love. Thus, his fixation with John Fraser's carelessly narcissistic Bosie is more palpable, as is his shame at embarrassing his adoring wife, Yvonne Mitchell. But he's always Peter Finch playing a celebrated sophisticate brought low by the vengeance of a boor – always the man with the green carnation, but never Oscar Wilde.

He is also upstaged by Lionel Jeffries, whose imperiously unhinged display as the Marquis of Queensberry belies his reputation as a comic character actor in the likes of *Two Way Stretch*. Ironically, Morley's nemesis was also essayed by a comic stalwart, Edward Chapman, who was Mr Grimsdale to Norman Wisdom's Pitkin. But James Mason failed to match Richardson's sadistic homophobia and the courtroom exchanges are as disappointing as the ones that Ken Hughes would later stage between Alec Guinness and Richard Harris in *Cromwell*. ★★★ **DP**

THE TRIP (1967)

Starring: *Peter Fonda (Paul Groves), Susan Strasberg (Sally Groves), Bruce Dern (John), Dennis Hopper (Max), Salli Sachese (Glenn), Katherine Walsh (Lulu)*
Director: *Roger Corman*
Screenwriter: *Jack Nicholson*
18/75 mins./Drama/USA

In Los Angeles, TV commercials director Paul Groves is introduced to LSD by a friend. He takes a trip, and spends a few hours hallucinating while exploring his own fractured mind.

Scripted by Jack Nicholson when he wasn't sure whether he wanted to stick with acting and directed by Roger Corman when he wanted to move on from Vincent Price movies, *The Trip* is an unusually simple idea: it just shows one man taking an LSD trip.

Free of most of the melodramatic trappings of the many acid freak-out exploitation films, it cuts between subjective representations of Paul's experiences and objective sequences showing how he appears to the straight world.

The former are moderately wild, with inevitable borrowings from Corman's Poe pictures (how many acidheads imagined encounters with mediaeval dwarves?), but the latter – depending on subtle playing from Fonda, LSD guide Dern and bystanders like housewife Barboura Morris, a child played by Corbin Bernsen's sister and waitress Luana Anders – are extremely credible and affecting.

An interesting, credible aspect of the movie is that it features square-dressing-and-talking drugs experimenters (Dennis Hopper, breaking the record for the use of the word 'man' in a speech, is an exception) rather than flamboyant hippie stereotypes. It also makes fine use of LA locations, borrowed hip homes (Dern has a swimming pool in his 'living room' – a phrase which makes Fonda fear the lounge has come to life) and authentic nightspot hang-outs from clubs to laundromats.

It may be that the secret of the film's commercial success was that it served as a substitute for acid to audiences who weren't willing to take the risk, but it probably stands as an honest account, though Corman protested the distributors' imposition of a fractured freeze frame to suggest that the protagonist has been irreparably damaged by his drug experience. ★★★★ **KN**

Inauspicious movie debuts

TOP10

1. Cuba Gooding Jr, Boy Getting Haircut, *Coming to America*
2. Sharon Stone, Pretty Girl on Train, *Stardust Memories*
3. Harrison Ford, Bellhop, *Dead Heat on a Merry-go-round*
4. Brad Pitt, Waiter, *No Man's Land*
5. Kevin Spacey, Subway Thief, *Heartburn*
6. Matthew McConnaughey, Guy #2, *My Boyfriend's Back*
7. Michael Douglas, Jeep Driver, *Cast A Giant Shadow*
8. Bruce Willis, Man Entering Diner, *The First Deadly Sin*
9. Pierce Brosnan, Last Victim, *The Carpathian Eagle*
10. Maggie Smith, Party Guest, *Child in the House*

A TRIP TO THE MOON (1902)

Starring: *Brunnet (Astronomer), Farjaut (Astronomer), Kelm (Astronomer), Georges Méliès (Prof. Barbenfoullis), Victor Andre, Jeanne D'Alcy, Henri Delannoy, Depierre*
Director: *Georges Méliès*
Screenwriter: *Georges Méliès, based on the novel* From The Earth To The Moon *by Jules Verne*
U/14 mins./Sci-Fi/France

Members of the Astronomic Club land on the moon in a cannon-launched rocket and encounter the malevolent King of the Moon and his Selenite army before escaping back to Earth and a heroes' welcome.

Considering how long it took the other narrative artforms to reach maturation, it's rather remarkable that cinema managed to produce a work of this sophistication within seven years of its invention. Much of the credit has to go to Georges Méliès, a stage illusionist who first used moving images as a novelty spectacle in his act. Working in a garden studio in the Parisian suburb of Montreuil, Méliès made around 500 films between 1897-1913 and, in the process, stumbled across such crucial narrative devices as the fade and the lap dissolve, as well as such effects as the matte, double-exposure and stop-motion – all of which he created in-camera.

Initially known for féeries or trick-shot films like *The Man With the India-Rubber Head*, Méliès also produced *actualités reconstituées* or historical recreations like *The Dreyfus Affair* (1899), which was his first multi-scene outing. But this adaptation of a Jules Verne novel was more ambitious than anything he had previously attempted and its 30 scenes ran for an unprecedented 825 feet or some 14 minutes, thus setting the standard length of films at one reel for the next few years.

Designed with his typical imaginative flamboyance, the scenes were essentially theatrical tableaux, which Méliès filmed front-on with a static camera to approximate the gaze of a patron in a prime seat in the auditorium. But, ever the showman, he littered the action with visual effects, such as the iconic shot of the rocket ship landing in the Man in the Moon's eye (which he achieved by moving the papier maché moon towards the camera on a dolly rather than the other way round) and the disappearance of the Selenites in a puff of smoke on being struck by the astronomers' umbrellas.

Yet, for all its ingenuity, this was still very much a rudimentary picture, with the action being linked by dissolves rather than cross-cuts within or between the individual scenes. But Méliès gave film a new fictional function and not only paved the way for such contemporaries as Edwin S. Porter and D.W. Griffith, but also for the later avant-garde. ★★★★★ **DP**

TRIUMPH OF THE WILL (TRIUMPH DES WILLENS) (1935)

Director: *Leni Riefenstahl*
Screenwriters: *Leni Riefenstahl, Walter Ruttmann*
Unrated/114 mins./Documentary/West Germany

A flagrantly propagandist, but visually astounding account of the 6th Nazi Party Congress at Nuremberg in 1934, as well as its attendant rallies of labour, youth and the blackshirts, which culminate in a memorial ceremony and a torchlight procession.

Leni Riefenstahl's record of the 1934 National Socialist rally at Nuremberg ranks among the most reviled films of all time. From its opening sequence, in which Adolf Hitler descends from the sunlit clouds in his plane and then seems to float through the streets as he stands saluting in his car, its pernicious content was consciously fashioned to depict the Führer in a messianic light. Indeed, such was the determination to present Hitler's triumph over the will of the German people that images of discernable individuals were gradually replaced by mass ranks of dehumanised subordination that symbolised the Volk's menial role in the grand Nazi design. No wonder Hitler dubbed this the 'incomparable glorification of the power and beauty of our movement'.

Few would deny that this is a magisterial piece of film-making. But it's impossible to divorce its technical and artistic brilliance from its hideous political connotations. Riefenstahl always denied party membership and pointed to Propaganda Minister Josef Goebbels' resentment at the licence she was accorded in producing an epic that his own units could never hope to emulate. Moreover, she always protested that she undertook the assignment with great reluctance, as she was keen to go to Spain to shoot *Tiefland* (which she eventually completed in the mid-1950s).

But Hitler had not only been impressed by her 1932 mountain film, *The Blue Light*, but he had also recognised the efficacy of her 1933 Nuremberg short, *Der Sieg des Glaubens*, which had been withdrawn because it featured Ernst Rohm, who had since been liquidated during the Night of the Long Knives. Consequently, he personally requested that she took over a project that had originally been destined for 'city symphony' pioneer and committed Nazi, Walter Ruttmann, and ordered his architect Albert Speer to choreograph the entire spectacle with her 30 cameras in mind.

Riefenstahl and cinematographer Sepp Allgeier shot 61 hours of footage during the six-day event, which took eight months to edit. The mystical contrasts in light and shade, the foregrounding of such potent symbols as the eagle and the swastika, and the rhythmic presentation of the fascistic pageantry could not have been bettered (and was much imitated in later Allied propaganda). But history dictates that this misguided masterpiece will forever live in infamy. ★★★★★ **DP**

TROUBLE IN PARADISE (1932)

Starring: *Miriam Hopkins (Lily Vautier), Kay Francis (Mariette Corlet), Herbert Marshall (Gaston Monescu/La Valle), Charlie Ruggles (The Major), Edward Everett Horton (François Filliba), C. Aubrey Smith (Adolph Giron), Robert Greig (Jacques The Butler), Georges Humbert (Waiter)*
Director: *Ernst Lubitsch*
Screenwriters: *Grover Jones, Samson Raphaelson based on the play* The Honest Finder *by Laszlo Aladar*
U/83 mins./Romance-Comedy/USA

Having fallen for the equally duplicitous Lily Vautier, gentleman thief Gaston Monescu sets about fleecing perfume heiress Mariette Colet, only to drift into love with her, too.

The most sophisticated comedy ever produced in Hollywood was loosely adapted from Laszlo Aladar's play *The Honest Finder*, which was itself based on the exploits of the notorious Hungarian swindler, Georges Manolescu, whose colourful career had already twice been filmed, most notably by the Russian actor Ivan Mosjoukine in 1929.

Ernst Lubitsch had a habit of taking unprepossessing stage properties and turning them into cinematic gold. But the imposition of the Production Code in 1934 ensured that he never surpassed the delicious indelicacy of this scintillating study of sexual intrigue and shameless duplicity.

Rejecting titles like *The Golden Widow*, *Thieves and Lovers* and *A Very Private Scandal* and Paramount's offer of such talents as Cary Grant, Lubitsch deliberately cast Herbert Marshall opposite Kay Francis and Miriam Hopkins, as he knew they had both previously been his lovers and the scorned frisson is simmeringly evident on the screen. But it's the famed Lubitsch Touch that makes this such a timeless delight.

The opening sequence mercilessly subverts the postcard image of Venice as a city of refined beauty by showing the aria 'O Solo Mio' being sung not by a gondolier but a garbage collector. But this is much more than an impish gag, as it efficiently establishes the theme of corruption and opulence that dictates Gaston's relationships with both Lily and Mariette. Similarly, the dinner sequence, in which Gaston and Lily pose as aristocrats only to spend the entire meal stealing each other's watches, wallets and jewellery, persuades us to empathise with these thoroughly reprehensible characters (something which her vague acknowledgement of the city's poor does for the otherwise hideously decadent Mariette).

The sublime opera parody and Marshall's respective shirt-sleeved and silhouetted seductions of Hopkins and Francis are equally assured. But there isn't a false step here, with Hans Dreier's Art Deco sets being as exquisite as Samuel Raphaelson's screenplay and the ensemble playing being as finely tuned as the dialogue, which often has the musicality of a recitative.

Lubitsch later wrote, 'As for style, I have done nothing better or as good as *Trouble in Paradise*'. And he was right. ★★★★★ **DP**

◑ THE TROUBLE WITH HARRY (1955)

Starring *Edmund Gwenn (Capt. Albert Wiles), John Forsythe (Sam Marlowe, the painter), Shirley Maclaine (Jennifer Rogers), Mildred Natwick (Miss Gravely), Mildred Dunnock (Mrs. Wiggs), Jerry Mathers (Arnie Rogers), Royal Dano (Calvin Wiggs), Parker Fennelly (Millionaire)*
Director: *Alfred Hitchcock*
Screenwriter: *John Michael Hayes, based on the novel by Jack Trevor Story*
PG/99 mins./Comedy/USA

A man's corpse is repeatedly buried and exhumed, after Captain Albert Wiles, artist Sam Marlowe and prim matron Miss Graveley learn that he is the estranged husband of their new neighbour, Jennifer Rogers.

Adapted with remarkable fidelity by John Michael Hayes from a short fable by Jack Trevor Story, this was one of Alfred Hitchcock's favourite pictures. Yet, for all its macabre whimsy, it would be wrong to see this simply as a droll entertainment, despite the geniality of the leading quartet, Robert Burks' gleaming autumnal vistas and Bernard Herrmann's jaunty score. Nor should it be dismissed as a one-gag wonder, as Harry's various burials and exhumations are merely the Macguffin that allows Hitchcock to discuss the weightier themes of faith, justice, passion and mortality.

Some critics have identified this as a resurrection story and used its vague references to Christian iconography to claim it was Hitchcock's treatise on religion. But, in fact, it's more a comment on those who use belief as a means of social control. Hypocrites never fare very well in Hitchcock's canon and, although they're admittedly thin on the New England ground, they are, nevertheless, denounced by implication throughout the film by the unabashed (if occasionally sniggering) discussion of those taboos of puritanical society, sex and death.

Few Hitchcock pictures are so laced with innuendo. But even more striking is the casual attitude towards death – not just on behalf of the four principals, but also on that of the director whose childhood terror of falling foul of the law is replaced by a barely suppressed glee at turning the disposal of a cadaver into a mischievous prank.

Perhaps the city boy in Hitchcock embraced the countryside's more relaxed attitude to death as part of the cycle of nature and that Harry was his pastoral variation on the trademark theme of suspense (albeit in a mild form) within the everyday. Certainly the picture's only surprise was in revealing what the debuting Shirley Maclaine whispered to John Forsythe as her cherished wish after he offers to buy her a gift – and even that reinforces the link between carnality and fatality, as her request for a double bed is made just as her ex-husband's body is left in the clearing awaiting its last and legitimate discovery. ★★★★ **DP**

◑ TROY (2004)

Starring: *Julian Glover (Triopas), Brian Cox (Agamemnon), Orlando Bloom (Paris), Brad Pitt (Achilles), Eric Bana (Hector), Diane Kruger (Helene), Sean Bean (Odysseus), Julie Christie (Thetis), Peter O'Toole (Priam), Brendan Gleeson (Menelaus)*
Director: *Wolfgang Petersen*
Screenplay: *David Benioff, based on the poem by Homer*
15/162 mins./Action/Adventure/War/History/USA

Trojan prince Paris steals Helen from the Spartan king, prompting the latter to go running to his brother, Agamemnon, king of the Greeks. With his imperialist bent, Agamemnon launches a full-scale war against Troy, which catapults his hero, Achilles, into confrontation with Trojan champion Hector.

The fiscal hawks at Warner Bros equipped Wolfgang Petersen with a $175 million-plus war chest to launch this film's flotilla of famous faces and bludgeoning battle sequences, yet beneath its muscle-bound, armoured shell, *Troy* is as hollow as its wooden horse.

Petersen would have launched a far more effective assault if he had deviated still further from his Homeric source: Troy is undone by *The Iliad*'s central conceit, which is too anachronistic. The director appears aware of this fact, weaving into the substantial downtime between set-pieces repeated assertions of the reason for the war – Helen and Paris' love – answering questions the audience has not raised, and thereby indicating a near-fatal lack of confidence in his source material.

That two powerful nations would go to war simply because Paris nicked Menelaus' girl found firm foundation in the age the tale was originally told, as a natural extension of the hero-cult.

This ancient concept ensured that the intended audience perceived the Homeric hard-men as heroes first, Trojans or Greeks second, their actions expressions of a now-extinct ideology. Today, fighting a war for love and honour seems mawkish and leaves the modern audience wondering which side to cheer.

Petersen does expand Brian Cox's delightfully spiteful Agamemnon, investing him with an imperial yearning that could have provoked the war. But the repeated affirmation of Paris and Helen's love igniting the campaign dilutes this war-mongering subtext.

Similarly, The Iliad's other great theme – the pathos of Achilles' fate – also fails to translate, with Petersen unsure how to handle this delicate premise. Again, it was the notion of hero-cult that underpinned Achilles' actions and Homer was facilitated in his tale by having the gods purvey his hero's destiny, adding a divine note to the emotional chord. Petersen, quite rightly, omits the Olympians, only introducing Thetis, Achilles' immortal mater, to relay her son's fate. But her visit is so fleeting that the import of her message dissipates as the crescendo looms, burdening Pitt with an impossible task.

Pitt makes full use of his many close-ups, his intensely physical form and heroic posturing encapsulating Achilles' enigmatic bravura, and if he fails to convince as the climax approaches, it's only because his motivation has been made forfeit. By contrast, Eric Bana's Trojan champion Hector, unshackled by Achilles' lofty premise, swashes his buckle as an embodiment of nobility that does command empathy.

Orlando Bloom's simpering turn is ideal for Paris and Bean and O'Toole provide much of the epic gravitas. The women, however, are less effective, and while Diane Kruger's Helen could launch a dinghy or two, she is far too insipid to launch a thousand ships. Which is a shame, as the thousand ships are a CG marvel, an example of Troy's awesome production values. The moment the two armies clash outside the walls rivals any battle in LOTR, and the individual combat, especially between Hector and Achilles, is mightily impressive. Through simple, if striking, fight choreography, Pitt's Achilles at last becomes a fully-realised cinematic take on a major hero. ★★★ **WL**

TRUE GRIT (1969)

Starring: *John Wayne (Marshall 'Rooster' Cogburn), Glen Campbell (La Boeuf), Kim Darby (Mattie Ross), Jeremy Slate (Emmett Quincy), Robert Duvall (Ned Pepper), Dennis Hopper (Moon)*
Director: *Henry Hathaway*
Screenwriter: *Marguerite Roberts, based on the novel by Charles Portis*
PG/128 mins./Western/USA

Awards: *Academy Awards – Best Actor (John Wayne)*

After her father is shot, and desperate for justice, Mattie Ross recruits a tough old marshal known as Rooster Cogburn, a wry character who comes complete with necessary grit to get a job done. They are joined by Texas Ranger La Boeuf, and head off to find the killer.

In the autumn of his career, assailed by ill-health as he was, John Wayne gave a series of defining performances that were amongst the most developed and genuinely warm of any of his great cowboys. With ageing, eye-patched rascal Rooster Cogburn, if less profoundly, Wayne is commentating both on his own fading position in the universe as well as reflecting on the nature of his career as Clint Eastwood later did with William Munny and *Unforgiven*.

Pairing the actor with the pretty and sparkling Kim Darby helped to bring out this refreshing human side. She was 22 at the time, but playing far younger, a girl, a tomboy, who is crazy-determined she will get vengeance for her slain pop. Darby is all squalls of passion, while Wayne's her spirit to keep keen, as much as she needs his wisdom to cut through her naiveté. The chemistry between them is near-perfect, giving the film a wry, colourful charge, and making it a film far more about the people than its essentially formulaic hunt-the-villain plot. It's less shrill and broadly funny than *Cat Ballou*, but certainly of a piece. Like Lee Marvin, Wayne would pick up an Oscar for his performance.

Elsewhere the performances aren't so fine-tuned, country and western singer Glen Campbell does a fairly hopeless job as the headstrong ranger who joins up with them, and Robert Duvall is unremarkable as their quarry Ned Pepper. Which points toward the fact Henry Hathaway's easy-riding movie, beautifully shot by cinematographer Lucien Ballard (who was responsible for that elegiac cloak over *The Wild Bunch*), is really just about placing the iconic Wayne in a specific light. The rich myth ebbing with the close of day, an idea that the film never overglorifies, but still has a closing shot that is a gesture of pure love. ★★★★ **IN**

TRUE LIES (1994)

Starring: *Arnold Schwarzenegger (Harry Tasker), Jamie Lee Curtis (Helen Tasker), Tom Arnold (Albert Gibson), Bill Paxton (Simon), Tia Carrere (Juno Skinner), Art Malik (Salim Abu Aziz), Eliza Dushku (Dana Tasker)*
Director: *James Cameron*
Screenwriter: *James Cameron, based on the screenplay* La Totale! *by Claude Zidi, Simon Michael, Didier Kaminka*
15/134 mins./Action/Comedy/USA
Awards – *Golden Globes – Best Comedy/Musical Actress*

When a secret agent learns of his wife's extra-marital affair, he pursues her and uses his intelligence resources in a job he kept secret from her.

Any film which features Arnold Schwarzenegger attempting to send himself up is usually a recipe for trouble – to wit, the box office performance of *Last Action Hero* or the lack of interest in his prosthetic pregnancy in *Junior*. *True Lies*, fortunately, is the exception to that rule – a glorious piece of self-parody that reunites Schwarzenegger with his Terminating partner James Cameron to startling effect. Arnie (complete with alarming sneer) is Harry Tasker, a Bond-derived spy capable of knocking off entire armies of villains with a single trusty Uzi 9mm, even though his wife Helen and daughter are convinced it's a mundane computer sales job that is bringing home the family bacon.

When a string of complicated coincidences lead Helen to the truth, the inevitable hell breaks loose and the two of them find themselves in one of those awkward save-the-planet type situations courtesy of the obligatory stereotypical insane Arab terrorists (led by Art Malik). If the whole thing does come across as politically incorrect at every turn, a situation fuelled by a middle sequence of latent and unsettling misogyny, it is rescued by Cameron's knack of pulling off standard-setting action scenes.

The final half-hour, in particular, is a remarkable tour de force that employs helicopters, out-of-control limos and a few Harrier jump jets thrown in for good measure and remains heart-stopping even for those who have already experienced it nine feet high in the cinema. What sets this apart from the average actioner is an over-the-top quality that makes it impossible to take seriously (a hilariously prolonged horseback chase, for example, is closer to something out of a *Naked Gun* movie than anything else). The net result is unbeatably good fun, helped along by that inherent fantasy that one man can create global mayhem without stopping to worry who's going to clean up afterwards. ★★★★ **CW**

Movie Trivia:
James Cameron (born 1954)

Who he is: Director with the biggest box-office, and budgets, in Hollywood. Futurist and technophile, known for his legendary temper as much as his progressive filmmaking.
Hallmarks: Groundbreaking special effects; jaw-dropping action; deep sea exploration; toughness towards actors and crew; post-Apocalyptic visions of the future; atomic bombs.
If you see one movie, see: *Titanic* (1997)

⦿ TRUE ROMANCE (1993)

Starring: *Christian Slater (Clarence Worley), Patricia Arquette (Alabama Whitman), Dennis Hopper (Clifford Worley), Val Kilmer (Elis), Gary Oldman (Drexl Spivey), Brad Pitt (Floyd), Christopher Walken (Vincenzo Coccotti), Samuel L. Jackson (Big Don), James Gandolfini (Virgil)*
Director: *Tony Scott*
Screenwriter: *Quentin Tarantino*
18/120 mins./Crime/Action/Drama/Romance/USA

Clarence falls for Alabama after meeting her at a late night movie screening. When he discovers she's a hooker, he decides to destroy her past – which has potentially fatal consequences for them both.

Quentin Tarantino's *True Romance* script is an elaborate, extended fantasy that sees a geeky shop assistant transformed into a great lover, a vengeful vigilante and, ultimately, a smooth criminal. Meanwhile, the story lacks any kind of emotional or moral consequence: the hero gets his father killed, the heroine guns down a cop during a drug deal gone sour, but they both drive off happily into the sunset, untainted by the mayhem they have left in their wake.

Are we expected to buy into this bloody fairytale? Are we supposed to like these self-obsessed, homicidal maniacs? The answer to both these questions is a resounding yes, because the wishes being fulfilled here belong to former geeky shop assistant Quentin Tarantino, and he had the talent to flesh out his fantasy with vividly-drawn characters spouting instantly classic dialogue during jaw-dropping set-pieces.

The 'I'd fuck Elvis' speech that introduces comic book clerk Clarence, the rooftop confession and declaration of love by Alabama, the showdown with Drexl, Virgil at the motel and, of course, the Sicilian scene are all hugely appealing to any budding hopeful. What Tarantino couldn't have known when he was scribbling away behind the counter at Video Archives, however, is that they would be equally attractive to established and, in some cases, legendary stars.

Despite his earlier reservations, Pitt signed on to play a bone idle stoner flatmate; the notoriously picky Gary Oldman sank his post-Dracula teeth into the role of a racially-confused pimp; and Chris Penn, Tom Sizemore and Samuel L. Jackson happily played virtual bit parts. Add never-to-be-bettered work from Christian Slater and Patricia Arquette to the mix, and you already have something special. But the genuinely great moments in *True Romance* belong to James Gandolfini, Dennis Hopper and Christopher Walken.

Even with an excellent screenplay and a rogues' gallery of protagonists waiting to be brought to life, any film needs the right director, and *True Romance* boasts an ideal helmer in the unlikely shape of Tony Scott. Who better than the director of *Top Gun* to bring an arrested adolescents fantasy to life? Scott verges on self-parody in terms of the gloss and pace he brings to proceedings, giving the movie a relentless energy that never allows the audience to stop and consider the absurdity of it all.

Alabama's execution of Virgil, complete with feral scream and lovingly photographed, blood-soaked breasts, earned the film notoriety and a run-in with the censors, although Scott's approach to the material is best summed up by another, less controversial creative decision. The script has Clarence's initial drug-hawking meeting with Elliot take place, unremarkably enough, in a zoo, but the director wanted something with a little more pizzazz, so he set the sequence on a rollercoaster. Tarantino is overstating the case when he compares Scott to undervalued auteurs of the past (Douglas Sirk he ain't), but there's no doubt he was perfect to orchestrate this wild ride. ★★★★ **RF**

⦿ TRULY MADLY DEEPLY (1991)

Starring: *Julie Stevenson (Nina), Alan Rickman (Jamie), Michael Maloney (Mark), Bill Paterson (Sandy), Christopher Roxycki (Titus)*
Director: *Anthony Minghella*
Screenwriter: *Anthony Minghella*
PG/102 mins./Romance/Drama/UK
Awards – *BAFTA – Best Original Screenplay*

Nina's grief for her dead lover is interrupted when his ghost appears and attempts to resume their relationship.

Dubbed by American critics as Blighty's answer to *Ghost*, this BBC-funded film explores in the reaction of Nina to the death of her cello-playing lover. Distraught and alone, and left with a rat-infested flat and a large therapy bill to pay, she is immediately thrown into a tangle of emotions when he miraculously reappears from the dead in her living room.

Actually made long before the success of the Swayze/Moore hit, and set in the less salubrious surroundings of a gloomy North London, it is more of a mood piece than a blockbuster. Stevenson carries the film well enough with an emotionally affecting and often uncomfortable portrayal of a woman facing the agony of bereavement, but the whole production shifts from an honest exploration of loss into a something more humorous when the morose ghostly Rickman appears.

In a brave directorial debut, Anthony Minghella tries to unfold the fact that rose-tinted memories of love are often more enthralling that the reality, but Rickman and his band of video-watching ghosts prevent this debate getting too serious. But what this lighter tone does allow is darker moments to really bite – there's a story Jamie tells about a three-year-old girl's ghost that is quite heart-breaking.

There are also strong supporting roles from Bill Paterson as Nina's amiable employer and Mark Maloney as a wayward admirer. ★★★ **WT**

⦿ THE TRUMAN SHOW (1998)

Starring: *Jim Carrey (Truman Burbank), Laura Linney (Meryl Burbank/Hannah Gill), Noah Emmerich (Marlon), Natascha McElhone (Lauren/Sylvia), Holland Taylor (Truman's Mother), Brian Delate (Truman's Father), Ed Harris (Christof)*
Director: *Peter Weir*
Screenwriter: *Andrew Niccol*
PG/103 mins./Sci-fi/Drama/Comedy/USA
Awards – *BAFTA – Best Production Design, Best Original Screenplay, David Lean Awards for Direction, Golden Globes – Best Score, Best Actor, Best Supporting Actor (Ed Harris)*

Truman lives is in a big studio with hidden cameras everywhere, and all his friends and people around him, are actors who play their roles in the most popular TV-series in the world. Truman thinks that he is an ordinary man and has no idea about how he is exploited. Until one day . . .

There are a number of powerful images in Peter Weir's end of the millennium masterpiece but one that really sticks in the mind, capturing as it does the central theme of *The Truman Show*, occurs only for a brief moment in the middle of a montage as 'creator' Christof describes Truman's development. We see a toddler in a playpen gazing upwards, apparently fascinated by a children's mobile. Fluffy shapes spin around to a tinkling nursery rhyme. But at the centre of the toy dangles the menacing shape of a camera lens and it's to this that the child's curious, slightly worried expression is directed. If one of the many themes of *The Truman Show* is betrayal then it is this shot that sums it up more eloquently than any other.

It's one of the ironies of science fiction movies that while they concern themselves with either the future or at least technology that doesn't yet exist, they generally have more to say about what's going on in the present than any of the other genres. By the end of the 90s, media saturation, anxiety over privacy, encroaching media power and, with virtual reality, the increasingly unreliable nature of the real world were the prevalent preoccupations. Peter Weir's film was not alone in broaching these themes. *The Matrix* took a different approach for a different audience. But it is Weir's film, which is certainly science fiction in that the technology required to create a whole artificial world for its protagonist is not (yet) possible, which caught the public's imagination, partly because of the sheer relevancy of the idea but also because of another element unusual in sci-fi, a performance of incredible warmth and vulnerability from Jim Carrey.

The conceit is pretty much summed up in a screaming voice-over at the beginning of the Tru Talk segment of the show itself. 'One-point-seven-million were there for his birth ... 220 countries tuned in for his first step ... An entire human life recorded on an intricate network of hidden cameras broadcast live and unedited 24 hours a day, seven days a week to an audience around the world!' Truman himself is only aware that he lives in Seahaven, an impossibly sundrenched, pastel-dappled island town which, owing to a carefully implanted fear of water, Truman cannot leave. (In fact the screenplay originally had Truman in a Se7en-style, grim rain-sodden city which Weir rejected, opting instead to shoot in a Florida retirement village.)

Starting quite literally with a falling star – a studio lamp marked Sirius 9 tumbles from the 'sky' – Truman begins to suspect that he is at the centre of a conspiracy. His wife insists on shouting product endorsements at the most inopportune moments, an elevator has no back walls revealing what looks suspiciously like a caterings service table surrounded by bored extras. Finally making a run for reality Truman is nearly killed by show creator Christof before opting for the real uncertainties of the world outside the TV studio instead of his ersatz existence.

Newspaper headlines like 'Who needs Europe?' rub shoulders with posters showing lightning striking planes ('It could happen to you!' reads the slogan) and hokey TV sitcoms which announce that 'You don't have to leave home to discover what the world's all about' all conspiring to counteract Burbank's curiosity. There's also tremendous fun to be had reading interpretations onto the movie. There's the 'Garden Of Eden in reverse' take in which Truman is Man fighting his way out of paradise, stopped by a terrified 'creator'. There's the anti-Capraesque angle, in which American smalltown life is not the very essence of perfection but stifling, repressive and false. There's even the fact that the whole premise is contained within its central character's moniker: the True Man's second name is Burbank, the LA suburb where the studios reside.

In *Truman* he creates a true hero for the times whose humanity shines even as he realises the extent to which he has been manipulated. It's easy to poke holes in the film. The show itself would in reality be deadly dull. The audience is as complicit in Truman's plight as Christof, yet they are presented sympathetically. And why does Christof attempt to make Truman stay once he has rumbled the game? But then, *The Truman Show* is best seen as a modern-day fable (and no one nit-picks the Hare And The Tortoise). It's a cautionary tale about the invasive, corrupting nature of a society that believes it has the right to watch everything. And it's a point that gets more, not less, prescient as we edge into the second millennium. With real-life shows like *Survivor* and *Big Brother* defining millennial TV and communications technology advancing with increasing rapidity, a real Truman Show becomes ever more likely. The events of Terry Gilliam's *Brazil* famously take place 20 minutes into the future. *The Truman Show* may be a lot closer than that. ★★★★★ **AS**

ⓘ THE TRUTH ABOUT CATS AND DOGS (1996)

Starring: *Uma Thurman (Noelle), Janeane Garofalo (Abby), Ben Chaplin (Brian), Jamie Foxx (Ed), James McCaffrey (Roy)*
Director: *Michael Lehmann*
Screenwriter: *Audrey Wells*
15/96 mins./Comedy/Romance/USA

A dowdy vet falls for a photographer but, afraid of rejection, persuades her super-model mate to pose as her and woo him instead.

After his career nearly expired with twin flops *Hudson Hawk* and *Airheads*, it was a relief to see *Heathers* man Michael Lehmann bound to the top of the American box office with this warm-hearted romantic comedy that's capped with a trio of winning performances. While the title ostensibly refers to a radio phone-in pet advice programme, it also plays on the eternal variations between men and women, with amusingly telling observations on what, whom and why we love.

Abby (Garofalo, charming in her first lead role) is short, dark and cuddly. Her neighbour Noelle is gorgeous, tall, thin and blonde. Abby is a smart, hilarious vet who dishes out pet advice on an LA radio station. Noelle is a model. It isn't hard to guess who gets all the male attention.

Then, one day, Brian rings Abby's show with a canine crisis and is taken by her personality. Attempting to meet her, he mistakes her babe buddy Noelle for the voice of his dreams. The women sustain the deception, creating all manner of complications – ranging from the wrong girl forced to give a turtle a rectal examination, to an awesomely embarrassing phone sex marathon.

While the ultimate lesson here is that what you see is not really what you get, it's arguably fatuous that the dazzling blonde should be dizzy as well, and somehow it all works out far too nicely to be true. But former DJ Audrey Wells' crafty screenplay brims with truths about the sexes, providing great lines for Garofalo, and great business for Thurman's confused waif, and cranks the feelgood factor up so high it's almost off the scale. In other words, there's plenty here to send you out purring. ★★★★ **AE**

ⓘ TSOTSI (2005)

Starring: *Presley Chweneyagae (Tsotsi), Mothusi Magano (Boston), Isreal Makoe (Tsotsi's father), Percy Matsemela (Sergeant Zuma), Nambitha Mpumlwana (Pumla Dube)*
Director: *Gavin Hood*
Screenwriter: *Gavin Hood, based on the novel by Athol Fugard*
15/94 mins./Drama/Crime/UK/South Africa

Awards – *Academy Awards – Best Foreign Language Film*

Tsotsi is an emotionally frozen street hoodlum punching and kicking his way round Soweto's shanty towns. When a carjacking goes wrong and he finds himself lumbered with the baby of a wealthy couple, the child begins to thaw his damaged soul – bringing confusion, trouble, and the possibility of some kind of redemption ...

Gavin Hood's third feature has inspired comparisons with *City Of God*, yet his harrowing look at six days in the life of a Soweto thug who accidentally kidnaps and grows attached to a tiny baby shares the weary compassion of 2005's *Crash* as much as the brutal desperation of Fernando Mereilles' acclaimed hit.

Hood cleverly interweaves elements of psychological thriller with a complex, layered character study, as Tsotsi (first-time actor Presley Chweneyagae) struggles to cope with his new companion, and the police close in on his trail. At times it's a difficult watch; the lead character is borderline psychotic in his inability to empathise with those around him, but it's testament to Chweneyagae's outstanding performance that such a frightening individual is understood and embraced by the audience, even as his actions repel.

Longest films ever shown TOP10

1. *The Cure For Insomnia* (1987), USA, 87hrs
2. *The Longest And Most Meaningless Movie In The World* (1970), UK, 48 hours
3. *The Burning Temple Of The Red Lotus Temple* (1931), China, 27 hrs
4. *Heimat 2* (1992), West Germany, 25 hrs 32 mins
5. **** (1967), USA, 25 hours
6. *Heimat* (1984), West Germany, 15hrs 40mins
7. *Berlin Alexanderplatz* (1980), West Germany/Italy, 15 hrs 21 mins
8. *The Journey* (1987), Sweden, 14 hrs 33 mins
9. *How Yukong Moved The Mountains* (1976), France, 12 hrs 43 mins
10. *Out 1: Noli Me Tangere* (1971), France, 12 hrs 9 mins

Shot largely in desaturated, sepia tones in Soweto's claustrophobic shanty towns, the raw energy of Tsotsi's existence is in neat contrast to the wealthy couple whose baby he has stolen. While some scenes (flashbacks to Tsotsi's AIDS-blighted childhood) are rushed and a little clumsy, Hood handles his material so deftly that a conclusion which could have been mawkish and sentimental is instead bittersweet, both painful and quietly affirming. ★★★★ **LB**

TUCKER: THE MAN AND HIS DREAM (1988)

Starring: *Jeff Bridges (Preston Thomas Tucker), Joan Allen (Vera Tucker), Martin Landau (Abe Karatz), Frederic Forrest (Eddie Dean), Mako (Jimmy Sakuyama), Elias Koteas (Alex Tremulis), Christian Slater (Junior Tucker), Nina Siemaszko (Marilyn Lee Tucker)*
Director: *Francis Coppola*
Screenwriters: *Arnold Schulman, David Seidler*
PG/110 mins./Drama/USA

The true life story of Preston Tucker, a maverick car designer who fought the car industry to create and manufacture his own dream car, The Tucker Torpedo.

It is impossible to ignore the parallels between the subject of this stylish biopic and its director, Francis Coppola. Just as Preston Tucker tried to forge his own factory to manufacture a range of luxury cars in opposition to the big 3 Detroit automobile companies, Coppola attempted to build his own studio – American Zoetrope – and create his own personal brand of cinema miles away from the spectre of Hollywood studio interference. That both men ultimately failed in their aspirations should make *Tucker: The Man And His Dream* a depressing experience, but in fact, it is a joyous celebration of the maverick American spirit, even if it never really gets under the skin of its flawed hero.

Jeff Bridges attacks the role of Tucker – part inventor, part con artist, all showman – with a mile-wide grin and an optimism that would make a Scientologist look morose. Cosseted by his big family and regular collaborators (more Coppola traits), Tucker's attempts to build his dream machine – a terrific-looking vehicle, it's special feature is a third headlight that turns in the same direction as the steering wheel – creating a prototype out of junkyard detritus, and then promoting the product to a sceptical public (the unveiling of the car sees a fire backstage) are engaging. Kudos here to an Oscar-nominated Martin Landau as Tucker's ageing right hand man, who adds a subtle counterpoint to Bridges' big performance.

But what really pulls you through the movie is its high style. Shot with all the sharpness and colours of a 1940s billboard, Vittorio Storaro's cinematography is sumptuous and endlessly imaginative, including a theatrical use of transitions between scenes that kidnap the breath.

If you wanted to nit-pick, you could argue that the film doesn't delve too deeply into Tucker's motivations or character – this is much more about the dream than the man – and Coppola ignores the darker undertones inherent in its story of thwarted ambition and the little man being crushed by huge corporations. But it remains a gorgeous entertaining evocation of both a fascinating period and a little-known American huckster. ★★★★ **IF**

TURNER & HOOCH (1989)

Starring: *Tom Hanks (Det. Scott Turner), Mare Winningham (Dr. Emily Carson), Craig T. Nelson (Chief Howard Hyde), Reginald VelJohnson (Det. David Sutton), Scott Paulin (Zack Gregory)*
Director: *Roger Spottiswoode*
Screenwriters: *Dennis Shyrack, Michael Blodgett, Daniel Petrie, Jr., Jim Cash, Jack Epps, Jr., based on a story by Shyack and Blodgett*
PG/97 mins./Comedy/USA

Tom Hanks plays a fastidious small town cop investigating a murder. Unfortunately his only witness is a beer-guzzling mastiff dog, Hooch. Much mayhem follows as the dog ignores Turner's house rules ('no begging, no crotch-sniffing') but wins him over with those bloodshot eyes.

Astonishingly it took five screenwriters to come up with this somewhat hackneyed tale.

There is never any doubt that Turner will initially be horrified, but then grudgingly respect and finally become inseparable from the slobbering mutt, or that the pair will clear up the case.

A romance with the unlikely town vet erodes the perfectionist in Turner and provides light relief from the antics of man and beast but really that's just to bulk out the running time.

A talented cast have here taken what is essentially a silly dog story with a predictable plot and made it into a tight, funny and thoroughly professional movie. Tom Hanks once again brings his glorious physical comic talent to bear in an unlikely movie – proving he's good enough to survive any film – and Hooch is equally wonderful. Fascinatingly ugly, his huge jowls shaking and dripping buckets of saliva, he deserves a special canine Oscar all of his own. ★★★ **KMc**

12 ANGRY MEN (1957)

Starring: *Henry Fonda (Juror No.8), Lee J. Cobb (Juror No.3), Jack Klugman (Juror No. 5), E.G. Marshall (Juror No.4), Jack Warden (Juror No.7), Ed Begley (Juror No. 10), John Fiedler (Juror No.2), Edward Binns (Juror No.6), Joseph Sweeney (Juror No.9)*
Director *Sidney Lumet*
Screenwriter: *Reginald Rose*
U/95 mins./Drama/USA

Awards – *BAFTA – Best Foreign Actor*

One man tries to change the opinion of the other eleven on the jury but it's going to be an uphill struggle.

You could jot the premise of *12 Angry Men* down on the back of the proverbial fag packet. The jury of a seemingly cut-and-dried murder case (a juvenile delinquent Hispanic accused of stabbing his father) are split eleven to one. Over the course of one sweltering hot day, the lone protestor gradually swings the jurors to his way of thinking, cutting away the prejudice and bald assumption from the evidence to reveal the doubt in the case. It remains one of the most thrilling and intelligent courtroom dramas ever made, commenting not only on the fallible procedures of law but on the dark recesses of the human heart. Judgment, it protests, is always clouded.

The idea was reputedly based on writer Reginald Rose's own experiences as a juror, which he turned into a teleplay. Hence, it was originally filmed for television's Studio One series in 1954 (Joseph Sweeney and George Voskovec actually appear in both versions). Henry Fonda was so taken with the subject matter he put his own money into a big screen remake – producing, starring and bringing in a little known director named Sidney Lumet. Such was Lumet's vibrancy and imagination for the project that in a long, illustrious career (including *Serpico* (1973) and *Prince Of The City* (1981) this remains his crowning piece.

Faced with the limitations of playing the entire drama in only a single room, Lumet keeps his camera dancing between his jurors as he stirs them up, sweating and irritable in the fierce New York heat. To imply the increasing claustrophobia of the situation, with each scene he slyly moves the walls in, the room getting tighter and tighter. But it is in the performances where the true dynamic rests. This is as much a movie about the acting process itself as anything else. The twelve brilliantly rich character actors on show have no names to work with, few props, and are confined to one set. All they can rely on is their own talent and Rose's magnificent writing to conjure vivid, realistic men. Never once does the film feel cramped or dull.

Class structure, intellectual snobbery and racism brew into heady conflict as the table is slowly but surely swung. Fonda's Juror No.8, an architect, allows his intelligence to rule his emotions, therefore he can clearly see the divide between factual evidence and foolish assumption. And from here the film expertly unravels each juror elaborating on their own stories (factually, in the 50s, women were not allowed to serve on juries) through the vessel of their 'anger' (in fact, only about eight of the jurors are demonstrably irate in any way, Fonda is the picture of self-control). Every one of them distinct and plausible:

Juror No.1 (Martin Balsam) – the foreman, insecure in the face of leading the room. Never at ease.

Juror No.2 (John Fielder) – a small, quiet accountant, amazed that anyone would want to hear his opinion.

Juror No.3 (Lee J. Cobb) – a boisterous, self-made businessman who becomes increasingly impassioned as his personal agenda emerges.

Juror No.4 (E.G. Marshall) – an arrogant stockbroker approaching the case with cold, hard logic.

Juror No.5 (Jack Klugman) – he recognises himself in the accused and, ironically, here lies his distrust.

Juror No.6 (Ed Binns) – again a quiet one, he is urgent to see justice done, but unable to express this need.

Juror No.7 (Jack Warden) – a swarthy, loud-mouthed baseball fan, eager to get the case done so he can get to the game, he is disinterested in the outcome.

Juror No.8 (Henry Fonda) – the calm, intellectual architect, who has 'reasonable doubt'.

Juror No.9 (Joseph Sweeney) – an old timer who, uniquely, sees the case from the point of view of the victim.

Juror No.10 (Ed Begley) – a man who votes guilty only because of his open antipathy to the boy's social status.

Juror No.11 (George Voskovec) – a methodical, clever immigrant watchmaker, who reasonably believes in the boy's guilt.

Juror No.12 (Robert Webber) – a smarmy ad exec, who sways with the majority.

It is a very romanticised view of jury service; the notion of winning over a sweaty room of bigots still fuels the dreams of even those about to tackle a case of tax fraud. But the film never fudges its points about the nature of reasonable doubt and the purity of the law. How the jury system will always be slave to petty prejudice and personality. It is also a film about men and what shapes them. The ephemera of life – names, job titles, ambitions – don't define us, but the various irrational paranoias, insecurities and wisdoms bred by experience. On such terms, the movie doesn't put a foot wrong – it even works as a murder mystery of sorts. We'll sensibly forget that William Friedkin remade the film for television with Tony Danza in 1997, to consider the fact that Lumet's classic was a box office failure (audiences, ironically, prejudiced against the apparent lack of excitement). It did, however, pick up three Oscar nominations for Picture, Adapted Screenplay and Actor, but lost out to *The Bridge On The River Kwai* on all counts. ★★★★★ **IN**

ⓘ TWELVE MONKEYS (1995)

Starring: *Bruce Willis (James Cole), Madeleine Stowe (Dr. Kathryn Railly), Brad Pitt (Jeffrey Goines), Christopher Plummer (Dr. Goines), Joseph Melito (Young Cole)*
Director: *Terry Gilliam*
Screenwriters: *David Peoples, Janet Peoples, based on the film* La Jetée *by Chris Marker*
15/129 mins./Sci-fi/Thriller/USA

Awards – *Empire Awards – Best Director, Golden Globes – Best Supporting Actor (Brad Pitt)*

An unknown and lethal virus has wiped out five billion people in 1996. In the year 2035 a convict reluctantly volunteers to be sent back in time to 1996 to gather information about the origin of the epidemic.

Terry Gilliam's genius as a filmmaker rests in his ability to create movies that are at once masterly and almost impossible to put up with. He crams each and every frame with brilliant touches and draws great performances from unusual actors, but he simultaneously presents a dark-funny vision of the world that regular people are never going to be able to get behind. *Brazil* may well be the ultimate full-strength Gilliam. Undoubtedly a masterpiece in its director-approved version, it nevertheless suffers from exactly the problem the callous studios recognised: it goes on for 20 minutes (albeit 20 brilliant minutes) beyond the human capacity to absorb such a dense vision.

After that, and the commercial catastrophe of *The Adventures Of Baron Munchausen*, Gilliam tried to readjust to a more human scale and shot a couple of pictures from scripts by other people. *Twelve Monkeys*, by David and Janet Peoples (*Blade Runner*, *Unforgiven* and, er, *Salute Of The Jugger*) is by no means Gilliam lite, but it is the one film in his canon that not only delivers the Kafka-meets-*MAD Magazine* nightmare but also a wholly absorbing emotional ride and a hugely complex plot that – against the odds – turns out to make perfect sense.

The Peoples take their *Twilight Zone*-ish plot nugget from Chris Marker's classic French short *La Jetée*, a film told almost entirely in a succession of still images with an overlaid soundtrack. It concerns a time traveller from the future who can build a link to the present because he retains a strong memory of an incident he witnessed at Orly airport as a child, which turns out to be the moment of his own death. Around this, and taking into account various disease scares (AIDS, Ebola, Hanta) of the mid-90s, the script weaves a labyrinthine tale of multiple time-jumps and a *Terminator*-style project on the part of a future civilisation the purpose of which is not to avert an apocalypse but to ensure that it's survivable.

In an underground hellhole of 2035 Philadelphia, prisoner Jack Cole is recruited by the authorities as a footsoldier in a desperate plan to visit the past and save the future. Cole is painfully blasted back in time to locate a sample of the virus which will appear in 1996 and wipe out most of humanity. But the haphazard nature of the time-travel process and the disorienting effects of the present on Cole's future-blunted psyche complicate his mission. As he is whipped back and forth between 1990, 1996, World War One and the future, Cole fixates not on saving the world but on psychiatrist Kathryn Railly, who manages to convince him it's all a delusion.

The horrible irony is that as soon as Cole starts rationalising the science fiction aspect of his dilemma as neurosis, Kathryn turns up physical evidence that suggests the opposite. Meanwhile, loony animal activist Jeffrey Goines, leader of the eco-terrorist sect 'Army Of 12 Monkeys', is planning a major coup, and the deadly *Omega Man*-type virus nestles in a laboratory run by Goines' father, waiting to be released.

The most recognisable Gilliamesque aspect of the film is the grotesque imagery (lots of brass and dirty polythene) of the futuristic scenes. But the strength of *Twelve Monkeys* is its heart. Willis does his best screen work ever in a daring, knockout performance which ranges from terrifying violent outbursts to a childishly desperate nostalgia for '20th Century music', and Stowe keeps up with him all the way as the plot noose draws tighter, easily shouldering the burden of representing everything in humanity worth saving. And the script keeps coming up with left-field twists: the lovers check into a sleazy hotel to sort out the plot, but just as their conversation is about to deliver vital exposition, an enraged pimp bursts into the room, convinced that Stowe is a high-class hooker poaching on his territory.

The film flirts with the notion that all we see is indeed a psychotic fantasy, and although initially disorientating, it pulls all its threads together at the half-way mark. From there on it transcends its trendy apocalypse gibberish superbly, offering up a last-minute realisation – cued by a glimpse of Hitchcock's *Vertigo* – of what perception might be for.

After a heart-rending finale at the airport, in which Cole dies in such a way as to imprint himself on the child witness who will grow up to be him, there's a sequence that takes two or three viewings to appreciate. Cole has been a stalking horse and the whole project is a set-up to get a future scientist onto a plane next to the already-infected 'Apocalypse nut' who is travelling the world, spreading the killer virus as he goes. The crucial sacrifice that saves the future is the handshake she forces upon him, which allows her to carry the virus home to 2035 in her own body. ★★★★★ **KN**

Movie Trivia: *Twelve Monkeys*

A brief clip from *The Andromeda Strain*, showing a monkey in the throes of death, can be seen on the dayroom television. Director Terry Gilliam, afraid that Brad Pitt wouldn't be able to pull off the nervous, rapid speech, took away his cigarettes to achieve the desired effect. Gilliam gave Bruce Willis a list of 'Willis acting clichés' not to be used during the film, including the 'steely blue eyes look'.

20,000 LEAGUES UNDER THE SEA (1954)

Starring: *Kirk Douglas (Ned Land), James Mason (Capt. Nemo), Paul Lukas (Prof. Pierre Aronnax), Peter Lorre (Conseil, His Assistant), Bob Wilke (1st mate of* Nautilus*), Carleton Young (John Howard)*
Director: *Richard Fleischer*
Screenwriter: *Earl Felton, based on novel by Jules Verne*
U/128 mins./Sci-fi/USA
Awards – *Academy Awards – Best Art Direction, Best Special Effects*

Three shipwrecked sailors are rescued by the mysterious Captain Nemo and taken on a fantastic underwater voyage. But gradually they learn that Nemo has sinister plans for the world.

Jules Verne, a prescient and brilliant novelist of the late 19th Century, is often dubbed the father of science fiction. He was the first to meld the traditions of the adventure story with the scientific and industrial revolution. And while his tales of exploration and discovery were far-reaching and exotic, there was a fascinating pessimism in his work – wary of rapid social changes, he inserted a warning against untapped scientific progress that predates Michael Crichton by a century. *20,000 Leagues Under The Sea* is easily his most cinematic book: extraordinary yet self-contained (the location is principally the seabed), it boasts four filmed versions including a George Méliès silent from 1907, Stuart Paton's 1916 version (one of the first movies ever shot underwater) and a 1997 TV mini-series featuring Michael Caine.

It is, however, Disney's dazzling 1954 spin that best captures Verne's imaginative sweep and dark, provocative undertones. Set in 1868 (the book was published in 1870) it follows the undersea adventures of three outsiders: salty seaman Ned Land (Douglas), scientific puritan Professor Pierre Aronnax (Paul Lukas) and his oddball sidekick Conseil (Lorre) who fall into the hands of Captain Nemo (Mason) and his fabulous submarine the *Nautilus*. It then adopts Verne's episodic style, flitting from encounter to encounter, before Nemo's idealism fragments into psychosis and the whole thing goes belly up.

The *Nautilus* itself is a design triumph (it gained immortality of sorts by being transformed into a Disneyland boat ride). Possessing an otherwordly, organic look – its spine of iron rivets hinting at elements of shark and alligator – it is presumed to be a sea monster by the Slavers traversing the ocean routes (a traditional 'backward' world, unable to divine a scientific explanation for the phenomenon). It's a beautiful, yet cruel underwater beast powered by Verne's prophetic notion of atomic power.

It was a huge scale production, still one of the most ambitious live action projects Disney has ever undertaken. The major stars and enormous special effects thrown into only the second Cinemascope film ever made predicted the advent of the blockbuster as much as the story predicted nuclear submarines. And it looked wonderful. The underwater scenes, filmed off the Bahamas, at the same location used for the 1916 version, invite you to marvel at man's exploration of new boundaries. 400 technicians were employed for the location shoot and the modelwork still stands up to close examination, although the squid attack, as fun as it is, has a touch of the Ed Woods. Fleischer went on to visualise more outlandish and terrifying scenarios in both *Fantastic Voyage* and *Soylent Green*. While Artist and Production Designer Harper Goff, who created special diving suits for the film and was instrumental in getting the green light from Walt, went on to the similarly creative 70s version of *Willy Wonka And The Chocolate Factory*.

While coupling the novel's concerns of science-unbounded with the then prevailing threat of nuclear war, the film also possesses an inner paranoia toward socialist ideals and progress which echoes the ongoing McCarthy witch hunts. Nemo's perfect world as metaphor for the Commies? Well it was the 50s, so it's no surprise he comes unstuck. Central to this is the refined, eloquent, dangerously ambiguous Captain Nemo. Mason fills the role with all his snaky, highbrow charm, turning in one of his most famous characterisations – his autocratic notions of a pure world hovers delicately between inspiration and mania. Aronnax gamely tries to persuade him to pass on his discoveries to the surface world, but Nemo has lost all sense of where his scientific ideals leave off and his lust for power begins (Verne's alarm bell – human nature will always corrupt pure scientific vision).

Still, this is Disney, and to maintain appeal to the kids (who were no doubt quite happy with the submarines and lunacy anyway) there are some attempts at comedy. Douglas spends his time mixing raw physicality with playing dumb and getting sloppy with a pet seal. He even ends up singing the suitably titled 'Whale Of A Tale'. Meanwhile Peter Lorre strives for craven but just ends up weird.

Ultimately, though, beyond the sermonising and whimsy, the enduring quality of this Disney epic is its simple, compelling sense of adventure. It rigorously upholds one of the most fundamental laws of cinema: it shows us something we've never seen before. And how. ★★★★ **IN**

⊙ 28 DAYS LATER (2002)

Starring: *Cillian Murphy (Jim), Naomie Harris (Selena Harris), Brendan Gleeson (Frank), Christopher Eccleston (Major Henry West), Luke Mably (Private Clifton)*
Director: *Danny Boyle*
Screenwriter: *Alex Garland*
18/113 mins./Sci-fi/Horror/Thriller/UK
Awards – *Empire Awards – Best British Film*

Misguided animal activists free some chimps from a research laboratory unknowingly setting off a chain of events which will see Britain overrun by zombies.

The last time a Brit tried to make a serious zombie movie, it turned out to be *Resident Evil* – a feeble, bloodless, scareless imitation of George Romero's *Living Dead* cycle. Here, Danny Boyle and novelist Alex Garland (doing a lot better by an original screenplay than in adapting *The Beach*) evoke Romero, as survivors try to cope with the evil walking dead and the gun-toting shreds of devastated authority – but they aren't content with mere pastiche.

For a start, they invoke the specifically British roots of this genre. Floating in the mind of *28 Days Later* are lasting cultural artifacts passed around or hotly discussed in British school playgrounds for decades: the novels of John Wyndham (the waking-up-in-a-deserted-hospital bit is a nod to *Day Of The Triffids*) and James Herbert (one scene hinges on a flood of rats); or the science shock TV series *Doomwatch* (don't trust the labcoats!) and *Survivors* (if everyone's dead, what's the point in surviving?).

Depopulated London, stunningly achieved by snatched digi-cam shots of empty streets and abandoned landmarks, with minimal CG employed, is a resonant location. It strikes chords with anyone who has ever wondered what the place would be like without people, and is embedded deep in the psyche by everything from H.G. Wells' *War Of The Worlds* to *Daleks: Invasion Earth 2150 AD*. An American film on this theme would start with the survivors gathering guns and using them as if they'd been fighting wars all their lives; here, even the toughest character – hardboiled chemist Selena – isn't that skilled at fending off zombies.

Survivalism is better represented by a tower block rooftop covered with a pathetic array of bright plastic buckets, basins and bins to catch rain that hasn't fallen. It proves that, even after the apocalypse, the weather will still be a national obsession and the scene sets up an unforgettable sudden thunderstorm to accompany the fast, gut-punch, brutal third act.

The power of the film is not that it hasn't been done before, but that it hasn't been done recently. Since the early 1970s, British movies have narrowed their focus to the problems of small groups of people, gnawing over microcosm genres like the gangster heist or romantic comedy. Here, we look at a bigger picture, intensifying the situation for a typically Boyle-like knot of antagonistic, uncomfortable characters. Headlines about Tony Blair and talk about *The Simpsons* insist that this future is just a step away, but forget the rave scene that might theoretically embrace such anarchy – here, the whole of Manchester is on fire and the only use for mood-altering drugs is to numb the mind to literally unbearable realities.

This may be a stylistic break with previous Boyle movies, but it has a similar structure (he likes games of two halves, with a collection of anecdotes setting up a more concentrated narrative). It even falls back on the essay topics of *The Beach*, as alternative society turns out to be flawed by reliance on brutality and vulnerable to sudden shark/zombie attacks.

Shot with Dogme-like camcorder veracity by Anthony Dod Mantle, the film has space for lyricism as the survivors briefly make it as happy campers in green, damp countryside. But it also pulls daring tricks with speeded-up motion and blobby bloodbursts to make the horror sequences genuinely jarring in a manner that marks a break with the more traditional effects style of, say, *Dog Soldiers*.

There is also room for the subtle, character-based chill: the scariest line is Eccleston's whispered, 'Slow down', a pregnant phrase overheard just as we realise how bad things really are.

If you look for flaws, they're there. Any film as rough-edged as this flirts with seeming amateurism, while the third act not only borrows almost wholesale from Romero's *Day Of The Dead* but hammers home the message about man's inherent inner rage a bit too forcefully. But the powerful, broad-strokes performances (both Murphy and Harris have been noticed by Hollywood since) recall an observation made of 1959 nuclear war movie, *On The Beach*: that it's impossible to judge the acting since what constitutes appropriate behaviour in this situation is anybody's guess. ★★★★ **KN**

⊙ 25TH HOUR (2002)

Starring: *Edward Norton (Monty Brogan), Phillip Seymour Hoffman (Jacob Elinsky), Barry Pepper (Frank Slaughtery), Rosario Dawson (Naturelle Riviera), Anna Paquin (Mary D'Annunzio), Brian Cox (James Brogan)*
Director: *Spike Lee*
Screenwriter: *David Benioff, from his novel*
15/135 mins./Crime/Drama/USA

A drug dealer spends the last day before turning himself in to the authorities – and an inevitable jail term – trying to make sense of his life so far.

How far can you take a metaphor before it sinks beneath the weight of its own self-importance? Spike Lee's latest is about a drug dealer cleaning up his act, so it's really about post-Giuliani New York and the effects of the ex-mayor's hard line attitude to crime. It's also about a drug dealer determined to ruin his pretty boy looks before he goes to prison, so it's really about the heterosexual male's fear of sodomy.

Then again, it's also about a drug dealer who finally accepts that the punishment being meted out to him is solely his responsibility, caused by his own past indiscretions, so it's really about the current political state of America. Under this reading, Monty is the USA, who can no longer blame his Latin American (i.e. Third World scapegoat) girlfriend for his woes, but must let his former Soviet (i.e. failing superpower) cohorts fight it out amongst themselves. Meanwhile he takes advice from his friends, a teacher (cultural heritage), a Wall Street broker (financial might) and his ex-fireman father (the hands that built America). Haven't quite worked out where the dog fits in yet.

Actually, the above interpretation isn't that ridiculous. There's a reason why Lee sets a key scene in an apartment overlooking Ground Zero, now a gaping wound in the street map and psyche of New York. David Benioff wrote his novel before 9/11, but his screenplay resonates with the sense of a city and its inhabitants shaken to their core.

Like Monty, everyone has to look deep within himself, weigh up his sins and, if necessary, pay his dues before redemption can be earned.

All of which makes *25th Hour* one of Lee's more thoughtful and timely works, one that tones down anger in favour of wider contemplation and a certain ambiguity when the final credits roll. Of course, the film could really just be about the surface story. And it wouldn't be any less enjoyable for that.

Lee's post-9/11 elegy to his home city has some obvious flaws – the teacher/pupil flirting sub-plot, the over-extended final reel fantasy life – but *25th Hour* proves that big ideas and an indie sensibility can still flourish inside the studio system. One of the more entertaining and thought-provoking Spike Lee Joints ... ★★★★ **AM**

⓪ 2046 (2004)

Starring: *Tony Leung Chiu Wai (Chow Mo Wan), Li Gong (Su Li Zhen), Takuya Kimura (Tak), Faye Wong (Wang Jing Wen), Ziyi Zhang (Bai Ling)*
Director: *Kar Wai Wong*
Screenwriter: *Kar Wai Wong*
12A/129 mins./Drama/Romance/China/France/Germany/Hong Kong

In the mid- 60s, on the rebound from an affair with a married woman, journalist Chow embarks on a series of doomed romances. In between flings, his obsession with the number of the room where he and the woman met inspires him to write *2046*, a sci-fi novel about a place where people go to forget . . .

After testing the patience of the Cannes festival organisers by delivering a visually arresting yet dense *2046* mere hours before its premiere, Hong Kong auteur Kar Wai Wong insisted that his five-years-in-the-making masterwork was ready for release. Which was bollocks. Instead, Mr. Pants-On-Fire almost entirely re-organised his baffling romance into something a little more orthodox, but definitely more engaging.

The result, a sort of sequel to Wong's 2000 arthouse smash *In The Mood For Love*, is well up to the director's usual standards. It's a hypnotic meditation on relationships based around a terrific central performance by longtime collaborator Tony Leung. Sporting a spiv's 'tache and leading a playboy's life, his Chow is a complex hero of sorts. He's charming, attentive and even sensitive, but capable of surprising emotional cruelty in his dealings with women, from mysterious, sophisticated gambler Su Li Zhen, to hopeful, guileless escort girl Bai Lin.

The latter is perhaps the film's greatest revelation. Bai Lin's hurt grounds this luminous, experimental movie in reality, while Zhang's turn earmarks her for stardom even more so than her breakout performance in *Crouching Tiger*. Without doubt, she is an actress of depth and versatility ★★★★ **DW**

⓪ 24 HOUR PARTY PEOPLE (2001)

Starring: *Steve Coogan (Tony Wilson), Lennie James (Alan Erasmus), Shirely Henderson (Lindsay Wilson), Paddy Considine (Rob Gretton), Andy Serkis (Martin Hannett), Sean Harris (Ian Curtis), Danny Cunningham (Shaun Ryder)*
Director: *Michael Winterbottom*
Screenwriter: *Frank Cottrell Boyce*
18/117 mins./Comedy/Biography/Music/UK

Manchester 76 – 92. The time of Tony Wilson, Factory Records and The Hacienda. The time of Joy Division, New Order and the Happy Mondays. The time of music, drugs and the birth of the rave scene.

Granada TV presenter Tony Wilson is standing on a hill outside Manchester. Attached to a hang-glider, he throws himself off, kamikaze-style. After a brief adrenalin rush and some genuinely dangerous moments, he crashes to the ground. 'It's symbolic – it works on two levels,' thinks the perceptive viewer, drawing parallels between this and the history of Wilson's music label, Factory Records. 'It's symbolic – it works on two levels,' says Steve Coogan, playing Wilson, talking directly to camera and stealing the audience's clever-clever thunder.

Barely two minutes into the movie, and director Michael Winterbottom has made a clean break from any by-the-rules 'biopic' approach to either Wilson, Factory or the whole Manchester scene from the late 70s to the early 90s. In one quick, self-referential move, he grants himself the freedom to mould the whole unruly subject into whatever shape he wants.

The finished product leans a bit too much towards the Tony Wilson/Steve Coogan Show to really do justice to such a vibrant era; at times, particularly when the floppy-lapelled TV presenter is up there in grainy glory, it's like Eric Idle playing Steve Coogan playing Alan Partridge playing Tony Wilson. But there's no doubt that this is a brave and brilliant movie that bristles with energy and attitude.

The tone shifts as the spotlight moves from Joy Division (and the unhappy suicide of Ian Curtis, brought brilliantly to life here by Sean Harris) to the Happy Mondays. The first half of the film is as intense and passionate as a night in with Curtis; the second is as shambolic and fun as a night out with Shaun Ryder.

If the film loses its focus in the later stages, it's because Winterbottom wants it to do so. Style reflects content as the director maintains a chaotic feel that is the Factory spirit in its most essential form. It's idealism and anarchy in a head-on collision; it's symbolic and it works on two levels. And, as the Mondays might say, Hallelujah to that. ★★★★ **AM**

Movie Trivia:
24 Hour Party People

The original Hacienda club was demolished in 2000 so, based mainly on no doubt distorted memories, a replica was built in a disused warehouse. Joy Division took their name from the concentration camp women kept aside for the 'use' of Nazi officers. Actor Steve Coogan apparently based his television character Alan Partridge on Tony Wilson years before the film was released.

⓪ 21 GRAMS (2003)

Starring: *Sean Penn (Paul Rivers), Benicio Del Toro (Jack Jordan), Naomi Watts (Cristina Peck), Charlotte Gainsbourg (Mary Rivers), Melissa Leo (Marianne Jordan), Clea DuVall (Claudia Williams)*
Director: *Alejandro Gonzalez Inarritu*
Screenwriter: *Guillermo Arriaga*
15/124 mins./Drama/Thriller/USA

An accident brings together a reformed ex-con, a grieving mother and a critically ill mathematician.

A slew of contemporary classics – *Out Of Sight*, *Memento*, *City Of God*, *The Usual Suspects*, pretty much everything by Quentin Tarantino – have exploited abrupt shifts in time or character perspective to dazzle or deceive the audience.

It's a technique founded in the work of Jean-Luc Godard and his fellow European New Wave auteurs, who used experimental narrative structures to highlight the essential artifice of film and unsettle the viewer. But with *21 Grams*, *Amores Perros* director Alejandro Gonzalez Inarritu and co-screenwriter Guillermo Arriaga have made a quantum leap, using a fragmented storytelling technique to involve, intrigue and, crucially, move the audience.

The resulting film is a genuinely thrilling emotional experience – often unbearably tense, occasionally heartbreakingly sad, ultimately uplifting but always, always riveting.

The basic premise seems simple enough – a tragic accident brings three disparate individuals together – but from such seemingly conventional material the filmmakers weave a complex tale, exploring issues of fate, guilt, revenge and redemption.

Sean Penn's directorial output (*The Indian Runner*, *The Crossing Guard*, *The Pledge*) has revealed his own preoccupation with these themes, so it's no surprise that his performance here is utterly compelling. With this film and *Mystic River*, for which he won an Oscar (although he could easily have been nominated for this), Penn is entering a golden period in his career, as he finally grows into the kind of role suited to his considerable gifts as an actor. As a young man, his undoubted intensity could often come across as adolescent angst or macho posturing. Now he exudes a world-weary gravitas worthy of pre-Method icons like Mitchum, Douglas or Lancaster.

In almost any other film, Penn's performance would be the standout, but his work here is matched by his co-stars'. Benicio Del Toro excels as ex-con Jack Jordan, whose acceptance of Jesus as his personal saviour makes him a pain in the ass to his much less fervent wife and kids. Jack's desire to do the right thing and face up to his culpability would ordinarily make him admirable, but the film is intelligent enough to point out the inherent selfishness of this moral code. The audience's relationship with the character is constantly alternating between sympathy and contempt, between affection and exasperation. Lesser actors would be weighed down by these contradictions; Del Toro uses them as fuel and takes flight.

With two such dominant alpha male presences in the film, it would be understandable if the lead actress failed to make much of an impact. The odds are further stacked against Naomi Watts since her character – the suburban soccer mom with a history of cocaine abuse – is confronted with a succession of revelations, and must 'do' shocked, outraged, grief-stricken, devastated.

Furthermore, the unconventional structure employed means that these 'big' scenes are interspersed with more intimate moments, calling for more subtle execution. She rises to every challenge, connecting with the audience on the emotional terms that are essential if we're to feel truly involved with the film's spiritual and philosophical elements. If Watts continues alternating work of the quality shown here – and in breakthrough *Mulholland Dr.* – with commercial hits like *The Ring* and *King Kong*, then the title 'finest actress of her generation' is hers for the taking.

The film has been described as a jigsaw puzzle, but that's not a suitable analogy. The individual pieces of a puzzle hold no value of their own, but every scene, every frame of *21 Grams* has real artistic merit. The editing, cinematography and use of music are all stunning and combine with the performances (main and supporting) to form a flawless whole. The film is less like a jigsaw and more like a great novel in which not a sentence, not a word, is wasted. Inarritu and his collaborators have created something astonishing, and your film journey will be incomplete if you miss it. ★★★★★ **RF**

◎ TWENTYFOURSEVEN (24 7) (1997)

Starring: *Bob Hoskins (Alan Darcy), Danny Nussbaum (Tim), Justin Brady (Gadget), James Hooton (Knighty), Darren Campbell (Daz)*
Director: *Shane Meadows*
Screenwriters: *Paul Fraser, Shane Meadows*
15/92 mins./Comedy/Drama/Sport/UK

A loner sets up a boxing club to give the disaffected Midlands housing estate troublemakers some sense of purpose.

Try this one for size. Make a film about boxing and shoot it in black-and-white. Bolster the soundtrack with classical music and then give it a subtext about redemption. What you get is *Raging Bull*, right? Well, not exactly. First time writer-director Shane Meadows has done just that, but he has created a film so resonant in character and bitter humour that Scorsese won't enter your head. In fact, you'll hardly notice the boxing at all.

The premise floats like a feather. A band of teenagers kill time on their Midland housing estate by drinking cheap lager, smoking bad weed and egging on their rival gang. Enter Darcy, a middle-aged loner (performed with burning intensity by Bob Hoskins) who knocks a fraction of sense into their thick skulls and involves them in a run-down boxing club. Funded by shifty business man Ronnie, Darcy unites both gangs to box against a local amateur team and, hopefully, instils some self respect into their vacant lives.

Of course it all ends on the ropes: parents object to their sons' imminent battering, drug use dampens ambition and love interests remain unrequited. Yet beneath the loneliness and squalor, Meadows has planted a seed of unremitting hope. In fact, moments of clear-cut genius blossom throughout. The *Blue Danube Waltz* sequence is breathtaking considering it was directed by a self-taught 26-year-old; and Hoskins caressing the fingerprint mark of his never-to-be lover is simply inspired. The naturalistic acting blends perfectly with Ashley Rowe's magnificent black-and-white photography making *TwentyFourSeven* the most challenging British debut in years. He may buck the trend for slick editing and dazzling set pieces but Meadows gives off a bold message: be a somebody, not a nobody. In other words, everyone over 15 should see this movie. ★★★★★ **JH**

◎ TWIN PEAKS FIRE WALK WITH ME (1992)

Starring: *Sheryl Lee (Laura Palmer), Ray Wise (Leland Palmer), Moira Kelly (Donna Hayward), David Bowie (Phillip Jeffries), Chris Issak (Special Agent Chester Desmond), Kyle MacLachlan (Special Agent Dale Cooper), Mädchen Amick (Shelly Johnson)*
Director: *David Lynch*
Screenwriters: *David Lynch, Robert Engels*
18/134 mins./Drama/USA

An FBI Agent and a forensic expert investigate the death of a young woman in an eerie American town.

If the extent of your *Twin Peaks* experience is spending a couple of episodes baffled by some dwarf talking backwards, then there is absolutely no point in checking this out for, with scant exposition, there is little here that makes anything remotely understandable.

If, however, you do subscribe to the view that David Lynch's Adventures In Logland are the work of a damned genius, the only course of action open is to disregard the negative advance word – boos and walkouts at its Cannes screening and zero box office in the US – and revel in the fact that *Twin Peaks: Fire Walk With Me*, 'prequel' to the small screen saga, will, with considerable style, exceed your wildest expectations.

In unconventional fashion, this divides into two quite separate parts : the first, a half-hour overture, playing like a self-contained episode, as FBI Agent Desmond (crooner Isaak, surprisingly good) and nerdish forensic expert Stanley investigate the death of Teresa Banks, zipping around the Fat Trout trailer park with its befuddled proprietor Carl Rodd.

It is only then, with this entree partially digested and all the characteristic humour exhausted, that the signature tune strikes up and events veer off into the main portion, a visually stunning and disturbing journey through the latter days of fallen angel Laura Palmer, the homecoming queen descending into a mire of prostitution and nose-candy – only reflected upon on TV, but here shown in full sordid detail – as things spiral to their cataclysmic conclusion, the point at which the series kicked off.

Darker than before – menacing Leland no longer the tragic character of the series, rather an out-and-out loony – this is also laced with minutiae that will have obsessive Peakies rubbing their hands with glee, as hitherto loose ends are tied up and some semblance of meaning – the notion of religious redemption – is proffered.

The absence of, among others, Sherilyn Fenn, Lara Flynn Boyle, the Great Northern Hotel, the police station and the sawmill, may disappoint, particularly when space has been made for new characters like oddball apparition Philip Jeffries (crooner David Bowie, unsurprisingly bad, mercifully brief), but this notwithstanding, Lynch's deeply weird revisitation is a triumph due to the sinister mood he creates, which, underscored by Angelo Badalamenti's haunting soundtrack, marks this as his darkest, most disturbing film to date. Pretentious codswallop? Quite probably. For devotees, however, it is nonetheless compulsive viewing. ★★★★ **JE**

t

Best selling soundtracks of all time

1. *The Bodyguard* (1992)–8million
2. *Saturday Night Fever* (1977)–7.5million
3. *Purple Rain* (1984)–6.5million
4. *Forrest Gump* (1994–6million
=5. *Dirty Dancing* (1987)–5.5million
=5. *Titanic* (1997)–5.5million
7. *The Lion King* (1994)–5million
8. *Top Gun* (1986)–4.5million
=9. *Grease* (1978)–4million
=9. *Footloose* (1984)–4million
11. *Waiting To Exhale* (1997)–3.5million

TWISTER (1996)

Starring: *Helen Hunt (Dr. Jo Harding), Bill Paxton (Bill Harding), Cary Elwes (Dr. Jonas Miller), Jamie Gertz (Dr. Melissa Reeves), Philip Seymour Hoffman (Dustin Davis)*
Director: *Jan de Bont*
Screenwriters: *Michael Crichton, Anne-Marie Martin*
PG/108 mins./Action/Adventure/USA
Awards – *BAFTA – Best Visual Effects, Razzie Awards – Worst Written Film Grossing Over $100 Million*

Two bands of rival scientists chase tornadoes across the American mid-West in twister season.

So tornadoes pass into the muse of one Michael Crichton, the reigning techno-king of Hollywood. And they make for rich pickings, indeed, for the science obsessed scribe: nature out-of-control, loads of accompanying technobabble, and the chance for huge screen-filling set-pieces.

But instead of channelling his premise of weather geeks careering across middle-American farmland in chase of the swirling masses of destruction into one of his populist novels, he decided (with the help of his wife Anne-Marie Martin) to make it straight into a movie. Computer generated tornadoes interacting with real-life actors? Cool idea. But could it be done?

Rope in one Jan De Bont, previously seen whipping a bus through LA's rush hour traffic, and the boys at Industrial Light & Magic and – hey presto – visual effects to smack the collective global gob. Their 'mission impossible' was accomplished. It's a shame such an effort was not afforded to the rather plodding storyline and lacklustre script. *Twister* is about one thing, and one thing alone: a thrill session. In that, it delivers tenfold.

The central hook is that a group of weatherfolk, dressed nattily in grunge gear, their four wheel-drives loaded with state-of-the-art equipment, are aiming to do the impossible and launch some sensors up inside a twister. This, for the sake of mankind, will allow them to predict their movements more quickly and hasten advanced warnings. Luckily for them, and the movie, it's about to be a double whammy of a tornado season.

And that, really, is all there is to it, plotwise. The team, led by the feisty Jo and her estranged hubbie Bill, chase the tornadoes, getting seriously up close and personal in the seemingly vain effort to get the early warning ultra-sensor 'Dorothy' in the twister's path.

There are attempts to add dimension: the spiky relations between the couple with Bill's new girl Melissa along for the ride, a formulaic but underused bad guy in Elwes' corporate-funded competitor and the rum nuttiness of the science-school dweebs of the team. But they're fooling no one. This is about the twisters, five of them, building up to the rip-roaring (literally) wham-bang conclusion.

Apart from the odd spot of shoddy matte-work, the effects do for wind what *Jurassic Park* did for dinosaurs. From the get-go we're launched into a high-speed chase – no buses, just jeeps and wind masses arbitrarily destroying farm buildings – and from there they just get bigger. The last 20 minutes predictably roll out that big gun, the F5 (top of the Fujita-Pearson Tornado Intensity Scale) leaving the audience suitably rapt by the sheer dynamism and flawless believability of it all.

De Bont knows about kinetics, he just lacks the skill to instil any lasting emotional level. Hunt and Paxton, valiant as they are, are simply ciphers to deliver us to the next thrill.

Twister is a disaster movie – houses collapse, cows fly, death looms – but a strange one where the victims are not unwittingly forced to face death, but, rather happily almost drunkenly imperil themselves like high-risk junkies (the compassionate subtext just doesn't rub). While it's hard to stir any sympathy for them, their excitement is infectious. Hence this film encompasses everything that is both grating and great about the blockbuster: it gives scant regard to character depth or dialogue while still being a must-see hoopla of computer trickery that weakens the knees and raises the neck-hairs. Like all white-knuckle rides, once you're done you fancy doing it all over again. ★★★ **IN**

TWO OR THREE THINGS I KNOW ABOUT HER (DEUX OU TROIS CHOSES QUE JE SAIS D'ELLE) (1966)

Starring: *Marina Vlady (Juliette Jeanson), Anny Duperey (Marianne), Roger Montsoret (Robert Janson), Jean Narboni (Roger), Christophe Bourseillier (Christophe), Raoul Levy (The American), Joseph Gehrard (M. Gehrard), Helena Bielicic (Girl In Bath)*
Director *Jean-Luc Godard*
Screenwriter: *Jean-Luc Godard, based on a letter from Catherine Vimonet that appeared in* Le Nouvel Observateur
15 90 mins./Drama/France

Juliette Jeanson has a child with her engineer husband Robert and seems to have a comfortable life. But, in order to keep up with her consumerist aspirations, she has to supplement the family income by working as a suburban prostitute.

Keen to accommodate former producer Georges de Beauregard's need for a quickie picture to extricate himself from a financial crisis, Jean-Luc Godard filmed this highly personal project simultaneously with the more disposable *Made In USA*. Ironically, this morning-afternoon division of labour echoed Juliette Jenson's switch from housewife to hooker in this biting, yet powerfully reflective study of the dehumanising effect of the media, town-planning, consumerism, chauvinism and our own inability to change the world around us.

Godard drew his inspiration from a Catharine Vimonet article in *Le Nouvel Observateur* about the suburban prostitutes known as 'les étoiles filantes'. But he reinforced his collage approach by including ideas and images that often contradicted as well as complemented each other. Indeed, from the opening shot, Godard challenges the viewer to rethink the very nature of cinema by introducing Marina Vlady as an actress from one side of her window and then as Juliette Jeanson, wife, mother and whore, from the other.

But while both Marina and Juliette could claim to be the 'Her' of the title, Godard is even more preoccupied by Paris, which he considers has similarly prostituted itself in the name of progress. Using shots of construction sites to emphasise the alienation of the citizenry, Godard attacks the city authorities who have permitted the creation of a *Metropolis* designed to entrap its inhabitants in a consumerist web whose comforts and conveniences lead only to debt and despair.

But he also puts the blame for this feeble surrender on to the pernicious forces of capitalism and American cultural imperialism, which are sugar-coated through advertisements that make tawdry and unnecessary products seem essential. Indeed, the US influence is everywhere – whether it's news of the escalating war in Vietnam on Robert's radio set or the cars, clothes and comestibles that Juliette desires – and it's impossible to discern whether Godard's red, white and blue colour scheme refers to the Tricoleur or the Stars'n'Stripes.

Yet, the film's most telling image is a contemplative close-up of a cup of coffee (riffed on by Scorsese in *Taxi Driver*), over which Godard confides his disillusion with society and himself. ★★★★ **DP**

ⓤ 2001: A SPACE ODYSSEY (1968)

Starring: *Keir Dullea (David Bowman), Gary Lockwood (Frank Poole), William Sylvester (Dr. Heywood Floyd), Daniel Richter (Moonwatcher), Leonard Rossiter (Smyslov)*
Director: *Stanley Kubrick*
Screenwriters: *Stanley Kubrick, Arthur C Clarke, based on a short story* The Sentinel *by Clarke*
U/139 mins./156 mins. (premiere cut)/Sci-fi/USA/UK

Awards: *Oscars – Best Special Effects, BAFTA – Best Art Direction, Best Cinematography, Best Sound Track*

In an alternatively imagined 2001, a computer threatens the lives of all on board a scientific space station and man and technology are locked in a symbolic struggle that began when the first ape discovered tools.

Of the many questions thrown up by *2001*, the most frequently asked is, quite simply, what the hell does it mean? It remains the most frequently asked because no one, least of all Stanley Kubrick, has ever furnished a satisfactory answer. In consequence, the film invites personal interpretation perhaps more readily than any other in the history of cinema.

One widely held theory is that it's about mankind's tenuous alliance with technology and how in freeing himself from enslavement to it, he is reborn to a higher plane of existence. And there is a thematic thread braided into the film's four chapters to support the idea.

The film opens with a breathtaking shot of the Earth, viewed from the dark side of the moon with the sun rising in the distance. All three are in perfect alignment. We later learn that when celestial bodies are seen in this configuration, it augurs a momentous event, and that is certainly the case here.

The first sequence, *The Dawn Of Man*, features the notorious man-apes, who are coaxed over a crucial evolutionary boundary by a mysterious alien monolith. At the monolith's bidding one of the apes, who are on the brink of extinction, hefts an animal bone above his head like a club, heralding the birth of Man's long and troubled relationship with technology. The club, almost immediately employed as a weapon of murder, is not only the means of man's salvation, but also of his potential destruction.

In the most celebrated match cut in cinema history, the man-ape throws his primitive club into the air where it transforms into a satellite orbiting the moon. Time has jumped forward four million years to 2001 AD.

The opening sequence of *TMA-1*, where the shuttle carrying NASA scientist Dr. Heywood Floyd docks with the space station, is probably the most famous in the film. It is a beautiful, languorous ballet of spacecraft wheeling against the stars, meticulously choreographed to the strains of *The Blue Danube*.

Floyd has been sent to investigate an alien artifact recently unearthed on the moon's surface – a four-million-year-old monolith, emitting an enormously powerful magnetic field. In another startling scene, Floyd and his team approach the monolith which suddenly lets out a piercing, siren shriek. It is announcing Man's arrival at a second key stage in his development: he is about to leave the safety of his own environment and reach out into the deep unknown.

The star of the third chapter, *Jupiter Mission: 18 Months Later* is, of course HAL, the hyper-intelligent computer who controls the expedition ship *Discovery* and in whose hands rests the fate of all on board. Although HAL is believed to be infallible, he makes an elementary technical error and, in an effort to cover his tracks, attempts to kill the two-man crew of the *Discovery* and their human cargo of scientists held in suspended animation.

Exactly why HAL screws up will be debated till Doomsday (the 1984, sequel 2010 proposed a fundamentally flawed solution) but the fact that he does and then retaliates with murderous intent is the turning point of the film. When HAL fails to kill astronaut Dave Bowman – who he knows has plotted against him – and Bowman methodically shuts down HAL's scheming data banks, Man has finally, after four million years, released himself from bondage to his tools.

HAL's death is an oddly moving scene, and loaded with significance. But it is not purely symbolic, as the extraordinary final chapter makes clear. As Bowman leaves the crippled *Discovery* in an escape pod, the film goes into hyperdrive. Jupiter and its moons are seen in alignment and the monolith reappears – a sure-fire tip that something big is about to happen. And, indeed, this is the moment chemically inclined members of *2001*'s original audience were waiting for. Underground magazines published guidelines on when to drop tabs of acid so they would kick in at precisely this point – Bowman's mind-blowing journey across the universe and the awesome light show that accompanies it. Here, the slow-burning narrative fuse touches off a powder keg of abstraction and colour-saturated psychedelia. It's a mesmerising ride.

At its end Bowman arrives in a weirdly stylised, luxuriously furnished room. In this room he encounters himself, first as an elderly man and then as a frail, wizened figure clearly close to death. Supine in bed, Bowman stretches out his hand – just as the man-ape and Dr. Floyd have done before him – to touch the monolith, which has appeared in the room. As he does so, the film's astonishing denouement is reached and the foetus of a Star Child manifests itself at his feet. Bowman – or his physical being at least – is gone, and as the monolith fills the screen we're back where we started with the Earth, the sun and the moon. But this time they're seen from the perspective of the Star Child, the symbol of Man's rebirth and his ultimate destiny.

Well, that's one theory. Some people think it's all about food. Either way there's a lot that is never explained – chiefly why an alien lifeforce should have decided to prod man's evolutionary urges in the first place. Is it a religious allegory? Is it a massive in-joke perpetrated by Kubrick and Arthur C. Clarke on messianic sci-fi fans? We'll never know, and that is all part of the fun. Whatever secret – if any – lies at the heart of *2001*, certain things are beyond question: it is a work of considerable genius and an unerringly satisfying, utterly unique cinematic experience. Even without the acid. ★★★★★ **SB**

ⓤ 2010 (1984)

Starring: *Roy Scheider (Dr. Heywood Floyd), Helen Mirren (Tanya Kirbuk), John Lithgow (Dr. Walter Curnow), Bob Balaban (Dr. R Chandra), Keir Dullea (Dave Bowman), Douglas Rain (voice of Hal 9000)*
Director: *Peter Hyams*
Screenwriter: *Peter Hyams, based on the novel by Arthur C. Clarke*
PG/116 mins./Sci-fi/USA

A sequel to *2001: A Space Odyssey* where a joint Soviet and US mission is launched to discover what happened to the *Discovery*. As the two nations cleave ever closer to war back on Earth, the crew make some startling discoveries of their own.

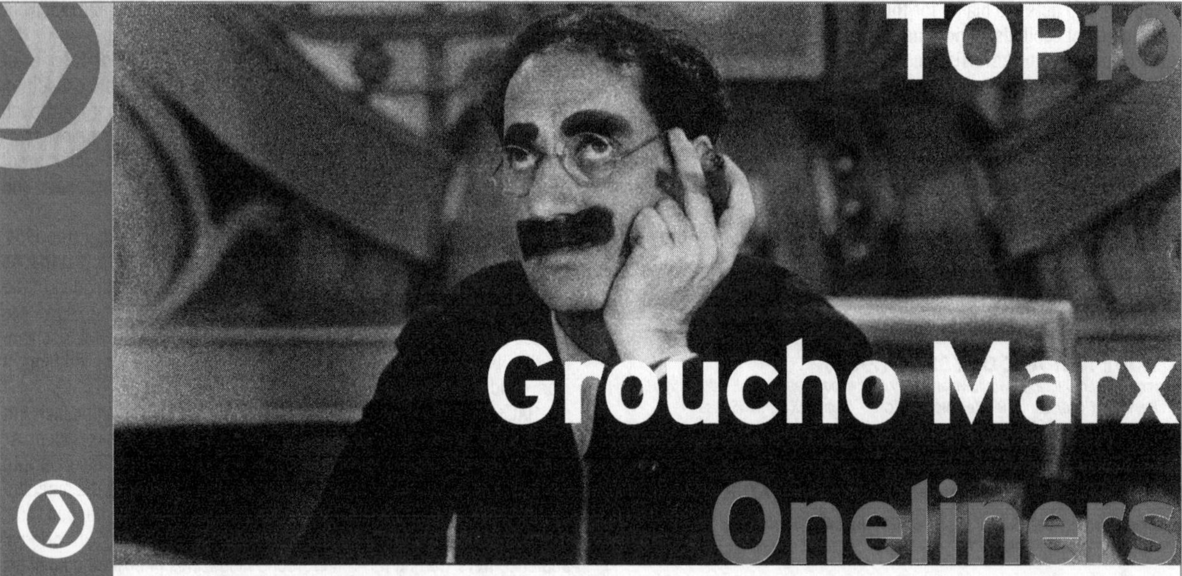

1 **'Remember, men, we're fighting for this woman's honour; which is probably more than she ever did.'**

2 **'I resign. I wouldn't want to be a member of any club that would have me as a member.'**

3 **'Once I shot an elephant in my pyjamas. How he got into my pyjamas, I'll never know.'**

4 **'Outside a dog, a book is a man's best friend. Inside a dog, it's too dark to read.'**

5 **'I was married by a judge. I should have asked for a jury.'**

6 **'If you want to see a comic strip, you should see me in the shower.'**

7 **'I could dance with you until the cows come home. On second thoughts, I'd rather dance with the cows until you come home.'**

8 **'Military intelligence is a contradiction in terms.'**

9 **'I never forget a face, but in your case I'll make an exception.'**

10 **'Those are my principles. If you don't like them, I have others.'**

As foolish exercises go, trying to hitch a lift on Kubrick's sublime stellar mysteries must count as one of the daftest ever. Still, author and Kubrick cohort Arthur C. Clarke (whose own explicatory tendencies were frustrated by the elusive director) had already penned the follow-up novel, so Hyams, at least, was equipped with a degree of credibility. And, if you manage to evade that looming shadow from the past, and take *2010* on its own sturdy merits, it turns out a half-decent, semi-considered sci-fi adventure.

Hyams was well aware what he was stepping into, citing it as an act of respect for Kubrick's genius, but this a film on a quest to explain whereas the original emanated a vague science of possibility. The mission for the crew of the *Leonov* – Scheider, Mirren (in typically icy form) and computer geek Balaban – must rewire the recently unplugged HAL to discover what happened to Bowman and Poole. And while tensions rise between the political factions (a thematically consistent note of man's tendency to war), wouldn't you know a certain black monolith rears its ugly, well, shape. And, without you knowing it, the film has become pretty exciting. The effects have a canny realism, the actors wear dark frowns and spout suitable jargon in good accents, while their boss, Hyams, bottles up the sci-fi rather than spinning it across the starfields in awe-inspiring dances of technology, granting the film a taut claustrophobia

Only at the close do the wheels come flying off. Why did it need to conclude with a morass of mock-Kubrickian vagaries (the aliens behind the monolith are as elusive as ever)? It's just a stark reminder of what this film is not. *2001* is a lustrous, dreamy work of mystery, *2010* a rusty but entertaining thriller. They're not really from the same universe. **★★★ IN**

U

⦿ U-TURN (1997)

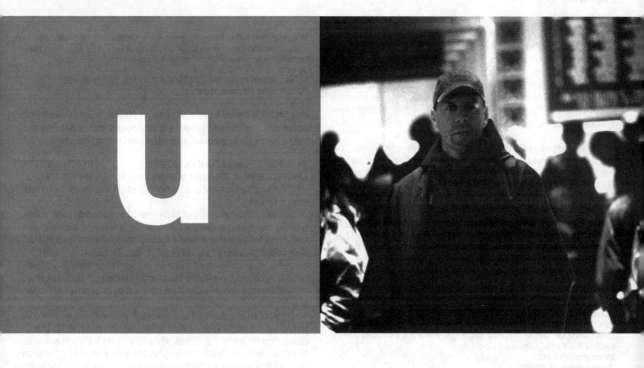

Starring: *Sean Penn (Bobby Cooper), Nick Nolte (Jake McKenna), Jennifer Lopez (Grace McKenna), Powers Boothe (Sheriff Virgil Potter), Claire Danes (Jenny), Joaquin Phoenix (Toby N. Tucker), Jon Voight (Blind Man), Billy Bob Thornton (Darrell)*
Director: *Oliver Stone*
Screenwriter: *John Ridley, based on his book*
18/125 mins./Crime/Drama/Thriller/USA

A drifter's car breaks down in a dead-end town and the locals seem to be conspiring to keep him there.

Having lost all sense of proportion with the over-inflated *Nixon*, Oliver Stone cuts back his budget and his post-NBK multimedia visuals to deliver a low-key, low-down, blacker-than-black comedy thriller. It's not the best film he's ever made, but certainly the best for a long while.

With more than a passing nod to John Dahl's *Red Rock West*, Stone's movie finds drifter Penn stuck in the arse-end of nowhere, his broken car in the garage, and two of his fingers seemingly missing.

What starts as a really bad day soon turns considerably worse under the frying temperatures of the noonday sun – deranged car mechanic Thornton won't give Penn his motor back, the local sheriff has his eye out for him, local vixen Lopez is on the tease, and her more-than-slightly possessive husband Nolte is none too chuffed with this new boy in town.

But soon, hubby is recruiting Penn to off the missus while she in turn is asking her newly bedded mate to do the same to hubby – who may well also be daddy (you know how these small towns are). Stone's direction seems generally reinvigorated by the reduced budget, with old Ollie out to prove his indie chops in inventive and often dazzling fashion. Having assembled an impressive cast, he's content to stand back and give them room to play, from the twisted humour of Thornton to the dark soul of Nolte to the luscious longings of Lopez. Penn, meanwhile, is superb – gradually falling apart through the course of the day, a man desperate to get out alive, with one eye on the road ahead and one on the buzzards circling above.

The plot does have obvious antecedents and Stone does betray himself with a few too many celeb cameos (just what is Liv Tyler doing standing in the back of that ticket office?). But for the most part, what you have here is a topnotch filmmaker getting back to basics and really delivering the goods. ★★★ **BM**

⦿ U2: RATTLE AND HUM (1988)

Starring: *as themselves: Bono, The Edge, Adam Clayton, Larry Mullen Jr., B.B. King, Phil Joanou*
Director: *Phil Joanou*
15/99 mins./Documentary/USA

A documentary that follows U2's tour of America, getting in touch with the country's musical roots, following the monster success of their album *The Joshua Tree*.

U2, bless them, were never going to be the best of subjects for the juice and splatter of the rockumentary. We're after infighting, scandal, the whiff of illict substances and the eternal blather of the gigantic ego, where this tight-knit quartet of God-fearing Dublin boys are more intent on waxing lyrical about authentic Americana, and raging against the injustices of the political state of their homeland. Phil Joanau's film neither tells us much that even the most casual of fans wouldn't already know, while unwittingly painting them as rather sensible. It comes across in doc-terms, unfortunately, as hagiography. Best then to approach what is an eloquent, beautifully shot movie (mixing colour with black and white stock) not as rock exposé but as a travelogue of a successful band's journey into America, punctuated by some excellent live footage.

There is also much pleasure to be had from watching the various members of U2 wrestle with the very concept of their own movie (they have since lightly regretted it as indulgence). Bono, the band's inevitable spokesman, is pointed and political and wry, happy to send up the other band members. Principally, the butt is stoic drummer Larry Mullen, who seems thoroughly pissed off with the whole carnival, although there's a gem of a moment, when the singer forces his indignant guitarist to just play chords when BB King turns up for a show: 'Um... yeah... well, uh, the Edge can do that'. The Edge, the band's musical brains, is the one who does most of the musing on the relationship between America's rock history and their own sound – although his conclusions feel a bit convenient given they have turned up on Elvis' lawn. Adam smiles pleasantly, and seems a bit above it all. Larry sullenly, and a tad sarcastically, mumbles: 'It's a musical journey.'

The gigs are where the film and U2 come alive. Renowned as one of the best live bands around, Joanou captures both the vitality – Bono's matchless engagement with an audience – and their versatility as they adapt to the huge size of these arenas, filling the voids with the tumbling landscape of their music. A gig played shortly after the tragic bombing in Enniskillen fires Bono into a speech of acid recrimination, a man enflamed against representing anything but peace: 'Fuck the revolution!' he cries, unable to help himself. It's a moment pure and unironc that confirms the band, apart from anything, are for real, the kind of electrifying passion that brought them to this station in the first place. ★★★ **IN**

ULZANA'S RAID (1972)

Starring: *Burt Lancaster (McIntosh), Bruce Davison (Lt. Garnett DeBuin), Jorge Luke (Ke-Ni-Tay), Richard Jaeckel (Sergeant), Joaquin Martinez (Ulzana), Lloyd Bochner (Capt. Charles Gates), Karl Swenson (Willy Rukeyser), Douglas Watson (Maj. Cartwright), Dran Hamilton (Mrs. Riordan), John Pearce (Corporal)*
Director: *Robert Aldrich*
Screenwriter: *Alan Sharp*
15/105 mins./Western/USA

Renegade Apache Ulzana breaks off the reservation and goes on a 'murder raid', pursued by a party of cavalrymen led by inexperienced young officer DeBuin with advice from a grizzled scout McIntosh.

One of the best Westerns of the 1970s, directed with grim efficiency and honesty by action man Robert Aldrich, from a peppery, complex script by unsung hero Alan Sharp (of *Night Moves* and *The Hired Hand*), it has great struggle-in-the-wilderness sequences as the barely-seen Apache warriors harry a US Cavalry troop in a hostile, mountain landscape.

Unlike many hippie-era Westerns, which reacted against the old cliché by presenting ridiculously pacifist and noble Indians, it doesn't flinch from the still-shocking business of the 'murder raid' (a trooper is commended for shooting a settler woman and himself rather than being taken captive by the torture-happy Ulzana) but the Apache are accorded a great deal of respect and understanding, and depicted as complex, interesting characters. In a classic exchange, Burt Lancaster's wise old scout says there's no point in hating Apaches for their cruelty because it would be 'like hating the desert because there's no water in it' and, when the newly-embittered Bruce Davison says that he *does* hate Apaches, observes 'it might not make you happy, but it sure won't make you lonesome'. Jorge Luke is especially strong as the cavalry's Indian scout, a relative of Ulzana, who is mistrusted by his white comrades but is literally incapably of going back on his word ('I sign paper') and emerges as the real hero of the film.

Tagline
To defeat the Apaches, they had to be just as savage.

As in many 1970s Westerns, there's a Vietnam parallel floating about in the 'lost patrol' storyline, but Ulzana's vision of well-intentioned but ignorant American military engagement with a violent culture in an alien landscape remains unsettlingly relevant. ★★★★★ **KN**

UMBERTO D (1952)

Starring: *Carlo Battisti (Umberto Domenico Ferrari), Maria Pia Casillo (Maria), Lina Gennari (Landlady), Alberto Albani Barbieri (Fiance), Elena Rea (Sister), Illeana Simonova (Surprised Woman), Memmo Carotenuto (Voice Of Light)*
Director: *Vittorio De Sica*
Screenwriter: *Cesare Zavattini, Vittorio De Sica from a story by Zavattini*
PG/89 mins./Drama/Italy

Despondent following a thwarted pensions protest, retired civil servant Umberto Domenico Ferrari decides to abandon his faithful dog Filke and his landlady's kindly pregnant maid, Maria, and commit suicide.

Screenwriter Cesare Zavattini had always contended that the ideal film would consist of 90 minutes of a man doing nothing and he came closest to fulfilling that austere ambition in this remarkable collaboration with Vittorio De Sica.

However, Undersecretary of State Giulio Andreotti didn't share their pride in this rigorous demonstration of the neo-realist aesthetic and announced legislation to withhold funding and exhibition licences from any film that presented Italy in a negative light. Consequently, Umberto D flopped at the box office and De Sica lost much of his personal investment. Yet, this remained his favourite film precisely because it eschewed sentimentality in exploring the everyday realities facing those on society's margins.

Umberto is essentially an unsympathetic character. He is more concerned with maintaining an outward appearance of respectability than in confronting his poverty and, thus, while he accepts Maria's concern, he fails to recognise her fears regarding her pregnancy and chides her when she lets his pet escape. Yet the detailed sequences in which he prepares for bed and she readies to face another day bind them together in pitiable need.

Yet, while De Sica employed a mostly non-professional cast (hiring University of Florence philology professor Carlo Battisti after encountering him *en route* to give a lecture), this was more an exercise in studio realism than street authenticity. He certainly shot sequences on location, but he spent most of his time at Cinecitta, where he had greater control over the bleak poetry of his imagery.

Thus, he and cinematographer G.R. Aldo were better able to exploit deep-focus techniques to place Umberto at the heart of his miserable existence and use the long hall of his tenement building, the tables at the soup kitchen and the rows of patients at the hospital to emphasise his isolation and insignificance. Even the rows of trees, as he and Filke wander into the distance after his failed suicide attempt, conspire to reinforce his endless entrapment in a hopeless situation and not even the sight of children playing could deflect from the harsh truth that both man and beast were enduring a dog's life. ★★★★ **DP**

THE UNBELIEVABLE TRUTH (1989)

Starring: *Adrienne Shelley (Audry Hugo), Robert Burke (Josh Hutton), Chris Cooke (Vic Hugo), Julia McNeal (Pearl), Katherine Mayfield (Liz Hugo)*
Director: *Hal Hartley*
Screenwriter: *Hal Hartley*
15/90 mins./Drama/USA

Recently released con Josh Hutton, who served time for murder, returns to his hometown and falls for local beauty Audry. But the town, especially Audry's father, are wary of Josh, unsure of the extent of Josh's crimes.

Hal Hartley is a low-key prince of an American filmmaker whose studies of small-town American life manage to be both lyrical and caustic, darkly comic fables of eccentrics and enigmas planted in the everyday. They usually get classified as offbeam, and there are leanings toward the bizzarro impulses of David Lynch, but for all his gentle whimsy Hartley's films do make a lot of sense. He's the Steve Soderbergh who never made it big. Thank God, because then we get terrific little movies like this.

Made on next to nothing, but still refreshingly ungrainy-looking, the film revolves around a central mystery – what is the extent of Josh's (Robert Burke) crimes in the past and is he still dangerous?-the latter an especially pertinent point given he has hooked up with the listless 17 year-old Audry. The outcomes, however, are never quite as important as typical films would have them, the plot being more of a framework for Hartley to hang his preoccupations upon: intellect, memory, love, guilt and the impending apocalypse. His characters define themselves against a doomy pessimism that sets them all as oddballs. Hartley just can't see conformity in the world, he may be allergic to it.

Robert Burke and the lovely Adrienne Shelley, give easy, lolling performances, characteristic of how Hartley (who directs-writes-edits and if you ask him nicely makes a great cup of coffee) manages a form of holistic filmmaking where everything becomes a necessary part of the seamless whole. It's drifty, dreamy quality that, contrary to the film's indie-cool ingredients, makes it eminently watchable and modern. ★★★★ **IN**

⊙ UNBREAKABLE (2000)

Starring: *Bruce Willis (David Dunn), Samuel L. Jackson (Elijah Price), Robin Wright Penn (Audrey Dunn), Spencer Treat Clark (Joseph Dunn)*
Director: *M. Night Shyamalan*
Screenwriter: *M. Night Shyamalan*
12/106 mins./Drama/Fantasy/Thriller/USA

David Dunn, a security guard with a failing marriage, is the sole survivor of a train derailment. Approached by Elijah Price, a dealer in comic book art who suffers from a rare brittle bone syndrome, Dunn comes to wonder whether Price's theory that he has superhuman abilities might hold water.

As the makers of *Blair Witch 2* discovered, the hardest gig in the movies is to follow up something that seemed to come from nowhere and took audiences by surprise. The second time around, everyone is ready for you.

Writer-director M. Night Shyamalan hasn't made an actual sequel to his breakthrough hit, *The Sixth Sense*, but he has reteamed with star Bruce Willis, come up with another story of everyday folk baffled by the supernatural (or at least, unknown-to-science), and returned to a Philadelphia presented as a wintery haunt of the bizarre yet transcendent.

This time round, Willis (in earnest, agonised, hair-free *Twelve Monkeys* mode) has the paranormal abilities, and a superbly un-typecast Samuel L. Jackson is the investigator who digs into someone else's strange life to prompt startling revelations about his own.

David Dunn is first seen on a train that is set to crash. Following the wreck, everyone else is dead, but not Dunn, who wanders ghost-like out of the hospital leaving behind doctors confused by the fact that he hasn't broken a single bone. He is accepted back into his family home by wife Audrey, who feels his survival is a sign they should give their faltering marriage another go, and adoring young son Joseph.

Before we meet Dunn, we're presented with some statistics about sales of comic books in America, and a 1961 prologue in which a black woman gives birth to a baby with such brittle bones that his arms and legs are broken during the delivery.

Elijah Price, nick-named 'Mr. Glass' at school, has grown up to be a strange combination of comic book geek, New Age zealot and crippled mastermind. Convinced that his own fragility represents one end of the spectrum of human possibilities, Elijah believes Dunn is his opposite, a real-life superhero archetype.

Many viewers won't be able to get past the premise, which means some audiences will treat the film as they would a real-life raving crank, but Shyamalan tackles his idea with almost no irony. Willis plays the realisation that he might be set apart from humanity with a quivering uncertainty, strikingly at odds with the bright-coloured glee of a Marvel or DC character.

The primal scene of Superman bouncing a bullet off his chest is rewritten as an amazing kitchen confrontation, as Joseph pulls the family gun on Dad (in front of Mum) in a desperate attempt to convince him that he really is unbreakable (surely Invulnerable would have been a more apt title).

Throughout, the film refers to comic book imagery – with Dunn's security guard slicker coming to look like a cape, and Price's gallery taking on elements of a Batcave-like lair – and the lectures on artwork and symbolism actually feed back into the plot.

The last act offers a terrific suspense-thriller scene (similar to the family-saving of *The Sixth Sense*), which is a self-contained sub-plot that slingshots a twist which may have been obvious all along. However, even those who can get past the 'Last Son of Krypton' plot may find the end unsatisfying, closing off developments rather than letting the premise expand into the mythic battle that is suggested. ★★★★ **KN**

⊙ UNCLE BUCK (1989)

Starring: *John Candy (Buck Russell), Jean Louisa Kelly (Tia Russell), Gaby Hoffman (Maizy Russell), Macaulay Culkin (Miles Russell), Amy Madigan (Chanice Kobolowski)*
Director: *John Hughes*
Screenwriter: *John Hughes*
PG/100 mins./Comedy/USA

It is with the greatest reluctance that Cindy Russell, lets her slobbish, unreliable brother-in-law Buck, babysit her three kids, after her father is hospitalised. Buck however will prove to be a revelation both to the kids and himself, as well as an unreliable slob.

A sort of cut-price *Parenthood* from the pen and megaphone of John Hughes, and thus is funny, sentimental and pointedly moral, made very easy on sensibilities thanks to the hulking congeniality of John Candy. It's the journey into adulthood once more that concerns glossy social commentator Hughes, here of a died-in-the-wool bachelor fully committed to the gospel of pizza and Bud, but through a rites-of-parental-passage will come to learn the value of family and pick up the tab on his faltering relationship with Amy Madigan.

Candy, who makes a charming asset out of his girth, works both ends of this trite deal considerably well. First, we have the trial by responsibility, as the big lummox causes mayhem in kitchen and laundry room. A fairly standard series of botched chores, turned into amusing skits by Buck's furious determination not to be the great oaf he clearly is. Pride, you see, is an issue. Naturally, the two small kids (one played by the still button-cute Macaulay Culkin from *Home Alone*) think he's like Santa Claus with a gambling habit. This, though, is above all things a Hughes parable, and we will need some teen angst to truly prove his mettle. So, Buck will rub up against eldest daughter Tia (Jean Louisa Kelly) currently detained by a regulation rebellious period. The main thrust of the movie seems to be the point these two will come to respect one another, and culminates in a decent sequence where Buck comes to her rescue with a power drill.

Tagline
He's crude.
He's crass.
He's family.

It all adheres to Hughes' limited worldview – that teens and families can be measured on some kind of sliding scale of good deeds and growing pains. Nonsense, basically, without any risk taking or taking up of the real potential for blacker comedy, but made beguiling and palatable by one of cinema's big-boned greats. ★★★ **IN**

UNDER CAPRICORN (1949)

Starring: *Ingrid Bergman (Lady Henrietta Flusky), Joseph Cotton (Sam Flusky), Michael Wilding (Hon. Charles Adare), Margaret Leighton (Mully), Cecil Parker (The Governor), Denis O'Dea (Mr Corrigan), Jack Watling (Winter), Harcourt Williams (The Coachman), John Ruddock (Mr. Potter), Bill Shine (Mr. Banks)*
Director: *Alfred Hitchcock*
Screenwriter: *James Bridie, based on the novel by Helen Simpson*
PG/117 mins./Drama/UK

Australia, 1831 and Charles Adare accompanies his governor uncle to Sydney and promptly falls for Lady Henrietta, the neglected Irish wife of ex-convict Samson Flusky, whose devoted housemaid Milly encourages her mistress's drinking in the hope of destroying the marriage.

Alfred Hitchcock's second outing for his Transatlantic Pictures company was adapted by the Scottish playwright James Bridie from a novel by Helen Simpson, who had co-written the 1929 thriller, *Enter Sir John*, on which Hitchcock had based *Murder*!.

Echoes of *Rebecca* reverberate through the action, as Ingrid Bergman's unhappy bride finds herself imprisoned in an imposing pile (whose name 'Minyago Yugilla' translates as 'Why Weepest Thou?') and imperilled by an envious domestic. But, despite the fact that *Under Capricorn* was Hitchcock's first British-made feature in a decade, it singularly failed to replicate the success of his Hollywood debut.

No sooner had Hitch arrived at Elstree Studios than an electricians' strike broke out and lingering resentments were exacerbated by his decision to shoot in complex long takes that placed additional pressure on the crew. The loss of a further fortnight to bad weather scarcely improved tempers and Hitchcock was then forced to complete the final scenes to a rigid deadline caused by the imminence of an incoming production. Having returned to Hollywood, Hitchcock and his partner Sidney Bernstein then squabbled via telegram over the cutting of the picture, which ended up costing $2.5 million.

Worse was to follow, however, as within days of the film's US opening, news broke of Bergman's adulterous affair with Roberto Rossellini (whom she had met during the shoot) and Catholic pressure groups demanded its immediate suppression. However, it was the bad press that caused the movie to flop and revert back to the bank that had financed it.

Yet, this acerbic historical is bleakly compelling. Jack Cardiff's Technicolor photography, Tom Morahan's sets, Roger Furse's costumes and John Addinsell's score were all splendid. Moreover, the action perfectly bore out Hitchcock's contention (which tellingly inverts Jean Renoir's belief that everyone has their reasons) that 'everything's perverted in a different way'. Thus, Henrietta has both beauty and a tendency to self-destruct; Flusky possesses decency, but no passion; Charles combines civility and covetousness; while Milly takes loyalty to the point where she's prepared to kill to prove it.

No classic, perhaps, but long overdue a critical re-evaluation. ★★★ **DP**

UNDER SIEGE (1992)

Starring: *Steven Seagal (Casey Ryback), Tommy Lee Jones (William Stannix), Gary Busey (Commander Krill), Erika Eleniak (Jordan Tate), Patrick O'Neal (Captain Adams)*
Director: *Andrew Davis*
Screenwriter: *J.F. Lawton*
15/98 mins./Action/Adventure/USA

***Die Hard* on a battleship with ex-Navy SEAL-cum-cook Steven Seagal heroically seeing off villains Tommy Lee Jones and Gary Busey who are hell-bent on pirating his ship's floating nuclear arsenal. Slam-bam no-brain entertainment.**

No one was pretending this was anything but a *Die Hard* rip-off styled to the, ahem, talents of Steve Seagal. Then, in the early 90s Segal had his place in the thinking of Hollywood, his stream of thick-headed action movies, mainly involving him kicking people and sneering (he has no other expression) with a voice that could be used to sandpaper logs, all made a decent amount of money. To challenge him would be to ruin him. Here is an actor totally unable to change gears, versatility an alien concept to the frozen features of his supercilious mug, vaguely reminiscent of a man permanently wearing a stocking mask. Perhaps, it is this supreme sense of nothing going on, that makes him seem so hard to beat. Here is not a man in up to his receding hairline like Bruce Willis' John McClane, but a man just waiting to kill some more people soon. Dangerously, you might want to consider that it is this reason why *Under Siege* is such fun.

That Tommy Lee Jones and Gary Busey are camping things up to high heaven as the villains certainly enables the film to have some characters. They play a pair of soured-American terrorists, bitching like old women, who seem to be named after plankton – Strannix and Krill. Erika Eleniak is purely on-hand as eye-candy, a fact announced by her topless entrance (one of cinema's most freeze-framed moments). And also, director Davis should take a lot of credit for mounting some gutsy action; blowing things up without letting it feel chaotic. He understands the rhythm of good brainless gung-ho, to build to the punch, and the chosen battleground, the USS *Alabama* dressed up as the USS *Missouri*, offers plenty of range for all the ensuing grappling.

We still all have to own up to the fact, it is not simply the fact this is such a professional piece of one-dimensional crap that gives it the kicks. There remains that something in Seagal's blank indomitability that veils the film in an efficient cool. You don't need to root for him – he's already won. It's an action film with all of the worry removed. No effort at all. ★★★ **IN**

UNFAITHFULLY YOURS (1948)

Starring: *Rex Harrison (Sir Alfred de Carter), Linda Darnell (Daphne de Carter), Barbara Lawrence (Barbara Henshler), Rudy Vallee (August Henshler), Kurt Kreuger (Anthony), Lionel Stander (Hugo Standoff), Edgar Kennedy (Detective Sweeney), Alan Bridge (House Detective)*
Director: *Preston Sturges*
Screenwriter: *Preston Sturges*
PG/105 mins./Comedy/USA

Convinced that his devoted wife, Daphne, is having an affair, conductor Sir Arthur de Carter envisions three ways of getting even while giving a concert. But each attempt at enacting his revenge goes horribly wrong.

Preston Sturges has been lionised by cinéastes, plagiarised by screenwriters and scrutinised by students. Yet he has never quite acquired the kudos of contemporaries like Ernst Lubitsch or Billy Wilder and part of the reason for this accidental anonymity lies with the critical and commercial failure of this structurally ambitious black comedy that, ironically, many have come to see as his masterpiece.

Sturges first conceived *The Symphony Story* in 1932 and it was hurriedly revived following the postponement of *The Beautiful Blonde from Bashful Bend* (1949). Known as *Improper Relations* and *Lover-in-Law* at various stages of its production, it came to reflect Sturges' own (equally specious) insecurities regarding his relationship with actress Frances

Movie Stars' First Jobs

TOP 10

1. Jim Carrey-Janitor
2. Sean Connery-Coffin polisher
3. Steven Spielberg-Fruit tree whitewasher
4. Danny DeVito-Hairdresser
5. Rob Schneider-Dishwasher at an ice cream parlour
6. Keanu Reeves-Skate sharpener at the local ice rink
7. Kevin Spacey-Stand-up comedian
8. Whoopi Goldberg-Makeup artist at a funeral parlour
9. Sylvester Stallone-Lion cage cleaner
10. Warren Beatty-Rat catcher

Ramsden, who was 24 years his junior. However, a back injury prevented her from taking a part that reached Linda Darnell via Gene Tierney, while Rex Harrison assumed the composite caricature of Sturges and Sir Thomas Beecham after James Mason discovered scheduling difficulties.

Neither star was considered box office and Fox chief Darryl F. Zanuck was hugely concerned that the average moviegoer wouldn't be able to follow the subtle shifts in perspective that accompanied Rossini's overture to *Semiramide*, Wagner's reconciliation theme from *Tannhäuser* and Tchaikovsky's opening to *Francesca da Rimini*.

Test screenings seemed to bear out his fears, with viewers either loving or loathing the dexterous blend of cultural satire, marital farce and unabashed slapstick. They were similarly divided on Harrison's deceptively easy switches from sneering and debonair to distraught and scheming and Darnell's ability to seem either devotedly innocent or coquettishly alluring depending on her husband's mood.

So, Zanuck personally supervised the excision of 20 minutes' footage. But the film was dealt a decisive blow when Harrison's mistress, Carole Landis, committed suicide and Fox decided that it would be in bad taste to distribute a comedy about a potential murder while its male star was embroiled in such a tragic, adulterous scandal. Consequently, this bold, erudite and hilariously macabre farce eventually emerged without the usual fanfare and promptly flopped, causing Sturges to lose his touch and spend his remaining decade unfulfilled in Europe. ★★★★ **DP**

UNFORGIVEN (1992)

Starring: *Clint Eastwood (William 'Bill' Munny), Gene Hackman (Little Bill Daggett), Morgan Freeman (Ned Logan), Richard Harris (English Bob), Frances Fisher (Strawberry Alice)*
Director: *Clint Eastwood*
Screenwriter: *David Webb Peoples*
15/131 mins./Western/USA

Awards – *Academy Awards – Best Supporting Actor (Gene Hackman), Best Director, Best Editing, Best Picture, BAFTA – Best Supporting Actor (Gene Hackman), Golden Globes – Best Director, Best Supporting Actor (Gene Hackman)*

Ageing gunman William Munny, recently widowed, is enticed into one last job to help a house of prostitutes wreak their revenge on a vicious cowboy who cut up the face of one of the girls. But violence takes its toll, even on the supposedly righteous.

In the end credit crawl of *Unforgiven* is a small note dedicating the film to 'Sergio and Don.' The message is clear: Eastwood's philosophical rumination on the history of the Old West is a paean to his mentors Sergio Leone and Don Siegal (the directors who created his iconic personas: The Man With No Name and Dirty Harry). It is a hymn to their legacy of uncompromising anti-heroism, and maybe a small prayer for forgiveness as he sets about re-evaluating their violent fantasy.

Blade Runner's David Webb Peoples wrote the script in 1976 when Eastwood picked it up discerning its resonance with his own career, ready to sit on it until he was old (and worn) enough to fit the bill for ageing William Munny, reformed killer, drawn back to his old ways by the lure of money and ultimately revenge. The set-up has an almost mundane practicality to it: a bounty set by vengeful prostitutes after one of their number has her face slashed by a drunk rancher. The sheriff of Big Whiskey, Little Bill (played with Oscar-wining class by the ineffable Gene Hackman) – raconteur, moralist, psychopath – faced with an influx of men of 'low character' clamps down hard.

Richard Harris, in a magnificent cameo, is English Bob, a pompous assassin dragging around a nervy biographer Beauchamp, who faces the full brutality of Bill's policing. Beauchamp finds himself purloined by the equally self-important sheriff – who gleefully dismantles his tales of rugged killers and their lethal habits.

The film plays a brilliant sleight-of-hand: it allows us to empathise with Munny, expectant he will rise into the Eastwood mould, but all the while a picture emerges of someone wholly despicable: 'a killer of women and children.' You accept it but don't defer your opinion, you still root for him unable to shed those preconceptions of history. Little Bill, ostensibly the villain, is a rigid upholder of the law – yet we come to despise his perverse moralism and misogyny.

Perceptions of heroism are constantly being muddied. Munny can barely mount his horse anymore, the young buck Sisco Kid who hounds him out of retirement is hopelessly myopic (he, too, has trouble seeing beyond the craggy legends of yore). Every act of violence carries an aftershock; the film is keen to assess the costs of killing as much for the killer as the victim. No-one dies clean: they struggle, whimpering to desultory, pathetic deaths (one is even shot taking a shit).

Cutting through the swaggering folklore upheld by Beauchamp's penny-dreadful novelettes (a metaphor for the glowing heroics of the old-school movie Western) murder is a costly business, it hurts, it drains the soul – there is an almost physical transformation in Munny as the darkness regains a hold and he becomes a cold-blooded murderer once more (the past has caught up with him, he is 'unforgiven'). In an extraordinary and pivotal scene, The Kid, drawing whiskey from an open bottle, finds it impossible to come to terms with the guilt that echoes from his actions (it transpires he is a virgin to the killing game).

With taciturn bluntness Munny cuts to the heart of the film's conscience. Munny: 'Hell of a thing, killin' a man. Take away all he's got and all he's ever gonna have.' Kid: 'Yeah, well, I guess he had it comin'.' Munny: 'We all got it comin', kid.' A man's sins will always catch up with him: we cannot escape ourselves. The climactic showdown is a sudden jolt from the measured solemnity that has come before it. Rasping and angry with whiskey coursing through his veins, Munny strides into the brothel where it all began to seek out Ned's killers and reap bloody revenge.

This is no glorious shoot-out but point blank assassination. But all the while Beauchamp's eyes continue to glitter as he begins to concoct legend out of truth. Which is exactly what most filmmakers have always done. Reputedly his swansong in the saddle, Eastwood has rent the veil of the Old

u

West, the mythological strata of America, to find something harder and truer.

This is a harsh, barbaric world striving to shape its future. It is also a fitting memoir to the myth-making of Eastwood's own career, here's an old man trying to let go of his past ('I ain't like that no more') but his past won't let go of him. *Unforgiven* won Best Film at the Oscars and Eastwood picked up Best Director. No one could argue. He had it coming. ★★★★★ **IN**

UNIVERSAL SOLDIER (1992)

Starring: *Jean-Claude Van Damme (Luc Deveraux/GR44), Dolph Lundgren (Andrew Scott/GR13), Ally Walker (Veronica Roberts), Ed O'Ross (Colonel Perry), Jerry Orbach (Dr. Christopher Gregor)*
Director: *Roland Emmerich*
Screenwriters: *Richard Rothstein, Christopher Leitch, Dean Devlin*
18/99 mins./Sci-fi/Action/Thriller/USA

Vietnam casualties Luc and Scott are resurrected by the government 23 years later and are turned into a killer anti-terrorist squad. But when their memories return Luc defects from the unit and psychopath Scott remembers a grudge from their 'Nam days and goes after his partner.

Take a pair of second-string hulks and give them the kind of budgetary back-up Arnie or Sly would expect, then set them loose on a script which mixes sci-fi, martial arts, exploding gas stations, sadistic wisecracks and post-Nam angst, and what you've got is *Universal Soldier*.

It opens in Vietnam in 1969 with a bleeding heart private scragging a psychopathic sergeant who has been collecting ears from innocent bystanders, then cuts to the present day when the deep-frozen dead have been revived for use in an experimental military programme whereby well-trained zombies are let loose with enormous weapons and deployed every time a terrorist incident threatens the integrity of the USA.

Naturally, a few wires get crossed and both the good and bad muscle-heads start reverting to their old personalities, Jean-Claude haring off across country with a lady journalist in tow in search of the truth about his resurrection, while Dolph slaughters all and sundry in an extended Nam flashback while giving out terrible one-liners ('I'm all ears') whenever he does anything especially violent.

Of course, while Jean-Claude – whose accent sounds more like something you'd expect from a soldier killed in Indochina in 1954 rather than Vietnam in 1969 – gets terribly sensitive en route to a reunion with his parents, Dolph, a foot and a hairstyle taller than the hero, gnashes his teeth at the prospect of a last-reel punch-up involving do-it-yourself steroids and a handy multi-pronged farm implement.

The action is interrupted only by pre-digested plot chunks and Linda Hamilton lookalike Ally Walker's fairly irritating hyperactivity, and both the he-men are given a chance to get away from their direct-to-video roots.

Van Damme, who is so proud of his bottom that he makes sure it appears in each of his films, does a sub-*RoboCop* bewildered act but cuts loose whenever he gets to show off his high kicks, while Lundgren, not really happy as the nice guy of his last few films, demonstrates that nature and his hairdresser have really cut him out to be a major Nazi genengineered baddie. Few Academy Awards but lots of ticket sales. ★★★ **KN**

UNITED 93 (2006)

Starring: *Ben Sliney, Christian Clemenson, Khalid Abdalla, Cheyenne Jackson, Trish Gates, Jamie Harding*
Director: *Paul Greengrass*
Screenwriter: *Paul Greengrass*
15/111 mins./Drama/History/France/UK/USA

September 11, 2001. Four planes are hijacked by extremist Muslim terrorists. As the world watches, two are flown into the World Trade Center, one into the Pentagon. But final plane United 93 never reaches its target in Washington DC, crashing in a field in Pennsylvania. This is a reconstruction of those events, and an account of how the passengers of United 93 took the tough decision to fight back.

During his live London stageshow in late 2002, controversy-baiting polemicist Michael Moore offered some rather disturbing reflections upon the events of 11 September the previous year. He pondered why nobody on either of the planes flown into the World Trade Center attempted to fight back – after all, they outnumbered their attackers, who were only armed with boxcutters. His conclusion? Most members of privileged Western society are too inclined to sit back and let the authorities sort it all out. Had either airliner been a plane-full of salt-of-the-earth miners or people from deprived inner-city areas, they would have fought back with little hesitation, Moore suggested.

'Unfair!' came the shouts of dissent from the stalls during the show's Q&A feedback session. And *United 93* director Paul Greengrass may as well have been among them. After all, wasn't it the passengers of that very flight – most of them, arguably, 'privileged' – who fought back as soon as they realised this wasn't a 'standard' hijack-and-make-demands affair, but rather an opening salvo in a terrifying new form of conflict? Of course, Moore wasn't merely trying to piss people off, he was intellectually tackling the awful events head-on. Similarly, Greengrass isn't out to antagonise, to deliberately solicit those cries of 'Too Soon!' which accompanied *United 93*'s Stateside trailer-screenings, but to try and, in his words, 'find meaning in the events of 9/11.'

In that sense, *United 93* makes an interesting companion piece to Moore's *Fahrenheit 9/11*. But where Moore focused on the slow and ultimately destructive Presidential knee-jerk, Greengrass deals with the 'real' people on the ground and in the air who had to make sense of the unthinkable and take tough, quick decisions. (Indeed, Dubya is notable only by his complete absence in Greengrass' film, with repeated references to everyone's inability to get a hold of him to confirm the 'rules of engagement'.)

The result is an astoundingly intense, pressure-cooker docudrama which plays out – horribly – in almost real-time. With its ugent handheld dynamic and nigh-on unbearable attention to mundane detail, this is reality that bites like a pitbull; we watch as the passengers of United 93 prepare to board at Gate 17, making final cellphone calls for the sake of killing time, politely avoiding eye-contact and smalltalking in the semi-hushed tones of the mildly tense air-commuter – all alongside the men who will ultimately kill them – and the feel of dread is so palpable as to make us nauseous.

Which hardly recommends Greengrass' movie as a night-out's entertainment. Because entertainment it most certainly is not. So what *is* its value? Is this really the IMPORTANT work its makers have insisted? Whether or not it's been made 'too soon' isn't really the point. The real question is: need it have been made at all? What precisely do we *learn* here?

Well, as an historical document which should be properly contextualised and handled with due care by future generations, it has plenty of value. Its most interesting moments take place in the various air-traffic and military command centres, as we watch while the realisation of what's happening hits. If there's a 'star' here, it's Federal Aviation Administration boss Ben Sliney (playing himself, no less), whose efforts to kick the military into gear, and his snap decision to ground more than 4,000 aircraft in the skies over the Eastern seaboard – all on his first day on the job – prove deeply impressive.

Then there's the film's arguable value as catharsis, giving us an unblinking, up-close portrayal of what it was like to be one of those passengers. These everyday people, each portrayed by a virtual unknown without a glimmer of fakeness, grasp the true gravity of their situation, make final calls to loved ones, organise a counter-attack and, while losing their own lives in the process, very possibly save countless others. Interestingly, despite all their families being behind this film, they're not presented as all-American heroes; rather, their primary concern appears to be self-preservation and, come the strike-back, there's almost a primal rush to be the first to put the boot in.

Yet in terms of provoking thought, *United 93* does fall short in one area: its presentation of the Al Qaeda hijackers. It opens with their mumblings of the Koran, boldly juxtaposes their prayers with those of the terrified passengers, and intriguingly makes the first line of translated terrorist dialogue, 'I love you' (via one of those departure lounge cellphone-calls). But in terms of trying to make sense of *why* this atrocity occurred, of what the hell was going on in their fundamentalist brains – very possibly the most crucial question of all – it achieves little. Perhaps we should add this year's Foreign Language Oscar-winner *Paradise Now* as a viewing companion. While an inferior movie to *United 93*, it at least offers more insight into where and how the kind of people responsible for 9/11 are formed. ★★★★★**DJ**

THE UNTOUCHABLES (1987)

Starring: *Kevin Costner (Eliot Ness), Sean Connery (Jim Malone), Charles Martin Smith (Agent Oscar Wallace), Andy Garcia (Agent George Stone), Robert De Niro (Al Capone)*
Director: *Brian De Palma*
Screenwriter: *David Mamet*
15/114 mins./Crime/Drama/USA

Awards – *Acacdemy Awards – Best Supporting Actor (Sean Connery), BAFTA – Best Score, Golden Globes – Best Supporting Actor (Sean Connery)*

Federal Agent Eliot Ness sets out to take out Al Capone; because of rampant corruption, he assembles a small, hand-picked team.

At the height of Prohibition, in 1930s America, Chicago was presided over by one Alfonso Capone. He ruled the town by the might of his fist, from the illegal speakeasy rackets right up through the ranks of the police and judicial system, holding them in thrall through bribery and blackmail. That was until the arrival of Eliot Ness, the incorruptible treasury agent assigned the role of bringing the Italian gangster to book. Faced with rank corruption, he surrounded himself with a team of cops dedicated to the cause: 'the Untouchables'. This is all bona fide history, a series of events that were finally drawn to a close when the psychotic mobster – himself seemingly untouchable – was finally snared for simple tax evasion. He died of syphilis eight years after his release from prison.

Eschewing any attempt at historical accuracy (although the last surviving real-life Untouchable Albert H. Wolff acted as an advisor) De Palma chose to reinterpret the Robert Stack television series of the early 60s rather than the actual events. This is a morally blunt comic-book world more akin to Western traditions than the complex milieu of gangsters. Yet, within its own context, *The Untouchables* is richly rewarding. It fuses the grandiose style of its director with a cool mix of established names (Connery, De Niro) and new stars (Costner, Garcia) and a feistily-exaggerated script from David Mamet ('Just like a Wop to bring a knife to a gunfight') to recreate history on a movie template. Big, bold, and hugely entertaining.

Sean Connery deservedly won an Oscar for his portrayal of (fictional) beat-cop Jim Malone who instils the requisite street-wisdom in Ness to defeat Capone – play him at his own game. Ebullient and wry, he wraps the Connery gravitas in an earthier, harder cloth. So convinced was De Palma that De Niro would turn him down for Capone, that he actually signed a deal with Bob Hoskins to take the role, having to pay him off ($200,000) when the Italian method genius assented. And in typical fashion, he gained weight, slicked back his hair and, in a relatively short amount of screen time, managed to charge the film with exuberant menace ('I'm talkin' about enthusiasms . . .' he sneers before smashing the brains out of a fumbling minion with a baseball bat). Costner was offered less: Ness is painted in strict lines – happily married, motivated by decency, leading by example – but the all-American masculinity with which he thrives fits the character like a glove.

The film has a pristine sense of place, a 1930s Chicago classify upholstered like a grand opera. Inverting the moralistic colours of tradition, the bad guys wear the white suits (especially depicted in Capone henchman Nitti's all-white get-up) and the heroes black. Much was made of Giorgio Armani designing the suits – a kind of functioning product placement – but De Niro, in fact, had suits knocked up by the very same tailors who made Capone's actual bespoke numbers. It is a world of tight lines, angular sets of doorways and windows as if in a comic strip (not a million miles from the stylized artifice of Warren Beatty's *Dick Tracy*). Meanwhile, the god-like Ennio Morricone infuses the spirit of the age with a heart-quickening score that drives the drama like an express train.

De Palma, ever the trickster even with mainstream material, delights in the flamboyance of his set-pieces. A sly POV shot of the assassin tracking Malone through his apartment spirals out into a glorious juxtaposition of a bloody, dying Malone crawling for safety, cross-cut with Capone's hypocritical tears to the strains of *I Pagliacci* at the Chicago opera. Most celebrated (justly) is the director's 'homage' to *Battleship Potemkin*'s Odessa Steps sequence. Set at Chicago's Union Station; where the remaining Untouchables gather to snatch Capone's bookkeeper out of a hail of bullets a pram tortuously bounces down a staircase in glorious slo-mo, it is an unforgettable slice of flashiness and pointed film history (if nothing else it brought the name Eisenstein to popcorn consumers). And, of course, there is De Palma's ever-present obsession with Hitchcock, with a facsimile of *Foreign Correspondent* in a shot of the good guys flying north in a twin-prop plane, a chase up a spiral staircase (a habitual motif) playing *Vertigo*, and the small girl blown to smithereens at the very beginning references the boy on a bus with a bomb from *Sabotage*.

The Untouchables is easily the most accessible of De Palma's work and remains (with the exception of *Mission: Impossible*) his most commercially successful movie. In stark contrast to the other gangster movies on show here, it is less concerned with the complex fabric of the crime unit than the earnest endeavours of the good guys. Bizarrely, this makes it a guilty pleasure. ★★★★ **IN**

URBAN LEGEND (1998)

Starring: *Alicia Witt (Natalie), Jared Leto (Paul), Rebecca Gayheart (Brenda), Michael Rosenbaum (Parker), Loretta Devine (Reese), Joshua Jackson (Damon), Robert Englund (Professor Wexler)*
Director: *Jamie Blanks*
Screenwriter: *Silvio Horta*
18/95 mins./Horror/Thriller/USA

A group of students studying urban legends are murdered one by one in very similar circumstances to the stories they discuss.

It was inevitable that once *Scream* set the teen horror bandwagon rolling, inferior rehashes would follow. To wit, *Urban Legend*, a film that takes the attractive young cast and bloody set pieces that initially attracted the punters to the *Scream* series, yet jettisons all the wit and style that made the Craven/ Williamson collaboration so distinctive.

It centres on Paul, Natalie, Brenda and their pals at university who all sit around and discuss urban legends – the modern ghost stories just about everyone has heard some variation on. Many of these variations stem from their rather over-zealous lecturer Professor Wexler (the inevitable Robert Englund). He teaches a class in Urban Legends revealing that this campus has its own legend – years before a killer went on a rampage through a now closed dorm building, killing several students along the way. Now it looks like the killer's back, and our attractive young cast are page one in his Most Likely To Get Butchered yearbook.

Despite a strong reputation for his early short movies, director Blanks delivers a wholly pedestrian feature debut in this by-numbers teen horror flick that could give you the impression *Scream* never really happened. (True, not all horror movies have to be ironic now but qualities like original or clever wouldn't go amiss). As ever with these movies, there's the odd impressive decapitation or blood-curdling dismemberment – John Neville's punctured Dean being just about the best – and while some of the cast, particularly Witt, are fresh-faced and appealing, Englund really has outstayed his welcome in the genre. At best, it could do for the fur-trimmed parka what *I Know What You Did Last Summer* did for the sou'wester, but that's about it. ★ **KN**

⊙ THE USUAL SUSPECTS (1995)

Starring: *Stephen Baldwin (Michael McManus), Gabriel Byrne (Dean Keaton), Benicio Del Toro (Fred Fenster), Kevin Pollak (Todd Hockney), Kevin Spacey (Roger 'Verbal' Kint), Chazz Palminteri (Dave Kujan), Pete Postlethwaite (Kobayashi)*
Director: *Bryan Singer*
Screenwriter: *Christopher McQuarrie*
18/106 mins./Crime/Thriller/Mystery/USA

Awards – *Academy Awards – Best Supporting Actor, Best Original Screenplay, BAFTA – Best Editing, Best Film, Best Original Screenplay, Empire – Best Debut (Bryan Singer)*

Five villains in New York are rounded up by police in an unconventional manner that worries them. After release, they get together for a spot of revenge, but someone else is controlling events.

The Usual Suspects arrived wearing a tag that read 'This year's *Reservoir Dogs*' but rapidly asserted its own identity and reputation. That was appropriate, since the core of this cracking cinematic confidence trick concerns the identification of a criminal mastermind and archfiend of spectacularly evil repute: who is Keyser Soze? The only real similarity between *Suspects* and *Dogs* is that five criminals are brought together to pull off a job snatching jewels. And there are shoot-'em-ups.

In the event, *The Usual Suspects* was so different from any other thriller of the 90s that cultdom beckoned instantly. With its mind-bogglingly convoluted plotting, Bryan Singer's confident, moody, stylish direction and the macho repartee ('Want a buckshot shampoo, chubby?'), this is an intrigue you love at first sight – unless you are infuriated by its being so very smugly clever and twisting and full of tricks. The greatest trick the filmmakers pulled was convincing audiences they had to see the film again, immediately. The illusion is that repeated viewing can unravel the mystery to complete satisfaction. The disillusion is that no matter how many times you see it, it doesn't make much more sense. The final shock twist revelation, a staggering blow to any and all expectations, makes the preceding 100 minutes even more unfathomable a tangled web of deceptions if you try to reason it out. It is more enjoyable not to try too hard.

Just accept that screenwriter Christopher McQuarrie, who won the Oscar, and Singer are a pair of smarty-pants, and enjoy the rollercoaster ride they engineered with such evident glee. To criticise them severely for being too clever is harsh, since successfully conning generally savvy, seen-it-all audiences is a rare feat. Terrific, enthralling viewing experiences are not necessarily neat and tidy; remember that no one, including novelist Raymond Chandler and his screen adapter William Faulkner, could ever remember or work out who the heck was supposed to have killed the chauffeur in *The Big Sleep* (1946).

Instead of being deceptively simple, this is deceptively complex. Five criminals with widely diverse rap sheets are brought together in a police holding cell to appear in a line-up. As it happens, none of them was involved with the crime for which they have been arrested: supposedly. The chance meeting, however, inspires them to pool their talents for a job. As befits a film premise inspired by an idea McQuarrie got (while standing in a cinema queue!) for the poster image (five guys in a line-up), everything hinges on this introductory gathering of the men. 'You don't put guys like that into a room together. Who knows what can happen?' Indeed.

Dean Keaton is an ex-cop, ex-con with a heavy rep for corruption, murder and faking his own death before re-emerging and going straight as a slick businessman with the support of his lawyer girlfriend Edie. McManus (Baldwin in his best role) is a 'top-notch entry man' and one hell of a shot. When later he lines up seven targets in his rifle sighting he scoffs, 'Oswald was a fag'. Fenster (Puerto Rican hunk Benicio Del Toro affecting a hilariously incomprehensible, mush-mouthed speech pattern) is his weirdo partner. Todd Hockney is 'good with explosives'. And Verbal 'Roger really, people say I talk too much' Kint (Spacey, seizing his first Oscar and vaulting to hottest character actor pre-eminence with this display) is 'a short con operator' and the loquacious cripple whose narrative is the thread to which we are directed to cling on to.

A hip, urban *Rashomon* (1950) with staccato bursts of violent, beautifully choreographed action, the film opens in 'San Pedro, California – last night' on a scene of carnage in which a mystery man in a suit executes Keaton. This 'objective' sequence will recur, revised, as Verbal's account and, reworked again, as the scene imagined by his dogged interrogator, Federal agent Dave Kujan, who is too fixated on his own theory of what transpired to 'stand back from it' and 'look at it right'. The viewer makes the same mistake, misdirected to participate rather than witness, to misjudge any version or sequence of events as objective and truthful. Very early on, when massacre survivor Verbal takes Kujan back to when, 'It all started back in New York six weeks ago...' Keaton is suspicious: 'There's no way they'd line five felons in the same row, no way.' This is a key point, but he lets it go and it isn't recalled until a second heist has proved a set-up and homicidal fiasco, delivering the profanely fretting crew into the hands of calmly menacing 'Limey' lawyer Kobayashi (Postlethwaite brazening out a transparently phoney moniker if ever there was one). He makes them an offer they can't refuse from the mysterious Mr. Soze. Singer delights in wizard sleights-of-hand, like camera dissolves into a swirling cup of coffee and a thrilling elevator shaft assassination that make one almost utterly forgetful of loose ends (if Soze's pathologically elaborate charade had the stated objective it's failed because that burn victim babbling in Hungarian in Intensive Care can supposedly identify him).

Tagline
Five criminals. One line-up. No coincidence.

The considerable contribution of John Ottman, performing the unusual double of deftly editing labyrinthine puzzle scenes and composing the brooding score, shouldn't be underestimated either. The ultimate accolade is that one can't say the film 'doesn't hold up' on seeing it again, and again. It doesn't add up, it doesn't hold true, but it remains a madly captivating bafflement. ★★★★★ **AE**

Gaps between orignal movie and sequel*

1. *The Wizard of Oz* (1939) to *Return to Oz* (1985) ... 46 years
2. *The Hustler* (1961) to *The Color Of Money* (1986) ... 25 years
3. *Carrie* (1976) to *The Rage: Carrie 2* (1999) ... 24 years
4. *Superman II* (1980) to *Superman Returns*† (2006) ... 26 years
5. *Psycho* (1960) to *Psycho 2* (1983) ... 23 years
6. *The Last Picture Show* (1971) to *Texasville* (1990) ... 19 years
7. *Chinatown* (1974) to *The Two Jakes* (1990) ... 16 years
8. *A Man And A Woman* (1966) to *A Man And A Woman, 20 Years Later* ... 20 years
9. *The Decline Of The American Empire* (1986) to *The Barbarian Invasions* (2003) ... 17 years
10. *Star Wars Episode III* (2005) and *Star Wars Episode IV* (1977) ... -28 years

*Not counting straight-to-DVD sequels

†It ignores III and IV, as should you

u

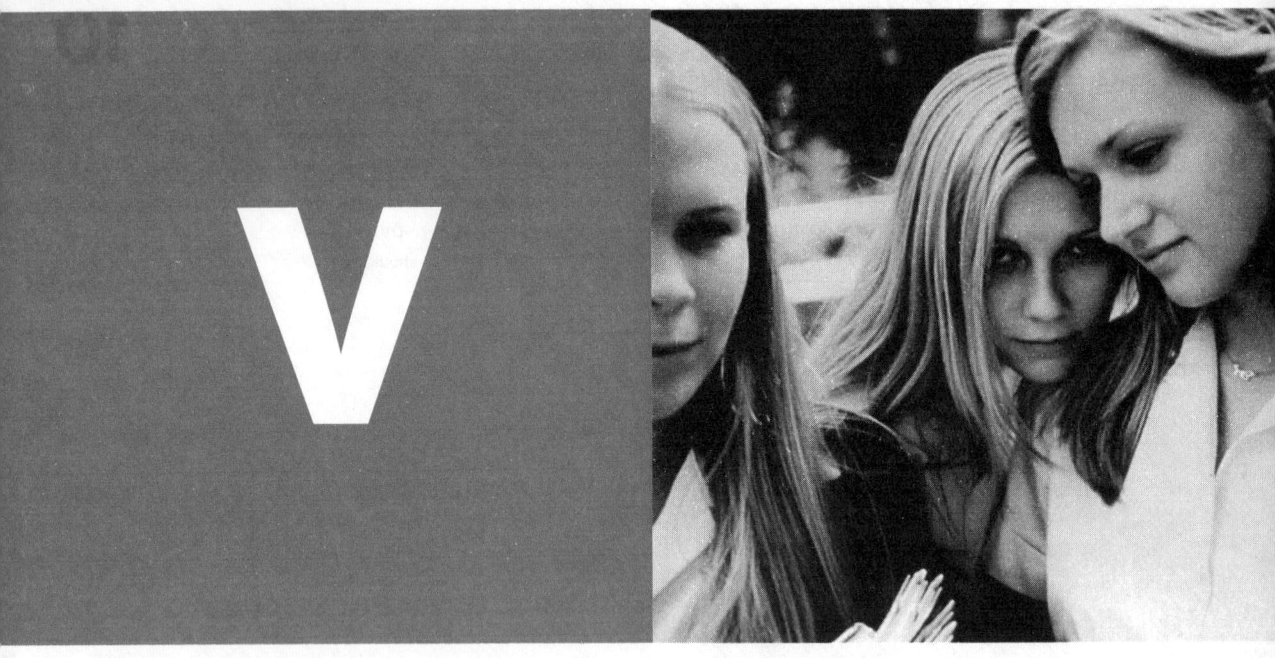

V FOR VENDETTA (2006)

Starring: *Natalie Portman (Evey), Hugo Weaving (V), Stephen Rea (Finch), Stephen Fry (Dietrich), John Hurt (Adam Sutler), Tim Pigott-Smith (Creedy), Rupert Graves (Dominic)*
Director: *James McTeigue*
Screenwriters: *Andy Wachowski, Larry Wachowski*
15/132 mins./Sci-fi/Thriller/USA/Germany

In the not-too-distant future, Britain has become a fascist, totalitarian state, its population cowed and apathetic. But the nation receives a wake-up call when mysterious masked terrorist 'V' blows up the Old Bailey and calls for the citizens to rise up against their oppressors.

Graphic novelist Alan Moore hasn't had much luck with the movie adaptations of his work: *The League Of Extraordinary Gentlemen* was downright risible and *From Hell* deeply so-so, while *Watchmen* – Moore's masterpiece – has stalled, spluttering somewhere in the pre-production netherworld. Or rather, it's fans of Alan Moore who haven't had much luck with movie adaptations of his work. The man himself has given up caring, and is so uninterested in this take on his 80s serial *V For Vendetta* that he declined any involvement and ordered his name off the credits. The irony being, this is the best Moore-to-big-screen translation yet.

Which does sound horribly like faint praise. But what marks *V* out from its Moore-ish predecessors is that it's been far less compromised by bottom-line concerns.

So much so that the result is decidedly uncommercial. Despite the trailer's promise of slo-mo action scenes with swooshing knives pirouetting through the air while bullet casings bounce artfully off concrete, this is no teen-pleasing slam-banger. Rather it's a very talky, deliberately paced political thriller; yes, V is handy with a stiletto, but said scenes occupy fewer than five minutes of screen time, while his preferred method of assassination is lethal injection; no need to draft in Yuen Wo-Ping to assist with that.

We have a protagonist whose face – eyes included – is hidden beneath an inexpressive Guy Fawkes mask throughout and who packs his lengthy monologues with as many multi-syllabled words as possible. We have a leading lady who spends half the film with an unflattering skinhead. And we have a plot which makes a hero of a man who wears bomb-belts and makes his political points turning major landmarks into fireworks displays.

That all these landmarks are found in London arguably makes *V For Vendetta* an even trickier sell in the UK. One sequence involves a tube train carriage packed with explosives... That's not going to go down well with a fair chunk of British cinemagoers. Yet we shouldn't get too hot under the collar, as all this is taking place in a nightmare UK of the future – a *Daily Mail* heaven of a nation, if you like: God-fearing, racially 'pure' and purged of all its sexual 'deviants'. In Moore's comics, this society was a post-apocalyptic reflection of Thatcher's Britain, Moore's way of launching a simplistic left-wing attack on the then-seemingly unyielding Conservative power-grip. In his world, the only justifiable response was that of an enlightened anarchist, a Fawkes for the modern era. Moore's *V For Vendetta*, Moore's politics, were firmly rooted in the 80s (where the writer obviously wants them to stay).

The Wachowskis' version is post-9/11 and proud of it. Their Britain is portrayed as a potential end-point for the current reactionary trend towards the restriction of personal liberty and for the Western media's fear-frenzy; avian flu and anti-Muslim sentiment are both mentioned while, crucially, V is never referred to as an anarchist, only as a terrorist. Still, the Fawkes parallels are played up (a prologue outlining the Gunpowder Plot has been included for the benefit of American audiences) and the brothers remain respectful of the material they're playing with; indeed, the comic's most powerful episode – we don't want to give it away; suffice to say it involves Natalie Portman's *Alien3* 'do – survives largely intact, providing one of the heftiest gut-punches you'll see in a movie this year.

Yet the film does have its problems. Debut helmer James McTeigue (former first assistant director to the Wachowskis and George Lucas) doesn't quite recapture the grimy, neo-Dickensian feel that characterised the comic, his future Britain largely looking rather plain and everyday – perhaps the point, but it leaves the picture feeling somewhat bereft of style. And while physically good casting for Evey, the doe-eyed innocent who has to conquer her fears just as the populace should to overwhelm their oppressors, Portman's accent flounders, trembling painfully at every vowel enunciation.

Opposite her, though, Hugo Weaving proves compelling as V, even if his performance is largely vocal. He has some clumsy moments to deal with (V's overly alliterative entrance speech is a dire scripting mis-step), but he overcomes them to make this borderline psychotic vigilante a memorable and unsettlingly charismatic anti-hero. Alan Moore may be snubbing Weaving's vicious cabaret, but that doesn't mean everyone else should. ★★★★ DJ

Movie Trivia: *V For Vendetta*

The domino scene, where Evey tips over dominoes to form a giant V, involved 22,000 dominoes and took 200 hours to set up. Natalie Portman worked with the same dialogue coach as Gwyneth Paltrow to perfect her English accent. James Purefoy was originally cast as V but was replaced by Hugo Weaving.

THE VALLEY OF GWANGI (1969)

Starring: *James Franciscus (Tuck Kirby), Gila Golan (T.J. Breckenridge), Richard Carlson (Champ Connors), Laurence Naismith (Prof. Horace Bromley), Freda Jackson (Tia Zorina)*
Director: *Jim O'Connolly*
Screenwriters: *William Bast, Julian More based on a story* Valley Of The Mist *by Willis H. O'Brien*
U/96 mins./Fantasy/USA

A team of cowboys, led by the impresario figure Tuck Kirby, capture a Tyrannosaurus Rex in a hidden valley in Mexico. They then decide to reveal it as the chief attraction in their circus with very bad results.

Jurassic Park with cowboys, or when Ray Harryhausen went West, what we have here is yet another fantasy action flick displaying that artist's remarkable talents for stop-motion creatures, intermingled with B-movie actors, that is otherwise fairly predictable hokum. There is the chance to locate an amusing double reading here about cowboy showmen looking for the biggest spectacle ever – something of a satire on Hollywood perhaps? But it's not really a film with subtlety or double-meanings on its mind, it's a film about the perils of keeping a pet dinosaur in a confined space. As people should know, it's just not fair.

And for those viewers who harbour a secret love for crackpot matinee madness such as this, it does enough to satisfy your lust for B-movie preposterousness. For one thing the Valley Of Gwangi, as in the locale of mystical creatures down Mexico way, is guarded over by some eco-conscious gypsies, who have classified the place as Forbidden. These conniving cowboys should know better. And you just know, once the T-Rex has been caught these gypsies will infiltrate the circus...

In real terms, that is real fantasy terms, falls short of *Clash Of The Titans* and *Jason And The Argonauts*, but still hosts some impressive fusion of stop-motion dinosaur and the real-life footage, but the acting is low grade even on this level, and the story far less intriguing than those recreations of bits and pieces of Greek legend. Director Jim O'Connolly is aiming to paraphrase the great passions of *King Kong*, but falls a long way short, but the final scenes of the dinosaur loose in a giant cathedral have an operatic quality that belies the thinness of the premise. ★★★ IN

VAN HELSING (2004)

Starring: *Hugh Jackman (Van Helsing), Kate Beckinsale (Anna Valerious), Richard Roxburgh (Count Vladislaus Dracula), Shuler Hensley (Frankenstein's Monster), Samuel West (Dr. Victor Frankenstein), Robbie Coltrane (Mr. Hyde)*
Director: *Stephen Sommers*
Screenwriter: *Stephen Sommers*
12A/130 mins./Action/Adventure/Horror/USA

Transylvania, late 19th century. Vatican-sponsored monster hunter Gabriel Van Helsing teams up with gypsy princess Anna Valerious to thwart Dracula, who is planning to unleash his evil spawn with the aid of Frankenstein's Monster and The Wolf Man.

Universal had a lot riding on *Van Helsing*. Aside from a tentpole $150 million summer blockbuster (and any potential sequels), the DVD reissue of the classic horror flicks, a computer game, a theme park ride, an animated prequel and a planned TV series were all to live or die by a mass audience embracing Stephen Sommers' monster mash-up.

Which might go some way to explaining why Sommers' follow-up to his *Mummy* pictures tries so damn hard to entertain: a blitzkrieg of CG monsters, voluptuous production values and Alan Silvestri musical bombast, the result reaches overload very quickly, squandering the potentially cool premise in a headlong assault of set-piece over story – and so killing many of the premature plans for the franchise.

Sommers sets his Cinema Of Excess manifesto from the outset, beginning with two prologues: the first a strikingly realised, black-and-white backstory for Dracula and pals – Sommers throws in every classic Universal trope, from Gothic castles, to angry villagers, to torchlight processions within the first two minutes – the second, the end of a previous Van Helsing mission in which Van The Man sees off Mr. Hyde in a full-on smackdown.

Yet rather than slowing down, we are thrown onto a runaway juggernaut of Event Sequences – Dracula's winged brides strafe Anna's village! The Wolf Man attacks! An escape by horse and carriage! Etc. etc. – that makes *Temple Of Doom* look like Tarkovsky.

There is an inescapable feeling that if Sommers had the confidence to jettison some of his action licks – do we really need to see our heroes swing across a CG castle so many times? – and put in some pauses for breath and character, Van Helsing would have been a much less wearing, more fulfilling experience.

Compounding the repetitive feel, the plot has a cyclical structure in which the events of the first half – Van Helsing must stop Dracula using The Wolf Man as a battery to revitalise his evil spawn – are practically repeated verbatim in the second half – Van Helsing must stop Dracula using Frankenstein's Monster as a battery to revitalise his evil spawn.

Potential points of affecting human drama – Van Helsing and Anna's growing attraction, Frankenstein's Monster's desire to live and the backstory between Van Helsing and Dracula – are squandered in the rush for the next pixel-packed punch.

Perhaps the biggest casualties of this kitchen sink-and-all mentality are the cast. Jackman, who, on paper, is the perfect modern matinée idol, is denied a single moment to inject character into his character, the minimal dialogue scenes tooled solely to forward what passes for a plot.

Adopting a borderline-camp East European accent, Beckinsale can do little with her vengeful vampire slayer. Only Richard Roxburgh is given space to etch a character, his Dracula, all flamboyant tics and hissy fits, coming on like a bassist from some defunct New Romantic outfit.

As a director, Sommers orchestrates with maximum hustle and bustle, his computer-controlled camera swooping and soaring with the winged Brides Of Dracula, his editing strategies juxtaposing storylines at a dizzying rate. But he has none of the relentless logic or beautifully-crafted artistry of a Zemeckis or Cameron.

Moreover, he has little idea how to develop dread or cultivate creepiness. For all its purported relationship to its fêted horror forebears, *Van Helsing* does not offer up anything like a genuine chill. ★★ IF

Ⓓ VANILLA SKY (2001)

Starring: *Tom Cruise (David Aames), Penelope Cruz (Sofia Serrano), Cameron Diaz (Julie Gianni), Kurt Russell (McCabe), Jason Lee (Brian Shelby), Noah Taylor (Edmund Ventura), Timothy Spall (Thomas Tipp)*
Director: *Cameron Crowe*
Screenwriter: *Cameron Crowe, from the film* Open Your Eyes *by Alejandro Amenábar, Mateo Gil*
15/130 mins./Fantasy/Thriller/USA

Charmed and charming David Aames, the princely heir to a publishing empire, is utterly captivated by Spanish dancer Sofia, to the distress of his carelessly discarded lover, Julie. The fateful consequences hurl him into a labyrinthine mystery of love, murder, conspiracy and revenge. But which of his memories are real, which a dream?

Tom Cruise loses his looks and his mind in Cameron Crowe's much-anticipated cover version of Alejandro Amenábar's 1997 psychological thriller, *Open Your Eyes*. The character of David Aames is effectively Jerry Maguire on a bad acid trip, with disfigurement and hallucinatory alienation wiping that winning, signature smirk off his face after the crisis.

Cruise is in fact more impossibly gorgeous than ever, between affecting stints brooding in a blank mask and tormented under remarkable prosthetics, and Crowe is confident enough in our continuing delight in looking at him to attempt his darkest, most ambitious and artiest work to date. Thankfully, speculative philosophy comes with haunting visual flourish and profundity is leavened with poignance and flashes of Crowe's customary warmth and humour.

To say much about the plot would be as cruel as the nightmarishly bizarre and relentlessly unsettling events that beset the protagonist, since much of the compelling intrigue and emotional impact come from putting some work into fathoming what is happening. Let it suffice to say that David is worn down from a cocksure man-about-town to a complete physical and mental wreck, fearful of 'inviting happiness in without a full body search'.

It's all carefully composed with suggestive references and allusions, alternating layers of dream, reality and confessional flashback related by the masked David to his understandably riveted psychologist (Russell, serving well as a baffled, tenacious interrogator on behalf of the audience).

Cruz, reprising her role from the Spanish original, meets the requirement of being enchanting, Diaz as 'the saddest woman to ever hold a martini' is unnervingly nuanced between perky seductiveness and menace, and the unbalancing act is sustained by a strong supporting cast that includes Timothy Spall, Noah Taylor and Tilda Swinton.

From the eerie opening sequence, Crowe and cinematographer John Toll use New York like an autumnal fairytale realm, with Monet skies and clues to the truth sprinkled through the set decoration. As usual Crowe's use of music (wife Nancy Wilson's score, interwoven with the likes of Dylan, R.E.M., Radiohead and a title song composed by Paul McCartney) adds bonus dividends.

No matter how sarcastically envious men might summarize the central character's problems – hmmm, Cruz or Diaz? Gosh, that would be torture – only a churl could find no sympathy with his guilt-wracked ordeal. ★★★★ AE

Ⓓ THE VANISHING (SPOORLOS) (1988)

Starring: *Bernard-Pierre Donnadieu (Raymond Lemorne), Gene Bervoets (Rex Hoffman), Johana ter Steege (Saskia Wagter), Gwen Eckhaus (Lieneke)*
Director: *George Sluizer*
Screenwriters: *George Sluizer, Tim Krabbe based on Krabbe's novel* The Golden Egg
12/107 mins./Thriller/

Three years after the disappearance of his girlfriend from a service station, the still-obsessed Rex Hoffman receives some postcards from someone who claims to be her abductor, saying that he is willing to reveal what happened to her. The writer, Raymond Lemorne, however, is playing a horribly sinister game.

A fantastically gripping and ultimately hugely disturbing Dutch thriller built around the very human torment of uncertainty – the agony of not knowing. It is also one successful enough to reap a chance to be remade, with its director intact, in Hollywood employing Jeff Bridges and Kiefer Sutherland over the local originals. A version that foolishly soft-peddles the story's grand reveal.

While there are the thriller staples of the psycho and the innocent kids under threat, George Sluizer is intent on investigating the psychological impulses inherent in both villain and survivor. Bernard-Pierre Donnadieu's Raymond is man divorced from emotion, and in his own head therefore, culpability for his actions or compassion for his fellow man. Yet, in a sickeningly eerie development, he has what seems a perfectly normal family life, with Sluzier focusing on the mundanity of his existence while we know he is on a chilling quest – the same as his director, to investigate how people deal with uncertainty and fear, to reduce his horrific, sociopathic actions to a science. It is a form of God-complex, we come to understand, a chance to break free of the predestination drummed into him as a child. In an about-face from usual thriller principles, such motives are revealed early on, it is his actions that will be kept secret, ready to spring on us with stunning precision.

As the dupe, the tortured man desperate at least to understand to get closure on the loss of his girlfriend, Gene Bervoets' Rex is a mess of fragged emotion, he is so weak, he becomes putty in Raymond's cold hands. And, amid grey, mordant images, an ordinary world harbouring deep, deep levels of menace, the film will wend its way to a conclusion that has become legend. The answer to what happened, impossible for us to reveal here, is devastating for character and watcher alike, enough to send you reeling, and to flood your nightmares with some very primal panics. Be warned. ★★★★ IN

Ⓓ VANITY FAIR (2005)

Starring: *Reese Witherspoon (Becky Sharp), Romola Garai (Amelia Sedley), Rhys Ifans (Dobby), James Purefoy (Rawdon Crawley), Gabriel Byrne (The Marquess of Steyne)*
Director: *Mira Nair*
Screenwriters: *Matthew Faulk, Mark Skeet, Julian Fellowes, based on the novel by William Makepeace Thackeray*
PG/141 mins./Drama/Comedy/USA/UK

Impoverished, ambitious Becky Sharp relies on her wits and good looks to move up through early 19th century society. Her fortunes become entangled with those of her genteel best friend Amelia Sedley, but when her plot to marry Amelia's brother fails she moves on to a titled family, hoping for better luck . . .

Once in a while, a film is announced that appears to have Oscar written all over it. Like Mira 'Monsoon Wedding' Nair's *Vanity Fair*, with its script by *Gosford Park* Academy Award-winner Julian Fellowes, which gives box office darling Reese Witherspoon a chance to show what she can really do. Despite the impressive pedigree, though, this take on William Makepeace Thackeray's satirical novel is flat and misguided.

It's not really like the world was crying out for another version – so far there have been six movies and three mini-series, and none of them have seared their way into the public consciousness in the way *Pride And Prejudice* has. 1935's *Becky Sharp*, starring Miriam Hopkins, at least had the distinction of being the first movie ever produced in Technicolor. This will go down in history, or rather probably won't, as the one with all that Indian stuff in it.

Nair's vision was to create a colonial Britain under the spell of the Raj, and Indian culture infuses many scenes. This new spirit is celebrated in the plot's parties – a picnic at Vauxhall is wild with monkeys and flowers, while a dance for royalty turns into a Bollywood-style production number. But all this rather dwarfs the plot. Look elsewhere for a primer guide to the text, as here it's truncated to the point of nonsense. What's more, while Becky's history spans 30 years, the characters never age and Becky herself seems to be eternally pregnant, probably because in real life Witherspoon was – celebrated by Nair in numerous close-ups of her leading lady's burgeoning chest.

The presentation of Becky's character is also flawed. Turning her from an anti-heroine (like, say, spitting vixen Scarlett O'Hara in *Gone With The Wind*) into a two-a-penny rom-com girl makes the final act hard to accept.

Tagline
All's fair in love and war.

There's an excellent supporting cast including James Purefoy, Bob Hoskins, Gabriel Byrne and Jim Broadbent, but there's also some crucial mis-casting, particularly Rhys Ifans as the pure-hearted Dobbin. As an interesting footnote, Natasha Little, who played Becky to great effect in the most recent BBC version, has a minor role in this one.

There's more amusement to be derived from the hope she'll elbow the Hollywood megastar out the way than can be found in the rest of the film. **★★ EC**

VELVET GOLDMINE (1998)

Starring: *Ewan McGregor (Curt Wild), Jonathan Rhys Meyers (Brian Slade), Toni Collette (Mandy Slade), Christian Bale (Arthur Stuart), Eddie Izzard (Jerry Devine)*
Director: *Todd Haynes*
Screenwriter: *Todd Haynes, from a story by Haynes, James Lyons*
15/118 mins./Drama/Music/UK/USA

Awards – *BAFTA – Best Costume Design*

This glam rock movie from American indie writer/director Todd Haynes somehow makes a pig's ear out of the silk purse that is the early 70s glitter era, contriving a ridiculous fiction when any number of true stories – not least the rise and fall of David Bowie's Ziggy Stardust – would have been better. But Haynes has a vision he'd like to share.

That vision follows the rise to glam superstardom of Brian Slade which ends with a faked death and mysterious disappearance. Ten years later, Mancunian journalist Arthur Stuart, working in New York, is asked to write a 'Whatever happened to Brian Slade?' story. It's a dream assignment for the former fan and so the film proceeds to tell in flashback both the stories of Slade and Stuart and how they briefly intertwined. On paper, fine; on celluloid, a *Rocky Horror Show* of nightmarish proportions.

After a fairy-tale voiceover opening which appears to link glam rock to Oscar Wilde and UFOs (but chiefly suggests the projectionist is showing a reel from another film), *Velvet Goldmine* quickly goes from bad to worse. Locations and period references are clumsily rendered, and the closest it comes to pitch-perfect style is in resembling a bad film actually made in the 70s – but *Stardust* is much better. Into the mix comes McGregor as Curt Wild, slurring his way through a reasonable Iggy Pop impersonation (although any actor who, with bare chest, long blond hair and tight trousers, couldn't manage one should hand back his Equity card). Bale copes well as a dour Northerner trying to overcome both his roots and his lines to fit into the London scene, and Rhys Meyers just Carries On Regardless as the script clunks on and on and on.

Only Collette (as Slade's distressed wife Mandy) and Eddie Izzard (as his brilliantly flamboyant manager) emerge with any dignity. Old classics in the soundtrack offer relief but the presence of a few rock'n'rollers (including members of Teenage Fan Club and Pulp) in stage scenes give it a credibility it doesn't deserve. The mystery twist is so obvious and dull, that long before the end is in sight, you'll only keep watching to see if it can get any worse. It does.

This might have worked if it had been played for laughs – but then The Comic Strip would have done it much better. **★ NJ**

VERA DRAKE (2004)

Starring: *Imelda Staunton (Vera), Richard Graham (George), Eddie Marsan (Reg), Anna Keaveney (Nellie), Alex Kelly (Ethel)*
Director: *Mike Leigh*
Screenwriter: *Mike Leigh*
12A/125 mins./Drama/History/UK

Awards – *BAFTA – Best Costume, Best Actress*

Islington, 1950. Charlady Vera bustles about keeping her family together and cheerfully helping others. She also performs discreet abortions for girls 'in trouble'. Eventually, this charitable sideline comes to the attention of the law and a prosecution threatens to break up the family.

V

Like *Topsy-Turvy*, this initially appears to be a break from the 'Mike Leigh style', being another period piece. Yet it's one that recreates the living memory of 1950, homing in on characters who could be the grandparents of the people in the director's other films. Vera offers a smile, kind words and endless soothing cups of tea as she provides support and motivation for friends and relations who might otherwise slide into feckless apathy.

Besides caring for her ancient mother and almost invisibly tidying wealthy homes, Vera matter-of-factly performs abortions most Friday afternoons at five (and, incidentally, demonstrates just how to perform a DIY termination). Disaster is inevitable and, when a client suffers complications, the police are called in. Vera's arrested, then retreats into a shell of shame as she's eased through the prosecution, trial and sentencing by not-unsympathetic authorities. It never overstresses subplots that put Vera's crimes in context, like the timid, date-raped upper-class girl going through a far more hypocritical system to procure an abortion (involving a hefty fee and a discreet stay in a private clinic) or the son's sideline in nylons used to get girls into bed and probably supply Vera with more customers.

Tagline
Wife.
Mother.
Criminal.

Though less comic than most Leigh films, there's an echo of that old wireless standby *The Glums* in the agonising courtship of Vera's lumpy daughter Ethel by terminally shy, scarf-wrapped Reg, with pauses as pregnant as the parade of desperate cameo girls. Also in the Leigh tradition is Vera's sister-in-law, one of his terrifyingly aspirational women, ruthlessly intent on scrubbing the proletarian taint from her family (and accent) and squandering her husband's earnings on new-fangled luxuries like a television set and a washing machine.

It catches exactly the drab, rationed, overly genteel-at-all-levels-of-society tone of the period (kudos to the location finder, set decorator and prop people). And the last act is almost unbearably affecting, with Staunton – like so many Leigh performers before her – going beyond the comic mannerisms to show naked pain. ★★★★ KN

⓪ VERONICA GUERIN (2003)

Starring: *Cate Blanchett (Veronica Guerin), Gerard McSorley (John Gilligan), Ciaran Hinds (John Traynor), Brenda Fricker (Bernadette Guerin)*
Director: *Joel Schumacher*
Screenwriters: *Carol Doyle, Mary Agnes Donoghue, from a story by Carol Doyle*
18/94 mins./Biography/Drama/USA/UK/Ireland

Veronica Guerin, a Dublin journalist, is murdered by two masked gunmen after being acquitted in court on charges of unpaid parking fines. In flashback, we learn that Guerin had been investigating a local drug ring – in particular a mysterious and very violent character named John Gilligan.

If the story of a crusading Irish journalist tangling with heavy-duty drug dealers sounds familiar, that's because Veronica Guerin's life and death were documented three years previously in *When The Sky Falls*. John Mackenzie's film, though, was hamstrung by one crucial fact: producer Jerry Bruckheimer had the rights to Guerin's life story sewn up, leaving Mackenzie to fudge the facts with a lead character called 'Sinead Hamilton' and an actress (Joan Allen) slightly too old for the part.

In this family-approved version, however, Cate Blanchett makes a much more appealing and less mythic heroine. She portrays Guerin as a highly complex individual, a suburban mum who loved her family and her football, but who made the mistake of believing her own hype as a bullet-proof newshound.

Schumacher handles the drama with surprising restraint and never shies away from the ugly truth of this violent world. The ending may be drawn out and over-sentimental, but this is a thoughtful interpretation of a very modern tragedy. ★★★ DW

⓪ VERTIGO (1958)

Starring: *James Stewart (Det. John 'Scottie' Ferguson), Kim Novak (Madeleine Elster/Judy Barton), Barbara Bel Geddes (Majorie 'Midge' Wood), Tom Helmore (Coroner), Raymond Bailey (Scottie's doctor)*
Director: *Alfred Hitchcock*
Screenwriters: *Alec Coppel, Samuel A. Taylor, based on the novel* D'entre les Morts *by Pierre Boileau, Thomas Narcejac*
PG/122 mins./Mystery/Thriller/USA

Scottie Ferguson is hired to watch ghost-like Madeleine Elster, a disturbed young woman. He falls in love, but his vertigo renders him powerless to prevent her suicidal leap from a bell-tower. Mentally scarred, he roams San Francisco until meeting Judy, a dead ringer for Madeleine, after which the truth slowly unravels.

Picture yourself on a rollercoaster at the highest peak of its circuit. That terrifying moment before your stomach plunges to hell is the best description of having vertigo. It's what Jimmy Stewart suffers from here, and it's what you'll experience leaving the theatre after watching Hitchcock's most disturbing masterpiece. Painstakingly restored from a destroyed 1958 negative to a majestic 70mm print by the team who renewed *Spartacus*, *Vertigo* can now terrify and seduce a whole new generation of cinemagoers, and still have enough intellectual clout to be one of, if not the finest, American movies ever made.

First and foremost it's a chilling thriller, but dig deeper and you'll uncover sinister references to Dante's *Inferno*, psychological colour codes and, most controversially, the master of suspense at last baring his soul on film. *Vertigo* presents the dizzy heights of many fabulous careers. Nice Guy Stewart has never been so complex and calculating, Novak never more mesmerising and Bernard Herrmann's score is magnificent. Even Saul Bass' whirling title credits have you gripping the arm-rest, but Hitchcock has stamped his personality on every scene. Using revolutionary techniques – the celebrated zoom-forward-track-back shot, the whodunnit giveaway, the scary downbeat ending – Hitchcock's obsessions with romantic love and female deception are exposed in this spine-tingling tale of mistaken identity. ★★★★ JH

⓪ VERY BAD THINGS (1998)

Starring: *Christian Slater (Robert Boyd), Cameron Diaz (Laura Garrety), Daniel Stern (Adam Berkow), Jeanne Tripplehorn (Lois Berkow), Jon Favreau (Kyle Fisher), Jeremy Piven (Michael Berkow)*
Director: *Peter Berg*
Screenwriter: *Peter Berg*
18/100 mins./Comedy/Crime/USA

After a stripper is accidentally killed during a stag party, the 'stags' go to desperate measures to cover up the tragedy.

For a while it looked like the next hot trend would be youthful ensemble black comedy, and this debut effort from writer-director Peter Berg – best known as a nice-but-dim character in the likes of *Shocker*, *Late For Dinner* and *The Last Seduction* – would stand as a transition between fringe efforts like *The Last Supper*, *Scream* and *Dead Man's Curve* and more mainstream, less extreme sick-coms. It feels like a bigger movie than any of its predecessors, with a shaky A-list cast and flamboyant effects, but is a little broader, blunter and less funny, with a tendency to rely too much on shtick we've seen already – especially as Christian Slater and Cameron Diaz play riffs on their roles in *Heathers* and *My Best Friend's Wedding*.

Revisiting the setting of early Tom Hanks comedy vehicle *Bachelor Party*, it starts out with yuppie bridegroom Keith nervously waiting in the church while flashing back to a stag weekend that got seriously out of hand. Along with his buddies – underachiever Charles, real estate psycho Robert Boyd, feuding brothers Man and Michael – Keith hits Las Vegas for the expected orgy of booze and drugs, but things go wrong when Man's bathroom romp with a stripper-hooker ends up with the girl dead and Boyd murders a security guard to cover up the killing. With the victims dismembered and buried in the desert, the gang gets increasingly paranoid and Boyd decides to clean house by killing anyone he thinks will crack and go to the cops.

The film has a real sense of a situation slipping out of control, with marvellous displays of hysteria matched by movie trickery that spreads the edginess to the audience. Stern, in particular, has a great freak-out moment and all the actors eagerly seize the chance to go into hyperdrive during the party and argument scenes. Though the premise is workable, Berg tends to have too many scenes turn into headache-inducing shouting matches with little verbal wit. Slater is excellent as the estate agent hopped up on Self-Actualisation therapy, but we've seen his act before, which leaves the surprises to Cameron Diaz, extending her range in a furious finale. Though the title means unimaginative critics are bound to tag it

TOP10 Band Names Inspired By Films

	Band	Film	Inspiration
1	Duran Duran	*Barbarella*	Villain played by Milo O'Shea
2	Travis	*Paris, Texas*	Anti-hero played by Harry Dean Stanton
3	Black Rebel Motorcycle Club	*The Wild One*	A posse of bike-riding hooligans
4	Black Sabbath	*Black Sabbath*	1963 horror movie with Boris Karloff
5	Mogwai	*Gremlins*	A gremlin before he turns nasty
6	Moloko	*A Clockwork Orange*	A milk drink
7	Nerfherder	*The Empire Strikes Back*	A creature mentioned in Princess Leia dialogue
8	Mudhoney	*Mudhoney*	A 1965 Russ Meyer film
9	They Might Be Giants	*They Might Be Giants*	A 1971 Sherlock Holmes movie
10	McFly	*Back To The Future*	Surname of hero

with the 'very bad film' label, it won't deserve such a drubbing – but it's not a very good one either. ★★★ **KN**

⊙ A VERY LONG ENGAGEMENT (UN LONG DIMANCHE DE FIANCAILLES) (2004)

Starring: *Audrey Tautou (Mathilde), Chantal Neuwirth (Benedicte), André Dussollier (Pierre-Marie Rouvières), Marion Cotillard (Tina Lombardi), Dominique Pinon (Ange Bassignano), Jodie Foster (Elodie Gordes)*
Director: *Jean-Pierre Jeunet*
Screenwriter: *Guillaume Laurant, based on the story adaptation by Jean-Pierre Jeunet, Guillaume Laurant, novel by Sébastien Japrisot*
15/133 mins./Drama/Romance/History/War/France/USA

Told that her sweetheart and fiancé has been court-martialled and sent, with four others, to the certain death of no-man's-land, orphaned dreamer Mathilde refuses to give up hope he will return. So begins her odyssey through the vile memories of World War I and across the pastures of rural France, to discover the truth of his crime and punishment, driven only by the power of her devotion.

As the commercially viable face of French cinema, the ever-beaming Jean-Pierre Jeunet could easily be dismissed as a gimmick merchant, a bravura showman who never breaks the skin of his movies. There's no doubt his style is as tricksy as a tea-time magic show: frenetic camera moves, baroque interchanges of flashbacks and forwards, stories embedded within stories, and whimsy up the wazoo – not to mention a penchant for the steam-punk décor of Jules Verne.

How his head must buzz with all the bells and whistles he can blare at his avid fans with each new fairy-tale. The frothy *Amélie*, the fantastic *The City Of Lost Children*, the murky satire of *Delicatessen* (let's forget *Alien: Resurrection*, his heavy dunk in the Hollywood pond) all swim with the vivid wonder of his imagination. With *A Very Long Engagement*, however, his strokes are far stronger and cut deeper. Not that he's pulled an entirely straight face. In classification terms alone, the film is hedging its bets as a war movie, a love story, a *Rashomon*-style memory game, an Agatha Christie-esque detective romp, a noir-ish revenge drama and a loamy comedy of French peasantry with an unfortunate tinge of the Stella Artois ads about its pastoral charm.

Yet, in the midst of his trademark brio, Jeunet invests this tall tale with a sharp reality. By the rain-washed opening credits' conclusion we've been introduced to the dark side – there's nothing fizzy about this brute vision of life and combat in the French trenches, in many ways as turbulent and destabilising as *Saving Private Ryan*'s Ohama Beach. The French maestro courageously rubs his light romance up against unflinching warfare – and the jarring cuts from windswept pastoral visions, as gilded as a Monet, to the deranged clutter of a killing field strike straight at the heart.

Tautou, still as slender as a pixie, is less spirited and inspired than in *Amélie*, having to lock her magical smile away in dogged frowns. Mathilde is headstrong, lamed by childhood polio, and prone to losing her rag, but determined to clutch at her love like a life raft. There's a wonderful recurring riff on how she tempts fate to reveal the truth, testing her hopes against absurd challenges (a dog spilling through a door, the time it takes for a car to pass), all of which, to a bet, return teasingly unanswered.

It is very long, but never dull, the mystery regularly spinning on its heel to veer off in a new direction. You half wonder whether the film can ever tie itself together again as it unveils yet more characters and subplots, all micro-detailed and often richly funny. In one heart-breaking sojourn, Jodie Foster takes on a fluent cameo, while elsewhere a Corsican whore launches her own parallel mission, murderously dispensing with French officers care of some cunning devices.

Some may not endure the story's wilful whirligigging, the pace is blinding, the flutter of names and moustaches dreadfully confusing, but the emotional drive couldn't be plainer. You care for Mathilde and you yearn for the truth, whatever form it might take. And as shadowy as the journey becomes, Jeunet, the optimist, also shows us a world of light. ★★★★ **IN**

⊙ VICTIM (1961)

Starring: *Dirk Bogarde (Melville Farr), Sylvia Syms (Laura), Dennis Price (Calloway), Anthony Nicholls (Lord Fulbrook), Peter Copley (Paul Mandrake), Norman Bird (Harold Doe), Peter McEnery (Barrett), Donald Churchill (Eddy), Derren Nesbitt (Sandy Youth), John Barrie (Det. Inspector Harris), John Cairney (Bridie)*
Director: *Basil Dearden*
Screenwriters: *Janet Green, John McCormick*
12/90 mins./Drama/UK

Barrister Melville Farr becomes the target of a blackmail ring who have already driven a homosexual friend to suicide. Farr works with the police to expose the blackmailers, but also has to admit to his wife that he has gay tendencies.

Daring in 1961, this now has its quaint side but remains a strong, unusual blackmail thriller. Having 'done' the race issue with *Sapphire*, another police procedural with an editorial, director Basil Dearden turns his attention to homosexual matters. Part of the trick of films like this is to play as a regular thriller so that the message gets through like the medicine in a spoonful of sugar – indeed, if the character played by Peter McEnery were a chorus girl, this could easily have been an *Edgar Wallace Presents ...* B picture.

Much of the interest comes from Dirk Bogarde, in a central performance that flirts with autobiography while presenting an almost caricature image of stiff-upper-lip British queer, painfully admitting to his cut-glass wife (Sims) that he really does have desires for 'the Boy' (McEnery). Normally swish character actors like Dennis Price, Norman Bird and Nigel Stock underplay as the gay blackmail victims, but the supposedly straight villains are weirdoes – Derren Nesbitt as a sneering, violent leather-boy and Mavis Viliers as a repressed spinster who is 'half avenging angel and half peeping tom' – who use the criminal status of homosexuals (under the Sodomy Laws then on the statutes) as a licence to extort.

Part of the bravery of the film is that it unusually dares to say that not only are some folks' attitudes wrong, but so (in this case) is the law of the land. The milieu of antique shops and cosy pick-up bars might be laughably genteel but it's still convincing. ★★★ **KN**

⊙ VICTOR/VICTORIA (1982)

Starring: *Julie Andrews (Victoria Grant/Victor Grazinski), James Garner (King Marchan), Robert Preston (Carroll 'Toddy' Todd), Lesley Ann Warren (Norma), Alex Karras (Squash Bernstein), John Rhys Davies (Andre Cassell), Graham Stark (Waiter), Peter Arne (Labisse), Sherloque Tanney (Bovin – the Detective)*
Director: *Blake Edwards*
Screenwriter: *Blake Edwards, based on the film* Viktor Und Viktoria *by Rheinhold Schüenzel and Hans Hömburg*
15/133 mins./Comedy-Musical/UK

Awards: *Academy Awards – Best Song Score*

Down on their luck in 1934 Paris, entertainers Victoria Grant and Carroll Todd hatch a scheme to pass her off as female impersonator Count Victor

Grezhinski. However, Chicago club owner King Marchand begins to fall for him/her, much to the dismay of his ditzy blonde lover Norma Cassady and macho bodyguard, Squash Bernstein.

In its heyday, the musical had been very much a cosy form of family entertainment. However, by the 1980s, a yen for the genre had become stereotypically synonomous with homosexuality. Consequently, Blake Edwards chose to stress the gay element that had lain dormant in previous adaptations of *Viktor Und Viktoria* in this calculating reworking that owed as much to Edouard Molinaro's *La Cage Aux Folles* (1978) as to Reinhold Schünzel's 1933 screwball musical.

Although Renate Muller still cross-dressed her way to celebrity in the original scenario, she got her break as a secret replacement for female impersonator Hermann Thimig. Moreover, London lothario Adolf Wohlbrück quickly discerns her true identity and puts her through a hellish macho initiation before declaring his love. In 1934, Victor Saville stuck closely to this storyline in tailoring it as *First A Girl* for Jessie Matthews and Sonny Hale, as did Karl Anton in his 1957 version with Annie Cordy.

But Blake Edwards opted to turn Robert Preston's mentor into a gay confidante and mock James Garner's growing disquiet about his feelings through macho henchman, Alex Karras. Thus, a sniggering sense of innuendo was introduced to a situation that already had a delicious ambiguity. Moreover, Edwards and Andrews insisted on using the picture to drive another nail into her detested Mary Poppins image, although this time they resisted the resort to momentary nudity that had made *S.O.B.* such a *succès de scandale*.

Andrews and Preston landed Oscar nominations in the film's unlikely haul of seven. But both the nominated Lesley Ann Warren and the overlooked Garner are infinitely more amusing in a double act that's part Clark Gable and Jean Harlow and part an inversion of Judy Holliday and Broderick Crawford's characters in *Born Yesterday*.

However, the least deserving recipients were Henry Mancini and Leslie Bricusse, who won the award for Best Song Score with a dismal collection of ditties that even riffed on the 'Lady of Seville' routine that Müller had performed with infinitely greater allure half a century before.

★★★ DP

⑩ VIDEODROME (1983)

Starring: *James Woods (Max Renn), Sonja Smits (Bianca O'Blivion), Deborah Harry (Nicki Brand), Peter Dvorsky (Harlan), Leslie Carlson (Barry Convex)*
Director: *David Cronenberg*
Screenwriter: *David Cronenberg*
18/84 mins./Horror/Fantasy/Thriller/USA

Lowlife cable TV operator Max Renn discovers a 'snuff TV' broadcast called Videodrome. But Videodrome is more than a TV show – it's an experiment that uses regular TV transmissions to permanently alter the viewer's perceptions by giving them brain damage.

A man and a woman begin to kiss. As they get more and more passionate their faces begin to liquefy and merge into one another, finally running off their skulls entirely. The molten mess slinks across the floor and up a bystander's leg who, screaming, proceeds to turn into goo himself. Fade to black...

Not, as it happens, a sequence that made it into David Cronenberg's *Videodrome* – effects director Rick Baker took one look at it in script form and realised there was no way his parsimonious $500,000 budget would stretch to this kind of latex lunacy (and, indeed, it would be a full decade before FX wunderkind Screaming Mad George would deliver a similar sequence in Brian Yuzna's horror satire *Society*) – but it's pretty typical of the twisted imagery coursing through the Canadian director's head as he sat in a rented office in downtown Toronto and worked on, what was then, a screenplay entitled *Network Of Blood*.

But if the sloppy snogging didn't get any further than Cronenberg's typewriter there was enough of his unique brand of fleshy surrealism in *Videodrome* to cement his reputation as the most challenging director working in horror (if that's an adequate word). It also, of course, sent detractors hurtling for the Basildon Bond to fire off letters to whoever might be able to stop him ever assaulting the screen, or their senses, again. Like the bulk of Cronenberg's work, *Videodrome* is impossible to adequately categorise. It perches on the cusp of sci-fi and horror – the story, such as it is, is pretty much sci-fi. A secret television signal is hidden behind extreme pornography – images of men and women chained to electrified clay walls being beaten and tortured, called Videodrome.

When TV executive MaxRenn is exposed to it it causes a brain tumour to develop which in turn generates increasingly bizarre hallucinations, visions that are the stuff of horror. A weird vagina-like wound appears on Renn's chest, videocassettes and his television develop veins and begin to pulsate; he imagines acts of violence that he doesn't appear to actually commit. Behind the signal are media expert Professor Brian O'Blivion, who exists only in the form of a giant library of videocassettes, and sinister businessman Barry Convex (Cronenberg remains the king of movie names, having delivered the likes of Strathis Borans, Adrian Tripod, Darryl Revok and Dr. Dan Keloid in his previous films) who intends to use the signal to form a new world order – a population composed entirely of the ultimate in telly addicts.

Videodrome is a perfect example of 'body horror' the sub-genre that Cronenberg invented with early movies like *Shivers* (1975), *Rabid* (1977) and *The Brood* (1979) and has since then pretty much made exclusively his own. His horrors are not bogeymen hiding in the dark with butcher knives or monsters from the pit of Hell. Cronenberg's terror derives from the human body and its capacity to be invaded by disease, to mutate and change uncontrollably. He once announced that he could perfectly well imagine a beauty contest for human internal organs or a disease of the week movie from a cancer's perspective.

Culturally *Videodrome* was right on the money. Made in 1982 and released in 83 it coincided perfectly with a period in which television was undergoing radical growth and change. In the UK not only was there the introduction of a fourth channel (Channel 4 in 1982) and the unimaginable phenomenon of breakfast TV (anyone under the age of 25 may find it difficult to believe that until Frank Bough, The Green Goddess and Selina Scott there was no television until schools programmes in the mid morning – we were a simple but happy people) but the video revolution was well under way with over 30 per cent of British households boasting a VCR, over twice the rate of America. Plus, the video nasties controversy was approaching boiling point with titles like *SS Experiment Camp* and *Cannibal Ferox* being removed from videoshop shelves by nervous cathode ray entrepreneurs. It was a hotbed of anxiety about the glowing retina in the corner of every living room and the government's inability to control what people saw on it. Ironically Cronenberg's movie, which deals with the very subject of censorship – and concludes that it inhibits progress – was the victim of censorship itself, with distributors, fearful of prosecution under the Video Recordings Act, cutting out whole sections.

After the intellectual and visual audacity of *Videodrome*, Cronenberg would retreat to the relative safety of Stephen King adaptation *The Dead Zone* (1983). It wasn't until *Crash* in 1995 that he produced anything nearly so provocative, and there have been failures like *Naked Lunch* (1991) and *M Butterfly* (1993) along the way. As critic Douglas Thompson eloquently put it, 'Anyone born and reckoning on dying needs to confront Cronenberg.' *Videodrome* seems as good a place as any to start.

★★★★ AS

⊙ A VIEW TO A KILL (1985)

Starring: *Roger Moore (James Bond), Christopher Walken (Max Zorin), Tanya Roberts (Stacey Sutton), Grace Jones (May Day), Patrick Macnee (Sir Godfrey Tibbett)*
Director: *John Glen*
Screenwriters: *Richard Maibaum, Michael G. Wilson, based on the novel by Ian Fleming*
PG/131 mins./Spy/UK-USA

Mysterious industrialist Max Zorin may be selling British microchip design to the Russians. When James Bond is sent to investigate, he discovers Zorin is not only stockpiling chips, he is also drilling dangerously close to the San Andreas Fault in California.

The last hurrah for Roger Moore as 007, and that nagging sense that retirement was long overdue is transformed into blatant evidence. No matter how hard they try, the difference between a podgy 58 year-old Moore and his stunt stand-ins was clear as day, and the love scenes with beaming but bland blonde Tanya Roberts is really quite yucky. The jib was up, he'd paid his dues, but this creaking Bond adventure is beyond redemption.

The plot is a failed attempt to rewire Goldfinger's global market meltdown strategy for the microchip business – relevant, perhaps, at the time but, frankly, boring in concept. Christopher Walken sleepwalks his way through playing smarmy Nazi geneticist Zorin, where you would think he would have a ball hamming it up as a Bond villain. Indeed, it is a rare moment when Grace Jones makes the biggest impression as an Amazonian (naturally) henchman called May Day. She gets to parachute off the Eiffel Tower, that's cool.

Director John Glen, with master stunt co-ordinator Vic Armstrong, strain every sinew to make the action exciting with fire-engine chase sequences in San Francisco and a grand finale on the Golden Gate Bridge, but no amount of smoke and mirrors can enable us to believe that Roger the Codger is really doing his bit for Queen and country. Although, you have to admit, Duran Duran wrote a cracking theme song. ★★ **IN**

⊙ THE VIKINGS (1958)

Starring: *Kirk Douglas (Einar), Tony Curtis (Eric), Ernest Borgnine (Ragnar), Janet Leigh (Morgana), James Donald (Egbert), Alexander Knox (Father Godwin)*
Director: *Richard Fleischer*
Screenwriters: *Edison Marshall, Dale Wasserman*
PG/114 mins./History/USA

Unbeknownst to the great warrior Einar and the shamed former slave Eric, they are, in fact, half-brothers. With a kingdom and princess for the taking in Northumbria, England, the good news will have to take a backseat to some major rivalry.

The other action epic that starred Kirk Douglas and Tony Curtis doesn't have quite the pedigree of the great *Spartacus*, but is still a rip-roaring adventure tale told with little authenticity whatsoever, but plenty of highly pleasurable grand old Hollywood ham. You're never quite convinced these guys, although Douglas' full-blooded and one-eyed tearaway gives it a good go, are the mead-guzzling, maiden ravishing ninth century stalwarts of macho legend. Curtis looks like he's just come out of the salon most of the time.

Rather than the big scope of traditional epic-making, this is resplendently comic-book, an unsurprising style given the director was Richard Fleischer, who cornered the market over the 50s and 60s in bottling boyhood fantasies as glossy Hollywood product (*20,000 Leagues Under The Sea, The Fantastic Voyage* et al). He aims to convey a snapshot of olde Viking life, with scenes of well researched shipbuilding and craftwork, and the usual swilling of mead and grasping of thick female thighs, but his psychology is one-dimensional and his actors keep things as broad as possible.

The plot has it that Einar and Eric are blood brothers deep down (some guff involving an amulet is the key), it's just a question of when they stop squabbling and make up, but Fleischer would rather have them fighting and leering after Janet Leigh's vulnerable English princess for most of the fast-paced picture. No bad thing, necessarily, when the scenery is as gorgeous as this and sword-fighting as thumpingly good as mounted here. ★★★ **IN**

⊙ VILLAGE OF THE DAMNED (1960)

Starring: *George Sanders (Gordon Zellaby), Barbara Shelley (Anthea Zellaby), Martin Stephens (David), Michael Gwynn (Major Alan Bernard), Laurence Naismith (Dr. Willers), Richard Warner (Harrington)*
Director: *Wolf Rilla*
Screenwriters: *Wolf Rilla, Stirling Silliphant, Ronald Kinnoch as George Barclay, from the novel* The Midwich Cuckoos *by John Wyndham*
12/77 mins./Sci-fi/Horror/UK

In the small English village of Midwich everybody and everything falls into a deep, mysterious sleep for several hours in the middle of the day. Some months later every woman capable of child-bearing is pregnant...

Ever since *The War Of The Worlds* (courtesy of H.G. Wells, not Cruise/Spielberg), the most reworked sub-genre of science fiction has been the invasion from outer space. In the 50s and 60s, any number of things came from other worlds to cause trouble on Earth – flying saucers, lone monsters on the rampage, body-snatching duplicates, humanoids with super-powers, giant disembodied brains, Daleks, intellectual carrots and Jerry Lewis.

Brit novelist John Wyndham came up with an original invasion in his novel *The Midwich Cuckoos*, in which the inhabitants of a small village all fall mysteriously asleep for a spell one morning and find when they wake up that all the women of child-bearing age are pregnant. When born, the children are at least half-alien; they are in telepathic contact with each other, and display maturing powers to influence and dominate ordinary folk, which forces the authorities to consider the uncomfortable notion of mass infanticide before the scary alien kids grow up and wipe out humankind.

Wolf Rilla's 1960 film, from a script by the American Stirling Silliphant (who uses a few incongrous Yank expressions – 'general store' for 'village shop'), is a low-key dramatisation of the Wyndham novel that could, perhaps, have done with another ten minutes running time. The first half of this brief picture deals with the Midwich blackout and the pregnancies, so the business with the children – which takes place over years of plot-time – often seems a little rushed, especially since there are a lot of secondary characters to cope with and the splendid Barbara Shelley (the most caring of the mothers) gets pushed into the background so her scientist husband (George Sanders) can shoulder the dramatic weight.

Nevertheless, it was such a sleeper success that a semi-sequel (*Children Of The Damned*) was made, and John Carpenter did a hash-job remake in 1995. His evil kids live in 90s California but still wear 60-vintage English school uniforms (and, though the remake is in colour, grey uniforms at that). The sleeping village set-up is classic *Quatermass* stuff. We see a tractor grinding around in a circle, an iron burning a hole in a dress, a record stuck in a groove, a cow collapsed in a field, a bus in a ditch and other vignettes, while boffin Gordon Zellaby (Sanders) and other interested parties – the army, a local GP, a bicycling bobby – test the limits of the phenomenon.

They rule out poison gas because the boundaries of the sleep zone are too sharp. A plane tries to fly over Midwich and crashes – in the novel, the pilot sees a flying saucer but the film eschews such trickery and leaves us to assume it's all been managed by a *Species*-like signal from outer space – and then everyone wakes up in convincing embarrassment, which gets odder as the pregnancies are announced. Here you get the sort of emotions American science fiction films, pitched at kiddies, just didn't do in the 50s and 60s: the awkward joy of the Zellabys (Sanders is much older than co-star Shelley) at an unexpected event; the meek terror of the teenage virgin confessing to a doctor; the rage of the sailor home after a year abroad to find his wife knocked up; the quiet solidarity of a pregnant mother and daughter who visit the clinic at the same time.

Once the kids are born, the film becomes a more conventional monster movie in which the threat is a malignant higher intelligence with no moral grounding. Here, what works is the shape the threat comes in: the Midwich children are the creepiest ever seen on film, with their identical blonde wigs (an unsettling effect is achieved by casting real-life brunette kids whose colouring is subtly wrong for their hair) and staring eyes (in some prints, a glowing effect was added). The polite spokesman for the group 'mind' is David, the Zellabys' son, played by Martin Stephens (also notable as Miles in *The Innocents*) but dubbed by a grown woman (it used to be a wireless convention to have actresses play children). Rilla hints at the children's human sides (they all solve a puzzle box to get chocolates) as well as a malevolence that would be scary in an alien but just might be even scarier from a human kid (Stephen's ghost of a smile after he forces a motorist to kill himself remains one of the nastiest shots in British cinema).

The plot gets out of hand rapidly, with rampaging mobs and committees of dignitaries debating the situation – we learn there were other villages in the frozen North (the Eskimos killed the blonde babies at birth) and Russia (the Soviets nuked the whole place) – but there's a great suspense finale as Zellaby, convinced that the children have to be destroyed, carries a bomb in his briefcase into the schoolroom and tries to think of a brick wall as the kids attempt to read his mind (we see the wall crumbling, a very effective depiction of a mental process), blocking them out until the disappointingly meagre explosion.

In true spread-the-unease fashion, the film ends with one of the first it-may-not-be-over endings (later to become a genre cliché): the glowing eyes of the children, superimposed over the fire, zap off into the skies, suggesting that killing the kids' bodies may not have wiped out their disembodied intelligence. ★★★★ **KN**

◑ VILLAIN (1971)

Starring: *Richard Burton (Vic Dakin), Ian McShane (Wolfe Lissner), Nigel Davenport (Bob Matthews), Donald Sinden (Gerald Draycott), Fiona Lewis (Venetia), Joss Ackland (Edgar Lewis)*
Director: *Michael Tuchner*
Screenwriters: *Dick Clement, Ian La Frenais, Al Lettieri, based on the novel* The Burden Of Proof *by James Barlow*
18/93 mins./Crime/Drama/UK

A gangster foolishly moves from the protection racket to armed robbery, hoping to impress the object of his affections.

If Richard Burton had made more films like this and fewer like *Cleopatra*, he would have been a major movie star rather than a tragic joke. As Vic Dakin, a London hard man who combines the characteristics of both Kray Twins, Burton is as distinctive a gangster for Britain as Cagney was for America or Alain Delon for France. A tough who gets a witness out of the way by telling her to make a cup of tea while he cuts her boyfriend's face off, Dakin is also devoted enough to take his dear old mum down to Brighton every weekend. His mistake comes in moving from his protection racket into armed robbery, not out of the traditional desire to expand his empire but because he is verging on middle-aged flabbiness and wants to get back into the action to impress his sometime love interest, Wolf.

Made just after *Get Carter*, Villain similarly updates the conventions of the British gangster movie into the 70s complete with flares, sideburns and seedy clubs. Written by Dick Clement and Ian La Frenais, its dialogue sounds a lot more authentic than that of TV's *The Sweeney* and the plot is a neatly-turned anecdote which pays off with a Burton speech that prefigures Al Pacino's great restaurant rant in *Scarface*.

Tuchner, who defected to US TV after this striking first film, marshals an awe-inspiring collection of British character actors who were later lured into sitcoms, cosy TV detectives or double glazing adverts. For your money, you get Joss Ackland as an ulcer-ridden gang boss, Nigel Davenport and Colin Welland as determined plods, McShane as a pimp-cum-rent boy, Donald Sinden as a sleazy MP caught in an extramarital orgy, Tony Selby and Del Henney as minders and Fiona Lewis as a high-class topless tart.

The London crime locations are acutely-observed and brilliantly used: the bungled smash and grab in an industrial estate is a treat, with Burton blinding a driver by squirting him with a Jif lemon and a booby-trapped suitcase full of cash extruding five-foot steel arms. Burton is truly creepy in a fascinating in-depth performance, consumed with hatred for the punters whose idea of a life is 'telly all week and screw the wife on Saturdays' as he self-destructs by always relying on weaklings who fall apart when the pressure is on. ★★★★ **KN**

◑ THE VIRGIN SPRING (JUNGFRUKALLAN) (1959)

Starring: *Max Von Sydow (Herr Töre), Brigitta Petterson (Karin Tore), Birgitta Valberg (Mareta Tore), Gunnel Lindblom (Ingeri), Axel Duberg (Thin Herdsmann), Tor Isedal (Mute Herdsman), Ove Porath (Boy), Allan Edwall (Beggar), Gudrun Brost (Frida), Oscar Ljung (Simon)*
Director: *Ingmar Bergman*
Screenwriter: *Ulla Isaksson, based on the 14th Century ballad* Tores Dotter I Vange
15/88 mins/Drama/Sweden

Awards: *Academy Awards – Best Foreign Language Film. Cannes Film Festival – Special Mention*

When his angelic daughter, Karin, is raped and murdered by a couple of goatherds, medieval Swedish farmer Töre purifies himself through purging before slaying the culprits and vowing to build a church on the site of Karin's ordeal.

Ingmar Bergman was in a particularly positive frame of mind when he embarked upon this daunting 13th-century parable. Indeed, he devised his comedy *The Devil's Eye* while Ulla Isaksson worked on her adaptation of a Nordic myth, whose many variations even included a physical manifestation in the form of the spring in the churchyard at Kärna. But, even though Bergman enjoyed the shoot, he came to dislike the film intensely, declaring it to be an 'aberration' and a 'lousy imitation of Kurosawa'.

Bergman's use of gliding tracking shots and the abrupt alternation between terse silence and pitiless violence certainly recalled the Japanese maestro's work. Moreover, *The Virgin Spring* shared *Rashomon*'s sense of moral ambiguity. But, its reliance on humble rustic symbolism more readily recalled such silent classics as *Terje Vigen* and *The Outlaw And His Wife*, which had been directed by Bergman's mentor, Victor Sjöström.

Replacing Gunnar Fischer (who was detained on a Disney movie in the Arctic), Sven Nykvist produced imagery that shifted between the lyrical and the Expressionist. But the film's resolutely simple design found echo in its artless, not to say, superficial psychology.

V

In retaining the structure of the original ballad, Isaksson's script also imported its acceding medieval attitude towards faith. Thus, rather than exploring the narrow divide between Christianity and paganism, Bergman ended up concentrating on more obvious contrasts between light and dark and Good and Evil. Töre's devotion to Karin, therefore, took on Freudian undertones, which were reinforced by his straddling of the birch sapling that he had uprooted in order to flagellate himself. Yet, the melodramatic and occasionally florid scenario wasn't able to support such incestuous implications without making them feel as histrionic as the sudden emergence of the spring (complete with celestial chorus after Töre vows to build a church on the site of Karin's murder) seemed atypically sentimental.

Presumably, it was this bathetic reconciliation of revenge and redemption that prompted the Academy to award the Oscar for Best Foreign Film. ★★★ **DP**

⑮ THE VIRGIN SUICIDES (1999)

Starring: *James Woods (Mr. Lisbon), Kathleen Turner (Mrs. Lisbon), Kirsten Dunst (Lux Lisbon), Josh Hartnett (Trip Fontaine), Michael Paré (Adult Trip Fontaine), Scott Glenn (Father Moody), Danny DeVito (Dr. Horniker)*
Director: *Sofia Coppola*
Screenwriter: *Sofia Coppola, based on the novel by Jeffrey Eugenides*
15/92 mins./Drama/USA

Five sisters, banned from dating, nethertheless captivate the local boys while concealing a sad secret.

Adapted from Jeffrey Eugenides' critically admired 1993 novel by Francis Coppola's daughter Sofia, this sultry tale of the five Lisbon sisters drowning in the sea of emotions that is adolescence, and the local boys they captivate, is a sultry, heady treat that, if not quite capturing the book's erotic intensity, certainly comes close.

Plotwise, *The Virgin Suicides* is very slight: born into a repressive, religious household, a brood of gorgeous, mysterious girls, banned from dating, parties and movies, have gone a bit bonkers – from permanently wearing a wedding dress to frenziedly flirting with anything in trousers. But these are no ordinary teen whims, as we see when, early on, the youngest sister, Cecilia, unsuccessfully slits her wrists in the bath, so setting in motion the tragic, inexorable breakdown of the family.

Yet, rather than spin a yarn, Coppola has created a film more about mood than substance, evoking the girls' sexual awakening with rich hues of yellow, gold and red and stunning visuals – especially a gorgeous dream-like sequence where the sisters frolic in a sun-kissed field of corn – complemented perfectly by a dreamily ethereal score by the French band Air.

Tagline
Beautiful, mysterious, haunting, invariably fatal. Just like life.

However, it's not all arty froth. A dry sense of humour runs through the film throwing into relief the build-up of muted hysteria that culminates in a genuinely shocking denouement. Playing superbly against type, Turner and Woods are a revelation as the girls' parents, and a smouldering Kirsten Dunst perfectly captures Lux Lisbon's seductive sexiness, while Hartnett manfully triumphs over a frighteningly silly haircut to convince as the rehab-bound school heart-throb who breaks Lux's heart.

Occasionally the thin plotting makes the lack of any discernible point more manifest. But whether *The Virgin Suicides* is a parable about what happens when you try to police sexuality, or a tribute to the memory of adolescence, or something else entirely, this remains a seductive tale that lingers long in the memory. ★★★★ **LB**

⑮ VIRIDIANA (1961)

Starring: *Sylvia Pinal (Viridiana), Francisco Rabal (Jorge), Fernando Rey (Don Jaime), Margaritta Lozano (Ramona), Victoria Zinny (Lucia), Teresa Rabal (Rita)*
Director: *Luis Buñuel*
Screenwriters: *Luis Buñuel, Julio Alejandro based on a story by Buñuel*
15/90 mins./Drama/Mexico-Spain

At the suggestion of her mother superior, innocent novitiate Viridiana pays a visit to her wealthy uncle, Don Jaime, only for him to rape her and commit suicide. Renouncing her vocation, she opens the estate that she has inherited with her illegitimate cousin, Jorge, to the local beggars, who proceed to take licentious advantage of their hospitality.

Despite a terror of women that dated back to his childhood, Luis Buñuel had always nursed a fantasy of drugging a beautiful woman who resembled the English Queen of Spain, Victoria Eugenia, and seducing her as she lay helpless before him. In developing this disquieting reverie, he had envisaged his victim as being a nun, who would breach the convent's rules of solitude by allowing society's detritus to sample its largesse, only for them to abuse her charity by turning the sanctuary into a grotesque parody of Leonardo Da Vinci's *Last Supper*, complete with an accompanying 'Hallelujah Chorus' from Handel's *Messiah*.

Quite how Spanish Under-Secretary of Cinema José Muñoz-Fontan failed to recognise this as a scurrilous satire on both the Francoist regime and the Catholic Church is one of film history's little miracles. But the fact that he had sufficient faith in the returning prodigal's integrity to allow the picture to screen unseen at Cannes, confidant that the changes to the screenplay that he had recommended had been made in full, suggests that something other than divine intervention had ensured that *Viridiana* won the Palme d'Or and restored Buñuel to the forefront of European art cinema.

What made Buñuel's triumph all the more ironically sweet was that this 'sacreligious and blasphemous' travesty (as the Vatican newspaper *L'Osservatore Romano* dubbed it) – which had been named after an obscure saint, who was always depicted with a crucifix, nails and a crown of thorns – was filmed in Madrid alongside Nicholas Ray's *King Of Kings*. But Buñuel's devastating parable shunned biblical opulence and clothed its outcasts in rags that had been purchased from street beggars, one of whom was cast as the drunken brute who tries to molest Silvia Pinal.

Such authenticity emphasised Buñuel's contention that 'we do not live in the best of all possible worlds'. But it also reinforced his unswerving determination to expose the hypocrisy of an institution that he believed had betrayed its flock by siding with the Fascists during the Civil War. Franco later claimed he couldn't understand the fuss *Viridiana* had generated. He clearly hadn't been paying attention. ★★★★★ **DP**

ⓟ I VITELLONI (1953)

Starring: *Franco Interlenghi (Moraldo Rubini), Alberto Sori (Alberto), Franco Fabrizi (Fausto Moretti), Leopoldo Trieste (Leopoldo Vannucci), Riccardo Fellini (Riccardo), Leonora Ruffo (Sandra Rubini)*
Director: *Federico Fellini*
Screenwriter: *Federico Fellini, based on a story by Fellini, Ennio Flaiano, Tullio Pinelli*
PG/103 mins./Drama/Italy/France

Five young men hang about in an Italian seaside town — Fausto marries the girl he has made pregnant, Leopoldo tries to write plays, Riccardo sings, Alberto makes jokes and Moraldo wonders whether he should leave.

TOP10

Blaxsploitation Taglines

1 'Women so hot with desire they melt the chains that enslave them!' – *The Big Bird Cage*

2 **'Men call him SAVAGE ... Women call him all the time.' – *Savage!***

3 'He's got The Man on the pan ... and he's gonna fry him good!' – *Black Jack*

4 **'Hail Caesar Godfather of Harlem ... the Cat with the .45 calibre Claws!' – *Black Caesar***

5 '6 feet 2 inches and all of it Dynamite!' – *Cleopatra Jones*

6 **'She's brown sugar and spice but if you don't treat her nice she'll put you on ice!' – *Foxy Brown***

7 'Every brother's friend. Every mother's enemy.' – *Black Samson*

8 **'Super sisters on cycles ... better move your butt when these ladies strut!' – *Darktown Strutters***

9 'Get back Jack – give him no jive ... he is the baaad'est cat in '75' – *The Candy Tangerine Man*

10 **'The Brother Man in the Motherland ... Shaft is stickin' it ... all the way.' – *Shaft in Africa***

V

This early Federico Fellini film, the first of his truly great movies, has been the model for many, many later autobiographies-on-celluloid in which auteur directors look back on the end of their growing-up years – the bunch-of-guys-hanging-out template is used exactly by George Lucas in *American Graffiti*, Martin Scorsese in *Mean Streets* and Barry Levinson in *Diner*.

The vitelloni ('young calves') are thirtyish, mostly unemployed, long-time pals who don't have much to do in their home town, too old to be kids but still uncertain about settling down or doing anything much. All of the five central characters represent aspects of Fellini's own character or history – the young husband who is not so much tempted to infidelity but unable to abandon the freedoms of the single life, the earnest would-be writer who impresses the maidservant next door but flees when an elderly gay actor makes a pass, the apparent leader (Sordi was the biggest star) who is basically a clown, and the sensitive young man who quietly gets on a train at the end and moves out into the wider world.

Made during the Italian neo-realist boom, it is rooted in observation of specific behaviour and 'realistic' detail but already Fellini is starting to dream of a more fantastical, carnivalesque cinema and find strange moments (a simpleton falling in love with a stolen angel statue) amid petty stories of infidelities and lost illusions.

It's as wistful and sad as it is funny and charming, with the first of Nino Rota's great scores to keep it burbling along. ★★★★ **KN**

ⓘ VIVA LAS VEGAS (1964)

Starring: *Elvis Presley (Lucky Jackson), Ann-Margret (Rusty Martin), Cesare Danova (Count Elmo Mancini), William Demarest (Mr. Martin), Nicky Blair (Shorty Fansworth)*
Director: *George Sidney*
Screenwriter: *Sally Benson*
U/84 mins./Musical/Romance/USA

Race driver Lucky Jackson pitches up in Las Vegas for a race but is forced to work as a waiter to earn money to fix his car when the engine breaks. Falling for local swimming pool attendant/dance teacher Rusty Martin only complicates things.

Elvis made thirty-one films in his lifetime (and managed to feature in many more after his death!) and to even the most hardened fan will admit that most of them – to use a technical term – suck.

Viva Las Vegas stands among the few that not only do not suck, but, actually, are rather good. Perhaps it was the chemistry between flame-haired Ann-Margret and Elvis (which continued off-screen and matured into a lifetime friendship – Ann-Margret was his only film co-star to attend his funeral). Certainly both of them seem to inject the film with a genuine sense of fun and sass which were sorely missing in some of his other dead-eyed film performances (including the excruciating *Kissing Cousins* released the same year). But it's also that *Viva Las Vegas* captured everything that has come to be synonymous which the legend himself.

This was the start of the idea of Elvis adding 'of Vegas' to his unofficial title of King of Rock 'n' Roll and he owned this city. The consummate showman effortlessly glides through the best set of songs in any Elvis movie from the titular 'Viva Las Vegas', wonderfully duelling with Ann-Margret in 'The Lady Loves Me' and making her shake everything she's got in the college gym – a memorably sight – to 'C'mon Everybody', and still leaves space for 'What Did I Say?' and 'Yellow Rose Of Texas'.

Although it became one of the best-grossing Elvis films ever, the soundtrack was pretty much chucked out by RCA, butchered of other highlights and it emerged later that more songs had been recorded for the film, which finally made it onto soundtrack recordings in the 1970s.

Viva Las Vegas also serves as a reminder of Presley's potential as an actor. Early performances in *King Creole* (1958) and *Flaming Star* (1960) – in a role that was intended for Marlon Brando – suggested he could have been more than a hack player, but his manager Colonel Tom Parker was more interesting in churning out cash cows. *Viva Las Vegas* showed that Presley, given the right partner, could move towards romantic comedy roles that might appeal to more than his fanbase. But Parker dismissed this film too, feeling someone like Ann-Margret was too much of a threat to Elvis' star status. It's a shame because pairing them again in something a little less lightweight could have been interesting. ★★★ **EC**

ⓘ VIVRE SA VIE (1962)

Starring: *Anna Karina (Nana), Sady Rebbot (Raoul), André S. Labarthe (Paul), Guylaine Schlumberger (Yvette), Gérard Hoffman (Le Chef), Monique Messine (Elizabeth), Paul Pavel (Journaliste), Dimitri Dineff (the Guy), Peter Kassovitz (Jeune Homme), Eric Schlumberger (Luigi), Brice Parain (The Philosopher)*
Director: *Jean-Luc Godard*
Screenwriter: *Jean-Luc Gôdard, Marcel Sacotte, based on the book* Où En Est La Prostitution *by Sacotte*
15/85 mins./Drama/France

Unable to pay her rent by working in a record shop, Nana becomes a prostitute. However, her pimp, Raoul, refuses to allow her to find happiness with a new lover and she is accidentally killed in a shootout.

From an artistic viewpoint, Jean-Luc Godard's fourth feature is a treasure trove of originals and reproductions, as the camera lingers on Anna Karina at her most bewitching. At one moment she's Lillian Gish, another Louise Brooks and another Renée Falconetti, whose performance in Carl Theodor Dreyer's *The Passion Of Joan Of Arc* moves her so deeply (perhaps because she was conscious of the fact that the actress drifted into prostitution after suffering a nervous breakdown). Yet Karina's descent from wannabe actress to chic hooker is studded with her own iconic moments, most of them involving cigarette smoke.

For Godard, however, this was clearly a difficult movie to make. It has both a B sensibility and a New Wave aura. But an wisp of sadness pervades the proceedings, as he realises he's virtually pimping for his own wife by presenting her as both madonna and whore.

Indeed, this is a film of conscious contradictions. It challenges cinematic preconceptions about the balance between text and image, while also questioning the nature of narrative by implying that this is simultaneously a documentary about prostitution, a drama about a woman trapped by fate and a study of Anna Karina playing such a character.

With its action being divided into 12 captioned segments, it also seems to be an experimental outing, which uses intense close-ups for seemingly insignificant incidents and distance shots for more dramatic moments. Yet Godard's depiction of Karina often has the romanticised glow of Hollywood glamour photography.

Similarly, Nana's killing seems random, yet she is surrounded by portents of death, such as the references to Alain Resnais' *Nuit Et Brouillard*, philosopher Brice Parain's account of Porthos the Musketeer's demise (which forms part of a diatribe on language's inadequacy as a means of communication) and her lover's rendition of Baudelaire's translation of Edgar Allan Poe's short story, *The Oval Portrait* (which was actually dubbed by Godard himself).

Less self-conscious, yet considerably more personal than any of his early films, this is Godard's forgotten masterpiece. Beautifully photographed by Raoul Coutard and scored by Michel Legrand, it simply makes cinema-going worthwhile. ★★★★★**DP**

W

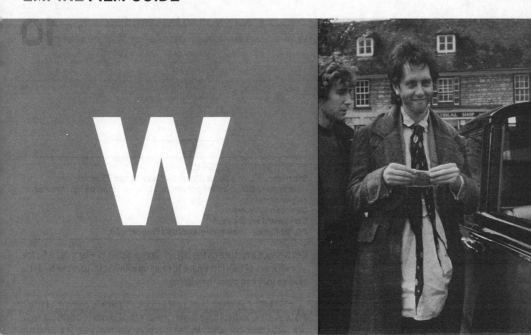

THE WAGES OF FEAR (LE SALAIRE DE LA PEUR) (1953)

Starring: *Yves Montand (Mario), Charles Vanel (M. Lo), Peter Van Eyck (Bimba), Antonio Centa (Camp Chief), Luis De Lima (Bernardo)*
Director: *Henri-Georges Clouzot*
Screenwriters: *Henri-Georges Clouzot, Jerome Germonimi, based on the novel by Georges Arnaud*
PG/147 mins./Adventure/Thriller/France
Awards: *BAFTA – Best Film from any source*

In a poor South American country, four drivers are asked to drive explosive nitroglycerine across 300 miles of rocky terrain.

In 1953, decades before the phrase 'high concept' was ever uttered, a French film received international distribution on the back of a simple, literally explosive premise. Henri-Georges Clouzot, later director of the great horror movie *Les Diaboliques*, found in George Arnaud's novel *Le Salaire de la Peur* what John Huston found in B. Traven's *The Treasure Of The Sierra Madre* – an action-adventure so spare and suspenseful that it comes over as more than a mere thriller.

Wages Of Fear has the force of an anecdote. An American outfit, Southern Oil Company, is drilling deep in the South American jungle, and the gushers have caught fire. The only way to beat the blaze is to blow it out 'like a candle, only you have to blow hard,' which means two lorryloads of highly unstable nitroglycerine have to be driven out to the fire. The only road from the depot to the disaster area runs through miles of treacherous terrain littered with dangerous turns, crumbling planks, falling rocks and ragged hardtop, and one good jolt will vaporise truck, nitro, drivers and a substantial swathe of the countryside. No union men can be asked to take suicide jobs, so company boss Big Bill O 'Brien (William Tubbs) recruits desperate souls from among the losers who haunt the nowhere town of Las Piedras, begging for work.

The first hour of this two-and-a-half-hour film, which was once trimmed severely for overseas release but is now usually seen complete, is all character stuff, introducing the doomed and the damned. The leads, fated to be unhappy partners, are Mario (Montand), a tough Corsican with a low-cut vest and a permanent fag drooping from his lips (even around the nitro), and Jo (Vanel), an older huckster whose sharp white suit and trim haircut-and-tache mark him as an operator with pretensions to style. The other drivers are sleek German Bimba (Van Eyck), who we take to be an ex-Nazi until he reveals that he spent the war in the salt mines as an enemy of the Reich, and tubby Italian Luigi (Folco Lulli), a building site foreman ordered to get a new job because of cement in his lungs. Mario rooms with Luigi and has an up-and-down relationship with gamine drudge Linda (Vera Clouzot), but neglects both when Jo comes to town.

On the road, Clouzot stages a string of unforgettable sequences. One stretch of ruined track can only be crossed by driving at under six miles an hour or over 40, no overtaking is possible. The truck in the rear takes the fast option while the lead lorry is forced to go slow, and a fender-bending bump will go off like Krakatoa. A mountain turn requires that the trucks back out onto a rickety wooden platform; the lighter first lorry barely makes it, giving Mario, in the second track, a truly sweaty moment that sends Jo cowering for the hills. A 50-ton boulder has fallen into the road, and Bimba calmly drains a litre of nitro into his thermos to blow it up, only remembering when the fuse is lit that this will rain pebbles all over the countryside and a few good hits on the cargo will set it off.

Finally, after the lead lorry has been detonated, Mario has to get the truck through a blast crater filled with oil from a ruptured pipeline, and the nerve-shredded Jo ('la mort qui marche') gets his leg stuck under the wheel. Clouzot is sometimes labelled a gimmicky filmmaker, taking properties so strong that even average direction will make them great. But since both his hits were remade and bungled by Hollywood (*Sorcerer*, William Friedkin's 1977 take on *Wages* and Jeremiah S. Chechik's *Diabolique* in 1996)

Actors Who Played Identical Twins — TOP10

1. Nicolas Cage-*Adaptation* (2002)
2. Jeremy Irons-*Dead Ringers* (1988)
3. Lindsay Lohan-*The Parent Trap* (1998)
4. Bette Davis-*Stolen Life* (1946); *Dead Ringer* (1964)
5. Lily Tomlin and Bette Midler-*Big Business* (1988)
6. Jean-Claude Van Damme-*Double Impact* (1991)
7. Eddie Murphy-*Bowfinger* (1999)
8. Leonardo DiCaprio-*The Man In The Iron Mask* (1998)
9. Elvis Presley-*Kissing Cousins* (1964)
10. Chris Rock-*Bad Company* (2002)

it's easier to appreciate the skills he brought to the table, especially his handling of neurotic, unlikeable characters who we are still compelled to identify with.

Wages Of Fear is so tense we don't even need to see the explosion when it comes (a blast of wind whips the tobacco out of the cigarette Jo is rolling for Mario), though both that wooden-turning area and (in the horribly ironic finale) the empty truck on the return trip are sent tumbling down the mountain, falling apart like matchstick models. Mario's thought for the day: 'And aren't we all the walking dead ?' ★★★★★ **KN**

WAIT UNTIL DARK (1967)

Starring: *Audrey Hepburn (Susie Hendrix), Alan Arkin (Harry Roat), Richard Crenna (Mike Talman), Efrem Zimbalist Jr. (Sam Hendrix)*
Director: *Terence Young*
Screenwriters: *Robert Howard-Carrington, Jane Howard Carrington based on the play by Frederick Knott*
12/107 mins./Thriller/USA

Susie Hendrix is blind, her husband is away on business, and three thugs are in her apartment looking for a doll stuffed with drugs. One of the thieves, their leader Harry Roat, is fully prepared to kill for the prize.

An outstanding thriller based on a stageplay (by Frederick Knott) that fits so much better on the screen because, as well as the expansive, cinema is really good at claustrophobia. The genius of the concept is to pitch its trio of villains, chasing a drug haul concealed in a doll placed on the heroine's now absent husband, against a blind woman. Not only is it the obvious vulnerability of the situation, it's the chance for manipulation as the hoods claims to be variously friends of sightless Susie's husband and the police on his trail.

Audrey Hepburn is cast to perfection as Susie, she is so frail and delicate, and flawlessly portrays the idea of women trapped in the prison cell of her own head. She pulls us in, charging us to protect her when there is nothing we can do. A devilish Alan Arkin leads Richard Crenna and Jack Weston as the nefarious thugs plying the con game, without knowing that their quarry (stashed in the house by a now dead colleague) is not there. It's a dilemma without a solution, another twist in this nightmare game.

Bond alumnus Terence Young plays some equally cruel visual tricks to torment the audience. He keeps his camera so tight into the action, the space feels to be shrinking; the film barely leaves the apartment keeping the tension wracked tight as a wire coil. There is some magnificent subtlety as Susie searches rooms to find out if she is alone, tortuous sequences played nearly silently. Yet, none of these brilliantly orchestrated scenes have anything on the finale, when Susie turns tables on her captors by smashing all the light-bulbs and plunging them all into blindness. The one place she has the advantage. ★★★★ **IN**

WAKING NED (1998)

Starring: *Ian Bannen (Jackie O'Shea), David Kelly (Michael O'Sullivan), Fionnula Flanagan (Annie O'Shea), Susan Lynch (Maggie O'Toole), James Nesbitt (Pig Finn), Paul Vaughan (Narrator)*
Director: *Kirk Jones*
Screenwriter: *Kirk Jones*
PG/91 mins./Comedy/Ireland/UK/France/USA

Ned has won a fortune on the lottery. Only problem is – he's dead. So the wily villagers of Tullymore have to come up with a scam to prove he's still alive so they can claim the winnings.

As 1994 Nic Cage vehicle *It Could Happen To You* and countless tabloid tales of misfortune have shown, the lure of six numbered balls is a topic rich with comic potential. And so it proves again here as one Saturday night, the glittery, golden finger of fate and a six million quid roll-over pot prods a tiny village in the south of Ireland.

Jackie O'Shea is determined to discover which of Tullymore's 52 inhabitants is suddenly rather well off. Plying his fellow villagers with wife Annie's chicken supper and a persuasive snifter of fermented barley, Jackie eventually twigs that the winner must be Ned Devine. But Ned's not well off at all, and won't be spending one penny of his massive windfall. Because Ned's dead. And with Lottery rep Jim Kelly (Brendan F. Dempsey) en route, the claim will die with him. Unless, of course, Jackie and best pal Michael can pull off a plan of guile, cunning and – well, let's call a spade a spade – fraud.

With its non-starry cast and such a modest premise, this could so easily have been dwarfed by the big screen, but it's a worthy feature and debutant Jones has a wealth of charming players, particularly in peripheral subplots such as whiffy pig farmer James Nesbitt's stop-start romance with single mum Susan Lynch. There's a wicked glint to his script, too, which always checks its warm-heartedness just short of sentimentality, and keeps a steady laugh count rolling.

Bannen and Kelly hurl themselves into this with the energy and exuberance of a pair of teenagers, and whether skinny-dipping at a picturesque cove or belting along lanes naked on a motorbike, the vim of these two twinkly-eyed and likeable old codgers is steeled with a wily determination.

It's this edge which hustled the movie deserved elbow room in the multiplexes alongside more expensive and cinematic productions, and as the twin revelations of a wonderfully unexpected pay-off prove, in the end there's no substitute for wit, invention and real, priceless humour. ★★★★ **DB**

WAKING LIFE (2001)

Starring: *Wiley Wiggins (Main Character), Ethan Hawke (Jesse), Julie Delpy (Celine), Steven Soderbergh*
Director: *Richard Linklater*
Screenwriter: *Richard Linklater*
15/96 mins./Animation/Drama/USA

A man walks through life as if in a dream, talking to a variety of people about the meaning of life and our perceptions of it.

Director Richard Linklater returned to the ground of his debut indie hit, *Slacker* – a series of rambling monologues and conversations, each delivered by the inhabitants of Austin, Texas.

However, *Waking Life*'s innovative twist is that it is filmed using digital cameras, with every frame then drawn over by a team of animators. This creates a dream-like effect that perfectly fits the film's theme: the nature of dreams versus reality.

As someone tells the unnamed protagonist, 'Most people just sleepwalk through their waking lives,' and the whole film is shown as a dream from which he can't wake. This is a film that is brimming with ideas and visual invention, but its occasional pretentiousness may prove too much for some. ★★★ **MT**

WALK THE LINE (2005)

Starring: *Joaquin Phoenix (Johnny Cash), Reese Witherspoon (June Carter), Ginnifer Goodwin (Vivian Cash), Robert Patrick (Ray Cash), Dallas Roberts (Sam Phillips)*
Director: *James Mangold*
Screenwriters: *Gill Dennis, James Mangold, based on the books* The Man In Black *by Johnny Cash,* Cash: An Autobiography *by Johnny Cash*
12A/136 mins./Drama/Biography/Romance/Music/USA

Awards – *Academy Awards – Best Actress, BAFTA – Best Actress, Best Sound, Golden Globes – Best Musical/Comedy, Best Actor, Best Actress*

After escaping an Arkansas cotton farm, singer Johnny Cash makes it all the way to Sun Records in Memphis, where he joins an illustrious roster that includes Elvis Presley. With a young family waiting back home, country-star-in-the-making Cash seems made – but will he throw it all away for two things he comes across while on the road: June Carter and drugs?

Musicians sing songs of three minutes and live lives in three acts. They all struggle to crack the big time, they all succumb to the temptations of the road and practically everyone manages to clean up in time for one final hit. Little wonder that ever since Elvis died on the crapper, the heady mix of pop and problems has excited almost as many TV movies as broken homes and bowel cancer.

And yet it is the particular misfortune of James Mangold's bubblegum biopic of country pioneer Johnny Cash to be released just 11 months after Taylor Hackford's glossy *Ray* snaffled a clutch of Oscar nominations and every conceivable acting award for star Jamie Foxx. The similarities between the two stories are striking: from the social and political upheaval of the American South in the post-War period, to the poor country boy haunted by guilt about the brother he lost, large chunks of the territory traversed here were mapped out by *Ray*. Like R'n'B innovator Ray Charles, Cash was a musical rebel determined to forge a new sound back when such things were possible, and just like Charles, the monumental Cash was very nearly undone by drugs.

Factor in the proximity and the superficial resemblance can become dazzling – expect critics to glibly cite this as yet another example of Hollywood's herd mentality (see *Volcano* vs. *Dante's Peak* etc.)

But hell, since we must be glib, the correct comparison is this: *Walk The Line* is the *Deep Impact* to *Ray*'s *Armageddon*. Where Hackford's film was an overblown, emotional blockbuster precision-engineered for Oscar- (rather than box-office) glory, Mangold's movie is a more composed affair, studiously focused on a slow-burning romance rather than straining to capture an entire life. As such, *Walk The Line* feels like a more rounded work; it may lack some of *Ray*'s pizzazz – heroin is a better villain than prescription speed – but it moves more smoothly and eventually arrives at a natural stopping place.

Interestingly, though, there is little to be made of the most obvious creative difference. Hackford's decision to have Foxx, an accomplished singer, mime to the inimitable Ray Charles proved to be a sound decision, but Mangold's riskier gamble – for the untested Phoenix and Witherspoon to provide all the vocals – also pays off handsomely. It is not so much that the pair's impressive impressions would ever fool a discerning ear, it is that the high-wire thrills tendered by watching amateurs stretch themselves on film is not so far from the buzz of live performance.

Walk The Line's greater reserve should endear it to any delicate palates who choked on *Ray*'s sentimental bluster, but in truth, both movies are fundamentally genre pictures elevated to a different league by two simple ingredients: a killer soundtrack and knockout performances.

For a life so chaotic and a star so singular, Mangold coughs up a structure so predictable it wouldn't look out of place on the Hallmark Channel. Much like those unstoppable Cash rhythms the narrative remains on rails, ticking off major life events and chalking up star cameos (Elvis! A namecheck for Bob Dylan!) without ever really bringing the Man In Black into the light. Then again, perhaps it all depends on how black you like it: as a psychological study of the complex Cash, *Walk The Line* is perfectly pat; as a celebration of the romance between Cash and Carter, it is perfectly sweet.

The appeal of the central couple is a direct result of tireless work from the two leads. Phoenix makes hay with the rich soil he's given to till, but if anyone suffers from close proximity to *Ray*, it is Phoenix. The broody actor is very good here – terrific, even – but, unlike Foxx, he is never astonishing.

Reese Witherspoon, though, comes mighty close. Witherspoon's June is a pistol – a sugar-rush of screwball energy and cornball Southern sass that's meticulously earthed with grace notes of sadness, hinting at the stolen childhood and broken marriages that all take place off screen. With a thin field confronting Witherspoon at the 2006 Oscars, this largely supporting role unsurprisingly nabbed major honours. ★★★★ **CK**

W

WALKABOUT (1971)

Starring: *Jenny Agutter (Girl), Luc Roeg (White Boy), David Gulpilil (Black Boy), John Meillon (Man)*
Director: *Nicolas Roeg*
Screenwriter: *Edward Bond, based on the novel by James Vance Marshall*
12/100 mins./Drama/UK

A sixteen-year old girl and her younger brother are stranded in the Australian outback after their father's suicide. The pair fall in with an aborigine youth.

Nicolas Roeg's second feature as director (and first solo effort) is deceptively simple: children from two different cultures survive in the desert. The title is an aboriginal term, referring to a time of reflection and testing spent apart from the tribe; the city kids' spell in the wild should serve as a walkabout of their own, but they only *almost* learn something which haunts the girl when she returns to her society to get on with ordinary life.

It's a deep film, but also elusive, accepting that some mysteries can never be solved – the story begins and ends with deaths we don't have enough information to 'understand'.

If the novel were remade conventionally, the picture would be full of exciting wilderness perils and go heavy on a *Blue Lagoon*-style affair between the repressed miss and the nature boy, but Roeg takes a more elliptical, enigmatic approach.

A drama of transformation and tragedy is played out through apparently thrown-away dialogue, footnote-like scenes which provide a 'civilised' contrast with wilderness behaviour (Gulpilil's spearing and bludgeoning of a kangaroo with a butcher impersonally chopping cuts of meat) and documentary footage of crawling lizards and swarming insects.

The normal skills associated with 'acting' aren't required and Roeg cast two of the major roles with players who had never acted before, the aborigine dancer Gulpilil and his own son Luc.

The film lives in the fantasies of a generation because Agutter, in and out of school uniform (she has a famous nude swim), emerged from her prim *Railway Children* image to be strikingly sensual. ★★★★★ **KN**

WALL STREET (1987)

Starring: *Charlie Sheen (Bud Fox), Michael Douglas (Gordon Gekko), Martin Sheen (Carl Fox), Daryl Hannah (Darien Taylor), Terence Stamp (Sir Larry Wildman), Sean Young (Kate Gekko), James Spader (Roger Barnes)*
Director: *Oliver Stone*
Screenwriters: *Stanley Weiser, Oliver Stone*
15/125 mins./Drama/USA

Awards – *Academy Awards – Best Actor (Michael Douglas), Golden Globes – Best Drama Actor, Razzie Awards – Worst Supporting Actress (Daryl Hannah)*

An impatient young stockbroker, Bud Fox, with no moral grounding and a desire to get rich whatever the cost, trades inside information and allows himself to be moulded into the fat-cat image of high-flyer Gordon Gekko. But Bud has harder lessons to learn . . .

Oliver Stone's indictment of the grasping yuppie ethos of the 80s took no prisoners, blasting fast-talking brokers, inside traders, corporate raiders, interior decorators, and sushi eaters in one energetic assault. Ironically, the domination of Michael Douglas, brilliantly bad-assed as arch-villain despoiler Gordon Gekko, so inspired wannabe Gekkos that the very lowliest of City twerps embraced his sartorial style from slicked-back hair to braces and his epigrams passed into the language: 'Greed is Good.' 'Lunch is for wimps.' 'If you need a friend, get a dog.' 'I create nothing; I own.' 'If you're not inside, you're outside.' 'Money isn't lost or gained, it's simply transferred.' 'A Player, or Nothing.' 'Money never sleeps, pal.'

This credo infects bushy-tailed broker Bud Fox with a mania. In his rush for the bucks he sidesteps loyalties, ethics and finally the law to acquire the penthouse, the offshore holdings and the Italian designer-dressed girl of his dreams. Fortunately for the sake of an upright moral he stays too long at the ball and gets turned back into a sadder but wiser pumpkin.

Buddy's rite of passage through the financial jungle is absorbing and even exciting even if you haven't a clue what the financial panjandrums are talking about half the time. Subtle this isn't; most of the characters, whether Bud's Honest, Hard Working manual labourer father (although played beautifully by Martin Sheen), Gekko's vacant wife, the Ethical Stockbroker (Hal Holbrook, presumably based on Stone's stockbroker father, to whom the film is dedicated), the Hotshot Lawyer or Bud's Greedy Tootsie are easily assimilated caricatures. Nevertheless Stone takes in a lot of plot and his many targets at an enthralling pace with style and Douglas' shark is a killer. ★★★★ **AE**

Movie Trivia:
Oliver Stone (born 1946)

Who he is: Yale dropout, Vietnam vet and former journalist. Hollywood's foremost conspiracy theorist. Mixes bohemian with political themes.
Hallmarks: Distrust of authority; controversy-baiting; frenetic editing and camera trickery; sense of outrage as an underlying theme; references to Vietnam; R-ratings.
If you see one movie, see: *Platoon* (1986)

WALLACE AND GROMIT: CURSE OF THE WERE-RABBIT (2005)

Starring: *the voices of: Peter Sallis (Wallace/Hutch), Ralph Fiennes (Victor Quartermaine), Helena Bonham Carter (Lady Campanula Tottington), Peter Kay (PC Mackintosh)*
Directors: *Steve Box, Nick Park*
Screenwriters: *Bob Baker, Steve Box, Mark Burton, based on characters by Nick Park*
U/85 mins./Animation/Adventure/Comedy/Family/UK

Awards – *Academy Awards – Best Animated Film, BAFTA – Alexander Korda Award for Best British Film, Empire Awards – Best Directors*

With just four days to go until Tottington's Giant Vegetable Competition, all is well with the village's vegetable crop, thanks to the watchful eye of Anti-Pesto, run by keen inventor Wallace and his loyal dog, Gromit. But when a mythical creature, known as the Were-Rabbit, starts terrorising the locals, the redoubtable duo find themselves in a fight unlike any they've faced before . . .

Three times Nick Park, the genius behind Aardman Animation, has gone to the Oscars. Three times he's worn a different coloured bow tie. Three times he's left with the little gold fella. Well, their first big-screen outing has added about 50 minutes to the running time, but thankfully that's all that's changed – for this consistently hilarious slice of Britannia also delivered his first Best Animated Feature Academy Award.

Of course, credit should also go to co-director Steve Box. For almost five years, the duo have locked themselves away to craft the first W&G tale since 1995's *A Close Shave*. That's a heck of a long time to keep gags fresh, but thanks to a beautifully modulated script, truly cinematic camerawork and editing, and astonishing animation, they've done it.

Were-Rabbit was funded by US behemoth DreamWorks Animation, yet it retains a charming homespun quality, fusing Ealing comedy tropes and Hammer horror conventions (don't be scared – the Were-Rabbit is as cute as a bag of Jessica Albas) into a near-dementedly British tone, augmented by a Pixar-level script that mixes killer sight gags, world-class punnery and ace one-liners.

However, the comedy is never indulged at the expense of the plot, which flies off in genuinely unexpected directions, culminating in a boundlessly inventive funfair chase sequence.

Tagline
Something wicked this way hops.

The supporting cast are clearly having fun but never overshadow the central pairing, Wallace enjoying a spot of romance, while Gromit gets all the cool action scenes. It's a tribute to Aardman that Gromit, who doesn't even have a mouth, conveys a cavalcade of emotion, from courage to suspicion to terror and, crucially, sadness, as Park uses those puppy dog eyes to elicit a few tears. ★★★★★ **CH**

Movie Trivia: Aardman Animation (established 1976)

What is it? Bristol-based animation studio, specialising in 'clay-mation' but also traditional and CG-animation. Defiantly British, popular worldwide.
Hallmarks: Wallace & Gromit; Creature Comforts; eccentric characters; thumbprints on clay characters; intricate and meticulously crafted Plasticine worlds.
If you see one movie, see: *Wallace & Gromit: The Curse of the Were-Rabbit* (2005)

THE WANDERERS (1979)

Starring: *Ken Wahl (Richie), John Friedrich (Joey), Karen Allen (Nina), Toni Kalem (Despie Galasso), Alan Rosenberg ('Turkey'), Jim Young (Buddy), Tony Ganios (Perry)*
Director: *Philip Kaufman*
Screenwriters: *Philip Kaufman, Rose Kaufman, from the novel by Richard Price*
18/117 mins./Drama/Action/USA

In the Bronx in 1963, the Wanderers – a working-class, mostly-Italian street gang – prepare for a rumble with their black rivals, the Del-Bombers.

This Philip Kaufman adaption of Richard Price's novel is a mutation of *American Graffiti* and *The Warriors.* With changin' times soundtracked extensively from doo-wop to Dylan and Kennedy getting shot at a crucial moment, it shows street gangs not as cool rebels but junior auxiliaries of the underworld types who run local communities.

In the slightly chilling finale, the more sensitive Wanderers, runty Joey and hulking Perry, head for San Francisco after writing off their rotten parents and the neighbourhood – while the smooth-talking gang-leader Richie, having knocked up the daughter (Toni Kalem) of the local bowling alley boss (Dolph Sweet), takes part in a defiant singalong of the gang's theme song, then heads out after a more unusual girl (Karen Allen), who goes to a folk club (where, inevitably, Dylan is playing) he cannot bring himself to enter, sending him back to the gang, the bowling alley, Kalem and the big Hawaiian shirt Sweet has given him ('don't worry, you'll grow into it').

There's gritty street comedy, with the lads meeting girls *Lemon Popsicle*-fashion by playing 'titty elbow' on the streets (Allen calls them on it), and strange side-tracks with surreal rival gangs: the Wongs, Orientals who can floor anyone with 'a judo chop'; the Baldies, shave-pates led by the mountainous but oddly dainty Erland Van Lidth der Jeude, whose 'ladies' auxiliary' consists of the rat-waif Linda Manz, and who wind up in the Marines, presumably to be packed off to Vietnam; and the silent, murderous Ducky Boys, who turn up like ghosts or zombies at the final game to precipitate a fight that unites the other hood factions. ★★★ **KN**

WAR AND PEACE (VOYNA I MIR) (1968)

Starring: *Ludmila Savelyeva (Natasha Rostov), Vyacheslav Tikhonov (Prince Andrew Bolkonsky), Sergei Bondarchuk (Pierre Bezukhov), Irina Skobtseva (Helene), Viktor Stanitsym (Ilya Andrevevich Rostov), Kira Golovko (Countess Roberts)*
Director: *Sergei Bondarchuk*
Screenwriters: *Sergei Bondarchuk, Vassili Soloviev based on the novel* Voyna I Mir *by Leo Tolstoy*
PG/434 mins./Historical Drama/USSR
Awards: *Academy Awards – Best Foreign Language Film*

The complex problems of the innocent Natasha Rostov, the arrogant Prince Andrew Bolkonsky and the idealistic Pierre Bezukhov, who is unhappily married to the manipulative Helene, are resolved by Napoleon's 1812 invasion of Russia.

In 1915, when Vladimir Gardin and Yakov Protazanov produced a 10-reel version of Leo Tolstoy's 1869 novel, it was hailed as the greatest motion picture ever produced in Russia. Half a century later, Sergei Bondarchuk surpassed their achievement with an epic that was so monumental that it had to be released in four two-hour episodes.

It was estimated to have cost between $40-100 million, making it the most expensive film made anywhere to date, and it proved one of the few domestic pictures of the Communist era to excel at the Soviet box office (earning Bondarchuk the Order of Lenin). Despite being cut to 373 and then 170 minutes for its dubbed English-language version, it dwarfed King Vidor's 1956 adaptation, with Henry Fonda and Audrey Hepburn, and deservedly won the Academy Award for Best Foreign Film.

Yet, *War And Peace* is never ranked among the master works of world cinema. It is regarded simply as an exercise in cultural propaganda, whose statistics are more impressive than its cinematic credentials.

It's worth repeating that 30 stars and 120,000 extras populated the 158 separate scenes that were played out against 272 sets, especially as the paintings, furnishings and props were borrowed from the country's finest museums to ensure the same authenticity that went into the making of the 6,000 military and 2,000 civilian costumes and the 60 French and Russian cannon.

However, Bondarchuk was less concerned with the scope and scale of the picture – even though the burning of Moscow and the Battle of Borodino were exemplars in movie logistics that were given additional visceral impact by the use of helicopter panoramas and dizzying subjective views. The director and his co-scenarist Vassili Soloviev were more interested in capturing the vibrant realism of Tolstoy's characters and his 'thoughts, emotions, philosophy and ideas'.

They succeeded largely through Bondarchuk's delicate handling of the human aspects of the drama and his accessible treatment of its complex politics. Some of the performances are deficient, but Bonadarchuk makes a solid Pierre and ballerina Ludmila Savelyeva is simply exquisite as Natasha.

Hence, this is long overdue a critical re-evaluation. ★★★★★ **DP**

THE WAR GAME (1965)

Starring: *Michael Aspel (Commentator), Peter Graham (Commentator)*
Director: *Peter Watkins*
Screenwriter: *Peter Watkins*
12/48 mins./Documentary/UK
Awards: *Academy Awards – Best Documentary Feature; BAFTA – Best Short Film, UN Award; Venice Film Festival – Special Prize*

A documentary about the effects on Great Britain of a nuclear war.

Made in 1965 for BBC-TV by Peter Watkins, using the mock-documentary techniques he had successfully used in the historical drama *Culloden*, this proved so controversial that the corporation refused to air it for three decades – though it won an Academy Award in the Best Documentary category and had a long, successful theatrical run which paradoxically made it far more accessible for many years than any number of less controversial BBC programme that were transmitted once and disappeared forever.

W

Watkins dares to contradict misinformation presented in numberless 'duck and cover'-style government civil defence propaganda efforts and makes a fair fist of showing how a nuclear exchange might happen and what its likely effects would be. Though dated in its Cold War politics, with a few Strangelovian talking heads adding a nearly comic touch, this remains chillingly convincing in its depiction of aspects of nuclear warfare rarely addressed by even the most hysterical 'awful warning' films: the psychological toll on survivors, especially those in the hard-pressed emergency services; the problems of evacuating the cities in a country still steeped in racial prejudice ('are they coloured?' asks a Kent housewife asked to billet refugees); the creation of a generation of orphans who 'don't want to be nothing' when they grow up.

Most controversial is the suggestion that after the attack 'ordinary people' will be in danger not from the communist supposed enemy but the armed remnants of their own military and police force. The images of British bobbies formed into firing squads, mercy-killing the grievously wounded or summarily-executing food rioters were calculated to be shocking. In 1984, director Mick Jackson and writer Barry Hines essentially updated *The War Game* as the even more despairing TV movie *Threads*. **★★★★ KN**

ⓞ WARGAMES (1983)

Starring: *Matthew Broderick (David Lightman), Dabney Coleman (Dr. John McKittrick), John Wood (Dr. Stephen Falken), Ally Sheedy (Jennifer Katherine Mack), Barry Corbin (Gen. Jack Beringer)*
Director: *John Badham*
Screenwriters: *Lawrence Lasker, Walter F. Parkes*
PG/114 mins./Thriller/USA

Awards: *BAFTA – Best Sound*

David Lightman, a whizz kid obsessed with computer games, manages by chance to connect into the Government's super-computer which controls the country's nuclear arsenal. Then the computer challenges him to a game of World War III, with David not realising it is the real thing.

Although personal computer technology has moved on in leaps and bounds since the clunky early 80s, making the crude machines on show here look the Spinning Jennys of the internet generation, this apocalyptic techno-thriller played out by teens still has a chilling grip. There is something frighteningly reminiscent of *2001*'s HAL about the robotic voice of the talking super-computer that challenges Matthew Broderick's David (the geek version of Ferris Bueller) to a game of Global Thermonuclear War – meaning the real thing. In a bleak gag, when David decides to nuke Las Vegas he ignites a countdown to oblivion. Quite a heavy thing for a kid to shoulder, but Broderick manages the terrible realisation with considerable restraint.

In 1983 the Cold War was still escalating, and the dread possibilities presented by the game carried a larger kick than they do today. With that HAL resonance it is clear to see off-and-on hack John Badham repeating Kubrick's dire warnings of technological take-overs in the confines of what is a preposterous but keenly thought out first half. Sadly, Badham feels it necessary to pluck David away from his computer screen for some ordinary chase sequences involving governmental agents and a tame romance with Ally Sheedy. And who needs the simpering message-making of the close?

But the tension is undeniable, the dire warning for boys glued to their computer games that they could bring about the end of the world, a sobering note for anyone of an impressionable age. Time to read a book? **★★★★ IN**

ⓞ THE WAR OF THE ROSES (1989)

Starring: *Michael Douglas (Oliver Rose), Kathleen Turner (Barbara Rose), Danny DeVito (Gavin D'Amato), Sean Astin (Josh at 17), Heather Fairfield (Carolyn at 17)*
Director: *Danny DeVito*
Screenwriter: *Michael Leeson, based on the novel by Warren Adler*
15/111 mins./Comedy/Drama/USA

The Roses, a couple who started out in life as a perfect match, descend over the years into a dogfight of a relationship. The story is told via the intermediary of a divorce lawyer . . .

Hollywood has traded off the Battle Of The Sexes since the 30s, but few, if any, movies have quite smashed the traditional boundaries of the convention in such an audacious way as *The War Of The Roses*. The verbal sparring of Tracy and Hepburn, say, pales into polite insignificance set next to the mesmerising anger and bitterness of Barbara and Oliver Rose. Here, perfect passion transmutes into perfect destruction in a diabolical dance of death, orchestrated as hilarious and shocking comedy. Danny DeVito's second directorial venture is framed in a structural device which has lawyer Oliver's former friend, partner and attorney telling the Roses' story to a new client who is considering divorce. This narrative undercutting creates a superb sense of anticipation as the next gripping instalment unfolds in what develops into a wholly intriguing tale of modern morals.

Tagline
Once in a lifetime comes a motion picture that makes you feel like falling in love all over again. This is not that movie.

The Roses are the Perfect Couple: following on their first idyllic encounter, at a Nantucket auction of objets d'art during their student days, they married and produced two children (one boy, one girl, natch). While Barbara cleaned and cooked and sewed and acquired The Dream House, Oliver steadily climbed the ladder of professional success, becoming a status-mad workaholic and growing very, very rich. Now, 17 years on, Barbara, her own sense of worth destroyed by Oliver's indifference, wants a divorce. He doesn't, and their wonderful home, which each stubbornly refuses to relinquish, became the battleground where the ensuing War is waged.

Working from a noticeably watertight and well-written screenplay by Michael Neeson (adapted from a novel by Warren Adler), DeVito delivers the blackest of black farces, charting the gradual disintegration of a relationship and demonstrating the violence – verbal, emotional and physical – that people can do to each other when their needs and desires gradually cease to correspond. DeVito's taste for exaggerated gestures does create the occasional credibility gap, as in the scene where Oliver deliberately sabotages a grand dinner party given by Barbara, a farcical progression that is at once crude and unbelievable.

For most of its 111 minutes, however, the film follows a parallel path of subtlety and perception, signposting the danger signals over the years, signals which are ignored by the protagonists until they find themselves in the eye of the self-created storm. Douglas presents a welcome return to form after the disappointing *Black Rain*, DeVito is terrific and Kathleen Turner has never been better. The scene where she reveals her frustrations in a loss-of-control monologue to a prospective housekeeper is pure magic. **★★★★ RK**

Movie Star Siblings

1. Rosanna, Patricia, Alexis and David Arquette
2. William, Alec, Steven and Daniel Baldwin
3. Warren Beatty and Shirley Maclaine
4. John and James Belushi
5. Macaulay, Kieran and Rory Culkin
6. Jake and Maggie Gyllenhaal
7. Casey and Ben Affleck
8. Owen, Luke and Andy Wilson
9. River, Summer and Joaquin Phoenix
10. Emilio Estevez and Charlie Sheen

WAR OF THE WORLDS (1953)

Starring: *Gene Barry (Dr. Clayton Forrester), Ann Robinson (Sylvia Van Buren), Les Tremayne (Maj. Gen. Mann), Robert Cornthwaite (Dr. Pryor), Sandro Giglio (Dr. Bilderbeck)*
Director: *Byron Haskin*
Screenwriter: *Barré Lyndon, based on the novel by H.G. Wells*
PG/81 mins./Sci-fi/Action/Drama/USA
Awards – *Academy Awards – Best Special Effects*

In the early 1950s, the Martians invade earth, their destructive power seemingly unstoppable.

Among many who seriously considered filming H.G. Wells' novel were Sergei Eisenstein, Cecil B. DeMille and Alfred Hitchcock. But, even when Orson Welles' 1938 radio adaptation made headlines, no Hollywood studio could work out how to do the special effects. The project languished until 1953, when Hungarian-born producer George Pal, who had made a career of 'puppetoon' shorts, convinced Paramount to finance the first big, all-in-colour, effects-heavy science fiction movie. Before Pal, rocketships and monsters were for cheapo Saturday matinee serials; after Pal, down to Lucas and Spielberg, they belonged in blockbuster releases.

Directed by Byron Haskin, who later did outstanding episodes of *The Outer Limits* and *Star Trek*, Pal's *War* followed Welles by relocating the story from Edwardian England to contemporary America. These Martians land not in Dorking but Southern California. Rather than tripods, they attack in sleek, somehow-beautiful manta-ray flying machines. Since the *concept* was star, Pal didn't cast, say, Charlton Heston and Rita Hayworth, opting for the more affordable, everyday Gene Barry, as a regular joe scientist who explains that all the energy at this barn dance could power a moon rocket, and the lovely Ann Robinson. One of many nods to the 53 classic in Steven Spielberg's retake is that Barry and Robinson reappear at the climax as the grandparents Tom Cruise has been trying to reach throughout the picture.

Taking the vague outline of the novel, plus its wonderful opening and closing passages (read by Sir Cedric Hardwicke), the film was nearly first in depicting a large-scale invasion from outer space, as opposed to the single incursion of *The Thing From Another World* (the cheaper *Invaders From Mars* pipped Pal by six months). In Cold War 1953, there was a chill to the scenes in which human military might, even the then-vaunted hydrogen bomb, prove useless against the merciless invaders. The screen is filled with devastation wrought upon American cities that had escaped two world wars unscathed, even as Europe and Japan were blitzed and bombed.

Pal opted to deliver only a glimpse of the Martians: in a creepy, stalking sequence (homaged by Spielberg, even down to repeated art direction features) set in the cellar of a ruined farmhouse where Barry and Robinson shrink first from a snake-necked alien probe and then bump into a short, spindle-armed Martian (played by ape impersonator Charles Gemora) with a bizarre trifurcate eye. Though it has still-shocking passages, like the riot of refugees that destroys much-needed scientific supplies, the 1953 *War* is so fondly remembered its colourful horrors take on a cosy, nostalgic glow. The material deserves many remakes but this particular invasion will always be loved by those who saw it in cinemas or on television at an impressionable age. ★★★ **KN**

WAR OF THE WORLDS (2005)

Starring: *Tom Cruise (Ray Ferrier), Dakota Fanning (Rachel Ferrier), Justin Chatwin (Robbie Ferrier), Miranda Otto (Mary Ann), Tim Robbins (Harlan Ogilvy)*
Director: *Steven Spielberg*
Screenwriters: *Josh Friedman, David Koepp, based on the novel by H.G. Wells*
12A/116 mins./Sci-fi/Action/Thriller/USA

Divorced dockworker Ray Ferrier is lumbered with his teenage son and young daughter for the weekend. Hardly a model dad, Ferrier is struggling to think of fun things to do. Not to worry, alien war machines have been buried under the ground for a million years and have chosen this Saturday to take over the world . . .

Around the point in Steven Spielberg's *War Of The Worlds* where the grunt-soldier ET bathes the cute blonde kid in yellow, *Close Encounters*-style God-light, seasoned 'berg-watchers may recall the heckle Homer J. Simpson once directed at greying rock institution The Who: 'No talk, no new stuff, just play the hits!'

'Tis no joke – after a couple of 'personal projects' failed to resume normal service at the box office, the world's most successful director was back in his summer-spectacle wheelhouse, crafting a blockbuster from *all* his favourite materials. And yet, while this delivered popcorn munchers and multiple bums on seats, remember this: the Indiana Jones guy is nearly 60 now, and the wars of the world weigh heavily upon his pleated brow.

As you would expect from an act with the richest repertoire in the biz, a Spielberg Best Of ... collection repays the ticket price very early doors. Dispensing with opening credits – currently de rigueur for Hollywood – *WOTW* busts out of its blocks, exhausting virtually all of the trailer footage in a breathless 25-minute sprint. (No interminable on-stage banter to rile Homer here.)

Indeed, before Spielberg groupies have had time to tick off 'broken home', 'precocious pre-teen' and 'blue-collar hero' from their prepared checklist, house cinematographer Janusz Kaminski is shooting the destruction of 'everytown USA' (notch up another tick) with a raw immediacy and random ferocity previously reserved for *Saving Private Ryan*. Spielberg, meanwhile, is busy banging the major chord marked 'tension' with a metronomic intensity not heard since Bruce the Shark went duh-dum.

And the hits keep on coming. For a solid hour, as the Ferrier family miraculously stay one step ahead of the Tripods, Spielberg keeps cranking out the sturm und drang beyond what might be expected – and perhaps past what most multiplexes will happily endure.

A few flashes of comedy dad from a decidedly unmannered Cruise aside, there is little *fun* to be had here, and certainly none of the good-natured bonhomie that made *Jaws* such a rollercoaster boat ride.

W

The effect is so striking that it can only be deliberate. In 1940, Welles (Orson) needed only Wells (Herbert George), a radio and some showmanship to scare a war-wary America witless. Some 65 years later, with the US shadow-boxing a less substantial foe, Spielberg requires a greater arsenal of parlour tricks to ram H.G. home but the result is similarly devastating.

Indeed, so terrifying and resonant is the surprise attack that one hopes George W. is next door watching *Dukes Of Hazzard* lest he cite this new 'alien threat' as a pretext to invade Iran.

The problem with one-note films, however, is that eventually said note goes flat, and here Spielberg is undone by a mixture of his own sensibilities (nothing breaks the tension like a sentimental aside), elements imported wholesale from the 107 year-old novel and, in one misjudged motif, sets stolen from Byron Haskin's 1953 Cold War classic (cineastes can quietly applaud the reproduced sound stage, everyone else will simply think it looks fake).

More damagingly, David Koepp's confident screenplay falters on a third act that even Wells wonks have always judged unsatisfactory, and a typically cloying conclusion seriously tests the goodwill amassed over the previous two hours. (Following similar fumbles on *Catch Me If You Can*, *Minority Report* and *The Terminal*, finishing movies on the right 'gracenote' – as studio suits will insist on calling it – has now become a major problem for Spielberg.)

And yet, ultimately, it is not the attenuated structure or occasionally sickly wicket that stand between *WOTW* and the front rank of Spielberg's matchless output – it is the slow sapping of what might best be described as total belief. As with *Ryan*'s Omaha beach, Spielberg's full focus is much more keenly felt in the opening onslaught than in the fightback that follows.

It's almost as if the veteran director is all too aware that America faces graver threats than previously imagined but no longer has complete conviction in allied victory, nor even, perhaps, in the continued right of her cause. Cynicism from that Indiana Jones guy – who'da thunk it? ★★★★ **CK**

Movie Trivia: *War Of The Worlds*

Gene Barry and Ann Robinson, who starred in the 1953 original, play Rachel and Robbie's grandparents at the end. During filming for the underwater sequences, Spielberg played the *Jaws* theme over the studios loudspeakers as a prank on Tom Cruise and Dakota Fanning. The sound of the Tripods' warning horn was created with a digitally enhanced didgeridoo.

THE WATCHER IN THE WOODS (1980)

Starring: *Bette Davis (Mrs. Aylwood), Lynn-Holly Johnson (Jan Curtis), Kyle Richards (Ellie Curtis), Carroll Baker (Helen Curtis), David McCallum (Paul Curtis)*
Directors: *John Hough, Vincent McEveety*
Screenwriters: *Brian Clemens, Rosemary Anne Sissons, Harry Spalding based on the novel by Florence Engel Randall*
PG/84 mins./Family/UK-USA

When American family the Curtises move into an old English house in the woods, their two daughters, Jan and Ellie, start witnessing strange apparitions out there among the trees. Then Ellie starts hearing the voice of a young girl who disappeared years before.

The only known sighting of a Disney horror film, this effective (for a while) things-that-go-bump-in-the-woods shocker has an appropriately twitchy quality to its clichés until it utterly unravels in the heavily reshot and confusing ending. Until then, we get plenty of elusive blue lights, mystery voices, mirrors without reflections, and exact triangular cracks in windows. Something weird is going on.

Well, when your rented house is owned by as cranky and gothic a creature as Mrs. Alywood (a weary and ancient Bette Davis in her final role) that shouldn't come as much of surprise. Anyway, moving into a lonely house in the middle of some dark woods is just asking for it. And, to be fair, John Hough (who would be fired from post-production) does a decent job at standard spooky atmospherics.

When not consumed by irritating histrionics, pretty Lynn-Holly Johnson and Kyle Richards are effective foils for the ghostly goings-on. Johnson's Ellie is the central figure convinced someone, or, indeed, something is watching from the woods (the clue is in the title) and when she hears of the strange disappearance of Mrs. Alywood's daughter thirty years makes the *Scooby Doo*-like assumption that both things must be connected. It does slow down a bit too much for endless walking hither and thither scenes in the woods, as we ebb toward the grand reveal, but the mystery proves strong enough to hold you.

Such a shame then that the ending is a shambles, a wash of extraneous special effects intending so spruce up the potential flashiness, that serve only to confuse rather than dazzle. ★★★ **IN**

WARLOCK (1989)

Starring: *Richard E. Grant (Giles Redferne), Julian Sands (The Warlock), Lori Singer (Kassandra), Kevin O'Brien (Chas), Mary Woronov (Channeller)*
Director: *Steve Miner*
Screenwriter: *David Twohy*
15/97 mins./Horror/USA

An evil Warlock has escaped capture and travelled through time to the late 20th Century, pursued by a witch finder from his own era.

Julian Sands, despite his roles in *The Killing Fields* and *Room With A View*, appeared in more than his share of clinkers. *Gothic* for one, in which he impersonated Percy Bysshe Shelley and was required to utter the astounding line 'Laudanum – I can handle it'.

It was a shrewd soul who cast the dashing young thespian as Warlock's eponymous evil doer. According to arch-enemy and one-man witch-buster Giles Redferne (*Withnail And I*'s Richard E. Grant), 'he's the rudest Warlock that ever travelled daylight,' which understates the case somewhat.

The movie gets into gear when the warlock, with Redferne in hot pursuit, crash lands into the pad of Kooky Kalifornian waitress Kassandra. In an effort to beat the warlock, Redferne forms an unlikely alliance with Kassandra, who's a little time-warped herself having aged 20 years overnight thanks to a beastly warlockian spell.

The couple take to the highway in Kassandra's clapped out wreck and follow the flying warlock first to the farm of some superstitious Amish folk ('A horse that sweats in the morning, milk that sours overnight – these are the signs') and back to Massachusetts for an exhausting climax.

Warlock is a hoot, the kind of hammy horror romp you wouldn't kick out of the video on a wet Wednesday night. ★★★ **EVP**

WATERWORLD (1995)

Starring: *Kevin Costner (Mariner), Jeanne Tripplehorn (Helen), Dennis Hopper (Deacon), Tina Majorino (Enola), Michael Jeter (Gregor)*
Director: *Kevin Reynolds*
Screenwriters: *Peter Rader, David Twohy*
12/129 mins./Sci-fi/Action/Adventure/USA
Awards – *Razzie Awards – Worst Supporting Actor (Dennis Hopper)*

In a future world where the entire planet seems to be covered by water, Mariner joins a young woman, Helen, and a girl, Enola, on a quest to find 'Dryland'.

The weight of expectation on Fishtar, Kevin's Gate, Wet Max (take your pick), meant you ccould almost smell the sadistic glee from those willing this $200 million bloater to turn belly-up. But, the bean counters at Universal apart, who cares? As for the real question – is it worth watching? – rest assured this action adventure is certainly a cut above your average over-hyped threequel, a quite impressive feat of filmmaking in which director Reynolds has not only created a whole capsule world of, well, water, but thrown in some spectacular stunts and sets unlike anything seen before.

In a futuristic scenario where land has become submerged, Costner is the lone Mariner, who drifts on his trimaran, quaffing his own urine and swimming about like the Man From Atlantis with some curious flap-like gills stuck behind his ears.

One thing leading to another, he ends up sharing his quarters with the rather comely Helen and a little girl Enola and it's off on a mission to seek terra firma, the mythic 'Dryland', its whereabouts detailed in a map tattooed on Enola's back. This, it transpires, is a good enough reason for arch villain Deacon and his band of marauding 'smokers' (so-called because they're fond of a tab or two) to set off in hot pursuit.

Hopper, of course, can always be relied upon for scenery chewing, and his off-the-peg baddie certainly makes up for the lack of flamboyance in Costner's unsympathetic hero. With water, water everywhere, the illusion of being (literally) all at sea is sustained throughout and the spectacular stunts (most notably a flying jet ski attack), and the sets themselves (like a huge floating pre-fab atoll), are a fair indication of where the odd bob or two was spent. Though, paradoxically, the best section of the film – the scenes on the trimaran – are also the least extravagant. Is the money up there on screen? Well, Universal at least made their cash back – and that boy Kevin swum well. ★★★★ **JD**

WAY OUT WEST (1937)

Starring: *Stan Laurel (Stan), Oliver Hardly (Ollie), James Finlayson (Mickey Finn), Sharon Lynne (Lola Marcel), Stanley Fields (Sheriff), Rosina Lawrence (Mary Roberts), James Mason (Anxious Patient)*
Director: *James W. Horne*
Screenwriters: *Charles Rogers, Felix Adler, James Parrott, from a story by Jack Javne and Charles Rogers*
U/65 mins/Comedy/USA

Stan and Ollie arrive in Brushwood Gulch to hand over the deeds to a gold mine to their dead pal's daughter, Mary Roberts. However, her scheming employers at the town saloon, Mickey Finn and his singer wife Lola Marcel, have other ideas.

Ruth Laurel apparently suggested that Stan and Ollie should make a comedy Western. No one had attempted anything similar since Buster Keaton's *Go West* (1925) and the boys were eminently well qualified, as not only had Oliver Hardy made silent Westerns, but Stan Laurel had also been one of Hollywood's most gifted parodists during the same period. But what set this enduringly popular romp apart from other movie spoofs was that Stan genuinely lampooned generic conventions rather than simply exploiting them as a convenient backdrop for situation or slapstick comedy. Thus, *Way Out West* was more wholly integrated than most Laurel and Hardy vehicles and this tautness left no room for the diversionary set-pieces that were too often shoehorned into their later features.

Yet, this genial picture was produced under the most trying circumstances. When he wasn't competing with other studios for a title (*You'd Be Surprised*, *Tonight's The Night* and *In The Money* all had to be discarded as they had already been copyrighted elsewhere), producer Hal Roach was squabbling with Stan over his new contract. He certainly needed the cash, too, as not only did Ruth walk out on him a week into the shoot, but his former vaudeville partner and self-proclaimed common-law wife Mael Laurel also arrived demanding alimony. Ollie's life was no less chaotic, as no sooner had his estranged spouse, Myrtle, sued for maintenance than his first wife, Madelyn, showed up destitute and demanding a new settlement.

But there's no evidence of such strife in the masterly saloon chase sequence, which Stan ends up spectating in pleats of helpless laughter having been tickled remorselessly by Sharon Lynne. Nor in the delightful dance routine the duo concocted to the Avalon Boys' number, 'At the Ball, That's All', or in the rendition of 'The Trail of the Lonesome Pine', which was recorded live (with the exception of Chill Wills' and Rosina Lawrence's bass and soprano interludes) and released as a single in the UK in 1975, when it reached No.2 in the charts. What's that about the tears of a clown?

Comic genius, pure and irresistibly simple. ★★★★★ **DP**

WAYNE'S WORLD (1992)

Starring: *Mike Myers (Wayne Campbell), Dana Carvey (Garth Algar), Rob Lowe (Benjamin Kane), Tia Carrere (Cassandra), Lara Flynn Boyle (Stacy)*
Director: *Penelope Spheeris*
Screenwriters: *Mike Myers, Bonnie Turner, Terry Turner, from characters created by Mike Myers*
PG/90 mins./Comedy/USA

Two slacker friends try to promote their public-access cable show

A cheaply-made, largely plot-free TV spin-off about a pair of heavy metal-obsessed teenagers, it is perhaps not surprising that *Wayne's World* was given something of a cool reception by American film critics when it appeared in 1992. What may puzzle future filmologists, however, is the bizarre way in which said critical community gave their verdict. *The Toronto Star*, for example, suggested that the Michael Myers/Dana Carvey vehicle was, 'A good idea for a movie – not.' In a similar vein, the *Star Tribune*'s scribe described the film as 'A surefire Oscar-winner and destined to become a Hollywood classic – not!' Finally, *The Village Voice* brusquely stated: 'Not!' Indeed, for a good six months it was simply impossible to escape the pair's 'not!' catchphrase – or, as *The New York Times*' William Safire described it in his 'On Language' column, 'the reversing addendum, or pseudo-Gaelic negative. Example: "I believe you -NOT!"'

Even leaving the planet provided no respite. 'Out in space a while back they were repairing a satellite,' Myers recalled shortly after the film's release. 'And one of the astronauts said, "Houston, I'm really enjoying myself – not!" I'm thinking, that's in space, that's not right! But the really surreal thing was when (then US President) George Bush said it. "Not" was something my brother used to say to torment me. And suddenly Bush is saying it to torment the free world.'

Yet, despite the one-time popularity of this particular 'reversing addendum' (not to mention other catchphrases such as 'Schwing!', 'Party on' and – who could forget – 'I think I've blown chunks') *Wayne's World* was a much, much sharper film than its critics would have their readers believe. Indeed, while its characters' hearts may belong to such rockers as Alice Cooper – who makes a hilarious cameo – its script owes far more to the anarchic tradition of British comedy.

'My parents are from Liverpool and moved to Canada in 1956,' says Myers. 'All my comic influences are from over there. People like Peter Sellers, Alec Guinness, *Python*, *The Goodies*, *Rutland Weekend Television*, *That Was The Week That Was*. We got a lot of British programmes in Canada and my father would really encourage us to watch that stuff with him. Then I moved over there for a while in 84 so I could be near all that. I saw some of the funniest acts I had ever seen before: Paul Merton, Alexei Sayle and, most particularly, a man who used to carve 27 different animals out of a block of ice. A man who I have never seen since.'

Together with his comedy partner Neil Mullarkey, the Canadian even appeared on the *Wide Awake Club* alongside Timmy Mallett. Myers' big break, however, came when he returned to America and was asked to join *Saturday Night Live* where together with Carvey he set about developing the characters of Wayne and Garth – two hapless small-town rock fans who broadcast a weekly cable access show.

'Wayne was based on me,' recalled Myers. 'I was into heavy metal and Ted Nugent, Zeppelin and Aerosmith. What you see onscreen is just what I was doing years ago. Hiking my underwear up the crack of my ass, rolling my stomach, all that intellectual stuff that came from being in the kitchen at parties impressing the girls. And wanna know something that'll surprise you? It worked.' But, when it came time to transplant the sketch to the big screen, Myers not only beefed up the cast to include Cooper, fellow SNL alumni Chris Farley and Rob Lowe – the latter in a career-reviving role as the evil TV executive who first buys up Wayne's show and then attempts to woo the babe-of-his-dreams Tia Carrere – but also increased its more surreal aspects, particularly during the concluding scenes where audiences are treated to a number of endings including 'sad', 'happy' and 'Scooby Doo.' In fact, just as the Pythons did before, Myers delighted in reminding audiences that they were watching a film as he messed around with subtitles or wrote a ludicrously expositional speech for Chris Farley's roadie character. The result was hugely popular – raking in over $110m at the American box office despite a meagre $14m budget – and established a template that Myers would go on to refine with both its sequel and the *Austin Powers* movies.

Finally, it also showed that, despite being almost 30 when he made the movie, Myers' acting powers are such that he could convincingly portray a character ten years younger. Not. ★★★ **CC**

⊙ THE WEDDING BANQUET (XIYAN) (1993)

Starring: *Winston Chao (Wai Tung), May Chin (Wei-Wei), Ah-Leh Gus (Mrs Gao), Sihung Lung (Mr. Gao), Mitchell Lichtenstein (Simon), Neal Huff (Steve), Jeffrey Howard (Street Musician), Anthony 'Iggy' Ingoglia (Restaurant Manager), Dion Birney (Andrew), Jeanne Kuo Chang (Wai Tung's Secretary).*
Director: *Ang Lee*
Screenwriters: *Ang Lee, Neil Peng*
15/106 mins./Comedy/Taiwan/USA

Gay yuppie Wai-Tung Gao, a naturalised American, has never come out to his Taiwanese parents. They pester him to give them a grandson so he proposes to Wei-Wei, a struggling artist who needs citizenship. When his parents insist on a huge ceremony, Chao has to pass off his doctor lover Simon as a live-in landlord and replace his muscle guy pin-ups with calligraphic scrolls.

Though an interesting attempt to discuss racial, national, sexual and generation identities and the conflicts that arise when the loyalties inherent in these groupings conflict, this early, small-scale Ang Lee film is mainly a wry, nicely observed romantic comedy. It is perhaps a little too soft sometimes – Wai-Tung and Simon have a relationship so idealised you'd never believe it if they were straight – but for the most part, the laughs keep coming as the enforced deceptions get more intricate. Considerably funnier and much more pointed than the similarly-plotted *La Cage aux Folles*, it has wonderfully farcical moments in the wedding feast that threatens never to end as a horde of guests invade the honeymoon suite to play mahjong and humiliate the happy couple.

But it also pulls off lovely smaller moments, as when Simon deftly teaches the inept Wei-Wei how to stir fry properly while the girl is trying to impress her future parents-in-law with her traditional Chinese kitchen skills. And the resolution shows everyone in a good light, as it comes out that no one is quite as bigoted as everyone else thinks they are. A gentle, surprising movie, this cross-cultural favourite advanced Lee towards the big leagues. ★★★★ **KN**

⊙ WEDDING CRASHERS (2005)

Starring: *Owen Wilson (John Beckwith), Vince Vaughn (Jeremy Grey), Christopher Walken (U.S. Treasury Secretary William Cleary), Rachel McAdams (Claire Cleary), Isla Fisher (Gloria Cleary), Jane Seymour (Kathleen Cleary)*
Director: *David Dobkin*
Screenwriters: *Steve Faber, Bob Fisher*
15/119 mins./128 mins (unrated version)/Comedy/USA

John Beckwith and Jeremy Grey have discovered that the perfect way to score with women is by gatecrashing romance-drenched weddings. Their perfect success rate is threatened, however, when they get too close to two bridesmaids and break their long-established 'Wedding Crashers code'.

This summertime rom-com was a mouthwatering prospect indeed: the Frat Pack's hippest stars – Owen Wilson and Vince Vaughn – teamed up as fast-talking rogues; an always-welcome comedy turn from Christopher Walken; and a flamboyant cameo from the daddy of Frat himself, Will Ferrell. To quote Vaughn from *Dodgeball*: 'I'm laughing already ...'

As it is, *Wedding Crashers* doesn't quite live up to its promise, but through no fault of its off-the-wall cast. Sharing an easy chemistry and free of the usual joker/straight-guy dynamic, Wilson and Vaughn quip, riff and banter to hilarious effect. And both get their fair share of money moments – the latter's muggings are particularly hysterical in a raunchy dinner-party sequence.

That the lead characters' cocksure confidence extends to the movie itself is its biggest weakness. While Vaughn and Wilson are adept at loose-limbed improvisation, that doesn't disguise the fact that the material they're funking up is pretty lazy. Sure, all Chris Walken has to do to score a laugh is narrow his reptilian eyes, but that's no reason not to give the man decent lines. In fact, the only supporting character who doesn't feel watered-down is Isla Fisher's nutso nympho – an unexpected, scene-stealing joy. There's enough good-natured energy to compensate, but this is no *Dodgeball*. ★★★ **NDS**

⊙ THE WEDDING SINGER (1998)

Starring: *Adam Sandler (Robbie Hart), Drew Barrymore (Julia Sullivan), Christine Taylor (Holly Sullivan), Allen Covert (Sammy), Matthew Glave (Glenn Guglia)*
Director: *Frank Coraci*
Screenwriter: *Tim Herlihy*
12/92 mins./Comedy/Romance/Music/USA

A wedding singer loses the desire for his chosen career after being ditched at the altar. Can waitress Julia re-kindle his interest?

Anybody still labouring under the illusion that the 70s was the decade style forgot should turn to the 80s for a true depiction of a time unbothered by fashion sense. And nowhere is the world of the spangly glove, the indescribable haircut or, indeed, *Miami Vice* chic more accurately captured onscreen than in The *Wedding Singer*. In fact, given that the average age of the 90s cinemagoer ranked them as teenagers of the 80s, this delightfully silly 1985-set nostalgia trip caused more cringes than the sight of polyester wing-collars or disco-era flared atrocities ever could.

Sandler, dispensing with the manic persona of Billy Madison and Happy Gilmore, here combines a lightweight comic touch with some surprising sensitivity as orphaned 'wedding singer' Robbie Hart. A failed rock star, he makes a living churning out Dead Or Alive covers at nuptial receptions.

Until, that is, he is left at the altar by foxy Linda, and suddenly the appeal of the job is lost on broken-hearted Robbie (culminating in a hysterical rendition of 'Love Stinks' at one wedding). He finds solace in waitress Julia and is smitten, but there's a snag: her own impending marriage to obnoxious 80s whizzkid Glenn, all pastel suits, DeLorean car and roving eye.

It's true to suggest that this simple boy-meets-girl story could have been set in any era. As it is, it's the unashamed overplaying of almost every tacky 80s fad that makes this such a joy to watch (and listen to), be it Glenn's wardrobe, Robbie's bad hair year or Alexis Arquette as crimped, face-painted band member George (geddit?), vying with John Turturro in *The Big Lebowski* for the most inspired support role of that year.

Add to this a script with a streak of clever cynicism and poignancy, a soundtrack of tunes you thought had long since departed to the vinyl graveyard and one of the most adorable screen pairings in ages in Sandler and Barrymore and the result is a film which, while hardly high art, is simply irresistible. ★★★★ **CW**

ⓓ WEEKEND (1967)

Starring: *Mireille Darc (Corinne), Jean Yanne (Roland), Jean-Pierre Kalfon (Leader Of FLSO), Valerie Lagrange (His Moll), Jean-Pierre Léaud (Saint-Just/Man In The Phone Booth), Yves Beneyton (Member of FLSO)*
Director: *Jean-Luc Godard*
Screenwriter: *Jean-Luc Godard*
18/103 mins./Drama/France-Italy

Unhappily married, cash-strapped bourgeois Corinne and Richard set off to visit her mother to borrow some money, only to find themselves caught in an endless traffic jam that soon turns out to be the least of their worries.

Jean-Luc Godard reached the cinematic crossroads with this audacious film, which sought to dispense with the paraphenalia of commercial movies in order to liberate the viewer from their conformist capitalist agenda. However, in decimating the illusion of screen reality, Godard managed only to replace it with an anti-structure that was every bit as politically driven and psychologically manipulative. He might have protested that he was not the author of *Weekend*, but it's impossible to escape his jaundiced views on the bourgeoisie and his contention that a brutalised society could only be purged by more extreme horrors. But, as failed polemics go, this one is a masterpiece.

The vendetta against linear narrative that had been fermenting throughout Godard's earlier work finally erupted here in a cascade of New Wave iconoclasm. Having declared it to be 'a film found on a rubbish tip', he proceeded to litter the action with captions that ranged from slogans to enigmatic pronouncements that opposed the purpose of screen calligraphy by confusing rather than clarifying the issue. Elsewhere he had characters speak directly to the camera, interview each other or launch into monologues, while others, like the French revolutionary St Just and the novelist Emily Brontë, were completely anachronistic.

The action was also packed with allusions to such features as Mauritz Stiller's *Gösta Berlings Saga*, Sergei Eisenstein's *Battleship Potemkin*, Nicholas Ray's *Johnny Guitar*, John Ford's *The Searchers* and Luis Buñuel's *The Exterminating Angel*, while Arizona Jules was a reference to both Jean Renoir's *Le Crime De Monsieur Lange* and François Truffaut's *Jules Et Jim*.

Moreover, Godard constantly drew attention to the filmicness of the picture. Fades misfired, colours were forced and the sprocket holes even appeared after one of film's many car crashes. Camera angles also occasionally seemed askew, while at other times they were rigorously controlled, such as the 360° shot during the Mozart lecture and the famous track past the endless traffic jam, which treated mundane and bizarre behaviour with equal indifference.

Scathingly satirical, recklessly poetic and bleakly surreal, this was a bloodcurdling howl of frustration at the state of both cinema and the world. ★★★★★ **DP**

ⓓ WEEKEND AT BERNIE'S (1989)

Starring: *Andrew McCarthy (Larry Wilson), Jonathan Silverman (Richard Parker), Catharine Mary Stewart (Gwen Saunders), Terry Kiser (Bernie Lomax)*
Director: *Ted Kotcheff*
Screenwriter: *Robert Klane*
12/97 mins./Comedy/USA

Two young dolts, Larry and Richard, trying to make their way up the corporate ladder, discover a major accounting error which they reveal to their boss Bernie. However, when he invites them to his beach house with the intention of murder, Bernie ends up dead and, caught in a panic, the boys desperately try and maintain the illusion Bernie is still alive.

A film whose very title became shorthand for the depths to which comedy, so-called comedy, can plumb, is going to struggle to win over the floating voter. And, apart from collectors of comedic aberrations, there is little to recommend this one-joke premise that hoped to turn Jonathan Silverman and Andrew McCarthy into the Bill and Ted of corporate climbers. Safe to say, it doesn't achieve that or anything else much.

The script is working toward the fraught pace of active farce, knitting together this pair of idiot suits, aiming to cut loose at their boss' summerhouse in the Hamptons, and their very dead boss. Murdered by the Mafia he was in leagues with, of course. That is merely the set-up, the joke, the only joke, is that Larry and Richard decide to have their weekend on the beach, and thus keep up the pretence that the late Bernie (when living played by smarm bucket Terry Kiser) is still in possession of mortal coil.

In other words, every single sicko-silly-undignifed gag you can do with a corpse, each one buffeting into the next without room for any to land. There could be some cheap laughs in stapling Bernie's toupee back in place but the idea of his mistress going in for sex with her deceased lover and not noticing is plain stupid. This kind of bad taste humour needs crafting, Ted Kotcheff just sprawls the mishap across the screen hoping the incongruity of dead body (which isn't on screen enough anyway) in living positions will get a giggle. It's hopelessly short of the mark, treating women as bimbos, and all else as clichés, with its leads ineffectively trying to muster some charm. Just like death and taxes, even more horrible sequels followed. ★ **IN**

WELCOME TO SARAJEVO (1997)

Starring: *Stephen Dillane (Michael Henderson), Woody Harrelson (Flynn), Marisa Tomei (Nina), Emira Nusevic (Emira), Kerry Fox (Jane Carson), Goran Visnjic (Risto Bavic), James Nesbitt (Gregg), Emily Lloyd (Annie McGee)*
Director: *Michael Winterbottom*
Screenwriter: *Frank Cottrell Boyce, based on the book by Michael Nicholson*
15/97 mins./Drama/War/UK/USA

A British journalist, covering the conflict in Sarajevo, finds it hard to remain dispassionate and uninvolved . . .

Guaranteed to stir up passions in all quarters, Michael Winterbottom's unlikely follow-on from the literary melancholia of *Jude* is a bristling, biting, fulminating depiction of TV journalists under fire in the besieged Sarajevo. It is, truth be known, partly based on the real life story of ITN TV journo Michael Nicholson and at its best you could swap fragmenting Sarajevo for sweaty Phnom Penh and the might of *The Killing Fields*. At its limpest, though, it scrambles around one-sided, intent on spelling out its inflammatory message with self-flattening bluntness.

Steve Dillane utilises the smile-free school of deadly earnest to great effect as Brit journo Henderson, bonding with his native driver, careering through bomb and sniper-fragged streets to grab up-to-the-moment reports and questioning his moral stance – can a journalist remain a bystander? In his case the answer is no, with a traumatised orphanage the focus of his exhalation. In particular a ten-year-old girl he eventually adopts and smuggles to the UK through a terrifying coach journey and the most wrenching scene of all – armed troops plucking screaming racially identified children from the busload. At such junctures *Welcome To Sarajevo* is a truly affecting experience, sobering and unblinking. And Winterbottom never lets us forget the reality base, intercutting stark television footage with the fiction, a stylistic gesture less trite than you would imagine.

There's also a set of superb performances to enjoy – Dillane's emotional turmoil, Tomei's neatly formed aid-worker and Woody Harrelson's American TV hack smothering his discord in a brash, hollow exterior the pick of the bunch. There is no way you can discount *Welcome To Sarajevo*, it is too deeply felt; an intelligent, passionate film documenting a smear on European history, but it too should have kept to more neutral ground – morals, politics and blame remain intertwined and confused. A film of extremes, then, by turns brash and simplistic and utterly powerful. See it. Then argue. ★★★★ **IN**

WELCOME TO THE DOLLHOUSE (1995)

Starring: *Heather Matarazzo (Dawn Wiener), Victoria Davis (Lolita), Christina Brucato (Cookie), Christina Vidal (Cynthia), Siri Howard (Chrissy)*
Director: *Todd Solondz*
Screenwriter: *Todd Solondz*
15/87 mins./Comedy/Drama/USA

Insightful look at an unattractive 7th grader as she struggles to cope with un-attentive parents, snobbish classmates, a smart older brother, an attractive younger sister, and her own insecurities.

For his debut effort, former English teacher Solondz takes the entire genre and turns it on its head, making a refreshing black comedy destined to provoke a nervous reaction among all those who couldn't wait to turn their back on the classroom for good.

Life for 11-year-old Dawn Wiener is far from easy, blessed as she is with an eye-damaging wardrobe, a worrying lack of social skills, and siblings (computer nerd brother, ballerina sister) more accomplished at everything and popular with her parents than she is.

Over the course of one nightmare school year she withstands constant taunts while her childish naiveté sees her strangely drawn to her brother's slacker friend Steve, an episode which results in a painfully embarrassing attempt to get into his hipsters. Most of the appeal hinges on Dawn as she lurches from one moment of pre-pubescent awkwardness to another buoyed by the thin hope that things might get better in high school, culminating in an inconclusive and rather unsatisfying denouement.

However, the humour is deliciously dark (upped a notch by some ironically placed classical music), and the all-too-familiar topics of peer group pressure and conformity tackled with sympathy, while Matarazzo (11 at the time of filming) offers up an astonishingly mature performance that suggests hers will be a name to watch. ★★★★ **CW**

WENT THE DAY WELL? (1942)

Starring: *Leslie Banks (Oliver Wilsford), C.V. France (The Vicar), Valerie Taylor (Nora Ashton), Marie Lohr (Mrs. Fraser), Basil Sydney (Kommandant Ortler), David Farrar (Lt. Jung), Harry Fowler (George Truscott), Frank Lawton (Tom Sturry), Edward Rigby (Bill Purvis), Elizabeth Allan (Peggy Pryde)*
Director: *Alberto Cavalcanti*
Screenwriters: *John Dighton, Angus MacPhail, Diana Morgan based on the short story* The Lieutenant Died Last *by Graham Greene*
PG/94 mins./War/UK

In World War Two, a unit of German shock troops disguise themselves as British soldiers and occupy a small English village in preparation for a full-scale invasion. The villagers see through the trick, and fight the invaders to the death.

Based on a Graham Greene short story and directed by the talented Alberto Cavalcanti, this still-underrated 1942 movie is framed by a supposed post-war setting as a local storyteller (Mervyn Johns) reminisces about what happened in Bramley Green on the night of the big Nazi invasion ('and you all know how that turned out'), noting the unusual presence of German names on gravestones in the churchyard.

It's pitched somewhere between paranoid fantasy and preparedness propaganda, putting forward the disquieting idea of a supposed military exercise which turns out to be for real. Betrayed by the quisling squire (Leslie Banks), the villagers gradually catch on that supposed British troops (led by the very stalwart David Farrar) are Germans in disguise (they cross their sevens) and mount effective, increasingly violent resistance. Though intended as a salute to the wartime spirit of the home front, there's something lastingly disturbing about the readiness with which these Ealing-type little Englanders turn into guerillas, as when a cheerful post mistress gores a Nazi to death with a letterspike or the local poacher becomes a rural Rambo.

The business of England invaded – reprised in *It Happened Here* and *The Eagle Has Landed* (which borrows quite a bit from *Went the Day Well?*) – is always disconcerting, and must have been especially so in wartime as skirmishes take place around a picturesque church and fierce fighting extends to the village shop and high street. A fine cast of familiar British character players, seen in numberless tamer films, get to play unusually intense scenes – Harry Fowler, Frank Lawton, Thora Hird, Marie Lohr, Elizabeth Allan, Patricia Hayes, Norman Shelley. ★★★★★ **KN**

WEST SIDE STORY (1961)

Starring: *Natalie Wood (Maria), Richard Beymer (Tony), Russ Tamblyn (Riff), Rita Moreno (Anita), George Chakiris (Bernardo)*
Directors: *Jerome Robbins, Robert Wise*
Screenwriter: *Ernest Lehman, based on a conception by Jerome Robbins, play by Arthur Laurents, from* Romeo and Juliet *by William Shakespeare (uncredited)*
PG/145 mins./Musical/Romance/USA

Awards – *Academy Awards – Best Supporting Actor (George Chakiris), Best Supporting Actress (Rita Moreno), Best Colour Art Direction-Set Direction, Best Colour Cinematography, Best Colour Costume, Best Director, Best Editing, Best Score, Best Picture, Best Sound, Golden Globes – Best Musical, Best Supporting Actor (George Chakiris), Best Supporting Actress (Rita Moreno)*

TOP10

Criticism of Films that are Beyond Criticism

1 **'I thought the photography quite good but nothing to write to Moscow about, the acting middling and the whole thing a little dull.'** James Agate on *Citizen Kane.*

2 **'So mincing as to border on baby talk.' Bosley Crowther on *It's A Wonderful Life***

3 'The old master has turned out another Hitchcock and bull story, in which the mystery is not so much who done it as who cares.' Time magazine on *Vertigo*

4 **'I sat cringing before Oz, which displays no trace of imagination, good taste or ingenuity.'** The New Yorker on *The Wizard of Oz*

5 'The jokes are tired and can often be seen dragging their feet towards us a mile off; when they finally arrive, we are more apt to commiserate than laugh.' – John Simon on *Annie Hall*

6 **'The only really satisfactory way to dispose of *Peeping Tom* would be to shovel it up and flush it swiftly down the nearest sewer. Even then, the stench would remain.' - Derek Hill on *Peeping Tom***

7 'For all of its good choices, there's something deeply wanting about Jackson's vision.' – Jason Clark on *The Fellowship Of The Ring*

8 **'Here is the ideal date movie, assuming you're dating a psychopath sadist with a high tolerance for dilly-dallying.' – Ralph Novak on *Reservoir Dogs***

9 'Disappointing. There is a feeling that it could have been so much more. Overlong and repetitious ....' (Variety on *The Searchers*)

10 **'No comedy dependent on men impersonating women can make friends and influence laughter for very long, certainly not for two hours.' (The Daily Mail on *Some Like It Hot*)**

In a musical reworking of *Romeo And Juliet*, 2nd in command for the Jets gang Tony falls in love with the sister of rival gang the Sharks' leader. Nobody approves, but nothing is going to keep these two apart

In 1957, playwright Arthur Laurents collaborated with Bernstein, Sondheim and choreographer Jerome Robbins on *West Side Story*, a show that followed *The Boys From Syracuse* and *Kiss Me Kate* in wrestling a Shakespeare plot into a Broadway musical.

Laurents set *Romeo And Juliet* against a New York gang war straight out of the headlines. His Montagues are the Jets, the 'American' gang – though a few tossed-off insults suggest they're mostly Polish with token Irish and Italian members.

Certainly, the gangs they've already beaten (the Harps and the Emeralds) sound Irish. In place of the Capulets, *West Side Story* brings on the Sharks, sharp and resentful lads recently arrived from Puerto Rico, hotly eager to match any force thrown against them.

The lovers are Maria, innocent sister of Shark leader Bernardo, and Tony, co-founder of the Jets but lately drifting into the straight life – given how keen Riff is to get Tony back in the gang, it's not difficult to perceive a gay subtext – and the duels of Shakespeare become gang 'rumbles' with switchblades.

United Artists, evidently keen on cutting in on MGM's position as the natural home of Broadway musicals, bought up the rights and got the film out in 1961. It won the Best Picture Oscar and nine additional statuettes, including an unprecedented shared award for direction plus supporting actor and actress nods for George Chakiris (Bernardo, though he had played Riff on stage) and Rita Moreno (as Bernardo's girl, Anita).

Like most Best Picture Oscar winners, it's too big a production to be perfect and its greatness floats in with a fair amount of lesser stuff. Neither Richard Beymer nor Natalie Wood could handle the songs, so their singing voices come from Jimmy Bryant and Marni Nixon.

Both castings are compromises: Tony was offered to Elvis Presley, but Colonel Tom Parker, with typical disregard for his client's career opportunities, turned it down, relegating The King to nonsensical children's films. Could Tupelo's finest have played a New Yorker? If his Southern twang were controlled, Presley would have been a lot more convincing in the fight scenes. Wood, in nut-brown makeup and thick accent, is an appealing if not remotely Hispanic Maria.

A possible reason for the Colonel's rejection is that Tony doesn't even get the best numbers. And *West Side Story* has more hit songs in it than *Chicago*, *Les Misérables* and the entire Andrew Lloyd Webber back-catalogue rolled up together. 'Gee, Officer Krupke!', banned by the BBC for its mentions of drug use ('Dear kindly judge, Your Honour, my parents treat me rough, with all their marijuana, they won't give me a puff') and sexual ambiguity ('My sister wears a moustache, my brother wears a dress, goodness gracious that's why I'm a mess'), is blazing satire, vintage 1957.

'I Feel Pretty', although sung by Nixon, allows Wood to be funny for a stretch rather than a saintly killjoy. If you wonder why the Academy handed out Oscars to Chakiris (a one-way ticket to Palookaville) and Moreno (the most explosive performer in the film), look no further than the standout song, 'America'.

On stage, this was a smaller number, with Anita's friends arguing with a conservative Puerto Rican girl. In the film, by matching the integrationist girls ('Free to be anything you choose') with the resentful boys ('Free to wait tables and shine shoes'), the conflict is more even, and we get a blazing musical battle at once celebration and indictment. A classic musical scene in a classic musical film. ★★★★★ **KN**

---

⑫ WESTWORLD (1973)

Starring: *Yul Brynner (The Gunslinger), Richard Benjamin (Peter Martin), James Brolin (John Blane), Norman Bartold (Medieval Knight), Alan Oppenheimer (Chief Supervisor), Victoria Shaw (Medieval Queen)*
Director: *Michael Crichton*
Screenwriter: *Michael Crichton*
15/85 mins./Sci-fi/Thriller/USA

An amusement park for rich vacationers gives its customers a way to live out their fantasies through the use of robots that provide anything they want. Two of the vacationers choose a Wild West adventure. However, after a computer breakdown, they find that they are now being stalked by a rogue robot gunslinger.

'When somebody tells me they're interested in directing,' Michael Crichton informed the *Sunday Express* back in 1979, 'I usually offer to take the day off and tell them how to do it. Orson Welles said you could learn all you need to know about film directing in four hours. But I think he was exaggerating a bit. I'd say a day was about right.'

The remarkable thing about this quote is not that Crichton genuinely seemed to believe what he was saying but that anyone should have asked his advice on being a director in the first place. For, while the Harvard-educated doctor is without peer as a writer of techno-thriller blockbusters, his reputation as a filmmaker remains less impressive. Indeed, most of the films he had directed before offering this quote (*Coma*, *The First Great Train Robbery*) are largely forgotten while the highlight of his subsequent work was to team Tom Selleck and KISS bassist Gene Simmons in the risible robots-go-mad *Runaway*.

In fact, Crichton's reputation as a filmmaker, such as it is, rests almost entirely on *Westworld* – an earlier robots-go-mad effort, albeit one vastly superior to *Runaway* despite not featuring the natural special effect that is Mr Simmons' tongue. Yet even *Westworld* is hardly without fault and certainly those early 70s viewers who left the cinema after an hour would not have regarded it as a classic. Nor could anyone really blame them.

Even the pre-credit sequence – in which a wooden interviewer asks returning holiday makers about their trip to the world's first robot-assisted resort – is stunningly dull. From there the 'action' switches to our nominal heroes, Richard Benjamin and James Brolin, who are just starting their own holiday at Delos, a theme park divided into three separate areas (West-, Roman- and Medievalworld) where for $1,000 a day visitors can enact their wildest fantasies thanks to the fact that everyone they shove, shoot or, indeed, shag is a robot.

After some initial reluctance from the uptight Benjamin, our faux cowpokes get into the swing of things, drinking, whoring and shooting town robo-gunslinger Yul Brynner like there's no tomorrow. Unfortunately, for them, there is a tomorrow. A tomorrow in which the robots will malfunction and slaughter everyone they can get their indestructible hands on. The ensuing mayhem gives as much relief to the viewer as it does distress to the dwindling numbers of onscreen humans. Upon its release one critic was moved to write that the film was 'An idea in search of a director' and, on the whole, it's difficult not to agree.

What makes *Westworld* such a great movie, however, is that in the climactic 20 minutes the 'idea' takes over completely as Brynner first shoots Brolin dead and then relentlessly pursues Benjamin across the entire theme park until finally being burned into oblivion (an early script suggestion which had the robot 'literally pulled apart' on a medieval rack was nixed at the last moment). It is a nightmarish, hallucinogenic, sequence in which Crichton's hamfisted scriptwriting matters not one jot because essentially there is no script – simply a helpless victim being pursued by an unreasoning angel of destruction.

Before *Westworld* 'baddies' nearly always had some motivation. The brilliance of Crichton's concept – subsequently aped in films such as *Halloween*, *Friday The 13th* and, most obviously, *The Terminator* – was to construct a situation in which death could neither be exhausted nor distracted by any amount of badinage. But despite the admitted genius of Crichton's idea, the film ultimately belongs to Brynner who, like Henry Fonda in *Once Upon A Time In The West*, was deliberately cast against type, an about-turn made more dramatic by Brynner somehow imbuing the role with a definite personality.

'At the beginning of every film I've taken on I've always said it was a walkover,' the actor explained while publicising the film. 'And by the time I get to the first day of shooting my part has become the most complex structure ever. It's my nature – I complicate my work.' While Brynner's cyborg may be both monstrous and motiveless it is also strangely human – a modern day Frankenstein's monster driven insane – something Crichton seems to be suggesting, by the inhumanity of the park's customers. He may not be the biggest or the baddest 'terminator' ever seen. But he remains among the best. ★★★★ **CC**

WHALE RIDER (2003)

Starring: *Keisha Castle-Hughes (Paikea), Pawiri Paratene (Koro), Vicky Haughton (Nanny Flowers), Cliff Curtis (Porourangi)*
Director: *Niki Caro*
Screenwriter: *Niki Caro, from the novel by Witi Ihimaera*
PG/101 mins./Drama/Adventure/New Zealand/Germany

Awards – *BAFTA – Children's Award (Best Film)*

A Maori community, which claims to descend from the whale rider, Paikea, needs a new chief. When stubborn leader Koro's son has twins and the boy dies, he refuses to accept his granddaughter, Pai, and blames the tribe's subsequent misfortunes on her birth. Can she prove him wrong?

The New Zealand Tourist Board must have been thrilled with this lovely looking culture-fest, jam-packed as it is with stunning coastal views, glorious sunshine and rare insights into Maori culture.

It sensitively (but occasionally ploddingly) explores the relationship between set-in-his-ways Koro and his eager-to-please granddaughter, whose adoration for him is harshly countered by his bitter disappointment with her.

As she's a girl, Pai (expertly played by unknown but Oscar-nominated Castle-Hughes) can't lead the tribe, so Koro's obsession with tradition sees him force a local crew of unsuitable lads into classes in the 'old ways.'

As he trains them in the art of being a warrior, Koro hopes that the new chief he so desires will reveal himself. But only Pai has the skills he's looking for.

Way more than just a Maori history class, the overriding feeling here is one of great enjoyment. Like a breath of fresh South Pacific air, director Caro combines classic themes with a little-seen cultural perspective to come up with an uplifting crowd-pleaser. ★★★★ **JH**

WHAT LIES BENEATH (2000)

Starring: *Harrison Ford (Dr. Norman Spencer), Michelle Pfeiffer (Claire Spencer), Diana Scarwid (Jody), Joe Morton (Dr. Drayton), James Remar (Warren Feuer), Miranda Otto (Mary Feuer)*
Director: *Robert Zemeckis*
Screenwriter: *Clark Gregg, based on a story by Gregg, Sarah Kernochan*
15/124 mins./Thriller/USA

The seemingly idyllic marriage between Claire Spencer and professor husband Norman begins to fragment when she starts to believe there is a ghost inhabiting their house. As the supernatural occurrences grow in ferocity, it becomes apparent that this strange spirit is not only real, but intent on revealing a terrible secret ... One which lies very close to home.

This wildly, but effectively, overwrought thriller – with added horror – arrived touting dazzling credentials: an idea by Steven Spielberg, directed by Robert Zemeckis, starring Harrison Ford and Michelle Pfeiffer. Under the weight of such a curtain call, the biggest surprise is, perhaps, that what emerges is no masterpiece, but a semi-sophisticated shocker, playfully homaging Hitchcock like a mechanical masterclass in doing 'genre'. The first hour is great fun.

Slowburning and suggestive, the mystery builds from all directions, with supernatural pointers, strange keys, a neighbour's wife going mysteriously absent, and various hints of a troubled past implying a myriad possibilities. All of it punctuated by classic 'Gotcha!' moments and black humour.

Pfeiffer – who carries the movie – looks svelte and vulnerable, and through the slow-slow-quick rhythm nicely evokes the fraught air of a poor soul simultaneously having to question her own sanity and the existence of the paranormal. Ford, who for the most part seems to be taking a surprising back seat, veers deliciously off his well-beaten path – although, for all those lusting after *Indy IV*, he is starting to look worryingly weatherworn. What we have, then, is a partnership of solid-as-oak stars not even breaking sweat with the demands of their director. Zemeckis, meanwhile, is having a whale of a time playing Hitch: blondes are abused; bathtubs and plugholes given frequent close-ups; while his camera twists and turns with voyeuristic lust. However, after an hour, we've been beaten over the head with so many jumps and jolts that they start to verge on the silly. But the skilful use of the motifs of the genre – mirrors, bodybags, water, blood – border on genius. It's such a shame his heart wasn't as occupied as his head.

It's in the midriff that the movie really sags. Domestic trauma takes over, events become talky and flat, while an encouraging red herring is abandoned far too early, and it seems that the much more enticing spooky stuff has just been forgotten. Nevertheless, it swings back round for the finale, a gripping, revelatory piece of artfully constructed schlock. Without giving too much away: a pick-up truck hitched to a yacht, a paralysis-inducing drug, a bathful of chilling water, a long-buried necklace and a decomposing corpse slot together with an almost unbearable sustained tension.

Yet it really doesn't add up to all that much. What lies beneath this masterful display of audience manipulation is a mightily confused film attempting a slice of everything: tricksy murderous thriller, beyond-the-grave spook story and *Sixth Sense*-style horror for grown-ups. It's an enjoyably giddy ride, certainly, but once you're back from the edge of your seat, you realise most of the creaks and groans are from the decomposing script. ★★★★ **IN**

WHAT'S NEW PUSSYCAT? (1965)

Starring: *Peter Sellers (Dr. Fritz Fassbender), Peter O'Toole (Michael James), Romy Schneider (Carole Werner), Capucine (Renée Lefebvre), Paula Prentiss (Liz), Woody Allen (Victor Shakapopolis), Ursula Andress (Rita), Richard Burton (Man In Bar)*
Director: *Clive Donner*
Screenwriter: *Woody Allen*
15/108 mins./Comedy/USA/France

Parisian fashion editor Michael Jones consults psychiatrist Fritz Fassbender, for, while he is engaged to Carol Werne, he can't resist the temptation of Rita, Liz and Renée.

W

When producer Charles K. Feldman purchased the rights to Hungarian Ladislas Bus-Fekete's play, *Lot's Wife*, he hoped to turn it into a vehicle for Cary Grant. However, Warren Beatty had assumed the lead by the time that Feldman caught Woody Allen's live act and offered him the chance to make his screenwriting debut.

Peeved by the pathetic fee, Allen also wrote himself the role of strip club wardrobe man, Victor Shakapopolis. But he made the mistake of ignoring I.A.L. Diamond's earlier attempt at an adaptation – for fear of being both swayed by its style and daunted by the expertise of Billy Wilder's longtime collaborator – and structured the scenario as a loose assemblage of gags and set-pieces, which bore more resemblance to a TV sketch show or a stand-up routine than a Hollywood narrative.

Initially, this didn't bother Feldman, as he had envisaged adopting a monochrome nouvelle vague-like approach. But Beatty (whose famous chat-up line had been commandeered for the title) disliked the anarchic style and resented Feldman's refusal to cast then-lover Leslie Caron as Carol. So, the highly unsuitable Peter O'Toole was hired as his replacement and he proceeded to ally himself with Peter Sellers in circumventing the script, which Allen had polished in conjunction with director, Clive Donner.

Keen to prove he still had it after the heart attack that had forced him to withdraw from *Kiss Me, Stupid*, Sellers insisted on boosting his part (which Allen had originally intended for Groucho Marx) in a series of self-indulgent improvisations that utterly altered the picture. Moreover, everyone seems to have an opinion about the much-amended ending, including Romy Schneider, who had a clause inserted into her contract blocking her marriage to a weed like Woody.

Allen managed to retain joke references to movies like *I Am a Fugitive from A Chain Gang*, *Moulin Rouge*, *Lust for Life*, *Dr. No* and *8 1/2*. But he followed threats to remove his name from the picture by disowning it – even though it actually explored several themes that would recur in his more mature work. ★★★ **DP**

WHAT'S UP, TIGER LILY? (1966)

Starring: *Tasuya Mihashi (Phil Moscowitz), Mie Hama (Terri Yaki), Akiko Wakabayashi (Suki Yai), Tadao Nakamaru (Shepherd Wong), Susumu Kurobe (Wing Fat), Woody Allen (Narrator/Host/Voice)*
Director: *Senkichi Taniguchi*
Screenwriters: *Kazuo Yamada, Woody Allen, Frank Buxton, Len Maxwell, Louise Lasser, Mickey Rose, Bryna Wilson, Julie Bennett*
PG/80 mins/Comedy/USA

Roguish Phil Moskowitz encounters scheming sisters Terry Yaki and Suki Yaki on his search for the recipe for the perfect egg salad.

In 1962, Roger Corman gave Francis Ford Coppola his first break in movies when, under the pseudonym Thomas Colchart, he reworked the Russian sci-fi movie *Nebo Zevet* (*The Heavens Call*) as the creature feature *Battle Beyond The Sun*. However, when Harry G. Saperstein attempted to release the 1964 Japanese James Bond pastiche *Kagi No Kagi* (*Key Of Keys*) as *Keg Of Powder*, heckling audiences ad libbed their own variations on the badly dubbed dialogue.

Desperate to recoup his $75,000 investment, Sapperstein decided to borrow the idea behind Jay Ward's TV show *Fractured Flickers*, in which Hans Conreid delivered parodic commentaries on melodramatic silents in a range of whacky accents. Quite why Woody Allen felt that he was the man to give Senkichi Taniguchi's programmer a comic lease of life is unclear, but the $66,000 fee probably had much to do with it. Moreover, it probably seemed like easy money, as Allen devised the gags during a brainstorming session with pals including Lenny Maxwell and Frank Buxton, as they rolled the Toho picture in a Manhattan hotel room.

There are some funny moments here. But Jimmy Murakami's opening credits, in which an animated Woody plucks names from the cleavages of posing pin-ups, was not one of them. However, Sapperstein, who had acquired the pioneering UPA studio from its Disney fugitive founder Stephen Bosustow, clearly felt the need to exploit his cartoon connections. The closing sequence was no less lame, as *Playboy* model China Lee teased an alternately disinterested and aroused Allen as he watched her stripping on TV. Much more amusing was the 'death is my bread and danger is my butter' routine, which anticipated the opening of *Manhattan*.

But Allen came to loathe the film and even tried to block its release when Sapperstein added 19 minutes from other Japanese movies (with Allen's voice dubbed by another actor) and two numbers by the Lovin' Spoonful. However, as with *What's New, Pussycat?*, Woody's negativity was out of step with the public's positive response and *Tiger Lily* became a cult hit. ★★ **DP**

WHAT EVER HAPPENED TO BABY JANE? (1962)

Starring: *Bette Davis (Baby Jane Hudson), Joan Crawford (Blanche Hudson), Victor Buono (Edwin Flagg), Wesley Addy (Marty McDonald)*
Director: *Robert Aldrich*
Screenwriter: *Lukas Heller, based on the novel by Henry Farrell*
18/127 mins./Drama/Horror/Thriller/USA

Awards – *Academy Awards – Best Black-and-White Costume*

Famed rivals Davis and Crawford get the knives out in a darkly comic psychodrama.

In a wickedly macabre tale of Hollywood woe, forgotten child star Baby Jane festers drunkenly in a mouldering manse with her memories and the invalid sister (Crawford's Blanche, the greater star, crippled in mysterious circumstances) she delights in tormenting.

The bizarrely appalling carry-on, like Jane's surprise din-din for Blanche, crackles with the real malice between longtime rivals Davis and Crawford. Davis' willingness – nay, avidity – to chew the scenery from under Crawford as a demented grotesque is scary in itself, but ageing screen queens don't get any gutsier.

This does well as psychodrama, black comedy or camp classic, and its success and five Oscar nominations prompted a rush of great old stars playing maniacs. If you haven't seen it, you might find it vaguely familiar from the many times it has been spoofed in film and television. ★★★★ **AE**

WHAT'S UP DOC? (1972)

Starring: *Barbra Streisand (Judy Maxwell), Ryan O'Neal (Dr. Howard Bannister), Madeline Kahn (Eunice Burns), Kenneth Mars (Hugh Simon), Austin Pendleton (Hugh Simon)*
Director: *Peter Bogandovich*
Screenwriters: *Buck Henry, David Newman, Robert Benton based on a story by Peter Bogandovich*
PG/94 mins./Comedy/USA

Dippy, unsatisfied music expert Howard Bannister comes to San Francisco with his bossy fiancée. Here he meets Judy Maxwell, a college dropout and whirlwind of a girl, and love, theft, conspiracy and all round chaos soon ensue.

The then hot director Peter Bogdanovich had landed himself a studio deal to make a movie with then hot stars Barbra Streisand and Ryan O'Neal. What he didn't have was a hot script. Or any script at all. So, he called screenwriters David Henry and Robert Benton (hot off *Bonnie And Clyde*) with the simple request that they provide him with a modern version of screwball classic *Bringing Up Baby*.

Most Expensive Movie Memorabilia — TOP 10

1. **Ruby slippers ...** ***Wizard of Oz*** **... £362,000**
2. **Marlon Brando's script ...** ***The Godfather*** **... £170,000**
3. **Clark Gable's script ...** ***Gone With The Wind*** **... £133,000**
4. **Aston Martin DB5 ...** ***Goldeneye*** **... £157,750**
5. **Rosebud sled ...** ***Citizen Kane*** **... £127,000**
6. **Tony Monero's white suit ...** ***Saturday Night Fever*** **... $78,800**
7. **Oddjob's bowler hat ...** ***Goldfinger*** **... £62,000**
8. **Charlie Chaplin's cane ...** ***Modern Times*** **... £47,800**
9. **Indy's whip ...** ***Indiana Jones*** **trilogy ... £27,600**
10. **Marilyn Monroe's 'Shimmy' dress ...** ***Some Like It Hot*** **... £19,800**

They come fairly close. With Bogdanovich directing with a lovely lightness of touch against a sunlit San Francisco (the perfect location for romantic comedies), and Barbra Streisand and Ryan O'Neal while never finding the sparkling energy of Katharine Hepburn and the prim exasperation of Cary Grant, working up a kooky charm more befitting of the hippy-era of the early 70s. Again, the pitch is the robust and amorous woman aiming to snare a shrinking violet of the male species. Streisand's Judy is part libertine, part nutcase, and alarmingly sexual, the actress never ever been so alive on the screen. O'Neal's doc is a music geek after a grant, his natural good looks and effervescence corseted by Bannister's frazzled over-education and self-importance.

For the plot to crackle with necessary screwballing mania, the script tosses up first Madeline Kahn's controlling fiancée Eunice as rival, then jewel thefts, matching luggage (yes, that staple), secret papers, prehistoric rocks and, of course, a grand chase sequence (de rigueur for San Fran) as well as a fabulous sequence at a banquet which the leads play under the table. Bogdanovich is busily paying reference to all his favourite flavours of humour efficiently packing them into the brief 94 minutes, hurtling from buffoonery and slapstick, to impersonations and word-play, and lets Babs have the one song to smooch up a romantic moment. It's never quite as tight or fierce as the original screwballers, but is fizzy and loveable and always worth watching. ★★★★ **IN**

WHEN HARRY MET SALLY ... (1989)

Starring: *Billy Crystal (Harry Burns), Meg Ryan (Sally Albright), Carrie Fisher (Marie), Bruno Kirby (Jess), Steven Ford (Joe)*
Director: *Rob Reiner*
Screenwriter: *Nora Ephron*
15/91 mins./Romance/Comedy/USA
Awards – *BAFTA – Best Original Screenplay*

Harry and Sally have known each other for years, and are very good friends, but they fear sex would ruin the friendship.

One of the most popular and popularly-imitated bits of contemporary movie lore comes from this film. Harry and Sally are chewing over sandwiches and the politics of sexual relationships in a crowded lunchroom when Sally noisily demonstrates that a man can't distinguish between a fake orgasm and the real thing. All that's required to conjure up the scene for anyone is to moan, grunt and scream the word yes 15 times and throw in some table banging for totally accurate effect. Her atypically uninhibited display rocketed Meg Ryan from winsome ingenue to star. But the fantastic punchline, the funniest line in the entire movie, is given not to either of the stars but to the director's mother. Estelle Reiner, wife of Carl, mother of Rob, and a former night-club singer, is the 'older woman customer' (as billed in the credits) who looks at the waiter after Sally has tucked into her side salad and deadpans, 'I'll have what she's having'. This is even funnier to women for whom select food items can be as good as sex.

When Harry Met Sally is the epitome of 80s Zeitgeist and the modern thirtysomething relationships romantic comedy, preoccupied with personality types and pop analysis rather than situation or plotting. A couple meet, don't hit it off, but in the course of their 12-year search for love re-connect to become confidantes, endlessly discussing their feelings, friendship and disappointments. The joke is always on them; the audience never loses confidence that all the cute, companionable chumming around with their honesty, lunches, late-night phone calls and strolls through the park will take them eventually, inevitably, into the bedroom and up the aisle.

The angle at which they are approached is the much-reiterated question 'Can men and women ever really be just good friends?' This is rather spuriously pushed as a burning contemporary issue (have none of them read, oh, say, Jane Austen's *Emma*?). Harry's contention (presumably also the conviction of director Reiner and famously embittered *Heartburn* writer Nora Ephron, whose divorce from journalist Carl Bernstein fuelled her new career as gender-differences savant), is borne out by the picture's climax and resolution. It's a resounding 'no'. The 'sex part' does get in the way, a consoling kiss escalating into a tumble, after which Sally goes into full-on commitment-demanding mode.

Thanks to the engaging leads, amusing dialogue and urban fairy-tale depiction of Manhattan (it's one of the last films shot by cinematographer Barry Sonnenfeld before he turned director), it's a charming, populist, Woody Allenesque affair in which goddess of cute Sally Albright and cynical, wisecracking Harry Burns play out their progress to classic love, crooned by Frank Sinatra, Ella Fitzgerald, Louis Armstrong and standards revivalist Harry Connick Jr. Meanwhile their best friends, Marie (Carrie Fisher, hers) and Jess (Bruno Kirby, his) couple without any of their hesitation or agonising in order to provide a balanced, two-person chorus for confidences, encouragement, and the story's most appealingly humorous element, the smart and knowing commentary on how 80s men view women and vice versa.

Highlights, apart from the orgasmic cafeteria routine, include Harry and Jess having a heart-to-heart while the men unconsciously rise up and down, up and down in the Mexican Wave at a football game and the representative character schtick like Sally's quirky food orders because she wants what she wants: 'I'd like the chef's salad, please, with the oil and vinegar on the side, and the apple pie à la mode. But I'd like the pie heated and I don't want the ice cream on top I want it on the side, and I'd like strawberry instead of vanilla if you have it. If not, then no ice cream just whipped cream but only if it's real; if it's out of a can then nothing.'

The timely script and the film's commerciality propelled screenwriter Ephron in the direction of movies for which *WHMS* was the blueprint. *Sleepless In Seattle*, *You've Got Mail* and other imitations have made a regular feature of the recurring movie reference (for *Casablanca* substitute *An Affair To Remember*, *The Dirty Dozen*, *The Godfather*), the Easy Listening soundtrack underlining scenes, the helpfully instructive best friends. Its influence can also be traced through 90s sitcoms like *Friends* and the Richard Curtis British romcom hit machine. Harry Burns is a gnomish Hugh

Grant without tics; Sally Albright is Bridget Jones' spiritual big sister – only she doesn't have any worries about her thighs. ★★★★★ **AE**

WHEN THE WIND BLOWS (1986)

Starring: the voices of: *Peggy Ashcroft (Hilda Bloggs), John Mills (Jim Bloggs), Robin Houston (Anouncer)*
Director: *Jimmy T. Murakami*
Screenwriter: *Raymond Briggs, from his comic book*
PG/80 mins./Animation/Drama/UK

The effects of a nuclear attack, as seen through the eyes of an elderly couple.

Subjects don't come much bigger than total species extinction and in the mid-80s, the imposing shadows thrown by the superpowers' volatile arsenal of nuclear warheads pretty much blackened the entire planet. With last-grip, nerve-stretched lunacies like Mutually Assured Destruction dominating US and Soviet policies, the standoff also had the vinegary whiff of desperate farce about it. War is hell but at least there are winners. In a nuclear conflict, everybody – and everything – loses. One big bang and we all fall down. Or, in the case of *When The Wind Blows*, fall-out.

While Mick Jackson's telemovie *Threads* remains the screen's most potent account of mass panic on apocalypse day, this British to-the-frame adaptation of Raymond Briggs' graphic novella is unquestionably the most humane. Say hello and wave goodbye then, to Jim and Hilda, our naive retired home counties couple who, on hearing of an imminent World War III, set about merrily obeying the ridiculous instructions from government protect and survive pamphlets. They whitewash the windows (to shield the radiation), stock up on supplies (a tin of Christmas pudding) and cheerfully anticipate a Blitz-style cosy-up sipping Ovaltine under Anderson shelters.

At first, it plays out like a black comedy – just as the bomb hits, dim Hilda goes to get the washing in – but as the insidious crackle of fall-out settles and the sickness sets in, the movie reveals its true nature: an unbearably intimate, gently accentuated tragedy with a tenacious pacifist streak. Blending 2D cells with 3D modelling, director Jimmy Murakami is technically adventurous but crucially, his connection to Briggs' material is total. In fact, with its working class nuances, droll dialogue and mundane aura, you sense that if Mike Leigh made cartoons, the results wouldn't be too far from this. Powerful stuff and in Brit-toon terms, a total one-off. ★★★★ **SC**

WHEN WE WERE KINGS (1996)

Starring: as themselves: *Muhammad Ali, George Foreman, Don King, James Brown, B.B. King, Mobutu Sese Seko, Spike Lee, Norman Mailer*
Director: *Leon Gast*
PG/83 mins./Documentary/History/Sport/USA

Awards – *Academy Awards – Best Documentary*

A documentary of the 1974 heavyweight championship bout in Zaire between champion George Foreman and underdog challenger Muhammad Ali.

Few gave Ali a prayer against George Foreman in Zaire in October 1974, back when Foreman was a 26-year-old fighting machine, who had pulverised Joe Frazier and Ken Norton, both of whom had beaten Ali.

Defeat, though, could mean the end of everything Ali had striven for. There could be only one winner. Ali was such a natural before the camera that the biggest problem facing director Gast must have been deciding which priceless press conference quips to omit.

In the end, he might have cut back on the footage of the music festival that ran for three days before the fight. While the concerts were organised to reinforce the cultural links between Africa and America, the clips of James Brown, BB King and The Spinners sit uncomfortably alongside the big fight which was motivated by anything but brotherly love.

Writers Norman Mailer and George Plimpton offer some astute recollections, but the most telling contribution comes from Spike Lee, who laments the fact that heroes are too transient in the modern world and that Ali's true achievement has been all but forgotten. One of the best and most emotionally affecting documentaries ever made. ★★★★★ **DP**

WHEN WORLDS COLLIDE (1951)

Starring: *Richard Derr (David Randall), Barbara Rush (Joyce Hendron), Peter Hanson (Dr. Tony Drake M.D.), John Hoyt (Sydney Stanton), Larry Keating (Dr. Cole Hendron)*
Director: *Rudolph Maté*
Screenwriter: *Sydney Boehm, based on the novel by Edwin Balmer and Philip Wylie*
PG/83 mins./Sci-fi/USA

Awards: *Academy Awards – Best Special Effects*

When a scientist realises a runaway star with a planet-sized object in its orbit has entered our solar system and is on course to collide with the Earth, he must convince the authorities to build a spacecraft to at least save a chosen few.

A sci-fi disaster movie, brimming with pessimism that predates more recent high-tech doom-mongering like *Armageddon* and *Deep Impact*, with its scenario of the world's end and how we, the poor beleaguered human face up to it. It's big, showy and pretentious, getting bogged down in chewy great lumps of philosophy and religiosity, while its science is scatterbrained, but there is still that charge of 50s paranoia that runs in its veins when the world must have felt a very vulnerable place. Most interesting, in Sydney Boehm's set-up (based up the novel by Edwin Balmer and Philip Wylie) is the notion of inevitability – no one is going to save the day, it's just a case of who will be allowed to survive.

The big disaster sequences boasted the finest in special effects for their day that, with age, take on a quaint quality no matter that you are supposed to be witnessing tidal waves, earthquakes and volcanos spewing up their innards, as the small planet first sweeps past Earth. The now iconic shots of New York flooded by waves (using superimposed images) was homaged, shall we say, by Roland Emmerich for his equally verbose *The Day After Tomorrow*.

The second half of the movie is the Noah's Ark scenario, as a rocket ship of '50s art deco design, is financed and constructed with room for animals and only 40 men and women. Which much wooden acting, and much turgid scenes of self-sacrifice, romantic clichés and warbling guilt, all the while the clock ticks and death looms. Richard Derr (as the handsome pilot), Barbara Rush and John Hoyt don't have the range to tap any great drama even in such a morbid possibility. It's tacky and melodramatic, but a fascinating insight into the preoccupations of the 50s rather than a look at some dread possibility of the future. ★★★ **IN**

WHERE EAGLES DARE (1968)

Starring: *Richard Burton (Major Jonathan Smith), Clint Eastwood (Lt. Morris Schaffer), Mary Ure (Mary Ellison), Patrick Wymark (Col. Wyatt Turner), Michael Horden (Adm. Rolland)*
Director: *Brian G. Hutton*
Screenwriter: *Alistair MacLean based on his own story*
PG/158 mins./War/UK/USA

When the Nazis capture a high ranking American general whose transport plane had crashed in enemy territory, a crack team of commandoes is sent to pluck him out of the mountaintop redoubt where he is held prisoner. But when one of their number is killed in the parachute drop, it becomes clear they may have a traitor in their midst and the mission may not have as clear an objective as it first seems.

A fine example of that war movie staple – the men on a mission caper, which could just as easily be dubbed the 'MacLean' given most of them are based on Alistair MacLean's popular boy's own adventure novels that while trivialising the violent truths of warfare, tend to be an absolute hoot anyway. This one was even scripted by the author, and is so far-fetched its po-faced façade nearly cracks, and, more unusually, proves to be as dense and complicated as a spy story, where only poor befuddled Clint Eastwood seems to stick on the side of good.

The set-up has all it could possibly need to fire-up its brash formula of action, adventure and intrigue: a crack team of commandoes sent to pluck a captured general from, you got it, an impregnable Nazi fortress stuck on the stop of an icy mountain accessed only by a cable car. Imagine the possibilities! Brian G. Hutton does, and rustles up some unforgettable stunt-work – the spectacular leap between cable cars has enflamed schoolboy imaginations and been instantly recalled long into adulthood. As a mission movie it has a keen atmosphere and a striking cast: Richard Burton gets most of the juicy dialogue, Eastwood just looks great in a stolen Nazi uniform, while good salts like Michael Horden and Patrick Wymark and fetching Ingrid Pitt fill out the requisite host of characters.

Where the film has become so famously confusing is in its cacophony of subplots and reversals – Burton's tricky major must swap sides fifteen times. Their quarry, the American general, has the plans for D-Day in his head that must not fall into German hands (is it easier to kill than rescue him?), then there is a rat in their camp (why-oh-why?), and what is sneaky Mary Ure doing parachuting in after the main team (apart from for some sexual tension)? All this requires reams of boggy exposition to be reeled off by Burton during a hilarious if pace-murdering sequence, and the real secret behind the whole mission just makes you want to throw bricks at the screen. You've had a rare old time getting there, though. ★★★ **IN**

WHILE YOU WERE SLEEPING (1995)

Starring: *Sandra Bullock (Lucy Eleanor Moderatz), Bill Pullman (Jack Callaghan), Peter Gallagher (Peter Callaghan), Peter Boyle (Ox Callaghan), Jack Warden (Saul), Glynis Johns (Elsie)*
Director: *John Turtletaub*
Screenwriters: *Daniel G. Sullivan, Fredric LeBow*
PG/103 mins./Romance/Comedy/USA

Lucy, a ticket booth worker in Chicago, lusts after a customer she sees every day. When he has an accident on her watch, she takes responsibility for getting him to hospital and his family accidentally assume she's his girlfriend

Sandra Bullock is Lucy, a lonely ticket booth worker for the Chicago Transit Authority, whose day revolves around the morning arrival of a gorgeous yuppie commuter. Every night she goes home, unwraps a TV dinner, bonds with her cat, and fights off the unwanted advances of her landlord's son. Coerced into working over Christmas, Lucy's dream man – she later learns his name is Peter – finally becomes more reality than she can cope with, when he's mugged on her platform and ends up on the tracks, leaving Lucy to step in and save him from the wheels of an oncoming train.

Later, at the hospital, Lucy is overheard by a nurse muttering to herself, 'I was going to marry him ...' and before you can say 'engagement party', Peter's eccentric family troop in and mistake her for his fiancée. It's a wonderful scene – fast, funny, totally implausible. Since Lucy is alone, weak-willed, and, more to the point, Peter is now in a coma, she plays along with the deception, warming to her surrogate family and they to her. All the while aware that one day she will be forced to come clean.

Then the arrival of Peter's less loaded, but far nicer brother, Jack, throws up another dilemma. Peter is not, she swiftly discovers, the Mr. Perfect she fantasised about, but a self-centred, conceited scumbag, who keeps pictures of himself in his wallet and only has one testicle. No, it's Jack who she really loves. What comes next is obvious, but the film is no less enchanting for it. Bullock is a delight, disarmingly kooky, pleasing to look at, and – as she has previously proved – a gifted comedic actress. Together with Pullman, she keeps the predictable plot chugging along nicely, and the corn pretty much on the cob. Pullman, so long the loser in celluloid love (think *Sleepless, Malice, Last Seduction*), finally – and it won't spoil your enjoyment to know – gets the girl. It's a mite pat and sentimental in parts, but this is romantic comedy, what do you expect? ★★★★ **MS**

WHISKY GALORE (1949)

Starring: *Basil Radford (Captain Paul Waggett), Catherine Lacey (Mrs. Waggett), Bruce Seton (Sergeant Odd), Joan Greenwood (Peggy Macroon), Wylie Watson (Joseph Macroon), Gabrielle Blunt (Catriona Macroon), Gordan Jackson (George Campbell)*
Director: *Alexander Mackendrick*
Screenwriters: *Angus MacPhail, Compton MacKenzie, based on the novel by MacKenzie*
PG/79 mins./Comedy/USA

Islanders on the Isle Of Eriskay in the Outer Hebrides discover 50,000 barrels of whiskey and, understandably, are keen to give them a good home

A classic tale of gentle anti-authoritarianism – the template also for 1998's *Waking Ned* – it was a natural for Ealing Studios whose head, Michael Balcon, outlined his company's theory about comedy thus: 'We take a character or group of characters and let them run up against either an untenable situation or an insoluble problem.' The problem for the islanders is Captain Waggett, the English leader of the island's Home Guard, opposed to the islander's looting and prepared to do everything to maintain law and order as he sees it. Balcon handed the job of producer to his publicity director, Monja 'Danny' Danischewsky.

The novice producer appointed a novice director, Alexander 'Sandy' Mackendrick, employed in Ealing as a writer. The American-born, Scottish-educated Mackendrick did have some limited experience of directing, having shot documentaries for the Ministry Of Information during the War. Understandably, as one of these was entitled *Kitchen Waste For Pigs* he preferred to regard *Whisky Galore!* as his first picture.

The pair settled on Eriskay's neighbouring island of Barra (rechristened Todday in the film) as their location and assembled their cast largely from Ealing's band of repertory regulars. Basil Radford was cast as Waggett, a similarly officious role to the one he took in *Passport To Pimlico*, while the part of the canniest of the islanders, Macroon, was taken by Wylie Watson. A young Gordon Jackson was cast as the mother-dominated George while Jean Cadell played the formidable matriarch to great comic effect. The film was also notable for ushering in a golden period in the career of Joan Greenwood, one of British film's most unsung – not to mention unreasonably attractive – actresses, who wrapped her husky voice around the Gaelic lilt of Macroon's daughter, Peggy.

W

Notwithstanding the talents of the cast, the shoot still threw up countless problems. Incessant rain limited outdoor filming drastically and caused the final budget to overrun by £20,000, a substantial amount for the permanently cash-strapped studio. Mackendrick, too, was dissatisfied with the quality of his work, later commenting, 'It looks like a home movie. It doesn't look like it was made by a professional at all. And it wasn't.'

More seriously, the Calvinist Mackendrick clashed with the Jewish Danischewsky over the film's moral message, with the director siding with Waggett while the producer went with the islanders. Partly to appease Mackendrick and moral guardians in the US, a rather unconvincing coda was tacked on declaring that the whisky soon ran out and the islanders returned to their former unhappiness. (In truth, there was no documentary evidence that the islanders ever went short of whisky again).

The film was released in June 1949, the same month as *Kind Hearts And Coronets*, stamping that year, which also saw the release of *Passport To Pimlico*, as Ealing comedy's annus mirabilis. The film's themes chimed with a country growing weary of rationing and austerity. As Michael Balcon later acknowledged, 'The country was tired of regulation and regimentation and there was a mild anarchy in the air.' Such anarchy wasn't shared in the US, however, where restrictions about endorsing alcoholic products, necessitated a name change to *Tight Little Island*. France, too, opted for a different title, namely *Whisky A Go-Go*.

Almost a decade later, Compton Mackenzie and Danischewsky attempted to return to their former glories with a sequel of sorts, *Rockets Galore!* wherein the islanders of Todday mobilised against a missile site being built there. The film failed to recapture its predecessor's charm. Intriguingly, however, Mackenzie might have found a more fertile sequel, had he stayed closer to his original source of inspiration. Papers released earlier this year show that the SS *Politician*, along with its whisky, was also carrying 290,000 Jamaican ten shilling notes. Over 75,000 of them were never unaccounted for, although many were presented in banks throughout the world suggesting they did not sink as authorities initially suggested. And one, at least, can be accounted for. A ten shilling note remains pinned above the bar in the main pub on the Isle Of Eriskay. A pub which was renamed The Politician, in tribute to the vessel which provided so much free inebriation and possible wealth.
★★★★★ **JN**

⦿ WHITE CHRISTMAS 1954)

Starring: *Bing Crosby (Bob Wallace), Danny Kaye (Phil Davis), Rosemary Clooney (Betty), Vera-Ellen (Judy), Dean Jagger (Gen. Waverly), Mary Wickers (Emma), John Brascia (Joe)*
Director: *Michael Curtiz*
Screenwriters: *Norman Krasna, Norman Panama, Melvyn Frank*
U/120 mins./Musical/USA

Sisters Betty and Judy Haynes misunderstand the motives of Bob Wallace and Phil Davis when they arrange a special variety show at the struggling Vermont ski lodge of their old wartime commander, General Waverly.

Despite not being able to read or write music and being incapable of composing in any key but F#, Irving Berlin knew from the moment he completed 'White Christmas' that he had written an enduring standard.

It was first performed on screen by Bing Crosby and Marjorie Fielding in *Holiday Inn* and Bing reprised it in his 1946 reunion with Fred Astaire, *Blue Skies*. However, it's best known in the context of this popular, if derivative musical, which became the genre's fifth most successful entry of the 1950s.

Donald O'Connor was to have partnered Crosby, but he broke his leg and had to be replaced by Danny Kaye for the comic sidekicking and John Brascia for choreographer Robert Alton's more demanding dance routines to 'Mandy' and 'Abraham'. However, Kaye holds his own with Vera-Ellen for 'The Best Things Happen When You're Dancing' and he contributes some typically pantomimic mugging to the Martha Graham parody, 'Choreography'.

But the songs don't rank among Berlin's best. Crosby croons happily to 'Count Your Blessings' and Rosemary Clooney delivers a mournful rendition of 'Love, You Didn't Do Right By Me'. But the majority of the numbers are presented in rehearsal or performance situations and, thus, don't always form an organic part of the narrative. The Haynes duet 'Sisters' admittedly explains the basis of their relationship (and Kaye and Crosby's later lip synch'd version is splendidly silly), while 'What Can You Do With a General?' sweetens Crosby's tele-appeal for the old unit to reform. But the latter is hardly up to the standard that Berlin set in *This Is the Army* (1943), while 'Gee, How I Wish I Were Back in the Army' smacks of that picture's biggest hit, 'Oh, How I Hate to Get Up in the Morning'.

Ultimately, a surfeit of plot prevents this otherwise genial entertainment from sparking, while Curtiz's studio-bound direction rather wastes the VistaVision widescreen on its debut outing. But how can you knock a movie that's still a festive institution over 50 years after its release?
★★★ **DP**

⦿ WHITE HEAT (1949)

Starring: *James Cagney (Arthur 'Cody' Jarrett), Virginia Mayo (Verna Jarrett), Edmond O'Brien (Vic Pardo/Hank Fallon), Margaret Wycherly (Ma Jarrett), Steve Cochran (Big Ed Somers)*
Director: *Raoul Walsh*
Screenwriters: *Ivan Goff, Ben Roberts, based on a story by Virginia Kellogg*
15/109 mins./Crime/Drama/USA

A psychopathic criminal with a mother complex makes a daring break from prison and leads his old gang in a chemical plant payroll heist. Shortly after the plan takes place, events take a crazy turn

It was over a decade since cinema had witnessed a genuine gangster. The imposition of the Production Code in 1934 had just about put paid to the violin case-carrying hood of the age, while nothing as unpatriotic as crime was allowed near American screens during World War II.

Increasingly affluent audiences didn't want to be reminded of the prohibition-depression era and, consequently, the very nature of movie crime changed. Instead of being career criminals with a killing complex and delusions of grandeur, the anti-heroes of the film noir boom were essentially decent saps who were led astray by their adverse post-war circumstances or tempted into indiscretion by a smouldering femme fatale.

So James Cagney was definitely bucking a trend when he decided to return to the gangster flick in mid-1949. Swallowing his pride, after the disappointing performance of Cagney Productions, he re-signed to Warner Brothers – the studio from which he had parted six years earlier – and allowed himself to be talked into Raoul Walsh's *White Heat*. However, this wasn't quite the capitulation it seemed. Such was Cagney's determination to shake his persona that since *The Roaring Twenties* (1939) he had refused to even read crime scripts. But, his desperate need for a hit after a string of misfires was equally pressing and so he agreed to work with the man who had so successfully remoulded Humphrey Bogart's screen image in *High Sierra* (1941).

Walsh planned to move Cagney out of his overly familiar tenements and into a rural setting more akin to a modern-day Western than an old-fashioned mob movie. Moreover, he was happy to acquiesce in Cagney's insistence on placing an emphasis on recent advances in scientific detection to ensure that the picture carried a 'crime does not pay' message. But screenwriters Ivan Goff and Ben Roberts were far more interested in the psychology of the psychotic. Thus, they sought to depict Cody Jarrett as a megalomaniac doomed by his own failings to destruction.

The inspiration for their story was Ma Barker, although they distilled the violent malevolence of her four sons into a single figure. As played by Margaret Wycherly, it's easy to see how such a mother could have engendered Cody's cynical, calculated approach to crime (especially bearing in mind the implied Oedipal nature of their relationship). But it's also intimated that Jarrett was born with the mental fragility that so frequently tipped him over the edge and, thus, made him marginally less morally responsible for his actions. Some critics have claimed he's an epileptic. But, whatever the cause of his mania, he is, like Hans Beckert in *M*, a victim of destiny.

The ferocity of Ma's hold over Jarrett is most clearly evident in the prison mess-hall sequence. Having learned of her death, he hurtles down the table lashing out at guards and cons alike in frenzied distress. The scene is rendered all the more shockingly realistic by the fact that not only did Cagney reproduce the pitiful screaming he remembered from his father's drinking bouts, but Walsh didn't tell the 300 or so extras what was going to happen, hence the genuine bewilderment in their expressions. The scene deeply disturbed Cagney, however, and after a preview screening he refused to watch the film ever again.

Yet for all the violence and anguish, there's also a dark undercurrent of comedy. It's almost as if Cagney were parodying his previous incarnations. Just as he pushed a grapefruit into Mae Clarke's face in *The Public Enemy* (1931), here he knocks Virginia Mayo off a chair as she shows off her new fur. Similarly, he also has a number of callous one-liners, none more heartless than the one which follows his silencing of a stool-pigeon's muffled cries as he riddles a car boot with lead – 'Oh, stuffy, huh? I'll give you a little air.' With its 13 slayings, *White Heat* was hot stuff for 1949, prompting Bosley Crowther of the *New York Times* to declare it was 'A cruelly vicious film', and that 'its impact upon the emotions of the unstable or impressionable is incalculable'. He was also prepared to concede that, 'Mr. Cagney achieves the fascination of a brilliant bullfighter at work, deftly engaging in the business of doing violence with economy and grace'.

Tagline
James Cagney is red-hot in White Heat!

Bridging the gap between the rise-and-fall pictures of the 1930s and the syndicate dramas that would dominate the 1950s, the film ends with a symbolic mushroom cloud, as Cody blows up a gas tank rather than be taken alive. It was also a token gesture on Cagney's behalf, as rarely again would he be such a potent screen force as this. ★★★★★ **DP**

WHITE HUNTER, BLACK HEART (1990)

Starring: *Clint Eastwood (John Wilson), Jeff Fahey (Pete Verrill), Charlotte Cornwell (Miss Wilding), Norman Lumsden (Butler George), George Dzundza (Paul Landers)*
Director: *Clint Eastwood*
Screenwriters: *Peter Viertel, James Bridges, Burt Kennedy based on the novel by Viertel*
PG/110 mins./Drama/USA

The thinly veiled story of John Huston's trip to Africa to shoot *The African Queen*. Once there the obstinate director, here christened John Wilson, becomes rather more intent on hunting elephants than actually starting filming.

The first thing you notice about this eloquent piece of Hollywood lore, rejigged as fiction and based on the novel by Peter Viertel (who wrote the script for *The African Queen*, and portrayed by Jeff Fahey as Pete Venill in the film), is how Clint Eastwood never shuts up. We've never known such dialogue to poor out of that normally taciturn face, spews of irascible tirades based on the rough candour of legend John Huston. It's not quite the right fit, Eastwood appears to be entertaining himself far more than anyone else.

There is a gruff sort of comedy to the film, which could just as easily be taken as a drama. Eastwood, who directs as well as stars, seems to find this encasement of Hollywood egomania a bit rum, so idly parodies the situation, this great lummox of a man who would rather bag himself a prize elephant than do what he is being paid for. The cast and crew idle, resting on the whims of their director too busy being macho to care about art or even filmmaking. Yet, Huston did create great film, including *The African Queen*.

There is Eastwood's usual fine polish, it certainly looks like its lounging around 1950s colonial Africa, and possesses that precise sense of self that he imbues into all his projects, which allows some other interesting parallels with the equally dominant Huston. Yet, beyond its sub-*Moby-Dick* buzz of one miserable old bugger versus an equally cantankerous force of nature (Wilson eventually squares off against a particular bull-male), it resists any greater sense of meaning, the moody trace of art that filled Eastwood's previous film *Bird*, or the resonance of his cowboy greats. ★★★ **IN**

WHO FRAMED ROGER RABBIT? (1988)

Starring: *Bob Hoskins (Eddie Valiant), Christopher Lloyd (Baron von Rotton), Joanna Cassidy (Dolores), Charles Fleischer (voice of Roger Rabbit/Benny The Cab/Greasy/Psycho), Stubby Kaye (Marvin Acme), Kathleen Turner (voice of Jessica Rabbit)*
Director: *Robert Zemeckis*
Screenwriters: *Jeffrey Price, Peter S. Seaman, based on the novel* Who Censored Roger Rabbit? *by Gary K. Wolf*
PG/99 mins./Animation/Comedy/Mystery/USA
Awards – *Academy Awards – Best Sound Effects Editing, Best Visual Effects, Best Editing, BAFTA – Best Special Effects*

Toon star Roger Rabbit is framed for murder and hires gumshoe Eddie Valiant to clear his name.

Part animation, part film noir, part slapstick comedy, part mismatched buddy movie, part postmodern treatise, director Robert Zemeckis' and executive producer Steven Spielberg's valentine to the cartoon heroes of their youth is all astonishing technical know-how in the service of infectious exuberance and pure wonder.

Mixing the indelible characterisations of Chuck Jones, Disney's beautiful animation and the screwball lunacy of Tex Avery, *Roger Rabbit* is a fitting tribute to the kind of fun you can only have with cinema.

Discovering the screenplay in the early 80s – the project was based on Gary K. Wolf's dark novel *Who Censored Roger Rabbit?*, which told of gumshoe Eddie Valiant's investigation of comic book character Roger Rabbit's murder – Zemeckis was entranced by the opening scene, in which 'toon characters walked off a cartoon set and into the real world.

Once Zemeckis was on board (Terry Gilliam had previously circled the project), he brightened the tone and transposed the action from the novel's contemporary setting to 1947, the golden age of cartoon making.

Where *Roger Rabbit* still amazes today is in just how much the cartoons feel part of the real world, rather than being pasted into it. Nifty mechanical effects (robotic arms, intricate wirework, sets built six feet off the floor to accommodate puppeteers) enabled props to be moved by cartoon characters – who were added in later – giving the dailies the appearance of an Invisible Man movie.

W

The interaction was helped significantly by Bob Hoskins, who sells the relationship between Valiant and Roger beautifully (and with few of the 'eyeline' problems that mar modern CG flicks).

It is one of the movie's greatest achievements that all the new 'toon characters more than hold their own with their classic counterparts – wisecracking New York cab Benny; Baby Herman, cute toddler on screen, cigar-chomping womaniser off it ('The problem is I've got 50 year-old lust and a three year-old dinky'); and, of course, Jessica, Roger's missus and femme fatale extraordinaire whose amazing anatomics describe parabolas that would induce cardiac arrest in a yak.

Spielberg personally negotiated with the myriad copyright holders to get animated stars from competing studios in the same picture. These ranged from big star turns – Daffy and Donald's hilarious piano duel ('That'th the latht time I work with anyone with a thpeech impediment'), Bugs and Mickey playing a cruel parachute gag on Valiant – to the tiniest cameos (Michigan J. Frog from Chuck Jones' 1955 short, *One Froggy Evening*).

When Eddie follows the mystery to the completely animated Toontown, the filmmaking process takes a 180-degree turn – here a real, live actor interacts with cartoon props and settings – and we are treated to a cavalcade of great cartoon characters, pratfalls and tropes, all flawlessly executed.

Yet the film has more to recommend it than techie jiggery-pokery and nostalgic pastiche. A sure-footed cinematic storyteller, Zemeckis marshals the narrative with tremendous discipline (the film noir plotline plays nice riffs on *Chinatown* as baddie Judge Doom – Christopher Lloyd – plans to demolish Toontown and build a freeway), never letting the stream of sight gags swamp the narrative.

Jeffrey Price and Peter S. Seaman's screenplay also finds a sly wit within the madness (when quizzed about his knowledge of showbusiness, Eddie replies, 'There's no business like it. No business I know.').

They also have the confidence to pause for the poignant: in the Ink And Paint Club, Valiant runs into a black-and-white Betty Boop who, working as a cigarette girl, laments, 'Times are tough since cartoons went to colour.' As she is immediately upstaged by the brassy arrival of Jessica, the film adds touching and bittersweet to a perfect and purely cinematic experience. ★★★★★ **IF**

WHO'S AFRAID OF VIRGINIA WOOLF? (1966)

Starring: *Elizabeth Taylor (Martha), Richard Burton (George), George Segal (Nick), Sandy Dennis (Honey)*
Director: *Mike Nichols*
Screenwriter: *Ernest Lehmann, based on the play by Edward Albee*
15/131 mins./Drama/USA
Awards: Academy Awards – *Best Actress (Elizabeth Taylor), Best Supporting Actress (Sandy Dennis), Best Art Direction-Set Decoration, Best Cinematography (Black And White), Best Costume Design (Black And White). BAFTA – Best Film From Any Source, Best British Actor (Richard Burton), Best British Actress (Elizabeth Taylor)*

Biology tutor Nick and his timid wife Honey become caught up in the nightly feuding between erudite, but brow-beaten historian George and his venomously vulgar wife, Martha, who also happens to be the daughter of the college president.

Despite having become the toast of New York by scooping three Tony awards in just four years, Mike Nichols was considered a surprising choice for debuting producer Ernest Lehman's adaptation of Edward Albee's corruscating stage play. Yet, as screenwriter, Lehmann had tailored the action to Nichols' strengths by confining the action (for all but one roadhouse sequence) to George and Martha's home and garden, so that he could concentrate on the intimate intensity of the drama and the power and poignancy of the performances.

Arthur Hill and Uta Hagen had played the quarrelling couple (who were named after the first American president and his wife) when the play opened on Broadway in 1962. Bette Davis had coveted the female lead and Albee wanted James Mason as her co-star. But Jack Lemmon, Robert Redford and Glenn Ford had all been linked with the role of George before Warners decided to cash-in on the notoriety of Elizabeth Taylor and Richard Burton's off-screen image and the stunt casting paid handsome dividends, as the $6 million project raked in around $15 million at the US box office.

The shoot had been far from easy, however, with Taylor (who had piled on the pounds for the part) struggling to cope with Nichols' exacting direction and his intrusive use of close-ups to capture every cruel jibe and wounded riposte as she and Burton cut deeply into each other's private misery. Indeed, some were to claim that the production placed the Burtons under such strain that their marriage never recovered. Sandy Dennis, however, suffered more than most, as she miscarried shortly after the picture wrapped.

Relentlessly filmed and edited by Haskell Wexler and Sam O'Steen, this is an excruciating, if often painfully funny experience. Arguing that it was vital to the picture's artistic integrity, Lehmann secured special permission from the Production Code guardians to retain the play's strong language and this shockingly free sense of expression doubtless contributed to the film's commercial appeal. Yet, ironically, it shared its haul of five Academy Awards with Fred Zinnemann's wholesome Thomas More drama, *A Man for All Seasons*. ★★★★ **DP**

THE WICKER MAN (1973)

Starring: *Edward Woodward (Sergeant Howie), Christopher Lee (Lord Summerisle), Diane Cilento (Miss Rose), Britt Ekland (Willow), Ingrid Pitt (Librarian)*
Director: *Robin Hardy*
Screenwriter: *Anthony Shaffer, based on his novel*
18/84 mins./117 mins. (director's cut)/Horror/Mystery/UK

Sgt. Howie travels to Summerisle to investigate the disappearance of a young girl. He discovers that the locals are weird and unhelpful, and becomes determined to get to the bottom of the disappearance.

When it comes to horror, as with much else, the British are a pretty repressed lot. The old Universal *Frankenstein* and *Dracula* of the 30s caused such a stir that a new H certificate was inaugurated. Later, the rash of drive-in movies of the 50s which were intended for adolescent audiences (*I Was A Teenage Werewolf* etc.) were slapped with X certificates and by the mid-80s Margaret Thatcher and *The Daily Mail* between them had conjured up the 'video nasties' scandal that was the latest episode in the continuing war on horror movies. As a result, British horror has generally bordered on the anaemic with Hammer dominating the home-grown industry, churning out movies that some critics will argue were innovative, but which for many didn't do what horror should – disturb and challenge.

There were however a few films that distanced themselves from the Hammer camp (and, indeed, from Hammer camp). Michael Powell's *Peeping Tom* (1960), Roman Polanski's *Repulsion* (1965) and Michael Reeves' *Witchfinder General* (1968) all delivered more intelligent, troubling horror. But standing head and shoulders above them all, dominating the landscape like its eponymous basketwork bloke, is the towering figure of *The Wicker Man*.

From the title sequence, in which we see a small plane flying over the desolate islands of the Hebrides accompanied by keening folk

Rappers Turned Actors

1. Will Smith (*I, Robot, Independence Day*)
2. Queen Latifah (*Chicago, Beauty Shop*)
3. Ice Cube (*Three Kings, Friday*)
4. LL Cool J (*Any Given Sunday, Deep Blue Sea*)
5. Mos Def (*Hitchhiker's Guide to the Galaxy, The Italian Job*)
6. Eminem (*8 Mile*)
7. Snoop Dogg (*Starsky & Hutch, Training Day*)
8. DMX (*Cradle 2 The Grave, Exit Wounds*)
9. 50 Cent (*Get Rich Or Die Tryin'*)
10. Eve (*The Woodsman*)

music, it's clear this is a horror movie that will take place not in the conventional shadows and nightime, but in bright sunlight. Like Kubrick's *The Shining* (which it predates by seven years) it's an opening sequence in which we see, from an aerial shot, a man – travelling to his doom. The man in this case is Sgt. Neil Howie, a policeman and devout Catholic sent to the remote island of Summerisle to investigate the disappearance of a child. From the moment he arrives he is assailed by images of paganism. Children dance round maypoles while the schoolteacher lectures on its phallic significance; sore throats are cured by holding toads in the mouth; naked girls jump over fires in fertility rituals and the landlord's daughter, played by 70s sex siren Britt Ekland, cavorts around her bedroom stark naked (or at least her top half does, Ekland requested an arse double, a fact that did not appease her boyfriend Rod Stewart who threatened to buy the negative and destroy it).

Stunt arse or not, she gives the unfortunate virgin copper something approaching a dose of the vapours. When he finally meets Lord Summerisle (Lee who, apart from a truly appalling mustard coloured rollneck sweater, delivers what may be the performance of his career), the de facto 'ruler' of the island, the horrified policeman is informed that the islanders have rejected Christianity and returned to the worship of the 'old gods'. It eventually dawns on Howie that part of the islanders' ritual is human sacrifice and that the missing girl may still be alive, on ice as it were, for the Mayday celebrations. But worse is to come, for Howie anyway, as we come to realise that it is not the girl who is to be sacrificed, but him.

The Wicker Man combines a host of compellingly horrific elements. The pagan imagery, of hobby horses, maypoles, the 'Green Man' pub and Mr. Punch, are all instantly recognisable as existing in our everyday lives, and particularly our childhoods (for some reason they have residual unnerving qualities, a bit like clowns), but screenwriter Anthony Shaffer's depiction of these elements as part of a living religion based upon fertility and sensuality, as opposed to the repression of Christianity, is the engine of the movie (and it is doubly appropriate that a repressed nation should make repression one of the subjects of its best horror movie).

In one eloquent sequence Howie watches naked girls conduct a fertility ritual. Disgusted, he asks if they have never heard of Jesus Christ. 'The son of a virgin, impregnated, I believe, by a ghost,' replies a quizzical Lord Summerisle. As writer Allan Brown has pointed out in his excellent book *Inside The Wicker Man*, the true strength of the story is that its presentation of religious dogma is frighteningly accurate. Both sides believe that they are unquestionably right and neither is willing, or even capable, of seeing the world from any other perspective. The final sequence, in which the swaying islanders sing their pagan hymn to the gods of the sea and the earth while inside the burning man Howie hysterically appeals to his own, remains one of the most disturbing in cinema. And the final shot, of the wicker man's head tumbling off to reveal the setting sun offers no relief.
★★★★★ **AS**

Movie Trivia: *The Wicker Man*

Christopher Lee agreed to appear in the film for free. Britt Ekland labelled Dumfries and Galloway in South West Scotland, where the film was shot, the 'bleakest place on Earth'. A model was used as a body double for Britt Ekland, who was pregnant by then boyfriend Rod Stewart at the time. To add insult to injury, she was also dubbed over, as her accent was unsuitable, something casting directors may have thought about before hiring her.

THE WILD ANGELS (1966)

Starring: *Peter Fonda (Heavenly Blues), Nancy Sinatra (Mike), Bruce Dern (Loser), Diane Ladd (Gaysh), Buck Taylor (Dear John), Norman Alden (Medic), Michael J. Pollard (Pigmy), Lou Procopio (Joint), Joan Shawlee (Momma Monahan), Marc Cavell (Frankenstein), Coby Denton (Bull Puckey), Frank Maxwell (Preacher), Gayle Hunnicutt (Suzie)*
Director: *Roger Corman*
Screenwriter: *Charles B. Griffith*
18/93 mins./Drama/USA

Heavenly Blues is president of a chapter of the Hells' Angels motorcycle gang. When Loser is shot by the cops, the Angels break him out of a hospital bed. Loser dies, and the gang gives him a major send-off.

Without Roger Corman's biker movie, there would be no *Easy Rider*, no *Five Easy Pieces*, no *Midnight Cowboy*. It's hard to tell whether the director intended a cheesy exploitation film crammed with sex and violence or a disenchanted, melancholy meditation on the inevitable failure of the American rebel ideal. Either way the film, taking up where Marlon Brando left off in *The Wild One*, is extraordinary.

An all-time great cast toplines showbiz kids Peter Fonda (in cool aviator shades) and Nancy Sinatra (sometimes in a nurse's uniform), plus Laura Dern's parents Bruce Dern and Diane Ladd and oddball presences like goofy Michael J. Pollard and flame-haired Brit Gayle Hunnicutt. After several reels of misbehaviour, it winds up with a bizarre funeral orgy as the Angels throw a party for deceased Dern, propping him up in the middle of a church (allowing the actor to do a terrific corpse act) while his girlfriend is respectfully gang-raped ('the Angels got themselves a new mama!') and Fonda's gang leader (addressed as 'Mr President' by his followers) gets fed up with the ways things are going and drops out of dropping-out.

Cool and crazy, this was a major commercial success, opening the way for dozens of similar cycle pictures (*Hells Angels On Wheels, Angels Hard As They Come, The Glory Stompers*, etc) but also opened the road for the counterculture films of the later 1960s and 70s. It features a great surf guitar score by Davie Allan and the Arrows. On its original

W

release, the Hells' Angels allegedly put a contract out on Corman's life. ★★★★ KN

WILD AT HEART (1990)

Starring: *Nicolas Cage (Sailor), Laura Dern (Lula), Willem Dafoe (Bobby Peru), Crispin Glover (Dell), Diane Ladd (Marietta Fortune), Isabella Rossellini (Perdita)*
Director: *David Lynch*
Screenwriter: *David Lynch, based on the novel by Barry Gifford*
18/119 mins./Drama/USA

Lula's mother is hysterical when her daughter takes off with jailbird Sailor and hires a hit man to track them down and bump off the boyfriend. Unaware of this, Lula and Sailor are gloriously happy journeying to California (and breaking his probation) but realise there is something wrong when they witness the death of a car-crash victim.

The mixture of catcalls and cheers – the latter in the clear majority – which greeted *Wild At Heart's* Palme D'Or win at Cannes in 1990 is a fair example of this extraordinary film's ability to delight and offend in equal measure. Basically, it all depends on just how you like your explicit sex, gratuitous violence and eardrum-busting rock music.

Whatever personal sensibilities may be ruffled, however, it is impossible to deny that what David Lynch produced was a weird and wonderful twist on the traditional road movie. Unlike his previous feature, *Blue Velvet*, where the emotional charge came from two ultra-normal characters suddenly pitched into a world of menacing evil, *Wild At Heart* starts out from a comic book situation and just gets crazier.

Sailor and Lula are young lovers fleeing south from her vengeful mother (histrionically played by Dern's real-life mum, Diane Ladd). In a fit of parental pique, Mum sets thoroughly weird hit man Bobby Peru on their trail, while a few other pursuers, among them Harry Dean Stanton and Isabella Rossellini, join in the chase. *Wild At Heart* is genuinely funny, with its warped humour serving to deflate the genuinely gory moments.

Nicolas Cage does a brilliant line in fat Elvis impersonations, Dern is wonderfully good as the hyperactive Lula, and Lynch's breathtaking imagination, surefooted direction and bizarre use of colour all add up to a genuine cinematic tour de force. ★★★★ KM

THE WILD BUNCH (1969)

Starring: *William Holden (Pike Bishop), Ernest Borgnine (Dutch Engstrom), Robert Ryan (Deke Thornton), Edmond O'Brien (Freddie Sykes), Warren Oates (Lyle Gorch), Jaime Sanchez (Angel), Ben Johnson (Tector Gorch)*
Director: *Sam Peckinpah*
Screenwriters: *Walon Green, Sam Peckinpah, from a story by Green, Roy N. Sickner*
18/138 mins./Action/Drama/Western/USA

Outlaws on the Mexican-U.S. frontier face the march of progress, the Mexican army and a gang of bounty hunters led by a former member while they plan a robbery of a U.S. army train

Few films can claim to do something that is truly original. But in the summer of 1969, while NASA was making the final preparations to put a man on the moon, Sam Peckinpah took his own small step for cinematic innovation. Exit wounds.

From the earliest days of cinema when ink-soaked pieces of rubber were fired from starting pistols, to Arthur Penn's groundbreaking *Bonnie And Clyde* with its explosive dance-of-death finale, numerous films had charted the destructive impact of the bullet to increasingly realistic effect. But it was Peckinpah who first showed on a cinema screen the morbid route taken by a bullet as it made its way into and out of a body. American television audiences, ironically, had already witnessed this most extreme lesson in ballistics the previous year with Brigadier General Nguyen Ngoc Loan's summary execution of a Viet Cong suspect.

The Wild Bunch did much to change the popular conception of the western. With a team of world-weary outlaws led by Pike Bishop supported by loyal lieutenant Dutch Engstrom and pursued by a relentless posse fronted by Deke Thornton, it shares more than a passing similarity with that other western of 1969, *Butch Cassidy And The Sundance Kid* (Cassidy's real gang were in fact known as The Wild Bunch). Peckinpah's producer on *The Wild Bunch*, Phil Feldman, had read William Goldman's screenplay and urged Warners to buy it, but they baulked at the $400,000 asking price. Similar material perhaps, but diametrically different in approach, *The Wild Bunch* made little effort to be likeable, with its heroes a group of cynical, greedy, washed-up outlaws supplying guns to the despots of a foreign country (Vietnam parallel, anyone?) before redeeming themselves in an orgiastically violent finale.

Peckinpah sought to breathe fresh life into the outlaw myth by focusing on Bishop's moral bankruptcy and redemption (an antidote to *Butch Cassidy*'s idealised, comic take). But just as that film is now best remembered for a song and a bike ride, *The Wild Bunch* has gained immortality through the two enormous gun battles which bookend the drama. The opening fight, when the gang ride into the town of Starbuck to rob the railroad offices where a posse of bounty-hunting gunmen await, is notable for the utterly indiscriminate carnage which follows. A Temperance Union group (surely no coincidence given Peckinpah's lifelong love of the bottle) march into the line of fire and innocent men and women are graphically gunned down along with the outlaws. Goaded later by a journalist at a press conference as to why he hadn't shown any children being torn apart, Peckinpah replied, 'Because I'm constitutionally unable to show a child in jeopardy.'

What Peckinpah could show, however, was a group of children laughing as they watched a scorpion being eaten alive by ants before setting them on fire, suggesting that violence is our innate original sin. (Look in vain for the 'No animals were harmed . . . ' disclaimer). Even this unsettling opening, however, was eclipsed by the firepower of the film's climactic shoot-out in Agua Verde, filmed in a disused winery near the Mexican town of Parras, an apt setting for such an inundation of claret. Having initially allowed one of their gang, Angel, to be captured and tortured by local warlord Mapache, the gang belatedly decide to rescue and the four walk into the tyrant's stronghold.

What ensues is unprecedented cinematic slaughter, the most visceral display of carnage ever committed to film. The promotional material for *The Wild Bunch* boasted that it used more bullets than the real Mexican revolution. Slightly tasteless, but it had a point. An estimated 90,000 rounds of blank ammunition were employed, and when the first day of shooting wrapped the company had run out of both ammo and fake blood. During the course of the shoot, Peckinpah sacked 22 crew members, *pour encourager les autres*. He raged that the squibs (small explosive charges filled with fake blood to simulate a gunshot) were not sufficiently realistic and demonstrated what he wanted with live gunshots. The props department responded by filling the squibs with more of the red stuff and raw meat.

Satisfied, Peckinpah insisted that actors wore them front and back to mark the entry and egress of every bullet. Although the film was cut behind Peckinpah's back, its set-pieces (marshalled by the director, but edited by Lou Lombardo and making extensive use of slo-mo) became the template for three decades of action. ★★★★★ JN

Movie Trivia: *The Wild Bunch*

Lou Lombardo, the film's editor, claimed that the film's original print contains some 3,643 editorial cuts. 10,000 squibs were used over twelve days during the shoot of the massacre/shootout, which was nicknamed the 'Battle of Bloody Porch' by the crew. The name 'The Wild Bunch' derived from Western outlaw Butch Cassidy's gang of fierce friends. Seven identical costumes for each actor were made by the costume department. All were ruined during the shoot.

THE WILD CHILD (L'ENFANT SAUVAGE) (1969)

Starring: *Jean-Pierre Cargol (Victor The Boy), François Truffaut (Dr. Jean Itard), Jean Daste (Prof. Phillippe Pinel), Françoise Seigner (Mme. Guerin), Paul Ville (Rémy), Claude Miller (M. Lemeri), Annie Miller (Mme. Lemeri), Pierre Fabre (Orderly At Institute)*
Director: *François Truffaut*
Screenwriter: *François Truffaut, Jean Gruault, based on* Mémoire Et Rapport Sur Victor De L'Aveyron *by Jean-Marc Gaspard Itard*
U/90 mins./Drama/France

Paris, 1797 and Dr. Jean Itard rescues a child of nature from public humiliation and, having named him Victor while studying him at an institution for deaf-mutes, he takes the boy to his country home to see if he will respond to civilising influences.

François Truffaut first encountered Dr. Jean Itard's *Mémoire Et Rapport Sur Victor De l'Aveyron* (1801-06) in 1966. The text clearly reflected with his own rather old-fashioned views on education, which prompted many to denounce *The Wild Child* for its dubious conservatism. But it also struck personal chords, as not only had Truffaut been rescued from himself as a youth by the critic André Bazin, but he had also become something of a father figure to Jean-Pierre Léaud during the production of *Les Quatre Cents Coups*.

In many ways, therefore, this was an inversion of Truffaut's first feature, as whereas Antoine Doinel had sought an escape from a society that didn't understand him, Victor slowly assimilated a system of values that had been irrelevant to his initial state of innocence. However, we never find out whether Victor was better off with his primitive unenlightenment or with this new mindset, in which he had to cope with feelings like nostalgia and rebellion that had been totally alien to him in the forest.

This ambiguity similarly made it difficult to separate Truffaut the man from both the character he played on screen and his young charge. Truffaut had benefited from an education and had learned how to communicate both in print and on celluloid. Yet all Itard had managed to teach Victor by the end of the picture was a sense of injustice that merely demonstrated him to be more instinctively human than merely animalistically malleable.

This conclusion intriguingly mirrors Truffaut's relationship with Jean-Pierre Cargol, a gypsy boy whom he had discovered on the same Montpellier streets that had provided the kids for his 1957 short, *Les Mistons*. Truffaut had originally intended to cast another non-professional as Itard, but he realised that it would be easier to direct Cargol if they were on the same side of the camera. Thus, the production became something of an experiment itself and its tone of scientific investigation was reinforced by the solemnly restrained shooting style, which was given an antiquated feel by Nestor Almendros' use of monochrome stock and framing devices associated with silent cinema. ★★★★ **DP**

THE WILD GEESE (1978)

Starring: *Richard Burton (Col. Allen Faulkner), Roger Moore (Lt. Shawn Flynn), Richard Harris (Capt. Rafer Janders), Hardy Kruger (Lt. Pieter Coetze), Stewart Granger (Sir Edward Matherson)*
Director: *Andrew V. McLaglen*
Screenwriter: *Reginald Rose*
15/134 mins./Adventure/UK

With the aim of overthrowing a wicked dictatorship in central Africa, a British multinational firm hires a small army of ageing mercenaries, led by Colonel Allen Faulkner, to rescue the preferred leader who has been unfairly imprisoned. But it is a mission that will be betrayed at the highest level.

Something of an old-boys get together for past-it action heroes with the reputations of heroic drinkers – heaven knows what it was like on set – that for all its Neanderthal posturing, thanks mainly to this crusty but likeable Brit cast and professional directing by no-mark Andrew V. McLaglen, remains a sneakily dumb pleasure.

You've got to get over a lot of nonsense to find its blunt treasure. That such a long-in-the-tooth gang would ever be sought out for mercenary action. That we should be rooting for mercenaries on some level anyway. That Richard Harris mawkish relationship with his son surely signals a bad outcome. That Hardy Kruger's racist soldier will learn the error of his ways as he carries Winston Ntshona's frail but noble leader on his back through the brush. And that the African foes will be treated like Zulu-like hoards of cannon fodder about as constructively defined as *Star Wars* Stormtroopers.

How is it then that we come to care? That the betrayed and, by now, very ragged gang of heroes make it to the supply plane and escape as the enemy hoards gradually close in. The second half of the film is actually quite thrilling, and the thing you can rely on with such stalwart character actors like these (Ronald Fraser, Stewart Granger and Jack Watson back up the leads with sturdy grimaces), is that they will deliver some rich, worthy characters for us to root for. When troopers we've come to care about perish, you'll be surprised to find a real tug on your heartstrings – the sequence where Harris' dignified captain can't quite get onto the moving plane is devastating for those not too intent on great acting. But even that doesn't mean we needed a sequel. ★★★ **IN**

THE WILD ONE (1953)

Starring: *Marlon Brando (Johnny), Mary Murphy (Kathie), Robert Keith (Harry Bleeker), Lee Marvin (Chino), Jay C. Flippen (Sheriff Singer), Peggy Maley (Mildred), Hugh Sanders (Charlie Thomas), Ray Teal (Frank Bleeker), John Brown (Bill Hannegan), Will Wright (Art Kleiner)*
Director: *Laszlo Benedek*
Screenwriter: *John Paxton, based on a story by Frank Rooney*
PG/79 mins./Drama/USA

The Black Rebel Motorcycle Club ride into the small California town of Wrightsville and party, irritating the solid citizens who become vengeance-crazed vigilantes. Johnny Strabler, head of the gang, falls for local girl Kathie and reforms, but takes a beating from the locals.

'What are you rebelling *against*?' a townie asks the leader of the pack, only to have him deliver a signature line for 1950s' juvenile delinquency by sneering 'What have you got?' This once-controversial item (banned in Britain for decades) from producer Stanley Kramer (always heavy on 'message' speeches) and director Laszlo Benedek founded the genre of biker gang movie, and offers a pouting, twitching Brando in an iconic leather jacket and Tom of Finland cap as the motorcycle crazy to beat.

It was sold at the time with the tagline 'that Streetcar man has a new desire!', but was actually a step down for the new-minted star, who brings all his method mumbling to this B-length Columbia quickie which wraps cartoonish social comment in exploitative scenes of tearaways tearing up the town, hassling the indignant straight citizens, ragging on the elder generation (though the hoods all seem well into their thirties) and stirring up the townsfolk into a lynching frenzy.

Typical of the wounded machismo often found in 1950s leading men is a scene in which Marlon is held down by the mob and brutalised, allowing the camera to linger lovingly on his beautifully bruised mug as he makes a slightly-sensitive thug seem like a martyr. It's a mix of impressive on-location cycle spills (the roaring-down-the-empty-road opening is still a grabber) and embarrassingly hokey rumbles on obvious poverty row sound-stages.

Lee Marvin is superbly grungy as a supporting troublemaker, and his character doesn't sell out by reforming for the love of a weedy but decent woman. ★★★ **KN**

WILD STRAWBERRIES (SMULTRONSTALLET) (1957)

Starring: *Victor Sjöström (Prof. Isak Borg), Bibi Andersson (Sara), Ingrid Thulin (Marianne Borg), Gunnar Björnstrand (Evald Borg), Julian Kindahl (Agda), Folke Sundquist (Anders), Björn Bjelvenstam (Viktor), Nalma Wifstrand (Isak's Mother)*
Director: *Ingmar Bergman*
Screenwriter: *Ingmar Bergman*
15/90 mins./Drama/Sweden

Awards: *Berlin Film Festival – FIPRESCO Prize (Victor Sjostrom), Golden Berlin Bear (Ingmar Bergman)*

Ageing medic Isak Borg travels by road with his daughter-in-law, Marianne, to receive an honorary degree and en route comes to recognise his faults and failings through a series of dreams, recollections and chance encounters.

Ingmar Bergman first had the idea for this cerebral road movie while standing at the door of his grandmother's house and wondering whether he'd re-enter childhood by stepping inside. The influence of Strindberg's *Dream Play* and Shakespeare's *King Lear* pervades proceedings, but the action is also full of personal details, with Isak Borg's mother being played by Bergman's ex-wife, Else Fisher, and many of the professor's character traits being inspired by Bergman's pastor father.

Bergman also quotes from Victor Sjöström's past by recalling his 1921 masterpiece, *The Phantom Carriage*, in the opening nightmare, which contains some of Bergman's most famous images. But this celebrated sequence is much more than a rattlebag of Expressionist symbolism. It establishes the tactic of anticipating events to come and reveals that, for all his ego, petulance and intolerant aloofness, Borg is a vulnerable figure who is worthy of our compassion.

This becomes clear once he sets off for Lund with Marianne, the daughter-in-law who shares his self-obsession and irritability and is anything but intimidated by him after spending years with his equally querulous son, Evald. However, they are not merely worthy foils for each other, they also represent birth and death, as Marianne is pregnant.

This doubling recurs when Borg wakes from his dream of idyllic summers past with his adored cousin Sara to meet her virtual reincarnation in Sara the hitcher, whose two pals remind Borg of himself and the brother who won Sara's heart.

Borg's unhappy marriage is mirrored by the feuding of the Almanns, whose bickering finally drives Marianne (doubtlessly reminded of her own domestic discord) to turf them out of the car. However, they return along with the other principals to witness Borg's final subconscious humiliation, in which he is finally forced to accept the flaws that have marred his existence. Yet, he's rewarded for his debasement with a final reverie, together with Sara and his parents beside a placid lake.

The winner of the Golden Bear at Berlin, *Wild Strawberries* now seems to creak in places. But its evocation of the nostalgia, dread and regret of old age remains as unsurpassed as Sjöström's miraculously sensitive performance. ★★★★ **DP**

WILD THINGS (1998)

Starring: *Matt Dillon (Sam Lombardo), Kevin Bacon (Sgt. Ray Duquette), Neve Campbell (Suzie Marie Toller), Denise Richards (Kelly Lanier Van Ryan), Daphne Rubin-Vega (Det. Gloria Perez), Robert Wagner (Tom Baxter), Bill Murray (Kenneth Bowden)*
Director: *John McNaughton*
Screenwriter: *Stephen Peters*
18/103 mins./Thriller/USA

A school counsellor is accused of raping a cheerleader, but is everything as it seems?

This self-consciously nouveau noir thriller quite fancies itself. It opens with fast aerial footage of the Everglades intercut with ominous-looking alligators – an area of great natural beauty with danger lurking beneath its seemingly picturesque surface, geddit? Blue Bay High School seems to have a stringent entry policy: statuesque boys and bosomy girls only. From the word go, hormones are in the air, and hunky 'guidance counsellor' Sam Lombardo is obviously the object of more than one schoolgirl crush.

Rich pompom girl Kelly Van Ryan (*Starship Troopers'* Richards) offers to wash his jeep, and a soap-sud come-on sequence follows – part *Cool Hand Luke*, part Wrigley's advert. The result: Sam allegedly rapes Kelly. Cue: Grishamesque courtroom drama, with seedy lawyer Bowden the only guy who'll take Sam's case (Kelly's mother is the rich and powerful Theresa Russell, her lawyer Robert Wagner). Throw in an over-zealous cop, his sultry partner Daphne Rubin-Vega and the star witness, 'swamp trash' Gothette Suzie and the pot's ready to boil over with intrigue, subterfuge and sexual tension. But the main ingredient is herring, served red.

With the court case apparently solved at the film's halfway mark, you may be sure nothing is as it seems, but screenwriter Stephen Peters (*Death Wish 5*) becomes so delighted with the power of an unexpected twist, the remaining 55 minutes amount to little more than an endless string of them. Granted, about three are genuinely surprising, but as double-cross becomes triple-cross becomes quadruple cross, it all gets awfully trying. And the script clangs along like a sack of bells, and even resorts to *Carry On*-style innuendo.

Only Campbell and Murray shine from the cast. Director McNaughton layers on flashy, *Angel Heart* colour-filters as if to compensate for his cheapo earlier work (*Henry: Portrait Of A Serial Killer*, mainly), and the much-hyped steamy sex is made ludicrous by Campbell's no-nudity clause. ★★ **AC**

WILD WILD WEST (1999)

Starring: *Will Smith (Capt. James West), Kevin Kline (Marshal Artemus Gordon/President Ulysses Grant), Kenneth Branagh (Dr. Arliss Loveless), Salma Hayek (Rita Escobar), M. Emmet Levine (Coleman)*
Director: *Barry Sonnenfeld*
Screenwriters: *S.S. Wilson, Brent Maddock, Jeffrey Price, Peter S. Seaman, from a story by Jim Thomas, John Thomas*
12/105 mins./Western/Action/Comedy/Sci-fi/USA

Awards – *Razzie Awards – Worst Director, Worst Original Song ('Wild Wild West'), Worst Picture, Worst Screen Couple (Kevin Kline, Will Smith), Worst Screenplay*

TOP10 Greatest Continuity Errors

1 *Star Wars* (1977)
A Stormtrooper hits his head running through a door.

2 *Ben-Hur* (1959)
One of the charioteers is seen wearing a wristwatch (although some claim it's a shadow).

3 *Mr and Mrs Smith* (2005)
Despite being set in New York, signs visible during the freeway chase clearly refer to LA.

4 *Raiders of the Lost Ark* (1981)
As Indy comes face-to-face with a hissing cobra, its reflection is clearly visible in the glass between them.

5 *Tristan + Isolde* (2006)
Isolde recites a poem by John Donne, written about 1000 years after the film is set.

6 *Commando* (1985)
The yellow Porsche is totally wrecked on the left-hand side after chasing down Sully – only suddenly it isn't.

7 *Carmen Jones* (1954)
As Carmen is walking through town, the camera and crew are clearly visible, reflected in a shop window.

8 *Pretty Woman* (1991)
For breakfast, Julia eats a pancake that turns into a croissant that turns back into an untouched pancake.

9 *Manhunter* (1986)
As Will Graham and son talk in a supermarket, and *without moving*, the products on the shelves behind them totally change.

10 *Titanic* (1997)
When Rose tries to cut the handcuffs off Jack's hands with an axe, you can clearly see the axe hit Jack's hand instead

W

A gunslinger teams up with a master of disguise to save America from evil Confederate Inventor Dr. Arliss Loveless.

At one particularly explosive stage in this eager-to-please holiday parade, an entire Western town is systematically blown to bits. Among the buildings demolished, one shop-sign clearly reads: Kasdan's Ironmongers. A sly reference perhaps to writer-director Lawrence Kasdan who, in 1985's *Silverado*, attempted to make an old-fashioned Western with new-fangled neuroses. Perhaps Barry Sonnenfeld is symbolically destroying Kasdan's stall, saying, 'No, this is how you modernise the seemingly moribund cowboy genre, sunshine!'

Reading anything into *Wild Wild West* is a bit like seeking the truth in a plate of alphabet spaghetti. Adapted from a spoofy 1960s TV show once described as '*Maverick* meets *The Man From UNCLE*' and assured a wham-bam, family-bucket July 4 opening by bankable star Will Smith, it was never going to be anything other than an expensive piece of gadget-driven hokum. Big star. Big effects. Big hit song. What could possibly go wrong?

Everything, if you believe virtually every critic in America. *WWW* has endured name-calling to embarrass any playground. It's not that bad, of course, but it's no Men In Black Hats – and that was surely the idea. In the aftermath of the Civil War, snake-hipped government gunslinger James West is teamed with boffinly master of disguise Artemus Gordon (a likeable Kline) at the behest of President Ulysses Grant (Kline again, for no good reason other than egomania or budget-capping). Aggrieved Confederate inventor Dr. Arliss Loveless has developed a vast weapon of mass destruction – the show-stopping mechanical Tarantula – with which he intends to create a Divided States Of America. Our heroes track him down in their customised train, picking up the vengeful beauty Rita along the way, and build to an effects-crazy duel in the Utah desert.

There's not much else to say about the story. It's merely an excuse for a truly dazzling fusion of modelwork, matte and CGI, exemplified by the screen-eating tarantula and Branagh's motorised wheelchair (Loveless, you see, is legless – a seamless digital illusion road-tested by Gary Sinise in *Forrest Gump*). Jules Verne-inspired, this is the past looking to the future, but fed by the present.

The smoke-spewing contraptions are satisfyingly rickety, satanic and sort of 19th-century-looking, but they still serve to unbalance the historical/mythical setting, as if the idea of Will Smith cleaning up the Old West wasn't sensational enough. As ever these days, it's a case of, 'Let me through, I'm an effects supervisor!' (Tellingly, outside of Branagh's panto silliness and Kline's incessant dressing-up, human performance seems to be positively discouraged – perhaps that's why M. Emmet Walsh is the only other half-recognisable supporting player).

It's a pity this supposed family entertainment exerts such laddish exuberance: pushed-up cleavages are everywhere you look and Hayek is insultingly called upon to do little more than be shapely (the scene where our heroes lasciviously ogle her exposed bottom is pure Benny Hill). The script veers uneasily between weak gags (Kline naming his flying machine the 'Air Gordon') and some spectacularly misjudged white guilt-tripping about slavery, as delivered by Smith, who must sweet-talk some rednecks to stop himself getting lynched at one especially uncomfy, apparently comedic juncture.

The kids in the audience with *Empire* just wanted him to fall in the mud again. Now that's funny. Tony Blair once complained that he had scars on his back from trying to precipitate change in the public sector. If that's the case, Will Smith must bear the marks of permanent spinal injury after carrying *Wild Wild West* to the box office, only to be swatted aside when the so-called 'mechanology' is on view. It's obviously a thankless task being a human in late-90s blockbusters. But then we're expected to pay for it. And what thanks do we get? ★★ **AC**

◎ WILLOW (1988)

Starring: *Val Kilmer (Madmarigan), Joanne Whalley (Sorsha), Warwick Davis (Willow Ufgood), Jean Marsh (Queen Bavmorda), Patricia Hayes (Fin Raziel)*
Director: *Ron Howard*
Screenwriters: *Bob Dolman, George Lucas*
PG/126 mins./Fantasy/USA

A diminutive nelwyn named Willow teams up with a wandering swordsman to protect a baby princess who has miraculously fallen into his care. It is foretold this baby girl will bring about the end of the rule of evil sorceress-queen Bavmorda.

While George Lucas' use of the *Lord Of The Rings* template for his original *Star Wars* trilogy can be viewed as the appropriation of storytelling traditions, this fantasy fable's familiarity to JRR Tolkien's famous novel is brazen theft. Lucas, however, only gets a story credit and producing duties here, handing directing reigns over to the middle-of-the-road solidity of Ron Howard. Even so, this special effects epic with its hobbity-tasting nelwyn hero (played by retired Ewok Warwick Davis) that shoplifts from any number of fantasy megastores apart from Middle-earth – The Bible, Narnia, Oz, He-man – feels anaemic and hollow.

No matter how much money has been spent on building olde worlde munchkin-sized villages, nor swashbuckling training devoted to transforming Val Kilmer into a reluctant Aragorn-alike, nor, indeed, effects time given over to two nine-inch comedy brownies (no, not the cakes or the little girls who get badges, Lucas was ripping off his own in these micro-versions of C-3PO and R2D2) there is no magic to be found. It is too stony-faced to carry the bouncy parody of *The Princess Bride*, and just way way short of Peter Jackson's God-sized *Rings* epics.

Howard doesn't seem to have the conviction; he's created a pretend-fantasy, embarrassed about its saggy clutch of whacky names and dreary concoctions. Sure, Joanne Whalley looks cute as warrior-babe Sorsha, there for Kilmer's waggish hero to romance, but Jean Marsh's scowling Malignant knock-off is cartoon-scary not real-scary and it takes an age to get to the big confrontation. All the while, ILM struggle to keep up with the demand for fairies, pixies, devil dogs, and trolls. ★★ **IN**

◎ WILLY WONKA AND THE CHOCOLATE FACTORY (1971)

Starring: *Gene Wilder (Willy Wonka), Jack Albertson (Grandpa Joe), Peter Ostrum (Charlie Bucket), Roy Kinnear (Mr. Henry Salt), Julie Dawn Cole (Veruca Salt)*
Director: *Mel Stuart*
Screenwriters: *David Seltzer, based on the book by Roald Dahl*
U/100 mins./Family/USA

The story of luckless Charlie who miraculously finds the last golden ticket in a chocolate bar, the chance to tour the mysterious chocolate factory belonging to the equally bizarre Willy Wonka. Alongside a group of other children, each with one guardian, Charlie will discover a world beyond his dreams.

Roald Dahl's immaculate morality tale is gloriously realised in this colourful fantasy with decent songs. It even manages to add to the original book, successfully giving the script a more movie-like dynamic in the addition of sinister Oslo Slugworth (Gunter Meisner) who might be manipulating events from the outside. But from tip to toe Mel Stuart turns Dahl's delicious fable into glowing cinema.

Surprisingly, Gene Wilder proves perfectly cast as the weird combination of the avuncular and the eccentric in Willy Wonka, just adding a layer of sinister to his aloof mad-inventor routine. Peter Ostrum's Charlie is rightly goody-goody but not mawkish, and across the troupe of brats and parental disasters everyone fits the bill of these gross creations. And those orange-skinned slave-imps the Oompa Loompas serve up all Dahl's witty warnings of the wages of naughtiness as magnificently choreographed tick-tock nursery-songs.

All this though pales in the face of Harper Goff's art direction. With the exteriors filmed in a fairy-tale Germany, the factory is a childhood fantasy turned madhouse, a trippy, sensuous micro-world that mixes temptation with moral burden that each winner will learn to their peril. Imagine room upon room where everything is edible, where rivers runs with chocolate milk, secret formulas are concocted for everlasting gobstoppers and golden geese lay chocolate eggs, all Dahl's genius is recreated in a primary coloured sheen like a giant sweet shop conjured up on LSD. The life lessons could be construed as trite, but with Anthony Newley and Leslie Bricusse's chirpy songs and the dark stabs of humour, even teasing feints of child torture, it never drifts too far into the sentimental. And better than Tim Burton's soppy rerun. ★★★★ **IN**

⊙ WINGS (1927)

Starring: *Clara Bow (Mary Preston), Charles 'Buddy' Rogers (Jack Powell), Richard Arlen (David Johnston), Jobyna Ralston (Sylvia Lewis), El Brendel (Herman Scwimpf), Richard Tucker (Air Commander), Gary Cooper (Cadet White)*
Director: *William A. Wellman*
Screenwriter: *Hope Loring, Louis D. Lighton, based on the story by John Monk Saunders*
Unrated/139 mins./War/USA

Awards: *Academy Awards – Best Picture, Best Engineering Effects*

Mary Preston loves Jack Powell, despite his infatuation with Sylvia Lewis, who only has eyes for David Armstrong. However, their romantic rivalries pale when they enlist in the Army Air Corps during the First World War.

Having survived being shot down while serving with the Lafayette Esquadrille during the Great War, William A. Wellman was the ideal director for this pioneering aerial combat picture. Although it paid its dues to the contention that 'war is hell', this was no pacifist tract like Rex Ingram's *The Four Horsemen Of The Apocalypse* or King Vidor's *The Big Parade*. Instead, it was a rousing adventure that sought to extol the gallantry and chivalry of the pilots who had made military history over the trenches.

In order to convey the viscerality of their derring-do, Wellman had cinematographer Harry Perry lash his cameras to the stunt planes to capture the terrifying perspective of a flyboy involved in a dog-fight, a bombing raid, the strafing of a stronghold or the pursuit and destruction of an enemy vehicle. Moreover, Wellman also employed the Magnascope widescreen process for the aerial sequences, which enhanced their sense of spectacle and realism. The Battle of St Mihiel was also meticulously staged, with Wellman spending 10 days choreographing and rehearsing his 60 planes and 3,500 extras. Indeed, veterans witnessing the first screenings anticipated the awed acclamations of authenticity that helped sell Steven Spielberg's *Saving Private Ryan* some 70 years later.

There's no question that these thrilling set-pieces helped *Wings* secure the first-ever Academy Award for Best Picture, as its storyline was lamentably novelettish and the acting inconsistent. El Brendel was typically embarrassing as the comic relief, while Richard Arlen's awkward inanimation was repeatedly emphasised by Charles 'Buddy' Rogers' handsome exuberance.

Yet Gary Cooper made a name for himself in a moving two-minute cameo, while Clara Bow produced a truly fascinating performance. Despite being top-billed, she essentially took a supporting role that contrasted sharply with the free-spirited flapper she had played in Clarence Badger's *It*. Yet, although she's mostly seen in sensible frocks and a nurse's uniform, Paramount was keen to cash in on her saucy image and so squeezed her into a plunging gown for the scene in which she poses as a Parisian floozie to spring the drunken Rogers from a military police cell. ★★★ **DP**

⊙ WINGS OF DESIRE (DER HIMMEL UBER BERLIN) (1987)

Starring: *Bruno Ganz (Damiel), Solvieg Dommartin (Marion), Otto Sandler (Cassiel), Curt Bois (Homer, the poet), Peter Falk (Der Filmstar)*
Director: *Wim Wenders*
Screenwriters: *Peter Handke, Richard Reitinger, Wim Wenders*
U/100 mins./Fantsy/Drama/West Germany-France
Awards: *Cannes Film Festival (Best Director)*

An angel tired of his immortal existence helping mankind from afar takes on mortal form to fulfil his feeling of love for a circus acrobat. He also discovers that he is not the only spiritual creature to have crossed over.

An elusive, poetic vision of Berlin before the Wall fell, an extraordinary, haunting piece that evades the hard edges of plot for a moody shimmer of ideas tracing lost souls about a cold city. Imagine the evocative, ghostly Americana of *Paris, Texas* transformed into an equally vivid Euro-vibe made up of a ruined tableau of Nazi trappings and silent streets shot in a celestial black and white. Both films mark a triumph for Wim Wenders, works that hover closer to poems or pieces of music than strict movies.

Here we have a world of invisible angels floating amongst us, and we follow Bruno Ganz's Damiel who seeks to taste human existence. There are those in this deadened city that are spiritual enough to detect traces of Damiel's passing, among them Peter Falk as an American actor who significantly is in the city to make a film about the Germans in wartime. But more important to Damiel is Marian, a circus acrobat who wears wings for her act to swing angel-like above awe-struck crowds, she in her pained solace has stirred this angel to consider shedding his spiritual form for the fulfilment of physical desires. The question of whether he will go through with it is as much of a plot as we get.

This is a film about dualities, separations, and disconnections set in a divided city, East and West held apart by a stone wall and vast gulfs of philosophy. The spiritual is cut off from the sensual, the Nazi past from this vague, uncertain present, but most of all we are separated from each other. Loneliness pervades every frame, but in the measured, inspired dialogue, Ganz's dreamy performance and the lovely, captivating images Wenders offers much to be hopeful about.

While Wenders served up a pseudo-sequel in 1993's *Faraway So Close* which only sporadically recaptured the magic, Hollywood served up a mawkish retread, *City Of Angels* with Nicolas Cage as the angel falling for Meg Ryan's heart surgeon. ★★★★★ **IN**

THE WITCHES OF EASTWICK (1987)

Starring: *Jack Nicholson (Daryl Van Horne), Cher (Alexandre Medford), Susan Sarandon (Jane Spofford), Michelle Pfeiffer (Sukie Ridgemont), Veronica Cartwright (Felicia Alden), Richard Jenkins (Clyde Alden)*
Director: *George Miller*
Screenwriters: *Michael Cristofer, based on the novel* The Witches Of Eastwick
18/118 mins./Comedy-Horror/USA

Awards: BAFTA – *Best Special Effects*

W

Three dissatisfied single women from the picturesque village of Eastwick, laughingly try to conjure a man to fulfil all their desires. Soon enough, Daryl Van Horne moves into the town, but he will have a strange effect on each of them, granting them strange powers and, as the lives of everyone in the whole town start to unravel, it becomes increasingly clear what Daryl's real identity might be.

In John Updike's ripe, witty novel of women's carnality in a rich little American backwater, it is hinted but never said that Daryl Van Horne, with his slippery pun of a name, is the Devil incarnate. In George Miller's loopy overcooked film version Jack Nicholson ultimately turns into a slobbery green special effect, a gloopy factory-made monster Satan hot-in from a B-movie. If there's a lesson on how Hollywood can misconstrue and reduce rich novels to middling films it's right there. For all it does right, and there is some bubbly satire early on in this shiny Eastwick, it is crushed by its cowardly recourse to cloddish sensation.

As the three divorcées who gather weekly to sup martinis and bewail their long-gone husbands and the lack of good men to satisfy their drying cravings, we have a triplet of mature Hollywood beauty: Cher, Susan Sarandon and Michelle Pfeiffer. They are fun and sexy, but already the film is working at remove from its own reality. For Daryl, the horny devil, on this level there really could only be Jack Nicholson and he wafts in on a wave of filthy-rich flamboyance and dripping grins to find their G-spots and give the witches powers to reap cynical havoc on this stuffy town that has sneered at their lonely spinsterdom.

Aussie director George Miller (of the *Mad Max* films) does little more than let the film flit classily between the sly black comedy of their reprisals and the looming threat that Jack's Satanic force is taking over them. Nicholson is having a ball as ever, but he's not working very hard, just giving that attractive impression that this zesty, insincere shade of cool is actually just his real personality. Miller is not sure what he is dealing with, a black comedy or a white horror movie? As he becomes ever more reliant on special effects and less and less on Michael Cristofer's bright script or Vilmos Zsigmond's crystal clean cinematography, the film empties of promise, leaving a catastrophic last act of cheap thrills signifying nothing. **★★ IN**

THE WITCHES (1990)

Starring: *Anjelica Huston (Miss Eva Ernst), Mai Zetterling (Helga Eveshim), Jasen Fischer (Luke Eveshim), Jane Horrocks (Miss Irvine), Anne Lambton (Woman in Black)*
Director: *Nicolas Roeg*
Screenwriter: *Allen Scott*
PG/91 mins./Family/UK

When a recently orphaned young scamp named Luke happens upon a secret witches' convention at an English hotel, he discovers they are plotting to rid the world of children. But before he can warn anyone they turn him into a mouse.

This mostly terrific Roald Dahl adaptation is down to the fact that left-leaning British master Nicolas Roeg, the man responsible for *Don't Look Now* and *The Man Who Fell To Earth*, is very much in tune with the devilish cunning of this black-hued novel. Hence, its one of the best, and most unnoticed, of recent kid-scaring (and therefore kid-pleasing) movies.

Screenwriter Allen Scott keeps most of Dahl's flip folklore intact. As young hero Luke's (a perky, likeable Jasen Fischer) Norwegian grandmother (Mai Zetterling) explains, with scrumptious detail, witches loathe children, they can't stand the smell of them, and they have square toes and wear masks to hide their real, hideous faces, landscapes of warts and wrinkles, enough to make any child squeal in revolted delight. It's high adventure and high grot all round, squirrelling about with humour and panache thanks to Roeg's dead-on handling of the material.

Casting Anjelica Huston as the chief witch was a coup. With her mask on she's slippery and sexy (and in a kids' movie as well), full of wicked, vampy vim as she delivers those twinkling lines. It's a magnificent performance, a black-clad variation on that ultimate fusion of Lady Macbeth and Cruella De Ville that mature actresses surely crave. The special effects, mainly animatronics, that serve to transform young Luke into a mouse are pretty good and used to best effect (i.e. not allowing them to govern the film's storytelling energy). And Roeg just keeps it buzzing along, equal parts funny and scary, ready to conclude in a near-operatic parade of pug-ugliness. **★★★★ IN**

WITCHFINDER GENERAL (1968)

Starring: *Vincent Price (Matthew Hopkins), Ian Ogilvy (Richard Marshall), Rupert Davies (John Lowes), Hilary Heath (Sarah Lowes), Robert Russell (John Stearne), Nicky Henson (Trooper Robert Swallow)*
Director: *Michael Reeves*
Screenwriters: *Tom Baker, Michael Reeves, based on the novel by Ronald Bassett, with additional scenes by Louis M. Heywood*
18/82 mins./Horror/UK

England is torn in civil strife as the Royalists battle the Parliamentary Party for control. Matthew Hopkins exploits the unrest by touring the land offering his services as a persecutor of witches.

Although Michael Reeves' film does feature one notable instance where a condemned witch is burned, he sets the tone immediately with an execution of quite a different stripe. Burning, you see, invariably adds a touch of melodrama. And if there's one thing this uncompromisingly brutal film eschews, it's melodrama.

The pre-title sequence makes this instantly apparent: on a bleak rural hillside, a man is building a gibbet. His hammer blows ring out through the surrounding countryside like a muted death knell. An old woman, wailing pitifully, is dragged up the hill by a small group of townsfolk, silent except for the murmuring priest at their head. The woman is brought to the gibbet and without ceremony is hanged. No last request, no pleas for mercy, no symbolic cleansing in the fire. She's just given the drop and left to dangle. It's a squalid, ignominious death. And one, it is clear, that is as mundane a feature of the unforgiving landscape as the wind and the rain.

The only other participant in this grim tableau is a man on horseback, who watches the execution from a distance. This is Matthew Hopkins, the self-styled witchfinder general of Civil War England. Something that is missing though, and which is conspicuously absent from the entire film, is any evidence of witchcraft or, indeed, of anything that could be construed as the practice of witchcraft. Hopkins, we soon learn, is little more than a sadistic mercenary who exploits the chaos of war to line his pockets and to satisfy a bloodthirsty religious fervour. The horror that pervades Reeves' extraordinary film is derived not from satanic ritual or the power of the occult but from the lurking evil that underpins the human condition.

Here the innocent are tortured and killed; the virtuous become vengeful and corrupted. The plot itself is straightforward enough – Hopkins, rampaging through the counties of East Anglia, ridding local communities of 'witches' for a fee, rapes the fiancée of young Parliamentary soldier Marshall and murders her uncle. The devastated Marshall swears vengeance and, consumed by hatred and grief, hunts down Hopkins. In the final shocking scene, he attacks the witchfinder in a frenzy with an axe. But he is denied revenge when his friend, in the spirit of mercy, shoots Hopkins.

'You took him away from me! You took him away from me' screams Marshall.

The story is strikingly told, and John Coquillon's cinematography is masterful. Just 24 years old, Reeves exhibits a maturity far beyond his years. It's no surprise that the film was heavily criticised on its release for gratuitous violence, but in fact he casts an unflinching eye over his barbaric subject matter, refusing to embellish the scenes of atrocity with any lurid flourishes.

In this, the violence is more disturbing – and less gratuitous – than any of Hammer's theatrical bloodletting. *Witchfinder General* was shot in Suffolk in the autumn of 1967. Enthusiasm compensated for a shoestring budget and the filmmakers gratefully accepted the generosity of Lee Electric, who provided lighting free of charge, and made good use of local facilities – the few sets that were built were housed in a disused WWII aircraft hangar which was rented for £50 a week. 'The film was a turning point in my life,' said Coquillon later. 'About two years after it was released, Don Siegel called his good friend Sam Peckinpah, inviting him to see, "an interesting number a couple of kids have made in Britain." ' Peckinpah was so impressed he employed Coquillon not only on *Straw Dogs*, but also on *Pat Garret And Billy The Kid*, *Cross Of Iron* and *The Osterman Weekend*.

Reeves had originally wanted Donald Pleasence for the role of Hopkins, but contractual obligations between Price and co-producers AIP ensured that the American actor got the part. And although he and Reeves fought tooth-and-claw during the shoot, it proved a fortuitous state of affairs for all concerned. Price turns in a stunning performance, substituting chilling malevolence for his usual camp posturing. He makes no attempt whatsoever at an English accent – probably a good thing – but he has a physicality that belies his age (he was 57) and conflicts effectively with his more familiar, languidly sinister persona. That said, and in spite of the on-set bickering with Reeves, he was gracious enough to give the young director due credit for the film's success.

A note on the title, incidentally. Purists maintain that the film should be referred to as *Matthew Hopkins: Witchfinder General*. And since the character's name does appear in the title sequence, albeit in smaller type and to the top right of the screen, they have a solid case. It's been truncated here for reasons of space. Following *Witchfinder General*, Reeves was seen as a rising star of the British film industry. He was inundated with scripts – Coquillon is adamant that he was offered *Easy Rider* by Peter Fonda – but few held any appeal. It wouldn't have made much difference if they had. Shortly after *Witchfinder* was released, and with only two other films to his credit, Michael Reeves was dead from a fatal dose of barbiturates. ★★★★★ **SB**

⊙ WITHNAIL AND I (1987)

Starring: *Richard E. Grant (Withnail), Paul McGann (I), Richard Griffiths (Monty), Ralph Brown (Danny), Michael Elphick (Jake)*
Director: *Bruce Robinson*
Screenwriter: *Bruce Robinson*
15/107 mins./Comedy/UK

Two down-on-their-luck actors find solace in drink and other substances. Seeking respite from their uneventful lives they escape up north to Withnail's uncle's stone cottage. Faced with no modern conveniences, a bunch of oddball locals, and a surprise visit from an amorous 'Uncle Monty', their wits are tested, along with their friendship.

Just as *Monty Python's Life Of Brian* (1979) is forever in danger of having its rare magic rubbed away by people drunkenly shouting out, 'We're the People's Front Of Judea!' in the Students' Union Bar, now the fate of *Withnail And I* rests in the unsafe hands of quote-reciting graduates demanding 'the finest wines available to humanity' and rolling Camberwell Carrots. But *Withnail* can take it. You probably even know someone who's played the *Withnail And I* drinking game (including the glug of Ronsonol), but even studenty idiocy on that scale cannot detract from the film's unique and lasting glory. Here is a comedy that, like *Spinal Tap*, *Brian* and *The Holy Grail*, improves with age and repeated viewings. Being able to quote great chunks of it does not impair the enjoyment – although doing so in mixed company may impair the enjoyment of others.

It's hard to imagine a time when it wasn't considered a national treasure (it was voted 29th in the BFFs Best British Movies poll in 1999, above *The Italian Job*, *Shakespeare In Love* and *Dr. No*) – indeed, a time when Richard E. Grant wasn't a much-loved public figure – but *Withnail And I* was a minor, underfunded anomaly in 1986, and Grant an unknown.

Bruce Robinson was an actor who'd been in Zeffirelli's *Romeo And Juliet* and Ken Russell's *The Music Lovers*, become disillusioned and allowed writing to take over. He actually penned *Withnail* as a novel in the winter of 1969/1970, while subsisting on discarded turnips and nicked milk in a dilapidated house in Camden Town with an old drama school chum called Vivian – the model for Withnail (The 'I' of the title was Robinson himself).

He turned his novel into a screenplay (not an easy job, he claimed) and because it was obviously so personal, producer Paul Heller encouraged Robinson to direct the film himself, even though he had no form in this department. The budget was set at a modest £1.1 million once former Beatle George Harrison had counted – the now defunct – Handmade Films in (he read the script on a flight to New York) and casting began. Grant famously clinched the Withnail part with a spirited rendition of the 'Fork it!' line, and Paul McGann had to promise to lose his Liverpool accent to become the unnamed Marwood ('And I'). If the wind had been blowing in another direction it could have been Daniel Day-Lewis as Withnail and Kenneth Branagh as I, although this is beyond the imagination, so born-to-it are Grant and McGann as the raddled eccentric and his sensitive foil.

The story is fairly slight – two out-of-work actors go to the country ('We've gone on holiday by mistake') where one is unsuccessfully pursued by the other's homosexual uncle and they return to North London when one of them gets an acting job. That's it. The entertainment lies in the texture – it's a comedy in that it's hilarious, but it is without actual jokes (in the normal sense) and is low on set-pieces (the urine test, the fishing expedition and ramming a chicken into a kettle are noble exceptions).

The laughs come from the fruity language – 'I've only had a few ales'; 'I mean to have you even if it must be by burglary'; 'Then the fucker will rue the day' and so on – the humanity (it's set in another decade but could be set any time), and of course the unrelenting squalor. Little wonder it strikes so many chords with those in higher education and squats. George Harrison and Handmade partner Denis O'Brien saw rushes before Robinson when the crew were shooting on location in the Lakes and apparently found the chicken scene 'as funny as cancer' – out of context – and wanted Uncle Monty to be more of a camp caricature to ensure easy laughs. To Robinson's credit, he stood his ground, and to theirs, they eventually left him to it. It is his self-belief that saw the unlikely project to fruition, his writing that made Grant's Withnail, Griffiths' Uncle Monty and Ralph Brown's befuddled Danny the dealer such memorable screen creations. Which is not to detract from the performances – these are actors who really 'get' the gags – just to say that *Withnail And I*'s genius flows from the written page.

In Grant's autobiography he recounts the 'ache in his gonads' after reading just two pages of Robinson's script; it really is worth consuming in book-form, not least for the evocative stage directions ('Dostoyevsky described hell as perhaps nothing more than a room with a chair in it. This room has several chairs'). That Robinson was capable of such priceless work and yet seems unable to quite match it again (1989's *How To Get Ahead In Advertising* was just too obvious and he had a disastrous foray into Hollywood with moribund serial killer flick *Jennifer Eight* in 1992) merely tells us that *Withnail* is an even rarer pleasure than it at first seems: a comedy that truly comes from the heart. It's criminal that – due to a no-points/flat fee deal – its author doesn't see a penny from video sales (the medium from whence its popularity grew) or from the 1996 cinematic re-release (Robinson wasn't even asked). Still, he keeps a sensational cellar, and imagine the size of his balls. ★★★★★ **AS**

Movie Trivia: *Withnail And I*

The film cost £1.1 million to make. Bruce Robinson received £1 for the script and £80,000 to direct it but reinvested £30,000. Although credited on screen only as 'I', Paul McGann's character is named as 'Marwood' in the script. In rehearsals, Withnail's lighter fluid can was actually filled with water. During the take, director Bruce Robinson substituted the water with vinegar to provoke a better reaction when Grant downed the contents. The Camberwell Carrot (big spliff) was actually made with herbal cigarettes.

WITHOUT A CLUE (1988)

Starring: *Michael Caine (Sherlock Holmes/Reginald Kincaid), Ben Kingsley (Dr. John Watson), Jeffrey Jones (Inspector Lestrade), Lysette Anthony (Leslie Giles), Paul Freeman (Moriarty), Nigel Davenport (Lord Smithwick), Pat Keen (Mrs Hudson), Peter Cook (Norman Greenhough), Tim Killick (Sebastian), Matthew Savage (Wiggins), John Warner (Peter Giles)*
Director: *Thom Eberhardt*
Screenwriters: *Garry Murphy, Larry Strawther*
PG/107 mins./Crime/Comedy/UK

Brilliant Dr Watson has hired washed-up actor Reginald Kincaid to impersonate Sherlock Holmes, the fictional genius Watson credits with his own crime-solving achievements. The partnership founders just as Scotland Yard needs the Great Detective to tackle a tricky counterfeiting scheme.

The basic joke of this would-be romp is that Kingsley's Watson is a genius while Caine's Sherlock is an alcoholic idiot, but that the clever doctor is now frustrated because his fictional creation is hailed as an infallible hero while he is always pushed out of the picture.

To really work, the film should have cast a leading man who might have made a good serious Holmes, but the lazy Caine is all too credible in his idiot act – in one of the best jokes, Watson covers up a faux pas by complementing 'Holmes' on his convincing disguise as a drunken lout – and so the laughs that should come in a flow only manage to trickle.

The plot is a trifle about forged bank-notes ruining the Empire, but is constructed to allow for the usual excursion by picturesque steam train to a clue-ridden holiday destination and some dirty deeds down by the docks. Though the leads coast through their routines, the supporting cast features an appropriately ratlike and embittered Inspector Lestrade from Jeffrey Jones, a winsomely duplicitous Victorian heroine from Lysette Anthony and a rather good goateed sadist Professor Moriarty from Paul Freeman.

It can't hold a magnifying glass to Billy Wilder's The Private Life of Sherlock Holmes, but as a Holmesian footnote it edges a deerstalker ahead of Gene Wilder's The Adventure of Sherlock Holmes' Smarter Brother and bests the Peter Cook-Dudley Moore Hound of the Baskervilles. Director Thom Eberhardt made an impression with the witty Night of the Comet, but this bland follow-up condemned him to career hell. ★★ **KN**

WITNESS (1985)

Starring: *Harrison Ford (Det. Cap. John Book), Kelly McGillis (Rachel Lapp), Josef Somner (Chief Paul Schaeffer), Lukas Haas (Samuel Lapp), Jan Rubes (Eli Lapp)*
Director: *Peter Weir*
Screenwriters: *William Kelley, Pamela Wallace, Earl. W. Wallace*
15/112 mins./Thriller/USA

Awards: Academy Awards – *Best Editing, Best Original Screenplay; BAFTA – Best Score*

When a young Amish boy, travelling with his mother, witnesses a murder at railway station, Detective John Book realises the perpetrators were corrupt policemen. To protect the boy, Book returns with them to their Amish community, where he must adjust to their strict lifestyle and to his growing feelings for the boy's mother.

Arguably Harrison Ford's finest performance, and one of the strongest thrillers to emerge from the heady gloss of the '80s, this is director Peter Weir at his most adept. That's because in many ways it is an anti-'80s film, its emphasis on character, cultural identity, mood and the diversity and conflicts of American life give it the weight and purpose of those expert policiers from the '70s. When the traditional gun-toting action finally arrives it's like a rude interruption. For this is an anti-thriller, much more about love than murder.

Weir is so good at containing big stars personas, and then drawing potent performances out of them. He has found depth in Mel Gibson, Robin Williams, and Jim Carrey, but with Ford he liberates him from iconography and lets John Book (what a solid, unshowy name) become an awkward, swagger-less, fascinating, lonely man – the anti-Indy. Weir also has such a feel for unusual locations, his films never bind us to the familiar. This strange corner of America might as well be Oz it is so closed off from the outside world, shunting the worldliness of electricity, music, standard clothing, normal pleasures. But this is not a parody, through Book's opening eyes, it highlights a purity in their way of life. There's one lovely montage in which the entire community erect a barn (spot the young Viggo Mortensen) a portrayal of communal harmony swelling to Maurice Jarre's soft, poetic score that matches the gentle rise of the countryside.

At heart, though, and heart is what matters in Weir's films, this is a romance. Kelly McGillis and Ford create a subtle, yearning chemistry. In one moment of poised perfection, Book spots the widow Rachel washing and their eyes meet, without a single caress the sexuality is more vivid and electrifying than any number of cheap fleshy tumbles. The action will arrive as the bad guys show up, and is as expertly handles as everything else in the movie, but you leave the film knowing it is about dignity, restraint, and the overriding theme in all Weir's films, about a man who comes to know himself. ★★★★★ **IN**

Movies That Sound Like Porn But Aren't

1. Shaft
2. X-Men
3. Deep Impact
4. Riding in Cars with Boys
5. Fanny and Alexander
6. Mother Jugs and Speed
7. Prize Puppies
8. Kiss Kiss Bang Bang
9. Stop! Or My Mom Will Shoot
10. Christie Malry's Own Double Entry

WITNESS FOR THE PROSECUTION (1957)

Starring: *Tyrone Power (Leonard Stephen Vole), Marlene Dietrich (Christine Helm/Vole), Charles Laughton (Sir Wilfrid Robarts), Elsa Lanchester (Miss Plimsoll), John Williams (Brogan Moore), Henry Daniell (Mayhew), Ian Wolfe (Carter)*
Director: *Billy Wilder*
Screenwriters: *Billy Wilder, Harry Kurnitz, Larry Marcus, based on the novel and the play by Agatha Christie*
U/114 mins./Mystery/USA

When Leonard Vole is charged with murder after inheriting a fortune from a wealthy widow, London barrister Sir Wilfrid Robarts agrees to take the case. However, the defendant's German refugee wife, Christine, stuns the court by testifying against him.

Although never as successful as *The Mousetrap*, Agatha Christie's 1953 play had, nevertheless, tallied 458 performances in London and 644 on Broadway before it was acquired by producer Edward Small. Joshua Logan seems to have been involved in the pre-production, but once Billy Wilder came on board the project changed dramatically.

Working with Harry Kurnitz, who had written whodunits under the pen name Marco Page, Wilder not only added edge to the dialogue, but he also bolstered the characterisation, which was never the Queen of Crime's strong point. In particular, Wilder shifted the emphasis away from Leonard Vole and on to Sir Wilfrid Robarts. This was partly because Charles Laughton was his favourite actor and Wilder had been keen to find a suitable project since their plans were dashed for a curio about an impoverished English aristocrat who ekes out a living as a wrestler named The Masked Marvel.

But, it also enabled Wilder to attempt a Hitchcock picture without drawing too many obvious parallels with his perennial 'wrong man' theme.

However, Hitchcock would never have so rigorously reined in his camera to allow the viewer to concentrate on both the twisting storyline and the performances. Wilder, on the other hand, tended to frame Laughton in isolation, especially within the courtroom, so that he could exploit such telling pieces of business as a trick with a monocle, which was just one of Wilder's interpolations to the screenplay.

Another was the character of Miss Plimsoll, the morbidly upbeat nurse whose insistence on getting Sir Wilfrid through the case mirrors his own determination to ascertain the truth. Doubtless drawing on their off-screen relationship, Laughton's wife, Elsa Lanchester, played the role to perfection and the pair thoroughly merited their Oscar nominations.

Tyrone Power (in what turned out to be his last completed assignment) and Marlene Dietrich are no less effective, however, with the latter defying her 55 years to recapture the femme fatalistic allure of her 1930s outings with another Viennese director, Josef Von Sternberg. **★★★★ DP**

THE WIZARD OF OZ (1939)

Starring: *Judy Garland (Dorothy Gale), Frank Morgan (Prof. Marvel/The Wizard Of Oz), Ray Bolger (Huck/The Scarecrow), Bert Lahr (Zeke/The Cowardly Lion), Jack Haley (Hickory/The Tin Man), Billie Burke (The Good Witch of the North), Margaret Hamilton (Miss Gulch/The Wicked Witch of the West/East)*
Director: *Victor Fleming*
Screenwriters: *Noel Langley, Florence Ryerson, Edgar Allan Woolf, based on the novel* The Wonderful Wizard of Oz *by L. Frank Baum*
U/97 mins./Fantasy/Adventure/Musical/USA

Awards – *Academy Awards – Best Original Score, Best Song ('Over The Rainbow')*

Dorothy, a young girl living on a farm in Kansas, is swept up, with her little dog, in a tornado and set down in a magical land. Making friends along the way, she sets out to find the mythical Wizard of Oz who is apparently the only one who has the power to send her home.

Over the course of film history, there's a lot of crap written about movies that speak to the child in us but this dazzling musical adaptation of L Frank Baum's novel – twisters, ruby slippers, yellow brick roads, you know the drill – genuinely hits on childish delights (the promise of adventure, the joy of finding new mates) and fears with effortless grace, warmth and imagination.

Chief among its pleasures are a clutch of hummable tunes ('We hear he is a whiz of a Wiz'), MGM's spectacular set design, a cute dog and the scariest villainess in cinema and the inimitable scarecrow-tin man-lion troika.

Sixty years on, the funny bits are still really funny (the cowardly lion's 'put 'em up'), the scary bits are really scary (the army of flying monkeys) and the evocation of innocent longing for a home far away – encapsulated in Garland's rendition of 'Over The Rainbow' – is beautifully pitched. Indeed, Garland, captured on the cusp of legend before traumas of stardom kicked in, provides the film's devastating emotional centre, an icon for homesick kiddies everywhere.

If you want a true barometer for greatness, just count the ways it has entered the culture: from references in David Lynch's *Wild At Heart* to the nexus of folklore that surrounds its making (rumours of munchkin behaviour are rife), Oz's influence is boundless. Spellbinding stuff. **★★★★★ IF**

Movie Trivia: *The Wizard of Oz*

Though only 17 at the time of release, during filming Judy Garland had to wear a corset to make her seem younger and more modest in the chest area. Shirley Temple was considered to play the part of Dorothy, but apparently her vocals just weren't up to it. Dorothy's ruby slippers were originally silver in the script. 'Over The Rainbow' was almost cut from the film, as producers thought it would be degrading for Judy Garland to sing in a barnyard. The yellow brick road originally showed up as green in the first prints.

⊙ WOLF (1994)

Starring: *Jack Nicholson (Will Randall), Michelle Pfeiffer (Laura Alden), James Spader (Stewart Swinton), Kate Nelligan (Charlotte Randall), Richard Jenkins (Det. Bridger)*
Director: *Mike Nichols*
Screenwriters: *Jim Harrison, Wesley Strick*
15/120 mins./Drama/Horror/Romance/USA

A publisher gets bitten by a wolf and soon develops canine characteristics.

Publisher Nicholson, struggling with personal and professional mid-life crises, runs into a wolf on a lonely road and gets bitten. Soon after, his senses become more acute, his teeth get sharper, he grows hairier and he becomes ruthless at the office. After flexing his new-found animal magnetism on rich dropout Pfeiffer, Jack starts roaming New York by night, ripping off muggers' fingers and howling at the full moon. Anyone who has seen more than half-a-dozen horror films will work out quickly that Nicholson has become a werewolf (a word the script coyly doesn't use), but big-name helmer Nichols and an A-list cast strangely seem to believe this is fresh meat.

Like all werewolves, this film is cursed by duality: despite the fervour a toothy Nicholson and an edible Pfeiffer bring to their roles, it's simply too ridiculous for a mainstream audience and too familiar for horror fans. As they pad ominously across the screen, plot developments will have genre cognoscenti checking off bits from *The Werewolf Of London*, *Curse Of The Werewolf*, *I Was A Teenage Werewolf* and *An American Werewolf In London*. And, going against the grain of recent bubbling rubber or morphing effects, the movie relies on Nicholson's growly face, minimally augmented by old-fashioned yak hair and dentures. It's a nice idea, but it won't scare anyone who has seen *The Howling*.

The first act, before Nicholson gets into hairy business, effectively juggles satire at the expense of the cut-throat publishing biz (Spader is wonderfully smarmy as Nicholson's stab-in-the-back protégé) with unease as Jack senses his new powers. There is a suggestion that Nichols is trying to do a remake of his last film, *Regarding Henry*, which was about a struggling New Yorker who suffers a trauma which induces a bizarre medical condition that changes his life around. While *Henry* was fuzzy, however, *Wolf* is sharp: by far the best scenes are those with Nicholson playing off the sneaky Spader and the genially tyrannical corporate raider (Christopher Plummer) who has taken over the firm. All seriousness evaporates when a mystic expert gives Nicholson an amulet that staves off the curse (this is a rip-off of the magic flower in 1935's *Werewolf Of London*, which also had a similar makeup for its star monster). And for a big, expensive, much rewritten movie, this has a remarkably dull finish: after a scrappy Wolf Man Meets The Wolf Man dust-up, one of the stars simply walks off into the woods and disappears, while the other does that glowing-eyed curse-lives-on shtick that has been a howling cliché for the last 30 years. ★★★ **KN**

⊙ WOLF CREEK (2005)

Starring: *John Jarratt (Mick Taylor), Cassandra Magrath (Liz Hunter), Kestie Morassi (Kristy Earl), Nathan Phillips (Ben Mitchell), Gordon Poole (Old Man)*
Director: *Greg McLean*
Screenwriter: *Greg McLean*
18/99 mins./Horror/Crime/Thriller/Australia

Three young travellers (an Aussie guy and two Brit girls) are making their way across the remote West-Australian outback, and run into car trouble. They're assisted by the likeable-but-odd Mick, who tows them back to his camp, and works on their vehicle while they rest. One of the girls awakes to find herself bound and gagged, and things are about to get a lot worse . . .

Opening with a True Crime Channel logo and the sombre header 'based on actual events', *Wolf Creek*'s overly keen to boast its based-on-reality credentials. Don't pay too much attention, though. Despite a faux post-script which unwisely enforces the impression that what we've just watched really happened, Greg McLean's raw slasher pic is about as based on fact as *The Texas Chainsaw Massacre*, drawing inspiration from various Oz multiple murderers (Ivan Milat, Bradley Murdoch, the Snowtown killers) rather than a single event. Just as well, really. With all the distressing brutality on display here, anything even faintly closer to real life would render this exploitation of the lowest order.

As it is, McLean turns in an upsettingly effective psycho-killer thriller, giving cinema its latest great bogeyman in the form of Mick Taylor, a creation which smartly inverts the Australian myth of the chirpy, tells-it-like-it-is, Outback-yomping bushman. Realised with sinister relish by the burly, silver-maned John Jarratt, who clearly revels in the archetype-corruption (McLean's script even cheekily throws in a few *Crocodile Dundee* references, including a horrifying – yet guiltily amusing – reference to the '*This* is a knife' gag), Taylor comes on like Steve Irwin's sadistic, Satanic uncle, a former vermin exterminator who now uses his skills to torture and kill unfortunate backpackers.

McLean refuses to follow the usual slasher formula, and as impressive a creation as Taylor is, he never becomes a cheerable anti-hero in the Freddy or Jason vein, casually offing a string of unconvincing teens until the only one left is a squealy but resourceful girl. Shot on hi-def DV with a Dogme 95 manifesto apparently close to hand, *Wolf Creek* proffers only three victims using a leisurely (perhaps too leisurely for the more impatient among us), docu-style set-up to let us get to know and like them. It's a process greatly aided by a trio of strong performances by Cassandra Macgrath, Kesti Morassi and Nathan Phillips (although the former two do need to work on their British accents) and it makes all that follows that much more unpleasant and distressing – deeply distressing. We'll spare you the scare-spoiling details, but for now just remember these words: 'Head on a stick . . .' ★★★★ **DJ**

⊙ THE WOLF MAN (1941)

Starring: *Claude Rains (Sir John Talbot), Warren William (Dr. Lloyd), Ralph Bellamy (Col. Paul Montford), Patric Knowles (Frank Andrews), Bela Lugosi (Bela), Marya Ouspenskaya (Maleva), Evelyn Ankers (Gwen Conliffe), J.M. Kerrigan (Charles Conliffe), Fay Helm (Jenny Williams), Lon Chaney Jr. (Lawrence Talbot), Forrester Harvey (Victor Twiddle)*
Director: *George Waggner*
Screenwriter: *Curt Siodmak*
PG/70 mins./Horror/USA

Lawrence Talbot returns to Wales, his homeland, and is bitten by a gypsy werewolf (Lugosi) he batters to death with a silver-headed cane. Under the influence of the full moon, Talbot turns into a wolf monster.

'Even a man who is pure at heart, and says his prayers by night, may become a wolf when the wolfbane blooms and the moon is full and bright.' Lon Chaney Junior became the premier horror star of the 1940s after this vehicle, which provided him with a signature role to match Bela Lugosi's Dracula and Boris Karloff's Frankenstein Monster.

It's a brisk, busy, overpopulated picture, set in a befuddling Hollywood idea of a Welsh village, which comes complete with a cathedral and a nearby gypsy camp and introduces a deal of business made up by screenwriter Curt Siodmak which has become accepted ancient folklore in dozens of subsequent lycanthropy movies.

In a poignant bit of baton-passing, the curse is passed on by Bela

Lugosi, whose position as a monster star was about to be ceded to Chaney. When the full moon rises, Talbot transforms into the last of Universal's truly classic monsters, with a faceful of yak-hair and canine fangs appearing in impressive lap-dissolve effects. The monster stalks through the wonderfully foggy fake forests to menace heroine Evelyn Ankers.

Claude Rains, as Chaney's father, gives it some dignity and pulls the puppyish Lon back on track, and there's wonderful work from Marya Ouspenskaya as the old gypsy woman who explains the tragic course of the plot. Nonsense, but vintage.

Chaney's Talbot returned in *Frankenstein Meets The Wolf Man*, in which Lugosi gets to play the Monster, and then teamed with Dracula, the Frankenstein Monster and sundry hunchbacks and mad doctors in *House of Frankenstein*, *House Of Dracula* and *Abbott And Costello Meet Frankenstein*. ★★★ **KN**

⓪ WOMAN OF THE DUNES (1964)

Starring: *Eiji Okada (Jumpei Niki), Kyoko Kishida (The Woman), Koji Mitsui, Hiroko Ito, Sen Yano, Ginzo Sekigushi, Kiyohiko Ichihara*
Director: *Hiroshi Teshigahara*
Screenwriter: *Kobo Abe based on his novel* Suna No Onna
18/147 mins./Drama/Japan
Awards: *Cannes Film Festival – Jury Special Prize*

Having missed his bus, Tokyo entomologist Jumpei Niki is offered lodging by a widow who entraps him in her shack at the bottom of a sand dune. Eventually, following several attempts to escape, he accepts his lot and remains to help the woman raise their child.

Hiroshi Teshigahara had wanted to film Kobo Abe's prize-winning novel on its publication in 1960. But while he was already a master painter, designer, sculptor and stage director, Teshigahara had only made a couple of short films and he decided to attempt an original Abe screenplay, *The Pitfall*, before embarking on what would become the most celebrated of their four collaborations.

In many ways, *Woman Of The Dunes* echoes *The Pitfall*'s emphasis on disappearance and the purpose of life. But this is also a Taoist parable about Japan's place in the world, as Niki wears Western clothing and his attitudes are resolutely modern. He is also obsessed with getting ahead and is as regimented in the conduct of his daily life as he is in his work. Everything is meticulously planned, yet his fascination with the wilderness causes him to miss his bus and strand himself in an environment that is as arid as his own existence.

We never see the city. But we hear it over the opening credits and the stamps on Niki's papers suggest that he enjoys escaping from it. Yet, he remains unaware of the dehumanising impact that it's had on him, as he initially treats the villagers and the widow with the same formal detachment with which he views his insects. Indeed, such is his polite arrogance that he singularly fails to recognise that he is every bit as insignificant as his specimens within his urban context.

However, Niki gradually comes to appreciate the benefits of his new situation, which frees him from the need to participate in an uphill struggle that is markedly more pointlessly Sisyphean than the imperative need to keep shovelling sand. It's only once he has accepted the awesome power of nature that he finds himself and, thus, rather than surrendering to his fate, he embraces it because he has finally realised that true freedom is not determined by physical limitation.

With its evocative textures sublimely captured by Hiroshi Segawa, the film won the Special Jury Prize at Cannes, although Teshigahara later cut back on the original 147-minute running time. ★★★★★ **DP**

⓪ WOMEN ON THE VERGE OF A NERVOUS BREAKDOWN (1988)

Starring: *Carmen Maura (Pepa), Antonio Banderas (Carlos), Fernando Guillen (Iván), Julietta Serrano (Lucia), Maria Barranco (Candela), Rossy de Palma (Marisa), Kiti Manver (Paulina)*
Director: *Pedro Almodóvar*
Screenwriter: *Pedro Almódovar*
15/98 mins./Drama/Spain

Having just discovered that she's pregnant, voice-over actress Pepa Marcos is dumped by her womanising lover Iván, whose disturbed wife Lucia sets out to exact revenge on Pepa, just as her son Carlos and his fiancée Marisa arrive to view Pepa's apartment.

Pedro Almodóvar's first mainstream hit was loosely based on Jean Cocteau's 1930 play, *La Voix Humaine*, although it also borrowed liberally from the works of Spanish dramatists Mihura and Jardiel Poncela, from Dorothy Parker's 'Anything Goes' essays, and from such Hollywood genre pictures as Jean Negulesco's *How to Marry A Millionaire*, Stanley Donen's *Funny Face* and Billy Wilder's *The Apartment*.

However, traces of George Cukor, Douglas Sirk, Nicholas Ray and Alfred Hitchcock are also readily evident in this gleeful melée of attitudes and styles whose audacity and vibrancy owes as much to a lingering sense of post-Franco exhilaration as to the 'couldn't care less' posture of the *pasota* generation that had informed Almodóvar's earlier features, including his debut, *Pepi, Luci, Bom And The Other Girls*, which had been completed largely thanks to Carmen Maura.

But for all its playful postmodernism, this is also a satirical treatise on the crisis of Spanish masculinity in the late 1980s. One of the main reasons why these women have been driven to the verge is that virtually every male character is portrayed as weak. Iván is ageing and inconstant; Carlos is ineffectual; the cabby (Guillermo Montesinos) is dependable, but camp; and Candela's boyfriend is a crazed Shiite terrorist.

But, in keeping with the classic woman's picture format, the female characters are surprisingly strong. Pepa, for example, is linked throughout with Joan Crawford – whom she dubs in a scene from *Johnny Guitar* – and although she's initially distraught at the prospect of having a child alone, she eventually takes control of her own desires and destiny.

Photographed in riotous colours by José Luis Alcaine, this is very much an ensemble farce. But Maura is superb as the resilient Pepa, whose accidental emancipation causes as much chaos as her drugged gazpacho. Almodóvar also excels, whether parodying TV commercials or sustaining the frantic pace and his £700,000 movie went on to gross over £3.5 million worldwide. ★★★★ **DP**

⓪ THE WOMEN (1939)

Starring *Norma Shearer (Mary Haines), Joan Crawford (Crystal Allen), Rosalind Russell (Sylvia Fowler), Mary Boland (Countess DeLave), Paulette Goddard (Miriam Aarons), Joan Fontaine (Peggy Day), Lucile Watson (Mrs. Moorehead)*
Director: *George Cukor*
Screenwriters: *Anita Loos, Jane Murfin, based on the play by Claire Boothe Luce*
U/132 mins./Comedy/USA

Having graciously surrendered her husband Stephen to shopgirl Crystal Allen, Park Avenue mother Mary Haines refuses to accept their marriage and sets out to expose her rival's affair with the singing cowboy who was once married to her friend, Countess DeLave.

Still feeling piqued at having been fired off *Gone With The Wind*, George Cukor took on this adaptation of Clare Boothe's stinging stage play to restore his reputation as Hollywood's finest director of actresses.

W

Lording it over a cast of 135 women – only two of whom, Marjorie Main and Phyllis Povah, were reprising their Broadway roles – he succeeded in coaxing one of the best ensemble displays since his own *Dinner At Eight* in 1933.

Having come through his own crisis of confidence, Cukor agreed to help Joan Crawford lobby for the role of Crystal, as she had recognised that her days as MGM's No.1 glamour star were dwindling and that she needed to extend her range. But, having browbeaten Louis B. Mayer and producer Hunt Stromberg into accepting his choice, Cukor then had to back down from casting Ilka Chase as the gossiping Sylvia Fowler and agree to the insertion of the Technicolor fashion parade, which he considered an embarrassment.

However, there were plenty more battles ahead. Crawford and Norma Shearer (who sought to sustain her status at the studio by playing on the fact that she was *wunderkind* Irving G. Thalberg's widow) bickered over billing and then refused to exchance a civil word for the remainder of the production, with Shearer having to plead with Cukor to prevent Crawford from knitting noisily as she delivered feed lines off camera. However, Rosalind Russell, who had landed the role of Sylvia, proved to be just as obstreperous and cried off sick until her co-star credit was confirmed.

But, once his cast had ceased cat-fighting (an apt description, since each character was associated with a symbolic animal), Cukor was able to persuade them to deliver performances that belied the two-dimensionality of Boothe's characterisation – which had scarcely been improved upon by screenwriter Jane Murfin, despite the fact she had been scripting woman's pictures since the silent era. However, Anita Loos managed to inject some bitchy grit into the proceedings after she was called in, ironically, to tone things down after complaints about the unlady-like language from the Breen Office. ★★★★ **DP**

WONDER BOYS (2000)

Starring: *Michael Douglas (Prof. Grady Tripp), Tobey Maguire (James Leer), Frances McDormand (Dean Sara Gaskell), Robert Downey Jr. (Terry Crabtree), Katie Holmes (Hannah Green), Rip Torn (Quentin 'Q' Morewood)*
Director: *Curtis Hanson*
Screenwriter: *Steven Kloves, based on the novel by Michael Chabon*
15/111 mins./Drama/Comedy/USA/Germany/UK/Japan
Awards – *Academy Awards – Best Original Song ('Things Have Changed'), Golden Globes – Best Original Song ('Things Have Changed')*

Preoccupied by his endless second novel, Professor Tripp's marriage is collapsing, as is his affair with college dean Sara. Matters come to a head one weekend, during which Tripp must negotiate predatory agent Crabtree, disturbed student James Leer, Marilyn Monroe's coat and a dead dog.

Curtis Hanson's breakthrough movie (let's forgive him such early endeavours as 1994's *The River Wild*) was hewn from the endlessly cinematic crime world of James Ellroy; shooting *L.A. Confidential* was mostly a matter of ironing out the Byzantine plot. Michael Chabon's *Wonder Boys*, however, presented a different challenge. A dense, introspective story of writer's block and literary rivalry, Chabon's novel is relatively untroubled by plot and handsomely burdened with character. By all accounts it should not translate into a good movie but, by sticking to his source material's strengths, Hanson, aided by Steve Kloves' erudite script and Bob Dylan's soundtrack, has gone one better: he's made a great movie.

Apparently, they don't make movies like this anymore. Don Simpson and his 'high concept' 80s juggernaut had, it seemed, killed off the 1970s' independent spirit (*Wonder Boys* plays like a joyous companion to Bob Rafelson's *Five Easy Pieces*). As this film illustrates, this is thankfully not so.

Unfortunately, we are all so spoiled, so spoon-fed, by the Simpson-style blockbuster, that the rarefied pleasures of *Wonder Boys* may escape you the first time around. Like all mood pieces, *Wonder Boys* requires a degree of patience – and if it fails to catch you in the right frame of mind, there is a real danger of, 'What was all that about?' syndrome. This movie refuses to grab you – it percolates into your conscious.

And yet *Wonder Boys* is that rare thing: a witty screenplay, unafraid of slapstick; a heart-felt drama, devoid of sentiment; and a complex story, presented with admirable simplicity. Hanson does not rely on tricks – everything is as it should be, the Pittsburgh interiors warm and the wintry exteriors bleak. He simply allows his actors room to breathe, and their subsequent work gives added impetus to the old argument that there should be an Oscar for ensemble performance.

A never-better Michael Douglas shoulders the movie as Grady Tripp, the dope-smoking literary professor hamstrung by a never-ending second novel. Douglas invests his academic with a dishevelled grace, rolling with the punches as his life slowly unravels over the course of a weekend. The aptly-named Tripp both stumbles and coasts along in an intoxicated haze, raising a wry eyebrow at the quixotic humanity he witnesses. Like almost everything in this elegantly understated movie, Douglas underplays, assaying a marijuana-mellow take on *Falling Down*'s D-Fens.

Elsewhere, Tobey Maguire is at his glassy-eyed, inscrutable best as troubled teen James Leer, while old-stagers Frances McDormand and Rip Torn eat up their limited screen time as Tripp's on-off love interest and literary adversary respectively. Only the requisitely cute Katie Holmes appears out of her depth, as alluring student Hannah Green. A pre-jail Robert Downey Jr., meanwhile, proves once and for all that Hollywood needs him this side of the bars. Indeed, it says much about the generosity of Douglas' performance that Downey's hugely entertaining literary agent is allowed to steal every scene.

Wonder Boys is not perfect; some sections drag, some characters refuse to come into focus. But it is a brave, important work which feels both timeless and contemporary. Of course, the point was so lost on the American public that the studio planned a post-award, glory re-release before the awards season even started. Don't make the same mistake – catch this minor masterpiece at the first opportunity. ★★★★★ **CK**

WONDERLAND (2003)

Starring: *Val Kilmer (John Holmes), Kate Bosworth (Dawn Schiller), Lisa Kudrow (Sharon Holmes), Josh Lucas (Ron Launius), Tim Blake Nelson (Billy Deverell), Dylan McDermott (David Lind), Christina Appelgate (Susan Launius)*
Director: *James Cox*
Screenwriters: *James Cox, Captain Mauzner, Todd Samovitz, D. Loriston Scott*
18/104 mins./Crime/Drama/Thriller/USA

Los Angeles, 1981: troubled porn star John Holmes is about to sell a stash of cocaine and skip town with his underage girlfriend when the police question him about his involvement in the brutal murder of four of his 'business colleagues' on Wonderland Avenue a few days earlier.

Since the success of *Boogie Nights*, mainstream films have realised that putting 'the other Hollywood' – namely LA's flourishing porn industry – under the microscope can often make for compelling cinema. In light of this, it was inevitable that we would get a film about the biggest name in the business. For while *Boogie Nights* was all about Dirk Diggler, *Wonderland*

TOP 10 Countries with most cinema screens

1. China	65,500	6. Spain	3,770
2. USA	36,764	7. UK	3,248
3. India	11,962	8. Italy	3,050
4. France	5,236	9. Canada	2,900
5. Germany	4,792	10. Japan	2,585

focuses on a legendary episode from the life of John Holmes, the person on whom Diggler was almost entirely based.

In the 70s, Holmes' charm – and also his enormous appendage – quickly took him to the top of the porn industry, but his immersion in cocaine culture tarnished his reputation and put his career in reverse.

Director James Cox's choice to play Holmes is so spot on, you cannot imagine anyone else in the role. Who could be better at playing a washed-up ex-star who had it and blew it than Val Kilmer, a washed-up ex-star who had it and blew it? Add into the equation that, just as with the much derided Kilmer, Holmes was not hugely popular amongst his peers, and what you have is perfect casting. And though Kilmer has in the past often been unappealing even when playing supposedly likeable characters, here – as the well-meaning but massively flawed fuck-up Holmes – he is not only amazingly good, but surprisingly sympathetic.

Supporting Kilmer is a raft of recognisable faces (from Dylan McDermott and Josh Lucas, to Carrie Fisher and Janeane Garofalo), but it is Kate Bosworth as Holmes' 15 year-old girlfriend Dawn who particularly impresses, giving a weighty and moving performance as a girl forced to grow up too soon, suggesting she's far more than just 'that girl from *Blue Crush*'.

Another of the film's positive aspects is its narrative style, reminiscent of Akira Kurosawa's *Rashomon*, which offers conflicting and incompatible versions of the 'truth' about the killings on Wonderland Avenue from each character. Presenting just one angle on an incident which has become part of the subculture folklore would have been to detract from its complexity and people's fascination with it; and moreover, it's not just a nod to Kurosawa, but also contributes to the film's freewheeling feel, generated by its pulsing energy and strong soundtrack. ★★★★ **ND**

Tagline
With a score this dirty, nobody gets away clean.

WONDERLAND (1999)

Starring: *Shirley Henderson (Debbie), Gina McKee (Nadia), Molly Parker (Molly), Ian Hart (Dan), John Simm (Eddie), Stuart Townsend (Tim)*
Director: *Michael Winterbottom*
Screenwriter: *Laurence Coriat*
15/104 mins./Drama/UK

Three sisters' lives unravel over five days in South London.

Covering five days in the lives of a South London family slowly fraying at the edges, *Wonderland* is a subtle, moving and evocative document of capital life at the end of the 90s. Boasting strong performances from all involved – with the sense that Shirley Henderson and Gina McKee in particular have relished the challenge of their front-line status – and a vaguely Dogme-like production approach (handheld footage shot on location with no artificial lighting or extras), the film manages to paint London in shaky, oversaturated colour while still managing to retain a sense of the city's inherent greyness.

Wonderland is built upon four inter-weaving plotlines concerning three sisters: the loveless and quietly desperate Nadia, forcing herself through the undignified process of lonely hearts dating; heavily pregnant Molly and partner Eddie, a fitted kitchen salesman with an overwhelming urge to ditch his day job; and white-trashy good-time girl Debbie (Henderson, with an impressively guttural South London accent), her half-neglected 11 year-old son and their dealings with his largely errant dad (a brilliantly scally Ian Hart).

Add to all this the suffocating, disintegrating marriage of their parents, Eileen and Bill, and the result is a patchwork narrative that collages poignant and dryly funny set-pieces, as the characters' lives unravel over one long weekend. But, performances aside, it's the high-production documentary quality of the film – the bingo hall scene where the pitted faces of real housewives are shot completely unawares, or the way that passers-by throw inquisitive stares at the camera – that brings a tangible sense of reality to the proceedings. Yet the gritty feel is given bizarre beauty, courtesy of Michael Nyman's score.

As a study of how loneliness and desperation can go painfully unnoticed as it's absorbed by the big city – the moment where a romantically ditched Nadia travels home on a bus full of revelry is one of the most moving – *Wonderland* is nothing less than a superb piece of filmmaking. ★★★★ **TD**

THE WOODSMAN (2005)

Starring: *Kevin Bacon (Walter), Kyra Sedgwick (Vicki), David Alan Grier (Bob), Eve (Mary-Kay), Benjamin Bratt (Carlos)*
Director: *Nicole Kassell*
Screenwriters: *Nicole Kassell, Steven Fechter, based on the play by Fechter*
15/87 mins./Drama/USA

Walter is a convicted paedophile who, on being released from prison, is rehoused a stone's throw from an elementary school. Taking a job at a sawmill, he meets Vicky, with whom he begins a relationship while coping with both the fear of being revealed and an aggressive supervising cop, Sergeant Lucas.

At first glance you'd be forgiven for wondering what it is with Kevin Bacon and child molesters. Not content with having pursued one as a cop in *Mystic River* and delivering an admirably unpleasant performance as a child rapist in *Sleepers*, he returns as yet another kiddie-fiddler in *The Woodsman*. But Bacon's performance as Walter, a convicted paedophile just released from prison, is of an entirely different order. It was undoubtedly one of the most impressive performances of the year, in one of 2005's most courageous films, and was shamefully neglected when it came to handing out gongs.

We shouldn't be too surprised: he has often been underrated – despite the Robbins/Penn fireworks it was Bacon's performance that ran away with *Mystic River*. Here he shows much of that same quiet control. Walter is a study in agonised self-loathing, both aware of the horror of his desires and at times utterly and apparently helplessly in their grip.

An easy watch it certainly is not. Two sequences particularly – both moments in which Walter either deliberately or by accident winds up in temptation's way – are excruciating. And for some, the humanising of predatory sex offenders will veer too close to becoming an apologia (it isn't here). In fact, in numerous Hollywood films paedophiles have become cinematic shorthand for pure, near-pantomimic evil; screenwriters need spend no time or effort exploring their characters, they simply serve plot. It's convenient and lazy and *The Woodsman* is a much-needed corrective.

If there is a slight failing, it's that the screenplay, possibly inevitably, backs off slightly towards the end, delivering if not a flat-packed farrago of redemption and forgiveness, something which nods far enough in that direction to suggest that the possibly more likely outcome would be just too much for audiences to bear.

Nicole Kassell directs her debut with the necessary understatement and support is good from both Kyra Sedgwick and Mos Def as a hostile cop. But it's Bacon's astonishing performance – in the midst of what, for the last two decades or so, has become a kind of persistent public hysteria – that is a quiet, challenging and ultimately discomfortingly human voice. ★★★★ **AS**

◑ WOODSTOCK (1970)

Starring: *as themselves: Richie Havens, Joan Baez, Janis Joplin, Joe Cocker, Jimi Hendrix, The Who, Crosby Stills & Nash, Santana, Sly & And The Family Stone*
Director: *Michael Wadleigh*
15/184 mins./Documentary/USA

Awards – *Academy Awards – Best Documentary Feature*

A documentary record of the '3 Days of Peace and Music' that took place on a remote farm in upstate New York and came to symbolise the end of the Swinging Sixties.

For one weekend in August 1969, Max Yasgur's farm in Sullivan County became the third largest community in New York State. No one had expected around 400,000 souls to descend on this tranquil backwater and the logistical chaos their presence caused was exacerbated by a downpour that reduced the fields to seas of mud. But such calamities only embellished the event's reputation and it eventually came to be seen as the decade's seminal happening.

Operating with 16 cameras, Mike Wadleigh and his crew shot 120 miles of footage over the three days. It doesn't matter that D.A. Pennebaker made a better job of a similar task in *Monterey Pop* or that the acts were on better form there. The Woodstock mythology has ensured that this has become the definitive concert film, although Martin Scorsese's presence among editor Thelma Schoonmaker's assistants hasn't done it much harm, either.

Wadleigh was only 27 when he embarked on the project and his coverage of political speeches by the likes of Martin Luther King and Bobby Kennedy could hardly have prepared him for mayhem that ensued. But, his fascination with people and their opinions is readily evident in the interviews that dot the action and even more so in some of the performances, as he captures the likes of Richie Havens, Joan Baez and Janis Joplin being genuinely caught in the moment rather than simply plugging their latest release.

The use of split screens becomes wearisome occasionally. But the grammar of recording live performance was still in its infancy and for every gimmicky moment there's a gem like Country Joe McDonald's 'I Feel Like I'm Fixin' to Die Rag', Joe Cocker's 'With a Little Help from My Friends' and Jimi Hendrix's iconic 'Star Spangled Banner'.

But reality intrudes on occasion, too, such as when the Port-o-San man casually mentions that his son is in Vietnam or when the newspaper headline behind the shopkeeper promises more revelations about the Sharon Tate murder, which would soon reveal the darker side of hippy culture.

This is a hugely overrated documentary, but it's still an important one. ★★★ **DP**

◑ WORKING GIRL (1988)

Starring: *Harrison Ford (Jack Trainer), Sigourney Weaver (Katharine Parker), Melanie Griffith (Tess McGill), Alec Baldwin (Mick Dugan), Joan Cusack (Cyn), Kevin Spacey (Bob Speck)*
Director: *Mike Nichols*
Screenwriter: *Kevin Wade*
15/112 mins./Romance/Comedy/Drama/USA

Awards – *Academy Awards – Best Original Song ('Let The River Run'), Golden Globes – Best Comedy/Musical, Best Original Song ('Let The River Run'), Best Comedy/Musical Actress, Best Supporting Actress*

Tess McGill is serving coffe and dressing badly until, one day, she decides to make something of herself. She ends up in the big city wheeling and dealing with the best of them and attracting the attention of a corporate Prince Charming.

The title could just as easily have been Cinderella Takes Manhattan, since this upbeat, urban fairy-tale of an oppressed secretary who gets to go – power-dressed – to the board room and meets Prince Charming is an unashamed comic fantasy. And very charming and cheerful it is, too, thanks largely to Melanie Griffith's delightful performance as the aspirational heroine from the wrong side of the Hudson River striving to 'be somebody'. Her sweet Tess is engaging throughout without becoming cloying or irritating – something of a miracle for an actress with an, apparently natural, itsy bitsy cute-little-girl voice.

Sigourney Weaver has a field day in her smaller, supporting role as the wicked stepmother, oops, make that 'bitch boss from hell', conniving, self-aggrandising and thunderstruck by her inevitable comeuppance. She must have relished the opportunity to swan about in designer clothes and loll fetchingly in silk lingerie sipping champagne like a witch in an American soap opera after her months up an African mountain with a bunch of smelly gorillas.

Harrison Ford as the uptown sex object is scarcely stretched but provides a relaxed, urbane air and hits the right, light note. In smaller roles there are two up-and-comers worth noting: Joan Cusack as Tess' sympathetic but unimaginative (except with her makeup) girlfriend is a born scene-stealer and Alec Baldwin (from *Beetlejuice*) as Tess' philandering boyfriend Mick is hot stuff.

The plotting of Tess' meteoric rise from coffee maker to merger mastermind is adroit, with director Mike Nichols careful to observe neat and amusing little details. But it does seem odd that such a supposedly smart cookie bent on self-improvement should look quite so tacky as she does at the beginning.

It's a little hard to see at this distance why a fairly simple fable seized people's fancies to the extent it did, but it's certainly entertaining and loses nothing on a TV screen. Presumably we little people still get a kick out of seeing the good girl become the belle of the ball. ★★★ **AE**

⊙ THE WORLD IS NOT ENOUGH (1999)

Starring: *Pierce Brosnan (James Bond), Sophie Marceau (Elektra King), Robert Carlyle (Victor 'Renard' Zokas), Denise Richards (Dr. Christmas Jones), Robbie Coltrane (Valentin Dmitrovich Zukovsky), Judi Dench (M), Desmond Llewelyn (Q), John Cleese (R), Samantha Bond (Miss Moneypenny)*
Director: *Michael Apted*
Screenwriters: *Neal Purvis, Robert Wade, Bruce Fierstein, based on a story by Purvis, Wade, characters by Ian Fleming*
12/128 mins./Action/Adventure/Thriller/UK/USA
Awards – *Empire Awards – Best Actor*

Bond is called in to protect a female oil magnate from assassination, but is the whole plot against her part of something very much bigger?

You know where you are with James Bond. Continuing the revival of the franchise established by the confident *GoldenEye* and slightly threatened by the somewhat wobbly *Tomorrow Never Dies*, this checks off all the boxes on the form with something like panache, if not actual inspiration.

All present and correct: pre-credits action (speedboat chase on the Thames) and plot set-up (at the Millennium Dome, no less); overblown title song (Garbage – the band, not the tune); semi-surreal title sequence (naked birds and oil wells); globe-trotting (Azerbaijan and Turkey); master villain with formidable henchman (the roles are cleverly scrambled a bit, though students of classical drama will note that the script tips the surprise early); bizarre handicap for Bond's main opponent (mad anarchist Carlyle has a bullet in his brain which makes him immune to pain and unafraid of death); recurring stooges (Dench's M, Desmond Llewellyn's Q, Samantha Bond's Moneypenny); cover girl babes with silly names (Marceau as Elektra King, Richards as Christmas Jones); attempted assassination set against picturesque landscape (hang-gliding bobsleigh killers attack Brosnan while out skiing); explosions and fights in giant sets (ex-Soviet missile silo, submarine sunk in the Bosphorus); high-stakes card-playing; double entendres (of Richards' character, during a clinch in Istanbul: 'I've always wanted to have Christmas in Turkey.'); torture and minor high-tech product placement (that *Moonraker* bit where the dignitaries call up Bond to find him, as it were, on the job, is recreated via the Internet and with heat-sensitive imaging).

Continuing the trend of hiring shaky A-list directors, this employs Apted – who probably worked hard on Brosnan exchanging pointed dialogue with pouting Marceau (who is very good in an unusual Bond Girl role) and baldie Carlyle (who could have been given a bit more business), but stood back and let second-unit specialists take over for the money-spinning scenes of helicopters dangling giant chainsaws and explosions chasing Bond out of tight spots.

The most cheerfully ridiculous aspect of the whole thing is, of course, Denise Richards as the sort of nuclear physicist who wears a cut-off T-shirt and short shorts while probing a leaky Soviet silo and has a habit of getting wet while talking about the insertion of plutonium rods. Bond is, after the 80s-style restraint of the Timothy Dalton period, thankfully back to being a reckless womaniser, but there's a distinct air of trying not to remind you of Austin Powers (even if Carlyle steals the 'Kreplachistan warhead' bit from *International Man Of Mystery*) which perhaps leads to a drabness of style.

The worst of it is the lumpen comedy, with John Cleese hauled in for a couple of scenes as Q's assistant, and would-be witty patter that constantly sounds as if Brosnan is reading it off the back of a cereal packet. Otherwise, the star has settled into the role, delivering precisely the required mix of unflappability, arrogance, heroism and smugness while not looking too uncomfortable in the clichés or a tuxedo. There are all sorts of ways of making the Bond movies more interesting – setting one in the early 50s of Ian Fleming's first novels, doing a story entirely in London with Bond as a detective, having him crack up entirely and become the villain – but after nearly 40 years of settling into a profitable, satisfying rut, they're probably never going to happen. In the meantime, we're likely to get one of these every couple of years, and it'd be a hard heart who didn't warm just a little to something so familiar, comforting and precision-made. ★★★ **KN**

⊙ W.R. MYSTERIES OF THE ORGANISM (1971)

Starring: *Milena Dravic (Milena), Ivica Vidovic (Vladymir Ilyich), Jagoda Kaloper (Jagoda), Tuli Kupferberg (US Soldier), Zoran Radmilovic (Radmilovic), Jackie Curtis (Herself), Miodrag Andric (Soldier)*
Director: *Dusan Makavejev*
Screenwriter: *Dusan Makavejev*
18/85 mins./Drama-Documentary/Yugoslavia/West Germany

Envying her roommate Jagoda's lack of sexual inhibiton, Yugoslav twentysomething Malena resists the attentions of fomer lover Radmilovic and tests her faith in the theories of Wilhelm Reich by sleeping with Russian ice skater Vladimir Ilyich, who is driven by the power of his orgasm to decapitate her with his skates.

Dusan Makavejev had read Wilhelm Reich's *Dialectical Materialism And Psychoanalysis* as a student and had been impressed by his contention that what Marx had done for economic society, Freud had done for the human organism. But he was also aware of the ironies within Reich's own career, which saw him exiled from both Soviet Russia and Nazi Germany for seeking to break down the barriers limiting creativity, only to be persecuted in the United States for being a medical charlatan. Indeed, the man who had given his life to love and liberty ended up dying alone in a federal prison in 1957, having had his books burned.

In 1969, Makavejev accepted a German television commission to make a programme about Reich's theories. But he soon realised that a documentary approach would not do them justice. So, he added a framing Yugoslav story to create a collage of factual and fictional elements that was designed to subvert repression through wit and hint at the joys that were possible through physical and psychological freedom. However, Makavejev was also keen for viewers to engage actively with the film and, thus, left many of the sequences unresolved so that they had to arrive at their own conclusions.

Unfortunately, the film's suppression in Eastern Europe and its limited distribution elsewhere (mostly as a porn flick) meant that few audiences were exposed to *W.R.*'s barrage of ideas. Typically, the critics were divided as to its meaning and described it variously as a political satire, an essay on applied sexology, a doomed romantic melodrama, an autobiographical fragment and a piece of agit-prop Pop Art. But most agreed that Makavejev had handled his material with comic and artistic assurance, particularly in his use of associational montage.

Yet in highlighting the mockery of Lenin, Stalin and Mao, the majority of Western commentators conveniently overlooked the fact that this was a morally balanced, as well as socially ennervating and visually poetic exercise, that also attacked America for its misuse of liberty and the casual manner in which it had allowed sex to be commercialised and harnessed to the capitalist cause. ★★★★ **DP**

⊙ THE WRONG MAN (1956)

Starring: *Henry Fonda (Manny Balestrero), Vera Miles (Rose Balestrero), Anthony Quayle (Frank O'Connor), Harold J. Stone (Lt. Bowers) Esther Minciotti (Mrs. Ballestero), Charles Cooper (Detective Matthews), Nehemiah Persoff (Gene Conforti),*
Director: *Alfred Hitchcock*
Screenwriters: *Maxwell Anderson, Angus Macphail, based on the* The True Story Of Christopher Emmanuel Balestrero
PG/105 mins./Crime/USA

W

Stork Club bassist Manny Balestrero is wrongfully accused of twice holding up an insurance office. Yet circumstances and the incompetence of his lawyer, Frank O'Connor, conspire against him and he's forced to face a trial alone after his wife, Rose, suffers a nervous breakdown.

Robert Montgomery had produced an NBC teleplay about the plight of Christopher Emmanuel Balestrero in 1954, with Robert Ellenstein in the lead. However, Alfred Hitchcock returned to Herbert Brean's 1953 *Life* magazine article, 'A Case of Identity', for this sombre drama, which chimed in so precisely with his trademark theme of the vicitimised Everyman that he made the picture without a fee.

In addition to trusted stalwart Angus MacPhail, Hitchcock hired playwright Maxwell Anderson to collaborate on the screenplay, as he had based his 1935 hit *Winterset* on the injustices inherent in the infamous Sacco-Vanzetti murder trial. But the most significant influence on the film's mood and mentality was Charles Dickens' *Bleak House*, which not only contained an interminable law suit, but which also focused on the confounding caprices of fate.

Indeed, such was Hitchcock's preoccupation with the ethereality of Manny's situation that he used the dissolve at regular intervals to suggest the fragility and transience of life, liberty and sanity. The freakish disappearance of the witnesses who could have given him an alibi is anticipated in the opening Stork Club sequences, in which the patrons seem to melt away during the course of the evening. But Hitch resorted to a similar device at the moment of redemption, as he follows Manny's prayer to the picture of Christ ('Emmanuel' means 'God With Us') with the superimposition of Henry Fonda's face on to that of the real culprit just as he is about to be apprehended by the courageous delicatessen owner.

Such religious overtones bind the film in to *I Confess* and *To Catch A Thief*. But Hitchcock was also keen to invert the conventions of the police procedural. Ever since his childhood, he had been terrified of the police and by presenting this true-life saga from the perspective of the protagonist rather than the interrogating officer, Hitch generated a new kind of suspense that revolved around a helpless individual waiting for mitigating evidence to emerge rather than a procactive hero who seeks out the real perpetrator.

Unfortunately, audiences failed to respond and this remains an undeservedly minor outing. ★★★★ **DP**

➂ WUTHERING HEIGHTS (1939)

Starring: *Merle Oberon (Cathy Linton), Laurence Olivier (Heathcliff), David Niven (Edgar Linton), Donald Crisp (Dr. Kenneth), Flora Robson (Ellen Dean), Hugh Williams (Hindley Earnshaw), Geraldine Fitzgerald (Isabella Linton), Leo G. Carroll (Joseph), Cecil Humphreys (Judge Linton)*
Director: *William Wyler*
Screenwriters: *Ben Hecht, Charles MacArthur, based on the novel by Emily Brontë*
U/103 mins./Romance/USA

Awards: *Academy Awards – Best Cinematography*

Inseperable as children, gypsy foundling Heathcliff drifts apart from Cathy Earnshaw after she pursues wealthy Edgar Linton to further her social ambitions. Returning a rich man, Heathcliff acquires the Earnshaw home of Wuthering Heights and marries Isabella Linton, to Cathy's terminal distress.

When Walter Wanger abandoned his scheme to adapt Emily Brontë's novel with Charles Boyer and Sylvia Sidney as Heathcliff and Cathy, he sold Ben Hecht and Charles MacArthur's treatment to fellow independent Samuel Goldwyn. On accepting the project, William Wyler lobbied for Bette Davis to play the tempestuous heroine, but Goldwyn was keen to boost his new star, Merle Oberon, and considered teaming her with Ronald Colman. Oberon, however, was keen to co-star with Douglas Fairbanks, Jr. and was furious when Goldwyn hired Laurence Olivier, especially as he wanted to play opposite his mistress, Vivien Leigh (who promptly rejected the supporting role of Isabella Linton and went off to make *Gone With the Wind*).

Unsurprisingly, therefore, this proved to be a fractious shoot. Wyler and Goldwyn fell out over John Huston's reworking of the scenario and the distressed look of Olivier's costume and makeup, as well as the ending, which was ultimately given an ethereal glow by H.C. Potter and a couple of stand-ins after Wyler flatly refused to indulge in such nonsensical romanticism. Despite having worked together perfectly amiably on *The Divorce Of Lady X*, Olivier and Oberon also began bickering, with Olivier calling the New Zealander an amateur after he accidentally spat at her in the throes of a love scene.

But while he recognised Oberon's shortcomings, Wyler was no more impressed by Olivier, whom he subjected to a public dressing down for mugging as though he were in Manchester Opera House. Olivier's retort that 'this anaemic little medium can't take great acting' elicited gales of laughter from the crew and he claimed never to have forgotten either this lesson in humility or Wyler's explanation of cinema's artistic potential.

The film itself epitomised Hollywood's attitude to so-called prestige projects. No expense was spared in its realisation, but over half of the novel was jettisoned in order to concentrate on the three-hankie melodrama at its core. Gregg Toland's Oscar-winning photography is superb and Wyler tells his story with typical assurance. But Goldwyn was always later to insist that 'I made it. Wyler only directed it.' ★★★ **DP**

➂ WYATT EARP (1994)

Starring: *Kevin Costner (Wyatt Earp), Dennis Quaid (Doc Holliday), Gene Hackman (Nicholas Earp), David Andrews (James Earp), Linden Asby (Morgan Earp)*
Director: *Lawrence Kasdan*
Screenwriters: *Dan Gordon, Lawrence Kasdan*
12/191 mins./212 mins. (extended cut)/Western/USA

Awards – *Razzie – Worst Actor, Worst Remake/Sequel*

The life of gunslinger Wyatt Earp, from boyhood through the Civil War and on to the infamous fight at the O.K. Corral.

The theme for the old Wyatt Earp TV series went 'Long may his fame, and long may his glory, and long may his story be told.' This long they could never have imagined, as this attempt to tell the Earp legend proves a somewhat overblown business that falls some way short of being truly epic.

Lawrence Kasdan simply doesn't make bad movies, however, and this handsomely-mounted effort to wed authenticity to classic Western themes is honourably watchable, if unexciting for its first two hours. But it strives too hard to inflate vignettes into Big Moments and music swells under 'significant' tableaux in an attempt to stir the senses as Kevin Costner's Earp strikes stolid poses like Scarlett O'Hara against pyrotechnic skies. Surprisingly it lets anticipated high-points like the gunfight at the O.K. Corral slip, reducing it to a (realistically, as it happens) scuffle in the street with baddies whose identities have never been established.

The screenplay, by Kasdan and Dan Gordon, begins in Wyatt's boyhood in the Civil War and jumps, with a variety of hair lengths for Costner, around the States through tragic first love, a youthful crime jag, and a spell slaughtering buffalo – Lt. Dunbar would be horrified! – to, eventually, his fabled career as a lawman in which Earp and his faithful crew of brothers and buddies acquire a merited reputation for brutality en route to their rendezvous with destiny and the Clanton gang in Tombstone.

We're an hour-and-a-half into the movie before Dennis Quaid materialises, marvellous as a gaunt, volatile Doc Holliday, dying of TB, but bringing the film to life. Indeed, alphabetically the credits promise a heck of a cast, but all of the characters are thinly sketched except Costner's Earp, with even Quaid under-used. Others – Gene Hackman as Pappa Earp, Isabella Rossellini as Doc's consort, Tom Sizemore as Bat Masterson – simply vanish, leading to the feeling that, despite its length, this has been mercilessly edited.

Most uncharacteristically from Kasdan there is a certain phoniness in the dialogue that frequently comes across as oration rather than conversation. Despite its length, the film is still confusing on salient details, and even the stoutest Costner fan's patience will be tested by Earp's in-need-of-redemption doings and family dynamics in the frankly tortuous third hour. Handsome to look at, and with some wonderful flourishes, this is by no means a disaster – just a disappointment from some of Hollywood's biggest talents. ★★★ **AE**

1 *Spellbound* (1945)
Dalí creates a wonderfully surreal sequence with giant eyes floating in the sky.

2 *A Nightmare On Elm Street* (1984)
Freddy attacks a teenage girl in her dreams.

3 *The Big Lebowski* (1998)
A musical number including Vikings and Saddam Hussein.

4 *Brazil* (1985)
Office drone dreams he's a winged warrior fighting mutants and giants.

5 *Mulholland Drive* (2001)
It's all a dream! Or some of it is! Or maybe none.

6 *An American Werewolf In London* (1981)
In a dream-within-a-dream, Nazi werewolves attack!

7 *Risky Business* (1983)
Boy dreams of naked blonde in the shower. But stylishly.

8 *Midnight Cowboy* (1969)
Rizzo's dreams crumble before his eyes.

9 *Un Chien Andalou* (1929)
The shocking image of an eyeball being slit with a razor.

10 *Wayne's World 2* (1993)
A naked Indian, and Jim Morrison, guide Wayne's fate.

X

⊙ X2 (2003)

Starring: *Hugh Jackman (Logan/Wolverine), Patrick Stewart (Professor Charles Xavier), Ian McKellen (Eric Lenshherr/Magneto), Famke Janssen (Jean Grey), James Marsden (Scott Summers/Cyclops), Halle Berry (Ororo Munroe/Storm), Anna Paquin (Rogue), Rebecca Romijn (Mystique), Alan Cumming (Nightcrawler/Kurt Wagner), Brian Cox (General William Stryker)*
Director: *Bryan Singer*
Screenwriters: *Dan Harris, Michael Dougherty, David Hayter, from a story by Hayter, Zak Penn, Bryan Singer, from characters by Stan Lee, Jack Kirby*
12/128 mins./Action/Adventure/Fantasy/USA

Following a mutant assassination attempt on the President, Colonel William Stryker initiates a war on mutants, specificially the superhero group, the X-Men. Now, they must join with their sworn enemy, Magneto, to survive; while Wolverine discovers that Stryker holds the key to his murky past . . .

Where would *X2* be without evolution? Three years ago, general consensus had it that the first *X-Men* movie, while enjoyable, was somehow lacking; that Bryan Singer, the *Usual Suspects* wunderkind, was patently uncomfortable working within the big bucks arena. Well, what a difference three years makes: for Singer has evolved. And as a result, *X2* is one of the finest comic book movies to date, and a film that in every conceivable way improves upon its predecessor.

Singer's evolution is confirmed in the astonishing opening sequence in which Alan Cumming's teleporting Nightcrawler attempts, under duress, to assassinate the American President. As he *bamfs* around, moving too fast for terrified Secret Service agents (and the camera itself) one thing is clear: Singer no longer has any hang-ups about handling action. Which is just as well, as *X2* redefines 'action-packed', including incidents both large (a suspenseful attack on the X-Mansion, during which Wolverine unleashes his berserker fury in truly iconic fashion) and small (a fiery conflagration at Iceman's family home). Spidey can sure swing, but, with a $50 million budget increase, this is the first comic book movie to really explore the potential of its heroes' powers. Halle Berry's Storm sets tornadoes on a pair of fighter jets in a cracking dogfight sequence. Jean Grey's telekinesis expands at a frightening rate. Professor X's telepathy has global consequences. Singer handles the diversity of powers superbly, assisted by cinematographer Tom Newton Sigel and editor/composer John Ottman, whose prudent pruning gives the film real momentum.

At 130 minutes, *X2* is some 37 minutes longer than the original, and Singer needs every second of it, for there's a lot to cram in. Amazingly, though, Singer avoids the 'too many cooks' syndrome that so tarnished the *Batman* films, while at the same time giving pretty much everyone – save James Marsden's Cyclops, sadly – something meaningful to do.

Jackman's Wolverine is again very much the focal point, and the hugely charismatic Aussie conveys Logan's growing anger and confusion about his shadowy past. Yet he's ably supported by the likes of Famke Janssen, subtly portraying Jean's struggle with her burgeoning powers, Rebecca Romijn-Stamos, having all sorts of fun in a beefed-up role as Mystique, and the old stagers McKellen and Stewart. And the newcomers don't disappoint, either. Aaron Stanford is all rebellious chic as the tormented, torn Pyro; Brian Cox's Stryker is so nefarious that he enables the audience to temporarily sympathise with Ian McKellen's Magneto; and Cumming's Nightcrawler is a delight.

X2 is also possessed of an emotional complexity that won't surprise comics fans, but will delight connoisseurs of the summer blockbuster. This film wears its heart on its sleeve, be it Wolverine's anguished search for his past (which kicks off with a chilling confrontation with his 'creator', the evil Stryker; and which takes in a savage scrap with Kelly Hu's similarly-clawed Lady Deathstrike), the poignant sequence in which Iceman 'comes out' to his family, or Magneto's corrupting influence upon the X-Men. The plot, in which hatred of a minority group threatens to spark a global war, is frighteningly topical and Singer doesn't flinch from showing that resolution often comes at a bitter price – albeit one which paves the way for a pleasingly inevitable *X3*.

Yet it's not all FX-augmented naval-gazing. Though it does get very dark, *X2* is unashamedly entertaining, with crowd-pleasing moments for geeks (the appearance of metal-skinned muscle man Colossus in full armoured form should benefit upholsterers everywhere) and non-geeks (a Nightcrawler-led mid-air rescue is exhilarating) alike. There's also a very welcome sly sense of humour, courtesy of a fine script by relative newcomers Mike Dougherty and Dan Harris, who manage to balance multiple storylines while maintaining continuity from the first movie.

There are problems – the third act sags a little under the sheer weight of storylines; while some of the expositional dialogue is a little heavy. However, this thought-provoking, scintillating and stylish flick has opened the summer of superheroes in fine style. *The Matrix Reloaded* may have better effects and *Hulk* may be more eye-catching, but as an overall package, *X2* is going to be hard to top. ★★★★ **CH**

XALA (1975)

Starring: *Thierno Leye (El Hadj Abdoukader Beye), Makhouredia Gueye (Minister Kebe), Mirian Niang (Rama), Illiamane Sagna (Modu), Seune Sambe (Adja Assatu)*
Director: *Ousmane Sembène*
Screenwriter: *Ousmane Sembène based on his own novel*
121/121 mins./Comedy/Drama/Senegal

In order to mark his appointment to the Chamber of Commerce, Senegalese bourgeois El Hadj Abdoukader Beye decides to take a third wife. But, having over-indulged at the ostentatious reception, he fails to consummate the union and his world collapses around him as he devotes himself to finding a cure for his impotence.

Having explored European racism in *The Black Girl*, African bureaucracy in *The Money Order* and imperial suppression in *Emitai*, Soviet-trained Senegalese director Ousmane Sembène turned to his own 1974 novel for this satirical exposé of Africa's post-colonial élite. Switching from the realism of what he called the 'cinema of placards', Sembène adopted an allegorical symbolism that was designed to show people the conditions under which they existed and suggest that the only way to escape from them was to take positive action.

Sembène scarcely veiled the contempt with which he depicted the leaders who betrayed their nation by driving out the French and promptly replacing their institutions with identical indigenous variations. They're all shown in Western suits and speaking French in private while pandering to the masses in the local Wolof dialect. They exploit their brothers by employing them as chauffeurs, whom they order to wash their white Mercedes in imported mineral water. And one even refuses to holiday in Spain any more because it's become so overrun with blacks.

Thus, El Hadj is not the guiltiest man in Dakar. But he revels in the luxury and status that his wealth has brought him and his disdain for the cripples and beggars whom he wanted removed from the streets results in the xala or curse that brings him so low that he has to subject himself to their scornful spittle in order to be shriven.

But, this is not just a treatise on post-colonialism and class. Sembène boldly uses his female characters to comment on Senegal's chauvinist patriarchy. El Hadj's first wife, Adja, evokes the pre-colonial past with her subservience and traditional dress, while Oumi, with her wigs, shades and plunging necklines, represents the imperial era, and Ngone symbolises the trophy rewards of independence. But his daughter, Rama, stands for the idealised future, with her preference for Wolof and local fashions being complemented by her moped and university education.

The populace certainly responded to Sembène's message, as *Xala* broke box-office records, while also being shown free to schoolchildren and villagers around Senegal. ★★★★★ **DP**

XANADU (1980)

Starring: *Olivia Newton-John (Kira), Gene Kelly (Danny McGuire), Michael Beck (Sonny Malone), James Sloyan (Simpson), Dimitra Arliss (Helena), Katie Hanley (Sandra), Fred McCarren (Richie), Ren Woods (Jo)*
Director: *Robert Greenwald*
Screenwriters: *Richard Christian Danus, Marc Reid Rubel*
PG/93 mins./Musical/USA

Awards – *Razzie Awards – Worst Director*

Album cover designer Sonny Malone and clarinettist-turned-construction tycoon Danny McGuire discover that they have both fallen for the same Muse, Kira – Danny back in the wartime Swing era and Sonny in the disco present.

Fresh from co-starring in *Grease*, the liveliest musical of the post-studio era and the genre's biggest ever commercial success, Olivia Newton-John made the mistake of trying to float a conceit that had already confounded Fred Astaire in *Yolanda And The Thief*, Rita Hayworth in *Down To Earth* and Ava Gardner in *One Touch Of Venus*.

Not even the presence of Gene Kelly, who was archly named after his character in *Cover Girl*, could elevate the stubbornly earthbound proceedings – not that he was allowed to, however. He got to rollerskate, as he had done in *It's Always Fair Weather*, and his duet with Olivia on 'Whenever You're Away From Me' is the film's highlight. But this was an Olivia Newton-John vehicle and Kelly was simply there to make her look good and lure the nostalgic away from their TV sets.

Of necessity, the plotline was risible. But Newton-John totally lacked the screen presence to carry off such an ethereal role. Moreover, her dramatic shortcomings were cruelly exacerbated by the inanimation of Michael Beck, as she was too often left to carry their scenes on her own. She made the most of tunes like ex-husband John Farrar's 'Magic' and the Jeff Lynne title theme (both of which charted well), but the inability to dance that had been disguised as best as possible in *Grease* was exposed by Kenny Ortega choreography that fell far short of the zeitgeist chic he managed to achieve in *Saturday Night Fever*.

However, *Xanadu's* gravest fault was its cynical resort to the Golden Age in a bid to appeal to the widest possible constituency. There was no real affection for the MGM style here, just an exploitative MTV-era pastiche that plugged gaps that the dismal pop of the late 1970s couldn't hope to fill.

Olivia met future husband Matt Lattanzi during the shoot (he played the younger Kelly). But she failed to learn anything from the film's failure and, three years later, played another heavenly messenger in her calamitous reunion with John Travolta, *Two Of A Kind*. ★★ **DP**

THE X-FILES (1998)

Starring: *David Duchovny (Agent Mulder), Gillian Anderson (Agent Scully), John Neville (Well-Manicured Man), William B. Davis (Cigarette-Smoking Man), Martin Landau (Dr. Alvin Kurtzwell)*
Director: *Rob Bowman*
Screenwriter: *Chris Carter, from a story by Carter, Frank Spotnitz*
15/117 mins./Sci-fi/Thriller/USA

Mulder and Scully are two FBI operatives who used to investigate the paranormal for the agency. When their bureau is shut down, they resume normal duties but are soon dragged back into stranger goings-on.

After five years and five series of televisual success which established *The X-Files* as a 'cult' phenomenon second only to *Star Trek*, it was all but inevitable that the series would eventually transfer to the big screen. Increasing TV ratings, shelves full of books and magazines, and – perhaps more significantly – extended length sell-through video releases have seen to that. But whereas those feature-length tapes have merely seen two or three episodes strung together as bridges between series, this movie had to be more, so much more.

Series creator Chris Carter and his preferred director Rob Bowman rose to the challenge and made a movie that disappointed few fans and, while not exactly standing as a landmark in cinema history, at least surprised the sceptics and give them an entertaining clue as to what all the fuss has been about.

Those anticipating an impenetrable plot after five years of back story should fear not – subtitles for the hard of paranormal are supplied. Wisely, Carter's screenplay has gone for intrigue and set pieces, all laced with enough in-jokes to keep the faithful happy without alienating the first-timers. And so proceedings begin in the frozen wastes of North Texas ... 35,000 years BC ... and a first human contact with an extra-terrestrial black plague. Fast forward to Texas today and its rediscovery (cue brief appearance for *Sling Blade* youngster Lucas Black). Step sideways for the first sight of agents Mulder and Scully, now on regular FBI duties after their special X-Files bureau has been closed, investigating a terrorist bomb scare. A sizeable bang and four corpses later, Mulder goes for an alleyway pee – against an *Independence Day* poster, hoho! – and meets Kurtzweil (an excellently tongue-in-cheek Landau) who tells him enough to warrant a two-hour movie. And that's all Empire is telling. The truth, however, is in there ...

While potentially apocalyptic, that truth is not exactly a jaw-dropping surprise and so instead the movie leans more on action boosted by a dozen or so walk-on characters familiar from the small screen. More importantly, it allows the simmering sexual chemistry between Mulder and Scully to come to the boil. Their relationship transfers well to the big screen – although it is difficult to tell whether their first scene's ludicrously contrived dialogue was written as a gag or a genuine piece of exposition.

Having established a global scenario, at times the film forsakes it for more of TV's Maglite beams, swooping helicopters and furtive glances between the leads. There's a horribly naff (but mercifully short) 'London, England' interlude and, midway, the style overtakes the content in a too easily resolved desert-based chase. But throughout, Bowman and director of photography Ward Russell see to it that that style looks good and the locations – especially the breathtaking snowy wastes of Antarctica – are frequently impressive. The shadowy syndicate with its 50-year plot, the mysterious tents and cornfields and the effects-fest ending (*Alien Resurrection* meets *ID4*) all add up to so much more than a TV show getting ideas above its station.

The X-Files can stand proud as a genuine movie with a beginning, a middle and an end, two charismatic leads and a franchise ahead of it. An impressive cinematic makeover that belies its TV roots. *X-Files* fans add one star to the following and trust no one who tells you any different. **★★★ NJ**

X-MEN (2000)

Starring: *Hugh Jackman (Logan/Wolverine), Patrick Stewart (Professor Charles Xavier), Ian McKellen (Eric Lensherr/Magneto), Famke Janssen (Jean Grey), James Marsden (Scott Summers/Cyclops), Halle Berry (Ororo Munroe/Storm), Anna Paquin (Rogue), Rebecca Romijn (Mystique)*
Director: *Bryan Singer*
Screenwriter: *David Hayter, from a story by Tom DeSanto, Bryan Singer, from characters by Stan Lee, Jack Kirby*
12/104 mins./Action/Adventure/Fantasy/USA
Awards – *Empire Awards – Best Director*

A group of super-powered humans must choose whether to fight for the good of mankind alongside Professor Xavier or to take over the planet with the power hungry Magneto.

With this kind of movie the whispering starts early, fervid fans (mis)reporting every little leak. For those net-heads who stopped to listen, the early buzz on Bryan Singer's adaptation of Marvel's bestselling comic imprint was poor. The director wasn't a fan (true). The production was mired in re-shoots (which blockbuster isn't?). And the final cut was strangely short (true again, although 90 minutes used to be considered an adequate running time for a movie).

Thankfully, it's time for the rumour-mongers to gracefully retire. The finished film is in, and – whisper it – it's not bad. Better than that, *X-Men* is actually pretty darn good.

The key decision in comic book adaptations amounts to this: how seriously do you treat your source material? It is possible to make a fun flick by employing an irreverent touch, but you only have to contrast Tim Burton's dark knight with Adam West's camp avenger to appreciate the difference.

Like Burton's *Batman* (1989), the X-Men go deep (they 'do' dark, too). A 60s comic born out of the civil rights movement, themes of prejudice and assimilation have always underpinned the cartoon adventures of these superpowerful mutants. Indeed, it's long been noted that the leading protagonists – teacher and telepath Professor Xavier and his nemesis Magneto – are basically Martin Luther King and Malcolm X. Appreciating the strength of this claim, Singer's first ace is to secure RSC alums Patrick Stewart and Ian McKellen as the two rivals, thereby lending the whole project some much-needed gravitas.

Singer's other trump card is Hugh Jackman's Wolverine. Deeply unimpressed and permanently grouchy, the new recruit to Xavier's superhero team is the perfect guide to the X-Men universe.

Whenever the script threatens to get silly, he will puncture the moment with a quip as sharp as his talons. He's also really, really hard. Between Jackman's physical presence and McKellen and Stewart's verbal jousting, it's fair to say that none of the other X-Men get much of a look in. Yet, perhaps that's just as well; if Singer and the only credited screenwriter, David Hayter, had paused to introduce back story on all ten characters, we might never have got started.

As it stands, the plot is breathtakingly simple – it amounts to little more than a line of dialogue, spoken about half-way through the film (to paraphrase: 'That's what Magneto's up to. We'd better stop him.'). Up until this point, everything is set-up; everything that follows qualifies as climax. Perhaps there was some fat on the original script, perhaps he even shot some rubbish, but Singer's 90-minute cut has excised all of it. What remains is lean, fast and over far too soon.

Tagline
Join the evolution.

Critically, Singer gets the details right. The production design is striking, the key special effects impressive and the set-pieces satisfying. And if the climax leaves you feeling short-changed, then all the more reason to watch the sequel. **★★★★ CK**

X-MEN: THE LAST STAND (2006)

Starring: *Hugh Jackman (Logan/Wolverine), Ian McKellen (Eric Lensherr/Magneto), Halle Berry (Ororo Munroe/Storm), Famke Janssen (Dr. Jean Grey/Phoenix), Patrick Stewart (Professor Charles Xavier), James Marsden (Scott Summers/Cyclops), Anna Paquin (Marie/Rogue)*
Director: *Brett Ratner*
Screenwriters: *Simon Kinberg, Zak Penn*
12A/104 mins./Fantasy/USA

X

Femme Fatales — TOP 10

1. Phyllis Dietrichson (Barbara Stanwyck), *Double Indemnity*
2. Matty Walker (Kathleen Turner), *Body Heat*
3. Brigid O'Shaughnessy (Mary Astor), *The Maltese Falcon*
4. Jessica Rabbit (Kathleen Turner, voice), *Who Framed Roger Rabbit?*
5. Catherine Tramell (Sharon Stone), *Basic Instinct*
6. Gilda (Rita Hayworth), *Gilda*
7. Cora Papadakis (Jessica Lange), *The Postman Always Rings Twice*
8. Rachael (Sean Young), *Blade Runner*
9. Xenia Onatopp (Famke Janssen), *GoldenEye*
10. Laura Dannon (Nora Zehetner), *Brick*

Mutants are on the verge of x-tinction, it seems, when US business Worthington Industries discovers a cure for mutation. This scientific breakthrough complicates and intensifies the battle – both physical and ideological – between Professor X's integration-friendly X-Men and the human-hating muties lead by Magneto ...

One reason why action franchises are so prone to ultimate failure is because it's so easy for them to collapse under their own weight. Each new installment feels it has to outdo the last, delivering bigger set pieces and cramming in more characters while such piffles as structure, pace, dialogue and all-round coherence are thrown to the wind. This was certainly true of the pre-Begins Batmans and the Christopher Reeve Supermans. But X-Men, like its fellow thoroughbred Marvel stablemate Spider-Man, has managed to withstand the added strain.

X2 was, above all, a masterful juggling/balancing act on the part of Bryan Singer. He expanded the X-universe while simultaneously taking us deeper into the characters - from frontline heroes like Wolverine down to supporting players like Iceman (Sean Ashmore) and Pyro (Aaron Stanford). Well, Brett Ratner's stepped onto the tightrope Singer vacated, and Fox/Marvel have chucked him even more juggling balls than Singer had to deal with. So we have the central cast's tussling with the whole 'cure' issue and their renewed mutant-versus-mutant battle, plus the drama surrounding now-schizo 'Grade Five' uber-mutant Jean Grey's return from her watery supposed-grave, plus all those little dramas that concern the teenie team, from Rogue's dilemma over whether or not to take the cure, to Iceman's relationship with Kitty Pryde.

Ratner's simply not gifted with Singer's versatility, and X3 lacks the sharp focus of its predecessor, as if unclear what exactly it should be doing when not delivering a set piece. The script, too, lacks the polish of Singer's second X, and even the esteemed Ian McKellen has trouble delivering a few of his clunkier lines with conviction. Meanwhile, Vinnie Jones as towering powerhouse Juggernaut is just wrong, wrong, WRONG.

However, two things rescue this so-called 'Last Stand': first, its shameless pandering to the fanboys. They're tossed plenty of little treats, including a glimpse (finally) inside the X-mansions Danger Room and the introduction of various new muties like Beast (Kelsey Grammar - excellent), Angel (Ben Foster - forgettable) and Leech (Cameron Bright). Oh, and if the words 'fastball special' mean anything to you, then rest assured Ratner's been thinking of you during the action scenes.

Which brings us to X3's second saving grace - those aforementioned set pieces. This is where Ratner gets it totally right. Whether it's that big show-off Magneto flying the Golden Gate bridge to Alcatraz, Wolverine and Beast going feral on a bunch of baddie mutants or Jean Grey telekinetically reducing people and buildings to their constituent atoms (nasty), there's enough smash-bang fun and CG-savvy here to justify the cost of your seat. Just don't go expecting it to get under your skin the way X2 did. ★★★ **DJ**

Movie Trivia: *X-Men The Last Stand*

Josh Holloway, Sawyer on *Lost*, turned down the role of Gambit as the characters were too similar. For the Golden Gate showdown, a 2,500ft replica was built of the bridge.

XXX (2002)

Starring: *Vin Diesel (Xander Cage), Asia Argento (Yelena), Marton Csokas (Yorgi), Samuel L. Jackson (Agent Augustus Gibbons), Michael Roof (Agent Toby Lee Shavers)*
Director: *Rob Cohen*
Screenwriter: *Rich Wilkes*
12A/15 (director's cut)/124 mins./132 mins. (director's cut)/Action/Adventure/USA

Having run out of suitable candidates for the American secret service, Agent Gibbons forcibly recruits extreme sports star Xander Cage, whom he threatens with prison if he doesn't co-operate. Cage is plunged into a Prague-set terrorist plot.

Rumour has it that a couple of years previous to this film, Vin Diesel was seen swanning around the Sundance Film Festival informing anyone who would listen – and given his physique, that was most people – that within a couple of years he would be a huge star.

For a while he seemed like he was right on the money, though quite how he did it remains a mystery. Roles in a low-budget sci-fi flick (*Pitch Black*) and then sleeper, *The Fast And The Furious*, weren't on the face of it any justification for the $20 million pay cheques he was demanding – and apparently getting.

xXx was supposedly the movie that would seal the deal and justify the hype.

It almost did – he's certainly the best thing in it – but it's a pity that he didn't choose a movie written and directed with a little more care for his megastar coming-out party.

Essentially *xXx* is James Bond stripped down for a generation that prefers thrash metal to John Barry. The film declares its revisionist intent in its first minutes by having a weak-chinned, tuxedo-clad 007-lookalike humiliatingly shot and borne aloft by an audience of writhing clubbers.

Enter Diesel, who couldn't be more unlike the Brit superspy. While Bond is a suave old Etonian naval commander, Cage is an anarchist extreme sports star with a penchant for cringeworthy anti-authoritarian lectures to webcam.

Tagline

A new breed of secret agent.

Bond is in it for 'Queen and Country', while Cage is blackmailed into it with the threat of jail. (His personal philosophy is deftly illustrated in one of the movie's few witty lines: 'If you're going to send someone to save the world – make sure they like it the way it is.') And while Bond is an inveterate womaniser, Diesel looks unaccountably uncomfortable during his on-screen clinches with Asia Argento – at one point his expression suggests that he's being invited to lock lips with the wrong end of Bella Emberg rather than one of Euro-cinema's more acknowledged hotties.

But the point of Diesel is not his acting ability but his sheer physical presence, and Rob Cohen puts it to reasonably good use in a couple of fantastically orchestrated action scenes – an early shot of Diesel 'surfing' a car off a bridge delivers the goods, as does a motorcycle chase in which Cohen brilliantly uses digital matting to keep his actors' faces in full view during stunt sequences that only a few years ago would have required the usual fudged medium and long-shots.

But the director unfortunately soon returns to the slightly inept, graceless style of filmmaking that typified *Dragonheart* and *The Skulls*. There's little of the goofy brio of *The Fast And The Furious* and screenwriter Rich Wilkes' screenplay threatens to run out of steam before delivering a denouement as damp as most of the movie's Prague locations are these days (and what the hell the bad guy has in mind constructing a submarine in landlocked Prague is never adequately explained).

All of which leaves us in the end with Vin, on whose ox-like shoulders the movie ends up almost completely resting. As a leading player, he just doesn't cut it, (by the lacklustre sequel *xXx: The Next Level*, he jumped ship to be replaced by Ice Cube), and those $20 million pay cheques didn't hang around for long either. ★★★ **AS**

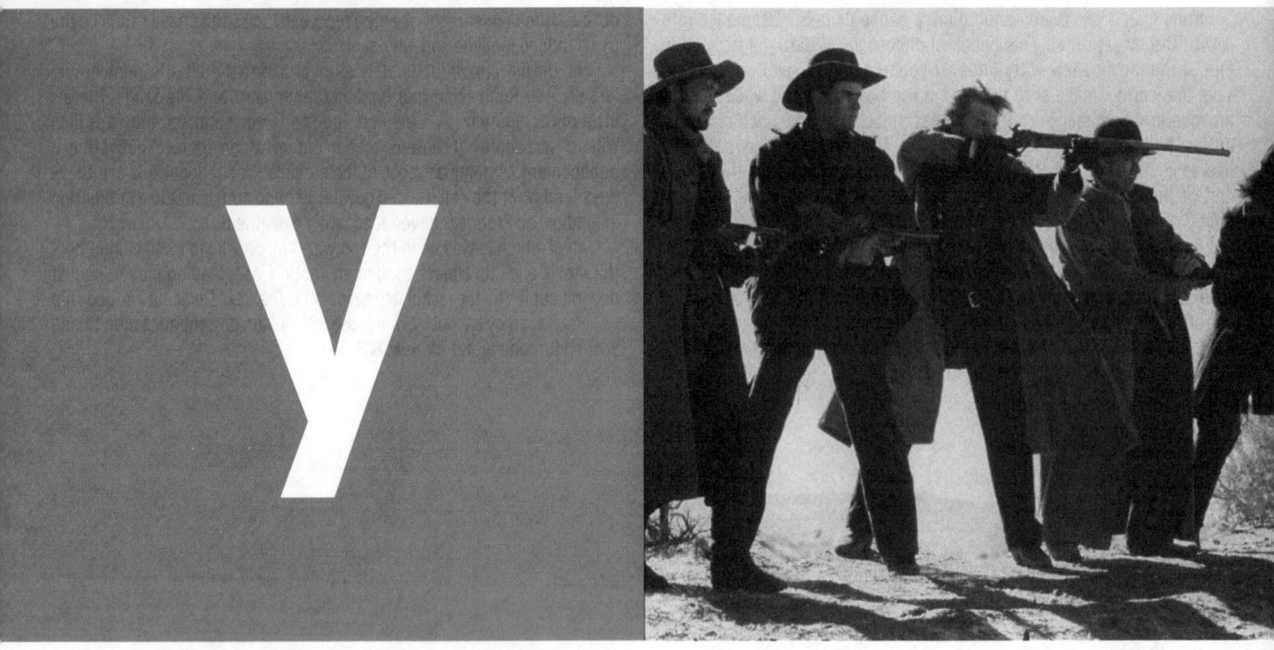

➂ THE YEAR OF LIVING DANGEROUSLY (1982)

Starring: *Mel Gibson (Guy Hamilton), Sigourney Weaver (Jill Bryant), Linda Hunt (Billy Kwan), Michael Murphy (Pete Curtis), Bill Kerr (Colonel Henderson)*
Director: *Peter Weir*
Screenwriters: *Peter Weir, David Williamson, C. J. Koch based on the novel by Koch*
PG/117 mins./Drama/Australia

Awards: *Academy Awards – Best Supporting Actress (Linda Hunt)*

Taking his first assignment, foreign correspondent Guy Hamilton lands in an Indonesia on the verge of revolution. Utilising the contacts of his photographer, Billy Kwan, who can bring him close to the action, as well as his affair with a female diplomat, he becomes the hottest reporter around. But the crises will bring him to a point where he can no longer simply report the news.

After their very productive relationship on *Gallipoli*, director Peter Weir and actor Mel Gibson reunited for this high-minded and atmospheric study of a reporter finding what he needs, a story, and what he hadn't foreseen, his own soul. With its echoes of Graham Greene's *The Quiet American*, the script is inevitably preachy and Weir's camera glowers over the injustices of President Sukarno's failing regime in late 1965, but the performances are strong and the drama gripping.

Gibson gives urgent life to this Aussie correspondent determined to make his mark, also embarking on a torrid affair with Sigourney Weaver's frosty diplomat. His pursuit of a story is at first a pursuit of personal glory as he manipulates those around him, but the country will come to wake him up. All about him the sweaty tangle of a nation in turmoil is pungently brought to life by Weir who shot in the Philippines. Yet, the centre of the film, its conscience and poetic voice, is Linda Hunt's half-Chinese dwarf photographer who freely quotes from Tolstoy and her people's need for some kind of salvation. It's a captivating, dynamic and unusual performance that deservedly won Hunt an Oscar working, as she was, even against gender.

Weir's contentions about the events that fermented in Indonesia in the mid-60s were called into question upon the film's release, and he had argued furiously with Christopher Koch upon whose novel the film was based, fixing on the now discounted contention that the CIA were behind the coup. But controversy aside, the film has weathered well, especially in Gibson's moving relationship with Hunt, the emergence of a man who has contended with politics and morality, but was only now engaging with the reality of people's lives. *The Killing Fields* may have made similar points about charging front-line journalists with nobility to greater acclaim, but this remains a powerful evocation of a nation's rage. ★★★★
IN

Tagline
A love caught in the fire of revolution.

➂ THE YEAR OF THE DRAGON (1985)

Starring: *Mickey Rourke (Stanley White), John Lone (Joey Tai), Araine (Tracy Tzu), Leonard Termo (Angelo Rizzo), Raymond J. Barry (Louis Bukowski)*
Director: *Michael Cimino*
Screenwriters: *Oliver Stone, Michael Cimino*
18/134 mins./Crime/USA

With a new, brutal boss heading up the Chinese mafia, tough-minded New York cop Stanley White is put in charge of Chinatown, a man left racist by his treatment in Vietnam. As both are fully willing to break their own codes of honour, a bloody clash awaits them.

His first film after the debacle of *Heaven's Gate* finds Michael Cimino bullish and clumsy. If that long, artful Western was precision as madness, this thriller charting the brute techniques of a racist cop is full of damnable self-righteousness and tough guy action. The plot, conceived and written by a young Oliver Stone, is restlessly complicated, but can be boiled down to a trite extension of the 'Nam fallout of *The Deer Hunter* – veteran soldier turned cop keeps his personal war going by taking on a Chinese gangster on his own turf. Mickey Rourke's decorated former hero is so conditioned in his bigotry he can't locate the difference between the Vietnamese and the Triad gang led by John Lone's Chinese murderer. White, mainly through an unconvincing relationship with Ariane's reporter, regales us with dull spiels of self-justification.

The film seethes with racism, so much so it is hard to decipher where Cimino and Stone are reflecting upon White's state of mind, and where they have spilled over into enrolling themselves by association. Their film has a mucky, murky, unclean feel, which assists in the building of tension, fired by Stone's terse dialogue, but still leaves a bad taste. Cimino gives it a thick, dense look, picked out by smears of neon. Everything from the style to the casting feels grubby and worn.

Not that Rourke or Lone don't fulfil their part of the deal, they are charismatic in opposite ways: one full of fire, the other ice. Rourke, especially, serves up that variety of smouldering anger all his own. It is also often forgotten how good Cimino is with an action sequence, hitting a Peckinpah-like frenzy with a shoot-out between White and two punkettes in a devastated Chinese restaurant, and the film takes on the lines of a Western showdown as White stalks his foe to New York's dockside. For all its sound and fury, it's messages on the chaos of race relations in America remain lumpy and leering. ★★ **IN**

YEELEN (1987)

Starring: *Issiaka Kane (Niankoro), Aoua Sangare (Attou), Niamanto Sanogo (Soma), Balla Moussa Keita (Rouma Boll), Soumba Traore (Mah), Ismailia Sarr (Boffing).*
Director: *Souleymane Cissé*
Screenwriter: *Souleymane Cissé*
PG/105 mins./Fantasy-Drama Mali/Burkina/Faso/France/West Germany

Threatened with death by his evil sorceror father, Soma, Bambara warrior Niankoro is urged by his doting mother to visit his father's twin, Djigui Diarra's, in order to acquire the wisdom and power that he will require for a supernatural showdown.

Set some time in the indeterminate past and derived from the Bambara people's ancient oral tradition, this is a highly stylised retelling of the classic Peulh or father-son feud story. Although strewn with such local concepts as Kôré (the speed of the human spirit) and Koma (the incarnation of celestial wisdom), it's also very much an Oedipal odyssey, in which a son abandoned at birth by his father is imperilled by the older man when he realises that the youth's maturing prowess will inevitably come to threaten his status. Reinforcing this sexuo-psychological link is the fact that Niankoro's doting mother urges the boy to consult his uncle about the best way of eliminating the patriarchal threat.

Yet, despite this universality, Cissé, who had trained in Moscow, was keen to break with the ethnographic approach that most European filmmakers took to African subjects. Thus, the film makes few concessions to non-African audiences, with either its enigmatic storytelling style or the symbolism of the characters and their situations.

Yet, notwithstanding its difficulties, there is clearly more imagination at work in this visionary study of light, fire, tradition, ritual, love and the landscape than any number of Hollywood fantasy features – which is all the more remarkable considering that Cissé struggled along on a meagre budget that was further strained by the death of the actor playing Soma and the need for retakes.

It's also more optimistic than many African films of the same period, as its celebration of the cycle of life and death suggests that we will all return to the brilliant innocence of our birth when we are reborn at the end of our days – just as the dawn restores the power removed from the Earth at sunset.

This last impression doubtlessly inspired one critic to dub Yeelen 'Africa's *2001*' – although the same review also recognised its Edenic idealism and compared it to 'science-fiction filmed by Louis Lumière'. Its reputation as 'the most beautifully photographed African film ever' was further bolstered by the Special Jury Prize at Cannes. But African cinema has all-too-rarely since attempted anything as ambitious since. ★★★★ **DP**

YELLOW SUBMARINE (1968)

Starring: as themselves: *John Lennon, Paul McCartney, George Harrison, Ringo Starr, the voices of: John Clive (John), Peter Batten (George), Paul Angelis (Ringo/Chief Blue Meanie), Dick Emery (Lord Mayor/Nowhere Man/Max), Lance Percival (Old Man)*
Director: *George Dunning*
Screenwriters: *Lee Minoff, Al Brodax, Erich Segal, Jack Mendelsohn, from the story by Lee Minoff, song by John Lennon, Paul McCartney*
U/86 mins./Animated/Music/Fantasy/Comedy/UK

John, Paul, George and Ringo travel to Pepperland to save the residents from music-hating Blue Meanies.

Probably the most fondly remembered of the four Beatles movies, *Yellow Submarine's* hallucinogenic, dazzling animation still looks pretty good three decades on, even away from the acid-enhanced glare of 1968. Now, this spruced-up version of the Fab Four's (literal) trip through a psychedelic universe in a big old sub works best as a reminder of just how influential the Beatles were.

The perfunctory story has John, Paul, George and Ringo attempting to rescue Pepperland, a music-loving community, from an invading army of Blue Meanies whose hatred of all things melodic is evident in their turning all the inhabitants to stone. They travel there in the titular U-boat, having one weird encounter after another: a universe filled entirely with holes, a timewarp that speeds up the ageing process, and so on. Plus, of course, there's a string of tuneful set pieces, from 'Nowhere Man' and 'Lucy In The Sky With Diamonds' to the title track.

None of it makes a great deal of sense and the plot loses steam after the first hour before rallying for the elaborate finale. But *Yellow Submarine's* deliriously silly humour, off the wall charm and wildly imaginative imagery (it might be billed as a family film, but there's some seriously scary stuff here) paper over any cracks in the storyline and most of the occasionally wayward vocal impersonations.

Perhaps most importantly, though, it paints a vivid and very welcome picture of a pop group actually having fun with their craft – which becomes evident when the real Beatles pop up at the end. A garish, gorgeous example of pop art at its finest, *Yellow Submarine's* reappearance should give a whole new generation a chance to discover the legends. ★★★★ **CW**

LES YEUX SANS VISAGE (EYES WITHOUT A FACE) (1959)

Starring: *Pierre Brasseur (Doctor Genessier), Alida Valli (Louise), Juliette Mayneil (Edna), Edith Scob (Christiane Genessier), François Guerin (Jacques Vernon), Alexandre Rignault (Inspector Parot)*
Director: *Georges Franju*
Screenwriter: *Pierre Gascar, from the novel by Jean Redon, adapted by Redon, Gascar, Pierre Boileau, Thomas Narcejac, Claude Sautet*
18/88 mins./Horror/France/Italy

Mad plastic surgeon Dr Genessier kidnaps young Parisiennes to serve as facial skin donors in a series of operations designed to restore the beauty of his daughter, who has been disfigured in a car accident.

A poetic horror classic, often imitated but never equalled. In 1959, Georges Franju was best known for documentaries about the horrors of the abattoir business (*Le Sang Des Bêtes*) and the early days of the cinema (Le Grand Méliès). *Eyes Without a Face* (known in heathen America as *Horror Chamber Of Dr Faustus*), his second feature film, is a strange combination of his earlier themes. Based on a novel by the Boileau-Narcejac team who had provided sources for Clouzot's *Les Diaboliques* and Hitchcock's *Vertigo*, this is at once an old-fashioned thriller shot through with the kind of surrealism that endeared French silent serials to the *avant-garde* and a forward-looking horror movie with an emphasis on the clinically gruesome.

Though a traditionally plodding police investigation explains it all, Franju's approach is to string together a series of extraordinary moments, alternating sheer sadism with a curious tenderness, in an attempt to create atmosphere rather than plot.

The victims are stalked by Genessier's raincoated assistant (a nastily-butch Alida Valli), a predator in a 2CV accompanied by an eerie Maurice Jarre waltz, and are thrown to a pack of vicious dogs when their usefulness is at an end. The operations (we actually see a face lifted off in glorious black and white) are gruesome and there is a dollop of *Grand Guignol* in the mix of mad dogs and mad docs.

Scob's mutilated angel is an amazing presence, floating through the film with birdlike grace in a long housecoat and an eerily blank mask.

Sharp as a scalpel, soft as a caress: a weird masterwork. ★★★★ **KN**

⊙ YOJIMBO (1961)

Starring: *Toshiro Mifune (Sanjuro Kuwabatake), Eijiro Tono (Gonji), Seizaburo Kawazu (Seibei), Isuzu Yamada (Orin), Hiroshi Tachikawa (Yochiro)*
Director: *Akira Kurosawa*
Screenwriters: *Akira Kurosawa, Ryuzo Kikushima, Hideo Oguni, from the novel Red Harvest by Dashiell Hammett*
PG/105 mins./Action/Drama/Japan

Yojimbo, a wandering samurai enters a rural town in nineteenth century Japan. After learning from the innkeeper that the town is divided between two gangsters, he plays one side off against the other.

To many, Akira Kurosawa's reputation rests on his samurai epics. But he was, in fact, a supremely versatile director. He started out in martial arts before tackling period dramas, social realism, hard-boiled crime and literary adaptations. But, before Yojimbo, he had never attempted a comedy. At first glance, this tale of a microcosmic civil war may not seem all that amusing.

Its setting is bleak, its scenario pitiful and its violence shocking. But set it against the films it influenced – including Sergio Leone's *Dollars* trilogy and the yakuza thrillers of Takeshi Kitano – and it's clear what kind of comedy we're dealing with. Since the discovery of his 1950 masterpiece, *Rashomon*, Kurosawa had been considered Japan's most Western film-maker. Indeed, such was his accessibility that John Sturges had aleady remade *Seven Samurai* as *The Magnificent Seven* while Kurosawa was developing *Yojimbo*. Yet the most distinctive influence on his visual style and his handling of storyline and theme was John Ford. Kurosawa even used Toshiro Mifune in much the same way that Ford used John Wayne.

It's ironic, therefore, that the film which brought Kurosawa his greatest domestic success owed so little to his mentor. *Yojimbo* is intimate to the point of claustrophobia. Its wit is wry, its characters flawed and its world-view uncompromisingly cynical. There was no room, therefore, for the grand sweep, broad humour and manly sentimentality that characterised Ford's work. Instead, Kurosawa drew on two of the new breed of Hollywood westerns, *High Noon* (1952) and *Shane* (1953), to produce what is essentially a psychological samurai flick. An itinerant swordslinger, Sanjuro (Mifune) goes where fate sends him. Following the promptings of a stick cast upon the wind, he enters a fortified village where the first thing he sees is a dog padding down the main street with a human hand in its mouth. The tone is set and it never wavers. Although he arrives like Shane (and, like Shane, will later deliver a worthy couple and their son from tyranny), Sanjuro's task is more like that facing Marshal Will Kane in *High Noon*. Courted by both sides in a feud between a silk merchant and his sake counterpart, he will be forced to risk his own life to save unworthy citizens from a crisis they've largely brought on themselves. But, unlike Kane, Sanjuro's motives are less than pure. No longer owing allegiance to a master, he's able to select from the bushido code at his convenience. Thus, he'll fight for money but he'll never take more than his due. Still, his amorality is nothing compared to the grotesque failings of his adversaries, several of whom have physical abnormalities to match their poisonous personalities.

Kurosawa had frequently explored the notion that the world was an irredeemable place. But *Yojimbo's* comic detachment enabled him to despair of the villagers without judging them. What he's condemning is the capitalist impulse that causes them to stake (and lose) everything in order to gain that little bit more. It may seem ironic that a wandering warrior should abjure a life of adventure. But his advice to the farmer's son he spares at the end of the climactic slaughter – to stay at home and make the best of what you've got – is the message Kurosawa hoped to impart to restlessly rebellious Japanese youth by slipping it in under the violence they'd paid to see.

Compared to latter genre outings like *Shogun Assassin* (1980), the bloodshed quotient may seem low. As much a thinker as a fighter, Sanjuro uses his knowledge of human nature to set the rivals against each other, thus decimating their numbers without undue risk to himself. Yet, when he does rouse himself, the ruthless efficiency of his swordsmanship ensures that the short, swift action sequences are utterly devastating. Confronted, early on, with a trio of hired thugs, each keen to show off their tattoos and prison records, he requires just three swiping blows to conquer them – one completely severing an arm, which falls to the ground still clutching its barely unsheathed sword. Thanks to this display of awesome power, Sanjuro will only need to fight once more: at the film's conclusion he mops up the handful of ne'er-do-wells who survive the onslaught that lays waste to the village.

Sanjuro watches from inside a sake barrel where he is recovering from the beating inflicted by the pistol-touting Unosuke for returning a reluctant concubine to her family. How typical that an act of charity should result in brutality. Maybe Kurosawa was admitting, after all, that you have to be bad to be the best. ★★★★★ **DP**

⊙ YOU CAN'T TAKE IT WITH YOU (1938)

Starring: *Jean Arthur (Alice Sycamore), Lionel Barrymore (Martin Vanderhof), James Stewart (Tony Kirby), Edward Arnold (Anthony P. Kirby), Mischa Auer (Kolenkhov), Anne Miller (Essie Carmichael) Spring Bylington (Penny Sycamore)*
Director: *Frank Capra*
Screenwriter: *Robert Riskin, based on the play by George S. Kaufman and Moss Hart*
U/126 mins./Comedy USA

Awards: *Academy Awards – Best Picture, Best Director*

Even though he resents munitions tycoon Anthony Kirby's plans to purchase his land, the head of an eccentric household, Martin Vanderhof, agrees to host a dinner party to facilitate granddaughter Alice Sycamore's courtship with Anthony Kirby, Jr. However, the guests arrive a day early ...

Frank Capra saw George S. Kaufman and Moss Hart's Pulitzer Prize-winning play while in New York to promote *Lost Horizon*. However, Columbia supremo Harry Cohn was less than impressed by Broadway producer Sam

Troy McLure* movies

1. *Leper In The Backfield*
2. *The Verdict Was Mail Fraud*
3. *Locker Room Towel Fight: The Blinding Of Harry Driscoll*
4. *Here Comes The Coastguard*
5. *Preacher With A Shovel*
6. *The President's Neck Is Missing*
7. *The Muppets Go Medieval*
8. *Dial M For Murderousness*
9. *My Darling Beefeater*
10. *Calling All Quakers*

*Legendary B movie star in *The Simpsons*

Harris' asking price and famously declared, 'I wouldn't shell out 200 Gs for the Second Coming!'. But Capra was on such a roll that Cohn paid up and was rewarded with Capra's third Oscar for Best Director and his second for Best Picture.

In its day, this was regarded as a joyous farce about a family whose wealth lay in love, health and the good opinion of its neighbours. Yet, this is a problematic film, from both a dramatic and political perspective.

Although he added mask and toymaker Mr Poppins (Donald Meek) to reinforce the air of whimisicality, Capra made few changes to the original text, as it chimed in so precisely with his perennial theme that money couldn't buy happiness. Yet, while he shifted the emphasis on to Kirby's munitions ambitions (some later claimed as a way of warning about the coming war), Capra adopted a highly naive approach to capitalism throughout this supposedly satirical romp.

Even though he had retired 30 years earlier, Grandpa Vanderhof still lives comfortably in a mansion and, apart from Alice's income from Kirby's coffers, he seems to have no visible means of financial support. So, despite his incessant tirades against the various 'isms' blighting society, one must conclude that he has a self-replenishing source of revenue, which tends to imply investments. Thus, he seems to have a stake in the very world of big business he has urged his shiftless family to reject – yet, when he finds himself in court, he appears reliant on the coppers that the townsfolk can muster.

Such clumsy plotting is compounded by the laziness of the characterisation, which reduces the Vanderhofs to buffoonish acolytes to Alice's Snow White. Her fond embarrassment about her relations and her willingness to marry into money are also conveniently glossed over.

This is often great fun, but it's also archly anarchic and inexpertly populist and prompts one to reconsider the Capra-corn canon with a new cynicism. ★★★ DP

YOU ONLY LIVE ONCE (1937)

Starring: *Sylvia Sidney (Joan Graham), Henry Fonda (Eddie Taylor), Barton MacLane (Stephn Whitney), Jean Dixon (Bonnie Graham), William Gargan (Father Dolan), Warren Hymer (Muggsy) Charles 'Chic' Sale (Ethan), Margaret Hamilton (Hester)*
Director: *Fritz Lang*
Screenwriters: *Gene Towne, Graham Baker based on a story by Towne*
12/86 mins.Crime/USA

Desperate to go straight after three spells in prison, Eddie Taylor finds his past catching up with him after marrying Joan Graham and he's wrongfully arrested for murder. However, he accidentally kills chaplain Fr. Dolan in attempting to escape from Death Row and goes on the run with his pregnant wife.

Several of Fritz Lang's German films had featured an evil genius. But, having been forced to flee Europe by just such a malevolent mastermind, he started to see the state and society at large as the real villains. Thus, he used his earliest Hollywood outings to champion the cause of the Everyman and exploit the latitude invariably granted to outsiders to offer pertinent insights into life in their adopted homelands.

Lang's US debut, *Fury*, had not been an easy experience, however, as he had deeply resented David O. Selznick's typical interference throughout the production. He was keen, therefore, to accept this commission from the easier-going Walter Wanger, although he had only been hired at the insistence of *Fury* star, Sylvia Sidney, who felt that he had had a raw deal at MGM.

Indeed, this was very much her project, as she had conceived the idea of doing a Bonnie and Clyde-style picture after novelist Theodore Dreiser told her about a magazine article he was writing about the notorious twosome. In fact, Sidney had already headlined a similar vehicle, *Mary Burns, Fugitive*, and Wanger even borrowed Paramount staffers Gene Towne and Graham Baker to rework the storyline.

But Lang quickly imparted his own personality upon proceedings and infuriated cinematographer Leon Shamroy with his insistence on repeated retakes to capture the precise image and emotion. Henry Fonda also resented Lang's meticulous approach and his tendency to use his stars as puppets rather than interpreters of character.

But, despite Fonda's claims that Lang required 16 weeks to complete the assignment, he actually took only 46 days (15 of which were devoted to retakes) and came in under budget. However, the film proved to be a commercial disappointment and, in his frustration, Lang blamed Fonda and Wanger for limiting his options.

Yet, Lang had been allowed to espouse a bleak realism that prevented the scenario from becoming overly melodramatic, while sentimentality was largely kept at bay by the cynical edge to Fonda's authentic sense of victimisation. But the emphasis on the futility of life ultimately proved too much for post-Depression audiences. ★★★★ DP

YOU ONLY LIVE TWICE (1967)

Starring: *Sean Connery (James Bond), Mie Hama (Kissy Suzuki), Tetsuro Tamba (Tiger Tanaka), Akiko Wakabayashi (Aki), Donald Pleasence (Ernst Stavro Blofeld), Bernard Lee (M)*
Director: *Lewis Gilbert*
Screenwriters: *Roald Dahl, Harold Jack Bloom based on the novel by Ian Fleming*
PG/117 mins./Spy-/UK-USA

After both US and Soviet space rockets are mysteriously hijacked, each blames the other, leaving the world on the brink of World War III. It takes James Bond to discover the culprit is his great foe Ernst Stavro Blofeld, who has a secret rocket-launching base hidden in a Japanese volcano.

'The firing power inside my crater is enough to annihilate a small army': if *Goldfinger* is held up as Bond perfected both in style and substance, *You Only Live Twice*, scripted with flashes of wild whimsy and spicy cross-cultural teases by Roald Dahl, is the *ne plus ultra* of the series. The one that fully embodies all the flamboyance of cinema's greatest character, and all the scope and brio of his adventures. Sean Connery may have been eying retirement, but he and Bond were by now moulded together, his sleek machismo indelibly imprinted on 007 forever.

Director Lewis Gilbert effortlessly marshals the intricacies of the plot (a nutty plan by SMERSH to ignite a world war), the exotic Japanese locations, and the extravagancies of having hundreds of ninja warriors abseiling into a huge enemy base unfathomably constructed in the belly of an extinct volcano (quite the engineering feat!). Special mention, therefore, should go to designer Ken Adams whose rock-hewn uber-lair, a potty cavernous playground of steel and concrete, has become the industry standard for villainous lairs everywhere.

Even so, the film never runs away with itself, to become some superhero projection. There is salty character work, as ever, between Bond and his superiors; a tender romance with Mie Hama's delightfully named Kissy Suzuki; and an excellent balance between global policing and top notch action (giro-copter Little Nelly defeating swarms of enemy choppers; a giant magnet, hung off of a helicopter is used to pluck an enemy car clean off the road) keep the plot motoring along to the best final act of any Bond movie.

That's before you even consider that pool of ravenous piranha, Donald Pleasence's proto-Dr. Evil performance as pussy-stroking Blofeld, and Bond felling an enemy cohort by firing a dart out of a cigarette. It may not be art, but it is genius. ★★★★★ **IN**

Movie Trivia: *You Only Live Twice*

Charles Gray who played Henderson in *YOLT* later played Blofeld in *Diamonds Are Forever*. Sean Connery's then wife Diane Cilento doubled for Mie Hama and Akika Wakabayashi in the swimming sequences as neither actress could swim. James Bond does not drive a car in the entire film.

YOU'VE GOT MAIL (1998)

Starring: *Meg Ryan (Kathleen Kelly), Tom Hanks (Joe Fox), Greg Kinnear (Frank Navasky), Parker Posey (Patricia Eden), Steve Zahn (George Pappas), Dave Chappelle (Kevin Scanlon)*
Director: *Nora Ephron*
Screenwriters: *Nora Ephron, Delia Ephron, from the film* The Shop Around The Corner *by Samson Raphaelson, from the play Parfumerie by Miklos Laszlo*

Corporate bookshop owner Joe and family friendly book shop owner Kathleen are romantic pen pals, unaware of the other's true identity. When Joe discovers the truth he decides to pursue Kathleen anyway . . . but will she still like him when she finds out the truth?

The third collaboration between Tom Hanks and Meg Ryan – after the forgotten flop of *Joe Versus The Volcano* and the mega success of *Sleepless In Seattle* – restakes their claim to be the monarchy of modern romantic comedy. An update of Ernst Lubitsch's James Stewart-Margaret Sullivan starrer *The Shop Around The Corner* (feuding co-workers are unwitting pen pal lovers) *You've Got Mail* attempts to imbue cold 90s technology with a warm fuzziness reserved for kids and kittens. And, in the face of well worn formula, it works. Kind of.

Echoing the contrivance of *Sleepless*' long distance romance, *You've Got Mail's* premise has a likeable, corny simplicity about it: corporate book shop owner Joe Fox is engaged in an e-mail relationship with Kathleen Kelly, proprietor of traditional, family run children's book store – cue Lubitsch nod – *The Shop Round The Corner*. Using cyberspace monikers – his NY152, hers Shopgirl – the two remain blissfully unaware of each other's real lives: chiefly that both are already in relationships – Joe with power-hungry book editor Patricia (a wasted Posey), Kathleen with egomaniacal columnist Frank and more pertinently that Joe is launching a massive bookstore opposite Kathleen's, potentially wiping out her charming, quaint little emporium.

The plot unravels with NY152 and Shopgirl becoming more emotionally embroiled via e-mail – the film leans heavily on images of the stars typing (never the stuff of great cinema) with Ephron displaying a keen, entertaining ear for the banality that traverses internet chat rooms – while, in the real world, Joe and Kathleen fight a war of attrition.

Unfortunately the development of the lightweight conceit is far too thin to sustain the running time. As ever, Ephron is good on the ammunition deployed in the battle of the sexes – there is an excellent running gag on the importance of *The Godfather* to men and *Pride And Prejudice* to women that has shades of *Sleepless In Seattle*'s *The Dirty Dozen* versus *An Affair To Remember* debate – yet the gags never really deliver the punch of the truly memorable. Moreover, the writing is let down by Ephron's broad, lazy direction: far too often, there is an overdependence on songs to supply the emotional core of each scene – indeed, the romantic pay-off, when it comes, is shockingly mismanaged.

Yet, the film's theme – the importance of the 'personal' touch, both in cyberspace or running bookstores – is seductively argued and the whole thing is winningly sweet-natured and attractively sentimental. Hanks, by sheer dint of his Tom Hanksness, invests Joe with a likeability and down-to-earth integrity whereas Ryan adds a vitality and steely streak to her customary ditzoid charms. Together, they are enormously ingratiating, a strong testament to the chemistry of star power. That said, as a loved up duo they should perhaps quit while they're just about ahead. ★★★ **IF**

YOUNG EINSTEIN (1989)

Starring: *Yahoo Serious (Albert Einstein), Odile Le Clezio (Marie Curie), John Howard (Preston Preston), Peewee Wilson (Mr. Einstein), Su Cruickshank (Mrs. Einstein)*
Director: *Yahoo Serious*
Screenwriters: *David Roach, Yahoo Serious*
PG/91 mins./Comedy/Australia

The tell of what would have happened if Albert Einstein had been born an Australian. The theory goes that he would have been a whacky inventor, finally figuring out a way of getting the bubbles in beer, an achievement that brings him to the world's attention, especially the rather attractive Marie Curie.

Less a revisionist history than a lolloping spoof with half an eye on playing funny with some famous scientific icons, this goofy Aussie comedy was attempting to export excitable homegrown funnyman Yahoo Serious as the next Paul Hogan. In real terms, the herky-jerky, I'm-a-bit-of-a-loony Mr. Serious (real name: Greg Pead) is nothing like the droll, dry-boned Hogan, but more along the lines of shrill, insistent, odd-pot games of Pee Wee Herman, and about as funny. Firm evidence that not all comedy travels well.

For all his Keaton-esque fumbling about, Serious (what irony in his moniker!) is firmly rooted in the clichés of the unreconstituted Australian male: he takes his baths in the outdoors, and in his dotty inventing brings about the surf board, the electric guitar (and thus rock'n'roll) and, most importantly, gets the bubbles into beer during which process he manages to split the atom. Against him is John Howard's scheming patent's clerk, while the love interest is Odile Le Clezio's unmemorable Marie Curie (a lame name gag).

The general stock of its comedy plays the familiar names and notions of scientific progress (the Wright Brothers, E=mc2, Edison, Freud, etc.) to the off-key tune of Serious' rock-flecked clowning (he also fancied himself as a singer back in Oz). But despite his pompadour of Sideshow Bob hair, his bottle thin frame and elastic features, his slapstick jinks are little more than a wan copy of any number of the great fools of cinema's yesteryear. So, the only thing that really ties this to the effervescent and hugely successful *Crocodile Dundee* is that it is a croc. ★★ **IN**

⦿ YOUNG FRANKENSTEIN (1974)

Starring: *Gene Wilder (Dr. Frederick Frankenstein), Peter Boyle (The Monster), Marty Feldman (Igor), Madeline Kahn (Elizabeth), Cloris Leachman (Frau Blucher), Teri Garr (Inge), Kenneth Mars (Police Inspector Hans Wilhelm Friedrich Kemp), Richard Haydn (Gerhard Falkstein), Liam Dunn (Mr. Hilltop)*
Director: *Mel Brooks*
Screenwriters: *Mel Brooks, Gene Wilder, based on the characters from Frankenstein by Mary Shelley*
PG/106 mins./Comedy/USA

Frederick Frankenstein inherits his grandfather's monster. Igor, his assistant, provides an abnormal brain, which leads to the usual problems.

Following Mel Brooks' unprecedented success with *Blazing Saddles*, he worked again with star (and, here, co-writer) Gene Wilder on another genre parody, this lovely-looking black and white homage to Universal's horror films in general and the first three Frankenstein films – *Frankenstein, Bride of Frankenstein* and (especially) *Son of Frankenstein* – in particular.

It's a more affectionate film than the hit-and-miss *Blazing Saddles*, which helps it through stretches of feeble jokes and Brooks' inability to come up with material worthy of his talented female cast members (here, Teri Garr, Cloris Leachman and Madeline Kahn). Nevertheless, it has an enormous amount of priceless, precious stuff – the snotty Frederick insisting his famous name is pronounced 'Fronkonsteen', 'Pardon me, boy, is this the Transylvania Station?', Wilder and Kenneth Mars reprising the darts game/verbal duel of Basil Rathbone and Lionel Atwill in *Son of Frankenstein*, Marty Feldman's moveable hump, the chiaroscuro bravura of a James Whale-style creation scene (complete with crackling vintage mad science equipment) and Peter Boyle as a hulking Monster with a zip in his neck who (unlike Karloff) is abused by a blind hermit (Gene Hackman) and a little girl and tries to demonstrate how unthreatening he is by duetting tunelessly with his creator in 'Puttin' on the Ritz'.

It benefits enormously from its luminous monochrome look, which perfectly catches the gothic shimmer of the best Universal films (Garr has never looked lovelier than in black and white) and an almost plaintive gypsy violin score, and is certainly a more respectful, honest homage to the great originals than, say, *The Munsters* or even *Abbott And Costello Meet Frankenstein*. ★★★★ **KN**

⦿ YOUNG GUNS (1988)

Starring: *Emilio Estevez (William H. Bonney), Kiefer Sutherland (Josiah Doc Scurlock), Lou Diamond Phillips (Jose Chavez y Chavez), Charlie Sheen (Richard Brewer), Casey Siesmasko (Charles Bowdre), Terence Stamp (John Tunstall)*
Director: *Christopher Cain*
Screenwriter: *John Fusco*
18/102 mins./Western/USA

When their mentor and father-figure John Tunstall is shot dead by a local cattle-rancher rival, his wards unite as deputies to arrest the villain who has the local sheriff in his pay. But when one of their number, Billy The Kid, shoots them dead instead the gang have to turn outlaw.

This noisy Brat Pack Western ends up suffocated by flip MTV editing and the frathouse atmosphere of a bunch of young actors having a gas hanging out and playing cowboys. In fact, the one thing this film never feels like is a real Western, just a giddy action flick bouncing to an endless succession of shoot-outs and horseback chases mounted with about as much similarity to the traditions of John Ford as the Marx Brothers. This is a cheesy, silly, smug movie.

Out of this parade of preened young actors, only really Emilio Estevez, who does have the best role of loose-hinged Billy The Kid, makes much impression. He plays it thick with beaming personality, but little sophistication – we learn nothing of this fabled killer. Then, the movie has nothing but its marketing gimmick to show for itself. Kiefer Sutherland mopes around a bit, Lou Diamond Philips displays the kind of charisma that would pioneer his career in straight to video dustbins, and Charlie Sheen (who was, ostensibly, the biggest star in the pack) looks out-of-sorts because he doesn't get any gags. Does anyone remember Casey Siesmasko? Didn't think so. Even Dermot Mulroney has been heard from since.

Tagline
Six reasons why the West was wild.

Although, set in the 1870s, Christopher Cain gives it the crisp, bland sheen of the 1980s, his landscapes are rather humdrum considering what is on offer, and his care and attention to character non-existent. Star-power made it grab enough attention to warrant a sequel, which on closer inspection turned out to be a better film, but it didn't take much.
★★ **IN**

⦿ YOUNG MR LINCOLN (1939)

Starring: *Henry Fonda (Abraham,Lincoln), Alice Brady (Abigail Clay), Marjorie Weaver (Mary Todd), Arleen Wheelan (Hannah Clay), Eddie Colins (Efe Turner), Pauline Moore (Ann Rutledge), Richard Cromwell (Matt Clay), Eddie Quillan (Adam Clay), Ward Bond (John Palmer Cass), Donald Meek (John Felder)*
Director: *John Ford*
Screenwriter: *Lamar Trotti*
U/100 mins./History Drama/USA
Awards: *Academy Awards – Best Original Story (Lamar Trotti)*

Adhering to the vow taken at the grave of his beloved Ann Rutledge, Illinois backwoodsman Abraham Lincoln becomes a lawyer and, in 1837, forges his reputation by defending Abigail Clay's sons, Matt and Adam, against a false murder charge.

Having just completed *Stagecoach*, his first film with John Wayne, director John Ford discarded notions of a remake of Jean Renoir's *La Grande Illusion* to embark on his first collaboration with his other favourite actor, Henry Fonda. Whereas Wayne would come to portray Ford's earthy action men, Fonda would reflect his sense of liberal decency – although both tended to play idealists who were intent on civilising America.

Lincoln's early career had already been chronicled in the sound era by D.W. Griffith in *Abraham Lincoln* and John Cromwell in *Abe Lincoln in Illinois*, with Walter Huston and Raymond Massey respectively bringing a more imposing presence to the role than Fonda could hope to emulate. Yet, his Honest Abe is a confident, almost patronising character who makes little effort to suppress the air of superiority he exhibits towards neighbours and adversaries alike. Moreover, he's not averse to duping them or exploiting their weaknesses and demonstrates an equal determination to succeed whether he's splitting rails, competing in a tug-of-war or arguing the law. Yet, while Lincoln wears his roots like a badge of honour that others are all the poorer for not possessing, he's sufficiently worldly to accept his fee from the widow who had come to represent a surrogate mother.

In revising Howard Estabrook's 1935 treatment, screenwriter Lamar Trotti added details from a trial that he had witnessed as a young journalist and sought to avoid a hagiographical depiction. Yet, Ford doesn't stray too far from popular preconceptions. Indeed, he uses the poem 'Mary Hanks' as an excuse for trading in myth rather than fact and, thus, created a new Lincoln legend that pertained for many years.

Y

Stars Who've Stripped For Playboy

1. Marilyn Monroe
2. Elizabeth Taylor
3. Jane Fonda
4. Catherine Deneuve
5. Brigitte Bardot
6. Kim Basinger
7. Melanie Griffith
8. Sharon Stone
9. Sophia Loren
10. Ursula Andress

Fonda's Abe is, therefore, a blend of human being and historical agent, who allows Ford frequently to anticipate the traits and events that would contribute to his greatness. However, Fox mogul Darryl F. Zanuck drew the line at the inclusion of a scene in which a young John Wilkes Booth encounters a top-hatted Abe riding his mule on leaving the theatre where he's playing *Hamlet*. ★★★★ **DP**

YOUNG SHERLOCK HOLMES (1985)

Starring: *Nicholas Rowe (Sherlock Holmes), Alan Cox (John Watson), Sophie Ward (Elizabeth Hardy), Anthony Higgins (Professor Rathe), Susan Fleetwood (Mrs. Dribb)*
Director: *Barry Levinson*
Screenwriter: *Chris Columbus, based on characters created by Sir Arthur Conan Doyle*
PG/109 mins./Mystery/USA

Two friends in an English boarding school, going by the names Sherlock Holmes and John Watson, discover a plot to murder British businessmen using a hallucinatory drug. The trail leads to the doorstep of an Egyptian cult.

While having nothing to do with Arthur Conan Doyle's great fiction, this Sherlock Holmes origin story is produced by the ineffable Steven Spielberg, written by Chris Columbus (who was responsible for *The Goonies*) and given real energy by director Barry Levinson. It lacks the sharpness and wit Spielberg might have granted it (it boasts trace elements of Indiana Jones, but the spruce special effects bring its bizarre riffs on hallucinations to dazzling life (death by pastries!) and Nicholas Rowe and Alan Cox are a likable match for literature's great detective partnership.

The London of the 1890s is everything Hollywood cliché has made it – streets suffocated by pea-soupers barely penetrated by gaslight. It's an effective world to plant a mystery such as this, which may test logic's outer reaches, but with its Egyptian motifs, murders and deranged drugs, possesses enough scares to enthral, especially with Rowe's eloquent chunks of exposition slowly putting the jigsaw together. Rowe also gets to romance the pretty Sophie Ward which may seem very un-Sherlock, meanwhile Watson is a bit bumbling and podgy (more Hollywood sidekick than anything), but as much as they are stereotypes, this is not trying to be anything but shiny, superficial entertainment constructed to a very familiar template: Indiana Jones-lite.

Tagline
Before a lifetime of adventure, they had the adventure of a lifetime.

Talking of which, with hindsight, and not that co-incidentally given Columbus wrote the script, this mix of magic and investigation now obviously harkens to the style of Harry Potter movies (Columbus directed the first two). Which makes it years ahead of its time. A boast doubled when you learn that it also boasts the first splicing of CG graphics with real-life action in a stained-glass knight springing to life. ★★★ **IN**

YOUR FRIENDS AND NEIGHBOURS (1998)

Starring: *Amy Brenneman (Mary), Aaron Eckhart (Barry), Catherine Keener (Terri), Nastassja Kinski (Cheri), Jason Patric (Cary), Ben Stiller (Jerry)*
Director: *Neil LaBute*
Screenwriter: *Neil LaBute*
18/95 mins./Drama/Comedy/USA

The intertwining lives of six self-obsessed, sexually dysfunctional yuppies – Mary and Barry, an unhappily married couple; Jerry and Kerri, an unhappily unmarried couple who stay together for convenience; Cheri, Kerri's lesbian lover and Cary, Barry's best friend, a demented, demonic hedonist.

Some time during the 90s, a cultural phenomenon occurred to millions of young couples around the globe. They started fantasising about the perfect world advertised in the TV show *Friends*. The fantasy soon became a corporate juggernaut that bombarded the public with exquisite images of this peaches 'n' cream lifestyle. But writer/director Neil LaBute, creator of the controversial *In The Company Of Men*, has squeezed the brakes down hard with a vicious, low-budget comedy showing exactly how couples really behave with each other.

The rules of the game remain the same. Six cute-looking friends exchange secrets and desires within their pristine middle-class world. The secrets, however, are a touch more shocking. There's Jerry and Terri (Stiller and Catherine Keener) whose relationship is under threat from Jerry's incessant urge to gabble during sex. There's Barry and Mary (Eckhart and Brenneman) whose marriage is stained with her frigidity and his wanking obsession. And then there's a superb Patric as one of the most immoral, malicious lovers committed to celluloid; and Nastassja Kinski, a clingy lesbian who needs to know the exact moment her bed partners orgasm.

The problems surface in the usual places: bookstores, art galleries, bistros and supermarkets. The difference, however, is in the brutally candid script. LaBute has crafted one of the most explicit and hilarious films of the year; it's a slow-moving affair, with little camera movement and only the merest hint of a soundtrack. Yet there are scenes of such wincing honesty that could get the most blissfully happy couples niggling. It's sexual warfare, but the weapons used are infidelity, stealth and deceit. And the jokes, pruned to perfection, are designed to kill. But if you want to improve your sex life, watch this movie. ★★★★ **JH**

Y TU MAMA TAMBIEN (AND YOUR MOTHER TOO) (2001)

Starring: *Ana Lopez Mercado (Ana Morelos), Diego Luna (Tenoch Iturbide), Gael García Bernal (Julio Zapata), Nathan Grinberg (Manuel Huerta), Veronica Langer (Maria Eugenia Calles de Hueta)*
Director: *Alfonso Cuaron*
Screenwriters: *Alfonso Cuaron, Carlos Cuaron*
18/105 mins./Drama/Mexico/USA

Y TU MAMA TAMBIEN (AND YOUR MOTHER TOO)

Two teenagers, Julio and Tenoch, persuade an older relative's attractive wife to accompany them on a journey to 'Heaven's Mouth', a beach they have just made up.

A sexy, funny road movie/coming-of-age tale, *And Your Mother Too* was a deservedly huge box office success in its home country of Mexico, as well as being the surprise hit of last year's London Film Festival and being both Oscar and BAFTA nominated.

The film tells the story of two teenagers, Julio and Tenoch, who persuade an older relative's attractive wife (Verdu) to accompany them on a journey to 'Heaven's Mouth', a beach they have just made up.

The usual rites-of-passage shenanigans inevitably ensue, but are given a subtle twist that keeps the film amusingly unpredictable. The performances are all spot-on (García Bernal and Luna are real-life best friends, and it shows) and director Cuarón makes great use of his gorgeous locations throughout. ★★★★ **MT**

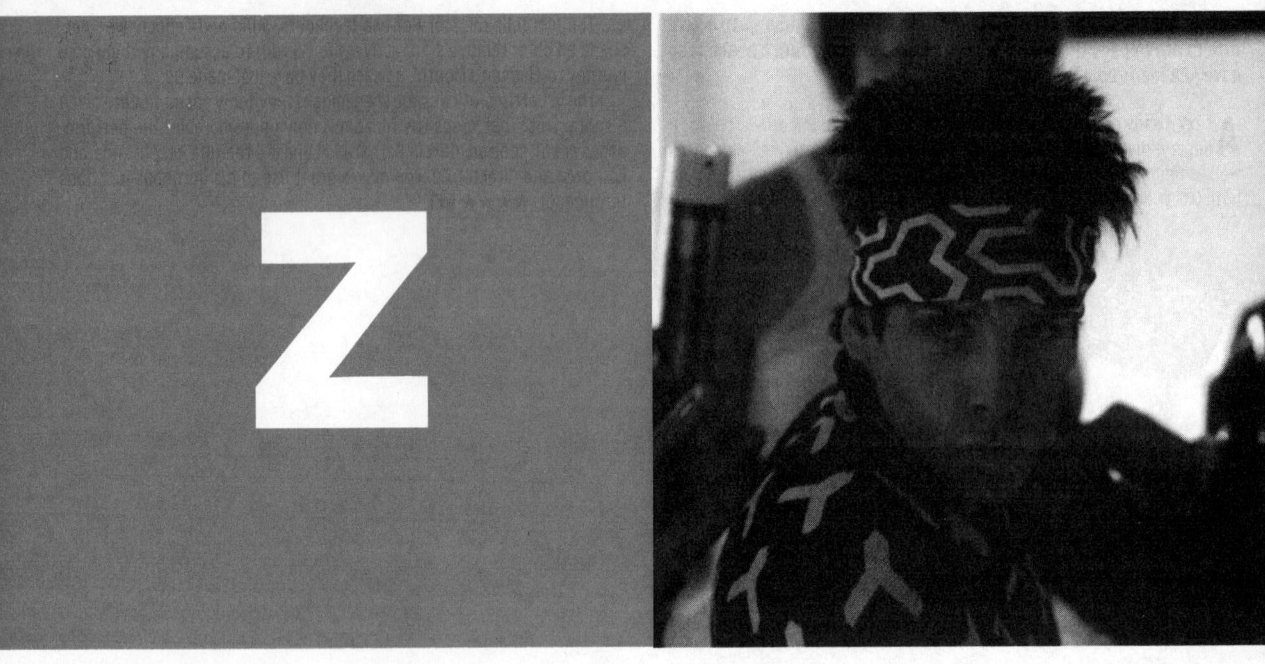

Z (1969)

Starring: *Yves Montand (The Deputy), Jean-Louis Trintignant (The Examining Magistrate), Irene Papas (Helene), Jacques Perrin (Photojournalist), Charles Denner (Manuel), François Perrier (Public Prosecutor), Pierre Dux (The General)*
Director: *Constantin Costa-Gavras*
Screenwriters: *Constantin Costa-Gavras, Jorge Semprum, based on the novel by Vassili Vassilikos*
15/127 mins./Drama/France-Algeria

Awards: *Academy Awards – Best Foreign Language Film, Best Film Editing. BAFTA – Best Music*

A deputy in an unnamed state is assassinated at a peace rally. An examining magistrate is appointed to conduct an inquiry and receives the assistance of a crusading photojournalist. But witnesses keep disappearing and the public prosecutor consistently strives to undermine the case.

As a Greek exile, whose father had been persecuted by the authorities, Costa-Gavras was determined to film Vassili Vassilikos' fictionalised account of the events that followed the assassination of liberal pacifist Gregorios Lambrakis at a demonstration against the installation of Polaris missiles on 22 May 1963. Keen to avoid a scandal, the right-wing Karamanlis government had appointed Judge Christos Sartzetakis to conduct an inquiry and it was soon clear that the Establishment had colluded in the conspiracy to remove Lambrakis before upcoming elections, lest he blocked the flow of bribes and armaments coming into Greece.

Although the murderers were tried in October 1966, the military coup of 21 April 1967 saw the restoration of officials dismissed in the affair and the torture and disbarment of Judge Sartzetakis. However, Lambrakis' followers continued to use the letter Z (meaning 'he lives') as a symbol of protest and Vassilikos adopted it for the title of his book.

Unable to raise funds in France, as the subject was deemed too political, Costa-Gavras and producer Jacques Perrin eventually struck a deal with Algerian backers and decided to shoot the film in accordance with its subtitle, 'The Anatomy of a Political Assassination'. Ditching supposition surrounding the case, such as the involvement of the CIA, Costa-Gavras stuck to proven facts so that the picture could not be accused of being propagandist.

However, there were those who denounced *Z* for lacking nuance, while others claimed that its unprecedented Oscar success was the result of it tapping into the cosy communal outrage that had followed the killings of the Kennedy brothers and Martin Luther King. There's no question that Costa-Gavras used the rapid cross-cutting between zooms, tracking shots and handheld footage to pitch the viewer into the heart of his thesis. But Raoul Coutard's photography and Françoise Bonnot's Oscar-winning editing were outstanding and exerted a considerable influence on the style of the political thrillers that liberal Hollywood produced during the Watergate era.

Banned by right-wing regimes worldwide, *Z* was finally released in Greece, to huge acclaim, following the fall of the Generals in 1974. ★★★★
DP

ZARDOZ (1974)

Starring: *Sean Connery (Zed), Charlotte Rampling (Consuella), Sara Kestelman (May), John Alderton (Friend), Sally Anne Newton (Avalow), Niall Buggy (Arthur Frayn), (Bosco Hogan) George Saden, Jessica Swift (Apathetic)*
Director: *John Boorman*
Screenwriter: *John Boorman*
15/105 mins./Sci-fi/UK-Ireland

In a future dystopia, the world is divided into the Brutals (Neanderthals forbidden to have sex) and the Immortals (cool sexy people who live forever) divided by a barrier in The Vortex. Meanwhile, Zed, an Exterminator of Brutals, raises his consciousness by reading L. Frank Baum's *The Wizard Of Oz*.

Most Annoying Movie Characters — TOP 10

1. DJ Ruby Rhod (Chris Tucker), *The Fifth Element* (1997)
2. Heather (Heather Donahue), *The Blair Witch Project* (1999)
3. Mr Freeze (Arnold Schwarzenegger), *Batman & Robin* (1997)
4. Mr Yunioshi (Mickey Rooney), *Breakfast At Tiffany's* (1961)
5. The Munchkins, *The Wizard Of Oz* (1939)
6. Carrie (Andie McDowell), *Four Weddings And A Funeral* (1994)
7. Prissy (Thelma Butterfly McQueen), *Gone With The Wind* (1939)
8. Forrest (Tom Hanks), *Forrest Gump* (1994)
9. Curly Sue (Alisan Porter), *Curly Sue* (1991)
10. Benjamin (Dustin Hoffman), *The Graduate* (1967)

You have to hand it to John Boorman. When he's brilliant, he's brilliant (*Point Blank*, *Deliverance*) but when he's terrible, he's *really terrible*. A fascinating reminder of what cinematic science fiction used to be like before *Star Wars*, this risible hodge-podge of literary allusions, highbrow porn, sci-fi staples, half baked intellectualism and a real desire to do something revelatory misses the mark by a hundred miles but has elements – its badness being one of them – that make it strangely compelling.

Burt Reynolds (who'd just come off *Deliverance* with Boorman) was originally earmarked for the role of Zed but declined, leaving the role open for Sean Connery who desperately wanted to shake off the mantle of Bond. The casting switch meant *Zardoz* offers the strange sight of a bemused looking James Bond strutting and preening around a futureworld (that looks a lot like Ireland) dressed in nothing but a nappy. But that is only the start of *Zardoz's* madness. Shockingly awful dialogue ('The Gun is good, the penis is evil!'), a mish mash of ludicrous ideas (the film desperately wants to say something about organized religion, it just doesn't know what), some truly bizarre performances (step forward John Alderton in a curly wig and Sara Kestelman who has an embarrassing bout of rumpy pumpy with Connery) all wrapped up in a cornucopia of bad special effects. If the movie has a saving grace it is Geoffery Unsworth's beautiful cinematography of striking Irish locations. But, by the end of the movie as Connery is turned into a fossil to the strains of Beethoven's 7th, you are in absolutely no doubt that you have just witnessed something extraordinary. And in case you were wondering, the title refers to a truncated play on 'The Wizard Of Oz'. It's that sort of movie. ★ **WT**

ZATOICHI (2003)

Starring: *Takeshi Kitano (Zatoichi/Ichi), Tadanobu Asano (Hattori Genosuke), Michiyo Ookusu (Aunt O-Ume), Gadarukanaru Taka (Shinkichi)*
Director: *Takeshi Kitano*
Screenwriter: *Takeshi Kitano, based on the novels by Kan Shimozawa*
18/116 mins./Action/Crime/Japan

A blind, itinerant masseur arrives in a feudal Japanese town during a turf war between rival clans and uses his intuitive swordsmanship to help an exploited vegetable seller, her hapless gambling nephew, and a pair of unusual geishas who are out to avenge the murder of their family.

The chambara, or swordplay film, has been a staple of Japanese cinema since Makino Shozo's *The Fight At Honno Temple* in 1908. Employing the duelling techniques developed in Kabuki theatre, these samurai and ronin adventures have considered such themes as duty and honour, while also utilising their period setting to explore contemporary issues.

Just as Hollywood churned out countless 'B' Westerns, so the Japanese studios of the 60s produced increasingly violent low-budget chambara for the youth market. Some heroes like Kyoshiro Nemuri and Hanzo the Blade are barely known in this country, but *The Lone Wolf & Cub* and *Zatoichi* are familiar thanks to the Warrior Films video collection.

However, little in the 26 *Zatoichi* vehicles that starred Shintaro Katsu can compare to the polish and panache of Takeshi Kitano's magnificent remake. In addition to turning in a blond-dyed display of Zen contemplation and vicious precision, actor-director Kitano combines cartoonish violence, broad pantomime and subtle asides with arresting visuals and exquisite period details to produce a piece of cult pulp that drips with arthouse style.

This is clearly his homage to a formative influence, in much the same way that *Crouching Tiger, Hidden Dragon* celebrated the martial arts movies of Ang Lee's youth. But while the severed limbs and gushing arteries are very much in evidence, what's so impressive about *Zatoichi* is the number of references it makes to Japan's master filmmakers.

The low-angle shots are reminiscent of Yasujiro Ozu; the sacrifices made by a selfless geisha recall the dramas of Kenji Mizoguchi; the effortless shifts in tone and quixotic intensity of the central character are worthy of Kon Ichikawa; the scale and pacing are pure Akira Kurosawa; the meticulous composition echoes Teinosuke Kinugasa; and the mistrust of wealth and power and the empathy with the under-classes reflect the concerns of Nagisa Oshima and Shohei Imamura.

Yet this isn't a pretentious scrapbook of bygone issues and styles. It's a complex and slow-burning clash between masterless samurai and lawless yakuza, which is as likely to meander into a slapstick set-piece as explode into visceral violence. Katsumi Yanagishima's photography is outstanding, while Keiichi Suzuki's percussive score informs such contrasting scenes as the peasants toiling in their field to the barnstorming festival finale, in which the cast join the dance troupe Stripes for a Busby Berkeley-like production number. ★★★★ **WL**

ZATHURA (2005)

Starring: *Jonah Bobo (Danny), Josh Hutcherson (Walter), Dax Shepard (Astronaut), Kristen Stewart (Lisa), Tim Robbins (Dad)*
Director: *Jon Favreau*
Screenwriters: *David Koepp, John Kamps*
PG/101 mins./Family/Adventure/Fantasy/USA

During a dull day at the house of their divorcé father, quarrelsome brothers Danny and Walter discover a musty old sci-fi boardgame. Once they start playing, the game's magic powers are unleashed and soon pop's house is spinning in space as they have to deal with errant robots and flesh-eating aliens.

Zathura is less of a sequel to Joe Johnston's *Jumanji* than a replay in the key of old-school sci-fi. Or, to be more accurate, it's another adaptation of a Chris Van Allsburg story, Allsburg having taken an ain't-broken-don't-fix approach, rather lazily repeating the same basic plot (kids discover magic boardgame, boardgame unleashes colourful chaos along with trapped ex-player, kids have to complete boardgame to end chaos). But do not fear the déjà vu, for *Zathura* rolls higher than its animal-packed predecessor.

Crucial to *Zathura*'s success is the way director Jon Favreau has taken his limitations and turned them into strengths. Clearly lacking the budget for big names and CGI splurging, Favreau worries more about character-fleshing and tension-building. Where *Jumanji* had Robin Williams yet again doing his tiresome manchild schtick, *Zathura* has no stars of note (although Tim Robbins does a good harried dad). And where *Jumanji* strained to impress with its unconvincing, digitally bred safari creatures rampaging out of the kids' house and across the screen, *Zathura* admirably relies more on physical fx and keeps things impressively contained.

With Danny and Walter's home whirling through the cosmos (in itself a magnificent, imagination-rousing image), it's less a case of things bursting from the inside-out, as in *Jumanji*, than breaking and blasting from the outside-in. So, for the most part, we stay within the building's crumbling walls, firmly sharing the kids' startled perspective. One scene involves a desperate, rocket-fuelled rescue attempt as one character is ejected into the inky vacuum. But where you'd normally expect a big, silly action set-piece you get only a small, nervous child watching it all happen off-screen. And it works. Favreau's less worried about trying to wow us with pyrotechnics than he is to have us share the brothers' adventure on a more personal level.

It would work *better*, though, if Favreau had cast stronger kiddie leads. As sensitive, clumsy younger brother Danny, Jonah Bobo is suitably crumpled and angelic, but he locks too easily into 'astonished gape' mode. As his jock-in-the-making sibling Walter, Josh Hutcherson is, by contrast, too inexpressive; yes, he has this amusing jaded-before-his-time air, but he really shouldn't look so blank when that killer robot's trying to tear him a new arse. With even marginally more astute child actors, the schmaltzier message moments (the importance of family, the wrongness of cheating) would be easier to swallow. Thankfully, though, they're balanced with enough inventive action to keep even the most attention-defecit pre-teen happy. ★★★ **DJ**

⓪ ZAZIE DANS LE METRO (1960)

Starring: *Catherine Demongeot (Zazie), Phillipe Noiret (Uncle Gabriel), Hubert Deschamps (Turnadot), Antoine Roblot (Charles), Annie Fratellini (Mado), Carlo Marlier (Albertine), Vittorio Caprioli (Trouscallion), Yvonne Clech (Mme. Mouaque)*
Director: *Louis Malle*
Screenwriters: *Louis Malle, Jean Paul Rappenau based on the book by Raymond Quenaeau*
15/86 mins./Comedy/France

While her mother visits her Parisian lover, 11 year-old Zazie is deposited with her female-impersonating Uncle Gabriel and drives him to distraction with her determination to ride on the Metro, despite the fact the system has been paralysed by a strike.

Having established a reputation for intense dramas, Louis Malle surprised everyone with this freewheeling adaptation of Raymond Queneau's 1959 novel, which had originally been slated as a project for René Clément. The book – which had also inspired a comic-strip and a stage play – had essentially been a series of elaborate word games, in which Queneau explored the efficacy of language through Parisian slang. But Malle and co-scenarist Jean-Paul Rappeneau sought to translate these verbal pyrotechnics into visual images and packed the picture with sight gags, trick shots, speed changes, superimpositions, jump cuts and references to other movies. However, this Left Bank blend of New Wave homage and lampoon divided the critics, with some commending its dazzling virtuosity, while others considered it to be a piece of self-conscious intellectual posturing and others still a chaotic mess.

François Truffaut declared Zazie to be 'madly ambitious and hugely courageous' and there's no denying the audacity of Malle's allusions to Ferdinand Zecca, Georges Méliès, Mack Sennett, Buster Keaton and Federico Fellini, among many others. But this was no mere grab-bag of bygone techniques, as Malle and cinematographer Henri Raichi successfully transformed Paris into the surreal playground that it clearly appeared in the tweenager's Alice in Wonderland imagination. Moreover, Uncle Gabriel's music-hall connections provided the perfect excuse for an evocation of old-fasioned illusionism, that prompted some to see him as a 'cinéma du papa' to his niece's nouvelle vague.

But while this may have represented a significant stylistic change of tack, Zazie explored the theme of a juvenile attempting to cope with the adult world to which Malle would return in *La Souffle Au Coeur*, *Lacombe, Lucien*, *Pretty Baby* and *Au Revoir Les Enfants*. Yet while these considerably more controversial films found international audiences, *Zazie*'s madcap humour didn't travel well. Indeed, it only proved a minor hit in France itself. However, it has since been acclaimed for its satirical digs at consumerism and American colonial imperialism and its gleefully inventive iconoclastic exuberance. ★★★★ **DP**

⓪ A ZED AND TWO NOUGHTS (1985)

Starring: *Andrea Ferreol (Alba Bewick), Brian Deacon (Oswald Deuce), Eric Deacon (Oliver Deuce), Frances Barber (Venus De Milo), Joss Ackland (Van Hoyten), Jim Davidson (Joshua Plate), Agnes Brulet (Beta Bewick)*
Director: *Peter Greenaway*
Screenwriter: *Peter Greenaway*
15/111 mins./Surreal Drama/UK/Netherlands

When the wives of identical twin zoologists Oswald and Oliver Deuce are killed in a freak car accident involving a white Ford Mercury and a swan, the pair become fascinated with death and decay, entering into a bizarre relationship with the mysterious Alba Bewick, the woman behind the wheel at the time of death.

In 1982, Peter Greenaway's *The Draughtsman's Contract* became a breakout arthouse hit and edged its marginal, idiosyncratic director towards the fringes of the mainstream. Yet as befitted Greenaway's *enfant terrible* credentials, the director's 1985 follow-up jettisoned all the commercial aspects of *Draughtsman's* (the murder mystery plot, the pretty locations, the catchy Michael Nyman tunes), opting instead for an emotionally sterile plotless meditation on grief and corporeality. It would be easy to reject *A Zed And Two Noughts* as pretentious claptrap – a recurring thread of the contemporary reviews invoked the parable of the Emperor's New Clothes – but, if taken in the right spirit, there is a sense of both cinema and playfulness at work that is often overlooked.

Even for Greenaway, the ingredients are bizarre. Shot in and around the Rotterdam Zoo (the title alludes to a whimsical spelling of 'zoo'), the movie begins with the aftermath of a swan crashing into a car leaving zoologist twins Oliver and Oswald Deuce bereaved. As a way of coping with the loss of their wives, the pair become driven to find out how long it takes for a corpse to rot (as you do) and so begin to make a series of time-lapse photography movies of objects decomposing – starting with an apple, building to crocodiles and zebras and ultimately onto human beings. Around this conceit, Greenaway has the twins seduced by the monoped Alba Bewick (who later has her other leg removed to attain symmetry), throws in a zoo hooker named Venus De Milo, intersperses natural history documentary footage narrated by David Attenborough and even finds room for a cameo for 'comedian' Jim 'Nick Nick' Davidson as an oick of a zookeeper.

This obviously isn't for every taste, takes a lot of effort to stay with and tonally is colder than a well-digger's arse. But that is to ignore *Zed*'s strengths. A painter as well as a filmmaker, Greenaway, collaborating with Cocteau's cameraman Sacha Vierny, turns every single shot into a memo-

Fictional Movie Presidents TOP10

1. Andrew Shepherd (Michael Douglas, *The American President*)
2. James Marshall (Harrison Ford, *Airforce One*)
3. Tom Beck (Morgan Freeman, *Deep Impact*)
4. Jackson Evans (Jeff Bridges, *The Contender*)
5. Merkin Muffley (Peter Sellers, *Dr. Strangelove*)
6. Thomas J. Whitmore (Bill Pullman, *Independence Day*)
7. The President (Donald Pleasence, *Escape From New York*)
8. Greg Stiltson (Martin Sheen, *The Dead Zone*)
9. James Dale (Jack Nicholson, *Mars Attacks!*)
10. Thomas Tug Benson (Lloyd Bridges, *Hot Shots Part Deux*)

rable image, marked out by sharp, synthetic colours, meticulously balanced compositions, imaginative daring lighting and carefully choreographed camera moves. This sense of high art is also present in Greenaway's penchant for visual puns and allusions to famous paintings (Vermeer in particular), particularly notions of twinning and symmetry. Moreover, *A Zed And Two Noughts* has a sly, dry sense of humour, a mischievous schoolboy's sense of the shocking (animal mutilations, hints at limbless sex) and Michael Nyman's driving pounding score adds momentum to knit the fragments together. Difficult it may be, but it is undouibtedly a feast for the eyes, ears and noggin. What more can you ask of movies than that? ★★★ **IF**

ZELIG (1983)

Starring: *Woody Allen (Leonard Zelig), Mia Farrow (Dr. Eudora Nesbitt Fletcher), John Buckwalter (Dr. Sindell), Patrick Horgan (The Narrator)*
Director: *Woody Allen*
Screenwriter: *Woody Allen*
PG/79 mins./Comedy/USA-South Africa-Netherlands

The mock-documentary account of the life of Leonard Zelig, a man so unassuming and maladroit he assumes the looks and speech of whoever is around him, managing to take part in some of the major events of world history.

This could be described as high concept Woody Allen, fixing the great comic writer's familiar philosophical preoccupations into a strange fictional documentary of a man who has no personal shape of his own, instead taking on the guise of any larger ego nearby. Allen's target is the pathology of the frail human psyche, how Zelig can only conform to what is around him, but whose complete inability to have a self makes him unique. Irony runs rife, and as the film stalks through history, shot in the style of those shuffling mock-aged newsreel edited together with the genuine articles, Allen skilfully weaves together the notion that Zelig is afflicted with an unknown disease – acute ordinariness, to an extent that makes him hugely influential, the anti-ego.

Zelig, played by Allen with both vacuity and versatility, plops in and out of history like a tumbleweed, every time a different person: an actor, a learned doctor, the son of a jazz musician. There is the teasing suggestion that, if anything, Zelig is exactly like an actor. Naturally, then, he becomes a celebrity, and is on hand at the pivotal joints of history itself from Babe Ruth's winning runs to Hitler's sinister rise to power. Allen is brilliantly superimposed into the archive footage, a chameleon, a trick later borrowed by *Forrest Gump*.

With Mia Farrow, starchy and poised, as the psychiatrist determined to cure him, the 20s setting accents the director's examination of human psychology – it was in its ascendancy during the era. And in a further irony still – there the onion layers of meaning that can picked off the film – the Jewish director even makes fun at intellectual posturing and over-analysis by having such big brains as Susan Sontag, Irving Howe and Saul Bellow comment knowingly on Zelig's dilemma.

Teeming with one-liners, humorous asides and references it is hilarious. The only problem the film faces is its own artifice. We are watching a hugely clever game that appears just that, impressive but mechanical. When the gears try to change – proposing that love could be the only answer to Zelig's shapelessness – the film suddenly feels forced. ★★★★ **IN**

Movie Trivia: *Zelig*

Mae Questel, the voice of Betty Boop, is the voice of Helen Kane singing 'Chameleon Days'. John Gielgud initially recorded the entire narration of the film but Allen dropped it as he felt Gielgud's voice was too grand for the film. The house in the closing scene is the same house used in Woody Allen's *A Midsummer Night's Sex Comedy*.

ZÉRO DE CONDUITE (ZERO FOR CONDUCT) (1933)

Starring: *Jean Daste, Robert Le Flon, Louis de Gonzague, Louis Lefebvre, Gilbert Pruchon, Gèrard de Bèdarieux, Constantin Goldstein-Kehler*
Director: *Jean Vigo*
Screenwriter: *Jean Vigo*
PG/44 mins./Drama/France

An absurd, oppressive school is rocked by an anarchic revolution on the part of the free-spirited pupils.

Jean Vigo's brief (44 minutes), startling feature prefigures Truffaut's *Les Quatre Cents Coups* in its sympathetic attitude to badly-behaved French children and Lindsay Anderson's *If ...* in its school revolution finale. The 1933 picture is also a development of the kind of surreal film-making Luis Buñuel and others were using to stir up riots in Paris back in the 20s and early 30s. Indeed, its commitment to filling up the minor offence book – the title refers to the marks for conduct its heroes continually earn – resulted in *Zéro De Conduite* being banned by the French censor until well after World War Two.

Given its reputation for rabble-rousing, it's actually a surprisingly gentle and lyrical film, absurd in its humour rather than vicious, as much in tune with Chaplin's world as Buñuel's. The teachers are bourgeois grotesques – a midget headmaster, a grossly fat science teacher – and a cross-section of grown-up authority figures are represented by dressed-up dummies in the big food fight finish, but all the children are monkeyish sprites, and the film allows their wonder and magic to take flight, with slow motion turning cigar smoke produced during an illicit gasping session and the unloosed feathers of a pillow-fight into hazy, fairytale images.

This is a very pro-child movie, and the only sympathetic adult is the teacher who enters into the spirit of things by larking around in lessons and produces a cartoon that comes to life.

Like Vigo's masterpiece *L'Atalante*, it manages to be subversive, charming and melancholy at the same time and, if it has been so often imitated as to seem less original than it was, still stands up as a miniature classic. ★★★★ **KN**

ZERO EFFECT (1998)

Starring: *Bill Pullman (Daryl Zero), Ben Stiller (Steve Arlo), Ryan O'Neal (Gregory Stark), Kim Dickens (Gloria Sullivan), Angela Featherstone (Jess)*
Director: *Jake Kasdan*
Screenwriter: *Jake Kasdan*
15/116 mins./Thriller/USA

Steve Arlo, a long-suffering lawyer, works for the neurotic, eccentric, brilliant private investigator Daryl Zero, who is hired by tycoon Gregory Stark to see off a blackmailing mystery woman.

It's a shame low-budget American indies don't do franchises, because this unusual but traditional detective story introduced a private eye who deserves his own series (Alan Cumming played Zero in a little-seen TV pilot, but nothing has been heard of the sleuth since). After decades of hard-boiled heroes, second-generation writer-director Jake Kasdan goes back to the classics to create a modern investigator on the Sherlock Holmes pattern, translating Conan Doyle's drug-using, personally distant violin virtuoso into Daryl, an amphetamine-popping, neurotically withdrawn bedroom guitar-player.

Like Holmes, Zero is a master of disguise (partly to submerge his own loser personality) and a whizz at deduction, with a repetoire of suggestive-sounding past cases to name-drop, like The Case of the Hired Gun Who Made Way Too Many Mistakes and The Case of the Guy Who Lied About His Age. In a case derived closely from Doyle's 'A Scandal in Bohemia', Zero ditches his justifiably-infuriated Watson-like sidekick to track down the blackmailing paramedic Gloria Sullivan and is then jogged out of his lifelong shell by the winning woman even as he realises his client is a far worse criminal than his quarry.

Kasdan perhaps takes a slightly too leisurely approach, but the film has enough incidental clevernesses (note the way O'Neal's character's backstory is a twisted rerun of his greatest hit, *Love Story*) to keep you hooked. Pullman, one of American cinema's most valuable players, is outstanding as the flawed genius, working in a sense of tragedy that makes this more than just a clever exercise.

Tagline
The world's most private detective.

A rare film to satisfy fans of classical mysteries (the illustrated deductions are perfect) and quirky-sad comedy-drama. ★★★★ **KN**

ZIEGFELD FOLLIES (1945)

Starring: *William Powell (The Great Ziegfeld), (as themselves): Fred Astaire, Lucille Ball, Judy Garland, Lena Horne, Esther Williams, Red Skelton, Gene Kelly, Fanny Brice, Edward Arnold*
Directors: *Vincente Minnelli, George Sidney, Charles Walters, Roy Del Ruth, Lemuel Ayers*
Screenwriters: *E.Y. Harburg, Jack McGowan, Guy Bolton Frank Sullivan, John Murray Anderson, Lemuel Ayers, Don Loper, Kay Thompson, Roger Edens, Hugh Martin, Ralph Blaine, William Noble, Wilkie Mahoney, Cal Howard, Erik Charell, Max Liebman, Bill Schorr, Harry Crane, Lou Holtz, Eddie Cantor, Allen Boretz, Edgar Allan Woolf, Phillip Rapp, Al Lewis, Joseph, Schrank, Robert Alton, Eugene Loring, Robert Lewis, Charles Walters, James O'Hanlon, David Freeman, Joseph Erons, Irving Brecher, Samson Raphaelson, Everett Freeman, Devery Freeman*
U/110 mins./Musical/USA

Florenz Ziegfeld looks down from heaven and plans a new musical revue featuring the biggest stars on the MGM lot.

Originally conceived to mark MGM's 20th anniversary, this musical extravaganza was confounded by its own ambitions and a surprising lack of leadership from the usually meticulous producer, Arthur Freed. Having spent $100,000 on acquiring the title of Florenz Ziegfeld's legendary Broadway spectaculars from his widow, Billie Burke, Louis B. Mayer gave Freed a $3 million budget and licence to create the most dazzling all-star revue ever assembled.

George Sidney was initially commissioned to direct, but it soon became clear that the project was spiralling out of control. Several sequences were aborted and many more were discarded following disastrous preview screenings. Among the casualties were sketches involving Katharine Hepburn and Jimmy Durante and two numbers reuniting Mickey Rooney and Judy Garland.

Vincente Minnelli was brought in for Garland's own number and he ended up supervising the remainder of the shoot, with the help of Norman Taurog. Garland herself was a replacement for Greer Garson, whose husband, Richard Ney, claimed that the 'Madame Crematon' routine was beneath her dignity. The Lone Ranger's horse, Silver, was similarly humiliated when *Life* magazine ran an article headlined, 'Silver is a sissy!' when he was decked in braids, bows and a pink ostrich feather for Lucille Ball's 'Bring on the Beautiful Girls' spot.

Indeed, only Fred Astaire really emerged from this misfire with much credit. The comedy skits, featuring the likes of Fanny Brice and Red Skelton, were deemed dated at the time and audiences had so little time for James Melton's tenor that his accompaniment to Esther Williams' aquatic ballet was removed.

Much has been made of Fred's teaming with Gene Kelly on 'The Babbitt and the Bromide', which he had first performed with his sister Adele in *Funny Face* in 1927. But while it's hardly either's best work, it's still an invaluable record of cinema's two finest hoofers jousting their contrasting styles.

Astaire's duets with Lucille Bremer on 'This Heart of Mine' and the sublime 'Limehouse Blues' were far superior. But a third pairing was abandoned when the bubble machine used for Kathryn Grayson's climactic 'There's Beauty Everywhere' filled the soundstage with noxious fumes. ★★★ **DP**

ZOMBIE FLESH EATERS (ZOMBI 2) (1979)

Starring: *Tisa Farrow (Annie Bowles), Ian McCulloch (Peter West), Richard Johnson (Dr. David Menard), Al Cliver (Brian Hull), Auretta Gay (Susan Barrett), Stefania D'Amario (Missey), Olga Karlatos (Paolo Menard)*
Director: *Lucio Fulci*
Screenwriter: *Elisa Briganti*
18/91 mins./Horror/Italy

A boat floats into New York harbour, inhabited only by a hulking, flesh-eating zombie. A journalist traces the trouble to the voodoo-haunted, zombie-overrun Caribbean island of Matoul.

This became semi-famous as one of the fabled 'video nasties', chiefly on the strength of a single, memorable bit of abuse in which a woman has her head pulled through a shattered door and a long shard of broken wood slowly pierces her eyeball.

The scene is not quite on a level with the eye-abuse of *Un Chien Andalou* in 1928, and in fact – though it's heretical to say so in fan circles – plays better in the BBFC-truncated version, which conveys the nasty idea but snips the footage before the ketchup-filled plastic novelty eye gets gored. Directed by the cheerful Italian hack Lucio Fulci as an imitation of George Romero's *Living Dead* films (it was passed off as a sequel to *Dawn Of The Dead* in Italy), this mixes melodramatic devices from the 30s with 1979-era

Movie Star Cameos In *Friends* TOP10

1. Julia Roberts (Chandler's school friend Susie 'Underpants' Moss)
2. Brad Pitt (Former fatty Will Colbert)
3. Reese Witherspoon (Rachel's sister Jill Green)
4. Bruce Willis (Paul Stevens, father of Ross' girlfriend)
5. George Clooney (Dr. Michael Mitchell)
6. Sean Penn (Phoebe's boyfriend Eric, who is also dating her twin sister)
7. Winona Ryder (Rachel's college friend Melissa)
8. Kathleen Turner (Chandler's drag queen dad)
9. Ben Stiller (Rachel's angry date Tommy)
10. Susan Sarandon (Soap star Jessica Lockhart)

hard gore as a whiskery Richard Johnson drinks himself insensible on an island while zombies gather outside his hut.

Some sequences are quite striking as the shambling undead emerge from their graves or advance menacingly and the serial-style silliness is sort of endearing, but Fulci's monotonous pacing and a few too many descents into total absurdity curtail the entertainment value.

Nice to see Mia Farrow's sister Tisa running away from flesh-eating monsters though, and few other films can claim anything to equal the dynamite scene in which an underwater zombie grapples with (and takes a bite out of) a surprised shark.

Various similar efforts have been passed off as *Zombi 3*, and Fulci proceded to more personal, occult-themed (but just as gory) pictures like *The Beyond* and *The House by the Cemetery*. ★★ **KN**

ZOOLANDER (2001)

Starring: *Ben Stiller (Derek Zoolander), Owen Wilson (Hansel), Christine Taylor (Matilda Jeffries), Will Ferrell (Mugatu), Milla Jovovich (Katinka), Jerry Stiller (Maury Ballstein), David Duchovny (J.P. Prewitt), Jon Voight (Larry Zoolander), Vince Vaughn (Luke Zoolander – uncredited)*
Director: *Ben Stiller*
Screenwriters: *Drake Sather, Ben Stiller, John Hamburg*
12/89 mins./Comedy/USA

With child labour 'under threat', the fashion industry talks male model Derek Zoolander into attempting an assassination. Can Derek hold out, with the help of a friendly female journalist, and his rival, Hansel?

Some actors practically guarantee quality: Kevin Spacey, for example (we'll ignore *Pay It Forward*, as indeed everyone should). Inversely, Chris Klein's name above the title is ominous indeed. Meanwhile, Will Ferrell is fast becoming a byword for patchy but funny all-star spoofs. watch him over-act wildly in *Jay And Silent Bob Strike Back*, and again here as the flamboyant fashion designer criminal mastermind, Mugatu. The message is clear: if you see Ferrell, stick around.

Stiller's first directorial effort since 1996's under-rated *The Cable Guy* is a mostly successful and unashamed attempt to make an utterly lunatic camp comedy, anchored superbly by its multi-tasking star. Based on a character Stiller debuted at the 1996 VH1 Fashion Awards (VH1 must have a sense of humour; it co-produced), *Zoolander* trades on the hold-the-front-page premise that male models are stupid. And so Stiller ladles on the hit-and-miss dumb jokes – including a priceless *2001* pisstake – thick and fast. Likewise the star cameos, the Stiller Rolodex proffering the likes of David Duchovny as a – ho! – conspiracy theorist, David Bowie as himself, Vince Vaughn as Zoolander's perpetually appalled, perpetually silent brother, and family members (Taylor is aka Mrs. Stiller, while Jerry Stiller – Daddy! – is Zoolander's crotchety agent). And, amidst the home video antics, Stiller dovetails perfectly with the unfathomably cool Wilson, so much so that you wish the 'world's top male models' (worth a laugh in itself) shared more screentime. And while *Zoolander*'s okay US performance may have killed a sequel, its close cousin *Austin Powers* (witness the zany tone, the incompetent, sex-obsessed hero and – blimey! – Will Ferrell) discovered hit status on DVD. If justice prevails, this will, too. ★★★ **CW**

Tagline
3% body fat.
1% brain activity.

ZORBA THE GREEK (1964)

Starring: *Anthony Quinn (Alexis Zorba), Alan Bates (Basil), Irene Papas (The Widow), Lila Kedrova (Mme. Hortense), George Foundas (Mavrandoni), Eleni Anousaki (Lola), Sotiris Moustakas (Mimithos), Takis Emmanuel (Manolakas), Yorgo Voyagis (Pavlo), Anna Kyriakou (Soul)*
Director: *Michael Cacoyannis*
Screenwriter: *Michael Cacoyannis, based on the novel by Niko Kazantzakis*
PG/142 mins./Drama/USA/Greece

Awards: *Academy Awards – Best Supporting Actress (Lila Kedrova), Best Art Direction-Set Decoration, Black And White, Best Black-and-White Cinematography*

Having failed in their attempt to work a Cretan lignite mine and respectively lost the Greek widow and French hotelier who loved them, uptight English writer Basil and larger-than-life peasant Alexis Zorba unite in a dance symbolising the distressing beauty of life.

Whether set in the ancient world of *Electra* or the modern environments of *Stella*, *A Girl in Black* and *A Matter of Dignity*, Michael Cacoyannis' best films had concentrated on the struggles of Greek women to survive the vissicitudes of a patriarchal society. But such concerns were largely relegated to the margins in this adaptation of Nikos Kazantzakis' best-selling novel, as Cacoyannis concentrated on the life-affirming friendship between Anthony Quinn's vulgar Greek peasant and Alan Bates' stiff English exile.

Yet, the real drama in this clumsy and occasionally leaden parable is to be found in the more melancholic experiences of Irene Papas' vilified widow and Lila Kedrova's pitiable French hooker, Madame Hortense.

Having spent the majority of his career playing a bewildering variety of ethnic types around Hollywood, Quinn finally found his alter ego in this dauntless opportunist, who treats every setback as the start of a new enterprise. Indeed, he even reprised the role in the short-lived Broadway musical, *Zorba*. But his tendency to overact frequently reduces his performance to caricature, as ironically, does Bates' resolute understatement.

Lila Kedrova, who was a late replacement for Simone Signoret, is equally culpable of striving too hard for effect. But her yearning for acceptance chimes in with Hortense's desperate need for respectability and genuine affection. However, the most affecting performance comes from Irene Papas, whose dignified reaction to both Bates' bashful attentions and the brutal consequences of their coupling alone approaches the sense of classical tragedy for which Cacoyannis consistently strives.

The film very much divided the critics, with those who applauded its vigorous embrace of life's pangs and pleasures being countered by others who denounced it as 'a painfully slow piece of pseudo-art'. It's best known now for Mikis Theodorakis's infectious bazouki music. But the Oscar-winning photography of Walter Lassally, who had worked with Cacoyannis three times before, is even more impressive, as it captures both the rugged beauty of the landscape, while also suggesting its influence on the unforgiving morality of its impoverished inhabitants. ★★★ **DP**

ZULU (1964)

Starring: *Stanley Baker (Lt. John Chard), Jack Hawkins (Rev. Otto Witt), Ulla Jacobsson (Margareta Witt), James Booth (Pvt. Henry Hook), Michael Caine (Lt. Gonville Bromhead), Nigel Green (Colour Sgt. Bourne)*
Director: *Cy Enfield*
Screenwriters: *John Prebble, Cy Endfield, based on a story by Prebble.*
PG/133 mins./War/Historical/UK

In 1879, a small British army contingent battle to defend their Natal outpost against 4000 Zulu warriors.

The defence of Rorke's Drift is one of the most revered episodes in British military history. After the battle of 22-23 January 1879, 11 men received the Victoria Cross, the British Empire's highest award for gallantry – the largest number of VCs ever awarded for a single engagement. In brutal contrast, the war opened with one of the greatest disasters ever suffered by the British army, when a Zulu surprise attack massacred an expeditionary force of 4000 souls (more than half of whom were native levies) at Isandlwana.

The Battle of Rorke's Drift, the following day, came to symbolise redemption for Britain. Along with the charge of the Light Brigade and Dunkirk, Rorke's Drift is one of the most terrible yet glorious moments that become enshrined in a nation's history. While the Isandlwana disaster is documented in the unloved *Zulu* prequel *Zulu Dawn* (1979), its precursor is seen as one of the greatest war films ever made.

And rightly so. *Zulu* is a movie of blazing colour, spectacular Natal scenery, gut-wrenching action and superb performances, not least from Michael Caine, who is 'introduced' here (presumably the 17 movies he'd previously appeared in didn't count).

Caine is brilliantly cast against type as the aristocratic Lieutenant Bromhead, while co-producer Stanley Baker takes the role of a lifetime as Lieutenant Chard who, despite being Bromhead's social inferior, assumes command of the outpost. Rebellious ranker Private Hook is memorably brought to life by James Booth, while Nigel Green's Colour Sergeant Bourne is a wonderfully understated portrait of the 'Ours is not to reason why' ethos.

In the politically correct 1990s the film fell from favour. The perceived spectacle of a tiny number of white imperialists triumphing over a barbarian horde of black savages was seen as implicitly racist. This could not be further from the truth. The Zulus are at all times depicted as resourceful and courageous, and the scenes in the royal kraal go some way to exploring Zulu society in all its complex vitality. The only overtly racist remark, from Bromhead, is promptly pounced on by Adendorff, a Boer: 'What the hell do you mean "cowardly blacks"? They died on your side, didn't they? And who do you think is coming to wipe out your little command? The Grenadier Guards?' The word Zulu has duly passed into the English language, coming to signify the noble, fearless warrior. 'They can run 50 miles in a day – run, mind you,' says Adendorff admiringly. 'And then fight the battle at the end.' Truly these are worthy – and terrifying – foes.

Perhaps more than any other film *Zulu* is about pure heroism. The British might be armed with rifles, but so are the Zulus, and in any case these slow-loading carbines are little use when you're outnumbered 40 to one and the enemy is already upon you.

Rorke's Drift was largely a battle of hand-to-hand combat and the crucial weapon was the bayonet. 'It's a short chamber Boxer Henry, point 4/5 calibre miracle,' announces Chard, ever the engineer. 'And the bayonet, sir,' replies Colour Sergeant Bourne. 'With some guts behind it.'

In some ways, Bourne is the key character in the film. He is the experienced old soldier, resolutely unflappable in the face of the Zulu onslaught, stoically mediating between the bickering officers, the frightened and bewildered rankers, and the troublemaking Hook. When the drunken Reverend Witt (Jack Hawkins) refuses to be pacified it is Bourne who confronts him with a dignified murmur: 'Be quiet now, will you, there's a good gentleman. You'll upset the lads.'

The battle scenes are simply astonishing, as the defending force of fewer than a hundred able-bodied men beat back wave after wave of seemingly invincible Zulu warriors. It's one of the best depictions of British military discipline brought to the screen this side of the documentary-style TV film *Bravo Two Zero* (1999), with painfully realistic reconstructions of man-to-man combat.

Far from being an imperialist fable, *Zulu* carries a palpable anti-war message. The British soldiers are apolitical to a man and the malingering Private Hook is downright subversive. 'Did I ever see a Zulu walk down the City Road?' he sneers, from his hospital bed. 'No. So what am I doing here?' After the battle, both Chard and Bromhead are consumed by self-disgust. 'Do you think I could stand this butcher's yard more than once?' is Chard's verdict. 'I came here to build a bridge.'

As a spectacular war film with a powerful moral dimension, *Zulu* predates Spielberg's *Saving Private Ryan* by more than three decades. Like the defence of Rorke's Drift itself, its legend grows with the passing of time. ★★★★★ **PR**

ZULU DAWN (1979)

Starring: *Burt Lancaster (Col. Durnford), Simon Ward (Lt. William Vereker), Denholm Elliot (Col. Pulleine), Peter Vaughan (Q.S.M. Bloomfield), Peter O'Toole (Gen. Lord Chelmsford), James Faulkner (Lt. Melvill)*
Director: *Douglas Hickox*
Screenwriters: *Cy Endfield, Anthony Story*
PG/115 mins./War/USA

The story of the 1879 British defeat at the Battle of Isandlwana in South Africa, where Zulu warriors crushed her Majesty's forces. A disaster that was put down to inept leadership.

Sixteen years after *Zulu*, this sturdy but inferior battle movie flips that film's stalwart heroics on their head to study the make-up of a towering defeat rather than last ditch victory. Despite all the visual similarities, the class conflicts among the soldiers, the florid, endless spill of the countryside, and the fact *Zulu*'s director Cy Endfield co-wrote the script from his own novel, thematically this film shares more in common with *Charge Of The Light Brigade* and its debate on the tragic folly of having idiots in charge. It is also set, historically, before the heroic stand of Rorke's Drift that makes *Zulu* a minor classic, so you could count this as a prequel, but there is no real need.

Aiming to give a more PC Zulu side of the story, director Douglas Hickox rather over-eggs his good manners. In its slow-build toward the big battle, he spends his time cross-cutting between the rituals of imperialist invader with their starchy table manners and social cruelties and some *National Geographic* swoops amongst real natives. But, for all the effort, the film never quite pitches you onto neutral ground, as we get to know this batch of British actors and Burt Lancaster as a pessimistic local guide.

In the camp of red coats, things are very predictable. There is the

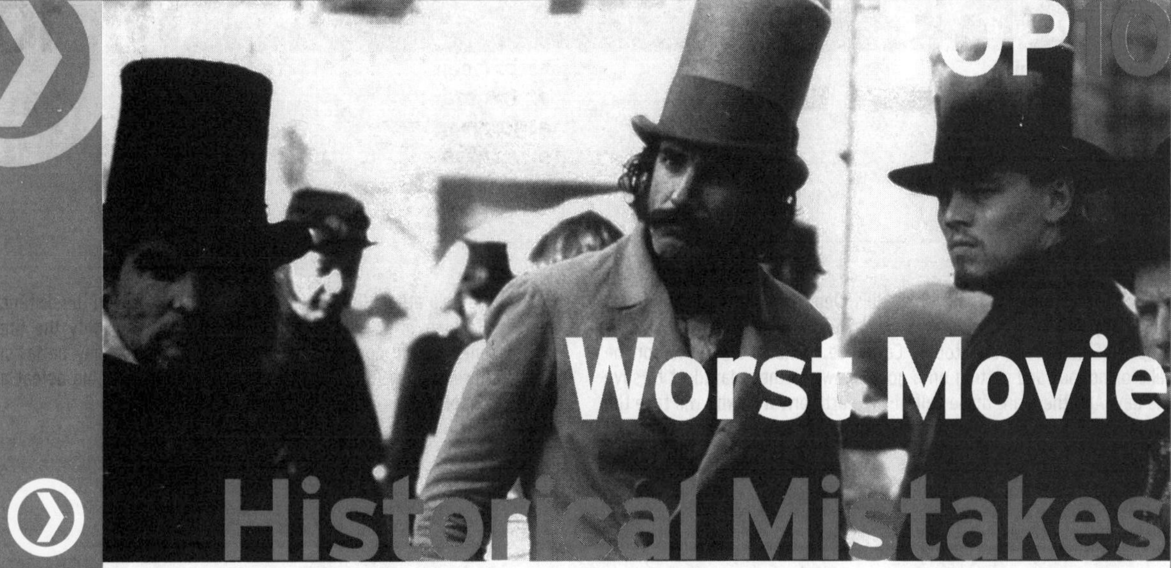

Worst Movie Historical Mistakes

1 *U-571* (2000)
The British captured the Enigma machine, not the Americans.

2 *The Patriot* (2000)
Mel Gibson's character's inspiration was a murderer – not mentioned by the movie.

3 *Gladiator* (2000)
Commodus was strangled by a slave, not killed in the arena.

4 *Robin Hood: Prince of Thieves* (1991)
Printing hadn't been invented yet – but there are wanted posters all over.

5 *Shane* (1953)
Like most Westerns, it's an all-white affair, despite the number of black people working in the Old West.

6 *Indiana Jones and the Last Crusade* (1989)
Indy flies across the Atlantic – a year before it was possible to do so – while two Germans read papers dated 1918.

7 *Jefferson in Paris* (1995)
Jefferson buys cloth by the metre, despite the fact that the metric system hadn't been invented. And in a Merchant-Ivory film too!

8 *From Hell* (2001)
Two people are lobotomised, despite the fact that the procedure was invented two years later, and that method not until 1945.

9 *Pearl Harbor* (2001)
In 1923, the two boys play in a crop duster – except the profession only developed post-1945, and the plane was built in 1937.

10 *Gangs of New York* (2003)
There were numerous appearances by things not available in 1860s New York - snooker, paperclips, bananas, Dobermans . . .

Z

Short Titles

1. *M* (1931/1951)
2. *O* (2001)
3. *Q* (1982)
4. *X* (1963)
5. *Z* (1968)
6. *CQ* (2001)
7. *FM* (1978)
8. IQ (1994)
9. *K2* (1991)
10. *P.J.* (1968)

stuffy top tier (Peter O'Toole, John Mills, Denholm Elliot) bungling local diplomacy and mismanaging their own. There are the dashingly heroic officers (Simon Ward, Christopher Cazenove, Nicholas Clay) who, for the sake of honour and putting on a good-show, do their darndest to save the day. And there are those salt-of-the-earth privates who will take the brunt of the Zulu attack (Bob Hoskins, Peter Vaughn). Given the distance from the making of *Zulu*, it is surprising how less almighty the final action scenes feel in comparison. The cinematography may be lavish, but the choreography of the fighting uninspired. It was a big defeat all round. ★★ **IN**

INDEX OF DIRECTORS

TThe following index lists the director of every film contained in the guide. Biographical dates are included where known.

C

Costa-Gavras, Constantin (1933 –): Z (1969), State Of Seige (1972), Mad City (1997), Music Box (1989)

Costner, Kevin (1955 –): Dances With Wolves (1990), The Postman (1997), Open Range (2003)

Coward, Noel (1899 – 1973): In Which We Serve (1942)

Cox, Alex (1954 –): Repo Man (1994)

Cox, James (1975 –): Wonderland (2003)

Crain , William (1949 –): Blacula (1972)

Craven, Wes (1939 –): The Hills Have Eyes (1977), A Nightmare On Elm Street (1984), The Serpent And The Rainbow (1987), The People Under The Stairs (1991), New Nightmare (1994), Scream (1996), Scream 2 (1997), Scream 3 (2000), Red Eye (2005)

Crichton, Charles (1910 – 1999): Dead Of Night (1945), The Lavender Hill Mob (1951)

Crichton, Michael (1942 –): The First Great Train Robbery (1978), Westworld (1971)

Cronenberg, David (1943 –): The Brood (1979), The Dead Zone (1983), Videodrome (1983), The Fly (1986), Dead Ringers (1988). Naked Lunch (1991), Crash (1996), ExisTenZ (1999), Spider (2002), A History Of Violence (2005)

Crowe, Cameron (1957 –): Say Anything (1989), Singles (1992), Jerry Maguire (1996), Vanilla Sky (2001), Almost Famous (2002), Elizabethtown (2005)

Crowley, John: Intermission (2003)

Crystal, Billy (1947 –): Mr, Saturday Night (1992)

Cuaron, Alfonso (1961 –): Y Tu Mama Tambien (2001), Harry Potter & The Prisoner Of Azkaban (2004)

Cukor, George (1899 – 1983): David Copperfield (1935), Sylvia Scarlett (1935), Camille (1937), Gone With The Wind (1939), The Women (1939), Philadelphia Story (1940), Gaslight (1944), Adam's Rib (1949), Born Yesterday (1950), Pat And Mike (1952), My Fair Lady (1964)

Cunningham, Sean S. (1941 –): Friday The 13th (1980)

Curtis, Richard (1956 –): Love Actually (2003)

Curtis-Hall, Vondie (1956 –): Glitter (2001)

Curtiz, Michael (1886 – 1962): Captain Blood (1935), The Adventures Of Robin Hood (1938), Angels With Dirty Faces (1938), Dodge City (1939), The Private Lives Of Elizabeth And Essex (1939), The Sea Hawk (1940), Casablanca (1942), Mildred Pierce (1945), White Christmas (1954)

D

DaCosta, Morton (1914 – 1989): The Music Man (1962)

Dahl, John (1956 –): Red Rock West (1992), The Last Seduction (1994)

Daldry, Stephen (1961 –): Billy Elliot (2000), The Hours (2002)

Daniel, Rod: Teen Wolf (1985)

Dante, Joe (1946 –): Piranha (1978), The Howling (1981), Gremlins (1984), The 'Burbs (1986), Innerspace (1987), Gremlins 2 : The New Batch (1990), Matinee (1993), Small Soldiers (1998), Looney Toons: Back In Action (2003)

Darabont, Frank (1959 –): The Shawshank Redemption (1994), The Green Mile (1999), The Majestic (2001)

Darnell, Eric: Antz (1998), Madagascar (2005)

Dassin, Jules (1911 –): Rififi (1955)

Davies, Terence (1945 –): The Long Day Closes (1992)

Davis, Andrew (1947 –): Under Siege (1992), The Fugitive (1993), A Perfect Murder (1998), Holes (2003)

Davis, Desmond (1926 –): Clash Of The Titans (1981)

Davis, John A.: Jimmy Neutron: Boy Genius (2001)

Davis, Tamra (1962 –): Guncrazy (1992)

Day, Robert (1922 –): The Rebel (1961)

De Bont, Jan (1943 –): Speed (1994), Twister (1996), Speed 2: Cruise Control (1997), The Haunting (1999), Lara Croft: Tomb Raider The Cradle Of Life (2003)

De Heer, Rolf (1951 –): Bad Boy Bubby (1993)

De La Iglesia, Alex (1965 –): Day Of The Beast (1995)

De Mille, Cecil B. (1881 – 1959): The Ten Commandments (1956)

De Palma, Brian (1940 –): Greetings (1968), Carrie (1976), Scarface (1983), Body Double (1984), Casualties Of Wat (1989). The Bonfire Of The Vanities (1990), Carlito's Way (1993), Mission: Impossible (1996)

De Sica, Vittorio (1902 – 1974): Bicycle Thieves (1948), Umberto D (1952), The Garden Of The Finzi-Continis (1971)

De Toth, Andre (1913 – 2002): House Of Wax (1953)

Dear, William (1944 –): Harry And The Hendersons (1997)

Dearden, Basil (1911 – 1971): Dead Of Night (1945), The Blue Lamp (1950), Victim (1961)

Del Toro, Gullermo (1964 –): Mimic (1997), Blade II (2002)

Demme, Jonathan (1944 –): Stop Making Sense (1984), Married To The Mob (1989), The Silence Of The Lambs (1991), Philadelphia (1993), The Manchurian Candidate (2004)

Demme, Ted (1963 – 2002): Beautiful Girls (1996)

Dey, Tom: Shanghai Noon (2000), Failure To Launch (2005)

Derrickson, Scott: The Exorcism Of Emily Rose (2005)

Despentes, Virginia: Baise-Moi (2000)

DeVito, Danny (1944 –): War Of The Roses (1989), Matilda (1996)

DiCillo, Tom (1954 –): Living In Oblivion (1995), Box Of Moonlight (1996)

Dieterle, William (1983 – 1972): The Hunchback Of Notre Dame (1939), The Life Of Emile Zola (1937)

Dippe, Mark A.Z. (1958 –): Spawn (1997)

Dmytryk, Edward (1908 – 1999): The Caine Mutiny (1954)

Docter, Peter: Monsters Inc. (2001)

Dobkin, David (1969 –): Shanghai Knights (2003), Wedding Crashers (2005)

Fleischer, Richard (1916 – 2006): The Narrow Margin (1952), 20, 000 Leagues Under The Sea (1954), The Vikings (1958), Fantasic Voyage (1966), Doctor Doolittle (1968), Soylent Green (1973), Conan The Destroyer (1984), Red Sonja (1985)

Fleming, Andrew: The Craft (1996), The In-Laws (2003)

Fleming, Victor (1899 – 1949): Gone With The Wind (1939), The Wizard Of Oz (1939)

Flemying, Gordon (1934 – 1995): Dr. Who And The Daleks (1965), Daleks Invasion Earth 2150 AD (1966)

Foley, James (1953 –): After Dark My Sweet (1990), Glengarry Glenn Ross (1992)

Fonda, Peter (1940 –): The Hired Hand (1971)

Forbes, Bryan (1926 –): The Stepford Wives (1975)

Ford, John (1894 –): Stagecoach (1939), Young Mr. Lincoln (1939), The Grapes Of Wrath (1940), How Green Was My Valley (1941), They Were Expendable (1945), My Cousin Vinny (1946), Fort Apache (1948), The Quiet Man (1952), Mister Roberts (1955), The Searchers (1956)

Forman, Milos (1932 –): One Flew Over The Cuckoo's Nest (1975), Hair (1979), Amadeus (1984), The People Vs Larry Flynt (1996), Man On The Moon (1999)

Forster, Marc: (1969 –): Monster's Ball (2001), Finding Neverland (2004)

Forsyth, Bill (1946 –): Gregory's Girl (1981), Local Hero (1983)

Forte, Lori: Ice Age (2002)

Fosse, Bob (1927 – 1987): Sweet Charity (1969), Cabaret (1972), Lenny (1974)

Foster, Jodie (1962 –): Little Man Tate (1991)

Fowler Jr., Gene (1917 – 1998): I Was A Teenage Werewolf (1957)

Frakes, Jonathan (1952 –): Star Trek: First Contact (1996), Star Trek: Insurrection (1998), Thunderbirds (2004)

Francis, Freddie (1917 –): Tales From The Crypt (1972)

Franju, Georges (1912 – 1987): Les Yeux Sans Visage (1959)

Frank, Melvyn (1913 – 1988): The Court Jester (1956)

Frankenheimer, John (1930 – 2002): The Manchurian Candidate (1962), Seconds (1966), Island Of Dr. Moreau (1996), Ronin (1998)

Franklin, Carl (1949 –): One False Move (1992),, Devil In A Blue Dress (1995)

Franklin, Richard (1948 –): Psycho II (1983)

Frears, Stephen (1941 –): Dangerous Liasons (1988), The Grifters (1990), Mary Reilly (1996), High Fidelity (2000), Dirty Pretty Things (2002), Mrs. Henderson Presents (2005)

Freeland, Thornton (1898 – 1987): Flying Down To Rio (1933)

French, Harold (1897 – 1997): Major Barbara (1941)

Frend, Charles (1909 – 1977): The Cruel Sea (1953)

Fresnadillo, Juan Carlos (1967 –): Intacto (2001)

Freund, Karl (1890 – 1969): The Mummy (1932)

Friedkin, William (1935 –): The French Connection (1971), The Exorcist (1973), To Live And Die To L.A. (1985)

Fritsch, Gunther Von (1906 – 1988): The Curse Of The Cat People (1944)

Fucqua, Antoine (1966 –): Trading Day (2001), King Arthur (2004)

Fuest, Robert (1927 –): The Abomminable Dr. Phibes (1971), Dr. Phibes Rides Again (1972)

Fukasaku, Kinji (1930 – 2003) : Battle Royale (2002)

Fulci, Lucio (1927 – 1996): Zombie Flesh Eaters (1979)

Fuller, Sam (1912 – 1997): Shock Corridor (1963), The Naked Kiss (1964), The Big Red One (1980)

Fulton, Keith: Lost In La Mancha (2002)

Furie, Sidney J. (1933 –): The Ipcress File (1965), Superman IV: The Quest For Peace (1987)

Fywell, Tim (1941 –): I Capture The Castle (2003)

G

Gabriel, Mike: Pocahontas (1995)

Gaghan, Stephen (1965 –): Syriana (2005)

Gallo, Vincent (1966 –): Buffalo 66 (1998)

Gance, Abel (1889 – 1981): Napoleon (1927)

Gans, Christophe (1960 –): Brotherhood Of The Wolf (2001)

Gast, Leon: When We Were Kings (1996)

Getino, Octavio (1935 –): The Hour Of The Furnaces (1965)

George, Terry: Hotel Rwanda (2004)

Geronimi, Clyde (1901 – 1989): Peter Pan (1953), Lady And The Tramp (1955), One Hundred And One Dalmatians (1961)

Gibbons, Cedric (1893 – 1960): Tarzan And His Mate (1934)

Gibson, Mel (1956 –): The Man Without A Face (1993), Braveheart (1995), The Passion Of Christ (2004)

Gilbert, Lewis (1920 –): Reach For The Sky (1956), Alfie (1966), You Only Live Twice (1967), The Spy Who Loved Me (1977), Moonraker (1979), Educating Rita (1983)

Gillespie, Jim: I Know What You Did Last Summer (1997)

Gilliam, Terry (1940 –): Monty Python And The Holy Grail (1975), Monty Python's Life Of Brian (1979), Time Bandits (1981), Monty Python's The Meaning Of Life (1983), Brazil (1985), The Adventures Of Baron Munchausen (1988), The Fisher King (1991), Twelve Monkeys (1995), Fear And Loathing In Las Vegas (1998), The Brothers Grimm (2005)

Gilliat, Sidney (1908 – 1994): Millions Like Us (1943)

Glaser, Paul Michael (1943 –): The Running Man (1987)

Glazer, Jonathan (1965 –): Sexy Beast (2000), Birth (2004)

Glebas, Francis: Fantasia 2000 (1999)

Helgeland, Brian: Payback (1998), A Knight's Tale (2001)

Henenlotter, Frank (1950 –): Basket Case (1982)

Henson, Jim (1936 – 1990): The Dark Crystal (1982), Labyrinth (1986), The Muppet Christmas Carol (1992)

Herek, Stephen (1958 –): Critters (1986), Bill & Ted's Excellent Adventure (1989), The Mighty Ducks (1992), Mr. Holland's Opus (1995), 101 Dalmatians (1997)

Herman, Mark (1954 –): Brassed Off (1996)

Herz, Michael: The Toxic Avenger (1985)

Herzog, Werner (1942 –): Aguirre, Wrath Of God (1972), The Enigma Of Kasper Hauser (1975), Fitzcarraldo (1982), Grizzly Man (2005)

Hessler, Gordon (1930 –): The Golden Voyage Of Sinbad (1974)

Hewitt, Peter (1965 –): Bill &Ted's Bogus Journey (1991)

Hickenlooper, George (1965–): Hearts Of Darkness: A Filmmakers Apocalypse (1991)

Hickox, Douglas (1929 – 1988): Theatre Of Blood (1973), Zulu Dawn (1979)

Hicks, Scott (1953 –): Shine (1996)

Hill, George Roy (1921 – 2002): Butch Cassidy And The Sundance Kid (1969), The Sting (1973)

Hill, Tim: Muppets From Space (1999)

Hill, Walter (1942 –): 48 Hours (1982), Another 48 Hrs. (1990), Last Man Standing (1996), Southern Comfort (1981), Streets Of Fire (1984)

Hillcoat, John (1961 –): The Proposition (2006)

Hiller, Arthur (1923 –): The In-Laws (1979)

Hitchcock, Alfred (1899 – 1980): The Lodger (1927), Blackmail (1929), The Man Who Knew Too Much (1934), The 39 Steps (1935), Sabotage (1936), The Lady Vanishes (1938), Foreign Correspondent (1940), Rebecca (1940), Mr. And Mrs. Smith (1941), Shadow Of A Doubt (1943), Lifeboat (1944), Saboteur (1945), Spellbound (1945), Notorious (1946), Rope (1948), Under Capricorn (1949), Stage Fright (1950), Strangers On A Train (1951), I Confess (1953), Dial M For Murder (1954), Rear Window (1954), To Catch A Thief (1955), The Trouble With Harry (1955), The Man Who Knew Too Much (1956), The Wrong Man (1956), Vertigo (1958), North By Northwest (1959), Psycho (1960), The Birds (1963), Marnie (1964), Frenzy (1972), Family Plot (1976)

Hirschbeigel, Oliver (1957): Das Experiment (2001), Downfall (2004)

Hodges, Mike (1932 –): Get Carter (1971), The Terminal Man (1974), Flash Gordon (1980), Croupier (1998)

Hogan, P.J. (1962 –): Muriel's Wedding (1994), My Best Friend's Wedding (1994)

Holland, Agneiszka (1948 –): Europa, Europa (1991)

Holland, Tom (1943 –): Fright Night (1985), Child's Play (1988)

Hooper, Tobe (1943 –): The Texas Chainsaw Massacre (1974), Poltergeist (1982), The Mangler (1995)

Honda, Ishiro (1911 – 1993): Godzilla (1954)

Hood, Gavin: Tsotsi (2005)

Hopkins, Stephen (1958 –): A Nightmare On Elm Street: The Dream Child (1989), Predator 2 (1990), Lost In Space (1998)

Hopper, Dennis (1936 –): Easy Rider (1968)

Horne, James W. (1880 – 1942): Way Out West (1937)

Hough, John (1941 –): Escape To Witch Mountain (1975), The Watcher In The Woods (1980)

Howard, Ron (1954 –): Splash (1984), Cocoon (1985), Willow (1988), Parenthood (1989), Backdraft (1991), Far And Away (1992). The Paper (1994), Apollo 13 (1995), A Beautiful Mind (2001), Cinderella Man (2005), The Da Vinci Code (2006)

Howitt, Peter (1957 –): Sliding Doors (1998), Johnny English (2003)

Hoyt, Harry O. (1885 – 1961): The Lost World (1925)

Huang, George: Swimming With Sharks (1994)

Hudson, Hugh (1936 –): Chariots Of Fire (1981), Greystoke: The Legend Of Tarzan, Lord Of The Apes (1984)

Hughes, Albert (1972 –) : Menace II Society (1993), Dead Presidents (1995), From Hell (2001)

Hughes, Allen (1972 –): Mean II Society (1993), Dead Presidents (1995), From Hell (2001)

Hughes, Bronwen: Forces Of Nature (1999), Stander (2003)

Hughes, Howard (1905 – 1976): Hell's Angels (1930), The Outlaw (1943)

Hughes, John (1950 –): The Breakfast Club (1985), Ferris Bueller's Day Off (1986), Planes, Trains And Automobiles (1987), Uncle Buck (1989)

Hughes, Ken (1922 – 2001): The Trials Of Oscar Wilde (1960), Casino Royale (1967), Chitty, Chitty, Bang, Bang (1968)

Humfress, Paul: Sebastiane (1976)

Hunt, Peter (1928 – 2002): On Her Majesty's Secret Service (1969)

Hunt, Pixote: Fantasia 2000 (1999)

Hunter, T. Hayes (1884 – 1944): The Ghoul (1933)

Hunter, Tim: River's Edge (1986)

Hurst, Brain Desmond (1900 – 1986): Scrooge (1951)

Huston, John (1906 – 1987): The Maltese Falcon (1941), Key Largo (1948), The Treasure Of The Sierra Madre (1948), The Asphalt Jungle (1950), The African Queen (1951), Moby Dick (1956), Casino Royale (1967), The Man Who Would Be King (1975), The Misfits (1961)

Hutton, Brian G. (1935 –): Where Eagles Dare (1968), Kelly's Heroes (1970)

Huyck, Willard: Howard The Duck (1986)

Hyams, Peter (1943 –): Capricorn One (1978), Outland (1981), 2010 (1984), Sudden Death (1996), End Of Days (1999)

Hytner, Nicholas (1956 –): The Madness Of King George (1994), The Crucible (1996), The Object Of My Affection (1998)

Kaufman, Philip (1936 –): Invasion Of The Body Snatchers (1978), The Wanderers (1979), The Right Stuff (1983), Henry And June (1990), Quills (2000)

Kaye, Tony (1952 –): American History X (1998)

Kazan, Elia (1909 – 2003): A Streetcar Named Desire (1951)

Keaton, Buster (1895 – 1966): Sherlock, Jr. (1924), The General (1927)

Kelly, Gene (1912 – 1996): On The Town (1949), Singin' In The Rain (1952), Hello, Dolly! (1969)

Kelly, Richard (1975 –): Donnie Darko (2001)

Kellogg, David (1952 –): Inspector Gadget (1999)

Kentis, Chris (1963 –): Open Water (2003)

Kenton, Erle C. (1896 – 1980): Island Of Lost Souls (1933)

Kershner, Irvin (1923 –): Never Say Never Again (1983), Star Wars Episode V: The Empire Strikes Back (1980)

Keshishian, Alek: In Bed With Madonna (1991)

Khan, Mehboob (1907 – 1964): Mother India (1957)

Kiarostami, Abbas: Ten (2002)

Kidd, Dylan: Rodger Dodger (2002)

Kidron, Beeban (1961 –): To Wong Foo, Thanks For Everything, Julie Newmar (1995), Bridget Jones – The Edge Of Reason (2004)

Kiersch, Fritz: Children Of The Corn (1984)

Kieslowski, Krzysztof (1941 – 1996): A Short Film About Killing (1987), A Short Film About Love (1987), The Double Life Of Veronique (1991), Three Colours Blue (1993), Three Colours White (1994), Three Colours Red (1994)

King, George (1899 – 1966): Sweeney Tood Or The Demon Barber Of Fleet Street (1936)

Kiriya , Kazuaki (1968 –) : Casshern (2004)

Kitano, Takeshi (1948 –): Sonatine (1993), Hana-Bi (1997), Zatoichi (2003)

Kleiser, Randal (1946 –): Grease (1978), The Blue Lagoon (1980), Flight Of The Navigator (1986)

Klimov, Elem (1933 – 2003): Come And See (1985)

Kloves, Steven (1960 –): The Fabulous Baker Boys (1989), Flesh And Bone (1993), Harry Potter And The Goblet Of Fire (2005)

Koepp, David (1964 –): Stir Of Echoes (1999)

Korda, Alexander (1893 – 1956): The Private Life Of Henry VIII (1933)

Koster, Henry (1905 – 1988): Harvey (1950), The Robe (1953)

Kotcheff, Ted (1931 –): Fun With Dick and Jane (1977), First Blood (1982), Weekend At Bernie's (1989)

Kovalyov, Igor (1963 –): The Rugrats Movie (1998)

Kramer, Stanley (1913 –2001): The Defiant Ones (1958), It's A Mad Mad Mad Mad World (1963)

Kubrick, Stanley (1928 – 1999): Killer's Kiss (1955), The Killing (1956), Spartacus (1960), Dr Strangelove Or How I Learned To Stop Worrying And Love The Bomb (1964), 2001: Space Odyssey (1968), A Clockwork Orange (1971), Barry Lyndon (1975), The Shining (1980), Full Metal Jacket (1987), Eyes Wide Shut (1999)

Kumble, Roger (1966 –): Cruel Intentions (1999), Just Friends (2005)

Kurosawa, Akira (1910 – 1998): Rashomon (1950), Ikiru (1952), Seven Samurai (1954), Throne Of Blood (1957), The Hidden Fortress (1958), Yojimbo (1961), Sanjuro (1962), High And Low (1963), Dersu Uzala (1975), Kagemusha (1980), Ran (1985)

Kusturica, Emir (1954 –); Time Of The Gypsies (1989), Black Cat, White Cat (1998)

Kwietniowski, Richard (1957 –): Love And Death On Long Island (1998)

L

LaBute, Neil (1963 –): In The Company Of Men (1997), Your Friends And Neighbours (1998), Nurse Betty (2000)

Lam, Ringo (1954 –): City On Fire (1997)

Lambert, Mary: Pet Sematary (1989)

Landis, John (1950 –): The Kentucky Fried Movie (1977), National Lampoon's Animal House (1978), The Blues Brothers (1980), An American Werewolf In London (1981), Trading Places (1983), Three Amigos! (1996), Blues Brothers 2000 (1998)

Lane, David: Thunderbirds Are Go (1966)

Lanfield, Sidney (1900 – 1972): The Hound Of The Baskervilles (1939), My Favourite Blonde (1942)

Lang, Fritz (1890 – 1976): Doctor Mabuse, The Gambler (1922), Die Nibelungen (1924), Metropolis (1927), M (1931), Fury (1936), You Only Live Once (1937), Scarlet Street (1945)

Lang, Walter (1896 – 1972): The King And I (1956)

Lanzmann, Claude (1925 –): Shoah (1985)

Lasseter, John (1957 –): Toy Story (1995), A Bug's Life (1998), Toy Story 2 (1999),

Lau, Ricky (1949 –): Mr. Vampire (1985)

Laughlin, Michael: Strange Invaders (1983)

Laughton, Charles (1899 – 1962): Night Of The Hunter (1955)

Launder, Frank (1906 – 1997): Millions Like Us (1943), The Happiest Days Of Your Life (1950), The Belles Of St. Trinians (1954)

Lawrence, Francis: Constantine (2005)

Lawrence, Ray: Lantana (2001)

LaZebnik, Philip: The Prince Of Egypt (1998)

Lean, David (1908 – 1991): Major Barbara (1941), This Happy Breed (1944), Brief Encounter (1945), Great Expectations (1946), Oliver Twist (1948), The Bridge On The River Kwai (1957), Lawrence Of The Arabia (1962), Doctor Zhivago (1965), Ryan's Daughter (1970), A Passage To India (1984)

Leder, Mimi (1957 –): Deep Impact (1998), The Peacemaker (1990)

Lee, Ang (1954 –): The Wedding Banquet (1993), Sense And Sensibility (1995), The Ice Storm (1997), Ride With The Devil (1999), Crouching Tiger, Hidden Dragon (2000), Hulk (2003), Brokeback Mountain (2005)

M

McBride, Jim (1941 –): The Big Easy (1987)

McCarey, Leo (1898 – 1969): Duck Soup (1933), An Affair To Remember (1957)

McCarthy, Thomas (1969 –): The Station Agent (2003)

McEveety, Vincent: The Watcher In The Woods (1980)

McG (1970 –): Charlie's Angels (2000)

McGraph , Joseph (1930 –): Casino Royale (1967)

McGrath, Tom: Madagascar (2005)

McGuigan, Paul (1963 –): Gangster No.1 (2000)

McKay, Adam (1968 –): Anchorman: The Legend Of Ron Burgundy (2004)

McLaglen, Andrew V. (1920 –): North Sea Hijack (1979)

McLean, Greg: Wolf Creek (2005)

McLeod, Norman Z. (1898 – 1964): Horse Feathers (1932), The Secret Of Walter Mitty (1947)

McNally, David: Coyote Ugly (2000)

McNaughton, John (1950 –): Henry: Portrait Of A Serial Killer (1986), Mad Dog And Glory (1993), Wild Things (1998)

McTeigue, James: V For Vendetta (2006)

McTiernan, John (1951 –): Predator (1987), Die Hard (1988), The Hunt For Red October (1990), The Last Action Hero (1993), Die Hard With A Vengeance (1995), The Thomas Crown Affair (1999), Basic (2003)

Madden, John (1949 –): Mrs. Brown (1997), Shakespeare In Love (1998), Captain Corelli's Mandolin (2001)

Magnoli, Albert: Purple Rain (1984)

Maguire, Sharon: Bridget Jones's Diary (2001)

Makin, Kelly: Mickey Blue Eyes (1999)

Mangold, James (1964 –): Walk The Line (2005)

Malick , Terrence (1943 –): Badlands (1973), Days Of Heaven (1978), The Thin Red Line (1998), The New World (2005)

Malkin, Kelly: Kids In The Hall: Brain Candy (1996)

Malle, Louis (1932 –): Les Amants (1952), Zazie Dans Le Metro (1960), Lacombe Lucien (1974), Au Revoir Les Enfants (1982), Atlantic City (1980)

Malone, William: House On Haunted Hill (1999)

Mamet, David (1947 –): House Of Games (1987), The Untouchables (1987), Homicide (1991), The Spanish Prisoner (1997)

Mamoulian, Rouben (1897 – 1987): Dr. Jekyll And Mr. Hyde (1932), Queen Christina (1933), The Mark Of Zorro (1940)

Mandel, Robert: F/X: Murder By Illusion (1986)

Mankiewicz, Joseph L. (1909 – 1993): The Ghost And Mrs. Muir (1947), All About Eve (1950), Guys And Dolls (1955), Suddenly, Last Summer (1959), Cleopatra (1963), Sleuth (1972)

Mankiewicz, Tom (1942 –): Dragnet (1987)

Mangold, James (1964 –): Cop Land (1997), Girl, Interrupted (1999)

Mann, Anthony (1906 – 1967): The Naked Spur (1953), El Cid (1961), The Glenn Miller Story (1953)

Mann, Daniel (1912 – 1991): Our Man Flint (1966)

Mann, Michael (1943 –): The Keep (1982), Manhunter (1986), Last Of The Mohicans (1992), Heat (1995), The Insider (1999), Ali (2001), Collateral (2004)

Marcel, Terry (1942 –): Hawk The Slayer (1980)

Margheriti, Antonio (1930 –): Flesh For Frankenstein (1973)

Marquand, Richard (1938 – 1987): Jagged Edge (1985)

Marshall, Frank (1947 –): Arachnophobia (1990), Alive (1992), Congo (1995)

Marshall, Garry (1934 –): Beaches (1988), Pretty Woman (1990)

Marshall , George (1891 – 1975): Destry Rides Again (1939)

Marshall, Neil (1970 –): Dog Soldiers (2002), The Descent (2005)

Marshall, Penny (1942 –): Big (1988), Awakenings (1990), A League Of Their Own (1992)

Marshall, Rob (1960 –): Chicago (2002), Memoirs Of A Geisha (2005)

Marston, Joshua: Maria Full Of Grace (2004)

Martinson, Leslie H. (1915 –): Batman (1966)

Marton, Andrew (1904 – 1992): King Solomon's Mines (1950)

Mate, Rudolph (1898 – 1964): When World's Collide (1951)

Mattinson, Burny: Basil, The Great Mouse Detective (1986)

May, Elaine (1932 –): A New Leaf (1971)

Maybury, John (1958 –): The Jacket (2005)

Mayfield, Les: California Man (1992)

Maylam, Tony: The Burning (1981)

Mazursky, Paul (1930 –): Harry And Tonto (1974), Scenes From A Mall (1991)

Meadows, Shane (1972 –): Twentyfourseven (1997), A Room For Romeo Brass (1999), Once Upon A Time In The Midlands (2002), Dead Man's Shoes (2004)

Medak, Peter (1937 –): Let Him Have It (1991)

Meins, Gus (1893 –): Babes In Toyland (1934)

Melies, Georges (1891 – 1938): A Trip To the Moon (1902)

Melville, Jean-Pierre (1917 – 1973): Les Enfants Terribles (1950)

Meirelles, Fernando (1955 –): Le Samourai (1967), City Of God (2002), The Constant Gardener (2005)

Mendes, Sam (1965 –): American Beauty (1999), Road To Perdition (2002), Jarhead (2005)

Menzel, Jiri (1938 –): Closely Observed Trains (1966)

Metter, Alan: Back To School (1986), Police Academy Mission To Moscow (1994)

N

Nispel, Marcus (1964 –): Texas Chainsaw Massacre (2003)

Noe, Gaspar (1963 –): Seul Contre Tous (1998), Irreversible (2002)

Nolan, Christopher (1970 –): Following (1998), Memento (2000), Insomnia (2002), Batman Begins (2005)

Noonan, Chris (1952 –): Babe (1995)

Norrington, Stephen (1964 –): Blade (1998), The League Of Extraordinary Gentleman (2003)

Noyce, Phillip (1950 –): Dead Calm (1989), Patriot Games (1992), Sliver (1993), Clear And Present Danger (1994), The Saint (1997), The Bone Collector (1999), The Quiet American (2002), Rabbit Proof Fence (2002)

Nugent, Elliott (1896 – 1980): The Cat And The Canary (1939)

Nuridsany, Claude: Microcosmos: Le People De L'Herbe (1996)

Nyby III, Christian: The Thing From Another World (1951)

O

O'Connolly, Jim (1926 – 1987): The Valley Of Gwangi (1969)

O'Donnell, Damien: East Is East (1999)

Oldman, Gary (1958 –): Nil By Mouth (1997)

Olivier, Laurence (1907 – 1989): Henry V (1944), Hamlet (1948), Richard III (1955)

Olmi, Ermanno: The Tree Of Wooden Clogs (1978)

Otomo, Katsuhiro (1954 –): Akira (1988)

Ophuls, Max (1902 – 1957): Letter From An Unknown Woman (1948), La Ronde (1950), Lola Montes (1955), The Sorrow And The Pity (1969)

Oshima, Nagisa (1932 –): Ai No Corrida (1976)

Othenin-Girard, Dominique: Halloween 5 (1989), Omen IV: The Awakening (1991)

Oz, Frank (1944 –): The Dark Crystal (1982), Dirty Rotten Scoundrels (1989), The Indian In The Cupboard (1995), Bowfinger (1999), The Stepford Wives (2004)

Ozon, Francois (1967 –); 8 Women (2001)

Ozu, Yasujiro (1903 – 1963): Tokyo Story (1953)

P

Pabst, G.W. (1885 – 1967): Pandora's Box

Pacino, Al (1940 –): Looking For Richard (1996)

Pakula, Alan J. (1928 – 1998): All The President's Men (1976), Presumed Innocent (1990), The Pelican Brief (1993), The Devil's Own (1997)

Pal, George (1908 – 1980): The Time Machine (1960)

Panama, Norman (1914 – 2003): The Court Jester (1956)

Pang, Danny (1965 –): The Eye (2002)

Pang, Oxide (1965 –): The Eye (2002)

Paradjanov, Sergei (1924 – 1990): Shadows Of Our Forgotten Ancestors (1964)

Paris, Jerry (1925 – 1986): Police Academy 3: Back In Training (1986)

Parisot, Dean: Galaxy Quest (1999)

Parajanov, Sergei (1924 – 1990): The Color Of Pomegranates (1968)

Park, Nick (1958 –): Chicken Run (2000), Wallace And Gromit: Curse Of The Were-Rabbit (2005)

Parker, Alan (1944 –): Bugsy Malone (1976), Angel Heart (1987), Mississipi Burning (1988), The Commitments (1991), Evita (1996)

Parker, Trey (1969 –): Cannibal! The Musical (1996), Orgazmo (1997), South Park: Bigger, Longer, Uncut (1999), Team America: World Police (2004)

Parker, Oliver (1960 –): The Importance Of Being Ernest (2002)

Parks, Gordon (1912 –): Shaft (1971)

Parrish, Robert (1916 – 1995): Casino Royale (1967)

Pascal, Gabriel (1894 – 1954): Major Barbara (1941)

Pasolini, Pier Paolo (1922 – 1975): Accatone (1961), The Gospel According To Matthew (1964), Theorem (1968), Salo, Or The 120 Days Of Sodom (1975)

Passer, Ivan (1933–): Cutter's Way (1981)

Past, Georg Wilhelm (1885 – 1967): The Threepenny Opera (1931)

Pawlikowski, Pawel (1957 –): The Last Resort (2000)

Payne, Alexander (1961 –): Election (1999), About Schmidt (2002), Sideways (2004)

Peckinpah , Sam (1925 – 1984): Major Dundee (1965), The Wild Bunch (1969), Straw Dogs (1971), The Getaway (1972), Cross Of Iron (1977), Convoy (1978)

Peebles, Mario Van: New Jack City (1991)

Peirce, Kimberly (1967 –): Boys Don't Cry (1999)

Pellington, Mark (1962 –): The Mothman Prophecies (2001)

Penn, Arthur (1922 –): Bonnie And Clyde (1968)

Penn, Sean (1960 –): The Pledge (2001)

Pepe, Louis: Lost In La Mancha (2002)

Peralta, Stacy (1957 –): Dogtown And Z Boys (2001)

Perennou, Marie: Microcosmos: Le People De L'Herbe (1996)

Perry, Frank (1930 – 1995): The Swimmer (1968)

Petersen, Wolfgang (1941 –): The NeverEnding Story (1984), Air Force One (1997), Das Boot (1981), In The Line Of Fire (1993), The Perfect Storm (2000), Troy (2004)

Petrie, Donald: Miss Congeniality (2000)

Philibert, Nicholas (1951 –): Etre Et Avoir (2002)

Phillips, Todd (1970 –): Road Trip (2000), Starsky And Hutch (2004)

Pichel, Irving (1891 – 1954): The Most Dangerous Game (1932), Destination Moon (1950)

Pinkaew, Prachya (1962 –): Ong-bak (2003)

Rilla, Wolf (1920 –): Village Of The Damned (1960)

Ritchie, Guy (1968 –): Smile (1975), Lock Stock And Two Smoking Barrels (1998), Snatch (2000), Revolver (2005)

Ritchie, Michael (1938 –): The Bad News Bears (1976), Prime Cut (1972), Fletch (1985), The Golden Child (1986)

Ritt, Martin (1914 – 1990): The Spy Who Came In From The Cold (1965)

Rivette, Jacques (1928 –): Celine And Juliet Go Boating (1974), La Belle Noiseuse (1991)

Roach, Jay (1957 –): Mystery Alaska (1991), Austin Powers International Man Of Mystery (1997), Austin Powers: The Spy Who Shagged Me (1999), Meet The Parents (2000), Austin Powers In Goldmember (2002), Meet The Fockers (2004)

Robinson, Angela (1971 –): Herbie: Fully Loaded (2005)

Robinson, Bruce (1946 –): Withnail And I (1987)

Robinson, Phil Alden (1950 –): Sneakers (1992), The Sum Of All Fears (2002)

Robbins, Jerome: West Side Story (1961)

Robbins, Matthew: Dragonslayer (1981), *batteries not included (1987)

Robbins, Tim (1958 –): Dead man Walking (1995), Cradle Will Rock (1999)

Robbins, Bill: Fantasia (1940)

Robinson, Phil Alden (1950 –): Field Of Dreams (1989)

Robson, Mark (1913 – 1978): Peyton Place (1957), Earthquake (1974)

Rockwell, Alexandre (1957 –): Four Rooms (1995)

Roddam, Franc (1946 –): Quadrophenia (1979)

Rodriguez, Robert (1968 –): El Mariachi (1992), Four Rooms (1995), Desperado (1995), From Dusk Till Dawn (1996), The Faculty (1998), Spy Kids (2001), Spy Kids 2: Island Of Lost Dreams (2002), Once Upon A Time In Mexico (2003), Spy Kids 3-D: Game Over (2003), Sin City (2005)

Roeg, Nicholas (1928 –): Performance (1970), Walkabout (1971), Don't Look Now (1973), The Man Who Fell To Earth (1976), Bad Timing (1980), Eureka (1984), The Witches (1990)

Rohmer, Eric (1920 –): Ma Nuit Chez Maud (1969), Claire's Knee (1970), Pauline At The Beach (1983), A Summer's Tale (1996)

Rogers, Charley (1887 – 1956): Babes In Toyland (1934)

Rogers, James B. : American Pie 2 (2001)

Rohmer, Eric (1920 –): An Autumn Tale (1998)

Romanek, Mark (1959 –): Static (1985), One Hour Photo (2002)

Romero, George A. (1940 –): Night Of The Living Dead (1968), Dawn Of The Dead (1978), Creepshow (1982), Land Of The Dead (2005)

Roos, Don (1955 –): The Opposite Of Sex (1998)

Rose, Bernard (1960 –): Paperhouse (1988), Candyman (1992)

Rose, Reginald: The Wild Geese (1978)

Rose, William (1920 – 2002): Genevieve (1953)

Rosen, Dan (1963 –): Dead Man's Curve (1998)

Rosenberg, Stuart (1927 –): Cool Hamd Luke (1967), The Amityville Horror (1979)

Rosenthal, Rick (1949 –): Halloween II (1981), Halloween: Resurrection (2002)

Ross, Gary (1956 –): Pleasantville (1998), Seabiscuit (2003)

Ross, Herbert (1927 – 2001): Play It Again, Sam (1972), The Last Of Sheila (1973), The Sunshine Boys (1975), The Seven Per Cent Solution (1976), California Suite (1978), Steel Magnolias (1989)

Rossellini, Roberto (1906 – 1977): Rome, Open City (1945)

Rossen, Robert (1908 – 1966): All The King's Men (1949), The Hustler (1961)

Roth, Eli (1972 –): Cabin Fever (2002), Hostel (2005)

Ruben, Joseph (1951 –): Sleeping With The Enemy (1991)

Rubin, Bruce Joel (1943 –): Ghost (1990), My Life (1993)

Rubin, Henry Alex: Murderball (2005)

Rudolph, Alan (1943 –): The Moderns (1988), Mrs. Parker And The Vicious Circle (1994)

Russell, Chuck, aka Russell, Charles (1952 –): A Nightmare On Elm Street, Part 3: Dream Warriors (1987), The Mask (1994), Scorpion King (2002)

Russell, David O. (1958 –): Spanking The Monkey (1994), Flirting with Disaster (1996), Three Kings (1999), I Heart Huckabees (2004)

Russell, Ken (1927 –): Altered States (1980)

Ruttmann, Walter (1887 – 1941): Berlin Symphony Of A City (1927). Triumph Of The Will (1935)

Rydell, Mark (1934 –): On Golden Pond (1981)

S

Sagal, Boris (1917 – 1981): The Helicopter Spies (1968), The Omega Man (1971)

Sagan, Leontine (1889 – 1974): Madchen In Uniform (1931)

Sakaguchi, Hironobu (1962 –): Final Fantasy: The Spirits Within (2001)

Saks, Gene (1921 –): The Odd Couple (1968)

Saldanha, Carlos (1965 –): Ice Age 2: The Meltdown (2006)

Salles, Walter (1956 –): Central Station (1998), Dark Water (2005)

Salva, Victor (1958 –): Jeepers Creepers (2001)

Salvatores, Gabriele (1950 –): Mediterraneo (1991)

Saltzman, Harry (1915 – 1994): Goldfinger (1964)

Sanchez, Eduardo (1968 –): The Blair Witch Project (1999)

Sandrich, Mark (1900 – 1945): The Gay Divorcee (1934), Follow The Fleet (1936)

Satterfield, Paul: Fantasia (1940)

Saura, Carlos (1932 –): Ay Carmela (1990)

Singer, Bryan (1965 –): The Usual Suspects (1995), Apt Pupil (1998), X-men (2000), X2 (2003)

Singleton, John (1968 –): Boyz N The Hood (1991)

Sinofsky, Bruce (1956 –): Metallica: Some Kind Of Monster (2004)

Siodmak, Robert (1900 – 1973): The Spiral Staircase (1946), The Crimson Pirate (1952)

Sirk, Douglas (1897 –): All That Heaven Allows (1955)

1963)

Sitch, Robert (1962 –): The Dish (2000)

Siu-Tung, Ching (1953 –): A Chinese Ghost Story (1987)

Sivan, Santosh: Asoka (2001)

Skoldbjaerg, Erik (1964 –): Insomnia (1997)

Skolnick, Barry: The Mean Machine (2001)

Sjoman, Vilgot (1924 – 2006): I Am Curious – Yellow (1967)

Sluizer, George (1932 –): The Vanishing (1988)

Smith, Chris (1970 –): American Movie (1999)

Smith, John N.: Dangerous Minds (1995)

Smith, Kevin (1970 –): Clerks (1994), Mallrats (1995), Chasing Amy (1997), Dogma (1999), Jay And Silent Bob Strike Back (2001), Jersey Girl (2004)

Smith, Mel (1952 –): The Tall Guy (1989), Radioland Murders (1994), Bean ((1997)

Soderbergh, Steven (1963 –): Sex, Lies And Videotape (1989), Kafka (1991), King Of Hill (1993), Out Of Sight (1998), The Limey (1999), Erin Brockovich (2000), Traffic (2000), Ocean's Eleven (2001), Solaris (2002), Ocean's 12 (2004)

Softley, Iain: Backbeat: 1994, Hackers (1995), K-Pax (2001), The Skeleton Key (2005)

Solanas, Fernando E. (1936 –): The Hours Of The Furnaces (1965)

Solondz, Todd (1960 –): Welcome To The Dollhouse (1995), Happiness (1998)

Sommers, Stephen (1962 –): Deep Rising (1998), The Mummy (1999), The Mummy Returns (2001), Van Helsing (2004)

Sonnenfeld, Barry (1953 –): The Addams Family (1991), Get Shorty (1995), Men In Black (1997), Wild Wild West (1999), Men In Black II

Spheeris, Penelope (1945 –): The Decline Of The Western Civilisation (1981), Wayne's World (1992)

Spicer, Brian: Mighty Morphin Power Rangers: The Movie (1995)

Spielberg, Steven (1946 –): Duel* (1971), The Sugarland Express (1974), Jaws (1975), Close Encounters Of The Third Kind (1977)

1941 (1979), Raiders Of The Lost Ark (1982), E.T. The Extra-Terrestrial (1982), Indiana Jones And The Temple Of Doom (1984), The Color Purple (1985), Empire Of The Sun (1987), Indiana Jones And The Last Crusade (1989), Always (1989), Hook (1991), Jurassic Park (1993), Schindler's List (1993), The Lost World Jurassic Park (1997), Amistad (1997), Saving Private Ryan (1998), A.I. Artificial Intelligence* (2001), Minority Report (2002), Catch Me If You Can (2002), The Terminal (2004), War Of The Worlds (2005), Munich (2005)

Spottiswoode, Roger (1943 –): Turner & Hooch (1989), Tomorrow Never Dies (1997)

Spurlock, Morgan (1970 –): Super Size Me (2004)

Stahl, John M. (1886 – 1950): Leave Her To Heaven (1945)

Stallone, Sylvester (1946 –): Rocky II (1979), Rocky III (1982), Rocky IV (1985)

Stanley, John Patrick (1950 –): Joe Versus The Volcano (1990)

Stanton, Andrew (1958 –): A Bug's Life (1998), Finding Nemo (2003)

Steers, Burr (1960 –): Igby Goes Down (2002)

Steinbach, Peter F.: Heimat (1984)

Stephani, Frederick: Flash Gordon (1936)

Stevens, George (1904 – 1975): A Place In The Sun (1951), Shane (1953), Giant (1956), The Diary Of Anne Frank (1959), The Greatest Story Ever Told (1965)

Stevenson, Robert (1905–1986): The Love Bug (1968), Bedknobs And Broomsticks (1971), Herbie Rides Again (1974), One Of Our Dinosaurs Is Missing (1975)

Stewart, David A. (1952 –): Honest (2000)

Stiller, Ben (1965 –): Reality Bites (1994), The Cable Guy (1996), Zoolander (2001)

Stillman, Whit (1951 –): Barcelona (1994), Whit Stillman (1988), Metropolitan (1990)

Streisand, Barbra (1942 –): The Mirror Has Two Faces (1996)

Stockwell, John (1961 –): Crazy/Beautiful (2001), Into The Blue (2005)

Stroham, Susan (1954 –): The Producers: The Movie Musical (2005)

Stone, Oliver (1946 –): Platoon (1986), Salvador (1986), Wall Street (1987), Talk Radio (1988), Born On The Fourth Of July (1989),The Doors (1991), JFK (1991), Heaven & Earth (1993), Natural Born Killers (1994), Nixon (1995), U-Turn (1997), Any Given Sunday (1999), Alexander (2004)

Story, Tim (1970 –): Barbershop (2002), Fantastic Four (2005)

Stuart, Mel (1928 –): Willy Wonka And The Chocolate Factory (1971)

Sturges, John (1911 – 1992): The Great McGinty (1940), Sullivan's Travels (1941), Bad Day At Black Rock (1955), The Magnificent Seven (1960), The Great Escape (1963), Ice Station Zebra (1968), The Eagle Has Landed (1976)

Sturges, Preston (1898 – 1959): Lady Eve (1941), The Palm Beach Story (1942), Hail The Conquering Hero (1944), The Miracle Of Morgan's Creek (1944), Unfaithfully Yours (1948)

Sukorov, Alexander (1951 –): Russian Ark (2002)

Suo, Masayuki (1956 –): Shall We Dance? (1996)

Sutherland , A. Edward (1895 – 1973): The Flying Deuces (1939)

Svankmajer, Jan (1934 –): Alice (1988)

Sverak, Jan (1965 –): Kolya (1996)

Verhoeven, Paul (1938 –): The Fourth Man (1983), Robocop (1987), Total Recall (1990), Basic Instinct (1992), Showgirls (1995), Starship Troopers (1997), Hollow Man (2000)

Vertov, Dziga (1896 – 1954): Man With A Movie Camera (1929)

Vidor, Charles (1918 – 1959): Gilda (1946)

Vidor, King (1894 – 1982): The Mask Of Fu Manchu (1932), Stella Dallas (1937)

Vigo, Jean (1905–1934): A Propos De Nice (1930), Zero De Conduite (1933), L'Atalante (1934)

Vigne, Daniel (1942 –): The Return Of Martin Guerre (1992)

Vinterberg, Thomas (1969 –) : Festen (1998)

Virgien, Norton: The Rugrats Movie (1998)

Visconti, Luchino (1906 – 1976): Ossessione (1942), Rocco And His Brothers (1960), The Leopard (1963)

Von Sternberg, Josef (1894 – 1969): The Blue Angel (1930) , Blonde Venus (1932), Shanghai Express (1932), The Scarlett Empress (1934)

Von Stroheim, Erich (1885 – 1957): Greed (1924), Queen Kelly (1929)

Von Trier, Lars (1956 –): Breaking The Waves (1996), The Idiots (1998), Dancer In The Dark (2000), Dogville (2003)

W

Wachowski, Andy (1967 –): Bound (1996), The Matrix (1999), Matrix Reloaded (2003), Matrix Revolutions (2003)

Wachowski, Larry (1965 –): Bound (1965), The Matrix (1999), Matrix Reloaded (2003), Matrix Revolutions (2003)

Wadleigh, Michael (1941 –): Woodstock (1970)

Waggner, George (1894 – 1984): The Wolf Man (1941)

Wajda, Andzej (1926 –): Ashes And Diamonds (1958), Man Of Marble (1977), Man Of Iron (1981)

Wallace, Tommy Lee: Halloween III: Season Of The Witch (1982)

Walsh, Raoul (1887 – 1980): The Roaring Twenties (1939), High Sierra (1941), They Died With Their Boots On (1941), White Heat (1949), The Naked And The Dead (1958)

Walters, Charles (1911 – 1982): High Society (1956)

Wanamaker, Sam (1919 – 1993): Sinbad And The Eye Of The Tiger (1977)

Wan, James: Saw (2004)

Wang, Wayne (1949 –): Blue In The Face (1995), Smoke (1995)

Ward, David S. (1945 –): Major League (1989)

Ward, Vincent (1956 –): The Navigator: A Mediaval Odyssey (1988), Map Of The Human Heart (1993)

Waters, John (1946 –): Pink Flamingos (1972), Hairspray (1988), Cry Baby (1990), Pecker (1998), Cecil B. Demented (2000)

Waters, Mark (1964 –): Freaky Friday (1993), Mean Girls (2004), Just Like Heaven (2005)

Watkins, Peter (1935 –): The War Game (1965)

Watt, Harry (1906 – 1987): Night Mail (1936)

Wayans, Keenan Ivory (1958 –): Scary Movie (2000)

Wayne, John (1907 – 1979): The Alamo (1960)

Webb, Jack (1920 – 1982): Pete Kelly's Blues (1955)

Webber, Peter: Girl With A Pearl Earring (2003)

Wedge, Chris (1958 –): Robots (2005)

Wegener, Paul: Der Golem (1920)

Weir, Peter (1941 –): Picnic At Hanging Rock (1975), Gallipoli (1981), The Year Of Living Dangerously (1982), Witness (1985), Dead Poet's Society (1989), Green Card (1990), Fearless (1993), The Truman Show (1998), Master And Commander: The Far Side Of The World (2003)

Weisman, Sam: George Of The Jungle (1997), The Out-Of-Towners (1999)

Weitz, Chris (1970 –): American Pie (1999), About A Boy (2002)

Weitz, Paul (1966 –): American Pie (1999), About A Boy (2002)

Welles, Orson (1915 – 1985): Citizen Kane (1941), The Magnificent Ambersons (1942), The Lady From Shanghai (1948), Macbeth (1948), Touch Of Evil (1958), The Trial (1962), Chimes At Midnight (1966)

Wellman, William A. (1896 – 1975): Wings (1927). The Public Enemy (1931)

Wenders, Wim (1945 –): Kings Of The Road (1976), The American Friend (1977), Paris, Texas (1984), Wings Of Desire (1987), The Buena Vista Social Club (1999)

West, Simon (1961) : Con Air (1997), Lara Croft: Tomb Raider (2001)

Werker, Alfred (1896 – 1975): The Adventures Of Sherlock Holmes (1939)

Whale, James (1889 – 1957): Frankenstein (1931), The Invisible Man (1933), Bride Of Frankenstein (1935), The Man In The Iron Mask (1939)

Whedon, Joss (1964 –): Serenity (2005)

Welan, Tim (1893 – 1957): The Thief Of Bagdad (1940)

Wickes, David: Sweeney! (1976)

Widen, Gregory: The Prophecy (1994)

Widerberg, Bo (1930 – 1997): Elvira Madigan (1967)

Wiene, Robert (1873 – 1938): The Cabinet Of Dr. Caligari (1920)

Wilcox, Fred M. (1907 – 1964): Lassie Come Home (1943), Forbidden Planet (1956)

Wilcox, Herbert (1892 – 1977): Spring In Park Lane (1948)

Wilder, Billy (1906 – 2002): Double Indemnity (1944), The Lost Weekend (1945), Sunset Boulevard (1950), Ace In The Hole (1951), Stalag 17 (1953), The Seven Year Itch (1955), Witness For The Prosecution (1957), The Spirit Of St. Louis (1957), Some Like It Hot (1959), The Apartment (1960), Irma La Douche (1963), Kiss Me, Stupid (1964), The Fortune Cookie (1966), The Private Life Of Sherlock Holmes (1970), Avanti (1972), The Front Page (1974)

STAR RATING INDEX

★★★★★

Stir Crazy
Stoned
Streets Of Fire
Subway
Sudden Death
Summer Holiday
Summer's Tale, A
Sunshine Boys, The
Sunshine State
Superman Iii
Supervixens
S.W.A.T.
Sweeney
Sweeney Todd Or The Demon Barber Of Fleet Street
Sweet Charity
Sweet Home Alabama
Sylvia Scarlett
Sympathy For Mr Vengeance
Take The Money And Run
Talented Mr. Ripley, The
Tales From The Crypt
Tango And Cash
Tarantula
Tarzan And His Mate
Tarzan The Ape Man
Tenebrae
Terminal Man, The
Terminator 3: Rise Of The Machine
Texas Chain Saw Massacre, The (2003)
This Boy's Life
Three Amigos!
Three Burials Of Melquiades Estrada
Three Men And A Little Lady
Threepenny Opera, The
Thunderball
Thunderbirds Are Go (1966)
Timecode
To Catch A Thief
To Live And Die In La
Tom Jones
Toys
Transamerica
Trials Of Oscar Wilde, The
Troy
Truly Madly Deeply
Turner And Hooch
Twister
2010
U Turn
U2 Rattle And Hum
Uncle Buck
Under Capricorn
Under Siege
Universal Soldier
Valley Of Gwangi
Veronica Guerin
Very Bad Things
Victim
Victor/Victoria
Vikings, The
Virgin Spring
Waking Life
Wanderers, The
War Of The Worlds, The (1953)
Watcher In The Woods, The
Warlock
Wayne's World
Wedding Crashers
What's New Pussycat
When Worlds Collide
Where Eagles Dare
White Christmas
White Hunter Black Heart
Wild Geese, The
Wild One, The
Wings
Wolf
Wolf Man, The
Woodstock
Working Girl
World Is Not Enough
Wuthering Heights
Wyatt Earp
X-Files, The
Xxx
You Can't Take It With You
You've Got Mail
Young Sherlock Holmes
Zathura
Ziegfield Follies
Zoolander
Zorba The Greek

★★

Absolute Beginners
Ace Ventura: Pet Detective
Against All Odds
Alamo, The
Alien Nation
Alien Vs. Predator
All The Right Moves
American Pie: The Wedding
Among Giants
Analyse That
Another 48 Hours
Any Which Way You Can
Around The World In 80 Days (2004)
Assassins
Astronaut's Wife, The
At The Earth's Core
Atlantis: The Lost Empire
Avengers, The
Bad Boys 2
Baise Moi
Barbershop
Basic Instinct 2: Risk Addiction
Basquiat
Batman & Robin
Batman Forever
Batteries Not Included
Battle For The Planet Of The Apes
Battlefield Earth
Be Cool
Beastmaster, The
Bewitched
Bhaji On The Beach
Bicentennial Man
Big Daddy
Bitter Moon
Blacula
Blood And Wine
Blue Lagoon, The
Blue Steel
Blues Brothers 2000
Body Of Evidence
Bone Collector, The
Bonfire Of The Vanities
Book Of Shadows: Blair Witch 2
Bound And Gagged
Braindead
Bram's Stoker's Dracula
Bridget Jones – Edge Of Reason
Brigadoon
Broken Arrow
Buck Rogers In The 25th Century
Burning, The
California Man
California Suite
Camelot
Carry On At Your Convenience
Carry On Behind
Carry On Camping
Carry On Follow That Camel
Carry On Girls
Carry On Henry
Carry On Jack
Carry On Loving
Carry On Sergeant
Charlie's Angels
Chronicles Of Riddick, The
Civil Action, A
Cleopatra
Conan The Destroyer
Condorman
Confessions Of A Window Cleaner
Congo
Dangerous Minds
Darkman
Day Of The Triffids, The
Days Of Thunder
Deep, The
Desperate Hours
Destination Moon
Dr Dolittle (1967)
Dr Doolittle (1998)
Dude, Where's My Car
Dukes Of Hazzard, The
Earth Girls At Easy
Earthquake
Elektra
Emerald Forest, The
Enter The Dragon
Entrapment
Escape From La
Exorcist Ii The Heretic
Exorcist Iii, The
Exorcist The Beginning
Fallen Angels
Fan, The
Fantasia
Fantastic Four, The
Firebox
First Knight
Fletch
Flintstones, The
Flirting With Disaster
For Your Eyes Only
Forces Of Nature
Four Rooms
Frankie And Johnny
Friday The 13th
G.I. Jane
Game, The
Gattaca
Gleaming The Cube
Godzilla (1997)
Gone In 60 Seconds
Greystoke, The Legend Of Tarzan, Lord Of The Apes
Halloween 2
Halloween 4
Hannibal
Harry And The Hendersons
Heaven And Earth
Hell's Angels
Henry And June
Herbie Fully Loaded
High Anxiety
Honest
Hook
Hot Shots!
House
House Of Wax (2005)
Hunger, The
Ice Station Zebra
Indian In The Cupboard, The
Inspector Gadget
Island Of Dr Moreau
Jesus Christ Superstar
Jewel Of The Nile
Jimmy Hollywood
Joe Vs. The Volcano
King Arthur
King Kong (1976)
King Of New York